CANADA

Alaska
(U.S.A)

REYKJAVÍK
ICELAND

OTTAWA

St Pierre &
Miquelon
(FRANCE)

UNITED STATES
OF AMERICA

Chicago

New York

WASHINGTON

Atlantic

Ocean

Los Angeles

Bermuda
(U.K.)

Pacific

Ocean

Hawaii
(U.S.A.)

MEXICO

BAHAMAS

Puerto
Rico
(U.S.A.)

Turks &
Caicos Is
(U.K.)

British Virgin Is (U.K.)
U.S. Virgin Is (U.S.A.)
Anguilla (U.K.)
ST KITTS & NEVIS
ANTIGUA & BARBUDA
Montserrat (U.K.)
Guadeloupe (FRANCE)
DOMINICA
Martinique (FRANCE)
ST LUCIA
BARBADOS
ST VINCENT & THE GRENADINES
GRENADA

CAPE
VERDE

Caymen Is.
(U.K.)

MEXICO
CITY

BELIZE

CUBA

JAMAICA

HAITI

HONDURAS

DOM.
REP.

Neth.
Ant.
(NETH.)

GUATEMALA
EL SALVADOR
NICARAGUA

Aruba
(NETH.)

MARSHALL
IS

COSTA RICA

CARACAS

TRINIDAD
& TOBAGO

PANAMA

VENEZUELA

GUYANA
SURINAME

BOGOTÁ

COLOMBIA

French Guiana
(FRANCE)

NAURU

QUITO
ECUADOR

KIRIBATI

SOLOMON
ISLANDS

TUVALU

Tokelau
(N.Z.)

BRAZIL

LIMA

PERU

Wallis &
Futuna Is
(FRANCE)

SAMOA

American
Samoa
(U.S.A.)

VANUATU

Cook Is
(N.Z.)

LA PAZ

BRASÍLIA

FIJI

TONGA

Niue
(N.Z.)

French Polynesia

BOLIVIA

PARAGUAY

Pitcairn Is
(U.K.)

Rio de Janeiro

ASUNCIÓN

São Paulo

...nia
CE)

CHILE

Norfolk Is.
(AUSTRALIA)

ARGENTINA

URUGUAY

NEW ZEALAND

SANTIAGO

BUENOS
AIRES

MONTEVIDEO

WELLINGTON

Falkland
Islands
(U.K.)

South Georgia & the
South Sandwich Islands
(U.K.)

THE EUROPA WORLD YEAR BOOK 2001

VOLUME I

PART ONE: INTERNATIONAL ORGANIZATIONS
PART TWO: AFGHANISTAN–JORDAN

EUROPA PUBLICATIONS
Taylor & Francis Group

First published 1926

ISBN 1-85743-100-6 (The Set)
1-85743-098-0 (Vol. I)
ISSN 0956-2273
Library of Congress Catalog Card Number 59-2942

Senior Editor: Joanne Maher

Statistics Editor: Andrew Thomas

Regional Editors: Imogen Bell, Lynn Daniel, Juliet Love, Joanne Maher,
Katharine Murison, Jacqueline West

International Organizations Editors: Catriona Appeatu Holman, Helen Canton

Technology Editor: Ian Preston

Assistant Editors: Camilla Chew, Katie Dawson, Lucy Dean, Helen Fox, Iain Frame,
Anthony Gladman, Dominic Heaney, Lauren Johnston, Christian Le Mière, David Lea,
Catriona Marcham, Colette Milward, Tiara Misquitta, Alison Neale, Wendy Parker,
Yoel Sano, Priya Shah, Nicola Stokes, Martyn Taylor

Editorial Co-ordinator: Mary Hill

Editorial Clerical Assistant: Fiona Vas

Typeset by UBL International and printed by Unwin Brothers Limited
The Gresham Press
Old Woking, Surrey

FOREWORD

THE EUROPA WORLD YEAR BOOK (formerly THE EUROPA YEAR BOOK: A WORLD SURVEY) was first published in 1926. Since 1960 it has appeared in annual two-volume editions, and has become established as an authoritative reference work, providing a wealth of detailed information on the political, economic and commercial institutions of the world.

Volume I contains a comprehensive listing of more than 1,650 international organizations and the first part of the alphabetical survey of countries of the world, from Afghanistan to Jordan. Volume II contains countries from Kazakhstan to Zimbabwe.

The International Organizations section gives extensive coverage to the United Nations and its related agencies and bodies. There are also detailed articles concerning some 60 other major international and regional organizations (including the World Trade Organization, the European Union and the North Atlantic Treaty Organization—NATO); entries for many affiliated organizations appear within these articles. In addition, briefer details of more than 1,000 other international organizations appear in a separate section which starts on page 279. A comprehensive Index of International Organizations can be found at the end of Volume I.

Each country is covered by an individual chapter, containing: an introductory survey including recent history, economic affairs, government, defence, social welfare, education, and public holidays; an economic and demographic survey using the latest available statistics on area and population, agriculture, forestry, fishing, industry, finance, trade, transport, tourism, the media, and education; and a directory section containing names, addresses and other useful facts about government, political parties, diplomatic representation, judiciary, religious groups, the media, telecommunications, banks, insurance, trade and industry, development organizations, chambers of commerce, industrial and trade associations, utilities, trade unions, transport and tourism.

Any important government changes (e.g. ministerial reorganizations and election results) that occur during the final stages of the production of the book and cannot, therefore, be incorporated in the appropriate chapters, may be found in Late Information, see p. xv.

Readers are referred to our eight regional surveys, AFRICA SOUTH OF THE SAHARA, CENTRAL AND SOUTH-EASTERN EUROPE, EASTERN EUROPE, RUSSIA AND CENTRAL ASIA, THE FAR EAST AND AUSTRALASIA, THE MIDDLE EAST AND NORTH AFRICA, SOUTH AMERICA, CENTRAL AMERICA AND THE CARIBBEAN, THE USA AND CANADA and WESTERN EUROPE, for additional information on the geography, history and economy of these areas. More detailed coverage of international organizations can be found in THE EUROPA DIRECTORY OF INTERNATIONAL ORGANIZATIONS.

The information is extensively revised and updated annually by a variety of methods, including direct mailing to all the institutions listed. Many other sources are used, such as national statistical offices, government departments and diplomatic missions. The editors thank the innumerable individuals and organizations throughout the world whose generous co-operation in providing current information for this edition is invaluable in presenting the most accurate and up-to-date material available.

June 2001.

ACKNOWLEDGEMENTS

The editors gratefully acknowledge particular indebtedness for permission to reproduce material from the following publications: the United Nations' *Demographic Yearbook*, *Statistical Yearbook* and *Industrial Commodity Statistics Yearbook*; the United Nations Educational, Scientific and Cultural Organization's *Statistical Yearbook*; the Food and Agriculture Organization of the United Nations' *Production Yearbook*, *Yearbook of Fishery Statistics* and *Yearbook of Forest Products*; the International Labour Office's *Yearbook of Labour Statistics*; the World Bank's *World Bank Atlas*, *Global Development Finance*, *World Development Report* and *World Development Indicators*; the International Monetary Fund's *International Financial Statistics* and *Government Finance Statistics Yearbook*; the World Tourism Organization's *Yearbook of Tourism Statistics*; and *The Military Balance 2000–2001*, a publication of the International Institute for Strategic Studies, Arundel House, 13–15 Arundel Street, London WC2R 3DX.

CONTENTS

* A complete Index of International Organizations is to be found on p. 2247.

CONTENTS

PART TWO
Afghanistan–Jordan

Index of International Organizations   2247

An Index of Territories is to be found at the end of Volume II.

ABBREVIATIONS

AB	Aktiebolag (Joint-Stock Company); Alberta	CA	California	Dec.	December
Abog.	Abogado (Lawyer)	CACM	Central American Common Market	Del.	Delegación
Acad.	Academician; Academy			Dem.	Democratic; Democrat
ACP	African, Caribbean and Pacific (countries)	Cad.	Caddesi (Street)	Dep.	Deputy
		CAP	Common Agricultural Policy	dep.	deposits
ACT	Australian Capital Territory	cap.	capital	Dept	Department
AD	anno Domini	Capt.	Captain	devt	development
ADB	African Development Bank; Asian Development Bank	CARICOM	Caribbean Community and Common Market	DF	Distrito Federal
				Dgo	Durango
ADC	aide-de-camp	CBSS	Council of Baltic Sea States	Diag.	Diagonal
Adm.	Admiral	CCL	Caribbean Congress of Labour	Dir	Director
admin.	administration	Cdre	Commodore	Div.	Division(al)
AfDB	African Development Bank	CEMAC	Communauté économique et monétaire de l'Afrique centrale	DM	Deutsche Mark
AG	Aktiengesellschaft (Joint-Stock Company)			DMZ	demilitarized zone
		Cen.	Central	DN	Distrito Nacional
AH	anno Hegirae	CEO	Chief Executive Officer	Doc.	Docent
a.i.	ad interim	CFA	Communauté Financière Africaine; Co-opération Financière en Afrique centrale	Dott.	Dottore
AID	(US) Agency for International Development			Dr	Doctor
				Dr.	Drive
AIDS	acquired immunodeficiency syndrome	CFP	Common Fisheries Policy; Communauté française du Pacifique; Comptoirs français du Pacifique	Dra	Doctora
				Dr Hab.	Doktor Habilitowany (Assistant Professor)
AK	Alaska				
Al.	Aleja (Alley, Avenue)			dr.(e)	drachma(e)
AL	Alabama	Chair.	Chairman/person/woman	Drs	Doctorandus
ALADI	Asociación Latinoamericana de Integración	Chih.	Chihuahua	DU	depleted uranium
		CI	Channel Islands	dwt	dead weight tons
Alt.	Alternate	Cia	Companhia		
AM	Amplitude Modulation	Cía	Compañía	E	East; Eastern
a.m.	ante meridiem (before noon)	CICP	Centre for International Crime Prevention	EBRD	European Bank for Reconstruction and Development
amalg.	amalgamated				
Apdo	Apartado (Post Box)	Cie	Compagnie		
APEC	Asia-Pacific Economic Co-operation	c.i.f.	cost, insurance and freight	EC	European Community
		C-in-C	Commander-in-Chief	ECA	(United Nations) Economic Commission for Africa
approx.	approximately	circ.	circulation		
Apt	Apartment	CIS	Commonwealth of Independent States	ECE	(United Nations) Economic Commission for Europe
AR	Arkansas				
AŞ	Anonim Şirketi (Joint-Stock Company)	CJD	Creutzfeldt-Jakob disease	ECLAC	(United Nations) Economic Commission for Latin America and the Caribbean
		cm	centimetre(s)		
A/S	Aktieselskab (Joint-Stock Company)	cnr	corner		
		CO	Colorado	ECO	Economic Co-operation Organization
ASEAN	Association of South East Asian Nations	Co	Company; County		
		c/o	care of	Econ.	Economist; Economics
asscn	association	Coah.	Coahuila	ECOSOC	(United Nations) Economic and Social Council
assoc.	associate	Col	Colonel		
ASSR	Autonomous Soviet Socialist Republic	Col.	Colima; Colonia	ECOWAS	Economic Community of West African States
		COMESA	Common Market for Eastern and Southern Africa		
asst	assistant			ECU	European Currency Unit
Aug.	August	Comm.	Commission; Commendatore	Edif.	Edificio (Building)
auth.	authorized	Commdr	Commander	edn	edition
Ave	Avenue	Commdt	Commandant	EEA	European Economic Area
Avda	Avenida (Avenue)	Commr	Commissioner	EFTA	European Free Trade Association
Avv.	Avvocato (Lawyer)	Cond.	Condiminio		
AZ	Arizona	Confed.	Confederation	e.g.	exempli gratia (for example)
		Cont.	Contador (Accountant)	EIB	European Investment Bank
BC	British Columbia	Corp.	Corporate	eKv	electron kilovolt
BC	before Christ	Corpn	Corporation	EMS	European Monetary System
Bd	Board	CP	Case Postale; Caixa Postal; Casella Postale (Post Box); Communist Party	EMU	economic and monetary union
Bd, Bld, Blv., Blvd	Boulevard			eMv	electron megavolt
				Eng.	Engineer; Engineering
b/d	barrels per day	CPSU	Communist Party of the Soviet Union	ERM	exchange rate mechanism
BFPO	British Forces' Post Office			ESACA	Emisora de Capital Abierto Sociedad Anónima
Bhd	Berhad (Public Limited Company)	Cres.	Crescent		
Bldg	Building	CSCE	Conference on Security and Co-operation in Europe	Esc.	Escuela; Escudos; Escritorio
Blvr	Bulevar			ESCAP	(United Nations) Economic and Social Commission for Asia and the Pacific
BP	Boîte postale (Post Box)	CSTAL	Confederación Sindical de los Trabajadores de América Latina		
br.(s)	branch(es)				
Brig.	Brigadier				
BSE	Bovine spongiform encephalopathy	CT	Connecticut	ESCWA	(United Nations) Economic and Social Commission for Western Asia
		CTCA	Confederación de Trabajadores Centro-americanos		
BSEC	(Organization of) Black Sea Economic Co-operation			esq.	esquina (corner)
		Cttee	Committee	est.	established; estimate; estimated
bte	boîte (box)	cu	cubic		
BTN	Brussels Tariff Nomenclature	cwt	hundredweight	etc.	et cetera
bul.	bulvar (boulevard)			EU	European Union
		DC	District of Columbia; Distrito Capital; Distrito Central	eV	eingetragener Verein
C	Centigrade			excl.	excluding
c.	circa; cuadra(s) (block(s))	DE	Departamento Estatal; Delaware	exec.	executive
				Ext.	Extension

F	Fahrenheit
f.	founded
FAO	Food and Agriculture Organization
f.a.s.	free alongside ship
Feb.	February
Fed.	Federation; Federal
FL	Florida
FM	frequency modulation
fmr(ly)	former(ly)
f.o.b.	free on board
Fr	Father
Fr.	Franc
Fri.	Friday
FRY	Federal Republic of Yugoslavia
ft	foot (feet)
FYRM	former Yugoslav republic of Macedonia
g	gram(s)
GA	Georgia
GATT	General Agreement on Tariffs and Trade
GCC	Gulf Co-operation Council
Gdns	Gardens
GDP	gross domestic product
Gen.	General
GeV	giga electron volts
GM	genetically modified
GmbH	Gesellschaft mit beschränkter Haftung (Limited Liability Company)
GMT	Greenwich Mean Time
GNP	gross national product
Gov.	Governor
Govt	Government
Gro	Guerrero
grt	gross registered tons
Gto	Guanajuato
GWh	gigawatt hours
ha	hectares
HE	His/Her Eminence; His/Her Excellency
hf	hlutafelag (Limited Company)
HI	Hawaii
HIPC	heavily indebted poor country
HIV	human immunodeficiency virus
hl	hectolitre(s)
HM	His/Her Majesty
Hon.	Honorary, Honourable
hp	horsepower
HQ	Headquarters
HRH	His/Her Royal Highness
HSH	His/Her Serene Highness
IA	Iowa
IBRD	International Bank for Reconstruction and Development (World Bank)
ICC	International Chamber of Commerce
ICFTU	International Confederation of Free Trade Unions
ICRC	International Committee of the Red Cross
ICTR	International Criminal Tribunal for Rwanda
ICTY	International Criminal Tribunal for the former Yugoslavia
ID	Idaho
IDA	International Development Association
IDB	Inter-American Development Bank
i.e.	id est (that is to say)
IFC	International Finance Corporation
IGAD	Intergovernmental Authority on Development
IL	Illinois
ILO	International Labour Organization/Office

IMF	International Monetary Fund
in (ins)	inch (inches)
IN	Indiana
Inc, Incorp.	
Incd	Incorporated
incl.	including
Ind.	Independent
INF	Intermediate-Range Nuclear Forces
Ing.	Engineer
Insp.	Inspector
Int.	International
Inzå.	Engineer
IPU	Inter-Parliamentary Union
Ir	Engineer
IRF	International Road Federation
irreg.	irregular
Is	Islands
ISIC	International Standard Industrial Classification
ITU	International Telecommunication Union
Iur.	Lawyer
Jal.	Jalisco
Jan.	January
Jnr	Junior
Jr	Jonkheer (Netherlands); Junior
Jt	Joint
kg	kilogram(s)
KG	Kommandit Gesellschaft (Limited Partnership)
kHz	kilohertz
KK	Kaien Kaisha (Limited Company)
km	kilometre(s)
Kom.	Komnata (Room)
kor.	korpus (block)
KS	Kansas
kv.	kvartal (apartment block); kvartira (apartment)
kW	kilowatt(s)
kWh	kilowatt hours
KY	Kentucky
LA	Louisiana
lauk	laukums (square)
lb	pound(s)
Lic.	Licenciado
Licda	Licenciada
LNG	liquefied natural gas
LPG	liquefied petroleum gas
Lt, Lieut	Lieutenant
Ltd	Limited
m	metre(s)
m.	million
MA	Massachusetts
Maj.	Major
Man.	Manager; managing
MB	Manitoba
mbH	mit beschränkter Haftung (with limited liability)
Mc/s	megacycles per second
MD	Maryland
ME	Maine
Me	Maître
mem.(s)	member(s)
MEP	Member of the European Parliament
Mercosul	Mercado Comum do Sul (Southern Common Market)
Mercosur	Mercado Común del Sur (Southern Common Market)
MEV, MeV	mega electron volts
Méx.	México
MFN	most favoured nation
mfrs	manufacturers
Mgr	Monseigneur; Monsignor
MHz	megahertz
MI	Michigan
MIA	missing in action

Mich.	Michoacán
MIGA	Multilateral Investment Guarantee Agency
Mil.	Military
Mlle	Mademoiselle
mm	millimetre(s)
Mme	Madame
MN	Minnesota
MO	Missouri
Mon.	Monday
Mor.	Morelos
MP	Member of Parliament
MS	Mississippi
MSS	Manuscripts
MT	Montana
MW	megawatt(s); medium wave
MWh	megawatt hour(s)
N	North; Northern
n.a.	not available
nab.	naberezhnaya (embankment, quai)
NAFTA	North American Free Trade Agreement
nám.	námětí (square)
Nat.	National
NATO	North Atlantic Treaty Organization
Nay.	Nayarit
NB	New Brunswick
NC	North Carolina
NCO	non-commissioned officer
ND	North Dakota
NE	Nebraska; North-East
NF	Newfoundland
NGO	non-governmental organization
NH	New Hampshire
NJ	New Jersey
NL	Nuevo León
NM	New Mexico
NMP	net material product
no	numéro, número (number)
no.	number
Nov.	November
nr	near
nrt	net registered tons
NS	Nova Scotia
NSW	New South Wales
NV	Naamloze Vennootschap (Limited Company); Nevada
NW	North-West
NY	New York
NZ	New Zealand
OAPEC	Organization of Arab Petroleum Exporting Countries
OAS	Organization of American States
OAU	Organization of African Unity
Oax.	Oaxaca
Oct.	October
OECD	Organisation for Economic Co-operation and Development
OECS	Organisation of Eastern Caribbean States
Of.	Oficina (Office)
OH	Ohio
OIC	Organization of the Islamic Conference
OK	Oklahoma
ON	Ontario
OPEC	Organization of the Petroleum Exporting Countries
opp.	opposite
OR	Oregon
Org.	Organization
ORIT	Organización Regional Interamericana de Trabajadores
OSCE	Organization for Security and Co-operation in Europe
p.	page
p.a.	per annum

ABBREVIATIONS

PA — Pennsylvania
Parl. — Parliament(ary)
pas. — passazh (passage)
per. — pereulok (lane, alley)
PE — Prince Edward Island
Perm. Rep. — Permanent Representative
PF — Postfach (Post Box)
PK — Post Box (Turkish)
Pl. — Plac (square)
pl. — platz; place; ploshchad (square)
PLC — Public Limited Company
PLO — Palestine Liberation Organization
p.m. — post meridiem (after noon)
PMB — Private Mail Bag
PNA — Palestinian National Authority
POB — Post Office Box
pp. — pages
PQ — Québec
PR — Puerto Rico
pr. — prospekt (avenue)
Pres. — President
PRGF — Poverty Reduction and Growth Facility
Prin. — Principal
Prof. — Professor
Propr — Proprietor
Prov. — Province; Provincial; Provinciale (Dutch)
prov. — provulok (lane)
PT — Perseroan Terbatas (Limited Company)
Pte — Private; Puente (Bridge)
Pty — Proprietary
p.u. — paid up
publ. — publication; published
Publr — Publisher
Pue. — Puebla
Pvt. — Private

Qld — Queensland
Qro — Querétaro
Q. Roo — Quintana Roo
q.v. — quod vide (to which refer)

Rag. — Ragioniere (Accountant)
Rd — Road
R(s) — rand; rupee(s)
reg., regd — register; registered
reorg. — reorganized
Rep. — Republic; Republican; Representative
Repub. — Republic
res — reserve(s)
retd — retired
Rev. — Reverend
RI — Rhode Island
RJ — Rio de Janeiro
Rm — Room
RN — Royal Navy
ro-ro — roll-on roll-off
RP — Recette principale
Rp.(s) — rupiah(s)
RSFSR — Russian Soviet Federative Socialist Republic
Rt — Right

S — South; Southern; San
SA — Société Anonyme, Sociedad Anónima (Limited Company); South Australia
SAARC — South Asian Association for Regional Co-operation

SAECA — Sociedad Anónima Emisora de Capital Abierto
SADC — Southern African Development Community
SAR — Special Administrative Region
SARL — Sociedade Anônima de Responsabilidade Limitada (Joint-Stock Company of Limited Liability)
Sat. — Saturday
SC — South Carolina
SD — South Dakota
Sdn Bhd — Sendirian Berhad (Private Limited Company)
SDR(s) — Special Drawing Right(s)
SE — South-East
Sec. — Secretary
Secr. — Secretariat
Sen. — Senior; Senator
Sept. — September
SER — Sua Eccellenza Reverendissima (His Eminence)
SFRY — Socialist Federal Republic of Yugoslavia
Sin. — Sinaloa
SITC — Standard International Trade Classification
SJ — Society of Jesus
SK — Saskatchewan
SLP — San Luis Potosí
SMEs — small and medium-sized enterprises
s/n — sin número (without number)
Soc. — Society
Sok. — Sokak (Street)
Son. — Sonora
Şos. — Şosea (Road)
SP — São Paulo
SpA — Società per Azioni (Joint-Stock Company)
Sq. — Square
sq — square (in measurements)
Sr — Senior; Señor
Sra — Señora
Srl — Società a Responsabilità Limitata (Limited Company)
SSR — Soviet Socialist Republic
St — Saint, Sint; Street
Sta — Santa
Ste — Sainte
str. — strada, stradă (street)
str-la — stradelă (street)
subs. — subscriptions; subscribed
Sun. — Sunday
Supt — Superintendent
sv. — Saint
SW — South-West

Tab. — Tabasco
Tamps — Tamaulipas
TAŞ — Turkiye Anonim Şirketi (Turkish Joint-Stock Company)
Tas — Tasmania
TD — Teachta Dàla (Member of Parliament)
tech., techn. — technical
tel. — telephone
TEU — 20-ft equivalent unit
Thur. — Thursday
TN — Tennessee
Treas. — Treasurer
Tue. — Tuesday
TV — television
TX — Texas

u. — utca (street)
u/a — unit of account
UAE — United Arab Emirates
UEE — Unidade Econômica Estatal
UEMOA — Union économique et monetaire ouest-africaine
UK — United Kingdom
ul. — ulica, ulitsa (street)
UM — ouguiya
UN — United Nations
UNCTAD — United Nations Conference on Trade and Development
UNDCP — United Nations International Drug Control Programme
UNDP — United Nations Development Programme
UNEP — United Nations Environment Programme
UNESCO — United Nations Educational, Scientific and Cultural Organization
UNHCHR — UN High Commissioner for Human Rights
UNHCR — United Nations High Commissioner for Refugees
UNICEF — United Nations Children's Fund
Univ. — University
UNRWA — United Nations Relief and Works Agency for Palestine Refugees in the Near East
USA — United States of America
USAID — United States Agency for International Development
USSR — Union of Soviet Socialist Republics
UT — Utah

VA — Virginia
VAT — Value-added Tax
VEB — Volkseigener Betrieb (Public Company)
v-CJD — variant Creutzfeldt-Jakob disease
Ven. — Venerable
Ver. — Veracruz
VHF — Very High Frequency
VI — (US) Virgin Islands
Vic — Victoria
viz. — videlicet (namely)
Vn — Veien (Street)
vol.(s) — volume(s)
VT — Vermont
vul. — vulitsa (street)

W — West; Western
WA — Western Australia; Washington (State)
WCL — World Confederation of Labour
Wed. — Wednesday
WEU — Western European Union
WFP — World Food Programme
WFTU — World Federation of Trade Unions
WHO — World Health Organization
WI — Wisconsin
WTO — World Trade Organization
WV — West Virginia
WY — Wyoming

yr — year
YT — Yukon Territory
Yuc. — Yucatán

INTERNATIONAL TELEPHONE CODES

To make international calls to telephone and fax numbers listed in *The Europa World Year Book*, dial the international code of the country from which you are calling, followed by the appropriate country code for the organization you wish to call (listed below), followed by the area code (if applicable) and telephone or fax number listed in the entry.

	Country code	+ or – GMT*
Afghanistan	93	+4½
Albania	355	+1
Algeria	213	+1
Andorra	376	+1
Angola	244	+1
Antigua and Barbuda	1 268	–4
Argentina	54	–3
Armenia	374	+4
Australia	61	+7 to +10
Australian External Territories:		
Australian Antarctic Territory	672	+3 to +10
Christmas Island	61	+10
Cocos (Keeling) Islands	61	+10
Norfolk Island	672	+11½
Austria	43	+1
Azerbaijan	994	+5
The Bahamas	1 242	–5
Bahrain	973	+3
Bangladesh	880	+6
Barbados	1 246	–4
Belarus	375	+2
Belgium	32	+1
Belize	501	–6
Benin	229	+1
Bhutan	975	+6
Bolivia	591	–4
Bosnia and Herzegovina	387	+1
Botswana	267	+2
Brazil	55	–3 to –4
Brunei	673	+8
Bulgaria	359	+2
Burkina Faso	226	0
Burundi	257	+2
Cambodia	855	+7
Cameroon	237	+1
Canada	1	–3 to –8
Cape Verde	238	–1
The Central African Republic	236	+1
Chad	235	+1
Chile	56	–4
China, People's Republic	86	+8
Special Administrative Regions:		
Hong Kong	852	+8
Macau	853	+8
China (Taiwan)	886	+8
Colombia	57	–5
The Comoros	269	+3
Congo, Democratic Republic	243	+1
Congo, Republic	242	+1
Costa Rica	506	–6
Côte d'Ivoire	225	0
Croatia	385	+1
Cuba	53	–5
Cyprus	357	+2
'Turkish Republic of Northern Cyprus'	90 392	+2
Czech Republic	420	+1
Denmark	45	+1
Danish External Territories:		
Faroe Islands	298	0
Greenland	299	–1 to –4
Djibouti	253	+3

	Country code	+ or – GMT*
Dominica	1 767	–4
The Dominican Republic	1 809	–4
East Timor	670	+8
Ecuador	593	–5
Egypt	20	+2
El Salvador	503	–6
Equatorial Guinea	240	+1
Eritrea	291	+3
Estonia	372	+2
Ethiopia	251	+3
Fiji	679	+12
Finland	358	+2
Finnish External Territory:		
Åland Islands	358	+2
France	33	+1
French Overseas Departments:		
French Guiana	594	–3
Guadeloupe	590	–4
Martinique	596	–4
Réunion	262	+4
French Overseas Collectivités Territoriales:		
Mayotte	269	+3
Saint Pierre and Miquelon	508	–3
French Overseas Territories:		
French Polynesia	689	–10
Wallis and Futuna Islands	681	+12
French Overseas Country:		
New Caledonia	687	+11
Gabon	241	+1
The Gambia	220	0
Georgia	995	+4
Germany	49	+1
Ghana	233	0
Greece	30	+2
Grenada	1 473	–4
Guatemala	502	–6
Guinea	224	0
Guinea-Bissau	245	0
Guyana	592	–4
Haiti	509	–5
Honduras	504	–6
Hungary	36	+1
Iceland	354	0
India	91	+5½
Indonesia	62	+7 to +8
Iran	98	+3½
Iraq	964	+3
Ireland	353	0
Israel	972	+2
Italy	39	+1
Jamaica	1 876	–5
Japan	81	+9
Jordan	962	+2
Kazakhstan	7	+6
Kenya	254	+3
Kiribati	686	+12
Korea, Democratic People's Republic (North Korea)	850	+9
Korea, Republic (South Korea)	82	+9
Kuwait	965	+3

	Country code	+ or − GMT*		Country code	+ or − GMT*
Kyrgyzstan	996	+5	Seychelles	248	+4
Laos	856	+7	Sierra Leone	232	0
Latvia	371	+2	Singapore	65	+8
Lebanon	961	+2	Slovakia	421	+1
Lesotho	266	+2	Slovenia	386	+1
Liberia	231	0	Solomon Islands	677	+11
Libya	218	+1	Somalia	252	+3
Liechtenstein	423	+1	South Africa	27	+2
Lithuania	370	+2	Spain	34	+1
Luxembourg	352	+1	Sri Lanka	94	+5½
Macedonia, former Yugoslav republic	389	+1	Sudan	249	+2
Madagascar	261	+3	Suriname	597	−3
Malawi	265	+2	Swaziland	268	+2
Malaysia	60	+8	Sweden	46	+1
Maldives	960	+5	Switzerland	41	+1
Mali	223	0	Syria	963	+2
Malta	356	+1	Tajikistan	992	+5
The Marshall Islands	692	+12	Tanzania	255	+3
Mauritania	222	0	Thailand	66	+7
Mauritius	230	+4	Togo	228	0
Mexico	52	−6 to −7	Tonga	676	+13
Micronesia, Federated States	691	+10 to +11	Trinidad and Tobago	1 868	−4
Moldova	373	+2	Tunisia	216	+1
Monaco	377	+1	Turkey	90	+2
Mongolia	976	+8	Turkmenistan	993	+5
Morocco	212	0	Tuvalu	688	+12
Mozambique	258	+2	Uganda	256	+3
Myanmar	95	+6½	Ukraine	380	+2
Namibia	264	+2	United Arab Emirates	971	+4
Nauru	674	+12	United Kingdom	44	0
Nepal	977	+5½	United Kingdom Crown		
The Netherlands	31	+1	Dependencies	44	0
Netherlands Dependencies:			United Kingdom Overseas		
Aruba	297	−4	Territories:		
Netherlands Antilles	599	−4	Anguilla	1 264	−4
New Zealand	64	+12	Ascension Island	247	0
New Zealand's Dependent and			Bermuda	1 441	−4
Associated Territories:			British Virgin Islands	1 284	−4
Cook Islands	682	−10½	Cayman Islands	1 345	−5
Niue	683	−11	Diego Garcia (British Indian		
Nicaragua	505	−6	Ocean Territory)	246	+5
Niger	227	+1	Falkland Islands	500	−4
Nigeria	234	+1	Gibraltar	350	+1
Norway	47	+1	Montserrat	1 664	−4
Norwegian External Territory:			Saint Helena	290	0
Svalbard	47	+1	Tristan da Cunha	2 897	0
Oman	968	+4	Turks and Caicos Islands	1 649	−5
Pakistan	92	+5	United States of America	1	−5 to −10
Palau	680	+9	United States Commonwealth		
Panama	507	−5	Territories:		
Papua New Guinea	675	+10	Northern Mariana Islands	1 670	+10
Paraguay	595	−4	Puerto Rico	1 787	−4
Peru	51	−5	United States External Territories:		
The Philippines	63	+8	American Samoa	684	−11
Poland	48	+1	Guam	1 671	+10
Portugal	351	0	United States Virgin Islands	1 340	−4
Qatar	974	+3	Uruguay	598	−3
Romania	40	+2	Uzbekistan	998	+5
The Russian Federation	7	+2 to +12	Vanuatu	678	+11
Rwanda	250	+2	Vatican City	39	+1
Saint Christopher and Nevis	1 869	−4	Venezuela	58	−4
Saint Lucia	1 758	−4	Viet Nam	84	+7
Saint Vincent and the Grenadines	1 784	−4	Yemen	967	+3
Samoa	685	−11	Yugoslavia	381	+1
San Marino	378	+1	Zambia	260	+2
São Tomé and Príncipe	239	0	Zimbabwe	263	+2
Saudi Arabia	966	+3			
Senegal	221	0			

* Time difference in hours + or − Greenwich Mean Time (GMT). The times listed compare the standard (winter) times. Some countries adopt Summer (Daylight Saving) Time — i.e. + 1 hour — for part of the year.

LATE INFORMATION

ANTIGUA AND BARBUDA (p. 463)
Government Changes
(May 2001)

Minister of Home Affairs, Urban Development and Renewal and Social Improvement, and Minister of Health: JOHN ST LUCE.

Minister of Justice and Legal Affairs, and Attorney-General: GRETEL THOM.

BRUNEI (p. 826)
Government Change
(May 2001)

Minister of Development: Dato' Seri Paduka Dr Haji AHMAD BIN Haji JUMAT (acting).

BULGARIA (p. 845)

Elections to the National Assembly took place on 17 June 2001. Preliminary results indicated that the National Movement Simeon II party took 42.73% of votes cast, the United Democratic Forces 18.17%, the Coalition for Bulgaria (comprising principally the Bulgarian Socialist Party) 17.14%, and the Turk Movement for Rights and Freedoms 7.45%. (No other party received the requisite 4% of votes cast to secure representation in the legislature.) Voter participation was estimated at 66.7%.

'TURKISH REPUBLIC OF NORTHERN CYPRUS' (p. 1288)
COUNCIL OF MINISTERS
(June 2001)

A coalition of the Ulusal Bırlık Partisi (UBP) and the Demokrat Parti (DP).

Prime Minister: DR DERVIŞ EROĞLU (UBP).

Deputy Prime Minister and Minister of State: SALİH COSAR (DP).

Minister of Foreign Affairs and Defence: TAHSIN ERTUĞRULOĞLU (UBP).

Minister of Finance: MEHMET BAYRAM (UBP).

Minister of the Interior, Rural Affairs and Housing: Dr MEHMET ALBAYRAK (UBP).

Minister of National Education and Culture: İLKAY KAMIL (UBP).

Minister of Agriculture and Forestry: İRSEN KÜÇÜK (UBP).

Minister of Communications and Works: SALİH MIROĞLU (UBP).

Minister of Labour, Social Security, Youth and Sports: Dr AHMET KAŞIF (DP).

Minister of Health and Social Welfare: Dr MUSTAFA ARABACIOĞLU (DP).

Minister of Tourism and the Environment: SERDAR DENKTAŞ (DP).

HONDURAS (p. 1889)
Government Change
(May 2001)

Minister of Public Works, Transport and Housing: SERGIO CANALES.

INDONESIA (p. 1996)
Government Changes
(June 2001)

Co-ordinating Minister for the Economy, Finance and Industry: BARHANUDDIN ABDULLAH.

Minister of Finance and State Enterprises Development: RIZAL RAMLI.

Minister of State for State Administrative Reforms: ANWAR SUPRIYADI.

IRAN (p. 2026)

At presidential elections held on 8 June 2001 the incumbent President Hojatoleslam Dr SAYED MUHAMMAD KHATAMI received 21,659,053 votes (76.9% of the total), defeating his principal rival, AHMAD TAVAKOLI, who took 4,387,112 votes (15.6%); there were eight other candidates.

ITALY (p. 2149)
COUNCIL OF MINISTERS
(June 2001)

A coalition of Forza Italia, Alleanza Nazionale (AN), Lega Nord, Cristiani Democratici Uniti (CDU), Centro Cristiano Democratico (CCD) and Independents (Ind.).

Prime Minister: SILVIO BERLUSCONI (Forza Italia).

Deputy Prime Minister: GIANFRANCO FINI (AN).

Minister of Foreign Affairs: RENATO RUGGIERO (Ind.).

Minister of Internal Affairs: CLAUDIO SCAJOLA (Forza Italia).

Minister of Justice: ROBERTO CASTELLI (Lega Nord).

Minister of Economy and Finance: GIULIO TREMONTI (Forza Italia).

Minister of Productive Activities: ANTONIO MARZANO (Forza Italia).

Minister of Education, Universities and Scientific Research: LETIZIA MORATTI (Ind.).

Minister of Labour and Welfare: ROBERTO MARONI (Lega Nord).

Minister of Defence: ANTONIO MARTINO (Forza Italia).

Minister of Agriculture and Forestry: GIANNI ALEMANNO (AN).

Minister of the Environment and Land Management: ALTERO MATTEOLI (AN).

Minister of Infrastructure and Transport: PIETRO LUNARDI (Ind.).

Minister of Health: GEROLAMO SIRCHIA (Ind.).

Minister of Culture: GIULIANO URBANI (Forza Italia).

Minister of Communications: MAURIZIO GASPARRI (AN).

Ministers without Portfolio:

Implementation of the Government Programme: GIUSEPPE PISANU (Forza Italia).

Public Function: FRANCO FRATTINI (Forza Italia).

European Union Affairs: ROCCO BUTTIGLIONE (CDU).

Technological Innovation: LUCIO STANCA (Ind.).

Regional Affairs: ENRICO LA LOGGIA (Forza Italia).

Equal Opportunities: STEFANIA PRESTIGIACOMO (Forza Italia).

Italians in the World: MIRKO TREMAGLIA (AN).

Reforms and Devolution: UMBERTO BOSSI (Lega Nord).

Relations with Parliament: CARLO GIOVANARDI (CCD).

PART ONE
International Organizations

THE UNITED NATIONS

Address: United Nations, New York, NY 10017, USA.

Telephone: (212) 963-1234; **fax:** (212) 963-4879; **internet:** www.un.org.

The United Nations was founded in 1945 to maintain international peace and security and to develop international co-operation in addressing economic, social, cultural and humanitarian problems.

The United Nations was a name devised by President Franklin D. Roosevelt of the USA. It was first used in the Declaration by United Nations of 1 January 1942, when representatives of 26 nations pledged their governments to continue fighting together against the Axis powers.

The United Nations Charter (see p. 18) was drawn up by the representatives of 50 countries at the United Nations Conference on International Organization, which met at San Francisco from 25 April to 26 June 1945. The representatives deliberated on the basis of proposals put forward by representatives of China, the USSR, the United Kingdom and the USA at Dumbarton Oaks in August–October 1944. The Charter was signed on 26 June 1945. Poland, not represented at the Conference, signed it later but nevertheless became one of the original 51 members.

The United Nations officially came into existence on 24 October 1945, when the Charter had been ratified by China, France, the USSR, the United Kingdom and the USA, and by a majority of other signatories. United Nations Day is celebrated annually on 24 October.

The UN's chief administrative officer is the Secretary-General, elected for a five-year term by the General Assembly on the recommendation of the Security Council. He acts in that capacity at all meetings of the General Assembly, the Security Council, the Economic and Social Council, and the Trusteeship Council, and performs such other functions as are entrusted to him by those organs. He is required to submit an annual report to the General Assembly and may bring to the attention of the Security Council any matter which, in his opinion, may threaten international peace.

Secretary-General (1997–2001): Kofi Annan (Ghana).

Membership

MEMBERS OF THE UNITED NATIONS

(with assessments for percentage contributions to the UN budget for 2000, and year of admission)

Country	Assessment	Year
Afghanistan	0.003	1946
Albania	0.003	1955
Algeria	0.086	1962
Andorra	0.004	1993
Angola	0.010	1976
Antigua and Barbuda	0.002	1981
Argentina	1.103	1945
Armenia	0.006	1992
Australia	1.483	1945
Austria	0.942	1955
Azerbaijan	0.011	1992
Bahamas	0.015	1973
Bahrain	0.017	1971
Bangladesh	0.010	1974
Barbados	0.008	1966
Belarus[1]	0.057	1945
Belgium	1.104	1945
Belize	0.001	1981
Benin	0.002	1960
Bhutan	0.001	1971
Bolivia	0.007	1945
Bosnia and Herzegovina[2]	0.005	1992
Botswana	0.010	1966
Brazil	1.471	1945
Brunei	0.020	1984
Bulgaria	0.011	1955
Burkina Faso	0.002	1960
Burundi	0.001	1962
Cambodia	0.001	1955
Cameroon	0.013	1960
Canada	2.732	1945
Cape Verde	0.002	1975
Central African Republic	0.001	1960
Chad	0.001	1960
Chile	0.136	1945
China, People's Republic[3]	0.995	1945
Colombia	0.109	1945
Comoros	0.001	1975
Congo, Democratic Republic (formerly Zaire)	0.007	1960
Congo, Republic	0.003	1960
Costa Rica	0.016	1945
Côte d'Ivoire	0.009	1960
Croatia[2]	0.030	1992
Cuba	0.024	1945
Cyprus	0.034	1960
Czech Republic[4]	0.107	1993
Denmark	0.692	1945
Djibouti	0.001	1977
Dominica	0.001	1978
Dominican Republic	0.015	1945
Ecuador	0.020	1945
Egypt	0.065	1945
El Salvador	0.012	1945
Equatorial Guinea	0.001	1968
Eritrea	0.001	1993
Estonia	0.012	1991
Ethiopia	0.006	1945
Fiji	0.004	1970
Finland	0.543	1955
France	6.545	1945
Gabon	0.015	1960
The Gambia	0.001	1965
Georgia	0.007	1992
Germany	9.857	1973
Ghana	0.007	1957
Greece	0.351	1945
Grenada	0.001	1974
Guatemala	0.018	1945
Guinea	0.003	1958
Guinea-Bissau	0.001	1974
Guyana	0.001	1966
Haiti	0.002	1945
Honduras	0.003	1945
Hungary	0.120	1955
Iceland	0.032	1946
India	0.299	1945
Indonesia	0.188	1950
Iran	0.161	1945
Iraq	0.032	1945
Ireland	0.224	1955
Israel	0.350	1949
Italy	5.437	1955
Jamaica	0.006	1962
Japan	20.573	1956
Jordan	0.006	1955
Kazakhstan	0.048	1992
Kenya	0.007	1963
Kiribati	0.001	1999
Korea, Democratic People's Republic	0.015	1991
Korea, Republic	1.006	1991
Kuwait	0.128	1963
Kyrgyzstan	0.006	1992
Laos	0.001	1955
Latvia	0.017	1991
Lebanon	0.016	1945
Lesotho	0.002	1966
Liberia	0.002	1945
Libya	0.124	1955
Liechtenstein	0.006	1990
Lithuania	0.015	1991
Luxembourg	0.068	1945
Macedonia, former Yugoslav republic[2]	0.004	1993
Madagascar	0.003	1960
Malawi	0.002	1964
Malaysia	0.183	1957
Maldives	0.001	1965
Mali	0.002	1960
Malta	0.014	1964
Marshall Islands	0.001	1991
Mauritania	0.001	1961
Mauritius	0.009	1968
Mexico	0.995	1945
Micronesia, Federated States	0.001	1991
Moldova	0.010	1992
Monaco	0.004	1993

Mongolia	. . . .	0.002	1961
Morocco	. . . .	0.041	1956
Mozambique	. . . . . .	0.001	1975
Myanmar	. . . .	0.008	1948
Namibia	. . . .	0.007	1990
Nauru	. . . .	0.001	1999
Nepal	. . . .	0.004	1955
Netherlands	. . . . . .	1.632	1945
New Zealand	. . . . .	0.221	1945
Nicaragua	. . . . . .	0.001	1945
Niger	. . . .	0.002	1960
Nigeria	. . . .	0.032	1960
Norway	. . . .	0.610	1945
Oman	. . . .	0.051	1971
Pakistan	. . . .	0.059	1947
Palau	. . . .	0.001	1994
Panama	. . . .	0.013	1945
Papua New Guinea	. . . .	0.007	1975
Paraguay	. . . . . .	0.014	1945
Peru	. . . .	0.099	1945
Philippines	. . . . . .	0.081	1945
Poland	. . . .	0.096	1945
Portugal	. . . . . .	0.431	1955
Qatar	. . . .	0.033	1971
Romania	. . . .	0.056	1955
Russia[5]	. . . .	1.077	1945
Rwanda	. . . .	0.001	1962
Saint Christopher and Nevis	. .	0.001	1983
Saint Lucia	. . . . . .	0.001	1979
Saint Vincent and the Grenadines	.	0.001	1980
Samoa (formerly Western Samoa)	. .	0.001	1976
San Marino	. . . . . .	0.002	1992
São Tomé and Príncipe	. . .	0.001	1975
Saudi Arabia	. . . . .	0.562	1945
Senegal	. . . .	0.006	1960
Seychelles	. . . . . .	0.002	1976
Sierra Leone	. . . . .	0.001	1961
Singapore	. . . . . .	0.179	1965
Slovakia[4]	. . . . . .	0.035	1993
Slovenia[2]	. . . . . .	0.061	1992
Solomon Islands	. . . .	0.001	1978
Somalia	. . . .	0.001	1960
South Africa	. . . . .	0.366	1945
Spain	. . . .	2.591	1955
Sri Lanka	. . . . . .	0.012	1955
Sudan	. . . .	0.007	1956
Suriname	. . . . . .	0.004	1975
Swaziland	. . . . . .	0.002	1968
Sweden	. . . .	1.079	1946
Syria	. . . .	0.064	1945
Tajikistan	. . . . . .	0.004	1992
Tanzania[6]	. . . . . .	0.003	1961
Thailand	. . . . . .	0.170	1946
Togo	. . . .	0.001	1960
Tonga	. . . .	0.001	1999
Trinidad and Tobago	. . .	0.016	1962
Tunisia	. . . .	0.028	1956
Turkey	. . . .	0.440	1945
Turkmenistan	. . . . .	0.006	1992
Tuvalu	. . . .	n.a.	2000
Uganda	. . . .	0.004	1962
Ukraine[1]	. . . . . .	0.190	1945
United Arab Emirates	. . .	0.178	1971
United Kingdom	. . . .	5.092	1945
USA	. . . .	25.000	1945
Uruguay	. . . .	0.048	1945
Uzbekistan	. . . . . .	0.025	1992
Vanuatu	. . . .	0.001	1981
Venezuela	. . . . . .	0.160	1945
Viet Nam	. . . . . .	0.007	1977
Yemen[7]	. . . .	0.010	1947/67
Yugoslavia[2]	. . . . . .	0.026	1945
Zambia	. . . .	0.002	1964
Zimbabwe	. . . . . .	0.009	1980

Total Membership: 189 (April 2001)

[1] Until December 1991 both Belarus and Ukraine were integral parts of the USSR and not independent countries, but had separate UN membership.

[2] Bosnia and Herzegovina, Croatia and Slovenia, previously republics within the Socialist Federal Republic of Yugoslavia, were each granted full UN membership in May 1992. Yugoslavia continued to exist (changing its official title to the Federal Republic of Yugoslavia in April 1992) but comprised only the two republics of Serbia and Montenegro. The remaining republic, Macedonia, declared itself a sovereign state in November 1991, and was admitted to the UN in April 1993 under the name of the former

Yugoslav republic of Macedonia. In September 1992 the UN General Assembly voted to suspend Yugoslavia from participation in its proceedings until the new Yugoslav state had applied and been accepted to fill the seat in the UN occupied by the former Yugoslavia; this was achieved in November 2000.

[3] From 1945 until 1971 the Chinese seat was occupied by the Republic of China (confined to Taiwan since 1949).

[4] Czechoslovakia, which had been a member of the UN since 1945, ceased to exist as a single state on 31 December 1992. In January 1993, as Czechoslovakia's legal successors, the Czech Republic and Slovakia were granted UN membership, and seats on subsidiary bodies that had previously been held by Czechoslovakia were divided between the two successor states.

[5] Russia assumed the USSR's seat in the General Assembly and its permanent seat on the Security Council (see p. 12) in December 1991, following the USSR's dissolution.

[6] Tanganyika was a member of the United Nations from December 1961 and Zanzibar was a member from December 1963. From April 1964 the United Republic of Tanganyika and Zanzibar continued as a single member, changing its name to United Republic of Tanzania in November 1964.

[7] The Yemen Arab Republic (admitted to the UN as Yemen in 1947) and the People's Democratic Republic of Yemen (admitted as Southern Yemen in 1967) merged to form the Republic of Yemen in May 1990.

Note: In December 2000 the UN General Assembly approved a reform of the system of assessment calculations for percentage contributions to the UN budget, to take effect from 2001 (see Finance).

SOVEREIGN COUNTRIES NOT IN THE UNITED NATIONS
(April 2001)

China (Taiwan)
Switzerland
Vatican City (Holy See)

Diplomatic Representation

MEMBER STATES' PERMANENT MISSIONS TO THE UNITED NATIONS
(with Permanent Representatives—May 2001)

Afghanistan: 360 Lexington Ave, 11th Floor, New York, NY 10017; tel. (212) 972-1212; fax (212) 972-1216; e-mail afgwatan@aol.com; Dr RAVAN A. G. FARHÁDI.

Albania: 320 East 79th St, New York, NY 10021; tel. (212) 249-2059; fax (212) 535-2917; e-mail albania@un.int; AGIM NESHO.

Algeria: 326 East 48th St, New York, NY 10017; tel. (212) 750-1960; fax (212) 759-9538; e-mail algeria@un.int; internet www.algeria-un.org; ABDALLAH BAALI.

Andorra: 2 United Nations Plaza, 25th Floor, New York, NY 10017; tel. (212) 750-8064; fax (212) 750-6630; e-mail andorra@un.int; JULI MINOVES TRIQUELL.

Angola: 125 East 73rd St, New York, NY 10021; tel. (212) 861-5656; fax (212) 861-9295; e-mail angola@un.int; ISMAEL ABRAÃO GASPAR MARTINS.

Antigua and Barbuda: 610 Fifth Ave, Suite 311, New York, NY 10020; tel. (212) 541-4117; fax (212) 757-1607; e-mail antigua@un.int; internet www.un.int/antigua; Dr PATRICK ALBERT LEWIS.

Argentina: 1 United Nations Plaza, 25th Floor, New York, NY 10017; tel. (212) 688-6300; fax (212) 980-8395; e-mail argentina@un.int; internet www.un.int/argentina; ARNOLDO M. LISTRE.

Armenia: 119 East 36th St, New York, NY 10016; tel. (212) 686-9079; fax (212) 686-3934; e-mail armenia@un.int; Dr MOVSES ABELIAN.

Australia: 150 East 42nd St, 33rd Floor, New York, NY 10017; tel. (212) 351-6600; fax (212) 351-6610; e-mail australia@un.int; internet www.un.int/australia; PENELOPE ANNE WENSLEY.

Austria: 823 United Nations Plaza, 8th Floor, New York, NY 10017; tel. (212) 949-1840; fax (212) 953-1302; e-mail austria@un.int; internet www.un.int/austria; GERHARD PFLANZELTER.

Azerbaijan: 866 United Nations Plaza, Suite 560, New York, NY 10017; tel. (212) 371-2559; fax (212) 371-2784; e-mail azerbaijan@un.int; internet www.un.int/azerbaijan; ELDAR G. KOULIEV.

Bahamas: 231 East 46th St, New York, NY 10017; tel. (212) 421-6925; fax (212) 759-2135; e-mail bahamas@un.int; ANTHONY CHARLES ROLLE.

Bahrain: 866 Second Ave, 14th/15th Floor, New York, NY 10017; tel. (212) 223-6300; fax (212) 319-0687; e-mail bahrain@un.int; JASSIM MOHAMMED BUALLAY.

Bangladesh: 821 United Nations Plaza, 8th Floor, New York, NY 10017; tel. (212) 867-3434; fax (212) 972-4038; e-mail bangladesh@un.int; internet www.un.int/bangladesh; F. A. SHAMIN AHMED.

Barbados: 800 Second Ave, 2nd Floor, New York, NY 10017; tel. (212) 867-8431; fax (212) 986-1030; e-mail barbados@un.int; JUNE YVONNE CLARKE.

Belarus: 136 East 67th St, New York, NY 10021; tel. (212) 535-3420; fax (212) 734-4810; e-mail belarus@un.int; internet www.un.int/belarus; SERGEI LING.

Belgium: 823 United Nations Plaza, 4th Floor, New York, NY 10017; tel. (212) 378-6300; fax (212) 681-7618; e-mail belgium@un.int; internet www.un.int/belgium; JEAN DE RUYT.

Belize: 800 Second Ave, Suite 400G, New York, NY 10017; tel. (212) 599-0233; fax (212) 599-3391; e-mail belize@un.int; MICHAEL ANTHONY ASHCROFT.

Benin: 4 East 73rd St, New York, NY 10021; tel. (212) 249-6014; fax (212) 734-4735; e-mail benin@un.int; JOËL WASSI ADECHI.

Bhutan: 2 United Nations Plaza, 27th Floor, New York, NY 10017; tel. (212) 826-1919; fax (212) 826-2998; e-mail bhutan@un.int; Lyonpo OM PRADHAN.

Bolivia: 211 East 43rd St, 8th Floor (Room 802), New York, NY 10017; tel. (212) 682-8132; fax (212) 682-8133; e-mail bolivia@un.int; Dr ROBERTO JORDÁN-PANDO.

Bosnia and Herzegovina: 866 United Nations Plaza, Suite 580, New York, NY 10017; tel. (212) 751-9015; fax (212) 751-9019; e-mail bosnia@un.int; internet www.un.int/bosnia; HUSEIN ZIVALJ.

Botswana: 103 East 37th St, New York, NY 10016; tel. (212) 889-2277; fax (212) 725-5061; e-mail botswana@un.int; LEGWAILA JOSEPH LEGWAILA.

Brazil: 747 Third Ave, 9th Floor, New York, NY 10017; tel. (212) 372-2600; fax (212) 371-5716; e-mail braun@lbrasonu.org; internet www.un.int/brazil; GELSON FONSECA, Jr.

Brunei: 771 First Ave, New York, NY 10017; tel. (212) 697-3465; fax (212) 697-9889; e-mail brunei@un.int; SERBINI ALI.

Bulgaria: 11 East 84th St, New York, NY 10028; tel. (212) 737-4790; fax (212) 472-9865; e-mail bulgaria@un.int; internet www.un.int/bulgaria; STEFAN TAFROV.

Burkina Faso: 115 East 73rd St, New York, NY 10021; tel. (212) 288-7515; fax (212) 772-3562; e-mail burkinafaso@un.int; MICHEL KAFANDO.

Burundi: 336 East 45th St, 12th Floor, New York, NY 10017; tel. (212) 499-0001; fax (212) 499-0006; e-mail burundi@un.int; MARC NTETURUYE.

Cambodia: 866 United Nations Plaza, Suite 420, New York, NY 10017; tel. (212) 223-0676; fax (212) 223-0425; e-mail cambodia@un.int; internet www.un.int/cambodia; BORITH OUCH.

Cameroon: 22 East 73rd St, New York, NY 10021; tel. (212) 794-2295; fax (212) 249-0533; e-mail cameroon@un.int; MARTIN BELINGA EBOUTOU.

Canada: 1 Dag Hammarskjöld Plaza, 885 Second Ave, 14th Floor, New York, NY 10017; tel. (212) 848-1100; fax (212) 848-1195; e-mail canada@un.int; internet www.un.int/canada; PAUL HEINBECKER.

Cape Verde: 27 East 69th St, New York, NY 10021; tel. (212) 472-0333; fax (212) 794-1398; e-mail capeverde@un.int; JOSÉ LUIS BARBOSA LEÃO MONTEIRO.

Central African Republic: 386 Park Ave South, Room 1114, New York, NY 10016; tel. (212) 679-8089; fax (212) 545-8326; e-mail caf@un.int; ANTONIO DEINDE FERNANDEZ.

Chad: 211 East 43rd St, Suite 1703, New York, NY 10017; tel. (212) 986-0980; fax (212) 986-0152; e-mail chad@un.int; LAOTEGGUEL-NODJI KOUMTOG.

Chile: 3 Dag Hammarskjöld Plaza, 305 East 47th St, 10th/11th Floor, New York, NY 10017; tel. (212) 832-3323; fax (212) 832-8714; e-mail chile@un.int; J. GABRIEL VALDES.

China, People's Republic: 350 East 35th St, New York, NY 10016; tel. (212) 655-6100; fax (212) 634-7626; e-mail china@un.int; internet www.un.fmprc.gov.cn/eng/index.html; WANG YINGFAN.

Colombia: 140 East 57th St, 5th Floor, New York, NY 10022; tel. (212) 355-7776; fax (212) 371-2813; e-mail colombia@un.int; internet www.un.int/colombia; ALFONSO VALDIVIESO.

Comoros: 420 East 50th St, New York, NY 10022; tel. (212) 972-8010; fax (212) 983-4712; e-mail comoros@un.int; Chargé d'affaires a.i. MAHMOUD MOHAMED ABOUD.

Congo, Democratic Republic: 866 United Nations Plaza, Suite 511, New York, NY 10017; tel. (212) 319-8061; fax (212) 319-8232; e-mail drcongo@un.int; internet www.un.int/drcongo; ATOKI CHRISTIAN ILEKA.

Congo, Republic: 14 East 65th St, New York, NY 10021; tel. (212) 744-7840; fax (212) 744-7975; e-mail congo@un.int; BASILE IKOUEBE.

Costa Rica: 211 East 43rd St, Room 903, New York, NY 10017; tel. (212) 986-6373; fax (212) 986-6842; e-mail costarica@un.int; BERND NIEHAUS.

Côte d'Ivoire: 46 East 74th St, New York, NY 10021; tel. (212) 717-5555; fax (212) 717-4492; e-mail ivorycoast@un.int; internet www.un.int/cotedivoire; CLAUDE STANISLAS BOUAH-KAMON.

Croatia: 820 Second Ave, 19th Floor, New York, NY 10017; tel. (212) 986-1585; fax (212) 986-2011; e-mail croatia@un.int; internet www.un.int/croatia; Dr IVAN SIMONOVIĆ.

Cuba: 315 Lexington Ave and 38th St, New York, NY 10016; tel. (212) 689-7215; fax (212) 779-1697; e-mail cuba@un.int; internet www.un.int/cuba; RAFAEL DAUSA CESPEDES.

Cyprus: 13 East 40th St, New York, NY 10016; tel. (212) 481-6023; fax (212) 685-7316; e-mail cyprus@un.int; internet www.un.int/cyprus; SOTIRIOS ZACKHEOS.

Czech Republic: 1109–1111 Madison Ave, New York, NY 10028; tel. (212) 535-8814; fax (212) 772-0586; e-mail czechrepublic@un.int; internet www.un.int/czechrepublic; VLADIMÍR GALUŠKA.

Denmark: 1 Dag Hammarskjöld Plaza, 885 Second Ave, 18th Floor, New York, NY 10017; tel. (212) 308-7009; fax (212) 308-3384; e-mail denmark@un.int; internet www.un.int/denmark; ELLEN LØJ.

Djibouti: 866 United Nations Plaza, Suite 4011, New York, NY 10017; tel. (212) 753-3163; fax (212) 223-1276; e-mail djibouti@nyct.net; ROBLE OLHAYE.

Dominica: 800 Second Ave, Suite 400H, New York, NY 10017; tel. (212) 949-0853; fax (212) 808-4975; e-mail dominica@un.int; SIMON PAUL RICHARDS.

Dominican Republic: 144 East 44th St, 4th Floor, New York, NY 10017; tel. (212) 867-0833; fax (212) 986-4694; e-mail dr@un.int; PEDRO PADILLA TONOS.

Ecuador: 866 United Nations Plaza, Room 516, New York, NY 10017; tel. (212) 935-1680; fax (212) 935-1835; e-mail ecuador@un.int; internet www.un.int/ecuador; MARIO ALEMÁN.

Egypt: 304 East 44th St, New York, NY 10017; tel. (212) 503-0300; fax (212) 949-5999; e-mail egypt@un.int; AHMED ABOUL GHEIT.

El Salvador: 46 Park Ave, New York, NY 10016; tel. (212) 679-1616; fax (212) 725-7831; e-mail elsalvador@un.int; JOSÉ ROBERTO ANDINO-SALAZAR.

Equatorial Guinea: 57 Magnolia Ave, Mount Vernon, NY 10553; tel. (914) 664-1882; fax (914) 667-6838; e-mail eqguinea@un.int; TEODORO BIYOGO NSUE.

Eritrea: 800 Second Ave, 18th Floor, New York, NY 10017; tel. (212) 687-3390; fax (212) 687-3138; e-mail eritrea@un.int; AHMED TAHIR BADURI.

Estonia: 600 Third Ave, 26th Floor, New York, NY 10016; tel. (212) 883-0640; fax (212) 883-0648; e-mail estonia@un.int; MERLE PAJULA.

Ethiopia: 866 Second Ave, 3rd Floor, New York, NY 10017; tel. (212) 421-1830; fax (212) 754-0360; e-mail ethiopia@un.int; internet www.un.int/ethiopia; FISSEHA YIMER.

Fiji: 630 Third Ave, 7th Floor, New York, NY 10017; tel. (212) 687-4130; fax (212) 687-3963; e-mail fiji@un.int; AMRAIYA NAIDU.

Finland: 866 United Nations Plaza, Suite 222, New York, NY 10017; tel. (212) 355-2100; fax (212) 759-6156; e-mail finland@un.int; internet www.un.int/finland; MARJATTA RASI.

France: 1 Dag Hammarskjöld Plaza, 245 East 47th St, 44th Floor, New York, NY 10017; tel. (212) 308-5700; fax (212) 421-6889; e-mail france@un.int; internet www.un.int/france; JEAN-DAVID LEVITTE.

Gabon: 18 East 41st St, 9th Floor, New York, NY 10017; tel. (212) 686-9720; fax (212) 689-5769; e-mail gabon@un.int; DENIS DANGUE RÉWAKA.

The Gambia: 800 Second Ave, Suite 400F, New York, NY 10017; tel. (212) 949-6640; fax (212) 808-4975; e-mail gambia@un.int; BABOU-CARR-BLAISE ISMAILA JAGNE.

Georgia: 1 United Nations Plaza, 26th Floor, New York, NY 10021; tel. (212) 759-1949; fax (212) 759-1832; e-mail georgia@un.int; internet www.un.int/georgia; Dr PETER P. CHKHEIDZE.

Germany: 871 United Nations Plaza, New York, NY 10017; tel. (212) 940-0400; fax (212) 940-0402; e-mail germany@un.int; internet www.germany-info.org/UN; Prof. Dr DIETER KASTRUP.

Ghana: 19 East 47th St, New York, NY 10017; tel. (212) 832-1300; fax (212) 751-6743; e-mail ghana@un.int; internet www.un.int/ghana; Chargé d'affaires a.i. NANA EFFAH-APENTENG.

Greece: 866 Second Ave, 13th Floor, New York, NY 10017; tel. (212) 888-6900; fax (212) 888-4440; e-mail greece@un.int; internet www.un.int/greece; ELIAS GOUNARIS.

Grenada: 800 Second Ave, Suite 400K, New York, NY 10017; tel. (212) 599-0301; fax (212) 599-1540; e-mail grenada@un.int; Dr LAMUEL A. STANISLAUS.

Guatemala: 57 Park Ave, New York, NY 10016; tel. (212) 679-4760; fax (212) 685-8741; e-mail guatemala@un.int; internet www.un.int/guatemala; GERT ROSENTHAL.

Guinea: 140 East 39th St, New York, NY 10016; tel. (212) 687-8115; fax (212) 687-8248; e-mail guinea@un.int; FRANÇOIS LONSENY FALL.

Guinea-Bissau: 211 East 43rd St, Room 704, New York, NY 10017; tel. (212) 338-9394; fax (212) 293-0264; e-mail guinea-bissau@un.int; Chargé d'affaires a.i. João Soares.

Guyana: 866 United Nations Plaza, Suite 555, New York, NY 10017; tel. (212) 527-3232; fax (212) 935-7548; e-mail guyana@un.int; (vacant).

Haiti: 801 Second Ave, Room 600, New York, NY 10017; tel. (212) 370-4840; fax (212) 661-8698; e-mail haiti@un.int; Pierre Lelong.

Honduras: 866 United Nations Plaza, Suite 417, New York, NY 10017; tel. (212) 752-3370; fax (212) 223-0498; e-mail honduras@un.int; Angel Edmundo Orellana Mercado.

Hungary: 227 East 52nd St, New York, NY 10022; tel. (212) 752-0209; fax (212) 755-5395; e-mail hungary@un.int; internet www.un.int/hungary; André Erdős.

Iceland: 800 Third Ave, 36th Floor, New York, NY 10022; tel. (212) 593-2700; fax (212) 593-6269; e-mail iceland@un.int; Thorsteinn Ingólfsson.

India: 235 East 43rd St, New York, NY 10017; tel. (212) 490-9660; fax (212) 490-9656; e-mail india@un.int; internet www.un.int/india; Kamalesh Sharma.

Indonesia: 325 East 38th St, New York, NY 10016; tel. (212) 972-8333; fax (212) 972-9780; e-mail indonesia@un.int; internet www.un.int/indonesia; Makmur Widodo.

Iran: 622 Third Ave, 34th Floor, New York, NY 10017; tel. (212) 687-2020; fax (212) 867-7086; e-mail iran@un.int; internet www.un.int/iran; Seyed Mohammad Hadi Nejad-Hosseinian.

Iraq: 14 East 79th St, New York, NY 10021; tel. (212) 737-4433; fax (212) 772-1794; e-mail iraq@un.int; internet www.iraqi-mission.org; Dr Saeed Hasan.

Ireland: 1 Dag Hammarskjöld Plaza, 885 Second Ave, 19th Floor, New York, NY 10017; tel. (212) 421-6934; fax (212) 752-4726; e-mail ireland@un.int; Richard Ryan.

Israel: 800 Second Ave, New York, NY 10017; tel. (212) 499-5510; fax (212) 499-5515; e-mail israel@un.int; internet www.israel-un.org; Yehuda Lancry.

Italy: 2 United Nations Plaza, 24th Floor, New York, NY 10017; tel. (212) 486-9191; fax (212) 486-1036; e-mail italy@un.int; internet www.italyun.org; Sergio Vento.

Jamaica: 767 Third Ave, 9th Floor, New York, NY 10017; tel. (212) 935-7509; fax (212) 935-7607; e-mail jamaica@un.int; internet www.un.int/jamaica; Patricia Durrant.

Japan: 866 United Nations Plaza, 2nd Floor, New York, NY 10017; tel. (212) 223-4300; fax (212) 751-1966; e-mail japan@un.int; internet www.un.int/japan; Yukio Sato.

Jordan: 866 United Nations Plaza, Suite 552, New York, NY 10017; tel. (212) 832-9553; fax (212) 832-5346; e-mail jordan@un.int; Prince Zeid Ra'ad Zeid al-Hussein.

Kazakhstan: 866 United Nations Plaza, Suite 586, New York, NY 10017; tel. (212) 230-1900; fax (212) 230-1172; e-mail kazakhstan@un.int; internet www.un.int/kazakhstan; Madina Jarbussynova.

Kenya: 866 United Nations Plaza, Room 486, New York, NY 10017; tel. (212) 421-4740; fax (212) 486-1985; e-mail kenya@un.int; Phares Michael Kuindwa.

Korea, Democratic People's Republic: 820 Second Ave, 13th Floor, New York, NY 10017; tel. (212) 972-3105; fax (212) 972-3154; dprk@un.int; Li Hyong-chol.

Korea, Republic: 335 East 45th St, New York, NY 10017; tel. (212) 439-4000; fax (212) 986-1083; e-mail korea@un.int; internet www.un.int/korea; Lee See-young.

Kuwait: 321 East 44th St, New York, NY 10017; tel. (212) 973-4300; fax (212) 370-1733; e-mail kuwait@kuwaitmission.com; internet www.kuwaitmission.com; Mohammad A. Abulhasan.

Kyrgyzstan: 866 United Nations Plaza, Suite 477, New York, NY 10017; tel. (212) 486-4214; fax (212) 486-5259; e-mail kyrgyzstan@un.int; Kamil Baialinov.

Laos: 317 East 51st St, New York, NY 10022; tel. (212) 832-2734; fax (212) 750-0039; e-mail laos@un.int; internet www.un.int/lao/laomission.html; Alounkeo Kittikhoun.

Latvia: 333 East 50th St, New York, NY 10022; tel. (212) 838-8877; fax (212) 838-8920; e-mail latvia@un.int; Dr Janis Priedkalns.

Lebanon: 866 United Nations Plaza, Room 531–533, New York, NY 10017; tel. (212) 355-5460; fax (212) 838-2819; e-mail lebanon@un.int; Chargé d'affaires a.i. Dr Higham Hamdan.

Lesotho: 204 East 39th St, New York, NY 10016; tel. (212) 661-1690; fax (212) 682-4388; e-mail lesotho@un.int; internet www.un.int/lesotho; Percy Metsing Mangoaela.

Liberia: 820 Second Ave, 13th Floor, New York, NY 10017; tel. (212) 687-1033; fax (212) 687-1035; e-mail liberia@un.int; Lami Kawah.

Libya: 309-315 East 48th St, New York, NY 10017; tel. (212) 752-5775; fax (212) 593-4787; e-mail libya@un.int; internet www.un.int/libya; Isa Ayad Baba.

Liechtenstein: 633 Third Avenue, 27th Floor, New York, NY 10017; tel. (212) 599-0220; fax (212) 599-0064; e-mail liechtenstein@un.int; internet www.un.int/liechtenstein; Claudia Fritsche.

Lithuania: 420 Fifth Ave, 3rd Floor, New York, NY 10018; tel. (212) 354-7820; fax (212) 354-7833; e-mail lithuania@un.int; internet www.un.int/lithuania; Gediminas Serksnys.

Luxembourg: 17 Beekman Pl., New York, NY 10022; tel. (212) 935-3589; fax (212) 935-5896; e-mail luxembourg@un.int; internet www.un.int/luxembourg; Hubert Wurth.

Macedonia, former Yugoslav republic: 866 United Nations Plaza, Suite 517, New York, NY 10017; tel. (212) 308-8504; fax (212) 308-8724; e-mail macedonia@un.int; Naste Calovski.

Madagascar: 820 Second Ave, Suite 800, New York, NY 10017; tel. (212) 986-9491; fax (212) 986-6271; e-mail madagascar@un.int; internet www.nyrepermad.org; Jean Delacroix Bakoniarivo.

Malawi: 600 Third Ave, 21st Floor, New York, NY 10016; tel. (212) 949-0180; fax (212) 599-5021; e-mail malawi@un.int; Yusuf McDadlly Juwayeyi.

Malaysia: 313 East 43rd St, New York, NY 10017; tel. (212) 986-6310; fax (212) 490-8576; email malaysia@un.int; internet www.un.int/Malaysia; Agam Hasmy.

Maldives: 800 Second Ave, Suite 400E, New York, NY 10017; tel. (212) 599-6195; fax (212) 661-6405; e-mail maldives@un.int; internet www.un.int/maldives; Hussain Shihab.

Mali: 111 East 69th St, New York, NY 10021; tel. (212) 737-4150; fax (212) 472-3778; e-mail mali@un.int; Moctar Ouane.

Malta: 249 East 35th St, New York, NY 10016; tel. (212) 725-2345; fax (212) 779-7097; e-mail malta@un.int; Walter Balzan.

Marshall Islands: 800 Second Ave, 18th Floor, New York, NY 10017; tel. (212) 983-3040; fax (212) 983-3202; e-mail marshallislands@un.int; Akeo A. Relang.

Mauritania: 211 East 43rd St, Suite 2000, New York, NY 10017; tel. (212) 986-7963; fax (212) 986-8419; e-mail mauritania@un.int; Mahfoudh Ould Deddach.

Mauritius: 211 East 43rd St, 15th Floor, New York, NY 10017; tel. (212) 949-0190; fax (212) 697-3829; e-mail mauritius@un.int; Anund Priyay Neewoor.

Mexico: 2 United Nations Plaza, 28th Floor, New York, NY 10017; tel. (212) 752-0220; fax (212) 688-8862; e-mail mexico@un.int; internet www.un.int/mexico; Manuel Tello.

Micronesia, Federated States: 820 Second Ave, Suite 17A, New York, NY 10017; tel. (212) 697-8370; fax (212) 697-8295; e-mail micronesia@un.int; Masao Nakayama.

Moldova: 573-577 Third Ave, New York, NY 10016; tel. (212) 682-3523; fax (212) 682-6274; e-mail moldova@un.int; internet www.un.int/modova; Dr Ion Botnaru.

Monaco: 866 United Nations Plaza, Suite 520, New York, NY 10017; tel. (212) 832-0721; fax (212) 832-5358; e-mail monaco@un.int; Jacques Louis Boisson.

Mongolia: 6 East 77th St, New York, NY 10021; tel. (212) 861-9460; fax (212) 861-9464; e-mail mongolia@un.int; internet www.un.int/mongolia; Jargalsaikhany Enkhsaikhan.

Morocco: 866 Second Ave, 6th and 7th Floors, New York, NY 10017; tel. (212) 421-1580; fax (212) 980-1512; e-mail morocco@un.int; Mohamed Bennouna.

Mozambique: 420 East 50th St, New York, NY 10022; tel. (212) 644-5965; fax (212) 644-5972; e-mail mozambique@un.int; internet www.un.int/mozambique; Carlos Dos Santos.

Myanmar: 10 East 77th St, New York, NY 10021; tel. (212) 535-1310; fax (212) 737-2421; e-mail myanmar@un.int; Kyaw Tint Swe.

Namibia: 135 East 36th St, New York, NY 10016; tel. (212) 685-2003; fax (212) 685-1561; e-mail namibia@un.int; internet www.un.int/namibia; Martin Andjaba.

Nauru: 800 Second Ave, Suite 400D, New York, NY 10017; tel. (212) 937-0074; fax (212) 937-0079; Vinci Neil Clodumar.

Nepal: 820 Second Ave, Suite 17B, New York, NY 10017; tel. (212) 370-3988; fax (212) 953-2038; e-mail nepal@un.int; internet www.un.int/nepal; Narendra Bikram Shah.

Netherlands: 235 East 45th St, 16th Floor, New York, NY 10017; tel. (212) 697-5547; fax (212) 370-1954; e-mail netherlands@un.int; internet www.un.int/netherlands; Dirk Jan van der Berg.

New Zealand: 1 United Nations Plaza, 25th Floor, New York, NY 10017; tel. (212) 826-1960; fax (212) 758-0827; e-mail newzealand@un.int; internet www.un.int/newzealand; Trevor Hughes.

Nicaragua: 820 Second Ave, 8th Floor, New York, NY 10017; tel. (212) 490-7997; fax (212) 286-0815; e-mail nicaragua@un.int; Eduardo J. Sevilla Somoza.

Niger: 417 East 50th St, New York, NY 10022; tel. (212) 421-3260; fax (212) 753-6931; e-mail niger@un.int; Ousmane Moutari.

Nigeria: 828 Second Ave, New York, NY 10017; tel. (212) 953-9130; fax (212) 697-1970; e-mail nigeria@un.int; ARTHUR C. I. MBANEFO.

Norway: 825 Third Ave, 39th Floor, New York, NY 10022; tel. (212) 421-0280; fax (212) 688-0554; e-mail delun.@mfa.no; internet www.un.int/norway; OLE PETER KOLBY.

Oman: 866 United Nations Plaza, Suite 540, New York, NY 10017; tel. (212) 355-3505; fax (212) 644-0070; e-mail oman@un.int; FUAD MUBARAK AL-HINAI.

Pakistan: 8 East 65th St, New York, NY 10021; tel. (212) 879-8600; fax (212) 744-7348; e-mail pakistan@un.int; internet www.un.int/pakistan; SHAMSHAD AHMAD.

Palau: New York; e-mail palau@un.int.

Panama: 866 United Nations Plaza, Suite 4030, New York, NY 10017; tel. (212) 421-5420; fax (212) 421-2694; e-mail panama@un.int; RAMÓN A. MORALES.

Papua New Guinea: 201 East 42nd St, Suite 405, New York, NY 10017; tel. (212) 557-5001; fax (212) 557-5009; e-mail png@un.int; PETER DICKSON DONIGI.

Paraguay: 211 East 43rd St, Suite 400, New York, NY 10017; tel. (212) 687-3490; fax (212) 818-1282; e-mail paraguay@un.int; JORGE LARA-CASTRO.

Peru: 820 Second Ave, Suite 1600, New York, NY 10017; tel. (212) 687-3336; fax (212) 972-6975; e-mail peru@un.int; JORGE VALDEZ.

Philippines: 556 Fifth Ave, 5th Floor, New York, NY 10036; tel. (212) 764-1300; fax (212) 840-8602; e-mail philippines@un.int; internet www.un.int/philippines; (vacant).

Poland: 9 East 66th St, New York, NY 10021; tel. (212) 744-2506; fax (212) 517-6771; e-mail poland@un.int; internet www.un.int/poland; JANUSZ STANCZYK.

Portugal: 866 Second Ave, 9th Floor, New York, NY 10017; tel. (212) 759-9444; fax (212) 355-1124; e-mail portugal@un.int; internet www.un.int/portugal; FRANCISCO SEIXAS DA COSTA.

Qatar: 809 United Nations Plaza, 4th Floor, New York, NY 10017; tel. (212) 486-9335; fax (212) 758-4952; e-mail qatar@un.int; Chargé d'affaires a.i. JAMAL NASSIR SULTAN AL-BADER.

Romania: 573–577 Third Ave, New York, NY 10016; tel. (212) 682-3273; fax (212) 682-9746; e-mail romania@un.int; internet www.un.int/romania; SORIN DUMITRU DUCARU.

Russia: 136 East 67th St, New York, NY 10021; tel. (212) 861-4900; fax (212) 628-0252; e-mail rusun@un.int; internet www.un.int/russia; SERGEI V. LAVROV.

Rwanda: 124 East 39th St, New York, NY 10016; tel. (212) 679-9010; fax (212) 679-9133; e-mail rwanda@un.int; ANASTASE GASANA.

Saint Christopher and Nevis: 414 East 75th St, 5th Floor, New York, NY 10021; tel. (212) 535-1234; fax (212) 535-6854; e-mail stkn@un.int; JOSEPH R. CHRISTMAS.

Saint Lucia: 800 Second Ave, 9th Floor, New York, NY 10017; tel. (212) 697-9360; fax (212) 697-4993; e-mail stlucia@un.int; internet www.un.int/stlucia; JULIAN ROBERT HUNTE.

Saint Vincent and the Grenadines: 801 Second Ave, 21st Floor, New York, NY 10017; tel. (212) 687-4490; fax (212) 949-5946; e-mail stvg@un.int; DENNIE M. J. WILSON.

Samoa: 800 Second Ave, Suite 400J, New York, NY 10017; tel. (212) 599-6196; fax (212) 599-0797; e-mail samoa@un.int; TUILOMA NERONI SLADE.

San Marino: 327 East 50th St, New York, NY 10022; tel. (212) 751-1234; fax (212) 751-1436; e-mail sanmarino@un.int; GIAN NICOLA FILIPPI BALESTRA.

São Tomé and Príncipe: 400 Park Ave, 7th Floor, New York, NY 10022; tel. (212) 317-0533; fax (212) 317-0580; e-mail stp@un.int; Chargé d'affaires a.i. DOMINGOS AUGUSTO FERREIRA.

Saudi Arabia: 405 Lexington Ave, 56th Floor, New York, NY 10017; tel. (212) 697-4830; fax (212) 983-4895; e-mail saudiarabia@un.int; internet www.un.int/saudiarabia; FAWZI BIN ABDUL MAJEED SHOBOKSHI.

Senegal: 238 East 68th St, New York, NY 10021; tel. (212) 517-9030; fax (212) 517-7628; e-mail senegal@un.int; IBRA DEGUÈNE KA.

Seychelles: 800 Second Ave, Room 400C, New York, NY 10017; tel. (212) 972-1785; fax (212) 972-1786; e-mail seychelles@un.int; CLAUDE MOREL.

Sierra Leone: 245 East 49th St, New York, NY 10017; tel. (212) 688-1656; fax (212) 688-4924; e-mail sierraleone@un.int; IBRAHIM M'BABA KAMARA.

Singapore: 231 East 51st St, New York, NY 10022; tel. (212) 826-0840; fax (212) 826-2964; e-mail singapore@un.int; internet www.mfa.gov.sg/newyork; KISHORE MAHBUBANI.

Slovakia: 866 United Nations Plaza, Suite 494, New York, NY 10017; tel. (212) 980-1558; fax (212) 980-3295; e-mail slovakia@un.int; PETER TOMKA.

Slovenia: 600 Third Ave, 24th Floor, New York, NY 10016; tel. (212) 370-3007; fax (212) 370-1824; e-mail slovenia@un.int; internet www.un.int/slovenia; Dr ERNEST PETRIČ.

Solomon Islands: 800 Second Ave, Suite 400L, New York, NY 10017; tel. (212) 599-6193; fax (212) 661-8925; e-mail solomonislands@un.int; JEREMIAH MANELE (Chargé d'affaires a.i.).

Somalia: 425 East 61st St, Suite 702, New York, NY 10021; tel. (212) 688-9410; fax (212) 759-0651; e-mail somalia@un.int; Chargé d'affaires a.i. FATUN MUHAMMAD HASSAN.

South Africa: 333 East 38th St, 9th Floor, New York, NY 10016; tel. (212) 213-5583; fax (212) 692-2498; e-mail southafrica@un.int; DUMISANA SHADRACK KUMALO.

Spain: 823 United Nations Plaza, 9th Floor, New York, NY 10017; tel. (212) 661-1050; fax (212) 949-7247; e-mail spain@un.int; internet www.spainun.org; INOCENCIO F. ARIAS.

Sri Lanka: 630 Third Ave, 20th Floor, New York, NY 10017; tel. (212) 986-7040; fax (212) 986-1838; e-mail srilanka@un.int; JOHN DE SARAM.

Sudan: 655 Third Ave, Suite 500-510, New York, NY 10017; tel. (212) 573-6033; fax (212) 573-6160; e-mail sudan@un.int; ELFATIH MOHAMED AHMED ERWA.

Suriname: 866 United Nations Plaza, Suite 320, New York, NY 10017; tel. (212) 826-0660; fax (212) 980-7029; e-mail suriname@un.int; SUBHAS CHANDRA MUNGRA.

Swaziland: 408 East 50th St, New York, NY 10022; tel. (212) 371-8910; fax (212) 754-2755; e-mail swaziland@un.int; CLIFFORD SIBUSIO MAMBA.

Sweden: 1 Dag Hammarskjöld Plaza, 885 Second Ave, 46th Floor, New York, NY 10017; tel. (212) 583-2500; fax (212) 832-0389; e-mail sweden@un.int; internet www.un.int/sweden; PIERRE SCHORI.

Syria: 820 Second Ave, 15th Floor, New York, NY 10017; tel. (212) 661-1313; fax (212) 983-4439; e-mail syria@un.int; Dr MIKHAIL WEHBE.

Tajikistan: 136 East 67th St, New York, NY 10021; tel. (212) 744-2196; fax (212) 472-7645; e-mail tajikistan@un.int; RASHID ALIMOV.

Tanzania: 205 East 42nd St, 13th Floor, New York, NY 10017; tel. (212) 972-9160; fax (212) 682-5232; e-mail tanzania@un.int; DAUDI NGELAUTWA MWAKAWAGO.

Thailand: 351 East 52nd St, New York, NY 10022; tel. (212) 754-2230; fax (212) 754-2535; e-mail thailand@un.int; ASDA JAYANAMA.

Togo: 112 East 40th St, New York, NY 10016; tel. (212) 490-3455; fax (212) 983-6684; e-mail togo@un.int; ROLAND YAO KPOTSRA.

Tonga: 800 Second Ave, Suite 400B, New York, NY 10017; tel. (212) 5996190; fax (212) 8084975; S. TU'A TAUMOEPEAU-TUPOU.

Trinidad and Tobago: 820 Second Ave, 5th Floor, New York, NY 10017; tel. (212) 697-7620; fax (212) 682-3580; e-mail tto@un.int; GEORGE W. McKENZIE.

Tunisia: 31 Beekman Pl., New York, NY 10022; tel. (212) 751-7503; fax (212) 751-0569; e-mail tunisia@un.int; NOUREDDINE MEJDOUB.

Turkey: 821 United Nations Plaza, 10th Floor, New York, NY 10017; tel. (212) 949-0150; fax (212) 949-0086; e-mail turkey@un.int; internet www.un.int/turkey; MEHMET UMIT PAMIR.

Turkmenistan: 866 United Nations Plaza, Suite 424, New York, NY 10021; tel. (212) 486-8908; fax (212) 486-2521; e-mail turkmenistan@un.int; AKSOLTAN T. ATAEVA.

Uganda: 336 East 45th St, New York, NY 10017; tel. (212) 949-0110; fax (212) 687-4517; e-mail uganda@un.int; internet www.un.int/uganda; Prof. MATIA MULAMBA SEMAKULA KIWANUKA.

Ukraine: 220 East 51st St, New York, NY 10022; tel. (212) 759-7003; fax (212) 355-9455; e-mail ukraine@un.int; internet www.un.int/ukraine; VOLODYMYR YELCHENKO.

United Arab Emirates: 747 Third Ave, 36th Floor, New York, NY 10017; tel. (212) 371-0480; fax (212) 371-4923; e-mail uae@un.int; MOHAMMAD JASIM SAMHAN.

United Kingdom: 1 Dag Hammarskjöld Plaza, 885 2nd Ave, New York, NY 10017; tel. (212) 745-9200; fax (212) 745-9316; e-mail uk@un.int; internet www.ukun.org; Sir JEREMY GREENSTOCK.

USA: 799 United Nations Plaza, New York, NY 10017; tel. (212) 415-4000; fax (212) 415-4443; e-mail usa@un.int; internet www.un.int/usa; JOHN S. NEGROPONTE (designate).

Uruguay: 747 Third Ave, 21st Floor, New York, NY 10017; tel. (212) 752-8240; fax (212) 593-0935; e-mail uruguay@un.int; internet www.un.int/uruguay; JORGE PÉREZ-OTERMIN.

Uzbekistan: 866 United Nations Plaza, Suite 326, New York, NY 10017; tel. (212) 486-4242; fax (212) 486-7998; e-mail uzbekistan@un.int; ALISHER VOHIDOV.

Vanuatu: 866 United Nations Plaza, 3rd Floor, New York, NY 10017; tel. (212) 425-9600; fax (212) 425-9653; e-mail vanuatu@un.int; Chargé d'affaires a.i. SELWYN ARUTANGAI.

Venezuela: 335 East 46th St, New York, NY 10017; tel. (212) 557-2055; fax (212) 557-3528; e-mail venezuela@un.int; internet www.un.int/venezuela; MILOS ALCALAY.

Viet Nam: 866 United Nations Plaza, Suite 435, New York, NY 10017; tel. (212) 644-0594; fax (212) 644-5732; e-mail vietnam@un.int; internet www.un.int/vietnam; NGUYEN THANH CHAU.

Yemen: 413 East 51st St, New York, NY 10022; tel. (212) 355-1730; fax (212) 750-9613; e-mail yemen@un.int; ABDALLA SALEH AL-ASHTAL.

Yugoslavia: 854 Fifth Ave, New York, NY 10021; tel. (212) 879-8700; fax (212) 879-8705; e-mail yugoslavia@un.int; internet www.un.int/yugoslavia; DEJAN SAHOVIĆ.

Zambia: 800 Second Ave, 9th Floor, New York, NY 10017; tel. (212) 972-7200; fax (212) 972-7360; e-mail zambianmission@msn.com; MWELWA C. MUSAMBACHI.

Zimbabwe: 128 East 56th St, New York, NY 10022; tel. (212) 980-9511; fax (212) 308-6705; e-mail zimbabwe@un.int; T. J. B. JOKONYA.

OBSERVERS

Non-member states, inter-governmental organizations, etc., which have received an invitation to participate in the sessions and the work of the General Assembly as Observers, maintaining permanent offices at the UN.

Non-member states

Holy See: 25 East 39th St, New York, NY 10016; tel. (212) 370-7885; fax (212) 370-9622; e-mail holysee@un.int; Most Rev. RENATO RAFFAELE MARTINO, Titular Archbishop of Segermes.

Switzerland: 633 Third Ave, 29th Floor, New York, NY 10017; tel. (212) 286-1540; fax (212) 286-1555; e-mail switzerland@un.int.; JENO C. A. STAEHELIN.

Inter-governmental organizations*

Asian-African Legal Consultative Committee: 404 East 66th St, Apt 12c, New York, NY 10021; tel. (212) 734-7608; e-mail aalcc@un.int; K. BHAGWAT-SINGH.

Caribbean Community: 97-40 62nd Drive, 15K, Rego Park, NY 11374-1336; tel. and fax (718) 896-1179; e-mail caribcomun@un.int; HAMID MOHAMMED.

Commonwealth Secretariat: 800 Second Ave, 4th Floor, New York, NY 10017; tel. (212) 599-6190; fax (212) 972-3970; e-mail chogrm@aol.com.

European Community: Delegation of the European Commission, 3 Dag Hammarskjöld Plaza, 12th Floor, 305 East 47th St, New York, NY 10017; tel. (212) 371-3804; fax (212) 758-2718; e-mail ec@un.int; Liaison Office of the General Secretariat of the Council of Ministers of the European Union, 345 East 46th St, 6th Floor, New York, NY 10017; tel. (212) 292-8600; fax (212) 681-6266; the Observer is the Permanent Representative to the UN of the country currently exercising the Presidency of the Council of Ministers of the European Union.

La Francophonie: 801 Second Ave, Suite 605, New York, NY 10017; tel. (212) 867-6771; fax (212) 867-3840; e-mail francophonie @un.int; RIDHA BOUABID.

International Organization for Migration: 122 East 42nd St, Suite 1610, New York, NY 10168; tel. (212) 681-7000; fax (212) 867-5887; e-mail unobserver@iom.int; ROBERT G. PAIVA.

International Seabed Authority: 1 United Nations Plaza, Room 1140, New York, NY 10017; tel. (212) 963-6470; fax (212) 963-0908.

International Tribunal for the Law of the Sea: 1 United Nations Plaza, Room 1140, New York, NY 10017, tel. (212) 963-6480; fax (212) 963-0908.

League of Arab States: 747 Third Ave, 35th Floor, New York, NY 10017; tel. (212) 838-8700; fax (212) 355-3909; e-mail las@un.int; Dr HUSSEIN A. HASSOUNA.

Organization of African Unity: 346 East 50th St, New York, NY 10022; tel. (212) 319-5490; fax (212) 319-7135; e-mail oau@un.int; AMADOU KÉBÉ.

Organization of the Islamic Conference: 130 East 40th St, 5th Floor, New York, NY 10016; tel. (212) 883-0140; fax (212) 883-0143; e-mail oic@un.int; internet www.un.int/oic; MOKHTAR LAMANI.

* The following inter-governmental organizations have a standing invitation to participate as Observers, but do not maintain permanent offices at the United Nations:
   African, Caribbean and Pacific Group of States
   African Development Bank
   Agency for the Prohibition of Nuclear Weapons in Latin America and the Caribbean
   Andean Community
   Association of Caribbean States
   Central American Integration System
   Commonwealth of Independent States
   Council of Europe
   Economic Co-operation Organization
   International Criminal Police Organization (Interpol)
   Latin American Economic System
   Latin American Parliament
   Organisation for Economic Co-operation and Development
   Organization for Security and Co-operation in Europe
   Organization of American States
   Permanent Court of Arbitration
   Pacific Islands Forum

Other observers

International Committee of the Red Cross: 801 Second Ave, 18th Floor, New York, NY 10017; tel. (212) 599-6021; fax (212) 599-6009; e-mail redcrosscommittee@un.int; SYLVIE JUNOD.

International Federation of Red Cross and Red Crescent Societies: 800 Second Ave, 3rd Floor, Suite 355, New York, NY 10017; tel. (212) 338-0161; fax (212) 338-9832; e-mail redcross@un.int; ENTCHO GOSPODINOV.

Palestine: 115 East 65th St, New York, NY 10021; tel. (212) 288-8500; fax (212) 517-2377; e-mail mission@palestine-un.org; internet www.palestine-un.org; Dr NASSER AL-KIDWA.

Sovereign Military Order of Malta: 416 East 47th St, 8th Floor, New York, NY 10017; tel. (212) 355-6213; fax (212) 355-4014; e-mail sm-malta@un.int; JOSÉ ANTONIO LINATI-BOSCH.

United Nations Information Centres/Services

Afghanistan: (temporarily inactive).

Algeria: 9A rue Emile Payen, Hydra, Algiers; tel. (2) 691212; fax (2) 692315; e-mail unic.dz@undp.org.

Argentina: Junín 1940, 1°, 1113 Buenos Aires; tel. (1) 803-7671; fax (1) 804-7545; e-mail buenosaires@unic.org.ar; internet www .unic.org.ar (also covers Uruguay).

Australia: POB 4045, 46-48 York St, 5th Floor, Sydney, NSW 2001; tel. (2) 9262-5111; fax (2) 9262-5886; e-mail unsyd@ozemail.com.au (also covers Fiji, Kiribati, Nauru, New Zealand, Samoa, Tonga, Tuvalu and Vanuatu).

Austria: POB 500, Vienna International Centre, 1400 Vienna; tel. (1) 26060-4666; fax (1) 26060-5899; e-mail unis@ununis.un.or.at; internet www.unis.unvienna.org (also covers Hungary, Slovakia and Slovenia).

Bahrain: POB 26004, Villa 131, Rd 2803, Segaya, Manama; tel. (973) 231-046; fax (973) 270-749; e-mail unic@batelco.com.bh (also covers Qatar and the United Arab Emirates).

Bangladesh: POB 3658, House 60, Rd 11A, Dhanmondi, Dhaka 1209; tel. (2) 8118600; fax (2) 8112343; e-mail unicdha@citechco.net.

Belgium: Montoyerstraat 14, 1000 Brussels; tel. (2) 289-28-90; fax (2) 502-40-61; e-mail unicbel@be.psinet.com; internet www.uno.be (also covers Luxembourg and the Netherlands).

Bolivia: Apdo 9072, Avda Mariscal, Santa Cruz No. 1350, La Paz; tel. (2) 358590; fax (2) 391368; e-mail unicbol@cos.pnud.bo.

Brazil: Palacio Itamaraty, Avda Marechal Floriano 196, 20080-002 Rio de Janeiro; tel. (21) 253-2211; fax (21) 233-5753; e-mail nacoes.unidas@openlink.com.br.

Burkina Faso: PB 135, ave Georges Konseiga, Secteur no 4, Ouagadougou; tel. (3) 306076; fax (3) 311322; e-mail cinu.oui@fasonet.bf (also covers Chad, Mali and Niger).

Burundi: PB 2160, ave de la Révolution 117, Bujumbura; tel. (2) 225018; fax (2) 241798; e-mail unicbuj@cni.cbinf.com.

Cameroon: PB 836, Immeuble Kamdem, rue Joseph Clère, Yaoundé; tel. 22-50-43; fax 23-51-73; e-mail unic@camnet.com (also covers the Central African Republic and Gabon).

Chile: Edif. Naciones Unidas, Avda Dag Hammarskjöld, Casilla 179-D, Santiago; tel. (2) 210-2000; fax (2) 208-1946; e-mail dpisantiago@eclac.cl.

Colombia: Apdo Aéreo 058964; Calle 100, No. 8A–55, Of. 815, Santafé de Bogotá 2; tel. (1) 257-6044; fax (1) 257-6244; e-mail santafe@ccmail.unicc.org (also covers Ecuador and Venezuela).

Congo, Democratic Republic: PB 7248, Batîment Deuxième République, blvd du 30 juin, Kinshasa; tel. (12) 33431; fax (871) 150-3261; amisi.ramazani@undp.org.

Congo, Republic: POB 13210, ave Foch, Case ORTF 15, Brazzaville; tel. 814447; fax 812744.

Czech Republic: Panská 5, 110 00 Prague 1; e-mail unicprg@terminal.cz; internet www.unicprague.cz.

Denmark: Midtermolen 3, 2100 Copenhagen Ø; tel. 35-46-73-00; fax 35-46-73-01; e-mail unic@un.dk; internet www.un.dk (also covers Finland, Iceland, Norway and Sweden).

Egypt: POB 982, World Trade Centre, 1191 Corniche El Nil, Boulak, Cairo; tel. (2) 5315593; fax (2) 3553705; e-mail unic.eg@undp.org; internet www.un.org.eg/unic (also covers Saudi Arabia).

El Salvador: (temporarily inactive).

Ethiopia: POB 3001, Africa Hall, Addis Ababa; tel. (1) 515826; fax (1) 510365; e-mail ecainfo@un.org.

France: 1 rue Miollis, 75732 Paris Cédex 15; tel. 1-45-68-10-00; fax 1-43-06-46-78; e-mail unic.paris@unesco.org; internet www.onu.fr.

Germany: 53175 Bonn, Haus Cartanjen, Martin-Luther-King-Str. 8; 53153 Bonn; tel. (228) 815-2770; fax (228) 815-2777; e-mail unic@uno.de; internet www.uno.de.

Ghana: POB 2339, Gamel Abdul Nassar/Liberia Roads, Accra; tel. (21) 666851; fax (21) 665578; e-mail unicar@ncs.com.gh (also covers Sierra Leone).

Greece: 36 Amalia Ave, 105 58; Athens; tel. (1) 5230640; fax (1) 5233639; e-mail unicgre@mbox.unicc.org; internet www.unic.gr (also covers Cyprus and Israel).

India: 55 Lodi Estate, New Delhi 110 003; tel. (11) 462-8877; fax (11) 462-0293; internet www.unic.org.in (also covers Bhutan).

Indonesia: Gedung Dewan Pers, 5th Floor, 32–34 Jalan Kebon Sirih, Jakarta; tel. (21) 3800292; fax (21) 3800274; e-mail unicjak@rad.net.id.

Iran: POB 15875-4557; 185 Ghaem Magham Farahani Ave, Tehran 15868; tel. (21) 873-1534; fax (21) 204-4523; e-mail iali@unic.un.or.ir.

Italy: Palazzetto Venezia, Piazza San Marco 50, 00186 Rome; tel. (06) 6785907; fax (06) 6789907; fax (06) 6997337; e-mail onuitalia@onuitalia.it; internet www.onuitalia.it (also covers the Holy See, Malta and San Marino).

Japan: UNU Bldg, 8th Floor, 53-70 Jingumae S-chome, Shibuya-ku, Tokyo 150 0001; tel. (3) 5467-4451; fax (3) 5467-4455; e-mail unictok@blue.ocn.ne.jp; internet www.unic.or.jp (also covers Palau).

Kenya: POB 30552, United Nations Office, Gigiri, Nairobi; tel. (2) 623292; fax (2) 624349 (also covers Seychelles and Uganda).

Lebanon: Riad es-Solh Sq., POB 4656, Chouran, Beirut; tel. (1) 981301; fax (1) 981516 (also covers Jordan, Kuwait and Syria).

Lesotho: POB 301; Letsie Rd, Food Aid Compound, behind Hotel Victoria, Maseru 100; tel. 312496; fax 310042; e-mail fo.lso@undp.org.

Libya: POB 286, Shara Muzzafar al-Aftas, Hay al-Andalous, Tripoli; tel. (21) 4777885; fax (21) 4777343; e-mail fo.lby@undp.org.

Madagascar: PB 1348, 22 rue Rainitovo, Antasahavola, Antananarivo; tel. (2) 24115; fax (2) 33315; internet www.onu.dts.mg.

Mexico: Presidente Masaryk 29, 6°, México 11 570, DF; tel. (5) 250-1364; fax (5) 203-8638; e-mail infounic@un.org.mx; internet www.cinu.org.mx (also covers Cuba and the Dominican Republic).

Morocco: PB 601, zankat Tarik Ibnou Zind (Angle rue Roudana) 6, Rabat; tel. (7) 7686-33; fax (7) 7683-77; internet www.cinu.org.ma.

Myanmar: POB 230, 6 Natmauk Rd, Yangon; tel. (1) 292619; fax (1) 292911; e-mail myanmar@undp.org.

Namibia: Private Bag 13351, Paratus Bldg, 372 Independence Ave, Windhoek; tel. (61) 233034; fax (61) 233036; e-mail unic@un.na.

Nepal: POB 107, UN House, Kathmandu; tel. (1) 524366; fax (1) 523991; e-mail registrynp@undp.org.

Nicaragua: Apdo 3260, Palacio de la Cultura, Managua; tel. (2) 664253; fax (2) 222362; e-mail cedoc@sdnnic.org.ni.

Nigeria: POB 1068, 17 Kingsway Rd, Ikoyi, Lagos; tel. 269-4886; fax (1) 269-934; e-mail uniclag@unic.org.ng.

Pakistan: POB 1107, House No. 26, 88th St, G-6/3, Islamabad; tel. (51) 270610; fax (51) 271856; e-mail unic@isb.paknet; com.pk; internet www.un.org.pk/unic/unic.htm.

Panama: POB 6-9083, El Dorado; Banco Central Hispano Edif., Calle Gerardo Ortega y Av. Samuel Lewis, Panama City; tel. (7) 233-0557; fax (7) 223-2198; e-mail cinup@sinfo.net; internet www.onu.org.pa/cinup.

Paraguay: Casilla de Correo 1107, Edif. City, 3°, Asunción; tel. (21) 493025; fax (21) 449611; e-mail unic@undp.org.py.

Peru: POB 14-0199, Lord Cochrane 130, San Isidro, Lima 27; tel. (1) 441-8745; fax (1) 441-8735; e-mail informes@uniclima.org.pe.

Philippines: NEDA Bldg, Ground Floor, 106 Amorsolo St, Legaspi Village, Makati City, Manila; tel. (2) 8920611; fax (2) 8163011; e-mail unic-mla@philonline.com (also covers Papua New Guinea and Solomon Islands).

Poland: 00-608 Warsaw, Al. Niepodległości 186; 02-514 Warsaw, POB 1; tel. (22) 8259245; fax (22) 8255785; internet www.unic.un.org.pl.

Portugal: Rua Latino Coelho No. 1, Edif. Aviz, Bloco A1, 10°, 1000 Lisbon; tel. (1) 319-0790; fax (1) 352-0559; e-mail lisbon@ccmail.unicc.org; internet www.onuportugal.pt.

Romania: POB 1-701, 16 Aurel Vlaic St, Bucharest; tel. (1) 2113242; fax (1) 2113506; e-mail unic@undp.ro.

Russia: 4/16 Glazovsky Per., Moscow; tel. (095) 241-2894; fax (095) 230-2138; e-mail dpi-moscow@unic.ru; internet www.unic.ru.

Senegal: PB 154, Immeuble UNESCO, 12 ave Roume, Dakar; tel. 823-30-70; fax 822-26-79; e-mail loum@sonatel.senet.net (also covers Cape Verde, Côte d'Ivoire, The Gambia, Guinea, Guinea-Bissau and Mauritania).

South Africa: Metro Park Bldg, 351 Schoeman St, POB 12677, Pretoria 0126; tel. (12) 320-1110; fax (12) 320-1122; e-mail unic@un.org.za.

Spain: Avda General Perón 32-1°, 28020 Madrid; tel. (91) 5558087; fax (91) 5971231; e-mail unicspa@mbox.unicc.org.

Sri Lanka: POB 1505, 202–204 Bauddhaloka Mawatha, Colombo 7; tel. (1) 580691; fax (1) 581116.

Sudan: POB 913, UN Compound, Gamma'a Ave, Khartoum; tel. (11) 773772; fax (11) 773722 (also covers Somalia).

Switzerland: Palais des Nations, 1211 Geneva 10; tel. (22) 917-2300, fax (22) 917-0030; e-mail dpi_geneva@unog.ch; internet www.unog.ch/unis/unis1.htm (also covers Bulgaria).

Tanzania: POB 9224, Old Boma Bldg, Morogoro Rd/Sokoine Drive, Dar es Salaam; tel. (51) 119510; fax (51) 112923; e-mail unic.urt@raha.com.

Thailand: ESCAP, United Nations Bldg, Rajdamnern Ave, Bangkok 10200; tel. (2) 288-1234; fax (2) 288-1000; (also covers Cambodia, Hong Kong, Laos, Malaysia, Singapore and Viet Nam).

Togo: PB 911, 107 blvd du 13 janvier, Lomé; tel. and fax 212306; e-mail cinu@rdd.tg (also covers Benin).

Trinidad and Tobago: POB 130, Bretton Hall, 16 Victoria Ave, Port of Spain; tel. 623-4813; fax 623-4332; e-mail unicpos@opus.co (also covers Antigua and Barbuda, the Bahamas, Barbados, Belize, Dominica, Grenada, Guyana, Jamaica, the Netherlands Antilles, Saint Christopher and Nevis, Saint Lucia, Saint Vincent and the Grenadines and Suriname).

Tunisia: PB 863, 61 blvd Bab-Benat, Tunis; tel. (1) 560-203; fax (1) 568-811; e-mail unic.tunis@planet.tn; internet www.unic-tunis.intl.tn.

Turkey: PK 407, 197 Atatürk Bulvarı, Ankara; tel. (312) 4268113; fax (312) 4689719; e-mail unic@un.org.tr; internet www.un.org.tr/unic.html.

United Kingdom: Millbank Tower, 21st Floor, 21-24 Millbank, London, SW1P 4QH; tel. (20) 7630-1981; fax (20) 7976-6478; e-mail info@uniclondon.org; internet www.unitednations.org.uk (also covers Ireland).

USA: 1775 K St, NW, Suite 400, Washington, DC 20006; tel. (202) 331-8670; fax (202) 331-9191; e-mail unicwash@unicwash.org; internet www.unicwash.org.

Yemen: POB 237, Handhal St, 4 Al-Boniya Arca, San'a; tel. (1) 274000; fax (1) 274043; e-mail unicyem@ynet.ye.

Zambia: POB 32905, Lusaka 10101; tel. (1) 228487; fax (1) 222958; unic@zamnet.zam (also covers Botswana, Malawi and Swaziland).

Zimbabwe: POB 4408, Sanders House, 2nd Floor, First St/Jason Moyo Ave, Harare; tel. (4) 777060; fax (4) 750476.

OTHER UNITED NATIONS OFFICES

Armenia: 375001 Yerevan, 14 Karl Libknekht St, 1st Floor; tel. and fax (2) 15-16-47; e-mail dpiarm@arminco.com; internet www.undpi.am.

Azerbaijan: 370001 Baku, 3 Isteglialiyat St; tel. and fax (12) 98-32-35; e-mail office@un.azeri.com.

Belarus: 220050 Minsk, 17 Kirov St, 6th Floor; tel. 2278149; fax 22260340; e-mail un_undp@un.minsk.by; internet www.un.minsk.by.

Eritrea: POB 5366, Andinet St, Zone 4 Admin. 07, Airport Rd, Asmara; tel. (1) 182166; fax (1) 1801081; e-mail fo.eri@undp.org.

Georgia: 380079 Tbilisi, Eristavi St 9; tel. (32) 998558; fax (32) 250271; e-mail registry.ge@undp.org.ge.

Kazakhstan: 480100 Almaty, c/o KIMEP, 4 Abai Ave; tel. (3272) 64-26-18; fax (3272) 64-26-08; e-mail vp@un.almaty.kz.

Ukraine: 252020 Kiev, 6 Klovsky Uzviz, 1; tel. (44) 293-34-12; fax (44) 293-26-07; e-mail fo.ukr@undp.org; internet www.un.kiev.ua.

Uzbekistan: 700029 Tashkent, 4 Taras Shevchenko St; tel. (371) 139-48-35; fax (371) 120-62-91; e-mail fouzb@fouzb.undp.org.

Finance

The majority of the UN's peace-keeping operations (q.v.) are financed separately from the UN's regular budget by assessed contributions from member states.

In recent years the UN has suffered financial difficulties, owing to an expansion of the organization's political and humanitarian activities and delay on the part of member states in paying their contributions. In 1993 the UN Secretary-General formulated a series of economy measures to be applied throughout the organization, in order to avert a financial crisis. However, the fragility of the UN's financial situation persisted, partly owing to delays in the process between approval of a peace-keeping operation and receipt of contributions for that budget. In 1997 a US business executive announced a donation of US $1,000m., to be paid in regular instalments over a 10-year period, to finance humanitarian and environmental programmes. A UN International Partnership Trust Fund was established to administer the donation. At 31 December 2000 members owed the UN some $2,258m., of which $222m. was for the regular budget, $1,989m. for peace-keeping operations and $47m. for international tribunals. During that month the General Assembly approved a restructuring of scale of assessment calculations, the methodology and accuracy of which had been contested in recent years, particularly by the USA, which owed about two-thirds of the unpaid contributions. For the period 2001–03 the level of US contributions to the regular annual budget was to be reduced from 25% to 22%, while annual contributions were to be raised for several nations with rapidly developing economies.

In 1997 the UN Secretary-General pledged to implement administrative reforms of the UN and proposed a reduction in the organization's budget. The budget for the two-year period 1998–99 amounted to US $2,532m., compared with the 1996–97 total of $2,712m. (later revised to $2,542m.). A Development Account was established in December 1997 under the Secretary-General's reform programme; administrative savings were to be channelled through this to finance development projects. In late 1999 the Secretary-General stated that a further reduction in the UN budget would compromise the organization's capacity to implement mandated activities. The budget for 2000–01 totalled $2,536m. Some 1,000 administrative posts were to be cut during this period.

TWO-YEAR BUDGET OF THE UNITED NATIONS (US $'000)

	2000–01
Overall policy-making, direction and co-ordination	473,645.3
Political affairs	231,586.3
International justice and law	55,386.8
International co-operation for development	268,767.9
Regional co-operation for development	347,230.4
Human rights and humanitarian affairs	123,613.1
Public information	143,605.5
Common support services	441,857.4
Internal oversight	19,220.6
Jointly-financed activities and special expenses	60,845.5
Capital expenditures	42,617.4
Staff assessment	314,248.0
Development Account	13,065.0
Total	**2,535,689.2**

United Nations Publications

Africa Recovery (quarterly).

Annual Report of the Secretary-General on the Work of the Organization.

Basic Facts About the United Nations.

Demographic Yearbook.

Development Update (2 a month).

Energy Statistics Yearbook.

Index to Proceedings (of the General Assembly; the Security Council; the Economic and Social Council; the Trusteeship Council).

Monthly Bulletin of Statistics.

Population and Vital Statistics Report (quarterly).

Statistical Yearbook.

The UN Chronicle (quarterly).

United Nations Disarmament Yearbook.

United Nations Juridical Yearbook.

World Economic and Social Survey.

Yearbook of the International Law Commission.

Yearbook of the United Nations.

Other UN publications are listed in the chapters dealing with the agencies concerned.

Secretariat

According to the UN Charter the Secretary-General is the chief administrative officer of the organization, and he may appoint further Secretariat staff as required. The principal departments and officers of the Secretariat are listed below. The chief administrative staff of the UN Regional Commissions and of all the subsidiary organs of the UN are also members of the Secretariat staff and are listed in the appropriate chapters. The Secretariat staff also includes a number of special missions and special appointments, including some of senior rank.

In November 2000 the total number of staff of the Secretariat holding appointments continuing for a year or more was approximately 13,891, including those serving away from the headquarters, but excluding staff working for the UN specialized agencies and subsidiary organs.

In July 1997 the Secretary-General initiated a comprehensive reform of the administration of the UN and abolished some 1,000 Secretariat posts. A Senior Management Group was established as part of a new Secretariat leadership and management structure, to enhance day-to-day efficiency and accountability. The reforms aimed to restructure the Secretariat's substantive work programme around the UN's five core missions, i.e. peace and security, economic and social affairs, development co-operation, humanitarian affairs and human rights. During 1997 the Centre for Human Rights and the Office of the High Commissioner for Human Rights were consolidated into a single office under the reform process, while a new Office for Drug Control and Crime Prevention was established, within the framework of the UN Office in Vienna, to integrate efforts to combat crime, drug abuse and terrorism. A new Office of the Iraq Programme was established in October to undertake and co-ordinate activities relating to the oil-for-food programme (see Security Council, p. 14). In December the General Assembly endorsed a recommendation of the Secretary-General to create the position of Deputy Secretary-General, who was to assist in the management of Secretariat operations, in particular the ongoing reform process, and represent the Secretary-General as required.

SECRETARY-GENERAL
KOFI ANNAN (Ghana).

DEPUTY SECRETARY-GENERAL
LOUISE FRÉCHETTE (Canada).

EXECUTIVE OFFICE OF THE SECRETARY-GENERAL
Under-Secretary-General, Chief of Staff: S. IQBAL RIZA (Pakistan).

Assistant Secretary-General, Special Adviser: JOHN G. RUGGIE.

Assistant Secretary-General, External Relations: GILLIAN SORENSEN (USA).

DEPARTMENT FOR DISARMAMENT AFFAIRS
Under-Secretary-General: JAYANTHA DHANAPALA (Sri Lanka).

DEPARTMENT OF ECONOMIC AND SOCIAL AFFAIRS
Under-Secretary-General: NITIN DESAI (India).

Assistant Secretary-General, Special Adviser on Gender Issues and the Advancement of Women: ANGELA KING (Jamaica).

Assistant Secretary-General, Policy Co-ordination and Inter-Agency Affairs: PATRIZIO CIVILI (Italy).

DEPARTMENT OF GENERAL ASSEMBLY AFFAIRS AND CONFERENCE SERVICES

Under-Secretary-General: JIN YONGJIAN (China).

Assistant Secretary-General: FEDERICO RIESCO (Chile).

DEPARTMENT OF MANAGEMENT

Under-Secretary-General: JOSEPH E. CONNOR (USA).

Assistant Secretary-General, Controller: JEAN-PIERRE HALBWACHS (Mauritius).

Assistant Secretary-General, Human Resources: RAFIAH SALIM (Malaysia).

Assistant Secretary-General, Central Support: TOSHIYUKI NIWA (Japan).

DEPARTMENT OF PEACE-KEEPING OPERATIONS

Under-Secretary-General: JEAN-MARIE GUÉHENNO (France).

Assistant Secretary-General: HÉDI ANNABI (Tunisia).

Assistant Secretary-General: HOCINE MEDILI (acting) (Algeria).

DEPARTMENT OF POLITICAL AFFAIRS

Under-Secretary-General: Sir KIERAN PRENDERGAST (United Kingdom).

Assistant Secretary-General: DANILO TÜRK (Slovenia).

Assistant Secretary-General: IBRAHIMA FALL (Senegal).

DEPARTMENT OF PUBLIC INFORMATION

Under-Secretary-General: (vacant).

OFFICE FOR THE CO-ORDINATION OF HUMANITARIAN AFFAIRS

Under-Secretary-General for Humanitarian Affairs and Emergency Relief Co-ordinator: KENZO OSHIMA (Japan).

OFFICE FOR DRUG CONTROL AND CRIME PREVENTION

Under-Secretary-General: PINO ARLACCHI (Italy).

OFFICE OF INTERNAL OVERSIGHT SERVICES

Under-Secretary-General: DILEEP NAIR (Singapore).

OFFICE OF THE IRAQ PROGRAMME

Assistant Secretary-General: BENON V. SEVAN (Cyprus).

OFFICE OF LEGAL AFFAIRS

Under-Secretary-General, The Legal Counsel: HANS CORELL (Sweden).

OFFICE OF SECURITY CO-ORDINATION

Assistant Secretary-General: BENON V. SEVAN (Cyprus).

OFFICE OF THE SPECIAL REPRESENTATIVE OF THE SECRETARY-GENERAL FOR CHILDREN AND ARMED CONFLICT

Under-Secretary-General: OLARA OTUNNU (Uganda).

OFFICE OF THE UNITED NATIONS HIGH COMMISSIONER FOR HUMAN RIGHTS

Address: Palais des Nations, 1211 Geneva 10, Switzerland.

Telephone: (22) 9179353; **fax:** (22) 9179012; **internet:** www.unhchr.ch.

High Commissioner: MARY ROBINSON (Ireland).

GENEVA OFFICE

Address: Palais des Nations, 1211 Geneva 10, Switzerland.

Telephone: (22) 9171234; 412962; **fax:** (22) 9170123; **internet:** www.unog.ch.

Director-General: VLADIMIR PETROVSKY (Russia).

NAIROBI OFFICE

Address: POB 30552, Nairobi, Kenya.

Telephone: (2) 623292; **fax:** (2) 624349.

Director-General: KLAUS TÖPFER (Germany).

VIENNA OFFICE

Address: Vienna International Centre, POB 500, 1400 Vienna, Austria.

Telephone: (1) 26060-4266; **fax:** (1) 26060-5819; **internet:** www.un.or.at.

Director-General: PINO ARLACCHI (Italy).

General Assembly

The General Assembly was established as a principal organ of the United Nations under the UN Charter (see p. 19). It first met on 10 January 1946. It is the main deliberative organ of the United Nations, and the only one composed of representatives of all the UN member states. Each delegation consists of not more than five representatives and five alternates, with as many advisers as may be required. The Assembly meets regularly for three months each year, and special sessions may also be held. It has specific responsibility for electing the Secretary-General and members of other UN councils and organs, and for approving the UN budget and the assessments for financial contributions by member states. It is also empowered to make recommendations (but not binding decisions) on questions of international security and co-operation.

After the election of its President and other officers, the Assembly opens its general debate, a three-week period during which the head of each delegation makes a formal statement of his or her government's views on major world issues. The Assembly then begins examination of the principal items on its agenda: it acts directly on a few agenda items, but most business is handled by the six Main Committees (listed below), which study and debate each item and present draft resolutions to the Assembly. After a review of the report of each Main Committee, the Assembly formally approves or rejects the Committee's recommendations. On designated 'important questions', such as recommendations on international peace and security, the admission of new members to the United Nations, or budgetary questions, a two-thirds majority is needed for adoption of a resolution. Other questions may be decided by a simple majority. In the Assembly, each member has one vote. Voting in the Assembly is sometimes replaced by an effort to find consensus among member states, in order to strengthen support for the Assembly's decisions: the President consults delegations in private to find out whether they are willing to agree to adoption of a resolution without a vote; if they are, the President can declare that a resolution has been so adopted.

Special sessions of the Assembly may be held to discuss issues which require particular attention (e.g. illicit drugs) and 'emergency special sessions' may also be convened to discuss situations on which the UN Security Council has been unable to reach a decision (for example, in 2000 on Israel's construction of new settlements in east Jerusalem). A special session of the Assembly entitled Gender Equality, Development and Peace for the 21st Century, reviewing the UN Fourth World Conference on Women, held at Beijing, People's Republic of China, in 1995, was convened in June 2000. During that month a special session reviewing the World Summit for Social Development, held at Copenhagen in 1995, was also convened. Two special sessions were scheduled to take place in June 2001: the first was to assess the outcome of the UN Conference on Human Settlements (Habitat II, held in Istanbul, Turkey, in 1996), and the second was to consider issues related to the global epidemic of HIV/AIDS. In September 2001 the General Assembly was to convene a special session on children, with the aim of reviewing progress made since the World Summit for Children, held in 1990, and the adoption in 1989 of the Convention on the Rights of the Child.

The Assembly's 55th session was designated as the Millennium Assembly. In early September 2000 a Millennium Summit of UN heads of state or government was convened to debate 'The Role of the United Nations in the 21st Century'. The Millennium Summit issued a declaration identifying the values, principles and goals that should guide the organization in key areas including peace, development, environment, human rights, protection of the vulnerable, and the special needs of the African continent; and specified six fundamental values underlying international relations: freedom; equality; solidarity; tolerance; respect for nature; and a sense of shared responsibility for the global economy and social development. Reform of the Security Council and the need for increased UN co-operation with the private sector, non-governmental organizations and civil society in pursuing its goals were addressed in the Declaration. It also requested regular reviews of the summit.

In September 1992 the Federal Republic of Yugoslavia (which in April had formally replaced the Socialist Federal Republic of Yugoslavia, although comprising only two of the six former Yugoslav republics) was suspended from the proceedings of the General Assembly. The Assembly required the new Yugoslav state to apply to occupy the former Yugoslavia's seat in the UN. This was achieved in November 2000. Following the successful conclusion of democratic elections, South Africa was readmitted to the Assembly in June 1994.

President of 55th Session (from September 2000): HARRI HOL-KERI (Finland).

MAIN COMMITTEES

There are six Main Committees, on which all members have a right to be represented. Each Committee includes an elected Chairperson and two Vice-Chairs.

First Committee: Disarmament and International Security.

Second Committee: Economic and Financial.

Third Committee: Social, Humanitarian and Cultural.

Fourth Committee: Special Political and Decolonization.

Fifth Committee: Administrative and Budgetary.

Sixth Committee: Legal.

OTHER SESSIONAL COMMITTEES

General Committee: f. 1946; composed of 28 members, including the Assembly President, the 21 Vice-Presidents of the Assembly and the Chairs of the six Main Committees.

Credentials Committee: f. 1946; composed of nine members elected at each Assembly session.

POLITICAL AND SECURITY MATTERS

Special Committee on Peace-keeping Operations: f. 1965; 34 appointed members.

Disarmament Commission: f. 1978 (replacing body f. 1952); 61 members.

UN Scientific Committee on the Effects of Atomic Radiation: f. 1955; 21 members.

Committee on the Peaceful Uses of Outer Space: f. 1959; 61 members; has a Legal Sub-Committee and a Scientific and Technical Sub-Committee.

Ad Hoc Committee on the Indian Ocean: f. 1972; 44 members.

Committee on the Exercise of the Inalienable Rights of the Palestinian People: f. 1975; 25 members.

Special Committee on the Implementation of the Declaration on Decolonization: f. 1961; 24 members.

DEVELOPMENT

Commission on Science and Technology for Development: f. 1992; 33 members.

Committee on Energy and Natural Resources Development: f. 1998; 24 members.

United Nations Environment Programme (UNEP) Governing Council: f. 1972; 58 members (see p. 96).

LEGAL QUESTIONS

International Law Commission: f. 1947; 34 members elected for a five-year term; originally established in 1946 as the Committee on the Progressive Development of International Law and its Codification.

Advisory Committee on the UN Programme of Assistance in Teaching, Study, Dissemination and Wider Appreciation of International Law: f. 1965; 25 members.

UN Commission on International Trade Law: f. 1966; 36 members.

Special Committee on the Charter of the United Nations and on the Strengthening of the Role of the Organization: f. 1975; composed of all UN members.

There is also a UN Administrative Tribunal and a Committee on Applications for Review of Administrative Tribunal Judgments.

ADMINISTRATIVE AND FINANCIAL QUESTIONS

Advisory Committee on Administrative and Budgetary Questions: f. 1946; 16 members appointed for three-year terms.

Committee on Contributions: f. 1946; 18 members appointed for three-year terms.

International Civil Service Commission: f. 1972; 15 members appointed for four-year terms.

Committee on Information: f. 1978, formerly the Committee to review UN Policies and Activities; 95 members.

There is also a Board of Auditors, Investments Committee, UN Joint Staff Pension Board, Joint Inspection Unit, UN Staff Pension Committee, Committee on Conferences, and Committee for Programme and Co-ordination.

Security Council

The Security Council was established as a principal organ under the United Nations Charter (see p. 20); its first meeting was held on 17 January 1946. Its task is to promote international peace and security in all parts of the world.

MEMBERS

Permanent members:

People's Republic of China, France, Russia, United Kingdom, USA.

The remaining 10 members are normally elected (five each year) by the General Assembly for two-year periods (five countries from Africa and Asia, two from Latin America, one from eastern Europe, and two from western Europe and others).

Non-permanent members as at 1 January 2001:

Bangladesh, Jamaica, Mali, Tunisia, Ukraine (term expires 31 December 2001).

Colombia, Ireland, Mauritius, Norway, Singapore (term expires 31 December 2002).

Rotation of the Presidency in 2001:

Singapore (January); Tunisia (February); Ukraine (March); United Kingdom (April); United States (May); Bangladesh (June); China (July); Colombia (August); France (September); Ireland (October); Jamaica (November); Mali (December).

ORGANIZATION

The Security Council has the right to investigate any dispute or situation which might lead to friction between two or more countries,

and such disputes or situations may be brought to the Council's attention either by one of its members, by any member state, by the General Assembly, by the Secretary-General or even, under certain conditions, by a state which is not a member of the United Nations.

The Council has the right to recommend ways and means of peaceful settlement and, in certain circumstances, the actual terms of settlement. In the event of a threat to or breach of international peace or an act of aggression, the Council has powers to take 'enforcement' measures in order to restore international peace and security. These include severance of communications and of economic and diplomatic relations and, if required, action by air, land and sea forces.

All members of the United Nations are pledged by the Charter to make available to the Security Council, on its call and in accordance with special agreements, the armed forces, assistance and facilities necessary to maintain international peace and security. These agreements, however, have not yet been concluded.

The Council is organized to be able to function continuously. The Presidency of the Council is held monthly in turn by the member states in English alphabetical order. Each member of the Council has one vote. On procedural matters decisions are made by the affirmative vote of any nine members. For decisions on other matters the required nine affirmative votes must include the votes of the five permanent members. This is the rule of 'great power unanimity' popularly known as the 'veto' privilege. In practice, an abstention by one of the permanent members is not regarded as a veto. Any member, whether permanent or non-permanent, must abstain from voting in any decision concerning the pacific settlement of a dispute to which it is a party. Any member of the UN that is party to a dispute under consideration by the Council may participate in the Council's discussions without a vote.

ACTIVITIES

In January 1992 the first ever summit meeting of the Security Council was convened, and was attended by the heads of state or government of 13 of its 15 members, and by the ministers of foreign affairs of the remaining two. The subject of the summit meeting, which was presented in a report drafted by the Secretary-General (entitled 'An Agenda for Peace') was the UN's role in preventive diplomacy, peace-keeping and peace-making.

Consideration of reform of the Security Council commenced in 1993 at the 48th Session of the General Assembly, which established a Working Group to assess the issue. In October 1994 a general debate of the General Assembly revealed widespread support for expanding the Security Council to 20 seats and awarding permanent membership to Japan and Germany. In March the President of the General Assembly formally introduced a proposal for reform, which envisaged a Council consisting of 24 members, including five new permanent members and four new non-permanent members. In September 2000 the UN Millennium Summit declared support for continued discussions on reform of the Council. A summit meeting of the Council convened during the Millennium Summit issued a declaration on ensuring an effective role for the Council in maintaining international peace and security, with particular reference to Africa.

During 2000 the Security Council continued to monitor closely all existing peace-keeping missions and the situations in countries where missions were being undertaken, and to authorize extensions of their mandates accordingly. The mandates of the UN Mission in the Central African Republic (MINURCA), the UN Civilian Police Mission in Haiti (MIPONUH) and the UN Mission of Observers in Tajikistan (UNMOT) were terminated in 2000, in February, March and May, respectively. In July 2000 the Council authorized the establishment of the UN Mission in Ethiopia and Eritrea (UNMEE, see below). (For details of UN observer missions and peace-keeping operations, see pp. 59–65.) In early 2001 the Council was also monitoring and supporting efforts to secure peace in Afghanistan, the Democratic Republic of the Congo (DRC), Cyprus, East Timor, Georgia, Kosovo and Metohija, the Middle East, Sierra Leone, Somalia, Tajikistan and Western Sahara.

In September 1998 a special meeting of the Security Council adopted a resolution to strengthen the effectiveness of arms embargoes imposed against regimes and rebel groups in Africa. In July 1998 a new series of sanctions, which had been authorized by the Security Council in June, entered into effect against the UNITA rebels in Angola, owing to their failure to implement earlier Council resolutions demanding compliance with the obligations of the peace process in that country. Accordingly, states were required to 'freeze' all UNITA funds held within their territory, to prevent any official contacts with UNITA leaders, and to prohibit the receipt or sale of diamonds from areas not under government control. In subsequent resolutions the Council continued to blame UNITA for the impasse in the peace process in Angola. In mid-1999 the Council established two expert panels to consider UNITA's banking arrangements and sources of funding, and to investigate its supplies of armaments and use of foreign mercenaries. The establishment of a new UN Office in Angola to assist capacitiy building, to promote human rights, and to liaise with the political, military and civilian authorities was approved by the Council in October. In April 2000 the Council authorized the establishment of a temporary monitoring mechanism to investigate alleged violations of the sanctions against UNITA. In July the Council declared its support for a peace accord signed between the conflicting parties in Sierra Leone, and in October it authorized the establishment of The UN Mission in Sierra Leone. In July 2000 the Council voted to prohibit the exportation of all rough diamonds from Sierra Leone that had not been officially certified by that country's Government. In the following month the Council requested that the Secretary-General hold negotiations with the Sierra Leone authorities regarding the proposed establishment of an international tribunal to try those accused of committing crimes against humanity in that country. The Council's sanctions committee organized a public hearing in mid-2000 to assess the role played in the conflict by the illicit diamond trade; the participants included representatives of interested states, regional and international organizations, the global diamond industry and of civil society, as well as individual experts. (It had become evident that the ongoing conflicts in Sierra Leone and Angola were fuelled by rebel groups' illegal exploitation of diamond resources and use of the proceeds derived therefrom to purchase armaments.) In December a panel of experts appointed by the Council issued a report on the connections between the illicit exportation of diamonds from Sierra Leone and the international trade in armaments. In March 2001 the Council banned the purchase of diamonds exported from Liberia, and demanded that the Liberian authorities refrain from purchasing so-called 'conflict diamonds' from illegal sources and cease providing

support to rebel organizations, with particular refererence to the main rebel grouping active in Sierra Leone. The Council re-imposed an embargo on the sale or supply of armaments to Liberia (a previous arms embargo, implemented in 1992, was terminated) and imposed a travel ban on high-level Liberian government officials and their spouses. In June 1999 the Council urged all parties to the conflict in the DRC to maintain a cease-fire and participate in a new round of negotiations for a peaceful settlement and, in the following month, it declared its support for a cease-fire agreement concluded in that country. In September the Council authorized the deployment of up to 90 military personnel to assist with the implemenation of the agreement. The formation of the UN Observer Mission in the DRC (MONUC) was approved at the end of November. During 2000 the Council resolved to appoint an expert panel to study the reported illegal exploitation of resources in the DRC. In February 1999 the Council urged countries to impose a voluntary embargo on the sale or supply of armaments to Eritrea or Ethiopia, owing to an escalation in the conflict between those countries; a mandatory arms embargo was imposed in May 2000. In July the Council authorized the creation of the UN Mission In Ethiopia and Eritrea to assist with the implementation of a cease-fire accord concluded by the two countries in June.

In March 1998 the Council voted to impose an arms embargo against the Federal Republic of Yugoslavia, in order to accelerate a dialogue between the Serbian authorities and separatist forces in the province of Kosovo and Metohija, with regard to its political status. In September, following an escalation of hostilities in Kosovo, the Council reiterated previous demands for an immediate cease-fire, and called for the withdrawal of Serbian forces, provision for the safe return of civilians who had been displaced by the recent fighting, and the initiation of negotiations on self-rule for the ethnic Albanians in Kosovo. The Council also determined to consider further action if its demands were ignored, but omitted any explicit authorization for military intervention in that region. In late March 1999 an emergency meeting of the Security Council was convened following the initiation of an aerial offensive by NATO against the Federal Republic of Yugoslavia, which aimed to accelerate a peace settlement on the political future of Kosovo. A draft resolution, presented by Russia, condemning the action and demanding an immediate end to the bombing was rejected by a majority of Council members. In May the Council expressed regret at the bombing of the embassy of the People's Republic of China in Belgrade, the Federal Republic of Yugoslavia, by NATO military aircraft, and urged NATO to conduct a full investigation. In June the Council approved Resolution 1244, which served as the legal basis of an international agreement to end the conflict in Kosovo. The resolution provided for the withdrawal of Yugoslav forces from the province under the supervision of a new international security presence, which was to co-ordinate the demilitarization of Kosovo and establish a safe environment for the returning population. It also provided for the establishment of a civilian operation (the UN Interim Administration in Kosovo and Metohija—UNMIK) to co-ordinate humanitarian assistance and economic rehabilitation, maintain law and order, and supervise the establishment of new democratic institutions.

In June 1999 the Council formally established a UN mission to organize and supervise an impending popular consultation on the political future of East Timor. In early September the Council met in emergency session in response to the escalation of violence that had followed the referendum, which had been held on 30 August. The Council demanded that Indonesian forces restore order in the territory, and resolved to send a high-level delegation to discuss the peaceful implementation of the outcome of the referendum with the Indonesian authorities. In mid-September, following the Indonesian Government's agreement to allow foreign troops into East Timor, the Council authorized the establishment of a multinational force to restore peace and security in the territory, to protect and support UN personnel, and to facilitate humanitarian assistance operations. In October the Council established the UN Transitional Administration in East Timor (UNTAET) as the sole legitimate authority in the territory with responsibility to supervise the period of transition to independence. The existing UN mission was incorporated into UNTAET. In February 2000 the multinational force was replaced by the military component of UNTAET.

In mid-October 1999 the Council issued a resolution in which it condemned suspected illegal terrorist-related activities undertaken in Taliban-controlled areas of Afghanistan, including the training of terrorists and, in particular, the shielding of those suspected of organizing the bomb attacks against the US embassies in Kenya and Tanzania in August 1998. The Council demanded that the main suspects be extradited for trial and resolved to impose punitive measures against the Taliban authorities if these conditions were not met within one month. Consequently, an embargo on all Taliban-controlled overseas funds and international flights of the national airline entered into effect on 14 November 1999. In December 2000 the Council authorized the imposition of an arms embargo on the area of Afghanistan under Taliban control, and resolved that all member states should 'freeze' the funds and assets of all individuals and entities accused of complicity in the 1998 terrorist bombings. In addition the Council banned the supply to the Taliban-controlled area of a specific chemical believed to be used there in the production of illegal narcotic drugs. The new sanctions took effect in January 2001. In March 1998 the Security Council held an open meeting to discuss sanctions that had been imposed against Libya in 1992 and 1993 as a consequence of that country's refusal to extradite for trial two people (alleged to be Libyan intelligence agents) suspected of bombing a US passenger airline over the United Kingdom in 1988. In August 1998 the Council endorsed a proposal to convene a trial under Scottish jurisdiction at a court in the Netherlands, and resolved to suspend all punitive measures against Libya once the authorities in that country had surrendered the suspects. In April 1999, following a period of intensive negotiations, facilitated by the South African President, Nelson Mandela, and representatives of the Saudi Arabian Government, Libya released the two suspects, who were escorted to the Netherlands by the UN's Legal Counsel. On their arrival, and transfer to Scottish custody, the suspension of sanctions against Libya came into effect. The trial commenced in May 2000; in January 2001 one of the accused was acquitted and the other found guilty of complicity in the bombing. A condition of the termination of the sanctions was that Libya should 'demonstrate by concrete actions its renunciation of terrorism'; as the Libyan authorities continued to deny any liability for the Lockerbie attack following the January 2001 verdict, the sanctions were not immediately fully withdrawn.

In December 1996 the Security Council approved the implementation of Resolution 986, which was adopted in April 1995, to provide for the limited sale of Iraqi petroleum to enable the purchase of humanitarian supplies and the provision of contributions to the UN Compensation Committee (which had been established to settle claims against Iraq resulting from the Gulf War). Exports of petroleum up to a value of US $1,000m. every 90 days were to be permitted under the agreement; the Council was responsible for renewing the mandate of the agreement and for approving contracts for the sale of petroleum and the purchase of food and medical goods. The Council monitored the situation in Iraq throughout 1997 and received regular reports from the UN Special Commission (UNSCOM), which had been established in 1991 to monitor the disposal of weapons. In mid-1997 the Council criticized Iraqi interference and non-compliance with UNSCOM activities. In October UNSCOM proposed that further punitive measures be imposed on Iraq to force the Government to disclose its weapons programme. The Council adopted a resolution to threaten the imposition of new sanctions; however, the People's Republic of China, France and Russia abstained from the vote. A few days later Iraq announced that all US members of UNSCOM were obliged to leave the country, and rejected the use of US surveillance aircraft in the inspection programme. The Council issued a condemnation of the expulsion order, but was divided on the means of retaliation. In mid-November the Council voted unanimously to impose a travel ban on all Iraqi officials deemed to be responsible for disrupting UNSCOM's operations. Iraq responded by implementing the expulsion of the US element of UNSCOM (having postponed the order pending negotiations), prompting the UN to withdraw almost all of the 97-member inspection team from the country in protest. UNSCOM resumed its activities in late November, following intensive diplomatic efforts. However, by early 1998 the contentious issues regarding the composition of UNSCOM, and Iraq's refusal to grant unrestricted access to a substantial number of sensitive sites throughout the country, remained unresolved. In late January the Iraqi Government requested a suspension of UNSCOM activities, pending a technical evaluation of Iraq's weaponry by a multinational team of experts. The US and United Kingdom Governments attempted to generate support among Security Council members and other Governments in the Gulf region for the use of force, in the event of Iraq's continued refusal to co-operate with the inspection process, in order to destroy any Iraqi facilities for the manufacture of chemical, biological and nuclear weapons. In mid-February the Security Council authorized the UN Secretary-General to visit Iraq, in an attempt to resolve the escalating diplomatic crisis without resort to military confrontation. The Secretary-General concluded a Memorandum of Understanding (MoU) with the Iraqi authorities allowing UNSCOM inspectors unrestricted access to the disputed sites within Iraq. The Security Council endorsed the agreement in early March, but threatened the 'severest measures' if Iraq failed to comply with the MoU. In February the Council approved a resolution expanding the so-called oil-for-food programme to allow for sales of petroleum up to a value of $5,256m. every 180 days (superseding a resolution to extend the programme at its existing level, which was authorized in December 1997). The new agreement entered into force on 1 June 1998, following the Secretary-General's approval of a new distribution plan. At the end of June the Council adopted a resolution permitting states to authorize the limited export of essential equipment to enable Iraq to increase its petroleum production. In August the Council criticized Iraq's decision to suspend co-operation with UN

weapons inspectors, owing to renewed concern on the part of the Iraqi Government that UNSCOM was obstructing the removal of UN sanctions. UNSCOM resolved to continue to monitor sites already inspected, but suspended all new inspection activities. At the end of October a diplomatic crisis again arose following an announcement by the Iraq authorities that they would end all co-operation with UNSCOM until the Security Council had reviewed the sanctions measures in force against Iraq and removed the current UNSCOM Chairman, as part of a complete restructuring of that body. The Council condemned Iraq's action as a violation of earlier resolutions, and of the MoU concluded in February, but reiterated its willingness to conduct a comprehensive review of sanctions, as proposed by the UN Secretary-General, if Iraq resumed co-operation. With no agreement having been reached, all UN personnel were withdrawn from Iraq in mid-November. The anticipated military strikes against Iraq, however, were averted at the last minute following Iraq's decision to allow UNSCOM to resume normal tasks. At the end of November reports circulated that Iraq was continuing to withhold requested documents and to restrict access to certain military sites. In mid-December UNSCOM's chairman, Richard Butler, reported to the Security Council regarding Iraq's continued failure to co-operate with UN inspectors and ordered the withdrawal of all UNSCOM personnel from Iraq. The US and United Kingdom Governments responded to Butler's report by conducting extensive airstrikes against Iraqi military targets; however, their action was condemned by some governments for having been undertaken without explicit Security Council authorization. US and British military aircraft subsequently continued to patrol no-fly zones in northern and southern Iraq and conducted several airstrikes against military sites. During 1999 the future of UNSCOM remained uncertain, amidst allegations that it was used illegally to provide intelligence information to the US Government. In January the Security Council decided to establish three panels to review the disarmament process in Iraq, to assess the impact of UN sanctions on the Iraqi people and to investigate Kuwaiti civilians still unaccounted for having been taken hostage in 1990. In October 1999 the Council agreed to permit Iraq to generate a further $3,040m. in the next 180-day period of the oil-for-food agreement, accounting for the shortfall of authorized revenue that had not yet been generated. In November Iraq temporarily suspended its exports of petroleum under the oil-for-food agreement, in protest at the short-term extensions of the programme granted by the Security Council. In mid-December the Council approved a six-month extension of the programme. A few days later it adopted a resolution establishing a new policy towards Iraq. The resolution provided for an unlimited ceiling on petroleum exports under the agreed humanitarian programme, and for a suspension of sanctions dependent upon Iraq's co-operation with a new arms inspection body, the UN Monitoring, Verification and Inspection Commission (UNMOVIC). UNMOVIC replaced UNSCOM in March 2000. At the end of March the Council doubled the maximum permitted revenue that Iraq might use to purchase petroleum industry spare parts and other equipment under the ongoing programme. In March 2000, during a Council meeting on Iraq, the Secretary-General stated that the oil-for-food programme represented a moral dilemma for the UN as it appeared insufficiently to meet the humanitarian requirements of the Iraqi population. The UN's economic sanctions, which no longer commanded widespread international support and had prompted the resignations (in October 1998 and March 2000) of two successive Chief UN Relief Co-ordinators for Iraq as well as continuing opposition within the Council from the People's Republic of China, France and Russia, were robustly challenged by the Iraqi regime during 2000 and early 2001. In November 2000 Iraq demanded the right to impose a surcharge on its exports under the oil-for-food programme, and in January 2001 an oil pipeline between Iraq and Syria was reportedly re-opened without recourse to the Council's sanctions committee. In early December 2000 the Iraqi regime, while agreeing the terms of the next (ninth) 180-day phase of the programme, temporarily suspended exports of petroleum once again during a dispute with the sanctions committee over the pricing mechanism for its oil sales. It was reported in mid-December that the Iraqi administration had implemented the illicit surcharge. The Council urged buyers of Iraqi oil not to pay the premium. By early March 2001 UNMOVIC inspectors had not yet been admitted to Iraq. Unsuccessful talks on ending the deadlock concerning weapons inspections took place in February; negotiations were to be resumed in April.

The imposition of sanctions by the Security Council as a means of targeting regimes and groupings that are deemed to threaten international peace and security has increased significantly in recent years and has been subjected to widespread scrutiny regarding enforceability and the potential adverse humanitarian consequences for general populations. In the latter respect the Council has, since 1999, incorporated clauses on humanitarian assessment in its resolutions; the sanctions that took effect against the Taliban in Afghanistan in January 2001 (see above) were the first to entail mandatory monitoring of the humanitarian impact. In 2000 a proposal was submitted to the Council regarding the establishment of a permanent body to monitor sanctions violations. The UN Secretary-General established a special committee in April 2000 to evaluate sanctions policy. A draft version of the committee's final report, issued in February 2001, recommended that future Security Council resolutions enforcing sanctions should clearly specify intended goals and targets, include incentives to reward partial compliance, and focus in particular on the finances of leaders. In August 1999 the Council adopted its first resolution concerned exclusively with the welfare of children in armed conflict, and in September it adopted a resolution on the protection of civilians in armed conflict. In July 2000 the Council adopted a resolution concerned with preventing the spread of HIV/AIDS among personnel deployed to peace-keeping operations. The Council welcomed the publication in August of a report by a panel of experts recommending extensive structural and management reforms of the UN's peace-keeping activites. In November the Council adopted a resolution in which it undertook to give future operations clear, credible and achievable mandates.

COMMITTEES

In April 2001 there were two **Standing Committees**, each composed of representatives of all Council member states:

Committee of Experts on Rules of Procedure (studies and advises on rule of procedure and other technical matters);

Committee on the Admission of New Members;

***Ad hoc* Committees**, which are established as needed, comprise all Council members and meet in closed session:

Security Committee on Council Meetings away from Headquarters.

Security Council Committee established pursuant to Resolution 1243 (2001) concerning Liberia.

Security Council Committee established pursuant to Resolution 1298 (2000) concerning the situation between Eritrea and Ethiopia;

Security Council Committee established pursuant to Resolution 1267 (1999) concerning Afghanistan;

Security Council Committee established pursuant to Resolution 1160 (1998) concerning Kosovo;

Security Council Committee established pursuant to Resolution 1132 (1997) concerning Sierra Leone;

Security Council Committee established pursuant to Resolution 918 (1994) concerning Rwanda;

Security Council Committee established pursuant to Resolution 864 (1993) concerning Angola;

Security Council Committee established pursuant to Resolution 751 (1992) concerning Somalia;

Security Council Committee established pursuant to Resolution 748 (1992) concerning Libya;

Governing Council of the UN Compensation Commission established by Security Council Resolution 692 (1991);

Security Council Committee established pursuant to Resolution 661 (1990) concerning the situation between Iraq and Kuwait.

INTERNATIONAL TRIBUNALS

In May 1993 the Security Council, acting under Article VII of the UN Charter, adopted Resolution 827, which established an *ad hoc* 'war crimes' tribunal. The so-called International Tribunal for the Prosecution of Persons Responsible for Serious Violations of International Humanitarian Law Committed in the Territory of the Former Yugoslavia (also referred to as the International Criminal Tribunal for the former Yugoslavia—ICTY) was inaugurated in The Hague, Netherlands, in November, comprising a prosecutor and 11 judges sitting in two trial chambers and one appeals chamber. In May 1998 the Security Council authorized the establishment of a third trial chamber, and the election of three new judges, in order to expand the capacity of the Tribunal. In November 2000 the Security Council authorized the enlargement of the appeals chamber and agreed to establish a reserve of 27 additional judges to serve as required. Public hearings were initiated in November 1994. The first trial proceedings commenced in May 1996, and the first sentence was imposed by the Tribunal in November. In July and November 1995 the Tribunal formally charged the Bosnian Serb political and military leaders Radovan Karadžić and Gen. Ratko Mladić, on two separate indictments, with genocide and crimes against humanity, and in July 1996 issued international warrants for their arrest. In April 2000 Momčilo Krajišnik, a senior associate of Karadžić, was detained by the ICTY, charged with genocide, war crimes and crimes against humanity. Biljana Plavšić, a further former Bosnian Serb political leader, surrendered to the Tribunal in January 2001, also indicted on charges of genocide, war crimes and crimes against

humanity. In the following month three Bosnian Serb former soldiers were convicted by the ICTY of utilizing mass rape and the sexual enslavement of women as instruments of terror in wartime. In mid-1998 the ICTY began investigating reported acts of violence against civilians committed by both sides in the conflict in the southern Serbian province of Kosovo and Metohija. In early 1999 there were reports of large-scale, organized killings, and expulsion of the local Albanian population by Serbian forces. In April ICTY personnel visited refugee camps in neighbouring countries in order to compile evidence of the atrocities, and obtained intelligence information from NATO members regarding those responsible for the incidents. In May the then President of the Federal Republic of Yugoslavia (FRY), Slobodan Milošević was indicted, along with three senior government ministers and the chief-of-staff of the army, charged with crimes against humanity and violations of the customs of war committed in Kosovo since 1 January 1999; international warrants were issued for their arrests. In June, following the establishment of an international force to secure peace in Kosovo, the ICTY established teams of experts to investigate alleged atrocities at 529 identified grave sites. The enforcement of arrests has been one of the principal difficulties confronting the Tribunal. By January 2001 eleven international arrest warrants remained to be enforced, including those against Karadžić, Mladić and Milošević. The new FRY administration, which had assumed power following legislative and presidential elections in late 2000, contested the impartiality of the ICTY, proposing that Milošević and other members of the former regime should be tried before a national court. At January 2001 some 98 individuals had been publicly indicted by the Tribunal (including 18 whose charges were subsequently removed and nine who had later died). Of the accused whose cases had been concluded by that time, four had been found guilty and sentenced and one had been acquitted on all charges.

President of the ICTY: CLAUDE JORDA (France).

Address: Public Information Unit, POB 13888, 2501 The Hague, Netherlands.

Telephone: (70) 512-5233; **fax:** (70) 512-5355; **internet:** www.un.org/icty.

In November 1994 the Security Council adopted Resolution 955, establishing an International Criminal Tribunal for Rwanda (ICTR) to prosecute persons responsible for genocide and other serious violations of humanitarian law that had been committed in Rwanda and by Rwandans in neighbouring states. The Tribunal was to consist of two three-member trial chambers and one appeals chamber, and was to be served by the same Prosecutor as that of the ICTY. Its temporal jurisdiction was limited to the period 1 January to 31 December 1994. In April 1998 the Security Council authorized the establishment of a third three-member trial chamber. The Security Council authorized the enlargement of the appeals chamber and approved the election of two further judges to the Tribunal in November 2000. The first plenary session of the Tribunal was held in The Hague in June 1995; formal proceedings at its permanent headquarters in Arusha, Tanzania, were initiated in November. The first trial of persons charged by the Tribunal commenced in January 1997, and sentences were imposed in July. During that year the proceedings of the ICTR were undermined by reports of mismanagement and the need for administrative reforms. In September 1998 the former Rwandan Prime Minister, Jean Kambanda, and a former mayor of Taba, Jean-Paul Akayesu, both Hutu extremists, were found guilty of genocide and crimes against humanity; Kambanda subsequently became the first person ever to be sentenced under the 1948 Convention on the Prevention and Punishment of the Crime of Genocide. In October 2000 the Tribunal rejected an appeal by Kambanda. In November 1999 the Rwandan Government temporarily suspended co-operation with the Tribunal in protest at a decision of the appeals chamber to release an indicted former government official owing to procedural delays. (The appeals chamber subsequently reversed this decision.) By November 2000 a total of 48 people had been indicted by the ICTR, of whom 44 were being detained in custody. Seven individuals had been sentenced by the Tribunal at January 2001.

President of the ICTR: NAVANETHEM PILLAY (South Africa).

Address: Arusha International Conference Centre, POB 6016, Arusha, Tanzania.

Telephone: (57) 4207; **fax:** (57) 4000; **e-mail:** public@un.org; **internet:** www.un.ictr.org.

Both Tribunals are supported by teams of investigators and human rights experts working in the field to collect forensic and other evidence in order to uphold indictments. Evidence of mass graves resulting from large-scale unlawful killings has been uncovered in both regions.

Chief Prosecutor: CARLA DEL PONTE (Switzerland).

Trusteeship Council

The Trusteeship Council (comprising the People's Republic of China—a non-active member until May 1989, France, Russia, the United Kingdom and the USA) was established to supervise United Nations Trust Territories through their administering authorities and to promote the political, economic, social and educational advancement of their inhabitants towards self-government or independence (see Charter, p. 24). On 1 October 1994 the last territory remaining under UN trusteeship, the Republic of Palau (part of the archipelago of the Caroline Islands), declared its independence under a compact of free association with the USA, its administering authority. The Security Council terminated the Trusteeship Agreement on 10 November, having determined that the objectives of the agreement had been fully attained. On 1 November the Trusteeship Council formally suspended its operations; thereafter it was to be convened on an extraordinary basis as required.

Economic and Social Council—ECOSOC

ECOSOC promotes world co-operation on economic, social, cultural and humanitarian problems. (See Charter, p. 22.)

MEMBERS

Fifty-four members are elected by the General Assembly for three-year terms: 18 are elected each year. Membership is allotted by regions as follows: Africa 14 members, western Europe and others 13, Asia 11, Latin America 10, eastern Europe 6.

President: MARTIN BELINGA-EBOUTOU (Cameroon).

ORGANIZATION

The Council, which meets annually for four to five weeks between May and July, alternately in New York and Geneva, is mainly a central policy-making and co-ordinating organ. It has a co-ordinating function between the UN and the specialized agencies, and also makes consultative arrangements with approved voluntary or non-governmental organizations which work within the sphere of its activities. The Council has functional and regional commissions to carry out much of its detailed work.

During 1999 ECOSOC pursued discussions with the IMF and World Bank regarding the socio-economic aspects of globalization and increased co-operation for development.

SESSIONAL COMMITTEES

Each sessional committee comprises the 54 members of the Council: there is a First (Economic) Committee, a Second (Social) Committee and a Third (Programme and Co-ordination) Committee.

FUNCTIONAL COMMISSIONS

Commission on Crime Prevention and Criminal Justice: f. 1992; aims to formulate an international convention on crime prevention and criminal justice; 40 members.

Commission on Human Rights: f. 1946; seeks greater respect for the basic rights of man, the prevention of discrimination and the protection of minorities; reviews specific instances of human rights violation and dispatches rapporteurs to investigate allegations of abuses in particular countries; provides policy guidance; works on declarations, conventions and other instruments of international law; meets annually for six weeks; 53 members. There is a Sub-Commission on the Promotion and Protection of Human Rights, comprising working groups on issues such as slavery, indigenous populations, detention and communications.

Commission on Narcotic Drugs: f. 1946; mainly concerned in combating illicit traffic; 53 members. There is a Sub-Commission on Illicit Drug Traffic and Related Matters in the Near and Middle East.

Commission on Population and Development: f. 1946; advises the Council on population matters and their relation to socio-economic conditions; 47 members.

Commission on Science and Technology for Development: f. 1992; works on the restructuring of the UN in the economic, social and related fields; 33 members.

Commission for Social Development: f. 1946 as the Social Commission; advises ECOSOC on issues of social and community development; 46 members.

Commission on the Status of Women: f. 1946; aims at equality of political, economic and social rights for women, and supports the right of women to live free of violence; 45 members.

Commission on Sustainable Development: f. 1993 to oversee integration into the UN's work of the objectives set out in 'Agenda 21', the programme of action agreed by the UN Conference on Environment and Development in June 1992; 53 members.

Statistical Commission: Standardizes terminology and procedure in statistics and promotes the development of national statistics; 24 members.

COMMITTEES AND SUBSIDIARY BODIES

Commission on Human Settlements: f. 1977.

Committee for Development Policy: f. 1965.

Committee on Energy and Natural Resources for Development: f. 1998.

Committee on Negotiations with Intergovernmental Agencies: f. 1946.

Committee on Non-Governmental Organizations: f. 1946.

Committee for Programme and Co-ordination: f. 1962.

REGIONAL COMMISSIONS
(see pp. 27–36)

Economic Commission for Africa—ECA.

Economic Commission for Europe—ECE.

Economic Commission for Latin America and the Caribbean—ECLAC.

Economic and Social Commission for Asia and the Pacific—ESCAP.

Economic and Social Commission for Western Asia—ESCWA.

RELATED BODIES

Board of Trustees of the International Research and Training Institute for Women (INSTRAW): 11 members (see p. 69).

International Narcotics Control Board: f. 1964; 13 members.

UNDP/UNFPA Executive Board: 36 members, elected by ECOSOC (see p. 45).

UNHCR Executive Committee: 53 members, elected by ECOSOC (see p. 52).

UNICEF Executive Board: 36 members, elected by ECOSOC (see p. 41).

WFP Executive Board: one-half of the 36 members are elected by ECOSOC, one-half by the FAO; governing body of the World Food Programme (see p. 70).

International Court of Justice

Address: Peace Palace, Carnegieplein 2, 2517 KJ The Hague, Netherlands.

Telephone: (70) 302-23-23; **fax:** (70) 364-99-28; **e-mail:** information@icj-cij.org; **internet:** www.icj-cij.org.

Established in 1945, the Court is the principal judicial organ of the UN. All members of the UN, and also Switzerland, are parties to the Statute of the Court. (See Charter, p. 24.)

THE JUDGES

(April 2001; in order of precedence)

	Term Ends*
President: GILBERT GUILLAUME (France)	2009
Vice-President: SHI JIUYONG (People's Republic of China)	2003
Judges:	
SHIGERU ODA (Japan)	2003
MOHAMMED BEDJAOUI (Algeria)	2006
RAYMOND RANJEVA (Madagascar)	2009
GÉZA HERCZEGH (Hungary)	2003
CARL-AUGUST FLEISCHHAUER (Germany)	2003
ABDUL G. KOROMA (Sierra Leone)	2003
VLADLEN S. VERESHCHETIN (Russia)	2006
ROSALYN HIGGINS (United Kingdom)	2009
GONZALO PARRA-ARANGUREN (Venezuela)	2009
PIETER H. KOOIJMANS (Netherlands)	2006
JOSÉ FRANCISCO REZEK (Brazil)	2006
AWN SHAWKAT AL-KHASAWNEH (Jordan)	2009
THOMAS BUERGENTHAL (USA)	2009

Registrar: PHILIPPE COUVREUR (Belgium)

* Each term ends on 5 February of the year indicated.

The Court is composed of 15 judges, each of a different nationality, elected with an absolute majority by both the General Assembly and the Security Council. Representation of the main forms of civilization and the different legal systems of the world are borne in mind in their election. Candidates are nominated by national panels of jurists.

The judges are elected for nine years and may be re-elected; elections for five seats are held every three years. The Court elects its President and Vice-President for each three-year period. Members may not have any political, administrative, or other professional occupation, and may not sit in any case with which they have been otherwise connected than as a judge of the Court. For the purposes of a case, each side—consisting of one or more States—may, unless the Bench already includes a judge with a corresponding nationality, choose a person from outside the Court to sit as a judge on terms of equality with the Members. Judicial decisions are taken by a majority of the judges present, subject to a quorum of nine Members. The President has a casting vote.

FUNCTIONS

The International Court of Justice operates in accordance with a Statute which is an integral part of the UN Charter. Only States may be parties in cases before the Court; those not parties to the Statute may have access in certain circumstances and under conditions laid down by the Security Council.

The Jurisdiction of the Court comprises:

1. All cases which the parties refer to it jointly by special agreement (indicated in the list below by a stroke between the names of the parties).

2. All matters concerning which a treaty or convention in force provides for reference to the Court. About 700 bilateral or multilateral agreements make such provision. Among the more noteworthy: Treaty of Peace with Japan (1951), European Convention for Peaceful Settlement of Disputes (1957), Single Convention on Narcotic Drugs (1961), Protocol relating to the Status of Refugees (1967), Hague Convention on the Suppression of the Unlawful Seizure of Aircraft (1970).

3. Legal disputes between States which have recognized the jurisdiction of the Court as compulsory for specified classes of dispute. Declarations by the following 62 States accepting the compulsory jurisdiction of the Court are in force: Australia, Austria, Barbados, Belgium, Botswana, Bulgaria, Cambodia (Kampuchea), Cameroon, Canada, Colombia, the Democratic Republic of the Congo, Costa Rica, Cyprus, Denmark, the Dominican Republic, Egypt, Estonia, Finland, The Gambia, Georgia, Greece, Guinea, Guinea-Bissau, Haiti, Honduras, Hungary, India, Japan, Kenya, Liberia, Liechtenstein, Luxembourg, Madagascar, Malawi, Malta, Mauritius, Mexico, Nauru, the Netherlands, New Zealand, Nicaragua, Nigeria, Norway, Pakistan, Panama, Paraguay, the Philippines, Poland, Portugal, Senegal, Somalia, Spain, Sudan, Suriname, Swaziland, Sweden, Switzerland, Togo, Uganda, the United Kingdom, Uruguay, and the Federal Republic of Yugoslavia.

Disputes as to whether the Court has jurisdiction are settled by the Court.

Judgments are without appeal, but are binding only for the particular case and between the parties. States appearing before the Court undertake to comply with its Judgment. If a party to a case fails to do so, the other party may apply to the Security Council, which may make recommendations or decide upon measures to give effect to the Judgment.

Advisory opinions on legal questions may be requested by the General Assembly, the Security Council or, if so authorized by the Assembly, other United Nations organs or specialized agencies.

Rules of Court governing procedure are made by the Court under a power conferred by the Statute.

In July 1993 the Court established a seven-member Chamber for Environmental Matters, in view of the world-wide expansion of environmental law and protection.

CONSIDERED CASES

Judgments

Since 1946 more than 80 cases have been referred to the Court by States. Some were removed from the list as a result of settlement or discontinuance, or on the grounds of a lack of basis for jurisdiction. Cases which have been the subject of a Judgment by the Court include: Monetary Gold Removed from Rome in 1943 (Italy v. France, United Kingdom and USA); Sovereignty over Certain Frontier Land (Belgium/Netherlands); Arbitral Award made by the King of Spain on 23 December 1906 (Honduras v. Nicaragua); Temple of Preah Vihear (Cambodia v. Thailand); South West Africa (Ethiopia and Liberia v. South Africa); Northern Cameroons (Cameroon v. United Kingdom); North Sea Continental Shelf (Federal Republic of Germany/Denmark and Netherlands); Appeal relating to the Jurisdiction of the ICAO Council (India v. Pakistan); Fisheries Jurisdiction (United Kingdom v. Iceland; Federal Republic of Germany v. Iceland); Nuclear Tests (Australia v. France; New Zealand v. France); Aegean Sea Continental Shelf (Greece v. Turkey); United States of America Diplomatic and Consular Staff in Tehran (USA v. Iran); Continental Shelf (Tunisia/Libya); Delimitation of the Maritime Boundary in the Gulf of Maine Area (Canada/USA); Continental Shelf (Libya/Malta); Application for revision and interpretation of the Judgment of 24 February 1982 in the case concerning the Continental Shelf (Tunisia v. Libya); Military and Paramilitary Activities in and against Nicaragua (Nicaragua v. USA); Frontier Dispute (Burkina Faso/Mali); Delimitation of Maritime Boundary (Denmark v. Norway); Maritime Boundaries (Guinea-Bissau v. Senegal); Elettronica Sicula SpA (USA v. Italy); Land, Island and Maritime Frontier Dispute (El Salvador/Honduras) (in one aspect of which Nicaragua was permitted to intervene); Delimitation of Maritime Boundary in the area between Greenland and Jan Mayen island (Denmark v. Norway); Maritime Delimitation and Territorial Questions between Qatar and Bahrain (Qatar v. Bahrain), aspects of which were still under consideration in 2001; Territorial Dispute (Libya/Chad); East Timor (Portugal v. Australia); the Gabčíkovo-Nagymaros Hydroelectric Project (Hungary v. Slovakia), aspects of which were still under consideration in 2001; Fisheries Jurisdiction (Spain v. Canada); and Delimitation of the Boundary around Kasikili Sedudu Island (Botswana v. Namibia).

Other cases remaining under consideration, or pending before the Court, in early 2001 were: cases brought by Libya against the United Kingdom and the USA concerning questions of interpretation and application of the 1971 Montreal Convention arising from the aerial incident at Lockerbie, United Kingdom, in 1988; a case brought by Iran against the USA concerning the destruction of oil platforms; cases brought by Bosnia and Herzegovina and Croatia against the Federal Republic of Yugoslavia concerning the application of the Convention on the Prevention and Punishment of the Crime of Genocide; a case brought by Cameroon against Nigeria concerning the land and maritime boundary between those two states, as well as a case concerning the interpretation of the Judgment of the Court on its jurisdiction in that case; a case concerning sovereignty over

Pulau Ligatan and Pulau Sipadan brought by Indonesia and Malaysia; a case brought by Guinea against the Democratic Republic of the Congo (DRC) concerning the treatment of a Guinean business executive, Ahmadou Sadio Diallo; a case brought by Germany against the USA concerning alleged violations of the 1963 Vienna Convention on Consular Relations with respect to the treatment of two German nationals; cases concerning the legality of the use of force brought by the Federal Republic of Yugoslavia (FRY) against Belgium, Canada, France, Germany, Italy, the Netherlands, Portugal and the United Kingdom; a case brought by the DRC against Uganda, regarding armed activities on the territory of the DRC; dispute between Nicaragua and Honduras concerning maritime delimitation in the Caribbean Sea; a case brought by Croatia against the FRY regarding alleged violations of the 1948 Convention on the Prevention and Punishment of the Crime of Genocide; and a case brought by the DRC against Belgium regarding the issuing by a Belgian examining judge of an international arrest warrant against a Congolese government minister.

Advisory Opinions

Matters on which the Court has delivered an Advisory Opinion at the request of the United Nations General Assembly, or an organ thereof, include the following: Condition of Admission of a State to Membership in the United Nations; Competence of the General Assembly for the Admission of a State to the United Nations; Interpretation of the Peace Treaties with Bulgaria, Hungary and Romania; International Status of South West Africa; Reservations to the Convention on the Prevention and Punishment of the Crime of Genocide; Effect of Awards of Compensation Made by the United Nations Administrative Tribunal (UNAT); Western Sahara; Application for Review of UNAT Judgment No. 333; Applicability of the Obligation to Arbitrate under Section 21 of the United Nations Headquarters Agreement of 26 June 1947 (relating to the closure of the Observer Mission to the United Nations maintained by the Palestine Liberation Organization).

An Advisory Opinion has been given at the request of the Security Council: Legal Consequences for States of the continued presence of South Africa in Namibia (South West Africa) notwithstanding Security Council resolution 276 (1970).

In 1989 (at the request of the UN Economic and Social Council—ECOSOC) the Court gave an Advisory Opinion on the Applicability of Article 6, Section 22, of the Convention on the Privileges and Immunities of the United Nations. The Court has also, at the request of UNESCO, given an Advisory Opinion on Judgments of the Administrative Tribunal of the ILO upon Complaints made against UNESCO, and on the Constitution of the Maritime Safety Committee of the Inter-Governmental Maritime Consultative Organization, at the request of IMCO. In July 1996 the Court delivered Advisory Opinions on the Legality of the Use by a State of Nuclear Weapons in Armed Conflict, requested by WHO, and on the Legality of the Use or Threat of Nuclear Weapons, requested by the UN General Assembly. In April 1999 the Court delivered an Advisory Opinion, requested by ECOSOC, on the Difference Relating to Immunity from Legal Process of a Special Rapporteur of the Commission on Human Rights.

Finance

The annual budget for the Court amounts to approximately US $11m., financed entirely by the United Nations.

Publications

Acts and Documents, No. 5 (contains Statute and Rules of the Court, the Resolution concerning its internal judicial practice and other documents).

Bibliography (annually).

Pleadings (Written Pleadings and Statements, Oral Proceedings, Correspondence): series.

Reports (Judgments, Opinions and Orders): series.

Yearbook.

Charter of the United Nations
(Signed 26 June 1945)

We the peoples of the United Nations determined

to save succeeding generations from the scourge of war, which twice in our lifetime has brought untold sorrow to mankind, and

to reaffirm faith in fundamental human rights, in the dignity and worth of the human person, in the equal rights of men and women and of nations large and small, and

to establish conditions under which justice and respect for the obligations arising from treaties and other sources of international law can be maintained, and

to promote social progress and better standards of life in larger freedom,

And for these ends

to practise tolerance and live together in peace with one another as good neighbours, and

to unite our strength to maintain international peace and security, and

to ensure, by the acceptance of principles and the institution of methods, that armed force shall not be used, save in the common interest, and

to employ international machinery for the promotion of the economic and social advancement of all peoples,

Have resolved to combine our efforts to accomplish these aims.

Accordingly, our respective Governments, through representatives assembled in the city of San Francisco, who have exhibited their full powers found to be in good and due form, have agreed to the present Charter of the United Nations and do hereby establish an international organization to be known as the United Nations.

I. PURPOSES AND PRINCIPLES

Article 1

The Purposes of the United Nations are:

1. To maintain international peace and security, and to that end: to take effective collective measures for the prevention and removal of threats to the peace, and for the suppression of acts of aggression or other breaches of the peace, and to bring about by peaceful means, and in conformity with the principles of justice and international law, adjustment or settlement of international disputes or situations which might lead to a breach of the peace:

2. To develop friendly relations among nations based on respect for the principle of equal rights and self-determination of peoples, and to take other appropriate measures to strengthen universal peace;

3. To achieve international co-operation in solving international problems of an economic, social, cultural, or humanitarian character, and in promoting and encouraging respect for human rights and for fundamental freedoms for all without distinction as to race, sex, language, or religion; and

4. To be a centre for harmonizing the accusations of nations in the attainment of these common ends.

Article 2

The Organization and its Members, in pursuit of the Purposes stated in Article 1, shall act in accordance with the following Principles.

1. The Organization is based on the principle of the sovereign equality of all its Members.

2. All Members, in order to ensure to all of them the rights and benefits resulting from membership, shall fulfil in good faith the obligations assumed by them in accordance with the present Charter.

3. All Members shall settle their international disputes by peaceful means in such a manner that international peace and security, and justice, are not endangered.

4. All Members shall refrain in their international relations from the threat or use of force against the territorial integrity or political independence of any state, or in any manner inconsistent with the Purposes of the United Nations.

5. All Members shall give the United Nations every assistance in any action it takes in accordance with the present Charter, and shall refrain from giving assistance to any state against which the United Nations is taking preventive or enforcement action.

6. The Organization shall ensure that states which are not Members of the United Nations act in accordance with these Principles so far as may be necessary for the maintenance of international peace and security.

7. Nothing contained in the present Charter shall authorize the United Nations to intervene in matters which are essentially within the domestic jurisdiction of any state or shall require the Members to submit such matters to settlement under the present Charter; but this principle shall not prejudice the application of enforcement measures under Chapter VII.

II. MEMBERSHIP

Article 3

The original Members of the United Nations shall be the states which, having participated in the United Nations Conference on International Organization at San Francisco, or having previously signed the Declaration by United Nations of January 1, 1942, sign the present Charter and ratify it in accordance with Article 110.

Article 4

1. Membership in the United Nations is open to all other peace-loving states which accept the obligations contained in the present Charter and, in the judgement of the Organization, are able and willing to carry out these obligations.

2. The admission of any such state to membership in the United Nations will be effected by a decision of the General Assembly upon the recommendation of the Security Council.

Article 5

A member of the United Nations against which preventive or enforcement action has been taken by the Security Council may be suspended from the exercise of the rights and privileges of membership by the General Assembly upon the recommendation of the Security Council. The exercise of these rights and privileges may be restored by the Security Council.

Article 6

A Member of the United Nations which has persistently violated the Principles contained in the present Charter may be expelled from the Organization by the General Assembly upon the recommendation of the Security Council.

III. ORGANS

Article 7

1. There are established as the principal organs of the United Nations: a General Assembly, a Security Council, an Economic and Social Council, a Trusteeship Council, an International Court of Justice, and a Secretariat.

2. Such subsidiary organs as may be found necessary may be established in accordance with the present Charter.

Article 8

The United Nations shall place no restrictions on the eligibility of men and women to participate in any capacity and under conditions of equality in its principal and subsidiary organs.

IV. THE GENERAL ASSEMBLY
Composition

Article 9

1. The General Assembly shall consist of all the Members of the United Nations.

2. Each Member shall have not more than five representatives in the General Assembly.

Functions and Powers

Article 10

The General Assembly may discuss any questions or any matters within the scope of the present Charter or relating to the powers and functions of any organs provided for in the present Charter, and, except as provided in Article 12, may make recommendations to the Members of the United Nations or to the Security Council or to both on any such questions or matters.

Article 11

1. The General Assembly may consider the general principles of co-operation in the maintenance of international peace and security, including the principles governing disarmament and the regulation of armaments, and may make recommendations with regard to such principles to the Members or to the Security Council or to both.

2. The General Assembly may discuss any questions relating to the maintenance of international peace and security brought before it by any Member of the United Nations, or by the Security Council, or by a state which is not a Member of the United Nations in

accordance with Article 35, paragraph 2, and, except as provided in Article 12, may make recommendations with regard to any such question to the state or states concerned or to the Security Council or both. Any such question on which action is necessary shall be referred to the Security Council by the General Assembly either before or after discussion.

3. The General Assembly may call the attention of the Security Council to situations which are likely to endanger international peace and security.

4. The powers of the General Assembly set forth in this Article shall not limit the general scope of Article 10.

Article 12

1. While the Security Council is exercising in respect of any dispute or situation the functions assigned to it in the present Charter, the General Assembly shall not make any recommendations with regard to that dispute or situation unless the Security Council so requests.

2. The Secretary-General, with the consent of the Security Council, shall notify the General Assembly at each session of any matters relative to the maintenance of international peace and security which are being dealt with by the Security Council and shall similarly notify the General Assembly, or the Members of the United Nations if the General Assembly is not in session, immediately the Security Council ceases to deal with such matters.

Article 13

1. The General Assembly shall initiate studies and make recommendations for the purpose of:

    (a) promoting international co-operation in the political field and encouraging the progressive development of international law and its codification;

    (b) promoting international co-operation in the economic, social, cultural, educational, and health fields, and assisting in the realization of human rights and fundamental freedoms for all without distinction as to race, sex, language, or religion.

2. The further responsibilities, functions and powers of the General Assembly with respect to matters mentioned in paragraph 1(b) above are set forth in Chapters IX and X.

Article 14

Subject to the provision of Article 12, the General Assembly may recommend measures for the peaceful adjustment of any situation, regardless of origin, which it deems likely to impair the general welfare or friendly relations among nations, including situations resulting from a violation of the provisions of the present Charter setting forth the Purposes and Principles of the United Nations.

Article 15

1. The General Assembly shall receive and consider annual and special reports from the Security Council; these reports shall include an account of the measures that the Security Council has decided upon or taken to maintain international peace and security.

2. The General Assembly shall receive and consider reports from the other organs of the United Nations.

Article 16

The General Assembly shall perform such functions with respect to the international trusteeship system as are assigned to it under Chapters XII and XIII, including the approval of the trusteeship agreements for areas not designated as strategic.

Article 17

1. The General Assembly shall consider and approve the budget of the Organization.

2. The expenses of the Organization shall be borne by the Members as apportioned by the General Assembly.

3. The General Assembly shall consider and approve any financial and budgetary arrangements with specialized agencies referred to in Article 57 and shall examine the administrative budgets of such specialized agencies with a view to making recommendations to the agencies concerned.

Voting

Article 18

1. Each Member of the General Assembly shall have one vote.

2. Decisions of the General Assembly on important questions shall be made by a two-thirds majority of the members present and voting. These questions shall include: recommendations with respect to the maintenance of international peace and security, the election of the non-permanent Members of the Security Council, the election of the Members of the Economic and Social Council, the election of Members of the Trusteeship Council in accordance with paragraph 1(c) of Article 86, the admission of new Members to the United Nations, the suspension of the rights and privileges of membership,

the expulsion of Members, questions relating to the operation of the trusteeship system, and budgetary questions.

3. Decisions on other questions, including the determination of additional categories of questions to be decided by a two-thirds majority, shall be made by a majority of the members present and voting.

Article 19

A Member of the United Nations which is in arrears in the payment of its financial contributions to the Organization shall have no vote in the General Assembly if the amount of its arrears equals or exceeds the amount of the contributions due from it for the preceding two full years. The General Assembly may, nevertheless, permit such a Member to vote if it is satisfied that the failure to pay is due to conditions beyond the control of the Member.

Procedure
Article 20

The General Assembly shall meet in regular annual sessions and in such special sessions as occasion may require. Special sessions shall be convoked by the Secretary-General at the request of the Security Council or of a majority of the members of the United Nations.

Article 21

The General Assembly shall adopt its own rules of procedure. It shall elect its President for each session.

Article 22

The General Assembly may establish such subsidiary organs as it deems necessary for the performance of its functions.

V. THE SECURITY COUNCIL
Composition
Article 23

1. The Security Council shall consist of 11 Members of the United Nations. The Republic of China*, France, the Union of Soviet Socialist Republics†, the United Kingdom of Great Britain and Northern Ireland, and the United States of America shall be permanent members of the Security Council. The General Assembly shall elect six other Members of the United Nations to be non-permanent members of the Security Council, due regard being specially paid, in the first instance to the contribution of Members of the United Nations to the maintenance of international peace and security and to the other purposes of the Organization, and also to equitable geographical distribution.

2. The non-permanent members of the Security Council shall be elected for a term of two years. In the first election of the non-permanent members, however, three shall be chosen for a term of one year. A retiring member shall not be eligible for immediate re-election.

3. Each member of the Security Council shall have one representative.

* From 1971 the Chinese seat in the UN General Assembly and its permanent seat in the Security Council were occupied by the People's Republic of China.

† In December 1991 Russia assumed the former USSR's seat in the UN General Assembly and its permanent seat in the Security Council.

Functions and Powers
Article 24

1. In order to ensure prompt and effective action by the United Nations, its Members confer on the Security Council primary responsibility for the maintenance of international peace and security, and agree that in carrying out its duties under this responsibility the Security Council acts on their behalf.

2. In discharging these duties the Security Council shall act in accordance with the Purposes and Principles of the United Nations. The specific powers granted to the Security Council for the discharge of these duties are laid down in Chapters VI, VII, VIII and XII.

3. The Security Council shall submit annual and, when necessary, special reports to the General Assembly for its consideration.

Article 25

The Members of the United Nations agree to accept and carry out the decisions of the Security Council in accordance with the present Charter.

Article 26

In order to promote the establishment and maintenance of international peace and security with the least diversion for armaments of the world's human and economic resources, the Security Council shall be responsible for formulating, with the assistance of the Military Staff Committee referred to in Article 47, plans to be submitted to the Members of the United Nations for the establishment of a system for the regulation of armaments.

Voting
Article 27

1. Each member of the Security Council shall have one vote.

2. Decisions of the Security Council on procedural matters shall be made by an affirmative vote of seven members.

3. Decisions of the Security Council on all other matters shall be made by an affirmative vote of seven members including the concurring votes of the permanent members; provided that, in decisions under Chapter VI, and under paragraph 3 of Article 52, a party to a dispute shall abstain from voting.

Procedure
Article 28

1. The Security Council shall be so organized as to be able to function continuously. Each member of the Security Council shall for this purpose be represented at all times at the seat of the Organization.

2. The Security Council shall hold periodic meetings at which each of its members may, if it so desires, be represented by a member of the government or by some other specially designated representative.

3. The Security Council may hold meetings at such places other than the seat of the Organization as in its judgment will best facilitate its work.

Article 29

The Security Council may establish such subsidiary organs as it deems necessary for the performance of its functions.

Article 30

The Security Council shall adopt its own rules of procedure, including the method of selecting its President.

Article 31

Any Member of the United Nations which is not a member of the Security Council may participate, without vote, in the discussion of any question brought before the Security Council whenever the latter considers that the interests of that Member are specially affected.

Article 32

Any Member of the United Nations which is not a member of the Security Council or any state which is not a Member of the United Nations, if it is a party to a dispute under consideration by the Security Council, shall be invited to participate, without vote, in the discussion relating to the dispute. The Security Council shall lay down such conditions as it deems just for the participation of a state which is not a Member of the United Nations.

VI. PACIFIC SETTLEMENT OF DISPUTES
Article 33

1. The parties to any dispute, the continuance of which is likely to endanger the maintenance of international peace and security, shall, first of all, seek a solution by negotiation, enquiry, mediation, conciliation, arbitration, judicial settlement, resort to regional agencies or arrangements, or other peaceful means of their own choice.

2. The Security Council shall, when it deems necessary, call upon the parties to settle their disputes by such means.

Article 34

The Security Council may investigate any dispute, or any situation which might lead to international friction or give rise to a dispute, in order to determine whether the continuance of the dispute or situation is likely to endanger the maintenance of international peace and security.

Article 35

1. Any Member of the United Nations may bring any dispute, or any situation of the nature referred to in Article 34, to the attention of the Security Council or of the General Assembly.

2. A state which is not a Member of the United Nations may bring to the attention of the Security Council or of the General Assembly any dispute to which it is a party if it accepts in advance, for the purposes of the dispute, the obligations of pacific settlement provided in the present Charter.

3. The proceedings of the General Assembly in respect of matters brought to its attention under this Article will be subject to the provisions of Articles 11 and 12.

Article 36

1. The Security Council may, at any stage of a dispute of the nature referred to in Article 33 or of a situation of like nature, recommend appropriate procedures or methods of adjustment.

2. The Security Council should take into consideration any procedures for the settlement of the dispute which have already been adopted by the parties.

3. In making recommendations under this Article the Security Council should also take into consideration that legal disputes should as a general rule be referred by the parties to the International Court of Justice in accordance with the provisions of the statute of the Court.

Article 37

1. Should the parties to a dispute of the nature referred to in Article 33, fail to settle it by the means indicated in that Article, they shall refer it to the Security Council.

2. If the Security Council deems that the continuance of the dispute is in fact likely to endanger the maintenance of international peace and security, it shall decide whether to take action under Article 36 or to recommend such terms of settlement as it may consider appropriate.

Article 38

Without prejudice to the provisions of Articles 33 to 37, the Security Council may, if all the parties to any dispute so request, make recommendations to the parties with a view to a pacific settlement of the dispute.

VII. ACTION WITH RESPECT TO THREATS TO THE PEACE, BREACHES OF THE PEACE, AND ACTS OF AGGRESSION

Article 39

The Security Council shall determine the existence of any threat to the peace, breach of the peace, or act of aggression and shall make recommendations, or decide what measures shall be taken in accordance with Articles 41 and 42, to maintain or restore international peace and security.

Article 40

In order to prevent an aggravation of the situation, the Security Council may, before making the recommendations or deciding upon the measures provided for in Article 39, call upon the parties concerned to comply with such provisional measures as it deems necessary or desirable. Such provisional measures shall be without prejudice to the rights, claims, or position of the parties concerned. The Security Council shall duly take account of failure to comply with such provisional measures.

Article 41

The Security Council may decide what measures not involving the use of armed force are to be employed to give effect to its decisions, and it may call upon the Members of the United Nations to apply such measures. These may include complete or partial interruption of economic relations and of rail, sea, air, postal, telegraphic, radio, and other means of communication, and the severance of diplomatic relations.

Article 42

Should the Security Council consider that measures provided for in Article 41 would be inadequate or have proved to be inadequate, it may take such action by air, sea, or land forces as may be necessary to maintain or restore international peace and security. Such action may include demonstrations, blockade, and other operations by air, sea, or land forces of Members of the United Nations.

Article 43

1. All Members of the United Nations, in order to contribute to the maintenance of international peace and security, undertake to make available to the Security Council, on its call and in accordance with a special agreement or agreements, armed forces, assistance, and facilities, including rights of passage, necessary for the purpose of maintaining international peace and security.

2. Such agreement or agreements shall govern the numbers and types of forces, their degree of readiness and general location, and the nature of the facilities and assistance to be provided.

3. The agreement or agreements shall be negotiated as soon as possible on the initiative of the Security Council. They shall be concluded between the Security Council and Members or between the Security Council and groups of Members and shall be subject to ratification by the signatory states in accordance with their respective constitutional processes.

Article 44

When the Security Council has decided to use force it shall, before calling upon a Member not represented on it to provide armed forces in fulfilment of the obligations assumed under Article 43, invite that Member, if the Member so desires, to participate in the decisions of the Security Council concerning the employment of contingents of that Member's armed forces.

Article 45

In order to enable the United Nations to take urgent military measures, Members shall hold immediately available national airforce contingents for combined international enforcement action. The strength and degree of readiness of these contingents and plans for their combined action shall be determined, within the limits laid down in the special agreement and agreements referred to in Article 43, by the Security Council with the assistance of the Military Staff Committee.

Article 46

Plans for the application of armed force shall be made by the Security Council with the assistance of the Military Staff Committee.

Article 47

1. There shall be established a Military Staff Committee to advise and assist the Security Council on all questions relating to the Security Council's military requirements for the maintenance of international peace and security, the employment and command of forces placed at its disposal, the regulation of armaments, and possible disarmament.

2. The Military Staff Committee shall consist of the Chiefs of Staff of the permanent members of the Security Council or their representatives. Any Member of the United Nations not permanently represented on the Committee shall be invited by the Committee to be associated with it when the efficient discharge of the Committee's responsibilities requires the participation of that Member in its work.

3. The Military Staff Committee shall be responsible under the Security Council for the strategic direction of any armed forces placed at the disposal of the Security Council. Questions relating to the command of such forces shall be worked out subsequently.

4. The Military Staff Committee, with the authorization of the Security Council and after consultation with appropriate regional agencies, may establish regional sub-committees.

Article 48

1. The action required to carry out the decisions of the Security Council for the maintenance of international peace and security shall be taken by all the Members of the United Nations or by some of them, as the Security Council may determine.

2. Such decisions shall be carried out by the Members of the United Nations directly and through their action in the appropriate international agencies of which they are members.

Article 49

The Members of the United Nations shall join in affording mutual assistance in carrying out the measures decided upon by the Security Council.

Article 50

If preventive or enforcement measures against any state are taken by the Security Council, any other state, whether a Member of the United Nations or not, which finds itself confronted with special economic problems arising from the carrying out of those measures shall have the right to consult the Security Council with regard to a solution of those problems.

Article 51

Nothing in the present Charter shall impair the inherent right of individual or collective self-defence if an armed attack occurs against a Member of the United Nations, until the Security Council has taken measures necessary to maintain international peace and security. Measures taken by Members in the exercise of this right of self-defence shall be immediately reported to the Security Council and shall not in any way affect the authority and responsibility of the Security Council under the present Charter to take at any time such action as it deems necessary in order to maintain or restore international peace and security.

VIII. REGIONAL ARRANGEMENTS

Article 52

1. Nothing in the present Charter precludes the existence of regional arrangements or agencies for dealing with such matters relating to the maintenance of international peace and security as are appropriate for regional action, provided that such arrangements or agencies and their activities are consistent with the Purposes and Principles of the United Nations.

2. The Members of the United Nations entering into such arrangements or constituting such agencies shall make every effort to achieve pacific settlement of local disputes through such regional agencies before referring them to the Security Council.

3. The Security Council shall encourage the development of pacific settlement of local disputes through such regional arrangements or by such regional agencies either on the initiative of the states concerned or by reference from the Security Council.

4. This Article in no way impairs the application of Articles 34 and 35.

Article 53

1. The Security Council shall, where appropriate, utilize such regional arrangements or agencies for enforcement action under its authority. But no enforcement action shall be taken under regional arrangements or by regional agencies without the authorization of the Security Council, with the exception of measures against any enemy state, as defined in paragraph 2 of this Article, provided for pursuant to Article 107 or in regional arrangements directed against renewal of aggressive policy on the part of any such state, until such time as the Organization may, on request of the Governments concerned, be charged with the responsibility for preventing further aggression by such a state.

2. The term enemy state as used in paragraph 1 of this Article applies to any state which during the Second World War has been an enemy of any signatory of the present Charter.

Article 54

The Security Council shall at all times be kept fully informed of activities undertaken or in contemplation under regional arrangements or by regional agencies for the maintenance of international peace and security.

IX. INTERNATIONAL ECONOMIC AND SOCIAL CO-OPERATION

Article 55

With a view to the creation of conditions of stability and well-being which are necessary for peaceful and friendly relations among nations based on respect for the principle of equal rights and self-determination of peoples, the United Nations shall promote:

(a) higher standards of living, full employment, and conditions of economic and social progress and development;

(b) solutions of international economic, social, health, and related problems; and international cultural and educational co-operation; and

(c) universal respect for, and observance of, human rights and fundamental freedoms for all without distinction as to race, sex, language, or religion.

Article 56

All Members pledge themselves to take joint and separate action in co-operation with the Organization for the achievement of the purposes set forth in Article 55.

Article 57

1. The various specialized agencies, established by intergovernmental agreement and having wide international responsibilities, as defined in their basic instruments, in economic, social, cultural, educational, health, and related fields, shall be brought into relationship with the United Nations in accordance with the provisions of Article 63.

2. Such agencies thus brought into relationship with the United Nations are hereinafter referred to as specialized agencies.

Article 58

The Organization shall make recommendations for the co-ordination of the policies and activities of the specialized agencies.

Article 59

The Organization shall, where appropriate, initiate negotiations among the states concerned for the creation of any new specialized agencies required for the accomplishment of the purposes set forth in Article 55.

Article 60

Responsibility for the discharge of the functions of the Organization set forth in this Chapter shall be vested in the General Assembly and, under the authority of the General Assembly, in the Economic and Social Council, which shall have for this purpose the powers set forth in Chapter X.

X. THE ECONOMIC AND SOCIAL COUNCIL

Composition

Article 61

1. The Economic and Social Council shall consist of 18 Members of the United Nations elected by the General Assembly.

2. Subject to the provisions of paragraph 3, six members of the Economic and Social Council shall be elected each year for a term of three years. A retiring member shall be eligible for immediate re-election.

3. At the first election, 18 members of the Economic and Social Council shall be chosen. The term of office of six members so chosen shall expire at the end of one year, and of six other members at the end of two years, in accordance with arrangements made by the General Assembly.

4. Each member of the Economic and Social Council shall have one representative.

Functions and Powers

Article 62

1. The Economic and Social Council may make or initiate studies and reports with respect to international economic, social, cultural, educational, health, and related matters and may make recommendations with respect to any such matters to the General Assembly, to the Members of the United Nations, and to the specialized agencies concerned.

2. It may make recommendations for the purpose of promoting respect for, and observance of, human rights and fundamental freedoms for all.

3. It may prepare draft conventions for submission to the General Assembly, with respect to matters falling within its competence.

4. It may call, in accordance with the rules prescribed by the United Nations, international conferences on matters falling within its competence.

Article 63

1. The Economic and Social Council may enter into agreements with any of the agencies referred to in Article 57, defining the terms on which the agency concerned shall be brought into relationship with the United Nations. Such agreements shall be subject to approval by the General Assembly.

2. It may co-ordinate the activities of the specialized agencies through consultation with and recommendations to such agencies and through recommendations to the General Assembly and to the Members of the United Nations.

Article 64

1. The Economic and Social Council may take appropriate steps to obtain regular reports from the specialized agencies. It may make arrangements with the Members of the United Nations and with specialized agencies to obtain reports on the steps taken to give effect to its own recommendations and to recommendations on matters falling within its competence made by the General Assembly.

2. It may communicate its observations on these reports to the General Assembly.

Article 65

The Economic and Social Council may furnish information to the Security Council and shall assist the Security Council upon its request.

Article 66

1. The Economic and Social Council shall perform such functions as fall within its competence in connection with the carrying out of the recommendations of the General Assembly.

2. It may, with the approval of the General Assembly, perform services at the request of Members of the United Nations and at the request of specialized agencies.

3. It shall perform such other functions as are specified elsewhere in the present Charter or as may be assigned to it by the General Assembly.

Voting

Article 67

1. Each member of the Economic and Social Council shall have one vote.

2. Decisions of the Economic and Social Council shall be made by a majority of the members present and voting.

Procedure

Article 68

The Economic and Social Council shall set up commissions in economic and social fields and for the promotion of human rights, and such other commissions as may be required for the performance of its functions.

Article 69

The Economic and Social Council shall invite any Member of the United Nations to participate, without vote, in its deliberations on any matter of particular concern to that Member.

Article 70

The Economic and Social Council may make arrangements for representatives of the specialized agencies to participate, without vote, in its deliberations and in those of the commissions established by it, and for its representatives to participate in the deliberations of the specialized agencies.

Article 71

The Economic and Social Council may make suitable arrangements for consultation with non-governmental organizations which are concerned with matters within its competence. Such arrangements may be made with international organizations and, where appropriate, with national organizations after consultation with the Member of the United Nations concerned.

Article 72

1. The Economic and Social Council shall adopt its own rules of procedure, including the method of selecting its President.

2. The Economic and Social Council shall meet as required in accordance with its rules, which shall include provision for the convening of meetings on the request of a majority of its members.

XI. NON-SELF-GOVERNING TERRITORIES

Article 73

Members of the United Nations which have or assume responsibilities for the administration of territories whose peoples have not yet attained a full measure of self-government recognize the principle that the interests of the inhabitants of these territories are paramount, and accept as a sacred trust the obligation to promote to the utmost, within the system of international peace and security established by the present Charter, the well-being of the inhabitants of these territories, and, to this end:

(a) to ensure, with due respect for the culture of the peoples concerned, their political, economic, social, and educational advancement, their just treatment, and their protection against abuses;

(b) to develop self-government, to take due account of the political aspirations of the peoples, and to assist them in the progressive development of their free political institutions, according to the particular circumstances of each territory and its peoples and their varying stages of advancement;

(c) to further international peace and security;

(d) to promote constructive measures of development, to encourage research, and to co-operate with one another and, when and where appropriate, with specialized international bodies with a view to the practical achievement of the social, economic, and scientific purposes set forth in this Article; and

(e) to transmit regularly to the Secretary-General for information purposes, subject to such limitations as security and constitutional considerations may require, statistical and other information, of a technical nature relating to economic, social, and educational conditions in the territories for which they are respectively responsible other than those territories to which Chapters XII and XIII apply.

Article 74

Members of the United Nations also agree that their policy in respect of the territories to which this Chapter applies, no less than in respect of their metropolitan areas, must be based on the general principles of good-neighbourliness, due account being taken of the interests and well-being of the rest of the world, in social, economic, and commercial matters.

XII. INTERNATIONAL TRUSTEESHIP SYSTEM

Article 75

The United Nations shall establish under its authority an international trusteeship system for the administration and supervision of such territories as may be placed thereunder by subsequent individual agreements. These territories are hereinafter referred to as trust territories.

Article 76

The basic objectives of the trusteeship system, in accordance with the Purposes of the United Nations laid down in Article 1 of the present Charter, shall be:

(a) to further international peace and security;

(b) to promote the political, economic, social, and educational advancement of the inhabitants of the trust territories, and their progressive development towards self-government or independence as may be appropriate to the particular circumstances of each territory and its peoples and the freely expressed wishes of the peoples concerned, and as may be provided by the terms of each trusteeship agreement;

(c) to encourage respect for human rights and for fundamental freedoms for all without distinction as to race, sex, language, or religion, and to encourage recognition of the interdependence of the peoples of the world; and

(d) to ensure equal treatment in social, economic, and commercial matters for all Members of the United Nations and their nationals, and also equal treatment for the latter in the administration of justice, without prejudice to the attainment of the foregoing objectives and subject to the provisions of Article 80.

Article 77

1. The trusteeship system shall apply to such territories in the following categories as may be placed thereunder by means of trusteeship agreements.

(a) territories now held under mandate;

(b) territories which may be detached from enemy states as a result of the Second World War; and

(c) territories voluntarily placed under the system by states responsible for their administration.

2. It will be a matter for subsequent agreement as to which territories in the foregoing categories will be brought under the trusteeship system and upon what terms.

Article 78

The trusteeship system shall not apply to territories which have become Members of the United Nations, relationship among which shall be based on respect for the principle of sovereign equality.

Article 79

The terms of trusteeship for each territory to be placed under the trusteeship system, including any alteration or amendment, shall be agreed upon by the states directly concerned, including the mandatory power in the case of territories held under mandate by a Member of the United Nations, and shall be approved as provided for in Articles 83 and 85.

Article 80

1. Except as may be agreed upon in individual trusteeship agreements, made under Articles 77, 79, and 81, placing each territory under the trusteeship system, and until such agreements have been concluded, nothing in this Chapter shall be construed in or of itself to alter in any manner the rights whatsoever of any states or any peoples or the terms of existing international instruments to which Members of the United Nations may respectively be parties.

2. Paragraph 1 of this Article shall not be interpreted as giving grounds for delay or postponement of the negotiation and conclusion of agreements for placing mandated and other territories under the trusteeship system as provided for in Article 77.

Article 81

The trusteeship agreement shall in each case include the terms under which the trust territory will be administered and designate the authority which will exercise the administration of the trust territory. Such authority, hereinafter called the administering authority, may be one or more states or the Organization itself.

Article 82

There may be designated, in any trusteeship agreement, a strategic area or areas which may include part or all of the trust territory to which the agreement applies, without prejudice to any special agreement or agreements made under Article 43.

Article 83

1. All functions of the United Nations relating to strategic areas, including the approval of the terms of the trusteeship agreements and of their alteration or amendment, shall be exercised by the Security Council.

2. The basic objectives set forth in Article 76 shall be applicable to the people of each strategic area.

3. The Security Council shall, subject to the provisions of the trusteeship agreements and without prejudice to security considerations, avail itself of the assistance of the Trusteeship Council to perform those functions of the United Nations under the trusteeship system relating to political, economic, social, and educational matters in the strategic areas.

Article 84

It shall be the duty of the administering authority to ensure that the trust territory shall play its part in the maintenance of international peace and security. To this end the administering authority may make use of volunteer forces, facilities, and assistance from the trust territory in carrying out the obligations towards the Security Council undertaken in this regard by the administering authority, as well as for local defence and the maintenance of law and order within the trust territory.

Article 85

1. The functions of the United Nations with regard to trusteeship agreements for all areas not designated as strategic, including the approval of the terms of the trusteeship agreements and of their alteration or amendment, shall be exercised by the General Assembly.

2. The Trusteeship Council, operating under the authority of the General Assembly, shall assist the General Assembly in carrying out these functions.

XIII. THE TRUSTEESHIP COUNCIL*

Composition

Article 86

1. The Trusteeship Council shall consist of the following Members of the United Nations:

(a) those Members administering trust territories:

(b) such of those Members mentioned by name in Article 23 as are not administering trust territories; and

(c) as many other Members elected for three-year terms by the General Assembly as may be necessary to ensure that the total number of members of the Trusteeship Council is equally divided between those Members of the United Nations which administer trust territories and those which do not.

2. Each member of the Trusteeship Council shall designate one specially qualified person to represent it therein.

Functions and Powers

Article 87

The General Assembly and, under its authority, the Trusteeship Council, in carrying out their functions, may:

(a) consider reports submitted by the administering authority;

(b) accept petitions and examine them in consultation with the administering authority;

(c) provide for periodic visits to the respective trust territories at times agreed upon with the administering authority; and

(d) take these and other actions in conformity with the terms of the trusteeship agreements.

Article 88

The Trusteeship Council shall formulate a questionnaire on the political, economic, social, and educational advancement of the inhabitants of each trust territory, and the administering authority for each trust territory within the competence of the General Assembly shall make an annual report to the General Assembly upon the basis of such questionnaire.

Voting

Article 89

1. Each member of the Trusteeship Council shall have one vote.

2. Decisions of the Trusteeship Council shall be made by a majority of the members present and voting.

Procedure

Article 90

1. The Trusteeship Council shall adopt its own rules of procedure, including the method of selecting its President.

2. The Trusteeship Council shall meet as required in accordance with its rules, which shall include provision for the convening of meetings on the request of a majority of its members.

Article 91

The Trusteeship Council shall, when appropriate, avail itself of the assistance of the Economic and Social Council and of the specialized agencies in regard to matters with which they are respectively concerned.

---

* On 1 October 1994 the Republic of Palau, the last remaining territory under UN trusteeship, became independent. The Trusteeship Council formally suspended operations on 1 November; subsequently it was to be convened, as required, on an extraordinary basis.

XIV. THE INTERNATIONAL COURT OF JUSTICE

Article 92

The International Court of Justice shall be the principal judicial organ of the United Nations. It shall function in accordance with the annexed Statute, which is based upon the Statute of the Permanent Court of International Justice and forms an integral part of the present Charter.

Article 93

1. All Members of the United Nations are *ipso facto* parties to the Statute of the International Court of Justice.

2. A state which is not a Member of the United Nations may become a party to the Statute of the International Court of Justice on condition to be determined in each case by the General Assembly upon the recommendation of the Security Council.

Article 94

1. Each Member of the United Nations undertakes to comply with the decision of the International Court of Justice in any case to which it is a party.

2. If any party to a case fails to perform the obligations incumbent upon it under a judgment rendered by the Court, the other party may have recourse to the Security Council, which may, if it deems necessary, make recommendations or decide upon measures to be taken to give effect to the judgment.

Article 95

Nothing in the present Charter shall prevent Members of the United Nations from entrusting the solution of their differences to other tribunals by virtue of agreements already in existence or which may be concluded in the future.

Article 96

1. The General Assembly or the Security Council may request the International Court of Justice to give an advisory opinion on any legal question.

2. Other organs of the United Nations and specialized agencies, which may at any time be so authorized by the General Assembly, may also request advisory opinions of the Court on legal questions arising within the scope of their activities.

XV. THE SECRETARIAT

Article 97

The Secretariat shall comprise a Secretary-General and such staff as the Organization may require. The Secretary-General shall be appointed by the General Assembly upon the recommendation of the Security Council. He shall be the chief administrative officer of the Organization.

Article 98

The Secretary-General shall act in that capacity in all meetings of the General Assembly, of the Security Council, of the Economic and Social Council, and of the Trusteeship Council, and shall perform such other functions as are entrusted to him by these organs. The Secretary-General shall make an annual report to the General Assembly on the work of the Organization.

Article 99

The Secretary-General may bring to the attention of the Security Council any matter which in his opinion may threaten the maintenance of international peace and security.

Article 100

1. In the performance of their duties the Secretary-General and the staff shall not seek or receive instructions from any government or from any other authority external to the Organization. They shall refrain from any action which might reflect on their position as international officials responsible only to the Organization.

2. Each Member of the United Nations undertakes to respect the exclusively international character of the responsibilities of the Secretary-General and the staff and not to seek to influence them in the discharge of their responsibilities.

Article 101

1. The staff shall be appointed by the Secretary-General under regulations established by the General Assembly.

2. Appropriate staffs shall be permanently assigned to the Economic and Social Council, the Trusteeship Council, and, as required, to other organs of the United Nations. These staffs shall form a part of the Secretariat.

3. The paramount consideration in the employment of the staff and in the determination of the conditions of service shall be the necessity of securing the highest standards of efficiency, competence, and

integrity. Due regard shall be paid to the importance of recruiting the staff on as wide a geographical basis as possible.

XVI. MISCELLANEOUS PROVISIONS

Article 102

1. Every treaty and every international agreement entered into by any Member of the United Nations after the present Charter comes into force shall as soon as possible be registered with the Secretariat and published by it.

2. No party to any such treaty or international agreement which has not been registered in accordance with the provisions of paragraph 1 of this Article may invoke that treaty or agreement before any organ of the United Nations.

Article 103

In the event of a conflict between the obligations of the Members of the United Nations under the present Charter and their obligations under any other international agreement, their obligations under the present Charter shall prevail.

Article 104

The Organization shall enjoy in the territory of each of its Members such legal capacity as may be necessary for the exercise of its functions and the fulfilment of its purposes.

Article 105

1. The Organization shall enjoy in the territory of each of its Members such privileges and immunities as are necessary for the fulfilment of its purposes.

2. Representatives of the Members of the United Nations and officials of the Organization shall similarly enjoy such privileges and immunities as are necessary for the independent exercise of their functions in connection with the Organization.

3. The General Assembly may make recommendations with a view to determining the details of the application of paragraphs 1 and 2 of this Article or may propose conventions to the Members of the United Nations for this purpose.

XVII. TRANSITIONAL SECURITY ARRANGEMENTS

Article 106

Pending the coming into force of such special agreements referred to in Article 43 as in the opinion of the Security Council enable it to begin the exercise of its responsibilities under Article 42, the parties to the Four-Nation Declaration signed at Moscow, October 30, 1943, and France, shall, in accordance with the provisions of paragraph 5 of that Declaration, consult with one another and as occasion requires with other Members of the United Nations with a view to such joint action on behalf of the Organization as may be necessary for the purpose of maintaining international peace and security.

Article 107

Nothing in the present Charter shall invalidate or preclude action, in relation to any state which during the Second World War has been an enemy of any signatory to the present Charter, taken or authorized as a result of that war by the Governments having responsibility for such action.

XVIII. AMENDMENTS

Article 108

Amendments to the present Charter shall come into force for all Members of the United Nations when they have been adopted by a vote of two-thirds of the members of the General Assembly and ratified in accordance with their respective constitutional processes by two-thirds of the Members of the United Nations, including all the permanent members of the Security Council.

Article 109

1. A General Conference of the Members of the United Nations for the purpose of reviewing the present Charter may be held at a date and place to be fixed by a two-thirds vote of the members of the General Assembly and by a vote of any seven members of the Security Council. Each Member of the United Nations shall have one vote in the conference.

2. Any alteration of the present Charter recommended by a two-thirds vote of the conference shall take effect when ratified in accordance with their respective constitutional processes by two-thirds of the Members of the United Nations including all the permanent members of the Security Council.

3. If such a conference has not been held before the tenth annual session of the General Assembly following the coming into force of the present Charter, the proposal to call such a conference shall be placed on the agenda of that session of the General Assembly, and

the conference shall be held if so decided by a majority vote of the members of the General Assembly and by a vote of any seven members of the Security Council.

XIX. RATIFICATION AND SIGNATURE

Article 110

1. The present Charter shall be ratified by the signatory states in accordance with their respective constitutional processes.

2. The ratifications shall be deposited with the Government of the United States of America, which shall notify all the signatory states of each deposit as well as the Secretary-General of the Organization when he has been appointed.

3. The present Charter shall come into force upon the deposit of ratifications by the Republic of China, France, the Union of Soviet Socialist Republics, the United Kingdom of Great Britain and Northern Ireland, and the United States of America, and by a majority of the other signatory states. A protocol of the ratifications deposited shall thereupon be drawn up by the Government of the United States of America which shall communicate copies thereof to all the signatory states.

4. The states signatory to the present Charter which ratify it after it has come into force will become original Members of the United Nations on the date of the deposit of their respective ratifications.

Article 111

The present Charter, of which the Chinese, French, Russian, English, and Spanish texts are equally authentic, shall remain deposited in the archives of the Government of the United States of America. Duly certified copies thereof shall be transmitted by that Government to the Governments of the other signatory states.

IN FAITH WHEREOF the representatives of the Governments of the United Nations have signed the present Charter.

DONE at the city of San Francisco the twenty-sixth day of June, one thousand nine hundred and forty-five.

Amendments

The following amendments to Articles 23 and 27 of the Charter came into force in August 1965.

Article 23

1. The Security Council shall consist of 15 Members of the United Nations. The Republic of China, France, the Union of Soviet Socialist Republics, the United Kingdom of Great Britain and Northern Ireland, and the United States of America shall be permanent members of the Security Council. The General Assembly shall elect 10 other Members of the United Nations to be non-permanent members of the Security Council, due regard being specially paid, in the first instance to the contribution of Members of the United Nations to the maintenance of international peace and security and to the other purposes of the Organization, and also to equitable geographical distribution.

2. The non-permanent members of the Security Council shall be elected for a term of two years. In the first election of the non-permanent members after the increase of the membership of the Security Council from 11 to 15, two of the four additional members shall be chosen for a term of one year. A retiring member shall not be eligible for immediate re-election.

3. Each member of the Security Council shall have one representative.

Article 27

1. Each member of the Security Council shall have one vote.

2. Decisions of the Security Council on procedural matters shall be made by an affirmative vote of nine members.

3. Decisions of the Security Council on all other matters shall be made by an affirmative vote of nine members including the concurring votes of the permanent members; provided that, in decisions under Chapter VI and under paragraph 3 of Article 52, a party to a dispute shall abstain from voting.

The following amendments to Article 61 of the Charter came into force in September 1973.

Article 61

1. The Economic and Social Council shall consist of 54 Members of the United Nations elected by the General Assembly.

2. Subject to the provisions of paragraph 3, 18 members of the Economic and Social Council shall be elected each year for a term of three years. A retiring member shall be eligible for immediate re-election.

3. At the first election after the increase in the membership of the Economic and Social Council from 27 to 54 members, in addition to the members elected in place of the nine members whose term of office expires at the end of that year, 27 additional members shall be elected. Of these 27 additional members, the term of office of nine members so elected shall expire at the end of one year, and of nine other members at the end of two years, in accordance with arrangements made by the General Assembly.

4. Each member of the Economic and Social Council shall have one representative.

The following amendment to Paragraph 1 of Article 109 of the Charter came into force in June 1968.

Article 109

1. A General Conference of the Members of the United Nations for the purpose of reviewing the present Charter may be held at a date and place to be fixed by a two-thirds vote of the members of the General Assembly and by a vote of any nine members of the Security Council. Each Member of the United Nations shall have one vote in the conference.

UNITED NATIONS REGIONAL COMMISSIONS

Economic Commission for Europe—ECE

Address: Palais des Nations, 1211 Geneva 10, Switzerland.
Telephone: (22) 9174444; **fax:** (22) 9170505; **e-mail:** info.ece@
unece.org; **internet:** www.unece.org.

The UN Economic Commission for Europe was established in 1947.
Representatives of all European countries, the USA, Canada, Israel
and central Asian republics study the economic, environmental and
technological problems of the region and recommend courses of
action. ECE is also active in the formulation of international legal
instruments and the setting of international standards.

MEMBERS

Albania	Liechtenstein
Andorra	Lithuania
Armenia	Luxembourg
Austria	Macedonia, former Yugoslav
Azerbaijan	republic
Belarus	Malta
Belgium	Moldova
Bosnia and Herzegovina	Monaco
Bulgaria	Netherlands
Canada	Norway
Croatia	Poland
Cyprus	Portugal
Czech Republic	Romania
Denmark	Russia
Estonia	San Marino
Finland	Slovakia
France	Slovenia
Georgia	Spain
Germany	Sweden
Greece	Switzerland
Hungary	Tajikistan
Iceland	Turkey
Ireland	Turkmenistan
Israel	Ukraine
Italy	United Kingdom
Kazakhstan	USA
Kyrgyzstan	Uzbekistan
Latvia	Yugoslavia

Organization

(April 2001)

COMMISSION

ECE, with ECAFE (now ESCAP), was the earliest of the five regional
economic commissions set up by the UN Economic and Social
Council. The Commission holds an annual plenary session and
several informal sessions, and meetings of subsidiary bodies are
convened throughout the year.
President: HARALD KREID (Austria).

SECRETARIAT

The secretariat services the meetings of the Commission and its
subsidiary bodies and publishes periodic surveys and reviews,
including a number of specialized statistical bulletins on timber,
steel, chemicals, housing, building, and transport (see list of publications below). It maintains close and regular liaison with the United
Nations Secretariat in New York, with the secretariats of the other
UN regional commissions and of other UN organizations, including
the UN Specialized Agencies, and with other intergovernmental
organizations. The Executive Secretary also carries out secretarial
functions for the executive body of the 1979 Convention on Long-
range Transboundary Air Pollution and its protocols. The ECE and
UN Secretariats also service the ECOSOC Committee of Experts on
the Transport of Dangerous Goods.
Executive Secretary: DANUTA HÜBNER (Poland).

Activities

The guiding principle of ECE activities is the promotion of sustainable development. Within this framework, ECE's main objectives
are to provide assistance to countries of central and eastern Europe

in their transition from centrally-planned to market economies and
to achieve the integration of all members into the European and
global economies. Environmental protection, transport, statistics,
trade facilitation and economic analysis are all principal topics in
the ECE work programme, which also includes activities in the
fields of timber, energy, trade, industry, and human settlements.

The 50th annual session of the ECE, held in April 1997, introduced
a programme of reform, reducing the number of principal subsidiary
bodies from 14 to seven, in order to concentrate resources on the
core areas of work listed below, assisted by sub-committees and
groups of experts. The Commission also determined to strengthen
economic co-operation within Europe and to enhance co-operation
and dialogue with other sub-regional organizations. In April 1998
the Commission decided to establish an *ad hoc* working group
to consider and develop practices for relations with the business
community.

Committee on Environmental Policy: Provides policy direction
for the ECE region and promotes co-operation among member governments in developing and implementing policies for environmental protection, rational use of natural resources, and sustainable
development; supports the integration of environmental policy into
sectoral policies; seeks solutions to environmental problems, particularly those of a transboundary nature; assists in strengthening
environmental management capabilities, particularly in countries
in transition; prepares ministerial conferences (normally held every
four years—1998: Århus, Denmark); develops and promotes the
implementation of international agreements on the environment;
and assesses national policies and legislation.

Committee on Human Settlements: Reviews trends and policies
in the field of human settlements; undertakes studies and organizes
seminars; promotes international co-operation in the field of housing
and urban and regional research; assists the countries of central
and eastern Europe, which are currently in the process of economic
transition, in reformulating their policies relating to housing, land
management, sustainable human settlements, and planning and
development.

Committee on Sustainable Energy: Exchanges information on
general energy problems; work programme comprises activities
including labelling classification systems and related legal and
policy frameworks; liberalization of energy markets, pricing policies
and supply security; development of regional sustainable energy
strategies for the 21st century; rational use of energy, efficiency and
conservation; energy infrastructure including interconnection of
electric power and gas networks; coal and thermal power generation
in the context of sustainable energy development; Energy Efficiency
2000 project; promotion and development of a market-based Gas
Industry in Economics in Transition—Gas Centre project; and technical assistance and operational activities in energy for the benefit
of countries with economies in transition.

Committee for Trade, Industry and Enterprise Development:
A forum for studying means of expanding and diversifying trade
among European countries, as well as with countries in other
regions, and for drawing up recommendations on how to achieve
these ends. Analyses trends, problems and prospects in intra-Euro-
pean trade; explores means of encouraging the flow of international
direct investment, including joint ventures, into the newly opening
economies of central and eastern Europe; promotes new or improved
methods of trading by means of marketing, industrial co-operation,
contractual guides, and the facilitation of international trade procedures (notably by developing and diffusing electronic data interchange standards and messages for administration, commerce and
transport—UNEDIFACT). In March 1997 ECE's Working Party on
the Facilitation of International Trade Procedures was transformed
into the Centre for the Facilitation of Procedures and Practices
for Administration, Commerce and Trade, which was intended to
develop harmonized procedures for international transactions and
to promote private sector activities.

Conference of European Statisticians: Promotes improvement
of national statistics and their international comparability in economic, social, demographic and environmental fields; promotes co-
ordination of statistical activities of European international organizations; and responds to the increasing need for international statistical co-operation both within the ECE region and between the region
and other regions. Works very closely with the OECD and the EU.

Inland Transport Committee: Promotes a coherent, efficient,
safe and sustainable transport system through the development

of international agreements, conventions and other instruments covering a wide range of questions relating to road, rail, inland water and combined transport, including infrastructure, border-crossing facilitation, road traffic safety, requirements for the construction of road vehicles and other transport regulations, particularly in the fields of transport of dangerous goods and perishable foodstuffs. Also considers transport trends and economics and compiles transport statistics. Assists central and eastern European countries in developing their transport systems and infrastructures.

Timber Committee: Regularly reviews markets for forest products; analyses long-term trends and prospects for forestry and timber; keeps under review developments in the forest industries, including environmental and energy-related aspects. Subsidiary bodies run jointly with the FAO deal with forest technology, management and training and with forest economics and statistics.

SUB-REGIONAL PROGRAMMES

Southeast European Co-operative Initiative—SECI: initiated in December 1996, in order to encourage co-operation among countries of the sub-region and to facilitate their access to the process of European integration. Nine *ad hoc* Project Groups have been established to undertake preparations for the following selected projects: trade facilitation; transport infrastructure, in particular road and rail networks; financial policies to promote small and medium-sized enterprises; co-operation to combat crime and corruption; energy efficiency demonstration zone networks; interconnection of natural gas networks; co-operation among securities markets; and the Danube recovery programme, incorporating the Danube River Basin and other international waterways and lakes. Activities are overseen by a SECI Agenda Committee and a SECI Business Advisory Council. Participating countries: Albania, Bosnia and Herzegovina, Bulgaria, Croatia, Greece, Hungary, the former Yugoslav republic of Macedonia, Moldova, Romania, Slovenia and Turkey.

Special Programme for the Economies of Central Asia—SPECA: initiated in March 1998 as a joint programme of the ECE and ESCAP. Aims to strengthen sub-regional co-operation, in particular in the following areas: the development of transport infrastructure and facilitation of cross-border activities; the rational use of energy and water; regional development and attraction of foreign investment; and development of multiple routes for pipeline transportation of hydrocarbons to global markets. Participating countries: Kazakhstan, Kyrgyzstan, Tajikistan, Turkmenistan and Uzbekistan.

Finance

ECE's budget for the two years 2000–01 was US $40.6m.

Publications

ECE Annual Report.
Annual Bulletin of Housing and Building Statistics for Europe.
Annual Bulletin of Steel Statistics for Europe.
Annual Bulletin of Transport Statistics for Europe.
The Chemical Industry.
Directory of Chemical Producers and Products.
The ECE in the Age of Change.
Economic Survey of Europe (3 a year).
Statistical Journal of the ECE (quarterly).
Statistics of Road Traffic Accidents in Europe.
Statistics of World Trade in Steel.
The Steel Market.
Timber Bulletin for Europe.
Transport Information.
Trends in Europe and North America: Statistical Yearbook of the ECE.
UN Manual of Tests and Criteria of Dangerous Goods.
UN Recommendations on the Transport of Dangerous Goods.
Women and Men in Europe and North America: Highlights (quarterly).

Series of studies on air pollution, the environment, forestry and timber, water, trade facilitation, industrial co-operation, energy, joint ventures, and economic reforms in eastern Europe.

Reports, proceedings of meetings, technical documents, codes of conduct, codes of practice, guide-lines to governments, etc.

Economic and Social Commission for Asia and the Pacific—ESCAP

Address: United Nations Bldg, Rajdamnern Ave, Bangkok 10200, Thailand.

Telephone: (2) 288-1234; **fax:** (2) 288-1000; **e-mail:** unisbkk.unescap@un.org; **internet:** www.unescap.org.

The Commission was founded in 1947 to encourage the economic and social development of Asia and the Far East; it was originally known as the Economic Commission for Asia and the Far East (ECAFE). The title ESCAP, which replaced ECAFE, was adopted after a reorganization in 1974.

MEMBERS

Afghanistan	Korea, Democratic	Papua New Guinea
Armenia	People's Republic	Philippines
Australia	Korea, Republic	Russia
Azerbaijan	Kyrgyzstan	Samoa
Bangladesh	Laos	Singapore
Bhutan	Malaysia	Solomon Islands
Brunei	Maldives	Sri Lanka
Cambodia	Marshall Islands	Tajikistan
China, People's	Micronesia, Federated	Thailand
Republic	States	Tonga
Fiji	Mongolia	Turkey
France	Myanmar	Turkmenistan
India	Nauru	Tuvalu
Indonesia	Nepal	United Kingdom
Iran	Netherlands	USA
Japan	New Zealand	Uzbekistan
Kazakhstan	Pakistan	Vanuatu
Kiribati	Palau	Viet Nam

ASSOCIATE MEMBERS

American Samoa	Hong Kong	Northern Mariana
Cook Islands	Macau	Islands
French Polynesia	New Caledonia	
Guam	Niue	

Organization

(April 2001)

COMMISSION

The Commission meets annually at ministerial level to examine the region's problems, to review progress, to establish priorities and to decide upon the recommendations of the Executive Secretary or the subsidiary bodies of the Commission.

Ministerial and intergovernmental conferences on specific issues may be held on an *ad hoc* basis with the approval of the Commission, although, from 1998, no more than one ministerial conference and five intergovernmental conferences may be held during one year.

COMMITTEES AND SPECIAL BODIES

The following advise the Commission and help to oversee the work of the Secretariat:

Committee on the Environment and Natural Resources Development: meets annually.

Committee on Regional Economic-Co-operation: meets every two years, with a high-level Steering Group, which meets annually to discuss and develop policy options.

Committee on Socio-economic Measures to Alleviate Poverty in Rural and Urban Areas: meets annually.

Committee on Statistics: meets every two years.

Committee on Transport, Communications, Tourism and Infrastructure Development: meets annually.

Special Body on Least-Developed and Land-locked Developing Countries: meets every two years.

Special Body on Pacific Island Developing Countries: meets every two years.

In addition, an Advisory Committee of permanent representatives and other representatives designated by members of the Commission functions as an advisory body.

SECRETARIAT

The Secretariat operates under the guidance of the Commission and its subsidiary bodies. It consists of two servicing divisions, covering administration and programme management, in addition to the following substantive divisions: Development research and policy analysis; International trade and industry; Environment and natural resources development; Social development; Population and rural and urban development; Transport, communications, tourism and infrastructure development; and Statistics.

The Secretariat also includes the ESCAP/UNCTAD Joint Unit on Transnational Corporations and the UN information services.

Executive Secretary: KIM HAK-SU (Republic of Korea).

SUB-REGIONAL OFFICE

ESCAP Pacific Operations Centre (EPOC): POB 503, Port Vila, Vanuatu; tel. 23458; fax 23921; e-mail escap@vanuatu.com.vu; f. 1984, to provide effective advisory and technical assistance at a sub-regional level and to identify the needs of island countries. Dir SAVENACA SIWATIBAU.

Activities

ESCAP acts as a UN regional centre, providing the only intergovernmental forum for the whole of Asia and the Pacific, and executing a wide range of development programmes through technical assistance, advisory services to governments, research, training and information.

In 1992 ESCAP began to reorganize its programme activities and conference structures in order to reflect and serve the region's evolving development needs. The approach that was adopted focused on regional economic co-operation, poverty alleviation through economic growth and social development, and environmental and sustainable development.

Regional Economic Co-operation. Provides technical assistance and advisory services, and aims to promote the exchange of experience and specialist knowledge in the trade, investment and technology sectors. ESCAP continues to assess issues arising from the implementation of World Trade Organization commitments and to assist least developed countries to undertake trade liberalization measures in accordance with national priorities. ESCAP promotes regional co-operation for enhancing trade efficiency, including electronic commerce, and increasing the exports of developing countries, in particular in the areas of commodities, textiles and products of small and medium-sized enterprises. Special emphasis is given to the needs of least developed, land-locked and island developing countries, and to economies in transition, in furthering their integration into the region's economy. In addition, the sub-programme aims to enhance institutional capacity-building, to promote private capital flows for trade-related investment, and to support the advancement of electronic commerce and other information technologies in the region.

Development research and policy analysis. Aims to increase the understanding of the economic and social development situation in the region, with particular attention given to sustainable economic growth, poverty alleviation, the integration of environmental concerns into macroeconomic decisions and policy-making processes, and enhancing the position of the region's disadvantaged economies. The sub-programme is responsible for the provision of technical assistance, and the production of relevant documents and publications.

Social development. The main objective of the sub-programme is to assess and respond to regional trends and challenges in social policy and human resources development, with particular attention to the planning and delivery of social services and training programmes for disadvantaged groups, including the poor, youths, women, the disabled, and the elderly. Implements global and regional mandates, such as the Programme of Action of the World Summit for Social Development and the Jakarta Plan of Action on Human Resources Development and Action for the Asian and Pacific Decade of Disabled Persons 1993–2002. In addition, the sub-programme aims to strengthen the capacity of public and non-government institutions to address the problems of marginalized social groups and to foster partnerships between governments, the private sector, community organizations and all other involved bodies. In 1998 ESCAP initiated a programme of assistance in establishing a regional network of Social Development Management Information Systems (SOMIS). Feasibility studies were conducted in three pilot countries in 1998–2000.

Population and rural and urban development. Aims to assess and strengthen the capabilities of local institutions in rural and urban development, as well as increasing the capacity of governmental and non-governmental organizations to develop new approaches to poverty alleviation and to support food security for rural households. Promotes the correct use of agro-chemicals in order to increase food supply and to achieve sustainable agricultural development and administers the Fertilizer Advisory Development and Information Network for Asia and the Pacific (FADINAP). Rural employment opportunities and the access of the poor to land, credit and other productive assets are also considered by the subprogramme. Undertakes technical co-operation and research in the areas of ageing, female economic migration and reproductive health, and prepares specific publications relating to population. Implements global and regional mandates, such as the Programme of Action of the International Conference on Population and Development. The Secretariat co-ordinates the Asia-Pacific Population Information Network (POPIN).

Environment and natural resources development. Concerned with strengthening national capabilities to achieve environmentally-sound and sustainable development by integrating economic concerns, such as the sustainable management of natural resources, into economic planning and policies. The sub-programme was responsible for implementation of the Regional Action Programme for Environmentally Sound and Sustainable Development for the period 1996–2000, adopted in November 1995. Other activities included the promotion of integrated water resources development and management, including water quality and a reduction in water-related natural disasters; strengthening the formulation of policies in the sustainable development of land and mineral resources; the consideration of energy resource options, such as rural energy supply, energy conservation and the planning of power networks; and promotion of the use of space technology applications for environmental management, natural disaster monitoring and sustainable development.

Transport, communications, tourism and infrastructure development. Aims to develop inter- and intra-regional transport links to enhance trade and tourism, mainly through implementation of an Asian Land Transport Infrastructure Development project. Other activities are aimed at improving the planning process in developing infrastructure facilities and services, in accordance with the regional action programme of the New Delhi Action Plan on Infrastructure Development in Asia and the Pacific, which was adopted at a ministerial conference held in October 1996, and at enhancing private sector involvement in national infrastructure development through financing, management, operations and risk-sharing. Aims to reduce the adverse environmental impact of the provision of infrastructure facilites and to promote more equitable and easier access to social amenities. Tourism concerns include the development of human resources, improved policy planning for tourism development, greater investment in the industry, and minimizing the environmental impact of tourism.

Statistics. Provides training and advice in priority areas, including national accounts statistics, gender statistics, population censuses and surveys, and the management of statistical systems. Supports co-ordination throughout the region of the development, implementation and revision of selected international statistical standards. Disseminates comparable socio-economic statistics, with increased use of the electronic media, promotes the use of modern information technology in the public sector and trains senior-level officials in the effective management of information technology.

Throughout all the sub-programmes, ESCAP aimed to focus particular attention on the needs and concerns of least developed, land-locked and island developing nations in the region.

CO-OPERATION WITH THE ASIAN DEVELOPMENT BANK

In July 1993 a memorandum of understanding was signed by ESCAP and the Asian Development Bank (ADB—q.v.), outlining priority areas of co-operation between the two organizations. These were: regional and sub-regional co-operation; issues concerning the least-developed, land-locked and island developing member countries; poverty alleviation; women in development; population; human resource development; the environment and natural resource management; statistics and data bases; economic analysis; transport and communications; and industrial restructuring and privatization. The two organizations were to co-operate in organizing workshops, seminars and conferences, in implementing joint projects, and in exchanging information and data on a regular basis.

ASSOCIATED BODIES

Asian and Pacific Centre for Transfer of Technology: Off New Mehrauli Rd, POB 4575, New Delhi 110 016, India; tel. (11) 6856276; fax (11) 6856274; e-mail postmaster@apctt.org; internet www.apctt.org; f. 1977 to assist countries of the ESCAP region by strengthening their capacity to develop, transfer and adopt technologies relevant to the region, and to identify and to promote regional technology development and transfer. Dir Dr JÜRGEN H. BISCHOFF. Publs *Asia Pacific Tech Monitor, VATIS Updates on Biotechnology, Food Processing, Ozone Layer Protection, Non-Conventional Energy,* and *Waste Technology* (each every 2 months), *International Technology and Business Opportunities Update* (quarterly).

ESCAP/WMO Typhoon Committee: c/o UNDP, POB 7285, ADC, Pasay City, Metro Manila, Philippines; tel. (632) 3733443; fax (2) 3733419; e-mail tcs@philonline.com.ph; f. 1968; an intergovernmental body sponsored by ESCAP and WMO for mitigation of typhoon damage. It aims at establishing efficient typhoon and flood warning systems through improved meteorological and telecommunication facilities. Other activities include promotion of disaster preparedness, training of personnel and co-ordination of research. The committee's programme is supported from national resources and also by UNDP and other international and bilateral assistance. Mems: Cambodia, People's Republic of China, Hong Kong, Japan, Democratic People's Republic of Korea, Republic of Korea, Laos, Macau, Malaysia, Philippines, Singapore, Thailand, USA, Viet Nam. Co-ordinator of Secretariat: Dr ROMAN L. KINTANAR.

Regional Co-ordination Centre for Research and Development of Coarse Grains, Pulses, Roots and Tuber Crops in the Tropics of Asia and the Pacific (CGPRT Centre): Jalan Merdeka 145, Bogor 16111, Indonesia; tel. (251) 343277; fax (251) 336290; e-mail cgprt@server.indo.net.id; internet www.cgprt.org.sg; f. 1981; initiates and promotes research, training and publications on the production, marketing and use of these crops. Dir HARUO INAGAKI. Publs *Palawija News* (quarterly), project reports, statistics, working paper series and monograph series.

Statistical Institute for Asia and the Pacific: 2-2 Wakaba 3-chome, Mihama-ku, Chiba-shi, Chiba 261-8787, Japan; tel. (43) 2999782; fax (43) 2999780; e-mail unsiap@ma.kcom.ne.jp; internet www1.kcom.ne.jp/~unsiap; f. 1970; trains government statisticians; prepares teaching materials, provides facilities for special studies and research of a statistical nature, assists in the development of training on official statistics in national and sub-regional centres. Dir LAU KAK EN.

WMO/ESCAP Panel on Tropical Cyclones: Technical Support Unit, Abhawa Bhaban, Agargon, Dhaka 1207, Bangladesh; f. 1973 to mitigate damage caused by tropical cyclones in the Bay of Bengal and the Arabian Sea; mems: Bangladesh, India, Maldives, Myanmar, Pakistan, Sri Lanka, Thailand.

Finance

For the two-year period 2000–01 ESCAP's regular budget, an appropriation from the UN budget, was US $57.0m. (compared with $67.5m. in 1998–99). The regular budget is supplemented annually by funds from various sources for technical assistance.

Publications

Annual Report.

Agro-chemicals News in Brief (quarterly).

Asia-Pacific Development Journal (2 a year).

Asia-Pacific in Figures (annually).

Asia-Pacific Population Journal (quarterly).

Asia-Pacific Remote Sensing and GIS Journal (2 a year).

Atlas of Mineral Resources of the ESCAP Region.

Confluence (water resources newsletter, 2 a year).

Economic and Social Survey of Asia and the Pacific (annually).

Environmental News Briefing (every 2 months).

ESCAP Energy News (2 a year).

ESCAP Human Resources Development Newsletter (2 a year).

ESCAP Population Data Sheet (annually).

ESCAP Tourism Newsletter (2 a year).

Fertilizer Trade Information Monthly Bulletin.

Foreign Trade Statistics of Asia and the Pacific (annually).

Government Computerization Newsletter (irregular).

Industry and Technology Development News for Asia and the Pacific (annually).

Poverty Alleviation Initiatives (quarterly).

Regional Network for Agricultural Machinery Newsletter (3 a year).

Small Industry Bulletin for Asia and the Pacific (annually).

Social Development Newsletter (2 a year).

Space Technology Applications Newsletter (quarterly).

Statistical Indicators for Asia and the Pacific (quarterly).

Statistical Newsletter (quarterly).

Statistical Yearbook for Asia and the Pacific.

Trade and Investment Information Bulletin (monthly).

Transport and Communications Bulletin for Asia and the Pacific (annually).

Water Resources Journal (quarterly).

Bibliographies; country and trade profiles; commodity prices; statistics.

Economic Commission for Latin America and the Caribbean—ECLAC

Address: Edif. Naciones Unidas, Avda Dag Hammarskjöld, Casilla 179D, Santiago, Chile.

Telephone: (2) 2102000; **fax:** (2) 2080252; **e-mail:** dpisantiago@eclac.cl; **internet:** www.eclac.org.

The UN Economic Commission for Latin America was founded in 1948 to co-ordinate policies for the promotion of economic development in the Latin American region. The current name of the Commission was adopted in 1984.

MEMBERS

Antigua and Barbuda	Costa Rica	Haiti
Argentina	Cuba	Honduras
Bahamas	Dominica	Italy
Barbados	Dominican Republic	Jamaica
Belize	Ecuador	Mexico
Bolivia	El Salvador	Netherlands
Brazil	France	Nicaragua
Canada	Grenada	Panama
Chile	Guatemala	Paraguay
Colombia	Guyana	Peru
		Portugal

Saint Christopher and Nevis	Spain	United Kingdom
Saint Lucia	Suriname	USA
Saint Vincent and the Grenadines	Trinidad and Tobago	Uruguay
		Venezuela

ASSOCIATE MEMBERS

Anguilla	Montserrat	Puerto Rico
Aruba	Netherlands Antilles	United States Virgin Islands
British Virgin Islands		

Organization

(April 2001)

COMMISSION

The Commission normally meets every two years in one of the Latin American capitals. The 27th session of the Commission was held in Oranjestad, Aruba in May 1998. The Commission has established the following permanent bodies:

Caribbean Development and Co-operation Committee.

Central American Development and Co-operation Committee.

Committee of High-Level Government Experts.

Committee of the Whole.

Regional Conference on the Integration of Women into the Economic and Social Development of Latin America and the Caribbean.

Regional Council for Planning.

SECRETARIAT

The Secretariat employs more than 500 staff and comprises the Office of the Executive Secretary; the Programme Planning and Operations Division; and the Office of the Secretary of the Commission. ECLAC's work programme is carried out by the following divisions: Economic Development; Social Development; International Commerce, Finance and Transportation; Productive and Entrepreneurial Development; Statistics and Economic Projections; Environment and Development; and Population. There is also a Woman and Development Unit, support divisions of documents and publications, and of administration, and an Economic and Social Documentation Centre (CLADES).

Executive Secretary: José Antonio Ocampo (Colombia).

Secretary of the Commission: Ernesto Ottone.

SUB-REGIONAL OFFICES

Caribbean: 63 Park St, Chic Bldg, 3rd Floor, POB 1113, Port of Spain, Trinidad and Tobago; tel. 623-5595; fax 623-8486; e-mail registry@eclacpos.org; internet www.searcher.eclacpos.org; f. 1956; covers non-Spanish-speaking Caribbean countries; Dir Len Ishmael.

Central America and Spanish-speaking Caribbean: Avda Presidente Masaryk 29, 11570 México, DF; tel. (5) 250-1555; fax (5) 531-1151; e-mail cepal@un.org.mx; internet www.un.org.mex/cepal; f. 1951; covers Central America and Spanish-speaking Caribbean countries; Dir Rómulo Caballeros.

There are also five national offices, in Santafé de Bogotá, Brasília, Buenos Aires, Montevideo and Washington, DC.

Activities

ECLAC collaborates with regional governments in the investigation and analysis of regional and national economic problems, and provides guidance in the formulation of development plans. Its activities include research; analysis; publication of information; provision of technical assistance; participation in seminars and conferences; training courses; and co-operation with national, regional and international organizations.

The 26th session of the Commission, which was held in San José, Costa Rica, in April 1996, considered means of strengthening the economic and social development of the region, within the framework of a document prepared by ECLAC's Secretariat, and adopted a resolution which defined ECLAC as a centre of excellence, charged with undertaking an analysis of specific aspects of the development process, in collaboration with member governments. The meeting also reviewed the impact on ECLAC of the ongoing process of reform throughout the UN system. The Commission agreed to establish an *ad hoc* working group to recommend a strategic framework for the Commission, to define priorities for a future work programme and to improve working relations between the Commission and member states. In May 1998 the 27th session of the Commission, held in Oranjestad, Aruba, approved the ongoing reform programme, and in particular efforts to enhance the effectiveness and transparency of ECLAC's activities. The main topics of debate at the meeting were public finances, fiscal management and social and economic development. The Commission adopted a Fiscal Covenant, incorporating measures to consolidate fiscal adjustment and to strengthen public management, democracy and social equity, which was to be implemented throughout the region and provide the framework for further debate at national and regional level. ECLAC's 28th session, convened in Mexico City in April 2000, debated a document prepared by the Secretariat which proposed that the pursuit of social equity, sustainable development and 'active citizenship' (with emphasis on the roles of education and employment) should form the basis of future policy-making in the region.

ECLAC works closely with other agencies within the UN system and with other regional and multinational organizations. ECLAC is co-operating with the OAS and the Inter-American Development Bank in the servicing of intergovernmental groups undertaking preparatory work for the establishment of a Free Trade Area of the Americas.

Latin American and Caribbean Institute for Economic and Social Planning—ILPES: Edif. Naciones Unidas, Avda Dag Hammarskjöld, Casilla 1567, Santiago, Chile; tel. (2) 2102506; fax (2) 2066104; e-mail pdekock@eclac.cl; f. 1962; supports regional governments through the provision of training, advisory services and research in the field of public planning policy and co-ordination. Dir José Antonio Ocampo.

Latin American Demographic Centre—CELADE: Edif. Naciones Unidas, Avda Dag Hammarskjöld, Casilla 179D, Santiago, Chile; tel. (2) 2102002; fax (2) 2080252; e-mail djaspers@eclac.cl; internet www.eclac.org/celade; f. 1957, became an integral part of ECLAC in 1975; provides technical assistance to governments, universities and research centres in demographic analysis, population policies, integration of population factors in development planning, and data processing; conducts three-month courses on demographic analysis for development and various national and regional seminars; provides demographic estimates and projections, documentation, data processing, computer packages and training. Dir Daniel S. Blanchard.

Finance

For the two-year period 2000–01 ECLAC's regular budget, an appropriation from the UN, amounted to US $78.9m. In addition, extra-budgetary activities are financed by governments, other organizations, and UN agencies, including UNDP, UNFPA and UNICEF.

Publications

Boletín del Banco de Datos del CELADE (annually).

Boletín demográfico (2 a year).

Boletín de Facilitación del Comercio y el Transporte (every 2 months).

CEPAL Review (Spanish and English, 3 a year).

CEPALINDEX (annually).

Co-operation and Development (Spanish and English, quarterly).

DOCPAL Resúmenes (population studies, 2 a year).

ECLAC Notes / Notas de la CEPAL (every 2 months).

Economic Panorama of Latin America (annually).

Economic Survey of Latin America and the Caribbean (Spanish and English, annually).

Foreign Investment in Latin America and the Caribbean.

Notas de Población (2 a year).

PLANINDEX (2 a year).

Preliminary Overview of the Economy of Latin America and the Caribbean (annually).

Social Panorama of Latin America (annually).

Statistical Yearbook for Latin America and the Caribbean (Spanish and English).

Studies, reports, bibliographical bulletins.

Economic Commission for Africa—ECA

Address: Africa Hall, POB 3001, Addis Ababa, Ethiopia.
Telephone: (1) 515826; **fax:** (1) 510365; **e-mail:** ecainfo@un.org; **internet:** www.uneca.org.

The UN Economic Commission for Africa was founded in 1958 by a resolution of the UN Economic and Social Council (ECOSOC) to initiate and take part in measures for facilitating Africa's economic development.

MEMBERS

Algeria	Eritrea	Niger
Angola	Ethiopia	Nigeria
Benin	Gabon	Rwanda
Botswana	The Gambia	São Tomé and
Burkina Faso	Ghana	Príncipe
Burundi	Guinea	Senegal
Cameroon	Guinea-Bissau	Seychelles
Cape Verde	Kenya	Sierra Leone
Central African	Lesotho	Somalia
Republic	Liberia	South Africa
Chad	Libya	Sudan
Comoros	Madagascar	Swaziland
Congo, Democratic	Malawi	Tanzania
Republic	Mali	Togo
Congo, Republic	Mauritania	Tunisia
Côte d'Ivoire	Mauritius	Uganda
Djibouti	Morocco	Zambia
Egypt	Mozambique	Zimbabwe
Equatorial Guinea	Namibia	

Organization

(April 2001)

COMMISSION

The Commission may only act with the agreement of the government of the country concerned. It is also empowered to make recommendations on any matter within its competence directly to the government of the member or associate member concerned, to governments admitted in a consultative capacity, and to the UN Specialized Agencies. The Commission is required to submit for prior consideration by ECOSOC any of its proposals for actions that would be likely to have important effects on the international economy.

CONFERENCE OF MINISTERS

The Conference, which meets every two years, is attended by ministers responsible for economic or financial affairs, planning and development of governments of member states, and is the main deliberative body of the Commission.

The Commission's responsibility to promote concerted action for the economic and social development of Africa is vested primarily in the Conference, which considers matters of general policy and the priorities to be assigned to the Commission's programmes, considers inter-African and international economic policy, and makes recommendations to member states in connection with such matters.

OTHER POLICY-MAKING BODIES

A Conference of Ministers of Finance and a Conference of Ministers responsible for economic and social development and planning meet in alternate years to formulate policy recommendations. Each is served by a committee of experts. Five intergovernmental committees of experts attached to the Sub-regional Development Centres (see below) meet annually and report to the Commission through a Technical Preparatory Committee of the Whole, which was established in 1979 to deal with matters submitted for the consideration of the Conference.

Seven other committees meet regularly to consider issues relating to the following policy areas: women and development; development information; sustainable development; human development and civil society; industry and private sector development; natural resources and science and technology; and regional co-operation and integration.

SECRETARIAT

The Secretariat provides the services necessary for the meeting of the Conference of Ministers and the meetings of the Commission's subsidiary bodies, carries out the resolutions and implements the programmes adopted there. It comprises an Office of the Executive Secretary, the African Centre for Women and the following eight divisions: Food Security and Sustainable Development; Development Management; Development Information Services; Regional Co-operation and Integration; Programme Planning, Finance and Evaluation; Economic and Social Policy; Human Resources and System Management; Conference and General Services.
Executive Secretary: Kingsley Y. Amoako (Ghana).

SUB-REGIONAL DEVELOPMENT CENTRES

Multinational Programming and Operational Centres (MULPOCs) were established, in 1977, to implement regional development programmes. In May 1997 the Commission decided to transform the MULPOCs into Sub-regional Development Centres (SRDCs) in order to enable member states to play a more effective role in the process of African integration and to facilitate the integration efforts of the other UN agencies active in the sub-regions. In addition, the SRDCs were to act as the operational arms of ECA at national and sub-regional levels: to ensure harmony between the objectives of sub-regional and regional programmes and those defined by the Commission; to provide advisory services; to facilitate sub-regional economic co-operation, integration and development; to collect and disseminate information; to stimulate policy dialogue; and to promote gender issues. In July 1997 it was reported that ECA intended to deploy 25% of its professional personnel in the SRDCs (up from 9%) and to allocate approximately 40% of its budget to the Centres.

Central Africa: POB 836, Yaoundé, Cameroon; tel. 23-14-61; fax 23-31-85; e-mail casrdc@camnet.cm; Dir Abdoulaye Niang.

Eastern Africa: POB 4654, Kigali, Rwanda; tel. 86545; fax 86546; e-mail easrdc@rwanda1.com; Dir Halidou Ouédraogo.

North Africa: POB 316, Tangier, Morocco; tel. (39) 322346; fax (39) 340357; e-mail srdc-na@uneca.org; Dir Abdelouahab Rezig.

Southern Africa: POB 30647, Lusaka, Zambia; tel. (1) 228503; fax (1) 236949; e-mail uneca@zamnet.zm; Dir Dr Robert M. Okello.

West Africa: POB 744, Niamey, Niger; tel. 72-29-61; fax 72-28-94; Dir Henri Soumah.

Activities

The Commission's activities are designed to encourage sustainable socio-economic development in Africa and to increase economic co-operation among African countries and between Africa and other parts of the world. The Secretariat is guided in its efforts by major regional strategies including the Abuja Treaty establishing the African Economic Community signed under the aegis of the Organization of African Unity and the UN New Agenda for the Development of Africa covering the period 1991–2000. ECA's main programme areas for the period 1996–2001 were based on an Agenda for Action, which was announced by the OAU Council of Ministers in March 1995 and adopted by African heads of state in June, with the stated aim of 'relaunching Africa's economic and social development'. The five overall objectives were to facilitate economic and social policy analysis and implementation; to ensure food security and sustainable development; to strengthen development management; to harness information for development; and to promote regional co-operation and integration. In all its activities ECA aimed to promote the themes of capacity-building and of fostering leadership and the empowerment of women in Africa. In May 1998 ECA's African Centre for Women inaugurated a new Fund for African Women's Development to support capacity-building activities.

DEVELOPMENT INFORMATION SYSTEMS

Until 1997 regional development information management was promoted through the Pan-African Development Information System (PADIS, established in 1980 and known until 1989 as the Pan-African Documentation and Information Service). In 1997 the Development Information Services Division (DISD) was created, with responsibility for co-ordinating the implementation of the Harnessing Information Technology for Africa project (in the context of the UN system-wide Special Initiative on Africa) and for the implementation of the African Information Society Initiative (AISI), a framework for creating an information and communications infrastructure; for overseeing quality enhancement and dissemination of statistical databases; for improving access to information by means of enhanced library and documentation services and output; and by strengthening geo-information systems for sustainable development. In addition, ECA encourages member governments to liberalize the telecommunications sector and stimulate imports of computers in order to enable the expansion of information technology throughout Africa. ECA manages the Information Technology Centre for Africa, based in Addis Ababa.

Regional statistical development activities are managed through the Co-ordinating Committee on African Statistical Development (CASD, established in 1992). The CASD facilitates the harmonization of statistical systems and methodologies at regional and national level; establishes mechanisms for the continuous exchange of information between governments, national agencies and regional and sub-regional bodies, and all bilateral and multilateral agencies; identifies and proposes new lines of action; and informs the Conference of African Planners, Statisticians and Population and Information Specialists (PSPI) on the progress of the Addis Ababa Plan of Action for Statistical Development in the 1990s (adopted in 1992). In May 1997 five task forces were established to undertake the CASD's activities; these covered the following areas: improving e-mail connectivity; monitoring the implementation of the Addis Ababa Plan of Action; strengthening statistical training programme for Africa (STPA) centres; assisting with the formation of census and household survey data service centres in two–five pilot countries, and with the establishment of a similar regional ECA service centre; and establishing live databases, comprising core macro and sectoral statistical indicators, initially as a pilot project in two–five countries, with eventual links to a regional database facility.

ECA assists its member states in (i) population data collection and data processing; (ii) analysis of demographic data obtained from censuses or surveys; (iii) training demographers at the Regional Institute for Population Studies (RIPS) in Accra, Ghana, and at the Institut de formation et de recherche démographiques (IFORD) in Yaoundé, Cameroon; (iv) formulation of population policies and integrating population variables in development planning, through advisory missions and through the organization of national seminars on population and development; and (v) dissemination of information through its *Newsletter, Demographic Handbook for Africa,* the *African Population Studies* series and other publications. The strengthening of national population policies was an important element of ECA's objective of ensuring food security in African countries. The Ninth PSPI was held in March 1996, in Addis Ababa, Ethiopia.

In August 2000 ECA hosted a preparatory workshop for the first Africa Knowledge Networks Forum (AKNF), which was scheduled to be convened, under ECA auspices, during 2001. The Forum was to facilitate co-operation in information-sharing and research between professional research and development networks, and also between these and policy-makers, educators, civil society organizations and the private sector. It was to provide technical support to the ADF process (see below).

DEVELOPMENT MANAGEMENT

ECA aims to assist governments, public corporations, universities and the private sector in improving their financial management; strengthening policy-making and analytical capacities; adopting measures to redress skill shortages; enhancing human resources development and utilization; and promoting social development through programmes focusing on youth, people with disabilities and the elderly. The Secretariat organizes training workshops, seminars and conferences at national, subregional and regional levels for ministers, public administrators and senior policy-makers, as well as for private and non-governmental organizations. ECA aims to increase the participation of women in economic development and incorporates this objective into its administrative activities and work programmes.

Following the failure to implement many of the proposals under the UN Industrial Development Decade for Africa (IDDA, 1980–90) and the UN Programme of Action for African Economic Recovery and Development (1986–90), a second IDDA was adopted by the Conference of African Ministers of Industry in July 1991. The main objectives of the second IDDA included the consolidation and rehabilitation of existing industries, the expansion of new investments, and the promotion of small-scale industries and technological capabilities. In June 1996 a conference, organized by ECA, was held in Accra, Ghana, with the aim of reviving private investment in Africa in order to stimulate the private sector and promote future economic development. In October 1999 the first African Development Forum (ADF) was held in Addis Ababa, Ethiopia. The ADF process was initiated by ECA to formulate an agenda for effective, sustainable development in African countries through dialogue and partnership between governments, academics, the private sector, donor agencies etc. It was intended that the process would focus towards an annual meeting concerned with a specific development issue. The first Forum was convened on the theme 'The Challenge to Africa of Globalization and the Information Age'. It reviewed the AISI (see above) and formulated country action plans and work programmes for 2000. The four issues addressed were: strengthening Africa's information infrastructure; Africa and the information economy; information and communication technologies for improved governance; and democratizing access to the information society. The second ADF, scheduled to be convened in October 2000 in Addis Ababa, on the theme 'AIDS: the Greatest Leadership Challenge', was to address the impact on Africa of the

human immunodeficiency virus (HIV) and acquired immunodeficiency syndrome (AIDS).

In 1997 ECA hosted the first of a series of meetings on good governance, in the context of the UN system-wide Special Initiative on Africa. The second African Governance Forum (AGF II) was held in Accra, Ghana, in June 1998. The Forum focused on accountability and transparency, which participants agreed were essential elements in promoting development in Africa and should involve commitment from both governments and civil organizations. AGF III was convened in June 1999 in Bamako, Mali, to consider issues relating to conflict prevention, management and governance. The fourth AGF, which took place in Kampala, Uganda, in September 2000, focused on parliamentary processes and their role in consolidating good governance on the continent.

ECONOMIC AND SOCIAL POLICY

The Economic and Social Policy division concentrates on the following areas: economic policy analysis, trade and debt, social policy and poverty analysis, and the co-ordination and monitoring of special issues and programmes. Monitoring economic and social trends in the African region and studying the development problems concerning it are among the fundamental tasks of the Commission, while the special issues programme updates legislative bodies regarding the progress made in the implementation of initiatives affecting the continent. Every year the Commission publishes the *Survey of Economic and Social Conditions in Africa* and the *Economic Report on Africa.*

The Commission gives assistance to governments in general economic analysis, fiscal, financial and monetary management, trade liberalization, regional integration and planning. The ECA's work on economic planning has been broadened in recent years, in order to give more emphasis to macro-economic management in a mixed economy approach: a project is being undertaken to develop short-term forecasting and policy models to support economic management. The Commission has also undertaken a major study of the informal sector in African countries. Special assistance is given to least-developed, land-locked and island countries which have a much lower income level than other countries and which are faced with heavier constraints. Studies are also undertaken to assist longer-term planning.

In May 1994 ECA ministers of economic and social development and of planning, meeting in Addis Ababa, adopted a *Framework Agenda for Building and Utilizing Critical Capacities in Africa.* The agenda aimed to identify new priority areas to stimulate development by, for example, strengthening management structures, a more efficient use of a country's physical infrastructure and by expanding processing or manufacturing facilities.

ECA aims to strengthen African participation in international negotiations. To this end, assistance has been provided to member states in the ongoing multilateral trade negotiations under the World Trade Organization; in the annual conferences of the IMF and the World Bank; in negotiations with the EU; and in meetings related to economic co-operation among developing countries. Studies have been prepared on problems and prospects likely to arise for the African region from the implementation of the Common Fund for Commodities and the Generalized System of Trade Preferences (both supervised by UNCTAD); the impacts of exchange-rate fluctuations on the economies of African countries; and on the long-term implications of different debt arrangements for African economies. ECA assists individual member states by undertaking studies on domestic trade, expansion of inter-African trade, transnational corporations, integration of women in trade and development, and strengthening the capacities of state-trading organizations. ECA encourages the diversification of production, the liberalization of cross-border trade and the expansion of domestic trade structures, within regional economic groupings, in order to promote intra-African trade. ECA also helps to organize regional and 'All-Africa' trade fairs.

In March/April 1997 the Conference of African Ministers of Finance, meeting in Addis Ababa, reviewed a new initiative of the World Bank and IMF to assist the world's 41 most heavily indebted poor countries, of which 33 were identified as being in sub-Saharan Africa. While the Conference recognized the importance of the involvement of multilateral institutions in assisting African economies to achieve a sustainable level of development, it criticized aspects of the structural adjustment programmes imposed by the institutions and advocated more flexible criteria to determine eligibility for the new initiative.

In 1997, with regard to social policy, ECA focused upon improving the socio-economic prospects of women through the promotion of social and legal equality, increasing opportunities for entering higher education and monitoring the prevalence of poverty.

FOOD SECURITY AND SUSTAINABLE DEVELOPMENT

In the early 1990s reports were compiled on the development, implementation and sound management of environmental programmes at national, sub-regional and regional levels. ECA members adopted a common African position for the UN Conference on Environment and Development, held in June 1992. In 1995 ECA published its first comprehensive report and statistical survey of human development issues in African countries. The *Human Development in Africa Report*, which was to be published every two years, aimed to demonstrate levels of development attained, particularly in the education and child health sectors, to identify areas of concern and to encourage further action by policy-makers and development experts. In 1997 ECA was actively involved in the promotion of food security in African countries and the study of the relationship between population, food security, the environment and sustainable development.

PROGRAMME PLANNING, FINANCE AND EVALUATION

ECA provides guidance in the formulation of policies towards the achievement of Africa's development objectives to the policy-making organs of the UN and OAU. It contributes to the work of the General Assembly and other specialized agencies by providing an African perspective in the preparation of development strategies. In March 1996 the UN announced a system-wide Special Initiative on Africa to mobilize resources and to implement a series of political and economic development objectives over a 10-year period. ECA's Executive Secretary is the Co-Chair, with the Administrator of the UNDP, of the Steering Committee for the Initiative.

REGIONAL CO-OPERATION AND INTEGRATION

The Regional Co-operation and Integration Division administers the transport and communications and mineral and energy sectors, in addition to its activities concerning the Sub-regional Development Centres (SRDCs—see above), the integrated development of transboundary water resources, and facilitating and enhancing the process of regional economic integration.

ECA was appointed lead agency for the second United Nations Transport and Communications Decade in Africa (UNTACDA II), covering the period 1991–2000. The principal aim of UNTACDA II was the establishment of an efficient, integrated transport and communications system in Africa. The specific objectives of the programme included: (i) the removal of physical and non-physical barriers to intra-African trade and travel, and improvement in the road transport sector; (ii) improvement in the efficiency and financial viability of railways; (iii) development of Africa's shipping capacity and improvement in the performance of Africa's ports; (iv) development of integrated transport systems for each lake and river basin; (v) improvement of integration of all modes of transport in order to carry cargo in one chain of transport smoothly; (vi) integration of African airlines, and restructuring of civil aviation and airport management authorities; (vii) improvement in the quality and availability of transport in urban areas; (viii) development of integrated regional telecommunications networks; (ix) development of broadcasting services, with the aim of supporting socio-economic development; and (x) expansion of Africa's postal network. ECA is the co-ordinator, with the World Bank, of a regional Road Maintenance Initiative, which was launched in 1988. By early 1996 13 African countries were receiving assistance under the initiative, which sought to encourage a partnership between the public and private sectors to manage and maintain road infrastructure more efficiently and thus to improve country-wide communications and transportation activities. The third African road safety congress was held in April 1997, in Pretoria, South Africa. The congress, which was jointly organized by ECA and the OECD, aimed to increase awareness of the need to adopt an integrated approach to road safety problems. During 1998/99 transport activities included consideration of a new African air transport policy, workshops on port restructuring, and regional and country analyses of transport trends and reforms.

The Fourth Regional Conference on the Development and Utilization of Mineral Resources in Africa, held in March 1991, adopted an action plan that included the formulation of national mineral exploitation policies; and the promotion of the gemstone industry, small-scale mining and the iron and steel industry. ECA supports the Southern African Mineral Resources Development Centre in Dar-es-Salaam, Tanzania, and the Central African Mineral Development Centre in Brazzaville, Republic of the Congo, which provide advisory and laboratory services to their respective member states.

ECA's Energy Programme provides assistance to member states in the development of indigenous energy resources and the formulation of energy policies to extricate member states from continued energy crises. In 1997 ECA strengthened co-operation with the World Energy Council and agreed to help implement the Council's African Energy Programme.

ECA assists member states in the assessment and use of water resources and the development of river and lake basins common to more than one country. ECA encourages co-operation between countries with regard to water issues and collaborates with other UN agencies and regional organizations to promote technical and economic co-operation in this area. ECA has been particularly active in efforts to promote the integrated development of the water resources of the Zambezi river basin and of Lake Victoria.

In all of its activities ECA aims to strengthen institutional capacities in order to support the process of regional integration, and aims to assist countries to implement existing co-operative agreements, for example by promoting the harmonization of macroeconomic and taxation policies and the removal of non-tariff barriers to trade.

ASSOCIATED BODY

Information Commmunications Technologies Centre for Africa (ICTCA): POB 3001, Addis Ababa, Ethiopia; tel. (1) 314520; fax (1) 515829; e-mail rhees@un.org; internet www.un.org.depts/tca; aims to strengthen the continent's communications infrastructure and promote the use of information and communications technologies in planning and policy-making; stages exhibitions and provides training facilities.

Finance

For the two-year period 2000–01 ECA's regular budget, an appropriation from the UN budget, was an estimated US $78.5m.

Publications

Africa in Figures.
African Statistical Yearbook.
African Trade Bulletin (2 a year).
African Women's Report (annually).
Compendium of Intra-African and Related Foreign Trade Statistics.
Directory of African Statisticians (every 2 years).
ECA Development Policy Review.
ECA Environment Newsletter (3 a year).
ECANews (monthly).
Economic Report on Africa (annually).
Focus on African Industry (2 a year).
GenderNet (annually).
Human Development in Africa Report (every 2 years).
Human Rights Education.
People First (2 a year).
Population of Africa: Data and Statistics.
Report of the Executive Secretary (every 2 years).
Survey of Economic and Social Conditions in Africa (annually).
Country reports, policy and discussion papers, reports of conferences and meetings, training series, working paper series.

Economic and Social Commission for Western Asia—ESCWA

Address: Riad es-Solh Sq., POB 11-8575, Beirut, Lebanon.
Telephone: (1) 981301; **fax:** (1) 981510; **e-mail:** unescwa@escwa.org.lb; **internet:** www.escwa.org.lb.

The UN Economic Commission for Western Asia was established in 1974 by a resolution of the UN Economic and Social Council (ECOSOC), to provide facilities of a wider scope for those countries previously served by the UN Economic and Social Office in Beirut (UNESOB). The name 'Economic and Social Commission for Western Asia' (ESCWA) was adopted in 1985.

MEMBERS

Bahrain	Palestine
Egypt	Qatar
Iraq	Saudi Arabia
Jordan	Syria
Kuwait	United Arab Emirates
Lebanon	Yemen
Oman	

Organization

(April 2001)

COMMISSION

The sessions of the Commission (held every two years) are attended by delegates from member states. Representatives of UN bodies and specialized agencies, regional organizations, other UN member states, and non-governmental organizations having consultative status with ECOSOC may attend as observers.

PREPARATORY COMMITTEE

The Committee, formerly the Technical Committee, has the task of reviewing programming issues and presenting recommendations in that regard to the sessions of the Commission. It is the principal subsidiary body of the Commission and functions as its policy-making structure. Six specialized inter-governmental committees have been established to consider specific areas of activity, to report on these to the Preparatory Committee and to assist the Committee in formulating ESCWA's medium-term work programmes.

Statistical Committee: established in 1992; meets every two years.
Committee on Social Development: established in 1994; meets every two years.
Committee on Energy: established in 1995; meets every two years.
Committee on Water Resources: established in 1995; meets annually.
Committee on Transport: established in 1997; meets every two years.
Committee on Liberalization of Foreign Trade and Economic Globalization: established in 1997; meets annually.

SECRETARIAT

The Secretariat comprises an Executive Secretary, a Deputy Executive Secretary, a Senior Adviser and Secretary of the Commission, an Information Services Unit and a Programme Planning and Co-ordination Unit. ESCWA's technical and substantive activities are undertaken by the following divisions: energy, natural resources and environment; social development issues and policies; economic development issues and policies; sectoral issues and policies; statistics; and technical co-operation.

Executive Secretary: MERVAT M. TALLAWY (Egypt).

Activities

ESCWA is responsible for proposing policies and actions to support development and to further economic co-operation and integration in western Asia. ESCWA undertakes or sponsors studies of economic social and development issues of the region, collects and disseminates information, and provides advisory services to member states in various fields of economic and social development. It also organizes conferences and intergovernmental and export group meetings and sponsors training workshops and seminars.

Much of ESCWA's work is carried out in co-operation with other UN bodies, as well as with other international and regional organizations, for example the League of Arab States (q.v.) the Co-operation Council for the Arab States of the Gulf (q.v.) and the Organization of the Islamic Conference (OIC, q.v.).

ESCWA works within the framework of medium-term plans, which are divided into two-year programmes of action and priorities. The biennium 1994–95 was considered to be a transitional period during which the Commission restructured its work programme. This restructuring focused ESCWA activities from 15 to five sub-programmes. A further reorganization of the sub-programmes was implemented in 1997 to provide the framework for activities in the medium-term period 1998–2001.

MANAGEMENT OF NATURAL RESOURCES AND ENVIRONMENT

The main objective of the sub-programme was to promote regional co-ordination and co-operation in the management of natural resources, in particular water resources and energy, and the protection of the environment. The sub-programme aimed to counter the problem of an increasing shortage of freshwater resources and deterioration in water quality resulting from population growth, agricultural land-use and socio-economic development, by supporting measures for more rational use and conservation of water resources, and by promoting public awareness and community participation in water and environmental protection projects. In addition, ESCWA aimed to assist governments in the formulation and implementation of capacity-building programmes and the development of surface and groundwater resources.

ESCWA supports co-operation in the establishment of electricity distribution and supply networks throughout the region and promotes the use of alternative sources of energy and the development of new and renewable energy technologies. Similarly, ESCWA promotes the application of environmentally sound technologies in order to achieve sustainable development, as well as measures to recycle resources, minimize waste and reduce the environmental impact of transport operations and energy use. Under the sub-programme ESCWA was to collaborate with national, regional and international organizations in monitoring and reporting on emerging environmental issues and to pursue implementation of Agenda 21, which was adopted at the June 1992 UN conference on Environment and Development, with particular regard to land and water resource management and conservation.

IMPROVEMENT OF THE QUALITY OF LIFE

ESCWA's key areas of activity in this sub-programme were population, human development, the advancement of women and human settlements, and, in particular, to pursue the implementation of recommendations relevant to the region of the four UN world conferences held on these themes during the mid-1990s.

ESCWA's objectives with regard to population were to increase awareness and understanding of links between population factors and poverty, human rights and the environment, and to strengthen the capacities of member states to analyse and assess demographic trends and migration. The main aim in the area of human development was to further the alleviation of poverty and to generate a sustainable approach to development through, for example, greater involvement of community groups in decision-making and projects to strengthen production and income-generating capabilities. The sub-programme incorporated activities to ensure all gender-related recommendations of the four world conferences could be pursued in the region, including support for the role of the family and assistance to organizations for monitoring and promoting the advancement of women. With regard to human settlements, the objectives of the sub-programme were to monitor and identify problems resulting from rapid urbanization and social change, to promote understanding and awareness of the problems and needs of human settlements, and to strengthen the capacity of governments in the region in formulating appropriate policies and strategies for sustainable human settlement development.

ECONOMIC DEVELOPMENT AND GLOBAL CHANGES

During the period 1998–2001 ESCWA aimed to support member states in their understanding of the process of globalization of the world economy and their participation in international trading negotiations and arrangements. ESCWA also aimed to strengthen the capacity of members in implementing economic reform policies, financial management and other structural adjustment measures, and to facilitate intra-regional trade, investment and capital movements.

CO-ORDINATION OF POLICIES AND HARMONIZATION OF NORMS AND REGULATIONS FOR SECTORAL DEVELOPMENT

This sub-programme was concerned with the harmonization of standards throughout the region in the areas of transport, industry, agriculture and technology. ESCWA aimed to promote co-operation among member states in transport and infrastructure policies and greater uniformity of safety and legal standards, the latter with a view to facilitating border crossings between countries in the region. ESCWA, similarly, aimed to assist local industries to meet regional and international standards and regulations, as well as to improve the competitiveness of industries through the development of skills and policies and greater co-operation with other national and regional support institutions. ESCWA strategies to develop the agricultural potential of member states included resource conservation activities, agricultural management, institution-building and harmonization of regulations and norms. In the field of technology the sub-programme was designed to strengthen the capabilities of member states, to promote the transfer of technologies, research and development activities, and to enhance collaboration in the production sector.

CO-ORDINATION AND HARMONIZATION OF STATISTICS AND INFORMATION DEVELOPMENT

In the medium-term ESCWA intended to develop the statistical systems of member states in order to improve the relevance and accuracy of economic and social data, and to implement measures to make the information more accessible to planners and researchers. ESCWA also aimed to promote the comparability of statistics, through implementation of various standard international systems and programmes, particularly focusing on a series of national population and housing censuses conducted in the region in 2000.

Finance

ESCWA's share of the UN budget for the two years 2000–01 was US $50.3m., compared with $49.5m. for the previous biennium.

Publications

All publications are annual, unless otherwise indicated.
Agriculture and Development in Western Asia.
External Trade Bulletin of the ESCWA Region.
National Accounts Studies of the ESCWA Region.
Population Bulletin of the ESCWA Region.
Prices and Financial Statistics in the ESCWA Region.
Socio-economic Data Sheet (every 2 years).
Statistical Abstract of the ESCWA Region.
Survey of Economic and Social Developments in the ESCWA Region.
Transport Bulletin.

OTHER UNITED NATIONS BODIES

Office for the Co-ordination of Humanitarian Affairs— OCHA

Address: United Nations Plaza, New York, NY 10017, USA.

Telephone: (212) 963-1234; **fax:** (212) 963-1312; **e-mail:** ochany@ un.org; **internet:** www.reliefweb.int/ocha_ol/.

OCHA was established in January 1998 as part of the UN Secretariat, with a mandate to co-ordinate international humanitarian assistance and to provide policy and other advice on humanitarian issues. It replaced the Department of Humanitarian Affairs, established in 1992.

Organization

(April 2001)

OCHA has headquarters in New York, and in Geneva, Switzerland, and it maintains a field presence in 22 locations. In 2000 there were 137 staff at the headquarters (of whom 50 were regular staff and 87 were extrabudgetary) and 111 field staff.

Under Secretary-General for Humanitarian Affairs and Emergency Relief Co-ordinator: KENZO OSHIMA (Japan).

Activities

OCHA's mandate is to work with UN agencies, governments, intergovernmental humanitarian organizations and non-governmental organizations to ensure that a prompt, co-ordinated and effective response to emergency situations is provided. OCHA reaches agreement with other UN bodies regarding the division of responsibilities, which may include field missions to assess requirements, organizing Consolidated Inter-agency Appeals for financial assistance, and mobilizing other resources. The Emergency Relief Co-ordinator is the principal adviser to the UN Secretary-General on humanitarian issues. He chairs an Inter-Agency Standing Committee (IASC), which co-ordinates and administers the international response to humanitarian disasters and to the development of relevant policies. The Co-ordinator also acts as Convener of the Executive Committee for Humanitarian Affairs, which provides a forum for humanitarian agencies, as well as the political and peace-keeping departments of the UN Secretariat, to exchange information on emergency situations and humanitarian issues.

OCHA monitors developments throughout the world and undertakes contingency planning to enable it to respond immediately to emergency situations. A Humanitarian Early Warning System (HEWS) has been established to assess indicators in order to identify the likelihood of a humanitarian crisis occurring in a certain area. An Integrated Regional Information Network (IRIN) was created in 1995 in Nairobi, Kenya, to disseminate information on the humanitarian situation in central and east Africa. Additional IRINs have since been established in Abidjan, Côte d'Ivoire, and Johannesburg, South Africa, in order to provide accurate information concerning developments in western and southern Africa. An IRIN for central Asia, operating from Islamabad, Afghanistan, was inaugurated in August 2000, and networks are also envisaged for south-eastern Europe and the Caucasus. A complementary service, ReliefWeb, which was launched in 1996, monitors crises and publishes the information obtained on the internet. IRIN and ReliefWeb together form part of OCHA's Policy, Analysis and Information Division, based in New York. In addition, OCHA holds a number of conferences and workshops.

OCHA administers a Disaster Response System, which monitors field situations, liaises with UN Resident Co-ordinators worldwide and undertakes disaster-preparedness activities. UN Disaster Assessment and Co-ordination (UNDAC) teams, established by OCHA with the aid of donor governments, are available for immediate deployment to help to determine requirements and to co-ordinate assistance in those countries affected by disasters, for example by establishing reliable telecommunications and securing other logistical support. OCHA maintains a Central Register of Disaster Management Capacities, which may be available for international assistance. In addition, emergency equipment and supplies are held in a warehouse in Pisa, Italy, ready for emergency dispatch. OCHA also issues Situation Reports to inform the international community of any emergency situation, the type and level of assistance required and action being undertaken.

In 1998 OCHA appealed for some US $2,160m. of assistance to support 12.8m. people in need of emergency relief. By the end of that year the international community had provided some $1,061m. in aid (including bilateral aid), of which $33m. was for OCHA's co-ordination activities in the field. The Consolidated Inter-agency Appeal Process (CAP) was established to organize a co-ordinated response to resource mobilization following humanitarian crises. Between 1992 and mid-1999 108 CAP appeals were launched, generating some US $13,300m. A Central Emergency Revolving Fund (CERF), under the authority of the Emergency Relief Co-ordinator, enables humanitarian agencies to provide an immediate response to emergencies, before donor contributions become available. Agencies borrowing from the fund are required to reimburse the amount loaned within a certain period of time, which is not to exceed one year. Between 1992 and mid-1999 the CERF was used 61 times, making disbursements totalling $135.7m.

Finance

OCHA's budgetary requirements for 2000 were an estimated US $45.5m., of which about $20.0m. was to be provided from the regular budget of the UN.

Publication

OCHA News (weekly).

Office for Drug Control and Crime Prevention—ODCCP

Address: Vienna International Centre, POB 500, A-1400 Vienna, Austria.

Telephone: (1) 26060-4266; **fax:** (1) 26060-5866; **e-mail:** odccp@odccp.org; **internet:** www.odccp.org.

The Office was established in November 1997 to strengthen the UN's integrated approach to issues relating to drug control, crime prevention and international terrorism. It comprises two principal components: the United Nations International Drug Control Programme and the Centre for International Crime Prevention, both headed by the ODCCP Executive Director.

In March 1999 a new UN Global Programme against Money Laundering (GPML) was established within the framework of the ODCCP to assist governments with formulating legislation against money laundering and establishing and maintaining appropriate frameworks to counter the problem. GPML activities include the provision of technical assistance, training, and the collection, research and analysis of crime data. The Programme, in collaboration with other governmental organizations, law enforcement agencies and academic institutions, co-ordinates the International Money Laundering Information Network (IMoLIN), an internet-based information resource. IMoLIN incorporates the Anti-Money Laundering International Database, a comprehensive database on money-laundering legislation throughout the world that constituted a key element in ODCCP activities in support of the elaboration of an

International Convention against Transnational Organized Crime, with a proposed set of guide-lines for the acceptable operation of offshore centres. At the first GPML Forum, held in the Cayman Islands in March 2000, the governments of 31 participating 'offshore' financial centres agreed in principle to adopt internationally-accepted standards of financial regulation and measures against money laundering.

ODCCP's Terrorism Prevention Branch, established in 1999, researches trends in terrorist activity and assists countries with improving their capabilities to investigate and prevent acts of terrorism. The Branch promotes international co-operation in combating the problem, is compiling a database on global terrorism, and has initiated a study into the connections between terrorist activity and other forms of crime.

Executive Director: PINO ARLACCHI (Italy).

UNITED NATIONS INTERNATIONAL DRUG CONTROL PROGRAMME—UNDCP

UNDCP was established in 1991 to co-ordinate the activities of all UN specialized agencies and programmes in matters of international drug control. The structures of the former Division of Narcotic Drugs, the UN Fund for Drug Abuse Control and the secretariat of the International Narcotics Control Board (see below) were integrated into the new body. Accordingly, UNDCP became the focal point for promoting the UN Decade Against Drug Abuse (1991–2000) and for assisting member states to implement the Global Programme of Action that was adopted by the General Assembly in 1990 with the objective of achieving an international society free of illicit drugs and drug abuse. At a special summit meeting of the UN General Assembly, held in June 1998, heads of state and representatives of some 150 countries adopted a global strategy, formulated on the basis of UNDCP proposals, to reduce significantly the production of illicit substances, by 2008, and to strengthen drug prevention, treatment and rehabilitation programmes, by 2003. UNDCP subsequently launched two programmes that aimed to facilitate the realization of these objectives by improving and standardizing the compilation and analysis of data. A four-year Global Monitoring Programme of Illicit Crops, covering the period January 2000–December 2003, was to employ a combination of satellite sensing (with the assistance of the European Space Agency, q.v.), aerial surveillance and ground-level surveys of regions known to have high levels of illicit crop cultivation, to provide a reliable collection and analysis mechanism for data on the production of illicit substances; governments were to be encouraged to use the information received in the formulation of comprehensive national monitoring systems. The Global Assessment Programme on Drug Abuse (GAP), also covering the period January 2000–December 2003, was to establish one global and nine regional drug abuse data systems to collect and evaluate data on the extent of and patterns of illegal substance abuse.

UNDCP serves as an international centre of expertise and information on drug abuse control, with the capacity to provide legal and technical assistance in relevant areas of concern. The Programme supports governments in efforts to strengthen their institutional capacities for drug control (for example, drug identification and drug law enforcement training) and to prepare and implement national drug control 'action plans'. Efforts to enhance regional co-operation in the control of narcotics are also supported. Through these national and regional strategies UNDCP aims to reduce the demand for illicit drugs, to suppress trafficking in these substances and to reduce the production of drugs, for example by creating alternative sources of income for farmers economically dependent on the production of illicit narcotic crops. This latter approach has been successfully applied in Laos, reducing the levels of opium cultivation, and in the coca-growing regions of Peru, Bolivia and Colombia.

UNDCP sponsors activities to generate public awareness of the harmful effects of drug abuse, as part of its efforts to reduce the demand for illicit drugs. In 1998 UNDCP established the Global Youth Network project, which aims to involve young people in drug-abuse prevention activities. UNDCP also works with governments, as well as non-governmental and private organizations, in the detection, treatment, rehabilitation and social reintegration of drug addicts. UNDCP undertakes research to monitor the drugs problem: for example, assessing the characteristics of drug-users and the substances being used, to help identify people at risk of becoming drug users and to enhance the effectiveness of national programmes to address the issue (see also the GAP, above).

UNDCP promotes implementation of the following major treaties which govern the international drug control system: the Single Convention on Narcotic Drugs (1961) and a Protocol amending the Convention (1972); the Convention on Psychotropic Substances (1971); and the UN Convention against Illicit Traffic in Narcotic Drugs and Psychotropic Substances (1988). Among other important provisions, these treaties aim to restrict severely the production of narcotic drugs, while ensuring an adequate supply for medical and scientific purposes, to prevent profits obtained from the illegal sale of drugs being diverted into legal usage and to secure the extradition of drug-traffickers and the transfer of proceedings for criminal prosecution. UNDCP assists countries to adapt their national legislation and drug policies to facilitate their compliance with these conventions and to enhance co-ordinated efforts with other governments to control the movement of drugs. UNDCP services meetings of the International Narcotics Control Board, an independent body responsible for promoting and monitoring government compliance with the provisions of the drug control treaties, and of the Commission on Narcotic Drugs, which, as a functional committee of ECOSOC (q.v.), is the main policy-making organ within the UN system on issues relating to international drug abuse control.

UNDCP co-operates closely with other international, regional and non-governmental organizations and maintains dialogue with agencies advocating drug abuse control. In April 1999 UNDCP became the seventh co-sponsor of the Joint UN Programme on HIV and AIDS (UNAIDS), which was established on 1 January 1996 by UNICEF, UNDP, UNFPA, UNESCO, WHO and the World Bank. UNDCP's participation was in recognition of the importance of international drug control efforts in preventing the spread of HIV/AIDS.

Finance

The UNDCP Fund receives an allocation from the regular budget of the UN, although voluntary contributions from member states and private organizations represent the majority of its resources. The regular budget for the two year period 2000–01 amounted to US \$14.45m., while the voluntary funded budget totalled \$157.5m.

Publications

Bulletin on Narcotics (quarterly).

Global Illicit Drug Trends.

ODCCP Update (quarterly).

Technical Series.

World Drug Report.

CENTRE FOR INTERNATIONAL CRIME PREVENTION—CICP

The CICP is the UN body responsible for crime prevention, criminal justice and criminal law reform. It the application of international standards and norms relating to these areas, for example the Minimum Rules for the Treatment of Prisoners, Conventions against Torture, and Other Cruel, Inhuman or Degrading Treatment or Punishment, and Safeguards Guaranteeing the Protection of the Rights of Those Facing the Death Penalty. The Centre provides member states with technical assistance to strengthen national capacities to establish appropriate legal and criminal justice systems and to combat transnational organized crime (see below). The CICP supports the Commission on Crime Prevention and Criminal Justice, a functional committee of ECOSOC which provides guidance in developing global anti-crime policies. In 1999 the CICP initiated three new programmes: a Global Programme against Corruption, a three-year Global Programme against Trafficking in Human Beings, and a Global Programme on Organized Crime, which aimed to analyse emerging transnational criminal organizations and assist countries to formulate strategies to combat the problem. The CICP supported member states in the preparation of the UN Convention against Transnational Organized Crime, which was adopted by the General Assembly in August 2000; the so-called Palermo Convention, with two additional Protocols on trafficking in human beings and the smuggling of migrants, was opened for signature in December at a UN conference on combating organized crime held in Sicily, Italy. Once ratified the Convention was to be monitored by the CICP.

The CICP promotes research and undertakes studies of new forms of crime prevention, in collaboration with the UN Interregional Crime and Justice Research Institute (UNICRI, q.v.). It also maintains a UN Crime and Justice Information Network database (UNCJIN), which provides information on national crime statistics, publications and links to other relevant intergovernmental agencies and research and academic institutes.

Finance

The Centre has an annual administrative budget of US $3.0m. Approximately $3m. is budgeted annually for projects.

Publications

Forum on Crime and Society.
Global Report on Crime and Justice.

The United Nations and Juvenile Justice: A Guide to International Standards and Best Practices.

Office of the United Nations High Commissioner for Human Rights—OHCHR

Address: Palais des Nations, 1211 Geneva 10, Switzerland.
Telephone: (22) 9179353; **fax:** (22) 9179012; **e-mail:** scrt.hchr@unog.ch; **internet:** www.unhchr.ch.

The Office is a body of the UN Secretariat and is the focal point for UN human rights activities. Since September 1997 it has incorporated the Centre for Human Rights.

Organization

(April 2001)

HIGH COMMISSIONER

In December 1993 the UN General Assembly decided to establish the position of a United Nations High Commissioner for Human Rights (UNHCHR) following a recommendation of the World Conference on Human Rights, held in Vienna, Austria, in June of that year. The High Commissioner, who is the UN official with principal responsibility for UN human rights activities, is appointed by the UN Secretary-General, with the approval of the General Assembly, for a four-year term in office, renewable for one term.

High Commissioner: MARY ROBINSON (Ireland).
Deputy to the High Commissioner: BERTRAND GANGAPERSAND RAMCHARAN (Guyana).

ADMINISTRATION

The work of the Office is conducted by the following branches: Research and Right to Development, responsible for human rights policy development, undertaking research and providing information to the High Commissioner and other human rights experts, working groups, etc.; Support Services, which provides administrative support to UN human rights mechanisms, including the Commission on Human Rights and its working groups, and the Sub-commission on the Promotion and Protection of Human Rights and its working groups; and Activities and Programmes, which conducts field operations, provides advice and technical assistance to governments, and implements special procedures relating to human rights concerns. The Office also comprises a Staff Office, an Administrative Section and a branch office in New York, USA.

FIELD PRESENCES

As the Office's involvement in field work has expanded, a substantial structure of field presences has developed to strengthen this aspect of the Office's work. In 2000 there were 27 field presences, covering the following areas: Abkhazia (Georgia), Afghanistan, Angola, Azerbaijan, Burundi, Cambodia, Central African Republic, Chad, Colombia, the Democratic Republic of the Congo, El Salvador, Gaza (Emerging Palestinian Autonomous Areas), Guatemala, Guinea-Bissau, Indonesia, Liberia, Madagascar, Malawi, Mongolia, Sierra Leone, Somalia, South Africa, Southern Africa, Uganda and the former Yugoslavia.

Activities

The mandate of the OHCHR incorporates the following functions and responsibilities: the promotion and protection of human rights throughout the world; the reinforcement of international co-operation in the field of human rights; the promotion of universal ratification and implementation of international standards; the establishment of a dialogue with governments to ensure respect for human rights; and co-ordination of efforts by other UN programmes and organs to promote respect for human rights. The Office may study and react to cases of serious violations of human rights, and

may undertake diplomatic efforts to prevent violations. It also produces educational and other information material to enhance understanding of human rights. The Office is the lead agency in undertaking preparations for the World Conference against Racism, Racial Discrimination, Xenophobia and Related Intolerance, scheduled to be convened in Durban, South Africa in August/September 2001.

OHCHR field offices and operations ('field presences'—see above) undertake a variety of activities, such as training and other technical assistance, support for Special Rapporteurs (usually appointed by the Commission on Human Rights), monitoring and fact-finding, and are increasingly a regular component of the Office's activities. In response to this development, the OHCHR has initiated a process of reviewing its activities in the field and of integrating them more effectively into the Office's overall structure and objectives.

The High Commissioner issues reports on human rights emergencies to the Commission on Human Rights. During 1999 the High Commissioner investigated allegations of gross violations of human rights in Kosovo and Metohija (the Federal Republic of Yugoslavia), Sierra Leone and East Timor, and reported on these to the Commission. In September the High Commissioner recommended the establishment of an international commission of inquiry to pursue consideration of the alleged abuses of human rights committed by the Indonesian authorities in East Timor during 1999. Within the framework of the interim administration in Kosovo, OHCHR was responsible for chairing a Joint Commission on Prisoners and Detainees, which met for the first time in September. In January 2000 OHCHR established a quick response desk to co-ordinate urgent appeals for assistance in addressing human rights emergencies.

TECHNICAL CO-OPERATION PROGRAMME

The UN Technical Co-operation Programme in the Field of Human Rights has been operational since 1955 to assist states, at their request, to strengthen their capacities in the observance of democracy, human rights, and the rule of law. The Programme has expanded significantly in recent years and is one of the key components of OHCHR's activities. Examples of work undertaken within the framework of the programme include training courses and workshops on good governance and the observance of human rights, expert advisory services on the incorporation of international human rights standards into national legislation and policies and on the formulation of national plans of action for the promotion and protection of human rights, fellowships, the provision of information and documentation, and consideration of promoting a human rights culture.

Finance

The Office is financed from the regular budget of the UN, as well as by a number of voluntary and trust funds. For 2001 some US $21.5m. was approved under the regular budget, while OHCHR appealed for $53.8m. in voluntary contributions.

Publications

Fact sheet series.
Human Rights Quarterly.
Human rights study series.
Professional training series.

Other reference material, reports, proceedings of conferences, workshops, etc.

United Nations Centre for Human Settlements—UNCHS (Habitat)

Address: POB 30030, Nairobi, Kenya.

Telephone: (2) 621234; **fax:** (2) 624266; **e-mail:** habitat@unchs.org; **internet:** www.unchs.org.

UNCHS (Habitat) was established in October 1978 to service the intergovernmental Commission on Human Settlements, and to serve as a focus for human settlements activities in the UN system.

Organization

(April 2001)

UN COMMISSION ON HUMAN SETTLEMENTS

The Commission (see ECOSOC, p. 16) is the governing body of UNCHS (Habitat). It meets every two years and has 58 members, serving for four years. Sixteen members are from Africa, 13 from Asia, six from eastern European countries, 10 from Latin America and 13 from western Europe and other countries.

CENTRE FOR HUMAN SETTLEMENTS

The Centre services the Commission on Human Settlements, implements its resolutions and ensures the integration and co-ordination of technical co-operation, research and policy advice. Its Work Programme incorporates the following priority areas, as defined by the Commission: Shelter and social services; Urban management; Environment and infrastructure; and Assessment, information and monitoring.

In 1992 the UN General Assembly designated UNCHS (Habitat) as the *ad hoc* secretariat for the Second UN Conference on Human Settlements, Habitat II, which was held in Istanbul, Turkey, in June 1996. As a result, most of the Centre's activities in recent years have been concerned with supporting the implementation of the Conference's objectives at global, regional, national and local levels.

Executive Director: Anna Kajumulo Tibaijuka (Tanzania).

Activities

UNCHS (Habitat) supports and conducts capacity-building and operational research, provides technical co-operation and policy advice, and disseminates information with the aim of strengthening the development and management of human settlements.

In June 1996 representatives of 171 national governments and of more than 500 municipal authorities attending Habitat II adopted a Global Plan of Action (the 'Habitat Agenda'), which incorporated detailed programmes of action to realize economic and social development and environmental sustainability, and endorsed the conference's objectives of ensuring 'adequate shelter for all' and 'sustainable human settlements development in an urbanizing world'. UNCHS (Habitat) was expected to provide the leadership and serve as a focal point for the implementation of the Agenda. It has consequently undertaken a process of restructuring its working methods and organization. In 1999 UNCHS (Habitat) approved a set of 23 resolutions to reduce poverty, improve shelter and environmental conditions, promote good governance, and improve the status of women. A special session of the UN General Assembly was to be held in June 2001 to report on the implementation of the recommendations of the Habitat II conference.

Following the June 1996 conference, UNCHS (Habitat) established a Global Urban Observatory to monitor implementation of the Habitat Agenda and to report on local and national plans of action, international and regional support programmes and ongoing research and development. The Observatory, which incorporates the Best Practices and Local Leadership Programme and the Urban Indicators Programme, operates through an international network of regional and national institutions, all of which provide local training in appropriate data collection methods and in the development, adoption and maintenance of reliable information systems.

UNCHS (Habitat) was the co-ordinating agency for the implementation of the Global Strategy for Shelter to the Year 2000 (GSS), adopted by the General Assembly in 1988. The GSS aimed to facilitate the construction and improvement of housing for all, in particular by and for the poorest in society, and promoted the use of legal and other incentives to encourage non-governmental parties to become engaged in housing and urban development.

Through its Women in Human Settlements Development Programme, which was established in 1990, UNCHS (Habitat) ensured that the issue of human settlements was included in the agenda of the UN Fourth World Conference on Women, which was held in Beijing, People's Republic of China, in September 1995, and successfully incorporated the right of women to ownership of land and property into the Global Platform for Action which resulted from the conference. An advisory board, the Huairou Commission, comprising women from 'grass-roots' groups, non-governmental organizations (NGOs), the UN and research and political institutions, has since been established to ensure a link between the Beijing and Habitat Agendas and the inclusion of gender issues in the follow-up to Habitat II.

The Centre participates in implementing the human settlements component of Agenda 21, which was adopted at the UN Conference on Environment and Development in June 1992, and is also responsible for the chapter of Agenda 21 that refers to solid waste management and sewage-related issues. UNCHS (Habitat) implements a programme entitled 'Localizing Agenda 21', to assist local authorities in developing countries to address local environmental and infrastructure-related problems. It also collaborates with national governments, private-sector and non-governmental institutions and UN bodies to achieve the objectives of Agenda 21. The Settlement Infrastructure and Environment Programme was initiated in 1992 to support developing countries in improving the environment of human settlements through policy advice and planning, infrastructure management and enhancing awareness of environmental and health concerns in areas such as water, sanitation, waste management and transport. An Urban Management Programme aims to strengthen the contribution of cities and towns in developing countries towards human development, including economic growth, social advancements, the reduction of poverty and the improvement of the environment. The Programme, which is active in 120 cities, is an international technical co-operation project, of which UNCHS (Habitat) is the executing agency, the World Bank is an associated agency, while UNDP provides core funding and monitoring. The Programme is operated through regional offices, in collaboration with bilateral and multilateral support agencies, and brings together national and local authorities, community leaders and representatives of the private sector to consider specific issues and solutions to urban problems. The related Safer Cities Programme was initiated in 1996. A Sustainable Cities Programme, operated jointly with UNEP, is concerned with incorporating environmental issues into urban planning and management, in order to ensure sustainable and equitable development. The Programme is active in some 20 cities worldwide, although a prepared series of policy guide-lines is used in many others. Some 95% of the Programme's resources are spent at city level to strengthen the capacities of municipal authorities and their public-, private- and community-sector partners in the field of environmental planning and management, with the objective that the concepts and approaches of the Programme are replicated throughout the region. UNCHS (Habitat) provides the secretariat of the Urban Environment Forum, which has been developed as a global network of city authorities, international agencies and other bodies concerned with exchanging information and policies in order to improve the urban environment. In addition, UNCHS (Habitat) supports training and other activities designed to strengthen management development (in particular in the provision and maintenance of services and facilities) at local and community level.

Increasingly UNCHS (Habitat) is being called upon to contribute to the relief, rehabilitation and development activities undertaken by the UN in areas affected by regional and civil conflict. UNCHS (Habitat) has been actively involved in the reconstruction of human settlements and other development activities in Afghanistan, and in 2000 was also contributing to reconstruction programmes in East Timor, Iraq, Mozambique, Rwanda and Somalia, as well as administering a new Housing and Property Directorate that was established in January 2000 in post-conflict Kosovo and Metohija, within the framework of the UN's interim administration in the province. UNCHS (Habitat) also provides assessment and technical support in the aftermath of natural disasters. Reconstruction and recovery activities are co-ordinated under the Risk and Disaster Management Programme.

Finance

The Centre's work programme is financed from the UN regular budget, the Habitat and Human Settlements Foundation and from

extra-budgetary resources. The approved budget for the two-year period 2000–01 amounted to US $23m.

Publications

Global Report on Human Settlements.

Habitat Debate (quarterly).

Technical reports and studies, occasional papers, bibliographies, directories.

United Nations Children's Fund—UNICEF

Address: 3 United Nations Plaza, New York, NY 10017, USA.

Telephone: (212) 326-7000; **fax:** (212) 888-7465; **e-mail:** netmaster@unicef.org; **internet:** www.unicef.org.

UNICEF was established in 1946 by the UN General Assembly as the UN International Children's Emergency Fund, to meet the emergency needs of children in post-war Europe and China. In 1950 its mandate was changed to respond to the needs of children in developing countries. In 1953 the General Assembly decided that UNICEF should continue its work, as a permanent arm of the UN system, with an emphasis on programmes giving long-term benefits to children everywhere, particularly those in developing countries. In 1965 UNICEF was awarded the Nobel Peace Prize.

Organization

(April 2001)

EXECUTIVE BOARD

The Executive Board, as the governing body of UNICEF, comprises 36 member governments from all regions, elected in rotation for a three-year term by ECOSOC. The Board establishes policy, reviews programmes and approves expenditure. It reports to the General Assembly through ECOSOC.

SECRETARIAT

The Executive Director of UNICEF is appointed by the UN Secretary-General in consultation with the Executive Board. The administration of UNICEF and the appointment and direction of staff are the responsibility of the Executive Director, under policy directives laid down by the Executive Board, and under a broad authority delegated to the Executive Director by the Secretary-General. In January 2001 there were some 5,600 UNICEF staff positions, of which about 86% were in the field.

Executive Director: Carol Bellamy (USA).

UNICEF REGIONAL OFFICES

UNICEF has a network of eight regional and 125 field offices serving more than 161 countries and territories. Its offices in Tokyo, Japan and Brussels, Belgium support fund-raising activities; UNICEF's supply division is administered from the office in Copenhagen, Demark. A research centre concerned with child development is based in Florence, Italy.

The Americas and the Caribbean: Edif. 868 Albrook, 1°, Panamá 5, Panama; tel. (507) 315-0552; fax (507) 315-0554; e-mail unicef@sinfo.net; internet www.unicef.org/panama.

Central and Eastern Europe, Commonwealth of Independent States and Baltic States: Palais des Nations, 1211 Geneva, Switzerland; tel. (22) 9095605; fax (22) 9095909.

East Asia and the Pacific: POB 2-154, Bangkok 10200, Thailand; tel. (2) 2805931; fax (2) 2803563; e-mail eapro@unicef.org.

Eastern and Southern Africa: POB 44145, Nairobi, Kenya; tel. (2) 621234; fax (2) 622678; e-mail nairobiro@unicef.org.

Europe: Palais des Nations, 1211 Geneva 10, Switzerland; tel. (22) 9095111; fax (22) 9095900.

Middle East and North Africa: POB 1551, UNICEF House, Tla'a al-Ali al Dahak Bin Soufian St, 11821 Amman, Jordan; tel. (6) 5539977; fax (6) 5538880; e-mail menaro@unicef.org.jo.

South Asia: POB 5815, Leknath Marg, Kathmandu, Nepal; tel. 417082; fax 419479; e-mail rosa@unicef.org.

West and Central Africa: BP 443, Abidjan 04, Côte d'Ivoire; tel. 213131; fax 227607; e-mail wcaro@unicef.org.

OTHER UNICEF OFFICES

UNICEF Innocenti Research Centre: Piazza SS. Annunziata 2, 50122 Florence, Italy; tel. (055) 2345258; fax (055) 244817; e-mail florence@unicef.org.

Belgium: POB 104, 1000 Brussels; tel. (2) 5132251; fax (2) 5132290; e-mail brussels@unicef.org; internet www.florence-icdc.org.

Denmark (UNICEF Supply Division): UNICEF Plads, Freeport 2100, Copenhagen; tel. (45) 35273527; fax (45) 35269421; e-mail supply@unicef.dk.

Japan: UN Bldg, 8th Floor, 53-70, Jingumae 5-chome, Shibuya-ku, Tokyo 150, Japan; tel. (3) 5467-4431; fax (3) 5467-4437; e-mail unicefjp@sepia.ocn.ne.jp.

NATIONAL COMMITTEES

UNICEF is supported by 37 National Committees, mostly in industrialized countries, whose volunteer members, numbering more than 100,000, raise money through various activities, including the sale of greetings cards. The Committees also undertake advocacy and awareness campaigns on a number of issues and provide an important link with the general public.

Activities

UNICEF is dedicated to the well-being of children and women and works for the realization and protection of their rights within the frameworks of the Convention on the Rights of the Child, which was adopted by the UN General Assembly in 1989 and by 2001 was almost universally ratified, and of the Convention on the Elimination of All Forms of Discrimination Against Women, adopted by the UN General Assembly in 1979. UNICEF promotes the full implementation of the Conventions. It also continues to provide relief and rehabilitation assistance in emergencies. Through its extensive field network in some 161 developing countries, areas and territories, UNICEF undertakes, in co-ordination with governments, local communities and other aid organizations, programmes in health, nutrition, education, water and sanitation, the environment, women in development, and other fields of importance to children. Emphasis is placed on low-cost, community-based programmes. UNICEF programmes are increasingly focused on supporting children and women during critical periods of their life, when intervention was determined to make a lasting difference, i.e. early childhood, the primary school years, adolescence and the reproductive years.

UNICEF was instrumental in organizing the World Summit for Children, held in September 1990 and attended by representatives from more than 150 countries, including 71 heads of state or government. The Summit produced a Plan of Action which recognized the rights of the young to 'first call' on their countries' resources and formulated objectives for the year 2000, including: (i) a reduction of the 1990 mortality rates for infants and children under five years by one-third, or to 50–70 per 1,000 live births, whichever is lower; (ii) a reduction of the 1990 maternal mortality rate by one-half; (iii) a reduction by one-half of the 1990 rate for severe malnutrition among children under the age of five; (iv) universal access to safe drinking water and to sanitary means of excreta disposal; and (v) universal access to basic education and completion of primary education by at least 80% of children. UNICEF supports the efforts of governments to achieve these objectives. In 2000 UNICEF planned to launch a new global initiative to promote a comprehensive approach to children's well-being which included survival, growth and development in early childhood, quality basic education for all, and adolescent health, development and participation.

UNICEF co-sponsored (with UNESCO, UNDP and the World Bank) the World Conference on Education for All, which was held in Thailand in March 1990, and has made efforts to achieve the objectives formulated by the conference, which include the elimination of disparities in education between boys and girls. Since the Conference an estimated 50m. more children had enrolled in primary schools in developing countries by 1999, however there was still concern at the lack of access to basic education and the drop-out rate. More than 110m. children world-wide, of whom nearly 60% are girls, are still deprived of basic education. Although about 90% of children start school, millions subsequently leave prematurely. UNICEF, in co-operation with the World Bank and UNDP, promotes quality education for all and aims to achieve universal access to basic education and completion of primary school education by at least 80% of children. UNICEF supports education projects in sub-Saharan Africa, South Asia and countries in the Middle East and North Africa. UNICEF implements a Girls' Education Programme in more than 60 developing countries, which aimed to increase the enrolment of girls in primary schools. In 1998 the African Girls' Education Initiative supported 4,200 schools and literacy centres in West and Central Africa.

Through UNICEF's efforts the needs and interests of children were incorporated into Agenda 21, which was adopted as a plan of action for sustainable development at the UN Conference on Environment and Development, held in June 1992. In mid-1997, at the UN General Assembly's Special Session on Sustainable Development, UNICEF highlighted the need to improve safe water supply, sanitation and hygiene as fundamental to fulfilment of child rights. In 1999 UNICEF continued to work with the World Bank to bring the benefits of safe water, sanitation and hygiene education to more than 250m. people in Africa. UNICEF also works with UNEP to promote environment issues of common concern and with the World Wide Fund for Nature to support the conservation of local ecosystems.

UNICEF aims to increase the level of development aid to developing countries, to ensure access to basic social services, and to help poor countries to obtain debt relief. UNICEF is the leading agency in promoting the 20/20 initiative, which was endorsed at the World Summit for Social Development, which took place in Copenhagen, Denmark, in March 1995. It aimed to encourage the governments of developing and donor countries to allocate at least 20% of their domestic budgets and official development aid respectively, to health care, primary education and low-cost safe water and sanitation. In October 1998 the progress of the initiative was discussed at a meeting held in Hanoi, Viet Nam. Representatives of UNICEF, other UN and international agencies and of governments attending the meeting also considered measures to improve the quality and impact of these basic social services and of using resources more efficiently and equitably.

UNICEF, which vigorously opposes the exploitation of children as a violation of their basic human rights, supports special projects to provide education, counselling and care for the estimated 250m. children between the ages of five and 14 years working in developing countries, many of whom are thought to be engaged in hazardous or exploitative labour. UNICEF played a major role at the World Congress against Commercial Sexual Exploitation of Children, held in Stockholm, Sweden, in 1996, which adopted a Declaration and Agenda for Action to end the sexual exploitation of children. UNICEF also actively participated in the International Conference on Child Labour held in Oslo, Norway, in November 1997. The Conference adopted an Agenda for Action to eliminate the worst forms of child labour, including slavery-like practices, forced labour, commercial sexual exploitation and the use of children in drugs-trafficking and other hazardous forms of work. UNICEF supports the 1999 ILO Worst Forms of Child Labour Convention, which aims at the prohibition and immediate elimination of the worst forms of child labour. In 1999 UNICEF launched a global initiative, Education as a Preventive Strategy Against Child Labour, with the aim of providing schooling to millions of children forced to work full time.

Child health is UNICEF's largest programme sector, accounting for some 32% of programme expenditure in 1998. UNICEF estimates that nearly 12m. children under five years of age die each year, mainly in developing countries, and the majority from largely preventable causes. UNICEF has worked with WHO and other partners to increase global immunization coverage against the following six diseases: measles, poliomyelitis, tuberculosis, diphtheria, whooping cough and tetanus. By 1999 more than 120 countries had achieved the objective of immunizing 80% of children against these diseases before their first birthday (compared with less than 5% in 1980), preventing more than 3m. child deaths each year. Nevertheless, tuberculosis remains the cause of some 250,000 child deaths annually. In January 2000 UNICEF, WHO, the World Bank and a number of public- and private-sector partners launched the Global Alliance for Vaccines and Immunization (GAVI), which aimed to protect children of all nationalities and socio-economic groups against vaccine-preventable diseases. GAVI's strategy included improving access to sustainable immunization services, expanding the use of existing vaccines, accelerating the development and

introduction of new vaccines and technologies and promoting immunization coverage as a focus of international development efforts. UNICEF and WHO also work in conjunction on the Integrated Management of Childhood Illness programme to control diarrhoeal dehydration, one of the largest causes of death among children under five years of age in the developing world. UNICEF-assisted programmes for the control of diarrhoeal diseases promote the low-cost manufacture and distribution of pre-packaged salts or home-made solutions. The use of 'oral rehydration therapy' rose from 17% in 1985 to nearly 70% in 2000, and is believed to prevent approximately 1.5m. child deaths each year. UNICEF also promotes the need to improve sanitation and access to safe water supplies in developing nations in order to reduce the risk of diarrhoea and other water-borne diseases (see 20/20 initiative, above). To control acute respiratory infections, which kill more than 1.9m. children under five years old each year, UNICEF works with WHO in training health workers to diagnose and treat the associated diseases in many developing countries. As a result, child deaths from pneumonia and other respiratory infections have been reduced by one-half since 1990. Some 750,000 children die from malaria every year. In October 1998 UNICEF, together with WHO, UNDP and the World Bank, inaugurated a new global campaign, Roll Back Malaria to fight the disease. UNICEF supports control programmes in more than 30 countries.

According to UNICEF estimates, almost one-third of children under five years of age are underweight, while each year malnutrition contributes to the deaths of almost 6m. children in that age group and leaves millions of others with physical and mental disabilities. More than 2,000m. people world-wide (mainly women and children in developing countries) are estimated to be deficient in one or more essential vitamins and minerals, such as vitamin A, iodine and iron. UNICEF supports national efforts to reduce malnutrition, for example, fortifying staple foods with micronutrients, widening women's access to education, improving household food security and basic health services, and promoting sound child-care and feeding practices. Since 1991 more than 15,000 hospitals in at least 132 countries had implemented the recommendations of UNICEF and WHO, entitled '10 steps to successful breast-feeding', to become 'baby-friendly'. In 1996 UNICEF expressed its concern at the impact of international economic embargoes on child health, citing as an example the extensive levels of child malnutrition recorded in Iraq. In early 1998 UNICEF remained actively concerned at the levels of child malnutrition and accompanying diseases in Iraq and in the Democratic People's Republic of Korea, which had suffered severe food shortages. During that year UNICEF worked to strengthen child-care facilities in those countries and operated nutritional rehabilitation centres. In October UNICEF published a report which highlighted the increasing incidence of poverty and child malnutrition throughout South and South-East Asia. In April UNICEF published a report entitled Generation in Jeopardy, concerned with the suffering of children as a result of war, poverty, disease and other social blights, particulary in areas of Africa and Eastern Europe.

UNICEF estimates that almost 600,000 women die every year during pregnancy or childbirth, largely because of inadequate maternal health care, while some 300m. women live with permanent injuries or chronic disabilities resulting from complications during pregnancy or childbirth. With its partners in the Safe Motherhood Initiative—UNFPA, WHO, the World Bank, the International Planned Parenthood Federation, the Population Council, and Family Care International—UNICEF promotes measures to reduce maternal mortality and morbidity, including improving access to quality reproductive health services, educating communities about safe motherhood and the rights of women, training midwives, and expanding access to family planning services.

During 1999 more than 2.5m. young people, aged 15 to 24 years, were infected with the human immunodeficiency virus (HIV), while some 1,300 children under 15 died as a result of AIDS every day. UNICEF attempts to reduce the risk of transmission during pregnancy and childbirth, and promotes HIV/AIDS education and prevention programmes, particularly among young people. It also supports programmes to assist the estimated 13m. children under the age of 15 who have lost one or both parents to AIDS since the epidemic began; 95% of these reside in sub-Saharan Africa. UNICEF works closely in this field with governments and co-operates with other UN agencies in the Joint UN Programme on HIV/AIDS (UNAIDS), which became operational on 1 January 1996.

UNICEF provides assistance to countries affected by violence and social disintegration, in particular to support the estimated 1m. children orphaned or separated from their parents and the 12m. children made homeless as a result of armed conflict in the past decade. In 1999 UNICEF adopted a Peace and Security Agenda to help guide international efforts in this field. In that year UNICEF extended emergency humanitarian assistance in several countries and areas affected by armed conflict, including Angola, Burundi,

Kosovo and Metohija, and Liberia. UNICEF also aims to assist ongoing development by supporting activities such as education (through 'Edukits') in refugee camps and the reconstruction of school buildings, and immunization programmes (the Fund co-operates with WHO to arrange 'days of tranquility' in order to facilitate the immunization of children in conflict zones). UNICEF supports psychosocial assistance activities and undertakes special programmes to assist traumatized children and help unaccompanied children to be reunited with parents or extended families. An estimated 300,000 children are involved in armed conflicts as soldiers, porters and forced labourers. UNICEF-supported programmes help to demobilize and rehabilitate former child soldiers in several countries, including Sierra Leone and Afghanistan, through counselling, education and job training. UNICEF is also encouraging all states to ratify the Optional Protocol to the Convention on the Rights of the Child on the involvement of children in armed conflict, which was adopted by the General Assembly in May 2000 and raises the minimum legal age for combatants from 15 to 18 years. The Fund also urges states to make unequivocal statements endorsing 18 as the minimum age of voluntary recruitment to the armed forces. UNICEF was an active participant in the so-called 'Ottawa' process (supported by the Canadian Government) to negotiate an international ban on anti-personnel land-mines which, it was estimated, kill and maim between 8,000 and 10,000 children every year. The so-called Convention on the Prohibition of the Use, Stockpiling, Production and Transfer of Anti-Personnel Mines and on their Destruction, was signed by 123 countries in December 1997, and entered into force in March 1999. By October 2000 the Convention had been ratified by 107 countries. UNICEF is committed to campaigning for its universal ratification and full implementation, and also supports mine-awareness campaigns.

Finance

UNICEF is funded by voluntary contributions from governments and non-governmental and private-sector sources. Total income in 1999 amounted to US \$1,118m., of which 61% was from governments and intergovernmental organizations. Total expenditure in 1998 amounted to \$882m.

UNICEF's income is divided between contributions for general resources, for supplementary funds and for emergencies. General resources are the funds available to fulfil commitments for co-operation in country programmes approved by the Executive Board, and to meet administrative and programme support expenditures. These funds amounted to US \$571m. in 1998. Contributions for supplementary funds are those sought by UNICEF from governments and intergovernmental organizations to support projects for which general resources are insufficient, or for relief and rehabilitation programmes in emergency situations. Supplementary funding in 1998 amounted to \$279m. Funding for emergencies in 1998 amounted to \$116m.

Publications

Facts and Figures (annually, in English, French and Spanish).

The State of the World's Children (annually, in Arabic, English, French, Russian and Spanish and about 30 other national languages).

UNICEF Annual Report (in English, French and Spanish).

UNICEF at a Glance (annually, in English, French and Spanish).

United Nations Conference on Trade and Development—UNCTAD

Address: Palais des Nations, 1211 Geneva 10, Switzerland.
Telephone: (22) 9071234; **fax:** (22) 9070057; **e-mail:** ers@unctad.org; **internet:** www.unctad.org.

UNCTAD was established in December 1964. It is the principal instrument of the UN General Assembly concerned with trade and development, and is the focal point within the UN system for integrated activities relating to trade, finance, technology, investment and sustainable development. It aims to maximize the trade and development opportunities of developing countries, in particular least-developed countries, and to assist them to adapt to the increasing globalization and liberalization of the world economy.

Organization

(April 2001)

CONFERENCE

The Conference is the organization's highest policy-making body and normally meets every four years at ministerial level in order to formulate major policy guide-lines and to decide on UNCTAD's forthcoming programme of work. Tenth session: Bangkok, Thailand, February 2000. All 188 UN member states are members of UNCTAD, while many intergovernmental and non-governmental organizations participate in its work as observers.

SECRETARIAT

The secretariat comprises the following Divisions: Globalization and Development Strategies; International Trade in Goods and Services and Commodities; Investment, Technology and Enterprise Development; Services Infrastructure for Development and Trade Efficiency. It also incorporates the Office of the Special Co-ordinator for Least Developed, Land-locked, and Small Island Developing States.

As well as servicing the Conference, the UNCTAD secretariat undertakes policy analysis; monitoring, implementation and follow-up of decisions of intergovernmental bodies; technical co-operation in support of UNCTAD's policy objectives; and information exchanges and consultations of various types. In October 1998 some 390 staff were employed at the secretariat.

Secretary-General: RUBENS RICÚPERO (Brazil).

TRADE AND DEVELOPMENT BOARD

The Trade and Development Board is the executive body of UNCTAD. It comprises elected representatives from 145 UNCTAD member states and is responsible for ensuring the overall consistency of UNCTAD's activities, as well as those of its subsidiary bodies. The Board meets for a regular annual session lasting about 10 days, at which it examines global economic issues. It also reviews the implementation of the Programme of Action for the Least-Developed Countries and the UN New Agenda for the Development of Africa in the 1990s (UNNADF), with particular attention given to lessons that may be drawn from successful development experiences. The final review of UNNADF was due to take place in 2002. The Board may also meet a further three times a year in order to address management or institutional matters.

COMMISSIONS

The ninth Conference (held at Midrand, South Africa in April/May 1996) approved the establishment of three Commissions to replace existing committees and working groups: the Commission on Trade in Goods and Services and Commodities; the Commission on Investment, Technology and Related Financial Issues; and the Commission on Enterprise, Business Facilitation and Development. UNCTAD also services the ECOSOC Commission on Science and Technology for Development (see below).

Activities

During the 1980s UNCTAD focused on its role in providing a forum for the negotiation of international agreements on commodities. (Such agreements are designed to ensure the stabilization of conditions in the trade of the commodities concerned.) UNCTAD's facilitation of international commodity agreements has subsequently continued but has been superseded as a priority by other activities (see below). Under UNCTAD's auspices agreements have been negotiated or renegotiated on cocoa (1975, 1980, 1986 and 1993), jute (1982 and 1989), olive oil (1986), rubber (1979, 1987 and 1995), sugar (1977 and 1992) and tin (1981). The establishment of the Common Fund for Commodities was agreed by UNCTAD in 1980, and the Fund came into operation in September 1989 (see p. 303). In 1994 the members of the International Tropical Timber Organization (see p. 305), meeting under UNCTAD auspices, decided to replace the International Tropical Timber Agreement of 1983 with

ITTA 1994. The new agreement entered into force in January 1997. In early 2001 UNCTAD was co-ordinating negotiations on the replacement of the existing International Cocoa Agreement, which was due to expire in September of that year, and on a new international arrangement for jute.

By the early 1990s several commodity agreements had lapsed and the conclusion of the GATT Uruguay Round of trade talks in December 1993 and the changes in international trading structures that had already taken place were deemed to necessitate a substantial reorientation of UNCTAD's role. Following restructuring agreed at the eighth session of the Conference in Cartagena, Colombia, in February 1992, further changes to UNCTAD's focus and organization were approved at the ninth Conference. In particular, UNCTAD was to give special attention to assisting developing countries in taking advantage of the increased liberalization of world trade under the GATT and World Trade Organization agreements (see p. 474). Concern was expressed that the world's poorest countries would be even further marginalized if they were not given additional support to enable them to begin to compete with more successful economies. During 1996 a Trust Fund for the Least Developed Countries was established, with an initial target figure of US $5m., with the aim of assisting those countries to become integrated into the world economy. UNCTAD has been mandated as the organ within the UN system responsible for negotiating a multilateral framework governing direct foreign investment that would protect the interests of the poorest countries, taking account of the work already undertaken by OECD in this area. In UNCTAD's revised approach, encouragement of foreign direct investment and of domestic private enterprise in developing countries and countries in transition have become central to the agency's work. UNCTAD is increasingly seeking the input and participation of non-governmental groups, such as academics, non-governmental organizations (NGOs) and business representatives, in its intergovernmental machinery, where appropriate. In November 1998 UNCTAD organized a Partners for Development summit meeting, with the aim of identifying development projects of interest to the private sector and facilitating co-operation between private companies, banks and development bodies. Some 2,700 representatives of the private sector, NGOs, academic institutions and governments from 172 countries attended the conference, which was held in Lyon, France. During the meeting the UNCTAD secretariat concluded 18 partnership agreements with private and public organizations, covering the following areas of activity: international transport; investment promotion; electronic commerce; the promotion of small and medium-sized enterprises and of entrepreneurship; conservation of biodiversity and sustainable development; and agricultural commodities. The 10th session of the Conference, held in February 2000 in Bangkok, Thailand, debated developmental strategies relating to globalization. The Conference issued the Bangkok Declaration, which stated the importance of promoting equitable and sustainable development in view of increasing global interdependence, trade liberalization and advances in technology. The Declaration emphasized commitment to a fair, non-discriminatory and fully-integrated multilateral trading system that would not tolerate the marginalization of the world's least developed economies, and urged that the next round of multilateral trade negotiations address development issues. The Declaration noted the need for increased policy coherence at national and international level, and for more effective co-operation and co-ordination among multilateral institutions. It recommended open debate on global development issues by all development partners, including the private sector, NGOs, academics and politicians. The Conference also adopted a plan of action which assessed the consequences of globalization for development, recommended measures to be implemented by the international community, and provided guide-lines for UNCTAD's future work programme.

The Commission on Trade in Goods and Services and Commodities examines ways of maximizing the positive impact of globalization and liberalization on sustainable development by assisting in the effective integration of developing countries into the international trading system. In the field of services, where developing countries suffer from deficiencies in the customs, financial and communications sectors, the Commission recommends ways for countries to overcome problems in these areas. In the field of commodities, the Commission promotes diversification, to reduce dependence on single commodities, transparency in commodity markets and the sustainable management of commodity resources. During the 1990s UNCTAD undertook research into the design and implementation of a multilateral system to trace emissions of so-called greenhouse gases. In June 1997, in co-operation with the Earth Council, UNCTAD established a Greenhouse Gas Emissions Trading Policy Forum. In June 1999 the International Emissions Trading Association (IETA) was established, sponsored by UNCTAD and the Earth Council. The IETA, which was envisaged as a successor to the Forum, comprised commercial companies, business organizations and regional and national trading associations, as well as invited international organizations, research institutes and NGOs. It was to serve as a forum for the exchange of information and ideas relating to international emissions trading and as a means of developing the market in emission permit trading, which was scheduled to be launched in 2008. During the initial phase of the IETA's operations UNCTAD provided temporary secretariat support.

The Commission on Investment, Technology and Related Financial Issues provides a forum to help general understanding of trends in the flow of foreign direct investment, which is considered one of the principal instruments for the integration of developing economies into the global system, and assists developing countries in improving their overall investment climate. The Commission examines issues related to competition law and assists developing countries in formulating competition policies. The Commission also undertakes the functions of the former ECOSOC Commission on International Investment and Transnational Corporations, which aimed to provide an understanding of the nature of foreign direct investment and transnational corporations, to secure effective international agreements and to strengthen the capacity of developing countries in their dealings with transnational corporations through an integrated approach, including research, information and technical assistance. A subsidiary body—the Intergovernmental Group of Experts on International Standards of Accounting and Reporting—aimed to improve the availability of information disclosed by transnational corporations. In November 1997 the UN General Assembly endorsed a proposal of the UN Secretary-General that the Group report directly through the UNCTAD Commission on Investment, Technology and Related Financial Issues.

The Commission on Enterprise, Business Facilitation and Development advises countries on policy-related issues and training activities concerning the development of entrepreneurship. It facilitates the exchange of experiences on the formulation and implementation of enterprise development strategies, including privatization, public-sector co-operation and the special problems relating to enterprise development in countries in economic transition.

UNCTAD is responsible for the Generalized System of Preferences (GSP), initiated in 1971, whereby a proportion of both agricultural and manufactured goods that are exported by developing countries receive preferential tariff treatment by certain developed countries, Russia and several central European countries. UNCTAD monitors changes in and amendments to national GSP schemes and reviews the use of these schemes by beneficiary developing countries. In addition, the Commission on Trade in Goods and Services and Commodities (see above) is responsible for providing a forum to examine the operation of schemes, the benefits they offer and the future role of the GSP. At November 1998 15 national GSP schemes were in operation, offered by 29 countries (including the 15 member countries of the European Union). Following the signing of the GATT Uruguay Round trade agreement in April 1994, UNCTAD estimated that the value of trade preferences for developing countries would be reduced, owing to a general reduction of tariffs. It advocated maintaining preferential margins for developing countries and extending GSP benefits to agricultural products and textiles from those countries after import quotas were eliminated, in accordance with the trade agreement.

Trade efficiency was discussed for the first time at the 1992 Conference, with computer-based technologies capable of substantially reducing the cost of transactions providing the focus. In 1994 a Global Trade Point Network (GTPNet), comprising an electronic network of trade-related information, was launched. The scheme, in which 120 countries were participating at November 1998, is monitored by the Commission on Enterprise, Business Facilitation and Development.

UNCTAD's work in the field of shipping and maritime activity resulted in the adoption of the UN Convention on a Code of Conduct for Liner Conferences (effective from 1983), which provides for the national shipping lines of developing countries to participate on an equal basis with the shipping lines of developed countries. Other UNCTAD initiatives have resulted in the adoption of the UN Convention on the Carriage of Goods by Sea (Hamburg Rules—1978), the UN Convention on International Multimodal Transport (1980), the UN Convention on Conditions for Registration of Ships (1986), and the International Convention on Maritime Liens and Mortgages. This last Convention was adopted in May 1993 in Geneva by a UN International Maritime Organization Conference of Plenipotentiaries, and its objectives were to encourage international uniformity in the field of maritime liens and mortgages and to improve conditions for ship financing. Technical co-operation and training projects, financed by UNDP and additional funds from bilateral donors, constitute an important component of UNCTAD's work in the fields of ports and multimodal transport and have resulted in the development of specialized courses. A software package Advance Cargo Information System (ACIS), enables shipping lines and railway companies to track the movement of cargo. Through the use of ACIS and the Automated System for Customs Data (ASYCUDA), operational in more than 80 countries, UNCTAD aims to enhance the effective exchange of information in order to counter customs fraud.

UNCTAD aims to give particular attention to the needs of the world's 49 least developed countries (LDCs—as defined by the

UN). The eighth session of the Conference requested that detailed analyses of the socio-economic situations and domestic policies of the LDCs, their resource needs, and external factors affecting their economies be undertaken as part of UNCTAD's work programme. The ninth session determined that particular attention be given to the problems of the LDCs in all areas of UNCTAD's work. The 10th session focused on the impact of globalization on developing economies and on means of improving trade opportunities for the LDCs. In its *Least Developed Countries Report 2000* UNCTAD urged a restructuring of international development co-operation. UNCTAD was the leading UN body involved in preparations for the Third UN Conference on the Least Developed Countries, which was scheduled to take place in Brussels, Belgium in May 2001.

UNCTAD provides assistance to developing countries in the area of debt-management, and in seeking debt relief from their creditors. UNCTAD is responsible for the software component of a joint programme with the World Bank to extend technical co-operation to developing countries in the field of debt management. The assistance is based on the development and distribution of software (the Debt Management and Financial Analysis System—DMFAS) designed to enable debtor countries to analyse data, make projections, and to plan strategies for debt repayment and reorganization. UNCTAD provides training for operators in the use of the software, and for senior officials, to increase their awareness of institutional reforms which might be necessary for effective debt management.

The Secretariat provided technical assistance to developing countries in connection with the Uruguay Round of multilateral trade negotiations (see WTO). The International Trade Centre in Geneva is operated jointly by WTO and UNCTAD.

Since May 1993 UNCTAD has serviced the ECOSOC Commission on Science and Technology for Development, which provides a forum for discussion of the following issues relating to science and technology for development: technology for small-scale economic activities to address the basic needs of low-income countries; gender implications of science and technology for developing countries; science and technology and the environment; the contribution of technologies to industrialization in developing countries; and the role of information technologies, in particular in relation to developing countries. The Commission meets every two years.

Finance

The operational expenses of UNCTAD are borne by the regular budget of the UN, and amount to approximately US $55m. annually. Technical co-operation activities, financed from extra-budgetary resources, amount to some $22m. annually.

Publications

Advanced Technology Assessment System Bulletin (occasional).
Guide to UNCTAD Publications (annually).
Handbook of Statistics (annually, also available on CD-ROM).
The Least Developed Countries Report (annually).
Monthly Commodity Price Bulletin.
Review of Maritime Transport (annually).
Trade and Development Report (annually).
Transnational Corporations (3 a year).
UNCTAD Commodity Yearbook.
UNCTAD News (6 a year).
World Investment Report (annually).

United Nations Development Programme—UNDP

Address: One United Nations Plaza, New York, NY 10017, USA.
Telephone: (212) 906-5315; **fax:** (212) 906-5364; **e-mail:** hq@undp.org; **internet:** www.undp.org.

The Programme was established in 1965 by the UN General Assembly. Its central mission is to help countries to eradicate poverty and achieve a sustainable level of human development.

Organization

(April 2001)

UNDP is responsible to the UN General Assembly, to which it reports through ECOSOC.

EXECUTIVE BOARD

The Executive Board is responsible for providing intergovernmental support to, and supervision of, the activities of UNDP and the UN Population Fund (UNFPA). It comprises 36 members: eight from Africa, seven from Asia, four from eastern Europe, five from Latin America and the Caribbean and 12 from western Europe and other countries.

SECRETARIAT

Offices and divisions at the Secretariat include: Planning and Resource Management; Development Policy Resources and External Affairs; Evaluation; Audit and Performance Review; Communications; and the Office of the Human Development Report. Five regional bureaux, all headed by an assistant administrator, cover: Africa; Asia and the Pacific; the Arab states; Latin America and the Caribbean; and Europe and the Commonwealth of Independent States. The Bureau for Resources and Strategic Partnerships facilitates co-operation with UNDP's development partners and serves as an information exchange for UNDP's other bureaux and offices.

Administrator: MARK MALLOCH BROWN (United Kingdom).
Associate Administrator: Dr ZÉPHIRIN DIABRÉ (Burkina Faso).

COUNTRY OFFICES

In almost every country receiving UNDP assistance there is an office, headed by the UNDP Resident Representative, who usually also serves as UN co-ordinator, responsible for the co-ordination of all UN technical assistance and operational development activities, advising the Government on formulating the country programme, ensuring that field activities are undertaken, and acting as the leader of the UN team of experts working in the country. The offices function as the primary presence of the UN in most developing countries.

Activities

As the world's largest source of grant technical assistance in developing countries, UNDP works with more than 150 governments and 40 international agencies in efforts to achieve faster economic growth and better standards of living throughout the developing world. Most of the work is undertaken in the field by the various United Nations agencies, or by the government of the country concerned. UNDP is committed to allocating some 87% of its core resources to low-income countries with an annual income per caput of less than US $750. Assistance is mostly non-monetary, comprising the provision of experts' services, consultancies, equipment and fellowships for advanced study abroad. In 1996 35% of spending on projects was for the services of personnel, 25% for subcontracts, 18% for equipment and 16% for training; the remainder was for other costs, such as maintenance of equipment. Most UNDP projects incorporate training for local workers. Developing countries themselves provide 50% or more of the total project costs in terms of personnel, facilities, equipment and supplies. At December 1996 there were 3,240 UN volunteer specialists and field workers, as well as 4,501 international experts and 5,703 national experts serving under UNDP. In that year UNDP awarded 13,393 fellowships for nationals of developing countries to study abroad.

In 1993 UNDP began to examine its role and effectiveness in promoting sustainable human development, an approach to economic growth that encompasses individual well-being and choice, equitable distribution of the benefits of development and conservation of the environment. In June 1994 the Executive Board endorsed a proposal of the UNDP Administrator to make sustainable human development the guiding principle of the organization. Within this framework there were to be the following priority objectives: poverty elimination; sustainable livelihoods; good governance; environmental protection and regeneration; and the advancement and empowerment of women. The allocation of programming resources has subsequently reflected UNDP's new agenda, with 26% of resources directed towards poverty eradication and livelihoods for the poor, 25% to capacity-building and governance, 24% to projects concerned with environmental resources and food security, and 23% to public resources management for sustainable human development (with 2% to other activities).

In 1994 the Executive Board also determined that UNDP should assume a more active and integrative role within the UN development system. This approach has been implemented by UNDP Resident Representatives, who usually also serve as UN Resident Co-ordinators, with responsibility for co-ordinating UN policies to achieve sustainable human development in consultation with other agencies, in particular UNEP, FAO and UNHCR. UNDP has increased its allocation of resources to training and skill-sharing programmes in order to promote this co-ordinating role. In late 1997 the UNDP Administrator was appointed to chair the UN Development Group, which was established as part of a series of structural reform measures initiated by the UN Secretary-General and which aimed to strengthen collaboration between some 20 UN funds, programmes and other development bodies. The Group promotes coherent policy at country level through the system of UN Resident Co-ordinators (see above), the Common Country Assessment mechanism (CCA, a country-based process for evaluating national development situations), and the UN Development Assistance Framework (UNDAF, the foundation for planning and co-ordinating development operations at country level, based on the CCA). UNDP's leading role within the process of UN reform has also been reflected in its own internal reform process, 'UNDP 2001', which focused on improving the methodology for planning, managing and reporting within a results-based management framework; UNDP 2001 was formally concluded in December 1999. In 1999 Results-Oriented Annual Reports (ROARs) were compiled for the first time by country offices and regional programmes. UNDP was to be the focus of UN efforts to reduce global poverty significantly by 2015, following pledges to this effect made at the Millennium Summit in September 2000.

UNDP aims to help governments to reassess their development priorities and to design initiatives for sustainable development. UNDP country officers support the formulation of national human development reports (NHDRs), which aim to facilitate activities such as policy-making, the allocation of resources and monitoring progress towards poverty eradiction and sustainable development. In addition, the preparation of Advisory Notes and Country Co-operation Frameworks by UNDP officials help to highlight country-specific aspects of poverty eradiction and national strategic priorities. In January 1998 the Executive Board adopted eight guiding principles relating to sustainable human development that were to be implemented by all country offices, in order to ensure a focus to UNDP activities. A network of Sub-regional Resource Facilities (SURFs) has been established to strengthen and co-ordinate UNDP's technical assistance services.

UNDP's activities to facilitate poverty eradication include support for capacity-building programmes and initiatives to generate sustainable livelihoods, for example by improving access to credit, land and technologies. In March 1996 UNDP launched the Poverty Strategies Initiative (PSI) to strengthen national capacities to assess and monitor the extent of poverty and to combat the problem. By the end of 1998 projects had been approved in 100 countries for funding under the PSI. All PSI projects were intended to involve representatives of governments, the private sector, social organizations and research institutions in policy debate and formulation. In early 1997 a UNDP scheme to support private-sector and community-based initiatives to generate employment opportunities, MicroStart, became operational with some US $41m. in initial funds. UNDP supports the Caribbean Project Development Facility and the Africa Project Development Facility, which are administered by the International Finance Corporation (q.v.) and which aim to develop the private sector in these regions in order to generate jobs and sustainable livelihoods.

Approximately one-quarter of all UNDP programme resources support national efforts to ensure efficient governance and to build effective relations between the state, the private sector and civil society, which are essential to achieving sustainable development. UNDP undertakes assessment missions to help ensure free and fair elections and works to promote human rights, an accountable and competent public sector, a competent judicial system and decentralized government and decision-making. Within the context of the UN Special Initiative on Africa, UNDP supports the Africa Governance Forum which convenes annually to consider aspects of governance and development. In July 1997 UNDP organized an International Conference on Governance for Sustainable Growth and Equity, which was held in New York, USA, and attended by more than 1,000 representatives of national and local authorities and the business and non-governmental sectors. At the Conference UNDP initiated a four-year programme to promote activities and to encourage new approaches in support of good governance. In May/June 1999 a World Conference on Governance was held in Manila, the Philippines, attended by some 1,000 government officials and representatives of the private sector and non-governmental organizations. UNDP sponsored a series of meetings held on the subject of Building Capacities for Governance. In April UNDP and the Office of the High Commissioner for Human Rights launched a joint programme to strengthen capacity-building in order to promote the integration of human rights issues into activities concerned with sustainable human development.

Within UNDP's framework of urban development activities the Local Initiative Facility for Urban Environment (LIFE) undertakes small-scale environmental projects in low-income communities, in collaboration with local authorities and community-based groups. Recent initiatives include canal and river improvement projects in Thailand, improvement of the urban environment in a suburb of Cairo, Egypt, and public-health improvements and the environmental rehabilitation of precipitous housing areas in Brazil. Other initiatives include the Urban Management Programme and the Public-Private Partnerships Programme for the Urban Environment which aimed to generate funds, promote research and support new technologies to enhance sustainable environments in urban areas. In November 1996 UNDP initiated a process of collaboration between city authorities world-wide to promote implementation of the commitments made at the 1995 Copenhagen summit for social development (see below) and to help to combat aspects of poverty and other urban problems, such as poor housing, transport, the management of waste disposal, water supply and sanitation. The first Forum of the so-called World Alliance of Cities Against Poverty was convened in October 1998, in Lyon, France. The second Forum took place in April 2000 in Geneva, Switzerland. UNDP supports the development of national programmes that emphasize the sustainable management of natural resources, for example through its Sustainable Energy Initiative, which promotes more efficient use of energy resources and the introduction of renewable alternatives to conventional fuels. UNDP is also concerned with forest management, the aquatic environment and sustainable agriculture and food security.

In the mid-1990s UNDP expanded its role in countries in crisis and with special circumstances, working in collaboration with other UN agencies to promote relief and development efforts, in order to secure the foundations for sustainable human development and thereby increase national capabilities to prevent or pre-empt future crises. In particular, UNDP was concerned to achieve reconciliation, reintegration and reconstruction in affected countries, as well as to support emergency interventions and management and delivery of programme aid. In 1995 the Executive Board decided that 5% of total UNDP core resources be allocated to countries in 'special development situations', i.e. urgently requiring major, integrated external support. Special development initiatives include the demobilization of former combatants, rehabilitation of communities for the sustainable reintegration of returning populations, the restoration and strengthening of democratic institutions, and clearance of anti-personnel land-mines. UNDP has established a mine action unit within its Emergency Response Division, in order to strengthen national de-mining capabilities. In December 1996 UNDP launched the Civilian Reconstruction Teams programme, creating some 5,000 jobs for former combatants in Liberia to work on the rehabilitation of the country's infrastructure. In December 1997 the UN General Assembly resolved to transfer the functions of natural disaster prevention, preparedness and mitigation to UNDP from the Department of Humanitarian Affairs (reorganized shortly afterwards as the Office for the Co-ordination of Humanitarian Affairs). Accordingly UNDP's Disaster Management Programme assumed responsibility for the UN's Disaster Management Training Programme.

UNDP is a co-sponsor, jointly with WHO, the World Bank, UNICEF, UNESCO, UNDCP and UNFPA, of a Joint UN Programme on HIV and AIDS, which became operational on 1 January 1996. UNAIDS co-ordinates UNDP's HIV and Development Programme. Within the UN system UNDP also has responsibility for co-ordinating activities following global UN conferences. In March 1995 government representatives attending the World Summit for Social Development, which was held in Copenhagen, Denmark, adopted the Copenhagen Declaration and a Programme of Action, which included initiatives to promote the eradication of poverty, to increase and reallocate official development assistance to basic social programmes and to promote equal access to education. With particular reference to UNDP, the Programme of Action advocated that UNDP support the implementation of social development programmes, co-ordinate these efforts through its field offices and organize efforts on the part of the UN system to stimulate capacity-building at local, national and regional levels. The PSI (see above) was introduced following the summit. A special session of the General Assembly to review the implementation of the summit's objectives was convened in June 2000. Following the UN Fourth World Conference on Women, held in Beijing, People's Republic of China, in September 1995, UNDP led inter-agency efforts to ensure the full participation of women in all economic, political and professional activities, and assisted with further situation analysis and training activities. (UNDP also created a Gender in Development Office to ensure that women participate more fully in UNDP-sponsored activities.) In June 2000 a special session of the General Assembly was convened to review the conference. UNDP played an important role, at both national and international levels, in preparing for the second UN Conference on Human Settlements (Habitat II), which was held in Istanbul, Turkey, in June 1996 (see the UN Centre for Human Settlements, p. 40). At the conference UNDP announced the establishment of a new facility, which was designed to promote private-sector investment in urban infrastructure. The facility was to be allocated initial resources of US $10m., with the aim of generating a total of $1,000m. from private sources for this sector.

Since 1990 UNDP has published an annual *Human Development Report*, incorporating a Human Development Index, which ranks countries in terms of human development, using three key indicators: life expectancy, adult literacy and basic income required for a decent standard of living. In 1997 a Human Poverty Index and a Gender-related Development Index, which assesses gender equality on the basis of life expectancy, education and income, were introduced into the Report for the first time. The 2000 Report focused on the relationship between human rights and human development. UNDP's *Poverty Report 2000* emphasized the importance of good governance as a fundamental condition of the eradication of poverty. In 1996 UNDP implemented its first corporate communications and advocacy strategy, which aimed to generate public awareness of the activities of the UN system, to promote debate on development issues and to mobilize resources by increasing public and donor appreciation of UNDP. A series of national and regional workshops was held, while media activities focused on the publication of the annual *Human Development Report* and the International Day for the Eradication of Poverty, held annually on 17 October. UNDP aims to use the developments in information technology to advance its communications strategy and to disseminate guide-lines and technical support throughout its country office network. The Bureau for Development Policy operates the Information Technology for Development Programme, which aims to promote sustainable human development through increased utilization of information and communications technologies globally. The Programme aims to establish technology access centres in developing countries. A Sustainable Development Networking Programme focuses on expanding internet connectivity in poorer countries through building national capacities and supporting local internet sites.

In October 1999 UNDP, in collaboration with an international communications company, Cisco Systems, organized NetAid, a series of international concerts held to improve awareness of Third World poverty, and broadcast live on the internet. Proceeds and donations generated by the initiative were to assist Kosovo refugees and the poorest African nations. An internet site linked to the initiative, www.netaid.org, has become a platform for co-ordinating fundraising and other activities aimed at alleviating poverty in the developing world.

Finance

UNDP is financed by the voluntary contributions of members of the United Nations and the Programme's participating agencies. Contributions from recipient governments, or third-party sources, to share the cost of projects constitute an increasingly significant portion of UNDP's total income. In 1996 total voluntary contributions amounted to US $2,186m., compared with some $1,842m. in 1995. Contributions to UNDP's core resources amounted to $844m. in 1996, compared with $927m. in 1995, while contributions to non-core funds, including cost-sharing arrangements, amounted to $1,342m. In 1996 estimated field programme expenditure under UNDP's core programme totalled $1,211m., of which $544m. was from general resources and $667m. cost-sharing contributions.

UNDP FIELD PROGRAMME EXPENDITURE BY REGION
(1996, UNDP core programme, US $ million)

Africa	248
Asia and the Pacific	196
Latin America and the Caribbean	613
Arab states	61
Europe and the CIS	43
Global and interregional	50
Total	**1,211***

* Including government cash counterpart contributions.

Publications

Annual Report.

Choices (quarterly).

Global Public Goods: International Co-operation in the 21st Century.

Human Development Report (annually, also available on CD-ROM).

Poverty Report (annually).

Associated Funds and Programmes

UNDP is the central funding, planning and co-ordinating body for technical co-operation within the UN system. A number of associated funds and programmes, financed separately by means of voluntary contributions, provide specific services through the UNDP network. UNDP manages a trust fund to promote economic and technical co-operation among developing countries.

Total expenditure of funds and programmes administered by UNDP amounted to an estimated US $263.3m. in 1996. The principal funds and programmes are listed below.

CAPACITY 21

UNDP initiated Capacity 21 at the UN Conference on Environment and Development, which was held in June 1992, to support developing countries in preparing and implementing policies for sustainable development. Capacity 21 promotes new approaches to development, through national development strategies, community-based management and training programmes. During 1998 programmes funded by Capacity 21 were under way in 52 countries.

GLOBAL ENVIRONMENT FACILITY—GEF

The GEF, which is managed jointly by UNDP, the World Bank and UNEP, began operations in 1991, with funding of US $1,500m. over a three-year period. Its aim is to support projects concerning climate change, the conservation of biological diversity, the protection of international waters, and reducing the depletion of the ozone layer in the atmosphere. UNDP is responsible for capacity-building, targeted research, pre-investment activities and technical assistance. UNDP also administers the Small Grants Programme of the GEF, which supports community-based activities by local non-governmental organizations. During the pilot phase of the GEF, in the period 1991–94, $242.5m. in funding was approved for 55 UNDP projects. In 1994 representatives of 34 countries agreed to provide $2,000m. to replenish GEF funds. In 1998 36 donor countries pledged $2,750m. for the next replenishment of GEF funds (GEF-2), covering the period 1 July 1998–30 June 2002. Negotiations for the third replenishment commenced in October 2000. At 30 June 2000 the GEF portfolio comprised 165 projects; 94 projects had been completed at that time.

Internet: www.gefweb.org.

MONTREAL PROTOCOL

UNDP assists countries to eliminate the use of ozone-depleting substances (ODS), in accordance with the Montreal Protocol to the Vienna Convention for the Protection of the Ozone Layer (see p. 98), through the design, monitoring and evaluation of ODS phase-out projects and programmes. In particular, UNDP provides technical assistance and training, national capacity-building and demonstration projects and technology transfer investment projects. The latter accounted for more than 75% of UNDP's activities in this area in 1994. At December 1998, through the Executive Committee of the Montreal Protocol, UNDP was assisting 64 countries in eliminating ozone-depleting substances.

OFFICE TO COMBAT DESERTIFICATION AND DROUGHT—UNSO

The Office was established following the conclusion, in October 1994, of the UN Convention to Combat Desertification in Those Countries Experiencing Serious Drought and/or Desertification, Particularly in Africa. It replaced the former UN Sudano–Sahelian Office (UNSO), while retaining the same acronym. UNSO is responsible for UNDP's role in desertification control and dryland management. Special emphasis is given to strengthening the environmental planning and management capacities of national institutions. During 1998 UNSO, in collaboration with other international partners, supported the implementation of the UN Convention in 55 designated countries.

Director: PHILIP DOBIE.

PROGRAMME OF ASSISTANCE TO THE PALESTINIAN PEOPLE—PAPP

PAPP is committed to strengthening newly-created institutions in the Israeli-occupied Territories and emerging Palestinian autonomous areas, to creating employment opportunities and to stimulating private and public investment in the area to enhance trade and export potential. Examples of PAPP activities include the following: construction of sewage collection networks and systems in the northern Gaza Strip; provision of water to 500,000 people in rural and urban areas of the West Bank and Gaza; construction of schools, youth and health centres; support to vegetable and fish traders through the construction of cold storage and packing facilities; and provision of loans to strengthen industry and commerce. Field programme expenditure in 1996 totalled US $47.1m.

UNITED NATIONS CAPITAL DEVELOPMENT FUND—UNCDF

The Fund was established in 1966 and became fully operational in 1974. It invests in poor communities in least-developed countries by providing economic and social infrastructure, credit for both agricultural and small-scale entrepreneurial activities, and local development funds which encourage people's participation as well as that of local governments in the planning and implementation of projects. UNCDF aims to promote the interests of women in community projects and to enhance their earning capacities. By 1999 56 countries had received UNCDF assistance. In 1998 the Fund nominated 15 countries in which to concentrate subsequent programmes. A Special Unit for Microfinance (SUM) was established in 1997 as a joint UNDP/UNCDF operation, to facilitate co-ordination between microcredit initiatives of the UN, and to support UNDP's MicroStart initiative. SUM was fully integrated into UNCDF in 1999. In May 1996 stable funding for the Fund was pledged by eight donors for a three-year period. UNCDF's annual programming budget amounts to some US $40m.

Internet: www.undp.org/uncdf.

Executive Secretary: NORMAND LAUZON.

UNITED NATIONS DEVELOPMENT FUND FOR WOMEN—UNIFEM

UNIFEM is the UN's lead agency in addressing the issues relating to women in development and promoting the rights of women worldwide. The Fund provides direct financial and technical support to enable low-income women in developing countries to increase earnings, gain access to labour-saving technologies and otherwise improve the quality of their lives. It also funds activities that include women in decision-making related to mainstream development projects. In 1998 UNIFEM approved 64 new projects and continued to support some 90 ongoing programmes in more than 100 countries. UNIFEM has supported the preparation of national reports in 30 countries and used the priorities identified in these reports and in other regional initiatives to formulate a Women's Development

Agenda for the 21st century. Through these efforts, UNIFEM played an active role in the preparation for the UN Fourth World Conference on Women, which was held in Beijing, People's Republic of China, in September 1995. In June 2000 UNIFEM participated at a special session of the General Assembly convened to review the conference, entitled Women 2000: Gender Equality, Development and Peace for the 21st Century (Beijing + 5). Programme expenditure in 1998 totalled US $18.3m.

Headquarters: 304 East 45th St, New York, NY 10017, USA; tel. (212) 906-6400; fax (212) 906-6705; internet www.unifem.undp.org.

Director: NOELEEN HEYZER (Singapore).

UNITED NATIONS VOLUNTEERS—UNV

The United Nations Volunteers is an important source of middle-level skills for the UN development system supplied at modest cost, particularly in the least-developed countries. Volunteers expand the scope of UNDP project activities by supplementing the work of international and host-country experts and by extending the influence of projects to local community levels. UNV also supports technical co-operation within and among the developing countries by encouraging volunteers from the countries themselves and by forming regional exchange teams comprising such volunteers. UNV is involved in areas such as peace-building, elections, human rights, humanitarian relief and community-based environmental programmes, in addition to development activities.

The UN International Short-term Advisory Programme, which is the private-sector development arm of UNV, has increasingly focused its attention on countries in the process of economic transition. Since 1994 UNV has administered UNDP's Transfer of Knowledge Through Expatriate Nationals (TOKTEN) programme, which was initiated in 1977 to enable specialists and professionals from developing countries to contribute to development efforts in their countries of origin through short-term technical assignments.

At 30 November 2000 3,160 UNVs were serving in 135 countries. The total number of people who had served under the initiative amounted to 20,642 at December 1999.

Headquarters: POB 260111, 53153 Bonn, Germany; tel. (228) 8152000; fax (228) 8152001; e-mail hq@unv.org; internet www.unv .org.

Executive Co-ordinator: SHARON CAPELING-ALAKIJA.

United Nations Environment Programme—UNEP

Address: POB 30552, Nairobi, Kenya.

Telephone: (2) 621234; **fax:** (2) 226890; **e-mail:** ipainfo@unep.org; **internet:** www.unep.org.

The United Nations Environment Programme was established in 1972 by the UN General Assembly, following recommendations of the 1972 UN Conference on the Human Environment, in Stockholm, Sweden, to encourage international co-operation in matters relating to the human environment.

Organization

(April 2001)

GOVERNING COUNCIL

The main functions of the Governing Council, which meets every two years, are to promote international co-operation in the field of the environment and to provide general policy guidance for the direction and co-ordination of environmental programmes within the UN system. It comprises representatives of 58 states, elected by the UN General Assembly, for four-year terms, on a regional basis. The Council is assisted in its work by a Committee of Permanent Representatives.

HIGH-LEVEL COMMITTEE OF MINISTERS AND OFFICIALS IN CHARGE OF THE ENVIRONMENT

The Committee was established by the Governing Council in April 1997, with a mandate to consider the international environmental agenda and to make recommendations to the Council on reform and policy issues. In addition, the Committee, comprising 36 elected members, was to provide guidance and advice to the Executive Director, to enhance UNEP's collaboration and co-operation with other multilateral bodies and to help to mobilize financial resources for UNEP.

SECRETARIAT

The Secretariat serves as a focal point for environmental action within the UN system. At October 1999 UNEP had 618 members of staff, of whom 284 were based at the organization's headquarters and 334 at regional and other offices.

Executive Director: Dr KLAUS TÖPFER (Germany).

REGIONAL OFFICES

Africa: POB 30552, Nairobi, Kenya; tel. (2) 624283; fax (2) 623928.

Asia and the Pacific: UN Bldg, 10th Floor, Rajdamnern Ave, Bangkok 10200, Thailand; tel. (2) 288-1870; fax (2) 280-3829.

Europe: 15 chemin des Anémones, 1219 Châtelaine, Geneva, Switzerland; tel. (22) 9171234; fax (22) 7973420; e-mail roe@unep.ch; internet www.unep.ch.

Latin America and the Caribbean: Blvd de los Virreyes 155, Lomas Virreyes, 11000 México, DF, Mexico; tel. (5) 2024841; fax (5) 2020950.

North America: 1707 H St NW, Washington, DC 20006, USA; tel. (202) 785-0465; fax (202) 785-2096; e-mail uneprona@un.org.

West Asia: Sheikh Rashid Bldg, 1st Floor, 244 Road No 2904, Area 329, Manama, Bahrain; tel. 276072; fax 276075; e-mail uneprowa@ batelco.com.bh.

OTHER OFFICES

Convention on International Trade in Endangered Species of Wild Fauna and Flora (CITES): 15 chemin des Anémones, 1219 Châtelaine, Geneva, Switzerland; tel. (22) 9178139; fax (22) 7973417; e-mail cites@unep.ch; internet www.cites.org; Sec.-Gen. WILLEM WOUTER WIJNSTEKERS (Netherlands).

Global Programme of Action for the Protection of the Marine Environment from Land-based Activities: POB 16227, 2500 The Hague, The Netherlands; tel. (70) 4114460; fax (70) 3456648; e-mail gpa@unep.nl; internet www.gpa.unep.org; Co-ordinator Dr VEERLE VANDEWEERD.

New York Office: DC-2 Bldg, Room 0803, 2 United Nations Plaza, New York, NY 10017, USA; tel. (212) 963-8210; fax (212) 963-7341; internet www.nyo.unep.org.

Regional Co-ordinating Unit for East Asian Seas: UN Bldg, 10th Floor, Rajdamnern Ave, Bangkok 10200, Thailand; tel. (2) 288-1860; fax (2) 281-2428; e-mail kirkman.unescap@un.org; Co-ordinator HUGH KIRKMAN.

Regional Co-ordinating Unit for the Caribbean Environment Programme: 14-20 Port Royal St, Kingston, Jamaica; tel. 9229267; fax 9229292; internet www.cep.unep.org; Co-ordinator NELSON ANDRADE.

Secretariat of the Basel Convention: CP 356, 15 chemin des Anémones, 1219 Châtelaine, Geneva, Switzerland; tel. (22) 9178218; fax (22) 7973454; e-mail sbc@unep.ch; internet www.unep.ch/basel; Officer-in-Charge PER BAKKEN.

Secretariat of the Convention on Biological Diversity: World Trade Centre, 393 St Jacques St West, Suite 300, Montréal, QC, Canada H2Y 1N9; tel. (514) 288-2220; fax (514) 288-6588; e-mail secretariat@biodiv.org; internet www.biodiv.org; Exec. Sec. HAMDALLAH ZEDAN.

Secretariat of the Multilateral Fund for the Implementation of the Montreal Protocol: 1800 McGill College Ave, 27th Floor, Montréal, QC, Canada H3A 3J6; tel. (514) 282-1122; fax (514) 282-0068; e-mail secretariat@unmfs.org; Chief OMAR EL-ARINI.

UNEP Arab League Liaison Office: 24 Iraq St, Mohandessin, Cairo, Egypt; tel. (2) 3361349; fax (2) 3370658.

UNEP/CMS (Convention on the Conservation of Migratory Species of Wild Animals) **Secretariat:** Martin-Luther-King-Str. 8, 53175 Bonn, Germany; tel. (228) 8152401; fax (228) 8152449; e-mail cms@unep.de; internet www.wcmc.org.uk/cms; Exec. Sec. ARNULF MÜLLER-HELMBRECHT.

UNEP Chemicals: International Environment House, 11–13 chemin des Anémones, 1219 Châtelaine, Geneva, Switzerland; tel. (22) 9171234; fax (22) 7973460; e-mail jwillis@unep.ch; internet www.chem.unep.ch; Dir JAMES B. WILLIS.

UNEP Co-ordinating Unit for the Mediterranean Action Plan (MEDU): Leoforos Vassileos Konstantinou 48, POB 18019, 11610 Athens, Greece; tel. (1) 7273100; fax (1) 7253196; e-mail unepmedu @unepmap.gr; internet www.unepmap.org; Co-ordinator LUCIEN CHABASON.

UNEP Division of Technology, Industry and Economics: Tour Mirabeau, 39–43, Quai André Citroën, 75739 Paris Cédex 15, France; tel. 1-44-37-14-50; fax 1-44-37-14-74; e-mail uneptic@unep.fr; internet www.uneptic.org/; Dir JACQUELINE ALOISI DE LARDEREL.

UNEP International Environmental Technology Centre: 2-110 Ryokuchi koen, Tsurumi-ku, Osaka 538-0036, Japan; tel. (6) 6915-4581; fax (6) 6915-0304; e-mail ietc@unep.or.jp; Dir STEVE HALLS.

UNEP Ozone Secretariat: POB 30552, Nairobi, Kenya; tel. (2) 623885; fax (2) 623913; e-mail ozoneinfo@unep.org; internet www.unep.ch/ozone/; Officer-in-Charge MICHAEL GRABER.

UNEP Secretariat for the UN Scientific Committee on the Effects of Atomic Radiation: Vienna International Centre, Wagramerstrasse 5, POB 500, 1400 Vienna, Austria; tel. (1) 26060-4330; fax (1) 26060-5902; e-mail burton.bennett@unvienna.un.or.at; Sec. BURTON G. BENNETT.

Activities

UNEP aims to maintain a constant watch on the changing state of the environment; to analyse the trends; to assess the problems using a wide range of data and techniques; and to promote projects leading to environmentally sound development. It plays a catalytic and co-ordinating role within and beyond the UN system. Many UNEP projects are implemented in co-operation with other UN agencies, particularly UNDP, the World Bank group, FAO, UNESCO and WHO. About 45 intergovernmental organizations outside the UN system and 60 international non-governmental organizations have official observer status on UNEP's Governing Council, and, through the Environment Liaison Centre in Nairobi, UNEP is linked to more than 6,000 non-governmental bodies concerned with the environment. UNEP also sponsors international conferences, programmes, plans and agreements regarding all aspects of the environment.

In February 1997 the Governing Council, at its 19th session, adopted a ministerial declaration (the Nairobi Declaration) on UNEP's future role and mandate, which recognized the organization as the principal UN body working in the field of the environment and as the leading global environmental authority, setting and overseeing the international environmental agenda. In June a Special Session of the UN General Assembly, referred to as the 'Earth Summit + 5', was convened to review the state of the environment and progress achieved in implementing the objectives of the UN

Conference on Environment and Development (UNCED) in Rio de Janeiro, Brazil, in June 1992. The meeting adopted a Programme for Further Implementation of Agenda 21 (a programme of activities to promote sustainable development, adopted by UNCED) in order to intensify efforts in areas such as energy, freshwater resources and technology transfer. The meeting confirmed UNEP's essential role in advancing the Programme and as a global authority promoting a coherent legal and political approach to the environmental challenges of sustainable development. An extensive process of restructuring and realignment of functions was subsequently initiated by UNEP, and a new organizational structure reflecting the decisions of the Nairobi Declaration was implemented during 1999.

In May 2000 UNEP sponsored the first annual Global Ministerial Environment Forum, held in Malmö, Sweden, and attended by environment ministers and other government delegates from more than 130 countries. Participants reviewed policy issues in the field of the environment and addressed issues such as the impact on the environment of population growth, the depletion of earth's natural resources, climate change and the need for fresh water supplies. The Forum issued the Malmö Declaration which identified the effective implementation of international agreements on environmental matters at national level as the most pressing challenge for policy makers. The Declaration emphasized the importance of mobilizing domestic and international resources and urged increased co-operation from civil society and the private sector in achieving sustainable development.

ENVIRONMENTAL ASSESSMENT AND EARLY WARNING

The Nairobi Declaration resolved that the strengthening of UNEP's information, monitoring and assessment capabilities was a crucial element of the organization's restructuring, in order to help establish priorities for international, national and regional action, and to ensure the efficient and accurate dissemination of emerging environmental trends and emergencies.

UNEP has developed an extensive network of collaborating centres to assist in its analysis of the state of the global environment. The outcome of its work, the first Global Environment Outlook (GEO-I), was published in January 1997. A second process of global assessment resulted in the publication of GEO-II in September 1999. UNEP has initiated a major Global International Waters Assessment to consider all aspects of the world's water-related issues, in particular problems of shared transboundary waters, and of future sustainable management of water resources. UNEP is also a sponsoring agency of the Joint Group of Experts on the Scientific Aspects of Marine Environmental Pollution and contributes to the preparation of reports on the state of the marine environment and on the impact of land-based activities on that environment. In November 1995 UNEP published a Global Biodiversity Assessment, which was the first comprehensive study of biological resources throughout the world.

UNEP's environmental information network includes the Global Resource Information Database (GRID), which converts collected data into information usable by decision-makers. The INFOTERRA programme facilitates the exchange of environmental information through an extensive network of national 'focal points'. By the end of 1998 178 countries were participating in the network. UNEP promotes public access to environmental information, as well as participation in environmental concerns, through the INFOTERRA initiative. UNEP aims to establish in every developing region an Environment and Natural Resource Information Network (ENRIN) in order to make available technical advice and manage environmental information and data for improved decision-making and action-planning in countries most in need of assistance. UNEP aims to integrate all its information resources in order to improve access to information and to promote the international exchange of information. This was to be achieved through the design and implementation of UNEPNET, which was to operate throughout the UN system and be fully accessible through the world-wide information networks. In addition, by late 1998, 15 so-called Mercure satellite systems were operational world-wide, linking UNEP offices and partner agencies.

UNEP's information, monitoring and assessment structures also serve to enhance early-warning capabilities and to provide accurate information during an environmental emergency. In 1997 and 1998 UNEP organized a series of meetings to assess the environmental damage resulting from forest fires in Indonesia and to consider measures to respond effectively to further incidents. In April 1998 an international meeting, convened under UNEP auspices in Geneva, Switzerland, approved US $10m. to finance an immediate package of measures aimed at extinguishing the most dangerous fires, preventing others from spreading and improving Indonesia's fire-fighting capabilities. UNEP was also concerned with other 'man-made' fires, in particular in Brazil where an extensive conflagration was threatening an indigenous reserve and a number of endangered species.

POLICY DEVELOPMENT AND LAW

UNEP aims to promote the development of policy tools and guidelines in order to achieve the sustainable management of the world environment. At a national level it assists governments to develop and implement appropriate environmental instruments and aims to co-ordinate policy initiatives. Training workshops in various aspects of environmental law and its applications are conducted. UNEP supports the development of new legal, economic and other policy instruments to improve the effectiveness of existing environmental agreements.

UNEP was instrumental in the drafting of a Convention on Biological Diversity (CBD) to preserve the immense variety of plant and animal species, in particular those threatened with extinction. The Convention entered into force at the end of 1993; by March 2001 180 countries were parties to the CBD. UNEP supports co-operation for biodiversity assessment and management in selected developing regions and for the development of strategies for the conservation and sustainable exploitation of individual threatened species (e.g. the Global Tiger Action Plan). UNEP also provides assistance for the preparation of individual country studies and strategies to strengthen national biodiversity management and research. In 1996 an *ad hoc* working group on biosafety was established to negotiate the conclusion of a protocol to the CBD to regulate international trade in living modified organisms (including genetically modified—GM—seeds and crops and pharmaceutical derivatives), in order to reduce any potential adverse effects on biodiversity and human health. An extraordinary session of the conference of parties to the CBD was convened in Cartagena, Colombia, in February 1999, to consider the provisional text formulated by the group and, if approved, to adopt its legally-binding provisions. The meeting, however, was suspended, owing to outstanding differences between the main producer countries and developing nations regarding the implications of the protocol on principles of free trade. An agreement on the so-called Cartagena Protocol was finally concluded at a meeting of parties to the CBD, held in Montreal, Canada, in January 2000. The Protocol permitted countries to ban imports of GM products if there were outstanding safety concerns, and provided for greater transparency in the description of products containing GM organisms, through a limited labelling system. By March 2001 the Protocol had been signed by 86 states and ratified by two.

In October 1994 87 countries, meeting under UN auspices, signed a Convention to Combat Desertification (see UNSO, p. 47), which aimed to provide a legal framework to counter the degradation of drylands. An estimated 75% of all drylands have suffered some land degradation, affecting approximately 1,000m. people in 110 countries. A second conference of the parties to the Convention was held in Dakar, Senegal, in December 1998, a third in Recife, Brazil, in November 1999, and a fourth in Bonn, Germany, in December 2000. UNEP continues to support the implementation of the Convention, as part of its efforts to protect land resources. UNEP also aims to improve the assessment of dryland degradation and desertification in co-operation with governments and other international bodies, as well as identifying the causes of degradation and measures to overcome these.

UNEP estimates that two-thirds of the world's population will suffer chronic water shortages by 2025, owing to rising demand for drinking water as a result of growing populations, decreasing quality of water because of pollution, and increasing requirements of industries and agriculture. UNEP provides scientific, technical and administrative support to facilitate the implementation and co-ordination of regional seas conventions and plans of action. UNEP promotes international co-operation in the management of river basins and coastal areas and for the development of tools and guidelines to achieve the sustainable management of freshwater and coastal resources. In particular, UNEP aims to control land-based activities, principally pollution, which affect freshwater resources, marine biodiversity and the coastal ecosystems of small-island developing states. In November 1995 110 governments adopted a Global Programme of Action for the Protection of the Marine Environment from Land-based Activities. UNEP aims to develop a similar global instrument to ensure the integrated management of freshwater resources, in order to address current and future needs. In 2000 UNEP, describing the unsustainable use of water as currently the most serious environmental and sustainable development issue, introduced a new Water Policy and Strategy, comprising assessment, management and co-ordination components.

In 1996 UNEP, in collaboration with FAO, began to work towards promoting and formulating a legally-binding international convention on prior informed consent (PIC) for hazardous chemicals and pesticides in international trade, extending a voluntary PIC procedure of information exchange undertaken by more than 100 governments since 1991. The Convention was adopted at a conference held in Rotterdam, Netherlands, in September 1998, and was to enter into force on being ratified by 50 signatory states. It aimed to reduce risks to human health and the environment by restricting the production, export and use of hazardous substances and enhancing information exchange procedures.

In conjunction with UNCHS (Habitat), UNDP, the World Bank and other regional organizations and institutions, UNEP promotes environmental concerns in urban planning and management through the Sustainable Cities Programme, as well as regional workshops concerned with urban pollution and the impact of transportation systems. In January 1994 UNEP inaugurated an International Environmental Technology Centre (IETC), with offices in Osaka and Shiga, Japan, in order to strengthen the capabilities of developing countries and countries with economies in transition to promote environmentally-sound management of cities and freshwater reservoirs through technology co-operation and partnerships.

UNEP has played a key role in global efforts to combat risks to the ozone layer, resultant climatic changes and atmospheric pollution. UNEP worked in collaboration with the World Meteorological Organization to formulate a Framework Convention on Climate Change, with the aim of reducing the emission of gases that have a warming effect on the atmosphere, and has remained an active participant in the ongoing process to review and enforce its implementation (see WMO, p. 115, for further details). UNEP was the lead agency in formulating the 1987 Montreal Protocol to the Vienna Convention for the Protection of the Ozone Layer (1985), which provided for a 50% reduction in the production of chlorofluorocarbons (CFCs) by 2000. An amendment to the Protocol was adopted in 1990, which required complete cessation of the production of CFCs by 2000 in industrialized countries and by 2010 in developing countries; these deadlines were advanced to 1996 and 2006, respectively, in November 1992. In 1997 the ninth Conference of the Parties (COP) to the Vienna Convention adopted a further amendment which aimed to introduce a licensing system for all controlled substances. The eleventh COP, meeting in Beijing, People's Republic of China, in November/December 1999, adopted the Beijing Amendment, which imposed tighter controls on the production and consumption of, and trade in, hydrochlorofluorocarbons. A Multilateral Fund for the Implementation of the Montreal Protocol was established in June 1990 to promote the use of suitable technologies and the transfer of technologies to developing countries. UNEP, UNDP, the World Bank and UNIDO are the sponsors of the Fund, which by early 1997 had financed 1,800 projects in 106 developing countries at a cost of US $565m. Commitments of $440m. were made to the fourth replenishment of the Fund, covering the three-year period 2000–02.

POLICY IMPLEMENTATION

UNEP's Division of Environmental Policy Implementation incorporates two main functions: technical co-operation and response to environmental emergencies.

With the UN Office for the Co-ordination of Humanitarian Assistance, UNEP has established an Environmental Emergencies Unit to mobilize and co-ordinate international assistance and expertise to countries facing disasters. It undertakes initial assessments of the situation, as well as post-conflict analysis, as required. In mid-1999 UNEP and the UN Centre for Human Settlements jointly established a Balkan Task Force to assess the environmental impact of NATO's aerial offensive against the Federal Republic of Yugoslavia. In November 2000 the Task Force led a field assessment to evaluate reports of environmental contamination by debris from NATO ammunition containing depleted uranium. During 2000 UNEP was involved in the implementation of a project on the mitigation and management of floods in China and conducted post-emergency assessments in Albania, Hungary, the former Yugoslav Republic of Macedonia, Romania and the Federal Republic of Yugoslavia regarding chemical spills; Mozambique and Venezuela (following floods); Guinea (on the impact of the refugee crisis); and Kenya (regarding drought).

UNEP, together with UNDP and the World Bank, is an implementing agency of the Global Environment Facility (GEF, see p. 47), which was established in 1991 as a mechanism for international co-operation in projects concerned with biological diversity, climate change, international waters and depletion of the ozone layer. UNEP services the Scientific and Technical Advisory Panel, which was established to provide expert advice on GEF programmes and operational strategies.

TECHNOLOGY, INDUSTRY AND ECONOMICS

The use of inappropriate industrial technologies and the widespread adoption of unsustainable production and consumption patterns have been identified as being inefficient in the use of renewable resources and wasteful, in particular in the use of energy and water. UNEP aims to encourage governments and the private sector to develop and adopt policies and practices that are cleaner and safer, make efficient use of natural resources, incorporate environmental costs, ensure the environmentally sound management of chemicals, and reduce pollution and risks to human health and the environment. In collaboration with other organizations and agencies UNEP works to define and formulate international guide-lines and agreements to address these issues. UNEP also promotes the transfer of appropriate technologies and organizes conferences and training workshops to provide sustainable production practices. Relevant information is disseminated through the International Cleaner Production Information Clearing House. UNEP, together with UNIDO, has established eight National Cleaner Production Centres to promote a preventive approach to industrial pollution control. In May 1999 representatives of some 33 countries signed an International Declaration on Cleaner Production, launched by UNEP in 1998, with a commitment to implement cleaner and more sustainable production methods and to monitor results.

UNEP provides institutional servicing to the Basel Convention on the Control of Transboundary Movements of Hazardous Wastes and their Disposal, which was adopted in 1989 with the aim of preventing the disposal of wastes from industrialized countries in countries that have no processing facilities. In March 1994 the second meeting of parties to the Convention agreed to ban exportation of hazardous wastes between OECD and non-OECD countries by the end of 1997.The third meeting of parties to the Convention, held in 1995, proposed that the ban should be incorporated into the Convention as an amendment; the resulting so-called Ban Amendment did not distinguish between OECD and non-OECD countries. The Ban Amendment required ratification by three-quarters of the 62 states present at the time of adoption before it could enter into effect. The fourth full meeting of parties to the Convention, held in February 1998, attempted to clarify the classification and listing of hazardous wastes, which was expected to stimulate further ratifications. By March 2001 the Ban Amendment had been ratified by 24 states. In December 1999 132 states adopted a Protocol to the Convention to address issues relating to liability and compensation for damages from waste exports. The governments also agreed to establish a multilateral fund to finance immediate clean-up operations following any environmental accident.

The UNEP Chemicals office was established to promote the sound management of hazardous substances, central to which was the International Register of Potentially Toxic Chemicals (IRPTC). UNEP aims to facilitate access to data on chemicals and hazardous wastes, in order to assess and control health and environmental risks, by using the IRPTC as a clearing house facility of relevant information and by publishing information and technical reports on the impact of the use of chemicals.

UNEP's OzonAction Programme works to promote information exchange, training and technological awareness. Its objective is to strengthen the capacity of governments and industry in developing countries to undertake measures towards the cost-effective phasing-out of ozone-depleting substances. UNEP also encourages the development of alternative and renewable sources of energy. To achieve this, UNEP is supporting the establishment of a network of centres to research and exchange information of environmentally-sound energy technology resources.

REGIONAL CO-OPERATION AND REPRESENTATION

UNEP maintains six regional offices. These work to initiate and promote UNEP objectives and to ensure that all programme formulation and delivery meets the specific needs of countries and regions. They also provide a focal point for building national, sub-regional and regional partnership and enhancing local participation in UNEP initiatives. Following UNEP's reorganization a co-ordination office was established at headquarters to promote regional policy integration, to co-ordinate programme planning, and to provide necessary services to the regional offices.

UNEP provides administrative support to several regional conventions, for example the Lusaka Agreement on Co-operative Enforcement Operations Directed at Illegal Trade in Wild Flora and Fauna, which entered into force in December 1996 having been concluded under UNEP auspices in order to strengthen the implementation of the Convention on Biological Diversity and the Convention on International Trade in Endangered Species (CITES) in Eastern and Central Africa. UNEP also organizes conferences, workshops and seminars at national and regional levels, and may extend advisory services or technical assistance to individual governments.

CONVENTIONS

UNEP aims to develop and promote international environmental legislation in order to pursue an integrated response to global environmental issues, to enhance collaboration among existing convention secetariats, and to co-ordinate support to implement the work programmes of international instruments.

UNEP has been an active participant in the formulation of several major conventions (see above). The Division of Environmental Conventions is mandated to assist the Division of Policy Development and Law in the formulation of new agreements or protocols to existing conventions. Following the successful adoption of the Rotterdam Convention in September 1998, UNEP played a leading role in formulating a multilateral agreement to reduce and ultimately eliminate the manufacture and use of Persistent Organic Pollutants (POPs), which are considered to be a major global environmental hazard. The agreement on POPs, concluded in December 2000 at a conference sponsored by UNEP in Johannesburg, South Africa, was expected to be opened for signature in May 2001.

UNEP has been designated to provide secretariat functions to a number of global and regional environmental conventions (see above for list of offices).

COMMUNICATION AND PUBLIC INFORMATION

UNEP's public education campaigns and outreach programmes promote community involvement in environmental issues. Further communication of environmental concerns is undertaken through the media, an information centre service and special promotional events, including World Environment Day, photograph competitions and the awarding of the Sasakawa Prize to recognize distinguished service to the environment by individuals and groups. In 1996 UNEP initiated a Global Environment Citizenship Programme to promote acknowledgment of the environmental responsibilities of all sectors of society.

Finance

UNEP derives its finances from the regular budget of the United Nations and from voluntary contributions to the Environment Fund. In February 1999 the Governing Council authorized a budget of US $120m. for the two-year period 2000–01, of which $100m. was for programme activities (see below), $14.4m. for management and administration, and $5m. for fund programme reserves.

APPROVED BUDGET FOR FUND PROGRAMME ACTIVITIES, 2000–01

	(US $'000)
Environmental Assessment and Early Warning.	24,000
Policy Development and Law	13,000
Policy Implementation .	7,000
Technology, Industry and Economics	23,000
Regional Co-operation and Representation .	20,500
Environment Conventions .	6,775
Communications and Public Information	5,725
Total .	100,000

Publications

Annual Report.

APELL Newsletter (2 a year).

Cleaner Production Newsletter (2 a year).

Climate Change Bulletin (quarterly).

Connect (UNESCO-UNEP newsletter on environmental degradation, quarterly).

Desertification Control Bulletin (2 a year).

EarthViews (quarterly).

Environment Forum (quarterly).

Environmental Law Bulletin (2 a year).

Financial Services Initiative (2 a year).

GEF News (quarterly).

Global Environment Outlook (annually).

GPA Newsletter.

IETC Insight (3 a year).

Industry and Environment Review (quarterly).

Leave it to Us (children's magazine, 2 a year).

Managing Hazardous Waste (2 a year).

Our Planet (quarterly).

OzonAction Newsletter (quarterly).

Tierramerica (4–6 a year).

Tourism Focus (2 a year).

UNEP Chemicals Newsletter (2 a year).

UNEP Update (monthly).

World Atlas of Desertification.

Studies, reports, legal texts, technical guide-lines, etc.

United Nations High Commissioner for Refugees—UNHCR

Address: CP 2500, 1211 Geneva 2 dépôt, Switzerland.

Telephone: (22) 7398502; **fax:** (22) 7397312; **e-mail:** hqpi00@unhcr.ch; **internet:** www.unhcr.ch.

The Office of the High Commissioner was established in 1951 to provide international protection for refugees and to seek durable solutions to their problems.

Organization

(April 2001)

HIGH COMMISSIONER

The High Commissioner is elected by the United Nations General Assembly on the nomination of the Secretary-General, and is responsible to the General Assembly and to the UN Economic and Social Council (ECOSOC).

High Commissioner: RUUD LUBBERS (Netherlands).

Deputy High Commissioner: MARY ANN WYRSCH (USA).

EXECUTIVE COMMITTEE

The Executive Committee of the High Commissioner's Programme, established by ECOSOC, gives the High Commissioner policy directives in respect of material assistance programmes and advice in the field of international protection. In addition, it oversees UNHCR's general policies and use of funds. The Committee, which comprises representatives of 53 states, both members and non-members of the UN, meets once a year.

ADMINISTRATION

Headquarters include the Executive Office, comprising the offices of the High Commissioner, the Deputy High Commissioner and the Assistant High Commissioner. There are separate offices for the Inspector General, the Special Envoy in the former Yugoslavia, and the Director of the UNHCR liaison office in New York. The other principal administrative units are the Division of Communication and Information, the Department of International Protection, the Division of Resource Management, and the Department of Operations, which is responsible for the five regional bureaux covering Africa; Asia and the Pacific; Europe; the Americas and the Caribbean; and Central Asia, South-West Asia, North Africa and the Middle East. At July 1999 there were 274 UNHCR field offices in 120 countries. At that time UNHCR employed 5,155 people, including short-term staff, of whom 4,265 (or 83%) were working in the field.

Activities

The competence of the High Commissioner extends to any person who, owing to well-founded fear of being persecuted for reasons of race, religion, nationality or political opinion, is outside the country of his or her nationality and is unable or, owing to such fear or for reasons other than personal convenience, remains unwilling to accept the protection of that country; or who, not having a nationality and being outside the country of his or her former habitual residence, is unable or, owing to such fear or for reasons other than personal convenience, is unwilling to return to it. Refugees who are assisted by other United Nations agencies, or who have the same rights or obligations as nationals of their country of residence, are outside the mandate of UNHCR.

In recent years there has been a significant shift in UNHCR's focus of activities. Increasingly UNHCR is called upon to support people who have been displaced within their own country (i.e. with similar needs to those of refugees but who have not crossed an international border) or those threatened with displacement as a result of armed conflict. In addition, it is providing greater support to refugees who have returned to their country of origin, to assist their reintegration, and is working to enable the local community to support the returnees. At December 1999 the refugee population world-wide totalled 11.7m. and UNHCR was concerned with a further 1.2m. asylum-seekers, 2.5m. recently returned refugees and 6.9m. others (of whom an estimated 4m. were internally displaced persons—IDPs).

INTERNATIONAL PROTECTION

As laid down in the Statute of the Office, one of the two primary functions of UNHCR is to extend international protection to refu-

gees. In the exercise of this function, UNHCR seeks to ensure that refugees and asylum-seekers are protected against *refoulement* (forcible return), that they receive asylum, and that they are treated according to internationally recognized standards. UNHCR pursues these objectives by a variety of means which include promoting the conclusion and ratification by states of international conventions for the protection of refugees. UNHCR promotes the adoption of liberal practices of asylum by states, so that refugees and asylum-seekers are granted admission, at least on a temporary basis.

The most comprehensive instrument concerning refugees that has been elaborated at the international level is the 1951 United Nations Convention relating to the Status of Refugees. This Convention, the scope of which was extended by a Protocol adopted in 1967, defines the rights and duties of refugees and contains provisions dealing with a variety of matters which affect the day-to-day lives of refugees. The application of the Convention and its Protocol is supervised by UNHCR. Important provisions for the treatment of refugees are also contained in a number of instruments adopted at the regional level. These include the OAU Convention of 1969 Governing the Specific Aspects of Refugee Problems, the European Agreement on the Abolition of Visas for Refugees, and the 1969 American Convention on Human Rights.

UNHCR has actively encouraged states to accede to the 1951 United Nations Refugee Convention and the 1967 Protocol: 139 states had acceded to either or both of these basic refugee instruments by July 2000. An increasing number of states have also adopted domestic legislation and/or administrative measures to implement the international instruments, particularly in the field of procedures for the determination of refugee status. Such measures provide an important guarantee that refugees will be accorded the standards of treatment which have been internationally established for their benefit. In recent years UNHCR has formulated a strategy designed to address the fundamental causes of refugee flows.

UNHCR has attempted to deal with the problem of military attacks on refugee camps, by formulating and encouraging the acceptance of a set of principles to ensure the safety of refugees. It also seeks to address the specific needs of refugee women and children.

ASSISTANCE ACTIVITIES

UNHCR assistance activities were formerly divided into General Programmes and Special Programmes. The latter were undertaken at the request of the UN General Assembly, the Secretary-General of the UN or member states, in response to a particular crisis. From January 2000 these were amalgamated under a single annual programme.

The first phase of an assistance operation uses UNHCR's capacity of emergency preparedness and response. This enables UNHCR to address the immediate needs of refugees at short notice, for example, by employing specially-trained emergency teams and maintaining stockpiles of basic equipment, medical aid and materials. A significant proportion of UNHCR expenditure is allocated to the next phase of an operation, providing 'care and maintenance' in stable refugee circumstances. This assistance can take various forms, including the provision of food, shelter, medical care and essential supplies. Also covered in many instances are basic services, including education and counselling.

POPULATIONS OF CONCERN TO UNHCR BY REGION* ('000 persons, at 31 December 1999)

	Refugees	Asylum-seekers	Returned refugees†	Others of concern‡	Total
Africa . . .	3,523	61	934	1,732	6,251
Asia . . .	4,782	25	618	1,885	7,309
Europe . .	2,608	473	952	3,252	7,286
Latin America .	61	2	6	21	90
North America .	636	606	—	—	1,242
Oceania . .	65	16	—	—	80
Total . . .	11,675	1,182	2,510	6,891	22,257

* In accordance with the regional classification of the UN's Department for Economic and Social Affairs, under which Africa includes countries of North Africa, and Asia incorporates Cyprus and Turkey and all countries of the Middle East not located on the African continent; Latin America covers Central and South America and the Caribbean.

† Refugees who have returned to their place of origin and remain of concern to UNHCR for a maximum period of two years.

‡ Mainly internally displaced persons (IDPs) and IDPs of concern to UNHCR who have returned to their place of origin and who remain of concern to UNHCR for a maximum of two years; also includes people who have received temporary protection and assistance outside their country, but who have not been formally recognized as refugees, as well as certain groups of war-affected populations and of countries of the former USSR who have not been granted a new nationality.

POPULATIONS OF CONCERN TO UNHCR BY COUNTRY* ('000 persons, at 31 December 1999)

	Refugees	Asylum-seekers	Returned refugees†	Others of concern†
Africa				
Algeria	165.2	—	—	—
Burundi	22.1	0.5	36.0	110.6
Congo, Democratic Republic	285.3	0.2	79.8	—
Congo, Republic	39.9	0.2	77.5	—
Côte d'Ivoire	138.4	0.7	—	—
Ethiopia	257.7	2.0	14.6	—
Guinea	501.5	0.4	—	—
Guinea-Bissau	7.1	—	5.3	265.0
Kenya	223.7	5.8	0.0	—
Liberia	96.3	0.0	297.0	204.2
Rwanda	34.4	1.8	49.2	626.1
Sierra Leone	6.6	0.0	198.1	500.0
Sudan	391.0	—	0.3	—
Tanzania	622.2	12.3	—	—
Uganda	218.2	0.2	1.2	—
Zambia	206.4	0.2	—	—
Asia				
Afghanistan	—	0.0	359.8	268.6
Armenia	296.2	0.0	0.0	—
Azerbaijan	221.6	0.4	—	569.6
China, People's Republic‡	293.3	0.0	—	—
East Timor	—	—	127.5	—
Georgia	5.2	—	1.8	279.2
India	180.0	0.0	—	—
Indonesia	162.5	0.0	—	—
Iran	1,835.7	—	—	—
Iraq	128.9	0.3	32.8	—
Kuwait	4.3	0.0	—	138.1
Nepal	127.9	0.0	—	—
Pakistan	1,202.0	0.5	—	—
Sri Lanka	0.0	—	0.2	612.5
Thailand	100.1	0.6	—	0.0
Europe				
Belarus	0.3	0.5	—	160.0
Bosnia and Herzegovina	65.6	0.0	161.0	882.5
Croatia	28.4	0.0	35.5	116.0
France	129.7	—	—	—
Germany	975.5	370.0	—	—
Netherlands	139.2§	—	—	—
Russia	80.1	1.1	0.0	1,408.3
Sweden	159.5§	7.9	—	—
Switzerland	82.3	34.8	—	—
Ukraine	2.7	3.0	—	260.0
United Kingdom	137.0§	128.6§	—	—
Yugoslavia	500.7	0.0	755.5	403.8
North America				
Canada	123.3§	24.7§	—	—
USA	513.0§	580.9§	—	—

* The list includes only those countries having 100,000 or more persons of concern to UNHCR.

† See table above for definitions.

‡ Excluding Hong Kong Special Administrative Region.

§ Figure estimated by UNHCR.

As far as possible, assistance is geared towards the identification and implementation of durable solutions to refugee problems—this being the second statutory responsibility of UNHCR. Such solutions generally take one of three forms: voluntary repatriation, local integration or resettlement in another country. Voluntary repatriation is increasingly the preferred solution, given the easing of political tension in many regions from which refugees have fled. Where voluntary repatriation is feasible, the Office assists refugees to overcome obstacles preventing their return to their country of origin. This may be done through negotiations with governments involved, or by prov-

iding funds either for the physical movement of refugees or for the rehabilitation of returnees once back in their own country.

ORIGIN OF MAJOR REFUGEE POPULATIONS AND PERSONS IN REFUGEE-LIKE SITUATIONS* ('000 persons, estimated at 31 December 1998)

Origin	Refugees
Afghanistan	2,633.9
Iraq	590.8
Burundi	500.0
Somalia	480.8
Bosnia and Herzegovina	471.6
Sierra Leone	411.0
Sudan	374.2
Eritrea	345.4
Croatia	334.6
Azerbaijan	328.5

* Information on the origin of refugees is not available for a number of, mainly industrialized, countries. Data exclude some 3.2m. Palestinian refugees who come under the mandate of UNRWA (q.v.). Palestinians who are outside the UNRWA area of operation, for example those in Iraq and Libya, are considered to be of concern to UNHCR.

When voluntary repatriation is not an option, efforts are made to assist refugees to integrate locally and to become self-supporting in their countries of asylum. This may be done either by granting loans to refugees, or by assisting them, through vocational training or in other ways, to learn a skill and to establish themselves in gainful occupations. One major form of assistance to help refugees re-establish themselves outside camps is the provision of housing. In cases where resettlement through emigration is the only viable solution to a refugee problem, UNHCR negotiates with governments in an endeavour to obtain suitable resettlement opportunities, to encourage liberalization of admission criteria and to draw up special immigration schemes. During 1998 21,210 refugees were resettled under UNHCR auspices.

In the early 1990s UNHCR aimed to consolidate efforts to integrate certain priorities into its programme planning and implementation, as a standard discipline in all phases of assistance. The considerations include awareness of specific problems confronting refugee women, the needs of refugee children, the environmental impact of refugee programmes and long-term development objectives. In an effort to improve the effectiveness of its programmes, UNHCR has initiated a process of delegating authority, as well as responsibility for operational budgets, to its regional and field representatives, increasing flexibility and accountability. In 1999 an Evaluation and Policy Analysis Unit was established to strengthen UNHCR's capacity to review systematically its operational effectiveness.

ASIA AND THE PACIFIC

In June 1989 an international conference was convened by UNHCR in Geneva to discuss the ongoing problem of refugees and displaced persons in and from the Indo-Chinese peninsula. The participants adopted the Comprehensive Plan of Action (CPA) for Indo-Chinese Refugees, which provided for the 'screening' of all Vietnamese arrivals in the region to determine their refugee status, the resettlement of 'genuine' refugees and the repatriation (described as voluntary 'in the first instance') of those deemed to be economic migrants. A steering committee of the international conference, representing 15 nations, met regularly to supervise the plan. In March 1996 UNHCR confirmed that it was to terminate funding for the refugee camps (except those in Hong Kong) on 30 June to coincide with the formal conclusion of the CPA; however, it pledged to support transitional arrangements regarding the completion of the repatriation process and maintenance of the remaining Vietnamese 'non-refugees' during the post-CPA phase-out period, as well as to continue its support for the reintegration and monitoring of returning nationals in Viet Nam and Laos. The prospect of forcible repatriation provoked rioting and violent protests in many camps throughout the region. By early July 16,800 Vietnamese remained in camps in Hong Kong, 4,000 in Indonesia, 3,700 in Thailand and 1,900 in the Philippines, with Malaysia and Singapore having completed the repatriation process. (At that time more than 88,000 Vietnamese and 22,000 Laotians had returned to their countries of origin under the framework of the CPA.) In late July the Philippines Government agreed to permit the remaining camp residents to settle permanently in that country. In September the remaining Vietnamese refugees detained on the island of Galang, in Indonesia, were repatriated, and in February 1997 the last camp for Vietnamese refugees in Thailand was formally closed. In mid-June of that year the main Vietnamese detention camp in Hong Kong was closed. However, the scheduled repatriation of all remaining Vietnamese (estimated at some 1,600 people qualifying as refugees and 700 non-refugees) before the transfer of sovereignty of the territory to the People's Republic of China on 30 June was not achieved. In early 1998 the Hong Kong authorities formally terminated the policy of granting a port of first asylum to Vietnamese 'boat people'. In February 2000 UNHCR, which had proposed the integration of the remaining Vietnamese as a final durable solution to the situation, welcomed a decision by the Hong Kong authorities to offer permanent residency status to the occupants of the last remaining Vietnamese detention camp (totalling 973 refugees and 435 'non-refugees'). By the end of May, when the camp was closed, more than 200 Vietnamese had failed to apply for residency. At 31 December 1999 UNHCR was providing assistance to a further 293,000 Vietnamese refugees in mainland People's Republic of China. In 1995, in accordance with an agreement concluded with the Chinese Government, UNHCR initiated a programme to redirect its local assistance to promote long-term self-sufficiency in the poorest settlements, including support for revolving-fund rural credit schemes.

The conclusion of a political settlement of the conflict in Cambodia in October 1991 made possible the eventual repatriation of some 370,000 Cambodian refugees and displaced persons. A land-mine survey was undertaken in order to identify the risk to returnees posed by unexploded mines (mine clearance was subsequently undertaken under UN auspices). The actual repatriation operation began in March 1992 and was completed in April 1993. At the same time, however, thousands of ethnic Vietnamese (of whom there were estimated to be 200,000 in Cambodia) were fleeing to Viet Nam, as a result of violence perpetrated against them by Cambodian armed groups. In March 1994, 25,000 supporters of the Khmers Rouges in Cambodia fled across the border into Thailand, following advances by government forces. The refugees were immediately repatriated by the Thai armed forces into Khmer Rouge territory, which was inaccessible to aid agencies. In July 1997 armed conflict between opposing political forces in northern Cambodia resulted in large-scale population movements. A voluntary repatriation programme was initiated in October to assist any refugee wishing to return. By 30 June 1998 some 5,595 Cambodians had been repatriated with UNHCR support, while a substantial number of others had returned in a spontaneous movement following a lull in the fighting in some border areas. In late March 1999 UNHCR announced that the last Cambodian refugees had left camps in Thailand, the majority having been repatriated to north-western Cambodia. A new UNHCR programme was initiated to monitor the welfare of returnees and assist in their reintegration.

A temporary cessation of hostilities between the Sri Lankan Government and Tamil separatists in early 1995 greatly facilitated UNHCR's ongoing efforts to repatriate Sri Lankan Tamils who had fled to India. However, later in that year an offensive by Sri Lankan government troops in the northern Jaffna peninsula caused a massive displacement of the local Tamil population and effectively ended the repatriation process. In India UNHCR had been concerned with verifying the voluntary nature of the repatriations, while in Sri Lanka itself UNHCR operated two 'Open Relief Centres' (established in 1990) to provide food, water and medical assistance and secure shelter for people unable to return to their home area. By 31 December 1999 there were 612,500 Sri Lankan IDPs of concern to UNHCR, and an estimated 66,400 Sri Lankan refugees remaining in India owing to the country's persisting political instability. India's total refugee population, of some 180,000 at December 1999, also included 98,000 refugees from the People's Republic of China (mainly Tibetans), and 14,500 Afghans.

In 1991–92 thousands of people of Nepalese ethnic origin living in Bhutan sought refuge from alleged persecution by fleeing to Nepal. By the end of 1999 their number totalled 107,600, of whom about 96,000 were receiving UNHCR assistance in the form of food, shelter, medical care, water and camp assistance. UNHCR has agreed to maintain its funding of the refugee camps, provided that negotiations between the two Governments, under the auspices of a high-level joint committee (established in 1993), continue. UNHCR has also made known its willingness to provide technical support for the verification of citizenship of the refugees, which was the principal issue precluding a resolution of the situation. In December 2000 Bhutan and Nepal reached reached agreement on a verification mechanism for the repatriation of refugees. At 31 December 1999 Nepal was also hosting some 20,300 refugees from Tibet.

From April 1991 increasing numbers of Rohingya Muslims in Myanmar fled into Bangladesh to escape the brutality and killings perpetrated by the Myanma armed forces. UNHCR launched an international appeal for financial aid for the refugees, at the request of Bangladesh, and collaborated with other UN agencies in providing humanitarian assistance. In May 1993 UNHCR and Bangladesh signed a memorandum of understanding, whereby UNHCR would be able to monitor the repatriation process of the estimated 270,000 Myanmar refugees and ensure that people were returning of their own free will. In November a memorandum of understanding, signed with the Myanma Government, secured UNHCR access to the returnees. The first refugees returned to Myanmar with UNHCR assistance at the end of April 1994. They were provided with a small amount of cash, housing grants and two months' food rations, and were supported by several small-scale reintegration projects. Despite disruption to the repatriation process owing to cyclone damage to repatriation facilities and attempts to prevent the spread of disease, by the end of December 1996 the Myanma refugee population in Bangladesh had declined to 30,578. UNHCR continued to monitor the estimated 219,282 returnees in Myanmar and to support their reintegration, for example through community-based agricultural activities and literacy and other education programmes. In January 1997 the Bangladesh and Myanma Governments agreed to conclude the mass repatriation programme by 31 March, later extended to August. In July, in advance of the revised deadline, Rohingya activists initiated a hunger-strike in protest at alleged efforts by the Bangladesh authorities to repatriate forcibly the remaining refugees. The repatriation process resumed in November 1998, although by the end of 1999 some 22,100 Myanma refugees still remained in camps in Bangladesh. Attempts by UNHCR to find a local solution for those unwilling to return to Myanmar have been met with resistance by the Bangladeshi Government.

In the early 1990s members of ethnic minorities in Myanmar attempted to flee attacks by government troops into Thailand; however, the Thai Government refused to recognize them as refugees or to offer them humanitarian assistance. Throughout 1997 the border camps were vulnerable to attacks by rival Karen (Kayin) factions and by Myanma Government forces. In December Thailand and Myanmar agreed to commence 'screening' the refugees to determine those who had fled persecution and those who were economic migrants. By the end of 1999 there were 99,700 people in camps along the Myanma–Thai border, the majority of whom were Karen refugees.

In April 1999, following the announcement by the Indonesian Government, in January, that it would consider a form of autonomy or independence for East Timor, some 26,000 Indonesian settlers left their homes as a result of clashes between opposing groups and uncertainty regarding the future of the territory. The popular referendum on the issue, conducted in late August, and the resulting victory for the independence movement, provoked a violent reaction by pro-integration militia. UNHCR staff, along with other international personnel, were forced to evacuate the territory in early September. At that time there were reports of forced mass deportations of Timorese to West Timor, while a large number of others fled their homes into remote mountainous areas of East Timor. In mid-September UNHCR staff visited West Timor to review the state of refugee camps, allegedly under the control of militia, and to persuade the authorities to permit access for humanitarian personnel. It was estimated that more than 250,000 East Timorese had fled to West Timor, of whom some 230,000 were registered in 28 camps at the end of September. At that time there were also an estimated 190,000–300,000 people displaced within East Timor, although the International Committee of the Red Cross estimated that a total of 800,000 people, or some 94% of the population, had been displaced, or deported, during the crisis. The arrival of multinational troops, from 20 September, helped to stabilize the region and enable the safe receipt and distribution of food supplies, prompting several thousands to return from hiding. Most homes, however, along with almost all other buildings in the capital, Dili, had been destroyed. In October UNHCR, together with the International Organization for Migration, initiated a repatriation programme for the refugees in West Timor. However, despite an undertaking by the Indonesian Government in mid-October that it would ensure the safety of all refugees and international humanitarian personnel, persistent intimidation by anti-independence militia impeded the registration and repatriation processes, particularly from early 2000. The operation was also hindered by the Indonesian Government's decision to reduce the provision of food aid to the camps from the beginning of July. UNHCR (which has established a working group to facilitate the implementation of the repatriation programme and to promote reconciliation and respect for human rights in East Timor) aimed to complete the operation by mid-2001, prior to the staging of legislative elections by the UN Transitional Administration in East Timor (UNTAET, q.v.). However, in early September 2000 UNHCR suspended its activities in West Timor, following the murder by militiamen of three of its personnel. A UN Security Council resolution, adopted soon afterwards, deplored this incident and strongly urged the Indonesian authorities to disable the militia and to guarantee the future security of refugees and humanitarian personnel. In mid-September UNTAET and the Indonesian Government signed a Memorandum of Understanding (MoU) on co-operation in resolving the refugee crisis; however, despite a subsequent operation by the Indonesian security forces to disarm the militia, intimidation of East Timorese refugees was reportedly persisting in early 2001. An estimated 80,000–100,000 East Timorese refugees were believed to remain in West Timorese camps at that time.

By mid-2000 hostilities between Muslim separatists and government forces in the autonomous Mindanao region of southern Philippines (which had escalated in March) had resulted in an estimated displaced population of 300,000.

CENTRAL ASIA, SOUTH-WEST ASIA, NORTH AFRICA AND THE MIDDLE EAST

From 1979, as a result of civil strife in Afghanistan, there was a massive movement of refugees from that country into Pakistan and Iran, creating the world's largest refugee population, which reached a peak of almost 6.3m. people in 1992. In 1988 UNHCR agreed to provide assistance for the voluntary repatriation of refugees, both in ensuring the rights of the returning population and in providing material assistance such as transport, immunization, and supplies of food and other essentials. In April 1992, following the establishment of a new Government in Afghanistan, refugees began to return in substantial numbers (hitherto only a small proportion had returned), although large numbers of people continued to flee into Pakistan as a result of continuing unrest. From October 1996 an escalation of hostilities in northern and western regions of Afghanistan resulted in further massive population displacement and in November UNHCR suspended its relief activities in the Afghan capital, Kabul, owing to mounting security concerns. Relief operations continued in other parts of the country. In Afghanistan UNHCR, with other UN agencies, has attempted to meet the immediate needs of IDPs and recent returnees, for example, by increasing rural water supply, initiating income-generation projects and providing food and tools. In Iran UNHCR has worked to ensure the voluntary nature of repatriation, while in Pakistan it has focused activities on strengthening refugees' capacity for self-sufficiency. During 1997 UNHCR operated a pilot scheme to organize group repatriations to specific areas in Afghanistan, under the protection of international observers; despite initial successes the scheme was suspended in late 1998, partly owing to lack of finance. In early 1998 UNHCR initiated a new monitoring system to evaluate the situation of returnees in Afghanistan. By 31 December 1998 93,000 refugees had returned, with UNHCR assistance, from Pakistan and 14,000 from Iran since the start of the year, bringing the total number of returnees to 4.2m. since 1988. In Afghanistan UNHCR, with other UN agencies, has attempted to meet the immediate needs of IDPs and recent returnees (totalling 359,800 returned refugees, 10,000 returned IDPs and 258,600 IDPs at 31 December 1999), for example, by increasing rural water supply, initiating income-generation projects and providing food and tools. In Iran UNHCR has worked to ensure the voluntary nature of repatriation, while in Pakistan it has focused activities on strengthening refugees' capacity for self-sufficiency. At the end of December 1999 a total of 1.3m. Afghan refugees remained in Iran, 1.2m. in Pakistan and 14,500 in India. However, the ongoing civil conflict and new population displacement has precluded a settlement of the Afghan refugee situation and has continued to cause immense difficulties in undertaking a comprehensive humanitarian operation in that country. From September 2000–March 2001 an estimated 170,000 Afghans fled to camps in Pakistan owing to prolonged severe drought and increasing insecurity in Afghanistan.

In late 1992 people began to flee civil conflict in Tajikistan and to seek refuge in Afghanistan. In 1993 an emergency UNHCR operation established a reception camp to provide the 60,000 Tajik refugees with basic assistance, and began to move them away from the border area to safety. In December a tripartite agreement was signed by UNHCR and the Tajik and Afghan Governments regarding the safety of refugees returning to Tajikistan. UNHCR monitored the repatriation process and provided materials for the construction of almost 20,000 homes. The repatriation process was concluded by the end of 1997. At the end of 1999, however, there were still 40,000 Tajik refugees remaining in other countries of the former USSR.

In March–May 1991, following the war against Iraq by a multinational force, and the subsequent Iraqi suppression of resistance in Kurdish areas in the north of the country, there was a massive movement of some 1.5m., mainly Kurdish, refugees, into Iran and Turkey. UNHCR was designated the principal UN agency to seek to alleviate the crisis. In May the refugees began to return to Iraq in huge numbers, and UNHCR assisted in their repatriation, establishing relief stations along their routes from Iran and Turkey. By the end of the year, however, negotiations between the Kurds and the Iraqi Government had broken down and refugees were once again entering Iran in large numbers, following the resumption of the violent suppression of Kurdish activists. In April 1994 UNHCR initiated a programme to provide food and relief assistance to Turkish Kurds who had fled into northern Iraq. In September 1996 fighting escalated among the Kurdish factions in northern Iraq. By the time a cease-fire agreement was concluded in November some 65,000 Iraqi Kurds had fled across the border into Iran. UNHCR, together with the Iranian Government, provided these new refugees with basic humanitarian supplies. By the end of the year, however, the majority of refugees had returned to Iraq, owing to poor conditions in the temporary settlements, security concerns at being located in the border region and pressure from the Iranian authorities. UNHCR announced

its intention to withdraw from the Atroush camp, which housed an estimated 15,000 Turkish Kurds, following several breaches of security in the camp, and expressed its concern at the political vacuum in the region resulting from the factional conflict. UNHCR proceeded to transfer 4,000 people to other local settlements and to provide humanitarian assistance to those refugees who had settled closer to Iraqi-controlled territory but who had been refused asylum. At 31 December 1999 the refugee population in Iraq amounted to 128,900, of whom about 32,000 were assisted by UNHCR. The total refugee population included some 60,000 Palestinians, 19,000 Iranian Kurds and 10,800 Turkish Kurds. In addition, there were 32,800 recently returned refugees in Iraq of concern to UNHCR. At that time there was still a substantial Iraqi refugee population in the region, totalling an estimated 521,200 of whom 510,000 were in Iran. At the end of 1999 Iran remained the principal country of asylum in the world, hosting some 1,835,700 refugees, mainly from Afghanistan and Iraq.

UNHCR co-ordinates humanitarian assistance for the estimated 165,000 Sahrawis registered as refugees in the Tindouf area of Algeria. Approximately 80,000 most vulnerable members of the Sahrawi refugee population receive direct assistance from UNHCR. In September 1997 an agreement was reached on implementing the 1991 Settlement Plan for the Western Sahara. Accordingly, UNHCR was to help organize the registration and safe return of up to 135,000 Sahrawi refugees who had been identified as eligible to vote in the referendum on the future of the territory (which was initially scheduled to be conducted in early December 1998 but subsequently postponed). In addition, UNHCR was to facilitate the reintegration of the returnees and monitor their rehabilitation.

In June 1992 people fleeing the civil war and famine in Somalia began arriving in Yemen in large numbers. UNHCR set up camps to accommodate some 50,000 refugees, providing them with shelter, food, water and sanitation. As a result of civil conflict in Yemen in mid-1994 a large camp in the south of the country was demolished and other refugees had to be relocated, while the Yemeni authorities initiated a campaign of forcible repatriation. During 1998–99 the refugee population in Yemen expanded owing to the influx of Somalis fleeing the ongoing civil conflict and the effects of heavy flooding which had devastated areas in the south of that country. At the end of 1999 Yemen was hosting 60,500 refugees, of whom 55,200 were from Somalia.

AFRICA

UNHCR has provided assistance to refugee populations in many parts of the continent where civil conflict, drought, extreme poverty, violations of human rights or environmental degradation had forced people to flee their countries. The majority of African refugees and returnees are located in countries that are themselves suffering major economic problems and are thus unable to provide the basic requirements of the uprooted people. Furthermore, UNHCR has often failed to receive adequate international financial support to implement effective relief programmes.

East Africa

The Horn of Africa, afflicted in the late 1980s and early 1990s by famine, separatist violence and ethnic conflict, experienced large-scale population movements. In 1992 UNHCR initiated a repatriation programme for the massive Somali and Ethiopian refugee populations in Kenya, which included assistance with reconstruction projects and the provision of food to returnees and displaced persons. The implementation by UNHCR of community-based projects, for example seed distribution, the establishment of a women's bakery co-operative and support for a brick production initiative, served as important instruments of assistance and of bringing stability to areas of returnee settlements. However, the continuing instability in north-western Somalia prevented a completion of the repatriation process, and resulted in further population displacement. From October 1997 severe flooding in southern areas of Somalia further hindered the repatriation of refugees. None the less, UNHCR and the authorities in north-western Somalia agreed to proceed with the repatriation process, with the aim of facilitating the speedy return of 100,000 Somalis, and to initiate projects to aid their reintegration. By late 2000 an estimated 111,877 Somali refugees were repatriated from Ethiopia under UNHCR auspices. Some spontaneous repatriation also took place. At 31 December 1999 there remained a total Somali refugee population of 464,300, of whom 180,900 were in Ethiopia and 141,100 were in Kenya. At the end of 1999 Ethiopia was still hosting a total of 257,000 refugees, while Kenya was hosting 223,700.

During the 1980s more than 900,000 Ethiopians fled to neighbouring countries. By November 1997 UNHCR estimated that some 600,000 Ethiopians had repatriated, either by spontaneous or organized movements. The voluntary repatriation operation of the estimated 50,000 Ethiopians remaining in Sudan was concluded in mid-1998. With effect from 1 March 2000 UNHCR withdrew the automatic refugee status of Ethiopians who left their country before 1991. From late 1999 until March 2000 transportation and rehabilitation assistance were offered to those concerned who wished to repatriate.

From 1992 some 500,000 Eritreans took refuge in Sudan as a result of separatist conflicts; however, by 1995 an estimated 125,000 had returned spontaneously, in particular following Eritrea's accession to independence in May 1993. A UNHCR repatriation programme to assist the remaining refugees, which had been delayed for various political, security and funding considerations, was initiated in November 1994. However, its implementation was hindered by a shortfall in donor funding and by disputes between the Eritrean and Sudanese Governments. At the end of 1999 Sudan still hosted a total of 391,000 refugees including 342,100 from Eritrea and 35,400 from Ethiopia. Renewed conflict between Ethiopia and Eritrea, which commenced in 1998, had, by mid-1999, resulted in the displacement of some 350,000 Eritreans and 300,000 Ethiopians. Meanwhile, UNHCR continued to negotiate with the Eritrean Government to permit an organized, voluntary repatriation of refugees from Sudan. In mid-2000, following an escalation of the conflict in May, UNHCR reported that some 95,000 Eritreans had sought refuge in Sudan, while smaller numbers had fled to Djibouti and Yemen. Consequently an operation to repatriate 160,000 long-term Eritrean refugees in Sudan (scheduled to commence in May) had been postponed. In view of the conclusion of a peace agreement between Eritrea and Ethiopia in June, UNHCR initiated an operation in December to repatriate the most recent wave of Eritrean refugees from Sudan. Owing to continuing unrest in Sudan itself some 462,000 Sudanese remained as refugees at 31 December 1999, mainly in the Central African Republic, the Democratic Republic of the Congo, Ethiopia, Kenya and Uganda. The Ugandan Government, hosting an estimated 200,600 of these refugees, has provided new resettlement sites and has supported refugee efforts to construct homes and cultivate crops in order to achieve some degree of self-sufficiency.

West Africa

In West Africa the refugee population increased by one-third during 1992 and the first half of 1993, with the addition of new refugees fleeing Togo, Liberia and Senegal. In accordance with a peace agreement, signed in July 1993, UNHCR was responsible for the repatriation of Liberian refugees who had fled to Guinea, Côte d'Ivoire and Sierra Leone during the civil conflict. The voluntary repatriation programme was to include substantial assistance to rebuild Liberia's infrastructure; UNHCR also began to provide emergency relief to displaced persons within the country. Persisting political insecurity prevented large-scale repatriation of Liberian refugees, and in mid-1996 UNHCR suspended its preparatory activities for a repatriation and reintegration operation, owing to an escalation in hostilities. In early 1997 the prospect of a peaceful settlement in Liberia prompted a spontaneous movement of refugees returning home, and in April UNHCR initiated an organized repatriation of Liberian refugees from Ghana. Improved security conditions in Liberia, following the establishment of a democratically-elected government in August and the consolidation of the peace settlement, were expected to accelerate the return of refugees and other displaced persons during 1998. In the event the process was hindered slightly by logistical difficulties and the persisting volatility of some border regions. During 1998 and 1999 an estimated Liberians 15,000 fled to Guinea from insecurity in the Lofa area of northern Liberia; meanwhile, UNHCR was forced to suspend its operations in Lofa. By the end of 1999 some 343,000 Liberians were reported to have returned, 128,200 with UNHCR assistance. UNHCR has organized quick impact projects to facilitate the reintegration of the returnees. At 31 December 1999 there were still some 281,700 Liberian refugees, of whom 135,600 were in Côte d'Ivoire and 129,100 in Guinea. At that time there were also some 297,000 recently returned Liberian refugees and 113,600 Liberian IDPs of concern to UNHCR. Mounting insecurity in southern Guinea from September 2000 (see below) accelerated the return of Liberian refugees from camps there.

Further large-scale population displacement in West Africa followed an escalation of violence in Sierra Leone in early 1995. By December 1996 there were nearly 370,000 Sierra Leonean refugees in Liberia and Guinea, while a further 654,600 internally displaced Sierra Leoneans were of concern to UNHCR. The repatriation of Sierra Leonean refugees from Liberia was initiated in February 1997; however, the programme was suspended in May, owing to renewed political violence, which forced UNHCR staff to evacuate the country, and the seizure of power by military forces. Thousands of people fled to other parts of the country, as well as to Guinea and Liberia, to escape the hostilities. Following the intervention of the ECOMOG multinational force (see ECOWAS p. 172) and the conclusion of a peace agreement in October, residents of the Sierra Leone capital, Freetown, who had been displaced by the conflict, began to return. In February 1998 ECOMOG troops took control of Freetown from the rebel military forces, and in the following month the elected President, Ahmed Tejan Kabbah, was reinstated as Head of State. None the less, large numbers of Sierra Leoneans continued to cross the border into neighbouring countries, owing to ongoing violence in the northern and eastern regions of the country and severe food shortages. In early

1999 anti-government forces again advanced on Freetown, prompting heavy fighting with ECOMOG troops and the displacement of thousands more civilians. In February a reported 200,000 people fled the town of Kenema in south-eastern Sierra Leone following attacks by rebel militia. In May a cease-fire agreement was concluded between the Government and opposition forces, and a formal peace accord was signed in early July under which the rebels were to be disarmed and demobilized; however, the agreement broke down in May 2000. The resumption of hostilities delayed a planned repatriation programme and displaced an estimated 50,000 thousand people from their homes. Meanwhile, persistent insecurity in northeastern and some border areas of Sierra Leone prompted further movements of Sierra Leonean refugees to Guinea during 2000. From September, however, unrest in southern Guinea caused some Sierra Leonean refugees who had been sheltering in camps there to repatriate (see below). At 31 December 1999 there were some 370,600 Sierra Leonean refugees in Guinea and 96,300 in Liberia. There were also 198,100 recently returned refugees in Sierra Leone of concern to UNHCR and an estimated displaced population of 500,000.

In August 2000 the security sitiuation in southern border areas of Guinea deteriorated owing to increasing insurgencies by rebels from Liberia and Sierra Leone, which displaced a large number of Guineans from their homes and also endangered an estimated 460,000 mainly Liberian and Sierra Leonean refugees (see above) accommodated in Guinean camps. In mid-September UNHCR and other aid organizations withdrew their international personnel and suspended food distribution in the area following the murder by armed rebels of a member of UNHCR staff. Insecurity, hunger and mounting hostility from elements of the local population subsequently led significant numbers of refugees to flee the unprotected camps. Many sought to reach northern Guinea, while some returned spontaneously to their countries of origin. Following an escalation in fighting between Guinean government forces and insurgent rebels in early December refugee movements intensified; however, it was reported that an estimated 180,000 refugees and 70,000 IDPs remained stranded without humanitarian assistance in the southwestern Bec de Perroquet area. Later in December UNHCR dispatched emergency teams to assist with the relocation of refugees who had escaped the conflict zone. In February 2001 the High Commissioner negotiated with the parties to the conflict for the establishment of a humanitarian 'lifeline' to enable the delivery of assistance to, and possible evacuation of, the refugees and IDPs trapped at Bec de Perroquet: conveys of food aid began to reach the area in early March.

In June 1998 UNHCR expressed concern at the outbreak of fighting in Guinea-Bissau, which had prompted the majority of the capital's population of some 300,000 to flee into the surrounding countryside and generated concern for the safety of the estimated 15,000 Senegalese refugees who had been based in camps in Guinea-Bissau since 1992. UNHCR staff attempted to monitor the movements of the population, and, despite the border between Guinea and Guinea-Bissau officially being declared closed, estimated that some 12,000 people crossed into the neighbouring country during June 1998. A cease-fire was agreed between the conflicting forces in August; however, there was renewed conflict in October prompting further population displacement. UNHCR staff attempted to distribute mosquito nets and other non-food supplies to the displaced population, but, along with other humanitarian personnel, they were repeatedly obliged to evacuate the country owing to the ongoing violence. A peace accord was concluded in November. During the first half of 1999 UNHCR repatriated all Guinea-Bissau refugees from Guinea. In early 1994 some 40,000 Tuareg nomads, who had fled from northern Mali into Burkina Faso, received protection and material assistance from two newly-established UNHCR field offices. During 1995 large numbers of the Malian refugee population (totalling some 175,000) returned spontaneously from camps in Mauritania, Burkina Faso and Algeria, owing to political developments in Mali. An organized repatriation of the remaining refugees was initiated in 1996. In November UNHCR signed an agreement with the Malian and Nigerien Governments establishing the conditions of repatriation of 25,000 Tuareg refugees living in Niger. By 31 December 1999 almost all Malian refugees in the region had repatriated, and there were 31,900 recently returned refugees of concern to UNHCR.

Central Africa

Since 1993 the Great Lakes region of Central Africa has experienced massive population displacement, causing immense operational challenges and demands on the resources of international humanitarian and relief agencies. In October of that year a military coup in Burundi prompted some 580,000 people to flee into Rwanda and Tanzania, although many had returned by early 1994. By May, however, an estimated 860,000 people from Burundi and Rwanda had fled to neighbouring states (following a resurgence of ethnic tension in both countries), including 250,000 mainly Rwandan Tutsi refugees who entered Tanzania over a 24-hour period in late April. In May UNHCR began an immediate operation to airlift emergency supplies to the refugees. Despite overcrowding in camps and a high incidence of cholera and dysentery (particularly in camps in eastern Zaire, where many thousands of Rwandan Hutus had sought refuge following the establishment of a new Rwandan Government in July) large numbers of refugees refused to accept UNHCR-assisted repatriation, owing to fears of reprisal ethnic killings. In September reports of mass ethnic violence, which were disputed by some UN agencies, continued to disrupt UNHCR's policy of repatriation and to prompt returnees to cross the border back into Zaire. Security in the refugee camps, which was undermined by the presence of military and political elements of the former Rwandan Government, remained an outstanding concern of UNHCR. A resurgence of violence in Burundi, in February 1995, provoked further mass population movements. However, in March the Tanzanian authorities, reportedly frustrated at the lack of international assistance for the refugees and the environmental degradation resulting from the camps, closed Tanzania's border with Burundi, thus preventing the admission into the country of some 100,000 Rwandan Hutu refugees who were fleeing camps in Burundi. While persisting disturbances in Rwanda disrupted UNHCR's repatriation programme, in April Rwandan government troops employed intimidation tactics to force some 90,000 internally displaced Hutus to leave a heavily-populated camp in the south-west of the country; other small camps were closed. In August the Zairean Government initiated a programme of forcible repatriation of the estimated 1m. Rwandan and 70,000 Burundian Hutu refugees remaining in the country, which prompted as many as 100,000 refugees to flee the camps into the surrounding countryside. Following widespread international condemnation of the forcible repatriation and expressions of concern for the welfare of the remaining refugees, the Zairean Government suspended the programme, having first received an assurance that UNHCR would assume responsibility for the repatriation of all the refugees by the end of 1995 (although in December the Government accepted that its deadline could not be achieved). In September Rwanda agreed to strengthen its reception facilities and to provide greater security and protection for returnees, in collaboration with UNHCR, in order to prepare for any large-scale repatriation. UNHCR, meanwhile, expanded its information campaign to promote the return of refugees, and enhanced its facilities at official border entry points. In December UNHCR negotiated an agreement between the Rwandan and Tanzanian authorities concerning the repatriation of the estimated 500,000 Rwandans remaining in camps in Tanzania. UNHCR agreed to establish a separate camp in north-west Tanzania in order to accommodate elements of the refugee population that might disrupt the repatriation programme. The repatriation of Rwandan refugees from all host countries was affected by reports of reprisals against Hutu returnees by the Tutsi-dominated Government in Rwanda. In February 1996 the Zairean Government renewed its efforts to accelerate the repatriation process, owing to concerns that the camps were becoming permanent settlements and that they were being used to train and rearm a Hutu militia. In July the Burundian Government forcibly repatriated 15,000 Rwandan refugees, having announced the closure of all remaining refugee camps. The repatriation programme, which was condemned by UNHCR, was suspended by the country's new military authorities, but only after many more thousands of refugees had been obliged to return to Rwanda and up to 30,000 had fled to Tanzania.

In October 1996 an escalation of hostilities between Zairean government forces, accused by Rwanda of arming the Hutu *Interahamwe* militia, and Zairean (Banyamulenge) Tutsis, who had been the focus of increasingly violent assaults, resulted in an extreme humanitarian crisis. Some 250,000 refugees fled 12 camps in the east of the country, including 90,000 Burundians who returned home. An estimated 500,000 refugees regrouped in Muganga camp, west of Goma, although with insufficient relief assistance, following the temporary evacuation of international aid workers. UNHCR appealed to all Rwandan Hutu refugees to return home, and issued assurances of the presence of human rights observers in Rwanda to enhance their security. In mid-November, with the apparent withdrawal of *Interahamwe* forces, and the advance of the Tutsi-dominated Alliance des forces démocratiques pour la libération du Congo–Zaïre (AFDL), more than 600,000 refugees unexpectedly returned to Rwanda; however, concern remained on the part of the international community for the substantial number of Rwandan Hutu refugees at large in eastern Zaire. Further mass movement of Rwandan refugee populations occurred in December, owing to the threat of forcible repatriation by the Tanzanian Government, which had announced its intention of closing all camps by the end of the year. UNHCR initiated a repatriation programme; however, 200,000 refugees, unwilling to return to Rwanda, fled their camps. The majority of the refugees were later identified by the Tanzanian national army and escorted to the Rwandan border. By the end of December some 483,000 refugees had returned to Rwanda from Tanzania.

In February 1997 violence in Zaire escalated, prompting some 56,000 Zaireans to flee into Tanzania and disrupting the distribution of essential humanitarian supplies to refugees remaining in Zaire. An estimated 170,000 refugees abandoned their temporary encampment at Tingi-Tingi, fearing attacks by the advancing AFDL forces.

About 75,000 reassembled at Ubundu, south of Kisangani, while the fate of the other refugees remained uncertain. In March and April reports of attacks on refugee camps, by AFDL forces and local Zaireans, resulted in large numbers of people fleeing into the surrounding countryside, with the consequent deaths of many of the most vulnerable members of the refugee population from disease and starvation. At the end of April the leader of the AFDL, Laurent-Désiré Kabila, ordered the repatriation of all Rwandan Hutu refugees by the UN within 60 days. Emergency air and land operations to evacuate some 185,000 refugees who had regrouped into temporary settlements were initiated a few days later. The repatriation process, however, was hindered by administrative and logistical difficulties and lack of co-operation on the part of the AFDL forces. By June an estimated 215,000 Rwandans were still missing or dispersed throughout the former Zaire (renamed the Democratic Republic of the Congo—DRC—by the AFDL in May). In the following months relations between the Kabila Government and UNHCR deteriorated as a result of several incidences of forcible repatriations of refugees to Rwanda and reports that the authorities were hindering a UN investigation into alleged abuses of the human rights of Rwandan Hutu refugees by AFDL forces. In August an agreement was concluded to provide for the voluntary repatriation of some 75,000 Congolese refugees remaining in Tanzania, under UNHCR supervision, and in December a tripartite agreement was signed to provide for the organized repatriation of the remaining Congolese refugees in Rwanda, with both Governments agreeing to observe strict conditions of security for the refugees on both sides of the border. Meanwhile, an estimated 40,000 refugees from the Republic of the Congo fled to the DRC in mid-1997, following a short-lived outbreak of civil conflict. In December a memorandum of understanding was signed by representatives of the two Governments and of UNHCR, providing for their immediate repatriation. UNHCR's concerns in the Great Lakes region in 1998 were to ensure the security of the returning refugee populations and to assist their reintegration and national reconciliation. UNHCR also resolved to work, in co-operation with UNDP and WFP, to rehabilitate areas previously inhabited by refugees in countries of asylum and undertook to repair roads, bridges and other essential transport infrastructure, improve water and sanitation facilities, and strengthen the education sector. However, the political stability of the region remained extremely uncertain. Fighting that erupted in August between DRC government forces and rebels (who were assisted by Burundian, Rwandan and Ugandan troops) escalated into prolonged civil war in which several regional governments became implicated. Although a cease-fire agreement was signed by all parties to the conflict in July 1999, this had not been fully implemented by early 2001. During late 1998 and throughout 1999 and 2000 substantial numbers of DRC nationals fled to neighbouring countries (mainly Tanzania and Zambia) or were displaced within the DRC. Meanwhile, the DRC, in turn, was hosting a significant foreign refugee population.

The major populations of concern to UNHCR in the Great Lakes region at 31 December 1999 were as follows: 626,100 IDPs in Rwanda; 285,300 refugees, and some 79,800 recently returned refugees, in the DRC; 50,000 IDPs in Burundi, as well as 36,000 returned refugees; and a refugee population of 622,200 remaining in Tanzania, which was also coping with new influxes of refugees, mainly from Burundi, but also from the DRC and Rwanda. UNHCR suspended all non-essential operations in Burundi from October 1999–April 2000, following the murder there of two UN personnel. In early 2001 UNHCR was providing education, environmental protection and healthcare programmes at camps in Tanzania.

From late 1998 intense fighting in the Republic of the Congo disrupted UNHCR humanitarian efforts in that country, causing 20,000 Congolese immediately to seek refuge in the DRC and leaving some 200,000 people displaced south-west of the capital, Brazzaville. Of these, 40,000 subsequently also fled to the DRC. UNHCR launched a repatriation operation in April 1999. However, fighting continued, and in July more than 12,000 Congolese refugees fled to Gabon. Following the agreement of a cease-fire in the Republic of the Congo in December, voluntary repatriations of Congolese refugees commenced in early 2000.

Southern Africa

In 1994 continuing civil conflict in Angola caused some 370,000 people to leave their home areas. Prior to the signing of a peace settlement in November, UNHCR provided assistance to 112,000 IDPs and returnees, although military activities, which hindered accessibility, undermined the effectiveness of the assistance programme. In mid-1995, following a consolidation of the peace process in Angola, UNHCR appealed for US $44m. to support the voluntary repatriation of Angolan refugees over a two-and-a-half-year operation. Implementation of the repatriation programme was delayed, however, reportedly owing to poor accommodation and other facilities for returnees, limited progress in confining and disarming opposition troops and the continued hazard of land-mines throughout the country. During 1997 an estimated 53,000 Angolans voluntarily returned from the DRC and Zambia, bringing the total returnees since mid-1995 to some 130,000. In November 1997 UNHCR resolved to implement an operation to provide for the repatriation and reintegration of the remaining Angolan refugees by June 1999. UNHCR allocated $15.7m. to support the repatriation process and other activities in Angola, including strengthening the country's road infrastructure, monitoring areas of return, reintegration projects and promoting links with other development programmes. In May 1998, however, the security situation in Angola deteriorated, and at the end of June UNHCR declared a temporary suspension of the repatriation operation. The renewed violence also resulted in further population displacement: by December at least 90,000 people had been displaced within Angola and 40,000 had fled to the DRC. By April 1999 a further 21,500 Angolan refugees had arrived in the DRC, and, from October a new influx of Angolan refugees, numbering more than 40,000, reached that country; at that time some 26,000 Angolans also crossed into Zambia, and 5,000 into Namibia. In early 2000 UNHCR resolved to expand its operations in Angola with a view to providing emergency humanitarian assistance to Angolan IDPs (estimated at that time to exceed 1.5m.). At December 1999 333,700 Angolan refugees were sheltering in neighbouring countries, including 163,100 in Zambia and 150,000 in the DRC. Refugee movements out of Angola continued during 2000.

THE AMERICAS AND THE CARIBBEAN

The International Conference on Central American Refugees — (CIREFCA), held in Guatemala in May 1989, adopted a plan of action for the voluntary repatriation of refugees in the region, and established national co-ordinating committees to assist in this process. At that time there were some 150,000 refugees receiving UNHCR assistance, and a further estimated 1.8m. other refugees and displaced persons. The repatriation process initiated by CIREFCA was formally concluded in June 1994. UNHCR's efforts in the region have subsequently emphasized legal issues and refugee protection, while assisting governments to formulate national legislation on asylum and refugees. At the end of 1998 the outstanding populations of concern to UNHCR in Central America were the 28,300 mainly Guatemalan refugees remaining in Mexico and some 7,500 recently returned Guatemalan refugees. At that time Costa Rica was hosting a refugee population of some 23,000, the majority of whom were from Nicaragua.

In 1999 the Colombian Government approved an operational plan proposed by UNHCR to address a massive population displacement that had arisen in that country in recent years (escalating from 1997), as a consequence of ongoing internal conflict and alleged human rights abuses committed by armed groups. By mid-2000 as many as 1.1m. IDPs were reported to require assistance, of whom many had congregated near Colombia's borders with Ecuador, Panama and Venezuela. In 2000 UNHCR was monitoring cross-border population movements, assisting with the implementation of an IDP registration plan, supporting a pilot early warning project to forecast future population movements, and providing training in emergency response to displacements. UNHCR was also co-operating with UNICEF (q.v.) to improve the provision of education to displaced children.

Canada and the USA are major countries of resettlement for refugees. UNHCR provides counselling and legal services for asylum-seekers in these countries. At 31 December 1999 the estimated refugee populations totalled 123,300 in Canada and 513,000 in the USA, while asylum-seekers numbered 24,730 and 580,900 respectively.

EUROPE

The political changes in eastern and central Europe during the early 1990s resulted in a dramatic increase in the number of asylum-seekers and displaced people in the region. UNHCR was the agency designated by the UN Secretary-General to lead the UN relief operation to assist those affected by the conflict in the former Yugoslavia. It was responsible for the supply of food and other humanitarian aid to the besieged capital of Bosnia and Herzegovina, Sarajevo, and to Muslim and Croatian enclaves in the country, under the armed escort of the UN Protection Force. Assistance was provided not only to Bosnian refugees in Croatia and displaced people within Bosnia and Herzegovina's borders, but also, in order to forestall further movements of people, to civilians whose survival was threatened. The operation was often seriously hampered by armed attacks (resulting, in some cases, in fatalities), distribution difficulties and underfunding from international donors. The Dayton peace agreement, which was signed in December 1995 bringing an end to the conflict, secured the right for all refugees and displaced persons freely to choose their place of residence within the new territorial arrangements of Bosnia and Herzegovina. Thus, the immediate effect of the peace accord was further population displacement, including a mass exodus of almost the entire Serb population of Sarajevo. Under the peace accord, UNHCR was responsible for

planning and implementing the repatriation of all Bosnian refugees and displaced persons, then estimated at 2m.; however, there were still immense obstacles to freedom of movement, in particular for minorities wishing to return to an area dominated by a different politico-ethnic faction. By the end of 1999 there was a total Bosnian refugee population of some 227,000, the majority of whom were in the Federal Republic of Yugoslavia (FRY). In addition, there were 161,000 recently returned refugees and 73,000 returned IDPs of concern to UNHCR in Bosnia and Herzegovina, as well as 809,500 IDPs who had yet to return home. Plans to accelerate reconstruction and rehabilitation efforts during 1999 were disrupted by events in the FRY (see below).

From March 1998 attacks by Serbian forces against members of a separatist movement in the southern Serbian province of Kosovo and Metohija resulted in large-scale population displacement. Of particular concern were some 50,000 people who had fled to the surrounding mountains, close to the Albanian border, without shelter or adequate provisions. In October the withdrawal of Serbian troops and the involvement of the international community in the provision of aid and monitoring of the situation in Kosovo was thought to have prompted substantial numbers to have returned home. However, in December there were reports of renewed attacks by Serbian forces on the local Albanian population, which persisted into 1999. The failure of peace negotiations prompted further displacement, and in late March an estimated 95,000 people fled their homes following the withdrawal of international observers of the OSCE and the commencement of a NATO operation, which aimed to halt the Serbian attacks and compel the FRY to agree to a peace settlement. By mid-April UNHCR estimated that up to 1.3m. Kosovar Albanians had been displaced since the fighting began in 1998, with reports that thousands had been forcibly expelled by Serbian troops in recent weeks. UNHCR attempted to provide emergency relief to the thousands of refugees who fled to neighbouring countries, and expressed concern for those remaining in the province, of whom up to 400,000 were thought to be living without shelter. In early April 1999 UNHCR condemned the decision of the authorities in the former Yugoslav republic of Macedonia (FYRM) forcibly to evacuate some 30,000 refugees from camps in Blace, near the FRY border, and subsequently to close the border to further refugees. At that time UNHCR helped to co-ordinate an international effort to evacuate substantial numbers of the refugees to third countries, and issued essential identity and travel documents. In Albania UNHCR funded transport to relocate an estimated 250,000 people from the border town of Kukës, where resources and the local infrastructure were strained by the massive population influx, to other sites throughout the country. At the start of June the Kosovar refugee population totalled some 443,300 people in Albania, 247,800 in the FYRM, 69,300 in Montenegro, and 21,700 in Bosnia and Herzegovina, while at least 40,000 had been temporarily resettled in more than 20 other countries. In mid-June, following a cease-fire accord and an agreement by the FRY to withdraw all forces and paramilitary units, UNHCR initiated a large-scale registration operation of Kosovar refugees and began to deliver emergency provisions to assist the displaced population within Kosovo. Despite warnings of anti-personnel devices and lack of shelter, UNHCR estimated that some 477,000 refugees had returned in a spontaneous repatriation movement by the end of June. Meanwhile, local Serbs began to move out of the province; by August an estimated 137,000 Serbs had left Kosovo, fearing reprisal attacks by returning ethnic Albanians. In September UNHCR estimated that one-third of all homes in Kosovo had been destroyed or seriously damaged during the conflict, prompting concerns regarding the welfare of returning refugees and IDPs in the coming winter months. UNHCR began to distribute 'shelter kits' to assist the process of reconstruction of homes, and proceeded to accelerate the distribution of blankets and winter clothing, as well as of fuel and other essential supplies, throughout Serbia and Montenegro. By the end of 1999 the majority of refugees had returned to Kosovo. In mid-2000 UNHCR scaled down its emergency humanitarian activities in Kosovo and provided a UN Humanitarian Co-ordinator to oversee the transition to reconstruction and development, in co-operation with the UN Interim Administration Mission in Kosovo (UNMIK).

In December 1992 UNHCR dispatched teams to establish offices in both Armenia and Azerbaijan to assist people displaced as a result of the war between the two countries and to provide immediate relief. A cease-fire was signed between the two sides in May 1994, although violations of the accord were subsequently reported and relations between the two countries remained tense. At the end of 1999 the region was still supporting a massive displaced population: including 296,200 Azerbaijani refugees in Armenia and 188,400 Armenians in Azerbaijan, and 569,600 IDPs of concern to UNHCR in Azerbaijan. UNHCR's humanitarian activities have focused on improving shelter, in particular for the most vulnerable among the refugee population, and promoting economic self-sufficiency and stability. In Georgia, where almost 300,000 people left their homes during the 1990s as a result of civil conflict that erupted in 1991, UNHCR has attempted to encourage income-generating activities among the displaced population, to increase the Georgian Government's capacity to support those people and to assist the rehabilitation of people returning to their areas of origin. During 1995 UNHCR pursued a process, initiated in the previous year, to establish a comprehensive approach to the problems of refugees, returnees, IDPs and migrants in the Commonwealth of Independent States. A regional conference convened in Geneva, Switzerland, in May 1996, endorsed a framework of activities aimed at managing migratory flows and at developing institutional capacities to prevent mass population displacements. At that time it was estimated that more than 9m. former citizens of the USSR had relocated since its disintegration as a result of conflict, economic pressures and ecological disasters.

In March 1995 UNHCR initiated an assistance programme for people displaced as a result of conflict in the separatist republic of Chechnya (Russian Federation), as part of a UN inter-agency relief effort, in collaboration with the International Committee of the Red Cross (ICRC, q.v.). UNHCR continued its activities in 1996, at the request of the Russian Government, at which time the displaced population within Chechnya and in the surrounding republics totalled 490,000. During 1997 UNHCR provided reintegration assistance to 25,000 people who returned to Chechnya, despite reports of sporadic violence. The security situation in the region deteriorated sharply in mid-1999, following a series of border clashes and incursions by Chechen separatist forces into the neighbouring republic of Dagestan. In September Russian military aircraft began an aerial offensive against suspected rebel targets in Chechnya, and at the end of the month ground troops moved into the republic. By November an estimated 225,000 Chechens had fled to neighbouring Ingushetia. UNHCR dispatched food supplies to assist these, but was unable to deploy inside Chechnya, owing to the adverse security situation. In late 2000 UNHCR assisted with the construction of the first tented camp to provide adequate winter shelter for Chechens in Ingushetia; many others were being sheltered in local homes. In January 2001 UNHCR temporarily suspended humanitarian convoys to Chechnya following the abduction there of an international aid worker. About 158,000 Chechens remained in Ingushetia in early 2001, while within Chechnya there were also significant numbers of IDPs.

CO-OPERATION WITH OTHER ORGANIZATIONS

UNHCR works closely with other UN agencies, intergovernmental organizations and non-governmental organizations (NGOs) to increase the scope and effectiveness of its emergency operations.

Within the UN system UNHCR co-operates, principally, with the World Food Programme in the distribution of food aid, UNICEF and the World Health Organization in the provision of family welfare and child immunization programmes, and UNDP in development-related activities and the preparation of guide-lines for the continuum of emergency assistance to development programmes. UNHCR also has close working relationships with the International Committee of the Red Cross and the International Organization for Migration. In 1999 UNHCR worked with 513 NGOs as 'implementing partners', enabling UNHCR to broaden the use of its resources while maintaining a co-ordinating role in the provision of assistance.

TRAINING

UNHCR organizes training programmes and workshops to enhance the capabilities of field workers and non-UNHCR staff, in the following areas: the identification and registration of refugees; people-orientated planning; resettlement procedures and policies; emergency response and management; security awareness; stress management; and the dissemination of information through the electronic media.

Finance

The United Nations' regular budget finances a proportion of UNHCR's administrative expenditure. The majority of UNHCR expenditure is funded by voluntary contributions. Prior to 2000 UNHCR's activities were designated as General Programmes and Special Programmes, with separate budgets. With effect from January 2000 these were unified under a single programme budget. Any further requirements identified following approval of the annual programme budget were to be managed in the form of Supplementary Programmes, to be funded by separate appeals. The programme budget for 2000 amounted to US $933.6m.

Publications

Refugees (quarterly, in English, French, German, Italian, Japanese and Spanish).
Refugee Survey Quarterly.
The State of the World's Refugees (every 2 years).
UNHCR Handbook for Emergencies.
Press releases, reports.

United Nations Peace-keeping Operations

Address: Department of Peace-keeping Operations, Room S-3727-B, United Nations, New York, NY 10017, USA.
Telephone: (212) 963-8079; **fax:** (212) 963-9222; **internet:** www.un.org/Depts/dpko/.

United Nations peace-keeping operations have been conceived as instruments of conflict control. The UN has used these operations in various conflicts, with the consent of the parties involved, to maintain international peace and security, without prejudice to the positions or claims of parties, in order to facilitate the search for political settlements through peaceful means such as mediation and the good offices of the Secretary-General. Each operation is established with a specific mandate, which requires periodic review by the Security Council. United Nations peace-keeping operations fall into two categories: peace-keeping forces and observer missions.

Peace-keeping forces are composed of contingents of military and civilian personnel, made available by member states. These forces assist in preventing the recurrence of fighting, restoring and maintaining peace, and promoting a return to normal conditions. To this end, peace-keeping forces are authorized as necessary to undertake negotiations, persuasion, observation and fact-finding. They conduct patrols and interpose physically between the opposing parties. Peace-keeping forces are permitted to use their weapons only in self-defence.

Military observer missions are composed of officers (usually unarmed), who are made available, on the Secretary-General's request, by member states. A mission's function is to observe and report to the Secretary-General (who, in turn, informs the UN Security Council) on the maintenance of a cease-fire, to investigate violations and to do what it can to improve the situation.

Peace-keeping forces and observer missions must at all times maintain complete impartiality and avoid any action that might affect the claims or positions of the parties. In January 1995 the UN Secretary-General presented a report to the Security Council, reassessing the UN's role in peace-keeping. The document stipulated

that UN forces in conflict areas should not be responsible for peace-enforcement duties, and included a proposal for the establishment of a 'rapid reaction' force which would be ready for deployment within a month of being authorized by the Security Council. In September 1997 the UN Secretary-General established a staff to plan and organize the formation of the so-called UN Stand-by Forces High Readiness Brigade (SHIRBRIG), to be based in Denmark. SHIRBRIG was declared available to the UN in January 2000; by that time Argentina, Austria, Canada, Denmark, Italy, the Netherlands, Norway, Poland, Romania and Sweden had formally committed troops to the force. SHIRBRIG became fully operational in late 2000 with the deployment of troops to the newly-authorized UN Mission in Ethiopia and Eritrea (UNMEE, see below). A Stand-by Arrangements System has been operational since 1994, to which some 88 countries had identified 147,900 troops as available for peace-keeping duties, as well as other services and equipment, by July 2000. In August 2000 a report on UN peace-keeping activities prepared by a team of experts appointed by the Secretary-General assessed the aims and requirements of peace-keeping operations and recommended several measures to improve the performance of the Department of Peace-Keeping Operations (DPKO), focusing on its planning and management capacity from the inception of an operation through to post-conflict peace-building activities, and on its rapid response capability. Proposed reforms included the establishment of a body to improve co-ordination of information and strategic analysis requirements; the promotion of partnership arrangements between member states (within the context of the Stand-by Arrangements System, see above) enabling the formation of several coherent multinational brigades, and improved monitoring of the preparedness of potential troop contributor nations, with a view to facilitating the effective deployment of most operations within 30 days of their authorization in a Security Council resolution; the adoption of 'on-call' reserve lists to ensure the prompt deployment of civilian police and specialists; the preparation of a global logistics support strategy; and a restructuring of the DPKO to improve administrative efficiency. The study also urged an increase in resources for funding peace-keeping operations and the adoption of a more flexible financing mechanism, and emphasized the importance of the UN's conflict prevention activities. In November the Security Council, having welcomed the report, adopted guide-lines aimed at improving its management of peace-keeping operations, including providing missions with clear and achievable mandates.

The UN's peace-keeping operations are financed by assessed contributions from member states (with the exception of two operations that are ongoing and financed through the regular budget of the UN). A significant expansion in the UN's peace-keeping activities during the early 1990s was accompanied by a perpetual financial crisis within the organization, as a result of the increased financial burden and the failure of member states to pay outstanding contributions. By 15 December 2000 unpaid contributions to the peace-keeping accounts amounted to US $1,990.4m.

By February 2001 the UN had undertaken a total of 54 peace-keeping operations, of which 13 were authorized in the period 1948–88 and 41 since 1988, reaching a peak in 1993 with a total deployment of more than 80,000 troops from 77 countries.

UNITED NATIONS DISENGAGEMENT OBSERVER FORCE—UNDOF

Headquarters: Camp Faouar, Syria.

Commander: Maj.-Gen. BO WRANKER (Sweden).

UNDOF was established for an initial period of six months by a UN Security Council resolution in May 1974, following the signature in Geneva of a disengagement agreement between Syrian and Israeli forces. The mandate has since been extended by successive resolutions. The initial task of the Force was to take over territory evacuated in stages by the Israeli troops, in accordance with the disengagement agreement, to hand over territory to Syrian troops, and to establish an area of separation on the Golan Heights.

UNDOF continues to monitor the area of separation; it carries out inspections of the areas of limited armaments and forces; uses its best efforts to maintain the cease-fire; and undertakes activities of a humanitarian nature, such as arranging the transfer of prisoners and war-dead between Syria and Israel. The Force operates exclusively on Syrian territory.

At 31 January 2001 the Force comprised 1,034 troops; it is assisted by approximately 80 military observers of UNTSO's Observer Group Golan, and supported by 124 international and local civilian personnel. Further UNTSO military observers help UNDOF in the performance of its tasks, as required. The General Assembly appropriated US $37.0m. to cover the cost of the operation for the period 1 July 2000–30 June 2001.

UNITED NATIONS INTERIM ADMINISTRATION MISSION IN KOSOVO—UNMIK

Headquarters: Priština, Kosovo, Yugoslavia.

Special Representative of the UN Secretary-General and Head of Mission: HANS HAEKKERUP (Denmark).

Principal Deputy Special Representative of the UN Secretary-General: GARY L. MATTHEWS (USA).

In June 1999 NATO suspended a 10-week aerial offensive against the Federal Republic of Yugoslavia, following an agreement by the Serbian authorities to withdraw all security and paramilitary forces from the southern province of Kosovo and Metohija, where Serbian repression of a separatist movement had prompted a humanitarian crisis and co-ordinated international action to resolve the conflict. On 10 June the UN Security Council adopted Resolution 1244, which outlined the terms of a political settlement for Kosovo and provided for the deployment of international civilian and security personnel. The security presence, termed the Kosovo Peace Implementation Force (KFOR), was to be led by NATO, while the UN was to oversee all civilian operations. UNMIK was established under the terms of Resolution 1244 as the supreme legal and executive authority in Kosovo, with responsibility for all civil administration and for facilitating the reconstruction and rehabilitation of the province as an autonomous region. For the first time in a UN operation other organizations were mandated to co-ordinate aspects of the mission in Kosovo, under the UN's overall jurisdiction. The four key elements of UNMIK were the interim civil administration; humanitarian affairs (led by UNHCR); democratization and institution-building (OSCE); and economic reconstruction (EU). An advance team, under a temporary interim administrator, accompanied the first deployment of KFOR troops, and civilian police officers began arriving in the province at the end of June. UNMIK and KFOR immediately established a Joint Implementation Commission

to co-ordinate and supervise the demilitarization of the Kosovo Liberation Army. UNMIK initiated a mass information campaign (and later administered new radio stations in Kosovo) to urge co-operation with the international personnel in the province and tolerance for all ethnic communities. A Mine Co-ordinating Centre supervised efforts to deactivate anti-personnel devices and to ensure the safety of the returning ethnic Albanian population. In mid-July the UN Secretary-General's permanent Special Representative took office, and chaired the first meeting of the Kosovo Transitional Council (KTC), which had been established by the UN as a multi-ethnic consultative organ, the highest political body under UNMIK, to help to restore law and order in the province and to reintegrate the local administrative infrastructure. In August a Joint Advisory Council on Legislative Matters was constituted, with representatives of UNMIK and the local judiciary, in order to consider measures to eliminate discrimination from the province's legal framework. At the end of July UNMIK personnel began to supervise customs controls at Kosovo's international borders. Other developments in the first few months of UNMIK's deployment included the establishment of joint commissions on energy and public utilities, education, and health, a Technical Advisory Commission on establishing a judiciary and prosecution service, and, in October, the establishment of a Fuel Supervisory Board to administer the import, sale and distribution of petroleum. Central financial institutions for the province were inaugurated in November. In the same month UNMIK established a Housing and Property Directorate and Claims Commission in order to resolve residential property disputes. In September the KTC agreed to establish a Joint Security Committee, in response to concerns at the escalation of violence in the province, in particular attacks on remaining Serbian civilians. In November the Special Representative appealed for additional funds and police officers to counter further ethnic violence. In mid-December the leaders of the three main political groupings in Kosovo agreed on a provisional power-sharing arrangement with UNMIK for the administration of Kosovo until the holding of municipal elections, scheduled to take place in 2000. The agreement on the so-called Kosovo-UNMIK Joint Interim Administrative Structure established an eight-member executive Interim Administrative Council and a framework of administrative departments. The KTC was to maintain its consultative role. In January 2000 UNMIK oversaw the inauguration of the Kosovo Protection Corps, a civilian agency comprising mainly former members of the newly-demilitarized Kosovo Liberation Army, which was to provide an emergency response service and a humanitarian assistance capacity, to assist in de-mining operations, and to contribute to rebuilding the local infrastructure. In August UNMIK, in view of its mandate to assist with the regeneration of the local economy, concluded an agreement with a multinational consortium to rehabilitate the important Trepca non-ferrous mining complex. During mid-2000 UNMIK organized the voter registration process for the forthcoming territory-wide municipal elections. These were held on 28 October with a strong voter turnout, although participation by minority communities was low. During 2000 UNMIK police and KFOR co-operated in conducting joint security operations; the establishment of a special security task force to combat ethnically-motivated political violence, comprising senior UNMIK police and KFOR members, was agreed in June.

At 1 January 2001 UNMIK comprised 4,411 civilian police officers, 39 military personnel, and an additional 1,150 international civilian personnel and 3,927 local civilian personnel. The General Assembly apportioned US $450.0m. to finance the operation during the period 1 July 2000–30 June 2001.

UNITED NATIONS INTERIM FORCE IN LEBANON—UNIFIL

Headquarters: Naqoura, Lebanon.

Commander: Maj.-Gen. SETH KOFI OBENG (Ghana).

UNIFIL was established by UN Security Council Resolution 425 in March 1978, following an invasion of Lebanon by Israeli forces. The force was mandated to confirm the withdrawal of Israeli forces, to restore international peace and security, and to assist the Government of Lebanon in ensuring the return of its effective authority in southern Lebanon. UNIFIL also extended humanitarian assistance to the population of the area, particularly following the second Israeli invasion of Lebanon in 1982. UNIFIL has provided civilians with food, water, fuel and medical and dental services.

In April 1992, in accordance with its mandate, UNIFIL completed the transfer of part of its zone of operations to the control of the Lebanese army. In April 1996 Israel initiated a large-scale offensive against suspected targets pertaining to the Hezbollah militia in southern Lebanon. During the offensive Israeli artillery shells struck a UNIFIL base at Qana, which was temporarily being used to shelter civilians displaced by the hostilities, resulting in the deaths of some 100 people. The UN Security Council condemned the attack and demanded the respect by all sides for UNIFIL's mandate and for the safety and freedom of movement of its troops. In May a UN inquiry concluded that the UN site had been deliberately targeted during the offensive, owing to the presence of Hezbollah activists in the camp. In June 1997 the UN General Assembly resolved that Israel should contribute US $1.8m. towards UNIFIL's operational costs, as compensation for the Qana incident.

In late March 1998 the Israeli Government announced that it recognized UN Security Council Resolution 425, requiring the unconditional withdrawal of its forces from southern Lebanon. It stipulated, however, that any withdrawal of its troops must be conditional on receiving security guarantees from the Lebanese authorities. A formal decision to this effect, adopted on 1 April, was rejected by the Lebanese and Syrian Governments. In mid-April 2000 the Israeli Government formally notified the UN Secretary-General of its intention to comply forthwith and in full with Resolution 425. Later in that month the UN Secretary-General dispatched a team of experts to study the technical aspects of the impending implementation of Resolution 425, and sent a delegation, led by both his Special Co-ordinator for the Middle East Peace Process, Terje Roed Larsen, and the Commander of UNIFIL, to consult with regional Governments and groupings. The withdrawal of Israeli troops commenced in mid-May, and the final contingent was reported to have left Lebanon on 24 May. Meanwhile, the Security Council endorsed an operational plan to enable UNIFIL to verify the withdrawal. All concerned parties were urged to co-operate with UNIFIL in order to ensure the full implementation of the resolution. In accordance with its mandate, UNIFIL was to be disbanded following the resumption by the Lebanese Government of effective authority and the normal responsibilities of a state throughout the area, including the re-establishment of law and order structures. In mid-June the UN Secretary-General confirmed that Israeli forces had been fully evacuated from southern Lebanon. (Soon afterwards UNIFIL reported several Israeli violations of the line of withdrawal: the Israeli Government agreed to rectify these by the end of July, and on 24 July the UN Secretary-General confirmed that no serious violations remained. Further violations of the line, however, were recorded in subsequent months.) From mid-2000 UNIFIL, reinforced with additional troops, patrolled the area vacated by the Israeli forces, monitored the line of withdrawal and continued to provide humanitarian assistance. From early August Lebanese security forces were stationed in the area, in co-operation with UNIFIL, although by January 2001 Lebanese military personnel had still not been deployed at the line of withdrawal. UNIFIL's mandate has been successively extended: in January 2001 the UN Security Council extended it further, until 31 July, and authorized a reduction in the Force's strength to 4,550 troops, to be effected by that date.

At 31 January 2001 the Force comprised 5,802 troops, assisted by some 50 military observers of UNTSO's Observer Group Lebanon, and also by some 483 international and local civilian staff. The General Assembly appropriation for the operation for the period 1 July 2000– 30 June 2001 amounted to US $233.6m.

UNITED NATIONS IRAQ-KUWAIT OBSERVATION MISSION—UNIKOM

Headquarters: Umm Qasr, Kuwait.

Commander: Maj.-Gen. JOHN A. VIZE (Ireland).

UNIKOM was established by a UN Security Council resolution (initially for a six-month period) in April 1991, to monitor a 200-km demilitarized zone along the border between Iraq and Kuwait. The task of the mission was to deter violations of the border, to monitor the Khawr 'Abd Allah waterway between Iraq and Kuwait, and to prevent military activity within the zone. In February 1993 the Security Council adopted a resolution to strengthen UNIKOM, following incursions into Kuwaiti territory by Iraqi personnel. The resolution enabled the use of physical action to prevent or redress violations of the demilitarized zone or the newly-defined boundary between Iraq and Kuwait. UNIKOM provides technical support to other UN operations in the area, particularly the Iraq–Kuwait Boundary Demarcation Commission, and has assisted with the relocation of Iraqi citizens from Kuwait, which was completed in February 1994.

At 31 January 2001 UNIKOM comprised 903 troops and 193 military observers, assisted by some 213 international and local civilian support staff. The UN General Assembly appropriated US $52.7m. for the maintenance of the mission for the period 1 July 2000–30 June 2001; two-thirds of UNIKOM's total costs are funded by voluntary contributions from Kuwait.

UNITED NATIONS MILITARY OBSERVER GROUP IN INDIA AND PAKISTAN— UNMOGIP

Headquarters: Rawalpindi, Pakistan (November–April), Srinagar, India (May–October).

Chief Military Observer: Maj.-Gen. MANUEL SAAVEDRA (Uruguay).

The Group was established in 1948 by UN Security Council resolutions aiming to restore peace in the region of Jammu and Kashmir, the status of which had become a matter of dispute between the Governments of India and Pakistan. Following a cease-fire which came into effect in January 1949, the military observers of UNMOGIP were deployed to assist in its observance. There is no periodic review of UNMOGIP's mandate. In 1971, following the signature of a new cease-fire agreement, India claimed that UNMOGIP's mandate had lapsed, since it was originally intended to monitor the agreement reached in 1949. Pakistan, however, regarded UNMOGIP's mission as unchanged, and the Group's activities have continued, although they have been somewhat restricted on the Indian side of the 'line of control', which was agreed by India and Pakistan in 1972.

At 1 January 2001 there were 46 military observers deployed on both sides of the 'line of control', supported by 62 international and local civilian personnel. The operation was allocated US $7.3m. from the regular budget of the UN for 2001.

UNITED NATIONS MISSION FOR THE REFERENDUM IN WESTERN SAHARA— MINURSO

Headquarters: el-Aaiún, Western Sahara.

Special Representative of the UN Secretary-General and Chief of Mission: WILLIAM EAGLETON (USA).

Personal Envoy of the UN Secretary-General: JAMES A. BAKER, III (USA).

Commander: Brig.-Gen. CLAUDE BUZE (BELGIUM).

In April 1991 the UN Security Council endorsed the establishment of MINURSO to verify a cease-fire in the disputed territory of Western Sahara (claimed by Morocco), which came into effect in September 1991, and to implement a settlement plan, involving the repatriation of Western Saharan refugees (in co-ordination with UNHCR), the release of all Sahrawi political prisoners, and and the organization of a referendum on the future of the territory. The referendum, originally envisaged for January 1992, was, however, postponed indefinitely. In 1992 and 1993 the Secretary-General's Special Representative organized negotiations between the Frente Popular para la Liberación de Saguia el Hamra y Río de Oro (Frente Polisario) and the Moroccan Government, who were in serious disagreement regarding criteria for eligibility to vote in the referendum (in particular, the Moroccan Government insisted that more than 100,000 members of ethnic groups who had been forced to leave the territory under Spanish rule prior to the last official census in 1974, the results of which were to be used as a basis for voter registration, should be allowed to participate in a referendum). Nevertheless, in March 1993 the Security Council advocated that further efforts should be made to compile a satisfactory electoral list and to resolve the outstanding differences on procedural issues. An Identification Commission was consequently established to begin the process of voter registration, although this was obstructed by the failure of the Moroccan Government and the Frente Polisario to pursue political dialogue. The identification and registration operation was formally initiated in August 1994; however, the process was complicated by the dispersed nature of the Western Saharan population. In December 1995 the UN Secretary-General reported that the identification of voters had stalled, owing to persistent obstruction of the process on the part of the Moroccan and Frente Polisario authorities; at the end of May 1996 the Security Council endorsed a recommendation of the Secretary-General to suspend the identification process until all sides demonstrate their willingness to co-operate with the mission. The Security Council decided that MINURSO's operational capacity should be reduced by 20%, with sufficient troops retained to monitor and verify the cease-fire.

In early 1997 the new Secretary-General of the UN, Kofi Annan, attempted to revive the possibility of an imminent resolution of the dispute, amid increasing concerns that the opposing authorities were preparing for a resumption of hostilities in the event of a collapse of the existing cease-fire, and appointed James Baker, a former US Secretary of State, as his Personal Envoy to the region.

In June Baker obtained the support of Morocco and the Frente Polisario, as well as Algeria and Mauritania (which border the disputed territory), to conduct further negotiations in order to advance the referendum process. Direct talks between senior representatives of the Moroccan Government and the Frente Polisario authorities were initiated later in that month, in Lisbon, Portugal, under the auspices of the UN, and attended by Algeria and Mauritania in an observer capacity. In September the two sides concluded an agreement which aimed to resolve the outstanding issues of contention and enable the referendum to be conducted in late 1998. The agreement included a commitment by both parties to identify eligible Sahrawi voters on an individual basis, in accordance with the results of the 1974 census, and a code of conduct to ensure the impartiality of the poll. In October 1997 the Security Council endorsed a recommendation of the Secretary-General to increase the strength of the mission, to enable it to supervise nine identification centres. The process of voter identification resumed in December 1997. The agenda for the settlement plan envisaged that the identification process would be followed by a process of appeal, the publication of a final list of voters, and then by a transitional period, under UN authority, during which all Sahrawi refugees would be repatriated. The referendum was scheduled to be conducted in December 1998. In January 1998 the Security Council approved the deployment of an engineering unit to support MINURSO in its demining activities. In April the Council extended MINURSO's mandate for a three-month period. At that time there were already significant delays apparent in the identification process, owing to ongoing disputes regarding the eligibility of members of three Saharan tribal groups. In July the Security Council extended MINURSO's mandate until mid-September, but warned that it would be terminated if either side significantly obstructed implementation of the settlement plan.

By early September 1998 the initial identification process had been completed, with a total of 147,350 voters identified, including 87,238 since December 1997. However, the issue of the eligibility of 65,000 members of the three disputed tribal groups remained unresolved. Later in September 1998 the UN Security Council extended MINURSO's mandate by 30 days, to enable the Personal Envoy of the Secretary-General to attempt to negotiate a solution to the problem. At the end of October the Council, extending MINURSO's mandate until mid-December, endorsed a series of measures proposed by the Secretary-General to advance the referendum, including a strengthened Identification Commission to consider requests from any applicant from the three disputed tribal groups on an individual basis. The proposals also incorporated the need for an agreement by both sides with UNHCR with regard to arrangements for the repatriation of refugees. In November, following a visit to the region by the Secretary-General, the Frente Polisario accepted the proposals, and in mid-March 1999 the Moroccan Government signed an agreement with the UN to secure the legal basis of the MINURSO operation, which was subsequently extended by the Security Council. In May the Council extended the mandate until mid-September. At the same time the Moroccan Government and the Frente Polisario agreed in principle to a draft plan of action for cross-border confidence measures. A new timetable envisaged the referendum being held on 31 July 2000. In July 1999 the UN published the first part of a provisional list of 84,251 qualified voters. The appeals process then commenced. In September the Mission's mandate was extended until mid-December. In late November almost 200 Moroccan prisoners of war were released by the Frente Polisario authorities, following a series of negotiations led by the Special Representative of the UN Secretary-General. The identification of applicants from the three disputed Saharan tribal groups was completed at the end of December 1999. In January 2000 the second part of the provisional list of qualified voters was issued, and a six-week appeals process ensued. In December 1999 the Security Council acknowledged that persisting disagreements obstructing the implementation of the settlement plan (mainly concerning the processing and analysis of appeals, the release of remaining prisoners and the repatriation of refugees) precluded any possibility of conducting the referendum before 2002. MINURSO's mandate was further extended successively in December 1999, in February, May, July and October 2000, and in February 2001.

The mission has headquarters in the north and south of the disputed territory, and there is a liaison office in Tindouf, Algeria, which was established in order to maintain contact with the Frente Polisario (which is based in Algeria) and the Algerian Government.

At 31 January 2001 MINURSO comprised 203 military observers, 27 troops and 31 civilian police observers, supported by 398 international and local civilian personnel. The General Assembly appropriation to cover the cost of the mission for the period 1 July 2000–30 June 2001 amounted to US $49.3m.

UNITED NATIONS MISSION IN BOSNIA AND HERZEGOVINA—UNMIBH

Headquarters: Sarajevo, Bosnia and Herzegovina.

Special Representative of the Secretary-General and Co-ordinator of UN Operations in Bosnia and Herzegovina: JACQUES PAUL KLEIN (USA).

Commissioner of the UN International Police Task Force: Gen. VINCENT COEURDEROY.

In February 1992 the UN established a Protection Force (UNPROFOR), in response to the escalating conflict in the former Yugoslavia, which became one of the largest operations ever mounted by the UN. UNPROFOR assumed responsibility for monitoring the withdrawal of anti-aircraft and heavy weapons by both Bosnian Muslims and Serbs to agreed locations within Bosnia and Herzegovina, the delivery of humanitarian assistance and monitoring compliance with the prohibition on military flights in Bosnian airspace. In December 1995 leaders of the warring parties in the former Yugoslavia signed a peace accord, which had been concluded in the previous month in Dayton, USA. UNPROFOR's mandate was terminated a few days later, when a new multinational force under NATO command (the Implementation Force—IFOR) assumed authority for implementation of the peace accord, for a 12-month period, on 20 December.

On 21 December 1995 the Security Council agreed on the establishment of the UN International Police Task Force (IPTF) and a UN civilian office, in accordance with the Dayton peace agreement. The operation subsequently became known as the UN Mission in Bosnia and Herzegovina (UNMIBH). The IPTF's tasks included: monitoring, observing and inspecting law enforcement activities in Bosnia and Herzegovina; the training of police officers and personnel; assessing threats to public order and advising on the capability of law enforcement agencies to deal with such threats; and accompanying the Bosnian police forces in the execution of their duties. The UN Co-ordinator was to exercise authority over the IPTF Commissioner and to co-ordinate other UN activities in Bosnia and Herzegovina relating to humanitarian relief and refugees, demining, elections and economic reconstruction. UNMIBH was to co-operate closely with IFOR and, later, with its successor operation, the Stabilization Force (SFOR), which became operational in December 1996. In early 1996 the UN was criticized for slow deployment of the IPTF: at the start of February fewer than 300 out of a total authorized strength of 1,721 police officers had arrived in the country. The Force was charged with maintaining an observer presence in Serb-dominated suburbs of Sarajevo that were due to come under the administration of the Bosnian Federation in March, a presence that was intended to provide encouragement to Serbs to stay in these areas. However, the vast majority of the Serbs took flight into the Republika Srpska prior to the transition of authority. In March the Security Council authorized the deployment of five military liaison officers, in order to strengthen liaison arrangements with IFOR. In August the mission reported failure on the part of Bosnian Federation police to protect political opponents of the Muslim nationalist Party of Democratic Action (PDA) from attacks by PDA loyalists in advance of the forthcoming all-Bosnia legislative elections. Prior to and during the elections, which were held in mid-September, the IPTF assisted IFOR in providing protection to refugees and displaced people returning to vote in their towns of origin. At the international conference to review implementation of the Dayton agreement, which was held in mid-November, it was agreed that the IPTF's mandate was to be strengthened, granting it enhanced powers to investigate the Bosnian police in both sectors of the country. In February 1997 the IPTF criticized police officers for using excessive force against civilians during recent unrest between the Muslim and Croat populations in Mostar. In the following month the Security Council demanded that the Mostar authorities suspend and prosecute those officers responsible for the attacks. Also in March the Council authorized the strengthening of the IPTF by an additional 186 police officers and 11 civilian monitors in order to monitor, restructure and train the local police force in the contested north-eastern city of Brčko, which was temporarily under international supervision. In August UNMIBH criticized the forcible evacuation of some 500 Bosniaks from the Muslim Croat Federation and initiated an investigation into the role of the local police in the incident. In Brčko, in August, 58 IPTF monitors had to be evacuated by SFOR troops after coming under attack by Bosnian Serbs demanding control of the local police station. During September UNMIBH co-operated with SFOR and an election monitoring group to assist safe and democratic voting in municipal elections in the Bosnian Federation, and monitored the movement of voters within the region and across boundary lines. In May 1998 the Security Council authorized the deployment of an additional 30 IPTF monitors to conduct a series of intensive training programmes for the local police in Bosnia and Herzegovina. In July the Security Council endorsed the establishment of a new programme, within

UNMIBH's mandate, to assess and monitor the judicial system in Bosnia and Herzegovina and to promote the rule of law. The Council authorized the deployment of 26 legal experts to undertake the programme. UNIMBH has endeavoured to ensure adequate minority representation in the Bosnian police in both sectors of the country. The Security Council has successively renewed UNMIBH's mandate, including that of the IPTF. In June 2000 the mission's mandate was extended until 21 June 2001.

At 1 January 2001 UNMIBH comprised 1,808 civilian police officers and five military liaison personnel, assisted by 1,772 international and local civilian personnel. The General Assembly appropriation for the period 1 July 2000 to 30 June 2001, which included the budgets of the UN Mission of Observers in Prevlaka and of UN liaison offices in Belgrade and Zagreb, amounted to US $158.7m.

UNITED NATIONS MISSION IN ETHIOPIA AND ERITREA—UNMEE

Headquarters: Asmara, Eritrea; Addis Ababa, Ethiopia.

Special Representative of the Secretary-General and Head of Mission: LEGWAILA JOSEPH LEGWAILA (Botswana).

Commander: Maj.-Gen. PATRICK C. CAMMAERT (Netherlands).

At the end of July 2000 the Security Council authorized the establishment of the UN Mission in Ethiopia and Eritrea (UNMEE) to facilitate compliance with and verify a cease-fire agreement that had been signed by the Governments of Eritrea and Ethiopia in mid-June (having been mediated by the Organization of African Unity, q.v.), with a view to settling a two-year border conflict between the two countries. In mid-September the Security Council authorized the deployment of up to 4,200 military personnel (including 220 military observers) to the operation, which was given an initial six-month mandate. The Security Council emphasized that UNMEE's mandate would be terminated on completion of the process to delimit and demarcate the Eritrea-Ethiopia border. In December the Eritrean and Ethiopian authorities concluded a full peace accord. In February 2001 the Military Co-ordination Commission (which had been established in accordance with the cease-fire accord and had met for the first time in December 2000) agreed a timetable to enable Eritrean and Ethiopian forces, monitored by UNMEE, to redeploy in order to establish a 25-km temporary security zone. Following the creation of the security zone UNMEE was to co-ordinate and provide technical assistance for demining activities in the vacated area and adjacent areas.

At 2 February 2001 UNMEE comprised 3,301 troops, 188 military observers and 226 international local and civilian personnel. The proposed budget for the mission amounted to US $150m. for the period 1 July 2000 until 30 June 2001.

UNITED NATIONS MISSION IN SIERRA LEONE—UNAMSIL

Headquarters: Freetown, Sierra Leone.

Special Representative of the Secretary-General and Chief of Mission: OLUYEMI ADENIJI (Nigeria).

Commander: Lt-Gen. DANIEL ISHMAEL OPANDE (Kenya).

In July 1998 the Security Council established a UN observer mission in Sierra Leone (UNOMSIL) to monitor the military and security situation in that country following the restoration of a democratically-elected government. UNOMSIL was authorized to oversee the disarmament and demobilization of former combatants, as well as the voluntary disarmament of members of the civilian defence force, and to assist in monitoring respect for international humanitarian law. The Special Representative, with the civilian component of the mission, was authorized to advise the Sierra Leonean authorities on police practice, training and reform, and to help to address the country's human rights needs. UNOMSIL was to work closely with forces of the Economic Community for West African States (ECOWAS) in promoting peace and national reconciliation. In January 1999, following a sudden escalation of hostilities, the UN Security Council extended the mandate of UNOMSIL for a further two months, although acknowledged that several UNOMSIL military observers, together with civilian support staff, would withdraw to Conakry, Guinea, until the security situation improved. In March the Security Council condemned the ongoing violation of human rights in Sierra Leone and urged all neighbouring countries to prevent the cross-border supply of armaments to anti-government forces. None the less, the Council extended the mission's mandate until mid-June and, subsequently, until mid-December. In August the Security Council authorized a provisional expansion of UNOMSIL of up to 210 military observers, in order to support the implementation of a peace agreement which had been signed by the parties to the Sierra Leone conflict in July, in Lomé, Togo. In October the Council authorized the establishment of the UN Mission in

Sierra Leone (UNAMSIL), comprising up to 6,000 military personnel, to help to consolidate peace in that country. UNAMSIL was mandated to co-operate with the Sierra Leonean Government and all other parties to enforce the cease-fire accord and Lomé peace agreement, to implement a plan for the disarmament and demobilization of all former combatants, and to facilitate the delivery of humanitarian assistance. The mission was to assume responsibility for all civilian, political and military components of UNOMSIL, the mandate of which was terminated with immediate effect. In February 2000 the Council expanded UNAMSIL's mandate to include the provision of security at key locations and government installations, assistance to the Sierra Leone law enforcement authorities, and the safekeeping and subsequent desposal of military equipment collected from former combatants. The Council also enlarged the mission's authorized strength from 6,000 to 11,100 military personnel. During early 2000, in contravention of the Lomé accord, Sierra Leone rebels repeatedly obstructed the implementation of the disarmament and demobilization plan. In May, following an attack on a contingent of UNAMSIL troops in the previous month, rebels killed several mission personnel and captured and detained a large number of others (reportedly as many as 500); these were all released later in the month. In response to the breakdown in security the United Kingdom deployed a force in Sierra Leone in early May, with a mandate to evacuate British nationals; the presence of the British troops was also regarded, however, as a deterrent to any escalation in rebel activities pending the arrival of UNAMSIL reinforcements. In mid-May the Security Council approved a further increase in the mission's authorized strength, providing for a total of 13,000 military personnel. In mid-July UNAMSIL mounted a successful operation to release 233 of its personnel, who had been surrounded by rebels in eastern Sierra Leone since the end of May. In August the Security Council recommended that the mission should be strengthened to enable it to secure approach routes to the Lungi and Freetown peninsulas and to counter continuing attacks by armed rebels. The Council asked the Secretary-General to assess the number of additional troops that would be required to achieve this. UNAMSIL's mandate has been successively extended at short intervals, most recently until 31 March 2001.

At 1 January 2001 UNAMSIL comprised 10,137 troops and 249 military observers, assisted by 34 civilian police and 399 international and local civilian personnel. The proposed budget for the mission amounted to US $504.4m. for the period 1 July 2000 until 30 June 2001.

UNITED NATIONS MISSION IN THE DEMOCRATIC REPUBLIC OF THE CONGO—MONUC

Headquarters: Kinshasa, Democratic Republic of the Congo.

Special Representative of the UN Secretary-General and Chief of Mission: KAMEL MORJANE (Tunisia).

Commander: Maj.-Gen. MOUNTAGA DIALLO (Senegal).

In August 1999 the UN Security Council authorized the deployment of up to 90 military liaison personnel to support implementation of a cease-fire agreement for the Democratic Republic of the Congo (DRC) which had been signed in Lusaka, Zambia, in July. Technical officers were also to be dispatched to Namibia, Rwanda, Uganda and Zimbabwe, all signatories of the Lusaka accord, to assess the security of any future UN presence in the sub-region. The Security Council approved the establishment of MONUC in late November. With an initial mandate until 1 March 2000, the mission was, in co-operation with a Joint Military Commission comprising representatives of the parties to the conflict, to oversee the implementation of the agreement, including monitoring the cease-fire and the disengagement of forces. The mission was also mandated to facilitate the delivery of humanitarian assistance. Initially MONUC was to comprise liaison and technical assessment officers, as well as other multidisciplinary personnel, previously authorized by the Council. In February 2000 the Security Council extended MONUC's mandate to the end of August and authorized the expansion of the mission to comprise up to 5,537 military personnel, including up to 500 observers. MONUC's mandate was subsequently further extended, to October, to December, and then to 15 June 2001. However, by February 2001 the Lusaka cease-fire accord had yet to be implemented and only a small contingent of MONUC observers had been deployed in the DRC. In mid-February the Security Council adopted a resolution demanding that the parties to the conflict commence the phased disengagement of their forces by mid-March and stipulating that plans for the full withdrawal of foreign troops and the disarmament, demobilization and resettlement of militia must be prepared and adopted by mid-May.

At 1 January 2001 MONUC comprised 24 troops and 183 military observers, assisted by 360 international and local civilian personnel.

The proposed budget for the mission amounted to US $141.3m. for the period 1 July 2000–30 June 2001.

UNITED NATIONS MISSION OF OBSERVERS IN PREVLAKA—UNMOP

Headquarters: Cavtat, Croatia.

Chief Military Observer: Col GRAEME ROGER WILLIAMS (New Zealand).

UNMOP was authorized by the Security Council in January 1996, following the termination of the mandate of the UN Confidence Restoration Operation, to assume responsibility for monitoring the demilitarization of the Prevlaka peninsula in Croatia, which had been occupied by the Serbian-dominated Yugoslav People's Army. UNMOP became operational on 1 February. While political tensions persisted throughout 1996, the UN Secretary-General reported that UNMOP's presence in the region had facilitated the process of bilateral negotiations between Croatia and the Federal Republic of Yugoslavia. In authorizing extensions of UNMOP's mandate in January and April 1997, the Security Council urged both parties to refrain from provocative actions in Prevlaka, to cease any violations of the demilitarized zone and to co-operate fully with UNMOP. The Council also reiterated the urgency of removing anti-personnel landmines from areas patrolled by UNMOP in order to improve the safety and security of the region and ensure freedom of movement to enable UNMOP to implement its mandate. By December it was reported that the demining process had been completed in the entire UN-controlled territory. UNMOP's mandate has subsequently been extended for six-month periods, most recently, despite concerns at the lack of substantive progress towards a settlement of the Prevlaka issue, until mid-July 2001.

At 1 January 2001 UNMOP comprised 27 military observers. The annual cost of UNMOP is included in the budget of the UN Mission in Bosnia and Herzegovina (see above).

UNITED NATIONS OBSERVER MISSION IN GEORGIA—UNOMIG

Headquarters: Sukhumi, Georgia.

Special Representative of the UN Secretary-General and Head of Mission: DIETER BODEN (Germany).

Chief Military Observer: Maj.-Gen. ANIS AHMED BAJWA (Pakistan).

UNOMIG was established in August 1993 to verify compliance with a cease-fire agreement, signed in July between the Government of Georgia and Abkhazian forces. The mission was the UN's first undertaking in the former USSR. In October the UN Secretary-General stated that a breakdown in the cease-fire agreement had invalidated UNOMIG's mandate. He proposed, however, to maintain, for information purposes, the eight-strong UNOMIG team in the city of Sukhumi, which had been seized by Abkhazian separatist forces in late September. In late December the Security Council authorized the deployment of additional military observers in response to the signing of a memorandum of understanding by the conflicting parties earlier that month. Further peace negotiations, which were conducted in January–March 1994 under the authority of the UN Secretary-General's Special Envoy, achieved no political consensus. While the Security Council approved new resolutions to prolong the existence of UNOMIG, the full deployment of a peace-keeping force remained dependent on progress in the peace process. In July the Security Council endorsed the establishment of a peace-keeping force, consisting of 3,000 troops from the Commonwealth of Independent States (CIS, q.v.), to verify a cease-fire agreement that had been signed in May. At the same time the Security Council increased the authorized strength of the mission from 88 to 136 military observers and expanded UNOMIG's mandate to incorporate the following tasks: to monitor and verify the implementation of the agreement and to investigate reported violations; to observe the CIS forces; to verify that troops and heavy military equipment remain outside the security zone and the restricted weapons zone; to monitor the storage of the military equipment withdrawn from the restricted zones; to monitor the withdrawal of Georgian troops from the Kodori Gorge region to locations beyond the Abkhazian frontiers; and to patrol regularly the Kodori Gorge. Peace negotiations were pursued in 1995, despite periodic outbreaks of violence in Abkhazia. In July 1996 the Security Council, extending UNOMIG's mandate, expressed its concern at the lack of progress being made towards a comprehensive political settlement in the region. The Council also urged the Abkhazian side to accelerate significantly the process of voluntary return of Georgian refugees and displaced persons to Abkhazia. In October the Council decided to establish a human rights office as part of UNOMIG. In May 1997 the Security Council issued a Presidential Statement urging greater efforts towards achieving a peaceful solution to the dispute. The Statement endorsed a proposal of the UN Secretary-General to strengthen the political element of UNOMIG to enable the mission to assume a more active role in furthering a negotiated settlement. In July direct discussions between representatives of the Georgian and Abkhazian authorities, the first in more than two years, were held under UN auspices. In early 1998 the security situation in Abkhazia deteriorated. Following an outbreak of violence in May the conflicting parties signed a cease-fire accord, which incorporated an agreement that UNOMIG and CIS forces would continue to work to create a secure environment to allow for the return of displaced persons to the Gali region of Abkhazia. In addition, the UN Security Council urged both parties to establish a protection unit to ensure the safety of UN military observers. In October 1999 seven UN personnel were held hostage for a short period in the Kodor Gorge area of Abkhazia. Two UNOMIG military observers were held hostage for several days in the Kodor Gorge region in June 2000 and, in December, the abduction and brief detention of two military observers was reported there; UNOMIG subsequently suspended patrols of that area. Reviewing the operation in January 2001 the UN Secretary-General urged the Abkhazian side to cease imposing restrictions on the mission's freedom of movement and expressed concern at the recent recurrent abductions of UNOMIG personnel. UNOMIG's mandate has been granted successive six-monthly extensions, the most recent of which was until 31 July 2001.

At 31 January 2001 UNOMIG comprised 103 military observers, supported by 240 international and local civilian personnel. The General Assembly budget appropriation for the mission for the period 1 July 2000–30 June 2001 amounted to US $30.0m.

UNITED NATIONS PEACE-KEEPING FORCE IN CYPRUS—UNFICYP

Headquarters: Nicosia, Cyprus.

Special Adviser to the UN Secretary-General: ALVARO DE SOTO (Peru).

Acting Special Representative of the UN Secretary-General and Chief of Mission: ZBIGNIEW WLOSOWICZ (Poland).

Commander: Maj.-Gen. VICTORY RANA (Nepal).

UNFICYP was established in March 1964 by a UN Security Council resolution (for a three-month period, subsequently extended) to prevent a recurrence of fighting between the Greek and Turkish Cypriot communities, and to contribute to the maintenance of law and order and a return to normal conditions. The Force controls a 180-km buffer zone, established (following the Turkish intervention in 1974) between the cease-fire lines of the Turkish forces and the Cyprus National Guard. The Force also performs humanitarian functions, such as facilitating the supply of electricity and water across the cease-fire lines, and offering emergency medical services. In August 1996 serious hostilities between elements of the two communities in the UN-controlled buffer zone resulted in the deaths of two people and injuries to many others, including 12 UN personnel. Following further intercommunal violence, UNFICYP advocated the prohibition of all weapons and military posts along the length of the buffer zone. The Force also proposed additional humanitarian measures to improve the conditions of minority groups living in the two parts of the island. A new series of direct negotiations between the leaders of the two communities was initiated, under the auspices of the UN Secretary-General's Special Adviser, in July 1997; however, the talks were suspended at the end of that year. In November 1999 the leaders of the two communities agreed to participate in proximity negotiations, to be mediated by the UN. The first round of these took place in New York, in December. A second and third round were convened in Geneva, Switzerland, in February and July 2000, respectively. A fourth round of proximity talks was held in New York in September and a fifth round in Geneva, in November.

At 1 January 2001 UNFICYP had an operational strength of 1,213 military personnel and 33 civilian police officers, supported by 187 international and local civilian staff. Over the period 1 July 2000–30 June 2001 the proposed cost of maintaining the force amounted to US $43.4m., of which some $23.1m. was to be met by assessed contributions from UN member states, with voluntary contributions from the Governments of Cyprus and of Greece to amount to $13.8m. and $6.5m. respectively.

UNITED NATIONS TRANSITIONAL ADMINISTRATION IN EAST TIMOR— UNTAET

Headquarters: Dili, East Timor.

Special Representative of the UN Secretary-General and Transitional Administrator: SÉRGIO VIEIRA DE MELLO (Brazil).

Commander: Lt-Gen. BOONSRANG NIUMPRADIT (Thailand).

In May 1999 Indonesia and Portugal signed an accord, under UN auspices, providing for a 'popular consultation' to determine the future status of East Timor, a former Portuguese colony which had been governed by Indonesia since 1976. The poll was to be organized by the UN, offering eligible voters a form of political autonomy or full independence from Indonesia, the outcome of which would then be endorsed by the Indonesian Government and implemented by a UN transitional authority. Under the agreement, Indonesia was to be responsible for maintaining peace and security in the territory and to ensure that voting was conducted without intimidation or violence, while the UN was to provide additional unarmed civilian and police personnel. In June the Security Council formally authorized the establishment of a UN Mission in East Timor (UNAMET), which was to comprise up to 280 police advisers and 50 military liaison officers, with an initial mandate until 31 August (later extended). The poll, which was initially scheduled for early August, was twice postponed, owing to security concerns; however, registration of voters commenced in mid-July. In late August the UN Security Council condemned the violent attacks and intimidatory tactics of militia groups favouring support for Indonesia, and acknowledged reports that Indonesian officers had failed to prevent the decline in law and order, but determined that the vote should proceed. The Council also resolved to expand UNAMET's presence in September to 460 police officers and 300 military liaison officers. The popular poll was conducted on 30 August. International and local UN staff supervised some 800 polling stations, established by UNAMET in 200 locations throughout the territory, and estimated that votes were cast by 98.6% of the 451,792 East Timorese who had been registered. The security situation in the territory declined dramatically following the popular consultation, and on 1 September the Security Council convened an emergency meeting to condemn, and demand the arrest of, those responsible for violent attacks on UN staff, pro-independence supporters and foreign journalists. The civil unrest and indiscriminate killings escalated after the announcement of the results of the poll, which identified some 78.5% of East Timorese voters in favour of independence, and resulted in mass population displacement. A further meeting of Security Council members, held on 5 September, resolved to send a five-member mission to discuss the situation with the Indonesian Government. The failure of a curfew, imposed by the Indonesian authorities a few days later, to restore security prompted the UN to evacuate almost all its remaining staff. In mid-September, following international condemnation of the situation and intense diplomatic pressure, the Indonesian Government reversed its earlier opposition to a proposal by the Australian Government and agreed to permit foreign troops to help restore order in East Timor. The Security Council subsequently authorized the establishment of a multinational force, under unified command, with a mandate to restore peace and security in the territory, until replaced by a UN peace-keeping operation. The so-called International Force for East Timor (INTERFET) was also mandated to protect and support UNAMET and to facilitate humanitarian operations. In late September INTERFET assumed formal control of the territory, while UNAMET re-established its headquarters in Dili. In late October, following ratification of the results of the popular poll by the Indonesian People's Consultative Assembly, the Security Council voted to estab-

lish a UN Transitional Administration in East Timor (UNTAET) to oversee the transition to independence and govern the territory on an interim basis. UNTAET was to exercise all judicial and executive authority in East Timor. The Transitional Administration's mandate authorized it to provide security and maintain law and order in the territory; to assume responsibility for the co-ordination and provision of humanitarian assistance; to establish an effective administration; to assist in the development of civil and social services and to promote capacity-building for self-government; and to assist in the creation of conditions for sustainable development. The responsibilities and personnel of UNAMET were incorporated into UNTAET. Military command was transferred from INTERFET to UNTAET in February 2000. In January 2001 the UN Secretary-General presented a report to the Security Council outlining recommendations to enable elections to a new permanent East Timorese legislative structure to be staged later in 2001 (these were subsequently scheduled for 30 August); the report envisaged the attainment of full independence for the territory by the end of the year. In late January an East Timorese court passed sentence on the first Indonesian militia member to be found guilty of crimes relating to the insecurity which had prevailed at the time of the popular referendum on the future of the territory. UNTAET's mandate (which had an initial duration until 31 January 2001) was extended in that month until 31 January 2002.

At 1 January 2001 UNTAET comprised 7,765 troops, 1,398 civilian police officers and 124 military observers, supported by 2,655 international and local civilian personnel. The cost of the operation for the period 1 July 2000–30 June 2001 was estimated at US $563m; this was to be funded mainly from assessed contributions, although a Trust Fund has been established to channel voluntary contributions for specific purposes.

UNITED NATIONS TRUCE SUPERVISION ORGANIZATION—UNTSO

Headquarters: Government House, Jerusalem.

Chief-of-Staff: Maj.-Gen. FRANCO GANGUZZA (Italy).

UNTSO was established initially to supervise the truce called by the UN Security Council in Palestine in May 1948 and has assisted in the application of the 1949 Armistice Agreements. Its activities have evolved over the years, in response to developments in the Middle East and in accordance with the relevant resolutions of the Security Council. There is no periodic renewal procedure for UNTSO's mandate.

UNTSO observers assist UN peace-keeping forces in the Middle East, at present UNIFIL and UNDOF (see above). There are small detachments of observers in Beirut, Lebanon and Damascus, Syria, as well as liaison offices in Amman, Jordan, and Gaza. In addition, UNTSO operates six outposts in the Sinai region of Egypt to maintain a UN presence there, and one at Ismailia, Egypt, in the area of the Suez canal. UNTSO observers have been available at short notice to form the nucleus of new peace-keeping operations.

The operational strength of UNTSO at 1 January 2001 was 150 military observers, supported by 118 international and local civilian staff. UNTSO expenditures are covered by the regular budget of the United Nations. The cost of the operation in 2001 was estimated to be US $22.8m.

United Nations Population Fund—UNFPA

Address: 220 East 42nd St, New York, NY 10017, USA.

Telephone: (212) 297-5020; **fax:** (212) 557-6416; **internet:** www.unfpa.org.

Created in 1967 as the Trust Fund for Population Activities, the UN Fund for Population Activities (UNFPA) was established as a Fund of the UN General Assembly in 1972 and was made a subsidiary organ of the UN General Assembly in 1979, with the UNDP Governing Council (now the Executive Board) designated as its governing body. In 1987 UNFPA's name was changed to the United Nations Population Fund (retaining the same acronym).

Organization
(April 2001)

EXECUTIVE DIRECTOR

The Executive Director, who has the rank of Under-Secretary-General of the UN, is responsible for the overall direction of the Fund, working closely with governments, other United Nations

bodies and agencies, and non-governmental and international organizations to ensure the most effective programming and use of resources in population activities.

Executive Director: THORAYA A. OBAID (Saudi Arabia).

EXECUTING AGENCIES

UNFPA provides financial and technical assistance to developing countries at their request. In many projects assistance is extended through member organizations of the UN system (in particular, FAO, ILO, UNESCO, WHO), although projects are executed increasingly by national governments themselves. The Fund may also call on the services of international, regional and national non-governmental and training organizations, as well as research institutions. In addition, eight UNFPA regional technical support teams, composed of experts from the UN, its specialized agencies and non-governmental organizations, assist countries at all stages of project/programme development and implementation.

FIELD ORGANIZATION

UNFPA operates field offices, each headed by an UNFPA Representative, in 105 countries. In other countries UNFPA uses UNDP's field structure of Resident Representatives as the main mechanism for performing its work. The field offices assist governments in formulating requests for aid and co-ordinate the work of the executing agencies in any given country or area. UNFPA has eight regional technical support teams (see above). At 1 January 2001 there were 628 UNFPA staff members in the field, of a world-wide total of 839.

Activities

The major functions of UNFPA, according to its mandate, are: to build up the capacity to respond to needs in population and family planning; to promote awareness of population problems in developed and developing countries and possible strategies to deal with them; to assist countries, at their request, in dealing with their population problems, in the forms and means best suited to the individual countries' needs; and to play a leading role in the UN system in promoting population programmes, and to co-ordinate projects supported by the Fund.

In co-operation with the UN Population Division, UNFPA played an important role in preparing for and conducting the International Conference on Population and Development (ICPD), held in Cairo, Egypt, in September 1994. UNFPA's then Executive Director, Dr Nafis Sadik, acted as Secretary-General of the Conference, which was attended by representatives of 182 countries. The ICPD adopted a Programme of Action, establishing the objectives to be pursued for the next 20 years (despite reservations recorded by the representatives of some predominantly Roman Catholic and Islamic countries, concerning sections which they regarded as endorsing abortion and sexual promiscuity). The Programme's objectives envisaged universal access to reproductive health and family planning services, a reduction in infant, child and maternal mortality, a life expectancy at birth of 75 years or more, and universal access to primary education for all children by 2015. The Programme emphasized the necessity of empowering and educating women, in order to achieve successful sustainable human development. Annual expenditure required for the implementation of the objectives was estimated to amount to US $17,000m. in 2000, increasing to $21,700m. in 2015: of these amounts, the international community or donor countries would need to contribute about one-third. During 1995 UNFPA undertook to redefine its programme directions, resource allocations and policy guide-lines in order to implement effectively the recommendations of the Cairo Conference Programme of Action. The Executive Board subsequently endorsed the following as core programme areas: Reproductive Health, including Family Planning and Sexual Health; Population and Development Strategies; and Advocacy (for example, human rights, education, basic health services and the empowerment of women). A special session of the UN General Assembly was held in June/July 1999 to assess progress in achieving the objectives of the ICPD and to identify priorities for future action. In February UNFPA organized a forum, held in The Hague, Netherlands, and attended by delegates from 177 countries, to review implementation of the ICPD Programme of Action in preparation for the special session. The forum's recommendations included greater funding for UNFPA activities, in particular for the prevention of HIV and AIDS, from governments as well as the private sector and non-governmental organizations, the incorporation of gender issues into social and development policies, greater involvement of women in decision-making processes, andstrengthened political commitment to the reproductive health ofadolescents.

UNFPA recognizes that improving reproductive health is an essential requirement for improving the general welfare of the population and the basis for empowering women and achieving sustainable social and economic development. The ICPD succeeded in raising the political prominence of reproductive health issues and stimulating consideration by governments of measures to strengthen and restructure their health services and policies. UNFPA encourages the integration of family planning into all maternal, child and other reproductive health care. Its efforts to improve the quality of these services include support for the training of health-care personnel and promoting greater accessibility. Many reproductive health projects focus on the reduction of maternal mortality, which was included as a central objective of the ICPD Programme and recognized as a legitimate element of international human rights instruments concerning the right to life/survival. The ICPD reported that the leading cause of maternal deaths (i.e. those related to pregnancy, which amount to about 600,000 each year) was unsafe abortions, and urged governments to confront the issue as a major public health concern. UNFPA is also concerned with reducing the use of abortion (i.e. its use as a means of family planning), and with preventing infertility, reproductive tract infections and sexually-transmitted diseases, including HIV and AIDS. Special attention is given to the specific needs of adolescents, for example through education and counselling initiatives, and to women in emergency situations. UNFPA distributes reproductive health supplies (including home delivery kits), with a focus on HIV-prevention, to regions affected by conflict or natural disaster. UNFPA also supports research into contraceptives and training in contraceptive technology. The Fund's Global Initiative on Reproductive Health Commodity Management (formerly known as the Global Initiative on Contraceptive Requirements and Logisitics Management Needs in Developing Countries) organizes in-depth studies on national contraceptive requirements and aims to ensure an adequate supply of contraceptives to developing countries. UNFPA is implementing a pilot project to encourage partnerships between private-sector interests and the governments of certain developing nations, with a view to making affordable commercial contraceptive products more easily available to consumers and thereby enabling governments to direct subsidies at the poorest sectors of society. In April 1998 UNFPA formally inaugurated a new pilot rural population control programme in the People's Republic of China, with a redefined emphasis on education and other methods to promote voluntary contraceptive use and reduce birth rates.

UNFPA helps countries to formulate and implement comprehensive population policies as a central part of any strategies to achieve sustainable development. The Fund aims to ensure that the needs and concerns of women are incorporated into development and population policies. Under this programme area UNFPA provides assistance and training for national statistical offices in undertaking basic data collection, for example censuses and demographic surveys. UNFPA also provides assistance for analysis of demographic and socio-economic data, for research on population trends and for the formulation of government policies. It supports a programme of fellowships in demographic analysis, data processing and cartography.

UNFPA's advocacy role is incorporated into all its programming activities in support of the objectives of the ICPD. Consequently, the Fund aims to encourage the participation of women at all levels of decision- and policy-making and supports programmes that improve the access of all girls and women to education and grant women equal access to land, credit and employment opportunities. UNFPA's annual *State of World Population Report* has consistently focused on the improved welfare of women as an issue of basic human rights; this includes the eradication of all forms of gender discrimination, entitlement to reproductive choice and the protection of women from sexual and domestic violence and coercion. (Gender equality is a fundamental principle of the UN Charter, q.v.) UNFPA helps to promote awareness of these objectives and to incorporate them into national programmes. In 1997 UNFPA appointed a special ambassador to generate international awareness of the dangers of female genital mutilation. UNFPA also has special programmes on youth, on ageing, on AIDS and on migration, and is currently increasing educational and research activities in the area of population and the environment. UNFPA attempts to increase awareness of the issue of population through regional and national seminars, publications (see below) and audio-visual aids, participation in conferences, and through a pro-active relationship with the mass media. In 1999 UNFPA promoted observance of 12 October as the symbolic day on which the world's population was estimated to reach 6,000m.

In 1995 UNFPA actively participated in the World Summit for Social Development, an international conference held in Copenhagen, Denmark, in March, and the UN Fourth World Conference on Women, held in Beijing, People's Republic of China, in September, at which the key concepts of the ICPD Programme were emphasized and reinforced. In 1996 UNFPA contributed to the second UN Conference on Human Settlements (Habitat II), which was held in Istanbul, Turkey, in June, by reporting on current trends in urbanization and population distribution and their link to human settlements. UNFPA is participating in the Special Initiative on Africa that was initiated by the UN Secretary-General in March 1996. UNFPA's principal involvement is to assist countries to implement efforts for reproductive health and to promote the integration of population considerations into development planning. UNFPA's Executive Director chairs the inter-agency Task Force on Basic Social Services for All, which was initially established to strengthen collaboration on implementing the ICPD Programme of Action through the UN Resident Co-ordinator System. In 1996 the Task Force assumed its current name with an expanded mandate to co-ordinate the follow-up to other global conferences. UNFPA also collaborates with other UN agencies and international experts to develop a reliable, multidisciplinary set of indicators to measure progress towards achieving the objectives of different conferences and to help formulate reproductive health programmes and monitor their success.

Finance

UNFPA is supported entirely by voluntary contributions from donor countries. In 1997 UNFPA's provisional income totalled US $319.9m. of which $290.1m. was for regular resources and $29.8m. for multi- and bilateral co-financing activities. Provisional project expenditure in 1997 totalled $214m., compared with $216.5m. in 1996. UNFPA's income for 1998 totalled $280.6m. Of total programme expenditure in 1998, about 60% was allocated to reproductive health care, 24% to population and development strategies and 16% to advocacy.

Publications

Annual Report.
AIDS Update (annually).
Dispatches (10 a year, in English, French and Spanish).
Inventory of Population Projects in Developing Countries around the World (annually in English and French).
Populi (quarterly, in English, French and Spanish).
State of World Population Report (annually).
Reports and reference works; videotapes and radio programmes.

United Nations Relief and Works Agency for Palestine Refugees in the Near East—UNRWA

Addresses: Gamal Abd an-Nasser St, Gaza City; Bayader Wadi Seer, POB 140157, Amman 11814, Jordan.
Telephone (Gaza City): (7) 6777333; **fax:** (7) 6777555.
Telephone (Amman): (6) 5826171; **fax:** (6) 5826177.
E-mail: unrwapio@unrwa.org; **internet:** www.un.org/unrwa/.

UNRWA was established by the UN General Assembly to provide relief, health, education and welfare services for Palestine refugees in the Near East, initially on a short-term basis. UNRWA began operations in May 1950 and, in the absence of a solution to the refugee problem, its mandate has subsequently been extended by the General Assembly, most recently until 30 June 2002.

Organization

(April 2001)

UNRWA employs an international staff of about 110 and nearly 22,000 local staff, mainly Palestine refugees. In mid-1996 the agency's headquarters were relocated, from Vienna, Austria, to Gaza and Jordan. The Commissioner-General is the head of all UNRWA operations and reports directly to the UN General Assembly. UNRWA has no governing body, but its activities are reviewed annually by a 10-member Advisory Commission comprising representatives of the governments of:

Belgium	Jordan	Turkey
Egypt	Lebanon	United Kingdom
France	Syria	USA
Japan		

Commissioner-General: PETER HANSEN (Denmark).

FIELD OFFICES

Each field office is headed by a director and has departments responsible for education, health and relief and social services programmes, finance, administration, supply and transport, legal affairs and public information.

Gaza: POB 61; Al Azhar Rd, Rimal Quarter, Gaza City; tel. (7) 2824508; fax (7) 6777444.
Jordan: POB 484; Al Zubeidi Bldg, Mustafa Bin Abdullah St, Tla'a Al-Ali, Amman; tel. (6) 5607194; fax (6) 5685476.
Lebanon: POB 947; Bir Hassan, Ghobeiri, Beirut; tel. (1) 603437; fax (1) 603443.
Syria: POB 4313; UN Compound, Mezzah Highway/Beirut Rd, Damascus; tel. (11) 6133035; fax (11) 6133047.
West Bank: POB 19149; Sheik Jarrah Qtr, Jerusalem; tel. (2) 5890400; fax (2) 5322714.

LIAISON OFFICES

Egypt: 2 Dar-el-Shifa St, Garden City, POB 227, Cairo; tel. (2) 354-8502; fax (2) 354-8504.
USA: 2 United Nations Plaza, Room DC 2-1755, New York, NY 10017; tel. (212) 963-2255; fax (212) 935-7899.

Activities

ASSISTANCE ACTIVITIES

Since 1950 UNRWA has been the main provider of relief, health, education and social services for Palestine refugees in Lebanon, Syria, Jordan, the West Bank and the Gaza Strip. For UNRWA's

purposes, a Palestine refugee is one whose normal residence was in Palestine for a minimum of two years before the 1948 conflict and who, as a result of the Arab–Israeli hostilities, lost his or her home and means of livelihood. To be eligible for assistance, a refugee must reside in one of the five areas in which UNRWA operates and be in need. A refugee's descendants who fulfil certain criteria are also eligible for UNRWA assistance. At 31 December 1998 UNRWA was providing essential services to 3,573,382 registered refugees (see table). Of these, an estimated 1,159,669 (33%) were living in 59 camps serviced by the Agency, while the remaining refugees had settled in the towns and villages already existing.

UNRWA's three principal areas of activity are education; health services; and relief and social services. Some 82% of the Agency's 2000 regular budget was devoted to these three operational programmes.

Education accounted for 54% of UNRWA's 2000 budget. In the 1998/99 school year there were 458,716 pupils enrolled in 650 UNRWA schools, and 13,915 educational staff. UNRWA also operated eight vocational and teacher-training centres, which provided a total of 4,632 training places. UNRWA awarded 891 scholarships for study at Arab universities in 1998/99. Technical co-operation for the Agency's education programme is provided by UNESCO.

Health services accounted for 18% of UNRWA's 2000 general fund budget. At the end of 1998 there were 122 primary health care units providing outpatient medical care, disease prevention and control, maternal and child health care and family planning services, of which 82 also offered dental care. At that time annual patient visits to UNRWA medical units numbered 7.0m., while the number of health staff totalled 3,484. UNRWA also operates a small hospital in the West Bank and offers assistance towards emergency and other secondary treatment, mainly through contractual agreements with non-governmental and private hospitals. Technical assistance for the health programme is provided by WHO.

Relief and social services accounted for 10% of UNRWA's general fund budget for 2000. These services comprise the distribution of food rations, the provision of emergency shelter and the organization of welfare programmes for the poorest refugees (at 31 December 1998 195,359 refugees, or 5.5% of the total registered refugee population, were eligible to receive special hardship assistance). In 1998 UNRWA provided technical and financial support to 70 women's programmes, 26 youth activity centres and 32 community-based rehabilitation centres.

In order to encourage Palestinian self-reliance the Agency issues grants to ailing businesses and loans to families who qualify as special hardship cases. Between 1983 and early 1993 608 such grants and loans were made. In 1991 UNRWA launched an income generation programme, which provides capital loans to small businesses and micro-enterprises with the objective of creating sustainable employment and eliminating poverty, particularly in the Occupied Territories. By 31 December 1998 18,053 loans, with a total estimated value of US $30.1m., had been issued to new and existing Palestinian-owned enterprises.

Following the signing of the Declaration of Principles by the Palestine Liberation Organization and the Israeli Government in September 1993, UNRWA initiated a Peace Implementation Programme (PIP) to improve services and infrastructure for Palestinian refugees. In September 1994 the first phase of the programme (PIP I) was concluded after the receipt of US $93.2m. in pledged donations. PIP I projects included the construction of 33 schools and 24 classrooms and specialized education rooms, the rehabilitation of 4,700 shelters, the upgrading of solid waste disposal facilities throughout the Gaza Strip and feasibility studies for two sewerage systems. It was estimated that these projects created more than 5,500 jobs in the Gaza Strip for an average period of four months each. By mid-1998 the total number of PIP projects, including those under the second phase of the programme (PIP II), amounted to 369, while funds received or pledged to the Programme totalled $221.7m.

Since 1993 UNRWA has been engaged in the construction, equipping and commissioning of a 232-bed hospital in Gaza, with funds from the European Union and its member states. Construction was finished in 1996. The hospital and an affiliated nursing college were to be integrated into the health care system of the Palestinian National Authority, once the process of commissioning had been completed.

AID TO DISPLACED PERSONS

After the renewal of Arab–Israeli hostilities in the Middle East in June 1967, hundreds of thousands of people fled from the fighting and from Israeli-occupied areas to east Jordan, Syria and Egypt. UNRWA provided emergency relief for displaced refugees and was additionally empowered by a UN General Assembly resolution to provide 'humanitarian assistance, as far as practicable, on an emergency basis and as a temporary measure' for those persons other than Palestine refugees who were newly displaced and in urgent need. In practice, UNRWA lacked the funds to aid the other displaced persons and the main burden of supporting them devolved on the Arab governments concerned. The Agency, as requested by the Government of Jordan in 1967 and on that Government's behalf, distributes rations to displaced persons in Jordan who are not registered refugees of 1948.

RECENT EMERGENCIES

Since 1982 UNRWA has managed a specially-funded operation in Lebanon, aimed at assisting refugees displaced by the continued civil conflict. In late 1986 and early 1987 fighting caused much destruction to Palestinian housing and UNRWA facilities in Lebanon, and an emergency relief operation was undertaken. In April 1996 UNRWA dispatched emergency supplies to assist some of the estimated 500,000 people displaced by renewed military activities in southern Lebanon.

In January 1991 (following the outbreak of war between Iraq and a multinational force whose aim was to enforce the withdrawal of Iraqi forces from Kuwait) the Israeli authorities imposed a curfew on Palestinians in the Israeli-occupied territories, and in February UNRWA began an emergency programme of food distribution to Palestinians who had thereby been prevented from earning a living. Following the conflict, Jordan absorbed more than 300,000 people fleeing Kuwait and other Gulf countries. Many of these people are eligible for UNRWA services.

In September 1992 an UNRWA mission was sent to Kuwait, following allegations of abuses of human rights perpetrated by the Kuwaiti authorities against Palestinian refugees living there. The mission was, however, limited to assessing the number of Palestinians from the Gaza Strip in Kuwait, who had been unable to obtain asylum in Jordan, since Jordan did not recognize Gazan identity documents.

STATISTICS

Refugees Registered with UNRWA (30 June 2000)

Country	Number	% of total
Jordan	1,570,192	42.0
Gaza Strip	824,622	22.1
West Bank	583,009	15.6
Syria	383,199	10.3
Lebanon	376,472	10.1
Total	**3,737,494**	**100.0**

Finance

UNRWA is financed almost entirely by voluntary contributions from governments and the European Union, the remainder being provided by UN bodies, non-governmental organizations, business corporations and private sources, which also contribute to extra-budgetary activities. UNRWA's general fund budget for 2000 amounted to US $300.9m.

Publication

Annual Report of the Commissioner-General of UNRWA.

United Nations Training and Research Institutes

UNITED NATIONS INSTITUTE FOR DISARMAMENT RESEARCH—UNIDIR

Address: Palais des Nations, 1211 Geneva 10, Switzerland.

Telephone: (22) 9173186; **fax:** (22) 9170176; **e-mail:** unidir@unog.ch; **internet:** www.unog.ch/unidir.

UNIDIR is an autonomous institution within the United Nations. It was established by the General Assembly in 1980 for the purpose of undertaking independent research on disarmament and related problems, particularly international security issues. UNIDIR's statute became effective on 1 January 1985.

The work of the Institute is based on the following objectives: to provide the international community with more diversified and complete data on problems relating to international security, the armaments race and disarmament in all fields, so as to facilitate progress towards greater global security and towards economic and social development for all peoples; to promote informed participation by all states in disarmament efforts; to assist ongoing negotiations on disarmament, and continuing efforts to ensure greater international security at a progressively lower level of armaments, in particular nuclear weapons, by means of objective studies and analyses; and to conduct long-term research on disarmament in order to provide a general insight into the problems involved and to stimulate new initiatives for negotiations.

The work programme of UNIDIR is reviewed annually and is subject to approval by its Board of Trustees. In early 2001 UNIDIR was conducting research and organizing seminars on a range of issues, including: peace-building and practical disarmament in West Africa; the costs of disarmament; contemporary issues in arms control and disarmament (the so-called Geneva Forum); development of the *UNIDIR Handbook on Arms Control*; tactical nuclear weapons; and fissile materials. Research projects are conducted within the Institute, or commissioned to individual experts or research organizations. For some major studies, multinational groups of experts are established. The Institute offers internships, in connection with its research programme. UNIDIR maintains a database on research institutes in the field of international security (Database on Research Institutes—DATARIs).

The Institute's budget for 1997 amounted to US $900,000. It is financed mainly by voluntary contributions from governments and public or private organizations. A contribution to the costs of the Director and staff may be provided from the UN regular budget.

The Director of UNIDIR reports annually to the General Assembly on the activities of the Institute. The UN Secretary-General's Advisory Board on Disarmament Studies functions as UNIDIR's Board of Trustees.

Director: PATRICIA LEWIS (United Kingdom).

Publications: *Disarmament Forum* (quarterly), *UNIDIR Newsletter* (quarterly); research reports (6 a year); research papers (irregular).

UNITED NATIONS INSTITUTE FOR TRAINING AND RESEARCH—UNITAR

Address: Palais des Nations, 1211 Geneva 10, Switzerland.

Telephone: (22) 9171234; **fax:** (22) 9178047; **e-mail:** info@unitar.org; **internet:** www.unitar.org.

UNITAR was established in 1963, as an autonomous body within the United Nations, in order to enhance the effectiveness of the latter body in achieving its major objectives. In recent years the main focus of the Institute has shifted to training, with basic research being conducted only if extra-budgetary funds are made available. Training is provided at various levels for personnel on assignments under the United Nations and its specialized agencies or under organizations operating in related fields. Training programmes comprise courses on multilateral diplomacy and the management of international affairs. Other training and capacity-building programmes, which are funded by special-purpose grants, are offered in issues relating to economic and social development, such as the application of environmental law; the legal aspects of debt, economic and financial management and public administration; chemicals and waste management; and climate change. Most training programmes are designed and conducted in Geneva.

UNITAR offers a fellowship programme in peace-making and preventive diplomacy to provide advanced training for international and national civil servants in conflict analysis and mediation. It also organizes, jointly with the UN Office for Legal Affairs, an annual fellowship programme in international law.

UNITAR is financed by voluntary contributions from UN member states, by donations from foundations and other non-governmental sources, and by income generated by its Reserve Fund.

Executive Director: MARCEL A. BOISARD (Switzerland).

UNITED NATIONS INTERNATIONAL RESEARCH AND TRAINING INSTITUTE FOR THE ADVANCEMENT OF WOMEN— INSTRAW

Address: Calle César Nicolás Pensón 102-A, POB 21747, Santo Domingo, Dominican Republic.

Telephone: (809) 685-2111; **fax:** (809) 685-2117; **e-mail:** instraw.hq.sd@codetel.net.do; **internet:** www.un-instraw.org.

The Institute was established by ECOSOC, and endorsed by the General Assembly, in 1976, following a recommendation of the World Conference on the International Women's Year (1975). INSTRAW provides training, conducts research and collects and disseminates relevant information in order to stimulate and to assist the advancement of women and their integration in the development process, both as participants and beneficiaries. During the two-year period 2001–02 INSTRAW's work programme focused on: building partnerships for gender equality; women and men in the information society; and the impact of globalization. In June 2000 INSTRAW inaugurated the Gender Awareness Information and Networking System (GAINS), an internet-based database on research and training materials.

INSTRAW is an autonomous body of the UN, funded by voluntary contributions from UN member states, inter- and non-governmental organizations, foundations and other private sources. An 11-member Board of Trustees meets annually to formulate the principles and guide-lines for the activities of INSTRAW and to consider the current work progamme and budget proposals, and reports to ECOSOC. INSTRAW maintains a liaison office at the UN Secretariat in New York.

Director: ELENI STAMIRIS.

Publications: *INSTRAW News* (2 a year); training materials, research studies.

UNITED NATIONS INTERREGIONAL CRIME AND JUSTICE RESEARCH INSTITUTE— UNICRI

Address: Viale Maestri del Lavoro 10, 10127 Turin, Italy.

Telephone: (11) 6537111; **fax:** (11) 6313368; **e-mail:** unicri@unicri.it; **internet:** www.unicri.it.

The Institute was established in 1968 as the United Nations Social Defence Research Institute. Its present name was adopted by a resolution of ECOSOC in 1989. The Institute undertakes research, training and information activities in the fields of crime prevention and criminal justice, at international, regional and national levels.

In collaboration with national governments, UNICRI aims to establish a reliable base of knowledge and information on organized crime; to identify strategies for the prevention and control of crime, within the framework of contributing to socio-economic development and protecting human rights; and to design systems to support policy formulation, implementation and evaluation. UNICRI organizes workshops and conferences, and promotes the exchange of information through its international documentation centre on criminology.

UNICRI is funded by the United Nations Crime Prevention and Criminal Justice Fund, which is financed by voluntary contributions from UN member states, non-governmental organizations, academic institutions and other concerned bodies.

Officer-in-Charge: ALBERTO BRADANINI (Italy).

UNITED NATIONS RESEARCH INSTITUTE FOR SOCIAL DEVELOPMENT—UNRISD

Address: Palais des Nations, 1211 Geneva 10, Switzerland.

Telephone: (22) 9173020; **fax:** (22) 9170650; **e-mail:** info@unrisd.org; **internet:** www.unrisd.org.

UNRISD was established in 1963 as an autonomous body within the United Nations, to conduct multi-disciplinary research into the social dimensions of contemporary problems affecting development.

The Institute aims to provide governments, development agencies, grass-roots organizations and scholars with a better understanding of how development policies and processes of economic, social and environmental change affect different social groups.

UNRISD research is undertaken in collaboration with a network of national research teams drawn from local universities and research institutions. UNRISD aims to promote and strengthen research capacities in developing countries. During the period 2000–03 its research programme was to include the following projects: gender, poverty and well-being; social policy in a development context; neoliberalism and institutional reform in East Asia; technocratic policy making and democratization; public sector reform and crisis-ridden states; community perspectives on urban governance; grassroots movements and initiatives for land reform; information technologies and social development; and business responsibility for sustainable development.

The Institute is supported by voluntary grants from governments, and also receives financing from other UN organizations, and from various other national and international agencies.

Director: THANDIKA MKANDAWIRE (Sweden).

Publications: *UNRISD Social Development News* (quarterly), discussion papers and monographs.

UNITED NATIONS UNIVERSITY—UNU

Address: 53–70, Jingumae 5-chome, Shibuya-ku, Tokyo 150-8925, Japan.

Telephone: (3) 3499-2811; **fax:** (3) 3499-2828; **e-mail:** mbox@hq.unu.edu; **internet:** www.unu.edu.

The University is sponsored jointly by the United Nations and UNESCO. It is an autonomous institution within the United Nations, guaranteed academic freedom by a charter approved by the General Assembly in 1973. It is governed by a 28-member University Council of scholars and scientists, of whom 24 are appointed by the Secretary-General of the UN and the Director-General of UNESCO (who, together with the Executive Director of UNITAR, are ex-officio members of the Council; the Rector is also on the Council). The University is not traditional in the sense of having students or awarding degrees, but works through networks of collaborating institutions and individuals. These include Associated Institutions (universities and research institutes linked with the UNU under general agreements of co-operation). The UNU undertakes multi-disciplinary research on problems of human survival, development and welfare that are the concern of the United Nations and its agencies, and works to strengthen research and training capabilities in developing countries. It provides post-graduate fellowships for scientists and scholars from developing countries, and conducts various training activities in association with its programme.

The UNU's research and training centres and programmes include the World Institute of Development Economics Research (UNU/WIDER) in Helsinki, Finland, the Institute for New Technologies (UNU/INTECH) in Maastricht, the Netherlands, the International Institute for Software Technology (UNU/IIST) in Macau, the UNU Institute for Natural Resources in Africa in Accra, Ghana (UNU/INRA—with a mineral resources unit in Lusaka, Zambia), the UNU Programme for Biotechnology in Latin America and the Caribbean (UNU/BIOLAC), based in Caracas, Venezuela, the UNU International Leadership Academy (UNU/ILA) in Amman, Jordan, the Institute of Advanced Studies (UNU/IAS), based in Tokyo, Japan, and the UNU International Network on Water, Environment and Health (UNU/INWEH) in Ontario, Canada.

The UNU is financed by voluntary contributions from UN member states. By May 1999 US $350m. had been pledged.

Rector: Prof. HANS J. A. VAN GINKEL (Netherlands).

Publication: *UNU Nexions* (regular newsletter).

UNIVERSITY FOR PEACE

Address: POB 138, Ciudad Colón, Costa Rica.

Telephone: 249-1072; **fax:** 249-1929; **e-mail:** info@upeace.org; **internet** www.upeace.org.

The University for Peace was established by the United Nations in 1980 to conduct research on, *inter alia*, disarmament, mediation, the resolution of conflicts, the preservation of the environment, international relations, peace education and human rights. The Council of the University (the governing body, comprising 15 members) was reconstituted in March 1999, meeting for the first time since 1994. In May 1999 the Council initiated a programme of extensive reforms. A Media and Peace Institute, affiliated to the University, was to be established in Paris, France in November 2001.

Rector and Chief Executive Officer: MARTIN LEES (United Kingdom).

Publications: *Dialogue, Infopaz.*

World Food Programme—WFP

Address: Via Cesare Giulio Viola 68, Parco dei Medici, 00148 Rome, Italy.

Telephone: (06) 6513-1; **fax:** (06) 6590-632; **e-mail:** wfpinfo @wfp.org; **internet:** www.wfp.org.

WFP, the food aid organization of the United Nations, became operational in 1963. It provides relief assistance to victims of natural and man-made disasters, and supplies food aid to people in developing countries with the aim of stimulating self-reliant communities.

Organization

(April 2001)

EXECUTIVE BOARD

At the end of 1995 the governing body of WFP, the 42-member Committee on Food Aid Policies and Programmes (CFA), was transformed into the WFP Executive Board, in accordance with a resolution of the UN General Assembly. The Board, comprising 36 members, held its first session in January 1996. It was to meet in at least three regular sessions each year.

SECRETARIAT

WFP's Executive Director is appointed jointly by the UN Secretary-General and the Director-General of FAO and is responsible for the management and administration of the Programme. At 31 December 1999 there were 5,248 WFP staff members, of whom about 80% were working in the field. WFP administers nine regional offices to provide operational, financial and management support at a more local level.

Executive Director: CATHERINE A. BERTINI (USA).

Activities

WFP is the only multilateral organization with a mandate to use food aid as a resource. It is the second largest source of assistance in the UN, after the World Bank group, in terms of actual transfers of resources, and the largest source of grant aid in the UN system. WFP handles more than one-third of the world's food aid. WFP is also the largest contributor to South–South trade within the UN system, through the purchase of food and services from developing countries. WFP's mission is to provide food aid to save lives in refugee and other emergency situations, to improve the nutrition and quality of life of vulnerable groups and to help to develop assets and promote the self-reliance of poor families and communities. WFP aims to focus its efforts on the world's poorest countries and to provide at least 90% of its total assistance to those designated as 'low-income food-deficit'. It also endeavours to address the specific nutritional needs of women and to increase their access to food and development resources. At the World Food Summit, held in November 1996, WFP endorsed the commitment to reduce by 50% the number of undernourished people, no later than 2015. In 1999 WFP delivered some 3.4m. metric tons of food assistance, reaching an estimated 89m. people in 82 countries.

In the early 1990s there was a substantial shift in the balance between emergency relief and development assistance provided by WFP, owing to the growing needs of victims of drought and other natural disasters, refugees and displaced persons. By 1994 two-thirds of all food aid was for relief assistance and one-third for development, representing a direct reversal of the allocations five years previously. In addition, there was a noticeable increase in aid given to those in need as a result of civil war, compared with commitments for victims of natural disasters. WFP has undertaken efforts to be prepared for emergency situations and to improve its capacity for responding effectively to situations as they arise. Through its Vulnerability Analysis and Mapping (VAM) project, WFP aims to identify potentially vulnerable groups by providing information on food security and the capacity of different groups for coping with shortages, and to enhance emergency contingency-planning and long-term assistance objectives. By 1999 VAM field units were operational in Angola, Bangladesh, Burkina Faso, Cambodia, the People's Republic of China, Ecuador, Ethiopia, India, Indonesia, Mozambique, Nicaragua, Pakistan, Sudan and Uganda. The key elements of WFP's emergency response capacity are its strategic stores of food and logistics equipment (maintained in Nairobi, Kenya, and Pisa, Italy), stand-by arrangements to enable the rapid deployment of personnel, communications and other essen-tial equipment, and the Augmented Logistics Intervention Team for Emergencies (ALITE), which undertakes capacity assessments and contingency-planning. A Crisis Support Facility was established at WFP Headquarters in 1996 in order to process information and assist co-ordination between WFP and other UN agencies working in Liberia. The Facility was reactivated in November to ensure an effective response to the humanitarian crisis in the former Zaire.

In 1999 some 70m. people received WFP humanitarian relief, of whom 29m. were refugees and internally displaced persons, and 41m. were victims of earthquakes, drought, floods and other natural disasters. Severe food shortages affected populations in 35 countries in 1999. In that year sub-Saharan Africa accounted for the largest share, some 44%, of total relief operational expenditure. The main populations of concern were in Angola, the Great Lakes region and Sierra Leone, which were affected by civil conflict, and in east Africa, where the people were affected by extreme climatic conditions and renewed conflict. During 1999 WFP provided assistance to 1.4m. Kosovar refugees, IDPs and returnees, and distributed emergency food aid or organized food-for-work rehabilitation initiatives for 500,000 people displaced by the unrest in East Timor. Assistance was also delivered to 1.3m. people displaced or otherwise affected by the ongoing conflict (aggravated by inclement climatic conditions) in Afghanistan. In December WFP approved an emergency operation to support 150,000 people displaced by insecurity in Chechnya. Food aid was supplied to 200,000 people following an earthquake in Colombia in January, to 230,000 people affected by cyclones in India in October, and to 150,000 people in Venezuela displaced from their homes by floods in December. WFP also provided emergency food assistance to 488,000 farmers and herders affected by severe drought in Jordan, Palestine and Syria during that year. In recent years WFP has been actively concerned with the food situation in the Democratic People's Republic of Korea (DPRK), which has required substantial levels of emergency food supplies, owing to natural disasters and consistently poor harvests. In September/October 1998 WFP, together with UNICEF and the EU, conducted the first random nation-wide nutritional survey in the DPRK, which identified some 16% of young children as suffering acute malnutrition and 60% suffering long-term malnutrition. By mid-1999 an estimated 1.5m.–3.5m. people had died of starvation in the DPRK since 1995. WFP initiated an emergency operation in the DPRK, covering the period July 1999–December 2000, with the aim of providing 877,000 metric tons of food aid to some 8m. people, at a cost of US $358m.

In accordance with a Security Council resolution providing for the limited sale of petroleum by the Iraqi Government in exchange for the purchase of essential humanitarian supplies, which came into effect in December 1996, WFP was mandated to establish an observation system to ensure the fair and efficient distribution of food throughout the country. WFP was also required to transport and distribute the food supplies to local populations in the north of Iraq. In October 1997 a joint FAO/WFP mission to Iraq reported extensive levels of malnutrition. In March 1998 WFP conducted a nutritional survey of children and women in Iraq, in an operation organized with the Iraqi Government and UNICEF. During 1998 WFP supervised the distribution of 4.8m. metric tons of food under the special operation in Iraq, at a cost of US $13.3m.

Through its development activities, WFP aims to alleviate poverty in developing countries by promoting self-reliant families and communities. Food is supplied, for example, as an incentive in development self-help schemes and as part-wages in labour-intensive projects of many kinds. In all its projects WFP aims to assist the most vulnerable groups and to ensure that beneficiaries have an adequate and balanced diet. Activities supported by the Programme include the settlement and resettlement of groups and communities; land reclamation and improvement; irrigation; forestry; dairy development; road construction; training of hospital staff; community development; and human resources development such as feeding expectant or nursing mothers and schoolchildren, and support for education, training and health programmes. During 1999 WFP supported 146 development projects, which benefited some 19m. people. Projects included rural development programmes in Bangladesh and Burkina Faso; a participatory rural land rehabilitation scheme in Ethiopia; a nutrition education and supplementary feeding programme in Guatemala; support for integrated child development services and for a forestry development scheme in India; rural primary school feeding programmes in Morocco; and land reclamation in northern Viet Nam.

Following a comprehensive evaluation of its activities, WFP is increasingly focused on linking its relief and development activities to provide a continuum between short-term relief and longer-term rehabilitation and development. In order to achieve this objective, WFP aims to integrate elements that strengthen disaster mitigation into development projects, including soil conservation, reafforest-ation, irrigation infrastructure and transport construction and re-habilitation and to promote capacity-building elements within relief operations, e.g. training, income-generating activities and environ-mental protection measures. In 1999 WFP approved 23 new Pro-tracted Relief and Recovery Operations (PRROs), where the emphasis is on fostering stability, rehabilitation and long-term development after an emergency. In all these operations, which are undertaken in collaboration with UNHCR and other international agencies, WFP is responsible for mobilizing basic food commodities and for related transport, handling and storage costs.

OPERATIONAL EXPENDITURE IN 1999, BY REGION AND TYPE* (US $ '000, provisional figures)

Region	Develop-ment	Relief	Special operations	Total (incl. others†)
Sub-Saharan Africa	83,658	509,492	11,647	633,021
Asia	100,803	370,195	5,317	479,830
Latin America and the Caribbean .	38,010	67,559	—	117,752
North Africa and the Middle East .	23,993	6,055	13,172	54,251
Europe and the CIS	—	136,055	4,012	139,079‡
Total	246,464	1,089,356	34,148	1,430,507§

* Excludes programme support and administrative costs.
† Trust fund expenditures.
‡ Includes adjustment.
§ Includes operational expenditures that cannot be apportioned by project operation.

Finance

The Programme is funded by voluntary contributions from donor countries and intergovernmental bodies such as the European Union. Contributions are made in the form of commodities, finance and services (particularly shipping). Commitments to the International Emergency Food Reserve (IEFR), from which WFP provides the majority of its food supplies, and to the Immediate Response Account of the IEFR (IRA) are also made on a voluntary basis by donors. WFP's total expenditure in 1999 (including non-operational costs) amounted to some US $1,568m.

Publications

Annual Report.
Food and Nutrition Handbook.
WFP in Action.

SPECIALIZED AGENCIES WITHIN THE UN SYSTEM

Food and Agriculture Organization
of the United Nations—FAO

Address: Viale delle Terme di Caracalla, 00100 Rome, Italy.
Telephone: (06) 57051; **fax:** (06) 5705-3152; **e-mail:** fao.hq@fao.org; **internet:** www.fao.org.

FAO, the first specialized agency of the UN to be founded after the Second World War, was established in Québec, Canada, in October 1945. The Organization aims to alleviate malnutrition and hunger, and serves as a co-ordinating agency for development programmes in the whole range of food and agriculture, including forestry and fisheries. It helps developing countries to promote educational and training facilities and the creation of appropriate institutions.

MEMBERS

181 members (including the European Union as a member organization): see Table on pp. 117–119.

Organization

(April 2001)

CONFERENCE

The governing body is the FAO Conference of member nations. It meets every two years, formulates policy, determines the Organization's programme and budget on a biennial basis, and elects new members. It also elects the Director-General of the Secretariat and the Independent Chairman of the Council. Every other year, FAO also holds conferences in each of its five regions (see below).

COUNCIL

The FAO Council is composed of representatives of 49 member nations, elected by the Conference for staggered three-year terms. It is the interim governing body of FAO between sessions of the Conference. The most important standing Committees of the Council are: the Finance and Programme Committees, the Committee on Commodity Problems, the Committee on Fisheries, the Committee on Agriculture and the Committee on Forestry.

SECRETARIAT

The total number of staff at FAO headquarters in September 1999 was 2,278, of whom 67 were associate experts, while staff in field, regional and country offices numbered 1,865, including 132 associate experts. Work is supervised by the following Departments: Administration and Finance; General Affairs and Information; Economic and Social Policy; Agriculture; Forestry; Fisheries; Sustainable Development; and Technical Co-operation.
Director-General: JACQUES DIOUF (Senegal).

REGIONAL OFFICES

Africa: UN Agency Bldg, North Maxwell Rd, POB 1628, Accra, Ghana; tel. (21) 666851; fax (21) 668427; e-mail fao-raf@fao.org; Regional Rep. B. F. DADA.

Asia and the Pacific: Maliwan Mansion, Phra Atit Rd, Bangkok 10200, Thailand; tel. (2) 281-7844; fax (2) 280-0445; e-mail fao-rap@fao.org; Regional Rep. R. B. SINGH.

Europe: Viale delle Terme di Caracalla, Room A-304, 00100 Rome, Italy; tel. (06) 570-54241; fax (06) 570-55634; Regional Rep. M. LINDAU.

Latin America and the Caribbean: Avda Dag Hammarskjöld 3241, Casilla 10095, Vitacura, Santiago, Chile; tel. (2) 337-2100; fax (2) 337-2102; e-mail fao-rlc@field.fao.org; internet www.rlc.fao.org; Regional Rep. GUSTAVO GORDILLO DE ANDA.

Near East: 11 El-Eslah el-Zerai St, Dokki, POB 2223, Cairo, Egypt; tel. (2) 3372229; fax (2) 7495981; e-mail fao-rne@field.fao.org; Regional Rep. ATIF YEHEYA BUKHARI.

In addition, the following Sub-regional Offices are operational: in Harare, Zimbabwe (for Southern and Eastern Africa); in Bridgetown, Barbados (for the Caribbean); in Tunis, Tunisia (for North Africa); in Budapest, Hungary (for Central and Eastern Europe); and in Apia, Samoa (for the Pacific Islands).

JOINT DIVISIONS AND LIAISON OFFICES

Joint ECA/FAO Agriculture Division: Africa Hall, POB 3001, Addis Ababa, Ethiopia; tel. (1) 510406; fax (1) 514416.

Joint ECE/FAO Timber Section: Palais des Nations, 1211 Geneva 10, Switzerland; tel. (22) 917-2874; fax (22) 917-0041.

Joint ESCWA/FAO Agriculture Division: POB 927115, Amman, Jordan; tel. (6) 606847; fax (6) 674261.

Joint IAEA/FAO Division of Nuclear Techniques in Food and Agriculture: Wagramerstrasse 5, 1400 Vienna, Austria; tel. (1) 2060-21610; fax (1) 2060-29946.

European Union: 21 ave du Boulevard, 1210 Brussels, Belgium; tel. (2) 203-8852; e-mail fao-lobr@field.fao.org; Dir M. R. DE MONTALEMBERT.

Japan: 6F Yokohama International Organizations Centre, Pacifico-Yokohama, 1-1-1, Minato Mirai, Nishi-ku, Yokohama 220-0012; tel. (45) 222-1101; fax (45) 222-1103.

North America: Suite 300, 2175 K St, NW, Washington, DC 20437, USA; tel. (202) 653-2400; fax (202) 653-5760; e-mail fao-lowa@fao.org; Dir C. H. RIEMENSCHNEIDER.

United Nations: Suite DC1-1125, 1 United Nations Plaza, New York, NY 10017, USA; tel. (212) 963-6036; fax (212) 963-5425; Dir HOWARD W. HJORT.

Activities

FAO aims to raise levels of nutrition and standards of living, by improving the production and distribution of food and other commodities derived from farms, fisheries and forests. FAO provides technical information, advice and assistance by disseminating information; acting as a neutral forum for discussion of food and agricultural issues; advising governments on policy and planning; and developing capacity directly in the field.

In November 1999 the FAO Conference identified the following areas of activity as FAO priorities for 2000–01: the Special Programme for Food Security; transboundary animal and plant pests and diseases; forest conservation; promotion of the Codex Alimentarius code on food standards; strengthening the technical co-operation programme (which funds 12% of FAO's field programme expenditure); and the implementation of a Programme Against African Trypanosomiasis. The Conference also approved a Strategic Framework for the period 2000–15, which emphasized national and international co-operation in pursuing the goals of the World Food Summit (see below). In October 1997 FAO organized its first televised fundraising event 'TeleFood', broadcast to an estimated 500m. viewers in some 70 countries. The initiative has subsequently been organized on an annual basis in order to raise public awareness of the problems of hunger and malnutrition. In November 1999 a TeleFood concert was held in Jamaica, which was broadcast around the world and on the internet. Since 1997 public donations to TeleFood have exceeded US $6m., financing more than 700 'grass-roots' projects in more than 100 countries. The projects have provided tools, seeds and other essential supplies directly to small-scale farmers, and have been especially aimed at helping women.

In November 1996 FAO hosted the World Food Summit, which was held in Rome and was attended by heads of state and senior government representatives of 186 countries. Participants approved the Rome Declaration on World Food Security and the World Food Summit Plan of Action, with the aim of halving the number of people afflicted by undernutrition, at that time estimated to total 828m. world-wide, by no later than 2015. A review conference to assess progress in achieving the goals of the summit was to be held in November 2001.

FAO's total field programme expenditure for 1999 was US $298m., compared with $278m. in 1998. An estimated 31% of field projects were in Africa, 20% in Asia and the Pacific, 11% in the Near East, 11% in Latin America and the Caribbean, 5% in Europe, and 22% were inter-regional or global.

AGRICULTURE

FAO's most important area of activity is crop production which annually accounts for about 24% of FAO's Field Programme expenditure. FAO assists developing countries in increasing agricultural production, by means of a number of methods, including improved seeds and fertilizer use, soil conservation and reforestation, better water resource management techniques, upgrading storage facilities, and improvements in processing and marketing. FAO places special emphasis on the cultivation of under-exploited traditional food crops, such as cassava, sweet potato and plantains.

In 1985 the FAO Conference approved an International Code of Conduct on the Distribution and Use of Pesticides, and in 1989 the Conference adopted an additional clause concerning 'Prior Informed Consent' (PIC), whereby international shipments of newly banned or restricted pesticides should not proceed without the agreement of importing countries. Under the clause, FAO aims to inform governments about the hazards of toxic chemicals and to urge them to take proper measures to curb trade in highly toxic agrochemicals while keeping the pesticides industry informed of control actions. In mid-1996 FAO, in collaboration with UNEP, publicized a new initiative which aimed to increase awareness of, and to promote international action on, obsolete and hazardous stocks of pesticides remaining throughout the world. In September 1998 a new legally-binding treaty on trade in hazardous chemicals and pesticides was adopted at an international conference held in Rotterdam, the Netherlands. The so-called Rotterdam Convention required that hazardous chemicals and pesticides banned or severely restricted in at least two countries should not be exported unless explicitly agreed by the importing country. It also identified certain pesticide formulations as too dangerous to be used by farmers in developing countries, and incorporated an obligation that countries halt national production of those hazardous compounds. The treaty was to enter into force on being ratified by 50 signatory states. FAO was co-operating with UNEP to provide an interim secretariat for the Convention. In July 1999 a conference on the Rotterdam Convention, held in Rome, established an Interim Chemical Review Committee with responsibility for recommending the inclusion of chemicals or pesticide formulations in the PIC procedure. By September the treaty had been signed by 60 states. As part of its continued efforts to reduce the environmental risks posed by over-reliance on pesticides, FAO has extended to other regions its Integrated Pest Management (IPM) programme in Asia and the Pacific on the adoption of safer and more effective methods of pest control, such as biological control methods and natural predators, such as spiders and wasps, to avert pests. In February 2001 FAO warned that some 30% of pesticides sold in developing countries did not meet internationally accepted quality standards.

FAO's Joint Division with the International Atomic Energy Agency (IAEA) tests controlled-release formulas of pesticides and herbicides that gradually free their substances and can limit the amount of agrochemicals needed to protect crops. The Joint FAO-IAEA Division is engaged in exploring biotechnologies and in developing non-toxic fertilizers (especially those that are locally available) and improved strains of food crops (especially from indigenous varieties). In the area of animal production and health, the Joint Division has developed progesterone-measuring and disease diagnostic kits, of which thousands have been delivered to developing countries. FAO's plant nutrition activities aim to promote nutrient management, such as the Integrated Plant Nutritions Systems (IPNS), which are based on the recycling of nutrients through crop production and the efficient use of mineral fertilizers.

The conservation and sustainable use of plant and animal genetic resources are promoted by FAO's Global System for Plant Genetic Resources, which includes five databases, and the Global Strategy on the Management of Farm Animal Genetic Resources. An FAO programme supports the establishment of gene banks, designed to maintain the world's biological diversity by preserving animal and plant species threatened with extinction. FAO, jointly with UNEP, has published a document listing the current state of global livestock genetic diversity. In June 1996 representatives of more than 150 governments convened in Leipzig, Germany, at a meeting organized by FAO (and hosted by the German Government) to consider the use and conservation of plant genetic resources as an essential means of enhancing food security. The meeting adopted a Global Plan of Action, which included measures to strengthen the development of plant varieties and to promote the use and availability of local varieties and locally-adapted crops to farmers, in particular following a natural disaster, war or civil conflict.

An Emergency Prevention System for Transboundary Animal and Plant Pests and Diseases (EMPRES) was established in 1994 to strengthen FAO's activities in the prevention, control and, where possible, eradication of pests and of highly contagious livestock diseases (which the system categorizes as epidemic diseases of strategic importance, such as rinderpest or foot-and-mouth; diseases requiring tactical attention at international or regional level, e.g. Rift Valley fever; and emerging diseases, e.g. bovine spongiform encephalopathy—BSE). EMPRES's initial priorities were locusts and rinderpest. During 1994 EMPRES published guide-lines on all aspects of desert locust monitoring, commissioned an evaluation of recent control efforts and prepared a concept paper on desert locust management. FAO has assumed responsibility for technical leadership and co-ordination of the Global Rinderpest Eradication Programme (GREP), which has the objective of eliminating the disease by 2010. Following technical consulations in late 1998, an Intensified

GREP was launched. In November 1997 FAO initiated a Programme Against African Trypanosomiasis, which aimed to counter the disease affecting cattle in almost one-third of Africa. EMPRES promotes Good Emergency Management Practices (GEMP) in animal health. The system is guided by the annual meeting of the EMPRES Expert Consultation.

In January 1999 the Committee on Agriculture recommended the development of a cross-sectoral programme on organic agriculture.

ENVIRONMENT

At the UN Conference on Environment and Development (UNCED), held in Rio de Janeiro, Brazil, in June 1992, FAO participated in several working parties and supported the adoption of Agenda 21, a programme of activities to promote sustainable development. FAO is responsible for the chapters of Agenda 21 concerning water resources, forests, fragile mountain ecosystems and sustainable agriculture and rural development.

FISHERIES

FAO's Fisheries Department consists of a multi-disciplinary body of experts who are involved in every aspect of fisheries development from coastal surveys, improvement of production, processing and storage, to the compilation and analysis of statistics, development of computer databases, improvement of fishing gear, institution-building and training. In November 1993 the FAO Conference adopted an agreement to improve the monitoring and control of fishing vessels operating on the high seas that are registered under 'flags of convenience'. These ships, amounting to an estimated 20% of all fishing vessels, are often able to avoid compliance with internationally accepted marine conservation and management measures. In March 1995 a ministerial meeting of fisheries adopted a Rome Consensus on World Fisheries, which identified a need for immediate action to eliminate overfishing and to rebuild and enhance depleting fish stocks. In November the FAO Conference adopted a Code of Conduct for Responsible Fishing, which incorporated many global fisheries and aquaculture issues (including fisheries resource conservation anddevelopment, fish catches, seafood and fish processing,commercialization, trade and research) to promote the sustainable development of the sector. In February 1999 the FAO Committee on Fisheries adopted new international measures, within the framework of the Code of Conduct, in order to reduce over-exploitation of the world's fish resources, as well as plans of action for the conservation and management of sharks and the reduction in the incidental catch of seabirds in longline fisheries. The voluntary measures were endorsed at a ministerial meeting, held in March and attended by representatives of some 126 countries, which issued a declaration to promote the implementation of the Code of Conduct and to achieve sustainable management of fisheries and aquaculture. In October a new Sustainable Fisheries Livelihoods Programme was initiated to assist 24 African countries to implement the Code of Conduct and to promote small-scale artisanal fishing projects. FAO promotes aquaculture as a valuable source of animal protein, and as an income-generating activity for rural communities. A new Programme of Fisheries Assistance for Small Island Developing States, which had been formulated by FAO in consultation with South Pacific member states and with the Alliance of Small Island States, was approved at a session of the Committee on Fisheries in March 1997. In 1996/97 FAO took part in 21 technical consultations on the management of marine resources. In addition, work on aquatic genetic resources was strengthened and studies were undertaken to monitor the impact of 'El Niño', a periodic warming of the tropical Pacific Ocean, on aquaculture in Latin America and Africa. In February 2000 FAO and the Network of Aquaculture Centres in Asia and the Pacific (NACA) jointly convened a Conference on Aquaculture in the Third Millennium, which was held in Bangkok, Thailand, and attended by participants representing more than 200 governmental and non-governmental organizations in 66 countries. The Conference debated global trends in aquaculture and future policy measures to ensure the sustainable development of the sector. In March 2001 the Committee on Fisheries established a Sub-committee on Aquaculture.

FORESTRY

FAO focuses on the contribution of forestry to food security, on effective and responsible forest management and on maintaining a balance between the economic, ecological and social benefits of forest resources. The Organization has helped to develop national forestry programmes and to promote the sustainable development of all types of forest. FAO's Forests, Trees and People Programme promotes the sustainable management of tree and forest resources, based on local knowledge and management practices, in order to improve the livelihoods of rural people in developing countries. A Strategic Plan for Forestry was approved in March 1999; its main objectives were to maintain the environmental diversity of forests, to realise the economic potential of forests and trees within a sustainable framework, and to expand access to information on forestry.

NUTRITION

The International Conference on Nutrition, sponsored by FAO and WHO, took place in Rome in December 1992. It approved a World Declaration on Nutrition and a Plan of Action, aimed at promoting efforts to combat malnutrition as a development priority. Since the conference, more than 100 countries have formulated national plans of action for nutrition, many of which were based on existing development plans such as comprehensive food security initiatives, national poverty alleviation programmes and action plans to attain the targets set by the World Summit for Children in September 1990. In October 1996 FAO, WHO and other partners jointly organized the first World Congress on Calcium and Vitamin D in Human Life, held in Rome. The Congress discussed methods to increase the intake of calcium and vitamin D by all members of the population in order to promote growth during childhood and adolescence and to reduce the prevalence of diseases such as osteoporosis, cancer and hypertension. In January 2001 a joint team of FAO and WHO experts issued a report concerning the allergenicity of foods derived from biotechnology (i.e. genetically modified—GM foods).

PROCESSING AND MARKETING

An estimated 20% of all food harvested is lost before it can be consumed, and in some developing countries the proportion is much higher. FAO helps reduce immediate post-harvest losses, with the introduction of improved processing methods and storage systems. It also advises on the distribution and marketing of agricultural produce and on the selection and preparation of foods for optimum nutrition. Many of these activities form part of wider rural development projects. Many developing countries rely on agricultural products as their main source of foreign earnings, but the terms under which they are traded are usually more favourable to the industrialized countries. FAO continues to favour the elimination of export subsidies and related discriminatory practices, such as protectionist measures that hamper international trade in agricultural commodities. FAO has organized regional workshops and national projects in order to help member states to implement World Trade Organization regulations, in particular with regard to agricultural policy, intellectual property rights, sanitary and phytosanitary measures, technical barriers to trade and the international standards of the Codex Alimentarius, and to consider the impact on member states of the ministerial decision concerning the possible negative effects of the reform programme on least-developed and net-food importing developing countries. FAO evaluates new market trends and helps to develop improved plant and animal quarantine procedures. In November 1997 the FAO Conference adopted new guide-lines on surveillance and on export certification systems in order to harmonize plant quarantine standards. In August 1999 FAO announced the establishment of a new forum, PhAction, to promote post-harvest research and the development of effective post-harvest services and infrastructure.

FOOD SECURITY

FAO's policy on food security aims to encourage the production of adequate food supplies, to maximize stability in the flow of supplies, and to ensure access on the part of those who need them. In 1994 FAO initiated a Special Programme for Food Security (SPFS), which was designed to assist low-income countries with a food deficit to increase food production and productivity as rapidly as possible, primarily through the widespread adoption by farmers of improved production technologies, with emphasis on areas of high potential. At September 2000 78 countries were categorized as 'low-income food-deficit', of which 42 were in Africa. In May of that year the SPFS was engaged in projects in 60 countries. A budget of US $10m. was allocated to the Programme for the two-year period 1998–99. In 1996 FAO was actively involved in the formulation of a Plan of Action on food security, adopted at the World Food Summit in November, and was to be responsible for monitoring and promoting its implementation. In March 1999, FAO signed agreements with the International Fund for Agricultural Development (IFAD) and WFP which aimed to increase co-operation within the framework of the SPFS. The Programme promotes South-South co-operation to improve food security and the exchange of knowledge and experience. By May 2000 14 bilateral co-operation agreements were in force, for example, between Viet Nam and Senegal, and India and Eritrea.

FAO's Global Information and Early Warning System (GIEWS), which become operational in 1975, maintains a database on and monitors the crop and food outlook at global, regional, national and sub-national levels in order to detect emerging food supply difficulties and disasters and to ensure rapid intervention in countries experiencing food supply shortages. It publishes regular reports on the weather conditions and crop prospects in sub-Saharan Africa and in the Sahel region and issues special alerts which describe the situation in countries or sub-regions experiencing food difficulties and recommends an appropriate international response. In October 1999 FAO published the first annual *State of Food Insecurity in the World*, based on data compiled by a new Food Insecurity and Vulnerability Information and Mapping Systems programme.

FAO INVESTMENT CENTRE

The Investment Centre was established in 1964 to help countries to prepare viable investment projects that will attract external financing. The Centre focuses its evaluation of projects on two fundamental concerns: the promotion of sustainable activities for land management, forestry development and environmental protection, and the alleviation of rural poverty. In 1998–99 76 projects were approved, representing a total investment of some US $4,670m.

EMERGENCY RELIEF

FAO works to rehabilitate agricultural production following natural and man-made disasters by providing emergency seed, tools, and technical and other assistance. Jointly with the United Nations, FAO is responsible for the World Food Programme (q.v.), which provides emergency food supplies and food aid in support of development projects. In 1997 more than 60 countries suffered the effects of heavy flooding or severe drought (occasionally, as in the case of Indonesia, followed by extensive forest fires), caused wholly or partially by the El Niño weather phenomenon. FAO attempted to help assess the damage to agricultural systems, to provide rehabilitation assistance and to initiate efforts to strengthen the resistance of agricultural sectors against future weather anomalies. In 1998 FAO was concerned at the possible effects of a converse climatic occurence, 'La Niña', caused by upswelling of cold water in areas of the Pacific Ocean. By 30 November FAO's Special Relief Operations Service had undertaken 96 new projects in 45 countries during that year, at a cost of US $93.3m. (53% in Africa, 23% in Asia and the Pacific, 10% in the Near East, 7% in Europe, and 7% in Latin America and the Caribbean).

INFORMATION

FAO functions as an information centre, collecting, analysing, interpreting and disseminating information through various media, including an extensive internet site. It issues regular statistical reports, commodity studies, and technical manuals in local languages (see list of publications below). Other materials produced by the FAO include information booklets, reference papers, reports of meetings, training manuals and audiovisuals.

FAO compiles and co-ordinates an extensive range of international databases on agriculture, fisheries, forestry, food and statistics, the most important of these being AGRIS (the International Information System for the Agricultural Sciences and Technology) and CARIS (the Current Agricultural Research Information System). Statistical databases include the GLOBEFISH databank and electronic library, FISHDAB (the Fisheries Statistical Database), FORIS (Forest Resources Information System), and GIS (the Geographic Information System). In addition, AGROSTAT PC has been designed to provide access to updated figures in six agriculture-related topics via personal computer. In 1996 FAO established a World Agricultural Information Centre (WAICENT), which offers wide access to agricultural data through the electronic media.

FAO Councils and Commissions

(Based at the Rome headquarters unless otherwise indicated.)

African Commission on Agricultural Statistics: c/o FAO Regional Office for Africa, POB 1628, Accra, Ghana: f. 1961 to advise member countries on the development and standardization of food and agricultural statistics; 37 member states.

African Forestry and Wildlife Commission: f. 1959 to advise on the formulation of forest policy and to review and co-ordinate its implementation on a regional level; to exchange information and advise on technical problems; 42 member states.

Asia and Pacific Commission on Agricultural Statistics: c/o FAO Regional Office, Maliwan Mansion, Phra Atit Rd, Bangkok 10200, Thailand; f. 1962 to review the state of food and agricultural statistics in the region and to advise member countries on the development and standardization of agricultural statistics; 25 member states.

Asia and Pacific Plant Protection Commission: c/o FAO Regional Office, Maliwan Mansion, Phra Atit Rd, Bangkok 10200, Thailand; f. 1956 (new title 1983) to strengthen international co-operation in plant protection to prevent the introduction and spread of destructive plant diseases and pests; 25 member states.

Asia-Pacific Fishery Commission: c/o FAO Regional Office, Maliwan Mansion, Phra Atit Rd, Bangkok 10200, Thailand; f. 1948 to develop fisheries, encourage and co-ordinate research, disseminate information, recommend projects to governments, propose standards in technique and management measures; 20 member states.

Asia-Pacific Forestry Commission: f. 1949 to advise on the formulation of forest policy, and review and co-ordinate its implementation throughout the region; to exchange information and advise on technical problems; 29 member states.

Caribbean Plant Protection Commission: f. 1967 to preserve the existing plant resources of the area.

Commission on African Animal Trypanosomiasis: f. 1979 to develop and implement programmes to combat this disease; 39 member states.

Commission for Controlling the Desert Locust in the Eastern Region of its Distribution Area in South West Asia: f. 1964 to carry out all possible measures to control plagues of the desert locust in Afghanistan, India, Iran and Pakistan.

Commission for Controlling the Desert Locust in the Near East: c/o FAO Regional Office for the Near East, POB 2223, Cairo, Egypt; f. 1967 to promote national and international research and action with respect to the control of the desert locust in the Near East.

Commission for Controlling the Desert Locust in North-West Africa: f. 1971 to promote research on control of the desert locust in NW Africa.

Commission on Fertilizers: f. 1973 to provide guidance on the effective distribution and use of fertilizers.

Commission for Inland Fisheries of Latin America: f. 1976 to promote, co-ordinate and assist national and regional fishery and limnological surveys and programmes of research and development leading to the rational utilization of inland fishery resources.

Commission on Plant Genetic Resources: f. 1983 to provide advice on programmes dealing with crop improvement through plant genetic resources.

European Commission on Agriculture: f. 1949 to encourage and facilitate action and co-operation in technological agricultural problems among member states and between international organizations concerned with agricultural technology in Europe.

European Commission for the Control of Foot-and-Mouth Disease: f. 1953 to promote national and international action for the control of the disease in Europe and its final eradication.

European Forestry Commission: f. 1947 to advise on the formulation of forest policy and to review and co-ordinate its implementation on a regional level; to exchange information and to make recommendations; 27 member states.

European Inland Fisheries Advisory Commission: f. 1957 to promote improvements in inland fisheries and to advise member governments and FAO on inland fishery matters.

FAO Regional Commission on Farm Management for Asia and the Far East: c/o FAO Regional Office, Maliwan Mansion, Phra Atit Rd, Bangkok 10200, Thailand; f. 1959 to stimulate and co-ordinate farm management research and extension activities and to serve as a clearing-house for the exchange of information and experience among the member countries in the region.

FAO/WHO Codex Alimentarius Commission: f. 1962 to make proposals for the co-ordination of all international food standards work and to publish a code of international food standards; 158 member states.

General Fisheries Council for the Mediterranean—GFCM: f. 1952 to develop aquatic resources, to encourage and co-ordinate research in the fishing and allied industries, to assemble and publish information, and to recommend the standardization of equipment, techniques and nomenclature.

Indian Ocean Fishery Commission: f. 1967 to promote national programmes, research and development activities, and to examine management problems; 41 member states.

International Poplar Commission: f. 1947 to study scientific, technical, social and economic aspects of poplar and willow cultivation; to promote the exchange of ideas and material between research workers, producers and users; to arrange joint research programmes, congresses, study tours; to make recommendations to the FAO Conference and to National Poplar Commissions.

International Rice Commission: f. 1948 to promote national and international action on production, conservation, distribution and consumption of rice, except matters relating to international trade; 61 member states.

Joint FAO/WHO/OAU Regional Food and Nutrition Commission for Africa: c/o FAO Regional Office for Africa, POB 1628, Accra, Ghana; f. 1962 to provide liaison in matters concerning food and nutrition, and to review food and nutritional problems in Africa; 43 member states.

Latin American and Caribbean Forestry Commission: f. 1948 to advise on formulation of forest policy and review and co-ordinate

its implementation throughout the region; to exchange information and advise on technical problems; 31 member states.

Near East Forestry Commission: f. 1953 to advise on formulation of forest policy and review and co-ordinate its implementation throughout the region; to exchange information and advise on technical problems; 20 member states.

Near East Regional Commission on Agriculture: c/o FAO Regional Office, POB 2223, Cairo, Egypt; f. 1983 to conduct periodic reviews of agricultural problems in the region; to promote the formulation and implementation of regional and national policies and programmes for improving production of crops and livestock; to strengthen the management of crops, livestock and supporting services and research; to promote the transfer of technology and regional technical co-operation; and to provide guidance on training and human resources development.

North American Forestry Commission: f. 1959 to advise on the formulation and co-ordination of national forest policies in Canada, Mexico and the USA; to exchange information and to advise on technical problems; three member states.

Regional Animal Production and Health Commission for Asia and the Pacific: c/o FAO Regional Office, Maliwan Mansion, Phra Atit Rd, Bangkok 10200, Thailand; f. 1973 to promote livestock development in general, and national and international research and action with respect to animal health and husbandry problems in the region; 14 member states.

Regional Commission on Land and Water Use in the Near East: f. 1967 to review the current situation with regard to land and water use in the region; to identify the main problems concerning the development of land and water resources which require research and study and to consider other related matters.

Regional Fisheries Advisory Commission for the South West Atlantic: f. 1961 to advise FAO on fisheries in the South West Atlantic area, to advise member countries (Argentina, Brazil and Uruguay) on the administration and rational exploitation of marine and inland resources; to assist in the collection and dissemination of data, in training, and to promote liaison and co-operation.

Western Central Atlantic Fishery Commission: f. 1973 to assist international co-operation for the conservation, development and utilization of the living resources, especially shrimps, of the Western Central Atlantic.

Finance

FAO's Regular Programme, which is financed by contributions from member governments, covers the cost of FAO's Secretariat, its Technical Co-operation Programme (TCP) and part of the cost of several special action programmes. The budget for the two years 2000–2001 was maintained at US $650m., the same amount as was approved for the previous biennium. Much of FAO's technical assistance programme is funded from extra-budgetary sources. The single largest contributor is the United Nations Development Programme (UNDP), which in 1999 accounted for $26m., or 8.7% of field project expenditures. More important are the trust funds that come mainly from donor countries and international financing institutions. They totalled $228m., or 76.5% of field project expenditures in 1999. FAO's contribution under the TCP (FAO's regular budgetary funds for the Field Programme) was $39m., or 13% of field project expenditures, while the Organization's contribution under the Special Programme for Food Security was $5m., or some 1.7% of the total $298m.

Publications

Animal Health Yearbook.

Commodity Review and Outlook (annually).

Environment and Energy Bulletin.

Fertilizer Yearbook.

Food Crops and Shortages (6 a year).

Food Outlook (5 a year).

Plant Protection Bulletin (quarterly).

Production Yearbook.

Quarterly Bulletin of Statistics.

The State of Food and Agriculture (annually).

The State of Food Insecurity in the World (annually).

The State of World Fisheries and Aquaculture (every two years).

The State of the World's Forests (every 2 years).
Trade Yearbook.
Unasylva (quarterly).
Yearbook of Fishery Statistics.

Yearbook of Forest Products.
World Animal Review (quarterly).
World Watch List for Domestic Animal Diversity.
Commodity reviews; studies; manuals.

International Atomic Energy Agency—IAEA

Address: POB 100, Wagramerstrasse 5, 1400 Vienna, Austria.
Telephone: (1) 26000; **fax:** (1) 26007; **e-mail:** official.mail@iaea.org; **internet:** www.iaea.org/worldatom.

The International Atomic Energy Agency (IAEA) is an intergovernmental organization, established in 1957 in accordance with a decision of the General Assembly of the United Nations. Although it is autonomous, the IAEA is administratively a member of the United Nations, and reports on its activities once a year to the UN General Assembly. Its main objectives are to enlarge the contribution of atomic energy to peace, health and prosperity throughout the world and to ensure, so far as it is able, that assistance provided by it or at its request or under its supervision or control is not used in such a way as to further any military purpose.

MEMBERS

131 members: see Table on pp. 117–119.

Organization

(April 2001)

GENERAL CONFERENCE

The Conference, comprising representatives of all member states, convenes each year for general debate on the Agency's policy, budget and programme. It elects members to the Board of Governors, and approves the appointment of the Director-General; it admits new member states.

BOARD OF GOVERNORS

The Board of Governors consists of 35 member states: 22 elected by the General Conference for two-year periods and 13 designated by the Board from among member states which are advanced in nuclear technology. It is the principal policy-making body of the Agency and is responsible to the General Conference. Under its own authority, the Board approves all safeguards agreements, important projects and safety standards. In 1999 the General Conference adopted a resolution on expanding the Board's membership to 43, to include 18 states designated as the most advanced in nuclear technology. The resolution required ratification by two-thirds of member states to come into effect.

SECRETARIAT

The Secretariat, comprising about 2,200 staff, is headed by the Director-General, who is assisted by six Deputy Directors-General. The Secretariat is divided into six departments: Technical Co-operation; Nuclear Energy; Nuclear Safety; Nuclear Sciences and Applications; Safeguards; Administration. A Standing Advisory Group on Safeguards Implementation advises the Director-General on technical aspects of safeguards.

Director-General: Dr MOHAMMAD EL-BARADEI (Egypt).

Activities

The IAEA's functions can be divided into two main categories: technical co-operation (assisting research on and practical application of atomic energy for peaceful uses); and safeguards (ensuring that special fissionable and other materials, services, equipment and information made available by the Agency or at its request or under its supervision are not used for any military purpose).

TECHNICAL CO-OPERATION AND TRAINING

The IAEA provides assistance in the form of experts, training and equipment to technical co-operation projects and applications worldwide, with an emphasis on radiation protection and safety-related activities. Training is provided to scientists, and experts and lecturers are assigned to provide specialized help on specific nuclear applications.

FOOD AND AGRICULTURE

In co-operation with FAO (q.v.), the Agency conducts programmes of applied research on the use of radiation and isotopes in fields including: efficiency in the use of water and fertilizers; improvement of food crops by induced mutations; eradication or control of destructive insects by the introduction of sterilized insects (radiation-based Sterile Insect Technique); improvement of livestock nutrition and health; studies on improving efficacy and reducing residues of pesticides, and increasing utilization of agricultural wastes; and food preservation by irradiation. The programmes are implemented by the Joint FAO/IAEA Division of Nuclear Techniques in Food and Agriculture and by the FAO/IAEA Agriculture Biotechnology Laboratory, based at Seibersdorf, Austria. A new laboratory at Seibersdorf, which was to serve as a Training and Reference Centre for food and pesticide-control activities, opened in mid-1999. The Centre was to support the implementation of national legislation and trade agreements ensuring the quality and safety of food products in international trade.

LIFE SCIENCES

In co-operation with the World Health Organization (WHO, q.v.), IAEA promotes the use of nuclear techniques in medicine, biology and health-related environmental research, provides training, and conducts research on techniques for improving the accuracy of radiation dosimetry.

In 1999 IAEA/WHO Network of Secondary Standard Dosimetry Laboratories (SSDLs) comprised 87 laboratories in 58 member states. The Agency's Dosimetry Laboratory performs dose inter-comparisons for both SSDLs and radiotherapy centres. The IAEA undertakes maintenance plans for nuclear laboratories; national programmes of quality control for nuclear medicine instruments; quality control of radioimmunoassay techniques; radiation sterilization of medical supplies; and improvement of cancer therapy.

PHYSICAL SCIENCES AND LABORATORIES

The Agency's programme in physical sciences includes industrial applications of isotopes and radiation technology; application of nuclear techniques to mineral exploration and exploitation; radio-pharmaceuticals; and hydrology, involving the use of isotope techniques for assessment of water resources. Nuclear data services are provided, and training is given for nuclear scientists from developing countries. The IAEA Laboratory at Seibersdorf, Austria, supports the Agency's research, radio-isotope and agriculture programmes, while the Safeguards Analytical Laboratory analyses nuclear fuel-cycle samples collected by IAEA safeguards inspectors. The IAEA Marine Environment Laboratory, in Monaco, studies radionuclides and other ocean pollutants. In July 1992 the EC, Japan, Russia and the USA signed an agreement to co-operate in the engineering design of an International Thermonuclear Experimental Reactor (ITER). The project aimed to demonstrate the scientific and technological feasibility of fusion energy, with the aim of providing a source of clean, abundant energy in the 21st century. An Extension Agreement, signed in 1998, provided for the continuation of the project.

NUCLEAR POWER

At the end of 1999 there were 433 nuclear power plants in operation in 32 countries throughout the world, with a total generating capacity of 349,063 MW, providing 2,401,160m. kWh. There were also 37 reactors under construction, in 14 countries. The Agency helps developing member states to introduce nuclear-powered electricity-generating plants through assistance with planning, feasibility studies, surveys of manpower and infrastructure, and safety measures. It publishes books on numerous aspects of nuclear power, and provides training courses on safety in nuclear power plants and other topics. An energy data bank collects and disseminates information on nuclear technology, and a power-reactor information system monitors the technical performance of nuclear power plants. There is increasing interest in the use of nuclear reactors for seawater desalination and radiation hydrology techniques to provide potable water.

RADIOACTIVE WASTE MANAGEMENT

The Agency provides practical help to member states in the management of radioactive waste. The Waste Management Advisory Programme (WAMAP) was established in 1987, and undertakes advisory missions in member states. A code of practice to prevent the illegal dumping of radioactive waste was drafted in 1989, and another on the international trans-boundary movement of waste was drafted in 1990. A ban on the dumping of radioactive waste at sea came into effect in February 1994, under the Convention on the Prevention of Marine Pollution by Dumping of Wastes and Other Matters (see IMO, p. 92). The IAEA was to determine radioactive levels, for purposes of the Convention, and provide assistance to countries for the safe disposal of radioactive wastes.

In September 1997 a Joint Convention on the Safety of Spent Fuel Management and on the Safety of Radioactive Waste Management was opened for signature. The first internationally-binding legal device to address such issues, the Convention was to ensure the safe storage and disposal of nuclear and radioactive waste, during both the construction and operation of a nuclear power plant, as well as following its closure. The Convention was to come into force 90 days after being ratified by 25 member states, 15 of which were to be in possession of an operational nuclear reactor. By mid-March 2001 these conditions had been met, ensuring the Convention's entry into force in June.

NUCLEAR SAFETY

The IAEA's nuclear safety programme encourages international co-operation in the exchange of information, promoting implementation of its safety standards and providing advisory safety services. It includes the IAEA International Nuclear Event Scale; the Incident Reporting System; an emergency preparedness programme; operational safety review teams; the 15-member International Nuclear Safety Advisory Group (INSAG); the Radiation Protection Advisory Team; and a safety research co-ordination programme. The safety review teams provide member states with advice on achieving and maintaining a high level of safety in the operation of nuclear power plants, while research programmes establish risk criteria for the nuclear fuel cycle and identify cost-effective means to reduce risks in energy systems. By the end of 1998 the review teams had conducted studies of operational safety at 100 plants. At that time 53 member states had agreed to report all nuclear events, incidents and accidents according to the International Nuclear Event Scale. In May the Director-General initiated a review of the Agency's nuclear strategy, proposing the development of national safety profiles, more active promotion of safety services and improved co-operation at governmental and non-governmental levels.

The revised edition of the Basic Safety Standards for Radiation Protection (IAEA Safety Series No. 9) was approved in 1994. The Nuclear Safety Standards programme, initiated in 1974 with five codes of practice and more than 60 safety guides, was revised in 1987 and again in 1995.

During 1998 there were some 250 technical co-operation projects under way in the field of nuclear safety and radiation protection. Missions visited about 50 countries to assist with radiation protection.

Following a serious accident at the Chornobyl (Chernobyl) nuclear power plant in Ukraine (then part of the USSR) in April 1986, two conventions were formulated by the IAEA and entered into force in October. The first, the Convention on Early Notification of a Nuclear Accident, commits parties to provide information about nuclear accidents with possible trans-boundary effects at the earliest opportunity (it had 85 parties by October 2000); and the second commits parties to endeavour to provide assistance in the event of a nuclear accident or radiological emergency (it had 81 parties by October 2000). During 1990 the IAEA organized an assessment of the consequences of the Chernobyl accident, undertaken by an international team of experts, who reported to an international conference on the effects of the accident, convened at the IAEA headquarters in Vienna in May 1991. In February 1993 INSAG published an updated report on the Chernobyl incident, which emphasized the role of design factors in the accident, and the need to implement safety measures in the RBMK-type reactor. In March 1994 an IAEA expert mission visited Chernobyl and reported continuing serious deficiencies in safety at the defunct reactor and the units remaining in operation. An international conference reviewing the radiological consequences of the accident, 10 years after the event, was held in April 1996, co-sponsored by the IAEA, WHO and the European Commission. Concerns over the reactor's safety persisted in 1998. The last of the Chernobyl plant's three operating units was officially closed in December 2000. The IAEA was to offer a wide range of assistance during Chernobyl's decommissioning period, the first stage of which was expected to have a duration of five years.

At the end of September 1999 the IAEA activated an Emergency Response Centre, following a serious incident at a fuel conversion facility in Tokaimura, Japan. The Centre was used to process information from the Japanese authorities and to ensure accurate reporting of the event. In mid-October a three-member IAEA team of experts visited the site to undertake a preliminary investigation into the causes and consequences of the accident.

An International Convention on Nuclear Safety was adopted at an IAEA conference in June 1994. The Convention applies to land-based civil nuclear power plants: adherents commit themselves to fundamental principles of safety, and maintain legislative frameworks governing nuclear safety. The Convention entered into force in October 1996, after having been signed by 65 states and ratified or otherwise approved by 26 states. The first Review Meeting of Contracting Parties to the Convention was held in April 1999. By October 2000 53 states had ratified the Convention.

In September 1997 more than 80 member states adopted a protocol to revise the 1963 Vienna Convention on Civil Liability for Nuclear Damage, fixing the minimum limit of liability for the operator of a nuclear reactor at 300m. Special Drawing Rights (SDRs, the accounting units of the IMF) in the event of an accident. The amended protocol also extended the length of time during which claims may be brought for loss of life or injury. The amended protocol had been signed by 14 countries and ratified by two at October 2000. A Convention on Supplementary Compensation for Nuclear Damage established a further compensatory fund to provide for the payment of damages following an accident; contributions to the Fund were to be calculated on the basis of the nuclear capacity of each member state. The Convention had 13 signatories and two contracting states by October 2000.

In July 1996 the IAEA co-ordinated a study on the radiological situation at the Mururoa and Fangatauta atolls, following the French nuclear test programmes in the South Pacific. Results published in May 1998 concluded there was no radiological health risk and that neither remedial action nor continued environmental monitoring was necessary.

The IAEA is developing a training course on measurement methods and risk analysis relating to the presence of depleted uranium (which can be used in ammunition) in post-conflict areas. In November 2000 IAEA specialists participated in a fact-finding mission organized by UNEP in Kosovo and Metohija, which aimed to assess the environmental and health consequences of the use of depleted uranium in ammunition by NATO during its aerial offensive against the Federal Republic of Yugoslavia in 1999.

DISSEMINATION OF INFORMATION

The International Nuclear Information System (INIS), which was established in 1970, provides a computerized indexing and abstracting service. Information on the peaceful uses of atomic energy is collected by member states and international organizations and sent to the IAEA for processing and dissemination (see list of publications below). The IAEA also co-operates with the FAO in an information system for agriculture (AGRIS) and with the World Federation of Nuclear Medicine and Biology, and the non-profit Cochrane Collaboration, in maintaining an electronic database of best practice in nuclear medicine. The IAEA Nuclear Data Section provides cost-free data centre services and co-operates with other national and regional nuclear and atomic data centres in the systematic world-wide collection, compilation, dissemination and exchange of nuclear reaction data, nuclear structure and decay data, and atomic and molecular data for fusion.

SAFEGUARDS

The Treaty on the Non-Proliferation of Nuclear Weapons (known also as the Non-Proliferation Treaty or NPT), which entered into force in 1970, requires each non-nuclear-weapon state (one which had not manufactured and exploded a nuclear weapon or other nuclear explosive device prior to 1 January 1967) which is a party to the Treaty to conclude a safeguards agreement with the IAEA. Under such an agreement, the state undertakes to accept IAEA safeguards on all nuclear material in all its peaceful nuclear activities for the purpose of verifying that such material is not diverted to nuclear weapons or other nuclear explosive devices. In May 1995 the Review and Extension Conference of parties to the NPT agreed to extend the NPT indefinitely, and reaffirmed support for the IAEA's role in verification and the transfer of peaceful nuclear technologies. At the next review conference, held in April/May 2000, the five nuclear-weapon states (see below) issued a joint statement pledging their commitment to the ultimate goal of complete nuclear disarmament under effective international controls. By January 2000 182 non-nuclear-weapon states and the five nuclear-weapon states had ratified and acceded to the Treaty, but a number of non-nuclear-weapon states had not complied, within the prescribed time-limit, with their obligations under the Treaty regarding the conclusion of the relevant safeguards agreement with the Agency.

The five nuclear-weapon states—the People's Republic of China, France, Russia, the United Kingdom and the USA—have concluded safeguards agreements with the Agency that permit the application of IAEA safeguards to all their nuclear activities, excluding those with 'direct national significance'. A Comprehensive Nuclear Test Ban Treaty (CTBT) was opened for signature in September 1996, having been adopted by the UN General Assembly. The Treaty was to enter into international law upon ratification by all 44 nations with known nuclear capabilities. A separate verification organization was to be established, based in Vienna. A Preparatory Commission for the treaty organization became operational in 1997. By March 2001 160 countries had signed the CTBT and 75 had ratified it, including 31 of the 44 states with nuclear capabilities. However, in October 1999 the US Senate rejected ratification of the CTBT.

The IAEA administers full applications of safeguards in relation to the Treaty for the prohibition of Nuclear Weapons in Latin America (Tlatelolco Treaty). By late 1998 31 of the 32 states party to the Tlatelolco Treaty had concluded safeguards agreements with the IAEA, as had all 11 signatories of the South Pacific Nuclear-Free Zone Treaty (Rarotonga Treaty). NPT safeguards agreements were in force with seven of the nine States party to the Treaty in the South-East Asia Nuclear-Weapon Free Zone (Treaty of Bangkok). In April 1996 an African Nuclear-Weapon Free Zone Treaty (the Pelindaba Treaty) was signed by 43 states at a ceremony in Cairo, Egypt. The IAEA provided technical and legal advice during the negotiations on the Treaty, which committed countries to renouncing the development, acquisition, testing or stationing of nuclear arms on their territories and prohibited all dumping of imported radioactive waste. The Treaty, as with the NPT and the other regional treaties, required and relied upon the IAEA safeguards systems. At the end of 1999 safeguards agreements were in force with 141 states. Of these, 71 states had declared nuclear activities and were under inspection.

In April 1992 the Democratic People's Republic of Korea (DPRK) ratified a safeguards agreement with the IAEA. In late 1992 and early 1993, however, the IAEA unsuccessfully requested access to two non-declared sites in the DPRK, where it was suspected that material capable of being used for the manufacture of nuclear weapons was stored. In March 1993 the DPRK announced its intention of withdrawing from the NPT: it suspended its withdrawal in June, but continued to refuse full access to its nuclear facilities for IAEA inspectors. In May 1994 the DPRK began to refuel an experimental nuclear power reactor at Yongbyon, but refused to allow the IAEA to analyse the spent fuel rods in order to ascertain whether plutonium had been obtained from the reactor for possible military use. In June the IAEA Board of Governors halted IAEA technical assistance to the DPRK (except medical assistance) because of continuous violation of the NPT safeguards agreements. In the same month the DPRK withdrew from the IAEA (though not from the NPT); however, it allowed IAEA inspectors to remain at the Yongbyon site to conduct safeguards activites. In October the Governments of the DPRK and the USA concluded an agreement whereby the former agreed to halt construction of two new nuclear reactors, on condition that it received international aid for the construction of two 'light water' reactors (which could not produce materials for the manufacture of nuclear weapons). The DPRK also agreed to allow IAEA inspections of all its nuclear sites, but only after the installation of one of the 'light water' reactors had been completed, a time lapse of at least five years. In November IAEA inspectors visited the DPRK to initiate verification of the suspension of the country's nuclear programme, in accordance with the agreement concluded in the previous month. Since 1995 the IAEA has pursued technical discussions with the DPRK authorities as part of the Agency's efforts to achieve the full compliance of the DPRK with the IAEA safeguards agreement. By the end of 1999 the canning of spent fuel rods from the Yongbyon nuclear power reactor was completed. However, little overall progress had been achieved, owing to the obstruction of inspectors by the authorities in that country, including their refusal to provide samples for analysis. The IAEA was unable to verify the suspension of the nuclear programme and declared that the DPRK continued to be in non-compliance with its NPT safeguards agreement. In March 1999 the USA concluded an accord with the DPRK to provide for inspection of a suspected nuclear facility near Yongbyon. Further negotiations were to be pursued to restrict the country's missile production programme.

In April 1991 the UN Security Council requested the IAEA to conduct investigations into Iraq's capacity to produce nuclear weapons, following the end of the war between Iraq and the UN-authorized, US-led multinational force. The IAEA was to work closely with a UN Special Commission of experts (UNSCOM, q.v.), established by the Security Council, whose task was to inspect and dismantle Iraq's weapons of mass destruction (including chemical and biological weapons). In July the IAEA declared that Iraq had violated its safeguards agreement with the IAEA by not submitting nuclear material and relevant facilities in its uranium-enrichment programme to the Agency's inspection. This was the first time that a state party to the NPT had been condemned for concealing a programme of this nature. In October the sixth inspection team, composed of UNSCOM and representatives of the IAEA, was reported to have obtained conclusive documentary evidence that Iraq had a programme for developing nuclear weapons. By February 1994 all declared stocks of nuclear-weapons-grade material had been removed from Iraq. Subsequently, the IAEA pursued a programme of long-term surveillance of nuclear activity in Iraq, under a mandate issued by the UN Security Council. In September 1996 Iraq sub-

mitted to the IAEA a 'full, final and complete' declaration of its nuclear activities. However, in September–October 1997 the IAEA recommended that Iraq disclose further equipment, materials and information relating to its nuclear programme. In April 1998 IAEA technical experts were part of a special group that entered eight presidential sites in Iraq to collect baseline data, in accordance with a Memorandum of Understanding concluded between the UN Secretary-General and the Iraqi authorities in February. The accord aimed to ensure full Iraqi co-operation with UNSCOM and IAEA personnel. In August, however, Iraq suspended co-operation with UN inspectors, which prevented IAEA from implementing its programme of ongoing monitoring and verification (OMV) activities. Iraq's action was condemned by the IAEA General Conference in September. In October IAEA reported that while there was no evidence of Iraq having produced nuclear weapons or having retained or obtained a capability for the production of nuclear weapons, the Agency was unable to guarantee that all items had been found. All IAEA inspectors were temporarily relocated from Iraq to Bahrain in November, in accordance with a decision to withdraw UNSCOM personnel owing to Iraq's failure to agree to resume co-operation. In March 2000 UNSCOM was replaced by a new arms inspection body, the UN Monitoring, Verification and Inspection Commission (UNMOVIC). Although the IAEA carried out an inventory verification of nuclear material at a site in Iraq in January 2000, pursuant to Iraq's NTP safeguards agreement, full inspection activities in conjunction with UNMOVIC remained suspended in early 2001.

In late 1997 the IAEA began inspections in the USA to verify the conversion for peaceful uses of nuclear material released from the military sector. In 1998 the United Kingdom announced that substantial quantities of nuclear material previously in its military programme would become available for verification under its voluntary offer safeguards agreement.

At the end of 1999 there were 900 nuclear facilities and locations containing nuclear material subject to IAEA safeguards. Of these, 587 were inspected in 1999, in a total of 2,495 inspections. Expenditure on the Safeguards Regular Budget for that year was US $92.8m., including extrabudgetary funds of $13.8m.

In June 1995 the Board of Governors approved measures to strengthen the safeguards system, including allowing inspection teams greater access to suspected nuclear sites and to information on nuclear activities in member states, reducing the notice time for inspections by removing visa requirements for inspectors and using environmental monitoring (i.e. soil, water and air samples) to test for signs of radioactivity. In April 1996 the IAEA initiated a programme to prevent and combat illicit trafficking of nuclear weapons, and in May 1998 the IAEA and the World Customs Organization (q.v.) signed a Memorandum of Understanding to enhance co-operation in the prevention of illicit nuclear trafficking. In May 1997 the Board of Governors adopted a model additional protocol approving measures to strengthen safeguards further, in order to ensure the compliance of non-nuclear-weapon states with IAEA commitments. The new protocol compelled member states to provide inspection teams with improved access to information concerning existing and planned nuclear activities, and to allow access to locations other than known nuclear sites within that country's territory. By March 2001 18 states had ratified additional protocols to their safeguards agreements.

NUCLEAR FUEL CYCLE

The Agency promotes the exchange of information between member states on technical, safety, environmental, and economic aspects of nuclear fuel cycle technology, including uranium prospecting and the treatment and disposal of radioactive waste; it provides assistance to member states in the planning, implementation and operation of nuclear fuel cycle facilities and assists in the development of advanced nuclear fuel cycle technology. Every two years, in collaboration with the OECD, the Agency prepares estimates of world uranium resources, demand and production.

Finance

The Agency is financed by regular and voluntary contributions from member states. Expenditure approved under the regular budget for 2000 amounted to some US $221.7m., and the target for voluntary contributions to finance the IAEA technical assistance and co-operation programme in 2000 was $73m. Expenditure approved under the regular budget for 2001 totalled $230.0m.

Publications

Annual Report.

IAEA Bulletin (quarterly).

IAEA Newsbriefs (every 2 months).

International Bank for Reconstruction and Development—IBRD (World Bank)

Address: 1818 H St, NW, Washington, DC 20433, USA.
Telephone: (202) 477-1234; **fax:** (202) 477-6391; **e-mail:** pic@worldbank.org; **internet:** www.worldbank.org.

The IBRD was established in December 1945. Initially it was concerned with post-war reconstruction in Europe; since then its aim has been to assist the economic development of member nations by making loans where private capital is not available on reasonable terms to finance productive investments. Loans are made either directly to governments, or to private enterprises with the guarantee of their governments. The World Bank, as it is commonly known, comprises the IBRD and the International Development Association (IDA, q.v.). The affiliated group of institutions, comprising the IBRD, the IDA, the International Finance Corporation (IFC, q.v.), the Multilateral Investment Guarantee Agency (MIGA, q.v.) and the International Centre for Settlement of Investment Disputes (ICSID, see below), is now referred to as the World Bank Group.

MEMBERS

There are 182 members: see Table on pp. 117–119. Only members of the International Monetary Fund (IMF, q.v.) may be considered for membership in the World Bank. Subscriptions to the capital stock of the Bank are based on each member's quota in the IMF, which is designed to reflect the country's relative economic strength. Voting rights are related to shareholdings.

Organization

(April 2001)

Officers and staff of the IBRD serve concurrently as officers and staff in the IDA. The World Bank has offices in Brussels, New York, Paris, London and Tokyo; regional missions in Nairobi (for eastern Africa) and Abidjan (for western Africa); and resident missions in more than 70 countries.

BOARD OF GOVERNORS

The Board of Governors consists of one Governor appointed by each member nation. Typically, a Governor is the country's finance minister, central bank governor, or a minister or an official of comparable rank. The Board normally meets once a year.

EXECUTIVE DIRECTORS

With the exception of certain powers specifically reserved to them by the Articles of Agreement, the Governors of the Bank have delegated their powers for the conduct of the general operations of the World Bank to a Board of Executive Directors which performs its duties on a full-time basis at the Bank's headquarters. There are 24 Executive Directors (see table below); each Director selects an Alternate. Five Directors are appointed by the five members having the largest number of shares of capital stock, and the rest are elected by the Governors representing the other members. The President of the Bank is Chairman of the Board.

The Executive Directors fulfil dual responsibilities. First, they represent the interests of their country or groups of countries. Second, they exercise their authority as delegated by the Governors in overseeing the policies of the Bank and evaluating completed projects. Since the Bank operates on the basis of consensus (formal votes are rare), this dual role involves frequent communication and consultations with governments so as to reflect accurately their views in Board discussions.

The Directors consider and decide on Bank policy and on all loan and credit proposals. They are also responsible for presentation to the Board of Governors at its Annual Meetings of an audit of accounts, an administrative budget, the *Annual Report* on the operations and policies of the World Bank, and any other matter that, in their judgement, requires submission to the Board of Governors. Matters may be submitted to the Governors at the Annual Meetings or at any time between Annual Meetings.

OFFICE OF THE PRESIDENT

President and Chairman of Executive Directors: JAMES D. WOLFENSOHN (USA).

Managing Directors: SVEN SANDSTRÖM (Sweden), SHENGMAN ZHANG (People's Republic of China), PETER L. WOICKE (Germany), JEFFREY GOLDSTEIN (USA), Dr MAMPHELA RAMPHELE (South Africa).

Corporate Secretary: CHEIKH IBRAHIMA FALL (Senegal).

OFFICES

New York Office and World Bank Mission to the United Nations: 809 United Nations Plaza, Suite 900, New York, NY 10017, USA; Special Rep. to UN CARLSTON B. BOUCHER.

European Office: 66 ave d'Iéna, 75116 Paris, France.

Brussels Office: 10 rue Montoyer, bte 16, 1000 Brussels, Belgium.

London Office: New Zealand House, 15th Floor, Haymarket, London, SW1Y 4TE, United Kingdom; Special Rep. to the UK, Ireland and OECD ANDREW ROGERSON.

Regional Mission in Eastern Africa: POB 30577, Nairobi; Hill Park Bldg, Upper Hill, Nairobi, Kenya; Chief HAROLD E. WACKMAN.

Regional Mission in Western Africa: angle rues Booker Washington/Jacques Aka, Cocody, BP 1850, Abidjan 01, Côte d'Ivoire; Chief SHIGEO KATSU.

Tokyo Office: Fukoku Seimei Bldg, 10th Floor, 2-2-2 Uchisaiwai-cho, Chiyoda-ku, Tokyo 100-0011, Japan; Dir SHUZO NAKAMURA.

Activities

FINANCIAL OPERATIONS

IBRD capital is derived from members' subscriptions to capital shares, the calculation of which is based on their quotas in the International Monetary Fund (q.v.). At 30 June 2000 the total subscribed capital of the IBRD was US $188,606m., of which the paid-in portion was $11,418m. (6.1%); the remainder is subject to call if required. Most of the IBRD's lendable funds come from its borrowing, on commercial terms, in world capital markets, and also from its retained earnings and the flow of repayments on its loans. IBRD loans carry a variable interest rate, rather than a rate fixed at the time of borrowing.

IBRD loans usually have a 'grace period' of five years and are repayable over 15 years or fewer. Loans are made to governments, or must be guaranteed by the government concerned, and are normally made for projects likely to offer a commercially viable rate of return. In 1980 the World Bank introduced structural adjustment lending, which (instead of financing specific projects) supports programmes and changes necessary to modify the structure of an economy so that it can restore or maintain its growth and viability in its balance of payments over the medium term.

The IBRD and IDA together made 223 new lending and investment commitments totalling US $15,276.2m. during the year ending 30 June 2000, compared with 276 (amounting to $28,994.1m.) in the previous year. During 1999/2000 the IBRD alone approved commitments totalling $10,918.6m. (compared with $22,182.3m. in the previous year), of which $3,898.1m. was allocated to Latin America and the Caribbean, $2,733.1m. to Europe and Central Asia, and $2,495.3m. to East Asia and the Pacific (see table). The largest borrower of IBRD funds in 1999/2000 was Turkey ($1,769.6m. for four projects), followed by the People's Republic of China ($1,672.5m.

EXECUTIVE DIRECTORS AND THEIR VOTING POWER (30 June 2000)

Executive Director	Casting Votes of	IBRD		IDA	
		Total votes	% of total	Total votes	% of total
Appointed:					
JAN PIERCY	USA	265,219	16.50	1,818,989	14.86
YUZO HARADA	Japan	127,250	7.92	1,301,679	10.63
HELMUT SCHAFFER	Germany	72,649	4.53	820,259	7.04
JEAN-CLAUDE MILLERON	France	69,647	4.34	497,297	4.27
STEPHEN PICKFORD	United Kingdom	69,647	4.34	582,514	5.00
Elected:					
RUTH BACHMAYER (Austria)	Austria, Belarus*, Belgium, Czech Republic, Hungary, Kazakhstan, Luxembourg, Slovakia, Slovenia, Turkey	76,720	4.77	522,649	4.27
PIETER STEK (Netherlands)	Armenia, Bosnia and Herzegovina, Bulgaria*, Croatia, Cyprus, Georgia, Israel, the former Yugoslav republic of Macedonia, Moldova, Netherlands, Romania*, Ukraine*	72,208	4.49	440,131	3.59
FEDERICO FERRER (Spain)	Costa Rica, El Salvador, Guatemala, Honduras, Mexico, Nicaragua, Panama, Spain, Venezuela*	68,475	4.26	252,488	2.06
TERRIE O'LEARY (Canada)	Antigua and Barbuda*, The Bahamas*, Barbados*, Belize, Canada, Dominica, Grenada, Guyana, Ireland, Jamaica*, Saint Christopher and Nevis, Saint Lucia, Saint Vincent and the Grenadines	62,217	3.87	519,218	4.24
MURILO PORTUGAL (Brazil)	Brazil, Colombia, Dominican Republic, Ecuador, Haiti, Philippines, Suriname*, Trinidad and Tobago	58,124	3.62	351,067	2.87
NEIL HYDEN (Australia)	Australia, Cambodia, Kiribati, Republic of Korea, Marshall Islands, Federated States of Micronesia, Mongolia, New Zealand, Papua New Guinea, Samoa, Solomon Islands,Vanuatu	55,800	3.47	368,942	3.01
GODFREY GAOSEB (Namibia)	Angola, Botswana, Burundi, Eritrea, Ethiopia, The Gambia, Kenya, Lesotho, Liberia, Malawi, Mozambique, Namibia*, Nigeria, Seychelles*, Sierra Leone, South Africa, Sudan, Swaziland, Tanzania, Uganda, Zambia, Zimbabwe	55,190	3.43	498,975	4.07
FRANCO PASSACANTANDO (Italy)	Albania, Greece, Italy, Malta*, Portugal	55,093	3.43	465,078	3.80
B. P. SINGH (India)†	Bangladesh, Bhutan, India, Sri Lanka	54,945	3.42	542,462	4.63
INAAMUL HAQUE (Pakistan)	Algeria, Ghana, Iran, Iraq, Morocco, Pakistan, Tunisia	54,052	3.36	248,528	2.03
FINN JØNCK (Denmark)†	Denmark, Estonia*, Finland, Iceland, Latvia, Lithuania*, Norway, Sweden	54,039	3.36	596,791	4.87
MATTHIAS MEYER (Switzerland)	Azerbaijan, Kyrgyzstan, Poland, Switzerland, Tajikistan, Turkmenistan*, Uzbekistan	46,096	2.87	413,995	3.38
ZHU XIAN	People's Republic of China	45,049	2.80	247,345	2.02
YAHYA ALYAHYA	Saudi Arabia	45,045	2.80	428,763	3.50
ANDREI BUGROV	Russia	45,045	2.80	34,397	0.28
KHALID AL-SAAD (Kuwait)	Bahrain*, Egypt, Jordan, Kuwait, Lebanon, Libya, Maldives, Oman, Qatar*, Syria, United Arab Emirates, Yemen	43,984	2.74	281,262	2.30
JANNES HUTAGALUNG (Indonesia)	Brunei*, Fiji, Indonesia, Laos, Malaysia, Myanmar, Nepal, Singapore*, Thailand, Tonga, Viet Nam	41,096	2.56	343,193	2.80
VALERIANO F. GARCÍA (Argentina)	Argentina, Bolivia, Chile, Paraguay, Peru, Uruguay*	37,499	2.33	230,533	1.88
BASSARY TOURÉ (Mali)	Benin, Burkina Faso, Cameroon, Cape Verde, Central African Republic, Chad, Comoros, Democratic Republic of the Congo, Republic of the Congo, Côte d'Ivoire, Djibouti, Equatorial Guinea, Gabon, Guinea, Guinea-Bissau, Madagascar, Mali, Mauritania, Mauritius, Niger, Rwanda, São Tomé and Príncipe, Senegal, Togo	32,252	2.01	368,063	3.01

Note: Afghanistan (550 votes in IBRD and 13,557 in IDA) and Somalia (802 votes in IBRD and 10,506 in IDA) did not participate in the 1998 regular election of Executive Directors; Palau (266 votes in IBRD and 504 in IDA) became a member after that election.

* Member of IBRD only (not IDA).

† Took office 7 August 2000.

for eight projects). Disbursements by the IBRD in the year ending 30 June 2000 amounted to $13,332m., compared with $18,205m. in the previous year. (For details of IDA operations, see separate chapter on IDA.) The reduction in lending in 1999/2000 was attributed to recovery from the effects of the economic crisis that erupted in Asia in mid-1997.

IBRD operations are supported by medium- and long-term borrowings in international capital markets. During the year ending 30 June 2000 the IBRD's net income amounted to US $1,991m.

The World Bank's primary objectives are the achievement of sustainable economic growth and the reduction of poverty in developing countries. In the context of stimulating economic growth the Bank promotes both private-sector development and human resource development and has attempted to respond to the growing demands by developing countries for assistance in these areas. The Bank's efforts to reduce poverty comprise two main elements: the compiling of country-specific assessments and the formulation of country assistance strategies (CASs) to review and guide the Bank's country programmes. Since August 1998 the Bank has published CASs, with the approval of the government concerned. In 1996/97 the Bank established a Poverty Sector Board, within the Poverty Reduction and Economic Management Network (see below), to direct the implementation of its poverty reduction efforts. A Committee

on Development Effectiveness addresses issues relating to the relevance and effectiveness of operations and monitors implementation of decisions taken by the Board of Governors on these matters.

In March 1997 the Board of Executive Directors endorsed a 'Strategic Compact', providing for a programme of reforms, to be implemented over a period of 30 months, to increase the effectiveness of the Bank in achieving its central objective of poverty reduction. The reforms, which aimed to increase the proportion of projects rated as satisfactory in development terms from 66% to 75% included greater decentralization of decision-making, and investment in front-line operations, enhancing the administration of loans, and improving access to information and co-ordination of Bank activities through a knowledge management system comprising four thematic networks: the Human Development Network; the Environmentally and Socially Sustainable Development Network; the Finance, Private Sector and Infrastructure Development Network; and the Poverty Reduction and Economic Management Network. In July the World Bank initiated a review to assess the economic and social impact of its work in developing countries. During 1997/98 the extreme financial difficulties confronting several Asian economies tested the Bank's capacity to respond effectively to major financial challenges and accelerated its process of internal reform. A Special Financial Operations Unit was established to help to alleviate the consequences of the crisis in all affected countries, while collaboration with external partners was enhanced. In 1998/99 the Bank's Executive Directors endorsed a Comprehensive Development Framework (CDF) to effect a new approach to development assistance based on partnerships and country responsibility, with an emphasis on the interdependence of the social, structural, human, governmental, economic and environmental elements of development. The Framework, which aimed to enhance the overall effectiveness of development assistance, was formulated after a series of consultative meetings, organized by the Bank and attended by representatives of governments, donor agencies, financial institutions, non-governmental organizations, the private sector and academics. By June 2000 13 countries were implementing pilot projects based on the CDF concept. In 1999/2000 the Bank focused strongly on the provision of advisory and analytical services to promote the effective use of its resources in recipient countries.

In June 1995 the World Bank joined other international donors (including regional development banks, other UN bodies, Canada, France, the Netherlands and the USA) in establishing a Consultative Group to Assist the Poorest (CGAP), which was to channel funds to the most needy through grass-roots agencies. An initial credit of approximately US $200m. was committed by the donors. The Bank manages the CGAP Secretariat, which is responsible for the administration of external funding and for the evaluation and approval of project financing. In addition, the CGAP was to provide training and information services on microfinance for policy-makers and practitioners.

In September 1996 the World Bank/IMF Development Committee endorsed a joint initiative to assist heavily indebted poor countries (HIPCs) to reduce their debt burden to a sustainable level, in order to make more resources available for poverty reduction and economic growth. A new Trust Fund was established by the World Bank in November to finance the initiative. The Fund, consisting of an initial allocation of US $500m. from the IBRD surplus and other contributions from multilateral creditors, was to be administered by IDA. Of the 41 HIPCs identified by the Bank, 33 were in sub-Saharan Africa. In April 1997 the World Bank and the IMF announced that Uganda was to be the first beneficiary of the initiative, enabling the Ugandan Government to reduce its external debt by some 20%, or an estimated $338m. In early 1999 the World Bank and IMF initiated a comprehensive review of the HIPC initiative. By April meetings of the Group of Seven industrialized nations (G-7) and of the governing bodies of the Bank and IMF indicated a consensus that the scheme needed to be amended and strengthened, in order to allow more countries to benefit from the initiative, to accelerate the process by which a country may qualify for assistance, and to enhance the effectiveness of debt relief. In June the G-7 and Russia, meeting in Cologne, Germany, agreed to increase contributions to the HIPC Trust Fund and to cancel substantial amounts of outstanding debt, and proposed more flexible terms for eligibility. In September the Bank and IMF reached an agreement on an enhanced HIPC scheme, with further revenue to be generated through the revaluation of a percentage of IMF gold reserves. Under the enhanced initiative it was agreed that, during the initial phase of the process to ensure suitability for debt relief, each applicant country should formulate a national poverty reduction strategy, presented in a Poverty Reduction Strategy Paper (PRSP), and should demonstrate prudent financial management in the implementation of the strategy for at least one year, with support from the IDA and IMF. In cases where there might be some delay in issuing a full PRSP, it was permissible for a country to submit a less detailed 'interim' PRSP (I-PRSP), in which it outlined its intent to compile the full document. PRSPs and I-PRSPs were to be made publicly available on the internet, with the country's consent. At the pivotal 'decision point' of the process, having thus developed and successfully applied the poverty reduction strategy, applicant countries still deemed to have an unsustainable level of debt were to qualify for interim debt relief from the IMF and IDA, as well as relief on highly concessional terms from other official bilateral creditors and multilateral institutions. During the ensuing 'interim period' countries were required successfully to implement further economic and social development reforms, as a final demonstration of suitability for securing full debt relief at the 'completion point' of the scheme. Data produced at the decision point was to form the base for calculating the final debt relief (in contrast to the original initiative, which based its calculations on projections of a country's debt stock at the completion point). In the majority of cases a sustainable level of debt was targeted at 150% of the net present value (NPV) of the debt in relation to total annual exports (compared with 200%–250% under the original initiative). Other countries with a lower debt-to-export ratio were to be eligible for assistance under the scheme, providing that their export earnings were at least 30% of GDP (lowered from 40% under the original initiative) and government revenue at least 15% of GDP (reduced from 20%). In May 2000 Uganda became the first country to reach completion point under the enhanced HIPC initiative. By February 2001 the Bank had reviewed PRSPs produced by four countries (Burkino

Faso, Mauritania, Tanzania and Uganda), and I-PRSPs prepared by 29 countries. Debt relief under the enhanced scheme had at that time been extended to 22 eligible countries, of which 18 were in Africa. Some eligible countries had delayed applying for assistance, owing to ongoing civil conflict or other insecurity. At 30 June 1999 a total of $3,355m. of debt relief in NPV terms had been agreed under the original initiative, of which the Bank's share was $801m.

In 2000 the World Bank, IMF, UN Secretariat and OECD issued a joint report entitled *A Better World for All*, which examined means of addressing the root causes of poverty and assessed the progress made by international institutions towards the achievement of poverty reduction objectives.

TECHNICAL ASSISTANCE

The provision of technical assistance to member countries has become a major component of World Bank activities. The economic sector and project analysis undertaken by the Bank in the normal course of its operations is the vehicle for considerable technical assistance. In addition, project loans and credits may include funds earmarked specifically for feasibility studies, resource surveys, management or planning advice, and training.

The Bank serves as an executing agency for projects financed by the UN Development Programme. It also administers projects financed by various trust funds.

Technical assistance (usually reimbursable) is also extended to countries that do not need Bank financial support, e.g. for training and transfer of technology. The Bank encourages the use of local consultants to assist with projects and stimulate institutional capability.

The Project Preparation Facility (PPF) was established in 1975 to provide cash advances to prepare projects that may be financed by the Bank. In December 1994 the PPF's commitment authority was increased from US $220m. to $250m. In 1992 the Bank established an Institutional Development Fund (IDF), which became operational on 1 July; the purpose of the Fund was to provide rapid, small-scale financial assistance, to a maximum value of $500,000, for capacity-building proposals.

In 1993 a task force was established to consider measures to reduce poverty in sub-Saharan Africa, in consultation with local and national experts, non-governmental organizations and government officials. The task force published its assessment of the situation in December 1996 and recommended that the Bank revise its lending strategy to emphasize poverty-reduction objectives and strengthen systematic monitoring of the poverty situation in all sub-Saharan African countries receiving World Bank assistance.

In March 1996 a new programme to co-ordinate development efforts in Africa was announced by the UN Secretary-General. The World Bank was to facilitate the mobilization of the estimated US $25,000m. required to achieve the objectives of the Special Initiative over a 10-year period. In addition, the Bank was to provide technical assistance to enable countries to devise economic plans (in particular following a period of civil conflict), agricultural development programmes and a common strategy for African countries to strengthen the management capacities of the public sector.

In April 1999 the World Bank and the IMF convened an international meeting of governments and agencies to review the immediate response of the international community to meet the humanitarian, economic and financial needs of the six Balkan countries most affected by the conflict in Kosovo and Metohija, a southern province of Serbia (Federal Republic of Yugoslavia). The meeting also aimed to consider areas for future co-operation and measures to promote economic recovery and growth in those countries.

ECONOMIC RESEARCH AND STUDIES

In the 1990s the World Bank's research, conducted by its own research staff, was increasingly concerned with providing information to reinforce the Bank's expanding advisory role to developing countries and to improve policy in the Bank's borrowing countries. The principal areas of current research focus on issues such as maintaining sustainable growth while protecting the environment and the poorest sectors of society, encouraging the development of the private sector, and reducing and decentralizing government activities.

Consultative Group on International Agricultural Research—CGIAR: founded in 1971 under the sponsorship of the World Bank, FAO and UNDP. The Bank is chairman of the Group (which includes governments, private foundations and multilateral development agencies) and provides its secretariat. In February 1995 UNEP was invited to become the fourth sponsoring member. The Group was formed to raise financial support for international agricultural research work for improving crops and animal production in the developing countries; it supports 16 research centres. Donations to the group's core research agenda totalled US $330m. in 1999. Exec. Sec. ALEXANDER VON DER OSTEN.

CO-OPERATION WITH OTHER ORGANIZATIONS

The World Bank co-operates closely with other UN bodies, at the project level, particularly in the design of social funds and social action programmes. It collaborates with the IMF in implementing economic adjustment programmes in developing countries. The Bank holds regular consultations with the European Union and OECD on development issues, and the Bank-NGO Committee provides an annual forum for discussion with non-governmental organizations (NGOs). In September 1995 the Bank initiated the Information for Development Programme (InfoDev) with the aim of fostering partnerships between governments, multilateral institutions and private-sector experts in order to promote reform and investment in developing countries through improved access to information technology. In 1997 a Partnerships Group was established to strengthen the Bank's work with development institutions, representatives of civil society and the private sector. The Group established a new Development Grant Facility, which became operational in October, to support partnership initiatives and to co-ordinate all of the Bank's grant-making activities. Also in 1997 the Bank, in partnership with the IMF, UNCTAD, UNDP, the World Trade Organization (WTO) and International Trade Commission, established an Integrated Framework for Trade-related Assistance to Least Developed Countries, at the request of the WTO, to assist those countries to integrate into the global trading system and improve basic trading capabilities.

Strengthening co-operation with external partners was a fundamental element of the Comprehensive Development Framework, which was adopted in 1998/99 (see above). During that year the Bank consolidated new partnerships in order to extend an effective international response to the financial crises which had affected several Asian countries from mid-1997. The Bank administered a US $40m. Trust Fund, established by the Asia-Europe Meeting (ASEM, see p. 223) and collaborated closely with the Japanese Government in its provision of assistance under the so-called Miyazawa initiative. In July 1999 the World Bank and European Commission organized an international conference to mobilize funds for post-conflict rehabilitation in Kosovo.

The Bank conducts co-financing and aid co-ordination projects with official aid agencies, export credit institutions, and commercial banks. During the year ending 30 June 1999 a total of 103 IBRD and IDA projects involved co-financers' contributions amounting to US $11,350m.

Global Environment Facility—GEF: founded in 1990 by the World Bank, UNDP and the UN Environment Programme, as a three-year pilot programme designed to provide grants for investment projects and technical assistance. The aim of the GEF is to assist developing countries in implementing projects that benefit the global (not just the local) environment. At the UN Conference on Environment and Development in June 1992, the GEF was recognized, in Agenda 21, as a source of funds to assist with activities benefiting the global environment, and was designated as the operator of the financial mechanism serving the conventions on climate change and biological diversity. In 1994 representatives of 34 countries agreed to provide US $2,000m. to replenish GEF funds. In 1998 36 donor countries pledged $2,750m. for the next replenishment of GEF funds (GEF-2), covering the period 1 July 1998–30 June 2002. Negotiations for the third replenishment commenced in October 2000. At 30 June 2000 the GEF portfolio comprised 165 projects; 94 projects had been completed at that time. CEO and Chair. MOHAMMED EL-ASHRY.

EVALUATION

The World Bank's Operations Evaluation Department studies and publishes the results of projects after a loan has been fully disbursed, so as to identify problems and possible improvements in future activities. A Quality Assurance Group monitors the effectiveness of the Bank's operations and performance.

In September 1993 the Bank's Board of Executive Directors agreed to establish an independent Inspection Panel, consistent with the Bank's objective of improving project implementation and accountability. The panel, which became operational in September 1994, was to conduct independent investigations and report on complaints concerning the design, appraisal and implementation of development projects supported by the Bank. By the end of 1999 the panel had received 14 formal requests for inspection. The three projects reviewed in 1999 concerned land reforms in Brazil, diamond mining

in Lesotho and a poverty reduction scheme in the People's Republic of China.

IBRD INSTITUTIONS

World Bank Institute—WBI: founded in March 1999 by merger of the Bank's Learning and Leadership Centre, previously responsible for internal staff training, and the Economic Development Institute (EDI), which had been established in 1955 to train government officials concerned with development programmes and policies. The new Institute aimed to emphasize the Bank's priority areas through the provision of training courses and seminars relating to poverty, crisis response, good governance and anti-corruption strategies. The Institute was also to take the lead in co-ordinating a process of consultation and dialogue with researchers and other representatives of civil society to examine poverty for a forthcoming *World Development Report*. Activities of the Institute in 1998/99 included a Clean Air Initiative for Latin American Cities, a new training programme for public officials responsible for financial sector supervision, and the establishment of a World Bank Learning Network. Under the EDI a World Links for Development programme was initiated to connect schools in developing countries with partner establishments in industrialized nations via the internet. Dir VINOD THOMAS (India).

International Centre for Settlement of Investment Disputes—ICSID: founded in 1966 under the Convention of the Settlement of Investment Disputes between States and Nationals of Other States. The Convention was designed to encourage the growth of private foreign investment for economic development, by creating the possibility, always subject to the consent of both parties, for a Contracting State and a foreign investor who is a national of another Contracting State to settle any legal dispute that might arise out of such an investment by conciliation and/or arbitration before an impartial, international forum. The governing body of the Centre is its Administrative Council, composed of one representative of each Contracting State, all of whom have equal voting power. The President of the World Bank is (*ex officio*) the non-voting Chairman of the Administrative Council.

At April 2001 133 countries had signed and ratified the Convention to become ICSID Contracting States. In late 2000 the total number of cases registered by the Centre stood at 81, of which 35 were pending. Sec.-Gen. KO-YUNG TUNG (Japan).

Publications

Abstracts of Current Studies: The World Bank Research Program (annually).

Annual Report on Operations Evaluation.

Annual Report on Portfolio Performance.

Annual Review of Development Effectiveness.

EDI Annual Report.

Global Commodity Markets (quarterly).

Global Development Finance (annually, also on CD-Rom).

Global Economic Prospects and Developing Countries (annually).

ICSID Annual Report.

ICSID Review—Foreign Investment Law Journal (2 a year).

Joint BIS-IMF-OECD-World Bank Statistics on External Debt (quarterly, also available on the internet at www.worldbank.org/data/jointdebt.html).

New Products and Outreach (EDI, annually).

News from ICSID (2 a year).

Research News (quarterly).

South Asia Rural Development Series.

Staff Working Papers.

Transition (every 2 months).

World Bank Annual Report.

World Bank Atlas (annually).

World Bank Catalog of Publications.

World Bank Economic Review (3 a year).

The World Bank and the Environment (annually).

World Bank Research Observer.

World Development Indicators (annually, also on CD-Rom).

World Development Report (annually, also on CD-Rom).

World Bank Statistics

LENDING OPERATIONS, BY PURPOSE
(projects approved, year ending 30 June 2000; US $ million)

	IBRD	IDA	Total
Agriculture	768.6	356.6	1,125.2
Economic policy	759.6	527.2	1,286.8
Education	215.3	468.7	684.0
Electric power and other energy	746.5	247.7	994.2
Environment	454.1	60.0	514.1
Finance	1,660.8	167.2	1,828.0
Health, nutrition and population	407.6	579.4	987.0
Mining and other extractive activities	54.5	—	54.5
Petroleum and gas	143.3	23.7	167.0
Private-sector development	5.0	216.3	221.3
Public-sector management	1,806.2	455.9	2,262.1
Social protection	716.6	384.4	1,101.0
Telecommunications	83.3	26.0	109.3
Transportation	1,155.1	534.9	1,690.0
Urban development	587.2	34.4	621.6
Water supply and sanitation	793.9	109.7	903.6
Multisector	561.0	165.5	726.5
Total	10,918.6	4,357.6	15,276.2

IBRD INCOME AND EXPENDITURE
(US $ million, year ending 30 June)

Revenue	1999	2000
Income from loans:		
Interest	7,535	8,041
Commitment charges	114	112
Income from investments and securities	1,975	1,759
Other income	134	133
Total income	9,758	10,045

Expenditure	1999	2000
Interest on borrowings	6,704	6,979
Amortization of issuance and prepayment costs	142	149
Interest on securities sold under repurchase agreements and payable-for-cash collateral received	36	4
Administrative expenses	975	945
Contributions to special programmes	129	126
Provision for loan losses	246	-166
Other financial expenses	8	17
Total	8,240	8,054
Operating income	1,518	1,991
Effects of accounting charge	—	—
Net income	1,518	1,991

IBRD LOANS AND IDA CREDITS APPROVED, BY SECTOR AND REGION (1 July 1999–30 June 2000; US $ million)

Sector	Africa	East Asia and Pacific	South Asia	Europe and Central Asia	Latin America and the Caribbean	Middle East and North Africa	Total
Agriculture	173.6	353.8	60.0	160.6	224.2	153.0	1,125.2
Economic policy	426.3	30.0	45.0	764.6	20.9	—	1,286.8
Education	159.7	5.0	200.0	22.6	77.5	219.2	684.0
Electric power and other energy	42.9	470.0	280.0	196.5	4.8	—	994.2
Environment	16.4	382.7	—	62.4	52.6	—	514.1
Finance	60.4	32.0	65.1	359.0	1,311.5	—	1,828.0
Health, nutrition and population	110.0	119.4	344.6	168.4	157.6	87.0	987.0
Mining and other extractive activities	—	10.0	—	44.5	—	—	54.5
Petroleum and gas	116.6	7.0	—	—	43.4	—	167.0
Private-sector development	200.6	—	—	—	4.8	15.9	221.3
Public-sector management	283.2	490.0	251.2	87.9	1,114.3	35.3	2,262.1
Social protection	139.4	100.0	111.0	35.0	640.6	75.0	1,101.0
Telecommunications	10.2	—	62.0	—	28.2	9.0	109.3
Transportation	256.2	629.2	582.1	207.5	—	15.0	1,690.0
Urban development	10.8	—	10.8	507.0	10.8	82.2	621.6
Water supply and sanitation	87.7	350.0	—	173.6	147.3	145.0	903.6
Multisector	65.0	—	100.5	252.5	225.0	83.5	726.5
Total	2,159.1	2,979.1	2,112.4	3,042.1	4,063.5	920.0	15,276.2
of which: IBRD	97.6	2,495.3	934.2	2,733.1	3,898.1	760.2	10,918.6
IDA	2,061.4	483.8	1,178.1	309.1	165.3	159.8	4,357.6
Number of operations	69	28	21	47	40	18	223

IBRD OPERATIONS AND RESOURCES, 1996–2000 (US $ million, years ending 30 June)

	1995/96	1996/97	1997/98	1998/99	1999/2000
Loans approved	14,656*	14,525	21,086	22,182	10,919
Gross disbursements	13,372*	13,998	19,232	18,205	10,918
Net disbursements†	1,213	2,094	n.a.	n.a.	n.a.
New medium- to long-term borrowings	10,883	15,139	n.a.	n.a.	n.a.
Net income	1,187	1,285	1,243	1,518	1,991
Subscribed capital	180,630	182,426	186,436	188,220	188,606
Statutory lending limit	197,785	198,705	202,209	205,292	206,992
Loans and callable guarantees outstanding	110,369	105,954	106,947	117,694	120,571

* Including refinanced/rescheduled overdue charges of US $167.8m. for Bosnia and Herzegovina.
† Including disbursements, repayments and prepayments to/from all members, including third-party repayments.
Source: *World Bank Annual Report 2000.*

International Development Association—IDA

Address: 1818 H Street, NW, Washington, DC 20433, USA.

Telephone: (202) 477-1234; **fax:** (202) 477-6391; **internet:** www.worldbank.org/ida.

The International Development Association began operations in November 1960. Affiliated to the IBRD (see above), IDA advances capital to the poorer developing member countries on more flexible terms than those offered by the IBRD.

MEMBERS

161 members: see Table on pp. 117–119.

Organization

(April 2001)

Officers and staff of the IBRD serve concurrently as officers and staff of IDA.

President and Chairman of Executive Directors: JAMES D. WOLFENSOHN (*ex officio*).

Activities

IDA assistance is aimed at the poorer developing countries (i.e. those with an annual GNP per head of less than US $885 in the financial year ending 30 June 2000 qualified for assistance in 2000/01). Under IDA lending conditions, credits can be extended to countries whose balance of payments could not sustain the burden of repayment required for IBRD loans. Terms are more favourable than those provided by the IBRD; credits are for a period of 35 or 40 years, with a 'grace period' of 10 years, and carry no interest charges. At 1 January 2001 78 countries were eligible for IDA assistance, including several small-island economies with a GNP per head greater than $925, but which would otherwise have little or no access to Bank funds, and 12 so-called 'blend borrowers' (such as India), which are entitled to borrow from both the IDA and IBRD.

IDA's total development resources, consisting of members' subscriptions and supplementary resources (additional subscriptions and contributions), are replenished periodically by contributions from the more affluent member countries. In November 1998 representatives of 39 donor countries agreed to provide US $11,600m. for the 12th replenishment of IDA funds, enabling total lending to amount to an estimated $20,500m. in the period July 1999–June 2002. The new IDA-12 resources were to be directed towards the following objectives: investing in people; promoting good governance; promoting broad-based growth;and protecting the environment. Discussions regarding the 13th replenishment of IDA funds commenced in February 2001.

During the year ending 30 June 2000 IDA credits totalling US $4,357.6m. were approved. Of total IDA assistance during that year, $2,061.4m. (47.3%) was for Africa, and $1,178.1m. (27.0%) for South Asia (see table on p. 83). The largest borrowers of IDA credits were India ($866.5m. for six projects) and Tanzania ($329.7m., also for six projects). IDA administers a Trust Fund, which was established in November 1996 as part of a World Bank/IMF initiative to assist heavily indebted poor countries (HIPCs, see IBRD).

Publication

Annual Report.

IDA OPERATIONS AND RESOURCES, 1996–2000 (US $ million, years ending 30 June)

	1995/96	1996/97	1997/98	1998/99	1999/2000
Commitments	6,861	4,622	7,508*	6,812*	4,358*
Disbursements	5,884	5,979	5,630	6,023	5,177

* Excluding HIPC development grants.

Source: *World Bank Annual Report 2000.*

International Finance Corporation—IFC

Address: 2121 Pennsylvania Ave, NW, Washington, DC 20433, USA.

Telephone: (202) 477-1234; **fax:** (202) 974-4384; **e-mail:** information@ifc.org; **internet:** www.ifc.org.

IFC was founded in 1956 as a member of the World Bank Group to stimulate economic growth in developing countries by financing private-sector investments, mobilizing capital in international financial markets, and providing technical assistance and advice to governments and businesses.

MEMBERS

174 members: see Table on pp. 117–119.

Organization

(April 2001)

IFC is a separate legal entity in the World Bank Group. Executive Directors of the World Bank also serve as Directors of IFC. The President of the World Bank is *ex officio* Chairman of the IFC Board of Directors, which has appointed him President of IFC. Subject to his overall supervision, the day-to-day operations of IFC are conducted by its staff under the direction of the Executive Vice-President.

PRINCIPAL OFFICERS

President: JAMES D. WOLFENSOHN (USA).

Executive Vice-President: PETER L. WOICKE (Germany).

REGIONAL AND INDUSTRY DEPARTMENTS

Seven Regional Departments cover: East Asia and the Pacific; South and Southeast Asia; Central Asia, the Middle East and North Africa; Central and Southern Europe; Europe; Latin America and the Caribbean; and sub-Saharan Africa. These aim to develop strategies for member countries, promote businesses, and strengthen relations with governments and the private sector. Industry Departments cover agribusiness; financial markets; chemicals, petrochemicals and fertilizers; corporate finance services; petroleum, gas and mining; power; and telecommunications, transportation and utilities.

REGIONAL AND RESIDENT MISSIONS

There are Regional and Resident Missions in Argentina, Australia, Brazil (for Latin America and the Caribbean), Cameroon (for Central Africa), People's Republic of China, Côte d'Ivoire (for West Africa), Egypt (for the Middle East), Ghana, Guatemala, India (for South and Southeast Asia), Kenya (for East Africa), Republic of Korea, Mexico, Morocco (for North Africa), Nigeria, Pakistan, the Philippines, Russia (for Europe), South Africa (for Southern Africa), Thailand, Turkey, Viet Nam and Zimbabwe. There are also Special Representatives in France, Germany, Japan and the United Kingdom, and other programme co-ordinators, managers and investment officers in more than 30 additional countries.

Activities

IFC provides financial support and advice for private-sector ventures and projects, and assists governments in creating conditions that stimulate the flow of domestic and foreign private savings and investment. Increasingly, IFC has worked to mobilize additional capital from other financial institutions. In all its activities IFC is guided by three major principles:

(i) The catalytic principle. IFC should seek above all to be a catalyst in helping private investors and markets to make good investments.

(ii) The business principle. IFC should function like a business in partnership with the private sector and take the same commercial risks, so that its funds, although backed by public sources, are transferred under market disciplines.

(iii) The principle of the special contribution. IFC should participate in an investment only when it makes a special contribution that supplements or complements the role of market operators.

IFC's authorized capital is US $2,450m. At 30 June 1999 paid-in capital was $2,349.8m. The World Bank was originally the principal source of borrowed funds, but IFC also borrows from private capital markets. IFC's net income amounted to $249.3m. in 1998/99, compared with $245.8m. in the previous year.

To be eligible for financing, projects must be profitable for investors, must benefit the economy of the country concerned, and must comply with IFC's environmental guide-lines. IFC may provide finance for a project that is partly state-owned, provided that there is participation by the private sector and that the project is operated on a commercial basis.

In the year ending 30 June 1999 project financing approved by IFC amounted to US $5,280m. for 255 projects (compared with $5,905m. for 304 projects in the previous year). Of the total approved, $3,505m. was for IFC's own account, while $1,775m. was in the form of loan syndications and underwriting of securities issues and investment funds by more than 100 participant banks and institutional investors. Generally, the IFC limits its financing to 5%–15% of the total cost of a project, but may take up to a 35% stake in a venture (although never as a majority shareholder). Disbursements for IFC's account amounted to $2,102m. (compared with $2,054m. in the previous year).

Projects approved during 1998/99 were located in 77 countries and regions. During that year IFC approved its largest ever project allocation, totalling some US $250m., in support of the establishment of a $750m. Asia Opportunity Fund, which aimed to assist corporate restructuring in Asian companies affected by financial instability. IFC also approved an investment for the first time in Saint Christopher and Nevis. The largest proportion of total financing by IFC was allocated to Latin America and the Caribbean (46%); Asia and the Pacific received 20%, Europe 17%, Central Asia, the Middle East and North Africa 9% and sub-Saharan Africa 7%. The Corporation invests in a wide variety of business and financial institutions in a broad range of sectors. In 1998/99 more than one-third of total financing approved (37%) was for financial services. Other financing was for infrastructure (15%), petroleum, gas and mining (15%), chemicals and petrochemicals (7%), cement and construction materials (6%), food and agribusiness (5%), manufacturing (4%) and others (11%).

During 1996/97 IFC inaugurated a three-year pilot programme, 'Extending IFC's Reach', which aimed to encourage private investment in 16 countries and regions (expanded to 20 in 1998/99) where adverse political conditions had previously limited IFC intervention. IFC has expanded its field-based activities in those countries in order to enhance local knowledge, strengthen relationships with government authorities and local businesses and improve access to IFC products and services. By 30 June 1999 IFC had approved 160 projects in 'Outreach' countries amounting to some US $1,000m., of which 67 investments, totalling $68.3m., were through a Small Enterprise Fund (SEF).

IFC offers risk-management services, assisting institutions in avoiding financial risks that arise from changes in interest rates, in exchange rates or in commodity prices. In 1998/99 IFC approved eight risk-management projects for companies and banks, bringing the total number of projects approved since the introduction of the service in 1990 to 83 in 35 countries.

IFC provides advisory services, particularly in connection with privatization and corporate restructuring, private infrastructure, and the development of capital markets. Under the Technical Assistance Trust Funds Program (TATF), established in 1988, IFC manages resources contributed by various governments and agencies to provide finance for feasibility studies, project identification studies and other types of technical assistance relating to project preparation. By 30 June 1999 the TATF had mobilized US $87m. through 26 trust funds, financing more than 700 technical assistance projects. The Foreign Investment Advisory Service (FIAS), established in 1986, is operated jointly by IFC and the IBRD: it provides advice on promoting foreign investment and strengthening the country's investment framework at the request of governments. During 1998/99 FIAS undertook projects and assignments in 33 countries.

IFC has helped to establish several regional facilities which aim to assist small-scale entrepreneurs to develop business proposals and generate funding for their projects. For each of the facilities listed below IFC is the executing agency. The Africa Project Development Facility (APDF) was established in 1986 by IFC, UNDP and the African Development Bank, and maintains offices in Cameroon, Côte d'Ivoire, Ghana, Kenya, South Africa and Zimbabwe. The South Pacific Project Facility, based in Sydney, Australia, was established in 1991. A separate office in Port Moresby, Papua New Guinea, was opened in 1997. The Facility is complemented by a Pacific Island Investment Fund, which was established by IFC in 1995. A Mekong Project Development Facility was inaugurated in 1995, specifically to support the development of small and medium-sized enterprises in Cambodia, Laos and Viet Nam. IFC also administers the Business Advisory Service for the Caribbean and Central America (BAS). In 1992 two locally-owned affiliates of the BAS were established—the Asesoría Empresarial Centroamericana in Costa Rica, to serve Central America, and Enterprise Development Ltd in Trinidad and Tobago, to serve the southern Caribbean and Guyana.

In 1989 IFC (with UNDP, the African Development Bank and other agencies and governments) began operating a new facility, the African Management Services Company (AMSCo), which helps to find qualified senior executives from around the world to work with African companies, assist in the training of local managers, and provide supporting services. By 31 December 1998 AMSCo had signed management contracts with companies in 23 countries. IFC's Africa Enterprise Fund (AEF) provides financial assistance to small and medium-sized enterprises. In 1995 a new facility, Enterprise Support Services for Africa (ESSA), was established, to provide technical and production assistance to businesses after they have secured financing. ESSA commenced operations in March 1996. In 1998/99 ESSA was expanded to be available throughout sub-Saharan Africa as part of APDF.

The dissolution of the USSR in 1991, and the transition to market economies there and in other central and eastern European countries, led to an increase in IFC activities in the region during the 1990s. In order to facilitate the privatization process in that region, the IFC has conducted several single-enterprise advisory assignments and has undertaken work to formulate models that can be easily replicated, notably for small-scale privatization and the privatization of agricultural land in Russia, Ukraine and Belarus.

Publications

Annual Report.

Emerging Stock Markets Factbook (annually).

Global Agribusiness (series of industry reports).

Impact (quarterly).

Lessons of Experience (series).

Results on the Ground (series).

Discussion papers and technical documents.

IFC OPERATIONS AND RESOURCES, 1990–99 (fiscal years ending 30 June)

	1990	1991	1992	1993	1994	1995	1996	1997	1998	1999
Approved investments										
Number of new projects . . .	122	152	167	185	231	213	264	276	304	255
Total financing (US $ million) . .	2,201	2,846	3,226	3,936	4,287	5,467	8,118	6,722	2,905	5,280
Total project costs* (US $ million) .	9,490	10,683	12,000	17,422	15,839	19,352	19,633	17,945	15,726	15,578
Disbursements (IFC's own account,										
US $ million)	1,001	1,249	1,114	1,106	1,537	1,808	2,053	2,003	2,054	2,102
Resources and income (US $ million)										
Borrowings	3,580	4,130	5,114	5,565	6,531	7,993	8,956	10,123	11,162	12,429
Paid-in capital	1,072	1,145	1,251	1,423	1,658	1,875	2,076	2,229	2,337	2,350
Retained earnings	792	957	1,138	1,280	1,538	1,726	2,071	2,503	2,749	2,998
Net income	157.0	165.9	180.2	141.7	258.2	188.0	345.8	431.9	245.8	249.3

* Including investment mobilized from other sources.
Source: *IFC Annual Report 1999.*

Multilateral Investment Guarantee Agency—MIGA

Address: 1818 H Street, NW, Washington, DC 20433, USA.
Telephone: (202) 473-6163; **fax:** (202) 522-2630; **internet:** www.miga.org.
MIGA was founded in 1988 as an affiliate of the World Bank. Its mandate is to encourage the flow of foreign direct investment to, and among, developing member countries, through the provision of political risk insurance and investment marketing services to foreign investors and host governments, respectively.

MEMBERS

At March 2001 MIGA had 154 member countries. Membership is open to all countries that are members of the World Bank.

Organization

(April 2001)

MIGA is legally and financially separate from the World Bank. It is supervised by a Council of Governors (comprising one Governor and one Alternate of each member country) and an elected Board of Directors (of no less than 12 members).
President: JAMES D. WOLFENSOHN (USA).
Executive Vice-President: MOTOMICHI IKAWA (Japan).

Activities

The convention establishing MIGA took effect in April 1988. Authorized capital was US $1,082m. In April 1998 the Board of Directors approved an increase in the Agency's capital base. A grant of $150m. was transferred from the IBRD as part of the package, while the capital increase (totalling $700m. callable capital and $150m. paid-in capital) was approved by MIGA's Council of Governors in April 1999. A three-year subscription period then commenced, covering the period April 1999–March 2002.
MIGA's purpose is to guarantee eligible investments against losses resulting from non-commercial risks, under four main categories:

(i) transfer risk resulting from host government restrictions on currency conversion and transfer;

(ii) risk of loss resulting from legislative or administrative actions of the host government;

(iii) repudiation by the host government of contracts with investors in cases in which the investor has no access to a competent forum;

(iv) the risk of armed conflict and civil unrest.

Before guaranteeing any investment, MIGA must ensure that it is commercially viable, contributes to the development process and is not harmful to the environment. During the fiscal year 1998/99 MIGA and IFC appointed the first Compliance Advisor and Ombudsman to consider the concerns of local communities directly affected by MIGA or IFC sponsored projects. In February 1999 the Board of Directors approved an increase in the amount of political risk insurance available for each project, from US $75m. to $200m., and increased the amount available to each host government from $350m. to $620m.

During the year ending 30 June 2000 MIGA issued 53 investment insurance contracts in 26 countries with a value of US $1,605m., compared with 72 contracts valued at $1,310m. in 1998/99. The amount of direct investment associated with the contracts totalled approximately $5,450m. (compared with $5,200m. in the previous year).

MIGA administers two investment guarantee trust funds, for Bosnia and Herzogovina and for the West Bank and Gaza Strip, to underwrite investment in post-conflict reconstruction activities.

MIGA also provides policy and advisory services to promote foreign investment in developing countries and in transitional economies, and to disseminate information on investment opportunities. In October 1995 MIGA established a new network on investment opportunities, which connected investment promotion agencies (IPAs) throughout the world on an electronic information network. The so-called IPA*net* aimed to encourage further investments among developing countries, to provide access to comprehensive information on investment laws and conditions and to strengthen links between governmental, business and financial associations and investors. A new version of IPA*net* was launched in 1997 (and can be accessed at www.ipanet.net). In June 1998 MIGA initiated a new internet-based facility, 'PrivatizationLink', to provide information on investment opportunities resulting from the privatization of industries in emerging economies.

Publications

Annual Report.
MIGA News (quarterly).

International Civil Aviation Organization—ICAO

Address: 999 University St, Montreal, QC H3C 5H7, Canada.
Telephone: (514) 954-8219; **fax:** (514) 954-6077; **e-mail:** icaohq@icao.int; **internet:** www.icao.int.

The Convention on International Civil Aviation was signed in Chicago in 1944. As a result, ICAO was founded in 1947 to develop the techniques of international air navigation and to help in the planning and improvement of international air transport.

MEMBERS

187 members: see Table on pp. 117–119.

Organization

(April 2001)

ASSEMBLY

Composed of representatives of all member states, the Assembly is the organization's legislative body and meets at least once every three years. It reviews the work of the organization, sets out the work programme for the next three years, approves the budget and determines members' contributions. The 33rd Assembly was scheduled to be held in October 2001.

COUNCIL

Composed of representatives of 33 member states, elected by the Assembly. It is the executive body, and establishes and supervises subsidiary technical committees and makes recommendations to member governments; meets in virtually continuous session; elects the President, appoints the Secretary-General, and administers the finances of the organization. The Council is assisted by the Air Navigation Commission (on technical matters), the Air Transport Committee (on economic matters), the Committee on Joint Support of Air Navigation Services and the Finance Committee. The functions of the Council are:

(i) to adopt international standards and recommended practices and incorporate them as annexes to the Convention on International Civil Aviation;

(ii) to arbitrate between member states on matters concerning aviation and implementation of the Convention;

(iii) to investigate any situation which presents avoidable obstacles to development of international air navigation;

(iv) to take whatever steps are necessary to maintain safety and regularity of operation of international air transport;

(v) to provide technical assistance to the developing countries under the UN Development Programme and other assistance programmes.

President of the Council: Dr ASSAD KOTAITE (Lebanon).

SECRETARIAT

The Secretariat, headed by a Secretary-General, is divided into five main divisions: the Air Navigation Bureau, the Air Transport Bureau, The Technical Co-operation Bureau, the Legal Bureau, and the Bureau of Administration and Services.

Secretary-General: RENATO CLAUDIO COSTA PEREIRA (Brazil).

REGIONAL OFFICES

Asia and Pacific: 252/1 Vipavadee Rangsit Rd, Ladyao, Chatuchak, POB 11, Bangkok 10900, Thailand.

Eastern and Southern Africa: Limuru Rd, Gigiri, POB 46294, Nairobi, Kenya.

Europe: 3 bis, Villa Emile-Bergerat, 92522 Neuilly-sur-Seine Cédex, France.

Middle East: Egyptian Civil Aviation Complex, Cairo Airport Rd, Cairo, Egypt.

North America, Central America and the Caribbean: Apdo Postal 5-377, CP 11590, México 5, DF, Mexico.

South America: Apdo 4127, Lima 100, Peru.

Western and Central Africa: BP 2356, Dakar, Senegal.

Activities

ICAO aims to ensure the safe and orderly growth of civil aviation; to encourage skills in aircraft design and operation; to improve airways, airports and air navigation; to prevent the waste of resources in unreasonable competition; to safeguard the rights of each contracting party to operate international air transport; and to prevent discriminatory practices. ICAO collects and publishes statistics relating to civil aviation. In the late 1990s ICAO implemented a Year 2000 Programme in order to address potential malfunctions, resulting from the date change at the start of the new century, of systems affecting the safety, regularity and efficiency of international civil aviation operations; under the programme regional contingency plans were harmonized and an extensive inventory of air traffic systems and aviation facilities was developed.

SAFETY AND SECURITY

ICAO aims to enhance all aspects of air safety and security. In 1998 a Global Aviation Safety Plan was initiated to promote new safety measures. A Programme for the Prevention of Controlled Flights into Terrain continued to be implemented. ICAO assists member countries to develop appropriate educational and training activities. It also supports programmes to assist the victims of aircraft accidents. The 32nd Assembly, held in September/October 1998, endorsed the establishment of a Universal Safety Oversight Programme, to provide for mandatory, systematic and harmonized safety audits regularly to be undertaken in member states. The Programme became operational on 1 January 1999 with the aim of auditing all member states over an initial three-year period. In October 1998 a protocol to the Chicago Convention, prohibiting the use of weapons against civil aircraft in flight, entered into effect, having been adopted in 1984 following an attack on a Korean Airlines passenger flight. During 2000 ICAO was preparing draft legislation concerning offences committed on board aircraft by unruly passengers (other than hijacking, sabotage etc., which are already governed by international legislation).

NAVIGATION

ICAO projects relating to navigation have included automated data interchange systems, all-weather navigation, obstacle clearances and the use of space technology in air navigation. In May 1998 an international conference was held in Rio de Janeiro, Brazil, to consider implementation of the Communications, Navigation, Surveillance, and Air Traffic Management (CNS/ATM) systems. The conference urged greater financing and co-operation between states to ensure that the CNS/ATM becomes the basis of a global ATM system. An Air Traffic Management Operational Concept Panel, which was to develop standards and recommend procedures for the development of an integrated ATM system, was convened for the first time in March/April 1999. In October 1998 the Assembly adopted a Charter on the Rights and Obligations of States relating to Global Navigation Satellite Systems (GNSS) to serve as an interim framework on the GNSS. A long-term legal framework on principles governing the GNSS, including a new international convention, remained under consideration.

ENVIRONMENT

International standards and guide-lines for noise certification of aircraft and international provisions for the regulation of aircraft engine emissions have been adopted and published in Annex 16 to the Chicago Convention. However, these remain under consideration. ICAO was recognized in the Kyoto Protocol to the Framework Convention on Climate Change as the global body through which industrialized nations were to pursue the limitation or reduction of so-called greenhouse gas emissions from international aviation. In 1998 ICAO's Committee on Aviation Environmental Protection recommended a reduction of 16% in the permissible levels of nitrogen oxides emitted by aircraft engines. The new limits, to be applicable to new engine designs from 2003, were adopted by the ICAO Council in early 1999. In January 2001 the Committee recommended several measures for review by the Council concerning aircraft noise mitigation; the proposals included a new noise standard, set at 10 decibels lower than the existing one, for new engine designs from 2006, and new take-off noise abatement procedures.

ICAO SPECIFICATIONS

These are contained in annexes to the Chicago Convention, and in three sets of Procedures for Air Navigation Services (PANS Documents). The specifications are periodically revised in keeping with developments in technology and changing requirements. The 18 annexes to the Convention include personnel licensing, rules relating to the conduct of flights, meteorological services, aeronautical charts, airground communications, safety specifications, identification, air-traffic control, rescue services, environmental protection, security and the transporting of dangerous goods. Technical Manuals and Circulars are issued to facilitate implementation.

ICAO REGIONAL PLANS

These set out the technical requirements for air navigation facilities in the nine ICAO regions; Regional Offices offer assistance (see addresses above). Because of growth in air traffic and changes in the pattern of air routes, the Plans are periodically amended. ICAO maintains a structure of Planning and Implementation Regional Groups.

TECHNICAL CO-OPERATION

ICAO's Technical Co-operation Bureau promotes the implementation of ICAO Standards and Recommended Practices, including the CNS/ATM and Safety Oversight Programmes, and assists developing countries in the execution of various projects, financed by UNDP and other sources.

ICAO works in close co-operation with other UN bodies, such as the World Meteorological Organization, the International Telecommunication Union, the Universal Postal Union, the World Health Organization and the International Maritime Organization. Non-governmental organizations which also participate in ICAO's work include the International Air Transport Association (q.v.), the Air-ports Council International (q.v.), the International Federation of Air Line Pilots' Associations (q.v.), and the International Council of Aircraft Owner and Pilot Associations.

Finance

ICAO is financed mainly by contributions from member states; the 32nd Session of the Assembly, held in September/October 1998, approved a budget of US $55.4m. for 2001.

Publications

Aircraft Accident Digest.
Annual Civil Aviation Report.
Civil Aviation Statistics of the World (annually).
ICAO Journal (10 a year, in English, French and Spanish; quarterly digest in Russian).
Lexicon of Terms.
Regional Air Navigation Plans.
Transition (CNS/ATM newsletter, quarterly).
Conventions, agreements, rules of procedures, regulations, technical publications and manuals.

International Fund for Agricultural Development—IFAD

Address: Via del Serafico 107, 00142 Rome, Italy.
Telephone: (06) 54591; **fax:** (06) 5043463; **e-mail:** ifad@ifad.org; **internet:** www.ifad.org.

IFAD was established in 1977, following a decision by the 1974 UN World Food Conference, with a mandate to combat hunger and eradicate poverty on a sustainable basis in the low-income, food-deficit regions of the world. Funding operations began in January 1978.

MEMBERS

161 members: see Table on pp. 117–119.

Organization

(April 2001)

GOVERNING COUNCIL

Each member state is represented in the Governing Council (the Fund's highest authority) by a Governor and an Alternate. Sessions are held annually with special sessions as required. The Governing Council elects the President of the Fund (who also chairs the Executive Board) by a two-thirds majority for a four-year term. The President is eligible for re-election.

EXECUTIVE BOARD

Consists of 18 members and 18 alternates, elected by the Governing Council, who serve for three years. The Executive Board is responsible for the conduct and general operation of IFAD and approves loans and grants for projects; it holds three regular sessions each year.

Following agreement on the fourth replenishment of the Fund's resources in February 1997, the governance structure of the Fund was amended. Former Category I countries (i.e. industrialized donor countries) were reclassified as List A countries and were awarded a greater share of the 1,800 votes in the Governing Council and Executive Board, in order to reflect their financial contributions to the Fund. Former Category II countries (petroleum-exporting developing donor countries) were reclassified as List B countries, while recipient developing countries, formally Category III countries, were termed as List C countries, and divided into three regional Sub-Lists. Where previously each category was ensured equal representation on the Executive Board, the new allocation of seats was as follows: eight List A countries, four List B, and two of each Sub-List C group of countries.

President and Chairman of Executive Board: LENNART BÅGE (Sweden).
Vice-President: JOHN WESTLEY (USA).

DEPARTMENTS

IFAD has three main administrative departments: the Economic Policy and Resource Strategy Department, the Programme Management Department (with five regional Divisions and a Technical Advisory Division); and the Management and Personnel Services Department (including Office of the Secretary, Management Information Systems, Personnel Division, and Administrative Services). At 31 December 1999 IFAD had 267 regular staff.

Activities

The Fund's objective is to mobilize additional resources to be made available on concessionary terms for agricultural development in developing member states. IFAD provides financing primarily for projects designed to improve food production systems and to strengthen related policies, services and institutions. In allocating resources IFAD is guided by: the need to increase food production in the poorest food-deficit countries; the potential for increasing food production in other developing countries; and the importance of improving the nutrition, health and education of the poorest people in developing countries, i.e. small-scale farmers, artisanal fishermen, nomadic pastoralists, indigenous populations, rural women, and the rural landless. All projects emphasize the participation of beneficiaries in development initiatives, both at the local and national level. IFAD is a leading repository in the world of knowledge, resources and expertise in the field of rural hunger and poverty alleviation. Through its technical assistance grants, IFAD aims to promote research and capacity-building in the agricultural sector, as well as the development of technologies to increase production and alleviate rural poverty. In recent years IFAD has been increasingly involved in promoting the use of communication technology to facilitate the exchange of information and experience among rural communities, specialized institutions and organizations and IFAD-sponsored projects.

IFAD is empowered to make both grants and loans. Grants are limited to 7.5% of the resources committed in any one financial year. Loans are available on highly concessional, intermediate and ordinary terms. Highly concessional loans carry no interest but have an annual service charge of 0.75% and a repayment period of 40 years, including a 10-year grace period. Intermediate term loans are subject to a variable interest charge, equivalent to 50% of the interest rate charged on World Bank loans, and are repaid over 20 years. Ordinary loans carry a variable interest charge equal to that charged by the World Bank, and are repaid over 15–18 years. Highly concessional loans form about two-thirds of the total lent annually by IFAD. To avoid duplication of work, the administration of loans, for the purposes of disbursements and supervision of project implementation, is entrusted to competent international financial institutions, with the Fund retaining an active interest. In order to increase the impact of its lending resources on food production, the Fund seeks as much as possible to attract other external donors and beneficiary governments as co-financiers of its projects.

At the end of 1999 total IFAD loans approved since 1978 amounted to US $6,489.1m. for 548 projects. During the same period the Fund approved 1,337 research and technical assistance grants, at a cost of $349.0m. In 1999 IFAD approved $432.7m. for 30 projects, as follows: $198.4m. for 14 projects in sub-Saharan Africa, (or 45.9% of the total committed in that year), $104.2m. for six operations in Asia and the Pacific (24.1%), $76.0m. for five projects in Latin America and the Caribbean (17.6%) and $54.1m. for five projects in the Near East and North Africa (12.5%). Technical assistance grants amounting to $29.6m. (for research, training and project preparation and development), were awarded, bringing the total financial assistance approved in 1999 to $462.3m., compared with $443.4m. in 1998.

IFAD's development projects usually include a number of components, such as infrastructure (e.g. improvement of water supplies, small-scale irrigation and road construction); input supply (e.g. improved seeds, fertilizers and pesticides); institutional support (e.g. research, training and extension services); and producer incentives (e.g. pricing and marketing improvements). IFAD also attempts to enable the landless to acquire income-generating assets: by increasing the provision of credit for the rural poor, it seeks to free them from dependence on the capital market and to generate productive activities.

The Fund supports projects that are concerned with environmental conservation, in an effort to alleviate poverty that results from the deterioration of natural resources. In addition, it extends environmental assessment grants to review the environmental consequences of projects under preparation.

In addition to its regular efforts to identify projects and programmes, IFAD organizes special programming missions to certain selected countries to undertake a comprehensive review of the constraints affecting the rural poor, and to help countries to design strategies for the removal of these constraints. In general, projects based on the recommendations of these missions tend to focus on institutional improvements at the national and local level to direct inputs and services to small farmers and the landless rural poor. Monitoring and evaluation missions are also sent to check the progress of projects.

In November 1995 IFAD organized a Conference on Hunger and Poverty, which was held in Brussels, Belgium, together with the World Bank, the European Commission, FAO, WFP and several European governments. The conference was attended by representatives from some 300 non-governmental organizations, and approved a programme of action to combat hunger and poverty.

In October 1997 IFAD was appointed to administer the Global Mechanism of the Convention to Combat Desertification in those Countries Experiencing Drought and Desertification, particularly in Africa, which entered into force in December 1996. The Mechanism was envisaged as a means of mobilizing and channelling resources for implementation of the Convention. A series of collaborative institutional arrangements were to be concluded between IFAD, UNDP and the World Bank in order to facilitate the effective functioning of the Mechanism.

In February 1998 IFAD inaugurated a new Trust Fund to complement the multilateral debt initiative for Heavily Indebted Poor Countries (HIPCs—see World Bank p. 81). The Fund was intended to assist IFAD's poorest members deemed to be eligible under the initiative to channel resources from debt repayments to communities in need. Also in 1998 the Executive Board endorsed a policy framework for the Fund's provision of assistance in post-conflict situations, with the aim of achieving a continuum from emergency relief to a secure basis from which to pursue sustainable development. In 1999 IFAD was involved in projects to combat problems resulting from civil conflict in Burundi, Cambodia, El Salvador, Guatemala and Sierra Leone.

During the late 1990s IFAD established several partnerships within the agribusiness sector, with a view to improving performance at project level, broadening access to capital markets, and encouraging the advancement of new technologies.

Finance

In accordance with the Articles of Agreement establishing IFAD, the Governing Council periodically undertakes a review of the adequacy of resources available to the Fund and may request members to make additional contributions. In 1997 the fourth replenishment of the Fund's resources, amounting to US $460m. over a three-year period, was successfully concluded. The administrative budget approved for 1998 amounted to $51.1m. The provisional budget for 1999 amounted to $55.0m.

Publications

Annual Report.
IFAD Update (2 a year).
Rural Poverty Report (annually).
Staff Working Papers (series).

International Labour Organization—ILO

Address: 4 route des Morillons, 1211 Geneva 22, Switzerland.
Telephone: (22) 7996111; **fax:** (22) 7988685; **internet:** www.ilo.org.

ILO was founded in 1919 to work for social justice as a basis for lasting peace. It carries out this mandate by promoting decent living standards, satisfactory conditions of work and pay and adequate employment opportunities. Methods of action include the creation of international labour standards; the provision of technical co-operation services; and research and publications on social and labour matters. In 1946 ILO became a specialized agency associated with the UN. It was awarded the Nobel Peace Prize in 1969.

MEMBERS

175 members: see Table on pp. 117–119.

Organization

(April 2001)

INTERNATIONAL LABOUR CONFERENCE

The supreme deliberative body of ILO, the Conference meets annually in Geneva, with a session devoted to maritime questions when necessary; it is attended by about 2,000 delegates, advisers and observers. National delegations are composed of two government delegates, one employers' delegate and one workers' delegate. Non-governmental delegates can speak and vote independently of the views of their national government. The conference elects the Governing Body and adopts International Labour Conventions and Recommendations. Every two years the Conference adopts the ILO Budget.

The President and Vice-Presidents hold office for the term of the Conference only.

GOVERNING BODY

ILO's executive council meets three times a year in Geneva to decide policy and programmes. It is composed of 28 government members, 14 employers' members and 14 workers' members. Ten seats are reserved for 'states of chief industrial importance': Brazil, the People's Republic of China, France, Germany, India, Italy, Japan, Russia, the United Kingdom and the USA. The remaining 18 are elected from other countries every three years. Employers' and workers' members are elected as individuals, not as national candidates.

Among the Committees formed by the Governing Body are: the Committee on Freedom of Association; the Programme, Financial and Administrative Committee; the Building Sub-Committee; the Committee on Legal Issues and International Labour Standards; the Sub-Committee on Multinational Enterprises; the Working Party on Policy regarding the Revision of Standards; the Committee on Employment and Social Policy; the Committee on Sectoral and Technical Meetings and Related Issues; the Committee on Technical Co-operation; and the Working Party on the Social Dimensions of the Liberalization of International Trade.

Chairman (2000–01): Celso N. Amorim (Brazil).
Employers' Vice-Chairman: Rolf Thüsing (Germany).
Workers' Vice-Chairman: William Brett (United Kingdom).

INTERNATIONAL LABOUR OFFICE

The International Labour Office is ILO's secretariat, operational headquarters and publishing house. It is staffed in Geneva and in the field by about 1,900 people of some 110 nationalities. Operations are decentralized to regional, area and branch offices in nearly 40 countries.

Director-General: Juan O. Somavía (Chile).

REGIONAL OFFICES

Regional Office for Africa: BP 3960, Abidjan 01, Côte d'Ivoire.
Regional Office for the Americas: Apdo Postal 3638, Lima 1, Peru.

Regional Office for Arab States: POB 11-4088, Beirut, Lebanon.
Regional Office for Asia and the Pacific: POB 2-349, Bangkok
10200, Thailand.

Activities

In 1999 ILO identified the following four principal themes as strategic objectives for its 2000–01 work programme: to promote and realize fundamental principles and rights at work; to create greater opportunities for women and men to secure decent employment and income; to enhance the coverage and effectiveness of social protection for all; and to strengthen tripartism and social dialogue.

FUNDAMENTAL PRINCIPLES AND RIGHTS AT WORK

One of ILO's primary functions is the adoption by the International Labour Conference of conventions and recommendations setting minimum labour standards. Through ratification by member states, conventions create binding obligations to put their provisions into effect. Recommendations provide guidance as to policy and practice. At June 2000 a total of 183 conventions and 191 recommendations had been adopted, ranging over a wide field of social and labour matters, including basic human rights such as freedom of association, abolition of forced labour, elimination of discrimination in employment promotion, training and the protection of workers. Together they form the International Labour Code. By 2000 more than 6,600 ratifications of the conventions had been registered by member states. The Committee of Experts on the Application of Conventions and Recommendations and the Conference Committee on the Application of Standards monitor the adoption of international labour standards. In June 1998 a Declaration establishing seven fundamental labour standards was adopted by the Conference. All member states were obliged to observe the four principles upon which these standards were based (see above), whether or not they had ratified the corresponding international conventions.

From 1996 ILO resolved to strengthen its efforts, working closely with UNICEF, to encourage member states to ratify and to implement relevant international standards on child labour. By late 2000 some 100 countries were taking part in ILO's International Programme for the Elimination of Child Labour (IPEC, established in 1992), with emphasis placed on the elimination of the most severe forms of labour such as hazardous working conditions and occupations, child prostitution and trafficking of children. In addition, IPEC gives special attention to children who are particularly vulnerable, for example those under 12 years of age.

In mid-2000 the Global Compact, an initiative of the UN Secretary-General, was inaugurated; this comprised leaders in the fields of business, labour and civil society who undertook to promote human rights, the fundamental principles of ILO, and protection of the environment.

DECENT EMPLOYMENT AND INCOME

ILO aims to monitor, examine and report on the situation and trends in employment throughout the world, and considers the effects on employment and social justice of economic trade, investment and related phenomena. In 1998 ILO estimated that some 1,000m. workers, or one-third of the world's labour force, were unemployed or underemployed. The impact on employment and related social issues of the financial crisis that affected several Asian economies from mid-1997 was of particular concern to ILO.

ILO's Employment and Training Department analyses and develops policies to promote the following objectives: full, productive and freely-chosen employment; a labour market that combines flexibility in the use of labour with employment security; enhanced employment opportunities for workers by adapting and improving their skills and competence through training; and the protection and access to employment of specific groups, such as women, youths, migrant workers and disabled persons; and the rehabilitation of workers exposed to drug and alcohol abuse.

ILO maintains technical relations with the IMF, the World Bank, OECD, the WTO and other international organizations on global economic issues, international and national strategies for employment, structural adjustment, and labour market and training policies. A number of employment policy reviews have been carried out by ILO within the framework of the UN Administrative Committee on Co-ordination Task Force on Full Employment and Sustainable Livelihoods.

SOCIAL PROTECTION FOR ALL

Access to an adequate level of social protection is recognized in ILO's 1944 Declaration of Philadelphia, as well as in a number of international labour standards, as a basic right of all individuals. ILO aims to enable countries to extend social protection to all groups in society and to improve working conditions and safety at work. The fundamental premise of ILO's new programme sector on economic and social security was that adequate security was essential for productive work and human dignity in the future global economy. It was to address the following concerns: why certain individuals and groups lack decent social security; how new schemes may be initiated in member countries to complement or replace existing social security systems; means of improving the governance and coverage of social protection programmes; identifying the constitutive elements of social security; and creating a balance between the flexible needs of the labour market with adequate social protection.

ILO extends direct technical assistance to member states in order to improve occupational safety and health, for example, through the development of management tools, monitoring and information services designed to prevent occupational accidents and diseases, and measures to protect the health and welfare of workers and the environment. ILO has also established a series of alliances and partnerships with governments, non-governmental organizations, social groups and human rights organizations to reinforce health and safety advocacy campaigns.

TRIPARTISM AND SOCIAL DIALOGUE

This area was identified as one of the four strategic objectives in order to concentrate and reinforce ILO's support for strengthening the process of tripartism, the role and activities of its tripartite constituents (i.e. governments, employers and workers' organizations), and, in particular, their capacity to engage in and to promote the use of social dialogue. ILO recognizes that the enactment of labour laws, and ensuring their effective enforcement, collective bargaining and other forms of co-operation are important means of promoting social justice. It aims to assist governments and employers' and workers' organizations to establish sound labour relations, to adapt labour laws to meet changing economic and social needs, and to improve labour administration.

INTERNATIONAL LABOUR CONFERENCE

87th Session: June 1999. Adopted the Worst Forms of Child Labour Convention, requiring signatory states to secure the prohibition and elimination of the most severe or hazardous forms of child labour. Also adopted a Recommendation urging any ratifying state to declare those activities to be criminal offences and to impose penal sanctions against the perpetrators. Adopted a Resolution condemning Myanmar for consistent violations of the Forced Labour Convention, which prevented that country from attending meetings or receiving technical assistance. Agreed that a revision of the Maternity Protection Convention (No 103) was appropriate. The situation of migrant workers remained under consideration.

88th Session: May/June 2000. Adopted the Maternity Protection Convention, 2000 (No 183), requiring signatory states to expand maternity protection to cover more categories of employment, including the informal sector; to extend statutory maternity leave from 12 to 14 weeks; to guarantee the right to leave from work prior to and after childbirth in cases of related complications or illness; to reimburse employers in respect of maternity leave through compulsory social insurance schemes, public funds or in another manner determined by national law or practice; and to permit short daily breaks from work for the purpose of breastfeeding. Held a special high-level meeting on the impact of HIV/AIDS on work, productivity and development, and discussed the social consequences of globalization. Adopted an unprecedented resolution threatening the imposition of punitive measures against Myanmar if it was still deemed to be contravening the Forced Labour Convention at 30 November 2000. (The sanctions were subsequently imposed.) Held a first discussion on drafting a new standard concerning health and safety in agriculture.

MEETINGS

Among meetings held during late 2000 and early 2001, in addition to the regular Governing Body sessions, were the Tripartite Meeting on Moving to Sustainable Agricultural Development through the Modernization of Agriculture and Employment in a Globalized Economy; the Tripartite Meeting on Labour Practices in the Footwear, Leather, Textiles and Clothing Industries; and the Tripartite Meeting on the Employment Impact of Mergers and Acquisitions in the Banking and Financial Services Sector.

INTERNATIONAL INSTITUTE FOR LABOUR STUDIES

Established in 1960 and based at ILO's Geneva headquarters, the Institute promotes the study and discussion of policy issues of concern to ILO and its constituents, i.e. government, employers and workers. The core theme of the Institute's activities is the interaction between labour institutions, development and civil society in a global economy. It identifies emerging social and labour issues by developing new areas for research and action, and encourages dialogue on social policy between the tripartite constituency of ILO and the international academic community and other experts. The Institute maintains research networks, conducts courses, seminars and social policy forums, and supports internships and visiting scholar and internship programmes.

INTERNATIONAL TRAINING CENTRE OF ILO

Address: Corso Unità d'Italia 125, 10127 Turin, Italy.

The Centre became operational in 1965. The ILO Director-General is Chairman of the Board of the Centre. It provides programmes for directors in charge of technical and vocational institutions, training officers, senior and middle-level managers in private and public enterprises, trade union leaders, and technicians, primarily from the developing regions of the world. Since 1991 the Centre has been increasingly used by UN agencies to provide training for improving the management of development and for building national capacities to sustain development programmes. In January 1996 a UN Staff College was established to improve staff training and to enhance collaboration among the various agencies and programmes of the UN.

Finance

The regular budget for the two years 2000–01 was US $467.5m.

Publications

(in English, French and Spanish unless otherwise indicated)

Bulletin of Labour Statistics (quarterly).

International Labour Review (quarterly).

International studies, surveys, works of practical guidance or reference on questions of social policy, manpower, industrial relations, working conditions, social security, training, management development, etc.

Key Indicators of the Labour Market.

Labour Law Documents (selected labour and social security laws and regulations; 3 a year).

Official Bulletin (3 a year).

Reports for the annual sessions of the International Labour Conference, etc. (also in Arabic, Chinese and Russian).

World Employment Report (every 2 years).

World Labour Report (every 2 years).

World of Work (magazine issued in several languages; 5 a year).

Yearbook of Labour Statistics.

Also maintains a database on international labour standards, ILOLEX, and a database on national labour law, NATLEX, in electronic form.

International Maritime Organization—IMO

Address: 4 Albert Embankment, London, SE1 7SR, United Kingdom.

Telephone: (20) 7735-7611; **fax:** (20) 7587-3210; **e-mail:** info@imo.org; **internet:** www.imo.org.

The Inter-Governmental Maritime Consultative Organization (IMCO) began operations in 1959, as a specialized agency of the UN to facilitate co-operation among governments on technical matters affecting international shipping. Its main functions are the achievement of safe and efficient navigation, and the control of pollution caused by ships and craft operating in the marine environment. IMCO became IMO in 1982.

MEMBERS

158 members and two associate members: see Table on pp. 117–119.

Organization

(April 2001)

ASSEMBLY

The Assembly consists of delegates from all member countries, who each have one vote. Associate members and observers from other governments and the international agencies are also present. Regular sessions are held every two years. The Assembly is responsible for the election of members to the Council and approves the appointment of the Secretary-General of the Secretariat. It considers reports from all subsidiary bodies and decides the action to be taken on them; it votes the agency's budget and determines the work programme and financial policy. The 21st regular session of the Assembly was held in London in November 1999.

The Assembly also recommends to members measures to promote maritime safety and to prevent and control maritime pollution from ships.

COUNCIL

The Council is the governing body of the Organization between the biennial sessions of the Assembly. Its members, representatives of 32 states, are elected by the Assembly for a term of two years. The Council appoints the Secretary-General; transmits reports by the subsidiary bodies, including the Maritime Safety Committee, to the Assembly, and reports on the work of the Organization generally; submits budget estimates and financial statements with comments and recommendations to the Assembly. The Council normally meets twice a year.

Facilitation Committee: Constituted by the Council in May 1972 as a subsidiary body, this Committee deals with measures to facilitate maritime travel and transport and matters arising from the 1965 Facilitation Convention. Membership is open to all IMO member states.

MARITIME SAFETY COMMITTEE

The Maritime Safety Committee is open to all IMO members. The Committee meets at least once a year and submits proposals to the Assembly on technical matters affecting the safety of shipping.

Sub-Committees:

Bulk Liquids and Gases*.	Safety of Navigation.
Carriage of Dangerous Goods,	Ship Design and Equipment.
Solid Cargoes and Containers.	Stability and Load Lines and
Fire Protection.	Fishing Vessel Safety.
Flag State Implementation*.	Standards of Training and
Radiocommunications and Search	Watchkeeping.
and Rescue.	

* Also sub-committees of the Marine Environment Protection Committee.

LEGAL COMMITTEE

Established by the Council in June 1967 to deal initially with problems connected with the loss of the tanker *Torrey Canyon*, and subsequently with any legal problems laid before IMO. Membership open to all IMO member states.

MARINE ENVIRONMENT PROTECTION COMMITTEE

Established by the eighth Assembly (1973) to co-ordinate IMO's work on the prevention and control of marine pollution from ships, and to assist IMO in its consultations with other UN bodies, and with international organizations and expert bodies in the field of marine pollution. Membership is open to all IMO members.

TECHNICAL CO-OPERATION COMMITTEE

Constituted by the Council in May 1972, this Committee evaluates the implementation of UN Development Programme projects for which IMO is the executing agency, and generally reviews IMO's technical assistance programmes. Its membership is open to all IMO member states.

SECRETARIAT

The Secretariat consists of the Secretary-General and a staff appointed by the Secretary-General and recruited on as wide a geographical basis as possible.

Secretary-General: William A. O'Neil (Canada).

Divisions of the Secretariat:

Administrative	Marine Environment
Conference	Maritime Safety
Legal Affairs and	Technical Co-operation
External Relations	

Activities

In addition to the work of its committees and sub-committees, the organization works in connection with the following Conventions, of which it is the depository:

Convention on Facilitation of International Maritime Traffic, 1965. Came into force in March 1967.

International Convention on Load Lines, 1966. Came into force in July 1968.

International Convention on Tonnage Measurement of Ships, 1969. Convention embodies a universal system for measuring ships' tonnage. Came into force in 1982.

International Convention relating to Intervention on the High Seas in Cases of Oil Pollution Casualties, 1969. Came into force in May 1975. A Protocol adopted in 1973 came into force in 1983.

International Convention on Civil Liability for Oil Pollution Damage, 1969. Came into force in June 1975.

Intenational Convention on the Establishment of an International Fund for Compensation for Oil Pollution Damage, 1971. Came into force in October 1978.

Convention relating to Civil Liability in the Field of Maritime Carriage of Nuclear Material, 1971. Came into force in 1975.

Special Trade Passenger Ships Agreement, 1971. Came into force in 1974.

Convention on the International Regulations for Preventing Collisions at Sea, 1972. Came into force in July 1977.

Convention on the Prevention of Marine Pollution by Dumping of Wastes and Other Matter, 1972. Came into force in August 1975. Extended to include a ban on low-level nuclear waste in November 1993; came into force in February 1994.

International Convention for Safe Containers, 1972. Came into force in September 1977.

International Convention for the Prevention of Pollution from Ships, 1973 (as modified by the Protocol of 1978). Came into force in October 1983. Extended to include regulations to prevent air pollution in September 1997; amendments will come into force 12 months after 15 countries whose combined fishing fleets constitute 50% of the world's merchant fleet have become parties thereto.

International Convention on Safety of Life at Sea, 1974. Came into force in May 1980. A Protocol drawn up in 1978 came into force in May 1981. Numerous extensions and amendments.

Athens Convention relating to the Carriage of Passengers and their Luggage by Sea, 1974. Came into force in April 1987.

Convention on the International Maritime Satellite Organization, 1976. Came into force in July 1979.

Convention on Limitation of Liability for Maritime Claims, 1976. Came into force in December 1986.

International Convention for the Safety of Fishing Vessels, Torremolinos, 1977. Will come into force 12 months after 15 countries whose combined fishing fleets constitute 50% of world fishing fleets of 24 metres in length and over have become parties thereto.

International Convention on Standards of Training, Certification and Watchkeeping for Seafarers, 1978. Came into force in April 1984; restructured by amendments that entered into force in February 1997.

International Convention on Maritime Search and Rescue, 1979. Came into force in June 1985.

Paris Memorandum of Understanding on Port State Control, 1982.

International Convention for the Suppression of Unlawful Acts against the Safety of International Shipping, 1988. Came into force in March 1992.

Protocol for the Suppression of Unlawful Acts against the Safety of Fixed Platform located on the Continental Shelf, 1988. Came into force in March 1992.

International Convention on Salvage, 1989. Came into force in July 1996.

International Convention on Oil Pollution, Preparedness, Response and Co-operation, 1990. Came into force on 13 May 1995.

International Convention on Liability and Compensation for Damage in Connection with the Carriage of Hazardous and Noxious Substances by Sea, 1996. Will come into force 18 months after 12 states of which four have not less than 2m. units of gross tonnage have become parties thereto.

ASSOCIATED INSTITUTES

IMO Maritime Law Institute—IMLI: POB 31, Msida, MSD 01, Malta; tel. 319343; fax 343092; e-mail imli@maltanet.net; internet www.imli.org; provides training for maritime lawyers. Dir Prof. DAVID ATTARD.

International Maritime Academy—IMA: via E. Weiss 15, 34127 Trieste, Italy; tel. (40) 350829; fax (40) 350322; e-mail imoima@imo-ima.org; internet www.imoima.org; provides postgraduate training for seafarers and onshore staff employed in maritime-related fields; Dir PIETRO MARIN.

Regional Marine Pollution Emergency Response Centre for the Mediterranean Sea—REMPEC: Manoel Island, GZR 03, Malta; tel. 337296; fax 339951; e-mail rempecdirector@waldonet.mt; internet www.rempec.org; f. 1976 as the Regional Oil Comnbating Centre for the Mediterranean Sea. Administered by IMO in conjunction with the Regional Seas Programme of the UN Environment Programme. Aims to develop measures to combat pollution in the Mediterranean. Dir ROBERTO PATRUNO.

World Maritime University—WMU: POB 500, Citadellsvägen 29, 201 24 Malmö, Sweden; tel. (40) 356300; fax (40) 128442; e-mail info@wmu.se; internet www.wmu.se; f. by IMO in 1983. It offers postgraduate courses in various maritime disciplines, mainly for students from developing countries. Rector K. LAUBSTEIN. Publs *WMU Newsletter, WMU Handbook*.

Finance

Contributions are received from the member states. The budget appropriation for the two years 2000–01 amounted to £36.61m.

Publications

IMO News (quarterly).
Numerous specialized publications, including international conventions of which IMO is depositary.

International Monetary Fund—IMF

Address: 700 19th St, NW, Washington, DC 20431, USA.
Telephone: (202) 623-7300; **fax:** (202) 623-6220; **e-mail:** publicaffairs@imf.org; **internet:** www.imf.org.

The IMF was established at the same time as the World Bank in December 1945, to promote international monetary co-operation, to facilitate the expansion and balanced growth of international trade and to promote stability in foreign exchange.

MEMBERS

183 members: see Table on pp. 117–119.

Organization

(April 2001)

Managing Director: HORST KÖHLER (Germany).
First Deputy Managing Director: STANLEY FISCHER (USA).
Deputy Managing Directors: SHIGEMITSU SUGISAKI (Japan); EDUARDO ANINAT (Chile).

BOARD OF GOVERNORS

The highest authority of the Fund is exercised by the Board of Governors, on which each member country is represented by a Governor and an Alternate Governor. The Board of Governors meets once a year, but the Governors may take votes by mail or other means between annual meetings. The Board of Governors has delegated many of its powers to the Executive Directors. However, the conditions governing the admission of new members, adjustment of quotas and the election of Executive Directors, as well as certain other important powers, remain the sole responsibility of the Board of Governors. The voting power of each member on the Board of Governors is related to its quota in the Fund (see p. 97).

In September 1999 the Board of Governors adopted a resolution to transform the Interim Committee of the Board of Governors (established 1974) into the International Monetary and Financial Committee (IMFC). The IMFC, which held its inaugural meeting in April 2000, comprises 24 members, representing the same countries or groups of countries as those on the Board of Executive Directors (see below). It reviews the international monetary system and advises the Board of Governors, but has no decision-making authority.

The Development Committee (the Joint Ministerial Committee of the Boards of Governors of the World Bank and the IMF on the Transfer of Real Resources to Developing Countries, created in 1974, with a structure similar to that of the IMFC) reviews development policy issues and financing requirements.

BOARD OF EXECUTIVE DIRECTORS

The 24-member Board of Executive Directors, responsible for the day-to-day operations of the Fund, is in continuous session in Washington, under the chairmanship of the Fund's Managing Director or Deputy Managing Directors. The USA, the United Kingdom, Germany, France and Japan each appoint one Executive Director, while the other 19 Executive Directors are elected by groups of the remaining countries. As in the Board of Governors, the voting power of each member is related to its quota in the Fund, but in practice the Executive Directors normally operate by consensus.

The Managing Director of the Fund serves as head of its staff, which is organized into departments by function and area. At 31 December 1999 the Fund staff employed 2,297 staff members (with a further 444 additional authorized staff positions) from 127 countries. In mid-1994 two new positions of Deputy Managing Director were created, bringing the total to three. This major structural development was approved by the Executive Board and reflected the increase in reponsibilities of that position, owing to the IMF's greatly enlarged membership.

Activities

The purposes of the IMF, as defined in the Articles of Agreement, are:

(i) To promote international monetary co-operation through a permanent institution which provides the machinery for consultation and collaboration on monetary problems.

(ii) To facilitate the expansion and balanced growth of international trade, and to contribute thereby to the promotion and maintenance of high levels of employment and real income and to the development of members' productive resources.

(iii) To promote exchange stability, to maintain orderly exchange arrangements among members, and to avoid competitive exchange depreciation.

(iv) To assist in the establishment of a multilateral system of payments in respect of current transactions between members and in the elimination of foreign exchange restrictions which hamper the growth of trade.

(v) To give confidence to members by making the general resources of the Fund temporarily available to them, under adequate safeguards, thus providing them with the opportunity to correct maladjustments in their balance of payments, without resorting to measures destructive of national or international prosperity.

(vi) In accordance with the above, to shorten the duration of and lessen the degree of disequilibrium in the international balances of payments of members.

In joining the Fund, each country agrees to co-operate with the above objectives. In accordance with its objective of facilitating the expansion of international trade, the IMF encourages its members to accept the obligations of Article VIII, Sections two, three and four, of the Articles of Agreement. Members that accept Article VIII undertake to refrain from imposing restrictions on the making of payments and transfers for current international transactions and from engaging in discriminatory currency arrangements or multiple currency practices without IMF approval. By March 2001 149 members had accepted Article VIII status.

In October 1995 the Interim Committee of the Board of Governors endorsed recent decisions of the Executive Board to strengthen IMF financial support to members requiring exceptional assistance. An Emergency Financing Mechanism was established to enable the IMF to respond swiftly to potential or actual financial crises, while additional funds were made available for short-term currency stabilization. (The Mechanism was activated for the first time in July 1997, in response to a request by the Philippines Government to reinforce the country's international reserves, and was subsequently used during that year to assist Thailand, Indonesia and the Republic of Korea, and, in July 1998, Russia.) Emergency assistance was also to be available to countries in a post-conflict situation, in addition to existing arrangements for countries having been affected by natural disasters, to facilitate the rehabilitation of their economies and to improve their eligibility for further IMF concessionary arrangements. During 1999/2000 the IMF extended emergency assistance totalling SDR 400m. to three countries—two in post-conflict situtations and Turkey, which received the largest ever emergency loan extended by the IMF, amounting to SDR 362m., following the earthquake that took place there in August 1999. In December 2000 the Federal Republic of Yugoslavia (FRY) was admitted to the IMF to succeed the former Socialist Federal Republic of Yugoslavia (whose membership had terminated in 1992); the Fund immediately approved a loan of SDR 116.9m. for post-conflict assistance to the FRY.

In December 1996 the IMF and the World Trade Organization (q.v.) signed a co-operation agreement which provided for increased consultation and exchanges of information and data between the

two organizations, and granted each organization observer status at certain of the other's decision-making bodies. In April 1997 the Interim Committee of the Board of Governors endorsed proposals to amend the Articles of Agreement to include the promotion of capital-account liberalization as a specific objective of the IMF and to extend the Fund's mandate to cover capital movements. The proposed amendment remained under consideration in 2000.

In mid-1997 the devaluation of the Thai baht, following intense speculation of the currency and market losses, initiated a period of severe financial and economic turmoil in several Asian countries. The widespread effect of the crisis dominated the work of the IMF in 1997/98 and placed a substantial strain on its financial resources: by August 1998 the Fund had disbursed approximately US $26,000m. to assist the countries most affected by the Asian crisis, i.e. Indonesia, the Republic of Korea and Thailand. The IMF led efforts to mobilize additional funding from international sources, and aimed to help restore confidence in those economies, to support structural reforms, including the reform of financial systems, and to address governance issues, such as links between commerce and government and the question of economic transparency. In April 1998 the Executive Board attempted to focus on discussions concerning the strengthening of the international monetary system by identifying the following fundamental approaches: reinforcing international and domestic financial systems; strengthening IMF surveillance; promoting greater availability and transparency of information regarding member countries' economic data and policies; emphasizing the central role of the IMF in crisis management; and establishing effective procedures to involve the private sector in forestalling or resolving financial crises. The Fund pursued its review and reform of the international financial architecture during 1998/99. Demands on IMF resources, however, remained heavy owing to the ongoing effects of the Asian financial crisis and economic upheavals in Russia, in mid-1998, and in Brazil, at the end of that year. In 1999/2000, as the effects of the Asian economic crisis abated, IMF lending was lower than in the previous financial year. During 1999/2000 the Fund implemented several measures in connection with its ongoing efforts to appraise and reinforce the global financial architecture, including the adoption by the Executive Board in March 2000 of a strengthened framework to safeguard the use of IMF resources and, in April, approval by the Board of the establishment of an independent evaluation office to complement the Fund's ongoing internal and external evaluation activities (see below). During 2000 the Fund established the IMF Center, in Washington, DC, which aimed to promote awareness and understanding of its activities.

SURVEILLANCE

Under its Articles of Agreement, the Fund is mandated to oversee the effective functioning of the international monetary system. Accordingly, the Fund aims to exercise firm surveillance over the exchange rate policies of member states and to assess whether a country's economic situation and policies are consistent with the objectives of sustainable development and domestic and external stability. The Fund's main tools of surveillance are regular, bilateral consultations with member countries conducted in accordance with Article IV of the Articles of Agreement, which cover fiscal and monetary policies, balance of payments and external debt developments, as well as policies that affect the economic performance of a country, such as the labour market, social and environmental issues and good governance, and aspects of the country's capital accounts, and finance and banking sectors. In addition, World Economic Outlook discussions are held, normally twice a year, by the Executive Board to assess policy implications from a multilateral perspective and to monitor global developments. The rapid decline in the value of the Mexican peso in late 1994 and the financial crisis in Asia, which became apparent in mid-1997, focused attention on the importance of IMF surveillance of the economies and financial policies of member states and prompted the Fund to enhance the effectiveness of its surveillance and to encourage the full and timely provision of data by member countries in order to maintain fiscal transparency. In April 1996 the IMF established the Special Data Dissemination Standard, which was intended to improve access to reliable economic statistical information for member countries that have, or are seeking, access to international capital markets. In March 1999 the IMF undertook to strengthen the Standard by the introduction of a new reserves data template. By March 2001 48 countries had subscribed to the Standard. In December 1997 the Executive Board approved a new General Data Dissemination System (GDDS), to encourage all member countries to improve the production and dissemination of core economic data. The operational phase of the GDDS commenced in May 2000. In April 1997, in an effort to improve the value of surveillance by means of increased transparency, the Executive Board agreed to the voluntary issue of Press Information Notices (PINs) (on the internet and in *IMF Economic Reviews*), following each member's Article IV consultation with the Board, to those member countries wishing to make public the Fund's views. Other background papers providing information on and analysis of economic developments in individual countries continued to be made available. In April 1998 the Interim Committee adopted a voluntary Code of Good Practices on Fiscal Transparency: Declaration of Principles, which aimed to increase the quality and promptness of official reports on economic indicators, and in September 1999 it adopted a Code of Good Practices on Transparency in Monetary and Financial Policies: Declaration of Principles. The IMF and World Bank jointly established a pilot Financial Sector Assessment Programme (FSAP) in May 1999, which aimed to promote greater global financial security through the preparation of confidential detailed evaluations of the financial sectors of individual countries. (The pilot included industrialized countries, emerging market economies and developing countries.) In March 2000 the Executive Board adopted a strengthened framework to safeguard the use of IMF resources. All member countries making use of Fund resources were to be required to publish annual central bank statements audited in accordance with internationally accepted standards. It was also agreed that any instance of intentional misreporting of information by a member country should be publicized. In the following month the Executive Board approved the establishment of an independent evaluation office to complement the Fund's ongoing internal and external evaluation activities. In August the Executive Board adopted a Code of Conduct to guide its activities.

SPECIAL DRAWING RIGHTS

The special drawing right (SDR) was introduced in 1970 as a substitute for gold in international payments. It was intended eventually to become the principal reserve asset in the international monetary system, although by 2000 this appeared unlikely to happen. SDRs are allocated to members in proportion to their quotas. The IMF has allocated a total of SDR 21,433m. since the SDR was created in 1970. In October 1996 the Executive Board agreed to a new allocation of SDRs in order to achieve their equitable distribution among member states (i.e. all members would have an equal number of SDRs relative to the size of their quotas). In particular, this was deemed necessary since 38 countries that had joined the Fund since the last allocation of SDRs in 1981 had not yet received any of the units of account. In September 1997 at the annual meeting of the Executive Board, a resolution approving a special allocation of SDR 21,400m. was passed, in order to ensure an SDR to quota ratio of 29.32%, for all member countries. The resolution was to come into effect following its acceptance by 60% of member countries, having 85% of the total voting power. By 31 December 2000 99 members (66.1% of the voting power) had ratified the amendment.

From 1974 to 1980 the SDR was valued on the basis of the market exchange rate for a basket of 16 currencies, belonging to the members with the largest exports of goods and services; since 1981 it has been based on the currencies of the five largest exporters (France, Germany, Japan, the United Kingdom and the USA), although the list of currencies and the weight of each in the SDR valuation basket is revised every five years. In January 1999 the IMF incorporated the new currency of the European Economic and Monetary Union, the euro, into the valuation basket; it replaced the French and German currencies, on the basis of their conversion rates with the euro as agreed by the EU. From 1 January 2001 the relative weights assigned to the currencies in the valuation basket were redistributed. The value of the SDR averaged US $1.3189 during 2000, and at 28 February 2001 stood at $1.2925.

The Second Amendment to the Articles of Agreement (1978) altered and expanded the possible uses of the SDR in transactions with other participants. These 'prescribed holders' of the SDRs have the same degree of freedom as Fund members to buy and sell SDRs and to receive or use them in loans, pledges, swaps, donations or settlement of financial obligations. In 2000/01 there were 15 'prescribed holders': the African Development Bank and the African Development Fund, the Arab Monetary Fund, the Asian Development Bank, the Bank of Central African States, the Bank for International Settlements, the Central Bank of West African States, the East African Development Bank, the Eastern Caribbean Central Bank, the European Central Bank, the International Bank for Reconstruction and Development and the International Development Association, the International Fund for Agricultural Development, the Islamic Development Bank, the Latin American Reserve Fund and the Nordic Investment Bank.

QUOTAS

Each member is assigned a quota related to its national income, monetary reserves, trade balance and other economic indicators. A member's subscription is equal to its quota and is payable partly in SDRs and partly in its own currency. The quota determines a member's voting power, which is based on one vote for each SDR 100,000 of its quota *plus* the 250 votes to which each member is entitled. A member's quota also determines its access to the financial resources of the IMF, and its allocation of SDRs.

Quotas are reviewed at intervals of not more than five years, to take into account the state of the world economy and members'

different rates of development. General increases were made in 1959, 1966, 1970, 1978, 1980 and 1984, while special increases were made for the People's Republic of China in April 1980, for a group of 11 members in December 1980, and for Saudi Arabia in April 1981. In June 1990 the Board of Governors authorized proposals for a Ninth General Review of quotas. Total quotas were to be increased by roughly 50% (depending on various factors). At the same time the Board of Governors stipulated that the quota increase could occur only after the Third Amendment of the IMF's Articles of Agreement had come into effect. The amendment provides for the suspension of voting and other related rights of members that do not fulfil their obligations under the Articles. By September 1992 the necessary proportion of IMF members had accepted the amendment, and it entered into force in November. The Tenth General Review of quotas was concluded in December 1994, with the Board recommending no further increase in quotas. However, the Board resolved to monitor closely the Fund's liquidity. In October 1996 the Fund's Managing Director advocated an increase in quotas under the latest review of at least two-thirds in the light of the IMF's reduced liquidity position. (The IMF had extended unprecedentedly large amounts in stand-by arrangements during the period 1995–96, notably to Mexico and Russia.) In January 1998 the Board of Governors adopted a resolution in support of an increase in quotas of 45%, subject to approval by member states constituting 85% of total quotas (as at December 1997). Sufficient consent had been granted by January 1999 to enable the Eleventh General Review of Quotas to enter into effect. At 26 March 2001 total quotas in the Fund amounted to SDR 212,401.1m.

RESOURCES

Members' subscriptions form the basic resource of the IMF. They are supplemented by borrowing. Under the General Arrangements to Borrow (GAB), established in 1962, the 'Group of Ten' industrialized nations (G-10—Belgium, Canada, France, Germany, Italy, Japan, the Netherlands, Sweden, the United Kingdom and the USA) and Switzerland (which became a member of the IMF in May 1992 but which had been a full participant in the GAB from April 1984) undertake to lend the Fund as much as SDR 17,000m. in their own currencies, to assist in fulfilling the balance-of-payments requirements of any member of the group, or in response to requests to the Fund from countries with balance-of-payments problems that could threaten the stability of the international monetary system. In 1983 the Fund entered into an agreement with Saudi Arabia, in association with the GAB, making available SDR 1,500m., and other borrowing arrangements were completed in 1984 with the Bank for International Settlements, the Saudi Arabian Monetary Agency, Belgium and Japan, making available a further SDR 6,000m. In 1986 another borrowing arrangement with Japan made available SDR 3,000m. In May 1996 GAB participants concluded an agreement in principle to expand the resources available for borrowing to SDR 34,000m., by securing the support of 25 countries with the financial capacity to support the international monetary system. The so-called New Arrangements to Borrow (NAB) was approved by the Executive Board in January 1997. It was to enter into force, for an initial five-year period, as soon as the five largest potential creditors participating in NAB had approved the initiative and the total credit arrangement of participants endorsing the scheme had reached at least SDR 28,900m. While the GAB credit arrangement was to remain in effect, the NAB was expected to be the first facility to be activated in the event of the Fund's requiring supplementary resources. In July 1998 the GAB was activated for the first time in more than 20 years in order to provide funds totalling US $6,300m. in support of an IMF emergency assistance package for Russia (the first time the GAB had been used for a non-participant). The NAB became effective in November, and was used for the first time as part of an extensive programme of support for Brazil, which was adopted by the IMF in early December.

DRAWING ARRANGEMENTS

Exchange transactions within the Fund take the form of members' purchases (i.e. drawings) from the Fund of the currencies of other members for the equivalent amounts of their own currencies. Fund resources are available to eligible members on an essentially short-term and revolving basis to provide members with temporary assistance to contribute to the solution of their payments problems. Before making a purchase, a member must show that its balance of payments or reserve position makes the purchase necessary. Apart from this requirement, reserve tranche purchases (i.e. purchases that do not bring the Fund's holdings of the member's currency to a level above its quota) are permitted unconditionally.

With further purchases, however, the Fund's policy of 'conditionality' means that a member requesting assistance must agree to adjust its economic policies, as stipulated by the IMF. All requests other than for use of the reserve tranche are examined by the Executive Board to determine whether the proposed use would be consistent with the Fund's policies, and a member must discuss

BOARD OF EXECUTIVE DIRECTORS (March 2001)

Director	Casting Votes of	Total Votes	%
Appointed:			
KARIN LISSAKERS	USA	371,743	17.16
YUKIO YOSHIMURA	Japan	133,378	6.16
BERND ESDAR	Germany	130,332	6.02
JEAN-CLAUDE MILLERON	France	107,635	4.97
STEPHEN PICKFORD	United Kingdom	107,635	4.97
Elected:			
WILLY KIEKENS (Belgium)	Austria, Belarus, Belgium, Czech Republic, Hungary, Kazakhstan, Luxembourg, Slovakia, Slovenia, Turkey	111,696	5.16
J. DE BEAUFORT WIJNHOLDS (Netherlands)	Armenia, Bosnia and Herzegovina, Bulgaria, Croatia, Cyprus, Georgia, Israel, the former Yugoslav republic of Macedonia, Moldova, Netherlands, Romania, Ukraine	105,412	4.87
HERNÁN OYARZÁBAL (Venezuela)	Costa Rica, El Salvador, Guatemala, Honduras, Mexico, Nicaragua, Spain, Venezuela	92,989	4.29
RICCARDO FAINI (Italy)	Albania, Greece, Italy, Malta, Portugal, San Marino	90,636	4.18
THOMAS A. BERNES (Canada)	Antigua and Barbuda, Bahamas, Barbados, Belize, Canada, Dominica, Grenada, Ireland, Jamaica, Saint Christopher and Nevis, Saint Lucia, Saint Vincent and the Grenadines	80,636	3.72
OLLI-PEKKA LEHMUSSAARI (Finland)	Denmark, Estonia, Finland, Iceland, Latvia, Lithuania, Norway, Sweden	76,276	3.53
MICHAEL J. CALLAGHAN (Australia)	Australia, Kiribati, Republic of Korea, Marshall Islands, Federated States of Micronesia, Mongolia, New Zealand, Palau, Papua New Guinea, Philippines, Samoa, Seychelles, Solomon Islands, Vanuatu	72,413	3.34
SULAIMAN M. AL-TURKEI	Saudi Arabia	70,105	3.24
CYRUS RUSTOMJEE (South Africa)	Angola, Botswana, Burundi, Eritrea, Ethiopia, The Gambia, Kenya, Lesotho, Liberia, Malawi, Mozambique, Namibia, Nigeria, Sierra Leone, South Africa, Sudan, Swaziland, Tanzania, Uganda, Zambia, Zimbabwe	69,968	3.23
DONO ISKANDAR DJOJOSUBROTO (Indonesia)	Brunei, Cambodia, Fiji, Indonesia, Laos, Malaysia, Myanmar, Nepal, Singapore, Thailand, Tonga, Viet Nam	68,229	3.15
A. SHAKOUR SHAALAN (Egypt)	Bahrain, Egypt, Iraq, Jordan, Kuwait, Lebanon, Libya, Maldives, Oman, Qatar, Syria, United Arab Emirates, Yemen	64,008	2.95
ALEKSEI V. MOZHIN	Russia	59,704	2.76
ROBERTO F. CIPPA (Switzerland)	Azerbaijan, Kyrgyzstan, Poland, Switzerland, Tajikistan, Turkmenistan, Uzbekistan	56,900	2.63
MURILO PORTUGAL (Brazil)	Brazil, Colombia, Dominican Republic, Ecuador, Guyana, Haiti, Panama, Suriname, Trinidad and Tobago	53,422	2.47
VIJAY L. KELKAR (India)	Bangladesh, Bhutan, India, Sri Lanka	52,112	2.41
ABBAS MIRAKHOR (Iran)	Algeria, Ghana, Iran, Morocco, Pakistan, Tunisia	51,793	2.39
WEI BENHUA	People's Republic of China	63,942	2.95
A. GUILLERMO ZOCCALI (Argentina)	Argentina, Bolivia, Chile, Paraguay, Peru, Uruguay	43,395	2.00
ALEXANDRE BARRO CHAMBRIER (Gabon)	Benin, Burkina Faso, Cameroon, Cape Verde, Central African Republic, Chad, Comoros, Republic of the Congo, Côte d'Ivoire, Djibouti, Equatorial Guinea, Gabon, Guinea, Guinea-Bissau, Madagascar, Mali, Mauritania, Mauritius, Niger, Rwanda, São Tomé and Príncipe, Senegal, Togo	25,169	1.16

Note: At 15 March 2001 member countries' votes totalled 2,166,601, while votes in the Board of Executive Directors totalled 2,159,528. The latter total does not include the votes of Afghanistan, Somalia and the Federal Republic of Yugoslavia, which did not participate in the 2000 election of Executive Directors; it also excludes the votes of the Democratic Republic of the Congo, whose voting rights were suspended with effect from 2 June 1994.

its proposed adjustment programme (including fiscal, monetary, exchange and trade policies) with IMF staff. Purchases outside the reserve tranche are made in four credit tranches, each equivalent to 25% of the member's quota; a member must reverse the transaction by repurchasing its own currency (with SDRs or currencies specified by the Fund) within a specified time. A credit tranche purchase is usually made under a 'Stand-by Arrangement' with the Fund, or under the Extended Fund Facility. A Stand-by Arrangement is normally of one or two years' duration, and the amount is made available in instalments, subject to the member's observance of 'performance criteria'; repurchases must be made within three-and-a-quarter to five years. An Extended Arrangement is normally of three years' duration, and the member must submit detailed economic programmes and progress reports for each year; repurchases must be made within four-and-a-half to 10 years. A member whose payments imbalance is large in relation to its quota may make use of temporary facilities established by the Fund using borrowed resources, namely the 'enlarged access policy' established in 1981, which helps to finance Stand-by and Extended Arrangements for such a member, up to a limit of between 90% and 110% of the member's quota annually. Repurchases are made within three-and-a-half to seven years. In October 1994 the Executive Board approved a temporary increase in members' access to IMF resources, on the basis of a recommendation by the Interim Committee. The annual access limit under IMF regular tranche draw-

ings, Stand-by Arrangements and Extended Fund Facility credits was increased from 68% to 100% of a member's quota, with the cumulative access limit remaining at 300% of quota. The arrangements were extended, on a temporary basis, in November 1997.

In addition, special-purpose arrangements have been introduced, all of which are subject to the member's co-operation with the Fund to find an appropriate solution to its difficulties. During late 1999 the Fund undertook a review of its non-concessional lending facilities. The Buffer Stock Financing Facility (BSFF), established in 1969 in order to enable members to pay their contributions to the buffer stocks which were intended to stabilize markets for primary commodities, was abolished in January 2000, having last been used in 1984. In January 2000 the Executive Board also resolved to eliminate the contingency component of the former Compensatory and Contingency Financing Facility, established in 1988, reforming it as the Compensatory Financing Facility (CCF). The CCF provides compensation to members whose export earnings are reduced as a result of circumstances beyond their control, or which are affected by excess costs of cereal imports. In December 1997 the Executive Board established a new Supplemental Reserve Facility (SRF) to provide short-term assistance to members experiencing exceptional balance-of-payments difficulties resulting from a sudden loss of market confidence. Repayments were to be made within one to one-and-a-half years of the purchase, unless otherwise extended by the Board. The SRF was activated immediately to provide SDR 9,950m.

to the Republic of Korea, as part of Stand-by Arrangement amounting to SDR 15,550m., the largest amount ever committed by the Fund. (With additional financing from governments and international institutions, the total assistance 'package' for the Republic of Korea reached an estimated $57,000m.) In July 1998 SDR 4,000m. was made available to Russia under the SRF and, in December, some SDR 9,100m. was extended to Brazil under the SRF as part of a new Stand-by Arrangement. In April 1999 an additional facility was established, for a two-year period, to provide short-term financing on similar terms to the SRF in order to prevent more stable economies being affected by adverse international financial developments and to maintain investor confidence. Under the Contingent Credit Lines (CCL), established in 1999, member countries were to have short-term access to up to 500% of their quota, subject to meeting various economic criteria stipulated by the Fund.

In April 1993 the Fund established the systemic transformation facility (STF) to assist countries of the former USSR and other economies in transition. The STF was intended to be a temporary facility to enable member countries to draw on financial assistance for balance-of-payments difficulties resulting from severe disruption of their normal trade and payments arrangements. Access to the facility was limited to not more than 50% of a member's quota, and repayment terms were equal to those for the extended Fund facility. The expiry date for access to resources under this facility was extended by one year from 31 December 1994, to the end of 1995. During the STF's period of operations purchases amounting to SDR 3,984m. were made by 20 countries.

In 1986 the Fund established a Structural Adjustment Facility (SAF) to provide balance-of-payments assistance on concessional terms to low-income developing countries. In November 1993 the Executive Board agreed that no new commitments would be made under the SAF. In 1987 the Fund established an Enhanced Structural Adjustment Facility (ESAF), which was to provide new resources of SDR 6,000m. (in addition to any amounts remaining undisbursed under the SAF), to assist the adjustment efforts of, in particular, heavily indebted countries. Eligible members were to develop a three-year adjustment programme (with assistance given jointly by staff of the Fund and of the World Bank) to strengthen the balance-of-payments situation and foster sustainable economic growth. In February 1994 a new period of operations of the ESAF became effective, following an agreement to enlarge the ESAF Trust (the funding source for ESAF arrangements) by transferring the bulk of resources from the Special Disbursement Account (SDA) of the SAF. The enlarged ESAF came into effect in February 1994, when the Executive Board accepted that sufficient contributions had been committed to the Loan and Subsidy Accounts of the ESAF Trust. The terms and conditions of the new Trust facility remained the same as those under the original ESAF, although the list of countries eligible for assistance was enlarged by six to 78 (subsequently extended to 80). The commitment period for lending from the ESAF Trust expired on 31 December 1996, with disbursements to be made through to the end of 1999. In September 1996 the Interim Committee of the Board of Governors endorsed measures to finance the ESAF for a further five-year (2000–04) period, after which the facility was to become self-sustaining. The interim period of the ESAF was to be funded mainly from bilateral contributions, but drawing on the Fund's additional resources as necessary. In November 2000 the ESAF was reformulated as the Poverty Reduction and Growth Facility (PRGF), with greater emphasis on poverty reduction and sustainable development as key elements of growth-orientated economic strategies. Assistance under the PRGF (for which 77 countries were deemed eligible) was to be carefully matched to specific national requirements. Prior to drawing on the facility each recipient country was, in collaboration with representatives of civil society, non-governmental organizations and bilateral and multilateral institutions, to develop a national poverty reduction strategy, which was to be presented in a Poverty Reduction Strategy Paper (PRSP). PRGF loans carry an interest rate of 0.5% per year and are repayable over 10 years, with a five-and-a-half-year grace period; each eligible country is normally permitted to borrow up to 140% of its quota (in exceptional circumstances the maximum access can be raised to 185%). A PGRF Trust replaced the former ESAF Trust.

The PRGF supports, through long-maturity loans and grants, IMF participation in a joint initiative, with the World Bank, to provide exceptional assistance to heavily indebted poor countries (HIPCs), in order to help them to achieve a sustainable level of debt management. The initiative was formally approved at the September 1996 meeting of the Interim Committee, having received the support of the 'Paris Club' of official creditors, which agreed to increase the relief on official debt from 67% to 80%. In all, 41 HIPCs were identified, of which 33 were in sub-Saharan Africa. In April 1997 Uganda was approved as the first beneficiary of the initiative (see World Bank, p. 81). Resources for the HIPC initiative are channelled through the PRGF Trust. In early 1999 the IMF and World Bank initiated a comprehensive review of the HIPC scheme, in order to consider modifications of the initiative and to strengthen the link between debt relief and poverty reduction. A consensus emerged among the financial institutions and leading industralized nations to enhance the scheme, in order to make it available to more countries, and to accelerate the process of providing debt relief. In September the IMF Board of Governors expressed its commitment to undertaking an off-market transaction of a percentage of the Fund's gold reserves (i.e. a sale, at market prices, to central banks of member countries with repayment obligations to the Fund, which were then to be made in gold), as part of the funding arrangements of the enhanced HIPC scheme; this was undertaken during the period December 1999–April 2000. Under the enhanced initiative it was agreed that countries seeking debt relief should first formulate, and successfully implement for at least one year, a national poverty reduction strategy (see above). In May 2000 Uganda became the first country to qualify for full debt relief under the enhanced scheme. By February 2001 debt relief under the enhanced initiative had been extended to 22 eligible countries, of which 18 were in Africa. At September 1999 IMF assistance under the original scheme in net present value terms amounted to $305m. of a total of $3,355m. of assistance committed, which had a nominal debt relief value of $6,770m.

During 1999/2000 the IMF approved funding commitments amounting to SDR 22,929m. in new arrangements. Of the total amount, SDR 15,706m. was committed under 11 Stand-by Arrangements, SDR 6,582m. under four Extended Arrangements, and SDR 641m. under 10 PRGF arrangements. During 1999/2000 members' purchases from the general resources account amounted to SDR 6,377m., compared with SDR 21,414m. in 1998/99, with the main users of IMF resources being Mexico, Indonesia and Brazil. Outstanding IMF credit at 28 February 2001 totalled SDR 50,158m., compared with SDR 56,026m.as at the previous year.

TECHNICAL ASSISTANCE

This is provided by special missions or resident representatives who advise members on every aspect of economic management. Specialized technical assistance is provided by the IMF's various departments, and accounted for some 15% of the administrative budget in 1998/99. The IMF Institute, founded in 1964, trains officials from member countries in financial analysis and policy, balance-of-payments methodology and public finance; it also gives assistance to national and regional training centres. In May 1998 an IMF—Singapore Regional Training Institute (an affiliate of the IMF Institute) was inaugurated, in collaboration with the Singaporean Government, in order to provide training for officials from the Asia-Pacific region. The IMF is a co-sponsor, with UNDP and the Japan administered account, of the Joint Vienna Institute, which was opened in the Austrian capital in October 1992 and which trains officials from former centrally-planned economies in various aspects of economic management and public administration. In January 1999 the IMF, in co-operation with the African Development Bank and the World Bank, announced the establishment of a Joint Africa Institute, in Abidjan, Côte d'Ivoire, which was to offer training to officials from African countries from the second half of the year. The IMF Institute also co-operates with other established regional training centres and institutes in order to refine its delivery of technical assistance and training services.

Publications

Annual Report.

Balance of Payments Statistics Yearbook.

Direction of Trade Statistics (quarterly and annually).

Finance and Development (quarterly, published jointly with the World Bank).

Government Finance Statistics Yearbook.

IMF Economic Reviews (3 a year).

IMF Survey (2 a month).

International Capital Markets: Developments, Prospects and Key Policy Issues.

International Financial Statistics (monthly and annually, also on CD-ROM).

Joint BIS-IMF-OECD-World Bank Statistics on External Debt (quarterly).

Staff Papers (quarterly).

World Economic Outlook (2 a year).

Occasional papers, economic and financial surveys, pamphlets, booklets.

Statistics

QUOTAS (SDR million)

	15 March 2001
Afghanistan*	(161.9) 120.4
Albania	48.7
Algeria	1,254.7
Angola	286.3
Antigua and Barbuda	13.5
Argentina	2,117.1
Armenia	92.0
Australia	3,236.4
Austria	1,872.3
Azerbaijan	160.9
Bahamas	130.3
Bahrain	135.0
Bangladesh	533.3
Barbados	67.5
Belarus	386.4
Belgium	4,605.2
Belize	18.8
Benin	61.9
Bhutan	6.3
Bolivia	171.5
Bosnia and Herzegovina	169.1
Botswana	63.0
Brazil	3,036.1
Brunei†	(215.2) 150.0
Bulgaria	640.2
Burkina Faso	60.2
Burundi	77.0
Cambodia	87.5
Cameroon	185.7
Canada	6,369.2
Cape Verde	9.6
Central African Republic	55.7
Chad	56.0
Chile	856.1
China, People's Republic‡	6,369.2
Colombia	774.0
Comoros	8.9
Congo, Democratic Republic*	(533.0) 291.0
Congo, Republic	84.6
Costa Rica	164.1
Côte d'Ivoire	325.2
Croatia	365.1
Cyprus	139.6
Czech Republic	819.3
Denmark	1,642.8
Djibouti	15.9
Dominica	8.2
Dominican Republic	218.9
Ecuador	302.3
Egypt	943.7
El Salvador	171.3
Equatorial Guinea	32.6
Eritrea	15.9
Estonia	65.2
Ethiopia	133.7
Fiji	70.3
Finland	1,263.8
France	10,738.5
Gabon	154.3
The Gambia	31.1
Georgia	150.3
Germany	13,008.2
Ghana	369.0
Greece	823.0
Grenada	11.7
Guatemala	210.2
Guinea	107.1
Guinea-Bissau	14.2
Guyana	90.9
Haiti†	(81.9) 60.7
Honduras	129.5
Hungary	1,038.4
Iceland	117.6
India	4,158.2
Indonesia	2,079.3
Iran	1,497.2
Iraq*	(1,188.4) 504.0
Ireland	838.4
Israel	928.2
Italy	7,055.5

	15 March 2001
Jamaica	273.5
Japan	13,312.8
Jordan	170.5
Kazakhstan	365.7
Kenya	271.4
Kiribati	5.6
Korea, Republic	1,633.6
Kuwait	1,381.1
Kyrgyzstan	88.8
Laos†	(52.9) 39.1
Latvia	126.8
Lebanon	203.0
Lesotho	34.9
Liberia*	(129.2) 71.3
Libya	1,123.7
Lithuania	144.2
Luxembourg	279.1
Macedonia, former Yugoslav republic	68.9
Madagascar	122.2
Malawi	69.4
Malaysia	1,486.6
Maldives	8.2
Mali	93.3
Malta	102.0
Marshall Islands†	(3.5) 2.5
Mauritania	64.4
Mauritius	101.6
Mexico	2,585.8
Micronesia, Federated States	5.1
Moldova	123.2
Mongolia	51.1
Morocco	588.2
Mozambique	113.6
Myanmar	258.4
Namibia	136.5
Nepal	71.3
Netherlands	5,162.4
New Zealand	894.6
Nicaragua	130.0
Niger	65.8
Nigeria	1,753.2
Norway	1,671.7
Oman	194.0
Pakistan	1,033.7
Palau	3.1
Panama	206.6
Papua New Guinea	131.6
Paraguay	99.9
Peru	638.4
Philippines	879.9
Poland	1,369.0
Portugal	867.4
Qatar	263.8
Romania	1,030.2
Russia	5,945.4
Rwanda	80.1
Saint Christopher and Nevis	8.9
Saint Lucia	15.3
Saint Vincent and the Grenadines	8.3
Samoa	11.6
San Marino	17.0
São Tomé and Príncipe	7.4
Saudi Arabia	6,985.5
Senegal	161.8
Seychelles	8.8
Sierra Leone	103.7
Singapore	862.5
Slovakia	357.5
Slovenia	231.7
Solomon Islands	10.4
Somalia*	(81.7) 44.2
South Africa	1,868.5
Spain	3,048.9
Sri Lanka	413.4
Sudan*	(315.1) 169.7
Suriname	92.1
Swaziland	50.7
Sweden	2,395.5
Switzerland	3,458.5
Syria	293.6
Tajikistan	87.0
Tanzania	198.9
Thailand	1,081.9

— continued	15 March 2001
Togo .	73.4
Tonga .	6.9
Trinidad and Tobago.	335.6
Tunisia .	286.5
Turkey .	964.0
Turkmenistan	75.2
Uganda .	180.5
Ukraine .	1,372.0
United Arab Emirates	611.7
United Kingdom .	10,738.5
USA .	37,149.3
Uruguay .	306.5
Uzbekistan .	275.6
Vanuatu .	17.0
Venezuela .	2,659.1
Viet Nam .	329.1
Yemen .	243.5
Yugoslavia, Federal Republic§ .	467.7

— continued	15 March 2001
Zambia .	489.1
Zimbabwe .	353.4

* At 15 March 2001 these members had overdue obligations and were therefore ineligible to consent to the increase in quotas under the Eleventh General Review (which came into effect in January 1999). The figures listed are those determined under previous reviews, while the figures in parentheses are the proposed Eleventh General Review quotas.

† At 15 March 2001 these members had not yet consented to their increased quotas under the Eleventh General Review. The proposed quotas are those in parentheses.

‡ The quota of the People's Republic of China was increased, at that country's request, from SDR 4,687.2m. to SDR 6,369.2m. on 8 February 2001.

§ In December 2000 the Federal Republic of Yugoslavia was admitted to the IMF, succeeding the former Socialist Federal Republic of Yugoslavia, whose membership of the Fund had been terminated in December 1992.

FINANCIAL ACTIVITIES (SDR million, year ending 30 April)

Type of Transaction	1994	1995	1996	1997	1998	1999
Total disbursements .	5,903	11,178	12,303	5,644	19,924	22,240
Purchases by facility (General Resources Account)* .	5,241	10,592	10,826	4,939	18,951	21,414
Stand-by and first credit tranche .	1,052	7,587	9,127	1,836	16,127	12,868
Compensatory and Contingency Financing Facility .	718	287	9	282	—	2,600
Extended Fund Facility.	746	1,595	1,554	2,820	2,824	5,947
Systemic Transformation Facility .	2,725	1,123	136	—	—	—
Loans under SAF/ESAF arrangements .	662	587	1,477	705	973	826
Special Disbursement Account resources .	68	19	185	—	—	—
ESAF Trust resources .	594	568	1,292	705	973	826
By region:						
Africa .	1,185	1,022	2,304	992	876	542
Asia .	690	383	367	181	16,446	8,918
Europe .	3,258	2,896	5,156	3,381	2,170	5,169
Middle East .	11	76	129	153	148	157
Western Hemisphere .	758	6,801	4,427	937	283	7,454
Repurchases and repayments .	4,509	4,231	7,100	7,196	4,385	11,091
Repurchases .	4,343	3,984	6,698	6,668	3,789	10,465
Trust Fund and SAF/ESAF loan repayments .	166	247	402	528	596	626
Total outstanding credit provided by Fund (end of year) .	29,889	36,837	42,040	40,488	56,026	67,175
Of which:						
General Resources Account .	25,533	32,140	36,268	34,539	49,701	60,651
Special Disbursement Account .	1,835	1,651	1,545	1,220	922	677
Administered Accounts						
Trust Fund .	105	102	95	90	90	89
ESAF Trust† .	2,416	2,944	4,132	4,639	5,314	5,758

* Excluding reserve tranche purchases.
† Including Saudi Fund for Development associated loans.

Source: *International Monetary Fund Annual Report 1999*.

International Telecommunication Union—ITU

Address: Place des Nations, 1211 Geneva 20, Switzerland.
Telephone: (22) 7305111; **fax:** (22) 7337256; **e-mail:** itumail@itu.int; **internet:** www.itu.int.

Founded in 1865, ITU became a specialized agency of the UN in 1947. It acts to encourage world co-operation in the use of telecommunication, to promote technical development, to harmonize national policies in the field, and to secure minimal costs for telecommunications products and services.

MEMBERS

189 member states: see Table on pp. 117–119. More than 600 scientific and technical companies, public and private operators, broadcasters and other organizations are also ITU members.

Organization

(April 2001)

PLENIPOTENTIARY CONFERENCE

The supreme organ of ITU; normally meets every four years. The main tasks of the Conference are to elect ITU's leadership, establish policies, revise the Convention (see below) and approve limits on budgetary spending.

WORLD CONFERENCES ON INTERNATIONAL TELECOMMUNICATIONS

The World Conferences on International Telecommunications are held at the request of members and after approval by the Plenipotentiary Conference. The World Conferences are authorized to review and revise the regulations applying to the provision and operation of international telecommunications services. As part of the 1993 restructuring of ITU, separate Conferences were to be held by three sectors (see below): Radiocommunication Conferences (to be held every two years); Telecommunication Standardization Assemblies (to be held every four years or at the request of one-quarter of ITU members); and Telecommunication Development Conferences (to be held every four years).

ITU COUNCIL

The Council meets annually in Geneva and is composed of 46 members elected by the Plenipotentiary Conference.

The Council ensures the efficient co-ordination and implementation of the work of the Union in all matters of policy, administration and finance, in the interval between Plenipotentiary Conferences, and approves the annual budget. It also co-ordinates the efforts of ITU to assist developing countries in the improvement of telecommunications equipment and networks.

GENERAL SECRETARIAT

The Secretary-General is elected by the Plenipotentiary Conference, and is responsible to it for the General Secretariat's work, and for the Union's administrative and financial services. The General Secretariat's staff totals about 712, representing 74 nationalities; the working languages are Arabic, Chinese, English, French, Russian and Spanish.
Secretary-General: YOSHIO UTSUMI (Japan).
Deputy Secretary-General: ROBERTO BLOIS MONTES DE SOUZA (Brazil).

Convention

The International Telecommunication Convention is the definitive convention of the Union, member countries being those that signed it in 1932 or acceded to it later. Since 1932 it has been superseded by new versions adopted at successive Plenipotentiary Conferences. At the Additional Plenipotentiary Conference held in December 1992, in Geneva, Switzerland, a new constitution and convention were signed. They entered into force on 1 July 1994, but the provisions relating to the new structure and functioning of ITU became effective on 1 March 1993. The Constitution contains the fundamental provisions of ITU, whereas the Convention contains other provisions which complement those of the Constitution and which, by their nature, require periodic revision.

The Constitution and Convention establish the purposes and structure of the Union, contain the general provisions relating to telecommunications and special provisions for radio, and deal with relations with the UN and other organizations. Both instruments

are further complemented by the administrative regulations listed below.

INTERNATIONAL TELECOMMUNICATIONS REGULATIONS

The International Telecommunications Regulations were adopted in 1988 and entered into force in 1990. They establish the general principles relating to the provision and operation of international telecommunication services offered to the public. They also establish rules applicable to administrations and recognized private operating agencies. Their provisions are applied to both wire and wireless telegraph and telephone communications in so far as the Radio Regulations do not provide otherwise.

RADIO REGULATIONS

The Radio Regulations, which first appeared in 1906, include general rules for the assignment and use of frequencies and the associated orbital positions for space stations. They include a Table of Frequency Allocations (governing the use of radio frequency bands between 9 kHz and 400 GHz) for the various radio services (*inter alia* radio broadcasting, television, radio astronomy, navigation aids, point-to-point service, maritime mobile, amateur).

The 1979 World Administrative Radio Conference undertook a complete revision of the radio spectrum allocation. Partial revisions were also made by subsequent world and regional administrative radio conferences, particularly with reference to space radiocommunications, using satellites.

Activities

In December 1992 an Additional Plenipotentiary Conference was held in Geneva, Switzerland, which agreed on reforms to the structure and functioning of ITU. As a result, ITU comprised three sectors corresponding to its main functions: standardization; radiocommunication; and development. In October 1994 the ordinary Plenipotentiary Conference, held in Kyoto, Japan, adopted ITU's first strategic plan. A second strategic plan, for the period 1999–2003, was adopted by the conference, convened in Minneapolis, USA, in October/November 1998. The plan recognized new trends and developments in the world telecommunication environment, such as globalization, liberalization, and greater competition, assessed their implications for ITU, and proposed new strategies and priorities to enable ITU to function effectively. The conference approved the active involvement of ITU in governance issues relating to the internet, and recommended that a World Summit on the Information Society be convened, given the rapid developments in that field. (This was subsequently scheduled to be held in 2003.) In 1999 an ITU Year 2000 Task Force pursued efforts to ensure that communications companies complied with measures to prevent any potential difficulties resulting from the millennium date change.

RADIOCOMMUNICATION SECTOR

The role of the sector is to ensure an equitable and efficient use of the radio-frequency spectrum by all radiocommunication services. The Radio Regulations are reviewed and revised by the sector's conferences. The technical work on issues to be considered by conferences is conducted by Radiocommunication Assemblies, on the basis of recommendations made by Study Groups. These groups of experts study technical questions relating to radiocommunications, according to a study programme formulated by the Assemblies. The Assemblies may approve, modify or reject any recommendations of the Study Groups, and are authorized to establish new groups and to abolish others. The procedural rules used in the application of the Radio Regulations were to be considered by a nine-member Radio Regulations Board, which may also perform duties relating to the allocation and use of frequencies and consider cases of interference. The Sector administers ITU's 'International Mobile Telecommunication-2000' initiative relating to third generation (3G) mobile communications systems, which aims to provide wireless access to the global telecommunication infrastructure through satellite and terrestrial systems. The 1998 Plenipotentiary Conference resolved to establish a working group open to members of the Sector to prepare recommendations concerning the submission and processing of charges of satellite networking filings..

The administrative work of the sector is the responsibility of the Radiocommunication Bureau, which is headed by an elected Director. The Bureau co-ordinates the work of Study Groups, provides administrative support for the Radio Regulations Board, and works alongside the General Secretariat to prepare conferences and to provide relevant assistance to developing countries. The Director is assisted by an Advisory Group.

Director: ROBERT W. JONES (Canada).

TELECOMMUNICATION STANDARDIZATION SECTOR

The sector was established to study technical, operational and tariff issues in order to standardize telecommunications throughout the world. The sector's conferences consider draft standards, referred to as Recommendations, which, if approved, establish ITU guidelines to guarantee the effective provision of telecommunication services. According to the priority given to different issues concerning draft standards, the conferences may maintain, establish or abolish Study Groups. Recommendations may be approved outside of the four-year interval between conferences if a Study Group concludes such action to be urgent. According to the 1999–2003 strategic plan, one of the priorities for the sector was to be the formulation of recommendations relating to Internet Protocol-based networks, as well as more general recommendations to keep pace with the rapid technological developments and expansion of market demand. A World Telecommunication Standardization Assembly was held in Montréal, Canada, in September/October 2000, to approve settlement rates for international connections. The meeting also approved the establishment of a management board to oversee the implementation of 3G mobile services. In June 1999 an ITU Study Group recommended implementing a scaled system of accounting rates based on telephone densities.

Preparations for conferences and other meetings of the sector are made by the Telecommunication Standardization Bureau (ITU-T). It administers the application of conference decisions, as well as relevant provisions of the International Telecommunications Regulations. The ITU-T is headed by an elected Director, who is assisted by an Advisory Group. The Director reports to conferences and to the ITU Council on the activities of the sector.

Director: HOULIN ZHAO (People's Republic of China).

TELECOMMUNICATION DEVELOPMENT SECTOR

The sector's objectives are to promote the development of telecommunication networks and services in developing countries, to facilitate the transfer of appropriate technologies and the use of resources by preferential credit arrangements, and to provide advice on issues specific to telecommunications. The sector operates as an executing agency for projects under the UN development system or other funding arrangements. In 1995 the ITU supported the establishment of an independent company, *World Tel*, which aimed to provide funding, technology and management assistance to telecommunications projects in low-income countries. The company's

first large-scale project, finalized in 1997, aimed to provide local telephone services in Mexico.

The sector holds conferences regularly to encourage international co-operation in the development of telecommunications, and to determine strategies for development. Conferences consider the result of work undertaken by Study Groups on issues of benefit to developing countries, including development policy, finance, network planning and operation of services. The sector aims to hold one world conference and one regional conference each in Africa, Asia and the Pacific, the Americas, Europe, and the Arab States every four years. The first World Telecommunications Development Conference was held in Buenos Aires, Argentina, in 1994; the second was convened in Valletta, Malta, in March 1998. The 1999–2003 strategic plan emphasized the need for the sector to enhance collaboration with the private sector and relevant organizations, especially at regional and sub-regional levels, and to promote new and more effective partnership arrangements in and between the public and private sectors. In early 2001 ITU published a report in which it identified securing effective interconnection regulation as a priority in overcoming the so-called global digital divide.

The administrative work of the sector is conducted by the Telecommunication Development Bureau, which may also study specific problems presented by a member state. The Director of the Bureau reports to conferences and the ITU Council, and is assisted by an Advisory Board.

Director: HAMEDOUN I. TOURÉ (Mali).

INFORMATION

ITU issues numerous technical and statistical publications (see below) and maintains a library and archives. It also offers the use of an on-line computer-based Telecom information exchange service (TIES), which provides access to ITU databases, document exchange, and other telecommunication information.

Finance

The 1998 Plenipotentiary Conference approved a maximum budget of 333.2m. Swiss francs for the two-year period 2000–01.

Publications

List of Publications (2 a year).
Telecommunication Journal (monthly in English, French and Spanish).
World Telecommunication Development Report.
Conventions, statistics, regulations, technical documents and manuals, conference documents.

United Nations Educational, Scientific and Cultural Organization—UNESCO

Address: 7 place de Fontenoy, 75352 Paris 07 SP, France.
Telephone: 1-45-68-10-00; **fax:** 1-45-67-16-90; **internet:** www.unesco.org.
UNESCO was established in 1946 'for the purpose of advancing, through the educational, scientific and cultural relations of the peoples of the world, the objectives of international peace and the common welfare of mankind'.

MEMBERS

188 members, and five associate members: see Table on pp. 117–119.

Organization

(April 2001)

GENERAL CONFERENCE

The supreme governing body of the Organization, the Conference meets in ordinary session once in two years and is composed of representatives of the member states.

EXECUTIVE BOARD

The Board, comprising 58 members, prepares the programme to be submitted to the Conference and supervises its execution; it meets twice or sometimes three times a year.

SECRETARIAT

Director-General: KOICHIRO MATSUURA (Japan).

CO-OPERATING BODIES

In accordance with UNESCO's constitution, national Commissions have been set up in most member states. These help to integrate work within the member states and the work of UNESCO.

PRINCIPAL REGIONAL OFFICES

Africa

Regional Office for Education in Africa: 12 ave Roume, BP 3311, Dakar, Senegal; tel. 823-50-82; fax 823-83-93; e-mail uhdak@unesco.org; Dir P. OBANYA.
Regional Office for Science and Technology for Africa: POB 30592, Nairobi, Kenya; tel. (2) 621234; fax (2) 215991; e-mail nairobi@unesco.org; internet www.unesco-nairobi.unon.org; f. 1965 to execute UNESCO's regional science programme, and to assist in the planning and execution of national programmes. Dir P. B. VITTA.

Arab States

Regional Office for Education in the Arab States: POB 5244, ave Cité Sportive, Beirut, Lebanon; tel. (1) 850075; fax (1) 824854; e-mail uhbei@unesco.org; internet www.unesco.org.lb; Dir V. BILLEH.
Regional Office for Science and Technology in the Arab States: 8 Abdel Rahman Fahmy St, Garden City, Cairo 11511,

Egypt; tel. (2) 3543036; fax (2) 3545296; e-mail uhcai@unesco.org; Dir Dr MOHAMED EL-DEEK (acting).

Asia and the Pacific

Principal Regional Office for Asia and the Pacific: 920 Sukhumvit Rd, POB 967, Bangkok 10110, Thailand; tel. (2) 391-0789; fax (2) 391-0866; e-mail uhbgk@unesco.org; internet www.unescobkk.org; Dir ZHOU NANZHAO.

Regional Office for Book Development in Asia and the Pacific: POB 2034, Islamabad 44000, Pakistan; tel. (51) 813308; fax (51) 825341; Dir M. M. KASEJU.

Regional Office for Science and Technology for South-East Asia: UN Building (2nd Floor), Jalan M. H. Thamrin 14, Tromol Pos 1273/JKT, Jakarta 10002, Indonesia; tel. (21) 3141308; fax (21) 3150382; e-mail uhjak@unesco.org; internet www.unesco.or.id; Dir Prof. STEPHEN HILL.

Europe and North America

European Centre for Higher Education (CEPES): Palatul Kretulescu, Stirbei Voda 39, 70732 Bucharest, Romania; tel. (1) 3159956; fax (1) 3123567; e-mail cepes@cepes.ro; internet www.cepes.ro; Dir JAN SADLAK.

Regional Office for Science and Technology for Europe: Palazzo Loredan degli Ambasciatori, 1262/a Dorsoduro, 30123 Venice, Italy; tel. (041) 522-5535; fax (041) 528-9995; e-mail roste@unesco.org; Dir Prof. PIERRE LASSERRE.

Latin America and the Caribbean

Caribbean Network of Educational Innovation for Development: POB 423, Bridgetown, St Michael, Barbados; tel. 4274771; fax 4360094; e-mail uhbri@unesco.org; Head of Office R. COLLEEN WINTER-BRAITHWAITE.

Regional Centre for Higher Education in Latin America and the Caribbean (CRESALC): Ave Los Chorros, c/c Calle Aceuducto, Edif. Asovincar, Altos de Sebucan, Apdo 68394, Caracas 1062 A, Venezuela; tel. (2) 286-0721; fax (2) 286-2039; e-mail uhcar@unesco.org; Dir L. YARZABAL.

Regional Office for Culture in Latin America and the Caribbean: Apdo 4158, Havana 4, Cuba; tel. (7) 32-7741; fax (7) 33-3144; e-mail uhldo@unesco.org; Dir GLORIA LÓPEZ MORALES.

Regional Office for Education in Latin America and the Caribbean: Calle Enrique Delpiano 2058, Plaza Pedro de Valdivia, Casilla 3187, Santiago, Chile; tel. (2) 2049032; fax (2) 2091875; e-mail uhstg@unesco.org; Dir A. MACHADO PINHEIRO.

Regional Office for Science and Technology for Latin America and the Caribbean: Avda Brasil 2697 P. 4, Casilla 859, 11300 Montevideo, Uruguay; tel. (2) 7072023; fax (2) 7072140; e-mail orcyt@unesco.org.uy; internet www.unesco.org.uy; Dir MIGUEL ANGEL ENRÍQUES.

Activities

UNESCO's overall work programme for 2000–01 comprised the following four major programmes (the same as for the previous biennium): Education for All Throughout Life; the Sciences in the Service of Development; Cultural Development: Heritage and Creativity; and Communication, Information and Informatics. Education for All Throughout Life was designated as the priority programme. The work programme also incorporated a transdisciplinary project — Towards a Culture of Peace — which aimed to promote the development of knowledge, attitudes and values that are conducive to peace. UNESCO was also responsible for co-ordinating activities relating to the International Year for the Culture of Peace, designated by the UN General Assembly to be observed in 2000. A Manifesto 2000 for a Culture of Peace and Non-violence, which was inaugurated in December 1998 at a celebration of the 50th anniversary of the Universal Declaration of Human Rights, had nearly 75m. signatories by March 2001.

EDUCATION

Since its establishment UNESCO has devoted itself to promoting education in accordance with principles based on democracy and respect for human rights.

In March 1990 UNESCO, with other UN agencies, sponsored the World Conference on Education for All. 'Education for All' was subsequently adopted as a guiding principle of UNESCO's contribution to development. The promotion of access to learning opportunities throughout an individual's life is a priority for UNESCO's 1996–2001 programme of activities. UNESCO aims, initially, to foster basic education for all. The second part of its strategy is to renew and diversify education systems, including updating curricular programmes in secondary education, strengthening science and technology activities and ensuring equal access to education for girls and women. In December 1993 the heads of government of nine

highly-populated developing countries (Bangladesh, Brazil, the People's Republic of China, Egypt, India, Indonesia, Mexico, Nigeria and Pakistan), meeting in Delhi, India, agreed to co-operate with the objective of achieving comprehensive primary education for all children and of expanding further learning opportunities for children and adults. By September 1999 all nine countries had officially signed the so-called Delhi Declaration. In November the General Conference urged for further support for new basic education projects targeting marginalized groups, including orphans, indigenous populations, refugees and the disabled. In endorsing the education programme for 2000–01 the Conference also emphasized the importance of information technologies, and the need to train teachers in the use of these, with the objective of providing educational opportunities to all. In April 2000 several UN agencies, including UNESCO and UNICEF, and other partners sponsored the World Education Forum, held in Dakar, Senegal, to assess international progress in achieving the goal of 'Education for All' and to adopt a strategy for further action, with the aim of ensuring universal basic education by 2015.

Within the UN system, UNESCO is responsible for providing technical assistance and educational services within the context of emergency situations. This includes providing education to refugees and displaced persons, as well as assistance for the rehabilitation of national education systems. In Palestine, UNESCO collaborates with UNRWA (q.v.) to assist with the training of teachers, educational planning and rehabilitation of schools.

UNESCO is concerned with improving the quality, relevance and efficiency of higher education. It assists member states in reforming their national systems, organizes high-level conferences for Ministers of Education and other decision-makers, and disseminates research papers. A World Conference on Higher Education was convened in October 1998 in Paris, France. The Conference adopted a World Declaration on Higher Education for the 21st Century, incorporating proposals to reform higher education, with emphasis on access to education, and educating for individual development and active participation in society. The Conference also approved a framework for Priority Action for Change and Development of Higher Education, which comprised guide-lines for governments and institutions to meet the objectives of greater accessibility, as well as improved standards and relevancy of higher education.

The International Institute for Educational Planning and the International Bureau of Education (see below) undertake training, research and the exchange of information on aspects of education. A UNESCO Institute for Education, based in Hamburg, Germany, researches literacy activities and the evolution of adult learning systems.

SCIENCE AND SOCIAL SCIENCES

In November 1999 the General Conference identified the following as priority areas of UNESCO science initiatives in 2000–01: combating poverty; science education; support for the integration of women in all fields of science and technology; the need for a future generations approach; environment and sustainable development; promotion of cultural diversity; the elaboration of an ethical framework for the application of scientific results; and access to scientific information. UNESCO was to continue to implement projects under the programme of the Sciences in the Service of Development, which was initiated in the previous biennium in order to foster the advancement, transfer and exchange of knowledge in the physical, natural, social and human sciences and to promote their application with the objective of improving the social and natural environment. The Conference also endorsed a Declaration on Science and the Use of Scientific Knowledge and an agenda for action, which had been adopted at the World Conference on Science, held in June/July 1999, in Budapest, Hungary.

UNESCO aims to improve the level of university teaching of the basic sciences through training courses, establishing national and regional networks and centres of excellence, and fostering co-operative research. In carrying out its mission, UNESCO relies on partnerships with non-governmental organizations and the world scientific communities. With the International Council of Scientific Unions and the Third World Academy of Sciences, UNESCO operates a short-term fellowship programme in the basic sciences and an exchange programme of visiting lecturers. In September 1996 UNESCO initiated a 10-year World Solar Programme, which aimed to promote the application of solar energy and to increase research, development and public awareness of all forms of ecologically-sustainable energy use.

In May 1997 the International Bioethics Committee, a group of 36 specialists who meet under UNESCO auspices, approved a draft version of a Universal Declaration on the Human Genome and Human Rights, in an attempt to provide ethical guide-lines for developments in human genetics. The Declaration, which identified some 100,000 hereditary genes as 'common heritage', was adopted by the UNESCO General Conference in November and committed states to promoting the dissemination of relevant scientific knowledge and co-operating in genome research. The November Conference also resolved to establish an 18-member World Commission on the Ethics of Scientific Knowledge and Technology to serve as a forum for the exchange of information and ideas and to promote dialogue between scientific communities, decision-makers and the public.

UNESCO has over the years established various forms of intergovernmental co-operation concerned with the environmental sciences and research on natural resources, in order to support the recommendations of the June 1992 UN Conference on Environment and Development and, in particular, the implementation of 'Agenda 21' to promote sustainable development. The International Geological Correlation Programme, undertaken jointly with the International Union of Geological Sciences, aims to improve and facilitate global research of geological processes. In the context of the International Decade for Natural Disaster Reduction (declared in 1990), UNESCO conducted scientific studies of natural hazards and means of mitigating their effects and organized several disaster-related workshops. The International Hydrological Programme considers scientific aspects of water resources assessment and management; and the Intergovernmental Oceanographic Commission (IOC, q.v.) focuses on issues relating to oceans, shorelines and marine resources, in particular the role of the ocean in climate and global systems. The IOC has been actively involved in the establishment of a Global Coral Reef Monitoring Network. An initiative on Environment and Development in Coastal Regions and in Small Islands is concerned with ensuring environmentally-sound and sustainable development by strengthening management of the following key areas: freshwater resources; the mitigation of coastline instability; biological diversity; and coastal ecosystem productivity.

UNESCO's Man and the Biosphere Programme supports a worldwide network of biosphere reserves (comprising 393 sites in 94 countries in March 2001), which aim to promote environmental conservation and research, education and training in biodiversity and problems of land use (including the fertility of tropical soils and the cultivation of sacred sites). Following the signing of the Convention to Combat Desertification in October 1994, UNESCO initiated an International Programme for Arid Land Crops, based on a network of existing institutions, to assist implementation of the Convention.

In 1994 UNESCO initiated an international social science research programme, the Management of Social Transformations (MOST), to promote capacity-building in social planning at all levels of decision-making. UNESCO sponsors several research fellowships in the social sciences. In other activities UNESCO promotes the rehabilitation of underprivileged urban areas, the research of sociocultural factors affecting demographic change, and the study of family issues.

UNESCO aims to assist the building and consolidation of peaceful and democratic societies. An international network of institutions and centres involved in research on conflict resolution is being established to support the promotion of peace. Other training, workshop and research activities have been undertaken in countries that have suffered conflict. The Associated Schools Project (ASPnet—comprising more than 6,700 institutions in 166 countries in 2001) has, for nearly 50 years, promoted the principles of peace, human rights, democracy and international co-operation through education. An International Youth Clearing House and Information Service (INFOYOUTH) aims to increase and consolidate the information available on the situation of young people in society, and to heighten awareness of their needs, aspirations and potential among public and private decision-makers. UNESCO's programme also focuses on the educational and cultural dimensions of physical education and sport and their capacity to preserve and improve health.

Fundamental to UNESCO's mission is the rejection of all forms of discrimination. It disseminates scientific information aimed at combating racial prejudice, works to improve the status of women and their access to education, and promotes equality between men and women.

Abdus Salam International Centre for Theoretical Physics: based in Trieste, Italy, the Centre brings together scientists from the developed and developing countries. With support from the Italian Government, the Centre has been operated jointly by the IAEA and UNESCO since 1970. At the end of 1995 administrative responsibility for the Centre was transferred to UNESCO, although IAEA remained a partner in the operations of the Centre. Each year it offers seminars followed by a research workshop, as well as short topical seminars, training courses, symposia and panels. Independent research is also carried out. The programme concentrates on condensed matter physics, high-energy physics, mathematics, physics of weather and climate, structure and nonlinear dynamics of the earth, and microprocessors; Dir Prof. MIGUEL A. VIRASORO (Argentina).

CULTURE

In undertaking efforts to preserve the world's cultural and natural heritage UNESCO has attempted to emphasize the link between

culture and development. The 2000–01 programme Cultural Development: Heritage and Creativity was to pursue UNESCO's objectives relating to the preservation and enhancement of cultural and natural heritage and promoting living cultures, in particular through the formulation of new national and international legislation (including an instrument on underwater cultural heritage), efforts to counter the illicit trafficking of cultural property, and the promotion of all forms of creativity.

UNESCO's World Heritage Programme, inaugurated in 1978, aims to protect historic sites and natural landmarks of outstanding universal significance, in accordance with the 1972 UNESCO Convention Concerning the Protection of the World Cultural and Natural Heritage, by providing financial aid for restoration, technical assistance, training and management planning. By December 2000 the 'World Heritage List' comprised 690 in 122 countries: for example, the Great Barrier Reef in Australia, the Galapagos Islands (Ecuador), Chartres Cathedral (France), the Taj Mahal at Agra (India), Auschwitz concentration camp (Poland), the historic sanctuary of Machu Picchu (Peru), Robben Island (South Africa), and the Serengeti National Park (Tanzania). UNESCO also maintains a 'List of World Heritage in Danger', comprising 30 sites at December 2000, in order to attract international attention to sites particularly at risk from the environment or human activities. In 1992 a World Heritage Centre was established to enable rapid mobilization of international technical assistance for the preservation of cultural sites. In addition, UNESCO supports efforts for the collection and safeguarding of humanity's non-material heritage, including oral traditions, music, dance and medicine. In co-operation with the International Council for Philosophy and Humanistic Studies, UNESCO is compiling a directory of endangered languages. In March 2001 UNESCO protested strongly against the reported destruction by order of the Taliban regime of two ancient monuments of Buddha at Bamiyan in Afghanistan.

UNESCO encourages the translation and publication of literary works, publishes albums of art, and produces records, audiovisual programmes and travelling art exhibitions. It supports the development of book publishing and distribution, including the free flow of books and educational material across borders, and the training of editors and managers in publishing. UNESCO is active in preparing and encouraging the enforcement of international legislation on copyright.

In December 1992 UNESCO established the World Commission on Culture and Development, to strengthen links between culture and development and to prepare a report on the issue. Within the context of the UN's World Decade for Cultural Development (1988–97) UNESCO launched the Silk Roads Project, as a multidisciplinary study of the interactions among cultures and civilizations along the routes linking Asia and Europe, and established an International Fund for the Promotion of Culture, awarding two annual prizes for music and the promotion of arts. In April 1999 UNESCO celebrated the completion of a major international project, the *General History of Africa*.

COMMUNICATION, INFORMATION AND INFORMATICS

UNESCO's communications programme comprises three interrelated components concerned with the flow of information: a commitment to ensuring the wide dissemination of information, through the development of communications infrastructures and without impediments to freedom of expression or of the press; promotion of greater access to knowledge through international co-operation in the areas of information, libraries and archives; and efforts to harness informatics for development purposes and strengthen member states' capacities in this field. Within this framework, activities include assistance towards the development of legislation, training programmes and infrastructures for the media in countries where independent and pluralistic media are in the process of emerging; assistance, through professional organizations, in the monitoring of media independence, pluralism and diversity; promotion of exchange programmes and study tours, especially for young communications professionals from the least developed countries and central and eastern Europe; and improving access and opportunities for women in the media. UNESCO's fourth major work programme for 2000–01 was entitled Towards a Communication and Information Society for All.

In regions affected by conflict UNESCO supports efforts to establish and maintain an independent media service. This strategy is largely implemented through an International Programme for the Development of Communication (IPDC—see below). In Cambodia, Haiti and Mozambique UNESCO participated in the restructuring of the media in the context of national reconciliation and in Bosnia and Herzegovina assisted in the development of independent media. In December 1998 the Israeli–Palestinian Media Forum was established, to foster professional co-operation between Israeli and Palestinian journalists. IPDC provides support to communication and media development projects in the developing world, including the establishment of news agencies and newspapers and training editorial and technical staff. Since its establishment in 1982 IPDC has provided more than US $75m. to finance some 600 projects.

The General Information Programme (PGI), which was established in 1976, provides a focus for UNESCO's activities in the fields of specialized information systems, documentation, libraries and archives. Under PGI, UNESCO aims to facilitate the elaboration of information policies and plans to modernize libraries and archives services; to encourage standardization; to train information specialists; and to establish specialized information networks. The objectives of the programme are accomplished by improving access to scientific literature; the holding of national seminars on information policies; the furthering of pilot projects, and preservation and conservation efforts under the Records and Archives Management Programme (RAMP); and the training of users of library and information services. UNESCO is participating in the reconstruction of the National and University Library in Bosnia and Herzegovina and in several national and regional projects to safeguard documentary heritage. PGI's mandate extends to trends and societal impacts of information technologies. In March 1997 the first International Congress on Ethical, Legal and Societal Aspects of Digital Information ('InfoEthics') was held in Monte Carlo, Monaco. At the second 'InfoEthics' Congress, held in October 1998, experts discussed issues concerning privacy, confidentiality and security in the electronic transfer of information. A World Commission on the Ethics of Scientific Knowledge and Technology, which had been approved by the 1997 General Conference, met for the first time in April 1999, in Oslo, Norway. UNESCO maintains an Observatory on the Information Society, which provides up-to-date information on the development of new information and communications technologies, and aims to raise awareness of related ethical, legal and societal issues.

UNESCO supports the development of computer networking and the training of informatics specialists, in particular through its Intergovernmental Informatics Programme (IIP). The Programme's priorities include training in informatics, software development and research, the modernization of public administration and informatics policies, and the development of regional computer networks. In November 1999 the General Conference resolved that PGI and IIP should merge; it was envisaged that this would be achieved in 2001.

Finance

UNESCO's activities are funded through a regular budget provided by contributions from member states and extrabudgetary funds from other sources, particularly UNDP, the World Bank, regional banks and other bilateral Funds-in-Trust arrangements. UNESCO co-operates with many other UN agencies and international non-governmental organizations.

UNESCO's Regular Programme budget for the two years 2000–01 was US $544.4m., the same as for the previous biennium. Extrabudgetary funds for 2000–01 were estimated at $250m.

Publications

(mostly in English, French and Spanish editions; Arabic, Chinese and Russian versions are also available in many cases)

Copyright Bulletin (quarterly).
International Review of Education (quarterly).
International Social Science Journal (quarterly).
Museum International (quarterly).
Nature and Resources (quarterly).
Prospects (quarterly review on education).
UNESCO Courier (monthly, in 27 languages).
UNESCO Sources (monthly).
UNESCO Statistical Yearbook.
World Communication Report.
World Educational Report (every 2 years).
World Heritage Review (quarterly).
World Information Report.
World Science Report (every 2 years).

Books, databases, video and radio documentaries, statistics, scientific maps and atlases.

INTERGOVERNMENTAL COMMITTEE FOR PHYSICAL EDUCATION AND SPORT

Address: 7 place de Fontenoy, 75352 Paris, France.

Established by UNESCO in 1978 to serve as a permanent intergovernmental body in the field of physical education and sport.

The Committee is composed of 30 representatives of member states of UNESCO, elected by the General Conference.

Among its many activities aimed at further development of physical education and sport throughout the world, the Committee is responsible for supervising the planning and implementation of UNESCO's programme of activities in physical education and sport, promoting international co-operation in this area and facilitating the adoption and implementation of an International Charter of physical education and sport.

INTERNATIONAL BUREAU OF EDUCATION—IBE

Address: POB 199, 1211 Geneva 20, Switzerland.

Telephone: (22) 9177800; **fax:** (22) 9177801; **e-mail:** doc.centre@ ibe.unesco.org; **internet:** www.ibe.unesco.org.

Founded in 1925, the IBE became an intergovernmental organization in 1929 and was incorporated into UNESCO in 1969. The Bureau's fundamental mission is to deal with matters concerning educational content, methods, and teaching/learning strategies. In addition, the IBE, as an observatory of educational trands and innovations, has assumed responsibilities in the field of educational information. It publishes a quarterly review of education and newsletter, in addition to various monographs and reference works. The Council of the IBE is composed of representatives of 28 member states of UNESCO, designated by the General Conference. The International Conference on Education is held periodically.

Director: CECILIA BRASLAVSKY (Argentina).

INTERNATIONAL INSTITUTE FOR EDUCATIONAL PLANNING—IIEP

Address: 7–9 rue Eugène Delacroix, 75116 Paris, France.

Telephone: 1-45-03-77-00; **fax:** 1-40-72-83-66; **e-mail:** informa tion@iiep.unesco.org; **internet:** www.unesco.org/iiep.

The Institute was established by UNESCO in 1963 to serve as a world centre for advanced training and research in educational planning. Its purpose is to help all member states of UNESCO in their social and economic development efforts, by enlarging the fund of knowledge about educational planning and the supply of competent experts in this field.

Legally and administratively a part of UNESCO, the Institute is autonomous, and its policies and programme are controlled by its own Governing Board, under special statutes voted by the General Conference of UNESCO.

A satellite office of the IIEP was opened in Buenos Aires, Argentina, in June 1998.

Director: GUDMUND HERNES.

INSTITUTE FOR INFORMATION TECHNOLOGIES IN EDUCATION

Address: 8 Kedrova St, 117292 Moscow, Russia.

Telephone: (95) 1292990; **fax:** (95) 1291225; **e-mail:** info@iite.ru; **internet:** www.unesco.artstyle.net/iite.

The Institute aims to formulate policies regarding the development of, and to support and monitor the use of, information and communication technologies in education. The Institute also conducts research and organizes training programmes.

Director: VLADIMIR KINELEV.

United Nations Industrial Development Organization—UNIDO

Address: Vienna International Centre, POB 300, 1400 Vienna, Austria.

Telephone: (1) 260260; **fax:** (1) 2692669; **e-mail:** unidoinfo@unido.org; **internet:** www.unido.org.

UNIDO began operations in 1967, as an autonomous organization within the UN Secretariat, and became a specialized agency of the UN in 1985. Its objective is to promote and accelerate sustainable industrial development in developing nations and countries with economies in transition. UNIDO aims to contribute to the stability of the global socio-economic system and promote equitable and sustainable industrialization.

MEMBERS

169 members: see Table on pp. 117–119.

Organization

(April 2001)

GENERAL CONFERENCE

The General Conference, which consists of representatives of all member states, meets once every two years. It is the chief policy-making organ of the Organization, and reviews UNIDO's policy concepts, strategies on industrial development and budget. The eighth General Conference was held in Vienna, Austria, in November/December 1999.

INDUSTRIAL DEVELOPMENT BOARD

The Board consists of 53 members elected by the General Conference for a four-year period. It reviews the implementation of the approved work programme, the regular and operational budgets and other General Conference decisions, and, every four years, recommends a candidate for the post of Director-General to the General Conference for appointment.

PROGRAMME AND BUDGET COMMITTEE

The Committee, consisting of 27 members elected by the General Conference for a two-year term, assists the Industrial Development Board in preparing work programmes and budgets.

SECRETARIAT

The Secretariat comprises the office of the Director-General and three divisions, each headed by a Managing Director: Investment Promotion and Institutional Capacity Building; Sectoral Support and Environmental Sustainability; and Field Operations and Administration. At December 2000 the Secretariat comprised 616 staff members.

Director-General: Carlos Alfredo Magariños (Argentina).

FIELD REPRESENTATION

At the end of 2000 UNIDO had field offices in 36 developing countries.

Activities

In its efforts to promote the advancement and integration of industry, UNIDO provides a global forum for addressing common obstacles to sustainable industrialization, for developing and assessing conventions, codes, norms and regulations, for disseminating new advances, policies and experiences in sustainable industrialization, for establishing international partnerships and networks and for developing comparable statistics and measures to provide criteria for industrial performance. In addition, UNIDO provides a range of services to governments, institutes and enterprises to enhance their capabilities to achieve UNIDO's overall aim of environmentally sustainable and equitable industrial development. The following three core competencies form the basis of UNIDO's services to promote sustainable industrialization, undertaken at policy, institutional and enterpreneural level: the encouragement of competitive economies; the development of a sound environment; and the promotion of productive employment. Client countries may select relevant aspects from these core elements to design an integrated and specific approach to a problem.

Between 1993 and 1998 UNIDO implemented a major restructuring programme in order to respond to changes in the global economy and industrial development. In December 1995 the General Conference, meeting in Vienna, Austria, approved the following set of development priorities, which formed the basis of a new conceptual and substantive framework for UNIDO activities:

(i) Promotion of economic co-operation between both developing and industrialized countries;

(ii) Dissemination of environmentally sustainable and energy-efficient industrial growth;

(iii) Development of small and medium-sized enterprises (SMEs);

(iv) Growth of global industrial competitiveness;

(v) Dissemination of new technologies;

(vi) Industrial development in rural areas;

(vii) Promotion of agro-industry in least-developed countries.

The seventh General Conference, held in December 1997, endorsed a Business Plan on the Future Role and Functions of UNIDO, which further defined the organization's functions and future priorities. The Plan regrouped UNIDO's activities into two main areas—Strengthening of industrial capacities and Cleaner and sustainable industrial development—which, together with an administrative component, was reflected in a revision of the organizational structure (see above). According to the Plan, activities were to be concentrated in support of the development and mainstreaming of SMEs (identified as the principal means for achieving equitable and sustainable industrial development) in support of agro-based industries and their integration into national industrial structures, and in least-developed countries, in particular in Africa, with emphasis on service provision at regional and sub-regional level. In December 1999, at its eighth session, the General Conference approved funding arrangements for a new strategy of developing integrated industrial service packages designed specifically for individual countries (41 of which had been finalized by the end of May 2000).

In 1996 UNIDO implemented a number of normative activities that aimed to assist the industrial sector in developing countries and in countries with economies in transition to compete for international business. Some of the activities undertaken were: co-operation with the International Organization for Standardization to establish internationally-recognized accreditation bodies in developing countries; the construction of a UNIDO Industrial Development Index to measure industrial development on the basis of various indicators; the preparation of UNIDO guide-lines for the classification and certification of industrial science and technology parks; and the assessment of industrial performance through the use of existing technological, environmental and social parameters.

Since 1993 much of UNIDO's assistance to governments, agencies and private industrial institutions has aimed at developing a strong private sector. The percentage of UNIDO's private-sector counterparts doubled between 1993 and 1996 to reach some 50%, while technical co-operation projects involving the private sector accounted for some 80% of all projects undertaken in 1996. UNIDO also works with the private sector in an advisory and co-operative function. In 1996 UNIDO launched the International Business Advisory Council (IBAC), composed of international industrialists whose role it is to advise UNIDO on means of approaching industrialization and promoting awareness of the Organization's work. In the same year UNIDO undertook an initiative to establish National Industrial Business Councils in 12 developing countries. The Councils aim to assist UNIDO in developing and funding joint programmes with the private sector and in recognizing industrial business achievements through the use of international standards and conventions. In the period 1996–98 UNIDO trained 7,505 people, assisted 38,477 small and medium-sized enterprises, and generated US $506m. in industrial investments, through some 634 projects. The first UNIDO Forum on Sustainable Industrial Development was held in December 1999.

UNIDO provides advice to governmental agencies and industrial institutions to improve the management of human resources. The Organization also undertakes training projects to develop human resources in specific industries, and aims to encourage the full participation of women in economic progress through gender awareness programmes and practical training to improve women's access to employment and business opportunities.

The 1995 Conference resolved that special attention was to be given to the industrialization of developing countries in Africa, and in October 1996 UNIDO formally inaugurated the Alliance for Africa's Industrialization, which constituted the industrial sector element of the UN system-wide special initiative on Africa. The programme was to promote development of the continent's natural resources, strengthen labour resources and build government capacities in order to exploit new global markets, in particular in the agro-industrial sector. During 1997 UNIDO helped to organize a number of conferences and forums to promote industrialization in developing countries. UNIDO supported the 13th Conference of African Ministers of Industry (Cami-13), held in Accra, Ghana, in May, which discussed methods to increase Africa's industrial development in the 21st century and to encourage greater participation by the private sector. UNIDO also sponsored an investment forum held in Yaoundé, Cameroon, in June, and a further UNIDO-sponsored forum was held in Abidjan, Côte d'Ivoire, in November, which concentrated on the potential impact of the Asian economic crisis on African economies.

UNIDO is increasingly involved in general environmental projects. As one of the four implementing agencies of the Multilateral Fund for the Implementation of the Montreal Protocol, UNIDO assists developing countries in efforts gradually to reduce the use of ozone-depleting substances. It is also involved in implementing the Kyoto Protocol of the Framework Convention on Climate Change (relating to greenhouse gas emissions) in old factories world-wide.

UNIDO also supports collaborative efforts between countries with complementary experience or resources in specific sectors. A network of investment and technology promotion offices publicizes investment opportunities, provide information to investors and promote business contacts between industrialized and developing countries and economies in transition. UNIDO is increasingly working to achieve investment promotion and transfer of technology and knowledge among developing countries. UNIDO maintains the UNIDO Exchange, an internet-based business intelligence network.

UNIDO supports regional networks and centres of excellence, including the International Centre for Genetic Engineering and Biotechnology, based in Trieste (Italy) and New Delhi (India), the International Centre for Sciences and High Technology, in Trieste, and the Centre for the Application of Solar Energy, in Perth, Australia.

Finance

The regular budget for the two years 2000–01 amounted to US $132.9m. There was an operational budget of some $28.3m. for the same period. In 2000 UNIDO's technical co-operation expenditure amounted to $70m. Allocations were received from UNDP, the Multilateral Fund for the Implementation of the Montreal Protocol on Substances that Deplete the Ozone Layer, the Global Environment Facility, and the Common Fund for Commodities. In addition, voluntary contributions from 25 member states amounted to $24.6m. The Industrial Development Fund is used by UNIDO to finance development projects that fall outside the usual systems of multilateral funding. In 2000 a total of $12.1m. was approved by the Fund.

Publications

Annual Report.

Environmental Technology Monitor (quarterly).

Industrial Africa (every 2 months).

Industrial Development for the 21st Century (every 2 months).

Industrial Development Global Report (annually).

International Yearbook of Industrial Statistics (annually).

The Globalization of Industry: Implications for Developing Countries Beyond 2000.

UNIDOScope (monthly).

World Information Directory of Industrial Technology and Investment Support Services.

Several other publications and databases; numerous working papers and reports (listed in *UNIDO Links* as they appear).

Universal Postal Union—UPU

Address: Case postale, 3000 Berne 15, Switzerland.

Telephone: (31) 3503111; **fax:** (31) 3503110; **e-mail:** info@upu.int; **internet:** www.upu.int.

The General Postal Union was founded by the Treaty of Berne (1874), beginning operations in July 1875. Three years later its name was changed to the Universal Postal Union. In 1948 the UPU became a specialized agency of the UN.

MEMBERS

189 members: see Table on pp. 117–119.

Organization

(April 2001)

CONGRESS

The supreme body of the Union is the Universal Postal Congress, which meets, in principle, every five years. Congress focuses on general principles and broad policy issues. It is responsible for the Constitution (the basic act of the Union), the General Regulations (which contain provisions relating to the application of the Constitution and the operation of the Union), changes in the provision of the Universal Postal Convention, approval of the strategic plan and budget parameters, formulation of overall policy on technical co-operation and for elections and appointments. Amendments to the Constitution are recorded in Additional Protocols, of which there are currently six. The 22nd Congress was held in Beijing, People's Republic of China, in August/September 1999; the 23rd Congress was to be held in Côte d'Ivoire in 2004.

COUNCIL OF ADMINISTRATION

The Council, created by the Seoul Congress, 1994, to replace the former Executive Council, meets annually at Berne. It is composed of a Chairman and representatives of 40 member countries of the Union elected by Congress on the basis of an equitable geographical distribution. It is responsible for supervising the affairs of the Union between Congresses. The Council also considers policies that may affect other sectors, such as standardization and quality of service, provides a forum for considering the implications of governmental policies with respect to competition, deregulation, and trade-in-service issues for international postal services, and considers intergovernmental aspects of technical co-operation. The Council approves the Union's budget, supervises the activities of the International Bureau and takes decisions regarding UPU contacts with other international agencies and bodies. It is also responsible for promoting and co-ordinating all aspects of technical assistance among member countries.

POSTAL OPERATIONS COUNCIL (POC)

As the technical organ of the UPU, the Council, which holds annual sessions and comprises 40 elected member countries, is responsible for the operational, economic and commercial aspects of international postal services. The POC has the authority to amend and enact the Detailed Regulations of the Universal Postal Convention, on the basis of decisions made at Congress. It promotes the studies undertaken by some postal services and the introduction of new postal products. It also prepares and issues recommendations for member countries concerning uniform standards of practice for technological, operational or other processes within its competence. The POC aims to assist national postal services to modernize postal products, including letter and parcel post, financial services and expedited mail services.

INTERNATIONAL BUREAU

The day-to-day administrative work of UPU is executed through the International Bureau, which provides secretariat and support facilities for the UPU's bodies. It serves as an instrument of liaison, information and consultation for the postal administration of the member countries and promotes technical co-operation among Union members. It also acts as a clearing house for the settlement of accounts between postal administrations for inter-administration charges related to the exchange of postal items and international reply coupons. The Bureau supports the technical assistance programmes of the UPU and serves as an intermediary between the UPU, the UN, its agencies and other international organizations, customer organizations and private delivery services. Increasingly the Bureau has assumed a greater role in certain areas of postal administration, for example, the application of Electronic Data Interchange (EDI) technology and the monitoring of quality of postal services world-wide.

Director-General of the International Bureau: THOMAS E. LEAVEY (USA).

Activities

The essential principles of the Union are the following:

   (i) to develop social, cultural and commercial communication between people through the efficient operation of the postal services;

   (ii) to guarantee freedom of transit and free circulation of postal items;

(iii) to ensure the organization, development and modernization of the postal services;

(iv) to promote and participate in postal technical assistance between member countries;

(v) to ensure the interoperability of postal networks by implementing a suitable policy of standardization;

(vi) to meet the changing needs of customers; and

(vii) to improve the quality of service.

In addition to the Constitution and the General Regulations, the Universal Postal Convention is also a compulsory Act of the UPU (binding on all member countries), in view of its importance in the postal field and historical value. The Convention and its Detailed Regulations contain the common rules applicable to the international postal service and provisions concerning letter- and parcel-post. The Detailed Regulations are agreements concluded by the national postal administrations elected by Congress to the POC. The POC is empowered to revise and enact these, taking into account decisions made at Congress.

The Postal Payment Services Agreement and its Regulations, adopted by the 1999 Beijing Congress to replace the former Money Orders, Giro and Cash-on-Delivery Agreements, is an optional arrangement that is not binding on all UPU member countries. Not all members have acceded to this Agreement.

Finance

The 1999 Beijing Congress agreed to replace the Union's annual budget with a biennial budget from 2001. The approved budget for 2001–02 amounted to 71.4m. Swiss francs. All of the UPU's regular budget expenses are financed by member countries, based on a contribution class system. Members are listed in 11 classes, establishing the proportion that they should pay.

Publications

Postal Statistics.

Union Postale (quarterly, in French, German, English, Arabic, Chinese, Spanish and Russian).

Other UPU publications are listed in *Liste des publications du Bureau international*; all are in French and English, some also in Arabic and Spanish.

World Health Organization—WHO

Address: Ave Appia, 1211 Geneva 27, Switzerland.
Telephone: (22) 7912111; **fax:** (22) 7910746; **e-mail:** info@who.ch; **internet:** www.who.int.

WHO, established in 1948, is the lead agency within the UN system concerned with the protection and improvement of public health.

MEMBERS

191 members and two associate members: see Table on pp. 117–119.

Organization

(April 2001)

WORLD HEALTH ASSEMBLY

The Assembly meets in Geneva, once a year; it is responsible for policy making and the biennial programme and budget; appoints the Director-General, admits new members and reviews budget contributions.

EXECUTIVE BOARD

The Board is composed of 32 health experts designated by, but not representing, their governments; they serve for three years, and the World Health Assembly elects 10–12 member states each year to the Board. It meets at least twice a year to review the Director-General's programme, which it forwards to the Assembly with any recommendations that seem necessary. It advises on questions referred to it by the Assembly and is responsible for putting into effect the decisions and policies of the Assembly. It is also empowered to take emergency measures in case of epidemics or disasters.

Chairman: Dr JÍMINEZ DE LA JARA (Chile).

SECRETARIAT

Director-General: Dr GRO HARLEM BRUNDTLAND (Norway).

Executive Directors: Dr ANARFI ASAMOAH-BAAH (Ghana), MARYAN BAQUEROT, Dr DAVID L. HEYMANN (USA), ANN KERN (Australia), Dr CHRISTOPHER MURRAY, Dr DAVID NABARRO (United Kingdom), Dr YASUHIRO SUZUKI (Japan), Dr TOMRIS TÜRMEN (Turkey), Dr DEREK YACH (South Africa).

REGIONAL OFFICES

Each of WHO's six geographical regions has its own organization consisting of a regional committee representing the member states and associate members in the region concerned, and a regional office staffed by experts in various fields of health.

Africa: (temporary office) Parirenyatwa Hospital, Mazoe St, POB BE 773, Belvedere, Harare, Zimbabwe; tel. (4) 707493; fax (4) 700742; e-mail regafro@whoafr.org; internet www.whoafr.org; Dir Dr EBRAHIM MALICK SAMBA (The Gambia).

Americas: Pan-American Sanitary Bureau, 525 23rd St, NW, Washington, DC 20037, USA; tel. (202) 974-3000; fax (202) 974-3663; e-mail postmaster@paho.org; internet www.paho.org; Dir Sir GEORGE ALLEYNE (Barbados).

Eastern Mediterranean: WHO Post Office, Abdul Razzak al Sanhouri St, Cairo (Nasr City)11371, Egypt; tel. (2) 6702535; fax (2) 6702492; e-mail emro@who.sci.eg; internet www.who.sci.eg; Dir Dr HUSSEIN ABDUL-RAZZAQ GEZAIRY.

Europe: 8 Scherfigsvej, 2100 Copenhagen Ø, Denmark; tel. (1) 39-17-17-17; fax (1) 39-17-18-18; e-mail postmaster@who.dk; internet www.who.dk; Dir Dr MARC DANZON (France).

South-East Asia: World Health House, Indraprastha Estate, Mahatma Gandhi Rd, New Delhi 110 002, India; tel. (11) 3317804; fax (11) 3318607; e-mail postmaster@who.ernet.in; internet www.who sea.org; Dir Dr UTON MUCHTAR RAFEI (Indonesia).

Western Pacific: POB 2932, Manila 1000, Philippines; tel. (2) 5288001; fax (2) 5211036; e-mail postmaster@who.org.ph; internet www.wpro.who.int; Dir Dr SHIGERU OMI (Japan).

Activities

WHO's objective is stated in the constitution as 'the attainment by all peoples of the highest possible level of health'. 'Health' is defined as 'a state of complete physical, mental and social well-being and not merely the absence of disease and infirmity'.

It acts as the central authority directing international health work, and establishes relations with professional groups and government health authorities on that basis.

It supports, on request from member states, programmes to promote health, prevent and control health problems, control or eradicate disease, train health workers best suited to local needs and strengthen national health systems. Aid is provided in emergencies and natural disasters.

A global programme of collaborative research and exchange of scientific information is carried out in co-operation with about 1,000 national institutions. Particular stress is laid on the widespread communicable diseases of the tropics, and the countries directly concerned are assisted in developing their research capabilities.

It keeps communicable and non-communicable diseases and other health problems under constant surveillance, promotes the exchange of prompt and accurate information and of notification of outbreaks of diseases, and administers the International Health Regulations. It sets standards for the quality control of drugs, vaccines and other substances affecting health.

It collects and disseminates health data and carries out statistical analyses and comparative studies in such diseases as cancer, heart disease and mental illness.

It receives reports on drugs observed to have shown adverse reactions in any country, and transmits the information to other member states.

It promotes improved environmental conditions, including housing, sanitation and working conditions. All available information on effects on human health of the pollutants in the environment is critically reviewed and published.

Co-operation among scientists and professional groups is encouraged, and the organization may propose international conventions and agreements. It assists in developing an informed public opinion on matters of health.

HEALTH FOR ALL

In May 1981 the 34th World Health Assembly adopted a Global Strategy in support of 'Health for all by the year 2000', which aimed to ensure the attainment by all citizens of the world of a level of health that would permit them to lead a socially and economically productive life. Primary health care was seen as the key to 'Health for all', with the following as minimum requirements:

Safe water in the home or within 15 minutes' walking distance, and adequate sanitary facilities in the home or immediate vicinity;

Immunization against diphtheria, pertussis (whooping cough), tetanus, poliomyelitis, measles and tuberculosis;

Local health care, including availability of at least 20 essential drugs, within one hour's travel;

Trained personnel to attend childbirth, and to care for pregnant mothers and children up to at least one year old.

The Ninth General Programme of Work, for the period 1996–2001, defined a policy framework for world action on health and the management and programme development of WHO itself. In May 1998 the World Health Assembly agreed that a new global strategy should be effected, through regional and national health policies. The so-called 'Health for all in the 21st century' initiative was to build on the primary health care approach of the 'Health for all' strategy, but was to strengthen the emphasis on quality of life, equity in health and access to health services.

In July 1998 Dr Gro Harlem Brundtland officially took office as the new Director-General of WHO. She immediately announced an extensive reform of the organization, including restructuring the WHO technical programmes into nine groups, or 'clusters', each headed by an Executive Director (see above). The groups were established within the framework of the following four main areas of activity: Combating ill health, incorporating Communicable Diseases and Non-communicable Diseases; Building healthy populations and communities, comprising the groups Health Systems and Community Health, Sustainable Development and Healthy Environments and Social Change and Mental Health; Sustained health, including the groups Health Technology and Pharmaceuticals and Evidence and Information for Policy; and Internal support—reaching out, comprising External affairs and Governing Bodies, and General Management. The impending merger of the Non-communicable Diseases and Social Change and Mental Health clusters was announced in March 2000.

COMMUNICABLE DISEASES

The Communicable Diseases group works to reduce the impact of infectious diseases world-wide through surveillance and response; prevention and control; eradication and elimination; and research and development. The group seeks to strengthen global monitoring of important communicable disease problems and to increase the organization's capacity to provide an effective response to those problems. WHO also aims to reduce the impact of other communicable diseases through intensive, routine, prevention and control and, where possible, through the elimination or eradication of specific infections. The group advocates a functional approach to disease control collaborating with other groups at all stages to provide an integrated response. In April 2000 WHO and several partner institutions in epidemic surveillance established a Global Outbreak Alert and Response Network.

One of WHO's major achievements was the eradication of smallpox. Following a massive international campaign of vaccination and surveillance (begun in 1958 and intensified in 1967), the last case was detected in 1977 and the eradication of the disease was declared in 1980. In May 1996 the World Health Assembly resolved that, pending a final endorsement, all remaining stocks of the smallpox virus were to be destroyed on 30 June 1999, although 500,000 doses of smallpox vaccine were to remain, along with a supply of the smallpox vaccine seed virus, in order to ensure that a further supply of the vaccine could be made available if required. In May 1999, however, the Assembly authorized a temporary retention of stocks of the virus until 2002. In 1988 the World Health Assembly declared its commitment to the similar eradication of poliomyelitis by the end of 2000 and launched the Global Polio Eradication Initiative. In August 1996 WHO, UNICEF and Rotary International, together with other national and international partners, initiated a campaign to 'Kick Polio out of Africa', with the aim of immunizing more than 100m. children in 46 countries against the disease over a three-year period. By the end of 1999 the number of reported polio cases world-wide had declined to over 7,000, from 35,000 in 1988 (the actual number of cases in 1988 was estimated at around 350,000). During 1999 and 2000 efforts to achieve the target date for eradication were intensified, in particular through the organization of large-scale National Immunization Days (NIDs). So-called 'days of tranquility' were negotiated in conflict zones to facilitate the implementation of NIDs. At the end of 2000 20 countries were still known or suspected of being polio endemic; of these, 16 were in Africa and four in Asia. In 2000 WHO adopted a strategic plan for the eradication of polio covering the period 2001–05, which envisaged the effective use of NIDs to secure global interruption of polio transmission by the end of 2002, with a view to achieving certification of the global eradication of polio by the end of 2005. Meanwhile, routine immunization services were to be strengthened.

The objective of providing immunization for all children by 1990 was adopted by the World Health Assembly in 1977. Six diseases (measles, whooping cough, tetanus, poliomyelitis, tuberculosis and diphtheria) became the target of the Expanded Programme on Immunization (EPI), in which WHO, UNICEF and many other organizations collaborated. As a result of massive international and national efforts, the global immunization coverage increased from 20% in the early 1980s to the targeted rate of 80% by the end of 1990. This coverage signified that more than 100m. children in the developing world under the age of one had been successfully vaccinated against the targeted diseases, the lives of about 3m. children had been saved every year, and 500,000 annual cases of paralysis as a result of polio had been prevented. In 1992 the Assembly resolved to reach a new target of 90% immunization coverage with the six EPI vaccines; to introduce hepatitis B as a seventh vaccine (with the aim of an 80% reduction in the incidence of the disease in children by 2001); and to introduce the yellow fever vaccine in areas where it occurs endemically.

In 1995 WHO established the Division of Emerging, Viral and Bacterial ('other communicable') Diseases Surveillance and Control to promote the development of national and international infrastructure and resources to recognize, monitor, prevent and control communicable diseases and emerging and re-emerging health problems, including anti-microbial resistance. WHO also aimed to promote applied research on the diagnosis, epidemiology, prevention and control of communicable diseases and emerging health problems. In July 1996 WHO launched an interagency initiative to control an outbreak of cerebrospinal meningitis in Africa, which caused some 15,000 deaths in the first half of that year. In January 1997 an International Co-ordinating Group (ICG) was established to ensure the optimum use and rapid provision of the 14m. doses of vaccine available for epidemic control in 1997, following the enormous demand of the previous year.

As a result of the reforms of the organization implemented from mid-1998, the Division of Control of Tropical Diseases was integrated into the Communicable Diseases cluster, providing active support for planning and implementing control programmes (based on global strategies for integrated tropical disease control) at regional, sub-regional and national levels. It assists with the mobilization of resources for disease control and the co-ordination of national and international participation. The group also promotes research and training that are directly relevant to control needs, and promotes the monitoring and evaluation of control measures.

A Special Programme for Research and Training in Tropical Diseases, sponsored jointly by WHO, UNDP and the World Bank, as well as by contributions from donor countries, was established in 1975, and involves a world-wide network of some 5,000 scientists working on the development and application of vaccines, new drugs, diagnostic kits and preventive measures, and an applied field research on practical community issues affecting the target diseases.

The Onchocerciasis Control Programme in West Africa (OCP) was initiated in 1974 to eliminate onchocerciasis, which can cause blindness, as a major public health problem and an impediment to socio-economic development in 11 countries of the region. In January 1996 a new initiative, the African Programme for Onchocerciasis Control (APOC), covering 19 countries outside West Africa, became operational, with funding co-ordinated by the World Bank and with WHO as the executing agency. In December 1994 WHO announced that the OCP was to be terminated by the end of 2002, by which time it was estimated that 40m. people would have been protected from the disease and 600,000 people prevented from blindness. In May 1999 WHO reported that the OCP, based in Ouagadougou, Burkina Faso, was to be transformed into a Multi-disease Surveillance Centre. The Onchocerciasis Elimination Programme in the Americas (OEPA), launched in 1992, co-ordinates work to control the disease in six endemic countries of Latin America. In January 1998 a new 20-year programme to eliminate lymphatic filariasis was initiated, with substantial funding and support from two major pharmaceutical companies, and in collaboration with the World Bank, the Arab Fund for Economic and Social Development and the governments of Japan, the United Kingdom and the USA. A regional intergovernmental commission is implementing a programme to eliminate South American trypanosomiasis ('Chagas disease', which causes the deaths of some 45,000 people each year and infects a further 16m.–18m.) from the Southern Cone region of Latin America; it is hoped that this goal will be achieved by 2010. The countries of the Andean region of Latin America initiated a plan for the elimination of transmission of Chagas disease in February 1997; a similar plan was launched by Central American governments in October.

A Ministerial Conference on Malaria, organized by WHO, was held in October 1992, attended by representatives from 102 member countries. The Conference adopted a plan of action for the 1990s for the control of the disease, which kills an estimated 1m. people every year and affects a further 300m.–500m. Some 90% of all cases are in sub-Saharan Africa. WHO assists countries where malaria is endemic to prepare national plans of action for malaria control in accordance with WHO's Global Malaria Control Strategy, which emphasized strengthening local capabilities, for example through training, for effective health control. In July 1998 WHO declared the control of malaria a priority concern, and in October formally launched the 'Roll Back Malaria' programme, in conjunction with UNICEF, the World Bank and UNDP. Emphasis was to be placed on strengthening local health systems and on the promotion of inexpensive preventative measures, including the use of bednets treated with insecticides. WHO, with several private- and public-sector partners, supports the development of more effective anti-malaria drugs and vaccines through the 'Medicines for Malaria' venture. An African Initiative for Malaria Control in the 21st Century, launched in 1999, aimed to reduce the prevalence of malaria in 42 African countries by as much as 50% by 2010.

In July 1994 WHO, together with the Sasakawa Memorial Health Foundation, organized an international conference on the elimination of leprosy. The conference adopted a declaration on their commitment to the elimination of leprosy (the reduction of the prevalence of leprosy to less than one case per 10,000 population) by 2000 and WHO established a Special Programme devoted to this objective. The use of a combination of three drugs (known as multi-drug therapy—MDT) has resulted in a reduction in the number of leprosy cases world-wide from 10m.–12m. in 1988 to 680,000 in 1999. In April 1999 WHO announced that the number of countries having more than one case of leprosy per 10,000 had declined from 122 in 1985 to 28. However, concern was expressed at the feasibility of the elimination target, in particular, given the large numbers of undetected cases of the disease. WHO reported that the continued use of MDT treatment over a period of five–10 years would result in an end to all transmission of the disease, except in India, which had more than one-half of the global total of active leprosy cases. In November 1999 WHO launched a new initiative, in collaboration with several governments and a major pharmaceutical company, to eradicate leprosy by the end of 2005. In July 1998 the Director-General of WHO and representatives of more than 20 countries, meeting in Yamoussoukro, Côte d'Ivoire, signed a declaration on the control of another mycobacterial disease, Buruli ulcer.

According to WHO estimates, one-third of the world's population carries the TB bacillus, and 2m.–3m. people die from the disease each year, prompting WHO, in 1993, to declare TB a global emergency. In 1995 WHO established a Global Tuberculosis Programme to address the challenges of the TB epidemic. WHO provides technical support to all member countries, with special attention given to those with high TB prevalence, to establish effective national tuberculosis control programmes. WHO's strategy for TB control includes the use of DOTS (direct observation treatment, short-course), standardized treatment guide-lines, and result accountability through routine evaluation of treatment outcomes. Simultaneously, WHO is encouraging research with the aim of further disseminating DOTS, adapting DOTS for wider use, developing new tools for prevention, diagnosis and treatment, and containing new threats such as the HIV/TB co-epidemic. In March 1999 WHO announced the launch of a new initiative, 'Stop TB', in co-operation with the World Bank, the US Government and a coalition of non-governmental organizations, which aimed to promote DOTS to ensure its use in 85% of cases by 2005, compared with some 16% in the late 1990s. However, inadequate control of DOTS in some areas, leading to partial and inconsistent treatments, has resulted in the development of drug-resistant and, often, incurable strains of the disease. The incidence of so-called multidrug-resistant TB (MDR-TB) strains, that are unresponsive to the two main anti-TB drugs, has risen in recent years. In early 2001 WHO estimated that 8m. new cases of TB were occurring world-wide each year, of which the largest concentration was in south-east Asia. It envisaged a substantial increase in new cases by 2005, mainly owing to the severity of the HIV/TB co-epidemic. TB is the principal cause of death for people infected with the HIV virus. In March 2001 the Global TB Drug Facility was launched under the 'Stop TB' initiative; this aimed to increase access to high-quality anti-TB drugs for sufferers in developing countries.

In June 2000 WHO released a report entitled 'Overcoming Antimicrobial Resistance', in which it warned that the misuse of antibiotics could render some common infectious illnesses unresponsive to treatment. At that time WHO issued guide-lines which aimed to mitigate the risks associated with the use of antimicrobials in livestock reared for human consumption.

NON-COMMUNICABLE DISEASES

The Non-communicable Diseases group comprises three departments responsible for the surveillance, prevention and management of uninfectious diseases (such as those arising from an unhealthy diet).

'Inter-Health', an integrated programme to combat non-communicable diseases, was initiated in 1990, with the particular aim of preventing an increase in the incidence of such diseases in developing countries.

WHO's programmes for diabetes mellitus, chronic rheumatic diseases and asthma assist with the development of national initiatives, based upon goals and targets for the improvement of early detection, care and reduction of long-term complications. They also monitor the global epidemiological situation and co-ordinate multinational research activities concerned with the prevention and care of non-communicable diseases. In mid-1998 WHO adopted a resolution on measures to be taken to combat these diseases, the prevalence of which was anticipated to increase, particularly in developing countries, owing to rising life expectancy and changes in lifestyles. For example, between 1995 and 2025 the number of adults affected by diabetes was projected to increase from 135m. to 300m. In February 1999 WHO initiated a new programme, 'Vision 2020: the Right to Sight', which aimed to eliminate avoidable blindness (estimated to be as much as 80% of all cases) by 2020. Blindness was otherwise predicted to increase by as much as twofold, owing to the increased longevity of the global population.

WHO's Cardiovascular Diseases Programme aims to prevent and control the major cardiovascular diseases, which are responsible for more than 14m. deaths each year. It is estimated that one-third of these deaths could have been prevented with existing scientific knowledge.

The Global Cancer Control Programme is concerned with the prevention of cancer, improving its detection and cure and ensuring care of all cancer patients in need. In 1998 a five-year programme to improve cancer care in developing countries was established, sponsored by private enterprises.

The WHO Human Genetics Programme manages genetic approaches for the prevention and control of common hereditary diseases and of those with a genetic predisposition representing a major health importance. The Programme also concentrates on the further development of genetic approaches suitable for incorporation into health care systems, as well as developing a network of international collaborating programmes.

HEALTH SYSTEMS AND COMMUNITY HEALTH

During 1998 WHO integrated its programmes relating to the health and development of children and adolescents, reproductive health and research (including HIV/AIDS and sexually transmitted diseases), women's health, and health systems within the Health Systems and Community Health group. The group's aim is to improve access to sustainable health care for all by strengthening health systems and fostering individual, family and community development. Activities include newborn care; child health, including promoting and protecting the health and development of the child through such approaches as promotion of breast-feeding and use of the mother-baby package, as well as care of the sick child, including diarrhoeal and acute respiratory disease control and support to women and children in difficult circumstances; the promotion of safe motherhood and maternal health; adolescent health, including the promotion and development of young people and the prevention of specific health problems; women, health and development, including addressing issues of gender, sexual violence, and harmful traditional practices; and human reproduction, including research related to contraceptive technologies and effective methods. In addition, WHO aims to provide technical leadership and co-ordination on reproductive health and to support countries in their efforts to ensure that people: experience healthy sexual development and maturation; have the capacity for healthy, equitable and responsible relationships; can achieve their reproductive intentions safely and healthily; avoid illnesses, diseases and injury related to sexuality and reproduction; and receive appropriate counselling, care and rehabilitation for diseases and conditions related to sexuality and reproduction.

In September 1997 WHO, in collaboration with UNICEF, formally launched a programme advocating the Integrated Management of Childhood Illness (IMCI), following successful regional trials in more than 20 developing countries during 1996–97. IMCI recognizes that pneumonia, diarrhoea, measles, malaria and malnutrition cause some 70% of the nearly 12m. childhood deaths each year, and recommends screening sick children for all five conditions, to obtain a more accurate diagnosis than may be achieved from the results of a single assessment. WHO's Division of Diarrhoeal and Acute Respiratory Disease Control encourages national programmes aimed at reducing childhood deaths as a result of diarrhoea, particularly through the use of oral rehydration therapy and preventive measures. The Division is also seeking to reduce deaths from pneumonia in infants through the use of a simple case-management strategy involving the recognition of danger signs and treatment with an appropriate antibiotic.

In December 1995 WHO's Global Programme on AIDS (Acquired Immunodeficiency Syndrome), which began in 1987, was concluded. A Joint UN Programme on the human immunodeficiency virus (HIV) and AIDS—UNAIDS—became operational on 1 January 1996, sponsored jointly by WHO, the World Bank, UNICEF, UNDP,

UNESCO and UNFPA. (The UN International Drug Control Programme became the seventh sponsoring agency of UNAIDS in 1999.) WHO established an Office of HIV/AIDS and Sexually-Transmitted Diseases in order to ensure the continuity of its global response to the problem, which included support for national control and education plans, improving the safety of blood supplies and improving the care and support of AIDS patients. In addition, the Office was to liaise with UNAIDS, which has its secretariat at WHO headquarters, and to make available WHO's research and technical expertise. In February 2000 WHO and UNAIDS launched a joint initiative to promote the development of a vaccine against HIV. In May the World Health Assembly adopted a resolution urging WHO member states to improve access to the prevention and treatment of HIV-related illnesses and to increase the availability and affordability of drugs. During that month WHO welcomed a decision by major pharmaceutical companies to lower the market cost of certain anti-HIV/AIDS drugs. At December 2000 an estimated 36.1m. adults and children world-wide were living with HIV/AIDS, of whom 5.3m. were newly infected during that year. By that time 21.8m. people, including 4.3m. children, had died of AIDS since the start of the epidemic. Some 95% of those known to be infected with HIV/AIDS live in developing countries.

By the late 1990s many countries had failed significantly to reduce inequalities in healthcare, to improve the health of poor and disadvantaged people or to improve the sustainability of health systems, owing to weak national health systems and the insufficient use of evidence-based, cost-effective treatment methods. In addition, there was a lack of systems to monitor improvements in health services and to determine overall changes in health. The Health Systems and Community Health group, therefore, aims to address these problems and works to ensure that treatment concerning children, adolescents and women, and reproductive health, HIV/AIDS and other sexually transmitted infections, is effectively provided. WHO assists countries to expand and improve the functioning of their health infrastructure in order to ensure wider access to care, hospital services and health education. It works with countries to ensure continuity and quality of care at all levels, by well-trained health personnel.

In March 1996 WHO's Centre for Health Development opened at Kobe, Japan. The Centre was to research health developments and other determinants to strengthen policy decision-making within the health sector.

SUSTAINABLE DEVELOPMENT AND HEALTHY ENVIRONMENTS

The Sustainable Development and Healthy Environment group comprises four departments that concentrate on: health in sustainable development; nutrition for health and development; protection of the human environment; and emergency and humanitarian action.

The group seeks to monitor the advantages and disadvantages for health, nutrition, environment and development arising from the process of globalization; to integrate the issue of health into poverty reduction programmes; and to promote human rights and equality. Adequate and safe food and nutrition is a priority programme area. WHO collaborates with FAO, the World Food Programme, UNICEF and other UN agencies in pursuing its objectives relating to nutrition and food safety. An estimated 780m. worldwide cannot meet basic needs for energy and protein, more than 2,000m. people lack essential vitamins and minerals, and 170m. children are estimated to be malnourished. In December 1992 WHO and FAO hosted an international conference on nutrition, at which a World Declaration and Plan of Action on Nutrition was adopted to make the fight against malnutrition a development priority. Following the conference, WHO promoted the elaboration and implementation of national plans of action on nutrition. WHO aims to support the enhancement of member states' capabilities in dealing with their nutrition situations, and addressing scientific issues related to preventing, managing and monitoring protein-energy malnutrition; micronutrient malnutrition, including iodine deficiency disorders, vitamin A deficiency, and nutritional anaemia; and diet-related non-communicable diseases such as cancer and heart disease. In 1990 the World Health Assembly resolved to eliminate iodine deficiency (causing mental handicap); a strategy of universal salt iodization was launched in 1993. In collaboration with other international agencies, WHO is implementing a comprehensive strategy for promoting appropriate infant, young child and maternal nutrition, and for dealing effectively with nutritional emergencies in large populations. Areas of emphasis include promoting healthcare practices that enhance successful breast-feeding; appropriate complementary feeding; refining the use and interpretation of body measurements for assessing nutritional status; relevant information, education and training; and action to give effect to the International Code of Marketing of Breast-milk Substitutes. WHO's food safety programme aims to protect human health against risks associated with biological and chemical contaminants and additives in food. With FAO, WHO establishes food standards (through the

work of the Codex Alimentarius Commission and its subsidiary committees) and evaluates food additives, pesticide residues and other contaminants and their implications for health. The programme provides expert advice on such issues as food-borne pathogens (e.g. listeria), production methods (e.g. aquaculture) and food biotechnology (e.g. genetic modification). In January 2001 a joint team of FAO and WHO experts issued a report concerning the allergenicity of foods derived from biotechnology (i.e. genetically modified—GM foods).

WHO's Programme for the Promotion of Environmental Health undertakes a wide range of initiatives to tackle the increasing threats to health and well-being from a changing environment, especially in relation to air pollution, water quality, sanitation, protection against radiation, management of hazardous waste, chemical safety and housing hygiene. Some 1,200m. people worldwide have no access to clean drinking water, while a further 2,900m. people are denied suitable sanitation systems. WHO helped launch the Water Supply and Sanitation Council in 1990 and regularly updates its *Guidelines for Drinking Water Quality*. In rural areas, the emphasis continues to be on the provision and maintenance of safe and sufficient water supplies and adequate sanitation, the health aspects of rural housing, vector control in water resource management, and the safe use of agrochemicals. In urban areas, assistance is provided to identify local environmental health priorities and to improve municipal governments' ability to deal with environmental conditions and health problems in an integrated manner; promotion of the 'Healthy City' approach is a major component of the Programme. Other Programme activities include environmental health information development and management, human resources development, environmental health planning methods, research and work on problems relating to global environment change, such as UV-radiation. A report considering the implications of climate change on human health, prepared jointly by WHO, WMO and UNEP, was published in July 1996. The WHO Global Strategy for Health and Environment, developed in response to the WHO Commission on Health and Environment which reported to the UN Conference on Environment and Development in June 1992, provides the framework for Programme activities. In January 2001 WHO sent a team of experts to Kosovo and Metohija (Federal Republic of Yugoslavia—FRY) to assess the potential impact on the health of the local population of exposure to depleted uranium, which had been used by NATO in ammunition during its aeriel offensive against the FRY in 1999.

WHO's work in the promotion of chemical safety is undertaken in collaboration with ILO and UNEP through the International Programme on Chemical Safety (IPCS), the Central Unit for which is located in WHO. The Programme provides internationally-evaluated scientific information on chemicals, promotes the use of such information in national programmes, assists member states in establishment of their own chemical safety measures and programmes, and helps them strengthen their capabilities in chemical emergency preparedness and response and in chemical risk reduction. In 1995 an Inter-organization Programme for the Social Management of Chemicals was established by UNEP, ILO, FAO, WHO, UNIDO and OECD, in order to strengthen international co-operation in the field of chemical safety. In 1998 WHO led an international assessment of the health risk from bendocine disruptors (chemicals which disrupt hormonal activities).

Within the UN system, WHO's Division of Emergency and Humanitarian Action co-ordinates the international response to emergencies and natural disasters in the health field, in close co-operation with other agencies and within the framework set out by the UN's Office for the Co-ordination of Humanitarian Affairs. In this context, WHO provides expert advice on epidemiological surveillance, control of communicable diseases, public health information and health emergency training. Its emergency preparedness activities include co-ordination, policy-making and planning, awareness-building, technical advice, training, publication of standards and guide-lines, and research. Its emergency relief activities include organizational support, the provision of emergency drugs and supplies and conducting technical emergency assessment missions. The Division's objective is to strengthen the national capacity of member states to reduce the adverse health consequences of disasters. In responding to emergency situations, WHO always tries to develop projects and activities that will assist the national authorities concerned in rebuilding or strengthening their own capacity to handle the impact of such situations. During 2000 emergency and humanitarian activities included support for cholera and malaria prevention in Mozambique, following severe floods in the early part of the year; the provision of medical supplies to an estimated 550,000 Eritreans displaced by the conflict between Eritrea and Ethiopia; advice to the authorities in Saudi Arabia and Yemen following outbreaks of Rift Valley fever; co-ordination of the international response to an outbreak of ebola (haemorraghagic) fever in Uganda, as well as the supply of protective equipment; and post-conflict reconstruction activities in East Timor.

SOCIAL CHANGE AND MENTAL HEALTH

The Social Change and Mental Health group comprises four departments: Health Promotion; Disability, Injury Prevention and Rehabilitation; Mental Health; and Substance Abuse. The group works to assess the impact of injuries, violence and sensory impairments on health, and formulates guide-lines and protocols for the prevention and management of mental problems. The Health Promotion department promotes decentralized and community-based health programmes and is concerned with developing new approaches to population ageing and encouraging healthy life-styles and self-care. It also seeks to relieve the negative impact of social changes such as urbanization, migration and changes in family structure upon health. Several health promotion projects have been undertaken, in collaboration between WHO regional and country offices and other relevant organizations, including: the Global School Health Initiative, to bridge the sectors of health and education and to promote the health of school-age children; the Global Strategy for Occupational Health, to promote the health of the working population and the control of occupational health risks; Community-based Rehabilitation, which aimed to provide a more enabling environment for people with disabilities; and a communication strategy to provide training and support for health communications personnel and initiatives.

In July 1997 the fourth International Conference on Health Promotion (ICHP) was held in Jakarta, Indonesia, where a declaration on 'Health Promotion into the 21st Century' was agreed. The fifth ICHP was convened in June 2000 in Mexico City, Mexico.

Mental health problems, which include unipolar and bipolar affective disorders, psychosis, epilepsy, dementia, Parkinson's disease, multiple sclerosis, drug and alcohol dependency, and neuropsychiatric disorders such as post-traumatic stress disorder, obsessive compulsive disorder and panic disorder, have been identified by WHO as significant global health problems. Although, overall, physical health has improved, mental, behavioural and social health problems are increasing, owing to extended life expectancy and improved child mortality rates, and factors such as war and poverty. WHO aims to address mental problems by increasing awareness of mental health issues and promoting improved mental health services and primary care.

The Substance Abuse department is concerned with problems of alcohol, drugs and other substance abuse. Within its Programme on Substance Abuse (PSA), which was established in 1990 in response to the global increase in substance abuse, WHO provides technical support to assist countries in formulating policies with regard to the prevention and reduction of the health and social effects of psychoactive substance abuse. PSA's sphere of activity includes epidemiological surveillance and risk assessment, advocacy and the dissemination of information, strengthening national and regional prevention and health promotion techniques and strategies, the development of cost-effective treatment and rehabilitation approaches, and also encompasses regulatory activities as required under the international drugs-control treaties in force.

The Tobacco or Health Programme, which was incorporated into the PSA in May 1994, aims to reduce the use of tobacco, by educating tobacco-users and preventing young people from adopting the habit. In 1996 WHO published its first report on the tobacco situation world-wide. According to WHO, about one-third of the world's population aged over 15 years smoke tobacco, which causes approximately 3.5m. deaths each year (through lung cancer, heart disease, chronic bronchitis and other effects). In 1998 the 'Tobacco Free Initiative', a major global anti-smoking campaign, was established. In May 1999 the World Health Assembly endorsed the formulation of a Framework Convention on Tobacco Control (FCTC) to help to combat the increase in tobacco use (although a number of tobacco growers expressed concerns about the effect of the convention on their livelihoods). The greatest increase in tobacco use was forecast to occur in developing countries.

HEALTH TECHNOLOGY AND PHARMACEUTICALS

WHO's Health Technology and Pharmaceuticals group is made up of three departments: Essential Drugs and Other Medicines; Vaccines and Other Biologicals; and Blood Safety and Clinical Technology. It promotes the development of drugs and vaccines, the self-sufficiency of immunization programmes and world-wide co-operation on blood safety.

The Department of Essential Drugs and Other Medicines promotes public health through the development of national drugs policies and global guide-lines and through collaboration with member countries to promote access to essential drugs, the rational use of medicines and compliance with international drug-control requirements. The department comprises four teams: Policy Access and Rational Use; the Drug Action Programme; Quality, Safety and the Regulation of Medicines; and Traditional Medicine.

The Policy Access and Rational Use team and the Drug Action Programme assist in the development and implementation by member states of pharmaceutical policies, in ensuring a supply of essential drugs of good quality at low cost, and in the rational use of

drugs. Other activities include global and national operational research in the pharmaceutical sector, and the development of technical tools for problem solving, management and evaluation. The Policy Access and Rational Use team also has a strong advocacy and information role, promulgated through a periodical, the *Essential Drugs Monitor*, an extensive range of technical publications, and an information dissemination programme targeting developing countries.

The Quality, Safety and Regulation of Medicines team supports national drug-regulatory authorities and drug-procurement agencies and facilitates international pharmaceutical trade through the exchange of technical information and the harmonization of internationally respected norms and standards. In particular, it publishes the *International Pharmacopoeia*, the *Consultative List of International Nonproprietary Names for Pharmaceutical Substances*, and annual and biennial reports of Expert Committees responsible for determining relevant international standards for the manufacture and specification of pharmaceutical and biological products in international commerce. It provides information on the safety and efficacy of drugs, with particular regard to counterfeit and substandard projects, to health agencies and providers of health care, and it maintains the pharmaceuticals section of the UN *Consolidated List of Products whose Consumption and/or Sale have been Banned, Withdrawn, Severely Restricted or Not Approved by Governments*. The *WHO Model List of Essential Drugs* is updated every two years and is complemented by corresponding model prescribing information; the 10th *Model List* was published in 1998 and identified 306 essential drugs.

The Traditional Medicine team encourages and supports member states in the integration of traditional medicine into national health-care systems and in the appropriate use of traditional medicine, in particular through the provision of technical guide-lines, standards and methodologies.

In January 1999 the Executive Board adopted a resolution on WHO's Revised Drug Strategy which placed emphasis on the inequalities of access to pharmaceuticals, and also covered specific aspects of drugs policy, quality assurance, drug promotion, drug donation, independent drug information and rational drug use. Plans of action involving co-operation with member states and other international organizations were to be developed to monitor and analyse the pharmaceutical and public health implications of international agreements, including trade agreements.

In September 1991 the Children's Vaccine Initiative (CVI) was launched, jointly sponsored by the Rockefeller Foundation, UNDP, UNICEF, the World Bank and WHO, to facilitate the development and provision of children's vaccines. The CVI has as its ultimate goal the development of a single oral immunization shortly after birth that will protect against all major childhood diseases. In 1998 the CVI reported that 4m. children die each year of diseases for which there were existing common vaccines. An International Vaccine Institute was established in Seoul, Republic of Korea, as part of the CVI, to provide scientific and technical services for the production of vaccines for developing countries. In September 1996 WHO, jointly with UNICEF, published a comprehensive survey, entitled *State of the World's Vaccines and Immunization*. In 1999 WHO, UNICEF, the World Bank and a number of public- and private-sector partners formed the Global Alliance for Vaccines and Immunization (GAVI), which aimed to expand the provision of existing vaccines and to accelerate the development and introduction of new vaccines and technologies, with the ultimate goal of protecting children of all nations and from all socio-economic backgrounds against vaccine-preventable diseases.

HEALTH DAYS

World Health Day is observed on 7 April every year, and is used to promote awareness of a particular health topic ('Stop Exclusion Dare to Care', relating to mental health, in 2001). World Leprosy Day is held every year on 30 January, World TB Day on 24 March, World No Tobacco Day on 31 May, World Heart Day on 24 September, World Mental Health Day on 10 October, World Diabetes Day, in association with the International Diabetes Federation, on 14 November, World AIDS Day on 1 December, and World Asthma Day on 11 December.

ASSOCIATED AGENCY

International Agency for Research on Cancer: 150 Cours Albert Thomas, 69372 Lyon Cédex 08, France; tel. 4-72-73-85-67; fax 4-72-73-85-75; e-mail gaudin@iarc.fr. Established in 1965 as a self-governing body within the framework of WHO, the Agency organizes international research on cancer. It has its own laboratories and runs a programme of research on the environmental factors causing cancer. Members: Argentina, Australia, Belgium, Brazil, Canada, Denmark, Finland, France, Germany, Italy, Japan, Netherlands, Norway, Sweden, Switzerland, United Kingdom, USA. Dir Dr PAUL KLEIHUES (Germany).

Finance

WHO's regular budget is provided by assessment of member states and associate members. An additional fund for specific projects is provided by voluntary contributions from members and other sources, including UNDP and UNFPA.

A regular budget of US $842.7m. was proposed for the two years 2000–01.

WHO budget appropriations by region, 2000–01*

Region	Amount ('000 US dollars)	% of total budget
Africa	176,822	20.98
Americas	77,725	9.22
South-East Asia	95,595	11.34
Europe	51,699	6.14
Eastern Mediterranean	85,869	10.19
Western Pacific	75,889	9.01
Headquarters	279,055	33.12
Total	842,654	100.00

* Provisional.

Publications

Bulletin of WHO (monthly).

Environmental Health Criteria.

International Digest of Health Legislation (quarterly).

International Statistical Classification of Diseases and Related Health Problems, Tenth Revision, 1992–1994 (versions in 37 languages).

Weekly Epidemiological Record.

WHO Drug Information (quarterly).

World Health Report (annually).

World Health Statistics Annual.

Technical report series; catalogues of specific scientific, technical and medical fields available.

World Intellectual Property Organization—WIPO

Address: 34 chemin des Colombettes, 1211 Geneva 20, Switzerland.
Telephone: (22) 3389111; **fax:** (22) 7335428; **e-mail:** wipo.mail@wipo.int; **internet:** www.wipo.int.

WIPO was established by a Convention signed in Stockholm in 1967, which came into force in 1970. It became a specialized agency of the UN in December 1974.

MEMBERS

175 members: see Table on pp. 117–119.

Organization

(April 2001)

GENERAL ASSEMBLY

The General Assembly is one of the three WIPO governing bodies, and is composed of all states that are party to the WIPO Convention and that are also members of any of the WIPO-administered Unions (see below). In February 2001 the Assembly comprised 163 members. The Assembly meets in ordinary session once every two years to agree on programmes and budgets. It elects the Director-General, who is the executive head of WIPO.

CONFERENCE

All member states are represented in the Conference, which meets in ordinary session once every two years to adopt budgets and programmes.

CO-ORDINATION COMMITTEE

Countries belonging to the Committee are elected from among the member states of WIPO, the Paris and Berne Unions, and, *ex officio*, Switzerland. At February 2001 there were 72 members of the Committee, including four *ad hoc* members and Switzerland. It meets in ordinary session once a year.

INTERNATIONAL BUREAU

The International Bureau, as WIPO's secretariat, prepares the meetings of the various bodies of WIPO and the Unions, mainly through the provision of reports and working documents. It organizes the meetings, and sees that the decisions are communicated to all concerned, and, as far as possible, that they are carried out.

The International Bureau implements projects and initiates new ones to promote international co-operation in the field of intellectual property. It acts as an information service and publishes reviews. It is also the depositary of most of the treaties administered by WIPO.
Director-General: Dr KAMIL IDRIS (Sudan).

Activities

WIPO is responsible for promoting the protection of intellectual property throughout the world. Intellectual property comprises two principal branches: industrial property (patents and other rights in technological inventions, rights in trademarks, industrial designs, appellations of origin, etc.) and copyright and neighbouring rights (in literary, musical, artistic, photographic and audiovisual works).

WIPO administers and encourages member states to sign and enforce, 21 international treaties relating to the protection of intellectual property (15 on industrial property and six on copyright), of which the most fundamental are the Paris Convention for the Protection of Industrial Property (1883) and the Berne Convention for the Protection of Literary and Artistic Works (1886). WIPO's main areas of activity are progressive development of international intellectual property law, global protection systems and services, and co-operation for development. The organization seeks to harmonize national intellectual property legislation and procedures, provide services for international applications for industrial property rights, exchange information on intellectual property, provide training and legal and technical assistance to developing countries, facilitate the resolution of private intellectual property disputes, and develop the use of information technology for storing, accessing and using valuable intellectual property information. The rapid advancement of digital communications networks has posed challenges regarding the protection and enforcement of intellectual property rights. WIPO has undertaken a range of initiatives to address the implications for copyright and industrial property law, and for electronic commerce transcending national jurisdictions. In 1998 WIPO established the Electronic Commerce Section to co-ordinate programmes and activities relating to the intellectual property aspects of electronic commerce. In September 1999 WIPO organized the first International Conference on Electronic Commerce and Intellectual Property.

PROGRESSIVE DEVELOPMENT OF INTERNATIONAL PROPERTY LAW

One of WIPO's major activities is the development and application of international norms and standards. The organization prepares new treaties and undertakes the revision of the existing treaties that it administers. WIPO administers international classifications established by treaties and relating to inventions, marks and industrial designs: periodically it reviews these to ensure their improvement in terms of coverage and precision. WIPO also carries out studies on issues in the field of intellectual property that could be the subject of model laws or guide-lines for implementation at national or international levels. The organization is increasingly active in harmonizing and simplifying procedures in order to make the registration of intellectual property more easily accessible. WIPO aims to keep pace with rapid developments in the intellectual property domain. Standing committees have been formed by member states to examine questions of substantive law or harmonization in the organization's main fields of activity and to ensure that the interests of member states are addressed promptly.

CO-OPERATION FOR DEVELOPMENT

WIPO aims to modernize national intellectual property systems. It offers assistance to increase the capabilities of developing countries to benefit from the international intellectual property framework, with a view to promoting the optimal use of human and other resources and thereby contributing to national prosperity. The WIPO Worldwide Academy, created in 1998, promotes the utilization of national intellectual property systems by strengthening human resource development programmes in intellectual property systems at national and regional levels. The Academy utilizes the internet, digital multimedia technology and video conferencing to better extend its reach to intellectual property and academic institutions around the world. It maintains a Distance Learning Center using on-line facilities. In January 2001 WIPO launched WIPONET, a global digital network of intellectual property information capable of transmitting confidential data.

WIPO advises countries on obligations under the World Trade Organization's agreement on Trade-Related Aspects of Intellectual Property Rights (TRIPS). The two organizations agreed on a joint technical co-operation initiative to assist developing countries to harmonize their national legislative and administrative structures in compliance with the TRIPS accord, by 1 January 2000 (the deadline was extended to 1 January 2006 for least developed countries).

GLOBAL PROTECTION SYSTEMS AND SERVICES

WIPO administers a small number of treaties, covering inventions (patents), trademarks and industrial designs, under which one international registration or filing has effect in any of the relevant signatory states. The services provided by WIPO under such treaties simplify the registration process and reduce the cost of making individual applications or filings in each country in which protection for a given intellectual property right is sought. The most widely used of these treaties is the Patent Co-operation Treaty (PCT), under which a single international patent application is valid in all signatory countries selected by the applicant. The PCT system has expanded rapidly in recent years. The corresponding treaties concerning the international registration of trademarks and industrial designs are, respectively, the Madrid Agreement (and its Protocol), and the Hague Agreement.

WIPO maintains the following international registration services:

International registration of trademarks: operating since 1893; during 1999 there were 20,072 registrations and renewals of trademarks; publ. *WIPO Gazette of International Marks* (monthly).

International deposit of industrial designs: operating since 1928; during 1998 6,464 deposits, renewals and prolongations of industrial designs were made; publ. *International Designs Bulletin* (monthly).

International registration of appellations of origin: operating since 1966; by 30 September 1997 740 appellations had been registered; publ. *Les appellations d'origine* (irreg.).

International applications for patents: operating since 1978; during 1999 74,023 record copies of international applications for patents under the Patent Co-operation Treaty (PCT) were received.

WIPO also maintains the WIPO Arbitration and Mediation Centre, which became operational on 1 October 1994, to facilitate the settlement of intellectual property disputes between private parties. The Centre also organizes arbitrator and mediator workshops and assists in the development of WIPO model contract clauses and industry-specific resolution schemes. In 1999 the Centre established an internet-based resolution facility to enhance its dispute resolution capabilities. The Centre operates a Domain Name Dispute Resolution Service, which reviews cases of conflict between trademarks and internet domain names.

PARIS AND BERNE CONVENTIONS

International Union for the Protection of Industrial Property (Paris Convention): the treaty was signed in Paris in 1883, and last revised in 1967; there were 160 members of the Union's Assembly at January 2001. Member states must accord to nationals and residents of other member states the same advantages under their laws relating to the protection of inventions, trademarks and other subjects of industrial property as they accord to their own nationals.

International Union for the Protection of Literary and Artistic Works (Berne Union): the treaty was signed in Berne in 1886 and last revised in 1971; there were 147 members of the Union's Assembly at January 2001. Members of the Union's Assembly must accord the same protection to the copyright of nationals of other member states as to their own. The treaty also prescribes minimum standards of protection, for example, that copyright protection generally continues throughout the author's life and for 50 years after. It includes special provision for the developing countries.

OTHER AGREEMENTS

(Status as on 15 January 2001, unless otherwise indicated)

International Protection of Industrial Property:

Madrid Agreement of 14 April 1891, for the Repression of False or Deceptive Indications of Source on Goods; 32 states party to the Agreement (at 15 April 2000).

Madrid Agreement of 14 April 1891, Concerning the International Registration of Marks; 67 states party to the Agreement.

The Hague Agreement of 6 November 1925, Concerning the International Deposit of Industrial Designs; 29 states party to the Agreement.

Nice Agreement of 15 June 1957, Concerning the International Classification of Goods and Services for the Purposes of the Registration of Marks; 65 states party to the Agreement.

Lisbon Agreement of 31 October 1958, for the Protection of Appellations of Origin and their International Registration; 20 states party to the Agreement.

Locarno Agreement of 8 October 1968, Establishing an International Classification for Industrial Designs; 39 states party to the Agreement.

Patent Co-operation Treaty of 19 June 1970 (PCT); 110 states party to the Treaty.

Strasbourg Agreement of 24 March 1971, Concerning the International Patent Classification (IPC); 47 states party to the Agreement.

Vienna Agreement of 12 June 1973, Establishing an International Classification of the Figurative Elements of Marks; 17 states party to the Agreement.

Budapest Treaty of 28 April 1977, on the International Recognition of the Deposit of Micro-organisms for the Purposes of Patent Procedure; 49 states party to the Treaty.

Nairobi Treaty of 26 September 1981, on the Protection of the Olympic Symbol; 40 states party to the Treaty.

Trademark Law Treaty of 27 October 1994; 26 states party to the Treaty 141.

Protocol Relating to the Madrid Agreement Concerning the International Registration of Marks, signed on 28 June 1989; 49 contracting states.

Treaty on Intellectual Property in Respect of Integrated Circuits, 1989; not yet entered into force.

Copyright Treaty, 1996; not yet entered into force.

Geneva Act of the Hague Agreement Concerning the International Registration of Industrial Designs, 1999; not yet entered into force.

Special International Protection of the Rights of Performers, Producers of Phonograms and Broadcasting Organizations ('Neighbouring Rights'):

Rome Convention, 26 October 1961, for the Protection of Performers, Producers of Phonograms and Broadcasting Organizations; 67 states party to the Convention.

Geneva Convention, 29 October 1971, for the Protection of Producers of Phonograms against Unauthorized Duplication of their Phonograms; 65 states party to the Convention (at March 2001).

Brussels Convention, 21 May 1974, Relating to the Distribution of Programme-carrying Signals Transmitted by Satellite; 24 states party to the Convention.

Performances and Phonograms Treaty, 1996; not yet entered into force.

Patent Law Treaty, 2000; not yet entered into force.

Finance

The budget for the two years 2000–2001 amounted to 409.7m. Swiss francs, compared with 383m. Swiss francs in 1998–99.

Publications

Annual Report.

Les appellations d'origine (irregular, in French).

Industrial Property and Copyright (monthly in English and French; bimonthly in Spanish).

Intellectual Property in Asia and the Pacific (quarterly in English).

International Designs Bulletin (monthly in English and French, also on CD-Rom).

Newsletter (irregular in Arabic, English, French, Portuguese, Russian and Spanish).

PCT Gazette (weekly in English and French).

PCT Newsletter (monthly in English).

WIPO Gazette of International Marks (monthly, in English and French, also on CD-Rom).

A collection of industrial property and copyright laws and treaties; a selection of publications related to intellectual property.

World Meteorological Organization—WMO

Address: 7 bis, ave de la Paix, CP 2300, 1211 Geneva 2, Switzerland. **Telephone:** (22) 7308111; **fax:** (22) 7308181; **e-mail:** ipa@gate way.wmo.ch; **internet:** www.wmo.ch.

The WMO was established in 1950 and was recognized as a Specialized Agency of the UN in 1951, operating in the fields of meteorology, climatology, operational hydrology and related fields, as well as their applications.

MEMBERS

185 members: see Table on pp. 117–119.

Organization

(April 2001)

WORLD METEOROLOGICAL CONGRESS

The supreme body of the Organization, the Congress, is convened every four years and represents all members; it adopts regulations, and determines policy, programme and budget. Thirteenth Congress: May 1999.

EXECUTIVE COUNCIL

The Council has 36 members and meets at least yearly to prepare studies and recommendations for the Congress; it supervises the implementation of Congress resolutions and regulations, informs members on technical matters and offers advice.

SECRETARIAT

The secretariat acts as an administrative, documentary and information centre; undertakes special technical studies; produces publications; organizes meetings of WMO constituent bodies; acts as a link between the meteorological and hydrometeorological services of the world, and provides information for the general public.

Secretary-General: Prof. G. O. P. OBASI (Nigeria).

REGIONAL ASSOCIATIONS

Members are grouped in six Regional Associations (Africa, Asia, Europe, North and Central America, South America and South-West Pacific), whose task is to co-ordinate meteorological activity within their regions and to examine questions referred to them by the Executive Council. Sessions are held at least once every four years.

TECHNICAL COMMISSIONS

The Technical Commissions are composed of experts nominated by the members of the Organization. Sessions are held at least once every four years. The Commissions cover the following areas: Basic Systems; Climatology; Instruments and Methods of Observation; Atmospheric Sciences; Aeronautical Meteorology; Agricultural Meteorology; Hydrology; Marine Meteorology.

Activities

WORLD WEATHER WATCH PROGRAMME

Combining facilities and services provided by the members, the Programme's primary purpose is to make available meteorological and related geophysical and environmental information enabling them to maintain efficient meteorological services. Facilities in regions outside any national territory (outer space, ocean areas and Antarctica) are maintained by members on a voluntary basis.

Antarctic Activities: co-ordinate WMO activities related to the Antarctic, in particular the surface and upper-air observing programme, plan the regular exchange of observational data and products needed for operational and research purposes, study problems related to instruments and methods of observation peculiar to the Antarctic, and develop appropriate regional coding practices. Contacts are maintained with scientific bodies dealing with Antarctic research and with other international organizations on aspects of Antarctic meteorology.

Data Management: This aspect of the Programme monitors the integration of the different components of the World Weather Watch (WWW) Programme, with the intention of increasing the efficiency of, in particular, the Global Observing System, the Global Data Processing System and the Global Telecommunication System. The Data Management component of the WWW Programme develops data handling procedures and standards for enhanced forms of data representation, in order to aid member countries in processing large volumes of meteorological data. It also supports the co-ordinated transfer of expertise and technology to developing countries.

Emergency Response Activities: assist national meteorological services to respond effectively to man-made environmental emergencies, particularly nuclear accidents, through the development, co-ordination and implementation of WMO/IAEA established procedures and response mechanisms for the provision and exchange of observational data and specialized transport model products.

Global Data Processing System: consists of World Meteorological Centres (WMCs) at Melbourne (Australia), Moscow (Russia) and Washington, DC (USA), 40 Regional/Specialized Meteorological Centres (RSMCs) and 187 National Meteorological Centres. The WMCs and RSMCs provide analyses, forecasts and warnings for exchange on the Global Telecommunications System. Some centres concentrate on the monitoring and forecasting of environmental quality and special weather phenomena, such as tropical cyclones, monsoons, droughts, etc., which have a major impact on human safety and national economies. These analyses and forecasts are designed to assist the members in making local and specialized forecasts.

Global Observing System: Simultaneous observations are made at more than 10,000 land stations. Meteorological information is also received from 3,000 aircraft, 7,000 ships, 600 drifting buoys, and nine polar orbiting and six geostationary meteorological satellites. About 160 members operate some 1,300 ground stations equipped to receive picture transmissions from geostationary and polar-orbiting satellites.

Global Telecommunication System: provides telecommunication services for the rapid collection and exchange of meteorological information and related data; consists of (a) the Main Telecommunication Network (MTN), (b) six Regional Meteorological Telecommunication networks, and (c) the national telecommunication networks. The system operates through 183 National Meteorological Centres, 29 Regional Telecommunications Hubs and the three WMCs.

Instruments and Methods of Observation Programme: promotes the world-wide standardization of meteorological and geophysical instruments and methods of observation and measurement to meet agreed accuracy requirements. It provides related guidance material and training assistance in the use and maintenance of the instruments.

System Support Activity: provides guidance and support to members in the planning, establishment and operation of the WWW. It includes training, technical co-operation support, system and methodology support, operational WWW evaluations, advanced technology support, an operations information service, and the WWW referral catalogue.

Tropical Cyclone Programme: established in response to UN General Assembly Resolution 2733 (XXV), aims at the development of national and regionally co-ordinated systems to ensure that the loss of life and damage caused by tropical cyclones and associated floods, landslides and storm surges are reduced to a minimum. The programme supports the transfer of technology, and includes five regional tropical cyclone bodies covering more than 60 countries, to improve warning systems and for collaboration with other international organizations in activities related to disaster mitigation.

WORLD CLIMATE PROGRAMME

Adopted by the Eighth World Meteorological Congress (1979), the World Climate Programme (WCP) comprises the following components: World Climate Data and Monitoring Programme (WCDMP), World Climate Applications and Services Programme (WCASP), World Climate Impact Assessment and Response Strategies Programme (WCIRP), World Climate Research Programme (WCRP). The WCP is supported by the Global Climate Observing System (GCOS), which provides comprehensive observation of the global climate system, involving a multi-disciplinary range of atmospheric, oceanic, hydrologic, cyrospheric and biotic properties and processes. In 1997/98 the GCOS was particularly active in monitoring the impact of the El Niño weather phenomenon on the climate system. The objectives of the WCP are: to use existing climate information to improve economic and social planning; to improve the understanding of climate processes through research, so as to determine the predictability of climate and the extent of man's influence on it; and to detect and warn governments of impending climate variations or changes, either natural or man-made, which may significantly affect critical human activities.

Co-ordination of the overall Programme is the responsibility of the WMO, along with direct management of the WCDMP and WCASP. The UN Environment Programme (UNEP, q.v.) has accepted responsibility for the WCIRP, while the WCRP is jointly administered by WMO, the International Council of Scientific

Unions (ICSU, q.v.) and UNESCO's Intergovernmental Oceanographic Commission. Other organizations involved in the Programme include FAO, WHO, and the Consultative Group on International Agricultural Research (CGIAR). The WCP Co-ordinating Committee co-ordinates the activities of the four components of the Programme and liaises with other international bodies concerned with climate. In addition, the WCP supports the WMO/UNEP Intergovernmental Panel on Climate Change and the implementation of international agreements, such as the UN Framework Convention on Climate Change (see below).

World Climate Applications and Services Programme (WCASP): promotes applications of climate knowledge in the areas of food production, water, energy (especially solar and wind energy), urban planning and building, human health, transport, tourism and recreation.

World Climate Data and Monitoring Programme (WCDMP): aims to make available reliable climate data for detecting and monitoring climate change for both practical applications and research purposes. The major projects are: the Climate Change Detection Project (CCDP); development of climate data bases; computer systems for climate data management (CLICOM); the World Data and Information Referral Service (INFOCLIMA); the Climate Monitoring System; and the Data Rescue (DARE) project.

World Climate Impact Assessment and Response Strategies Programme (WCIRP): aims to make reliable estimates of the socio-economic impact of climate changes, and to assist in forming national policies accordingly. It concentrates on: study of the impact of climate variations on national food systems; assessment of the impact of man's activities on the climate, especially through increasing the amount of carbon dioxide and other radiatively active gases in the atmosphere; and developing the methodology of climate impact assessments.

World Climate Research Programme (WCRP): organized jointly with the Intergovernmental Oceanographic Commission of UNESCO and the ICSU, to determine to what extent climate can be predicted, and the extent of man's influence on climate. Its three specific objectives are: establishing the physical basis for weather predictions over time ranges of one to two months; understanding and predicting the variability of the global climate over periods of several years; and studying the long-term variations and the response of climate to natural or man-made influence over periods of several decades. Studies include: changes in the atmosphere caused by emissions of carbon dioxide, aerosols and other gases; the effect of cloudiness on the radiation balance; the effect of ground water storage and vegetation on evaporation; the Arctic and Antarctic climate process; and the effects of oceanic circulation changes on the global atmosphere. The 10-year Tropical Ocean and Global Atmosphere Project, which ended in 1994, developed forecasting techniques used to monitor the climate phenomenon, El Niño, in 1997–98.

ATMOSPHERIC RESEARCH AND ENVIRONMENT PROGRAMME

This major programme aims to help members to implement research projects; to disseminate relevant scientific information; to draw the attention of members to outstanding research problems of major importance, such as atmospheric composition and environment changes; and to encourage and help members to incorporate the results of research into operational forecasting or other appropriate techniques, particularly when such changes of procedure require international co-ordination and agreement.

Global Atmosphere Watch (GAW): This is a world-wide system that integrates most monitoring and research activities involving the measurement of atmospheric composition, and is intended to serve as an early warning system to detect further changes in atmospheric concentrations of 'greenhouse' gases, changes in the ozone layer and in long-range transport of pollutants, including acidity and toxicity of rain, as well as the atmospheric burden of aerosols. The instruments of these globally standardized observations and related research are a set of 22 global stations in remote areas and, in order to address regional effects, some 200 regional stations measuring specific atmospheric chemistry parameters, such as ozone and acid deposition. GAW is the main contributor of data on chemical composition and physical characteristics of the atmosphere to the GCOS. Through GAW, WMO has collaborated with the UN Economic Commission for Europe (ECE) and has been responsible for the meteorological part of the Monitoring and Evaluation of the Long-range Transmission of Air Pollutants in Europe. In this respect, WMO has arranged for the establishment of two Meteorological Synthesizing Centres (Oslo, Norway, and Moscow, Russia) which provide daily analysis of the transport of pollution over Europe. GAW also gives attention to atmospheric chemistry studies, prepares scientific assessments and encourages integrated environmental monitoring. Quality Assurance Science Activities Centres have been established to ensure an overall level

of quality in GAW. Atmospheric composition information is maintained by and available through a series of six GAW World Data Centres. GAW operates the GAW Urban Environment Meteorological Research Programme (GURME), which assists National Meteorological and Hydrological Services (NMHSs) in dealing with regional and urban pollution monitoring forecasting, through the provision of guide-lines and information on the requisite measuring and modelling infrastructures, and by bringing together NMHSs, regional and local administrations and health authorities. GURME is being developed in co-operation with the World Health Organization.

Physics and Chemistry of Clouds and Weather Modification Research Programme: encourages scientific research on cloud physics and chemistry, with special emphasis on interaction between clouds and atmospheric chemistry, as well as weather modification such as precipitation enhancement ('rain-making') and hail suppression. It provides information on world-wide weather modification projects, and guidance in the design and evaluation of experiments. It also studies the chemistry of clouds and their role in the transport, transformation and dispersion of pollution.

Tropical Meteorology Research Programme: aims at the promotion and co-ordination of members' research efforts into such important problems as monsoons, tropical cyclones, meteorological aspects of droughts in the arid zones of the tropics, rain-producing tropical weather systems, and the interaction between tropical and mid-latitude weather systems. This should lead to a better understanding of tropical systems and forecasting, and thus be of economic benefit to tropical countries.

Weather Prediction Research Programmes: The programmes assist members in exchanging the results of research on weather prediction and long-range forecasting by means of international conferences and technical reports and progress reports on numerical weather prediction, in order to improve members' weather services. The Programme on Very Short- and Short-range Weather Prediction Research is designed to promote and co-ordinate research activities by members, with a view to improving forecast accuracy over a period extending to three or four days. The Programme on Medium- and Long-range Weather Prediction Research is aimed at the improvement and better co-ordination of members' research activities in weather prediction beyond day four, including monthly and seasonal forecasting.

APPLICATIONS OF METEOROLOGY PROGRAMME

Agricultural Meteorology Programme: the study of weather and climate as they affect agriculture and forestry, the selection of crops and their protection from disease and deterioration in storage, soil conservation, phenology and physiology of crops and productivity and health of farm animals; the Commission for Agricultural Meteorology supervises the applications projects and also advises the Secretary-General in his efforts to co-ordinate activities in support of food production. There are also special activities in agrometeorology to monitor and combat drought and desertification, to apply climate and real-time weather information in agricultural planning and operations, and to help improve the efficiency of the use of human labour, land, water and energy in agriculture; close co-operation is maintained with FAO, centres of CGIAR and UNEP.

Aeronautical Meteorology Programme: to provide operational meteorological information required for safe, regular and efficient air navigation, as well as meteorological assistance to non-real-time activities of the aviation industry. The objective is to ensure the world-wide provision of cost-effective and responsive meteorological services, in support of safe, regular and efficient aviation operations. The programme is implemented at global, regional and national levels by the Commission for Aeronautical Meteorology (CAeM) playing a major role, taking into account relevant meteorological developments in science and technology, studying aeronautical requirements for meteorological services, promoting international standardization of methods, procedures and techniques, and considering requirements for basic and climatological data as well as aeronautical requirements for meteorological observations and specialized instruments and enhanced understanding and awareness of the impact of aviation on the environment. Activities under this programme are carried out, where relevant, with the International Civil Aviation Organization (ICAO, q.v.) and in collaboration with users of services provided to aviation.

Marine Meteorology and Associated Oceanographic Activities Programme: operational monitoring of the oceans and the maritime atmosphere; collection, exchange, archival recording and management of marine data; processing of marine data, and the provision of marine meteorological and oceanographic services in support of the safety of life and property at sea and of the efficient and economic operation of all sea-based activities. The joint WMO/Intergovernmental Oceanographic Commission (IOC) Technical Commission for Oceanography and Marine Meteorology (JCOMM) has broad responsibilities in the overall management of the programme. Many programme elements are undertaken jointly with the IOC, within the context of JCOMM, and also of the Global Ocean Observing System (GOOS). Close co-operation also occurs with the International Maritime Organization (IMO, q.v.), as well as with other bodies both within and outside the UN system.

World Weather Research Programme: Promotes the development and application of improved weather forecasting techniques. The Programme is primarily concerned with predicting weather events that have the potential to cause considerable socio-economic dislocation. Advances in forecasting capability are pursued through a combination of improved scientific understanding (attained by means of field experiments and research), forecast technique development, the demonstration of new forecasting capabilities, and the transfer of these advances to all members in conjunction with related training.

HYDROLOGY AND WATER RESOURCES PROGRAMME

The overall objective of this major programme is to apply hydrology to meet the needs of sustainable development and use of water and related resources; for the mitigation of water-related disasters; and to ensure effective environment management at national and international levels. The Programme consists of the following mutually supporting component programmes:

Programme on Basic Systems in Hydrology (BSH): Provides a framework for the majority of the scientific and technical aspects of WMO activities in hydrology and water resources. The BSH covers the collection, transmission and storage of data, the implementation of the Hydrological Operational Multipurpose System (HOMS), and the development of the World Hydrological Cycle Observing System (WHYCOS).

Programme on Forecasting and Applications in Hydrology (FAH): Covers aspects of the Hydrology and Water Resources Programme relating to hydrological modelling and forecasting, and to the application of hydrology in studies of global change. The FAH organizes activities in support of water resources development and management, and hazard mitigation, and conducts studies on climate change and environmental protection. The Programme is linked to the World Climate and Tropical Cyclone programmes.

Programme on Sustainable Development of Water Resources (SDW): Encourages the full participation of hydrological services in national planning and in the implementation of actions pursuant to the recommendations of the United Nations Conference on Environment and Development (UNCED, held in Rio de Janeiro, Brazil, in 1992), and of its review conference in 1997.

Programme on Capacity Building in Hydrology and Water Resources (CBH): Provides a framework under which National Hydrological Services (NHSs) can request advice and assistance. Supports NHSs' capacity-building efforts.

Programme on Water-related Issues (WRI): Maintains WMO's important role in international activities relating to water resource assessment and hydrological forecasting. Collaborates with other UN agencies, and conducts joint activities with international river basin commissions and with scientific and technical non-governmental organizations.

Specific suppport for the transfer of operational technology is provided through the Hydrological Operational Multipurpose System (HOMS).

Other WMO programmes contain hydrological elements, which are closely co-ordinated with the Hydrology and Water Resources Programme. These include the Tropical Cyclone Programme, the World Climate Programme, and the Global Energy and Water Budget Experiment of the World Climate Research Programme.

EDUCATION AND TRAINING PROGRAMME

The overall objective of this programme is to assist members in developing adequately trained staff to meet their responsibilities for providing meteorological and hydrological information services.

Activities include surveys of the training requirements of member states, the development of appropriate training programmes, the monitoring and improvement of the network of WMO Regional Meteorological Training Centres, the organization of training courses, seminars and conferences and the preparation of training materials. The Programme also arranges individual training programmes and the provision of fellowships. There are about 500 trainees in any one year. About 300 fellowships are awarded annually. Advice is given on training materials, resources and expertise between members. A Panel of Experts on Education and Training was set up by the Executive Council to serve as an advisory body on all aspects of technical and scientific education and of training in meteorology and operational hydrology.

TECHNICAL CO-OPERATION PROGRAMME

The objective of the WMO Technical Co-operation Programme is to assist developing countries in improving their meteorological and hydrological services so that they can serve the needs of their people more effectively. This is through improving, *inter alia*, their early warning systems for severe weather; their agricultural-meteorological services, to assist in more reliable and fruitful food production; and the assessment of climatological factors for economic planning. At a regional level the Programme concentrates on disaster prevention and mitigation. In 2000 the cost of the assistance to developing countries, administered or arranged by the Technical Co-operation Programme, was US $16.6m.

United Nations Development Programme (UNDP): WMO provides assistance in the development of national meteorological and hydrological services, in the application of meteorological and hydrological data to national economic development, and in the training of personnel. Assistance in the form of expert missions, fellowships and equipment was provided to 18 countries in 2000 at a cost of US $2.6m., financed by UNDP.

Voluntary Co-operation Programme (VCP): WMO assists members in implementing the World Weather Watch Programme to develop an integrated observing and forecasting system. Member governments contribute equipment, services and fellowships for training, in addition to cash donations. During 2000 167 projects in 778 countries received support under the VCP, while 124 short-term and 78 long-term fellowships were being implemented in the framework of the programme. Contributions to the VCP totalled US $8.4m. in 2000.

WMO also carries out assistance projects under Trust Fund arrangements, financed by national authorities, either for activities in their own country or in a beneficiary country and managed by UNDP, the World Bank and UNEP. Such arrangements provided one-third of total Programme funds in 2000.

Financial support from WMO's regular budget for fellowships, group training, technical conferences and study tours amounted to US $800,000 in 2000.

CO-OPERATION WITH OTHER BODIES

As a Specialized Agency of the UN, WMO is actively involved in the activities of the UN system. In addition, WMO has concluded a number of formal agreements and working arrangements with international organizations both within and outside the UN system, at the intergovernmental and non-governmental level. As a result, WMO participates in major international conferences convened under the auspices of the UN or other organizations.

Intergovernmental Panel on Climate Change (IPCC): established in 1988 by UNEP and WMO; comprises some 3,000 scientists as well as other experts and representatives of all UN member governments. Approximately every five years the IPCC assesses all available scientific, technical and socio-economic information on anthropogenic climate change. IPCC provides, on request, scientific, technical and socio-economic advice to the parties to the Conference of the Parties to the UN Framework Convention on Climate Change (UNFCCC) and to its subsidiary bodies, and compiles reports on specialized topics, such as *Aviation and the Global Atmosphere* and *Regional Impacts of Climate Change*. The IPCC informs and guides, but does not prescribe, policy. In December 1995 the IPCC presented evidence to 120 governments, demonstrating 'a discernible human influence on global climate'. In early 2001 the Panel issued its *Third Assessment Report*, in which it confirmed this finding and presented new and strengthened evidence attributing most global climate warming over the past 50 years to human activities.

Secretariat of the UN Framework Convention on Climate Change: Haus Carstanjen, Martin-Luther-King-Strasse 8, 53175 Bonn, Germany; tel. (228) 815-1000; fax (228) 815-1999; e-mail secretariat@unfccc.de; internet www.unfccc.de. WMO and UNEP worked together to formulate the Convention, in response to the first report of the IPCC, issued in August 1990, which predicted an increase in the concentration of 'greenhouse' gases (i.e. carbon dioxide and other gases that have a warming effect on the atmosphere) owing to human activity. The UNFCCC was signed in May 1992 and formally adopted at the UN Conference on Environment and Development, held in June. It entered into force in March 1994. It commited countries to submitting reports on measures being taken to reduce the emission of greenhouse gases and recommended stabilizing these emissions at 1990 levels by 2000; however, this was not legally-binding. In July 1996, at the second session of the Conference of the Parties (COP) of the Convention, representatives of developed countries declared their willingness to commit to legally-binding objectives for emission limitations in a specified timetable. Multilateral negotiations ensued to formulate a mandatory treaty on greenhouse gas emissions. At the third COP, held in Kyoto, Japan, in December 1997, 38 industrial nations endorsed mandatory reductions of emissions of the six most harmful gases by an average of 5.2% from 1990 levels, between 2008 and 2012. The agreement was to enter into force on being ratified by countries representing 55% of the world's carbon dioxide emissions in 1990. The fourth COP, convened in Buenos Aires, Argentina, in November 1998, adopted a plan of action to promote implementation of the Kyoto Protocol, through further detailed consideration of measures designed to reduce gas emissions. These included the Clean Development Mechanism, by which industrialized countries may obtain credits towards achieving their reduction targets by assisting developing countries to implement emission-reducing measures, and a system of trading emission quotas. The meeting also agreed on the need to formulate an effective compliance mechanism; however, discussion on the voluntary participation by developing countries in the Kyoto Protocol was postponed. The fifth COP to pursue negotiations on implementation of the Kyoto Protocol, held in Bonn, Germany, in October/November 1999, adopted guide-lines for the technical review of national gas emissions inventories submitted by industrialized countries. The sixth COP, convened in November 2000 at The Hague, Netherlands, aimed to finalize operational details for commitments on emissions reductions under the Kyoto Protocol. However, the Conference was stalled by a lack of consensus on several technical matters, including the formulation of the compliance mechanism, and adequately defining a provision of the Protocol under which industrialized countries may obtain credits towards achieving their reduction targets in respect of the absorption of emissions resulting from activities in the so-called land-use, land-use change and forestry (LULUCF) sector. Further, informal, talks were held in Ottawa, Canada, in early December. The sixth COP was to reconvene in May/June 2001. In late March, however, the USA (the most prolific national producer of harmful gas emissions) announced that it would not ratify the Kyoto Protocol, thereby placing in doubt the future efficacy of the agreement.

INTERNATIONAL DAY

World Meteorological Day is observed every year on 23 March. The theme in 2001 was 'Volunteers for Weather, Climate and Water'.

Finance

WMO is financed by contributions from members on a proportional scale of assessment. The assessed regular budget for the four years 2000–03 was 248.8m. Swiss francs; additional expenditure of 3.5m. Swiss francs was also authorized to be used for high priority activities. Outside this budget, WMO implements a number of projects as executing agency for the UNDP or else under trust-fund arrangements.

Publications

Annual Report.
Statements on the Status of the Global Climate.
WMO Bulletin (quarterly in English, French, Russian and Spanish).
Reports, technical regulations, manuals and notes and training publications.

Membership of the United Nations and its Specialized Agencies

(at April 2001)

	UN	IAEA	IBRD	IDA	IFC	IMF	FAO[1]	IFAD[2]	IMO[3]	ICAO[4]	ILO	ITU[5]	UNESCO[6]	UNIDO	UPU[7]	WHO[8]	WMO[9]	WIPO
Afghanistan	x	x	x	x	x	x	x	x		x	x	x	x	x	x	x	x	
Albania	x	x	x	x	x	x	x	x	x	x	x	x	x	x	x	x	x	x
Algeria	x	x	x	x	x	x	x	x	x	x	x	x	x	x	x	x	x	x
Andorra	x									x		x	x		x	x		x
Angola	x		x	x	x	x	x	x		x	x	x	x	x	x	x	x	x
Antigua and Barbuda	x		x		x	x		x	x	x	x	x	x		x	x	x	x
Argentina	x	x	x	x	x	x	x	x	x	x	x	x	x	x	x	x	x	x
Armenia	x	x	x	x	x	x	x	x	x	x	x	x	x	x	x	x	x	x
Australia	x	x	x	x	x	x	x	x	x	x	x	x	x	x	x	x	x	x
Austria	x	x	x	x	x	x	x	x	x	x	x	x	x	x	x	x	x	x
Azerbaijan	x		x	x	x	x	x	x	x	x	x	x	x	x	x	x	x	x
Bahamas	x		x		x	x	x		x	x	x	x	x	x	x	x	x	x
Bahrain	x		x		x	x	x		x	x	x	x	x	x	x	x	x	x
Bangladesh	x	x	x	x	x	x	x	x	x	x	x	x	x	x	x	x	x	x
Barbados	x		x	x	x	x	x	x		x	x	x	x	x	x		x	x
Belarus	x	x	x		x	x				x	x	x	x	x	x	x	x	x
Belgium	x	x	x	x	x	x	x	x	x	x	x	x	x	x	x	x	x	x
Belize	x		x	x	x	x	x	x	x	x	x	x	x	x	x	x	x	x
Benin	x		x	x	x	x	x	x	x	x	x	x	x	x	x	x	x	x
Bhutan	x		x	x	x	x	x	x				x	x	x	x	x	x	x
Bolivia	x	x	x	x	x	x	x	x	x	x	x	x	x	x	x	x	x	x
Bosnia and Herzegovina	x	x	x	x	x	x	x	x	x	x	x	x	x	x	x	x	x	x
Botswana	x		x	x	x	x	x	x		x	x	x	x	x	x	x	x	x
Brazil	x	x	x	x	x	x	x	x	x	x	x	x	x	x	x	x	x	x
Brunei	x		x			x			x	x		x			x	x		x
Bulgaria	x		x			x		x		x			x			x	x	x
Burkina Faso	x	x	x	x	x	x	x		x	x	x	x	x	x	x	x	x	x
Burundi	x		x	x	x	x	x	x		x	x	x	x	x	x	x	x	x
Cambodia	x	x	x	x	x	x	x	x	x	x	x	x	x	x	x	x	x	x
Cameroon	x	x	x	x	x	x	x	x	x	x	x	x	x	x	x	x	x	x
Canada	x	x	x	x	x	x	x	x	x	x	x	x		x	x	x	x	x
Cape Verde	x		x	x	x	x	x	x	x	x	x	x	x	x	x	x	x	x
Central African Republic	x		x	x	x	x	x	x	x	x	x	x	x	x	x	x	x	x
Chad	x		x	x	x	x	x	x		x	x	x	x	x	x	x	x	x
Chile	x	x	x	x	x	x	x	x	x	x	x	x	x	x	x	x	x	x
China, People's Republic	x	x	x	x	x	x	x	x	x	x	x	x	x	x	x	x	x	x
Colombia	x	x	x	x	x	x	x	x	x	x	x	x	x	x	x	x	x	x
Comoros	x		x	x	x	x	x	x	x	x	x	x	x	x	x	x	x	
Congo, Democratic Republic	x	x	x	x	x	x	x	x	x	x	x	x	x	x	x	x	x	
Congo, Republic	x		x	x	x	x	x	x	x	x	x	x	x	x	x	x	x	x
Costa Rica	x	x	x	x	x	x	x	x	x	x	x	x	x	x	x	x	x	x
Côte d'Ivoire	x	x	x	x	x	x	x	x	x	x	x	x	x	x	x	x	x	x
Croatia	x	x	x	x	x	x	x	x	x	x	x	x	x	x	x	x	x	x
Cuba	x	x					x	x	x	x	x	x	x	x	x	x	x	x
Cyprus	x	x	x	x	x	x	x	x	x	x	x	x	x	x	x	x	x	x
Czech Republic	x	x	x	x	x	x	x		x	x	x	x	x	x	x	x	x	x
Denmark	x	x	x	x	x	x	x	x	x	x	x	x	x	x	x	x	x	x
Djibouti	x		x	x	x	x	x	x		x	x	x	x	x	x	x	x	x
Dominica	x		x	x	x	x	x	x		x	x	x	x		x	x	x	x
Dominican Republic	x	x	x	x	x	x	x	x	x	x	x	x	x	x	x	x	x	x
Ecuador	x	x	x	x	x	x	x	x	x	x	x	x	x	x	x	x	x	x
Egypt	x	x	x	x	x	x	x	x	x	x	x	x	x	x	x	x	x	x
El Salvador	x	x	x	x	x	x	x	x	x	x	x	x	x	x	x	x	x	x
Equatorial Guinea	x		x	x	x	x	x	x	x	x	x	x	x	x	x	x		x
Eritrea	x		x	x	x	x	x	x		x	x	x	x	x	x	x	x	x
Estonia	x	x	x		x	x	x		x	x	x	x	x	x	x	x	x	x
Ethiopia	x		x	x	x	x	x	x		x	x	x	x	x	x	x	x	x
Fiji	x		x	x	x	x	x	x	x	x	x	x	x		x	x	x	x
Finland	x	x	x	x	x	x	x	x	x	x	x	x	x	x	x	x	x	x
France	x	x	x	x	x	x	x	x	x	x	x	x	x	x	x	x	x	x
Gabon	x	x	x	x	x	x	x	x	x	x	x	x	x	x	x	x	x	x
The Gambia	x		x	x	x	x	x	x	x	x	x	x	x	x	x	x	x	x
Georgia	x	x	x	x	x	x	x		x	x	x	x	x	x	x	x	x	x
Germany	x	x	x	x	x	x	x	x	x	x	x	x	x	x	x	x	x	x
Ghana	x	x	x	x	x	x	x	x	x	x	x	x	x	x	x	x	x	x
Greece	x	x	x		x	x	x		x	x	x	x	x	x	x	x	x	x
Grenada	x		x	x	x	x	x		x	x	x	x	x		x	x		x
Guatemala	x	x	x	x	x	x	x	x	x	x	x	x	x	x	x	x	x	x

continued

	UN	IAEA	IBRD	IDA	IFC	IMF	FAO[1]	IFAD[2]	IMO[3]	ICAO[4]	ILO	ITU[5]	UNESCO[6]	UNIDO	UPU[7]	WHO[8]	WMO[9]	WIPO
Guinea	x		x	x	x	x	x	x	x	x	x	x	x	x	x	x	x	x
Guinea-Bissau	x		x	x	x	x	x	x	x	x	x	x	x	x	x	x	x	x
Guyana	x		x	x	x	x	x	x	x	x	x	x	x	x	x	x	x	x
Haiti	x	x	x	x	x	x	x	x	x	x	x	x	x	x	x	x	x	x
Honduras	x	x	x	x	x	x	x	x	x	x	x	x	x	x	x	x	x	x
Hungary	x	x	x	x	x	x	x	x	x	x	x	x	x	x	x	x	x	x
Iceland	x	x	x	x	x	x	x		x	x	x	x	x		x	x	x	x
India	x	x	x	x	x	x	x	x	x	x	x	x	x	x	x	x	x	x
Indonesia	x	x	x	x	x	x	x	x	x	x	x	x	x	x	x	x	x	x
Iran	x	x	x	x	x	x	x	x	x	x	x	x	x	x	x	x	x	x
Iraq	x	x	x	x	x	x	x	x	x	x	x	x	x	x	x	x	x	x
Ireland	x	x	x	x	x	x	x	x	x	x	x	x	x	x	x	x	x	x
Israel	x	x	x	x	x	x	x	x	x	x	x	x	x	x	x	x	x	x
Italy	x	x	x	x	x	x	x	x	x	x	x	x	x	x	x	x	x	x
Jamaica	x	x	x	x		x	x	x	x	x	x	x	x	x	x	x	x	x
Japan	x	x	x	x	x	x	x	x	x	x	x	x	x	x	x	x	x	x
Jordan	x	x	x	x	x	x	x	x	x	x	x	x	x	x	x	x	x	x
Kazakhstan	x	x	x	x	x	x	x	x	x	x	x	x	x	x	x	x	x	x
Kenya	x	x	x	x	x	x	x	x	x	x	x	x	x	x	x	x	x	x
Kiribati	x		x	x	x	x			x			x	x	x		x	x	
Korea, Democratic People's Republic	x						x		x	x		x	x	x	x	x	x	x
Korea, Republic	x	x	x	x	x	x	x	x	x	x	x	x	x	x	x	x	x	x
Kuwait	x	x	x	x	x	x	x	x	x	x	x	x	x	x	x	x	x	x
Kyrgyzstan	x		x	x	x	x	x		x		x	x	x	x	x	x	x	x
Laos	x		x	x	x	x	x	x		x	x	x	x	x	x	x	x	x
Latvia	x	x	x	x	x	x	x			x	x	x	x	x	x			x
Lebanon	x	x	x	x	x	x	x	x	x	x	x	x	x	x	x	x	x	x
Lesotho	x		x	x	x	x	x	x		x	x	x	x	x	x	x	x	x
Liberia	x		x	x	x	x	x	x	x	x	x	x	x	x	x	x	x	x
Libya	x		x	x	x	x	x	x	x	x	x	x	x	x	x	x	x	x
Liechtenstein	x	x										x				x	x	x
Lithuania	x	x	x		x	x	x		x	x	x	x	x	x	x	x	x	x
Luxembourg	x	x	x	x	x	x	x	x	x	x	x	x	x	x	x	x	x	x
Macedonia, former Yugoslav republic	x		x	x	x	x	x	x	x	x	x	x	x	x	x	x	x	x
Madagascar	x	x	x	x	x	x	x	x	x	x	x	x	x	x	x	x	x	x
Malawi	x		x	x	x	x	x	x	x	x	x	x	x	x	x	x	x	x
Malaysia	x	x	x	x	x	x	x	x	x	x	x	x	x	x	x	x	x	x
Maldives	x		x	x	x	x	x	x	x	x	x	x	x	x	x	x	x	x
Mali	x	x	x	x	x		x	x		x	x	x	x	x	x	x	x	x
Malta	x	x	x				x	x	x	x	x	x	x	x	x	x	x	x
Marshall Islands	x	x	x		x	x			x	x		x			x			
Mauritania	x		x	x	x	x	x	x	x	x	x	x	x	x	x	x	x	x
Mauritius	x	x	x	x	x	x	x	x	x	x	x	x	x	x	x	x	x	x
Mexico	x	x	x	x	x	x	x	x	x	x	x	x	x	x	x	x	x	x
Micronesia, Federated States of	x		x	x	x	x				x		x			x		x	
Moldova	x	x	x	x	x	x	x		x	x	x	x	x	x	x	x	x	x
Monaco	x	x							x	x		x	x		x	x	x	x
Mongolia	x	x	x	x	x	x	x	x	x	x	x	x	x	x	x	x	x	x
Morocco	x	x	x	x	x	x	x	x	x	x	x	x	x	x	x	x	x	x
Mozambique	x		x	x	x	x	x	x	x	x	x	x	x	x	x	x	x	x
Myanmar	x	x	x	x	x	x	x	x	x	x	x	x	x	x	x	x	x	
Namibia	x		x		x	x	x	x	x	x	x	x	x	x	x	x	x	x
Nauru	x									x		x			x	x		
Nepal	x		x	x	x	x	x	x	x	x	x	x	x	x	x	x	x	x
Netherlands	x	x	x	x	x	x	x	x	x	x	x	x	x	x	x	x	x	x
New Zealand	x	x	x	x	x	x	x	x	x	x	x	x	x	x	x	x	x	x
Nicaragua	x	x	x	x	x	x	x	x	x	x	x	x	x	x	x	x	x	x
Niger	x	x	x	x	x	x	x	x		x	x	x	x	x	x	x	x	x
Nigeria	x	x	x	x	x	x	x	x	x	x	x	x	x	x	x	x	x	x
Norway	x	x	x	x	x	x	x	x	x	x	x	x	x	x	x	x	x	x
Oman	x		x	x	x	x	x	x	x	x	x	x	x	x	x	x	x	x
Pakistan	x	x	x	x	x	x	x	x	x	x	x	x	x	x	x	x	x	x
Palau	x		x	x	x	x	x		x	x		x		x		x		
Panama	x	x	x	x	x	x	x	x	x	x	x	x	x	x	x	x	x	x
Papua New Guinea	x		x	x	x	x	x	x	x	x	x	x	x	x	x	x	x	x
Paraguay	x	x	x	x	x	x	x	x	x	x	x	x	x	x	x	x	x	x
Peru	x	x	x	x	x	x	x	x	x	x	x	x	x	x	x	x	x	x
Philippines	x	x	x	x	x	x	x	x	x	x	x	x	x	x	x	x	x	x
Poland	x	x	x	x	x	x	x		x	x	x	x	x	x	x	x	x	x
Portugal	x	x	x	x	x	x	x		x	x	x	x	x	x	x	x	x	x
Qatar	x	x	x	x	x	x	x	x	x	x	x	x	x	x	x	x	x	x
Romania	x	x	x		x	x	x	x		x	x	x	x	x	x	x	x	x
Russia	x	x	x	x	x	x			x	x	x	x	x	x	x	x	x	x
Rwanda	x		x	x	x	x	x	x		x	x	x	x	x	x	x	x	x
Saint Christopher and Nevis	x		x	x	x	x	x	x		x		x		x	x	x		x

continued

	UN	IAEA	IBRD	IDA	IFC	IMF	FAO[1]	IFAD[2]	IMO[3]	ICAO[4]	ILO	ITU[5]	UNESCO[6]	UNIDO	UPU[7]	WHO[8]	WMO[9]	WIPO
Saint Lucia	x		x	x	x	x	x	x	x	x	x	x	x	x	x	x	x	x
Saint Vincent and the Grenadines	x		x	x		x	x	x	x	x	x	x	x	x	x	x		x
Samoa	x		x	x	x		x	x	x	x	x		x	x		x	x	x
San Marino	x		x			x	x		x	x	x	x	x		x	x	x	x
São Tomé and Príncipe	x		x	x		x	x	x	x	x	x	x	x	x	x	x	x	x
Saudi Arabia	x	x	x	x	x	x	x	x	x	x	x	x	x	x	x	x	x	x
Senegal	x	x	x	x	x	x	x	x	x	x	x	x	x	x	x	x	x	x
Seychelles	x		x		x	x	x	x	x	x	x	x	x	x	x	x	x	x
Sierra Leone	x	x	x	x	x	x	x	x	x	x	x	x	x	x	x	x	x	x
Singapore	x	x	x		x	x			x	x	x	x				x	x	x
Slovakia	x	x	x	x	x	x	x		x	x	x	x	x	x	x	x	x	x
Slovenia	x	x	x	x	x	x	x		x	x	x	x	x	x	x	x	x	x
Solomon Islands	x		x	x	x	x	x	x	x	x	x	x	x	x	x	x	x	x
Somalia	x		x	x	x	x	x	x	x	x	x	x	x	x	x	x	x	x
South Africa	x	x	x	x	x	x	x	x	x	x	x	x	x	x	x	x	x	x
Spain	x	x	x	x	x	x	x	x	x	x	x	x	x	x	x	x	x	x
Sri Lanka	x	x	x	x	x	x	x	x	x	x	x	x	x	x	x	x	x	x
Sudan	x	x	x	x	x	x	x	x	x	x	x	x	x	x	x	x	x	x
Suriname	x		x			x	x	x	x	x	x	x	x	x	x	x	x	x
Swaziland	x		x	x	x	x	x	x	x	x	x	x	x	x	x	x	x	x
Sweden	x	x	x	x	x	x	x	x	x	x	x	x	x	x	x	x	x	x
Switzerland		x	x	x	x	x	x	x	x	x	x	x	x	x	x	x	x	x
Syria	x	x	x	x	x	x	x	x	x	x	x	x	x	x	x	x	x	x
Tajikistan	x		x	x	x	x	x		x	x	x	x	x	x	x	x	x	x
Tanzania	x		x	x	x	x	x	x	x	x	x	x	x	x	x	x	x	x
Thailand	x	x	x	x	x	x	x	x	x	x	x	x	x	x	x	x	x	x
Togo	x		x	x	x	x	x	x	x	x	x	x	x	x	x	x	x	x
Tonga	x		x	x	x	x	x	x	x	x	x	x	x		x	x	x	x
Trinidad and Tobago	x		x	x	x	x	x	x	x	x	x	x	x	x	x	x	x	x
Tunisia	x	x	x	x	x	x	x	x	x	x	x	x	x	x	x	x	x	x
Turkey	x	x	x	x	x	x	x	x	x	x	x	x	x	x	x	x	x	x
Turkmenistan	x		x		x	x			x	x	x	x	x	x	x	x		x
Tuvalu	x											x			x	x		
Uganda	x	x	x	x	x	x	x	x			x	x	x	x	x	x	x	x
Ukraine	x	x	x		x	x			x	x	x	x	x	x	x	x	x	x
United Arab Emirates	x	x	x	x	x	x	x	x	x	x	x	x	x	x	x	x	x	x
United Kingdom	x	x	x	x	x	x	x	x	x	x	x	x	x	x	x	x	x	x
USA	x	x	x	x	x	x	x	x	x	x	x	x			x	x	x	x
Uruguay	x	x	x		x	x	x	x	x	x	x	x	x	x	x	x	x	x
Uzbekistan	x	x	x	x	x	x				x	x	x	x	x	x	x	x	x
Vanuatu	x		x	x	x	x	x		x		x	x	x	x	x	x	x	
Vatican City		x										x			x			x
Venezuela	x	x	x		x	x	x	x	x	x	x	x	x	x	x	x	x	x
Viet Nam	x	x	x	x	x	x	x	x	x	x	x	x	x	x	x	x	x	x
Yemen	x	x	x	x	x	x	x	x	x	x	x	x	x	x	x	x	x	x
Yugoslavia, Federal Republic	x	x				x	x	x	x	x	x	x	x	x	x	x	x	x
Zambia	x	x	x	x	x	x	x	x		x	x	x	x	x	x	x	x	x
Zimbabwe	x	x	x	x	x	x	x	x	x	x	x	x	x	x	x	x	x	x

[1] The Cook Islands, Niue and the European Union are members of FAO.

[2] The Cook Islands is a member of IFAD.

[3] Hong Kong and Macau are associate members of IMO.

[4] The Cook Islands is a member of ICAO.

[5] Members also include British Overseas Territories, French Overseas Territories and United States Territories.

[6] The Cook Islands and Niue are members of UNESCO; Aruba, the British Virgin Islands, the Cayman Islands, Macau and the Netherlands Antilles are associate members.

[7] Members also include British Overseas Territories and the Netherlands Antilles and Aruba.

[8] The Cook Islands and Niue are members of WHO; Puerto Rico and Tokelau are associate members.

[9] Members also include British Caribbean Territories, the Cook Islands, French Polynesia, Hong Kong, Macau, the Netherlands Antilles and Aruba, New Caledonia and Niue.

AFRICAN DEVELOPMENT BANK—ADB

Address: rue Joseph Anoma, 01 BP 1387, Abidjan 01, Côte d'Ivoire.
Telephone: 20-20-44-44; **fax:** 20-20-40-06; **e-mail:** comuadb
@afdb.org; **internet:** www.afdb.org.

Established in 1964, the Bank began operations in July 1966, with the aim of financing economic and social development in African countries.

AFRICAN MEMBERS

Algeria	Equatorial Guinea	Namibia
Angola	Eritrea	Niger
Benin	Ethiopia	Nigeria
Botswana	Gabon	Rwanda
Burkina Faso	The Gambia	São Tomé and
Burundi	Ghana	Príncipe
Cameroon	Guinea	Senegal
Cape Verde	Guinea-Bissau	Seychelles
Central African	Kenya	Sierra Leone
Republic	Lesotho	Somalia
Chad	Liberia	South Africa
Comoros	Libya	Sudan
Congo,	Madagascar	Swaziland
Democratic	Malawi	Tanzania
Republic	Mali	Togo
Congo, Republic	Mauritania	Tunisia
Côte d'Ivoire	Mauritius	Uganda
Djibouti	Morocco	Zambia
Egypt	Mozambique	Zimbabwe

There are also 24 non-African members.

Organization

(April 2001)

BOARD OF GOVERNORS

The highest policy-making body of the Bank. Each member country nominates one Governor, usually its Minister of Finance and Economic Affairs, and an alternate Governor or the Governor of its Central Bank. The Board meets once a year. It elects the Board of Directors and the President.

BOARD OF DIRECTORS

The Board consists of 18 members (of whom six are non-African), elected by the Board of Governors for a term of three years, renewable once; it is responsible for the general operations of the Bank. The Board meets on a weekly basis.

OFFICERS

The President is responsible for the organization and the day-to-day operations of the Bank under guidance of the Board of Directors. The President is elected for a five-year term and serves as the Chairman of the Board of Directors. Three Vice-Presidents are responsible for Operations, Finance and Planning, and Corporate Management.

The Bank's operational activities are divided into five regional departments (for northern, southern, eastern, western and central Africa), departments for central operations and for the private sector, and units for co-operation and for environment and sustainable development.

Executive President and Chairman of Board of Directors: OMAR KABBAJ (Morocco).

Vice-President (Finance and Planning): AHMED M. F. BAHGAT (Egypt).

Vice-President (Administration and Corporate Management): CHANEL BOUCHER (Canada).

Vice-President (Operations): CYRIL ENWEZE (Nigeria).

Secretary-General: PHILIBERT AFRIKA (Rwanda).

FINANCIAL STRUCTURE

The ADB Group of development financing institutions comprises the African Development Fund (ADF) and the Nigeria Trust Fund (NTF), which provide concessional loans, and the African Development Bank itself. The group uses a unit of account (UA), which, at 31 July 2000, was valued at US $1.3134.

The capital stock of the Bank was at first exclusively open for subscription by African countries, with each member's subscription consisting of an equal number of paid-up and callable shares. In 1978, however, the Governors agreed to open the capital stock of the Bank to subscription by non-regional states on the basis of

nine principles aimed at maintaining the African character of the institution. The decision was finally ratified in May 1982, and the participation of non-regional countries became effective on 30 December. It was agreed that African members should still hold two-thirds of the share capital, that all loan operations should be restricted to African members, and that the Bank's President should always be an African national. In May 1998 the Board of Governors approved an increase in capital of 35%, and resolved that the non-African members' share of the capital be increased from 33.3% to 40%. In 1999 the ADB's authorized capital was US $29,983m. At the end of 1999 subscribed capital was $22,976m. (of which the paid-up portion was $2,712m.).

Activities

At the end of 1999 total loan and grant approvals by the ADB Group since the beginning of its operations amounted to US $36,280m. Of that amount agriculture received the largest proportion of assistance (23.3%), while public utilities received 20.4%, transport 16.3%, industry 15.8%, multi-sector activities 14.2%, and social projects 10.0%. In 1999 the group approved 93 loans and grants amounting to $1,696m.

A new credit policy, adopted in May 1995, effectively disqualified 39 low-income regional members, deemed to be non-creditworthy, from receiving non-concessional ADB financing, in an attempt to reduce the accumulation of arrears. The ADB Group estimated that its capital requirements for the period 1997–2001 would amount to US $46,500m. to allow for greater flexibility in its lending. In September 1997 the Bank approved an initial UA 133m. to establish a Supplementary Financing Mechanism, which aimed to assist countries eligible for ADF funds to meet interest payments on outstanding Bank debt. Since 1996 the Bank has supported international efforts to address the problems of heavily indebted poor countries (HIPCs) (see World Bank, p. 81). The ADB's initial contribution to the HIPC initiative, approved in April 1997, was an amount up to UA 230m., to be generated over the period 1997–2003.

The ADB contributed funds for the establishment in 1986 of the Africa Project Development Facility, which assists the private sector in Africa by providing advisory services and finance for entrepreneurs: it is managed by the International Finance Corporation (IFC—see p. 84). In 1989 the ADB, in co-ordination with IFC and UNDP, created the African Management Services Company (AMSCo) which provides management support and training to private companies in Africa.

The Bank also provides technical assistance to regional member countries in the form of experts' services, pre-investment feasibility studies, and staff training; much of this assistance is financed through bilateral aid funds contributed by non-African member states. The Bank's African Development Institute provides training for officials of regional member countries in order to enhance the management of Bank-financed projects and, more broadly, to strengthen national capacities for promoting sustainable development. In 1990 the ADB established the African Business Round Table (ABR), which is composed of the chief executives of Africa's leading corporations. The ABR aims to strengthen Africa's private sector, promote intra-African trade and investment, and attract foreign investment to Africa. The ABR is chaired by the ADB's Executive President. At its fourth annual meeting, held in Arusha, Tanzania, in March 1994, the ABR resolved to establish an African Investment Bank, in co-operation with the ADB, which was to provide financial services to African companies. In November 1999 a Joint Africa Institute, which had been established by the Bank, the World Bank and the IMF, was formally inaugurated in Abidjan, Côte d'Ivoire. The Institute aimed to enhance training opportunities in economic policy and management and to strengthen capacity-building in the region.

In 1990 a Memorandum of Understanding for the Reinforcement of Co-operation between the Organization of African Unity (OAU—q.v.), the UN's Economic Commission for Africa (q.v.) and the ADB was signed by the three organizations. A joint secretariat supports co-operation activities between the organizations. In 1999 a Co-operation Agreement was formally concluded between the Bank and the Common Market for Eastern and Southern Africa (COMESA —q.v.).

AFRICAN DEVELOPMENT BANK (ADB)

The Bank makes loans at a variable rate of interest, which is adjusted twice a year (the rate was 7.16% per year at December 1999), plus a commitment fee of 0.75%. Loan approvals amounted to US $1,065.5m. for 23 loans in 1999. Since October 1997 new fixed and floating rate loans have also been made available.

Summary of Bank Group Activities (US $ million)

	1998	1999	Cumulative total*
ADB loans			
Number	18	23	795
Amount approved	931.92	1,065.48	22,930.08
Disbursements	618.96	700.62	15,562.83
ADF loans and grants			
Number	115	70	1,474
Amount approved	810.49	630.14	13,029.16
Disbursements	623.88	504.94	8,740.47
NTF loans			
Number	—	—	58
Amount approved	—	—	320.27
Disbursements	6.73	10.27	227.51
Group total			
Number	133	93	2,327
Amount approved	1,742.41	1,695.62	36,279.51
Disbursements	1,249.58	1,215.83	24,530.81

* Since the initial operations of the three institutions (1967 for ADB, 1974 for ADF and 1976 for NTF).

Source: *Annual Report 1999*.

AFRICAN DEVELOPMENT FUND (ADF)

The Fund commenced operations in 1974. It grants interest-free loans to low-income African countries for projects with repayment over 50 years (including a 10-year grace period) and with a service charge of 0.75% per annum. Grants for project feasibility studies are made to the poorest countries.

In 1991 a sixth replenishment of the Fund's resources amounting to US $3,340m. was approved for 1991–93. Negotiations for the seventh replenishment of the Fund's resources commenced in May 1993. However, in May 1994, donor countries withheld any new funds owing to dissatisfaction with the Bank's governance. In May 1996, following the implementation of various institutional reforms to strengthen the Bank's financial management and decision-making capabilities and to reduce its administrative costs, an agreement was concluded on the seventh replenishment of the ADF. Donor countries pledged some $2,690m. for the period 1996–98. An additional allocation of $420m. was endorsed at a special donors' meeting held in Osaka, Japan, in June. The ADF aimed to offer concessional assistance to 42 African countries over the period 1996–98. The seventh replenishment provided for the establishment of an ADF Microfinance Initiative (AMINA), initially for a two-year period, to support small-scale capacity-building projects. In January 1999 negotiations on the eighth replenishment of the Fund were concluded with an agreement to provide additional resources amounting to $3,437m. The replenishment was approved by the Board of Governors in May, and came into effect in December.

In 1999 70 ADF loans and grants were approved amounting to US $630m.

NIGERIA TRUST FUND (NTF)

The Agreement establishing the Nigeria Trust Fund was signed in February 1976 by the Bank and the Government of Nigeria. The Fund is administered by the Bank and its loans are granted for up to 25 years, including grace periods of up to five years, and carry 0.75% commitment charges and 4% interest charges. The loans are intended to provide financing for projects in co-operation with other lending institutions. The Fund also aims to promote the private sector and trade between African countries by providing information on African and international financial institutions able to finance African trade.

In 1996, the last time the facility was used, the Fund approved one loan amounting to US $8.63m., bringing the total amount committed since operations began to $320.27m. for 58 loans. During 1999 negotiations on a revised Agreement and replenishment of the Fund's resources were reported to have been concluded.

ASSOCIATED INSTITUTIONS

The ADB actively participated in the establishment of five associated institutions:

Africa Reinsurance Corporation—Africa-Re: Reinsurance House, 46 Marina, PMB 12765, Lagos, Nigeria; tel. (1) 2663323; fax (1) 2668802; e-mail africare@hyperia.com; f. 1977; started operations in 1978; its purpose is to foster the development of the insurance and reinsurance industry in Africa and to promote the growth of national and regional underwriting capacities; auth. cap. US $50m., of which the ADB holds 10%. There are 12 directors, one appointed by the Bank. Mems: 41 countries, the ADB, and some 90 insurance and reinsurance cos. Man. Dir BAKARY KAMARA.

Group Loan and Grant Approvals by Country
(millions of UA)

Country	1998	1999	Cumulative total*
Algeria	156.71	157.46	1,650.67
Angola	—	—	294.14
Benin	—	12.27	277.53
Botswana	—	—	324.93
Burkina Faso	16.37	10.00	304.89
Burundi	—	8.59	275.96
Cameroon	21.46	21.95	577.35
Cape Verde	3.00	0.13	148.22
Central African Republic	—	—	139.39
Chad	12.41	21.10	293.64
Comoros	—	—	64.74
Congo, Democratic Republic	—	—	936.20
Congo, Republic	—	—	277.83
Côte d'Ivoire	81.09	32.67	1,031.55
Djibouti	7.05	—	90.95
Egypt	35.44	53.55	1,488.24
Equatorial Guinea	2.20	—	67.19
Eritrea	1.07	—	37.59
Ethiopia	118.66	—	1,044.27
Gabon	17.11	—	596.81
Gambia	0.76	5.65	175.40
Ghana	16.30	16.16	587.47
Guinea	0.85	—	457.18
Guinea Bissau	—	—	157.26
Kenya	25.69	15.50	526.29
Lesotho	13.30	6.05	265.85
Liberia	—	—	153.25
Madagascar	26.61	26.10	401.51
Malawi	46.07	24.24	509.75
Mali	1.40	21.94	411.41
Mauritania	2.18	23.02	263.26
Mauritius	—	—	151.95
Morocco	227.20	19.60	2,710.08
Mozambique	30.10	74.21	673.17
Namibia	28.11	7.10	62.13
Niger	46.08	—	210.50
Nigeria	—	36.51	1,939.38
Rwanda	46.64	—	278.41
São Tomé and Príncipe	—	4.20	93.78
Senegal	11.09	24.75	433.89
Seychelles	—	7.09	89.50
Sierra Leone	—	9.21	167.96
Somalia	—	—	150.40
South Africa	—	82.59	196.79
Sudan	—	—	349.80
Swaziland	—	11.11	200.04
Tanzania	19.43	28.15	635.21
Togo	1.20	12.18	170.68
Tunisia	104.67	262.97	2,419.55
Uganda	34.33	32.54	573.74
Zambia	1.87	33.77	572.55
Zimbabwe	—	118.23	726.15
Total	1,165.04	1,212.00	26,636.38

* Since the initial operation of the three institutions (1967 for ADB, 1974 for ADF and 1976 for NTF).

African Export-Import Bank—Afreximbank: POB 404 Gezira, Cairo 11568; World Trade Centre Bldg, 1191 Corniche el-Nil, Cairo 11221, Egypt; tel. (2) 5780282; fax (2) 5780277; e-mail mail@afreximbank.com; internet www.afreximbank.com; f. 1993; aims to increase the volume of African exports and to expand intra-African trade by financing exporters and importers directly and indirectly through trade finance institutions, such as commercial banks; auth. cap. US $750m.; paid-up cap. $145.4m. (Dec. 1998). Pres. CHRISTOPHER C. EDORDU; Exec. Vice-Pres. JEAN-LOUIS EKRA. Publ. *Annual Report*.

Association of African Development Finance Institutions—AADFI: c/o ADB, 01 BP 1387, Abidjan 01, Côte d'Ivoire; tel. 20-40-90; fax 22-73-44; e-mail adfi@africaonline.co.ci; f. 1975; aims to promote co-operation among financial institutions in the region in matters relating to economic and social development, research, project design, financing and the exchange of information. Mems: 92 in 43 African and non-African countries. Pres. GERSHOM MUMBA; Sec.-Gen. Dr MAGATTE WADE.

Shelter-Afrique (Société pour l'habitat et le logement territorial en Afrique): Longonot Rd, POB 41479, Nairobi, Kenya; tel. (2) 722305; fax (2) 722024; e-mail info@shelter.co.ke; f. 1982 to finance housing in ADB mem. countries. Share cap. is US $300m., held by 40 African countries, the ADB, Africa-Re and the Commonwealth

Development Corpn; Chair. PAUL M. N'KOUE-N'KONGO; Man. Dir P. M'BAYE.

Société Internationale Financière pour les Investissements et le Développement en Afrique—SIFIDA: 22 rue François-Perréard, BP 310, 1225 Chêne-Bourg/Geneva, Switzerland; tel. (22) 8692000; fax (22) 8692001; e-mail headoffice@sifida.com; internet www.sifida.com; f. 1970 by 120 financial and industrial institutions, including the ADB and the IFC. Following a restructuring at the end of 1995, the main shareholders are the Banque Nationale de Paris (BNP), SFOM (itself owned by BNP and Dresdner Bank) and the six banking affiliates of BNP/SFOM in West and Central Africa. SIFIDA is active in the fields of project and trade finance in Africa and also provides financial advisory services, notably in the context of privatizations and debt conversion; auth. cap. US $75m., subscribed cap. $12.5m. Chair. VIVIEN LÉVY-GARBOUA; Man. Dir PHILIPPE SÉCHAUD. Publ. *African Banking Directory* (annually).

Publications

Annual Report.

ADB Today (every 2 months).

African Development Report (annually).

African Development Review.

Basic Information (annually).

Economic Research Papers.

Quarterly Operational Summary.

Statistical Handbook (annually).

Summaries of operations in each member country and various background documents.

ANDEAN COMMUNITY OF NATIONS
(COMUNIDAD ANDINA DE NACIONES—CAN)

Address: Avda Paseo de la República 3895, San Isidro, Lima 27; Casilla 18-1177, Lima 18, Peru.

Telephone: (1) 4111400; **fax:** (1) 2213329; **e-mail:** contacto@comunidadandina.org; **internet:** www.comunidadandina.org.

The organization was established in 1969 as the Acuerdo de Cartagena (the Cartagena Agreement), also referred to as the Grupo Andino (Andean Group) or the Pacto Andino (Andean Pact). In March 1996 member countries signed a Reform Protocol of the Cartagena Agreement, in accordance with which the Andean Group was superseded in August 1997 by the Andean Community of Nations (CAN, generally referred to as the Andean Community). The Andean Community was to promote greater economic, commercial and political integration under a new Andean Integration System (Sistema Andino de Integración), comprising the organization's bodies and institutions. The Community covers an area of 4,710,000 sq km, with some 111m. inhabitants.

MEMBERS

Bolivia   Colombia   Ecuador   Peru   Venezuela

Note: Chile withdrew from the Andean Group in 1976. Panama has observer status with the Community.

Organization
(April 2001)

ANDEAN PRESIDENTIAL COUNCIL

The presidential summits, which had been held annually since 1989, were formalized under the 1996 Reform Protocol of the Cartagena Agreement as the Andean Presidential Council. The Council provides the political leadership of the Community.

COMMISSION

The Commission consists of a plenipotentiary representative from each member country, with each country holding the presidency in turn. The Commission is the main policy-making organ of the Andean Community, and is responsible for co-ordinating Andean trade policy.

COUNCIL OF FOREIGN MINISTERS

The Council of Foreign Ministers meets annually or whenever it is considered necessary, to formulate common external policy and to co-ordinate the process of integration.

GENERAL SECRETARIAT

The General Secretariat (formerly the Junta) is the body charged with implementation of all guide-lines and decisions issued by the bodies listed above. It submits proposals to the Commission for facilitating the fulfilment of the Community's objectives. Members are appointed for a three-year term. They supervise technical officials assigned to the following Departments: External Relations, Agricultural Development, Press Office, Economic Policy, Physical

Integration, Programme of Assistance to Bolivia, Industrial Development, Programme Planning, Legal Affairs, Technology. Under the reforms agreed in March 1996 the Secretary-General is elected by the Council of Foreign Ministers and has enhanced powers to adjudicate in disputes arising between member states.

Secretary-General: SEBASTIÁN ALEGRETT (Venezuela).

PARLIAMENT

Parlamento Andino: Carrera 7ª, No. 13–58, Oficina 401, Santafé de Bogotá, Colombia; tel. (1) 284-4191; fax (1) 284-3270; e-mail pandino@cable.net.co; internet www.parlamentoandino.org; f. 1979; comprises five members from each country, and meets in each capital city in turn; makes recommendations on regional policy. In April 1997 a new protocol was adopted which provided for the election of members by direct and universal voting. Sec.-Gen. Dr RUBÉN VÉLEZ NÚÑEZ.

COURT OF JUSTICE

Tribunal de Justicia de la Comunidad Andina: Calle Roca 450 y 6 de deciembre, Quito, Ecuador; tel. (2) 529998; fax (2) 565007; e-mail tjca@impsat.net.ec; internet www.altesa.net/tribunal; f. 1979, began operating in 1984; a protocol approved in May 1996 modified the Court's functions; its main responsibilities are to resolve disputes among member countries and interpret community legislation. It comprises five judges, one from each member country, appointed for a renewable period of six years. The Presidency is assumed annually by each judge in turn, by alphabetical order of country. Pres. Dr RUBEN HERDOIZA MERA (Ecuador).

Activities

In May 1979, at Cartagena, Colombia, the Presidents of the five member countries signed the 'Mandate of Cartagena', which envisaged greater economic and political co-operation, including the establishment of more sub-regional development programmes (especially in industry). In May 1989 the Group undertook to revitalize the process of Andean integration, by withdrawing measures that obstructed the programme of trade liberalization, and by complying with tariff reductions that had already been agreed upon. In May 1991, in Caracas, Venezuela, a summit meeting of the Andean Group agreed the framework for the establishment of a free-trade area on 1 January 1992 (achieved in February 1993) and for an eventual Andean common market (see below, under Trade).

In March 1996 heads of state, meeting in Trujillo, Peru, affirmed member countries' commitment to combating drugs trafficking and indirectly condemned the decision of the USA to 'decertify' the Colombian anti-narcotics campaign (and thus to suspend financial assistance to that country). At the same meeting, member countries agreed to a substantial restructuring of the Andean Group. The heads of state signed the Reform Protocol of the Cartagena Agreement, providing for the establishment of the Andean Community of Nations, which was to have more ambitious economic and political objectives than the Group. Consequently, in August 1997 the Andean

Community was inaugurated, and the Group's Junta was replaced by a new General Secretariat, headed by a Secretary-General with enhanced executive and decision-making powers. The initiation of these reforms was designed to accelerate harmonization in economic matters, particularly the achievement of a common external tariff. In September 1996 the Group agreed to negotiate a free-trade agreement with the Mercado Común del Sur (Mercosur—see p. 284). (Disunity among the Andean nations had been evident in June, when Bolivia had agreed to enter into free-trade negotiations with Mercosur on a unilateral basis, thus becoming an associate member of that grouping.) In April 1997 the Peruvian Government announced its intention to withdraw from the Cartagena Agreement, owing to disagreements about the terms of Peru's full integration into the Community's trading system. Later in that month the heads of state of the four other members attended a summit meeting, in Sucre, Bolivia, and reiterated their commitment to strengthening regional integration. A high-level group of representatives was established to pursue negotiations with Peru regarding its future relationship with the Community (agreement was reached in June—see below).

The 10th presidential summit, held in Guayaquil, Ecuador, in April 1998, reiterated the objective of creating a common market and defined specific measures to achieve this, including efforts to promote the Community, to strengthen joint institutions and physical infrastructure, and to formulate a common foreign policy. The 12th presidential summit, convened at Lima, Peru, in June 2000, approved official guide-lines to enable the establishment of the proposed common market by 2005 (see below). In April 2001 Venezuela announced that it intended to apply for membership of Mercosur (while retaining its membership of the Community).

TRADE

Trade within the group increased by about 37% annually between 1978 and 1980. A council for customs affairs met for the first time in January 1982, aiming to harmonize national legislation within the group. In December 1984 the member states launched a new common currency, the Andean peso, aiming to reduce dependence on the US dollar and to increase regional trade. The new currency was to be backed by special contributions to the Fondo Andino de Reservas (now the Fondo Latinoamericano de Reservas) amounting to US $80m., and was to be 'pegged' to the US dollar, taking the form of financial drafts rather than notes and coins. In May 1986 a new formula for trade among member countries was agreed, in order to restrict the number of products exempted from trade liberalization measures to 40 'sensitive' products.

The 'Caracas Declaration' of May 1991 provided for the establishment of an Andean free-trade area, which entered into effect (excluding Peru—see below) in February 1993. Heads of state also agreed in May 1991 to create a common external tariff (CET), to standardize member countries' trade barriers in their dealings with the rest of the world, and envisaged the eventual creation of an Andean common market. In December heads of state defined four main levels of external tariffs (between 5% and 20%). The conclusion of negotiations, however, was subsequently delayed, notably by Ecuador's request for numerous exceptions and by a deterioration in relations between Peru and Venezuela during 1992 (following the suspension of the Peruvian Constitution in April), which halted progress completely. In August the Group approved a request by Peru for the suspension of its rights and obligations under the Pact, thereby enabling the other members to proceed with negotiations on the CET. Peru was readmitted as a full member of the Group in 1994, but participated only as an observer in the ongoing negotiations.

In November 1994 ministers of trade and integration, meeting in Quito, Ecuador, concluded a final agreement on a four-tier structure of external tariffs (although Bolivia was to retain a two-level system). The CET agreement, which came into effect in February 1995, covered 90% of the region's imports (the remainder to be incorporated by 1999, later extended to June 2000), which were to be subject to the following tariff bands: 5% for raw materials; 10%–15% for semi-manufactured goods; and 20% for finished products. In order to reach an agreement, special treatment and exemptions were granted, while Peru, initially, was to remain a 'non-active' member of the accord: Bolivia was to maintain external tariffs of 5% and 10%, Ecuador was permitted to apply the lowest rate of 5% to 990 items and was granted an initial exemption from tariffs on 400 items, while Colombia and Venezuela were granted 230 items to be subject to special treatment for four years. In June 1997 an agreement was concluded to ensure Peru's continued membership of the Community, which provided for that country's integration into the free-trade area. The Peruvian Government determined to eliminate customs duties on some 2,500 products with immediate effect, and it was agreed that the process be completed by 2005. However,

negotiations were to continue with regard to the replacement of Peru's single tariff on products from outside the region with the Community's scale of external duties.

In May 1999 the Community adopted a policy on border integration and development, which aimed to prepare the border regions of member countries for the envisaged free circulation of people, goods, capital and services, and had the general objective of consolidating subregional security. Community heads of state, meeting in June 2000 at the 12th Andean presidential summit, approved official guide-lines for the creation of an Andean common market by the end of 2005, and agreed a programme of related measures to be implemented during 2000/01.

EXTERNAL RELATIONS

In September 1995 heads of state of member countries identified the formulation of common positions on foreign relations as an important part of the process of relaunching the integration initiative. A Protocol Amending the Cartagena Agreement was signed in June 1997 to confirm the formulation of a common foreign policy. During 1998 the General Secretariat held consultations with government experts, academics, representatives of the private sector and other interested parties to help formulate a document on guide-lines for a common foreign policy. The guide-lines, establishing the principles, objectives and mechanisms of a common foreign policy, were approved by the Council of Foreign Ministers in 1999. The 12th Andean presidential summit, held in June 2000, expressed support for the ongoing formulation and implementation of the policy. A Council on Trade and Investment between the Andean Community and the USA has been established to strengthen the trading relations between the two parties. A co-operation agreement between the European Union and Andean Group was signed in April 1993. A Euro-Andean Forum is held periodically to promote co-operation, trade and investment between the two communities. In February 1998 the Community signed a co-operation and technical assistance agreement with the EU in order to combat drugs trafficking. In March 2000 the Community concluded an agreement to establish a political consultation and co-operation mechanism with the People's Republic of China.

In April 1998, at the 10th Andean presidential summit, an agreement was signed with Panama establishing a framework for negotiations providing for the conclusion of a free-trade accord by the end of 1998 and Panama's eventual associate membership of the Community. Also in April 1998 the Community signed a framework agreement with Mercosur on the establishment of a free-trade accord. The process of extending trade preferences was to commence in October 1998, and the agreement was to become fully effective by January 2000. Negotiations between the two sides, however, were delayed during 1998, owing to differences regarding tariff reductions and the items to be covered by the accord. Bilateral agreements between the countries of the two groupings were extended. In January 1999 representatives of the Community and Mercosur pledged to complete the first stage of negotiations of the free-trade agreement by 31 March; this, however, was not achieved. It was agreed, in March, that the duration of bilateral trade arrangements would be extended and that the Community would initiate negotiations to conclude a free-trade area with Brazil. A preferential tariff agreement was concluded between Brazil and the Community in July; the accord entered into effect, for a period of two years, in mid-August. In August 2000 a preferential tariff agreement concluded with Argentina entered into force. The Community commenced negotiations on drafting a preferential tariff agreement with (jointly) El Salvador, Guatemala and Honduras in March of that year. In September leaders of the Community and Mercosur, meeting at a summit of Latin American heads of state, determined to relaunch negotiations, with a view to establishing a free-trade area by 1 January 2002.

In March 1998 ministers of trade from 34 countries, meeting in San José, Costa Rica, concluded an agreement on the structure of negotiations for the establishment of a Free Trade Area of the Americas (FTAA). The process was formally initiated by heads of state, meeting in Santiago, Chile, in the following month. The Community negotiated as a bloc to obtain chairmanship of three of the nine negotiating groups: on market access (Colombia), on competition policy (Peru), and on intellectual property (Venezuela). The Community insisted that the final declaration issued by the meeting include recognition that the varying levels of development of the participating countries should be taken into consideration throughout the negotiating process.

In August 1999 the Secretary-General of the Community visited Guyana in order to promote bilateral trading opportunities and to strengthen relations with the Caribbean Community. The Community held a meetings on trade relations with the Caribbean Community during 2000.

INDUSTRY

Negotiations began in 1970 for the formulation of joint industrial programmes, particularly in the petrochemicals, metal-working and motor vehicle sectors, but disagreements over the allocation of different plants, and the choice of foreign manufacturers for co-operation, prevented progress and by 1984 the more ambitious schemes had been abandoned. Instead, emphasis was to be placed on assisting small and medium-sized industries, particularly in the agro-industrial and electronics sectors, in co-operation with national industrial organizations.

An Andean Agricultural Development Programme was formulated in 1976 within which 22 resolutions aimed at integrating the Andean agricultural sector were approved. In 1984 the Andean Food Security System was created to develop the agrarian sector, replace imports progressively with local produce, and improve rural living conditions. In April 1998 the Presidential Council instructed the Commission, together with ministers of agriculture, to formulate an Andean Common Agricultural Policy, including measures to harmonize trade policy instruments and legislation on animal and plant health. The 12th Andean presidential summit, held in June 2000, authorized the adoption of the concluded Policy and the enforcement of a plan of action for its implementation.

In May 1987 member countries signed the Quito Protocol, modifying the Cartagena Agreement, to amend the strict rules that had formerly been imposed on foreign investors in the region. The Protocol entered into force in May 1988. Accordingly, each government was to decide which sectors were to be closed to foreign participation, and the period within which foreign investors must transfer a majority shareholding to local investors was extended to 30 years (37 years in Bolivia and Ecuador). In March 1991 the Protocol was amended, with the aim of further liberalizing foreign investment and stimulating an inflow of foreign capital and technology. External and regional investors were to be permitted to repatriate their profits (in accordance with the laws of the country concerned) and there was no stipulation that a majority shareholding must eventually be transferred to local investors. A further directive, adopted in March, covered the formation of 'Empresas Multinacionales Andinas' (multinational enterprises) in order to ensure that at least two member countries have a shareholding of 15% or more of the capital, including the country where the enterprise was to be based. These enterprises were entitled to participate in sectors otherwise reserved for national enterprises, subject to the same conditions as national enterprises in terms of taxation and export regulations, and to gain access to the markets of all member countries.

In November 1988 member states established a bank, the Banco Intermunicipal Andino, which was to finance public works.

In May 1995 the Group initiated a programme to promote the use of cheap and efficient energy sources and greater co-operation in the energy sector. The programme planned to develop a regional electricity grid.

TRANSPORT AND COMMUNICATIONS

The Andean Community (formerly Andean Group) has pursued efforts to improve infrastructure throughout the region. In 1983 the Commission formulated a plan to assist land-locked Bolivia, particularly through improving roads connecting it with neighbouring countries and the Pacific Ocean. An 'open skies' agreement, giving airlines of member states equal rights to airspace and airport facilities within the grouping, was signed in May 1991. In June 1998 the Commission approved the establishment of an Andean Commission of Land Transportation Authorities, which was to oversee the operation and development of land transportation services. Similarly, an Andean Committee of Water Transportation Authorities has been established to ensure compliance with Community regulations regarding ocean transportation activities. The Community aims to facilitate the movement of goods throughout the region by the use of different modes of transport ('multimodal transport') and to guarantee operational standards. It also intends to harmonize Community transport regulations and standards with those of Mercosur countries.

In August 1996 a regulatory framework was approved for the development of a commercial Andean satellite system. In December 1997 the General Secretariat approved regulations for granting authorization for the use of the system; the Commission subsequently granted the first Community authorization to an Andean multinational enterprise (Andesat), comprising 48 companies from all five member states. The system was expected to be fully operational from mid-2002. In 1994 the Community initiated efforts to establish a digital technology infrastructure throughout the Community: the resulting Andean Digital Corridor comprises ground, under water and satellite routes providing a series of cross-border interconnections between the member countries. The Andean

Internet System, which aims to provide internet protocol-based services throughout the Community, was operational in Colombia, Ecuador and Venezuela in 2000, and was to be extended to all five member countries from early 2001. In May 1999 the Andean Committee of Telecommunications Authorities agreed to remove all restrictions to free trade in telecommunications services (excluding sound broadcasting and television) by 1 January 2002. The Committee also determined to formulate provisions on interconnection and the safeguarding of free competition and principles of transparency within the sector.

Asociación de Empresas de Telecomunicaciones de la Comunidad Andina—ASETA: Calle La Pradera 510 y San Salvador, Casilla 10-1106042, Quito, Ecuador; tel. (2) 563-812; fax (2) 562-499; e-mail info@aseta.org; internet www.aseta.org.ec; f. 1974; co-ordinates improvements in national telecommunications services, in order to contribute to the further integration of the countries of the Andean Community. Sec.-Gen. MARCELO LÓPEZ ARJONA.

SOCIAL INTEGRATION

Several formal agreements and institutions have been established within the framework of the grouping to enhance social development and welfare (see below). The Community aims to incorporate these bodies into the process of enhanced integration and to promote greater involvement of representatives of the civil society. In May 1999 the 11th Andean presidential summit adopted a 'multidimensional social agenda' focusing on job creation and on improvements in the fields of education, health and housing throughout the Community. In June 2000 the 12th presidential summit instructed the Andean institutions to prepare individual programmes aimed at consolidating implementation of the Community's integration programme and advancing the development of the social agenda.

INSTITUTIONS

Consejo Consultivo Empresarial Andino (Andean Business Advisory Council): Paseo de la Republica 3895, Lima, Peru; tel. (1) 4111400; fax (1) 2213329; e-mail rsuarez@comunidadandina.org; first meeting held in November 1998; a consultative institution within the framework of the Sistema Andino de Integración; comprises elected representatives of business organizations; advises Community ministers and officials on integration activities affecting the business sector.

Consejo Consultivo Laboral Andino (Andean Labour Advisory Council): Edif. José Vargas, Avda Andres Eloy Blanco, Los Caobos, Caracas, Venezuela; tel. (2) 9872501; fax (2) 9866394; a consultative institution within the framework of the Sistema Andino de Integración; comprises elected representatives of labour organizations; advises Community ministers and officers on related labour issues.

Convenio Andrés Bello (Andrés Bello Agreement): Paralela Autopista Norte, Avda 13 85–60, Santafé de Bogotá, Colombia; tel. (1) 6181701; fax (1) 6100139; e-mail ecobello@col1.telecom.com.co; internet www.cab.int.co; f. 1970, modified in 1990; aims to promote integration in the educational, technical and cultural sectors. Mems: Bolivia, Chile, Colombia, Ecuador, Panama, Peru, Spain, Venezuela.

Convenio Hipólito Unanue (Hipólito Unanue Agreement): Edif. Cartagena, Paseo de la República 3832, 3°, Lima, Peru; tel. (1) 2210074; fax (1) 4409285; e-mail postmaster@conhu.org.pe; internet www.conhu.org.pe; f. 1971 on the occasion of the first meeting of Andean ministers of health; aims to enhance the development of health services, and to promote regional co-ordination in areas such as environmental health, disaster preparedness and the prevention and control of drug abuse.

Convenio Simón Rodríguez (Simón Rodríguez Agreement): Luis Felipe Borja s/n, Edif. Géminis, 9°, Quito, Ecuador; tel. (2) 5453774; promotes a convergence of social and labour conditions throughout the Community, for example, working hours and conditions, employment and social security policies, and to promote the participation of workers and employers in the sub-regional integration process.

Corporación Andina de Fomento—CAF (Andean Development Corporation): Torre CAF, Avda Luis Roche, Altamira, Apdo 5086, Caracas, Venezuela; tel. (2) 2092111; fax (2) 2092394; e-mail sede@caf.com; internet www.caf.com; f. 1968, began operations in 1970; aims to encourage the integration of the Andean countries by specialization and an equitable distribution of investments. It conducts research to identify investment opportunities, and prepares the resulting investment projects; gives technical and financial assistance; and attracts internal and external credit. Auth. cap. US $3,000m., subscribed or underwritten by the governments of member countries, or by public, semi-public and private-sector institutions authorized by those governments. The Board of Directors comprises representatives of each country at ministerial level.

Mems: the Andean Community, Brazil, Chile, Jamaica, Mexico, Panama, Paraguay, Trinidad and Tobago, and 22 private banks in the Andean region. Exec. Pres. ENRIQUE GARCÍA RODRÍGUEZ (Bolivia).

Fondo Latinoamericano de Reservas—FLAR (Latin American Reserve Fund): Edif. Banco de Occidente, Edif. Banco de Occidente, Carrera 13, No. 27–47, 10°, Santafé de Bogotá, Colombia; tel. (1) 2858511; fax (1) 2881117; e-mail agamarra@bloomberg.net; internet www.flar.net; f. 1978 as the Fondo Andino de Reservas to support the balance of payments of member countries, provide credit, guarantee loans, and contribute to the harmonization of monetary and financial policies; adopted present name in 1991, in order to allow the admission of other Latin American countries. In 1992 the Fund began extending credit lines to commercial for export financing. It is administered by an Assembly of the ministers of finance and economy of the member countries, and a Board of Directors comprising the Presidents of the central banks of the member states. In

October 1995 it was agreed to expand the Fund's capital from US $800m. to $1,000m.; the increase became effective on 30 June 1997. Exec. Pres. ROBERTO GUARNIERI (Venezuela); Sec.-Gen. ANA MARÍA CARRASQUILLA (Colombia).

Universidad Andina Simón Bolívar (Simón Bolívar Andean University): Calle Real Audiencia 73, POB 608-33, Sucre, Bolivia; tel. (64) 60265; fax (64) 60833; e-mail uasb@uasb.edu.bo; internet www.uasb.edu.bo; f. 1985; institution for postgraduate study and research; promotes co-operation between other universities in the Andean region.

Publications

Gaceta Oficial del Acuerdo de Cartagena.
Trade and Investment Guide.
Treinta Años de Integración Andina.

ARAB FUND FOR ECONOMIC AND SOCIAL DEVELOPMENT—AFESD

Address: POB 21923, Safat, 13080 Kuwait.
Telephone: 4844500; **fax:** 4815760; **e-mail:** hq@arabfund.org; **internet:** www.arabfund.org.
Established in 1968 by the Economic Council of the Arab League, the Fund began its operations in 1974. It participates in the financing of economic and social development projects in the Arab states.

MEMBERSHIP

Twenty-one members (see table of subscriptions below).

Organization

(April 2001)

BOARD OF GOVERNORS

The Board of Governors consists of a Governor and an Alternate Governor appointed by each member of the Fund. The Board of Governors is considered as the General Assembly of the Fund, and has all powers.

BOARD OF DIRECTORS

The Board of Directors is composed of eight Directors elected by the Board of Governors from among Arab citizens of recognized experience and competence. They are elected for a renewable term of two years.

LOANS BY MEMBER, 1999

Member	Project	Amount (KD million)
Algeria . .	Al Hamma power-generating station	30.0
Bahrain. .	Hidd industrial area	25.0
	Housing project (second loan)	20.0
Djibouti. .	Modernization of Boulaos power-generating station (phase II)	3.0
Egypt . .	Construction of flat steel plant	17.0
Jordan . .	Prince Hamza hospital	23.0
Libya . .	Submarine fibre optic cable	12.5
Mauritania .	Construction/rehabilitation of 33 small dams near Achram	3.5
Morocco. .	Ait Hamou dam and Agadir water supply	17.0
	Muhammad V airport development	10.0
Palestine .	Rural development	3.0
Syria . .	Latakia–Ariha motorway	30.0
	Modernization of communications system (subscribers' networks)	30.0
Tunisia .	Tunis–Bizerta motorway	24.0
Yemen . .	San'a sanitation networks	18.0
Total		**266.0**

The Board of Directors is charged with all the activities of the Fund and exercises the powers delegated to it by the Board of Governors.

Director-General and Chairman of the Board of Directors: ABDLATIF YOUSUF AL-HAMAD.

FINANCIAL STRUCTURE

In 1982 the authorized capital was increased from 400m. Kuwaiti dinars (KD) to KD 800m., divided into 80,000 shares having a value of KD 10,000 each. At the end of 1999 paid-up capital was KD 663.04m.

SUBSCRIPTIONS (KD million, December 1999)*

Algeria . . .	64.78	Oman	17.28
Bahrain . .	2.16	Palestine . . .	1.10
Djibouti . .	0.02	Qatar . . .	6.75
Egypt . .	40.50	Saudi Arabia . .	159.07
Iraq . . .	31.76	Somalia . .	0.21
Jordan . . .	17.30	Sudan . . .	11.06
Kuwait . .	169.70	Syria . . .	24.00
Lebanon . .	2.00	Tunisia . .	6.16
Libya . . .	59.85	United Arab Emirates .	28.00
Mauritania . .	0.82	Yemen . . .	4.52
Morocco . .	16.00		
		Total	**663.04**

* 100 Kuwaiti dinars = US $328.5 (December 1999).

Activities

Pursuant to the Agreement Establishing the Fund (as amended in 1997 by the Board of Governors), the purpose of the Fund is to contribute to the financing of economic and social development projects in the Arab states and countries by:

1. Financing economic development projects of an investment character by means of loans granted on concessionary terms to governments and public enterprises and corporations, giving preference to projects which are vital to the Arab entity, as well as to joint Arab projects.

LOANS BY SECTOR, 1999

Sector	Amount (KD million)	%
Agriculture and rural development . .	6.5	2.4
Energy	33.0	12.4
Industry and mining	42.0	15.8
Transport and telecommunications . .	106.5	40.0
Water and sewerage	35.0	13.2
Other	43.0	16.2
Total	**266.0**	**100.0**

2. Financing private sector projects in member states by providing all forms of loans and guarantees to corporations and enterprises (possessing juridical personality), participating in their equity capital, and providing other forms of financing and the requisite financial, technical and advisory services, in accordance with such regulations and subject to such conditions as may be prescribed by the Board of Directors.

3. Forming or participating in the equity capital of corporations possessing juridical personality, for the implementation and financing of private sector projects in member states, including the provision and financing of technical, advisory and financial services.

4. Establishing and administering special funds with aims compatible with those of the Fund and with resources provided by the Fund or other sources.

5. Encouraging, directly or indirectly, the investment of public and private capital in a manner conducive to the development and growth of the Arab economy.

6. Providing expertise and technical assistance in the various fields of economic development.

The Fund co-operates with other Arab organizations such as the Arab Monetary Fund, the League of Arab States and OAPEC in preparing regional studies and conferences, and acts as the secretariat of the Co-ordination Group of Arab National and Regional Development Institutions. These organizations also work together to produce a *Unified Arab Economic Report*, which considers economic and social developments in the Arab states.

By the end of 1999 the Fund had made 388 loans, to finance 318 projects in 17 countries, since the beginning of its operations. The total value of these loans was KD 3,294.2m. Disbursements amounted to KD 1,950.4m. by the end of 1999.

During 1999 the Fund approved 15 loans totalling KD 266m. for projects in 11 Arab countries and Palestine (see table above).

The total number of technical assistance grants provided by the end of 1999 was 609, with a value of KD 71.1m. During 1999 38 new grants, totalling KD 6.3m., were approved, mainly for institutional support and training, education and research, seminars and conferences, and feasibility studies and project preparation.

ARAB MONETARY FUND

Address: Arab Monetary Fund Bldg, Corniche Rd, POB 2818, Abu Dhabi, United Arab Emirates.

Telephone: (2) 215000; **fax:** (2) 326454.

The Agreement establishing the Arab Monetary Fund was approved by the Economic Council of Arab States in Rabat, Morocco, in April 1976 and entered into force on 2 February 1977.

MEMBERS

Algeria	Oman
Bahrain	Palestine
Djibouti	Qatar
Egypt	Saudi Arabia
Iraq*	Somalia*
Jordan	Sudan*
Kuwait	Syria
Lebanon	Tunisia
Libya	United Arab Emirates
Mauritania	Yemen
Morocco	

* From July 1993 loans to Iraq, Somalia and Sudan were suspended as a result of their failure to repay debts to the Fund totalling US $603m. By the end of 1998 the arrears amounted to AAD 197.3m. (or some $833.4m.). Sudan was readmitted in April 2000, having settled arrears of $214m.

Organization

(April 2001)

BOARD OF GOVERNORS

The Board of Governors is the highest authority of the Arab Monetary Fund. It formulates policies on Arab economic integration and liberalization of trade among member states. With certain exceptions, it may delegate to the Board of Executive Directors some of its powers. The Board of Governors is composed of a governor and a deputy governor appointed by each member state for a term of five years. It meets at least once a year; meetings may also be convened at the request of half the members, or of members holding half of the total voting power.

BOARD OF EXECUTIVE DIRECTORS

The Board of Executive Directors exercises all powers vested in it by the Board of Governors and may delegate to the Director-General such powers as it deems fit. It is composed of the Director-General and eight non-resident directors elected by the Board of Governors. Each director holds office for three years and may be re-elected.

DIRECTOR-GENERAL

The Director-General of the Fund is appointed by the Board of Governors for a renewable five-year term, and serves as Chairman of the Board of Executive Directors.

The Director-General supervises a Committee on Loans and a Committee on Investments to make recommendations on loan and investment policies to the Board of Executive Directors, and is required to submit an Annual Report to the Board of Governors.

Director-General and Chairman of the Board of Executive Directors: Dr JASSIM ABDULLAH AL-MANNAI.

FINANCE

The Arab Accounting Dinar (AAD) is a unit of account equivalent to 3 IMF Special Drawing Rights. (The average value of the SDR in 1999 was US $1.3673.)

Each member paid, in convertible currencies, 5% of the value of its shares at the time of its ratification of the Agreement and another 20% when the Agreement entered into force. In addition, each member paid 2% of the value of its shares in its national currency regardless of whether it is convertible. The second 25% of the capital was to be subscribed by the end of September 1979, bringing the total paid-up capital in convertible currencies to AAD 131.5m. An increase in requests for loans led to a resolution by the Board of Governors in April 1981, giving members the option of paying the balance of their subscribed capital. This payment became obligatory in July 1981, when total approved loans exceeded 50% of the already paid-up capital in convertible currencies. In April 1983 the authorized capital of the Fund was increased from AAD 288m. to AAD 600m. The new capital stock comprised 12,000 shares, each having the value of AAD 50,000. At the end of 1998 total paid-up capital was AAD 324.1m.

CAPITAL SUBSCRIPTIONS
(million Arab Accounting Dinars, 31 December 1998)

Member	Paid-up capital
Algeria	42.40
Bahrain	5.00
Djibouti	0.25
Egypt	32.00
Iraq	42.40
Jordan	5.40
Kuwait	32.00
Lebanon	5.00
Libya	13.44
Mauritania	5.00
Morocco	15.00
Oman	5.00
Palestine	2.16
Qatar	10.00
Saudi Arabia	48.40
Somalia	4.00
Sudan	10.00
Syria	7.20
Tunisia	7.00
United Arab Emirates	19.20
Yemen	15.40
Total	324.09*

* Excluding Palestine's share, which was deferred by a Board of Governors' resolution in 1978.

Activities

The creation of the Arab Monetary Fund was seen as a step towards the goal of Arab economic integration. It assists member states in balance of payments difficulties, and also has a broad range of aims.

The Articles of Agreement define the Fund's aims as follows:

(*a*) to correct disequilibria in the balance of payments of member states;

(*b*) to promote the stability of exchange rates among Arab currencies, to render them mutually convertible, and to eliminate restrictions on current payments between member states;

(*c*) to establish policies and modes of monetary co-operation to accelerate Arab economic integration and economic development in the member states;

(*d*) to tender advice on the investment of member states' financial resources in foreign markets, whenever called upon to do so;

(*e*) to promote the development of Arab financial markets;

(*f*) to promote the use of the Arab dinar as a unit of account and to pave the way for the creation of a unified Arab currency;

(*g*) to co-ordinate the positions of member states in dealing with international monetary and economic problems; and

(*h*) to provide a mechanism for the settlement of current payments between member states in order to promote trade among them.

The Arab Monetary Fund functions both as a fund and a bank. It is empowered:

(*a*) to provide short- and medium-term loans to finance balance of payments deficits of member states;

(*b*) to issue guarantees to member states to strengthen their borrowing capabilities;

(*c*) to act as intermediary in the issuance of loans in Arab and international markets for the account of member states and under their guarantees;

(*d*) to co-ordinate the monetary policies of member states;

(*e*) to manage any funds placed under its charge by member states;

(*f*) to hold periodic consultations with member states on their economic conditions; and

(*g*) to provide technical assistance to banking and monetary institutions in member states.

Loans are intended to finance an overall balance of payments deficit and a member may draw up to 75% of its paid-up subscription, in convertible currencies, for this purpose unconditionally (automatic loans). A member may, however, obtain loans in excess of this limit, subject to agreement with the Fund on a programme aimed at reducing its balance of payments deficit (ordinary and extended loans, equivalent to 175% and 250% of its quota respectively). From 1981 a country receiving no extended loans was entitled to a loan under the Inter-Arab Trade Facility (discontinued in 1989) of up to 100% of its quota. In addition, a member has the right to borrow up to 50% of its paid-up capital in order to cope with an unexpected deficit in its balance of payments resulting from a decrease in its exports of goods and services or a large increase in its imports of agricultural products following a poor harvest (compensatory loans). Over the period 1978–98, 105 loans were extended to 12 member countries.

Automatic and compensatory loans are repayable within three years, while ordinary and extended loans are repayable within five and seven years respectively. Loans are granted at concessionary and uniform rates of interest which increase with the length of the period of the loan. In 1988 the Fund's executive directors agreed to modify their policy on lending, placing an emphasis on the correction of economic imbalances in recipient countries.

At the end of 1998 total approved loans amounted to AAD 733.8m., of which AAD 705.7m. had been disbursed and AAD 506.4m. repaid. During 1998 the Fund approved two loans, amounting to AAD 15.0m., under a new Structural Adjustment Facility established in 1996.

The Fund also provides technical assistance to its member countries. Such assistance is furnished through either the provision of

LOANS APPROVED, 1978–98

Type of loan	Number of loans	Amount (AAD '000)
Automatic	53	257,775
Ordinary	11	104,566
Compensatory	11	72,485
Extended	17	219,206
Structural Adjustment Facility . . .	2	15,023
Inter-Arab Trade Facility (cancelled in 1989)	11	64,730
Total	105	733,785

LOANS APPROVED, 1998

Borrower	Type of loan	Amount (AAD million)
Jordan	Structural Adjustment Facility	3.910
Yemen	Structural Adjustment Facility	11.113
Total		15.023

experts to the country concerned or in the form of specialized training of officials of member countries. In view of the increased importance of this type of assistance, the Fund established, in 1988, the Economic Policy Institute (EPI) which offers regular training courses and specialized seminars for middle-level and senior staff, respectively, of financial and monetary institutions of the Arab countries. On 1 April 1999 the Fund signed a memorandum of understanding with the International Monetary Fund to establish a joint regional training programme.

TRADE PROMOTION

Arab Trade Financing Program (ATFP): POB 26799, Arab Monetary Fund Bldg, 7th Floor, Corniche Rd, Abu Dhabi, United Arab Emirates; tel. (2) 6316999; fax (2) 6316793; e-mail atfphq@atfp.org.ae; internet www.atfp.org.ae; f. 1989 to develop and promote trade between Arab countries and to enhance the competitive ability of Arab exporters; operates by extending lines of credit to Arab exporters and importers through national agencies (some 121 agencies designated by the monetary authorities of 18 Arab countries at early 2001). The Arab Monetary Fund provided 50% of ATFP's authorized capital of US $500m.; participation was also invited from private and official Arab financial institutions and joint Arab/foreign institutions. ATFP administers the Inter-Arab Trade Information Network (IATIN), and organizes Buyers-Sellers meetings to promote Arab goods. Chair. and Chief Exec. Dr JASSIM ABDULLAH AL-MANNAI. Publs *Annual Report* (Arabic and English), *IATIN Quarterly Bulletin* (Arabic).

Publications

Annual Report.

Arab Countries: Economic Indicators (annually).

Cross Exchange Rates of Arab Currencies (annually).

Foreign Trade of Arab Countries (annually).

Joint Arab Economic Report (annually).

Money and Credit in Arab Countries.

National Accounts of Arab Countries (annually).

Balance of Payments and Public Debt of Arab Countries (annually).

AMF Publications Catalog (annually).

Reports on commodity structure (by value and quantity) of member countries' imports from and exports to other Arab countries; other studies on economic, social, management and fiscal issues.

ASIA-PACIFIC ECONOMIC CO-OPERATION—APEC

Address: 438 Alexandra Rd, 14th Floor, Alexandra Point, Singapore 119958.

Telephone: 2761880; **fax:** 2761775; **e-mail:** info@mail.apecsec.org.sg; **internet:** www.apecsec.org.sg.

Asia-Pacific Economic Co-operation (APEC) was initiated in November 1989, in Canberra, Australia, as an informal consultative forum. Its aim is to promote multilateral economic co-operation on issues of trade and investment.

MEMBERS

Australia	Japan	Philippines
Brunei	Korea, Republic	Russia
Canada	Malaysia	Singapore
Chile	Mexico	Taiwan*
China, People's Republic	New Zealand	Thailand
Hong Kong	Papua New Guinea	USA
Indonesia	Peru	Viet Nam

* Admitted as Chinese Taipei.

Organization

(April 2001)

ECONOMIC LEADERS' MEETINGS

The first meeting of APEC heads of government was convened in November 1993, in Seattle, USA. Subsequently, each annual meeting of APEC ministers of foreign affairs and of economic affairs has been followed by an informal gathering of the leaders of the APEC economies, at which the policy objectives of the grouping are discussed and defined. The 2000 meeting was held in Bandar Seri Begawan, Brunei, in November, and the 2001 meeting was scheduled to be held in Shanghai, People's Republic of China.

MINISTERIAL MEETINGS

APEC ministers of foreign affairs and ministers of economic affairs meet annually. These meetings are hosted by the APEC Chair, which rotates each year, although it was agreed, in 1989, that alternate Ministerial Meetings were to be convened in an ASEAN member country. A Senior Officials' Meeting (SOM) convenes regularly between Ministerial Meetings to co-ordinate and to administer the budgets and work programmes of APEC's committees and working groups. Other meetings of ministers are also held on a regular basis to enhance co-operation in specific areas.

SECRETARIAT

In 1992 the Ministerial Meeting, held in Bangkok, Thailand, agreed to establish a permanent secretariat to support APEC activities, and approved an annual budget of US $2m. The Secretariat became operational in February 1993. The Executive Director is appointed from the member economy chairing the group and serves a one-year term. A Deputy Executive Director is appointed by the member economy designated to chair APEC in the following year.

Executive Director: ZHANG YAN (People's Republic of China).

Deputy Executive Director: RICARDO VILLANUEVA-HALLAL (Mexico).

COMMITTEES AND GROUPS

Budget and Management Committee (BAC): f. 1993 as Budget and Administrative Committee, present name adopted 1998; advices APEC senior officials on budgetary, administrative and managerial issues. The Committee reviews the operational budgets of APEC committees and groups, evaluates their effectiveness and conducts assessments of group projects.

Committee on Trade and Investment (CTI): f. 1993 on the basis of a Declaration signed by ministers meeting in Seattle, USA, in order to facilitate the expansion of trade and the development of a liberalized environment for investment among member countries. The CTI undertakes initiatives to improve the flow of goods, services and technology in the region. In May 1997 an APEC Tariff Database was inaugurated, with sponsorship from the private sector. A new Market Access Group was established in 1998 to administer CTI activities concerned with non-tariff measures.

Economic Committee: f. 1994 following an agreement, in November, to transform the existing *ad hoc* group on economic trends and issues into a formal committee. The Committee aims to enhance APEC's capacity to analyse economic trends and to research and report on issues affecting economic and technical co-operation in the region. In addition, the Committee is considering the environmental and development implications of expanding population and economic growth.

Sub-Committee on Economic and Technical Co-operation: f. 1998 to assist the SOM with the co-ordination of APEC's economic and technical co-operation programme (ECOTECH); monitors and evaluates project implementation.

In addition, the following Working Groups promote and co-ordinate practical co-operation between member countries in different activities: Trade promotion; Industrial science and technology; Human resources development; Energy; Marine resource conservation; Telecommunications; Transport; Tourism; Agricultural Co-operation; Small and Medium Enterprises (SMEs); and Fisheries. (See below for more detailed information.)

ADVISORY COUNCIL

APEC Business Advisory Council (ABAC): Equitable Card Center Bldg, 8th Floor, 203 Salcedo St, Legaspi Village, Makati City 1229, Philippines; tel. (2) 8436001; fax (2) 8454832; e-mail abacsec@equitable.equicom.com; internet www.abaconline.org; an agreement to establish ABAC, comprising up to three representatives of the private sector from each APEC member economy, was concluded at the Ministerial Meeting held in November 1995. The first meeting of ABAC was convened in June 1996 in Manila, the Philippines. At the meeting, ABAC resolved to accelerate the liberalization of regional trade and agreed to focus its activities on infrastructure, SMEs and human resource development, regional communications and finance and cross-border investment. In 1998 ABAC focused on measures to alleviate the effects of the financial crisis in Asia, in particular by enhancing confidence in the private sector, as well as other efforts to support SMEs, to develop electronic commerce in the region and to advise on APEC plans of action. In 1999 ABAC aimed to continue to promote capital flows into Asia, to restructure unpaid corporate debts, to recapitalize banks and to develop domestic debt or bond markets. Priorities in 2000 included the promotion of best practices in national financial systems; consolidating efforts towards developing domestic debt markets; continuing to support SMEs; supporting APEC initiatives relating to e-commerce, the liberalization of air services and developing a food system for member countries; and developing the potential of the internet as an inexpensive instrument of learning in APEC states. Chair. QIN XIAO (People's Republic of China).

Activities

APEC was initiated in 1989 as a forum for informal discussion between the then six ASEAN members and their six dialogue partners in the Pacific, and, in particular, to promote trade liberalization in the Uruguay Round of negotiations, which were being conducted under the General Agreement on Tariffs and Trade (GATT). The Seoul Declaration, adopted by ministers meeting in the Republic of Korea in November 1991, defined the objectives of APEC (see below).

ASEAN countries were initially reluctant to support any more formal structure of the forum, or to admit new members, owing to concerns that it would undermine ASEAN's standing as a regional grouping and be dominated by powerful non-ASEAN economies. In August 1991 it was agreed to extend membership to the People's Republic of China, Hong Kong and Taiwan (subject to conditions imposed by the People's Republic of China, including that a Taiwanese official of no higher than vice-ministerial level should attend the annual meeting of ministers of foreign affairs). Mexico and Papua New Guinea acceded to the organization in November 1993, and Chile joined in November 1994. The summit meeting held in November 1997 agreed that Peru, Russia and Viet Nam should be admitted to APEC at the 1998 meeting, but imposed a 10-year moratorium on further expansion of the grouping.

In September 1992 APEC ministers agreed to establish a permanent secretariat. In addition, the meeting created an 11-member non-governmental Eminent Persons Group (EPG), which was to assess trade patterns within the region and propose measures to promote co-operation. At the Ministerial Meeting in Seattle, USA, in November 1993, members agreed on a framework for expanding trade and investment among member countries, and to establish a permanent committee (the CTI, see above) to pursue these objectives.

In August 1994 the EPG proposed the following timetable for the liberalization of all trade across the Asia-Pacific region: negotiations for the elimination of trade barriers were to commence in 2000 and be completed within 10 years in developed countries, 15 years in newly-industrialized economies and by 2020 in developing countries.

Trade concessions could then be extended on a reciprocal basis to non-members in order to encourage world-wide trade liberalization rather than isolate APEC as a unique trading bloc. In November 1994 the meeting of APEC heads of government adopted the Bogor Declaration of Common Resolve, which endorsed the EPG's timetable for free and open trade and investment in the region by the year 2020. Other issues incorporated into the Declaration included the implementation of GATT commitments in full and strengthening the multilateral trading system through the forthcoming establishment of the World Trade Organization (WTO), intensifying development co-operation in the Asia-Pacific region and expanding and accelerating trade and investment programmes.

During 1995 meetings of APEC officials and other efforts to substantiate the trade liberalization agreement revealed certain differences among members regarding the timetable and means of implementing the measures, which were to be agreed upon at the 1995 Economic Leaders' Meeting. The principal concern, expressed notably by the USA, focused on whether tariff reductions were to be achieved by individual trade liberalization plans or based on some reciprocal or common approach. In August the EPG issued a report, to be considered at the November Leaders' Meeting, which advocated acceleration of tariff reductions and other trade liberalization measures agreed under GATT, the establishment of a dispute mediation service to reduce and settle regional trade conflicts and a review of new trade groupings within the APEC region. Further proposals for the implementation of the Bogor Declaration objectives were presented, in September, by the Pacific Business Forum, comprising APEC business representatives. The recommendations included harmonization of product quality, the establishment of one-stop investment agencies in each APEC country, training and technology transfers and the implementation of visa-free business travel by 1999. In November 1995 the Ministerial Meeting decided to dismantle the EPG, and to establish an APEC Business Advisory Council (ABAC) consisting of private-sector representatives.

In November 1995 APEC heads of government, meeting in Osaka, Japan, adopted an Action Agenda as a framework to achieve the commitments of the Bogor Declaration. Part One of the Agenda identified action areas for the liberalization of trade and investment and the facilitation of business, for example customs procedures, rules of origin and non-tariff barriers. It incorporated agreements that the process was to be comprehensive, consistent with WTO commitments, comparable among all APEC economies and non-discriminatory. Each member economy was to ensure the transparency of its laws, regulations and procedures that affect the flow of goods, services and capital among APEC economies and to refrain from implementing any trade protection measures. A second part of the Agenda was to provide a framework for further economic and technical co-operation between APEC members in areas such as energy, transport, infrastructure, SMEs and agricultural technology. In order to resolve a disagreement concerning the inclusion of agricultural products in the trade liberalization process, a provision for flexibility was incorporated into the Agenda, taking into account diverse circumstances and different levels of development in APEC member economies. Liberalization measures were to be implemented from January 1997 (i.e. three years earlier than previously agreed) and were to be subject to annual reviews. A Trade and Investment Liberalization and Facilitation Special Account was established to finance projects in support of the implementation of the Osaka Action Agenda. In May 1996 APEC senior officials met in Cebu, the Philippines, to consider the medium-term Individual Action Plans (IAPs) of tariff reductions, which had been submitted by all members, and to achieve some coherent approach to tariff liberalization prior to the Leaders' Meeting in November.

In November 1996 the Economic Leaders' Meeting, held in Subic Bay, the Philippines, approved the Manila Action Plan for APEC (MAPA), which had been formulated at the preceding Ministerial Meeting, held in Manila. MAPA incorporated the IAPs and other collective measures aimed at achieving the trade liberalization and co-operation objectives of the Bogor Declaration (see above), as well as the joint activities specified in the second part of the Osaka Agenda. Heads of government also endorsed a US proposal to eliminate tariffs and other barriers to trade in information technology products by 2000 and determined to support efforts to conclude an agreement to this effect at the forthcoming WTO conference; however, they insisted on the provision of an element of flexibility in achieving trade liberalization in this sector.

The 1997 Economic Leaders' Meeting, held in Vancouver, Canada, in November, was dominated by concern at the financial instability that had affected several Asian economies during 1997. The final declaration of the summit meeting endorsed a framework of measures which had been agreed by APEC deputy ministers of finance and central bank governors at an emergency meeting convened in the previous week in Manila, the Philippines (the so-called Manila Framework for Enhanced Asian Regional Co-operation to Promote Financial Stability). The meeting, attended by representatives of the IMF, the World Bank and the Asian Development Bank, committed all member economies receiving IMF assistance to undertake specified economic and financial reforms, and supported the establishment of a separate Asian funding facility to supplement international financial assistance (although this was later rejected by the IMF). APEC ministers of finance and governors of central banks were urged to accelerate efforts for the development of the region's financial and capital markets and to liberalize capital flows in the region. Measures were to include strengthening financial market supervision and clearing and settlement infrastructure, the reform of pension systems, and promoting co-operation among export credit agencies and financing institutions. The principal item on the Vancouver summit agenda was an initiative to enhance trade liberalization, which, the grouping insisted, should not be undermined by the financial instability in Asia. At the earlier Ministerial Meeting the following nine economic sectors had been identified for 'early voluntary sectoral liberalization' ('EVSL'): environmental goods and services; fish and fish products; forest products; medical equipment and instruments; toys; energy; chemicals; gems and jewellery; and telecommunications. The heads of government subsequently requested the authorities in each member state to formulate details of tariff reductions in these sectors by mid-1998, with a view to implementing the measures in 1999. (In June 1998, however, ministers of trade, meeting in Malaysia, failed to conclude an agreement on early tariff reductions, in part owing to Japan's reluctance to liberalize trade in fish and forest products.) In Vancouver APEC Economic Leaders declared their support for an agreement to liberalize financial services (which was successfully negotiated under the auspices of the WTO in December 1997) and for the objective of reducing the emission of 'greenhouse gases', which was under consideration at a global conference, held in Kyoto, Japan, in December.

In May 1998 APEC finance ministers met in Canada to consider the ongoing financial and economic crisis in Asia and to review progress in implementing efforts to alleviate the difficulties experienced by several member economies. The ministers agreed to pursue activities in the following three priority areas: capitalmarket development, capital account liberalization and strengthening financial systems (including corporate governance). The region's economic difficulties remained the principal topic of discussion at the Economic Leaders' Meeting, which was held in Kuala Lumpur, Malaysia, in November. A final declaration reiterated their commitment to co-operation in pursuit of sustainable economic recovery and growth, in particular through the restructuring of financial and corporate sectors, promoting and facilitating private-sector capital flows, and efforts to strengthen the global financial system. The meeting endorsed a proposal of ABAC to establish a partnership for equitable growth, which aimed to enhance business involvement in APEC's programme of economic and technical co-operation. Other initiatives approved included an Agenda of APEC Science and Technology Industry Co-operation into the 21st Century (for which the People's Republic of China announced it was to establish a special fund), and an Action Programme on Skills and Development in APEC. Japan's persisting opposition to a reduction of tariffs in the fish and forestry sectors prevented final approval of the EVSL scheme, and it was agreed to refer the proposals to the WTO for consideration. Substantive progress at the meeting was further hindered by political differences within the grouping regarding human rights, and in particular, the treatment by the Malaysian authorities of the imprisoned former Deputy Prime Minister, Anwar Ibrahim. A declaration of support for the democratic reform movement in Malaysia by the US representative, Vice-President Gore, dominated discussions at the start of the summit meeting and provoked a formal complaint from the Malaysian Government.

In September 1999 political dialogue regarding the civil conflict in East Timor dominated the start of the annual meetings of the grouping, held in Auckland, New Zealand, although the issue remained separate from the official agenda. Ministers of foreign affairs, convened in emergency session, declared their support for the establishment of a multinational force, under UN auspices, to restore peace in the territory and determined to provide humanitarian and technical assistance to facilitate the process of reconstruction and rehabilitation. The Economic Leaders' Meeting considered measures to sustain the economic recovery in Asia and endorsed the APEC Principles to Enhance Competition and Regulatory Reform (for example, transparency, accountability, non-discrimination) as a framework to strengthen APEC markets and to enable further integration and implementation of the IAPs. Also under discussion was the forthcoming round of multilateral trade negotiations, to be initiated by the WTO. The heads of government proposed the objective of completing a single package of trade agreements within three years and endorsed the abolition of export subsidies for agricultural products. The meeting determined to support the efforts of the People's Republic of China, Russia, Taiwan and Viet Nam to accede to WTO membership.

The Economic Leaders' Meeting for 2000, held in Brunei in November, urged that an agenda for the now-stalled round of multilateral trade negotiations should be formulated without further delay. The heads of government endorsed an Action Agenda to promote the utilization of advances in information and communications technologies in member economies, for the benefit of all citizens. The meeting adopted the aim of tripling the number of people in the region with access to the internet by 2005, and determined to co-operate with business and education sector interests to attract investment and expertise in the pursuit of this goal. A proposal that the Democratic People's Republic of Korea be permitted to participate in APEC working groups was approved at the meeting.

WORKING GROUPS

APEC's structure of working groups aims to promote practical and technical co-operation in specific areas, and to help to implement individual and collective action plans in response to the directives of the Economic Leaders. APEC recognizes sustainable development as a key issue cross-cutting all forum activities. In 1997 APEC leaders declared their commitment to the integration of women into the mainstream of APEC activities.

Agricultural Technical Co-operation: Formally established as an APEC Expert's Group in 1996, and incorporated into the system of working groups in 2000. The group aims to enhance the role of agriculture in the economic growth of the region and to promote co-operation in the following areas: conservation and utilization of plant and animal genetic resources; research, development and extension of agricultural biotechnology; processing, marketing, distribution and consumption of agricultural products; plant and animal quarantine and pest management; development of an agricultural finance system; sustainable agriculture; and agricultural technology transfer and training.

Energy: Responsible for the development of the energy component of the 1995 Action Agenda. APEC ministers responsible for energy convened for the first time in 1996 to discuss major energy challenges confronting the region and to provide guidance for the working group. Accordingly, the group's main objectives were determined as being to enhance regional energy security and to improve the fuel supply market for the power sector; to develop and implement programmes of work for promoting the adoption of environmentally-sound energy technologies and promoting private-sector investment in regional power infrastructure; to develop energy efficiency guidelines; and to standardize testing facilities and results. In March 1999 the group resolved to establish a business network to improve relations and communications with the private sector. The first meeting of the network took place in April. In October 1998 APEC energy ministers, meeting in Okinawa, Japan, emphasized the role of the sector in stimulating economic activity and the need to develop infrastructure, to improve energy efficiency and to accelerate the development of natural gas reserves. In May 2000 energy ministers, meeting in San Diego, USA, launched the APEC 21st Century Renewable Energy Initiative, which aimed to encourage co-operation in and advance the utilization of renewable energy technologies, envisaging the establishment of a Private Sector Renewable Energy Forum.

Fisheries: Aims to maximize the economic benefits and sustainability of fisheries resources for all APEC members. In 1996 the group initiated a four-year study on trade and investment liberalization in the sector, in the areas of tariffs, non-tariff barriers and investment measures and subsidies. In 1997 the group organized two technical workshops on seafood inspection systems, and conducted a workshop addressing destructive fishing techniques, in particular cyanide fishing, in an effort to conserve natural resources and to protect the marine environment. The first APEC Aquaculture Forum, which considered the sustainable development of aquaculture in the region and the development of new markets for APEC fish products, was held in Taipei, Taiwan, in June 1998. In May 1999 new guide-lines were adopted to encourage the participation of the private sector in the activities of the working group. The group's first business forum was convened in July 2000.

Human Resources Development: Comprises three (formerly five) networks which promote co-operation in different areas of human resources, training and education: the Capacity Building Network, with a focus on human capacity building, including management and technical skills development and corporate governance; the Education Network, promoting effective learning systems and supporting the role of education in advancing individual, social and economic development; and the Labour and Social Protection Network, concerned with promoting social integration through the strengthening of labour markets, the development of labour market information and policy, and improvements in working conditions and social safety net frameworks. The working group undertakes activities through these networks to implement ministerial and leaders' directives and the 'Medium Term Strategic Priorities', which were formulated in January 1997. A voluntary network of APEC Study Centers links higher education and research institutions throughout member economies concerned with the APEC process.

In January 1998 the working group established a Task Force on the Human Resource and Social Impacts of the Financial Crisis. Private-sector participation in the working group has been strengthened by the establishment of a network of APEC senior executives responsible for human resources management.

Industrial Science and Technology: Aims to contribute to sustainable development in the region, improve the availability of information, enhance human resources development in the sector, improve the business climate, promote policy dialogue and review and facilitate networks and partnerships. Accordingly, the group has helped to establish an APEC Virtual Centre for Environmental Technology Exchange in Japan; a Science and Technology Industrial Parks Network; an International Molecular Biology Network for the APEC Region; an APEC Centre for Technology Foresight, based in Thailand; and the APEC Science and Technology Web, an online database.

Marine Resource Conservation: Promotes initiatives within APEC to protect the marine environment and its resources. In 1996 a five-year project was initiated for the management of red tide and harmful algal blooms in the APEC region. An APEC Action Plan for Sustainability of the Marine Environment was adopted by ministers responsible for the environment, meeting in June 1997. The Plan aimed to promote regional co-operation and an integrated approach to coastal management, the prevention, reduction and control of marine pollution, and sustainable development. The group promotes these objectives through research, training, information exchange and the promotion of partnerships with the private sector. It also supports efforts to establish an Ocean Research Network of centres of excellence in the Pacific. In December 1997 the group organized a workshop, in Hong Kong, on the impact of destructive fishing practices on the marine environment. A workshop was held in Australia, in April 1998, on preventing maritime accidents and pollution in the Pacific region. In April 1999 the group organized a training course, held in Hong Kong, on the satellite remote sensing of algal blooms. Strategies to encourage private-sector participation in promoting the sustainable management of marine resource were endorsed by the working group in June 2000.

Small and Medium Enterprises: The group was established in 1995, as the Ad Hoc Policy Level Group on Small and Medium Enterprises (PLG-SME), with a temporary mandate to oversee all APEC activities relating to SMEs. It supported the establishment of an APEC Centre for Technical Exchange and Training for Small and Medium Enterprises, which was inaugurated at Los Baños, near Manila, the Philippines, in September 1996. The group was resdesignated as a working group, with permanent status, in 2000.

Telecommunications: Incorporates four steering groups concerned with different aspects of the development and liberalization of the sector—Liberalization; Business facilitation; Development co-operation; and Human resource development. Activities guided by directives of ministers responsible for telecommunications, who first met in 1995, in the Republic of Korea, and adopted a Seoul Declaration on Asia Pacific Information Infrastructure (APII). The second ministerial meeting, held in Gold Coast, Australia, in September 1996, adopted more detailed proposals for liberalization of the sector in member economies. In June 1998 ministers, meeting in Singapore, agreed to remove technical barriers to trade in telecommunications equipment (although Chile and New Zealand declined to sign up to the arrangement). At their fourth meeting, convened in May 2000 in Cancún, Mexico, telecommunications ministers approved a programme of action which included measures to bridge the 'digital divide' between developed and developing member economies, and adopted the APEC Principles on International Charging Arrangements for Internet Services and the APEC Principles of Interconnection.

Tourism: Aims to achieve long-term sustainability of the tourism industry, in environmental and social terms, through human resources development, greater involvement of the private sector in policy formation, liberalizing trade in services associated with tourism to facilitate investment and movement within the region, and using tourism to achieve sustainable economic development. In 1998 the group initiated a project to assess the impact of the Asian financial crisis on regional tourism and to identify strategies to counter any negative effects. The first meeting of APEC ministers of tourism, held in the Republic of Korea in July 2000, adopted the Seoul Declaration on the APEC Tourism Charter.

Trade Promotion: Aims to promote trade, as a key aspect of regional economic co-operation, through activities to enhance trade financing, skills and training, information and networking (for example, through the establishment of APEC Net, providing information to the business community via the internet, accessible at www.apecnet.org.sg), and co-operation with the private sector and public agencies, including trade promotion organizations. Organizes an APEC International Trade Fair, the third of which was held in

Kuala Lumpur, Malaysia, in November 1998. The fourth Trade Fair was held in Jakarta, Indonesia, in October 2000.

Transportation: Undertakes initiatives to enhance the efficiency and safety of the regional transportation system, in order to facilitate the development of trade. The working group focuses on three main areas: improving the competitiveness of the transportation industry; safe and environmentally-sound transportation system; and human resources development, including training, research and education. The group has published surveys, directories and manuals on all types of transportation systems, and has compiled an inventory on regional co-operation on oil spills preparedness and response arrangements. A Road Transportation Harmonization Project aims to provide the basis for common standards in the automotive industry in the Asia-Pacific region.

Publications

APEC Business Travel Handbook.
APEC Economic Outlook (annually).
APEC Energy Statistics (annually).
Foreign Direct Investment and APEC Economic Integration (irregular).
Guide to the Investment Regimes of the APEC Member Economies.
Key APEC Documents (annually).
The State of Economic and Technical Co-operation in APEC.
Trade and Investment Liberalization in APEC.
Working group reports, regional directories, other irregular surveys.

ASIAN DEVELOPMENT BANK—ADB

Address: 6 ADB Ave, Mandaluyong City 0401, Metro Manila, Philippines; POB 789, 0980 Manila, Philippines.
Telephone: (2) 6324444; **fax:** (2) 6362442; **e-mail:** information@ mail.asiandevbank.org; **internet:** www.adb.org.

The ADB commenced operations in December 1966. The Bank's principal functions are to provide loans and equity investments for the economic and social advancement of its developing member countries, to give technical assistance for the preparation and implementation of development projects and programmes and advisory services, to promote investment of public and private capital for development purposes, and to respond to requests from developing member countries for assistance in the co-ordination of their development policies and plans.

MEMBERS

There are 43 member countries and territories within the ESCAP region and 16 others (see list of subscriptions below).

Organization

(April 2001)

BOARD OF GOVERNORS

All powers of the Bank are vested in the Board, which may delegate its powers to the Board of Directors except in such matters as admission of new members, changes in the Bank's authorized capital stock, election of Directors and President, and amendment of the Charter. One Governor and one Alternate Governor are appointed by each member country. The Board meets at least once a year.

BOARD OF DIRECTORS

The Board of Directors is responsible for general direction of operations and exercises all powers delegated by the Board of Governors, which elects it. Of the 12 Directors, eight represent constituency groups of member countries within the ESCAP region (with about 65% of the voting power) and four represent the rest of the member countries. Each Director serves for two years and may be re-elected.

Three specialized committees (the Audit Committee, the Budget Review Committee and the Inspection Committee), each comprising six members, assist the Board of Directors in exercising its authority with regard to supervising the Bank's financial statements, approving the administrative budget, and reviewing and approving policy documents and assistance operations.

The President of the Bank, though not a Director, is Chairman of the Board.

Chairman of Board of Directors and President: TADAO CHINO (Japan).
Vice-President (Region East): JOSEPH EICHENBERGER (USA).
Vice-President (Finance and Administration): JOHN LINTJER (Netherlands).
Vice-President (Region West): MYOUNG-HO SHIN (Republic of Korea).

ADMINISTRATION

The Bank had 1,961 staff at June 2000.

A major reorganization of the ADB's administrative and operational structure came into effect on 1 January 1995, in order to strengthen the Bank's regional and country focus. The offices of the General Auditor, Operations Evaluation, Strategy and Policy, and Environment and Social Development report directly to the President of the

Bank. The three Vice-Presidents are responsible for the following departments and divisions: Programmes (West), Agriculture and Social Sectors, Infrastructure, Energy and Financial Sectors, the Private Sector Group, the Economics and Development Resource Centre; Programmes (East), Agriculture and Social Sectors, Infrastructure, Energy and Financial Sectors, the Office of Co-financing Operations, the Office of Pacific Operations, Central Operations Services; and, the Office of the Secretary, the Office of the General Counsel, Budget, Personnel and Management Systems, Office of Administrative Services, Controller's Department, Treasurer's Department, the Office of External Relations, the Office of Information Systems and Technology, and the North American, European and Japanese Representative Offices.

There are Resident Missions in Bangladesh, Cambodia, the People's Republic of China, India, Indonesia, Kazakhstan, Kyrgyzstan, Laos, Mongolia, Nepal, Pakistan, Sri Lanka, Uzbekistan and Viet Nam. In addition, there is a South Pacific Regional Mission, based in Vanuatu, Representative Offices in Tokyo, Japan, Frankfurt am Main, Germany (for Europe), and Washington, DC, USA (for North America), and a country office in the Philippines. So-called Extended Missions are located in Papua New Guinea and Thailand, and a Special Liaison Office has been established in East Timor.

Secretary: B. N. LOHANI.
General Counsel: GERALD SUMIDA.

INSTITUTE

ADB Institute—ADBI: Kasumigaseki Bldg, 8th Floor, 2–5 Kasumigaseki 3-chome, Chiyoda-ku, Tokyo 100-0011, Japan; tel. (3) 3593-5500; fax (3) 3593-5571; e-mail webmaster@adbi.org; internet www.adbi.org; f. 1997 as a subsidiary body of the ADB to research and analyse long-term development issues and to disseminate development practices through training and other capacity-building activities. Dean MASARU YOSHITOMI (Japan).

FINANCIAL STRUCTURE

The Bank's ordinary capital resources (which are used for loans to the more advanced developing member countries) are held and used entirely separately from its Special Funds resources (see below). A fourth General Capital Increase (GCI IV), amounting to US $26,318m. (or some 100%), was authorized in May 1994. At the final deadline for subscription to GCI IV, on 30 September 1996, 55 member countries had subscribed shares amounting to US $24,675.4m.

At 31 December 1999 the position of subscriptions to the capital stock was as follows: authorized US $47,945m.; subscribed US $47,597m.

The Bank also borrows funds from the world capital markets. Total borrowings during 1999 amounted to US $5,186m. (compared with US $9,617m. in 1998).

In July 1986 the Bank abolished the system of fixed lending rates, under which ordinary operations loans had carried interest rates fixed at the time of loan commitment for the entire life of the loan. Under the new system the lending rate is adjusted every six months, to take into account changing conditions in international financial markets.

SPECIAL FUNDS

The Asian Development Fund (ADF) was established in 1974 in order to provide a systematic mechanism for mobilizing and administering resources for the Bank to lend on concessional terms to the least-developed member countries. In 1998 the Bank revised the terms of ADF. Since 1 January 1999 all new project loans are repayable within 32 years, including an eight-year grace period, while quick-disbursing programme loans have a 24-year maturity, also including an eight-year grace period. The previous annual service charge was redesignated as an interest charge, including a portion to cover administrative expenses. The new interest charges on all loans are 1%–1.5% per annum. At 31 December 1999 total ADF loans approved amounted to US $22,760m., while cumulative disbursements from ADF resources totalled US $15,393m.

Successive replenishments of the Fund's resources amounted to US $809m. for the period 1976–78, US $2,150m. for 1979–82, US $3,214m. for 1983–86, US $3,600m. for 1987–90, and US $4,200m. for 1992–95. In January 1997 donor countries concluded an agreement for a seventh replenishment of the Fund's resources, which incorporated an agreed figure of US $6,300m. for ADF operations during the period 1997–2000 and recommendations that new donor contributions initially amount to US $2,610m. and that the commitment authority from non-donor resources total US $3,300m., almost double the level set in the previous replenishment. In September 2000 25 donor countries pledged US $2,910m. towards the ADF's eighth replenishment (ADF VIII), which totalled US $5,650m. and covered the period 2000–04; repayments of earlier ADF loans were to provide the remaining US $2,740m.

The Bank provides technical assistance grants from its Technical Assistance Special Fund (TASF). By the end of 1999, the Fund's total resources amounted to US $809.2m., of which US $692.9m. had been utilized or committed. The Japan Special Fund (JSF) was established in 1988 to provide finance for technical assistance by means of grants, in both the public and private sectors. The JSF aims to help developing member countries restructure their economies, enhance the opportunities for attracting new investment, and recycle funds. The Japanese Government had committed a total of 86,500m. yen (equivalent to some US $745m.) to the JSF by the end of 1999 (of which US $675m. had been utilized). In March 1999 an Asian Currency Crisis Support Facility was launched as an independent component of the JSF. It was to be administered by the Bank to provide additional technical assistance and interest payment assistance to countries most affected by financial instability. The Japanese Government, as the sole financier of the fund, contributed 12,500m. yen (some US $104.4m.) to the new Facility in 1999. The Japanese Government also funds the ADB Institute Special Fund, which was established to finance the initial operations of the new Institute (see above). By 31 December 1999 cumulative commitments to the Special Fund amounted to 4,300m. yen (or US $34.7m.).

Activities

Loans by the ADB are usually aimed at specific projects. In responding to requests from member governments for loans, the Bank's staff assesses the financial and economic viability of projects and the way in which they fit into the economic framework and priorities of development of the country concerned. In 1987 the Bank adopted a policy of lending in support of programmes of sectoral adjustment, not limited to specific projects; such loans were not to exceed 15% of total Bank public sector lending. In 1999 the Board of Directors increased the ceiling on programme lending to 20% of the annual total. In 1985 the Bank decided to expand its assistance to the private sector, hitherto comprising loans to development finance institutions, under government guarantee, for lending to small and medium-sized enterprises; a programme was formulated for direct financial assistance, in the form of equity and loans without government guarantee, to private enterprises. In addition, the Bank was to increase its support for financial institutions and capital markets and, where appropriate, give assistance for the privatization of public sector enterprises. In 1992 a Social Dimensions Unit was established as part of the central administrative structure of the Bank, which contributed to the Bank's increasing awareness of the importance of social aspects of development as essential components of sustainable economic growth. During the early 1990s the Bank also aimed to expand its role as project financier by providing assistance for policy formulation and review and promoting regional co-operation, while placing greater emphasis on individual country requirements.

Under the Bank's Medium-Term Strategic Framework for the period 1995–98 the following concerns were identified as strategic development objectives: promoting economic growth; reducing poverty; supporting human development (including population planning); improving the status of women; and protecting the environment. Accordingly, the Bank resolved to promote sound development management, by integrating into its operations and projects the promotion of governance issues, such as capacity-building, legal frameworks and openness of information. During 1995 the Bank introduced other specific policy initiatives including a new co-financing and guarantee policy to extend the use of guarantees and to provide greater assistance to co-financiers in order to mobilize more effectively private resources for development projects; a commitment to assess development projects for their impact on

SUBSCRIPTIONS AND VOTING POWER*
(31 December 1999)

Country	Subscribed capital (% of total)	Voting power (% of total)
Regional:		
Afghanistan	0.034	0.372
Australia	5.908	5.071
Azerbaijan	0.454	0.708
Bangladesh	1.042	1.179
Bhutan	0.006	0.350
Cambodia	0.050	0.385
China, People's Republic	6.579	5.608
Cook Islands	0.003	0.347
Fiji	0.069	0.400
Hong Kong	0.556	0.790
India	6.464	5.516
Indonesia	5.560	4.793
Japan	15.934	13.092
Kazakhstan	0.823	1.004
Kiribati	0.004	0.348
Korea, Republic	5.143	4.459
Kyrgyzstan	0.305	0.589
Laos	0.014	0.356
Malaysia	2.780	2.569
Maldives	0.004	0.348
Marshall Islands	0.003	0.347
Micronesia, Federated States	0.004	0.348
Mongolia	0.015	0.357
Myanmar	0.556	0.790
Nauru	0.004	0.348
Nepal	0.150	0.465
New Zealand	1.568	1.599
Pakistan	2.224	2.124
Papua New Guinea	0.096	0.421
Philippines	2.433	2.291
Samoa	0.003	0.348
Singapore	0.347	0.623
Solomon Islands	0.007	0.350
Sri Lanka	0.592	0.818
Taiwan	1.112	1.234
Tajikistan	0.292	0.579
Thailand	1.390	1.457
Tonga	0.004	0.348
Tuvalu	0.001	0.346
Uzbekistan	0.688	0.895
Vanuatu	0.007	0.350
Viet Nam	0.348	0.624
Sub-total	63.580	65.347
Non-regional:		
Austria	0.347	0.623
Belgium	0.347	0.623
Canada	5.341	4.617
Denmark	0.347	0.623
Finland	0.347	0.623
France	2.376	2.246
Germany	4.417	3.878
Italy	1.845	1.821
Netherlands	1.047	1.183
Norway	0.347	0.623
Spain	0.347	0.623
Sweden	0.347	0.623
Switzerland	0.596	0.822
Turkey	0.347	0.623
United Kingdom	2.085	2.013
USA	15.934	13.092
Sub-total	36.420	34.653
Total	100.000	100.000

* Turkmenistan became a member on 31 August 2000.

the local population and to avoid all involuntary resettlement where possible; the establishment of a formal procedure for grievances, under which the Board may authorize an inspection of a project, by an independent panel of experts, at the request of the affected community or group; and a policy to place greater emphasis on the development of the private sector, through the Bank's lending commitments and technical assistance activities. During 1997 the Bank attempted to refine its policy on good governance by emphasizing the following two objectives: assisting the governments of developing countries to create conditions conducive to private-sector investment, for example through public-sector management reforms; and assisting those governments to identify and secure large-scale and long-term funding, for example through the establishment of joint public-private ventures and the formulation of legal frameworks. In 1998 the Bank further extended its governance policy by means of a new anticorruption strategy.

The currency instability and ensuing financial crises affecting many Asian economies in the second half of 1997 and in 1998 prompted the Bank to reflect on its role in the region. The Bank resolved to strengthen its activities as a broad-based development institution, rather than solely as a project financier, through lending policies, dialogue, co-financing and technical assistance. A Task Force on Financial Sector Reform was established to review the causes and effects of the regional financial crisis. The Task Force identified the Bank's initial priorities as being to accelerate banking and capital market reforms in member countries, to promote market efficiency in the financial, trade and industrial sectors, to promote good governance and sound corporate management, and to alleviate the social impact of structural adjustments. In mid-1999 the Bank approved a technical assistance grant to establish an internet-based Asian Recovery Information Centre , within a new Regional Monitoring Unit, which aimed to facilitate access to information regarding the economic and social impact of the Asian financial crisis, analyses of economic needs of countries, reform programmes and monitoring of the economic recovery process. In November the Board of Directors approved a new overall strategy objective of poverty reduction, which was to be the principal consideration for all future Bank lending, project financing and technical assistance.The strategy incorporated key aims of supporting sustainable, grass-roots based economic growth, social development and good governance. The Board also approved a health sector policy, to concentrate resources on basic primary healthcare, and initiated reviews of the Bank's private sector strategy and the efficiency of resident missions.

In 1999 the Bank approved 66 loans in 52 projects amounting to US \$4,978.6m. (compared with US \$5,982.5m. for 66 loans in 57 projects in 1998). Loans from ordinary capital resources in 1999 totalled US \$3,908.1m., while loans from the ADF amounted to US \$1,070.5m. Private-sector operations approved amounted to US \$153.9m., which included direct loans without government guarantee of US \$146.5m. and equity investments of US \$7.4m. The largest proportion of assistance, amounting to some 28% of total lending was allocated to social infrastructure projects, including water supply and sanitation, education, and housing. Disbursements of loans during 1999 amounted to US \$4,823.6m., bringing cumulative disbursements to a total of US \$54,275.0m.

In 1999 grants approved for technical assistance (e.g. project preparation, consultant services and training) amounted to

US \$172.9m. for 315 projects, with US \$88.0m. deriving from the Bank's ordinary resources and the TASF, US \$61.0m. from the JSF, US \$10.5m. from the newly-established ACCSF, and US \$13.5m. from bilateral and multilateral sources. The Bank's Operations Evaluation Office prepares reports on completed projects, in order to assess achievements and problems. In 1997 the Bank adopted several new initiatives to evaluate and classify project performance and to assess the impact on development of individual projects. In April 2000 the Bank announced that, from 2001, some new loans would be denominated in local currencies, in order to ease the repayment burden on recipient economies.

The Bank co-operates with other international organizations active in the region, particularly the World Bank group, the IMF, UNDP and APEC, and participates in meetings of aid donors for developing member countries. In 1996 the Bank signed a memorandum of understanding with the UN Industrial Development Organization (UNIDO), in order to strengthen co-operation between the two organizations. A new policy concerning co-operation with non-governmental organizations was approved by the Bank in 1998.

Finance

Internal administrative expenses amounted to US \$193.5m. in 1999, and were projected to total US \$215.4m. in 2000.

Publications

ADB Business Opportunities (monthly).

ADB Institute Newsletter.

ADB Research Bulletin (2 a year).

ADB Review (6 a year).

Annual Report.

Asian Development Outlook (annually).

Asian Development Review (2 a year).

Key Indicators of Developing Asian and Pacific Countries (annually).

Law and Policy Reform Bulletin (annually).

Loan, Technical Assistance and Private Sector Operations Approvals (monthly).

Project Profiles for Commercial and Export Credits Co-financing (quarterly).

Studies and reports, guide-lines, sample bidding documents, staff papers.

Statistics

BANK ACTIVITIES BY SECTOR

	Loan Approvals (US \$ million)		
	1999		1968–99
Sector	Amount	%	%
Agriculture and natural resources	430.40	8.65	18.76
Energy	719.00	14.44	21.47
Finance	69.30	1.39	15.53
Industry and non-fuel minerals.	407.00	8.18	3.40
Social infrastructure	1,386.62	27.85	16.16
Transport and communications.	993.00	19.95	19.50
Multi-sector and others.	973.25	19.54	5.17
Total	4,978.57	100.00	100.00

LENDING ACTIVITIES BY COUNTRY (US $ million)

Country	Loans approved in 1999		
	Ordinary Capital	ADF	Total
Bangladesh	82.00	250.00	332.00
Bhutan.	—	10.00	10.00
Cambodia	—	88.00	88.00
China, People's Republic . .	1,258.50	—	1,258.50
India	625.00	—	625.00
Indonesia	1,020.00	—	1,020.00
Kyrgyzstan. . . .	—	72.00	72.00
Laos	—	25.60	25.60
Maldives	—	8.00	8.00
Marshall Islands . . .	—	9.25	9.25
Mongolia	—	50.00	50.00
Nepal	—	50.00	50.00
Pakistan	307.00	95.80	402.80
Papua New Guinea . .	88.80	20.00	108.80
Philippines	88.00	—	88.00
Sri Lanka	35.00	148.80	183.80
Tajikistan	—	25.00	25.00
Thailand	363.82	—	363.82
Tuvalu	—	4.00	4.00
Vanuatu	—	2.00	2.00
Viet Nam	40.00	155.00	195.00
Regional	—	57.00	57.00
Total	3,908.12	1,070.45	4,978.57

LENDING ACTIVITIES (in %)

Country	1993–97		1998–99	
	Ordinary Capital	ADF	Ordinary Capital	ADF
Bangladesh	0.2	21.0	1.1	21.1
Bhutan	—	0.3	—	0.8
Cambodia	—	2.5	—	4.3
China, People's Republic .	23.3	—	27.6	—
Cook Islands . . .	—	0.2	—	—
Fiji	0.2	—	—	—
India	13.2	—	9.8	—
Indonesia	22.2	3.6	32.1	—
Kazakhstan . . .	1.6	0.8	—	—
Kiribati	—	—	—	0.5
Korea, Republic . . .	18.3	—	—	—
Kyrgyzstan	—	3.5	—	6.6
Laos	—	5.8	—	2.2
Malaysia	0.9	—	—	—
Maldives	—	0.2	—	0.7
Marshall Islands . . .	—	0.5	—	0.4
Micronesia, Federated States . . .	—	0.5	—	—
Mongolia	—	4.8	—	2.4
Nauru	—	—	0.1	—
Nepal	0.2	5.2	—	7.5
Pakistan	4.1	20.5	3.4	4.6
Papua New Guinea . .	0.2	0.6	1.2	1.0
Philippines	6.7	3.1	10.5	0.4
Samoa	—	0.0	—	0.4
Solomon Islands . .	—	0.0	—	1.3
Sri Lanka	0.0	7.8	0.5	16.2
Tajikistan	—	—	—	2.2
Thailand	8.5	—	11.2	—
Tonga	—	0.2	—	—
Tuvalu	—	—	—	0.2
Uzbekistan . . .	0.3	0.3	1.3	—
Vanuatu	—	0.1	—	1.1
Viet Nam	0.1	18.2	—	16.5
Regional	—	—	0.8	9.6
Total	100.0	100.0	100.0	100.0
Value (US $ million) .	21,903.8	7,214.4	4,995.4	987.1

Source: *ADB Annual Report 1999.*

ASSOCIATION OF SOUTH EAST ASIAN NATIONS—ASEAN

Address: 70A Jalan Sisingamangaraja, POB 2072, Jakarta 12110, Indonesia.

Telephone: (21) 7262991; **fax:** (21) 7398234; **e-mail:** public@ asean.or.id; **internet:** www.aseansec.org.

ASEAN was established in August 1967 at Bangkok, Thailand, to accelerate economic progress and to increase the stability of the South-East Asian region.

MEMBERS

Brunei	Malaysia	Thailand
Cambodia	Myanmar	Viet Nam
Indonesia	Philippines	
Laos	Singapore	

Organization

(April 2001)

SUMMIT MEETING

The highest authority of ASEAN, bringing together the heads of government of member countries. The first meeting was held in Bali, Indonesia, in February 1976. In 1992 it was agreed that summit meetings were to be held every three years, with an interim informal gathering of heads of government convened at least once. The 30th anniversary of the founding of ASEAN was commemorated at an informal summit meeting held in Kuala Lumpur, Malaysia, in December 1997. The sixth summit meeting was convened in Hanoi, Viet Nam, in December 1998 and the seventh meeting was scheduled to be held in Brunei, in 2001. Informal summit meetings were convened in Manila, Philippines, in November 1999, and in Singapore, in November 2000.

MINISTERIAL MEETINGS

The ASEAN Ministerial Meeting (AMM), comprising ministers of foreign affairs of member states, meets annually, in each member country in turn, to formulate policy guide-lines and to co-ordinate ASEAN activities. These meetings are followed by 'post-ministerial conferences' (PMCs), where ASEAN ministers of foreign affairs meet with their counterparts from countries that are 'dialogue partners' (see below) as well as from other countries. Ministers of economic affairs also meet once a year, to direct ASEAN economic co-operation. Joint Ministerial Meetings, consisting of ministers of foreign affairs and of economic affairs are convened prior to a summit meeting, and may be held at the request of either group of ministers. Other ministers meet regularly to promote co-operation in different sectors. Ministerial meetings are serviced by the committees described below.

STANDING COMMITTEE

The Standing Committee normally meets every two months. It consists of the minister of foreign affairs of the host country and ambassadors of the other members accredited to the host country.

SECRETARIATS

A permanent secretariat was established in Jakarta, Indonesia, in 1976 to form a central co-ordinating body. The Secretariat comprises the following four bureaux: economic co-operation; functional co-operation; ASEAN co-operation and dialogue relations; and AFTA. The Secretary-General holds office for a five-year term, and is assisted by two Deputy Secretaries-General. In each member country day-to-day work is co-ordinated by an ASEAN National Secretariat.

Secretary-General: RODOLFO CERTEZA SEVERINO (Philippines).

Deputy Secretaries-General: TRAN DUC MINH (Viet Nam), AHMAD MOKHTAR SELAT (Malaysia).

COMMITTEES AND SENIOR OFFICIALS' MEETINGS

Relevant ministerial meetings are serviced by the following three Committees: Culture and Information; Science and Technology; and Social Development. ASEAN political co-operation is directed by a Senior Officials' Meeting. Economic co-operation activities are administered by a Senior Economic Officials' Meeting. Other groups of senior officials meet to direct ASEAN activities concerned with drug issues and the environment. Matters relating to the civil service are considered by an ASEAN Conference (held every two years). ASEAN's various work programmes and activities are also supported by a network of subsidiary technical bodies comprising sub-committees, expert groups, *ad hoc* working groups and working parties.

To support the conduct of relations with other countries and international organizations, ASEAN committees (composed of heads of diplomatic missions) have been established in 15 foreign capitals: those of Australia, Belgium, Canada, the People's Republic of China, France, Germany, India, Japan, the Republic of Korea, New Zealand, Pakistan, Russia, Switzerland, the United Kingdom and the USA.

Activities

ASEAN was established in 1967 with the signing of the ASEAN Declaration, otherwise known as the Bangkok Declaration, by the ministers of foreign affairs of Indonesia, Malaysia, the Philippines, Singapore and Thailand. Brunei joined the organization in January 1984, shortly after attaining independence. Viet Nam was admitted as the seventh member of ASEAN in July 1995. Laos and Myanmar joined in July 1997 and Cambodia was formally admitted in April 1999, fulfilling the organization's ambition to incorporate all 10 countries in the sub-region.

TRADE

A Basic Agreement on the Establishment of ASEAN Preferential Trade Arrangements was concluded in 1977, but by mid-1987 the system covered only about 5% of trade between member states, since individual countries were permitted to exclude any 'sensitive' products from preferential import tariffs. In December 1987 the meeting of ASEAN heads of government resolved to reduce such exclusions to a maximum of 10% of the number of items traded and to a maximum of 50% of the value of trade, over the next five years (seven years for Indonesia and the Philippines).

In January 1992 heads of government, meeting in Singapore, signed an agreement to create an 'ASEAN Free Trade Area' (AFTA), by 2008. In accordance with the agreement, a common effective preferential tariff (CEPT) scheme came into effect in January 1993. The CEPT covered all manufactured products, including capital goods, and processed agricultural products (which together accounted for two-thirds of intra-ASEAN trade), but was to exclude unprocessed agricultural products. Tariffs were to be reduced to a maximum of 20% within a period of five to eight years and to 0%–5% during the subsequent seven to 10 years. Fifteen categories were designated for accelerated tariff reduction, including vegetable oils, rubber products, textiles, cement and pharmaceuticals. Member states were, however, still to be permitted exclusion for certain 'sensitive' products. In October 1993 ASEAN trade ministers agreed to modify the CEPT, with only Malaysia and Singapore having adhered to the original tariff reduction schedule. The new AFTA programme, under which all member countries except Brunei were scheduled to begin tariff reductions from 1 January 1994, substantially enlarged the number of products to be included in the tariff-reduction process and reduced the list of products eligible for protection. In September 1994 ASEAN ministers of economic affairs agreed to accelerate the implementation of AFTA: tariffs were to be reduced to 0%–5% within seven to 10 years, or within five to eight years for products designated for accelerated tariff cuts. In July 1995 Viet Nam was admitted as a member of ASEAN and was granted until 2006 to implement the AFTA trade agreements (this deadline was subsequently advanced to 2003). In September 1995 ASEAN economic affairs ministers, meeting in Brunei, advocated a further acceleration of the tariff reduction deadline, to 2000. The ministers emphasized the importance of maintaining momentum in trade

liberalization, in order to ensure ASEAN's continued relevance in relation to other regional groupings. In December 1995 heads of government, convened in Bangkok, agreed to maintain the objective of achieving AFTA by 2003, while pursuing efforts to eliminate or reduce tariffs to less than 5% on the majority of products by 2000. Liberalization was to be extended to certain service industries, including banking, telecommunications and tourism. In July 1997 Laos and Myanmar became members of ASEAN and were granted a 10-year period, from 1 January 1998, to comply with the AFTA schedule. (This deadline was subsequently advanced to 2005.) In December 1997 ASEAN leaders again agreed to accelerate the implementation of AFTA, but without specifying any new target date. Meeting in Hanoi, Viet Nam, in December 1998, heads of government approved a Statement on Bold Measures, detailing ASEAN's strategies to deal with the economic crisis that had prevailed in the region since late 1997. These included incentives to attract investors, for example a three-year exemption on corporate taxation, accelerated implementation of the ASEAN Investment Area (see below), and advancing the AFTA deadline, for the original six members, to 2002, with some 85% of products to be covered by the arrangements by 2000, and 90% by 2001. It was envisaged that the original six members and the new members would achieve the elimination of all tariffs by 2015 and 2018 respectively. The Hanoi Plan of Action, which was also adopted at the meeting as a framework for the development of the organization over the period 1999–2004, incorporated a series of measures aimed at strengthening macroeconomic and financial co-operation and enhancing greater economic integration. In April 1999 Cambodia, on being admitted as a full member of ASEAN, signed an agreement to implement the tariff reduction programme over a 10-year period, commencing 1 January 2000. Cambodia also signed a declaration endorsing the commitments of the 1998 Statement on Bold Measures. In May 2000 Malaysia was granted a special exemption to postpone implementing tariff reductions on motor vehicles for two years from 1 January 2003.

In June 1996 ASEAN's Working Group on Customs Procedures completed a draft legal framework for regional co-operation in order to simplify and to harmonize customs procedures, legislation and product classification. The customs agreement was to complement AFTA in facilitating intra-ASEAN trade. It was signed in March 1997 at the inaugural meeting of ASEAN finance ministers. (Laos and Myanmar signed the customs agreement in July 1997, and Cambodia assented to it in April 1999.)

During 1991 ASEAN ministers discussed a proposal made by the Malaysian Government for the formation of an economic grouping, to be composed of ASEAN members, the People's Republic of China, Hong Kong, Japan, the Republic of Korea and Taiwan. In July 1993 ASEAN ministers of foreign affairs agreed a compromise, whereby the grouping was to be a caucus within APEC, although it was to be co-ordinated by ASEAN's meeting of economy ministers. In July 1994 ministers of foreign affairs of nine prospective members of the group held their first informal collective meeting; however, no progress was made towards forming the proposed East Asia Economic Caucus. There was renewed speculation on the formation of an East Asian grouping following the onset of the Asian financial crisis of the late 1990s. At an informal meeting of leaders of ASEAN countries, China, Japan and the Republic of Korea, held in November 1999, all parties (designating themselves 'ASEAN + 3') issued a Joint Statement on East Asian Co-operation, in which they agreed to strengthen regional unity and addressed the long-term possibility of establishing an East Asian common market and currency. Meeting in May 2000 ASEAN + 3 ministers of economic affairs agreed to establish an enhanced currency swap mechanism in order to defend member economies against future financial crises. In July ASEAN + 3 ministers of foreign affairs convened an inaugural formal summit in Bangkok, Thailand, and in October ASEAN + 3 economic affairs ministers agreed to hold their hitherto twice-yearly informal meetings on an institutionalized basis. In November an informal meeting of ASEAN +3 leaders approved further co-operation in various sectors and initiated a feasibility study into a proposal to establish a regional free trade area.

SECURITY

In 1971 ASEAN members endorsed a declaration envisaging the establishment of a Zone of Peace, Freedom and Neutrality (ZOPFAN) in the South-East Asian region. This objective was incorporated in the Declaration of ASEAN Concord, which was adopted at the first summit meeting of the organization, held in Bali, Indonesia, in February 1976. (The Declaration also issued guidelines for co-operation in economic development and the promotion of social justice and welfare.) Also in February 1976 a Treaty of Amity and Co-operation was signed by heads of state, establishing principles of mutual respect for the independence and sovereignty of all nations, non-interference in the internal affairs of one another and settlement of disputes by peaceful means. The Treaty was amended in December 1987 by a protocol providing for the accession of Papua New Guinea and other non-member countries in the region; it was reinforced by a second protocol, signed in July 1998.

In January 1992 ASEAN leaders agreed that there should be greater co-operation on security matters within the grouping, and that ASEAN's post-ministerial conferences (PMCs) should be used as a forum for discussion of questions relating to security with its dialogue partners and other countries. In July 1992 the ASEAN Ministerial Meeting issued a statement calling for a peaceful resolution of the dispute concerning the strategically significant Spratly Islands in the South China Sea, which are claimed, wholly or partly, by the People's Republic of China, Taiwan, Viet Nam, Brunei, Malaysia and the Philippines. (In February China had introduced legislation that defined the Spratly Islands as belonging to its territorial waters.) The ministers proposed a code of international conduct for the South China Sea, to be based on the principles contained in ASEAN's Treaty of Amity and Co-operation. At the ensuing PMC ASEAN requested the USA to maintain a military presence in the region, to compensate for the departure of its forces from the Philippines. The USA affirmed its commitment to maintaining the balance of security in South-East Asia. However, the issue of sovereignty of the Spratly Islands remained unresolved, and tensions in the region heightened in early 1995 owing to Chinese occupation of part of the disputed territory. Viet Nam's accession to ASEAN in July 1995, bringing all the Spratly Islands claimants except China and Taiwan into the grouping, was expected to strengthen ASEAN's position of negotiating a multilateral settlement on the islands. In mid-1999 ASEAN established a special committee to formulate a code of conduct to be observed by all claimants to the Spratly Islands. Proposals under consideration were a ban on the building of all new structures, which had been the cause of escalating tensions in 1998, and a declaration rejecting the use of force to resolve disputes. A draft code of conduct was approved in November 1999. China, insisting that it would adopt the proposed code only as a set of guide-lines and not as a legally-binding document, resolved not to attempt to strengthen its presence on the islands and, in March 2000, participated in discussions with ASEAN officials concerning the document.

In December 1995 ASEAN heads of government, meeting in Bangkok, signed a treaty establishing a South-East Asia Nuclear-Weapon Free Zone (SEANWFZ). The treaty was also signed by Cambodia, Myanmar and Laos. It was extended to cover the offshore economic exclusion zones of each country. On ratification by all parties, the Treaty was to prohibit the manufacture or storage of nuclear weapons within the region. Individual signatories were to decide whether to allow port visits or transportation of nuclear weapons by foreign powers through territorial waters. The Treaty entered into force on 27 March 1997. ASEAN senior officials were mandated to oversee implementation of the Treaty pending the establishment of a permanent monitoring committee. In July 1999 the People's Republic of China and India agreed to observe the terms of the SEANWFZ.

In July 1997 ASEAN ministers of foreign affairs reiterated their commitment to the principle of non-interference in the internal affairs of other countries. However, the group's efforts in Cambodia (see below) marked a significant shift in diplomatic policy towards one of 'constructive intervention', which had been proposed by Malaysia's Deputy Prime Minister in recognition of the increasing interdependence of the region. At the Ministerial Meeting, held in July 1998, Thailand's Minister of Foreign Affairs, supported by his Philippine counterpart, proposed that the grouping formally adopt a policy of 'flexible engagement'. The proposal, based partly on concerns that the continued restrictions imposed by the Myanmar authorities on dissident political activists was damaging ASEAN relations with its dialogue partners, was to provide for the discussion of the affairs of other member states when they have an impact on neighbouring countries. While rejecting the proposal, other ASEAN ministers agreed to pursue a more limited version, referred to as 'enhanced interaction', and to maintain open dialogue within the grouping. In September 1999 the unrest prompted by the popular referendum on the future of East Timor and resulting humanitarian crisis highlighted the unwillingness of some ASEAN member states to intervene in other member countries and undermined the political unity of the grouping. A compromise agreement, whereby countries were to act on an individual basis rather than as representatives of ASEAN, was formulated prior to an emergency meeting of ministers of foreign affairs, held during the APEC meetings in Auckland, New Zealand. Malaysia, the Philippines, Singapore and Thailand declared their support for the establishment of a multinational force to restore peace in East Timor and committed troops to participate in the Australian-led operation. Myanmar and Viet Nam, however, remained opposed to intervention in the territory. At their informal summit in November 1999 heads of state approved the establishment of an ASEAN Troika, with a view to providing a rapid response mechanism in the event of a regional crisis. The Troika, which was to be constituted as an *ad hoc* body comprising the foreign ministers of the Association's current, previous and future chairmanship, was to present recommendations to the meeting of foreign ministers.

In June 1999 the first meeting was convened, at ministerial level, to consider issues relating to transnational crime and to strengthen regional co-operation to combat the problem. Regular meetings of senior officials and ministers have subsequently been held.

ASEAN Regional Forum (ARF): In July 1993 the meeting of ASEAN ministers of foreign affairs sanctioned the establishment of a forum that was to discuss and co-operate on security issues within the region, and in particular was to ensure the involvement of the People's Republic of China in regional dialogue. The ARF was informally initiated during that year's PMC, comprising the ASEAN countries, its dialogue partners (at that time—Australia, Canada, the EC, Japan, the Republic of Korea, New Zealand and the USA), as well as the People's Republic of China, Laos, Papua New Guinea, Russia and Viet Nam. The first formal meeting of the ARF was conducted in July 1994, following the Ministerial Meeting held in Bangkok, Thailand, and it was agreed that the ARF be convened on an annual basis. The 1995 meeting, held in Brunei, in August, attempted to define a framework for the future of the ARF. It was perceived as evolving in three stages: the promotion of confidence-building (including disaster relief and peace-keeping activities); the development of preventive diplomacy; and the elaboration of approaches to conflict. The 19 ministers of foreign affairs attending the meeting (Cambodia participated for the first time) recognized that the ARF was still in the initial stage of implementing confidence-building measures. The ministers, having conceded to a request by China not to discuss explicitly the Spratly Islands, expressed concern at overlapping sovereignty claims in the region. In a further statement, the ministers urged an 'immediate end' to the testing of nuclear weapons, then being undertaken by the French Government in the South Pacific region. The third ARF, convened in July 1996, which was attended for the first time by India and Myanmar, agreed a set of criteria and guiding principles for the future expansion of the grouping. In particular, it was decided that the ARF would only admit as participants countries that have a direct influence on the peace and security of the East Asia and Pacific region. The meeting supported the efforts of all claimants to territories in the South China Sea to resolve any disputes in accordance with international law, and recognized the importance of ending all testing of nuclear weapons in the region. The ARF that was held in July 1997 reviewed progress being made in developing the first two 'tracks' of the ARF process, through the structure of inter-sessional working groups and meetings. The Forum's consideration of security issues in the region was dominated by concern at the political situation in Cambodia; support was expressed for ASEAN mediation to restore stability within that country. Myanmar and Laos attended the ARF for the first time. Mongolia was admitted into the ARF at its meeting in July 1998. The meeting condemned the recent testing of nuclear weapons in the region, but declined to criticize specifically India and Pakistan as the two countries involved. In July 1999 the ARF warned the Democratic People's Republic of Korea (DPRK) not to conduct any further testing of missiles over the Pacific. At the seventh meeting of the ARF, convened in Bangkok, Thailand, in July 2000, the DPRK was admitted to the Forum.

EXTERNAL RELATIONS

ASEAN's external relations have been pursued through a dialogue system, initially with the objective of promoting co-operation in economic areas with key trading partners. The system has been expanded in recent years to encompass regional security concerns and co-operation in other areas, such as the environment. The ARF (see above) emerged from the dialogue system, and more recently the formalized discussions of ASEAN with Japan, China and the Republic of Korea has evolved as a separate process with its own strategic agenda.

European Union: In March 1980 a co-operation agreement was signed between ASEAN and the European Community (EC, as the EU was known prior to its restructuring on 1 November 1993), which provided for the strengthening of existing trade links and increased co-operation in the scientific and agricultural spheres. A Joint Co-operation Committee met in November (and annually thereafter); it drew up a programme of scientific and technological co-operation, approved measures to promote contacts between industrialists from the two regions, and agreed on EC financing of ASEAN regional projects. An ASEAN-EC Business Council was launched in December 1983, and three European Business Information Councils have since been established, in Malaysia, the Philippines and Thailand, in order to promote private sector co-operation. The first meeting of ministers of economic affairs from ASEAN and EC member countries took place in October 1985. In 1986 a joint group of experts on trade was set up, to examine problems of access to ASEAN markets and similar matters, and in 1987 joint investment committees were established in all the ASEAN capital cities. In December 1990 the Community adopted new guide-lines on development co-operation, with an increase in assistance to Asia, and a change in the type of aid given to ASEAN members, emphasizing training, science and technology and venture capital, rather than assistance for rural development. In October 1992 the EC and ASEAN agreed to promote further trade between the regions, as well as bilateral investment, and made a joint declaration in support of human rights. In October 1995 an ASEAN-EU Eminent Persons Group was established to consider the future direction of ASEAN-EU relations. An EU-ASEAN Junior Managers Exchange Programme was initiated in November 1996, as part of efforts to promote co-operation and understanding between the industrial and business sectors in both regions. In May 1995 ASEAN and EU senior officials endorsed an initiative to strengthen relations between the two economic regions within the framework of an Asia-Europe Meeting of heads of government (ASEM). The first ASEM was convened in Bangkok, Thailand, in March 1996, at which leaders approved a new Asia-Europe Partnership for Greater Growth (see EU, p. 204). The second ASEM summit meeting, held in April 1998, focused heavily on economic concerns. In February 1997 ministers of foreign affairs of countries participating in ASEM met in Singapore. Despite ongoing differences regarding human rights issues, in particular concerning ASEAN's granting of full membership status to Myanmar and the situation in East Timor (which precluded the conclusion of a new co-operation agreement), the Ministerial Meeting issued a final joint declaration, committing both sides to strengthening co-operation and dialogue on economic, international and bilateral trade, security and social issues. A protocol to the 1980 co-operation agreement was signed, enabling the participation of Viet Nam in the dialogue process. In November 1997 a session of the Joint Co-operation Committee was postponed and later cancelled, owing to a dispute concerning objections by the EU to the participation of Myanmar. A compromise agreement, allowing Myanma officials to attend meetings as 'silent' observers, was concluded in November 1998. However, a meeting of the Joint Co-operation Committee, scheduled to take place in January 1999, was again cancelled, owing to controversy over perceived discrimination by the EU against Myanmar's status. The meeting was finally convened in Bangkok, Thailand, in late May. In December 2000 an ASEAN-EU Ministerial Meeting was held in Vientiane, Laos. Both sides agreed to pursue dialogue and co-operation and issued a joint declaration which accorded support for the efforts of the UN Secretary-General's special envoy towards restoring political dialogue in Myanmar. Myanmar agreed to permit an EU delegation to visit the country, and opposition leaders, in early 2001.

People's Republic of China: Efforts to develop consultative relations between ASEAN and China were initiated in 1993. Joint Committees on economic and trade co-operation and on scientific and technological co-operation were subsequently established. The first formal consultations between senior officials of the two sides were held in April 1995. Despite ASEAN's continued concern at China's territorial claims to the Spratly Islands in the South China Sea, efforts were pursued to strengthen relations between the two sides, and in July 1996 China was admitted to the PMC as a full dialogue partner. In February 1997 a Joint Co-operation Committee was established to co-ordinate the China-ASEAN dialogue and all aspects of relations between the two sides. Relations between the two sides were further strengthened by the decision to establish a joint business council to promote bilateral trade and investment. China participated in the informal summit meeting that was held in December, at the end of which both sides issued a joint statement affirming their commitment to resolving regional disputes through peaceful means. A second meeting of the Joint Co-operation Committee was held in March 1999. China was a participant in the first official ASEAN + 3 meeting of foreign ministers, which was convened in July 2000 (see above). In November the informal summit meeting agreed to establish a working group to consider future economic co-operation and free trade opportunities between ASEAN and China.

Japan: The ASEAN-Japan Forum was established in 1977 to discuss matters of mutual concern in trade, investment, technology transfer and development assistance. The first ever meeting between ASEAN economic ministers and the Japanese Minister of International Trade and Industry was held in October 1992. At this meeting, and subsequently, ASEAN requested Japan to increase its investment in member countries and to make Japanese markets more accessible to ASEAN products in order to reduce the trade deficit with Japan. Japan agreed to extend ASEAN's privileges under its generalized system of tariffs until 2001. Since 1993 ASEAN-Japanese development and cultural co-operation has expanded under schemes including the Inter-ASEAN Technical Exchange Programme, the Japan-ASEAN Co-operation Promotion Programme and the ASEAN-Japan Friendship Programme. In December 1997 Japan, attending the informal summit meeting in Malaysia, agreed to improve market access for ASEAN products and to provide training opportunities for more than 20,000 young people in order to help develop local economies. In December 1998 ASEAN heads of government welcomed a Japanese initiative, announced in October, to allocate US $30,000m. to promote economic recovery in the region. At the same time the Japanese Prime Minister announced a further package of $5,000m. to be available as conces-

sionary loans for infrastructure projects. In mid-2000 a new Japan-ASEAN General Exchange Fund (JAGEF) was established to promote and facilitate the transfer of technology, investment and personnel. In November 1999 Japan, along with the People's Republic of China and the Republic of Korea, attending an informal summit meeting of ASEAN, agreed to strengthen economic and political co-operation with the ASEAN countries, to enhance political and security dialogue, and to implement joint infrastructure and social projects. Japan participated in the first official ASEAN + 3 meeting of foreign ministers, which was convened in July 2000.

Other countries: Under the ASEAN-Australia Development (formerly Economic) Co-operation Programme, Australia gives financial support for ASEAN activities, and a joint Business Council was set up in 1980. A fourth phase of the Programme was initiated in April 1999, with assistance amounting to $A45m. Co-operation relations with New Zealand are based on the Inter-Institutional Linkages Programme and the Trade and Investment Promotion Programme, which mainly provide assistance in forestry development, dairy technology, veterinary management and legal aid training. An ASEAN-New Zealand Joint Management Committee was initiated in November 1993, in order to oversee the implementation of co-operation projects. The USA gives assistance for the development of small and medium-sized businesses and other projects, and supports a Center for Technology Exchange. In 1990 ASEAN and the USA established an ASEAN-US Joint Working Group, whose purpose is to review ASEAN's economic relations with the USA and to identify measures by which economic links could be strengthened. ASEAN-Canadian co-operation projects include fisheries technology, the telecommunications industry, use of solar energy, and a forest seed centre. A Joint Planning and Monitoring Committee was established in 1994 (and met for the first time in October 1995) to oversee projects at the planning and implementation levels. In July 1991 the Republic of Korea was accepted as a 'dialogue partner', and in December a joint ASEAN-Korea Chamber of Commerce was established. During 1995 co-operation projects concerned with human resources development, science and technology, agricultural development and trade and investment policies were implemented. The Republic of Korea participated in ASEAN's informal summit meetings in December 1997 and November 1999 (see above), and took part in the first official ASEAN + 3 meeting of foreign ministers, which was convened in July 2000.

In July 1993 both India and Pakistan were accepted as sectoral partners: sectoral partners can participate in ASEAN meetings on certain sectors such as trade, transport and communications and tourism. An ASEAN-India Business Council was established, and met for the first time, in New Delhi, in February 1995. In December 1995 the ASEAN summit meeting agreed to enhance India's status to that of a full dialogue partner; India was formally admitted to the PMC in July 1996. In July 1998 India rejected a proposal that Pakistan attend that month's ARF to discuss issues relating to both countries' testing of nuclear weapons. An ASEAN-Pakistan joint Business Council met for the first time in February 2000.

In March 2000 the first ASEAN-Russia business forum opened in Kuala Lumpur, Malaysia. East Timor was granted observer status at the AMM which took place in July, amid speculation that it might be admitted to ASEAN following the attainment of full independence.

Indo-China: In 1981 ASEAN sponsored a UN conference on Kampuchea, and gave assurances that it would not, as a group, supply arms to any faction. In 1988–89 'informal' meetings were held by representatives of Viet Nam, Laos, ASEAN and the Kampuchean factions to discuss a possible political settlement in Kampuchea. ASEAN participated in the international conference on Cambodia (as it was now known) which was held in Paris, France, in July/August 1989, and in further negotiations held in Jakarta, Indonesia, in February 1990, neither of which achieved a political settlement. In July ASEAN ministers urged the formation of a Supreme National Council (SNC), on which the Vietnamese-supported Government of Cambodia and the three opposition groups would be represented. A UN proposal for the formation of an SNC and the holding of elections, under UN supervision, was accepted by all the Cambodian factions in September. Following the mass return of Cambodian refugees and displaced people in 1992–93, ASEAN and Japan provided technical experts to assist in the resettlement of the returnees. In July 1994 ASEAN ministers of foreign affairs and their dialogue partner counterparts agreed to provide military training in order to assist the Cambodian Government in consolidating its position. In July 1995 Cambodia was accorded observer status. Subsequent co-operation focused on issues relating to Cambodia's future admission to the grouping as a full member. In May 1997 ASEAN ministers of foreign affairs confirmed that Cambodia, together with Laos and Myanmar, was to be admitted to the grouping in July of that year. In mid-July, however, Cambodia's membership was postponed owing to the deposition of Prince Ranariddh, and the resulting civil unrest. Later in that month Cambodia's *de facto* leader, Second Prime Minister Hun Sen, agreed to ASEAN's pursuit of a mediation role in restoring stability in the country and in preparing for democratic elections. In early August the ministers of foreign affairs of Indonesia, the Philippines and Thailand, representing ASEAN, met Hun Sen to confirm these objectives. A team of ASEAN observers joined an international monitoring mission to supervise the election held in Cambodia in July 1998. International approval of the conduct of the election, and consequently of Hun Sen's victory, prompted ASEAN to agree to reconsider Cambodia's admission into the Association. In December, following the establishment of a coalition administration in Cambodia, the country was welcomed, by the Vietnamese Government, as the 10th member of ASEAN, despite an earlier meeting of ministers of foreign affairs which failed to reach a consensus decision. Its formal admission took place on 30 April 1999.

In July 1992 Viet Nam and Laos signed ASEAN's Treaty on Amity and Co-operation: subsequently, the two countries participated in ASEAN meetings and committees as observers. Viet Nam was admitted as a full member of ASEAN in July 1995. In July 1994 an official delegation from Myanmar attended the annual Ministerial Meeting, having been invited by the host Thai Government on the basis of ASEAN's policy of pursuing limited 'constructive engagement' with Myanmar in order to encourage democracy in that country. In July 1995 Myanmar signed ASEAN's Treaty on Amity and Co-operation. In July 1996 ASEAN granted Myanmar observer status and admitted it to the ARF, despite the expression of strong reservations by (among others) the Governments of Australia, Canada and the USA, owing to the human rights situation in Myanmar. In November ASEAN heads of government, attending an informal summit meeting in Jakarta, Indonesia, agreed to admit Myanmar as a full member of the grouping at the same time as Cambodia and Laos. While Cambodia's membership was postponed, Laos and Myanmar were admitted to ASEAN in July 1997.

In June 1996 ministers of ASEAN countries, and of the People's Republic of China, Cambodia, Laos and Myanmar adopted a framework for ASEAN-Mekong Basin Development Co-operation. The initiative aimed to strengthen the region's cohesiveness, with greater co-operation on issues such as drugs-trafficking, labour migration and terrorism, and to facilitate the process of future expansion of ASEAN. Groups of experts and senior officials were to be convened to consider funding issues and proposals to link the two regions, including a gas pipeline network, rail links and the establishment of a common time zone. In December 1996 the working group on rail links appointed a team of consultants to conduct a feasibility study of the proposals. The completed study was presented at the second ministerial conference on ASEAN-Mekong Basin Development Co-operation, which was convened in Hanoi, Viet Nam, in July 2000.

INDUSTRY

The ASEAN Industrial Co-operation (AICO) scheme, initiated in 1996, encourages companies in the ASEAN region to undertake joint manufacturing activities. Products derived from an AICO arrangement benefit immediately from a preferential tariff rate of 0%–5%. The AICO scheme superseded the ASEAN industrial joint venture scheme, established in 1983. The ASEAN-Chambers of Commerce and Industry (CCI) aims to enhance ASEAN economic and industrial co-operation, and the participation in these activities of the private sector. In March 1996 a permanent ASEAN-CCI secretariat became operational at the ASEAN Secretariat. The ASEAN Consultative Committee on Standards and Quality (ACCSQ) aims to promote the understanding and implementation of quality concepts, which are considered to be important in strengthening the economic development of a member state and in helping to eliminate trade barriers. ACCSQ comprises three working groups: standards and information, conformance and assessment, and testing and calibration. In September 1994 the ACCSQ was recognized by the International Organization for Standardization as the standards organization for South-East Asia. In 1995 ACCSQ began to consider the elimination of technical barriers to trade, in order to facilitate the implementation of AFTA. In September 1994 an *ad hoc* Working Group on Intellectual Property Co-operation was established, with a mandate to formulate a framework agreement on intellectual property co-operation and to strengthen ASEAN activities towards intellectual property protection in the region. ASEAN aimed to establish, by 2004, a regional electronic database to strengthen the administration of intellectual property.

In 1988 the ASEAN Fund was established, with capital of US $150m. (of which US $15m. was contributed by the Asian Development Bank), to provide finance for portfolio investments in ASEAN countries, in particular for small and medium-sized enterprises (SMEs). The Hanoi Plan of Action, which was adopted by ASEAN heads of state in December 1998, incorporated a series of initiatives to enhance the development of SMEs, including training and technical assistance, co-operation activities and greater access to information.

FINANCE, BANKING AND INVESTMENT

In 1987 heads of government agreed to accelerate regional co-operation in this field, in order to support intra-ASEAN trade and investment; they adopted measures to increase the role of ASEAN currencies in regional trade, to assist negotiations on the avoidance of double taxation, and to improve the efficiency of tax and customs administrators. An ASEAN Reinsurance Corporation was established in 1988, with initial authorized capital of US $10m. In December 1995 the summit meeting proposed the establishment of an ASEAN Investment Area (AIA). Other measures to attract greater financial resource flows in the region, including an ASEAN Plan of Action for the Promotion of Foreign Direct Investment and Intra-ASEAN Investment, were implemented during 1996. In February 1997 ASEAN central bank governors agreed to strengthen efforts to combat currency speculation through the established network of foreign-exchange repurchase agreements. However, from mid-1997 several Asian currencies were undermined by speculative activities. Subsequent unsuccessful attempts to support the foreign-exchange rates contributed to a collapse in the value of financial markets in some countries and to a reversal of the region's economic growth, at least in the short term, while governments undertook macro-economic structural reforms. In early December ASEAN ministers of finance, meeting in Malaysia, agreed to liberalize markets for financial services and to strengthen surveillance of member country economies in order to help prevent further deterioration of the regional economy. The ministers also endorsed a proposal for the establishment of an Asian funding facility to provide emergency assistance in support of international credit and structural reform programmes. At the informal summit meeting held later in December ASEAN leaders issued a joint statement in which they expressed the need for mutual support to counter the region's financial crisis and urged greater international assistance to help overcome the situation and address the underlying problems. The heads of government also resolved to accelerate the implementation of the AIA in order to promote intra-ASEAN trade and to attract foreign direct investment. In July 1998 the ASEAN Ministerial Meeting endorsed the decisions of finance ministers, taken in February, to promote greater use of regional currencies for trade payments and to establish an economic surveillance mechanism. In October ministers of economic affairs, meeting in Manila, the Philippines, signed a framework agreement on the AIA, which was expected to provide for equal treatment of domestic and other ASEAN direct investment proposals within the grouping by 2010, and of all foreign investors by 2020. The meeting also confirmed that the proposed ASEAN Surveillance Process (ASP) to monitor the economic stability and financial systems of member states would be implemented with immediate effect, and would require the voluntary submission of economic information by all members to a monitoring committee, to be based in Jakarta, Indonesia. The ASP and the framework agreement on the AIA were incorporated into the Hanoi Plan of Action, adopted by heads of state in December 1998. The AIA was to be implemented by means of individual and collective action plans according to the following schedules: Co-operation and facilitation; Promotion and awareness; and Liberalization. The summit meeting also resolved to accelerate reforms, particularly in the banking and financial sectors, in order to strengthen the region's economies, and to promote the liberalization of the financial services sector. In March 1999 ASEAN ministers of trade and industry, meeting in Phuket, Thailand, as the AIA Council, agreed to open their manufacturing, agriculture, fisheries, forestry and mining industries to foreign investment. Investment restrictions affecting those industries were to be eliminated by 2003 in most cases, although Laos and Viet Nam were granted until 2010 to eliminate restrictions. In addition, ministers adopted a number of measures to encourage investment in the region, including access to three-year corporate income-tax exemptions, and tax allowances of 30% for investors. The AIA agreement formally entered into force in June 1999, having been ratified by all member countries.

AGRICULTURE, FISHERIES AND FORESTRY

In October 1983 a ministerial agreement on fisheries co-operation was concluded, providing for the joint management of fish resources, the sharing of technology, and co-operation in marketing. In July 1994 a Conference on Fisheries Management and Development Strategies in the ASEAN region, held in Bangkok, Thailand, resolved to enhance fish production through the introduction of new technologies, aquaculture development, improvements of product quality and greater involvement by the private sector.

Co-operation in forestry is focused on joint projects, funded by ASEAN's dialogue partners, which include a Forest Tree Seed Centre, an Institute of Forest Management and the ASEAN Timber Technology Centre. In April 1995 representatives of the ASEAN Secretariat and private-sector groups met to co-ordinate the implementation of a scheme to promote the export of ASEAN agricultural and forestry products.

ASEAN holds an emergency rice reserve, amounting to 53,000 metric tons, as part of its efforts to ensure food security in the region. There is an established ASEAN programme of training and study exchanges for farm workers, agricultural experts and members of agricultural co-operatives. During 1998 ASEAN was particularly concerned with the impact of the region's economic crisis on the agricultural sector, and of the possible effects of climatic change. In September ministers of agriculture and forestry, meeting in Hanoi, Viet Nam, endorsed a Strategic Plan of Action on ASEAN Co-operation in Food, Agriculture and Forestry for the period 1999–2004. The Plan focused on programmes and activities aimed at enhancing food security, and the international competitiveness of ASEAN food, agriculture and forestry products, promoting the sustainable use and conservation of natural resources, encouraging greater involvement by the private sector in the food and agricultural industry, and strengthening joint approaches on international and regional issues. An ASEAN Task Force has been established to harmonize regulations on agricultural products derived from biotechnology. In December 1998 heads of state resolved further to improve food security in the region by establishing an ASEAN Food Security Information Service to enhance the capacity of member states to forecast and manage food supplies and the use of basic commodities.

MINERALS AND ENERGY

In April 1994, a meeting of the ASEAN economic ministers on energy co-operation recognized the significance of energy and power development in sustaining the overall growth of the region's economies. A medium-term programme of action on energy co-operation, for the period 1995–99, included measures to promote energy efficiency, the diversification of energy sources, training and research activities, and the exchange of information on energy policies among ASEAN members. In 1990 efforts to establish an ASEAN electricity grid were initiated. The ASEAN Centre of Energy (ACE), based in Jakarta, Indonesia, provides an energy information network, promotes the establishment of interconnecting energy structures among ASEAN member countries, supports the development of renewable energy resources and encourages co-operation in energy efficiency and conservation. An ASEAN energy business forum is held annually and attended by representatives of the energy industry in the private and public sectors.

A Framework of Co-operation in Minerals was adopted by an ASEAN working group of experts in August 1993. The group has also developed a programme of action for ASEAN co-operation in the development and utilization of industrial minerals to promote the exploration and development of mineral resources in ASEAN member countries, the transfer of mining technology and expertise, the participation of the private sector in industrial mineral production. The programme of action is implemented by an ASEAN Regional Development Centre for Mineral Resources, which also conducts workshops and training programmes relating to the sector.

TRANSPORT AND COMMUNICATIONS

ASEAN aims to promote greater co-operation in the transport and communications sector, and in particular to develop multi-modal transport; achieve interoperability and interconnectivity in telecommunications; harmonize road transport laws and regulations; improve air space management; develop ASEAN legislation for the carriage of dangerous goods and waste by land and sea; and human resources development. The summit meeting, held in December 1998, agreed to develop a trans-ASEAN transportation network by 2000, comprising principal routes for the movement of goods and people. (The deadline for the full implementation of the agreement was subsequently advanced to the end of 2000.) In September 1999 ASEAN ministers of transport and communications resolved to establish working groups to strengthen co-operation within the sector and adopted a programme of action for further development of the sector in the period 1999–2004.

SCIENCE AND TECHNOLOGY

The Hanoi Plan of Action, adopted in December 1998, envisaged a series of measures aimed at promoting development in the fields of science and technology, including the establishment of networks of science and technology centres of excellence and academic institutions, the creation of a technology scan mechanism, the promotion of public- and private-sector co-operation in scientific and technological (particularly information technology) activities, and an increase in research on strategic technologies. ASEAN supports co-operation in food science and technology, meteorology and geophysics, microelectronics and information technology, biotechnology, non-conventional energy research, materials science and technology and marine science. There is an ASEAN Science Fund, used to finance policy studies in science and technology and to support information exchange and dissemination.

In October 1999 an e-ASEAN initiative was launched, which aimed to promote and co-ordinate electronic commerce and internet utilization. In November 2000 the informal meeting of ASEAN heads of government approved an e-ASEAN Framework Agreement to further the aims of the initiative. The Agreement incorporated commitments to develop and strengthen the region's information infrastructure and to accelerate tariff reduction on information technology products (with the aim of eliminating all tariffs in the sector by 2010).

ENVIRONMENT

A ministerial meeting on the environment, held in April 1994, approved an ASEAN Strategic Plan of Action on the Environment for the period 1994–98, which established long-term objectives on environmental quality and standards for the ASEAN region and aimed to enhance joint action to address environmental concerns. At the same time the ministers adopted standards for air quality and river water which were to be achieved by all ASEAN member countries by 2010. In June 1995 ministers agreed to co-operate in order to counter the problems of transboundary pollution. In December 1997 ASEAN heads of state endorsed a Regional Haze Action Plan to address the environmental problems resulting from forest fires, which had afflicted several countries in the region throughout that year. A Haze Technical Task Force undertook to implement the plan in 1998, with assistance from the UN Environment Programme, and was to assist members to formulate national haze action plans. In March ministers of the environment requested international financial assistance to help to mitigate the dangers of forest fires in Indonesia, which had suffered an estimated US $1,000m. in damages in 1997 as a result of the fires (of an estimated total of US $1,300m. suffered by the region as a whole, mainly resulting from health problems and the effects on tourism). Sub-regional fire-fighting arrangement working groups for Sumatra and Borneo were established in April 1998, and in May the Task Force organized a regional workshop to strengthen ASEAN capacity to prevent and alleviate the haze caused by the extensive fires. A pilot project of aerial surveillance of the areas in the region most at risk of forest fires was initiated in July. In December heads of government resolved to establish an ASEAN Regional Research and Training Centre for Land and Forest Fire Management by 2004. Other environmental objectives approved at the meeting included: implementation of a water conservation programme by 2001; greater co-operation in the integrated protection and management of coastal zones; establishment of a regional centre or network for the promotion of environmentally-sound technologies by 2004; and formation and adoption of an ASEAN protocol on access to genetic resources by 2003. An ASEAN Regional Centre for Biodiversity Conservation was established in February 1999.

SOCIAL DEVELOPMENT

ASEAN concerns in social development include youth development, the role of women, health and nutrition, education, labour affairs and disaster management. In December 1993 ASEAN ministers responsible for social affairs adopted a Plan of Action for Children, which provided a framework for regional co-operation for the survival, protection and development of children in member countries. An ASEAN task force on AIDS has been created, and its first meeting was held in Jakarta in March 1993.

ASEAN supports efforts to combat drug abuse and illegal drugs-trafficking. It aims to promote education and drug-awareness campaigns throughout the region, and administers a project to strengthen the training of personnel involved in combating drug concerns. In October 1994 a meeting of ASEAN Senior Officials on Drug Matters approved a three-year plan of action on drug abuse, which provided a framework for co-operation in four priority areas: preventive drug education; treatment and rehabilitation; law enforcement; and research. In July 1998 ASEAN ministers of foreign affairs signed a Joint Declaration for a Drug-Free ASEAN, which envisaged greater co-operation among member states, in particular in information exchange, educational resources and legal procedures, in order to eliminate the illicit production, processing and trafficking of narcotic substances by 2020. (This deadline was subsequently advanced to 2015.)

In December 1998 ASEAN leaders approved a series of measures aimed at mitigating the social impact of the financial and economic crises which had affected many countries in the region. Plans of Action were to be implemented on ASEAN Rural Development and Poverty Eradication, and Social Safety Nets, which aimed to protect the most vulnerable members of society. The summit meeting also emphasized the need to promote job generation as a key element of strategies for economic recovery and growth. In November 2000 heads of government endorsed an Initiative for ASEAN Integration, which aimed to reduce economic disparities within the region through effective co-operation, in particular in training and other educational opportunities.

TOURISM

National Tourist Organizations from ASEAN countries meet regularly to assist in co-ordinating the region's tourist industry, and a

Tourism Forum is held annually to promote the sector. The first formal meeting of ASEAN ministers of tourism was held in January 1998, in Cebu, the Philippines. The meeting adopted a Plan of Action on ASEAN Co-operation in Tourism, which aimed to promote intra-ASEAN travel, greater investment in the sector, joint marketing of the region as a single tourist destination and environmentally sustainable tourism. The second meeting of ASEAN ministers of tourism was held in Singapore in January 1999. Ministers agreed to appoint country co-ordinators to implement various initiatives, including the designation of 2002 as 'Visit ASEAN Millennium Year'; research to promote the region as a tourist destination in the 21st century, and to develop a cruise-ship industry; and the establishment of a network of ASEAN Tourism Training Centres to develop new skills and technologies in the tourism industry by 2001. The third meeting of tourism ministers, held in Bangkok, Thailand, in January 2000, agreed to reformulate the Visit ASEAN Millennium Year initiative as a long-term Visit ASEAN campaign.

CULTURE AND INFORMATION

Regular workshops and festivals are held in visual and performing arts, youth music, radio, television and films, and print and interpersonal media. In addition, ASEAN administers a News Exchange and provides support for the training of editors, journalists and information officers. In July 1997 ASEAN ministers of foreign affairs endorsed the establishment of an ASEAN Foundation to promote awareness of the organization and greater participation in its activities; this was inaugurated in July 1998.

Publications

Annual Report of the ASEAN Standing Committee.

ASEAN Investment Report (annually).

ASEAN Journal on Science and Technology for Development (2 a year).

ASEAN Update (6 a year).

Business ASEAN (6 a year).

Information Series and *Documents Series*.

BANK FOR INTERNATIONAL SETTLEMENTS—BIS

Address: Centralbahnplatz 2, 4002 Basel, Switzerland.

Telephone: (61) 2808080; **fax:** (61) 2809100; **e-mail:** emailmaster@bis.org; **internet:** www.bis.org.

The Bank for International Settlements was founded pursuant to the Hague Agreements of 1930 to promote co-operation among national central banks and to provide additional facilities for international financial operations.

Organization

(April 2001)

GENERAL MEETING

The General Meeting is held annually in June and is attended by representatives of the central banks of countries in which shares have been subscribed. At January 2001 the central banks of the following authorities were entitled to attend and vote at General Meetings of the BIS: Argentina, Australia, Austria, Belgium, Brazil, Bulgaria, Canada, the People's Republic of China, the Czech Republic, Denmark, Estonia, Finland, France, Germany, Greece, Hong Kong, Hungary, Iceland, India, Ireland, Italy, Japan, the Republic of Korea, Latvia, Lithuania, Malaysia, Mexico, the Netherlands, Norway, Poland, Portugal, Romania, Russia, Saudi Arabia, Singapore, Slovakia, South Africa, Spain, Sweden, Switzerland, Thailand, Turkey, the United Kingdom and the USA. The European Central Bank became a shareholder in December 1999. The legal status of the Yugoslav issue of the Bank's capital remains in suspense. However, new shares have been issued, on an interim basis, to the central banks of four of the successor states of the former Yugoslavia, i.e. Bosnia and Herzegovina, Croatia, the former Yugoslav republic of Macedonia and Slovenia, pending a comprehensive settlement of all outstanding issues.

BOARD OF DIRECTORS

The Board of Directors is responsible for the conduct of the Bank's operations at the highest level, and comprises the Governors in office of the central banks of Belgium, France, Germany, Italy, the United Kingdom and the USA, each of whom appoints another member of the same nationality. The statutes also provide for the election to the Board of not more than nine Governors of other member central banks: those of Canada, Japan, the Netherlands, Sweden and Switzerland are elected members of the Board.

Chairman of the Board and President of the Bank: URBAN BÄCKSTRÖM (Sweden).

MANAGEMENT

General Manager: ANDREW CROCKETT (United Kingdom).

The Bank has a staff of about 500 employees, from 35 countries. In July 1998 the BIS inaugurated its first overseas administrative unit, the Representative Office for Asia and the Pacific, which was based in Hong Kong. In March 2001 an agreement was reached to open a Representative Office for the Americas in Mexico City, Mexico.

Activities

The BIS is an international financial institution whose role is to promote international monetary and financial co-operation, and to fulfil the function of a 'central banks' bank'. Although it has the legal form of a company limited by shares, it is an international organization governed by international law, and enjoys special privileges and immunities in keeping with its role (a Headquarters Agreement was concluded with Switzerland in 1987). The participating central banks were originally given the option of subscribing the shares themselves or arranging for their subscription in their own countries: thus the BIS also has some private shareholders, but they have no right of participation in the General Meeting. Some 86% of the total share capital is in the hands of central banks and 14% is held by private shareholders. In January 2001 an extraordinary general meeting amended the Bank's statutes to restrict ownership to central banks. Accordingly, all shares held by private shareholders were to be repurchased at a specified rate of compensation.

FINANCE

The authorized capital of the Bank is 1,500m. gold francs, divided into 600,000 shares of 2,500 gold francs each.

Statement of Account*
(In gold francs; units of 0.29032258 . . . gram of fine gold—Art. 4 of the Statutes; 31 March 2000)

Assets		%
Gold (bars)	2,265,425,772	3.03
Cash on hand and on sight		
a/c with banks	11,382,465	0.02
Treasury bills	7,853,868,515	10.49
Time deposits and advances . .	43,094,217,297	57.59
Securities at term . . .	21,408,027,645	28.61
Miscellaneous	202,744,017	0.27
Total	74,835,665,711	100.00

Liabilities		%
Authorized cap.: 1,500,000,000		
Issued cap.: 1,292,912,500		
viz. 529,165 shares of which		
25% paid up	330,728,125	0.44
Reserves	2,911,547,717	3.89
Deposits (gold)	2,820,208,609	3.77
Deposits (currencies) . . .	65,903,655,555	88.06
Miscellaneous	2,814,867,462	3.76
Dividend payable on 1 July . .	54,658,243	0.07
Total	74,835,665,711	100.0

* Assets and liabilities in US dollars are converted at a fixed rate of US $208 per fine ounce of gold (equivalent to 1 gold franc = $1.94149 . . .) and all other items in currencies on the basis of market rates against the US dollar.

BANKING OPERATIONS

The BIS assists central banks in managing and investing their monetary reserves: in 2000 some 120 international financial institutions and central banks from all over the world had deposits with the BIS, representing around 7% of world foreign exchange reserves.

The BIS uses the funds deposited with it partly for lending to central banks. Its credit transactions may take the form of swaps against gold; covered credits secured by means of a pledge of gold or marketable short-term securities; credits against gold or currency deposits of the same amount and for the same duration held with the BIS; unsecured credits in the form of advances or deposits; or standby credits, which in individual instances are backed by guarantees given by member central banks. In addition, the Bank undertakes operations in foreign exchange and in gold, both with central banks and with the markets.

In 1982, faced with the increasingly critical debt situation of some Latin American countries and the resultant threat to the viability of the international financial system, the BIS granted comparatively large-scale loans to central banks that did not number among its shareholders: the central banks of Argentina, Brazil and Mexico were granted bridging loans pending the disbursement of balance-of-payments credits extended by the IMF. These facilities amounted to almost US $3,000m., all of which had been repaid by the end of 1983. The Bank subsequently made similar loans, but with decreasing frequency. Since 1990 the BIS has contributed funds to bridging facilities arranged for the central banks of Venezuela, Guyana, Hungary, Romania, the former Yugoslav republic of Macedonia, Mexico (in 1995) and Thailand (in August 1997). Within the framework of an international financial programme, approved in support of the Brazilian economy in late 1998, the Bank was to co-ordinate a credit facility of up to $13,280m. in favour of the Banco Central do Brasil. Funds were provided with the backing or guarantee of 19 central banks; the load was repaid in full in April 2000.

The BIS also engages in traditional types of investment: funds not required for lending to central banks are placed in the market as deposits with commercial banks and purchases of short-term negotiable paper, including Treasury bills. Such operations constitute a major part of the Bank's business.

Because the central banks' monetary reserves must be available at short notice, they can only be placed with the BIS at short term, for fixed periods and with clearly defined repayment terms. The BIS has to match its assets to the maturity structure and nature of its commitments, and must therefore conduct its business with special regard to maintaining a high degree of liquidity.

The Bank's operations must be in conformity with the monetary policy of the central banks of the countries concerned. It is not permitted to make advances to governments or to open current accounts in their name. Real estate transactions are also excluded.

INTERNATIONAL MONETARY CO-OPERATION

Governors of central banks meet for regular discussions at the BIS to co-ordinate international monetary policy and ensure orderly conditions on the international financial markets. There is close co-operation with the IMF and the World Bank. The BIS participates in meetings of the so-called Group of 10 (G-10) industrialized nations (see IMF p. 94), which has been a major forum for discussion of international monetary issues since its establishment in 1962. Governors of central banks of the G-10 countries convene for regular Basle Monthly Meetings. In 1971 a Standing Committee of the G-10 central banks was established at the BIS to consider aspects of the development of Euro-currency markets. In February 1999 the G-10 renamed the body as the Committee on the Global Financial System, and approved a revised mandate to undertake systematic short-term monitoring of global financial system conditions; longer-term analysis of the functioning of financial markets; and the articulation of policy recommendations aimed at improving market functioning and promoting stability. The Committee was to meet four times a year.

In 1974 the Governors of central banks of the G-10 set up the Basle Committee on Banking Supervision (whose secretariat is provided by the BIS) to co-ordinate banking supervision at the international level. The Committee pools information on banking supervisory regulations and surveillance systems, including the supervision of banks' foreign currency business, identifies possible danger areas and proposes measures to safeguard the banks' solvency and liquidity. An International Conference of Banking Supervisors is held every two years. In 1997 the Committee published new guide-lines, entitled Core Principles for Effective Banking Supervision, that were intended to provide a comprehensive set of standards to ensure sound banking. In 1998 the Committee was concerned with the development and implementation of the Core Principles, particularly given the ongoing financial and economic crisis affecting several Asian countries and instability of other major economies. A Financial Stability Institute was established in 1998,

jointly by the BIS and Basle Committee, to enhance the capacity of central banks and supervisory bodies to implement aspects of the Core Principles, through the provision of training programmes and other policy workshops. The Committee was a sponsor of the Joint Year 2000 Council, which aimed to ensure an effective response to the technological difficulties resulting from the millennium date change and to supervise banks' compliance with adopted strategies.

In February 1999 ministers of finance and governors of the central banks of the Group of Seven (G-7) industrialized nations approved the establishment of a Financial Stability Forum to strengthen co-operation among the world's largest economies and economic bodies, to improve the monitoring of international finance and to prevent a recurrence of the economic crises of 1997 and 1998. The General Manager of the BIS was appointed to chair the Forum for an initial three-year term. The first meeting of the Forum, comprising representatives of G-7 ministries of finance and central banks, and of international financial institutions and regulatory bodies, took place at the headquarters of the IMF in Washington, DC, USA, in April 1999. Three working groups were established to study aspects of highly leveraged, or unregulated, institutions, offshore financial centres, and short-term capital flows. In November the Forum constituted additional groups to review deposit insurance schemes and to consider measures to promote implementation of international standards.

The Bank organizes and provides the secretariat for periodic meetings of experts, such as the Group of Computer Experts, the Committee on Payment and Settlement Systems, the Group of Experts on Monetary and Economic Data Bank Questions, which aims to develop a data bank service for the G-10 central banks and the BIS, and the Committee of Experts on Gold and Foreign Exchange, which monitors financial market developments.

Since January 1998 the BIS has hosted the secretariat of the International Association of Insurance Supervisors, established in 1994. The Association aims to promote co-operation within the insurance industry with regard to effective supervision and the development of domestic insurance markets.

RESEARCH

The Bank's Monetary and Economic Department conducts research, particularly into monetary and financial questions; collects and publishes data on securities markets and international banking developments; and organizes a data bank for central banks. The BIS Annual Report provides an independent analysis of monetary and economic developments. Statistics on international banking and on external indebtedness are also published regularly.

AGENCY AND TRUSTEE FUNCTIONS

Throughout its history the BIS has undertaken various duties as Trustee Fiscal Agent or Depository with regard to international loan agreements. From October 1986 the BIS performed the functions of Agent for the private European Currency Unit (ECU) clearing and settlement system, in accordance with the provisions of successive agreements concluded between the then ECU Banking Association (now Euro Banking Association—EBA), based in Paris, and the BIS. This arrangement was terminated following the introduction of the euro on 1 January 1999, when the ECU clearing system was replaced by a new euro clearing system of the EBA. At that time 62 banks had been granted the status of clearing bank by the EBA.

In April 1994 the BIS assumed new functions in connection with the rescheduling of Brazil's external debt, which had been agreed by the Brazilian Government in November 1993. In accordance with two collateral pledge agreements, the BIS acts in the capacity of Collateral Agent to hold and invest collateral for the benefit of the holders of certain US dollar-denominated bonds, maturing in 15 or 30 years, which have been issued by Brazil under the rescheduling arrangements. The Bank acts in a similar capacity for Peru, in accordance with external debt agreements concluded in November 1996 and a collateral agreement signed with the BIS in March 1997, and for Côte d'Ivoire, under a restructuring agreement signed in May 1997 and collateral agreement signed in March 1998.

Publications

Annual Report (in English, French, German and Italian).

Quarterly Review: International Banking and Financial Market Developments (English, French, German and Italian).

The BIS Consolidated International Banking Statistics (every 6 months).

Joint BIS-IMF-OECD-World Bank Statistics on External Debt (quarterly).

Regular OTC Derivatives Market Statistics (every 6 months).

Central Bank Survey of Foreign Exchange and Derivatives Market Activity (3 a year).

CARIBBEAN COMMUNITY AND COMMON MARKET—CARICOM

Address: Bank of Guyana Building, POB 10827, Georgetown, Guyana.
Telephone: (2) 69281; **fax:** (2) 67816; **e-mail:** carisec3@caricom.org; **internet:** www.caricom.org.

CARICOM was formed in 1973 by the Treaty of Chaguaramas, signed in Trinidad, as a movement towards unity in the Caribbean; it replaced the Caribbean Free Trade Association (CARIFTA), founded in 1965. A revision of the Treaty of Chaguaramas (by means of nine separate Protocols) was undertaken in the 1990s, to institute greater regional integration and to establish a single Caribbean market and economy.

MEMBERS

Anguilla*	Jamaica
Antigua and Barbuda	Montserrat
Bahamas†	Saint Christopher and Nevis
Barbados	Saint Lucia
Belize	Saint Vincent and the Grenadines
British Virgin Islands*	Suriname
Dominica	Trinidad and Tobago
Grenada	Turks and Caicos Islands*
Guyana	

* The British Virgin Islands and the Turks and Caicos Islands were granted associate membership in 1991; Anguilla's application for associate membership was approved in July 1998 and formally implemented in July 1999.
† The Bahamas is a member of the Community but not the Common Market.
Note: Haiti was accepted as a full member of the Community in July 1997, although the final terms and conditions of its accession had yet to be concluded; it was invited to participate in the deliberations of all the organs and bodies of the Community in the interim. The terms for Haiti's accession were agreed in July 1999. Aruba, Bermuda, the Cayman Islands, Colombia, the Dominican Republic, Mexico, the Netherlands Antilles, Puerto Rico and Venezuela have observer status with the Community.

Organization

(April 2001)

HEADS OF GOVERNMENT CONFERENCE AND BUREAU

The Conference is the final authority of the Community and determines policy. It is responsible for the conclusion of treaties on behalf of the Community and for entering into relationships between the Community and international organizations and states. Decisions of the Conference are generally taken unanimously. Heads of government meet annually, although inter-sessional meetings may be convened.

At a special meeting of the Conference, held in Trinidad and Tobago in October 1992, participants decided to establish a Heads of Government Bureau, with the capacity to initiate proposals, to update consensus and to secure the implementation of CARICOM decisions. The Bureau became operational in December, comprising the Chairman of the Conference, as Chairman, as well as the incoming and outgoing Chairmen of the Conference, and the Secretary-General of the Conference, in the capacity of Chief Executive Officer.

COMMUNITY COUNCIL OF MINISTERS

In October 1992 CARICOM heads of government agreed that a Caribbean Community Council of Ministers should be established to replace the existing Common Market Council of Ministers as the second highest organ of the Community. Protocol I amending the Treaty of Chaguaramas, to restructure the organs and institutions of the Community, was formally adopted at a meeting of CARICOM heads of government in February 1997 and was signed by all member states in July. The inaugural meeting of the Community Council of Ministers was held in Nassau, the Bahamas, in February 1998. The Council consists of ministers responsible for community affairs, as well as other government ministers designated by member states, and is responsible for the development of the Community's strategic planning and co-ordination in the areas of economic integration, functional co-operation and external relations.

MINISTERIAL COUNCILS

The principal organs of the Community are assisted in their functions by the following bodies, established under Protocol I amending the Treaty of Chaguaramas: the Council for Trade and Economic Development (COTED); the Council for Foreign and Community Relations (COFCOR); the Council for Human and Social Development (COHSOD); and the Council for Finance and Planning (COFAP). The Councils are responsible for formulating policies, promoting their implementation and supervising co-operation in the relevant areas.

SECRETARIAT

The Secretariat is the main administrative body of the Caribbean Community. The functions of the Secretariat are: to service meetings of the Community and of its Committees; to take appropriate follow-up action on decisions made at such meetings; to carry out studies on questions of economic and functional co-operation relating to the region as a whole; to provide services to member states at their request in respect of matters relating to the achievement of the objectives of the Community.
Secretary-General: EDWIN W. CARRINGTON (Trinidad and Tobago).
Deputy Secretary-General: Dr CARLA BARNETT (Belize).

Activities

REGIONAL INTEGRATION

In 1989 CARICOM heads of government established the 15-member West Indian Commission to study regional political and economic integration. The Commission's final report, submitted in July 1992, recommended that CARICOM should remain a community of sovereign states (rather than a federation), but should strengthen the integration process and expand to include the wider Caribbean region. It recommended the formation of an Association of Caribbean States (ACS), to include all the countries within and surrounding the Caribbean Basin (see p. 306). The Heads of Government Conference that was held in October 1992 established an Inter-Governmental Task Force, which was to undertake preparations for a reorientation of CARICOM. In February 1993 it presented a draft Charter of Civil Society for the Community, which set out principles in the areas of democracy, government, parliament, freedom of the press and human rights. The Charter was signed by Community heads of government in February 1997. Suriname was admitted to the organization in July 1995. In July 1997 the Heads of Government Conference agreed to admit Haiti as a member, although the terms and conditions of its accession had yet to be negotiated. In February 2001 heads of government resolved to establish a CARICOM Office in Haiti. In November 1997 the Secretaries-General of CARICOM and the ACS signed a Co-operation Agreement to formalize the reciprocal procedures through which the organizations work to enhance and facilitate regional integration.

In August 1998 CARICOM and the Dominican Republic signed a free-trade accord, covering trade in goods and services, technical barriers to trade, government procurement, and sanitary and phytosanitary measures and standards. A protocol to the agreement was signed in April 2000, following the resolution of differences concerning exempted items. The accord was ratified by the Dominican Republic in February 2001.

In July 1999 CARICOM heads of government endorsed proposals to establish a Caribbean Court of Justice, which, it was provisionally agreed, would be located in Port of Spain, Trinidad and Tobago. The Court was intended to replace the Judicial Committee of the Privy Council as the Court of Final Appeal for those countries recognizing its jurisdiction, and was also to adjudicate on trade disputes and on the interpretation of the CARICOM Treaty. An agreement establishing the Court was formally signed by 10 member countries in February 2001.

CO-ORDINATION OF FOREIGN POLICY

The co-ordination of foreign policies of member states is listed as one of the main objectives of the Community in its founding treaty. Activities include: strengthening member states' position in international organizations; joint diplomatic action on issues of particular interest to the Caribbean; joint co-operation arrangements with third countries and organizations; and the negotiation of free-trade agreements with third countries and other regional groupings. This last area of activity has assumed increasing importance since the agreement in 1994 by almost all the governments of countries in the Americas to establish a 'Free Trade Area of the Americas' (FTAA) by 2005. In April 1997 CARICOM inaugurated a Regional Negotiating Machinery body to co-ordinate the region's external negotiations. The main focus of activities was to be the establishment of the FTAA, ACP relations with the EU, and multilateral trade negotiations under the WTO.

In 1990 a working group was established with Brazil, Colombia and Venezuela to consider ways of developing regional economic co-operation, including greater self-sufficiency in food, joint exploration for mineral resources, joint trading policies, and co-operation in communications and transport systems. In July 1991 Venezuela applied for membership of CARICOM, and offered a non-reciprocal free-trade agreement for CARICOM exports to Venezuela, over an initial five-year period. In October 1993 the newly-established Group of Three (Colombia, Mexico and Venezuela) signed joint agreements with CARICOM and Suriname on combating drugs trafficking and environmental protection. In June 1994 CARICOM and Colombia concluded an agreement on trade, economic and technical co-operation, which, *inter alia*, gives special treatment to the least-developed CARICOM countries. CARICOM has observer status in the Latin American Rio Group (see p. 318).

In 1992 Cuba applied for observer status within CARICOM, and in July 1993 a joint commission was inaugurated to establish closer ties between CARICOM and Cuba. In July 1997 the heads of government agreed to pursue consideration of a free-trade accord between the Community and Cuba. In February 1992 ministers of foreign affairs from CARICOM and Central American states met to discuss future co-operation, in view of the imminent conclusion of the North American Free Trade Agreement (NAFTA, see p. 240) between the USA, Canada and Mexico. It was agreed that a consultative forum would be established to discuss the possible formation of a Caribbean and Central American free-trade zone. In October 1993 CARICOM declared its support for NAFTA, but requested a 'grace period', during which the region's exports would have parity with Mexican products, and in March 1994 requested that it should be considered for early entry into NAFTA. In July 1996 the heads of government expressed strong concern over the complaint lodged with the World Trade Organization (WTO) by the USA, Ecuador, Guatemala and Honduras regarding the European Union's import regime on bananas, which gives preferential access to bananas from the ACP countries (see the EU, p. 207). CARICOM requested the US Government to withdraw its complaint and to negotiate a settlement. Nevertheless, WTO panel hearings on the complaint were initiated in September. Banana producers from the ACP countries were granted third-party status, at the insistence of the Eastern Caribbean ambassador to the EU, Edwin Laurent. In December a special meeting of the Heads of Government Conference was convened, in Barbados, in order to formulate a common position on relations with the USA, in particular with respect to measures to combat illegal drugs-trafficking, following reports that the US Government was planning to impose punitive measures against certain regional authorities, owing to their perceived failure to implement effective controls on illicit drugs. The Conference confirmed the need for comprehensive co-operation and technical assistance to combat the problem, but warned that any adverse measures implemented by the USA would undermine CARICOM–US relations. The Conference decided to establish a Caribbean Security Task Force to help formulate a single regional agreement on maritime interdiction, incorporating agreements already concluded by individual members.

In May 1997 CARICOM heads of government met the US President, Bill Clinton, to discuss issues of mutual concern. A partnership for prosperity and security was established at the meeting, and arrangements were instituted for annual consultations between the ministers of foreign affairs of CARICOM countries and the US Secretary of State. However, the Community failed to secure a commitment by the USA to grant the region's exports 'NAFTA-parity' status, or to guarantee concessions to the region's banana industry, following a temporary ruling of the WTO, issued in March, upholding the US trade complaint. The WTO ruling was confirmed in May and endorsed by the WTO dispute settlement body in September. The USA's opposition to a new EU banana policy (which was to terminate the import licensing system, extending import quotas to 'dollar' producers, while maintaining a limited duty-free quota for Caribbean producers) was strongly criticized by CARICOM leaders, meeting in July 1998. In March 1999 the 10th Inter-Sessional meeting of the Conference of Heads of Government, held in Paramaribo, Suriname, issued a statement condemning the imposition by the USA of sanctions against a number of EU imports, in protest at the revised EU banana regime, and the consequences of this action on Caribbean economies, and agreed to review its co-operation with the USA under the partnership for prosperity and security.

During 1998 CARICOM was particularly concerned by the movement within Nevis to secede from its federation with Saint Christopher. In July heads of government agreed to dispatch a mediation team to the country (postponed until September). The Heads of Government Conference held in March 1999 welcomed the establishment of a Constitutional Task Force by the local authorities to prepare a draft constitution, on the basis of recommendations of a previous constitutional commission and the outcome of a series of public meetings. In July 1998 heads of government expressed concern at the hostility between the Government and opposition groupings in Guyana. The two sides signed an agreement, under CARICOM auspices, and in September a CARICOM mediation mission visited Guyana to promote further dialogue. CARICOM has declared its support for Guyana in its territorial disputes with Venezuela and Suriname. In June 2000 CARICOM initiated negotiations following Suriname's removal of petroleum drilling equipment from Guyanan territorial waters. In March 2000 heads of government issued a statement supporting the territorial integrity and security of Belize in that country's ongoing border dispute with Guatemala. CARICOM subsequently urged both countries to implement the provisions of an agreement signed in November.

ECONOMIC CO-OPERATION

The Caribbean Community's main field of activity is economic integration, by means of a Caribbean Common Market which replaced the former Caribbean Free Trade Association. The Secretariat and the Caribbean Development Bank undertake research on the best means of facing economic difficulties, and meetings of the Chief Executives of commercial banks and of central bank officials are also held with the aim of strengthening regional co-operation. In October 1998 the CARICOM Bureau requested an urgent assessment of the impact on the region of the financial and economic instability apparent in several major economies.

During the 1980s the economic difficulties of member states hindered the development of intra-regional trade. At the annual Conference held in June/July 1987, the heads of government agreed to dismantle all obstacles to trade within CARICOM by October 1988. This was implemented as planned, but included a three-year period of protection for 17 products from the member countries of the Organisation of Eastern Caribbean States (OECS, see p. 309).

In July 1984 heads of government agreed to establish a common external tariff (CET) on certain products, in order to protect domestic industries, although implementation of the CET was considerably delayed (see below). They also urged the necessity of structural adjustment in the economies of the region, including measures to expand production and reduce imports. In 1989 the Conference of Heads of Government agreed to implement, by July 1993, a series of measures to encourage the creation of a single Caribbean market. These included the establishment of a CARICOM Industrial Programming Scheme; the inauguration of the CARICOM Enterprise Regime; abolition of passport requirements for CARICOM nationals travelling within the region; full implementation of the rules of origin and the revised scheme for the harmonization of fiscal incentives; free movement of skilled workers; removal of all remaining regional barriers to trade; establishment of a regional system of air and sea transport; and the introduction of a scheme for regional capital movement. A CARICOM Export Development Council, established in November 1989, undertook a three-year export development project to stimulate trade within CARICOM and to promote exports outside the region.

In August 1990 CARICOM heads of government mandated the governors of CARICOM members' central banks to begin a study of the means to achieve a monetary union within CARICOM; they also institutionalized meetings of CARICOM ministers of finance and senior finance officials, to take place twice a year.

The initial deadline of 1 January 1991 for the establishment of a CET was not achieved, and in July a new deadline of 1 October was set for those members which had not complied—Antigua and Barbuda, Belize, Montserrat, Saint Christopher and Nevis and Saint Lucia, whose governments feared that the tariff would cause an increase in the rate of inflation and damage domestic industries. This deadline was later (again unsuccessfully) extended to February 1992. The tariff, which imposed a maximum level of duty of 45% on imports (compared with a maximum rate of 20% imposed by members of the Andean Group and the Central American Common Market), was also criticized by the World Bank, the IMF and the US Government as being likely to reduce the region's competitiveness. At a special meeting, held in October 1992, CARICOM heads of government agreed to reduce the maximum level of tariffs to between 30% and 35%, to be in effect by 30 June 1993 (the level was to be further lowered, to 25%–30% by 1995). The Bahamas, however, was not party to these trading arrangements (since it is a member of the Community but not of the Common Market), and Belize was granted an extension for the implementation of the new tariff levels. At the Heads of Government Conference, held in July 1995 in Guyana, Suriname was admitted as a full member of CARICOM and acceded to the treaty establishing the Common Market. It was granted until 1 January 1996 for implementation of the tariff reductions.

The 1995 Heads of Government Conference approved additional measures to promote the single market. The free movement of skilled workers (mainly graduates from recognized regional institutions) was to be permitted from 1 January 1996. At the same time an agreement on the mutual protection and provision of social security benefits was to enter into force. The meeting also agreed to implement the 'open-sky' agreement enabling all CARICOM-owned and -controlled airlines to operate freely within the region.

In July 1996 the heads of government decided that CARICOM ministers of finance, central bank governors and planning agencies should meet more frequently to address single market issues and agreed to extend the provisions of free movement to sports people, musicians and others working in the arts and media. In July 1997 the heads of government, meeting in Montego Bay, Jamaica, agreed to accelerate economic integration, with the aim of completing a single market by 1999. It was noted that, as of 1 July 1997, all member states except Antigua and Barbuda had implemented the second phase of the CET, while four countries had implemented phase three, comprising a tariff of 0%–25%. At the meeting 11 member states signed Protocol II amending the Treaty of Chaguaramas, which constituted a central element of a CARICOM Single Market and Economy (CSME), providing for the right to establish enterprises, the provision of services and the free movement of capital and labour throughout participating countries. A regional collaborative network was established to promote the CSME. At June 2000 Protocol II had been signed and provisionally applied by 13 member states, and ratified by two. In February 2001 heads of government agreed to establish a new high-level sub-committee to accelerate the establishment of the CSME and to promote its objectives. The sub-committee was to be supported by a Technical Advisory Council, comprising representatives of the public and private sectors.

In July 1998, at the meeting of heads of government, held in Saint Lucia, an agreement was signed with the Insurance Company of the West Indies to accelerate the establishment of a Caribbean Investment Fund, which was to mobilize foreign currency from extra-regional capital markets for investment in new or existing enterprises in the region. Some 60% of all funds generated were to be used by CARICOM countries and the remainder by non-CARICOM members of the ACS. The Fund was expected to become operational in 2000, with funds of US $150m.

INDUSTRY AND ENERGY

CARICOM aims to promote the development of joint ventures in exporting industries (particularly the woodwork, furniture, ceramics and foundry industries) through an agreement (reached in 1989) on an industrial programming scheme. Work on an investors' guide for each member state was completed in 1984. CARICOM's Export Development Council gives training and consultancy services to regional manufacturers. Regional manufacturers' exhibitions (CARIMEX) are held every three years. The Caribbean Trade Information System (CARTIS) comprises computer databases covering country and product profiles, trade statistics, trade opportunities, institutions and bibliographical information; it links the national trade centres of CARICOM members. A protocol relating to the CARICOM Industrial Programming Scheme (CIPS), approved in 1988, is the Community's instrument for promoting the co-operative development of industry in the region. Protocol III amending the Treaty of Chaguaramas, with respect to industrial policy, was opened for signature in July 1998. At June 2000 it had been signed and provisionally applied by 13 member states, and ratified by one.

The Secretariat has established a national standards bureau in each member country to harmonize technical standards, and supervises the metrication of weights and measures. In 1999 CARICOM members agreed to establish a new Regional Organization of Standards and Quality to develop common regional standards and resolve disputes.

The CARICOM Alternative Energy Systems Project provides training, assesses energy needs and conducts energy audits. Efforts in regional energy development are directed at the collection and analysis of data for national energy policy documents.

TRANSPORT, COMMUNICATIONS AND TOURISM

A Caribbean Confederation of Shippers' Councils represents the interests of regional exporters and importers. In July 1990 the Caribbean Telecommunications Union was established to oversee developments in regional telecommunications.

In 1988 a Consultative Committee on Caribbean Regional Information Systems (CCCRIS) was established to evaluate and monitor the functioning of existing information systems and to seek to co-ordinate and advise on the establishment of new systems.

A Summit of Heads of Government on Tourism, Trade and Transportation was held in Trinidad and Tobago, in August 1995, to which all members of the ACS and regional tourism organizations were invited. In 1997 CARICOM heads of government considered a number of proposals relating to air transportation, tourism, human resource development and capital investment, which had been identified by Community ministers of tourism as critical issues in the sustainable development of the tourist industry. The heads of government requested ministers to meet regularly to develop tourism

policies, and in particular to undertake an in-depth study of human resource development issues in early 1998. A new fund to help train young people from the region in aspects of the tourist industry was inaugurated in July 1997, in memory of the former Prime Minister of Jamaica, Michael Manley. A regional summit on tourism, in recognition of the importance of the industry to the economic development of the region, was scheduled to be held in July 2001. In July 1999 heads of government signed Protocol VI amending the Treaty of Chaguaramas providing for a common transportation policy, with harmonized standards and practices, which was to be an integral component of the development of a single market and economy.

AGRICULTURE

In 1985 the New Marketing Arrangements for Primary Agricultural Products and Livestock were instituted, with the aim of increasing the flow of agricultural commodities within the region. A computer-based Caribbean Agricultural Marketing Information System was initiated in 1987.

At the CARICOM summit meeting in July 1996 it was agreed to undertake wide-ranging measures in order to modernize the agricultural sector and to increase the international competitiveness of Caribbean agricultural produce. The CARICOM Secretariat was to support national programmes with assistance in policy formulation, human resource development and the promotion of research and technology development in the areas of productivity, marketing, agri-business and water resources management. During 1997 CARICOM Governments continued to lobby against a complaint lodged at the WTO with regard to the EU's banana import regime (offering favourable conditions to ACP producers—see above) and to generate awareness of the economic and social importance of the banana industry to the region. Protocol V amending the Treaty of Chaguaramas, which was concerned with agricultural policy, was opened for signature by heads of government in July 1998. At June 2000 it had been signed and provisionally applied by 13 member states, and ratified by one.

HEALTH AND EDUCATION

In 1986 CARICOM and the Pan-American Health Organization launched 'Caribbean Co-operation in Health' with projects to be undertaken in six main areas: environmental protection, including the control of disease-bearing pests; development of human resources; chronic non-communicable diseases and accidents; strengthening health systems; food and nutrition; maternal and child health care; and population activities. In 2001 CARICOM was to co-ordinate a new regional partnership to reduce the spread and impact of HIV and AIDS in member countries. A Caribbean Environmental Health Institute (see below) aims to promote collaboration among member states in all areas of environmental management and human health.

CARICOM educational programmes have included the improvement of reading in schools through assistance for teacher-training; and ensuring the availability of low-cost educational material throughout the region. A strategy for developing and improving technical and vocational education and training within each member state and throughout the region was completed and published in 1990. In July 1997 CARICOM heads of government adopted the recommendations of a ministerial committee, which identified priority measures for implementation in the education sector. These included the objective of achieving universal, quality secondary education and the enrolment of 15% of post-secondary students in tertiary education by 2005, as well as improved training in foreign languages and science and technology.

EMERGENCY ASSISTANCE

A Caribbean Disaster Emergency Response Agency (CDERA) was established in 1991 to co-ordinate immediate disaster relief, primarily in the event of hurricanes (see Institutions, below). During 1997 CARICOM Governments remained actively concerned with the situation in Montserrat, which had suffered a series of massive volcanic eruptions. At the Heads of Government Conference in July, the Community pledged humanitarian, economic and technical assistance and resolved to help mobilize external assistance from regional and international donor countries and institutions. In March 1998 CARICOM heads of government agreed to establish a team, comprising representatives of the CARICOM Secretariat, CDERA and the Caribbean Development Bank, to assist the Montserrat Government in formulating programmes to provide a secure future for the island. In November the Community determined to support the countries of Central America in their reconstruction and rehabilitation efforts following the devastation caused by 'Hurricane Mitch', and to co-ordinate the provision of immediate humanitarian assistance by CARICOM member countries.

INSTITUTIONS

The following are among the institutions formally established within the framework of CARICOM.

Assembly of Caribbean Community Parliamentarians: c/o CARICOM Secretariat; an intergovernmental agreement on the establishment of a regional parliament entered into force in August 1994; inaugural meeting held in Barbados, in May 1996. Comprises up to four representatives of the parliaments of each member country, and up to two of each associate member. It aims to provide a forum for wider community involvement in the process of integration and for enhanced deliberation on CARICOM affairs; authorized to issue recommendations for the Conference of Heads of Government and to adopt resolutions on any matter arising under the Treaty of Chaguaramas.

Caribbean Agricultural Research and Development Institute—CARDI: UWI Campus, St Augustine, Trinidad and Tobago; tel. 645-1205; fax 645-1208; e-mail infocentre@cardi.org; internet www.cardi.org; f. 1975; aims to support the development of profitable and sustainable business systems and enterprises through its scientific, technological and information activities; provides training, a Caribbean agricultural information service, and technology and business advisory services. Exec. Dir HAYDEN BLADES. Publs *CARDI Update, Procicaribe News, CARDI Annual Report*, technical bulletin series.

Caribbean Centre for Development Administration—CARICAD: ICB Bldg, Roebuck St, St Michael, Barbados; tel. 4278535; fax 4361709; e-mail caricad@caribsurf.com; f. 1980; aims to assist governments in the reform of the public sector and to strengthen their managerial capacities for public administration; promotes the involvement of the private sector, non-governmental organizations and other bodies in all decision-making processes. Exec. Dir Dr I. GOMES.

Caribbean Disaster Emergency Response Agency—CDERA: The Garrison, St Michael, Barbados; tel. 436-9651; fax 437-7649; e-mail cdera@caribsurf.com; internet www.cdera.org. For activities, see Emergency Assistance above. Regional Co-ordinator JEREMY COLLYMORE.

Caribbean Environmental Health Institute—CEHI: POB 1111, The Morne, Castries, St Lucia; tel. 4522501; fax 4532721; e-mail cehi@candw.lc; internet www.cehi.org.lc; f. 1980 (began operations in 1982); provides technical and advisory services to member states in formulating environmental health policy legislation and in all areas of environmental management (for example, solid waste management, water supplies, beach and air pollution, and pesticides control); promotes, collates and disseminates relevant research; conducts courses, seminars and workshops throughout the region. Exec. Dir VINCENT SWEENEY.

Caribbean Food and Nutrition Institute: UWI Campus, St Augustine, Trinidad and Tobago; tel. 662-7025; fax 662-5511; f. 1967 to serve the governments and people of the region and to act as a catalyst among persons and organizations concerned with food and nutrition through research and field investigations, training in nutrition, dissemination of information, advisory services and production of educational material. Mems: all English-speaking Caribbean territories, including the mainland countries of Belize and Guyana. Dir Dr FITZROY HENRY. Publs *Cajanus* (quarterly), *Nyam News* (monthly), *Nutrient-Cost Tables* (quarterly), educational material.

Caribbean Food Corporation—CFC: 30 Queen's Park West, Post Office Bag 264B, Port of Spain, Trinidad and Tobago; tel. 622-5827; fax 622-4430; e-mail cfc@trinidad-net; f. 1976 (began operations in 1979); implements joint-venture projects with investors from the private and public sectors to enhance regional food self-sufficiency and reduce the need for food imports. Man. Dir E. C. CLYDE PARRIS.

Caribbean Meteorological Organization—CMO: POB 461, Port of Spain, Trinidad and Tobago; tel. 624-4481; fax 623-3634; e-mail hqcmo@tstt.net.tt; f. 1951 to co-ordinate regional activities in meteorology, operational hydrology and allied sciences; became an associate institution of CARICOM in 1983. Comprises a headquarters unit, a Council of Government Ministers, the Caribbean Meteorological Foundation and the Caribbean Institute for Meteorology and Hydrology, located in Barbados. Mems: govts of 16 countries and territories represented by the National Meteorological and Hydro-meteorological Services. Co-ordinating Dir T. W. SUTHERLAND.

ASSOCIATE INSTITUTIONS

Caribbean Development Bank: POB 408, Wildey, St Michael, Barbados; tel. 431-1600; fax 426-7269; e-mail info@caribank.org; internet www.caribank.org; f. 1969 to stimulate regional economic growth through support for agriculture, industry, transport and other infrastructure, tourism, housing and education; subscribed cap. US $687.2m. (Dec. 1999). In 1999 net approvals totalled $146.6m. for 16 projects; at the end of 1999 cumulative grant and loan disbursements totalled $1,275.0m. The Special Development Fund was replenished in 1996. Mems: CARICOM states, and Canada, Cayman Islands, the People's Republic of China, Colombia, France, Germany, Italy, Mexico, United Kingdom, Venezuela. Pres. Prof. COMPTON BOURNE (from 1 May 2001).

Caribbean Law Institute: University of the West Indies, Cave Hill Campus, POB 64, Bridgetown, Barbados; tel. 417-4560; fax 417-4138.

Other Associate Institutions of CARICOM, in accordance with its constitution, are the University of Guyana and the University of the West Indies.

Publication

Annual Report.

CENTRAL AMERICAN INTEGRATION SYSTEM

(SISTEMA DE LA INTEGRACIÓN CENTROAMERICANA—SICA)

Address: blvd de la Orden de Malta 470, Santa Elena, Antiguo Cuscatlán, San Salvador, El Salvador.

Telephone: 289-6131; **fax:** 289-6124; **e-mail:** sgsica@sicanet.org.sv; **internet:** www.sicanet.org.sv.

Founded in December 1991, when the heads of state of six Central American countries signed the Protocol of Tegucigalpa to the agreement establishing the Organization of Central American States (f. 1951), creating a new framework for regional integration. A General Secretariat of the Sistema de la Integración Centroamericana (SICA) was inaugurated in February 1993 to co-ordinate the process of political, economic, social cultural and environmental integration and to promote democracy and respect for human rights throughout the region.

MEMBERS

Costa Rica	Guatemala	Nicaragua
El Salvador	Honduras	Panama

OBSERVERS

Belize	Dominican Republic	Taiwan

Organization

(April 2001)

SUMMIT MEETINGS

The meetings of heads of state of member countries serve as the supreme decision-making organ of SICA.

COUNCIL OF MINISTERS

Ministers of Foreign Affairs of member states meet regularly to provide policy direction for the process of integration.

CONSULTATIVE COMMITTEE

The Committee comprises representatives of business organizations, trade unions, academic institutions and other federations concerned with the process of integration in the region. It is an integral element of the integration system and assist the Secretary-General in determining the policies of the organization.

GENERAL SECRETARIAT

The General Secretariat of SICA was established in February 1993 to co-ordinate the process of enhanced regional integration. It comprises the following divisions: inter-institutional relations; research and co-operation; legal and political affairs; economic affairs; and communications and information.

In September 1997 Central American Common Market (CACM) heads of state, meeting in the Nicaraguan capital, signed the Managua Declaration in support of further regional integration and the establishment of a political union. A commission was to be established to consider all aspects of the policy and to formulate a timetable for the integration process. In February 1998 SICA heads of state resolved to establish a Unified General Secretariat to integrate the institutional aspects of SICA (see below) in a single office, to be located in San Salvador. The process was ongoing in 2000.

Secretary-General: Dr OSCAR SANTAMARÍA.

SPECIALIZED TECHNICAL SECRETARIATS

Secretaría Ejecutiva de la Comisión Centroamericana de Ambiente y Desarrollo: blvd de la Orden de Malta 470, Santa Elena, Antiguo Cuscatlán, San Salvador, El Salvador; tel. 289-6131; fax 289-6124; internet www.ccad.org.gt; f. 1989 to enhance collaboration in the promotion of sustainable development and environmental protection. Exec. Sec. MAURICIO CASTRO.

Secretaría General de la Coordinación Educativa y Cultural Centroamericana: 175m. norte de la esquina oeste del ICE, Sabana Norte, San José, Costa Rica; tel. 232-3783; fax 231-2366; f. 1982; promotes development of regional programmes in the fields of education and culture. Sec.-Gen. MARVIN HERRERA ARAYA.

Secretaría Permanente del Tratado General de Integración Económica Centroamericana—SIECA: 4A Avda 10–25, Zona 14, Apdo Postal 1237, 01901 Guatemala City, Guatemala; tel. (2) 3682319; fax (2) 3681071; e-mail sieca@pronet.net.gt; internet www.sieca.org.gt; f. 1960 to assist the process of economic integration and the establishment of a Central American Common Market (see below). Sec.-Gen. RÓGER HAROLDO RODAS MELARA.

Secretaría Técnica del Consejo de Integración Social—SISCA: blvd de la Orden de Malta 470, Santa Elena, Antiguo Cuscatlán, San Salvador, El Salvador; tel. 289-6131; fax 289-6124; e-mail hmorgado@sicanet.org.sv; Dir-Gen. Dr HUGO MORGADO.

OTHER SPECIALIZED SECRETARIATS

Secretaria de Integración Turística Centroamericana—SITCA: blvd de la Orden de Malta 470, Santa Elena, Antiguo Cuscatlán, San Salvador, El Salvador; tel. 289-6131; fax 289-6124; e-mail econtreras@sicanet.org.sv; f. 1965 to develop regional tourism activities; Sec.-Gen. EDGARDO CONTRERAS SCHNEIDER.

Secretaría del Consejo Agropecuario Centroamericano—SCAC: Sede del IICA, Apdo Postal 55-2200 Coronado, San José, Costa Rica; tel. 216-0303; fax 216-0285; e-mail rguillen@iica.ac.cr; f. 1991 to determine and co-ordinate regional policies and programmes relating to agriculture and agroindustry. Sec-Gen. RÓGER GUILLÉN BUSTOS.

Secretaría Ejecutiva del Consejo Monetario Centroamericano—CMCA (Central American Monetary Council): Ofiplaza del Este, Edif. C, 75m. oeste de la Rotonda la Bandera, San Pedro Montes de Oca, Apdo 5438, 1000 San José, Costa Rica; tel. 280-9522; fax 280-9511; e-mail secma@sol.racsa.co.cr; internet www.cmca.or.ca; f. 1964 by the presidents of Central American central banks, to co-ordinate monetary policies. Exec. Sec. MIGUEL CHORRO. Publs *Boletín Estadístico* (annually), *Informe Económico* (annually).

Secretaría Ejecutiva de la Comisión Centroamericana de Transporte Marítimo—COCATRAM: Cine Cabrera 2c. arriba y 2½ al sur, Apdo 2423, Managua, Nicaragua; tel. (2) 222754; fax (2) 222759; e-mail cocatram@ibw.com.ni; f. 1981; Exec. Sec. LIANA ZÚÑIGA DE CÁCERES.

PARLIAMENT

Address: 12A Avda 33-04, Zona 5, Guatemala City, Guatemala.

Telephone: (2) 339-0466; **fax:** (2) 334-6670; **e-mail:** cdpar@parlacen.org.gt; **internet:** www.parlacen.org.gt.

Founded 1989 within the framework of the Central American Common Market. Comprises representatives of El Salvador, Guatemala, Honduras, Nicaragua and Panama. In February 1998 heads of state of member countries resolved to limit the number of deputies to 10–15 from each country.

President: HUGO GIRAUD (Panama).

COURT OF JUSTICE

Address: Kilómetro 17½ Carretera Norte, contiguo a la TANIC, Managua, Nicaragua.

Telephone: 233-2128; **fax:** 233-2135; **e-mail:** cortecen@tmx.com.ni; **internet:** www.ccj.org.ni.

Tribunal authorized to consider disputes relating to treaties agreed within the regional integration system. In February 1998 Central American heads of state agreed to limit the number of magistrates in the Court to one per country.

AD HOC INTERGOVERNMENTAL SECRETARIATS

Comisión de Ciencia y Tecnología de Centroamérica y Panamá (Comission for Science and Technology in Central America and Panama): Col. Palmira, Avda República de Brasil 2231, Apdo Postal 4458, Tegucigalpa, Honduras; tel. and fax 232-5669; f. 1976; Pres. GERARDO ZEPEDA.

Consejo Centroamericano de Instituciones de Seguridad Social—COCISS: Caja de Seguridad Social, Panamá, Panama; tel. 261-7264; f. 1992; Pres. Dr MARIANELA MORALES.

Consejo del Istmo Centroamericano de Deportes y Recreación: 5009-1000 San José, Costa Rica; tel. 257-8770; fax 222-5003; f. 1992; Pres. HILDA GONZÁLEZ.

Secretaría Ejecutiva del Consejo Centroamericana de Vivienda y Asentamientos Humanos (Central American Council on Housing and Human Settlements): Avda la Paz 244, Tegucigalpa, Honduras; tel. 236-5804; fax 236-6560; f. 1992; Dir Dr CONCEPCIÓN RAMOS.

Secretaría Ejecutiva del Consejo de Electrificación de América Central: Apdo Postal 10032, San José, Costa Rica; tel. 220-7562; fax 220-8232; e-mail ceac@ns.ice.go.cr; f. 1985; Dir LUIS BUJÁN.

OTHER REGIONAL INSTITUTIONS

Finance

Banco Centroamericano de Integración Económica—BCIE (Central American Bank for Economic Integration): Blvd Suyapa, Contigua a Banco de Honduras, Apdo Postal 772, Tegucigalpa, Honduras; tel. 228-2243; fax 228-2185; e-mail jose_manuel_pacas@bcie.hn; f. 1961 to promote the economic integration and balanced economic development of member countries; finances public and private development projects, particularly those related to industrialization and infrastructure. By June 1993 cumulative lending amounted to US $3,217m., mainly for roads, hydroelectricity projects, housing and telecommunications. Auth. cap. $2,000m. Regional mems: Costa Rica, El Salvador, Honduras, Nicaragua; Non-regional mems: Argentina, the People's Republic of China, Colombia, Mexico. Pres. JOSÉ ALEJANDRO ARÉVALO. Publs *Annual Report, Revista de la Integración y el Desarrollo de Centroamérica*.

Public Administration

Centro de Coordinación para la Prevención de Desastres Naturales en América Central—CEPREDENAC: Howard, Edif. 707, Panamá, Panama; tel. 3160065; fax 3160074; e-mail secretariat@cepredenac.org; internet www.cepredenac.org; Dir LUIS ROLANDO DURÁN VARGAS.

Comisión Centroamericana Permanente para la Erradicación de la Producción, Tráfico, Consumo y Uso Ilícitos de Estupefacientes y Sustancias Psicotrópicas—CCP: Edif. de Comisiones, 1°, Tegucigalpa, Honduras; tel. 237-0568; fax 238-3960. Pres. Dr CARLOS SOSA COELLO.

Instituto Centroamericano de Administración Pública—ICAP (Central American Institute of Public Administration): POB 10025-1000, De la Heladería Pops en Curridabat 100m. sur y 50 oeste, San José, Costa Rica; tel. 234-1011; fax 225-2049; e-mail icapcr@sol.racsa.co.cr; internet www.icap.ac.cr; f. 1954 by the five Central American Republics and the United Nations, with later participation by Panama. The Institute aims to train the region's public servants, provide technical assistance and carry out research leading to reforms in public administration. Dir Dr HUGO ZELAYA CÁLIX.

Secretaría Ejecutiva de la Comisión Regional de Recursos Hidráulicos: Blvd Rohrmoser, Pavas, Apdo Postal 21-2300, Curridabat, San José, Costa Rica; tel. 231-5791; fax 296-0047; e-mail crrhcr@sol.racsa.co.cr; f. 1966. Mems: Belize, Costa Rica, El Salvador, Guatemala, Honduras, Nicaragua, Panama; Exec. Dir MAX CAMPOS O.

Education and Health

Comité Coordinador Regional de Instituciones de Agua Potable y Saneamiento de Centro América, Panamá y República Dominicana—CAPRE: De la casa Italia, 100m. al sur y 100 al este, diagonal a farmacia Umaña, Barrio Francisco Peralta, San Pedro de Montes de OCA, San José, Costa Rica; tel. 280-4460; fax 280-4414; e-mail capregtz@sol.racsa.co.cr; f. 1979; Dir LILIANA ARCE UMAÑA.

Consejo Superior Universitario Centroamericano—CSUCA (Central American University Council): Apdo 37, Ciudad Universitaria Rodrigo Facio, 2060 San José, Costa Rica; tel. 225-2744; fax 234-0071; e-mail rsol@cariari.ucr.ac.cr; internet www.csuca.ac.cr;

f. 1948 to guarantee academic, administrative and economic autonomy for universities and to encourage regional integration of higher education; maintains libraries and documentation centres; Council of 32 mems. Mems: 16 universities, in Belize, Costa Rica (four), El Salvador, Guatemala, Honduras (two), Nicaragua (four) and Panama (three). Sec.-Gen. Dr RICARDO SOL ARRIAZA (El Salvador). Publs *Estudios Sociales Centroamericanas* (quarterly), *Cuadernos de Investigación* (monthly), *Carta Informativa de la Secretaría General* (monthly).

Instituto de Nutrición de Centroamérica y Panamá—INCAP (Institute of Nutrition of Central America and Panama): Apdo 1188, Carretera Roosevelt, Zona 11, 01901 Guatemala City, Guatemala; tel. (2) 4723762; fax (2) 4736529; e-mail hdelgado@incap.org.gt; f. 1949 to promote the development of nutritional sciences and their application and to strengthen the technical capacity of member countries to reach food and nutrition security; provides training and technical assistance for nutrition education and planning; conducts applied research; disseminates information. Maintains library (including about 600 periodicals). Administered by the Pan American Health Organization (PAHO) and the World Health Organization. Mems: CACM mems and Belize and Panama. Dir Dr HERNÁN L. DELGADO. Publ. *Annual Report*.

Organismo Internacional Regional de Sanidad Agropecuaria—OIRSA (International Regional Organization of Plant Protection and Animal Health): Calle Ramón Belloso, Final Pasaje Isolde, Col Escalón, Apdo Postal 61, San Salvador, El Salvador; tel. 263-

1123; fax 263-1128; e-mail oirsa@ns1.oirsa.org.sv; internet www.ns1.oirsa.org.sv; f. 1953 for the prevention of the introduction of animal and plant pests and diseases unknown in the region; research, control and eradication programmes of the principal pests present in agriculture; technical assistance and advice to the ministries of agriculture and livestock of member countries; education and qualification of personnel. Mems: Belize, Costa Rica, Dominican Republic, El Salvador, Guatemala, Honduras, Mexico, Nicaragua, Panama. Exec. Dir Dr CELIO HUMBERTO BARRETO.

Transport and Communications

Comisión Técnica de las Telecomunicaciones de Centroamérica—COMTELCA (Technical Commission for Telecommunications in Central America): Col. Palmira, Edif. Alpha, Avda Brasil, Apdo 1793, Tegucigalpa, Honduras; tel. 220-6666; fax 220-1197; e-mail dgeneral@comtelca.hn; internet www.comtelca.hn; f. 1966 to co-ordinate and improve the regionaltelecommunications network. Dir-Gen. HÉCTOR LEONEL RODRÍGUEZ MILLA.

Corporación Centroamericana de Servicios de Navegación Aérea—COCESNA (Central American Air Navigation Service Corporation): Apdo 660, Aeropuerto de Toncontín, Tegucigalpa, Honduras; tel. 233-1143; fax 233-1219; e-mail gergral@cocesna.hn; f. 1960; offers radar air traffic control services, aeronautical telecommunications services, flight inspections and radio assistance services for air navigation; administers the Central American Aeronautical School. Gen. Man. EDUARDO MARÍN JIMENEZ.

Central American Common Market—CACM (Mercado Común Centroamericano)

CACM was established by the Organization of Central American States under the General Treaty of Central American Economic Integration (Tratado General de Integración Económica Centroamericana) signed in Managua (Nicaragua) on 13 December 1960. It was ratified by all countries by September 1963. It now forms a subsystem of the Sistema de la Integración Centroamericana (SICA, see above).

MEMBERS

Costa Rica	El Salvador	Nicaragua
Guatemala	Honduras	

Organization
(April 2001)

MINISTERIAL MEETINGS

The organization's policy is formulated by regular meetings of the Council of Ministers for Economic Integration (COMIECO), meetings of other ministers, and of presidents of central banks, also play an important part.

PERMANENT SECRETARIAT

Secretaría Permanente del Tratado General de Integración Económica Centroamericana—SIECA: 4A Avda 10-25, Zona 14, Apdo 1237, 01901 Guatemala City, Guatemala; tel. 268-2151; provides institutional support for the Common Market, supervises the correct implementation of the legal instruments of economic integration, carries out relevant studies at the request of the Common Market authorities, and arranges meetings. There are departments covering the working of the Common Market; negotiations and external trade policy; external co-operation; systems and statistics; finance and administration. There is also a unit for co-operation with the private sector and finance institutions and a legal consultative committee.

Secretary-General: HAROLDO RODAS MELGAR.

Activities

The General Treaty envisaged the eventual liberalization of intra-regional trade and the establishment of a free-trade area and a customs union. Economic integration in the region, however, has been hampered by ideological differences between governments, difficulties in internal supply, protectionist measures by overseas markets, external and intra-regional debts, adverse rates of exchange and high interest rates. Regular meetings of senior customs officials aim to increase co-operation, to develop a uniform termin-

ology, and to recommend revisions of customs legislation. CACM member-countries also aim to pursue a common policy in respect of international trade agreements on commodities, raw materials and staples.

Under the Convention for Fiscal Incentives for Industrial Development, which came into operation in 1969, a wide range of tax benefits are applied to various categories of industries in the region, to encourage productivity. SIECA carries out studies on the industrial sector, compiles statistics, and provides information to member governments. It also analyses energy consumption in the region and assists governments in drawing up energy plans, aiming to reduce dependence on imported petroleum.

A co-ordinating commission supervises the marketing of four basic crops (maize, rice, beans and sorghum), recording and forecasting production figures and recommending minimum guarantee prices. Information on other crops is also compiled. A permanent commission for agricultural research and extension services monitors and co-ordinates regional projects in this field.

An agreement to establish a Central American Monetary Union was signed in 1964, with the eventual aim of establishing a common currency and aligning foreign exchange and monetary policies. The Central American Monetary Council, comprising the presidents of the member states' central banks, meets regularly to consider monetary policy and financial affairs. A Fund for Monetary Stabilization provides short-term financial assistance to members facing temporary balance-of-payments difficulties.

Trade within the region increased in value from US $33m. in 1960 to $1,129m. in 1980, but subsequently diminished every year until 1986, when it amounted to $406m. The decline was due to a number of factors: low prices for the region's main export commodities, and heavy external debts, both resulting in a severe shortage of foreign exchange, and intra-regional trade 'freezes' provoked by debts amounting to $700m. at mid-1986 (Guatemala and Costa Rica being the chief creditors, and Nicaragua and El Salvador the main debtors). In January 1986 a new CACM tariff and customs agreement came into effect, imposing standard import duties for the whole region (aimed at discouraging the import of non-essential goods from outside the region), and a uniform tariff nomenclature. Honduras, however, continued to insist on bilateral tariff agreements with other member countries. Honduras subsequently signed a temporary free-trade agreement with all the other member states. From 1987 intra-regional trade increased steadily and reached an estimated $1,840m. in 1997.

In June 1990 the presidents of the five CACM countries signed a declaration welcoming peace initiatives in El Salvador, Guatemala and Nicaragua, and appealing for a revitalization of CACM, as a means of promoting lasting peace in the region. In December the presidents committed themselves to the creation of an effective common market, proposing the opening of negotiations on a comprehensive regional customs and tariffs policy by March 1991, and the introduction of a regional 'anti-dumping' code by December 1991. They requested the support of multilateral lending institutions through investment in regional development, and the cancellation or rescheduling of member countries' debts.

In February 1993 the European Community (EC) signed a new framework co-operation agreement with the CACM member states extending the programme of economic assistance and political dialogue initiated in 1984; a further co-operation agreement with the European Union (as the EC had become) was signed in early 1996.

In October 1993 the presidents of the CACM countries and Panama signed a protocol to the 1960 General Treaty, committing themselves to full economic integration in the region (with a common external tariff of 20% for finished products and 5% for raw materials and capital goods) and creating conditions for increased free trade. The countries agreed to accelerate the removal of internal non-tariff barriers, but no deadline was set. Full implementation of the protocol was to be 'voluntary and gradual', owing to objections on the part of Costa Rica and Panama. In May 1994, however, Costa Rica committed itself to full participation in the protocol. In March 1995 a meeting of the Central American Monetary Council discussed and endorsed a reduction in the tariff levels from 20% to 15% and from 5% to 1%. However, efforts to adopt this as a common policy were hindered by the implementation of these tariff levels by El Salvador on a unilateral basis, from 1 April, and the subsequent modifications by Guatemala and Costa Rica of their external tariffs.

In May 1997 the heads of state of CACM member countries, together with the Prime Minister of Belize, conferred with the US President, Bill Clinton, in San José, Costa Rica. The leaders resolved to establish a Trade and Investment Council to promote trade relations; however, Clinton failed to endorse a request from CACM members that their products receive preferential access to US markets, on similar terms to those from Mexico agreed under the NAFTA accord. During the 1990s the Central American Governments pursued negotiations to conclude free-trade agreements with Mexico, Panama and the members of the Caribbean Community and

Common Market (CARICOM). Nicaragua signed a bilateral accord with Mexico in December (Costa Rica already having done so in 1994). El Salvador, Guatemala and Honduras jointly concluded a free-trade arrangement with Mexico in May 2000; this was to enter into effect in January 2001. In November 1997, at a special summit meeting of CACM heads of state, an agreement was reached with the President of the Dominican Republic to initiate a gradual process of incorporating that country into the process of Central American integration, with the aim of promoting sustainable development throughout the region. The first sectors for increased co-operation between the two sides were to be tourism, health, investment promotion and air transport. A free-trade accord with the Dominican Republic was concluded in April 1998, and formally signed in November.

In November 1998 Central American heads of state held an emergency summit meeting to consider the devastation in the region caused by 'Hurricane Mitch'. The Presidents urged international creditors to write off the region's estimated debts of US $16,000m. to assist in the economic recovery of the countries worst-affected. They also reiterated requests for preferential treatment for the region's exports within the NAFTA framework. In October 1999 heads of state adopted a strategic framework for the period 2000–04 to strengthen the capacity for the physical, social, economic and environmental infrastructure of Central American countries to withstand the impact of natural disasters. In particular, programmes for the integrated management and conservation of water resources, and for the prevention of forest fires were to be implemented.

Publications

Anuario Estadístico Centroamericano de Comercio Exterior.
Carta Informativa (monthly).
Cuadernos de la SIECA (2 a year).
Estadísticas Macroeconómicas de Centroamérica (annually).
Series Estadísticas Seleccionadas de Centroamérica (annually).

COMMON MARKET FOR EASTERN AND SOUTHERN AFRICA—COMESA

Address: COMESA Centre, Ben Bella Rd, POB 30051, 101101 Lusaka, Zambia.

Telephone: (1) 229725; **fax:** (1) 225107; **e-mail:** comesa@comesa.int; **internet:** www.comesa.int.

COMESA was formally inaugurated in 1994 as a successor to the Preferential Trade Area for Eastern and Southern Africa (PTA), which was established in 1981.

MEMBERS*

Angola	Malawi
Burundi	Mauritius
Comoros	Namibia
Congo, Democratic Republic	Rwanda
Djibouti	Seychelles
Egypt	Sudan
Eritrea	Swaziland
Ethiopia	Uganda
Kenya	Zambia
Madagascar	Zimbabwe

* Tanzania withdrew from COMESA in September 2000.

Organization

(April 2001)

AUTHORITY

The Authority of the Common Market is the supreme policy organ of COMESA, comprising heads of state or of government of member countries. The inaugural meeting of the Authority took place in Lilongwe, Malawi, in December 1994. The fifth summit meeting was held in Grand Baie, Mauritius, in May 2000.

COUNCIL OF MINISTERS

Each member government appoints a minister to participate in the Council. The Council monitors COMESA activities, including supervision of the Secretariat, recommends policy direction and development, and reports to the Authority.

A Committee of Governors of Central Banks advises the Authority and the Council of Ministers on monetary and financial matters.

COURT OF JUSTICE

The COMESA treaty envisaged the establishment of a sub-regional Court of Justice, to replace the former PTA Tribunal, with authority to settle disputes between member states and to adjudicate on matters concerning the interpretation of the treaty. In June 1998 COMESA heads of state announced the appointment of seven judges to serve in the Court.

President: AKILANO AKIWUMI (Kenya) (acting).

SECRETARIAT

In 1998 the administrative structure of COMESA was undergoing a process of restructuring, according to which the existing 12 divisional areas were to be consolidated into the following four divisions: Trade, customs and monetary affairs; Investment promotion and private sector development; Infrastructure development; and Information.

Secretary-General: J. E. O. (ERASTUS) MWENCHA (Kenya).

Activities

The COMESA treaty was signed by member states of the PTA in November 1993 and was scheduled to come into effect on being ratified by 10 countries. COMESA formally succeeded the PTA in December 1994 (by which time it had received 12 ratifications), with the aim of strengthening the process of regional economic integration that had been initiated under the PTA, in order to help member states achieve sustainable economic growth.

In May 1999 COMESA established a Free Trade Area Committee to facilitate and co-ordinate preparations for the establishment of the Common Market envisaged under the COMESA treaty. A special summit of COMESA heads of state, held in October 2000, established the free-trade area, with nine initial members: Djibouti, Egypt, Kenya, Madagascar, Malawi, Mauritius, Sudan, Zambia and Zimbabwe. The Seychelles was due to join the free-trade area in mid-2001, while Burundi, Eritrea and Rwanda were expected to form a subsequent wave of applicants. Trading practices within the free-trade area were fully liberalized, including the elimination of non-tariff barriers, thereby enabling the free internal movement of goods, services and capital. It was envisaged that a regional customs union would be established by 2004, with a common external tariff set at 0%, 5%, 15% and 30% for, respectively, capital goods, raw materials, intermediate goods and final goods. COMESA also plans to form an economic community (entailing monetary union and the free movement of people between member states) by 2025. COMESA aims to formulate a common investment procedure to promote domestic, cross-border and direct foreign investment by ensuring the free movement of capital, services and labour. Heads of regional investment agencies, meeting in August 2000, developed a plan of action for the creation of a Common Investment Agency to facilitate the establishment of a Common Investment Area, in accordance with recommendations by the Authority.

The PTA aimed to facilitate intra-regional trade by establishing a clearing house to deal with credit arrangements and balance of payments issues. The clearing house became operational in February 1984 using the unit of account of the PTA (UAPTA) as its currency. (The UAPTA was valued at the rate of the IMF special drawing rights.) The clearing house, based in Harare, Zimbabwe, remained an integral part of the COMESA infrastructure, although its role was diminished by the liberalization of foreign exchange markets in the majority of member countries. In April 1997 the Authority endorsed a proposal to replace UAPTA with a COMESA dollar (CMD), to be equivalent to the value of the US currency. An Automated System of Customs Data (ASYCUDA) has been established to facilitate customs administration in all COMESA member states. Through support for capacity-building activities and the establishment of other specialized institutions (see below) COMESA aims to reinforce its objectives of regional integration. A COMESA Telecommunications Company (COMTEL) was registered in May 2000, although it did not immediately commence operations.

Co-operation programmes have been implemented by COMESA in the industrial, agricultural, energy and transport and communications sectors. A regional food security programme aimed to ensure adequate food supplies at all times. In 1997 COMESA Heads of State advocated that the food sector be supported by the immediate implementation of an irrigation action plan for the region. The organization also supports the establishment of common agricultural standards and phytosanitary regulations throughout the region in order to stimulate trade in food crops. Other initiatives include a road customs declaration document, a regional customs bond guarantee scheme, third party motor vehicle insurance scheme and travellers cheques in the UAPTA unit of currency. A Trade Information Network co-ordinates information on the production and marketing of goods manufactured and traded in the region. COMESA is implementing the new COMESA Information Network, which aims to develop the utilization by member states of advanced information and communication technologies. The first meeting of representatives of business communities in COMESA countries was held in November 1997, and the first COMESA trade fair was held in Nairobi, Kenya, in May 1999. The first COMESA economic forum was held in Cairo, Egypt, in February 2000.

Since its establishment there have been concerns on the part of member states, as well as other regional non-member countries, in particular South Africa, of adverse rivalry between COMESA and the Southern African Development Community (SADC, q.v.) and of a duplication of roles. In December 1996 and January 1997 respectively, Lesotho and Mozambique suspended their membership of COMESA and announced their intention to withdraw from the organization owing to concerns that their continued participation in COMESA was incompatible with their SADC membership. Lesotho subsequently terminated its membership. Tanzania withdrew from COMESA in September 2000, reportedly also in view of its dual

commitment to that organization and to the SADC. The summit meeting of COMESA heads of state held in May 2000 expressed support for an ongoing programme of co-operation by the secretariats of COMESA and SADC, aimed at reducing the duplication of roles between the two organizations, and urged further mutual collaboration.

COMESA INSTITUTIONS

COMESA Association of Commercial Banks: 12 Victoria Ave, Unit House (GF), Private Bag 271, Blantyre, Malawi; tel. (4) 621503; fax (4) 621204; aims to strengthen co-operation between banks in the region; organizes training activities; conducts studies to harmonize banking laws and operations; initiated a project to combat bank fraud and money laundering in December 2000. Mems: commercial banking orgs in Burundi, Ethiopia, Malawi, Rwanda, Sudan, Uganda.

COMESA Leather and Leather Products Institute—LLPI: POB 2358, Addis Ababa, Ethiopia; tel (1) 431318; fax (1) 615755; e-mail comesa.llpi@telecom.net.et; internet www.leathernet.com/comesa/llpi; f. 1990 as the PTA Leather Institute. Mems: Govts of 16 COMESA mem. states; Dir Dr ROBERT ARUNGA.

COMESA Metallurgical Industries Association (COMESAMIA): Kampala, Uganda; f. 1999; aims to advance capabilities in the production, processing and marketing of metals and allied engineering products, and to develop co-operation and networking in the sector.

Compagnie de réassurance de la Zone d'échanges préférentiels—ZEP-RE (PTA Reinsurance Co): Anniversary Towers, University Way, POB 42769, Nairobi, Kenya; tel. (2) 212792; fax (2) 224102; e-mail zep-re@africaonline.co.ke; f. 1992 (began operations on 1 January 1993); provides local reinsurance services and training to personnel in the insurance industry; auth. cap. CMD 27.3m.; Man. Dir S. M. LUBASI.

Eastern and Southern African Trade and Development Bank: NSSF Bldg, 23rd Floor, Bishop's Rd, POB 48596, Nairobi, Kenya; tel. (2) 712260; fax (2) 711510; e-mail infoserv@ptabank.co.ke; internet www.ptabank.co.ke; f. 1983 as PTA Development Bank; aims to mobilize resources and finance COMESA activities to foster regional integration; promotes investment and co-financing within the region; shareholders 16 COMESA mem. states and the African Development Bank; cap. p.u. SDR 63.7m. (Dec. 1998); Pres. Dr MICHAEL GONDWE.

Federation of National Associations of Women in Business — FEMCOM: c/o COMESA Secretariat; f. 1993 to provide links between female business executives throughout the region and to promote greater awareness of relevant issues at policy level. FEMCOM was to be supported by a Revolving Fund for Women in Business.

Finance

COMESA is financed by member states. Its administrative budget for 1996 amounted to US $4m. In April 1997 COMESA heads of state concluded that the organization's activities were being undermined by lack of resources, and determined to expel countries which fail to pay membership dues over a five-year period.

Publications

Annual Report of the Council of Ministers.

Asycuda Newsletter.

COMESA Journal.

COMESA Trade Directory (annually).

COMESA Trade Information Newsletter (monthly).

Demand/supply surveys, catalogues and reports.

THE COMMONWEALTH

Address: Commonwealth Secretariat, Marlborough House, Pall Mall, London, SW1Y 5HX, United Kingdom.
Telephone: (20) 7839-3411; **fax:** (20) 7930-0827; **e-mail:** info@commonwealth.int; **internet:** www.thecommonwealth.org.

The Commonwealth is a voluntary association of 54 independent states, comprising about one-quarter of the world's population. It includes the United Kingdom and most of its former dependencies, and former dependencies of Australia and New Zealand (themselves Commonwealth countries).

The evolution of the Commonwealth began with the introduction of self-government in Canada in the 1840s; Australia, New Zealand and South Africa became independent before the First World War. At the Imperial Conference of 1926 the United Kingdom and the Dominions, as they were then called, were described as 'autonomous communities within the British Empire, equal in status', and this change was enacted into law by the Statute of Westminster, in 1931.

The modern Commonwealth began with the entry of India and Pakistan in 1947, and of Sri Lanka (then Ceylon) in 1948. In 1949, when India decided to become a republic, the Commonwealth Heads of Government agreed to replace allegiance to the British Crown with recognition of the British monarch as Head of the Commonwealth, as a condition of membership. This was a precedent for a number of other members (see Heads of State and Heads of Government, below).

MEMBERS*

Antigua and Barbuda	Kenya	Samoa
Australia	Kiribati	Seychelles
Bahamas	Lesotho	Sierra Leone
Bangladesh	Malawi	Singapore
Barbados	Malaysia	Solomon Islands
Belize	Maldives	South Africa
Botswana	Malta	Sri Lanka
Brunei	Mauritius	Swaziland
Cameroon	Mozambique	Tanzania
Canada	Namibia	Tonga
Cyprus	Nauru	Trinidad and Tobago
Dominica	New Zealand	Tuvalu
Fiji	Nigeria	Uganda
The Gambia	Pakistan	United Kingdom
Ghana	Papua New Guinea	Vanuatu
Grenada	Saint Christopher and Nevis	Zambia
Guyana	Saint Lucia	Zimbabwe
India	Saint Vincent and the Grenadines	
Jamaica		

* Ireland, South Africa and Pakistan withdrew from the Commonwealth in 1949, 1961 and 1972 respectively. In October 1987 Fiji's membership was declared to have lapsed (following the proclamation of a republic there). It was readmitted in October 1997, but was suspended from participation in meetings of the Commonwealth in June 2000. Pakistan rejoined the Commonwealth in October 1989; however, it was suspended from participation in meetings in October 1999. South Africa rejoined in June 1994. Nigeria's membership was suspended in November 1995; it formally resumed membership in May 1999, when a new civilian government was inaugurated.Tuvalu, previously a special member of the Commonwealth with the right to participate in all activities except full Meetings of Heads of Government, became a full member of the Commonwealth in September 2000.

Dependencies and Associated States

Australia:
  Ashmore and Cartier Islands
  Australian Antarctic Territory
  Christmas Island
  Cocos (Keeling) Islands
  Coral Sea Islands Territory
  Heard Island and the McDonald Islands
  Norfolk Island
New Zealand:
  Cook Islands
  Niue
  Ross Dependency
  Tokelau
United Kingdom:
  Anguilla
  Bermuda

British Antarctic Territory
British Indian Ocean Territory
British Virgin Islands
Cayman Islands
Channel Islands
Falkland Islands
Gibraltar
Isle of Man
Montserrat
Pitcairn Islands
St Helena
  Ascension
  Tristan da Cunha
South Georgia and the South Sandwich Islands
Turks and Caicos Islands

HEADS OF STATE AND HEADS OF GOVERNMENT

At April 2001 21 member countries were monarchies and 33 were republics. All Commonwealth countries accept Queen Elizabeth II as the symbol of the free association of the independent member nations and as such the Head of the Commonwealth. Of the 33 republics, the offices of Head of State and Head of Government were combined in 22: Botswana, Cameroon, Cyprus, The Gambia, Ghana, Guyana, Kenya, Kiribati, Malawi, Maldives, Mozambique, Namibia, Nauru, Nigeria, Seychelles, Sierra Leone, South Africa, Sri Lanka, Tanzania, Uganda, Zambia and Zimbabwe. The two offices were separated in the remaining 11: Bangladesh, Dominica, Fiji, India, Malta, Mauritius, Pakistan, Samoa, Singapore, Trinidad and Tobago and Vanuatu.

Of the monarchies, the Queen is Head of State of the United Kingdom and of 15 others, in each of which she is represented by a Governor-General: Antigua and Barbuda, Australia, the Bahamas, Barbados, Belize, Canada, Grenada, Jamaica, New Zealand, Papua New Guinea, Saint Christopher and Nevis, Saint Lucia, Saint Vincent and the Grenadines, Solomon Islands and Tuvalu. Brunei, Lesotho, Malaysia, Swaziland and Tonga are also monarchies, where the traditional monarch is Head of State.

The Governors-General are appointed by the Queen on the advice of the Prime Ministers of the country concerned. They are wholly independent of the Government of the United Kingdom.

HIGH COMMISSIONERS

Governments of member countries are represented in other Commonwealth countries by High Commissioners, who have a status equivalent to that of Ambassadors.

Organization

(April 2001)

The Commonwealth is not a federation: there is no central government nor are there any rigid contractual obligations such as bind members of the United Nations.

The Commonwealth has no written constitution but its members subscribe to the ideals of the Declaration of Commonwealth Principles unanimously approved by a meeting of heads of government in Singapore in 1971. Members also approved the 1977 statement on apartheid in sport (the Gleneagles Agreement); the 1979 Lusaka Declaration on Racism and Racial Prejudice; the 1981 Melbourne Declaration on relations between developed and developing countries; the 1983 New Delhi Statement on Economic Action; the 1983 Goa Declaration on International Security; the 1985 Nassau Declaration on World Order; the Commonwealth Accord on Southern Africa (1985); the 1987 Vancouver Declaration on World Trade; the Okanagan Statement and Programme of Action on Southern Africa (1987); the Langkawi Declaration on the Environment (1989); the Kuala Lumpur Statement on Southern Africa (1989); the Harare Commonwealth Declaration (1991); the Ottawa Declaration on Women and Structural Adjustment (1991); the Limassol Statement on the Uruguay Round of multilateral trade negotiations (1993); the Millbrook Commonwealth Action Programme on the Harare Declaration (1995); the Edinburgh Commonwealth Economic Declaration (1997); and the Fancourt Commonwealth Declaration on Globalization and People-centred Development (1999).

MEETINGS OF HEADS OF GOVERNMENT

Meetings are private and informal and operate not by voting but by consensus. The emphasis is on consultation and exchange of views for co-operation. A communiqué is issued at the end of every meeting. Meetings are held every two years in different capitals in the Commonwealth. The 1999 meeting was held in Durban, South Africa, in November, and the 2001 meeting was to be held in Brisbane, Australia.

OTHER CONSULTATIONS

Meetings at ministerial and official level are also held regularly. Since 1959 finance ministers have met in a Commonwealth country in the week prior to the annual meetings of the IMF and the World Bank. Meetings on education, legal, women's and youth affairs are held at ministerial level every three years. Ministers of health hold annual meetings, with major meetings every three years, and ministers of agriculture meet every two years. Ministers of trade, labour and employment, industry, science and the environment also hold periodic meetings.

Senior officials—cabinet secretaries, permanent secretaries to heads of government and others—meet regularly in the year between meetings of heads of government to provide continuity and to exchange views on various developments.

In November 1999 the heads of government meeting established a Commonwealth High Level Review Group to review the role and activities of the Commonwealth. In 2000 the Group initiated a programme of consulations to proceed with its mandate and established a working group of experts to consider the Commonwealth's role in supporting information technology capabilities in member countries.

COMMONWEALTH SECRETARIAT

The Secretariat, established by Commonwealth heads of government in 1965, operates as an international organization at the service of all Commonwealth countries. It organizes consultations between governments and runs programmes of co-operation. Meetings of heads of government, ministers and senior officials decide these programmes and provide overall direction.

The Secretariat is headed by a secretary-general (elected by heads of government), assisted by three deputy secretaries-general. One deputy is responsible for political affairs, one for economic and social affairs, and one for development co-operation (including the Commonwealth Fund for Technical Co-operation—see below). The Secretariat comprises 12 Divisions in the fields of political affairs; legal and constitutional affairs; information and public affairs; administration; economic affairs; human resource development; gender and youth affairs; science and technology; economic and legal advisory services; export and industrial development; management and training services; and general technical assistance services. It also includes a non-governmental organizations desk and a unit for strategic planning and evaluation.

Secretary-General: DONALD (DON) C. MCKINNON (New Zealand).

Deputy Secretary-General (Political): KRISHNAN SRINIVASAN (India).

Deputy Secretary-General (Economic and Social): Dame VERONICA SUTHERLAND (United Kingdom).

Deputy Secretary-General (Development Co-operation): WINSTON A. COX (Barbados).

Activities

INTERNATIONAL AFFAIRS

In October 1991 heads of government, meeting in Harare, Zimbabwe, issued the Harare Commonwealth Declaration, in which they reaffirmed their commitment to the Commonwealth Principles declared in 1971, and stressed the need to promote sustainable development and the alleviation of poverty. The Declaration placed emphasis on the promotion of democracy and respect for human rights and resolved to strengthen the Commonwealth's capacity to assist countries in entrenching democratic practices. The meeting also welcomed the political reforms introduced by the South African Government to end the system of apartheid and urged all South African political parties to commence negotiations on a new constitution as soon as possible. The meeting endorsed measures on the phased removal of punitive measures against South Africa. 'People-to-people' sanctions (including consular and visa restrictions, cultural and scientific boycotts and restrictions on tourism promotion) were removed immediately, with economic sanctions to remain in place until a constitution for a new democratic, non-racial state had been agreed. A sports boycott, first imposed in 1977, would continue to be repealed on a sport-by-sport basis, as each sport in South Africa became integrated and non-racial. The embargo on the supply of armaments would remain in place until a post-apartheid, democratic regime had been firmly established in South Africa. In December a group of six eminent Commonwealth citizens was dispatched to observe multi-party negotiations on the future of South Africa and to assist the process where possible. In October 1992, in a fresh attempt to assist the South African peace process, a Commonwealth team of 18 observers was sent to monitor political violence in the country. A second phase of the Commonwealth Mission to South Africa (COMSA) began in February 1993, comprising 10 observers with backgrounds in policing, the law, politics and public life. COMSA issued a report in May in which it urged a concerted effort to build a culture of political tolerance in South Africa. In a report on its third phase, issued in December, COMSA appealed strongly to all political parties to participate in the transitional arrangements leading to democratic elections. In October the Commonwealth heads of government, meeting in Limassol, Cyprus, agreed that a democratic and non-racial South Africa would be invited to join the organization. They endorsed the removal of all economic sanctions against South Africa, but agreed to retain the

arms embargo until a post-apartheid, democratic government had been established.

In November 1995 Commonwealth heads of government, convened in New Zealand, formulated and adopted the Millbrook Commonwealth Action Programme on the Harare Declaration, to promote adherence by member countries to the fundamental principles of democracy and human rights (as proclaimed in the 1991 Declaration). The Programme incorporated a framework of measures to be pursued in support of democratic processes and institutions, and actions to be taken in response to violations of the Harare Declaration principles, in particular the unlawful removal of a democratically-elected government. A Commonwealth Ministerial Action Group on the Harare Declaration (CMAG) was to be established to implement this process and to assist the member country involved to comply with the Harare principles. On the basis of this Programme, the leaders suspended Nigeria from the Commonwealth with immediate effect, following the execution by that country's military Government of nine environmental and human rights protesters and a series of other violations of human rights. The meeting determined to expel Nigeria from the Commonwealth if no 'demonstrable progress' had been made towards the establishment of a democratic authority by the time of the next summit meeting. In addition, the Programme formulated measures to promote sustainable development in member countries, which was considered to be an important element in sustaining democracy, and to facilitate consensus-building within the international community. Earlier in the meeting a statement was issued declaring the 'overwhelming majority' of Commonwealth governments to be opposed to nuclear-testing programmes being undertaken in the South Pacific region. However, in view of events in Nigeria, the issue of nuclear testing and disagreement among member countries did not assume the significance anticipated.

In December 1995 CMAG convened for its inaugural meeting in London. The Group, comprising the ministers of foreign affairs of Canada, Ghana, Jamaica, Malaysia, New Zealand, South Africa, the United Kingdom and Zimbabwe, commenced by considering efforts to restore democratic government in the three Commonwealth countries under military regimes, i.e. The Gambia, Nigeria and Sierra Leone. At the second meeting of the Group, in April 1996, ministers commended the conduct of presidential and parliamentary elections in Sierra Leone and the announcement by The Gambia's military leaders to proceed with a transition to civilian rule. In June a three-member CMAG delegation visited The Gambia to reaffirm Commonwealth support of the transition process in that country and to identify possible areas of further Commonwealth assistance. In August the Gambian authorities issued a decree removing the ban on political activities and parties, although shortly afterwards prohibited certain parties and candidates involved in political life prior to the military take-over from contesting the elections. CMAG recommended that in such circumstances there should be no Commonwealth observers sent to either the presidential or parliamentary elections, which were held in September 1996 and January 1997 respectively. Following the restoration of a civilian Government in early 1997, CMAG requested the Commonwealth Secretary-General to extend technical assistance to The Gambia in order to consolidate the democratic transition process. In April 1996 it was noted that the human rights situation in Nigeria had continued to deteriorate. CMAG, having pursued unsuccessful efforts to initiate dialogue with the Nigerian authorities, outlined a series of punitive and restrictive measures (including visa restrictions on members of the administration, a cessation of sporting contacts and an embargo on the export of armaments) that it would recommend for collective Commonwealth action in order to exert further pressure for reform in Nigeria. Following a meeting of a high-level delegation of the Nigerian Government and CMAG in June, the Group agreed to postpone the implementation of the sanctions, pending progress on the dialogue. (Canada, however, determined, unilaterally, to impose the measures with immediate effect; the United Kingdom did so in accordance with a decision of the European Union to implement limited sanctions against Nigeria.) A proposed CMAG mission to Nigeria was postponed in August, owing to restrictions imposed by the military authorities on access to political detainees and other civilian activists in that country. In September the Group agreed to proceed with the visit and to delay further a decision on the implementation of sanction measures. CMAG, without the participation of the representative of the Canadian Government, undertook its ministerial mission in November. In July 1997 the Group reiterated the Commonwealth Secretary-General's condemnation of a military coup in Sierra Leone in May, and decided to suspend that country's participation in meetings of the Commonwealth pending the restoration of a democratic government.

In October 1997 Commonwealth heads of government, meeting in Edinburgh, the United Kingdom, endorsed CMAG's recommendation that the imposition of sanctions against Nigeria be held in abeyance pending the scheduled completion of a transition programme towards democracy by October 1998. It was also agreed that

CMAG be formally constituted as a permanent organ to investigate abuses of human rights throughout the Commonwealth. Jamaica and South Africa were to be replaced as members of CMAG by Barbados and Botswana, respectively.

In March 1998 CMAG, at its ninth meeting, commended the efforts of the Economic Community of West African States in restoring the democratically-elected Government of President Ahmed Tejan Kabbah in Sierra Leone, and agreed to remove all restrictions on Sierra Leone's participation in Commonwealth activities. Later in that month, a representative mission of CMAG visited Sierra Leone to express its support for Kabbah's administration and to consider the country's needs in its process of reconstruction. At the CMAG meeting held in October members agreed that Sierra Leone should no longer be considered under the Group's mandate; however, they urged the Secretary-General to continue to assist that country in the process of national reconciliation and to facilitate negotiations with opposition forces to ensure a lasting cease-fire.

In April 1998 the Nigerian military leader, Gen. Sani Abacha, confirmed his intention to conduct a presidential election in August, but indicated that, following an agreement with other political organizations, he was to be the sole candidate. In June, however, Abacha died suddenly. His successor, Gen. Abdulsalam Abubakar, immediately released several prominent political prisoners, and in early July agreed to meet with the Secretaries-General of the UN and the Commonwealth to discuss the release of the imprisoned opposition leader, Chief Moshood Abiola. Abubakar also confirmed his intention to abide by the programme for transition to civilian rule by October. In mid-July, however, shortly before he was to have been liberated, Abiola died. The Commonwealth Secretary-General subsequently endorsed a new transition programme, which provided for the election of a civilian leader in May 1999. In October 1998 CMAG, convened for its 10th formal meeting, acknowledged Abubakar's efforts towards restoring a democratic government and recommended that member states begin to remove sanctions against Nigeria and that it resume participation in certain Commonwealth activities. The Commonwealth Secretary-General subsequently announced a programme of technical assistance to support Nigeria in the planning and conduct of democratic elections. Staff teams from the Commonwealth Secretariat observed local government, and state and governorship elections, held in December and in January 1999, respectively. A 23-member Commonwealth Observer Group was also dispatched to Nigeria to monitor the preparations and conduct of legislative and presidential elections, held in late February. While the Group reported several deficiencies and irregularities in the conduct of the polling, it confirmed that, in general, the conditions had existed for free and fair elections and that the elections were a legitimate basis for the transition of power to a democratic, civilian government. In April CMAG voted to readmit Nigeria to full membership on 29 May, upon the installation of the new civilian administration.

In 1999 the Commonwealth Secretary-General appointed a Special Envoy to broker an agreement in order to end a civil dispute in Honiara, Solomon Islands. An accord was signed in late June, and it was envisaged that the Commonwealth would monitor its implementation. In October a Commonwealth Multinational Police Peace Monitoring Group was stationed in Solomon Islands; this was superseded by a Commonwealth Multinational Police Assistance Force in January 2000. Following further internal unrest, however, CMAG, in June, determined to send a new mission to Solomon Islands in order to facilitate negotiations between the opposing parties, to convey the Commonwealth's concern and to offer assistance. The Commonwealth welcomed the peace accord concluded in Solomon Islands in October, and extended its support to the International Peace Monitoring Team which was to be established to oversee implementation of the peace accords. In June 1999 an agreement was concluded between opposing political groups in Zanzibar, having been facilitated by the good offices of the Secretary-General; however, this was only partially implemented.

In mid-October 1999 a special meeting of CMAG was convened to consider the overthrow of the democratically-elected Government in Pakistan in a military coup. The meeting condemned the action as a violation of Commonwealth principles and urged the new authorities to declare a timetable for the return to democratic rule. CMAG also resolved to send a four-member delegation, comprising the ministers of foreign affairs of Barbados, Canada, Ghana and Malaysia, to discuss this future course of action with the military regime. Pakistan was suspended from participation in meetings of the Commonwealth with immediate effect. The suspension, pending the restoration of a democratic government, was endorsed by heads of government, meeting in November, who requested that CMAG keep the situation in Pakistan under review. At the meeting, held in Durban, South Africa, CMAG was reconstituted to comprise the ministers of foreign affairs of Australia, Bangladesh, Barbados, Botswana, Canada, Malaysia, Nigeria and the United Kingdom. It was agreed that no country would serve for more than two consecutive two-year terms. CMAG was requested to remain actively involved in the post-conflict development and rehabilitation of Sierra Leone and the process of consolidating peace. In addition, it was urged to monitor persistent violations of the Harare Declaration principles in all countries. Heads of government also agreed to establish a new ministerial group on Guyana and to reconvene a ministerial committee on Belize, in order to facilitate dialogue in ongoing territorial disputes with neighbouring countries.

In June 2000, following the overthrow in May of the Fijian Government by a group of armed civilians, and the subsequent illegal detention of members of the elected administration, CMAG suspended Fiji's participation in meetings of the Commonwealth pending the restoration of democratic rule. In September, upon the request of CMAG, the Secretary-General appointed a Special Envoy to support efforts towards political dialogue and a return to democratic rule in Fiji. The Special Envoy under took his first visit in December.

In March 2001 CMAG resolved to send a ministerial mission to Zimbabwe, in order to relay to the government the Commonwealth's concerns at the ongoing violence and abuses of human rights in that country, as well as to discuss the conduct of parliamentary elections and extend technical assistance. The mission was rejected by the Zimbabwean Government.

Political Affairs Division: assists consultation among member governments on international and Commonwealth matters of common interest. In association with host governments, it organizes the meetings of heads of government and senior officials. The Division services committees and special groups set up by heads of government dealing with political matters. The Secretariat has observer status at the United Nations, and the Division manages a joint office in New York to enable small states, which would otherwise be unable to afford facilities there, to maintain a presence at the United Nations. The Division monitors political developments in the Commonwealth and international progress in such matters as disarmament, the concerns of small states, dismantling of apartheid and the Law of the Sea. It also undertakes research on matters of common interest to member governments, and reports back to them. The Division is involved in diplomatic training and consular co-operation.

In 1990 Commonwealth heads of government mandated the Division to support the promotion of democracy by monitoring the preparations for and conduct of parliamentary, presidential or other elections in member countries at the request of national governments. By the end of 2000 the Commonwealth had dispatched more than 30 electoral missions in accordance with this mandate. Observer groups monitored legislative elections in Zimbabwe in June 2000, in Sri Lanka during October, and in Trinidad and Tobago in December. A Commonwealth observer mission was also dispatched to Zanzibar in October to attend concurrent legislative and presidential elections, and it was agreed that Commonwealth officials would be present at local elections to be held in Pakistan over a six-month period from December. In March 2001 an observer group monitored the organization and conduct of a general election in Guyana. In the same month representatives of the Commonwealth Secretary-General were sent to Uganda and to St Vincent and the Grenadines, to be present at a presidential and general election respectively.

A new expert group on good governance and the elimination of corruption in economic management convened for its first meeting in May 1998. In November 1999 Commonwealth heads of government endorsed a Framework for Principles for Promoting Good Governance and Combating Corruption, which had been drafted by the group.

LAW

Legal and Constitutional Affairs Division: promotes and facilitates co-operation and the exchange of information among member governments on legal matters. It administers, jointly with the Commonwealth of Learning, a distance training programme for legislative draftsmen and assists governments to reform national laws to meet the obligations of international conventions. The Division organizes the triennial meeting of ministers, Attorneys General and senior ministry officials concerned with the legal systems in Commonwealth countries. It has also initiated four Commonwealth schemes for co-operation on extradition, the protection of material cultural heritage, mutual assistance in criminal matters and the transfer of convicted offenders within the Commonwealth. It liaises with the Commonwealth Magistrates' and Judges' Association, the Commonwealth Legal Education Association, the Commonwealth Lawyers' Association (with which it helps to prepare the triennial Commonwealth Law Conference for the practising profession), the Commonwealth Association of Legislative Counsel, and with other international non-governmental organizations. The Division provides in-house legal advice for the Secretariat. The quarterly *Commonwealth Law Bulletin* reports on legal developments in and beyond the Commonwealth.

The Division's Commercial Crime Unit assists member countries to combat financial and organized crime, in particular transborder criminal activities, and promotes the exchange of information regarding national and international efforts to combat serious commercial crime through a quarterly publication, *Commonwealth Legal Assistance News,* and the *Crimewatch* bulletin. A Human Rights Unit aims to assist governments to strengthen national institutions and other mechanisms for the protection for human rights. It also organizes training workshops and promotes the exchange of relevant information among member countries.

ECONOMIC CO-OPERATION

In October 1997 Commonwealth heads of government, meeting in Edinburgh, the United Kingdom, signed an Economic Declaration that focused on issues relating to global trade, investment and development and committed all member countries to free-market economic principles. The Declaration also incorporated a provision for the establishment of a Trade and Investment Access Facility within the Secretariat in order to assist developing member states in the process of international trade liberalization and promote intra-Commonwealth trade.

In May 1998 the Commonwealth Secretary-General appealed to the Group of Eight industrialized nations to accelerate and expand the initiative to ease the debt burden of the most heavily indebted poor countries (HIPCs) (see World Bank and IMF). However, the Group failed to endorse the so-called 'Mauritius Mandate', adopted by Commonwealth finance ministers, meeting in Mauritius, in September 1997, which stipulated that by 2000 all eligible HIPCs should have in progress measures to reduce their external debt. In October 1998 Commonwealth finance ministers, convened in Ottawa, Canada, reiterated their appeal to international financial institutions to accelerate the HIPC initiative. The meeting also issued a Commonwealth Statement on the global economic crisis and endorsed several proposals to help to counter the difficulties experienced by several countries. These measures included a mechanism to enable countries to suspend payments on all short-term financial obligations at a time of emergency without defaulting, assistance to governments to attract private capital and to manage capital market volatility, and the development of international codes of conduct regarding financial and monetary policies and corporate governance. In March 1999 the Commonwealth Secretariat hosted a joint IMF-World Bank conference to review the HIPC scheme and initiate a process of reform. In November Commonwealth heads of government, meeting in South Africa, declared their support for measures undertaken by the World Bank and IMF to enhance the HIPC initiative. At the end of an informal retreat the leaders adopted the Fancourt Commonwealth Declaration on Globalization and People-Centred Development, which emphasized the need for a more equitable spread of wealth generated by the process of globalization, and expressed a renewed commitment to the elimination of all forms of discrimination, the promotion of people-centred development and capacity-building, and efforts to ensure developing countries benefit from future multilateral trade liberalization measures.

Economic Affairs Division: organizes and services the annual meetings of Commonwealth ministers of finance and the ministerial group on small states and assists in servicing the biennial meetings of heads of government and periodic meetings of environment ministers. It engages in research and analysis on economic issues of interest to member governments and organizes seminars and conferences of government officials and experts. The Division undertook a major programme of technical assistance to enable developing Commonwealth countries to participate in the Uruguay Round of multilateral trade negotiations and has assisted the African, Caribbean and Pacific (ACP) group of countries in their trade negotiations with the European Union. It continues to help developing countries to strengthen their links with international capital markets and foreign investors. The Division also services groups of experts on economic affairs that have been commissioned by governments to report on, among other things, protectionism; obstacles to the North-South negotiating process; reform of the international financial and trading system; the debt crisis; management of technological change; the special needs of small states; the impact of change on the development process; environmental issues; women and structural adjustment; and youth unemployment. In February 1998 the Commonwealth Secretariat hosted the first Inter-Governmental Organizations Meeting to promote co-operation between small island states and the formulation of a unified policy approach to international fora. A second meeting was convened in March 2001, where discussions focused on the forthcoming WTO ministerial meeting and the OECD's harmful tax initiative. The Economic Affairs Division co-ordinates the Secretariat's environmental work and manages the Iwokrama International Centre for Rainforest Conservation and Development.

The Division played a catalytic role in the establishment of a Commonwealth Equity Fund, initiated in September 1990, to allow developing member countries to improve their access to private institutional investment, and promoted a Caribbean Investment

Fund. The Division supported the establishment of a Commonwealth Private Investment Initiative (CPII) to mobilize capital, on a regional basis, for investment in newly-privatized companies and in small and medium-sized businesses in the private sector. The first regional fund under the CPII was launched in July 1996. The Commonwealth Africa Investment Fund (Comafin), was to be managed by the United Kingdom's official development institution, the Commonwealth Development Corporation, to assist businesses in 19 countries in sub-Saharan Africa, with initial resources of US $63.5m. In August 1997 a fund for the Pacific Islands was launched, with an initial capital of $15.0m. A $200m. South Asia Regional Fund was established at the Heads of Government Meeting in October. In October 1998 a fund for the Caribbean states was inaugurated, at a meeting of Commonwealth finance ministers.

HUMAN RESOURCES

Human Resource Development Division: consists of two departments concerned with education and health. The Division co-operates with member countries in devising strategies for human resource development.

The **Education Department** arranges specialist seminars, workshops and co-operative projects, and commissions studies in areas identified by ministers of education, whose three-yearly meetings it also services. Its present areas of emphasis include improving the quality of and access to basic education; strengthening the culture of science, technology and mathematics education in formal and non-formal areas of education; improving the quality of management in institutions of higher learning and basic education; improving the performance of teachers; strengthening examination assessment systems; and promoting the movement of students between Commonwealth countries. The Department also promotes multi-sectoral strategies to be incorporated in the development of human resources. Emphasis is placed on ensuring a gender balance, the appropriate use of technology, promoting good governance, addressing the problems of scale particular to smaller member countries, and encouraging collaboration between governments, the private sector and other non-governmental organizations.

The **Health Department** organizes ministerial, technical and expert group meetings and workshops, to promote co-operation on health matters, and the exchange of health information and expertise. The Department commissions relevant studies and provides professional and technical advice to member countries and to the Secretariat. It also supports the work of regional health organizations and promotes health for all people in Commonwealth countries.

Gender and Youth Affairs Division: consists of the Gender Affairs Department and the Commonwealth Youth Affairs Department.

The **Gender Affairs Department** is responsible for the implementation of the 1995 Commonwealth Plan of Action on Gender and Development, which was endorsed by the Heads of Government in order to achieve gender equality in the Commonwealth. The main objective of the Plan is to ensure that gender is incorporated into all policies, programmes, structures and procedures of member states and of the Commonwealth Secretariat. The Department is also addressing specific concerns such as the integration of gender issues into national budgetary processes, increasing the participation of women in politics and conflict prevention and resolution, and the promotion of human rights, including the elimination of violence against women and girls.

The **Youth Affairs Department** administers the Commonwealth Youth Programme (CYP), funded through separate voluntary contributions from governments, which seeks to promote the involvement of young people in the economic and social development of their countries. The CYP was awarded a budget of £2.1m. for 1998/99. It provides policy advice for governments and operates regional training programmes for youth workers and policymakers through its centres in Africa, Asia, the Caribbean and the Pacific. It conducts a Youth Study Fellowship scheme, a Youth Project Fund, a Youth Exchange Programme (in the Caribbean), and a Youth Service Awards Scheme, holds conferences and seminars, carries out research and disseminates information. In May 1995 a Commonwealth Youth Credit Initiative was launched, in order to provide funds, training and advice to young entrepreneurs. In May 1998 a Commonwealth ministerial meeting, held in Kuala Lumpur, Malaysia, approved a new Plan of Action on Youth Empowerment to the Year 2005.

SCIENCE

Science and Technology Division: is partially funded and governed by the Commonwealth Science Council, consisting of 35 member governments, which aims to enhance the scientific and technological capabilities of member countries, through co-operative research, training and the exchange of information. Current priority areas of work are concerned with the promotion of sustainable development and cover biological diversity and genetic resources, water resources, and renewable energy.

TECHNICAL CO-OPERATION

Commonwealth Fund for Technical Co-operation (CFTC): f. 1971 to facilitate the exchange of skills between member countries and to promote economic and social development. It is administered by the Commonwealth Secretariat and financed by voluntary subscriptions from member governments. The CFTC responds to requests from member governments for technical assistance, such as the provision of experts for short- or medium-term projects, advice on economic or legal matters, in particular in the areas of natural resources management and public-sector reform, and training programmes. The CFTC also administers the Langkawi awards for the study of environmental issues, which is funded by the Canadian Government. The CFTC budget for 1998/99 amounted to £20.5m.

CFTC activities are implemented by the following divisions:

Economic and Legal Advisory Services Division: serves as an in-house consultancy, offering advice to governments on macro-economic and financial management, capital market and private-sector development, debt management, the development of natural resources, and the negotiation of maritime boundaries and fisheries access agreements;

Export and Industrial Development Division: advises on all aspects of export marketing and the development of tourism, industry, small businesses and enterprises. Includes an Agricultural Development Unit, which provides technical assistance in agriculture and renewable resources;

General Technical Assistance Services Division: provides short- and long-term experts in all fields of development;

Management and Training Services Division: provides integrated packages of consultancy and training to enhance skills in areas such as public sector reform and the restructuring of enterprises, and arranges specific country and overseas training programmes.

The Secretariat also includes an Administration Division, a Strategic Planning and Evaluation Unit, and an Information and Public Affairs Division, which produces information publications, and radio and television programmes, about Commonwealth co-operation and consultation activities.

Finance

The Secretariat's budget for 1998/99 was £10.5m. Member governments meet the cost of the Secretariat through subscriptions on a scale related to income and population.

Publications

Commonwealth Currents (quarterly).
Commonwealth Declarations 1971–91.
Commonwealth Organisations (directory).
The Commonwealth Today.
In Common (quarterly newsletter of the Youth Programme).
International Development Policies (quarterly).
Link In to Gender and Development (2 a year).
Notes on the Commonwealth (series of reference leaflets).
Report of the Commonwealth Secretary-General (every 2 years).
The Commonwealth Yearbook.
Numerous reports, studies and papers (catalogue available).

Commonwealth Organizations

(In the United Kingdom, unless otherwise stated.)

PRINCIPAL BODIES

Commonwealth Foundation: Marlborough House, Pall Mall, London, SW1Y 5HY; tel. (20) 7930-3783; fax (20) 7839-8157; e-mail geninfo@commonwealth.int; internet www.commonwealthfoundation.com; f. 1966; intergovernmental body promoting people-to-people interaction, and collaboration within the non-governmental sector of the Commonwealth; supports non-governmental organizations, professional associations and Commonwealth arts and culture. Awards an annual Commonwealth Writers' Prize. Funds are provided by Commonwealth govts. Chair. GRACA MACHEL (Mozambique); Dir COLIN BELL (United Kingdom). Publ. *Common Path* (quarterly).

The Commonwealth of Learning (COL): 1285 West Broadway, Suite 600, Vancouver, BC V6H 3X8, Canada; tel. (604) 775-8200; fax (604) 775-8210; e-mail info@col.org; internet www.col.org; f. 1987 by Commonwealth Heads of Government to promote the devt and sharing of distance education and open learning resources, including materials, expertise and technologies, throughout the Commonwealth and in other countries; implements and assists with national and regional educational programmes; acts as consultant to international agencies and national governments; conducts seminars and studies on specific educational needs. COL is financed by Commonwealth governments on a voluntary basis; in 1999 heads of government endorsed an annual core budget for COL of US $9m. Pres. Dato' Prof. GAJARAJ DHANARAJAN (Malaysia). Publs *Connections*, *EdTech News*.

The following represents a selection of other Commonwealth organizations:

AGRICULTURE AND FORESTRY

Commonwealth Forestry Association: c/o Oxford Forestry Institute, South Parks Rd, Oxford, OX1 3RB; tel. (1865) 271037; fax (1865) 275074; e-mail cfa_ox@hotmail.com; f. 1921; produces, collects and circulates information relating to world forestry and promotes good management, use and conservation of forests and forest lands throughout the world. Mems: 1,000. Chair. Dr J. S. MAINI. Publs *International Forestry Review* (quarterly), *Commonwealth Forestry News* (quarterly), *Commonwealth Forestry Handbook* (irregular).

Standing Committee on Commonwealth Forestry: Forestry Commission, 231 Corstorphine Rd, Edinburgh, EH12 7AT; tel. (131) 314-6137; fax (131) 334-0442; e-mail libby.jones@forestry.gov.uk; f. 1923 to provide continuity between Confs, and to provide a forum for discussion on any forestry matters of common interest to mem. govts which may be brought to the Cttee's notice by any member country or organization; 54 mems. 1997 Conference: Victoria Falls, Zimbabwe; 2001 Conference: Perth, Australia. Sec. LIBBY JONES. Publ. *Newsletter* (quarterly).

COMMONWEALTH STUDIES

Institute of Commonwealth Studies: 28 Russell Sq., London, WC1B 5DS; tel. (20) 7862-8844; fax (20) 7862-8820; e-mail ics@sas.ac.uk; internet www.sas.ac.uk/commonwealthstudies/; f. 1949 to promote advanced study of the Commonwealth; provides a library and meeting place for postgraduate students and academic staff engaged in research in this field; offers postgraduate teaching. Dir Prof. PAT CAPLAN. Publs *Annual Report, Collected Seminar Papers, Newsletter, Theses in Progress in Commonwealth Studies*.

COMMUNICATIONS

Commonwealth Telecommunications Organization: Clareville House, 26–27 Oxendon St, London, SW1Y 4EL; tel. (20) 7930-5516; fax (20) 7930-4248; e-mail info@cto.int; internet www.cto.int; f. 1967; aims to enhance the development of telecommunications in Commonwealth countries and contribute to the communications infrastructure required for economic and social devt, through a devt and training programme. Exec. Dir Dr DAVID SOUTER. Publ. *CTO Briefing* (3 a year).

EDUCATION AND CULTURE

Association of Commonwealth Universities (ACU): John Foster House, 36 Gordon Sq., London, WC1H 0PF; tel. (20) 7380-6700; fax (20) 7387-2655; e-mail info@acu.ac.uk; internet www.acu.ac.uk; f. 1913; organizes major meetings of Commonwealth universities and their representatives; publishes factual information about Commonwealth universities and access to them; acts as a liaison office and general information centre and provides a recruitment advertising and publicity service; hosts a management consultancy service; supplies secretariats for the Commonwealth Scholarship Comm., the Marshall Aid Commemoration Comm. and the Commonwealth Universities Study Abroad Consortium; administers various other fellowship and scholarship programmes. Mems: 480 universities in 36 Commonwealth countries or regions. Sec.-Gen. Prof. MICHAEL GIBBONS. Publs include: *Commonwealth Universities Yearbook, ACU Bulletin* (5 a year), *Report of the Council of the ACU* (annually), *Awards for University Teachers and Research Workers, Awards for Postgraduate Study at Commonwealth Universities, Awards for First Degree Study at Commonwealth Universities, Awards for University Administrators and Librarians, Who's Who of Executive Heads: Vice-Chancellors, Presidents, Principals and Rectors*, Student Information Papers (study abroad series).

Commonwealth Association for Education in Journalism and Communication—CAEJC: c/o Faculty of Law, University of Western Ontario, London, ON N6A 3K7, Canada; tel. (519) 6613348; fax (519) 6613790; e-mail caejc@julian.uwo.ca; f. 1985; aims to foster high standards of journalism and communication education and research in Commonwealth countries and to promote co-operation among institutions and professions. c. 700 mems in 32 Commonwealth countries. Pres. Prof. SYED ARABI IDID (Malaysia); Sec. Prof. ROBERT MARTIN (Canada). Publ. *CAEJAC Journal* (annually).

Commonwealth Association of Science, Technology and Mathematics Educators—CASTME: c/o Education Dept, Human Resource Development Division, Commonwealth Secretariat, Marlborough House, Pall Mall, London, SW1Y 5HX; tel. (20) 7747-6282; fax (20) 7747-6287; e-mail v.goel@commonwealth.int; f. 1974; special emphasis is given to the social significance of education in these subjects. Organizes an Awards Scheme to promote effective teaching and learning in these subjects, and biennial regional seminars. Pres. Sir HERMANN BONDI; Hon. Sec. Dr VED GOEL. Publ. *CASTME Journal* (quarterly).

Commonwealth Council for Educational Administration and Management: c/o International Educational Leadership Centre, School of Management, Lincoln University Campus, Brayford Pool, Lincoln, LN6 7TS; tel. (1522) 886071; fax (1522) 886023; e-mail athody@lincoln.ac.uk; f. 1970; aims to foster quality in professional development and links among educational administrators; holds nat. and regional confs, as well as visits and seminars. Mems: 24 affiliated groups representing 3,000 persons. Pres. Prof. ANGELA THODY; Sec. GERALDINE BRISTOW. Publs *Managing Education Matters* (2 a year), *International Studies in Educational Administration* (2 a year).

Commonwealth Institute: 230 Kensington High St, London, W8 6NQ; tel. (20) 7603-4535; fax (20) 7602-7374; e-mail info@commonwealth.org.uk; internet www.commonwealth.org.uk; f. 1893 as the Imperial Institute; restructured as an independent pan-Commonwealth agency Jan. 2000; governed by a Bd of Trustees elected by the Bd of Governors; Commonwealth High Commissioners to the United Kingdom act as ex-officio Governors; the Inst. houses a Commonwealth Resource and Literature Library and a Conference and Events Centre; supplies educational resource materials and training throughout the United Kingdom; provides internet services to the Commonwealth; operates as an arts and conference centre, running a Commonwealth-based cultural programme; a new five-year strategic plan, entitled 'Commonwealth 21', was inaugurated in 1998. Chair. DAVID A. THOMPSON; Chief Exec. DAVID FRENCH. Publ. *Annual Review.*

League for the Exchange of Commonwealth Teachers: 7 Lion Yard, Tremadoc Rd, London, SW4 7NQ; tel. (20) 7498-1101; fax (20) 7720-5403; e-mail lectcom_exchange@compuserve.com; internet www.lect.org.uk; f. 1901; promotes educational exchanges between teachers in Australia, the Bahamas, Barbados, Bermuda, Canada, Guyana, India, Jamaica, Kenya, Malawi, New Zealand, Pakistan, South Africa and Trinidad and Tobago. Dir ANNA TOMLINSON. Publs *Annual Report, Exchange Teacher* (annually).

HEALTH

Commonwealth Medical Association: BMA House, Tavistock Sq., London, WC1H 9JP; tel. (20) 7272-8492; fax (20) 7272-1663; e-mail office@commat.org; internet www.commat.org; f. 1962 for the exchange of information; provision of tech. co-operation and advice; formulation and maintenance of a code of ethics; provision of continuing medical education; devt and promotion of health education programmes; and liaison with WHO and the UN on health issues; meetings of its Council are held every three years. Mems: medical asscns in Commonwealth countries. Sec. Dr J. D. J. HAVARD. Publ. *CommonHealth* (quarterly).

Commonwealth Pharmaceutical Association: 1 Lambeth High St, London, SE1 7JN; tel. (20) 7820-3399 ext. 303; fax (20) 7582-3401; e-mail eharden@rpsgb.org.uk; f. 1970 to promote the interests of pharmaceutical sciences and the profession of pharmacy in the Commonwealth; to maintain high professional standards, encourage links between members and the creation of nat. asscns; and to facilitate the dissemination of information. Holds confs (every four years) and regional meetings. Mems: 39 pharmaceutical asscns. Sec. PHILIP E. GREEN. Publ. *Quarterly Newsletter.*

Commonwealth Society for the Deaf: 34 Buckingham Palace Rd, London, SW1W 0RE; tel. (20) 7233-5700; fax (20) 7233-5800; e-mail sound.seekers@btinternet.com; internet www.sound-seekers.org.uk; promotes the health, education and general welfare of the deaf in developing Commonwealth countries; encourages and assists the development of educational facilities, the training of teachers of the deaf, and the provision of support for parents of deaf children; organizes visits by volunteer specialists to developing countries; provides audiological equipment and organizes the training of audiological maintenance technicians; conducts research into the causes and prevention of deafness. CEO Brig. J. A. DAVIS. Publ. *Annual Report.*

Sight Savers International (Royal Commonwealth Society for the Blind): Grosvenor Hall, Bolnore Rd, Haywards Heath, West Sussex, RH16 4BX; tel. (1444) 446600; fax (1444) 446688; e-mail information@sightsaversint.org.uk; internet www.sightsavers.org.uk; f. 1950 to prevent blindness and restore sight in developing countries, and to provide education and community-based training for incurably blind people; operates in collaboration with local part-

ners, with high priority given to training local staff; Chair. DAVID THOMPSON; Dir RICHARD PORTER. Publ. *Horizons* (newsletter, 3 a year).

INFORMATION AND THE MEDIA

Commonwealth Broadcasting Association: 17 Fleet St, London, EC4Y 1AA; tel. (20) 7583-5550; fax (20) 7583-5549; e-mail cba@cba.org.uk; internet www.oneworld.org/cba; f. 1945; gen. confs are held every two years (2002: Manchester, United Kingdom). Mems: 100 in 57 countries. Pres. BOB O'REILLY; Sec.-Gen. ELIZABETH SMITH. Publs *Commonwealth Broadcaster* (quarterly), *Commonwealth Broadcaster Directory* (annually).

Commonwealth Institute: see under Education.

Commonwealth Journalists Association: 17 Nottingham St, London, W1M 3RD; tel. (20) 7486-3844; fax (20) 7486-3822; internet www.ozemail.com.au/~pwessels/cja.html; f. 1978 to promote co-operation between journalists in Commonwealth countries, organize training facilities and confs, and foster understanding among Commonwealth peoples. Pres. MURRAY BURT; Exec. Dir IAN GILLHAM.

Commonwealth Press Union (Asscn of Commonwealth Newspapers, News Agencies and Periodicals): 17 Fleet St, London, EC4Y 1AA; tel. (20) 7583-7733; fax (20) 7583-6868; e-mail 106156.3331@compuserve.com; f. 1950; promotes the welfare of the Commonwealth press; provides training for journalists and organizes biennial confs. Mems: c. 1,000 newspapers, news agencies, periodicals in 42 Commonwealth countries. Dir ROBIN MACKICHAN. Publs *CPU News, Annual Report.*

LAW

Commonwealth Lawyers' Association: c/o The Law Society, 114 Chancery Lane, London, WC2A 1PL; tel. (20) 7320-5772; fax (20) 7831-0057; e-mail cla@lawsociety.org.uk; internet www.commonwealthlawyers.com; f. 1983 (fmrly the Commonwealth Legal Bureau); seeks to maintain and promote the rule of law throughout the Commonwealth, by ensuring that the people of the Commonwealth are served by an independent and efficient legal profession; upholds professional standards and promotes the availability of legal services; assists in organizing the triennial Commonwealth law confs. Pres. (1999–2001) CYRUS DAS; Exec. Sec. HELEN POTTS. Publs *The Commonwealth Lawyer, Clarion.*

Commonwealth Legal Advisory Service: c/o British Institute of International and Comparative Law, Charles Clore House, 17 Russell Sq., London, WC1B 5JP; tel. (20) 7862-5151; fax (20) 7862-5152; e-mail info@biicl.org; financed by the British Institute and by contributions from Commonwealth govts; provides research facilities for Commonwealth govts and law reform commissions.

Commonwealth Legal Education Association: c/o Legal and Constitutional Affairs Division, Commonwealth Secretariat, Marlborough House, Pall Mall, London, SW1Y 5HX; tel. (20) 7747-6415; fax (20) 7747-6406; e-mail clea@commonwealth.int; internet www.clea.org.uk; f. 1971 to promote contacts and exchanges and to provide information regarding legal education. Gen. Sec. JOHN HATCHARD. Publs *Commonwealth Legal Education Association Newsletter* (3 a year), *Directory of Commonwealth Law Schools* (every 2 years).

Commonwealth Magistrates' and Judges' Association: Uganda House, 58/59 Trafalgar Sq., London, WC2N 5DX; tel. (20) 7976-1007; fax (20) 7976-2395; e-mail info@cmja.org; internet www.cmja.org; f. 1970 to advance the administration of the law by promoting the independence of the judiciary, to further education in law and crime prevention and to disseminate information; confs and study tours; corporate membership for asscns of the judiciary or courts of limited jurisdiction; assoc. membership for individuals. Pres. DAVID ARMATI; Sec.-Gen. Dr KAREN BREWER. Publ. *Commonwealth Judicial Journal* (2 a year).

PARLIAMENTARY AFFAIRS

Commonwealth Parliamentary Association: Westminster House, Suite 700, 7 Millbank, London, SW1P 3JA; tel. (20) 7799-1460; fax (20) 7222-6073; e-mail hq.sec@comparlhq.org.uk; internet www.comparlhq.org.uk; f. 1911 to promote understanding and co-operation between Commonwealth parliamentarians; organization: Exec. Cttee of 32 MPs responsible to annual Gen. Assembly; 148 brs throughout the Commonwealth; holds annual Commonwealth Parliamentary Confs and seminars; also regional confs and seminars; Sec.-Gen. ARTHUR DONAHOE. Publ. *The Parliamentarian* (quarterly).

PROFESSIONAL AND INDUSTRIAL RELATIONS

Commonwealth Association of Architects: 66 Portland Pl., London, W1N 4AD; tel. (20) 7490-3024; fax (20) 7253-2592; e-mail caa@gharchitects.demon.co.uk; internet www.archexchange.org; f. 1964; an asscn of 38 socs of architects in various Commonwealth countries. Objects: to facilitate the reciprocal recognition of professional qualifications; to provide a clearing house for information on architectural practice, and to encourage collaboration. Plenary confs every three years; regional confs are also held. Exec. Dir TONY GODWIN. Publs *Handbook, Objectives and Procedures: CAA Schools Visiting Boards, Architectural Education in the Commonwealth* (annotated bibliography of research), *CAA Newsnet* (2 a year), a survey and list of schools of architecture.

Commonwealth Association for Public Administration and Management—CAPAM: 1075 Bay St, Suite 402, Toronto, ON M5S 2B1, Canada; tel. (416) 920-3337; fax (416) 920-6574; e-mail capam@capam.ca; internet www.comnet.mt/capam/; f. 1994; aims to promote sound management of the public sector in Commonwealth countries and to assist those countries undergoing political or financial reforms. An international awards programme to reward innovation within the public sector was introduced in 1997, and was to be awarded every 2 years. Pres. Dr ZOLA SKWEYIYA (South Africa); Exec. Dir ART STEVENSON (Canada).

Commonwealth Trade Union Council: Congress House, 23–28 Great Russell St, London, WC1B 3LS; tel. (20) 7631-0728; fax(20) 7436-0301; e-mail info@commonwealthtuc.org; internet www.commonwealthtuc.org; f. 1979; links trade union national centres (representing more than 30m. trade union mems) throughout the Commonwealth; promotes the application of democratic principles and core labour standards, works closely with other international trade union orgs. Dir ANNIE WATSON. Publ. *Annual Report.*

SCIENCE AND TECHNOLOGY

Commonwealth Engineers' Council: c/o Institution of Civil Engineers, One Great George St, London, SW1P 3AA; tel. (20) 7222-7722; fax (20) 7222-7500; e-mail international@ice.org.uk; f. 1946; the Council meets every two years to provide an opportunity for engineering institutions of Commonwealth countries to exchange views on collaboration; there is a standing cttee on engineering education and training; organizes seminars on related topics. Sec. J. A. WHITWELL.

Commonwealth Geological Surveys Forum: c/o Commonwealth Science Council, CSC Earth Sciences Programme, Marlborough House, Pall Mall, London, SW1Y 5HX; tel. (20) 7839-3411; fax (20) 7839-6174; e-mail comsci@gn.apc.org; f. 1948 to promote collaboration in geological, geochemical, geophysical and remote sensing techniques and the exchange of information. Geological Programme Officer Dr SIYAN MALOMO.

SPORT

Commonwealth Games Federation: Walkden House, 3–10 Melton St, London, NW1 2EB; tel. (20) 7383-5596; fax (20) 7383-5506; e-mail commonwealthgamesfederation@abtinternet.com; internet www.commonwealthgames-fed.org; the Games were first held in 1930 and are now held every four years; participation is limited to competitors representing the mem. countries of the Commonwealth; to be held in Manchester, United Kingdom, in 2002. Mems: 72 affiliated bodies. Pres. HRH The Earl of WESSEX; Chair. MICHAEL FENNELL.

YOUTH

Commonwealth Youth Exchange Council: 7 Lion Yard, Tremadoc Rd, London, SW4 7NQ; tel. (20) 7498-6151; fax (20) 7720-5403; e-mail mail@cyec.demon.co.uk; f. 1970; promotes contact between groups of young people of the United Kingdom and other Commonwealth countries by means of educational exchange visits, provides information for organizers and allocates grants; 224 mem. orgs. Dir V. S. G. CRAGGS. Publs *Contact* (handbook), *Exchange* (newsletter), *Safety and Welfare* (guide-lines for Commonwealth Youth Exchange groups).

Duke of Edinburgh's Award International Association: Award House, 7-11 St Matthew St, London, SW1P 2JT; tel. (20) 7222-4242; fax (20) 7222-4141; e-mail sect@intaward.org; internet www.intaward.org; f. 1956; offers a programme of leisure activities for young people, comprising Service, Expeditions, Physical Recreation, and Skills; operates in more than 60 countries (not confined to the Commonwealth). International Sec.-Gen. PAUL ARENGO-JONES. Publs *Award World* (2 a year), *Annual Report*, handbooks and guides.

MISCELLANEOUS

British Commonwealth Ex-Services League: 48 Pall Mall, London, SW1Y 5JG; tel. (20) 7973-7263; fax (20) 7973-7308; links the ex-service orgs in the Commonwealth, assists ex-servicemen of the Crown and their dependants who are resident abroad; holds triennial confs. Grand Pres. HRH The Duke of EDINBURGH; Sec.-Gen. Lt-Col S. POPE. Publ. *Annual Report.*

Commonwealth Countries League: 14 Thistleworth Close, Isleworth, Middlesex, TW7 4QQ; tel. (20) 8737-3572; fax (20) 8568-2495; f. 1925 to secure equal opportunities and status between men and women in the Commonwealth, to act as a link between Commonwealth women's orgs, and to promote and finance secondary education of disadvantaged girls of high ability in their own countries, through the CCL Educational Fund; holds meetings with speakers and an annual Conf., organizes the annual Commonwealth Fair for fund-raising; individual mems and affiliated socs in the Commonwealth. Sec.-Gen. SHEILA O'REILLY. Publ. *CCL Newsletter* (3 a year).

Commonwealth War Graves Commission: 2 Marlow Rd, Maidenhead, Berks, SL6 7DX; tel. (1628) 634221; fax (1628) 771208; e-mail general.enq@cwgc.org; internet www.cwgc.org; f. 1917 (as Imperial War Graves Commission); responsible for the commemoration in perpetuity of the 1.7m. members of the Commonwealth Forces who died during the wars of 1914–18 and 1939–45; provides for the marking and maintenance of war graves and memorials at some 23,000 locations in 150 countries. Mems: Australia, Canada, India, New Zealand, South Africa, United Kingdom. Pres. HRH The Duke of KENT; Dir-Gen. R. KELLAWAY.

Joint Commonwealth Societies' Council: c/o Royal Commonwealth Society, 18 Northumberland Ave, London, WC2N 5BJ; tel. (20) 7930-6733; fax (20) 7930-9705; e-mail jcsc@rcsint.org; internet www.rcsint.org; f. 1947; provides a forum for the exchange of information regarding activities of mem. orgs which promote understanding among countries of the Commonwealth; co-ordinates the distribution of the Commonwealth Day message by Queen Elizabeth, organizes the observance of the Commonwealth Day and produces educational materials relating to the occasion; mems: 16 unofficial Commonwealth orgs and four official bodies. Chair. Sir PETER MARSHALL; Sec. GWENDOLYN WHITE.

Royal Commonwealth Society: 18 Northumberland Ave, London, WC2N 5BJ; tel. (20) 7930-6733; fax (20) 7930-9705; e-mail info@rcsint.org; internet www.rcsint.org; f. 1868; to promote international understanding of the Commonwealth and its people; organizes meetings and seminars on topical issues, and cultural and social events; library housed by Cambridge University Library. Chair. Sir MICHAEL McWILLIAM; Dir STUART MOLE. Publs *Annual Report, Newsletter* (3 a year), conference reports.

Royal Over-Seas League: Over-Seas House, Park Place, St James's St, London, SW1A 1LR; tel. (20) 7408-0214; fax (20) 7499-6738; f. 1910 to promote friendship and understanding in the Commonwealth; club houses in London and Edinburgh; membership is open to all British subjects and Commonwealth citizens. Chair. Sir GEOFFREY ELLERTON; Dir-Gen. ROBERT F. NEWELL. Publ. *Overseas* (quarterly).

The Victoria League for Commonwealth Friendship: 55 Leinster Sq., London, W2 4PW; tel. (20) 7243-2633; fax (20) 7229-2994; f. 1901; aims to further personal friendship among Commonwealth peoples and to provide hospitality for visitors; maintains Student House, providing accommodation for students from Commonwealth countries; has brs elsewhere in the UK and abroad. Pres. HRH Princess MARGARET, Countess of SNOWDON; Chair. COLIN WEBBER; Gen. Sec. JOHN ALLAN. Publ. *Annual Report.*

THE COMMONWEALTH OF INDEPENDENT STATES—CIS

Address: 220000 Minsk, Kirava 17, Belarus.
Telephone: (172) 22-35-17; **fax:** (172) 27-23-39; **e-mail:** postmaster@www.cis.minsk.by; **internet:** www.cis.minsk.by.

The Commonwealth of Independent States is a voluntary association of 12 (originally 11) states, established at the time of the collapse of the USSR in December 1991.

MEMBERS

Armenia	Moldova
Azerbaijan	Russia
Belarus	Tajikistan
Georgia	Turkmenistan
Kazakhstan	Ukraine
Kyrgyzstan	Uzbekistan

Note: Azerbaijan signed the Alma-Ata Declaration (see below), but in October 1992 the Azerbaijan legislature voted against ratification of the foundation documents by which the Commonwealth of Independent States had been founded in December 1991. Azerbaijan, however, formally became a member of the CIS in September 1993, after the legislature voted in favour of membership. Georgia was admitted to the CIS in December 1993.

Organization

(April 2001)

COUNCIL OF HEADS OF STATE

This is the supreme body of the CIS, on which all the member states of the Commonwealth are represented at the level of head of state, for discussion of issues relating to the co-ordination of Commonwealth activities and the development of the Minsk Agreement. Decisions of the Council are taken by common consent, with each state having equal voting rights. The Council meets no less than twice a year, although an extraordinary meeting may be convened on the initiative of the majority of Commonwealth heads of state.

COUNCIL OF HEADS OF GOVERNMENT

This Council convenes for meetings no less than once every three months; an extraordinary sitting may be convened on the initiative of a majority of Commonwealth heads of government. The two Councils may discuss and take necessary decisions on important domestic and external issues and may hold joint sittings.

Working and auxiliary bodies, composed of authorized representatives of the participating states, may be set up on a permanent or interim basis on the decision of the Council of Heads of State and the Council of Heads of Government.

CIS EXECUTIVE COMMITTEE

The Committee was established by the Council of Heads of State in April 1999 to supersede the existing Secretariat, the Inter-state Economic Committee and other working bodies and committees, in order to improve the efficient functioning of the organization.

Executive Secretary and Chairman of the Executive Committee: YURII YAROV.

Activities

On 8 December 1991 the heads of state of Belarus, Russia and Ukraine signed the Minsk Agreement, providing for the establishment of a Commonwealth of Independent States. Formal recognition of the dissolution of the USSR was incorporated in a second treaty, signed by 11 heads of state in the then Kazakh capital, Alma-Ata (Almaty), later in that month.

In March 1992 a meeting of the CIS Council of Heads of Government decided to establish a commission to examine the resolution that 'all CIS member states are the legal successors of the rights and obligations of the former Soviet Union'. Documents relating to the legal succession of the Soviet Union were signed at a meeting of Heads of State in July. In April an agreement establishing an Inter-parliamentary Assembly (IPA), signed by Armenia, Belarus, Kazakhstan, Kyrgyzstan, Russia, Tajikistan and Uzbekistan, was published. The first Assembly was held in Bishkek, Kyrgyzstan, in September, attended by delegates from all these countries, with the exception of Uzbekistan. By March 2001 the IPA, which maintains close co-operation with international institutions, such as the Council of Europe (q.v.) and the OSCE (q.v.), comprised 10 CIS member states.

A CIS Charter was formulated at the meeting of the heads of state in Minsk, Belarus, in January 1993. The Charter, providing for a defence alliance, an inter-state court and an economic co-ordination committee, was to serve as a framework for closer co-operation and was signed by all of the members except Moldova, Turkmenistan and Ukraine.

In November 1995, at the Council of Heads of Government meeting, Russia expressed concern at the level of non-payment of debts by CIS members (amounting to an estimated US $5,800m.), which, it said, was hindering further integration. At the meeting of the Council in April 1996 a long-term plan for the integrated development of the CIS, incorporating measures for further socio-economic, military and political co-operation was approved.

In March 1997 the then Russian President, Boris Yeltsin, admitted that the CIS institutional structure had failed to ameliorate the severe economic situation of certain member states. Nevertheless, support for the CIS as an institution was reaffirmed by the participants during the meeting. At the heads of state meeting held in Chişinău, Moldova, in October, Russia was reportedly criticized by the other country delegations for failing to implement CIS agreements, for hindering development of the organization and for failing to resolve regional conflicts. Russia, for its part, urged all member states to participate more actively in defining, adopting and implementing CIS policies. In 1998 the issue of reform of the CIS was seriously addressed. The necessity of improving the activities of the CIS and of reforming its bureaucratic structure was emphasized at the meeting of heads of state in April. However, little in the way of reform was achieved at the meeting and it was decided not to adopt any declaration relating to the discussions. Reform of the CIS was also the main item on the agenda of the eleventh IPA, held in June. It was agreed that an essentially new institution needed to be created, taking into account the relations between the states in a new way. The IPA approved a decision to sign the European Social Charter; a declaration of co-operation between the Assembly and the OSCE Parliamentary Assembly (q.v.) was also signed. In the same month the first plenary meeting of a special forum, convened to address issues of restructuring the CIS, was held. Working groups were to be established to co-ordinate proposals and draft documents. However, in October reform proposals drawn up by 'experienced specialists' and presented by the Executive Secretary were unanimously rejected as inadequate by the 12 member states. In March 1999 Boris Yeltsin, acting as Chairman of the Council of Heads of State, dismissed the Executive Secretary, Boris Berezovskii, owing to alleged misconduct and neglect of duties. The decision was endorsed by the Council of Heads of Government meeting in early April. The Council also adopted guide-lines for restructuring the CIS and for the future development of the organization. Economic co-operation was to be a priority area of activity, and in particular, the establishment of a free-trade zone. Vladimir Putin, then acting President of the Russian Federation, was elected as the new Chairman of the Council of Heads of Government at a CIS summit held in Moscow in January 2000.

Member states of the CIS have formed alliances of various kinds among themselves, thereby potentially undermining the unity of the Commonwealth. In March 1996 Belarus, Kazakhstan, Kyrgyzstan and the Russian Federation signed the Quadripartite Treaty for greater integration. This envisaged the establishment of a 'New Union', based, initially on a common market and customs union and was to be open to all CIS members and the Baltic states. In April 1996 Belarus and Russia signed the Treaty on the Formation of a Community of Sovereign Republics (CSR), which provided for extensive economic, political and military co-operation. In April 1997 the two countries signed a further Treaty of Union and, in addition, initialled the Charter of the Union, which detailed the procedures and institutions designed to develop a common infrastructure, a single currency and a joint defence policy within the CSR, with the eventual aim of 'voluntary unification of the member states'. The Charter was signed in May and ratified by the respective legislatures the following month. The Union's Parliamentary Assembly, comprising 36 members from the legislature of each country, convened in official session for the first time shortly afterwards. In December 2000 the Presidents of Belarus and Russia signed an accord providing for the adoption by Belarus of the Russian currency from 1 January 2005, and for the introduction of a new joint Union currency by 1 January 2008. Azerbaijan, Georgia, Moldova and Ukraine co-operated increasingly during the late 1990s as the so-called GUAM Group; Uzbekistan joined in April 1999, creating GUUAM. In October 1997 the GUAM countries agreed collectively to establish a Eurasian Trans-Caucasus transportation corridor. The group agreed in September 2000 to convene regular annual summits of member countries' heads of state, and to organize meetings of ministers of foreign affairs at least twice a year.

ECONOMIC AFFAIRS

At a meeting of the Council of Heads of Government in March 1992 agreement was reached on repayment of the foreign debt of the former USSR. Agreements were also signed on pensions, joint tax policy and the servicing of internal debt. In May an agreement on repayment of inter-state debt and the issue of balance-of-payments statements was signed by the heads of government, meeting in Tashkent, Uzbekistan. In July it was decided to establish an economic court in Minsk.

The CIS Charter, formulated in January 1993 and signed by seven of the 10 member countries, provided for the establishment of an economic co-ordination committee. In February, at a meeting of the heads of foreign economic departments, a Foreign Economic Council was formed. All states, with the exception of Turkmenistan, signed a declaration of support for increased economic union at a meeting of the heads of state in May. At a further meeting, held in September, agreement on a framework for economic union, including the gradual removal of tariffs and creation of a currency union was reached, although Ukraine and Turkmenistan did not sign the accord. Turkmenistan was subsequently admitted as a full member of the economic union in December 1993 and Ukraine as an associate member in April 1994.

At the Council of Heads of Government meeting in September 1994 all member states, except Turkmenistan, agreed to establish an Inter-state Economic Committee to implement economic treaties adopted within the context of an economic union. The establishment of a payments union to improve the settlement of accounts was also agreed. Heads of state, meeting in the following month, resolved that the Inter-state Economic Committee would be located in Moscow, with Russia contributing the majority of administrative costs in exchange for 50% of the voting rights. The first session of the Committee was held in November. In April 1998 CIS heads of state resolved to incorporate the functions of the Committee, along with those of other working bodies and sectional committees, into a new CIS Executive Committee.

In October 1997 seven heads of government signed a document on implementing the 'concept for the integrated economic development of the CIS' which had been approved in March. The development of economic co-operation between the member states was a priority task of the special forum on reform held in June 1998. In the same month an economic forum, held in St Petersburg, Russia, acknowledged the severe economic conditions prevailing in certain CIS states.

BANKING AND FINANCIAL AFFAIRS

In February 1992 CIS heads of state agreed to retain the rouble as the common currency for trade between the republics. However, in July 1993, in an attempt to control inflation, notes printed before 1993 were withdrawn from circulation and no new ones were issued until January 1994. Despite various agreements to recreate the 'rouble zone', including a protocol agreement signed in September 1993 by six states, it effectively remained confined to Tajikistan, which joined in January 1994, and Belarus, which joined in April. Both those countries proceeded to introduce national currencies in May 1995. In January 1993, at the signing of the CIS Charter, all 10 member countries endorsed the establishment of an inter-state bank to facilitate payments between the republics and to co-ordinate monetary-credit policy. Russia was to hold 50% of shares in the bank, but decisions were to be made only with a two-thirds majority approval.

TRADE

Agreement was reached on the free movement of goods between republics at a meeting of the Council of Heads of State in February 1992, and in April 1994 an agreement on the creation of a free-trade zone within the CIS was signed. In July a council of the heads of customs committees, meeting in Moscow, approved a draft framework for customs legislation in CIS countries, to facilitate the establishment of a free-trade zone. The framework was approved by all the participants, with the exception of Turkmenistan. In April 1999 CIS heads of state signed a protocol to the 1994 free-trade area accord, which aimed to accelerate economic co-operation. In June 2000 the Council of Heads of State adopted a schedule for the implementation of priority measures related to the establishment of the free-trade zone.

At the first session of the Inter-state Economic Committee in November 1994 draft legislation regarding a customs union was approved. In March 1998 Russia, Belarus, Kazakhstan and Kyrgyzstan signed an agreement establishing a customs union, which was to be implemented in two stages: firstly, the removal of trade restrictions and the unification of trade and customs regulations; followed by the integration of economic, monetary and trade policies

(see above). The establishment of a customs union and the strengthening of intra-CIS trade were objectives endorsed by all participants, with the exception of Georgia, at the Council of Heads of Government meeting held in March 1997. In February 1999 Tajikistan signed the 1998 agreement to become the fifth member of the customs union. In October 1999 the heads of state of the five member states reiterated their political determination to implement the customs union and approved a programme to harmonize national legislation to create a single economic space. In October 2000 the heads of government of the five member states of the customs union signed a treaty establishing the Eurasian Economic Community; under the new structure, to be governed by an interstate council based in Astana, Kazakhstan, member states aimed to formulate a unified foreign economic policy, and collectively to pursue the creation of the planned single economic space. In the following month the five member governments signed an agreement enabling visa-free travel within the Community. (Earlier in 2000 Russia had withdrawn from a CIS-wide visa-free travel arrangement agreed in 1992.) In December 2000 member states of the Community adopted several documents aimed at facilitating economic co-operation.

DEFENCE

An Agreement on Armed Forces and Border Troops was concluded on 30 December 1991, at the same time as the Agreement on Strategic Forces. This confirmed the right of member states to set up their own armed forces and appointed Commanders-in-Chief of the Armed Forces and of the Border Troops, who were to elaborate joint security procedures. In February 1992 an agreement was signed stipulating that the commander of the strategic forces was subordinate to the Council of Heads of States. Eight states agreed on a unified command for general-purpose (i.e. non-strategic) armed forces for a transitional period of two years. Azerbaijan, Moldova and Ukraine resolved to establish independent armed forces.

In January 1992 Commissions on the Black Sea Fleet (control of which was disputed by Russia and Ukraine) and the Caspian Flotilla (the former Soviet naval forces on the Caspian Sea) were established. The defence and stability of CIS external borders and the status of strategic and nuclear forces were among topics discussed at the meeting of heads of state and of government, in Bishkek, in October. The formation of a defence alliance was provided for in the CIS Charter formulated in January 1993 and signed by seven of the 10 member countries; a proposal by Russia to assume control of all nuclear weapons in the former USSR was rejected at the same time.

In June 1993 CIS defence ministers agreed to abolish CIS joint military command and to abandon efforts to maintain a unified defence structure. The existing CIS command was to be replaced, on a provisional basis, by a 'joint staff for co-ordinating military co-operation between the states of the Commonwealth'. It was widely reported that Russia had encouraged the decision to abolish the joint command, owing to concerns at the projected cost of a CIS joint military structure and support within Russia's military leadership of bilateral military agreements with the country's neighbours. In December the Council of Defence Ministers agreed to establish a secretariat to co-ordinate military co-operation as a replacement to the joint military command. In November 1995 the Council of Defence Ministers authorized the establishment of a Joint Air Defence System, to be co-ordinated largely by Russia. By early 1998 all member states, except Azerbaijan and Moldova, were participating in the system (Armenia, Georgia, Kyrgyzstan and Uzbekistan joined in January). Air defence forces were to be set up in Tajikistan in 1998 and a CIS combat duty system was to be created in 1999–2005. A meeting of the Council of Defence Ministers in Moscow, in December 1998, approved a plan for further development of the system. Russia and Belarus were also in the process of establishing a joint air-defence unit in the context of the CSR (see above).

In August 1996 the Council of Defence Ministers condemned what it described as the political, economic and military threat implied in any expansion of NATO (q.v.). The statement was not signed by Ukraine. The eigthth plenary session of the IPA, held in November, urged NATO countries to abandon plans for the organization's expansion. In September the first meeting of the inter-state commission for military economic co-operation was held; a draft agreement on the export of military projects and services to third countries was approved.

The basic principles of a programme for greater military and technical co-operation were approved by the Council of Defence Ministers in March 1997. In April 1998 the Council proposed drawing up a draft programme for military and technical co-operation between member countries and also discussed procedures advising on the use and maintenance of armaments and military hardware. Draft proposals relating to information security for the military were approved by the Council in December. It was remarked that the inadequate funding of the Council was a matter for concern and that the CIS states had failed to fulfil their military co-operation plan for 1998.

REGIONAL SECURITY

At a meeting of heads of government in March 1992 agreements on settling inter-state conflicts were signed by all participating states (except Turkmenistan). At the same meeting an agreement on the status of border troops was signed by five states. In May a five-year Collective Security Agreement was signed. In July further documents were signed on collective security and it was agreed to establish joint peacemaking forces to intervene in CIS disputes. In April 1999 Armenia, Belarus, Kazakhstan, Kyrgyzstan, Russia and Tajikistan signed a protocol to extend the Collective Security Agreement for a further five-year period.

In September 1993 the Council of Heads of State agreed to establish a Bureau of Organized Crime, to be based in Moscow. A meeting of the Council of Border Troop Commanders in January 1994 prepared a report on the issue of illegal migration and drug trade across the extenal borders of the CIS; Moldova, Georgia and Tajikistan did not attend. A programme to combat organized crime within the CIS was approved by heads of government, meeting in Moscow, in April 1996. In March 2001 CIS interior ministers agreed to strengthen co-operation in combating transnational organized crime, in view of reportedly mounting levels of illicit drugs trafficking in the region.

In February 1995 a non-binding memorandum on maintaining peace and stability was adopted by heads of state, meeting in Almaty. Signatories were to refrain from applying military, political, economic or other pressure on another member country, to seek the peaceful resolution of border or territorial disputes and not to support or assist separatist movements active in other member countries. In April 1998 the Council of Defence Ministers approved a draft document proposing that coalition forces be provided with technical equipment to enhance collective security.

In June 1998, at a session of the Council of Border Troop Commanders, some 33 documents were signed relating to border co-operation. A framework protocol on the formation and expedient use of a border troops reserve in critical situations was discussed and signed by several participants. A register of work in scientific and engineering research carried out in CIS countries in the interests of border troops was also adopted.

The fourth plenary session of the IPA in March 1994 established a commission for the resolution of the conflicts in the secessionist regions of Nagornyi Karabakh (Azerbaijan) and Abkhazia (Georgia) and endorsed the use of CIS peace-keeping forces. In the following month Russia agreed to send peace-keeping forces to Georgia, and the dispatch of peace-keeping forces was approved by the Council of Defence Ministers in October. The subsequent session of the IPA in October adopted a resolution to send groups of military observers to Abkhazia and to Moldova. The inter-parliamentary commission on the conflict between Abkhazia and Georgia proposed initiating direct negotiations with the two sides in order to reach a peaceful settlement.

In December 1994 the Council of Defence Ministers enlarged the mandate of the commander of the CIS collective peace-keeping forces in Tajikistan: when necessary CIS military contingents were permitted to engage in combat operations without the prior consent of individual governments. At the Heads of State meeting in Moscow in January 1996 Georgia's proposal to impose sanctions against Abkhazia was approved, in an attempt to achieve a resolution of the conflict. Provisions on arrangements relating to collective peace-keeping operations were approved at the meeting; the training of military and civilian personnel for these operations was to commence in October. In March 1997 the Council of Defence Ministers agreed to extend the peace-keeping mandates for CIS forces in Tajikistan and Abkhazia (following much disagreement, the peace-keepers' mandate in Abkhazia was further renewed in October). At a meeting of the Council in January 1998 a request from Georgia that the CIS carry out its decisions to settle the conflict with Abkhazia was added to the agenda. The Council discussed the promotion of military co-operation and the improvement of peace-making activities, and declared that there was progress in the formation of the collective security system, although the situation in the North Caucasus remained tense. In April President Yeltsin requested that the Armenian and Azerbaijani presidents sign a document to end the conflict in Nagornyi Karabakh; the two subsequently issued a statement expressing their support for a political settlement of the conflict. A document proposing a settlement of the conflict in Abkhazia was also drawn up, but the resolutions adopted were not accepted by Abkhazia. Against the wishes of the Abkhazian authorities, the mandate for the CIS troops in the region was extended to cover the whole of the Gali district. The mandate expired in July 1998, but the forces remained in the region while its renewal was debated. In April 1999 the Council of Heads of State agreed to a retrospective extension of the operation's mandate; the mandate has subsequently continued to be renewed at six-monthly intervals, most recently until 31 July 2001. The mandate of the CIS peace-keeping operation in Tajikistan was terminated in June 2000. In February 2001 it was reported that regulations had been drafted for the inistitution of a CIS Special Envoy for the Settlement of Conflicts.

An emergency meeting of heads of state in October 1996 discussed the renewed fighting in Afghanistan and the threat to regional security. The participants requested the UN Security Council to adopt measures to resolve the conflict. The eighth plenary session of the IPA in November reiterated the call for a cessation of hostilities in the country. In June 1998 the IPA approved the Kyrgyzstan parliament's appeal for a peace settlement in Afghanistan.

A meeting of the Council of Ministers of Internal Affairs was held in Tashkent, Uzbekistan, in June 1998; President Leonid Kuchma of Ukraine signed a decree approving his country's membership of the Council. A number of co-operation agreements were signed, including a framework for the exchange of information between CIS law-enforcement agencies. The Council also decided to maintain its contact with Interpol.

In May 2000 the leaders of Russia, Armenia, Belarus, Kazakhstan, Kyrgyzstan and Tajikistan pledged to strengthen military co-operation in view of the perceived continuing threat to their security from the Taliban regime in Afghanistan. It was reported that a mechanism had been approved that would enable parties to the Collective Security Treaty to purchase arms from Russia at special rates. In October the parties to the Collective Security Treaty signed an agreement on the Status of Forces and Means of Collective Security Systems, establishing a joint rapid deployment function. Joint military forces were to be assembled to combat insurgencies, with particular reference to trans-border terrorism from Afghanistan, and also to deter trans-border illegal drugs trafficking (see above). The establishment of a CIS anti-terrorism centre was approved by the Council of Heads of Government in December.

LEGISLATIVE CO-OPERATION

An agreement on legislative co-operation was signed at an Inter-Parliamentary Conference in January 1992; joint commissions were established to co-ordinate action on economy, law, pensions, housing, energy and ecology. The CIS Charter, formulated in January 1993, provided for the establishment of an inter-state court. In October 1994 a Convention on the rights of minorities was adopted at the meeting of the Heads of State. In May 1995, at the sixth plenary session of the IPA, several acts to improve co-ordination of legislation were approved, relating to migration of labour, consumer rights, and the rights of prisoners of war.

The creation of a Council of Ministers of Internal Affairs was approved at the Heads of State meeting in January 1996; the Council was to promote co-operation between the law-enforcement bodies of member states. At the 10th plenary session of the IPA in December 1997 14 laws, relating to banking and financial services, education, ecology and charity were adopted. At the IPA session held in June 1998 10 model laws relating to social issues were approved, including a law on obligatory social insurance against production accidents and occupational diseases, and on the general principles of regulating refugee problems.

OTHER ACTIVITIES

The CIS has held a number of discussions relating to the environment. In July 1992 agreements were concluded to establish an Inter-state Ecological Council. The 10th plenary session of the IPA in December 1997 appealed to international organizations, parliaments and governments to participate in defeating an international convention on ecological safety.

In July 1992 it was agreed to establish an Inter-state Television and Radio Company (ITRC). In February 1995 the IPA established a Council of Heads of News Agencies, in order to promote the concept of a single information area. In December 1997 the IPA expressed concern about the dissemination of misleading or inaccurate information, particularly via the internet.

A Petroleum and Gas Council was created at a Heads of Government meeting in March 1993, to guarantee energy supplies and to invest in the Siberian petroleum industry. The Council was to have a secretariat based in Tyumen, Siberia. In the field of civil aviation, the inter-state economic committee agreed in February 1997 to establish an Aviation Alliance to promote co-operation between the countries' civil aviation industries.

CO-OPERATION COUNCIL FOR THE ARAB STATES OF THE GULF

Address: POB 7153, Riyadh 11462, Saudi Arabia.
Telephone: (1) 482-7777; **fax:** (1) 482-9089; **internet:** www.gcc-sg.org.
More generally known as the Gulf Co-operation Council (GCC), the organization was established on 25 May 1981 by six Arab states.

MEMBERS

Bahrain	Oman	Saudi Arabia
Kuwait	Qatar	United Arab Emirates

Organization

(April 2001)

SUPREME COUNCIL

The Supreme Council is the highest authority of the GCC, comprises the heads of member states and meets annually in ordinary session, and in emergency session if demanded by two or more members. The Presidency of the Council is undertaken by each state in turn, in alphabetical order. The Supreme Council draws up the overall policy of the organization; it discusses recommendations and laws presented to it by the Ministerial Council and the Secretariat General in preparation for endorsement. The GCC's charter provides for the creation of a commission for the settlement of disputes between member states, to be attached to and appointed by the Supreme Council. In December 1997 the Supreme Council authorized the establishment of a 30-member Consultative Council, appointed by member states, to act as an advisory body.

MINISTERIAL COUNCIL

The Ministerial Council consists of the foreign ministers of member states, meeting every three months, and in emergency session if demanded by two or more members. It prepares for the meetings of the Supreme Council, and draws up policies, recommendations, studies and projects aimed at developing co-operation and co-ordination among member states in various spheres.

SECRETARIAT GENERAL

The Secretariat assists member states in implementing recommendations by the Supreme and Ministerial Councils, and prepares reports and studies, budgets and accounts. The Secretary-General is appointed by the Supreme Council for a renewable three-year term. In March 1996 the Ministerial Council approved a proposal that, in future, the position of Secretary-General be rotated among member states, in order to ensure equal representation. Assistant Secretary-Generals are appointed by the Ministerial Council upon the recommendation of the Secretary General. All member states contribute in equal proportions towards the budget of the Secretariat.

Secretary-General: Sheikh JAMIL IBRAHIM ALHEJAILAN (Saudi Arabia).
Assistant Secretary-General for Political Affairs: Dr HAMAD ALI AS-SULAYTI (Bahrain).
Assistant Secretary-General for Economic Affairs: AJLAN BEN ALI AL-KUWARI (Qatar).
Assistant Secretary-General for Military Affairs: Maj.-Gen. FALEH ABDULLAH ASH-SHATTI (Kuwait).

Activities

The GCC was established following a series of meetings of foreign ministers of the states concerned, culminating in an agreement on the basic details of its charter on 10 March 1981. The Charter was signed by the six heads of state on 25 May. It describes the organization as providing 'the means for realizing co-ordination, integration and co-operation' in all economic, social and cultural affairs.

ECONOMIC CO-OPERATION

In November 1982 GCC ministers drew up a 'unified economic agreement' covering freedom of movement of people and capital, the abolition of customs duties, technical co-operation, harmonization of banking regulations and financial and monetary co-ordination. At the same time GCC heads of state approved the formation of a Gulf Investment Corporation, to be based in Kuwait (see below). Customs duties on domestic products of the Gulf states were abolished in March 1983, and new regulations allowing free movement of workers and vehicles between member states were also introduced. A common minimum customs levy (of between 4% and 20%) on foreign imports was imposed in 1986. In May 1992 GCC trade ministers announced the objective of establishing a GCC common market by 2000. In September 1992 GCC ministers reached agreement on the application of a unified system of tariffs by March 1993. A meeting of the Supreme Council, held in December 1992, however, decided to mandate GCC officials to formulate a plan for the introduction of common external tariffs, to be presented to the Council in December 1993. Only the tax on tobacco products was to be standardized from March 1993, at a rate of 50% (later increased to 70%). In April 1994 ministers of finance agreed to pursue a gradual approach to unifying tariffs, which was to be achieved according to a schedule over two to three years. A technical committee, which had been constituted to consider aspects of establishing a customs union, met for the first time in June 1998. In December the Supreme Council requested that ministers of finance conclude an agreement on a unified customs tariff before the end of 1999, and resolved that a customs union should become effective in March 2001. In November 1999 the Supreme Council concluded an agreement to establish the customs union by 1 March 2005. The arrangement required all member states to amend their tariff levels to 5.5% on basic commodities and 7.5% on other commodities. A unified legal system for customs was to be enforced in 2002.

In February 1987 the governors of the member states' central banks agreed in principle to co-ordinate their rates of exchange, and this was approved by the Supreme Council in November. It was subsequently agreed to link the Gulf currencies to a 'basket' of other currencies. In April 1993 GCC central bank governors agreed to establish a joint banking supervisory committee, in order to devise rules for GCC banks to operate in other member states. They also decided to allow Kuwait's currency to become part of the GCC monetary system that was established following Iraq's invasion of Kuwait in order to defend the Gulf currencies. In December 1997 GCC heads of state authorized the guide-lines that had been formulated to enable national banks to establish operations in other GCC states. These were to apply only to banks established at least 10 years previously with a share capital of more than US $100m. In December 2000 the Supreme Council determined to establish a GCC single currency, although a timescale for its implementation was not decided.

TRADE AND INDUSTRY

In 1982 a ministerial committee was formed to co-ordinate trade policies and development in the region. Technical subcommittees were established to oversee a strategic food reserve for the member states, and joint trade exhibitions (which were generally held every year until responsibility was transferred to the private sector in 1996). In November 1986 the Supreme Council approved a measure whereby citizens of GCC member states were enabled to undertake certain retail trade activities in any other member state, with effect from 1 March 1987. The ministerial committee in charge of trade also forms the board of directors of the GCC Authority for Standards and Metrology, which approves minimum standards for goods produced in or imported to the region.

In 1985 the Supreme Council endorsed a common industrial strategy for the GCC states. It approved regulations stipulating that priority should be given to imports of GCC industrial products, and permitting GCC investors to obtain loans from GCC industrial development banks. In November 1986 resolutions were adopted on the protection of industrial products, and on the co-ordination of industrial projects, in order to avoid duplication. In March 1989 the Ministerial Council approved the Unified GCC Foreign Capital Investment Regulations, which aimed to attract foreign investment and to co-ordinate investments amongst GCC countries. Further guide-lines to promote foreign investment in the region were formulated during 1997. In December 1999 the Supreme Council amended the conditions determining rules of origin on industrial products in order to promote direct investment and intra-Community trade. In December 1992 the Supreme Council endorsed Patent Regulations for GCC member states to facilitate regional scientific and technological research. A GCC Patent Office for the protection of intellectual property in the region, was established in 1998.

In December 1998 the Supreme Council discussed the adverse effects on members' economies deriving from the decline in worldwide petroleum prices. The Council urged members to comply with the petroleum production reductions pledged earlier in the year (see OPEC, p. 269), with the aim of promoting market stability. Other petroleum-producing countries were requested to make similar production commitments. In September 2000 GCC member states (which by then were benefiting economically from increased oil revenues) were reported to have announced their preparedness to resume higher petroleum production, with a view to lowering global prices, in response to protests in a number of non-oil-producing countries against high fuel costs. However, in view of a subsequent significant fall in global petroleum prices, the GCC Council supported reductions in production pledged by OPEC in early 2001, aimed at achieving a target band for the reference price of US $25–$28 per barrel.

In September 2000 GCC ministers of commerce agreed to establish a technical committee to promote the development of electronic commerce and trade among member states.

In 1997 GCC ministers of planning determined to formulate a regional population strategy. In December 2000 the Supreme Council agreed gradually to limit, by means of the imposition of quotas and deterrent taxation measures, the numbers of foreign workers admitted to member states, in order to redress the current demographic imbalance resulting from the large foreign population resident in the region (believed to comprise more than one-third of the overall population).

AGRICULTURE

A unified agricultural policy for GCC countries was endorsed by the Supreme Council in November 1985. Between 1983 and 1990 ministers also approved proposals for harmonizing legislation relating to water conservation, veterinary vaccines, insecticides, fertilizers, fisheries and seeds. A permanent committee on fisheries aims to co-ordinate national fisheries policies, to establish designated fishing periods and to undertake surveys of the fishing potential in the Arabian (Persian) Gulf. Co-operation in the agricultural sector also extends to consideration of the water resources in the region. In February 2001 GCC ministers of water and electricity determined to formulate a common water policy for the region, which experiences annual shortfalls of water.

TRANSPORT, COMMUNICATIONS AND INFORMATION

During 1985 feasibility studies were undertaken on new rail and road links between member states, and on the establishment of a joint coastal transport company. A scheme to build a 1,700-km railway to link all the member states and Iraq (and thereby the European railway network) was postponed, owing to its high cost (estimated at US $4,000m.). In November 1993 ministers agreed to request assistance from the International Telecommunication Union on the establishment of a joint telecommunications network, which had been approved by ministers in 1986. The region's telecommunications systems were to be integrated through underwater fibre-optic cables and a satellite-based mobile telephone network. In the mid-1990s GCC ministers of information began convening on a regular basis with a view to formulating a joint external information policy. In November 1997 GCC interior ministers approved a simplified passport system to facilitate travel between member countries.

ENERGY

In 1982 a ministerial committee was established to co-ordinate hydrocarbons policies and prices. Ministers adopted a petroleum security plan to safeguard individual members against a halt in their production, to form a stockpile of petroleum products, and to organize a boycott of any non-member country when appropriate. In December 1987 the Supreme Council adopted a plan whereby a member state whose petroleum production was disrupted could 'borrow' petroleum from other members, in order to fulfil its export obligations.

During the early 1990s proposals were formulated to integrate the electricity networks of the six member countries. In the first stage of the plan the networks of Saudi Arabia, Bahrain, Kuwait and Qatar would be integrated; those of the United Arab Emirates (UAE) and Oman would be interconnected and finally linked to the others in the second stage, to be completed by 2003. In December 1997 GCC heads of state declared that work should commence on the first stage of the plan, under the management of an independent authority. The estimated cost of the project was more than US $6,000m. However, it was agreed not to invite private developers to participate in construction of the grid, but that the first phase of the project be financed by member states (to contribute 35% of the estimated $2,000m. required), and by loans from commercial banking and international monetary institutions. The so-called Gulf Council Interconnection Authority was established in mid-1999, with its headquarters in Dammam, Saudi Arabia.

REGIONAL SECURITY

Although no mention of defence or security was made in the original charter, the summit meeting which ratified the charter also issued a statement rejecting any foreign military presence in the region. The Supreme Council meeting in November 1981 agreed to include defence co-operation in the activities of the organization: as a result, defence ministers met in January 1982 to discuss a common security policy, including a joint air defence system and standardization of weapons. In November 1984 member states agreed to form the Peninsula Shield Force for rapid deployment against external aggression, comprising units from the armed forces of each country under a central command to be based in north-eastern Saudi Arabia.

In October 1987 (following an Iranian missile attack on Kuwait, which supported Iraq in its war against Iran) GCC ministers of foreign affairs issued a statement declaring that aggression against one member state was regarded as aggression against them all. In December the Supreme Council approved a joint pact on regional co-operation in matters of security. In August 1990 the Ministerial Council condemned Iraq's invasion of Kuwait as a violation of sovereignty, and demanded the withdrawal of all Iraqi troops from Kuwait. The Peninsula Shield Force was not sufficiently developed to be deployed in defence of Kuwait. During the crisis and the ensuing war between Iraq and a multinational force which took place in January and February 1991, the GCC developed closer links with Egypt and Syria, which, together with Saudi Arabia, played the most active role among the Arab countries in the anti-Iraqi alliance. In March the six GCC nations, Egypt and Syria formulated the 'Declaration of Damascus', which announced plans to establish a regional peace-keeping force. The Declaration also urged the abolition of all weapons of mass destruction in the area, and recommended the resolution of the Palestinian question by an international conference. In June Egypt and Syria, whose troops were to have formed the largest proportion of the peace-keeping force, announced their withdrawal from the project, reportedly as a result of disagreements with the GCC concerning the composition of the proposed force and the remuneration involved. A meeting of ministers of foreign affairs of the eight countries took place in July, but agreed only to provide mutual military assistance when necessary. In September 1992 the signatories of the Damascus Declaration adopted a joint statement on regional questions, including the Middle East peace process and the dispute between the UAE and Iran (see below), but rejected an Egyptian proposal to establish a series of rapid deployment forces which could be called upon to defend the interests of any of the eight countries. A meeting of GCC ministers of defence in November agreed to maintain the Peninsula Shield Force. In November 1993 GCC ministers of defence approved a proposal for the significant expansion of the force and for the incorporation of air and naval units. Ministers also agreed to strengthen the defence of the region by developing joint surveillance and early warning systems. A GCC military committee was established, and convened for the first time in April 1994, to discuss the implementation of the proposals. However, the expansion of the Peninsula Shield Force was not implemented. Joint military training exercises were conducted by forces of five GCC states (excluding Qatar) in northern Kuwait in March 1996. In December 1997 the Supreme Council approved plans that had been authorized by defence ministers in November for linking the region's military telecommunications networks and establishing a common early warning system. In December 2000 GCC leaders signed an agreement on enhancing the grouping's defence capability. The joint defence pact formally commited member states to defending any other member state from external attack, envisaging the expansion of the Peninsula Shield Force from 5,000 to 22,000 troops and the creation of a new rapid deployment function within the force. In March 2001 the GCC member states inaugurated the first phase of the long-envisaged joint air defence system.

In 1992 Iran extended its authority over the island of Abu Musa, which it had administered under a joint arrangement with the UAE since 1971. In September 1992 the GCC Ministerial Council condemned Iran's continued occupation of the island and efforts to consolidate its presence, and reiterated support of UAE sovereignty over Abu Musa, as well as the largely uninhabited Greater and Lesser Tunb islands (also claimed by Iran). All three islands are situated at the approach to the Strait of Hormuz, through which petroleum exports are transported. In December 1994 the GCC supported the UAE's request that the dispute be referred to the International Court of Justice.

In late September 1992 a rift within the GCC was caused by an incident on the disputed border between Saudi Arabia and Qatar. Qatar's threat to boycott a meeting of the Supreme Council in December was allayed at the last minute as a result of mediation efforts by the Egyptian President. At the meeting, which was held in UAE, Qatar and Saudi Arabia agreed to establish a joint commission to demarcate the disputed border. The resolution of border disputes was the principal concern of GCC heads of state when they convened for their annual meeting in December 1994, in Bahrain. The Kuwaiti leader proposed the establishment of a GCC framework for resolving border disputes, consisting of bilateral negotiations between the concerned parties, mediated by a third GCC state.

In November 1994 a security agreement, to counter regional crime and terrorism, was concluded by GCC states. The pact, however, was not signed by Kuwait, which claimed that a clause concerning the extradition of offenders was in contravention of its constitution; Qatar did not attend the meeting, held in Riyadh, owing to its ongoing dispute with Saudi Arabia (see above). At the summit meeting in December GCC heads of state expressed concern at the increasing incidence of Islamic extremist violence throughout the region. In April 1995 GCC interior ministers convened to discuss ongoing civil unrest in Bahrain; the ministers collectively supported measures adopted by the Bahraini Government to secure political and civil stability. The continuing unrest in Bahrain and the involvement of the Iranian Government in Bahraini domestic affairs remained issues of concern for the GCC throughout 1995 and 1996.

During 1995 the deterioration of relations between Qatar and other GCC states threatened to undermine the Council's solidarity. In December Qatar publicly displayed its dissatisfaction at the appointment, without a consensus agreement, of Saudi Arabia's nominee as the new Secretary-General by failing to attend the final session of the Supreme Council, held in Muscat, Oman. However, at a meeting of ministers of foreign affairs in March 1996, Qatar endorsed the new Secretary-General, following an agreement on future appointment procedures, and reasserted its commitment to the organization. In June Saudi Arabia and Qatar agreed to reactivate a joint technical committee in order to finalize the demarcation of their mutual border. In December Qatar hosted the annual GCC summit meeting; however, Bahrain refused to attend, owing to Qatar's 'unfriendly attitude' and a long-standing dispute between the two countries (referred by Qatar to the International Court of Justice in 1991) concerning the sovereignty of the Hawar islands, and of other islands, maritime and border areas. The issue dominated the meeting, which agreed to establish a four-member committee to resolve the conflicting sovereignty claims. In January 1997 the ministers of foreign affairs of Kuwait, Oman, Saudi Arabia and the UAE, meeting in Riyadh, formulated a seven-point memorandum of understanding to ease tensions between Bahrain and Qatar. The two countries refused to sign the agreement; however, in March both sides announced their intention to establish diplomatic relations at ambassadorial level. In March 2001 the International Court of Justice ruled on the dispute between Bahrain and Qatar concerning the sovereignty of the Hawar Islands and other territorial boundaries, awarding Bahrain sovereignty of the Hawar islands, while supporting Qatar's sovereignty of other disputed territories; the GCC welcomed the judgement, which was accepted by the Governments of both countries.

In May 1997 the Ministerial Council, meeting in Riyadh, expressed concern at Turkey's cross-border military operation in northern Iraq and urged a withdrawal of Turkish troops from Iraqi territory. In December the Supreme Council reaffirmed the need to ensure the sovereignty and territorial integrity of Iraq. At the same time, however, the Council expressed concern at the escalation of tensions in the region, owing to Iraq's failure to co-operate with the UN Special Commission (UNSCOM). The Council also noted the opportunity to strengthen relations with Iran, in view of political developments in that country. In mid-February 1998 the US Defense Secretary visited each of the GCC countries in order to generate regional support for any punitive military action against Iraq, given that country's obstruction of UN weapons inspectors. Kuwait was the only country to declare its support for the use of force (and to permit the use of its bases in military operations against Iraq), while other member states urged a diplomatic solution to the crisis. Qatar pursued a diplomatic initiative to negotiate directly with the Iraqi authorities, and in mid-February the Qatari Minister of Foreign Affairs became the most senior GCC government official to visit Iraq since 1990. The GCC supported an agreement concluded between the UN Secretary-General and the Iraqi authorities at the end of February 1998, and urged Iraq to co-operate with UNSCOM in order to secure an end to the problem and a removal of the international embargo against the country. This position was reiterated by the Supreme Council in December. In April 2000 the Ministerial Council issued a statement in which it held the Iraqi administration solely responsible for the suffering of its population, on the grounds of its continuing refusal to co-operate with the UN (which had replaced UNSCOM by a new arms inspection body, the UN Monitoring, Verification and Inspection Commission—UNMOVIC, in December 1999). In December 2000 Kuwait and Saudi Arabia rejected a proposal by the Qatari Government (supported by the UAE) that the GCC should soften its policy on Iraq and demand the immediate removal of the international embargo against that country. During that month the Supreme Council determined to establish a committee with the function of touring Arab states to explain the GCC's Iraq policy.

The GCC has condemned repeated military exercises conducted by Iran in the waters around the disputed islands of Abu Musa and Greater and Lesser Tunb as a threat to regional security and a violation of the UAE's sovereignty. Nevertheless, member countries have pursued efforts to strengthen relations with Iran. In May 1999 President Khatami undertook a state visit to Qatar, Saudi Arabia and Syria, prompting concern on the part of the UAE that its support within the GCC and the solidarity of the grouping were being undermined. In June a meeting of GCC ministers of foreign affairs was adjourned, owing to reported disagreements between Saudi Arabia and the UAE. Diplomatic efforts secured commitments, issued by both countries later in that month, to co-operate fully within the GCC. In early July the Ministerial Council reasserted GCC support of the UAE's sovereignty claim over the three disputed islands and determined to establish a committee, comprising the ministers of foreign affairs of Oman, Qatar and Saudi Arabia and the GCC Secretary-General, to resolve the dispute. In December the Supreme Council extended the mandate of the committee to establish a mechanism for direct negotiations between UAE and Iran. Iran, however, refused to co-operate with the committee; consequently, the committee's mandate was terminated in January 2001. In March 2001 the Ministerial Council demanded that Iran cease the construction of buildings for settlement on the disputed islands, and reiterated its support for the UAE's sovereignty claim.

EXTERNAL RELATIONS

In June 1988 an agreement was signed by GCC and European Community (EC) ministers on economic co-operation; this took effect from January 1990. Working groups were subsequently established to promote co-operation in several specific areas, including business, energy, the environment and industry. In March 1990, at the first annual meeting of a Joint Co-operation Council, established under the accord, GCC and EC ministers of foreign affairs undertook to hold negotiations on a free-trade agreement. Discussions commenced in October. Prior to such an agreement entering into effect, the GCC was to adopt a unified structure of customs duties. In early 1992 the co-operation accord was jeopardized by the GCC's opposition to the EC's proposed tax on fossil fuels (intended to reduce pollution). With the new US administration proposing a similar energy tax, in March 1993 GCC oil ministers threatened to restrict the supply of petroleum (the GCC countries control some 45% of the world's petroleum reserves) in retaliation. In October 1995 a conference was held in Muscat, Oman, which aimed to strengthen economic co-operation between European Union (EU, as the restructured EC was now known) and GCC member states, and to promote investment in both regions. In December 1997 GCC heads of state condemned statements issued by the European Parliament, as well as by other organizations, regarding human rights issues in member states and insisted they amounted to interference in GCC judicial systems. In late 1999 the GCC Supreme Council agreed to establish a customs union—a precondition of the proposed GCC-EU free-trade agreement—by March 2005 (see above). Free-trade negotiations were continuing in early 2001.

In December 1991 GCC ministers of finance and of foreign affairs approved the establishment of an Arab Development Fund, which aimed to create greater political and economic stability in the region, and in particular was intended to assist Egypt and Syria, as a reward for their active military part in the Gulf War and their major role in the security force envisaged by the Declaration of Damascus. A starting capital of US $10,000m. was originally envisaged for the Fund, although by mid-1992 only $6,500m. had been pledged, with reports that the project had been scaled down. In May 1993 ministers of finance from the GCC states, Egypt and Syria, meeting in Qatar, failed to agree on the level of contributions to the Fund.

In September 1994 GCC ministers of foreign affairs decided to end the secondary and tertiary embargo on trade with Israel. In February 1995 a ministerial meeting of signatories of the Damascus Declaration adopted a common stand, criticizing Israel for its refusal to renew the nuclear non-proliferation treaty. In December 1996 the foreign ministers of the Damascus Declaration states, convened in Cairo, requested the USA to exert financial pressure on Israel to halt the construction of settlements on occupied Arab territory.

In June 1997 ministers of foreign affairs of the Damascus Declaration states agreed to pursue efforts to establish a free-trade zone throughout the region, which they envisaged as the nucleus of a future Arab common market. (Meanwhile, the League of Arab States (q.v.) has also initiated efforts to create a Greater Arab Free Trade Area.)

The GCC-USA Economic Dialogue, which commenced in 1985, convenes periodically as a government forum to promote co-operation between the GCC economies and the USA. Since the late 1990s private-sector interests have been increasingly represented at sessions of the Dialogue. It was announced in March 2001 that a business forum was to be established under the auspices of the Dialogue, to act as a permanent means of facilitating trade and investment between the GCC countries and the USA.

INVESTMENT CORPORATION

Gulf Investment Corporation (GIC): Joint Banking Center, Kuwait Real Estate Bldg, POB 3402, Safat 13035, Kuwait; tel.

2431911; fax 2448894; e-mail gic@gic.com.kw; internet www.gic
.com.kw; f. 1983 by the six member states of the GCC, each contributing US \$350m. of the total capital of \$2,100m.; total assets
\$19,500m. (1999), dep. \$8,135m. (1995); investment chiefly in the
Gulf region, financing industrial projects (including pharmaceuticals, chemicals, steel wire, aircraft engineering, aluminium, dairy
produce and chicken-breeding). GIC provides merchant banking and
financial advisory services, and in 1992 was appointed to advise
the Kuwaiti Government on a programme of privatization. Chair.
IBRAHIM ABDUL-KARIM; Gen. Man. HISHAM A. RAZZUQI. Publ. *The GIC
Gazetteer* (annually).

Gulf International Bank: POB 1017, Al-Dowali Bldg, 3 Palace
Ave, Manama 317, Bahrain; tel. 534000; fax 522633; e-mail

info@gib.com.bh; internet www.gibonline.com; f. 1976 by the six
GCC states and Iraq; became a wholly-owned subsidiary of the
GIC (without Iraqi shareholdings) in 1991; in April 1999 a merger
with Saudi Investment Bank was concluded; cap. US \$1,000m.,
dep. \$13,277m., total assets \$15,679.4m. (Dec. 1999). Chair.
IBRAHIM ABDUL-KARIM; Gen. Man. Dr ABDULLAH AL-KUWAIZ.

Publications

GCC News (monthly).

At-Ta'awun (periodical).

COUNCIL OF ARAB ECONOMIC UNITY

Address: 1191 Corniche en-Nil, 12th Floor, POB 1, Mohammed
Fareed, Cairo, Egypt.

Telephone: (2) 5755321; **fax:** (2) 5754090.

Established in 1957 by the Economic Council of the League of Arab
States (q.v.). The first meeting of the Council was held in 1964.

MEMBERS

Egypt	Palestine
Iraq	Somalia
Jordan	Sudan
Libya	Syria
Mauritania	Yemen

Organization

(April 2001)

COUNCIL

The Council consists of representatives of member states, usually
ministers of economy, finance and trade. It meets twice a year;
meetings are chaired by the representative of each country for
one year.

GENERAL SECRETARIAT

Entrusted with the implementation of the Council's decisions and
with proposing work plans, including efforts to encourage participation by member states in the Arab Economic Unity Agreement. The
Secretariat also compiles statistics, conducts research and publishes
studies on Arab economic problems and on the effects of major world
economic trends.

General Secretary: Dr AHMED GOWEILI (Egypt).

COMMITTEES

There are seven standing committees: preparatory, follow-up and
Arab Common Market development; Permanent Delegates; budget;
economic planning; fiscal and monetary matters; customs and trade
planning and co-ordination; statistics. There are also seven *ad
hoc* committees, including meetings of experts on tariffs, trade
promotion and trade legislation.

Activities

The Council undertakes to co-ordinate measures leading to a customs union subject to a unified administration; conduct market
and commodity studies; assist with the unification of statistical
terminology and methods of data collection; conduct studies for the
formation of new joint Arab companies and federations; and to
formulate specific programmes for agricultural and industrial co-
ordination and for improving road and railway networks.

ARAB COMMON MARKET

Based on a resolution passed by the Council in August 1964; its
implementation was to be supervised by the Council and does not
constitute a separate organization. Customs duties and other taxes
on trade between the member countries (Egypt, Iraq, Jordan, Libya,
Mauritania, Syria and Yemen) were to be eliminated in annual
stages. The second stage was to be the adoption of a full customs
union, and ultimately all restrictions on trade between the member
countries, including quotas, and restrictions on residence, employment and transport, were to be abolished. In practice, however, the

trading of national products was not freed from all monetary,
quantitative and administrative restrictions.

Between 1978 and 1989, the following measures were undertaken
by the Council for the development of the Arab Common Market:
introduction of flexible membership conditions for the least developed Arab states (Mauritania, Somalia, Sudan and Yemen);
approval in principle of a fund to compensate the least developed
countries for financial losses incurred as a result of joining the Arab
Common Market; approval of legal, technical and administrative
preparations for unification of tariffs levied on products imported
from non-member countries; formation of a committee of ministerial
deputies to deal with problems in the application of market rulings
and to promote the organization's activities and adoption of unified
customs legislation and of an integrated programme aimed at enhancing trade between member states and expanding members'
productive capacity.

Meanwhile, Arab League member states have pursued other
attempts to liberalize intra-Arab trade. In 1981 18 member states
of the League signed an Agreement to Facilitate and Develop Trade
Among Arab Countries, which envisaged negotiation of the full
exemption of tariffs and non-tariff measures for manufactured and
semi-manufactured goods; implementation of this agreement was,
however, postponed. Egypt, Iraq, Jordan and Yemen formed the
Arab Co-operation Council (q.v.) in February 1989, with a view to
accelerating progress towards an Arab Common Market. Implementation of the Common Market initiative appeared to gain new
momentum following the adoption in February 1997 by 18 Arab
League member states of the Executive Programme of the Agreement to Facilitate and Develop Trade Among Arab Countries, reactivating the 1981 accord with a view to creating a Greater Arab Free
Trade Area. The Agreement, which was to be implemented through
the League's Economic and Social Council, envisaged the gradual
elimination by 2007 of tariff and non-tariff barriers on trade between
states parties, at a rate of 10% per year, commencing on 1 January 1998.

MULTILATERAL AGREEMENTS

The Council has initiated the following multilateral agreements
aimed at achieving economic unity:

Agreement on Basic Levels of Social Insurance.

Agreement on Reciprocity in Social Insurance Systems.

Agreement on Labour Mobility.

Agreement on Organization of Transit Trade.

Agreement on Avoidance of Double Taxation and Elimination of
Tax Evasion.

Agreement on Co-operation in Collection of Taxes.

Agreement on Capital Investment and Mobility.

Agreement on Settlement of Investment Disputes between Host
Arab Countries and Citizens of Other Countries.

JOINT VENTURES

A number of multilateral organizations in industry and agriculture
have been formed on the principle that faster development and
economies of scale may be achieved by combining the efforts of
member states. In industries that are new to the member countries,
Arab Joint Companies are formed, while existing industries are co-
ordinated by the setting up of Arab Specialized Unions. The unions
are for closer co-operation on problems of production and marketing,
and to help companies deal as a group in international markets. The
companies are intended to be self-supporting on a purely commercial
basis; they may issue shares to citizens of the participating countries.
The joint ventures are:

Arab Joint Companies:

Arab Company for Drug Industries and Medical Appliances: POB 925161, Amman, Jordan; tel. (6) 5821618; fax (6) 5821649; e-mail acdima@go.com.jo; f. 1976.

Arab Company for Industrial Investment: POB 3385, Alwiyah, Baghdad, Iraq; tel. 718-9215; fax 718-0710.

Arab Company for Livestock Development: POB 5305, Damascus, Syria; tel. 666037.

Arab Mining Company: POB 20198, Amman, Jordan; tel. (6) 5663148; fax (6) 5684114; e-mail armico@go.com.jo; f. 1974.

Specialized Arab Unions and Federations:

Arab Co-operative Federation: POB 57640, Baghdad, Iraq; tel. (1) 888-8121; f. 1985.

Arab Federation for Paper, Printing and Packaging Industries: POB 5456, Baghdad, Iraq; tel. (1) 887-2384; fax (1) 886-9639; f. 1977; 250 mems.

Arab Federation of Chemical Fertilizers Producers: Cairo, Egypt; f. 1976.

Arab Federation of Engineering Industries: POB 509, Baghdad, Iraq; tel. (1) 776-1101.

Arab Federation of Shipping: POB 1161, Baghdad, Iraq; tel. (1) 717-4540; fax (1) 717-7243; f. 1979; 22 mems.

Arab Federation of Leather Industries: POB 2188, Damascus, Syria; f. 1978.

Arab Federation of Textile Industries: POB 620, Damascus, Syria.

Arab Federation of Travel Agents: POB 7090, Amman, Jordan.

Arab Seaports Federation: Alexandria, Egypt; f. 1977.

Arab Sugar Federation: POB 195, Khartoum, Sudan; f. 1977.

Arab Union for Cement and Building Materials: POB 9015, Damascus, Syria; tel. (11) 6118598; fax (11) 6111318; e-mail aucbm@net.sy; internet www.aucbm.org; f. 1977; 22 mem. countries, 100 mem. cos.

Arab Union for Information Technology.

Arab Union of Fish Producers: POB 15064, Baghdad, Iraq; tel. (1) 551-1261; f. 1976.

Arab Union of Food Industries: POB 13025, Baghdad, Iraq; f. 1976.

Arab Union of Hotels and Tourism: Beirut, Lebanon; f. 1994.

Arab Union of Land Transport: POB 926324, Amman 11110, Jordan; tel. (6) 5663153; fax (6) 5664232; f. 1978.

Arab Union of the Manufacturers of Pharmaceuticals and Medical Appliances: POB 81150, Amman 11181, Jordan; tel. (6) 4654306; fax (6) 4648141; f. 1986.

Arab Union of Railways: POB 6599, Aleppo, Syria; tel. (21) 220302; f. 1979.

General Arab Insurance Federation: POB 611, 11511 Cairo, Egypt; tel. (2) 5743177; fax (2) 5762310; f. 1964.

General Union of Arab Agricultural Workers and Co-operatives: Tripoli, Libya; f. 1993.

Union of Arab Contractors: Cairo, Egypt; f. 1995.

Union of Arab Investors: Cairo, Egypt; f. 1995.

Publications

Annual Bulletin for Arab Countries' Foreign Trade Statistics.
Annual Bulletin for Official Exchange Rates of Arab Currencies.
Arab Economic Unity Bulletin (2 a year).
Demographic Yearbook for Arab Countries.
Economic Report of the General Secretary (2 a year).
Guide to Studies prepared by Secretariat.
Progress Report (2 a year).
Statistical Yearbook for Arab Countries.
Yearbook for Intra-Arab Trade Statistics.
Yearbook of National Accounts for Arab Countries.

COUNCIL OF BALTIC SEA STATES—CBSS

Address: Strömsberg, POB 2010, 103 11 Stockhölm, Sweden.
Telephone: (8) 440-19-20; **fax:** (8) 440-19-44; **e-mail:** cbss@baltinfo .org; **internet:** www.baltinfo.org/CBSS.htm.

The Council of Baltic Sea States (CBSS) was established in 1992 to intensify co-operation between member states.

MEMBERS

Denmark	Iceland	Poland
Estonia	Latvia	Russia
Finland	Lithuania	Sweden
Germany	Norway	

The European Commission also has full membership status.

Organization

(April 2001)

PRESIDENCY

The presidency is occupied by heads of government for one year, on a rotating basis. Informal summit meetings of heads of government take place on an irregular basis, according to requirements.

COUNCIL

The Council comprises the ministers of foreign affairs of each member state and a representative of the European Commission. The Council meets annually and aims to serve as a forum for guidance and overall co-ordination among participating states. The minister of foreign affairs of the presiding country is responsible for co-ordinating the Council's activities between ministerial sessions.

COMMITTEE OF SENIOR OFFICIALS—CSO

The Committee consists of senior officials of the ministries of foreign affairs of the member states and of the European Commission. It serves as a discussion forum for matters relating to the work of the Council and undertakes inter-sessional activities. The Chairman of the Committee, from the same country serving as President of the CBSS, meets regularly with the previous and future Chairmen. The so-called Troika aims to maintain information co-operation, promote better exchange of information, and ensure more effective decision-making.

SECRETARIAT

In October 1998 the presidency inaugurated a permanent secretariat in Stockholm. The tasks of the secretariat include the preparation of summit meetings, annual sessions of ministers of foreign affairs, and other meetings of high-level officials and experts, the provision of technical support to the presidency regarding the implementation of plans, maintaining contacts with other sub-regional organizations, and strengthening awareness of the Council and its activities.

Secretary-General: JACEK STAROSCIAK (Poland).

COMMISSIONER ON DEMOCRATIC DEVELOPMENT

Address: Amagertorv 14², POB 1165, 1010 Copenhagen K, Denmark.

Telephone: 33-91-22-88; **fax:** 33-91-22-96; **e-mail:** mail@cbsscommissioner.org; **internet:** www.cbss-commissioner.org.

The ministerial session held in May 1994 agreed to appoint an independent Commissioner on democratic institutions and human rights to serve a three-year term of office, from October of that year. In July 1997, at the sixth ministerial session held in Riga, the Commissioner's term of office was extended by a further three years. The ninth ministerial session, held in Bergen in June 2000, renewed the Commissioner's mandate until September 2003. The Commissioner is based in Copenhagen, Denmark.

Commissioner on Democratic Development: HELLE DEGN (Denmark).

Activities

The CBSS was established in March 1992 as a forum to enhance and strengthen co-operation between countries in the Baltic Sea region. At a meeting of the Council in Kalmar, Sweden, in July 1996, ministers adopted an Action Programme as a guide-line for CBSS activities. The main programme areas covered stable and participatory political development; economic integration and prosperity; and protection of the environment. The third summit meeting of CBSS heads of government, held at Kolding, Denmark, in April

2000, agreed to consolidate all regional intergovernmental, multilateral co-operation, and to strengthen collaboration at municipality and county levels.

At the first Baltic Sea States summit, held in Visby, Sweden, in May 1996, heads of government agreed to establish a Task Force on organized crime to counter drugs-trafficking, strengthen judicial co-operation, increase the dissemination of information, impose regional crime-prevention measures, improve border controls and provide training. In January 1998 the second summit meeting, convened in Riga, Latvia, agreed to extend the mandate of the Task Force until the end of 2000 and to enhance co-operation in the areas of civic security and border control. In April 2000 the third summit prolonged the Task Force's mandate further, until the end of 2004.

The Council has founded a number of working groups, comprising experts in specific fields, which aim to report on and recommend action on issues of concern to the Council. In early 2001 there were three groups working under the auspices of the CSO: the working group on assistance to democratic institutions, based in Riga, Latvia; the working group on economic co-operation, based in Bonn, Germany; and the working group on nuclear and radiation safety, based in Helsinki, Finland. The Swedish Special Group originated as a working group with a mandate to support the elimination of the sexual exploitation of children for commercial purposes in the Baltic Sea region. The Group helped to organize a conference on the subject held in Tallinn, Estonia, in September 1998.

In July 1998 ministers of trade of member states met in Vilnius, Lithuania, to discuss the development of small and medium-sized enterprises. Ministers agreed to strengthen links between member states, to implement measures to increase access to information in the region and to improve procedures for commercial border crossings.

In January 2001 the CBSS Council agreed to establish a secretariat to implement Baltic 21, the regional variant (adopted by the CBSS in 1998) of 'Agenda 21', the programme of action agreed by the UN Conference on Environment and Development, held in Rio de Janeiro, Brazil, in June 1992. Baltic 21 comprised a programme of 30 projects throughout the region, which aim to promote sustainable development in the agriculture, forestry and fisheries, energy, industry, tourism, transport, and spatial planning sectors. The first Baltic Sea area forum of non-governmental organizations was scheduled to be convened by the CBSS in Lübeck, Germany, in late May 2001.

Finance

The Council is financed by contributions of the governments of its 11 member states.

Publication

Newsletter (monthly).

THE COUNCIL OF EUROPE

Address: 67075 Strasbourg Cédex, France.

Telephone: 3-88-41-20-00; **fax:** 3-88-41-27-81; **e-mail:** point_i@coe.int; **internet:** www.coe.int.

The Council was founded in May 1949 to achieve a greater unity between its members, to facilitate their social progress and to uphold the principles of parliamentary democracy, respect for human rights and the rule of law. Membership has risen from the original 10 to 43.

MEMBERS*

Albania	Liechtenstein
Andorra	Lithuania
Armenia	Luxembourg
Austria	Macedonia, former Yugoslav
Azerbaijan	republic
Belgium	Malta
Bulgaria	Moldova
Croatia	Netherlands
Cyprus	Norway
Czech Republic	Poland
Denmark	Portugal
Estonia	Romania
Finland	Russia
France	San Marino
Georgia	Slovakia
Germany	Slovenia
Greece	Spain
Hungary	Sweden
Iceland	Switzerland
Ireland	Turkey
Italy	Ukraine
Latvia	United Kingdom

* Bosnia and Herzegovina, Monaco and the Federal Republic of Yugoslavia have applied for full membership. In addition, Belarus has applied for membership; however, at March 2001 its application was not under consideration owing to its domestic political situation. The Holy See, Canada, Japan, Mexico and the USA have observer status with the organization.

Organization

(April 2001)

COMMITTEE OF MINISTERS

The Committee consists of the ministers of foreign affairs of all member states (or their deputies); it decides with binding effect all matters of internal organization, makes recommendations to governments and draws up conventions and agreements; it also discusses matters of political concern, such as European co-operation, compliance with member states' commitments, in particular

concerning the protection of human rights, and considers possible co-ordination with other institutions, such as the European Union (EU) and the Organization for Security and Co-operation in Europe (OSCE). The Committee usually meets in May and November each year.

CONFERENCES OF SPECIALIZED MINISTERS

There are 19 Conferences of specialized ministers, meeting regularly for intergovernmental co-operation in various fields.

PARLIAMENTARY ASSEMBLY

President: Lord RUSSELL-JOHNSTON (United Kingdom).

Chairman of the Socialist Group: PETER SCHIEDER (Austria).

Chairman of the Group of the European People's Party: RENÉ VAN DER LINDEN (Netherlands).

Chairman of the European Democratic (Conservative) Group: DAVID ATKINSON (United Kingdom).

Chairman of the Liberal Democratic and Reformers' Group: KRIISTINA OJULAND (Estonia).

Chairman of the Unified European Left Group: JAAKKO LAAKSO (Finland).

Members are elected or appointed by their national parliaments from among the members thereof; political parties in each delegation follow the proportion of their strength in the national parliament. Members do not represent their governments; they speak on their own behalf. At March 2001 the Assembly had 301 members (and 301 substitutes): 18 each for France, Germany, Italy, Russia and the United Kingdom; 12 each for Poland, Spain, Turkey and Ukraine; 10 for Romania; seven each for Belgium, the Czech Republic, Greece, Hungary, the Netherlands and Portugal; six each for Austria, Azerbaijan, Bulgaria, Sweden and Switzerland; five each for Croatia, Denmark, Finland, Georgia, Moldova, Norway and Slovakia; four each for Albania, Armenia, Ireland and Lithuania; three each for Cyprus, Estonia, Iceland, Latvia, Luxembourg, the former Yugoslav republic of Macedonia, Malta and Slovenia; and two each for Andorra, Liechtenstein and San Marino. Israel, Canada and Mexico have permanent observer status, while Belarus, Bosnia and Herzegovina and the Federal Republic of Yugoslavia have been granted special 'guest status'. (Belarus's special status was suspended in January 1997.)

The Assembly meets in ordinary session once a year. The session is divided into four parts, held in the last full week of January, April, June and September. The Assembly submits Recommendations to the Committee of Ministers, passes Resolutions, and discusses reports on any matters of common European interest. It is also a consultative body to the Committee of Ministers, and elects the Secretary-General, the Deputy Secretary-General, the Secretary-General of the Assembly, the Council's Commissioner for Human Rights, and the members of the European Court of Human Rights.

Standing Committee: Represents the Assembly when it is not in session, and may adopt Recommendations to the Committee of Ministers and Resolutions on behalf of the Assembly. Consists of the President, Vice-Presidents, Chairmen of the Political Groups, Chairmen of the Ordinary Committees and Chairmen of national delegations. Meets usually three times a year.

Ordinary Committees: political; economic and development; social, health and family affairs; legal and human rights; culture and education; environment, regional planning and local authorities; migration, refugees and demography; rules of procedure and immunities; monitoring; equal opportunities.

CONGRESS OF LOCAL AND REGIONAL AUTHORITIES OF EUROPE—CLRAE

The Congress was established in 1994, incorporating the former Standing Conference of Local and Regional Authorities, in order to protect and promote the political, administrative and financial autonomy of local and regional European authorities by encouraging central governments to develop effective local democracy. The Congress comprises two chambers—a Chamber of Local Authorities and a Chamber of Regions—with a total membership of 301 elected representatives (and 301 elected substitutes). Annual sessions are mainly concerned with local government matters, regional planning, protection of the environment, town and country planning, and social and cultural affairs. A Standing Committee, drawn from all national delegations, meets between plenary sessions of the Congress. Four Statutory Committees (Institutional; Sustainable Development; Social Cohesion; Culture and Education) meet twice a year in order to prepare texts for adoption by the Congress.

The Congress advises the Council's Committee of Ministers and the Parliamentary Assembly on all aspects of local and regional policy and co-operates with other national and international organizations representing local government. The Congress monitors implementation of the European Charter of Local Self-Government, which was opened for signature in 1985 and provides common standards for effective local democracy. Other legislative guide-lines for the activities of local authorities and the promotion of democracy at local level include the 1980 European Outline Convention on Transfrontier Co-operation, and its Additional Protocol which was opened for signature in 1995, a Convention on the Participation of Foreigners in Public Life at Local Level (1992), and the European Charter for Regional or Minority Languages (1992). In addition, the European Urban Charter defines citizens' rights in European towns and cities, for example in the areas of transport, urban architecture, pollution and security.

President: LLIBERT CUATRECASAS (Spain).

SECRETARIAT

Secretary-General: Dr WALTER SCHWIMMER (Austria).

Deputy Secretary-General: HANS CHRISTIAN KRÜGER (Germany).

Secretary-General of the Parliamentary Assembly: BRUNO HALLER (France).

Activities

In an effort to harmonize national laws, to put the citizens of member countries on an equal footing and to pool certain resources and facilities, the Council has concluded a number of conventions and agreements covering particular aspects of European co-operation. Since 1989 the Council has undertaken to increase co-operation with all countries of the former Eastern bloc and to facilitate their accession to the organization. In October 1997 heads of state or government of member countries convened for only the second time (the first meeting took place in Vienna, in October 1993—see below) with the aim of formulating a new social model to consolidate democracy throughout Europe. The meeting endorsed a Final Declaration and an Action Plan, which established priority areas for future Council activities, including fostering social cohesion; protecting civilian security; promoting human rights; enhancing joint measures to counter cross-border illegal trafficking; and strengthening democracy through education and other cultural activities. In addition, the meeting generated renewed political commitment to the Programme of Action against Corruption, which has become a key element of Council activities.

HUMAN RIGHTS

The promotion and development of human rights is one of the major tasks of the Council of Europe. The European Convention for the Protection of Human Rights and Fundamental Freedoms (European Convention on Human Rights) was opened for signature in 1950. The Steering Committee for Human Rights is responsible for intergovernmental co-operation in the field of human rights and fundamental freedoms; it works to strengthen the effectiveness of systems for protecting human rights, to identify potential threats and challenges to human rights, and to encourage education and provide information on the subject. The Committee has been responsible for the elaboration of several conventions and other legal instruments including most recently Protocol (No. 12) of the European Convention on Human Rights, adopted in June 2000, which enforces a general prohibition of discrimination.

The Committee was responsible for the preparation of the European Ministerial Conference on Human Rights, held in Rome in November 2000, which commemorated the 50th anniversary of the adoption of the European Convention on Human Rights. Delegates addressed issues such as the protection of human rights during armed conflicts and in situations of national crisis; the abolition of the death penalty during times of war, etc.

At the Council's first meeting of heads of state and of government, held in Vienna, Austria, in October 1993, members agreed to draw up a new Protocol to the European Convention on Human Rights to establish cultural rights of minorities and to draw up a new Framework Convention for the protection of national minorities. (Work on the Additional Protocol, however, was suspended in 1996.) The Framework Convention was adopted by the Council's Committee of Ministers in November 1994 and opened for signature on 1 February 1995. It entered into force on 1 February 1998 as the first ever legally-binding instrument devoted to the general protection of national minorities. In addition, the Convention obliged all parties to implement domestic legislation and programmes to fulfil the objectives of the instrument and to submit regular reports, to an 18-member Advisory Committee, on their implementation of the Convention. At March 2001 the Framework Convention had been ratified by 33 states.

The 1993 Vienna summit meeting also agreed to restructure the control mechanism for the protection of human rights, mainly the procedure for the consideration of cases, in order to reduce the length of time before a case is concluded. As a result, Protocol (No. 11) to the European Convention on Human Rights was opened for signature by member states in May 1994. The then existing institutions (i.e. the European Commission of Human Rights and the European Court of Human Rights) were consequently replaced in November 1998 (when Protocol No. 11 entered into force) by a single Court, working on a full-time basis.

The second summit meeting of the Council's heads of state and government, held in Strasbourg, France, in October 1997, welcomed a proposal to institute a Council of Europe Commissioner for Human Rights to promote respect for human rights in member states; this office was established by a resolution of the Council's Committee of Ministers in May 1999.

Commissioner for Human Rights: ALVARO GIL-ROBLES (Spain).

European Court of Human Rights

The Court has compulsory jurisdiction and is competent to consider complaints lodged by states party to the European Convention and by individuals, groups of individuals or non-governmental organizations claiming to be victims of breaches of the Convention's guarantees. The Court comprises one judge for each contracting state (i.e. 41 in May 2000). The Court sits in three-member Committees, empowered to declare applications inadmissible in the event of unanimity and where no further examination is necessary, seven-member Chambers, and a 17-member Grand Chamber. Chamber judgments become final three months after delivery, during which period parties may request a rehearing before the Grand Chamber, subject to acceptance by a panel of five judges. Grand Chamber judgments are final. At March 2001 17,024 applications were pending before the Court.

President: LUZIUS WILDHABER (Switzerland).

Registrar: MICHELE DE SALVIA (Italy).

European Committee for the Prevention of Torture and Inhuman or Degrading Treatment or Punishment—CPT

The Committee was established under the 1987 Convention for the Prevention of Torture as an integral part of the Council of Europe's system for the protection of human rights. The Committee, comprising independent experts, aims to examine the treatment of persons deprived of their liberty with a view to strengthening, if necessary, the protection of such persons from torture and from inhuman or degrading treatment or punishment. It conducts periodic visits to prisons, detention centres, and all other sites where persons are deprived of their liberty by a public authority, in all states parties to the Convention, and may also undertake *ad hoc* visits when the Committee considers them necessary. By March 2001 the Committee had undertaken 79 periodic visits and 34 *ad hoc* visits. After each visit the Committee drafts a report of its findings and any further advice or recommendations, based on dialogue and co-operation.

President: SILVIA CASALE (United Kingdom).

European Social Charter

The European Social Charter, in force since 1965, is the counterpart of the European Convention on Human Rights, in the field of protection of economic and social rights. A revised Charter, which amended existing guarantees and incorporated new rights, was opened for signature in May 1996, and entered into force on 1 July 1999. At January 2001 the Charters were applied in 28 member states guaranteeing fundamental rights in all aspects of national social policies. These relate to conditions of employment (such as the prohibition on the employment of children, non-discrimination in employment, the right to decent working conditions and a fair remuneration and trade union rights), and of social cohesion (such as the right to social security and assistance, and the rights of families, migrants and elderly persons to legal, social and economic protection). A supervisory procedure provides for the examination of each contracting party's practical application of the rights guaranteed. The European Committee of Social Rights, composed of independent experts undertakes a legal assessment of national legislation, regulations and practices within the content of the Charter. The Committee of Ministers may then, if it considers it to be appropriate given economic and social factors, address a recommendation to the state concerned, asking it to comply with the Charter. Its decisions are prepared by a Governmental Committee, composed of representatives of each Contracting Party. An Additional Protocol (1995), providing for a system of collective complaints, entered into force on 1 July 1998 and permits trade unions, employers' organizations and NGOs to lodge complaints against perceived contraventions of the Charter.

President of the European Committee of Social Rights: STEIN EVJU (Norway).

RACISM AND INTOLERANCE

In October 1993 heads of state and of government, meeting in Vienna, resolved to reinforce a policy to combat all forms of intolerance, in response to the increasing incidence of racial hostility and intolerance towards minorities in European societies. A European Commission against Racism and Intolerance (ECRI) was established by the summit meeting to analyse and assess the effectiveness of legal, policy and other measures taken by member states to combat these problems. It became operational in March 1996. Members of ECRI are designated by governments on the basis of their recognized expertise in the field, although participate in the Commission in an independent capacity. ECRI undertakes activities in three programme areas: country-by-country approach; work on general themes; and ECRI and civil society. In the first area of activity, ECRI analyses the situation regarding racism and intolerance in each of the member states, in order to advise governments on measures to combat these problems. In December 1998 ECRI completed a first round of reports for all Council members. A follow-up series of reports were to be prepared during the four-year period 1999–2002. ECRI's work on general themes includes the preparation of policy recommendations and guide-lines on issues of importance to combating racism and intolerance. ECRI also collects and disseminates examples of good practices relating to these issues. Under the third programme area ECRI aims to disseminate information and raise awareness of the problems of racism and intolerance among the general public.

A Committee on the Rehabilitation and Integration of People with Disabilities supports co-operation between member states in this field and undertakes studies in order to promote legislative and administrative action.

MEDIA AND COMMUNICATIONS

Article 10 of the European Convention on Human Rights (freedom of expression and information) forms the basis for the Council of Europe's mass media activities. Implementation of the Council of Europe's work programme concerning the media is undertaken by the Steering Committee on the Mass Media (CDMM), which comprises senior government officials and representatives of professional organizations, meeting in plenary session twice a year. The CDMM is mandated to devise concerted European policy measures and appropriate legal instruments. Its underlying aims are to further freedom of expression and information in a pluralistic democracy, and to promote the free flow of information and ideas. The CDMM is assisted by various specialist groups and committees. Policy and legal instruments have been developed on subjects including: exclusivity rights; media concentrations and transparency of media ownership; protection of journalists in situations of conflict and tension; independence of public-service broadcasting; protection of rights holders; legal protection of encrypted television services; media and elections; protection of journalists' sources of information; and the independence and functions of broadcasting regulatory authorities. These policy and legal instruments (mainly in the form on non-binding recommendations addressed to member governments) are complemented by the publication of studies, analyses and seminar proceedings on topics of media law and policy. The CDMM has also prepared a number of international binding legal instruments, including the European Convention on Transfrontier Television (adopted in 1989 and ratified by 22 countries by

March 2001), the European Convention on the legal protection of services based on or consisting of conditional access, and the European Convention relating to questions on copyright law and other rights in the context of transfrontier broadcasting by satellite (ratified by two countries and signed by seven other member states and the European Community by March 2001). CDMM areas of activity in 2001 included: self-regulation of internet services; credibility of information desseminated online; media and privacy; and regulation of digital broadcasting services.

SOCIAL COHESION

In June 1998, the Committee of Ministers established the European Committee for Social Cohesion (CDCS). The CDCS has the following responsibilities: to prepare proposals for a strategy for social cohesion, to co-ordinate, guide and stimulate co-operation between member States with a view to promoting social cohesion in Europe (by, for example, the regular exchange of views, information and good practice) and to promoting the social standards embodied in the European Social Charter and other Council of European instruments, including the European Code of Social Security. The CDCS is also responsible for executing the terms of reference of the European Code of Social Security, the European Convention on Social Security and the European Agreement on 'au pair' Placement. The CDCS initiated a series of activities in 1999, in particular to promote social standards, and to facilitate access to social rights (such as rights to employment, housing, social protection) and a Programme for Children.

The European Code of Social Security and its Protocol entered into force in 1968; by March 2001 the Code and Protocol had been ratified by Belgium, Germany, Luxembourg, the Netherlands, Norway, Portugal and Sweden, while the Code alone had been ratified by Cyprus, the Czech Republic, Denmark, France, Greece, Ireland, Italy, Spain, Switzerland, Turkey and the United Kingdom. These instruments set minimum standards for medical care and the following benefits: sickness, old-age, unemployment, employment injury, family, maternity, invalidity and survivor's benefit. A revision of these instruments, aiming to provide higher standards and greater flexibility, was completed for signature in 1990 and had been signed by 14 states at March 2001.

The European Convention on Social Security, in force since 1977, now applies in Austria, Belgium, Italy, Luxembourg, the Netherlands, Portugal, Spain and Turkey; most of the provisions apply automatically, while others are subject to the conclusion of additional multilateral or bilateral agreements. The Convention is concerned with establishing the following four fundamental principles of international law on social security: equality of treatment, unity of applicable legislation, conservation of rights accrued or in course of acquisition, and payment of benefits abroad. In 1994 a Protocol to the Convention, providing for the enlargement of the personal scope of the Convention, was opened for signature. By March 2001 it had been signed by Austria, Greece, Luxembourg and Portugal.

HEALTH

Through a series of expert committees, the Council aims to ensure constant co-operation in Europe in a variety of health-related fields, with particular emphasis on patients' rights, for example: equity in access to health care, quality assurance, health services for institutionalized populations (prisoners, elderly in homes), discrimination resulting from health status and education for health. These efforts are supplemented by the training of health personnel.

Improvement of blood transfusion safety and availability of blood and blood derivatives has been ensured through European Agreements and guide-lines. Advances in this field and in organ transplantation are continuously assessed by expert committees.

Eighteen states co-operate in a Partial Agreement to protect the consumer from potential health risks connected with commonplace or domestic activities. The committees of experts of the Public Health Committee provide the scientific base for national and international regulations regarding products which have a direct or indirect impact on the human food chain, pesticides, pharmaceuticals and cosmetics.

In the co-operation group to combat drug abuse and illicit drugs trafficking (Pompidou Group), 31 states work together, through meetings of ministers, officials and experts, to counteract drug abuse. The Group follows a multidisciplinary approach embracing in particular legislation, law enforcement, prevention, treatment, rehabilitation and data collection.

The Convention on the Elaboration of a European Pharmacopoeia (establishing legally binding standards for medicinal substances, auxiliary substances, pharmaceutical preparations, vaccines for human and vetinary use and other articles) entered into force in eight signatory states in May 1974: in March 2001 28 states and the European Union were parties to the Convention. WHO and 16 European and non-European states participate as observers in the sessions of the European Pharmacopoeia Commission. A network of official control laboratories for human and veterinary medicines was established in 1995, open to all signatory countries to the Convention and observers at the Pharmacopoeia Commission. The fourth edition of the European Pharmacopoeia (published in early 2001) includes some 1,800 harmonized European standards, or 'monographs', 300 general methods of analysis and 1,000 reagents.

In April 1997 the first international convention on biomedicine was opened for signature at a meeting of health ministers of member states, in Oviedo, Spain. The so-called Convention for the Protection of Human Rights and the Dignity of Human Beings with Respect to the Applications of Biology and Medicine incorporated provisions on scientific research, the principle of informed patient consent, organ and tissue transplants and the prohibition of financial gain and disposal of a part of the human body. It entered into force on 1 November 1999. An Additional Protocol to the Convention, with regard to the prohibition of medical cloning of human beings, was approved by Council heads of state and government in October 1997 and was opened for signature in January 1998. In 2000 work was ongoing to draft protocols relating to the transplantation of human organs and tissue, medical research, protection of the human embryo and foetus and genetics.

POPULATION AND MIGRATION

The European Convention on the Legal Status of Migrant Workers, in force since 1983, has been ratified by France, Italy, the Netherlands, Norway, Portugal, Spain, Sweden and Turkey. The Convention is based on the principle of equality of treatment for migrant workers and the nationals of the host country as to housing, working conditions, and social security. The Convention also upholds the principle of the right to family reunion. An international consultative committee, representing the parties to the Convention, monitors the application of the Convention.

In 1996 the European Committee on Migration concluded work on a project entitled 'The Integration of Immigrants: Towards Equal Opportunities' was concluded and the results were presented at the sixth conference of European ministers responsible for migration affairs, held in Warsaw, Poland. At the conference a new project, entitled 'Tensions and Tolerance: Building better integrated communities across Europe' was initiated; it was concluded in 1999. The Committee was responsible for activities concerning Roma/ Gypsies in Europe, in co-ordination with other relevant Council of Europe bodies. The Committee is also jointly responsible, with the *ad hoc* Committee of Experts on the legal aspects of territorial asylum, refugees and stateless persons, for the examination of migration issues arising at the pan-European level.

The European Population Committee, an intergovernmental committee of scientists and government officials responsible for population matters, monitors and analyses population trends throughout Europe and informs governments, research centres and the public of demographic developments and their impact on policy decisions. It compiles an annual statistical review of demographic developments (covering 46 European states) and publishes the results of studies on population issues, such as the demographic characteristics of national minorities in certain European states (Vol. I–1998), internal migration and regional population dynamics (1999), fertility and new types of households and family formation in Europe, and demographic trends and the labour market (2000). Future publications were to include studies on trends in mortality and differential mortality in Europe, the demographic characteristics of immigrant populations, the demographic consequences of economic transition in the countries of central and eastern Europe, and the demographic implications of social exclusion.

COUNCIL OF EUROPE DEVELOPMENT BANK

A Council of Europe Social Development Fund was created in 1956 (as the Resettlement Fund). Its primary aim was to finance projects to benefit refugees, migrants and displaced persons, and victims of natural or ecological disasters. As a secondary objective, it also funds social projects involving job creation, vocational training, social housing, education, health, the protection of the environment, and the protection and rehabilitation of the historic heritage. In November 1999 the Fund was renamed the Council of Europe Development Bank. At September subscribed capital amounted to €1,401m., while total loans granted since the Fund's inception amounted to €12,210m.

EQUALITY BETWEEN WOMEN AND MEN

The Steering Committee for Equality between Women and Men (CDEG—an intergovernmental committee of experts) is responsible for encouraging action at both national and Council of Europe level to promote equality of rights and opportunities between the two sexes. Assisted by various specialist groups and committees, the CDEG is mandated to establish analyses, studies and evaluations, to examine national policies and experiences, to work out concerted policy strategies and measures for implementing equality and, as necessary, to prepare appropriate legal and other instruments. It is also responsible for preparing the European Ministerial Conferences on Equality between Women and Men. The main areas of CDEG activities are the comprehensive inclusion of the rights of women (for example, violence against women, forced prostitution, reproductive rights) within the context of human rights; the issue of equality and democracy, including the promotion of the participation of women in political and public life; projects aimed at studying the specific equality problems related to cultural diversity, migration and minorities; positive action in the field of equality between men and women and the mainstreaming of equality into all policies and programmes at all levels of society. In October 1998 the Committee of Ministers adopted a recommendation to member states on gender mainstreaming.

LEGAL MATTERS

The European Committee on Legal Co-operation develops co-operation between member states in the field of law, with the objective of harmonizing and modernizing public and private law, including administrative law and the law relating to the judiciary. The Committee is responsible for expert groups which consider issues relating to administrative law, efficiency of justice, family law, nationality, information technology and data protection. Numerous conventions and Recommendations have been adopted, and followed up by appropriate committees or groups of experts, on matters which include: information on foreign law; children born out of wedlock; adoption; nationality; animal protection; administrative law; custody of children; data protection; legal aid; and the legal status of non-governmental organizations.

An *ad hoc* Committee of Legal Advisors on Public and International Law (CAHDI), comprising the legal advisors of ministers of foreign affairs of member states and of several observer states, is authorized to examine questions of public international law, and to exchange and, if appropriate, to co-ordinate the views of member states. Recent activities of the CAHDI include the preparation of a Recommendation on reaction to inadmissible reservations to international treaties, and publication of a report on a pilot project relating to state practice with regard to state succession and recognition in the period 1989–1994. An *ad hoc* Committee of Experts on the Legal Aspects of Territorial Asylum, Refugees and Stateless Persons (CAHAR) proposes solutions to practical and legal problems relating to its area of expertise, formulates appropriate legal instruments, reviews relevant national and international developments and adopts Recommendations. The CAHAR has adopted a series of opinions for the Committee of Ministers on the situation of refugees and displaced persons in the CIS, on access to asylum by EU citizens, and on the human rights of refugees and asylum-seekers in Europe. It works closely with other international bodies, in particular UNHCR and the Council's Parliamentary Assembly.

With regard to crime, the European Committee on Crime Problems has prepared conventions on such matters as extradition, mutual assistance, recognition and enforcement of foreign judgments, the transfer of proceedings, the suppression of terrorism, the transfer of prisoners, the compensation to be paid to victims of violent crime, and search, seizure and confiscation of the proceeds from crime. A new Criminal Convention on Corruption was opened for signature in January 1999, and a Civil Law Convention against Corruption was opened for signature in November. In May a new monitoring organ, the Group of States against Corruption (GRECO), became operational.

A Criminological Scientific Council, composed of specialists in law, psychology, sociology and related sciences, advises the Committee and organizes criminological research conferences and colloquia. A Council for Penological Co-operation organizes regular high-level conferences of directors of prison administration and is responsible for collating statistical information on detention and community sanctions in Europe. The Council prepared new European Prison Rules in 1987 and European Rules on Community Sanctions (alternatives to imprisonment) in 1992.

In May 1990 the Committee of Ministers adopted a Partial Agreement to establish the European Commission for Democracy through Law, to be based in Venice, Italy. The Commission is composed of legal and political experts and is concerned with the guarantees offered by law in the service of democracy. In particular, it may supply opinions upon request, made through the Committee of Ministers, by the Parliamentary Assembly, the Secretary-General or any member states of the Council of Europe. Other states and international organizations may request opinions with the consent of the Committee of Ministers. The Commission may also conduct research on its own initiative. In 1999 the Commission was working on the following issues: constitutional justice; constitutional reforms; electoral law and national minorities; self-determination and secession in constitutional law; federated and regional entities and international treaties; and the prohibition of political parties. The Commission has pursued its activities through the UniDem (University for Democracy) programme of seminars and maintains its own website (at venice.coe.int/).

The promotion of local and regional democracy and of decentralized transfrontier co-operation constitutes a major aim of the Council's intergovernmental programme of activities. The Steering Committee on Local and Regional Democracy (CDLR) serves as a forum for representatives of member states to exchange information and pursue co-operation in order to promote the decentralization of powers, in accordance with the European Charter on Local Self-Government. The CDLR aims to improve the legal, institutional and financial framework of local democracy and to encourage citizen participation in local and regional communities. It prepares comparative studies and national reports, and issues guide-lines to promote the implementation of the principles of subsidiarity and solidarity, and is responsible for formulating or finalizing drafts of legal texts in the field of local and regional democracy. The work of the CDLR constitutes a basis for the provision of aid to central and eastern European countries under the ADACS-Local Government Programme. The policy of the Council of Europe on transfrontier co-operation between territorial communities or authorities is implemented through two committees. A Select Committee of Experts on Transfrontier Co-operation (LR-R-CT), composed of national experts, aims to monitor the implementation of the European Outline Convention on Transfrontier Co-operation between Territorial Communities or Authorities; to make proposals for the elimination of obstacles, in particular of a legal nature, to transfrontier and interterritorial co-operation; and to compile 'best practice' examples of transfrontier co-operation in various fields of activity. A Committee of Advisers for the development of transfrontier co-operation in central and eastern Europe is composed of three members representing, respectively, the Secretary-General, the Committee of Ministers and the Congress of Local and Regional Authorities of Europe. Its task is to guide the promotion of transfrontier co-operation in central and eastern European countries, with a view to fostering good neighbourly relations between the frontier populations, especially in particularly sensitive regions. Its programme comprises: conferences and colloquies designed to raise awareness on the Outline Convention; meetings in border regions between representatives of local communities with a view to strengthening mutual trust; and restricted meetings with national and local representatives responsible for preparing the legal texts for ratification and/or implementation of the Outline Convention.

EDUCATION, CULTURE AND HERITAGE

The European Cultural Convention covers education, culture, heritage, sport and youth. Programmes on education, higher education, culture and cultural heritage are managed by the Council for Cultural Co-operation, assisted by four specialized committees.

The education programme consists of projects on 'Education for democratic citizenship', 'Learning and teaching about the history of Europe in the 20th century', 'Language policies for a multilingual and multicultural Europe', and 'Education strategies for social cohesion and democratic security'. Other activities include: the annual European Schools Day Competition, organized in co-operation with the EU; the In-service Educational Staff Training Programme; the Network for School Links and Exchanges; and the European Secondary School Students Exchange Programme. The Council's main contribution in the field of higher education is its activity on the recognition of qualifications and mobility of students and staff. The Council of Europe/UNESCO Convention on the Recognition of Qualifications Concerning Higher Education in the European Region was adopted in 1997 and entered into force on 1 February 1999. Practical recognition work is conducted within the framework of a European Network of National Information Centres (ENIC) network on academic recognition and mobility. Other activities include a legislative reform programme; lifelong learning for equity and social cohesion; universities as sites of citizenship and civic responsibility; and techical co-operation and assistance to South-East Europe, in particular Bosnia and Herzegovina and Kosovo and Metohija.

In December 2000 the Committee of Ministers adopted a Declaration on Cultural Diversity, formulated in consultation with other organizations (including the European Union and UNESCO), which created a framework for developing a European approach to valuing cultural diversity.

In the field of cultural policy, a series of surveys of national policies are conducted (for example, on Croatia and Portugal in 1998 and Romania in 1999). Since 1998 this series has been complemented by 'transversal' policy reviews, for example on national cultural institutions and on cultural policy and cultural diversity. A Research and Development Unit for cultural policies became operational in 1997 with responsibility for the improvement, accuracy and circulation of information concerning European cultural policies. During 1999 reviews of national book policies were undertaken in Albania, Estonia and Lithuania. Guide-lines have been formulated on library legislation and policy in Europe, and in early 2000 work was ongoing on the preparation of guide-lines on book development and electronic publishing, and on a European policy on access to archives. Two main archive projects were being undertaken at early 2000—the computerization of the Komintern Archives in Moscow,

Russia, and the reconstitution of archival sources relating to Polish history. In 1998 the Council initiated a new four-year assistance programme to support cultural development in South-East Europe (the MOSAIC project). A similar plan, the STAGE project, for countries of the Caucasus became operational in 2000.

The European Convention on Cinematographic Co-production was opened for signature in October 1992. The Eurimages support fund helps to finance co-production of films. Conventions for the Protection of the Architectural Heritage and the Protection of the Archaeological Heritage provide a legal framework for European co-operation in these areas. The Cultural Heritage Committee promotes discussion on measures relating to heritage and consolidating democracy in Europe, the formulation of strategies for sustainable development, and on national experience and policies concerning conservation and enhancement of the European cultural heritage. In September 1999 a new campaign was inaugurated to promote co-operation and to generate awareness of the common heritage of Europe. In 1996 the European Conference of Ministers responsible for cultural heritage resolved to establish a network for the dissemination of information, using the electronic media, on heritage policies in states party to the European Cultural Convention. The network was initiated as a pilot scheme, covering six countries, in 1999. It was being developed by the European Foundation for Heritage Skills, which aimed to develop practical co-operation among professionals of all European countries.

YOUTH

In 1972 the Council of Europe established the European Youth Centre (EYC) in Strasbourg. A second residential centre was created in Budapest in 1995. The centres, run with and by international non-governmental youth organizations representing a wide range of interests, provide about 50 residential courses a year (study sessions, training courses, symposia). A notable feature of the EYC is its decision-making structure, by which decisions on its programme and general policy matters are taken by a Programming Committee composed of an equal number of youth organizations and government representatives.

The European Youth Foundation (EYF) aims to provide financial assistance to European activities of non-governmental youth organizations and began operations in 1973. Since that time more than 380 organizations have received financial aid for carrying out international activities, while more than 210,000 young people have participated in meetings supported by the Foundation. The European Steering Committee for Intergovernmental Co-operation in the Youth Field conducts research in youth-related matters and prepares for ministerial conferences.

SPORT

The Committee for the Development of Sport, founded in November 1977, administers the Sports Fund. Its activities concentrate on the implementation of the European Sports Charter; the role of sport in society (e.g. medical, political, ethical and educational aspects); the provision of assistance in sports reform to new member states in central and eastern Europe; and the practice of sport (activities, special projects, etc.). The Committee is also responsible for preparing the conference of European ministers responsible for sport. In 1985 the Committee of Ministers adopted the European Convention on Spectator Violence and Misbehaviour at Sports Events. A Charter on Sport for Disabled Persons was adopted in 1986, an Anti-Doping Convention in 1989, and a Code of Sports Ethics in 1992. During the period 1996–2000 the Committee for the Development of Sport implemented an Action Plan for Bosnia and Herzegovina, entitled 'Rehabilitation through Sport'.

ENVIRONMENT AND SUSTAINABLE DEVELOPMENT

In 1995 a pan-European biological and landscape diversity strategy, formulated by the Committee of Ministers, was endorsed at a ministerial conference of the UN Economic Commission for Europe, which was held in Sofia, Bulgaria. The strategy was to be implemented jointly by the Council of Europe and UNEP, in close co-operation with the European Community. In particular, it provided for implementation of the Convention on Biological Diversity.

At January 2001 43 states and the European Community had ratified a Convention on the Conservation of European Wildlife and Natural Habitats, which entered into force in June 1982 and gives total protection to 693 species of plants, 89 mammals, 294 birds, 43 reptiles, 21 amphibians, 115 freshwater fishes, 111 invertebrates and their habitats. The Convention established a network of protected areas known as the 'Emerald Network'. The Council's NATUROPA Centre provides information and documentation on the environment, through periodicals and campaigns such as the Europe Nature Conservation Year (1995). The Council awards the European Diploma for protection of areas of European significance, supervises a network of biogenetic reserves, and maintains 'red lists' of threatened animals and plants.

Regional disparities constitute a major obstacle to the process of European integration. Conferences of ministers of regional planning are held to discuss these issues. In 1997 they adopted a set of principles concerning the outlook for sustainable development and its implication for Europe beyond the year 2000.

EXTERNAL RELATIONS

Agreements providing for co-operation and exchange of documents and observers have been concluded with the United Nations and its agencies, and with most of the European inter-governmental organizations and the Organization of American States. Particularly close relations exist with the EU, OECD, and the OSCE. Relations with non-member states, other organizations and non-governmental organizations are co-ordinated by the Directorate General of Political Affairs.

Israel, Canada and Mexico are represented in the Parliamentary Assembly by observer delegations, and certain European and other non-member countries participate in or send observers to certain meetings of technical committees and specialized conferences at intergovernmental level. Full observer status with the Council was granted to the USA in 1995, to Canada and Japan in 1996 and to Mexico in 1999. The Holy See has had a similar status since 1970.

The European Centre for Global Interdependence and Solidarity (the 'North–South Centre') was established in Lisbon, Portugal, in 1990, in order to provide a framework for European co-operation in this area and to promote pluralist democracy and respect for human rights. The Centre is co-managed by parliamentarians, governments, non-governmental organizations and local and regional authorities. Its activities are divided into three programmes: public information and media relations; education and training for global interdependence; and dialogue for global partnership. The Centre organizes workshops, seminars and training courses on global interdependence and convenes international colloquies on human rights.

During the early 1990s the Council of Europe established a structure of programmes to assist the process of democratic reform in central and eastern European countries that had formerly been under communist rule. In October 1997 the meeting of heads of state or of government of Council members agreed to extend the programmes as the means by which all states are assisted to meet their undertakings as members of the Council. These specific co-operation programmes were mainly concerned with the development

of the rule of law; the protection and promotion of human rights; and strengthening local democracy. A scheme of Democratic Leadership Programmes has also been established for the training of political leaders. Within the framework of the co-operation programme 19 information and documentation centres have been established in 14 countries of Central and Eastern Europe. Council offices in Belgrade, Mostar, Podgorica, Priština, Sarajevo and Tirana support the implementation of the co-operation programmes in Albania, Bosnia and Herzegovina and the Federal Republic of Yugoslavia. A secretariat representation to co-ordinate the Council's contribution to the UN operation in Kosovo was established in the capital of Kosovo and Metohija, Priština, in mid-1999.

Finance

The budget is financed by contributions from members on a proportional scale of assessment (using population and gross domestic product as common indicators). The 2001 budget totalled £146.3m.

Publications

Activities and achievements (in 17 languages).
Activities Report (in French and English).
Annual Report of the Council for Cultural Co-operation.
Catalogue of Publications (annually).
Congress of Local and Regional Authorities of Europe Newsletter (6 a year).
Europa40plus (electronic newsletter, monthly, in English and French).
European Cultural Diary (annually).
European Heritage (2 a year, in English, French and German).
The Europeans (electronic bulletin of the Parliamentary Assembly).
Naturopa (3 a year, in 15 languages).
Official Gazette of the Council of Europe (monthly, in English and French).
Sports Information Bulletin (quarterly).
Strategy Bulletin (6 a year, in 5 languages).

ECONOMIC COMMUNITY OF WEST AFRICAN STATES—ECOWAS

Address: ECOWAS Secretariat and Conference Centre, 60 Yakubu Gowon Crescent, Asokoro, Abuja, Nigeria.
Telephone: (9) 3147647; **fax:** (9) 3147646; **e-mail:** info@ecowas-mail.net; **internet:** www.ecowas.int.

The Treaty of Lagos, establishing ECOWAS, was signed in May 1975 by 15 states, with the object of promoting trade, co-operation and self-reliance in West Africa. Outstanding protocols bringing certain key features of the Treaty into effect were ratified in November 1976. Cape Verde joined in 1977. A revised ECOWAS treaty, designed to accelerate economic integration and to increase political co-operation, was signed in July 1993.

MEMBERS*

Benin	Ghana	Niger
Burkina Faso	Guinea	Nigeria
Cape Verde	Guinea-Bissau	Senegal
Côte d'Ivoire	Liberia	Sierra Leone
The Gambia	Mali	Togo

*Mauritania withdrew from ECOWAS in December 2000.

Organization

(April 2001)

AUTHORITY OF HEADS OF STATE AND GOVERNMENT

The Authority is the supreme decision-making organ of the Community, with responsibility for its general development and realization of its objectives. The Chairman is drawn from the member states in turn. In August 1997 ECOWAS heads of state decided that the Authority (previously convened on an annual basis) should meet

twice each year to enhance monitoring and co-ordination of the Community's activities.

COUNCIL OF MINISTERS

The Council consists of two representatives from each country; a chairman is drawn from each country in turn. It meets at least twice a year, and is responsible for the running of the Community.

EXECUTIVE SECRETARIAT

The Executive Secretary is elected for a four-year term, which may be renewed once only.
Executive Secretary: LANSANA KOUYATÉ (Guinea).

SPECIALIZED TECHNICAL COMMISSIONS

There are eight commissions, comprising representatives of each member state, which prepare Community projects and programmes in the following areas:

  (i) Food and Agriculture;
  (ii) Industry, Science and Technology, and Energy;
  (iii) Environment and Natural Resources;
  (iv) Transport, Communications, and Tourism;
  (v) Trade, Customs, Taxation, Statistics, and Money and Payments;
  (vi) Political, Judicial and Legal Affairs, Regional Security, and Integration;
  (vii) Human Resources, Information, and Social and Cultural Affairs; and
  (viii) Administration and Finance.

ECOWAS PARLIAMENT

The inaugural session of the 120-member ECOWAS Parliament, based in Abuja, Nigeria, was convened in November 2000. Members of the Parliament are elected for five-year terms. Each ECOWAS member state is allocated a minimum of five seats; the distribution of the remaining 45 seats is proportionate to the relative sizes of member states' populations. There is a co-ordinating Administrative Bureau, comprising a Speaker, elected for a five-year term of office, and other elected officials who serve renewable one-year terms. There are 13 Technical Committees covering the Parliament's areas of activity, including defence and security, economics and finance, energy, environment and natural resources, foreign affairs, human rights, laws and regulations, rural development, transport and communications, and women's and children's affairs.

Speaker: Prof. ALI NOUHOUM DIALLO (Mali).

ECOWAS FUND FOR CO-OPERATION, COMPENSATION AND DEVELOPMENT

Address: BP 2704, blvd du 13 Janvier, Lomé, Togo.

Telephone: 216864; **fax:** 218684; **e-mail:** info-fund@ecowas-mail.net; **internet:** www.ecowas-fund.org.

The Fund is administered by a Board of Directors. The chief executive of the Fund is the Managing Director, who holds office for a renewable term of four years. There is a staff of 100. The authorized cap. of the Fund is US $500m.; paid-up cap. totalled $66.5m. at Dec. 1997. In 1988 agreements were reached with the African Development Bank and the Islamic Development Bank on the co-financing of projects and joint training of staff. Efforts have been initiated to enhance the Fund's financial resources, by opening its capital to non-regional participants. At a summit of ECOWAS heads of state and government in December 1999 it was announced that the Fund was to be converted into an Investment and Development Bank, which was to have two divisions, a Regional Investment Bank and a Regional Development Fund.

Managing Director: DRABO D. BARTHELAMY (acting).

Activities

ECOWAS aims to promote co-operation and development in economic, social and cultural activity, particularly in the fields for which specialized technical commissions (see above) are appointed, to raise the standard of living of the people of the member countries, increase and maintain economic stability, improve relations among member countries and contribute to the progress and development of Africa. ECOWAS is committed to abolishing all obstacles to the free movement of people, services and capital, and to promoting: harmonization of agricultural policies; common projects in marketing, research and the agriculturally-based industries; joint development of economic and industrial policies and elimination of disparities in levels of development; and common monetary policies. The ECOWAS treaty provides for compensation for states whose import duties are reduced through trade liberalization and contains a clause permitting safeguard measures in favour of any country affected by economic disturbances through the application of the treaty.

Slow progress in achieving many of ECOWAS' aims has been attributed to some member governments' lack of commitment, shown by their reluctance to implement policies at the national level, their failure to provide the agreed financial resources, and the absence of national links with the Secretariat; to the high cost of compensating loss of customs revenue; and to the existence of numerous other intergovernmental organizations in the region (in particular the Union économique et monétaire ouest-africaine—UEMOA, q.v., which replaced the francophone Communauté économique de l'Afrique de l'ouest in 1994). In early 2001, however, in respect of the latter obstacle to progress, ECOWAS and UEMOA were jointly planning to create a single monetary zone (see below). In March 2000 the ECOWAS Authority discussed using the community levy (see Finance, below) as a solidarity fund for reimbursing member states for customs revenue lost due to implementation of the trade liberalization programme. During the 1990s ECOWAS' activities were increasingly dominated by its efforts to secure peace in Liberia, and later in Sierra Leone (see below). At a summit meeting in December 1999 ECOWAS heads of state appealed to external development partners for assistance with the implementation of their ongoing programme to establish a single monetary zone (see below). In October 2000 ECOWAS and the European Union (EU) held their first joint high-level meeting, at which the EU pledged financial support for ECOWAS' economic integration programme.

A revised treaty for the Community was drawn up by an ECOWAS Committee of Eminent Persons in 1991–92, and was signed at the ECOWAS summit conference that took place in Cotonou, Benin, in July 1993. The treaty, which was to extend economic and political co-operation among member states, designates the achievement of a common market and a single currency as economic objectives, while in the political sphere it envisages the establishment of a

West African Parliament, an economic and social council and an ECOWAS Court of Justice to replace the existing Tribunal and enforce Community decisions. The treaty also formally assigned the Community with the responsibility of preventing and settling regional conflicts. At the summit meeting, held in Abuja, Nigeria, in August 1994, ECOWAS heads of state and government signed a protocol agreement for the establishment of a regional parliament. The meeting also adopted a Convention on Extradition of non-political offenders. The new ECOWAS treaty entered into effect in August 1995, having received the required number of ratifications. A draft protocol providing for the creation of a mechanism for the prevention, management and settlement of conflicts, and for the maintenance of peace in the region, was approved by ECOWAS heads of state and government in December 1999. The protocol establishing the ECOWAS Parliament came into effect in March 2000. The inaugural session of the parliament was held in Abuja, Nigeria, in November. It was envisaged that the ECOWAS Court of Justice would become operational during 2001; in January of that year the court's seven judges were sworn in, for a five-year renewable term of office. By December 2000 the revised ECOWAS treaty had been ratified by 13 member states (all but Cape Verde, Guinea Bissau and Mauritania; Mauritania left the grouping at the end of that month).

TRADE AND MONETARY UNION

Under the founding ECOWAS treaty elimination of tariffs and other obstructions to trade among member states, and the establishment of a common external tariff, were planned over a transitional period of 15 years, from 1975. At the 1978 Conference of Heads of State and Government it was decided that from May 1979 no member state might increase its customs tariff on goods from another member. This was regarded as the first step towards the abolition of customs duties within the Community. During the first two years import duties on intra-community trade were to be maintained, and then eliminated in phases over the next eight years. Quotas and other restrictions of equivalent effect were to be abolished in the first 10 years. It was envisaged that in the remaining five years all differences between external customs tariffs would be abolished.

In 1980 ECOWAS heads of state and government decided to establish a free-trade area for unprocessed agricultural products and handicrafts from May 1981. Tariffs on industrial products made by specified community enterprises were also to be abolished from that date, but implementation was delayed by difficulties in defining the enterprises. From 1 January 1990 tariffs were eliminated on 25 listed items manufactured in ECOWAS member states. Over the ensuing decade, tariffs on other industrial products were to be eliminated as follows: the 'most-developed' countries of ECOWAS (Côte d'Ivoire, Ghana, Nigeria and Senegal) were to abolish tariffs on 'priority' products within four years and on 'non-priority' products within six years; the second group (Benin, Guinea, Liberia, Sierra Leone and Togo) were to abolish tariffs on 'priority' products within six years, and on 'non-priority' products within eight years; and the 'least-developed' members (Burkina Faso, Cape Verde, The Gambia, Guinea-Bissau, Mali and Niger) were to abolish tariffs on 'priority' products within eight years and on 'non-priority' products within 10 years. By 1997 an estimated 400 industrial goods had been approved under the trade liberalization scheme.

In 1990 ECOWAS heads of state and government agreed to adopt measures that would create a single monetary zone and remove barriers to trade in goods that originated in the Community. ECOWAS regards monetary union as necessary to encourage investment in the region, since it would greatly facilitate capital transactions with foreign countries. In September 1992 it was announced that, as part of efforts to enhance monetary co-operation and financial harmonization in the region, the West African Clearing House was to be restructured as the West African Monetary Agency (WAMA, see p. 311). As a specialized agency of ECOWAS, WAMA was to be responsible for administering an ECOWAS exchange rate system (EERS) and for establishing the single monetary zone. A credit guarantee scheme and travellers' cheque system were to be established in association with the EERS. The agreement founding WAMA was signed by the Governors of the central banks of ECOWAS member states, meeting in Banjul, The Gambia, in March 1996. In July the Authority agreed to impose a common value-added tax (VAT) on consumer goods, in order to rationalize indirect taxation and to stimulate greater intra-Community trade. In August 1997 ECOWAS heads of state and government appointed an *ad hoc* monitoring committee to promote and oversee the implementation of trade liberalization measures and the establishment of a single monetary zone by 2000. (This deadline was subsequently revised to 1 January 2004.) The meeting also authorized the introduction of the regional travellers' cheque scheme. In March 1998 senior customs officials of ECOWAS countries agreed to harmonize customs policies and administrations, in order to facilitate intra-Community trade, and to pursue the objective of establishing a common external tariff by 2000. (This deadline was not met. The ECOWAS Authority summit held in December 2000 in Bamako, Mali, determined that the harmonization of member countries' tariff structures should be accelerated to facilitate the implementation of the planned customs union.) In October 1998 the travellers' cheque scheme was formally inaugurated at a meeting of ECOWAS heads of state. The cheques were to be issued by WAMA in denominations of a West African Unit of Account and convertible into each local currency at the rate of one Special Drawing Right (SDR—see IMF p. 94). The cheques entered into circulation on 1 July 1999. In April 2000 seven, predominantly anglophone, ECOWAS member states—Cape Verde, Gambia, Ghana, Guinea, Liberia, Nigeria and Sierra Leone—agreed to establish by 1 January 2003 a second West African monetary union to co-exist alongside UEMOA, which unites eight, mainly francophone, ECOWAS member states. The two complementary monetary unions were expected to harmonize their economic programmes, with a view to effecting a merger prior to the planned creation of a single West African Monetary Zone (WAMZ) in 2004. The proposed merger of the two monetary unions was outlined in an action plan adopted by ECOWAS and UEMOA in February 2000.

In December 1992 ECOWAS ministers agreed on the institutionalization of an ECOWAS trade fair, in order to promote trade liberalization and intra-Community trade. The first trade fair, which was held in Dakar, Senegal, in May/June 1995, was attended by some 400 private businesses from the 16 member states. A second trade fair was staged in Accra, Ghana, in March 1999.

TRAVEL, TRANSPORT AND COMMUNICATIONS

In 1979 ECOWAS heads of state signed a Protocol relating to free circulation of the region's citizens and to rights of residence and establishment of commercial enterprises. The first provision (the right of entry without a visa) came into force in 1980. An optional ECOWAS travel certificate, valid for travel within the Community in place of a national passport, was established in July 1985. The second provision of the 1979 Protocol, allowing unlimited rights of residence, was signed in 1986 (although Nigeria indicated that unskilled workers and certain categories of professionals would not be allowed to stay for an indefinite period) and came into force in 1989. The third provision, concerning the right to establish a commercial enterprise in another member state was signed in 1990. In July 1992 the ECOWAS Authority formulated a Minimum Agenda for Action for the implementation of Community agreements regarding the free movement of goods and people, for example the removal of non-tariff barriers, the simplification of customs and transit procedures and a reduction in the number of control posts on international roads. By mid-1996 the ECOWAS summit meeting observed that few measures had been adopted by member states to implement the Minimum Agenda, and emphasized that it remained a central element of the Community's integration process. In April 1997 the Gambian and Senegalese finance and trade officials concluded an agreement on measures to facilitate the export of goods via Senegal to neighbouring countries, in accordance with ECOWAS protocols relating to inter-state road transit arrangements. A Brown Card scheme, providing a recognized third-party liability insurance throughout the region, was operational in 1998. An Inter-State Road Transit Authority has been established. A prototype ECOWAS passport was prepared during 2000; the prompt circulation of the passport in member states was urged by the Authority at its summit in December. Following the introduction of the ECOWAS passport national passports were to be gradually eliminated over a period of five years; the ECOWAS travel certificate was to remain in operation.

In February 1996 ECOWAS and several private-sector partners established ECOAIR Ltd, based in Abuja, Nigeria, which was to develop a regional airline.

In August 1996 the initial phase of a programme to improve regional telecommunications was reported to have been completed. Some US $35m. had been granted for project financing in eight ECOWAS countries. A second phase of the programme (INTELCOM II), which aimed to modernize and expand the region's telecommunications services, was initiated by ECOWAS heads of state in August 1997. A West African Telecommunications Regulators' Association was established, under the auspices of ECOWAS, in September 2000.

A programme for the development of an integrated regional road network was adopted in 1980. Under the programme, two major trans-regional roads were to be completed: the Trans-Coastal Highway, linking Lagos, Nigeria, with Nouackchott, Mauritania (4,767 km); and the Trans-Sahelian Highway, linking Dakar, Senegal, with N'Djamena, Chad (4,633 km). By the end of 2000 about 83% of the trans-coastal route was reportedly complete, and about 87% of the trans-Sahelian route.

ECONOMIC AND INDUSTRIAL DEVELOPMENT

In November 1984 ECOWAS heads of state and government approved the establishment of a private regional investment bank, to be known as Ecobank Transnational Inc. The bank, which was based in Lomé, Togo, opened in March 1988. ECOWAS has a 10%

share in the bank. By the end of 2000 Ecobank affiliates were operating in 11 member countries.

The West African Industrial Forum, sponsored by ECOWAS, is held every two years to promote regional industrial investment. Community ministers of industry are implementing an action plan on the formulation of a West African Industrial Master Plan identifying strategies for stimulating regional economic development and attracting external investment.

In September 1995 Nigeria, Ghana, Togo and Benin resolved to develop a gas pipeline to connect Nigerian gas supplies to the other countries. In August 1999 the participating countries, together with two petroleum companies operating in Nigeria, signed an agreement on the financing and construction of the pipeline, which was expected to become operational in 2002. During 2000 a Community initiative to connect the electricity supply networks throughout the region was under consideration. The implementation of a planned energy exchange scheme, known as the West African Power Pool Project, is envisaged as a means of efficiently utilizing the region's hydro-electricity and thermal power capabilities by transferring power from surplus producers to countries unable to meet their energy requirements. ECOWAS is developing an initiative aimed at promoting the use of renewable energy resources.

REGIONAL SECURITY

In 1990 a Standing Mediation Committee was formed to mediate disputes between member states. Member states reaffirmed their commitment to refrain from aggression against one another at a summit conference in 1991. The revised ECOWAS treaty, signed in July 1993, incorporates a separate provision for regional security, requiring member states to work towards the maintenance of peace, stability and security.

In December 1997 an extraordinary meeting of ECOWAS heads of state and government was convened in Lomé, Togo, to consider the future stability and security of the region. It was agreed that a permanent mechanism be established for conflict prevention and the maintenance of peace. ECOWAS leaders also reaffirmed their commitment to pursuing dialogue to prevent conflicts, co-operating in the early deployment of peace-keeping forces and implementing measures to counter trans-border crime and the illegal trafficking of armaments and drugs. At the meeting ECOWAS leaders acknowledged ECOMOG's role in restoring constitutional order in Liberia and expressed their appreciation of the force's current efforts in Sierra Leone (see below). In March 1998 ECOWAS ministers of foreign affairs, meeting in Yamoussoukro, Côte d'Ivoire, resolved that ECOMOG should become the region's permanent peace-keeping force, and upheld the decision of heads of state regarding the establishment of a new body, which should be used to observe, analyse and monitor the security situation in the West African region. Ministers agreed to undertake a redefinition of the command structure within the organization in order to strengthen decision-making and the legal status of the ECOMOG force.

In July 1998 ECOWAS ministers of defence and of security adopted a draft mechanism for conflict management, peace-keeping and security, which provided for ECOWAS intervention in the internal affairs of member states, where a conflict or military uprising threatened the region's security. In October the ECOWAS Authority determined to implement a renewable three-year ban on the import, export or manufacture of small armaments in order to enhance the security of the sub-region. The Authority also issued a declaration on the control and prevention of drug abuse, agreeing to allocate US $150,000 to establish an Eco-Drug Fund to finance regional activities in countering substance abuse.

The summit meeting of ECOWAS heads of state and government held in December 1999 in Lomé, Togo, approved a draft protocol to the organization's treaty, providing for the establishment of a Permanent Mechanism for the Prevention, Management and Settlement of Conflicts and the Maintenance of Peace in the Region, as envisaged at their conference in December 1997, and for the creation in connection with the Mechanism of a Mediation and Security Council, to comprise representatives of 10 member states, elected for two-year terms. ECOMOG (see below) was to be transformed from an *ad hoc* cease-fire monitoring group into a permanent standby force available for immediate deployment to avert emerging conflicts in the region.

Peace-keeping operations

In August 1990 an ECOWAS Cease-fire Monitoring Group (ECOMOG—initially comprising about 4,000 troops from The Gambia, Ghana, Guinea, Nigeria and Sierra Leone) was dispatched to Liberia in an attempt to enforce a cease-fire between conflicting factions there, to restore public order, and to establish an interim government, until elections could be held. In November a temporary cease-fire was agreed by the protagonists in Liberia, and an interim president was installed by ECOMOG. Following the signature of a new cease-fire agreement a national conference, organized by ECOWAS in March 1991, established a temporary government, pending elections to be held in early 1992. In June 1991 ECOWAS established a committee (initially comprising representatives of five member states, later expanded to nine) to co-ordinate the peace negotiations. In September, at a meeting in Yamoussoukro, Côte d'Ivoire, held under the aegis of the ECOWAS committee, two of the rival factions in Liberia agreed to encamp their troops in designated areas and to disarm under ECOMOG supervision. During the period preceding the proposed elections, ECOMOG was to occupy Liberian air and sea ports, and create a 'buffer zone' along the country's border with Sierra Leone. By September 1992, however, ECOMOG had been unable either to effect the disarmament of two of the principal military factions, the National Patriotic Front of Liberia (NPFL) and the United Liberation Movement of Liberia for Democracy (ULIMO), or to occupy positions in substantial areas of the country, as a result of resistance on the part of the NPFL. The proposed elections were consequently postponed indefinitely.

In October 1992 ECOMOG began offensive action against NPFL positions, with a campaign of aerial bombardment. In November ECOWAS imposed a land, sea and air blockade on the NPFL's territory, in response to the Front's refusal to comply with the Yamoussoukro accord of October 1991. In April 1993 ECOMOG announced that the disarmament of ULIMO had been completed, amid widespread accusations that ECOMOG had supported ULIMO against the NPFL, and was no longer a neutral force. An ECOWAS-brokered cease-fire agreement was signed in Cotonou, Benin, in July, and took effect on 1 August. In September a 300-member UN observer mission (UNOMIL) was established in Liberia to work alongside ECOMOG in monitoring the process of disarming troops, as well as to verify the impartiality of ECOMOG.

In September 1994 leaders of Liberia's main military factions, having negotiated with representatives of ECOWAS, the Organization of African Unity (OAU, q.v.) and the UN, signed an amendment to the Cotonou Agreement in Akosombo, Ghana. The accord provided for a new five-member Council of State, in the context of a cease-fire, as a replacement to the expired interim executive authority, and established a new timetable for democratic elections. In early 1995 negotiations to secure a peace settlement, conducted under ECOWAS auspices, collapsed, owing to disagreement on the composition of a new Council of State. In May, in an attempt to ease the political deadlock, ECOWAS heads of state and of government met leaders of the six main warring factions. Under continuing pressure from the international community, the leaders of the Liberian factions signed a new peace accord, in Abuja, Nigeria, in August. This political development led to renewed efforts on the part of ECOWAS countries to strengthen ECOMOG, and by October Burkina Faso, Nigeria, Ghana and Guinea had pledged troop contributions to increase the force strength from 7,268 to 12,000. In accordance with the peace agreement, ECOMOG forces, with UNOMIL, were to be deployed throughout Liberia and along its borders to prevent the flow of arms into the country and to monitor the disarmament of the warring parties. In December an attack on ECOMOG troops, by a dissident ULIMO faction (ULIMO–J), disrupted the deployment of the multinational forces and the disarmament process, which was scheduled to commence in mid-January 1996. At least 16 members of the peace-keeping force were killed in the fighting that ensued. Clashes between ECOMOG and the ULIMO–J forces continued in the west of the country in late December 1995 and early January 1996, during which time 130 Nigerian members of ECOMOG were held hostage. In April, following a series of violations of the cease-fire, serious hostilities erupted in the Liberian capital, Monrovia, between government forces and dissident troops. An initial agreement to end the fighting, negotiated under ECOWAS auspices, was unsuccessful; however, it secured the release of several civilians and soldiers who had been taken hostage during the civil disruption. Later in April a further cease-fire agreement was concluded, under the aegis of the US Government, the UN and ECOWAS. In May ministers of foreign affairs of the countries constituting the ECOWAS Committee of Nine advocated that all armed factions be withdrawn from Monrovia and that ECOMOG troops be deployed throughout the capital in order to re-establish the city's 'safe-haven' status. According to the Committee's demands, all property, armaments and equipment seized unlawfully from civilians, ECOMOG and other international organizations during the fighting were to be returned, while efforts to disarm the warring factions and to pursue the restoration of democracy in the country were to be resumed. At the end of May the deployment of ECOMOG troops was initiated. In August a new cease-fire accord was signed by the leaders of the principal factions in Liberia, which envisaged the completion of the disarmament process by the end of January 1997, with elections to be held in May. The disarmament process began in November 1996, and by the end of January 1997 ECOMOG confirmed that 23,000 of the targeted 30,000–35,000 soldiers had been disarmed (the original estimate of 60,000 troops having been revised, disputed by both faction leaders and ECOMOG officials once movement between factions was taken into account). The deadline for disarmament was extended by seven days, during which time a further 1,500 soldiers

were reported to have been disarmed. However, vigilante attacks by remaining armed faction fighters persisted. In February, at the end of a meeting of the Committee of Nine, it was announced that presidential and legislative elections would be held on 30 May (later revised to 19 July). ECOMOG was to withdraw from Liberia six months after the election date, until which time it had proposed to offer security for the incoming government and to provide training for a new unified Liberian army. The Committee also agreed, in consultation with the Council of State, to replace the existing Electoral Commission with a new Commission comprising seven members, to reflect all aspects of Liberian society. The Chairman would be selected from among the seven, in consultation with ECOWAS, which along with the UN and the OAU, would act as a 'technical adviser' to the Commission. ECOMOG deployed additional troops, who were joined by other international observers in ensuring that the elections were conducted in the necessary conditions of security. In early August several ECOWAS leaders celebrated the democratic transition of power in Liberia at the inauguration of Charles Taylor (formerly leader of the NPFL) as the newly-elected President. Later in that month ECOWAS heads of state agreed that the ECOMOG force in Liberia was to be reconstituted and would henceforth assist in the process of national reconstruction, including the restructuring of the armed and security forces, and the maintenance of security; it was further envisaged that ECOMOG's mandate (officially due to expire on 2 February 1998) would be extended in agreement with the Liberian Government. A Status of Forces Agreement, which defined ECOMOG's post-conflict responsibilities (i.e. capacity-building and maintenance of security) and imposed conditions on the peace-keeping forces remaining in the country, was signed by the Liberian Government and ECOWAS in June 1998. Relations with the Taylor administration, however, deteriorated, owing to accusations that ECOMOG was providing assistance to opposition groupings. The tense political situation, therefore, and the need for greater resources in Sierra Leone, resulted in ECOMOG transferring its headquarters from Monrovia to Freetown in Sierra Leone. The transfer was reported to have been completed by October, with just two ECOMOG battalions remaining in Liberia. The ECOMOG mission in Liberia was effectively terminated in October 1999 when the final declared stocks of rebel armaments were destroyed. In August 1999 a regional meeting was convened, under ECOWAS auspices, to attempt to defuse escalating tensions between Liberia and Guinea following an incursion into northern Liberia by Guinean rebel forces earlier in that month. In September representatives of eight member countries determined to establish a monitoring body to supervise the border region between Guinea, Liberia and Sierra Leone.

Insecurity in the border region between Guinea, Liberia and Sierra Leone escalated in the latter part of 2000, particularly in southern Guinea, which was increasingly subjected to insurgencies by Sierra Leonean RUF rebels (see below), combated forcefully by Guinean troops, and prompting massive displacement of and severe hardship for the local population, which included significant numbers of refugees who had fled unrest in Liberia and Sierra Leone. Relations between the three countries deteriorated swiftly, amidst mutual accusations and counter-accusations concerning the provision of external support for dissidents in their respective territories. Allegations that the RUF rebels were supported by the Liberian authorities were the subject of a report issued by an independent UN panel of experts in December. During that month the ECOWAS Authority approved the deployment of a 1,700-strong ECOMOG interposition force to act as a buffer in the Guinea-Liberia-Sierra Leone border region, in order to deter the rebel activity and thereby alleviate the ongoing humanitarian crisis. (In early October the grouping's newly-formed Mediation and Security Council had authorized the deployment of a military observer mission to the area.) Meanwhile, the governments of the three countries agreed to disarm rebel groups and to prevent these from entering neighbouring countries from their territories. However, the political crisis subsequently intensified, leading to the expulsion by Liberia, in March 2001, of the Guinean and Sierra Leonean ambassadors. By early April the Presidents of Guinea and Liberia, who opposed the proposed intervention, had both failed to sign the Status of Force Agreement necessary to enable the deployment of the ECOMOG troops.

In May 1997 the democratically-elected Sierra Leonean leader, President Ahmed Tejan Kabbah, was overthrown by a military coup involving officers of the national army and RUF rebels. Nigerian forces based in Sierra Leone as part of a bilateral defence pact attempted to restore constitutional order. Their numbers were strengthened by the arrival of more than 700 Nigerian soldiers and two naval vessels which had been serving under the ECOMOG mandate in neighbouring Liberia. At the end of June ECOWAS ministers of foreign affairs, convened in Conakry, Guinea, agreed to pursue the objective of restoring a democratic government in Sierra Leone through dialogue and the imposition of economic sanctions. In July a five-member ECOWAS committee, comprising the foreign ministers of Côte d'Ivoire, Ghana, Guinea, Liberia and Nigeria, together with representatives of the OAU, negotiated an agreement with the so-called Armed Forces Revolutionary Council (AFRC) in Sierra Leone to establish an immediate cease-fire and to pursue efforts towards the restoration of constitutional order. In August ECOWAS heads of state reaffirmed the Community's condemnation of the removal of President Kabbah and officially endorsed a series of punitive measures against the AFRC authorities in order to accelerate the restoration of democratic government. The meeting mandated ECOMOG to maintain and monitor the cease-fire and to prevent all goods, excepting essential humanitarian supplies, from entering that country. It was also agreed that the committee on Sierra Leone include Liberia and be convened at the level of heads of state. In October the UN Security Council imposed an embargo on the sale or supply of armaments to Sierra Leone and authorized ECOWAS to ensure implementation of these measures. In September ECOMOG forces fired on container ships in the port of Freetown, which were suspected of violating the economic embargo. Clashes occurred between ECOMOG troops and AFRC/RUF soldiers, in particular around the area of Freetown's Lungi international airport which had been seized by ECOMOG; further ECOMOG air attacks against commercial and military targets were also conducted, with the aim of upholding the international sanctions and in self-defence. Despite the escalation in hostilities, the ECOWAS Committee of Five pursued negotiations with the military authorities, and at the end of October both sides signed a peace agreement, in Conakry, Guinea, providing for an immediate end to all fighting and the reinstatement of Kabbah's Government by April 1998; all combatants were to be disarmed and demobilized under the supervision of a disarmament committee comprising representatives of ECOMOG, the military authorities and local forces loyal to President Kabbah. In November 1997, however, the peace process was undermined by reports that ECOMOG forces had violated the cease-fire agreement following a series of air raids on Freetown, which ECOMOG claimed to have been in retaliation for attacks by AFRC/RUF-operated anti-aircraft equipment, and a demand by the AFRC authorities that the Nigerian contingent of ECOMOG leave the country. In mid-February 1998, following a series of offensive attacks against forces loyal to the military authorities, ECOMOG assumed control of Freetown and arrested several members of the AFRC/RUC regime. Some 50 AFRC officials were arrested by troops serving under ECOMOG on arrival at James Spriggs Payne Airport in Liberia, prompting protests from the Liberian Government at the Nigerian military intervention. An 11-member supervisory task force, which included the ECOMOG Commander, was established in Sierra Leone to maintain order, pending Kabbah's return from exile. ECOMOG troops subsequently also monitored the removal of the embargo against the use of the airport and port facilities in Freetown. Kabbah returned to Sierra Leone in March and installed a new administration. It was agreed that ECOMOG forces were to remain in the country in order to ensure the full restoration of peace and security, to assist in the restructuring of the armed forces and to help to resolve the problems of the substantial numbers of refugees and internally displaced persons. In early May ECOWAS Chiefs of Staff, meeting in Accra, Ghana, urged member states to provide more troops and logistical support to strengthen the ECOMOG force in Sierra Leone (at that time numbering some 10,000 troops), which was still involved in ongoing clashes with remaining rebel soldiers in eastern regions of the country. In July the UN established an Observer Mission in Sierra Leone (UNOMSIL), whose officers were to monitor the cease-fire, mainly in areas secured by ECOMOG troops. In October ECOMOG transferred its headquarters to Freetown, in order, partly, to reinforce its presence in the country. In January 1999 rebel soldiers attacked the capital and engaged in heavy fighting with ECOMOG forces, amid reports that the Liberian Government was supporting the rebels. Nigeria dispatched several thousand additional troops to counter the rebel advance and to secure the border with Liberia. In February, however, once ECOMOG had regained control of Freetown, the Nigerian Government expressed its desire to withdraw all its troops from the peace-keeping force by May, owing to financial restraints. Efforts to negotiate a peace settlement were initiated, with the Chairman of ECOWAS at that time, President Gnassingbe Eyadéma of Togo, actively involved in mediation between the opposing groups, despite persisting reports of fighting between ECOMOG and rebel soldiers in areas east of the capital. A cease-fire agreement was concluded in May, and a political settlement was signed, by Kabbah and the RUF leader, in Lomé, Togo, in July. ECOMOG's mandate in Sierra Leone was adapted to support the consolidation of peace in that country and national reconstruction. In October UNOMSIL was replaced by the UN Mission in Sierra Leone (UNAMSIL), which was to assist with the implementation of the Lomé accord and to assume many of the functions then being performed by ECOMOG, including the provision of security at Lungi international airport and at other key installations, buildings and government institutions in the Freetown area. In consequence the ECOMOG contingent was withdrawn in April 2000. However, following a resurgence of RUF violence in April and May, when as many as 500 members of UNAMSIL (which had not been deployed to full strength) were

captured by the rebels, ECOWAS heads of government agreed to reinforce the UN peace-keeping operation with some 3,000 regional troops. A UN Security Council mission to Sierra Leone in September recommended the establishment of a mechanism to co-ordinate the formulation and implementation by the UN, ECOWAS, the Sierra Leone Government and other parties of a unified strategy to resolve the insecurity in Sierra Leone.

In July 1998 ECOWAS ministers of defence and of foreign affairs met to consider the political unrest in Guinea-Bissau, following an unsuccessful attempt by rebel soldiers, in June, to overthrow the Government of President João Vieira, and urged both sides to co-operate in negotiating a settlement. An ECOWAS Committee of Seven on Guinea-Bissau (comprising the ministers of foreign affairs of Burkina Faso, Côte d'Ivoire, The Gambia, Ghana, Guinea, Nigeria and Senegal) was established and met for the first time in August. In late August, following mediation by ECOWAS representatives and a contact group of the Comunidade dos Países de Língua Portuguesa (CPLP, q.v.), which had secured an initial cease-fire, an agreement was signed by the conflicting parties providing for an end to hostilities, the reopening of the international airport to facilitate the provision of humanitarian supplies, and for independent supervision of the cease-fire agreement. ECOWAS subsequently held discussions with the CPLP in order to co-ordinate efforts to secure peace in Guinea-Bissau. In late October ECOWAS heads of state endorsed the deployment of ECOMOG forces in Guinea-Bissau. On 1 November the two sides in the dispute, meeting in Abuja, Nigeria, signed a peace accord under ECOWAS auspices, which reinforced the August cease-fire and incorporated an agreement to establish a government of national unity. ECOMOG forces were to replace all foreign troops, mainly Senegalese, currently in Guinea-Bissau, supervise the security of the border region between those two countries, and enable humanitarian organizations to have free access to those needing assistance. In addition ECOMOG was to be responsible for monitoring the conduct of presidential and legislative elections, scheduled to be held in 1999. In early February President Vieira and the rebel leader Gen. Manè signed a cease-fire accord, under ECOWAS auspices. A new Government of National Unity was established later in that month and an ECOMOG Interposition Force began to be dispatched to Guinea-Bissau. In early May, however, President Vieira was ousted by the rebel forces. Meeting later in that month, in Lomé, Togo, ECOWAS ministers of foreign affairs condemned the overthrow of Vieira. They resolved to withdraw the ECOMOG contingent, at that time numbering 600 troops from Benin, Gabon, Niger and Togo, owing to the political developments and lack of finances. By early June all ECOMOG troops had left Guinea-Bissau.

ECOWAS supported the establishment by the OAU in July 2000 of a committee, comprising the foreign ministers of 10 OAU member countries, which was mandated to address the ongoing political crisis in Côte d'Ivoire.

The initiation of a planned ECOWAS enquiry into the evident link between illicit trading in diamonds and ongoing rebel activity in the region, particularly emanating from Liberia and Sierra Leone, was pending in early 2001.

ENVIRONMENTAL PROTECTION

ECOWAS promotes implementation of the UN Convention on Desertification Control and supports programmes initiated at national and sub-regional level within the framework of the treaty. Together with the Permanent Inter-State Committee on Drought Control in the Sahel (CILSS, q.v.), ECOWAS has been designated as a project leader for implementing the Convention in West Africa. Other environmental initiatives include a regional meteorological project to enhance meteorological activities and applications, and in particular to contribute to food security and natural resource management in the sub-region. ECOWAS pilot schemes have formed the basis of integrated control projects for the control of floating weeds in five water basins in West Africa, which had hindered the development of the local fishery sectors. A rural water supply programme aims to ensure adequate water for rural dwellers in order to improve their living standards. The first phase of the project focused on schemes to develop village and pastoral water points in Burkina Faso, Guinea, Mali, Niger and Senegal, with funds from various multilateral donors.

AGRICULTURE AND FISHING

An Agricultural Development Strategy was adopted in 1982, aiming at sub-regional self-sufficiency by the year 2000. The strategy included plans for selecting seeds and cattle species, and called for solidarity among member states during international commodity negotiations. A transhumance certification scheme, to facilitate the monitoring of animal movement and animal health surveillance and protection in the sub-region, was under preparation in 1997.

In November 1995 an agro-industrial forum, jointly organized by ECOWAS and the EU, was held in Dakar, Senegal. The forum aimed to facilitate co-operation between companies in the two regions, to develop the agro-industrial sector in West Africa and to promote business opportunities.

In February 2001 ECOWAS ministers of agriculture adopted an action plan for the formulation of a common agricultural policy, as envisaged under the ECOWAS treaty.

SOCIAL PROGRAMME

Four organizations have been established within ECOWAS by the Executive Secretariat: the Organization of Trade Unions of West Africa, which held its first meeting in 1984; the West African Youth Association; the West African Universities' Association; and the West Africa Women's Association (whose statutes were approved by a meeting of ministers of social affairs in May 1987). Regional sports competitions are held annually. In 1987 ECOWAS member states agreed to establish a West African Health Organization (WAHO) by merger of the existing West African Health Community (q.v.) and the Organization for Co-ordination and Co-operation in the Struggle against Endemic Diseases; operational arrangements for the impending inauguration of WAHO were discussed by a meeting of Community health ministers held in November 2000.

INFORMATION AND MEDIA

In March 1990 ECOWAS ministers of information formulated a policy on the dissemination of information about ECOWAS throughout the region and the appraisal of attitudes of its population towards the Community. The ministers established a new information commission. In November 1991 a conference on press communication and African integration, organized by ECOWAS, recommended the creation of an ECOWAS press card, judicial safeguards to protect journalists, training programmes for journalists and the establishment of a regional documentation centre and data bank. In November 1994 the commission of social and cultural affairs, meeting in Lagos, Nigeria, endorsed a series of measures to promote west African integration. These included special radio,

television and newspaper features, sporting events and other competitions or rallies. In December 2000 the Council of Ministers approved a new policy on the dissemination of information about the Community's activities.

Finance

ECOWAS is financed by contributions from member states, although there is a poor record of punctual payment of dues, which has hampered the work of the Secretariat. Arrears in contributions to the Secretariat were reported to total US $37m. at September 2000. Under the revised treaty, ECOWAS was to receive revenue from a community tax, based on the total value of imports from member countries. In July 1996 the summit meeting approved a protocol on a community levy, providing for the imposition of a 0.5% tax on the value of imports from a third country. In August 1997 the Authority of Heads of State and Government determined that the community levy should replace budgetary contributions as the organization's principal source of finance. The protocol came into force in January 2000, having been ratified by nine member states. By December the protocol had been ratified by 11 member states, and was being implemented by six of these, as well as by two states (Benin and Senegal) which were applying the protocol prior to ratifying it.

The provisional budget for 2001 amounted to approximately US $9m.

Publications

Annual Report.
Contact.
ECOWAS National Accounts.
ECOWAS News.
West African Bulletin.

ECONOMIC CO-OPERATION ORGANIZATION—ECO

Address: 1 Golbou Alley, Kamranieh St, POB 14155-6176, Tehran, Iran.

Telephone: (21) 2831731; **fax:** (21) 2831732; **e-mail:** registry@ecosecretariat.org; **internet:** www.ecosecretariat.org.

The Economic Co-operation Organization (ECO) was established in 1985 as the successor to the Regional Co-operation for Development, founded in 1964.

MEMBERS

Afghanistan	Kyrgyzstan	Turkey
Azerbaijan	Pakistan	Turkmenistan
Iran	Tajikistan	Uzbekistan
Kazakhstan		

The 'Turkish Republic of Northern Cyprus' has been granted special guest status.

Organization

(April 2001)

SUMMIT MEETING

The first summit meeting of heads of state and of government of member countries was held in Tehran in February 1992. Summit meetings are held at least once every two years. The sixth summit meeting was convened in Tehran in June 2000.

COUNCIL OF MINISTERS

The Council of Ministers, comprising ministers of foreign affairs of member states, is the principal policy- and decision-making body of ECO. It meets at least once a year.

COUNCIL OF PERMANENT REPRESENTATIVES

Permanent representatives or Ambassadors of member countries accredited to Iran meet regularly to formulate policy for consideration by the Council of Ministers and to promote implementation of decisions reached at ministerial or summit level.

REGIONAL PLANNING COUNCIL

The Council, comprising senior planning officials or other representatives of member states, meets annually. It is responsible for

reviewing programmes of activity and evaluating results achieved, and for proposing future plans of action to the Council of Ministers.

SECRETARIAT

The Secretariat is headed by a Secretary-General, who is supported by two Deputy Secretaries-General. The following Directorates administer and co-ordinate the main areas of ECO activities: Trade; Transport and communications; Energy, minerals and environment; Industry and agriculture (to be renamed Human Development); Project research; and Economic research and statistics.

Secretary-General: Dr ABDULRAHIM GAVAHI (Iran).

Activities

The Regional Co-operation for Development (RCD) was established in 1964 as a tripartite arrangement between Iran, Pakistan and Turkey, which aimed to promote economic co-operation between member states. ECO replaced the RCD in 1985, and seven additional members were admitted to the Organization in November 1992. The main areas of co-operation are transport (including the building of road and rail links), telecommunications and post, trade and investment, energy (including the interconnection of power grids in the region), minerals, environmental issues, industry, and agriculture. ECO priorities and objectives for each sector are defined in the Quetta Plan of Action and the İstanbul Declaration; an Almaty Outline Plan, which was adopted in 1993, is specifically concerned with the development of regional transport and communication infrastructure.

In 1990 an ECO College of Insurance was inaugurated. A joint Chamber of Commerce and Industry was established in 1993. The third ECO summit meeting, held in Islamabad, Pakistan, in March 1995, concluded formal agreements on the establishment of several other regional institutes and agencies: an ECO Trade and Development Bank, in İstanbul, Turkey, a joint shipping company, airline, and an ECO Cultural Institute, all to be based in Iran, and an ECO Reinsurance Company and an ECO Science Foundation, with headquarters in Pakistan. In addition, heads of state and of government endorsed the creation of an ECO eminent persons group and signed the following two agreements in order to enhance and facilitate trade throughout the region: the Transit Trade Agreement (which entered into force in December 1997) and the Agreement on the Simplification of Visa Procedures for Businessmen of ECO Countries (which came into effect in March 1998).

In September 1996, at an extraordinary meeting of the ECO Council of Ministers, held in Izmir, Turkey, member countries signed a revised Treaty of Izmir, the Organization's fundamental charter. An extraordinary summit meeting, held in Ashgabat, Turkmenistan, in May 1997, adopted the Ashgabat Declaration, emphasizing the importance of the development of the transport and communications infrastructure and the network of transnational petroleum and gas pipelines through bilateral and regional arrangements in the ECO area. In May 1998, at the fifth summit meeting, held in Almaty, Kazakhstan, ECO heads of state and of government signed a Transit Transport Framework Agreement and a memorandum of understanding to help combat the cross-border trafficking of illegal goods. The meeting also agreed to establish an ECO Educational Institute in Ankara, Turkey. The sixth ECO summit meeting, held in June 2000 in Tehran, Iran, encouraged member states to participate in the development of information and communication technologies through the establishment of a database of regional educational and training institutions specializing in that field and of an ECO Intra-regional Network (ECONET). The ECO heads of state and government also reconfirmed their commitment to the Ashgabat Declaration and urged the completion of the necessary formalities for the creation of the planned ECO Trade and Development Bank and ECO Reinsurance Company.

Convening in conference for the first time in early March 2000, ECO ministers of trade signed a Framework Agreement on ECO Trade Co-operation, which established a basis for the expansion of intra-regional trade. The Framework Agreement envisaged the eventual adoption of an ECO Trade Agreement (ECOTA), providing for the gradual elimination of regional tariff and non-tariff barriers between member states.

ECO staged its third trade fair in Bandar Anzali, Iran, in July 1998, and the fourth trade fair was held in Karachi, Pakistan, in April 2000. ECO has co-operation agreements with several UN agencies and other international organizations in development-related activities. An ECO-UN International Drug Control Programme (UNDEP) Project on Drug Control and Co-ordination Unit commenced operations in Tehran in July 1999. ECO has been granted observer status at the UN, OIC and WTO.

Finance

Member states contribute to a centralized administrative budget.

Publication

ECO Annual Economic Report.

EUROPEAN BANK FOR RECONSTRUCTION AND DEVELOPMENT—EBRD

Address: One Exchange Square, 175 Bishopsgate, London, EC2A 2EH, United Kingdom.

Telephone: (20) 7338-6000; **fax:** (20) 7338-6100; **internet:** www.ebrd.com.

The EBRD was founded in May 1990 and inaugurated in April 1991. Its object is to contribute to the progress and the economic reconstruction of the countries of central and eastern Europe which undertake to respect and put into practice the principles of multiparty democracy, pluralism, the rule of law, respect for human rights and a market economy.

MEMBERS

Countries of Operations:

Albania	Lithuania
Armenia	Macedonia, former Yugoslav
Azerbaijan	republic
Bosnia and Herzegovina	Moldova
Belarus	Mongolia
Bulgaria	Poland
Croatia	Romania
Czech Republic	Russia
Estonia	Slovakia
Georgia	Slovenia
Hungary	Tajikistan
Kazakhstan	Turkmenistan
Kyrgyzstan	Ukraine
Latvia	Uzbekistan

EU members*:

Austria	Italy
Belgium	Luxembourg
Denmark	Netherlands
Finland	Portugal
France	Spain
Germany	Sweden
Greece	United Kingdom
Ireland	

EFTA members:

Iceland	Norway
Liechtenstein	Switzerland

Other countries:

Australia	Malta
Canada	Mexico
Cyprus	Morocco
Egypt	New Zealand
Israel	Turkey
Japan	USA
Republic of Korea	

* The European Community and the European Investment Bank are also shareholder members in their own right.

Note: In December 2000 the Board of Governors approved the application of Yugoslavia to become a member of the Bank.

Organization

(April 2001)

BOARD OF GOVERNORS

The Board of Governors, to which each member appoints a Governor and an alternate, is the highest authority of the EBRD.

BOARD OF DIRECTORS

The Board is responsible for the organization and operations of the EBRD. The Governors elect 23 directors for a three-year term and a President for a term of four years. Vice-Presidents are appointed by the Board on the recommendation of the President.

ADMINISTRATION

The EBRD's operations are conducted by its Banking Department, headed by the First Vice-President. The other departments are: Finance; Personnel and Administration; Project Evaluation, Operation Support and Nuclear Safety; Internal Audit; Communications; and Offices of the Secretary-General, the General Counsel and the Chief Economist. A structure of country teams, industry teams and operations support units oversee the implementation of projects. The EBRD has 29 Resident Offices or other offices in all of its countries of operations. There were some 1,207 staff at the end of 1999.

President: JEAN LEMIERRE (France).

First Vice-President: CHARLES FRANK (USA) (until 31 Aug. 2001).

Activities

In April 1996 EBRD shareholders, meeting in Sofia, Bulgaria, agreed to increase the Bank's capital from ECU 10,000m. to ECU 20,000m., to enable the Bank to continue, and to enhance, its lending programme (the ECU was replaced by the euro, with an equivalent value, from 1 January 1999). It was agreed that 22.5% of the ECU 10,000m. of new resources, was to be paid-up, with the remainder as 'callable' shares. Contributions were to be paid over a 13-year period from April 1998. By 31 December 1999 the final stages of the capital increase were complete, with 56 of the 60 members, representing 97% of the Bank's capital, having deposited their instruments of subscription to the capital increase.

The Bank aims to assist the transition of the economies of central and eastern European countries towards a market economy system, and to encourage private enterprise. The Agreement establishing the EBRD specifies that 60% of its lending should be for the private sector, and that its operations do not displace commercial sources of finance. The Bank helps the beneficiaries to undertake structural and sectoral reforms, including the dismantling of monopolies, decentralization, and privatization of state enterprises, to enable these countries to become fully integrated in the international economy. To this end, the Bank promotes the establishment and improvement of activities of a productive, competitive and private nature, particularly small and medium-sized enterprises (SMEs), and works to strengthen financial institutions. It mobilizes national and foreign capital, together with experienced management teams, and helps to develop an appropriate legal framework to support a market-orientated economy. The Bank provides extensive financial services, including loans, equity and guarantees. The EBRD's founding Agreement specifies that all operations are to be undertaken in the context of promoting environmentally sound and sustainable development. It undertakes environmental audits and impact assessments in areas of particular concern, which enable the Bank to incorporate environmental action plans into any project approved for funding. An Environment Advisory Council assists with the development of policy and strategy in this area.

The economic crisis in Russia, in August 1998, undermined the viability of many proposed projects and adversely affected the Bank's large portfolio of Russian investments. In March 1999, partly in response to the region's economic difficulties, the Board of Directors approved a new medium-term strategy for 2000–03, which focused on advancing the process of transition. Key aspects of the strategy were to develop a sound financial sector and investment climate in its countries of operations; to provide leadership for the development of SMEs; to promote infrastructure development; and to ensure a balanced and focused project portfolio. In September a specific strategy to promote SMEs, through an expanded level of financing, an improved investment climate and the development of new support networks, was approved by the Board.

In the year ending 31 December 1999 the EBRD approved 88 operations, involving funds of € 2,162m., of which some€ 1,039m. (48%) was for countries at the early or intermediate stages of transition. During 1999 34% of all project financing committed was allocated to the financial sector, in order to support the development and restructuring of sound financial institutions and to make more funds available, through banks and local intermediaries, for small-scale private enterprises. A Trade Facilitation Programme, which extends bank guarantees in order to promote trading capabilities in the region, was expanded during 1999. The second largest area of project financing in that year was transport, accounting for €315m. of committed funds, of which the main focus was improvements to and development of local railway infrastructure. During 1999 the Bank participated in international efforts to secure economic and political stability in the Balkans, following the conflict in Kosovo. The Bank formulated a South Eastern Europe Action Plan to develop its specific role of promoting investment into the region and assisting its economic recovery.

A high priority is given to attracting external finance for Bank-sponsored projects, in particular in countries at advanced stages of transition, from government agencies, international financial institutions, commercial banks and export credit agencies. In 1999 those sources provided co-financing funds amounting to €1,465m. The EBRD's Technical Co-operation Funds Programme (TCFP) aims to facilitate access to the Bank's capital resources for countries of operations by providing support for project preparation, project implementation and institutional development. In 1999 the EBRD committed €89.4m. to finance 289 consultancy assignments under the TCFP, bringing the total amount committed since 1991 to €646.8m. for 2,381 assignments. Resources for technical co-operation originate from regular TCFP contributions, specific agreements and contributions to Special Funds. The Baltic Investment Programme, which is administered by Nordic countries, consists of two special funds to co-finance investment and technical assistance projects in the private sectors of Baltic states. The Funds are open to contributions from all EBRD member states. The Russia Small Business Special Funds, established in October 1993, support local SMEs through similar investment and technical co-operation activities. Other financing mechanisms that the EBRD uses to address the needs of the region include Regional Venture Funds, which invest equity in privatized companies, in particular in Russia, and provide relevant management assistance, and the Central European Agency Lines, which disburse lines of credit to small-scale projects through local intermediaries. A TurnAround Management Programme (TAM) provides practical assistance to senior managers of industrial enterprises to facilitate the expansion of businesses in a market economy. A Business Advisory Services programme complements TAM by undertaking projects to improve competitiveness, strategic planning, marketing and financial management in SMEs, particularly in countries seeking accession to the EU. In April 1999 the Bank and the European Commission launched a new SME Finance

Facility, with committed funds of €125m., to provide equity and loan financing for SMEs in the accession countries.

In February 1993 the Group of Seven (G-7) industrialized countries officially proposed the establishment of a Nuclear Safety Account (NSA) to fund a multilateral programme of action for the improvement of safety in nuclear power plants of the former eastern bloc. The NSA, which is administered by the EBRD, was approved by the Bank's Board of Directors in March, and extended for further three-year periods in both April 1996 and April 1999. At the end of 1999 14 countries and the European Community had pledged funds amounting to some €261m. to the NSA. At that time projects to improve plants in Bulgaria, Lithuania, Russia and Ukraine had been approved, while short-term safety improvements had been completed.

In 1997 the G-7, together with the European Community and Ukraine, endorsed the creation of a supplemental multilateral funding mechanism to assist Ukraine in repairing the protective sarcophagus covering the faulty Chernobyl (Chornobyl) reactor, under the Chernobyl Unit 4 Shelter Implementation Plan (SIP).

PROJECT FINANCING COMMITTED BY SECTOR

	1999		Cumulative to 31 Dec. 1999	
	Number	Amount (€ million)	Number	Amount (€ million)
Agribusiness .	9	222	55	871
Energy efficiency . .	1	34	7	171
Financial institutions .	32	735	247	4,165
Municipal and environmental infrastructure	7	161	21	556
Natural resources .	5	180	30	1,146
Power and energy utilities . .	4	155	30	1,162
Property, tourism and shipping . .	5	102	36	565
Telecommunications, informatics and media .	7	180	44	1,330
Transport . .	12	315	59	1,952
Total (including others) . .	88	2,162	624	13,745

PROJECT FINANCING COMMITTED BY COUNTRY

	1999		Cumulative to 31 Dec. 1999	
	Number	Amount (€ million)	Number	Amount (€ million)
Albania . . .	3	41	11	93
Armenia . .	0	1	3	82
Azerbaijan . .	3	41	10	254
Belarus . . .	—	—	7	170
Bosnia and Herzegovina .	2	7	9	82
Bulgaria . . .	3	27	24	325
Croatia . . .	4	44	25	565
Czech Republic .	3	205	27	642
Estonia . .	5	46	33	315
Georgia . . .	4	44	12	172
Hungary . .	4	117	54	1,106
Kazakhstan . .	4	183	11	507
Kyrgyzstan . .	1	6	10	162
Latvia . . .	3	29	19	252
Lithuania . .	3	62	17	249
Macedonia, former Yugoslav republic	4	47	11	179
Moldova . . .	1	0	12	133
Poland . . .	6	147	76	1,398
Romania . .	5	134	46	1,456
Russia . . .	6	164	85	2,723
Slovakia . .	3	70	22	481

— continued	1999		Cumulative to 31 Dec. 1999	
	Number	Amount (€ million)	Number	Amount (€ million)
Slovenia . .	1	40	20	329
Tajikistan . .	2	3	4	14
Turkmenistan .	1	63	4	154
Ukraine. .	7	243	29	832
Uzbekistan . .	3	131	14	519
Regional . .	8	267	30	553
Total . .	**88**	**2,162**	**624**	**13,745**

Note: Operations may be counted as fractional numbers if multiple sub-loans are grouped under one framework agreement.

Source: EBRD, *Annual Report 1999*.

The EBRD's Board of Directors approved the participation of the Bank in September 1997. The rules of the so-called Chernobyl Shelter Fund, which the EBRD was to administer, were approved in November and the Fund became operational in the following month. In 1995 the G-7 requested that the Bank fund the completion of two new nuclear reactors in Ukraine, to provide alternative energy sources to the Chernobyl power-station, which, it was agreed, was to shut down in December 2000. A study questioning the financial viability of the proposed reactors threatened funding in early 1997; a second survey, carried out by the EBRD, pronounced the plan viable, although environmental groups continued to dispute the proposals. By late November 1999, with an agreement on funding arrangements for the two new facilities still not reached, the Ukrainian authorities resumed power generation at one of the Chernobyl reactors. In December 2000 the Bank approved a loan for the completion of the nuclear facilities, although it was to be conditional on Ukraine undertaking a restructuring of its electricity sector, as well as the conduct of a safety check of the redundant Chernobyl power station.

Publications

Annual Report.
Environments in Transition (2 a year).
Transition Report (annually).

EUROPEAN FREE TRADE ASSOCIATION—EFTA

Address: 9-11 rue de Varembé, 1211 Geneva 20, Switzerland.
Telephone: (22) 7491111; **fax:** (22) 7339291.

Established in 1960, EFTA aimed to bring about free trade in industrial goods and to contribute to the liberalization and expansion of world trade. EFTA now serves as the structure through which three of its members participate in the European Economic Area (EEA), together with the 15 member states of the European Union (q.v.).

MEMBERS

Iceland	Norway
Liechtenstein	Switzerland

Three founder members subsequently left EFTA and joined the European Community (EC): Denmark (1973), the United Kingdom (1973) and Portugal (1986). Finland, formerly an associate member of EFTA, became a full member on 1 January 1986. Liechtenstein joined EFTA as a full member in September 1991, having hitherto had associate status through its customs union with Switzerland. Austria, Sweden (both founder members) and Finland left the Association on 31 December 1994 to become members of the European Union (as the EC had been restyled).

Organization

(April 2001)

EFTA COUNCIL

The Council is EFTA's governing body. The Chair is held for six months by each country in turn. The Council's decisions are binding on member states and must be unanimous. The Council is assisted by a substructure of committees and working groups.

EFTA STANDING COMMITTEES

Board of Auditors.
Budget Committee.
Committee of Members of Parliament of the EFTA Countries.
Committee of Origin and Customs Experts.
Committee on Technical Barriers to Trade.
Committee on Third Country Relations.
Committee of Trade Experts.
Consultative Committee.
Economic Committee.
Steering Committee of the Portuguese Fund.

MATTERS RELATED TO THE EEA

The treaty establishing the EEA, which entered into force in 1994, provided for an institutional structure to enhance its operations. An EEA Council, comprising ministers of all signatory countries, provides policy direction, while a Joint Committee, comprising representatives of the EFTA states in the EEA, the European Commission and EU member states, is responsible for the day-to-day management of EEA matters. A Standing Committee serves as the forum of consultation within EFTA, consisting of representatives from Iceland, Liechtenstein and Norway and observers from Switzerland. It is assisted by five Subcommittees and a number of Working Groups. An independent EFTA Surveillance Authority and an EFTA Court have also been established to provide judicial control.

SECRETARIAT

Address: 74 rue de Trèves, 1040 Brussels, Belgium.
Telephone: (2) 286-17-11; **fax:** (2) 286-17-50; **e-mail:** eftamailbox@secrbru.efta.be; **internet:** www.efta.be.
Secretary-General: WILLIAM ROSSIER (Switzerland).

Activities

The creation of a single market including all the countries in Western Europe was the ultimate objective of EFTA when it was created in 1960. Member states were, however, not ready or able to accept the far-reaching political and economic implications of joining the EC, which was established in 1958. EFTA's first target, the creation of free trade in industrial goods between its members, was achieved by the end of 1966. By 1991 tariffs or import duties had been removed on all imports except agricultural products.

In 1972 EFTA member states signed bilateral agreements with the EC, which established free trade in most industrial goods between them from 1 July 1977. The last restrictions on free industrial trade were abolished from 1 January 1984. In April of that year ministers from all EFTA and EC member countries agreed on general guidelines for developing the EFTA-EC relationship. Their Declaration (known as the Luxembourg Declaration) recommended intensified efforts to improve the free circulation of industrial products between their countries, and closer co-operation beyond the framework of the free-trade agreements, in fields such as education, the environment, social policy, and research and development. In March 1989 the EFTA heads of government issued a declaration reaffirming their commitment to establish a European Economic Area (EEA), consisting of all the member states of EFTA and the EC. Formal negotiations on the establishment of the EEA commenced in June 1990, and the Agreement was signed in Oporto, Portugal, in May 1992. In December a Swiss referendum voted to oppose ratification of the EEA treaty. The ministers of trade of the remaining 18 member countries, however, signed an adjustment protocol in March 1993, allowing the EEA to be established without Switzerland. The EEA entered into force on 1 January 1994. Liechtenstein joined the EEA on 1 May 1995, having amended its customs union agreement and secured the support of the majority of its population in a national referendum. The EEA Agreement provided for the removal of all restrictions on the movement of goods, persons, services and capital within the area, effectively extending the internal market of the EU to the three EFTA countries within the EEA. In addition, the Agreement provided for co-operation in areas such as the environment, social policy, education and training, tourism, culture, consumer protection and small and medium-sized enterprises. To maintain homogeneity within the EEA, the Agreement is amended on a continuous basis to ensure that relevant EU legislation is extended to the EFTA EEA grouping.

Although Portugal left EFTA in 1985, EFTA decided to maintain an industrial development fund (established in 1976) for that country, for the 25-year period originally foreseen. EFTA has concluded free-trade agreements with Turkey, in December 1991; with Czechoslovakia in March 1992 (with protocols on succession with the Czech Republic and Slovakia in April 1993); with Israel in September 1992; with Poland and Romania in December 1992; with Bulgaria and Hungary in March 1993; with Slovenia in July 1995, and with Estonia, Latvia and Lithuania in December of that year; with Morocco (which was granted a 12-year transitional period to phase out customs duties) in June 1997; with the Palestinian Authority in November 1998; with the former Yugoslav Republic of Macedonia in June 2000, and with Mexico in November of that year. In addition, declarations on co-operation (with a view to securing a free-trade agreement) are in force with Albania (signed in December 1992); with Egypt and Tunisia (December 1995); with Jordan and Lebanon (June 1997); and with Croatia, Ukraine and the Co-operation Council for the Arab States of the Gulf (June 2000). Formal negotiations on instigating a free-trade agreement were initiated with Cyprus in March 1998, with Canada in October of that year (upon completion, this accord would form the first transatlantic trade agreement between Europe and North America); and with Chile in December 2000.

Finance

Net budget for 1999: 19.2m. Swiss francs.

Publications

EFTA Annual Report.
EFTA Bulletin.
EFTA Traders' ABC (CD-Rom).
Factsheets, legal documents.

EUROPEAN SPACE AGENCY—ESA

Address: 8–10 rue Mario Nikis, 75738 Paris Cédex 15, France.
Telephone: 1-53-69-76-54; **fax:** 1-53-69-75-60; **internet:** www.esa.int.

ESA was established in 1975 to provide for, and to promote, European co-operation in space research and technology, and their applications, for exclusively peaceful purposes. It replaced the European Space Research Organisation (ESRO) and the European Launcher Development Organisation (both founded in 1962).

MEMBERS*

Austria	Netherlands
Belgium	Norway
Denmark	Portugal
Finland	Spain
France	Sweden
Germany	Switzerland
Ireland	United Kingdom
Italy	

* Canada has signed an agreement for close co-operation with ESA, including representation on the ESA Council.

Organization
(April 2001)
Director-General: ANTONIO RODOTÀ (Italy).

COUNCIL

The Council is composed of representatives of all member states. It is responsible for formulating policy and meets at ministerial or delegate level.

PROGRAMME BOARDS AND COMMITTEES

The Council is assisted in its work by six specialized Programme Boards, which oversee the management of the following ESA activities: Communication Satellite Programmes; Satellite Navigation; Earth Observation; Microgravity; Ariane Launcher; and Manned Spaceflight. The other principal bodies of the ESA administrative structure are the Committees for Long-term Space Policy, Administration and Finance, Industrial Policy, Science Programme and International Relations.

ESA CENTRES

European Space Research and Technology Centre—ESTEC: Noordwijk, Netherlands. ESA's principal technical establishment, at which the majority of project teams are based, together with the space science department and the technological research and support engineers; provides the appropriate testing and laboratory facilities.

European Space Operations Centre—ESOC: Darmstadt, Germany. Responsible for all satellite operations and the corresponding ground facilities and communications networks.

European Space Research Institute—ESRIN: Frascati, Italy. Responsible for the corporate exploitation of Earth observation data from space.

European Astronaut Centre—EAC: Porz-Wahn, Germany. Co-ordinates all European astronaut activities, including the training of astronauts. In 1996 the Centre began to develop computer-based training courses for the ESA aspects of the International Space Station.

ESA also helps to maintain the Space Centre at Kourou, French Guyana, which is used for the Ariane launchers.

ESA had a total of some 1,700 permanent staff at February 2001.

Activities

ESA's tasks are to define and put into effect a long-term European space policy of scientific research and technological development and to encourage all members to co-ordinate their national programmes with those of ESA to ensure that Europe maintains a competitive position in the field of space technology. ESA's basic activities cover studies on future projects, technological research, shared technical investments, information systems and training programmes. These, and the science programme, are mandatory activities to which all members must contribute; other programmes are optional and members may determine their own level of participation. In November 2000 the ESA Council and the Council of the European Union Research Council adopted parallel resolutions endorsing a European strategy for space. The strategy, which had been jointly prepared in 1999 and was entitled *Europe and Space: A New Chapter*, aimed to strengthen the foundation for European space activities; advance scientific knowledge; and to use the technical capabilities developed in connection with space activities to secure wider economic and social benefits.

ESA is committed to pursuing international co-operation to achieve its objectives of developing the peaceful applications of space technology. ESA works closely with both the US National Aeronautics and Space Administration (NASA) and the Russian Space Agency. More recently it has developed a co-operative relationship with Japan, in particular in data relay satellites and the exchange of materials for the International Space Station. ESA has also concluded co-operation agreements with the Czech Republic, Greece, Hungary, Poland and Romania, providing for technical training and joint projects in the field of space science, Earth observation and telecommunications. ESA assists other developing and transitional countries to expand their space activities. It works closely with other international organizations, in particular the European Union and EUMETSAT (q.v.). ESA has observer status with the UN Committee on the Peaceful Uses of Outer Space and co-operates closely with the UN's Office of Outer Space Affairs, in particular through the organization of a training and fellowship programme.

SCIENCE

The first European scientific space programmes were undertaken under the aegis of ESRO, which launched seven satellites during 1968–72. The science programmes are mandatory activities of the Agency and form the basis of co-operation between member states. The first astronomical satellite (COS-B) was launched by ESA in August 1975. By the end of 2000 ESA had launched 17 scientific satellites and probes, among the most successful being the Giotto probe, launched in 1985 to study the composition of Halley's comet and reactivated in 1990 to observe the Grigg-Skjellerup comet in July 1992, and Hipparcos, which, between 1989 and 1993, determined the precise astronomic positions and distances of more than 1m. stars. In November 1995 ESA launched the Infrared Space Observatory, which has successfully conducted pre-planned scientific studies providing data on galaxy and star formation and on interstellar matter. ESA is collaborating with NASA in the Ulysses space project (a solar polar mission), the Solar and Helispheric Observatory (SOHO), launched in 1995 to study the internal structure of the sun, and the Hubble Space Telescope. In October 1997 the Huygens space probe was launched under the framework of a joint NASA–ESA project (the Cassini/Huygens mission) to study the planet Saturn and its largest moon, Titan. In December 1999 the X-Ray Multimirror Mission (XMM–Newton) was launched from Kourou, French Guyana. It was envisaged that XMM–Newton, the most powerful x-ray telescope ever placed in orbit, would investigate the origin of galaxies, the formation of black holes, etc. Four cluster satellites, launched from Baikonur, Russia, in July/August 2000, were, in association with SOHO, to explore the interaction between the Earth's magnetic field and electrically-charged particles transported on the solar wind.

ESA's space missions are an integral part of its long-term science programme, Horizon 2000, which was initiated in 1984. In 1994 a new set of missions was defined, to enable the inclusion of projects using new technologies and participation in future international space activities, which formed the Horizon 2000 Plus extension covering the period 2005–16. Together they are called Horizons 2000.

The main projects being developed under the science programme in 2001 included the International Gamma-Ray Astrophysical Laboratory (Integral), scheduled to be launched in April 2002; the Rosetta spacecraft, which was to research Comet 46 P/Wirtanen and was due to be launched in early 2003; the Mars Express spacecraft, which aimed to map and search for water on Mars, and was to be launched in 2003; and the Herschel Space Observatory, which was to investigate the formation of stars and galaxies, and was to be launched in 2007.

OBSERVATION OF THE EARTH AND ITS ENVIRONMENT

ESA has contributed to the understanding and monitoring of the Earth's environment through its satellite projects. Since 1977 ESA has launched seven Meteosat spacecraft into geosynchronous orbit, which have provided continuous meteorological data, mainly for the purposes of weather forecasting. The Meteosat systems are financed and owned by EUMETSAT, but were operated by ESA until December 1995. ESA and EUMETSAT have collaborated on the development of a successor to the Meteosat weather satellites (Meteosat Second Generation) to provide enhanced geostationary data coverage. The first satellite was to be launched in 2002. ESA and EUMETSAT have also begun development of the METOP/EPS (EUMETSAT Polar System) programme, to provide observations from polar orbit. The first METOP satellite was scheduled for launch in 2003.

In 1991 ESA launched the ERS–1 satellite, which carried sophisticated instruments to measure the Earth's surface and its atmosphere. A second ERS satellite was launched in April 1995 with the specific purpose of measuring the stratospheric and tropospheric ozone. ENVISAT, the largest and most advanced European-built observation satellite, was scheduled to be launched in the latter half of 2001 from Kourou, French Guyana. ENVISAT was to provide a detailed assessment of the impact of human activities on the Earth's atmosphere, and land and coastal processes, and to monitor exceptional natural events, such as volcanic eruptions.

In June 1998 the ESA Council approved the initiation of activities related to the Living Planet Programme, designed to increase understanding of environmental issues. In May 1999 the Council committed funds for a research mission, Cryosat, to be undertaken, in order to study the impact of global warming on polar ice caps. Cryosat was due to be launched in 2003. The Council also approved funding for the definition phase of the Global Navigation Satellite System (GNSS-2, or 'Galileo') programme, to be developed through a public-private partnership with the European Commission, users and industry. Future missions also include the Gravity Field and Steady-State Ocean Circulation Explorer (GOCE), scheduled to be launched in 2005; the GOCE mission was to use a unique measurement technique to recover geodetic precision data on the Earth's gravity field.

TELECOMMUNICATIONS

ESA commenced the development of communications satellites in 1968. These have since become the largest markets for space use and have transformed global communications, with more than 100 satellites circling the Earth for the purposes of telecommunications. The main series of operational satellites developed by ESA are the European Communications Satellites (ECS), based on the original orbital test satellite and used by EUTELSAT, and the Maritime

Communications Satellites (MARECS), which have been leased for operations to INMARSAT (q.v.).

In 1989 ESA launched an experimental civilian telecommunications satellite, Olympus, to develop and demonstrate new broadcasting services. An Advanced Relay and Technology Mission Satellite (ARTEMIS) has been developed by ESA to test and operate new telecommunications techniques, and in particular to enable the relay of information directly between satellites. ARTEMIS was scheduled to be launched in 2001. In 1998 ESA, together with the EU and EUROCONTROL (q.v.), continued to implement a satellite-based navigation system to be used for civilian aircraft and maritime services, similar to the two existing systems operational for military use. ESA was also working with the EU and representatives of the private sector to enhance the region's role in the development of electronic media infrastructure to meet the expanding global demand. In May 1999 the Council approved funding for a satellite multimedia programme, Artes 3, which aimed to support the development of satellite systems and services for delivering information through high-speed internet access.

LAUNCHERS

In 1973 several European Governments adopted a programme to ensure that the future ESA had independent access to space, and determined to co-ordinate knowledge gained through national programmes to develop a space launcher. The resulting Ariane rocket was first launched in December 1979. The project, which incorporated four different launchers during the 1980s, subsequently became an essential element of ESA's programme activities and, furthermore, developed a successful commercial role in placing satellites into orbit. From 1985 ESA worked to develop Ariane–5, which was to be the prototype for future launchers. The third and final qualification flight took place in October 1998. Ariane–5 successfully completed its first year of service in 2000. Ariane–5 was to be upgraded by 2005 to enable it to lift into geostationary orbit a payload of 11m. metric tons (compared with the current limit of 6.5m. tons). In December 2000 the ESA Council approved the Vega Small Launcher Development programme and the P80 Advanced Solid Propulsion Stage Demonstrator programme. The Vega programme was to support small payloads of up to 1,500 kg for polar earth orbit missions at 700 m. The first Vega launch was due to take place in 2005. The Agency also operates the Future Launch Techologies Programme (FLTP), which studies concepts and technology requirements for future reusable launch vehicles (RLVs).

MANNED SPACEFLIGHT AND MICROGRAVITY

European astronauts and scientists have gained access to space through Spacelab, which ESA developed and contributed as part of the US Space Shuttle Programme, and through joint missions on the Russian space station, Mir. The Spacelab project enabled ESA to conduct research in life and material sciences under microgravity conditions. ESA has an ongoing programme of research in microgravity, and in 1997 initiated a new project to develop the facilities required for microgravity experiments to be conducted on the Columbus Laboratory module of the International Space Station (ISS). ESA is a partner in the ISS, which was initiated by the US Government in 1984, and was subsequently developed as a joint project between five partners—Canada, Europe, Japan, Russia and the USA. ESA's main contributions to the ISS are the Columbus Laboratory (due to be launched in 2004); and the Automated Transfer Vehicle—ATV (due to be launched by Ariane–5, with the first flight scheduled for 2003), which is to provide logistical support to the Space Station. ESA is also co-operating with NASA on developing a prototype Crew Return Vehicle (CRV), known as the X-38.

Finance

All member states contribute to ESA's mandatory programme activities, on a scale based on their national income, and are free to decide on their level of commitment in optional programmes, such as telecommunications, the Ariane project and future space station and platform projects. The 2001 budget totalled about €2,800m., including €637m. (22.8%) for manned spaceflight, €593m. (21.2%) for launchers; €459m. (16.4%) for Earth observation programmes, and €363m. (13.0%) for the science programme.

Publications

ESA Annual Report.
ECSL News (quarterly).
ESA Bulletin (quarterly).
Earth Observation Quarterly.
Microgravity News (3 a year).
Preparing for the Future (quarterly).
Reaching for the Skies (quarterly).
Scientific and technical reports, brochures, training manuals, conference proceedings.

THE EUROPEAN UNION—EU

No final decision has been made on a headquarters for the Union. Meetings of the principal organs take place in Brussels, Luxembourg and Strasbourg.

The European Coal and Steel Community (ECSC) was created by a treaty signed in Paris on 18 April 1951 (effective from 25 July 1952) to pool the coal and steel production of the six original members (see below). It was seen as a first step towards a united Europe. The European Economic Community (EEC) and European Atomic Energy Community (Euratom) were established by separate treaties signed in Rome on 25 March 1957 (effective from 1 January 1958), the former to create a common market and to approximate economic policies, the latter to promote growth in nuclear industries. The common institutions of the three Communities were established by a treaty signed in Brussels on 8 April 1965 (effective from 1 July 1967).

The EEC was formally changed to the European Community (EC) under the Treaty on European Union (effective from 1 November 1993), although in practice the term EC had been used for several years to describe the three Communities together. The new Treaty established a European Union (EU), which introduced citizenship thereof and aimed to increase intergovernmental co-operation in economic and monetary affairs; to establish a common foreign and security policy; and to introduce co-operation in justice and home affairs. The EU was placed under the supervision of the European Council (comprising Heads of State or Government of member countries), while the EC continued to exist, having competence in matters relating to the Treaty of Rome and its amendments.

MEMBERS

Austria	Germany*	Netherlands*
Belgium*	Greece	Portugal
Denmark	Ireland	Spain
Finland	Italy*	Sweden
France*	Luxembourg*	United Kingdom

* Original members. Denmark, Ireland and the United Kingdom joined on 1 January 1973, and Greece on 1 January 1981. In a referendum held in February 1982, the inhabitants of Greenland voted to end their membership of the Community, entered into when under full Danish rule. Greenland's withdrawal took effect from 1 February 1985. Portugal and Spain became members on 1 January 1986. Following the reunification of Germany in October 1990, the former German Democratic Republic immediately became part of the Community, although a transitional period was to be allowed before certain Community legislation took effect there. Austria, Finland and Sweden became members on 1 January 1995.

Note: In February 2000 the 14 other members of the EU suspended bilateral political relations with Austria, following the formation in that country of a coalition government including the far right-wing Freedom Party of Austria. Relations with Austria were restored in September.

PERMANENT REPRESENTATIVES OF MEMBER STATES

Austria: 30 ave de Cortenbergh, 1040 Brussels; tel. (2) 234-53-00; fax (2) 235-63-00; e-mail austria.press@pophost.eunet.be; GREGOR WOSCHNAGG.

Belgium: 62 rue Belliard, 1040 Brussels; tel. (2) 233-21-11; fax (2) 233-10-75; e-mail belgoeurop@skynet.be; FRANS VAN DAELE.

Denmark: 73 rue d'Arlon, 1040 Brussels; tel. (2) 233-08-11; fax (2) 230-93-84; e-mail eu-rep@brubee.um.dk; POUL SKYTTE CHRISTOF-FERSEN.

Finland: 100 rue de Trèves, 1040 Brussels; tel. (2) 287-84-11; fax (2) 287-84-00; ANTTI SATULI.

France: 14 place de Louvain, 1000 Brussels; tel. (2) 229-82-11; fax (2) 229-82-82; e-mail firstname.lastname@diplomatie.fr; internet www.rpfrance.org; PIERRE VIMONT.

Germany: 19–21 rue J. de Lalaing, 1040 Brussels; tel. (2) 238-18-11; fax (2) 238-19-78; Dr WILHELM SCHÖNFELDER.

Greece: 25 rue Montoyer, 1000 Brussels; tel. (2) 551-56-11; fax (2) 551-56-51; e-mail mea.bruxelles@rp-grece.be; ARISTIDE AGATHOCLES.

Ireland: 89–93 rue Froissart, 1040 Brussels; tel. (2) 230-85-80; fax (2) 230-32-03; e-mail reppermirl@online.be; DENIS O'LEARY.

Italy: 9 rue du Marteau, 1000 Brussels; tel. (2) 220-04-11; fax (2) 219-34-49; SILVIO FAGIOLO.

Luxembourg: 75 ave de Cortenbergh, 1000 Brussels; tel. (2) 737-56-00; fax (2) 737-56-10; e-mail secretariat@rpue.etat.lu; NICOLAS SCHMIT.

Netherlands: 48 ave Herrmann Debroux, 1160 Brussels; tel. (2) 679-15-11; fax (2) 679-17-75; Dr BERNHARD R. BOT.

Portugal: 12 ave de Cortenbergh, 1040 Brussels; tel. (2) 286-42-00; fax (2) 231-00-26; e-mail reper@reper.portugal.be; VASCO VALENTE.

Spain: 52 blvd du Régent, 1000 Brussels; tel. (2) 509-86-11; fax (2) 511-19-40; FRANCISCO JAVIER CONDE DE SARO.

Sweden: 30 square de Meeûs, 1000 Brussels; tel. (2) 289-56-11; fax (2) 289-56-00; e-mail representationen.bryssel@foreign.ministry.se; GUNNAR LUND.

United Kingdom: 10 ave D'Auderghem, 1040 Brussels; tel. (2) 287-82-11; fax (2) 287-83-98; internet ukrep.fco.gov.uk; Sir NIGEL SHEINWALD.

PERMANENT MISSIONS TO THE EUROPEAN UNION, WITH AMBASSADORS
(April 2001)

Afghanistan: 32 ave Raphaël, 75016 Paris, France; tel. 1-45-25-05-29; fax 1-45-24-46-87; Chargé d'affaires a.i.: MEHRABODIN MASSTAN.

Albania: 42 rue Alphonse Hottat, 1050 Brussels; tel. (2) 640-35-44; fax (2) 640-31-77; e-mail amba.brux@skynet.be; FERIT HOXHA.

Algeria: 209 ave Molière, 1050 Brussels; tel. (2) 343-50-78; fax (2) 343-51-68; MUHAMMAD LAMARI.

Andorra: 10 rue de la Montagne, 1000 Brussels; tel. (2) 513-28-06; fax (2) 513-07-41; e-mail meri.mateu@skynet.be; MERITXELL MATEU I PI.

Angola: 182 rue Franz Merjay, 1180 Brussels; tel. (2) 346-18-80; fax (2) 344-08-94; JOSÉ GUERREIRO ALVES PRIMO.

Antigua and Barbuda: 100 rue des Aduatiques, 1040 Brussels; tel. (2) 733-43-28; fax (2) 735-72-37; e-mail ecs.embassies@skynet.be; EDWIN P. J. LAURENT.

Argentina: 225 ave Louise (7e étage), Boîte 2, 1050 Brussels; tel. (2) 648-93-71; fax (2) 648-08-04; JUAN JOSÉ URANGA.

Armenia: 157 rue Franz Merjay, 1060 Brussels; tel. and fax (2) 346-56-67; V. CHITECHIAN.

Australia: 6–8 rue Guimard, 1040 Brussels; tel. (2) 286-05-00; fax (2) 230-68-02; e-mail pub.affs.brussels@dfat.gov.au; internet www.austemb.be; DONALD KENYON.

Bahamas: 10 Chesterfield St, London, W1X 8AH, United Kingdom; tel. (20) 7408-4488; fax (20) 7499-9937; e-mail bahamas.hicom.lon@cableinet.co.uk; BASIL G. O'BRIEN.

Bangladesh: 29–31 rue Jacques Jordaens, 1000 Brussels; tel. (2) 640-55-00; fax (2) 646-59-98; MUHAMMAD ZAMIR.

Barbados: 78 ave Gén. Lartigue, 1200 Brussels; tel. (2) 732-17-37; fax (2) 732-32-66; e-mail embar@pophost.eunet.be; internet www.foreign.barbadosgov.org; MICHAEL I. KING.

Belize: 100 rue des Aduatiques, 1040 Brussels; tel. (2) 732-62-04; fax (2) 732-62-46; e-mail ecs.embassies@skynet.be; EDWIN P. J. LAURENT.

Benin: 5 ave de l'Observatoire, 1180 Brussels; tel. (2) 375-06-74; fax (2) 375-83-26; ABOUDOU SALIOU.

Bhutan: 17–19 chemin du Champ d'Anier, 1209 Geneva, Switzerland; tel. (22) 7990890; fax (22) 7990899; e-mail mission.bhutan.ties.itu.int; BAP KESANG.

Bolivia: 176 ave Louise, Boîte 6, 1050 Brussels; tel. (2) 627-00-10; fax (2) 647-47-82; e-mail embolbrus@arcadis.be; ARTURO LIEBERS BALDIVIESO.

Bosnia and Herzegovina: 9 rue Paul Lauters, 1000 Brussels; tel. (2) 644-00-47; fax (2) 644-16-98; e-mail mission.bih.brussels@euronet.be; VITOMIR MILES RAGUZ.

Botswana: 169 ave de Tervueren, 1150 Brussels; tel. (2) 735-20-70; fax (2) 735-63-18; SASALA CHASALA GEORGE.

Brazil: 30 ave F.D. Roosevelt, 1050 Brussels; tel. (2) 640-20-40; fax (2) 648-80-40; e-mail braseuropa@compuserve.com; JORIO DAUSTER MAGALHÃES E SILVA.

Brunei: 238 ave F. D. Roosevelt, 1050 Brussels; tel. (2) 675-08-78; fax (2) 672-93-58; e-mail kedutaan-brunei.brussels@skynet.be; Dato' KASSIM DAUD.

Bulgaria: 7 ave Moscicki, 1180 Brussels; tel. (2) 374-84-68; fax (2) 374-91-88; e-mail missionlog@village.eunet.be; ANTOINETTE PRIMATA-ROVA.

Burkina Faso: 16 place Guy d'Arezzo, 1180 Brussels; tel. (2) 345-99-12; fax (2) 345-06-12; e-mail ambassade.burkina@skynet.be; KADRÉ DÉSIRÉ OUÉDRAOGO.

Burundi: 46 square Marie-Louise, 1040 Brussels; tel. (2) 230-45-35; fax (2) 230-78-83; e-mail ambassade.burundi@skynet.be; internet www.burundi.gov.bi; LÉONIDAS NDORICIMPA.

Cameroon: 131–133 ave Brugmann, 1190 Brussels; tel. (2) 345-18-70; fax (2) 344-57-35; ISABELLE BASSONG.

Canada: 2 ave de Tervueren, 1040 Brussels; tel. (2) 741-06-60; fax (2) 741-06-29; internet www.dfait-maeci.gc.ca/eu-mission; JEAN-PIERRE JUNEAU.

Cape Verde: 29 ave Jeanne, 1050 Brussels; tel. (2) 643-62-70; fax (2) 646-33-85; JOSÉ LUÍS ROCHA.

Central African Republic: 416 blvd Lambermont, 1030 Brussels; tel. (2) 242-28-80; fax (2) 215-13-11; ARMAND GUY ZOUNGUERE-SOKAMBI.

Chad: 52 blvd Lambermont, 1030 Brussels; tel. (2) 215-19-75; fax (2) 216-35-26; Chargé d'affaires a.i.: IDRISS ADJIDEYE.

Chile: 13 blvd St Michel, 1040 Brussels; tel. (2) 743-36-60; fax (2) 736-49-94; e-mail misue@skynet.be; GONZALO ARENAS-VALVERDE.

China, People's Republic: 443–445 ave de Tervueren, 1150 Brussels; tel. (2) 771-33-09; fax (2) 779-28-95; SONG MINGJIANG.

Colombia: 96A ave F.D. Roosevelt, 1050 Brussels; tel. (2) 649-56-79; fax (2) 646-54-91; e-mail colombia@emcolbru.org; ROBERT ARENAS BONILLA.

Comoros: 27 chemin des Pins, 1180 Brussels; tel. (2) 218-41-43; fax (2) 218-69-84; e-mail ambassade.comores@skynet.be; AMOÏSS ASSOUMANI.

Congo, Democratic Republic: 30 rue Marie de Bourgogne, 1040 Brussels; tel. (2) 513-66-10; fax (2) 514-04-03; JUSTINE M'POYO-KASA VUBU.

Congo, Republic: 16–18 ave F. D. Roosevelt, 1050 Brussels; tel. (2) 648-38-56; fax (2) 648-42-13; JACQUES OBIA.

Costa Rica: 489 ave Louise (4e étage), 1050 Brussels; tel. (2) 640-55-41; fax (2) 648-31-92; e-mail embcrbel@infonie.be; MARIO FERNÁNDEZ-SILVA.

Côte d'Ivoire: 234 ave F. D. Roosevelt, 1050 Brussels; tel. (2) 672-95-77; fax (2) 672-04-91; ANET N'ZI NANAN KOLIABO.

Croatia: 50 ave des Arts, Boîte 14, 1000 Brussels; tel. (2) 500-09-20; fax (2) 512-03-38; ŽELJKO MATIĆ.

Cuba: 77 rue Robert Jones, 1180 Brussels; tel. (2) 343-00-20; fax (2) 344-96-91; RENé MUJICA CANTELAR.

Cyprus: 2 square Ambiorix, 1000 Brussels; tel. (2) 735-35-10; fax (2) 735-45-52; e-mail chypre.pio.bxl@skynet.be; internet www.pio.gov.cy; GEORGE ZODIATES.

Czech Republic: 15 rue Caroly, 1050 Brussels; tel. (2) 213-01-11; fax (2) 213-01-85; e-mail eu.brussels@embassy.mzv.cz; LIBOR SECKA.

Djibouti: 26 rue Emile-Menier, 75116 Paris, France; tel. 1-47-27-49-22; fax 1-45-53-52-53; OMAR MOUINE ROBLEH.

Dominica: 100 rue des Aduatiques, 1040 Brussels; tel. (2) 733-43-28; fax (2) 735-72-37; e-mail ecs.embassies@skynet.be; EDWIN P. J. LAURENT.

Dominican Republic: 12 ave Bel Air, 1180 Brussels; tel. (2) 346-49-35; fax (2) 346-51-52; CLARA JOSELYN QUIÑONES RODRÍGUEZ.

Ecuador: 363 ave Louise, 1050 Brussels; tel. (2) 644-30-50; fax (2) 644-28-13; ALFREDO PINOARGOTE CEVALLOS.

Egypt: 44 ave Léo Errera, 1180 Brussels; tel. (2) 345-52-53; fax (2) 343-65-33; MUHAMMAD CHABANE.

El Salvador: 171 ave de Tervueren, 1150 Brussels; tel. (2) 733-04-85; fax (2) 735-02-11; JOAQUÍN RODEZNA MUNGUIA.

Equatorial Guinea: 17 ave Jupiter, 1190 Brussels; tel. (2) 346-25-09; fax (2) 346-33-09; AURÉLIO MBA OLO ANDEME.

Eritrea: 15–17 ave de Wolvendael, 1180 Brussels; tel. (2) 374-44-34; fax (2) 372-07-30; e-mail eebb@pophost.eunet.be; ANDEBRHAN WELDEGIORGIS.

Estonia: 1–3 rue Marie-Thérèse, 1000 Brussels; tel. (2) 227-39-10; fax (2) 227-39-25; e-mail eu.all@eu.estemb.be; PRIIT KOLBRE.

Ethiopia: 231 ave de Tervueren, Brussels; tel. (2) 771-32-94; fax (2) 771-49-14; PETER GABRIEL ROBLEH.

Fiji: 66 ave de Cortenbergh (7e étage), Boîte 7, 1000 Brussels; tel. (2) 736-90-50; fax (2) 736-14-58; ISIKELI ULUINAIRAI MATAITOGA.

Gabon: 112 ave Winston Churchill, 1180 Brussels; tel. (2) 340-62-10; fax (2) 346-46-69; e-mail bs.175335@skynet.be; JEAN-ROBERT GOULONGANA.

The Gambia: 126 ave F. D. Roosevelt, 1050 Brussels; tel. (2) 640-10-49; fax (2) 646-32-77; e-mail gambianmission@hotmail.com; ALICU M. NGUM.

Georgia: 15 rue Vergote, 1030 Brussels; tel. (2) 732-85-50; fax (2) 732-85-47; e-mail geoemb.bru@skynet.be; ZURAB ABACHIDZE.

Ghana: 7 blvd Gén. Wahis, 1030 Brussels; tel. (2) 705-66-53; fax (2) 705-66-53; e-mail head@ghembassy.arc.be; NANA OYE-MANSA YEBOAA.

Grenada: 123 rue de Laeken, 1000 Brussels; tel. (2) 223-73-03; fax (2) 223-73-07; FABIAN A. REDHEAD.

Guatemala: 185 ave Winston Churchill, 1180 Brussels; tel. (2) 345-90-58; fax (2) 344-64-99; e-mail obguab@infoboard.be; EDMOND MULET LESIEUR.

Guinea: 75 ave Roger Vandendriessche, 1150 Brussels; tel. (2) 771-01-26; fax (2) 762-60-36; MAMADOU BOBO CAMARA.

Guinea-Bissau: 70 ave F. D. Roosevelt, 1050 Brussels; tel. (2) 647-08-90; fax (2) 640-43-12; Chargé d'affaires a.i.: JOSÉ FONSECA.

Guyana: 12 ave du Brésil, 1000 Brussels; tel. (2) 675-62-16; fax (2) 675-55-98; e-mail embassy.guyana@skynet.be; HAVELOCK R. H. BREWSTER.

Haiti: 160A ave Louise, Boîte 4, 1050 Brussels; tel. (2) 649-73-81; fax (2) 640-60-80; YOLETTE AZOR-CHARLES.

Holy See: 5–9 ave des Franciscains, 1150 Brussels; tel. (2) 762-20-05; fax (2) 762-20-32; Apostolic Nuncio: Most Rev. PIER LUIGI CELATA, Titular Archbishop of Doclea.

Honduras: 3 ave des Gaulois (5e étage), 1040 Brussels; tel. (2) 734-00-00; fax (2) 735-26-26; IVÁN ROMERO MARTÍNEZ.

Hungary: 44 ave du Vert Chasseur, 1180 Brussels; tel. (2) 372-08-00; fax (2) 372-07-84; e-mail titkarsag@humisbeu.be; ENDRE JUHÁSZ.

Iceland: 74 rue de Trèves, 1040 Brussels; tel. (2) 286-17-00; fax (2) 286-17-70; e-mail icemb.brussel@utn.stjr.is; internet www.islande.be; GUNNAR SNORRI GUNNARSSON.

India: 217 chaussée de Vleurgat, 1050 Brussels; tel. (2) 640-91-40; fax (2) 648-96-38; e-mail eoibru@mail.skynet.be; C. DASGUPTA.

Indonesia: 38 blvd de la Woluwe, 1200 Brussels; tel. (2) 779-09-15; fax (2) 772-82-10; POEDJI KOENTARSO.

Iran: 415 ave de Tervueren, 1150 Brussels; tel. (2) 762-37-45; fax (2) 762-39-15; e-mail eiri.bxl@skynet.be; ABOLGHASEM DELFI.

Iraq: 23 ave des Aubépines, 1180 Brussels; tel. (2) 374-59-92; fax (2) 374-76-15; Chargé d'affaires a.i.: MAHDI S. HAMOUDI.

Israel: 40 ave de l'Observatoire, 1180 Brussels; tel. (2) 373-55-00; fax (2) 373-56-17; HARRY KNEY-TAL.

Jamaica: 2 ave Palmerston, 1000 Brussels; tel. (2) 230-11-70; fax (2) 230-37-09; e-mail emb.jam.brussels@skynet.be; DOUGLAS ANTHONY CLIVE SAUNDERS.

Japan: 5–6 Sq. de Meeûs, 1000 Brussels; tel. (2) 500-77-11; fax (2) 513-32-41; internet www.jmission-eu.be; ATSUSHI TOKINOYA.

Jordan: 104 ave F. D. Roosevelt, 1050 Brussels; tel. (2) 640-77-55; fax (2) 640-27-96; Dr UMAYYA TOUKAN.

Kazakhstan: 30 ave Van Bever, 1180 Brussels; tel. (2) 374-95-62; fax (2) 374-50-91; AKHMETZHAN S. YESIMOV.

Kenya: 208 ave Winston Churchill, 1180 Brussels; tel. (2) 340-10-40; fax (2) 340-10-50; e-mail kenbrussels@hotmail.com; PETER OLE NKURAIYIA.

Kiribati: c/o Ministry of Foreign Affairs, POB 68, Bairiki, Tarawa; tel. 21342; fax 21466.

Korea, Republic: 173–175 chaussée de la Hulpe, 1170 Brussels; tel. (2) 675-57-77; fax (2) 675-52-21; LEE JAI CHUN.

Kuwait: 43 ave F. D. Roosevelt, 1050 Brussels; tel. (2) 647-79-50; fax (2) 646-12-98; AHMAD A. AL-EBRAHIM.

Kyrgyzstan: 133 rue Tenbosch, 1050 Brussels; tel. (2) 534-63-99; fax (2) 534-23-25; CHINGIZ TOREKULOVICH AITMATOV.

Laos: 74 ave Raymond Poincaré, 75116 Paris, France; tel. 1-45-53-02-98; fax 1-47-57-27-89; KHAMPHAN SIMMALAVONG.

Latvia: 39–41 rue d'Arlon, Boîte 6, 1000 Brussels; tel. (2) 282-03-60; fax (2) 282-03-69; e-mail missioneu@mfa.gov.lv; ANDRIS PIEBALGS.

Lebanon: 2 rue Guillaume Stocq, 1050 Brussels; tel. (2) 645-77-60; fax (2) 645-77-69; FAWZI FAWAZ.

Lesotho: 45 blvd Général Wahis, 1030 Brussels; tel. (2) 705-39-76; fax (2) 705-67-79; R. V. LECHESA.

Liberia: 50 ave du Château, 1081 Brussels; tel. (2) 414-73-17; fax (2) 411-09-12; Dr CECIL T. O. BRANDY.

Libya: 28 ave Victoria, 1050 Brussels; tel. (2) 649-21-12; HAMED AHMED ELHOUDERI.

Liechtenstein: 1 Place du Congrès, 1000 Brussels; tel. (2) 229-39-00; fax (2) 219-35-45; e-mail ambassade.liechtenstein@bbru.llv.li; Prince NIKOLAUS VON LIECHTENSTEIN.

Lithuania: 51 ave des Cinq Bonniers, 1150 Brussels; tel. (2) 771-01-40; fax (2) 771-45-97; ROMUALDAS KOLONAITIS.

Madagascar: 297 ave de Tervueren, 1150 Brussels; tel. (2) 770-17-26; fax (2) 772-37-31; e-mail ambamad@ambassademadagascar.be; internet www3.itu.ch/mission/Madagascar; JEAN OMER BERIZIKY.

Malawi: 15 rue de la Loi, 1040 Brussels; tel. (2) 231-09-80; fax (2) 231-10-66; JULIE NANYONI MPHANDE.

Malaysia: 414A ave de Tervueren, 1150 Brussels; tel. (2) 776-03-40; fax (2) 762-67-67; e-mail embassy.malaysia@euronet.be; Dato' M. M. SATHIAH.

Maldives: 212 East 47th St, Apt 15B, New York, NY 10017, USA; tel. (212) 688-0776.

Mali: 487 ave Molière, 1050 Brussels; tel. (2) 345-74-32; fax (2) 344-57-00; AHMED MOHAMED AG HAMANI.

Malta: 44 rue Jules Lejeune, 1050 Brussels; tel. (2) 343-01-95; fax (2) 343-01-06; Victor Camilleri.

Mauritania: 6 ave de la Colombie, 1050 Brussels; tel. (2) 672-47-47; fax (2) 672-20-51; Boullah Ould Mogueye.

Mauritius: 68 rue des Bollandistes, 1040 Brussels; tel. (2) 733-99-88; fax (2) 734-40-21; e-mail ambmaur@skynet.be; S. Gunessee.

Mexico: 94 ave F.D. Roosevelt, 1050 Brussels; tel. (2) 629-07-11; fax (2) 644-08-19; e-mail mex-ue@pophost.eunet.be; Jaime Zabludovsky Kuper.

Mongolia: 18 ave Besme, 1190 Brussels; tel. (2) 344-69-74; fax (2) 344-32-15; e-mail embassy.mongolia@skynet.be; internet users.skynet.be/mongolia; Shukher Altangerel.

Morocco: 29 blvd Saint-Michel, 1040 Brussels; tel. (2) 736-11-00; fax (2) 734-64-68; e-mail sifamabruxe@infoboard.be; Chargé d'affaires a.i.: Abdeljalil Saubry.

Mozambique: 97 blvd Saint-Michel, 1040 Brussels; tel. (2) 736-25-64; fax (2) 735-62-07; e-mail embamoc.bru@euronet.be; Álvaro Manuel Trinidade da Silva.

Myanmar: Schumannstrasse 112, 53113 Bonn, Germany; tel. (228) 210091; fax (228) 219316; U Tun Ngwe.

Namibia: 454 ave de Tervueren, 1150 Brussels; tel. (2) 771-14-10; fax (2) 771-96-89; e-mail nam.emb@brutele.be; Dr Zedekia Josef Ngavirue.

Nepal: 68 ave Winston Churchill, 1180 Brussels; tel. (2) 346-26-58; fax (2) 344-13-61; e-mail rne.bru@skynet.be; Kedar Bhakta Shrestha.

New Zealand: 47–48 blvd du Régent, 1000 Brussels; tel. (2) 512-10-40; fax (2) 513-48-56; e-mail nzembbru@compuserve.com; Dell Higgie.

Nicaragua: 55 ave de Wolvendael, 1180 Brussels; tel. (2) 375-64-34; fax (2) 375-71-88; Alvaro Porta Bermúdez.

Niger: 78 ave F. D. Roosevelt, 1050 Brussels; tel. (2) 648-61-40; fax (2) 648-27-84; Housseini Abdou-Saleye.

Nigeria: 288 ave de Tervueren, 1150 Brussels; tel. (2) 762-52-00; fax (2) 762-37-63; Alaba Cornelius Abiodun Adeboyeio Ogunsanwo.

Norway: 17 rue Archimède, 1000 Brussels; tel. (2) 234-11-11; fax (2) 234-11-50; Einar M. Bull.

Oman: 50 ave d'Iéna, 75116 Paris, France; tel. 1-47-23-01-63; fax 1-47-23-77-10; Muhammad bin Sultan al-Busaidi.

Pakistan: 57 ave Delleur, 1170 Brussels; tel. (2) 673-80-07; fax (2) 675-83-94; e-mail parepbru_econ@infoboard.be; Saidulla Khan Dehlavi.

Panama: 390–392 ave Louise, 1050 Brussels; tel. (2) 649-07-29; fax (2) 648-92-16; e-mail panama@antrasite.be; Chargé d'affaires a.i.: Elena Barletta de Nottebohm.

Papua New Guinea: 430 ave de Tervueren, 1150 Brussels; tel. (2) 779-08-26; fax (2) 772-70-88; Gabriel Koiba Pepson.

Paraguay: 475 ave Louise (12e étage), 1050 Brussels; tel. (2) 649-90-55; fax (2) 647-42-48; Manuel María Cáceres.

Peru: 179 ave de Tervueren, 1150 Brussels; tel. (2) 733-33-19; fax (2) 733-48-19; e-mail embassy.of.peru@unicall.be; José Urrutia.

Philippines: 297 ave Molière, 1050 Brussels; tel. (2) 340-33-77; fax (2) 345-64-25; e-mail bleu.pe@skynet.be; Clemencio F. Montesa.

Poland: 282–284 ave de Tervueren, 1150 Brussels; tel. (2) 777-72-00; fax (2) 777-72-97; e-mail 101642.2616@compuserve.com; Jan Truszczynski.

Qatar: 71 ave F. D. Roosevelt, 1050 Brussels; tel. (2) 640-29-00; fax (2) 648-40-78; e-mail qatar@infonie.be; Chargé d'affaires a.i.: Mohamed al-Haiyki.

Romania: 107 rue Gabrielle, 1180 Brussels; tel. (2) 344-41-45; fax (2) 344-24-79; e-mail rommis@pophost.eunet.be; Alexandru Herlea.

Russia: 56 ave Louis Lepoutre, 1060 Brussels; tel. (2) 343-03-39; fax (2) 346-24-53; e-mail misrusce@interpac.be; Vasilii Likhachen.

Rwanda: 1 ave des Fleurs, 1150 Brussels; tel. (2) 763-07-02; fax (2) 763-07-53; e-mail rwanda.info@la.be; internet www.rwanda.net; Manzi Bakuramurza.

Saint Christopher and Nevis: 100 rue des Aduatiques, 1040 Brussels; tel. (2) 733-43-28; fax (2) 735-72-37; e-mail ecs.embassies@skynet.be; Edwin P. J. Laurent.

Saint Lucia: 100 rue des Aduatiques, 1040 Brussels; tel. (2) 733-43-28; fax (12) 735-72-37; e-mail ecs.embassies@skynet.be; Edwin P. J. Laurent.

Saint Vincent and the Grenadines: 100 rue des Aduatiques, 1040 Brussels; tel. (2) 733-43-28; fax (12) 735-72-37; e-mail ecs.embassies@skynet.be; Edwin P. J. Laurent.

Samoa: 123 ave F. D. Roosevelt, Boîte 14, 1050 Brussels; tel. (2) 660-84-54; fax (2) 675-03-36; e-mail samoa.emb.bxl@skynet.be; Tauilii Uili Meredith.

San Marino: 62 ave F.D. Roosevelt, 1050 Brussels; tel. (2) 644-22-24; fax (2) 644-20-57; Savina Zafferani.

São Tomé and Príncipe: 175 ave de Tervueren, 1150 Brussels; tel. and fax (2) 734-88-15; e-mail ambassade.sao.tome@skynet.be; Chargé d'affaires a.i.: Armindo de Brito Fernandes.

Saudi Arabia: 45 ave F. D. Roosevelt, 1050 Brussels; tel. (2) 649-20-44; fax (2) 647-24-92; Nassir al-Alassaf.

Senegal: 196 ave F. D. Roosevelt, 1050 Brussels; tel. (2) 673-00-97; fax (2) 675-04-60; Saloum Kande.

Seychelles: 51 ave Mozart, 75016 Paris, France; tel. 1-42-30-57-47; fax 1-42-30-57-40; e-mail ambsey@aol.com; Callixte François-Xavier d'Offay.

Sierra Leone: 410 ave de Tervueren, 1150 Brussels; tel. (2) 771-00-53; fax (2) 771-82-30; Peter J. Kuyembeh.

Singapore: 198 ave F. D. Roosevelt, 1050 Brussels; tel. (2) 660-29-79; fax (2) 660-86-85; e-mail amb.eu@singembbru.be; A. Selverajah.

Slovakia: 79 ave Cortenbergh, 1000 Brussels; tel. (2) 743-68-11; fax (2) 743-68-88; e-mail slovakmission@pmsreu.be; Juraj Migas.

Slovenia: 30 ave Marnix, 1000 Brussels; tel. (2) 512-44-66; fax (2) 512-09-97; e-mail mission.bruxelles@mzz-dkp.sigor.si; Marko Kranjec.

Solomon Islands: 13 ave de L'Yser, Boîte 3, 1040 Brussels; tel. (2) 732-70-85; fax (2) 732-68-85; Robert Sisilo.

Somalia: 26 rue Dumont d'Urville, 75116 Paris, France; tel. 1-45-00-76-51; (vacant).

South Africa: 26 rue de la Loi, Boîtes 7–8, 1040 Brussels; tel. (2) 285-44-00; fax (2) 285-44-87; e-mail samission@village.uunet.be; Dr Elias Links.

Sri Lanka: 27 rue Jules Lejeune, 1050 Brussels; tel. (2) 344-53-94; fax (2) 344-67-37; e-mail sri.lanka@euronet.be; N. Navaratnarajah.

Sudan: 124 ave F. D. Roosevelt, 1050 Brussels; tel. (2) 647-51-59; fax (2) 648-34-99; Galal Hassan Atabani.

Suriname: 379 ave Louise, 1050 Brussels; tel. (2) 640-11-72; fax (2) 646-39-62; e-mail sur.amb.bru@online.be; Chargé d'affaires a.i.: Jane R. Nanhu.

Swaziland: 188 ave Winston Churchill, 1180 Brussels; tel. (2) 347-47-71; fax (2) 347-46-23; Dr Thembayena Annastasia Dlamini.

Switzerland: 53 rue d'Arlon, Boîte 9, 1040 Brussels; tel. (2) 286-13-11; fax (2) 230-45-09; e-mail vertretung@brm.rep.admin.ch; Dante Martinelli.

Syria: 3 ave F. D. Roosevelt, 1050 Brussels; tel. (2) 648-01-35; fax (2) 646-40-18; (vacant).

Tanzania: 363 ave Louise (7e étage), 1050 Brussels; tel. (2) 640-65-00; fax (2) 646-80-26; Ali Abeid Aman Karume.

Thailand: 2 square du Val de la Cambre, 1050 Brussels; tel. (2) 640-68-10; fax (2) 648-30-60; e-mail thaibxl@pophost.eunet.be; internet www.waw.be/rte-be; Surapong Posayanond.

Togo: 264 ave de Tervueren, 1150 Brussels; tel. (2) 770-17-91; fax (2) 771-50-75; Eliott Latevi-Atcho Lawson.

Tonga: 36 Molyneux St, London, W1H 6AB, United Kingdom; tel. (20) 7724-5828; fax (20) 7723-9074; e-mail tongahicommission@btinternet.com; 'Akosita Fineanganofo.

Trinidad and Tobago: 14 ave de la Faisanderie, 1150 Brussels; tel. (2) 762-94-15; fax (2) 772-27-83; (vacant).

Tunisia: 278 ave de Tervueren, 1150 Brussels; tel. (2) 771-73-95; fax (2) 771-94-33; Tahar Sioud.

Turkey: 4 rue Montoyer, 1000 Brussels; tel. (2) 513-28-36; fax (2) 511-0450; e-mail turkdelegeu@euronet.be; Nihat Akyol.

Tuvalu: c/o Prime Minister's Office, Vaiaku, Funafuti, Tuvalu.

Uganda: 317 ave de Tervueren, 1150 Brussels; tel. (2) 762-58-25; fax (2) 763-04-38; Kamima Ntambi.

Ukraine: 7 rue Guimard, 1040 Brussels; tel. (2) 511-46-09; fax (2) 512-40-45; Boris Hudyma.

United Arab Emirates: 73 ave F. D. Roosevelt, 1050 Brussels; tel. (2) 640-60-00; fax (2) 646-24-73; e-mail emirates.bxl@infonie.be; Abdel Hadi Abdel Wahid al-Khaja.

USA: 40 blvd du Régent, Boîte 3, 1000 Brussels; tel. (2) 500-27-74; fax (2) 512-57-20; e-mail useu@usinfo.be; internet www.useu.be; Richard L. Morningstar.

Uruguay: 22 ave F. D. Roosevelt, 1050 Brussels; tel. (2) 640-11-69; fax (2) 648-29-09; e-mail uruemb@euronet.be; Guillermo Valles.

Vanuatu: c/o Prime Minister's Office, POB 110, Port Vila, Vanuatu.

Venezuela: 10 ave F. D. Roosevelt, 1050 Brussels; tel. (2) 639-03-40; fax (2) 647-88-20; Luis Xavier Grisanti.

Viet Nam: 130 ave de la Floride, 1180 Brussels; tel. (2) 374-91-33; fax (2) 374-93-76; Huynh Anh Dzung.

Yemen: 114 ave F. D. Roosevelt, 1050 Brussels; tel. (2) 646-52-90; fax (2) 646-29-11; Gazem A. K. al-Aghbari.

Yugoslavia: 11 ave Emile Demot, 1000 Brussels; tel. (2) 649-83-65; fax (2) 649-08-78; Dragoslav Jovanović.

Zambia: 469 ave Molière, 1060 Brussels; tel. (2) 343-56-49; fax (2) 347-43-33; ISAIAH ZIMBA CHABALA.

Zimbabwe: 11 square Joséphine Charlotte, 1200 Brussels; tel. (2) 762-58-08; fax (2) 762-96-05; SIMBARASHE S. MUMBENGEGWI.

Union Institutions

Originally each of the Communities had its own Commission (High Authority in the case of the ECSC) and Council, but a treaty transferring the powers of these bodies to a single Commission and a single Council came into effect in 1967.

EUROPEAN COMMISSION

Address: 200 rue de la Loi, 1049 Brussels, Belgium.

Telephone: (2) 299-11-11; **fax:** (2) 295-01-38; **internet:** europa .eu.int/comm/index_en.htm.

MEMBERS OF THE COMMISSION
(with their responsibilities: April 2001)

President: ROMANO PRODI (Italy): Secretariat General; Forward Studies Unit; Legal Service; Media and Communication.

Vice-Presidents:

NEIL KINNOCK (United Kingdom): Administrative reform; Personnel and administration; Linguistic services; Protocol and security; Internal Audit Service.

LOYOLA DE PALACIO (Spain): Relations with the European Parliament; Relations with the Committee of the Regions, the Economic and Social Committee, and the Ombudsman; Transport, including trans-European networks; Energy.

Other Members:

MARIO MONTI (Italy): Competition.

FRANZ FISCHLER (Austria): Agriculture and rural development; Fisheries.

ERKKI LIIKANEN (Finland): Enterprise; Competitiveness; Innovation; Information Society.

FRITS BOLKESTEIN (Netherlands): Internal market; Financial services; Customs; Taxation.

PHILIPPE BUSQUIN (Belgium): Science, research and development; Joint Research Centre.

PEDRO SOLBES MIRA (Spain): Economic and financial affairs; Monetary matters; Statistical office.

POUL NIELSON (Denmark): Development aid and co-operation; Humanitarian Aid office.

GÜNTER VERHEUGEN (Germany): Enlargement process, including the pre-accession strategy.

CHRISTOPHER PATTEN (United Kingdom): External relations; Common foreign and security policy; Delegations to non-member countries; Common service for external relations.

PASCAL LAMY (France): Trade policy and instruments of trade policy.

DAVID BYRNE (Ireland): Public health; Consumer protection.

MICHEL BARNIER (France): Regional policy; Cohesion fund; Intergovernmental Conference.

VIVIANE REDING (Luxembourg): Citizens' Europe; Transparency; Education and culture; Publications office.

MICHAELE SCHREYER (Germany): Budget; Financial control; Fraud prevention.

MARGOT WALLSTRÖM (Sweden): Environment; Nuclear safety.

ANTÓNIO VITORINO (Portugal): Freedom, security and justice.

ANNA DIAMANTOPOULOU (Greece): Employment and social affairs; Equal opportunities.

The functions of the Commission are fourfold: to ensure the application of the provisions of the Treaties and of the provisions enacted by the institutions of the Communities in pursuance thereof; to formulate recommendations or opinions in matters which are the subject of the Treaties, where the latter expressly so provides or where the Commission considers it necessary; to dispose, under the conditions laid down in the Treaties, of a power of decision of its own and to participate in the preparation of acts of the Council of the European Union and of the European Parliament; and to exercise the competence conferred on it by the Council of the European Union for the implementation of the rules laid down by the latter.

The Commission may not include more than two members having the nationality of the same state; the number of members of the Commission may be amended by a unanimous vote of the Council of the European Union. In the performance of their duties, the members of the Commission are forbidden to seek or accept instruc-

tions from any Government or other body, or to engage in any other paid or unpaid professional activity.

The members of the Commission are nominated by the Governments of the member states acting in common agreement normally for a renewable term of five years. From January 1995, under the terms of the Treaty on European Union, the nominated President and other members of the Commission must be approved as a body by the European Parliament before they can take office. Once approved, the Commission may nominate one or two of its members as Vice-President. Any member of the Commission, if he or she no longer fulfils the conditions required for the performance of his or her duties, or commits a serious offence, may be declared removed from office by the Court of Justice. The Court may furthermore, on the petition of the Council of the European Union or of the Commission itself, provisionally suspend any member of the Commission from his or her duties. The European Parliament has the authority to dismiss the entire Commission.

In January 1999 Commissioners accused of mismanagement and corruption retained their positions following a vote of censure by Parliament. However, Parliament proceeded to appoint a five-member Committee of Independent Experts to investigate allegations of fraud, mismanagement and nepotism within the Commission. In early March two new codes of conduct for Commissioners were announced. On 15 March the Committee published a report that criticized the Commission's failure to control the administration and to take responsibility for the budget and other measures implemented by each department. The report also identified individual Commissioners as guilty of nepotism and mismanagement and proposed the establishment of a new independent unit to investigate fraud. As a consequence of the report the Commission agreed, collectively, to resign, although Commissioners were to retain their positions, and exercise limited duties, until their successors were appointed. In late March EU heads of state and of government nominated Romano Prodi, the former Italian Prime Minister, as the next President of the Commission. His appointment was endorsed by the outgoing Parliament in early May, but it required formal ratification by the newly-constituted Parliament, which was scheduled to convene for the first time in July, following elections in June. Prodi's appointment, and the team of Commissioners that he had appointed in the interim, were duly ratified by Parliament in September. However, Parliament made ratification subject to conditions, forming the foundation of a future inter-institutional agreement between itself and the Commission: while it did not lose any of its powers, the Commission undertook to be more open in its future dealings with the Parliament. In February 2000 Prodi issued a mission statement proposing a radical restructuring of the EU's system of governance, including a redistribution of responsibilities between EU, national, regional and local authorities.

ADMINISTRATION

Offices are at the address of the European Commission: 200 rue de la Loi, 1049 Brussels, Belgium; tel. (2) 299-11-11; fax (2) 295-01-38; internet europa.eu.int/comm/index_en.htm (unless otherwise stated).

GENERAL SERVICES

Secretariat-General of the Commission: Sec.-Gen. DAVID O'SULLIVAN.

Statistical Office (EUROSTAT): Bâtiment Jean Monnet, rue Alcide de Gasperi, 2920 Luxembourg; tel. 4301-33-107; fax 4301-33-015; e-mail media.support@eurostat.cec.be; internet europa.eu.int/eurostat.html; Dir-Gen. YVES FRANCHET.

Press and Communication: Dir JONATHAN FAULL.

Office for Official Publications of the European Union (EUROP): 2 rue Mercier, 2985 Luxembourg; tel. 2929-1; fax 4957-19; e-mail europ@opoce.cec.be; internet eur-op.eu.int; Dir-Gen. THOMAS L. CRANFIELD.

POLICIES

Agriculture: Dir-Gen. JOSÉ MANUEL SILVA RODRÍGUEZ.

Competition: Dir-Gen. ALEXANDER SCHAUB.

Economics and Financial Affairs: Dir-Gen. GIOVANNI RAVISIO.

Education and Culture: Dir-Gen. NIKOLAUS VAN DER PAS.

Employment and Social Affairs: Dir-Gen. ODILE QUINTIN.

Energy and Transport: Dir-Gen. FRANÇOIS LAMOUREUX.

Enterprise: Dir-Gen. FABIO COLASANTI.

Environment: Dir-Gen. JAMES CURRIE.

Fisheries: Dir-Gen. STEFFEN SMIDT.

Health and Consumer Protection: Dir-Gen. ROBERT COLEMAN.

Information Society: Dir-Gen. ROBERT VERRUE.

Internal Market: Dir-Gen. JOHN F. MOGG.

Joint Research Centre: Dir-Gen. FINBARR MCSWEENEY.

Justice and Home Affairs: Dir-Gen. ADRIAN FORTESCUE.
Regional Policy: Dir-Gen. GUY CRAUSER.
Research: Dir-Gen. ACHILLEAS MITSOS.
Taxation and Customs Union: Dir-Gen. MICHEL VANDEN ABEELE.

EXTERNAL RELATIONS

Common Service for External Relations: Dir-Gen. DANIELA TRAMACERE.

Development: Dir-Gen. JACOBUS RICHELLE.

Enlargement: Dir-Gen. ENEKO LANDÁBURU ILLARRAMENDI.

EuropeAid - Co-operation Office: Dir-Gen. GIORGIO BONACCI.

External Relations: Dir-Gen. GUY LEGRAS.

European Community Humanitarian Office (ECHO): Dir COSTANZA ADINOLFI.

Trade: Dir-Gen. MOGENS PETER CARL.

INTERNAL SERVICES

Budget: Dir-Gen. JEAN-PAUL MINGASSON.
European Anti-fraud Office: Dir-Gen. FRANZ-HERMANN BRUENER.
Financial Control: Dir-Gen. EDITH KITZMANTEL.
Joint Interpreting and Conference Service: Head of Service MARCO BENEDETTI.
Legal Service: Dir-Gen. (vacant).
Personnel and Administration: Dir-Gen. HORST REICHENBACH.
Translation Service: Dir-Gen. a.i. BRIAN McCLUSKEY.

THE EUROPEAN COUNCIL

The heads of state or of government of the member countries meet at least twice a year, in the member state which currently exercises the presidency of the Council of the European Union, or in Brussels.

Until 1975 summit meetings were held less frequently, on an *ad hoc* basis, usually to adopt major policy decisions regarding the future development of the Community. In answer to the evident need for more frequent consultation at the highest level, it was decided at the summit meeting in Paris, in December 1974, to hold the meetings on a regular basis, under the rubric of the European Council. There was no provision made for the existence of the European Council in the Treaty of Rome, but its position was acknowledged and regularized in the Single European Act (1987). Its role was further strengthened in the Treaty on European Union, which entered into force on 1 November 1993. As a result of the Treaty, the European Council became directly responsible for common policies within the fields of Common Foreign and Security Policy and Justice and Home Affairs.

COUNCIL OF THE EUROPEAN UNION

General Secretariat: 175 rue de la Loi, 1048 Brussels, Belgium.
Telephone: (2) 285-61-11; **fax:** (2) 285-73-97; **e-mail:** public.relations@consilium.eu.int; **internet:** ue.eu.int.

The Council of the European Union (until 1994 known formally as the Council of Ministers of the European Community and still frequently referred to as the Council of Ministers) is the only institution that directly represents the member states. It is the Community's principal decision-making body, acting on proposals made by the Commission, and is responsible for ensuring the co-ordination of the general economic policies of the member states and for taking the decisions necessary to implement the Treaties. The Council is composed of representatives of the member states, each Government delegating to it one of its members, according to the subject to be discussed. These meetings are generally referred to as the Agriculture Council, Telecommunications Council, etc. The Foreign Affairs, Economics and Finance ('ECOFIN') and Agriculture Councils normally meet once a month. The office of President is exercised for a term of six months by each member of the Council in rotation (January–June 2001: Sweden; July–December: Belgium). Meetings of the Council are convened and chaired by the President, acting on his or her own initiative or at the request of a member or of the Commission.

The Treaty of Rome prescribed three types of voting: simple majority, qualified majority and unanimity. The votes of its members are weighted as follows: France, Germany, Italy and the United Kingdom 10; Spain 8; Belgium, Greece, the Netherlands and Portugal 5; Austria and Sweden 4; Denmark, Finland and Ireland 3; Luxembourg 2. Out of a total number of votes of 87, 62 are required for a qualified majority decision, making 26 votes sufficient for a blocking minority. During negotiations for enlargement of the EU, an agreement was reached, in March 1994, on new rules regulating voting procedures in the expanded Council, in response to concerns on the part of Spain and the United Kingdom that their individual

influence would be diminished. Under the 'Ioannina compromise' (named after the Greek town where the agreement was concluded) 23–25 opposing votes were to be sufficient to continue debate of legislation for a 'reasonable period' until a consensus decision is reached. Amendments to the Treaty of Rome (the Single European Act), effective from July 1987, restricted the right of 'veto', and were expected to accelerate the development of a genuine common market: they allowed proposals relating to the dismantling of barriers to the free movement of goods, persons, services and capital to be approved by a majority vote in the Council, rather than by a unanimous vote. Unanimity would still be required, however, for certain areas, including harmonization of indirect taxes, legislation on health and safety, veterinary controls, and environmental protection; individual states would also retain control over immigration rules, prevention of terrorism and drugs-trafficking. The Treaty of Amsterdam, which came into force on 1 May 1999, extended the use of qualified majority voting to limited policy areas.

The Single European Act introduced a 'co-operation procedure' whereby a proposal adopted by a qualified majority in the Council must be submitted to the European Parliament for approval: if the Parliament rejects the Council's common position, unanimity shall be required for the Council to act on a second reading, and if the Parliament suggests amendments, the Commission must re-examine the proposal and forward it to the Council again. A 'co-decision procedure' was introduced in 1993 by the Treaty on European Union. The procedure allows a proposal to be submitted for a third reading by a so-called 'Conciliation Committee', composed equally of Council representatives and members of the European Parliament. The Treaty of Amsterdam was to simplify the co-decision procedure, and extend it to matters previously resolved under the co-operation procedure, although the latter was to remain in place for matters concerning economic and monetary union.

Under the Treaty of Amsterdam, the Secretary-General of the Council was also to take the role of 'High Representative', responsible for the co-ordination of common foreign and security policy. The Secretary-General was to be supported by a policy planning and early warning unit. In June 1999 Javier Solana Madariaga, at that time Secretary-General of NATO, was designated as the first Secretary-General of the Council.

The Treaty of Nice, initialled in February 2001, addresses institutional issues that remained outstanding under the Treaty of Amsterdam and which had to be settled before the enlargement of the EU from 2003, and various other issues not directly connected with enlargement. The main focus of the Treaty is the establishment of principles governing the new distribution of seats in the European Parliament, the new composition of the Commission and a new definition of qualified majority voting within the European Council. It stipulates that, with effect from the appointment of the next European Commission, in January 2005, the five largest member states (France, Germany, Italy, Spain and the United Kingdom) will lose their present right each to nominate two Commissioners. Instead, all member states will be entitled to nominate one member of the Commission, which may be enlarged to an upper limit of 26 Commissioners. Were the number of EU member states to expand beyond 26, the Council would set a limit on Commission membership, at 26 Commissioners or fewer, to be appointed on a rotational basis. The powers of the President of the Commission were to be enhanced. The new weighting system for existing members' votes within the European Council, effective from 1 January 2005, was designated as follows: France, Germany, Italy and the United Kingdom 29; Spain 27; Netherlands 13; Greece, Belgium and Portugal 12; Sweden and Austria 10; Denmark, Finland and Ireland 7; Luxembourg 4. Of the total number of 237 votes (based on the current 15 member states), a majority of 169 (71.3%) would be required for the adoption of a decision by the Council. The number of weighted votes needed for the adoption of a decision (referred to as the 'qualified majority threshold') was to be reassessed on the accession of each new member state. Qualified majority voting was to be applied to 30 additional policy areas that were presently subject to national vetos. The Treaty also provides for a major reform of the EU's legal system, and for changes to the rules on decision-making within the European Central Bank and the European Investment Bank. Under the terms of the Treaty some alterations are made to the EU's common foreign and security policy, mainly entailing an increased role for the EU in crisis prevention and conflict management activities. In December 2000 EU heads of state or government had reached agreement on the development of a regional military rapid response capability (the so-called Rapid Reaction Force—RRF). During that month EU leaders also signed a European Charter of Fundamental Rights; this was not incorporated into the Treaty of Nice, however, and so was not to be legally binding in member states. The Treaty of Nice requires ratification by member states' legislatures or approval by national popular referendums prior to its entry into force.

PERMANENT REPRESENTATIVES

Preparation and co-ordination of the Council's work is entrusted to a Committee of Permanent Representatives (COREPER), meeting in Brussels, consisting of the ambassadors of the member countries to the Union. A staff of national civil servants assists each ambassador.

ADMINISTRATION

Offices are at the address of the Council of the European Union: 175 rue de la Loi, 1048 Brussels, Belgium; tel. (2) 285-61-11; fax (2) 285-73-97; e-mail public.relations@consilium.eu.int; internet ue .eu.int.

Secretariat-General of the Council: Sec.-Gen. JAVIER SOLANA MADARIAGA.

Secretary-General's Private Office: Dir and Head of Cabinet ALBERTO NAVARRO GONZÁLEZ.

Legal Service: Dir-Gen. (Juriconsult of the Council) JEAN-CLAUDE PIRIS.

Directorates-General:

A (Administration Protocol): Dir-Gen. VITTORIO GIFFO.

B (Agriculture and Fisheries): Dir-Gen. NIELS HENRIK SLIBEN.

C (Internal Market; Customs Union, Industrial Policy, Telecommunications, Information Society, Research Energy, Transport): Dir-Gen. KLAUS GRETSCHMANN.

E* (External Economic Relations and Common Foreign and Security Policy): Dirs-Gen. BRIAN L. CROWE, CORNELIS STEKE-LENBURG.

F (Relations with the European Parliament, the Economic and Social Committee and the Committee of the Regions; Institutional Affairs; Budget and Staff Regulations; Information Policy; Transparency; Public Relations): Dir-Gen. ANGEL BOIXAREU CARRERA.

G (Economic and Financial Affairs; European Monetary Union—EMU): Dir-Gen. SIXTEN KORKMAN.

H (Justice and Home Affairs): Dir-Gen. CHARLES ELSEN.

I (Environmental and Consumer Protection; Civil Protection; Health and Food Legislation; Drug Addiction; AIDS): Dir-Gen. KERSTIN NIBLAEUS.

J (Social Policy; Employment; Regional Policy and Economic and Social Cohesion; Education and Youth; Culture; Audio-visual Media): Dir-Gen. MARC LEPOIVRE.

*Directorate-General D no longer exists.

EUROPEAN PARLIAMENT

Address: Centre Européen, Plateau du Kirchberg, 2929 Luxembourg.

Telephone: 4300-1; **fax:** 4300-7009; **internet:** www.europarl .eu.int.

PRESIDENT AND MEMBERS
(April 2001)

President: NICOLE FONTAINE (France).

Members: 626 members, apportioned as follows: Germany 99 members; France, Italy and the United Kingdom 87 members each; Spain 64; the Netherlands 31; Belgium, Greece and Portugal 25 each; Sweden 22; Austria 21; Denmark and Finland 16 each; Ireland 15; Luxembourg 6. Members are elected for a five-year term by direct universal suffrage by the citizens of the member states. Members sit in the Chamber in political, not national, groups.

The tasks of the European Parliament are: amending legislation, scrutinizing the Union budget and exercising a measure of democratic control over the executive organs of the European Communities, the Commission and the Council. It has the power to dismiss the Commission by a vote of censure (see above). Increases in parliamentary powers have been brought about through amendments to the Treaty of Rome. The Single European Act, which entered into force on 1 July 1987, introduced, in certain circumstances where the Council normally adopts legislation through majority voting, a co-operation procedure involving a second parliamentary reading, enabling Parliament to amend legislation. Community agreements with third countries require parliamentary approval. The Treaty on European Union, which came into force in November 1993, introduced the co-decision procedure, permitting a third parliamentary reading (see Council of the European Union, above). The Treaty also gives Parliament the right to veto legislation, and allows Parliament a vote of approval for a new Commission. Parliament appoints the European Ombudsman, who investigates reports of maladministration in Community institutions. The Treaty

of Amsterdam, which entered into force in May 1999, expanded and simplified Parliament's legislative role.

Political Groupings

	Distribution of seats (April 2001)
Group of the European People's Party . . .	232
Party of European Socialists	181
European Liberal Group	52
Green/European Free Alliance	46
Confederal Group of the European United Left-Nordic Green Left	42
Union for a Europe of the Nations . . .	21
Technical Group of Independent Members . .	19
The Europe of Democracies and Diversities . .	19
Non-attached	14
Total	**626**

Parliament has an annual session, divided into about 12 one-week meetings, normally held in Strasbourg, France. The session opens with the March meeting. Committees and political group meetings and additional sittings of Parliament are held in Brussels.

The budgetary powers of Parliament (which, with the Council, forms the Budgetary Authority of the Communities) were increased to their present status by a treaty of 22 July 1975. Under this treaty, it can amend non-agricultural spending and reject the draft budget, acting by a majority of its members and two-thirds of the votes cast.

The Parliament is run by a Bureau comprising the President, 14 Vice-Presidents elected from its members by secret ballot to serve for two-and-a-half years, and the four members of the College of Quaestors. Elections to the Bureau took place most recently in June 1999. Parliament has 20 specialized committees, which deliberate on proposals for legislation put forward by the Commission before Parliament's final opinion is delivered by a resolution in plenary session.

There are Standing Committees on Foreign Affairs, Security, and Defence Policies; Agriculture and Rural Development; Budgets; Budgetary Control; Economic and Monetary Affairs and Industrial Policy; Research, Technological Development and Energy; External Economic Relations; Legal Affairs and Citizens' Rights; Social Affairs and Employment; Regional Policy; Transport and Tourism; Environment, Public Health and Consumer Protection; Culture, Youth, Education and the Media; Development and Co-operation; Fisheries; Rules of Procedure, the Verification of Credentials and Immunities; Institutional Affairs; Petitions; Women's Rights; Civil Liberties and Internal Affairs.

The first direct elections to the European Parliament took place in June 1979, and Parliament met for the first time in July. The second elections were held in June 1984 (with separate elections held in Portugal and Spain in 1987, following the accession of these two countries to the Community), the third in June 1989, the fourth in June 1994. Direct elections to the European Parliament were held in Sweden in September 1995, and in Austria and Finland in October 1996. The fifth European Parliament was elected in June 1999.

COURT OF JUSTICE OF THE EUROPEAN COMMUNITIES

Address: Palais de la Cour de Justice, 2925 Luxembourg.

Telephone: 4303-1; **fax:** 4303-2600; **internet:** www.curia.eu.int.

The task of the Court of Justice is to ensure the observance of law in the interpretation and application of the Treaties setting up the three Communities. The 15 Judges and the nine Advocates General are appointed for renewable six-year terms by the Governments of the member states. The President of the Court is elected by the Judges from among their number for a renewable term of three years. The majority of cases are dealt with by one of the six chambers, each of which consists of a President of Chamber and two or four Judges. The Court may sit in plenary session in cases of particular importance or when a member state or Community institution that is a party to the proceedings so requests. The Court has jurisdiction to award damages. It may review the legality of acts (other than recommendations or opinions) of the Council, the Commission or the European Central Bank, of acts adopted jointly by the European Parliament and the Council and of Acts adopted by Parliament and intended to produce legal effects *vis-à-vis* third parties. It is also competent to give judgment on actions by a member state, the Council or the Commission on grounds of lack of competence, of infringement of an essential procedural requirement, of infringement of a Treaty or of any legal rule relating to its application, or of misuse of power. The Court of Justice may hear appeals, on a point of law only, from the Court of First Instance.

The Court is also empowered to hear certain other cases concerning the contractual and non-contractual liability of the Communities and disputes between member states in connection with the objects of the Treaties. It also gives preliminary rulings at the request of national courts on the interpretation of the Treaties, of Union legislation, and of the Brussels Convention on Jurisdiction and the Enforcement of Judgments in Civil and Commercial Matters. During 1999 541 new cases were brought before the Court, of which 255 were cases referred to it for preliminary rulings by the national courts of the member states and 72 were appeals from the Court of First Instance. In the same period 235 judgments were delivered and 395 cases completed.

Composition of the Court (in order of precedence, as at April 2001):

GIL CARLOS RODRÍGUEZ IGLESIAS (Spain), President of the Court of Justice.

CLAUS CHRISTIAN GULMANN (Denmark), President of the Third and Sixth Chambers.

ANTONIO MARIO LA PERGOLA (Italy), President of the Fourth and Fifth Chambers.

DÁMASO RUIZ-JARABO COLOMER (Spain), First Advocate General.

MELCHIOR WATHELET (Belgium), President of the First Chamber.

VASSILIOS SKOURIS (Greece), President of the Second Chamber.

FRANCIS JACOBS (United Kingdom), Advocate General.

DAVID ALEXANDER OGILVY EDWARD (United Kingdom), Judge.

JEAN-PIERRE PUISSOCHET (France), Judge.

PHILIPPE LÉGER (France), Advocate General.

PETER JANN (Austria), Judge.

LEIF SEVÓN (Finland), Judge.

ROMAIN SCHINTGEN (Luxembourg), Judge.

SIEGBERT ALBER (Germany), Advocate General.

JEAN MISCHO (Luxembourg), Advocate General.

FIDELMA O'KELLY MACKEN (Ireland), Judge.

NINON COLNERIC (Germany), Judge.

STIG VON BAHR (Sweden), Judge.

ANTONIO TIZZANO (Italy), Advocate General.

JOSÉ NARCISO DA CUNHA RODRIGUES (Portugal), Judge.

CHRISTIAAN WILLEM ANTON TIMMERMANS (Netherlands), Judge.

LEENDERT A. GEELHOED (Netherlands), Advocate General.

CHRISTINE STIX-HACKL (Austria), Advocate General.

ROGER GRASS (France), Registrar.

COURT OF FIRST INSTANCE OF THE EUROPEAN COMMUNITIES

Address: blvd Konrad Adenauer, 2925 Luxembourg.

Telephone: 4303-1; **fax:** 4303-2100; **internet:** www.curia.eu.int.

By a decision of 24 October 1988, as amended by decisions of 8 June 1993 and 7 March 1994, the European Council, exercising powers conferred upon it by the Single European Act, established a Court of First Instance with jurisdiction to hear and determine cases brought by natural or legal persons and which had hitherto been dealt with by the Court of Justice.

Composition of the Court of First Instance (in order of precedence, as at April 2001):

BO VESTERDORF (Denmark), President of the Court of First Instance.

PERNILLA LINDH (Sweden), President of Chamber.

JOSEF AZIZI (Austria), President of Chamber.

PAOLO MENGOZZI (Italy), President of Chamber.

ARJEN W. H. MEIJ (Netherlands), President of Chamber.

RAFAEL GARCÍA-VALDECASAS Y FERNÁNDEZ (Spain), Judge.

KOENRAAD LENAERTS (Belgium), Judge.

VIRPI E. TIILI (Finland), Judge.

ANDRÉ POTOCKI (France), Judge.

RUI MANUEL GENS DE MOURA RAMOS (Portugal), Judge.

JOHN D. COOKE (Ireland), Judge.

MARC JAEGER (Luxembourg), Judge.

JÖRG PIRRUNG (Germany), Judge.

MIHALIS VILARAS (Greece), Judge.

NICHOLAS JAMES FORWOOD (United Kingdom), Judge.

HANS JUNG (Germany), Registrar.

COURT OF AUDITORS OF THE EUROPEAN COMMUNITIES

Address: 12 rue Alcide De Gasperi, 1615 Luxembourg.

Telephone: 4398-45410; **fax:** 4398-46430; **e-mail:** euraud@eca.eu.int; **internet:** www.eca.eu.int.

The Court of Auditors was created by the Treaty of Brussels, which was signed on 22 July 1975, and commenced its duties in late 1977. It was given the status of an institution on a par with the Commission, the Council, the Court of Justice and the Parliament by the Treaty on European Union. It is the institution responsible for the external audit of the resources managed by the three Communities and the European Union. It consists of 15 members who are appointed for six-year terms by unanimous decision of the Council of the European Union, after consultation with the European Parliament. The members elect the President from among their number for a term of three years.

The Court is organized and acts as a collegiate body. It adopts its decisions by a majority of its members. Each member, however, has a direct responsibility for the audit of certain sectors of Union activities.

The Court examines the accounts of all expenditure and revenue of the European Communities and of any body created by them in so far as the relevant constituent instrument does not preclude such examination. It examines whether all revenue has been received and all expenditure incurred in a lawful and regular manner and whether the financial management has been sound. The audit is based on records, and if necessary is performed directly in the institutions of the Communities, in the member states and in other countries. In the member states the audit is carried out in co-operation with the national audit bodies. The Court of Auditors draws up an annual report after the close of each financial year. The Court provides the Parliament and the Council with a statement of assurance as to the reliability of the accounts, and the legality and regularity of the underlying transactions. It may also, at any time, submit observations on specific questions (usually in the form of special reports) and deliver opinions at the request of one of the institutions of the Communities. It assists the European Parliament and the Council in exercising their powers of control over the implementation of the budget, in particular in the framework of the annual discharge procedure, and gives its prior opinion on the financial regulations, on the methods and procedure whereby the budgetary revenue is made available to the Commission, and on the formulation of rules concerning the responsibility of authorizing officers and accounting officers and concerning appropriate arrangements for inspection.

President: JAN O. KARLSSON (Sweden).

Audit Group I: BERNHARD FRIEDMAN; KALLIOPI NIKOLAOU; MÁIRE GEOGHEGAN-QUINN.

Audit Group II: GIORGIO CLEMENTE, JØRGEN MOHR, FRANÇOIS COLLING, JEAN-FRANÇOIS BERNICOT.

Audit Group III: HUBERT WEBER, MAARTEN ENGWIRDA, JUAN MANUEL FABRA VALLÉS.

Audit Group IV: JOHN WIGGINS, ROBERT REYNDERS, VITOR MANUEL DA SILVA CADEIRA.

Audit Development and Reports (ADAR) Group: JAN O. KARLSSON.

Statement of Assurance (SoA) Group: AUNUS SALMI.

Secretary-General: EDOUARD RUPPERT.

EUROPEAN CENTRAL BANK

Address: 60066 Frankfurt am Main, Kaiserstr. 29, Postfach 160319, Germany.

Telephone: (69) 13440; **fax:** (69) 13446000; **internet:** www.ecb.int.

The European Central Bank (ECB) was formally established on 1 June 1998, replacing the European Monetary Institute, which had been operational since January 1994. The Bank has the authority to issue the single currency, the euro, which replaced the European Currency Unit (ECU) on 1 January 1999, at the beginning of Stage III of Economic and Monetary Union (EMU), in accordance with the provisions of the Treaty on European Union ('the Maastricht Treaty'). The Bank's leadership is provided by a six-member executive board, appointed for a non-renewable term of eight years (it should be noted that the Statute of the European System of Central Banks —ESCB— provides for a system of staggered appointments to the first executive board for members other than the President in order to ensure continuity), which is responsible for the preparation of meetings of the governing council, the implementation of monetary policy in accordance with the guide-lines and decisions laid down by the governing council and for the current business of the ECB. The ECB and the national central banks of EU member states together comprise the ESCB. The governing council of the ESCB, which consists of ECB executive board members and the governors of central banks of countries participating in EMU, meets twice a month. The general council comprises the President, the Vice-President and the governors of the central banks of all EU member states.

President: WILLEM (WIM) F. DUISENBERG (Netherlands).

Vice-President: CHRISTIAN NOYER (France).

Executive Board: SIRKKA HÄMÄLÄINEN (Finland), OTMAR ISSING (Germany), TOMMASO PADOA-SCHIOPPA (Italy), EUGENIO SOMINGO SOLANS (Spain).

EUROPEAN INVESTMENT BANK

Address: 100 blvd Konrad Adenauer, 2950 Luxembourg.

Telephone: 4379-1; **fax:** 4377-04; **e-mail:** info@eib.org; **internet:** www.eib.org.

The European Investment Bank (EIB) was created in 1958 by the six founder member states of the European Economic Community. At December 1998 the capital subscribed by the 15 member states totalled ECU 62,013m., of which 7.5% was paid-in or to be paid-in. In June 1998 the Board of Governors agreed to increase subscribed capital to €100,000m., from January 1999. Capital structure at 31 December 2000 was as follows: France, Germany, Italy and the United Kingdom 17.8% each; Spain 6.5%; Belgium and the Netherlands 4.9% each; Sweden 3.3%; Denmark 2.5%; Austria 2.4%; Finland 1.4%; Greece 1.3%; Portugal 0.9%; Ireland 0.6%; Luxembourg 0.1%. The bulk of the EIB's resources comes from borrowings, principally public bond issues or private placements on capital markets inside and outside the Union. In 2000 the Bank borrowed €29,002m., compared with €28,334m. in 1999. Some 72% of resources raised in 2000 was in EU currencies.

The EIB's principal task, defined by the Treaty of Rome, is to work on a non-profit basis, making or guaranteeing loans for investment projects which contribute to the balanced and steady development of EU member states. Throughout the Bank's history, priority has been given to financing investment projects which further regional development within the Community. The EIB also finances projects that improve communications, protect and improve the environment, promote urban development, strengthen the competitive position of industry and encourage industrial integration within the Union, support the activities of small and medium-sized enterprises (SMEs), and help ensure the security of energy supplies. The EIB also provides finance for developing countries in Africa, the Caribbean and the Pacific, under the terms of the Lomé Convention (q.v.); for countries in the Mediterranean region, under co-operation agreements; and for countries in central and eastern Europe.

The European Investment Fund (EIF) was founded in 1994 by the EIB (which was to provide 40% of the Fund's ECU 2,000m. authorized capital), the European Communities (EC—represented by the Commission; 30%) and a group of 77 banks and financial institutions from throughout the EU (30%). The EIF's purpose is to assist SMEs and provide guarantees for the long-term financing of European infrastructure projects, particularly for Trans-European Networks (TENs) in the fields of transport, energy transmission and telecommunications. By the end of 1999 cumulative guarantee operations signed by the EIF totalled €2,784.4m. A European Technology Faculty (ETF) was established in November 1997 to support investment in SMEs. The EIF was to invest up to ECU 125m. in the ETF over a three-year period. In June 1999 the EIB established a Balkans Task Force to evaluate investment requirements and identify priority infrastructure projects in south-eastern Europe.

In 2000 total financing contracts signed by the EIB, both inside and outside the European Union, amounted to €36,033m., compared with €31,800m. in 1999. Loans agreed for projects within member states in 2000 totalled €30,644m. In 1999 transport accounted for 32.1%, energy 7.9%, industry and services 7.8% and telecommunications 7.7%. Operations outside the Union totalled €5,389m., compared with €4,035m. in 1999.

The Board of Governors of the EIB, which usually meets only once a year, lays down general directives on credit policy, approves the annual report and accounts and decides on capital increases. The Board of Directors has sole power to take decisions in respect of loans, guarantees and borrowings. Its members are appointed by the Governors for a renewable five-year term following nomination by the member states. The Bank's President presides over meetings of the Board of Directors. The day-to-day management of operations is the responsibility of the Management Committee, which is the EIB's collegiate executive body and recommends decisions to the Board of Directors. It comprises the President and seven Vice-Presidents, nominated for six-year terms by the Board of Directors and approved by the Board of Governors. The Audit Committee, which reports to the Board of Governors regarding the management of operations and the maintenance of the Bank's accounts, is an independent body comprising three members who are appointed by the Board of Governors for a renewable three-year term.

Board of Governors: One minister (usually the minister of finance) from each member state.

Board of Directors: Twenty-five directors and 13 alternates (senior officials from finance or economic ministries, public-sector banks or credit institutions), appointed for a renewable five-year term, of whom 24 and 12 respectively are nominated by the member states; one director and one alternate are nominated by the Commission of the European Communities.

FINANCE CONTRACTS SIGNED

	1999		2000	
Recipient	Amount (ECU million)	%	Amount (€ million)	%
Austria . . .	606	2.2	735	2.4
Belgium . . .	226	0.8	503	1.6
Denmark . . .	898	3.2	991	3.2
Finland . . .	576	2.1	525	1.7
France. . .	4,295	15.5	3,323	10.8
Germany . . .	5,534	19.9	6,038	19.7
Greece . . .	1,436	5.2	1,712	5.6
Ireland . . .	87	0.3	419	1.4
Italy . . .	4,053	14.6	5,640	18.4
Luxembourg . . .	105	0.4	200	0.7
Netherlands . . .	311	1.1	260	0.8
Portugal . . .	1,603	5.8	1,852	6.0
Spain . . .	4,048	14.6	4,199	13.7
Sweden . . .	544	2.0	621	2.0
United Kingdom . .	3,348	12.1	3,303	10.8
Other* . . .	97	0.3	321	1.0
EU total . . .	**27,765**	**100.0**	**30,644**	**100.0**
ACP-Overseas countries and territories . .	341	8.5	401	7.4
South Africa . .	150	3.7	140	2.6
Mediterranean . .	802	19.9	1,214	22.5
Balkans . .	60	1.5	154	2.9
Latin America and Asia . .	310	7.7	532	9.9
Candidate countries . .	2,373	58.8	2,948	54.7
Non-EU total . .	**4,035**	**100.0**	**5,839**	**100.0**
Total	**31,800**	**—**	**36,033**	**—**

* Projects of direct benefit to the Union but located outside the member states.

Management Committee:

President: PHILIPPE MAYSTADT.

Vice-Presidents: WOLFGANG ROTH, MASSIMO PONZELLINI, EWALD NOWOTNY, FRANCIS MAYER, PETER SEDGWICK, ISABEL MARTÍN CASTELLÁ, MICHAEL G. TUTTY.

CONSULTATIVE BODIES
ECONOMIC AND SOCIAL COMMITTEE

Address: 2 rue Ravenstein, 1000 Brussels.

Telephone: (2) 546-90-11; **fax:** (2) 513-48-93; **internet:** www.esc .eu.int.

The Committee is advisory and is consulted by the Council of the European Union or by the European Commission, particularly with regard to agriculture, free movement of workers, harmonization of laws and transport, as well as legislation adopted under the Euratom Treaty. In certain cases consultation of the Committee by the Commission or the Council is mandatory. In addition, the Committee has the power to deliver opinions on its own initiative.

The Committee has 222 members: 24 each from France, Germany, Italy and the United Kingdom, 21 from Spain, 12 each from Austria, Belgium, Greece, the Netherlands, Portugal and Sweden, nine from Denmark, Finland and Ireland, and six from Luxembourg. One-third represent employers, one-third employees, and one-third various interest groups (e.g. agriculture, small enterprises, consumers). The Committee is appointed for a renewable term of four years by the unanimous vote of the Council of the European Union. Members are nominated by their governments, but are appointed in their personal capacity and are not bound by any mandatory instructions. The Committee is served by a permanent and independent General Secretariat, headed by the Secretary-General.

President: BEATRICE RANGONI MACHIAVELLI (Italy).

Vice-Presidents: AINA MARGARETA REGNELL (Sweden), JOSLY PIETTE (Belgium).

Secretary-General: PATRICK VENTURINI.

COMMITTEE OF THE REGIONS

Address: 79 rue Belliard, 1040 Brussels.

Telephone: (2) 282-22-11; **fax:** (2) 282-20-85; **internet:** www.cor .eu.int.

The Treaty on European Union provided for a committee to be established, with advisory status, comprising representatives of regional and local bodies throughout the EU. The first meeting of the Committee was held in March 1994. It may be consulted on EU proposals concerning economic and social cohesion, trans-European networks, public health, education and culture, and may issue an opinion on any issue with regional implications. The Committee meets in plenary session five times a year.

The number of members of the Committee is equal to that of the Economic and Social Committee (see above). Members are appointed for a renewable term of four years by the Council, acting unanimously on the proposals from the respective member states. The Committee elects its principal officers from among its members for a two-year term, most recently to serve 16 February 2000–25 January 2002.

President: JOZEF (JOS) CHABERT (Belgium).

First Vice-President: Prof. Dr MANFRED DAMMEYER (Germany).

ECSC CONSULTATIVE COMMITTEE

Address: Bâtiment Jean Monnet, 2920 Luxembourg.

Telephone: 4301-32846; **fax:** 4301-34455.

The Committee is advisory and is attached to the Commission. It advises the Commission on matters relating to the coal and steel industries of the Union. Its members are appointed by the Council of the European Union for two years and are not bound by any mandate from the organizations that designated them in the first place.

There are 108 members representing, in equal proportions, producers, workers and consumers and dealers in the coal and steel industries.

President: GIOVANNI PEREGO (Italy).

Vice President: RUPRECHT VONDRAN (Germany).

OTHER ADVISORY COMMITTEES

There are advisory committees dealing with all aspects of EU policy. Consultation with some committees is compulsory in the procedure for drafting EC legislation.

In addition to the consultative bodies listed above there are several hundred special interest groups representing every type of interest within the Union. All these hold unofficial talks with the Commission.

OTHER INSTITUTIONS

European Environment Agency (EEA): 6 Kongens Nytorv, 1050 Copenhagen K, Denmark; tel. 33-36-71-00; fax 33-36-71-99; e-mail eea@eea.eu.int; internet www.eea.eu.int.

Became operational in 1994, having been approved in 1990, to gather and supply information to assist the implementation of Community policy on environmental protection and improvement. In 1999 the Agency's budget amounted to €18.2m. The Agency publishes a report on the state of the environment every three years.

Chairman of the Management Board: KEES ZOETMAN (Netherlands).

Chairman of the Scientific Committee: Prof. PHILIPPE BOURDEAU (Belgium).

Executive Director: DOMINGO JIMÉNEZ-BELTRÁN (Spain).

European Monitoring Centre for Drugs and Drug Addiction (EMCDDA): Palacete Mascarenhas, Rua da Cruz de Sta. Apolónia 23–25, 1149 Lisbon, Portugal; tel. (1) 21811-30-00; fax (1) 21811-17-11; e-mail info@emcdda.org; internet www.emcdda.org.

Became fully operational at the end of 1995, with the aim of providing member states with objective, reliable and comparable information on drugs and drug addiction in order to assist in combatting the problem. The Centre co-operates with other European and international organizations and non-Community countries. The Centre publishes an *Annual Report on the State of the Drugs Problem in Europe*. A newsletter, *Drugnet Europe*, is published every two months.

Chairman of the Management Board: FRANZ-JOSEF BINDERT (Germany).

Executive Director: GEORGES ESTIEVENART (France).

European Agency for the Evaluation of Medicinal Products (EMEA): 7 Westferry Circus, Canary Wharf, London, E14 4HB, United Kingdom; tel. (20) 7418-8400; fax (20) 7418-8416; e-mail mail@emea.eudra.org; internet www.emea.eu.int.

Established in 1993 for the authorization and supervision of medicinal products for human and veterinary use. In 2000 the Agency's proposed budget was €50.36m.

Chairman of the Management Board: STRACHAN HEPPELL (United Kingdom).

Chairman of the Scientific Committee for Proprietary Medicinal Products (CPMP): Prof. JEAN-MICHEL ALEXANDRE.

Chairman of the Scientific Committee for Veterinary Medicinal Products (CVMP): Dr REINHARD KROKER (Germany).

Executive Director: FERNAND SAUER (France).

European Training Foundation (ETF): Villa Gualino, Viale Settimio Severo 65, 10133 Turin, Italy; tel. (011) 630-22-22; fax (011) 630-22-00; e-mail info@etf.eu.int; internet www.etf.int.

Established in 1995 with the aim of contributing to the development of the vocational training systems of designated central and eastern European countries. In 1998 the Foundation's responsibilities were extended to include certain non-member Mediterranean countries.

Director: PETER G. M. DE ROOIJ.

European Foundation for the Improvement of Living and Working Conditions: Wyattville Rd, Loughlinstown, Shankill, Co Dublin, Ireland; tel. (1) 204-3100; fax (1) 282-6456; e-mail.postmaster@eurofound.ie; internet www.eurofound.eu.int.

Established in 1975 to develop strategies for the medium- and long-term improvement of living and working conditions. The Foundation publishes a regular newsletter.

Chairman of the Administrative Board: J. W. VAN DEN BRAAK.

Director: RAYMOND-PIERRE BODIN.

Office for Harmonization in the Internal Market (Trade Marks and Designs) (OHIM): Avda de Europa 4, 03080 Alicante, Spain; tel. (96) 513-91-00; fax (96) 513-91-73; e-mail information@oami.eu.int; internet www.oami.eu.int.

Established in 1993 to promote and control trade marks and designs throughout the European Union.

Chairman of the Administrative Board: JOSÉ MOTA MAIA (Portugal).

Chairman of the Budget Committee: Dr RENZO ANTONINI (Italy).

President: JEAN-CLAUDE COMBALDIEU.

Activities of the Community

AGRICULTURE

Co-operation in the Community is at its most highly-organized in the area of agriculture. The objectives of the Common Agricultural Policy (CAP) are described in the Treaty of Rome. The markets for agricultural products have been progressively organized following three basic principles: (i) unity of the market (products must be able to circulate freely within the Community and markets must be organized according to common rules); (ii) Community preference (products must be protected from low-cost imports and from fluctuations on the world market); (iii) common financial responsibility: the European Agricultural Guidance and Guarantee Fund (EAGGF) finances, through its Guarantee Section, all public expenditure intervention, storage costs, marketing subsidies and export rebates.

Agricultural prices are, in theory, fixed each year at a common level for the Community as a whole, taking into account the rate of inflation and the need to discourage surplus production of certain commodities. Export subsidies are paid to enable farmers to sell produce at the lower world market prices without loss. These subsidies account for some 50% of agricultural spending. When market prices of certain cereals, sugar, some fruits and vegetables, dairy produce and meat fall below a designated level the Community intervenes, and buys a certain quantity which is then stored until prices recover. During the 1980s expanding production led to food surpluses, costly to maintain, particularly in dairy produce, beef, cereals and wine, and to the destruction of large quantities of fruit and vegetables.

Agriculture is by far the largest item on the Community budget, accounting for about two-thirds of annual expenditure, mainly for supporting prices through the EAGGF Guarantee Section (appropriations for which amounted to €40,994m., or 44% of total commitment appropriations, in 2000). A system of 'stabilizers' was introduced in February 1988, imposing an upper limit on the production of certain products. Any over-production would result in a decrease in the guaranteed intervention price for the following year. Similar 'stabilizers' were later imposed on production of oilseeds, protein feed crops, wine, sugar, fruit and vegetables, tobacco, olive oil, cotton and mutton.

In 1990 the CAP came under attack in the 'Uruguay Round' of negotiations on the General Agreement on Tariffs and Trade (GATT, see WTO). The US Government demanded massive reductions in the EC's agricultural and export subsidies, on the grounds that they disrupted world markets. In November Community ministers of agriculture agreed to accept proposals by the Commission for a reduction of 30% in agricultural subsidies over a 10-year period. In 1990 increasing surpluses of cereals, beef and dairy products were again reported, and a decline in international wheat prices increased the cost to the Community of exporting surplus wheat. In May 1992, on the basis of proposals made by the Commission in 1991, ministers adopted a number of reforms, which aimed to transfer the Community's agricultural support from upholding prices to maintaining farmers' incomes, thereby removing the incentive to over-produce. Intervention prices were reduced by 29% for cereals, 15% for beef and poultry, and 5% for dairy products. Farmers were to be compensated for the price reductions by receiving additional grants, which, in the case of crops, took the form of a subsidy per hectare of land planted. To qualify for these subsidies, arable farmers (except for those with the smallest farms) were to be obliged to remove 15% of their land from cultivation (the 'set-aside' scheme). Incentives were to be given for alternative uses of the withdrawn land (e.g. forestry). The reform meant that prices payable for cereals would be reduced to the level of those prevailing in the international market.

In May 1992 the US Government threatened to impose a large increase in import tariffs on European products, in retaliation against subsidies paid by the EC to oilseed producers, which, the US Government claimed, led to unfair competition for US exports of soya beans. In November, however, agreement was reached between the USA and the European Commission: the USA agreed that limits should be imposed on the area of EC land on which cultivation of oilseed was permitted. The USA also agreed to accept a reduction of 21% in the volume and 36% in the value of the EC's subsidized exports of farm produce, over a six-year period (the amounts being based on average production during 1986–90). These agreements formed the basis of the GATT agricultural accord which was concluded as part of the Uruguay Round trade agreement in mid-December 1993.

The Commission estimated that between September 1992 and the end of July 1993, as a result of the turmoil in the exchange rate mechanism (see below), an extra ECU 1,500m. was spent in price support payments to farmers. In February 1995 ministers adopted a new agrimonetary regime, which limited the amount of compensation paid to farmers as a result of currency fluctuations. Further amendments, introduced in June, abandoned the existing common exchange rate, used to calculate compensation payments, and introduced two rates: one for currencies linked to the Deutsche Mark and one for all other EU currencies. Attempts by some member states to reform the system further were unsuccessful, and in October ministers agreed that national governments would be permitted to compensate farmers who had suffered loss of income as a result of currency fluctuations. In June 1997 it was reported that cereal farmers had been over-compensated by some ECU 8,500m. over the previous four years as a result of inaccurate price-reduction forecasts. In June 1995 the guaranteed intervention price for beef was decreased by 5%, and that for cereals by 7.5%. In September ministers agreed to reduce the level of compulsory 'set-aside' for 1996/97 to 10%, in response to much lower food surpluses in the EU and high world prices for cereal crops. In July 1996 agriculture ministers agreed on a further reduction in the 'set-aside' rate for cereals to 5%. Fruit and vegetable production subsidies were fixed at no more than 4% of the value of total marketed production, rising to 4.5% in 1999. The aim was to improve competitiveness in the European market and avoid the widespread destruction of surplus fruit and vegetables that had taken place in recent years. The Commission is allowed to recover from member states sums that they have paid out under the CAP without sufficient guarantees of legitimacy or without adequate regard to control and verification. In May 1998 the Commission announced that it was to recover ECU 308m. paid to member states in 1994 and in February 1999 the Commission decided to recover a further €493m., mainly relating to spending in 1995.

In July 1994 Community ministers adopted measures to prevent the spread of the disease bovine spongiform encephalopathy (BSE) by imposing strict controls on carcass beef trade, extending the time-scale for the prohibition of exports from diseased herds from two years to six years. The agreement temporarily resolved a dispute whereby Germany had attempted to impose a unilateral ban on beef exports from the United Kingdom, provoking that country to seek a judicial ruling on the action by the European Court of Justice. Despite a relaxation in the rules to allow the export of UK beef from any animal under 30 months old, three German Länder imposed a ban on UK beef imports. New fears about possible links between BSE and Creutzfeldt-Jakob disease (CJD), which affects humans, led to a collapse in consumer confidence in the European beef market in early 1996. In March the Commission accepted that member countries could unilaterally stop imports of UK beef on health grounds, pending a decision by a committee of scientific and veterinary experts from all member states. By late March 12 EU countries had banned UK beef imports, and at the end of the month the Commission agreed a ban on exports from the United Kingdom of live cattle, beef and beef products. In late May the UK Government proposed a programme of selective slaughter as a means of eradicating BSE from the national herd. At the European Council meeting held in June, the United Kingdom agreed to the slaughter of 120,000 animals born since 1989, and to implement new national legislation to ensure that meat and bonemeal were excluded from the manufacture of animal feeds. In return, the ban on UK beef exports would be gradually removed. By July European beef con-

sumption had fallen by an average of 11%, with the largest decrease, 30%, recorded in Germany. At the end of 1996 the Commission was estimated to have spent some ECU 1,500m., including ECU 850m. as compensation paid to beef farmers, on dealing with the consequences of the BSE crisis. Meanwhile, the UK Government abandoned the planned cull, proposing instead a much smaller slaughter scheme. This provoked widespread anger in other EU member states, and in July the European Court of Justice rejected the UK Government's application for the beef export ban to be suspended.

In August 1996 evidence emerged that BSE could be transmitted from cows to their calves. In December the UK Government yielded to the European Commission's demand for an additional cull of more than 100,000 cattle. The Commission also stated that the United Kingdom was to submit plans for a certified BSE-free herd scheme, to provide computerized evidence that cattle herds had had no contact with other animals infected with BSE, before a phased removal of the embargo could begin. In June 1997 the United Kingdom's plans for monitoring and preventing BSE were judged by the Commission to be inadequate. However, in September the Scientific Veterinary Committee confirmed that a successful automated certified herd scheme had been used in Northern Ireland for nine years. In July 1997 the United Kingdom was reported to the Commission to have engaged in the illegal export of beef, while in late June the Commission commenced infringement proceedings against 10 EU countries accused of evading the full implementation of hygiene procedures for the eradication of BSE. In July agriculture ministers voted, by a narrow margin, to introduce a complete ban on the use, for any purpose, of 'specified risk materials' (SRMs), i.e. those most likely to carry BSE, from cattle, sheep and goats. In August the USA requested that US tallow manufacturers be temporarily exempted from the ban, claiming that the USA was free from BSE and that compliance with the new regulations could cause shortages within the pharmaceutical and cosmetics industries. In December the USA announced the extension of an existing ban on EU beef and lamb, in a move that was considered by some to be retaliatory. The Commission voted to postpone the introduction of the ban on SRMs from January 1998 until April (later delayed until January 1999), as a result of opposition from a number of EU member states, particularly Germany, in addition to that from the USA. In December 1997, in protest at the delay, the United Kingdom imposed a unilateral ban on imports of all beef products breaching UK meat safety regulations. In May 1998 the Commission agreed to ease the export ban on British beef, to allow the export of deboned beef from Northern-Irish herds certified as BSE-free for eight years, from June. Production and dispatch of the meat was to be carried out by approved plants. In November the Agriculture Council agreed to repeal the ban on exports of UK beef, when it endorsed the United Kingdom's Date-based Export Scheme. The Commission subsequently approved the Scheme, which permitted the export of deboned beef produced from animals born after August 1996 and tracked by an official monitoring system. In October 1998, however, Portugal was banned from exporting beef and live cattle, following a two-fold increase in reported cases of BSE, to some 69 between May and November of that year (compared with about 1,800 confirmed cases in the United Kingdom from January). The ban on beef exports was to expire after nine months, unless concerns about meat safety remained, while the ban on cattle exports was to be reviewed after 18 months. (In July 1999 the EU Veterinary Committee agreed to prolong for a further six months from 1 August the embargo on exports of Portuguese beef.)

In July 1999 the United Kingdom was deemed to have met all of the conditions pertaining to the lifting of the ban on its beef exports, and the European Commission announced that exports would be permitted to resume from 1 August. However, the French Government remained unconvinced that UK beef no longer presented any threat to consumers, citing, in support of this view, the recommendation of the French statutory Food Safety Agency on 1 October that it would be premature to resume imports of UK beef. In mid-October the UK Prime Minister warned that the United Kingdom would take legal action if France did not lift its unilateral embargo, and on 22 October the UK Minister of Agriculture, Food and Fisheries encouraged British consumers to boycott French food products in protest at France's continued failure to comply with the Commission's decision. On 29 October an EU scientific committee announced that it saw no reason, in the light of the recommendation of the French Food Safety Agency, to revise its earlier endorsement of the safety of UK beef. France did, however, continue to receive some support from Germany. On 30 October seven of the 16 German Länder announced their opposition to any hasty lifting of the ban on UK beef. By the end of 1999 France's unilateral ban remained in place (the German Government claimed that only bureaucratic reasons were preventing the resumption of UK beef exports to Germany) and, in the face of a threat of legal action by the Commission, it was reported that the French Government planned to initiate legal proceedings against the Commission for its alleged failure adequately to protect consumer health. On 4 January 2000 the

Commission commenced legal action against the French Government at the European Court of Justice.

The number of confirmed cases of BSE in France and Ireland increased significantly during 2000, while reported cases in Portugal also remained at a high level in 1999 and 2000. In November 2000 the first case of the disease in a German-bred animal was announced, prompting the resignation of two government ministers in that country. By January 2001 incidences of BSE infection had been reported in 11 of the 15 member countries. The BSE epidemic in the United Kingdom had eased progressively since its peak in 1993, although in early 2001 approximately 30 suspected cases were still being reported every week. In December 2000, as an emergency measure to boost dwindling confidence in European beef, agriculture ministers determined to ban from the regional food chain (with effect from 1 January 2001) all cattle aged more than 30 months, unless these had been tested and proven not to be infected with the disease. An EU-wide six-month ban on the use of meat and bonemeal in animal feed was also adopted, effective from 1 January 2001.

From February 2001 the European Union imposed a temporary ban on imports of livestock products from the United Kingdom, following an outbreak of foot-and-mouth disease on farms in that country.

In April 1999 a dispute arose between the EU and the USA after the EU announced plans to ban all imports of US beef. The EU took this decision after traces of growth hormones were found in imported meat that was supposed to be hormone-free. In May the EU informed the World Trade Organization (WTO) that it would not be able to lift the ban it applied to imports of US hormone-treated beef by 13 May 1999, as the WTO had ordered that it should. The USA was reported to be planning to apply sanctions to some European exports as a retaliatory measure. The USA has also accused the EU of excessive caution with regard to the restrictions that it imposes on genetically-modified (GM) crops and food products derived from or containing them. In October the EU ruled that food products which were labelled as 'GM-free' could contain as much as 1% of GM material. In June the USA impounded all imports of European pork and poultry. The USA took this action because of the possibility that these imports might have been contaminated by a carcinogen, dioxin, extremely high levels of which had been discovered in some Belgian supplies of animal feedstuffs. The European Commission had already prohibited the sale of some Belgian food products.

In June 1995 the Agriculture Council agreed to new rules on the welfare of livestock during transport. The agreement, which came into effect in 1996, limited transport of livestock to a maximum of eight hours in any 24-hour period, and stipulated higher standards for their accommodation and care while in transit. In January 1996 the Commission proposed a ban on veal crates, which was to come into effect from January 1998. In June 1999 EU agriculture ministers agreed to end battery egg production within the EU by 2012.

During 1995–97 there was widespread speculation that the CAP would have to undergo dramatic reform to prevent possible economic problems, in particular following the proposed expansion of the EU into the less agriculturally-developed countries of central and eastern Europe. In March 1998 the Commission outlined firm proposals for reform of the CAP as part of its 'Agenda 2000', concerning the enlargement of the EU and the Community's budget for 2000–2006, published in July 1997. The plans envisaged imposing limits on subsidies and reductions of up to 30% in guaranteed prices, to allow compliance with WTO rules. In June 1998 the Commission adopted proposals to introduce new agrimonetary arrangements for a period of three years from January 1999, owing to the launch of the euro. The arrangements were to compensate farmers in those EU member states not participating in the process of economic and monetary union for currency fluctuations until 2002. Farmers in countries taking part in EMU were also to be compensated for reductions in prices and aid payments resulting from the abolition of currency differentials. In June 1998 the Council agreed upon reforms to the tobacco and olive oil subsidy regimes. The changes abolished guaranteed prices for olive oil and eliminated production aid for small-scale producers, despite earlier protests from Spain. In addition, aid for hemp farmers was reduced. The 'set-aside' rate for 1999–2000 was increased to 10%, to prevent intervention stocks from rising to unacceptable levels. (In 1997 the cereals surplus amounted to 14m. metric tons.) In March 1999 EU ministers of agriculture reached a compromise agreement on reform of the CAP, which proposed reductions of up to 20% in guaranteed prices and increases in milk quotas from 2003/04. The plans were approved by heads of state and of government later that month, although they were modified to include less dramatic reductions in the guaranteed prices for cereals and to delay reforms to the dairy sector until 2005/06. According to the final agreement on the reforms, guaranteed prices for cereals were to be reduced by 7.5% in both 2000 and 2001, and the 'set-aside' rate was to be fixed at 10% until 2006. Guaranteed prices for beef were to be abolished and the 'basic price' offered for the meat was to decrease by a total of 20% over a three-year period from 2000. Direct annual payments to farmers were to be increased, thereby compensating farmers for the reductions in guaranteed

prices and removing incentives for over-production. A proposed limit on payments made to farmers, which was to have prevented large-scale producers from receiving excessive compensation, failed to win approval. The CAP budget was expected to stabilize at some €4,500m. until 2006, although some officials expressed concern that the reforms were not sufficiently far-reaching to achieve this aim.

FISHERIES

The Common Fisheries Policy (CFP) came into effect in January 1983 after seven years of negotiations, particularly concerning the problem of access to fishing-grounds. In 1973 a 10-year agreement had been reached, whereby member states could have exclusive access to waters up to six nautical miles (11.1 km) or, in some cases, 12 miles from their shores; 'historic rights' were reserved in certain cases for foreign fishermen who had traditionally fished within a country's waters. In 1977 the Community set up a 200-mile (370-km) fishing zone around its coastline (excluding the Mediterranean) within which all members would have access to fishing. The 1983 agreement confirmed the 200-mile zone and allowed exclusive national zones of six miles with access between six and 12 miles from the shore for other countries according to specified 'historic rights'. Rules furthering conservation (e.g. standards for fishing tackle) are imposed under the policy, with checks by a Community fisheries inspectorate. Total allowable catches are fixed annually by species, divided into national quotas under the renewable Multi-annual Guidance Programme (MAGP). In 1990 it was reported that stocks of certain species of fish in EC waters had seriously diminished, and a reduction in quotas was agreed, together with the imposition of a compulsory eight-day period in each month during which fishermen in certain areas (chiefly the North Sea) would stay in port, with exemptions for fishermen using nets with larger meshes that would allow immature fish to escape. In 1992 the compulsory non-fishing period was increased to 135 days between February and December (with similar exemptions). In December of that year EC ministers agreed to extend the CFP for a further 10-year period. In March 1998 the Commission began a review of the CFP, in preparation for a report on the development of the CFP after 2002, which was to be presented in 2001.

The proposals put forward in May 1996 by the European Commission for the fourth MAGP, covering 1997–2002, envisaged catch reductions of up to 40% for species most at risk, and set targets and detailed rules for restructuring fishing fleets in the EU. The draft MAGP IV failed to gain approval at the meeting of fisheries ministers held in November 1996. In particular, the proposed reduction in the number of fishing vessels provoked anger in many member countries. The UK Government, in October, insisted that it would not accept additional limits on catches without action to stop 'quota-hopping', in which UK-registered boats are bought by operators in other EU countries (mainly Spain and the Netherlands), which are thus able to gain part of the UK fishing quotas. (In mid-1998 the UK Government received approval from the Commission to introduce new licensing conditions from 1 January 1999 that would compel the owners of boats involved in 'quota-hopping' to establish economic links with the United Kingdom. The new restrictions required UK-registered vessels to land one-half of their catch in the United Kingdom, to employ a crew of whom the majority are resident in the United Kingdom or to incur a set level of operating expenditure in that country.) In April 1997, following a number of concessions by the Commission, ministers approved MAGP IV. The programme fixed catch reductions at 30% for species most at risk and at 20% for other over-fished species. In December 1996 ministers agreed upon the establishment of a satellite monitoring system, which was to be used to verify the fishing activities of boats greater than 20 m in length. The new system was introduced from 1 June 1998. In July it was agreed that funds of ECU 39.4m. were to be made available for monitoring activities, including the purchase of inspection boats and the provision of onshore centres for the management of satellite-monitoring activities. In June the Council had overcome long-standing objections from a number of member states and adopted a ban on the use of drift nets in the Atlantic Ocean and the Mediterranean Sea, in an attempt to prevent the unnecessary deaths of marine life such as dolphins and sharks. The ban, which was to be introduced in January 2002, would partially implement a 1992 UN resolution demanding a complete cessation of drift-net fishing. A series of compensatory measures was to be implemented to rectify any short-term detrimental impact on fishing fleets.

In December 1999 fisheries ministers agreed to implement a reduction of almost 40% in the total EU catch in 2000, with the principal objective of saving stocks in the North and Irish Seas. For some species these had been scientifically assessed as dangerously low. The Commission had demanded an even more severe reduction, including a total ban on fishing for cod in these areas. In December 2000 fisheries ministers adopted a further severe reduction in the EU catch for 2001, including a 45% cut in the total permissible catch of North Sea cod. An emergency 11-week ban on deep-sea cod fishing over about 40,000 sq miles of the North Sea area was introduced in February 2001 in order to combat the effects of overfishing.

The organization of fish marketing involves common rules on quality and packing, and a system of guide prices established annually by the Council. Fish are withdrawn from the market if prices fall too far below the guide price, and compensation may then be paid to the fishermen. Export subsidies are paid to enable the export of fish onto the lower-priced world market, and import levies are imposed to prevent competition from low-priced imports. A new import regime took effect from May 1993. The regime enabled regional fishermen's associations to increase prices to a maximum of 10% over the Community's reference price, although this was to apply to both EU and imported fish.

Agreements have been signed with other countries (Norway, Sweden, Canada and the USA) allowing reciprocal fishing rights and other advantages, and with some African countries which receive assistance in strengthening their fishing industries in return for allowing EU boats to fish in their waters. Following the withdrawal of Greenland from the Community in February 1985, Community vessels retained fishing rights in Greenland waters, in exchange for financial compensation. In 1992 fisheries agreements with Estonia, Latvia, Lithuania and Argentina were initialled; and in 1993 an agreement was reached with Mauritania to benefit Spanish fishermen in the Canary Islands. Under a four-year agreement signed with Morocco in November 1995, the size of catches by EU vessels fishing in Moroccan waters was to be reduced by 20%–40% for various species, and the EU was to provide financial compensation for Morocco amounting to ECU 355m. Morocco decided that it would not renew the fishing agreement with the EU in November 1999, but, rather, seek to renegotiate it. In 1995 relations with Canada were severely strained by a dispute concerning Spanish boats, which, Canada claimed, were breaking rules, established by the Northwest Atlantic Fisheries Organization (q.v.), to prevent overfishing of Greenland halibut. In mid-April the EU and Canada reached agreement on an increased quota for EU fishermen, and extra inspection and surveillance measures were introduced to ensure that fishing limits were observed. Following the publication of an independent scientific report in April 1996, which warned that herring stocks were in danger of being totally eradicated, the EU and Norway agreed an emergency measure to reduce by 50% catches in the North Sea and the waters around Denmark. In June 1997 the Commission voted to counteract the 'dumping' of low-cost Norwegian salmon imports on the EU market, by accepting a five-year accord, negotiated with the Norwegian Government, compelling Norway to sell its salmon at a fixed minimum price and to set its export growth to the EU at no more than 12% in the first year, and 10% per year thereafter. Norway also agreed to a voluntary increase in the export duty on Norwegian salmon imports.

In December 1994 the EU fisheries ministers concluded a final agreement on the revised CFP, allowing Spain and Portugal to be integrated into the CFP by 1 January 1996. A compromise accord was reached regarding access to waters around Ireland and off south-west Great Britain (referred to as the 'Irish box') by means of which up to 40 Spanish vessels were granted access to 80,000 sq miles of the 90,000 sq mile area. However, the accord was strongly opposed by Irish and British fishermen. In April 1995 seven Spanish vessels were seized by the Irish navy, allegedly for fishing illegally in the Irish Sea. In October fisheries ministers agreed a regime to control fishing in the 'Irish box', introducing stricter controls, and instituting new surveillance measures. In October 1999 the UK government lost a legal appeal against a decision that required it to pay compensation to Spanish trawler owners who had been illegally prevented from exploiting UK fishing quotas by legislation enacted in 1988.

SCIENCE AND TECHNOLOGY

In the amendments to the Treaty of Rome, effective from July 1987, a section on research and technology was included for the first time, defining the extent of Community co-operation in this area. Most of the funds allocated to research and technology are granted to companies or institutions that apply to participate in EU research programmes. The fourth framework programme (1994–98) included new areas: research into transport systems, socio-economic projects concerning the urban environment, social exclusion and education. The programme aimed to focus on important technologies of benefit to industry, and to improve dissemination of research and development findings. In January 1996 the Commission proposed that additional research funds for the programme, should be concentrated on five priority areas: aeronautics, clean cars, multimedia software, intermodal transport and environmental technologies. In December 1997 the European Parliament and the Council authorized additional funding for research on transmissible spongiform encephalopathies. The fifth framework programme, covering the period 1999–2002, was proposed by the Commission in April 1997. The programme aimed to focus on the economic and social priorities of those living in the EU and on strengthening the capacity of the EU for scientific and technological research. In January 1998 it was suggested that the new programme should concentrate on four main areas: preservation of the ecosystem, management of living resources, the information society and competitive and sustainable growth. A budget of €14,960m. was allocated to the programme. In 1998 research and development projects were allocated a total of ECU 2,999.3m. in the EU budget. In July the Commission proposed that the 11 candidate countries for EU membership should have the opportunity to contribute to the fifth framework programme. An EU economic summit convened in March 2000 agreed on a programme to ensure internet access for all schoolchildren by 2001. It was also decided that the cost of access to the internet in the Community should be substantially reduced, and that the EU should adopt legislation providing a legal framework for electronic commerce.

The Community's own Joint Research Centre (JRC), following a reorganization in 1996, comprises seven institutes, based at Ispra (Italy), Geel (Belgium), Karlsruhe (Germany), Seville (Spain) and Petten (Netherlands). The institutes' work covers: nuclear measurements; transuranium elements; advanced materials; remote sensing applications; the environment; systems engineering and informatics; safety technology; and prospective technological studies. Proposed funding for the JRC under the fifth framework programme amounted to €815m.

The European Strategic Research Programme for Research and Development in Information Technology ('ESPRIT'), inaugurated in 1984, concentrates on five key areas: advanced micro-electronics; software technology; advanced information processing; office automation; and computer integrated manufacturing. The programme is financed half by the EU and half by the participating research institutes, universities and industrial companies. In November 1997 a research project to develop technology to improve the methods used to locate and deactivate landmines under the ESPRIT programme was announced by the Commission.

The Community supports biotechnological research, aiming to promote the use of modern biology in agriculture and industry. In 1998 the EU's biotechnology programme ('BRIDGE') involved 154 projects with a budget of ECU 138m. Funding for 456 biotechnology projects was approved between 1994 and mid-1998. Other programmes have focused on agro-industrial research, and food sciences and technology.

In 1985 the Council adopted a programme of basic research in industrial technologies ('BRITE'), aiming to develop new methods for the benefit of existing industries, such as aeronautics, chemicals, textiles and metalworking. A 'Euram' research programme covered raw materials and advanced materials. BRITE/Euram III, on industrial and materials technologies, covered three areas in 1997: the development of production technologies for industry in the future; materials and technologies for the design of new products; and technologies for transportation.

In March 1996 research–industry task forces established by the Commission presented a report identifying priority topics for European research: the car of tomorrow; educational software and multimedia; new generation aircraft; vaccines and viral diseases; trains and railway systems of the future; intermodal transport; maritime systems; and environment, with a particular focus on water. An action plan to encourage innovation was approved in November by the Commission. The plan aimed to create a legal, regulatory and financial framework more favourable to innovation, and to strengthen links between business and research.

In July 1997 the European Parliament approved the Life Patent Directive, a proposal aiming to harmonize European rules on gene patenting in order to promote research into genetic diseases, despite objections regarding the ethical implications.

Research in the fields of energy, the environment and telecommunications is described below under the appropriate headings.

The EU also co-operates with non-member countries (particularly EFTA states) in bilateral research projects. The Commission and 19 European countries (including the members of the EU as individuals) participate in the 'Eureka' programme of research in advanced technology. The Community research and development information service ('Cordis') disseminates findings in this field and comprises eight databases. The 'Value' programme funds the publication and dissemination of technical reports from specific research projects. From 1994 a European Technology Assessment Network (ETAN) was developed in order to improve the dissemination of technological research findings.

ENERGY

The treaty establishing the European Atomic Energy Community ('Euratom') came into force on 1 January 1958, to encourage the growth of the nuclear energy industry in the Community by conducting research, providing access to information, supplying nuclear fuels, building reactors and establishing common laws and procedures for the nuclear industry. A common market for nuclear materials was introduced in 1959, and there is a common insurance scheme against nuclear risks. In 1977 the Commission began granting loans on behalf of Euratom to finance investment in nuclear power stations and the enrichment of fissile materials. An agreement with the International Atomic Energy Authority entered into force in 1977, to facilitate co-operation in research on nuclear safeguards and controls. The EU's Joint Research Centre (see under Science and Technology) conducts research on nuclear safety and the management of radioactive waste. The fifth framework programme for research and technological development (1999–2002) allocated €1,260m. for Euratom research projects.

The Joint European Torus (JET) is an experimental thermo-nuclear machine designed to pioneer new processes of nuclear fusion, using the 'Tokamak' system of magnetic confinement to heat gases to very high temperatures and bring about the fusion of tritium and deuterium nuclei. Switzerland is also a member of the JET project. Since 1974 work has been proceeding at Culham in the United Kingdom, and the project was formally inaugurated in April 1984. In 1988 work began with representatives of Japan, the former USSR and the USA on the joint design of an International Thermonuclear Experimental Reactor (ITER). Construction of a demonstration reactor was not expected to begin in the short term.

The Commission has consistently urged the formation of an effective overall energy policy. The 'Thermie' programme, initiated in 1990, fosters the development of new technologies in the energy sector; in 1997 it supported 286 energy projects at a cost of ECU 136.1m. and in 1998 the Commission was to provide funds of a further ECU 140m. The five-year 'SAVE' programme, introduced in 1991, emphasized the improvement of energy efficiency, reduction of the energy consumption of vehicles, and the use of renewable energy. A second five-year programme, SAVE II, was initiated in 1995. It was to continue the work of the first programme, and also aimed to establish energy efficiency as a criterion for all EU projects.

In 1990 Community legislation on the completion of the 'internal energy market' was adopted: it aimed to encourage the sale of electricity and gas across national borders in the Community, by opening national networks to foreign supplies, obliging suppliers to publish their prices, and co-ordinating investment in energy. Energy ministers reached agreement in June 1996 on rules for the liberalization of the electricity market, which was to be carried out progressively. Twenty-five per cent of the market was to be opened up from 19 February 1999, rising to about 33% by 2003. Belgium and Ireland were to implement the agreement in 2000, and Greece was to be exempt until 2001. In November 1999 the Commission commenced legal action against France and Luxembourg for their alleged failure to open their electricity markets by February 1999. In December 1997 the Council agreed rules to allow the gas market to be opened up in three stages, over a period of 10 years. At least 33% of the market was to be liberalized within five years, with the proportion rising to some 42% after 10 years. In the first instance those consuming 25m. cu m of gas per annum were to be eligible to benefit from liberalization, but this threshold was to decrease to 15m. cu m within five years and to 5m. cu m within 10 years. The scheme was to allow the largest gas suppliers to receive temporary exemptions from trade liberalization if the presence of competitors should cause demand for supplies to drop below the amount which the distributor was contracted to purchase in the long term.

In October 1990 the Council agreed that emissions of carbon dioxide should be stabilized at their 1990 level by 2000. It established the ALTENER programme, which aimed to increase the contribution of renewable energy sources (RES) within the Community. The programme finished at the end of 1997, having supported 278 projects since 1993, at a cost of ECU 26.9m. A replacement programme for 1998–2002, ALTENER II, was allocated a budget of ECU 22m. for the first two-year period. A green paper on ways of promoting RES in the EU was issued in November 1996. These sources (such as wind, solar, biomass and small-scale hydropower) provided less than 6% of total energy produced in the EU at that time. In May 1998 the Council committed the EU to increasing the use of RES to 12% by 2010, following the publication of a report by the Commission in late 1997. The paper also proposed a strategy which could result in a reduction in carbon dioxide emissions of 402 metric tons each year by 2010, along with significant savings on fuel costs and employment opportunities. In December 1997, in the context of the third conference of the parties to the UN Framework Convention on Climate Change (held in Kyoto, Japan), the EU adopted a target to reduce greenhouse gas emissions by 8% between 2008 and 2012, in comparison with 1990 levels.

Energy ministers from the EU member states and 12 Mediterranean countries agreed at a meeting held in June 1996 in Trieste, Italy, to develop a Euro-Mediterranean gas and electricity network. The first Euro-Mediterranean Energy Forum was held in May 1997.

In 1997 it was agreed to help a number of eastern European countries to overcome energy problems by means of the Interstate Oil and Gas to Europe programme (INOGATE), which was to receive ECU 50m. over a five-year period in order to improve energy flows in eastern Europe and increase the access of newly-independent countries to European markets. INOGATE forms part of the TACIS programme (see under External Relations). In the same year a programme for the Optimal Use of Energy Resources in Latin America (ALURE) began to undertake projects in that region.

INDUSTRY

Industrial co-operation was the earliest activity of the Community. The treaty establishing the European Coal and Steel Community (ECSC) came into force in July 1952, and by the end of 1954 nearly all barriers to trade in coal, coke, steel, pig-iron and scrap iron had been removed. The ECSC treaty was due to expire in July 2002, and in 1991 the Council agreed that, by that date, the provisions of the ECSC treaty should be incorporated in the EEC treaty, on the grounds that it was no longer appropriate to treat the coal and steel sectors separately.

In the late 1970s and 1980s measures were adopted to restructure the steel industry in response to a dramatic reduction in world demand for steel. These included production capacity quotas and a reduction of state subsidies. In November 1992 the Commission announced a three-year emergency programme to further restructure the industry, following a reduction of 30% in steel prices over the previous two years. In December 1993 ministers approved aid totalling ECU 7,000m. to achieve a further reduction in annual capacity at a number of state-owned steel plants. The industry failed to achieve the required reduction in capacity of 19m. metric tons, and in October 1994 the Commission decided to abandon the restructuring plan, although the social measures, which allocated ECU 240m. to compensate for job losses, were to be maintained. Capital expenditure in the steel industry amounted to ECU 3,312m. in 1995, some 21.6% higher than in 1994, and it continued to increase in 1996. Output of crude steel totalled 155.8m. tons in 1995, reversing the downward trend of previous years. Coal production continued to decline in 1998. The ECSC operating budget for 1998 was set at ECU 219m. In December 1996 the Commission adopted a new code on steel aid, for the period 1997–2002, which stipulated the conditions whereby member states may grant aid to steel companies, namely for research and development, for environmental protection and for full or partial closures of capacity. In October 1997 the Commission announced plans to finance, using ECSC reserves, research of benefit to the coal and steel industries amounting to some ECU 40m. each year, after the expiry of the ECSC Treaty in 2002.

The European textile and clothing industry has been seriously affected by overseas competition over an extended period. The Community participates in the Multi-fibre Arrangement (MFA, see WTO), to limit imports from low-cost suppliers overseas. A proposal by the Commission in October 1996 to accelerate liberalization of the textiles and clothing market in the EU provoked anger among industry leaders in member states, because no reciprocal concessions, in the form of removal of trade barriers, were being obtained from the major textile-exporting countries in other parts of the world. The Commission planned to include several 'sensitive' categories in the second stage of the MFA phasing-out of trade barriers, which was to start in January 1998. These categories include woollen yarns and fabrics, gloves, and synthetic ropes. A proposal by the Commission to impose duties of between 3% and 36% on imports of unfinished cotton fabrics, to counter alleged 'dumping' by several developing countries, was opposed by a majority of EU member states. The proposal aimed to help weaving industries (mainly in France and Italy), which had been adversely affected by the developing countries' practice of sharply undercutting their prices. Duties were provisionally introduced, for a period of six months, in late 1996. In March 1998 provisional duties of between 14% and 32.5% were imposed on imports of unbleached cotton from six countries, despite opposition by nine EU member states. Ministers of foreign affairs voted to remove duties in October.

Production in EU member states' shipyards has fallen drastically since the 1970s, mainly as a result of competition from shipbuilders in the Far East. In the first half of the 1980s a Council directive allowed for subsidies to help to reorganize the shipbuilding industry and to increase efficiency, but subsequently rigorous curbs on state aid to the industry were introduced. The permitted maximum percentage of state aid for shipbuilding was reduced from 28% of the value of each vessel in 1987 to 9% in 1992. In July 1994 the EU signed an accord with Japan, the USA, the Republic of Korea and the Nordic countries to end subsidies to the shipbuilding industry from 1996, subject to ratification by member states. Subsidies available in several EU countries in 1996 were higher than the official ceiling, and state aid was also given for industrial restructuring (for example, for modernization of east German shipyards) and for rescuing state-owned yards in difficulties (as was the case in Spain). In October 1997 the Commission proposed to maintain state aid until the end of 2000.

The Commission has made a number of proposals for the development of the information technology industry in Europe, particularly in view of the superiority of Japan and the USA in the market for advanced electronic circuits. The ESPRIT research programme (see under Science and Technology) aims to build the technological foundations for a fully competitive European industry. The INFO

2000 programme (1996–99) aims to promote development of the European multi-media industry, focusing on electronic publishing and interactive information services. In April 1998 the Commission proposed that the WTO should discuss the expanding electronic trade sector, in order to clarify international rules.

Harmonization of national company law to form a common legal structure has led to the adoption of directives concerning disclosure of information, company capital, internal mergers, the accounts of companies and of financial institutions, division of companies, the qualification of auditors, single-member private limited companies, mergers, take-over bids, and the formation of joint ventures. The Community Patent Convention was signed in 1975, subject to ratification by all member states. In June 1997 the Commission published a consultative document containing proposals that aimed to simplify the European patent system through the introduction of a unitary Community patent, thereby removing the need to file patent applications with individual member states. In 1996 EU member states filed 34,608 patents. An Office for Harmonization in the Internal Market (OHIM), based in Alicante, Spain, was established in December 1993, and is responsible for the registration of Community trade marks and ensuring that they receive uniform protection throughout the EU. Numerous directives have been adopted on the technical harmonization and standardization of products (e.g. on safety devices in motor vehicles, labelling of foodstuffs and of dangerous substances, and classification of medicines). In July 1998 the European Court of Justice ruled that the sale of 'grey imports' (often designer-label clothing), imported into the EU without the permission of the trade-mark holder, was in contravention of EU law.

The liberalization of Community public procurement formed an important part of the establishment of the internal market. A directive on public supplies contracts (effective from January 1989, or from March 1992 in Greece, Portugal and Spain) stipulated that major purchases of supplies by public authorities should be offered for tender throughout the community; while public contracts for construction or civil engineering works in excess of ECU 5m. were to be offered for tender throughout the EC from July 1990 (March 1992 for Greece, Portugal and Spain). From January 1993 the liberalization of procurement was extended to include public utilities in the previously excluded sectors of energy, transport, drinking-water and telecommunications. In mid-1998 business leaders proposed introducing independent ombudsmen to monitor the operation of public procurement throughout the EU and to verify its compliance with competition rules.

In September 1990 new regulations entered into force concerning mergers of large companies that might create unfair competition. In July 1996 the Commission proposed an extension of its authority to oversee merger operations, to include smaller mergers and joint ventures overseen by national regulators. The Commission planned to have authority over operations involving companies with combined global turnover of more than ECU 2,000m. and turnover within the EU of ECU 150m.; however, the proposal was widely opposed.

The Business Co-operation Centre, established in 1973, supplies information to businesses and introduces businesses from 70 different countries wishing to co-operate or form links. The Business Co-operation Network (BC-Net) links enterprises, both public and private, that wish to form alliances with others (e.g. licensing agreements), on a confidential basis. In September 1995 a Commission report outlined proposals to improve the business environment for small and medium-sized enterprises (SMEs) in the EU, by improving fiscal policies and access to finance, in addition to introducing measures aimed at reducing delays in payments and the costs of international transactions. The European Investment Bank (see p. 307) provides finance for small businesses by means of 'global loans' to financial intermediaries. A mechanism providing small businesses with subsidized loans was approved by ministers in April 1992. In March 1996 the Commission agreed new guide-lines for state aid to SMEs. Aid for the acquisition of patent rights, licences, expertise, etc., would now be allowed at the same level as that for tangible investment. In July 1997 the I-TEC scheme was inaugurated, with a budget of ECU 7.5m., to encourage SMEs to invest in new technology. By mid-1998 I-TEC had facilitated investments amounting to over ECU 250m. A network of 39 Euro Info Centres (EICs — aimed particularly at small businesses) began work in 1987, and a total of 227 EICs and 21 Euro Info Correspondence Centres were in operation in 1997.

A review of industry, published in early 1996, showed that EU companies were losing world market share in many areas, especially in electronics, mechanical engineering and automotive equipment. A study, published by the Commission in October, criticized the fact that, since 1960, only 10m. jobs in industry had been created in the EU (half the number created in Japan and less than one-fifth the number in the USA). The study cited high costs of labour, telecommunications and energy as being major contributory factors in the EU's declining share of export markets. Ministers of industry, meeting in November, decided to promote the use of benchmarking techniques to improve the competitiveness of European industry.

They also reached political agreement on the third multiannual programme (1997–2000) for SMEs, reducing the budget from ECU 140m. to ECU 127m.

In November 2000 the European Commission filed a lawsuit with the WTO against two US tobacco companies accused of complicity in illicit cigarette smuggling, and requested the WTO to impose sanctions on the USA for allegedly granting illegal tax concessions to national exporters.

TELECOMMUNICATIONS

In 1990 proposals were adopted by the Council on the co-ordinated introduction of a European public paging system and of cellular digital land-based mobile communications. In 1991 the Council adopted a directive requiring member states to liberalize their rules on the supply of telecommunications terminal equipment, thus ending the monopolies of national telecommunications authorities. In the same year the Council adopted a plan for the gradual introduction of a competitive market in satellite communications. In October 1995 the Commission adopted a directive liberalizing the use of cable telecommunications, requiring members states to permit a wide range of services, in addition to television broadcasts, on such networks. The EU market for mobile telephone networks was opened to full competition as a result of a directive adopted by the Commission in January 1996, according to which member states were to abolish all exclusive and special rights in this area, and establish open and fair licensing procedures for digital services. The number of subscribers to cellular networks in the EU grew from 12m. to more than 20m. during 1995. The telecommunications market was to be fully deregulated by 1998, although extensions to the deregulation schedule were agreed for a number of member states. In October 1997 the Commission announced plans to commence legal proceedings against those member states which had not yet adopted the legislation necessary to permit the liberalization of the telecommunications market. Spain agreed to bring forward the full deregulation of its telecommunications market from January 2003 to 1998, which meant that all the major EU telecommunications markets were open to competition from 1998. In March 2000 the EU resolved that telecommunications markets throughout the Community should be fully liberalized and integrated by 2002.

In July 1998 the Commission identified 14 cases of unfair pricing after commencing an investigation into the charges imposed by telecommunications companies for interconnection between fixed and mobile telephone networks. In December the Commission suspended some of its investigations, after a number of companies introduced price reductions.

In 1987 the Community began a joint programme of research and development in advanced communications technology in Europe (RACE), aiming to establish an integrated broad-band telecommunications network. The successor programme, Advanced Communications Technologies and Services (ACTS), became effective in September 1994.

THE SCHENGEN AGREEMENT AND TRANSPORT POLICY

Measures on the abolition of customs formalities at intra-community frontiers were completed by mid-1991, and entered into force in January 1993. However, disagreements remained among member governments concerning the free movement of persons: discussions continued in 1992 on the abuse of open frontiers by organized crime, particularly for drugs-trafficking; on extradition procedures; and on rules of asylum and immigration. In June 1990 Belgium, France, Germany, Luxembourg and the Netherlands, meeting in Schengen, Luxembourg, signed a Convention to implement an earlier agreement (concluded in 1985 at the same location), abolishing frontier controls on the free movement of persons from 1993. Delay in the establishment of the Schengen Information System (SIS), providing a computer network on criminals and illegal immigrants for use by the police forces of signatory states, resulted in postponement of implementation of the new agreement. Seven countries agreed to implement the Agreement with effect from March 1995 (Belgium, France, Germany, Luxembourg, the Netherlands, Portugal and Spain). Frontier controls at airports on those travelling between the seven countries were dismantled during a three-month transition period, which ended on 1 July 1995. However, after that date the French Government announced that it would retain land-border controls for a further six months, claiming that drugs-trafficking and illegal immigration had increased as a result of the Agreement. In March 1996 France decided to lift its border controls with Spain and Germany while maintaining controls on borders with the Benelux countries, mainly because of its anxieties about drugs being brought in from the Netherlands via Belgium and Luxembourg. Italy joined the 'Schengen Group' in October 1997, and Austria was to join in December. Border controls for both countries were removed in 1998. Denmark, Finland and Sweden (and non-EU members Norway and Iceland) were admitted as observers of the accord from 1 May 1996. The latter agreement was framed in such a way as to enable the three countries to accede to the Schengen Agreement in the future without adversely affecting the border-free zone provided by the Nordic Passport Union (see Nordic Council, p. 237). In April 1998 Sweden voted to join the 'Schengen Group'. Denmark and Finland were also reported to be making preparations for membership. In March 1999 signatories of the Schengen accords on visa-free border crossings began to waive visa requirements with Estonia, Latvia and Lithuania. In June 1997 the Commission published details of an action plan to achieve a single market, which envisaged the abolition of all EU internal border controls by 1 January 1999. The Treaty of Amsterdam, which came into effect on 1 May 1999, incorporated the so-called Schengen *'acquis'* (comprising the 1985 Agreement, 1990 Convention and additional Accession Protocols and executive decisions), in order to integrate it into the framework of the EU. The Treaty permitted the United Kingdom and Ireland to maintain permanent jurisdiction over their borders and rules of asylum and immigration. Countries acceding to the EU after 2000 were automatically to adhere to the Schengen arrangements.

The establishment of a common transport policy is stipulated in the Treaty of Rome, with the aim of gradually standardizing national regulations which hinder the free movement of traffic within the Community, such as the varying safety and licensing rules, diverse restrictions on the size of lorries, and frontier-crossing formalities. In 1986 transport ministers agreed on a system of Community-wide permits for commercial vehicles, to facilitate the crossing of frontiers, and in 1993 they agreed on measures concerning road haulage. A common tax system for trucks using EC roads was to lead to full liberalization of road 'cabotage' (whereby road hauliers may provide services in the domestic market of another member state) by 1998. In 1991 directives were adopted by the Council on the compulsory use of safety belts in vehicles weighing less than 3.5 metric tons. Further regulations applying to minibuses and coaches were to be introduced, following approval by the Commission in mid-1996. In May 1998 ministers of transport approved legislation to compel member governments to clear serious obstructions, such as truck blockades, which hinder the free movement of goods, and so disrupt the operation of a single market.

In July 1998 the Commission proposed harmonizing transport costs, to link the cost of using air services, ports, railways and roads to the social costs they incur. Under the plans, vehicles weighing more than 12 metric tons were to be charged for each km travelled, and existing charges were to be removed. The new charges were to be introduced during 2001–2004.

In the late 1980s ministers of transport approved measures to contribute to the liberalization of air transport within the Community. In 1990 ministers agreed to make further reductions in guaranteed quotas for a country's airlines on routes to another country, and to liberalize air cargo services. In 1992 they approved an 'open skies' arrangement that would allow any EC airline to operate domestic flights within another member state (with effect from 1 April 1997). In June 1996 the ministers of transport approved a limited mandate for the Commission to negotiate an 'open skies' agreement with the USA, under which a common EU–US aviation area would be created. However, the USA wished to negotiate on the basis of a full mandate. In October 1998 ministers failed to award a full mandate to the Commission. In November the Commission filed a case with the European Court of Justice, accusing eight member countries that had reached bilateral 'open skies' agreements with the USA of distorting competition to the disadvantage of EU airlines. The Commission was also initiating legal action against agreements made with the USA by Iceland, Norway and Switzerland. In July 1994, despite the recommendations of a 'Committee of Wise Men' (established by the Commission in 1993) for tighter controls on subsidies awarded to airlines, as part of efforts to increase competitiveness within the industry, the Commission approved substantial subsidies that had been granted by the French and Greek governments to their respective national airlines. Subsequently the Commission specified that state assistance could be granted to airlines 'in exceptional, unforeseen circumstances, outside the control of the company'. In June 1998 the European Court of Justice declared the subsidies awarded by the French Government illegal. However, in the following month the Commission stated that the subsidies were valid, since they had been accompanied by restructuring measures and certain competition guarantees.

In 1986 progress was made towards the establishment of a common maritime transport policy, with the adoption of regulations on unfair pricing practices, safeguard of access to cargoes, application of competition rules, and the eventual elimination of unilateral cargo reservation and discriminatory cargo-sharing arrangements. In December 1990 the Council approved, in principle, the freedom for shipping companies to provide maritime transport anywhere within the Community.

In April 1998 the Commission published a report on railway policy, with the aim of achieving greater harmonization, the regulation of state subsidies and the progressive liberalization of the rail-freight market. The Commission proposed the immediate liberalization of 5% of the market, increasing to 15% after five years and to 25%

after 10 years. In October 1999 EU transport ministers concluded an agreement that was regarded as a precursor to the full liberalization of the rail-freight market. The agreement provided for the extension of access to a planned Trans-European Rail Freight Network (TERFN). Officials had reportedly been instructed to devise a charging system that would ensure 'optimum competitiveness'. Ministers also approved the Commission's plan to expedite the implementation of its proposals to harmonize rail networks. Meanwhile, France, Belgium and Luxembourg were thought likely to oppose the full liberalization of the rail-freight market, even though the sector's share of the total freight market has declined from some 30% in 1970 to about 14%.

The PACT (pilot action for combined transport) scheme was instigated in 1992 and had funded 65 combined transport projects (where goods are moved by at least two forms of transport without unloading) on 22 routes by July 1996, when the Commission approved plans to extend the programme from 1997 to 2001, with an additional budget of ECU 35m.

A Commission report on growth, competitiveness and employment, issued in December 1993, proposed the establishment of trans-European networks (TENs) to improve transport, telecommunications and energy infrastructure throughout the Community. Most of the finance for the schemes is provided by individual member states, although by mid-1997 some ECU 3,000m. had been made available from the EU budget. In June 1998 the Commission revealed that three of 14 priority projects identified were expected to be completed by 2000. The projects were: a suspension bridge between Denmark and Sweden; an Irish railway, linking Cork to Larne via Dublin and Belfast; and an airport in Milan, Italy. The Commission planned to increase the TENs budget to €5,000m. during 2000–2006. In April 1997 plans to extend the TENs scheme into central and eastern Europe were disclosed. ECU 100m. was to be provided for such projects under the PHARE (Poland/Hungary Aid for Restructuring of Economies) assistance programme (see under External Relations). A project to develop a motorway providing a Berlin–Kiev link began in May, aided by a grant of ECU 68m. from the PHARE programme.

In December 1997 the Council adopted a directive on postal services defining the level of service to be provided throughout the EU and establishing a timetable for the liberalization of postal services.

JUSTICE AND HOME AFFAIRS

Under the Treaty on European Union, EU member states undertook to co-operate in the areas of justice and home affairs, particularly in relation to the free movement of people between member states. Issues of common interest were defined as asylum policy; border controls; immigration; drug addiction; fraud; judicial co-operation in civil and criminal matters; customs co-operation; and police co-operation for the purposes of combating terrorism, drugs-trafficking and other serious forms of international crime. A European Police Office (Europol), to facilitate the exchange of information between police forces, was to be established in The Hague, the Netherlands. The special Europol unit dealing with the trafficking of illicit drugs and nuclear and radioactive materials began work in 1994. Europol later had its mandate extended to cover illegal immigrants, stolen vehicles and paedophilia. A European Council meeting in June 1996 had resolved outstanding disagreements relating to the establishment of Europol and the Europol Convention finally entered into force on 1 October 1998, after ratification by member states. Europol was allocated a budget of ECU 6.8m. and in January 1999 its mandate was further extended to include terrorist activities. The EU convention on extradition, signed by ministers of justice in September 1996 prior to ratification by national governments, simplified and accelerated procedures, reduced the number of cases where extradition can be refused, and made it easier to extradite members of criminal organizations. In November 1997 the Commission proposed an extension to European law to allow civil and commercial judgments made in the courts of member states to be enforced across the whole of the EU. In June 1998 the Council and ministers from the 11 countries applying for EU membership approved a pre-accession agreement on combating organized crime. In February 1994 the Commission issued a document concerning the formulation of a comprehensive EU policy on asylum and immigration. In September 1995, as part of a policy of achieving a common visa regime for non-EU nationals, ministers agreed a common list of 101 countries, citizens of which required visas to enter the EU. Further progress on this issue was delayed by the desire of some member states to retain existing bilateral visa agreements.

EDUCATION, CULTURE AND BROADCASTING

The Treaty of Rome, although not covering education directly, gave the Community the role of establishing general principles for implementing a common vocational training policy. The Treaty on European Union urged greater co-operation on education policy, including the encouragement of exchanges and mobility for students and teachers, and of distance learning, and development of European studies.

The postgraduate European University Institute was founded in Florence in 1972, with departments of history, economics, law and political and social sciences, together with a European Policy Unit and a European Culture Research Centre. In 2000 there were some 450 research students. The Commission provided ECU 4.75m. towards the Institute's budget for 1997. In April 1998 202 research and teaching projects were approved for EU universities, including the establishment of 25 Jean Monnet European Centres of Excellence. Work on the projects was to begin in October 1998.

In September 1980 an educational information network, 'Eurydice', began operations, with a central unit in Brussels and national units providing data on the widely varying systems of education within member states. In 1987 the Council adopted a European Action Scheme for the Mobility of University Students ('Erasmus'). The scheme was expanded to include EFTA member states from 1992. The 'Lingua' programme promoted the teaching of foreign languages in the Community, with a budget of ECU 200m. for 1990–94. From 1 January 1995 the Erasmus and Lingua schemes were incorporated into a new Community programme, Socrates, which was to be effective during 1995–99, with a budget of ECU 850m. The programme aims to pursue the Community's activities of promoting co-operation and the exchange of information between member states with regard to education, as well as the mobility of students, especially in higher education. In 1997 Erasmus supported educational exchanges for 180,000 students and 30,000 teachers. During 1998–99 24 countries were to take part in the Erasmus scheme, which had a budget of ECU 116m. The Trans-European Mobility Programme for University Studies (TEMPUS) was launched in 1990 to foster co-operation between institutions of higher education and their counterparts in central and eastern Europe, as part of their wider aid programme to those countries (see below). By May 1993 TEMPUS had supported 637 projects, involving more than 10,000 teachers and 6,400 students in 1,800 institutions. Under the second phase of the scheme (TEMPUS II) for 1994–98 the former Soviet republics were eligible to participate in the scheme. It also sought to provide support for the restructuring of higher education in countries of central and eastern Europe participating in the PHARE programme (see under External Relations). In 1975 a European Centre for the Development of Vocational Training (CEDEFOP) was established in Berlin, Germany. The centre relocated to Thessaloniki, Greece, in 1995. The priority areas for 1997–2000 were identified as: promoting access to skills and lifelong learning; monitoring developments in member states; and support for European mobility. From 1 January 1995 the Leonardo da Vinci programme for vocational training became effective, with a budget of ECU 620m. for 1995–99.

In December 1998 the Council agreed education, training and youth programmes for 2000–06. Socrates was to have a budget of €1,150m. and the Leonardo da Vinci programme was allocated €1,550m. The TEMPUS scheme was to incorporate a third phase, TEMPUS III, which was to extend its co-operation with central and eastern European countries.

Under the Community's programme for conserving the European architectural heritage, 100 projects were approved in 1995, with a budget of ECU 4.7m. In March 1995 the Commission initiated the Raphael programme, which aimed to promote the cultural heritage of Europe, by developing links between cultural institutions and improving training. The programme had a budget of ECU 30m. for the period 1997–2000. In 1998 the Kaleidoscope programme, which encourages European cultural exchanges and other cultural projects, supported 147 projects at a total cost of ECU 8m. The programme's budget for 1996–98 was ECU 26.5m. In 1996 the Ariane programme was established to promote reading and to provide public access to books. In January 1999 the Commission selected 192 projects to receive funding under the Ariane programme in that year. In September 1998 ministers had agreed to extend its existing cultural programmes until the end of 1999, when the Culture 2000 framework programme for 2000–04 was to replace the Raphael, Kaleidoscope and Ariane programmes. It was envisaged that the framework programme would concentrate on the following themes: legislation of benefit to cultural projects; the cultural aspects of existing support policies; and the incorporation of culture into the field of external relations.

A programme to improve awareness of information technology, promote understanding of the 'Information Society', and identify opportunities for the use of new technologies, particularly in relation to disadvantaged social groups, was proposed by the Commission in December 1996. The ECU 45m. programme was to operate during 1997–2001. A further information technology scheme was initiated in September 1997, with a budget of ECU 13m., to examine new methods for the promotion of learning among children aged between four and eight years. The scheme formed part of the ESPRIT research programme (see under Science and Technology).

In 1989 ministers of foreign affairs adopted a directive (television without frontiers) establishing minimum standards for television programmes which could be broadcast freely throughout the Community: limits were placed on the amount of time devoted to advertisements, a majority of programmes broadcast were to be from the Community, where practicable, and governments were to be allowed to forbid the transmission of programmes considered morally harmful. The 'Media' programme was introduced in 1991 to provide financial support to the television and film industry. During 1991–95 it provided funds for some 5,000 projects, including professional training, the production of programmes and films with a European dimension and the transnational distribution of programmes. A second programme, 'Media II', was initiated in January 1996 with a planned budget of ECU 310m. for 1996–2000. In 1993 ministers approved a measure to ensure copyright protection for television programmes broadcast across borders by means of satellite and cable transmission. In March 1998 the Commission published a report suggesting that the regulatory framework of broadcasting rules might require amendment in the future, owing to the increasing convergence of the television, telecommunications and information technology industries.

SOCIAL POLICY

The Single European Act, which entered into force in 1987, added to the original Treaty of Rome articles which emphasized the need for 'economic and social cohesion' in the Community, i.e. the reduction of disparities between the various regions, principally through the existing 'structural funds'–the European Regional Development Fund, the European Social Fund, and the Guidance Section of the European Agricultural Guidance and Guarantee Fund (for details of these funds, as well as the Cohesion Fund, which became operational in 1993, see p. 209). In 1988 the Council declared that Community operations through the structural funds, the European Investment Bank and other financial instruments should have five priority objectives: (i) promoting the development and structural adjustment of the less-developed regions (where gross domestic product per caput is less than 75% of the Community average); (ii) converting the regions, frontier regions or parts of regions seriously affected by industrial decline; (iii) combating long-term unemployment among people above the age of 25; (iv) providing employment for young people (aged under 25); (v) with a view to the reform of the common agricultural policy: speeding up the adjustment of agricultural structures and promoting the development of rural areas. 'Agenda 2000', concerning the Community's budget after 2000, which was published in July 1997, envisaged a reform of the structural funds. Political agreement on 'Agenda 2000' was reached in March 1999.

In 1989 the Commission proposed a Charter on the Fundamental Social Rights of Workers (Social Charter), covering freedom of movement, fair remuneration, improvement of working conditions, the right to social security, freedom of association and collective wage agreements, the development of participation by workers in management, and sexual equality. The Charter was approved by the heads of government of all Community member states except the United Kingdom in December. On the insistence of the United Kingdom, the chapter on social affairs of the Treaty on European Union, negotiated in December 1991, was omitted from the Treaty to form a separate protocol. In May 1997 the new UK Government approved the Social Charter, which was to be incorporated into the Treaty of Amsterdam, signed in October. The Treaty, which entered into force in May 1999, also included a new chapter on employment.

A number of Community directives have been adopted on equal rights for women in pay, access to employment and social security, and the Commission has undertaken legal proceedings against several member states before the European Court of Justice for infringements. In 1991–95 the third Community Action Programme on the Promotion of Equal Opportunities for Women was undertaken, involving action by national governments in combating unemployment among women; bringing about equal treatment for men and women in occupational social schemes (e.g. sick pay and pensions) and in self-employed occupations, including agriculture; and legislation on parental leave. The first EU meeting on female employment was held in Belfast, the United Kingdom, in May 1998. A Fourth Action Programme, with a budget of ECU 30m. for the five-year period 1996–2000, aimed to ensure that the question of equality is integrated into all relevant policy issues. In 1997 Daphne, a programme to combat domestic violence, was launched. The programme's proposed budget for 2000–04 was €25m. In December 1997 the Council adopted a directive on sex discrimination cases, whereby the plaintiff and defendant were to share the burden of proof. Legislation was to be introduced by 1 January 2000. Numerous directives on health and safety in the workplace have been adopted by the Community. The creation of a Major Accident Hazards Bureau (MAHB) was announced by the Commission in February 1996. Based at the Joint Research Centre at Ispra in Italy, its purpose is to help prevent industrial accidents in the EU. In June 1993 the Working Time directive was approved, restricting the working week to 48 hours, except where overtime arrangements are agreed with trade unions. In October ministers adopted a directive limiting the number of hours worked by young people. The United Kingdom secured a dispensation to delay implementation of these latter measures for four years. The directive, which also prescribed minimum rest periods and a minimum of four weeks' paid holiday a year, had to be implemented by 23 November 1996. Certain categories of employee were exempt from the maximum 48-hour week rule, including those in the transport sector, fishermen and junior hospital doctors, but in December 1998 the Commission proposed extending the directive to cover those groups. In September 1994 ministers adopted the first directive to be approved under the Social Charter, concerning the establishment of mandatory works councils in multinational companies. After lengthy negotiations, it was agreed that the legislation was to be applied in companies employing more than 1,000 people, of whom 150 worked in at least two EU member states. The United Kingdom was excluded from the directive; however, UK companies operating in other European countries were to participate in the scheme (although without counting UK-based employees towards the applicability thresholds). The directive came into force in September 1996. In November 1998 the Commission proposed a directive to compel companies employing more than 50 staff to consult workers about decisions likely to cause significant organizational or contractual changes. In April 1996 the Commission proposed that part-time, fixed-term and temporary employees should receive comparable treatment to permanent, full-time employees. A directive ensuring equal treatment for part-time employees was adopted by the Council in December 1997. The directive on parental leave, the second directive to be adopted under the Social Charter, provided for a statutory minimum of three months' unpaid leave to allow parents to care for young children, and was adopted in June 1996. In December 1997, following the UK Government's approval of the Social Charter in May, the Council adopted amendments extending the two directives to include the United Kingdom.

The European Confidence Pact for Employment was launched by the Commission in January 1996 as a comprehensive strategy to combat unemployment involving a common approach by public authorities, employers and employees. An employment body, EURES, launched in November 1994, operates as a network of 450 advisers who have access to two European databases listing job vacancies in the EU and in Norway and Iceland. During 1996–97 EURES assisted more than 1m. people. (Its website can be accessed at europa.eu.int/jobs/eures.) In November 1998 the Commission proposed that national public employment services should have greater involvement with EURES. The rate of unemployment across the Community averaged 9.8% of the labour force at November 1998. An employment summit was held in Luxembourg in November 1997, with the aim of promoting job creation. The conference focused on four themes: employability, entrepreneurship, equal opportunities and adaptability, and committed member governments to providing training or work placements for unemployed young people within six months, and for the long-term unemployed within 12 months. Member states also agreed to reduce taxation on labour-intensive service industries from 1 July 1998, and to produce a national action plan for employment. In April 1998 a Social Action Plan for 1998–2000 was adopted by the Commission. It concentrated on three main areas: the promotion of jobs, skills and mobility; the changing world of work; and the development of an inclusive society. In January 1999 the Commission proposed simplifying the existing social security system to ensure that the entitlements of people moving between EU countries were protected.

EU activities regarding disability include the HELIOS programme for disabled people, which focuses on the issues of mobility, integration and independence and a 'technology initiative for disabled and elderly people' (TIDE), which aims to develop technologies that improve the living conditions of the groups concerned.

The European Voluntary Service (EVS) was established in 1996 as a pilot scheme to enable young people aged 18–25 to take part in a range of projects of benefit to the community in a country other than their own. EVS was allocated a budget of ECU 47.5m. for 1998–99. In June 1998 the Council agreed to issue 'Europasses' to record vocational training carried out in other EU member states. In July 1999 the Euro-Mediterranean Youth Programme was inaugurated. The programme had initially been adopted by the Commission in October 1998 and was to receive funding of €6m. over two years, plus grants worth €3.7m. from the Youth for Europe and EVS programmes.

The European Foundation for the Improvement of Living and Working Conditions (Dublin), established in 1975, undertakes four-year research programmes. Under the Treaty on European Union, the EU assumed responsibility for addressing the problem of drug addiction, and a European Monitoring Centre for Drugs and Drug Addiction was established in Lisbon, Portugal, in 1995 (see 'Other Institutions'). A programme to promote co-operation between member states in action against drug dependency was adopted by

ministers of health, meeting in November 1996. The ECU 27m. programme covered the period 1996–2000.

CONSUMER PROTECTION

The Community's second Consumer Protection Programme was approved by the Council in 1981, based on the principles of the first programme: protection of health and safety; standardization of rules for food additives and packaging; rules for machines and equipment; and authorization procedures for new products. The programme also included measures for monitoring the quality and durability of products, improving after-sales services, legal remedies for unsatisfactory goods and services, and the encouragement of consumer associations.

In 1993 a three-year action plan was inaugurated, with the aim of strengthening consumer power in the single market. The plan's priorities were: to consolidate legislation; to improve dissemination of consumer information; to facilitate access to small claims' courts; and to increase customer security in cross-frontier payments and after-sales services. The Consumers' Consultative Council represents European consumers' organizations, and gives opinions on consumer matters. In October 1996 the Commission issued a plan for 1997–98 containing some new priorities, including the protection of consumer interests in the supply of public utilities, improving consumer confidence in foodstuffs, strengthening consumer representation and developing consumer policies in central and eastern Europe. A new framework programme was planned for 1999–2003.

In November 1996 ministers approved a Commission directive which would enable a consumer body in one member state to take action in another in connection with breaches of certain EU laws such as those on consumer credit, package holidays, and misleading advertising. In April 1998 the Council agreed to introduce two-year guarantees on consumer goods purchased in any EU country.

In February 1997 the Commission extended the function of its directorate-general on consumer policy to incorporate consumer health protection, in order to ensure that sufficient importance be given to food safety, particularly owing to consumer concerns resulting from the BSE crisis (see under Agriculture). In June the Commission announced that a Scientific Steering Committee was to be established to provide advice regarding consumer health issues. In July 1998 an Institute for Health and Consumer Protection, attached to the Commission's Joint Research Centre, was established to improve research on that subject. In January 2000, in order to improve food safety and restore consumer confidence, the Commission formally proposed the creation of an all-European, independent food safety agency in 2002.

ENVIRONMENT POLICY

The Community's fifth environmental action programme (1993–2000), entitled 'Towards Sustainability', aimed to address the root causes of environmental degradation, by raising public awareness and changing the behaviour of authorities, enterprises and the general public. The programme targets the following sectors: industry (aiming for improved resource management and production standards); energy (reducing emissions of carbon dioxide and other pollutants, by improving energy efficiency); transport (investment in public transport, cleaner fuels); agriculture (reducing pollution, encouraging tree-planting); and tourism (controls on new and existing tourist developments).

Directives have been adopted, obliging member states to introduce regulations on air and water pollution (e.g. 'acid rain', pollution by fertilizers and pesticides, and emissions from vehicles), the transport of hazardous waste across national boundaries, waste treatment, noise abatement and the protection of natural resources; and guaranteeing freedom of access to information on the environment held by public authorities. The fifth environmental action programme focuses on anticipating environmental problems, with initiatives expected on improved resource management by industry, more effective management of mass tourism, and the development of environmental policies in agriculture.

The Community's programme of research and technological development on the environment, carried out on a shared-cost basis by various scientific institutions, covers the EU's participation in global change programmes; technologies and engineering for the environment; research on economic and social aspects of environmental issues; and technological and natural hazards. The programme is open to all European countries. A separate programme covers research in marine science and technology. In 1990 the EC established a European Environment Agency (EEA, see p. 189) to monitor environmental issues. The agency became operational in November 1994.

In 1996 the LIFE programme was established as a financial instrument to promote the development and implementation of environmental policy. LIFE funds priority activities in EU member states and provides technical assistance to countries in central and eastern Europe and the Mediterranean. In 1997 LIFE supported

211 projects. In 1998 LIFE was allocated ECU 96.6m. to finance 201 projects in the EU and an additional 4.7m. ECU was provided to finance projects outside the EU. In January 1999 it was proposed to extend the LIFE programme into 2000–04, with a budget of €613m. (The LIFE programme has a website giving details of its activities, which can be found at europa.eu.int/comm/life/home.htm.)

In 1985 the Community (and a number of individual member states) ratified the Vienna Convention for the Protection of the Ozone Layer, and in 1987 the Community signed a protocol to the treaty, controlling the production of chlorofluorocarbons. In 1990 ministers of the environment undertook to ban the production of chlorofluorocarbons by mid-1997; the introduction of the ban was brought forward to 1996. In July 1998 the Commission proposed committing EU countries to the progressive elimination of remaining ozone-depleting substances by 2001, by introducing a ban on the sale and use of CFCs and imposing production limits on HCFCs, which were originally introduced to replace CFCs. In 1990 ministers agreed to stabilize emissions of carbon dioxide, believed to be responsible for 'global warming', at 1990 levels by 2000 (2005 for the United Kingdom). In December 1997, at the third conference of parties to the UN Framework Convention on Climate Change (held in Kyoto, Japan), agreement was reached to reduce emissions of six greenhouse gases by 8% between 2008 and 2012 in member states, in comparison with 1990 levels. In June 1998 ministers of the environment agreed upon individual emission targets for each EU member state. The agreement allows a number of less industrialized countries to increase gas emissions. In May 1999 the Commission urged EU member states to redouble their efforts to reduce emissions of greenhouse gases. It was reported that while in 2000 emissions levels were expected to fall, approximately, to those prevailing in 1990, thereafter they were likely to rise again failing appropriate action.

The Eco-Management and Audit Scheme (EMAS) is a voluntary scheme, launched in April 1995, in which participating industrial companies undergo an independent audit of their environmental performance.

In June 1996 the Commission agreed a strategy, drawn up in collaboration with the European petroleum and car industries, for reducing harmful emissions from road vehicles by between 60% and 70% by 2010. In late June 1998 EU member states reached an 'auto-oil' agreement to reduce air pollution. The agreement committed member states to the progressive elimination of leaded petrol by 2000 (with limited exemptions until 2005). From 2000 petrol-powered road vehicles were to be fitted with 'on-board diagnostic' systems (OBDs) to monitor emissions. Diesel vehicles were to be installed with OBD systems by 2005. In July the Commission announced plans to decrease pollution from nuclear power stations by reducing emissions of sulphur dioxides, nitrogen oxides and dust by one-half.

An action programme for the protection and management of groundwater resources was adopted by the Commission in July 1997. Member states were to be asked to prepare national programmes to identify, map and protect groundwater resources. In December the Council agreed upon a target to reduce the volume of waste disposed in landfill sites.

Rules governing the sale of genetically modified (GM) foods were agreed by ministers in November 1996, despite objections from some countries, principally Germany and Austria, and strong opposition from environmental campaigners. In May 1998 measures were adopted to compel member countries to label food products containing GM soya and maize. In December 1999 EU environment ministers urged the adoption of stringent global regulations to govern trade in GM commodities. In April 2000 the EU Commission established a team of experts to advise on controversial biotechnology issues, including GM food production. A draft directive on new regulations covering the testing, planting and sale of GM products was approved by the European Parliament in February 2001.

A regulation revising EU laws on trade in wild animals and plants was adopted by ministers of the environment in December 1996. It was to tighten controls and improve enforcement of restrictions on trade in endangered species. In mid-1999 the EU was reported to be threatening to withhold structural fund payments from some member states if they did not implement the habitats directive and establish protected environmental areas and nature reserves.

In early 1999 a conflict arose between the EU and the USA over the introduction of new EU legislation to curb aircraft noise. Initially, the EU proposed to prevent aircraft fitted with hush kits from flying in the EU after 1 April 2002 unless they were already operating there before 1 April 1999. However, the legislation was subsequently amended in order to avert the threat of a temporary boycott of some European flights by the US authorities.

FINANCIAL SERVICES AND CAPITAL MOVEMENTS

A directive on Community banking, adopted in 1977, laid down common prudential criteria for the establishment and operation of banks in member states. A second banking directive, adopted in 1989, aimed to create a single community licence for banking,

thereby permitting a bank established in one member country to open branches in any other. The directive entered into force on 1 January 1993. Related measures were subsequently adopted with the aim of ensuring the capital adequacy of credit institutions, and the prevention of 'money-laundering' by criminals. In September 1993 ministers approved a directive on a bank deposit scheme to protect account-holders: banks were to be obliged to raise protection to 90% on the first ECU 20,000 in an account from 1 January 1995.

In 1992 the third insurance co-ordination directives, relating to life assurance and non-life insurance, were adopted, creating a framework for an integrated Community insurance market. The directives provide greater access to insurance companies and customers to the European market, guarantee greater protection for purchasers of life assurance policies and prohibit substantive control of rates. The directives came into effect on 1 July 1994.

In May 1993 ministers adopted a directive on investment services, which (with effect from 1 January 1996) allows credit institutions to offer investment services in any member state, on the basis of a licence held in one state.

In late 1999 the Commission put forward proposals to remove tax barriers and investment restrictions affecting cross-border pension schemes. At present, variations among the member states in the tax liability of contributions to supplementary pension schemes obstruct the transfer of pension rights from one state to another, contradicting the Treaty of Rome's principles of free movement of labour, capital and services.

Freedom of capital movement and the creation of a uniform financial area were regarded as vital for the completion of the internal market by 1992. In 1987, as part of the liberalization of the flow of capital, a Council directive came into force, whereby member states were obliged to remove restrictions on three categories of transactions: long-term credits related to commercial transactions; acquisition of securities; and the admission of securities to capital markets. In June 1988 the Council of Ministers approved a directive whereby all restrictions on capital movements (financial loans and credits, current and deposit account operations, transactions in securities and other instruments normally dealt in on the money market) were removed by 1 July 1990 (although a number of countries were permitted to exercise certain restrictions until the end of 1992). In September 1995 the Council adopted measures to eliminate excessive fees and delays in transfers of funds between banks in member states. In November 1997 the Commission adopted proposals to co-ordinate tax policy among member states. The measures included a code of conduct on corporate taxation and were to lead to the simplification of methods used to transfer royalty and interest payments between member countries and to prevent the withholding of taxes. In February 1999 Parliament endorsed a proposal by the Commission to harmonize taxation further, through the co-ordination of savings taxes. However, the EU's efforts in this respect were opposed by the United Kingdom on the grounds that the proposed new legislation (among other things, banks would be obliged to collect a withholding tax of at least 20% on cross-border payments of interest to individuals within the EU) would threaten the future of the international bond market, which is principally based in London. At the summit meeting of EU leaders held in Helsinki, Finland, in December 1999, it was agreed to postpone the introduction of the new tax on savings for a period of six months, in response to the United Kingdom's objections.

ECONOMIC CO-OPERATION

A report on the economic situation is presented annually by the Commission, analysing recent developments and short- and medium-term prospects. Economic policy guide-lines for the following year are adopted annually by the Council.

The following objectives for the end of 1973 were agreed by the Council in 1971, as the first of three stages towards European economic and monetary union:

the narrowing of exchange rate margins to 2.25%; creation of a medium-term pool of reserves; co-ordination of short- and medium-term economic and budgetary policies; a joint position on international monetary issues; harmonization of taxes; creation of the European Monetary Co-operation Fund (EMCF); creation of the European Regional Development Fund.

The narrowing of exchange margins (the 'snake') came into effect in 1972; but Denmark, France, Ireland, Italy and the United Kingdom later floated their currencies, with only Denmark permanently returning to the arrangement. Sweden and Norway also linked their currencies to the 'snake'; but Sweden withdrew from the arrangement in August 1977, and Norway withdrew in December 1978.

The European Monetary System (EMS) came into force in March 1979, with the aim of creating closer monetary co-operation, leading to a zone of monetary stability in Europe, principally through an exchange rate mechanism (ERM), supervised by the ministries of finance and the central banks of member states. Not all Community members participated in the ERM: Greece did not join, Spain joined only in June 1989, the United Kingdom in October 1990 and Portugal in April 1992. To prevent wide fluctuations in the value of members' currencies against each other, the ERM fixed for each currency a central rate in European Currency Units (ECUs, see below), based on a 'basket' of national currencies; a reference rate in relation to other currencies was fixed for each currency, with established fluctuation margins (until July 1993 6% for the Portuguese escudo and the Spanish peseta, 2.25% for others). Central banks of the participating states intervened by buying or selling currencies when the agreed margin was likely to be exceeded. Each member placed 20% of its gold reserves and dollar reserves respectively into the EMCF, and received a supply of ECUs to regulate central bank interventions. Short- and medium-term credit facilities were given to support the balance of payments of member countries. The EMS was initially put under strain by the wide fluctuations in the exchange rates of non-Community currencies and by the differences in economic development among members, which led to nine re-alignments of currencies in 1979–83. Subsequently greater stability was achieved, with only two realignments of currencies between 1984 and 1988. In September 1992, however, the Italian and Spanish currencies were devalued, by 7% and 5% respectively, within the ERM, and Italian and British membership was suspended; in November the Portuguese and Spanish currencies were both devalued by 6% within the ERM. In May 1993 the Spanish and Portuguese currencies were further devalued (by 8% and 6.5%, respectively). In late July, as a result of intensive currency speculation on European financial markets (forcing the weaker currencies to the very edge of their permitted margins), the ERM almost collapsed. In response to the crisis, EC finance ministers decided to widen the fluctuation margins allowed for each currency to 15%, except in the cases of Germany and the Netherlands, which agreed to maintain their currencies within the original 2.25% limits. The 15% margins were regarded as allowing for so much fluctuation in exchange rates as to represent a virtual suspension of the ERM; however, some countries, notably France and Belgium, expressed determination to adhere as far as possible to the original 'bands' in order to fulfil the conditions for eventual monetary union. In practice, during 1994, most currencies remained within the former 2.25% and 6% bands. Austria became a member of the EMS in January 1995, and its currency was subject to ERM conditions. While Sweden decided to remain outside the EMS, Finland joined in October 1996. In November the Italian lira was readmitted to the ERM.

In September 1988 a committee (chaired by Jacques Delors, the President of the European Commission, and comprising the governors of member countries' central banks, representatives of the European Commission and outside experts) was established to discuss European monetary union. The resulting 'Delors plan' was presented to heads of government in June 1989, and they agreed to begin the first stage of the process of monetary union—the drafting of a treaty on the subject—in 1990. The Intergovernmental Conference on Economic and Monetary Union was initiated in December 1990, and continued to work (in parallel with the Intergovernmental Conference on Political Union) throughout 1991, with monthly meetings at ministerial level. The Intergovernmental Conference was responsible for the drafting of the economic and monetary provisions of the Treaty on European Union, which was agreed by the European Council in December 1991 and which came into force on 1 November 1993. The principal feature of the Treaty's provisions on economic and monetary union (EMU) was the gradual introduction of a single currency, to be administered by a single central bank. During the remainder of Stage I, member states were to adopt programmes for the 'convergence' of their economies and ensure the complete liberalization of capital movements. Stage II began on 1 January 1994, and included the establishment of a European Monetary Institute (EMI), replacing the EMCF and comprising governors of central banks and a president appointed by heads of government. Heads of government were to decide, not later than 31 December 1996, whether a majority of member states fulfilled the necessary conditions for the adoption of a single currency: if so, they were to establish a date for the beginning of Stage III, but if no date for this had been set by the end of 1997, Stage III was to begin on 1 January 1999, and was to be confined to those members which did fulfil the necessary conditions. After the establishment of a starting date for Stage III, the European Central Bank (ECB) and a European System of Central Banks were to be set up to replace the EMI. During Stage III, exchange rates were to be irrevocably fixed, and a single currency introduced. Member states that had not fulfilled the necessary conditions for the adoption of a single currency would be exempt from participating. The United Kingdom was to be allowed to make a later, separate decision on whether to proceed to Stage III, while Denmark reserved the right to submit its participation in Stage III to a referendum. The near-collapse of the ERM in July 1993 cast serious doubts on the agreed timetable for monetary union, although in October the EC heads of government reaffirmed their commitment to their objective.

In December 1995 the European Council, meeting in Madrid, confirmed that Stage III of Economic and Monetary Union was to begin on 1 January 1999. The economic conditions for member states wishing to enter Stage III (including an annual budget deficit of no more than 3% of annual gross domestic product—GDP—and total public debt of no more than 60% of annual GDP) were also confirmed. The meeting decided that the proposed single currency would be officially known as the 'euro'. Participants in EMU were to be selected in early 1998, on the basis of economic performance during 1997. In October 1996 the Commission issued a draft regulation on a proposed 'stability pact', intended to ensure that member countries maintained strict budgetary discipline during Stage III of monetary union. Another draft regulation formed the legal framework for the euro, confirming that it would be the single currency of participating countries from 1 January 1999. During a transitional period of up to three years, national currencies would remain in circulation, having equivalent legal status to the euro. The communication outlined the main features of a new ERM, which would act as a 'waiting room' for countries preparing to join the single currency. Member countries remaining outside the monetary system, whether or not by choice, would still be part of the single market.

Although all 15 members of the EU endorsed the principle of monetary union, with France and Germany the most ardent supporters, certain countries were known to have political doubts about joining. In October 1997 both the United Kingdom and Sweden confirmed that they would not participate in EMU from 1999. Denmark was also to remain outside the single currency.

Technical preparations for the euro were confirmed during a meeting of the European Council in Dublin in December 1996. The heads of government endorsed the new ERM and the legal framework for the euro and agreed to the proposed 'stability pact'. Controversy arose in May 1997 over plans by the German Government to revalue gold reserves in an apparent attempt to modify figures for its 1997 budget. In June the European Council, meeting in Amsterdam, reached final agreement on the content of the 'stability pact', which included a resolution on growth. In March 1998 the Commission and the EIB published reports on the progress made by member states towards the fulfilment of convergence criteria. The Commission concluded that Greece alone failed to satisfy the necessary conditions. However, the EIB warned that Italy and Belgium, with public-debt ratios of over 100% of GDP, had made insufficient progress towards the reduction of debt levels. In March Greece was admitted to the ERM, causing a 14% devaluation of its national currency. In early May 1998 heads of state and of government confirmed that Greece failed to fulfil the conditions required for the adoption of a single currency from 1999, and that 11 countries would take part in Stage III of EMU. After substantial debate, the European Council agreed to appoint Willem Duisenberg, governor of the central bank of the Netherlands, as the President of the new ECB. Duisenberg was to be succeeded by Jean-Claude Trichet, governor of the French central bank, before the end of the usual eight-year term. The Vice-President and the remaining four members of the ECB's executive board were also appointed. The meeting agreed that existing ERM central rates were to be used to determine the final rates of exchange between national currencies and the euro, which were to be adopted on 1 January 1999. The ECB, which was established on 1 June 1998 and ceremonially launched on 30 June, was to be accountable to a European Forum, comprising members of the European Parliament (MEPs) and chairmen of the finance committees of the national parliaments of EU member countries. Euro-XI, an informal grouping of the ministers of finance of member states participating in EMU, met for the first time in June 1998. The euro was to be represented at an international level by a delegation involving the Council of Ministers, the Commission and the ECB. In September Sweden and the United Kingdom came under pressure to join the successor to the ERM, ERM2, launched on 1 January 1999, as a precondition of future participation in EMU. In October 1998 ministers discussed Greece's convergence programme for 1998–2001. The programme sought to allow Greece to join the single currency from 1 January 2001. On 31 December 1998 the ECOFIN Council adopted the conversion rates for the national currencies of the countries participating in the single currency. The euro was formally launched on 1 January 1999. Both Greece and Denmark joined ERM2. On 1 January 2001 Greece became the twelfth EU member state to adopt the single currency in the first enlargement of the euro area since its inception.

The euro

With the creation of the European Monetary System (EMS) a new monetary unit, the European Currency Unit (ECU) was adopted. Its value and composition were identical to those of the European Unit of Account (EUA) already used in the administrative fields of the Community. The ECU was a composite monetary unit, in which the relative value of each currency was determined by the gross national product and the volume of trade of each country.

The ECU, which was assigned the function of the unit of account used by the European Monetary Co-operation Fund, was also used as the denominator for the exchange rate mechanism; as the denominator for operations in both the intervention and the credit mechanisms; and as a means of settlement between monetary authorities of the European Community.

From April 1979 onwards the ECU was also used as the unit of account for the purposes of the common agricultural policy. From 1981 it replaced the EUA in the general budget of the Community; the activities of the European Development Fund under the Lomé Convention; the balance sheets and loan operations of the European Investment Bank; and the activities of the European Coal and Steel Community.

In June 1985 measures were adopted by the governors of the Community's central banks, aiming to strengthen the EMS by expanding the use of the ECU, for example by allowing international monetary institutions and the central banks of non-member countries to become 'other holders' of ECUs.

In June 1989 it was announced that, with effect from 20 September, the Portuguese and Spanish currencies were to be included in the composition of the ECU. From that date the amounts of the national currencies included in the composition of the ECU were 'weighted' as follows (in percentages): Belgian franc 7.6; Danish krone 2.45; French franc 19.0; Deutsche Mark 30.1; Greek drachma 0.8; Irish pound 1.1; Italian lira 10.15; Luxembourg franc 0.3; Netherlands guilder 9.4; Portuguese escudo 0.8; Spanish peseta 5.3; United Kingdom pound sterling 13.0. The composition of the ECU 'basket' of currencies was 'frozen' with the entry into force of the Treaty on European Union on 1 November 1993. This was not affected by the accession to the EU of Austria, Finland and Sweden; consequently those countries' currencies were not represented in the ECU 'basket'.

As part of Stage III of the process of economic and monetary union (EMU), the ECU was replaced by a single currency, the euro (€), on 1 January 1999, at a conversion rate of 1:1.

Designs for the euro bank notes, and the symbol for the single currency, were presented by the EMI in December 1996, and designs for the euro coins were presented in June 1997. The notes and coins would not be in circulation until 2002, and the euro was gradually to replace the national currencies of participating countries in the first half of that year. EU finance ministers subsequently agreed that national currencies should be replaced by the euro during the first two months of 2002. In May 1998 the French Government began minting the new euro coins. However, changes to the specifications of euro coins were proposed in July, to aid the identification of 10- and 50-cent coins by the visually impaired and vending machines.

In April 1998 ministers agreed that banks should make no charge for the conversion of accounts or payments of national currency into euros, during a transitional period. In July agreement was reached with trade and consumer groups to establish a voluntary scheme to allow retailers to display prices in euros and to accept payments made in euros without imposing any additional charges. Retailers taking part in the scheme were to display a logo to show their compliance with a code of practice on the single currency. In the same month the Commission proposed measures to combat the counterfeiting of euros. In October the ECB agreed to introduce an analysis centre for counterfeit currency, with a database accessible to national central banks. A payments settlement system, called Target (Trans-European Automated Real-time Gross Settlement Express Transfer), was introduced for countries participating in EMU on 4 January 1999. In the same month the public debt of those countries was converted into euros. A borrowing scheme worth €2,000m. was also agreed, to enable the Commission to issue euro-denominated bonds on behalf of the EU or Euratom.

The euro's value in national currencies is calculated and published daily. Its value on 1 February 1999 was US $1.1305. By mid-1999 the value of the euro had declined by some 12% against the US dollar compared with its value on introduction. The decline was attributed to the relatively high degree of economic growth taking place in the USA compared to rates in the euro-zone. In March the Commission had revised down to 2.2% its forecast of economic growth in the 11 member states participating in Stage III of EMU, compared with a forecast of 2.6% made in October 1998. Signs of economic recovery, especially in Germany, led to the strengthening of the euro against the US dollar in the second half of 1999. However, this renewal of confidence in the euro was not sustained, prompting the ECB to raise interest rates four times during the six months to May 2000. In September the monetary authorities of the USA and Japan intervened jointly with the ECB in exchange markets because of their concern about the impact of the weakness of the euro on the world economy.

In March 2000 Belgium, France and the Netherlands announced the pending merger of their stock exchanges, to form a joint exchange, EURONEXT, with a view to facilitating cross-border euro commerce.

External Relations

The EU has diplomatic relations in its own right with many countries, and with international organizations, and participates as a

body in international conferences on trade and development, such as the 'Uruguay Round' of trade negotiations, under the General Agreement on Tariffs and Trade (GATT—see WTO, p. 292). It has observer status at the United Nations. Agreements have been signed with numerous countries and groups of countries, allowing for co-operation in trade and other matters. Association agreements were initially signed between the EC and other European countries for the purpose of customs union or possible accession. After the decline of Communism in eastern Europe in 1989, it was decided that the new states, many of which expressed a desire to become full members of the EC, should be offered association status in the first instance. The resulting agreements are known as 'Europe Agreements'. Co-operation agreements are less comprehensive, and seek to facilitate economic co-operation with both European and non-European countries. Prior to 1989 they represented the preferred form of relationship with eastern European countries. The Union is also a party to various international conventions (in some of these to the exclusion of the individual member states).

Under the Single European Act, which came into force on 1 July 1987 (amending the Treaty of Rome), it was formally stipulated for the first time that member states should inform and consult each other on foreign policy matters (as was already, in practice, often the case).

The Treaty on European Union, which came into force on 1 November 1993, provided for joint action by member governments in matters of foreign and security policy, and envisaged the eventual formation of a common defence policy, with the possibility of a common defence force. The Western European Union (WEU, q.v.), to which all EU members except Denmark, Greece and Ireland belong, was to be developed as the 'defence component' of the Union, but member states' existing commitments to NATO were to be honoured. Common foreign and security policy is the province of the EU (as opposed to the EC), and decisions in this field are made by the European Council and the Council of the European Union.

The Treaty of Amsterdam, which entered into force on 1 May 1999, aimed to strengthen the concept of a Common Foreign and Security Policy within the Union and incorporated a process of common strategies to co-ordinate external relations with a third party. Accordingly, a High Representative was to be appointed to represent the EU at international meetings. In late March representatives of the Commission and NATO held a joint meeting, for the first time, to discuss the conflict in the southern Serbian republic of Kosovo (see below). In April a meeting of NATO heads of state and of government determined that its equipment, personnel and infrastructure would be available to any future EU military operation.

CENTRAL AND EASTERN EUROPE

ASSOCIATION COUNCILS:

EC–POLAND (Europe Agreement entered into force 1 February 1994); EC–HUNGARY (Europe Agreement entered into force 1 February 1994); EC–CZECH REPUBLIC (Europe Agreement entered into force 1 February 1995); EC–ROMANIA (Europe Agreement entered into force 1 February 1995); EC–BULGARIA (Europe Agreement entered into force 1 February 1995); EC–SLOVAKIA (Europe Agreement entered into force 1 February 1995); EC–ESTONIA (Europe Agreement entered into force 1 February 1998); EC–LATVIA (Europe Agreement entered into force 1 February 1998); EC–LITHUANIA (Europe Agreement entered into force 1 February 1998); EC–SLOVENIA (Europe Agreement entered into force 1 February 1999).

CO-OPERATION COUNCIL:

EC–YUGOSLAVIA (Agreement entered into force 8 April 1983—suspended in 1991).

During the late 1980s the extensive political changes and reforms in eastern European countries led to a strengthening of links with the EC. Agreements on trade and economic co-operation were concluded with Hungary (1988), Poland (1989), the USSR (1989), Czechoslovakia (1988—on trade only—and 1990), Bulgaria (1990), the German Democratic Republic (GDR—1990) and Romania (1990). In July 1989 the EC was entrusted with the co-ordination of aid from member states of the Organisation for Economic Co-operation and Development (OECD) to Hungary and Poland ('Operation PHARE'—Poland/Hungary Aid for Restructuring of Economies): this programme was subsequently extended to include Albania, Bulgaria, the Czech Republic, Slovakia, Romania and the Baltic states. Community heads of government agreed in December 1989 to establish a European Bank for Reconstruction and Development (EBRD, q.v.), with participation by member states of the OECD and the Council for Mutual Economic Assistance, to promote investment in eastern Europe; the EBRD began operations in April 1991. In June 1995 the European Council agreed to provide total funding under the PHARE programme of ECU 6,693m. to central and eastern European countries in the period 1995–99.

In August 1991 the EC formally recognized the independence of the Baltic republics (Estonia, Latvia and Lithuania), and in December the PHARE programme was extended to them. Trade and co-operation agreements with the three Baltic states were signed in May 1992. In 1991 the EC established a programme providing technical assistance to the Commonwealth of Independent States (TACIS). In 1994 Mongolia also became eligible for assistance. The programme aimed to assist in the development of successful market economies and to foster pluralism and democracy, by providing expertise and training. In 1996–99 ECU 2,224m. was to be made available under the TACIS programme. The programme's proposed budget for 2000–06 was €4,000m.

'Europe Agreements' between the EC and Czechoslovakia, Hungary and Poland were signed in December 1991, with the aim of establishing a free-trade area within 10 years and developing political co-operation (see above). In April 1994 Hungary and Poland submitted formal applications for EU membership. In June 1991 the EC established diplomatic relations with Albania, and in May 1992 an agreement on trade and co-operation was signed. Europe Agreements were initialled with Romania in October, and with Bulgaria in March 1993 (see above). In June the European Council approved measures to accelerate the opening of EC markets to goods from central and eastern European countries, with customs duties on many industrial items to be removed by the end of 1994. In September 1993 a co-operation agreement with Slovenia came into force. A Europe Agreement was signed in 1996 (see above) and Slovenia then formally applied for EU membership. The Interim Agreement, implementing the agreement signed in June, was due to come into force on 1 January 1997 and provided for the gradual establishment of a free-trade area during a transitional period of six years. In June 1996 the Commission decided that 2002 was the earliest probable date for the Czech Republic, Poland and Hungary to become members of the EU. This decision which also applies to Estonia and Slovenia, was reaffirmed in late 1999.

In February 1994 the EU Council of Ministers agreed to pursue closer economic and political relations with Ukraine, following an agreement by that country to renounce control of nuclear weapons on its territory. A partnership and co-operation agreement was signed by the two sides in June. In December EU ministers of finance approved a loan totalling ECU 85m., conditional on Ukraine's implementation of a strategy to close the Chernobyl (Chornobyl) nuclear power plant. An Interim Trade Agreement with Ukraine came into force in February 1996. In mid-1999 Ukraine's President announced that the Chernobyl plant would be closed in 2000 if the EBRD confirmed its decision to finance the completion of alternative power-generating facilities. A partnership and co-operation agreement was successfully concluded with Russia at the European Council meeting of heads of government in June 1994. An Interim Agreement on trade concessions was initiated in July 1995, after a six-month delay, owing to EU disapproval of Russia's violent repression of an independence movement in Chechnya. This agreement came into effect in February 1996, giving EU exporters improved access to the Russian market for specific products, and at the same time abolishing quantitative restrictions on some Russian exports to the EU. A partnership and co-operation agreement with Russia came into effect in December 1997. In November 1998 the Commission prepared food aid measures for Russia amounting to ECU 400m., in response to the financial crisis there. In mid-1999 the EU expressed its deep concern at the renewed fighting between Russian and Chechen armed forces in Chechnya, and urged Russia to seek a political solution to the conflict. Partnership and co-operation agreements were signed with Kazakhstan in January 1995, with Kyrgyzstan in February 1995, with Georgia, Armenia and Azerbaijan in January 1996 and with Uzbekistan in July 1996. Free-trade agreements with the Baltic states were finalized by the EU in July 1994, and came into effect on 1 January 1995. In June 1995 the EU concluded Europe Agreements with the three Baltic states (see above). In October Latvia submitted a formal application for EU membership. In December Estonia and Lithuania also submitted membership applications. A partnership agreement with Moldova entered into force in July 1998.

In May 1994 a Conference on Stability in Europe was convened in Paris to discuss the prevention of ethnic and territorial conflicts in central and eastern Europe. In particular, the conference sought to secure bilateral 'good-neighbour' accords between nine European countries that were regarded as potential future members of the EU (Bulgaria, the Czech Republic, Estonia, Hungary, Latvia, Lithuania, Poland, Romania and Slovakia). These countries, together with EU member states and other European countries (including Belarus, Moldova, Russia and Ukraine), signed a 'Stability Pact' in Paris in March 1995.

In March 1997 the Commission agreed to extend the PHARE programme in order to provide specific assistance to applicant countries in central and eastern Europe, by helping such countries to implement the reforms required to fulfil the criteria for EU membership. In July the Commission published a report, entitled 'Agenda 2000', which proposed that accession negotiations should commence with the Czech Republic, Estonia, Hungary, Poland and Slovenia, while it was recommended that discussions with Bulgaria, Latvia, Lithuania, Romania and Slovakia be deferred, owing to the need for further economic or democratic reform in those countries. The report acknowledged that it was also necessary for the EU to be restructured in order to ensure its successful operation following expansion, after the failure of negotiations leading to the Treaty of Amsterdam, approved in June, to reach agreement upon the issue of institutional reform. Ministers of foreign affairs, meeting in Luxembourg in December, endorsed the 'Agenda 2000' proposals, and membership negotiations commenced on 31 March 1998. A European Conference took place in the same month, attended by representatives of applicant countries. Also in March, the Commission approved Accession Partnerships to support preparations for accession, by identifying priority areas where progress should be made and providing financial assistance. Accession negotiations at ministerial level commenced on 10 November with the first group of applicant countries. In late 1999 it was agreed to initiate accession negotiations with Bulgaria, Latvia, Lithuania, Romania and Slovakia; these commenced in February 2000.

Following the introduction on 1 July 1990 of monetary, economic and social union between the Federal Republic of Germany and the GDR, and the formal integration of the two countries on 3 October, Community legislation was introduced within the former GDR over a transitional period.

A co-operation agreement was signed with Yugoslavia in 1980 (but not ratified until April 1983), allowing tariff-free imports and Community loans. New financial protocols were signed in 1987 and 1991. However, EC aid was suspended in July 1991, following the declarations of independence by the Yugoslav republics of Croatia and Slovenia, and the subsequent outbreak of civil conflict. Efforts were made in the ensuing months by EC ministers of foreign affairs to negotiate a peaceful settlement between the Croatian and Serbian factions, and a team of EC observers was maintained in Yugoslavia from July onwards, to monitor successive cease-fire agreements. In October the EC proposed a plan for an association of independent states, to replace the Yugoslav federation: this was accepted by all the Yugoslav republics except Serbia, which demanded a redefining of boundaries to accommodate within Serbia all predominantly Serbian areas. In November the application of the Community's co-operation agreements with Yugoslavia was suspended (with exemptions for the republics which co-operated in the peace negotiations). In January 1992 the Community granted diplomatic recognition to the former Yugoslav republics of Croatia and Slovenia, and in April it recognized Bosnia and Herzegovina, while withholding recognition from Macedonia (owing to pressure from the Greek Government, which feared that the existence of an independent Macedonia would imply a claim on the Greek province of the same name). In May EC ambassadors were withdrawn from Belgrade, in protest at Serbia's support for aggression by Bosnian Serbs against other ethnic groups in Bosnia and Herzegovina, and in the same month the Community imposed a trade embargo on Serbia and Montenegro.

New proposals for a settlement of the Bosnian conflict, submitted by EC and UN mediators in 1993, were accepted by the Bosnian Croats and by the Bosnian Government in March, but rejected by the Bosnian Serbs. In June the European Council pledged more rigorous enforcement of sanctions against Serbia. In July, at UN/EC talks in Geneva, all three parties to the Bosnian war agreed on a plan to divide Bosnia and Herzegovina into three separate republics; however, the Bosnian Government rejected the proposals for the share of territory to be allotted to the Muslims.

In April 1994, following a request from EU ministers of foreign affairs, a Contact Group, consisting of France, Germany, the United Kingdom, the USA and Russia, was initiated to undertake peace negotiations. The following month ministers of foreign affairs of the USA, Russia and the EU (represented by five member states) jointly endorsed a proposal to divide Bosnia and Herzegovina in proportions of 49% to the Bosnian Serbs and 51% to the newly-established Federation of Muslims and Croats. The proposal was rejected by the Bosnian Serb assembly in July and had to be abandoned after the Muslim-Croat Federation withdrew its support subsequent to the Bosnian Serb vote. In July the EU formally assumed political control of Mostar, a town in southern Bosnia and Herzegovina, in order to restore the city's administrative infrastructure and secure peace.

Negotiations towards a trade and co-operation agreement with Croatia began in June 1995, but talks were suspended in early August, following Croatia's military offensive in the Krajina region, which was strongly criticized by the EU. Despite some criticism of US policy towards the former Yugoslavia, in September the EU supported US-led negotiations in Geneva to devise a plan to end the conflict in Bosnia and Herzegovina. The plan closely resembled the previous proposals of the Contact Group: two self-governing entities were to be created within Bosnia and Herzegovina, with 51% of territory being allocated to the Muslim-Croat Federation, and 49% to Bosnian Serbs. The proposals were finally agreed after negotiations in Dayton, USA, in November 1995, and an accord was signed in Paris in December. In September EU ministers endorsed a plan to provide financial aid valued at some US $2,000m. to Bosnia and Herzegovina and other parts of the former Yugoslavia for post-war reconstruction. In January 1996 the EU announced its intention to recognize Yugoslavia (Serbia and Montenegro), despite the opposition of the USA. In September 1998 EU observers criticized the management of a general election in Bosnia and Herzegovina. In November the Commission proposed exceptional assistance of ECU 60m. to aid growth and employment in that country. During 1996–99 the EU allocated ECU 1,000m. for the repatriation of refugees, restructuring the economy and technical assistance, in addition to ECU 1,000m. in humanitarian aid provided since the beginning of the conflict in the former Yugoslavia.

In December 1993 six member states of the EU formally recognized the former Yugoslav republic of Macedonia (FYRM) as an independent state, but in February 1994 Greece imposed a commercial embargo against the FYRM, on the grounds that the use of the name and symbols (e.g. on the state flag) of 'Macedonia' was a threat to Greek national security. In March, however, ministers of foreign affairs of the EU decided that the embargo was in contravention of EU law, and in April the Commission commenced legal proceedings in the European Court of Justice against Greece. In September 1995 Greece and the FYRM began a process of normalizing relations, after the FYRM agreed to change the design of its state flag. In October Greece ended its economic blockade of the FYRM, and in November the Council of the European Union authorized the Commission to begin negotiating a trade and co-operation agreement with the FYRM, which entered into force in January 1998.

In March 1997 the EU sent two advisory delegations to Albania to help to restore order after violent unrest and political instability erupted in that country. A request by the Albanian Government for the deployment of EU peace-keeping troops was refused, but it was announced in early April that the EU was to provide humanitarian aid of some ECU 2m., to be used for emergency relief in Albania.

In 1998 the escalation of violence in Kosovo and Metohija, a southern Serbian province of Yugoslavia, between Serbs and the ethnic Albanian majority, prompted the imposition of sanctions by EU ministers of foreign affairs. In March ministers agreed to impose an arms embargo, to halt export credit guarantees to Yugoslavia and to restrict visas for Serbian officials. A ban on new investment in the region was imposed in June. In the same month military observers from the EU, Russia and the USA were deployed to Kosovo. In July an EU diplomatic delegation assessed the impact of the latest outbreak of violence in the region. In September the EU agreed to deny JAT, the Yugoslav airline, landing rights in EU countries. In October the Yugoslav Government allowed a team of international experts to investigate atrocities in the region, under an EU mandate. Several EU countries participated in the NATO military offensive against Yugoslavia, which was initiated in March 1999 owing to the continued repression of ethnic Albanians in Kosovo by Serbian forces. In early April EU ministers of foreign affairs formally endorsed NATO's objectives. Later in that month ministers approved a new series of punitive measures, including an embargo on the sale or supply of petroleum to the Yugoslav authorities and an extension of a travel ban on Serbian official and business executives. At the same time, ministers resolved to formulate a new plan to consolidate peace, security and economic stability in the countries of South-East Europe. EU humanitarian assistance was extended to provide relief for the substantial numbers of refugees who fled Kosovo amid the escalating violence, in particular to assist the Governments of Albania and the FYRM, while several countries agreed to provide asylum for those most at risk. By early May an estimated 25,000 refugees had been transported from camps in the FYRM, of whom more than 9,000 had been given shelter in Germany. In June EU foreign ministers approved the withdrawal of €150m. from unused budget resources in order to fund reconstruction in Kosovo and assist the return of refugees to the province. On 28 July the first donor conference for Kosovo was held, under the auspices of the Commission and the World Bank. It was reported that the EU had already provided aid worth €378m. through its 'Echo' humanitarian assistance programme; and that the Commission planned to implement a €500m.-aid programme for Kosovo in 2000. The Commission was to seek the approval of the member states for the provision, in the form of loans and grants, of €380m. in balance-of-payments support to Bulgaria, Romania and the FYRM, in order to alleviate economic difficulties resulting from the crisis in Kosovo. In June 1999 the EU, in conjunction with the Group of Seven industrialized nations and Russia (the G-8), regional governments and other organizations concerned with the stability of the region, launched the Stability Pact for South-Eastern Europe, which was placed under the auspices of the OSCE. For its part, the EU had proposed to offer customized stabilization and association agreements to Albania, Bosnia, Croatia, Macedonia and Yugoslavia, provided that they fulfilled certain conditions. In September EU foreign ministers agreed to ease sanctions in force against Kosovo and Montenegro. In October the EU began to implement an 'Energy for

Democracy' initiative, with the objective of supplying some €5m.-worth of heating oil to Serbian towns controlled by groups in opposition to the Yugoslav President Slobodan Milošević. After a lengthy delay, the first delivery of oil was made in early December to the town of Nis, regarded as a stronghold of the Serbian opposition. In February 2000 the EU suspended its ban on the Yugoslav national airline. However, the restrictions on visas for Serbian officials were reinforced.

OTHER EUROPEAN COUNTRIES

The members of the European Free Trade Association (EFTA) concluded bilateral free trade agreements with the EEC and the ECSC during the 1970s. On 1 January 1984 the last tariff barriers were eliminated, thus establishing full free trade for industrial products between the Community and EFTA members. Some EFTA members subsequently applied for membership of the EC: Austria in 1989, Sweden in 1991, and Finland, Switzerland and Norway in 1992. Formal negotiations on the creation of a 'European Economic Area' (EEA), a single market for goods, services, capital and labour among EC and EFTA members, began in June 1990, and were concluded in October 1991. The agreement was signed in May 1992 (after a delay caused by a ruling of the Court of Justice of the EC that a proposed joint EC-EFTA court, for adjudication in disputes, was incompatible with the Treaty of Rome; EFTA members then agreed to concede jurisdiction to the Court of Justice on cases of competition involving both EC and EFTA members, and to establish a special joint committee for other disputes). In a referendum in December Swiss voters rejected ratification of the agreement, and the remaining 18 countries signed an adjustment protocol in March 1993, allowing the EEA to be established without Switzerland (which was to have observer status). The EEA entered into force on 1 January 1994. Formal negotiations on the accession to the EU of Austria, Finland and Sweden began on 1 February, and those on Norway's membership started on 1 April. Negotiations were concluded with Austria, Finland and Sweden on 1 March 1994, and with Norway on 16 March, having been delayed by issues concerning the fisheries sector. Heads of government of the four countries signed treaties of accession to the EU in June, which were to come into effect from 1995, subject to approval by a national referendum in each country. Accession to the EU was endorsed by the electorates of Austria, Finland and Sweden in June, October and November respectively. Norway's accession was rejected by a referendum conducted at the end of November. Austria, Finland and Sweden became members of the EU on 1 January 1995. Liechtenstein, which became a full member of EFTA in September 1991, joined the EEA on 1 May 1995. Negotiations conducted with Switzerland since 1992 on the formulation of a new bilateral economic arrangement proceeded slowly. The main obstacles to an agreement concerned Switzerland's work permit quotas for EU citizens, and the weight limit on trucks passing through its territory. In December 1996 it was reported that Switzerland had agreed to phase out the use of work permit quotas within six years of a treaty being signed. In early December 1998 political agreement was reached with Switzerland to abolish the weight limit and instead impose road-haulage charges on trucks weighing 40 metric tons or more. Later in that month an interim trade agreement was concluded.

THE MIDDLE EAST AND THE MEDITERRANEAN

ASSOCIATION COUNCILS:

EC–GREECE (Agreement signed in 1961—joined the EC in 1972); EC–TURKEY (Agreement entered into force 1 December 1964); EC–MALTA (Agreement entered into force 1 April 1971); EC–CYPRUS (Agreement entered into force 1 June 1973); EC–ISRAEL (Agreement signed in November 1995); EC–MOROCCO (Agreement signed in February 1996); EC–JORDAN (Agreement signed in November 1997).

CO-OPERATION COUNCILS:

EC–ALGERIA (Agreement entered into force 1 November 1978); EC–MOROCCO (Agreement entered into force 1 November 1978—succeeding an Association Agreement signed in March 1969); EC–TUNISIA (Agreement entered into force 1 November 1978—succeeding an Association Agreement signed in March 1969); EC–EGYPT (Agreement entered into force 1 November 1978); EC–JORDAN (Agreement entered into force 1 November 1978); EC–SYRIA (Agreement entered into force 1 November 1978); EC–LEBANON (Agreement entered into force 1 November 1978); EC–ISRAEL (Agreement entered into force 1 November 1978); EC–GULF STATES (Agreement signed in June 1988); EC–YEMEN (Agreement negotiated with the Yemen Arab Republic in 1984; extended agreement to cover the Republic of Yemen entered into force 1 February 1995; new draft agreement signed in November 1998).

The association agreements signed with Greece, Turkey, Malta and Cyprus established free access to the Community market for

European Union

most industrial products and tariff reductions for most agricultural products. Annexed were financial protocols under which the Community was to provide concessional finance. Aid to Turkey was suspended, owing to human rights violations following the coup in 1980. In 1987 Turkey applied for membership of the Community. In 1989 the European Commission stated that, for formal negotiations on Turkish membership to take place, it would be necessary for Turkey to restructure its economy, improve its observance of human rights, and harmonize its relations with Greece. Negotiations in early 1995 to conclude a customs union agreement with Turkey were obstructed by the opposition of Greece. In early March, however, Greece removed its veto on the customs union, having received assurance on the accession of Cyprus to the EU. Ratification of the agreement by the European Parliament was delayed until mid-December, owing to concern over issues of human rights, in particular the policies of the Turkish Government towards the Kurdish population in Turkey. Under the agreement, Turkey was to receive some ECU 1,400m. in grants and loans in 1995–99. In July 1990 Cyprus and Malta made formal applications to join the Community. In June 1993 the European Commission approved the eligibility of both countries to join the community, but in November 1996 Malta's new Government announced its intention to 'freeze' its application. In September 1998, following the return to power of a Nationalist government, Malta renewed its membership application. In February 1999 the Commission recommended the initiation of membership negotiations; these commenced in February 2000. In 1996 and 1997 the EU, along with the USA, took part in extensive diplomatic activity to facilitate Cyprus' accession as a single entity. In March 1997 Turkey received assurances that its application for membership would be considered on equal terms with that of any other country. However, in July the Commission published 'Agenda 2000', a report which recommended that accession negotiations should begin with the (Greek) Cypriot Government, while talks with Turkey were to be postponed indefinitely. In December ministers of foreign affairs, meeting in Luxembourg, endorsed the report's proposals. Detailed accession talks with Cyprus began on 10 November 1998. From August 1999, when a devastating earthquake struck northwestern Turkey, a *rapprochement* began to take place between Greece and Turkey. Greece lifted its longstanding veto on disbursements of aid to Turkey and the EU made a loan of €600m. to the Turkish government to assist reconstruction. This improvement in relations culminated, at the Helsinki summit meeting of EU leaders in December, in a formal invitation to Turkey to present its candidacy for EU membership. A trade agreement with Andorra entered into force on 1 January 1991, establishing a customs union for industrial products, and allowing duty-free access to the EC for certain Andorran agricultural products. Negotiations on a similar agreement with San Marino were concluded in December 1991.

Co-operation agreements with Israel, the Maghreb countries (Algeria, Morocco and Tunisia) and the Mashreq countries (Egypt, Jordan, Lebanon and Syria) covered free access to the Community market for industrial products, customs preferences for certain agricultural products, and financial aid in the form of grants and loans from the European Investment Bank. The co-operation agreement negotiated with the Republic of Yemen was non-preferential. In November 1998 a new draft accord, incorporating commitments to democratic principles and a respect for human rights, was signed. In July 1987 Morocco applied to join the Community, but its application was rejected on the grounds that it is not a European country. An association agreement signed with Tunisia, which entered into force in March 1998, aimed to eliminate duties and other trade barriers on most products over a transitional 12-year period. In the short term the agreement provided for an increase in quotas for certain agricultural exports from Tunisia to the EU. In early 1998 EU delegations visited Algeria to express concern at the escalation of violence in that country. In October the EU agreed to commence negotiations with the Algerian Government, with the aim of concluding an association agreement and co-operating to combat terrorism. Preliminary negotiations towards association agreements have also taken place with Egypt and Syria, although formal authorization to conclude an agreement with Syria was only granted by EU heads of government in December 1997.

Three protocols were negotiated in 1987 on assistance to Israel for the period 1987–91; however, approval of these protocols was delayed by the European Parliament until October 1988, as a protest against Israel's response to unrest in the occupied territories of the West Bank and the Gaza Strip. In January 1989 the Community and Israel eliminated the last tariff barriers to full free trade for industrial products. An association agreement signed in 1995 established more extensive political dialogue between the two parties and provided trade concessions. In September 1993, following the signing of the Israeli-Palestine Liberation Organization (PLO) peace agreement, the EC committed ECU 33m. in immediate humanitarian assistance. In addition, a five-year assistance programme for the period 1994–98 was proposed, which was to consist of ECU 500m. in grants and loans to improve the economic and social infrastructure in the Occupied Territories. In October 1996 ministers

of foreign affairs agreed to appoint a special envoy to the Middle East in order to promote a peaceful settlement. A Euro-Mediterranean Interim Association Agreement on Trade and Co-operation was signed with the PLO in January 1997 and entered into force in July. The agreement confirmed existing trade concessions offered to the Palestinians since 1986 and provided for free trade to be introduced during an initial five-year period. During 1998 diplomatic relations between Israel and the EU deteriorated. In May the Israeli Prime Minister insisted that any EU role in the Middle East peace process would be unacceptable if the European Commission proceeded with a threat to ban disputed agricultural products from being imported into the EU. Additionally, the European Commission was critical of Israel's perceived obstruction of Palestinian trade. In April 1998 the EU and the Palestinian National Authority (PNA) signed a security co-operation agreement, which provided for regular meeetings to promote joint efforts on security issues, in particular in combating terrorism. In March 1999 EU heads of state and government urged Israel to fulfil within one year the 'unqualified Palestinian right' to independence. Israel was strongly critical of what it perceived as an ultimatum and stated that the EU had reduced its scope as a mediator in the Middle East peace process. In April the European Parliament demanded an investigation into the handling of Commission funds to Palestinian-controlled areas of the West Bank and Gaza. At that time the EU was reported to be the largest donor to the PNA.

Talks were held with Iran in April 1992 on the establishment of a co-operation accord. In December the Council of Ministers recommended that a 'critical dialogue' be undertaken with Iran, owing to the country's significance to regional security. In April 1997 the 'critical dialogue' was suspended and ambassadors were recalled from Iran, following a German court ruling that found the Iranian authorities responsible for ordering the murder of four Kurdish dissidents in Berlin in 1992. Later that month ministers of foreign affairs resolved to restore diplomatic relations with Iran, in order to protect the strong trading partnership. However, diplomatic relations were not resumed until November, as EU ministers reversed their decision to return diplomats to Tehran, owing to the Iranian Government's reluctance to readmit the German and Dutch ambassadors. In February 1998 EU ministers of foreign affairs removed the ban on high-level contacts with Iran, in an attempt to strengthen dialogue with that country. In August 1999 the Iranian ministry of foreign affairs acknowledged an improvement in EU-Iranian relations since the election of Muhammad Khatami as President.

In June 1995 the European Council endorsed a proposal by the Commission to reform and strengthen the Mediterranean policy of the EU. The initiative envisaged the establishment of a Euro-Mediterranean Economic Area (EMEA) by 2010, preceded by a gradual liberalization of trade within the region. The Council approved financial support amounting to ECU 4,685.5m. for the Maghreb and Mashreq agreement countries, as well as for Israel (including the Palestinian Territories), Cyprus, Malta, Turkey and Libya, for the period 1995–99. In November 1995 representatives of these countries (with the exception of Libya) and the EU finalized agreement on the EMEA at a conference held in Barcelona, Spain. In April 1997 a second Euro-Mediterranean Conference of ministers of foreign affairs was held in Malta. In September 1998 the Commission proposed measures to extend the single market to the Mediterranean countries and sought to formulate common rules on customs and taxation, free movement of goods, public procurement, intellectual property, financial services, data protection and accounting. A third Euro-Mediterranean Conference of ministers of foreign affairs was held in Stuttgart, Germany in April 1999, and a fourth in Marseilles, France in November 2000.

An agreement between the EC and the countries of the Gulf Co-operation Council (GCC) provided for co-operation in industry, energy, technology and other fields. Negotiations on a full free-trade pact began in October 1990, but it was expected that any agreement would involve transition periods of some 12 years for the reduction of European tariffs on 'sensitive products' (i.e. petrochemicals). In November 1999 the GCC Supreme Council agreed to establish a customs union (a precondition of the proposed EU-GCC free-trade agreement) by March 2005. Free-trade negotiations were continuing in 2000.

Contacts with the Arab world in general take place within the framework of the 'Euro-Arab Dialogue', established in 1973 to provide a forum for discussion of economic issues through working groups on specific topics. Following a decision in 1989 to reactivate the Dialogue, meetings were suspended in 1990 as a result of Iraq's invasion of Kuwait. In April 1992 senior EC and Arab officials agreed to resume the process.

LATIN AMERICA

A non-preferential trade agreement was signed with Uruguay in 1974, and economic and commercial co-operation agreements with Mexico in 1975 and Brazil in 1980. A five-year co-operation agreement with the members of the Central American Common Market and with Panama entered into force in 1987, as did a similar agreement with the member countries of the Andean Group (now the Andean Community). Co-operation agreements were signed with Argentina and Chile in 1990, and in that year tariff preferences were approved for Bolivia, Colombia, Ecuador and Peru, in support of those countries' efforts to combat drugs-trafficking. In May 1992 an interinstitutional co-operation agreement was signed with the Southern Common Market (Mercosur); in June the EC and the member states of the Andean Group (Bolivia, Colombia, Ecuador, Peru and Venezuela) initialled a new co-operation agreement, which was to broaden the scope of economic and development co-operation and enhance trade relations, and a new co-operation agreement was signed with Brazil. In April 1997 the EU extended further trade benefits to the countries of the Andean Community. In July 1993 the EC introduced a tariff regime to limit the import of bananas from Latin America, in order to protect the banana-producing countries of the ACP group, linked to the EC by the Lomé Convention (see below). In June 1995 a Commission communication advocated greater economic co-operation with Cuba. This policy was strongly supported by a resolution of the European Parliament in January 1996, but was criticized by the US Government, which continued to maintain an economic embargo against Cuba (see Canada and the USA, below). In July 1997 the EU and Mexico concluded a co-operation agreement and an interim agreement on trade. The accords were signed in December. In November 1998 formal negotiations were commenced with Mexico, towards a more extensive free-trade agreement, which was to cover economic co-operation, drugs-trafficking and human rights issues. In November 1999 the EU and Mexico concluded a free-trade agreement which, on implementation, will lead to the removal of all tariffs on bilateral trade in industrial products by 2007.

In April 1994 ministers of foreign affairs of the EU and the Rio Group (q.v.) held their fourth meeting since formal dialogue was initiated in 1990. A final declaration issuing from the meeting, in São Paulo, Brazil, consisted of a joint commitment to protect human rights and to promote social development and the principles of free trade. The Rio Group ministers, however, rejected any imposition of social or environmental conditional terms on trading agreements.

In late December 1994 the EU and Mercosur signed a joint declaration that aimed to promote trade liberalization and greater political co-operation. In September 1995, at a meeting in Montevideo, Uruguay, a framework agreement on the establishment of a free-trade regime between the two organizations was initialled. The agreement was formally signed in December. In July 1998 the Commission voted to commence negotiations towards an interregional agreement with Mercosur and Chile, which would strengthen existing co-operation agreements. Negotiations were initiated in April 2000.

ASIA AND AUSTRALASIA

CO-OPERATION COUNCIL:

EC–VIET NAM (Agreement entered into force 1 June 1996).

Non-preferential co-operation agreements were signed with Bangladesh, India, Pakistan and Sri Lanka between 1973 and 1986. A trade agreement was signed with the People's Republic of China in 1978, and renewed in May 1985. A co-operation agreement was signed with the countries of the Association of South East Asian Nations (ASEAN) in 1980. In October 1992 the EC and ASEAN reached a further agreement on co-operation between the two groupings in spite of Portugal's threat to veto the agreement in protest at the killing of demonstrators in East Timor by Indonesian security forces in November 1991. (See p. 136 for the EU's relations with ASEAN.) In June 1989, following the violent repression of the Chinese pro-democracy movement by the Chinese Government, the EC imposed economic sanctions on China. In October 1990 it was decided that relations with China should be 'progressively normalized'. In November 1994 a China-Europe International Business School was initiated in Shanghai. The EU has supported China's increased involvement in the international community and, in particular, its application for membership of the WTO. In October 1997 senior EU representatives signed a memorandum of understanding with China on future co-operation. The first EU-China meeting of heads of government was convened in April 1998. In November the President of the Commission made an official visit to China and urged that country to remove trade restrictions imposed on European products. In the same month the EU and Hong Kong signed a co-operation agreement to combat drugs-trafficking and copyright piracy. The agreement was the first international accord to be signed by the territory since its reversion to Chinese sovereignty in July 1997. At the second Asia-Europe meeting (ASEM, see below) of foreign ministers in March 1999 criticism of China's human rights record was rejected by the Chinese minister of foreign affairs. In April negotiations between the EU and China regarding China's admission to the WTO were abandoned after the accidental bombing by NATO forces of the Chinese embassy in Belgrade, Yugoslavia.

Negotiations resumed in January 2000. The second EU-China summit meeting was held in December 1999, in Beijing. At the meeting, among other things, EU leaders urged the Chinese Government to abandon its use of capital punishment. A bilateral trade agreement between the EU and China was concluded in May 2000, removing a major barrier to China's accession to the WTO. In October 1997 the EU and the Republic of Korea signed an agreement regarding a reciprocal opening of markets for telecommunications equipment, following a protracted dispute, which had led the EU to lodge a complaint with the WTO. In September 1997, however, the Commission submitted a further complaint to the WTO, accusing the Republic of Korea of tax discrimination against European spirits exporters. In the same month the EU joined the Korean Peninsular Energy Development Organization (KEDO), an initiative to increase nuclear safety and reduce the risk of nuclear proliferation from the energy programme of the Democratic People's Republic of Korea (DPRK). In September 1999, for the first time ever, ministerial-level discussions took place between the EU and the DPRK at the United Nations General Assembly. In June 1992 the EC signed trade and co-operation agreements with Mongolia and Macau, with respect for democracy and human rights forming the basis of envisaged co-operation. A co-operation accord was formally signed with Viet Nam in July 1995, under which the EU agreed to increase quotas for Vietnamese textile products, to support the country's efforts to join the WTO and to provide aid for environmental and public management projects. The agreement, which entered into force on 1 June 1996, incorporated a commitment by Viet Nam to guarantee human rights and a procedure for the gradual repatriation of some 40,000 Vietnamese refugees from Germany, who had lost their legal status after German reunification. A permanent EU mission to Viet Nam was established in February 1996. In July 1996 a European Business Information Centre was opened in Malaysia, with the object of promoting trade. In October the EU imposed strict limits on entry visas for Myanmar officials, because of Myanmar's refusal to allow the Commission to send a mission to investigate allegations of forced labour. In March 1997 EU ministers of foreign affairs agreed to revoke Myanmar's special trade privileges under the Generalized System of Preferences (GSP). In November a meeting of EU and ASEAN officials was postponed, owing to Myanmar's insistence (then as a full member of the ASEAN grouping) that it attend with full observer status. With no agreement having been concluded, the meeting was again postponed in July 1998 and in January 1999. In early 2000 the EU continued to impose the suspension of humanitarian aid and an arms embargo against Myanmar. Non-preferential co-operation agreements were signed with Laos and Cambodia in April 1997. The agreement with Laos entered into force on 1 December; the agreement with Cambodia was postponed owing to adverse political developments in that country. In 1998 the EU provided financial assistance to support preparations for a general election in Cambodia, and dispatched observers to monitor the election, which was held in July. In September 1999 the EU briefly imposed an arms embargo against Indonesia, which was at that time refusing to permit the deployment of an international peace-keeping force in East Timor.

Textiles exports by Asian countries have caused concern in the EU, owing to the depressed state of its textiles industry. In 1982 bilateral negotiations were held under the Multi-fibre Arrangement (MFA, see WTO) with Asian producers, notably Hong Kong, the Republic of Korea and Macau. Agreements were eventually reached involving reductions in clothing quotas and 'anti-surge' clauses to prevent flooding of European markets. In 1986 new bilateral negotiations were held and agreements were reached with the principal Asian textile exporters, for the period 1987–91 (later extended to December 1993, when the 'Uruguay Round' of GATT negotiations was finally concluded): in most cases a slight increase in quotas was permitted. Under the conclusions of the Uruguay Round, the MFA was to be progressively eliminated over a 10-year period. In January 1995 bilateral textiles agreements, signed by the EU with India, Pakistan and the People's Republic of China, specified certain trade liberalization measures to be undertaken, including an increase of China's silk export quota to 38,000 metric tons and a removal of trade barriers on small-business and handloom textile products from India, while including commitments from the Asian countries for greater efforts to combat textile and design fraud. In October 1997 the EU agreed to increase Viet Nam's textile quotas by some 30%, in exchange for improved market access for EU exports. The agreement was ratified in September 1998. In March 1998 the European Commission, for the third time, imposed provisional six-month duties on unbleached cotton from the People's Republic of China, Egypt, India, Indonesia, Pakistan and Turkey, in response to claims by European textile manufacturers that those countries were selling products at lower prices in Europe than in their domestic markets. In July the Commission proposed that these punitive 'anti-dumping' duties be imposed for a period of at least five years (although Turkey was to be excluded from the ruling). However, the Commission's proposal was rejected by EU ministers of foreign affairs in October.

The first Asia-Europe meeting (ASEM) was held in March 1996 in Bangkok, Thailand. A wide range of political, economic and co-operation issues was discussed by representatives of the EU member countries and 10 east Asian countries. It was agreed to launch an Asia-Europe Partnership for Greater Growth, in order to expand trade, investment and technology transfer. An Asia-Business Forum was to be formed, as well as an Asia-Europe Foundation in Singapore to promote educational and cultural exchanges. The EU-Korea Framework Agreement was initialled, and Malaysia was appointed to oversee the building of an integrated Asian electric rail network to link Singapore to Europe via China. Issues of human and labour rights threatened to provoke confrontation, but this was averted by the topics being relegated to a single sentence in the final statement. The second ASEM summit, convened in the United Kingdom in April 1998, was dominated by economic and financial concerns, and both sides' declared intention to prevent a return to protectionist trading policies. A special statement, issued at the end of the meeting, identified the need for economic reform in individual countries and for a reinforcement of international financial institutions. The meeting established an ASEM Trust Fund, under the auspices of the World Bank, to alleviate the social impact of the financial crisis. Other initiatives adopted by ASEM were an Asia-Europe Co-operation Framework to co-ordinate political, economic and financial co-operation, a Trade Facilitation Action Plan, and an Investment Promotion Action Plan, which incorporated a new Investment Experts Group. The meeting resolved to promote efforts to strengthen relations in all areas, and to establish a series of working bodies to promote specific areas of co-operation; however it was decided not to establish a permanent secretariat for the ASEM arrangement.

Numerous discussions have been held since 1981 on the Community's increasing trade deficit with Japan, and on the failure of the Japanese market to accept more European exports. In July 1991 the heads of government of Japan and of the EC signed a joint declaration on closer co-operation in both economic and political matters. In the same month an agreement was reached on limiting exports of Japanese cars to the EC until the end of 1999. The agreement did not include vehicles produced in Europe by Japanese companies. In October 1995 the EU secured an agreement to establish a WTO dispute panel to consider Japan's trade restrictions on alcohol, which were subsequently judged to discriminate against European manufacturers of alcoholic spirits. Japan's restrictive trading practices in several sectors, and its treatment of foreign shipping companies using Japanese ports, was a source of disagreement between the EU and Japan during much of 1996. However, the fifth annual meeting between the EU and Japan, held in Tokyo in September, appeared to facilitate more constructive dialogue. The European office of the EU-Japan Industrial Co-operation Centre was opened in Brussels in June 1996; the Centre, which was established in 1987 as a joint venture between the Japanese Government and the European Commission, sought to boost industrial co-operation between the EU and Japan and foster business contacts between companies and universities. The Vulcanus programme, launched in June 1995 by the European Commission and the Japanese Ministry of International Trade and Industry, aims to foster links with Japan through the hosting of Japanese advanced students by European companies.

Regular consultations are held with Australia at ministerial level. In January 1996 the Commission proposed a framework agreement to formalize the EU's trade and political relationship with Australia. However, in September negotiations were suspended, following the Australian Government's objections to the human rights clause contained in all EU international agreements. In June 1997 a joint declaration was signed, committing both sides to greater political, cultural and economic co-operation. Despite intensive negotiations between the EU and the New Zealand Government in 1996, no conclusion was reached regarding import duties. In March 1997 New Zealand took the case to the WTO, which later ruled against the EU. A joint declaration detailing areas of co-operation and establishing a consultative framework to facilitate the development of these was signed in May 1999.

CANADA AND THE USA

A framework agreement for commercial and economic co-operation between the Community and Canada was signed in Ottawa in 1976. It was superseded in 1990 by a Declaration on EC-Canada Relations. In 1995 relations with Canada were strained as a result of a dispute regarding fishing rights in the north-west Atlantic Ocean. An agreement on a new division of quotas between EU and Canadian fishermen was concluded in April (see above under Fisheries). In February 1996 the Commission proposed closer ties with Canada, and an action plan including early warning to avoid trade disputes, elimination of trade barriers, and promotion of business contacts. An action plan and joint political declaration were signed in December. In 1996 and 1997 negotiations took place over the use of leg-hold traps in the Canadian hunting and fur industry. In July 1997 an agreement was reached, limiting their use.

A number of specific agreements have been concluded between the Community and the USA: a co-operation agreement on the peaceful use of atomic energy entered into force in 1959, and agreements on environmental matters and on fisheries came into force in 1974 and 1984 respectively. Additional agreements provide for co-operation in other fields of scientific research and development, while bilateral contacts take place in many areas not covered by a formal agreement.

The USA has frequently criticized the Common Agricultural Policy, which it sees as creating unfair competition for American exports by its system of export refunds and preferential agreements. A similar criticism has been levelled at Community subsidies to the steel industry. In October 1985 and September 1986 agreements were reached on Community exports of steel to the USA until September 1989 (subsequently extended until March 1992). In January 1993 the USA announced the imposition of substantial duties on imports of steel from 19 countries, including seven EC member states, as an 'anti-dumping' measure. Meanwhile, a further trade dispute emerged between the EC and the USA regarding the liberalization of public procurement of services (e.g. telecommunications, transport and power). In early December the EC and the USA undertook intensive trade negotiations, which facilitated the conclusion of GATT's Uruguay Round of talks by the deadline of 15 December.

A 'Transatlantic Declaration' on EC-US relations was agreed in November 1990: the two parties agreed to consult each other on important matters of common interest, and to increase formal contacts. A new Trans-Atlantic Agenda for EU-US relations was signed by the US President and the Presidents of the European Commission and European Council at a meeting in Madrid, Spain, in December 1995. In October 1996 EU ministers of foreign affairs agreed to pursue in the WTO a complaint regarding the effects on European businesses of the USA's trade embargo against Cuba, formulated in the Helms-Burton Act. In April 1997 the EU and the USA approved a temporary resolution of the Helms-Burton dispute, whereby the US Administration was to limit the application of sanctions in return for a formal suspension of the WTO case. In mid-1996 the US Congress had adopted legislation imposing an additional trade embargo (threatening sanctions against any foreign company investing more than US $40m. in energy projects in a number of prescribed states, including Iran and Libya, the presence of which further complicated the EU-US debate in September 1997, when a French petroleum company, Total, provoked US anger, owing to its proposed investment in an Iranian natural gas project. In May 1998 an EU-USA summit meeting reached agreement on a 'Trans-Atlantic Economic Partnership' (TEP), to remove technical trade barriers, eliminate industrial tariffs, establish a free-trade area in services, and further liberalize measures relating to government procurement, intellectual property and investment. The agricultural and audio-visual sectors were to be excluded from the agreement. Initial objections from France were overcome when the EU and the USA reached a resolution to the dispute on sanctions legislation. The USA agreed to exempt European companies from the trade embargo on Iran and Libya, and to seek congressional approval for an indefinite waiver for the Helms-Burton Act, thereby removing the threat of sanctions from Total. The EU had allowed the WTO case to lapse in April, but it warned that a new WTO panel would be established if the USA took action against European companies trading with Cuba. In return, the EU agreed to increase co-operation in combating terrorism and the proliferation of weapons of mass destruction and to discourage investment in expropriated property. Following approval by the Council in November, it was agreed that implementation of the TEP would begin in advance of an EU-USA summit meeting in December.

In July 1997 the EU became involved in intensive negotiations with the US aircraft company, Boeing, over fears that its planned merger with McDonnell Douglas would harm European interests. In late July the EU approved the merger, after Boeing accepted concessions including an agreement to dispense with exclusivity clauses for 20-year supply contracts and to maintain McDonnell Douglas as a separate company for a period of 10 years. In June the EU and the USA agreed to introduce a mutual recognition agreement, which was to enable goods (including medicines, pharmaceutical products, telecommunications equipment and electrical apparatus) undergoing tests in Europe to be marketed in the USA or Canada without the need for further testing. In May 1997 the WTO upheld a US complaint against the EU's ban on imports of hormone-treated beef, which had led to a retaliatory US ban on meat imports from the EU. Negotiations took place in 1998 regarding the enforcement of European meat hygiene regulations (see under Agriculture), the reform of the EU's banana import regime (see Lomé Convention, below) and the application of a data protection law, which empowers national regulators to stop the transfer of personal information to countries judged to have inadequate data protection arrangements (including the USA). In July the Commission submitted a complaint to the WTO regarding tax exemptions granted to US companies exporting goods via subsidiaries established in tax-free countries (foreign sales corporations). Trading relations between the USA and EU deteriorated in early 1999, with regard to the disputes over the banana import regime, the EU ban on US beef imports, and new directives on acceptable levels of noise from commercial aircraft.

GENERALIZED PREFERENCES

In July 1971 the Community introduced a system of generalized tariff preferences (GSP) in favour of developing countries, ensuring duty-free entry to the EC of all otherwise dutiable manufactured and semi-manufactured industrial products, including textiles—but subject in certain circumstances to preferential limits. Preferences, usually in the form of a tariff reduction, are also offered on some agricultural products. In 1980 the Council agreed to the extension of the scheme for a second decade (1981–90): at the same time it adopted an operational framework for industrial products, which gives individual preferential limits based on the degree of competitiveness of the developing country concerned. From the end of 1990 an interim scheme was in operation, pending the introduction of a revised scheme based on the outcome of the 'Uruguay Round' of GATT negotiations on international trade (which were finally concluded in December 1993). Since 1977 the Community has progressively liberalized GSP access for the least-developed countries by according them duty-free entry on all products and by exempting them from virtually all preferential limits. In 1992–93 the GSP was extended to Albania, the Baltic states, the CIS and Georgia; in September 1994 it was extended to South Africa.

In December 1994 the European Council adopted a revised GSP to operate during 1995–98. It provided additional trade benefits to encourage the introduction by governments of environmentally sound policies and of internationally-recognized labour standards. Conversely, a country's preferential entitlement could be withdrawn, for example, if it undertook forced labour. Under the new scheme preferential tariffs amounted to 85% of the common customs duty for very sensitive products (for example, most textile products), and 70% or 35% for products classified as sensitive (for example, chemicals, electrical goods). The common customs duty was suspended for non-sensitive products (for example, paper, books, cosmetics). In accordance with the EU's foreign policy objective of focusing on the development of the world's poorest countries, duties were eliminated in their entirety for 49 least-developed countries. Duties were also suspended for a further five Latin American countries, conditional on the implementation of campaigns against the production and trade of illegal drugs.

In September 1998 the Commission proposed a new GSP for 1999–2001, which largely extended the existing scheme unchanged.

AID TO DEVELOPING AND NON-EU COUNTRIES

The main channels for Community aid to developing countries are the Lomé Convention (see below) and the Mediterranean Financial Protocols, but technical and financial aid, and assistance for refugees, training, trade promotion and co-operation in industry, energy, science and technology is also provided to about 30 countries in Asia and Latin America. The EC International Investment Partners facility, established in 1988, promotes private-sector investment in Asian, Latin American and Mediterranean countries, especially in the form of joint ventures. The European Community Humanitarian Office (ECHO) was established in 1991 with a mandate to co-ordinate emergency aid provided by the Community and became fully operational in early 1993. ECHO finances operations conducted by non-governmental organizations and international agencies, with which it works in partnership. In 1997 the EU provided humanitarian aid worth ECU 438m. The main areas of operation were Burundi, the Democratic Republic of the Congo, the Republic of the Congo, Rwanda and Tanzania (ECU 172m.) and the former Yugoslavia (ECU 132m., of which 84% was used for operations in Bosnia and Herzegovina). In June 1995 EU finance ministers agreed to contribute ECU 500m. during 1996–99 to fund the European Reconstruction and Development Programme for South Africa. In April 1999 ECHO signed a framework partnership agreement with the International Federation of Red Cross and Red Crescent Societies to promote effective co-operation in the provision of humanitarian assistance.

EU-ACP PARTNERSHIP

The First Lomé Convention (Lomé I), which was concluded at Lomé, Togo, in February 1975 and came into force on 1 April 1976, replaced the Yaoundé Conventions and the Arusha Agreement. Lomé I was designed to provide a new framework of co-operation, taking into account the varying needs of developing African, Caribbean and Pacific (ACP) countries. The Second Lomé Convention came into force on 1 January 1981. The Third Lomé Convention came into force on 1 March 1985 (trade provisions) and 1 May 1986 (aid). The Fourth Lomé Convention, which had a 10-year commitment period, was signed in December 1989: its trade provisions entered into force on 1 March 1990, and the remainder entered into force in September 1991. In June 2000, meeting in Cotonou, Benin, EU and ACP heads of state and government concluded a new 20-year partnership accord with 77 ACP states. The so-called Cotonou Agreement was to enter into effect once it had been ratified by the European Parliament and by the ACP national legislatures.

ACP-EU Institutions

Council of Ministers: one minister from each signatory state; one co-chairman from each of the two groups; meets annually.

Committee of Ambassadors: one ambassador from each signatory state; chairmanship alternates between the two groups; meets at least every six months.

Joint Assembly: EU and ACP are equally represented; attended by parliamentary delegates from each of the ACP countries and an equal number of members of the European Parliament; one co-chairman from each of the two groups; meets twice a year.

Secretariat of the ACP-EU Council of Ministers: 175 rue de la Loi, 1048 Brussels; tel. (2) 285-61-11; fax (2) 285-74-58.

Centre for the Development of Industry (CDI): 52 ave Herrmann Debroux, 1160 Brussels, Belgium; tel. (2) 679-18-11; fax (2) 675-26-03; e-mail director@cdi.be; internet www.cdi.be; f. 1977 to encourage and support the creation, expansion and restructuring of industrial companies (mainly in the fields of manufacturing and agro-industry) in the ACP states by promoting co-operation between ACP and European companies, in the form of financial, technical or commercial partnership, management contracts, licensing or franchise agreements, sub-contracts, etc.; Dir SURENDRA SHARMA.

Technical Centre for Agricultural and Rural Co-operation: Postbus 380, 6700 AJ Wageningen, Netherlands; tel. (317) 467100; fax (317) 460067; e-mail cta@cta.nl; internet www.agricta.org; f. 1983 to provide ACP states with better access to information, research, training and innovations in agricultural development and extension; Dir CARL B. GREENIDGE.

ACP Institutions

ACP Council of Ministers.

ACP Committee of Ambassadors.

ACP Secretariat: ACP House, 451 ave Georges Henri, Brussels, Belgium; tel. (2) 743-06-00; fax (2) 735-55-73; e-mail info@acpsec.org; internet www.acpsec.org; Sec.-Gen. JEAN-ROBERT GOULONGANA (Gabon).

The ACP States (parties to the Fourth Lomé Convention as of December 1999)

Angola	Eritrea
Antigua and Barbuda	Ethiopia
Bahamas	Fiji
Barbados	Gabon
Belize	The Gambia
Benin	Ghana
Botswana	Grenada
Burkina Faso	Guinea
Burundi	Guinea-Bissau
Cameroon	Guyana
Cape Verde	Haiti
Central African Republic	Jamaica
Chad	Kenya
Comoros	Kiribati
Congo, Democratic Republic	Lesotho
Congo, Republic	Liberia
Côte d'Ivoire	Madagascar
Djibouti	Malawi
Dominica	Mali
Dominican Republic	Mauritania
Equatorial Guinea	Mauritius

Mozambique
Namibia
Niger
Nigeria
Papua New Guinea
Rwanda
Saint Christopher and Nevis
Saint Lucia
Saint Vincent and the
 Grenadines
Samoa
São Tomé and Príncipe
Senegal
Seychelles
Sierra Leone

Solomon Islands
Somalia
South Africa*
Sudan
Suriname
Swaziland
Tanzania
Togo
Tonga
Trinidad and Tobago
Tuvalu
Uganda
Vanuatu
Zambia
Zimbabwe

*Partial membership (see below).

Under Lomé I, the Community committed ECU 3,052.4m. for aid and investment in developing countries, through the European Development Fund (EDF) and the European Investment Bank (EIB). Provision was made for over 99% of ACP (mainly agricultural) exports to enter the EC market duty free, while certain products which compete directly with Community agriculture, such as sugar, were given preferential treatment but not free access. The Stabex (Stabilization of Export Earnings) scheme was designed to help developing countries to withstand fluctuations in the price of their agricultural products, by paying compensation for reduced export earnings.

The Second Lomé Convention (1981–85) envisaged Community expenditure of ECU 5,530m.: it extended some of the provisions of Lomé I, and introduced new fields of co-operation, including a scheme (Sysmin) to safeguard exports of mineral products.

Lomé III made commitments of ECU 8,500m., including loans of ECU 1,100m. from the EIB. Innovations included an emphasis on agriculture and fisheries, and measures to combat desertification; assistance for rehabilitating existing industries or sectoral improvements; improvements in the efficiency of the Stabex system (now covering a list of 48 agricultural products) and of Sysmin; simplification of the rules of origin of products; the promotion of private investment; co-operation in transport and communications; cultural and social co-operation; restructuring of emergency aid; and more efficient procedures for technical and financial assistance.

The Fourth Lomé Convention was to cover the period 1990–99 (subsequently extended to February 2000). The budget for financial and technical co-operation for 1990–95 amounted to ECU 12,000m., of which ECU 10,800m. was from the EDF (including ECU 1,500m. for Stabex and ECU 480m. for Sysmin) and ECU 1,200m. from the EIB. The budget for the second five years was ECU 14,625m., of which ECU 12,967m. was from the EDF, and ECU 1,658m. from the EIB. Under Lomé IV, the obligation of most of the ACP states to contribute to the replenishment of STABEX resources, including the repayment of transfers made under the first three Conventions, was removed. In addition, special loans made to ACP member countries were to be cancelled, except in the case of profit-orientated businesses. Other innovations included the provision of assistance for structural adjustment programmes (amounting to ECU 1,150m.); increased support for the private sector, environmental protection, and control of growth in population; and measures to avoid increasing the recipient countries' indebtedness (e.g. by providing Stabex and Sysmin assistance in the form of grants, rather than loans).

On 1 July 1993 the EC introduced a regime covering the import of bananas into the Community. This was designed to protect the banana industries of ACP countries (mostly in the Caribbean), which were threatened by the availability of cheaper bananas, produced by countries in Latin America. The new regime guaranteed 30% of the European market to ACP producers, and established an annual quota of 2m. metric tons for bananas imported from Latin America, which would incur a uniform duty of 20%, while imports above this level were to be subject to a tariff of ECU 850 per ton. In February 1994 a dispute panel of GATT upheld a complaint, brought by five Latin American countries, that the EU banana import regime was in contravention of free-trade principles. An agreement was reached in March, under which the EU increased the annual quota for Latin American banana imports to 2.1m. tons with effect from October 1994, and to 2.2m. tons in 1995. However, in 1995 the USA, supported by Guatemala, Honduras and Mexico (and subsequently by Ecuador), filed a complaint with the WTO against the EU's banana regime. In May 1997 the WTO concluded that the EU banana import regime violated 19 free-trade regulations. The EU appealed against the ruling in July, but in September the WTO's dispute settlement body endorsed the original verdict. However, the allocation of preferential tariffs to ACP producers, covered by a waiver since late 1994, was upheld. In October 1997 the EU agreed to amend its banana import regime to comply with the WTO ruling. An arbitration report, published in January 1998, compelled the EU to implement changes by 1 January 1999. In June 1998 EU ministers of agriculture approved a reform of the import regime, providing for two separate

COMMITMENTS MADE UNDER THE LOMÉ CONVENTION (ECU million)

	1995	1996*
Trade promotion	57.6	8.7
Cultural and social development	163.8	69.5
Education and training	40.7	38.6
Water engineering, urban infrastructure		
and housing	65.8	22.7
Health	57.3	8.1
Economic infrastructure (transport and		
communications)	236.8	104.3
Development of production	471.2	122.9
Rural production	93.4	24.6
Industrialization	286.3	51.7
Campaigns on specific themes[1] . . .	91.5	46.5
Exceptional aid, Stabex	334.2	121.3
Rehabilitation	161.0	47.2
Disasters	33.7	–9.7
Stabex	131.1	78.8
AIDS	9.6	3.9
Refugees and returnees	–1.2	1.0
Other[2]	256.5	170.0
Total	**1,520.0**	**596.7**

* Provisional figures.
[1] Including desertification and drought, natural disasters, major endemic and epidemic diseases, hygiene and basic health, endemic cattle diseases, energy-saving research, sectoral imports programmes and long-term operations.
[2] Including information and documentation, seminars, programmes and general technical co-operation, general studies, multi-sectoral programmes, delegations, public buildings and project-linked multi-sectoral technical co-operation (all projects).

Source: European Commission, *General Report* (1996).

quota systems, granting Latin American producers greater access to the European market, with a quota of 2.53m. tons (at a tariff of ECU 75 per ton), while ACP countries would have a quota of 857,000 tons (tariff-free). The quota systems, which were to apply from 1 January 1999, were approved by the Commission in October. However, in November the USA proposed the imposition of duties of 100% on a number of European imports, in protest at the reform, which it continued to regard as discriminatory and incompatible with WTO provisions. In February 1999 the EU requested that a WTO panel be established to investigate the validity of the clause of the US Trade Act that permitted the imposition of retaliatory sanctions (considered by the EU to be in breach of the WTO dispute settlement procedure). In March, however, the USA imposed provisional measures against a diverse range of EU products, prompting the EU to issue a complaint with the WTO. In April an arbitration panel of the WTO confirmed that the EU had failed to conform its banana regime with WTO rules and formally authorized the USA to impose trade sanctions, valued at US $191.4m. In November the Commission proposed a radical reform of the EU's banana regime, involving the gradual dismantling of the existing quota system and its replacement with a tariff system that would open the banana market to other competitors. However, US trade representatives indicated that the USA would find the reforms unacceptable. A satisfactory accord, involving the adoption by the EU of a new system of licences and quotas to cover the period 2001–06 and the introduction of a new tariff-only system from 2006, was eventually reached by the EU and USA in April 2001, subject to approval by EU member states; the USA consequently agreed to suspend its punitive trade sanctions.

In September 1993 the Community announced plans to revise and strengthen its relations with the ACP countries under the Lomé Convention. In May 1994 representatives of EU member states and ACP countries initiated the mid-term review of Lomé IV. The Community reiterated its intention to maintain the Convention as an aid instrument but emphasized that stricter conditions relating to the awarding of aid would be imposed, based on standards of human rights, human resource development and environmental protection. However, negotiations between EU and ACP states were adjourned in February 1995, owing to disagreements among EU states concerning reimbursement of the EDF in the period 1995–2000. In June the European Council agreed to provide ECU 14,625m. for the second phase of Lomé IV, of which ECU 12,967m. was to be allocated from the EDF and ECU 1,658m. in loans from the EIB. Agreement was also reached on revision of the 'country-of-origin' rules for manufactured goods, a new protocol on the sustainable management of forest resources and a joint declaration on support for the banana industry. The agreement was subsequently endorsed by an EU-ACP ministerial group, and the revised Convention was signed in November, in Mauritius. In March

1997 the Commission proposed granting debt relief assistance of ECU 25m. each year for the period 1997–2000 to the 11 heavily-indebted poor countries (as identified by the World Bank and the IMF) forming part of the ACP group. Funding was to be used to support international efforts to reduce debt and encourage the economic prospects of such countries.

In June 1995 negotiations opened with a view to concluding a wide-ranging trade and co-operation agreement with South Africa, including the eventual creation of a free-trade area (FTA). The accord was approved by heads of state and of government in March 1999, after agreement was reached to eliminate progressively, over a 12-year period, the use of the terms 'port' and 'sherry' to describe South African fortified wines. The accord provided for the removal of duties from about 99% of South Africa's industrial exports and some 75% of its agricultural products within 10 years, while South Africa was to liberalize its market for some 86% of EU industrial goods (with protection for the motor vehicle and textiles industries), within a 12-year period. The accord also introduced increased development assistance for South Africa after 1999. Implementation of the accord was delayed in January 2000 after some member states refused to ratify it unless South Africa also agreed to abandon the use of names such as 'ouzo' and 'grappa'. A duty-free quota for exports of South African wine was suspended pending a resolution. The dispute was eventually resolved in February. In March 1997 the Commission approved a Special Protocol for South Africa's accession to the Lomé Convention, and in April South Africa attained partial membership. Full membership was withheld, as South Africa was not regarded as, in all respects, a developing country, and was therefore not entitled to aid provisions. A special provision was introduced into the revised Lomé Convention to allow Somalia to accede, should constitutional government be established in that country prior to the expiry of the Convention.

Intensive debate took place from 1995 on the future of relations between the ACP states and the EU, in view of the increasingly global nature of the EU's foreign policies, and particular the growing emphasis it was placing on relations with central and eastern Europe and countries of the Mediterranean rim. In November 1996 the Commission published a consultative document to consider the options for future ACP-EU relations. The document focused on the areas of trade, aid and politics, and included proposals to encourage competitiveness, to support private-sector investment and to enhance democracy. The report suggested abolishing or restructuring Stabex and Sysmin, and considered altering the grouping of the ACP states for the purpose of implementing economic agreements. The ultimate aim of the document was to foster conditions in which the EU and the ACP countries could co-exist as equal partners. In November 1997 the first summit of heads of state of ACP countries was held in Libreville, Gabon. The ACP council of ministers prepared a mandate for negotiations towards a renewed Lomé Convention, which was approved by the Commission in January 1998. The Joint Assembly of ACP ministers, meeting in Mauritius in April, and the ACP-EU Council of Ministers, meeting in Barbados in May, discussed proposals for future ACP-EU relations after the expiry of Lomé IV. The ACP states emphasized that they should be regarded as a single entity, with recognition for the individual requirements of each region, and that any renewed partnership should continue to support the elimination of poverty as its main objective. In late June EU ministers of foreign affairs approved preliminary directives for the negotiation of a new partnership agreement, based on proposals to replace existing trade privileges with regional free-trade areas by 2015. Additional financial support was to be made available to promote the development of the private sector in ACP states. However, any country unwilling to participate in a free-trade area arrangement would be granted trading privileges equivalent to its existing situation, and the poorest states were to be permitted to export goods to the EU tariff-free. The ministers agreed to allow Cuba to participate in the negotiations, with observer status, but emphasized that their decision would have no influence on any future accession discussions should Cuba wish to join the Lomé Convention. In November 1998 Cuba formally applied for full membership. A successor convention to Lomé IV, covering the period 2000–20, was signed in Cotonou, Benin, in June 2000. The principal objective of the Cotonou Agreement is the reduction of poverty through political dialogue, development aid and closer economic and trade co-operation. In the first five years of the agreement's 20-year term it is envisaged that the EDF will grant development assistance of €13,500m. The main focus of this assistance will be to support the ACP member countries in their attempts to create balanced macroeconomic conditions, expand the private sector and improve the quality and scope of social services. The system of trade preferences pertaining under the Lomé conventions is to be gradually replaced by new economic partnerships based on the progressive and reciprocal removal of trade barriers. Under the terms of the Cotonou Agreement the EU would negotiate free-trade arrangements with the most developed ACP countries during 2000–08; these would be structured around a system of free-trade zones. An assessment to be conducted in 2004 would identify those mid-

BUDGET EXPENDITURE APPROPRIATIONS FOR THE ACTIVITIES OF THE EUROPEAN COMMISSION
(ECU million)

	1998	1999
Administration		
Expenditure relating to persons working with the institution . . .	1,712.1	1,760.8
Buildings, equipment and miscellaneous operating expenditure .	319.2	312.6
Expenditure resulting from special functions carried out by the institution	249.5	256.7
Data-processing	93.9	93.9
Staff and administrative expenditure of EC delegations	202.6	213.9
Interinstitutional co-operation, services and activities	74.5	73.9
Decentralized expenditure	192.5	211.1
Total	2,844.3	2,923.0
Operations		
EAGGF Guarantee Section . . .	40,437.0	40,940.0
Structural operations, other agricultural and regional operations, transport and fisheries	28,712.5	30,658.5
Training, youth, culture, audiovisual media, information and other social operations	725.4	741.0
Energy, Euratom nuclear safeguards and environment	182.2	198.4
Consumer protection, internal market, industry and trans-European networks	795.6	883.1
Research and technological development	3,047.6	2,990.2
External actions	4,666.9	4,275.3
Common foreign and security policy . .	20.3	23.0
Repayments, guarantees and reserves .	437.0	346.0
Other Community institutions . . .	1,660.3	1,579.3
Operations—Total	80,684.8	82,634.8
Grand total	83,529.2	85,557.7

Note: The funds allocated to the other Community institutions were to be supplemented by the institutions' own resources.

ranking ACP nations also capable of entering into such free-trade deals. Meanwhile, the least-developed ACP nations were to benefit from an EU initiative to allow free access for most of their products by 2005. The preferential agreements currently in force would be retained initially (phase I), in view of a waiver granted by the WTO; thereafter ACP–EU trade was to be gradually liberalized over a period of 12–15 years (phase II). It was envisaged that Stabex and Sysmin would be eliminated gradually.

Finance
THE COMMUNITY BUDGET

The general budget of the European Union covers all EEC and Euratom expenditure and the administrative expenditure of the ECSC. The Commission is responsible for implementing the budget. (The ECSC, like the EIB, has its own resources and conducts its own financial operations.) Under the Council decision of 24 June 1988 all revenue (except that expressly designated for supplementary research and technological development programmes) is used without distinction to finance all expenditure, and all budget expenditure must be covered in full by the revenue entered in the budget. Any amendment of this decision requires the unanimous approval of the Council and must be ratified by the member states. The Treaty of Rome requires member states to release funds to cover the appropriations entered in the budget.

Each Community institution draws up estimates of its expenditure, and sends them to the Commission before 1 July of the year preceding the financial year (1 January–31 December) in question. The Commission consolidates these estimates in a preliminary draft budget, which it sends to the Council by 1 September. Expenditure is divided into two categories: that necessarily resulting from the Treaties (compulsory expenditure) and other (non-compulsory) expenditure. The draft budget must be approved by a qualified majority in the Council, and presented to Parliament by 5 October. Parliament may propose modifications to compulsory expenditure, and may (within the limits of the 'maximum rate of increase', dependent on growth of member states' gross national product—GNP—and budgets) amend non-compulsory expenditure. The budget must normally be declared finally adopted 75 days after the draft is presented to Parliament. If the budget has not been adopted by the beginning of the financial year, monthly expenditure may amount to one-twelfth of the appropriations adopted for the previous year's budget. The Commission may (even late in the year during which the budget is being executed) revise estimates of revenue and expenditure, by presenting supplementary and/or amending budgets.

Expenditure under the general budget is financed by 'own resources', comprising agricultural duties (on imports of agricultural produce from non-member states), customs duties, application of value-added tax (VAT) on goods and services, and (since 1988) a levy based on the GNP of member states. Member states are obliged to collect 'own resources' on the Community's behalf. From May 1985 arrangements were introduced for the correction of budgetary imbalances, as a result of which the United Kingdom received compensation in the form of reductions in VAT payments. In 1988 it was decided by the Community's heads of government to set a maximum amount for 'own resources' that might be called up in any one year.

REVENUE (ECU million)

Source of revenue	1998	1999
Agricultural duties .	1,101.8	1,054.5
Sugar and isoglucose levies .	1,069.8	1,080.0
Customs duties .	13,504.8	13,215.4
Own resources collection costs .	−1,567.8	−1,535.0
VAT own resources .	32,752.8	30,374.2
GNP-based own resources .	34,501.6	39,260.0
Balance of VAT and GNP own resources from previous years .	988.7	n.a.
Budget balance from previous year .	960.0	1,400.0
Other revenue .	668.1	708.6
Total .	**83,967.1**	**85,557.7**

Source: European Commission, *General Report* (1998).

MEMBER STATES' PAYMENTS

Country (ECU million)	Contribution for 1998	% of total
Austria .	2,067.6	2.5
Belgium .	3,047.7	3.7
Denmark .	1,635.4	2.0
Finland .	1,122.1	1.3
France .	14,064.7	17.0
Germany .	22,668.7	27.3
Greece .	1,324.0	1.6
Ireland .	817.7	1.0
Italy .	10,600.7	12.8
Luxembourg .	183.6	0.2
Netherlands .	4,867.2	5.9
Portugal .	1,112.2	1.3
Spain .	5,405.8	6.5
Sweden .	2,296.3	2.8
United Kingdom .	11,647.3	14.1
Total .	**82,861.1**	**100.0**

The general budget contains the expenditures of the six main Community institutions—the Commission, the Council, Parliament, the Court of Justice, the Court of Auditors, and the Economic and Social Committee and the Committee of the Regions—of which Commission expenditure (covering administrative costs and expenditure on operations) forms the largest proportion. The Common Agricultural Policy accounts for about 50% of total expenditure, principally in agricultural guarantees. In 1988 it was decided (as part of a system of budgetary discipline agreed by the Council) that the rate of increase in spending on agricultural guarantees between 1988 and a given year was not to exceed 74% of the growth rate of Community GNP during the same period. In December 1992 it was agreed to increase the upper limit on Community expenditure from 1.2% of the EC's combined GNP to 1.27% in 1999. 'Agenda 2000', concerning financial arrangements for the period 2000–2006, proposed maintaining the limit at 1.27% from 2000. In December 1994, taking into account the enlargement of the EU to 15 countries (from 1 January 1995) it was agreed to set a level of maximum expenditure at ECU 75,500m. in 1995, increasing to ECU 87,000m. in 1999, at constant 1992 prices. Agenda 2000 proposed that maximum annual expenditure would increase to €104,600m. at 1999 prices, by 2006.

STRUCTURAL FUNDS

The Community's 'structural funds' comprise the Guidance Section of the European Agricultural Guidance and Guarantee Fund, the European Regional Development Fund, the European Social Fund and the Cohesion Fund. There is also a financial instrument for fisheries guidance, commitments for which amounted to ECU 308.2m. in 1997. In accordance with the Single European Act (1987), reforms of the Community's structural funds were adopted by the Council with effect from 1 January 1989, with the aim of more accurate identification of priority targets, and greater selectivity to enable action to be concentrated in the least-favoured regions (see Social Policy, p. 196). In December 1992 it was agreed that total 'structural' expenditure would be increased to ECU 30,000m. per year by 1999, at constant 1992 prices. Commitments in the 1998 budget totalled ECU 30,482m. 'Agenda 2000', which was approved by the Council in March 1999, provided for the reform of the structural funds to make available some €213,000m. for 2000–2006, at 1999 prices.

Cohesion Fund

The Treaty on European Union and its protocol on economic and social cohesion provided for the establishment of a 'cohesion fund', which began operating on 1 April 1993, with a budget of ECU 1,500m. for the first year. This was to subsidize projects in the fields of the environment and trans-European energy and communications networks in member states with a per caput GNP of less than 90% of the Community average (in practice, this was to mean Greece, Ireland, Portugal and Spain). Commitments under the fund in the budget appropriations for 2000 amounted to $2,615m. The fund's total budget for the period 1993–99 was ECU 15,500m.

European Agricultural Guidance and Guarantee Fund (EAGGF)—Guidance Section

Created in 1962, the European Agricultural Guidance and Guarantee Fund is administered by the Commission. The Guidance section covers expenditure on Community aid for projects to improve farming conditions in the member states. It includes aid for poor rural areas and the structural adjustment of rural areas, particularly in the context of the reform of the common agricultural policy (CAP). This aid is usually granted in the form of financial contributions to programmes also supported by the member governments themselves. Commitments of ECU 2,578.7m. were budgeted for in 1997.

European Regional Development Fund—ERDF

Payments began in 1975. The Fund is intended to compensate for the unequal rate of development in different regions of the Community, by encouraging investment and improving infrastructure in 'problem regions'. The 1997 budget included an allocation of ECU 10,069.9m. for the Fund's commitments.

European Social Fund

Internet: europa.eu.int/comm/dgo5/esf/en/index.htm.

The Fund (established in 1960) provides resources with the aim of combating long-term unemployment and facilitating the integration into the labour market of young people and the socially disadvantaged. It also supports schemes to help workers to adapt to industrial changes. The 1997 budget allocated ECU 4,058.8m. for the Fund's commitments. The fund's total budget for the period 1994–99 was ECU 47,000m.

Publications*

Bulletin of the European Union (10 a year).

The Courier (every 2 months, on ACP-EU affairs).

European Economy (every 6 months, with supplements).

European Voice (weekly).

General Report on the Activities of the European Union (annually).

Official Journal of the European Communities.

Publications of the European Communities (quarterly).

EUR-Lex Website (treaties, legislation and judgments, europa.eu.int/ eur-lex/en/index.html).

Information sheets, background reports and statistical documents.

* Most publications are available in all the official languages of the Union. They are obtainable from the Office for Official Publications of the European Communities, 2 rue Mercier, 2985 Luxembourg; tel. 29291; fax 495719; e-mail europ@opoce.cec.be; internet eur-op.e-u.int.

THE FRANC ZONE

Address: Direction Générale des Services Etrangers (Service de la Zone Franc), Banque de France, 39 rue Croix-des-Petits-Champs, 75049, Paris Cédex 01, France.

Telephone: 1-42-92-31-46; **fax:** 1-42-92-39-88.

MEMBERS

Benin	Equatorial Guinea
Burkina Faso	French Republic*
Cameroon	Gabon
Central African Republic	Guinea-Bissau
Chad	Mali
The Comoros	Niger
Republic of the Congo	Senegal
Côte d'Ivoire	Togo

* Metropolitan France, Mayotte, St Pierre and Miquelon and the Overseas Departments and Territories.

The Franc Zone embraces all those countries and groups of countries whose currencies are linked with the French franc at a fixed rate of exchange and who agree to hold their reserves mainly in the form of French francs and to effect their exchange on the Paris market. Each of these countries or groups of countries has its own central issuing bank and its currency is freely convertible into French francs. This monetary union is based on agreements concluded between France and each country or group of countries.

Apart from Guinea and Mauritania, all of the countries that formerly comprised French West and Equatorial Africa are members of the Franc Zone. The former West and Equatorial African territories are still grouped within the currency areas that existed before independence, each group having its own currency issued by a central bank.

A number of states left the Franc Zone during the period 1958–73: Guinea, Tunisia, Morocco, Algeria, Mauritania and Madagascar.

The Comoros, formerly a French Overseas Territory, did not join the Franc Zone following its unilateral declaration of independence in 1975. However, francs CFA were used as the currency of the new state and the Institut d'émission des Comores continued to function as a Franc Zone organization. In 1976 the Comoros formally assumed membership. In July 1981 the Banque centrale des Comores replaced the Institut d'émission des Comores, establishing its own currency, the Comoros franc. The island of Mayotte, however, has remained under French administration as an Overseas Collectivité Territoriale, using the French franc as its unit of currency.

Equatorial Guinea, a former Spanish possession, joined the Franc Zone in January 1985, and Guinea-Bissau, a former Portuguese territory, joined in May 1997.

During the late 1980s and early 1990s the economies of the African Franc Zone countries were adversely affected by increasing foreign debt and by a decline in the prices paid for their principal export commodities. The French Government, however, refused to devalue the franc CFA, as recommended by the IMF. In 1990 the Franc Zone governments agreed to develop economic union, with integrated public finances and common commercial legislation. In April 1992, at a meeting of Franc Zone ministers, a treaty was signed on the insurance industry whereby a regulatory body for the industry was to be established: the Conférence Intrafricaine des Marchés d'Assurances (CIMA). Under the treaty, which was to be effective from 31 December 1992, a council of Franc Zone ministers responsible for the insurance industry was also to be established with its secretariat in Libreville, Gabon. (A code of conduct for members of CIMA came into effect in early 1995.) At the meeting held in April 1992 ministers also agreed that a further council of ministers was to be created with the task of monitoring the social security systems in Franc Zone countries. A programme drawn up by Franc Zone finance ministers concerning the harmonization of commercial legislation in member states through the establishment of l'Organisation pour l'Harmonisation du Droit des Affaires en Afrique (OHADA), was approved by the Franco-African summit in October. A treaty to align corporate and investment regulations was signed by 11 member countries at the annual meeting with France in October 1993. Devaluations of the franc CFA and the Comoros franc were agreed by CFA central banks in January 1994 (see below). Following the devaluation the CFA countries embarked on programmes of economic adjustment, including restrictive fiscal and wage policies and other monetary, structural and social measures, designed to stimulate growth and to ensure eligibility for development assistance from international financial institutions. France established a special development fund of FFr 300m. to alleviate the immediate social consequences of the devaluation, and announced substantial debt cancellations. In April the French Government announced assistance amounting to FFr 10,000m. over three years

to Franc Zone countries undertaking structural adjustment programmes. The IMF, which had strongly advocated a devaluation of the franc CFA, and the World Bank approved immediate soft-credit loans, technical assistance and cancellations or rescheduling of debts. In June 1994 heads of state (or representatives) of African Franc Zone countries convened in Libreville, Gabon, to review the effects of the currency realignment. The final communiqué of the meeting urged further international support for the countries' economic development efforts. In April 1995 Franc Zone finance ministers, meeting in Paris, recognized the positive impact of the devaluation on agricultural export sectors, in particular in west African countries, though central African countries, it was noted, were still afflicted by serious economic difficulties. In September the Franc Zone member countries and the French Government agreed to establish a research and training institution, Afristat, which was to support national statistical organizations in order to strengthen economic management capabilities in participating states. In April 1997 finance ministers met to review the economies of member states. Capital entries (private investment and public development aid) along with tax and wage policies and an increase in exports were found to have contributed to economic growth. Improvements were continuing within a programme supported by the IMF and the World Bank, though ministers stated that economic development efforts were not sufficiently supported by the private sector, with the average rate of investment remaining at 10% of GDP. The adoption of a charter to encourage private investors was discussed, but postponed pending an investigation into proposals made by UEMOA and CEMAC. The co-operation agreement permitting Guinea-Bissau's membership of the Franc Zone, to come into effect on 2 May, was also signed. In the same month delegates from OHADA met donors in Guinea-Bissau, aiming to raise funds worth US $50m. over a 12-year period, to allow them to train commercial court judges, provide information for businesses and cover administration costs. In April 1998 the annual meeting of finance ministers was dominated by discussions regarding the future of the Franc Zone and possible currency devaluations resulting from the introduction of a European single currency, the euro, within the framework of a European economic and monetary union, in which France was scheduled to participate when it entered into effect on 1 January 1999. In July 1998 the European Commission recommended that all convertibility arrangements concluded between France and the Franc Zone countries be preserved after the introduction of the euro, and that member countries maintain the fixed parity of the franc CFA (and of the Comoros franc). These arrangements consequently remained in effect after 1 January 1999. In February 2000 UEMOA and ECOWAS (q.v) adopted an action plan for the proposed creation, by 1 January 2004, of a single West African Monetary Zone (see below), effectively entailing the assimilation of UEMOA into the larger regional organization.

EXCHANGE REGULATIONS

Currencies of the Franc Zone are freely convertible into the French franc at a fixed rate, through 'operations accounts' established by agreements concluded between the French Treasury and the individual issuing banks. It is backed fully by the French Treasury, which also provides the issuing banks with overdraft facilities.

The monetary reserves of the CFA countries are normally held in French francs in the French Treasury. However, the Banque centrale des états de l'Afrique de l'ouest (BCEAO) and the Banque des états de l'Afrique centrale (BEAC) are authorized to hold up to 35% of their foreign exchange holdings in currencies other than the franc. Exchange is effected on the Paris market. Part of the reserves earned by richer members can be used to offset the deficits incurred by poorer countries.

Regulations drawn up in 1967 provided for the free convertibility of currency with that of countries outside the Franc Zone. Restrictions were removed on the import and export of CFA banknotes, although some capital transfers are subject to approval by the governments concerned.

When the French Government instituted exchange control to protect the French franc in May 1968, other Franc Zone countries were obliged to take similar action in order to maintain free convertibility within the Franc Zone. The franc CFA was devalued following devaluation of the French franc in August 1969. Since March 1973 the French authorities have ceased to maintain the franc-US dollar rate within previously agreed margins, and, as a result, the value of the franc CFA has fluctuated on foreign exchange markets in line with the French franc.

In August 1993, as a result of the financial turmoil regarding the European exchange rate mechanism and the continuing weakness of the French franc, the BCEAO and the BEAC decided to suspend repurchasing of francs CFA outside the Franc Zone. Effectively this signified the withdrawal of guaranteed convertibility of the franc CFA with the French franc. In January 1994 the franc CFA was devalued by 50%, and the Comoros franc by 33.3%.

CURRENCIES OF THE FRANC ZONE

French franc (= 100 centimes): used in Metropolitan France, in the Overseas Departments of Guadeloupe, French Guiana, Martinique, Réunion, and in the Overseas Collectivités Territoriales of Mayotte and St Pierre and Miquelon.

1 franc CFA = 1 French centime. CFA stands for Communauté financière africaine in the West African area and for Coopération financière en Afrique centrale in the Central African area. Used in the monetary areas of West and Central Africa respectively.

1 Comoros franc = 1.333 French centimes (1 French franc = 75 Comoros francs). Used in the Comoros, where it replaced the franc CFA in 1981.

1 franc CFP = 5.5 French centimes. CFP stands for Comptoirs français du Pacifique. Used in New Caledonia, French Polynesia and the Wallis and Futuna Islands.

WEST AFRICA

Union économique et monétaire ouest-africaine—UEMOA: BP 543, Ouagadougou, Burkina Faso; tel. 31-88-73; fax 31-88-72; e-mail commission@uemoa.bf; internet www.uemoa.int; f. 1994; replaced the Communauté économique de l'Afrique de l'ouest–CEAO; promotes regional monetary and economic convergence, and aims to improve regional trade by facilitating the movement of labour and capital between member states. The first meeting of heads of state of UEMOA member countries, held in May 1996 in Ouagadougou, agreed to establish a customs union with effect from 1 January 1998. A preferential tariff scheme, eliminating duties on most local products and reducing by 30% import duties on many Community-produced industrial goods, became operational on 1 July 1996; in addition, from 1 July, a community solidarity tax of 0.5% was imposed on all goods from third countries sold within the Community, in order to strengthen UEMOA's capacity to promote economic integration. (This was increased to 1% in December 1999.) In June 1997 the second meeting of UEMOA heads of state and government agreed to reduce import duties on industrial products originating in the Community by a further 30%. The meeting also confirmed that Côte d'Ivoire's stock exchange was to be transformed into a regional institution serving the UEMOA sub-region, in order to further economic integration (see below). At the meeting UEMOA heads of state adopted a declaration on peace and security in the region. In November UEMOA ministers of finance, meeting in extraordinary session, agreed to postpone the establishment of a customs union until 1 January 2000. In March 1998 an inter-parliamentary committee, recognized as the predecessor of a UEMOA legislature, was inaugurated in Mali. In August 1999 the committee adopted a draft treaty on the establishment of a UEMOA parliament. On 1 January 2000, according to schedule, internal tariffs were eliminated on all local products (including industrial goods) and a joint external tariff system, reportedly in five bands of between 0% and 20%, was imposed on goods deriving from outside the new customs union. Guinea-Bissau was excluded from the arrangement owing to its unstable political situation. The UEMOA member countries also belong to ECOWAS and, in accordance with an action plan adopted by the two organizations in February 2000, aim to harmonize UEMOA's economic programme with that of a planned second West African monetary union, scheduled to be established in January 2003 by the remaining—mainly anglophone—ECOWAS member states. A merger of the two complementary monetary unions is then envisaged, prior to the planned creation in January 2004 of the West African Monetary Zone. Under this new agenda the ECOWAS Parliament, inaugurated in November 2000, was to supersede UEMOA's initiative to establish a subregional legislature. Mems: Benin, Burkina Faso, Côte d'Ivoire, Guinea-Bissau, Mali, Niger, Senegal and Togo. Chair. Gen. GNAS-SINGBE EYADÉMA (Togo).

Union monétaire ouest-africaine—UMOA (West African Monetary Union): established by Treaty of November 1973, entered into force 1974; in 1990 the UMOA Banking Commission was established, which is responsible for supervising the activities of banks and financial institutions in the region, with the authority to prohibit the operation of a banking institution. UMOA constitutes an integral part of UEMOA.

Banque centrale des états de l'Afrique de l'ouest—BCEAO: ave Abdoulaye Fadiga, BP 3108, Dakar, Senegal; tel. 839-05-00; fax 823-93-35; e-mail akangni@bceao.int; internet www.bceao.int; f. 1962; central bank of issue for the mems of UEMOA; cap. and res 844,377m. francs CFA (Dec. 1999). Mems: Benin, Burkina Faso, Côte d'Ivoire, Guinea Bissau, Mali, Niger, Senegal and Togo. Gov. CHARLES KONAN BANNY (Côte d'Ivoire); Sec.-Gen. MICHEL K. KLOUSSEH (Togo). Publs *Annual Report, Notes d'Information et Statistiques*

(monthly), *Annuaire des banques, Bilan des banques et établissements financiers* (annually).

Banque ouest-africaine de développement—BOAD: 68 ave de la Libération, BP 1172, Lomé, Togo; tel. 21-42-44; fax 21-52-67; e-mail boadsiege@boad.org; internet www.boad.org; f. 1973 to promote the balanced development of mem. states and the economic integration of West Africa; auth. cap. 35,000m. francs CFA, subscribed cap. 33,680m. francs CFA (Dec. 2000). A Guarantee Fund for Private Investment in West Africa, established jtly by BOAD and the European Investment Bank, was inaugurated in Dec. 1994. The Fund aims to guarantee medium- and long-term credits to private sector businesses in the region. Mems: Benin, Burkina Faso, Côte d'Ivoire, Guinea-Bissau, Mali, Niger, Senegal, Togo. Pres. Dr YAYI BONI (Benin); Vice-Pres. ALPHA TOURÉ. Publs *Rapport Annuel, BOAD en Bref* (quarterly).

Bourse Régionale des Valeurs Mobilières—BRVM: 18 ave Joseph Anoma, BP 3802, Abidjan 01, Côte d'Ivoire; tel. 32-66-85; fax 32-66-84; f. 1998; Pres. LAMASEH ALEXIS LOOKY; Man. KOKOU GOZAN (acting).

CENTRAL AFRICA

Communauté économique et monétaire de l'Afrique centrale—CEMAC: BP 969, Bangui, Central African Republic; tel. and fax 61-21-35; e-mail sgudeac@intnet.cf; internet www.socatel .intnet.cf/accueil1.html; f. 1998; formally inaugurated as the successor to the Union douanière et économique de l'Afrique centrale (UDEAC, f. 1966) at a meeting of heads of state held in Malabo, Equatorial Guinea, in June 1999; aims to promote the process of sub-regional integration within the framework of an economic union and a monetary union; CEMAC was also to comprise a parliament and sub-regional tribunal. UDEAC established a common external tariff for imports from other countries and administered a common code for investment policy and a Solidarity Fund to counteract regional disparities of wealth and economic development. Mems: Cameroon, Central African Republic, Chad, Republic of the Congo, Equatorial Guinea, Gabon. Sec.-Gen. JEAN NKUETE.

At a summit meeting in December 1981, UDEAC leaders agreed in principle to form an economic community of Central African states (Communauté économique des états d'Afrique centrale—CEEAC), to include UDEAC members and Burundi, Rwanda, São Tomé and Príncipe and Zaire (now Democratic Republic of the Congo). CEEAC (q.v.) began operations in 1985.

Banque de développement des états de l'Afrique centrale—BDEAC: place du Gouvernement, BP 1177, Brazzaville, Republic of the Congo; tel. 81-18-85; fax 81-18-80; f. 1975; cap. 20,095m. francs CFA (June 1998); shareholders: Cameroon, Central African Republic, Chad, Republic of the Congo, Gabon, Equatorial Guinea, ADB, BEAC, France, Germany and Kuwait; Chair. AHMED LAMINE ALI; Gen. Man. EMMANUEL DOKOUNA.

Banque des états de l'Afrique centrale—BEAC: ave Mgr François Xavier Vogt, BP 1917, Yaoundé, Cameroon; tel. 23-40-30; fax 23-33-29; f. 1973 as the central bank of issue of Cameroon, the Central African Republic, Chad, Republic of the Congo, Equatorial Guinea and Gabon; a monetary market, incorporating all national financial institutions of the BEAC countries, came into effect on 1 July 1994; cap. 45,000m. francs CFA (Dec. 1998). Gov. JEAN-FÉLIX MAMALEPOT. Publs *Rapport annuel, Etudes et statistiques* (monthly).

CENTRAL ISSUING BANKS

Banque centrale des Comores: place de France, BP 405, Moroni, Comoros; tel. (73) 1002; fax (73) 0349; e-mail bcc@snpt.km; f. 1981; cap. 1,100m. Comoros francs (Dec. 1997); Gov. SAÏD AHMED SAÏD ALI.

Banque centrale des états de l'Afrique de l'ouest: see above.

Banque des états de l'Afrique centrale: see above.

Banque de France: 39 rue Croix-des-Petits-Champs, BP 140-01, 75049 Paris Cédex 01, France; tel. 1-42-92-42-92; fax 1-42-96-04-23; internet www.banque-france.fr; f. 1800; bank of issue for Metropolitan France; Gov. JEAN-CLAUDE TRICHET; Dep. Govs HERVÉ HANNOUN; JEAN-PAUL REDOUIN.

Institut d'émission des départements d'outre-mer—IEDOM: 5 rue Roland Barthes, 75598 Paris Cédex 12, France; tel. 1-53-44-41-41; fax 1-44-87-99-62; internet www.iedom-ieom.com; f. 1959; issuing authority for the French Overseas Departments and the French Overseas Collectivités Territoriales of St Pierre and Miquelon, and Mayotte; Dir-Gen. ANTOINE POUILLIEUTE; Dir GILLES AUDREN.

Institut d'émission d'outre-mer—IEOM: 5 rue Roland Barthes, 75598 Paris Cédex 12, France; tel. 1-53-44-41-41; fax 1-44-87-99-62; internet www.iedom-ieom.com; f. 1966; issuing authority for the French Overseas Territories; Pres. DENIS FERMAN; Dir-Gen. ANTOINE POUILLIEUTE; Dir FULVIO MAZZÉO.

FRENCH ECONOMIC AID

France's connection with the African Franc Zone countries involves not only monetary arrangements, but also includes comprehensive

French assistance in the forms of budget support, foreign aid, technical assistance and subsidies on commodity exports.

Official French financial aid and technical assistance to developing countries is administered by the following agencies:

Agence française de développement—AFD: 5 rue Roland Barthes, 75598 Paris Cédex 12, France; tel. 1-53-44-31-31; fax 1-44-87-99-39; e-mail com@afd.fr; internet www.afd.fr/; f. 1941; fmrly the Caisse française de développement—CFD; French development bank which lends money to member states and former member states of the Franc Zone and several other states, and executes the financial operations of the FAC (see below). Following the devaluation of the franc CFA in January 1994, the French Government cancelled some 25,000m. French francs in debt arrears owed by member states to the CFD. The CFD established a Special

Fund for Development and the Exceptional Facility for Short-term Financing to help alleviate the immediate difficulties resulting from the devaluation. A total of FFr 4,600m. of financial assistance was awarded to Franc Zone countries in 1994. In early 1994 the CFD made available funds totalling 2,420m. francs CFA to assist the establishment of CEMAC (see above). Serves as the secretariat for the Fonds français pour l'environnement mondial (f. 1994). Dir-Gen. ANTOINE POUILLIEUTE.

Fonds de Solidarité Prioritaire (FSP): 20 rue Monsieur, 75007 Paris, France; tel. 1-53-69-00-00; fax 1-53-69-43-82; f. 2000, taking over from the Fonds d'aide et de coopération (f. 1959) the administration of subsidies and loans from the French Government to the former French African states. FSP is administered by the Ministry of Co-operation, which allocates budgetary funds to it.

INTER-AMERICAN DEVELOPMENT BANK—IDB

Address: 1300 New York Ave, NW, Washington, DC 20577, USA.

Telephone: (202) 623-1000; **fax:** (202) 623-3096; **internet:** www.iadb.org.

The Bank was founded in 1959 to promote the individual and collective development of Latin American and Caribbean countries through the financing of economic and social development projects and the provision of technical assistance. Membership was increased in 1976 and 1977 to include countries outside the region.

MEMBERS

Argentina	Ecuador	Norway
Austria	El Salvador	Panama
Bahamas	Finland	Paraguay
Barbados	France	Peru
Belgium	Germany	Portugal
Belize	Guatemala	Slovenia
Bolivia	Guyana	Spain
Brazil	Haiti	Suriname
Canada	Honduras	Sweden
Chile	Israel	Switzerland
Colombia	Italy	Trinidad and
Costa Rica	Jamaica	Tobago
Croatia	Japan	United Kingdom
Denmark	Mexico	USA
Dominican	Netherlands	Uruguay
Republic	Nicaragua	Venezuela

Organization

(April 2001)

BOARD OF GOVERNORS

All the powers of the Bank are vested in a Board of Governors, consisting of one Governor and one alternate appointed by each member country (usually ministers of finance or presidents of central banks). The Board meets annually, with special meetings when necessary. The 42nd annual meeting of the Board of Governors took place in Santiago, Chile, in March 2001.

BOARD OF EXECUTIVE DIRECTORS

The Board of Executive Directors is responsible for the operations of the Bank. It establishes the Bank's policies, approves loan and technical co-operation proposals that are submitted by the President of the Bank, and authorizes the Bank's borrowings on capital markets.

There are 12 executive directors and 12 alternates. Each Director is elected by a group of two or more countries, except the Directors representing Canada and the USA. The USA holds 30% of votes on the Board, in respect of its contribution to the Bank's capital. The Board has four standing committees, relating to: Policy and evaluation; Organization, human resources and board matters; Budget, financial policies and audit; and Programming. A steering committee was established in 1997. A new Office of Evaluation and Oversight, reporting directly to the Board, was established in 2000 as part of a reorganization of the Bank's evaluation system.

ADMINISTRATION

In 1994 the Bank reorganized its administrative structure, in order to improve management accountability and efficiency, to strengthen

country focus and regional co-operation and to address the region's priorities. The Bank currently comprises three Regional Operations Departments, as well as the following departments: Finance; Legal; Research; Integration and Regional Programmes; Private Sector; External Relations; Sustainable Development; Information Technology and General Services; Strategic Planning and Budget; and Human Resources. In addition, there is an Office of the Chief Economist, an Evaluation Office, an Office of the Multilateral Investment Fund, and an External Relations Advisor. The Bank has country offices in each of its borrowing member states, and special offices in Paris, France and in Tokyo, Japan. At the end of 2000 there were 1,719 Bank staff (excluding the Board of Executive Directors and the Evaluation Office). The administrative budget for 2000 amounted to US $346.8m.

President: ENRIQUE V. IGLESIAS (Uruguay).

Executive Vice-President: K. BURKE DILLON (USA).

Activities

Loans are made to governments, and to public and private entities, for specific economic and social development projects and for sectoral reforms. These loans are repayable in the currencies lent and their terms range from 12 to 40 years. Total lending authorized by the Bank by the end of 2000 amounted to US $106,607m. During 2000 the Bank approved loans totalling $5,266m., compared with $9,486m. in 1999. Disbursements on authorized loans amounted to $7,069m. in 2000, compared with $8,387m. in the previous year.

The subscribed ordinary capital stock, including inter-regional capital, which was merged into it in 1987, totalled US $100,959.4m. at the end of 2000, of which $4,340.7m. was paid-in and $96,618.7m. was callable. The callable capital constitutes, in effect, a guarantee of the securities which the Bank issues in the capital markets in order to increase its resources available for lending. Replenishments are usually made every four years. In July 1995 the eighth general increase of the Bank's authorized capital was ratified by member countries: the Bank's resources were to be increased by $41,000m. to $102,000m.

In 2000 the Bank borrowed the equivalent of US $8,139m. on the international capital markets, bringing total borrowings outstanding to more than $41,394m. at the end of the year. During 2000 net earnings amounted to $846m. in ordinary capital resources and $135m. from the Fund for Special Operations (see below), and at the end of that year the Bank's total reserves were $8,591m.

The Fund for Special Operations enables the Bank to make concessional loans for economic and social projects where circumstances call for special treatment, such as lower interest rates and longer repayment terms than those applied to loans from the ordinary resources. The Board of Governors approved US $200m. in new contributions to the Fund in 1990, and in 1995 authorized $1,000m. in extra resources for the Fund. During 2000 the Fund made 22 loans totalling $297m., compared with loans amounting to $417m. in the previous year.

In January 1993 a Multilateral Investment Fund was established, as an autonomous fund administered by the Bank, to promote private sector development in the region. The 21 Bank members who signed the initial draft agreement in 1992 to establish the Fund pledged to contribute US $1,200m. The Fund's activities are undertaken through three separate facilities concerned with technical co-operation, human resources development and small enterprise development. In 2000 a specialist working group, established to consider MIF operations, recommended that it target its resources on the following core areas of activity: small business development; microenterprise; market functioning; and financial and capital markets. During 2000 the Fund approved $115m. for 78 projects, including $10m. to support the establishment of a special contingency fund for the rehabilitation of small businesses following natural disasters, bringing the cumulative total approved to $661m. for 386 projects since the Fund began operations.

In 1998 the Bank agreed to participate in a joint initiative by the International Monetary Fund and the World Bank to assist heavily indebted poor countries (HIPCs) to maintain a sustainable level of debt (see p. 81). Four member countries were eligible for assistance under the initiative (Bolivia, Guyana, Honduras and Nicaragua). Also in 1998, following projections of reduced resources for the Fund for Special Operations, borrowing member countries agreed to convert about US $2,400m. in local currencies held by the Bank, in order to maintain a convertible concessional Fund for poorer countries, and to help to reduce the debt-servicing payments under the HIPC initiative. In mid-2000 a committee of the Board of Governors endorsed a financial framework for the Bank's participation in an Enhanced HIPC Initiative, which aimed to broaden the eligibility criteria and accelerate the process of debt reduction. The Bank's total contribution to the initiative was estimated to be $1,100m.

In late 1998 the Board of Governors endorsed the establishment of an Emergency Loan Programme, for a one-year period, in order to help to mitigate the effects of the global financial crisis. Funds totalling US $9,000m. were to be made available under the Programme, which was to enable the bank to make large disbursements under special terms. Two emergency loans were approved in 1998, including a loan to Argentina for $2,500m., the largest amount ever approved by the Bank. In December the Bank established an emergency Consultative Group for the Reconstruction and Transformation of Central America to co-ordinate assistance to countries that had suffered extensive damage as a result of Hurricane Mitch. The Bank hosted the first meeting of the Group in the same month, which was attended by government officials, representatives of donor agencies and non-governmental organizations and academics. A total of $6,200m. was pledged in the form of emergency aid, longer-term financing and debt relief. A second meeting of the Group was held in May 1999, in Stockholm, Sweden, at which the assistance package was increased to some $9,000m., of which the Bank and World Bank committed $5,300m. In March 2001 the Consultative Group convened, in Madrid, Spain, to promote integration and foreign investment in Central America. The meeting, organized by the Bank, was also used to generate $1,300m. in commitments from international donors to assist emergency relief and reconstruction efforts in El Salvador following an earthquake earlier in the year.

An increasing number of donor countries have placed funds under the Bank's administration for assistance to Latin America, outside the framework of the Ordinary Resources and the Bank's Special Operations. These trust funds, totalling some 58 in 2000, include the Social Progress Trust Fund (set up by the USA in 1961); the Venezuelan Trust Fund (set up in 1975); the Japan Special Fund (1988); and other funds administered on behalf of Austria, Belgium, Canada, Denmark, Finland, France, Israel, Italy, Japan, the Netherlands, Norway, Portugal, Spain, Sweden, Switzerland, the United Kingdom and the EU. A Program for the Development of Technical Co-operation was established in 1991, which is financed by European countries and the EU. Total cumulative lending from all these trust funds was $1,724.4m. for loans approved by the end of 2000, of which $1,650.4m. had been disbursed. During 2000 projects involved cofinancing by bilateral and multilateral sources amounting to $1,888.5m., of which $1,329.7m. was provided by the World Bank.

Following the capital increase approved in 1989, the Bank was to undertake sectoral lending for the first time, devoting up to 25% of its financing in 1990–93 to loans which would allow countries to make policy changes and improve their institutions. An environmental protection division was also formed in 1989. In December 1993 a task force presented a report on the Bank's operations to the Board of Executive Directors, which recommended greater responsibility for country offices throughout the project cycle; greater emphasis on development results, as opposed to lending targets; increased training for the personnel involved in implementing projects; and increased lending to social and poverty reduction programmes. A high-level Social Agenda Policy Group was created in 1993 to investigate the most effective means of supporting social reform in borrowing countries. In 1994 the Bank established an Independent Investigation Mechanism to assess Bank-financed projects, at the request of populations likely to be directly affected, in terms of their policy design and management. Under the eighth general increase of the Bank's resources priority areas of operation were designated as poverty reduction and social equity; modernization of state organs; and the environment. During 1995 an inter-departmental working group on poverty was established, in order to identify policies and projects likely to be effective in reducing poverty. In 1997 an inter-departmental working group was established with the aim of helping member countries to combat corruption and to promote transparency in the Bank's own lending procedures.

The Bank provides technical co-operation to help member countries to identify and prepare new projects, to improve loan execution, to strengthen the institutional capacity of public and private agencies, to address extreme conditions of poverty and to promote small- and micro-enterprise development. The Bank has established a special co-operation programme to facilitate the transfer of experience and technology among regional programmes. In 2000 the Bank approved 356 technical co-operation operations, totalling US $66.7m., mainly financed by income from the Fund for Special Operations and donor trust funds. The Bank supports the efforts of the countries of the region to achieve economic integration and has provided extensive technical support for the formulation of integration strategies in the Andean, Central American and Southern Cone regions. The Bank is also supporting the initiative to establish a Free Trade Area of the Americas (FTAA) by 2005 and has provided technical assistance, developed programming strategies and produced a number of studies on relevant integration and trade issues.

INSTITUTIONS

Instituto para la Integración de América Latina y el Caribe (Institute for the Integration of Latin America and the Caribbean): Esmeralda 130, 16° and 17°, 1035 Buenos Aires, Argentina; tel. (1) 4320-1850; fax (1) 4320-1865; e-mail int/inl@iadb.org; internet www.iadb.org/intal; f. 1965 under the auspices of the Inter-American Development Bank; forms part of the Bank's Integration and Regional Programmes Department. The Institute undertakes research on all aspects of regional integration and co-operation and issues related to international trade, hemispheric integration and relations with other regions and countries of the world. Activities come under four main headings: regional and national technical co-operation projects on integration; policy fora; integration fora; and journals and information. A Documentation Center holds 100,000 documents, 12,000 books and 400 periodical titles. Dir JUAN JOSÉ TACCONE. Publs *Integración y Comercio/Integration and Trade* (3 a year), *Carta Mensual/Monthly Newsletter, Informe Mercosur/Mercosur Report* (2 a year).

Inter-American Institute for Social Development—INDES: 1300 New York Ave, NW, Washington, DC, 20057, USA; internet www.iadb.org/indes; commenced operations in 1995; aims to support the training of senior officials from public sector institutions and organizations involved with social policies and social services. INDES organizes specialized sub-regional courses and seminars and national training programmes. It produces teaching materials and also serves as a forum for the exchange of ideas on social reform. By the end of 2000 INDES had provided training for some 5,000 people.

Inter-American Investment Corporation—IIC: 1300 New York Ave, NW, Washington, DC 20057, USA; tel. (202) 623-3900; fax

Distribution of loans (US $ million)

Sector	2000	%	1961–2000	%
Productive Sectors				
Agriculture and fisheries . .	165	3.1	11,973	11.2
Industry, mining and tourism	311	5.9	10,577	9.9
Science and technology . .	133	2.5	1,676	1.6
Physical Infrastructure				
Energy	437	8.3	16,415	15.4
Transportation and communications . . .	435	8.3	12,827	12.0
Social Sectors				
Sanitation	145	2.8	9,015	8.5
Urban development . . .	685	13.0	6,655	6.2
Education	271	5.2	4,467	4.2
Social investment . . .	618	11.7	7,427	7.0
Health	10.6	0.2	2,139	2.0
Environment	142	2.7	1,493	1.4
Microenterprise . . .	0	0.0	386	0.4
Other				
Public-sector reform and modernization . . .	1,885	35.8	17,710	16.6
Export financing . . .	17	0.3	1,546	1.4
Other	12	0.2	2,302	2.2
Total	**5,266**	**100.0**	**106,607**	**100.0**

Source: *Annual Report, 2000.*

(202) 623-2360; e-mail iicmail@iadb.org; internet www. iadb.org/iic; f. 1986 as a legally autonomous affiliate of the Inter-American Development Bank, to promote the economic development of the region; commenced operations in 1989. The IIC's initial capital stock was US $200m., of which 55% was contributed by developing member nations, 25.3% by the USA, and the remainder by non-regional members. In total, the IIC has 37 shareholders (26 Latin American and Caribbean countries, eight European countries, Israel, Japan and the USA). Emphasis is placed on investment in small and medium-sized enterprises without access to other suitable sources of equity or long-term loans. In 2000 the IIC approved equity investments and loans totalling $143m. for 19 transactions. In that year the Board of Governors of the IADB agreed to increase the IIC's capital by $500m. Gen. Man. JACQUES ROGOZINSKI. Publ. *Annual Report* (in English, French, Portuguese and Spanish).

Publications

Annual Report (in English, Spanish, Portuguese and French).

Annual Report on the Environment and Natural Resources (in English and Spanish).

Economic and Social Progress in Latin America (annually, in English and Spanish).

IDB América (monthly, English and Spanish).

IDB Projects (10 a year, in English).

Proceedings of the Annual Meeting of the Boards of Governors of the IDB and IIC (in English, Spanish, Portuguese and French).

The IDB (monthly, in English and Spanish).

Brochure series, occasional papers, working papers, reports.

INTERGOVERNMENTAL AUTHORITY ON DEVELOPMENT—IGAD

Address: BP 2653, Djibouti.

Telephone: 354050; **fax:** 356994; **e-mail:** igad@intnet.dj.

The Intergovernmental Authority on Development (IGAD) was established in 1996 to supersede the Intergovernmental Authority on Drought and Development (IGADD), founded in 1986 to co-ordinate measures to combat the effects of drought and desertification and attain regional food security.

MEMBERS

Djibouti	Kenya	Sudan
Eritrea	Somalia	Uganda
Ethiopia		

Organization

(April 2001)

ASSEMBLY

The Assembly, consisting of heads of state and of government of member states, is the supreme policy-making organ of the Authority. It holds a summit meeting at least once a year. The eighth Assembly meeting of heads of state and of government was held in Khartoum, Sudan in November 2000. The chairmanship of the Assembly rotates among the member countries on an annual basis.

Chairman (2000/01): Lt-Gen. OMAR HASSAN AHMAD AL-BASHIR (Sudan).

COUNCIL OF MINISTERS

The Council of Ministers is composed of the minister of foreign affairs and one other minister from each member state. It meets at least twice a year and approves the work programme and the annual budget of the Secretariat.

COMMITTEE OF AMBASSADORS

The Committee of Ambassadors comprises the ambassadors or plenipotentiaries of member states to Djibouti. It convenes as regularly as required to advise and assist the Executive Secretary concerning the interpretation of policies and guide-lines and the realization of the annual work programme.

SECRETARIAT

The Secretariat, the executive body of IGAD, is headed by the Executive Secretary, who is appointed by the Assembly for a term of four years, renewable once. In addition to the Office of the Executive Secretary, the Secretariat comprises the following three divisions: Agriculture and Environment; Economic Co-operation; and Political and Humanitarian Affairs.

Executive Secretary: Dr ATALLA HAMAD BASHIR (Sudan).

Activities

IGADD was established in 1986 by Djibouti, Ethiopia, Kenya, Somalia, Sudan and Uganda, to combat the effects of aridity and desertification, as a result of the severe drought and famine that had affected the Horn of Africa during the early 1980s. Eritrea became a member of IGADD in September 1993, following its proclamation as an independent state. In April 1995, at an extraordinary summit meeting held in Addis Ababa, Ethiopia, heads of state and of government resolved to reorganize and expand the Authority. In March 1996 IGAD was endorsed to supersede IGADD, at a second extraordinary summit meeting of heads of state and of government, held in Nairobi, Kenya. The meeting led to the adoption of an agreement for a new organizational structure and the approval of an extended mandate to co-ordinate and harmonize policy in the areas of economic co-operation and political and humanitarian affairs, in addition to its existing responsibilities for food security and environmental protection.

IGAD aims to achieve regional co-operation and economic integration. To facilitate this IGAD assists the governments of member states to maximize resources and co-ordinates efforts to initiate and implement regional development programmes and projects. In this context, IGAD promotes the harmonization of policies relating to agriculture and natural resources, communications, customs, trade and transport; the implementation of pro-grammes in the fields of social sciences, research, science and technology; and effective participation in the global economy. Meetings between IGAD foreign affairs ministers and the IGAD Joint Partners' Forum, comprising the grouping's donors, are convened periodically to discuss issues such as food security and humanitarian affairs.

FOOD SECURITY AND ENVIRONMENTAL PROTECTION

IGAD seeks to achieve regional food security, the sustainable development of natural resources and environmental protection, and to encourage and assist member states in their efforts to combat the consequences of drought and other natural and man-made disasters. The region suffers from recurrent droughts, which severely impede crop and livestock production. Natural and man-made disasters increase the strain on resources, resulting in annual food deficits. About 80% of the IGAD sub-region is classified as arid or semi-arid, and some 40% of the region is unproductive, owing to severe environmental degradation. Priority areas of activity to improve food security and preserve natural resources during 1997–2001 included: the introduction of remote-sensing services; a Marketing Information System and a Regional Integrated Information System; the establishment of training and credit schemes for fishermen; research into the sustainable production of drought-resistant, high-yielding crop varieties; transboundary livestock disease control and vaccine production; the control of environmental pollution; the promotion of alternative sources of energy in the home; the management of integrated water resources; the promotion of community-based land husbandry; training programmes in grain marketing; and the implementation of the International Convention to Combat Desertification.

ECONOMIC CO-OPERATION

The Economic Co-operation division concentrates on the development of a co-ordinated infrastructure for the region, in particular in the areas of transport and communications, to promote foreign, cross-border and domestic trade and investment opportunities. IGAD seeks to harmonize national transport and trade policy and thereby facilitate the free movement of people, goods and services.

The improvements to infrastructure also aim to facilitate more timely interventions to conflicts, disasters and emergencies in the sub-region. Projects to be undertaken by the end of 2001 included: the construction of missing segments of the Trans-African Highway and the Pan African Telecommunications Network; the removal of barriers to trade and communications; improvements to ports and inland container terminals; and the modernization of railway and telecommunications services. In November 2000 the IGAD Assembly determined to establish an integrated rail network connecting all member countries. In addition, the heads of state and government considered the possibility of drafting legislation to facilitate the expansion of intra-IGAD trade.

POLITICAL AND HUMANITARIAN AFFAIRS

The field of political and humanitarian affairs focuses on conflict prevention, management and resolution through dialogue. The division's primary aim is to restore peace and stability to member countries affected by conflict, in order that resources may be diverted for development purposes. Efforts have been pursued to strengthen capacity for conflict prevention and to relieve humanitarian crises. In September 1995 negotiations between the Sudanese Government and opposition leaders were initiated, under the auspices of IGAD, with the aim of resolving the conflict in southern Sudan; these have subsequently been reconvened periodically. In March 2001 IGAD's mediation committee on southern Sudan, chaired by President Daniel arap Moi of Kenya, publicized a seven-point plan for a peaceful settlement of the conflict. In May–August 2000 a conference aimed at securing peace in Somalia was convened in Arta, Djibouti, under the auspices of IGAD. The conference appointed a transitional Somali legislature, which then elected an interim national president. The eighth summit of IGAD heads of state and government, held in Khartoum, Sudan, in November, welcomed the conclusion in September of an agreement of reconciliation between the new Somali interim administration and a prominent opposition alliance, and determined that those member countries that neighboured Somalia (Djibouti, Ethiopia and Kenya) should co-operate in assisting the process of reconstruction and reconciliation in that country. The summit appointed a special envoy to implement IGAD's directives concerning the Somali situation. Following the violent escalation of a border dispute between Eritrea and Ethiopia in mid-1998 IGAD supported efforts by the Organization of African Unity (q.v.) to mediate a cease-fire between the two sides. This was achieved in mid-2000.

Publications

Agromet Bulletin (quarterly).

Annual Report.

Food Situation Report (quarterly).

IGAD News (2 a year).

Proceedings of the Summit of Heads of State and Government.

Reports of the Council of Ministers' Meetings.

INTERNATIONAL CHAMBER OF COMMERCE—ICC

Address: 38 Cours Albert 1er, 75008 Paris, France.

Telephone: 1-49-53-28-28; **fax:** 1-49-53-29-42; **e-mail:** icc@iccwbo.org; **internet:** www.iccwbo.org.

The ICC was founded in 1919 to promote free trade and private enterprise, provide practical services and represent business interests at governmental and inter-governmental levels.

MEMBERS

At the end of 1998 membership consisted of about 5,500 individual corporations and 1,700 organizations (mainly trade and industrial organizations and chambers of commerce). National Committees or Groups have been formed in some 70 countries and territories to co-ordinate ICC objectives and functions at the national level.

Argentina	Hong Kong	Philippines
Australia	Hungary	Poland
Austria	Iceland	Portugal
Bahrain	India	Russia
Bangladesh	Indonesia	Saudi Arabia
Belgium	Iran	Senegal
Brazil	Ireland	Singapore
Burkina Faso	Israel	South Africa
Canada	Italy	Spain
Chile	Japan	Sri Lanka
China, People's	Jordan	Sweden
Republic	Korea, Republic	Switzerland
Colombia	Kuwait	Syria
Cuba	Lebanon	Taiwan*
Cyprus	Lithuania	Thailand
Czech Republic	Luxembourg	Togo
Denmark	Mexico	Tunisia
Ecuador	Morocco	Turkey
Egypt	Netherlands	Ukraine
Finland	New Zealand	United Kingdom
France	Nigeria	USA
Germany	Norway	Uruguay
Ghana	Pakistan	Venezuela
Greece	Peru	Yugoslavia

* Admitted as Chinese Taipei.

Organization

(April 2001)

COUNCIL

The Council is the governing body of the organization. It meets twice a year and is composed of members nominated by the National Committees. Ten direct members, from countries where no National Committee exists, may also be invited to participate. The Council elects the President and Vice-President for terms of two years.

President: RICHARD D. McCORMICK (USA).

EXECUTIVE BOARD

The Executive Board consists of 15–30 members appointed by the Council on the recommendation of the President and nine *ex-officio* members. Members serve for a three-year term, one-third of the members retiring at the end of each year. It ensures close direction of ICC activities and meets at least three times each year.

INTERNATIONAL SECRETARIAT

The ICC secretariat is based at International Headquarters in Paris, with additional offices maintained in Geneva and New York principally for liaison with the United Nations and its agencies. The Secretary-General is appointed by the Council on the recommendation of the Executive Board.

Secretary-General: MARIA LIVANOS CATTAUI (SWITZERLAND).

NATIONAL COMMITTEES AND GROUPS

Each affiliate is composed of leading business organizations and individual companies. It has its own secretariat, monitors issues of concern to its national constituents, and draws public and government attention to ICC policies.

CONGRESS

The ICC's supreme assembly, to which all member companies and organizations are invited to send senior representatives. Congresses are held regulary, in a different place on each occasion, with up to 2,000 participants. The 32nd Congress took place in Shanghai, People's Republic of China, in April 1997 and the 33rd Congress was held in Budapest, Hungary, in May 2000, on the theme of 'The New Europe in the World Economy'.

CONFERENCES

ICC Conferences was created in 1996 to disseminate ICC expertise in the fields of international arbitration, trade, banking and commercial practice, by means of a world-wide programme of conferences and seminars.

Activities

The various Commissions of the ICC (listed below) are composed of at least 500 practising business executives and experts from all sectors of economic life, nominated by National Committees. ICC recommendations must be adopted by a Commission following consultation with National Committees, and then approved by the Council or Executive Board, before they can be regarded as official ICC policies. Meetings of Commissions are generally held twice a year. Working Parties are frequently constituted by Commissions to undertake specific projects and report back to their parent body. Officers of Commissions, and specialized Working Parties, often meet in the intervals between Commission sessions. The Commissions produce a wide array of specific codes and guide-lines of direct use to the world business community; draw up statements and initiatives for presentation to governments and international bodies; and comment constructively and in detail on proposed actions by intergovernmental organizations that are likely to affect business.

ICC works closely with other international organizations. ICC members, the heads of UN economic organizations and the OECD convene for annual discussions on the world economy. The Commission on International Trade and Investment Policy campaigns against protectionism in world trade and in support of the World Trade Organization (WTO, q.v.). The ICC also works closely with the European Union, commenting on EU directives and making recommendations on, for example, tax harmonization and laws relating to competition.

ICC plays a part in combating international crime connected with commerce through its Commercial Crime Services, based in London, United Kingdom, and Kuala Lumpur, Malaysia. These comprise: the Commercial Crime Bureau; the International Maritime Bureau, which combats maritime fraud, including insurance fraud and the theft of cargoes; and the Counterfeiting Intelligence Bureau, established in 1985 to investigate counterfeiting in trade-marked goods, copyrights and industrial designs. Commercial disputes are submitted to the ICC International Court of Arbitration. The Court received some 541 requests for arbitration in 2000. In January 1997 the ICC opened its first regional office, in the Hong Kong Special Administrative Region. The office now also provides the secretariat for the Hong Kong, China Business Council, established in December 1998 to promote the region's business interests abroad.

In 1998 the ICC continued to develop rules and guide-lines relating to electronic transactions, including guide-lines for ethical advertising on the internet and for data protection. In September it presented model clauses for company contracts involving the electronic transfer of personal information. The Geneva Business Dialogue was held in Switzerland in September. The primary subjects discussed were the importance of globalization in business and the need to avoid protectionist reactions to economic upheaval. In September 1999 ICC published a fully revised and updated version of the standard commercial terms for international sales contracts, Incoterms 2000, which define the responsibilities of buyers and sellers.

Policy and Technical Commissions:

Commission on Air Transport
Commission on Banking Technique and Practice
Commission on Energy
Commission on Environment
Commission on Extortion and Bribery
Commission on Financial Services
Commission on Insurance
Commission on Intellectual and Industrial Property
Commission on International Arbitration
Commission on International Commercial Practice
Commission on International Trade and Investment Policy
Commission on Law and Practices Relating to Competition
Commission on Maritime and Surface Transport
Commission on Marketing, Advertising and Distribution
Commission on Taxation
Commission on Telecommunications and Information Technologies

Bodies for the Settlement of Disputes:

International Centre for Technical Expertise
International Court of Arbitration
International Maritime Arbitration Organization

Other Bodies:

ICC Centre for Maritime Co-operation
ICC Commercial Crime Bureau
ICC Corporate Security Services
ICC Counterfeiting Intelligence Bureau
ICC Cybercrime Unit
ICC Institute of International Business Law and Practice
ICC International Maritime Bureau
ICC-WTO Economic Consultative Committee
Institute of World Business Law
International Bureau of Chambers of Commerce

Finance

The International Chamber of Commerce is a private organization financed partly by contributions from National Committees and other members, according to the economic importance of the country which each represents, and partly by revenue from fees for various services and from sales of publications.

Publications

Annual Report.
Business World (electronic magazine).
Documentary Credits Insight (quarterly).
Handbook.
ICC Contact (newsletter).
ICC International Court of Arbitration Bulletin.
IGO Report.
Numerous publications on general and technical business and trade-related subjects.

INTERNATIONAL CONFEDERATION OF FREE TRADE UNIONS—ICFTU

Address: 5 blvd Roi Albert II, 1210 Brussels, Belgium.

Telephone: (2) 224-02-11; **fax:** (2) 201-58-15; **e-mail:** internet po@icftu.org; **internet:** www.icftu.org.

ICFTU was founded in 1949 by trade union federations which had withdrawn from the World Federation of Trade Unions (see p. 291). It aims to promote the interests of working people and to secure recognition of workers' organizations as free bargaining agents; to reduce the gap between rich and poor; and to defend fundamental human and trade union rights. During 1996 it campaigned for the adoption by the World Trade Organization of a social clause, with legally-binding minimum labour standards. In 1998 it participated in negotiations on the introduction of ethical codes of conduct into global corporations in the energy sector. In early 2001 ICTFU launched a two-year campaign to promote the eradication of child labour; the agricultural sector, believed to employ about 70% of all child labourers, was to be targeted in particular. See also the World Confederation of Labour (p. 289).

MEMBERS

221 organizations in 148 countries with 155m. members (April 2001).

Organization

(April 2001)

WORLD CONGRESS

The Congress, the highest authority of ICFTU, normally meets every four years. The 16th Congress was held in Brussels, Belgium, in June 1996. The 17th Congress met in Durban, South Africa, in April 2000.

Delegations from national federations vary in size according to membership. The Congress examines past activities, maps out future plans, elects the Executive Board and the General Secretary, considers the functioning of the regional machinery, examines financial reports and social, economic and political situations. It works through plenary sessions and through technical committees which report to the plenary sessions.

EXECUTIVE BOARD

The Board meets not less than once a year, for about three days, usually at Brussels, or at the Congress venue; it comprises 53 members elected by Congress and nominated by areas of the world. The General Secretary is an *ex-officio* member. After each Congress the Board elects a President and at least seven Vice-Presidents.

The Board considers administrative questions; hears reports from field representatives, missions, regional organizations and affiliates, and makes resultant decisions; and discusses finances, applications for affiliation, and problems affecting world labour. It elects a steering committee of 19 to deal with urgent matters between Board meetings.

President: FACKSON SHAMENDA (ZAMBIA).

PERMANENT COMMITTEES

Steering Committee. Administers the General Fund, comprising affiliation fees, and the International Solidarity Fund, constituting additional voluntary contributions.

Economic and Social Committee.

Human and Trade Union Rights Committee.

*ICFTU/ITS Working Party on Trade Union Education.

*ICFTU/ITS Occupational Health, Safety, and the Environment Working Party.

*ICFTU/ITS Working Party on Multinational Companies.

Peace, Security and Disarmament Committee.

Youth Committee.

Women's Committee.

*A joint body of the ICFTU and International Trade Secretariats.

SECRETARIAT

The headquarters staff numbers 75, comprising some 25 different nationalities.

The six departments are: Economic and Social Policy; Trade Union Rights; Projects, Co-ordination and Education (comprising units for Projects and Trade Union Education); Equality (including Youth); Finance and Administration; Press and Publications. There are also the Co-ordination Unit for Central and Eastern Europe, the Electronic Data Processing Unit, Personnel, Co-ordination and Regional Liaison Desks for the Americas, Africa and Asia.

General Secretary: WILLIAM (BILL) JORDAN (United Kingdom).

BRANCH OFFICES

ICFTU Geneva Office: 46 ave Blanc, 1202 Geneva, Switzerland; tel. (22) 7384202; fax (22) 7381082; e-mail icftu-ge@geneva.icftu.org; Dir DAN CUNNIAH.

ICFTU Moscow Office: Leninsky Prospekt 42, 117119 Moscow, Russia; tel. (95) 9387356; fax (95) 9387304; e-mail icftumos@cq.ru.

ICFTU United Nations Office: Room 404, 104 East 40th St, New York, NY 10016, USA; tel. (212) 986-1820; fax (212) 972-9746; e-mail icftuny@igc.org; Perm. Rep. GEMMA ADABA.

There are also Permanent Representatives accredited to FAO (Rome) to the UN, UNIDO and IAEA (Vienna) and to UNEP and UNCHS (Habitat) (Nairobi).

REGIONAL ORGANIZATIONS

ICFTU African Regional Organization—AFRO: POB 67273, Ambank House, 14th Floor, University Way, Nairobi, Kenya; tel. (2) 221357; fax (2) 215072; e-mail info@ictfu.afro.org; f. 1957. Mems: 5m. workers in 36 African countries; Pres. MADIA DIOP (Senegal); Gen. Sec. ANDREW KAILEMBO (Tanzania).

ICFTU Asian and Pacific Regional Organization—APRO: 73 Bras Basah Rd, 4th Floor, Singapore 189556; tel. (65) 2226294; fax (65) 2217380; e-mail gs@icftu-apro.org; internet www.icftu-apro.org; f. 1951. Mems: 33m. in 38 orgs in 29 countries. Pres. KENNETH G. DOUGLAS; Gen. Sec. NORIYUKI SUZUKI.

Inter-American Regional Organization of Workers—ORIT: Edif. José Vargas, Avda Andrés Eloy Blanco No 2, 15°, Los Caobos, Caracas, Venezuela; tel. (2) 578-3538; fax (2) 578-1702; e-mail sec-genorit@cantv.net; internet www.orit-ciosl.org; f. 1951. Mems: national unions in 28 countries and territories. Pres. A. MADARIAGA; Gen. Sec. LUIS A. ANDERSON.

There are Field Representatives in various parts of Africa. In addition, a number of Project Planners for development co-operation travel in different countries.

Finance

Affiliated federations pay a standard fee of €161.8 (2001) (2002 fee: €165.1), or its equivalent in other currencies, per 1,000 members per annum, which covers the establishment and routine activities of the ICFTU headquarters in Brussels, and partly subsidizes the regional organizations.

An International Solidarity Fund was set up in 1956 to assist unions in developing countries, and workers and trade unionists victimized by repressive political measures. It provides legal assistance and supports educational activities. In cases of major natural disasters affecting workers token relief aid is granted.

Publications

Survey of Violations of Trade Union Rights (annually).

Trade Union World (official journal, monthly).

These periodicals are issued in English, French and Spanish. In addition the Congress report is issued in English. Numerous other publications on labour, economic and trade union training have been published in various languages.

Associated International Trade Secretariats

Education International—EI: 5 blvd Roi Albert II (8ème étage), 1210 Brussels, Belgium; tel. (2) 224-06-11; fax (2) 224-06-06; e-mail headoffice@ei-ie.org; internet www.ei-ie.org; f. 1993 by merger of the World Confederation of Organizations of the Teaching Profession (f. 1952) and the International Federation of Free Teachers' Unions (f. 1951). Mems: 294 national orgs of teachers' trade unions representing 23m. members in 152 countries and territories. Holds Congress (every three years): July 2001 in Kathmandu, Nepal. Pres. MARY HATWOOD FUTRELL (USA); Sec.-Gen. FRED VAN LEEUWEN (Netherlands). Publs *EI Monitor* (monthly), *Education International* (quarterly) (both in English, French and Spanish).

International Federation of Building and Woodworkers—IFBWW: 54 route des Acacias, POB 1412, 1227 Carouge, Switzerland; tel. (22) 827-37-77; fax (22) 827-37-70; e-mail info@ifbww.org; internet www.ifbww.org; f. 1934. Mems: 285 national unions with a membership of more than 11.0m. workers in 124 countries. Organization: Congress, Executive Committee. Pres. ROEL DE VRIES (Netherlands); Sec.-Gen. ULF ASP (Sweden). Publ. *Bulletin* (8 a year).

International Federation of Chemical, Energy, Mine and General Workers' Unions—ICEM: 109 ave Emile de Béco, 1050 Brussels, Belgium; tel. (2) 626-20-20; fax (2) 648-43-16; e-mail icem@geo2.poptel.org.uk; internet www.icem.org; f. 1995 by merger of the International Federation of Chemical, Energy and General Workers' Unions (f. 1907) and the Miners' International Federation (f. 1890). Mems: 403 trade unions covering approximately 20m. workers in 115 countries. Main sectors cover energy industries; chemicals; pharmaceuticals and biotechnology; mining and extraction; pulp and paper; rubber; ceramics; glass; building materials; and environmental services. Pres. JOHN MAITLAND; Gen. Sec. FRED HIGGS. Publs *ICEM Info* (quarterly), *ICEM Focus on Health, Safety and Environment* (2 a year), *ICEM Update* (Irregular).

International Federation of Journalists—IFJ: 266 rue Royale, 1210 Brussels, Belgium; tel. (2) 223-22-65; fax (2) 219-29-76; e-mail ifj@icj.org; internet www.ifj.org; f. 1952 to link national unions of professional journalists dedicated to the freedom of the press, to defend the rights of journalists, and to raise professional standards; it conducts surveys, assists in trade union training programmes, organizes seminars and provides information; it arranges fact-finding missions in countries where press freedom is under pressure, and issues protests against the persecution and detention of journalists and the censorship of the mass media; Holds Congress (every three years): June 2001 in Seoul, Republic of Korea. Mems: 143 unions in 104 countries, comprising 450,000 individuals. Pres. CHRIS WARREN (Australia); Gen. Sec. AIDAN WHITE (UK). Publ. *IFJ Direct Line* (every two months).

International Metalworkers' Federation—IMF: CP 1516, Route des Acacias 54 bis, 1227 Geneva, Switzerland; tel. (22) 3085050; fax

International Olympic Committee

(22) 3085055; e-mail info@imfmetal.org; internet www.imfmetal.org; f. 1893. Mems: national orgs covering 23m. workers in 193 unions in 101 countries. Holds Congress (every four years); has six regional offices; seven industrial departments; World Company Councils for unions in multinational corporations. Pres. K. ZWICKEL (Germany); Gen. Sec. MARCELLO MALENTACCHI. Publs *IMF NewsBriefs* (weekly), *Metal World* (quarterly).

International Textile, Garment and Leather Workers' Federation—ITGLWF: rue Joseph Stevens 8 (Boîte 4), 1000 Brussels, Belgium; tel. (2) 512-26-06; fax (2) 511-09-04; e-mail itglwf@compuserve.com; f. 1970. Mems: 220 unions covering 10m. workers in 110 countries. Holds Congress (every four years): June 2001 in Norrköping, Sweden. Pres. PETER BOOTH (UK); Gen. Sec. NEIL KEARNEY (Ireland). Publ. *ITGLWF Newsletter* (quarterly).

International Transport Workers' Federation—ITF: 49-60 Borough Rd, London, SE1 1DS, United Kingdom; tel. (20) 7403-2733; fax (20) 7357-7871; e-mail mail@itf.org.uk; internet www.itf.org.uk; f. 1896. Mems: national trade unions covering 5m. workers in 579 unions in 132 countries. Holds Congress (every four years); has eight Industrial Sections. Pres. UMRAOMAL PURDIT (India); Gen. Sec. DAVID COCKROFT (UK). Publ. *ITF News* (every two months).

International Union of Food, Agricultural, Hotel, Restaurant, Catering, Tobacco and Allied Workers' Associations—IUF: 8 rampe du Pont-Rouge, 1213 Petit-Lancy, Switzerland; tel. (22) 7932233; fax (22) 7932238; e-mail iuf@iuf.org; internet www.iuf.org; f. 1920. Mems: 331 affiliated organizations covering about 2.6m

workers in 112 countries. Holds Congress (every five years). Pres. FRANK HURT (USA); Gen. Sec. RON OSWALD. Publs bi-monthly bulletins.

Public Services International—PSI: 45 ave Voltaire, BP9, 01211 Ferney-Voltaire Cédex, France; tel. 4-50-40-64-64; fax 4-50-40-73-20; e-mail psi@world-psi.org; internet www.world-psi.org; f. 1907; Mems: 585 unions and professional associations covering 20m. workers in 146 countries. Holds Congress (every five years). Pres. WILLIAM LUCY (USA); Gen. Sec. HANS ENGELBERTS (Netherlands). Publ. *Focus* (quarterly).

Union Network International—UNI: 8-10 ave Reverdil, 1260 Nyon, Switzerland; tel. (22) 3652100; fax (22) 3652121; e-mail contact@union-network.org; internet www.union-network.org; f. 2000 by merger of Communications International (CI), the International Federation of Commercial, Clerical, Professional and Technical Employees (FIET), the International Graphical Federation (IGF), and Media and Entertainment International (MEI). Mems: 800 unions in more than 140 countries, representing 15.5m. people. Activities cover the following 12 sectors: commerce; electricity; finance; graphical; hair and beauty; professional and information technology staff; media, entertainment and the arts; postal; property services; social insurance and private health care; telecommunications; and tourism. First World Congress scheduled to be convened in Berlin, Germany, in September 2001. Pres. KURT VAN HAAREN (Germany); Gen. Sec. PHILIP JENNINGS (United Kingdom). Publs *UNI-info* (quarterly), *UNInet News* (monthly).

INTERNATIONAL OLYMPIC COMMITTEE

Address: Château de Vidy, 1007 Lausanne, Switzerland.
Telephone: (21) 6216111; **fax:** (21) 6216216; **internet:** www.olympic.org.

The International Olympic Committee was founded in 1894 to ensure the regular celebration of the Olympic Games.

Organization

(April 2001)

INTERNATIONAL OLYMPIC COMMITTEE

The International Olympic Committee (IOC) is a non-governmental international organization comprising 123 members, who are representatives of the IOC in their countries and not their countries' delegates to the IOC. The members meet in session at least once a year. In accordance with reforms adopted in December 1999, the Committee was to comprise a maximum of 115 members, including 15 active Olympic athletes, 15 National Olympic Committee presidents, 15 International Sports Federation presidents, and 70 other individuals. A nominations committee has been established under the reform programme to select qualified candidates to stand for election to the IOC.

The IOC is the final authority on all questions concerning the Olympic Games and the Olympic movement. There are 199 recognized National Olympic Committees, which are the sole authorities responsible for the representation of their respective countries at the Olympic Games. The IOC may give recognition to International Federations which undertake to adhere to the Olympic Charter, and which govern sports that comply with the IOC's criteria.

An International Council for Arbitration for Sport (ICAS) has been established. ICAS administers the Court of Arbitration for Sport which hears cases brought by competitors.

EXECUTIVE BOARD

The session of the IOC delegates to the Executive Board the authority to manage the IOC's affairs. The President of the Board is elected for an eight-year term, and is eligible for re-election once for an additional term of four years. The Vice-Presidents are elected for four-year terms, and may be re-elected after a minimum interval of four years. Members of the Board are elected to hold office for four years. The Executive Board generally meets four to five times per year.

President: JUAN ANTONIO SAMARANCH (Spain).
Vice-Presidents: RICHARD KEVAN GOSPER (Australia); THOMAS BACH

(Germany); ANITA DEFRANTZ (USA); KÉBA MBAYE (Senegal).

Members of the Board:
UN YONG KIM (Republic of Korea)
MARC HODLER (Switzerland)
JACQUES ROGGE (Belgium)
ZHENLIANG HE (People's Republic of China)
GUNILLA LINDBERG (Sweden)
FRANCO CARRARO (Italy)

ETHICS COMMISSION

In March 1999 an extraordinary meeting of the IOC approved the establishment of an independent Ethics Commission to develop and monitor rules and principles to guide the selection of hosts for the Olympic Games, and the organization and execution of the Games. The eight-member Commission, which is responsible to the Executive Board, comprises three IOC members. The Commission aims to strengthen the Olympic Movement by ensuring adherence to the principles of the Olympic Charter and a new IOC code of conduct, by promoting positive ethics, and by providing transparency, accountability and an effective response to ethical issues. The Commission held its first meeting in Lausanne, Switzerland, in May.

Chairman: KÉBA MBAYE.

Other IOC commissions include the Olympic Games Co-ordination Commission; the Commission for Culture and Olympic Education; and the Athletics Commission.

ADMINISTRATION

The administration of the IOC is under the authority of the Director-General and the Secretary-General, who are appointed by the Executive Board, on the proposal of the President.

Director-General: FRANÇOIS CARRARD.
Secretary-General: FRANÇOISE ZWEIFEL.

Activities

The fundamental principles of the Olympic movement are:

Olympism is a philosophy of life, exalting and combining, in a balanced whole, the qualities of body, will and mind. Blending sport with culture and education, Olympism seeks to create a way of life based on the joy found in effort, the educational value of good example and respect for universal fundamental ethical principles.

Under the supreme authority of the IOC, the Olympic movement encompasses organizations, athletes and other persons who agree to be guided by the Olympic Charter. The criterion for belonging to the Olympic movement is recognition by the IOC.

The goal of the Olympic movement is to contribute to building a peaceful and better world by educating youth through sport practised without discrimination of any kind and in the Olympic spirit, which requires mutual understanding with a spirit of friendship, solidarity and fair-play.

The activity of the Olympic movement is permanent and universal. It reaches its peak with the bringing together of the athletes of the world at the great sport festival, the Olympic Games.

The Olympic Charter is the codification of the fundamental principles, rules and bye-laws adopted by the IOC. It governs the organization and operation of the Olympic movement and stipulates the conditions for the celebration of the Olympic Games.

In March 1998, at a meeting organized with other international sports governing bodies, it was agreed to form a working group to defend the principle of self-regulation in international sports organizations, against possible interference by the EU. At a meeting in August methods of containing the increase in drugs abuse in sport were discussed. In January 1999, following publication of the results of an investigation into allegations of corruption and bribery, six members of the Committee were recommended for expulsion while investigations into the conduct of other officials were to be pursued. In March an extraordinary session of the IOC was convened, at which the six Committee members were expelled for violating rules relating to Salt Lake City's bid to host the Olympic Winter Games in 2002 (four other members had already resigned, while Executive Board member Un Yong Kim had received disciplinary action). The President of the IOC retained his position after receiving a vote of confidence. The session approved far-reaching reforms, including the introduction of an interim procedure to select the host city for the Winter Games in 2006, by means of which an election college was to choose two finalists from the six cities submitting bids. Visits by IOC members to any of the bid cities were prohibited. In addition, the meeting approved the establishment of an independent Ethics Commission to oversee cities' bids to host the Olympic Games (see above) and an IOC 2000 Commission to review the bidding process after 2006 and the internal structure of the organization. A declaration on drugs and sport was also adopted by the meeting. In November 1999, an independent World Anti-Doping Agency (WADA) was established by the IOC. In December the IOC adopted 50 reforms proposed by the IOC 2000 Commission during the Extraordinary 110th Session. The changes aimed to create a more open, responsive and accountable organization, and included the elimination of member visits to bid cities, the application of terms of office, limiting the expansion of the Summer Games, and the election of 15 active athletes to the IOC membership. In 2000, prior to the Sydney 'Summer' Olympic Games, held in September of that year, WADA conducted about 2,200 out-of-competition drugs tests, involving competitors from more than 80 nations and supplementing significantly the IOC's ongoing out-of-competition drugs testing programme. The Agency established a 15-member team of independent observers to oversee doping control operations at the Sydney Games. A new president of the IOC's Executive Board was to be elected at the 112th Session, scheduled to be held in Moscow, Russia, in July 2001.

ASSOCIATED AGENCY

World Anti-Doping Agency (WADA): f. 1999 to promote and co-ordinate efforts to achieve drug-free sport; has five committees:

Ethics and Education; Finance and Administration; Health, Medical and Research; Legal; Standards and Harmonization; Chair. RICHARD W. POUND; Sec.-Gen. HARRI SYVÄSALMI.

THE GAMES OF THE OLYMPIAD

The Olympic Summer Games take place during the first year of the Olympiad (period of four years) which they are to celebrate. They are the exclusive property of the IOC, which entrusts their organization to a host city seven years in advance.

1896	Athens	1960	Rome
1900	Paris	1964	Tokyo
1904	St Louis	1968	Mexico City
1908	London	1972	Munich
1912	Stockholm	1976	Montreal
1920	Antwerp	1980	Moscow
1924	Paris	1984	Los Angeles
1928	Amsterdam	1988	Seoul
1932	Los Angeles	1992	Barcelona
1936	Berlin	1996	Atlanta
1948	London	2000	Sydney
1952	Helsinki	2004	Athens
1956	Melbourne		

The programme of the Games must include at least 15 of the total number of Olympic sports (sports governed by recognized International Federations and admitted to the Olympic programme by decision of the IOC at least seven years before the Games). The Olympic summer sports are: archery, athletics, badminton, baseball, basketball, boxing, canoeing, cycling, equestrian sports, fencing, football, gymnastics, handball, field hockey, judo, modern pentathlon, rowing, sailing, shooting, softball, swimming (including water polo and diving), table tennis, tae kwondo, tennis, triathlon, volleyball, weight-lifting, wrestling.

OLYMPIC WINTER GAMES

The Olympic Winter Games comprise competitions in sports practised on snow and ice. From 1994 onwards, they were to be held in the second calendar year following that in which the Games of the Olympiad take place.

1924	Chamonix	1964	Innsbruck
1928	St Moritz	1968	Grenoble
1932	Lake Placid	1972	Sapporo
1936	Garmisch-Partenkirchen	1976	Innsbruck
1948	St Moritz	1980	Lake Placid
1952	Oslo	1984	Sarajevo
1956	Cortina d'Ampezzo	1988	Calgary
1960	Squaw Valley	1992	Albertville
1994	Lillehammer	2002	Salt Lake City
1998	Nagano	2006	Turin

The Winter Games may include skiing, skating, ice hockey, bobsleigh, luge, curling and biathlon.

Finance

The operational budget for the International Olympic Committee for 1998 was 37,240m. Swiss francs.

Publication

Olympic Review.

INTERNATIONAL ORGANIZATION FOR MIGRATION—IOM

Address: 17 route des Morillons, CP 71, 1211 Geneva 19, Switzerland.

Telephone: (22) 7179111; **fax:** (22) 7986150; **e-mail:** uinfo@iom.int; **internet:** www.iom.int.

The Intergovernmental Committee for Migration (ICM) was founded in 1951 as a non-political and humanitarian organization with a predominantly operational mandate, including the handling of orderly and planned migration to meet specific needs of emigration and immigration countries; and the processing and movement of refugees, displaced persons and other individuals in need of international migration services to countries offering them resettlement opportunities. In 1989 ICM's name was changed to the International Organization for Migration (IOM). IOM was admitted as an observer to the UN General Assembly in October 1992.

MEMBERS

Albania	El Salvador	Pakistan
Algeria	Finland	Panama
Angola	France	Paraguay
Argentina	Germany	Peru
Armenia	Greece	Philippines
Australia	Guatemala	Poland
Austria	Guinea	Portugal
Bangladesh	Guinea-Bissau	Romania
Belgium	Haiti	Senegal
Belize	Honduras	Slovakia
Benin	Hungary	Slovenia
Bolivia	Israel	South Africa
Bulgaria	Italy	Sri Lanka
Burkina Faso	Japan	Sudan
Canada	Jordan	Sweden
Chile	Kenya	Switzerland
Colombia	Korea, Republic	Tajikistan
Costa Rica	Kyrgyzstan	Tanzania
Côte d'Ivoire	Latvia	Thailand
Croatia	Liberia	Tunisia
Cyprus	Lithuania	Uganda
Czech Republic	Luxembourg	USA
Denmark	Mali	Uruguay
Dominican	Morocco	Venezuela
Republic	Netherlands	Yemen
Ecuador	Nicaragua	Zambia
Egypt	Norway	

Observers: Afghanistan, Belarus, Bhutan, Bosnia and Herzegovina, Brazil, Cambodia, Cape Verde, Democratic Republic of the Congo, Republic of the Congo, Cuba, Estonia, Ethiopia, Georgia, Ghana, Holy See, India, Indonesia, Iran, Ireland, Jamaica, Kyrgyzstan, Madagascar, Malta, Mexico, Moldova, Mozambique, Namibia, New Zealand, Papua New Guinea, Russia, Rwanda, San Marino, São Tomé and Príncipe, Somalia, Sovereign Military Order of Malta, Spain, Turkey, Turkmenistan, Ukraine, United Kingdom, Viet Nam, Yugoslavia, Zimbabwe. In addition, some 49 international governmental organizations hold observer status with IOM.

Organization

(April 2001)

IOM is governed by a Council which is composed of representatives of all member governments, and has the responsibility for making final decisions on policy, programmes and financing. An Executive Committee of nine member governments elected by the Council prepares the work of the Council and makes recommendations on the basis of reports from the Sub-Committee on Budget and Finance and the Sub-Committee on the Co-ordination of Transport. IOM had a network of more than 80 offices in 2000.

Director General: BRUNSON McKINLEY (USA).

Deputy Director General: NDIORO NDIAYE (Senegal).

Activities

IOM aims to provide assistance to member governments in meeting the operational challenges of migration, to advance understanding of migration issues, to encourage social and economic development through migration and to work towards effective respect of the human dignity and well-being of migrants. It provides a full range of migration assistance to, and sometimes *de facto* protection of, migrants, refugees, displaced persons and other individuals in need of international migration services. This includes recruitment, selection, processing, medical examinations, and language and cultural orientation courses, placement, activities to facilitate reception and integration and other advisory services. IOM co-ordinates its refugee activities with the UN High Commissioner for Refugees (UNHCR, q.v.) and with governmental and non-governmental partners. In May 1997 IOM and UNHCR signed a memorandum of understanding which aimed to facilitate co-operation between the two organizations. During 1999 IOM transported and assisted some 430,684 people, of whom 409,663 were humanitarian migrants, 13,731 national migrants and 7,290 were registered as qualified human resources. Since it commenced operations in February 1952 IOM has provided assistance to an estimated 11m. migrants.

IOM programmes are divided into four main areas.

HUMANITARIAN MIGRATION

Under its humanitarian migration programmes, IOM provides assistance to persons fleeing conflict situations, to refugees being resettled in third countries or repatriated, to stranded individuals and unsuccessful asylum seekers returning home, to internally and externally displaced persons, to other persons compelled to leave their homelands, to individuals seeking to reunite with other members of their families and to migrants involved in regular migration. IOM provides these individuals with secure, reliable, cost-effective services, including counselling, document processing, medical examination, transportation, language training, and cultural orientation and integration assistance. In addition, IOM organizes temporary evacuation for medical treatment where necessary.

Humanitarian migration activities also include the provision of emergency assistance to persons affected by conflict and post-conflict situations. IOM offers its services to vulnerable populations in need of evacuation, resettlement or return, both in the initial phases of an emergency and during the transition from emergency humanitarian relief, through a period of rehabilitation, to longer-term reconstruction and development efforts. Between 1996 and 1998 more than 160,000 Bosnians were assisted to return voluntarily under IOM auspices. In late 1998 IOM mobilized all available resources in the Central American region in an attempt to provide shelter to the thousands of displaced people who lost their homes as a result of 'Hurricane Mitch'.

From April–June 1999 IOM co-operated with UNHCR and the OSCE to facilitate the evacuation of refugees from Kosovo and Metohija, a southern Serbian province of Yugoslavia, following an escalation of violence against the local Albanian population by Serbian forces and the initiation of a NATO military offensive. The joint Humanitarian Evacuation Programme included land transportation to move substantial numbers of refugees away from overcrowded camps in the border region of the former Yugoslav republic of Macedonia (FYRM), and the provision of charter flights to evacuate those refugees most at need to third countries. IOM was also involved in implementing a programme to register the refugees in Albania, the FYRM and Montenegro, and to reissue identification documents where necessary. Other activities being undertaken by IOM personnel included medical screening of refugees and trauma assessment and rehabilitation. Following the end of the conflict, in June, IOM co-ordinated the return movement of refugees and worked with the UN mission and UNHCR to assist returnees to move to their final destination in Kosovo. From July 1999–December 2000 IOM assisted some 170,000 Kosovars to return to the province.

In response to the violence and humanitarian crisis which followed the popular consultation conducted in East Timor in late August 1999, IOM formulated an East Timor Assistance Programme, comprising specific projects such as the assisted return of refugees, emergency transport, and the provision of shelter materials. During October 1999–December 2000 IOM assisted 115,000 East Timorese to return to the territory from camps in West Timor, and participated in rehabilitation and reconstruction activities. The repatriation operation was suspended temporarily during September–November 2000, following the murder by Indonesian militiamen in September of three UNHCR personnel in West Timor.

A joint IOM/UNHCR programme to facilitate the return of a projected 100,000 Afghan refugees from Iran commenced in April 2000. In early 2001 IOM was assisting with the repatriation of Sierra Leonean refugees from Guinea, following an escalation of violence in the south of that country which had rendered refugee camps vulnerable to attack and largely inaccessible to humanitarian aid agencies.

In recent years IOM has increasingly assisted in the return home and reintegration of demobilized soldiers, police officials, and their dependents. In 1997 IOM provided assistance to demobilized soldiers and their families in Angola; by the end of that year IOM had helped to resettle 40,621 soldiers and 107,197 dependents. The assistance programme continued in 1998, when IOM launched a major appeal for funding of the initiative. However, at the end of March 1999 IOM ended its work in Angola, owing to a lack of resources and a deterioration of the security situation in that country. IOM was also involved in the resettlement of demobilized forces in Guatemala in 1998. In mid-1999 IOM established an Information Counselling and Referral Service (ICRS) to undertake the registration of former combatants in Kosovo and assist their rehabilitation. From July–November 1999 the ICRS registered 25,723 demobilized soldiers from the Kosovo Liberation Army; during that period IOM helped 4,122 of the former combatants to start their own businesses or to find other permanent employment.

MIGRATION FOR DEVELOPMENT

IOM's programmes of migration for development aim to contribute towards alleviating economic and social problems through recruitment and selection of high-level workers and professionals to fill positions in priority sectors of the economy in developing countries for which qualified persons are not available locally (particularly in Latin America and Africa), taking into account national development priorities as well as the needs and concerns of receiving communities. Under the programmes for the Transfer of Qualified Human Resources IOM screens candidates, identifies employment opportunities and provides reintegration assistance. Selection Migration programmes help qualified professionals migrate to countries in need of specific expertise when the country cannot find the required skills from within or through the return of nationals. Integrated Experts programmes provide temporary expatriate expertise to states for up to six years: these experts transfer their skills to their working partners and contribute directly to productive output. Programmes of Intraregional Co-operation in the field of qualified human resources encourage collective self-reliance among developing countries by fostering the exchange of governmental experts and the transfer of professionals and technicians within a given region. IOM maintains recruitment offices throughout the world. In November 1996 IOM established a Return of Qualified Nationals (RQN) programme to facilitate the employment of refugees returning to Bosnia and Herzegovina. By December 1998 more than 600 professionals had been placed in jobs in that country. An RQN has been established for East Timor, and a programme to encourage the Return and Reinitegration of Qualified Afghan Nationals in the Health and Education Sectors is under way. In addition, IOM operates a Return of Qualified African Nationals scheme. IOM and the EU jointly fund a scheme to support Rwandan students abroad and encourage their return to Rwanda.

TECHNICAL CO-OPERATION

Through its technical co-operation programmes IOM offers advisory services on migration to governments, intergovernmental agencies and non-governmental organizations. They aim to assist in the formation and implementation of effective and coherent migration policy, legislation and administration. IOM technical co-operation also focuses on capacity building projects such as training courses for government migration officials, and analysis of and suggestions for solving emerging migration problems. In August 1999 IOM was responsible for organizing voting in the popular consultation in East Timor in five external areas (i.e. Indonesia, Macau, Mozambique, Portugal and the USA) under UN auspices. IOM was also responsible for registering Kosovars resident abroad and for co-ordinating voting by these at the municipal elections held under UN auspices in Kosovo in October 2000.

MIGRATION DEBATE, RESEARCH AND INFORMATION

IOM furthers the understanding of migration through regional and international seminars and conferences which bring together those concerned with migration issues in order to develop practical solutions on current migration problems. Recent topics have included migrant women, migrant trafficking, migration and development, undocumented migrants, the impact of migration on social structures, migration and health. In the area of healthcare, IOM is working with UNAIDS on a project aimed at improving knowledge of the impact of migration on the spread of HIV. In September 1999 IOM and UNAIDS signed a co-operation framework to promote awareness on HIV/AIDS issues relating to displaced populations, and to ensure the needs of migrants are incorporated into national and regional AIDS strategies. In October IOM and WHO signed an agreement to strengthen collaborative efforts to improve the health care of migrants.

Research on migration relates not only to the migration process but also to the specific situation and needs of the migrant as an individual human being. IOM has developed mechanisms to gather information on potential migrants' attitudes and motivations, as well as on situations which could lead to irregular migration flows. Trends in international migration point to information as an essential resource for individuals making life-changing decisions about migrating; for governments setting migration policies; for international, regional or non-governmental organizations designing migration programmes; and for researchers, the media and individuals analyzing and reporting on migration. IOM gathers information on migration to meet these growing demands. It also designs and implements information campaigns which provide potential migrants with a more accurate picture of migration realities, in order to prevent unsuccessful or unnecessary migration.

INTERNATIONAL CENTRE FOR MIGRATION AND HEALTH

Address: 11 route du Nant-d'Avril, 1214 Geneva, Vernier, Switzerland; **tel.:** (22) 7831080; **fax:** (22) 7831087; **e-mail:** icmh@worldcom.ch; internet www.icmh.ch.

Established in March 1995, by IOM and the University of Geneva, with the support of WHO, to respond to the growing needs for information, documentation, research, training and policy development in migration health; designated a WHO collaborating centre, in August 1996, for health-related issues among people displaced by disasters.

Co-ordinator: Dr MANUEL CARBALLO.

Finance

The approved IOM budget for 2000 amounted to US $208.4m. for operations and 34.1m. Swiss francs for administration.

Publications

International Migration (quarterly).

IOM Latin American Migration Journal (3 a year, in English and Spanish).

IOM News (quarterly, in English, French and Spanish).

IOM News – North American Supplement.

Migration and Health (quarterly).

Report by the Director General (in English, French and Spanish).

Trafficking in Migrants (quarterly).

World Migration Report (annual).

Research reports, *IOM Info Sheets,* surveys and studies.

INTERNATIONAL RED CROSS AND RED CRESCENT MOVEMENT

The International Red Cross and Red Crescent Movement is a worldwide independent humanitarian organization, comprising three components: the International Committee of the Red Cross (ICRC), founded in 1863; the International Federation of Red Cross and Red Crescent Societies (the Federation), founded in 1919; and National Red Cross and Red Crescent Societies working mainly at national level in 176 countries.

Organization

INTERNATIONAL CONFERENCE

The supreme deliberative body of the Movement, the Conference comprises delegations from the ICRC, the Federation and the National Societies, and of representatives of States Parties to the Geneva Conventions (see below). The Conference's function is to determine the general policy of the Movement and to ensure unity in the work of the various bodies. It usually meets every four to five years, and is hosted by the National Society of the country in which it is held. The 26th International Conference, due to be held in November/December 1991 in Budapest, Hungary, was postponed; it was finally convened in December 1995, in Geneva, Switzerland. The 27th International Conference was held in Geneva in October/November 1999.

STANDING COMMISSION

The Commission meets at least twice a year in ordinary session. It promotes harmony in the work of the Movement, and examines matters which concern the Movement as a whole. It is formed of two representatives of the ICRC, two of the Federation, and five members of National Societies elected by the Conference.

COUNCIL OF DELEGATES

The Council comprises delegations from the National Societies, from the ICRC and from the Federation. The Council is the body where the representatives of all the components of the Movement meet to discuss matters that concern the Movement as a whole.

In November 1997 the Council adopted an Agreement on the organization of the activities of the Movement's components. The Agreement aimed to promote increased co-operation and partnership between the Movement's bodies, clearly defining the distribution of tasks between agencies. In particular, the Agreement aimed to ensure continuity between international operations carried out in a crisis situation and those developed in its aftermath.

Fundamental Principles of the Movement

Humanity. The International Red Cross and Red Crescent Movement, born of a desire to bring assistance without discrimination to the wounded on the battlefield, endeavours, in its international and national capacity, to prevent and alleviate human suffering wherever it may be found. Its purpose is to protect life and health and to ensure respect for the human being. It promotes mutual understanding, friendship, co-operation and lasting peace amongst all peoples.

Impartiality. It makes no discrimination as to nationality, race, religious beliefs, class or political opinions. It endeavours to relieve the suffering of individuals, being guided solely by their needs, and to give priority to the most urgent cases of distress.

Neutrality. In order to continue to enjoy the confidence of all, the Movement may not take sides in hostilities or engage in controversies of a political, racial, religious or ideological nature.

Independence. The Movement is independent. The National Societies, while auxiliaries in the humanitarian services of their governments and subject to national laws, must retain their autonomy so that they may always be able to act in accordance with the principles of the Movement.

Voluntary Service. It is a voluntary relief movement not prompted by desire for gain.

Unity. There can be only one Red Cross or Red Crescent Society in any one country. It must be open to all. It must carry on its humanitarian work throughout the territory.

Universality. The International Red Cross and Red Crescent Movement, in which all National Societies have equal status and share equal responsibilities and duties in helping each other, is worldwide.

International Committee of the Red Cross—ICRC

Address: 19 avenue de la Paix, 1202 Geneva, Switzerland.

Telephone: (22) 7346001; **fax:** (22) 7332057; **e-mail:** press.gva@icrc.org; **internet:** www.icrc.org.

Founded in 1863, the ICRC is at the origin of the Red Cross and Red Crescent Movement, and co-ordinates all international humanitarian actvities conducted by the Movement in situations of conflict. New statutes of the ICRC, incorporating a revised institutional structure, were adopted in June 1998 and came into effect in July.

Organization

(April 2001)

INTERNATIONAL COMMITTEE

The ICRC is an independent institution of a private character composed exclusively of Swiss nationals. Members are co-opted, and their total number may not exceed 25. The international character of the ICRC is based on its mission and not on its composition.

President: JAKOB KELLENBERGER.

Vice-Presidents: Prof. JACQUES FORSTER; ANNE PETITPIERRE.

ASSEMBLY

Under the new decision-making structures, approved in 1998, the Assembly was defined as the supreme governing body of the ICRC. It formulates policy, defines the Committee's general objectives and strategies, oversees its activities, and approves its budget and accounts. The Assembly is composed of the members of the ICRC, and is collegial in character. The President and Vice-Presidents of the ICRC hold the same offices in the Assembly.

ASSEMBLY COUNCIL

The Council (formally the Executive Board) is a subsidiary body of the Assembly, to which the latter delegates certain of its responsibilities. It prepares the Assembly's activities and takes decisions on matters within its competence. The Council is composed of five members elected by the Assembly and is chaired by the President of the ICRC.

Members: JAKOB KELLENBERGER, ERNST A. BRUGGER, Prof. JACQUES FORSTER, LISELOTTE KRAUS-GURNY, JAKOB NÜESCH.

DIRECTORATE

Comprising four members appointed by the Assembly, the Directorate is the executive body of the ICRC, overseeing the efficient running of the organization and responsible for the application of the general objectives and institutional strategies decided by the Assembly.

Director-General: PAUL GROSSRIEDER.

Members: JEAN-DANIEL TAUXE (Director of Operations), FRANÇOIS BUG-
NION (Director for International Law and Communication), JACQUES
STROUN (Director of Human Resources and Finance).

Activities

The International Committee of the Red Cross was founded in 1863
in Geneva, by Henry Dunant and four of his friends. The original
purpose of the Committee was to promote the foundation, in every
country, of a voluntary relief society to assist wounded soldiers on the
battlefield (the origin of the National Societies of the Red Cross or Red
Crescent), as well as the adoption of a treaty protecting wounded
soldiers and all those who come to their rescue. The mission of the
ICRC was progressively extended through the Geneva Conventions
(see below). The present activities of the ICRC consist in giving legal
protection and material assistance to military and civilian victims of
wars (international wars, internal strife and disturbances) and in
promoting and monitoring the application of international humanitarian law. The ICRC takes into account the legal standards and the
specific cultural, ethical and religious features of the environment in
which it operates. It aims to influence the conduct of all actual and
potential perpetrators of violence by seeking direct dialogue with combatants. In 1990 the ICRC was granted the status of an observer at
the United Nations General Assembly.

As well as providing medical aid and emergency food supplies in
many countries, the ICRC plays an important part in monitoring
prison conditions, in tracing missing persons, and in disseminating
humanitarian principles in an attempt to protect non-combatants
from violence. In January 1991 the World Campaign for the Protection
of War Victims was initiated. This campaign aimed to draw attention
to the large numbers of civilians who are killed or injured as a result
of armed conflict in which they are not directly involved. At the end of
August 1993 the ICRC held an international conference at which a
Declaration for the Protection of War Victims was adopted to confirm
adherence to the fourth Geneva Convention. In December 1995 the
26th International Conference of the Red Cross and Red Crescent was
held in Geneva. It considered the following main themes: protection
of the civilian population in periods of armed conflict; international
humanitarian law applicable to armed conflicts at sea; principles and
action in international humanitarian assistance and protection;
strengthening national capacities to provide humanitarian and development assistance; and protection to the most vulnerable. At the same
time the ICRC presented a new Advisory Service, which was intended
to assist national authorities in their implementation of humanitarian law and to provide a basis for consultation, analysis and harmonization of legislative texts. It became fully operational in January
1996. A Documentation Centre for exchanging information on what
national measures exist and what is being done to promote the law in
the different states has been established. It is open to all states and
National Societies, as well as interested institutions and the general
public. The ICRC fully supported efforts to establish a permanent
International Criminal Court, with the authority to try serious violations of international humanitarian law. A Statute on the establishment of the Court was signed in July 1998 by representatives of 120
countries, meeting in Rome, Italy, under UN auspices. (At February
2001 the Statute had 139 signatories and had been ratified by 29
states.)

In 1996 the ICRC launched the 'Avenir' project to define the organization's future role, in recognition of significant changes in the world
situation and the consequent need for changes in humanitarian
action. Four main priorities were identified: improving the status of
international humanitarian action and knowledge of and respect for
humanitarian law; carrying out humanitarian action in closer proximity to victims, with long-term plans and identified priorities; strengthening dialogue with all parties (including launching joint appeals
with other organizations if necessary, and the establishment of a
combined communication and information dissemination unit); and
increasing the ICRC's efficiency. The Assembly endorsed the plan
of action in April 1998. In November 1999 the 27th International
Conference of the Red Cross and Red Cross adopted a plan of action
for the movement for the four-year period 2000–03. The plan incorporated the following three main objectives: to strengthen respect for
international humanitarian law, including the conformity of weapons
with legal guide-lines, in order to protect victims of armed conflict; to
improve national and international preparedness to respond effectively to disaster situations, as well as to improve mechanisms of co-
operation and protection of humanitarian personnel working in the
field; and strategic partnerships to improve the lives of vulnerable
people through health initiatives, measures to reduce discrimination
and violence, and strengthening National Societies' capacities and
their co-operation with other humanitarian organizations.

In April 1993 the ICRC organized a symposium in Montreux, Switzerland, to consider the use of anti-personnel mines. The ICRC has

continued to convene experts to consider the issue in the context of
incorporating the use of anti-personnel mines into the review of the
1980 UN Convention on prohibitions or restrictions on the use of
conventional weapons. In February 1994 the ICRC issued a report for
the review of the Convention. This included a recommendation for the
adoption of an additional protocol on the use of laser weapons, which
cause permanent blindness or irreparable damage; in October 1995 a
session of the Review Conference on the Convention adopted a Protocol, which, as a binding instrument of humanitarian law, prohibits
the use and transfer of these weapons. In May 1996 the Conference
approved an amended protocol on prohibitions or restrictions on the
use of land-mines. The ICRC subsequently resolved to continue its
efforts to achieve a world-wide ban on the use of land-mines, and other
anti-personnel devices. In October the ICRC supported an International Strategy Conference, organized by the Canadian Government
in Ottawa, which was the first formal meeting of states committed to
a comprehensive ban on land-mines. In September 1997 the ICRC
participated in an international conference, held in Oslo, Norway, at
which a Convention was adopted, prohibiting 'the use, stockpiling,
production and transfer of anti-personnel mines' and ensuring their
destruction. The treaty was opened for signature in December and
became legally-binding on 1 March 1999 for the 66 states that had
ratified it. By April 2001 the treaty had been ratified by 111 states. In
April 1998 the Swiss Government established a Geneva International
Centre for Humanitarian Demining, in co-operation with the United
Nations and the ICRC, to co-ordinate the destruction of land-mines
world-wide.

In 1995 the ICRC adopted a 'Plan of Action concerning Children in
Armed Conflicts', to promote the principle of non-recruitment and
non-participation in armed conflict of children under the age of 18
years. A co-ordinating group was established, with representatives of
the individual National Societies and the International Federation of
Red Cross and Red Crescent Societies. The UN Commission of Human
Rights invited the ICRC to participate in drafting the Optional Protocol to the Convention on the Rights of the Child (adopted and opened
for signature by the UN General Assembly in May 2000), which will
raise from 15 to 18 the minimum age for recruitment in armed conflict.
The ICRC also co-operated with the UN to draw up the 'Guiding
Principles on Internal Displacement', finalized in early 1998.

Examples of recent ICRC activities include the following:

Africa: visits to detainees; food and medical assistance, including
public health services, war surgery, assistance for victims of land-
mines, programmes for the rehabilitation of the disabled, food distribution; agricultural and veterinary programmes to improve the self-
sufficiency of vulnerable and displaced populations; and tracing activities to unite separated relatives. Major operations in 2000 and early
2001 covered the Democratic Republic of the Congo, Republic of the
Congo, Eritrea, Ethiopia, Guinea and Sierra Leone. From September
2000–April 2001 the ICRC undertook an emergency operation to provide food aid and other essential items to 96,000 Guineans displaced
from their homes in southern Guinea by fighting between Guinean
government forces and mainly Sierra Leonean rebels. An operation
to provide further assistance to vulnerable members of the displaced
and returning populations (such as unaccompanied children and the
elderly) commenced immediately afterwards.

Latin America: protection and relief activities for civilian population, prisoners of war and detainees in the context of civil conflict, as
well as in various situations of internal violence; the dissemination of
the fundamental principles of international humanitarian law, in
particular in the training of armed forces. In 1998 the ICRC also
provided assistance for those affected by adverse climatic conditions
resulting from 'El Niño' and collaborated with national societies in
Central America to assist victims of 'Hurricane Mitch'. In 1999 the
ICRC aimed to provide emergency assistance to about 171,000 people
displaced by the ongoing conflict in Colombia. In that country the
ICRC has distributed basic food supplies; provided health care and
organized vaccination campaigns; supplied tools and seeds to facilitate crop production by local populations suffering food shortages;
and enabled communication between separated family members.

Asia: protection of detainees and prisoners; tracing missing relatives
among families affected by armed conflict (including the reunification
of families separated by the insecurity that escalated in East Timor
in 1999, see below); in Afghanistan the ICRC provides the following
assistance to people internally displaced by the ongoing conflict and
to those affected by a combination of severe drought and harsh winter
weather: food and other relief supplies for vulnerable elements of the
population; assistance to medical facilities and the manufacture and
fitting of prosthetic limbs for amputees; rehabilitation of irrigation
and sanitation systems; and the provision of seeds, seedlings, fertilizers and agricultural implements, advice on crop production, and
training for smallholders and farmers. Other recipients of humanitarian assistance by the ICRC in 2000 and early 2001 included 10,450
people displaced by conflict on the Philippine island of Mindanao, and

displaced populations in Kalimantan, Indonesia, in Solomon Islands, and on the Sri Lankan island of Jaffna. The ICRC was also involved in the manufacture and fitting of prosthetic limbs for amputees in Cambodia; the reception and care of freed hostages who had been captured during the attempted coup in Fiji in mid-2000; and in providing humanitarian relief in the aftermath of an earthquake that affected Gujarat, India, in early 2001. The ICRC has provided assistance to those affected by the 1999 unrest in East Timor, and fully finances a 210-bed hospital in the territory's capital, Dili.

Middle East: visits to detainees in Israel, the Israeli-occupied territories and the Autonomous Territories and monitoring the implementation of the fourth Geneva Convention; visits to detainees and prisoners in Bahrain, Iraq, Jordan, Kuwait, Yemen, Morocco and the Western Sahara; rehabilitation, sanitation and orthopaedic programmes in Iraq; acting as a neutral intermediary in the search for people missing since the 1991 Gulf War. During the period 1980–2000 the ICRC supervised the repatriation of more than 97,500 Iraqi prisoners of war from Iran. In August 1999 the ICRC provided assistance to Turkey, following an earthquake that left some 130,000 people homeless. In October the ICRC resumed its inspection of prisons in Algeria, which had been suspended in 1992. In early 2000 the ICRC organized a regional conference of high-ranking military commanders concerning the role of the armed forces in disseminating the basic principles of the law of armed conflict, and also assisted with the co-ordination of a regional seminar on landmines. Following the withdrawal of Israeli troops from southern Lebanon in May the ICRC increased its field presence in that area, focusing particularly on the provision of medical supplies and assistance. Activities were intensified in East Jerusalem, Gaza and the West Bank in late 2000 and early 2001, in view of escalating insecurity.

Europe and Transcaucasia: medical aid, protection of civilian population, relief assistance, support to local hospitals and visits to detainees in the former Yugoslavia, Albania, Armenia, Azerbaijan and Georgia; tracing activities in the former Yugoslavia; promoting awareness of the dangers of anti-personnel devices; assistance to persons in Chechnya and the surrounding republics affected by the outbreak of hostilities with Russian authorities in late 1994; and for victims of the crisis in Kosovo and Metohija (Serbia, Yugoslavia). In March 1998 the ICRC temporarily withdrew from Kosovo, following threats to its staff. In late March 1999 the ICRC again withdrew from Kosovo owing to the deteriorating security situation in the province. In June the ICRC was able to resume its operations. In neighbouring countries the ICRC provided emergency relief to the hundreds of thousands of refugees fleeing the province and remained actively concerned for the safety and welfare of the civilian population throughout the region, including those displaced or affected by NATO's aerial offensive within the Federal Republic of Yugoslavia. The ICRC co-ordinated tracing procedures in order to reunite refugee families including through refugee databases on internet sites. In June 2000 the ICRC issued a *Book of Missing Persons in Kosovo*, listing people reported missing in the province since January 1998. From late 1999 the ICRC undertook humanitarian activities in Ingushetia for refugees fleeing the renewed conflict in adjoining Chechnya. Operations to assist the displaced population within Chechnya were suspended in early 2001 following the murder by rebels of an international humanitarian aid worker.

THE GENEVA CONVENTIONS

In 1864, one year after its foundation, the ICRC submitted to the states called to a Diplomatic Conference in Geneva a draft international treaty for 'the Amelioration of the Condition of the Wounded in Armies in the Field'. This treaty was adopted and signed by twelve states, which thereby bound themselves to respect as neutral wounded soldiers and those assisting them. This was the first Geneva Convention.

With the development of technology and weapons, the introduction of new means of waging war, and the manifestation of certain phenomena (the great number of prisoners of war during World War I; the enormous number of displaced persons and refugees during World War II; the internationalization of internal conflicts in recent years) the necessity was felt of having other international treaties to protect new categories of war victims. The ICRC, for more than 134 years, has been the leader of a movement to improve and complement international humanitarian law.

There are now four Geneva Conventions, adopted on 12 August 1949: I—to protect wounded and sick in armed forces on land, as well as medical personnel; II—to protect the same categories of people at sea, as well as the shipwrecked; III—concerning the treatment of prisoners of war; IV—for the protection of civilians in time of war; and there are two Additional Protocols of 8 June 1977, for the protection of victims in international armed conflicts (Protocol I) and in non-international armed conflicts (Protocol II).

By October 2000 189 states were parties to the Geneva Conventions; 157 were parties to Protocol I and 150 to Protocol II.

In April 2000 a joint working group on the emblems of the National Red Cross and Red Crescent Societies recommended the formulation of a Third Additional Protocol to the Geneva Conventions, designating a new official emblem so that National Societies could be recognized in countries that did not wish to be represented by either current symbol or did not wish to choose between the two.

Finance

The ICRC's work is financed by a voluntary annual grant from governments parties to the Geneva Conventions, voluntary contributions from National Red Cross and Red Crescent Societies and by gifts and legacies from private donors. The ICRC's budgets for 2000 amounted to some 1,080.3m. Swiss francs. Of the 'headquarters' budget of 144.5m. Swiss francs, 55.4% was allocated to field support services and 23.7% to the development, promotion and implementation of international humanitarian law. The field budget for 2000 amounted to 935.8m. Swiss francs. Operations in Africa were allocated 40.2% of the field budget.

Publications

Annual Report (editions in English, French and Spanish).
The Geneva Conventions: texts and commentaries.
ICRC News (weekly, French, English, Spanish and German editions).
International Review of the Red Cross (quarterly in French and English; annually in Russian, Arabic and Spanish).
The Protocols Additional.
Yearbook of International Humanitarian Law (annually).
Various publications on subjects of Red Cross interest (medical studies, international humanitarian law, etc.), some in electronic form.

International Federation of Red Cross and Red Crescent Societies

Address: 17 chemin des Crêts, Petit-Saconnex, CP 372, 1211 Geneva 19, Switzerland.

Telephone: (22) 7304222; **fax:** (22) 7330395; **e-mail:** secretariat@ifrc.org; **internet:** www.ifrc.org.

The Federation was founded in 1919 (as the League of Red Cross Societies). It works on the basis of the Principles of the Red Cross and Red Crescent Movement to inspire, facilitate and promote all forms of humanitarian activities by the National Societies, with a view to the prevention and alleviation of human suffering, and thereby contribute to the maintenance and promotion of peace in the world. The Federation acts as the official representative of its member societies in the field. The Federation maintains close relations with many intergovernmental organizations, the United Nations and its Specialized Agencies, and with non-governmental organizations. It has permanent observer status with the United Nations.

MEMBERS

National Red Cross and Red Crescent Societies in 176 countries in April 2001, with a total of 105m. members and volunteers.

Organization

(April 2001)

GENERAL ASSEMBLY

The General Assembly is the highest authority of the Federation and meets every two years in commission sessions (for development, disaster relief, health and community services, and youth) and plenary sessions. It is composed of representatives from all National Societies that are members of the Federation.

President: Dr ASTRID NØKLEBYE HEIBERG (Norway).

EXECUTIVE COUNCIL

The Council, which meets every six months, is composed of the President of the Federation, nine Vice-Presidents and 16 National Societies elected by the Assembly. Its functions include the implementation of decisions of the General Assembly; it also has powers to act between meetings of the Assembly.

ASSEMBLY AND FINANCE COMMISSIONS

Development Commission.
Disaster Relief Commission.
Finance Commission.
Health and Community Services Commission.
Youth Commision.

The Advisory Commissions meet, in principle, twice a year, just before the Executive Council. Members are elected by the Assembly under a system that ensures each Society a seat on one Commission.

SECRETARIAT

The Secretariat assumes the statutory responsibilities of the Federation in the field of relief to victims of natural disasters, refugees and civilian populations who may be displaced or exposed to abnormal hardship. In addition, the Secretariat promotes and co-ordinates assistance to National Societies in developing their basic structure and their services to the community. In 1999 there were some 250 employees at the Secretariat from more than 50 countries.

Secretary-General: DIDIER J. CHERPITEL (France).

Activities

DISASTER RESPONSE

The Federation supports the establishment of emergency response units, which aim to act effectively and independently to meet the needs of victims of natural or man-made disasters. The units cover basic health care provision, referral hospitals, water sanitation, logistics, telecommunications and information units. The Federation advises National Societies in relief health. In the event of a disaster the following areas are covered: communicable disease alleviation and vaccination; psychological support and stress management; health education; the provision of medicines; and the organization of mobile clinics and nursing care. The Societies also distribute food and clothing to those in need and assist in the provision of shelter and adequate sanitation facilities and in the management of refugee camps.

DEVELOPMENT

The Federation undertakes capacity-building activities with the National Societies to train and develop staff and volunteers and to improve management structures and processes, in particular in the area of disaster-preparedness. Blood donor programmes are often undertaken by National Societies, sometimes in conjuction with WHO. The Federation supports the promotion of these programmes and the implementation of quality standards. Other activities in the health sector aim to strengthen existing health services and promote community-based health care and first aid; the prevention of HIV/AIDS and substance abuse; and health education and family planning initiatives. The Federation also promotes the establishment and development of education and service programmes for children and for other more vulnerable members of society, including the elderly and disabled. Education projects support the promotion of humanitarian values.

Finance

The permanent Secretariat of the Federation is financed by the contributions of member Societies on a pro-rata basis. Each relief action is financed by separate, voluntary contributions, and development programme projects are also financed on a voluntary basis.

Publications

Annual Report.

Handbook of the International Red Cross and Red Crescent Movement (with the ICRC).

Red Cross, Red Crescent (quarterly, English, French and Spanish).

Weekly News.

World Disasters Report (annually).

Newsletters on several topics; various guides and manuals for Red Cross and Red Crescent activities.

INTERNATIONAL SEABED AUTHORITY

Address: 14–20 Port Royal St, Kingston, Jamaica.
Telephone: 922-9105; **fax:** 922-0195; **e-mail:** postmaster@isa.org.jm; **internet:** www.isa.org.jm.
The Authority was established in November 1994, upon the entry into force of the 1982 United Nations Convention on the Law of the Sea.

Organization

(April 2001)

ASSEMBLY

The Assembly is the supreme organ of the Authority, consisting of representatives of all member states. It formulates policies, approves the budget and elects Council members. The first session of the Assembly was initiated in November 1994 and was continued at a meeting in February/March 1995. The session was concluded in August 1995, having failed to reach agreement on the composition of the Council (see below) and to elect a Secretary-General of the Authority. In March 1996 the Assembly concluded the first part of its second session, having constituted the 36-member Council and elected, by consensus, the first Secretary-General of the Authority. The seventh session of the Assembly was due to be held in July 2001.

COUNCIL

The Council acts as the executive organ of the Authority. It consists of 36 members, of whom 18 are elected from four 'major interest groups'—the four states who are the largest investors in sea-bed minerals, the four major importers of sea-bed minerals, the four major land-based exporters of the same minerals, and six developing countries representing special interests—while 18 are elected on the principle of equitable representation. The Council aims to reach decisions by consensus agreement, failing which a vote may be conducted, although any decision has to be approved by the majority within each of the four member groups, or chambers.

LEGAL AND TECHNICAL COMMISSION

The 21-member Commission (originally it was to comprise 15 members) assists the Council by making recommendations concerning sea-bed activities, assessing the environmental implications of activities in the area and proposing measures to protect the marine environment. Under the terms of the agreement on the implementation of Part XI of the Convention, the Commission was to undertake the functions of a proposed economic planning commission until the Council decides otherwise or until the approval of the first work plan for mineral exploitation of the deep sea-bed. These functions include reviewing trends and factors affecting supply, demand and prices of materials that may be derived from the deep sea-bed area. The main task of the Commission between 1996 and 1998 was the elaboration of draft regulations on prospecting and exploration for polymetallic nodules in the deep sea-bed area; the draft was adopted by the sixth session of the Assembly in July 2000; exploration contracts were subsequently to be issued to seven contractors. In 1999 the Legal and Technical Commission commenced work on compiling guide-lines for assessing the potential environmental consequences of recovering polymetallic nodules.

FINANCE COMMITTEE

The Committee, comprising 15 members, was established to make recommendations to the Assembly and the Council on all financial and budgetary issues.

SECRETARIAT

The Secretariat provides administrative services to all the bodies of the Authority and implements the relevant work programmes. It comprises the Office of the Secretary-General, Offices of Resources and Environmental Monitoring, Legal Affairs, and Administration and Management. Under the terms of the agreement on the implementation of Part XI of the Convention (see below), the Secretariat was to undertake the functions of the Enterprise, which was to carry out deep sea-bed mining operations, through joint ventures.
Secretary-General: SATYA N. NANDAN (Fiji).

Activities

The Authority is the organization through which states party to the Law of the Sea Convention organize and control activities in the international sea-bed area beyond the limits of national jurisdiction, particularly with a view to administering the mineral resources of that area. It functions as an autonomous international organization in relationship with the UN. All states party to the Convention are members of the Authority.

The third UN Conference on the Law of the Sea (UNCLOS) began its work in 1973, with the aim of regulating maritime activities by defining zones and boundaries, ensuring fair exploitation of resources, and providing machinery for settlement of disputes. Negotiations, involving more than 160 countries, continued until April 1982, when the Conference finally adopted the UN Convention on the Law of the Sea: 130 states voted in its favour, while the USA, Israel, Turkey and Venezuela voted against, and there were 17 abstentions, including the then Federal Republic of Germany, the USSR and the United Kingdom. The Convention was opened for signing in December for a two-year period. By 1984 159 states had signed, but the USA, the United Kingdom and the Federal Republic of Germany refused to sign. The 60th ratification of the Convention was received in November 1993, and by April 2001 135 states had ratified, acceded or succeeded to the Convention. The main provisions of the Convention are as follows:

Coastal states are allowed sovereignty over their territorial waters of up to 12 nautical miles in breadth; foreign vessels are to be allowed 'innocent passage' through these waters.

Ships and aircraft of all states are allowed 'transit passage' through straits used for international navigation.

Archipelagic states (composed of islands) have sovereignty over a sea area enclosed by straight lines drawn between the outermost points of the islands.

Coastal states have sovereign rights in a 200-mile exclusive economic zone with respect to natural resources and jurisdiction over certain activities (such as protection and preservation of the environment), and rights over the adjacent continental shelf up to 350 miles from the shore under specified circumstances.

All states have freedom of navigation, overflight, scientific research and fishing on the high seas, but must co-operate in measures to conserve living resources.

A 'parallel system' is to be established for exploiting the international sea-bed, where all activities are to be supervised by the International Seabed Authority.

States are bound to control pollution and co-operate in forming preventive rules, and incur penalties for failing to combat pollution.

Marine scientific research in the zones under national jurisdiction is subject to the prior consent of the coastal state, but consent may be denied only under specific circumstances.

States must submit disputes on the application and interpretation of the Convention to a compulsory procedure entailing decisions binding on all parties. An International Tribunal for the Law of the Sea is to be established.

The USA and other industrialized nations witheld their support, owing to Part XI of the Convention, concerning the provisions for exploitation of the international ocean bed, and particularly the minerals to be found there (chiefly manganese, cobalt, copper and nickel), envisaged as the 'common heritage of mankind'. It was argued that those countries which possess adequate technology for deep-sea mining would be insufficiently represented in the new Authority; the operations of private mining consortia, according to the objectors, would be unacceptably limited by the stipulations that their technology should be shared with a supranational mining venture (the 'Enterprise'), and that production should be limited in order to protect land-based mineral producers. In July 1994 the UN General Assembly adopted an agreement amending the implementation of Part XI of the Convention. Under the new agreement, which aimed to counter the objections of the industrialized nations, there was to be no mandatory transfer of technology, the Enterprise was to operate according to commercial principles and there were to be no production limits, although a compensation fund was to assist land-based producers adversely affected by sea-bed mining. The agreement entered into force in July 1996. An agreement on the implementation of the provisions of the Convention relating to the conservation and management of straddling and highly migratory fish stocks was opened for signature in December 1995 and was to enter into force after ratification by 30 countries.

In August 1998 discussions began, under the auspices of the Authority, relating to the recovery of polymetallic nodules from the international sea-bed. The Authority has held a series of workshops on this and other issues. In 2001 the Authority was organizing a workshop on the development of a standardized system of data interpretation.

Finance

The Authority's budget is the responsibility of the Finance Committee. The budget for the Authority for 2000 was US $5.3m. A budget of $10.5m. was approved for the period 2001–02. The administrative expenses of the Authority are met by assessed contributions of its members.

Publications

Handbook 2000
Selected decisions and documents of sessions of the Authority; rules of procedure, etc.

Associated Institutions

The following were also established under the terms of the Convention:

Commission on the Limits of the Continental Shelf: Division for Ocean Affairs and the Law of the Sea, Room DC2-0450, United Nations, New York, NY 10017, USA; tel. (212) 963-3951; fax (212) 963-5847; e-mail doalos@un.org; internet www.un.org/Depts/los; 21 members of the Commission were elected, for a five-year term, in March 1997; responsible for making recommendations regarding the establishment of the outer limits of the continental shelf of a coastal state, where the limit extends beyond 200 nautical miles (370 km).

International Tribunal for the Law of the Sea: Am internationalen Seegerichtshof 1, Hamburg, Germany; tel. (40) 356070; fax (40) 35607245; e-mail itlos@itlos.org; inaugurated in Oct. 1996; 21 judges; responsible for interpreting the Convention and ruling on disputes brought by states party to the Convention on matters within its jurisdiction. Registrar: GRITAKUMAR E. CHITTY.

INTER-PARLIAMENTARY UNION—IPU

Address: CP 438, 1211 Geneva 19, Switzerland.
Telephone: (22) 9194150; **fax:** (22) 9194160; **e-mail:** postbox@mail.ipu.org; **internet:** www.ipu.org.
Founded in 1889, the IPU aims to promote peace, co-operation and representative democracy by providing a forum for multilateral political debate between representatives of national parliaments.

MEMBERS

National parliaments of 141 sovereign states; five international parliamentary associations (Associate Members).

Organization

(April 2001)

INTER-PARLIAMENTARY CONFERENCE

The Conference is the main statutory body of the IPU, comprising eight to 10 representatives from each member parliament. It meets twice a year to discuss current issues in world affairs and to make political recommendations. Other specialized conferences may also be held. The Conference is assisted by four plenary Study Committees on Political Questions: International Security and Disarmament; Parliamentary, Juridical and Human Rights Questions; Economic and Social Questions; and Education, Science, Culture and the Environment.

INTER-PARLIAMENTARY COUNCIL

The Council comprises two representatives of each member parliament, usually from different political groups. It is responsible for approving membership and the annual programme and budget of the IPU, and for electing the Secretary-General. The Council may consider substantive issues and adopt resolutions and policy statements, in particular on the basis of recommendations from its subsidiary bodies.
President: NAJMA HEPTULLA (India).

MEETING OF WOMEN PARLIAMENTARIANS

The Meeting is a mechanism for co-ordination between women parliamentarians. Since 1975 the Meeting has been convened twice a year, on the occasion of IPU statutory meetings, to discuss subjects of common interest, to formulate strategies to develop the IPU's women's programme, to strengthen their influence within the organization and to ensure that women are elected to key positions. The Meeting is assisted by a Co-ordinating Committee.

SUBSIDIARY BODIES

In addition to the thematic Study Committees of the IPU Conference, various other committees and groups undertake and co-ordinate IPU activities in specific areas. All these bodies are subsidiary to the IPU Council:
Committee on the Human Rights of Parliamentarians
Committee for Sustainable Development
Committee on Middle East Questions
Group of Facilitators for Cyprus
Committee to Promote Respect for International and Humanitarian Law

CSCM Process and CSCM Co-ordinating Committee (concerned with security and co-operation in the Mediterranean)
Co-ordinating Committee of the Meeting of Women MPs
Gender Partnership Group

EXECUTIVE COMMITTEE

The Committee, comprising 12 members and presided over by the President of the Council, oversees the administration of the IPU and advises the Council on membership, policy and programme, and any other matters referred to it.

SECRETARIAT

Secretary-General: ANDERS B. JOHNSSON (Sweden).

Activities

PROMOTION OF REPRESENTATIVE DEMOCRACY

This is one of the IPU's core areas of activity, and covers a wide range of concerns, such as democracy, gender issues, human rights and ethnic diversity, parliamentary action to combat corruption, and links between democracy and economic growth. In September 1997 the Council adopted a Universal Declaration on Democracy. The IPU subsequently published a study entitled *Democracy: Its Principles and Achievements.*

The IPU administers a Programme for the Study and Promotion of Representative Institutions, which aims to improve knowledge of the functioning of national parliaments by gathering and disseminating information on their constitutional powers and responsibilities, structure, and membership, and on the electoral systems used. The IPU also organizes international seminars and gatherings for parliamentarians, officials, academics and other experts to study the functioning of parliamentary institutions. A Technical Co-operation Programme aims to mobilize international support in order to improve the capabilities, infrastructure and technical facilities of national parliaments and enhance their effectiveness. Under the Programme, the IPU may provide expert advice on the structure of legislative bodies, staff training, and parliamentary working procedures, and provide technical equipment and other resources. In 1999 technical assistance projects were implemented in Burundi, Ethiopia, Fiji, Gabon, The Gambia, Kyrgyzstan, Laos, Malawi, Viet Nam and Yemen.

IPU teams of observers have overseen elections in Namibia, in 1989, in Cambodia, 1993, and in El Salvador, in 1994. Their duties included observing the process of voter registration, the election campaign and voting, and verifying the results. In 1993 the Council resolved that the IPU be present at all national elections organized, supervised or verified by the United Nations. The IPU has reported on the rights and responsibilities of election observers and issued guide-lines on the holding of free and fair elections. These include a *Declaration on Criteria for Free and Fair Elections,* together with a study on the subject, and Codes of Conduct for Elections.

The IPU maintains a special database (PARLINE) on parliaments of the world, giving access to information on the structure and functioning of all existing parliaments, and on national elections. It conducts regular world studies on matters regarding the structure and functioning of parliaments. It also maintains a separate database (PARLIT) comprising literature from around the world on constitutional, electoral and parliamentary matters.

In August/September 2000 the IPU organized the first international conference of speakers of national parliaments.

INTERNATIONAL PEACE AND SECURITY

The IPU aims to promote conflict resolution and international security through political discussion. Certain areas of conflict are monitored by the Union on an ongoing basis (for example, Cyprus and the Middle East), while others are considered as they arise. In recent years, the IPU has been particularly concerned with the situation in the former Yugoslavia, and has condemned incidents of violations of humanitarian law and supported efforts to improve the lives of those affected by the conflict. In April 1998 the Union adopted an emergency resolution on the situation in Kosovo and Metohija, southern Serbia. An extensive programme of activities is undertaken by the IPU with regard to the Mediterranean region. In June 1992 the first Conference on Security and Co-operation in the Mediterranean (CSCM) took place; the objectives outlined at the Conference have been integrated as a structured process of the IPU. A second CSCM was held in Valetta, Malta, in November 1995, and a third was convened at Marseilles, France, in March/April 2000. Intermediary thematic meetings are held between plenary conferences, while consultations among parties to the CSCM process take place every six months.

The IPU has worked constantly to promote international and regional efforts towards disarmament, as part of the process of enhancing peace and security. Issues that have been discussed by the Conference include nuclear non-proliferation, a ban on testing of nuclear weapons, and a global register of arms transfers.

SUSTAINABLE DEVELOPMENT

The Committee for Sustainable Development guides the IPU's work in this area, with a broad approach of linking economic growth with social, democratic, human welfare and environmental considerations. Issues of world economic and social development on which the IPU has approved recommendations include employment in a globalizing world, the globalization of economy and liberalization of trade, Third World debt and its impact on the integration of those countries affected into the process of globalization, international mass migration and other demographic problems, and the right to food. The IPU co-operates with programmes and agencies of the UN, in particular in the preparation of major socio-economic conferences, including the World Summit for Social Development, which was held in Copenhagen, Denmark, in March 1995, the Fourth World Conference on Women, held in Beijing, People's Republic of China, in September 1995, and the World Food Summit, held in Rome, Italy, in November 1996. In September 1996 a tripartite meeting of parliamentary, governmental and inter-governmental representatives, convened at the UN headquarters in New York, considered legislative measures to pursue the objectives of the World Summit for Social Development; a follow-up meeting was held in March 1999. In November/December 1998 the IPU, in co-operation with FAO, organized an Inter-Parliamentary Conference concerned with 'Attaining the World Food Summit's Objectives through a Sustainable Development Strategy'.

Activities to protect the environment are undertaken within the framework of sustainable development. In 1984 the first Inter-Parliamentary Conference on the Environment, convened in Nairobi, Kenya, advocated the inclusion of environmental considerations into the development process. The IPU was actively involved in the preparation of the UN Conference on Environment and Development (UNCED), which was held in Rio de Janeiro, Brazil, in June 1992. Subsequently the IPU's environment programme has focused on implementing the recommendations of UNCED, and identifying measures to be taken at parliamentary level to facilitate that process. The IPU also monitors the actual measures taken by national parliaments to pursue the objective of sustainable development, as well as emerging environmental problems. In 1997 the IPU published the *World Directory of Parliamentary Bodies for Environment*.

HUMAN RIGHTS AND HUMANITARIAN LAW

The IPU frequently considers human rights issues and makes relevant recommendations at its statutory Conferences and during specialized meetings, and aims to incorporate human rights concerns, including employment, the rights of minorities, and gender issues, in all areas of activity. A five-member Committee on the Human Rights of Parliamentarians is responsible for the consideration of complaints relating to alleged violations of the human rights of members of parliament, for example state harassment, arbitrary arrest and detention, unfair trail and violation of parliamentary immunity, based on a procedure adopted by the IPU in 1976. The Committee conducts hearings and site missions to investigate a complaint and communicates with the authorities of the country concerned. If no settlement is reached at that stage, the Committee may then publish a report for the Inter-Parliamentary Council and submit recommendations on specific measures to be adopted. By the end of 1998 1,097 cases had been declared admissible, in 87 countries, of which the majority had reached a satisfactory settlement, often through the support of IPU member parliaments.

The IPU works closely with the International Committee of the Red Cross to uphold respect for international humanitarian law. It supports the implementation of the Geneva Conventions and their Additional Protocols, and the adoption of appropriate national legislation. In 1995 the Council adopted a special resolution to establish a reporting mechanism at the parliamentary level to ensure respect for international humanitarian law. Consequently IPU initiated a world survey on legislative action regarding the application of international humanitarian law, as well as efforts to ban anti-personnel land-mines. In April and September 1998 the Council adopted special resolutions on parliamentary action to secure the entry into force and implementation of the Convention on the Prohibition of the Use, Stockpiling, Production and Transfer of Anti-personnel Mines and on their Destruction, which was signed by representatives of some 120 countries meeting in Ottawa, Canada, in December 1997. Further resolutions to that effect were adopted by the Inter-Parliamentary Conference in October 1999 and in April 2001.

In 1998 the IPU published a *World Directory of Parliamentary Human Rights Bodies*.

WOMEN IN POLITICS

The IPU aims to promote the participation of women in the political and parliamentary decision-making processes, and, more generally, in all aspects of society. It organizes debates and events on these issues and compiles a statistical database on women in politics, compiled by regular world surveys. The IPU also actively addresses wider issues of concern to women, such as literacy and education, women in armed conflicts, women's contribution to development, and women in the electoral process. The eradication of violence against women was the subject of a special resolution adopted by the Conference in 1991. The Meeting of Women MPs has monitored efforts by national authorities to implement the recommendations outlined in the resolution. In 1996 the IPU promoted the Framework for Model Legislation on Domestic Violence, formulated by the UN Special Rapporteur on the issue, which aimed to assist national parliaments in preparing legislation to safeguard women. At the Fourth World Conference on Women, held in Beijing, in September 1995, the IPU organized several events to bring together parliamentarians and other leading experts, diplomats and officials to promote the rights of women and of children. In February 1997 the IPU organized a Specialized Inter-Parliamentary Conference, in New Delhi, India, entitled 'Towards partnership between men and women in politics'. Following the Conference the IPU decided to establish a Gender Partnership Group, comprising two men and two women, within the Executive Committee, to ensure that IPU activities and decisions serve the interests and needs of all members of the population. The Group was authorized to report to the IPU Council.

The IPU aims to promote the importance of women's role in economic and social development and their participation in politics as a democratic necessity, and recognizes the crucial role of the media in presenting the image of women. Within the context of the 1997 New Delhi Conference, the IPU organized a second Round Table on the Image of Women Politicians in the Media (the first having been convened in November 1989). The debate urged fair and equal representation of women politicians by the media and for governments to revise their communications policies to advance the image of female parliamentarians.

EDUCATION, SCIENCE AND CULTURE

Activities in these sectors are often subject to consideration by statutory Conferences. Resolutions of the Conference have focused on the implementation of educational and cultural policies designed to foster greater respect for demographic values, adopted in April 1993; on bioethics and its implications world-wide for human rights protection, adopted in April 1995; and on the importance of education and culture as prerequisites for securing sustainable development (with particular emphasis on the education of women and the application of new information technologies), necessitating their high priority status in national budgets, adopted in April 2001. Specialized meetings organized by the IPU have included the Asia and Pacific Inter-Parliamentary Conference on 'Science and technology for regional sustainable development', held in Tokyo, Japan, in June 1994, and the Inter-Parliamentary Conference on 'Education, science, culture and communication on the threshold of the 21st century', organized jointly with UNESCO, and held in Paris, France, in June 1996.

Finance

The IPU is financed by its members from public funds. The 2001 annual budget totalled 10m. Swiss francs. In addition external financial support, primarily from UNDP, is received for some special activities.

Publications

Chronicle of Parliamentary Elections (annually).
Handbook for Parliamentarians: Respect for International Humanitarian Law.
Inter-Parliamentary Bulletin (2 a year).
World Directory of Parliaments (annually).
Other reports, documents, conference proceedings.

ISLAMIC DEVELOPMENT BANK

Address: POB 5925, Jeddah 21432, Saudi Arabia.
Telephone: (2) 6361400; **fax:** (2) 6366871; **e-mail:** archives@isdb.org.sa; **internet:** www.isdb.org.

The Bank is an international financial institution that was established following a conference of Ministers of Finance of member countries of the Organization of the Islamic Conference (OIC, q.v.), held in Jeddah in December 1973. Its aim is to encourage the economic development and social progress of member countries and of Muslim communities in non-member countries, in accordance with the principles of the Islamic *Shari'a* (sacred law). The Bank formally opened in October 1975.

MEMBERS

There are 53 members.

Organization

(April 2001)

BOARD OF GOVERNORS

Each member country is represented by a governor, usually its Minister of Finance, and an alternate. The Board of Governors is the supreme authority of the Bank, and meets annually.

BOARD OF EXECUTIVE DIRECTORS

The Board consists of 14 members, seven of whom are appointed by the seven largest subscribers to the capital stock of the Bank; the remaining seven are elected by Governors representing the other subscribers. Members of the Board of Executive Directors are elected for three-year terms. The Board is responsible for the direction of the general operations of the Bank.
President of the Bank and Chairman of the Board of Executive Directors: Dr Ahmed Mohamed Ali.
Bank Secretary: Dr Abderrahim Omrana.

REGIONAL OFFICES

Kazakhstan: c/o Director, External Aid Co-ordination Dept, 93–95 Ablay-Khan Ave, 480091 Almaty; tel. (3272) 62-18-68; fax (3272) 69-61-52; Dir Zhankyn Kakimzkanova.
Malaysia: Level 11, Front Wing, Bank Industri, Jalan Sultan Ismail, POB 13671, 50818 Kuala Lumpur; tel. (3) 2946627; fax (3) 2946626; Dir Dr Muhammad Siddik.
Morocco: 177 Ave John Kennedy, Souissi 10105, POB 5003, Rabat; tel. (7) 757191; fax (7) 775726; Dir Dr Marwan Seifuddin.

FINANCIAL STRUCTURE

The authorized capital of the Bank is 6,000m. Islamic Dinars (divided into 600,000 shares, having a value of 10,000 Islamic Dinars each). The Islamic Dinar (ID) is the Bank's unit of account and is equivalent to the value of one Special Drawing Right of the IMF (SDR 1 = US $1.2925 at 28 February 2001).
Subscribed capital amounts to ID 4,000m.

Activities

The Bank adheres to the Islamic principle forbidding usury, and does not grant loans or credits for interest. Instead, its methods of project financing are: provision of interest-free loans (with a service fee), mainly for infrastructural projects which are expected to have a marked impact on long-term socio-economic development; provision of technical assistance (e.g. for feasibility studies); equity participation in industrial and agricultural projects; leasing operations, involving the leasing of equipment such as ships, and instal-

SUBSCRIPTIONS (million Islamic Dinars, as at December 1998)

Afghanistan	5.00		Maldives	2.50
Albania	2.50		Mali	4.92
Algeria	124.26		Mauritania	4.92
Azerbaijan	4.92		Morocco	24.81
Bahrain	7.00		Mozambique	2.50
Bangladesh	49.29		Niger	12.41
Benin	4.92		Oman	13.78
Brunei	12.41		Pakistan	124.26
Burkina Faso	12.41		Palestine	9.85
Cameroon	12.41		Qatar	49.23
Chad	4.92		Saudi Arabia	997.17
Comoros	2.50		Senegal	12.42
Djibouti	2.50		Sierra Leone	2.50
Egypt	49.23		Somalia	2.50
Gabon	14.77		Sudan	19.69
The Gambia	2.50		Suriname	2.50
Guinea	12.41		Syria	5.00
Guinea-Bissau	2.50		Tajikistan	2.50
Indonesia	124.26		Togo	2.50
Iran	349.97		Tunisia	9.85
Iraq	13.05		Turkey	315.47
Jordan	19.89		Turkmenistan	2.50
Kazakhstan	2.50		Uganda	12.41
Kuwait	496.64		United Arab	
Kyrgyzstan	2.50		Emirates	283.03
Lebanon	4.92		Yemen	24.81
Libya	400.00		**Total**	**3,763.77**
Malaysia	79.56			

ment sale financing; and profit-sharing operations. Funds not immediately needed for projects are used for foreign trade financing. Under the Import Trade Financing Operations (ITFO) scheme, funds are used for importing commodities for development purposes (i.e. raw materials and intermediate industrial goods, rather than consumer goods), with priority given to the import of goods from other member countries (see table). The Longer-term Trade Financing Scheme (LTTFS) was introduced in 1987/88 to provide financing for the export of non-traditional and capital goods. During AH 1419 the LTTFS was renamed the Export Financing Scheme (EFS). In addition, the Special Assistance Waqf Fund (which was established with effect from 7 May 1997, formerly the Special Assistance Account) provides emergency aid and other assistance, with particular emphasis on education in Islamic communities in non-member countries. A Special Account for least-developed member countries aims to assist these countries by providing loans on concessionary terms. Loans financed by this Account are charged an annual service fee of 0.75%, compared with 2.5% for ordinary loans, and have a repayment period of 25–30 years, compared with 15–25 years.

By 16 April 1999 the Bank had approved a total of ID 4,306.61m. for project financing and technical assistance, a total of ID 10,606.58m. for foreign trade financing, and ID 378.92m. for special assistance operations, excluding amounts for cancelled operations. During the Islamic year 1419 (8 May 1998 to 16 April 1999) the Bank approved a total of ID 1,299.70m., for 212 operations.

The Bank approved 37 loans in the year ending 16 April 1999, amounting to ID 159.05m. (compared with 31 loans, totalling ID 133.90m., in the previous year). These loans supported projects concerned with infrastructural improvements, for example of roads, canals, sewerage, water-supply and rural electrification, the construction of schools and health centres, and agricultural developments.

During AH 1419 the Bank approved 29 technical assistance operations for 19 countries (as well as three regional projects) in the form of grants and loans, amounting to ID 5.90m.

Operations approved, Islamic year 1419 (8 May 1998–16 April 1999)

Type of operation	Number of operations	Total amount (million Islamic Dinars)
Ordinary operations . . .	98	525.28
Project financing . . .	69	519.39
Technical assistance . . .	29	5.90
Trade financing operations* .	65	766.45
Waqf Fund operations . . .	49	7.97
Total†	212	1,299.70

* Including ITFO, the EFS, the Islamic Bank's Portfolio and the UIF.
† Excluding cancelled operations.

Project financing and technical assistance by sector, Islamic year 1419

Sector	Number of Operations	Amount (million Islamic Dinars)	%
Agriculture and agro-industry	24	76.72	14.6
Industry and mining . . .	3	33.09	6.3
Transport and communications . . .	14	67.61	12.9
Public utilities . . .	20	155.58	29.9
Social sectors	24	109.12	20.8
Other*	13	83.16	15.8
Total†	98	525.28	100.0

* Mainly approved amounts for Islamic banks.
† Excluding cancelled operations.

Import trade financing approved during the Islamic year 1419 amounted to ID 629.78m. for 36 operations in 11 member countries. By the end of that year cumulative import trade financing amounted to ID 8,851.44m., of which 38.1% was for imports of crude petroleum, 27.1% for intermediate industrial goods, 8.0% for vegetable oil and 5.8% for refined petroleum products. Export financing approved under the EFS amounted to ID 47.99m. for 15 operations in eight countries in AH 1419. In the same year the Bank's Portfolio for Investment and Development, established in AH 1407 (1986–87), approved 17 operations amounting to US $321m. (or approximately ID 218.56m.). Since its introduction, the Portfolio has approved net financing operations amounting to $1,817m.

During AH 1419 the Bank approved 49 special assistance operations, amounting to ID 7.97m., providing assistance primarily in the education sector, as well as emergency relief; of the total financing, 27 operations provided for Muslim communities in 18 non-member countries.

The Bank's scholarships programme sponsored 459 students from seven member and 30 non-member countries during the year to 16 April 1999. The Merit Scholarship Programme, initiated in AH 1412 (1991–92), aims to develop scientific, technological and research capacities in member countries through advanced studies and/or research. By AH 1419 (1998–99) 134 scholars from 38 member countries had been placed in academic centres of excellence in Australia, Europe and the USA under the programme; a further 15 scholarships were awarded in AH 1420. In December 1997 the Board of Executive Directors approved a new scholarship programme designed specifically to assist scholars from least-developed member countries to study for a masters degree in science and technology. Some 20 scholarships were allocated in AH 1419, and it was expected that a total of 190 would be awarded by AH 1423. The Bank's Programme for Technical Co-operation aims to mobilize technical capabilities among member countries and to promote the exchange of expertise, experience and skills through expert missions, training, seminars and workshops. During AH 1419 96 projects were implemented under the programme. The Bank also undertakes the distribution of meat sacrificed by Muslim pilgrims: in AH 1419 meat from approximately 469,150 animals was distributed to the needy in 24 countries.

During the year ending 16 April 1999 the Bank's disbursements totalled ID 535m., bringing the total cumulative disbursements since the Bank began operations to ID 10,139m.

The Bank's Unit Investment Fund (UIF) became operational in 1990, with the aim of mobilizing additional resources and providing a profitable channel for investments conforming to *Shari'a*. The initial issue of the UIF was US $100m., which has subsequently been increased to $325m. The Fund finances mainly private-sector industrial projects in middle-income countries. The UIF also finances short-term trade financing operations: four were approved in AH 1419, amounting to $17.60m. In October 1998 the Bank announced the establishment of a new fund to invest in infrastructure projects in member states. The Bank committed $250m. to the fund, which was to comprise $1,000m. equity capital and a $500m. Islamic financing facility. In September 1999 the Bank's Board of Executive Directors approved the establishment of an Islamic Corporation for the Development of the Private Sector, which was scheduled to commence operations in 2000.

SUBSIDIARY ORGANS

Islamic Corporation for the Insurance of Investment and Export Credit—ICIEC: POB 15722, Jeddah 21454, Saudi Arabia; tel. (2) 6445666; fax (2) 6379504; e-mail idb.iciec@isdb.org.sa; internet www.iciec.org; f. 1994; aims to promote trade and the flow of investments among member countries of the OIC through the provision of export credit and investment insurance services; auth. cap. ID 100m., subscribed cap. ID 91.2m. (April 1999). Man. Dr ABDEL RAHMAN A. TAHA. Mems: 23 OIC member states.

Islamic Research and Training Institute: POB 9201, Jeddah 21413, Saudi Arabia; tel. (2) 6361400; fax (2) 6378927; e-mail mal-jarhi@isdb.org.sa; internet www.irti.org; f. 1982 to undertake research enabling economic, financial and banking activities to conform to Islamic law, and to provide training for staff involved in development activities in the Bank's member countries. The Institute also organizes seminars and workshops, and holds training courses aimed at furthering the expertise of government and financial officials in Islamic developing countries. Dir Dr MABID ALI AL-JARHI. Publs *Annual Report*, *Journal of Islamic Economic Studies*, various research studies, monographs, reports.

Publication

Annual Report.

LATIN AMERICAN INTEGRATION ASSOCIATION—LAIA

(ASOCIACIÓN LATINOAMERICANA DE INTEGRACIÓN—ALADI)

Address: Cebollatí 1461, Casilla 577, 11000 Montevideo, Uruguay.

Telephone: (2) 4001121; **fax:** (2) 4090649; **e-mail:** sgaladi@aladi.org; **internet:** www.aladi.org.

The Latin American Integration Association was established in August 1980 to replace the Latin American Free Trade Association, founded in February 1960.

MEMBERS

Argentina	Colombia	Paraguay
Bolivia	Cuba	Peru
Brazil	Ecuador	Uruguay
Chile	Mexico	Venezuela

Observers: People's Republic of China, Costa Rica, Dominican Republic, El Salvador, Guatemala, Honduras, Italy, Nicaragua,

Panama, Portugal, Romania, Russia, Spain and Switzerland; also the UN Economic Commission for Latin America and the Caribbean (ECLAC), the UN Development Programme (UNDP), the European Union, the Inter-American Development Bank, the Organization of American States, the Andean Development Corporation, the Inter-American Institute for Co-operation on Agriculture and the Latin American Economic System.

Organization

(April 2001)

COUNCIL OF MINISTERS

The Council of Ministers of Foreign Affairs is responsible for the adoption of the Association's policies. It meets when convened by the Committee of Representatives.

EVALUATION AND CONVERGENCE CONFERENCE

The Conference, comprising plenipotentiaries of the member governments, assesses the Association's progress and encourages negotiations between members. It meets when convened by the Committee of Representatives.

COMMITTEE OF REPRESENTATIVES

The Committee, the permanent political body of the Association, comprises a permanent and a deputy representative from each member country. Permanent observers have been accredited by 15 countries and eight international organizations (see above). The Committee is the main forum for the negotiation of ALADI's initiatives and is responsible for the correct implementation of the Treaty and its supplementary regulations. There are the following auxiliary bodies:

Advisory Commission on Customs Valuation.

Advisory Commission on Financial and Monetary Affairs.

Advisory Council for Export Financing.

Advisory Council for Customs Matters.

Budget Commission.

Commission for Technical Support and Co-operation.

Council for Financial and Monetary Affairs: comprises the Presidents of member states' central banks, who examine all aspects of financial, monetary and exchange co-operation.

Council on Transport for Trade Facilitation.

Entrepreneurial Advisory Council.

Labour Advisory Council.

Meeting of Directors of National Customs Administrations.

Nomenclature Advisory Commission.

Sectoral Councils.

Tourism Council.

GENERAL SECRETARIAT

The General Secretariat is the technical body of the Association; it submits proposals for action, carries out research and evaluates activities. The Secretary-General is elected for a three-year term. There are two Assistant Secretaries-General.

Secretary-General: JUAN FRANCISCO ROJAS PENSO (Venezuela).

Activities

The Latin American Free Trade Association (LAFTA) was an intergovernmental organization, created by the Treaty of Montevideo in February 1960 with the object of increasing trade between the Contracting Parties and of promoting regional integration, thus contributing to the economic and social development of the member countries. The Treaty provided for the gradual establishment of a free-trade area, which would form the basis for a Latin American Common Market. Reduction of tariff and other trade barriers was to be carried out gradually until 1980.

By 1980, however, only 14% of annual trade among members could be attributed to LAFTA agreements, and it was the richest states which were receiving most benefit. In June it was decided that LAFTA should be replaced by a less ambitious and more flexible organization, the Latin American Integration Association (Asociación Latinoamericana de Integración—ALADI), established by the 1980 Montevideo Treaty, which came into force in March 1981, and was fully ratified in March 1982. Instead of across-the-board tariff cuts, the Treaty envisaged an area of economic preferences, comprising a regional tariff preference for goods originating in member states (in effect from 1 July 1984) and regional and partial scope agreements (on economic complementation, trade promotion, trade in agricultural goods, scientific and technical co-operation, the environment, tourism, and other matters), taking into account the different stages of development of the members, and with no definite timetable for the establishment of a full common market.

The members of ALADI are divided into three categories: most developed (Argentina, Brazil and Mexico); intermediate (Chile, Colombia, Peru, Uruguay and Venezuela); and least developed (Bolivia, Cuba—which joined the Association in August 1999, Ecuador and Paraguay), enjoying a special preferential system. In 2000 the value of exports within ALADI amounted to US $43,202m., compared with $34,776m. in 1999. The countries of the Southern Common Market (Mercosur) accounted for more than one-half of this total. By 2004 75% of all intra-ALADI trade was expected to be free of trade restrictions.

Certain LAFTA institutions were retained and adapted by ALADI, e.g. the Reciprocal Payments and Credits Agreement (1965, modified in 1982) and the Multilateral Credit Agreement to Alleviate Temporary Shortages of Liquidity, known as the Santo Domingo Agreement (1969, extended in 1981 to include mechanisms for counteracting global balance-of-payments difficulties and for assisting in times of natural disaster).

By August 1998 98 agreements had entered into force. Seven were 'regional agreements' (in which all 11 member countries participate). These agreements included a regional tariff preference agreement, whereby members allow imports from other member states to enter with tariffs 20% lower than those imposed on imports from other countries, and a Market Opening Lists agreement in favour of the three least developed member states, which provides for the total elimination of duties and other restrictions on imports of certain products. The remaining 91 agreements were 'partial scope agreements' (in which two or more member states participate), including: renegotiation agreements (pertaining to tariff cuts under LAFTA); trade agreements covering particular industrial sectors; the agreements establishing Mercosur (q.v.) and the Group of Three (G3); and agreements covering agriculture, gas supply, tourism, environmental protection, books, transport, sanitation and trade facilitation. A new system of tariff nomenclature, based on the 'harmonized system', was adopted from 1 January 1990 as a basis for common trade negotiations and statistics. General regimes on safeguards and rules of origin entered into force in 1987.

The Secretariat convenes meetings of entrepreneurs in various private industrial sectors, to encourage regional trade and co-operation. In early 2001 ALADI conducted a survey on small and medium-sized enterprises in order to advise the Secretary-General in formulating a programme to assist those businesses and enhance their competitiveness.

A feature of ALADI is its 'outward' projection, allowing for multilateral links or agreements with Latin American non-member countries or integration organizations, and with other developing countries or economic groups outside the continent. In February 1994 the Council of Ministers of Foreign Affairs urged that ALADI should become the co-ordinating body for the various bilateral, multilateral and regional accords (the Andean Community, Mercosur and G3 etc.), with the aim of eventually forming a region-wide common market. The General Secretariat initiated studies in preparation for a programme to undertake this co-ordinating work. At the same meeting in February there was a serious disagreement regarding the proposed adoption of a protocol to the Montevideo Treaty to enable Mexico to participate in the North American Free Trade Agreement (NAFTA), while remaining a member of ALADI. Brazil, in particular, opposed such a solution. However, in June the first Interpretative Protocol to the Montevideo Treaty was signed by the Ministers of Foreign Affairs: the Protocol allows member states to establish preferential trade agreeements with developed nations, with a temporary waiver of the most-favoured nation clause (article 44 of the Treaty), subject to the negotiation of unilateral compensation.

Mercosur (which comprises Argentina, Brazil, Paraguay and Uruguay, with Chile and Bolivia as associate members) aims to conclude free-trade agreements with the other members of ALADI. In March 2001 ALADI signed a co-operation agreement with the Andean Community to facilitate the exchange of information and consolidate regional and sub-regional integration.

Publications

Empresarios en la Integración (monthly, in Spanish).

Noticias ALADI (monthly, in Spanish).

Estadísticas y Comercio (quarterly, in Spanish).

Reports, studies, brochures, texts of agreements.

LEAGUE OF ARAB STATES

Address: POB 11642, Arab League Bldg, Tahrir Square, Cairo, Egypt.

Telephone: (2) 5750511; **fax:** (2) 5775626.

The League of Arab States (more generally known as the Arab League) is a voluntary association of sovereign Arab states, designed to strengthen the close ties linking them and to co-ordinate their policies and activities and direct them towards the common good of all the Arab countries. It was founded in March 1945.

MEMBERS

Algeria	Lebanon	Somalia
Bahrain	Libya	Sudan
Comoros	Mauritania	Syria
Djibouti	Morocco	Tunisia
Egypt	Oman	United Arab
Iraq	Palestine*	Emirates
Jordan	Qatar	Yemen
Kuwait	Saudi Arabia	

* Palestine is considered an independent state, and therefore a full member of the League.

Organization

(May 2001)

COUNCIL

The supreme organ of the Arab League, the Council consists of representatives of the member states, each of which has one vote, and a representative for Palestine. Unanimous decisions of the Council shall be binding upon all member states of the League; majority decisions shall be binding only on those states which have accepted them.

The Council may, if necessary, hold an extraordinary session at the request of two member states. Invitations to all sessions are extended by the Secretary-General. The ordinary sessions are presided over by representatives of the member states in turn.

The Council is supported by technical and specialized committees which advise on financial and administrative affairs, information affairs and legal affairs. In addition, specialized ministerial councils have been established to formulate common policies for the regulation and the advancement of co-operation in the following areas: information; home affairs; legal affairs; health; housing; social affairs; transport; the youth and sports sectors; environmental affairs; and telecommunications.

GENERAL SECRETARIAT

The administrative and financial offices of the League. The Secretariat carries out the decisions of the Council, and provides financial and administrative services for the personnel of the League. General departments comprise: the Bureau of the Secretary-General, Arab Affairs, Economic Affairs, International Affairs, Palestine Affairs, Legal Affairs, Military Affairs, Social and Cultural Affairs, Information Affairs and Financial and Administrative Affairs. In addition, there are Units for Internal Auditing and Institutional Development, a Documentation and Information Centre, Arab League Centres in Tunis and, for Legal and Judicial Research, in Beirut, and a Principal Bureau for the Boycott of Israel, based in Damascus, Syria (see below).

The Secretary-General is appointed by the League Council by a two-thirds' majority of the member states, for a five-year, renewable term. He appoints the Assistant Secretaries-General and principal officials, with the approval of the Council. He has the rank of ambassador, and the Assistant Secretaries-General have the rank of ministers plenipotentiary.

Secretary-General: AMR MUHAMMAD MOUSSA (Egypt).

DEFENCE AND ECONOMIC CO-OPERATION

Groups established under the Treaty of Joint Defence and Economic Co-operation, concluded in 1950 to complement the Charter of the League.

Arab Unified Military Command: f. 1964 to co-ordinate military policies for the liberation of Palestine.

Economic and Social Council: to compare and co-ordinate the economic policies of the member states; supervises the activities of the Arab League's specialized agencies. The Council is composed of ministers of economic affairs or their deputies; decisions are taken by majority vote. The first meeting was held in 1953.

Joint Defence Council: supervises implementation of those aspects of the treaty concerned with common defence. Composed of foreign and defence ministers; decisions by a two-thirds' majority vote of members are binding on all.

Permanent Military Commission: established 1950; composed of representatives of army general staffs; main purpose: to draw up plans of joint defence for submission to the Joint Defence Council.

ARAB DETERRENT FORCE

Created in June 1976 by the Arab League Council to supervise successive attempts to cease hostilities in Lebanon, and afterwards to maintain the peace. The mandate of the Force has been successively renewed. The Arab League Summit Conference in October 1976 agreed that costs were to be paid in the following percentage contributions: Saudi Arabia and Kuwait 20% each, the United Arab Emirates 15%, Qatar 10% and other Arab states 35%.

OTHER INSTITUTIONS OF THE LEAGUE

Other bodies established by resolutions adopted by the Council of the League:

Administrative Tribunal of the Arab League: f. 1964; began operations 1966.

Arab Fund for Technical Assistance to African Countries: f. 1975 to provide technical assistance for development projects by providing African and Arab experts, grants for scholarships and training, and finance for technical studies.

Higher Auditing Board: comprises representatives of seven member states, elected every three years; undertakes financial and administrative auditing duties.

Investment Arbitration Board: examines disputes between member states relating to capital investments.

Special Bureau for Boycotting Israel: POB 437, Damascus, Syria; f. 1951 to prevent trade between Arab countries and Israel, and to enforce a boycott by Arab countries of companies outside the region that conduct trade with Israel.

SPECIALIZED AGENCIES

All member states of the Arab League are also members of the Specialized Agencies, which constitute an integral part of the Arab League. (See also entries on the Arab Fund for Economic and Social Development, the Arab Monetary Fund, the Council of Arab Economic Unity and the Organization of Arab Petroleum Exporting Countries.)

Arab Academy for Science, Technology and Maritime Transport: POB 1029, Alexandria, Egypt; tel. (3) 5602388; fax (3) 5622525; internet www.aast.eduf. 1975 as Arab Maritime Transport Academy; provides specialized training in marine transport, engineering, technology and management. Dir-Gen. Dr GAMAL ED-DIN MOUKHTAR. Publs *Maritime Research Bulletin* (monthly), *Journal of the Arab Academy for Science, Technology and Maritime Transport* (2 a year).

Arab Administrative Development Organization—ARADO: POB 2692 Al-Horreia, Heliopolis, Cairo, Egypt; tel. (2) 4175401; fax (2) 4175407; e-mail arado@arado.org; internet www.arado.org; f. 1961 (as Arab Organization of Administrative Sciences), although became operational in 1969; administration development, training, consultancy, research and studies, information, documentation; promotes Arab and international co-operation in administrative sciences; includes Arab Network of Administrative Information; 20 Arab state members; Library of 26,000 volumes, 400 periodicals. Dir-Gen. Dr MOHAMED IBRAHIM AT-TWAIJRI. Publs *Arab Journal of Administration* (biannual), *Management Newsletter* (quarterly), research series, training manuals.

Arab Atomic Energy Agency—AAEA: 4 rue Mouaouiya ibn Abi Soufiane, al-Menzah 8, POB 402, 1004 Tunis, Tunisia; tel. (1) 709464; fax (1) 711330; e-mail aaea@aaea.org.tn; f. 1988 to co-ordinate research into the peaceful uses of atomic energy. Dir-Gen. Prof. Dr MAHMOUD NASREDDINE (Lebanon). Publs *The Atom and Development* (quarterly), other publs in the field of nuclear sciences and their applications in industry, biology, medicine, agriculture, food irradiation and seawater desalination.

Arab Bank for Economic Development in Africa (Banque arabe pour le développement économique en Afrique—BADEA): Sayed Abd ar-Rahman el-Mahdi St, POB 2640, Khartoum, Sudan; tel. (11) 773646; fax (11) 770660; e-mail badea@badea.org; internet www.badea.org; f. 1973 by Arab League; provides loans and grants to African countries to finance development projects; paid-up cap. US $1,500m. (Dec. 1999). In 1999 the Bank approved loans and grants totalling $119.5m. By the end of 2000 total loans and grants approved since funding activities began in 1975 amounted to $2,298.1m. Subscribing countries: all countries of Arab League, except the Comoros, Djibouti, Somalia and Yemen; recipient countries: all countries of Organization of African Unity (q.v.), except those belonging to the Arab League. Chair. AHMAD ABDALLAH AL-AKEIL (Saudi Arabia); Dir-Gen. MEDHAT SAMI LOTFY (Egypt). Publs *Annual Report, Co-operation for Development* (quarterly), Studies on Afro-Arab co-operation, periodic brochures.

Arab Centre for the Study of Arid Zones and Dry Lands — ACSAD: POB 2440, Damascus, Syria; tel. (11) 5743087; fax (11) 5743063; e-mail ruacsad@net.sy; f. 1971 to conduct regional research and development programmes related to water and soil resources, plant and animal production, agro-meteorology, and socio-economic studies of arid zones. The Centre holds conferences and training courses and encourages the exchange of information by Arab scientists. Dir-Gen. Dr HASSAN SEOUD.

Arab Industrial Development and Mining Organization: rue France, Zanagat Al Khatawat, POB 8019, Rabat, Morocco; tel. (7) 772600; fax (7) 772188; e-mail aidmo@arifonet.org.ma; internet www.arifonet.org.ma; f. 1990 by merger of Arab Industrial Development Organization, Arab Organization for Mineral Resources and Arab Organization for Standardization and Metrology. Comprises a 13-member Executive Council, a High Consultative Committee of Standardization, a High Committee of Mineral Resources and a Co-ordination Committee for Arab Industrial Research Centres; a Ministerial Council, of ministers of member states responsible for industry, meets every two years. Dir-Gen. TALA'AT AD-DAFER. Publs *Arab Industrial Development* (monthly and quarterly newsletters).

Arab Labour Organization: POB 814, Cairo, Egypt; f. 1965 for co-operation between member states in labour problems; unification of labour legislation and general conditions of work wherever possible; research; technical assistance; social insurance; training, etc.; the organization has a tripartite structure: governments, employers and workers. Dir-Gen. IBRAHIM GUDIR. Publs *ALO Bulletin* (monthly), *Arab Labour Review* (quarterly), *Legislative Bulletin* (annually), series of research reports and studies concerned with economic and social development issues in the Arab world.

Arab League Educational, Cultural and Scientific Organization—ALECSO: POB 1120, Tunis, Tunisia; tel. (1) 784-466; fax (1) 784-965; e-mail alecsolibrary@yahoo.fr; internet www.alecso.org/alecso/index.htm; f. 1970 to promote and co-ordinate educational, cultural and scientific activities in the Arab region. Regional units: Arab Centre for Arabization, Translation, Authorship, and Publication—Damascus, Syria; Institute of Arab Manuscript—Cairo, Egypt; Institute of Arab Research and Studies—Cairo, Egypt; Khartoum Institute for Arabic Language—Khartoum, Sudan; and the Arabization Co-ordination Bureau—Rabat, Morocco. Dir-Gen. MOHAMED AL-MILI IBRAHIMI (Algeria). Publs *Arab Journal of Culture, Arab Journal of Science, Arab Bulletin of Publications, Statistical Yearbook, Journal of the Institute of Arab Manuscripts, Arab Magazine for Information Science.*

Arab Organization for Agricultural Development: St no. 7, Al-Amarat, POB 474, Khartoum, Sudan; tel. (11) 472176; fax (11) 471402; e-mail aoad@sudanmail.net; internet www.aoad.org; f. 1970; began operations in 1972 to contribute to co-operation in agricultural activities, and in the development of natural and human resources for agriculture; compiles data, conducts studies, training and food security programmes; includes Arab Institute of Forestry and Range, Arab Centre for Information and Early Warning, and Arab Centre for Agricultural Documentation. Dir-Gen. Dr YAHIA BAKOUR. Publs *Agricultural Statistics Yearbook, Annual Report on Agricultural Development, the State of Arab Food Security* (annually), *Agriculture and Development in the Arab World* (quarterly), *Accession Bulletin* (every 2 months), *AOAD Newsletter* (monthly), *Arab Agricultural Research Journal, Arab Journal for Irrigation Water Management* (2 a year).

Arab Satellite Communications Organization—ARABSAT: King Fahd Express Rd (Ollaya St), POB 1038, Riyadh, 11431 Saudi Arabia; tel. (1) 4820000; fax (1) 4887999; e-mail albidnah@arabsat.com; internet www.arabsat.com; f. 1976; regional satellite telecommunications organization providing television, telephone and data exchange services to members and private users; operates three satellites, which cover all Arab and Mediterranean countries, controlled by a Primary Control Station in Dirab, Saudi Arabia, and a Secondary Control Facility, based in Dkhila, Tunisia. Dir-Gen. SAAD IBN ABD AL-AZIZ AL-BIDNAH (Saudi Arabia).

Arab States Broadcasting Union—ASBU: POB 250, 1080 Tunis Cedex; 6 rue des Entrepreneurs, zone industrielle Charguia 2, Ariana Aéroport, Tunisia; tel. (1) 703854; fax (1) 704203; f. 1969 to promote Arab fraternity, co-ordinate and study broadcasting subjects, to exchange expertise and technical co-operation in broadcasting; conducts training and audience research. Mems: 23 Arab radio and TV stations and eight foreign associates. Sec.-Gen. RAOUF BASTI. Publ. *ASBU Review* (quarterly).

Inter-Arab Investment Guarantee Corporation: POB 23568, Safat 13096, Kuwait; tel. 4844500; fax 4815741; f. 1975; insures Arab investors for non-commercial risks, and export credits for commercial and non-commercial risks; undertakes research and other activities to promote inter-Arab trade and investment; auth. cap. 25m. Kuwaiti dinars (Dec. 1995). Mems: 22 Arab governments. Dir-Gen. MAMOUN IBRAHIM HASSAN. Publs *News Bulletin* (monthly), *Arab Investment Climate Report* (annually).

External Relations

ARAB LEAGUE OFFICES AND INFORMATION CENTRES ABROAD

Established by the Arab League to co-ordinate work at all levels among Arab embassies abroad.

Austria: Grimmelshausengasse 12, 1030 Vienna.

Belgium: 89 ave de l'Uruguay, 1000 Brussels.

China, People's Republic: 14 Liang Male, 1-14-2 Tayuan Diplomatic Building, Beijing 100600.

Ethiopia: POB 5768, Addis Ababa.

France: 36 rue Fortuny, 75017 Paris.

Germany: Rheinallee 23, 53173 Bonn.

India: B-8/19 Vasant Vihar, New Delhi.

Italy: Piazzale delle Belle Arti 6, 00196 Rome.

Russia: 28 Koniouch Kovskaya, 132242 Moscow.

Spain: Paseo de la Castellana 180, 60°, 28046 Madrid.

Switzerland: 9 rue du Valais, 1202 Geneva.

Tunisia: 93 ave Louis Braille, el-Khadra, 1003 Tunis.

United Kingdom: 52 Green St, London, W1Y 3RH.

USA: 1100 17th St, NW, Suite 602, Washington, DC 20036; 17 Third Ave, 35th Floor, New York, NY 10017 (UN Office).

Record of Events

1945	Pact of the Arab League signed, March.
1946	Cultural Treaty signed.
1950	Joint Defence and Economic Co-operation Treaty.
1952	Agreements on extradition, writs and letters of request, nationality of Arabs outside their country of origin.
1953	Formation of Economic and Social Council. Convention on the privileges and immunities of the League.
1954	Nationality Agreement.
1956	Agreement on the adoption of a Common Tariff Nomenclature.
1962	Arab Economic Unity Agreement.
1964	First Summit Conference of Arab kings and presidents, Cairo, January. First meeting of Arab Economic Unity Council, June. Arab Common Market Agreement endorsed by the Council, August. Second Summit Conference welcomed establishment of Palestine Liberation Organization (PLO), September.
1965	Arab Common Market established, January.
1969	Fifth Summit Conference, Rabat. Call for mobilization of all Arab nations against Israel.
1977	Tripoli Declaration, December. Decision of Algeria, Iraq, Libya and Yemen PDR to boycott League meetings in Egypt in response to President Sadat's visit to Israel.
1979	Council meeting resolved to withdraw Arab ambassadors from Egypt; to recommend severance of political and diplomatic relations with Egypt; to suspend Egypt's membership of the League on the date of the signing of the peace treaty with Israel; to transfer the headquarters of the League to Tunis; to condemn US policy regarding its role in concluding the Camp David agreements and the peace treaty; to halt all bank loans, deposits, guarantees or facilities, as well as all financial or technical contributions and aid to Egypt; to prohibit trade exchanges with the Egyptian state and with private establishments dealing with Israel.
1981	In November the 12th Summit Conference, held in Fez, Morocco, was suspended after a few hours, following disagreement over a Saudi Arabian proposal known as the Fahd Plan, which included not only the Arab demands on behalf of the Palestinians, as approved by the UN General Assembly, but also an implied *de facto* recognition of Israel.
1982	The 12th Summit Conference was reconvened in September.

It adopted a peace plan, which demanded Israel's withdrawal from territories occupied in 1967, and removal of Israeli settlements in these areas; freedom of worship for all religions in the sacred places; the right of the Palestinian people to self-determination, under the leadership of the PLO; temporary supervision for the west bank and the gaza strip; the creation of an independent Palestinian state, with Jerusalem as its capital; and a guarantee of peace for all the states of the region by the UN Security Council.

1983 The summit meeting due to be held in November was postponed owing to members' differences of opinion concerning Syria's opposition to Yasser Arafat's chairmanship of the PLO, and Syrian support of Iran in the war against Iraq.

1984 In March an emergency meeting established an Arab League committee to encourage international efforts to bring about a negotiated settlement of the Iran–Iraq war. In May ministers of foreign affairs adopted a resolution urging Iran to stop attacking non-belligerent ships and installations in the Gulf region: similar attacks by Iraq were not mentioned.

1985 In August an emergency Summit Conference was boycotted by Algeria, Lebanon, Libya, Syria and Yemen PDR, while of the other 16 members only nine were represented by their heads of state. Two commissions were set up to mediate in disagreements between Arab states (between Jordan and Syria, Iraq and Syria, Iraq and Libya, and Libya and the PLO).

1986 In July King Hassan of Morocco announced that he was resigning as chairman of the next League Summit Conference, after criticism by several Arab leaders of his meeting with the Israeli Prime Minister earlier that month. A ministerial meeting, held in October, condemned any attempt at direct negotiation with Israel.

1987 An extraordinary Summit Conference was held in November, mainly to discuss the war between Iran and Iraq. Contrary to expectations, the participants unanimously agreed on a statement expressing support for Iraq in its defence of its legitimate rights, and criticizing Iran for its procrastination in accepting the UN Security Council Resolution 598 of July, which had recommended a cease-fire and negotiations on a settlement of the conflict. The meeting also stated that the resumption of diplomatic relations with Egypt was a matter to be decided by individual states.

1988 In June a Summit Conference agreed to provide finance for the PLO to continue the Palestinian uprising in Israeli-occupied territories. It reiterated a demand for the convening of an international conference, attended by the PLO, to seek to bring about a peaceful settlement in the Middle East (thereby implicitly rejecting recent proposals by the US Government for a conference that would exclude the PLO).

1989 In January an Arab League group, comprising six ministers of foreign affairs, began discussions with the two rival Lebanese governments on the possibility of a political settlement in Lebanon. At a Summit Conference, held in May, Egypt was readmitted to the League. The Conference expressed support for the chairman of the PLO, Yasser Arafat, in his recent peace proposals made before the UN General Assembly, and reiterated the League's support for proposals that an international conference should be convened to discuss the rights of Palestinians: in so doing, it accepted UN Security Council Resolutions 242 and 338 on a peaceful settlement in the Middle East and thus gave tacit recognition to the State of Israel. The meeting also supported Arafat in rejecting Israeli proposals for elections in the Israeli-occupied territories of the West Bank and the Gaza Strip. A new mediation committee was established, with a six-month mandate to negotiate a cease-fire in Lebanon, and to reconvene the Lebanese legislature with the aim of holding a presidential election and restoring constitutional government in Lebanon. In September the principal factions in Lebanon agreed to observe a cease-fire, and the surviving members of the Lebanese legislature (originally elected in 1972) met at Ta'if, in Saudi Arabia, in October, and approved the League's proposed 'charter of national reconciliation'.

1990 In May a Summit Conference, held in Baghdad, Iraq (which was boycotted by Syria and Lebanon), criticized recent efforts by Western governments to prevent the development of advanced weapons technology in Iraq. In August an emergency Summit Conference was held to discuss the invasion and annexation of Kuwait by Iraq. Twelve members (Bahrain, Djibouti, Egypt, Kuwait, Lebanon, Morocco, Oman, Qatar, Saudi Arabia, Somalia, Syria and the United Arab Emirates) approved a resolution condemning Iraq's action, and demanding the withdrawal of Iraqi forces from Kuwait and the reinstatement of the Government. The 12 states expressed support for the Saudi Arabian Government's invitation to the USA to send forces to defend Saudi Arabia; they also agreed to impose economic sanctions on Iraq, and to provide troops for an Arab defensive force in Saudi Arabia. The remaining member states, however, condemned the presence of foreign troops in Saudi Arabia, and their ministers of foreign affairs refused to attend a meeting, held at the end of August, to discuss possible solutions to the crisis. The dissenting countries also rejected the decision, taken earlier in the year, to return the League's headquarters from Tunis to Cairo. None the less, the official transfer of the League's headquarters to Cairo took place on 31 October. In November King Hassan of Morocco urged the convening of an Arab Summit Conference, in an attempt to find an 'Arab solution' to Iraq's annexation of Kuwait. However, the divisions in the Arab world over the issue meant that conditions for such a meeting could not be agreed.

1991 The first meeting of the Arab League since August 1990 took place in March, attended by representatives of all 21 member nations, including Iraq. Discussion of the recently-ended war against Iraq was avoided, in an attempt to re-establish the unity of the League. In September, despite deep divisions between member states, it was agreed that a committee should be formed to co-ordinate Arab positions in preparation for the US-sponsored peace talks between Arab countries and Israel. (In the event, an *ad hoc* meeting, attended by Egypt, Jordan, Syria, the PLO, Saudi Arabia—representing the Gulf Co-operation Council (GCC), and Morocco—representing the Union of the Arab Maghreb, was held in October, prior to the start of the talks.) In December the League expressed solidarity with Libya, which was under international pressure to extradite two government agents who were suspected of involvement in the explosion which destroyed a US passenger aircraft over Lockerbie, United Kingdom, in December 1988.

1992 The League attempted to mediate between the warring factions in Somalia. In March the League appointed a committee to seek to resolve the disputes between Libya and the USA, the United Kingdom and France over the Lockerbie bomb and the explosion which destroyed a French passenger aircraft over Niger in September 1989. The League condemned the UN's decision, at the end of March, to impose sanctions against Libya, and appealed for a negotiated solution. In September the League's Council issued a condemnation of Iran's alleged occupation of three islands in the Persian (Arabian) Gulf that were claimed by the United Arab Emirates, and decided to refer the issue to the UN.

1993 In April the Council approved the creation of a committee to consider the political and security aspects of water supply in Arab countries. In the same month the League pledged its commitment to the Middle East peace talks, but warned that Israel's continued refusal to repatriate the Palestinians based in Lebanon remained a major obstacle to the process. The League sent an official observer to the independence referendum in Eritrea, held in April. In September the Council admitted the Comoros as the 22nd member of the League. Following the signing of the Israeli-PLO peace accord in September the Council convened in emergency session, at which it approved the agreement, despite opposition from some members, notably Syria. In November it was announced that the League's boycott of commercial activity with Israel was to be maintained.

1994 The League condemned a decision of the GCC, announced in late September, to end the secondary and tertiary trade embargo against Israel, by which member states refuse to trade with international companies which have investments in Israel. A statement issued by the League insisted that the embargo could be removed only on the decision of the Council. Earlier in September the Council endorsed a recommendation that the UN conduct a census of Palestinian refugees, in the absence of any such action taken by the League.

1995 In March Arab ministers of foreign affairs approved a resolution urging Israel to renew the Nuclear Non-Proliferation Treaty (NPT). The resolution stipulated that failure by Israel to do so would cause Arab states to seek to protect legitimate Arab interests by alternative means. In May an extraordinary session of the Council condemned a decision by Israel to confiscate Arab-owned land in East Jerusalem for resettlement. Arab heads of state and government were scheduled to convene in emergency session later in that month to formulate a collective response to the action. However, the meeting was postponed, following an announcement by the Israeli Government that it was suspending its expropriation plans. In September the Council discussed plans for a regional court of justice and for an Arab Code of Honour to prevent the use of force in disputes between Arab states. The Council expressed its support for the Algerian Government in its efforts to combat Muslim separatist violence. In October the League was reported to be in financial difficulties, owing to the non-payment of contributions by seven member states. At that time undisputed arrears amounted to US $80.5m. In November the Arab League dispatched 44 observers to oversee elections in Algeria as part of an international monitoring team.

1996   In March, following protests by Syria and Iraq that extensive construction work in southern Turkey was restricting water supply in the region, the Council determined that the waters of the Euphrates and Tigris rivers be shared equitably between the three countries. In April an emergency meeting of the Council issued a further endorsement of Syria's position in the dispute with Turkey. The main objective of the meeting, which was convened at the request of Palestine, was to attract international attention to the problem of radiation from an Israeli nuclear reactor. The Council requested an immediate technical inspection of the site by the UN, and further demanded that Israel be obliged to sign the NPT to ensure the eradication of its nuclear weaponry. In June a Summit Conference was convened, the first since 1990, in order to formulate a united Arab response to the election, in May, of a new government in Israel and to the prospects for peace in the Middle East. At the Conference, which was attended by heads of state of 13 countries and senior representatives of seven others (Iraq was excluded from the meeting in order to ensure the attendance of the Gulf member states), Israel was urged to honour its undertaking to withdraw from the Occupied Territories, including Jerusalem, and to respect the establishment of an independent Palestinian state, in order to ensure the success of the peace process. A final communiqué of the meeting warned that Israeli co-operation was essential to prevent Arab states' reconsidering their participation in the peace process and the re-emergence of regional tensions. Meanwhile, there were concerns over increasing inter-Arab hostility, in particular between Syria and Jordan, owing to the latter's relations with Israel and allegations of Syrian involvement in recent terrorist attacks against Jordanian targets. In early September the League condemned US missile attacks against Iraq as an infringement of that country's sovereignty. In addition, it expressed concern at the impact on Iraqi territorial integrity of Turkish intervention in the north of Iraq. Later in September the League met in emergency session, following an escalation of civil unrest in Jerusalem and the Occupied Territories. The League urged the UN Security Council to prevent further alleged Israeli aggression against the Palestinians. In November the League criticized Israel's settlement policy, and at the beginning of December convened in emergency session to consider measures to end any expansion of the Jewish population in the West Bank and Gaza.

1997   In March the Council met in emergency session, in response to the Israeli Government's decision to proceed with construction of a new settlement at Har Homa (Jabal Abu-Ghunaim) in East Jerusalem. The Council pledged its commitment to seeking a reversal of the decision and urged the international community to support this aim. At the end of March ministers of foreign affairs of Arab League states agreed to end all efforts to secure normal diplomatic relations with Israel (although binding agreements already in force with Egypt, Jordan and Palestine were exempt) and to close diplomatic offices and missions while construction work continued in East Jerusalem. In addition, ministers recommended reactivating the economic boycott against Israel until comprehensive peace was achieved in the region and suspending Arab participation in the multilateral talks that were initiated in 1991 to further the peace process. Earlier in the year, in February, the Economic and Social Council adopted the Executive Programme of the (1981) Agreement to Facilitate and Develop Trade Among Arab Countries, with a view to creating a Greater Arab Free Trade Area, which aimed to facilitate and develop inter-Arab trade through the reduction and eventual elimination of customs duties over a 10-year period (at a rate of 10% per year), with effect from 1 January 1998. The Council agreed to supervise the implementation of the free trade agenda and formally to review its progress twice a year. In June a 60-member delegation from the Arab League participated in an international mission to monitor legislative elections in Algeria. In the same month the League condemned Turkey's military incursion into northern Iraq and demanded a withdrawal of Turkish troops from Iraqi territory. In September ministers of foreign affairs of member states advocated a gradual removal of international sanctions against Libya, and agreed that member countries should

permit international flights to leave Libya for specific humanitarian and religious purposes and when used for the purposes of transporting foreign nationals. Ministers also voted to pursue the decision, adopted in March, not to strengthen relations with Israel. Several countries urged a formal boycott of the forthcoming Middle East and North Africa economic conference, in protest at the lack of progress in the peace process (for which the League blamed Israel, which was due to participate in the conference). However, the meeting upheld a request by the Qatari Government, the host of the conference, that each member should decide individually whether to attend. In the event, only seven Arab League countries participated in the conference, which was held in Doha in mid-November, while the Secretary-General of the League decided not to attend as the organization's official representative. In November the League criticized the decision of the US Government to impose economic sanctions against Sudan. The League also expressed concern at the tensions arising from Iraq's decision not to co-operate fully with UN weapons inspectors, and held several meetings with representatives of the Iraqi administration in an effort to secure a peaceful conclusion to the impasse.

1998   In early 1998 the Secretary-General of the League condemned the use or threat of force against Iraq and continued to undertake diplomatic efforts to secure Iraq's compliance with UN Security Council resolutions. The League endorsed the agreement concluded between the UN Secretary-General and the Iraqi authorities in late February, and reaffirmed its commitment to facilitating the eventual removal of the international embargo against Iraq. A meeting of the Council in March, attended by ministers of foreign affairs of 16 member states, rejected Israel's proposal to withdraw from southern Lebanon, which was conditional on the deployment by the Lebanese Government of extra troops to secure Israeli territory from attack, and, additionally, urged international support to secure Israel's withdrawal from the Golan Heights. In April Arab League ministers of the interior and of justice signed an agreement to strengthen Arab co-operation in the prevention of terrorism, incorporating security and judicial measures, such as extradition arrangements and the exchange of evidence. The agreement was to enter into effect 30 days after being ratified by at least seven member countries. In August the League denounced terrorist bomb attacks against the US embassies in Kenya and Tanzania. Nevertheless, it condemned US retaliatory military action, a few days later, against suspected terrorist targets in Afghanistan and Sudan, and endorsed a request by the Sudanese Government that the Security Council investigate the incident. In the same month the USA and United Kingdom accepted a proposal of the Libyan Government, supported by the Arab League, that the suspects in the Lockerbie case be tried in The Hague, Netherlands, under Scottish law. In September the Council discussed the conditions for the suspension of sanctions against Libya. Other items concluded by the Council were condemnation of Turkey's military co-operation with Israel, support for efforts to maintain unity in the Comoros, rejection of further Israeli construction in the Golan Heights, and a request that the UN dispatch a fact-finding mission to examine conditions in the Israeli-occupied territories and alleged violations of Palestinian property rights. In November, following an escalation of tensions between the Iraqi authorities and UN weapons inspectors, the Secretary-General reiterated the League's opposition to the use of force against Iraq, but urged Iraq to maintain a flexible approach in its relations with the UN. The League condemned the subsequent bombing of strategic targets in Iraq, conducted by US and British military aircraft from mid-December, and offered immediate medical assistance to victims of the attacks. An emergency summit meeting of the League was scheduled to be held at the end of December, further to a request by the Yemeni Government to formulate a unified Arab response to the bombings; however, it was postponed, reportedly at the request of Gulf Arab states.

1999   The postponed emergency meeting of ministers of foreign affairs was held in late January, attended by representatives of 18 member states. The meeting expressed concern at the military response to the stand-off between Iraq and the UN. However, the Iraqi delegation withdrew from the meeting in protest at the final statement, which included a request that Iraq recognize Kuwait's territorial integrity and comply with UN Security Council resolutions before sanctions may be removed. The meeting agreed to establish a seven-member *ad hoc* committee to consider the removal of punitive measures against Iraq within the framework of UN resolutions. In March the League's Council determined that member states would suspend sanctions imposed against Libya, once arrangements for the trial of the suspects in the Lockerbie case had been finalized. (The suspects were transferred to a detention centre in the Netherlands in early April, whereupon the UN Security Council suspended its sanctions against Libya.) The meeting also expressed support for a UN resolution convening an international conference to facilitate the implementation of agreements applying to Israel and the Occupied Territories, condemned Israel's refusal to withdraw from the Occupied Territories without a majority vote in favour from its legislature, as well as its refusal to resume the peace negotiations with Lebanon and Syria that had ended in 1996, and advocated the publication of evidence of Israeli violence against Palestinians. The Council considered other issues, including the need to prevent further Israeli expansion in Jerusalem and the problem of Palestinian refugees, and reiterated demands for international support to secure Israel's withdrawal from the Golan Heights. In May the League expressed its concern at the political situation in the Comoros, following the removal of the government and establishment of a new military regime in that country at the end of April. In June the League condemned an Israeli aerial attack on Beirut and southern Lebanon. In September Iraq chaired a meeting of the Ministerial Council for the first time since 1990. The meeting considered a range of issues, including the Middle East peace process, US military aid to Israel, and a dispute with the Walt Disney corporation regarding a forthcoming exhibition which appeared to depict Jerusalem as the capital of Israel. Later in September an extraordinary meeting of League senior media and information officials was convened to discuss the latter issue. Negotiations with representatives of Disney were pursued and the implied threat of an Arab boycott of the corporation was averted following assurances that the exhibition would be apolitical. In October the Secretary-General of the League condemned the Mauritanian authorities for concluding an agreement with Israel to establish diplomatic relations. In November the League, in conjunction with the Arab Monetary Fund and the Palestinian Monetary Authority, convened a symposium on the planned issuance of a Palestinian currency. The League demanded that Israel compensate Palestinians for alleged losses incurred by their enforced use of the Israeli currency. The League reported in December that it was owed some US $135m. in arrears by its members, announcing that only six of the 22 states were up-to-date with their contributions. In late December, prior to a short-lived resumption of Israeli-Syrian peace negotiations, the League reaffirmed its full support for Syria's position.

2000   In February the League strongly condemned an Israeli aerial attack on southern Lebanon; the League's Council changed the venue of its next meeting, in March, from its Cairo headquarters to Beirut as a gesture of solidarity with Lebanon. During March the Secretary-General of the League expressed regret over Iraq's failure to join the *ad hoc* committee established in early 1999 (see above) and also over Iraq's refusal to co-operate with the recently established UN Monitoring, Verification and Inspection Commission (UNMOVIC). The League welcomed the withdrawal of Israeli forces from southern Lebanon in May, although in mid-June it questioned the UN's official verification of the operation, citing reported continuing territorial violations by Israeli troops. In late June the League concluded a co-operation accord with UNHCR; the two bodies agreed to exchange documents and data. Meeting in early September League foreign ministers approved a draft amendment to the League's charter, providing for an annual summit conference of heads of state to take place every March. In addition, resolutions were passed urging international bodies to avoid participating in conferences in Jerusalem, reiterating a threatened boycott of a US chain of restaurants which was accused of operating a franchise in an Israeli settlement in the West Bank, and opposing an Israeli initiative for a Jewish emblem to be included as a symbol of the International Red Cross and Red Crescent Movement. At an emergency summit convened in late October in response to mounting insecurity in Jerusalem and the Occupied Territories, 15 Arab heads of state, senior officials from six countries and Yasser Arafat,

the Palestinian National Authority leader, strongly rebuked Israel, which was accused of inciting the ongoing violent disturbances by stalling the progress of the peace process. The summit determined to 'freeze' co-operation with Israel, requested the formation of an international committee to conduct an impartial assessment of the situation, urged the UN Security Council to establish a mechanism to bring alleged Israeli 'war' criminals to trial, and requested the UN to approve the creation of an international force to protect Palestinians residing in the Occupied Territories. The summit also endorsed the establishment of an 'Al-Aqsa Fund', with a value of US $800m., which was to finance initiatives aimed at promoting the Arab and Islamic identity of Jerusalem, and a smaller 'Jerusalem Intifada Fund' to support the families of Palestinians killed in the unrest. A follow-up committee was subsequently established to implement the resolutions adopted by the emergency summit. Iraq and Somalia both participated in the gathering, each sending high-level representation to a summit meeting of the League for the first time since 1990. The first ever summit meeting of Arab leaders' wives was held in mid-November; it determined to convene every two years. Periodically during 2000 the League reiterated its condemnation of the ongoing aerial attacks by the United Kingdom and the USA against strategic targets in Iraq (initiated in December 1998, see above).

2001   In early January a meeting of League foreign ministers reviewed a proposed framework agreement, presented by outgoing President Clinton of the USA, which aimed to resolve the continuing extreme tension between the Israeli and Palestinian authorities. The meeting agreed that the issues dominating the stalled Middle East peace process should not be redefined, strongly objecting to a proposal that, in exchange for Palestinian assumption of control over Muslim holy sites in Jerusalem, Palestinians exiled at the time of the foundation of the Israeli state in 1948 should forgo their claimed right to return to their former homes. At the end of January, following the completion of the trial in The Hague, Netherlands, of the two Libyans accused of complicity in the Lockerbie case (one of whom was found guilty and one of whom was acquitted), the Arab League Secretary-General urged the UN Security Council fully to terminate the sanctions against Libya that had been suspended in 1999. Meeting in mid-March the League's Council pledged that member states would not consider themselves bound by the (inactive) UN sanctions. The Council also reiterated the League's opposition to the economic sanctions maintained by the USA against Sudan, welcomed the political *rapprochement* achieved in Comoros in February, and accused Iran of threatening regional security by conducting military manoeuvres on the three disputed islands in the Persian (Arabian) Gulf that were also claimed by the United Arab Emirates. In late March the League's first annual summit meeting of heads of state was convened, in Amman, Jordan. The summit issued the Amman Declaration, which emphasized the promotion of Arab unity, and demanded the reversal of Israel's 1967 occupation of Arab territories and the removal of the UN sanctions against Iraq. The Declaration also urged all member states to accelerate implementation of the Greater Arab Free Trade Area initiative. (It was reported prior to the summit that 15 of the League's 22 member states were making sufficient progress in realizing the requisite trade liberalization measures.) Heads of state attending the summit meeting requested that the League consider means of reactivating the now relaxed Arab economic boycott of Israel, and agreed that the Jordanian King should mediate contacts between Iraq and Kuwait. At the summit Amr Moussa, hitherto Egypt's minister of foreign affairs, was appointed as the League's new Secretary-General.

Publications

Arab Perspectives—Sh'oun Arabiyya (monthly).
Journal of Arab Affairs (monthly).
Bulletins of treaties and agreements concluded among the member states, essays, regular publications circulated by regional offices.

NORDIC COUNCIL

Address: Store Strandstraede 18, 1255 Copenhagen K, Denmark.
Telephone: 33-96-04-00; **fax:** 33-11-18-70; **internet:** www.norden
.org.

The Nordic Council was founded in 1952 for co-operation between the Nordic parliaments and governments. The four original members were Denmark, Iceland, Norway and Sweden; Finland joined in 1955, and the Faroe Islands and Åland Islands were granted representation in 1970 within the Danish and Finnish delegations respectively. Greenland had separate representation within the Danish delegation from 1984. Co-operation was first regulated by a Statute, and subsequently by the Helsinki Treaty of 1962. The Nordic region has a population of about 24m.

MEMBERS

Denmark (with the autonomous territories of the Faroe Islands and Greenland)	Finland (with the autonomous territory of the Åland Islands) Iceland	Norway Sweden

Organization
(April 2001)

COUNCIL

The Nordic Council is not a supranational parliament, but a forum for co-operation between the parliaments and governments of the Nordic countries. The Nordic Council of Ministers (see below) co-ordinates the activities of the governments of the Nordic countries when decisions are to be implemented.

The Council comprises 87 members, elected annually by and from the parliaments of the respective countries (Denmark 16 members; Faroes 2; Greenland 2; Finland 18; Åland 2; Iceland 7; Norway 20; Sweden 20). The various parties are proportionately represented in accordance with their representation in the national parliaments. Sessions of the Council consider proposals submitted by Council members, by the Council of Ministers or national governments. The sessions also follow up the outcome of past decisions and the work of the various Nordic institutions. The Plenary Assembly, which convenes once a year, is the highest body of the Nordic Council. Government representativesparticipate in the Assembly, but do not have the right to vote.

The Council has initiated and overseen extensive efforts to strengthen Nordic co-operation at the political, economic and social level.

The intensification of co-operation among European countries, particularly since the mid-1980s, and the dissolution of the former Soviet Union created new challenges for the Nordic Council and Council of Ministers. In 1995 the Nordic Council, meeting in Reykjavík, Iceland, endorsed new guide-lines for policy and administrative reform, in response to the region's political developments. Subsequently the Council's activities have focused on the following three areas: intra-Nordic co-operation, with the emphasis on cultural, education and research co-operation; co-operation with the EU and the European Economic Area, where the aim was jointly to promote Nordic values and interests in a broader European context; and co-operation with the Adjacent Areas, i.e. the Baltic States, north-west Russia and the Arctic Area/Barents Sea, where Nordic governments are committed to furthering democracy, security and sustainable development.

STANDING COMMITTEES

Council members are assigned to the following Standing Committees, corresponding to the Council's three pillars for co-operation: the Committee on Nordic Affairs; the Committee on the Adjacent Areas; and the Committee on European Affairs.

PRESIDIUM

The day-to-day work of the Nordic Council is directed by a Presidium, consisting of 13 members of national legislatures. The Presidium is the Council's highest decision-making body between sessions. The Presidium secretariat is headed by a Council Director. Each delegation to the Nordic Council has a secretariat at its national legislature.

Publications

Note: the titles listed below are joint publications of the Nordic Council and Nordic Council of Ministers.

Norden the Top of Europe (monthly newsletter in English, German and French).

The Nordic Council.

Politik i Norden (newsletter, in the languages of the region).

Yearbook of Nordic Statistics (in English, Finnish and Swedish).

Books and pamphlets on Nordic co-operation; summaries of Council sessions.

NORDIC COUNCIL OF MINISTERS

Address: Store Strandstraede 18, 1255 Copenhagen K, Denmark.
Telephone: 33-96-02-00; **fax:** 33-96-02-02; **internet:** www.norden
.org.

The Governments of Denmark, Finland, Iceland, Norway and Sweden co-operate through the Nordic Council of Ministers. This co-operation is regulated by the Treaty of Co-operation between Denmark, Finland, Iceland, Norway and Sweden of 1962 (amended in 1971, 1974, 1983, 1985, 1993 and 1995) and the Treaty between Denmark, Finland, Iceland, Norway and Sweden concerning cultural co-operation of 1971 (amended in 1983 and 1985). Although the Prime Ministers do not meet formally within the Nordic Council of Ministers, they have decided to take a leading role in overall Nordic co-operation. The Ministers of Defence and Foreign Affairs do not meet within the Council of Ministers. These ministers, however, meet on an informal basis.

MEMBERS

Denmark   Finland   Iceland   Norway   Sweden
Greenland, the Faroe Islands and the Åland Islands also participate as autonomous regions.

Organization
(April 2001)

COUNCIL OF MINISTERS

The Nordic Council of Ministers holds formal and informal meetings and is attended by ministers with responsibility for the subject

under discussion. Each member state also appoints a minister in its own cabinet as Minister for Nordic Co-operation.

Decisions of the Council of Ministers must be unanimous, except for procedural questions, which may be decided by a simple majority of those voting. Abstention constitutes no obstacle to a decision. Decisions are binding on the individual countries, provided that no parliamentary approval is necessary under the constitution of any of the countries. If such approval is necessary, the Council of Ministers must be so informed before its decision.

Meetings are concerned with: agreements and treaties, guidelines for national legislation, recommendations from the Nordic Council, financing joint studies, setting up Nordic institutions.

The Council of Ministers reports each year to the Nordic Council on progress in all co-operation between member states, as well as on future plans.

SECRETARIAT

The Office of the Secretary-General is responsible for co-ordination and legal matters (including co-ordination of work related to the European integration process and to the development of eastern Europe).

The work of the Secretariat is divided into the following departments:

Cultural and educational co-operation, research, advanced education, computer technology;

Budget and administration;

Environmental protection, finance and monetary policy, fisheries, industry and energy, regional policy, agriculture and forestry; Information;

Labour market issues, social policy and health care, occupational environment, consumer affairs, equal opportunities.

Secretary-General: SØREN CHRISTENSEN (Denmark).

COMMITTEES

Nordic Co-operation Committee: for final preparation of material for the meetings of Ministers of Nordic Co-operation.

Senior Executives' Committees: prepare the meetings of the Council of Ministers and conduct research at its request. There are a number of sub-committees. The Committees cover the subjects listed under the Secretariat (above).

Activities

ECONOMIC CO-OPERATION

Economic co-operation is undertaken in the following areas: freer markets for goods and services; measures on training and employment; elimination of trade barriers; liberalization of capital movements; research and development; export promotion; taxes and other levies; and regional policy.

Nordic Development Fund: f. 1989; supports activities by national administrations for overseas development with resources amounting to SDR 500m.

Nordic Environmental Finance Corporation (NEFCO): f. 1990 to finance environmental projects in Central and Eastern Europe; cap. €80m.; administers the Nordic Environmental Development Fund (NEDF, authorized in 1999 to finance environmental projects in the Barents Sea and Baltic Sea areas during 1999–2003).

Nordic Industrial Fund: f. 1973 to provide grants, subsidies and loans for industrial research and development projects of interest to more than one member country.

Nordic Investment Bank (NIB): f. under an agreement of December 1975 to provide finance and guarantees for the implementation of investment projects and exports; cap. €384.3m., dep. €11,564.5m. (Dec. 1999). The main sectors of the Bank's activities are energy, metal and wood-processing industries (including petroleum extraction) and manufacturing. In 1982 a separate scheme for financing investments in developing countries was established. In 1997 an Environmental Loan Facility was established to facilitate environmental investments in the Nordic Adjacent Areas.

Nordic Project Fund (NoPEF): f. 1982 to strengthen the international competitiveness of Nordic exporting companies, and to promote industrial co-operation in international projects (e.g. in environmental protection).

NORDTEST: f. 1973 as an inter-Nordic agency for technical testing and standardization of methods and of laboratory accreditation.

RELATIONS WITH THE EU AND EASTERN EUROPE

In 1991 the theme 'Norden in Europe' was regarded as an area of high priority for the coming years by the Council. Nordic co-operation was to be used to co-ordinate member countries' participation in the western European integration process, based on EC and EC/EFTA co-operation. Since 1995, when Finland and Sweden acceded to the European Union (joining Denmark, already a member of that organization), Europe and the EU have been an integrated part of the work of Nordic co-operation.

Since 1991 the Nordic Council of Ministers has developed its co-operation relating to the Baltic countries and north-west Russia, in order to contribute to peace, security and stability in Europe. Co-operation measures aim to promote democracy, the establishment of market economies, respect for civil rights and the responsible use of resources in these areas. The Nordic 'Working Programme of the Adjacent Areas' comprises the following three major components: Nordic Information Offices in Tallinn, Riga, Vilnius and St Petersburg, which co-ordinate Nordic projects and activities, promote regional contact at all levels and provide information about the Nordic countries in general and Nordic co-operation specifically; the Nordic-Baltic Scholarship Scheme, which awards grants to students, teachers, scientists, civil servants and parliamentarians; and the Nordic Council of Ministers Project Activities, which in 1997 was to fund 31 projects within the cultural, educational, industrial, housing, agricultural and environmental sectors.

The Nordic Council of Ministers proposed a resolution that was adopted by the Nordic Council in January 2001 urging the formulation of a Nordic strategy for sustainable development in the region and adjacent areas over the period 2001–20.

COMMUNICATIONS AND TRANSPORT

The main areas of co-operation have been concerned with international transport, the environment, infrastructure, road research, transport for the disabled and road safety.

EMPLOYMENT

In 1954 an agreement entered into force on a free labour market between Denmark, Finland, Norway and Sweden. Iceland became a party to the agreement in 1982 and the Faroe Islands in 1992. In 1982 an agreement on worker training and job-oriented rehabilitation came into effect. There is a joint centre for labour market training at Övertorneå in Sweden. A convention on the working environment was signed in 1989. The Nordic Institute for Advanced Training in Occupational Health is based in Helsinki, Finland.

GENDER EQUALITY

A Nordic co-operation programme on equality between women and men began in 1974. The main areas of co-operation have been working conditions, education, social welfare and family policy, housing and social planning, and women's participation in politics. In 1995–2000 the main areas of concern were the integration of equality aspects into all areas of society (i.e. 'mainstreaming'), the role of men, and the means of securing equal access for women and men to economic and political processes.

ENVIRONMENT

A Nordic Strategy for the Environment was adopted in February 1996 to constitute the overall guide-lines for Nordic co-operation in this field over the period 1996–2000. In the Nordic region priority was to be given to nature conservation and the integration of environmental considerations into sectors such as fisheries, agriculture and forestry, finance and energy. Support for the solution of environmental problems was accorded high priority in relation to the areas adjacent to the Nordic region, with monitoring and assessment the key elements of its strategy for the Arctic region. The Nordic countries promote a high level of ambition as the basis for the environmental work conducted in the EU and at an international level.

ENERGY AND INDUSTRY

Co-operation in the energy sector focuses on energy-saving, energy and the environment, the energy market, and the introduction of new and renewable sources of energy.

CONSUMER AFFAIRS

The main areas of co-operation are in safety legislation, consumer education and information and consumers' economic and legal interests.

FOOD AND NUTRITION

Co-operation in this sector began in 1982, and includes projects in food legislation, diet and nutrition, toxicology, risk evaluation and food controls.

AGRICULTURE AND FISHERIES

In 1995 a five-year programme for Nordic co-operation in agriculture and forestry was approved for the period 1996–2000, identifying the following as areas of future co-operation activities: quality production; management of genetic resources; development of regions dependent on agriculture and forestry; and sustainable forestry. Efforts to develop co-operation in both the fisheries and agriculture and forestry sectors have been undertaken with the aim of integrating environmental aspects into the relevant policies and strategies. The four-year programme of co-operation in the Nordic fisheries sector for 1997–2000 aimed to strengthen fisheries regulation, management, and research and development. It emphasized the environmental aspects of the industry, such as the influence of land-based pollution on the sea and the integration of environmentally-compatible techniques into fishing and the on-shore industry.

LAW

The five countries have similar legal systems and tend towards uniformity in legislation and interpretation of law. Much of the preparatory committee work within the national administrations on new legislation involves consultation with the neighbour countries.

Citizens of one Nordic country working in another are in many respects given the status of nationals. In all the Nordic countries they already have the right to vote in local elections in the country of residence. The changing of citizenship from one Nordic country to another has been simplified, and legislation on marriage and on children's rights amended to achieve the greatest possible parity.

There are special extradition facilities between the countries and further stages towards co-operation between the police and the courts have been adopted. In October 1996 justice ministers of the Nordic countries agreed to strengthen police co-operation in order to counter an increase in violent crime perpetrated by gangs. Emphasis is also placed on strengthening co-operation to combat the sexual abuse of children.

There is a permanent Council for Criminology and a Nordic Institute for Maritime Law in Oslo.

REGIONAL POLICY

Under a joint programme, covering the period 1995–99, the Council of Ministers agreed to develop cross-border co-operation between the Nordic countries and co-operation with the EU and the Baltic countries and to give greater priority to exchanging knowledge and information.

SOCIAL WELFARE AND HEALTH

Existing conventions and other co-operation directives ensure that Nordic citizens have the same rights, benefits and obligations in each Nordic country, with regard to sickness, parenthood, occupational injury, unemployment, disablement and old-age pension. Uniform provisions exist concerning basic pension and supplementary pension benefits when moving from one Nordic country to another. In June 1993 Nordic representatives signed an agreement providing for a common Nordic labour market for health professionals. Numerous joint initiatives have been undertaken in the social welfare and health sectors within the framework of the co-operating institutions.

Institutions:
Nordic Centre for the Development of Aids and Appliances for the Handicapped;
Nordic Committee on Disability;
Nordic Committee on Social Security Statistics;
Nordic Council for Alcohol and Drug Research, Helsinki, Finland;
Nordic Council on Medicines, Uppsala, Sweden;
Nordic Education Programme for Social Service Development, Gothenburg, Sweden;
Nordic Medico-statistical Committee;
Nordic School of Public Health, Gothenburg, Sweden;
Nordic Staff Training Centre for Deaf-blind Services, Dronninglund, Denmark;
Scandinavian Institute of Dental Materials.

EDUCATIONAL AND SCIENTIFIC CO-OPERATION

Education: Nordic co-operation in the educational field includes the objective content and means of education, the structure of the educational system and pedagogical development work.

The Nordic Council of Ministers finances the following co-operating bodies, permanent institutions and joint programmes:
Nordic-Baltic Scholarship Scheme
Nordic Folk Academy
Nordic Institute in Finland
Nordic Language and Literature Courses
NORDPLUS (Nordic Programme for Mobility of University Students and Teachers)
Nordic programmes for mobility of pupils, students, and teachers at primary and secondary school level (NORDPLUS-Junior and others)
Nordic School Data Network
Nordic Summer University
Programme of Action for Nordic Language Co-operation
Steering Committee for Nordic Co-operation on General and Adult Education
Steering Committee for Nordic Co-operation in Higher Education
Steering Committee for Nordic Educational Co-operation (primary and secondary school)

Research: Nordic co-operation in research comprises information on research activities and research findings, joint research projects, joint research institutions, the methods and means in research policy, the organizational structure of research and co-ordination of the national research programmes.

Much of the research co-operation activities at the more permanent joint research institutions consists of establishing science contacts in the Nordic areas by means of grants, visiting lecturers, courses and symposia.

The research institutions and research bodies listed below receive continuous financial support via the Nordic cultural budget. In many cases, these joint Nordic institutions ensure a high international standard that would otherwise have been difficult to maintain at a purely national level.

Nordic Academy for Advanced Study
Nordic Committee for Bioethics
Nordic Council for Scientific Information and Research Libraries
Nordic Institute of Asian Studies
Nordic Institute of Maritime Law
Nordic Institute for Theoretical Physics
Nordic Programme for Arctic Research
Nordic Sami Institute
Nordic Science Policy Council
Nordic Vulcanological Institute
Research Programme on the Nordic Countries and Europe

Cultural activities: Cultural co-operation is concerned with artistic and other cultural exchange between the Nordic countries; activities relating to libraries, museums, radio, television, and film; promotion of activities within organizations with general cultural aims, including youth and sports organizations; the improvement of conditions for the creative and performing arts; and encouragement for artists and cultural workers. Exhibitions and performances of Nordic culture are organized abroad.

Joint projects include:
Fund for Mobility of Young Nordic Artists—SLEIPNIR
Nordic Amateur Theatre Council
Nordic Art Centre
Nordic Co-operation in Athletics
Nordic Council Literature Prize
Nordic Council Music Prize
Nordic Documentation Centre for Mass Communication Research
Nordic Film and Television Fund
Nordic House in the Faroe Islands
Nordic House in Reykjavík
Nordic Institute in Åland
Nordic Institute of Contemporary Art
Nordic Institute in Greenland
Nordic Literature and Libraries Committee
Nordic Music Committee
Nordic Theatre and Dance Committee
Nordic Visual Art Committee
Steering Committee on Culture and Mass Media
Steering Committee on Nordic Cultural Projects Abroad

NORDIC CULTURAL FUND

The Nordic Cultural Fund was established through a separate agreement between the governments of the Nordic countries in 1966, and began operating in 1967, with the aim of supporting the needs of cultural life in the Nordic countries. A Board of 11 members administers and distributes the resources of the Fund and supervises its activities. Five of the members are appointed by the Nordic Council and five by the Nordic Council of Ministers (of culture and education), for a period of two years. The autonomous territories (the Åland islands, the Faroe Islands and Greenland) are represented by one member on the Board, appointed alternately by the Nordic Council and the Nordic Council of Ministers. The Fund is located within and administered by the Secretariat of the Nordic Council of Ministers. It considers applications for assistance for research, education and general cultural activities; grants may also be awarded for the dissemination of information concerning Nordic culture within and outside the region.

Finance

Joint expenses are divided according to an agreed scale in proportion to the relative national product of the member countries. The 2001 budget of the Nordic Council of Ministers amounted to 752m. Danish kroner. Various forms of co-operation are also financed directly from the national budgets.

NORTH AMERICAN FREE TRADE AGREEMENT—NAFTA

Canadian section: Royal Bank Centre, 90 Sparks St, Suite 705, Ottawa, ON, K1P 5B4; **tel.:** (613) 992-9388: **fax:** (613) 992-9392.

Mexican section: Blvd Adolfo López Mateos 3025, 2°, Col Héroes de Padierna, 10700 Mexico, DF; **tel.:** (5) 629-9630; **fax:** (5) 929-9637.

US section: 14th St and Constitution Ave, NW, Room 2061, Washington, DC 20230; **tel.:** (202) 482-5438; **fax:** (202) 482-0148.

E-mail: info@nafta-sec-alena.org; **internet:** www.nafta-sec-alena.org.

The North American Free Trade Agreement (NAFTA) grew out of the free-trade agreement between the USA and Canada that was signed in January 1988 and came into effect on 1 January 1989. Negotiations on the terms of NAFTA, which includes Mexico in the free-trade area, were concluded in October 1992 and the Agreement was signed in December. The accord was ratified in November 1993 and entered into force on 1 January 1994. The NAFTA Secretariat is composed of national sections in each member country.

MEMBERS

Canada	Mexico	USA

MAIN PROVISIONS OF THE AGREEMENT

Under NAFTA almost all restrictions on trade and investment between Canada, Mexico and the USA were to be gradually removed over a 15-year period. Most tariffs were eliminated immediately on agricultural trade between the USA and Mexico, with tariffs on 6% of agricultural products (including corn, sugar, and some fruits and vegetables) to be abolished over the 15 years. Tariffs on automobiles and textiles were to be phased out over 10 years in all three countries. Mexico was to open its financial sector to US and Canadian investment, with all restrictions to be removed by 2007. Barriers to investment were removed in most sectors, with exemptions for petroleum in Mexico, culture in Canada and airlines and radio communications in the USA. Mexico was to liberalize government procurement, removing preferential treatment for domestic companies over a 10-year period. In transport, heavy goods vehicles were to have complete freedom of movement between the three countries by 2000. An interim measure, whereby transport companies could apply for special licences to travel further within the borders of each country than the existing limit of 20 miles (32 km), was postponed in December 1995, shortly before it was scheduled to come into effect. The postponement was due to concerns, on the part of the US Government, relating to the implementation of adequate safety standards by Mexican truck-drivers. The 2000 deadline for the free circulation of heavy goods vehicles was not met, owing to the persistence of these concerns. In February 2001, however, a five-member NAFTA panel of experts appointed to adjudicate on the dispute ruled that the USA was violating the Agreement. The panel demanded that the US authorities consider entry applications from Mexican-based truck companies on an individual basis. In April 1998 the fifth meeting of the three-member ministerial Free Trade Commission (see below), held in Paris, France, agreed to remove tariffs on some 600 goods, including certain chemicals, pharmaceuticals, steel and wire products, textiles, toys, and watches, from 1 August. As a result of the agreement, a number of tariffs were eliminated as much as 10 years earlier than had been originally planned.

In the case of a sudden influx of goods from one country to another that adversely affects a domestic industry, the Agreement makes provision for the imposition of short-term 'snap-back' tariffs.

Disputes are to be settled in the first instance by intergovernmental consultation. If a dispute is not resolved within 30 to 40 days, a government may call a meeting of the Free Trade Commission. In October 1994 the Commission established an Advisory Committee on Private Commercial Disputes to recommend procedures for the resolution of such disputes. If the Commission is unable to settle the issue a panel of experts in the relevant field is appointed to adjudicate. In June 1996 Canada and Mexico announced their decision to refer the newly-enacted US 'Helms-Burton' legislation on trade with Cuba to the Commission. They claimed that the legislation, which provides for punitive measures against foreign companies that engage in trade with Cuba, imposed undue restrictions on Canadian and Mexican companies and was, therefore, in contravention of NAFTA. However, at the beginning of 1997 certain controversial provisions of the Helms-Burton legislation were suspended for a period of six months by the US administration. In April these were again suspended, as part of a compromise agreement with the European Union. The relevant provisions continued to be suspended at six-monthly intervals, and remained suspended in

early 2001. An Advisory Committee on Private Commercial Disputes Regarding Agricultural Goods was formed in 1998.

In December 1994 NAFTA members issued a formal invitation to Chile to seek membership of the Agreement. Formal discussions on Chile's entry began in June 1995, but were stalled in December when the US Congress failed to approve 'fast-track' negotiating authority for the US Government, which was to have allowed the latter to negotiate a trade agreement with Chile, without risk of incurring a line-by-line veto from the US Congress. In February 1996 Chile began high-level negotiations with Canada on a wide-ranging bilateral free-trade agreement. Chile, which already had extensive bilateral trade agreements with Mexico, was regarded as advancing its position with regard to NAFTA membership by means of the proposed accord with Canada. The bilateral agreement, which provided for the extensive elimination of customs duties by 2002, was signed in November 1996 and ratified by Chile in July 1997. However, in November 1997 the US Government was obliged to request the removal of the 'fast-track' proposal from the legislative agenda, owing to insufficient support within Congress.

In April 1998 heads of state of 34 countries, meeting in Santiago, Chile, agreed formally to initiate the negotiating process to establish a Free Trade Area of the Americas (FTAA). The US Government had originally proposed creating the FTAA through the gradual extension of NAFTA trading privileges on a bilateral basis. However, the framework agreed upon by ministers of trade of the 34 countries, meeting in March, provided for countries to negotiate and accept FTAA provisions on an individual basis and as part of a sub-regional economic bloc. It was envisaged that the FTAA would exist alongside the subregional associations, including NAFTA. The negotiating process was scheduled to be concluded in Mexico City on 31 December 2004, at which time the co-ordinating FTAA Trade Negotiations Committee was to be presided over jointly by Brazil and the USA.

ADDITIONAL AGREEMENTS

During 1993, as a result of domestic pressure, the new US Government negotiated two 'side agreements' with its NAFTA partners, which were to provide safeguards for workers' rights and the environment. A Commission for Labour Co-operation was established under the North American Agreement on Labour Co-operation (NAALC) to monitor implementation of labour accords and to foster co-operation in that area. The North American Commission for Environmental Co-operation (NACEC) was initiated to combat pollution, to ensure that economic development was not environmentally damaging and to monitor compliance with national and NAFTA environmental regulations. Panels of experts, with representatives from each country, were established to adjudicate in cases of alleged infringement of workers' rights or environmental damage. The panels were given the power to impose fines and trade sanctions, but only with regard to the USA and Mexico; Canada, which was opposed to such measures, was to enforce compliance with NAFTA by means of its own legal system. In 1995 the North American Fund for Environmental Co-operation (NAFEC) was established. NAFEC, which is financed by the NACEC, supports community environmental projects.

In February 1996 the NACEC consented for the first time to investigate a complaint brought by environmentalists regarding non-compliance with domestic legislation on the environment. Mexican environmentalists claimed that a company that was planning to build a pier for tourist ships (a project that was to involve damage to a coral reef) had not been required to supply adequate environmental impact studies. The NACEC was limited to presenting its findings in such a case, as it could only make a ruling in the case of complaints brought by one NAFTA government against another. The NACEC allocates the bulk of its resources to research undertaken to support compliance with legislation and agreements on the environment. However, in October 1997 the council of NAFTA ministers of the environment, meeting in Montréal, Canada, approved a new structure for the NACEC's activities. The NACEC's main objective was to be the provision of advice concerning the environmental impact of trade issues. It was also agreed that the Commission was further to promote trade in environmentally-sound products and to encourage private-sector investment in environmental trade issues.

With regard to the NAALC, National Administration Offices have been established in each of the three NAFTA countries in order to monitor labour issues and to address complaints about non-compliance with domestic labour legislation. However, punitive measures in the form of trade sanctions or fines (up to US $20m.)

may only be imposed in the specific instances of contravention of national legislation regarding child labour, a minimum wage or health and safety standards. A Commission for Labour Co-operation has been established (see below) and incorporates a council of ministers of labour of the three countries.

In August 1993 the USA and Mexico agreed to establish a Border Environmental Co-operation Commission (BECC) to assist with the co-ordination of projects for the improvement of infrastructure and to monitor the environmental impact of the Agreement on the US–Mexican border area, where industrial activity was expected to intensify. The Commission is located in Ciudad Juárez, Mexico. By April 2000 the BECC had certified 44 projects, at a cost of US \$949.3m. In October 1993 the USA and Mexico concluded an agreement to establish a North American Development Bank (NADB or NADBank), which was mandated to finance environmental and infrastructure projects along the US–Mexican border.

North American Commission for Environmental Co-operation (NACEC): 393 rue St Jacques West, Bureau 200, Montréal, QC H2Y IN9, Canada; tel. (514) 350-4300; fax (514) 350-4314; e-mail info@ccemtl.org; internet www.cec.org; f. 1994; Exec. Dir JANINE FERRETI; Dir GREG BLOCK. Publ. *Annual Report.*

Commission for Labour Co-operation: One Dallas Center, 350 N. St Paul 2424, Dallas, TX 75201-4240, USA; tel. (214) 754-1100; fax (214) 754-1199; e-mail info@naalc.org; internet www.naalc.org; f. 1994; Exec. Dir JOHN MCKENNIREY. Publ. *Annual Report.*

North American Development Bank (NADB or NADBank): 203 St Mary's, Suite 300, San Antonio, TX 78205, USA; tel. (210) 231-8000; fax (210) 231-6232; internet www.nadbank.org. At April 2001 the NADB had authorized capital of US \$3,000m., subscribed equally by Mexico and the USA, of which \$450m. was paid-up; Man. Dir RAUL RODRIGUEZ (Mexico). Publ. *Annual Report, NADBank News.*

NORTH ATLANTIC TREATY ORGANIZATION—NATO

Address: blvd Léopold III, 1110 Brussels, Belgium.

Telephone: (2) 707-41-11; **fax:** (2) 707-45-79; **e-mail:** nato-doc@hq.nato.int; **internet:** www.nato.int.

The Atlantic Alliance was established on the basis of the 1949 North Atlantic Treaty as a defensive political and military alliance of a group of European states (then numbering 10) and the USA and Canada. The Alliance aims to provide common security for its members through co-operation and consultation in political, military and economic fields, as well as scientific, environmental, and other non-military aspects. The objectives of the Alliance are implemented by NATO. Following the collapse of the communist governments in central and eastern Europe, from 1989 onwards, and the dissolution of the Warsaw Pact (which had hitherto been regarded as the Alliance's principal adversary) in 1991, NATO has undertaken a fundamental transformation of its structures and policies to meet the new security challenges in Europe.

MEMBERS*

Belgium	Hungary	Poland
Canada	Iceland	Portugal
Czech Republic	Italy	Spain
Denmark	Luxembourg	Turkey
France	Netherlands	United Kingdom
Germany	Norway	USA
Greece		

* Greece and Turkey acceded to the Treaty in 1952, and the Federal Republic of Germany in 1955. France withdrew from the integrated military structure of NATO in 1966, although remaining a member of the Atlantic Alliance; in 1996 France resumed participation in some, but not all, of the military organs of NATO. Spain acceded to the Treaty in 1982, but remained outside the Alliance's integrated military structure until 1999. The Czech Republic, Hungary and Poland were formally admitted as members of NATO in March 1999.

Organization

(April 2001)

NORTH ATLANTIC COUNCIL

The Council, the highest authority of the Alliance, is composed of representatives of the 16 member states. It meets at the level of Permanent Representatives, ministers of foreign affairs, or heads of state and government, and, at all levels, has effective political and decision-making authority. Ministerial meetings are held at least twice a year. Occasional meetings of defence ministers are also held. At the level of Permanent Representatives the Council meets at least once a week.

The Secretary-General of NATO is Chairman of the Council, and each year a minister of foreign affairs of a member state is nominated honorary President, following the English alphabetical order of countries.

Decisions are taken by common consent and not by majority vote. The Council is a forum for wide consultation between member governments on major issues, including political, military, economic and other subjects, and is supported by the Senior or regular Political Committee, the Military Committee and other subordinate bodies.

PERMANENT REPRESENTATIVES

Belgium: THIERRY DE GRUBEN
Canada: DAVID WRIGHT
Czech Republic: KAREL KOVANDA

Denmark: NIELS EGELUND
France: PHILIPPE GUELLUY
Germany: GEBHARDT VON MOLTKE
Greece: VASSILIS KASKARELIS
Hungary: JÁNOS HERMANI
Iceland: GUNNAR PÁLSSON
Italy: AMEDEO DE FRANCHIS
Luxembourg: JEAN-JACQUES KASEL
Netherlands: Dr NICOLAAS HENDRIK BIEGMANN
Norway: HANS JACOB BIÖRN LIAN
Poland: ANDRZEJ TOWPIK
Portugal: FERNANDO ANDRESEN-GUIMARÃES
Spain: JUAN PRAT Y COLL
Turkey: ONUR ÖYMEN
United Kingdom: Sir DAVID G. MANNING
USA: ALEXANDER R. VERSHBOW

Note: NATO partner countries are represented by heads of diplomatic missions or liaison officers located at NATO headquarters.

DEFENCE PLANNING COMMITTEE

Most defence matters are dealt with in the Defence Planning Committee, composed of representatives of all member countries except France. The Committee provides guidance to NATO's military authorities and, within the field of its responsibilities, has the same functions and authority as the Council. Like the Council, it meets regularly at ambassadorial level and assembles twice a year in ministerial sessions, when member countries are represented by their ministers of defence.

NUCLEAR PLANNING GROUP

Defence ministers of countries participating in the Defence Planning Committee meet regularly in the Nuclear Planning Group (NPG) to discuss specific policy issues relating to nuclear forces, such as safety, deployment issues, nuclear arms control and proliferation. The NPG is supported by a Staff Group, composed of representatives of all members participating in the NPG, which meets at least once a week.

OTHER COMMITTEES

There are also committees for political affairs, economics, military medical services, armaments, defence review, science, the environment, infrastructure, logistics, communications, civil emergency planning, information and cultural relations, and civil and military budgets. In addition, other committees consider specialized subjects such as NATO pipelines, air traffic management, etc. Since 1992 most of these committees consult on a regular basis with representatives from central and eastern European countries.

INTERNATIONAL SECRETARIAT

The Secretary-General is Chairman of the North Atlantic Council, the Defence Planning Committee and the Nuclear Planning Group. He is the head of the International Secretariat, with staff drawn from the member countries. He proposes items for NATO consultation and is generally responsible for promoting consultation and co-operation in accordance with the provisions of the North Atlantic Treaty. He is empowered to offer his help informally in cases of disputes between member countries, to facilitate procedures for settlement.

Secretary-General: Lord ROBERTSON OF PORT ELLEN (United Kingdom).

Deputy Secretary-General: SERGIO BALANZINO (Italy), (from 1 July 2001) ALESSANDRO MINUTO RIZZO (Italy).

There is an Assistant Secretary-General for each of the operational divisions listed below.

PRINCIPAL DIVISIONS

Division of Political Affairs: maintains political liaison with national delegations and international organizations. Prepares reports on political subjects for the Secretary-General and the Council, and provides the administrative structure for the management of the Alliance's political responsibilities, including disarmament and arms control. Asst Sec.-Gen. Dr KLAUS-PETER KLAIBER (Germany).

Division of Defence Planning and Operations: studies all matters concerning the defence of the Alliance, and co-ordinates the defence review and other force planning procedures of the Alliance. Asst Sec.-Gen. Dr EDGAR BUCKLEY (United Kingdom).

Division of Defence Support: promotes the most efficient use of the Allies' resources in the production of military equipment and its standardization. Asst Sec.-Gen. ROBERT BELL (USA).

Division of Security Investment, Logistics and Civil Emergency Planning: supervises the technical and financial aspects of the security investment programme. Provides guidance, co-ordination and support to the activities of NATO committees or bodies active in the field of consumer logistics and civil emergency planning. Asst Sec.-Gen. ØIVIND BAEKKEN (Norway).

Division of Scientific and Environmental Affairs: advises the Secretary-General on scientific matters of interest to NATO. Responsible for promoting and administering scientific exchange programmes between member countries, research fellowships, advanced study institutes and special programmes of support for the scientific and technological development of less-advanced member countries. Asst Sec.-Gen. YVES SILLARD (France).

Military Organization

MILITARY COMMITTEE

Composed of the allied Chiefs-of-Staff, or their representatives, of all member countries: the highest military body in NATO under the authority of the Council. Meets at least twice a year at Chiefs-of-Staff level and remains in permanent session with Permanent Military Representatives. It is responsible for making recommendations to the Council and Defence Planning Committee and Nuclear Planning Group on military matters and for supplying guidance on military questions to Supreme Allied Commanders and subordinate military authorities.

In December 1995 France agreed to rejoin the Military Committee, which it formally left in 1966.

Chairman: Adm. GUIDO VENTURONI (Italy).

INTERNATIONAL MILITARY STAFF

Director: Lt-Gen. O. L. KANDBORG (Norway).

COMMANDS

Allied Command Europe (ACE): Casteau, Belgium—Supreme Headquarters Allied Powers Europe—SHAPE. Supreme Allied Commander Europe—SACEUR: Gen. JOSEPH W. RALSTON (USA).

Allied Command Atlantic (ACLANT): Norfolk, Virginia, USA. Supreme Allied Commander Atlantic—SACLANT: Gen. WILLIAM F. KERNAN (USA).

Activities

The common security policy of the members of the North Atlantic Alliance is to safeguard peace through the maintenance of political solidarity and adequate defence at the lowest level of military forces needed to deter all possible forms of aggression. Each year, member countries take part in a Defence Review, designed to assess their contribution to the common defence in relation to their respective capabilities and constraints. Allied defence policy is reviewed periodically by ministers of defence.

Since the 1980s the Alliance has been actively involved in co-ordinating policies with regard to arms control and disarmament issues designed to bring about negotiated reductions in conventional forces, intermediate and short-range nuclear forces and strategic nuclear forces. A Verification Co-ordinating Committee was established in 1990.

Political consultations within the Alliance take place on a permanent basis, under the auspices of the North Atlantic Council (NAC), on all matters affecting the common security interests of the member countries, as well as events outside the North Atlantic Treaty area.

Co-operation in scientific and technological fields as well as co-operation on environmental challenges takes place in the NATO Science Committee and in its Committee on the Challenges of Modern Society. Both these bodies operate an expanding international programme of science fellowships, advance study institutes and research grants.

At a summit meeting of the Conference on Security and Co-operation in Europe (CSCE, now renamed as the Organization for Security and Co-operation in Europe, OSCE, see p. 252) in November 1990, the member countries of NATO and the Warsaw Pact signed an agreement limiting Conventional Armed Forces in Europe (CFE), whereby conventional arms would be reduced to within a common upper limit in each zone. The two groups also issued a Joint Declaration, stating that they were no longer adversaries and that none of their weapons would ever be used 'except in self-defence'. Following the dissolution of the USSR in December 1991, the eight former Soviet republics with territory in the area of application of the CFE Treaty committed themselves to honouring its obligations in June 1992. The Treaty entered retroactively into full force from 17 July 1992 (Armenia was unable to ratify it until the end of July, and Belarus until the end of October). In March 1992, under the auspices of the CSCE, the ministers of foreign affairs of the NATO and of the former Warsaw Pact countries (with Russia, Belarus, Ukraine and Georgia taking the place of the USSR) signed the 'Open Skies' treaty. Under this treaty, aerial reconnaissance missions by one country over another were to be permitted, subject to regulation. At the summit meeting of the OSCE in December 1996 the signatories of the CFE Treaty agreed to begin negotiations on a revised treaty governing conventional weapons in Europe. In July 1997 the CFE signatories concluded an agreement on Certain Basic Elements for Treaty Adaptation, which provided for substantial reductions in the maximum levels of conventional military equipment at national and territorial level, replacing the previous bloc-to-bloc structure of the Treaty.

In October 1991 NATO defence ministers endorsed the US decision to withdraw and destroy all its nuclear artillery shells and nuclear warheads for its short-range ballistic missiles in Europe. The ministers also agreed to reduce NATO's stock of airborne nuclear bombs by 50%. These and other measures were to reduce NATO's nuclear arsenal in Europe by 80%.

An extensive review of NATO's structures was initiated in June 1990, in response to the fundamental changes taking place in central and eastern Europe. In November 1991 NATO heads of government, convened in Rome, recommended a radical restructuring of the organization in order to meet the demands of the new security environment, which was to involve further reductions in military forces in Europe, active involvement in international peace-keeping operations, increased co-operation with other international institutions and close co-operation with its former adversaries, the USSR and the countries of eastern Europe. The basis for NATO's new force structure was incorporated into a new Strategic Concept, which was adopted in the Rome Declaration issuing from the summit meeting. The concept provided for the maintenance of a collective defence capability, with a reduced dependence on nuclear weapons. Substantial reductions in the size and levels of readiness of NATO forces were undertaken, in order to reflect the Alliance's strictly defensive nature, and forces were reorganized within a streamlined integrated command structure. Forces were categorized into immediate and rapid reaction forces (including the ACE Rapid Reaction Corps—ARRC, which was inaugurated in October 1992), main defence forces and augmentation forces, which may be used to reinforce any NATO region or maritime areas for deterrence, crisis management or defence. Discussions on a new command structure were hindered during 1997 by bilateral disagreements within the Alliance, notably between the United Kingdom and Spain regarding Spanish restrictions on the use of Gibraltar for military manoeuvres. In early December the United Kingdom withdrew its opposition to the establishment of a NATO command in Spain, enabling the Military Committee to approve a new command structure. The NAC, meeting at ministerial level in mid-December, endorsed the new military structure, which envisaged a reduction in the number of NATO command headquarters from 65 to 20, and instructed the military authorities of the Alliance to formulate a plan for the transitional process. During 1998 work was undertaken on the formulation of a new Strategic Concept, reflecting the changing security environment and defining NATO's future role and objectives, which recognized a broader sphere of influence of NATO in the 21st century and confirmed NATO to be the principal generator of security in the Euro-Atlantic area. It emphasized NATO's role in crisis management and a renewed commitment to partnership and dialogue. The document was approved at a special summit meeting, convened in Washington, USA, in April 1999, to commemorate the 50th anniversary of the Alliance. A separate initiative was approved to assist member states to adapt their defence capabilities to meet changing security requirements, for example improving the means of troop deployment and equipping and protecting forces. A High-Level Steering Group was established to oversee implementation of the Defence Capabilities Initiative. The meeting also determined to improve co-ordination on issues relating to weapons of mass destruction through the establishment a separate centre at NATO headquarters. The Washington meeting, which had been envisaged as a celebration of NATO's achievements since its foundation, was, however, dominated by consideration of the situation in the southern Serbian province of Kosovo and Metohija and the conduct of its military offensive against the Federal Republic of Yugoslavia, initiated in late March (see below).

In January 2001 NATO established an *ad hoc* working committee in response to concerns expressed by several member governments regarding the health implications of the use of depleted uranium munitions during the Alliance's military intervention in the Balkans. The committee was to co-ordinate the compilation of information regarding the use of depleted uranium and to co-operate with the Yugoslav authorities in the rehabilitation of the local environment. An extraordinary meeting of chiefs of military medical services, including surgeons-general and medical experts, was also convened to consider the issue.

In January 1994 NATO heads of state and government welcomed the entry into force of the Maastricht Treaty, establishing the European Union (EU, superseding the EC). The Treaty included an agreement on the development of a common foreign and security policy, which was intended to be a mechanism to strengthen the European pillar of the Alliance. In May 1995 NATO's ministers of foreign affairs supported a decision by Council of Ministers of the Western European Union (WEU) to improve the Union's operational capabilities through new mechanisms and force structures, which could be employed within the framework of NATO. In November the first memorandum of understanding between the two organizations was signed, to provide for full access to each other's communications capabilities; and in May 1996 NATO and WEU signed a security agreement concerning the safeguarding of classified material provided by either organization.

In June 1996 NATO ministers of foreign affairs reached agreement on the implementation of the 'Combined Joint Task Force (CJTF) concept', which had been adopted in January 1994. Measures were to be taken to establish the 'nuclei' of these task forces at certain NATO headquarters, which would provide the basis for missions that could be activated at short notice for specific purposes such as crisis management and peace-keeping. It was also agreed to make CJTFs available for operations undertaken by WEU. In conjunction with this, WEU was to be permitted to make use of Alliance hardware and capabilities (in practice, mostly belonging to the USA) subject to the endorsement of the NAC. This development represented the evolving construction of a European Security and Defence Identity (ESDI) within NATO. The summit meeting, held in April 1999, confirmed NATO's willingness to establish a direct NATO-EU relationship. In February 2000 the first joint NATO-WEU crisis management exercise was conducted. However, in accordance with decisions taken by the EU in late 1999 and 2000 to implement a common security and defence policy, it was agreed that routine NATO-WEU consultation mechanisms were to be suspended. In order to support an integrated security structure in Europe, NATO co-operates with the OSCE and has provided assistance for the development of the latter's conflict prevention and crisis management activities.

PARTNERSHIPS

In May 1997 a Euro-Atlantic Partnership Council (EAPC) was inaugurated as a successor to the North Atlantic Co-operation Council (NACC), that had been established in December 1991 to provide a forum for consultation on political and security matters with the countries of central and eastern Europe, including the former Soviet republics. An EAPC Council was to meet monthly at ambassadorial level and twice a year at ministerial level. It was to be supported in its work by a steering committee and a political committee. The EAPC was to pursue the NACC Work Plan for Dialogue, Partnership and Co-operation and incorporate it into a new Work Plan, which was to include an expanded political dimension of consultation and co-operation among participating states. The Partnership for Peace (PfP) programme, which was established in January 1994 within the framework of the NACC, was to remain an integral element of the new co-operative mechanism. The PfP incorporated practical military and defence-related co-operation activities that had originally been part of the NACC Work Plan. Participation in the PfP requires an initial signature of a framework agreement, establishing the common principles and objectives of the partnership, the submission of a presentation document, indicating the political and military aspects of the partnership and the nature of future co-operation activities, and thirdly, the development of individual partnership programmes establishing country-specific objectives. In June 1994 Russia, which had previously opposed the strategy as being the basis for future enlargement of NATO, signed the PfP framework document, which included a declaration envisaging an 'enhanced dialogue' between the two sides. Despite its continuing opposition to any enlargement of NATO, in May 1995 Russia agreed to sign a PfP Individual Partnership Programme, as well as a framework document for NATO-Russian dialogue and co-operation beyond the PfP. During 1994 a Partnership Co-ordination Cell (PCC), incorporating representatives of all partnership coun-

tries, became operational in Mons, Belgium. The PCC, under the authority of the NAC, aims to co-ordinate joint military activities and planning in order to implement PfP programmes. The first joint military exercises with countries of the former Warsaw Pact were conducted in September. NATO began formulating a PfP Status of Forces Agreement (SOFA) to define the legal status of Allies' and partners' forces when they are present on each other's territory; the PfP SOFA was opened for signature in June 1995. The new EAPC was to provide a framework for the development of an enhanced PfP programme, which NATO envisaged would become an essential element of the overall European security structure. Accordingly, the military activities of the PfP were to be expanded to include all Alliance missions and incorporate all NATO committees into the PfP process, thus providing for greater co-operation in crisis management, civil emergency planning and training activities. In addition, all PfP member countries were to participate in the CJTF concept through a structure of Partners Staff Elements, working at all levels of the Alliance military structure. Defence ministers of NATO and partner countries (some 27 in late 1997) were to meet regularly to provide the political guidance for the enhanced Planning and Review Process of the PfP. In December NATO ministers of foreign affairs endorsed an EAPC Action Plan for 1998–2000 to enhance the co-ordination and transparency of activities between participating states. The ministers also approved the establishment of a Euro-Atlantic Disaster Response Co-ordination Centre (EDRCC), and a non-permanent Euro-Atlantic Disaster Response Unit. The EDRCC was inaugurated in June 1998 and immediately commenced operations to provide relief to ethnic Albanian refugees fleeing the conflict in the Serbian province of Kosovo. In November the NAC approved the establishment of a network of PfP training centres, the first of which was inaugurated in Ankara, Turkey. The centres were a key element of a Training and Education Programme, which was endorsed at the summit meeting in April 1999. During 2000 *ad hoc* working groups were convened to consider EAPC involvement in global humanitarian action against mines, the challenge of small arms and light weapons, and prospects for regional co-operation in South-Eastern Europe and in the Caucasus.

The enlargement of NATO, through the admission of new members from the former USSR and eastern and central European countries, was considered to be a progressive means of contributing to the enhanced stability and security of the Euro-Atlantic area. In December 1996 NATO ministers of foreign affairs announced that invitations to join the Alliance would be issued to some former eastern bloc countries during 1997. The NATO Secretary-General and member governments subsequently began intensive diplomatic efforts to secure Russia's tolerance of these developments. It was agreed that no nuclear weapons or large numbers of troops would be deployed on the territory of any new member country in the former Eastern bloc. In May 1997 NATO and Russia signed the Founding Act on Mutual Relations, Co-operation and Security, which provided for enhanced Russian participation in all NATO decision-making activities, equal status in peace-keeping operations and representation at the Alliance headquarters at ambassadorial level, as part of a recognized shared political commitment to maintaining stability and security throughout the Euro-Atlantic region. A NATO-Russian Permanent Joint Council was established under the Founding Act, and met for the first time in July; the Council provided each side the opportunity for consultation and participation in the other's security decisions, but without a right of veto. The Council's work programme for 1998 focused on political consultations, a series of workshops and seminars and co-operation by military experts. In March 1999 Russia condemned NATO's military action against the Federal Republic of Yugoslavia and announced the suspension of all relations within the framework of the Founding Act, as well as negotiations on the establishment of a NATO mission in Moscow. Meetings of the Permanent Joint Council were held during 2000, and in February 2001 the NATO Secretary-General agreed with the then acting Russian President a joint statement of commitment to pursuing dialogue and co-operation.

In May 1997 NATO ministers of foreign affairs, meeting in Sintra, Portugal, concluded an agreement with Ukraine providing for enhanced co-operation between the two sides; the so-called Charter on a Distinctive Relationship was signed at the NATO summit meeting held in Madrid, Spain, in July. In May 1998 NATO agreed to appoint a permanent liaison officer in Ukraine to enhance co-operation between the two sides and assist Ukraine to formulate a programme of joint military exercises. The first NATO-Ukraine meeting at the level of heads of state took place in April 1999.

The Madrid summit meeting in July 1997 endorsed the establishment of a Mediterranean Co-operation Group to enhance NATO relations with Egypt, Israel, Jordan, Mauritania, Morocco and Tunisia. The Group was to provide a forum for regular political dialogue between the two groupings and to promote co-operation in training, scientific research and information exchange. In April 1999 NATO heads of state endorsed measures to strengthen the so-called Mediterranean Dialogue. Algeria joined the Mediterranean Dialogue in February 2000.

In July 1997 heads of state and government formally invited the Czech Republic, Hungary and Poland to begin accession negotiations, with the aim of extending membership to those countries in April 1999. During 1997 concern was expressed on the part of some member governments with regard to the cost of expanding the Alliance; however, in November the initial cost of incorporating the Czech Republic, Hungary and Poland into NATO was officially estimated at US $1,300m. over a 10-year period, which was widely deemed to be an acceptable figure. Accession Protocols for the admission of those countries were signed in December and required ratification by all member states. The three countries formally became members of NATO in March 1999. In April the NATO summit meeting, held in Washington, DC, USA, initiated a new Membership Action Plan to extend practical support to aspirant member countries and to formalize a process of reviewing applications. Albania, Bulgaria, Estonia, Latvia, Lithuania, Romania, Slovakia, Slovenia and the former Yugoslav republic of Macedonia were participating in the Membership Action Plan in 2000.

PEACE-KEEPING ACTIVITIES

During the 1990s NATO increasingly developed its role as a mechanism for peace-keeping and crisis management. In June 1992 NATO ministers of foreign affairs, meeting in Oslo, Norway, announced the Alliance's readiness to support peace-keeping operations under the aegis of the CSCE on a case-by-case basis: NATO would make both military resources and expertise available to such operations. In July NATO, in co-operation with WEU, undertook a maritime operation in the Adriatic Sea to monitor compliance with the UN Security Council's resolutions imposing sanctions against the Yugoslav republics of Serbia and Montenegro. In October NATO was requested to provide, staff and finance the military headquarters of the United Nations peace-keeping force in Bosnia and Herzegovina, the UN Protection Force in Yugoslavia (UNPROFOR). In December NATO ministers of foreign affairs expressed the Alliance's readiness to support peace-keeping operations under the authority of the UN Security Council; in that month NATO began formal military planning of operations designed to help bring an end to hostilities in Bosnia and Herzegovina. From April 1993 NATO fighter and reconnaissance aircraft began patrolling airspace over Bosnia and Herzegovina in order to enforce the UN prohibition of military aerial activity over the country. In addition, from July NATO aircraft provided protective cover for UNPROFOR troops operating in the 'safe areas' established by the UN Security Council. In August the NAC endorsed operational plans to conduct air attacks, at the request of the UN, to defend and deter attacks on the designated 'safe areas'. In February 1994 NATO conducted the first of several aerial strikes against artillery positions that were violating heavy-weapons exclusion zones imposed around 'safe areas' and threatening the civilian populations. Throughout the conflict the Alliance also provided transport, communications and logistics to support UN humanitarian assistance in the region.

The peace accord for the former Yugoslavia, which was initialled in Dayton, USA, in November 1995, and signed in Paris in December, provided for the establishment of a NATO-led Implementation Force (IFOR) to ensure compliance with the treaty, in accordance with a strictly defined timetable and under the authority of a UN Security Council mandate. In early December a joint meeting of allied foreign and defence ministers endorsed the military structure for the peace mission, entitled Operation Joint Endeavour, which was to involve approximately 60,000 troops from 31 NATO and non-NATO countries. The Operation was to include a Russian contingent, under an agreement that granted Russia access to the consultation and decision-making processes affecting participating troops. The mission was to be under the overall authority of the Supreme Allied Commander Europe (ACE), with the Commander of the ACE Rapid Reaction Corps providing command on the ground. IFOR, which constituted NATO's largest military operation ever, formally assumed responsIbility for peace-keeping in Bosnia and Herzegovina from the UN on 20 December.

By mid-1996 the military aspects of the Dayton peace agreement had largely been implemented under IFOR supervision, including the withdrawal of former warring parties to behind agreed lines of separation and the release of prisoners of war. Territory was exchanged between the two Bosnian 'entities', although IFOR was criticized for failing to prevent widespread destruction in suburbs of Sarajevo that were being vacated by Bosnian Serbs on the transfer of the districts to Bosnian Federation control. Substantial progress was achieved in the demobilization of soldiers and militia and in the cantonment of heavy weaponry. However, in August and September the Bosnian Serbs obstructed IFOR weapons inspections and the force was obliged to threaten the Serbs with strong military retaliation to secure access to the arms sites. During 1996 IFOR personnel undertook many activities relating to the civilian reconstruction of Bosnia and Herzegovina, including the repair of roads, railways and bridges; reconstruction of schools and hospitals; delivery of emergency food and water supplies; and emergency medical transportation. IFOR also co-operated with, and provided logist-

ical support for, the Office of the High Representative of the International Community in Bosnia and Herzegovina, which was charged with overseeing implementation of the civilian aspects of the Bosnian peace accord. IFOR assisted the OSCE in preparing for and overseeing the all-Bosnia legislative elections that were held in September, and provided security for displaced Bosnians who crossed the inter-entity boundary in order to vote in their towns of origin. In December NATO ministers of foreign affairs approved a follow-on operation, with an 18-month mandate, to be known as the Stabilization Force (SFOR). SFOR was to be about one-half the size of IFOR, but was to retain 'the same unity of command and robust rules of engagement' as the previous force. However, NATO failed to give SFOR an increased mandate to pursue and arrest indicted war criminals, whose prosecution at the International Criminal Tribunal for the Former Yugoslavia (ICTY, see p. 15). in The Hague, was widely regarded as essential for the success of the Bosnian peace process. SFOR became operational on 20 December. Its principal objective was to maintain a safe environment at a military level to ensure that the civil aspects of the Dayton peace accord could be fully implemented, including the completion of the de-mining process, the repatriation of refugees and preparations for municipal elections. In July 1997 NATO heads of government expressed their support for a more determined implementation of SFOR's mandate permitting the arrest of people sought by the ICTY if they were discovered within the normal course of duties. A few days later troops serving under SFOR seized two former Serb officials who had been indicted on charges of genocide. SFOR has subsequently undertaken this objective as part of its operational activities. From mid-1997 SFOR assisted efforts by the Bosnian Serb President, Biljana Plavšić, to maintain the security and territorial integrity of the Republika Srpska in the face of violent opposition from nationalist supporters of the former President, Radovan Karadžić, based in Pale. In August NATO authorized SFOR to use force to prevent the use of the local media to incite violence, following attacks on multinational forces by Serb nationalists during attempts to regain control of police buildings. In October SFOR seized radio and television transmitters, which had allegedly been exploited by Karadžić supporters. In November SFOR provided the general security framework, as well as logistical and communications assistance, in support of the OSCE's supervision of legislative elections that were conducted in the Republika Srpska. In December NATO ministers of defence confirmed that SFOR would be maintained at its current strength of some 31,000 troops, subject to the periodic six-monthly reviews. In February 1998 NATO resolved to establish within SFOR a specialized unit to respond to civil unrest and uphold public security. At the same time the NAC initiated a series of security co-operation activities to promote the development of democratic practices and defence mechanisms in Bosnia and Herzegovina. In October 1999 the NAC formally agreed to implement a reduction in SFOR's strength to some 20,000 troops, as well as a revision of its command structure, in response to the improved security situation in Bosnia and Herzegovina. The reforms were approaching completion in early 2001.

In March 1998 an emergency session of the NAC was convened at the request of the Albanian Government, which was concerned at the deteriorating security of its border region with the Serbian province of Kosovo and Metohija, following intensified action by the Kosovo Liberation Army (KLA) and retaliatory attacks by Serbian security forces. Diplomatic efforts were pursued to contain and resolve the conflict, at the same time as NATO undertook consideration of military options. In mid-June NATO defence ministers authorized the formulation of plans for airstrikes against Serbian targets. A few days later some 80 aircraft dispatched from 15 NATO bases flew close to Albania's border with Kosovo, in an attempt to demonstrate the Alliance's determination to prevent further reprisals agianst the ethnic Albanian population. Military exercises involving 1,700 troops from 11 NATO countries, as well as from Albania, Lithuania and Russia, were conducted in Albania in August. In September NATO defence ministers urged a diplomatic solution to the conflict, but insisted that, with an estimated 50,000 refugees living without shelter in the mountainous region bordering Albania, their main objective was to avert a humanitarian disaster. In late September the UN Security Council issued a resolution (1199) demanding an immediate cease-fire in Kosovo, the withdrawal of the majority of Serbian military and police forces, co-operation by all sides with humanitarian agencies, and the initiation of political negotiations on some form of autonomy for the province. Plans for NATO airstrikes were finalized in early October. However, the Russian Government remained strongly opposed to the use of force and there was concern among some member states whether there was sufficient legal basis for NATO action without further UN authorization. Nevertheless, in mid-October, following Security Council condemnation of the humanitarian situation in Kosovo, the NAC agreed on limited airstrikes against Serbian targets, with a 96-hour delay on the 'activation order'. At the same time the US envoy to the region, Richard Holbrooke, concluded an agreement with President Milošević to implement the conditions of UN Resolution 1199. A 2,000-member international observer force, under the auspices of the OSCE, was to be established to monitor compliance with the agreement, supported by a NATO Co-ordination Unit, based in the former Yugoslav republic of Macedonia (FYRM), to assist with aerial surveillance. In mid-November NATO ambassadors approved the establishment of a 1,200–1,800 strong multinational force, under French command, to assist in any necessary evacuation of OSCE monitors. A NATO Kosovo Verification Command Centre was established in Kumanovo, north-east FYRM, in late November; however, President Milošević warned that the dispatch of foreign troops into Kosovo would be treated as an act of aggression.

In mid-January 1999 NATO ambassadors convened in an emergency session following the discovery of the bodies of 45 ethnic Albanians in the Kosovan village of Racak. The meeting demanded that Serbia co-operate with an inquiry into the incident by the Prosecutor of the ICTY, guarantee the security and safety of all international personnel, withdraw security forces (which had continued to undertake offensives within Kosovo), and uphold the cease-fire. Intensive diplomatic efforts, co-ordinated by the six-country 'Contact Group' on the former Yugoslavia, succeeded in bringing both sides in the dispute to talks on the future of Kosovo. During the first stage of negotiations, held in Rambouillet, France, a provisional framework for a political settlement was formulated, based on a form of autonomy for Kosovo (to be reviewed after a three-year period), and incorporating a mandate for a NATO force of some 28,000 troops to monitor its implementation. The talks were suspended in late February with neither side having agreed to the accord. On the resumption of negotiations in mid-March representatives of the KLA confirmed that they would sign the peace settlement. President Milošević, however, continued to oppose the establishment of a NATO force in Kosovo and, despite further diplomatic efforts by Holbrooke, declined to endorse the agreement in accordance with a deadline imposed by the Contact Group. Amid reports of renewed Serbian violence against Albanian civilians in Kosovo, the NAC subsequently reconfirmed its support for NATO military intervention.

On 24 March 1999 an aerial offensive against the Federal Republic of Yugoslavia was initiated by NATO, with the declared aim of reducing that country's capacity to commit attacks on the Albanian population. The first phase of the allied operation was directed against defence facilities, followed, a few days later, by the second phase which permitted direct attacks on artillery positions, command centres and other military targets in a declared exclusion zone south of the 44th parallel. The escalation of the conflict prompted thousands of Albanians to flee Kosovo, while others were reportedly forced from their homes by Serbian security personnel, creating massive refugee populations in neighbouring countries. In early April NATO ambassadors agreed to dispatch some 8,000 troops, as an ACE Mobile Force Land operation (entitled 'Operation Allied Harbour'), to provide humanitarian assistance to the estimated 300,000 refugees in Albania at that time and to provide transportation to relieve overcrowded camps, in particular in border areas. Refugees in the FYRM were to be assisted by the existing NATO contingent (numbering some 12,000 troops by early April), which was permitted by the authorities in that country to construct new camps for some 100,000 displaced Kosovans. An additional 1,000 troops were transferred from the FYRM to Albania in mid-May in order to construct a camp to provide for a further 65,000 refugees. In mid-April NATO ministers of foreign affairs, meeting in special session, expressed extreme concern at the refugee situation throughout the region. The ministers also clarified the conditions necessary to halt the offensive, which included Serbia's agreement to an international military presence in Kosovo, provision for the safe return of all refugees and an undertaking to work on the basis of the Rambouillet accord. Russia continued to pursue diplomatic efforts to secure a peaceful settlement to the conflict, however, Milošević's reported agreement to allow an unarmed international force in Kosovo, conditional on the immediate end to the NATO campaign, was dismissed by NATO governments. From early April there was increasing evidence of civilian casualties resulting from NATO's aerial bombing of transport, power and media infrastructure and suspected military targets. In mid-April NATO initiated an inquiry following the bombing of a convoy of lorries which resulted in the deaths of some 69 refugees. In the following month NATO was obliged to apologise to the authorities of the People's Republic of China after the accidental bombing of its embassy in Belgrade. At the same time there was widespread concern among governments at increasing evidence of systematic killings and ethnic violence being committed by Serbian forces within Kosovo, and at the estimated 100,000 Albanian men unaccounted for among the massive displaced population. NATO's 50th anniversary summit meeting, held in Washington, USA, in late April, was dominated by consideration of the conflict and of the future stability of the region. A joint statement declared the determination of all Alliance members to increase economic and military pressure on President Milošević to withdraw forces from Kosovo. In particular, the meeting agreed to prevent shipments of petroleum reaching Serbia through Mon-

tenegro, to complement the embargo imposed by the EU and a new focus of the bombing campaign which aimed to destroy the fuel supply within Serbia. However, there was concern on the part of several NATO governments on the legal and political aspects of implementing the embargo. The meeting failed to adopt a unified position on the use of ground forces, which many expert commentators insisted, throughout the campaign, were necessary to secure NATO's objectives. In May ministers of foreign affairs of the Group of Seven industrialized nations and Russia (the G-8) agreed on general principles for a political solution, which was to form the basis of UN Security Council resolution. Later in that month NATO estimated that a future Kosovo Peace Implementation Force (KFOR), installed to guarantee a settlement, would require at least 48,000 troops. Following further intensive diplomatic efforts to secure a cease-fire in Kosovo, on 9 June a Military Technical Agreement was signed between NATO and the Federal Republic of Yugoslavia, incorporating a timetable for the withdrawal of all Serbian security personnel. On the following day the UN Security Council adopted Resolution 1244, which authorized an international security presence in Kosovo, under NATO, and an international civilian presence, the UN Interim Administration Mission in Kosovo (UNMIK). The NAC subsequently suspended the airstrike campaign, which, by that time, had involved some 38,000 sorties. KFOR was organized into six brigades, under the leadership of France, Germany, Italy, USA and the United Kingdom (with responsibility for two brigades). An initial force of 20,000 troops entered Kosovo on 12 June. A few days later an agreement was concluded with Russia, whose troops had also entered Kosovo and taken control of Pristina airport, which provided for the joint responsibility of the airstrip with a NATO contingent and for the participation of some 3,600 Russian troops in KFOR, reporting to the country command in each sector. On 20 June the withdrawal of Yugoslav troops from Kosovo was completed, providing for the formal ending of NATO's campaign. The KLA undertook to demilitarize and transform the force, as required under Resolution 1244, which was reported to have been achieved in September. KFOR's immediate responsibility was to provide a secure environment to facilitate the safe return of refugees, and, pending the full deployment of UNMIK, to assist the reconstruction of infrastructure and civil and political institutions. In addition, NATO troops were to assist personnel of the international tribunal to investigate sites of alleged violations of human rights and mass graves. From August an escalation of ethnic violence and deterioration of law and order in some parts of the province was an outstanding concern. In January 2000 NATO agreed that the Eurocorps defence force (see under WEU) would assume command of KFOR headquarters in April. At that time KFOR's main concerns were to protect the minority populations, maintain security and reintegrate members of the KLA into civilian life. KFOR was also to continue to work closely with UNMIK in the provision of humanitarian aid, the rehabilitation of infrastructure and the development of civil administration. In February an emergency meeting of the NAC was convened to review the situation in the divided town of Titova Mitrovica, northern Kosovo, where violent clashes had occurred between the ethnic populations and five people had died during attempts by KFOR to impose order. The NAC expressed its determination to reinforce KFOR's troop levels. In September KFOR undertook to protect ethnic Serbians who were eligible to vote in a general election in the Federal Republic of Yugoslavia, and in the following month KFOR worked with OSCE and UN personnel to maintain a secure environment and provide logistical assistance for the holding of municipal elections in Kosovo. During the year KFOR attempted to prevent the movement and stockpiling of illegal armaments in the region. In November there was a marked deterioration in the security situation in Kosovo, and KFOR attempted to halt several outbreaks of cross-border violence. In February 2001 NATO conducted negotiations with the Yugoslav Government regarding new security arrangements to prevent further attacks on the local population in southern Serbia and to counter illegal arms-trafficking. In early March Albanian separatists in the FYRM escalated their campaign in the north of that country. KFOR troops attempted to prevent Kosovo Albanians from supporting the rebels, fighting as the National Liberation Army (NLA), in order to avert further violence and instability. NATO dispatched military and political missions to meet with the Macedonian authorities, and agreed that Serbian troops were to be permitted to enter the ground safety zone in the Presevo valley (bordering on Kosovo and the FYRM) to strengthen security and prevent it becoming a safe haven for the rebel fighters. The Secretary-General also requested an additional 1,400 troops from member countries to reinforce border security. In mid-March the NLA seized strategic positions around Tetovo, in north-west FYRM. After several days of conflict Macedonian troops initiated an offensive against the rebel strongholds, prompting thousands of Albanians to flee into Kosovo.

Nato Agencies

1. Civilian production and logistics organizations responsible to the NAC:

Central European Pipeline Management Agency—CEPMA: BP 552, 78005 Versailles, France; tel. 1-39-24-49-00; fax 1-39-55-65-39; f. 1957 as the Central European Operating Agency; responsible for the 24-hour operation of the Central European Pipeline System and its storage and distribution facilities.

Nato Airborne Early Warning and Control Programme Management Organisation—NAPMO: c/o Akerstraat 7, 6445 CL Brunssum, Netherlands; fax (45) 5254373; f. 1978 to manage the procurement aspects of the NATO Airborne Early Warning and Control System.

NATO Consultation, Command and Control Organization—NC3O: 1110 Brussels, Belgium; tel. (2) 707-43-58; fax (2) 708-87-70; f. 1997 by restructuring of the NATO Communications and Information Systems Organization and the Tri-Service Group on Communications and Electronics; incorporates the former Allied Data Systems Interoperability Agency, the Allied Naval Communications Agency and the Allied Tactical Communications Agency; decides on policies and interoperability, supervises planning and implementation, and operates and maintains communications and information systems for tactical and strategic integrated services, including voice, data, fax, video (tele)conferencing and automated command and control capability for crisis management, consultation of the NATO nations and the command and control of NATO forces.

NATO C3 Agency: Responsible for planning, design, systems engineering, technical support and procurements; operates from Brussels and offices in The Hague.

NATO CIS Operating and Support Agency—NACOSA: Maintains NATO's communications and information system (CIS). Responsible for the NATO Communications and Information Systems School, based in Latina, Italy.

NATO EF 2000 and Tornado Development, Production and Logistics Management Agency—NETMA: Insel Kammerstrasse 12–14, Postfach 1302, 82008 Unterhaching, Germany; tel. (89) 666800; fax (89) 6668055; replaced the NATO Multirole Combat Aircraft (MRCA) Development and Production Management Agency (f. 1969) and the NATO European Fighter (EF) Aircraft Development, Production and Logistics Management Agency (f. 1987); responsible for the joint development and production of the European Fighter Aircraft and the MRCA (Tornado).

NATO HAWK Management Office: 26 rue Galliéni, 92500 Rueil-Malmaison, France; tel. 1-47-08-75-00; fax 1-47-52-10-99; f. 1959 to supervise the multinational production and upgrading programmes of the HAWK surface-to-air missile system in Europe; Gen. Man. A. BOCCHI.

NATO Helicopter Design and Development Production and Logistics Management Agency—NAHEMA: Le Quatuor, Bâtiment A, 42 route de Galice, 13082 Aix-en-Provence Cédex 2, France; tel. 4-42-95-92-00; fax 4-42-64-30-50.

NATO Maintenance and Supply Agency—NAMSA: 8302 Capellen, Luxembourg; fax 30-87-21; f. 1958; supplies spare parts and logistic support for a number of jointly-used weapon systems, missiles and electronic systems; all member nations except Iceland participate.

2. Responsible to the Military Committee:

Allied Communications Security Agency—ACSA: Brussels, Belgium; f. 1953.

Military Agency for Standardization—MAS: 1110 Brussels, Belgium; tel. (2) 707-55-76; fax (2) 707-57-18; e-mail mas@hq.nato.int; f. 1951 to foster NATO standardization in order to increase the combined operational effectiveness of the Alliance's military forces.

NATO Defense College—NADEFCOL: Via Giorgio Pelosi 1, 00143 Rome-Cecchiguola, Italy; tel. (06) 505259; f. 1951 to train officials for posts in NATO organizations or in national ministries.

NATO Frequency Management Sub-Committee—FMSC: 1100 Brussels, Belgium; tel. (2) 707-55-28; replaced the Allied Radio Frequency Agency (f. 1951); the FMSC is the frequency authority of the Alliance and establishes and co-ordinates all policy concerned with the military use of the radio frequency spectrum.

Research and Technology Organization—RTO: BP 25, 7 rue Ancelle, 92201 Neuilly-sur-Seine Cédex, France; tel. 1-55-61-22-00; fax 1-55-61-22-99; e-mail mailbox@rta.nato.int; f. 1998 by merger of the Advisory Group for Aerospace Research and Development and the Defence Research Group; brings together scientists and engineers from member countries for exchange of information and research co-operation (formally established 1998); provides scientific and technical advice for the Military Committee, for other NATO bodies and for member nations; comprises a Research and Technology Board and a Research and Technology Agency, responsible for implementing RTO's work programme.

3. Responsible to Supreme Allied Commander Atlantic (SACLANT):

NATO SACLANT Undersea Research Centre—SACLANTCEN: Viale San Bartolomeo 400, 19138 La Spezia, Italy; tel. (0187) 5271; fax (0187) 527420; e-mail library@saclantc.nato.int; internet www.saclantc.nato.int; f. 1959 to conduct research in support of NATO operational requirements in antisubmarine warfare and mine counter-measures.

4. Responsible to Supreme Allied Commander Europe (SACEUR):

NATO (SHAPE) School: Am Rainenbichl 54, 82487 Oberammergau, Germany; tel. (88) 224477; fax (88) 221035; e-mailpostmaster@natoschool-shape.de; f. 1975; acts as a centre for training military and civilian personnel of NATO countries, and, since 1991, for officials from partner countries, in support of NATO policies, operations and objectives.

Finance

As NATO is an international, not a supra-national, organization, its member countries themselves decide the amount to be devoted to their defence effort and the form which the latter will assume. Thus, the aim of NATO's defence planning is to develop realistic military plans for the defence of the alliance at reasonable cost. Under the annual defence planning process, political, military and economic factors are considered in relation to strategy, force requirements and available resources. The procedure for the co-ordination of military plans and defence expenditures rests on the detailed and comparative analysis of the capabilities of member countries. All installations for the use of international forces are financed under a common-funded infrastructure programme. In accordance with the terms of the Partnership for Peace strategy, partner countries undertake to make available the necessary personnel, assets, facilities and capabilities to participate in the programme. The countries also share the financial cost of military exercises in which they participate. The administrative (or 'civil') budget amounted to US $157m. in 1998. The total military budget approved for 1998 amounted to $680m. (excluding the costs of assignment of military personnel, met by the contributing countries).

Publications

NATO publications (in English and French, with some editions in other languages) include:
NATO Basic Fact Sheets.
NATO Final Communiqués.
NATO Handbook.
NATO Review (quarterly in 11 languages; annually in Icelandic).
NATO Update (weekly, electronic version only).
Economic and scientific publications.

ORGANISATION FOR ECONOMIC CO-OPERATION AND DEVELOPMENT—OECD

Address: 2 rue André-Pascal, 75775 Paris Cédex 16, France.

Telephone: 1-45-24-82-00; **fax:** 1-45-24-85-00; **e-mail:** webmaster@oecd.org; **internet:** www.oecd.org.

OECD was founded in 1961, replacing the Organisation for European Economic Co-operation (OEEC) which had been established in 1948 in connection with the Marshall Plan. It constitutes a forum for governments to discuss, develop and attempt to co-ordinate their economic and social policies. The Organisation aims to promote policies designed to achieve the highest level of sustainable economic growth, employment and increase in the standard of living while maintaining financial stability, and to contribute to economic expansion in member and non-member states and to the expansion of world trade.

MEMBERS

Australia	Hungary	Norway
Austria	Iceland	Poland
Belgium	Ireland	Portugal
Canada	Italy	Slovakia
Czech Republic	Japan	Spain
Denmark	Republic of Korea	Sweden
Finland	Luxembourg	Switzerland
France	Mexico	Turkey
Germany	Netherlands	United Kingdom
Greece	New Zealand	USA

The European Commission also takes part in OECD's work.

Organization

(April 2001)

COUNCIL

The governing body of OECD is the Council, at which each member country is represented. The Council meets from time to time (usually once a year) at the level of government ministers, the Chairmanship being rotated among member states. It also meets regularly at official level, when it comprises the Secretary-General and the Permanent Representatives of member states to OECD. It is responsible for all questions of general policy and may establish subsidiary bodies as required to achieve the aims of the Organisation. Decisions and recommendations of the Council are adopted by mutual agreement of all its members.

Heads of Permanent Delegations (with ambassadorial rank):

Australia: ANTHONY HINTON
Austria: KARL SCHRAMEK
Belgium: RÉGINE DE CLERCQ
Canada: SUZANNE HURTUBISE
Czech Republic: JAROMÍR PRIVRATSKY
Denmark: FLEMMING HEDEGAARD
Finland: JORMA JULIN
France: JOËLLE BOURGEOIS
Germany: WERNER KAUFMANN-BÜHLER
Greece: SPYROS LIOUKAS
Hungary: BÉLA KÁDÁR
Iceland: SIGRIDUR ASDIS SNAEVARR
Ireland: PATRICK O'CONNOR
Italy: ALESSANDRO VATTANI
Japan: MUTSUYOSHI NISHIMURA
Republic of Korea: DUCK-SOO HAN
Luxembourg: JEAN-MARC HOSCHEIT
Mexico: JAVIER ARRIGUNAGA
Netherlands: FRANZ ENGERING
New Zealand: RICHARD GRANT
Norway: PER LUDVIG MAGMUS
Poland: JAN WORONIECKI
Portugal: ANA MARTINHO
Slovakia: DUSAN BELLA
Spain: ELENA PISONERO RUIZ
Sweden: ANDERS FERM
Switzerland: WILLIAM JAGGI
Turkey: ULUÇ ÖZÜLKER
United Kingdom: CHRISTOPHER CRABBIE
USA: AMY BONDURANT

Participant with Special Status:

European Commission: JOHN MADDISON (United Kingdom).

EXECUTIVE COMMITTEE

The Executive Committee prepares the work of the Council. It is also called upon to carry out specific tasks where necessary. In addition to its regular meetings, the Committee meets occassionally in special sessions attended by senior government officials.

SECRETARIAT

The Council, the committees and other bodies in OECD are assisted by an independent international secretariat headed by the Secretary-General. An Executive Director is responsible for the management of administrative support services. Some 1,850 staff were employed in the secretariat in January 2000.

Secretary-General: DONALD J. JOHNSTON (Canada).

Deputy Secretaries-General: THORVALD MOE (Norway), HERWIG SCHLÖGL (Germany), SEIICHI KONDO (Japan), SALLY SHELTON-COLBY (USA).

Executive Director: JEAN-JACQUES NOREAU (Canada).

AUTONOMOUS AND SEMI-AUTONOMOUS BODIES

Centre for Educational Research and Innovation—CERI: f. 1968; includes all member countries. Dir THOMAS J. ALEXANDER (see also under Education, Employment, Labour and Social Affairs, below).

Club du Sahel: f. 1976; an informal forum of donor countries and member states of the Permanent Inter-State Committee on Drought Control in the Sahel (see p. 309). Dir JACQUELINE DAMON.

Development Centre: f. 1962; includes most member countries and Argentina, Brazil and Chile. Pres. JORGE BRAGA DE MACEDO (Portugal) (see also under Development Co-operation, below).

European Conference of Ministers of Transport (see p. 359).

International Energy Agency (see p. 250).

Nuclear Energy Agency (see p. 251).

Activities

The greater part of the work of OECD, which covers all aspects of economic and social policy, is prepared and carried out in about 200 specialized bodies (Committees, Working Parties, etc.); all members are normally represented on these bodies, except on those of a restricted nature.

ECONOMIC POLICY

The main organ for the consideration and direction of economic policy among the member countries is the Economic Policy Committee, which comprises governments' chief economic advisors and central bankers, and meets two or three times a year to review the economic and financial situation and policies of member countries. It has several working parties and groups, the most important of which are Working Party No. 1 on Macro-Economic and Structural Policy Analysis, Working Party No. 3 on Policies for the Promotion of Better International Payments Equilibrium, and the Working Group on Short-Term Economic Prospects.

The Economic and Development Review Committee, comprising all member countries, is responsible for the annual examination of the economic situation and macro economic and structural policies of each member country. A report is issued every 12 to 18 months on each country, after an examination carried out by the Committee; this process of peer review has been extended also to other branches of the Organisation's work (agriculture, environment, manpower and social affairs, scientific policy and development aid efforts).

STATISTICS

Statistical data and related methodological information are collected from member governments and, where possible, consolidated, or converted into an internationally comparable form. The Statistics Directorate maintains data required for macroeconomic forecasting, i.e. national accounts, the labour force, foreign trade, prices, output, and monetary, financial, industrial and other short-term statistics. Specialist directorates collect and maintain other databases. In 2000 the principal concerns of the Directorate were to: improve the supply of statistical information to analysts and policy-makers within and outside the Organisation; develop international statistical standards, systems and classifications, in collaboration with other international agencies; and provide a mechanism for the improved co-ordination of statistical activities within the Organisation and with other agencies.

DEVELOPMENT CO-OPERATION

The Development Assistance Committee (DAC) is the principal body through which the Organisation deals with issues relating to co-operation with developing countries and is one of the key forums in which the major bilateral donors work together to increase their effectiveness in support of sustainable development. Guided by the Development Partnerships Strategy formulated in 1996, the DAC's mission is to foster co-ordinated, integrated, effective and adequately financed international efforts in support of sustainable economic and social development. Recognizing that developing countries themselves are ultimately responsible for their own development, the DAC concentrates on how international co-operation can contribute to the population's ability to overcome poverty and participate fully in society. Principal activities include: adopting authoritative policy guide-lines; conducting periodic critical reviews of members' programmes of development co-operation; providing a forum for dialogue, exchange of experience and the building of international consensus on policy and management issues; and publishing statistics and reports on aid and other resource flows to developing countries and countries in transition. A working set of indicators of development progress has been established by the DAC, in collaboration with experts from the UN agencies, the World Bank and developing countries.

The OECD Development Centre was established in 1962 to provide a focal point within the Organisation for analysis and policy dialogue on economic and social aspects of development in Africa, Asia, Latin America, the Caribbean and the Middle East. The Centre informs member countries of emerging issues and offers developing countries objective, in-depth analyses, with a view to promoting constructive policy reform. It serves as an intermediary between OECD and the developing countries by promoting the exchange of ideas and information. Research and dialogue activities are orientated towards topics with a high priority on the agenda of policy-makers. The Centre's work programme for 1999–2000, entitled 'The Sustainability of Economic Policy Reform', focused on four main themes: Financial Crises and Structural Implications; Implementation of the Development Partnerships Strategy; Sustainable Development; Globalization, Social Cohesion and Demography.

The Club du Sahel provides an informal framework for dialogue and co-operation between Sahelian countries, donor governments, and concerned organizations. Its work programme has evolved since its establishment to reflect the most pressing needs and concerns of the sub-region. In the late 1990s the principal issues under consideration were demographic change; regional economic development; environmental restoration; food crisis prevention; globalization; and the emergence of civil society.

In a report to the Secretary-General in late 1997 an advisory group on the environment, comprising non-governmental experts, recommended that OECD should evolve into the principal inter-governmental organization providing the analytical and comparative framework of policy necessary for industrialized countries to make the transition to sustainable development. At a meeting in April 1998 ministers from member countries reiterated that the achievement of sustainable development was a priority, and recommended wide-ranging projects over the forthcoming three years in areas relating to technology, the effects of climate change, the environmental impact of subsidies, and the creation of indicators of sustainability, in order comprehensively to address the economic, social and environmental dimensions of sustainable development.

In May 1999 the Executive Committee in Special Session considered OECD's role in South-East Europe once a peace settlement had been agreed on the future of Kosovo and Metohija, in southern Serbia. The Committee determined that OECD should collaborate with the World Bank, IMF and other agencies to promote economic and social development in countries bordering the Federal Republic of Yugoslavia, in order to strengthen political stability throughout the region.

PUBLIC MANAGEMENT

The Public Management Committee, and its secretariat, the Public Management Service (PUMA) are concerned with issues of governance, including: the formulation of policies and their implementation; the allocation of resources; the renewal of the institutions of state; and questions of accountability, consultation and transparency. PUMA serves as a forum for senior officials responsible for the central management systems of government, providing information, analysis and recommendations on public management and governing capacity. A joint initiative of OECD and the EU, operating within PUMA, supports good governance in countries of Central and Eastern Europe. The so-called Support for Improvement in Governance and Management (SIGMA) programme advises countries on improving their administrative efficiency and promotes the adherence of public sector staff to democratic values and ethics and respect for the rule of law. SIGMA also helps to strengthen capacities at the level of central government to address the challenges of EU integration, and greater global interdependence.

CO-OPERATION WITH NON-MEMBER ECONOMIES

The Centre for Co-operation with Non-Members (CCNM) was established in January 1998, by merger of the Centre for Co-operation with Economies in Transition (founded in 1990) and the Liaison and Co-ordination Unit. It serves as the focal point for the development of policy dialogue with non-member economies, managing multi-country, thematic, regional and country programmes. An Emerging Market Economy Forum brings together non-member economies engaged in market-oriented policy reform of interest to members. Recent topics discussed included tax evasion, the regulation of securities markets and foreign direct investment policy. In 1998 a programme addressing issues arising from financial instability in East Asia was instituted within the Centre. There is also a Transition Economy Programme, which covers a broad range of economic and social policy issues, as well as structural adjustment, and aims to provide insights into policy design and implementation. Country and regional programmes were in place for Bulgaria, China, Romania, Russia, Slovenia and the Baltic States in 2000.

Non-member economies are invited, on a selective basis by the CCNM, to participate in or observe the work of certain OECD committees and working parties. The Centre also provides a limited range of training activities in support of policy implementation and institution building. Five multilateral tax centres provide workshops and seminars for senior officials in tax administration and policy. OECD, through the CCNM, co-sponsors the Centre for Private Sector Development in İstanbul, Turkey, with the Turkish and German Governments. This assists various countries to develop the necessary framework and policies for a market economy and integration into the world economy. The CCNM also sponsors the Joint Vienna Institute (see IMF, p. 96), which offers a variety of administrative, economic and financial management courses to participants from transition economies. The Centre co-operates with a number of other international organizations.

INTERNATIONAL TRADE

OECD's Trade Committee supports the continued liberalization and efficient operation of the multilateral trading system, with the aim of contributing to the expansion of world trade on a non-discriminatory basis. Its activities include examination of issues concerning trade relations among member countries as well as relations with non-member countries, and consideration and discussion of trade measures taken by a member country which adversely affect another's interests. The Committee also considers the challenges that are presented to the existing international trading system by financial or economic instability, the process of globalization of production and markets and the ensuing deeper integration of national economies. OECD provided support to the multilateral trade negotiations conducted under the General Agreement on Tariffs and Trade (GATT), assisting member countries to analyse the effects of the trade accords and promoting its global benefits. Following the conclusion of the negotiations in December 1993, and the entry into force of the World Trade Organization (WTO) agreements in 1995, OECD has continued to study and assess aspects of the international trade agenda, such as integrating emerging market economies into the international trading system, trade and environment, trade and competition policy, trade and investment and trade and industry. In November 1999 OECD published a report on the impact of further trade liberalization on developing countries, in preparation for the next round of multilateral trade negotiations, which were initiated by WTO later in that month.

FINANCIAL, FISCAL AND ENTERPRISE AFFAIRS

Promoting the efficient functioning of markets and enterprises and strengthening the multilateral framework for trade and investment is the responsibility of a number of OECD Committees under the Directorate for Financial, Fiscal and Enterprise Affairs. The Committee on Capital Movements and Invisible Transactions monitors the implementation of the Codes of Liberalization of Invisible Transactions and of Capital Movements as legally binding norms for all member countries. The Committee on International Investment and Multinational Enterprises is reviewing the OECD Guide-lines for Multinational Enterprises, a corporate Code of Conduct recommended by OECD member governments, business and labour units. A Declaration on International Investment and Multinational Enterprises, while non-binding, contains commitments on the conduct and treatment of foreign-owned enterprises established in member countries. Negotiations on a Multilateral Agreement on Investment (MAI), initiated by OECD ministers in 1995 to provide a legal framework for international investment, broke down in October 1998, although 'informal consultation' on the issue was to continue. OECD has initiated an extensive work programme on investment policy issues for the 21st century.

The Committee on Competition Law and Policy promotes the harmonization of national competition policies, co-operation in competition law enforcement, common merger reporting rules and pro-competitive regulatory reform. The Committee on Financial Markets exercises surveillance over recent developments, reform measures and structural and regulatory conditions in financial markets. It aims to promote international trade in financial services, to encourage the integration of non-member countries into the global financial system, and to improve financial statistics. The Committee on Fiscal Affairs has recently focused its efforts on the tax implications of the globalization of national economies. Its activities include promoting the removal of tax barriers and monitoring the implementation and impact of major tax reforms, as well as developing a neutral tax framework for electronic commerce. The Insurance Committee monitors andsurveys structural changes and reform measures in insurance markets.

In May 1997 the OECD Council endorsed plans to introduce a global ban on the corporate bribery of public officials. In December ministers from 33 member and non-member countries signed the OECD Convention on Bribery of Foreign Public Officials in International Business Transactions. The Convention entered into force in February 1999. By April 2001 the Convention had been ratified by 31 countries. A monitoring framework was established to ensure conformity. In May ministers endorsed a set of OECD Principles for Corporate Governance, which covered of ownership and control of corporate entities, the rights of shareholders, the role of stakeholders, transparency, disclosure and the responsibilities of boards. OECD was collaborating with the World Bank and other organizations to promote good governance world-wide, for example through regional meetings. OECD provides the secretariat for the Financial Action Task Force on Money Laundering (q.v.).

FOOD, AGRICULTURE AND FISHERIES

The Committee for Agriculture reviews major developments in agricultural policies, deals with the adaptation of agriculture to changing economic conditions, elaborates forecasts of production and market prospects for the major commodities, promotes the use of sustainable practices in the sector, assesses implications of world developments in food and agriculture for member countries' policies and evaluates progress towards the integration of the agro-food sector into the multilateral trading system. A separate Fisheries Committee carries out similar tasks in its own sector, and, in particular, analyses the consequences of policy measures with a view to promoting responsible and sustainable fisheries.

TERRITORIAL DEVELOPMENT

The Territorial Development Service assists central governments with the design and implementation of more effective, area-based strategies, encourages the emergence of locally driven initiatives for economic development, and promotes better integration of local and national approaches. Territorial policies have recently emphasized the need to mobilize local resources to enhance regional competitiveness and to create employment. The Service comprises two intergovernmental bodies—the Local Economic and Employment Development Committee and the Territorial Development Policy Committee—which share an overall work programme emphasizing the need for innovative policy initiatives and exchange of knowledge in a wide range of policies, such as entrepreneurship and technology diffusion and issues of social exclusion and urban deprivation.

ENVIRONMENT

The OECD Environment Directorate works in support of the Environment Policy Committee (EPOC) on environmental issues. In April 1998 environment ministers of member countries agreed upon a set of 'Shared Goals for Action', with four principal aims: to promote strong national policies and effective regulatory structures for the protection of the natural environment and human health; to promote an integrated policy approach, encouraging coherence among economic, environmental and social policies; to strengthen international co-operation in meeting global and regional environmental commitments; and to support participation, transparency, the provision of information and accountability in environmental policy-making at all levels. The Environment Directorate's work programme for the two year period 1999–2000 outlined 12 main activities consistent with these goals and the Organisation's priorities. There were three new activities: the Environmental Outlook and Strategy aspect, which aimed to establish a conceptual and quantitative foundation for the programme on sustainable development; the work on Sustainable Consumption Patterns, to support member countries in efforts to achieve more sustainable patterns of consumption; and the project on Increasing Resource Efficiency, to assist members and non-members in developing approaches to managing resources more efficiently. Other aspects of the work programme address issues such as climate change, the promotion of environmentally sustainable transport, and the management of transborder movements of waste. An important element of the programme concentrates on chemicals and biotechnology, specifically, on the risks to health and the environment from chemicals. The Environment Directorate also provides the secretariat for the Environmental Action Programme Task Force of the Environment for Europe process, which encourages countries in Eastern Europe and the CIS to take environmental issues into consideration in the process of economic restructuring. A further part of the environment programme considers environmental data, indicators and measurement of performance. The first cycle of a programme of Environmental Performance Reviews of all OECD countries was completed in 1999. By December 28 OECD member countries had been assessed.

SCIENCE, TECHNOLOGY AND INDUSTRY

The principal objective of the Directorate for Science, Technology and Industry is to assist member countries in formulating and implementing policies that optimize the contribution of science, technology, industrial development and structural change to economic growth, employment and social development. The Committee for Scientific and Technological Policy reviews national and international policy issues relating to science and technology. It provides indicators and analysis on emerging trends in these fields, identifies and promotes best practices, and offers a forum for dialogue. Important themes include: the management and reform of science systems; the development of policies to promote the innovative capacity of members' economies; and policy responses to the globalization of science and technology.

A Working Party on Biotechnology was established in 1993 and its mandate was renewed in 1998. Among the priority topics in its most recent work programme were scientific and technological infrastructure, and the relation of biotechnology to sustainable industrial development. In June 1999 it was requested to undertake a study of aspects of biotechnology with respect to food safety. In 1992 a Megascience Forum was established to bring together senior science policy-makers for consultations regarding large scientific projects and programmes. It was succeeded, in 1999, by a Global Science Forum. In 1999 work was proceeding on the establishment of a Global Biodiversity Information Forum to collate, co-ordinate and disseminate data on biodiversity.

The Committee for Information, Computer and Communications Policy monitors developments in telecommunications and information technology and their impact on competitiveness and productivity, with a new emphasis on technological and regulatory convergence. It also promotes the development of new rules (e.g. guide-lines on information security) and analyses trade and liberalization issues. In 1998 the Committee concentrated on issues related to electronic commerce, and played a leading role in the preparation of the Ministerial Conference on this subject in October. In December 1999 the OECD Council approved a set of Guide-lines for Consumer Protection in the Context of Electronic Commerce, which had been prepared by the Committee on Consumer Policy.

The Industry Committee regularly reviews issues of competitiveness in industry and policies for private sector development in member and selected non-member economies. The Committee is particularly concerned with the issues of globalization, regulatory reform, intangible investments and business services, corporate governance, small and medium-sized enterprises (SMEs) and the role of industry in sustainable development. A business and industry policy forum exists for senior policy-makers and representatives of the business sector to address topical issues. A working party on SMEs conducts an ongoing review of the contribution of SMEs to growth and employment and a comparative assement of best practice policies. Databases enabling internationally comparable monitoring of structural change in areas of science and technology, investment, production, employment and trade were being prepared by a working party on statistics in 1998/99.

A Programme of Co-operation in the Field of Research on Road Transport and its Intermodal Linkages examines a range of issues related primarily to the institutional and economic aspects of advanced logistics, freight transport, intelligent transport systems and asset management. The programme also maintains two databases on road transport research and road safety. The Maritime Transport and Steel Committees aim to promote multilateral solutions to sectoral friction and instability based on the definition and monitoring of rules. In June 1994 negotiations between leading shipbulding nations, conducted under OECD auspices, concluded a multilateral agreement to end state subsidies to the industry. However, continued failure by the US Congress to ratify the agreement disrupted its entry into force.

EDUCATION, EMPLOYMENT, LABOUR AND SOCIAL AFFAIRS

The Employment, Labour and Social Affairs Committee is concerned with the development of labour market and selective employment policies to ensure the utilization of human capital at the highest possible level and to improve the quality and flexibility of working life, as well as the effectiveness of social policies; it plays a central role in addressing OECD's concern to reduce high and persistent unemployment through the creation of high-quality jobs. The Committee's work covers such issues as the role of women in the economy, industrial relations, international migration and the development of an extensive social data base. The Committee also carries out single-country and thematic reviews of labour-market policies and social assistance systems. In addition, it has assigned a high priority to work on the policy implications of an ageing population and on indicators of human capital investment. The Education Committee analyses policies for education and training at all levels, carries out education and training policy reviews, conducts an international adult literacy survey, and produces education data and indicators. Together, the Employment, Labour and Social Affairs and Education Committees seek to provide for the greater integration of labour market and educational policies and the prevention of social exclusion.

OECD's Centre for Educational Research and Innovation (CERI) promotes the development of research activities in education together with experiments of an advanced nature designed to test innovations in educational systems and to stimulate research and development. A programme for the production of policy-oriented and comparable indicators of student achievement on a regular basis was established in 1998, in order to provide a profile of the knowledge, skills and competencies of students towards the end of compulsory schooling and information on how such skills relate to important social, economic and educational variables. A Programme on Educational Building provides analysis and advice on the management of educational facilities and infrastructure, while the Programme on Institutional Management in Higher Education focuses on the relation between higher education policy and the management of institutions in the sector.

RELATIONS WITH OTHER INTERNATIONAL ORGANIZATIONS

Under a Protocol signed at the same time as the OECD Convention, the European Commission generally takes part in the work of OECD. EFTA may also send representatives to OECD meetings. Formal relations exist with a number of other international organizations, including the ILO, FAO, IMF, IBRD, UNCTAD, IAEA and the Council of Europe. A few non-governmental organizations have been granted consultative status, notably the Business and Industry Advisory Committee to OECD (BIAC) and the Trade Union Advisory Committee to OECD (TUAC).

Finance

In 1998 OECD's total budget amounted to 1,300m. French francs, of which some 75% was funded by regular contributions from member states and the remainder by special income or project participants.

Publications

Activities of OECD (Secretary-General's Annual Report).
Agricultural Outlook (annually).
Energy Balances (quarterly).
Energy Prices and Taxes (quarterly).
Financial Market Trends (3 a year).
Financial Statistics (Part 1 (domestic markets): monthly; Part 2 (international markets): monthly; Part 3 (OECD member countries): 25 a year).
Foreign Trade Statistics (monthly).
Higher Education Management (3 a year).
Indicators of Industrial Activity (quarterly).
Joint BIS-IMF-OECD-World Bank Statistics on External Debt (quarterly).
Main Developments in Trade (annually).
Main Economic Indicators (monthly).
National Accounts Quarterly.
OECD Economic Outlook (2 a year).
OECD Economic Studies (2 a year).
OECD Economic Surveys (every 12 to 18 months for each country).
OECD Employment Outlook (annually).
The OECD Observer (every 2 months).
Oil and Gas Statistics (quarterly).
PEB Exchange (newsletter of the Programme on Educational Building, 3 a year).
Quarterly Labour Force Statistics.
Science, Technology, Industry Review (2 a year).
Short-term Economic Indicators: Transition Economies (quarterly).
Numerous specialized reports, working papers, books and statistics on economic and social subjects (about 130 titles a year, both in English and French) are also published.

International Energy Agency—IEA

Address: 9 rue de la Fédération, 75739 Paris Cédex 15, France.

Telephone: 1-40-57-65-00; **fax:** 1-40-57-65-59; **e-mail:** info@iea.org; **internet:** www.iea.org.

The Agency was established by the OECD Council in 1974 to develop co-operation on energy questions among participating countries.

MEMBERS

Australia	Greece	Norway*
Austria	Hungary	Portugal
Belgium	Ireland	Spain
Canada	Italy	Sweden
Czech Republic	Japan	Switzerland
Denmark	Republic of Korea	Turkey
Finland	Luxembourg	United Kingdom
France	Netherlands	USA
Germany	New Zealand	

The European Commission is also represented.

*Norway participates in the IEA under a special arrangement.

Organization

(April 2001)

GOVERNING BOARD

Composed of ministers or senior officials of the member governments. Decisions may be taken by a weighted majority on a number of specified subjects, particularly concerning emergency measures and the emergency reserve commitment; a simple weighted majority is required for procedural decisions and decisions implementing specific obligations in the agreement. Unanimity is required only if new obligations, not already specified in the agreement, are to be undertaken.

The Governing Board is assisted by a Coal and an Oil Industry Advisory Board, composed of industrial executives.

SECRETARIAT

The Secretariat comprises the following four Offices: Long-Term Co-operation and Policy Analysis; Non-member Countries; Oil Markets and Emergency Preparedness; and Energy Efficiency, Technology and Research and Development.

Executive Director: ROBERT PRIDDLE (United Kingdom).

Activities

The Agreement on an International Energy Programme was signed in November 1974 and formally entered into force in January 1976. The Programme commits the participating countries of the International Energy Agency to share petroleum in emergencies, to strengthen their long-term co-operation in order to reduce dependence on petroleum imports, to increase the availability of information on the petroleum market and to develop relations with the petroleum-producing and other petroleum-consuming countries.

An emergency petroleum-sharing plan has been established, and the IEA ensures that the necessary technical information and facilities are in place so that it can be readily used in the event of a reduction in petroleum supplies. The IEA undertakes emergency response reviews and workshops, and publishes an Emergency Management Manual to facilitate a co-ordinated response to a severe disruption in petroleum supplies. A separate division monitors and reports on short-term developments in the petroleum market. It also considers other related issues, including international crude petroleum pricing, petroleum trade and stock developments and investments by major petroleum-producing countries.

The IEA Long-Term Co-operation Programme is designed to strengthen the security of energy supplies and promote stability in world energy markets. It provides for co-operative efforts to conserve energy, to accelerate the development of alternative energy sources by means of both specific and general measures, to strengthen research and development of new energy technologies and to remove legislative and administrative obstacles to increased energy supplies. Regular reviews of member countries' efforts in the fields of energy conservation and accelerated development of alternative energy sources assess the effectiveness of national programmes in relation to the objectives of the Agency.

The IEA also reviews the energy situation in non-member countries, in particular the petroleum-producing countries of the Middle East and central and eastern European countries. In the latter states the IEA has provided technical assistance for the development of national energy legislation and energy efficiency projects. The IEA has entered into co-operation agreements with Russia, the People's Republic of China and India.

The IEA aims to contribute to the energy security of member countries through energy technology and research and development projects, in particular those concerned with energy efficiency, conservation and protection of the environment. The IEA promotes international collaboration in this field and the participation of energy industries to facilitate the application of new technologies, through effective transfer of knowledge, technology innovation and training. Member states adopt Implementing Agreements, which provide mechanisms for collaboration and information exchange in specific areas, for example electric vehicle technologies, electric demand-side management and photovoltaic power systems. Non-member states are encouraged to participate in these Agreements. The Agency sponsors conferences, symposia and workshops to further enhance international co-operation among member and non-member countries.

Publications

Coal Information (annually).
Electricity Information (annually).
Natural Gas Information (annually).
Oil Information (annually).
Oil Market Report (monthly).
World Energy Outlook (annually).
Reports, studies, statistics, country reviews.

OECD Nuclear Energy Agency—NEA

Address: Le Seine Saint-Germain, 12 blvd des Îles, 92130 Issy-les-Moulineaux, France.

Telephone: 1-45-24-82-00; **fax:** 1-45-24-11-10; **e-mail:** nea@nea.fr; **internet:** www.nea.fr.

The NEA was established in 1958 to further the peaceful uses of nuclear energy. Originally a European agency, it has since admitted OECD members outside Europe.

MEMBERS

All members of OECD (except New Zealand and Poland).

Organization

(April 2001)

STEERING COMMITTEE FOR NUCLEAR ENERGY

Meets twice a year. Comprises senior representatives of member governments, presided over by a chairman.

SECRETARIAT

Director-General: LUIS ENRIQUE ECHAVARRI (Spain).
Deputy Director-General: SAMUEL THOMPSON (USA).

MAIN COMMITTEES

Committee on Nuclear Regulatory Activities;
Committee on Radiation Protection and Public Health;
Committee on the Safety of Nuclear Installations;
Committee for Technical and Economic Studies on Nuclear Energy Development and the Fuel Cycle;
Group of Governmental Experts on Third Party Liability in the Field of Nuclear Energy;
Nuclear Science Committee;
Radioactive Waste Management Committee.

NEA DATA BANK

The Data Bank was established in 1978, as a successor to the Computer Programme Library and the Neutron Data Compilation Centre. The Data Bank develops and supplies data and computer programmes for nuclear technology applications to users in laboratories, industry, universities and other areas of interest. Under the supervision of the Nuclear Science Committee, the Data Bank collates integral experimental data, and functions as part of a network of data centres to provide direct data services. It was responsible for co-ordinating the development of the Joint Evaluation Fission and Fusion (JEFF) data reference library, and works with the Radioactive Waste Management Division of the NEA to develop the Thermochemical Database project.

Activities

The main purpose of the Agency is to promote international co-operation and develop consensus opinions within the OECD area for the development and application of nuclear power for peaceful purposes through international research and development projects and exchange of scientific and technical experience and information. It aims to contribute to the development of nuclear energy as a safe, economical and environmentally acceptable energy source. The Agency maintains a continual survey with the co-operation of other organizations, notably the International Atomic Energy Agency (IAEA, see p. 76), of world uranium resources, production and demand, and of economic and technical aspects of the nuclear fuel cycle.

A major part of the Agency's work is devoted to the safety and regulation of nuclear power, including co-operative studies and projects related to the prevention of nuclear accidents and the long-term safety of radioactive waste disposal systems. It is also concerned with the harmonization of nuclear legislation and the dissemination of information on nuclear law issues. In 1997 two new legal instruments were adopted, under the auspices of the IAEA: the Protocol to Amend the Vienna Convention on Civil Liability for Nuclear Damage and the Convention on Supplementary Compensation for Nuclear Damage. A Nuclear Development Committee provides members with statistics and analysis on nuclear resources, economics, technology and prospects. The NEA also co-operates with non-member countries of central and eastern Europe and the CIS in areas such as nuclear safety, radiation protection and nuclear law.

JOINT PROJECTS

Decommissioning of Nuclear Installations: this co-operative programme, set up in 1985, provides for an exchange of scientific and technical information to develop the operational experience and data base needed for the future decommissioning of large nuclear power plants and other nuclear fuel cycle facilities. The Programme is administered by a Liaison Committee, while technical discussions and exchanges are undertaken in the context of a Technical Advisory Group. In early 2001 the Programme comprised 31 projects in 13 countries.

Halden Reactor Project: Halden, Norway; experimental boiling heavy water reactor, which became an OECD project in 1958. From 1964, under successive agreements with participating countries, the reactor has been used for long-term testing of water reactor fuels and for research into automatic computer-based control of nuclear power stations. Some 100 nuclear energy research institutions and authorities in 20 countries support the project.

Incident Reporting System—IRS: introduced in 1980 to exchange experience in operating nuclear power plants in OECD member countries and to improve nuclear safety by facilitating feedback of this experience to nuclear regulatory authorities, utilities and manufacturers. Since 1995 the IRS has operated in conjunction with the IAEA.

Information System on Occupational Exposure—ISOE: initiated in 1992; ISOE databases contain annual collective dose information on 397 reactors in some 27 countries; the system also contains information from 39 nuclear reactors which are either defunct or actively decommissioning.

Lower Head Failure Project: initiated in 1999; aims to provide experimental data on lower head deformation and failure phenomena; uses prototypic material and geometry to simulate conditions. Several OECD countries are participating in this project, which was to last for three years.

OECD-IPSN CABRI Water Loop Project: revised programme initiated in 1999; addresses reactivity-initiated accidents involving high burn-up fuel.

Plasma Project: initiated in 1999; co-operative international research project aimed at developing a plant safety monitoring and assessment system for use with WER reactors.

Rasplav Project: initiated in 1994, in Moscow, Russia, to study the behaviour of molten core material in a reactor pressure vessel during a severe accident. Seventeen countries participate in the project. The second three-year phase of the project began in July 1997. A final presentation was held November 2000.

Scorpio Project: initiated in 1996, in agreement with the Japanese Science and Technology Agency and in co-operation with the Halden Reactor Project, the Scorpio Project aims to improve the surveillance capabilities for WER reactor cores in various operational conditions. The surveillance system is installed at the Dukovang Nuclear Power

Plant in the Czech Republic, for the purpose of developing a general framework for WER-type reactors.

Finance

The Agency's annual budget amounts to 75m. French francs.

Publications

Annual Report.

NEA Newsletter (2 a year).

Newsletter on International Nuclear Data Measurement Activities (annually).

Nuclear Law Bulletin (2 a year).

Publications on a range of issues relating to nuclear energy, reports and proceedings.

ORGANIZATION FOR SECURITY AND CO-OPERATION IN EUROPE—OSCE

Address: 1010 Vienna, Kärntner Ring 5–7, Austria.

Telephone: (1) 514-36-0; **fax:** (1) 514-36-105; **e-mail:** info@osce.org; **internet:** www.osce.org.

The OSCE was established in 1972 as the Conference on Security and Co-operation in Europe (CSCE), providing a multilateral forum for dialogue and negotiation. It produced the Helsinki Final Act of 1975 on East–West relations (see below). The areas of competence of the CSCE were expanded by the Charter of Paris for a New Europe (1990), which transformed the CSCE from an *ad hoc* forum to an organization with permanent institutions, and the Helsinki Document 1992 (see 'Activities'). In December 1994 the summit conference adopted the new name of OSCE, in order to reflect the Organization's changing political role and strengthened secretariat. The OSCE has 55 participating states and comprises all the recognized countries of Europe, and Canada, the USA and all the former republics of the USSR.

PARTICIPATING STATES

Albania	Greece	Portugal
Andorra	Hungary	Romania
Armenia	Iceland	Russia
Austria	Ireland	San Marino
Azerbaijan	Italy	Slovakia
Belarus	Kazakhstan	Slovenia
Belgium	Kyrgyzstan	Spain
Bosnia and	Latvia	Sweden
Herzegovina	Liechtenstein	Switzerland
Bulgaria	Lithuania	Tajikistan
Canada	Luxembourg	Turkey
Croatia	Macedonia, former	Turkmenistan
Cyprus	Yugoslav republic	Ukraine
Czech Republic	Malta	United Kingdom
Denmark	Moldova	USA
Estonia	Monaco	Uzbekistan
Finland	Netherlands	Vatican City (Holy
France	Norway	See)
Georgia	Poland	Yugoslavia*
Germany		

* The Federal Republic of Yugoslavia, suspended from the CSCE in July 1992, was admitted to the OSCE in November 2000.

Organization

(April 2001)

SUMMIT CONFERENCES

Heads of state or government of OSCE participating states normally meet every two years to set priorities and political orientation of the Organization. The most recent conference was held in İstanbul, Turkey, in November 1999.

MINISTERIAL COUNCIL

The Ministerial Council (formerly the Council of Foreign Ministers) comprises ministers of foreign affairs of member states. It is the

central decision-making and governing body of the OSCE and meets at least once a year.

SENIOR COUNCIL

The Senior Council (formerly the Council of Senior Officials—CSO) is responsible for the supervision, management and co-ordination of OSCE activities. Member states are represented by senior political officers, who convene at least twice a year in Prague, Czech Republic, and once a year as the Economic Forum.

PERMANENT COUNCIL

The Council, which is based in Vienna, is responsible for day-to-day operational tasks. Members of the Council, comprising the permanent representatives of member states to the OSCE, convene weekly. The Council is the regular body for political consultation and decision-making, and may be convened for emergency purposes.

FORUM FOR SECURITY CO-OPERATION—FSC

The FSC, comprising representatives of delegations of member states, meets weekly in Vienna to negotiate and consult on measures aimed at strengthening security and stability throughout Europe. Its main objectives are negotiations on arms control, disarmament, and confidence- and security-building; regular consultations and intensive co-operation on matters related to security; and the further reduction of the risks of conflict. The FSC is also responsible for the implementation of confidence- and security-building measures (CSBMs); the preparation of seminars on military doctrine; the holding of annual implementation assessment meetings; and the provision of a forum for the discussion and clarification of information exchanged under agreed CSBMs.

CHAIRMAN-IN-OFFICE—CIO

The CIO is vested with overall responsibility for executive action. The position is held by a minister of foreign affairs of a member state for a one-year term. The CIO may be assisted by a troika, consisting of the preceding, current and succeeding chairpeople; *ad hoc* steering groups; or personal representatives, who are appointed by the CIO with a clear and precise mandate to assist the CIO in dealing with a crisis or conflict.

Chairman-in-Office: MIRCEA DAN GEOANA (Romania).

SECRETARIAT

In 2000 the Secretariat was restructured on the basis of two departments: the Conflict Prevention Centre (including an Operations Centre), which focuses on the support of the CIO in the implementation of OSCE policies, in particular the monitoring of field activities and co-operation with other international bodies; and the Department for Support Services and Budget, responsible for technical and administrative support activities. The OSCE maintains an office in Prague, Czech Republic, which assists with documentation and information activities, and a liaison office in Central Asia, based in Tashkent, Uzbekistan.

The position of Secretary-General was established in December 1992 and the first appointment to the position was made in June

1993. The Secretary-General is the representative of the CIO and is responsible for the management of OSCE structures and operations.

Secretary-General: JÁN KUBIŠ (Slovakia).

HIGH COMMISSIONER ON NATIONAL MINORITIES

Address: POB 20062, 2500 EB The Hague, Netherlands.
Telephone: (70) 3125500; **fax:** (70) 3635910; **e-mail:** hcnm@hcnm.org.

The establishment of the office of High Commissioner on National Minorities was proposed in the 1992 Helsinki Document, and endorsed by the Council of Foreign Ministers in Stockholm in December 1992. The role of the High Commissioner is to identify ethnic tensions that might endanger peace, stability or relations between OSCE participating states, and to promote their early resolution. The High Commissioner may issue an 'early warning' for the attention of the Senior Council of an area of tension likely to degenerate into conflict. The High Commissioner is appointed by the Ministerial Council, on the recommendation of the Senior Council, for a three-year term.

High Commissioner: MAX VAN DER STOEL (Netherlands).

OFFICE FOR DEMOCRATIC INSTITUTIONS AND HUMAN RIGHTS—ODIHR

Address: Aleje Ujazdowskie 19, 00-517 Warsaw, Poland.
Telephone: (22) 520-06-00; **fax:** (22) 520-06-05; **e-mail:** office@ odihr.osce.waw.pl; **internet:** www.osce.odihr.org.

The ODIHR, which was originally called the Office for Free Elections with a mandate to promote multiparty democracy, was assigned major new tasks under the Helsinki Document 1992, including responsibility for promoting human rights, democracy and the rule of law. The Office provides a framework for the exchange of information on and the promotion of democracy-building, respect for human rights and elections within OSCE states. In addition, it co-ordinates the monitoring of elections and provides expertise and training on constitutional and legal matters.

Director: GÉRARD STOUDMANN (Switzerland).

OFFICE OF THE REPRESENTATIVE ON FREEDOM OF THE MEDIA

Address: 1010 Vienna, Kärntner Ring 5–7, Austria.
Telephone: (1) 512-21-450; **fax:** (1) 512-21-459; **e-mail:** pmfom@ osce.org; **internet:** www.osce.org/inst/fom.

The office was founded in 1998 to strengthen the implementation of OSCE commitments regarding free, independent and pluralistic media.

Representative: FREIMUT DUVE (Germany).

PARLIAMENTARY ASSEMBLY

Address: Rådhusstraede 1, 1466 Copenhagen K, Denmark.
Telephone: 33-37-80-40; **fax:** 33-37-80-30; **e-mail:** osce@oscepa.dk; **internet:** www.oscepa.com.

The OSCE Parliamentary Assembly, which is composed of 317 parliamentarians from 55 participating countries, was inaugurated in July 1992, and meets annually. The Assembly comprises a Standing Committee, a Bureau and three General Committees and is supported by a Secretariat in Copenhagen, Denmark.

President: ADRIAN SEVERIN (Romania).

Secretary-General: R. SPENCER OLIVER.

OSCE Related Bodies

COURT OF CONCILIATION AND ARBITRATION

Address: 266 route de Lausanne, 1292 Chambesy, Geneva, Switzerland.
Telephone: (22) 7580025; **fax:** (22) 7582510.

The establishment of the Court of Conciliation and Arbitration was agreed in 1992 and effected in 1994. OSCE states that have ratified the OSCE Convention on Conciliation and Arbitration may submit a dispute to the Court for settlement by the Arbitral Tribunal or the Conciliation Commission.

JOINT CONSULTATIVE GROUP (JCG)

The states that are party to the Treaty on Conventional Armed Forces in Europe (CFE), which was concluded within the CSCE framework in 1990, established the Joint Consultative Group (JCG). The JCG, which meets in Vienna, addresses questions relating to compliance with the Treaty; enhancement of the effectiveness of the Treaty; technical aspects of the Treaty's implementation; and disputes arising out of its implementation. There are currently 30 states participating in the JCG.

OPEN SKIES CONSULTATIVE COMMISSION

The Commission represents all states parties to the 1992 Treaty on Open Skies, and promotes its implementation. Its regular meetings are serviced by the OSCE secretariat.

Activities

In July 1990 heads of government of the NATO member countries proposed to increase the role of the CSCE 'to provide a forum for wider political dialogue in a more united Europe'. In November heads of government of the participating states signed the Charter of Paris for a New Europe, which undertook to strengthen pluralist democracy and observance of human rights, and to settle disputes between participating states by peaceful means. At the summit meeting the Treaty on Conventional Armed Forces in Europe (CFE), which had been negotiated within the framework of the CSCE, was signed by the member states of NATO (q.v.) and of the Warsaw Pact. The Treaty limits non-nuclear air and ground armaments in the signatory countries. It was decided at the same meeting to establish a secretariat in Prague, Czechoslovakia, which was opened in February 1991. (The secretariat was moved to Vienna, Austria, in 1993.) It was also decided to create a Conflict Prevention Centre, which was established in Vienna, Austria, in March 1991, and an Office for Free Elections (later renamed the Office for Democratic Institutions and Human Rights), which was established in Warsaw, Poland, in July. In April parliamentarians from the CSCE countries agreed on the creation of a pan-European parliamentary assembly. Its first session was held in Budapest, Hungary, in July 1992.

The Council of Foreign Ministers met for the first time in Berlin, Germany, in June 1991. The meeting adopted a mechanism for consultation and co-operation in the case of emergency situations, to be implemented by the Council of Senior Officials (CSO, which was subsequently renamed the Senior Council). A separate mechanism regarding the prevention of the outbreak of conflict was also adopted, whereby a country can demand an explanation of 'unusual military activity' in a neighbouring country. These mechanisms were utilized in July in relation to the armed conflict in Yugoslavia between the Republic of Croatia and the Yugoslav Government. The CSCE appealed to all parties involved in the conflict to uphold a cease-fire. In mid-August a meeting of the CSO resolved to reinforce the CSCE's mission in Yugoslavia considerably and requested all the parties involved in the conflict to begin negotiations as a matter of urgency. In September the CSO agreed to impose an embargo on the export of armaments to Yugoslavia. In October the CSO resolved to establish an observer mission to monitor the observance of human rights in Yugoslavia.

The third Review CSCE Conference on Human Dimensions (the CSCE term used with regard to issues concerning human rights and welfare) was held in Moscow in September 1991. The Conference formulated an accord which empowers CSCE envoys to investigate reported abuses of human rights in any CSCE country, either at the request of the country concerned, or if six participating states deem such an investigation necessary. In 1993 the First Implementation Meeting on Human Dimension Issues took place; meetings were subsequently held biannually. The Meeting, for which the ODIHR serves as a secretariat, provides a forum for the exchange of news regarding OSCE commitments in the fields of human rights and democracy. The Fifth Meeting took place in Warsaw, Poland, in October 2000. Since 1999 the ODIHR has been particularly concerned with combating trafficking in human beings.

In January 1992 the Council of Foreign Ministers agreed that the Conference's rule of decision-making by consensus was to be altered to allow the CSO to take appropriate action against a participating state 'in cases of clear and gross violation of CSCE commitments'. This development was precipitated by the conflict in Yugoslavia, where the Yugoslav Government was held responsible by the majority of CSCE states for the continuation of hostilities. It was also agreed at the meeting that the CSCE should undertake fact-finding and conciliation missions to areas of tension, with the first such mission to be sent to Nagornyi Karabakh, the largely Armenian-populated enclave in Azerbaijan.

In March 1992 CSCE participating states reached agreement on a number of confidence-building measures, including commitments to exchange technical data on new weapons systems; to report activation of military units; and to prohibit military activity involving very large numbers of troops or tanks. Later in that month at a meeting of the Council of Foreign Ministers, which opened the Helsinki Follow-up Conference, the members of NATO and the former members of the Warsaw Pact (with Russia, Belarus, Ukraine and Georgia taking the place of the USSR) signed the Open Skies Treaty. Under the treaty, aerial reconnaissance missions by one country over another were permitted, subject to regulation. An Open Skies Consultative Commission was subsequently established (see above).

The Federal Republic of Yugoslavia (Serbia and Montenegro) was suspended from the CSCE immediately prior to the summit meeting of heads of state and government that took place in Helsinki, Finland, in July 1992. The meeting adopted the Helsinki Document 1992, in which participating states defined the terms of future CSCE peace-keeping activities. Conforming broadly to UN practice, peace-keeping operations would be undertaken only with the full consent of the parties involved in any conflict and only if an effective cease-fire were in place. The CSCE may request the use of the military resources of NATO, WEU, the EU, the CIS or other international bodies. (NATO and WEU had recently changed their constitutions to permit the use of their forces for CSCE purposes.) The Helsinki Document declared the CSCE a 'regional arrangement' in the sense of Chapter VIII of the UN's Charter, which states that such a regional grouping should attempt to resolve a conflict in the region before referring it to the Security Council. In December 1993 a Permanent Committee (now renamed the Permanent Council) was established in Vienna, providing for greater political consultation and dialogue through its weekly meetings. In December 1994 the summit conference endorsed the organization's role as the primary instrument for early warning, conflict prevention and crisis management in the region, and adopted a 'Code of Conduct on Politico-Military Aspects of Security', which set out principles to guide the role of the armed forces in democratic societies. The summit conference that was held in Lisbon, Portugal, in December 1996 agreed to adapt the CFE Treaty, in order to further arms reduction negotiations on a national and territorial basis. The conference also adopted the 'Lisbon Declaration on a Common and Comprehensive Security Model for Europe for the 21st Century' (see below), committing all parties to pursuing measures to ensure regional security. A Security Model Committee was established and began to meet regularly during 1997 to consider aspects of the Declaration, including the identification of risks and challenges to future European security; enhancing means of joint co-operative action within the OSCE framework in the event of non-compliance with OSCE commitments by participating states; considering other new arrangements within the OSCE framework that could reinforce security and stability in Europe; and defining a basis of co-operation between the OSCE and other relevant organizations to co-ordinate security enforcement. In November 1997 the Office of the Representative on Freedom of the Media was established in Vienna, to support the OSCE's activities in this field.

In November 1999 OSCE heads of state and of government, convened in İstanbul, Turkey, signed a new Charter for European Security, which aimed to formalize existing norms regarding the observance of human rights and to strengthen co-operation with other organizations and institutions concerned with international security. The Charter focused on measures to improve the operational capabilities of the OSCE in early warning, conflict prevention, crisis management and post-conflict rehabilitation. Accordingly, Rapid Expert Assistance and Co-operation (REACT) teams were to be established to enable the organization to respond rapidly to requests from participating states for assistance in crisis situations. At the meeting a revised CFE Treaty was also signed, providing for a stricter system of limitations and increased transparency, which was to be open to other OSCE states not currently signatories. The US and EU governments determined to delay ratification of the Agreement of the Adaptation of the Treaty until Russian troop levels in the Caucasus had been reduced.

In April 2000 the OSCE High Commissioner on National Minorities issued a report reviewing the problems confronting Roma and Sinti populations in OSCE member states. The Federal Republic of Yugoslavia (suspended from the CSCE in 1992, see above) was admitted to the OSCE in November, following the election of Vojislav Koštunica as president. In that month an OSCE Document on Small Arms and Light Weapons was adopted, aimed at curtailing the spread of armaments in member states. The REACT programme became operational in April 2001.

OSCE MISSIONS AND FIELD ACTIVITIES

In December 1994 OSCE heads of state and government authorized the establishment of a 3,000-strong peace-keeping force for the Nagornyi Karabakh region, which was the focus of a conflict between Armenia and Azerbaijan. However, in the absence of a formal cease-fire and the start of peace negotiations, the proposed force was not dispatched. The OSCE continued to provide a framework for discussions between the two countries through its 11-nation Minsk Group, which from early 1997 was co-chaired by France, Russia and the USA. In October 1997 Armenia and Azerbaijan reached agreement on OSCE proposals for a political settlement; however, the concessions granted by the Armenian President, Levon Ter-Petrossian, which included the withdrawal of troops from certain strategic areas of Nagornyi Karabakh precipitated his resignation in February 1998. The proposals were rejected by his successor, Robert Kocharian. Nevertheless, meetings of the Minsk Group continued in 1998 and both countries expressed their willingness to recommence negotiations. The then CIO, Bronisław Geremek, met with the leaders of both countries in November and persuaded them

to exchange prisoners of war. The Azeri President, however, rejected a new proposal to settle the dispute.

In January 1995 Russia agreed to an OSCE proposal to send a fact-finding mission to assist in the conflict between the Russian authorities and an independence movement in Chechnya. The mission criticized the Russian army for using excessive force against Chechen rebels and civilians; reported that violations of human rights had been perpetrated by both sides in the conflict; and urged Russia to enforce a cease-fire in Groznyi to allow the delivery of humanitarian supplies by international aid agencies to the population of the city. An OSCE Assistance Group mediated between the two sides, and, in July, brokered a cease-fire agreement between the Russian military authorities in Chechnya and the Chechen rebels. A further peace accord was signed, under the auspices of the OSCE, in May 1996, but the truce was broken in July. A more conclusive cease-fire agreement was signed by the two parties to the conflict in August. In January 1997 the OSCE assisted in the preparation and monitoring of general elections conducted in Chechnya. The Assistance Group remained in the territory to help with post-conflict rehabilitation, including the promotion of democratic institutions and respect for human rights. In September 1999, following a resurgence of separatist activity, Russian launched a military offensive against Chechnya. In early November an OSCE mission arrived in the neighbouring republic of Ingushetia to assess the condition and needs of the estimated 200,000 refugees who had fled the hostilities; however, the officials were prevented by the Russian authorites from travelling into Chechnya. The issue dominated the OSCE summit meeting, held in İstanbul, Turkey, later in that month. The meeting insisted upon a political solution to the conflict and called for an immediate cease-fire. An agreement was reached with the Russian President to allow the CIO to visit the region, and on an OSCE role in initiating political dialogue. Owing to the intensification of hostilities the Assistance Group relocated on a temporary basis to Moscow. From January 2000 an OSCE observer mission was deployed at the border between Chechnya and Georgia.

In late 1996 the OSCE declared the constitutional referendum held in Belarus in November to be illegal and urged that country's Government to ensure political freedoms and respect for human rights. An OSCE fact-finding mission visited Belarus in April 1997 and recommended the establishment of a permanent presence in the country, to assist with the process of democratization. This was established in February 1998. In October the OSCE Parliamentary Assembly formed an *ad hoc* Committee on Belarus, to act as a working group to support and intensify the organization's work in the country. The OSCE/ODIHR declared legislative elections held in Belarus in October 2000 not to have been conducted freely and fairly.

In March 1997 the OSCE dispatched a fact-finding mission to Albania to help restore political and civil stability, which had been undermined by the collapse of national pyramid saving schemes at the start of the year. An agreement was negotiated between Albania's President Sali Berisha and opposition parties to hold elections in mid-1997 and to establish a government of national reconciliation. At the end of March the Permanent Council agreed to establish an OSCE Presence in Albania, and confirmed that the organization should provide the framework for co-ordinating other international efforts in the country. OSCE efforts focused on reaching a political consensus on new legislation for the conduct of the forthcoming elections. Voting took place in June/July, with 500 OSCE observers providing technical electoral assistance and helping to monitor the voting. In March 1998 the OSCE Presence was mandated to monitor the country's borders with the Kosovan region of southern Serbia and to prevent any spillover effects from the escalating crisis. This role was reduced following the political settlement for Kosovo and Metohija concluded in mid-1999. In June 1998 the OSCE observed local elections in Albania. It became the Co-Chair, with the EU, of the Friends of Albania group, which then brought together countries and international bodies concerned with the situation in Albania for the first time in September. In October a decision was taken by the Permanent Council to enhance the Presence's role in border-monitoring activities. With other organizations, the OSCE was involved in the preparation of the country's draft constitution, finalized in October, and an ODIHR Election Observation Mission was established to observe the referendum on the constitution held in November. The OSCE Presence in Albania has subsequently provided advice and support to the Albanian Government regarding democratization, the rule of law, the media, human rights, election preparation and monitoring, and the development of civil society. The Presence is also monitoring the Government's weapons collection programme.

Under the Dayton peace accords for the former Yugoslavia, which were concluded in late 1995, the OSCE was assigned the tasks of supervising post-war Bosnian elections; drafting arms-control agreements for the former Yugoslavia; and monitoring the observance of human rights in Bosnia and Herzegovina. The OSCE mission to organize and oversee the Bosnian national elections, which were held on 14 September 1996, was the largest-ever operation undertaken by the organization, with some 1,200 electoral observers deployed. The OSCE subsequently monitored Bosnian municipal elections, twice rescheduled by the organization and eventually held in September 1997, and the elections to the National Assembly of the Serb Republic and to the Bosnian Serb presidency in November. In 1998 the mission was charged with organizing the second post-war general elections in Bosnia and Herzegovina (comprising elections to the legislature of Bosnia and Herzegovina, the Federation and the Serb Republic, and to the presidencies of Bosnia and Herzegovina and the Serb Republic). The mission assisted with the registration of voters and, in September, was responsible for the supervision of the elections at polling stations within and outside the country. The final results of the election to the Bosnian Serb presidency were delayed, owing to the unexpected victory of an extreme nationalist, Nikola Poplasen, which, it was feared, could jeopardize the peace process. The OSCE immediately emphasized the necessity of maintaining the process. It also insisted on the need to transfer responsibility for the electoral process to the national authorities for future elections. In March 1999 the OSCE initiated an educational campaign relating to new election laws. However a permanent electoral legal framework had not been approved by the time of legislative elections held in November 2000; the OSCE was therefore active in both preparing and monitoring these. Progress was made from 1995 in the area of arms control, under the Agreement on Regional Arms Control, with confidence- and security-building measures implemented and excess armaments reduced.

In April 1997 the OSCE monitored legislative and municipal elections in Croatia, including the Eastern Slavonia, Baranja and Western Srem (Sirmium) region under UN administration. In June the Permanent Council agreed to increase the OSCE Presence in Croatia, and to enhance the mission's capacity to protect human rights, in particular the rights of minorities, and to monitor the implementation of legislation and other commitments concerning the return and treatment of refugees and displaced persons, under a new mandate extending until 31 December 1998. In March 1998, following the integration of the disputed region into Croatia, the OSCE criticized the conditions imposed by the Croatian Government for the return of Serb refugees, stating that the right to return to one's own country was inalienable and must not depend on the fulfilment of conditions. In October the mission to Croatia assumed the responsibilities of the United Nations Police Support Group (UNPSG). The OSCE Police Monitoring Group, comprising a maximum of 120 unarmed OSCE civilian police monitors, was deployed in the region, representing the Organization's first police-monitoring role. The Group was terminated in October 2000, although the OSCE was to continue to advise on and monitor police activities in Croatia. The OSCE was also to be responsible for monitoring the border regions, with particular concern for customs activities. The OSCE/ODIHR monitored legislative and presidential elections held in Croatia in January 2000.

In Yugoslavia the OSCE was invited to verify the results of elections held in Serbia in November 1996; it also monitored the presidential poll in Montenegro in October 1997. In mid-1998 the OSCE was involved in the mediation effort to resolve the conflict between the Serbian authorities and ethnic Albanian separatists in the formerly autonomous province of Kosovo and Metohija. In October, following months of diplomatic effort and the threat of NATO air strikes, Yugoslav President Slobodan Milošević agreed to comply with UN Security Council Resolution 1199, which required an immediate cease-fire, Serbian troop withdrawals, the commencement of meaningful peace negotiations, and unrestricted access for humanitarian aid. Under a peace plan proposed by the US special envoy, Richard Holbrooke, President Milošević agreed to the formation of a 2,000-member OSCE Kosovo Verification Mission (KVM) to monitor compliance, in addition to surveillance flights by unarmed NATO aircraft. The KVM was to patrol the region to ensure the withdrawal of Serbian military and police units, and to oversee the safe return of refugees and the non-harassment of ethnic Albanian inhabitants. It was also to monitor border control activities and accompany police units in Kosovo, when necessary, to assist them to perform their normal policing roles. The mission was guaranteed free access through the area and aimed to open offices in all of Kosovo's 29 regions. Examples of progress and non-compliance were to be reported to the OSCE Permanent Council, the UN Security Council and other organizations. The mission's mandate was formally established on 25 October 1998 for a period of one year. Upon achievement of a political settlement defining the area's self-government, and its subsequent implementation, the KVM was to be responsible for supervising elections in Kosovo, assisting in the establishment of democratic institutions and developing a Kosovo police force. The long-term mission was accepted in return for the eventual removal of Yugoslavia's suspension from the OSCE. However, sporadic fighting continued in the province, and the monitoring force began unofficially to assume a peace-keeping role. In January 1999 the KVM successfully negotiated for the release of eight Yugoslav soldiers held hostage by the separatist forces. Later

in that month following the KVM's denunciation of the killing of some 45 ethnic Albanians by Serbian security forces in the village of Racak, President Milošević ordered the head of the mission, William Walker, to leave the region. This was later revoked. Meanwhile, OSCE monitors were forced to withdraw from Racak under fire from Serbian troops. An emergency meeting of the OSCE in Vienna agreed to maintain the mission. However, on 19 March, following the failure of negotiations to resolve the crisis, the CIO decided to evacuate the 1,380 unarmed monitors to the former Yugoslav republic of Macedonia, owing to the deteriorating security situation in Kosovo. NATO commenced an aerial offensive against Yugoslavia in late March. In early April the CIO condemned the mass expulsion of ethnic Albanians from Kosovo and other violations of human rights committed by Serbian forces. Later in the same month the CIO, at a meeting of a ministerial troika attended by the Secretary-General, announced that the OSCE was willing to assist in the implementation of a political settlement in Kosovo. The OSCE was also concerned with measures to prevent the crisis affecting the other Balkan states. Within the framework of a political settlement for Kosovo, which was formally concluded in June, the OSCE (whose Mission in Kosovo—OMIK was established in July) was responsible for democracy- and institution-building under the auspices of the UN Interim Administration Mission for Kosovo (UNMIK). OSCE monitors were deployed to assess the human rights situation throughout the region, and in August a new OSCE-administered police training school was inaugurated. Later in the year the OSCE commenced the training of judicial and administrative officers. At that time the OSCE mission consisted of 1,400 personnel. In December the OSCE published a report on the situation in Kosovo, which confirmed that Serbian forces had conducted systematic abuses of human rights but also raised suspicion against the KLA for organizing retribution attacks against Serbian civilians later in the year. In June 2000 the OSCE founded the Kosovo Law Centre, to provide technical assistance to the legal community, with a view to promoting democratic principles and human rights. The Department for Democratic Governance and Civil Society, established in the following month by UNMIK, was to be administered by OMIK. In August an Ombudsperson, nominated by OMIK, was appointed to a new Office of the Ombudsperson, which became operational in November: the role of the Ombudsperson was to investigate and mediate claims of human rights violations arising within Kosovo. The OSCE was responsible for registering about 1m. voters prior to municipal elections that were held in Kosovo in October. By that month some 1,700 police officers had graduated from the OSCE-administered police-training school.

In March 2000 the OSCE adopted a Regional Strategy for South-Eastern Europe, aimed at enhancing co-operation amongst its presences in the region. The OSCE was actively involved in co-ordinating the Stability Pact for South-Eastern Europe, which was initiated, in June 1999, as a collaborative plan of action by the EU, Group of Seven industrialized nations and Russia (the G-8), regional governments and other organizations concerned with the stability of the region. (This can be accessed at www.stabilitypact.org.) A meeting of participants in the Pact was convened to coincide with the OSCE summit meeting, held in November.

During 1998 the High Commissioner on National Minorities advised Latvia on the development of liberal amendments to its citizenship law, which were presented to parliament in June. The OSCE closely observed the referendum on these amendments, which took place in October, and continued to monitor the implementation of the amendments, following their approval by the electorate. In January 1999, for the first time, the OSCE refused to dispatch official observers to monitor presidential elections in a member state, owing to concerns about the legitimacy of elections held in Kazakhstan. In December the OSCE and ODIHR decided not to deploy a mission to observe parliamentary elections in Turkmenistan owing to an inadequate legislative framework, and in January 2000 an observer mission was not dispatched to monitor the presidential election held in Uzbekistan, on the grounds that the choice of candidates was insufficient. In October the OSCE/ODIHR concluded that the presidential election held in that month in Kyrgyzstan had not been conducted fairly and freely.

In early 2001 there were long-term OSCE missions, with the objectives of conflict prevention and crisis management, in Bosnia and Herzegovina, Croatia, Estonia, Georgia, Latvia, the former Yugoslav republic of Macedonia, Moldova, Tajikistan, the Federal Republic of Yugoslavia (Serbia), and Kosovo. The OSCE also operated field activities in Albania, Belarus, Chechenya (temporarily based in Moscow) and Ukraine, and maintained offices in Yerevan (Armenia) and Baku (Azerbaijan), and Centres in Almaty (Kazakhstan), Ashgabad (Turkmenistan), Bishkek (Kyrgyzstan) and Tashkent (Uzbekistan). The OSCE also has institutionalized structures to assist in the implementation of certain bilateral agreements. At the end of 1999 there were OSCE representatives to the Russian-Latvian Joint Commission on Military Pensioners; the Estonian Government Commission on Military Pensioners; and the Joint Committee on the Skrunda Radar Station.

Japan, the Republic of Korea and Thailand have the status of 'partners for co-operation' with the OSCE, while Algeria, Egypt, Israel, Jordan, Morocco and Tunisia are 'Mediterranean partners for co-operation'. Consultations are held with these countries in order to discuss security issues of common concern.

Finance

All activities of the institutions, negotiations, *ad hoc* meetings and missions are financed by contributions from member states. The

proposed budget for 2001 amounted to €190m., of which some 82% was allocated to OSCE missions and field activities.

Publications

Annual Report of the Secretary-General.

Decision Manual (annually).

OSCE Handbook (annually).

OSCE Newsletter (monthly).

ORGANIZATION OF AFRICAN UNITY—OAU

Address: POB 3243, Addis Ababa, Ethiopia.

Telephone: (1) 517700; **fax:** (1) 513036; **internet** www.oau-oua.org.

The Organization was founded in 1963 to promote unity and solidarity among African states.

FORMATION

There were various attempts at establishing an inter-African organization before the OAU Charter was drawn up. In November 1958 Ghana and Guinea (later joined by Mali) drafted a Charter which was to form the basis of a Union of African States. In January 1961 a conference was held at Casablanca, attended by the heads of state of Ghana, Guinea, Mali, Morocco, and representatives of Libya and of the provisional government of the Algerian Republic (GPRA). Tunisia, Nigeria, Liberia and Togo declined the invitation to attend. An African Charter was adopted and it was decided to set up an African Military Command and an African Common Market.

Between October 1960 and March 1961 three conferences were held by French-speaking African countries, at Abidjan, Brazzaville and Yaoundé. None of the 12 countries which attended these meetings had been present at the Casablanca Conference. These conferences led eventually to the signing in September 1961, at Tananarive, of a charter establishing the Union africaine et malgache, later the Organisation commune africaine et mauricienne (OCAM).

In May 1961 a conference was held at Monrovia, Liberia, attended by the heads of state or representatives of 19 countries: Cameroon, Central African Republic, Chad, Congo Republic (ex-French), Côte d'Ivoire, Dahomey, Ethiopia, Gabon, Liberia, Madagascar, Mauritania, Niger, Nigeria, Senegal, Sierra Leone, Somalia, Togo, Tunisia and Upper Volta. They met again (with the exception of Tunisia and with the addition of the ex-Belgian Congo Republic) in January 1962 at Lagos, Nigeria, and set up a permanent secretariat and a standing committee of finance ministers, and accepted a draft charter for an Organization of Inter-African and Malagasy States.

It was the Conference of Addis Ababa, held in 1963, which finally brought together African states despite the regional, political and linguistic differences which divided them. The foreign ministers of 32 African states attended the Preparatory Meeting held in May: Algeria, Burundi, Cameroon, Central African Republic, Chad, Congo (Brazzaville) (now Republic of the Congo), Congo (Léopoldville) (now Democratic Republic of the Congo), Côte d'Ivoire, Dahomey (now Benin), Ethiopia, Gabon, Ghana, Guinea, Liberia, Libya, Madagascar, Mali, Mauritania, Morocco, Niger, Nigeria, Rwanda, Senegal, Sierra Leone, Somalia, Sudan, Tanganyika (now Tanzania), Togo, Tunisia, Uganda, the United Arab Republic (Egypt) and Upper Volta (now Burkina Faso).

The topics discussed by the meeting were: (i) creation of the Organization of African States; (ii) co-operation among African states in the following fields: economic and social; education, culture and science; collective defence; (iii) decolonization; (iv) apartheid and racial discrimination; (v) effects of economic grouping on the economic development of Africa; (vi) disarmament; (vii) creation of a Permanent Conciliation Commission; and (viii) Africa and the United Nations.

The Heads of State Conference which opened on 23 May drew up the Charter of the Organization of African Unity, which was then signed by the heads of 30 states on 25 May 1963. The Charter was essentially functional and reflected a compromise between the concept of a loose association of states favoured by the Monrovia Group and the federal idea supported by the Casablanca Group, and in particular by Ghana.

MEMBERS*

Algeria	Eritrea	Nigeria
Angola	Ethiopia	Rwanda
Benin	Gabon	São Tomé and
Botswana	The Gambia	Príncipe
Burkina Faso	Ghana	Senegal
Burundi	Guinea	Seychelles
Cameroon	Guinea-Bissau	Sierra Leone
Cape Verde	Kenya	Somalia
Central African	Lesotho	South Africa
Republic	Liberia	Sudan
Chad	Libya	Swaziland
The Comoros	Madagascar	Tanzania
Congo, Democratic	Malawi	Togo
Republic†	Mali	Tunisia
Congo, Republic	Mauritania	Uganda
Côte d'Ivoire	Mauritius	Zambia
Djibouti	Mozambique	Zimbabwe
Egypt	Namibia	
Equatorial Guinea	Niger	

* The Sahrawi Arab Democratic Republic (SADR–Western Sahara) was admitted to the OAU in February 1982, following recognition by 26 of the then 50 members, but its membership was disputed by Morocco and other states which claimed that a two-thirds majority was needed to admit a state whose existence was in question. Morocco withdrew from the OAU with effect from November 1985.

† Known as Zaire between 1971 and 1997.

Organization

(April 2001)

ASSEMBLY OF HEADS OF STATE

The Assembly of Heads of State and Government meets annually to co-ordinate policies of African states. Resolutions are passed by a two-thirds majority, procedural matters by a simple majority. A chairman is elected at each meeting from among the members, to hold office for one year.

Chairman (2000/01): Gen. GNASSINGBE EYADÉMA (Togo).

COUNCIL OF MINISTERS

Consists of ministers of foreign affairs and others and meets twice a year, with provision for extraordinary sessions. Each session elects its own Chairman. Prepares meetings of, and is responsible to, the Assembly of Heads of State.

GENERAL SECRETARIAT

The permanent headquarters of the organization. It carries out functions assigned to it in the Charter of the OAU and by other agreements and treaties made between member states. Departments: Political; Finance; Education, Science, Culture and Social Affairs; Economic Development and Co-operation; Administration and Conferences. The Secretary-General is elected for a four-year term by the Assembly of Heads of State.

Secretary-General: SALIM AHMED SALIM (Tanzania).

ARBITRATION COMMISSION

Commission of Mediation, Conciliation and Arbitration: Addis Ababa; f. 1964; consists of 21 members elected by the Assembly of Heads of State for a five-year term; no state may have more than one member; has a Bureau consisting of a President and two Vice-Presidents, who shall not be eligible for re-election. Its task is to hear and settle disputes between member states by peaceful means.

SPECIALIZED COMMISSIONS

There are specialized commissions for economic, social, transport and communications affairs; education, science, culture and health; defence; human rights; and labour.

Finance

Member states contribute in accordance with their United Nations assessment. No member state is assessed for an amount exceeding 20% of the yearly regular budget of the Organization. The budget for 2001–02 was US $31m. At February 2001 member states owed some $39m. in outstanding contributions. By that time the following countries had had their voting rights in the Organization suspended owing to outstanding arrears: Burundi, Central African Republic, Chad, Comoros, Democratic Republic of the Congo, Equatorial Guinea, Guinea-Bissau, Liberia, Niger, São Tomé and Príncipe, Seychelles, and Sierra Leone.

Principal Events, 1989–2001

1989

Jan.   A meeting on apartheid, organized by the OAU, resulted in the formation of an African Anti-Apartheid Committee.

May   The OAU Chairman undertook a mission of mediation between the governments of Mauritania and Senegal, following ethnic conflict between the citizens of the two countries.

July   The Assembly of Heads of State discussed the Namibian independence process, and urged that the UN should ensure that the forthcoming elections there would be fairly conducted. They reiterated requests that an international conference on Africa's substantial external debt should be held.

Sept.–   The newly-elected OAU Secretary-General, Salim Ahmed
Dec.   Salim, attempted to mediate in the dispute between Mauritania and Senegal. In November a mediation committee, comprising representatives of six countries, visited Mauritania and Senegal.

1990

March   A monitoring group was formed by the OAU to report on events in South Africa. The OAU urged the international community to continue imposing economic sanctions on South Africa.

July   The Assembly of Heads of State reviewed the implications for Africa of recent socio-economic and political changes in Eastern Europe, and of the European Community's progress towards monetary and political union.

1991

June   The Assembly of Heads of State signed the Abuja Treaty on the creation of an African Economic Community (AEC). The Treaty was to enter into force after ratification by two-thirds of OAU member states. The Community was to be established by 2025, beginning with a five-year stage during which measures would be taken to strengthen existing economic groupings. The meeting also established a committee of heads of state to assist national reconciliation in Ethiopia; and gave a mandate to the OAU Secretary-General to undertake a mission to assist in restoring political stability in Somalia.

1992

Feb.–   The OAU was involved, together with the UN and the
March   Organization of the Islamic Conference (OIC, q.v.), in mediation between the warring factions in Mogadishu, Somalia. The OAU subsequently continued to assist in efforts to achieve a peace settlement in Somalia.

May   An OAU mission was dispatched to South Africa to monitor the continued violence in that country.

June–   Proposals were advanced at the Assembly of Heads of
July   State, held in Dakar, Senegal, for a mechanism to be established within the OAU for 'conflict management, prevention and resolution'. These proposals were accepted in principle, but operational details were to be elaborated at a later stage.

Oct.   The *Ad Hoc* Committee on Southern Africa met in Gaborone, Botswana, to discuss a report compiled by a team of OAU experts on practical steps to be taken towards the democratization of South Africa. Plans to send a mission to monitor the Mozambican peace accord were announced.

1993

Feb.   A session of the Council of Ministers discussed the OAU's serious financial crisis. The meeting agreed to allocate US $250,000 to the creation of a conflict prevention bureau, and a further $250,000 for the purposes of monitoring elections.

May   A Pan-African Conference on Reparations for the suffering caused by colonialism in Africa, organized by the OAU together with the Nigerian Government, was held in Abuja. The Conference appealed to those countries which had benefited from the colonization of Africa and the use of Africans as slaves (particularly European countries and the USA) to make reparations to Africans and their descendants, either in the form of capital transfers, or cancellation of debt.

June   Eritrea was admitted as the 52nd member of the OAU. The 29th Assembly of Heads of State resolved to establish a mechanism for conflict prevention and resolution. The mechanism's primary objective was to be anticipation and prevention of conflict. In cases where conflicts had already occurred, the OAU was to undertake peace-making and peace-building activities, including the deployment of civilian or military monitoring missions. However, in the case of a conflict seriously degenerating, assistance would be sought from the United Nations.

July   A seminar on the AEC was held in Addis Ababa, Ethiopia, concerned with the popularization of the treaty establishing the Community. Lack of resources emerged as one of the main barriers to the actual creation of the Community.

Sept.   The OAU announced the immediate removal of economic sanctions against South Africa, following the approval by that country's Parliament of a bill to establish a transitional executive council prior to the democratic elections, scheduled to be conducted in April 1994.

Oct.   The OAU Secretary-General condemned an attempted military coup in Burundi, in which the President and six Cabinet ministers were killed, and the subsequent civil unrest.

Nov.   A summit conference of African ministers of foreign affairs, conducted in Addis Ababa, resolved to establish a 200-member OAU protection and observation mission to Burundi, and appealed for international financial and material support to assist the mission. The ministers approved the principles for the establishment of a mechanism for conflict prevention, management and resolution. The meeting suggested that 5% of the OAU budget, but not less than US $1m., be allocated for an OAU Peace Fund to finance the mechanism, and that $0.5m. be made available for 1993.

Dec.   A meeting of 11 African Heads of State approved the establishment of the Peace Fund and called for contributions from the international community. A draft statement of the mechanism for conflict prevention, management and resolution, issued by the OAU Secretary-General, expressed support for the efforts to resolve the conflict in Somalia and emphasized the need to promote national reconciliation.

1994

Feb.   The Council of Ministers reaffirmed its support for the results of elections in Burundi, which were conducted in 1993, and endorsed the establishment of an OAU mission to promote dialogue and national reconciliation in that country. The Council condemned anti-government forces for the escalation of violence in Angola.

April   The OAU mission to South Africa participated as observers of the electoral process. An OAU delegation visited Nigeria and Cameroon to investigate the border dispute between the two countries.

May   South Africa was admitted as the 53rd member of the OAU.

June   Consultations with each of the conflicting parties in Rwanda were conducted by the OAU. The Assembly of Heads of State, meeting in Tunis, approved a code of conduct for inter-African relations, in order to strengthen political consultation and co-operation for the promotion of security and stability in the region. Nine countries were nominated to serve on the central committee (organ) of the mechanism for conflict prevention, management and resolution. The military component of the OAU mission in Burundi was now deployed in that country, and its mandate was extended until mid-September. (The mission was subsequently granted three-monthly extensions of its mandate.)

Nov.   The Secretary-General, noting the Organization's serious financial situation, warned that most activities of the regular budget for 1994/95 would have to be suspended. Certain sanctions were to be imposed on any country that had not paid its contribution in full by 1 June 1995.

1995

March   An extraordinary session of the Council of Ministers, held in Cairo, Egypt, adopted an Agenda for Action, which aimed to stimulate African economic and social development. The document emphasized the importance of peace, democratic government and stability in achieving development targets. It also assessed Africa's role in the world economy and the need for structural reforms of countries' economies, in particular in view of agreements reached under the GATT Uruguay Round of trade negotiations. The OAU, together with representatives of the UN and the Commonwealth Secretariat, dispatched a special mission to Sierra Leone, in order to assess means of facilitating the peace process in that country.

April   A meeting of the conflict mechanism's central organ, held in Tunis, Tunisia, reviewed OAU peace initiatives. The meeting urged OAU member states to offer humanitarian aid to consolidate the peace process in Angola and for further OAU assistance for the rehabilitation and reconstruction of Somalia. A seminar, organized jointly by the OAU and the International Committee of the Red Cross, assembled military and civil experts in Yaoundé, Cameroon, to discuss the issue of land-mines.

May   An 81-member OAU observer group was deployed to monitor a general election in Ethiopia. The group confirmed that the electoral process had been 'free and fair'.

June   At the 31st Assembly of Heads of State, held in Addis Ababa, Ethiopia, the Secretary-General observed that the OAU's peace-keeping role had been severely affected by the failure of member states to pay their contributions. Sanctions were to be imposed on those countries which had failed to pay 25% of their arrears by the end of June. (Liberia and Somalia were exempted from this deadline.) The meeting endorsed a proposal to establish a conflict management centre, provisionally in Cairo, Egypt, to strengthen the OAU's role in conflict prevention. The situation in warring African countries was discussed, as well as the problem of large-scale refugee and displaced populations in the region. In addition, member states urged the international community to end the application of sanctions against Libya.

Sept.   An extraordinary meeting of the conflict mechanism's central organ condemned the attempted assassination of Egypt's President Mubarak prior to the Heads of State meeting in June. The committee censured Sudan for protecting the alleged perpetrators of the attack and for supporting other terrorist elements in the country.

Oct.   OAU observers monitored the conduct of elections in Zanzibar and attempted to mediate between the parties when the vote failed to secure a decisive result.

Nov.   A 50-member OAU observer group was deployed to monitor elections in Algeria, as part of an international team.

1996

Feb.   The Council of Ministers reiterated the OAU's readiness to promote and support dialogue and reconciliation in Burundi. However, the meeting did not support military intervention in that country, despite a UN report proposing international co-operation with the OAU to establish a stand-by force for Burundi.

March   The UN Secretary-General launched a system-wide Special Initiative on Africa, which was based on the development objectives outlined in the OAU Agenda for Action (see above). Funds were to be allocated under the Initiative to strengthen the OAU's capacity for conflict prevention, management and resolution.

May-   The OAU assisted the International Peace Academy to
June   conduct a meeting of international organizations, in Cape Town, South Africa, to promote the OAU's conflict mechanism, under the theme of 'Civil Society and Conflict Management in Africa'.

July   The 32nd Assembly of Heads of State agreed to support a plan, formulated earlier that month by the Governments of Tanzania, Uganda and Ethiopia, to send troops to Burundi in a peace-keeping capacity. The Assembly requested logistical and financial support from the international community for the initiative. In a separate declaration OAU leaders expressed their support for Boutros

Boutros-Ghali's candidacy for a second term as the UN Secretary-General. The endorsement was opposed by the President of Rwanda, Pasteur Bizimungu, who condemned the lack of UN protection afforded to his country during the civil unrest in 1994. At the end of July, following a military coup in Burundi, the OAU endorsed a decision of seven east and central African states to impose economic sanctions against the new regime.

Oct.   The OAU Secretary-General cautiously endorsed a US proposal to establish an African military force for the protection of civilian populations in areas of conflict. A regional committee of the OAU declared its support for the continuation of the economic embargo against Burundi.

Nov.   An OAU delegation, meeting with the heads of state of eight African countries in Nairobi, Kenya, supported the establishment of an international humanitarian force, to be sent to Zaire (although this was never deployed).

Dec.   The OAU President, in an attempt to overcome the impasse reached regarding the election of a new UN Secretary-General (owing to US opposition to Boutros-Ghali), confirmed that African nations should propose alternative candidates for the position.

1997

Jan.   The UN and the OAU appointed Muhamed Sahnoun as a joint Special Representative for the Great Lakes Region.

Feb.   The 65th session of the Council of Ministers, meeting in Libya, expressed its support of that country in the face of sanctions imposed upon it by the international community. The OAU welcomed the newly-elected Secretary-General of the UN, the Ghanaian, Kofi Annan. The situation in Zaire was discussed and an extraordinary summit of the OAU's conflict management mechanism was scheduled for March. Further donations to the OAU Peace Fund were requested.

March   A special summit of the OAU Organ on conflict prevention, management and resolution, which was attended by delegations from both the Zairean Government and the rebel AFDL forces, called for an immediate cease-fire and concluded a provisional agreement for negotiations between the two sides based on a five-point plan that had been formulated by Sahnoun and approved by the UN Security Council in February.

June   The Assembly of Heads of State, meeting in Harare, Zimbabwe, condemned the military coup in Sierra Leone, which took place in May, and endorsed the intervention of ECOMOG troops in order to restore a democratic government in that country. The OAU stated that future coups in the continent would not be tolerated, and the importance of universal human rights to be established across Africa was reiterated throughout the meeting. The first meeting between ministers of the OAU and the European Union was held in New York, USA. The inaugural meeting of the African Economic Community took place.

July   The UNDP donated US $3m. to the OAU conflict management mechanism. An OAU observer group was deployed to monitor elections in Liberia.

Aug.   The OAU appointed a special envoy to the Comoros, Pierre Yere, following a declaration of independence by separatists on the islands of Nzwani and Mwali.

Oct.   Chiefs of Defence Staff, meeting in Harare, Zimbabwe, proposed a series of measures to strengthen the capacity of African countries to lead peace-keeping missions in the region, which included the establishment of operations, training and early-warning units.

Nov.   A group of OAU military observers was reported to have been dispatched to the Comoros.

Dec.   The OAU organized an international conference, held in Addis Ababa, Ethiopia, which aimed to resolve the dispute between the Comoran Government and the secessionists and to initiate a process of political dialogue. In a separate meeting OAU ministers of justice adopted a protocol approving the creation of a permanent African court of human rights (based on the African Charter of Human and People's Rights, signed in 1981).

1998

Feb.   The OAU concluded an agreement with La Francophonie (q.v.) to co-operate in economic and cultural areas.

March   The OAU declared its support for ECOWAS efforts in restoring President Ahmed Tejan Kabbah to power in Sierra Leone. A nine-member OAU ministerial mission visited the Comoros in an attempt to further a peaceful solution to the dispute; however, it was prevented from conducting discussions with the separatist leaders in Nzwani.

June   Fighting between Eritrea and Ethiopia dominated discussions at the 34th Assembly of Heads of State, held in Burkina Faso. It was agreed to send a delegation to attempt to resolve the dispute. The Assembly also considered economic issues affecting the region, and resolved to disregard certain economic and humanitarian sanctions imposed against Libya, owing to that country's refusal to release two people suspected of the bombing of a US aircraft over the United Kingdom in 1988. The OAU leaders reiterated their support for the proposal of the Libyan authorities that the suspects be tried in a neutral venue. The OAU agreed to establish a seven-member International Panel of Eminent Personalities to examine all aspects of the genocide that occurred in Rwanda in 1994; a special trust fund was to be established to finance its activities. (The Panel met for the first time in October.)

July   An OAU delegation conducted discussions with the Eritrean and Ethiopian authorities in an attempt to conclude a peace settlement. The OAU Secretary-General also expressed support for efforts to negotiate a settlement between the conflicting parties in Guinea-Bissau.

Aug.   The OAU expressed its concern at the escalating violence in the Democratic Republic of the Congo (DRC), in particular the involvement of armed forces from other countries in the region, and resolved to send a mission to negotiate a cease-fire. An OAU ministerial committee (comprising representatives of Burkina Faso, Djibouti and Zimbabwe) pursued efforts to negotiate an accord between Eritrea and Ethiopia. The proposed OAU framework agreement was based on a US-Rwandan peace plan, presented to both sides in June, and included implementation of an immediate cease-fire, the initiation of peace discussions and recognition of the positions prior to the start of hostilities in May. At the end of August delegates of the SADC held talks at OAU headquarters, and urged an immediate cease-fire by all sides in the Congolese conflict.

Sept.   The OAU Secretary-General supported a request of the Sudanese Government for an international commission of inquiry to be established to examine the US airstrike on a pharmaceutical plant in Khartoum, in retaliation to terrorist bombing incidents in August.

Nov.   A meeting of the OAU mediation committee on the Eritrean/Ethiopian dispute was held in Ouagadougou.

Dec.   A special meeting of the conflict resolution mechanism, at the level of heads of state, was held to pursue a peace settlement in the DRC. The ongoing Eritrean-Ethiopian dispute and the unstable security situation in Angola were also considered. A Special OAU Ministerial Meeting on Refugees, Returnees and Internally Displaced Persons was convened, in Khartoum; the meeting urged member states to implement efforts to mitigate problems associated with the mass movement of populations, and to promote humanitarian assistance efforts.

1999

Feb.   A high-level OAU delegation, including the Chairman and Secretary-General, replaced the previous ministerial committee on a visit to Eritrea, following that country's refusal to negotiate with a representative of Djibouti. In early February an OAU delegation conducted talks with representatives of the Nzwani separatist factions and the Government of the Comoros; however, the negotiations failed to conclude an agreement on a political settlement to the conflict or on the establishment of an OAU peace-keeping mission.

March   An OAU mission visited the authorities in Ethiopia and Eritrea to pursue efforts towards settling the conflict. The Chairman of the OAU cancelled a special summit meeting on African conflict scheduled to take place at the end of March, owing to controversy over the extension of invitations to rebel leaders from those countries affected by civil conflict. A meeting of the Council of Ministers appointed the President of Zambia, Frederick Chiluba, to co-ordinate efforts to resolve the conflict in the DRC. The meeting also imposed sanctions against eight countries that had failed to pay their annual contributions to the Organization for two years. The sanctions denied nationals from those countries the right to vote or to work at the OAU offices, which resulted in a substantial reduction in personnel at OAU headquarters.

April   The first OAU conference on human rights, at ministerial level, was convened in Mauritius. An inter-island conference was held, under OAU auspices, in Antananarivo,

Madagascar, to conclude arrangements for a new political union in the Comoros. At the end of the month, however, the Government of the Comoros was removed by army officers following renewed unrest. The OAU condemned the coup, but urged the Nzwani representatives to sign the agreed framework.

May   The OAU announced the withdrawal of the military component of its observer mission in the Comoros. A new round of talks with the heads of government of Eritrea and Ethiopia was initiated to provide for a cessation of hostilities.

July   The summit meeting, held in Algiers, was concerned with the economic development of Africa and prospects for greater integration, as well as ongoing conflicts in the region. The meeting requested the Secretary-General to send a fact-finding mission to Somalia to assess its post-conflict needs. The OAU also appointed a senior Algerian army general to chair a Joint Military Commission in the DRC, which was to be established according to the terms of a peace accord signed earlier in July. Heads of state declared that the Organization would not recognize any authority in a member state which assumed power illegally. An African convention for the prevention and combating of terrorism was signed, which included provisions for the exchange of information to help counter terrorism and for signatory states to refrain from granting asylum to terrorists. The meeting also declared that 2000 was to be the Year of Peace, Security and Solidarity in Africa.

Sept.   An extraordinary summit meeting was convened in Sirte, Libya, at the request of the Libyan leader Col al-Qaddafi, in order to promote African unity and to demonstrate African solidarity with Libya. The meeting determined to establish an African Union, based on the principles and objectives of the OAU. A new charter was to be adopted by 2001. In addition, heads of state declared their commitment to accelerating the establishment of regional institutions, including an African parliament, court of justice, and central bank, as well as the implementation of an economic and monetary union. The Ethiopian Government rejected the final technical arrangements for implementation of the framework peace plan, which had been approved by Eritrea in August, on the grounds that they did not ensure the return of disputed territories to their status prior to the start of the conflict.

Oct.   A conference on Industrial Partnerships and Investment in Africa was held in Dakar, Senegal, jointly organized by OAU with UNIDO, the ECA, the African Development Bank, and the Alliance for Africa's Industrialization.

Dec.   The OAU Chairman, President Bouteflika of Algeria, urged the removal of UN sanctions against Libya. The OAU condemned the military's seizure of power in Côte d'Ivoire.

2000

Feb.   The OAU imposed economic sanctions against the Nzwani separatists in the Comoros, including the immobilization of their overseas assets, and urged the co-operation of OAU members in implementing these. The OAU dispatched a special envoy to mediate between Eritrea and Ethiopia; the Ethiopian adminstration reiterated its dissatisfaction with the technical arrangements (deemed no longer negotiable by the OAU) for the framework peace plan, which in other respects it was prepared to approve.

March   An OAU conference unanimously approved a peace plan for Somalia that had been drafted in late 1999 by the Djibouti President (and then IGAD Chairman), Ismael Omar Gelleh. Further punitive measures were imposed against the Nzwani separatists in the Comoros, including the suspension of telephone communications, and restrictions on oil deliveries and on sea and air traffic.

April   The OAU participated in an EU–Africa summit, held in Cairo, Egypt.

May   In early May an initiative by the OAU's special envoy to mediate indirect communications ('proximity talks') between Eritrea and Ethiopia failed, and was followed by a serious escalation of their conflict. The OAU urged an immediate cessation of hostilities and commitment from both sides to pursuing a peaceful resolution. Indirect negotiations, mediated by the OAU and envoys of the EU and USA, resumed in late May.

June   The OAU, EU and USA continued to mediate proximity talks between Eritrea and Ethiopia, culminating, in mid-June, in the conclusion of a cease-fire agreement, which was formalized at Algiers. The Algiers accord stipulated the immediate cessation of hostilities and withdrawal by both sides to the positions that had been held prior to the commencement of the conflict. Meanwhile, a UN peace-keeping force was to be deployed to supervise the disputed border area. Subsequently negotiations were to be convened on the implementation of the OAU framework agreement. Following the conclusion of the accord an OAU Liaison Mission in Ethiopia and Eritrea—OLMEE—was established. During the month a committee comprising 10 OAU heads of state was appointed to address the ongoing political insecurity in Côte d'Ivoire.

July   At the annual summit meeting, held at Lomé, Togo, 27 OAU heads of state signed the draft Constituent Act of the African Union, concerning the establishment of the proposed African Union, agreed in September 1999. The Constituent Act was to enter into force following ratification by two-thirds of member states' legislatures. It was envisaged that the Union would be inaugurated, and would thus replace the OAU, one year after the endorsement of the Act. The terms of the draft Act provided for the institution of a supreme body, an executive council of foreign ministers, and a court of justice. The summit adopted a resolution in support of the ongoing Somali peace and reconciliation conference convened in Arta, Djibouti, under the auspices of IGAD. At the end of July the OAU announced that it was to send observers to the Horn of Africa to monitor the implementation of the Algiers ceasefire accord.

Sept. A special envoy appointed by the Secretary-General to address the conflict in Sierra Leone visited several West African leaders for consultations regarding the situation in that country.

Oct.   The OAU declined to dispatch a team of observers to monitor presidential elections held in Côte d'Ivoire, following failure by that country's government to accept the mediation attempts of the OAU 'Committee of 10'. The Secretary-General subsequently declared that the elections had not been conducted freely and fairly and urged that the electoral process be repeated. An OAU observer team monitoring concurrent legislative and presidential elections staged in Zanzibar at the end of the month identified numerous electoral irregularities and refused to endorse the official results. (Legislative and presidential elections held at that time in mainland Tanzania were declared free and fair.)

Nov.   A draft protocol for the establishment of a Pan-African Parliament, with a consultative function, was adopted by 41 member states; the protocol was to enter into effect following ratification by a majority of states. An OAU special representative was appointed to a military co-ordination commission jointly established by the OAU and UN under the terms of Algiers accord, to facilitate the conflict settlement process in Eritrea and Ethiopia. During the month the Secretary-General expressed concern over mounting insecurity in southern Guinea.

Dec.   At the beginning of the month the OAU adopted the Bamako Declaration, concerning arresting the circulation of small arms on the continent. The Organization refused to dispatch observers to monitor legislative elections that were held in Côte d'Ivoire in early December. Following continued mediation efforts by the OAU a formal peace agreement was concluded by Eritrea and Ethiopia in Algiers in mid-December.

2001

Feb.   The OAU endorsed a framework agreement for reconciliation initialled in mid-February, at Fomboni on the island of

Mwali, by the Comoros Government and former dissident factions; consequently, at the end of the month, the punitive economic sanctions imposed on the former Nzwani separatists in February 2000 were suspended. The Council of Ministers urged all Somali faction leaders who had not participated in the Arta peace conference convened in mid-2000 to support ongoing efforts towards reconciliation in that country.

March The OAU's fifth extraordinary summit, convened at the start of the month in Sirte, Libya, discussed progress towards the proposed establishment of the African Union. The Union was officially declared, in anticipation of promptly securing the ratification of the Constituent Act by the requisite two-thirds majority. By mid-March the Act had been ratified by 34 member states.

Specialized Agencies

African Accounting Council: POB 11223, Kinshasa, Democratic Republic of the Congo; tel. (12) 33567; f. 1979; provides assistance to institutions in member countries on standardization of accounting; promotes education, further training and research in accountancy and related areas of study. Publ. *Information and Liaison Bulletin* (every two months).

African Bureau for Educational Sciences: 29 ave de la Justice, BP 1764, Kinshasa I, Democratic Republic of the Congo; tel. (12) 22006; f. 1973 to conduct educational research. Publs *Bulletin d'Information* (quarterly), *Revue africaine des sciences de l'éducation* (2 a year), *Répertoire africain des institutions de recherche* (annually).

African Civil Aviation Commission—AFCAC: 15 blvd de la République, BP 2356, Dakar, Senegal; tel. 839-93-93; fax 823-26-61; e-mail cafac@telecomplus.sn; internet www.afcac-cafac.sn; f. 1969 to encourage co-operation in all civil aviation activities; promotes co-ordination and better utilization and development of African air transport systems and the standardization of aircraft, flight equipment and training programmes for pilots and mechanics; organizes working groups and seminars, and compiles statistics. Pres. Capt. SHETTIMA ABBA GANA (Nigeria); Sec. A. CHEIFFOU (acting).

Pan-African News Agency—PANA: BP 4650, Dakar, Senegal; tel. 824-14-10; fax 824-13-90; internet www.africanews.org/PANA; regional headquarters in Khartoum, Sudan; Lusaka, Zambia; Kinshasa, Democratic Republic of the Congo; Lagos, Nigeria; Tripoli, Libya; began operations in May 1983; receives information from national news agencies and circulates news in English and French. Following financial problems, plans to restructure the agency at a cost of US $4.7m., in order to allow shares to be held by the private sector, were announced in June 1997. Capital was to be increased by 25,000 shares, while the agency was to be renamed PANA Presse. Co-ordinator BABACAR FALL. Publ. *PANA Review*.

Pan-African Postal Union—PAPU: POB 6026, Arusha, Tanzania; tel. (27) 2508603; fax (27) 2503913; e-mail papu@habar'i.co.tz; f. 1980 to extend members' co-operation in the improvement of postal services. Sec.-Gen. JILANI BEN HADDADA. Publ. *PAPU Bulletin*.

Pan-African Railways Union: BP 687, Kinshasa, Democratic Republic of the Congo; tel. (12) 23861; f. 1972 to standardize, expand, co-ordinate and improve members' railway services; the ultimate aim is to link all systems; main organs: Gen. Assembly, Exec. Bd, Gen. Secr., five tech. cttees. Mems in 30 African countries.

Pan-African Telecommunications Union: POB 7248, Kinshasa, Democratic Republic of the Congo; f. 1977; co-ordinates devt of telecommunications networks and services in Africa.

Supreme Council for Sports in Africa: BP 1363, Yaoundé, Cameroon; tel. and fax 23-95-80; Sec.-Gen. Dr AWOTURE ELEYAE (Nigeria). Publs *SCSA News* (6 a year), *African Sports Movement Directory* (annually).

ORGANIZATION OF AMERICAN STATES—OAS

(ORGANIZACIÓN DE LOS ESTADOS AMERICANOS—OEA)

Address: 17th St and Constitution Ave, NW, Washington, DC 20006, USA.

Telephone: (202) 458-3000; **fax:** (202) 458-3967; **e-mail:** pi@oas.org; **internet:** www.oas.org.

The OAS was founded at Bogotá, Colombia, in 1948 (succeeding the International Union of American Republics, founded in 1890) to foster peace, security, mutual understanding and co-operation among the nations of the Western Hemisphere.

MEMBERS

Antigua and Barbuda	Guyana
Argentina	Haiti
Bahamas	Honduras
Barbados	Jamaica
Belize	Mexico
Bolivia	Nicaragua
Brazil	Panama
Canada	Paraguay
Chile	Peru
Colombia	Saint Christopher and Nevis
Costa Rica	Saint Lucia
Cuba*	Saint Vincent and the Grenadines
Dominica	Suriname
Dominican Republic	Trinidad and Tobago
Ecuador	USA
El Salvador	Uruguay
Grenada	Venezuela
Guatemala	

* The Cuban Government was suspended from OAS activities in 1962.

Permanent Observers: Algeria, Angola, Austria, Belgium, Bosnia and Herzegovina, Bulgaria, Croatia, Cyprus, Czech Republic, Denmark, Egypt, Equatorial Guinea, Finland, France, Germany, Ghana, Greece, the Holy See, Hungary, India, Ireland, Israel, Italy, Japan, Kazakhstan, the Republic of Korea, Latvia, Lebanon, Morocco, the Netherlands, Norway, Pakistan, Poland, Portugal, Romania, Russia, Saudi Arabia, Spain, Sri Lanka, Sweden, Switzerland, Thailand, Tunisia, Turkey, Ukraine, the United Kingdom, Yemen and the European Union.

Organization

(April 2001)

GENERAL ASSEMBLY

The Assembly meets annually and may also hold special sessions when convoked by the Permanent Council. As the supreme organ of the OAS, it decides general action and policy.

MEETINGS OF CONSULTATION OF MINISTERS OF FOREIGN AFFAIRS

Meetings are convened, at the request of any member state, to consider problems of an urgent nature and of common interest to member states, or to serve as an organ of consultation in cases of armed attack or other threats to international peace and security. The Permanent Council determines whether a meeting should be convened and acts as a provisional organ of consultation until ministers are able to assemble.

PERMANENT COUNCIL

The Council meets regularly throughout the year at OAS headquarters. It is composed of one representative of each member state with the rank of ambassador; each government may accredit alternate representatives and advisers and when necessary appoint an interim representative. The office of Chairman is held in turn by each of the representatives, following alphabetical order according to the names of the countries in Spanish. The Vice-Chairman is determined in the same way, following reverse alphabetical order. Their terms of office are three months.

The Council acts as an organ of consultation and oversees the maintenance of friendly relations between members. It supervises the work of the OAS and promotes co-operation with a variety of other international bodies including the United Nations. The official languages are English, French, Portuguese and Spanish.

INTER-AMERICAN COUNCIL FOR INTEGRAL DEVELOPMENT—CIDI

The Council was established in 1996, replacing the Inter-American Economic and Social Council and the Inter-American Council for Education, Science and Culture. Its aim is to promote co-operation among the countries of the region, in order to accelerate economic and social development. CIDI's work focuses on eight areas: social development and education; cultural development; the generation of productive employment; economic diversification, integration and trade liberalization; strengthening democratic institutions; the exchange of scientific and technological information; the development of tourism; and sustainable environmental development. An Executive Secretary for Integral Development provides CIDI with technical and secretarial services.

Executive Secretary: RONALD SCHEMAN (USA).

Inter-American Agency for Co-operation and Development: f. November 1999 as a subsidiary body of CIDI to accelerate the development of Latin America and the Caribbean through technical co-operation and training programmes. In particular, the Agency aimed to formulate strategies for mobilizing external funds for OAS co-operation initiatives; establish criteria for the promotion and exchange of co-operation activities; prepare co-operation accords and evaluate project requests and results; and review mechanisms for promoting scholarships and professional exchange programmes. The Executive Secretary for Integral Development serves as the Agency's Director-General.

GENERAL SECRETARIAT

The Secretariat, the central and permanent organ of the Organization, performs the duties entrusted to it by the General Assembly, Meetings of Consultation of Ministers of Foreign Affairs and the Councils.

Secretary-General: CÉSAR GAVIRIA TRUJILLO (Colombia).

Assistant Secretary-General: LUIGI R. EINAUDI (USA).

INTER-AMERICAN COMMITTEES AND COMMISSIONS

Inter-American Juridical Committee: Rua Senador Vergueiro 81, Rio de Janeiro, RJ 22230-000, Brazil; tel. (21) 558-3204; fax (21) 558-4600; e-mail cjioea@trip.com.br; composed of 11 jurists, nationals of different member states, elected for a period of four years, with the possibility of re-election. The Committee's purposes are: to serve as an advisory body to the Organization on juridical matters; to promote the progressive development and codification of international law; and to study juridical problems relating to the integration of the developing countries in the hemisphere, and, in so far as may appear desirable, the possibility of attaining uniformity in legislation. Sec. MANOEL TOLOMEI MOLETTA.

Inter-American Commission on Human Rights: 1889 F St, NW, Washington, DC 20006, USA; tel. (202) 458-6002; fax (202) 458-3992; e-mail cidhoea@oas.org; internet www.cidh.oas.org; f. 1960. The Commission comprises seven members. It promotes the observance and protection of human rights in the member states of the OAS; it examines and reports on the human rights situation in member countries, and provides consultative services. Exec. Sec. JORGE TAIANA.

Inter-American Court of Human Rights: Apdo Postal 6906-1000, San José, Costa Rica; tel. 234-0581; fax 234-0584; e-mail corteidh@racsa.co.cr; internet www.corteidh-oea.nu.or.cr/ci; f. 1978, as an autonomous judicial institution whose purpose is to apply and interpret the American Convention on Human Rights (which entered into force in 1978: at November 1998 the Convention had been ratified by 25 OAS member states, of which 18 had accepted the competence of the Court). The Court comprises seven jurists from OAS member states. Pres. ANTÔNIO CANÇADO TRINDADE; Sec. MANUEL E. VENTURA-ROBLES.

Inter-American Drug Abuse Control Commission—CICAD: 1889 F St, NW, Washington, DC 20006-4499, USA; tel. (202) 458-3178; fax (202) 458-3658; e-mail cicad@oas.org; internet www.cicad.oas.org; f. 1986 by the OAS to promote and facilitate multilateral co-operation in the control and prevention of the trafficking, production and use of illegal drugs, and related crimes. Mems 34 countries. Exec. Sec. DAVID R. BEALL. Publs *Statistical Survey* (annually), *Directory of Governmental Institutions Charges with the Fight Against the Illicit Production, Trafficking, Use and*

Abuse of Narcotic Drugs and Psychotropic Substances (annually), *Evaluation of Progress in Drug Control* (annually).

Inter-American Telecommunication Commission: 1889 F St, NW, Washington, DC 20006, USA; tel. (202) 458-3004; fax (202) 458-6854; e-mail citel@oas.org; f. 1993; Exec. Sec. CLOVIS BAPTISTA.

Inter-American Committee on Ports: 1889 F St, NW, Washington, DC 20006, USA; tel. and fax (202) 458-3871; e-mail cgallegos@oas.org; f. 1998 to further OAS activities in the sector (previously undertaken by Inter-American port conferences); aims to develop and co-ordinate member state policies in port administration and management. The first meeting of the Committee took place in October 1999; three technical advisory groups were established to advise on port operations, port security, and navigation safety and environmental protection. An Executive Board meets annually. Sec. CARLOS GALLEGOS.

Activities

In December 1994 the first Summit of the Americas was convened in Miami, USA. The meeting endorsed the concept of a Free Trade Area of the Americas (FTAA), and also approved a Plan of Action to strengthen democracy, eradicate poverty and promote sustainable development throughout the region. The OAS subsequently embarked on an extensive process of reform and modernization to strengthen its capacity to undertake a lead role in implementing the Plan. The Organization realigned its priorities in order to respond to the mandates emerging from the Summit and developed a new institutional framework for technical assistance and co-operation, although many activities continued to be undertaken by the specialized or associated organizations of the OAS (see below). In 1998, following the second Summit of the Americas, held in April, in Santiago, Chile, the OAS established an Office of Summit Follow-Up, in order to strengthen its servicing of the meetings, and to co-ordinate tasks assigned to the Organization. The third Summit was to be convened in Quebec City, Canada, in April 2001.

TRADE AND ECONOMIC INTEGRATION

A trade unit was established in 1995 in order to strengthen the Organization's involvement in trade issues and the process of economic integration, which became a priority area following the first Summit of the Americas. The unit was to provide technical assistance in support of the establishment of the FTAA, and to co-ordinate activities between regional and sub-regional integration organizations. In 2000 the unit was providing technical support to six of the nine FTAA negotiating groups, relating to the following areas: investment; services; dispute settlement; intellectual property rights; subsidies, anti-dumping and countervailing duties; and competition policy.

The unit operates in consultation with a Special Committee on Trade, which was established in 1993 comprising high-level officials representing each member state. The Committee studies trade issues, provides technical analyses of the economic situation in member countries and the region, and prepares reports for ministerial meetings of the FTAA. The OAS also administers an Inter-American Foreign Trade Information System which facilitates the exchange of information.

DEMOCRACY AND CIVIL SOCIETY

Two principal organs of the OAS, the Inter-American Commission on Human Rights and the Inter-American Court of Human Rights, work to secure respect for human rights in all member countries. The OAS aims to encourage more member governments to accept jurisdiction of the Court. The OAS also collaborates with member states in the strengthening of representative institutions within government and as part of a democratic civil society.

Through its unit for the promotion of democracy, established in 1990, the OAS provides electoral technical assistance to member states and undertakes missions to observe the conduct of elections. By late 2000 the OAS had conducted 53 electoral missions in 18 countries. In March 2001 OAS observers monitored parliamentary elections in St Vincent and the Grenadines, and in April a team of 50 experts observed the general election in Peru. The OAS also supports societies in post-conflict situations and recently-installed governments to promote democratic practices. In 1993 the OAS participated in a joint civil mission with the UN in Haiti in order to promote respect for human rights and the re-establishment of a democratically-elected government.

In June 1991 the OAS General Assembly approved a resolution on representative democracy, which authorized the Secretary-General to summon a session of the Permanent Council in cases where a democratically-elected government had been overthrown or democratic procedures abandoned in member states. The Council could then convene an *ad hoc* meeting of ministers of foreign affairs to consider the situation. The procedure was invoked following political developments in Haiti, in September 1991, and Peru, in April 1992. Ministers determined to impose trade and diplomatic sanctions against Haiti and sent missions to both countries. The resolution was incorporated into the Protocol of Washington, amending the OAS charter, which was adopted in December 1992 and entered into force in September 1997. A high-level OAS mission was dispatched to Peru in June 2000 to assist with the process of 'strengthening its institutional democratic system', following allegations that the Peruvian authorities had manipulated the re-election of that country's President in May. The mission subsequently co-ordinated negotiations between the Peruvian Government and opposition organizations. In August the OAS Secretary-General undertook the first of several high-level missions to negotiate with the authorities in Haiti in order to resolve the political crisis resulting from a disputed general election in May. (An OAS electoral monitoring team was withdrawn from Haiti in July prior to the second round of voting owing to concern at procedural irregularities.) In January 2001, following a meeting with the Haitian Prime Minister, the Assistant Secretary-General recommended that the OAS renew its efforts to establish a dialogue between the government, opposition parties and representatives of civil society in that country.

An OAS Mine-Clearing Assistance Programme in Central America was established in 1992, as part of efforts to facilitate the social and economic rehabilitation of the region. By 1999 the programme had provided training for 250 de-mining experts and assisted countries in the clearance of some 28,000 anti-personnel devices. Technical support was provided by the Inter-American Defense Board (see below).

The OAS has formulated an Inter-American Programme of Co-operation to Combat Corruption in order to address the problem at national level and, in 1996, adopted a Convention against Corruption. The first conference of the parties to the treaty was scheduled to be held in Buenos Aires, Argentina, in May 2001. By March of that year the treaty had been ratified by 21 member states. A working group on transparency aims to promote accountability throughout the public sector and supports national institutions responsible for combating corruption. In 1997 the OAS organized a meeting of experts to consider measures for the prevention of crime. The meeting adopted a work programme which included commitments to undertake police training in criminology and crime investigation, to exchange legal and practical knowledge, and to measure crime and violence in member countries.

REGIONAL SECURITY

In 1991 the General Assembly established a working group to consider issues relating to the promotion of co-operation in regional security. A Special Commission on Hemispheric Security was subsequently established, while two regional conferences have been held on security and confidence-building measures. Voluntary practices agreed by member states include the holding of border meetings to co-ordinate activities, co-operation in natural disaster management, and the exchange of information on military exercises and expenditure. From 1995 meetings of ministers of defence have been convened regularly, which provide a forum for discussion of security matters. In June 2000 the OAS General Assembly, convened in Windsor, Canada, established a Fund for Peace in support of the peaceful settlement of territorial disputes.

The OAS is actively involved in efforts to combat the abuse and trafficking of illegal drugs. In 1996 members approved a Hemispheric Anti-drug Strategy, reiterating their commitment to combating the problem. In 1998 the Inter-American Drug Abuse Control Commission established a Multilateral Evaluation Mechanism (MEM) to measure aspects of the drug problem and to co-ordinate an evaluation process under which national plans of action to combat drugs trafficking were to be formulated. The first hemispheric drugs report was published by MEM in January 2001 and in February 34 national reports produced under MEM were issued together with a series of recommendations for action. Since 1996 an OAS group of experts has undertaken efforts to assist countries in reducing the demand for illegal substances. Activities include the implementation of prevention programmes for street children; the development of communication strategies; and education and community projects relating to the prevention of drug dependence.

The first Specialized Inter-American Conference on Terrorism was held in Lima, Peru, in April 1996. A Declaration and Plan of Action were adopted, according to which member states agreed to co-operate and implement measures to combat terrorism and organized crime. A second conference was held in Mar del Plata, Argentina, in 1998. Member states recommended the establishment of an Inter-American Committee against Terrorism to implement decisions relating to judicial, police and intelligence co-operation.

SOCIAL DEVELOPMENT AND EDUCATION

In June 1996 the OAS established a specialized unit for social development and education to assist governments and social institutions of member states to formulate public policies and implement initiatives relating to employment and labour issues, education development, social integration and poverty elimination. It was also to provide technical and operational support for the implementation of inter-American programmes in those sectors, and to promote the exchange of information among experts and professionals working in those fields. In June 1997 the OAS approved an Inter-American Programme to Combat Poverty. The unit serves as the technical secretariat for annual meetings on social development that were to be convened within the framework of the Programme. The unit also administers the Social Networks of Latin America and the Caribbean project, and its co-ordinating committee, which promotes sub-regional co-operation to combat poverty and discrimination. In 1999 the unit was to implement a project funded by the Inter-American Development Bank to place interns and trainees within the Social Network institutions and to promote exchanges between the institutions.

The first meeting of ministers of education of the Americas was held in Brasília, Brazil, in July 1998, based on the mandate of the second Summit of the Americas. The meeting approved an Inter-American Education Programme, formulated by the unit for social development and education, which incorporated the following six priority initiatives: education for priority social sectors; strengthening educational management and institutional development; education for work and youth development; education for citizenship and sustainability in multicultural societies; training in the use of new technologies in teaching the official languages of the OAS; and training of teachers and education administrators. Other programmes in the education sector are undertaken with international agencies and non-governmental organizations.

The OAS supports member states to formulate and implement programmes to promote productive employment and vocational training, to develop small businesses and other employment generation initiatives, and to regulate labour migration. In 1998 the OAS initiated the Labour Market Information System project, which aimed to provide reliable and up-to-date indicators of the labour situation in member countries, to determine the impact of economic policy on the labour situation, and to promote the exchange of information among relevant national and regional institutions. Labour issues were addressed by the second Summit of the Americas, and, following an Inter-American Conference of Labour Ministers, held in Viña del Mar, Chile, in October 1998, two working groups were established to consider the globalization of the economy and its social and labour dimension and the modernization of the state and labour administration.

SUSTAINABLE DEVELOPMENT AND THE ENVIRONMENT

In 1996 a summit meeting on social development adopted a plan of action, based on the objectives of the UN Conference on the Environment and Development, which was held in Rio de Janeiro, Brazil, in June 1992. The OAS was to participate in an inter-agency group to monitor implementation of the action plan. The OAS has subsequently established new financing mechanisms and networks of experts relating to aspects of sustainable development. Technical co-operation activities include multinational basin management; a strategic plan for the Amazon; natural disaster management; and the sustainable development of border areas in Central America and South America. In December 1999 the Inter-American Council for Integral Development approved a policy framework and recommendations for action of a new Inter-American Strategy for Public Participation in Decision-making for Sustainable Development.

The following initiatives have also been undertaken: a Caribbean Disaster Mitigation Project, to help those countries to counter and manage the affects of natural disasters; a Post-Georges Disaster Mitigation initiative specifically to assist countries affected by Hurricane Georges; a Natural Hazards Project to provide a general programme of support to assess member states' vulnerability, to provide technical assistance and training to mitigate the effects of a disaster, and to assist in the planning and formulation of development and preparedness policies; the Renewable Energy in the Americas initiative to promote co-operation and strengthen renewable energy and energy efficiency; an Inter-American Water Resources Network, which aims to promote collaboration, training and the exchange of information within the sector; and a Water Level Observation Network for Central America to provide support for coastal resources management, navigation and disaster mitigation in the countries affected by Hurricane Mitch.

SCIENCE AND TECHNOLOGY

The OAS supports and develops activities to contribute to the advancement of science and technology throughout the Americas, and to promote its contribution to social and sustainable development. In particular, it promotes collaboration, dissemination of information and improved communication between experts and institutions working in the sector. Specialized bodies and projects have been established to promote activities in different fields, for example metrology; co-operation between institutions of accreditation, certification and inspection; the development of instruments of measurements and analysis of science and technology; chemistry; the development of technical standardization and related activities; and collaboration between experts and institutions involved in biotechnology and food technology. The OAS also maintains an information system to facilitate access to databases on science and technology throughout the region.

TOURISM AND CULTURE

A specialized unit for tourism was established in 1996 in order to strengthen and co-ordinate activities for the sustainable development of the tourism industry in the Americas. The unit supports regional and sub-regional conferences and workshops, as well as the Inter-American Travel Congress, which was convened for the first time in 1993 to serve as a forum to formulate region-wide tourism policies. The unit also undertakes research and analysis of the industry.

In 1998 the OAS approved an Inter-American Programme of Culture to support efforts being undertaken by member states and to promote co-operation in areas such as cultural diversity; protection of cultural heritage; training and dissemination of information; and the promotion of cultural tourism. The OAS also assists with the preparation of national and multilateral cultural projects, and co-operates with the private sector to protect and promote cultural assets and events in the region.

COMMUNICATIONS

In June 1993 the OAS General Assembly approved the establishment of an Inter-American Telecommunication Commission. The body has technical autonomy, within the statute and mandate agreed by the Assembly. It aims to facilitate and promote the development of communications in all member countries, in collaboration with the private sector and other organizations, and serves as the principal advisory body of the OAS on matters related to telecommunications.

Finance

The OAS budget for 2001, approved by the General Assembly in mid-2000, amounted to US $84.4m.

Publications

(in English and Spanish)

Américas (6 a year).
Annual Report.
Catalog of Publications (annually).
Ciencia Interamericana (quarterly).
La Educación (quarterly).
Statistical Bulletin (quarterly).
Numerous cultural, legal and scientific reports and studies.

Specialized Organizations and Associated Agencies

Inter-American Children's Institute: Avda 8 de Octubre 2904, Montevideo, Uruguay; tel. (2) 4872150; fax (2) 4873242; e-mail iinpiinfa@redfacil.com.uy; internet www.iin.org.uy; f. 1927; promotes the regional implementation of the Convention on the Rights of the Child, assists in the development of child-oriented public policies; promotes co-operation between states; and aims to develop awareness of problems affecting children and young people in the region. The Institute organizes workshops, seminars, courses, training programmes and conferences on issues relating to children, including, for example, the rights of children, children with disabilities, and the child welfare system. It also provides advisory services, statistical data and other relevant information to authorities and experts throughout the region. Dir-Gen. RODRIGO QUINTANA (Chile). Publs *Boletín* (quarterly), *IINfancia* (2 a year).

Inter-American Commission of Women: 1889 F St, NW, Suite 880 Washington, DC 20006, USA; tel. (202) 458-6084; fax (202)

458-6094; f. 1928 for the extension of civil, political, economic, social and cultural rights for women. In 1991 a Seed Fund was established to provide financing for grass-roots projects consistent with the Commission's objectives. Pres. INDRANIE CHANDARPAL (Guyana); Exec. Sec. CARMEN LOMELLIN.

Inter-American Defense Board: 2600 16th St, NW, Washington, DC 20441, USA; tel. (202) 939-6600; works in liaison with member governments to plan and train for the common security interests of the western hemisphere; operates the Inter-American Defense College. Chair. Maj.-Gen. CARL H. FREEMAN (USA).

Inter-American Indigenous Institute: Av. de las Fuentes 106, Col. Jardines del Pedregal 01900 México, DF, Mexico; tel. (5) 595-8410; fax (5) 652-0089; f. 1940; conducts research on the situation of the indigenous peoples of America; assists the exchange of information; promotes indigenist policies in member states aimed at the elimination of poverty and development within Indian communities, and to secure their position as ethnic groups within a democratic society. Dir Dr JOSÉ MANUEL DEL VAL (Mexico); Exec. Co-ordinator EVANGELINA MENDIZABAL. Publs *América Indígena* (quarterly), *Anuario Indigenista*.

Inter-American Institute for Co-operation on Agriculture: Apdo 55–2200 Coronado, San José, Costa Rica; tel. 229-0222; fax 229-4741; f. 1942 (as the Inter-American Institute of Agricultural Sciences: new name 1980); supports the efforts of member states to improve agricultural development and rural well-being; encourages co-operation between regional organizations, and provides a forum for the exchange of experience. Dir-Gen. CARLOS AQUINO GONZÁLEZ (Dominican Republic). Publ. *Comuniica* (quarterly).

Pan American Development Foundation—PADF: 2600 16th St, NW, Washington, DC 20009-4202, USA; tel. (202) 458-3969; fax (202) 458-6316; f. 1962 to improve economic and social conditions in Latin America and the Caribbean through providing low-interest credit for small-scale entrepreneurs, vocational training, improved health care, agricultural development and reafforestation, and strengthening local non-governmental organizations; provides emergency disaster relief and reconstruction assistance. Mems: foundations and institutes in 35 countries. Pres. JACK HELLER; Exec. Dir BOB MOORE. Publ. *PADF Newsletter* (2 a year).

Pan American Health Organization: 525 23rd St, NW, Washington, DC 20037, USA; tel. (202) 974-3000; fax (202) 974-3663; e-mail webmaster@paho.org; internet www.paho.org; f. 1902; co-ordinates regional efforts to improve health; maintains close relations with national health organizations and serves as the Regional Office for the Americas of the World Health Organization. Dir Sir GEORGE ALLEYNE (Barbados).

Pan-American Institute of Geography and History: Ex-Arzobispado 29, 11869 México, DF, Mexico; tel. (5) 277-5888; fax (5) 271-6172; e-mail ipgh@laneta.apc.org; internet www.spin.com.mx/~ipgh; f. 1928; co-ordinates and promotes the study of cartography, geophysics, geographyand history; it provides technical assistance, conducts training at research centres, distributes publications, and organizes technical meetings. Chair. Dr JORGE SALVADOR LARA (Ecuador); Sec.-Gen. CHESTER ZELAYA GOODMAN (Costa Rica). Publs *Boletín Aéreo* (quarterly), *Revista Cartográfica* (2 a year), *Revista Geográfica* (2 a year), *Revista Historia de América* (2 a year), *Revista de Arqueología Americana* (2 a year), *Revista Geofísica* (2 a year), *Folklore Americano* (2 a year), *Boletín de Antropología Americana* (2 a year).

ORGANIZATION OF ARAB PETROLEUM EXPORTING COUNTRIES—OAPEC

Address: POB 20501, Safat 13066, Kuwait.

Telephone: 4844500; **fax:** 4815747; **e-mail:** oapec@qualitynet.net; **internet:** www.oapec.org.

OAPEC was established in 1968 to safeguard the interests of members and to determine ways and means for their co-operation in various forms of economic activity in the petroleum industry. In 1998 member states accounted for 26.2% of total world petroleum production and 9.7% of total global natural gas output.

MEMBERS

Algeria	Kuwait	Saudi Arabia
Bahrain	Libya	Syria
Egypt	Qatar	United Arab Emirates
Iraq		

Organization

(April 2001)

MINISTERIAL COUNCIL

The Council consists normally of the ministers of petroleum of the member states, and forms the supreme authority of the Organization, responsible for drawing up its general policy, directing its activities and laying down its governing rules. It meets twice yearly, and may hold extraordinary sessions. Chairmanship is on an annual rotation basis.

EXECUTIVE BUREAU

Assists the Council to direct the management of the Organization, approves staff regulations, reviews the budget, and refers it to the Council, considers matters relating to the Organization's agreements and activities and draws up the agenda for the Council. The Bureau comprises one senior official from each member state. Chairmanship is by rotation. The Bureau convenes at least three times a year.

GENERAL SECRETARIAT

Secretary-General: ABDULAZIZ A. AL-TURKI (Saudi Arabia).

Besides the Office of the Secretary-General, there are four departments: Finance and Administrative Affairs, Information and Library, Technical Affairs and Economics. The last two form the Arab Centre for Energy Studies (which was established in 1983). At the end of 1999 there were 17 professional staff members and 36 general personnel at the General Secretariat.

JUDICIAL TRIBUNAL

The Tribunal comprises seven judges from Arab countries. Its task is to settle differences in interpretation and application of the OAPEC Agreement, arising between members and also between OAPEC and its affiliates; disputes among member countries on petroleum activities falling within OAPEC's jurisdiction and not under the sovereignty of member countries; and disputes that the Ministerial Council decides to submit to the Tribunal.

President: FARIS ABDUL AL-WAGAYAN.

Registrar: Dr RIAD RASHAD AL-DAOUDI.

Activities

OAPEC co-ordinates different aspects of the Arab petroleum industry through the joint undertakings described below. It co-operates with the League of Arab States and other Arab organizations, and attempts to link petroleum research institutes in the Arab states. It organizes or participates in conferences and seminars, many of which are held jointly with non-Arab organizations in order to enhance Arab and international co-operation.

OAPEC provides training in technical matters and in documentation and information. The General Secretariat also conducts technical and feasibility studies and carries out market reviews. It provides information through a library, 'databank' and the publications listed below.

The invasion of Kuwait by Iraq in August 1990, and the subsequent international embargo on petroleum exports from Iraq and Kuwait, severely disrupted OAPEC's activities. In December the OAPEC Council decided to establish temporary headquarters in Cairo while Kuwait was under occupation. The Council resolved to reschedule overdue payments by Iraq and Syria over a 15-year period, and to postpone the Fifth Arab Energy Conference from mid-1992 to mid-1994. The Conference was held in Cairo, Egypt, in May 1994, attended by OAPEC ministers of petroleum and energy, senior officials from nine other Arab states and representatives of regional and international organizations. In June OAPEC returned to its permanent headquarters in Kuwait. The Sixth Conference was held in Damascus, Syria, in May 1998, with the theme of 'Energy and Arab Co-operation'. The seventh conference was scheduled to be convened in May 2002, in Cairo, Egypt.

Finance

The 2000 budget amounted to 1,450,000 Kuwaiti dinars (KD). A budget of 117,200 KD was approved for the Judicial Tribunal for 2001.

Publications

Annual Statistical Report.
Energy Resources Monitor (quarterly, Arabic).
OAPEC Monthly Bulletin (Arabic and English editions).
Oil and Arab Co-operation (quarterly, Arabic).
Secretary-General's Annual Report (Arabic and English editions).
Papers, studies, conference proceedings.

OAPEC-Sponsored Ventures

Arab Maritime Petroleum Transport Company—AMPTC: POB 22525, Safat 13086, Kuwait; tel. 4844500; fax 4842996; f. 1973 to undertake transport of crude petroleum, gas, refined products and petro-chemicals, and thus to increase Arab participation in the tanker transport industry; auth. cap. US $200m. Gen. Man. SULAYMAN AL-BASSAM.

Arab Petroleum Investments Corporation—APICORP: POB 9599, Dammam 31423, Saudi Arabia; tel. (3) 887-0555; fax (3) 887-0505; e-mail info@apicorp-arabia.com; internet www.apicorp-arabia.com; f. 1975 to finance investments in petroleum and petro-chemicals projects and related industries in the Arab world and in developing countries, with priority being given to Arab joint ventures. Projects financed include gas liquefaction plants, petrochemicals, tankers, oil refineries, pipelines, exploration, detergents, fertilizers and process control instrumentation; auth. cap. US $1,200m.; subs. cap. $460m. (31 Dec. 1996). Shareholders: Kuwait, Saudi Arabia and United Arab Emirates (17% each), Libya (15%), Iraq and Qatar (10% each), Algeria (5%), Bahrain, Egypt and

Syria (3% each). Chair. ABDULLAH A. AZ-ZAID; Gen. Man. RASHEED AL-MARAJ.

Arab Company for Detergent Chemicals—ARADET: POB 27864, el-Monsour, Baghdad, Iraq; tel. (1) 541-9893; f. 1981 to implement two projects in Iraq; APICORP and the Iraqi Government each hold 32% of shares in the co; auth. cap. 72m. Iraqi dinars.

Arab Petroleum Services Company—APSCO: POB 12925, Tripoli, Libya; tel. (21) 45861; fax (21) 3331930; f. 1977 to provide petroleum services through the establishment of companies specializing in various activities, and to train specialized personnel; auth. cap. 100m. Libyan dinars; subs. cap. 15m. Libyan dinars. Chair. AYAD HUSSEIN AD-DALI; Gen. Man. ISMAIL AL-KORAITLI.

Arab Drilling and Workover Company: POB 680, Suani Rd, km 3.5, Tripoli, Libya; tel. (21) 800064; fax (21) 805945; f. 1980; auth. cap. 12m. Libyan dinars; Gen. Man. MUHAMMAD AHMAD ATTIGA.

Arab Geophysical Exploration Services Company—AGESCO: POB 84224, Airport Rd, Tripoli, Libya; tel. (21) 4804863; fax (21) 4803199; f. 1985; auth. cap. 12m. Libyan dinars; Gen. Man. AYAD HUSSEIN AD-DALI.

Arab Well Logging Company—AWLCO: POB 6225, Baghdad, Iraq; tel. (1) 541-8259; f. 1983; provides well-logging services and data interpretation; auth. cap. 7m. Iraqi dinars.

Arab Petroleum Training Institute—APTI: POB 6037, Al-Tajeyat, Baghdad, Iraq; tel. (1) 523-4100; fax (1) 521-0526; f. 1978 to provide instruction in many technical and managerial aspects of the oil industry. From Dec. 1994 the Institute was placed under the trusteeship of the Iraqi Government; the arrangement was scheduled to come to an end in Dec. 1998. Dir HAZIM A. AS-SULTAN.

Arab Shipbuilding and Repair Yard Company—ASRY: POB 50110, Hidd, Bahrain; tel. 671111; fax 670236; e-mail asryco@batel-co.com.bh; internet www.asry.net; f. 1974 to undertake repairs and servicing of vessels; operates a 500,000 dwt dry dock in Bahrain; two floating docks operational since 1992; cap. (auth. and subs.) US $340m. Chair. Sheikh DAIJ BIN KHALIFA AL-KHALIFA; Chief Exec. MOHAMED M. AL-KHATEEB.

ORGANIZATION OF THE BLACK SEA ECONOMIC CO-OPERATION—BSEC

Address: İstinye Cad. Müşir Fuad Paşa Yalısı, Eski Tersane 80860 İstinye-İstanbul, Turkey.

Telephone: (212) 229-63-30; **fax:** (212) 229-63-36; **e-mail:** bsec@turk.net; **internet:** www.bsec.gov.tr.

The Black Sea Economic Co-operation (BSEC) was established in 1992 to strengthen regional co-operation, particularly in the field of economic development. In June 1998, at a summit meeting held in Yalta, Ukraine, participating countries signed the BSEC Charter, thereby officially elevating the BSEC to regional organization status. The Charter entered into force on 1 May 1999, at which time the BSEC formally became the Organization of the Black Sea Economic Co-operation, retaining the same acronym.

MEMBERS

Albania	Georgia	Russia
Armenia	Greece	Turkey
Azerbaijan	Moldova	Ukraine
Bulgaria	Romania	

Note: Observer status has been granted to Austria, Egypt, France, Germany, Israel, Italy, Poland, Slovakia and Tunisia. The BSEC Business Council, International Black Sea Club, and the Energy Charter Conference also have observer status. Iran, the former Yugoslav republic of Macedonia, the Federal Republic of Yugoslavia and Uzbekistan have applied for full membership.

Organization

(April 2001)

PRESIDENTIAL SUMMIT

The Presidential Summit, comprising heads of state or government of member states, represents the highest authority of the body.

COUNCIL

The Council of Ministers of Foreign Affairs is BSEC's principal decision-making organ. Ministers meet at least once a year to review progress and to define new objectives.

PARLIAMENTARY ASSEMBLY

The Parliamentary Assembly, consisting of the representatives of the national parliaments of member states, was created in February 1993 to provide a legal basis for the implementation of decisions within the BSEC framework. It comprises three committees concerning economic, commercial, technological and environmental affairs; legal and political affairs; and cultural, educational and social affairs.

PERMANENT INTERNATIONAL SECRETARIAT

The Secretariat commenced operations in March 1994. Its tasks are, primarily, of an administrative and technical nature, and include the maintenance of archives, and the preparation and distribution of documentation.

Secretary-General: VALERI CHECHELASHVILI (Georgia).

Activities

In June 1992, at a summit meeting held in İstanbul, heads of state and of government signed the summit declaration on BSEC, and adopted the Bosphorus statement, which established a regional structure for economic co-operation. The grouping attained regional organization status in May 1999 (see above). The organization's main areas of co-operation include transport and communications; information technology; the standardization and certification of products; energy; the mining and processing of raw materials; tourism; agriculture and agro-industry; health care and pharmaceuticals; sustainable development; environmental protection; and science and technology. In order to promote regional co-operation, the organization also aims to strengthen the business environment by providing support for small and medium-sized enterprises; facilitating closer contacts between businesses in member countries; progressively eliminating obstacles to the expansion of trade; creating appropriate conditions for investment and industrial co-operation, in particular through the avoidance of double taxation and the promotion and protection of investments; encouraging the dissemination of information concerning international tenders organized by member states; and promoting economic co-operation in free-trade zones.

A BSEC Business Council was established in İstanbul in December 1992 by the business communities of member states. It has observer status at the BSEC, and aims to identify private and public investment projects, maintain business contacts and develop programmes in various sectors. A Black Sea Trade and Development Bank was inaugurated in early 1998, in Thessaloniki, Greece, as the organization's main funding institution, to finance and implement joint regional projects. It began operations on 1 July 1999. The European Bank for Reconstruction and Development (EBRD, see p. 176) was entrusted as the depository for all capital payments made prior to its establishment. A BSEC Co-ordination Centre,

located in Ankara, Turkey, aims to promote the exchange of statistical and economic information. In September 1998 a Black Sea International Studies Centre was inaugurated in Athens, Greece, in order to undertake research concerning the BSEC, in the fields of economics, industry and technology. The transport ministers of BSEC member states adopted a Transport Action Plan in March 2001, which envisaged reducing the disparities in regional transport systems and integrating the BSEC regional transport infrastructure with wider international networks and projects.

A Black Sea Environment Programme (BSEP), funded by the Global Environment Facility (q.v., managed jointly by UNDP, UNEP and the World Bank) and the European Union, was launched in 1993 and terminated in January 1998. A Strategic Action Plan for the Rehabilitation and Protection of the Black Sea (BSSAP), formulated by the BSEP and also to be supported by the Global Environment Facility, was signed by Bulgaria, Georgia, Romania, Russia, Turkey and Ukraine in October 1996. It was envisaged that the BSSAP would be implemented by the permanent secretariat of the Commission of the Convention on the Protection of the Black Sea against Pollution; by early 2001, however, this had not yet been established owing to financial constraints, and so the BSSAP was being co-ordinated by a temporary programme implementation unit.

ORGANIZATION OF THE ISLAMIC CONFERENCE—OIC

Address: Kilo 6, Mecca Rd, POB 178, Jeddah 21411, Saudi Arabia.
Telephone: (2) 680-0800; **fax:** (2) 687-3568; **e-mail:** info@oic-oci.org; **internet:** www.oic-oci.org.

The Organization was formally established in May 1971, when its Secretariat became operational, following a summit meeting of Muslim heads of state at Rabat, Morocco, in September 1969, and the Islamic Foreign Ministers' Conference in Jeddah in March 1970, and in Karachi, Pakistan, in December 1970.

MEMBERS

Afghanistan*	Indonesia	Palestine
Albania	Iran	Qatar
Algeria	Iraq	Saudi Arabia
Azerbaijan	Jordan	Senegal
Bahrain	Kazakhstan	Sierra Leone
Bangladesh	Kuwait	Somalia
Benin	Kyrgyzstan	Sudan
Brunei	Lebanon	Suriname
Burkina Faso	Libya	Syria
Cameroon	Malaysia	Tajikistan
Chad	Maldives	Togo
The Comoros	Mali	Tunisia
Djibouti	Mauritania	Turkey
Egypt	Morocco	Turkmenistan
Gabon	Mozambique	Uganda
The Gambia	Niger	United Arab
Guinea	Nigeria†	Emirates
Guinea-Bissau	Oman	Uzbekistan
Guyana	Pakistan	Yemen

* Afghanistan's membership of the OIC was suspended in 1996, following the occupation of that country's capital, Kabul, by the Taliban.
† Nigeria renounced its membership in May 1991; however, the OIC has not formally recognized this decision.

Note: Observer status has been granted to Bosnia and Herzegovina, the Central African Republic, Côte d'Ivoire, Thailand, the Muslim community of the 'Turkish Republic of Northern Cyprus', the Moro National Liberation Front (MNLF) of the southern Philippines, the United Nations, the Non-Aligned Movement, the League of Arab States, the Organization of African Unity, the Economic Co-operation Organization, the Union of the Arab Maghreb and the Co-operation Council for the Arab States of the Gulf.

Organization
(April 2001)

SUMMIT CONFERENCES

The supreme body of the Organization is the Conference of Heads of State, which met in 1969 at Rabat, Morocco, in 1974 at Lahore,

Pakistan, and in January 1981 at Mecca, Saudi Arabia, when it was decided that summit conferences would be held every three years in future. Ninth Conference: Doha, Qatar, November 2000.

CONFERENCE OF MINISTERS OF FOREIGN AFFAIRS

Conferences take place annually, to consider the means for implementing the general policy of the Organization, although they may also be convened for extraordinary sessions.

SECRETARIAT

The executive organ of the Organization, headed by a Secretary-General (who is elected by the Conference of Ministers of Foreign Affairs for a four-year term, renewable only once) and four Assistant Secretaries-General (similarly appointed).
Secretary-General: Dr ABDELOUAHED BELKEZIZ (Morocco).

At the summit conference in January 1981 it was decided that an International Islamic Court of Justice should be established to adjudicate in disputes between Muslim countries. Experts met in January 1983 to draw up a constitution for the court; however, by early 2001 it was not yet in operation.

SPECIALIZED COMMITTEES

Al-Quds Committee: f. 1975 to implement the resolutions of the Islamic Conference on the status of Jerusalem (Al-Quds); it meets at the level of foreign ministers; maintains the Al-Quds Fund; Chair. King MUHAMMAD VI of Morocco.

Standing Committee for Economic and Commercial Co-operation (COMCEC): f. 1981; Chair. AHMET NECDET SEZER; (Pres. of Turkey).

Standing Committee for Information and Cultural Affairs (COMIAC): f. 1981. Chair. ABDOULAYE WADE (Pres. of Senegal).

Standing Committee for Scientific and Technological Co-operation (COMSTECH): f. 1981; Chair. MOHAMMAD RAFIQ TARAR (Pres. of Pakistan).

Islamic Commission for Economic, Cultural and Social Affairs: f. 1976.

Islamic Peace Committee.

Permanent Finance Committee.

Other committees comprise the Committee of Islamic Solidarity with the Peoples of the Sahel, the Six-Member Committee on the Situation of Muslims in the Philippines, the Six-Member Committee on Palestine, the *ad hoc* Committee on Afghanistan, and the OIC contact groups on Bosnia and Herzegovina, and Kosovo; Jammu and Kashmir; and Sierra Leone.

Activities

The Organization's aims, as proclaimed in the Charter that was adopted in 1972, are:

(i) To promote Islamic solidarity among member states;

(ii) To consolidate co-operation among member states in the economic, social, cultural, scientific and other vital fields, and to arrange consultations among member states belonging to international organizations;

(iii) To endeavour to eliminate racial segregation and discrimination and to eradicate colonialism in all its forms;

(iv) To take necessary measures to support international peace and security founded on justice;

(v) To co-ordinate all efforts for the safeguard of the Holy Places and support of the struggle of the people of Palestine, and help them to regain their rights and liberate their land;

(vi) To strengthen the struggle of all Muslim people with a view to safeguarding their dignity, independence and national rights; and

(vii) To create a suitable atmosphere for the promotion of co-operation and understanding among member states and other countries.

The first summit conference of Islamic leaders (representing 24 states) took place in 1969 following the burning of the Al Aqsa Mosque in Jerusalem. At this conference it was decided that Islamic governments should 'consult together with a view to promoting close co-operation and mutual assistance in the economic, scientific, cultural and spiritual fields, inspired by the immortal teachings of Islam'. Thereafter the foreign ministers of the countries concerned met annually, and adopted the Charter of the Organization of the Islamic Conference in 1972.

At the second Islamic summit conference (Lahore, Pakistan, 1974), the Islamic Solidarity Fund was established, together with a committee of representatives which later evolved into the Islamic Commission for Economic, Cultural and Social Affairs. Subsequently, numerous other subsidiary bodies have been set up (see below).

ECONOMIC CO-OPERATION

A general agreement for economic, technical and commercial co-operation came into force in 1981, providing for the establishment of joint investment projects and trade co-ordination. This was followed by an agreement on promotion, protection and guarantee of investments among member states. A plan of action to strengthen economic co-operation was adopted at the third Islamic summit conference in 1981, aiming to promote collective self-reliance and the development of joint ventures in all sectors. In May 1993 the OIC committee for economic and commercial co-operation, meeting in İstanbul, agreed to review and update the 1981 plan of action.

A meeting of ministers of industry was held in February 1982, and agreed to promote industrial co-operation, including joint ventures in agricultural machinery, engineering and other basic industries. The fifth summit conference, held in 1987, approved proposals for joint development of modern technology, and for improving scientific and technical skills in the less developed Islamic countries. In December 1988 it was announced that a committee of experts, established by the OIC, was to draw up a 10-year programme of assistance to developing countries (mainly in Africa) in science and technology.

In 1991 22 OIC member states signed a framework agreement concerning the introduction of a system of trade preferences among member states. It was envisaged that, if implemented, this would represent the first step towards the eventual establishment of an Islamic common market. In 2000 an OIC group of experts was considering the implications of the proposed creation of such a common market.

CULTURAL CO-OPERATION

The Organization supports education in Muslim communities throughout the world, and was instrumental in the establishment of Islamic universities in Niger and Uganda (see below). It organizes seminars on various aspects of Islam, and encourages dialogue with the other monotheistic religions. Support is given to publications on Islam both in Muslim and Western countries.

HUMANITARIAN ASSISTANCE

Assistance is given to Muslim communities affected by wars and natural disasters, in co-operation with UN organizations, particularly UNHCR. The countries of the Sahel region (Burkina Faso, Cape Verde, Chad, The Gambia, Guinea, Guinea-Bissau, Mali, Mauritania, Niger and Senegal) receive particular attention as victims of drought. In April 1993 member states pledged US $80m. in emergency assistance for Muslims affected by the war in Bosnia and Herzegovina (see below for details of subsequent assistance). In April 1999 the OIC resolved to send humanitarian aid to assist the displaced ethnic Albanian population of Kosovo and Metohija, in southern Serbia. During 2000 several member states were providing humanitarian assistance to the Muslim population affected by the ongoing conflict in Chechnya.

POLITICAL CO-OPERATION

Since its inception the OIC has called for vacation of Arab territories by Israel, recognition of the rights of Palestinians and of the Palestine Liberation Organization (PLO) as their sole legitimate representative, and the restoration of Jerusalem to Arab rule. The 1981 summit conference called for a *jihad* (holy war—though not necessarily in a military sense) 'for the liberation of Jerusalem and the occupied territories'; this was to include an Islamic economic boycott of Israel. In 1982 Islamic ministers of foreign affairs decided to establish Islamic offices for boycotting Israel and for military co-operation with the PLO. The 1984 summit conference agreed to reinstate Egypt (suspended following the peace treaty signed with Israel in 1979) as a member of the OIC, although the resolution was opposed by seven states.

The fifth summit conference, held in January 1987, discussed the continuing Iran–Iraq war, and agreed that the Islamic Peace Committee should attempt to prevent the sale of military equipment to the parties in the conflict. The conference also discussed the conflicts in Chad and Lebanon, and requested the holding of a United Nations conference to define international terrorism, as opposed to legitimate fighting for freedom.

In August 1990 a majority of ministers of foreign affairs condemned Iraq's recent invasion of Kuwait, and demanded the withdrawal of Iraqi forces. In August 1991 the Conference of Ministers of Foreign Affairs obstructed Iraq's attempt to propose a resolution demanding the repeal of economic sanctions against the country. The sixth summit conference, held in Senegal in December 1991, reflected the divisions in the Arab world that resulted from Iraq's invasion of Kuwait and the ensuing war. Twelve heads of state did not attend, reportedly to register protest at the presence of Jordan and the PLO at the conference, both of which had given support to Iraq. Disagreement also arose between the PLO and the majority of other OIC members when a proposal was adopted to cease the OIC's support for the PLO's *jihad* in the Arab territories occupied by Israel, in an attempt to further the Middle East peace negotiations.

In August 1992 the UN General Assembly approved a non-binding resolution, introduced by the OIC, that requested the UN Security Council to take increased action, including the use of force, in order to defend the non-Serbian population of Bosnia and Herzegovina (some 43% of Bosnians being Muslims) from Serbian aggression, and to restore its 'territorial integrity'. The OIC Conference of Ministers of Foreign Affairs, which was held in Jeddah, Saudi Arabia, in December, demanded anew that the UN Security Council take all necessary measures against Serbia and Montenegro, including military intervention, in accordance with Article 42 of the UN Charter, in order to protect the Bosnian Muslims. In February 1993 the OIC appealed to the Security Council to remove the embargo on armaments to Bosnia and Herzegovina with regard to the Bosnian Muslims, to allow them to defend themselves from the Bosnian Serbs, who were far better armed.

A report by an OIC fact-finding mission, which in February 1993 visited Azad Kashmir while investigating allegations of repression of the largely Muslim population of the Indian state of Jammu and Kashmir by the Indian armed forces, was presented to the 1993 Conference. The meeting urged member states to take the necessary measures to persuade India to cease the 'massive human rights violations' in Jammu and Kashmir and to allow the Indian Kashmiris to 'exercise their inalienable right to self-determination'. In September 1994 ministers of foreign affairs, meeting in Islamabad, Pakistan, urged the Indian Government to grant permission for an OIC fact-finding mission, and for other human rights groups, to visit Jammu and Kashmir (which it had continually refused to do) and to refrain from human rights violations of the Kashmiri people. The ministers agreed to establish a contact group on Jammu and Kashmir, which was to provide a mechanism for promoting international awareness of the situation in that region and for seeking a peaceful solution to the dispute. In December OIC heads of state approved a resolution condemning reported human rights abuses by Indian security forces in Kashmir.

In July 1994 the OIC Secretary-General visited Afghanistan and proposed the establishment of a preparatory mechanism to promote national reconciliation in that country. In mid-1995 Saudi Arabia, acting as a representative of the OIC, pursued a peace initiative for Afghanistan and issued an invitation for leaders of the different factions to hold negotiations in Jeddah.

A special ministerial meeting on Bosnia and Herzegovina was held in July 1993, at which seven OIC countries committed themselves to making available up to 17,000 troops to serve in the UN Protection Force in the former Yugoslavia (UNPROFOR). The meeting also decided to dispatch immediately a ministerial mission to persuade influential governments to support the OIC's demands for the removal of the arms embargo on Bosnian Muslims and the convening of a restructured international conference to bring about a political solution to the conflict. At the end of September 1994 ministers of foreign affairs of nine countries constituting the OIC contact group on Bosnia and Herzegovina, meeting in New York, resolved to prepare an assessment document on the issue, and to establish an alliance with its Western counterpart (comprising France, Germany, Russia, the United Kingdom and the USA). The two groups met in Geneva, Switzerland, in January 1995. In December 1994 OIC heads of state, convened in Morocco, proclaimed that the UN arms embargo on Bosnia and Herzegovina could not be applied to the Muslim authorities of that Republic. The Conference also resolved to review economic relations between OIC member states and any country that supported Serbian activities. An aid fund was established, to which member states were requested to contribute between US $500,000 and US $5m., in order to provide further humanitarian and economic assistance to Bosnian Muslims. In relation to wider concerns the conference adopted a Code of Conduct for Combating International Terrorism, in an attempt to control Muslim extremist groups. The code commits states to ensuring that militant groups do not use their territory for planning or executing terrorist activity against other states, in addition to states refraining from direct support or participation in acts of terrorism. In a further resolution the OIC supported the decision by Iraq to recognize Kuwait, but advocated that Iraq comply with all UN Security Council decisions.

In July 1995 the OIC contact group on Bosnia and Herzegovina (at that time comprising Egypt, Iran, Malaysia, Morocco, Pakistan, Saudi Arabia, Senegal and Turkey), meeting in Geneva, declared the UN arms embargo against Bosnia and Herzegovina to be 'invalid'. Several Governments subsequently announced their willingness officially to supply weapons and other military assistance to the Bosnian Muslim forces. In September a meeting of all OIC ministers of defence and foreign affairs endorsed the establishment of an 'assistance mobilization group' which was to supply military, economic, legal and other assistance to Bosnia and Herzegovina. In a joint declaration the ministers also demanded the return of all territory seized by Bosnian Serb forces, the continued NATO bombing of Serb military targets, and that the city of Sarajevo be preserved under a Muslim-led Bosnian Government. In November the OIC Secretary-General endorsed the peace accord for the former Yugoslavia, which was concluded, in Dayton, USA, by leaders of all the conflicting factions, and reaffirmed the commitment of Islamic states to participate in efforts to implement the accord. In the following month the OIC Conference of Ministers of Foreign Affairs, convened in Conakry, Guinea, requested the full support of the international community to reconstruct Bosnia and Herzegovina through humanitarian aid as well as economic and technical co-operation. Ministers declared that Palestine and the establishment of fully-autonomous Palestinian control of Jerusalem were issues of central importance for the Muslim world. The Conference urged the removal of all aspects of occupation and the cessation of the construction of Israeli settlements in the occupied territories. In addition, the final statement of the meeting condemned Armenian aggression against Azerbaijan, registered concern at the persisting civil conflict in Afghanistan, demanded the elimination of all weapons of mass destruction and pledged support for Libya (affected by the US trade embargo).

In December 1996 OIC ministers of foreign affairs, meeting in Jakarta, Indonesia, urged the international community to apply pressure on Israel in order to ensure its implementation of the terms of the Middle East peace process. The ministers reaffirmed the importance of ensuring that the provisions of the Dayton Peace Agreement for the former Yugoslavia were fully implemented, called for a peaceful settlement of the Kashmir issue, demanded that Iraq fulfil its obligations for the establishment of security, peace and stability in the region and proposed that an international conference on peace and national reconciliation in Somalia be convened. The ministers elected a new Secretary-General, Azeddine Laraki, who confirmed that the organization would continue to develop its role as an international mediator. In March 1997, at an extraordinary summit held in Pakistan, OIC heads of state and of government reiterated the organization's objective of increasing international pressure on Israel to ensure the full implementation of the terms of the Middle East peace process. An 'Islamabad Declaration' was also adopted, which pledged to increase co-operation between members of the OIC. In June the OIC condemned the decision by the US House of Representatives to recognize Jerusalem as the Israeli capital. The Secretary-General of the OIC issued a statement rejecting the US decision as counter to the role of the USA as sponsor of the Middle East peace plan. In December OIC heads of state attended the eighth summit conference, held in Iran. The Tehran Declaration, issued at the end of the conference, demanded the 'liberation' of the Israeli-occupied territories and the creation of an autonomous Palestinian state. The conference also appealed for a cessation of the conflicts in Afghanistan, and between Armenia and Azerbaijan. It was requested that the UN sanctions against Libya be removed and that the US legislation threatening sanctions against foreign companies investing in certain countries (including Iran and Libya), introduced in July 1996, be dismissed as invalid. In addition, the Declaration encouraged the increased participation of women in OIC activities.

In early 1998 the OIC appealed for an end to the threat of US-led military action against Iraq arising from a dispute regarding access granted to international weapons inspectors. The crisis was averted by an agreement concluded between the Iraqi authorities and the UN Secretary-General in February. In March OIC ministers of foreign affairs, meeting in Doha, Qatar, requested an end to the international sanctions against Iraq. Additionally, the ministers urged all states to end the process of restoring normal trading and diplomatic relations with Israel pending that country's withdrawal from the occupied territories and acceptance of an independent Palestinian state. In April the OIC, jointly with the UN, sponsored new peace negotiations between the main disputing factions in Afghanistan, which were conducted in Islamabad, Pakistan. In early May, however, the talks collapsed and were postponed indefinitely. In September the Secretaries-General of the OIC and UN agreed to establish a joint mission to counter the deteriorating security situation along the Afghan–Iranian border, following the large-scale deployment of Taliban troops in the region and consequent military manoeuvres by the Iranian authorities. They also reiterated the need to proceed with negotiations to conclude a peaceful settlement in Afghanistan.In December the OIC appealed for a diplomatic solution to the tensions arising from Iraq's withdrawal of co-operation with UN weapons inspectors, and criticized subsequent military air-strikes, led by the USA, as having been conducted without renewed UN authority.

In early April 1999 ministers of foreign affairs of the countries comprising OIC's contact group met to consider the crisis in Kosovo. The meeting condemned Serbian atrocities being committed against the local Albanian population and urged the provision of international assistance for the thousands of people displaced by the conflict. The group resolved to establish a committee to co-ordinate relief aid provided by member states. The ministers also expressed their willingness to help to formulate a peaceful settlement and to participate in any subsequent implementation force. In June an OIC Parliamentary Union was inaugurated: its founding conference was convened in Tehran, Iran.

In early March 2000 the OIC mediated contacts between the parties to the conflict in Afghanistan, with a view to reviving peace negotiations. Talks, held under OIC auspices, ensued in May. In November OIC heads of state attended the ninth summit conference, held in Doha, Qatar. In view of the significant deterioration in relations between Israel and the Palestinian Authority during late 2000, the summit issued a Declaration pledging solidarity with the Palestinian cause and accusing the Israeli authorities of implementing large-scale systematic violations of human rights against Palestinians. The summit also issued the Doha Declaration, which reaffirmed commitment to the OIC Charter and undertook to modernize the organization's organs and mechanisms. Both the elected Government of Afghanistan and the Taliban sent delegations to the Doha conference. The summit determined that Afghanistan's official participation in the OIC, suspended in 1996, should not yet be reinstated.

Finance

The OIC's activities are financed by mandatory contributions from member states. The budget for 2000/01 totalled US $11.4m.

SUBSIDIARY ORGANS

Islamic Centre for the Development of Trade: Complexe Commercial des Habous, ave des FAR, BP 13545, Casablanca, Morocco; tel. (2) 314974; fax (2) 310110; e-mail icdt@icdt.org; internet www.icdt.org; f. 1983 to encourage regular commercial contacts, harmonize policies and promote investments among OIC mems. Dir-Gen. RACHDI ALLAL. Publs *Tijaris: International and Inter-Islamic Trade Magazine* (quarterly), *Inter-Islamic Trade Report* (annually).

Islamic Institute of Technology (IIT): GPO Box 3003, Board Bazar, Gazipur 1704, Dhaka, Bangladesh; tel. (2) 980-0960;fax (2) 980-0970; e-mail dg@iit.dhaka.edu; internet www.iitoic-dhaka.edu; f. 1981 to develop human resources in OIC mem. states, with special reference to engineering, technology, tech. and vocational education and research; 224 staff and 1,000 students; library of 23,000 vols. Dir-Gen. Prof. Dr M. ANWAR HOSSAIN. Publs *News Bulletin* (annually), annual calendar and announcement for admission, reports, human resources development series.

Islamic Jurisprudence Academy: Jeddah, Saudi Arabia; f. 1982. Sec.-Gen. Sheikh MOHAMED HABIB BELKHOJAH.

Islamic Solidarity Fund: c/o OIC Secretariat, POB 178, Jeddah 21411, Saudi Arabia; tel. (2) 680-0800; fax (2) 687-3568; f. 1974 to meet the needs of Islamic communities by providing emergency aid and the finance to build mosques, Islamic centres, hospitals, schools and universities. Chair. Sheikh NASIR ABDULLAH BIN HAMDAN; Exec. Dir ABDULLAH HERSI.

Islamic University of Niger: BP 11507, Niamey, Niger; tel. 723903; fax 733796; f. 1984; provides courses of study in *Shari'a* (Islamic law) and Arabic language and literature; also offers courses in pedagogy and teacher training; receives grants from Islamic Solidarity Fund and contributions from OIC member states. Rector Prof. ABDELALI OUDHRIRI.

Islamic University in Uganda: POB 2555, Mbale, Uganda; tel. (45) 33502; fax (45) 34452; e-mail iuiu@info.com.co.ug; Kampala Liaison Office: POB 7689, Kampala; tel. (41) 236874; fax (41) 254576; f. 1988 to meet the educational needs of Muslim populations in English-speaking African countries; mainly financed by OIC. Principal Officer Prof. MAHDI ADAMU.

Research Centre for Islamic History, Art and Culture (IRCICA): POB 24, Beşiktaş 80692, İstanbul, Turkey; tel. (212) 2591742; fax (212) 2584365; e-mail ircica@superonline.com; internet www.ircica.org; f. 1980; library of 50,000 vols. Dir-Gen. Prof. Dr EKMELEDDÍN İHSANOĞLU. Publs *Newsletter* (3 a year), monographical studies.

Statistical, Economic and Social Research and Training Centre for the Islamic Countries: Attar Sok 4, GOP 06700, Ankara, Turkey; tel. (312) 4686172; fax (312) 4673458; e-mail sesrtcic@tr-net.net.tr; internet www.sesrtcic.org; f. 1978. Dir-Gen. ERDINÇ ERDÜN.

SPECIALIZED INSTITUTIONS

International Islamic News Agency (IINA): King Khalid Palace, Madinah Rd, POB 5054, Jeddah, Saudi Arabia; tel. (2) 665-8561; fax (2) 665-9358; e-mail iina@ogertel.com; internet www.islamicnews.org; f. 1972. Dir-Gen. ABDULWAHAB KASHIF.

Islamic Educational, Scientific and Cultural Organization (ISESCO): Ave Attine, Hay Ryad, BP 2275, Rabat 10104, Morocco; tel. (7) 772433; fax (7) 777459; e-mail cid@isesco.org.ma; internet www.isesco.org.ma; f. 1982. Dir-Gen. Dr ABDULAZIZ BIN OTHMAN AL-TWAIJRI. Publs *ISESCO Newsletter* (quarterly), *Islam Today* (2 a year), *ISESCO Triennial*.

Islamic States Broadcasting Organization (ISBO): POB 6351, Jeddah 21442, Saudi Arabia; tel. (2) 672-1121; fax (2) 672-2600; f. 1975. Sec.-Gen. HUSSEIN AL-ASKARY.

AFFILIATED INSTITUTIONS

International Association of Islamic Banks (IAIB): King Abdulaziz St, Queen's Bldg, 23rd Floor, Al-Balad Dist, POB 23425, Jeddah 21426, Saudi Arabia; tel. (2) 643-1276; fax (2) 644-7239; f. 1977 to link financial institutions operating on Islamic banking principles; activities include training and research; mems: 192 banks and other financial institutions in 34 countries. Sec.-Gen. SAMIR A. SHAIKH.

Islamic Chamber of Commerce and Industry: POB 3831, Clifton, Karachi 75600, Pakistan; tel. (21) 5874756; fax (21) 5870765; e-mail icci@icci-oic.org; internet www.icci.org.pk/islamic/main.html; f. 1979 to promote trade and industry among member states; comprises nat. chambers or feds of chambers of commerce and industry. Sec.-Gen. AQEEL AHMAD AL-JASSEM.

Islamic Committee for the International Crescent: c/o OIC, Kilo 6, Mecca Rd, POB 178, Jeddah 21411, Saudi Arabia; tel. (2) 680-0800; fax (2) 687-3568; f. 1979 to attempt to alleviate the suffering caused by natural disasters and war. Sec.-Gen. Dr AHMAD ABDALLAH CHERIF.

Islamic Solidarity Sports Federation: POB 6040, Riyadh 11442, Saudi Arabia; tel. and fax (1) 482-2145; f. 1981. Sec.-Gen. Dr MOHAMMAD SALEH GAZDAR.

Organization of Islamic Capitals and Cities—OICC: POB 13621, Jeddah 21414, Saudi Arabia; tel. (2) 698-1953; fax (2) 698-1053; e-mail oiccorg@icc.net.sa; f. 1980 to promote and develop co-operation among OICC mems, to preserve their character and heritage, to implement planning guide-lines for the growth of Islamic cities and to upgrade standards of public services and utilities in those cities. Sec.-Gen. OMAR ABDULLAH KADI.

Organization of the Islamic Shipowners' Association: POB 14900, Jeddah 21434, Saudi Arabia; tel. (2) 663-7882; fax (2) 660-4920; e-mail oisa@sbm.net.sa; f. 1981 to promote co-operation among maritime cos in Islamic countries. In 1998 mems approved the establishment of a new commercial venture, the Bakkah Shipping Company, to enhance sea transport in the region. Sec.-Gen. Dr ABDULLATIF A. SULTAN.

ORGANIZATION OF THE PETROLEUM EXPORTING COUNTRIES—OPEC

Address: Obere Donaustrasse 93, 1020 Vienna, Austria.

Telephone: (1) 211-12-279; **fax:** (1) 214-98-27; **e-mail:** info@opec.org; **internet:** www.opec.org.

OPEC was established in 1960 to link countries whose main source of export earnings is petroleum; it aims to unify and co-ordinate members' petroleum policies and to safeguard their interests generally. The OPEC Fund for International Development is described on p. 273.

OPEC's share of world petroleum production was 40.8% in 1999 (compared with 44.7% in 1980 and 54.7% in 1974). It is estimated that OPEC members possess more than 75% of the world's known reserves of crude petroleum, of which about two-thirds are in the Middle East. In 1999 OPEC members possessed about 43.2% of known reserves of natural gas.

MEMBERS

Algeria	Kuwait	Saudi Arabia
Indonesia	Libya	United Arab Emirates
Iran	Nigeria	Venezuela
Iraq	Qatar	

Organization

(April 2001)

CONFERENCE

The Conference is the supreme authority of the Organization, responsible for the formulation of its general policy. It consists of representatives of member countries, who examine reports and recommendations submitted by the Board of Governors. It approves the appointment of Governors from each country and elects the Chairman of the Board of Governors. It works on the unanimity principle, and meets at least twice a year.

BOARD OF GOVERNORS

The Board directs the management of the Organization; it implements resolutions of the Conference and draws up an annual budget. It consists of one governor for each member country, and meets at least twice a year.

MINISTERIAL MONITORING COMMITTEE

The Committee (f. 1988) is responsible for monitoring price evolution and ensuring the stability of the world petroleum market. As such, it is charged with the preparation of long-term strategies, including the allocation of quotas to be presented to the Conference. The Committee consists of all national representatives, and is normally convened four times a year. A Ministerial Monitoring Sub-committee, reporting to the Committee on production and supply figures, was established in 1993.

ECONOMIC COMMISSION

A specialized body operating within the framework of the Secretariat, with a view to assisting the Organization in promoting stability in international prices for petroleum at equitable levels; consists of a Board, national representatives and a commission staff; meets at least twice a year.

SECRETARIAT

Secretary-General: Dr ALÍ RODRÍGUEZ ARAQUE (Venezuela).

Research Division: comprises three departments:

Data Services Department: Maintains and expands information services to support the research activities of the Secretariat and those of member countries; collects, collates and analyses statistical information and provides essential data for forecasts and estimates necessary for OPEC medium- and long-term strategies.

Energy Studies Department: Energy Section monitors, forecasts and analyses developments in the energy and petrochemical industries and their implications for OPEC, and prepares forecasts of demands for OPEC petroleum and gas. Petroleum Section assists the Board of the Economic Commission in determining the relative values of OPEC crude petroleum and gases and in developing alternative methodologies for this purpose.

Economics and Finance Department: Comprises the Economics Section and a Finance Section. Analyses and reports on economic and financial developments relevant to the world energy market and the deliberations of the Economic Commission Board and the Conference, including world trade, international monetary movements, Third World debt, the financial performance of petroleum companies and oil revenues of member states.

Division Director: Dr SHOKRI M. GHANEM (Libya).

Administration and Human Resources Department: Responsible for all organization methods, provision of administrative services for all meetings, personnel matters, budgets, accounting and internal control; reviews general administrative policies and industrial relations practised throughout the oil industry; **Head:** Dr TALAL DEHRAB (Kuwait).

Public Relations and Information Department: Concerned with communicating OPEC objectives, decisions and actions; produces and distributes a number of publications, films, slides and tapes; and disseminates news of general interest regarding the Organization and member countries on energy and other related issues. Operates a daily on-line news service, the OPEC News Agency (OPECNA). An OPEC Library contains an extensive collection of energy-related publications; **Head:** FAROUK U. MUHAMMED (Nigeria).

Legal Office: Provides legal advice, supervises the Secretariat's legal commitments, evaluates legal issues of concern to the Organization and member countries, and recommends appropriate action; **Legal Officer:** DOLORES DOBARRO DE TORRES (Venezuela).

Office of the Secretary-General: Provides the Secretary-General with executive assistance in maintaining contacts with governments, organizations and delegations, in matters of protocol and in the preparation for and co-ordination of meetings; **Officer-in-Charge:** DOLORES DOBARRO DE TORRES (Venezuela).

Record of Events

1960   The first OPEC Conference was held in Baghdad in September, attended by representatives from Iran, Iraq, Kuwait, Saudi Arabia and Venezuela.

1961   Second Conference, Caracas, January. Qatar was admitted to membership; a Board of Governors was formed and statutes agreed.

1962   Fourth Conference, Geneva, April and June. Protests were addressed to petroleum companies against price cuts introduced in August 1960. Indonesia and Libya were admitted to membership.

1965   In July the Conference reached agreement on a two-year joint production programme, implemented from 1965 to 1967, to limit annual growth in output to secure adequate prices.

1967   Abu Dhabi was admitted to membership.

1969   Algeria was admitted to membership.

1970   Twenty-first Conference, Caracas, December. Tax on income of petroleum companies was raised to 55%.

1971   A five-year agreement was concluded in February between the six producing countries in the Gulf and 23 international petroleum companies (Teheran Agreement). Nigeria was admitted to membership.

1972   In January petroleum companies agreed to adjust petroleum revenues of the largest producers after changes in currency exchange rates (Geneva Agreement).

1973   OPEC and petroleum companies concluded an agreement whereby posted prices of crude petroleum were raised by 11.9% and a mechanism was installed to make monthly adjustments to prices in future (Second Geneva Agreement). Negotiations with petroleum companies on revision of the Teheran Agreement collapsed in October, and the Gulf states unilaterally declared 70% increases in posted prices, from US $3.01 to $5.11 per barrel. In December the Conference resolved to increase the posted price by nearly 130%, to $11.65 per barrel, from 1 January 1974. Ecuador was admitted to full membership and Gabon became an associate member.

1974   As a result of Saudi opposition to the December price increase, prices were held at current level for first quarter (and subsequently for the remainder of 1974). Abu Dhabi's membership was transferred to the United Arab Emirates (UAE). A meeting in June increased royalties charged to petroleum companies from 12.5% to 14.5% in all member states except Saudi Arabia. A meeting in September increased gov-

ernmental take by about 3.5% through further increases in royalties on equity crude to 16.67% and in taxes to 65.65%, except in Saudi Arabia.

1975   OPEC's first summit meeting of heads of state or government was held in Algiers in March. Gabon was admitted to full membership. A ministerial meeting in September agreed to raise prices by 10% for the period until June 1976.

1976   The OPEC Fund for International Development was created in May. In December 11 member states endorsed a rise in basic prices of 10% as of 1 January 1977, and a further 5% rise as of 1 July 1977. However, Saudi Arabia and the UAE decided to raise their prices by 5% only.

1977   Following an earlier waiver by nine members of the 5% second stage of the price increase, Saudi Arabia and the UAE announced in July that they would both raise their prices by 5%. As a result, a single level of prices throughout the organization was restored. Because of continued disagreements between the 'moderates', led by Saudi Arabia and Iran, and the 'radicals', led by Algeria, Libya and Iraq, the Conference, held in December, was unable to settle on an increase in prices.

1978   The June Conference agreed that price levels should remain stable until the end of the year. In December it was decided to raise prices in four instalments, in order to compensate for the effects of the depreciation of the US dollar. These would bring a rise of 14.5% over nine months, but an average increase of 10% for 1979.

1979   At an extraordinary meeting in March members decided to raise prices by 9%. In June the Conference agreed minimum and maximum prices which seemed likely to add between 15% and 20% to import bills of consumer countries. The December Conference agreed in principle to convert the OPEC Fund into a development agency with its own legal personality.

1980   In June the Conference decided to set the price for a marker crude at US $32 per barrel, and that the value differentials which could be added above this ceiling (on account of quality and geographical location) should not exceed $5 per barrel. The planned OPEC summit meeting in Baghdad in November was postponed indefinitely because of the Iran–Iraq war, but the scheduled ministerial meeting went ahead in Bali in December, with both Iranians and Iraqis present. A ceiling price of $41 per barrel was fixed for premium crudes.

1981   In May attempts to achieve price reunification were made, but Saudi Arabia refused to increase its US $32 per barrel price unless the higher prices charged by other countries were lowered. Most of the other OPEC countries agreed to cut production by 10% so as to reduce the surplus. An emergency meeting in Geneva in August again failed to unify prices, although Saudi Arabia agreed to reduce production by 1m. barrels per day (b/d). In October OPEC countries agreed to increase the Saudi marker price to $34 per barrel, with a ceiling price of $38 per barrel.

1982   In March an emergency meeting of petroleum ministers was held in Vienna and agreed (for the first time in OPEC's history) to defend the Organization's price structure by imposing an overall production ceiling of 18m. b/d. At the same time Saudi Arabia announced a reduction in its own production to 7m. b/d. In December the Conference agreed to limit OPEC production to 18.5m. b/d in 1983 but postponed the allocation of national quotas pending consultations among the respective governments.

1983   In January an emergency meeting of petroleum ministers, fearing a collapse in world petroleum prices, decided to reduce the production ceiling to 17.5m. b/d, but failed to agree on individual production quotas or on adjustments to the differentials in prices charged for the high-quality crude petroleum produced by Algeria, Libya and Nigeria compared with that produced by the Gulf States. In February Nigeria cut its prices to US $30 per barrel, following a collapse in its production. To avoid a 'price war' OPEC set the official price of marker crude at $29 per barrel, and agreed to maintain existing price differentials at the level agreed on in March 1982, with the temporary exception that the differentials for Nigerian crudes should be $1 more than the price of the marker crude. It also agreed to maintain the production ceiling of 17.5m. b/d and allocated quotas for each member country except Saudi Arabia, which was to act as a 'swing producer' to supply the balancing quantities to meet market requirements.

1984   In October the production ceiling was lowered to 16m. b/d. In December price differentials for light (more expensive) and heavy (cheaper) crudes were slightly altered in an attempt to counteract price-cutting by non-OPEC producers, particularly Norway and the United Kingdom.

1985 In January members (except Algeria, Iran and Libya) effectively abandoned the marker price system. During the year production in excess of quotas by OPEC members, unofficial discounts and barter deals by members, and price cuts by non-members (such as Mexico, which had hitherto kept its prices in line with those of OPEC) contributed to a weakening of the market.

1986 During the first half of the year petroleum prices dropped to below US $10 per barrel. In April ministers agreed to set OPEC production at 16.7m. b/d for the third quarter of 1986 and at 17.3m. b/d for the fourth quarter. Algeria, Iran and Libya dissented. Discussions were also held with non-member countries (Angola, Egypt, Malaysia, Mexico and Oman), which agreed to co-operate in limiting production, although the United Kingdom declined. In August all members, with the exception of Iraq (which demanded to be allowed the same quota as Iran and, when this was denied it, refused to be a party to the agreement), agreed upon a return to production quotas, with the aim of cutting production to 14.8m. b/d (about 16.8m. b/d including Iraq's production) for the ensuing two months. This measure resulted in an increase in prices to about $15 per barrel, and was extended until the end of the year. In December members (with the exception of Iraq) agreed to return to a fixed pricing system at a level of $18 per barrel as the OPEC reference price, with effect from 1 February 1987. OPEC's total production for the first half 1987 was not to exceed 15.8m. b/d.

1987 In June, with prices having stabilized, the Conference decided that production during the third and fourth quarters of the year should be limited to 16.6m. b/d (including Iraq's production). However, total production continued to exceed the agreed levels. In December ministers decided to extend the existing agreement for the first half of 1988, although Iraq, once more, refused to participate.

1988 By March prices had fallen below US $15 per barrel. In April non-OPEC producers offered to reduce the volume of their petroleum exports by 5% if OPEC members would do the same. Saudi Arabia, however, refused to accept further reductions in production, insisting that existing quotas should first be more strictly enforced. In June the previous production limit (15.06m. b/d, excluding Iraq's production) was again renewed for six months, in the hope that increasing demand would be sufficient to raise prices. By October, however, petroleum prices were below $12 per barrel. In November a new agreement was reached, limiting total production (including that of Iraq) to 18.5m. b/d, with effect from 1 January 1989. Iran and Iraq finally agreed to accept identical quotas.

1989 In June (when prices had returned to about US $18 per barrel) ministers agreed to increase the production limit to 19.5m. b/d for the second half of 1989. However, Kuwait and the UAE indicated that they would not feel bound to observe this limit. In September the production limit was again increased, to 20.5m. b/d, and in November the limit for the first half of 1990 was increased to 22m. b/d.

1990 In May members resolved to adhere more strictly to the agreed production quotas, in response to a sharp decline in prices. By late June, however, it was reported that total production had decreased by only 400,000 b/d, and prices remained at about US $14 per barrel. In July Iraq threatened to take military action against Kuwait unless it reduced its petroleum production. In the same month OPEC members agreed to limit output to 22.5m. b/d. In August Iraq invaded Kuwait, and petroleum exports by the two countries were halted by an international embargo. Petroleum prices immediately increased to exceed $25 per barrel. Later in the month an informal consultative meeting of OPEC ministers placed the July agreement in abeyance, and permitted a temporary increase in production of petroleum, of between 3m. and 3.5m. b/d (mostly by Saudi Arabia, the UAE and Venezuela). In September and October prices fluctuated in response to political developments in the Gulf region, reaching a point in excess of $40 per barrel in early October, but falling to about $25 per barrel by the end of the month. In December a meeting of OPEC members voted to maintain the high levels of production and to reinstate the quotas that had been agreed in July, once the Gulf crisis was over. During the period August 1990–February 1991 Saudi Arabia increased its petroleum output from 5.4m. to 8.5m. b/d. Seven of the other OPEC states also produced in excess of their agreed quotas.

1991 In March, in an attempt to reach the target of a minimum reference price of US $21 per barrel, ministers agreed to reduce production from 23m. b/d to 22.3m. b/d, although Saudi Arabia refused to return to its pre-August 1990 quota.

In June ministers decided to maintain the ceiling of 22.3m. b/d into the third quarter of the year, since Iraq and Kuwait were still unable to export their petroleum. In September it was agreed that OPEC members' production for the last quarter of 1991 should be raised to 23.65m. b/d, and in November the OPEC Conference decided to maintain the increased production ceiling during the first quarter of 1992. From early November, however, the price of petroleum declined sharply, with demand less than anticipated as a result of continuing world recession and a mild winter in the northern hemisphere.

1992 The Ministerial Monitoring Committee, meeting in February, decided to impose a production ceiling of 22.98m. b/d with immediate effect. The agreement was, however, repudiated by both Saudi Arabia, which stated that it would not abide by its allocated quota of 7.9m. b/d, and Iran, unhappy that the production ceiling had not been set lower. In May it was agreed to continue the production restriction of 22.98m. b/d during the third quarter of 1992. Kuwait, which was resuming production in the wake of the extensive damage inflicted on its oil-wells by Iraq during the Gulf War, was granted a special dispensation to produce without a fixed quota. During the first half of 1992 member states' petroleum output consistently exceeded agreed levels, with Saudi Arabia and Iran (despite its stance on reducing production) the principal over-producers. In June, at the UN Conference on Environment and Development, OPEC's Secretary-General expressed its member countries' strong objections to the tax on fossil fuels (designed to reduce pollution) proposed by the EC. In September negotiations between OPEC ministers in Geneva were complicated by Iran's alleged annexation of Abu Musa and two other islands in the territorial waters of the UAE. However, agreement was reached on a production ceiling of 24.2m. b/d for the final quarter of 1992, in an attempt to raise the price of crude petroleum to the OPEC target of US $21 per barrel. At the Conference, held in late November, Ecuador formally resigned from OPEC, the first country ever to do so, citing as reasons the high membership fee and OPEC's refusal to increase Ecuador's quota. The meeting agreed to restrict production to 24.58m. b/d for the first quarter of 1993 (24.46m. b/d, excluding Ecuador).

1993 In mid-February a quota was set for Kuwait for the first time since the onset of the Gulf crisis. Kuwait agreed to produce 1.6m. b/d (400,000 less than current output) from 1 March, on the understanding that this would be substantially increased in the third quarter of the year. The quota for overall production from 1 March was set at 23.58m. b/d. A Ministerial Monitoring Sub-committee was established to supervise compliance with quotas. In June OPEC ministers decided to 'roll over' the overall quota of 23.58m. b/d into the third quarter of the year. However, Kuwait rejected its new allocation of 1.76m. b/d, demanding a quota of at least 2m. b/d. In July discussions between Iraq and the UN on the possible supervised sale of Iraqi petroleum depressed petroleum prices to below US $16 per barrel. The Monitoring Sub-committee urged member states to adhere to their production quotas (which were exceeded by a total of 1m. b/d in July). At the end of September an extraordinary meeting of the Conference agreed on a raised production ceiling of 24.52m. b/d, to be effective for six months from 1 October. Kuwait accepted a quota of 2m. b/d, which brought the country back into the production ceiling mechanism. Iran agreed on an allocation of 3.6m. b/d, while Saudi Arabia consented to freeze production at current levels, in order to support petroleum prices which remained persistently low. In November the Conference rejected any further reduction in production. Prices subsequently fell below $14, owing partly to a decision by Iraq to allow the UN to monitor its weapons programme (a move that would consequently lead to a repeal of the UN embargo on Iraqi petroleum exports).

1994 In March ministers opted to maintain the output quotas, agreed in September 1993, until the end of the year, and urged non-OPEC producers to freeze their production levels. (Iraq failed to endorse the agreement, since it recognizes only the production agreement adopted in July 1990.) At the meeting Saudi Arabia resisted a proposal from Iran and Nigeria, both severely affected by declines in petroleum revenue, to reduce its production by 1m. b/d in order to boost prices. In June the Conference endorsed the decision to maintain the existing production ceiling, and attempted to reassure commodity markets by implying that the production agreement would remain in effect until the end of 1994. Ministers acknowledged that there had been a gradual increase in petroleum prices in the second quarter of the year, with an average basket price of US $15.6 per barrel for that period. Political disruption in Nigeria, including a strike by petroleum workers, was considered to be the principal factor contributing to the price per barrel rising above $19 in August. In November OPEC ministers endorsed a proposal by Saudi Arabia to maintain the existing production quota, of 24.52m. b/d, until the end of 1995.

1995   In January it was reported that Gabon was reconsidering its membership of OPEC, owing to difficulties in meeting its budget contribution. During the first half of the year Gabon consistently exceeded its quota of 287,000 b/d, by 48,000 b/d, and the country failed to send a delegate to the ministerial Conference in June. At the Conference ministers expressed concern at OPEC's falling share of the world petroleum market. The Conference criticized the high level of North Sea production, by Norway and the United Kingdom, and urged collective production restraint in order to stimulate prices. In November the Conference agreed to extend the existing production quota, of 24.52m. b/d, for a further six months, in order to stabilize prices. During the year, however, output remained in excess of the production quotas, some 25.58m. b/d.

1996   The possibility of a UN-Iraqi agreement permitting limited petroleum sales dominated OPEC concerns in the first half of the year and contributed to price fluctuations in the world markets. By early 1996 output by OPEC countries was estimated to be substantially in excess of quota levels; however, the price per barrel remained relatively buoyant (the average basket price reaching US $21 in March), owing largely to unseasonal cold weather in the northern hemisphere. In May a memorandum of understanding was signed between Iraq and the UN to allow the export of petroleum, up to a value of $2,000m. over a six-month period, in order to fund humanitarian relief efforts within that country. In June the Conference agreed to increase the overall output ceiling by 800,000 b/d, i.e. the anticipated level of exports from Iraq in the first six months of the agreement. A proposal, endorsed by Iran, to raise the individual country quotas failed to win support, while a comprehensive reduction in output, in order to accommodate the Iraqi quota without adjusting the existing production ceiling, was also rejected, notably by Saudi Arabia and Venezuela. At the meeting Gabon's withdrawal from the Organization was confirmed. As a result of these developments, the new ceiling was set at 25.03m. b/d. Independent market observers expressed concern that, without any formal agreement to reduce overall production and given the actual widespread violation of the quota system, the renewed export of Iraqi petroleum would substantially depress petroleum prices. However, the markets remained stable as implementation of the UN-Iraqi agreement was delayed. In September the monitoring group acknowledged that members were exceeding their production quotas, but declined to impose any punitive measures (owing to the steady increase in petroleum prices). In late November the Conference agreed to maintain the existing production quota for a further six months. Also in November, Iraq accepted certain disputed technical terms of the UN agreement, enabling the export of petroleum to commence in December.

1997   During the first half of the year petroleum prices declined, reaching a low of US $16.7 per barrel in early April, owing to the Iraqi exports, depressed world demand and persistent overproduction. In June the Conference agreed to extend the existing production ceiling, of 25.03m. b/d, for a further six-month period. Member states resolved to adhere to their individual quotas in order to reduce the cumulative excess production of an estimated 2m. b/d; however, Venezuela, which (some sources claimed) was producing almost 800,000 b/d over its quota of 2.4m. b/d, declined to co-operate. An escalation in political tensions in the Gulf region in October, in particular Iraq's reluctance to co-operate with UN inspectors, prompted an increase in the price of crude petroleum to some $21.2 per barrel. Price fluctuations ensued, although there was a general downward trend. In November the OPEC Conference, meeting in Jakarta, approved a proposal by Saudi Arabia, to increase the overall production ceiling by some 10%, with effect from 1 January 1998, in order to meet the perceived stable world demand and to reflect more accurately current output levels. At the same time the Iranian Government announced its intention to increase its production capacity and maintain its share of the quota by permitting foreign companies to conduct petroleum exploration in Iran.

1998   A decline in petroleum prices at the start of the year caused widespread concern, and speculation that this had resulted from the decision to increase production to 27.5m. b/d, coinciding with the prospect of a decline in demand from Asian economies that had been undermined by extreme financial difficulties and of a new Iraqi agreement with the UN with

provision for increased petroleum exports. A meeting of the Monitoring Sub-committee, in late January, urged members to implement production restraint and resolved to send a monitoring team to member states to encourage compliance with the agreed quotas. In February the UN Security Council approved a new agreement permitting Iraq to export petroleum valued at up to US $5,200m. over a six-month period, although the Iraqi Government insisted that its production and export capacity was limited to $4,000m. Indonesia requested an emergency meeting of ministers to discuss this development and the ongoing decline in petroleum prices. Saudi Arabia rejected the proposal unless member states agreed to adhere to their quotas, with particular reference to Venezuela, which was still OPEC's largest over-producer. In March Saudi Arabia, Venezuela and Mexico announced a joint agreement to reduce domestic production by 300,000 b/d, 200,000 b/d and 100,000 b/d respectively, with effect from 1 April, and agreed to co-operate in persuading other petroleum producing countries to commit to similar reductions. At the end of March an emergency ministerial meeting ratified the reduction proposals (the so-called 'Riyadh Pact'), which amounted to 1.245m. b/d pledged by OPEC members and 270,000 b/d by non-member states. Nevertheless, prices remained low, with over-production, together with lack of market confidence in member states' willingness to comply with the restricted quotas, an outstanding concern. In June Saudi Arabia, Venezuela and Mexico reached agreement on further reductions in output of some 450,000 b/d. Later in that month the Conference, having reviewed the market situation, agreed to implement a new reduction in total output of some 1.36m b/d, with effect from 1 July, reducing the total production target for OPEC members to 24.387m. b/d. Iran, which had been criticized for not adhering to the reductions agreed in March, confirmed that it would reduce output by 305,000 b/d. At the meeting, which was also attended by senior officials from Mexico, Oman and Russia, Saudi Arabia proposed the establishment of a new *ad hoc* grouping of the world's largest petroleum producers, in order to monitor output and support price initiatives. In early August petroleum prices fell below $12 per barrel. In September the Kuwaiti authorities, which advocated further production cuts, arranged meetings with Saudi Arabia and Qatar, and later with the petroleum ministers of Algeria, Iran, Oman and the UAE, to discuss the situation in the petroleum markets, and to co-ordinate efforts to stabilize and uphold petroleum prices. In that month Iraq's petroleum production reached an estimated 2.4m. b/d, contributing to concerns of over-supply in the world market. In early November OPEC members attending a conference of the parties to the UN Framework Convention on Climate Change, held in Buenos Aires, Argentina, warned that they would claim compensation for any lost revenue resulting from initiatives to limit the emission of 'greenhouse gases' and reduce the consumption of petroleum. Later in November OPEC ministers, meeting in Vienna, resolved to maintain the existing production levels, but improve compliance. Subsequently, despite the escalation of tensions between the UN and Iraqi authorities, prices remained consistently around the level of $11 per barrel. Air strikes conducted by the USA and United Kingdom against strategic targets in Iraq in mid-December were not considered to have interrupted petroleum supplies and therefore had little impact on prices. Lost export earnings by OPEC member states as a result of the depressed oil prices amounted to some $50,000m. in 1998.

1999   In March ministers from Algeria, Iran, Mexico, Saudi Arabia and Venezuela, meeting in The Hague, the Netherlands, agreed further to reduce petroleum production, owing to the continued weakness of the global market. Subsequently, petroleum prices rose by nearly 40%, after reaching the lowest price of US $9.9 per barrel in mid-February. Later in March OPEC confirmed a new reduction in output of 2.104m. b/d from 1 April, including commitments from non-OPEC members Mexico, Norway, Oman and Russia to decrease production by a total of 388,000 b/d. The agreement envisaged a total production target for OPEC member countries of 22.976m. b/d. Actual output in April was estimated at 26.38m. b/d (compared with 27.72m. in March), which contributed to prices reaching $17 per barrel. Prices continued to fluctuate, however, owing to concern at Iraq's potential production capacity. By June total production by OPEC member states (excluding Iraq) had declined to a reported 23.25m. b/d. The evidence of almost 90% compliance with the new production quotas contributed to market confidence that stockpiles of petroleum would be reduced, and resulted in sustained price increases. At the end of July a meeting of the Ministerial Monitoring Sub-committee confirmed that adherence to the production quotas in the period April to June had been strong, but reiterated the need to maintain the total production level at least until March 2000 given that the year's average basket price was under $14 per barrel and markets remained volatile. In late August 1999 Saudi Arabia, Mexico and Venezuela agreed to extend production reductions until March 2000. In September 1999 OPEC ministers confirmed that the existing quotas would be maintained for a further six-month period. At the end of September the reference price for petroleum rose above $24, its highest level since January 1997. Prices remained buoyant during the rest of the year; however, there was increasing speculation at whether the situation was sustainable. At the end of November Iraq temporarily suspended its petroleum exports, totalling some 2.2m. b/d, pending agreement on a new phase of the 'oil-for-food' arrangement and concern at the lack of progress on the removal of international sanctions.

2000 In March petroleum prices attained their highest level since the 1990 Gulf crisis; the reference price briefly exceeded US $34, representing more than a threefold increase over early 1999 price levels. At the end of that month OPEC ministers, meeting in Vienna, agreed to raise output by 1.45m. b/d, in order to ease supply shortages and thereby contain the surge in prices, with a view to restoring these to a more moderate level. A further increase in production, of 500,000 b/d, was approved by member states in June, to take effect from July (contingent on the reference price continuing to exceed $28 for 20 consecutive days). Prices remained high, reaching $34.6 in early September and leading to intense international pressure on OPEC to resolve the situation. OPEC ministers immediately announced that an increase in production of 800,000 b/d would take effect from 1 October and indicated that, were the reference price still to exceed $28 at the end of that month, an additional increase in output would be implemented. It was noted that a target band of $22–$28 per barrel was envisaged as an acceptable price level. The production agreement was supported by five non-OPEC member countries: Angola, Mexico, Norway, Oman and Russia. In late September both the Group of Seven industrialized nations (G-7) and the IMF issued warnings about the potential economic and social consequences of sustained high petroleum prices. Meanwhile the US administration agreed to release part of its strategic petroleum reserve. Towards the end of the month OPEC heads of state or government, convened at their first summit since 1975, issued the so-called 'Caracas Declaration' in which they resolved to promote market stability by developing 'remunerative, stable and competitive' pricing policies in conjunction with implementing a production policy that would secure OPEC member states an equitable share of world supply; by strengthening co-operation between the organization and other oil-exporting nations; and by developing communication between petroleum producers and consumers. The declaration also affirmed the organization's commitment to environmentally sound practice and to promoting sustainable global economic growth, social development and the eradication of poverty;

supported research in technical and scientific fields; expressed concern that government taxation policies significantly inflate the end cost of petroleum; and agreed to convene future heads of state summits at regular five-yearly intervals on an institutionalized basis. By the end of September petroleum prices had declined to just above $30 per barrel; this was attributed in part to an announcement by the Saudi Arabian Government that it would consider unilaterally raising output if prices were to remain at a high level. However, the decline in prices was short-lived, as the political crisis in the Middle East prompted a further series of increases: by 12 October the London Brent crude price exceeded $35 per barrel for the first time since 1990. From 31 October an additional increase in production, of 500,000 b/d was implemented, as planned for in early September. Meeting in mid-November the Conference appointed Dr Alí Rodríguez Araque, the Venezuelan minister of energy and mines, as the new OPEC Secretary-General, with effect from January 2001. Addressing the Conference, Rodríguez identified the following contributory factors to the high level of petroleum prices other than the relationship between production and price levels: a decline in recent years in the refining capacity of the USA (the world's largest market), the high national taxes on consumption (particularly within the European Union), and price distortions deriving from speculation on futures markets. Attending the sixth conference of parties to the UN Framework Convention on Climate Change later in November OPEC reiterated its concern over the lost revenue that limits on 'greenhouse gas' emissions and reduced petroleum consumption would represent for member states, estimating this at $63,000m. per year.

2001 In mid-January, with a view to stabilizing petroleum prices that by now had fallen back to around $25 per barrel, the Conference agreed to implement a reduction in production of 1.5m. b/d, to take effect on 1 February. A further reduction, of 1m. b/d, effective from 1 April, was approved by the Conference in mid-March.

Finance

The budget for 2001 amounted to 194.8m. Austrian Schilling, of which 29.8m. Schilling was to be financed by transfer from the Reserve Fund and the balance was to be contributed by member states.

Publications

Annual Report.
Annual Statistical Bulletin.
Monthly Oil Market Report.
OPEC Bulletin (monthly).
OPEC Review (quarterly).
Reports, information papers, press releases.

OPEC FUND FOR INTERNATIONAL DEVELOPMENT

Address: POB 995, 1011 Vienna, Austria.
Telephone: (1) 515-64-0; **fax:** (1) 513-92-38; **e-mail:** info@opecfund.org; **internet:** www.opecfund.org.
The Fund was established by OPEC member countries in 1976.

MEMBERS
Member countries of OPEC (q.v.).

Organization
(April 2001)

ADMINISTRATION
The Fund is administered by a Ministerial Council and a Governing Board. Each member country is represented on the Council by its minister of finance. The Board consists of one representative and one alternate for each member country.
Chairman, Ministerial Council: Dr BAMBANG SUDIBYO (Indonesia).
Chairman, Governing Board: Dr SALEH AL-OMAIR (Saudi Arabia).

Director-General of the Fund: Dr YESUFU SEYYID ABDULAI (Nigeria).

FINANCIAL STRUCTURE
The resources of the Fund, whose unit of account is the US dollar, consist of contributions by OPEC member countries, and income received from operations or otherwise accruing to the Fund.
The initial endowment of the Fund amounted to US $800m. Its resources have been replenished three times, and have been further increased by the profits accruing to seven OPEC member countries through the sales of gold held by the International Monetary Fund. The pledged contributions to the OPEC Fund amounted to $3,435.0m. at the end of 1999, and paid-in contributions totalled $2,880.9m.

Activities

The OPEC Fund for International Development is a multilateral agency for financial co-operation and assistance. Its objective is to reinforce financial co-operation between OPEC member countries and other developing countries through the provision of financial support to the latter on appropriate terms, to assist them in their economic and social development. The Fund was conceived as a collective financial facility which would consolidate the assistance extended by its member countries; its resources are additional to those already made available through other bilateral and multilateral aid agencies of OPEC members. It is empowered to:

(*i*) Provide concessional loans for balance-of-payments support;

(*ii*) Provide concessional loans for the implementation of development projects and programmes;

(*iii*) Make contributions and/or provide loans to eligible international agencies; and

(*iv*) Finance technical assistance and research through grants.

The eligible beneficiaries of the Fund's assistance are the governments of developing countries other than OPEC member countries, and international development agencies whose beneficiaries are developing countries. The Fund gives priority to the countries with the lowest income.

The Fund may undertake technical, economic and financial appraisal of a project submitted to it, or entrust such an appraisal to an appropriate international development agency, the executing national agency of a member country, or any other qualified agency. Most projects financed by the Fund have been co-financed by other development finance agencies. In each such case, one of the co-financing agencies may be appointed to administer the Fund's loan in association with its own. This practice has enabled the Fund to extend its lending activities to 105 countries over a short period of time and in a simple way, with the aim of avoiding duplication and complications. As its experience grew, the Fund increasingly

OPEC FUND COMMITMENTS AND DISBURSEMENTS IN 1999 (US $ million)

	Commitments	Disbursements
Public-sector lending operations:	287.55	141.57
Project financing	277.95	131.57
Programme financing	—	10.00
HIPC initiative financing*	9.60	—
Private-sector lending operations	29.50	—
Lines of credit	29.50	—
Grant Programme:	3.44	3.71
Technical assistance	1.95	2.46
Research and other activities	0.54	0.20
Emergency aid	0.95	1.05
Total	320.48	145.28

* Heavily Indebted Poor Countries initiative, jointly implemented by the International Monetary Fund and World Bank.

Project loans approved in 1999 (US $ million)

	Loans approved
Sector:	
Transportation	66.08
Agriculture and agro-industry	44.23
Education	42.93
Health	37.35
Water supply and sewerage	10.00
Energy	37.34
Multisectoral	40.02
Total	277.95
Region*:	
Africa	155.40
Asia	86.05
Europe	4.50
Latin America and the Caribbean	32.00

* A total of 45 loans was approved for projects in 39 countries, benefiting 20 countries in Africa, 13 in Asia, five in Latin America and the Caribbean, and one in Europe.

resorted to parallel, rather than joint financing, taking up separate project components to be financed according to its rules and policies. In addition, it started to finance some projects completely on its own. These trends necessitated the issuance in 1982 of guide-lines for the procurement of goods and services under the Fund's loans, allowing for a margin of preference for goods and services of local origin or originating in other developing countries: the general principle of competitive bidding is, however, followed by the Fund. The loans are not tied to procurement from Fund member countries or from any other countries. The margin of preference for goods and services obtainable in developing countries is allowed on the request of the borrower and within defined limits. Fund assistance in the form of programme loans has a broader coverage than project lending. Programme loans are used to stimulate an economic sector or sub-sector, and assist recipient countries in obtaining inputs, equipment and spare parts. Besides extending loans for project and programme financing and balance of payments support, the Fund also undertakes other operations, including grants in support of technical assistance and other activities (mainly research), and financial contributions to other international institutions. In 1998 the Fund began to extend lines of credit to support private-sector activities in beneficiary countries; six such operations were approved in 1999.

The Fund's thirteenth lending programme, covering a two-year period effective from 1 January 1998, aimed, in particular, to target 72 developing countries. By the end of December 1999 the Fund had extended 825 loans since operations began in 1976, totalling US $4,270.2m., of which $3,231.1m. (or 75.7%) was for project financing, $724.2m. (17.0%) was for balance-of-payments support, $305.3m. (7.1%) was for programme financing and $9.6m. (0.2%) was allocated as financing for the Heavily Indebted Poor Countries (HIPC) initiative (see World Bank, p. 81). The Fund's fourteenth lending programme, covering the period 2000–01, commenced on 1 January 2000.

Direct loans are supplemented by grants to support technical assistance, food aid and research. By the end of December 1999 507 grants, amounting to US $242.7m., had been extended, including $83.6m. to the Common Fund for Commodities (established by the UN Conference on Trade and Development—UNCTAD), $41.8m. in support of emergency relief operations and a special contribution of $20m. to the International Fund for Agricultural Development (IFAD). In addition, the OPEC Fund had committed $971.8m. to other international institutions by the end of 1999, comprising OPEC members' contributions to the resources of IFAD, and irrevocable transfers in the name of its members to the IMF Trust Fund. By the end of 1999 68.3% of total commitments had been disbursed.

During the year ending 31 December 1999 the Fund's total commitments amounted to US $320.5m. (compared with $160.1m. in 1998). These commitments included 45 project loans, amounting to $277.9m., and two loans, totalling $9.6m., to finance debt-relief under the HIPC initiative. The largest proportion of project loans (23.8%) was to support improvements in the transportation sector in eight countries and included road upgrading in Cameroon, Ethiopia, Ghana, Kenya, Togo and Zimbabwe, improvements to port facilities in Djibouti, and the rehabilitation of a section of railway line in Myanmar. Agriculture and agro-industry loans, amounting to 15.9%, supported integrated rural development projects in Burundi, Guatemala and Mali, soil fertility improvement in Jordan and irrigation schemes in the Democratic People's Republic of Korea and Mozambique. The education sector received 15.5% of loans, financing improved access to basic education in Albania and Mali, the construction of educational establishments in Côte d'Ivoire, Senegal and Zambia, the production and distribution of textbooks in Tajikistan, the restructuring of Sri Lanka's vocational training system, and improvements to vocational education and the purchase of equipment in Tanzania. The health and energy sectors each received 13.4% of project loans. Other loans, including multisector loans, amounted to 18% of the total.

During 1999 the Fund approved US $3.44m. for 28 grants, of which $2.0m. was for technical assistance activities, $538,000 for research, and $950,000m. to support four emergency humanitarian operations.

Publications

Annual Report (in Arabic, English, French and Spanish).
OPEC Aid and OPEC Aid Institutions—A Profile (annually).
OPEC Fund Newsletter (3 a year).

PACIFIC COMMUNITY

Address: BP D5, 98848 Nouméa Cédex, New Caledonia.

Telephone: 26-20-00; **fax:** 26-38-18; **e-mail:** spc@spc.int; **internet:** www.spc.org.nc/.

In February 1947 the Governments of Australia, France, the Netherlands, New Zealand, the United Kingdom, and the USA signed an agreement to establish the South Pacific Commission, which came into effect in July 1948. (The Netherlands withdrew from the Commission in 1962, when it ceased to administer the former colony of Dutch New Guinea, now Irian Jaya, also known as West Papua, part of Indonesia.) In October 1997 the 37th South Pacific Conference, convened in Canberra, Australia, agreed to rename the organization the Pacific Community, with effect from 6 February 1998. The Secretariat of the Pacific Community (SPC) services the Community, and provides technical advice, training and assistance in economic, social and cultural development to 22 countries and territories of the Pacific region. It serves a population of about 6.8m., scattered over some 30m. sq km, more than 98% of which is sea.

MEMBERS

American Samoa	Niue
Australia	Northern Mariana Islands
Cook Islands	Palau
Fiji	Papua New Guinea
France	Pitcairn Islands
French Polynesia	Samoa
Guam	Solomon Islands
Kiribati	Tokelau
Marshall Islands	Tonga
Federated States of	Tuvalu
Micronesia	United Kingdom
Nauru	USA
New Caledonia	Vanuatu
New Zealand	Wallis and Futuna Islands

Organization
(April 2001)

CONFERENCE OF THE PACIFIC COMMUNITY

The Conference is the governing body of the Community (replacing the former South Pacific Conference) and is composed of representatives of all member countries and territories. The main responsibilities of the Conference, which meets annually, are to appoint the Director-General, to determine major national or regional policy issues in the areas of competence of the organization and to note changes to the Financial and Staff Regulations approved by the Committee of Representatives of Governments and Administrations (CRGA).

COMMITTEE OF REPRESENTATIVES OF GOVERNMENTS AND ADMINISTRATIONS (CRGA)

This Committee comprises representatives of all member states and territories, having equal voting rights. It meets annually to consider the work programme evaluation conducted by the Secretariat and to discuss any changes proposed by the Secretariat in the context of regional priorities; to consider and approve any policy issues for the organization presented by the Secretariat or by member countries and territories; to consider applicants and make recommendations for the post of Director-General; to approve the administrative and work programme budgets; to approve amendments to the Financial and Staff Regulations; and to conduct annual performance evaluations of the Director-General.

SECRETARIAT

The Secretariat is headed by a Director-General and two Deputy Directors-General, based in Suva and Nouméa. Three administrative Divisions cover Land Resources, Marine Resources and Social Resources. The Secretariat also provides information services, including library facilities, publications, translation and computer services. The organization has about 250 staff members.

Director-General: LOURDES PANGELINAN (Guam).

Deputy Directors-General: Dr JIMMIE RODGERS (Solomon Islands), YVES CORBEL (France).

Regional Office: Private Mail Bag, Suva, Fiji; tel. 370733; fax 370021; e-mail spcsuva@spc.org.fj.

Activities

The SPC provides, on request of its member countries, technical assistance, advisory services, information and clearing-house ser-

vices. The organization also conducts regional conferences and technical meetings, as well as training courses, workshops and seminars at the regional or country level. It provides small grants-in-aid and awards to meet specific requests and needs of members. In November 1996 the Conference agreed to establish a specific Small Islands States fund to provide technical services, training and other relevant activities. The Conference also endorsed a series of organizational reforms, on the basis of a review conducted earlier in the year. The Pacific Community oversees the maritime programme and telecommunications policy activities of the Pacific Islands Forum Secretariat (q.v.).

LAND RESOURCES

The SPC's agriculture programme, which is based in Suva, Fiji, aims to promote land and agricultural management practices that are both economically and environmentally sustainable; to strengthen national capabilities to reduce losses owing to crop pests (insects, pathogens and weeds) and animal diseases already present, and to prevent the introduction of new pests and diseases; to facilitate trade through improved quarantine procedures; and to improve access to, and use of, sustainable development information for all. The programme incorporates the following four main policy units: general agriculture, including advice and specific activities in crop diversification, such as coconut technology development, and the provision of agricultural training; plant protection, through the implementation of regional research and technical support projects; animal health and animal production; and the provision of advice and information on agricultural concerns and sustainable development. A Pacific Regional Agricultural Programme (PRAP), funded by the European Union, was introduced by eight member states in 1990. The SPC administers a Pacific Islands Forests and Trees Support Project, which is concerned with natural forest management and conservation, agroforestry and development and the use of tree and plant resources, and a regional project relating to the sustainable management of forests and agroforesty. Maritime activities are also covered by the Land Resources Division.

The SPC office in Suva, Fiji, administers a Community Education Training Centre (CETC), which conducts a seven-month training course for up to 36 women community workers annually, with the objective of training women in methods of community development so that they can help others to achieve better living conditions for island families and communities. A Regional Media Centre provides training, technical assistance and production materials in all areas of the media for member countries and territories, Community work programmes, donor projects and regional non-governmental organizations. The Centre comprises a radio broadcast unit, a graphic design and publication unit and a TV and video unit.

MARINE RESOURCES

The SPC aims to support and co-ordinate the sustainable development and management of inshore fisheries resources in the region, to undertake scientific research in order to provide member governments with relevant information for the sustainable development and management of tuna and billfish resources in and adjacent to the South Pacific region, and to provide data and analytical services to national fisheries departments. The main components of the Community's fisheries activities are the Coastal Fisheries Programme (CFP) and the Oceanic Fisheries Programme (OFP). The CFP is divided into the following sections: fishery assessment; sustainable fishery development; womens' fishery development (assisting women from coastal fishing communities to participate more effectively in, and benefit from, fisheries activities, particularly in the post-harvest processing industry); post-harvest development (offering advice and training in order to improve handling practices, storage, seafood product development, quality control and marketing); training and education; information and networking; and programme support and management. The OFP consists of the following three sections: statistics and monitoring; tuna ecology and biology; and stock assessment and modelling. The statistics and monitoring section maintains a database of industrial tuna fisheries in the region. The OFP contributed research and statistical information to a multilateral high-level conference that was convened in Majuro, the Marshall Islands, in June 1997, to formulate a framework for the conservation and management of highly migratory fish stocks in the Western and Central Pacific.

SOCIAL RESOURCES

A Community Health Programme aims to implement health promotion programmes; to assist regional authorities to strengthen health information systems and to promote the use of new technology for health information development and disease control (for example, through the Public Health Surveillance and Disease Control Programme); to promote efficient health services management; and to help all Pacific Islanders to attain a level of health and quality of life that will enable them to contribute to the development of their communities. The Community Health Services also work in the areas of non-communicable diseases and nutrition (with particular focus on the high levels of diabetes and heart disease in parts of the region); environmental health, through the improvement of water and sanitation facilities; and reducing the incidence of HIV/AIDS and other sexually-transmitted diseases (STDs). The SPC has initiated, with funding from the European Union, a project to prevent AIDS and STDs among young people based on peer education and awareness. The Division is responsible for implementing a Pacific Regional Vector-Borne Diseases Project that was established in 1996, with particular emphasis on Fiji, Vanuatu and the Solomon Islands.

A Statistics Programme assists governments and administrations in the region to provide effective and efficient national statistical services through the provision of training activities, a statistical information service and other advisory services. A Regional Conference of Statisticians facilitates the integration and co-ordination of statistical services throughout the region.

The Population and Demography Programme aims to assist governments effectively to utilize and incorporate data into the formulation of development policies and programmes and to provide technical support in population, demographic and development issues to member governments, other SPC programmes and organizations active in the region. The Programme organizes national workshops in population and development planning, provides short-term professional attachments, undertakes demographic research and analysis and disseminates information.

The Rural Development Programme promotes active participation of the rural population and encourages the use of traditional practices and knowledge in the formulation of rural development projects and income-generating activities. The Rural Technology Programme (incorporating the Rural Energy Development Programme) aims to provide technical assistance, advice and monitoring of pilot regional programmes, with emphasis on technologies to generate renewable energy in rural areas, to help achieve environmentally-sustainable development.

The Pacific Youth Resource Bureau provides non-formal education and support for youth, community workers and young adults in community development subjects and provides grants to help young people find employment. It also advises and assists the Pacific Youth Council in promoting a regional youth identity. The SPC implements its cultural affairs and conservation programme mainly through the Council of Pacific Arts. A Pacific Women's Resource Bureau aims to promote the social, economic and cultural advancement of women in the region by assisting governments and regional organizations to include women in the development planning process. The Bureau also provides technical and advisory services, advocacy and management support training to groups concerned with women in development and gender and development, and supports the production and exchange of information regarding women.

A Cultural Programme was established in 1996 to preserve and promote the cultural heritage of the Pacific Islands. The Programme assists with the training of librarians, archivists and researchers and promotes instruction in local languages, history and art at schools in member states and territories.

Finance

The organization's budget is divided into administrative and work programme budgets. The administrative budget is funded by assessed contributions from member states, while the work programme is financed in part by assessed contributions, but in the main by voluntary contributions from industrialized member governments, other governments, aid agencies and other sources. The approved administrative budget for 2000 amounted to US $2.5m.

Publications

Annual Report.
Fisheries Newsletter (quarterly).
Pacific Aids Alert Bulletin (quarterly).
Pacific Island Nutrition (quarterly).
Regional Tuna Bulletin (quarterly).
Report of the Conference of the Pacific Community.
Women's Newsletter (quarterly).

Technical publications, statistical bulletins, advisory leaflets and reports.

PACIFIC ISLANDS FORUM

MEMBERS

Australia	Niue
Cook Islands	Palau
Fiji	Papua New Guinea
Kiribati	Samoa
Marshall Islands	Solomon Islands
Federated States of	Tonga
Micronesia	Tuvalu
Nauru	Vanuatu
New Zealand	

Note: New Caledonia was admitted as an observer at the Forum in 1999.

The Pacific Islands Forum (which changed its name from South Pacific Forum in October 2000) was founded as the gathering of Heads of Government of the independent and self-governing states of the South Pacific. Its first meeting was held on 5 August 1971, in Wellington, New Zealand. It provides an opportunity for informal discussions to be held on a wide range of common issues and problems and meets annually or when issues require urgent attention. The Forum has no written constitution or international agreement governing its activities nor any formal rules relating to its purpose, membership or conduct of meeting. Decisions are always reached by consensus, it never having been found necessary or desirable to vote formally on issues. In October 1994 the Forum was granted observer status by the General Assembly of the United Nations.

Since 1989 each Forum has been followed by 'dialogues' with representatives of other countries with a long-term interest in and commitment to the region. In October 1995 the Forum Governments suspended France's 'dialogue' status, following that country's resumption of the testing of nuclear weapons in French Polynesia. France was reinstated as a 'dialogue partner' in September 1996. In 2001 'dialogue partners' comprised Canada, the People's Republic of China, France, Japan, Malaysia, Philippines, the United Kingdom, the USA, the Republic of Korea and the European Union.

The South Pacific Nuclear-Free Zone Treaty (Treaty of Rarotonga), prohibiting the acquisition, stationing or testing of nuclear weapons in the region, came into effect in December 1986, following ratification by eight states. The USSR signed the protocols to the treaty (whereby states possessing nuclear weapons agree not to use or threaten to use nuclear explosive devices against any non-nuclear party to the Treaty) in December 1987 and ratified them in April 1988; the People's Republic of China did likewise in December 1987 and October 1988 respectively. The other three major nuclear powers, however, intimated that they did not intend to adhere to the Treaty. In July 1993 the Forum petitioned the USA, the United Kingdom and France, asking them to reconsider their past refusal to sign the Treaty in the light of the end of the 'Cold War'. In July 1995, following the decision of the French Government to resume testing of nuclear weapons in French Polynesia, members of the Forum resolved to increase diplomatic pressure on the three Governments to sign the Treaty. In October the United Kingdom, the USA and France announced their intention to accede to the Treaty, by mid-1996. While the decision was approved by the Forum, it urged the Governments to sign with immediate effect, thus accelerating the termination of France's testing programme. Following France's decision, announced in January 1996, to end the programme four months earlier than scheduled, representatives of the Governments of the three countries signed the Treaty in March.

In 1990 five of the Forum's smallest island member states formed an economic sub-group to address their specific concerns, in particular economic disadvantages resulting from a poor resource base, absence of a skilled work-force and lack of involvement in world markets. In September 1997 the 28th Forum, convened in Rarotonga, the Cook Islands, endorsed the inclusion of the Marshall Islands as the sixth member of the Smaller Island States sub-group. Representatives of the grouping, which also includes Kiribati, the Cook Islands, Nauru, Niue and Tuvalu, meet regularly. In February 1998 senior Forum officials, for the first time, met with representatives of the Caribbean Community and the Indian Ocean Commission, as well as other major international organizations, to discuss means to enhance consideration and promotion of the interests of small island states.

The 21st Forum, held in August 1990 in Vanuatu, criticized the US Government's proposal to use the US external territory of Johnston Atoll for the destruction of chemical weapons. The meeting urged industrialized countries to reduce the emission of gases that contribute to the so-called 'greenhouse effect', or warming of the earth's atmosphere. A ministerial committee was established to monitor political developments in New Caledonia, in co-operation with the French authorities.

The 22nd Forum took place in Pohnpei, Federated States of Micronesia, in July 1991. It issued a strong condemnation of French testing of nuclear weapons in the region. The Forum examined the report of the ministerial committee on New Caledonia, and instructed the committee to visit New Caledonia annually. However, this proposal was rejected by the French Government.

The 23rd Forum, held in Honiara, Solomon Islands, in July 1992, welcomed France's suspension of its nuclear-testing programme until the end of the year, but urged the French Government to make the moratorium permanent. Forum members discussed the decisions made at the UN Conference on Environment and Development held in June, and approved the Cook Islands' proposal to host a 'global conference for small islands'. The Niue Fisheries Surveillance and Law Enforcement Co-operation Treaty was signed by members, with the exception of Fiji, Kiribati and Tokelau, which were awaiting endorsement from their legislatures. The treaty provides for co-operation in the surveillance of fisheries resources and in defeating drugs-trafficking and other organized crime. Forum leaders also adopted a separate declaration on future priorities in law enforcement co-operation.

At the 24th Forum, held in Yaren, Nauru, in August 1993 it was agreed that effective links needed to be established with the broader Asia-Pacific region, with participation in Asia-Pacific Economic Co-operation (APEC), where the Forum has observer status, to be utilized to the full. The Forum urged an increase in intra-regional trade and asked for improved opportunities for Pacific island countries exporting to Australia and New Zealand. New Caledonia's right to self-determination was supported. Environmental protection measures and the rapid growth in population in the region, which was posing a threat to economic and social development, were also discussed by the Forum delegates.

The 25th Forum was convened in Brisbane, Australia, in August 1994 under the theme of 'Managing Our Resources'. In response to the loss of natural resources as well as of income-earning potential resulting from unlawful logging of timber by foreign companies, Forum members agreed to impose stricter controls on the exploitation of forestry resources and to begin negotiations to standardize monitoring of the region's resources. The Forum also agreed to strengthen its promotion of sustainable exploitation of fishing stocks, reviewed preparations of a convention to control the movement and management of radioactive waste within the South Pacific and discussed the rationalization of national airlines, on a regional or sub-regional basis, to reduce operational losses.

The 26th Forum, held in Madang, Papua New Guinea, in September 1995, was dominated by extreme hostility on the part of Forum Governments to the resumption of testing of nuclear weapons by France in the South Pacific region. The decision to recommence testing, announced by the French Government in June, had been instantly criticized by Forum Governments. The 26th Forum reiterated their demand that France stop any further testing, and also condemned the People's Republic of China for conducting nuclear tests in the region. The meeting endorsed a draft Code of Conduct on the management and monitoring of indigenous forest resources in selected South Pacific countries, which had been initiated at the 25th Forum; however, while the six countries concerned committed themselves to implementing the Code through national legislation, its signing was deferred, owing to an initial unwillingness on the part of Papua New Guinea and Solomon Islands. The Forum did adopt a treaty to ban the import into the region of all radioactive and other hazardous wastes, and to control the transboundary movement and management of these wastes (the so-called Waigani Convention). The Forum agreed to reactivate the ministerial committee on New Caledonia, comprising Fiji, Nauru and Solomon Islands, which was to monitor political developments in that territory prior to its referendum on independence, scheduled to be held in 1998. In addition, the Forum resolved to implement and pursue means of promoting economic co-operation and long-term development in the region. In December 1995 Forum finance ministers, meeting in Port Moresby, Papua New Guinea, discussed the issues involved in the concept of 'Securing Development Beyond 2000' and initiated an assessment project to further trade liberalization efforts in the region.

The 27th Forum, held in Majuro, the Marshall Islands, in September 1996, supported the efforts of the French Government to improve relations with countries in the South Pacific and agreed to readmit France to the post-Forum dialogue. The Forum meeting recognized the importance of responding to the liberalization of the global trading system by reviewing the region's economic tariff policies, and of assisting members in attracting investment for the development of the private sector. The Forum advocated that a meeting of economy ministers of member countries be held each year. The Forum was also concerned with environmental issues: in particular, it urged the

ratification and implementation of the Waigani Convention by all member states, the formulation of an international, legally-binding agreement to reduce gas emissions, and the promotion of regional efforts to conserve marine resources and to protect the coastal environment. The Forum requested the ministerial committee on New Caledonia, which had visited the territory in July, to pursue contacts with all parties and to continue to monitor preparations for the 1998 referendum.

In July 1997 the inaugural meeting of Forum economy ministers was convened in Cairns, Australia. It formulated an Action Plan to encourage the flow of foreign investment into the region by committing members to economic reforms, good governance and the implementation of multilateral trade and tariff policies. The meeting also commissioned a formal study of the establishment of a free-trade agreement between Forum island states. The 28th Forum, held in Rarotonga, the Cook Islands, in September, considered the economic challenges confronting the region. However, it was marked by a failure to conclude a common policy position on mandatory targets for the emission of so-called 'greenhouse gases', which some members considered to be a threat to low-lying islands in the region, owing to an ongoing dispute between Australia and other Forum Governments.

The 29th Forum, held in Pohnpei, Federated States of Micronesia, in August 1998, considered the need to pursue economic reforms and to stimulate the private sector and foreign investment in order to ensure economic growth. Leaders reiterated their support for efforts to implement the economic Action Plan and to develop a framework for a free-trade agreement, and endorsed specific recommendations of the second Forum Economic Ministers Meeting, which was held in Fiji, in July, including the promotion of competitive telecommunications markets, the development of information infrastructures and support for a new economic vulnerability index at the UN to help determine least developed country status. The Forum was also concerned with environmental issues, notably the shipment of radioactive wastes, the impact of a multinational venture to launch satellites from the Pacific, the need for ongoing radiological monitoring of the Mururoa and Fangataufa atolls, and the development of a South Pacific Whale Sanctuary. The Forum adopted a Statement on Climate Change, which urged all countries to ratify and implement the gas emission reductions agreed upon in December 1997 (the so-called Kyoto Protocol of the UN Framework Convention on Climate Change), and emphasized the Forum's commitment to further measures for verifying and enforcing emission limitation.

In October 1999 the 30th Forum, held in Koror, Palau, endorsed in principle the establishment of a regional free-trade area (FTA), which had been approved at a special ministerial meeting held in June. The FTA was to be implemented from 2002 over a period of eight years for developing member countries and 10 years for smaller island states and least developed countries. The Forum requested officials from member countries to negotiate the details of a draft agreement on the FTA (the so-called Pacific Regional Trade Agreement), including possible extensions of the arrangements to Australia and New Zealand. The heads of government adopted a Forum Vision for the Pacific Information Economy, which recognized the importance of information technology infrastructure for the region's economic and social development and the possibilities for enhanced co-operation in investment, job creation, education, training and cultural exchange. Forum Governments also expressed concern at the shipment of radioactive waste through the Pacific and determined to pursue negotiations with France, Japan and the United Kingdom regarding liability and compensation arrangements; confirmed their continued support for the multinational force and UN operations in East Timor; and urged more countries to adopt and implement the Kyoto Protocol to limit the emission of 'greenhouse gases'. In addition, the Forum agreed to rename the grouping (hitherto known as the South Pacific Forum) the Pacific Islands Forum, to reflect the expansion of its membership since its establishment; the new designation took effect at the 31st Forum, which was convened in Tarawa, Kiribati, at the end of October 2000.

At the 31st Forum the heads of government discussed the escalation in regional insecurity that had occurred since the previous Forum. Concern was expressed over the unrest that prevailed during mid-2000 in Fiji and Solomon Islands, and also over ongoing political violence in the Indonesian province of Irian Jaya (West Papua). The Forum adopted the Biketawa Declaration, which outlined a mechanism for responding to any future such crises in the region while urging members to undertake efforts to address the fundamental causes of instability. The detrimental economic impact of the disturbances in Fiji and Solomon Islands was noted. The Forum observed that significant progress had been achieved in the negotiation of the draft legal text of the Pacific Regional Trade Agreement. The Forum also considered a proposal to establish a Regional Financial Information Sharing Facility, and welcomed the adoption in September of the Convention on the Conservation and Management of Highly Migratory Fish Stocks in the Western and Central Pacific, which aimed to establish a regime for the sustainable management of tuna resources. Support for the prompt implementation of the Kyoto Protocol was reiterated.

Pacific Islands Forum Secretariat

Address: Private Mail Bag, Suva, Fiji.
Telephone: 312600; **fax:** 301102; **e-mail:** info@forumsec.org.fj;
internet: www.forumsec.org.fj.

The South Pacific Bureau for Economic Co-operation (SPEC) was established by an agreement signed on 17 April 1973, at the third meeting of the South Pacific Forum (now Pacific Islands Forum) in Apia, Western Samoa (now Samoa). SPEC was renamed the South Pacific Forum Secretariat in 1988; this, in turn, was redesignated as the Pacific Islands Forum Secretariat in October 2000.

Organization

(April 2001)

FORUM OFFICIALS COMMITTEE

The Forum Officials Committee is the Secretariat's executive board. It comprises representatives and senior officials from all member countries. It meets twice a year, immediately before the meetings of the Pacific Islands Forum and at the end of the year, to discuss in detail the Secretariat's work programme and annual budget.

SECRETARIAT

The Secretariat undertakes the day-to-day activities of the Forum. It is headed by a Secretary-General, with a staff of some 70 people drawn from the member countries. The Secretariat comprises the following four Divisions: Corporate Services; Development and Economic Policy; Trade and Investment; and Political and International Affairs.

Secretary-General: NOEL LEVI (Papua New Guinea).
Deputy Secretary-General: IOSEFA MAIAVA (Samoa).

Activities

The Secretariat's aim is to enhance the economic and social well-being of the people of the South Pacific, in support of the efforts of national governments.

The Secretariat's trade and investment services extend advice and technical assistance to member countries in policy, development, export marketing, and information dissemination. Trade policy activities are mainly concerned with improving private sector policies, for example investment promotion, assisting integration into the world economy, and the development of businesses. The Secretariat aims to assist both island governments and private sector companies to enhance their capacity in the development and exploitation of export markets, product identification and product development. A trade exhibition was held in French Polynesia in 1997, and support was granted to provide for visits to overseas trade fairs and the development of promotional materials. Other trade activities in 1997 included capacity-building in new technologies, business marketing workshops, and technical assistance to improve the cost and efficiency of petroleum management by member countries. Two trade missions, to the Republic of Korea and Taiwan, were undertaken to generate mutual awareness of business opportunities. The Trade and Investment Division of the Secretariat also co-ordinates the activities of the regional trade offices located in Australia, New Zealand and Japan (see below). The establishment of a representative trade office in the People's Republic of China was envisaged in 2001.

The South Pacific Regional Trade and Economic Co-operation Agreement (SPARTECA), which came into force in 1981, aims to redress the trade deficit of the South Pacific countries with Australia and New Zealand. It is a non-reciprocal trade agreement under which Australia and New Zealand offer duty-free and unrestricted access or concessional access for specified products originating from the developing island member countries of the Forum. In 1985 Australia agreed to further liberalization of trade by abolishing (from the beginning of 1987) duties and quotas on all Pacific products except steel, cars, sugar, footwear and garments. In August 1994 New Zealand expanded its import criteria under the agreement by reducing the rule of origin requirement for garment products from 50% to 45% of local content. In response to requests from Fiji, Australia agreed to widen its interpretation of the agreement by accepting as being of local content manufactured products that consist of goods and components of 50% Australian content. A new Fiji/Australia Trade and Economic Relations Agreement (FATERA) was concluded in March 1999 to complement SPARTECA and compensate for certain trade benefits that were in the process of being withdrawn.

The Political and International Affairs Division of the Secretariat organizes and services the meetings of the Forum, disseminates its views, administers the Forum's observer office at the United Nations, and aims to strengthen relations with other regional and international organizations, in particular APEC and ASEAN. The Division's other main concern is to promote regional co-operation in law enforcement and legal affairs, and it provides technical support for the drafting of legal documents and for law enforcement capacity-building. In 1997 the Secretariat undertook an assessment to survey the need for specialist training in dealing with money laundering in member countries. In recent years the Forum Secretariat has been concerned with assessing the legislative reforms and other commitments needed to ensure implementation of the 1992 Honiara Declaration on Law Enforcement Co-operation. The Division assists member countries to ratify and implement the 1988 UN Convention against Illicit Trafficking in Narcotic Drugs and Psychotropic Substances, and administered a South Pacific Police Customs Drug Enforcement Project until 1997. In December 1998 the Secretariat initiated a five-year programme to strengthen regional law enforcement capabilities, in particular to counter cross-border crimes such as money-laundering, drugs-trafficking and smuggling. All member states, apart from Australia and New Zealand, were to participate in the initiative.

The Secretariat helps to co-ordinate environmental policy. With support from the Australian Government, it administers a network of stations to monitor sea-levels and climate change throughout the Pacific region. In 1998 the Secretariat hosted a preparatory meeting for Forum delegates to help establish a common position on climate change issues prior to the fourth Conference of the Parties to the Framework Convention on Climate Change, which was held in Buenos Aires, Argentina, in November.

The Development and Economic Policy Division of the Secretariat aims to co-ordinate and promote co-operation in development activities and programmes throughout the region. The Division administers a Short Term Advisory Service, which provides consultancy services to help member countries meet economic development priorities, and a Fellowship Scheme to provide practical training in a range of technical and income-generating activities. A Small Island Development Fund aims to assist the economic development of this sub-group of member countries (i.e. the Cook Islands, Kiribati, the Marshall Islands, Nauru, Niue and Tuvalu) through project financing. A separate fellowship has also been established to provide training to the Kanak population of New Caledonia, to assist in their social, economic and political development. The Division aims to assist regional organizations to identify development priorities and to provide advice to national governments on economic analysis, planning and structural reforms.

The Secretariat services the Pacific Group Council of ACP states receiving assistance from the EU (q.v.), and in early 1993 a joint unit was established within the Secretariat headquarters to assist Pacific ACP countries and regional organizations in submitting projects to the EU for funding. In October 1994 the Secretariat signed an agreement with representatives of the EU for the establishment of a Pacific Regional Agricultural Programme. The four-year programme was to be funded under the Lomé IV Pacific Regional Programme, with the aim of improving agricultural productivity in the region.

The South Pacific Forum (now Pacific Islands Forum) established the Pacific Forum Line and the Association of South Pacific Airlines (see below), as part of its efforts to promote co-operation in regional transport. On 1 January 1997 the work of the Forum Maritime Programme, which included assistance for regional maritime training and for the development of regional maritime administrations and legislation, was transferred to the regional office of the South Pacific Commission (renamed the Pacific Community from February 1998) at Suva. At the same time responsibility for the Secretariat's civil aviation activities was transferred to individual countries, to be managed at a bilateral level. Telecommunications policy activities were also transferred to the then South Pacific Commission at the start of 1997. In May 1998 ministers responsible for aviation in member states approved a new regional civil aviation policy, which envisaged liberalization of air services, common safety and security standards and provisions for shared revenue.

Finance

The Governments of Australia and New Zealand each contribute some 37% of the annual budget and the remaining amount is shared by the other member Governments. Extra-budgetary funding is contributed mainly by Australia, New Zealand, Japan, the EU and France. Forum officials approved a budget of $F 11.9m. for the Secretariat's 2000 work programme.

Publications

Annual Report.
Forum News (quarterly).

South Asian Association for Regional Co-operation

Forum Trends.
Forum Secretariat Directory of Aid Agencies.
South Pacific Trade Directory.
SPARTECA (guide for Pacific island exporters).
Reports of meetings; profiles of Forum member countries.

Associated and Affiliated Organizations

Association of South Pacific Airlines—ASPA: POB 9817, Nadi Airport, Nadi, Fiji; tel. 723526; fax 720196; f. 1979 at a meeting of airlines in the South Pacific, convened to promote co-operation among the member airlines for the development of regular, safe and economical commercial aviation within, to and from the South Pacific. Mems: 17 regional airlines, two associates. Pres. RICHARD GATES; Sec.-Gen. GEORGE E. FAKTAUFON.

Forum Fisheries Agency—FFA: POB 629, Honiara, Solomon Islands; tel. (677) 21124; fax (677) 23995; e-mail info@ffa.int; internet www.ffa.int; f. 1979 to promote co-operation in fisheries among coastal states in the region; collects and disseminates information and advice on the living marine resources of the region, including the management, exploitation and development of these resources; provides assistance in the areas of law (treaty negotiations, drafting legislation, and co-ordinating surveillance and enforcement), fisheries development, research, economics, computers, and information management. A Vessel Monitoring System, to provide automated data collection and analysis of fishing vessel activities throughout the region, was inaugurated by the FFA in 1998. On behalf of its member countries, the FFA administers a multilateral fisheries treaty, under which vessels from the USA operate in the region, in exchange for an annual payment. Dir VICTORIO UHERBELAU. Publs *FFA News Digest* (every two months), *FFA Reports*.

Pacific Forum Line: POB 796, Auckland, New Zealand; tel. (9) 356-2333; fax (9) 356-2330; e-mail info@pflnz.co.nz; f. 1977 as a joint venture by South Pacific countries, to provide shipping services to meet the special requirements of the region; operates three container vessels; conducts shipping agency services in Australia, Fiji, New Zealand and Samoa, and stevedoring in Samoa. Chair. T. TUFUI; CEO W. J. MACLENNAN.

Pacific Islands Centre—PIC: Sotobori Sky Bldg, 5th Floor, 2-11 Ichigayahonmura-cho, Shinjuku-ku,, Tokyo 162-0845, Japan; tel. (3) 3268-8419; fax (3) 3268-6311; f. 1996 to promote and to facilitate trade, investment and tourism among Forum members and Japan. Dir HIDEO FUJITA.

South Pacific Trade Commission (Australia Office): Suite 3003, Piccadilly Tower, 133 Castlereagh St, Sydney, NSW 2000, Australia; tel. (2) 9283-5933; fax (2) 9283-5948; e-mail info@sptc.gov.au; internet www.sptc.gov.au; f. 1979; assists Pacific Island Governments and business communities to identify market opportunities in Australia and promotes investment in the Pacific Island countries. Senior Trade Commr AIVU TAUVASA (Papua New Guinea).

South Pacific Trade Commission (New Zealand Office): Flight Centre, 48 Emily Pl., Auckland, New Zealand; tel. (9) 3020465; fax (9) 3776642; e-mail parmeshc@sptc.org.nz; internet www.sptc.org.nz.

SOUTH ASIAN ASSOCIATION FOR REGIONAL CO-OPERATION—SAARC

Address: POB 4222, Kathmandu, Nepal.
Telephone: (1) 221785; **fax:** (1) 227033; **e-mail:** saarc@saarc-sec.org; **internet:** www.saarc-sec.org.
The South Asian Association for Regional Co-operation (SAARC) was formally established in 1985 in order to strengthen and accelerate regional co-operation, particularly in economic development.

MEMBERS

Bangladesh	Nepal
Bhutan	Pakistan
India	Sri Lanka
Maldives	

Organization
(April 2001)

SUMMIT MEETING
Heads of state and of government of member states represent the body's highest authority, and a summit meeting is normally held annually.

COUNCIL OF MINISTERS
The Council of Ministers comprises the ministers of foreign affairs of member countries, who meet twice a year. The Council may also meet in extraordinary session at the request of member states. The responsibilities of the Council include formulation of policies, assessing progress and confirming new areas of co-operation.

STANDING COMMITTEE
The Committee consists of the secretaries of foreign affairs of member states. It has overall responsibility for the monitoring and co-ordination of programmes and financing, and determines priorities, mobilizes resources and identifies areas of co-operation. It usually meets twice a year, and submits its reports to the Council of Ministers. The Committee is supported by an *ad hoc* Programming Committee made up of senior officials, who meet to examine the budget of the Secretariat, confirm the Calendar of Activities and resolve matters assigned to it by the Standing Committee.

TECHNICAL COMMITTEES
SAARC comprises 11 technical committees covering: agriculture and forestry; education, culture and sports; health, population and child welfare; environment and meteorology; rural development (including the SAARC Youth Volunteers Programme—SYVOP); tourism; transport; science and technology; communications; women in development; and the prevention of drugs-trafficking and drug abuse. Each committee is headed by a representative of a member state.

SECRETARIAT
The Secretariat was established in January 1987 to co-ordinate and oversee SAARC activities. It comprises the Secretary-General and a Director from each member country. The Secretary-General is appointed by the Council of Ministers, after being nominated by a member state. The ninth summit meeting of heads of state and of government, held in Malé, Maldives, in 1997, extended the Secretary-General's term of office from two to three years. The Director is nominated by member states and appointed by the Secretary-General for a term of three years, although this may be increased in special circumstances.
Secretary-General: NIHAL RODRIGO (Sri Lanka).

Activities

In August 1993 ministers of foreign affairs of seven countries, meeting in New Delhi, India, adopted a Declaration on South Asian Regional Co-operation and launched an Integrated Programme of Action, which identified the main areas for regional co-operation. The first summit meeting of heads of state and of government, held in Dhaka, Bangladesh, in December 1985, resulted in the signing of the Charter of the South Asian Association for Regional Co-operation (SAARC).

SAARC is committed to improving quality of life in the region by accelerating economic growth, social progress and cultural development; promoting self-reliance; encouraging mutual assistance; increasing co-operation with other developing countries; and co-operating with other regional and international organizations. The SAARC Charter stipulates that decisions should be made unanimously, and that 'bilateral and contentious issues' should not be discussed. Regular meetings, at all levels, are held to further co-operation in areas covered by the Technical Committees (see above). A priority objective is the eradication of poverty in the region, and in 1993 SAARC endorsed an Agenda of Action to help achieve this. A framework for exchanging information on poverty eradication has also, since, been established.

A Committee on Economic Co-operation (CEC), comprising senior trade officials of member states, was established in July 1991 to monitor progress concerning trade and economic co-operation issues. In the same year the summit meeting approved the creation of an inter-governmental group to establish a framework for the promotion of specific trade liberalization measures. A SAARC Chamber of Commerce (SCCI) became operational in 1992, with headquarters in Karachi, Pakistan. (The SCCI headquarters were subsequently transferred to Islamabad, Pakistan.) In April 1993 ministers signed a SAARC Preferential Trading Arrangement (SAPTA) which came into effect in December 1995. By early 2001 three rounds of trade negotiations had been held under SAPTA, and more than 3,400 products had been identified as eligible for preferential trade tariffs. In December 1995 the Council resolved that the ultimate objective for member states should be the establishment of a South Asian Free Trade Area (SAFTA), superseding SAPTA. An *ad hoc* inter-governmental expert group was constituted to formulate a framework to realize SAFTA. In January 1996 the first SAARC Trade Fair was held, in New Delhi, India, to promote intra-SAARC commerce. A second trade fair was held at Colombo, Sri Lanka, in 1998. The third SAARC Trade Fair was to be held in Islamabad, Pakistan, in late April 2001.

An Agricultural Information Centre was founded in 1988, in Dhaka, Bangladesh, to serve as a central institution for the dissemination of knowledge and information in the agricultural sector. It maintains a network of centres in each member state, which provide for the efficient exchange of technical information and for strengthening agricultural research. An agreement establishing a Food Security Reserve to meet emergency food requirements was signed in November 1987, and entered into force in August 1988. The Board of the Reserve meets annually to assess the food security of the region. At mid-1998 the Reserve contained some 241,580 metric tons of grain. Other regional institutions include the SAARC Tuberculosis Centre in Thimi, Nepal, which opened in July 1992 with the aim of preventing and reducing the prevalence of the disease in the region through the co-ordination of tuberculosis control programmes, research and training; a SAARC Documentation Centre, established in New Delhi in May 1994; and a SAARC Meteorological Research Centre which opened in Dhaka in January 1995. A Human Resource Development Centre was established in Islamabad, Pakistan in 1999. Regional funds include a SAARC-Japan Special Fund established in September 1993. One-half of the fund's resources, which were provided by the Japanese Government, was to be used to finance projects identified by Japan, and one-half was to be used to finance projects identified by SAARC member states. The eighth SAARC summit meeting, held in New Delhi in May 1996, established a South Asian Development Fund, comprising a Fund for Regional Projects, a Regional Fund and a fund for social development and infrastructure building.

A SAARC Youth Volunteers Programme (SYVOP) enables young people to work in other member countries in the agriculture and forestry sectors. By early 1997 seven such projects had been organized. The Programme is part of a series of initiatives designed to promote intra-regional exchanges and contact. A Youth Awards Scheme to reward outstanding achievements by young people was inaugurated in 1996. The theme selected for recognition in 1999 was 'Creative Skills'. Founded in 1987, the SAARC Audio-visual Exchange Programme (SAVE) broadcasts radio and television programmes on social and cultural affairs to all member countries, twice a month, in order to disseminate information about SAARC and its members. The first South Asian festival was held in India in 1992. A Visa Exemption Scheme, exempting 21 specified categories of person from visa requirements, with the aim of promoting closer regional contact, became operational in March 1992. A SAARC citizens forum promotes interaction among the people of South Asia. In addition, SAARC operates a fellowships, scholarships and chairs scheme and a scheme for the promotion of organized tourism.

At the third SAARC summit, held in Kathmandu in November 1987, member states signed a regional convention on measures to counteract terrorism. The convention, which entered into force in August 1988, commits signatory countries to the extradition or prosecution of alleged terrorists and to the implementation of preventative measures to combat terrorism. Monitoring desks for terrorist and drugs offences have been established to process information relating to those activities. The first SAARC conference on co-operation in police affairs, attended by the heads of the police forces of member states, was held in Colombo in July 1996. The conference discussed the issues of terrorism, organized crime, the extradition of criminals, drugs-trafficking and drug abuse. A convention on narcotic drugs and psychotropic substances was signed during the fifth SAARC summit meeting, held in Malé in 1990. The convention entered into force in September 1993, following its ratification by member states.

SAARC co-operates with other regional and international organizations. In February 1993 SAARC signed a memorandum of understanding with UNCTAD, whereby both parties agreed to exchange information on trade control measures regionally and in 50 developed and developing countries, respectively, in order to increase transparency and thereby facilitate trade. SAARC has also signed co-operation agreements with UNICEF, UNDP, UNDCP, the European Union, ESCAP, the International Telecommunication Union, the Asia Pacific Telecommunity, the Colombo Plan and the Canadian International Development Agency.

The 10th SAARC summit meeting was convened in Colombo, Sri Lanka, in July 1998. The 11th summit, scheduled to be held in November 1999 in Kathmandu, Nepal, was postponed indefinitely owing to a deterioration in relations between India and Pakistan.

Finance

The national budgets of member countries provide the resources to finance SAARC activities. The Secretariat's annual budget is shared among member states according to a specified formula.

Publications

SAARC News (monthly).
SPECTRUM (irregular).

Regional Apex Bodies

Association of Persons of the Legal Communities of the SAARC Countries—SAARCLAW: 129 Hulftsdorp St, Colombo 12, Sri Lanka; tel. (1) 433411; fax (1) 436328; e-mail saarclaw@ntc.net.np; internet www.saarclaw.org; f. 1991; recognized as a SAARC regional apex body in July 1994; aims to enhance exchanges and co-operation amongst the legal communities of the sub-region and to promote the development of law. Pres. LAXMAN ARYAL (Nepal); Sec.-Gen. BHARAT RAJ UPRETI (Nepal).

SAARC Chamber of Commerce and Industry (SCCI): House 5, St 59, F-8/4, Islamabad, Pakistan; tel. (51) 2281395; fax (51) 2281390; e-mail saarc@isb.comsats.net.pk; internet www.saarcnet.com/saarcnet.org/index.htm; f. 1992; promotes economic and trade co-operation throughout the sub-region and greater interaction between the business communities of member countries; organizes SAARC Economic Co-operation Conferences and Trade Fairs. Pres. QASIM IBRAHIM (Maldives); Sec.-Gen. SYED ABUL HASAN.

Other recognized regional bodies include the South Asian Association for Regional Co-operation of Architects, the Association of Management Development Institutions, the SAARC Federation of University Women, the South Asian Federation of Accountants and the Association of SAARC Speakers and Parliamentarians.

SOUTHERN AFRICAN DEVELOPMENT COMMUNITY—SADC

Address: SADC Bldg, Private Bag 0095, Gaborone, Botswana.
Telephone: 351863; **fax:** 372848; **e-mail:** sadcsec@sadc.int.

The first Southern African Development Co-ordination Conference (SADCC) was held at Arusha, Tanzania, in July 1979, to harmonize development plans and to reduce the region's economic dependence on South Africa. On 17 August 1992 the 10 member countries of the SADCC signed a treaty establishing the Southern African Development Community (SADC), which replaced the SADCC. The treaty places binding obligations on member countries, with the aim of promoting economic integration towards a fully developed

common market. A tribunal was to be established to arbitrate in the case of disputes between member states arising from the treaty. By September 1993 all of the member states had ratified the treaty; it came into effect on 5 October.

MEMBERS

Angola	Malawi	South Africa
Botswana	Mauritius	Swaziland
Congo, Democratic	Mozambique	Tanzania
Republic	Namibia	Zambia
Lesotho	Seychelles	Zimbabwe

Organization

(April 2001)

SUMMIT MEETING

The meeting is held at least once a year and is attended by heads of state and government or their representatives. It is the supreme policy-making organ of the SADC and is responsible for the appointment of the Executive Secretary.

COUNCIL OF MINISTERS

Representatives of SADC member countries at ministerial level meet at least once a year. In addition, special meetings of sectoral committees of ministers are held to co-ordinate regional policy in a particular field by, for example, ministers of energy and ministers of transport.

STANDING COMMITTEE OF OFFICIALS

The Committee, comprising senior officials, usually from the ministry responsible for economic planning or finance, acts as the technical advisory body to the Council. It meets at least once a year. Members of the Committee also act as a national contact point for matters relating to SADC.

SECRETARIAT

Executive Secretary: Dr Pakereesamy ('Prega') Ramsamy (Mauritius).

SECTORAL CO-ORDINATION OFFICES

Each member state has a responsibility to promote and co-ordinate regional policies and programmes in specific areas on behalf of the organization as a whole. Accordingly, the Sectoral Co-ordinating Units are part of national governments and administered by the civil service of that country. Sectoral Commissions and Centres are regional institutions, which are established and supported by all member states.

Agricultural Research and Training: Private Bag 0033, Gaborone, Botswana; tel. 328780; fax 328965; e-mail dar@info.bw; Dir Dr L. M. Mazhani.

Culture, Information and Sport: Avda Francisco Orlando Magumbwe 780, 10th Floor, POB 1154, Maputo, Mozambique; tel. (1) 497944; fax (1) 497943; e-mail sacis@sadc.uem.mz; Dir Renato Matusse.

Employment and Labour: POB 31969, Lusaka, Zambia; tel. (1) 251719; fax (1) 252095; Dir C. J. Chanda.

Energy: rua Gil Vicente No. 2, CP 2876, Luanda, Angola; tel. (2) 345288; fax (2) 343003; e-mail sadc_elec@ebonet.net; internet www.ebonet.net/sadc; Dir Antonio Henrique da Silva.

Environment and Land Management: Ministry of Agriculture and Co-operatives, POB 24, Maseru 100, Lesotho; tel. 323561; fax 310349; Dir Bataung Leleka.

Finance and Investment: Private Bag X115, Pretoria, 0001, South Africa; tel. (12) 3155653; fax (12) 3219580; Dir Sechocha Makhoalibe.

Food, Agriculture and Natural Resources: 43 Robson Manyika Ave, POB 4046, Harare, Zimbabwe; tel. (4) 736051; fax (4) 795345; e-mail fstau@fanr-sadc.org.zw; Dir Reginald Mugwara.

Human Resources Development: Ministry of Public Service and Information, POB 5873, Mbabane, Swaziland; tel. 4046344; fax 4046407; e-mail sadchrd@realnet.co.sz; Dir Ennet Nkambule.

Industry and Trade: POB 9491, Dar es Salaam, Tanzania; tel. (51) 31455; fax (51) 46919; Dir Abrahim Pallangyo.

Inland Fisheries, Wildlife and Forestry: Ministry of Forestry, Fisheries and Environmental Affairs, Private Bag 350, Lilongwe 3, Malawi; tel. 782600; fax 780260; Dir D. Kambauwa.

Livestock Production and Animal Disease Control: Private Bag 0032, Gaborone, Botswana; tel. 350620; fax 303744; Dir M. Fanikiso.

Marine Fisheries and Resources: Private Bag 13355, Windhoek, Namibia; tel. (61) 2053911; fax (61) 235269; Dir Z. A. Ishitile.

Mining: Ministry of Mines and Mineral Development, Chilufya Mulenga Rd, POB 31969, 10101 Lusaka, Zambia; tel. (1) 254043; fax (1) 252095; e-mail sadc-mcu@zamnet.zm; internet www.sadcmining.org.zm; Dir C. J. Chanda.

Southern African Centre for Co-operation in Agricultural Research (SACCAR): Private Bag 00108, Gaborone, Botswana; tel. 328847; fax 328806; Dir K. Molapong.

Southern African Transport and Communications Commission (SATCC): CP 2677, Maputo, Mozambique; tel. (1) 427202; fax (1) 420213; e-mail director@satcc.org; internet www.satcc.org; Dir E. H. Msolomba.

Tourism: c/o Ministry of Tourism and Leisure, Air Mauritius Centre, Level 12, Pres. J. F. Kennedy St, Port Louis, Mauritius; tel. 210-1329; fax 208-6776; e-mail mot@intnet.mu; Dir Susy Eduard.

Water: c/o Ministry of Natural Resources, POB 426, Maseru 100, Lesotho; tel. 323163; fax 310250.

Note: In November 2000 the SADC determined to restructure its system of sectors; these were to be re-organized into four clusters, as follows: trade, industry, finance and investment; infrastructure and services; food, agriculture and natural resources; and social and human development and special programmes. A multisectoral sub-committee on HIV/AIDS was established in December 1999.

Activities

In July 1979 the first Southern African Development Co-ordination Conference was attended by delegations from Angola, Botswana, Mozambique, Tanzania and Zambia, with representatives from donor governments and international agencies. In April 1980 a regional economic summit conference was held in Lusaka, Zambia, and the Lusaka Declaration, a statement of strategy entitled 'Southern Africa: Towards Economic Liberation', was approved, together with a programme of action allotting specific studies and tasks to member governments (see list of co-ordinating offices, above). The members aimed to reduce their dependence on South Africa for rail and air links and port facilities, imports of raw materials and manufactured goods, and the supply of electric power. In 1985, however, an SADCC report noted that since 1980 the region had become still more dependent on South Africa for its trade outlets, and the 1986 summit meeting, although it recommended the adoption of economic sanctions against South Africa, failed to establish a timetable for doing so.

In January 1992 a meeting of the SADCC Council of Ministers approved proposals to transform the organization (by then expanded to include Lesotho, Malawi, Namibia and Swaziland) into a fully integrated economic community, and in mid-August the treaty establishing the SADC (see above) was signed. South Africa became a member of the SADC in August 1994, thus strengthening the objective of regional co-operation and economic integration. Mauritius became a member in August 1995. In September 1997 SADC heads of state agreed to admit the Democratic Republic of the Congo and Seychelles as members of the Community.

A possible merger between the SADC and the Preferential Trade Area for Eastern and Southern African States (PTA), which consisted of all the members of the SADC apart from Botswana and had similar aims of enhancing economic co-operation, was rejected by the SADC's Executive Secretary in January 1993. He denied that the two organizations were duplicating each other's work, as had been suggested. In August 1994 SADC heads of state, meeting in Gaborone, Botswana, advocated that, in order to minimize any duplication of activities, the PTA be divided into two sections: a southern region, incorporating all SADC members, and a northern region. It was emphasized that there would not be a merger between the two groupings. However, concerns of regional rivalry with the PTA's successor, the Common Market for Eastern and Southern Africa (COMESA, q.v.), persisted. In August 1996 an SADC–COMESA ministerial meeting advocated the continued separate functioning of the two organizations. A programme of co-operation between the secretariats of the SADC and COMESA, aimed at reducing all duplication of roles between the two organizations, was ongoing in 2000.

In September 1994 the first meeting of ministers of foreign affairs of the SADC and the European Union (EU) was held in Berlin, Germany. The two sides agreed to establish working groups to promote closer trade, political, regional and economic co-operation. In particular, a declaration issued from the meeting specified joint objectives, including a reduction of exports of weapons to southern Africa and of the arms trade within the region, promotion of investment in the region's manufacturing sector and support for democracy at all levels. A consultative meeting between representatives of the SADC and EU was held in February 1995, in Lilongwe, Malawi, at which both groupings resolved to strengthen security in the southern African region. The meeting proposed initiating mechanisms to prevent conflicts and to maintain peace, and agreed to organize a conference to address the problems of drugs-trafficking and cross-border crime in the region. A second SADC–EU ministerial meeting, held in Namibia in October 1996, endorsed a Regional Indicative Programme to enhance co-operation between the two organizations over the next five years. The third ministerial meeting took place in Vienna, Austria, in November 1998. In September 1999 the SADC signed a co-operation agreement with the US Government, which incorporated measures to promote US investment in the region, and commitments to support HIV/AIDS assessment and prevention programmes, and to assist member states to develop environmental protection capabilities. The fourth SADC–EU ministerial meeting, convened in Gaborone, Botswana, in November 2000, adopted a joint declaration on the control of small arms and light weapons in the SADC region. The meeting also emphasized that the termination of illicit trading in diamonds would be a major contributory factor in resolving the ongoing conflicts in Angola and the Democratic Republic of the Congo—DRC (see below).

In April 1997 the SADC announced the establishment of a Parliamentary Forum to promote democracy, human rights and good governance throughout the region. Membership was to be open to national parliaments of all SADC countries, and was to offer fair representation for women. Representatives were to serve for a period of five years. The Parliamentary Forum, with its headquarters in Windhoek, Namibia, was to receive funds from member parliaments, governments and charitable and international organizations. In September SADC heads of state endorsed the establishment of the Forum as an autonomous institution.

The SADC has adopted a strategic framework and programme of action for tackling HIV/AIDS, which are endemic in the region. In December 1999 a multisectoral sub-committee on HIV/AIDS was established.

The SADC expressed support for the legislation on land acquisition passed in Zimbabwe in April 2000 that permitted the state to acquire land from white settlers for redistribution to beneficiaries from the indigenous population, with payment of compensation only in respect of 'improvements' (i.e. farm buildings, irrigation schemes, machinery etc).

REGIONAL SECURITY

In November 1994 SADC ministers of defence, meeting in Arusha, Tanzania, approved the establishment of a regional rapid-deployment peace-keeping force, which could be used to contain regional conflicts or civil unrest in member states. In April 1997 a training programme was held, which aimed to inform troops from nine SADC countries of UN peace-keeping doctrines, procedures and strategies. The exercise took place in Zimbabwe at a cost of US \$900,000, provided by the British Government and the Zimbabwe National Army. A peace-keeping exercise involving 4,000 troops was held in South Africa, in April 1999. An SADC Mine Action Committee has been established to monitor and co-ordinate the process of removing anti-personnel land devices from countries in the region.

In June 1996 SADC heads of state and government, meeting in Gaborone, Botswana, inaugurated a new Organ on Politics, Defence and Security, which was expected to enhance co-ordination of national policies and activities in these areas. The objectives of the body were, *inter alia*, to safeguard the people and development of the region against instability arising from civil disorder, inter-state conflict and external aggression; to undertake conflict prevention, management and resolution activities, by mediating in inter-state and intra-state disputes and conflicts, pre-empting conflicts through an early-warning system and using diplomacy and peace-keeping to achieve sustainable peace; to promote the development of a common foreign policy, in areas of mutual interest, and the evolution of common political institutions; to develop close co-operation between the police and security services of the region; and to encourage the observance of universal human rights, as provided for in the charters of the UN and OAU. The summit meeting elected the Zimbabwean President, Robert Mugabe, to chair the Organ. The Zambian President, Frederick Chiluba, failed to attend the meeting, owing to his Government's concern that the new body was empowered to interfere in the country's internal affairs. In October the Organ convened, at summit level, to consider measures to promote the peace process in Angola; however, there were disagreements within SADC regarding the future status of the security Organ either as an integrated part of the community (favoured by South Africa) or as a more autonomous body (supported by Zimbabwe).

In August 1998 the Zimbabwean Government convened a meeting of the heads of state of seven SADC member states to discuss the escalation of civil conflict in the DRC and the threat to regional security, with Rwanda and Uganda reportedly having sent troops to assist anti-government forces. Later in that month ministers of defence and defence officials of several SADC countries declared their support for an initiative of the Zimbabwean Government to send military assistance to the forces loyal to President Kabila in the DRC. South Africa, which did not attend the meeting, rejected any military intervention under SADC auspices and insisted that the organization would pursue a diplomatic initiative. Zimbabwe, Angola and Namibia proceeded to send troops and logistical support to counter rebel Congolese forces. The Presidents of those countries failed to attend an emergency meeting of heads of state, convened by President Mandela of South Africa, which called for an immediate cease-fire and presented a 10-point-peace plan. A further emergency meeting, held in early September and attended by all SADC leaders, agreed to pursue negotiations for a peaceful settlement of the conflict. Some unity within the grouping was restored by Mandela's endorsement of the objective of supporting Kabila as the legitimate leader in the DRC. Furthermore, at the annual SADC summit meeting, held in Mauritius, it was agreed that discussion of the report on the security Organ, scheduled to have been presented to the conference, would be deferred to a specially convened summit meeting (although no date was agreed). Talks attended by Angola,

the DRC, Namibia, Rwanda, Uganda, Zambia and Zimbabwe, conducted in mid-September, in Victoria Falls, agreed in principle on a cease-fire in the DRC but failed to conclude a detailed peace accord. Fighting continued to escalate, and in October Zimbabwe, Angola and Namibia resolved to send reinforcements to counter the advancing rebel forces. Meanwhile, in September representatives of the SADC attempted to mediate between government and opposition parties in Lesotho amidst a deteriorating security situation in that country. At the end of the month, following an attempt by the Lesotho military to seize power, South Africa, together with Botswana, sent troops into Lesotho to restore civil order. The operation was declared to have been conducted under SADC auspices, however it prompted widespread criticism owing to the troops' involvement in heavy fighting with opposition forces. A committee was established by SADC to secure a cease-fire in Lesotho. Also at the end of September SADC chiefs of staff agreed that the Community would assist the Angolan Government to eliminate the UNITA movement, owing to its adverse impact on the region's security. In mid-October an SADC ministerial team, comprising representatives of South Africa, Botswana, Mozambique and Zimbabwe, negotiated an accord between the opposing sides in Lesotho providing for the conduct of democratic elections. The withdrawal of foreign troops from Lesotho was initiated at the end of April 1999, and was reported to have been completed by mid-May.

During the first half of 1999 Zambia's President Chiluba pursued efforts, under SADC auspices, to negotiate a political solution to the conflict in the DRC. Troops from the region, in particular from Angola and Zimbabwe, remained actively involved in the struggle to uphold Kabila's administration. SADC ministers of defence and of foreign affairs convened in Lusaka, in late June, in order to secure a cease-fire agreement. An accord was finally signed in July between Kabila, leaders of the rebel forces and foreign allies of both sides. All foreign troops were to be withdrawn within nine months according to a schedule to be drawn up by the UN, OAU and a Joint Military Commission. However, the troop withdrawal did not commence until February 2001. In August 2000 proposals were announced (strongly supported by South Africa — see above) to develop the Organ for Politics, Defence and Security as a substructure of the SADC, with subdivisions for defence and international diplomacy, to be chaired by a member country's head of state, working within a troika system.

TRANSPORT AND COMMUNICATIONS

At the SADC's inception transport was seen as the most important area to be developed, on the grounds that, as the Lusaka Declaration noted, without the establishment of an adequate regional transport and communications system, other areas of co-operation become impractical. Priority was to be given to the improvement of road and railway services into Mozambique, so that the landlocked countries of the region could transport their goods through Mozambican ports instead of South African ones. The Southern African Transport and Communications Commission (SATCC) was established, in Maputo, Mozambique, in order to undertake SADC's activities in this sector. The successful distribution of emergency supplies in 1992/93, following a severe drought in the region, was reliant on improvements made to the region's infrastructure. The facilities of 12 ports in southern Africa, including South Africa, were used to import some 11.5m. metric tons of drought-related commodities, and the SADC co-ordinated six transport corridors to ensure unobstructed movement of food and other supplies. During 1995 the SATCC undertook a study of regional transport and communications to provide a comprehensive framework and strategy for future courses of action. A task force was also established to identify measures to simplify procedures at border crossings throughout southern Africa. In 1996 the SATCC Road Network Management and Financing Task Force was established.

In 1996/97 174 of the SADC's 407 development projects were in the transport and communications sector, amounting to US \$6,474.4m., or 80% of total project financing. These projects aimed to address missing links and over-stretched sections of the regional network, as well as to improve efficiency, operational co-ordination and human resource development, such as management training projects. Other sectoral objectives were to ensure the compatibility of technical systems within the region and to promote the harmonization of regulations relating to intra-regional traffic and trade. In 1997 Namibia announced plans, supported by the SADC, to establish a rail link with Angola in order to form a trade route similar to that created in Mozambique, on the western side of southern Africa. In March 1998 the final stage of the trans-Kalahari highway, linking ports on the east and west coasts of southern Africa, was officially opened. In July 1999 a 317-km rail link between Bulawayo, Zimbabwe, and the border town of Beitbridge, administered by the SADC as its first build-operate-transfer project, was opened.

The SADC promotes greater co-operation in the civil aviation sector, in order to improve efficiency and to reverse a steady decline in the region's airline industries. Within the telecommunications sector efforts have been made to increase the capacity of direct exchange lines and international subscriber dialling (ISD) services. In January 1997 the Southern African Telecommunications Regional Authority (SATRA), a regulatory authority, was established. An SADC Expedited Mail Service operates in the postal services sector. The SATCC's Technical Unit oversees the region's meteorological services and issues a regular *Drought-Watch for Southern Africa* bulletin, a monthly *Drought Overview* bulletin and forewarnings of impending natural disasters.

FOOD, AGRICULTURE AND NATURAL RESOURCES

The food, agriculture and natural resources sector covers eight sub-sectors: agricultural research and training; inland fisheries; forestry; wildlife; marine fisheries and resources; food security; livestock production and animal disease control; and environment and land management. The importance of this sector is evident in the fact that, according to SADC figures, agriculture contributes one-third of the region's GNP, accounts for 26% of total earnings of foreign exchange and employs some 80% of the labour force. The sector's principal objectives are regional food security, agricultural development and natural resource development.

The Southern African Centre for Co-operation in Agricultural Research (SACCAR), was established in Gaborone, Botswana, in 1985. It aims to strengthen national agricultural research systems, in order to improve management, increase productivity, promote the development and transfer of technology to assist local farmers, and improve training. Examples of activity include: a sorghum and millet improvement programme; a land and water management research programme; a root crop research network; agroforestry research, implemented in Malawi, Tanzania, Zambia and Zimbabwe; and a grain legume improvement programme, comprising separate research units for groundnuts, beans and cowpeas. The SADC's Plant Genetic Resources Centre was established in 1988, near Lusaka, Zambia, to collect, conserve and utilize indigenous and exotic plant genetic resources and to develop appropriate management practices.

The sub-sector for livestock production and animal disease control aims to improve breeding methods in the region through the Management of Farm Animal Genetic Research Programme. It also seeks to control diseases such as contagious bovine pleuropneumonia, foot and mouth disease and heartwater through diagnosis, monitoring and vaccination programmes. An *Animal Health Mortality Bulletin* is published, as is a monthly *Animal Disease Situation Bulletin*, which alerts member states to outbreaks of disease in the region.

The sector aims to promote inland and marine fisheries as an important, sustainable source of animal protein. Marine fisheries are also considered to be a potential source of income of foreign exchange. In May 1993 the first formal meeting of SADC ministers of marine fisheries convened in Namibia, and it was agreed to hold annual meetings. In April 1997 it was agreed that Namibia would co-ordinate the establishment of inspectorates to monitor and control marine fisheries in the region for a period of five years. The development of fresh water fisheries is focused on aquaculture projects, and their integration into rural community activities. The environment and land management sub-sector is concerned with sustainability as an essential quality of development. It aims to protect and improve the health, environment and livelihoods of people living in the southern African region; to preserve the natural heritage and biodiversity of the region; and to support regional economic development on a sustainable basis. The sector also focuses on capacity-building, training, regional co-operation and the exchange of information in all areas related to the environment and land management. It administers an SADC Environmental Exchange Network, which was established in 1995, and the Community's Land Degradation and Desertification Control Programme. The sector also undertakes projects for the conservation and sustainable development of forestry and wildlife.

Under the food security programme, the Harare-based Regional Early Warning System aims to anticipate and prevent food shortages through the provision of information relating to the food security situation in member states. As a result of the drought crisis experience, SADC member states have agreed to inform the food security sector of their food and non-food requirements on a regular basis, in order to assess the needs of the region as a whole. A regional food reserve project was also to be developed.

WATER

Following the severe drought in the region in 1991/92, the need for water resource development became a priority. The water sector was established as a separate administrative unit in August 1996, although the terms of reference of the sector were only formally approved by the Council, meeting in Windhoek, Namibia, in Feb-

ruary 1997. The sector aims to promote the equitable distribution and effective management of water resources, in order to address the concern that many SADC member countries may be affected by future droughts and water scarcity. In April a workshop was held in Swaziland concerning the implementation of a new SADC Protocol on Shared Watercourse Systems. The involvement of the private sector in the region's water policies was under consideration at the Round Table Conference on Integrated Water Resources Development in October 1998.

ENERGY

Areas of activity in the energy sector include: joint petroleum exploration, training programmes for the petroleum sector and studies for strategic fuel storage facilities; promotion of the use of coal; development of hydroelectric power and the co-ordination of SADC generation and transmission capacities; new and renewable sources of energy, including pilot projects in solar energy; assessment of the environmental and socio-economic impact of wood-fuel scarcity and relevant education programmes; and energy conservation. In July 1995 SADC energy ministers approved the establishment of a Southern African Power Pool, whereby all member states were to be linked into a single electricity grid. (Several grids are already integrated and others are being rehabilitated.) At the same time, ministers endorsed a Protocol to promote greater co-operation in energy development within the SADC. On receiving final approval and signature by member states, the Protocol was to replace the energy sector with an Energy Commission, responsible for 'demand-side' management, pricing, ensuring private-sector involvement and competition, training and research, collecting information, etc. The sector administers a joint SADC Petroleum Exploration Programme. In September 1997 heads of state endorsed an Energy Action Plan to proceed with the implementation of co-operative policies and strategies in four key areas of energy: trade, information exchange, training and organizational capacity-building, and investment and financing. A technical unit of the Energy Commission was to be responsible for implementation of the Action Plan.

TRADE, INDUSTRY AND MINING

Under the treaty establishing the SADC, efforts were to be undertaken to achieve regional economic integration. The trade and industry sector aims to facilitate this by the creation of an enabling investment and trade environment in SADC countries, the establishment of a single regional market, by progressively removing barriers to the movement of goods, services and people, and the promotion of cross-border investment. The sector supports programmes for industrial research and development and standardization and quality assurance. A sector of finance and investment has been established to mobilize industrial investment resources and to co-ordinate economic policies and the development of the financial sector. During 1995 work continued on the preparation of two Protocols on trade co-operation and finance and investment, which were to provide the legal framework for integration. In August 1996 SADC member states (except Angola) signed a Protocol providing for the establishment of a regional free-trade area, through the gradual elimination of tariff barriers over an eight-year period, at a summit meeting held in Lesotho. In September 1999 representatives of the private sector in SADC member states, meeting in Mauritius, agreed to establish an Association of SADC Chambers of Commerce. In accordance with a revised schedule, announced in May 2000, the SADC free-trade area was launched in September of that year, comprising the 11 member states that had ratified the Protocol by that time (all but Angola, the DRC and Seychelles). It was envisaged, under the new timescale, that all intra-SADC trade tariffs would be removed by 2012, with about 85% to be withdrawn by 2008.

In January 1992 a five-year strategy for the promotion of mining in the region was approved, with the principal objective of stimulating local and foreign investment in the sector to maximize benefits from the region's mineral resources. In December 1994 the SADC held a mining forum, jointly with the EU, in Lusaka, Zambia, with the aim of demonstrating to potential investors and promoters the possibilities of mining exploration in the region. A second mining investment forum was held in Lusaka in December 1998. Other objectives of the mining sector are the improvement of industry training, increasing the contribution of small-scale mining, reducing the illicit trade in gemstones and gold, increasing co-operation in mineral exploration and processing, and minimizing the adverse impact of mining operations on the environment. At the summit meeting, held in September 1997, SADC heads of state signed a Protocol providing for the harmonization of policies and programmes relating to the development and exploitation of mineral resources in the region.

HUMAN RESOURCES DEVELOPMENT

The SADC helps to supply the region's requirements in skilled manpower by providing training in the following categories: high-level managerial personnel; agricultural managers; high- and medium-level technicians; artisans; and instructors. The Technical Committee on Accreditation and Certification aims to harmonize and strengthen the education and training systems in the SADC through initiatives such as the standardization of curricula and examinations. The sector also aims to determine active labour market information systems and institutions in the region, improve education policy analysis and formulation, and address issues of teaching and learning materials in the region. It administers an Intra-regional Skills Development Programme. The sector has initiated a programme of distance education to enable greater access to education, and operates the SADC's scholarship and training awards programme. In September 1997 heads of state, meeting in Blantyre, Malawi, endorsed the establishment of a Gender Department within the Secretariat to promote the advancement and education of women. At the same time representatives of all member countries (except Angola) signed a Protocol on Education and Training, which was to provide a legal framework for co-operation in this sector.

EMPLOYMENT AND LABOUR

The sector was founded in 1996, and is co-ordinated by Zambia. It seeks to promote employment and harmonize legislation concerning labour and social protection. Its activities include: the implementation of International Labour Standards, the improvement of health and safety standards in the workplace, combating child labour and the establishment of a statistical database for employment and labour issues.

CULTURE, SPORT AND INFORMATION

A culture and information sector was established in 1990, and is co-ordinated by Mozambique. Following the ratification of the treaty establishing the Community, the sector was expected to emphasize regional socio-cultural development as part of the process of greater integration. The SADC Press Trust was established, in Harare, Zimbabwe, to disseminate information about the SADC and to articulate the concerns and priorities of the region. Public education initiatives have commenced to encourage the involvement of people in the process of regional integration and development, as well as to promote democratic and human rights' values. In 1998 a new project —'Information 21'— was to be implemented under the sector, in collaboration with the SADC secretariat and the Southern African Research and Documentation Centre (q.v.), which aimed to promote community-building and greater participation in decision-making at all levels of government. Efforts to harmonize legislation in order to prevent breaches of copyright were underway in early 1999. A four-year programme, entitled the SADC Festival on Arts and Culture, was initiated in 1994. Events included a theatre festival, held in Maputo, Mozambique, in June 1997, a visual arts and crafts regional exposition, in Namibia, in April 1998, and a dance festival in Mauritius in 1999.

TOURISM

The sector aims to promote tourism within the context of national and regional socio-economic development objectives. It comprises four components: tourism product development; tourism marketing and research; tourism services; and human resources development and training. The SADC has promoted tourism for the region at trade fairs in Europe, and has initiated a project to provide a range of promotional material and a regional tourism directory. By September 1993 a project to design a standard grading classification system for tourist accommodation in the region was completed, with the assistance of the World Tourism Organization, and the Council approved its implementation. A new five-year development strategy for tourism in the region was initiated in 1995, the key element of which was the establishment of a new tourism body, to be administered jointly by SADC officials and private-sector operators. The Regional Tourism Organization for Southern Africa (RETOSA) was to assist member states to formulate tourism promotion policies and strategies. A legal charter for the establishment of RETOSA was signed by ministers of tourism in September 1997. During 1999 a feasibility study on the development of the Upper Zambezi basin as a site for eco-tourism was initiated.

FINANCE AND INVESTMENT

In July 1998 a Banking Association was officially constituted by representatives of SADC member states. The Association was to establish international banking standards and regional payments systems, organize training and harmonize banking legislation in the region. In April 1999 governors of SADC central banks determined to strengthen and harmonize banking procedures and technology in order to facilitate the financial integration of the region. Efforts to harmonize stock exchanges in the region were also initiated in 1999.

Finance

The SADC's administrative budget for 1998, approved by the Council in February, amounted to US $12.5m., financed mainly by contributions from member states. At February 1998 members owed some $4.5m. in unpaid arrears.

Publications

SACCAR Newsletter (quarterly).
SADC Annual Report.
SADC Energy Bulletin.
SADC Today (six a year)
SATCC Bulletin (quarterly).
SKILLS.
SPLASH.

SOUTHERN COMMON MARKET— MERCOSUR/MERCOSUL

(MERCADO COMÚN DEL SUR/MERCADO COMUM DO SUL)

Address: Edif. Mercosur, Dr Luis Piera 1992, 1°, Montevideo, Uruguay.
Telephone: (2) 4029024; **fax:** (2) 4080557; **e-mail:** informatica@mercosur.org.uy; **internet:** www.mercosur.org.uy.

Mercosur (known as Mercosul in Portuguese) was established in March 1991 by the heads of state of Argentina, Brazil, Paraguay and Uruguay with the signature of the Treaty of Asunción. The primary objective of the Treaty is to achieve the economic integration of member states by means of a free flow of goods and services between member states, the establishment of a common external tariff, the adoption of common commercial policy, and the co-ordination of macroeconomic and sectoral policies. The Ouro Preto Protocol, which was signed in December 1994, conferred on Mercosur the status of an international legal entity with the authority to sign agreements with third countries, group of countries and international organizations.

MEMBERS

| Argentina | Brazil | Paraguay | Uruguay |

Chile and Bolivia are associate members.

Organization

(April 2001)

COMMON MARKET COUNCIL

The Common Market Council (Consejo Mercado Común) is the highest organ of Mercosur and is responsible for leading the integration process and for taking decisions in order to achieve the objectives of the Asunción Treaty.

COMMON MARKET GROUP

The Common Market Group (Grupo Mercado Común) is the executive body of Mercosur and is responsible for implementing concrete measures to further the integration process.

TRADE COMMISSION

The Trade Commission has competence for the area of joint commercial policy and, in particular, is responsible for monitoring the operation of the common external tariff (see below). The Brasília

Protocol may be referred to for the resolution of trade disputes between member states.

JOINT PARLIAMENTARY COMMISSION

The Joint Parliamentary Commission (Comisión Parlamentaria Conjunto) is made up of parliamentarians from the member states and is charged with accelerating internal national procedures to implement Mercosur decisions, including the harmonization of country legislation.

CONSULTATIVE ECONOMIC AND SOCIAL FORUM

The Consultative Economic and Social Forum is made up of representatives from the business community and trade unions in the member countries and has a consultative role in relation to Mercosur.

ADMINISTRATIVE SECRETARIAT

Director: SANTIAGO GONZÁLEZ CRAVINO (Argentina).

Activities

Mercosur's free-trade zone entered into effect on 1 January 1995, with tariffs removed from 85% of intra-regional trade. A regime of gradual removal of duties on a list of special products was agreed, with Argentina and Brazil given four years to complete this process while Paraguay and Uruguay were allowed five years. Regimes governing intra-zonal trade in the automobile and sugar sectors remained to be negotiated. Mercosur's customs union also came into force at the start of 1995, comprising a common external tariff of 0–20%. A list of exceptions from the common external tariff was also agreed; these products were to lose their special status and be subject to the general tarification concerning foreign goods by 2006. The value of intra-Mercosur trade was estimated to have tripled during the period 1991–95 and was reported to have amounted to US $20,300m. in 1998.

In June 1995 Mercosur ministers responsible for the environment held a meeting at which they agreed to harmonize environmental legislation and to form a permanent sub-group of Mercosur. At the summit meeting held in December 1995 presidents affirmed the consolidation of free trade as Mercosur's 'permanent and most urgent goal'. To this end they agreed to prepare norms of application for Mercosur's customs code, accelerate paper procedures and increase the connections between national computerized systems. It was also agreed to increase co-operation in the areas of agriculture, industry, mining, energy, communications, transport and tourism, and finance. At this meeting Argentina and Brazil reached an accord aimed at overcoming their dispute regarding the trade in automobiles between the two countries. They agreed that cars should have a minimum of 60% domestic components and that Argentina should be allowed to complete its balance of exports of cars to Brazil, which had earlier imposed a unilateral quota on the import of Argentine cars.

In May 1996 Mercosur parliamentarians met with the aim of harmonizing legislation on patents in member countries. In December Mercosur heads of state, meeting in Fortaleza, Brazil, approved agreements on harmonizing competition practices (by 2001), on the integration of educational opportunities for postgraduates and human resources training, on the standardization of trading safeguards applied against third-country products (by 2001) and for intra-regional cultural exchanges. An Accord on Sub-regional Air Services was signed at the meeting (including by the heads of state of Bolivia and Chile) to liberalize civil transport throughout the region. In addition, the heads of state endorsed texts on consumer rights that were to be incorporated into a Mercosur Consumers' Defence Code and agreed to consider the establishment of a bank to finance the integration and development of the region.

In June 1996 the Joint Parliamentary Commission agreed that Mercosur should endorse a 'Democratic Guarantee Clause', whereby a country would be prevented from participation in Mercosur unless democratic, accountable institutions were in place. The clause was adopted by Mercosur heads of state at the summit meeting that was held in San Luis de Mendoza, Argentina, later in the month. The presidents approved the entry into Mercosur of Bolivia and Chile as associate members. An Economic Complementation Accord with Bolivia, which includes Bolivia in Mercosur's free-trade zone, but not in the customs union, was signed in December 1995 and was to come into force on 1 January 1997. In December 1996 the Accord was extended until 30 April 1997, when a free-trade zone between Bolivia and Mercosur was to become operational. Measures of the free-trade agreement, which was signed in October 1996, were to be implemented over a transitional period commencing on 28 February 1997 (revised from 1 January). Chile's Economic

Complementation Accord with Mercosur entered into effect on 1 October 1996, with duties on most products to be removed over a 10-year period (Chile's most sensitive products were given 18 years for complete tariff elimination). Chile was also to remain outside the customs union, but was to be involved in other integration projects, in particular infrastructure projects designed to give Mercosur countries access to both the Atlantic and Pacific Oceans (Chile's Pacific coast was regarded as Mercosur's potential link to the economies of the Far East).

In June 1997 the first meeting of tax administrators and customs officials of Mercosur member countries was held, with the aim of enhancing information exchange and promoting joint customs inspections. During 1997 Mercosur's efforts towards regional economic integration were threatened by Brazil's adverse external trade balance and its Government's measures to counter the deficit, which included the imposition of import duties on certain products. In November the Brazilian Government announced that it was to increase its import tariff by 3%, in a further effort to improve its external balance. The measure was endorsed by Argentina as a means of maintaining regional fiscal stability. The new external tariff, which was to remain in effect until 31 December 2000, was formally adopted by Mercosur heads of state at a meeting held in Montevideo, Uruguay, in December 1997. At the summit meeting a separate Protocol was signed providing for the liberalization of trade in services and government purchases over a 10-year period. In order to strengthen economic integration throughout the region, Mercosur leaders agreed that Chile, while still not a full member of the organization, be integrated into the Mercosur political structure, with equal voting rights. In December 1998 Mercosur heads of states agreed on the establishment of an arbitration mechanism for disputes between members, and on measures to standardize human, animal and plant health and safety regulations throughout the grouping. In March 1998 the ministers of the interior of Mercosur countries, together with representatives of the Governments of Chile and Bolivia, agreed to implement a joint security arrangement for the border region linking Argentina, Paraguay and Brazil. In particular, the initiative aimed to counter drugs trafficking, money laundering and other illegal activities in the area.

In January 1999 economic instability in Brazil, and its Government's decision effectively to devalue the national currency, the real, added pressures to relations within Mercosur. The grouping's efforts at integration were further undermined, in March, by political instability within Paraguay. As a consequence of the devaluation of its currency Brazil's important automotive industry became increasingly competitive, to the detriment of that of Argentina. In April Argentina imposed tariffs on imports of Brazilian steel and, in July, the Argentine authorities approved a decree permitting restrictions on all imports from neighbouring countries, in order to protect local industries, prompting Brazil to suspend negotiations to resolve the trading differences between the two countries. Argentina withdrew the decree a few days later, but reiterated its demand for some form of temporary safeguards on certain products as compensation for their perceived loss of competitiveness resulting from the devalued real. An extraordinary meeting of the Common Market Council was convened, at Brazil's request, in early August, in order to discuss the dispute, as well as measures to mitigate the effects of economic recession throughout the sub-region. However, little progress was achieved and the bilateral trade dispute continued to undermine Mercosur. Argentina imposed new restrictions on textiles and footwear, while, in September, Brazil withdrew all automatic import licences for Argentine products, which were consequently to be subject to the same quality control, sanitary measures and accounting checks applied to imports from non-Mercosur countries. The volume of intra-Mercosur trade shrank during 1999 as a consequence of the continuing dispute. In January 2000, however, the Argentinian and Brazilian Governments agreed to refrain from adopting potentially divisive unilateral measures and resolved to accelerate negotiations on the resolution of ongoing differences. In early March Mercosur determined to promote and monitor private accords to cover the various areas of contention, and also established a timetable for executing a convergence of regional macroeconomic policies (to which the grouping had recommitted itself at a summit meeting in December 1999). In June 2000 Argentina and Brazil signed a bilateral automobile agreement, however a new sectoral trade regime failed to be approved by the summit meeting held later in that month. The Motor Vehicle Agreement, incorporating new tariffs and a nationalization index, was endorsed by all Mercosur leaders at a meeting convened in Florianopolis, Brazil, in December. The significant outcome of that meeting was the approval of criteria, formulated by Mercosur finance ministers and central bank governors, determining monetary and fiscal targets to achieve economic convergence. Annual inflation

INTERNATIONAL ORGANIZATIONS

Western European Union

rates were to be no higher than 5% in 2002-2005, and reduced to 4% in 2006 and 3% from 2007 (with an exception for Paraguay). Public debt was to be reduced to 40% of GDP by 2010, and fiscal deficits were to be reduced to no more than 3% of GDP by 2002. The targets aimed to promote economic stability throughout the region, as well as to reduce competitive disparities affecting the unity of the grouping. The meeting also recommended the formulation of social indicators to facilitate achieving targets in the reduction of poverty and the elimination of child labour. Political debate surrounding the meeting, however, was dominated by the announcement of the Chilean Government that it had initiated bilateral free trade discussions with the USA, which was considered, in particular by the Brazilian authorities, to undermine Mercosur's unified position at multilateral free trade negotiations. Procedures to incorporate Chile as a full member of Mercosur were suspended. In early 2001 Argentina imposed several emergency economic measures to strengthen its economy, in contradiction of Mercosur's external tariffs. External commentators speculated on whether the grouping could withstand such unilateral policies.

EXTERNAL RELATIONS

In December 1995 Mercosur and the EU signed a framework agreement for commercial and economic co-operation, which provided for co-operation in the economic, trade, industrial, scientific, institutional and cultural fields and the promotion of wider political dialogue on issues of mutual interest. In June 1997 Mercosur heads of state, convened in Asunción, Paraguay, reaffirmed the group's intention to pursue trade negotiations with the EU, Mexico and the Andean Community, as well as to negotiate as a single economic bloc in discussions with regard to the establishment of a Free Trade Area of the Americas (FTAA). Chile and Bolivia were to be incorporated into these negotiations.   During 1997 negotiations to establish a free-trade accord with the Andean Community were hindered by differences regarding schedules for tariff elimination and Mercosur's insistence on a local content of 60% to qualify for rules of origin preferences. However, in April 1998 the two groupings signed an accord which committed them to the establishment of a free-trade area by January 2000. It was agreed that negotiations would commence later in 1998 on the elimination of tariffs and other restrictions to trade, measures to expand and diversify commercial activity between countries of the two groups and on the formulation of a legal and institutional framework for co-operation and economic and physical integration. In October it was reported that Mercosur was to extend existing bilateral trade agreements with the Andean Community until 31 March 1999. Negotiations in early 1999 failed to conclude an agreement on preferential tariffs between the two blocs (intended to be a basis for the establishment of a free-trade area) and the existing arrangements were again extended on a bilateral basis. At the end of March the Andean Community agreed

to initiate free-trade negotiations with Brazil; a preferential tariff agreement was concluded in July. In August 2000 a similar agreement between the Community and Argentina entered into force. In September leaders of Mercosur and the Andean Community, meeting at a summit of Latin American heads of state, determined to relaunch negotiations, with a view to establishing a free-trade area by 1 January 2002. In December 1997 the Mercosur summit meeting failed to conclude a single trading policy with Mexico, although Argentina, Paraguay and Uruguay resolved to extend the existing bilateral trade preferences with that country beyond their expiry at the end of the year. In January 1998 Brazil and Mexico agreed to pursue regular dialogue on bilateral and regional trade issues.

In March 1998 ministers of trade of 34 countries agreed a detailed framework for negotiations to establish the FTAA by 2005. Mercosur secured support for its request that a separate negotiating group be established to consider issues relating to agriculture, as one of nine key sectors to be discussed. The FTAA negotiating process was formally initiated by heads of state of the 34 countries meeting in Santiago, Chile in April 1998. In June Mercosur and Canada signed a Trade and Investment Co-operation Arrangement, which aimed to remove obstacles to trade and to increase economic co-operation between the two signatories. In July the European Commission proposed obtaining a mandate to commence negotiations with Mercosur and Chile towards a free-trade agreement, which, it was envisaged would provide for the elimination of tariffs over a period of 10 years. However, Mercosur requested that the EU abolish agricultural subsidies as part of any accord. Negotiations between Mercosur, Chile and the EU commenced in April 2000. In November it was announced that specific discussion of tariff reductions and market access was to be initiated in July 2001. In September 2000 heads of state of the Andean Community and Mercosur announced their intention to conclude free trade negotiations by 2002. In December 2000 Mercosur leaders also determined to pursue a formalized political dialogue with the Andean grouping. The summit meeting was attended by the President of South Africa, and it was agreed that Mercosur would initiate free trade negotiations with that country.

Finance

In December 1996 the Mercosur summit meeting approved an annual budget of US $1.2m. for the Mercosur secretariat, to be contributed by the four full member countries.

Publication

Boletín Oficial del Mercosur (quarterly).

WESTERN EUROPEAN UNION—WEU

Address: 4 rue de la Régence, 1000 Brussels, Belgium
Telephone: (2) 500-44-11; **fax:** (2) 511-35-19; **e-mail:** ueo.presse@skynet.be; **internet:** www.weu.int.
Based on the Brussels Treaty of 1948, the Western European Union (WEU) was set up in 1955 as an intergovernmental organization for European co-operation in the field of security and defence. In the 1990s WEU was being developed as the defence component of the European Union, and as the means of strengthening the European pillar of the Atlantic Alliance under NATO. However, from 1999 the EU was committed to the formulation of a common European security and defence policy, incorporating the main crisis management responsibilities of WEU, making the future role of WEU uncertain.

MEMBERS*

Belgium	Luxembourg
France	Netherlands
Germany	Portugal
Greece	Spain
Italy	United Kingdom

* WEU has invited the other members of the EU to join the organization and has invited other European members of NATO to become Associate Members to enable them to participate fully in WEU activities. In November 1992 Denmark and Ireland took up observer status and on 1 January 1995 Austria, Finland and Sweden became Observers following their accession to the EU.

Associate partnership status was granted to Iceland, Norway and Turkey in November 1992, to Bulgaria, the Czech Republic, Estonia, Hungary, Latvia, Lithuania, Poland, Romania and Slovakia in May 1994, to Slovenia in June 1996, and to the Czech Republic, Hungary and Poland in March 1999.

Organization

(April 2001)

COUNCIL

The Council is the WEU's main body, responsible for addressing all security and defence matters within WEU's remit. It is organized so as to be able to function on a permanent basis and may be convened at any time at the request of a member state. The Council of Ministers, comprising ministers of defence and of foreign affairs, meets usually once every six months in the country holding the WEU presidency. The Permanent Council, chaired by the WEU Secretary-General, is the central body responsible for day-to-day management of the organization and for assigning tasks to and co-ordinating the activities of the various working groups. It is composed of permanent representatives, supported by military delegates, and meets as often as required (normally once a week). The presidency of the Council is rotated between member states on a six-monthly basis.

286

MILITARY COMMITTEE

In May 1997 WEU ministers agreed to establish a WEU Military Committee. The necessary implementing measures were taken at a ministerial meeting in Erfurt, Germany, in November and came into effect in 1998. The new Military Committee is the senior authority in WEU, operating under the authority of the Council. The Committee consists of Chiefs of Defence Staff who are represented in permanent session by a Military Delegates Committee, under a permanent chairman. A military staff, WEU's only permanent military element, was inaugurated in May 1998, comprising a Director, support staff, a planning cell and a Situation Centre; in November 2000, however, WEU ministers confirmed that the military staff was to cease activities.

SECRETARIAT-GENERAL

Secretary-General: Dr Javier Solana Madariaga (Spain).

SUBSIDIARY BODIES

WEU Institute for Security Studies: 43 ave du Président Wilson, 75775 Paris Cédex 16, France; tel. 1-53-67-22-00; fax 1-47-20-81-78; e-mail weu_iss@compuserve.com; internet www.weu.int/institute; f. 1990; Dir Nicole Gnesotto (France).

WEU Satellite Centre: Avda de Cádiz, Edif. 457, Base Aérea de Torrejón, 28850 Torrejón de Ardoz, Madrid, Spain; tel. (91) 6786000; fax (91) 6786006; e-mail info@weusc.es; internet www.weu.int/satellite/en; imagery for the general surveillance of areas of interest to WEU, used, for example, in support of treaty verification, arms control, maritime surveillance and environmental monitoring; Dir Fernando Davara (Spain).

In accordance with the development of a common European security and defence system the above institutions were to remain under WEU responsibility until the establishment of appropriate EU agencies, scheduled to become operational in 2002.

ASSEMBLY

Address: 43 ave du Président Wilson, 75775 Paris Cédex 16, France; tel. 1-53-67-22-00; fax 1-53-67-22-01; e-mail assembly@weu.int; internet www.weu.int/assembly/welcome.html.

The Assembly of Western European Union is composed of the representatives of the Brussels Treaty powers to the Parliamentary Assembly of the Council of Europe. It meets at least twice a year, usually in Paris. The Assembly may proceed on any matter regarding the application of the Brussels Treaty and on any matter submitted to the Assembly for an opinion by the Council. Resolutions may be adopted in cases where this form is considered appropriate. When so directed by the Assembly, the President transmits such resolutions to international organizations, governments and national parliaments. An annual report is presented to the Assembly by the Council. In March 2000 an extraordinary meeting of the Assembly determined to initiate a process of transforming the body into the European Security and Defence Assembly (ESDA). In 2001 the Assembly was functioning as the WEU Assembly and the interim ESDA.

President: Klaus Buehler (Germany).

PERMANENT COMMITTEES OF THE ASSEMBLY

There are permanent committees on: Defence Questions and Armaments; General Affairs; Scientific Questions; Budgetary Affairs and Administration; Rules of Procedure and Privileges; and Parliamentary and Public Relations.

Activities

The Brussels Treaty was signed in 1948 by Belgium, France, Luxembourg, the Netherlands and the United Kingdom. It foresaw the potential for international co-operation in Western Europe and provided for collective defence and collaboration in economic, social and cultural activities. Within this framework, NATO and the Council of Europe (see chapters) were formed in 1949.

On the collapse in 1954 of plans for a European Defence Community, a nine-power conference was convened in London to try to reach a new agreement. This conference's decisions were embodied in a series of formal agreements drawn up by a ministerial conference held in Paris in October. The agreements entailed: arrangements for the Brussels Treaty to be strengthened and modified to include the Federal Republic of Germany and Italy, the ending of the occupation regime in the Federal Republic of Germany, and the invitation to the latter to join NATO. These agreements were ratified on 6 May 1955, on which date the seven-power Western European Union came into being. WEU was reactivated in October 1984

by restructuring its organization and by holding more frequent ministerial meetings, in order to harmonize members' views on defence questions, arms control and disarmament, developments in East-West relations, Europe's contribution to the Atlantic alliance, and European armaments co-operation.

In April 1990 ministers of foreign affairs and defence discussed the implications of recent political changes in central and eastern Europe, and mandated WEU to develop contacts with democratically elected governments there. In June 1992 an extraordinary meeting of WEU's Ministerial Council with the ministers of defence and foreign affairs of Hungary, Czechoslovakia, Poland, Romania, Bulgaria, Estonia, Latvia and Lithuania agreed on measures to enhance co-operation. The ministers were to meet annually, while a forum of consultation was to be established between the WEU Council and the ambassadors of the countries concerned, which was to meet at least twice a year. The focus of consultations was to be the security structure and political stability of Europe; the future development of the CSCE (now the OSCE); and arms control and disarmament, in particular the implementation of the Treaty on Conventional Armed Forces in Europe (the CFE Treaty) and the 'Open Skies' Treaty (see NATO for both). In May 1994 the Council of Ministers, meeting in Luxembourg, issued the Kirchberg Declaration, according the nine countries concerned (including the Czech Republic and Slovakia, which were the legal successors to Czechoslovakia) the status of Associate Members of WEU, thereby suspending the forum of consultation.

The EC Treaty on European Union, which was agreed at Maastricht, in the Netherlands, in December 1991, and entered into force on 1 November 1993, referred to WEU as an 'integral part of the development of European Union' and requests WEU 'to elaborate and implement decisions and actions of the Union which have defence implications'. The Treaty also committed EU member countries to the 'eventual framing of a common defence policy which might in time lead to a common defence'. A separate declaration, adopted by WEU member states in Maastricht, defined WEU's role as being the defence component of the European Union but also as the instrument for strengthening the European pillar of the Atlantic Alliance, thus maintaining a role for NATO in Europe's defence and retaining WEU's identity as distinct from that of the EU. In January 1993 WEU's Council and Secretariat-General moved to Brussels (from Paris and London, respectively), in order to promote closer co-operation with both the EU and NATO, which have their headquarters there.

In June 1992 WEU ministers of defence and foreign affairs convened in Petersberg, Germany, to consider the implementation of the Maastricht decisions. The resulting Declaration was significant in defining WEU's operational role. Member states declared that they were prepared to make available military units from the whole spectrum of their conventional armed forces for military tasks conducted under the authority of WEU. In addition to contributing to the common defence in accordance with Article V of the modified Brussels Treaty, three categories of missions have been identified for the possible employment of military units under the aegis of WEU: humanitarian and rescue tasks; peace-keeping tasks; and crisis management, including peace-making. Missions of this kind are often described as 'Petersberg tasks'. The Petersberg Declaration stated that the WEU was prepared to support peace-keeping activities of the CSCE and UN Security Council on a case-by-case basis. A WEU planning cell was established in Brussels in October, which was to be responsible for preparing contingency plans for the employment of forces under WEU auspices for humanitarian operations, peace-keeping and crisis-management activities. It was expected that the same military units identified by member states for deployment under NATO would be used for military operations under WEU: this arrangement was referred to as 'double-hatting'. In May 1995 WEU ministers, convened in Lisbon, Portugal, agreed to strengthen WEU's operational capabilities through new structures and mechanisms, including the establishment of a politico-military group to advise on crises and crisis management, a Situation Centre able to monitor WEU operations and support decisions taken by the Council, and an Intelligence Section within the planning cell. WEU rules of engagement, with a view to implementing the missions identified in the Petersberg Declaration, were to be formulated.

In January 1994 NATO heads of state gave their full support to the development of a European Security and Defence Identity (ESDI) and to the strengthening of WEU. They declared their readiness to make collective assets of the Alliance available for WEU operations, and endorsed the concept of Combined Joint Task Forces (CJTFs), which was to provide separable, but not separate, military capabilities that could be employed by either organization. In May 1996 NATO and WEU signed a security agreement, which provided for the protection and shared use of classified information. In June NATO ministers, meeting in Berlin, Germany, agreed on a framework of measures to enable the implementation of the CJTF concept and the development of an ESDI within the Alliance. WEU was to be permitted to request the use of a CJTF headquarters for an operation under its command and to use Alliance planning capabilities and military infrastructure. In May 1998 the Council of both organizations approved a set of consultation arrangements as a guide to co-operation in a crisis situation. A framework document on principles and guide-lines for detailed practicalities of cases where NATO assets and/or capabilities were loaned to WEU was subsequently prepared.

In November 1994 a WEU ministerial meeting in Noordwijk, the Netherlands, adopted a set of preliminary conclusions on the formulation of a common European defence policy. The role and place of WEU in further European institutional arrangements were addressed by the EU's Intergovernmental Conference, which commenced in March 1996. The process was concluded in June 1997 with agreement having been reached on the Treaty of Amsterdam (see EU chapter). The Treaty, which was signed in October and entered into force on 1 May 1999, confirmed WEU as providing the EU with access to operational capability for undertaking the Petersberg tasks, which were incorporated into the revised Treaty. It advocated enhanced EU-WEU co-operation and referred to the possible integration of the WEU into the EU, should the European Council so decide (the United Kingdom being the main opponent). Following the entry into force of the Treaty of Amsterdam WEU and the EU approved a set of arrangements for enhanced co-operation. In June the EU determined to strengthen its common security and defence policy, and initiated a process of assuming direct responsibility for the Petersburg tasks. Javier Solana was appointed as the EU's first High Representative for foreign and security policy, and subsequently named as the new WEU Secretary-General, providing for the highest level of co-operation between the two organizations. In November WEU ministers adopted a series of recommendations, based on the results of an audit of assets, to enable European countries to respond rapidly to conduct crisis management operations, to enhance collective capabilities in strategic intelligence and planning, and to strengthen military air, sea and transport equipment and capabilities for use in humanitarian and peace-keeping operations. In November 2000 WEU ministers confirmed that the EU was to assume control of its crisis management responsibilities, with extensive implications to the organization and role of WEU. The only key aspect of WEU's existing mandate to remain was to be commitments relating to collective defence.

In the early 1990s WEU's operational capabilities were substantially developed. From mid-July 1992 warships and aircraft of WEU members undertook a monitoring operation in the Adriatic Sea, in co-ordination with NATO, to ensure compliance with the UN Security Council's resolutions imposing a trade and armaments embargo on Serbia and Montenegro. In mid-November the UN Security Council gave the NATO/WEU operation the power to search vessels suspected of attempting to flout the embargo. In June 1993 the Councils of WEU and NATO agreed to establish a unified command for the operation, which was to implement a Security Council resolution to strengthen the embargo against Serbia and Montenegro. Under the agreement, the Councils were to exert joint political control, and military instructions were to be co-ordinated within a joint *ad hoc* headquarters. In April WEU ministers offered civil assistance to Bulgaria, Hungary and Romania in enforcing the UN embargo on the Danube, and a monitoring mission began operations in June. In June 1996 the NATO/WEU naval monitoring mission in the Adriatic Sea was suspended, following the decision of the UN Security Council to remove the embargo on the delivery of armaments to the former Yugoslavia. At that time more than 73,000 ships had been challenged, and 5,800 inspected, under the operation. WEU provides assistance for the administration of Mostar, Bosnia and Herzegovina, for which the EU assumed responsibility in July 1994.

In May 1997 WEU dispatched a Multinational Advisory Police Element (MAPE) to Albania to provide training and advice on restructuring the police force in that country. By the end of 1999 a new State Police Law, formulated with MAPE's support, had been ratified by the Albanian legislature, while some 3,000 police officers had been trained at centres in Tirana and Dürres and through field programmes. In February the WEU Council approved plans for an enhanced MAPE, with greater geographical coverage and operational mobility, with an initial mandate until April 2000. MAPE was being conducted by WEU at the request of the EU, enabling a large part of the costs to be met from the EU budget. In accordance with EU provisions to develop a common defence policy, responsibility for the mission was expected to be transferred to the EU in 2001. In response to the escalation of conflict in the Serbian province of Kosovo and Metohija in 1999, MAPE assisted the Albanian authorities to establish an Emergency Crisis Group to help to administer and to assist the massive refugee population which entered Albania in March and April. In November 1998, in response to a request by the EU, the WEU Satellite Centre initiated a mission of 'general security surveillance' of the Kosovo region. Since July 1999 the Centre has focused on the completion of a digital map, or geographic information system (GIS), of the entire region, which may be used to assist aspects of the reconstruction and de-mining efforts being undertaken in Kosovo.

In April 1999 WEU and Croatia signed an agreement to establish a WEU De-mining Assistance Mission (WEUDAM) in that country, upon a request by the Council of the EU. WEUDAM, which commenced activities in May, was to provide advice, technical expertise and training to the Croatian Mine Action Centre, initially for a period of one year. In November 2000 WEU ministers agreed to continue the work of WEUDAM until its existing mandate expired, on 9 May 2001.

In May 1992 France and Germany announced their intention to establish a joint defence force, the 'Eurocorps', which was to be based in Strasbourg, France, and which was intended to provide a basis for a European army under the aegis of WEU. This development caused concern among some NATO member countries, particularly the USA and United Kingdom, which feared that it represented a fresh attempt (notably on the part of France, which is outside NATO's military structure) to undermine the Alliance's role in Europe. In November, however, France and Germany stated that troops from the joint force could serve under NATO military command. This principle was recognized in an agreement signed in January 1993, which established links between the proposed joint force and NATO's military structure. In June Belgium opted to participate in the Eurocorps. In December Spain agreed to provide troops for the force. Luxembourg agreed to participate in May 1994. Eurocorps formally became operational on 30 November 1995. In June 1999 EU ministers decided that Eurocorps was to be transformed into a rapid reaction force, under EU authority. In May 1995 France, Italy, Spain and Portugal announced the establishment of two new forces, which were to be at the disposal of WEU as well as NATO and the UN: EUROFOR, consisting of up to 14,000 ground troops, to be based in Florence, Italy; and EUROMARFOR, a maritime force serving the Mediterranean. A number of other multinational forces are also designated as forces answerable to WEU (FAWEU) or that were to be available to WEU: the Multinational Division (Central), comprising Belgium, Germany, the Netherlands and the United Kingdom; the Headquarters of the First German-Netherlands Corps; the United Kingdom-Netherlands Amphibious Force; the Spanish-Italian Amphibious Force; and the European Air Group (EAG), comprising Belgium, France, Germany, Italy, Netherlands, Spain and the United Kingdom.

Publications

Account of the Session (WEU Assembly, 2 a year).
Annual Report of the Council.
Assembly of Western European Union: Texts adopted and Brief Account of the Session (2 a year).
Assembly documents and reports.

WORLD CONFEDERATION OF LABOUR—WCL

Address: 33 rue de Trèves, 1040 Brussels, Belgium.

Telephone: (2) 285-47-00; **fax:** (2) 230-87-22; **e-mail:** info@cmt-wcl.org; **internet:** www.cmt-wcl.org.

Founded in 1920 as the International Federation of Christian Trade Unions (IFCTU); reconstituted under present title in 1968. (See also the International Confederation of Free Trade Unions and the World Federation of Trade Unions.)

MEMBERS

Affiliated national federations and trade union internationals; about 26m. members in 113 countries.

Organization

(April 2001)

CONGRESS

The supreme and legislative authority, which convenes every four years (December 1997: Bangkok, Thailand). Congress consists of delegates from national confederations and trade internationals. Delegates have votes according to the size of their organization. Congress receives official reports, elects the Executive Board, considers the future programme and any proposals.

CONFEDERAL BOARD

The Board meets annually, and consists of 38 members (including 18 representatives of national confederations and 11 representatives of trade internationals) elected by Congress from among its members for four-year terms. It issues executive directions and instructions to the Secretariat.

SECRETARIAT-GENERAL

Secretary-General: WILLY THYS (Belgium).

REGIONAL AND OTHER OFFICES

Africa: Democratic Organization of African Workers' Trade Unions (ODSTA), BP 4401, Route International d'Atakpamé, Lomé, Togo; tel. 250710; fax 256113; e-mail odsta@fé.tg. Pres. F. KIKONGI.

Asia: Brotherhood of Asian Trade Unionists (BATU), 1943 Taft Avenue, 1004 Malate, Manila, Philippines; tel. (2) 500709; fax (2) 5218335; e-mail batunorm@iconn.con.ph. Pres. J. TAN.

Latin America: Latin-American Confederation of Workers (CLAT), Apdo 6681, Caracas 1010, Venezuela; tel. (32) 720794; fax (32) 720463; e-mail clat@telcel.net.ve; internet www.clat.org. Sec.-Gen. EDUARDO GARCÍA.

North America: c/o National Alliance of Postal and Federal Employees, 1628 11th St, NW, Washington, DC 20001, USA; tel. (202) 939-6325; fax (202) 939-6389; e-mail napte@patriot.net.

Eastern Europe Liaison Office: Bucharest, Splaiul Independentei, nr 202, cam. 324, Sector 6, Romania; tel. and fax (1) 3101586; e-mail cmtest@rtel.alfa.ro.

Geneva Liaison Office: CP 122, 1 rue de Varembé, 1211 Geneva 20, Switzerland; tel. (22) 7482080; fax (22) 7482088.

INTERNATIONAL INSTITUTES OF TRADE UNION STUDIES

Africa: Fondation panafricaine pour le développement économique, social et culturel (Fopadesc), Lomé, Togo.

Asia: BATU Social Institute, Manila, Philippines.

Latin America:
Instituto Andino de Estudios Sociales, Lima, Peru.
Instituto Centro-Americano de Estudios Sociales (ICAES), San José, Costa Rica.
Instituto del Cono Sur (INCASUR), Buenos Aires, Argentina.
Instituto de Formación del Caribe, Willemstad, Curaçao, Netherlands Antilles.
Universidad de Trabajadores de América Latina (UTAL).

Finance

Income is derived from affiliation dues, contributions, donations and capital interest.

Publications

Tele-flash (every 2 weeks).
Labor magazine (quarterly).

Reports of Congresses; Study Documents.

International Trade Union Federations

Federation of Professional Sportsmen: Chaussée de Haecht 579, 1031 Brussels, Belgium; tel. (2) 246-35-41; fax (2) 246-35-42. Sec. MARCEL VAN MOL.

International Federation of Textile and Clothing Workers—IFTC: 27 Koning Albertlaan, 9000 Ghent, Belgium; tel. (9) 222-57-01; fax (9) 220-45-59; e-mail piet.nelissen@cmt-wcl.org; f. 1901. Mems: unions covering 800,000 workers in 39 countries. Organization: Congress (every three years), Board, Exec. Committee, Pres. JACQUES JOURET (Belgium); Gen. Sec. BART BRUGGEMAN (Netherlands).

International Federation of Trade Unions of Employees in Public Service—INFEDOP: 33 rue de Trèves, 1040 Brussels, Belgium; tel. (2) 230-38-65; fax (2) 231-14-72; e-mail info@infedop_eurofedop.com; f. 1922. Mems: national federations of workers in public service, covering 4m. workers. Organization: World Congress (at least every five years), World Confederal Board (meets every year), 10 Trade Groups, Secretariat. Pres. GUY RASNEUR (Belgium); Sec.-Gen. BERT VAN CAELENBERG (Belgium). Publ. *Servus* (monthly).

European Federation of Employees in Public Services—EUROFEDOP: 33 rue de Trèves, 1040 Brussels, Belgium; tel. (2) 230-38-65; fax (2) 231-14-72; e-mail info@infedop_eurofedop.com; Chair. GUY RASNEUR (Belgium); Sec.-Gen. BERT VAN CAELENBERG (Belgium).

International Federation of Trade Unions of Transport Workers—FIOST: Galerie Agora, 105 rue du Marché aux Herbes, bte 40, 1000 Brussels, Belgium; tel. (2) 549-07-62; fax (2) 512-85-91; e-mail freddy.pools@cmt-wcl.org; f. 1921. Mems: national federations in 28 countries covering 600,000 workers. Organization: Congress (every four years), Committee (meets twice a year), Executive Board. Pres. MICHEL BOVY (Belgium); Exec. Sec. FREDDY POOLS (Belgium). Publ. *Labor* (6 a year).

World Confederation of Teachers—WCL: 33 rue de Trèves, 1040 Brussels, Belgium; tel. (2) 285-47-29; fax (2) 230-87-22; e-mail wct@cmt-wcl.org; internet www.wctcsme.org; f. 1963. Mems: national federations of unions concerned with teaching. Organization: Congress (every four years), Council (at least once a year), Steering Committee. Pres. LOUIS VAN BENEDEN; Sec.-Gen. GASTON DE LA HAYE.

World Federation of Agriculture, Food, Hotel and Allied Workers—WFAFW: 33 rue de Trèves, 1040 Brussels, Belgium; tel. (2) 230-60-90; fax (2) 230-87-22; e-mail fmtaa@cmt-wcl.org; f. 1982 (merger of former World Federation of Agricultural Workers and World Federation of Workers in the Food, Drink, Tobacco and Hotel Industries). Mems: national federations covering 2,800,000 workers in 38 countries. Organization: Congress (every five years), World Board, Daily Management Board. Pres. ADRIAN COJOCARUN (Romania); Exec. Sec. JOSÉ GÓMEZ CERDA (Dominican Republic).

World Federation of Building and Woodworkers Unions—WFBW: 33 rue de Trèves, 1040 Brussels, Belgium; tel. (2) 285-47-33; fax (2) 230-87-22; e-mail piet.nelissen@cmt-wcl.org; f. 1936. Mems: national federations covering 2,438,000 workers in several countries. Organization: Congress, Bureau, Permanent Secretariat. Pres. JACKY JACKERS; Sec.-Gen. DICK VAN DE KAMP (Netherlands). Publ. *Bulletin.*

World Federation of Clerical Workers—WFCW: 33 rue de Trèves, 1040 Brussels, Belgium; tel. (2) 285-47-00; fax (2) 230-87-22; e-mail piet.nelissen@cmt-wcl.org; f. 1921. Mems: national federations of unions and professional associations covering 700,000 workers in 57 countries. Organization: Congress (every four years), Council, Executive Board, Secretariat. Pres. ROEL ROTSHUIZEN (Netherlands); Sec. PIET NELISSEN. Publ. *Labor*.

World Federation of Industry Workers—WFIW: 33 rue de Trèves, 1040 Brussels, Belgium; e-mail piet.nelissen@cmt-wcl.org;

f. 1985. Mems: regional and national federations covering about 600,000 workers in 45 countries. Organization: Congress (every five years), World Board (every year), Executive Committee, six World Trade Councils. Pres. JAAP WIENEN; Gen. Sec. ALFONS VAN GENECHTEN. Publ. *Labor*.

WORLD COUNCIL OF CHURCHES—WCC

Address: 150 route de Ferney, POB 2100, 1211 Geneva 2, Switzerland.

Telephone: (22) 7916111; **fax:** (22) 7910361; **e-mail:** info@wcc-coe.org; **internet:** www.wcc-coe.org.

The Council was founded in 1948 to promote co-operation between Christian Churches and to prepare for a clearer manifestation of the unity of the Church.

MEMBERS

There are 342 member Churches in more than 120 countries. Chief denominations: Anglican, Baptist, Congregational, Lutheran, Methodist, Moravian, Old Catholic, Orthodox, Presbyterian, Reformed and Society of Friends. The Roman Catholic Church is not a member but sends official observers to meetings.

Organization

(April 2001)

ASSEMBLY

The governing body of the World Council, consisting of delegates of the member Churches, it meets every seven or eight years to frame policy and consider some main themes. It elects the Presidents of the Council, who serve as members of the Central Committee. The eighth Assembly was held at Harare, Zimbabwe, in December 1998.

Presidium: Dr AGNES ABOUM (Kenya), Rev KATHRYN K. BANNISTER (USA), Bishop JABEZ L. BRYCE (Fiji), His Eminence CHRYSOSTOMOS OF EPHESUS (Greece), Dr MOON-KYU KANG (Republic of Korea), Bishop FEDERICO J. PAGURA (Argentina), Bishop EBERHARDT RENZ (Germany), His Holiness IGNATIUS ZAKKA I (Syria).

CENTRAL COMMITTEE

Appointed by the Assembly to carry out its policies and decisions, the Committee consists of 158 members chosen from Assembly delegates. It meets every 12 to 18 months.

The Central Committee comprises the Programme Committee and the Finance Committee. Within the Programme Committee there are advisory groups on issues relating to communication, women, justice, peace and creation, youth, ecumenical relations, and inter-religious relations. There are also five commissions and boards.

Moderator: His Holiness ARAM I, Catholicos of Cilicia (Armenian Apostolic Church, Lebanon).

Vice-Moderators: Justice SOPHIA O. A. ADINYIRA (Ghana), Dr MARION S. BEST (Canada).

EXECUTIVE COMMITTEE

Consists of the Presidents, the Officers and 20 members chosen by the Central Committee from its membership to prepare its agenda, expedite its decisions and supervise the work of the Council between meetings of the Central Committee. Meets every six months.

GENERAL SECRETARIAT

The General Secretariat implements the policies laid down by the WCC, and co-ordinates the work of the programme units described below. The General Secretariat is also responsible for the Ecumenical Centre Library and an Ecumenical Institute, at Bossey, which provides training in ecumenical leadership.

General Secretary: Rev. Dr KONRAD RAISER (Germany).

Activities

Following the Assembly in Harare in December 1998 the work of the WCC was restructured. Activities were grouped into four 'clusters':

RELATIONSHIPS

The cluster group on relationships carries out the Council's work in promoting unity and community. There are teams on Church and Ecumenical Relations; Relations and Ecumenical Sharing; Inter-religious Relations and Dialogue; and International Relations. Two programmes—Action by Churches Together (ACT) and the Ecumenical Church Loan Fund (ECLOF)—are included in this grouping.

ISSUES AND THEMES

This grouping, dealing with issues and themes encompassed by the aims of the Council, comprises four teams: Faith and Order; Mission and Evangelism; Justice, Peace, Creation; and Education and Ecumenical Formation.

COMMUNICATION

The Communication cluster unites those parts of the Council involved in the provision of public information, documentation, and the production of publications.

FINANCE, SERVICES AND ADMINISTRATION

This grouping comprises the following teams: Finance, Human Resources, Income Monitoring and Development, Computer Information Services, and Building Services.

Finance

The main contributors to the WCC's budget are the churches and their agencies, with funds for certain projects contributed by other organizations. The 1999 budget amounted to 53.9m. Swiss francs.

Publications

Catalogue of periodicals, books and audio-visuals.

Current Dialogue (2 a year).

Echoes (2 a year).

Ecumenical News International (weekly).

Ecumenical Review (quarterly).

International Review of Mission (quarterly).

Ministerial Formation (quarterly).

Overcoming Violence (quarterly).

WCC News (quarterly).

WCC Yearbook.

WORLD FEDERATION OF TRADE UNIONS—WFTU

Address: Branická 112, 14701 Prague 4, Czech Republic.
Telephone: (2) 44462140; **fax:** (2) 44461378; **e-mail:** wftu@login.cz; **internet:** www.wftu.cz.

The Federation was founded in 1945, on a world-wide basis. A number of members withdrew from the Federation in 1949 to establish the International Confederation of Free Trade Unions (see p. 216). (See also the World Confederation of Labour, p. 289.)

MEMBERS

Affiliated or associated national federations (including the six Trade Unions Internationals) in 126 countries representing some 135m. individuals.

Organization

(April 2001)

WORLD TRADE UNION CONGRESS

The Congress meets every five years. It reviews WFTU's work, endorses reports from the executives, and elects the General Council. The size of the delegations is based on the total membership of national federations. The Congress is also open to participation by non-affiliated organizations. The 14th Congress was held in New Delhi, India, in March 2000.

GENERAL COUNCIL

The General Council meets three times between Congresses, and comprises members and deputies elected by Congress from nominees of national federations. Every affiliated or associated organization and Trade Unions International has one member and one deputy member.

The Council receives reports from the Presidential Council, approves the plan and budget and elects officers.

PRESIDENTIAL COUNCIL

The Presidential Council meets twice a year and conducts most of the executive work of WFTU. It comprises a President, elected each year from among its members, the General Secretary and 18 Vice-Presidents.

SECRETARIAT

The Secretariat consists of the General Secretary, and six Deputy General Secretaries. It is appointed by the General Council and is responsible for general co-ordination, regional activities, national trade union liaison, press and information, administration and finance.

WFTU has regional offices in New Delhi, India (for the Asia-Pacific region), Havana, Cuba (covering the Americas), Dakar, Senegal (for Africa), Damascus, Syria (for the Middle East) and in Moscow, Russia (covering the CIS countries).

General Secretary: ALEKSANDR ZHARIKOV (Russia).

Finance

Income is derived from affiliation dues, which are based on the number of members in each trade union federation.

Publication

Flashes from the Trade Unions (fortnightly, in English, French and Spanish; monthly in Arabic and Russian).

Trade Unions Internationals

The following autonomous Trade Unions Internationals (TUIs) are associated with WFTU:

Trade Unions International of Agriculture, Food, Commerce, Textile and Allied Workers: c/o POB 50, Central International Post, Moscow, Russia; tel. and fax (95) 938-82-63; f. 1997 by merger of the TUI of Agricultural, Forestry and Plantation Workers (f. 1949), the TUI of Food, Tobacco, Hotel and Allied Industries Workers (f. 1949), the TUI of Workers in Commerce (f. 1959) and the TUI of Textile, Clothing, Leather and Fur Workers (f. 1949). Pres. FREDDY HUCK (France); Gen. Sec. DMITRII DOZORIN (Russia).

Trade Unions International of Public and Allied Employees: 4 Windsor Pl., New Delhi 110 001, India; tel. (11) 3311829; fax (11) 3311849; internet www.tradeunionindia.org; f. 1949. Mems: 34m. in 152 unions in 54 countries. Branch Commissions: State, Municipal, Postal and Telecommunications, Health, Banks and Insurance. Gen. Sec. SUKOMAL SEN (India) (acting). Publ. *Information Bulletin* (in three languages).

Trade Unions International of Transport Workers: Tengerszem U. 21/B, 1142 Budapest, Hungary; tel. (1) 2511282; fax (1) 2524921; f. 1949. Mems: 160 unions from 67 countries. Pres. NASR ZARIF MOUHREZ (Syria); Gen. Sec. JÓZSEF TÓTH. Publ. *TUI Reporter* (every 2 months, in English and Spanish).

Trade Unions International of Workers of the Building, Wood and Building Materials Industries (Union Internationale des Syndicats des Travailleurs du Bâtiment, du Bois et des Matériaux de Construction—UITBB): Box 281, 00101 Helsinki, Finland; tel. (9) 6931130; fax (9) 6931020; e-mail rguitbb@kaapeli.fi; internet ww.uitbb.org; f. 1949. Mems: 78 unions in 60 countries, grouping 17m. workers. Sec.-Gen. JOSÉ DINIS. Publ. *Bulletin*.

Trade Unions International of Workers in the Energy, Metal, Chemical, Oil and Related Industries: c/o 3a Calle del Maestro Antonio Caso 45, Col. Tabacatera, 06470 Mexico City, Mexico; internet www.uis-tui.org; f. 1998 by merger of the TUI of Chemical, Oil and Allied Workers (f. 1950), the TUI of Energy Workers (f. 1949) and the TUI of Workers in the Metal Industry (f. 1949). Gen. Sec. ROSENDO FLORES FLORES (Mexico).

World Federation of Teachers' Unions: 4 Windsor Pl., New Delhi 110 001, India; tel. (11) 3311829; fax (11) 3311849; f. 1946. Mems: 132 national unions of teachers and educational and scientific workers in 85 countries, representing over 25m. individuals. Pres. LESTURUGE ARIYAWANSA (Sri Lanka); Gen. Sec. MRINMOY BHATTACHARYYA (India). Publ. *FISE-Infos* (quarterly, in English, French and Spanish).

WORLD TRADE ORGANIZATION—WTO

Address: Centre William Rappard, rue de Lausanne 154, 1211 Geneva, Switzerland.

Telephone: (22) 7395111; **fax:** (22) 7314206; **e-mail:** enquiries@wto.org; **internet:** www.wto.org.

The WTO is the legal and institutional foundation of the multilateral trading system. It was established on 1 January 1995, as the successor to the General Agreement on Tariffs and Trade (GATT).

MEMBERS*

Albania	Georgia	Nigeria
Angola	Germany	Norway
Antigua and	Ghana	Oman
Barbuda	Greece	Pakistan
Argentina	Grenada	Panama
Australia	Guatemala	Papua New Guinea
Austria	Guinea	Paraguay
Bahrain	Guinea-Bissau	Peru
Bangladesh	Guyana	Philippines
Barbados	Haiti	Poland
Belgium	Honduras	Portugal
Belize	Hong Kong	Qatar
Benin	Hungary	Romania
Bolivia	Iceland	Rwanda
Botswana	India	Saint Christopher
Brazil	Indonesia	and Nevis
Brunei	Ireland	Saint Lucia
Bulgaria	Israel	Saint Vincent and
Burkina Faso	Italy	the Grenadines
Burundi	Jamaica	Senegal
Cameroon	Japan	Sierra Leone
Canada	Jordan	Singapore
Central African	Kenya	Slovakia
Republic	Korea, Republic	Slovenia
Chad	Kuwait	Solomon Islands
Chile	Kyrgyzstan	South Africa
Colombia	Latvia	Spain
Congo, Democratic	Lesotho	Sri Lanka
Republic	Liechtenstein	Suriname
Congo, Republic	Luxembourg	Swaziland
Costa Rica	Macau	Sweden
Côte d'Ivoire	Madagascar	Switzerland
Croatia	Malawi	Tanzania
Cuba	Malaysia	Thailand
Cyprus	Maldives	Togo
Czech Republic	Mali	Trinidad and
Denmark	Malta	Tobago
Djibouti	Mauritania	Tunisia
Dominica	Mauritius	Turkey
Dominican Republic	Mexico	Uganda
Ecuador	Mongolia	United Arab
Egypt	Morocco	Emirates
El Salvador	Mozambique	United Kingdom
Estonia	Myanmar	USA
Fiji	Namibia	Uruguay
Finland	Netherlands	Venezuela
France	New Zealand	Zambia
Gabon	Nicaragua	Zimbabwe
The Gambia	Niger	

* The European Community also has membership status.

Note: In early 2001 the application of Lithuania had been approved and was awaiting ratification; a further 28 governments had requested to join the WTO, and their applications were under consideration by accession working parties.

Organization

(April 2001)

MINISTERIAL CONFERENCE

The Ministerial Conference is the highest authority of the WTO. It is composed of representatives of all WTO members at ministerial level, and may take decisions on all matters under any of the multilateral trade agreements. The Conference is required to meet at least every two years. The fourth Conference was scheduled to be convened in Doha, Qatar, in November 2001.

GENERAL COUNCIL

The General Council, which is also composed of representatives of all WTO members, is required to report to the Ministerial Conference and conducts much of the day-to-day work of the WTO. The Council convenes as the Dispute Settlement Body, to oversee the trade dispute settlement procedures, and as the Trade Policy Review Body, to conduct regular reviews of the trade policies of WTO members. The Council delegates responsibility to three other major Councils: for trade-related aspects of intellectual property rights, for trade in goods and for trade in services.

SECRETARIAT

The WTO Secretariat comprises some 534 staff. Its responsibilities include the servicing of WTO delegate bodies, with respect to negotiations and the implementation of agreements, undertaking accession negotiations for new members and providing technical support and expertise to developing countries. In July 1999 member states reached a compromise agreement on the appointment of a new Director-General, having postponed the decision several times after failing to achieve the required consensus. Two candidates were appointed to serve consecutive three-year terms-in-office. New procedures for the appointment of officers were expected to be negotiated.

Director-General: MICHAEL MOORE (New Zealand); (from Sept. 2002) SUPACHAI PANITCHPAKDI (Thailand).

Deputy Directors-General: (until Aug. 2002) ANDREW STOLER (USA), ABLASSE OUÉDRAOGO (Burkina Faso), PAUL-HENRI RAVIER (France), MIGUEL RODRÍGUEZ MENDOZA (Venezuela).

Activities

The Final Act of the Uruguay Round of GATT multilateral trade negotiations, which were concluded in December 1993, provided for extensive trade liberalization measures and for the establishment of a permanent structure to oversee international trading procedures. The Final Act was signed in April 1994, in Marrakesh, Morocco. At the same time a separate accord, the Marrakesh Declaration, was signed by the majority of GATT contracting states, endorsing the establishment of the WTO. The essential functions of the WTO are: to administer and facilitate the implementation of the results of the Uruguay Round; to provide a forum for multilateral trade negotiations; to administer the trade dispute settlement procedures; to review national trade policies; and to co-operate with other international institutions, in particular the IMF and World Bank, in order to achieve greater coherence in global economic policy-making.

The WTO Agreement contains some 29 individual legal texts and more than 25 additional Ministerial declarations, decisions and understandings, which cover obligations and commitments for member states. All these instruments are based on a few fundamental principles, which form the basis of the WTO Agreement. An integral part of the Agreement is 'GATT 1994', an amended and updated version of the original GATT Agreement of 1947, which was formally concluded at the end of 1995. Under the 'most-favoured nation' (MFN) clause, members are bound to grant to each other's products treatment no less favourable than that accorded to the products of any third parties. A number of exceptions apply, principally for customs unions and free-trade areas and for measures in favour of and among developing countries. The principle of 'national treatment' requires goods, having entered a market, to be treated no less favourably than the equivalent domestically-produced goods. Secure and predictable market access, to encourage trade, investment and job creation, may be determined by 'binding' tariffs, or customs duties. This process means that a tariff level for a particular product becomes a commitment by a member state, and cannot be increased without compensation negotiations with its main trading partners. Other WTO agreements also contribute to predictable trading conditions by demanding commitments from member countries and greater transparency of domestic laws and national trade policies. By permitting tariffs, whilst adhering to the guide-lines of being non-discriminatory, the WTO aims to promote open, fair and undistorted competition.

The WTO aims to encourage development and economic reform among the increasing number of developing countries and countries with economies in transition participating in the international trading system. These countries, particularly the least-developed states, have been granted transition periods and greater flexibility to implement certain WTO provisions. Industrial member countries are encouraged to assist developing nations by their trading conditions and by not expecting reciprocity in trade concession negotiations. In addition, the WTO operates a limited number of technical assistance programmes, mostly relating to training and the provision of information technology.

Finally, the WTO Agreement recognizes the need to protect the environment and to promote sustainable development. A new Committee on Trade and Environment was established to identify the relationship between trade policies, environmental measures and sustainable development and to recommend any appropriate modifications of the multilateral trading provisions. There was much contention over the compatibility of environmental and free-trade concerns in 1998, which was highlighted by a dispute settlement relating to shrimp-fishing in Asia (see below).

At the end of the Uruguay Round a 'built-in' programme of work for the WTO was developed. In addition, the Ministerial Conferences in December 1996 and May 1998 addressed a range of issues. The final declaration issued from the Ministerial Conference in December 1996 incorporated a text on the contentious issue of core labour standards, although it was emphasized that the relationship between trade and labour standards was not part of the WTO agenda. The text recognized the International Labour Organization's competence in establishing and dealing with core labour standards and endorsed future WTO/ILO co-operation. The declaration also included a plan of action on measures in favour of the world's least-developed countries, to assist these countries in enhancing their trading opportunities. The second Conference, convened in May 1998, decided against imposing customs duties on international electronic transactions, and agreed to establish a comprehensive work programme to address the issues of electronic commerce. The Conference also supported the creation of a framework of international rules to protect intellectual property rights and provide security and privacy in transactions. Developing countries were assured that their needs in this area would be taken into account. Members agreed to begin preparations for the launch of comprehensive talks on global trade liberalization. In addition, following repeated mass public demonstrations against free trade, it was agreed to try to increase the transparency of the WTO and improve public understanding of the benefits of open global markets.

Formal negotiations on the agenda of a new multilateral trade 'round', which was scheduled to be launched at the third Ministerial Conference, to be held in Seattle, USA, in late November/December 1999, commenced in September. While it was confirmed that further liberalization of agriculture and services was to be considered, no consensus was reached (in particular between the Cairns Group of countries and the USA, and the EU, supported by Japan) on the terms of reference or procedures for these negotiations prior to the start of the Conference. In addition, developing countries criticized renewed efforts, mainly by the USA, to link trade and labour standards and to incorporate environmental considerations into the discussions. Efforts by the EU to broaden the talks to include investment and competition policy were also resisted by the USA. The conduct of the Ministerial Conference was severely disrupted by public demonstrations by a diverse range of interest groups concerned with the impact of WTO accords on the environment, workers' rights and developing countries. The differences between member states with regard to a formal agenda failed to be resolved during extensive negotiations, and the Conference was suspended. At a meeting of the General Council, convened later in December, member countries reached an informal understanding that any agreements concluding on 31 December would be extended. Meanwhile, the Director-General attempted to maintain a momentum for proceeding with a new round of trade negotiations, although it was considered unlikely to be initiated before 2001. In February 2000 the General Council agreed to resume talks with regard to agriculture and services, and to consider difficulties in implementing the Uruguay Accord, which was a main concern of developing member states. The Council also urged industrialized nations to pursue an earlier initiative to grant duty-free access to the exports of least developed countries. In May the Council resolved to initiate a series of Special Sessions to consider implementation of existing trade agreements, and approved more flexible provisions for implementation of TRIPS (see below), as part of ongoing efforts to address the needs of developing member states and strengthen their confidence in the multilateral trading system. During 2001 negotiations were to be pursued to reach a near conclusive agreement on trade liberalization prior to the fourth Conference, scheduled to be held in November.

At the 1996 Conference representatives of some 28 countries signed a draft Information Technology Agreement (ITA), which aimed to eliminate tariffs on the significant global trade in IT products by 2000. By late February 1997 some 39 countries, representing the required 90% share of the world's IT trade, had consented to implement the ITA. It was signed in March, and was to cover the following main product categories: computers; telecommunications products; semiconductors or manufacturing equipment; software; and scientific instruments. Tariff reductions in these sectors were to be undertaken in four stages, commencing in July, and subsequently on 1 January each year, providing for the elimination of all tariffs by the start of 2000. In February 1999 the WTO announced plans to investigate methods of removing non-tariff barriers to trade in IT products, such as those resulting from non-standardization of technical regulations. A one-year work programme on non-tariff measures was approved by the Committee of Participants on the Expansion of Trade in IT Products in November 2000.

AGRICULTURE

The Final Act of the Uruguay Round extended previous GATT arrangements for trade in agricultural products through new rules and commitments to ensure more predictable and fair competition in the sector. All quantitive measures limiting market access for agricultural products were to be replaced by tariffs (i.e. a process of 'tariffication'), enabling more equal protection and access opportunities. All tariffs on agricultural items were to be reduced by 36% by developed countries, over a period of six years, and by 24% by developing countries (excluding least-developed member states) over 10 years. A special treatment clause applied to 'sensitive' products (mainly rice) in four countries, for which limited import restrictions could be maintained. Efforts to reduce domestic support measures for agricultural products were to be based on calculations of total aggregate measurements of support (Total AMS) by each member state. A 20% reduction in Total AMS was required by developed countries over six years, and 13% over 10 years by developing countries. No reduction was required of least-developed countries. Developed member countries were required to reduce the value and quantity of direct export subsidies by 36% and 21% respectively (on 1986–90 levels) over six years. For developing countries these reductions were to be two-thirds those of developed nations, over 10 years. A specific concern of least-developed and net-food importing developing countries, which had previously relied on subsidized food products, was to be addressed through other food aid mechanisms and assistance for agricultural development. The situation was to be monitored by WTO's Committee on Agriculture. Negotiations on the further liberalization of agricultural markets were part of the WTO 'built-in' programme for 2000 or earlier, but remained a major area of contention. In March 2000 negotiations on market access in the agricultural sector commenced, under an interim chairman owing to a disagreement among participating states. By March 2001 125 countries had issued proposals for the next stage of negotiations.

The Agreement on the Application of Sanitary and Phytosanitary Measures aims to regulate world-wide standards of food safety and animal and plant health in order to encourage the mutual recognition of standards and conformity, so as to facilitate trade in these products. The Agreement includes provisions on control inspection and approval procedures. In September 1997, in the first case to be brought under the Agreement, a dispute panel of the WTO ruled that the EU's ban on imports of hormone-treated beef and beef products from the USA and Canada was in breach of international trading rules. In January 1998 the Appellate Body upheld the panel's ruling, but expressed its support for restrictions to ensure food standards if there was adequate scientific evidence of risks to human health. The EU maintained the ban, against resistance from the USA, while it carried out scientific risk assessments. In early 1999 the USA proposed a labelling scheme to resolve the dispute, while the WTO reaffirmed its decision that the EU was obliged to remove all restrictions by mid-May unless there was scientific evidence to justify the action. In early May the European Commission published a study which supported its concerns of the existence of hormone residues in meat declared to be clear of those products, and resolved not to remove the ban. At the same time the USA issued a provisional list of EU products that were to be subject to retaliatory measures.

TEXTILES AND CLOTHING

From 1974 the Multi-fibre Arrangement (MFA) provided the basis of international trade concerning textiles and clothing, enabling the major importers to establish quotas and protect their domestic industries, through bilateral agreements, against more competitive low-cost goods from developing countries. MFA restrictions that were in place on 31 December 1994 were carried over into the new agreement and were to be phased out through integration into GATT 1994, under which they would be subject to the same rules applying to other industrial products. This was to be achieved in four stages: products accounting for 16% of the total volume of textiles and clothing imports (at 1990 levels) were to be integrated from 1 January 1995; a further 17% on 1 January 1998; and not less than a further 18% on 1 January 2002, with all remaining products to be integrated by 1 January 2005.

TRADE IN SERVICES

The General Agreement on Trade in Services (GATS), which was negotiated during the GATT Uruguay Round, is the first set of multilaterally-agreed and legally-enforceable rules and disciplines ever negotiated to cover international trade in services. The GATS comprises a framework of general rules and disciplines, annexes addressing special conditions relating to individual sectors and national schedules of market access commitments. A Council for Trade in Services oversees the operation of the agreement.

The GATS framework consists of 29 articles, including the following set of basic obligations: total coverage of all internationally-traded services; national treatment, i.e. according services and service suppliers of other members no less favourable treatment than that accorded to domestic services and suppliers; MFN treatment (see above), with any specific exemptions to be recorded prior to the implementation of the GATS, with a limit of 10 years duration; transparency, requiring publication of all relevant national laws and legislations; bilateral agreements on recognition of standards and qualifications to be open to other members who wish to negotiate accession; no restrictions on international payments and transfers; progressive liberalization to be pursued; and market access and national treatment commitments to be bound and recorded in national schedules. These schedules, which include exemptions to the MFN principles, contain the negotiated and guaranteed conditions under which trade in services is conducted and are an integral part of the GATS.

Annexes to the GATS cover the movement of natural persons, permitting governments to negotiate specific commitments regarding the temporary stay of people for the purpose of providing a service; the right of governments to take measures in order to ensure the integrity and stability of the financial system; the role of telecommunications as a distinct sector of economic activity and as a means of supplying other economic activities; and air transport services, excluding certain activities relating to traffic rights.

At the end of the Uruguay Round governments agreed to continue negotiations in the following areas: basic telecommunications, maritime transport, movement of natural persons and financial services. The Protocol to the GATS relating to movement of natural persons was concluded in July 1995. In May 1996 the USA withdrew from negotiations to conclude an agreement on maritime transport services. At the end of June the participating countries agreed to suspend the discussions and to recommence negotiations in 2000. At the end of July 1995 some 29 members signed an interim agreement to grant greater access to the banking, insurance, investment and securities sectors from August 1996. Negotiations to strengthen the agreement and to extend it to new signatories (including the USA, which had declined to sign the agreement, claiming lack of reciprocity by some Asian countries) commenced in April 1997. A final agreement was successfully concluded in mid-December: 102 countries endorsed the elimination of restrictions on access to the financial services sectors from 1 March 1999, and agreed to subject those services to legally-binding rules and disciplines. Further negotiations were scheduled to commence in 2000. In late January 1999 some 35 signatory states had yet to ratify the financial services agreement, and its entry into force was postponed. Negotiations on trade in basic telecommunications began in May 1994 and were scheduled to conclude in April 1996. Before the final deadline, however, the negotiations were suspended, owing to US concerns, which included greater access to satellite telecommunications markets in Asia and greater control over foreign companies operating from the domestic markets. An agreement was finally concluded by the new deadline of 15 February 1997. Accordingly the largest telecommunications markets, i.e. the USA, the EU and Japan, were to eliminate all remaining restrictions on domestic and foreign competition in the industry by 1 January 1998 (although delays were granted to Spain, until December 1998, Ireland, until 2000, and Greece and Portugal, until 2003). The majority of the 69 signatories to the accord also agreed on common rules to ensure that fair competition could be enforced by the WTO disputes settlement mechanism, and pledged their commitment to establishing a regulatory system for the telecommunications sector and guaranteeing transparency in government licensing. The agreement entered into force on 5 February 1998, having been rescheduled, owing to the delay on the part of some signatory countries (then totalling 72 states) in ratifying the accord and incorporating the principles of industry regulation into national legislation.

INTELLECTUAL PROPERTY RIGHTS

The WTO Agreement on Trade-Related Aspects of Intellectual Property Rights (TRIPS) recognizes that widely varying standards in the protection and enforcement of intellectual property rights and the lack of multilateral disciplines dealing with international trade in counterfeit goods have been a growing source of tension in international economic relations. The TRIPS agreement aims to ensure that nationals of member states receive equally favourable treatment with regard to the protection of intellectual property and that adequate standards of intellectual property protection exist in all WTO member countries. These standards are largely based on the obligations of the Paris and Berne Conventions of WIPO (see p. 112), however, the agreement aims to expand and enhance these where necessary, for example: computer programmes, to be protected as literary works for copyright purposes; definition of trade marks eligible for protection; stricter rules of geographical indications of consumer products; a 10-year protection period for industrial designs; a 20-year patent protection available for all inventions;

tighter protection of layout design of integrated circuits; and protection for trade secrets and 'know-how' with a commercial value.

Under the agreement member governments are obliged to provide procedures and remedies to ensure the effective enforcement of intellectual property rights. Civil and administrative procedures outlined in the TRIPS include provisions on evidence, injunctions, judicial authority to order the disposal of infringing goods, and criminal procedures and penalties, in particular for trade-mark counterfeiting and copyright piracy. A one-year period was envisaged for developed countries to bring their legislation and practices into conformity with the agreement. Developing countries were to do so in five years (or 10 years if an area of technology did not already have patent protection) and least-developed countries in 11 years. A Council for Trade-Related Property Rights monitors the compliance of governments with the agreement and its operation. During 2000 the implementation of TRIPS was one the key areas of contention among WTO members. In November WTO initiated a review of TRIPS, although this was expected to consider alteration of the regime rather than of its implementation. At that time some 70 developing countries were failing to apply TRIPS rules.

LEGAL FRAMEWORK

In addition to the binding agreements mentioned above, WTO aims to provide a comprehensive legal framework for the international trading system. Under GATT 1994 'anti-dumping' measures were permitted against imports of a product with an export price below its normal value, if these imports were are likely to cause damage to a domestic industry. The WTO agreement provides for greater clarity and more-detailed rules determining the application of these measures and determines settlement procedures in disputes relating to anti-dumping actions taken by WTO members. In general, anti-dumping measures were to be limited to five years. WTO's Agreement on Subsidies and Countervailing Measures is intended to expand on existing GATT agreements. It classifies subsidies into three categories: prohibited, which may be determined by the Dispute Settlement Body and must be immediately withdrawn; actionable, which must be withdrawn or altered if the subsidy is found to cause adverse effects on the interests of other members; and non-actionable, for example subsidies involving assistance to industrial research, assistance to disadvantaged regions or adaptation of facilities to meet new environmental requirements. The Agreement also contains provisions on the use of duties to offset the effect of a subsidy (so-called countervailing measures) and establishes procedures for the initiation and conduct of investigations into this action. Countervailing measures must generally be terminated within five years of their imposition. Least-developed countries, and developing countries with gross national product per capita of less than US $1,000, are exempt from disciplines on prohibited export subsidies; however, these were to be eliminated by 2003 in all other developing countries and by 2002 in countries with economies in transition.

WTO members may take safeguard actions to protect a specific domestic industry from a damaging increase of imported products. However, the WTO agreement aims to clarify criteria for imposing safeguards, their duration (normally to be no longer than four years, which may be extended to eight years) and consultations on trade compensation for the exporting countries. At 1 December 1995 50 member states had notified the Committee on Safeguards of the WTO Secretariat of their existing domestic safeguard legislations, as required under the agreement. Any measures to protect domestic industries through voluntary export restraints or other market-sharing devices were to be phased out by the end of 1998, or a year later for one specific safeguard measure, subject to mutual agreement of the members directly concerned. Safeguard measures are not applicable to products from developing countries as long as their share of imports of the product concerned does not exceed 3%.

Further legal arrangements act to ensure the following: that technical regulations and standards (including testing and certification procedures) do not create unnecessary obstacles to trade; that import licensing procedures are transparent and predictable; that the valuation of goods for customs purposes are fair and uniform; that GATT principles and obligations apply to import preshipment inspection activities; the fair and transparent administration of rules of origin; and that no investment measures which may restrict or distort trade may be applied. A Working Group on Notification Obligations and Procedures aims to ensure that members fulfil their notification requirements, which facilitate the transparency and surveillance of the trading rules.

PLURILATERAL AGREEMENTS

The majority of GATT agreements became multilateral obligations when the WTO became operational in 1995; however, four agreements, which have a selective group of signatories, remained in effect. These so-called plurilateral agreements, the Agreement on Trade in Civil Aircraft, the Agreement on Government Procurement, the International Dairy Agreement and the International Bovine Meat Agreement, aim to increase international co-operation and fair and open trade and competition in these areas. Each of the agreements establish their own management bodies, which are required to report to the General Council.

TRADE POLICY REVIEW MECHANISM

The mechanism, which was established provisionally in 1989, was given a permanent role in the WTO. Through regular monitoring and surveillance of national trade policies the mechanism aims to increase the transparency and understanding of trade policies and practices and to enable assessment of the effects of policies on the world trading system. In addition, it records efforts made by governments to bring domestic trade legislation into conformity with WTO provisions and to implement WTO commitments. Reviews are conducted in the Trade Policy Review Body on the basis of a policy statement of the government under review and an independent report prepared by the WTO Secretariat. Under the mechanism the world's four largest traders, the European Union, the USA, Japan and Canada, were to be reviewed every two years. Special groups were established to examine new regional free-trade arrangements and the trade policies of acceding countries. In February 1996 a single Committee on Regional Trade Agreements was established, superseding these separate working parties. The Committee aimed to ensure that these groupings contributed to the process of global trade liberalization and to study the implications of these arrangements on the multilateral system. At the Ministerial Conference held in December 1996 it was agreed to establish a new working group to conduct a study of transparency in government procurement practices.

SETTLEMENT OF DISPUTES

A separate annex to the WTO agreement determines a unified set of rules and procedures to govern the settlement of all WTO disputes, substantially reinforcing the GATT procedures. WTO members are committed not to undertake unilateral action against perceived violations of the trade rules, but to seek recourse in the dispute settlement mechanism and abide by its findings.

The first stage of the process requires bilateral consultations between the members concerned in an attempt to conclude a mutually-acceptable solution to the issue. These may be undertaken through the good offices and mediation efforts of the Director-General. Only after a consultation period of 60 days may the complainant ask the General Council, convened as the Dispute Settlement Body (DSB), to establish an independent panel to examine the case, which then does so within the terms of reference of the agreement cited. Each party to the dispute submits its arguments and then presents its case before the panel. Third parties which notify their interest in the dispute may also present views at the first substantive meeting of the panel. At this stage an expert review group may be appointed to provide specific scientific or technical advice. The panel submits sections and then a full interim report of its findings to the parties, who may then request a further review involving additional meetings. A final report should be submitted to the parties by the panel within six months of its establishment, or within three months in cases of urgency, including those related to perishable goods. Final reports are normally adopted by the DSB within 60 days of issuance. In the case of a measure being found to be inconsistent with the relevant WTO agreement, the panel recommends ways in which the member may bring the measure into conformity with the agreement. However, under the WTO mechanism either party has the right to appeal against the decision and must notify the DSB of its intentions before adoption of the final report. Appeal proceedings, which are limited to issues of law and the legal interpretation covered by the panel report, are undertaken by three members of the Appellate Body within a maximum period of 90 days. The report of the Appellate Body must be unconditionally accepted by the parties to the dispute (unless there is a consensus within the DSB against its adoption). If the recommendations of the panel or appeal report are not implemented immediately, or within a 'reasonable period' as determined by the DSB, the parties are obliged to negotiate mutually-acceptable compensation pending full implementation. Failure to agree compensation may result in the DSB authorizing the complainant to suspend concessions or obligations against the other party. In any case the DSB monitors the implementation of adopted recommendations or rulings, while any outstanding cases remain on its agenda until the issue is resolved. In May 1997 a WTO dispute panel upheld a complaint against the EU's banana import regime (brought by Ecuador, Guatemala, Honduras, Mexico and the USA in 1996), which granted preferential market access to Caribbean-produced goods. An appeal was rejected. In late 1998 the USA alleged that the EU had failed to comply with the panel's ruling and announced its intention to impose punitive measures against a series of European products. The legality of the action, in the absence of any panel ruling on the modified import arrangements (which entered into force on 1 January 1999), was disputed by several member governments and generated intensive consideration of the dispute procedures. In March, at the request of the EU, the WTO authorized the establishment of a panel to investigate the validity of a section of US trade legislation that permitted the imposition of duties, on the basis that it was incompatible with existing procedures authorized by the WTO. The EU also brought a complaint against the imposition of 100% tariffs on 15 products, of which the US Government issued formal notification earlier in that month. In early April a WTO panel upheld US claims that the modified banana regime was discriminatory and permitted trade measures to compensate for losses incurred by US companies, the first time punitive measures had been approved by the WTO, although that figure was set at US \$191.4m. annually, compared with \$520m. originally claimed. In April 2001, following approval of a new EU quota system, to remain in effect until 2006, the USA agreed to suspend its trade sanctions. Disputes under consideration in 2000 included the USA's prohibition of certain shrimp and shrimp products from India, Malaysia, Pakistan and Thailand, a complaint brought by the EU against US restrictions on imports of wheat gluten, US duties on imports of steel (brought by the Republic of Korea), and levies imposed by Chile on alcoholic spirits (brought by the EU and the USA). By late March 2001 228 trade complaints had been notified to the WTO (on some 178 different issues) since 1995, 47 Appellate Body or panel reports had been adopted, 36 cases were inactive or had been settled, while 16 cases remained active at that time.

CO-OPERATION WITH OTHER ORGANIZATIONS

WTO is mandated to pursue co-operation with the IMF and the World Bank, as well as with other multilateral organizations, in order to achieve greater coherence in global economic policy-making. In November 1994 the preparatory committee of the WTO resolved not to incorporate the new organization into the UN structure as a specialized agency. Instead, co-operation arrangements with the IMF and World Bank were to be developed. In addition, efforts were pursued to enhance co-operation with UNCTAD in research, trade and technical issues. The Directors-General of the two organizations agreed to meet at least twice a year in order to develop the working relationship. In particular, co-operation was to be undertaken in WTO's special programme of activities for Africa, which aimed to help African countries expand and diversify their trade and benefit from the global trading system. Since 1997 WTO has co-operated with the IMF, ITC, UNCTAD, UNDP and World Bank in an Integrated Framework for trade-related technical assistance to least developed countries. In 2000 WTO led efforts to enhance activities under this grouping.

International Trade Centre UNCTAD/WTO: Palais des Nations, 1211 Geneva 10, Switzerland; tel. (22) 7300111; fax (22) 7334439; e-mail itcreg@intracen.org; internet www.intracen.org; f. 1964 by GATT; jointly operated with the UN (through UNCTAD) since 1968; ITC works with developing countries in product and market development, the development of trade support services, trade information, human resource development, international purchasing and supply management, and needs assessment and programme design for trade promotion. Publs *International Trade Forum* (quarterly), market studies, handbooks etc.

Executive Director: J. DENIS BÉLISLE.

Finance

The WTO's 2000 budget amounted to 125m. Swiss francs, financed mainly by contributions from members in proportion to their share of total trading conducted by WTO members.

Publications

Annual Report (2 volumes).
International Trade Statistics (annually).
WTO Focus (monthly).

OTHER INTERNATIONAL ORGANIZATIONS

OTHER INTERNATIONAL ORGANIZATIONS

Agriculture, Food, Forestry and Fisheries

(For organizations concerned with agricultural commodities, see Commodities, p. 303)

African Timber Organization—ATO: BP 1077, Libreville, Gabon; tel. 732928; fax 734030; e-mail oab-gabon@internetgabon.com; f. 1976 to enable members to study and co-ordinate ways of ensuring the optimum utilization and conservation of their forests. Mems: Angola, Cameroon, Central African Republic, Democratic Republic of the Congo, Republic of the Congo, Côte d'Ivoire, Equatorial Guinea, Gabon, Ghana, Liberia, Nigeria, São Tomé and Príncipe, Tanzania. Sec.-Gen. PAUL NGATSE-OBALA. Publs *ATO Information Bulletin* (quarterly), *International Magazine of African Timber* (2 a year).

Asian Vegetable Research and Development Center: POB 42, Shanhua, Tainan 741, Taiwan; tel. (6) 5837801; fax (6) 5830009; e-mail avrdcbox@netra.avrdc.org.tw; internet www.avrdc.org.tw; f. 1971; aims to enhance the nutritional well-being and raise the incomes of the poor in rural and urban areas of developing countries, through improved varieties and methods of vegetable production, marketing and distribution, taking into account the need to preserve the quality of the environment; the Centre has an experimental farm, laboratories, gene-bank, greenhouses, quarantine house, insectarium, library and weather station and provides training for research and production specialists in tropical vegetables; exchanges and disseminates vegetable germplasm through regional centres in the developing world; serves as a clearing-house for vegetable research information and undertakes scientific publishing. Mems: Australia, France, Germany, Japan, Republic of Korea, Philippines, Taiwan, Thailand, USA. Dir-Gen. Dr SAMSON C. S. TSOU. Publs *Technical Bulletin, Proceedings, Centerpoint* (3 a year).

CAB International (CABI): Wallingford, Oxon, OX10 8DE, United Kingdom; tel. (1491) 832111; fax (1491) 833508; e-mail cabi@cabi.org; internet www.cabi.org; f. 1929 as the Imperial Agricultural Bureaux (later Commonwealth Agricultural Bureaux); current name adopted in 1985; inter-governmental organization which aims to improve human welfare world-wide through the generation, dissemination and application of scientific knowledge in support of sustainable development. It places particular emphasis on forestry, human health and the management of natural resources, with priority given to the needs of developing countries. CABI compiles and publishes extensive information (in a variety of print and electronic forms) on aspects of agriculture, forestry, veterinary medicine, the environment and natural resources, Third World rural development, leisure, recreation and tourism, human nutrition, and human health. Maintains regional centres in Kenya, Malaysia, Pakistan, Switzerland and Trinidad and Tobago. Mems: 40 countries. Dir-Gen. Dr DENIS BLIGHT.

CABI Bioscience: Bakeham Lane, Egham, Surrey, TW20 9TY, United Kingdom; tel. (1491) 829080; fax (1491) 829100; e-mail bioscience@cabi.org; internet www.cabi.org/bioscience; f. 1998 by integration of the capabilities and resources of the following four CABI scientific institutions: International Institute of Biological Control; International Institute of Entomology; International Institute of Parasitology; International Mycological Institute; undertakes research, consultancy, training, capacity-building and institutional development in sustainable pest management, biosystematics and molecular biology, ecological applications and environmental and industrial microbiology. There are CABI Bioscience centres in Kenya, Malaysia, Pakistan, Switzerland, Trinidad and the United Kingdom.

Collaborative International Pesticides Analytical Council Ltd—CIPAC: c/o Dr A. Martijn, 't Gotink 7, 7261 VE Ruurlo, Netherlands; tel. and fax (573) 452851; e-mail martijn.ruurlonl@freeler.nl; internet www.cipac.org; f. 1957 to organize international collaborative work on methods of analysis for pesticides used in crop protection. Mems: in 46 countries. Chair. Dr W. DOBRAT (Germany); Sec. Dr A. MARTIJN (Netherlands).

Dairy Society International—DSI: 7185 Ruritan Drive, Chambersburg, PA 17201, USA; tel. (717) 375-4392; f. 1946 to foster the extension of dairy and dairy industrial enterprise internationally through an interchange and dissemination of scientific, technological, economic, dietary and other relevant information; organizer and sponsor of the first World Congress for Milk Utilization. Mems: in 50 countries. Pres. JAMES E. CLICK (USA); Man. Dir G. W. WEIGOLD (USA). Publs *DSI Report to Members, DSI Bulletin, Market Frontier News, Dairy Situation Review.*

Desert Locust Control Organization for Eastern Africa: POB 30023, Nairobi, Kenya; tel. (2) 501704; fax (2) 505137; e-mail delco@insightkenya.com; f. 1962 to promote effective control of desert locust in the region and to conduct research into the locust's environment and behaviour; conducts pesticides residue analysis; assists member states in the monitoring and extermination of other migratory pests such as the quelea-quelea (grain-eating birds), the army worm and the tsetse fly; bases at Asmara (Eritrea), Dire Dawa (Ethiopia), Mogadishu and Hargeisa (Somalia), Nairobi (Kenya), Khartoum (Sudan), Arusha (Tanzania), Kampala (Uganda) and Djibouti. Mems: Djibouti, Eritrea, Ethiopia, Kenya, Somalia, Sudan, Tanzania, Uganda. Dir PETER O. ODHO (acting); Co-ordinator J. M. GATIMU. Publs *Desert Locust Situation Reports* (monthly), *Annual Report*, technical reports.

European and Mediterranean Plant Protection Organization: 1 rue Le Nôtre, 75016 Paris, France; tel. 1-45-20-77-94; fax 1-42-24-89-43; e-mail hq@eppo.fr; internet www.eppo.org; f. 1951, present name adopted in 1955; aims to promote international co-operation between government plant protection services and in preventing the introduction and spread of pests and diseases of plants and plant products. Mems: governments of 43 countries and territories. Chair. OLIVER FELIX; Dir-Gen. Dr I. M. SMITH. Publs *EPPO Bulletin, Data Sheets on Quarantine Organisms, Guidelines for the Efficacy Evaluation of Pesticides, Crop Growth Stage Keys, Summary of the Phytosanitary Regulations of EPPO Member Countries, Reporting Service.*

European Association for Animal Production (Fédération européenne de zootechnie): Via A. Torlonia 15A, 00161 Rome, Italy; tel. (06) 44238013; fax (06) 44241466; e-mail zoorec@mnet.it; f. 1949 to help improve the conditions of animal production and meet consumer demand; holds annual meetings. Mems: associations in 37 member countries. Pres. Prince P. ZU SOLMS-LICH (Germany). Publ. *Livestock Production Science* (16 a year).

European Association for Research on Plant Breeding—EUCARPIA: c/o POB 315, 6700 AH Wageningen, Netherlands; tel. (317) 482838; e-mail marjo.dejeu@pv.dpw.wag-ur.nl; internet www.eucarpia.org; f. 1956 to promote scientific and technical co-operation in the plant breeding field. Mems: 1,000 individuals, 64 corporate mems; 12 sections and several working groups. Pres. Dr G. R. MACKAY (UK); Sec. Dr Ir M. J. DE JEU (Netherlands). Publ. *Bulletin.*

European Confederation of Agriculture: 23 rue de la Science, 1040 Brussels, Belgium; tel. (2) 230-43-80; fax (2) 230-46-77; e-mail cea@pophost.eunet.be; f. 1889 as International Confederation, re-formed in 1948 as European Confederation; represents the interests of European agriculture in the international field; social security for independent farmers and foresters in the member countries; currently giving priority to developing relations with the countries of central and eastern Europe. Mems: 300 mems. from 30 countries. Pres. HANS JONSSON (Sweden); Gen. Sec. CHRISTOPHE HÉMARD (France). Publs *CEA Dialog, Annual Report.*

European Grassland Federation: c/o Dr W. H. Prins, Hollandseweg 382, 6705 BE Wageningen, Netherlands; tel. (317) 416386; fax (317) 416386; e-mail egf-secr@pckassa.com; internet www.europeangrassland.org; f. 1963 to facilitate and maintain liaison between European grassland organizations and to promote the interchange of scientific and practical knowledge and experience; general meeting is held every two years and symposia at other times. Mems: 29 full and eight corresponding member countries in Europe. Pres. Dr CHRISTIAN HUYGHE; Sec. Dr W. H. PRINS. Publ. *Proceedings (Grassland Science in Europe).*

European Livestock and Meat Trading Union: 81A rue de la Loi, 1040 Brussels, Belgium; tel. (2) 230-46-03; fax (2) 230-94-00; e-mail uecbv@pophost.eunet.be; internet uecbv.eunet.be; f. 1952 to study problems of the European livestock and meat trade and inform members of all legislation affecting it, and to act as an international arbitration commission; conducts research on agricultural markets, quality of livestock, and veterinary regulations. Mems: national organizations in Austria, Belgium, Czech Republic, Denmark, Finland, France, Germany, Greece, Hungary, Ireland, Italy, Luxembourg, Netherlands, Norway, Poland, Portugal, Spain, Sweden, Switzerland, United Kingdom; corresponding mems in Croatia, Estonia, Russia, Slovakia, Slovenia and Federal Republic of Yugoslavia; and the European Association of Livestock Markets. Pres. L. SPANGHERO; Sec.-Gen. J.-L. MERIAUX.

Inter-American Association of Agricultural Librarians, Documentalists and Information Specialists (Asociación Interamericana de Bibliotecarios, Documentalistas y Especialistas en Información Agrícolas—AIBDA): c/o IICA-CIDIA, Apdo 55-2200 Coronado, Costa Rica; tel. 216-0290; fax 216-0291; e-mail cmolesti@iica.ac.cr; internet www.iica.ac.cr; f. 1953 to promote professional improvement of its members through technical publications and meetings, and to promote improvement of library services in agricultural sciences. Mems: about 400 in 29 countries and territories. Pres. MAGDA SAUDÍ; Exec. Sec. CARLOS J. MOLESTINA; Publs *Boletín Informativo* (3 a year), *Boletín Especial* (irregular), *Revista AIBDA* (2 a year), *AIBDA Actualidades* (4 or 5 a year).

Inter-American Tropical Tuna Commission—IATTC: Scripps Institution of Oceanography, 8604 La Jolla Shores Drive, La Jolla, CA 92037-1508, USA; tel. (858) 546-7100; fax (858) 546-7133; e-mail rallen@iattc.org; internet www.iattc.org; f. 1950; two programmes, the Tuna-Billfish Programme and the Tuna-Dolphin Programme. The Tuna-Billfish Programme investigates the biology of the tunas and related species of the eastern Pacific Ocean to determine the effects of fishing and natural factors on the stocks of tunas and billfish, and recommends appropriate conservation measures to maintain stocks at levels which will afford maximum sustainable catches; the Tuna-Dolphin Programme monitors dolphin levels and the number of deaths caused to dolphins by tuna-fishers, in order to recommend measures to maintain dolphin stocks; promotes fishing methods that avoid the needless killing of dolphins; investigates the effect of various fishing methods on different species of fish and other aquatic animals. Mems: Costa Rica, Ecuador, El Salvador, France, Guatemala, Japan, Mexico, Nicaragua, Panama, USA, Vanuatu, Venezuela. Dir ROBIN L. ALLEN; Publs *Bulletin* (irregular), *Annual Report*.

International Association for Cereal Science and Technology—ICC: Wiener Strasse 22A, POB 77, 2320 Schwechat, Austria; tel. (1) 707-72-02; fax (1) 707-72-04; e-mail gen.sec@icc.or.at; internet www.icc.or.at; f. 1955 (as the International Association for Cereal Chemistry; name changed 1986); aims to promote international co-operation in the field of cereal science and technology through the dissemination of information and the development of standard methods of testing and analysing products. Mems: 50 mem. states. Sec.-Gen. Dr HELMUT GLATTES (Austria).

International Association for Vegetation Science: IBN-DLO, POB 47, 6700 AA Wageningen, Netherlands; tel. (317) 477914; fax (317) 424988; e-mail j.h.j.schaminee@alterra.wagur.nl; internet www.iavs.org; f. 1938. Mems: 1,330 from 70 countries. Chair. Prof. Dr E. O. BOX; Gen Sec. Dr J. H. J. SCHAMINÉE. Publs *Phytocoenologia*, *Journal of Vegetation Science, Applied Vegetation Science*.

International Association of Agricultural Economists: 1211 West 22nd St, Suite 216, Oak Brook, IL 60523-2197, USA; tel. (630) 571-9393; fax (630) 571-9580; e-mail iaae@farmfoundation.org; internet www.iaae-agecon.org; f. 1929 to foster development of the sciences of agricultural economics and further the application of the results of economic investigation in agricultural processes and the improvement of economic and social conditions relating to agricultural and rural life. Mems: in 96 countries. Pres. JOACHIM VON BRAUN; Sec. and Treas. WALTER J. ARMBRUSTER (USA). Publs *Agricultural Economics* (8 a year), *IAAE Newsletter* (2 a year).

International Association of Agricultural Information Specialists: c/o Margot Bellamy, 14 Queen St, Dorchester-on-Thames, Oxon OX10 7HR, United Kingdom; tel. (1865) 340054; e-mail margot.bellamy@fritillary.demon.co.uk; f. 1955 to promote agricultural library science and documentation, and the professional interests of agricultural librarians and documentalists; affiliated to the International Federation of Library Associations. Mems: 600 in 84 countries. Pres. Dr JAN VAN DER BURG (Netherlands); Sec.-Treas. MARGOT BELLAMY (UK). Publs *Quarterly Bulletin, World Directory of Agricultural Information Resource Centres*.

International Association of Horticultural Producers: Postbus 200, 2700 AG Zoetermeen, Netherlands; tel. (79) 3470707; fax (79) 3470404; e-mail pt@tuinbouw.nl; internet www.aiph.org.uk; f. 1948; represents the common interests of commercial horticultural producers in the international field by frequent meetings, regular publications, press-notices, resolutions and addresses to governments and international authorities; authorizes international horticultural exhibitions. Mems: national associations in 25 countries. Pres. B. WERNER; Gen. Sec. Dr J. B. M. ROTTEVEEL. Publ. *Yearbook of International Horticultural Statistics*.

International Bee Research Association: 18 North Rd, Cardiff, CF10 3DT, United Kingdom; tel. (29) 2037-2409; fax (29) 2066-5522; e-mail ibra@cardiff.ac.uk; internet www.cf.ac.uk/ibra; f. 1949 to further bee research and provide an information service for bee scientists and bee-keepers world-wide. Mems: 1,200 in 130 countries. Dir RICHARD JONES; Asst Dir Dr PAMELA MUNN. Publs *Bee World*

(quarterly), *Apicultural Abstracts* (quarterly), *Journal of Apicultural Research* (quarterly).

International Centre for Integrated Mountain Development: POB 3226, Kathmandu, Nepal; tel. (1) 525313; fax (1) 524509; e-mail dits@icimod.org.np; internet www.icimod.org.sg; f. 1983 with the primary objective of promoting the sustained well-being of mountain communities through effective socioeconomic development policies and programmes, and through the sound management of fragile mountain habitats, especially in the Hindu Kush-Himalayan region, covering all or parts of Afghanistan, Bangladesh, Bhutan, China, India, Myanmar, Nepal and Pakistan; international staff of 30; Dir-Gen. EGBERT PELINCK.

International Centre for Tropical Agriculture (Centro Internacional de Agricultura Tropical—CIAT): Apdo Aéreo 6713, Cali, Colombia; tel. (2) 445-0000; fax (2) 445-0073; e-mail ciat@cgnet.com; internet www.ciat.cgiar.org; f. 1967 to contribute to the alleviation of hunger and poverty in tropical developing countries by using new techniques in agriculture research and training; focuses on production problems of the tropics concentrating on field beans, cassava, rice and tropical pastures. Dir-Gen. Dr JOACHIM VOSS. Publs *Annual Report, Growing Affinities* (2 a year), *Pasturas Tropicales* (3 a year), catalogue of publications.

International Commission for the Conservation of Atlantic Tunas—ICCAT: Calle Corazón de Maria 8, 28020 Madrid, Spain; tel. (91) 4165600; fax (91) 4152612; internet www.iccat.es; f. 1969 under the provisions of the International Convention for the Conservation of Atlantic Tunas (1966) to maintain the populations of tuna and tuna-like species in the Atlantic Ocean and adjacent seas at levels that will permit the maximum sustainable catch; collects statistics, conducts studies. Mems: 24 contracting parties. Chair. J. BARANANO; Exec. Sec. Dr A. RIBEIRO LIMA (Portugal). Publs *ICCAT Newsletter, Statistical Bulletin* (annually), *Data Record* (annually).

International Commission of Sugar Technology: c/o Dr H. van Malland, 97199 Ochsenfurt, Marktbreiter Str. 74, Germany; tel. (9331) 91450; fax (9331) 91462; f. 1949 to discuss investigations and promote scientific and technical research work. Pres. of Scientific Cttee. Dr JAN MAARTEN DE BRUIJN (Netherlands); Sec.-Gen. Dr HENK VAN MALLAND.

International Committee for Animal Recording: Villa del Ragno, Via Nomentana 134, 00161 Rome, Italy; tel. (06) 86329141; fax (06) 86329263; e-mail icar@eap.org; internet www.icar.org; f. 1951 to extend and improve the work of recording and to standardize methods. Mems: in 40 countries. Pres. Dr JOSEPH CRETTENAND (Switzerland).

International Crops Research Institute for the Semi-Arid Tropics—ICRISAT: Patancheru, Andhra Pradesh, India; tel. (40) 596161; fax (40) 241239; e-mail icrisat@cgiar.org; internet wwwicrisat.org; f. 1972 as world centre for genetic improvement of sorghum, millet, pigeonpea, chickpea and groundnut, and for research on the management of resources in the world's semi-arid tropics with the aim of reducing poverty and protecting the environment; research covers all physical and socio-economic aspects of improving farming systems on unirrigated land. Dir Dr WILLIAM D. DAR (Philippines). Publs *ICRISAT Report* (annually), *SAT News* (2 a year), *International Chickpea and Pigeonpea Newsletter, International Arachis Newsletter, International Sorghum and Millet Newsletter* (annually), information and research bulletins.

International Dairy Federation: 41 Square Vergote, 1030 Brussels, Belgium; tel. (2) 733-98-88; fax (2) 733-04-13; e-mail info@fil-idf.org; internet www.fil-idf.org; f. 1903 to link all dairy associations in order to encourage the solution of scientific, technical and economic problems affecting the dairy industry. Mems: national committees in 34 countries. Dir. Gen. E. HOPKIN (UK). Publs *Bulletin of IDF, IDF Standards*.

International Federation of Agricultural Producers—IFAP: 60 rue St Lazare, 75009 Paris, France; tel. 1-45-26-05-53; fax 1-48-74-72-12; e-mail info@ifap.org; internet www.ifap.org; f. 1946 to represent, in the international field, the interests of agricultural producers; to exchange information and ideas and help develop understanding of world problems and their effects upon agricultural producers; to encourage sustainable patterns of agricultural development; holds conference every two years. National farmers' organizations and agricultural co-operatives of 60 countries are represented in the Federation. Pres. GERARD DOORNBOS (Netherlands); Sec.-Gen. DAVID KING. Publs *The World Farmer* (bimonthly), *Proceedings of General Conferences*.

International Federation of Beekeepers' Associations—APIMONDIA: Corso Vittorio Emanuele 101, 00186 Rome, Italy; tel. and fax (06) 6852286; e-mail apimondia@mclink.it; internet www.beekeeping.org/apimondia; f. 1949; collects and brings up to date documentation concerning international beekeeping; studies the particular problems of beekeeping through its permanent committees; organizes international congresses, seminars, symposia and meetings; stimulates research into new techniques for more economical results; co-operates with other international organizations interested in beekeeping, in particular with FAO. Mems: 56 associations from 52 countries. Pres. RAYMOND BORNECK; Sec.-Gen. RICCARDO JANNONI-SEBASTIANINI. Publs *Apiacta* (quarterly, in English, French, German and Spanish), *Dictionary of Beekeeping Terms*, AGROVOC (thesaurus of agricultural terms), studies.

International Hop Growers' Convention: c/o Inštitut za hmeljarstvo in pivovarstvo, POB 51, 3310 Žalec, Slovenia; tel. (63) 715214; fax (63) 717163; e-mail martin.pavlovic@uni-lj.si; internet www.hmelj-giz.si/ihgc/; f. 1950 to act as a centre for the collection of data on hop production, and to conduct scientific, technical and economic commissions. Mems: national associations in Australia, Belgium, Bulgaria, the People's Republic of China, Czech Republic, France, Germany, New Zealand, Poland, Portugal, Russia, Slovakia, Slovenia, South Africa, Spain, Ukraine, United Kingdom, USA, Federal Republic of Yugoslavia. Pres. MARTIN JOLLY; Gen. Sec. Dr MARTIN PAVLOVIČ. Publ. *Hopfen-Rundschau* (fortnightly).

International Institute for Beet Research: 195 ave de Tervueren, 1150 Brussels, Belgium; tel. (2) 737-70-90; fax (2) 737-70-99; e-mail mail@iirb.org; f. 1932 to promote research and exchange of information, by organizing meetings and study groups. Mems: 600 in 33 countries. Pres. of the Admin. Council J-J. MISONNE; Sec.-Gen. R. BECKERS.

International Institute of Tropical Agriculture—IITA: Oyo Rd, PMB 5320, Ibadan, Nigeria; tel. (2) 241-2626; fax (2) 241-2221; e-mail iita@cgiar.org; internet www.iita.org; f. 1967; principal financing arranged by the Consultative Group on International Agricultural Research (CGIAR), co-sponsored by the FAO, the IBRD and the UNDP. The research programmes comprise crop management, improvement of crops (cereals, legumes and root crops) and plant protection and health; training programme for researchers in tropical agriculture; library of 75,000 vols and data base of 115,180 records; also administers six agro-ecological research stations. Dir-Gen. Dr LUKAS BRADER. Publs *Annual Report, IITA Research* (quarterly), technical bulletins, research reports.

International Livestock Research Institute—ILRI: POB 30709, Nairobi, Kenya; tel. (2) 632311; fax (2) 631499; e-mail ilri-kenya@cgiar.org; internet www.cgiar.org/ilri; f. 1995, to supersede the International Laboratory for Research on Animal Diseases and the International Livestock Centre for Africa; conducts laboratory and field research on animal health (in particular, animal trypanosomiasis and theileriosis), the conservation of genetic resources, production systems analysis, natural resource management, livestock policy analysis and strengthening national research capacities; undertakes training programmes for scientists and technicians; specialized science library. Dir Dr HANK FITZHUGH. Publs *Annual Report, Livestock Research for Development* (newsletter, 2 a year).

International Maize and Wheat Improvement Centre—CIMMYT: Apdo Postal 6-641, 06600 México, DF, Mexico; tel. (5) 804-2004; fax (5) 804-7588; e-mail cimmyt@cgiar.org; internet www.cimmyt.mx; conducts world-wide research programme for sustainable increase in production of maize, wheat and triticale in developing countries. Dir-Gen. Prof. TIMOTHY REEVES.

International Organization for Biological Control of Noxious Animals and Plants: IOBC Permanent Secretariat, AGROPOLIS, Ave Agropolis, 34394 Montpellier Cédex 5, France; e-mail iobc@agropolis.fr; f. 1955 to promote and co-ordinate research on the more effective biological control of harmful organisms; re-organized in 1971 as a central council with world-wide affiliations and six largely autonomous regional sections: the West Palaearctic (North Africa, the Middle East and most of Europe), the East Palaearctic (Eastern Europe and Russia), the Neartic (North America), the Neo-Tropical (Central and South America), Tropical Africa, and Asia and the Pacific. Pres. Dr J. WAAGE (UK); Sec.-Gen. Dr E. WAJNBERG (France). Publs *BioControl, Newsletter*.

International Organization of Citrus Virologists: c/o C. N. Roistacher, Dept of Plant Pathology, Univ. of California, Riverside, CA 92521-0122, USA; tel. (909) 684-0934; fax (909) 684-4324; e-mail chester.r@worldnet.att.net; f. 1957 to promote research on citrus virus diseases at international level by standardizing diagnostic techniques and exchanging information. Mems: 250. Chair. R. F. LEE; Sec. CHESTER N. ROISTACHER.

International Red Locust Control Organization for Central and Southern Africa: POB 240252, Ndola, Zambia; tel. (2) 615684; fax (2) 614285; e-mail locust@zamnet.zm; f. 1971 to control locusts in eastern, central and southern Africa, and assists in the control of African army-worm and quelea-quelea. Mems: eight countries. Dir Dr A. D. GADABU. Publs *Annual Report, Monthly Report* and scientific reports.

International Rice Research Institute—IRRI: DAPO Box 7777, Metro Manila, Philippines; tel. (2) 8450563; fax (2) 8911292; e-mail irri@cgiar.org; internet www.cgiar.org/irri; f. 1960; conducts research on rice, aiming to develop technology that is of environmental, social and economic benefit, and to enhance national rice research systems; maintains a library to collect and provide access to the world's technical rice literature; publishes and disseminates research results; conducts regional rice research projects in co-operation with scientists in rice-producing countries; offers training in rice research methods and techniques; organizes international conferences and workshops and operates Riceworld, a museum and learning centre about rice and rice-related culture and research. Dir-Gen. Dr RONALD CANTRELL. Publs *Annual Report, Rice Literature Update, Hotline, Facts about IRRI, News about Rice and People, International Rice Research Notes*..

International Seed Testing Association—ISTA: Zürichstrasse 50, Postfach 308, 8303 Bassersdorf, Switzerland; tel. (1) 8386060; fax (1) 8386001; e-mail executive.office@ista.ch; internet www.seedtest.org; f. 1906 (reconstituted 1924) to promote uniformity and accurate methods of seed testing and evaluation in order to facilitate efficiency in production, processing, distribution and utilization of seeds; organizes triennial congresses, meetings, workshops, symposia and training courses. Mems: 72 countries. Exec. Officer Dr M. MUSCHICK; Hon. Sec. Treas. Prof. A. LOVATO (Italy). Publs *Seed Science and Technology* (3 a year), *ISTA News Bulletin* (3 a year).

International Sericultural Commission: 25 quai JeanJacques Rousseau, 69350 La Mulatière, France; tel. 4-78-50-41-98; fax 4-78-86-09-57; f. 1948 to encourage the development of silk production. Library of 1,215 vols. Mems: governments of Brazil, Egypt, France, India, Indonesia, Japan, Lebanon, Madagascar, Romania, Thailand, Tunisia, Turkey. Sec.-Gen. Dr GÉRARD CHAVANCY (France). Publ. *Sericologia* (quarterly).

International Service for National Agricultural Research—ISNAR: Laan van Nieuw Oost Indie 133, 2593 BM The Hague, Netherlands; tel. (70) 349-61-00; fax (70) 381-96-77; e-mail isnar@cgiar.org; internet www.cgiar.org/isnar; f. 1980 by the Consultative Group on International Agricultural Research (q.v.) to strengthen national agricultural research systems in developing countries by promoting appropriate research policies, sustainable research institutions, and improved research management; provides advisory service, training, research services and information. Chair. MOÏSE MENSAH; Dir-Gen. STEIN BIE.

International Society for Horticultural Science: Decroylaan 42, POB 500, 3001 Leuven, Belgium; tel. (16) 22-94-27; fax (16) 22-94-50; e-mail info@ishs.org; internet www.ishs.org; f. 1959 to co-operate in the research field. Mems: 54 member countries, 265 organizations, 3,050 individuals. Pres. Prof. Dr C. D. BRICKELL (UK); Exec. Dir Ir Jozef VAN ASSCHE (Belgium). Publs *Chronica Horticulturae* (quarterly), *Acta Horticulturae, Scientia Horticulturae* (monthly), *Horticultural Research International*.

International Union of Forest Research Organizations—IUFRO: 1131 Vienna, Seckendorff-Gudent-Weg 8, Austria; tel. (1) 877-01-51; fax (1) 877-93-55; e-mail iufro@forvie.ac.at; f. 1892. Mems: 700 organizations in 115 countries, involving more than 15,000 scientists. Pres. Prof. RISTO SEPPÄLÄ (Finland); Sec. HEINRICH SCHMUTZEN-HOFER (Austria). Publs *Annual Report, IUFRO News* (quarterly), *IUFRO World Series, IUFRO Occasional Paper Series* (occasional).

International Union for the Protection of New Plant Varieties—UPOV: c/o 34 chemin des Colombettes, 1211 Geneva 20, Switzerland; tel. (22) 3389153; fax (22) 7330336; e-mail upov.mail@wipo.org; internet www.upov.int/; f. 1961 by the International Convention for the Protection of New Varieties of Plants (entered into force 1968, revised in 1972, 1978 and 1991). Aims to protect intellectual property rights of plant breeders and to harmonize legislation in the field. Admin. support provided by WIPO (q.v.). Signatory states: 47 (March 2001). Sec.-Gen. Dr KAMIL IDRIS.

International Union of Soil Sciences: c/o University of Agriculture, Gregor-Mendel-Strasse 33, 1180 Vienna, Austria; tel. (1) 478-9107; fax (1) 478-9110; e-mail iusss@edv1.boku.ac.at; internet ww.17wcss.ku.ac.th; f. 1924. Mems: 8,000 individuals and associations in 163 countries. Pres. Dr SOMPONG THEERAWONG; Sec.-Gen. Prof. Dr W. E. H. BLUM (Austria). Publ. *Bulletin* (2 a year).

International Whaling Commission—IWC: The Red House, 135 Station Rd, Impington, Cambridge, CB4 9NP, United Kingdom; tel. (1223) 233971; fax (1223) 232876; e-mail secretariat@iwcoffice.com; internet www.iwcoffice.org; f. 1946 under the International Convention for the Regulation of Whaling, for the conservation of the world whale stocks; aims to review the regulations covering the operations of whaling, to encourage research relating to whales and whaling, to collect and analyse statistical information and to study and disseminate information concerning methods of increasing whale stocks; a ban on commercial whaling was passed by the Commission in July 1982, to take effect three years subsequently (although, in some cases, a phased reduction of commercial operations was not completed until 1988). An assessment of the effects on whale stocks of this ban was under way in the early 1990s, and a revised whale-management procedure was adopted in 1992, to be implemented only after the development of a complete whale management scheme, including arrangements for data collection and an inspection and monitoring scheme; Iceland left the IWC in June 1992 and Norway resumed commercial whaling in 1993. Mems: governments of 40 countries. Chair. Prof. BO FERNHOLM (Sweden); Sec. Dr NICOLA GRANDY. Publ. *Annual Report*.

Joint Organization for the Control of Desert Locust and Bird Pests (Organisation commune de lutte anti-acridienne et de lutte antiaviaire—OCLALAV): BP 1066, route des Pères Maristes, Dakar, Senegal; tel. 832-32-80; fax 832-04-87; f. 1965 to destroy insect pests, in particular the desert locust, and grain-eating birds, in particular the quelea-quelea, and to sponsor related research projects. Mems: Benin, Burkina Faso, Cameroon, Chad, Côte d'Ivoire, The Gambia, Mali, Mauritania, Niger, Senegal. Dir-Gen. ABDULLAHI OULD SOUEÏD AHMED. Publ. *Bulletin* (monthly).

North Pacific Anadromous Fish Commission: 889 W. Pender St, Suite 502, Vancouver, BC V6C 3B2, Canada; tel. (604) 775-5550; fax (604) 775-5577; e-mail secretariat@npafc.org; f. 1993. Mems: Canada, Japan, Russia, USA. Exec. Dir VLADIMIR FEDORENKO. Publs *Annual Report, Newsletter* (2 a year), *Statistical Yearbook, Scientific Bulletin.*

Northwest Atlantic Fisheries Organization: POB 638, Dartmouth, NS B2Y 3Y9, Canada; tel. (902) 468-5590; fax (902) 468-5538; e-mail nafo@fox.nstn.ca; internet www.cafo.ca; f. 1979 (formerly International Commission for the Northwest Atlantic Fisheries); aims at optimum use, management and conservation of resources, promotes research and compiles statistics. Pres. E. OLTUSKI (Cuba); Exec. Sec. Dr L. I. CHEPEL. Publs *Annual Report, Statistical Bulletin, Journal of Northwest Atlantic Fishery Science, Scientific Council Reports, Scientific Council Studies, Sampling Yearbook, Proceedings.*

World Association for Animal Production: Via A. Torlonia 15A, 00161 Rome, Italy; tel. (06) 44238013; fax (06) 44241466; e-mail zoorec@rmnet.it; internet www.waap.it; f. 1965; holds world conference on animal production every five years; encourages, sponsors and participates in regional meetings, seminars and symposia. Pres. AKKE J. VAN DER ZJIPP (Netherlands); Sec.-Gen. JEAN GEORGES BOYAZOGLLI (Greece). Publ. *News Items* (2 a year).

World Association of Veterinary Food-Hygienists: Federal Institute for Health Protection of Consumers and Veterinary Medicine (BgVV), Diedersdorfer Weg 1, 12277 Berlin, Germany; tel. (30) 8412-2101; fax (30) 8412-2951; e-mail p.teufel@bgvv.de; f. 1955 to promote hygienic food control and discuss research. Mems: national asscns in 40 countries. Pres. Prof. PAUL TEUFEL; Sec. Treas. Dr L. ELLERBROEK.

World Association of Veterinary Microbiologists, Immunologists and Specialists in Infectious Diseases: Ecole Nationale Vétérinaire d'Alfort, 7 ave du Général de Gaulle, 94704 Maisons-Alfort Cédex, France; tel. 1-43-96-70-21; fax 1-43-96-70-22; f. 1967 to facilitate international contacts in the fields of microbiology, immunology and animal infectious diseases. Pres. Prof. CH. PILET (France). Publs *Comparative Immunology, Microbiology and Infectious Diseases.*

World Ploughing Organization—WPO: Søkildevej 17, 5270 Odense N, Denmark; tel. 65-97-80-06; fax 65-93-24-40; e-mail ht@flbf.dk; internet www.worldploughing.org; f. 1952 to promote World Ploughing Contest in a different country each year, to improve techniques and promote better understanding of soil cultivation practices through research and practical demonstrations; arranges tillage clinics world-wide to improve the use of new techniques. Affiliates in 30 countries. Gen. Sec. CARL ALLESO. Publ. *WPO Handbook* (annually).

World's Poultry Science Association: c/o Dr P. C. M. Simons, Centre for Applied Poultry Research, 'Het Spelderholt', POB 31, 7360 AA Beekbergen, Netherlands; tel. (55) 506-6534; fax (55) 506-4858; e-mail p.c.m.simons@pp.agro.nl; internet www.wpsa.com; f. 1912 to exchange knowledge in the industry, to encourage research and teaching, to publish information relating to production and marketing problems; to promote World Poultry Congresses and co-operate with governments. Mems: individuals in 95 countries, branches in 55 countries. Pres. Dr PETER HUNTON (Canada); Sec. Dr P. C. M. SIMONS (Netherlands). Publ. *The World Poultry Science Journal* (quarterly).

World Veterinary Association: Rosenlunds Allé 8, 2720 Vanlose, Denmark; tel. 38-71-01-56; fax 38-71-03-22; e-mail wva@ddd.dk; internet www.worldvet.org; f. 1959 as a continuation of the International Veterinary Congresses; organizes quadrennial congress. Mems: organizations in 76 countries and 19 organizations of veterinary specialists as associate members. Pres. Dr JIM EDWARDS (New Zealand); Exec. Sec. Dr LARS HOLSAAE. Publs *WVA Bulletin, World Veterinary Directory.*

Arts and Culture

Europa Nostra—Pan-European Federation for Heritage: Lange Voorhout 35, 2514 EC The Hague, Netherlands; tel. (70) 3024050; fax (70) 3617865; e-mail office@europanostra.org; internet www.europanostra.org; f. 1963; a large grouping of organizations and individuals concerned with the protection and enhancement of the European architectural and natural heritage and of the European environment; has consultative status with the Council of Europe. Mems: 216 mem. organizations, more than 150 associate mems, more than 40 supporting bodies, more than 1,000 individual mems. Pres. HRH The Prince Consort of Denmark; Exec. Pres. DANIEL CARDON DE LICHTBUER (Belgium); Sec.-Gen. SNESKA QUAEDVLIEG-MIHAILOVIĆ.

European Association of Conservatoires, Music Academies and Music High Schools: c/o Music House International Centre for Music and Music Education, POB 005, 3500 AV Utrecht, Netherlands; tel. (30) 236-12-42; fax (30) 236-12-90; e-mail aecinfo@aecinfo.org; internet www.aecinfo.org; f. 1953 to establish and foster contacts and exchanges between members. Mems: 133; 14 associate mems. Pres. IAN HORSBRUGH; Gen. Sec. JOHANNES JOHANSSON.

European Centre for Culture (Centre Européen de la Culture): Maison de l'Europe, 120B rue de Lausanne, 1202 Geneva, Switzerland; tel. (22) 7322803; fax (22) 7384012; e-mail cecge@vtx.ch; internet www.europeans.ch; f. 1950 to contribute to the union of Europe by encouraging cultural pursuits, providing a meeting place, and conducting research in the various fields of European Studies; holds conferences and training on European subjects, European documentation and archives. Pres. JEAN-FRED BOURQUIN (Switzerland). Publ. *Newsletter* (3 a year).

European Society of Culture: Guidecca 54P (Calle Michelangelo, Villa Hériot), 30133 Venice, Italy; tel. (041) 5230210; fax (041) 5231033; e-mail soceurcultur@flashnet.it; f. 1950 to unite artists, poets, scientists, philosophers and others through mutual interests and friendship in order to safeguard and improve the conditions required for creative activity; library of 10,000 volumes. Mems: national and local centres, and 2,000 individuals, in 60 countries. Pres. Prof. VINCENZO CAPPELLETTI (Italy); Gen. Sec. Dott. MICHELLE CAMPAGNOLO-BOUVIER.

Inter-American Music Council (Consejo Interamericano de Música—CIDEM): 2511 P St NW, Washington, DC 20007, USA; f. 1956 to promote the exchange of works, performances and information in all fields of music, to study problems relative to music education, to encourage activity in the field of musicology, to promote folklore research and music creation, to establish distribution centres for music material of the composers of the Americas, etc. Mems: national music societies of 33 American countries. Sec.-Gen. EFRAÍN PAESKY.

International Association of Art: Maison de l'UNESCO, 1 rue Miollis, 75732 Paris Cédex 15, France; tel. 1-45-68-26-55; fax 1-45-67-22-87; f. 1954. Mems: 104 national committees. Pres. UNA WALKER; Sec.-Gen. J. C. DE SALINS. Publ. *IAA Newsletter* (quarterly).

International Association of Art Critics: 11 rue Berryer, 75008 Paris, France; tel. 1-42-56-17-53; fax 1-42-56-08-42; f. 1949 to increase co-operation in plastic arts, promote international cultural exchanges and protect the interests of members. Mems: 4,062 in 77 countries. Pres. KIM LEVIN (USA); Sec.-Gen. RAMON TIO BELLIDO (France). Publs *Annuaire, Newsletter* (quarterly).

International Association of Bibliophiles: Bibliothèque nationale de France, 58 rue Richelieu, 75084 Paris Cédex 02, France; fax 1-47-03-77-57; f. 1963 to create contacts between bibliophiles and to encourage book-collecting in different countries; to organize or encourage congresses, meetings, exhibitions, the award of scholarships, the publication of a bulletin, yearbooks, and works of reference or bibliography. Mems: 450. Pres. CONDE DE ORGAZ (Spain); Sec.-Gen. JEAN-MARC CHATELAIN (France). Publ. *Le Bulletin du Bibliophile.*

International Association of Literary Critics: 38 rue du Faubourg St-Jacques, 75014 Paris, France; tel. 1-53-10-12-13; fax 1-53-10-12-12; f. 1969; national centres in 34 countries; organizes congresses. Pres. ROBERT ANDRÉ. Publ. *Revue* (2 a year).

International Association of Museums of Arms and Military History—IAMAM: c/o Dr C. Gaier, Musée d'Armes de Liège, Quai de Maastricht 8, 4000 Liège, Belgium; tel. (4) 221-94-16; fax (4) 221-94-01; f. 1957; links museums and other scientific institutions with public collections of arms and armour and military equipment, uniforms, etc.; triennial conferences and occasional specialist symposia. Mems: 252 institutions in 50 countries. Pres. CLAUDE GAIER (Belgium); Sec.-Gen. JAN PIET PUYPE (Netherlands). Publ. *The Mohonk Courier.*

International Board on Books for Young People—IBBY: Nonnenweg 12, Postfach, 4003 Basel, Switzerland; tel. (61) 2722917; fax (61) 2722757; e-mail ibby@eye.ch; internet www.ibby.org; f. 1953 to support and link bodies in all countries connected with children's book work; to encourage the distribution of good children's books; to promote scientific investigation into problems of juvenile books; presents the Hans Christian Andersen Award every two years to a living author and a living illustrator whose work is an outstanding contribution to juvenile literature, and the IBBY-Asahi Reading Promotion Award annually to an organization that has made a significant contribution towards the encouragement of reading; sponsors International Children's Book Day (2 April). Mems: national sections and individuals in more than 60 countries. Pres. TAYO SHIMA (Japan); Sec. LEENA MAISSEN. Publs *Bookbird* (quarterly, in English), *Congress Papers, IBBY Honour List* (every 2 years); special bibliographies.

International Centre for the Study of the Preservation and Restoration of Cultural Property—ICCROM: Via di San Michele 13, 00153 Rome, Italy; tel. (06) 585-531; fax (06) 5855-3349; e-mail iccrom@iccrom.org; internet www.iccrom.org; f. 1959; assembles documents on preservation and restoration of cultural property; stimulates research and proffers advice; organizes missions of experts;

Arts and Culture

undertakes training of specialists and heritage conservation world-wide. Mems: 98 countries. Dir-Gen. Dr NICHOLAS STANLEY-PRICE (United Kingdom). Publ. *Newsletter* (annually, English and French).

International Centre of Films for Children and Young People—Centre international des films pour les enfants et les jeunes—CIFEJ: 3774 rue Saint-Denis, Bureau 200, Montréal, QC H2W 2M1, Canada; tel. (514) 284-9388; fax (514) 284-0168; e-mail info@cifej.com; internet www.cifej.com; f. 1955; a clearing house for information about: entertainment films (cinema and television) for children and young people, influence of films on the young, and regulations in force for the protection and education of young people; promotes production and distribution of suitable films and their appreciation. The CIFEJ prize is awarded at selected film festivals. Mems: 163 mems from 53 countries. Exec. Dir JO-ANNE BLOUIN. Publ. *CIFEJ Info* (monthly).

International Committee for the Diffusion of Arts and Literature through the Cinema (Comité international pour la diffusion des arts et des lettres par le cinéma—CIDALC): 24 blvd Poissonnière, 75009 Paris, France; tel. 1-42-46-13-60; f. 1930 to promote the creation and release of educational, cultural and documentary films and other films of educational value in order to contribute to closer understanding between peoples; awards medals and prizes for films of exceptional merit. Mems: national committees in 19 countries. Pres. JEAN-PIERRE FOUCAULT (France); Sec.-Gen. MARIO VERDONE (Italy). Publs *Annuaire CIDALC, Cinéma éducatif et culturel.*

International Comparative Literature Association: c/o Paola Mildonian, Letterature Comparate, Dipartim. di Studi Anglo-Americani e Ibero-Americani, Università Ca'Foscari-Venezia, Ca'Garzoni, S. Marco 3417, 30124 Venice, Italy; tel. (041) 257-8427; fax (041) 257-8476; e-mail pamildo@unive.it; internet www.byu.edu/ icla/; f. 1954 to work for the development of the comparative study of literature in modern languages. Member societies and individuals in 78 countries. Pres. KOJI KAWAMOTO. Publ. *ICLA Bulletin* (2 a year).

International Confederation of Societies of Authors and Composers—World Congress of Authors and Composers: 11 rue Kepler, 75116 Paris, France; tel. 1-53-57-34-00; fax 1-53-57-34-10; e-mail cisac@cisac.org; internet www.cisac.org; f. 1926 to protect the rights of authors and composers; organizes biennial congress. Mems: 173 member societies from 91 countries. Sec.-Gen. ERIC BAPTISTE.

International Council of Graphic Design Associations—ICOGRADA: POB 5, Forest 2, 1190, Brussels, Belgium; tel. (2) 344-58-43; fax (2)344-71-38; e-mail secretariat@icograda.org; internet www.icograda.org; f. 1963; aims to raise standards of graphic design, to exchange information, and to organize exhibitions and congresses; maintains library, slide collection and archive. Mems: 62 associations in 38 countries. Pres. DAVID GROSSMAN (Israel); Sec.-Gen. MARTHA BATEMAN (South Africa). Publs *Newsletter* (quarterly), *Regulations and Guidelines governing International Design Competitions, Model Code of Professional Conduct* and other professional documents.

International Council of Museums—ICOM: Maison de l'UNESCO, 1 rue Miollis, 75732 Paris Cédex 15, France; tel. 1-47-34-05-00; fax 1-43-06-78-62; e-mail secretariat@icom.org; internet www.icom.org; f. 1946 to further international co-operation among museums and to advance museum interests; maintains with UNESCO the organization's documentation centre. Mems: 15,000 individuals and institutions from 139 countries. Pres. JACQUES PEROT (France); Sec.-Gen. MANUS BRINKMAN (Netherlands). Publ. *ICOM News—Nouvelles de l'ICOM—Noticias del ICOM* (quarterly).

International Council on Monuments and Sites—ICOMOS: 49–51 rue de la Fédération, 75015 Paris, France; tel. 1-45-67-67-70; fax 1-45-66-06-22; e-mail secretariat@icomos.org; internet www.international.icomos.org; f. 1965 to promote the study and preservation of monuments and sites; to arouse and cultivate the interest of public authorities, and people of every country in their monuments and sites and in their cultural heritage; to liaise between public authorities, departments, institutions and individuals interested in the preservation and study of monuments and sites; to disseminate the results of research into the problems, technical, social and administrative, connected with the conservation of the architectural heritage, and of centres of historic interest; holds triennial General Assembly and Symposium. Mems: c. 6,000; 18 international committees, 90 national committees. Pres. Dr MICHAEL PETZET (Germanya); Sec.-Gen. JEAN-LOUIS LUXEN (Belgium). Publs *ICOMOS Newsletter* (quarterly), *Scientific Journal* (quarterly).

International Federation for Theatre Research: c/o Flat 9, 118 Avenue Rd, London, W3 8QG, United Kingdom; tel. (20) 8608-1550; fax (20) 8679-3488; e-mail bsnglton@tcd.ie; internet www.tcd.ie/iftr; f. 1955 by 21 countries at the International Conference on Theatre History, London. Pres. Prof. JOSETTE FÉRAL; Joint Secs-Gen. DAVID WHITTON, Prof. CHRISTIANE PAGE. Publs *Theatre Research International* (in association with Oxford University Press) (3 a year), *Bulletin* (2 a year).

International Federation of Film Archives—FIAF: c/o Christian Dimitriu, rue Defacqz 1, 1000 Brussels, Belgium; tel. (2) 538-30-65; fax (2) 534-47-74; e-mail info@fiafnet.org; internet www.fiaf-net.org; f. 1938 to encourage the creation of audio-visual archives in all countries for the collection and conservation of the moving image heritage of each land; to facilitate co-operation and exchanges between these film archives; to promote public interest in the art of the cinema; to aid research in this field and to compile new documentation; conducts research; publishes manuals, etc.; holds annual congresses. Mems in 60 countries. Pres. IVAN TRUJILLO BOLIO (Mexico); Sec.-Gen. ROGER SMITHER (UK). Publ. *Journal of Film Preservation* (2 a year).

International Federation of Film Producers' Associations: 9 rue de l'Echelle, 75002 Paris, France; tel. 1-44-77-97-50; fax 1-42-56-16-52; e-mail infos@fiapf.org; internet fiapf.org; f. 1933 to represent film production internationally, to defend its general interests and promote its development; to study all cultural, legal, economic, technical and social problems of interest to the activity of film production. Mems: national associations in 23 countries. Pres. AURELIO DE LAURENTIIS (Italy); Dir-Gen. ANDRÉ CHAUBEAU (France).

International Institute for Children's Literature and Reading Research (Internationales Institut für Jugendliteratur und Leseforschung): 1040 Vienna, Mayerhofgasse 6, Austria; tel. (1) 50503-59; fax (1) 50503-5917; e-mail kidlit@netway.at; internet www.kidlit.nwy.at; f. 1965 as an international documentation, research and advisory centre of juvenile literature and reading; maintains specialized library; arranges conferences and exhibitions; compiles recommendation lists. Mems: individual and group members in 28 countries. Pres. Dr HILDE HAWLICEK; Dir KARIN HALLER. Publs *1000 & 1 Buch* (quarterly and 1 special issue).

International Institute for Conservation of Historic and Artistic Works: 6 Buckingham St, London, WC2N 6BA, United Kingdom; tel. (20) 7839-5975; fax (20) 7976-1564; e-mail iicon@compuserve.com; internet www.iiconservation.org; f. 1950. Mems: 3,350 individual, 450 institutional members. Pres. ANDREW ODDY; Exec. Sec. PERRY SMITH. Publ. *Studies in Conservation* (quarterly).

International Liaison Centre for Cinema and Television Schools (Centre international de liaison des écoles de cinéma et de télévision): 8 rue Thérésienne, 1000 Brussels, Belgium; tel. (2) 511-98-39; fax (2) 511-98-39; e-mail hverh.cilect@skynet.be; internet www.cilect.org; f. 1955 to link higher teaching and research institutes and to improve education of makers of films and television programmes; organizes conferences, student film festivals, training programme for developing countries. Mems: 107 institutions in 52 countries. Pres. CATERINA D'AMICO (Italy); Exec. Sec. HENRY VERHASSELT (Belgium). Publ. *Newsletter*.

International Music Council—IMC: Maison de l'UNESCO, 1 rue Miollis, 75732 Paris Cédex 15, France; tel. 1-45-68-25-50; fax 1-43-06-87-98; e-mail imc_cim@compuserve.com; internet www.unesco.org/imc; f. 1949 to foster the exchange of musicians, music (written and recorded), and information between countries and cultures; to support traditional music, contemporary composers and young professional musicians. Mems: 30 international non-governmental organizations, national committees in 65 countries. Pres. FRANS DE RUITER (Netherlands); Sec.-Gen. GUY HUOT.

Members of IMC include:

European Festivals Association: 120B rue de Lausanne, 1202 Geneva, Switzerland; tel. (22) 7386873; fax (22) 7384012; e-mail geneva@eurofestival.net; internet www.eurofestival.net; f. 1952; aims to maintain high artistic standards and the representative character of art festivals; holds annual General Assembly. Mems: 88 regularly-held music festivals in 29 European countries, Israel, Japan, Lebanon and Mexico. Pres. FRANS DE RUITER. Publ. *Festivals* (annually).

International Association of Music Libraries, Archives and Documentation Centres—IAML: c/o Cataloguing Dept, Carleton Univ. Library, 1125 Colonel By Drive, Ottawa, ON K1S 5B6, Canada; tel. (613) 520-2600; fax (613) 520-3583; e-mail alison-hall@carleton.ca; internet www.cilea.it/music/iame/iamchome.htm; f. 1951. Mems: 2,003 institutions and individuals in 58 countries. Pres. PAMELA THOMPSON (UK); Sec.-Gen. ALISON HALL (Canada). Publ. *Fontes artis musicae* (quarterly).

International Council for Traditional Music: Dept of Music—MC 1815, Columbia University, 2960 Broadway, New York, NY 10027, USA; tel. (212) 678-0332; fax (212) 678-2513; e-mail ictm@compuserve.com; f. 1947 (as International Folk Music Council) to further the study, practice, documentation, preservation and dissemination of traditional music of all countries; conferences held every two years. Mems: 1,350. Pres. Dr KRISTER MALM (Sweden); Sec.-Gen. Prof. DIETER CHRISTENSEN (USA). Publs *Yearbook for Traditional Music, Bulletin* (2 a year), *Directory of Traditional Music* (every 2 years).

International Federation of Musicians: 21 bis rue Victor Massé, 75009 Paris, France; tel. 1-45-26-31-23; fax 1-45-26-31-57; e-mail fimparis2@compuserve.com; f. 1948 to promote and protect the interests of musicians in affiliated unions; promotes international exchange of musicians. Mems: 50 unions totalling 200,000 individuals in 43 countries. Pres. JOHN MORTON (UK); Gen. Sec. JEAN VINCENT (France).

International Music Centre (Internationales Musikzentrum—IMZ): 1230 Vienna, Speisinger Str. 121–127, Austria; tel. (1) 889-03-15; fax (1) 889-03-15-77; e-mail office@imz.at; internet www.imz.at; f. 1961 for the study and dissemination of music through the technical media (film, television, radio, gramophone); organizes congresses, seminars and screenings on music in the audio-visual media; courses and competitions to strengthen the relationship between performing artists and the audio-visual media. Mems: 110 ordinary mems and 30 associate mems in 33 countries, including 50 broadcasting organizations. Pres. HENK VAN DER MEULEN (Netherlands); Sec.-Gen. FRANZ A. PATAY (Austria). Publ. *IMZ-Bulletin* (6 a year in English).

International Society for Contemporary Music: c/o Gaudeamus, Swammerdamstraat 38, 1091 RV Amsterdam, Netherlands; tel. (20) 6947349; fax (20) 6947258; e-mail info@iscm.nl; f. 1922 to promote the development of contemporary music and to organize annual World Music Days. Member organizations in 48 countries. Pres. ARNE MELLNAS; Sec.-Gen. HENK HEUVELMANS.

Jeunesses Musicales International: Palais des Beaux-Arts, 10 rue Royale, 1000 Brussels, Belgium; tel. (2) 513-97-74; fax (2) 514-47-55; e-mail mail@jmi.net; internet www.jmi.net; f. 1945 to enable young people to develop, through music, across all boundaries and to stimulate contacts between member countries. Mems: organizations in 40 countries. Sec.-Gen. DAG FRANZÉN.

World Federation of International Music Competitions: 104 rue de Carouge, 1205 Geneva, Switzerland; tel. (22) 3213620; fax (22) 7811418; e-mail fmcim@iprolink.ch; internet www.wfimc.org; f. 1957 to co-ordinate the arrangements for affiliated competitions, to exchange experience, etc.; a General Assembly is held every May. Mems: 107. Pres. MARIANNE GRANVIG; Sec.-Gen. RENATE RONNEVELD.

International PEN (A World Association of Writers): 9–10 Charterhouse Bldgs, Goswell Rd, London, EC1M 7AT, United Kingdom; tel. (20) 7253-4308; fax (20) 7253-5711; e-mail intpen@dircon.co.uk; internet www.oneworld.org/internatpen; f. 1921 to promote co-operation between writers. There are 129 centres throughout the world, with total membership about 13,500. International Pres. HOMERO ARIDJIS; International Sec. TERRY CARLBOM. Publ. *PEN International* (2 a year in English, French and Spanish, with the assistance of UNESCO).

International Theatre Institute—ITI: Maison de l'UNESCO, 1 rue Miollis, 75732 Paris Cédex 15, France; tel. 1-45-68-26-50; fax 1-45-66-50-40; e-mail iti@unesco.org; internet iti-worldwide.org; f. 1948 to facilitate cultural exchanges and international understanding in the domain of the theatre; conferences, publications, etc. Mems: 87 member nations, each with an ITI national centre. Pres. KIM JEONG-OK (Republic of Korea); Sec.-Gen. ANDRÉ-LOUIS PERINETTI.

Organization of World Heritage Cities: 56 Saint-Pierre St, Suite 401, Quebec City, QC, G1K 4AI, Canada; tel. (418) 692-0000; fax (418) 692-5558; e-mail secretariat@ovpm.org; internet www.ovpm.org; f. 1993; aims to assist cities inscribed on the UNESCO World Heritage List to implement the Convention concerning the Protection of the World Cultural and Natural Heritage (1972); promotes co-operation between city authorities, in particular in the management and sustainable development of historic sites. A General Assembly, comprising the mayors of member cities, meets at least every two years. Mems: 164 cities world-wide. Sec.-Gen. D. S. MYRVOLL (acting).

Pan-African Writers' Association—PAWA: PAWA House, Roman Ridge, Accra, Ghana; tel. (21) 773062; fax (21) 773042; e-mail pawa@ghana.com; f. 1989 to link African creative writers, defend the rights of authors and promote awareness of literature. Sec.-Gen. ATUKWEI OKAI (Ghana); Dep. Sec.-Gen. MAHAMADU TRAORÉ DIOP (Senegal).

Royal Asiatic Society of Great Britain and Ireland: 60 Queen's Gardens, London, W2 3AF, United Kingdom; tel. (20) 7724-4742; e-mail royalasiaticsociety@btinternet.com; internet www.royalasiatic-society.co.uk; f. 1823 for the study of history and cultures of the East. Mems: c. 1,000, branch societies in Asia. Pres. Prof. A. J. STOCKWELL; Sec. A. P. THOMAS. Publ. *Journal* (3 a year).

Society of African Culture: 25 bis rue des Ecoles, 75005 Paris, France; tel. 1-43-54-15-88; fax 1-43-25-96-67; f. 1956 to create unity and friendship among scholars in Africa for the encouragement of their own cultures. Mems: national asscns and individuals in 44 countries and territories. Pres. AIMÉ CÉSAIRE; Sec.-Gen. CHRISTIANE YANDÉ DIOP. Publ. *La Revue Présence Africaine* (2 a year).

United Towns Organization: 60 rue de la Boétie, 75008 Paris, France; tel. 1-53-96-05-80; fax 1-53-96-05-81; e-mail cites.unies@wanadoo.fr; f. 1957 by Le Monde Bilingue (f. 1951); aims to set up permanent links between towns throughout the world, leading to social, cultural, economic and other exchanges favouring world peace, understanding and development; involved in sustainable development and environmental activities at municipal level; mem. of the Habitat II follow-up group. Mems: 4,000 local and regional authorities

throughout the world. World Pres. DABY DIAGNE; Dir-Gen. MICHEL BESCOND. Publs *Cités Unies* (quarterly, French, English and Spanish), *Newsletter* (3 a year in English, French, Italian and Spanish).

World Crafts Council: 52 Archbishop Mathias's Rd, R.A. Puram, Chennai 600-028, India; tel. (44) 4337999; fax (44) 4327931; e-mail arvimee@vsnl.com; f. 1964; aims to strengthen the status of crafts as a vital part of cultural life, to link crafts people around the world, and to foster wider recognition of their work. Mems: national organizations in more than 87 countries. Pres. VIJAYA RAJAN. Publs *Annual Report, Newsletter* (2 a year).

Commodities

African Groundnut Council: Trade Fair Complex, Badagry Expressway Km 15, POB 3025, Lagos, Nigeria; tel. (1) 880982; fax (1) 887811; f. 1964 to advise producing countries on marketing policies. Mems: The Gambia, Mali, Niger, Nigeria, Senegal, Sudan. Chair. MUSTAFA BELLO; Exec. Sec. Elhadj MOUR MAMADOU SAMB (Senegal). Publ. *Groundnut Review*.

African Oil Palm Development Association—AFOPDA: 15 BP 341, Abidjan 15, Côte d'Ivoire; tel. 25-15-18; f. 1985; seeks to increase production of, and investment in, palm oil. Mems: Benin, Cameroon, Democratic Republic of the Congo, Côte d'Ivoire, Ghana, Guinea, Nigeria, Togo. Exec. Sec. BAUDELAIRE SOUROU.

African Petroleum Producers' Association—APPA: POB 1097, Brazzaville, Republic of the Congo; tel. 83-64-38; fax 83-67-99; f. 1987 by African petroleum-producing countries to reinforce co-operation among regional producers and to stabilize prices; council of ministers responsible for the hydrocarbons sector meets twice a year. Mems: Algeria, Angola, Benin, Cameroon, Democratic Republic of the Congo, Republic of the Congo, Côte d'Ivoire, Egypt, Equatorial Guinea, Gabon, Nigeria. Publ. *APPA Bulletin* (2 a year).

Asian and Pacific Coconut Community: POB 1343, 3rd Floor, Lina Bldg, Jalan H. R. Rasuna Said Kav. B7, Kuningan, Jakarta 10002, Indonesia; tel. (21) 5221712; fax (21) 5221714; e-mail apcc@indo.net.id; internet www.apcc.org.sg; f. 1969 to promote, co-ordinate, and harmonize all activities of the coconut industry towards better production, processing, marketing and research. Mems: Fiji, India, Indonesia, Malaysia, Federated States of Micronesia, Papua New Guinea, Philippines, Samoa, Solomon Islands, Sri Lanka, Thailand, Vanuatu, Viet Nam; assoc. mem.: Palau. Exec. Dir NORBERTO M. BOCETA. Publs *Cocomunity* (2 a month), *CORD* (2 a year), *Statistical Yearbook, Cocoinfo International* (2 a year).

Association of Coffee Producing Countries: Suite B, 5th Floor, 7/10 Old Park Lane, London, W1Y 3LJ, United Kingdom; tel. (20) 7493-4790; fax (20) 7355-1690; e-mail info@acpc.org; internet www.acpc.org; f. 1993; aims to co-ordinate policies of coffee production and to co-ordinate the efforts of producer countries to secure a stable situation in the world coffee market. Mems 29 African, Asian and Latin American countries. Pres. Ambassador RUBENS ANTÔNIO BARBOSA (Brazil); Sec.-Gen. ROBÉRIO OLIVEIRA SILVA.

Association of Natural Rubber Producing Countries—ANRPC: Bangunan Getah Asli, 148 Jalan Ampang, 7th Floor, 50450 Kuala Lumpur, Malaysia; tel. (3) 2611900; fax (3) 2613014; f. 1970 to co-ordinate the production and marketing of natural rubber, to promote technical co-operation amongst members and to bring about fair and stable prices for natural rubber. A joint regional marketing system has been agreed in principle. Seminars, meetings and training courses on technical and statistical subjects are held. Mems: India, Indonesia, Malaysia, Papua New Guinea, Singapore, Sri Lanka, Thailand. Sec.-Gen. GNOH CHONG HOCK. Publs *ANRPC Statistical Bulletin* (quarterly), *ANRPC Newsletter*.

Association of Tin Producing Countries—ATPC: Menara Dayabumi, 4th Floor, Jalan Sultan Hishamuddin, 50050 Kuala Lumpur, Malaysia; tel. (3) 2747620; fax (3) 2740669; e-mail atpc@tm.net.my; f. 1983; promotes co-operation in marketing of tin, supports research, compiles and analyses data. The headquarters scheduled to be moved to Rio de Janeiro, Brazil. Mems: Bolivia, Brazil, People's Republic of China, Democratic Republic of the Congo, Malaysia, Nigeria; observers: Peru, Viet Nam. Exec. Sec. MOHAMED ZARIF MOHAMED ZAMAN (Malaysia).

Cocoa Producers' Alliance: POB 1718, Western House, 8–10 Broad St, Lagos, Nigeria; tel. (1) 2635506; fax (1) 2635684; f. 1962 to exchange technical and scientific information; to discuss problems of mutual concern to producers; to ensure adequate supplies at remunerative prices; to promote consumption. Mems: Brazil, Cameroon, Côte d'Ivoire, Dominican Republic, Ecuador, Gabon, Ghana, Malaysia, Nigeria, São Tomé and Príncipe, Togo, Trinidad and Tobago. Sec.-Gen. DJEUMO SILAS KAMGA.

Common Fund for Commodities: Postbus 74656, 1070 BR, Amsterdam, Netherlands; tel. (20) 575-4949; fax (20) 676-0231; e-mail managing.director@common-fund.org; internet www.common-fund.org; f. 1989 as the result of an UNCTAD agreement; finances commodity development measures such as research, marketing, productivity improvements and vertical diversification, with the aim of increasing the long-term competitiveness of particular commodities; paid-in capital US $165m. Mems 104 countries and the EC, OAU and COMESA. Man. Dir (also Chief Exec. and Chair.) ROLF BOEHNKE.

European Aluminium Association: 12 ave de Broqueville, 1150 Brussels, Belgium; tel. (2) 755-63-11; fax (2) 779-05-31; e-mail eaa@eaa.be; f. 1981 to encourage studies, research and technical co-operation, to make representations to international bodies and to assist national associations in dealing with national authorities. Mems: individual producers of primary aluminium, 18 national groups for wrought producers, the Organization of European Aluminium Smelters, representing producers of secondary aluminium, and the European Aluminium Foil Association, representing foil rollers and converters. Chair. KURT WOLFENSBERGER; Sec.-Gen. DICK DERMER. Publs *Annual Report, EAA Quarterly Report.*

European Association for the Trade in Jute and Related Products: Adriaan Goekooplaan 5, 2517 JX The Hague, Netherlands; tel. (70) 354-68-11; fax (70) 351-27-77; e-mail jute@verbondgroothandel.nl; f. 1970 to maintain contacts between national associations and carry out scientific research; to exchange information and to represent the interests of the trade. Mems: enterprises in Belgium, Denmark, France, Germany, Italy, Netherlands, Spain, Sweden, Switzerland, United Kingdom. Sec.-Gen. H. J. J. KRUIPER.

European Committee of Sugar Manufacturers: 182 ave de Tervueren, 1150 Brussels, Belgium; tel. (2) 762-07-60; fax (2) 771-00-26; e-mail cefs@cefs.org; internet www.ib.be.cefs; f. 1954 to collect statistics and information, conduct research and promote co-operation between national organizations. Mems: national associations in Austria, Belgium, Denmark, Finland, France, Germany, Greece, Ireland, Italy, Netherlands, Portugal, Spain, Sweden, Switzerland, United Kingdom. Pres. RENATO PICCO; Dir-Gen. J. L. BARJOL.

Group of Latin American and Caribbean Sugar Exporting Countries—GEPLACEA: Paseo de la Reforma 1030, Lomas de Chapultepec, México DF 11000, Mexico; tel. (5) 20-97-11; fax (5) 20-50-89; e-mail geplacea@mail.internet.com.mx; internet www.geplacea.ipn.mx; f. 1974 to serve as a forum of consultation on the production and sale of sugar; to contribute to the adoption of agreed positions at international meetings on sugar; to provide training and the transfer of technology; to exchange scientific and technical knowledge on agriculture and the sugar industry; to co-ordinate the various branches of sugar processing; to co-ordinate policies of action in order to achieve fair and remunerative prices. Mems: 23 Latin American and Caribbean countries (accounting for about 45% of world sugar exports and 66% of world cane sugar production). Exec. Sec. LUIS PONCE DE LEÓN.

Inter-African Coffee Organization—IACO: BP V210, Abidjan, Côte d'Ivoire; tel. 20-21-61-31; fax 20-21-62-12; e-mail oiac-iaco@aviso.ci; f. 1960 to adopt a common policy on the marketing of coffee; aims to collaborate on research, in particular through the establishment of the African Coffee Research Network, and improvement in the quality of exports. Mems: 25 coffee-producing countries in Africa. Chair. GILBERTO BUTA LUTUCUTA (Angola); Sec.-Gen. JOSEFA LEONEL CORREIA SACKO (Angola).

International Cadmium Association: 42 Weymouth St, London, W1N 3LQ, United Kingdom; tel. (20) 7499-8425; fax (20) 7486-4007; f. 1976; covers all aspects of the production and use of cadmium and its compounds; includes almost all producers and users of cadmium outside the USA. Chair. JEAN FEUILLAT (Belgium); Dir J. K. ATHERTON (UK).

International Cocoa Organization—ICCO: 22 Berners St, London, W1P 3DB, United Kingdom; tel. (20) 7637-3211; fax (20) 7631-0114; e-mail exec.dir@icco.org; internet www.icco.org; f. 1973 under the first International Cocoa Agreement, 1972 (renewed in 1975 and 1980; the fourth agreement entered into force in January 1987; it was extended, without its economic clauses, for two years from October 1990, and again to 30 September 1993). ICCO supervises the implementation of the agreement, and provides member governments with conference facilities and up-to-date information on the world cocoa economy and the operation of the agreement (price-stabilizing activities were suspended in March 1990). Negotiations on a fifth agreement were concluded in July 1993, under the auspices of UNCTAD, which came into force in February 1994 (the agreement was extended for a further 2 years from 1 October 1999). Mems: 19 exporting countries and 23 importing countries; and the European Union. Exec. Dir EDOUARD KOUAMÉ (Côte d'Ivoire); Council Chair. 2000–01 Cdr DJIKALOU SAINT-CYR (Côte d'Ivoire). Publs *Quarterly Bulletin of Cocoa Statistics, Annual Report, World Cocoa Directory, Cocoa Newsletter,* studies on the world cocoa economy.

International Coffee Organization: 22 Berners St, London, W1P 4DD, United Kingdom; tel. (20) 7580-8591; fax (20) 7580-6129; e-mail info@ico.org; internet www.ico.org; f. 1963 under the International Coffee Agreement, 1962, which was renegotiated in 1968, 1976, 1983 and 1994. The objectives of the 1994 Agreement are to improve international co-operation and provide a forum for intergovernmental consultations on coffee matters; to facilitate international trade in coffee by the collection, analysis and dissemination of statistics; to act as a centre for the collection, exchange and publication of coffee information; to promote studies in the field of coffee; and to encourage an increase in coffee consumption. Mems: 44 exporting and 18 importing countries. Chair. of Council FERDINANDO MASSIMO (Italy); Exec. Dir CELSIUS A. LODDER (Brazil).

International Confederation of European Sugar Beet Growers: 29 rue du Général Foy, 75008 Paris, France; tel. 1-44-69-41-80; fax 1-42-93-28-93; f. 1925 to act as a centre for the co-ordination and dissemination of information about beet sugar production and the industry; to represent the interests of sugar beet growers at an international level. Member associations in Austria, Belgium, Czech Republic, Denmark, Finland, France, Germany, Greece, Hungary, Ireland, Italy, Netherlands, Poland, Portugal, Romania, Slovakia, Spain, Sweden, Switzerland, United Kingdom. Pres. J. KIRSCH (Germany); Sec.-Gen. H. CHAVANES (France).

International Cotton Advisory Committee: 1629 K St, NW, Suite 702, Washington, DC 20006, USA; tel. (202) 463-6660; fax (202) 463-6950; e-mail secretariat@icac.org; internet www.icac.org; f. 1939 to observe developments affecting the world cotton situation; to collect and disseminate statistics; to suggest to the governments represented any measures for the furtherance of international collaboration in maintaining and developing a sound world cotton economy; and to provide a forum for international discussions on cotton prices. Mems: 40 countries. Exec. Dir Dr TERRY TOWNSEND (USA). Publs *Cotton: Review of the World Situation, Cotton: World Statistics, The ICAC Recorder.*

International Grains Council: 1 Canada Sq., Canary Wharf, London, E14 5AE, United Kingdom; tel. (20) 7513-1122; fax (20) 7513-0630; e-mail igc@igc.org.uk; internet www.igc.org.uk; f. 1949 as International Wheat Council, present name adopted in 1995; responsible for the administration of the Grains Trade Convention of the International Grains Agreement, 1995; aims to further international co-operation in all aspects of trade in grains, to promote international trade in grains, and to secure the freest possible flow of this trade in the interests of members, particularly developing member countries; and to contribute to the stability of the international grain market; acts as forum for consultations between members, and provides comprehensive information on the international grain market and factors affecting it. Mems: 28 countries and the EU. Exec. Dir. G. DENIS. Publs *World Grain Statistics* (annually), *Wheat and Coarse Grain Shipments* (annually), *Report for the Fiscal Year* (annually), *Grain Market Report* (monthly), *Grain Market Indicators* (weekly).

International Jute Organization—IJO: 145 Monipuriparu, Old Airport Rd, Dhaka 1215, Bangladesh; tel. (2) 9125581; fax (2) 9125248; e-mail ijoinf@bdmail.net; f. 1984 in accordance with an agreement made by 48 producing and consuming countries in 1982, under the auspices of UNCTAD (new agreement negotiated in 1989, expiring in April 2000); aimed to improve the jute economy and the quality of jute and jute products through research and development projects and market promotion. Entered an 18-month period of liquidation in April 2000; successor org. under consideration by the International Jute Study Group. Mems: three exporting and 20 importing countries, as well as the European Union. Publs *Jute* (quarterly), *Annual Report.*

International Lead and Zinc Study Group: 2 King St, London, SW1Y 6QP, United Kingdom; tel. (20) 7484-3300; fax (20) 7930-4635; e-mail root@ilzsg.org; internet www.ilzsg.org; f. 1959, for intergovernmental consultation on world trade in lead and zinc; conducts studies and provides information on trends in supply and demand. Mems: 28 countries. Chair. A. IGNATOW (Canada); Sec.-Gen. DON SMALE. Publ. *Lead and Zinc Statistics* (monthly).

International Molybdenum Association: 2 Baron's Gate, 33 Rothschild Rd, London, W4 5HT, United Kingdom; tel. (20) 8742-2274; fax (20) 8742-7345; e-mail itia.imoa@compuserve.com; internet www.imoa.org.uk/; f. 1989; collates statistics, promotes the use of molybdenum, monitors health and environmental issues. Mems: 49. Pres. R. S. DE CESARE; Sec.-Gen. MICHAEL MABY.

International Natural Rubber Organization—INRO: POB 10374, 50712 Kuala Lumpur, Malaysia; tel. (3) 2486466; fax (3) 2486485; e-mail inro@po.jaring.my; internet www.inro.com.my/inro; f. 1980 to stabilize natural rubber prices by operating a buffer stock, and to seek to ensure an adequate supply, under the International Natural Rubber Agreement (1979), which entered into force in April 1982, and was extended for two years in 1985; a second agreement came into effect in 1988, to expire in Dec. 1993 but was extended to Dec. 1995; a third agreement was adopted in Feb. 1995 and entered into effect in 1997. By Oct. 1999 Malaysia, Thailand and Sri Lanka had confirmed their intention to withdraw from the organization owing to its failure to support market prices, and a decision was taken to terminate the International Natural Rubber Agreement and to disband the organization. A special session of INRO, held in Dec., made arrangements for the disposal of the existing buffer stocks; all sales and deliveries were to be completed by 30 June 2001. Mems: 17 importing countries (including the European Union) and six exporting countries (Côte d'Ivoire, Indonesia, Malaysia, Nigeria, Sri Lanka and Thailand).

International Olive Oil Council: Príncipe de Vergara 154, 28002 Madrid, Spain; tel. (91) 59033638; fax (91) 5631263;e-mail iooc@internationaloliveoil.org; internet www.internationaloliveoil.org; f. 1959 to administer the International Agreement on Olive Oil and Table Olives, which aims to promote international co-operation in connection with problems of the world economy for olive products; to prevent unfair competition; to encourage the production and consumption of, and international trade in, olive products, and to reduce the disadvantages due to fluctuations of supplies on the market. Mems: of the 1986 Agreement (Fourth Agreement, amended and extended in 1993): eight mainly producing countries, one mainly importing country, and the European Commission. Dir FAUSTO LUCHETTI. Publs *Information Sheet of the IOOC* (fortnightly, French and Spanish), *OLIVAE* (5 a year, in English, French, Italian and Spanish), *National Policies for Olive Products* (annually).

International Pepper Community: 4th Floor, Lina Bldg, Jalan H. R. Rasuna Said, Kav. B7, Kuningan, Jakarta 12920, Indonesia; tel. (21) 5224902; fax (21) 5224905; e-mail ipc@indo.net.id; internet www.ipcnet.org; f. 1972 for promoting, co-ordinating and harmonizing all activities relating to the pepper economy. Mems: six exporting countries (Brazil, India, Indonesia, Malaysia, Federated States of Micronesia, Papua New Guinea, Sri Lanka, Thailand), 30 importing countries. Exec. Dir Dr K. P. G. MENON. Publs *Pepper Statistical Yearbook, International Pepper News Bulletin* (quarterly), *Directory of Pepper Exporters, Directory of Pepper Importers, Weekly Prices Bulletin, Pepper Market Review*.

International Platinum Association: 60313 Frankfurt-am-Main, Kroegerstr. 5, Germany; tel. (69) 287941; fax (69) 283601; links principal producers and fabricators of platinum. Pres. EDWARD HASLAM; Man. Dir MARCUS NURDIN.

International Rubber Study Group: Heron House, 109–115 Wembley Hill Rd, Wembley, HA9 8DA, United Kingdom; tel. (20) 8903-7727; fax (20) 8903-2848; e-mail irsg@compuserve.com; internet www.rubberstudy.org; f. 1944 to provide a forum for the discussion of problems affecting synthetic and natural rubber and to provide statistical and other general information on rubber. Mems: 18 governments. Sec.-Gen. Dr A. F. S. BUDIMAN (Indonesia). Publs *Rubber Statistical Bulletin* (monthly), *International Rubber Digest* (monthly), *Proceedings of International Rubber Forums* (annually), *World Rubber Statistics Handbook, Key Rubber Indicators, Rubber Statistics Yearbook* (annually), *Rubber Economics Yearbook* (annually), *Outlook for Elastomers* (annually).

International Silk Association: 34 rue de la Charité, 69002 Lyon, France; tel. 4-78-42-10-79; fax 4-78-37-56-72; e-mail isa-silk.ais-sole@wanadoo.fr; f. 1949 to promote closer collaboration between all branches of the silk industry and trade, develop the consumption of silk and foster scientific research; collects and disseminates information and statistics relating to the trade and industry; organizes biennial Congresses. Mems: employers' and technical organizations in 40 countries. Pres. MICHELE CANEPA (Italy); Gen. Sec. R. CURRIE. Publs *ISA Newsletter* (monthly), congress reports, standards, trade rules, etc.

International Spice Group: c/o International Trade Centre (UNCTAD/WTO), 54–56 rue de Montbrillant, 1202 Geneva, Switzerland; tel. (22) 730-01-01; fax (22) 730-02-54; e-mail itcreg@intracen.org; f. 1983 to provide forum for producers and consumers of spices, and to attempt to increase the consumption of spices. Mems: 33 producer countries, 15 importing countries. Chair. HERNAL HAMILTON (Jamaica).

International Sugar Organization: 1 Canada Sq., Canary Wharf, London, E14 5AA, United Kingdom; tel. (20) 7513-1144; fax (20) 7513-1146; e-mail exdir@ isosugar.org; internet wwwisosugar.org; administers the International Sugar Agreement (1992); the agreement does not include measures for stabilizing markets. Mems: 58 countries. Exec. Dir Dr P. BARON. Publs *Sugar Year Book, Monthly Statistical Bulletin, Market Report and Press Summary, Quarterly Market Review*, seminar proceedings.

International Tea Committee Ltd: Sir John Lyon House, 5 High Timber St, London, EC4V 3NH, United Kingdom; tel. (20) 7248-4672; fax (20) 7329-6955; e-mail inteacom@globalnet.co.uk; internet www.intteacomm.co.uk; f. 1933 to administer the International Tea Agreement; now serves as a statistical and information centre; in 1979 membership was extended to include consuming countries. Producer Mems: national tea boards or associations of Bangladesh, India, Indonesia, Japan, Kenya, Malawi, Sri Lanka, Zimbabwe; Consumer Mems: United Kingdom Tea Assn, Tea Assn of the USA Inc., Comité Européen du Thé and the Tea Council of Canada; Assoc. Mems: Netherlands and UK ministries of agriculture, Cameroon Development Corpn. Chair. M. J. BUNSTON. Publs *Annual Bulletin of Statistics, Monthly Statistical Summary*.

International Tea Promotion Association: POB 20064, Tea Board of Kenya, Nairobi, Kenya; tel. (2) 220241; fax (2) 331650; f. 1979. Mems: Bangladesh, Indonesia, Kenya, Malawi, Mauritius, Mozambique, Tanzania, Uganda. Chair. GEORGE M. KIMANI; Liaison Officer NGOIMA WA MWAURA. Publ. *International Tea Journal* (2 a year).

International Tobacco Growers' Association: Apdo 5, 6001-081 Castelo Branco, Portugal; tel. (72) 325901; fax (72) 325906; e-mail itga@mail.telepac.pt; internet www.tobaccoleaf.org; f. 1984 to provide forum for the exchange of views and information of interest to tobacco producers. Mems: 22 countries producing over 80% of the world's internationally traded tobacco. Pres. MARCELO QUEVEDO (Argentina); Exec. Dir ANTONIO ABRUNHOSA (Portugal). Publs *Tobacco Courier* (quarterly), *Tobacco Briefing*.

International Tropical Timber Organization—ITTO: International Organizations Center, 5th Floor, Pacifico-Yokohama, 1-1-1, Minato-Mirai, Nishi-ku, Yokohama 220, Japan; tel. (45) 223-1110; fax (45) 223-1111; e-mail itto@itto.or.jp; internet www.itto.or.jp; f. 1985 under the International Tropical Timber Agreement (1983); a new treaty, ITTA 1994, came into force in 1997; provides a forum for consultation and co-operation between countries that produce and consume tropical timber; facilitated progress towards 'the objective for the year 2000' (all trade in tropical timber to be derived from sustainably managed resources) financed by a special Bali Partnership Fund; conducts research and development, reafforestation and forest management, further processing of tropical timber in producing countries, and establishment of market intelligence and economic information; no economic provision is made for price stabilization. Mems: 26 producing and 26 consuming countries and the EU. Exec. Dir Dr FREEZAILAH BIN CHE YEOM (Malaysia). Publs *Annual Review, Market Information Service* (every 2 weeks), *Tropical Forest Update* (quarterly).

International Tungsten Industry Association: 2 Baron's Gate, 33 Rothschild Rd, London, W4 5HT, United Kingdom; tel. (20) 8742-2274; fax (20) 8742-7345; e-mail itiaimoa@compuserve.com; internet www.itia.org.uk/; f. 1988 (fmrly Primary Tungsten Asscn, f. 1975); promotes use of tungsten, collates statistics, prepares market reports, monitors health and environmental issues. Mems: 51. Pres. S. OGURA; Sec.-Gen. MICHAEL MABY.

International Vine and Wine Office: 18 rue d'Aguesseau, 75008 Paris, France; tel. 1-44-94-80-80; fax 1-42-66-90-63; e-mail oiv@oiv.int; internet www.oiv.int; f. 1924 to study all the scientific, technical, economic and human problems concerning the vine and its products; to spread knowledge by means of its publications; to assist contacts between researchers and establish international research programmes. Mems: 45 countries. Dir-Gen. GEORGES DUTRUC-ROSSET. Publs *Bulletin de l'OIV* (every 2 months), *Lettre de l'OIV* (monthly), *Lexique de la Vigne et du Vin, Recueil des méthodes internationales d'analyse des vins, Code international des Pratiques oenologiques, Codex oenologique international*, numerous scientific publications.

Lead Development Association International: 42 Weymouth St, London, W1N 3LQ, United Kingdom; tel. (20) 7499-8422; fax (20) 7493-1555; e-mail eng@ldaint.org; internet www.ldaint.org; f. 1956; provides authoritative information on the use of lead and its compounds. Financed by lead producers and users in the United Kingdom, Europe and elsewhere. Dir Dr D. N. WILSON (UK).

Regional Association of Oil and Natural Gas Companies in Latin America and the Caribbean (Asociación Regional de Empresas de Petróleo y Gas Natural en América Latina y el Caribe—ARPEL): Javier de Viana 2345, Casilla de correo 1006, 11200 Montevideo, Uruguay; tel. (2) 4006993; fax (2) 4009207; e-mail arpel@adinet.com.uy; internet www.arpel.org; f. 1965 as the Mutual Assistance of the Latin American Oil Companies; aims to initiate and implement activities for the development of the oil and natural gas industry in Latin America and the Caribbean; promotes the expansion of business opportunities and the improvement of the competitive advantages of its members; promotes guide-lines in support of competition in the sector; and supports the efficient and sustainable exploitation of hydrocarbon resources and the supply of products and services. Works in co-operation with international organizations, governments, regulatory agencies, technical institutions, universities and non-governmental organizations. Mems: state enterprises in Argentina, Bolivia, Brazil, Canada, Chile, Colombia, Costa Rica, Cuba, Ecuador, Jamaica, Mexico, Nicaragua, Paraguay, Peru, Suriname, Trinidad and Tobago, Uruguay, Venezuela. Sec.-Gen. ANDRÉS TIERNO ABREU. Publ. *Boletín Técnico*.

Sugar Association of the Caribbean (Inc.): c/o Caroni (1975) Ltd, Brechin Castle, Conva, Trinidad; tel. 636-2449; fax 636-2847; f. 1942. Mems: national sugar cos of Barbados, Belize, Guyana, Jamaica and Trinidad and Tobago, and Sugar Asscn of St Kitts–Nevis–Anguilla. Chair. KARL JAMES. Sec. AZIZ MOHAMMED. Publs *SAC Handbook, SAC Annual Report, Proceedings of Meetings of WI Sugar Technologists*.

Union of Banana-Exporting Countries—UPEB: Apdo 4273, Bank of America, piso 7, Panamá 5, Panama; tel. 263-6266; fax 264-8355; e-mail iicapan@pan.gbm.net; f. 1974 as an intergovernmental agency to assist the cultivation and marketing of bananas and secure prices; collects statistics and compiles bibliographies. Mems: Colombia, Costa Rica, Guatemala, Honduras, Nicaragua, Panama, Venezuela. Exec. Dir J. ENRIQUE BETANCOURT. Publs *Informe UPEB, Fax UPEB, Anuario de Estadísticas,* bibliographies.

West Africa Rice Development Association—WARDA: 01 BP 2551 Bouaké 01, Côte d'Ivoire; tel. 31-63-45-14; fax 31-63-47-14; e-mail warda@cgiar.org; internet www.cgiar.org/warda; f. 1971; aims to contribute to food security and poverty eradication in poor rural and urban populations, particularly in West and Central Africa, through research, partnerships, capacity strengthening and policy support on rice-based systems, and in ways that promote sustainable agricultural development based on environmentally-sound management of natural resources; maintains research stations in Côte d'Ivoire, Nigeria and Senegal; four research programmes—Rainfed rice, Irrigated rice, Policy support, and Systems development and technology transfer; provides training and consulting services; revenue: US $10.3m. in 1998. WARDA is a member of the network of agricultural research centres supported by the Consultative Group on International Agricultural Research (CGIAR, q.v.). Mems: Benin, Burkina Faso, Cameroon, Chad, Côte d'Ivoire, The Gambia, Ghana, Guinea, Guinea-Bissau, Liberia, Mali, Mauritania, Niger, Nigeria, Senegal, Sierra Leone, Togo. Dir-Gen. Dr KANAYO F. NWANZE (Nigeria). Publs *Annual Report, Current Contents at WARDA* (monthly), *Programme Report, Advances in Rice Research,* proceedings, leaflets, brochures.

West Indian Sea Island Cotton Association (Inc.): c/o Barbados Agricultural Development Corporation, Fairy Valley, Christ Church, Barbados. Mems: organizations in Antigua-Barbuda, Barbados, Jamaica, Montserrat and St Christopher and Nevis. Pres. E. LER. ROACH; Sec. MICHAEL I. EDGHILL.

World Federation of Diamond Bourses: 62 Pelikaanstraat, 2018 Antwerp, Belgium; tel. (3) 234-07-78; fax (3) 226-40-73; e-mail wfdb@iway.be; f. 1947 to protect the interests of affiliated organizations and their individual members and to settle or arbitrate in disputes. Mems: 24 bourses in 15 countries. Pres. A. FISCHLER (Belgium); Sec.-Gen. G. GOLDSCHMIDT (Belgium).

World Gold Council: 45 Pall Mall, London, SW1Y 5JG, United Kingdom; tel. (20) 7930-5171; fax (20) 7839-6561; internet www.gold .org; f. 1987 as world-wide international association of gold producers, to promote the demand for gold. Chair. D. M. MORLEY; Chief Exec. HARUKO FUKUDA (Japan).

Zinc Development Association: 42 Weymouth St, London, W1N 3LQ, United Kingdom; tel. (20) 7499-6636; fax (20) 7493-1555; e-mail enq@zda.org; provides authoritative advice on the uses of zinc, its alloys and its compounds; maintains a library in collaboration with the Lead Development Association (q.v.). Affiliate: Zinc Pigment Development Association. Financed by zinc producers and users in Europe and North America. Chair. P. NEATBY (UK).

Development and Economic Co-operation

African Capacity Building Foundation: Southampton Life Centre, 7th Floor, Jason Moyo Ave/Second St, POB 1562, Harare, Zimbabwe; tel. (4) 702931; fax (4) 702915; e-mail root@acbf.co.zw; internet www.acbf-pact.org; f. 1991 by the World Bank, UNDP, the African Development Bank, African and non-African governments; assists African countries to strengthen and build local capacity in economic policy analysis and development management. Exec. Sec. ABEL L. THOAHLANE.

African Training and Research Centre in Administration for Development (Centre africain de formation et de recherche administratives pour le développement—CAFRAD): ave Mohamed V, BP 310, Tangier, 90001 Morocco; tel. 942652; fax 325785; e-mail cafrad@cafrad.org; internet www.cafrad.org; f. 1964 by agreement between Morocco and UNESCO; undertakes research into administrative problems in Africa, documentation of results, provision of a consultation service for governments and organizations; holds frequent workshops for training of senior civil servants; prepares the Biennial Pan-African Conference of Ministers of the Civil Service. Mems: 35 African countries. Chair. M'HAMED EL KHALIFA; Dir-Gen. Prof. TIJJANI MUHAMMAD BANDE (acting). Publs *African Administrative Studies* (2 a year), *Research Studies, CAFRAD News* (2 a year, in English, French and Arabic).

Afro-Asian Rural Development Organization—AARDO: No. 2, State Guest Houses Complex, Chanakyapuri, New Delhi 110 021, India; tel. (11) 6877783; fax (11) 6115937; e-mail aardohq@nde .vsnl.net.in; internet www.aardo.org; f. 1962 to act as a catalyst for co-operative restructuring of rural life in Africa and Asia; and to explore collectively opportunities for co-ordination of efforts for promoting welfare and eradicating hunger, thirst, disease, illiteracy and poverty among the rural people. Activities include collaborative research on development issues; training; the exchange of information; international conferences and seminars; and awarding 100 individual training fellowships at nine institutes in Egypt, India, Japan, the Republic of Korea and Taiwan. Mems: 12 African, 14 Asian countries, and one African associate. Sec.-Gen. Dr BAHAR MUNIP. Publs *Afro-Asian Journal of Rural Development. Annual Report, Journal of Rural Reconstruction* (2 a year), *AARDO Newsletter* (2 a year).

Agence Intergouvernementale de la Francophonie: 13 quai André Citroën, 75015 Paris, France; tel. 1-44-37-33-00; fax 1-45-79-14-98; internet www.francophonie.org; f. 1970 as l'Agence de coopération culturelle et technique; promotes co-operation among French-speaking countries in the areas of education, culture, science and technology; implements decisions of the Sommet francophone (q.v.); technical and financial assistance has been given to projects in every member country, mainly to aid rural people. Mems: 50 countries and territories. Gen. Dir ROGER DEHAYBE (Belgium). Publs *Journal de l'Agence de la Francophonie* (6 a year).

Amazonian Co-operation Council: f. 1978 by signature of the Amazon Region Co-operation Treaty; aims to promote the harmonious development of the Amazon territories of signatory countries; Lima Declaration on Sustainable Development signed by ministers of foreign affairs in December 1995. Mems: Bolivia, Brazil, Colombia, Ecuador, Guyana, Peru, Suriname, Venezuela.

Arab Authority for Agricultural Investment and Development—AAAID: POB 2102, Khartoum, Sudan; tel. 784924; fax 772600; f. 1976 to accelerate agricultural development in the Arab world and to ensure food security; acts principally by equity participation in agricultural projects in Iraq, Sudan and Tunisia; signed a co-operation agreement with IFAD in Nov. 2000. Mems: Algeria, Egypt, Iraq, Jordan, Kuwait, Mauritania, Morocco, Oman, Qatar, Saudi Arabia, Somalia, Sudan, Syria, Tunisia, United Arab Emirates. Pres. ABDULKARIM AL-AMRI. Publ. *Annual Report.*

Arab Co-operation Council: POB 2640, Khartoum, Sudan; tel. (11) 73646; f. 1989 to promote economic co-operation between member states, including free movement of workers, joint projects in transport, communications and agriculture, and eventual integration of trade and monetary policies. Mems: Egypt, Iraq, Jordan, Yemen.

Arab Gulf Programme for the United Nations Development Organizations—AGFUND: POB 18371, Riyadh 11415, Saudi Arabia; tel. (1) 4418888; fax (1) 4412962; e-mail info@agfund.org; internet www.agfund.org; f. 1981 to provide grants for projects in mother and child care carried out by United Nations organizations, Arab non-governmental organizations and other international bodies, and co-ordinate assistance by the nations of the Gulf; financing comes mainly from member states, all of which are members of OPEC. Mems: Bahrain, Iraq, Kuwait, Oman, Qatar, Saudi Arabia, UAE. Pres. HRH Prince TALAL IBN ABD AL-AZIZ AL-SAUD.

Arctic Council: c/o Ministry of Foreign Affairs, Unit for Northern Dimension, POB 176, 00161 Helsinki, Finland; tel. (9) 1341-6187; fax (9) 1341-6120; e-mail johanna.lammi@formin.fi; internet www.arctic-council.org; f. 1996 to promote co-ordination of activities in the Arctic region, in particular in the areas of education, development and environmental protection. Mems: govts of eight circumpolar countries.

Association of Caribbean States—ACS: 11–13 Victoria Ave, POB 660, Port of Spain, Trinidad and Tobago; tel. 623-2783; fax 623-2679; e-mail mail@acs-aec.org; internet www.acs-aec.org; f. 1994 by the Governments of the 13 CARICOM countries (q.v.) and Colombia, Costa Rica, Cuba, the Dominican Republic, El Salvador, Guatemala, Haiti, Honduras, Mexico, Nicaragua, Suriname and Venezuela. Aims to promote economic integration and co-operation in the region; to co-ordinate participation in multilateral forums; to undertake concerted action to protect the environment, particularly the Caribbean Sea; and to co-operate in the areas of science and technology, health, transport, education and culture. Policy is determined by a Ministerial Council and implemented by a Secretariat based in Port of Spain, Trinidad and Tobago. The Fourth Ordinary Meeting of the Ministerial Council was held in Bridgetown, Barbados in December 1998. The Ministers urged States to study the Draft Regional Co-operation Agreement on Natural Disasters in preparation for the 1999 Summit. In April 1999 a second Summit of Heads of State and Government was convened in Santo Domingo, Dominican Republic; a Declaration of Santo Domingo, a Plan of Action and a Declaration of the Caribbean Zone of Sustainable Tourism were signed. The Sixth Ordinary Meeting of the Council was held in San Pedro Sula, Honduras, in December 2000. Mems: 25 signatory states, three associate members, and a further 14 countries have observer status. Sec.-Gen. Prof. Dr NORMAN GIRVAN (Jamaica).

Association of Development Financing Institutions in Asia and the Pacific—ADFIAP: Skyland Plaza, 2nd Floor, Sen. Gil J.

Puyat Ave, Majati City, Metro Manila, 1200 Philippines; tel. (2) 816-1672; fax (2) 817-6498; e-mail inquire@adfiap.org; internet www.adfiap.org; f. 1976 to promote the interests and economic development of the respective countries of its member institutions, through development financing. Mems: 81 institutions in 35 countries. Chair. ASWIN KONGSIRI (Thailand); Sec.-Gen. ORLANDO P. PEÑA (Philippines). Publs *Asian Banking Digest, Journal of Development Finance* (2 a year), *ADFIAP Newsletter,* surveys.

Benelux Economic Union: 39 rue de la Régence, 1000 Brussels, Belgium; tel. (2) 519-38-11; fax (2) 513-42-06; e-mail sg@benelux.be; f. 1960 to bring about the economic union of Belgium, Luxembourg and the Netherlands; aims to introduce common policies in the field of cross-border co-operation and establish co-operation in the harmonization of standards and intellectual property legislation; structure comprises: Committee of Ministers; Council; Court of Justice; Consultative Inter-Parliamentary Council; the Economic and Social Advisory Council; and the General Secretariat; Sec.-Gen. Dr B. M. J. HENNEKAM (Netherlands). Publs *Benelux Newsletter, Bulletin Benelux.*

Caritas Internationalis (International Confederation of Catholic Organizations for charitable and social action): Palazzo San Calisto, 00120 Città del Vaticano; tel. (06) 69887197; fax (06) 69887237; e-mail caritas.internationalis@caritas.va; f. 1950 to study problems arising from poverty, their causes and possible solutions; national member organizations undertake assistance and development activities. The Confederation co-ordinates emergency relief and development projects, and represents members at international level. Mems: 156 national orgs. Pres. Mgr AFFONSO GREGORY, Bishop of Imperatriz (Brazil); Sec.-Gen. DUNCAN MACLAREN. Publs *Caritas Matters* (quarterly), *Emergency Calling* (2 a year).

Caribbean Council for Europe: Westminster Palace Gardens, Suite 18, 1–7 Artillery Row, London, SW1P 1RR, United Kingdom; tel. (20) 7799-1521; e-mail caribbean@compuserve.com; f. 1992 by the Caribbean Association of Industry and Commerce and other regional organizations, to represent the interests of the Caribbean private sector in the European Union; organizes regular Europe/Caribbean Conference. Chair. YESU PERSAUD; Exec. Dir DAVID JESSOP.

Central European Free Trade Association: internet www.ijs.si/cefta; f. 1992, entered into force 1993; free-trade agreement covering a number of sectors. Mems: Bulgaria, Czech Republic, Hungary, Poland, Romania, Slovakia, Slovenia.

Colombo Plan: Bank of Ceylon Merchant Tower, 28 St Michael's Rd, Colombo 03, Sri Lanka; tel. (1) 564448; fax (1) 564531; e-mail cplan@slt.lk; internet www.colombo-plan.org; f. 1950 by seven Commonwealth countries, to encourage economic and social development in Asia and the Pacific. The Plan comprises the Programme for Public Administration, to provide training for officials in the context of a market-orientated economy; the Programme for Private Sector Development, which organizes training programmes to stimulate the economic benefits of development of the private sector; a Drug Advisory Programme, to encourage regional co-operation in efforts to control drug-related problems, in particular through human resources development; a programme to establish a South-South Technical Co-operation Data Bank, to collate, analyse and publish information in order to facilitate south-south co-operation; and a Staff College for Technician Education (see below). All programmes are voluntarily funded; developing countries are encouraged to become donors and to participate in economic and technical co-operation activities among developing members. Mems: 24 countries. Sec.-Gen. U. SARAT CHANDRAN (India). Publs *Annual Report, Colombo Plan Focus* (quarterly), Consultative Committee proceedings (every 2 years).

Colombo Plan Staff College for Technician Education: POB 7500, Domestic Airport Post Office, NAIA, Pasay City 1300, Metro Manila, Philippines; tel. (2) 6310991; fax (2) 6310996; e-mail cpsc@skyinet.net; internet www.cpsc.org.ph; f. 1973 with the support of member Governments of the Colombo Plan; aims to enhance the development of technician education systems in developing member countries. Dir Dr BERNARDO F. ADIVISO. Publ. *CPSC Quarterly.*

Communauté économique des états de l'Afrique centrale—CEEAC (Economic Community of Central African States): BP 2112, Libreville, Gabon; tel. 73-35-48; f. 1983; operational 1 January 1985; aims to promote co-operation between member states by abolishing trade restrictions, establishing a common external customs tariff, linking commercial banks, and setting up a development fund, over a period of 12 years; combat drug abuse; and to promote regional security. Budget (1998): US $1.82m. Mems: Angola, Burundi, Central African Repub., Chad, the Democratic Repub. of the Congo, the Repub. of the Congo, Equatorial Guinea, Gabon, Rwanda and São Tomé and Príncipe. Sec.-Gen. LOUIS-SYLVAIN GOMA (Republic of the Congo).

Community of the Sahel-Saharan States (Communauté des Etats du Sahel et du Sahara—CEN-SAD): Tripoli, Libya; f. 1997; fmrly known as COMESSA; aims to strengthen co-operation between signatory states; established a joint commission with the OAU, in 1998, to support mediation in the conflicts between Eritrea and Ethiopia; mems. Burkina Faso, Central African Republic, Chad, Djibouti, Egypt, Eritrea, The Gambia, Libya, Mali, Morocco, Niger, Nigeria, Senegal, Sudan, Tunisia. Sec.-Gen. ALMADANI AL-AZHARI (Libya).

Conseil de l'Entente (Entente Council): 01 BP 3734, Abidjan 01, Côte d'Ivoire; tel. 33-28-35; fax 33-11-49; f. 1959 to promote economic development in the region. The Council's Mutual Aid and Loan Guarantee Fund (Fonds d'Entraide et de Garantie des Emprunts) finances development projects, including agricultural projects, support for small and medium-sized enterprises, vocational training centres, research into new sources of energy and building of hotels to encourage tourism. A Convention of Assistance and Co-operation was signed in February 1996. Holds annual summit: 2000 in Kara, Togo, in March. Fund budget (1999): 2,074m. francs CFA. Mems: Benin, Burkina Faso, Côte d'Ivoire, Niger, Togo. Sec.-Gen. PAUL KOUAMÉ. Publ. *Rapport d'activité* (annually).

Communauté économique du bétail et de la viande (CEBV) du Conseil de l'Entente (Livestock and Meat Economic Community of the Entente Council): 01 BP 638 Ouagadougou, Burkina Faso; tel. 30-62-67; fax 30-62-68; e-mail cebv@cenatrin.bf; internet www.cenatrin.bf/cebv; f. 1970 to promote the production, processing and marketing of livestock and meat; negotiates between members and with third countries on technical and financial co-operation and co-ordinated legislation; attempts to co-ordinate measures to combat drought and cattle diseases. Mems: states belonging to the Conseil de l'Entente. Exec. Sec. Dr ELIE LADIKPO.

Council of American Development Foundations—SOLIDA-RIOS: Calle 6 No. 10 Paraiso, Apdo Postal 620, Santo Domingo, Dominican Republic; tel. (809) 549-5111; fax (809) 544-0550; e-mail solidarios@codetel.net.do; f. 1972; exchanges information and experience, arranges technical assistance, raises funds to organize training programmes and scholarships; administers development fund to finance programmes carried out by members through a loan guarantee programme; provides consultancy services. Member foundations provide technical and financial assistance to low-income groups for rural, housing and microenterprise development projects. Mems: 18 institutional mems in 14 Latin American and Caribbean countries. Pres. MERCEDES P. DE CANALDA; Sec.-Gen. ISABEL C. ARANGO. Publs *Solidarios* (quarterly), *Annual Report.*

Developing Eight — D-8: Musir Fuad Pasa Yalisi, Eski Tersane, Emirgan, Cad. 90, Istinye 80860, İstanbul, Turkey; tel. (212) 2275513; fax (212) 2275519; e-mail edoffice@d8net.org; internet www.d8net.org; inaugurated at a meeting of heads of state in June 1997; aims to foster economic co-operation between member states and to strengthen the role of developing countries in the global economy; project areas include trade and industry, agriculture, poverty alleviation, human resources development, science and technology, telecommunications and information, rural development, finance (including banking and privatization), energy, environment, and health. Third Summit meeting, convened in Cairo, Egypt, in Feb. 2001, discussed reducing trade barriers amongst member states and considered the impact of external debt on member economies. Mems: Bangladesh, Egypt, Indonesia, Iran, Malaysia, Nigeria, Pakistan, Turkey. Exec. Dir AYHAN KAMEL.

East African Community—EAC: Arusha International Conference Centre, POB 1096, Arusha, Tanzania; tel. (57) 4253; fax (57) 4255; e-mail eac@eachq.org; internet www.eachq.org; f. Jan. 2001, following the adoption of a treaty on political and economic integration (signed in November 1999) by the heads of state of Kenya, Tanzania and Uganda, replacing the Permanent Tripartite Commission for East African Co-operation (f. 1993) and reviving the former East African Community (f. 1967; dissolved 1977); initial areas for co-operation were to be trade and industry, security, immigration, transport and communications, and promotion of investment; further objectives were the elimination of trade barriers and ensuring the free movement of people and capital within the grouping. Sec.-Gen. FRANCIS KIRIMI MUTHAURA.

Economic Community of the Great Lakes Countries (Communauté économique des pays des Grands Lacs—CEPGL): POB 58, Gisenyi, Rwanda; tel. 61309; fax 61319; f. 1976; main organs: annual Conference of Heads of State, Council of Ministers of Foreign Affairs, Permanent Executive Secretariat, Consultative Commission, Security Commission, three Specialized Technical Commissions. There are four specialized agencies: a development bank, the Banque de Développement des Etats des Grands Lacs (BDEGL) at Goma, Democratic Republic of the Congo; an energy centre at Bujumbura, Burundi; the Institute of Agronomic and Zootechnical Research, Gitega, Burundi; and a regional electricity company (SINELAC) at Bukavu, Democratic Republic of the Congo. Two extraordinary summit meetings were held in 1994 to discuss security concerns in the region and efforts to revive economic co-operation activities. Mems: Burundi, the Democratic Republic of the Congo, Rwanda. Publs *Grands Lacs* (quarterly review), *Journal* (annually).

Food Aid Committee: c/o International Grains Council, 1 Canada Square, Canary Wharf, London, E14 5AE, United Kingdom; tel. (20) 7513-1122; fax (20) 7513-0630; e-mail igc-fac@igc.org.uk; internet www.igc.org.uk; f. 1967; responsible for administration of the Food Aid Convention—FAC (1999), a constituent element of the International Grains Agreement (1995); the FAC aims to make available appropiate levels of food aid on a consistent basis, maximize the impact and effectiveness of such assistance, and provide a framework for co-operation, co-ordination and information-sharing among members on matters related to food aid. The 23 donor members are pledged to supply a minimum of approximately 5m. metric tons of food annually to developing countries and territories, mostly as gifts: in practice aid has usually exceeded 8m. tons annually. Secretariat support is provided by the International Grains Council (q.v.). Exec. Dir G. DENIS. Publ. *Report on shipments* (annually).

Gambia River Basin Development Organization (Organisation de mise en valeur du fleuve Gambie—OMVG): BP 2353, 13 passage Leblanc, Dakar, Senegal; tel. 822-31-59; fax 822-59-26; e-mail omvg@telecomplus.sn; f. 1978 by Senegal and The Gambia; Guinea joined in 1981 and Guinea-Bissau in 1983. A masterplan for the integrated development of the Kayanga/Geba and Koliba/Corubal river basins has been developed, encompassing a projected natural resources management project; work on a hydraulic development plan for the Gambia river commenced in late 1996 and was completed in mid-1998; a pre-feasibility study on connecting the national electric grids of the four member states has been completed, and a feasibility study for the construction of the proposed Sambangalou hydroelectric dam, providing for energy transmission to all member states, was scheduled to commence in mid-2001 and to conclude by late 2002; maintains documentation centre. Exec. Sec. MAMADOU NASSIROU DIALLO.

Group of Three—G3: f. 1993 by Colombia, Mexico and Venezuela to remove restrictions on trade between the three countries. The trade agreement covers market access, rules of origin, intellectual property, trade in services, and government purchases, and entered into force in early 1994. Tariffs on trade between member states were to be removed on a phased basis. Co-operation was also envisaged in employment creation, the energy sector and the fight against cholera.

Indian Ocean Commission—IOC: Q4, Ave Sir Guy Forget, BP 7, Quatre Bornes, Mauritius; tel. 425-9564; fax 425-2709; e-mail coi7@intnet.mu; internet www.coi.intnet.mu; f. 1982 to promote regional co-operation, particularly in economic development; principal projects under way in the early 1990s (at a cost of 11.6m. francs CFA) comprised tuna-fishing development, protection and management of environmental resources and strengthening of meteorological services, with assistance principally from the EU, UN Environment Programme and World Bank; tariff reduction is also envisaged. Permanent technical committees cover: tuna-fishing; regional industrial co-operation; regional commerce; tourism; environment; maritime transport; handicrafts; labour; education; telecommunication; culture; sports. The IOC organizes an annual regional trade fair. Mems: Comoros, France (representing the French Overseas Department of Réunion), Madagascar, Mauritius, Seychelles. Sec.-Gen. CAABI E. MOHAMED. Publ. *La Gazette de la Commission de l'Océan Indien.*

Indian Ocean Rim Association for Regional Co-operation—IOR-ARC: Sorèce House, 14 Angus Rd, Vacoas, Mauritius; tel. 698-3979; fax 697-5390; e-mail iorarchq@intnet.mu; the first intergovernmental meeting of countries in the region to promote an Indian Ocean Rim initiative was convened in March 1995; charter to establish the Asscn signed at a ministerial meeting in March 1997; aims to promote regional economic co-operation through trade, investment, infrastructure, tourism, science and technology. Mems: Australia, Bangladesh, India, Indonesia, Iran, Kenya, Madagascar, Malaysia, Mauritius, Mozambique, Oman, Seychelles, Singapore, South Africa, Sri Lanka, Tanzania, Thailand, United Arab Emirates and Yemen. Chair. Dr LEONARDO SIMÃO (Mozambique); Sec.-Gen. KAILASH RUHEE (Mauritius).

Inter-American Planning Society (Sociedad Interamericana de Planificación—SIAP): c/o Revista Interamericana de Planificación, Casilla 01-05-1978, Cuenca, Ecuador; tel. (7) 823-860; fax (7) 823-949; f. 1956 to promote development of comprehensive planning as a continuous and co-ordinated process at all levels. Mems: institutions and individuals in 46 countries. Pres. Arq. HERMES MARROQUÍN (Guatemala); Exec. Sec. LUIS E. CAMACHO (Colombia). Publs *Correo Informativo* (quarterly), *Inter-American Journal of Planning* (quarterly).

International Bank for Economic Co-operation—IBEC: 107815 GSP Moscow B-78, 11 Masha Poryvaeva St, Russia; tel. (95) 975-38-61; fax (95) 975-22-02; f. 1963 by members of the Council for Mutual Economic Assistance (dissolved in 1991), as a central institution for credit and settlements; following the decision in 1989–91 of most member states to adopt a market economy, the IBEC abandoned its system of multilateral settlements in transfer-

able roubles, and (from 1 January 1991) began to conduct all transactions in convertible currencies. The Bank provides credit and settlement facilities for member states, and also acts as an international commercial bank, offering services to commercial banks and enterprises. Authorized capital € 400m., paid-up capital €143.5m. (Dec. 1998). Mems: Bulgaria, Cuba, Czech Republic, Hungary, Mongolia, Poland, Romania, Russia, Slovakia, Viet Nam. Chair. VITALI S. KHOKHLOV; Man. Dirs V. SYTNIKOV, S. CONSTANTINESCU.

International Co-operation for Development and Solidarity—CIDSE: 16 rue Stévin, 1000 Brussels, Belgium; tel. (2) 230-77-22; fax (2) 230-70-82; e-mail postmaster@cidse.org; internet www.cidse.org; f. 1967 to link Catholic development organizations and assist in co-ordination of projects, co-ordinating advocacy and lobbying and providing information. Mems: 14 Catholic agencies in 13 countries and territories. Pres. JUSTIN KILCULLEN; Sec.-Gen. JEF FELIX.

International Investment Bank: 107078 Moscow, 7 Masha Poryvaeva St, Russia; tel. (95) 975-40-08; fax (95) 975-20-70; f. 1970 by members of the CMEA (q.v.) to grant credits for joint investment projects and the development of enterprises; following the decision in 1989–91 of most member states to adopt a market economy, the Bank conducted its transactions (from 1 January 1991) in convertible currencies, rather than in transferable roubles. The Bank focuses on production and scientific and technical progress. By the end of 1996 the Bank had approved financing of some ECU 7,000m. for 159 projects. Authorized capital ECU 1,300m., paid-up capital ECU 214.5m., reserves ECU 835.4m. (Dec. 1997). Mems: Bulgaria, Cuba, Czech Republic, Hungary, Mongolia, Poland, Romania, Russia, Slovakia, Viet Nam.

Lake Chad Basin Commission: BP 727, N'Djamena, Chad; tel. 52-41-45; fax 52-41-37; e-mail lcbc@intnet.td; f. 1964 to encourage co-operation in developing the Lake Chad region and to promote the settlement of regional disputes. Work programmes emphasize the regulation of the utilization of water and other natural resources in the basin; the co-ordination of natural resources development projects and research; in 1988–92 a border demarcation exercise concerning all five member states was conducted. Annual summit of heads of state. Budget 400m. francs CFA. Mems: Cameroon, Central African Republic, Chad, Niger, Nigeria. Exec. Sec. BOBBOÏ JAURO ABUBAKAR. Publ. *Bibliographie générale de la cblt* (2 a year).

Latin American Association of Development Financing Institutions (Asociación Latinoamericana de Instituciones Financieras para el Desarrollo—ALIDE): Apdo Postal 3988, Paseo de la República 3211, Lima 100, Peru; tel. (1) 442-2400; fax (1) 442-8105; e-mail sg@alide.org.pe; internet www.alide.org.pe; f. 1968 to promote co-operation among regional development financing bodies. Mems: 62 active, 8 associate and 8 collaborating (banks and financing institutions and development organizations in 22 Latin American countries, Slovenia and Spain). Sec.-Gen. ROMMEL ACEVEDO. Publs *ALIDE Bulletin* (6 a year), *ALIDENOTICIAS Newsletter* (monthly), *Annual Report, Latin American Directory of Development Financing Institutions.*

Latin American Economic System (Sistema Económico Latinoamericano—SELA): Apdo 17035, Avda Francisco de Miranda, Centro Empresarial Parque del Este, 1°, La Carlota, Caracas 1017, Venezuela; tel. (212) 202-5111; fax (212) 238-8923; e-mail difusion@sela.org; internet www.sela.org; f. 1975 by the Panama Convention; aims to accelerate the economic and social development of its members through intra-regional co-operation, and to provide a permanent system of consultation and co-ordination in economic and social matters; conducts studies; provides library, information service and data bases on regional co-operation. The Latin American Council meets annually at ministerial level and high-level regional consultation and co-ordination meetings are held; there is also a Permanent Secretariat. Mems: 28 countries. The following organizations have also been created within SELA:

Latin American and Caribbean Trade Information and Foreign Trade Support Programme (PLACIEX): Lima, Peru.
Latin American Fisheries Development Organization (OLDEPESCA): Lima, Peru.
Latin American Handicraft Co-operation Programme (PLACART): Caracas, Venezuela.
Latin American Technological Information Network (RITLA): Brasilia, Brazil.
Perm. Sec. OTTO BOYO (Chile). Publs *Capítulos del SELA* (quarterly), *SELA Newsletter* (monthly), *Strategic Issues* (monthly).

Liptako-Gourma Integrated Development Authority: POB 619, ave M. Thevenond, Ouagadougou, Burkina Faso; tel. (3) 30-61-48; f. 1972; scope of activities includes water infrastructure, telecommunications and construction of roads and railways; in 1986 undertook study on development of water resources in the basin of the Niger river (for hydroelectricity and irrigation). Mems: Burkina Faso, Mali, Niger. Dir-Gen. GISANGA DEMBÉLÉ (Mali).

Mano River Union: Private Mail Bag 133, Delco House, Lightfoot Boston St, Freetown, Sierra Leone; tel. (22) 226883; f. 1973 to establish a customs and economic union between member states to accelerate development via integration. A common external tariff was instituted in October 1977. Intra-union free trade was officially introduced in May 1981, as the first stage in progress towards a customs union. An industrial development unit was set up in 1980 to identify projects and encourage investment. Construction of the Monrovia-Freetown-Conakry highway was partially completed by 1990. The Union was inactive for three years until mid-1994, owing to disagreements regarding funding. In January 1995 a Mano River Centre for Peace and Development was established, which was to be temporarily based in London. The Centre aims to provide a permanent mechanism for conflict prevention and resolution, and monitoring of human rights violations, and to promote sustainable peace and development following a peaceful resolution of the conflicts currently under way in the region. Decisions are taken at meetings of a joint ministerial council formed by the ministers of member states. Mems: Guinea, Liberia, Sierra Leone. Dir Dr KABINEH KOROMAH (Sierra Leone).

Mekong River Commission: 364 M. V. Preah Monivong, Sangkat Phsar Doerm Thkouv, Khan Chamkar Mon, POB 1112, Phnom Penh, Cambodia; tel. (23) 720979; fax (23) 720972; e-mail mrcs@mrcmekong.org; f. 1995, as successor to the Committee for Co-ordination of Investigations of the Lower Mekong Basin (f. 1957); aims to promote and co-ordinate the sustainable development, utilization and conservation of the resources of the Mekong River Basin for navigational and non-navigational purposes, in order to assist the social and economic development of member states, while at the same time preserving the ecological balance of the basin. Provides scientific information and policy advice; supports the implementation of strategic programmes and activities; organizes an annual donor consultative group meeting; maintains regular dialogue with Myanmar and the People's Republic of China. Mems: Cambodia, Laos, Thailand, Viet Nam. CEO JOERN KRISTENSEN.

Niger Basin Authority (Autorité du bassin du Niger): BP 729, Niamey, Niger; tel. 723102; fax 735310; f. 1964 (as River Niger Commission; name changed 1980) to harmonize national programmes concerned with the River Niger Basin and to execute an integrated development plan; activities comprise: statistics; navigation regulation; hydrological forecasting; environmental control; infrastructure and agro-pastoral development; and arranging assistance for these projects. Mems: Benin, Burkina Faso, Cameroon, Chad, Côte d'Ivoire, Guinea, Mali, Niger, Nigeria. Exec. Sec. OTHMAN MUSTAPHA (Nigeria). Publ. *Bulletin.*

Organisation of Eastern Caribbean States—OECS: POB 179, Morne Fortune, Castries, Saint Lucia; tel. 452-2537; fax 453-1628; e-mail oesec@oecs.org; internet www.oecs.org; f. 1981 by the seven states which formerly belonged to the West Indies Associated States (f. 1966). Aims to promote the harmonized development of trade and industry in member states; single market created on 1 January 1988. Principal institutions are: the Authority of Heads of Government (the supreme policy-making body), the Foreign Affairs Committee, the Defence and Security Committee, and the Economic Affairs Committee. There is also an Export Development and Agricultural Diversification Unit—EDADU (based in Dominica). Mems: Antigua and Barbuda, Dominica, Grenada, Montserrat, Saint Christopher and Nevis, Saint Lucia, Saint Vincent and the Grenadines; assoc. mems: Anguilla, British Virgin Islands. Dir-Gen. SWINBURNE LESTRADE.

Organization for the Development of the Senegal River (Organisation pour la mise en valeur du fleuve Sénégal—OMVS): 46 rue Carnot, BP 3152, Dakar, Senegal; tel. 823-45-30; fax 823-47-62; e-mail omvs.sphc@telecomplus.sn; f. 1972 to use the Senegal river for hydroelectricity, irrigation and navigation. The Djama dam in Senegal provides a barrage to prevent salt water from moving upstream, and the Manantali dam in Mali is intended to provide a reservoir for irrigation of about 375,000 ha of land and for production of hydroelectricity and provision of year-round navigation for ocean-going vessels. In 1997 two companies were formed to manage the dams: Société de Gestion de l'Energie de Manantali (SOGEM) and Société de Gestion et d'Exploitation du Barrage de Djama (SOGED). Work began in 1997 on a hydro-electric power station on the Senegal River: international donors provided US $440m. for the project which was due for completion in 2001. Mems: Mali, Mauritania, Senegal; Guinea has held observer status since 1987. Chair. MAAOUYA OULD SID'AHMED TAYA.

Organization for the Management and Development of the Kagera River Basin (Organisation pour l'aménagement et le développement du bassin de la rivière Kagera): BP 297, Kigali, Rwanda; tel. (7) 84665; fax (7) 82172; f. 1978; envisages joint development

and management of resources, including the construction of an 80-MW hydroelectric dam at Rusumo Falls, on the Rwanda-Tanzania border, a 2,000-km railway network between the four member countries, road construction (914 km), and a telecommunications network between member states (financed by US $16m. from the African Development Bank). A tsetse-fly control project began in 1990. Budget (1992) $2m. Mems: Burundi, Rwanda, Tanzania, Uganda. Exec. Sec. JEAN-BOSCO BALINDA.

Pacific Basin Economic Council—PBEC: 900 Fort St, Suite 1080, Honolulu, HI 96813, USA; tel. (808) 521-9044; fax (808) 521-8530; e-mail info@pbec.org; internet www.pbec.org; f. 1967; an association of business representatives which aims to promote business opportunities in the region in order to enhance overall economic development; to advise governments and to serve as a liaison between business leaders and government officials; encourages business relationships and co-operation among members; holds business symposia. Mems: 20 country committees (Australia, Canada, Chile, People's Republic of China, Colombia, Ecuador, Hong Kong, Indonesia, Japan, Republic of Korea, Malaysia, Mexico, New Zealand, Peru, Philippines, Russia, Taiwan, Thailand, USA). Chair. KOSAKU INABA; Sec.-Gen. ROBERT G. LEES.

Pacific Economic Co-operation Council—PECC: 4 Nassim Rd, Singapore 258372; tel. 7379823; fax 7379824; e-mail peccsec@pacific .net.sg; internet www.pecc.net; f. 1980; an independent, policy-orientated organization of senior research, government and business representatives from 23 economies in the Asia-Pacific region; aims to foster economic development in the region by providing a forum for discussion and co-operation in a wide range of economic areas; general meeting every 2 years. Mems: Australia, Brunei, Canada, Chile, the People's Republic of China, Colombia, Ecuador, Hong Kong, Indonesia, Japan, the Republic of Korea, Malaysia, Mexico, Mongolia (assoc.mem.), New Zealand, Peru, Philippines, Russia, Singapore, Taiwan, Thailand, USA, Viet Nam and the South Pacific Forum; French Pacific Territories (assoc. mem.); Dir-Gen. MIGNON CHAN MAN-JUNG. Publs *PECC E-Newsletter* (electronic newsletter, 2 a week), *Pacific Economic Outlook* (annually), *Pacific Food Outlook* (-annually).

Pan-African Institute for Development—PAID: BP 4056, Douala, Cameroon; tel. 42-10-61; fax 42-43-35; e-mail ipd.sg@camnet .cm; f. 1964; gives training to people involved with development at grassroots, intermediate and senior levels coming from African countries (48 countries in 1998); emphasis in education is given to: development management and financing; agriculture and rural development; gender and development; promotion of small and medium-sized enterprises; training policies and systems; environment, health and community development; research, support and consultancy services; and specialized training. There are four regional institutes: Central Africa (Douala), Sahel (Ouagadougou, Burkina Faso) (French-speaking), West Africa (Buéa, Cameroon), Eastern and Southern Africa (Kabwe, Zambia) (English-speaking), and a European office in Geneva. Sec.-Gen. MICHEL ONGOLO-NDONGO. Publs *Newsletter* (2 a year), *Annual Progress Report, PAID Report* (quarterly).

Permanent Inter-State Committee on Drought Control in the Sahel—CILSS: POB 7049, Ouagadougou, Burkina Faso; tel. 306758; fax 306757; e-mail cilss@fasonet.bf; f. 1973; works in co-operation with UN Sudano-Sahelian Office (UNSO, q.v.); aims to combat the effects of chronic drought in the Sahel region (where the deficit in grain production was estimated at 1.7m. metric tons for 1988), by improving irrigation and food production, halting deforestation and creating food reserves; maintains Institut du Sahel at Bamako (Mali) and centre at Niamey (Niger). Budget (2000): 9,506.1m. francs CFA, of which 318.5m. francs CFA was to be provided by mems. Mems: Burkina Faso, Cape Verde, Chad, The Gambia, Guinea-Bissau, Mali, Mauritania, Niger, Senegal. Chair. (1997–2000) Pres. YAHYA A. J. J. JAMMEH (The Gambia); Exec. Sec. MOUSSA BENGA. Publ. *Reflets Sahéliens* (quarterly).

Population Council: 1 Dag Hammarskjöld Plaza, New York, NY 10017, USA; tel. (212) 339-0500; fax (212) 755-6052;e-mail pubinfo @popcouncil.org; internet www.popcouncil.org; f. 1952; aims to improve reproductive health and achieve a balance between people and resources; analyses demographic trends; conducts biomedical research to develop new contraceptives; works with private and public agencies to improve the quality and scope of family planning and reproductive health services; helps governments to design and implement population policies; communicates results of research. Five regional offices, in India, Mexico, Egypt, Kenya and Senegal, and 15 country offices. Additional office in Washington, DC, USA, carries out world-wide operational research and activities for reproductive health and the prevention of HIV and AIDS. Chair. ELIZABETH J. McCORMACK; Pres. LINDA MARTIN. Publs *Studies in Family Planning* (quarterly), *Population and Development Review* (quarterly), *Population Briefs* (quarterly).

Society for International Development: Via Panisperna 207, 00184 Rome, Italy; tel. (06) 4872172; fax (06) 4872170;e-mail info@

sidint.org; internet www.sidint.org; f. 1957; a global network of individuals and institutions concerned with development that is participative, pluralistic and sustainable; mobilizes and strengthens civil society groups by actively building partnerships among them and with other sectors; fosters local initiatives and new forms of social experimentation. Mems: over 3,000 in 115 countries and 60 local chapters. Pres. ENRIQUE IGLESIAS; Sec.-Gen. ROBERTO SAVIO. Publs *Development* (quarterly), *Bridges* (bimonthly newsletter).

South Centre: Chemin du Champ-d'Anier 17–19, BP 228, 1211 Geneva 19, Switzerland; tel. (22) 7918050; fax (22) 7988531; e-mail south@southcentre.org; internet www.southcentre.org; f. 1990 as a follow-up mechanism of the South Commission (f. 1987); 1995 established as an intergovernmental body that aims to promote South–South solidarity and co-operation by generating ideas and action-oriented proposals on major policy issues for consideration by collective institutions and intergovernmental organizations of the South and individual governments. Chair. (vacant). Publ. *South Letter* (quarterly).

Union of the Arab Maghreb (Union du Maghreb arabe—UMA): 26–27 rue Okba, Agdal, Rabat, Morocco; tel. (7) 772668; fax (7) 772693; e-mail uma@mtds.com; internet www.maghrebarabe.org; f. 1989; aims to encourage joint ventures and to create a single market; structure comprises a council of heads of state (meeting annually), a council of ministers of foreign affairs, a consultative council of 30 delegates from each country, a UMA judicial court, and four specialized ministerial commissions. Chairmanship rotates annually between heads of state. By 1995 joint projects that had been approved or were under consideration included: free movement of citizens within the region; joint transport undertakings, including road and railway improvements; establishment of the Maghreb Investment and Foreign Trade Bank to fund joint agricultural and industrial projects (with a capital of US $500m.); and the creation of a customs union. In April 1994 the Supreme Council agreed to undertake measures to establish a free trade zone, and to set up a Maghrebian Agency for Youth Tourism and a Maghrebian Union of Sport. In 1992 UMA adopted the Maghrebian Charter for Environment Protection and Sustainable Development. In September 1999 the Sub-regional Action Programme to Combat Desertification in the Maghreb was inaugurated. Sec.-Gen. MOHAMED AMAMOU (Tunisia). Mems: Algeria, Libya, Mauritania, Morocco, Tunisia.

Vienna Institute for Development and Co-operation (Wiener Institut für Entwicklungsfragen und Zusammenarbeit): Weyrgasse 5, 1030 Vienna, Austria; tel. (1) 713-35-94; fax (1) 713-35-94-73; e-mail vidc@magnet.at; internet www.oneworld.at; f. 1987 (fmrly Vienna Institute for Development, f. 1964); disseminates information on the problems and achievements of developing countries; encourages increased aid-giving and international co-operation; conducts research. Pres. FRANZ VRANITZKY; Dir ERICH ANDLIK. Publs *Report Series, Echo.*

Economics and Finance

African Centre for Monetary Studies: 15 blvd Franklin Roosevelt, BP 4128, Dakar, Senegal; tel. 821-93-80; fax 822-73-43; e-mail caem@syfed.refer.sn; began operations 1978; aims to promote better understanding of banking and monetary matters; to study monetary problems of African countries and the effect on them of international monetary developments; seeks to enable African countries to co-ordinate strategies in international monetary affairs. Established as an organ of the Association of African Central Banks (AACB) as a result of a decision by the OAU Heads of State and Government. Mems: all mems of AACB (q.v.). Chair. Dr PAUL A. OGWUMA (Nigeria); Dir MAMADOU SIDIBE (acting).

African Insurance Organization: BP 5860, Douala, Cameroon; tel. 42-47-58; fax 43-20-08; e-mail aio@sprynet.com; internet www.africaninsurance.org; f. 1972 to promote the expansion of the insurance and reinsurance industry in Africa, and to increase regional co-operation; holds annual conference, (2000: Abuja, Nigeria), periodic seminars and workshops, and arranges meetings for reinsurers, brokers, consultant and regulators in Africa; has established African insurance 'pools' for aviation, petroleum and fire risks, and has created associations of African insurance educators, supervisory authorities and insurance brokers and consultants. Sec.-Gen. YOSEPH ASEFFA.

Asian Clearing Union—ACU: c/o Central Bank of the Islamic Republic of Iran, POB 11365/8531, Tehran, Iran; tel. (21) 2842076; fax (21) 2847677; e-mail acusecret@irenet.net; f. 1974 to provide clearing arrangements, whereby members settle payments for intra-regional transactions among the participating central banks, on a multilateral basis, in order to economize on the use of foreign exchange and promote the use of domestic currencies in trade transactions among developing countries; part of ESCAP's Asian trade expansion programme; the Central Bank of Iran is the Union's agent; in September 1995 the ACU unit of account was changed from SDR to US dollars, with effect from 1 January 1996. Mems:

central banks of Bangladesh, Bhutan, India, Iran, Myanmar, Nepal, Pakistan, Sri Lanka. Sec.-Gen. MOHAMMAD FIROUZDOR. Publs *Annual Report, Newsletter* (monthly).

Asian Reinsurance Corporation: 17th Floor, Tower B, Chamnan Phenjati Business Center, 65 Rama 9 Rd, Huaykwang, Bangkok 10320, Thailand; tel. (2) 245-2169; fax (2) 248-1377; e-mail asianre@loxinfo.co.th; f. 1979 by ESCAP with UNCTAD, to operate as a professional reinsurer, giving priority in retrocessions to national insurance and reinsurance markets of member countries, and as a development organization providing technical assistance to countries in the Asia-Pacific region; cap. (auth.) US $15m., (p.u.) $5m. Mems: Afghanistan, Bangladesh, Bhutan, People's Republic of China, India, Iran, Republic of Korea, Philippines, Sri Lanka, Thailand. Gen. Man. A. S. MALABANAN.

Association of African Central Banks: 15 blvd Franklin Roosevelt, BP 4128, Dakar, Senegal; tel. 821-93-80; fax 822-73-43; f. 1968 to promote contacts in the monetary and financial sphere in order to increase co-operation and trade among member states; to strengthen monetary and financial stability on the African continent. Mems: 36 African central banks representing 47 states. Chair. Dr PAUL A. OGWUMA (Nigeria).

Association of African Tax Administrators: POB 13255, Yaoundé, Cameroon; tel. 22-41-57; fax 23-18-55; f. 1980 to promote co-operation in the field of taxation policy, legislation and administration among African countries. Mems: 20 states. Exec. Sec. OWONA PASCAL-BAYLON.

Association of Asian Confederation of Credit Unions: POB 24-171, Bangkok 10240, Thailand; tel. (2) 374-3170; fax (2) 374-5321; e-mail accuran@ksc.th.com; internet www.aaccu.net; links and promotes credit unions in Asia, provides research facilities and training programmes. Mems in Bangladesh, Hong Kong, Indonesia, Japan, Republic of Korea, Malaysia, Philippines, Sri Lanka, Taiwan, Thailand. Gen. Man. RANJITH HETTIARACHICHI. Publs *ACCU News* (every 2 months), *Annual Report and Directory.*

Association of European Institutes of Economic Research (Association d'instituts européens de conjoncture économique): 3 place Montesquieu, 1348 Louvain-la-Neuve, Belgium; tel. (10) 47-41-52; fax (10) 47-39-45; e-mail olbrechts@ires.ucl.ac.be; f. 1955; provides a means of contact between member institutes; organizes two meetings yearly, at which discussions are held on the economic situation and on a special theoretical subject. Mems: 40 institutes in 20 European countries. Admin. Sec. PAUL OLBRECHTS.

Central Asian Bank for Co-operation and Development: 115A Abay, Almaty, Kazakhstan; tel. (2) 422737; fax (2) 428627; f. 1994; to support trade and development in the sub-region. Auth. cap. US $9m. Mems: Kazakhstan, Kyrgyzstan, Uzbekistan.

Centre for Latin American Monetary Studies (Centro de Estudios Monetarios Latinoamericanos): Durango 54, Col. Roma, Del. Cuauhtémoc, 06700 México, DF, Mexico; tel. and fax (5) 533-03-00; e-mail cemlainf@mail.internet.com.mx.; f. 1952; organizes technical training programmes on monetary policy, development finance, etc., applied research programmes on monetary and central banking policies and procedures, regional meetings of banking officials. Mems: 31 associated members (Central Banks of Latin America and the Caribbean), 28 co-operating members (supervisory institutions of the region and non-Latin American Central Banks). Dir SERGIO GHIGLIAZZA. Publs *Bulletin* (every 2 months), *Monetaria* (quarterly), *Money Affairs* (2 a year).

Comité Européen des Assurances: 3 bis rue de la Chaussée d'Antin, 75009 Paris, France; tel. 1-44-83-11-83; fax 1-47-70-03-75; internet www.cea.assur.org; f. 1953 to represent the interests of European insurers, to encourage co-operation between members, to allow the exchange of information and to conduct studies. Mems: national insurance associations of 29 countries. Pres. PETER ECKERT (Switzerland); Sec.-Gen. FRANCIS LOHEAC (France). Publs *CEA INFO—Euro Brief* (every 2 months), *European Insurance in Figures* (annually), *The European Life Insurance Market* (annually).

Eastern Caribbean Central Bank: POB 89, Basseterre, St Christopher and Nevis; tel. 465-2537; fax 466-8954; e-mail eccberu@caribsurf.com; f. 1983 by OECS governments; maintains regional currency (Eastern Caribbean dollar) and advises on the economic development of member states. Mems: Anguilla, Antigua and Barbuda, Dominica, Grenada, Montserrat, Saint Christopher and Nevis, Saint Lucia, Saint Vincent and the Grenadines. Gov. DWIGHT VENNER.

Econometric Society: Dept of Economics, Northwestern University, Evanston, IL 60208, USA; tel. (847) 491-3615; internet www.econometricsociety.org; f. 1930 to promote studies that aim at a unification of the theoretical-quantitative and the empirical-quantitative approach to economic problems. Mems: 7,000. Exec. Dir and Sec. JULIE P. GORDON. Publ. *Econometrica* (6 a year).

European Federation of Finance House Associations—Eurofinas: 267 ave de Tervueren, 1150 Brussels, Belgium; tel. (2) 778-05-60; fax (2) 778-05-79; f. 1959 to study the development of instalment credit financing in Europe, to collate and publish instalment credit statistics, to promote research into instalment credit practice; mems: finance houses and professional associations in Austria, Belgium, Finland, France, Germany, Ireland, Italy, Netherlands, Norway, Portugal, Spain, Sweden, Switzerland, United Kingdom. Chair. GREGORIO D'OTTAVIANO (Italy); Sec.-Gen. MARC BAERT. Publs *Eurofinas Newsletter* (monthly), *Annual Report, Study Reports.*

European Federation of Financial Analysts Societies: 3 rue d'Antin, 75002 Paris, France; tel. 1-42-98-02-00; fax 1-42-98-02-02; f. 1962 to co-ordinate the activities of all European associations of financial analysts. Biennial congress: Barcelona, Spain, 1996. Mems: 10,700 in 17 societies. Chair. J.-G. DE WAEL.

European Financial Management and Marketing Association: 16 rue d'Aguesseau, 75008 Paris, France; tel. 1-47-42-52-72; fax 1-47-42-56-76; e-mail info@efma.com; internet www.efma.com; f. 1971 to link financial institutions by organizing seminars, conferences and training sessions and an annual Congress and World Convention, and by providing information services and publications. Mems: 145 European financial institutions. Pres. ALFREDO SÁENZ ABAD; Sec.-Gen. MICHEL BARNICH (acting). Publ. *Newsletter.*

European Private Equity and Venture Capital Association: Minervastraat 6, 1930 Zaventem, Belgium; tel. (2) 715-00-20; fax (2) 725-07-04; e-mail evca@evca.com; internet www.evca.com; f. 1983 to link private equity and venture capital companies within Europe and to encourage joint investment projects, particularly in support of small and medium-sized businesses; holds annual symposium, seminars and training courses. Mems: over 750 in more than 35 countries. Chair. ARI TOLPPANEN; Sec.-Gen. JAVIER ECHARRI.

Fédération Internationale des Bourses de Valeurs—FIBV (International Federation of Stock Exchanges): 22 boulevard de Courcelles, 75017 Paris, France; tel. 1-44-01-05-45; fax 1-47-54-94-22; f. 1961; assumes a leadership role in advocating the benefits of self-regulation in the regulatory process, offers a platform for closer collaboration between member exchanges, promotes enhanced ethical and professional behaviour in the securities industry. Mems: 51 and 42 corresponding exchanges. Pres. MANUEL ROBLEDA; Sec-Gen. GERRIT H. DE MAREZ OYENS.

Financial Action Task Force on Money Laundering—FATF: 37 bis blvd Suchet, 75016 Paris, France; tel. 1-45-24-79-45; fax 1-45-24-17-60; f. 1989 to develop and promote policies to combat money laundering; formulated a set of Recommendations for member countries to implement; established regional task forces in the Caribbean and Asia-Pacific. Mems: 26 countries, the European Commission, and the Co-operation Council for the Arab States of the Gulf. Exec. Sec. PATRICK MOULETTE.

Fonds Africain de Garantie et de Co-opération Economique—FAGACE (African Guarantee and Economic Co-operation Fund): BP 2045, Cotonou, Benin; tel. 300376; fax 300284; commenced operations in 1981; guarantees loans for development projects, provides loans and grants for specific operations and supports national and regional enterprises. Cap. 7,750m. francs CFA. Mems: Benin, Burkina Faso, Central African Republic, Côte d'Ivoire, Mali, Niger, Rwanda, Senegal, Togo. Dir-Gen. SOULEYMANE GADO.

International Accounting Standards Board—IASB: 30 Cannon St, London, EC4M, United Kingdom; tel. (20) 7353-0565; fax (20) 7353-0562; e-mail iasb@iasb.org.uk; internet www.iasb.org.uk; f. 1973 as International Accounting Standards Committee, reorganized and present name adopted 2001; aims to develop, in the public interest, a single set of high-quality, uniform, clear and enforceable global accounting standards requiring the submission of high-quality, transparent and comparable information in financial statements and other financial reporting, in order to assist participants in world-wide capital markets and other end-users to make informed decisions on economic matters; aims also to promote the use and rigorous application of these global accounting standards, and to bring about the convergence of these with national accounting standards. Chair. and CEO Sir DAVID TWEEDIE. Publs *IASB Insight* (quarterly), *Bound Volume of International Accounting Standards* (annually), *Interpretations of International Accounting Standards.*

International Association for Research in Income and Wealth: Dept of Economics, New York University, 269 Mercer St, Room 700, New York, NY 10003, USA; tel. (212) 924-4386; fax (212) 366-5067; e-mail iariw@fasecon.econ.nyu.edu; internet www.econ .nyu.edu/dept/iariw; f. 1947 to further research in the general field of national income and wealth and related topics by the organization of biennial conferences and by other means. Mems: approx. 425. Chair. ANNE HARRISON; Exec. Sec. JANE FORMAN (USA). Publ. *Review of Income and Wealth* (quarterly).

International Bureau of Fiscal Documentation: H. J. Wenckebachweg 201, POB 20237, 1096 AS Amsterdam, Netherlands; tel. (20) 5540100; fax (20) 6228658; e-mail info@ibfd.nl; internet www.ibfd.nl; f. 1938 to supply information on fiscal law and its application; library on international taxation. Pres. J. F. AVERY JONES; Man. Dir H. M. A. L. HAMAEKERS. Publs *Bulletin for International Fiscal Documentation, Asia Pacific Tax Bulletin, Derivatives and Financial Instru-*

ments, European Taxation, International VAT Monitor, Supplementary Service to European Taxation (all monthly), *Tax News Service* (fortnightly); studies, data bases, regional tax guides.

International Centre for Local Credit: Koninginnegracht 2, 2514 AA The Hague, Netherlands; tel. (70) 3750850; fax (70) 3454743; e-mail centre@bng.nl; f. 1958 to promote local authority credit by gathering, exchanging and distributing information and advice on member institutions and on local authority credit and related subjects; studies important subjects in the field of local authority credit. Mems: 22 financial institutions in 14 countries. Pres. F. NARMON (Belgium); Sec.-Gen. P. P.VAN BESOUW(Netherlands). Publs *Bulletin, Newsletter* (quarterly).

International Economic Association: 23 rue Campagne Première, 75014 Paris, France; tel. 1-43-27-91-44; fax 1-42-79-92-16; e-mail iea@iea-world.org; f. 1949 to promote international collaboration for the advancement of economic knowledge and develop personal contacts between economists, and to encourage provision of means for the dissemination of economic knowledge. Member associations in 59 countries. Pres. Prof. ROBERT SOLOW; Sec.-Gen. Prof. JEAN-PAUL FITOUSSI (France).

International Federation of Accountants: 535 Fifth Ave, 26th Floor, New York, NY 10017, USA; tel. (212) 286-9344; fax (212) 286-9570; internet www.ifac.org; f. 1977 to develop a co-ordinated world-wide accounting profession with harmonized standards. Mems: 143 accountancy bodies in 104 countries. Pres. FRANK HARDING; Gen. Dir JOHN GRUNER (USA). Publ. *Codification of International Standards on Auditing.*

International Fiscal Association: World Trade Center, POB 30215, 3001 DE Rotterdam, Netherlands; tel. (10) 4052990; fax (10) 4055031; e-mail n.gensecr@ifa.nl; internet www.ifa.nl; f. 1938 to study international and comparative public finance and fiscal law, especially taxation; holds annual congresses. Mems in 90 countries and national branches in 45 countries. Pres. S. O. LODIN (Sweden); Sec.-Gen. J. FRANS SPIERDIJK (Netherlands). Publs *Cahiers de Droit Fiscal International, Yearbook of the International Fiscal Association, IFA Congress Seminar Series.*

International Institute of Public Finance: University of the Saar, PO Box 151150, 66041 Saarbrücken, Germany; fax (681) 302-4369; e-mail sec@iipf.net; internet www.iipf.net; f. 1937; a private scientific organization aiming to establish contacts between people of every nationality, whose main or supplementary activity consists in the study of public finance; holds one meeting a year devoted to a certain scientific subject. Pres. HIROFUMI SHIBATA (JAPAN).

International Organization of Securities Commissions—IOSCO; CP 171, Tour de la Bourse, 800 Square Victoria, Suite 4210, Montréal, QC H4Z 1C8, Canada; tel. (514) 875-8278; fax (514) 875-2669; e-mail mail@oicv.iosco.org; internet www.iosco.org; f. 1983 to facilitate co-operation between securities and futures regulatory bodies at the international level. Mems: 163 agencies. Sec.-Gen. PETER CLARK. Publ. *IOSCO News* (3 a year).

International Securities Market Association: Rigistr. 60, PO Box, 8033 Zürich, Switzerland; tel. (1) 3634222; fax (1) 3637772; f. 1969 for discussion of questions relating to the international securities market, to issue rules governing their functions, and to maintain a close liaison between the primary and secondary markets in international securities. Mems: 838 banks and major financial institutions in 48 countries. Chair. RIJNHARD W. F. VAN TETS (Netherlands); Chief Exec. and Sec.-Gen. JOHN L. LANGTON (Switzerland). Publs *International Bond Manual*, daily Eurobond listing, electronic price information, weekly Eurobond guide, ISMA formulae for yield, members' register, ISMA quarterly comment, reports, etc.

International Union for Housing Finance: Suite 400, 111 East Wacker Drive, Chicago, IL 60601-4389, USA; tel. (312) 946-8200; fax (312) 946-8202; e-mail iuhf@wwa.com; internet www.housingfinance.org; f. 1914 to foster world-wide interest in savings and home-ownership and co-operation among members; to encourage comparative study of methods and practice in housing finance; to encourage appropriate legislation on housing finance. Mems: 350 in 71 countries, 8 regional affiliates. Sec.-Gen. DONALD R. HOLTON. Publs *Housing Finance International* (quarterly), *Directory, International Housing Finance Factbook* (every 2 years), *IUHFI Newsletter* (3 a year).

Latin American Banking Federation (Federación Latino-americana de Bancos—FELABAN): Apdo Aéreo 091959, Santafé de Bogotá, DE8, Colombia; tel. (1) 621-8617; fax (1) 621-8021; f. 1965 to co-ordinate efforts towards a wide and accelerated economic development in Latin American countries. Mems: 19 Latin American national banking associations. Pres. of Board MILTON AYON WONG; Sec.-Gen. Dra MARICIELO GLEN DE TOBÓN (Colombia).

West African Monetary Agency: 11–13 ECOWAS St, PMB 218, Freetown, Sierra Leone; tel. 224485; fax 223943; e-mail wama@sierratel.sl; f. 1975 as West African Clearing House; administers transactions between its 10 member central banks in order to promote sub-regional trade and monetary co-operation; administers

ECOWAS travellers' cheques scheme. Mems: Banque Centrale des Etats de l'Afrique de l'Ouest (serving Benin, Burkina Faso, Côte d'Ivoire, Guinea-Bissau, Mali, Niger, Senegal, Togo) and the central banks of Cape Verde, The Gambia, Ghana, Guinea, Liberia, Mauritania, Nigeria and Sierra Leone. Dir-Gen. ANTOINE M. F. NDIAYE (Senegal). Publ. *Annual Report.*

World Council of Credit Unions—WOCCU: POB 2982, 5710 Mineral Point Rd, Madison, WI 53705, USA; tel. (608) 231-7130; fax (608) 238-8020; e-mail mail@woccu.org; internet www.woccu.org; f. 1970 to link credit unions and similar co-operative financial institutions and assist them in expanding and improving their services; provides technical and financial assistance to credit union associations in developing countries. Mems: 35,000 credit unions in 86 countries. CEO CHRISTOPHER BAKER. Publs *WOCCU Annual Report, Perspectives* (quarterly).

World Savings Banks Institute: 11 rue Marie Thérèse, 1000 Brussels, Belgium; tel. (2) 211-11-11; fax (2) 211-11-99; internet www.savings-banks.com/wsbi; f. 1924 as International Savings Banks Institute, present name and structure adopted in 1994; promotes co-operation among members and the development of savings banks world-wide. Mems: 107 banks and asscns in 88 countries. Pres. MANUEL PIZARRO (Spain). Publs *Annual Report, International Savings Banks Directory, Perspectives* (8–10 a year).

Education

African Association for Literacy and Adult Education: POB 50768, Finance House, 6th Floor, Loita St, Nairobi, Kenya; tel. (2) 222391; fax (2) 340849; f. 1984, combining the former African Adult Education Association and the AFROLIT Society (both f. 1968); aims to promote adult education and literacy in Africa, to study the problems involved, and to allow the exchange of information; programmes are developed and implemented by 'networks' of educators; holds Conference every three years. Mems: 28 national education associations and 300 institutions in 33 countries. Chair. (vacant). Publs *The Spider Newsletter* (quarterly, French and English), *Journal* (2 a year).

Agence Universitaire de la Francophonie (AUPELF–UREF): BP 400, succ. Côte-des-Neiges, Montréal, QC H3S 2S7, Canada; tel. (514) 343-6630; fax (514) 343-2107; e-mail rectorat@aupelf.refer.org; internet www.aupelf-uref.org; f. 1961; aims: documentation, co-ordination, co-operation, exchange. Mems: 391 institutions. Pres. ARTHUR BODSON (Canada); Dir-Gen. and Rector MICHEL GUILLOU (France). Publs *Universités* (quarterly), *UREF Actualités* (every 2 months), directories (Francophone universities, Professors from francophone universities, Departments of French studies worldwide).

Asian Confederation of Teachers: 2nd Floor, Wisma DTC, 3455-B Jalan Sultansh Zainab, 15050 Kota Bharu, Kelatan, Malaysia; f. 1990. Pres. MUHAMMAD MUSTAPHA; Sec.-Gen. LAM WAH-HUI.

Association for Childhood Education International: 11501 Georgia Ave, Suite 315, Wheaton, MD 20902, USA; tel. (301) 942-2443; fax (301) 942-3012; f. 1892 to work for the education of children (from infancy through early adolescence) by promoting desirable conditions in schools, raising the standard of teaching, co-operating with all groups concerned with children, informing the public of the needs of children. Mems: 12,000. Pres. SUE WORTHAM; Exec. Dir GERALD C. ODLAND. Publs *Childhood Education* (6 a year), *ACEI Exchange Newsletter* (6 a year), *Journal of Research in Childhood Education* (2 a year), books on current educational subjects (3 a year).

Association Montessori Internationale: Koninginneweg 161, 1075 CN Amsterdam, Netherlands; tel. (20) 6798932; e-mail ami@xs4all.nl; f. 1929 to propagate the ideals and educational methods of Dr Maria Montessori on child development, without racial, religious or political prejudice; organizes training courses for teachers in 15 countries. Pres. RENILDE MONTESSORI; Sec. MARY P. HAYES. Publ. *Communications* (quarterly).

Association of African Universities: POB 5744, Accra North, Ghana; tel. (21) 774495; fax (21) 774821; f. 1967 to promote exchanges, contact and co-operation among African university institutions and to collect and disseminate information on research and higher education in Africa. Mems: 132 university institutions. Sec.-Gen. Prof. NARCISO MATOS (Mozambique). Publs *AAU Newsletter* (3 a year), *Directory of African Universities* (every 2 years).

Association of Arab Universities: POB 401, Jubeyha, Amman, Jordan; tel. (6) 5345131; fax (6) 5332994; e-mail secgen@aaru.edu.jo; internet www.aaru.edu.jo; f. 1964. Mems: 137 universities. Sec.-Gen. Dr MARWAN RASIM KAMAL. Publ. *AARU Bulletin* (annually and quarterly, in Arabic).

Association of Caribbean University and Research Institutional Libraries—ACURIL: Apdo postal 23317, San Juan 00931, Puerto Rico; tel. 764-0000; fax 763-5685; e-mail vtorres@upracd.upr-

.clu.edu; f. 1968 to foster contact and collaboration between member universities and institutes; conferences, meetings, seminars, etc.; circulation of information through newsletters, bulletins; facilitates co-operation and the pooling of resources in research; encourages exchange of staff and students. Mems: 250. Exec.-Sec. ONEIDA R. ORTIZ. Publ. *Newsletter* (2 a year).

Association of South-East Asian Institutions of Higher Learning—ASAIHL: Secretariat, Ratasastra Bldg 2, Chulalongkorn University, Henri Dunant Rd, Bangkok 10330, Thailand; tel. (2) 251-6966; fax (2) 253-7909; f. 1956 to promote the economic, cultural and social welfare of the people of South-East Asia by means of educational co-operation and research programmes; and to cultivate a sense of regional identity and interdependence; collects and disseminates information, organizes discussions. Mems: 160 university institutions in 14 countries. Pres. Prof. Tan Sri Dr SYED JALALUDIN SYED SALIM; Sec.-Gen. Dr NINNAT OLANVORAVUTH. Publs *Newsletter, Handbook* (every 3 years).

Caribbean Council of Legal Education: Mona Campus, Kingston 7, Jamaica; tel. 92-71899; fax 92-73927; f. 1971; responsible for the training of members of the legal profession. Mems: govts of 15 countries and territories.

Caribbean Examinations Council: The Garrison, St Michael 20, Barbados; tel. 436-6261; fax 429-5421; f. 1972; develops syllabuses and conducts examinations. Mems: govts of 16 English-speaking countries and territories.

Catholic International Education Office: 60 rue des Eburons, 1000 Brussels, Belgium; tel. (2) 230-72-52; fax (2) 230-97-45; e-mail oiec@pophost.eunet.be; internet www.ciateq.mx/~maria/oiec; f. 1952 for the study of the problems of Catholic education throughout the world; co-ordination of the activities of members; and representation of Catholic education at international bodies. Mems: 98 countries, 16 assoc. mems, 13 collaborating mems, 5 corresponding mems. Pres. Mgr CESARE NOSIGLIA; Sec.-Gen. ANDRÉS DELGADO HERNÁNDEZ. Publs *OIEC Bulletin* (every 3 months in English, French and Spanish), *OIEC Tracts on Education.*

Catholic International Federation for Physical and Sports Education: 22 rue Oberkampf, 75011 Paris, France; tel. 1-43-38-50-57; f. 1911 to group Catholic associations for physical education and sport of different countries and to develop the principles and precepts of Christian morality by fostering meetings, study and international co-operation. Mems: 14 affiliated national federations representing about 3.5m. members. Pres. ACHILLE DIEGENANT (Belgium); Sec.-Gen. CLÉMENT SCHERTZINGER (France).

Comparative Education Society in Europe: Institut für Augemeine Pädagogik, Humboldt-Universität zu Berlin, Unter den Linden 6, 10099 Berlin, Germany; tel. (30) 20934094; fax (30) 20931006; e-mail juergen.schriewer@educat.hu-berlin.de; f. 1961 to promote teaching and research in comparative and international education; the Society organizes conferences and promotes literature. Mems in 49 countries. Pres. Prof. J. SCHRIEWER (Belgium); Sec. and Treasurer Prof. M. A. PEREYRA (Spain). Publ. *Newsletter* (quarterly).

European Association for the Education of Adults: Pere Vergés 1, 08020 Barcelona, Spain; tel. (93) 2780294; fax (93) 2780174; e-mail eaea@mx3.redestb.es; internet www.vsy.fi/eaea; f. 1953 as a clearing-house and centre of co-operation for all groups concerned with adult education in Europe. Mems: 150 in 18 countries. Pres. P. FEDERIGHI (Italy); Publs *Conference Reports, Directory of Adult Education Organisations in Europe, Newsletter, Survey of Adult Education Legislation, Glossary of Terms.*

European Cultural Foundation: Jan van Goyenkade 5, 1075 HN Amsterdam, Netherlands; tel. (20) 6760222; fax (20) 6752231; e-mail eurocult@eurocult.org; internet www.eurocult.org; f. 1954 as a non-governmental organization, supported by private sources, to promote activities of mutual interest to European countries, concerning culture, education, environment, East-West cultural relations, media, cultural relations with the countries of the Mediterranean, issues regarding cultural pluralism; national committees in 23 countries; transnational network of institutes and centres: European Institute of Education and Social Policy, Paris; Institute for European Environmental Policy, London, Madrid and Berlin; Association for Innovative Co-operation in Europe (AICE), Brussels; EURYDICE Central Unit (the Education Information Network of the European Community), Brussels; European Institute for the Media, Düsseldorf; European Foundation Centre, Brussels; Fund for Central and East European Book Projects, Amsterdam; Institute for Human Sciences, Vienna; East West Parliamentary Practice Project, Amsterdam; Centre Européen de la Culture, Geneva. A grants programme, for European co-operation projects is also conducted. Pres. HRH Princess MARGRIET of the Netherlands; Sec.-Gen. Dr R. STEPHAN. Publs *Annual Report, Newsletter* (3 a year).

European Federation for Catholic Adult Education: Bildungshaus Mariatrost, Kirchbergstrasse 18, A-8044 Graz, Austria; tel. (316) 39-11-31-35; fax (316) 39-11-31-30; f. 1963 to strengthen international contact between members, to assist international research and practical projects in adult education; to help communications between its members and other international bodies; holds conference every two years. Pres. Prof. Mag. KARL KALCSICS (Austria).

European Foundation for Management Development: 88 rue Gachard, 1050 Brussels, Belgium; tel. (2) 629-08-10; fax (2) 629-08-11; e-mail info@efmd.be; internet www.efmd.be; f. 1971 through merger of European Association of Management Training Centres and International University Contact for Management Education; aims to help improve the quality of management development and disseminate information within the economic, social and cultural context of Europe and promote international co-operation. Mems: more than 390 institutions in 41 countries world-wide (26 in Europe). Dir-Gen. ERIC CORNUEL. Publs *Forum* (3 a year), *Guide to European Business Schools and Management Centres* (annually).

European Union of Arabic and Islamic Scholars: c/o Dipartimento di studi e ricerche su Africa e Paesi arabi, Istituto universitario orientale, Piazza S. Domenico Maggiore 12, 80134 Naples, Italy; tel. (081) 5517840; fax (081) 5515386; f. 1964 to organize congresses of Arabic and Islamic Studies; congresses are held every two years. Mems: 300 in 28 countries. Pres. Prof. URBAIN VERMEULEN (Belgium); Sec. Prof. CARMELA BAFFIONI (Italy).

European University Association—EUA: 10 rue du Conseil Général, 1211 Geneva 4, Switzerland; tel. (22) 3292644; fax (22) 3292821; e-mail info@eua.unige.ch; internet www.unige.ch/eua/; f. 2001 by merger of the Association of European Universities and the Confederation of EU Rectors' Conferences; holds conferences, a General Assembly, and training seminars for university executive heads; also involved in various programmes: new technologies to help universities face new teaching methods; an Academic Task Force to mobilize the support needed by war-damaged universities; institutional evaluation of quality management strategies; transatlantic dialogue between leaders of European and North American universities; a history of the university in Europe in four volumes; a joint university programme on institutional development with Latin American universities (*Columbus*). Mems: 543 universities and associate members in 44 countries. Sec.-Gen. Dr ANDRIS BARBLAN. Publs *EUA-Info, EUA-Action, EUAdoc, EUAguide.*

Graduate Institute of International Studies (Institut universitaire de hautes études internationales): POB 36, 132 rue de Lausanne, Geneva, Switzerland; tel. (22) 9085700; fax (22) 9085710; e-mail info@hei.unige.ch; internet heiwww.unige.ch; f. 1927 to establish a centre for advanced studies in international relations of the present day, juridical, historical, political and economic. Library of 147,000 vols. Dir Prof. PETER TSCHOPP; Sec.-Gen. Dr DANIEL WARNER.

Inter-American Centre for Research and Documentation on Vocational Training (Centro Interamericano de Investigación y Documentación sobre Formación Profesional—CINTERFOR): Avda Uruguay 1238, Casilla de correo 1761, Montevideo, Uruguay; tel. (2) 920557; fax (2) 921305; e-mail dirmvd@cinterfor.org.uy; internet www.cinterfor.org.uy; f. 1964 by the International Labour Organization (q.v.) for mutual help among the Latin American and Caribbean countries in planning vocational training; services are provided in documentation, research, exchange of experience; holds seminars and courses. Dir PEDRO DANIEL WEINBERG. Publs *Bulletin* (quarterly), *Documentation* (2 a year), *Herramientas para la transformación, Trazos de la formación*, studies, monographs and technical office papers.

Inter-American Confederation for Catholic Education (Confederación Interamericana de Educación Católica—CIEC): Calle 78 No 12–16 (ofna 101), Apdo Aéreo 90036, Santafé de Bogotá 8 DE, Colombia; tel. (1) 255-3676; fax (1) 255-0513; e-mail ciec@latino.net.co; internet www.ciec.to; f. 1945 to defend and extend the principles and rules of Catholic education, freedom of education, and human rights; organizes congress every three years. Pres. ADRIANO PACIFICO TOMASI; Sec. Gen. MARIA CONSTANZA ARANGO. Publ. *Educación Hoy.*

International Association for Educational and Vocational Guidance—IAEVG: c/o Linda Taylor, Kent Careers Services, 2nd Floor, 35 Earl St, Maidstone, Kent, ME14 1LG, United Kingdom; tel. (1622) 200711; fax (1622) 751157; e-mail linda.taylor@kentcareers.co.uk; f. 1951 to contribute to the development of vocational guidance and promote contact between persons associated with it. Mems: 40,000 from 60 countries. Pres. Dr BERNHARD JENSCHKE (Germany); Sec.-Gen. LINDA TAYLOR (UK). Publs *Bulletin* (2 a year), *Newsletter* (3 a year).

International Association for the Development of Documentation, Libraries and Archives in Africa: Villa 2547 Dieuppeul II, BP 375, Dakar, Senegal; tel. 824-09-54; f. 1957 to organize and develop documentation and archives in all African countries. Mems: national asscns, institutions and individuals in 48 countries. Sec.-Gen. ZACHEUS SUNDAY ALI (Nigeria).

International Association of Educators for World Peace: POB 3282, Mastin Lake Station, Huntsville, AL 35810, USA; tel. (256) 534-5501; fax (256) 536-1018; e-mail mercieca@hiwaay.net; internet www.earthportals.com/portal_messenger/mercieca.html; f. 1969 to develop the kind of education which will contribute to the promotion of peaceful relations at personal, community and international levels, to communicate and clarify controversial views in order to achieve maximum understanding and to help put into practice the Universal Declaration of Human Rights. Mems: 35,000 in 102 countries. Pres. Dr CHARLES MERCIECA (USA); Exec. Vice-Pres. RAJWANT SINGH SIDHU (UK); Sec.-Gen. Dr SURYA NATH PRASAD (India). Publs *Peace Progress* (annually), *IAEWP Newsletter* (6 a year), *Peace Education* (2 a year), *UN News*(monthly).

International Association of Papyrologists: Fondation Egyptologique Reine Elisabeth, Parc du Cinquantenaire 10, 1000 Brussels, Belgium; tel. (2) 741-73-64; e-mail amartin@ulb.ac.be; internet www.ulb.ac.be/assoc/aip; f. 1947; Mems: about 400. Pres. Prof. LUDWIG KOENEN (USA); Sec. Prof. ALAIN MARTIN (Belgium).

International Association of Physical Education in Higher Education: Institut Supérieur d'Éducation Physique, Bâtiment B21, Université de Liège au Sart Tilman, 4000 Liège, Belgium; tel. (4) 366-38-90; fax (4) 366-29-01; e-mail mpieron@ulg.ac.be; f. 1962; organizes congresses, exchanges, and research in physical education. Mems: institutions in 51 countries. Sec.-Gen. Dr MAURICE PIERON.

International Association of Universities—IAU/International Universities Bureau—IUB: 1 rue Miollis, 75732 Paris Cédex 15, France; tel. 1-45-68-25-45; fax 1-47-34-76-05; e-mail iau@unesco.org; internet www.unesco.org/iau; f. 1950 to allow co-operation at the international level among universities and other institutions of higher education; provides clearing-house services and operates the joint IAU/UNESCO Information Centre on Higher Education; conducts meetings and research on issues concerning higher education. Mems: about 700 universities and institutions of higher education in some 150 countries, 31 international and national university organizations. Pres. HANS VAN GINKEL; Sec.-Gen. FRANZ EBERHARD. Publs *Higher Education Policy* (quarterly), *IAU Newsletter* (every 2 months), *International Handbook of Universities* (every 2 years), *Issues in Higher Education* (monographs), *World Academic Database* (CD-ROM, annually), *World List of Universities* (every 2 years).

International Association of University Professors and Lecturers—IAUPL: c/o F. Mauro, 18 rue du Docteur Roux, 75015 Paris, France; f. 1945 for the development of academic fraternity amongst university teachers and research workers; the protection of independence and freedom of teaching and research; the furtherance of the interests of all university teachers; and the consideration of academic problems. Mems: federations in 17 countries. Sec.-Gen. F. MAURO.

International Baccalaureate Organization—IBO: Route des Morillons 15, Grand-Saconnex 1218, Geneva, Switzerland; tel. (22) 7917740; fax (22) 7910277; e-mail ibhq@ibo.org; internet www.ibo.org; f. 1967 to plan curricula and an international university entrance examination, the International Baccalaureate, recognized by major universities world-wide; offers the Primary Years Programme for children aged between 3 and 12, the Middle Years Programme for students in the 11–16 age range, and the Diploma Programme for 17–18 year olds; Mems: over 1,180 participating schools in 101 countries. Pres. of Council GREG CRAFTER (Australia); Dir-Gen. GEORGE WALKER.

International Council for Adult Education: 720 Bathurst St, Suite 500, Toronto, Canada ON M5S 2R4; tel. (416) 588-1211; fax (416) 588-5725; e-mail icae@web.net; internet www.web.net/icae; f. 1973 to promote the education of adults in relation to the need for healthy growth and development of individuals and communities; undertakes research and training; organizes seminars, the exchange of information, and co-operative publishing; maintains resource centre with extensive material on literacy, adult education and development education; General Assembly meets every four years. Mems: seven regional organizations and 95 national associations in 80 countries. Pres. PAUL BÉLANGER. Publs *Convergence, ICAE News.*

International Council for Open and Distance Education—ICDE: Gjerdrums Vei 12, 0484 Oslo, Norway; tel. 22-02-81-70; fax 22-02-81-61; e-mail icde@icde.no; internet www.icde.org; f. 1938 (name changed 1982); furthers distance (correspondence) education by promoting research, encouraging regional links, providing information and organizing conferences. Mems: institutions, corporations and individuals in 120 countries. Pres. MOLLY CORBETT BROAD (USA); Sec.-Gen. REIDAR ROLL (Norway). Publ. *Open Praxis* (2 a year).

International Federation for Parent Education: 1 ave Léon Journault, 92311 Sèvres Cédex, France; tel. 1-45-07-21-64; fax 1-46-26-69-27; f. 1964 to gather in congresses and colloquia experts from different scientific fields and those responsible for family education in their own countries and to encourage the establishment of family education where it does not exist. Mems: 120. Pres. MONEEF GUITOUNI (Canada). Publ. *Lettre de la FIEP* (2 a year).

International Federation of Catholic Universities (Fédération internationale d'universités catholiques—FIUC): 21 rue d'Assas, 75270 Paris Cédex 06, France; tel. 1-44-39-52-26; fax 1-44-39-52-28; e-mail sgfiuc@bureau.fiuc.org; internet www.fiuc.org/; f. 1948; to ensure a strong bond of mutual assistance among all Catholic universities in the search for truth; to help to solve problems of growth and development, and to co-operate with other international organizations. Mems: 191 in 41 countries. Pres. Rev. JAN PETERS (Netherlands); Sec.-Gen. GUY-RÉAL THIVIERGE (Canada). Publ. *Quarterly Newsletter*.

International Federation of Library Associations and Institutions—IFLA: POB 95312, 2509 CH The Hague, Netherlands; tel. (70) 3140884; fax (70) 3834827; e-mail ifla@ifla.org; internet www.ifla.org; f. 1927 to promote international co-operation in librarianship and bibliography. Mems: 155 associations, 1,120 institutions and 370 individual members in 153 countries. Pres. CHRISTINE DESCHAMPS; Sec.-Gen. ROSS SHIMMON. Publs *IFLAAnnual Report, IFLA Directory, IFLA Journal, International Cataloguing and Bibliographic Control* (quarterly), *IFLA Professional Reports*.

International Federation of Organizations for School Correspondence and Exchange: Via Torino 256, 10015 Ivrea, Italy; tel. (0125) 234433; fax (0125) 234761; e-mail fioces@ipfs.org; internet ipfs.org/fioces.htm; f. 1929; aims to contribute to the knowledge of foreign languages and civilizations and to bring together young people of all nations by furthering international scholastic correspondence. Mems: comprises 78 national bureaux of scholastic correspondence and exchange in 21 countries. Pres. ALBERT V. RUTTER (Malta); Gen. Sec. LIVIO TONSO (Italy).

International Federation of Physical Education (Fédération internationale d'éducation physique—FIEP): c/o Prof. Robert Decker, 7–9 rue du X Octobre, 7243 Bereldange, Luxembourg; tel. and fax 33-94-81; f. 1923; studies physical education on scientific, pedagogic and aesthetic bases in order to stimulate health, harmonious development or preservation, healthy recreation, and the best adaptation of the individual to the general needs of social life; organizes international congresses and courses, and awards research prize. Mems: from 112 countries. Vice-Pres. (Europe) Prof. ROBERT DECKER. Publ. *FIEP Bulletin* (trilingual edition in French, English and Spanish, 3 a year).

International Federation of Teachers of Modern Languages: Seestrasse 247, 8038 Zürich, Switzerland; tel. (1) 4855251; fax (1) 4825054; f. 1931; holds meetings on every aspect of foreign-language teaching; has consultative status with UNESCO. Mems: 33 national and regional language associations and six international unilingual associations (teachers of English, French, German, Italian and Spanish). Pres. MICHAEL CANDELIER; Sec.-Gen. DENIS CUNNINGHAM. Publ. *FIPLV World News* (quarterly in English, French and Spanish).

International Federation of University Women: 8 rue de l'Ancien Port, 1201 Geneva, Switzerland; tel. (22) 7312380; fax (22) 7380440; e-mail ifuw@ifuw.org; internet www.ifuw.org; f. 1919 to promote understanding and friendship among university women of the world; to encourage international co-operation; to further the development of education; to represent university women in international organizations; to encourage the full application of members' skills to the problems which arise at all levels of public life. Affiliates: 66 national associations with over 180,000 mems. Pres. LINDA F. SOUTER (Canada). Publs *IFUW News* (6 a year), triennial report.

International Federation of Workers' Education Associations: c/o AOF Postboks 8703, Youngstorget, 0028 Oslo 1, Norway; tel. 23-06-12-88; fax 23-06-12-70; e-mail jmehlum@online.no; internet www.ifwea.org; f. 1947 to promote co-operation between non-governmental bodies concerned with workers' education, through clearing-house services, exchange of information, publications, international seminars, conferences, summer schools, etc. Pres. DAN GALLIN (Switzerland); Gen. Sec. JAN MEHLUM (Norway).

International Institute for Adult Literacy Methods: POB 19395/6194, 5th Floor, Golfam St, 19156 Tehran, Iran; tel. (21) 2220313; f. 1968 by UNESCO and the Government of Iran, to collect, analyse and distribute information on activities concerning methods of literacy training and adult education; sponsors seminars; maintains documentation service and library on literacy and adult education. Dir Dr MOHAMMAD REZA HAMIDIZADE. Publs *Selection of Adult Education Issues* (monthly), *Adult Education and Development* (quarterly), *New Library Holdings* (quarterly).

International Institute of Philosophy—IIP (Institut international de philosophie—IIP): 8 rue Jean-Calvin, 75005 Paris, France; tel. 1-43-36-39-11; e-mail inst.intern.philo@wanadoo.fr; f. 1937 to clarify fundamental issues of contemporary philosophy in annual meetings and to promote mutual understanding among thinkers of different backgrounds and traditions; a maximum of 115 members are elected, chosen from all countries and representing different tendencies. Mems: 96 in 35 countries. Pres. JAAKKO HINTIKKA (Finland); Sec.-Gen. P. AUBENQUE (France). Publs *Bibliography of Philosophy* (quarterly), *Proceedings* of annual meetings, *Chroniques, Philosophy and World Community* (series), *Philosophical Problems Today, Controverses philosophiques*.

International Institute of Public Administration: 2 ave de l'Observatoire, 75272 Paris Cédex 06; tel. 1-44-41-85-00; fax 1-44-

41-86-19; e-mail iiap.bib@wanadoo.fr; f. 1966; trains high-ranking civil servants from abroad; administrative, economic, financial and diplomatic programmes; Africa, Latin America, Asia, Europe and Near East departments; research department, library of 80,000 vols; Documentation Centre. Dir M. MAUS. Publs *Revue française d'administration publique* (quarterly).

International Reading Association: 800 Barksdale Rd, POB 8139, Newark, DE 19714-8139, USA; tel. (302) 731-1600; fax (302) 731-1057; internet www.reading.org; f. 1956 to improve the quality of reading instruction at all levels, to promote the habit of lifelong reading, and to develop every reader's proficiency. Mems: 90,000 in 99 countries. Pres. CAROL M. SANTA; Publs *The Reading Teacher* (8 a year), *Journal of Adolescent and Adult Literacy* (8 a year), *Reading Research Quarterly, Lectura y Vida* (quarterly in Spanish), *Reading Today* (6 a year).

International Schools Association—ISA: CIC CASE 20, 1211 Geneva 20, Switzerland; tel. (22) 7336717; f. 1951 to co-ordinate work in international schools and promote their development; member schools maintain the highest standards and accept pupils of all nationalities, irrespective of race and creed. ISA carries out curriculum research; convenes annual conferences on problems of curriculum and educational reform; organizes occasional teachers' training workshops and specialist seminars. Mems: 85 schools throughout the world. Pres. BERT TIMMERMANSAN. Publs *Education Bulletin* (2 a year), *ISA Magazine* (annually), *Conference Report* (annually), curriculum studies (occasional).

International Society for Business Education: 3550 Anderson St, Madison, WI 53704-2599, USA; tel. (608) 837-7518; fax (608) 834-1301; e-mail lkantine@prodigy.net; internet www.siec-isbe.org; f. 1901 to encourage international exchange of information and organize international courses and congresses on business education; 2,200 mems, national organizations and individuals in 21 countries. Pres. MICHAELA FEVERSTEIN (Germany); Gen. Sec. G. LEE KANTIN (USA). Publ. *International Review for Business Education*.

International Society for Education through Art: c/o Peter Hermans, Citogroep, POB 1109, 6801 BC Arnhem, Netherlands; fax (26) 3521202; e-mail insea@citogroep.nl; internet www.insea.org; f. 1951 to unite art teachers throughout the world, to exchange information and to co-ordinate research into art education; organizes international congresses and exhibitions of children's art. Pres. DIEDERIK SCHöNAU (Netherlands). Publ. *INSEA News* (3 a year).

International Society for Music Education: ICRME, University of Reading, Bulmershe Court, Reading, RG6 1HY, United Kingdom; tel. (118) 9318846; fax (118) 9318846; e-mail e.smith@reading.ac.uk; internet www.isme.org; f. 1953 to organize international conferences, seminars and publications on matters pertaining to music education; acts as advisory body to UNESCO in matters of music education. Mems: national committees and individuals in 60 countries. Pres. EINAR SOLBU (Norway); Sec.-Gen. JOAN THERENS (Canada). Publs *ISME Newsletter, Journal*.

International Society for the Study of Medieval Philosophy: Collège Mercier, place du Cardinal Mercier 14, 1348 Louvain-la-Neuve, Belgium; tel. (10) 47-48-07; fax (10) 47-82-85; e-mail siepm @isp.vcp.ac.be; internet www.isp.ucl.ac.be/isp/siepm/siepm.html; f. 1958 to promote the study of medieval thought and the collaboration between individuals and institutions concerned in this field; organizes international congresses. Mems: 576. Pres. Prof. DAVID LUSCOMBE (United Kingdom); Sec. Prof. JACQUELINE HAMESSE (Belgium). Publ. *Bulletin de Philosophie Médiévale* (annually).

International Youth Library (Internationale Jugendbibliothek): 81247 Munich, Schloss Blutenburg, Germany; tel. (89) 8912110; fax (89) 8117553; e-mail bib@ijb.de; internet www.ijb.de; f. 1949, since 1953 an associated project of UNESCO, to promote the international exchange of children's literature and to provide study opportunities for specialists in children's books; maintains a library of 510,000 volumes in about 130 languages. Dir Dr BARBARA SCHARIOTH. Publs *The White Ravens, IJB Report*, catalogues.

League of European Research Libraries—LIBER: c/o Prof. Elmar Mittler, Göttingen Univ. Library, 37070 Göttingen, Germany; tel. (551) 395212; fax (551) 395222; e-mail mittler@mail.sub.uni-goettingen.def. 1971 to establish close collaboration between the general research libraries of Europe, and national and university libraries in particular; and to help in finding practical ways of improving the quality of the services these libraries provide. Mems: 310 libraries and individuals in 33 countries. Pres. Prof. ELMAR MITTLER; Sec. Dr TOBY BAINTON (UK). Publ. *LIBER Quarterly*.

Organization of Ibero-American States for Education, Science and Culture (Organización de Estados Iberoamericanos para la Educación, la Ciencia y la Cultura): Centro de Recursos Documentales e Informáticos, Calle Bravo Murillo, No 38, 28015 Madrid, Spain; tel. (91) 594-44-42; fax (91) 594-32-86; e-mail oeimad@oei.es; internet www.oei.es; f. 1949 (as the Ibero-American Bureau of Education); promotes peace and solidarity between member countries, through education, science, technology and culture; provides information, encourages exchanges and organizes training courses; the

General Assembly (at ministerial level) meets every four years. Mems: governments of 20 countries. Sec.-Gen. FRANCISCO JOSÉ PIÑÓN. Publ. *Revista Iberoamericana de Educacion* (quarterly).

Organization of the Catholic Universities of Latin America (Organización de Universidades Católicas de América Latina—ODUCAL): c/o Dr J. A. Tobías, Universidad del Salvador, Viamonte 1856, CP 1056, Buenos Aires, Argentina; tel. (1) 813-1408; fax (1) 812-4625; f. 1953 to assist the social, economic and cultural development of Latin America through the promotion of Catholic higher education in the continent. Mems: 43 Catholic universities in Argentina, Bolivia, Brazil, Chile, Colombia, Dominican Republic, Ecuador, Guatemala, Mexico, Panama, Paraguay, Peru, Puerto Rico, Uruguay, Venezuela. Pres. Dr JUAN ALEJANDRO TOBÍAS (Argentina); Publs *Anuario, Sapientia, Universitas.*

Southeast Asian Ministers of Education Organization—SEAMEO: Darakarn Bldg, 920 Sukhumvit Rd, Bangkok 10110, Thailand; tel. (2) 391-0144; fax (2) 381-2587; e-mail secretariat@seameo.org; internet www.seameo.org; f. 1965 to promote co-operation among the Southeast Asian nations through projects in education, science and culture; SEAMEO has 14 regional centres including: BIOTROP for tropical biology, in Bogor, Indonesia; INNOTECH for educational innovation and technology; an Open-Learning Centre in Indonesia; RECSAM for education in science and mathematics, in Penang, Malaysia; RELC for languages, in Singapore; RIHED for higher education development in Bangkok, Thailand; SEARCA for graduate study and research in agriculture, in Los Baños, Philippines; SPAFA for archaeology and fine arts in Bangkok, Thailand; TROPMED for tropical medicine and public health with regional centres in Indonesia, Malaysia, Philippines and Thailand and a central office in Bangkok; VOCTECH for vocational and technical education; and the SEAMO Training Centre in Ho Chi Minh City, Viet Nam. Mems: Brunei, Cambodia, Indonesia, Laos, Malaysia, Philippines, Singapore, Thailand, Viet Nam. Assoc. mems: Australia, Canada, France, Germany, Netherlands, New Zealand. Pres. TEO CHEE HEAN (Singapore); Dir Dr SUPARAK RACHAINTRA. Publs *Annual Report, SEAMEO Horizon.*

Union of Latin American Universities (Unión de Universidades de América Latina—UDUAL): Edificio UDUAL, Apdo postal 70-232, Ciudad Universitaria, Del. Coyoacán, 04510 México, DF, Mexico; tel. (5) 622-0991; fax (5) 616-1414; f. 1949 to organize the interchange of professors, students, research fellows and graduates and generally encourage good relations between the Latin American universities; arranges conferences, conducts statistical research; centre for university documentation. Mems: 165 universities. Pres. Dr JORGE BROVETO (Uruguay); Sec.-Gen. Dr ABELARDO VILLEGAS (Mexico). Publs *Universidades* (2 a year), *Gaceta UDUAL* (quarterly), *Censo* (every 2 years).

Universal Esperanto Association: Nieuwe Binnenweg 176, 3015 BJ Rotterdam, Netherlands; tel. (10) 4361044; fax (10) 4361751; e-mail uea@inter.nl.net; internet www.uea.org; f. 1908 to assist the spread of the international language, Esperanto, and to facilitate the practical use of the language. Mems: 62 affiliated national associations and 19,750 individuals in 120 countries. Pres. KEPPEL E. ENDERBY (Australia); Gen. Sec. MICHELA LIPARI (Italy). Publs *Esperanto* (monthly), *Kontakto* (every 2 months), *Jarlibro* (yearbook), *Esperanto Documents.*

World Association for Educational Research: Université de Sherbrooke, Sherbrooke, QC J1K 2R1, Canada; e-mail ylenoir@courrier.usherb.ca; f. 1953, present title adopted 1977; aims to encourage research in educational sciences by organizing congresses, issuing publications, the exchange of information, etc. Member societies and individual members in 50 countries. Pres. Prof. Dr Y. LENOIR.

World Education Fellowship: 22A Kew Gardens, Kew, Richmond, TW9 3HD, United Kingdom; tel. (20) 8940-0131; f. 1921 to promote education for international understanding, and the exchange and practice of ideas together with research into progressive educational theories and methods. Sections and groups in 20 countries. Chair. CHRISTINE WYKES; Sec. ROSEMARY CROMMELIN. Publ. *The New Era in Education* (3 a year).

World Union of Catholic Teachers (Union Mondiale des Enseignants Catholiques—UMEC): Piazza San Calisto 16, 00120 Città del Vaticano; tel. 698-87286; f. 1951; encourages the grouping of Catholic teachers for the greater effectiveness of the Catholic school, distributes documentation on Catholic doctrine with regard to education, and facilitates personal contacts through congresses, seminars, etc., nationally and internationally. Mems: 32 organizations in 29 countries. Pres. ARNOLD BACKX; Sec.-Gen. MICHAEL EMM. Publ. *Nouvelles de l'UMEC.*

World University Service—WUS: 383 Los Jardines, Nuñoa, Santiago de Chile, Chile; tel. (2) 272375; fax (2) 2724002; f. 1920; links students, faculty and administrators in post-secondary institutions concerned with economic and social development, and seeks to protect their academic freedom and autonomy; seeks to extend technical, personal and financial resources of post-secondary institutions to under-developed areas and communities; provides scholarships at university level for refugees, displaced people, and returnees, and supports informal education projects for women; the principle is to assist people to improve and develop their own communities. WUS is independent and is governed by an assembly of national committees. Pres. CALEB FUNDANGA (Zambia); Sec.-Gen. XIMENA ERAZO. Publs *WUS News, WUS and Human Rights* (quarterly).

Environmental Conservation

BirdLife International: Wellbrook Ct, Girton Rd, Cambridge, CB3 0NA, United Kingdom; tel. (1223) 277318; fax (1223) 277200; e-mail birdlife@birdlife.org.uk; internet www.birdlife.net; f. 1922 as the International Council for Bird Preservation; a global partnership of organizations that determines status of bird species throughout the world and compiles data on all endangered species; identifies conservation problems and priorities; initiates and co-ordinates conservation projects and international conventions. Partners in 60 countries; representatives in around 31 more. Chair. GERARD A. BERTRAND; Dir Dr MICHAEL RANDS (UK). Publs *Bird Red Data Book, World Birdwatch* (quarterly), *Bird Conservation Series* and study reports.

Friends of the Earth International: Prins Hendrikkade 48, POB 19199, 1000 GD Amsterdam, Netherlands; tel. (20) 6221369; fax (20) 6392181; e-mail foeint@antenna.nl; internet www.xs4all-nl/~foeint; f. 1971 to promote the conservation, restoration and rational use of the environment and natural resources through public education and campaigning. Mems: 56 national groups. Publ. *FoE Link* (6 a year).

Greenpeace International: Keizersgracht 176, 1016 DW Amsterdam, Netherlands; tel. (20) 5236222; fax (20) 5236200; e-mail greenpeaceinternational@green2.greenpeace.org; internet www.greenpeace.org; f. 1971 to campaign for the protection of the environment; aims to bear witness to environmental destruction, and to demonstrate solutions for positive change. Mems: offices in 34 countries. Chair. CORNELIA DURRANT; Exec. Dir GERD LEIPOLD.

Independent World Commission on the Oceans—IWCO: c/o Palácio de Belém, 1300 Lisbon, Portugal; tel. (1) 3637141; fax (1) 3636603; e-mail secretariat@world-oceans.org; internet www.world-oceans.org; f. 1995 to study ways of protecting maritime resources and coastal areas. Chair. MÁRIO SOARES.

International Commission for the Protection of the Rhine: 56002 Koblenz, Hohenzollernstrasse 18, POB 200253, Germany; tel. (261) 12495; fax (261) 36572; e-mail sekretariat@iksr.de; internet www.iksr.org; f. 1950 to prepare and commission research to establish the nature of the pollution of the Rhine; to propose measures of protection, ecological rehabilitation and flood prevention of the Rhine to the signatory governments. Mems: 23 delegates from France, Germany, Luxembourg, Netherlands, Switzerland and the EU. Pres. A. JACOBOVITZ DE SZEGED; Sec. J. H. OTERDOOM. Publ. *Annual Report.*

International Council on Metals and the Environment: 294 Albert St, Suite 506, Ottawa, ON K1P 6E6, Canada; tel. (613) 235-4263; fax (613) 235-2865; e-mail info@icme.com; internet www.icme.com; f. 1991 by metal-producing and mining companies to promote responsible environmental practices and policies in the mining, use, recycling and disposal of metals. Mems: companies from six continents. Chair. DOUGLAS YEARLEY (USA);Sec.-Gen. GARY NASH (Canada). Publ. *ICME Newsletter* (quarterly).

South Pacific Regional Environment Programme—SPREP: POB 240, Apia, Samoa; tel. 21929; fax 20231; e-mail sprep@sprep.org.ws; internet www.sprep.org.ws; f. 1978 by the South Pacific Commission (where it was based), the South Pacific (now Pacific Islands) Forum, ESCAP and UNEP; formally established as an independent institution in June 1993 when members signed the *Agreement Establishing SPREP*; aims to promote regional co-operation in environmental matters, to assist members to protect and improve their shared environment, and to help members to work towards sustainable development; adopted the Action Plan for Managing the Environment of the South Pacific Region 1997–2000, in November 1996; responsible for implementation of the South Pacific Biodiversity Conservation Programme, a five-year project funded by the UN's Global Environment Facility. Mems: 22 Pacific islands, Australia, France, New Zealand, USA. Dir TAMARII P. TUTANGATA (Cook Islands). Publs *SPREP Newsletter* (quarterly), *CASOLink* (quarterly), *La letter de l'environnement* (quarterly), *South Pacific Sea Level and Climate Change Newsletter* (quarterly).

Wetlands International Africa, Europe, Middle East (AEME): Droevendaalsteeg 3A, POB 7002, 6700 CA Wageningen, Netherlands; tel. (317) 478884; fax (317) 478885; e-mail post@wetlands.agro.nl; internet www.wetlands.org; f. 1995 by merger of several regional wetlands organizations; aims to sustain and restore wetlands, their resources and biodiversity through research, information exchange and conservation activities; promotes implementation of the 1971 Ramsar Convention on Wetlands. Exec. Dir JAMES

McCuaig. Publs *Wetlands* (2 a year), other studies, technical publications, manuals, proceedings of meetings.

World Conservation Union—IUCN: rue Mauverney 28, 1196 Gland, Switzerland; tel. (22) 9990001; fax (22) 9990002; e-mail mail@ iucn.org; internet www.iucn.org; f. 1948, as the International Union for Conservation of Nature and Natural Resources; supports partnerships and practical field activities to promote the conservation of natural resources, to secure the conservation of nature, and especially of biological diversity, as an essential foundation for the future; to ensure wise use of the earth's natural resources in an equitable and sustainable way; to guide the development of human communities towards ways of life in enduring harmony with other components of the biosphere, developing programmes to protect and sustain the most important and threatened species and eco-systems and assisting governments to devise and carry out national conservation strategies; maintains a conservation library and documentation centre and units for monitoring traffic in wildlife. Mems: 79 governments, 112 government agencies, 68 international non-governmental organizations and 692 national non-governmental organizations, from a total of 141 countries; 37 non-voting affiliate mems. Pres. YOLANDA KAKABADSE (Ecuador); Dir-Gen. SIMON STUART. Publs *World Conservation Strategy, Caring for the Earth, Red List of Threatened Plants, Red List of Threatened Species, United Nations List of National Parks and Protected Areas, World Conservation* (quarterly).

World Society for the Protection of Animals: 89 Albert Embankment, London, SE1 7TP, United Kingdom; tel. (20) 7793-0540; fax (20) 7793-0208; e-mail wspa@wspa.org.uk; internet www.wspa.org. uk; f. 1981, incorporating the World Federation for the Protection of Animals (f. 1950) and the International Society for the Protection of Animals (f. 1959); promotes animal welfare and conservation by humane education, practical field projects, international lobbying and legislative work. Chief Exec. ANDREW DICKSON.

World Wide Fund for Nature—WWF: ave de Mont-Blanc, 1196 Gland, Switzerland; tel. (22) 3649111; fax (22) 3643239; e-mail userid@wwfnet.org; internet www.panda.org; f. 1961 (as World Wildlife Fund); aims to conserve nature and ecological processes by preserving genetic, species and ecosystem diversity; to ensure the sustainable use of resources; to reduce pollution and wasteful consumption of resources and energy. Mems: 27 national organizations, and five associates. Pres. Prof. RUUD LUBBERS (Netherlands); Dir-Gen. Dr CLAUDE MARTIN. Publs *Annual Report, WWF News* (quarterly).

Government and Politics

African Association for Public Administration and Management: POB 48677, Nairobi, Kenya; tel. (2) 52-19-44; fax (2) 52-18-45; e-mail aapam@africaonline.co.ke; f. 1971 to provide senior officials with a forum for the exchange of ideas and experience, to promote the study of professional techniques and encourage research in particular African administrative problems. Mems: over 500 corporate and individual. Pres Dr ROBERT DODOO; Sec.-Gen. HUDSON M. BIGOGO. Publs *Newsletter* (quarterly), *Annual Seminar Report, African Journal of Public Administration and Management,* studies.

Afro-Asian Peoples' Solidarity Organization—AAPSO: 89 Abdel Aziz Al-Saoud St, POB 11559-61 Manial El-Roda, Cairo, Egypt; tel. (2) 3636081; fax (2) 3637361; e-mail aapso@idsc.gov.eg; f. 1958; acts among and for the peoples of Africa and Asia in their struggle for genuine independence, sovereignty, socio-economic development, peace and disarmament. Mems: national committees and affiliated organizations in 66 countries and territories, assoc. mems in 15 European countries. Pres. Dr MOURAD GHALEB; Sec.-Gen. NOURI ABD AR-RAZZAK HUSSEIN (Iraq). Publs *Solidarity Bulletin* (monthly), *Development and Socio-Economic Progress* (quarterly), *Human Rights Newsletter* (6 a year).

Agency for the Prohibition of Nuclear Weapons in Latin America and the Caribbean (Organismo para la Proscripción de las Armas Nucleares en la América Latina y el Caribe—OPANAL): Temístocles 78, Col. Polanco, CP 11560, México, DF, Mexico; tel. (5) 280-4923; fax (5) 280-2965; f. 1969 to ensure compliance with the Treaty for the Prohibition of Nuclear Weapons in Latin America (Treaty of Tlatelolco), 1967; to ensure the absence of all nuclear weapons in the application zone of the Treaty; to contribute to the movement against proliferation of nuclear weapons; to promote general and complete disarmament; to prohibit all testing, use, manufacture, acquisition, storage, installation and any form of possession, by any means, of nuclear weapons. The organs of the Agency comprise the General Conference, meeting every two years, the Council, meeting every two months, and the secretariat. Holds General Conference every two years. Mems: 30 states which have fully ratified the Treaty: Antigua and Barbuda, Argentina, Bahamas, Barbados, Belize, Bolivia, Brazil, Chile, Colombia, Costa Rica, Dominica, Dominican Republic, Ecuador, El Salvador, Grenada, Guatemala, Haiti, Honduras, Jamaica, Mexico, Nicaragua, Panama, Paraguay, Peru, Saint Vincent and the Grenadines, Suriname, Trinidad and Tobago, Uruguay and Venezuela. The Treaty has two

additional Protocols: the first signed and ratified by France, the Netherlands, the United Kingdom and the USA; the second signed and ratified by China, the USA, France, the United Kingdom and Russia. Sec.-Gen. ENRIQUE ROMÁN-MOREY (Peru).

Alliance of Small Island States—AOSIS: c/o 800 Second Ave, Suite 400D, New York, NY 10017, USA; tel. (212) 599-6196; fax (212) 599-0797; f. 1990 as an *ad hoc* intergovernmental grouping to focus on the special problems of small islands and low-lying coastal developing states. Mems: 43 island nations. Chair. TUILOMA NERONI SLADE (Samoa). Publ. *Small Islands, Big Issues.*

ANZUS: c/o Dept of Foreign Affairs and Trade, Locked Bag 40, Queen Victoria Terrace, Canberra, ACT 2600, Australia; tel. (2) 6261-9111; fax (2) 6273-3577; internet www.dfat.gov.au; the ANZUS Security Treaty was signed in 1951 by Australia, New Zealand and the USA, and ratified in 1952 to co-ordinate partners' efforts for collective defence for the preservation of peace and security in the Pacific area, through the exchange of technical information and strategic intelligence, and a programme of exercises, exchanges and visits. In 1984 New Zealand refused to allow visits by US naval vessels that were either nuclear-propelled or potentially nuclear-armed, and this led to the cancellation of joint ANZUS military exercises: in 1986 the USA formally announced the suspension of its security commitment to New Zealand under ANZUS. Instead of the annual ANZUS Council meetings, bilateral talks were subsequently held every year between Australia and the USA. ANZUS continued to govern security relations between Australia and the USA, and between Australia and New Zealand; security relations between New Zealand and the USA were the only aspect of the treaty to be suspended. Senior-level contacts between New Zealand and the USA resumed in 1994.

Association of Secretaries General of Parliaments: c/o Committee Office, House of Commons, London, SW1, United Kingdom; tel. (20) 7219-3259; f. 1938; studies the law, practice and working methods of different Parliaments and proposes measures for improving those methods and for securing co-operation between the services of different Parliaments; operates as a consultative body to the Inter-Parliamentary Union (q.v.), and assists the Union on subjects within the scope of the Association. Mems: about 200 representing about 90 countries. Pres. JACQUES OLLÉ-LAPRUNE (France); Sec. Y. AZAD (UK). Publ. *Constitutional and Parliamentary Information* (2 a year).

Atlantic Treaty Association: 10 rue Crevaux, 75116 Paris, France; tel. 1-45-53-28-80; fax 1-47-55-49-63; e-mail atasg@noos.fr; f. 1954 to inform public opinion on the North Atlantic Alliance and to promote the solidarity of the peoples of the North Atlantic; holds annual assemblies, seminars, study conferences for teachers and young politicians. Mems: national associations in the 19 member countries of NATO (q.v.); 18 assoc. mems from central and eastern Europe, one observer mem. Chair. ALAN LEE WILLIAMS (United Kingdom); Sec.-Gen. ANTÓNIO BORGES DE CARVALHO (Portugal).

Baltic Council: f. 1993 by the Baltic Assembly comprising 60 parliamentarians from Estonia, Latvia and Lithuania; Council of Ministers of the three Baltic countries to co-ordinate policy in the areas of foreign policy, justice, the environment, education and science.

Celtic League: 11 Hilltop View, Farmhill, Braddan, Isle of Man; tel. (1624) 627128; e-mail b.moffatt@advsys.co.im; internet www.manxman.co.im/cleague/index.html; f. 1961 to foster co-operation between the six Celtic nations (Ireland, Scotland, Man, Wales, Cornwall and Brittany), especially those who are actively working for political autonomy by non-violent means; campaigns politically on issues affecting the Celtic countries; monitors military activity in the Celtic countries; co-operates with national cultural organizations to promote the languages and culture of the Celts. Mems: approx. 1,400 individuals in the Celtic communities and elsewhere. Chair. CATHAL Ó LUAIN; Gen. Sec. J. B. MOFFAT. Publ. *Carn* (quarterly).

Central European Initiative—CEI: c/o Ambassador Paul Hartig, CEI Executive Secretariat, Via Genova 9, 34132 Trieste, Italy; tel. (040) 7786777; fax (040) 360640; internet ceinet.org; f. 1989 as 'Pentagonal' group of central European countries (Austria, Czechoslovakia, Italy, Hungary, Yugoslavia); became 'Hexagonal' with the admission of Poland in July 1991; present name adopted in March 1992, when Croatia and Slovenia replaced Yugoslavia as members (Bosnia and Herzegovina and the former Yugoslav republic of Macedonia subsequently became members); the Czech Republic and Slovakia became separate mems in January 1993; Albania, Belarus, Bulgaria, Romania and Ukraine joined the CEI in June 1996 and Moldova in November; aims to encourage regional and bilateral co-operation, working within the OSCE (q.v.).

Christian Democrat International: 16 rue de la Victoire, Boîte 1, 1060 Brussels, Belgium; tel. (2) 537-13-22; fax (2) 537-93-48; f. 1961 to serve as a platform for the co-operation of political parties of Christian Social inspiration. Mems: parties in 64 countries (of which 47 in Europe). Pres. JAVIER RUPÉREZ. Publs *DC-Info* (quarterly), *Human Rights* (5 a year), *Documents* (quarterly).

Comunidade dos Países de Língua Portuguesa (Community of Portuguese-Speaking Countries): rua S. Caetano 32, 1200 Lisbon, Portugal; tel. (1) 392-8560; fax (1) 392-8588; f. 1996; aims to produce close political, economic, diplomatic and cultural links between Portuguese-speaking countries and to strengthen the influence of the Lusophone commonwealth within the international community. Undertook efforts to negotiate a cease-fire agreement in Guinea-Bissau in mid-1998. Mems: Angola, Brazil, Cape Verde, Guinea-Bissau, Mozambique, Portugal, São Tomé e Príncipe; East Timor has observer status. Exec. Sec. Dr DULCE MARIA PEREIRA .

Eastern Regional Organization for Public Administration—EROPA: One Burgundy Plaza, Suite 12M, 307 Katipunan Ave, Loyola Heights, Quezon City 1105, Metro Manila, Philippines; tel. (2) 433-8175; fax (2) 434-9223; e-mail eropa@eropa.org.ph; internet www.eropa.org.ph; f. 1960 to promote regional co-operation in improving knowledge, systems and practices of governmental administration to help accelerate economic and social development; organizes regional conferences, seminars, special studies, surveys and training programmes. There are three regional centres: Training Centre (New Delhi), Local Government Centre (Tokyo), Development Management Centre (Seoul). Mems: 12 countries, 102 organizations/groups, 418 individuals. Chair. CORAZON ALMA G. DE LEON (Philippines); Sec.-Gen. PATRICIA A. STO TOMAS (Philippines). Publs *EROPA Bulletin* (quarterly), *Asian Review of Public Administration* (2 a year).

European Movement: 25 Square de Meeus, 1040 Brussels, Belgium; tel. (2) 508-30-88; fax (2) 512-66-73; e-mail secretariat@europeanmovement.skynet.be; f. 1947 by a liaison committee of representatives from European organizations, to study the political, economic and technical problems of a European Union and suggest how they can be solved; to inform and lead public opinion in the promotion of integration. Conferences have led to the creation of the Council of Europe, College of Europe, etc. Mems: national councils and committees in Austria, Belgium, Croatia, Cyprus, Czech Republic, Denmark, France, Germany, Greece, Hungary, Ireland, Italy, Luxembourg, former Yugoslav republic of Macedonia, Malta, Netherlands, Norway, Poland, Portugal, Romania, Slovakia, Slovenia, Spain, Switzerland, Turkey, United Kingdom, Yugoslavia; and several international social and economic organizations. Pres. JOSÉ MARIA GIL-ROBLES (Spain); Sec.-Gen. PIER VIRGILIO DASTOLI (Italy).

European Union of Women—EUW: 2 Pittakou St, 10558 Athens, Greece; tel. (1) 3314847; fax (1454) 3314817; e-mail fpetralia@parliament.gr; f. 1955 to increase the influence of women in the political and civic life of their country and of Europe. Mems: national organizations in 21 countries. Chair. FANNY PALLI; Sec.-Gen. VASSO KOLLIA.

European Young Christian Democrats—EYCD: 16 rue de la Victoire, 1060 Brussels, Belgium; tel. (2) 537-41-47; fax (2) 534-50-28; f. 1947; holds monthly seminars and meetings for young political leaders; conducts training in international political matters. Mems: 28 national organizations in 25 European countries. Pres. ENRICO LETTA (Italy); Sec.-Gen. MARC BERTRAND (Belgium). Publ. *EYCD File* (6 a year).

La Francophonie: 28 rue de Bourgogne, 75007 Paris, France; tel. 1-44-11-12-50; fax 1-44-11-12-76; political grouping of French-speaking countries; conference of heads of state convened every two years to promote co-operation throughout the French-speaking world (1999: Moncton, Canada). Mems: Governments of 51 countries. Sec.-Gen. BOUTROS BOUTROS-GHALI (Egypt).

Gulf of Guinea Commission (Commission du Golfe de Guinée—CGG): f. Nov. 1999 to promote co-operation among member countries and the peaceful and sustainable development of natural resources in the sub-region. Mems: Angola, Cameroon, the Repub. of the Congo, Equatorial Guinea, Gabon, Nigeria, Sao Tomé e Principe.

Hansard Society: St Philips Bldg North, LSE, Sheffield St, London, WC2A 2EX, United Kingdom; tel. (20) 7955-7459; fax (20) 7955-7492; e-mail hansard@hansard.lse.ac.uk; internet www.hansardsociety.org.uk; f. 1944 as Hansard Society for Parliamentary Government; aims to promote political education and research and the informed discussion of all aspects of modern parliamentary government. Dir SHELAGH DIPLOCK. Publ. *Parliamentary Affairs—A Journal of Comparative Politics* (quarterly).

Inter-African Socialists and Democrats: 6 rue al-Waquidi 1004, al-Menzah IV, Tunis, Tunisia; tel. 231-138; f. 1981 (as Inter-African Socialist Organization; name changed 1988). Sec.-Gen. SADOK FAYALA (Tunisia).

International Alliance of Women: 9/10 Queen St, Melbourne, Vic 3000, Australia; tel. (3) 9629-3653; fax (3) 9629-2904; e-mail toddsec@surfnetcity.com.au; f. 1904 to obtain equality for women in all fields and to encourage women to take up their responsibilities; to join in international activities. Mems: 78 national affiliates in 67 countries. Pres. PATRICIA GILES. Publ. *International Women's News* (quarterly).

International Association for Community Development: 179 rue du Débarcadère, 6001 Marcinelle, Belgium; tel. (71) 44-72-78; fax (71) 47-11-04; organizes annual international colloquium for community-based organizations. Sec.-Gen. PIERRE ROZEN. Publ. *IACD Newsletter* (2 a year).

International Commission for the History of Representative and Parliamentary Institutions: c/o John Rogister, Dept of History, 43–46 North Bailey, Durham DH1 3EX, United Kingdom; fax (191) 374-4754; f. 1936. Mems: 300 individuals in 31 countries. Pres. JOHN ROGISTER (UK); Sec. JOHN H. GREVER (USA). Publs *Parliaments, Estates and Representation* (annually), studies.

International Democrat Union: 32 Smith Sq., London, SW1P 3HH, United Kingdom; tel. (20) 7984-8052; fax (20) 7976-0486; e-mail rnormington@idu.org; internet www.idu.org; f. 1983; group of centre-right political parties; holds conference every six months. Mems: political parties in 35 countries, four assoc. mems. Exec. Sec. RICHARD NORMINGTON.

International Federation of Resistance Movements: c/o R. Maria, 5 rue Rollin, 75005 Paris, France; tel. 1-43-26-84-29; f. 1951; supports the medical and social welfare of former victims of fascism; works for peace, disarmament and human rights, against fascism and neo-fascism. Mems: 82 national organizations in 29 countries. Pres. ALIX LHOTE (France); Sec.-Gen. Prof. ILYA KREMER (Russia). Publs *Feuille d'information* (in French and German), *Cahier d'informations médicales, sociales et juridiques* (in French and German).

International Institute for Peace: Möllwaldplatz 5, 1040 Vienna, Austria; tel. (1) 504-43-76; fax (1) 505-32-36; f. 1957; non-governmental organization with consultative status at ECOSOC (see UN) and UNESCO; studies interdependence as a strategy for peace, conflict prevention and the transformation of central and eastern Europe. Mems: individuals and corporate bodies invited by the executive board. Pres. ERWIN LANC (Austria); Dir Prof. LEV VORONKOV (Russia). Publs *Peace and the Sciences* (quarterly, in English), occasional papers (2 or 3 a year, in English and German).

International Institute for Strategic Studies: Arundel House, 13–15 Arundel St, London, WC2R 3DX, United Kingdom; tel. (20) 7379-7676; fax (20) 7836-3108; e-mail iiss@iiss.org; internet www.iiss.org; f. 1958; concerned with the study of the role of force in international relations, including problems of international strategy, the ethnic, political and social sources of conflict, disarmament and arms control, peace-keeping and intervention, defence economics, etc.; independent of any government. Mems: 3,000. Dir Dr JOHN M. W. CHIPMAN. Publs *Survival* (quarterly), *The Military Balance* (annually), *Strategic Survey* (annually), *Adelphi Papers* (10 a year), *Strategic Comments* (10 a year).

International Lesbian and Gay Association—ILGA: 81 rue Marché-au-charbon, 1000 Brussels 1, Belgium; tel. and fax (2) 502-24-71; e-mail ilga@ilga.org; f. 1978; works to remove legal, social and economic discrimination against homosexual and bisexual women and men, and transexuals, throughout the world; co-ordinates political action at an international level; co-operates with other supportive movements. 2000 world conference: Rome, Italy. Mems: 350 national and regional associations in 75 countries. Secs-Gen. PHUMI MTETWA, KURSAD KAHRAMANOGLU. Publ. *ILGA Bulletin* (quarterly), *GBLT Human Rights Annual Report*.

International Peace Bureau: 41 rue de Zürich, 1201 Geneva, Switzerland; tel. (22) 7316429; fax (22) 7389419; e-mail mailbox@ipb .org.org; internet www.ipb.org; f. 1892; promotes international co-operation for general and complete disarmament and the non-violent solution of international conflicts; co-ordinates and represents peace movements at the UN; conducts projects on the abolition of nuclear weapons and the role of non-governmental organizations in conflict prevention/resolution. Mems: 188 peace organizations in 53 countries. Pres. CORA WEISS; Sec.-Gen. COLIN ARCHER. Publ. *IPB News* (quarterly), *IPB Geneva News*.

International Political Science Association: c/o Prof. John Coakley, Dept. of Politics, Univ. College Dublin, Belfield, Dublin 4, Ireland; tel. (1) 706-8182; fax (1) 706-1171; e-mail ipsa@ucd.ie; internet www.ucd.ie/~ipsa/index.html; f. 1949; aims to promote the development of political science. Mems: 41 national associations, 100 institutions, 1,350 individual mems. Pres. Prof. THEODORE J. LOWI (USA); Sec.-Gen. JOHN COAKLEY. Publs *Participation* (3 a year), *International Political Science Abstracts* (6 a year), *International Political Science Review* (quarterly).

International Union of Local Authorities: POB 90646, 2509 LP, The Hague, Netherlands; tel. (70) 3066066; fax (70) 3500496; e-mail iula@iula-hq.nl; internet www.iula.org; f. 1913 to promote local government, improve local administration and encourage popular participation in public affairs. Activities include organization of a biennial international congress; operation of specific 'task forces' (Association Capacity–Building, Women in Local Government, Information Technology); development of intermunicipal relations to provide a link between local authorities of countries; maintenance of a permanent office for the collection and distribution of information on municipal affairs. Mems in over 110 countries; seven regional sections. Pres. MAX NG'ANDWE (Zambia); Sec.-Gen. JACQUES JOBIN.

International Union of Young Christian Democrats—IUYCD: 16 rue de la Victoire, 1060 Brussels, Belgium; tel. (2) 537-77-51; fax (2) 534-50-28; f. 1962. Mems: national organizations in 59 countries and territories. Sec.-Gen. MARCOS VILLASMIL (Venezuela). Publs *IUYCD Newsletter* (fortnightly), *Debate* (quarterly).

Inuit Circumpolar Conference: 170 Laurier Ave West, Suite 504, Ottawa, ON K1P 5V5, Canada; tel. (613) 563-2642; fax (613) 565-3089; f. 1977 to protect the indigenous culture, environment and rights of the Inuit people (Eskimoes), and to encourage co-operation among the Inuit; conferences held every three years. Mems: Inuit communities in Canada, Greenland, Alaska and Russia. Pres. ROSE-MARIE KUPTANA. Publ. *ICC Arctic Policy Review*.

Jewish Agency for Israel: POB 92, 48 King George St, Jerusalem, Israel; tel. (2) 6202297; fax (2) 6202412; e-mail elibir@jazo.org.il; internet www.jafi.org.il; f. 1929; reconstituted 1971 as an instrument through which world Jewry could develop a national home. Constituents are: World Zionist Organization, United Israel Appeal, Inc. (USA), and Keren Hayesod. Chair. Exec. SALLAI MERIDOR; Chair. Bd. ALEX GRASS.

Latin American Parliament (Parlamento Latinoamericano): Avda Auro Soares de Moura Andrade 564, São Paulo, Brazil; tel. (11) 38246325; fax (11) 38246324; internet www.parlatino.org; f. 1965; permanent democratic institution, representative of all existing political trends within the national legislative bodies of Latin America; aims to promote the movement towards economic, political and cultural integration of the Latin American republics, and to uphold human rights, peace and security. Publs *Acuerdos, Resoluciones de las Asambleas Ordinarias* (annually), *Revista del Parlamento Latinoamericano* (annually); statements and agreements.

Liberal International: 1 Whitehall Place, London, SW1A 2HD, United Kingdom; tel. (20) 7839-5905; fax (20) 7925-2685; e-mail li@worldlib.org; internet www.worldlib.org/li/; f. 1947; world union of 83 liberal parties in 58 countries; co-ordinates foreign policy work of member parties, and promotes freedom, tolerance, democracy, international understanding, protection of human rights and market-based economics; has consultative status at ECOSOC of United Nations and the Council of Europe. Pres. ANNEMIE NEYTS-UYTTEBROECK; Sec.-Gen. JAN WEIJERS. Publ. *London Aerogramme* (monthly).

Nato Parliamentary Assembly: 3 place du Petit Sablon, 1000 Brussels, Belgium; tel. (2) 513-28-65; fax (2) 514-18-47; internet www.naa.be; f. 1955 as the NATO Parliamentarians' Conference; name changed 1966 to North Atlantic Assembly; renamed as above 1999; the inter-parliamentary assembly of the North Atlantic Alliance; holds two plenary sessions a year and meetings of committees (Political, Defence and Security, Economic, Scientific and Technical, Civilian Affairs) where parliamentarians from North America, western Europe and eastern Europe (associate delegates) examine the problems confronting the Alliance and European security issues in general. Pres. RAFAEL ESTRELLA; Sec.-Gen. SIMON LUNN (United Kingdom).

Non-aligned Movement: c/o Permanent Representative of South Africa to the UN, 333 East 38th St, 9th Floor, New York, NY 10016, USA (no permanent secretariat); tel. (212) 213-5583; fax (212) 692-2498; f. 1961 by a meeting of 25 Heads of State, aiming to link countries which refused to adhere to the main East-West military and political blocs; co-ordination bureau established in 1973; works for the establishment of a new international economic order, and especially for better terms for countries producing raw materials; maintains special funds for agricultural development, improvement of food production and the financing of buffer stocks; 'South Commission' (q.v.) promotes co-operation between developing countries; seeks changes in the United Nations to give developing countries greater decision-making power; in October 1995 member states urged the USA to lift its economic embargo against Cuba; summit conference held every three years, 12th conference of heads of state and government was held in Durban, South Africa, in 1998. Mems: 113 countries (at Sept. 1998).

Open Door International (for the Economic Emancipation of the Woman Worker): 16 rue Américaine, 1060 Brussels, Belgium; tel. (2) 537-67-61; f. 1929 to obtain equal rights and opportunities for women in the whole field of work. Mems in 10 countries. Hon. Sec. ADÈLE HAUWEL (Belgium).

Organization for the Prohibition of Chemical Weapons—OPCW: Johan de Wittlaan 32, 2517JR The Hague, Netherlands; tel. (70) 4163300; fax (70) 3063535; e-mail mediabr@opcw.org; internet www.opcw.org; f. 1997 to oversee implementation of the Chemical Weapons Convention, which aims to ban the development, production, stockpiling and use of chemical weapons. The Convention was negotiated under the auspices of the UN Conference on Disarmament and opened for signature in January 1993; it entered into force in April 1997, at which time the OPCW was inaugurated. Governed by an Executive Council, comprising representatives of 41 States Parties, elected on a regional basis; undertakes mandatory inspections of member states party to the Convention. Provisional 1999 budget: US $69m. Dir-Gen. JOSÉ MAURICIO BUSTANI (Brazil).

Organization of Solidarity of the Peoples of Africa, Asia and Latin America (Organización de Solidaridad de los Pueblos de Africa, Asia y América Latina—OSPAAAL): Apdo 4224 y 6130, Calle C No 670 esq. 29, Vedado, Havana 10400, Cuba; tel. (7) 30-5136; fax (7) 33-3985; f. 1966 at the first Conference of Solidarity of the Peoples of Africa, Asia and Latin America, to unite, co-ordinate and encourage national liberation movements in the three continents, to oppose foreign intervention in the affairs of sovereign states, colonial and neo-colonial practices, and to fight against racialism and all forms of racial discrimination; favours the establishment of a new international economic order. Mems: organizations in Angola, Republic of the Congo, Guatemala, Guinea, Democratic People's Republic of Korea, Palestine, Puerto Rico, South Africa, Syria and Viet Nam. Sec.-Gen. Dr RAMÓN PEZ FERRO. Publ. *Tricontinental* (quarterly).

Organization of the Cooperatives of America (Organización de las Cooperativas de América): Apdo postal 241263, Carrera 11, No. 86-32 Of. 101, Santafé de Bogotá, DC, Colombia; tel. (1) 610-3296; fax (1) 610-1912; f. 1963 for improving socio-economic, cultural and moral conditions through the use of the co-operative system; works in every country of the continent; regional offices sponsor plans of activities based on the most pressing needs and special conditions of individual countries. Mems: organizations in 23 countries and territories. Pres. Dr ARMANDO TOVAR PARADA; Exec. Sec. Dr CARLOS JULIO PINEDA. Publs *OCA News* (monthly), *América Cooperativa* (3 a year).

Parliamentary Association for Euro-Arab Co-operation: 21 rue de la Tourelle, 1040 Brussels, Belgium; tel. (2) 231-13-00; fax (2) 231-06-46; e-mail paeac@medea.be; internet www.medea.be; f. 1974 as an association of 650 parliamentarians of all parties from the national parliaments of the Council of Europe countries and from the European Parliament, to promote friendship and co-operation between Europe and the Arab world; Executive Committee holds annual joint meetings with Arab Inter-Parliamentary Union; represented in Council of Europe, Western European Union and European Parliament; works for the progress of the Euro-Arab Dialogue and a settlement in the Middle East which takes into account the national rights of the Palestinian people. Joint Chair. ROSELYNE BACHELOT (France), HENNING GJELLEROD (Denmark); Sec.-Gen. JEAN-MICHEL DUMONT (Belgium). Publs *Information Bulletin* (quarterly), *Euro-Arab and Mediterranean Political Fact Sheets* (2 a year).

Party of European Socialists: 60 rue Wiertz, 1047 Brussels, Belgium; tel. (2) 284-29-78; fax (2) 230-17-66; e-mail pes@pes.org; internet www.pes.org; f. 1974 as the Confederation of the Socialist Parties of the EC; affiliated to the Socialist International (q.v.). Mems: 21 full member parties, two associate, 17 with observer status. Chair. RUDOLF SCHARPING (Germany); Sec.-Gen. JEAN FRANÇOIS VALLIN (France).

Rio Group: f. 1987 at a meeting in Acapulco, Mexico, of eight Latin American government leaders, who agreed to establish a 'permanent mechanism for joint political action'; additional countries subsequently joined the Group (see below); holds annual summit meetings at presidential level. At the ninth presidential summit (Quito, Ecuador, September 1995) a 'Declaration of Quito' was adopted, which set out joint political objectives, including the strengthening of democracy; combating corruption, drugs-production and -trafficking and 'money laundering'; and the creation of a Latin American and Caribbean free trade area by 2005 (supporting the efforts of the various regional groupings). Opposes US legislation (the 'Helms-Burton' Act), which provides for sanctions against foreign companies that trade with Cuba; also concerned with promoting sustainable development in the region, the elimination of poverty, and economic and financial stability. The Rio Group holds annual ministerial conferences with the European Union. Mems: Argentina, Bolivia, Brazil, Chile, Colombia, Ecuador, Mexico, Panama, Paraguay, Peru, Uruguay, Venezuela.

Socialist International: Maritime House, Clapham, London, SW4 0JW, United Kingdom; tel. (20) 7627-4449; fax (20) 7720-4448; e-mail socint@gn.apc.org; internet www.gn.apc.org/socint; f. 1864; the world's oldest and largest association of political parties, grouping democratic socialist, labour and social democratic parties from every continent; provides a forum for political action, policy discussion and the exchange of ideas; works with many international organizations and trades unions (particularly members of ICFTU, q.v.); holds Congress every three years; the Council meets twice a year, and regular conferences and meetings of party leaders are also held; committees and councils on a variety of subjects and in different regions meet frequently. Mems: 66 full member parties, 25 consultative and 8 observer parties in 85 countries. There are three fraternal organizations and nine associated organizations, including: the Party of European Socialists (PES), the Group of the PES at the European Parliament and the International Federation of the

Socialist and Democratic Press (q.v.). Pres. ANTONIO GUTTERES (Portugal); Gen. Sec. LUIS AYALA (Chile); Publ. *Socialist Affairs* (quarterly).

International Falcon Movement—Socialist Educational International: 3 rue Quinaux, 1030 Brussels, Belgium; tel. (2) 215-79-27; fax (2) 245-00-83; e-mail ifm-sei@infonie.be; f. 1924 to promote international understanding, develop a sense of social responsibility and to prepare children and adolescents for democratic life; co-operates with several institutions concerned with children, youth and education. Mems: about 1m.; 62 co-operating organizations in all countries. Pres. JESSI SÖRENSEN (Denmark); Sec.-Gen. ODETTE LAMBERT (Belgium). Publs *IFM-SEI Bulletin* (quarterly), *IFM-SEI Documents*, *Flash Infos* (6 a year), *Asian Regional Bulletin, Latin American Regional Bulletin*.

International Union of Socialist Youth: 1070 Vienna, Neustiftgasse 3/13, Austria; tel. (1) 523-12-67; fax (1) 523-12-679; e-mail iusy@iusy.org; internet www.iusy.org; f. 1907 as Socialist Youth International (present name from 1946) to educate young people in the principles of free and democratic socialism and further the co-operation of democratic socialist youth organizations; conducts international meetings, symposia, etc. Mems: 134 youth and student organizations in 100 countries. Pres. ALVARO ELIZALDE SOTO; Gen. Sec. LISA PELLING. Publs *IUSY Newsletter, FWG News, IUSY—You see us in Action*.

Socialist International Women: Maritime House, Old Town, Clapham, London, SW4 0JW, United Kingdom; tel. (20) 7627-4449; fax (20) 7720-4448; e-mail socintwomen@gn.apc.org; internet socintwomen.org.uk; f. 1907 to strengthen relations between its members, to exchange experience and views, to promote the understanding among women of the aims of democratic socialism, to promote programmes to oppose any discrimination in society and to work for human rights in general and for development and peace. Mems: 131 organizations. Pres. DOLORS RENAU; Gen. Sec. MARLÈNE HAAS. Publ. *Women and Politics* (quarterly).

Stockholm International Peace Research Institute—SIPRI: Signalistgatan 9, 169 70 Solna, Sweden; tel. (8) 655-97-00; fax (8) 655-97-33; e-mail sipri@sipri.se; internet www.sipri.se; f. 1966; studies relate to international security and arms control, e.g. conflict and crisis management, peace-keeping and regional security, conventional and nuclear arms control, chemical and biological warfare, production and transfer of arms, military expenditure, etc. About 50 staff mems, half of whom are researchers. Dir Dr ADAM DANIEL ROTFELD (Poland); Chair. ROLF EKENS (Sweden). Publs *SIPRI Yearbook: Armaments, Disarmament and International Security*, monographs and research reports.

Transparency International: Otto-Suhr-Allee 97-99, 10585 Berlin, Germany; tel. (30) 3438200; fax (30) 34703912; e-mail ti@transparency.de; internet www.transparency.de; f. 1993; aims to promote governmental adoption of anti-corruption practices and accountability at all levels of the public sector; aims to ensure international business transactions conducted with integrity and without resort to corrupt practices. Formulates an annual Corruption Perception Index and a Bribe Payers Index. An International Anti-Corruption Conference is held every two years. Chair. Dr PETER EIGEN.

Trilateral Commission: 345 East 46th St, New York, NY 10017, USA; tel. (212) 661-1180; fax (212) 949-7268; e-mail admin@trilateral.org; internet www.trilateral.org; (also offices in Paris and Tokyo); f. 1973 by private citizens of western Europe, Japan and North America, to encourage closer co-operation among these regions on matters of common concern; by analysis of major issues the Commission seeks to improve public understanding of such problems, to develop and support proposals for handling them jointly, and to nurture the habit of working together in the 'trilateral' area. The Commission issues 'task force' reports on such subjects as monetary affairs, political co-operation, trade issues, the energy crisis and reform of international institutions. Mems: about 335 individuals eminent in academic life, industry, finance, labour, etc.; those currently engaged as senior government officials are excluded. Chairmen PAUL A. VOLCKER, OTTO Graf LAMBSDORFF, YOTANO KOBAYASHI; Dirs CHARLES B. HECK, PAUL REVAY, TADASHI YAMAMOTO. Publs *Task Force Reports, Triangle Papers*.

Unrepresented Nations' and Peoples' Organization—UNPO: Javastraat, 40A, 2585 AP, Netherlands; tel. (70) 360-3318; fax (70) 360-3346; e-mail unpo@unpo.nl; internet www.unpo.org; f. 1991 to provide an international forum for indigenous and other unrepresented peoples and minorities; provides training in human rights, law, diplomacy and public relations to UNPO members; provides conflict resolution services. Mems: 50 peoples and minorities. Gen.-Sec. HELEN CORBETT. Publs *UNPO News, UNPO Yearbook*.

War Resisters' International: 5 Caledonian Rd, London, N1 9DX, United Kingdom; tel. (20) 7278-4040; fax (20) 7278-0444; e-mail warresisters@gn.apc.org; internet www.gn.apc.org/warresisters; f. 1921; encourages refusal to participate in or support wars or

military service, collaborates with movements that work for peace and non-violent social change. Mems: approx. 150,000. Chair. JOANNE SHEEHAN; Sec. ROBERTA BACIC. Publ. *Peace News* (quarterly).

Women's International Democratic Federation: c/o 'Femmes solidaires', 25 rue du Charolais, 75012 Paris, France; tel. 1-40-01-90-90; fax 1-40-01-90-81; e-mail fdif@fdif.eu.org; internet www.fdif.eu.org; f. 1945 to unite women regardless of nationality, race, religion and political opinion, so that they may work together to win and defend their rights as citizens, mothers and workers, to protect children and to ensure peace and progress, democracy and national independence. Structure: Congress, Secretariat and Executive Committee. Mems: 180 organizations in 101 countries as well as individual mems. Pres. SYLVIE JAN (France); Vice-Pres. MAYADA ABBASSI (Palestine). Publs *Women of the Whole World* (6 a year), *Newsletter*.

World Council of Indigenous Peoples: 100 Argyle Ave, 2nd Floor, Ottawa, K2P 1B6, Canada; tel. (613) 230-9030; fax (613) 230-9340; f. 1975 to promote the rights of indigenous peoples and to support their cultural, social and economic development. The Council comprises representatives of indigenous organizations from five regions: North, South and Central America, Pacific-Asia and Scandinavia; a general assembly is held every three years. Pres. CONRADO JORGE VALIENTE. Publ. *WCIP Newsletter* (4–6 a year).

World Disarmament Campaign: 45–47 Blythe St, London, E2 6LN, United Kingdom; tel. (20) 7729-2523; f. 1980 to encourage governments to take positive and decisive action to end the arms race, acting on the four main commitments called for in the Final Document of the UN's First Special Session on Disarmament; aims to mobilize people of every country in a demand for multilateral disarmament, to encourage consideration of alternatives to the nuclear deterrent for ensuring world security, and to campaign for a strengthened role for the UN in these matters. Chair. Dr FRANK BARNABY, Dr TONY HART. Publ. *World Disarm!* (6 a year).

World Federalist Movement: 777 UN Plaza, New York, NY 10017, USA; tel. (212) 599-1320; fax (212) 599-1332; e-mail wfm@igc.apc.org; f. 1947 to achieve a just world order through a strengthened United Nations; to acquire for the UN the authority to make and enforce laws for peaceful settlement of disputes, and to raise revenue under limited taxing powers; to establish better international co-operation in areas of environment, development and disarmament and to promote federalism throughout the world. Mems: 25,000 in 41 countries. Pres. Sir PETER USTINOV; Exec. Dir WILLIAM R. PACE. Publ. *World Federalist News* (quarterly).

World Federation of United Nations Associations—WFUNA: c/o Palais des Nations, 1211 Geneva 10, Switzerland; tel. (22) 7330730; fax (22) 7334838; f. 1946 to encourage popular interest and participation in United Nations programmes, discussion of the role and future of the UN, and education for international understanding. Plenary Assembly meets every two years; WFUNA founded International Youth and Student Movement for the United Nations (q.v.). Mems: national associations in 80 countries. Pres. HASHIM ABDUL HALIM (India); Sec.-Gen. L. H. HORACE PERERA (Sri Lanka) (acting). Publ. *WFUNA News*.

World Peace Council: 94 rue Jean-Pierre Timbaud, 75011 Paris, France; tel. 1-40-12-09-12; fax 1-40-11-57-87; e-mail 100144.1501@compuserve.com; f. 1950 at the Second World Peace Congress, Warsaw. Principles: the prevention of nuclear war; the peaceful co-existence of the various socio-economic systems in the world; settlement of differences between nations by negotiation and agreement; complete disarmament; elimination of colonialism and racial discrimination; respect for the right of peoples to sovereignty and independence. Mems: Representatives of national organizations, groups and individuals from 140 countries, and of 30 international organizations; Executive Committee of 40 mems elected by world assembly held every 3 years. Pres. ALBERTINA SISULU; Exec. Sec. LYSIANE ALEZARD. Publ. *Peace Courier* (monthly).

Industrial and Professional Relations

See also the chapters on ICFTU, WCL and WFTU.

Arab Federation of Petroleum, Mining and Chemicals Workers: POB 5339, Tripoli, Libya; tel. (2) 608501; fax (2) 608989; f. 1961 to establish industrial relations policies and procedures for the guidance of affiliated unions; promotes establishment of trade unions in the relevant industries in countries where they do not exist. Publs *Arab Petroleum* (monthly), specialized publications and statistics.

European Association for Personnel Management: c/o CIPD, IPD House, Camp Rd, Wimbledon, London, SW19 4UX; tel. (20) 8263-3273; fax (20) 8262-3806; e-mail f.wilson@ipd.co.uk; internet www.eapm.org; f. 1962 to disseminate knowledge and information concerning the personnel function of management, to establish and maintain professional standards, to define the specific nature of personnel management within industry, commerce and the public services, and to assist in the development of national associations. Mems: 22 national associations. Pres. CHRISTOPH SCHAUB (Switzerland); Sec.-Gen. GEOFF ARMSTRONG (United Kingdom).

European Civil Service Federation: Ave d'Aderghem, 1040 Brussels, Belgium; tel. (2) 230-84-33; fax (2) 230-69-05; f. 1962 to foster the idea of a European civil service of staff of international organizations operating in western Europe or pursuing regional objectives; upholds the interests of civil service members. Mems: local cttees in 12 European countries and individuals in 66 countries. Sec.-Gen. L. RIJNOUDT. Publ. *Eurechos.*

European Construction Industry Federation: 66 ave Louise, 1050 Brussels, Belgium; tel. (2) 514-55-35; fax (2) 511-02-76; e-mail info@fiec.org; internet www.fiec.org; f. 1905 as International European Construction Federation; present name adopted 1999; Mems: 31 national employers' organizations in 24 countries. Pres. FRANCO NOBILI (Italy); Dir-Gen. ULRICH PAETZOUD. Publs *Annual Report, Construction Activity in Europe.*

European Federation of Conference Towns: POB 182, 1040 Brussels, Belgium; tel. (2) 732-69-54; fax (2) 732-58-62; e-mail efct@efct.com; internet www.caefct.com; lays down standards for conference towns; provides advice and assistance to its members and other organizations holding conferences in Europe; undertakes publicity and propaganda for promotional purposes; helps conference towns to set up national centres. Exec. Dir ALINE LEGRAND.

European Federation of Lobbying and Public Affairs (Fédération Européenne du Lobbying et Public Affairs—FELPA): rue du Trône 61, 1050 Brussels, Belgium; tel. (2) 511-74-30; fax (2) 511-12-84; aims to enhance the development and reputation of the industry; encourages professionals active in the industry to sign a code of conduct outlining the ethics and responsibilities of people involved in lobbying or public relations work with the institutions of the EU. Pres. Y. DE LESPINAY.

European Industrial Research Management Association—EIRMA: 34 rue de Bassano, 75008 Paris, France; tel. 1-53-23-83-10; fax 1-47-20-05-30; e-mail info@eirma.asso.fr; internet www.eirma.asso.fr; f. 1966 under auspices of the OECD (q.v.); a permanent body in which European science-based firms meet to consider approaches to industrial innovation, support research and development, and take joint action to improve performance in their various fields. Mems: 160 in 21 countries. Pres. LARS-GÖRAN ROSENGREN. Gen. Sec. ANDREW DEARING. Publs *Annual Report, Conference Reports, Working Group Reports, Workshop Reports.*

European Trade Union Confederation (Confédération Européenne des Syndicats): 5 blvd du Roi Albert II, 1210 Brussels, Belgium; tel. (2) 224-04-11; fax (2) 224-04-54; e-mail etuc@etuc.org; internet www.etuc.org; f. 1973; comprises 74 national trade union confederations and 15 European industrial federations in 33 European countries, representing 60m. workers; holds congress every four years (1999—Helsinki, Finland). Gen. Sec. EMILIO GABAGLIO.

Federation of International Civil Servants' Associations: Palais des Nations, 1211 Geneva 10, Switzerland; tel. (22) 917-3150; fax (22) 917-0660; e-mail ficsa@ficsa.org; f. 1952 to co-ordinate policies and activities of member associations and unions, to represent staff interests before inter-agency and legislative organs of the UN and to promote the development of an international civil service. Mems: 26 associations and unions consisting of staff of UN organizations, 2 associate mems from non-UN organizations, 25 consultative associations and 17 inter-organizational federations with observer status. Pres. BERNHARD P. GRANDJEAN; Gen. Sec. ANDRÉ J. HEITZ. Publs *Annual Report, FICSA Newsletter, FICSA Update, FICSA circulars.*

Graphical International Federation: Valeriusplein 30, 1075 BJ Amsterdam, Netherlands; tel. (20) 671-32-79; fax (20) 675-13-31; f. 1925. Mems: national federations in 15 countries, covering 100,000 workers. Pres. L. VAN HAUDT (Belgium); Sec.-Gen. R. E. VAN KESTEREN (Netherlands).

International Association of Conference Interpreters: 10 ave de Sécheron, 1202 Geneva, Switzerland; tel. (22) 9081540; fax (22) 7324151; e-mail aiic@compuserve.com; internet www.aiic.net; f. 1953 to represent professional conference interpreters, ensure the highest possible standards and protect the legitimate interests of members. Establishes criteria designed to improve the standards of training and recognizes schools meeting the required standards. Has consultative status with the UN and several of its agencies. Mems: 2,300 in 53 countries. Pres. MALICK SY (Switzerland); Exec. Sec. JOSYANE CRISTINA. Publs *Code of Professional Conduct, Yearbook* (listing interpreters), etc.

International Association of Conference Translators: 15 route des Morillons, 1218 Le Grand-Saconnex, Geneva, Switzerland; tel. (22) 7910666; fax (22) 7885644; e-mail secretariat@aitc.ch; internet www.aitc.ch; f. 1962; represents revisers, translators, précis writers and editors working for international conferences and organizations, to protect the interests of those in the profession and help maintain

high standards; establishes links with international organizations and conference organizers. Mems: 419 in 33 countries. Pres. GENEVIÈVE SÉRIOT (Switzerland); Exec. Sec. MICHEL BOUSSOMMIER (France). Publs *Directory, Bulletin.*

International Association of Crafts and Small and Medium-Sized Enterprises—IACME: c/o Centre patronal, CP 1215, 1001 Lausanne, Switzerland; tel. (21) 796-33-54; fax (21) 796-33-11; e-mail info@centrepatronal.ch; f. 1947 to defend undertakings and the freedom of enterprise within private economy, to develop training, to encourage the creation of national organizations of independent enterprises and promote international collaboration, to represent the common interests of members and to institute exchange of ideas and information. Mems: organizations in 26 countries. Chair. MARIO SECCA; Gen. Sec. JACQUES DESGRAZ.

International Association of Medical Laboratory Technologists: Adolf Fredriks Kyrkogata 11, 111 37 Stockholm, Sweden; tel. (8) 10-30-31; fax (8) 10-90-61; e-mail margareta.haag@iamlt.org; internet www.iamlt.org; f. 1954 to allow discussion of matters of common professional interest; aims to promote globally the highest standards in the delivery of care, of professional training, and ethical and professional practices; develops and promotes active professional partnerships in health care at the international level; promotes and encourages participation of members in international activities; holds international congress every second year. Mems: 180,000 in 40 countries. Pres. MARTHA HJÁLMARSDÓTTIR; Exec. Dir MARGARETA HAAG. Publs *MedTecInternational* (2 a year), *Newsletter* (6 a year).

International Association of Mutual Insurance Companies: 114 rue La Boëtie, 75008 Paris, France; tel. 1-42-25-84-86; fax 1-42-56-04-49; e-mail alsam@wanadoo.fr; f. 1963 for the establishment of good relations between its members and the protection of the general interests of private insurance based on the principle of mutuality. Mems: over 250 in 25 countries. Pres. E. J. ALDEWEIRELDT (Belgium); Sec.-Gen. A. TEMPELAERE (France). Publs *Mutuality* (2 a year), *AISAM Dictionary, Newsletter* (3 a year).

International Federation of Actors: Guild House, Upper St Martin's Lane, London, WC2H 9EG, United Kingdom; tel. (20) 7379-0900; fax (20) 7379-8260; e-mail office@fia-actors.com; internet www.fia-actors.com; f. 1952. Mems: 100 performers' unions in 70 countries. Pres. TOMAS BOLME (Sweden); Gen. Sec. KATHERINE SAND.

International Federation of Air Line Pilots' Associations: Interpilot House, Gogmore Lane, Chertsey, Surrey, KT16 9AP, United Kingdom; tel. (1932) 571711; fax (1932) 570920; e-mail admin@ifalpa.org; internet ifalpa.org; f. 1948 to aid in the establishment of fair conditions of employment; to contribute towards safety within the industry; to provide an international basis for rapid and accurate evaluation of technical and industrial aspects of the profession. Mems: 93 associations, over 100,000 pilots. Pres. Capt. R. J. MCINNIS; Exec. Dir CATHY BILL.

International Federation of Business and Professional Women: Studio 16, Cloisters Business Centre, 8 Battersea Park Rd, London, SW8 4BG, United Kingdom; tel. (20) 7738-8323; fax (20) 7622-8528; e-mail bpwihq@cscom; internet www.bpwintl.com; f. 1930 to promote interests of business and professional women and secure combined action by them. Mems: national federations, associate clubs and individual associates, totalling more than 200,000 mems in over 100 countries. Pres. SYLVIA G. PERRY; Exec. Dir JANIC BANCROFT. Publ. *BPW News International* (monthly).

International Industrial Relations Association: c/o International Labour Office, 1211 Geneva 22, Switzerland; tel. (22) 7996841; fax (22) 7998541; e-mail mennie@ilo.org; f. 1966 to encourage development of national associations of specialists, facilitate the spread of information, organize conferences, and to promote internationally planned research, through study groups and regional meetings; a World Congress is held every three years. Mems: 39 associations, 47 institutions and 1,100 individuals. Pres. Prof. MANFRED WEISS; Sec. Prof.TAYO FASHOYIN. Publs *IIRA Bulletin* (3 a year), *IIRA Membership Directory, IIRA Congress proceedings.*

International Organisation of Employers—IOE: 26 chemin de Joinville, BP 68, 1216 Cointrin/Geneva, Switzerland; tel. (22) 7981616; fax (22) 7988862; f. 1920, reorganized 1948; aims to establish and maintain contacts between members and to represent their interests at the international level; to promote free enterprise; and to assist the development of employers' organizations. General Council meets annually; there is an Executive Committee and a General Secretariat. Mems: 122 federations in 119 countries. Chair. JEAN-JACQUES OECHSLIN (France); Sec.-Gen. COSTAS KAPARTIS (Cyprus). Publ. *The Free Employer.*

International Organization of Experts—ORDINEX: 19 blvd Sébastopol, 75001 Paris, France; tel. 1-40-28-06-06; fax 1-40-28-03-13; e-mail contact@ordinex.org; internet www.ordinex.org; f. 1961 to establish co-operation between experts on an international level. Mems: 600. Pres. ALI EL KAÏBI (Tunisia); Sec.-Gen. PIERRE ROYER (France). Publ. *General Yearbook.*

Law

International Public Relations Association—IPRA: Cardinal House, 7 Wolsey Rd, Kingston-upon-Thames, KT8 9EL, United Kingdom; tel. (20) 8481-7634; fax (20) 8481-7648; e-mail iprasec@compuserve.com; internet www.ipranet.org; f. 1955 to provide for an exchange of ideas, technical knowledge and professional experience among those engaged in international public relations, and to foster the highest standards of professional competence. Mems: 750 in 73 countries. Sec.-Gen. FRANS VOORHOEVE. Publs *Newsletter* (6 a year), *Frontline 21* (quarterly), *Members' Manual* (annually).

International Society of City and Regional Planners—ISo-CaRP: Mauritskade 23, 2514 HD The Hague, Netherlands; tel. (70) 3462654; fax (70) 3617909; e-mail secretariat@isocarp.org; internet www.isocarp.org; f. 1965 to promote better planning practice through the exchange of knowledge. Holds annual international congress (2000—Mexico). Mems: 450 in 64 countries. Pres. Prof. IR MAX VAN DEN BERG (Netherlands); Sec.-Gen. Prof. Dr MILICA BAJÍC BRKOVIC (Federal Republic of Yugoslavia). Publs *News Bulletin* (quarterly), *Bulletin* (2 a year); seminar and congress reports.

International Union of Architects: 51 rue Raynouard, 75016 Paris, France; tel. 1-45-24-36-88; fax 1-45-24-02-78; e-mail uia@uia.architects.org; internet www.uia-architects.org; f. 1948; holds triennial congress. Mems: 106 countries. Pres. VASSILIS SGOUTAS (Greece); Sec.-Gen JEAN-CLAUDE RIGUET (France). Publ. *Lettre d'informations* (monthly).

Latin American Federation of Agricultural and Food Industry Workers (Federación Latinoamericana de Trabajadores Campesinos y de la Alimentación): Avda Baralt esq. Conde a Padre Cierra, Edificio Bapgel, 4°, Oficina 42, Apdo 1422, Caracas 1010A, Venezuela; tel. (2) 863-2447; fax (2) 720463; e-mail lassofeltaca@cantv.net; f. 1961 to represent the interests of agricultural workers and workers in the food and hotel industries in Latin America. Mems: national unions in 28 countries and territories. Sec.-Gen. JOSÉ LASSO. Publ. *Boletín Luchemos* (quarterly).

Nordic Industry Workers' Federation (Nordiska Industriarbetarefederationen—NIF): Olof Palmes gata 11, 5th Floor, Box 1114, 111 81 Stockholm, Sweden; tel. (8) 7868500; fax (8) 105968; e-mail henning.carlsson.nif@industrifacket.se; f. 1901; promotes collaboration between affiliates representing workers in the chemicals, energy, garment, manufacturing, mining, paper and textile sectors in Denmark, Finland, Iceland, Norway and Sweden; supports sister unions economically and in other ways in labour market conflicts. Mems: 400,000 in 17 unions. Pres. SUNE EKBÅGE (Sweden); Sec. ARNE LÖKKEN (Sweden).

Organisation of African Trade Union Unity—OATUU: POB M386, Accra, Ghana; tel. (21) 772574; fax (21) 772621; f. 1973 as a single continental trade union org., independent of international trade union organizations; has affiliates from all African trade unions. Congress, composed of four delegates from all affiliated trade union centres, meets at least every four years as supreme policy-making body; General Council, composed of one representative from all affiliated trade unions, meets annually to implement Congress decisions and to approve annual budget. Mems: trade union movements in 52 independent African countries. Sec.-Gen. HASSAN SUNMONU (Nigeria). Publ. *Voices of African Workers*.

Pan-African Employers' Confederation: c/o Mauritius Employers' Federation, Cerné House, 13 la chaussée, Port Louis, Mauritius; tel. 212-1599; fax 212-6725; e-mail mef@intnet.mu; f. 1986 to link African employers' organizations and to represent them at the UN, the ILO and the OAU. Sec.-Gen. AZAD JEETUN (Mauritius).

World Federation of Scientific Workers: 1–7 Great George St, London, SW1P 3AA, United Kingdom; tel. (20) 7222-7722; e-mail 100764.1427@compuserve.com; f. 1946 to improve the position of science and scientists, to assist in promoting international scientific co-operation and to promote the use of science for beneficial ends; studies and publicizes problems of general, nuclear, biological and chemical disarmament; surveys the position and activities of scientists. Member organizations in 37 countries, totalling over 500,000 mems. Sec.-Gen. S. DAVISON (UK). Publ. *Scientific World* (quarterly in English, Esperanto, German and Russian).

World Movement of Christian Workers—WMCW: 124 blvd du Jubilé, 1080 Brussels, Belgium; tel. (2) 421-58-40; fax (2) 421-58-49; e-mail mmtc@skynet.be; internet www.mmtc-wmcw-wbca.be; f. 1961 to unite national movements that advance the spiritual and collective well-being of workers; general assembly every four years. Mems: 47 affiliated movements in 39 countries. Sec.-Gen. NORBERT KLEIN. Publ. *Infor-WMCW*.

World Union of Professions (Union mondiale des professions libérales): 38 rue Boissière, 75116 Paris, France; tel. 1-44-05-90-15; fax 1-44-05-90-17; e-mail info@umpl.com; internet www.umpl.com; f. 1987 to represent and link members of the liberal professions. Mems: 27 national inter-professional organizations, two regional groups and 12 international federations. Pres. LUIS EDUARDO GAUTERIO GALLO; Sec.-Gen. HENRY SALMON.

Law

African Bar Association: 29/31 Obafemi Awolowo Way, Ikeja, Lagos, Nigeria (temporary address); tel. (1) 4936907; fax (1) 7752202; f. 1972; aims to uphold the rule of law, to maintain the independence of the judiciary, and to improve legal services. Pres. PETER ALA ADJETY (Ghana); Sec.-Gen. FEMI FELANA (Nigeria).

African Society of International and Comparative Law: Private Bag 520, Kairaba ave KSMD, Banjul, The Gambia; tel. 375476; fax 375469; f. 1986; promotes public education on law and civil liberties; aims to provide a legal aid and advice system in each African country, and to facilitate the exchange of information on civil liberties in Africa. Ninth annual conference: Abidjan, Côte d'Ivoire, 1997. Pres. MOHAMED BEDJAOUI; Sec. EMILE YAKPO (Ghana). Publs *Newsletter* (every 2 months), *African Journal of International and Comparative Law* (quarterly).

Asian-African Legal Consultative Committee: E-66, Vasant Marc, Vasant Vihar, New Delhi 110057, India; tel. (11) 6152251; fax (11) 6152041; e-mail aalcc@vsnl.com; internet www.aalcc.org; f. 1956 to consider legal problems referred to it by member countries and to be a forum for Afro-Asian co-operation in international law and economic relations; provides background material for conferences, prepares standard/model contract forms suited to the needs of the region; promotes arbitration as a means of settling international commercial disputes; trains officers of member states; has permanent UN observer status. Mems: 45 states. Pres. FAROUK SEIF EL-NASR (Egypt); Sec.-Gen. Dr WAFIK ZAHER KAMIL (Egypt).

Council of the Bars and Law Societies of the European Union—CCBE: 45 rue de Trèves, 1040 Brussels, Belgium; tel. (2) 234-65-10; fax (2) 234-65-11; e-mail ccbe@ccbe.org; internet www.ccbe.org; f. 1960; the officially recognized representative organization for the legal profession in the European Union and European Economic Area; liaises between the bars and law societies of member states and represents them before the European institutions; also maintains contact with other international organizations of lawyers. The CCBE's principal objective is to study all questions affecting the legal profession in member states and to harmonize professional practice. Mems: 18 delegations (representing some 500,000 European lawyers), and observers from Cyprus, the Czech Republic, Estonia, Hungary, Poland, Romania, Slovakia, Slovenia, Switzerland and Turkey. Pres. RUPERT WOLF; Sec.-Gen. VALÉRIE BAUER.

Hague Conference on Private International Law: Scheveningseweg 6, 2517 KT The Hague, Netherlands; tel (70) 3633303; fax (70) 3604867; e-mail secretariat@hcch.net; internet www.hcch.net; f. 1893 to work for the unification of the rules of private international law, Permanent Bureau f. 1955. Mems: 32 European and 15 other countries. Sec.-Gen. J. H. A. VAN LOON.

Institute of International Law (Institut de Droit international): IUHEI, 132 rue de Lausanne, CP 36, 1211 Geneva 21, Switzerland; tel. (22) 9085720; fax (22) 9085710; e-mail gerardi@hei.unige.ch; f. 1873 to promote the development of international law by endeavouring to formulate general principles in accordance with civilized ethical standards, and by giving assistance to genuine attempts at the gradual and progressive codification of international law. Mems: limited to 132 members and associates from all over the world. Sec.-Gen. CHRISTIAN DOMINICÉ (Switzerland). Publ. *Annuaire de l'Institut de Droit international*.

Inter-African Union of Lawyers: 12 rue du Prince Moulay Abdullah, Casablanca, Morocco; tel. (2) 271017; fax (2) 204686; f. 1980; holds congress every three years. Pres. ABDELAZIZ BENZAKOUR (Morocco); Sec.-Gen. FRANÇOIS XAVIER AGONDJO-OKAWE (Gabon). Publ. *L'avocat africain* (2 a year).

Inter-American Bar Association: 1211 Connecticut Ave, NW, Suite 202, Washington, DC 20036, USA; tel. (202) 466-5944; fax (202) 466-9546; internet www.uaba.org; f. 1940 to promote the rule of law and to establish and maintain relations between associations and organizations of lawyers in the Americas. Mems: 90 associations and 3,500 individuals in 27 countries. Pres. CAYETANO POVOLO; Sec.-Gen. LOUIS G. FERRAND (USA). Publs *Newsletter* (quarterly), *Conference Proceedings*.

Intergovernmental Committee of the Universal Copyright Convention: Division of Creativity, Cultural Industries and Copyright, UNESCO, 7 place de Fontenoy, 75700 Paris, France; tel. 1-45-68-47-05; fax 1-45-68-55-89; e-mail r.sye@unesco.org; established to study the application and operation of the Universal Copyright Convention and to make preparations for periodic revisions of this Convention; and to study any other problems concerning the international protection of copyright, in co-operation with various international organizations. Mems: 18 states. Publ. *Copyright Bulletin* (quarterly).

International Association for the Protection of Industrial Property—AIPPI: Tödistrasse 16, 8027 Zürich 27, Switzerland; tel. (1) 2805880; fax (1) 2805885; e-mail mail@aippi.org; internet www.aippi.org; f. 1897 to encourage legislation regarding the international protection of industrial property and the development and extension of international conventions, and to make comparative studies of existing legislation with a view to its improvement and unification; holds triennial congress. Mems: 8,200 (national and regional groups and individual mems) in 108 countries. Exec. Pres. J. MICHAEL DOWLING (Australia); Sec.-Gen. VINCENZO M. PEDRAZZINI (Switzerland). Publs *Yearbook*, reports.

International Association of Democratic Lawyers: 21 rue Brialmont, 1210 Brussels, Belgium; tel. and fax (2) 223-33-10; e-mail iadl@ist.cerist.dz; f. 1946 to facilitate contacts and exchange between lawyers, to encourage study of legal science and international law and support the democratic principles favourable to maintenance of peace and co-operation between nations; promotes the preservation of the environment; conducts research on labour law, private international law, agrarian law, etc.; consultative status with UN. Mems: in 96 countries. Pres. AMAR BENTOUMI (Algeria); Sec.-Gen. JITENDRA SHARMA (India). Publ. *International Review of Contemporary Law*, in French, English and Spanish (2 a year).

International Association of Juvenile and Family Court Magistrates: 175 Andersonstown Rd, Belfast, BT11 9EA, Northern Ireland; f. 1928 to consider questions concerning child welfare legislation and to encourage research in the field of juvenile courts and delinquency. Activities: international congress, study groups and regional meetings. Mems: 23 national associations. Pres. LUCIEN BEAULIEU (Canada).

International Association of Law Libraries: POB 5709, Washington, DC 20016-1309, USA; tel. (804) 924-3384; fax (804) 982-2232; e-mail mber@loc.gov; internet www.iall.org; f. 1959 to encourage and facilitate the work of librarians and others concerned with the bibliographic processing and administration of legal materials. Mems: 600 from more than 50 countries (personal and institutional). Pres. LARRY B. WENGER (USA); Sec. MARIE-LOUISE H. BERNAL (USA). Publ. *International Journal of Legal Information* (3 a year).

International Association of Legal Sciences (Association internationale des sciences juridiques): c/o CISS, 1 rue Miollis, 75015 Paris, France; tel. 1-45-68-25-59; fax 1-43-06-87-98; f. 1950 to promote the mutual knowledge and understanding of nations and the increase of learning by encouraging throughout the world the study of foreign legal systems and the use of the comparative method in legal science. Governed by a president and an executive committee of 11 members known as the International Committee of Comparative Law. National committees in 47 countries. Sponsored by UNESCO. Pres. Prof. WLADIMIR TOUMANOV (Russia); Sec.-Gen. M. LEKER (Israel).

International Association of Penal Law: 41 rue Bonado, 640000 Pau, France; tel. 5-59-98-08-24; fax 5-59-27-24-56; e-mail aidp-pau@infonie.fr; f. 1924 to establish collaboration between those from different countries who are working in penal law, studying criminology, and promoting the theoretical and practical development of an international penal law. Mems: 1,800. Pres. Prof. M. C. BASSIOUNI; Sec.-Gen. Dr H. EPP. Publ. *Revue Internationale de Droit Pénal* (2 a year).

International Bar Association: 271 Regent St, London, W1R 7PA, United Kingdom; tel. (20) 7629-1206; fax (20) 7409-0456; internet www.ibanet.org; f. 1947; a non-political federation of national bar associations and law societies; aims to discuss problems of professional organization and status; to advance the science of jurisprudence; to promote uniformity and definition in appropriate fields of law; to promote administration of justice under law among peoples of the world; to promote in their legal aspects the principles and aims of the United Nations. Mems: 154 member organizations in 164 countries, 17,500 individual members in 173 countries. Pres. KLAUS BÖHLHOFF (Germany); Exec. Dir PAUL HODDINOTT (UK). Publs *International Business Lawyer* (11 a year), *International Bar News* (3 a year), *International Legal Practitioner* (quarterly), *Journal of Energy and Natural Resources Law* (quarterly).

International Commission of Jurists: POB 216, 81A ave de Châtelaine, 1219 Châtelaine/Geneva, Switzerland; tel. (22) 9793800; fax (22) 9793801; e-mail info@icj.org; internet www.icj.org; f. 1952 to promote the understanding and observance of the rule of law and the protection of human rights throughout the world; maintains Centre for the Independence of Judges and Lawyers (f. 1978); contributes to the elaboration of international human rights instruments and their adoption and implementation by governments. Mems: 81 sections and affiliates. Pres. Justice CLAIRE L'HEUREUX-DUBÉ (Canada); Sec.-Gen. LOUISE DOSWALD-BECK. Publs *CIJL Yearbook, The Review, ICJ Newsletter*, special reports.

International Commission on Civil Status: 3 place Arnold, 67000 Strasbourg, France; e-mail ciec-sg@ciec1.org; internet www.ciec1.org; f. 1950 for the establishment and presentation of legislative documentation relating to the rights of individuals, and research on means of simplifying the judicial and technical administration concerning civil status. Mems: governments of Austria, Belgium, Croatia, France, Germany, Greece, Hungary, Italy, Luxembourg, Netherlands, Poland, Portugal, Spain, Switzerland, Turkey,

United Kingdom. Pres. B. VERSCHRAEGEN (Belgium); Sec.-Gen. P. LAGARDE (France).

International Copyright Society: 81667 Munich, Rosenheimer Strasse 11, Germany; tel. (89) 4800300; fax (89) 48003969; f. 1954 to enquire scientifically into the natural rights of the author and to put the knowledge obtained to practical application all over the world, in particular in the field of legislation. Mems: 393 individuals and corresponding organizations in 52 countries. Pres. Prof. Dr REINHOLD KREILE; Gen. Sec. Dr MARTIN VOGEL. Publs *Schriftenreihe* (61 vols), *Yearbook*.

International Council of Environmental Law: 53113 Bonn, Adenauerallee 214, Germany; tel. (228) 2692240; fax (228) 2692250; e-mail 100651.317@compuserve.com; f. 1969 to exchange information and expertise on legal, administrative and policy aspects of environmental questions. Exec. Governors Dr WOLFGANG BURHENNE, Dr ABDULBAR AL-GAIN. Publs *Directory, References, Environmental Policy and Law, International Environmental Law—Multilateral Treaties*, etc.

International Criminal Police Organization—INTERPOL: BP 6041, 69411 Lyon Cédex 06, France; tel. 4-72-44-70-00; fax 4-72-44-71-63; internet www.interpol.int; f. 1923, reconstituted 1946; aims to promote and ensure the widest possible mutual assistance between police forces within the limits of laws existing in different countries, to establish and develop all institutions likely to contribute to the prevention and suppression of ordinary law crimes; co-ordinates activities of police authorities of member states in international affairs, centralizes records and information regarding international criminals; operates a telecommunications network of 176 stations. The General Assembly is held annually. Mems: official bodies of 177 countries. Sec.-Gen. RAYMOND E. KENDALL (United Kingdom). Publs *International Criminal Police Review* (6 a year), *International Crime Statistics, Stolen Works of Art* (CD rom), *Interpol Guide to Vehicle Registration Documents* (annually).

International Customs Tariffs Bureau: 38 rue de l'Association, 1000 Brussels, Belgium; tel. (2) 501-87-74; fax (2) 218-30-25; e-mail bitd@euronet.be; internet www.bitd.org; the executive instrument of the International Union for the Publication of Customs Tariffs; f. 1890, to translate and publish all customs tariffs in five languages—English, French, German, Italian, Spanish. Mems: 71. Pres. JAN DE BOCK (Belgium); Dir DAVID DAVIES (UK). Publs *International Customs Journal, Annual Report*.

International Development Law Institute: Via di San Sebastianello 16, 00187 Rome, Italy; tel. (06) 6979261; fax (06) 6781946; e-mail idli@idli.org; internet www.idli.org; f. 1983; designs and conducts courses and seminars for lawyers, legal advisors and judges from developing countries, central and eastern Europe and the former USSR; also provides in-country training workshops; training programme addresses legal skills, international commercial law, economic law reform, governance and the role of the judiciary. Dir-Gen. WILLIAM T. LORIS.

International Federation for European Law—FIDE: Via Nicolò Tartaglia 5, 00197 Rome, Italy; fax (06) 8080731; f. 1961 to advance studies on European law among members of the European Community by co-ordinating activities of member societies and by organizing conferences every two years. Mems: 12 national associations. Pres. FRANCESCO CAPOTORIL; Sec.-Gen. Prof. P.-C. MÜLLER-GRAFF.

International Federation of Senior Police Officers: 26 rue Cambacères, 75008 Paris, France; tel. 1-49-27-40-67; fax 1-49-24-01-13; f. 1950 to unite policemen of different nationalities, adopting the general principle that prevention should prevail over repression, and that the citizen should be convinced of the protective role of the police; seeks to develop methods, and studies problems of traffic police. Set up International Centre of Crime and Accident Prevention, 1976. Established International Association against Counterfeiting, 1994. Mems: 34 national organizations. Sec.-Gen. JEAN-PIERRE HAVRIN (France). Publ. *International Police Information* (every 3 months, French, German and English).

International Institute for the Unification of Private Law—UNIDROIT: Via Panisperna 28, 00184 Rome, Italy; tel. (06) 696211; fax (06) 69941394; e-mail unidroit.rome@unidroit.org; internet www.unidroit.org; f. 1926 to undertake studies of comparative law, to prepare for the establishment of uniform legislation, to prepare drafts of international agreements on private law and to organize conferences and publish works on such subjects; holds international congresses on private law and meetings of organizations concerned with the unification of law; library of 215,000 vols. Mems: governments of 58 countries. Pres. LUIGI FERRARI BRAVO (Italy); Sec.-Gen. Prof. Dr HERBERT KRONKE (Germany). Publs *Uniform Law Review* (quarterly), *Digest of Legal Activities of International Organizations*, etc.

International Institute of Space Law—IISL: 3–5 rue Mario Nikis, 75015 Paris, France; tel. 1-45-67-42-60; fax 1-42-73-21-20; e-mail rtmasson@cyberway.com.sg; internet www.iafastro.com; f. 1959 at the XI Congress of the International Astronautical Federation; organizes annual Space Law colloquium; studies juridical and sociological aspects of astronautics and makes awards. Mems: individuals from many countries. Pres. NANDARI JASENTULYIANA (acting). Publs *Proceedings of Annual Colloquium on Space Law, Survey of Teaching of Space Law in the World*.

International Juridical Institute: Permanent Office for the Supply of International Legal Information, Spui 186, 2511 BW, The Hague, Netherlands; tel. (70) 3460974; fax (70) 3625235; e-mail iji@worldonline.nl; f.1918 to supply information on any matter of international interest, not being of a secret nature, respecting international, municipal and foreign law and the application thereof. Pres. A. V. M. STRUYCKEN; Dir A. L. G. A. STILLE.

International Law Association: Charles Clore House, 17 Russell Sq., London, WC1B 5DR, United Kingdom; tel. (20) 7323-2978; fax (20) 7323-3580; e-mail secretariat@ila-hq.org; internet www.ila-hq.org; f. 1873 for the study and advancement of international law, public and private; the promotion of international understanding and goodwill. Mems: 4,000 in 51 regional branches; 25 international cttees. Pres. Prof. HUNGDAH CHIU (Taiwan); Chair. Exec. Council Lord SLYNN OF HADLEY (UK); Sec.-Gen. DAVID J. C. WYLD (UK).

International Maritime Committee (Comité Maritime International): Markgravestraat 9, 2000 Antwerp, Belgium; tel. (3) 227-35-26; fax (3) 227-35-28; e-mail admin@cmi-imc.org; f. 1897 to contribute to the unification of maritime law by means of conferences, publications, etc. and to encourage the creation of national associations; work includes drafting of conventions on collisions at sea, salvage and assistance at sea, limitation of shipowners' liability, maritime mortgages, etc. Mems: national associations in 50 countries. Pres. PATRICK GRIGGS (UK). Publs *CMI Newsletter, Year Book*.

International Nuclear Law Association: 29 sq. de Meeûs, 1000 Brussels, Belgium; tel. (2) 547-58-41; fax (2) 503-04-40; e-mail aidn.inla@skynet.be; f. 1972 to promote international studies of legal problems related to the peaceful use of nuclear energy; holds conference every two years. Mems: 500 in 30 countries. Sec.-Gen. V. VERBRAEKEN.

International Penal and Penitentiary Foundation: c/o Dr K. Hobe, Bundesministerium der Justiz, 10104 Berlin, Germany; tel. (30) 20259226; fax (30) 20259525; f. 1951 to encourage studies in the field of prevention of crime and treatment of delinquents. Mems in 23 countries (membership limited to three people from each country) and corresponding mems. Pres. JORGE DE FIGUEIREDO DIAS (Portugal); Sec.-Gen. KONRAD HOBE (Germany).

International Police Association—IPA: 1 Fox Rd, West Bridgford, Nottingham, NG2 6AJ, United Kingdom; tel. (115) 945-5985; fax (115) 982-2578; e-mail isg@ipa-iac.org; internet www.ipa-iac.org; f. 1950 to exchange professional information, create ties of friendship between all sections of police service, organize group travel, studies, etc. Mems: 291,000 in more than 58 countries. International Sec.-Gen. A. F. CARTER.

International Society for Labour Law and Social Security: CP 500, 1211 Geneva 22, Switzerland; tel. (22) 7996343; fax (22) 7998542; e-mail servaisjm@ilo.org; internet www.ilo.org/isllss; f. 1958 to encourage collaboration between specialists; holds World Congress every three years as well as irregular regional congresses (Europe, Africa, Asia and Americas). Mems: 66 national associations of labour law officers. Pres. Prof. ROGER BLANPAIN (Belgium); Sec.-Gen. J.-M. SERVAIS (Belgium).

International Union of Latin Notaries (Unión Internacional del Notariado Latino): Via Locatelli 5, 20124 Milan, Italy; f. 1948 to study and standardize notarial legislation and promote the progress, stability and advancement of the Latin notarial system. Mems: organizations and individuals in 68 countries. Sec. EMANUELE FERRARI. Publ. *Revista Internacional del Notariado* (quarterly), *Notarius International*.

Law Association for Asia and the Pacific—LAWASIA: GPO Box 3275, NT House, 11th Floor, 22 Mitchell St, Darwin, Northern Territory 0800, Australia; tel. (8) 8946-9500; fax (8) 8946-9505; e-mail lawasia@lawasia.asn.au; internet lawasia.asn.au; f. 1966; provides an international, professional network for lawyers to update, reform and develop law within the region; comprises five Sections and 21 Standing Committees in Business Law and General Practice areas which organize speciality conferences. Also holds a biennial conference (2001: Christchurch, New Zealand). Mems: national orgs in 23 countries; 2,500 mems in 55 countries. Sec.-Gen. (acting) JANET NEVILLE (Australia). Publs *Directory* (annually), *LAWASIA Update* (quarterly), *Directory* (annually), *Journal* (annually).

Permanent Court of Arbitration: Peace Palace, Carnegieplein 2, 2517 KJ The Hague, Netherlands; tel. (70) 3024165; fax (70) 3024167; e-mail bureau@pca-cpa.org; internet www.pca-cpa.org; f. by the Convention for the Pacific Settlement of International Disputes (1899, 1907) to enable immediate recourse to be made to arbitration for international disputes which cannot be settled by diplomacy, to facilitate the solution of disputes by international inquiry and conciliation commissions. Mems: governments of 89 countries. Sec.-Gen. TJACO VAN DEN HOUT (Netherlands).

Society of Comparative Legislation: 28 rue Saint-Guillaume, 75007 Paris, France; tel. 1-44-39-86-23; fax 1-44-39-86-28; e-mail slc@sky.fr; internet www.legiscompare.com; f. 1869 to study and compare laws of different countries, and to investigate practical means of improving the various branches of legislation. Mems: 600 in 48 countries. Pres. GUY CANIVET (France); Sec.-Gen. MARIE-ANNE GALLOT LE LORIER (France). Publ. *Revue Internationale de Droit Comparé* (quarterly).

Union Internationale des Avocats (International Association of Lawyers): 25 rue du Jour, 75001 Paris, France; tel. 1-44-88-55-66; fax 1-44-88-55-77; e-mail uiacentre@wanadoo.fr; internet www.uianet.org; f. 1927 to promote the independence and freedom of lawyers, and defend their ethical and material interests on an international level; to contribute to the development of international order based on law. Mems: 250 asscns and 3,000 lawyers in over 120 countries. Pres. MIGUEL ESTRADA SAMANO (Mexico); Exec. Dir MARIE-PAUL RICHARD.

Union of Arab Jurists: POB 6026, Al-Mansour, Baghdad, Iraq; tel. (1) 8840051; fax (1) 8849973; f. 1975 to facilitate contacts between Arab lawyers, to safeguard the Arab legislative and judicial heritage; to encourage the study of Islamic jurisprudence; and to defend human rights. Mems: national jurists asscns in 15 countries. Sec.-Gen. SHIBIB LAZIM AL-MALIKI. Publ. *Al-Hukuki al-Arabi* (Arab Jurist).

Union of International Associations: 40 rue Washington, 1050 Brussels, Belgium; tel. (2) 640-41-09; fax (2) 643-61-99; e-mail uia@uia.be; internet www.uia.org/; f. 1907, present title adopted 1910; aims to facilitate the evolution of the activities of the world-wide network of non-profit organizations, especially non-governmental and voluntary associations; collects information on such organizations and makes this information available; promotes research on the legal, administrative and other problems common to these associations. Mems: 200 in 54 countries. Sec.-Gen. JACQUES RAEYMAECKERS (Belgium). Publs *Transnational Associations* (6 a year), *International Congress Calendar* (quarterly), *Yearbook of International Organizations, International Organization Participation* (annually), *Global Action Network* (annually), *Encyclopedia of World Problems and Human Potential, Documents for the Study of International Non-Governmental Relations, International Congress Science* series, *International Association Statutes* series, *Who's Who in International Organizations*.

World Jurist Association—WJA: 1000 Connecticut Ave, NW, Suite 202, Washington, DC 20036, USA; tel. (202) 466-5428; fax (202) 452-8540; e-mail wja@worldjurist.org; internet www.worldjurist.org; f. 1963; promotes the continued development of international law and legal maintenance of world order; holds biennial world conferences, World Law Day, demonstration trials; organizes research programmes. Mems: lawyers, jurists and legal scholars in 155 countries. Pres. DANIEL J. MONACO (USA); Exec. Vice-Pres. MARGARETHA M. HENNEBERRY (USA). Publs *The World Jurist* (English, every 2 months), Research Reports, *Law and Judicial Systems of Nations,* 3rd revised edn (directory), *World Legal Directory, Law / Technology* (quarterly), *World Law Review* Vols I–V (World Conference Proceedings), *The Chief Justices and Judges of the Supreme Courts of Nations* (directory), etc.

World Association of Judges—WAJ: 1000 Connecticut Ave, NW, Suite 202, Washington, DC 20036, USA; tel. (202) 466-5428; fax (202) 452-8540; e-mail wja@worldjurist.org; f. 1966 to advance the administration of judicial justice through co-operation and communication among ranking jurists of all countries. Pres. Prince BOLA AJIBOLA (Nigeria).

World Association of Law Professors—WALP: 1000 Connecticut Ave, NW, Suite 202, Washington, DC 20036, USA; tel. (202) 466-5428; fax (202) 452-8540; e-mail wja@worldjurist.org; internet www.worldjurist.org; f. 1975 to improve scholarship and education in dealing with matters related to international law. Pres. SERAFIN V. C. GUINGONA (Philippines).

World Association of Lawyers—WAL: 1000 Connecticut Ave, NW, Suite 202, Washington, DC 20036, USA; tel. (202) 466-5428; fax (202) 452-8540; e-mail wja@worldjurist.org; internet www.worldjurist.org; f. 1975 to develop international law and improve lawyers' effectiveness in dealing with it. Pres. JACK STREETER (USA).

Medicine and Health

Council for International Organizations of Medical Sciences—CIOMS: c/o WHO, ave Appia, 1211 Geneva 27, Switzerland; tel. (22) 7913467; fax (22) 7913111; e-mail cioms@who.ch; internet www.cioms.ch; f. 1949; general assembly every three years. Mems: 67 organizations. Pres. Prof. JOHN H. BRYANT; Sec.-Gen. Prof. J. E. IDÁNPÁÁN-HEIKKILÄ. Publs *Reports on Drug Development and Use, Proceedings of CIOMS Conferences, International Nomenclature of Diseases*.

MEMBERS OF CIOMS

Members of CIOMS include the following:

FDI World Dental Federation: 7 Carlisle St, London, W1V 5RG, United Kingdom; tel. (20) 7935-7852; fax (20) 7486-0183; internet www.fdi.org.uk; f. 1900. Mems: 129 national dental associations and 29 affiliates. Pres. Dr Katsuo Tsurumaki (Japan); Exec. Dir Dr P. A. Zillén (Sweden). Publs *International Dental Journal* (every 2 months) and *FDI World* (every 2 months).

International Association for the Study of the Liver: c/o Prof. June W. Halliday, Queensland Institute of Medical Research, The Bancroft Centre, PO Royal Brisbane Hospital, Brisbane, Australia 4029; tel. (7) 3362-0373; fax (7) 3362-0191; e-mail jhallid@tpgi.com.au; internet www.powerup.com.au/~iasl; Pres. Dr John L. Gollan; Sec. Prof. June W. Halliday.

International Association of Allergology and Clinical Immunology: Health Science Center, State Univ. of New York at Stony Brook, Stony Brook, NY 11794, USA; tel. (414) 276-6445; fax (414) 276-3349; f. 1945 to further work in the educational, research and practical medical aspects of allergic and immunological diseases; 1997 Congress: Cancun, Mexico. Mems: 42 national societies. Pres. Albert Oehling (Spain); Sec.-Gen. Allen Kaplan (USA); Exec. Sec. R. Iber (USA). Publ. *Allergy and Clinical Immunology News* (6 a year).

International College of Surgeons: 1516 N. Lake Shore Drive, Chicago, IL 60610, USA; tel. (312) 642-3555; fax (312) 787-1624; e-mail info@icsglobal.org; internet www.icsglobal.org; f. 1935, as a world-wide federation of surgeons and surgical specialists for the advancement of the art and science of surgery, to create a common bond among the surgeons of all nations and promote the highest standards of surgery without regard to nationality, creed, or colour; sends teams of surgeons to developing countries to teach local surgeons; provides research and scholarship grants, organizes surgical congresses around the world; manages the International Museum of Surgical Science in Chicago. Mems: about 10,000 in 112 countries. Pres. Prof. Chun-Jean Lee (Taiwan); Exec. Dir Max Downham (USA). Publ. *International Surgery* (quarterly).

International Diabetes Federation: 1 rue Defacqz, 1000 Brussels, Belgium; tel. (2) 538-55-11; fax (2) 538-51-14; e-mail idf@idf.org; internet www.idf.org; f. 1949 to help in the collection and dissemination of information regarding diabetes and to improve the welfare of people suffering from that disease. Mems: 175 assocns in 138 countries. Pres. Sir George Alberti; Exec. Dir Marta Levy. Publs *Diabetes Voice, Bulletin of the IDF* (quarterly).

International Federation of Clinical Neurophysiology: c/o Prof. G. Caruso, Clinica Neurologica, Univ. di Napoli 'Federico II', Via S. Panini 5, 80131 Naples, Italy; tel. (081) 746-3793; fax (081) 546-9861; f. 1949 to attain the highest level of knowledge in the field of electro-encephalography and clinical neurophysiology in all the countries of the world. Mems: 48 organizations. Pres. Prof. Marc Nuwer; Sec. Prof. Hiroshi Shibasaki. Publs *The EEG Journal* (monthly), *Evoked Potentials* (every 2 months), *EMG and Motor Control* (every 2 months).

International Federation of Oto-Rhino-Laryngological Societies: Oosterveldlaan 24, 2610 Wilrijk, Belgium; tel. and fax (3) 443-36-11; e-mail ifos@uia.ua.ac.be; internet www.ifosworld.org; f. 1965 to initiate and support programmes to protect hearing and prevent hearing impairment; Congresses every four years. Pres. G. J. McCafferty (Australia); Sec.-Gen. P. W. Alberti. Publ. *IFOS Newsletter* (quarterly).

International Federation of Surgical Colleges: c/o Prof. S. W. A. Gunn, La Panetiere, 1279 Bogis-Bossey, Switzerland; tel. (22) 7762161; fax (22) 7766417; e-mail muldoon@mail.med.upenn.edu; f. 1958 to encourage high standards in surgical training; co-operates with the World Health Organization in developing countries; conducts international symposia; receives volunteers to serve as surgical teachers in developing countries; provides journals and text books for needy medical schools; offers travel grants. Mems: colleges or associations in 77 countries, and 420 individual associates. Pres. Prof. Jonathan Meakins (Canada); Hon. Sec. Prof. S. W. A. Gunn. Publ. *World Journal of Surgery*.

International League of Associations for Rheumatoloy: c/o Dr J. Sergent, Chief Medical Officer, Vanderbilt Univ., 3810 Nashville, TN 37232-5545, USA; tel. (615) 343-9324; fax (615) 343-6478; f. 1927 to promote international co-operation for the study and control of rheumatic diseases; to encourage the foundation of national leagues against rheumatism; to organize regular international congresses and to act as a connecting link between national leagues and international organizations. Mems: 13,000. Pres. Dr Roberto Arinoviche (Chile); Sec.-Gen. Dr John Sergent (USA). Publs *Annals of the Rheumatic Diseases* (in the UK), *Revue du Rhumatisme* (in France), *Reumatismo* (in Italy), *Arthritis and Rheumatism* (in the USA), etc.

International Leprosy Association (ILA): c/o ALM, 1 ALM Way, Greenville, SC 29601, USA; tel. (864) 271-7040; fax (864) 271-7062; e-mail amlep@leprosy.org; f. 1931 to promote international co-operation in work on leprosy, from which some 1m. people still suffer; holds congress every five years (2002: Brazil). Pres. Dr Yo Yuasa (Japan); Sec. Dr Pieter Feenstra (Netherlands). Publ. *International Journal of Leprosy and Other Mycobacterial Diseases* (quarterly).

International Pediatric Association: c/o Univ. of Rochester School of Medicine and Dentistry, Dept. of Pediatrics (Rm 4-8104), 601 Elmwood, Rochester NY 14642-8777, USA; tel. (716) 275-0225; fax (716) 273-1038; f. 1912; holds triennial congresses and regional and national workshops. Mems: 135 national paediatric societies in 131 countries, 9 regional affiliate societies, 9 paediatric specialty societies. Pres. Prof. Gavin C. Arneil (United Kingdom); Exec. Dir Dr Robert J. Haggerty. Publ. *International Child Health* (quarterly).

International Rhinologic Society: c/o Prof. Clement, ENT-Dept, AZ-VUB, Laarbeeklaan 101, 1090 Brussels, Belgium; tel. (2) 477-60-02; fax (2) 477-64-23; e-mail knoctp@az.vub.ac.be; f. 1965; holds congress every four years. Pres. IY. Park (Republic of Korea); Sec. Prof. P. A. R. Clement (Belgium). Publ. *Rhinology*.

International Society of Audiology: University Hospital Rotterdam, Audiological Centre, Molewaterplein 40, 3015 GD Rotterdam, Netherlands; tel. (10) 463-4586; fax (10) 463-3102; e-mail verschuure@kno.fgg.eur.nl; f. 1952. Mems: 300 individuals. Pres. Prof. G. Mencher; Gen. Sec. Dr J. Verschuure. Publ. *Audiology* (every 2 months).

International Society of Dermatopathology: 1398 Semoran Blvd, Suite 102, Casselberry, FL 32707, USA; tel. (407) 678-5563; e-mail isdpoffice@aol.com; f. 1958; holds quinquennial congress. Pres. Dr Jorge Sanchez; Sec. Dr Lorenzo Cerroni.

International Society of Internal Medicine: Dept. of Medicine, Regionalspital, 4900 Langenthal, Switzerland; tel. (62) 9163102; fax (62) 9164155; e-mail r.streuli@sro.ch; internet www.acponline.org/isim; f. 1948 to encourage research and education in internal medicine. Mems: 51 national societies, 3,000 individuals in 54 countries. Congresses: Kyoto, Japan 2002; Granada, Spain 2004. Pres. Prof. Josef E. Johnson (USA); Sec. Prof. Rolf A. Streuli (Switzerland).

International Society of Physical and Rehabilitation Medicine: c/o Dr J. Jimenez, 600 University Ave, Rm 215, Toronto, M5G 1XJ, Canada; f. 1999 by merger of International Federation of Physical Medicine and Rehabilitation (f. 1952) and International Rehabilitation Medicine Association (f. 1968); World Congress to be held in Amsterdam, the Netherlands, in 2001. Mems in 68 countries.

International Union against Cancer: 3 rue du Conseil Général, 1205 Geneva, Switzerland; tel. (22) 8091811; fax (22) 8091810; e-mail info@uicc.org; internet www.uicc.org; f. 1933 to promote on an international level the campaign against cancer in its research, therapeutic and preventive aspects; organizes International Cancer Congress every four years; administers the American Cancer Society UICC International Fellowships for Beginning Investigators (ACSBI), the Astrzeneco and Novartis UICC Translational Cancer Research Fellowships (TCRP), the UICC International Cancer Technology Transfer Fellowships (ICRETT), the Yamagiwa-Yoshida Memorial UICC International Cancer Study Grants (YY), the Trish Greene UICC International Oncology Nursing Fellowships (IONF), the UICC Asia-Pacific Cancer Society Training Grants (APCASOT), and the Latin America UICC COPES Training and Education Fellowship (LACTEF); conducts worldwide programmes of campaign organization, public education and patient support, detection and diagnosis, epidemiology and prevention, professional education, tobacco and cancer, treatment of cancer and tumour biology. Mems: voluntary national organizations, private or public cancer research and treatment organizations and institutes and governmental agencies in more than 80 countries. Pres. Dr E. Robinson (Israel); Sec.-Gen. Dr S. Kvinnsland (Norway); Exec. Dir I. Mortarol(Switzerland). Publs *UICC International Directory of Cancer Institutes and Organizations* (electronic version), *International Journal of Cancer* (36 a year), *UICC News* (quarterly), *International Calendar of Meetings on Cancer* (2 a year).

Latin American Association of National Academies of Medicine: Col 7 No 60–15, Santafé de Bogotà, Colombia; tel. (1) 2493122; fax (1) 2128670; f. 1967. Mems: nine national Academies. Pres. Dr Plutarco Naranjo (Peru); Sec. Dr Alberto Cárdenas-Escovar (Colombia).

Medical Women's International Association: 44141 Dortmund, Wilhelm-Brand-Str.3, Germany; e-mail mwia@aol.com; internet members.aol.com/mwia/index.htm; f. 1919 to facilitate contacts between medical women and to encourage their co-operation in matters connected with international health problems. Mems: national associations in 43 countries, and individuals. Pres. Shelley Ross (Canada); Sec.-Gen. Dr Waltraud Diekhaus (Germany). Publ. *MWIA UPDATE* (3 a year).

Organisation panafricaine de lutte contre le SIDA—OPALS: 15/21 rue de L'Ecole de Médecine, 75006 Paris, France; tel. 1-43-26-72-28; fax 1-43-29-70-93; f. 1988; disseminates information relating to the treatment and prevention of AIDS; provides training of medical personnel; promotes co-operation between African medical centres and specialized centres in the USA and Europe. Publ. *OPALS Liaison*.

World Federation for Medical Education: University of Edinburgh Centre for Medical Education, 11 Hill Square, Edinburgh, EH8 9DR, United Kingdom; tel. (131) 650-6209; fax (131) 650-6537; f. 1972; promotes and integrates medical education world-wide; links regional and international associations, and has official relations with WHO, UNICEF, UNESCO, UNDP and the World Bank. Pres. Prof. H. J. WALTON.

World Federation of Associations of Paediatric Surgeons: c/o Prof. J. Boix-Ochoa, Clinica Infantil 'Vall d'Hebrón', Departamento de Cirugía Pediátrica, Valle de Hebrón, s/n, Barcelona 08035, Spain; f. 1974. Mems: 50 associations. Pres. Prof. W. MAIER; Sec. Prof. J. BOIX-OCHOA.

World Federation of Neurology: 12 Chandos St, London, W1M 9DE, United Kingdom; tel. (20) 7323-4011; fax (20) 7323-4012; e-mail wfnlondon@aol.com; f. 1955 as International Neurological Congress, present title adopted 1957. Aims to assemble members of various congresses associated with neurology, and organize co-operation of neurological researchers. Organizes Congress every four years. Mems: 23,000 in 70 countries. Pres. Dr J. F. TOOLE (USA); Sec.-Treas. Dr R. GODWIN-AUSTEN (UK); Administrator K. M. NEWTON (UK). Publs *Journal of the Neurological Sciences, World Neurology* (quarterly).

World Heart Federation: 34 rue de l'Athénée, CP 117, 1211 Geneva 12, Switzerland; tel. (22) 3476755; fax (22) 3471028; e-mail admin@worldheart.org; internet www.worldheart.org; f. 1978 as International Society and Federation of Cardiology, through merger of the International Society of Cardiology and the International Cardiology Federation; name changed as above 1998; aims to promote the study, prevention and relief of cardiovascular diseases through scientific and public education programmes and the exchange of materials between its affiliated societies and foundations and with other agencies having related interests. Organizes world congresses every four years. Mems: national cardiac societies and heart foundations in 84 countries. Pres. Dr MARIO MARANHAO (Brazil); Sec. Dr J. G. PAPP (Hungary). Publs *CVD Prevention, Heartbeat* (quarterly).

World Medical Association: 13 chemin du Levant, 01210 Ferney-Voltaire, France; tel. 4-50-40-75-75; fax 4-50-40-59-37; e-mail info@wma.net; internet www.wma.net; f. 1947 to achieve the highest international standards in all aspects of medical education and practice, to promote closer ties among doctors and national medical associations by personal contact and all other means, to study problems confronting the medical profession and to present its views to appropriate bodies. Structure: annual General Assembly and Council (meets twice a year). Mems: 73 national medical associations. Pres. Dr E. TSUBOI; Sec.-Gen. Dr DELON HUMAN (South Africa). Publ. *The World Medical Journal* (6 a year).

World Organization of Gastroenterology: II Medizinische Klinik und Poliklinik der Technischen Universität München, Ismaninger Str. 22, 81675 Munich, Germany; tel. (89) 41402250; fax (89) 41404871; f. 1958 to promote clinical and academic gastroenterological practice throughout the world, and to ensure high ethical standards. Mems in 80 countries. Pres. MEINHARD CLASSEN.

World Psychiatric Association: Mt Sinai School of Medicine, Fifth Ave and 100th St, 1093, New York, NY 10029-6574, USA; tel. (212) 241-6133; fax (212) 426-0437; e-mail wpa@dti_net; internet www.wpanet.org; f. 1961 for the exchange of information concerning the problems of mental illness and the strengthening of relations between psychiatrists in all countries; organizes World Psychiatric Congresses and regional and inter-regional scientific meetings. Mems: 150,000 psychiatrists in 100 countries. Pres. Prof. JUAN J. LÓPEZ-IBOR (Spain); Sec.-Gen. Prof JUAN ENRIQUE MEZZICH (USA).

ASSOCIATE MEMBERS OF CIOMS

Associate members of CIOMS include the following:

Asia Pacific Academy of Ophthalmology: c/o Prof. Arthur S. M. Lim, Eye Clinic Singapura, 6A Napier Rd, 02-38 Gleneagles Annexe Block Gleneagles Hospital, Singapore 258500; tel. 466-6666; fax 733-3360; f. 1956; holds congress every two years. Pres. S. SELVARAJAH (Malaysia); Sec.-Gen. Prof. ARTHUR S. M. LIM (Singapore).

International Association of Medicine and Biology of the Environment: c/o 115 rue de la Pompe, 75116 Paris, France; tel. 1-45-53-45-04; fax 1-45-53-41-75; e-mail celine.abbou@free.fr; f. 1971 with assistance from the UN Environment Programme; aims to contribute to the solution of problems caused by human influence on the environment; structure includes 13 technical commissions. Mems: individuals and organizations in 73 countries. Hon. Pres. Prof. R. DUBOS; Pres. Dr C. ABBOU.

International Committee of Military Medicine: Hôpital Militaire Reine Astrid, rue Bruyn, 1120 Brussels, Belgium; tel. (2) 264-43-48; fax (2) 264-43-67; f. 1921. Mems: official delegates from 94 countries. Pres. Dr R. SCHLÖGEL (Austria); Sec.-Gen. Col Dr J. SANABRIA (Belgium). Publ. *Revue Internationale des Services de Santé des Forces Armées* (quarterly).

International Congress on Tropical Medicine and Malaria: congress held every four years to work towards the solution of the problems concerning malaria and tropical diseases; 1996 congress: Japan. Pres. Dr S. SORNMANI.

International Council for Laboratory Animal Science—ICLAS: Canadian Council on Animal Care, 315-350 Albert Street, Ottawa, ON, K1R 1B1, Canada; tel. (613) 238-4031 ext. 28; fax (613) 238-2837; e-mail gdemers@bart.ccac.ca; internet www.iclas.org; f. 1956. Pres. Prof. STEVEN PAKES (USA); Sec.-Gen. Dr GILLES DEMERS (Canada).

International Federation of Clinical Chemistry and Laboratory Medicine: 30 rue Lionnois, 54000 Nancy, France; tel. 3-83-35-26-16; fax 3-83-32-13-22; e-mail thirion@ifccts.unancy.fr; internet www.ifcc.org; f. 1952. Mems: 78 national societies (about 33,000 individuals) and 33 corporate mems. Pres. Prof. M. MÜLLER (Austria); Sec. Dr R. BAIS (Australia). Publs *Journal* (electronic version), *Annual Report*.

International Medical Society of Paraplegia: National Spinal Injuries Centre, Stoke Mandeville Hospital, Aylesbury, Bucks, HP21 8AL, United Kingdom; tel. (1296) 315866; fax (1296) 315870; e-mail imsop@bucks.net; internet www.imsop.org.uk; Pres. Prof. T. IKATA; Hon. Sec. Prof. J. J. WYNDALE. Publ. *Spinal Cord*.

International Society of Blood Transfusion: Gateway House, Picadilly South, Manchester M60 7LP, United Kingdom; tel. (161) 236-2263; fax (161) 236-0519; f. 1937. Mems: about 1,300 in 100 countries. Pres. S. LEONG (Hong Kong); Sec.-Gen. H. GUNSON (UK). Publ. *Transfusion Today* (quarterly).

Rehabilitation International: 25 East 21st St, New York, NY 10010, USA; tel. (212) 420-1500; fax (212) 505-0871; f. 1922 to improve the lives of disabled people through the exchange of information and research on equipment and methods of assistance; organizes international conferences and co-operates with UN agencies and other international organizations. Mems: organizations in 92 countries. Pres. Dr ARTHUR O'REILLY; Sec.-Gen. SUSAN PARKER. Publs *International Rehabilitation Review, Rehabilitación* (2 a year).

Transplantation Society: c/o Dr Felix Rapaport, PR Transplant Program, University Hospital, Health Science Centre, State Univ. of New York at Stony Brook, Stony Brook, NY 11794-8192, USA; tel. (516) 444-2209; fax (516) 444-3831; e-mail rapaport@surg.som .sunysb.edu; Sec. EDUARDO A. SANTIAGO-DELPÍN.

World Federation of Associations of Clinical Toxicology Centres and Poison Control Centres: c/o Prof. Jacques Descotes, Centre anti-poisons, Pavilion N, Hôpital Edouard Herriot, 69009 Lyon, France. Pres. Prof. A. FURTADO RAHDE; Sec. Prof. JACQUES DESCOTES.

OTHER ORGANIZATIONS

Aerospace Medical Association: 320 So. Henry St, Alexandria, VA 22314, USA; tel. (703) 739-2240; fax (703) 739-9652; e-mail rrayman@asma.org; f. 1929 as Aero Medical Association; to advance the science and art of aviation and space medicine; to establish and maintain co-operation between medical and allied sciences concerned with aerospace medicine; to promote, protect, and maintain safety in aviation and astronautics. Mems: individual, constituent and corporate in 75 countries. Pres. ROGER F. LANDRY (USA); Exec. Dir RUSSELL B. RAYMAN (USA). Publ. *Aviation Space and Environmental Medicine* (monthly).

Asian-Pacific Dental Federation: 242 Tanjong Katong Rd, Singapore 437030; tel. 3453125; fax 3442116; e-mail bibi@pacific.net.sg; f. 1955 to establish closer relationship among dental associations in Asian and Pacific countries and to encourage research on dental health in the region; holds congress every year. Mems: 19 national associations. Sec.-Gen. Dr OLIVER HENNEDIGE. Publ. *Asian Dentist* (every 2 months).

Association for Paediatric Education in Europe: c/o Dr Claude Billeaud, Dept. Néonatal Médicine, Maternité-CHU Pellegrin, 33076 Bordeaux Cédex, France; fax 5-56-79-61-56; e-mail claude.billeaud-@neonata.u-bordeaux2.fr; internet www.atinternet.com/apee; f. 1970 to promote research and practice in educational methodology in paediatrics. Mems: 127 in 20 European countries. Pres. Dr JUAN BRINES (Spain); Sec.-Gen. Dr CLAUDE BILLEAUD (France).

Association of National European and Mediterranean Societies of Gastroenterology—ASNEMGE: c/o Mrs A. C. M. van Dijk-Meijer, Wolkendek 5, 3454 TG De Meern, Netherlands; tel. (30) 6667400; fax (30) 6622808; e-mail info@asnemge.org; internet www.asnemge.org; f. 1947 to facilitate the exchange of ideas between gastroenterologists and disseminate knowledge; organizes International Congress of Gastroenterology every four years. Mems in 37 countries, national societies and sections of national medical societies. Pres. Prof. COLM D'MORAÍN (Ireland); Sec. Prof. JØRGEN RASK-MADSEN (Denmark).

Balkan Medical Union: 1 rue G. Clémenceau, 70148 Bucharest, Romania; tel. (1) 6137857; fax (1) 3121570; f. 1932; studies medical problems, particularly ailments specific to the Balkan region, to promote a regional programme of public health; enables exchange of information between doctors in the region; organizes research programmes and congresses. Mems: doctors and specialists from Albania, Bulgaria, Cyprus, Greece, Moldova, Romania, Turkey and the former Yugoslav republics. Pres. Prof. NIKI AGNANTIS (Greece); Sec.-Gen. (1997–2000) Prof. Dr VASILE CÂNDEA (Romania). Publs *Archives de l'union médicale Balkanique* (quarterly), *Bulletin de l'union médicale Balkanique* (6 a year), *Annuaire*.

European Association for Cancer Research: c/o P. Saunders, Cancer Research Laboratories, University of Nottingham, University Park, Nottingham, NG7 2RD, United Kingdom; tel. and fax (115) 9515114; e-mail paul.saunders@nottingham.ac.uk; internet www.oncoweb.com/EACR; f. 1968 to facilitate contact between cancer research workers and to organize scientific meetings in Europe. Mems: over 3,000 in more than 40 countries in and outside Europe. Pres. E. OLAH; Sec. Dr HELGA ÖGMUNDSDÓTTIR (Iceland).

European Association for the Study of Diabetes: 40223 Düsseldorf, Merowingerstr. 29, Germany; tel. (211) 316738; fax (211) 3190987; e-mail easd@uni-duesseldorf.de; internet www.easd.org; f. 1965 to support research in the field of diabetes, to promote the rapid diffusion of acquired knowledge and its application; holds annual scientific meetings within Europe. Mems: 6,000 in 101 countries, not confined to Europe. Pres. Prof. J. NERUP (Denmark); Exec. Dir Dr VIKTOR JOERGENS. Publ. *Diabetologia* (13 a year).

European Association of Radiology: c/o Prof. Dr P. Vock, Institut für Diagnostische Radiologie der Universität Bern, Inselspital, 3010 Bern, Switzerland; tel. (31) 632-24-35; fax (31) 632-48-74; e-mail p.vock@insel.unibe.ch; f. 1962 to develop and co-ordinate the efforts of radiologists in Europe by promoting radiology in both biology and medicine, studying its problems, developing professional training and establishing contact between radiologists and professional, scientific and industrial organizations. Mems: national associations in 38 countries. Sec.-Gen. Prof. Dr PETER VOCK.

European Association of Social Medicine: Corso Vittorio Emanuele 92, 10121 Turin, Italy; f. 1953 to provide co-operation between national associations of preventive medicine and public health. Mems: associations in 10 countries. Pres. Dr JEAN-PAUL FOURNIER (France); Sec.-Gen. Prof. Dr ENRICO BELLI (Italy).

European Brain and Behaviour Society: c/o Dr S. J. Sara, UPMC, Institut des Neurosciences, 9 quai St Bernard, 75005 Paris, France; fax 1-44-27-32-51; e-mail ebbs@snv.jussieu.fr; internet www.ebbs-science.org; f. 1969; holds two conferences a year. Pres. WOLFROM SCHULTZ; Sec.-Gen. Dr SUSAN J. SARA. Publ. *Newsletter*.

European Federation of Internal Medicine: c/o Dr Davidson, Royal Sussex County Hospital, Eastern Rd, Brighton, United Kingdom; tel. (1273) 696955; fax (1273) 684554; internet www.efim.org; f. 1969 as European Asscn of Internal Medicine (present name adopted 1996); aims to promote internal medicine on the ethical, scientific and professional level; to bring together European specialists and establish communication between them; to organize congresses and meetings; and to provide information. Mems: 400 in 20 European countries. Sec. Dr CHRISTOPHER DAVIDSON. Publ. *European Journal of Internal Medicine* (quarterly).

European Health Management Association: Vergemount Hall, Clonskeagh, Dublin 6, Ireland; tel. (1) 2839299; fax (1) 2838653; e-mail pcberman@ehma.org; internet www.ehma.org; f. 1966; aims to improve health care in Europe by raising standards of managerial performance in the health sector; fosters co-operation between health service organizations and institutions in the field of health-care management education and training. Mems: 225 in 30 countries. Pres. Dr PETER BAECKSTRÖM; Dir PHILIP C. BERMAN. Publs *Newsletter*, *Eurobriefing* (quarterly).

European League against Rheumatism: Witikonerstr. 15, 8032 Zürich, Switzerland; tel. (1) 3839690; fax (1) 3839810; f. 1947 to co-ordinate research and treatment of rheumatic complaints, conducted by national societies; holds an annual congress. Mems in 41 countries. Exec. Sec. F. WYSS. Publ. *Annals of the Rheumatic Diseases*.

European Organization for Caries Research—ORCA: c/o Lutz Stösser, Dept of Preventive Dentistry, Dental School of Erfurt, Univ. of Jena, Nordhauser Str. 78, 99089 Erfurt, Germany; tel. (361) 7411205; e-mail stoesser@zmkh.ef.uni-jena.de; f. 1953 to promote and undertake research on dental health, encourage international contacts, and make the public aware of the importance of care of the teeth. Mems: research workers in 23 countries. Pres. (from July 2001) Prof. BIRGIT ANGMAR-MANSSON (Sweden); Sec.-Gen. Prof. L. STÖSSER (Germany).

European Orthodontic Society: Flat 20, 49 Hallam St, London, W1W 6JN, United Kingdom; tel. (20) 7935-2795; fax (20) 7323-0410; e-mail eoslondon@compuserve.com; f. 1907 (name changed in 1935) to advance the science of orthodontics and its relations with the collateral arts and sciences. Mems: 2,491 in 80 countries. Sec. Prof. J. MOSS. Publ. *European Journal of Orthodontics* (6 a year).

European Union of Medical Specialists: 20 ave de la Couronne, Brussels 1050, Belgium; tel. (2) 649-51-64; fax (2) 640-37-30; e-mail uems@skynet.be; internet www.uems.be; f. 1958 to safeguard the interests of medical specialists. Mems: two representatives each from Austria, Belgium, Denmark, Finland, France, Germany, Greece, Iceland, Ireland, Italy, Luxembourg, Netherlands, Norway, Portugal, Spain, Sweden, Switzerland, United Kingdom. Pres. Dr C. TWOMEY (Ireland); Sec.-Gen. Dr C. LEIBBRANDT (Netherlands).

Eurotransplant International Foundation: POB 2304, 2301 CH Leiden, Netherlands; tel. (71) 5795795; fax (71) 5790057; internet www.eurotransplant.nl; f. 1967; co-ordinates the exchange of organs for transplants in Austria, Belgium, Germany, Luxembourg, Netherlands and Slovenia; keeps register of almost 15,000 patients with all necessary information for matching with suitable donors in the shortest possible time; organizes transport of the organ and the transplantation; collaboration with similar organizations in western and eastern Europe. Dirs Dr B. COHEN, Dr G. G. PERSIJN.

Federation of French-Language Obstetricians and Gynaecologists (Fedération des gynécologues et obstetriciens de langue française): Clinique Baudelocque, 123 blvd de Port-Royal, 75674 Paris Cédex 14, France; tel. 1-42-34-11-43; fax 1-42-34-12-31; f. 1920 for the scientific study of phenomena having reference to obstetrics, gynaecology and reproduction in general. Mems: 1,500 in 50 countries. Pres. Prof. H. RUF (France); Gen. Sec. Prof. J. R. ZORN (France). Publ. *Journal de Gynécologie Obstétrique et Biologie de la Reproduction* (8 a year).

Federation of the European Dental Industry: 50858 Cologne, Kirchweg 2, Germany; tel. (221) 9486280; fax (221) 483428; f. 1957 to promote the interests of the dental industry. Mems: national associations in Austria, Belgium, Denmark, Germany, Italy, Netherlands, Spain, Sweden, Switzerland, United Kingdom. Pres. and Chair. Dr J. EBERLEIN (Germany); Sec. HARALD RUSSEGGER (Germany).

General Association of Municipal Health and Technical Experts: 83 ave Foch, BP 3916, 75761 Paris Cédex 16, France; tel. 1-53-70-13-53; fax 1-53-70-13-40; e-mail aghtm@aghtm.org; internet www.aghtm.org; f. 1905 to study all questions related to urban and rural health—the control of preventable diseases, disinfection, distribution and purification of drinking water, construction of drains, sewage, collection and disposal of household refuse, etc. Mems in 35 countries. Dir.-Gen. ALAIN LASALMONIE (France). Publ. *TSM-Techniques, Sciences, Méthodes* (monthly).

Inter-American Association of Sanitary and Environmental Engineering: Rua Nicolau Gagliardi 354, 05429-010 São Paulo, SP, Brazil; tel. (11) 3212-4080; fax (11)3814-2441; e-mail aidis@unisys.com.br; internet www.aidis.org.br; f. 1948 to assist the development of water supply and sanitation. Mems: 32 countries. Exec. Dir LUIZ AUGUSTO DE LIMA PONTES. Publs *Revista Ingeniería Sanitaria* (quarterly), *Desafío* (quarterly).

International Academy of Aviation and Space Medicine: 21 Antares Dr., Suite 112, Nepean, ON K2E 7T8, Canada; tel. (613) 228-9345; fax (613) 228-0242; e-mail g.takahashi@sympatico.ca; f. 1955 to facilitate international co-operation in research and teaching in the fields of aviation and space medicine. Mems: in 41 countries. Sec.-Gen. Dr GEORGE TAKAHASHI.

International Academy of Cytology: 79104 Freiburg, Burgunderstr. 1, Germany; tel. (761) 292-3801; fax (761) 292-3802; internet www.cytology-iac.org; f. 1957 to facilitate international exchange of information on specialized problems of clinical cytology, to stimulate research and to standardize terminology. Mems: 2,400. Pres. HARUBUMI KATO; Sec. VOLKER SCHNEIDER. Publs *Acta Cytologica, Analytical and Quantitative Cytology and Histology* (both every 2 months).

International Agency for the Prevention of Blindness: L. V. Prasad Eye Institute, L. V. Prasad Marg, Banjara Hills, Hyderabad 500 034, India; tel. (40) 3545389; fax (40) 3548271; e-mail IAPB_SECT/eye@lvp.lvpeye.stph.net; f. 1975; overarching organization whose objectives include advocacy and information sharing on prevention of blindness; aims to encourage the formation of national prevention of blindness committees and programmes; in official relationship with WHO. Pres. Dr HANNAH FAAL; Sec.-Gen. Dr GULLAPALLI N. RAO. Publ. *IAPB News*.

International Anatomical Congress: c/o Prof. Dr Wolfgang Kühnel, Institut für Anatomie, Medizinische Universität zu Lübeck, Ratzeburger Allee 160, 23538 Lübeck, Germany; tel. (451) 500-4030; fax (451) 500-4034; e-mail buchuel@anet.mu-luebeck.de; internet www.anet.mu-luebeck.de/anetpes.html; f. 1903; runs congresses for anatomists from all over the world to discuss research, teaching methods and terminology in the fields of gross and microscopical anatomy, histology, cytology, etc. Pres. J. ESPERENCA-PINE (Portugal); Sec.-Gen. Prof. Dr WOLFGANG KÜHNEL (Germany). Publ. *Annals of Anatomy*.

International Association for Child and Adolescent Psychiatry and Allied Professions: c/o Prof. Kosuke Yamazaki, Tokai Univ. School of Medicine, Dept of Psychiatry, Bohseidai, Isehara, Kanagawaken 259 11, Japan; tel. (463) 93-1121; fax (463) 94-5532;

Medicine and Health

f. 1937 to promote scientific research in the field of child psychiatry by collaboration with allied professions. Mems: national associations and individuals in 44 countries. Sec.-Gen. Prof. KOSUKE YAMAZAKI. Publs *The Child in the Family (Yearbook of the IACAPP), Newsletter*.

International Association for Dental Research: 1619 Duke St, Alexandria, VA 22314, USA; tel. (703) 548-0066; fax (703) 548-1883; e-mail research@iadr.com; internet www.iadr.com; f. 1920 to encourage research in dentistry and related fields, and to publish the results; holds annual meetings, triennial conferences and divisional meetings. Pres. Dr SALLY MARSHALL; Exec. Dir Dr ELI SCHWARZ.

International Association of Agricultural Medicine and Rural Health: Saku Central Hospital, 197 Usuda-machi, Minami-saku-Gun, Nagano 384-0301, Japan; tel. (267) 82-3131; fax (267) 82-7533; e-mail sakuchp@valley.or.jp; internet www.valley.ne.jp/sakuchp/; f. 1961 to study the problems of medicine in agriculture in all countries and to prevent the diseases caused by the conditions of work in agriculture. Mems: 405. Pres. Prof. J. TÉNYI (Hungary); Sec.-Gen. Dr SHOSUI MATSUSHIMA (Japan) (acting).

International Association of Applied Psychology: c/o Prof. J. M. Prieto, Colegio Oficial de Psicólogos, Cuesta de San Vicente 4, 5-28008 Madrid, Spain; e-mail iaap@cop.es; internet www.iaapsy.org; f. 1920, present title adopted in 1955; aims to establish contacts between those carrying out scientific work on applied psychology, to promote research and the adoption of measures contributing to this work. Mems: 2,200 in 94 countries. Pres. Prof. C. D. SPIELBERGER (USA); Sec.-Gen. Prof. J. M. PRIETO (Spain). Publ. *Applied Psychology: An International Review* (quarterly).

International Association of Asthmology—INTERASMA: c/o Prof. Hugo Neffen, Irigoyen Freyre 2670, 3000 Santa Fé, Argentina; tel. (42) 453-7638; fax (42) 456-9773; e-mail interasm@neffen.satlink.net; f. 1954 to advance medical knowledge of bronchial asthma and allied disorders. Mems: 1,100 in 54 countries. Pres. Prof. GAETANO MELILLO (Italy); Sec./Treas. Prof. H. NEFFEN. Publs *Journal of Investigative Allergology and Clinical Immunology* (every 2 months), *Allergy and Clinical Immunology International* (every 2 months).

International Association of Gerontology: Centre for Ageing Studies, Flinders Univ. of S. Australia, Lafter Dr., Science Park, Bedford Park, S. Australia; tel. (618) 8201-7552; fax (618) 8201-7551; e-mail iag@flinders.edu.au; internet www.cas.flinders.edu.au/iag; f. 1950 to promote research and training in all fields of gerontology and to protect interests of gerontologic societies and institutions. Holds World Congress every four years. Mems: 60 national societies in 51 countries. Pres. Prof. GARY ANDREWS; Sec.-Gen. Prof. MARY LUSZCZ. Publ. *International Newsletter* (2 a year).

International Association of Group Psychotherapy: c/o Dr E. Hopper, 11 Heath Mansions, The Mount, London, NW3 6SN, United Kingdom; f. 1954; holds congresses every three years. Mems: in 35 countries. Pres. Dr E. HOPPER; Sec. Dr C. SANDAHL (Sweden). Publs *Newsletter, Yearbook of Group Psychotherapies*.

International Association of Hydatidology: Florida 460, Piso 3, 1005 Buenos Aires, Argentina; tel. (1) 4324-4700; fax (1) 4325-8231; f. 1941. Mems: 1,200 in more than 40 countries. Pres. Dr RAÚL UGARTE ARTOLA (Uruguay); Sec.-Gen. Prof. Dr JORGE ALFREDO (Argentina). Publs *Archivos Internacionales de la Hidatidosis* (every 2 years), *Boletín de Hidatidosis* (quarterly).

International Association of Logopedics and Phoniatrics: 43 Louis de Savoie, 1110 Morges, Switzerland; fax (21) 3209300; f. 1924 to promote standards of training and research in human communication disorders in all countries, to establish information centres and communicate with kindred organizations. Mems: 125,000 in 60 societies from 54 countries. Pres. Dr EWA SÖDERPALM. Publ. *Folia Phoniatrica et Logopedica* (6 a year).

International Association of Oral and Maxillofacial Surgeons: 9700 W. Bryn Mawr, Suite 210, Rosemont, ILL 60018-5701, USA; tel. (847) 678-9370; fax (847) 678-9380; e-mail lsavler@iaoms.org; f. 1963 to advance the science and art of oral and maxillofacial surgery; organizes biennial international conference. Mems: over 3,000. Pres. JOHN HELFRICK (USA); Exec. Dir VICTOR MONCARZ (Canada). Publs *International Journal of Oral and Maxillofacial Surgery* (every 2 months), *Newsletter* (every 6 months).

International Brain Research Organization—IBRO: 51 blvd de Montmorency, 75016 Paris, France; tel. 1-46-47-92-92; fax 1-45-20-60-06; e-mail ibro@wanadoo.fr; internet www.ibro.org; f. 1958 to further all aspects of brain research. Mems: 45 corporate, 16 academic and 51,000 individual. Pres. Prof. T. N. WIESEL (USA); Sec.-Gen. Prof. A. J. AGUAYO (Canada). Publs *IBRO News, Neuroscience* (bi-monthly).

International Bronchoesophagological Society: Mayo Clinic, 13400 E. Shea Blvd, Scottsdale, AZ 85259, USA; f. 1951 to promote by all means the progress of bronchoesophagology and to provide a forum for discussion among broncho-esophagologists of various specialities; holds congress every three years. Mems: 500 in 37 countries. Exec. Sec. Dr DAVID SANDERSON.

International Bureau for Epilepsy: POB 21, 2100 AA Heemstede, Netherlands; tel. (23) 5237411; fax (23) 5470119; e-mail ibe@xs4all.nl; internet www.ibe-epilepsy.org; f. 1961 to collect and disseminate information about social and medical care for people with epilepsy; to organize international and regional meetings; to advise and answer questions on social aspects of epilepsy. Mems: 59 national epilepsy organizations. Sec.-Gen. ESPER CAVALHEIRO. Publ. *International Epilepsy News* (quarterly).

International Cell Research Organization: c/o UNESCO, SC/BES/LSC, 1 rue Miollis, 75015 Paris, France; e-mail icro@unesco.org; internet www.unesco.org/icro; f. 1962 to create, encourage and promote co-operation between scientists of different disciplines throughout the world for the advancement of fundamental knowledge of the cell, normal and abnormal; organizes every year 10 to 12 international laboratory courses on modern topics of cell and molecular biology and biotechnology for young research scientists in important research centres all over the world. Mems: 400. Pres. Prof. J. E. ALLENDE (Chile); Exec. Sec. Prof. G. N. COHEN (France).

International Centre for Diarrhoeal Disease Research (ICDDR), Bangladesh: GPO Box 128, Dhaka 1000, Bangladesh; tel. (2) 8811751; fax (2) 8823116; e-mail info@icddrb.org; internet www.icddrb.org; f. 1960; undertakes research, training and information dissemination on diarrhoeal diseases, child health and child survival, reproductive health, women's health, nutrition, emerging infectious diseases, environmental health, vaccine evaluation and case management, with particular reference to developing countries; supported by 55 governments and international organizations. Dir Prof. DAVID SACK. Publs *Annual Report, Journal of Health, Population and Nutrition* (quarterly), *Glimpse* (quarterly), *Shasthya Sanglap* (3 a year), *DISC Bulletin* (weekly), scientific reports, working papers, monographs.

International Chiropractors' Association: 1110 North Glebe Rd, Suite 1000, Arlington, VA 22201, USA; tel. (703) 528-5000; f. 1926 to promote advancement of the art and science of chiropractic. Mems: 7,000 individuals in addition to affiliated associations. Pres. FRED BARGE; Exec. Vice-Pres. RON HENRIKSON. Publs *International Review of Chiropractic* (every 2 months), *ICA Today* (every 2 months).

International Commission on Occupational Health: Dept of Community, Occupational and Family Medicine, MD3, National University of Singapore, 16 Medical Drive, Singapore 117597; tel. (65) 8744915; fax (65) 7791489; e-mail icohsg@singnet.com.sg; internet www.icoh.org.sg; f. 1906 (present name 1985) to study and prevent pathological conditions arising from industrial work; arranges congresses on occupational medicine and the protection of workers' health; provides information for public authorities and learned societies. Mems: 1,944 from 89 countries. Pres. Prof. BENGT KNAVE (Sweden); Sec.-Gen. Prof. CHIA KEE SENG (Singapore). Publ. *Newsletter* (electronic version).

International Commission on Radiological Protection—ICRP: 17116 Stockholm, Sweden; tel. (8) 729-72-75; fax (8) 729-72-98; e-mail jack.valentin@ssi.se; internet www.icrp.org; f. 1928 to provide technical guidance and promote international co-operation in the field of radiation protection; committees on Radiation Effects, Doses from Radiation Exposure, Protection in Medicine, and the Application of Recommendations. Mems: about 70. Chair. Prof. R. H. CLARKE (UK); Scientific Sec. Dr J. VALENTIN (Sweden). Publ. *Annals of the ICRP*.

International Committee of Catholic Nurses: 43 Square Vergote, 1040 Brussels, Belgium; tel. (2) 732-10-50; fax (2) 734-84-60; f. 1933 to group professional Catholic nursing associations; to represent Christian thought in the general professional field at international level; to co-operate in the general development of the profession and to promote social welfare. Mems: 49 full, 20 corresponding mems. Pres. R. LAI; Gen. Sec. AN VERLINDE. Publ. *Nouvelles / News / Nachrichten* (3 a year).

International Council for Physical Activity and Fitness Research—ICPAFR: Faculty of Physical Education and Physiotherapy, Catholic Univ. of Leuven, 3001 Heverlee (Leuven), Belgium; tel. (16) 32-90-83; fax (16) 32-91-97; e-mail albrecht.claessens@flok.kuleuven.ac.be; f. 1964 to construct international standardized physical fitness tests, to encourage research based upon the standardized tests and to encourage research to enhance participation in physical activity. Mems: some 35 countries. Pres. Prof. ALBRECHT L. CLAESSENS (Belgium); Sec. Treas. Prof. ANDREW HILLS (Australia).

International Council of Nurses—ICN: 3 place Jean-Marteau, 1201 Geneva, Switzerland; tel. (22) 8090100; fax (22) 8090101; f. 1899 to allow national associations of nurses to share their common interests, working together to develop the contribution of nursing to the promotion of health. Quadrennial congresses are held. Mems: 112 national nurses' associations. Pres. (from June 2001) CHRISTINE HANCOCK (UK); Exec. Dir JUDITH OULTON. Publ. *The International Nursing Review* (6 a year, in English).

International Cystic Fibrosis (Mucoviscidosis) Association: POB 2290, 5600 MD Eindhoven, Netherlands; tel. (40) 2502444; fax (40) 2502445; e-mail steenkamer.gina@kpmg.nl; internet www.icfma.org; f. 1964 to disseminate current information on cystic fibrosis in those areas of the world where the disease occurs and to stimulate the work of scientific and medical researchers attempting to discover its cure. Conducts annual medical symposia. Mems: 54 national organizations; 14 associate mems. Pres. HERMAN WEGGEN (Netherlands); Sec. GINA STEENKAMER (Netherlands).

International Epidemiological Association—IEA: Suite 840, 111 Market Place, Baltimore, MD 21202-6709, USA; tel. (410) 223-1600; fax (410) 223-1620; e-mail harmenia@jhsph.edu; f. 1954. Mems: 2,237. Pres. and Chair. Dr RODOLFO SARACCI; Sec. Prof. HAROUTUNE ARMENIAN. Publ. *International Journal of Epidemiology* (6 a year).

International Federation for Medical and Biological Engineering: c/o Prof. Jos A. E. Spaan, Faculty of Medicine, Meibergdreef 15, 1105 AZ Amsterdam, Netherlands; tel. (20) 566-5200; fax (20) 691-7233; e-mail ifmbe@amc.uva.nl; internet www.vub.vub.oc.be/~ifmbe/ifmbe-html; f. 1959. Mems: organizations in 40 countries. Sec.-Gen. Prof. JOS A. E. SPAAN (Netherlands).

International Federation for Medical Psychotherapy: c/o Prof. E. Heim, Tannackstr. 3, 3653 Oberhofen, Switzerland; tel. and fax (33) 2431141; e-mail senf-blum@t-online.de; f. 1946 to further research and teaching of psychotherapy and to organize international congresses. Mems: some 6,000 psychotherapists from around 40 countries, 36 societies. Pres. Dr EDGAR HEIM (Switzerland); Sec.-Gen. Prof. Dr WOLFGANG SENE (Germany).

International Federation of Fertility Societies—IFFS: c/o CSI, 337 rue de la Combe Caude, 34090 Montpellier, France; tel. 4-67-63-53-40; fax 4-67-41-94-27; e-mail algcsi@mnet.fr; internet www.mnet.fr/iffs; f. 1951 to study problems of fertility and sterility. Sec.-Gen. Prof. BERNARD HEDON. Publ. *Newsletter*(2 a year).

International Federation of Gynecology and Obstetrics—FIGO: 70 Wimpole St, London, W1X 8AG, United Kingdom; tel. (20) 7224-3270; fax (20) 7935-0736; e-mail secret@figo.win-uk.net; internet www.figo.org; f. 1954; aims to improve standards in gynaecology and obstetrics, to promote better health care for women, and to facilitate the exchange of information and perfect methods of teaching. Membership: national societies in 100 countries. Pres. Dr SHIRISH S. SHETH (India); Sec.-Gen. Prof. G. BENAGIANO (Italy). Publ. *International Journal of Obstetrics and Gynecology.*

International Federation of Multiple Sclerosis Societies: 10 Heddon St, London, W1R 7LJ, United Kingdom; tel. (20) 7734-9120; fax (20) 7287-2587; e-mail info@ifmss.org.uk; internet www.ifmss.org.uk; f. 1965 to co-ordinate the work of 38 national multiple sclerosis organizations throughout the world, to encourage scientific research in this and related neurological diseases, to aid member societies in helping individuals who are in any way affected as a result of these diseases, to collect and disseminate information and to provide counsel and active help in furthering the development of voluntary national multiple sclerosis organizations. Pres. PETER SCHWEITZER; Chief Exec. CHRISTINE PURDY. Publs *Making Connections* (annually), *MS Research in Progress* (every 2 years), *MS Management* (2 a year), *Therapeutic Claims in MS* (annually).

International Federation of Ophthalmological Societies: c/o Dr Bruce E. Spivey, Spivey International, One Beekman Pl., New York, NY 10022, USA; fax (212) 326-8773; internet www.icoph.org; f. 1953; holds international congress every four years. Pres. Prof. A. NAKAJIMA (Japan); Sec. Dr BRUCE E. SPIVEY.

International Hospital Federation: 46–48 Grosvenor Gdns, London, SW1W 0EB, United Kingdom; tel. (20) 7881-9222; fax (20) 7881-9223; e-mail 101662.1262@compuserve.com; f. 1947 for information exchange and education in hospital and health service matters; represents institutional health care in discussions with WHO; conducts conferences and courses on management and policy issues. Mems in five categories: national hospital and health service organizations; professional associations, regional organizations and individual hospitals; individual mems; professional and industrial mems; honorary mems. Dir-Gen. Prof. PER-GUNNAR SVENSSON. Publs *Yearbook, Journal, Newsletter.*

International League against Epilepsy: c/o Prof. Peter Wolf, Klinik Mara I, Epilepsie-Zentrum Bethel, Maraweg 21, 33617 Bielefeld, Germany; tel. (521) 144-4897; fax (521) 144-4637; e-mail ilae-secretariat@mara.de; f. 1909 to link national professional associations and to encourage research, including classification and anti-epileptic drugs; collaborates with the International Bureau for Epilepsy (q.v.) and with WHO. Mems: 72 associations. Pres. JEROME ENGEL, Jr (USA); Sec.-Gen. P. WOLF.

International Narcotics Control Board—INCB: 1400 Vienna, POB 500, Austria; tel. (1) 260-60-42-77; fax (1) 260-60-58-67; e-mail secretariat@incb.org; internet www.incb.org; f. 1961 by the Single Convention on Narcotic Drugs to supervise the implementation of the drug control treaties by governments. Mems: 13 individuals.

Pres. HAMID GHODSE (Iran); Sec. HERBERT SCHAEPE (Germany). Publ. *Annual Report* (with three technical supplements).

International Opticians' Association: 6 Hurlingham Business Park, Sulivan Rd, London, SW6 3DU, United Kingdom; tel. (20) 7736-0088; fax (20) 7731-5531; e-mail general@abcb.org.uk; f. 1951 to promote the science of, and to maintain and advance standards and effect co-operation in optical dispensing.

International Organization for Medical Physics: c/o Prof. Gary D. Fullerton, UTHSCSA, Dept of Radiology, MSC 7800, 7703 Floyd Curl Drive, San Antonio, TX 78229-3900, USA; tel. (210) 567-5551; fax (210) 567-5549; e-mail iomp@uthscsa.edu; internet www.iomp.org; f. 1963 to organize international co-operation in medical physics, to promote communication between the various branches of medical physics and allied subjects, to contribute to the advancement of medical physics in all its aspects and to advise on the formation of national organizations. Mems: national organizations of medical physics in more than 70 countries. Pres. Prof. OSKAR CHORNICKI (Poland); Sec.-Gen. Prof. GARY FULLERTON. Publ. *Medical Physics World.*

International Pharmaceutical Federation: POB 84200, 2508 AE The Hague, Netherlands; tel. (70) 3021970; fax (70) 3021999; e-mail int.pharm.fed@fip.nl; f. 1912; aims to represent and serve pharmacy and pharmaceutical sciences world-wide; holds Assembly of Pharmacists every two years, International Congress every year. Mems: 86 national pharmaceutical organizations in 62 countries, 55 associate, supportive and collective mems, 4,000 individuals. Dir A. H. M (TON) HOEK (Netherlands). Publ. *International Pharmacy Journal* (every 2 months).

International Psycho-Analytical Association: Broomhills, Woodside Lane, London, N12 8UD, United Kingdom; tel. (20) 8446-8324; fax (20) 8445-4729; e-mail ipa@ipa.org.uk; internet www.ipa@ipa.org.uk; f. 1908 to hold meetings to define and promulgate the theory and teaching of psychoanalysis, to act as a forum for scientific discussions, to control and regulate training and to contribute to the interdisciplinary area which is common to the behavioural sciences. Mems: 10,000. Pres. Dr OTTO KERNBERG; Sec. Dr ROBERT TYSON. Publs *Bulletin, Newsletter.*

International Society for Cardiovascular Surgery: 13 Elm St, Manchester, MA 01944-1314, USA; tel. (978) 526-8330; fax (978) 526-4018; e-mail iscvs@prri.com; f. 1950 to stimulate research in the diagnosis and therapy of cardiovascular diseases and to exchange ideas on an international basis. Sec.-Gen. Dr LAZAR J. GREENFIELD (USA). Publ. *Cardiovascular Surgery.*

International Society for Oneiric Mental Imagery Techniques: c/o Odile Dorkel, 56 rue Sedaine, 75011 Paris, France; tel. 1-47-00-16-63; a group of research workers, technicians and psychotherapists using oneirism techniques under waking conditions, with the belief that a healing action cannot be dissociated from the restoration of creativity. Mems: in 17 countries. Pres. ODILE DORKEL (France); Sec.-Gen. JEAN-FRANÇOIS CESARO (France).

International Society of Art and Psychopathology: c/o Dr G. Roux, 27 rue du mal Joffre, 64000 Pau, France; tel. and fax 5-59-27-69-74; e-mail sipearther@aol.com; internet mageos.ifrance.com/art-therapy/art-therapy/sipe.htm; f. 1959 to bring together the various specialists interested in the problems of expression and artistic activities in connection with psychiatric, sociological and psychological research, as well as in the use of methods applied to other fields than that of mental illness. Mems: 625. Pres. Dr G. ROUX (France); Sec.-Gen. J. L. SUDRES (France).

International Society of Developmental Biologists: c/o Dr Paul T. van der Saag, Hubrecht Laboratorium/Netherlands Institute for Developmental Biology, Uppsalalaan 8, 3584 CT, Utrecht, Netherlands; tel. (30) 2510-211; e-mail directie@niob.knaw.nl; f. 1911 as International Institute of Embryology. Aims to promote the study of developmental biology and to promote international co-operation among the investigators in this field. Mems: 850 in 33 countries. Pres. Prof. WALTER GEHRING (Switzerland); Sec.-Treas. Prof. SIEGFRIED DE LAAT (Netherlands). Publ. *Mechanisms of Development.*

International Society of Lymphology: POB 245063, University of Arizona, 1501 North Campbell Ave, Room 4406, Tucson, AZ 85724-5063, USA; tel. (520) 626-6118; fax (520) 626-0822; e-mail lymph@u.arizona.edu; f. 1966 to further progress in lymphology through personal contact and exchange of ideas among members. Mems: 400 in 43 countries. Pres. C. PAPENDIECK (Argentina); Sec.-Gen. M. H. WITTE (USA). Publ. *Lymphology* (quarterly).

International Society of Neuropathology: c/o Prof. Hannu Kalimo, Dept of Pathology, Turku University Hospital, 20520 Turku, Finland; tel. (2) 2611685; fax (2) 3337456; e-mailhkalimo@mailhost.utu.fi. Pres. Prof. SAMUEL LUDWIN (Canada); Sec.-Gen. Prof. HANNU KALIMO.

International Society of Orthopaedic Surgery and Traumatology: 40 rue Washington, 1050 Brussels, Belgium; tel. (2) 648-68-23; fax (2) 649-86-01; f. 1929; world congresses are convened every three years. Mems: 102 countries, 3,000 individuals. Pres.

Medicine and Health

RAINER KOTZ (Austria); Sec.-Gen. ANTHONY J. HALL (UK). Publ. *International Orthopaedics* (every 2 months).

International Society of Radiology: 7910 Woodmont Ave, Suite 800, Bethesda, Maryland 20814-3095, USA; tel. (301) 657-2652; fax (301) 907-8768; f. 1953 to promote radiology world-wide. International Commissions on Radiation Units and Measurements (ICRUM), on Radiation Protection (ICRP), and on Radiological Education (ICRE); organizes biannual International Congress of Radiology; collaborates with WHO. Mems: more than 50 national radiological societies. Pres. C.-G. SANDERTSKÖJOLD-NORDENSTAM; Sec.-Gen. FRANCISCO ARREDONDO.

International Society of Surgery: Netzibodenstr. 34, POB 1527, 4133 Pratteln, Switzerland; tel. (61) 8159666; fax (61) 8114775; e-mail surgery@iss-sic.ch; internet www.iss-sic.ch; f. 1902; organizes congresses: 39th World Congress of Surgery (Centennial Congress), Brussels, Belgium, August 2001. Mems: 4,000. Admin. Dir. VICTOR BERTSCHI; Sec.-Gen. Prof. J. RÜDIGER SIEWERT. Publ. *World Journal of Surgery* (monthly).

International Union against Tuberculosis and Lung Disease: 68 blvd St Michel, 75006 Paris, France; tel. 1-44-32-03-60; fax 1-43-29-90-87; e-mail iuatldparis@compuserve.com; f. 1920 to co-ordinate the efforts of anti-tuberculosis and respiratory disease associations, to mobilize public interest, to assist control programmes and research around the world, to collaborate with governments and WHO and to promote conferences. Mems: associations in 165 countries, 3,000 individual mems. Pres. Prof. S. SUPCHAROEN; Exec. Dir Dr NILS BILLO. Publs *The International Journal of Tuberculosis and Lung Disease* (in English with summaries in French and Spanish; incl. conference proceedings), *Newsletter*.

International Union for Health Promotion and Education: Immeuble le Berry, 2 rue Auguste Comte, 92170 Vanves, France; tel. 1-46-45-00-59; fax 1-46-45-00-45; e-mail iuhpemcl@worldnet.fr; internet www.iuhpe.org; f. 1951; provides an international network for the exchange of practical information on developments in health promotion and education; promotes research into effective methods and techniques in health promotion and education and encourages professional training in health promotion and education for health workers, teachers, social workers and others; holds a World Conference on Health Promotion and Health Education every three years, and also holds regional conferences and seminars. Mems: in more than 90 countries. Pres. Dr SPENCER HAGARD (UK). Publ. *International Journal of Health Promotion and Education* (quarterly, in English, French and Spanish).

International Union of Therapeutics: c/o Prof. A. Pradalier, Hôpital Louis Mourier, 178 rue des Renouillers, 92700 Colombes, France; tel. 1-47-60-67-05; e-mail secretariat.medecine4@lmr.ap-hop-paris.fr; f. 1934; international congress held every other year. Mems: 500 from 22 countries. Pres. Prof. A. PRADALIER; Gen. Sec. Prof. P. LECHAT.

Middle East Neurosurgical Society: c/o Dr Fuad S. Haddad, Neurosurgical Department, American University Medical Centre, POB 113-6044, Beirut, Lebanon; tel. (1) 347348; fax (1) 342517; e-mail gfhaddad@aub.edu.lb; f. 1958 to promote clinical advances and scientific research among its members and to spread knowledge of neurosurgery and related fields among all members of the medical profession in the Middle East. Mems: 684 in nine countries. Pres. Dr FUAD S. HADDAD; Hon. Sec. Dr GEDEON MOHASSEB.

Organization for Co-ordination and Co-operation in the Struggle against Endemic Diseases (Organisation de coordination et de coopération pour la lutte contre les grandes endémies—OCCGE): 01 BP 153, Bobo-Dioulasso 01, Burkina Faso; tel. 97-01-55; fax 97-00-99; e-mail sq@pegase.occge.bf; f. 1960; conducts research, provides training and maintains a documentation centre and computer information system. Mems: governments of Benin, Burkina Faso, Côte d'Ivoire, Mali, Mauritania, Niger, Senegal, Togo. Sec.-Gen. Prof. ABDOULAYE RHALY. Publs *Rapport annuel*, *OCCGE Info* (3 a year), *Bulletin Bibliographique* (quarterly).

Research centres:

Centre de Recherches sur les Méningites et les Schistosomiases: BP 10 887, Niamey, Niger; tel. 75-20-45; fax 75-31-80; e-mail chippaux@ird.ne; internet www.ird.fr.cermes; f. 1978; Dir J. P. CHIPPAUX.

Centre Muraz: 01 BP 153, Bobo-Dioulasso 01, Burkina Faso; tel. 97-01-02; fax 97-04-57; e-mail direction.muraz@fasonet.bf; f. 1939; multi-disciplinary research centre with special interest in biology and epidemiology of tropical diseases and training of health workers. Dir Prof. PHILIPPE VAN DE PERRE.

Centre Régional de Recherches entomologiques: Cotonou, Benin.

Institut de Recherche sur la Tuberculose et les Infections respiratoires aigües: Nouakchott, Mauritania.

Institut d'ophtalmologie tropicale africaine—IOTA: BP 248, Bamako, Mali; tel. 22-34-21; fax 22-51-86; e-mail iota@iota-

occge.org;f. 1953; eye care, clinical, operational and epidemiological research, training; Dir Dr AUZEMERY.

Institut Marchoux: BP 251, Bamako, Mali; tel. 22-51-31; fax 22-28-45; research, epidemiology and training on leprosy, dermatology, surgery. Dir Prof. MAMADOU HAMET CISSÉ.

Institut Pierre Richet: BP 1500, Bouaké 01, Côte d'Ivoire; tel. 63-37-46; fax 63-27-38; e-mail carneval@bouake2.orsrom.ci; f. 1974; research on trypanosomiasis, onchocerciasis, malaria and vector control; maintains a geographical information system; Dir Dr PIERRE CARNEVALE.

Office de Recherches sur l'Alimentation et la Nutrition africaine: BP 2089, Dakar, Senegal; tel. 822-58-92; Dir Dr MAKHTAR N'DIAYE.

In 1990 it was announced that the West African Health Community was to be amalgamated with the Organization for Co-ordination and Co-operation in the Struggle against Endemic Diseases to form the West African Health Organization, covering all the member states of ECOWAS (subject to ratification by member states).

Organization for Co-ordination in the Struggle against Endemic Diseases in Central Africa (Organisation de coordination pour la lutte contre les endémies en Afrique Centrale—OCEAC): BP 288, Yaoundé, Cameroon; tel. 23-22-32; fax 23-00-61; e-mail oceac@mnet.cm; f. 1965 to standardize methods of controlling endemic diseases, to co-ordinate national action, and to negotiate programmes of assistance and training on a regional scale. Mems: Cameroon, Central African Republic, Chad, Republic of the Congo, Equatorial Guinea, Gabon. Pres. L. ESSO (Cameroon); Sec.-Gen. Dr AUGUSTE BILONGO MANENE. Publ. *Bulletin de Liaison et de Documentation* (quarterly).

Pan-American Association of Ophthalmology: 1301 South Bowen Rd, Suite 365, Arlington, TX 76013, USA; tel. (817) 265-2831; fax (817) 275-3961; e-mail paao@flash.net; f. 1939 to promote friendship and dissemination of scientific information among the profession throughout the Western Hemisphere; holds biennial congress (1999: Florida, USA). Mems: national ophthalmological societies and other bodies in 39 countries. Pres. Dr PAUL R. LICHTER (Chile); Exec. Dir Dr FRANCISCO MARTINEZ CASTRO (Mexico). Publs *The Pan American* (2 a year), *El Noticiero* (quarterly).

Pan-Pacific Surgical Association: 2000 L. St, NW, Suite 200, Washington, DC 20036, USA; tel. (202) 416-1866; fax (202) 416-1867; e-mail ppsa@slackinc.com; internet www. ppsa.org; f. 1929 to bring together surgeons to exchange scientific knowledge relating to surgery and medicine, and to promote the improvement and standardization of hospitals and their services and facilities; congresses are held every two years. Mems: 2,716 regular, associate and senior mems from 44 countries. Chair. ALLAN KUNIMOTO.

Society of French-speaking Neuro-Surgeons (Société de neuro-chirurgie de langue française): Hôpital d'Enfants de la Timone, 13385 Marseille, France; f. 1949; holds annual convention and congress. Mems: 700 in numerous countries. Pres. M. CHOUX (France); Sec. J. LAGARRIGUE (France). Publ. *Neuro-Chirurgie* (6 a year).

World Association for Disaster and Emergency Medicine—WADEM: c/o Marvin L. Birnbaum, E5/615 CSC, 600 Highland Avenue, Madison, WI 53791-9744, USA; tel. (608) 263-2069; fax (608) 265-3037; e-mail mlb@medicine.wisc.edu; internet www.pdm.medicine.wisc.edu; f. 1976 to improve the world-wide delivery of emergency and humanitarian care in mass casualty and disaster situations through training, symposia, and publications. Mems: 600 in 62 countries. Hon. Sec. Prof. W. DICK (Germany). Publ. *Prehospital and Disaster Medicine*.

World Association of Societies of (Anatomic and Clinical) Pathology—WASP: c/o Japan Clinical Pathology Foundation for International Exchange, Sakura-Sugamo Bldg 7F, Sugamo 2-11-1, Toshima-ku, Tokyo 170, Japan; tel. (3) 3918-8161; fax (3) 3949-6168; f. 1947 to link national societies and to co-ordinate their scientific and technical means of action; and to promote the development of anatomic and clinical pathology, especially by convening conferences, congresses and meetings, and by the interchange of publications and personnel. Membership: 54 national associations. Pres. PETER B. HERDSON; Sec. WALTER TIMPERLEY. Publ. *Newsletter* (quarterly).

World Confederation for Physical Therapy: 4A Abbots Pl., London, NW6 4NP, United Kingdom; tel. (20) 7328-5448; fax (20) 7624-7579; f. 1951; represents physical therapy internationally; encourages high standards of physical therapy education and practice; promotes exchange of information among members, and the development of a scientific professional base through research; aims to contribute to the development of informed public opinion regarding physical therapy. Mems: 67 organizations. Pres. Prof. D. P. G. TEAGER; Sec.-Gen. B. J. MYERS. Publ. *Newsletter* (2 a year).

World Council of Optometry—WCO: 8360 Old York West, 4th Floor, Elkins Park, PA 19027, USA; e-mail wco@pco.edu; internet www.worldoptometry.org; f. 1927 to co-ordinate efforts to provide a good standard of ophthalmic optical (optometric) care throughout the world; enables exchange of ideas between different countries; a large part of its work is concerned with optometric education, and advice upon standards of qualification. The WCO also interests itself in legislation in relation to optometry throughout the world. Mems: 70 optometric organizations in 47 countries and four regional groups. Exec. Dir Dr ANTONY DI STEFANO. Publ. *Interoptics* (quarterly).

World Federation for Mental Health: 1021 Prince St, Alexandria, VA 22314, USA; tel. (703) 838-7543; fax (703) 519-7648; e-mail wfmh@erols.com; internet www.wfmh.org; f. 1948 to promote among all nations the highest possible standard of mental health; to work with agencies of the United Nations in promoting mental health; to help other voluntary associations in the improvement of mental health services. Mems: 250 national or international associations in 115 countries. Pres. Dr AHMED EL-AZAYEM; Sec.-Gen. Prof. Dr MARTEN DE VRIES. Publs *Newsletter* (quarterly), *Annual Report*.

World Federation of Hydrotherapy and Climatotherapy: Cattedra di Terapia Med. E Medic. Termal, Università degli Studi, via Cicognara 7, 20129 Milan, Italy; tel. (02) 733880; fax (02) 70100398; f. 1947 as International Federation of Thermalism and Climatism; present name adopted 1999. Mems in 36 countries. Pres. M. NIKOLAI A. STOROJENKO; Gen. Sec. Prof. UMBERTO SOLIMENE.

World Federation of Neurosurgical Societies: c/o Prof. Edward R. Laws, Dept. of Neurological Surgery, Univ. of Virginia, Box 212, Health Science Center, Charlottesville, VA 22908, USA; tel. (804) 924-2650; fax (804) 924-5894; f. 1957 to assist the development of neurosurgery and to help the formation of associations; to assist the exchange of information and to encourage research. Mems: 57 societies representing 56 countries. Pres. Prof. ARMANDO BASSO; Sec. Prof. EDWARD R. LAWS, Jr.

World Federation of Occupational Therapists: c/o Carolyn Webster, Disabilities Services Comm., PO Box 441, West Perth, 6872 Western Australia, Australia; tel. (8) 9426-9200; fax (8) 9490-5223; e-mail wfot@multiline.com.au; internet wfot.org.au; f. 1952 to further the rehabilitation of the physically and mentally disabled by promoting the development of occupational therapy in all countries; to facilitate the exchange of information and publications; to promote research in occupational therapy; international congresses are held every four years. Mems: national professional associations in 50 countries, with total membership of approximately 100,000. Pres. CAROLYN WEBSTER (Australia); Hon. Sec. CLEPHANE HUME (UK). Publ. *Bulletin* (2 a year).

World Federation of Public Health Associations: c/o Allen Jones, APHA, 800 I St, NW, Washington, DC 20001-3710, USA; tel. (202) 777-2487; fax (202) 777-2534; e-mail allen.jones@apha.org; internet www.apha.org; f. 1967. Triennial Congress: Beijing, People's Republic of China, 2000. Mems: 61 national public health associations. Exec. Sec. ALLEN JONES (USA). Publs *WFPHA News* (in English), and occasional technical papers.

World Federation of Societies of Anaesthesiologists—WFSA: Imperial House, 8th Floor, 15–19 Kingsway, London, WC2B 6TH, United Kingdom; tel. (20) 7836-5652; fax (20) 7836-5616; e-mail wfsa@compuserve.com; internet www.nda.ox.ac.uk/wfsa; f. 1955 to make available the highest standards of anaesthesia to all peoples of the world. Mems: 106 national societies. Pres. Dr K. BROWN (Australia); Sec. Dr A. E. E. MEURSING; Publs *World Anaesthesia Newsletter* (2 a year), *Annual Report*.

Posts and Telecommunications

African Posts and Telecommunications Union: Brazzaville, Republic of the Congo; f. 1961 to improve postal and telecommunication services between member administrations. Mems: 11 countries. Sec.-Gen. MAHMOUDOU SAMOURA.

Arab Permanent Postal Commission: c/o Arab League Bldg, Tahrir Sq., Cairo, Egypt; tel. (2) 5750511; fax (2) 5775626; f. 1952; aims to establish stricter postal relations between the Arab countries than those laid down by the Universal Postal Union, and to pursue the development and modernization of postal services in member countries. Publs *APU Bulletin* (monthly), *APU Review* (quarterly), *APU News* (annually).

Arab Telecommunications Union: POB 2397, Baghdad, Iraq; tel. (1) 555-0642; f. 1953 to co-ordinate and develop telecommunications between member countries; to exhange technical aid and encourage research; promotes establishment of new cable telecommunications networks in the region. Sec.-Gen. ABDUL JAFFAR HASSAN KHALAF IBRAHIM AL-ANI. Publs. *Arab Telecommunications Union Journal* (2 a year), *Economic and Technical Studies*.

Asia-Pacific Telecommunity: No. 12/49, Soi 5, Chaengwattana Rd, Thungsonghong, Bangkok 10210, Thailand; tel. (2) 573-0044; fax (2) 573-7479; e-mail aptmail@aptsec.org; internet www.aptsec .org;. 1979 to cover all matters relating to telecommunications in the region. Mems: Afghanistan, Australia, Bangladesh, Brunei, the People's Republic of China, India, Indonesia, Iran, Japan, the Republic of Korea, Laos, Malaysia, Maldives, Myanmar, Nauru, Nepal, Pakistan, the Philippines, Singapore, Sri Lanka, Thailand, Viet Nam; assoc. mems: Cook Islands, Hong Kong; two affiliated mems each in Indonesia, Japan and Thailand, three in the Republic of Korea, four in Hong Kong, one in Maldives and six in the Philippines. Exec. Sec. JONG-SOON LEE.

Asian-Pacific Postal Union: Post Office Bldg, 1000 Manila, Philippines; tel. (2) 470760; fax (2) 407448; f. 1962 to extend, facilitate and improve the postal relations between the member countries and to promote co-operation in the field of postal services. Mems: 23 countries. Dir JORGE SARMIENTO. Publs *Annual Report, Exchange Program of Postal Officials, APPU Newsletter*.

European Conference of Postal and Telecommunications Administrations: Ministry of Transport and Communications, Odos Xenofontos 13, 10191 Athens, Greece; tel. (1) 9236494; fax (1) 9237133; f. 1959 to strengthen relations between member administrations and to harmonize and improve their technical services; set up Eurodata Foundation, for research and publishing. Mems: 26 countries. Sec. Z. PROTOPSALTI. Publ. *Bulletin*.

European Telecommunications Satellite Organization—EUTELSAT: 70 rue Balard, 75502, Paris Cédex 15, France; tel. 1-53-98-47-47; fax 1-53-98-37-00; internet www.eutelsat.com/; f. 1977 to operate satellites for fixed and mobile communications in Europe; operates an eight-satellite system, incorporating four EUTELSAT I and four EUTELSAT II satellites. Mems: public and private telecommunications operations in 47 countries. Dir-Gen. GIULIANO BERRETTA.

INMARSAT—International Mobile Satellite Organization: 99 City Rd, London, EC1Y 1AX, United Kingdom; tel. (20) 7728-1000; fax (20) 7728-1044; internet www.inmarsat.org; f. 1979, as International Maritime Satellite Organization, to provide (from February 1982) global communications for shipping via satellites on a commercial basis; satellites in geo-stationary orbit over the Atlantic, Indian and Pacific Oceans provide telephone, telex, facsimile, telegram, low to high speed data services and distress and safety communications for ships of all nations and structures such as oil rigs; in 1985 the operating agreement was amended to include aeronautical communications, and in 1988 amendments were approved which allow provision of global land-mobile communications. In April 1999 INMARSAT was transferred to the private sector and became a limited company; an intergovernmental secretariat was to be maintained to monitor INMARSAT's public service obligations. Mems: 86 countries. Chair. RICHARD VOS; Dir of Secretariat JERZY VONAU (Poland).

International Telecommunications Satellite Organization—INTELSAT: 3400 International Drive, NW, Washington, DC 20008-3098, USA; tel. (202) 944-6800; fax (202) 944-7860; f. 1964 to establish a global commercial satellite communications system. Assembly of Parties attended by representatives of member governments, meets every two years to consider policy and long-term aims and matters of interest to members as sovereign states. Meeting of Signatories to the Operating Agreement held annually. Twenty-four INTELSAT satellites in geosynchronous orbit provide a global communications service; INTELSAT provides most of the world's overseas traffic. In 1998 INTELSAT agreed to establish a private enterprise, incorporated in the Netherlands, to administer six satellite services. Mems: 143 governments. Dir-Gen. and Chief Exec. CONNY KULLMAN (Sweden).

Pacific Telecommunications Council: 2454 S. Beretania St, 302 Honolulu, HI 96826, USA; tel. (808) 941-3789; fax (808) 944-4874; e-mail info@ptc.org; f. 1980 to promote the development, understanding and beneficial use of telecommunications and information systems/services throughout the Pacific region; provides forum for users and providers of communications services; sponsors annual conference and seminars. Mems: 650 (corporate, government, academic and individual). Pres. JANE HURD; Exec. Dir HOYT ZIA. Publ. *Pacific Telecommunications Review* (quarterly).

Postal Union of the Americas, Spain and Portugal (Unión Postal de las Américas, España y Portugal): Calle Cebollatí 1468/70, 1°, Casilla de Correos 20.042, Montevideo, Uruguay; tel. (2) 4000070; fax (2) 405046; internet www.upaepadinet.com.uy; f. 1911 to extend, facilitate and study the postal relationships of member countries. Mems: 27 countries. Sec.-Gen. MARIO FELMER KLENNER (Chile).

Press, Radio and Television

Asia-Pacific Broadcasting Union—ABU: POB 1164, 59700 Kuala Lumpur, Malaysia; tel. (3) 22823592; fax (3) 22825292; e-mail sg@abu.org.my; internet www.abu.org.my; f. 1964 to foster and co-ordinate the development of broadcasting in the Asia-Pacific area, to develop means of establishing closer collaboration and co-operation among broadcasting orgs, and to serve the professional needs of broadcasters in Asia and the Pacific; holds annual General

Assembly. Mems: 45 full, 31 additional and 26 associates in 51 countries and territories. Pres. KATSUJI EBISAWA (Japan); Sec.-Gen. HUGH LEONARD. Publs *ABU News* (every 2 months), *ABU Technical Review* (every 2 months).

Association for the Promotion of the International Circulation of the Press—DISTRIPRESS: 8002 Zürich, Beethovenstrasse 20, Switzerland; tel. (1) 2024121; fax (1) 2021025; e-mail info@distripress.ch; internet www.distripress.ch; f. 1955 to assist in the promotion of the freedom of the press throughout the world, supporting and aiding UNESCO in promoting the free flow of ideas. Organizes meetings of publishers and distributors of newspapers, periodicals and paperback books, to promote the exchange of information and experience among members. Mems: 458. Pres. ALFRED HEINTZE (Germany); Man. HEINZ E. GRAF (Switzerland). Publs *Distripress Gazette*, *Who's Who*.

Association of European Journalists: 5300 Bonn 2, Kastanienweg 26, Germany; tel. and fax (228) 321712; f. 1963 to participate actively in the development of a European consciousness; to promote deeper knowledge of European problems and secure appreciation by the general public of the work of European institutions; and to facilitate members' access to sources of European information. Mems: 1,500 individuals and national associations in 15 countries. Sec.-Gen. GUENTHER WAGENLEHNER.

Association of Private European Cable Operators: 1 blvd Anspach, boîte 25, 1000 Brussels, Belgium; tel. (2) 223-25-91; fax (2) 223-06-96; f. 1995 aims to promote the interests of independent cable operators and to ensure exchange of information on cable and telecommunications; carries out research on relevant technical and legal questions. Mems: 27 organizations in 19 countries. Pres. M. DE SUTTER.

Broadcasting Organization of Non-aligned Countries—BONAC: c/o Cyprus Broadcasting Corpn, POB 4824, 1397 Nicosia, Cyprus; tel. (2) 422231; fax (2) 314050; e-mail rik@cybc.com.cy; f. 1977 to ensure an equitable, objective and comprehensive flow of information through broadcasting; Secretariat moves to the broadcasting organization of host country. Mems: in 102 countries.

European Alliance of Press Agencies: c/o Agence Belga, rue F. Pelletier 8B, 1030 Brussels, Belgium; tel. (2) 743-13-11; fax (2) 735-18-74; e-mail dir@belganews.be; f. 1957 to assist co-operation among members and to study and protect their common interests; annual assembly. Mems in 30 countries. Sec.-Gen. RUDI DE CEUSTER.

European Broadcasting Union—EBU: CP 45, Ancienne-Route 17A, 1218 Grand-Saconnex, Geneva, Switzerland; tel. (22) 7172111; fax (22) 7472200; e-mail ebu@ebu.ch; internet www.ebu.ch; f. 1950 in succession to the International Broadcasting Union; a professional association of broadcasting organizations, supporting the interests of members and assisting the development of broadcasting in all its forms; activities include the Eurovision news and programme exchanges and the Euroradio music exchanges. Mems: 69 active (European) in 50 countries, and 46 associate in 29 countries. Pres. ARNE WESSBERG (Finland); Sec.-Gen. JEAN BERNARD MÜNCH (Switzerland). Publs *EBU Technical Review* (annually), *Diffusion* (quarterly).

IFRA: Washingtonplatz 1, 64287 Darmstadt, Germany; tel. (6151) 7336; fax (6151) 733800; e-mail info@ifra.com; internet www.ifra.com; f. 1961 as Inca-Fiej Research Asscn to develop methods and techniques for the newspaper industry; to evaluate standard specifications for raw materials for use in newspaper production; to investigate economy and quality improvements for newspaper printing and publishing. Mems: more than 1,300 newspapers, 400 suppliers. Pres. MURDOCH MacLENNAN; Man. Dir G. W. BOETTCHER. Publ. *Newspaper Techniques* (monthly in English, French and German).

Inter-American Press Association (Sociedad Interamericana de Prensa): Jules Dubois Bldg, 1801 SW 3rd Ave, Miami, FL 33129, USA; tel. (305) 634-2465; fax (305) 635-2272; e-mail info@sipiapa.org; internet www.sipiapa.org; f. 1942 to guard the freedom of the press in the Americas; to promote and maintain the dignity, rights and responsibilities of the profession of journalism; to foster a wider knowledge and greater interchange among the peoples of the Americas. Mems: 1,400. Exec. Dir JULIO E. MUÑOZ. Publ. *IAPA News*.

International Association of Broadcasting (Asociación Internacional de Radiodifusión—AIR): Cnel Brandzen 1961, Office 402, 11200 Montevideo, Uruguay; tel. (2) 408-8129; fax (2) 408-8121; e-mail airiab@distrinet.com.uy; f. 1946 to preserve free and private broadcasting; to promote co-operation between the corporations and public authorities; to defend freedom of expression. Mems: national associations of broadcasters. Pres. Dr LUIS H. TARSITANO; Dir-Gen. Dr HÉCTOR OSCAR AMENGUAL. Publ. *La Gaceta de AIR* (every 2 months).

International Association of Sound and Audiovisual Archives: c/o Albrecht Häfner, Südwestrundfunk, Documentation and Archives Dept, 76522 Baden-Baden, Germany; tel. (7221) 9293487; fax (7221) 9294199; e-mail albrecht.haefner@swr.de;

internet www.llgc.org.uk/iasa; f. 1969; supports the professional exchange of sound and audiovisual documents, and fosters international co-operation between audiovisual archies in all field, in particular in the areas of acquisition, documentation, access, exploitation copyright, and preservation; holds annual conference. Mems: 380 individuals and institutions in 48 countries. Sec.-Gen. ALBRECHT HÄFNER. Publs. *IASA Journal* (2 a year), *IASA Information Bulletin* (quarterly).

International Catholic Union of the Press (Union catholique internationale de la presse—UCIP): 37–39 rue de Vermont, Case Postale 197, 1211 Geneva 20, Switzerland; tel. (22) 7340017; fax (22) 7340053; e-mail helo@ucip.ch; internet www.ucip.ch; f. 1927 to link all Catholics who influence public opinion through the press, to inspire a high standard of professional conscience and to represent the interest of the Catholic press at international organizations. Mems: Federation of Catholic Press Agencies, Federation of Catholic Journalists, Federation of Catholic Dailies, Federation of Catholic Periodicals, Federation of Teachers in the Science and Technics of Information, Federation of Church Press Associations, Federation of Book Publishers, eight regional asscns. Pres. RERESA EE-CHOOI; Sec.-Gen. JOSEPH CHITTILAPPILLY (India). Publ. *UCIP-Information*.

International Council for Film, Television and Audiovisual Communication: 1 rue Miollis, 75732 Paris Cédex 15, France; tel. 1-45-68-48-55; fax 1-45-67-28-40; f. 1958 to arrange meetings and co-operation generally. Mems: 36 international film and television organizations. Pres. JEAN ROHCH; Sec.-Gen. Dr ROBERT E. KALMAN. Publ. *Letter of Information* (monthly).

International Council of French-speaking Radio and Television Organizations (Conseil international des radios-télévisions d'expression française): 52 blvd Auguste-Reyers, 1044 Brussels, Belgium; tel. (2) 732-45-85; fax (2) 732-62-40; f. 1978 to establish links between French-speaking radio and television organizations. Mems: 46 organizations. Sec.-Gen. ABDELKADER MARZOUKI (Tunisia).

International Federation of Press Cutting Agencies: Streulistr. 19, POB 8030 Zürich, Switzerland; tel. (1) 3888200; fax (1) 3888201; e-mail fibep@swissline.ch; f. 1953 to improve the standing of the profession, prevent infringements, illegal practices and unfair competition; and to develop business and friendly relations among press cuttings agencies throughout the world. Annual meeting, 1999: Malta. Mems: 71 agencies. Pres. XAVIER DE MONREDON (France); Gen. Sec. Dr DIETER HENNE (Switzerland).

International Federation of the Cinematographic Press—FIPRESCI: Schleissheimerstr. 83, 80797 Munich, Germany; tel. (89) 182303; fax (89) 184766; e-mail keder@fipresci.org; internet www.fipresci.org; f. 1930 to develop the cinematographic press and promote cinema as an art; organizes international meetings and juries in film festivals. Mems: national organizations or corresponding members in 68 countries. Pres. DEREK MALCOLM (UK); Sec.-Gen. KLAUS EDER (Germany).

International Federation of the Periodical Press—FIPP: Queen's House, 55/56 Lincoln's Inn Fields, London, WC2A 3LJ, United Kingdom; tel. (20) 7404-4169; fax (20) 7404-4170; e-mail info@fipp.com; internet www.fipp.com; f. 1925; works through national associations to promote optimum conditions for the development of periodical publishing; fosters formal and informal alliances between magazine publishers. Mems: 35 national asscns representing 2,500 publishing cos and 75 international publishing cos and assoc. mems. Pres. and CEO PER R. MORTENSEN; Chair. AXEL GANZ (Germany). Publ. *Magazine World* (6 a year).

International Federation of the Socialist and Democratic Press: CP 737, 20101 Milan, Italy; tel. (02) 8050105; f. 1953 to promote co-operation between editors and publishers of socialist newspapers; affiliated to the Socialist International (q.v.). Mems: about 100. Sec. UMBERTO GIOVINE.

International Institute of Communications: Tavistock House South, Tavistock Sq., London, WC1H 9LF, United Kingdom; tel. (20) 7388-0671; fax (20) 7380-0623; f. 1969 (as the International Broadcast Institute) to link all working in the field of communications, including policy makers, broadcasters, industrialists and engineers; holds local, regional and international meetings, undertakes research and publishes journal. Mems: over 1,000 corporate, institutional and individual. Pres. HENRI PIGEAT; Exec. Dir VICKI MACLEOD.

International Maritime Radio Association: South Bank House, Black Prince Rd, London, SE1 7SJ, United Kingdom; tel. (20) 7587-1245; fax (20) 7587-1436; e-mail secgen@cirm.org; internet www.cirm.org; f. 1928 to study and develop means of improving marine radio communications and radio aids to marine navigation. Mems: over 70 organizations and companies are involved in marine electronics in the areas of radio communications and navigation. The member companies are located in the major maritime nations of the world. Pres. G. SEUTIN (Belgium); Sec.-Gen. and Chair. of Technical Cttee Capt. C. K. D. COBLEY.

International Organization of Journalists: Calle Mayor 81, Madrid 28013, Spain; tel. (91) 24224243; fax (91) 24223853; f. 1946 to defend the freedom of the press and of journalists and to promote their material welfare. Activities include the maintenance of international training centres and international recreation centres for journalists. Mems: national organizations and individuals in 120 countries. Pres. ARMANDO S. ROLLEMBERG; Sec.-Gen. GERARD GATINOT. Publs *The World of Journalists* (quarterly, in English, French and Spanish), *IOJ Newsletter* (2 a month, in Arabic, English, French, Russian and Spanish).

International Press Institute—IPI: Spiegelgasse 2/29, 1010 Vienna, Austria; tel. (1) 5129011; fax (1) 5129014; e-mail ipi@ freemedia.at; internet www.freemedia.at; f. 1951 as a non-governmental organization of editors, publishers and news broadcasters who support the principles of a free and responsible press; activities: defence of press freedom, regional meetings of members, training programmes, research and library; annual World Congress. Mems: about 2,000 from 110 countries. Pres. HUGO BUETLER (Switzerland); Dir JOHANN FRITZ (Austria). Publs *IPI Global Journalist* (quarterly), *World Press Freedom Review* (annually).

International Press Telecommunications Council: Royal Albert House, Sheet St, Windsor, Berks, SL4 1BE, United Kingdom; tel. (1753) 705051; fax (1753) 831541; e-mail m_director_iptc@dial.pipex.com; internet www.iptc.org/iptc; f. 1965 to safeguard and promote the interests of the Press on all matters relating to telecommunications; keeps its members informed of current and future telecommunications developments; to act as the news information formal standards body. The Council meets three times a year and maintains four committees and 10 working parties. Mems: 44 press associations, newspapers, news agencies and industry vendors. Chair. PETER MÜLLER; Man. Dir DAVID ALLEN. Publs *IPTC Spectrum* (annually), *IPTC Mirror* (monthly).

Latin-American Catholic Press Union: Apdo Postal 17-21-178, Quito, Ecuador; tel. (2) 548046; fax (2) 501658; f. 1959 to co-ordinate, promote and improve the Catholic press in Latin America. Mems: national asscns and local groups in most Latin American countries. Pres. ISMAR DE OLIVEIRA SOARES (Brazil); Sec. CARLOS EDUARDO CORTÉS (Colombia).

Organization of Asia-Pacific News Agencies—OANA: c/o Xinhua News Agency, 57 Xuanwumen Xidajie, Beijing 100803, People's Republic of China; tel. (10) 3074762; fax (10) 3072707; f. 1961 to promote co-operation in professional matters and mutual exchange of news, features, etc. among the news agencies of Asia and the Pacific via the Asia-Pacific News Network (ANN). Mems: Anadolu Ajansi (Turkey), Antara (Indonesia), APP (Pakistan), Bakhtar (Afghanistan), BERNAMA (Malaysia), BSS (Bangladesh), ENA (Bangladesh), Hindustan Samachar (India), IRNA (Iran), ITAR-TASS (Russia), Kaz-TAG (Kazakhstan), KABAR (Kyrgyzstan), KCNA (Korea, Democratic People's Republic), KPL (Laos), Kyodo (Japan), Lankapuvath (Sri Lanka), Montsame (Mongolia), PNA (Philippines), PPI (Pakistan), PTI (India), RSS (Nepal), Samachar Bharati (India), TNA (Thailand), UNB (Bangladesh), UNI (India), Viet Nam News Agency, Xinhua (People's Republic of China), Yonhap (Republic of Korea). Pres. GUO CHAOREN; Sec.-Gen. YU JIAFU.

Press Foundation of Asia: POB 1843, S & L Bldg, 3rd Floor, 1500 Roxas Blvd, Manila, Philippines; tel. (2) 598633; fax (2) 5224365; e-mail pfa@pressasia.org; internet www.pressasia.org; f. 1967; an independent, non-profit making organization governed by its newspaper members; acts as a professional forum for about 200 newspapers in Asia; aims to reduce cost of newspapers to potential readers, to improve editorial and management techniques through research and training programmes and to encourage the growth of the Asian press; operates *Depthnews* feature service. Mems: 200 newspapers. Exec. Chair. EUGENIO LOPEZ (Philippines); Dir-Gen. MOCHTAR LUBIS (Indonesia). Publs *Pressasia* (quarterly), *Asian Women* (quarterly).

Reporters sans Frontières: 5 rue Geoffroy Marie, 75009 Paris, France; tel. 1-44-83-84-84; fax 1-45-23-11-51; e-mail rsf@rsf.fr; internet www.rsf.fr; f. 1985 to defend press freedoms throughout the world; generates awareness of violations of press freedoms and supports journalists under threat or imprisoned as a result of their work. Mems in 77 countries. Dir ROBERT MÉNARD. Publs *Annual Report, Quarterly Digest, La Lettre de Reporters sans Frontières* (monthly).

Union of National Radio and Television Organizations of Africa—URTNA: 101 rue Carnot, BP 3237, Dakar, Senegal; tel. 821-16-25; fax 822-51-13; e-mail urtnadkr@telecomplus.sn; f. 1962; co-ordinates radio and television services, including monitoring and frequency allocation, the exchange of information and coverage of national and international events among African countries; maintains programme exchange centre (Nairobi, Kenya), technical centre (Bamako, Mali), a centre for rural radio studies (Ouagadougou, Burkina Faso) and a centre for the exchange of television news in Algiers, Algeria. Mems: 48 organizations and six associate members. Sec.-Gen. ABDELHAMID BOUKSANI. Publ. *URTNA Review* (English and French, 2 a year).

World Association for Christian Communication—WACC: 357 Kennington Lane, London, SE11 5QY, United Kingdom; tel. (20) 7582-9139; fax (20) 7735-0340; e-mail wacc@wacc.org.uk; internet www.wacc.org.uk; f. 1975; WACC seeks to promote human dignity, justice and peace through freedom of expression and the democratization of communication. It offers professional guidance on communication policies and interprets developments in and consequences of global communication methods. WACC works towards the empowerment of women and assists the training of Christian communicators. Mems: more than 800 corporate and personal mems in 115 countries, organized in eight regional assocs. Pres. ALBERT VAN DEN HEUVEL; Gen.-Sec. CARLOS A. VALLE. Publs *Action* newsletter (10 a year), *Media Development* (quarterly), *Communication Resource, Media and Gender Monitor* (both occasional).

World Association of Newspapers: 25 rue d'Astorg, 75008 Paris, France; tel. 1-47-42-85-00; fax 1-47-42-49-48; e-mailtbalding@wan .asso.fr; internet www.wan-press.org; f. 1948 to defend the freedom of the press, to safeguard the ethical and economic interests of newspapers and to study all questions of interest to newspapers at international level. Mems: 66 national newspaper asscns, individual newspaper executives in 93 countries, 17 news agencies and seven regional and world-wide press groups. Pres. BENGT BRAUN (Sweden); Dir-Gen. TIMOTHY BALDING. Publ. *Newsletter*.

Religion

Agudath Israel World Organisation: Hacherut Sq., POB 326, Jerusalem 91002, Israel; tel. (2) 5384357; fax (2) 5383634; f. 1912 to help solve the problems facing Jewish people all over the world in the spirit of the Jewish tradition; holds World Rabbinical Council (every five years), and an annual Central Council comprising 100 mems nominated by affiliated organizations. Mems: over 500,000 in 25 countries. Chair. J. M. ABRAMOWITZ (Jerusalem). Publs *Hamodia* (Jerusalem weekly newspaper), *Jewish Tribune* (London, weekly), *Jewish Observer* (New York, monthly), *Dos Yiddishe Vort* (New York, monthly), *Coalition* (New York), *Perspectives* (Toronto, monthly), *La Voz Judia* (Buenos Aires, monthly), *Jüdische Stimme* (Zürich, monthly).

All Africa Conference of Churches—AACC: POB 14205, Waiyaki Way, Nairobi, Kenya; tel. (2) 441483; fax (2) 443241; e-mail aacc-secretariat@maf.org; f. 1958; an organ of co-operation and continuing fellowship among Protestant, Orthodox and independent churches and Christian Councils in Africa. 1997 Assembly: Addis Ababa, Ethiopia. Mems: 147 churches and affiliated Christian councils in 39 African countries. Pres. The Very Rev. Prof. KWESI DICKSON (Ghana); Gen. Sec. Canon CLEMENT JANDA (Uganda). Publs *ACIS/APS Bulletin, ACLCA News, Tam Tam*.

Alliance Israélite Universelle: 45 rue La Bruyère, 75425 Paris Cédex 09, France; tel. 1-53-32-88-55; fax 1-48-74-51-33; e-mail info@aiu.org; internet www.aiu.org; f. 1860 to work for the emancipation and moral progress of the Jews; maintains 40 schools in eight countries; library of 120,000 vols. Mems: 8,000 in 16 countries. Pres. ADY STEG; Dir JEAN-JACQUES WAHL (France). Publs *Les Cahiers de l'Alliance Israélite Universelle* (3 a year, in French), *Les Cahiers du Judaïsme, The Alliance Review* (in English).

Bahá'í International Community: Bahá'í World Centre, POB 155, 31 001 Haifa, Israel; tel. (4) 8358394; fax (4) 8313312; e-mail opi@bwc.org; internet www.bahai.org; f. 1844 in Persia to promote the unity of mankind and world peace through the teachings of the Bahá'í religion, including the equality of men and women and the elimination of all forms of prejudice; maintains schools for children and adults worldwide, and maintains educational and cultural radio stations in the USA, Asia and Latin America; has 32 publishing trusts throughout the world. Governing body: Universal House of Justice (nine mems elected by 182 National Spiritual Assemblies). Mems: in 129,949 centres (190 countries and 45 dependent territories or overseas departments). Sec.-Gen. ALBERT LINCOLN (USA). Publs *Bahá'í World* (annually), *One Country* (quarterly, in 6 languages).

Baptist World Alliance: 6733 Curran St, McLean, VA 22101-6005, USA; tel. (703) 790-8980; fax (703) 893-5160; e-mail bwa@bwanet .org; f. 1905; aims to unite Baptists, lead in evangelism, respond to people in need and defend human rights. Mems: 191 Baptist unions and conventions comprising 42m. people in 200 countries and territories. Pres. Dr NILSON DO AMARAL FANINI (Brazil); Gen. Sec. Dr DENTON LOTZ. Publ. *The Baptist World* (quarterly).

Caribbean Conference of Churches: POB 616, Bridgetown, Barbados; tel. (246) 427-2681; fax (246) 429-2075; e-mail cccbdos@cariaccess.com; f. 1973; holds Assembly every five years; conducts study and research programmes and supports education and community projects. Mems: 34 churches. Gen. Sec. GERARD GRANADO.

Christian Conference of Asia: Pak Tin Village, Mei Tin Rd, Shatin, NT, Hong Kong; tel. 26911068; fax 26924378; e-mail cca@hk.super.net; f. 1957 (present name adopted 1973) to promote co-operation and joint study in matters of common concern among the Churches of the region and to encourage interaction with other regional Conferences and the World Council of Churches. Mems: 119 churches and 16 national councils of churches. Gen. Sec. Dr FELICIANO V. CARIÑO. Publ. *CCA News* (quarterly).

Christian Peace Conference: 130 11, Prague 3, POB 136, Proko-pova 4, Czech Republic; tel. (2) 22781800; fax (2) 22781801; e-mail cpc.off@iol.cz; f. 1958 as an international movement of theologians, clergy and lay-people, aiming to bring Christendom to recognize its share of guilt in both world wars and to dedicate itself to the service of friendship, reconciliation and peaceful co-operation of nations, to concentrate on united action for peace and justice, and to co-ordinate peace groups in individual churches and facilitate their effective participation in the peaceful development of society. It works through five continental associations, regional groups and member churches in many countries. Moderator Dr SERGIO ARCE MARTÍNEZ; Co-ordinator Rev. BRIAN G. COOPER. Publs *CPC INFORMATION* (8 a year in English and German), occasional *Study Volume*.

Conference of European Churches—CEC: POB 2100, 150 route de Ferney, 1211 Geneva 2, Switzerland; tel. (22) 7916111; fax (22) 7916227; e-mail reg@cec-kek.org; internet www.cec-kek.org; f. 1959 as a regional ecumenical organization for Europe and a meeting-place for European churches, including members and non-members of the World Council of Churches; assemblies every few years. Mems: 128 Protestant, Anglican, Orthodox and Old Catholic churches in all European countries. Gen. Sec. Rev. Dr KEITH CLEMENTS. Publs *Monitor*, CEC communiqués.

Conference of International Catholic Organizations: 37–39 rue de Vermont, 1202 Geneva, Switzerland; tel. (22) 7338392; f. 1927 to encourage collaboration and agreement between the different Catholic international organizations in their common interests, and to contribute to international understanding; organizes interna-tional assemblies and meetings to study specific problems. Perm-anent commissions deal with human rights, the new international economic order, social problems, the family health, education, etc. Mems: 36 Catholic international organizations. Administrator PAUL MORAND (Switzerland).

Consultative Council of Jewish Organizations—CCJO: 420 Lexington Ave, New York, NY 10170, USA; tel. (212) 808-5437; f. 1946 to co-operate and consult with the UN and other international bodies directly concerned with human rights and to defend the cultural, political and religious rights of Jews throughout the world. Sec.-Gen. WARREN GREEN (USA).

European Baptist Federation: Postfach 610340, 22423 Hamburg, Germany; tel. (40) 5509723; fax (40) 5509725; e-mail office@ebf.org; f. 1949 to promote fellowship and co-operation among Baptists in Europe; to further the aims and objects of the Baptist World Alliance; to stimulate and co-ordinate evangelism in Europe; to provide for consultation and planning of missionary work in Europe and else-where in the world. Mems: 49 Baptist Unions in European countries and the Middle East. Pres. DAVID COFFEY; Sec.-Treas. Rev. KARL-HEINZ WALTER (Germany).

European Evangelical Alliance: Wilhelmshoeher Allee 258, 34131 Kassel, Germany; tel. (561) 3149711; fax (561) 9387520; e-mail 100341.550@compuserve.com; internet www.hfe.org; f. 1953 to promote understanding and co-operation among evangelical Chris-tians in Europe and to stimulate evangelism. Mems: 25 national alliances from 24 countries, 6 pan-European asscns. Pres. DEREK COPLEY (UK); Sec. GORDON SHOWELL-ROGERS.

Friends World Committee for Consultation: 4 Byng Pl., London, WC1E 7JH, United Kingdom; tel. (20) 7388-0497; fax (20) 7383-4644; e-mail fwccworldofficelondon@compuserve.com; internet www.quaker.org/fwcc/; f. 1937 to encourage and strengthen the spiri-tual life within the Religious Society of Friends (Quakers); to help Friends to a better understanding of their vocation in the world; to promote consultation among Friends of all countries; representation at the United Nations as a non-governmental organization. Mems: appointed representatives and individuals from 70 countries. Gen. Sec. ELIZABETH DUKE. Publs *Friends World News* (2 a year), *Calendar of Yearly Meetings* (annually), *Quakers around the World* (hand-book).

International Association for Religious Freedom—IARF: 2 Market St, Oxford OX1 3EF, United Kingdom; tel. (1865) 202-744; fax (1865) 202-746; e-mail iarf@interfaith-center.org; internet www.iarf-religiousfreedom.net; f. 1900 as a world community of religions, subscribing to the principle of openness and to respect for fundamental human rights; conducts intercultural encounters, inter-religious dialogues, a social service network and development programme. Regional conferences and triennial congress. Mems: 70 groups in 25 countries. Pres. YUKITAKA YAMAMOTO (Japan); Gen. Sec. Rev. Dr ROBERT TRAER (UK). Publ. *IARF World* (2 a year).

International Association of Buddhist Studies: c/o Prof. Oskar von Hinüber, Orientalisches Seminar, Indologie, Humboldtstr. 5, Freiburg 79085, Germany; tel. (761) 203-3158; fax (761) 203-3152; f. 1976; holds international conference every three or four years;

supports studies of Buddhist religion, philosophy and literature. Gen. Sec. OSKAR VON HINÜBER. Publ. *Journal* (2 a year).

International Council of Christians and Jews: 64629 Hep-penheim, Werlestrasse 2, Postfach 1129, Germany; tel. (6252) 5041; fax (6252) 68331; e-mail iccj_buberhouse@t-online.de; f. 1955 to promote mutual respect and co-operation; holds annual interna-tional colloquium, seminars, meetings for young people and for women; forum for Jewish–Christian–Muslim relations established. Mems: national councils in 29 countries. Pres. Rabbi Prof. DAVID ROSEN; Sec.-Gen. Rev. FRIEDHELM PIEPER.

International Council of Jewish Women: 24–32 Stephenson Way, London, NW1 2JW, United Kingdom; tel. (20) 7388-8311; fax (20) 7387-2110; e-mail hq@icjw.demon.co.uk; internet www.icjw.org.uk; f. 1912 to promote friendly relations and under-standing among Jewish women throughout the world; campaigns for human and women's rights, exchanges information on community welfare activities, promotes volunteer leadership, sponsors field work in social welfare, co-sponsors the International Jewish Women's Human Rights Watch and fosters Jewish education. Mems: affiliates totalling over 1.5m. members in 46 countries. Pres. JUNE JACOBS. Publs *Newsletter, Links around the World* (2 a year, English and Spanish), *International Jewish Women's Human Rights Watch* (2 a year).

International Fellowship of Reconciliation: Spoorstraat 38, 1815 BK Alkmaar, Netherlands; tel. (72) 512-30-14; fax (72) 515-11-02; e-mail office@ifor.org; internet www.ifor.org; f. 1919; interna-tional, spiritually-based movement committed to active non-violence as a way of life and as a means of transformation, to build a culture of peace and non-violence. Branches, affiliates and groups in more than 50 countries. Int. Pres. VIRGINIA BARON (USA). Publs *Reconcilia-tion International* (quarterly), *Patterns in Reconciliation , Cross the Lines* (3 a year, in English, French and Spanish), occasional paper series.

International Humanist and Ethical Union: 47 Theobald's Rd, London, WC1X 8SP, United Kingdom; tel. (20) 7831-4817; fax (20) 7404-8641; internet www.iheu.org; f. 1952 to bring into association all those interested in promoting ethical and scientific humanism and human rights. Mems: national organizations and individuals in 37 countries. Exec. Dir BABU R. R. GOGINENI. Publ. *International Humanist News* (quarterly).

International Organization for the Study of the Old Testa-ment: Faculteit der Godgeleerdheid, POB 9515, 2300 RA Leiden, Netherlands; tel. (71) 5272577; fax (71) 5272571; f. 1950. Holds triennial congresses. Pres. Prof. E. JENNI (Switzerland); Sec. Prof. A. VAN DER KOOIJ (Netherlands). Publ. *Vetus Testamentum* (quarterly).

Latin American Council of Churches (Consejo Latinoamericano de Iglesias—CLAI): Casilla 17-08-8522, Calle Inglaterra 943 y Mar-iana de Jesús, Quito, Ecuador; tel. and fax (2) 553996; e-mail israel@clai.ecuanex.net.ec; f. 1982. Mems: 147 churches in 19 coun-tries. Gen. Sec. Rev. ISRAEL BATISTA.

Latin American Episcopal Council: Apartado Aéreos 5278 y 51086, Santafé de Bogotá, Colombia; tel. (1) 612-1620; fax (1) 612-1929; f. 1955 to study the problems of the Roman Catholic Church in Latin America and to co-ordinate Church activities. Mems: the Episcopal Conferences of Central and South America and the Carib-bean. Pres. Archbishop OSCAR ANDRÉS RODRÍGUEZ MARADIAGA (Hond-uras). Publ. *CELAM* (6 a year).

Lutheran World Federation: 150 route de Ferney, POB 2100, 1211 Geneva 2, Switzerland; tel. (22) 7916111; fax (22) 7988616; e-mail info@lutheranworld.org; internet www.lutheranworld.org; f. 1947; communion of 128 Lutheran Churches of 70 countries. Current activities: inter-church aid; relief work in various areas of the globe; service to refugees including resettlement; aid to missions; theological research, conferences and exchanges; scholarship aid in various fields of church life; inter-confessional dialogue with Roman Catholic, Seventh-day Adventist, Anglican and Orthodox churches; Christian communications projects and international news and information services; Ninth Assembly: Hong Kong, 1997. Pres. Rt Rev. Dr CHRISTIAN KRAUSE (Germany); Gen. Sec. Rev. Dr ISHMAEL NOKO (Zimbabwe). Publs *Lutheran World Information* (English and German, every 2 weeks), *LWF Today* and *LWF Documentation* (both irregular).

Middle East Council of Churches: Makhoul St, Deep Bldg, POB 5376, Beirut, Lebanon; tel. and fax (1) 344894; f. 1974. Mems: 28 churches. Pres Pope SHENOUDAH III, Patriarch PETROS VII PAPAPETRO, Rev. Dr SELIM SAHYOUNI, Archbishop KYRILLOS BUSTROS; Gen. Sec. Rev. Dr RIAD JARJOUR. Publs *MECC News Report* (monthly), *Al Montada News Bulletin* (quarterly, in Arabic), *Courrier oecuménique du Moyen-Orient* (quarterly), *MECC Perspectives* (3 a year).

Moral Re-Armament: POB 3, 1211 Geneva 20, Switzerland; tel. (22) 7330920; fax (22) 7330267; e-mail media@caux.ch; internet www.caux.ch; other international centres at Panchgani, India, Petropolis, Brazil, London and Tirley Garth, UK, and Gweru, Zim-babwe; f. 1921; aims: a new social order for better human relations and the elimination of political, industrial and racial antagonism. Legally incorporated bodies in 20 countries. Pres. of Swiss foundation CORNELIO SOMMARUGA. Publs *Changer* (French, 6 a year), *For a Change* (English, 6 a year), *Caux Information* (German, monthly).

Muslim World League (Rabitat al-Alam al-Islami): POB 537–538, Makkah, Saudi Arabia; tel. (2) 5422733; fax (2) 5436619; e-mail mwlhq@aol.com; internet www.arab.net/mwl; f. 1962; aims to advance Islamic unity and solidarity, and to promote world peace and respect for human rights; provides financial assistance for education, medical care and relief work; has 30 offices throughout the world. Sec.-Gen. Sheikh Prof. Dr ABD' ALLAH BIN SALEH EL-OBEID. Publs *Majalla al-Rabita* (monthly, Arabic), *Akhbar al-Alam al Islami* (weekly, Arabic), *Journal* (monthly, English).

Opus Dei (Prelature of the Holy Cross and Opus Dei): Viale Bruno Buozzi 73, 00197 Rome, Italy; tel. (06) 808961; f. 1928 by Blessed Josemaría Escrivá de Balaguer to spread, at every level of society, a profound awakening of consciences to the universal calling to sanctity and apostolate in the course of members' own professional work. Mems: 81,954 Catholic laypeople and 1,734 priests. Prelate Most Rev. JAVIER ECHEVARRÍA. Publ. *Romana, Bulletin of the Prelature* (every six months).

Pacific Conference of Churches: POB 208, 4 Thurston St, Suva, Fiji; tel. 311277; fax 303205; e-mail pacific@is.com.fj; f. 1961; organizes assembly every five years, as well as regular workshops, meetings and training seminars throughout the region. Mems: 36 churches and councils. Moderator Pastor REUBEN MAGEKON; Gen. Sec. Rev. VALAMOTU PALU.

Pax Romana International Catholic Movement for Intellectual and Cultural Affairs—ICMICA; and International Movement of Catholic Students—IMCS: 15 rue du Grand-Bureau, POB 315, 1211 Geneva 24, Switzerland; tel. (22) 8230707; fax (22) 8230708; e-mail miicmica@paxromana.int.ch; internet www.pax-romana.org; f. 1921 (IMCS), 1947 (ICMICA), to encourage in members an awareness of their responsibilities as people and Christians in the student and intellectual milieux; to promote contacts between students and graduates throughout the world and co-ordinate the contribution of Catholic intellectual circles to international life. Mems: 80 student and 60 intellectual organizations in 80 countries. ICMICA—Pres. MARY J. MWINGIRA (Tanzania); Gen. Sec. ANSELMO LEE SEONG-HOON (Republic of Korea); IMCS—Gen. Secs WALTER PRYSTHON (Brazil), ROLAND RANAIVOARISON (Madagascar). Publ. *Convergence* (3 a year).

Salvation Army: International HQ, 101 Queen Victoria St, London, EC4P 4EP, United Kingdom; tel. (20) 7332-0022; fax (20) 7236-4981; e-mail websa@salvationarmy.org; internet www.salvationarmy.org.uk; f. 1865 to spread the Christian gospel and relieve poverty; emphasis is placed on the need for personal discipleship, and to make its evangelism effective it adopts a quasi-military form of organization. Social, medical and educational work is also performed in the 107 countries where the Army operates. Pres. Gen. JOHN GOWANS; Chief of Staff Commissioner JOHN LARSSON. Publs 132 periodicals in 31 languages.

Soroptimist International: 87 Glisson Rd, Cambridge, CB1 2HG, United Kingdom; tel. (1223) 311833; fax (1223) 467951; e-mail sorophq@dial.pipex.com; internet www.sorop.org/; f. 1921; aims to strive for the advancement of the status of women, high ethical standards, human rights for all, equality and development of peace through international goodwill, understanding and friendship. Convention held every 4 years, 2003: Sydney, Australia. Mems: 95,000 in 3,000 clubs in 121 countries and territories. International Pres. JANE ZIMMERMAN (Australia); Exec. Officer JANET BILTON. Publ. *International Soroptimist* (quarterly).

Theosophical Society: Adyar, Chennai 600 020, India; tel. (44) 4915552; fax (44) 4902706; e-mail theossoc@satyam.net.in; internet www.ts-adyar.org; f. 1875; aims at universal brotherhood, without distinction of race, creed, sex, caste or colour; study of comparative religion, philosophy and science; investigation of unexplained laws of nature and powers latent in man. Mems: 35,000 in 70 countries. Pres. RADHA S. BURNIER; Int. Sec. DOLORES GAGO. Publs *The Theosophist* (monthly), *Adyar News Letter* (quarterly), *Brahmavidya* (annually).

United Bible Societies: 7th Floor, Reading Bridge House, Reading, RG1 8PJ, United Kingdom; tel. (118) 950-0200; fax (118) 950-0857; e-mail jphillips@ubs-wsc.org; internet www.biblesociety.org; f. 1946; co-ordinates the translation, production and distribution of the Bible by Bible Societies world-wide. Mems: 136 Bible Societies in more than 200 countries. Pres. Dr SAMUEL ESCOBAR (Peru/USA); Gen. Sec. Rev. FERGUS MACDONALD (UK). Publs *United Bible Societies Bulletin, The Bible Translator* (quarterly), *Publishing World* (3 a year), *Prayer Booklet* (annually), *Special Report* (3 or 4 a year), *World Report* (monthly).

Watch Tower Bible and Tract Society: (British section) The Ridgeway, London, NW7 1RN, United Kingdom; tel. (20) 8906-2211; fax (20) 8959-3855; e-mail pr@wtbts.org.uk; internet www.watchtower.org; f. 1881; 110 branches; serves as legal agency for Jehovah's Witnesses, whose membership is 6m. Pres. MILTON G. HENSCHEL; Sec. and Treas. LYMAN SWINGLE. Publs *The Watchtower* (2 a month, in 140 languages), *Awake!* (2 a month, in 83 languages).

World Alliance of Reformed Churches (Presbyterian and Congregational): Box 2100, 150 route de Ferney, 1211 Geneva 2, Switzerland; tel. (22) 7916240; fax (22) 7916505; e-mail sn@warc.ch; internet www.warc.ch; f. 1970 by merger of WARC (Presbyterian) (f. 1875) with International Congregational Council (f. 1891) to promote fellowship among Reformed, Presbyterian and Congregational churches. Mems: 214 churches in 106 countries. Pres. Prof. CHOAN-SENG SONG; Gen. Sec. Revd Dr SETRI NYOMI (Ghana). Publs *Reformed World* (quarterly), *Up-Date*.

World Christian Life Community: Borgo S. Spirito 8, Casella Postale 6139, 00195 Rome, Italy; tel. (06) 6868079; e-mail mcvx.wclc@agora.stm.it; f. 1953 as World Federation of the Sodalities of our Lady (first group founded 1563) as a lay movement (based on the teachings of Ignatius Loyola) to integrate Christian faith and daily living. Mems: groups in 55 countries representing about 100,000 individuals. Pres. JOSÉ MARÍA RIERA; Exec. Sec. GILLES MICHAUD. Publ. *Progressio* (in English, French, Spanish).

World Conference on Religion and Peace: 777 United Nations Plaza, New York, NY 10017, USA; tel. (212) 687-2163; fax (212) 983-0566; f. 1970 to co-ordinate education and action of various world religions for world peace and justice. Mems: religious organizations and individuals in 100 countries. Sec.-Gen. Dr WILLIAM VENDLEY. Publ. *Religion for Peace*.

World Congress of Faiths: 2 Market St, Oxford, OX1 3EF, United Kingdom; tel. (1865) 202751; fax (1865) 202746; f. 1936 to promote a spirit of fellowship among mankind through an understanding of each other's religion, to bring together people of all nationalities, backgrounds and creeds in mutual respect and tolerance, to encourage the study and understanding of issues arising out of multi-faith societies, and to promote welfare and peace. Mems: about 800. Vice-Pres Rev. Dr EDWARD CARPENTER, Prof. KEITH WARD; Chair. MARCUS BRAYBROOKE. Publ. *World Faiths Encounter* (3 a year).

World Evangelical Fellowship: 141 Middle Rd 05-05, GSM Bldg, Singapore 188976, Singapore; tel. 3397900; fax 3383756; e-mail 100012.345@compuserve.com; f. 1951, on reorganization of World Evangelical Alliance (f. 1846); an int. grouping of national and regional bodies of evangelical Christians; encourages the organization of national fellowships and assists national mems in planning their activities. Mems: national evangelical asscns in 110 countries. International Dir AUGUSTIN B. VENCER, Jr. Publs *Evangelical World* (monthly), *Evangelical Review of Theology* (quarterly).

World Fellowship of Buddhists: 616 Benjasiri Pk, Soi Medhinivet off Soi Sukhumvit 24, Bangkok 10110, Thailand; tel. (2) 661-1284; fax (2) 661-0555; e-mail wfb-hq@asianet.co.th; internet www.wfb-hq.org; f. 1950 to promote strict observance and practice of the teachings of the Buddha; holds General Conference every 2 years; 140 regional centres in 37 countries. Pres. PHAN WANNAMETHEE; Hon. Sec.-Gen. Dr NANTASARN SEESALAB. Publs *WFB Journal* (6 a year), *WFB Review* (quarterly), *WFB Newsletter* (monthly), documents, booklets.

World Hindu Federation: c/o Dr Jogendra Jha, Pashupati Kshetra, Kathmandu, Nepal; tel. (1) 470182; fax (1) 470131; e-mail hem@karki.com.np; f. 1981 to promote and preserve Hindu philosophy and culture; to protect the rights of Hindus, particularly the right to worship. Executive Board meets annually. Mems: in 45 countries and territories. Sec.-Gen. Dr JOGENDRA JHA (Nepal). Publ. *Vishwa Hindu* (monthly).

World Jewish Congress: 501 Madison Ave, New York, NY 10022, USA; tel. (212) 755-5770; fax (212) 755-5883; f. 1936; a voluntary association of representative Jewish communities and organizations throughout the world, aiming to foster the unity of the Jewish people and to ensure the continuity and development of their heritage. Mems: Jewish communities in 84 countries. Pres. EDGAR M. BRONFMAN; Sec.-Gen. ISRAEL SINGER. Publs *Gesher* (Hebrew quarterly, Israel), *Boletín Informativo OJI* (fortnightly, Buenos Aires).

World Methodist Council: International Headquarters, POB 518, Lake Junaluska, NC 28745, USA; tel. (704) 456-9432; fax (704) 456-9433; e-mail wmc6@juno.com; internet www.worldmethodistcouncil.org; f. 1881 to deepen the fellowship of the Methodist peoples, to encourage evangelism, to foster Methodist participation in the ecumenical movement, and to promote the unity of Methodist witness and service. Mems: 75 churches in 130 countries, comprising 32m. individuals. Gen. Sec. JOE HALE (USA). Publ. *World Parish* (6 a year).

World Sephardi Federation: 13 rue Marignac, 1206 Geneva, Switzerland; tel. (22) 3473313; fax (22) 3472839; f. 1951 to strengthen the unity of Jewry and Judaism among Sephardi and Oriental Jews, to defend and foster religious and cultural activities of all Sephardi and Oriental Jewish communities and preserve their spiritual heritage, to provide moral and material assistance where necessary and to co-operate with other similar organizations. Mems: 50

communities and organizations in 33 countries. Pres. NESSIM D. GAON; Sec.-Gen. SHIMON DERY.

World Student Christian Federation: 5 route des Morillons, Grand-Saconnex, 1218 Geneva, Switzerland; tel. (22) 7988953; fax (22) 7982370; e-mail wscf@worldcom.ch; internet www.wscf.net; f. 1895 to proclaim Jesus Christ as Lord and Saviour in the academic community, and to present students with the claims of the Christian faith over their whole life. Gen. Assembly every four years. Mems: 67 national Student Christian Movements, and 34 national correspondents. Chair. Rev. EJIKE OKORD (Nigeria); Secs-Gen. BEATE FAGERLI (Norway), LAWRENCE BREW (Ghana).

World Union for Progressive Judaism: 633 Third Ave, New York, NY 10017, USA; tel. (212) 249-0100; fax (212) 650-4099; f. 1926; promotes and co-ordinates efforts of Reform, Liberal, Progressive and Reconstructionist congregations throughout the world; supports new congregations; assigns and employs rabbis; sponsors seminaries and schools; organizes international conferences; maintains a youth section. Mems: organizations and individuals in 30 countries. Pres. AUSTIN BEUTEL; Exec. Dir Rabbi RICHARD G. HIRSCH (Israel). Publs *News Updates, International Conference Reports, European Judaism* (bi-annual).

World Union of Catholic Women's Organisations: 18 rue Notre-Dame-des-Champs, 75006 Paris, France; tel. 1-45-44-27-65; fax 1-42-84-04-80; e-mail wucwoparis@wanadoo.fr; f. 1910 to promote and co-ordinate the contribution of Catholic women in international life, in social, civic, cultural and religious matters. Mems: 20m. Pres. MARÍA EUGENIA DÍAZ DE PFENNICH (Mexico); Sec.-Gen. GILLIAN BADCOCK (UK). Publ. *Newsletter* (quarterly, in four languages).

Science

International Council for Science—ICSU: 51 blvd de Montmorency, 75016 Paris, France; tel. 1-45-25-03-29; fax 1-42-88-94-31; e-mail secretariat@icsu.org; internet www.icsu.org; f. 1919 as International Research Council; present name adopted 1931; new statutes adopted 1996; to co-ordinate international co-operation in theoretical and applied sciences and to promote national scientific research through the intermediary of affiliated national organizations; General Assembly of representatives of national and scientific members meets every three years to formulate policy. The following committees have been established: Cttee on Science for Food Security, Scientific Cttee on Antarctic Research, Scientific Cttee on Oceanic Research, Cttee on Space Research, Scientific Cttee on Water Research, Scientific Cttee on Solar-Terrestrial Physics, Cttee on Science and Technology in Developing Countries, Cttee on Data for Science and Technology, Programme on Capacity Building in Science, Scientific Cttee on Problems of the Environment, Steering Cttee on Genetics and Biotechnology and Scientific Cttee on International Geosphere-Biosphere Programme. The following services and Inter-Union Committees and Commissions have been established: Federation of Astronomical and Geophysical Data Analysis Services, Inter-Union Commission on Frequency Allocations for Radio Astronomy and Space Science, Inter-Union Commission on Radio Meteorology, Inter-Union Commission on Spectroscopy, Inter-Union Commission on Lithosphere. National mems: academies or research councils in 98 countries; Scientific mems and assocs: 26 international unions (see below) and 28 scientific associates. Pres. W. ARBER; Sec.-Gen. H. A. MOONEY. Publs *ICSU Yearbook, Science International* (quarterly), *Annual Report*.

UNIONS FEDERATED TO THE ICSU

International Astronomical Union: 98 bis blvd d'Arago, 75014 Paris, France; tel. 1-43-25-83-58; fax 1-43-25-26-16; e-mail iau@iap.fr; internet www.iau.org; f. 1919 to facilitate co-operation between the astronomers of various countries and to further the study of astronomy in all its branches. Mems: organizations in 65 countries, and 9,000 individual mems. Pres. FRANCO PACINI (Italy); Gen. Sec. HANS RICKMAN (Sweden). Publs *IAU Information Bulletin* (2 a year), *Symposia Series* (6 a year), *Highlights* (every 3 years).

International Geographical Union—IGU: Dept of Geography, University of Bonn, 53115 Bonn, Meckenheimer Allee 166, Germany; tel. (228) 739287; fax (228) 739272; e-mail secretariat@igu.bn.eunet.be; internet www.helsinki.fi/science/igu; f. 1922 to encourage the study of problems relating to geography, to promote and co-ordinate research requiring international co-operation, and to organize international congresses and commissions. Mem. countries: 83, and 11 associates. Pres. Prof. BRUNO MESSERLI (Switzerland); Sec.-Gen. Prof. ECKART EHLERS (Germany). Publ. *IGU Bulletin* (2 a year).

International Mathematical Union: c/o Institute for Advanced Study (IAS), Olden Lane, Princeton, NJ 08540, USA; e-mail imu@ias.edu; f. 1952 to support and assist the International Congress of Mathematicians and other international scientific meetings or conferences; to encourage and support other international mathematical activities considered likely to contribute to the development

of mathematical science—pure, applied or educational. Mems: 63 countries. Pres. Prof. JACOB PALIS; Sec.-Gen. Prof. PHILLIP GRIFFITHS.

International Union for Physical and Engineering Sciences in Medicine: c/o Prof. G. Fullerton, UTHSCSA, Dept of Radiology, MSC 7800, 7703 Floyd Curl Drive, San Antonio, TX 78229-3900, USA; tel. (210) 567-5551; fax (210) 567-5549; e-mail fullerton@uthscsa.edu; internet www.iupesm.org; f. 1980 by its two constituent orgs (International Federation for Medical and Biological Engineering, see p.516, and International Organization for Medical Physics, see p.517); promotes international co-operation in health care science and technology and represents the professional interests of members; organizes seminars, workshops, scientific conferences; World Congress held every three years (2003: Sydney, Australia). Sec.-Gen. Prof. GARY FULLERTON (USA). Publs *IUPESM Newsletter* (2 a year), Congress proceedings.

International Union for Pure and Applied Biophysics: School of Biochemistry and Molecular Biology, University of Leeds, Leeds, LS2 9JT, United Kingdom; tel. (113) 2333023; fax (113) 2333167; e-mail a.c.t.north@leeds.ac.uk; internet www.iupab.org; f. 1961 to organize international co-operation in biophysics and promote communication between biophysics and allied subjects, to encourage national co-operation between biophysical societies, and to contribute to the advancement of biophysical knowledge. Mems: 50 adhering bodies. Pres. I. PECHT (Israel); Sec.-Gen. Prof. A. C. T. NORTH (UK). Publ. *Quarterly Reviews of Biophysics*.

International Union of Biochemistry and Molecular Biology: Institute for Biophysical Chemistry and Biochemistry, Technical University Berlin, Franklinstr. 29, 10587 Berlin, Germany; tel. (30) 31424205; fax (30) 31424783; e-mail kleinkauf@chem.tu-berlin.de; f. 1955 to sponsor the International Congresses of Biochemistry, to co-ordinate research and discussion, to organize co-operation between the societies of biochemistry and molecular biology, to promote high standards of biochemistry and molecular biology throughout the world and to contribute to the advancement of biochemistry and molecular biology in all its international aspects. Mems: 65 bodies. Pres. W. WHELAN (USA); Gen. Sec. Prof. Dr H. KLEINKAUF (Germany).

International Union of Biological Sciences: 51 blvd de Montmorency, 75016 Paris, France; tel. 1-45-25-00-09; fax 1-45-25-20-29; e-mail iubs@paris7.jussieu.fr; f. 1919. Mems: 43 national bodies, 86 scientific bodies. Exec. Dir Dr T. YOUNES. Publs *Biology International* (2 a year, plus special issues), *IUBS Monographs, IUBS Methodology, Manual Series*.

International Union of Crystallography: c/o M. H. Dacombe, 2 Abbey Sq., Chester, CH1 2HU, United Kingdom; tel. (1244) 345431; fax (1244) 344843; f. 1947 to facilitate international standardization of methods, of units, of nomenclature and of symbols used in crystallography; and to form a focus for the relations of crystallography to other sciences. Mems in 40 countries. Pres. Prof. H. SCHENK (Netherlands); Gen. Sec. S. LARSEN (Denmark); Exec. Sec. M. H. DACOMBE. Publs *Acta Crystallographica, Journal of Applied Crystallography, Journal of Synchroton Radiation, International Tables for Crystallography, World Directory of Crystallographers, IUCr/OUP Crystallographic Symposia, IUCr/OUP Monographs on Crystallography, IUCr/OUP Texts on Crystallography*.

International Union of Food Science and Technology: 522 Maple Ave, Oakville, Ontario, L6J 2J4, Canada; tel. (905) 815-1926; fax (905) 815-1574; e-mail iufost@inforamp-net; internet home.inforamp.net/-iufost; f. 1970; sponsors international symposia and congresses. Mems: 60 national groups. Pres. Prof. WALTER SPIESS (Germany); Sec.-Gen. JUDITH MEECH (Canada). Publ. *IUFOST Newsline* (3 a year).

International Union of Geodesy and Geophysics—IUGG: Cires Campus Box 216, University of Colorado, Boulder, CO 80309, USA; tel. (303) 497-51-47; fax (303) 497-36-45; e-mail jjoselyn@cisnes.colorado.edu; internet www.obs-mip.fr/uggi/; f. 1919; federation of seven associations representing Geodesy, Seismology and Physics of the Earth's Interior, Physical Sciences of the Ocean, Volcanology and Chemistry of the Earth's Interior, Hydrological Sciences, Meteorology and Atmospheric Physics, Geomagnetism and Aeronomy, which meet at the General Assemblies of the Union. In addition, there are Joint Committees of the various associations either among themselves or with other unions. The Union organizes scientific meetings and also sponsors various permanent services, to collect, analyse and publish geophysical data. Mems: in 75 countries. Pres. Prof. MASARU KONO (Japan); Sec.-Gen. Dr JOANN JOSELYN (USA). Publs *IUGG Yearbook, Journal of Geodesy* (quarterly), *IASPEI Newsletter* (irregular), *Bulletin Volcanologique* (2 a year), *Hydrological Sciences Journal* (quarterly), *Bulletin de l'Association Internationale d'Hydrologie Scientifique* (quarterly), *IAMAP News Bulletin* (irregular).

International Union of Geological Sciences—IUGS: c/o Norges Geologiske Unders+kelse, N-7491 Trondheim, Norway; tel. 73-90-40-40; fax 73-50-22-30; e-mail iugs.secretariat.ngu.no; internet www.iugs.org/; f. 1961 to encourage the study of geoscientific problems, facilitate international and inter-disciplinary co-operation in geology and related sciences, and support the quadrennial International Geological Congress. IUGS organizes international meetings and co-sponsors joint programmes, including the International Geological Correlation Programme (with UNESCO). Mems from 114 countries. Pres. Prof. ED DE MULDER (Netherlands); Sec.-Gen. Prof. A. BORIANI (Italy).

International Union of Immunological Societies: Dept of Surgery, University of Edinburgh Medical School, Teviot Place, Edinburgh, EH8 9AG, United Kingdom; tel. (131) 650-3557; fax (131) 667-6190; f. 1969; holds triennial international congress. Mems: national societies in 50 countries and territories. Pres. TOMIO TADA; Sec.-Gen. KEITH JAMES.

International Union of Microbiological Societies—IUMS: c/o Prof. John S. Mackenzie, Dept. of Microbiology, University of Queensland, Brisbane QLD 4072, Australia; tel. (7) 3365-4648; fax (7) 3365-6265; e-mail jmac@biosci.uq.edu.au; f. 1930. Mems: 106 national microbiological societies. Pres. P. HELENA MÄKELÄ (Finland); Sec.-Gen. Prof. JOHN S. MACKENZIE. Publs *International Journal of Systematic Bacteriology* (quarterly), *International Journal of Food Microbiology* (every 2 months), *Advances in Microbial Ecology* (annually), Archives of Virology.

International Union of Nutritional Sciences: c/o Prof. Galal, UCLA School of Public Health, International Health Program, 10833 Le Conte Ave, POB 951772, Los Angeles, CA 90095-1772, USA; tel. (310) 2069639; fax (310) 7941805; e-mail ogalal@ucla.edu; f. 1946 to promote international co-operation in the scientific study of nutrition and its applications, to encourage research and exchange of scientific information by holding international congresses and issuing publications. Mems: 67 organizations. Pres. Dr B. A. UNDERWOOD (USA); Sec.-Gen. Prof. OSMAN M. GALAL. Publs *Annual Report, IUNS Directory, Newsletter*.

International Union of Pharmacology: c/o Prof. Paul M. Vanhoutte, 6 pl. des Pléiades, 92415 Courbevoie Cédex, France; tel. 1-55-72-61-23; fax 1-55-72-72-76; f. 1963 to promote international co-ordination of research, discussion and publication in the field of pharmacology, including clinical pharmacology, drug metabolism and toxicology; co-operates with WHO in all matters concerning drugs and drug research; holds international congresses. Mems: 54 national and three regional societies. Pres. W. W. FLEMING (USA); Sec.-Gen. Prof.PAUL M. VANHOUTTE(France). Publ. *PI (Pharmacology International)*.

International Union of Physiological Sciences: IUPS Secretariat, LGN, Bâtiment CERVI, Hôpital de la Pitié-Salpêtrière, 83 blvd de l'Hôpital, 75013 Paris, France; tel. 1-42-17-75-37; fax 1-42-17-75-75; e-mail svorsoni@infobiogen.fr; f. 1955. Mems: 50 national, six assoc., four regional, two affiliated and 14 special mems. Pres. Prof. EWALD WEIBEL (Switzerland); Sec. Prof. DENIS NOBLE.

International Union of Psychological Science: c/o Prof. P. L.-J. Ritchie, Ecole de psychologie, Université d'Ottawa, 145 Jean-Jacques-Lussier, CP 450, Succ. A, Ottawa, ON KIN 6N5, Canada; tel (613) 562-5289; fax (613) 562-5169; e-mail pritchie@uottawa.ca; internet www.aix1.uottawa.ca~pritchie; f. 1951 to contribute to the development of intellectual exchange and scientific relations between psychologists of different countries. Mems: 64 national and 10 affiliate orgs. Pres. Prof. GÉRY D'YDEWALLE (Belgium); Sec.-Gen. Prof. P. L.-J. RITCHIE (Canada). Publs *International Journal of Psychology* (quarterly), *The IUPsyS Directory* (irregular), *Psychology CD Rom Resource File* (annually).

International Union of Pure and Applied Chemistry—IUPAC: Bldg 19, 104 T. W. Alexander Dr., Research Triangle Park, POB 13757, NC 27709-3757, USA; tel. (919) 485-8700; fax (919) 485-8706; e-mail secretariat@iupac.org; internet www.iupac.org; f. 1919 to organize permanent co-operation between chemical associations in the member countries, to study topics of international importance requiring standardization or codification, to co-operate with other international organizations in the field of chemistry and to contribute to the advancement of all aspects of chemistry. Biennial General Assembly. Mems: in 44 countries. Pres. Dr A. HAYES (UK); Sec.-Gen. Dr E. D. BECKER (USA). Publs *Chemistry International* (bi-monthly), *Pure and Applied Chemistry* (monthly).

International Union of Pure and Applied Physics: CEN Saclay, 91191 Gif-sur-Yvette Cédex, France; tel. 1-69-08-84-18; fax 1-69-08-76-36; e-mail turlay@hep.saclay.cea.fr; f. 1922 to promote and encourage international co-operation in physics. Mems: in 46 countries. Pres. B. RICHTER (USA); Sec.-Gen. Dr RENÉ TURLAY (France).

International Union of Radio Science: c/o INTEC, University of Ghent, Sint-Pietersnieuwstraat 41, 9000 Ghent, Belgium; tel. (9) 264-33-20; fax (9) 264-42-88; e-mail ursi@intec.rug.ac.be; internet www.intec.rug.ac.be/ursi; f. 1919 to stimulate and co-ordinate, on an international basis, studies, research, applications, scientific exchange and communication in the fields of radio science. Aims to encourage and promote international activity in radio science and its applications for the benefit of humanity; to encourage the adoption of common methods of measurement, and the standardization of

measuring instruments used in scientific work; to stimulate and co-ordinate studies; and to represent radio science at national and international levels. There are 47 national committees. Pres. Prof. H. MATSUMOTO (Japan); Sec.-Gen. Prof. P. LAGASSE (Belgium). Publs *The Radio Science Bulletin* (quarterly), *Proceedings of General Assemblies* (every 3 years), *Handbook on Radiopropagation related to Satellite Communications in Tropical and Subtropical Countries, Review of Radio Science* (every 3 years).

International Union of the History and Philosophy of Science: Division of the History of Science (DHS): Centre d'Histoire des Sciences et des Techniques, 5 quai Banning, 4000 Liège, Belgium; tel. (4) 366-94-79; fax (4) 366-94-47; e-mail chst@ulg.ac.be; Division of the History of Logic, Methodology and Philosophy of Science (DLMPS): 161 rue Ada, 34392 Montpellier, France; f. 1956 to promote research into the history and philosophy of science. DHS has 44 national committees and DLMPS has 35 committees. DHS Council: Pres. Prof. B. V. SUBBARAYAPPA (India); Sec. Prof. R. HALLEUX (Belgium). DLMPS Council: Pres. Prof. M. RABIN (Israel); Sec.-Gen. Prof. D. WESTERSTAHL (Sweden).

International Union of Theoretical and Applied Mechanics: c/o Prof. Michael A. Hayes, Mathematical Physics Dept, University College Dublin, Belfield, Dublin 4, Ireland; tel. and fax (1) 706-1172; e-mail iutam@ucd.ie; internet www.iutam.org; f. 1947 to form a link beween persons and organizations engaged in scientific work (theoretical or experimental) in mechanics or in related sciences; to organize international congresses of theoretical and applied mechanics, through a standing Congress Committee, and to organize other international meetings for subjects falling within this field; and to engage in other activities meant to promote the development of mechanics as a science. Mems: from 49 countries. Pres. Prof. W. SCHIEHLEN (Germany); Sec.-Gen. Prof. M. HAYES (Ireland). Publs *Annual Report, Newsletter*.

International Union of Toxicology: c/o Dept of Environmental and Occupational Health, University of Pittsburgh, Pittsburgh, PA 15238, USA; tel. (412) 967-6530; fax (412) 967-6611; e-mail mhk@pitt.edu; internet www.toxicology.org/iutox; f. 1980 to foster international co-operation among toxicologists and to promote worldwide acquisition, dissemination and utilization of knowledge in the field; sponsor International Congresses, and other education programmes. Mems: 37 national societies. Sec.-Gen. MERYL H. KAROL. Publs *IUTOX Newsletter,* Congress proceedings.

OTHER ORGANIZATIONS

Association for the Taxonomic Study of the Flora of Tropical Africa: National Botanic Garden of Belgium, Domein van Bouchout, 1860 Meise, Belgium; tel. (2) 260-09-28; fax (2) 260-08-45; e-mail rammeloo@br.fgov.be; f. 1950 to facilitate co-operation and liaison between botanists engaged in the study of the flora of tropical Africa south of the Sahara including Madagascar; maintains a library. Mems: about 800 botanists in 63 countries. Sec.-Gen. Prof. J. RAMMELOO. Publs *AETFAT Bulletin* (annually), *Proceedings*.

Association of European Atomic Forums—FORATOM: 15–17 rue Belliard, 1040 Brussels, Belgium; tel. (2) 502-45-95; fax (2) 502-39-02; e-mail foratom@skynet.be; internet www.foratom.org; f. 1960; holds periodical conferences. Mems: atomic 'forums' in Austria, Belgium, Czech Republic, Finland, France, Germany, Italy, Netherlands, Spain, Sweden, Switzerland and the United Kingdom. Pres. JEAN-PIERRE ROUGEAU; Sec.-Gen. Dr W.-J. SCHMIDT-KÜSTER. Publ. *Almanac* (annually).

Association of Geoscientists for International Development—AGID: Institute of Geoscience, University of São Paulo, 11348 São Paulo, 05422-970 Brazil; tel. (11) 818-4232; fax (11) 818-4207; e-mail abmacedo@usp.br; internet agid.igc.usp.br; f. 1974 to encourage communication between those interested in the application of the geosciences to international development; to give priority to the developing countries in these matters; to organize meetings and publish information; affiliated to the International Union of Geological Sciences (q.v.) and the Economic and Social Council of the United Nations. Mems: in 149 countries (2,000 individuals, and 57 institutions). Pres. S. D. LIMAYE; Sec. A. J. REEDMAN; Exec. Dir A. B. MACEDO. Publs *AGID Update Newsletter* (2 a year), *Geoscience and Development* (annually).

Council for the International Congresses of Entomology: c/o FAO, POB 3700 MCPO, 1277 Makati, Philippines; tel. (2) 8134229; fax (2) 8127725; f. 1910 to act as a link between quadrennial congresses and to arrange the venue for each congress; the committee is also the entomology section of the International Union of Biological Sciences (q.v.). Chair. Dr M. J. WHITTAM (Australia); Sec. Dr J. OLIVER (USA).

European Association of Geoscientists and Engineers—EAGE: c/o EAGE Business Office, 3990 DB Houten, Netherlands; tel. (30) 6354055; fax (30) 6343524; e-mail eage@eage.nl; internet www.eage.nl; f. 1997 by merger of European Asscn of Exploration Geophysicists and Engineers (f. 1951) and the European Asscn of Petroleum Geoscientists and Engineers (f. 1988); these two organizations have become, respectively, the Geophysical and the Petroleum Divisions of the EAGE; aims to promote the applications of geoscience and related subjects, to foster communication, fellowship and co-operation between those working or studying in the fields; organizes conferences, workshops, education programmes and exhibitions and seeks global co-operation with other organizations having similar objectives. Mems approx. 5,400 in 95 countries throughout the world. Pres. M. PELTONIEMI; Sec. J.-C. GROSSET. Publs *Geophysical Prospecting* (6 a year), *First Break* (monthly), *Petroleum Geoscience* (quarterly).

European Molecular Biology Organization—EMBO: Meyerhofstr. 1, Postfach 1022.40, 69012 Heidelberg, Germany; tel. (6221) 383031; fax (6221) 384879; e-mail embo@embo.org; internet www.embo.org; f. 1962 to promote collaboration in the field of molecular biology; to establish fellowships for training and research; established a European Molecular Biology Laboratory where a majority of the disciplines comprising the subject are represented. Mems: 965. Exec. Dir Prof. FRANK GANNON. Publ. *EMBO Journal* (24 a year).

European Organization for Nuclear Research—CERN: European Laboratory for Particle Physics, 1211 Geneva 23, Switzerland; tel. (22) 7676111; fax (22) 7676555; internet www.cern.ch; f. 1954 to provide for collaboration among European states in nuclear research of a pure scientific and fundamental character; the work of CERN is for peaceful purposes only and concerns subnuclear, high-energy and elementary particle physics; it is not concerned with the development of nuclear reactors or fusion devices. Council comprises two representatives of each member state. Major experimental facilities: Proton Synchrotron (of 25–28 GeV), Super Proton Synchrotron (of 450 GeV), and a Large Electron-Positron Collider (LEP) of 27 km circumference (of 94 GeV per beam). Budget (1998) 875m. Swiss francs. Mems: Austria, Belgium, Bulgaria, Czech Republic, Denmark, Finland, France, Germany, Greece, Hungary, Italy, Netherlands, Norway, Poland, Portugal, Slovakia, Spain, Sweden, Switzerland, United Kingdom; Observers: Israel, Japan, Russia, Turkey, USA, European Commission, UNESCO. Dir-Gen. LUCIANO MAIANI (Italy). Publs *CERN Courier* (monthly), *Annual Report, Scientific Reports.*

European-Mediterranean Seismological Centre: c/o LDG, BP 12, 91680 Bruyères-le-Châtel, France; tel. 1-69-26-78-14; fax 1-69-26-70-00; e-mail csem@mail.csem.fr; f. 1976 for rapid determination of seismic hypocentres in the region; maintains data base. Mems: institutions in 21 countries. Pres. C. BROWITT; Sec.-Gen. F. RIVIERE. Publ. *Newsletter* (two a year).

Federation of Arab Scientific Research Councils: POB 13027, Al Karkh/Karadat Mariam, Baghdad, Iraq; tel. (1) 8881709; fax (1) 8866346; f. 1976 to encourage co-operation in scientific research, to promote the establishment of new institutions and plan joint regional research projects. Mems: national science bodies in 15 countries. Sec.-Gen. Dr TAHA AL-NUEIMI. Publs *Journal of Computer Research, Journal of Environmental and Sustained Development, Journal of Biotechnology.*

Federation of Asian Scientific Academies and Societies—FASAS: c/o Indian National Science Academy, Bahadur Shah Zafar Marg, New Delhi 110 002, India; tel. (11) 3232066; fax (11) 3235648; e-mail insa@giasdlo1.vsnl.net.in; f. 1984 to stimulate regional co-operation and promote national and regional self-reliance in science and technology, by organizing meetings, training and research programmes and encouraging the exchange of scientists and of scientific information. Mems: national scientific academies and societies from Afghanistan, Australia, Bangladesh, People's Republic of China, India, Republic of Korea, Malaysia, Nepal, New Zealand, Pakistan, Philippines, Singapore, Sri Lanka, Thailand. Pres. Prof. C. S. DAYRIT (Philippines); Sec. Prof. INDIRA NATH (India).

Federation of European Biochemical Societies: c/o Institute of Cancer Biology and Danish Centre for Human Genome Research, Danish Cancer Society, Strandoulevarden 49, 2100 Copenhagen Ø, Denmark; tel. 3525-7363; fax 3525-7376; e-mail febs@cancer.dk; internet www.febs.unibe.ch; f. 1964 to promote the science of biochemistry through meetings of European biochemists, provision of fellowships and advanced courses and issuing publications. Mems: 40,000 in 34 societies. Chair. Prof. G. DIRHEIMER; Sec.-Gen. Prof. JULIO E. CELIS. Publs *European Journal of Biochemistry, FEBS Letters, FEBS Bulletin.*

Foundation for International Scientific Co-ordination (Fondation 'Pour la science', Centre international de synthèse): 12 rue Colbert, 75002 Paris, France; tel. 1-42-97-50-68; fax 1-42-97-46-46; e-mail synthese@libertysurf.fr; internet synthese.pour-le-science.org; f. 1925. Dirs MICHEL BLAY, ERIC BRIAN; Publs *Revue de Synthèse, Revue d'Histoire des Sciences, Semaines de Synthèse, L'Evolution de l'Humanité.*

Intergovernmental Oceanographic Commission: UNESCO, 1 rue Miollis, 75732 Paris Cédex 15, France; tel. 1-45-68-39-83; fax 1-45-68-58-10; f. 1960 to promote scientific investigation of the nature and resources of the oceans through the concerted action of its members. Mems: 127 governments. Chair. SU JILAN (China); Exec. Sec. Dr PATRICIO BERNAL. Publs *IOC Technical Series* (irregular), IOC *Manuals and Guides* (irregular), *IOC Workshop Reports* (irregular) and *IOC Training Course Reports* (irregular), annual reports.

International Academy of Astronautics—IAA: 6 rue Galilee, POB 1268–16, 75766 Paris Cédex 16, France; tel. 1-47-23-82-15; fax 1-47-23-82-16; f. 1960; fosters the development of astronautics for peaceful purposes, holds scientific meetings and makes scientific studies, reports, awards and book awards; maintains 19 scientific cttees and a multilingual terminology data base (20 languages). Mems: 681, and 382 corresponding mems, in basic sciences, engineering sciences, life sciences and social sciences, from 57 countries. Sec.-Gen. Dr JEAN-MICHEL CONTANT. Publ. *Acta Astronautica* (monthly).

International Association for Biologicals: CP 456, 1211 Geneva 4, Switzerland; fax (22) 702-93-55; e-mail biostandards@aiabs.org; internet www.iabs.org; f. 1955 to connect producers and controllers of immunological products (sera, vaccines, etc.) for the study and the development of methods of standardization; supports international organizations in their efforts to solve problems of standardization. Mems: 500. Pres. J. PETRICCIANI (USA); Sec.-Gen. D. GAUDRY (France). Publs *Newsletter* (quarterly), *Biologicals* (quarterly).

International Association for Earthquake Engineering: Kenchiku Kaikan, 3rd Floor, 5-26-20, Shiba, Minato-ku, Tokyo 108, Japan; tel. (3) 453-1281; fax (3) 453-0428; f. 1963 to promote international co-operation among scientists and engineers in the field of earthquake engineering through exchange of knowledge, ideas and results of research and practical experience. Mems: national cttees in 49 countries. Pres. SHELDON CHERRY (Canada); Sec.-Gen. Dr TSUNEO KATAYAMA.

International Association for Ecology—INTECOL: Lunigiana Museum of Natural History, 54011 Aulla, Italy; tel. (0187) 400252; fax (0187) 420727; e-mail afarina@tamnet.it; f. 1967 to provide opportunities for communication between ecologists world-wide; to co-operate with organizations and individuals having related aims and interests; to encourage studies in the different fields of ecology; affiliated to the International Union of Biological Sciences (q.v.). Mems: 35 national and international ecological societies, and 1,000 individuals. Pres. J. A. LEE (UK); Sec.-Gen. A. FARINA (Italy).

International Association for Mathematical Geology: c/o T. A. Jones, POB 2189, Houston, TX 77252-2189, USA; tel. (713) 431-6546; fax (713) 431-6336; internet www.iamg.org; f. 1968 for the preparation and elaboration of mathematical models of geological processes; the introduction of mathematical methods in geological sciences and technology; assistance in the development of mathematical investigation in geological sciences; the organization of international collaboration in mathematical geology through various forums and publications; educational programmes for mathematical geology; affiliated to the International Union of Geological Sciences (q.v.). Mems: c. 600. Pres. Dr R. A. OLEA (USA); Sec.-Gen. Dr T. A. JONES (USA). Publs *Mathematical Geology* (8 a year), *Computers and Geosciences* (10 a year), *Natural Resources Research* (quarterly), *Newsletter* (2 a year).

International Association for Mathematics and Computers in Simulation: c/o Free University of Brussels, Automatic Control, CP 165, 50 ave F. D. Roosevelt, 1050 Brussels, Belgium; tel. (2) 650-20-97; fax (2) 650-35-64; f. 1955 to further the study of mathematical tools and computer software and hardware, analogue, digital or hybrid computers for simulation of soft or hard systems. Mems: 1,100 and 27 assoc. mems. Pres. R. VICHNEVETSKY (USA); Sec. Prof. RAYMOND HANUS. Publs *Mathematics and Computers in Simulation* (6 a year), *Applied Numerical Mathematics* (6 a year), *Journal of Computational Acoustics.*

International Association for the Physical Sciences of the Ocean—IAPSO: POB 820440, Vicksburg, MS 39182-0440, USA; tel. (601) 636-1363; fax (601) 629-9640; e-mail camfield@vicksburg.com; internet www.olympus.net/IAPSO; f. 1919 to promote the study of scientific problems relating to the oceans and interactions occurring at its boundaries, chiefly in so far as such study may be carried out by the aid of mathematics, physics and chemistry; to initiate, facilitate and co-ordinate research; to provide for discussion, comparison and publication; affiliated to the International Union of Geodesy and Geophysics (q.v.). Mems: 81 member states. Pres. PAOLA RIZZOLI; Sec.-Gen. Dr FRED E. CAMFIELD (USA). Publ. *Publications Scientifiques* (irregular).

International Association for Plant Physiology—IAPP: c/o Dr D. Graham, Div. of Food Science and Technology, CSIRO, POB 52, North Ryde, NSW, Australia 2113; tel. (2) 9490-8333; fax (2) 9490-3107; e-mail douglasgraham@dfst.csiro.au; f. 1955 to promote the development of plant physiology at the international level through congresses, symposia and workshops, by maintaining communication with national societies and by encouraging interaction between plant physiologists in developing and developed countries; affiliated to the International Union of Biological Sciences (q.v.). Pres. Prof. S. MIYACHI; Sec.-Treas. Dr D. GRAHAM.

International Association for Plant Taxonomy: c/o Prof. Tod F. Stuessy, Institut für Botanik und Botanischer Garten, Universität Wien, Rennweg 14, A-1030 Wien, Austria; f. 1950 to promote the development of plant taxonomy and encourage contacts between people and institutes interested in this work; affiliated to the International Union of Biological Sciences (q.v.). Mems: institutes and individuals in 85 countries. Publs *Taxon* (quarterly), *Regnum vegetabile* (irregular).

International Association of Botanic Gardens: c/o Prof. J. E. Hernández-Bermejo, Córdoba Botanic Garden, Avda de Linneo, s/n, 14004 Córdoba, Spain; tel. (957) 200077; fax (957) 295333; f. 1954 to promote co-operation between scientific collections of living plants, including the exchange of information and specimens; to promote the study of the taxonomy of cultivated plants; and to encourage the conservation of rare plants and their habitats; affiliated to the International Union of Biological Sciences (q.v.). Pres. Prof. KUNIO IWATSUKI (Japan); Sec. Prof. J. ESTEBAN HERNÁNDEZ-BERMEJO (Spain).

International Association of Geodesy: Dept of Geophysics, Juliane Maries Vej 30, 2100 Copenhagen Oe, Denmark; tel. (45) 3532-0582; fax (45) 3536-5357; e-mail iag@gfy.ku.dk; internet www.gfy.ku.dk/~iag/; f. 1922 to promote the study of all scientific problems of geodesy and encourage geodetic research; to promote and co-ordinate international co-operation in this field; to publish results; affiliated to the International Union of Geodesy and Geophysics (q.v.). Mems: national committees in 73 countries. Pres. F. SANSÓ (Italy); Sec.-Gen. C. C. TSCHERNING (Denmark). Publs *Journal of Geodesy, Travaux de l'AIG.*

International Association of Geomagnetism and Aeronomy—IAGA: c/o Dr JoAnn Joselyn, NOAA Space Environment Center, 325 Broadway, Boulder, CO 80303, USA; tel. (303) 497-5147; fax (303) 494-0980; e-mail jjoselyn@sec.noaa.gov; f. 1919 for the study of questions relating to geomagnetism and aeronomy and the encouragement of research; holds General and Scientific Assemblies every two years; affiliated to the International Union of Geodesy and Geophysics (IUGG, q.v.). Mems: the countries which adhere to the IUGG. Pres. M. KONO (Japan); Sec.-Gen. Dr JOANN JOSELYN. Publs *IAGA Bulletin* (including annual *Geomagnetic Data*), *IAGA News* (annually).

International Association of Hydrological Sciences: Dept of Geography, Wilfrid Laurier Univ., Waterloo, ON N2L 3C5, Canada; tel. (519) 884-1970; fax (519) 846-0968; e-mail 44iahs@mach1.wlu.ca; internet www.wlu.ca/~wwwiahs/index.html; f. 1922 to promote co-operation in the study of hydrology and water resources. Pres. Dr J. C. RODDA (UK); Sec.-Gen. Dr GORDON J. YOUNG (Canada). Publs *Journal* (every 2 months), *Newsletter* (3 a year).

International Association of Meteorology and Atmospheric Sciences—IAMAS: Dept of Physics, Univ. of Toronto, Toronto, ON M5S 1A7, Canada; f. 1919; permanent commissions on atmospheric ozone, radiation, atmospheric chemistry and global pollution, dynamic meteorology, polar meteorology, clouds and precipitation, climate, atmospheric electricity, planetary atmospheres and their evolution, and meteorology of the upper atmosphere; general assemblies held once every four years; special assemblies held once between general assemblies; affiliated to the International Union of Geodesy and Geophysics (q.v.). Pres. Prof. R. DUCE (USA); Sec.-Gen. Prof. R. LIST (Canada).

International Association of Sedimentologists: c/o Prof. A. Strasser, Institut de Géologie, Pérolles, 1700 Fribourg, Switzerland; tel. (26) 3008978; fax (26) 3009742; e-mail andreas.strasser@unifr.ch; internet www.blackwell-science.com/uk/society/ias; f. 1952; affiliated to the International Union of Geological Sciences (q.v.). Mems: 2,200. Pres. Prof. M. E. TUCKER (UK); Gen. Sec. Prof. A. STRASSER (Switzerland). Publ. *Sedimentology* (every 2 months).

International Association of Theoretical and Applied Limnology (Societas Internationalis Limnologiae): Dept of Biology, University of Alabama, Tuscaloosa, AL 35487-0206, USA; tel. (205) 348-1793; fax (205) 348-1403; e-mail rwetzel@biology.as.ua.edu; internet www.limnology.org; f. 1922; study of physical, chemical and biological phenomena of lakes and rivers; affiliated to the International Union of Biological Sciences (q.v.). Mems: about 3,200. Pres. G. E. LIKENS (USA); Gen. Sec. and Treas. ROBERT G. WETZEL (USA).

International Association of Volcanology and Chemistry of the Earth's Interior—IAVCEI: Geophysical Institute, University of Alaska Fairbanks, POB 757320, Fairbanks, AK 99775, USA; tel. (907) 474-7131; fax (907) 474-5618; f. 1919 to examine scientifically all aspects of volcanology; affiliated to the International Union of Geodesy and Geophysics (q.v.). Pres. R. S. J. SPARKS (UK); Sec.-Gen. S. R. McNUTT (USA). Publs *Bulletin of Volcanology, Catalogue of the Active Volcanoes of the World, Proceedings in Volcanology.*

International Association of Wood Anatomists: USDA Forest Service, Forest Products, Laboratory, 1 Gifford Pinchot Drive, Madison WI 53705-2398, USA; tel. (608) 231-9200; fax (608) 231-9508; f. 1931 for the purpose of study, documentation and exchange of information on the structure of wood; holds annual conference.

Mems: 650 in 68 countries. Exec. Sec. REGIS B. MILLER. Publ. *IAWA Journal.*

International Astronautical Federation—IAF: 3–5 rue Mario-Nikis, 75015 Paris, France; tel. 1-45-67-42-60; fax 1-42-73-21-20; e-mail iaf@wanadoo.fr; internet www.iafastro.com; f. 1950 to foster the development of astronautics for peaceful purposes at national and international levels. The IAF has created the International Academy of Astronautics (IAA) and the International Institute of Space Law (IISL). Mems: 153 national astronautical societies in 45 countries. Pres. Dr TOMIFUMI GODAI (Japan); Exec. Sec. CLAUDE GOURDET.

International Biometric Society: c/o Prof. E. Baráth, Chair. of Statistics, 2103 Gödöllö, Hungary; tel. (28) 410-694; fax (28) 430-336; f. 1947 for the advancement of quantitative biological science through the development of quantitative theories and the application, development and dissemination of effective mathematical and statistical techniques; the Society has 16 regional organizations and 17 national groups, is affiliated with the International Statistical Institute and the World Health Organization, and constitutes the Section of Biometry of the International Union of Biological Sciences (q.v.). Mems: over 6,000 in more than 70 countries. Pres. Prof. SUE WILSON (Australia); Sec. Prof. E. BARÁTH (Hungary). Publs *Biometrics* (quarterly), *Biometric Bulletin* (quarterly), *Journal of Agricultural, Biological and Environmental Statistics* (quarterly).

International Botanical Congress: c/o Dr Peter Hoch, Missouri Botanical Garden, PO Box 299, St Louis, MO 63166-0299, USA; tel. (314) 577-5175; fax (314) 577-9589; e-mail ibc16@mobot.org; f. 1864 to inform botanists of recent progress in the plant sciences; the Nomenclature Section of the Congress attempts to provide a uniform terminology and methodology for the naming of plants; other Divisions deal with developmental, metabolic, structural, systematic and evolutionary, ecological botany; genetics and plant breeding; 1999 Congress: St Louis; affiliated to the International Union of Biological Sciences (q.v.). Sec. Dr PETER HOCH.

International Bureau of Weights and Measures: Pavillon de Breteuil, 92312 Sèvres Cédex, France; tel. 1-45-07-70-70; fax 1-45-34-20-21; e-mail info@bipm.org; internet www.bipm.org; f. 1875 for the international unification of physical measures; establishment of fundamental standards and of scales of the principal physical dimensions; preservation of the international prototypes; determination of national standards; precision measurements in physics. Mems: 49 states. Pres. J. KOVALEVSKY (France); Sec. R. KAARLS (Netherlands).

International Cartographic Association: 136 bis rue de Grenelle, 75700 Paris 07 SP, France; tel. 1-43-98-82-95; fax 1-43-98-84-00; f. 1959 for the advancement, instigation and co-ordination of cartographic research involving co-operation between different nations. Particularly concerned with furtherance of training in cartography, study of source material, compilation, graphic design, drawing, scribing and reproduction techniques of maps; organizes international conferences, symposia, meetings, exhibitions. Mems: 80 nations. Pres. MICHAEL WOOD. Publ. *ICA Newsletter* (2 a year).

International Centre of Insect Physiology and Ecology: POB 30772, Nairobi, Kenya; tel. (2) 861680; fax (2) 803360; e-mail icipe@africaonline.co.ke; f. 1970; specializes in research and development of environmentally sustainable and affordable methods of managing tropical arthropod plant pests and disease vectors, and in the conservation and utilisation of biodiversity of insects of commercial and ecological importance; organizes training programmes. Dir-Gen. Dr HANS RUDOLPH HERREN. Publs *Insect Science and its Application* (quarterly), *Annual Report*, training manuals, technical bulletins, newsletter.

International Commission for Optics: Institut d'Optique/CNRS, POB 147, 91403 Orsay Cédex, France; tel. 1-69-35-87-41; fax 1-69-35-87-00; internet www.ico-optics.org; f. 1948 to contribute to the progress of theoretical and instrumental optics, to assist in research and to promote international agreement on specifications; Gen. Assembly every three years. Mems: committees in 42 territories, and four international societies. Pres. Prof. A. H. GUEUTHER (USA); Sec.-Gen. Dr P. CHAVEL (France). Publ. *ICO Newsletter.*

International Commission for Plant-Bee Relationships: c/o Prof. I. Williams, Entomology-Nematology Dept, Rothamsted Experimental Station, Harpenden, Herts, AL5 2JQ, United Kingdom; e-mail ingrid.williams@bbsrc.ac.uk; f. 1950 to promote research and its application in the field of bee botany, and collect and spread information; to organize meetings, etc., and collaborate with scientific organizations; affiliated to the International Union of Biological Sciences (q.v.). Mems: 175 in 34 countries. Pres. Prof. INGRID WILLIAMS; Sec. Dr J. N. TASEI.

International Commission for the Scientific Exploration of the Mediterranean Sea (Commission internationale pour l'exploration scientifique de la mer Méditerranée—CIESM): 16 blvd de Suisse, 98000 Monaco; tel. 93-30-38-79; fax 92-16-11-95; internet www.ciesm.org; f. 1919 for scientific exploration and sustainable management of the Mediterranean Sea; includes 6 scientific committees. Mems: 23 member countries, 2,500 scientists. Pres. SAS The

Prince RAINIER III of MONACO; Sec.-Gen. Prof. F. DOUMENGE; Dir-Gen. Prof. F. BRIAND.

International Commission on Physics Education: c/o Prof. J. Barojas, POB 55534, 09340 México DF, Mexico; tel. (5) 686-35-19; f. 1960 to encourage and develop international collaboration in the improvement and extension of the methods and scope of physics education at all levels; collaborates with UNESCO and organizes international conferences. Mems: appointed triennially by the International Union of Pure and Applied Physics. Sec. Prof. J. BAROJAS.

International Commission on Radiation Units and Measurements—ICRU: 7910 Woodmont Ave, Suite 800, Bethesda, MD 20814, USA; tel. (301) 657-2652; fax (301) 907-8768; e-mail icru@icru.org; f. 1925 to develop internationally acceptable recommendations regarding: (1) quantities and units of radiation and radioactivity, (2) procedures suitable for the measurement and application of these quantities in clinical radiology and radiobiology, (3) physical data needed in the application of these procedures. Makes recommendations on quantities and units for radiation protection (see below, International Radiation Protection Association). Mems: from about 18 countries. Chair. A. ALLISY; Sec. R. S. CASWELL. Publs *Reports*.

International Commission on Zoological Nomenclature: c/o The Natural History Museum, Cromwell Rd, London, SW7 5BD, United Kingdom; tel. (20) 7942-5653; e-mail iczn@nhm.ac.uk; internet www.iczn.org; f. 1895; has judicial powers to determine all matters relating to the interpretation of the International Code of Zoological Nomenclature and also plenary powers to suspend the operation of the Code where the strict application of the Code would lead to confusion and instability of nomenclature; the Commission is responsible also for maintaining and developing the Official Lists and Official Indexes of Names in Zoology; affiliated to the International Union of Biological Sciences (q.v.). Pres. Prof. A. MINELLI (Italy); Exec. Sec. Dr P. K. TUBBS (UK). Publs *Bulletin of Zoological Nomenclature* (quarterly), *International Code of Zoological Nomenclature, Official Lists and Indexes of Names in Zoology, Towards Stability in the Names of Animals*.

International Council for Scientific and Technical Information: 51 blvd de Montmorency, 75016 Paris, France; tel. 1-45-25-65-92; fax 1-42-15-12-62; e-mail icsti@dial.oleane.com; internet www.icsti.org; f. 1984 as the successor to the International Council of Scientific Unions Abstracting Board (f. 1952); aims to increase accessibility to scientific and technical information; fosters communication and interaction among all participants in the information transfer chain. Mems: 50 organizations. Pres. DAVID RUSSON (UK); Gen. Sec. MARIE WALLIN (Sweden).

International Council for the Exploration of the Sea—ICES: Palægade 2–4, 1261 Copenhagen K, Denmark; tel. 33-15-42-25; fax 33-93-42-15; e-mail ices.info@ices.dk; internet www.ices.dk; f. 1902 to encourage and facilitate marine research on the utilization and conservation of living resources and the environment in the North Atlantic Ocean and its adjacent seas; to publish and disseminate results of research; to advise member countries and regulatory commissions. Gen. Sec. D. de G. GRIFFITH. Publs *ICES Journal of Marine Science, ICES Marine Science Symposia, ICES Fisheries Statistics, ICES Cooperative Research Reports, ICES Oceanographic Data Lists and Inventories, ICES Techniques in Marine Environmental Sciences, ICES Identification Leaflets for Plankton, ICES Identification Leaflets for Diseases and Parasites of Fish and Shellfish, ICES/CIEM Information*.

International Council of Psychologists: Dept. of Psychology, Southwest Texas State University, San Marcos, TX 78666, USA; tel. (512) 245-7605; fax (512) 245-3153; f. 1941 to advance psychology and the application of its scientific findings throughout the world; holds annual conventions. Mems: 1,200 qualified psychologists. Sec.-Gen. Dr JOHN M. DAVIS. Publs *International Psychologist* (quarterly), *World Psychology* (quarterly).

International Council of the Aeronautical Sciences: 66 route de Verneuil, BP 3002, 78133 Les Mureaux Cédex, France; tel. 1-39-06-34-23; fax 1-39-06-36-15; e-mail secr.exec@icas.org; internet www.icas.org; f. 1957 to encourage free interchange of information on all phases of mechanical flight; holds biennial Congresses. Mems: national associations in 27 countries. Pres. JEAN-PIERRE MAREC (France); Exec. Sec. CLEMENT DOUSSET (France).

International Earth Rotation Service: Central Bureau, Paris Observatory, 61 ave de l'Observatoire, 75014 Paris, France; tel. 1-40-51-22-26; fax 1-40-51-22-91; e-mail iers@obspm.fr; f. 1988 (fmrly International Polar Motion Service and Bureau International de l'Heure); maintained by the International Astronomical Union and the International Union of Geodesy and Geophysics; defines and maintains the international terrestrial and celestial reference systems; determines earth orientation parameters (terrestrial and celestial co-ordinates of the pole and universal time) connecting these systems; monitors global geophysical fluids; organizes collec-

tion, analysis and dissemination of data. Pres. Directing Bd Prof. C. REIGBER.

International Federation for Cell Biology: c/o Dr Ivan Cameron, Dept of Cellular and Structural Biology, Univ. of Texas Health Science Center, 7703 Floyd Curl Drive, San Antonio, Texas 78229, USA; f. 1972 to foster international co-operation, and organize conferences. Pres. Dr JUDIE WALTON; Sec.-Gen. Dr IVAN CAMERON. Publs *Cell Biology International* (monthly), reports.

International Federation of Operational Research Societies: c/o Loretta Peregrina, Richard Ivey School of Business, University of Western Ontario, London, ON N6A 3K7, Canada; tel. (519) 661-4220; fax (519) 661-3485; e-mail ifors@ivey.uwo.ca; f. 1959 for development of operational research as a unified science and its advancement in all nations of the world. Mems: about 30,000 individuals, 44 national societies, four kindred societies. Pres. Prof. PAOLO TOTH (Italy); Sec. LORETTA PEREGRINA. Publs *International Abstracts in Operational Research, IFORS Bulletin, International Transactions in Operational Research*.

International Federation of Science Editors: School for Scientific Communication, Abruzzo Science Park, Via Antica Arischia 1, 67100 L'Aquila, Italy; tel. (0862) 3475308; fax (0862) 3475213; e-mail miriam.balaban@aquila.infn.it; f. 1978; links editors in different branches of science with the aim of improving scientific writing, editing, ethics and communication internationally. Pres. MIRIAM BALABAN (Italy).

International Federation of Societies for Electron Microscopy: Dept of Materials, Univ. of Oxford, Parks Rd, Oxford, OX1 3PH, United Kingdom; tel (18650) 273654; fax (1865) 283329; e-mail david.cockayne@materials.ox.ac.uk; f. 1955. Mems: representative organizations of 40 countries. Pres. Prof. A. HOWIE (UK); Gen.-Sec. D. J. H. COCKAYNE (Australia).

International Food Information Service—IFIS: UK Office (IFIS Publishing), Lane End House, Shinfield Rd, Shinfield, Reading, RG2 9BB, United Kingdom; tel. (118) 988-3895; fax (118) 988-5065; e-mail ifis@ifis.org; internet www.ifis.org; f. 1968; board of governors comprises two members each from CAB-International (UK), Bundesministerium für Landwirtschaft, Ernährung und Forsten (represented by Deutsche Landwirtschafts-Gesellschaft e.V.) (Germany), the Institute of Food Technologists (USA), and the Centrum voor Landbouwpublikaties en Landbouwdocumentaties (Netherlands); collects and disseminates information on all disciplines relevant to food science, food technology and human nutrition. Man. Dir Prof. J. D. SELMAN. Publ. *Food Science and Technology Abstracts* (monthly, also available via the internet and on CD-ROM).

International Foundation of the High-Altitude Research Stations Jungfraujoch and Gornergrat: Sidlerstrasse 5, 3012 Berne, Switzerland; tel. (31) 6314052; fax (31) 6314405; e-mail louise.wilson@phim.unibe.ch; internet www.ifjungo.ch; f. 1931; international research centre which enables scientists from many scientific fields to carry out experiments at high altitudes. Six countries contribute to support the station: Austria, Belgium, Germany, Italy, Switzerland, United Kingdom. Pres. Prof. E. FLÜCKIGER.

International Glaciological Society: Lensfield Rd, Cambridge, CB2 1ER, United Kingdom; tel. (1223) 355974; fax (1223) 336543; e-mail int_glaciol_soc@compuserve.com; internet www.spri.cam.ac.uk/igs/home.htm; f. 1936 to stimulate interest in and encourage research into the scientific and technical problems of snow and ice in all countries. Mems: 850 in 30 countries. Pres. Dr R. A. BINDSCHADLER; Sec.-Gen. C. S. L. OMMANNEY. Publs *Journal of Glaciology* (quarterly), *Ice* (News Bulletin—3 a year), *Annals of Glaciology*.

International Hydrographic Organization: 4 quai Antoine 1er, BP 445, Monte Carlo, 98011 Monaco; tel. 93-10-81-00; fax 93-10-81-40; e-mail info@ihb.mc; internet www.iho.shom.fr; f. 1921 to link the hydrographic offices of its member governments and co-ordinate their work with a view to rendering navigation easier and safer on all the seas of the world; to obtain as far as possible uniformity in charts and hydrographic documents; to foster the development of electronic chart navigation; to encourage the adoption of the best methods of conducting hydrographic surveys and improvements in the theory and practice of the science of hydrography, and to encourage surveying in those parts of the world where accurate charts are lacking; to extend and facilitate the application of oceanographic knowledge for the benefit of navigators and specialists in marine sciences; to render advice and assistance to developing countries upon request, facilitating their application for financial aid from UNDP and other aid organizations for creation or extension of their hydrographic capabilities; to fulfil the role of world data centre for bathymetry; provides IHO Data Centre for Digital Bathymetry; organizes quinquennial conference. Mems: 66 states. Directing Committee: Pres. Rear-Adm. GIUSEPPE ANGRISANO (Italy); Dir Rear-Adm. N. GUY (South Africa). Publs *International Hydrographic Bulletin* (monthly), *IHO Yearbook*.

International Institute of Refrigeration: 177 blvd Malesherbes, 75017 Paris, France; tel. 1-42-27-32-35; fax 1-47-63-17-98; e-mail

Science

iifiir@ibm.net; internet www.iifiir.org; f. 1908 to further the development of the science of refrigeration and its applications on a worldwide scale; to investigate, discuss and recommend any aspects leading to improvements in the field of refrigeration; maintains FRIDOC data-base (available on CD-ROM). Mems: 61 national, 1,500 associates. Dir FRANÇOIS BILLIARD (France). Publs *Bulletin* (every 2 months), *International Journal of Refrigeration* (8 a year), books, proceedings, recommendations.

International Mineralogical Association: Institute of Mineralogy, University of Marburg, 3550 Marburg, Germany; tel. 28-5617; fax 285831; f. 1958 to further international co-operation in the science of mineralogy; affiliated to the International Union of Geological Sciences (q.v.). Mems: national societies in 31 countries. Sec. Prof. S. S. HAFNER.

International Organization of Legal Metrology: 11 rue Turgot, 75009 Paris, France; tel. 1-48-78-12-82; fax 1-42-82-17-27; f. 1955 to serve as documentation and information centre on the verification, checking, construction and use of measuring instruments, to determine characteristics and standards to which measuring instruments must conform for their use to be recommended internationally, and to determine the general principles of legal metrology. Mems: governments of 50 countries. Dir B. ATHANÉ (France). Publ. *Bulletin* (quarterly).

International Palaeontological Association: c/o Prof. D. L. Bruton, Paleontologisk Museum, Box 1172 Blindern, 0318 Oslo, Norway; tel. 2285-1668; fax 2285-1810; e-mail d.l.bruton@nhm.uio.no; internet ipa.geo.ukans.edu; f. 1933; affiliated to the International Union of Geological Sciences and the International Union of Biological Sciences (q.v.). Pres. Dr J. TALENT (Australia); Sec.-Gen. D. L. BRUTON (Norway). Publs *Lethaia* (quarterly), *Directory of Paleontologists of the World, Directory of Fossil Collectors of the World*.

International Peat Society: Vapaudenkatu 12, 40100 Jyväskylä, Finland; tel. (14) 3385440; fax (14) 3385410; e-mail ips@peatsociety.fi; internet www.peatsociety.fi; f. 1968 to encourage co-operation in the study and use of mires, peatlands, peat and related material, through international meetings, research groups and the exchange of information. Mems: 18 Nat. Cttees, research institutes and other organizations, and individuals from 35 countries. Pres. GERRY HOOD (Canada); Sec.-Gen. RAIMO SOPO (Finland). Publs *Peatlands International* (2 a year), *International Peat Journal* (annually).

International Phonetic Association—IPA: Dept of Linguistics, University of Victoria, POB 3045, Victoria, V8W 3P4, Canada; e-mail esling@uvic.ca; internet www.arts.gla.ac.uk/ipa/ipa.html; f. 1886 to promote the scientific study of phonetics and its applications. Mems: 1,000. Pres. K. KOHLER (Germany). Publ. *Journal* (2 a year).

International Photobiology Association: c/o Dr Tom Dubbelman, POB 9503, 2300 RA Leiden, Netherlands; tel. (71) 5276053; fax (71) 5276125; e-mail t.m.a.r.dubbelman@mcb.medfac.leidenuniv.nl; f. 1928; stimulation of scientific research concerning the physics, chemistry and climatology of non-ionizing radiations (ultraviolet, visible and infra-red) in relation to their biological efffects and their applications in biology and medicine; 18 national committees represented; affiliated to the International Union of Biological Sciences (q.v.). International Congresses held every four years. Pres. Prof. PILL SOON SONG; Sec.-Gen. Dr TOM DUBBELMAN.

International Phycological Society: c/o Harbor Branch Oceanographic Institution, 5600 Old Dixie Highway, Fort Pierce, FL 34946, USA; fax (561) 468-0757; e-mail hanisak@hboi.edu; f. 1961 to promote the study of algae, the distribution of information, and international co-operation in this field. Mems: about 1,000. Pres. C. J. BIRD; Sec. M. D. HANISAK. Publ. *Phycologia* (every 2 months).

International Primatological Society: c/o Dr D. Fragaszy, Dept of Psychology, Univ. of Georgia, Athens, GA 30602, USA; tel. (706) 542-3036; fax (706) 542-3275; e-mail doree@arches.uga.edu; f. 1964 to promote primatological science in all fields. Mems: about 1,500. Pres. Dr T. NISHIDA; Sec.-Gen. Dr D. FRAGASZY.

International Radiation Protection Association—IRPA: POB 662, 5600 AR Eindhoven, Netherlands; tel. (40) 247-33-55; fax (40) 243-50-20; e-mail irpa.exof@sbd.tue.nl; f. 1966 to link individuals and societies throughout the world concerned with protection against ionizing radiations and allied effects, and to represent doctors, health physicists, radiological protection officers and others engaged in radiological protection, radiation safety, nuclear safety, legal, medical and veterinary aspects and in radiation research and other allied activities. Mems: 16,000 in 42 societies. Pres. Prof. K. DUFTSCMID (Austria); Sec.-Gen. C. J. HUYSKENS (Netherlands). Publ. *IRPA Bulletin*.

International Society for General Semantics: POB 728, Concord, CA 94522, USA; tel. (925) 798-0311; e-mail isgs@generalsemantics.org; internet www.generalsemantics.org; f. 1943 to advance knowledge of and inquiry into non-Aristotelian systems and general semantics. Mems: 2,000 individuals in 40 countries. Pres. CHARLES RUSSELL, Jr (USA); Exec. Dir PAUL D. JOHNSTON (USA).

International Society for Human and Animal Mycology—ISHAM: Mycology Unit, Women's and Children's Hospital, N. Adelaide 5006, Australia; tel. (8) 8204-7365; fax (8) 8204-7589; e-mail dellis@mad.adelaide.edu.au; f. 1954 to pursue the study of fungi pathogenic for man and animals; holds congresses (2003 Congress: San Antonio, USA). Mems: 1,100 from 70 countries. Pres. Prof. M. R. McGINNIS; Gen. Sec. Dr D. H. ELLIS. Publ. *Medical Mycology* (6 a year).

International Society for Rock Mechanics: c/o Laboratório Nacional de Engenharia Civil, 101 Av. do Brasil, 1799 Lisboa Codex, Portugal; tel. (21) 8482131; fax (21) 8497660; e-mail isrm@lnec.pt; internet www.lnec.pt/isrm; f. 1962 to encourage and co-ordinate international co-operation in the science of rock mechanics; to assist individuals and local organizations to form national bodies; to maintain liaison with organizations that represent related sciences, including geology, geophysics, soil mechanics, mining engineering, petroleum engineering and civil engineering. The Society organizes international meetings and encourages the publication of the results of research in rock mechanics. Mems: c. 6,000. Pres. Prof. SHUNSUKE SAKURAI; Sec.-Gen. JOSÉ DELGADO RODRIGUES. Publ. *News Journal* (3 a year).

International Society for Stereology: c/o Dr Jens R. Nyengaard, Stereological Research Laboratory, Bartholin Bldg, Aarhus Univ., 8000 Arhus C, Denmark; tel. 89-49-36-54; fax 89-49-36-50; e-mail stereo@svfcd.aau.dk; internet www.health.aau.dk/stereology/iss; f. 1962; an interdisciplinary society gathering scientists from metallurgy, geology, mineralogy and biology to exchange ideas on three-dimensional interpretation of two-dimensional samples (sections, projections) of their material by means of stereological principles; tenth Congress: Melbourne, Australia, 1999. Mems: 300. Pres. BENTE PAKKENBERG; Treas. JENS R. NYENGAARD.

International Society for Tropical Ecology: c/o Botany Dept, Banaras Hindu University, Varanasi, 221 005 India; tel. (542) 317099; fax (542) 317074; f. 1956 to promote and develop the science of ecology in the tropics in the service of humanity; to publish a journal to aid ecologists in the tropics in communication of their findings; and to hold symposia from time to time to summarize the state of knowledge in particular or general fields of tropical ecology. Mems: 500. Sec. Prof. J. S. SINGH (India); Editor Prof. K. P. SINGH. Publ. *Tropical Ecology* (2 a year).

International Society of Biometeorology: Dept of Physical Geography, Div. of Environmental and Life Sciences, Macquarie Univ., Sydney, NSW 2109, Australia; tel. (2) 9850-8399; fax (2) 9850-8420; e-mail paul.beggs@mq.edu.au; internet www.biometeorology.org; f. 1956 to unite all biometeorologists working in the fields of agricultural, botanical, cosmic, entomological, forest, human, medical, veterinarian, zoological and other branches of biometeorology. Mems: 350 individuals, nationals of 46 countries. Pres. Dr PETER HÖPPE (Germany); Sec. Dr PAUL J. BEGGS (Australia). Publs *Biometeorology* (Proceedings of the Congress of ISB), *International Journal of Biometeorology* (quarterly), *Biometeorology Bulletin*.

International Society of Criminology (Société Internationale de Criminologie): 4 rue Ferrus, 75014 Paris, France; tel. 1-45-88-00-23; fax 1-45-88-96-40; e-mail crim.sic@wanadoo.fr; f. 1934 to promote the development of the sciences in their application to the criminal phenomenon. Mems: in 63 countries. Sec.-Gen. GEORGES PICCA. Publ. *Annales internationales de Criminologie* .

International Union for Quaternary Research—INQUA: Dept of Soil and Water Sciences, Agricultural University of Norway, POB 3028, 1432, Aas, Norway; e-mail sylvi.haldorsen@ijvf.nlh.no; internet inqua.nlh.no; f. 1928 to co-ordinate research on the Quaternary geological era throughout the world; holds congress every four years (2003: Reno, USA, in August). Sec.-Gen. Prof. SYLVI HALDORSEN (Norway); Administrative Sec. GERRY KROON (Netherlands).

International Water Association: Alliance House, 12 Caxton St, London SW1H 0QS, United Kingdom; tel. (20) 7654-5500; fax (20) 7654-5555; e-mail water@iwahq.org.uk; internet www.iwahq.org.uk; f. 1999 by merger of the International Water Services Association and the International Association on Water Quality; aims to encourage international communication, co-operative effort, and a maximum exchange of information on water quality management through conferences, electronic media, and publication of research reports. Mems: approx. 9,000. Co-Pres VINCENT BATH (South Africa), PIET ODENDAAL (South Africa); Exec. Dir ANTHONY MILBURN (UK). Publs *Water Research* (monthly), *Water Science and Technology* (24 a year), *Water Quality International* (6 a year), *Yearbook, Scientific and Technical Reports*.

Nordic Molecular Biology Association: c/o Prof. Bjursell, Institute of Molecular Biology, Univ. of Göteborg, Göteborg, Sweden; organizes congress every two years, symposia. Mems: 1,000 in Denmark, Finland, Iceland, Norway, Sweden. Chair. Prof. GUNNAR BJURSELL; Sec. LENE SVITH. Publ. *NOMBA Bulletin* (2 a year).

Pacific Science Association: 1525 Bernice St, POB 17801, Honolulu, HI 96817; tel. (808) 848-4139; fax (808) 847-8252; e-mail psa@bishop.bishop.hawaii.org; f. 1920 to promote co-operation in the study of scientific problems relating to the Pacific region, more particularly those affecting the prosperity and well-being of Pacific peoples; sponsors Pacific Science Congresses and Inter-Congresses. Mems: institutional representatives from 35 areas, scientific societies, individual scientists. Ninth Inter-Congress: Taipei, Taiwan, Nov. 1998; 19th Congress: Sydney, Australia, 1997. Pres. Dr AKITA ARIMA (Japan); Exec. Sec. Dr LUCIUS G. ELDREDGE. Publ. *Information Bulletin* (2 a year).

Pan-African Union of Science and Technology: POB 2339, Brazzaville, Republic of the Congo; tel. 832265; fax 832185; f. 1987 to promote the use of science and technology in furthering the development of Africa; organizes triennial congress. Pres. Prof. EDWARD AYENSU; Sec.-Gen. Prof. LÉVY MAKANY.

Pugwash Conferences on Science and World Affairs: 63A Great Russell St, London, WC1B 3BJ, United Kingdom; tel. (20) 7405-6661; fax (20) 7831-5651; e-mail pugwash@qmw.ac.uk; internet www.pugwash.org; f. 1957 to organize international conferences of scientists to discuss problems arising from development of science, particularly the dangers to mankind from weapons of mass destruction. Mems: national Pugwash groups in 38 countries. Pres. Sir MICHAEL ATIYAH; Sec.-Gen. Prof. GEORGE RAHJENS. Publs *Pugwash Newsletter* (quarterly), *Annals of Pugwash*, proceedings of Pugwash conferences, monographs.

Scientific, Technical and Research Commission—STRC: Nigerian Ports Authority Bldg, PMB 2359, Marina, Lagos, Nigeria; tel. (1) 2633430; fax (1) 2636093; e-mail oaustrc@rcl.nig.com; f. 1965 to succeed the Commission for Technical Co-operation in Africa (f. 1954). Supervises the Inter-African Bureau for Animal Resources (Nairobi, Kenya), the Inter-African Bureau for Soils (Lagos, Nigeria) and the Inter-African Phytosanitary Commission (Yaoundé, Cameroon) and several joint research projects. The Commission provides training in agricultural man., and conducts pest control programmes. Exec. Sec. Dr ROBERT N. MSHANA.

Unitas Malacologica (Malacological Union): c/o Dr P. B. Mordan, The Natural History Museum, Science Depts, Zoology: Mollusca, Cromwell Rd, London, SW7 5BD, United Kingdom; tel. (20) 7938-9359; fax (20) 7938-8754; e-mail p.mordan@nhm.ac.uk; f. 1962 to further the study of molluscs; affiliated to the International Union of Biological Sciences (q.v.); holds triennial congress. Mems: 400 in over 30 countries. Pres. Prof. L. VON SALVINI-PLAWEN (Austria); Sec. Dr PETER B. MORDAN (UK). Publ. *UM Newsletter* (2 a year).

World Organisation of Systems and Cybernetics—WOSC: c/o Prof. R. Vallée, 2 rue de Vouillé, 75015 Paris, France; tel. and fax 1-45-33-62-46; f. 1969 to act as clearing-house for all societies concerned with cybernetics and systems, to aim for the recognition of cybernetics as fundamental science, to organize and sponsor international exhibitions of automation and computer equipment, congresses and symposia, and to promote and co-ordinate research in systems and cybernetics; sponsors an honorary fellowship and awards a Norbert Wiener memorial gold medal. Mems: national and international societies in 30 countries. Pres. Prof. S. BEER (UK); Dir-Gen. Prof. R. VALLÉE (France). Publs *Kybernetes, the International Journal of Cybernetics and Systems*.

Social Sciences

International Council for Philosophy and Humanistic Studies—ICPHS: Maison de l'UNESCO, 1 rue Miollis, 75732 Paris Cédex 15, France; tel. 1-45-68-26-85; fax 1-40-65-94-80; f. 1949 under the auspices of UNESCO to encourage respect for cultural autonomy by the comparative study of civilization and to contribute towards international understanding through a better knowledge of humanity; to develop international co-operation in philosophy, humanistic and kindred studies and to encourage the setting up of international organizations; to promote the dissemination of information in these fields; to sponsor works of learning, etc. Mems: organizations (see below) representing 145 countries. Pres. JEAN D'ORMESSON (France); Sec.-Gen. TILO SCHABERT (Germany). Publs *Bulletin of Information* (biennially), *Diogenes* (quarterly).

UNIONS FEDERATED TO THE ICPHS

International Academic Union: Palais des Académies, 1 rue Ducale, 1000 Brussels, Belgium; tel. (2) 550-22-00; fax (2) 550-22-05; f. 1919 to promote international co-operation through collective research in philology, archaeology, art history, history and social sciences. Mems: academic institutions in 49 countries. Pres. M. CAVINESS (USA); Secs J.-L. DE PAEPE, L. HOUZIAUX.

International Association for the History of Religions: c/o Prof. Armin W. Geertz, Institut for Religionsvidenskab, Aarhus Universitet, Taasingegade 3, 8000 Aarhus C, Denmark; tel. 89-42-23-06; fax 86-13-04-90; e-mail geertz@teologi.au.dk; internet www.iahr.dk; f. 1950 to promote international collaboration of scholars, to organize congresses and to stimulate research. Mems: 33 countries. Pres. PETER ANTES; Gen. Sec.Prof. ARMIN W. GEERTZ.

International Committee for the History of Art: 13 rue de Seine, 75006 Paris, France; e-mail philippe.senechal@inha.fr; internet www.esteticas.unam.mx/ciha; f. 1930 by the 12th International Congress on the History of Art, for collaboration in the scientific study of the history of art. International congress every four years, and at least two colloquia between congresses. Mems: National Committees in 34 countries. Pres. Prof. STEPHEN BANN (United Kingdom); Sec. PHILIPPE SENECHAL (France). Publ. *Bibliographie d'histoire de l'Art* (quarterly).

International Committee of Historical Sciences: Bâtiment Laplace, École Normale Supérieure de Cachan, 94235 Cachan Cédex, France; e-mail cish@ihtp-cnrs.ens-cachan.fr; f. 1926 to work for the advancement of historical sciences by means of international co-ordination; an international congress is held every five years. Mems: 53 national committees, 22 affiliated international organizations and 18 internal commissions. Pres. IVAN T. BEREND (USA); Sec.-Gen. FRANÇOIS BÉDARIDA (France). Publ. *Bulletin d'Information du CISH*.

International Congress of African Studies: c/o International African Institute, School of Oriental and African Studies, Thornhaugh St, London, WC1H OXG, United Kingdom; tel. (20) 7898-4420; fax (20) 7898-4419; e-mail iai@soas.ac.uk; f. 1962.

International Federation for Modern Languages and Literatures: c/o D. A. Wells, Dept of German, Birkbeck College, Malet St, London, WC1E 7HX, United Kingdom; tel. (20) 7631-6103; fax (20) 7383-3729; e-mail d.wells@bbk.ac.uk; f. 1928 to establish permanent contact between historians of literature, to develop or perfect facilities for their work and to promote the study of modern languages and literature. Congress every three years. Mems: 19 associations, with individual mems in 98 countries. Sec.-Gen. D. A. WELLS (UK).

International Federation of Philosophical Societies: c/o I. Kuçuradi, Ahmet Rasim Sok. 8/4, Çankaya, 06550 Ankara, Turkey; tel. (312) 2351219; fax (312) 2978300; e-mail ioanna@fisp.org.tr; internet www.fisp.org.tr; f. 1948 under the auspices of UNESCO, to encourage international co-operation in the field of philosophy; holds World Congress of Philosophy every five years. Mems: 125 societies from 50 countries; 27 international societies. Pres. IOANNA KUÇURADI (Turkey); Sec.-Gen. PETER KEMP (Denmark). Publs *Newsletter, International Bibliography of Philosophy, Chroniques de Philosophie, Contemporary Philosophy, Philosophical Problems Today, Philosophy and Cultural Development*.

International Federation of Societies of Classical Studies: c/o Prof. F. Paschoud, 6 chemin aux Folies, 1293 Bellevue, Switzerland; tel. (22) 7742656; fax (22) 7742734; e-mail zosime@isuisse.com; f. 1948 under the auspices of UNESCO. Mems: 79 societies in 44 countries. Pres. C. J. CLASSEN; Sec. Prof. F. PASCHOUD (Switzerland). Publs *L'Année Philologique, Thesaurus linguae Latinae*.

International Musicological Society: CP 1561, 4001 Basel, Switzerland; fax (1) 9231027; e-mail imsba@swissonline.ch; internet www.ims-online.ch; f. 1927; international congresses every five years. Pres. LÁSZLÓ SOMFAI; Sec.-Gen. Dr DOROTHEA BAUMANN (Switzerland). Publ. *Acta Musicologica* (2 a year).

International Union for Oriental and Asian Studies: Közraktar u. 12A 11/2, 1093 Budapest, Hungary; f. 1951 by the 22nd International Congress of Orientalists under the auspices of UNESCO, to promote contacts between orientalists throughout the world, and to organize congresses, research and publications. Mems: in 24 countries. Sec.-Gen. Prof. GEORG HAZAI. Publs *Philologiae Turcicae Fundamenta, Materialien zum Sumerischen Lexikon, Sanskrit Dictionary, Corpus Inscriptionum Iranicarum, Linguistic Atlas of Iran, Matériels des parlers iraniens, Turcology Annual, Bibliographie égyptologique*.

International Union of Anthropological and Ethnological Sciences: c/o Dr P. J. M. Nas, Faculty of Social Sciences, Univ. of Leiden, Wassenaarseweg 52, POB 9555, 2300 RB Leiden, Netherlands; tel. (71) 5273992; fax (71) 5273619; e-mail nas@rulfsw.leidenuniv.nl; f. 1948 under the auspices of UNESCO; has 19 international research commissions. Mems: institutions and individuals in 100 countries. Pres. Prof. ERIC SUNDERLAND (UK); Sec.-Gen. Dr P. J. M. NAS (Netherlands). Publ. *IUAES Newsletter* (3 a year).

International Union of Prehistoric and Protohistoric Sciences: c/o Prof. J. Bourgeois, Dept of Archaeology and Ancient History of Europe, University of Ghent, Blandijnberg 2, 9000 Ghent, Belgium; tel. (9) 264-41-06; fax (9) 264-41-73; e-mail jean.bourgeois@rug.ac.be; f. 1931 to promote congresses and scientific work in the fields of pre- and proto-history. Mems: 120 countries. Pres. Prof. P. BONENFANT (Belgium); Sec.-Gen. Prof. J. BOURGEOIS (Belgium).

Permanent International Committee of Linguists: Instituut voor Nederlandse Lexicologie, Matthias de Vrieshof 2, 2311 BZ Leiden, Netherlands; tel. (71) 5141648; fax (71) 5272115; e-mail secretariaat@inl.nl; f. 1928; to further linguistic research, to co-ordinate activities undertaken for the advancement of linguistics, and to make the results of linguistic research known internationally; holds Congress every five years. Mems: 48 countries and two international linguistic organizations. Pres. S. A. Wurm (Australia); Sec.-Gen. P. G. J. van Sterkenburg (Netherlands). Publ. *Linguistic Bibliography* (annually).

OTHER ORGANIZATIONS

African Social and Environmental Studies Programme: Box 4477, Nairobi, Kenya; tel. (2) 747960; fax (2) 740817; f. 1968; develops and disseminates educational material on social and environmental studies, and education for all in eastern and southern Africa. Mems: 18 African countries. Chair. Prof. William Senteza-Kajubi; Exec. Dir Prof. Peter Muyanda Mutebi. Publs *African Social Studies Forum* (2 a year), teaching guides.

Arab Towns Organization—ATO: POB 68160, Kaifan 71962, Kuwait; tel. 4849705; fax 4849322; e-mail ato@ato.net; f. 1967; aims to promote co-operation and the exchange of expertise with regard to urban administration; to improve the standard of municipal services and utilities in Arab towns; and to preserve the character and heritage of Arab towns. Administers an Institute for Urban Development (AUDI), based in Riyadh, Saudi Arabia, which provides training and research for municipal officers; the Arab Towns Development Fund, to provide financial assistance to help member towns implement projects; and the ATO Award, to encourage the preservation of Arab architecture. Mems: 413 towns. Dir-Gen. Mohammed Abdul Hamid al-Saqr; Sec.-Gen. Abd al-Aziz Y. al-Adasani. Publ. *Al-Madinah Al-Arabiyah* (every 2 months).

Association for the Study of the World Refugee Problem—AWR: Piazzale di Porta Pia 121, 00198 Rome, Italy; tel. (06) 44250159; f. 1951 to promote and co-ordinate scholarly research on refugee problems. Mems: 475 in 19 countries. Pres. Franco Foschi (Italy); Sec.-Gen. Aldo Clemente (Italy). Publs *AWR Bulletin* (quarterly, in English, French, Italian and German), treatises on refugee problems (17 vols).

Council for the Development of Social Science Research in Africa—CODESRIA: BP 3304, Dakar, Senegal; tel. 825-98-22; fax 824-12-89; e-mail codesria@telecomplus.sn; f. 1973; promotes research, provides conferences, working groups and information services. Mems: research institutes and university faculties in African countries. Exec. Sec. Achille Mbembe. Publs *Africa Development* (quarterly), *CODESRIA Bulletin* (quarterly), *Index of African Social Science Periodical Articles* (annually), directories of research.

Council for Research in Values and Philosophy: c/o Prof. G. F. McLean, School of Philosophy, Catholic University of America, Washington, DC 20064, USA; tel. and fax (202) 319-6089; e-mail cuarvp@cua.edu; internet www.crvp.org. Mems: 33 teams from 24 countries. Pres. Prof. Kenneth L. Schmitz (Canada); Sec.-Gen. Prof. George F. McLean (USA).

Eastern Regional Organisation for Planning and Housing: POB 10867, 50726 Kuala Lumpur, Malaysia; tel. (3) 718-7068; fax (3) 718-3931; f. 1958 to promote and co-ordinate the study and practice of housing and regional town and country planning. Offices in Japan, India and Indonesia. Mems: 57 organizations and 213 individuals in 28 countries. Sec.-Gen. John Koh Seng Siew. Publs *EAROPH News and Notes* (monthly), *Town and Country Planning* (bibliography).

English-Speaking Union of the Commonwealth: Dartmouth House, 37 Charles St, Berkeley Sq., London, W1J 5ED, United Kingdom; tel. (20) 7529-1550; fax (20) 7495-6108; e-mail esu@esu.org; internet www.esu.org; f. 1918 to promote international understanding between Britain, the Commonwealth, the United States and Europe, in conjunction with the ESU of the USA. Mems: 70,000 (incl. USA). Chair. Lord Alan Watson; Dir-Gen. Valerie Mitchell. Publ. *Concord*.

European Association for Population Studies: POB 11676, 2502 AR The Hague, Netherlands; tel. (70) 3565200; fax (70) 3647187; e-mail eaps@nidi.nl; internet www.nidi.nl/eaps; f. 1983 to foster research and provide information on European population problems; organizes conferences, seminars and workshops. Mems: demographers from 40 countries. Exec. Sec. Vera Holman. Publ. *European Journal of Population / Revue Européenne de Démographie* (quarterly).

European Society for Rural Sociology: c/o C. Ray, Centre for Rural Economy, Univ. of Newcastle upon Tyne, NE1 7RU, United Kingdom; tel. (191) 222-6460; fax (191) 222-6720; e-mail christopher .ray@newcastle.ac.uk; f. 1957 to further research in, and co-ordination of, rural sociology and provide a centre for documentation of information. Mems: 300 individuals, institutions and associations in 29 European countries and nine countries outside Europe. Pres. Dr Hilary Tovey (Ireland); Sec. Christopher Ray (United Kingdom). Publ. *Sociologia Ruralis* (quarterly).

Experiment in International Living: POB 595, Main St, Putney, VT 05346, USA; tel. (802) 387-4210; fax (802) 387-5783; e-mail federation@experiment.org; internet www.experiment.org; f. 1932 as an international federation of non-profit educational and cultural exchange institutions, to create mutual understanding and respect among people of different nations, as a means of furthering peace. Mems: organizations in 20 countries. Dir Robin Bitters.

International African Institute: School of Oriental and African Studies, Thornhaugh St, Russell Sq., London, WC1H 0XG, United Kingdom; tel. (20) 7898-4420; fax (20) 7898-4419; e-mail iai@soas .ac.uk; internet www.oneworld.org/iai; f. 1926 to promote the study of African peoples, their languages, cultures and social life in their traditional and modern settings; international seminar programme brings together scholars from Africa and elsewhere; links scholars so as to facilitate research projects, especially in the social sciences. Mems: 1,500 in 97 countries. Chair. Prof. V. Y. Mudimbe; Dir Prof. Paul Spencer. Publs *Africa* (quarterly), *Africa Bibliography* (annually).

International Association for Mass Communication Research: c/o Prof. Dr Cees J. Hamelink, IAMCR Administrative Office, Baden Powellweg 109-111, 1069 LD Amsterdam, Netherlands; tel. (20) 6101581; fax (20) 6104821; f. 1957 to stimulate interest in mass communication research and the dissemination of information about research and research needs, to improve communication practice, policy and research and training for journalism, to provide a forum for researchers and others involved in mass communication to meet and exchange information. Mems: over 2,000 in 65 countries. Pres. Prof. Dr Cees J. Hamelink (Netherlands); Sec.-Gen. Dr Robin Cheesman (Denmark).

International Association of Applied Linguistics: c/o Prof. Andrew D. Cohen, Dept of ESL, 331e Nolte Center, University of Minnesota, 315 Pillsbury Drive SE, Minneapolis, MN 55455, USA; tel. (612) 624-3806; fax (612) 624-4579; e-mail adcohen@tc.umn.edu; internet www.aila.ac; f. 1964; organizes seminars on applied linguistics, and a World Congress every three years. Mems: associations in 38 countries. Pres. Prof. Christopher Candlin (Hong Kong); Sec.-Gen. Prof. Andrew D. Cohen (USA). Publs *AILA Review* (annually), *AILA News* (2 a year).

International Association of Metropolitan City Libraries—INTAMEL: c/o Frances Schwenger, Metropolitan Toronto Reference Library, 789 Yonge St, Toronto, ON M4W 2G8, Canada; tel. (416) 393-7215; fax (416) 393-7229; f. 1967. Mems: 93 libraries in 28 countries. Sec. and Treas. Frances Schwenger.

International Committee for Social Sciences Information and Documentation: c/o Dr A. F. Marks, Herengracht 410 (Swidoc), 1017BX Amsterdam, Netherlands; tel. (20) 6225061; fax (20) 6238374; f. 1950 to collect and disseminate information on documentation services in social sciences, to help improve documentation, to advise societies on problems of documentation and to draw up rules likely to improve the presentation of all documents. Members from international associations specializing in social sciences or in documentation, and from other specialized fields. Sec.-Gen. Arnaud F. Marks (Netherlands). Publs *International Bibliography of the Social Sciences* (annually), *Newsletter* (2 a year).

International Council on Archives: 60 rue des Francs-Bourgeois, 75003 Paris, France; tel. 1-40-27-63-06; fax 1-42-72-20-65; e-mail secretariat@ica.cia.org; internet www.ica.org; f. 1948. Mems: 1,574 in 176 countries and territories; work includes conservation, training, automation, development of standards for description of archives; 10 regional branches. Pres. Elisa de Santos (Spain); Sec.-Gen. Joan van Albada. Publ. *Archivum* (5 a year).

International Ergonomics Association: BP 2025, 3500 HA Utrecht, Netherlands; tel. (30) 35-44-55; fax (30) 35-76-39; f. 1957 to bring together organizations and persons interested in the scientific study of human work and its environment; to establish international contacts among those specializing in this field, co-operate with employers' associations and trade unions in order to encourage the practical application of ergonomic sciences in industries, and promote scientific research in this field. Mems: 17 federated societies. Pres. Ilkka Kuorinka (Finland); Sec.-Gen. Prof. D. P. Rookmaaker. Publ. *Ergonomics* (monthly).

International Federation for Housing and Planning: Wassenaarseweg 43, 2596 CG The Hague, Netherlands; tel. (70) 3244557; fax (70) 3282085; e-mail ifhp.nl@inter.nl.net; internet www.ifhp.org; f. 1913 to study and promote the improvement of housing, the theory and practice of town planning inclusive of the creation of new agglomerations and the planning of territories at regional, national and international levels; world congress and international conference held every 2 years. Mems: 200 organizations and 300 individuals in 65 countries. Pres. Irene Wiese-von Ofen (Germany); Sec.-Gen. E. E. van Hylckama Vlieg (Netherlands). Publ. *Newsletter* (quarterly).

International Federation of Institutes for Socio-religious Research: 1 place Montesquieu, Bte 13, 1348 Louvain-la-neuve, Belgium; e-mail gendebien@anso.ucl.ac.be; f. 1958; federates centres engaged in undertaking scientific research in order to analyse and discover the social and religious phenomena at work in contemporary society. Mems: institutes in 26 countries. Pres. Canon Fr. Houtart (Belgium); Sec. F. Gendebien. Publ. *Social Compass (International Review of Sociology of Religion)* (quarterly, in English and French).

International Federation of Social Science Organizations: Via dei Laghi 14, 00198 Rome, Italy; tel. and fax (06) 8848943; f. 1979 to assist research and teaching in the social sciences, and to facilitate co-operation and enlist mutual assistance in the planning and evaluation of programmes of major importance to members. Mems: 23 organizations. Pres. Prof. CARMENCITA T. AGUILAR; Sec.-Gen. Prof. J. BLAHOZ. Publs *Newsletter, International Directory of Social Science Organizations*.

International Federation of Vexillological Associations: Box 580, Winchester, MA 01890, USA; tel. (781) 729-9410; fax (781) 721-4817; e-mail vexor@mediaone.net; f. 1967 to promote through its member organizations the scientific study of the history and symbolism of flags, and especially to hold International Congresses every two years and sanction international standards for scientific flag study. Mems: 42 institutions and associations in 27 countries. Pres. Prof. MICHEL LUPANT (Belgium); Liaison Officer WHITNEY SMITH. Publs *Recueil* (every 2 years), *The Flag Bulletin* (every 2 months), *Info FIAV* (every 4 months).

International Institute for Ligurian Studies: Via Romana 39, 18012 Bordighera, Italy; tel. (0184) 263601; fax (0184) 266421; e-mail istituto@üsl.it; internet www.üsl.it; f. 1947 to conduct research on ancient monuments and regional traditions in the north-west arc of the Mediterranean (France and Italy). Library of 80,000 vols. Mems: in France, Italy, Spain, Switzerland. Dir Prof. CARLO VARALDO (Italy).

International Institute of Administrative Sciences: 1 rue Defacqz, 1000 Brussels, Belgium; tel. (2) 538-91-65; fax (2) 537-97-02; e-mail iias@iiasiisa.be; internet www.iiasiisa.be; f. 1930 for comparative examination of administrative experience in the various countries; research and programmes for improving administrative law and practices and for technical assistance; library of 15,000 vols; consultative status with UN, UNESCO and ILO; international congresses. Mems: 46 mem. states, 55 national sections, 9 international governmental organizations, 51 corporate mems, 13 individual members. Pres. IGNACIO PICHARDO PAGAZA (Mexico); Dir-Gen. GIANCARLO VILELLA (Italy). Publs *International Review of Administrative Sciences* (quarterly), *Newsletter* (3 a year).

International Institute of Sociology: c/o Facoltà di Scienze Politiche, Università di Roma 'La Sapienza', Piazzale A. Moro 5, 00185 Rome, Italy; tel. (06) 3451017; fax (06) 3451017; f. 1893 to enable sociologists to meet and study sociological questions. Mems: 300, representing 45 countries. Pres. PAOLO AMMASSARI (Italy); Gen. Sec. ALAN HEDLEY. Publ. *The Annals of the IIS*.

International Numismatic Commission: Coins and Medals Dept, British Museum, London, WC1B 3DG, United Kingdom; tel. (20) 7323-8227; fax (20) 7323-8171; f. 1936; enables co-operation between scholars studying coins and medals. Mems: numismatic organizations in 35 countries. Pres. A. BURNETT; Sec. M. AMANDRY.

International Peace Academy: 777 United Nations Plaza, New York, NY 10017, USA; tel. (212) 687-4300; fax (212) 983-8246; e-mail ipa@ipacademy.org; internet www.ipacademy.org/; f. 1970 to promote the prevention and settlement of armed conflicts between and within states through policy research and development; educates government officials in the procedures needed for conflict resolution, peace-keeping, mediation and negotiation, through international training seminars and publications; off-the-record meetings are also conducted to gain complete understanding of a specific conflict. Chair. RITA E. HAUSER; Pres. OLARA A. OTUNNU. Publs *Annual Report, Newsletter* (2 a year).

International Peace Research Association: c/o Copenhagen Peace Research Institute, University of Copenhagen, Fredericiagade 18, 1310 Copenhagen, Denmark; tel. 3345-5052; fax 3345-5060; e-mail bmoeller@copn.dk; internet www.copn.dk/ipra/ipra.html; f. 1964 to encourage interdisciplinary research on the conditions of peace and the causes of war. Mems: 150 corporate, five regional branches, 1,000 individuals, in 93 countries. Pres. URSULA OSWALD (Mexico); Sec.-Gen. BJOERN MOELLER (Denmark). Publ. *IPRA Newsletter* (quarterly).

International Social Science Council—ISSC: Maison de l'UNESCO, 1 rue Miollis, 75732 Paris Cédex 15, France; tel. 1-45-68-25-58; fax 1-45-66-76-03; e-mail issclak@unesco.org; internet www.unesco.org/ngo/issc; f. 1952; aims to promote the advancement of the social sciences throughout the world and their application to the major problems of the world; the spread of co-operation at an international level between specialists in the social sciences. ISSC has a Senior Board; and programmes on International Human Dimensions of Global Environmental Change (IHDP), co-sponsored by the International Council of Scientific Unions (q.v.), and Comparative Research on Poverty (CROP). Mems: 14 associations (listed below), 17 national organizations, 16 associate member organizations. Pres. KURT PAWLIK (Germany); Sec.-Gen. LESZEK A. KOSINSKI (Canada).

Associations Federated to the ISSC

(details of these organizations will be found under their appropriate category elsewhere in the International Organizations section)

International Society of Social Defence and Humane Criminal Policy: c/o Centro nazionale di prevenzione e difesa sociale, Piazza Castello 3, 20121 Milan, Italy; tel. (02) 86460714; fax (02) 72008431; e-mail cnpds.ispac@iol.it; f. 1945 to combat crime, to protect society and to prevent citizens from being tempted to commit criminal actions. Mems: in 34 countries. Pres. SIMONE ROZES (France); Sec.-Gen. EDMONDO BRUTI LIBERATI (Italy). Publ. *Cahiers de défense sociale* (annually).

International Sociological Association: c/o Faculty of Political Sciences and Sociology, Universidad Complutense, 28223 Madrid, Spain; tel. (91) 3527650; fax (91) 3524945; e-mail isa@sis.ucm.es; internet www.ucm.es/info/isa; f. 1949 to promote sociological knowledge, facilitate contacts between sociologists, encourage the dissemination and exchange of information and facilities and stimulate research; has 53 research committees on various aspects of sociology; holds World Congresses every four years (15th Congress: Brisbane, Australia, 2002). Pres. A. MARTINELLI (Italy); Exec. Sec. IZABELA BARLINSKA. Publs *Current Sociology* (3 a year), *International Sociology* (quarterly), *Sage Studies in International Sociology* (based on World Congress).

International Statistical Institute: POB 950, Prinses Beatrixlaan 428, 2270 AZ Voorburg, Netherlands; tel. (70) 3375737; fax (70) 3860025; e-mail isi@cbs.nl; internet www.cbs.nl/isi; f. 1885; devoted to the development and improvement of statistical methods and their application throughout the world; administers among others a statistical education centre in Calcutta in co-operation with the Indian Statistical Institute; executes international research programmes. Mems: 2,000 ordinary mems; 10 hon. mems; 110 ex-officio mems; 75 corporate mems; 45 affiliated organizations; 32 national statistical societies. Pres. J.-L. BODIN; Dir Permanent Office M. P. R. VAN DEN BROECKE. Publs *Bulletin of the International Statistical Institute* (proceedings of biennial sessions), *International Statistical Review* (3 a year), *Short Book Reviews* (3 a year), *Statistical Theory and Method Abstracts* (quarterly), *ISI Newsletter* (3 a year), *Directories* (every 2 years).

International Studies Association: Social Science 324, Univ. of Arizona, Tucson, AZ 85721, USA; tel. (520) 621-7715; fax (520) 621-5780; e-mail isa@u.arizona.edu; internet www.isanet.org; f. 1959; links those whose professional concerns extend beyond their own national boundaries (government officials, representatives of business and industry, and scholars). Mems: 3,500 in 60 countries. Pres. MICHAEL BRECHER; Exec. Dir THOMAS J. VOLGY. Publs *International Studies Quarterly, International Studies Perspectives, International Studies Review, ISA Newsletter*.

International Union for the Scientific Study of Population: 34 rue des Augustins, 4000 Liège, Belgium; tel. (4) 222-40-80; fax (4) 222-38-47; e-mail iussp@iussp.org; internet www.iussp.org; f. 1928 to advance the progress of quantitative and qualitative demography as a science. Mems: 1,917 in 121 countries. Pres. JOSÉ ALBERTO M. DE CARVALHO. Publs *IUSSP Bulletin* and books on population.

Mensa International: 15 The Ivories, 6–8 Northampton St, London, N1 2HY, United Kingdom; tel. (20) 7226-6891; fax (20) 7226-7059; internet www.mensa.org/mensa-international; f. 1946 to identify and foster intelligence for the benefit of humanity. Members are individuals who score in a recognized intelligence test higher than 98% of people in general: there are 100,000 mems world-wide. Exec. Dir E. J. VINCENT (UK). Publ. *Mensa International Journal* (monthly).

Third World Forum: 39 Dokki St, POB 43, Orman, Cairo, Egypt; tel. (2) 3488092; fax (2) 3480668; e-mail isabry@idsc1.gov.eg; f. 1973 to link social scientists and others from the developing countries, to discuss alternative development policies and encourage research; undertaking Egypt 2020 research project. Regional offices in Egypt, Mexico, Senegal and Sri Lanka. Mems: individuals in more than 50 countries. Chair. ISMAIL-SABRI ABDALLA.

World Association for Public Opinion Research: c/o University of Nebraska-Lincoln, UNL Gallup Research Center, 200 N 11th St, Lincoln, NE 68588-0241, USA; tel. (402) 458-2030; fax (402) 458-

Social Welfare and Human Rights

2038; e-mail wapor@unl.edu; internet www.wapor.org; f. 1947 to establish and promote contacts between persons in the field of survey research on opinions, attitudes and behaviour of people in the various countries of the world; to further the use of objective, scientific survey research in national and international affairs. Mems: 450 from 72 countries. Man. Dir RENAE REIS. Publs *WAPOR Newsletter* (quarterly), *International Journal of Public Opinion* (quarterly).

World Society for Ekistics: c/o Athens Centre of Ekistics, 24 Strat. Syndesmou St, 106 73 Athens, Greece; tel. (1) 3623216; fax (1) 3629337; e-mail ekistics@otenet.gr; f. 1965; aims to promote knowledge and ideas concerning human settlements through research, publications and conferences; to recognize the benefits and necessity of an inter-disciplinary approach to the needs of human settlements. Pres. Prof. UDO E. SIMONIS; Sec.-Gen. P. PSOMOPOULOS.

Social Welfare and Human Rights

African Commission on Human and People's Rights: Kairaba Ave, POB 673, Banjul, The Gambia; tel. 392962; fax 390764; f. 1987; meets twice a year for 10 days in March and Oct.; the Commission comprises 11 members. Its mandate is to monitor compliance with the African Charter on Human and People's Rights (ratified in 1986), and it investigates claims of human rights abuses perpetrated by govts that have ratified the Charter. Claims may be brought by other African govts, the victims themselves, or by a third party. Sec. GERMAIN BARICAKO (Burundi).

Aid to Displaced Persons and its European Villages: 35 rue du Marché, 4500 Huy, Belgium; tel. (85) 21-34-81; f. 1957 to carry on and develop work begun by the Belgian association Aid to Displaced Persons; aims to provide material and moral aid for refugees; European Villages established at Aachen, Bregenz, Augsburg, Berchem-Ste-Agathe, Spiesen, Euskirchen, Wuppertal as centres for refugees. Pres. LUC DENYS (Belgium).

Amnesty International: 1 Easton St, London, WC1X 0DW, United Kingdom; tel. (20) 7413-5500; fax (20) 7956-1157; e-mail amnestyis-@amnesty.org; internet www.amnesty.org/; f. 1961; an independent world-wide movement, campaigning impartially for the release of all prisoners of conscience, fair and prompt trials for all political prisoners, the abolition of torture and the death penalty and the end of extrajudicial executions and 'disappearances'; also opposes abuses by opposition groups (hostage-taking, torture and arbitrary killings); financed by donations. Mems: 1m. represented by 7,500 local groups, youth and student groups and other specialist groups, in more than 100 countries and territories; nationally organized sections in 56 countries. Sec.-Gen. PIERRE SANÉ (Senegal); (from mid-2001) IRENE KHAN (Bangladesh). Publs *International Newsletter* (monthly), *Annual Report*, other country reports.

Anti-Slavery International: Thomas Clarkson House, The Stableyard, Broomgrove Rd, London, SW9 7TL, United Kingdom; tel. (20) 7501-8920; fax (20) 7738-4110; e-mail antislavery@antislavery.org; internet www.antislavery.org; f. 1839 to eradicate slavery and forced labour in all their forms, to generate awareness of such abuses, to promote the well-being of indigenous peoples, and to protect human rights in accordance with the Universal Declaration of Human Rights, 1948. Mems: 1,800 members in 30 countries. Chair. REGGIE NORTON; Dir MIKE DOTTRIDGE. Publs *Annual Report, Anti-Slavery Reporter* (quarterly), special reports on research.

Associated Country Women of the World: Clutha House, 10 Storey's Gate, London, SW1P 3AY, United Kingdom; tel. (20) 7834-8635; f. 1933; aims to aid the economic and social development of countrywomen and home-makers of all nations; to promote international goodwill and understanding; and to work to alleviate poverty, and promote good health and education. Mems: several million. Gen. Sec. ANNA FROST. Publ. *The Countrywoman* (quarterly).

Association Internationale de la Mutualité (International Association for Mutual Benefit Societies): 50 rue d'Arlon, 1000 Brussels, Belgium; tel. (2) 234-57-00; fax (2) 234-57-08; e-mail aim.secretariat-@skynet.be; internet www.hurisc.org/aim; f. 1950; aims to promote and reinforce access to health care by developing the sound management of mutualities. Mems: 44 federations of mutualities in 28 countries. Pres. MICHEL SCHMITE (Luxembourg); Dir WILLY PALM (Belgium).

Aviation sans frontières—ASF: Brussels National Airport, Brucargo 706, POB 7339, 1931 Brucargo, Belgium; tel. (2) 751-24-70; fax (2) 751-24-71; e-mail office@asfbelgium.org; f. 1980 to make available the resources of the aviation industry to humanitarian organizations, for carrying supplies and equipment at minimum cost, both on long-distance flights and locally. Pres. PHILIPPE DEHENNIU; Gen. Man. ALAIN PEETERS.

Catholic International Union for Social Service: 31 rue de la Citronelle, 1348 Louvaine-la-Neuve, Belgium; tel. (10) 45-25-13; f.

1925 to develop social service on the basis of Christian doctrine; to unite Catholic social schools and social workers' associations in all countries to promote their foundation; to represent at the international level the Catholic viewpoint as it affects social service. Mems: 172 schools of social service, 26 associations of social workers, 52 individual members. Exec. Sec. ALEXANDRE CARLSON. Publs *Service Social dans le monde* (quarterly), *News Bulletin, Bulletin de Liaison, Boletín de Noticias* (quarterly).

Co-ordinating Committee for International Voluntary Service—CCIVS: Maison de l'UNESCO, 1 rue Miollis, 75732 Paris Cédex 15, France; tel. 1-45-68-49-36; fax 1-42-73-05-21; e-mail ccivs-@unesco.org; internet www.unesco.org/ccivs; f. 1948 to co-ordinate youth voluntary service organizations all over the world. Organizes seminars and conferences; publishes relevant literature; undertakes planning and execution of projects in collaboration with UNESCO, the UN, the EU etc; and generates funds for member organizations' projects. Affiliated mems: 140 orgs in more than 90 countries. Pres. G. ORSINI; Dir S. COSTANZO-SOW . Publs *News from CCIVS* (3 a year), *The Volunteer's Handbook,* other guides, handbooks and directories.

EIRENE—International Christian Service for Peace: 56503 Neuwied, Postfach 1322, Germany; tel. (2631) 83790; fax (2631) 31160; e-mail eirene-int@eirene.org; internet www.eirene.org; f. 1957; works in Africa and Latin America (professional training, apprenticeship programmes, agricultural work and co-operatives), Europe and the USA (volunteer programmes in co-operation with peace groups). Gen. Sec. ECKEHARD FRICKE.

European Federation of the Elderly—EURAG: Wielandgasse 9, 1 Stock, 8010 Graz, Austria; tel. (316) 81-46-08; fax (316) 81-47-67; e-mail eurag.europe@aon.at; internet www.eurag.org; f. 1962, as the European Federation for the Welfare of the Elderly (present name adopted 1996), for the exchange of experience among member associations; practical co-operation among member organizations to achieve their objectives in the field of ageing; representation of the interests of members before international organizations; promotion of understanding and co-operation in matters of social welfare; to draw attention to the problems of old age. Mems: organizations in 33 countries. Pres. EDMÉE MANGERS-ANEN (Luxembourg); Sec.-Gen. GREGOR HAMMERL (Austria). Publs (in English, French, German and Italian) *EURAG Newsletter* (quarterly), *EURAG Information* (monthly).

Federation of Asian Women's Associations—FAWA: Centro Escolar University, 9 Mendiola St, San Miguel, Manila, Philippines; tel. (2) 741-04-46; f. 1959 to provide closer relations, and bring about joint efforts among Asians, particularly among the women, through mutual appreciation of cultural, moral and socio-economic values. Mems: 415,000. Pres. MADELEINE BORDALLO (Guam); Sec. EVELINA McDONALD (Guam). Publ. *FAWA News Bulletin* (quarterly).

Interamerican Conference on Social Security (Conferencia Interamericano de Seguridad Social—CISS): Calle San Ramon s/n esq. Avda San Jerónimo, Unidad Independencia, Col. San Jerónimo Lídice, Deleg. Magdalena Contreras, CP 10100 México DF, Mexico; tel. (5) 595-01-77; fax (5) 683-85-24; e-mail ciss@data.net.mx; internet www.ciss.org.mx; f. 1942 to contribute to the development of social security in the countries of the Americas and to co-operate with social security institutions. CISS bodies are: the General Assembly, the Permanent Interamerican Committee on Social Security, the Secretariat General, six American Commissions of Social Security and the Interamerican Center for Social Security Studies. Mems: 77 social security institutions in 38 countries. Pres. Dr SANTIAGO LEVY ALGAZI (Mexico); Sec.-Gen. Dr JOSÉ LUIS STEIN VELASCO (Mexico) (acting). Dir of the Interamerican Center for Social Security Studies Dr LUIS JOSÉ MARTÍNEZ VILLALBA (Uruguay). Publs *Social Security Journal / Seguridad Social* (every 2 months), monographs, study series.

International Abolitionist Federation: 16 rue Cassette, 75006 Paris, France; f. 1875 for the abolition of the organization and exploitation of prostitution by public authorities, sex discrimination, and for the rehabilitation of the victims of traffic and prostitution; holds international congress every three years and organizes regional conferences to raise awareness regarding the cultural, religious and traditional practices which affect adversely the lives of women and children. Affiliated organizations in 17 countries. Corresponding mems in 40 countries. Pres. BRIGITTE POLONOVSKI (Switzerland); Exec. Sec. HÉLÈNE SACKSTEIN (France). Publ. *IAF Information* (3 a year).

International Association against Noise: Hirschenplatz 7, 6004 Lucerne, Switzerland; tel. (41) 4103013; fax (41) 4109093; f. 1959 to promote noise-control at an international level; to promote co-operation and the exchange of experience and prepare supranational measures; issues information, carries out research, organizes conferences, and assists national anti-noise associations. Mems: four, and one associate mem. Pres. KAREL NOVOTNÝ (Czech Republic); Sec. Dr WILLY AECHERLI (Switzerland).

International Association of Children's International Summer Villages—CISV International Ltd: Mea House, Ellison

Pl., Newcastle upon Tyne, NE1 8XS, United Kingdom; tel. (191) 232-4998; fax (191) 261-4710; e-mail cisvio@dial.pipex.com; internet www.cisv.org; f. 1950 to promote peace, education and cross-cultural friendship; conducts International Camps for children and young people mainly between the ages of 11 and 19. Mems: some 49,000. International Pres. DAVID LISTER; Sec.-Gen. GABRIELLE MANDELL. Publs *CISV News, Annual Report, Local Work Magazine, Interspectives* (all annually).

International Association for Education to a Life without Drugs (Internationaler Verband für Erziehung zu suchtmittel-freiem Leben—IVES): c/o Uljas Syväniemi, Haiharankatu 15 G 64, 33710 Tampere, Finland; e-mail uljas.syvaniemi@koti.tpo.ti; f. 1954 (as the International Association for Temperance Education) to promote international co-operation in education on the dangers of alcohol and drugs; collection and distribution of information on drugs; maintains regular contact with national and international organizations active in these fields; holds conferences. Mems: 77,000 in 10 countries. Pres. ULJAS SYVÄNIEMI; Sec. DAG MAGNE JOHANNESSEN.

International Association for Suicide Prevention: c/o Ms M. Campos, IASP Central Administrative Office, 1725 West Harrison St, Suite 955, Chicago, IL 60612, USA; tel. (312) 942-7208; fax (312) 942-2177; f. 1960 to establish an organization where individuals and agencies of various disciplines and professions from different countries can find a common platform for interchange of acquired experience, literature and information about suicide; disseminates information; arranges special training; encourages and carries out research; organizes the Biennial International Congress for Suicide Prevention. Mems: 340 individuals and societies, in 55 countries of all continents. Pres. Dr DIEGO DE LEO. Publ. *Crisis* (quarterly).

International Association of Schools of Social Work: 1010 Vienna, Palais Palfy, Josefplatz 6, Austria; tel. (1) 513-4297; fax (1) 513-8468; f. 1928 to provide international leadership and encourage high standards in social work education. Mems: 1,600 schools of social work in 70 countries, and 25 national associations of schools. Pres. Dr RALPH GARBER (Canada); Sec.-Gen. VERA MEHTA (India). Publs *International Social Work* (quarterly), *Directory of Members, IASSW News.*

International Association of Workers for Troubled Children and Youth: 22 rue Halévy, 59000 Lille, France; tel. 3-20-93-70-16; fax 3-20-09-18-39; e-mail aieji@nordnet.fr; f. 1951 to promote the profession of specialized social workers for troubled children and youth; to provide a centre of information about child welfare and encourage co-operation between the members; 1997 Congress: Brescia, Italy. Mems: national and regional public or private associations from 22 countries and individual members in many other countries. Pres. GUSTAVO VELASTEGUI (France); Sec.-Gen. LARS STEINOV (Denmark).

International Catholic Migration Commission: CP 96, 37–39 rue de Vermont, POB 96, 1211 Geneva 20, Switzerland; tel. (22) 9191020; fax (22) 9191048; e-mail secretariat@icmc.pingnet.ch; f. 1951; offers migration aid programmes to those who are not in a position to secure by themselves their resettlement elsewhere; grants interest-free travel loans; assists refugees on a world-wide basis, helping with all social and technical problems. Sub-committees dealing with Europe and Latin America. Mems: in 85 countries. Pres. Prof. STEFANO ZAMAGNI (Italy); Sec.-Gen. WILLIAM CANNY (USA). Publ. *Annual Report.*

International Christian Federation for the Prevention of Alcoholism and Drug Addiction: 20A Ancienne Route, Apt. No 42, 1218 Grand-Saconnex, Geneva, Switzerland; tel. (22) 7888158; fax (22) 7888136; e-mail jonathan@iprolink.ch; f. 1960, reconstituted 1980 to promote world-wide education and remedial work through the churches, to co-ordinate Christian concern about alcohol and drug abuse, in co-operation with the World Council of Churches and WHO. Chair. KARIN ISRAELSSON (Sweden); Gen. Sec. JONATHAN N. GNANADASON.

International Civil Defence Organization: POB 172, 10–12 chemin de Surville, 1213 Petit-Lancy 2, Geneva, Switzerland; tel. (22) 8796969; fax (22) 8796979; e-mail icdo@icdo.org; internet www.icdo.org; f. 1931, present statutes in force 1972; aims to intensify and co-ordinate on a world-wide scale the development and improvement of organization, means and techniques for preventing and reducing the consequences of natural disasters in peacetime or of the use of weapons in time of conflict. Sec.-Gen. SADOK ZNAÏDI (Tunisia). Publs *International Civil Defence Journal* (quarterly, in English, French, Spanish, Russian and Arabic).

International Commission for the Prevention of Alcoholism and Drug Dependency: 12501 Old Columbia Pike, Silver Spring, MD 20904-6600 USA; tel. (301) 680-6719; fax (301) 680-6090; f. 1952 to encourage scientific research on intoxication by alcohol, its physiological, mental and moral effects on the individual, and its effect on the community; tenth World Congress, Stavanger, Norway, 1997. Mems: individuals in 120 countries. Exec. Dir THOMAS R. NESLUND. Publ. *ICPA Quarterly.*

International Council of Voluntary Agencies—ICVA: 48 Chemin du Grand-Montfleury, 1290 Versoix, Switzerland; tel. (22) 9509600; fax (22) 9509609; e-mail secretariat@icva.ch; internet www.icva.ch; f. 1962 to provide a forum for voluntary humanitarian and development agencies. Mems: 78 non-governmental organizations. Chair. ANDERS LADEKARL; Co-ordinator ED SCHENKENBERG VAN MIEROP; Publ. *Newsletter* (available on website).

International Council of Women: c/o 13 rue Caumartin, 75009 Paris, France; tel. 1-47-42-19-40; fax 1-42-66-26-23; e-mailicw-cif@wanadoo.fr; f. 1888 to bring together in international affiliation Nat. Councils of Women from all continents for consultation and joint action in order to promote equal rights for men and women and the integration of women in development and in decision-making; five standing committees. Mems: 78 national councils. Pres. PNINA HERZOG; Sec.-Gen. MARIE-CHRISTINE LAFARGUE.

International Council on Alcohol and Addictions: CP 189, 1001 Lausanne, Switzerland; tel. (21) 3209865; fax (21) 3209817; e-mail icaa@pingnet.ch; f. 1907; organizes training courses, congresses, symposia and seminars in different countries. Mems: affiliated organizations in 74 countries, as well as individual members. Pres. Dr IBRAHIM AL-AWAJI (Saudi Arabia); Exec. Dir Dr EVA TONGUE (UK). Publs *ICAA News* (quarterly), *Alcoholism* (2 a year).

International Council on Disability: c/o Rehabilitation International, 25 East 21st St, New York, NY 10010, USA; tel. (212) 420-1500; f. 1953 to assist the UN and its specialized agencies to develop a well co-ordinated international programme for rehabilitation of the handicapped. Mems: 66 organizations. Pres. SHEIKH AL-GHANIM; Sec.-Gen. SUSAN HAMMERMAN.

International Council on Jewish Social and Welfare Services: 75 rue de Lyon, 1211 Geneva 13, Switzerland; tel. (22) 3449000; fax (22) 3457013; f. 1961; functions include the exchange of views and information among member agencies concerning the problems of Jewish social and welfare services including medical care, old age, welfare, childcare, rehabilitation, technical assistance, vocational training, agricultural and other resettlement, economic assistance, refugees, migration, integration and related problems; representation of views to governments and international organizations. Mems: six national and international organizations. Exec. Sec. CHERYL MARINER.

International Council on Social Welfare: 380 St Antoine St West, Suite 3200, Montreal H2Y 3X7, Canada; tel. (514) 287-3280; fax (514) 287-9702; e-mail icsw@icsw.org; internet www.icsw.org; f. 1928 to provide an international forum for the discussion of social work and related issues; to promote interest in social welfare; holds international conference every two years; provides documentation and information services. Mems: 45 national committees, 12 international organizations and 33 other organizations. Pres. JULIAN DISNEY (Australia); Exec. Dir STEPHEN KING (UK). Publ. *Social Development Review* (quarterly).

International Dachau Committee: 95 ave des Ortolans, 1170 Brussels, Belgium; f. 1958 to perpetuate the memory of the political prisoners of Dachau; to manifest the friendship and solidarity of former prisoners whatever their beliefs or nationality; to maintain the ideals of their resistance, liberty, tolerance and respect for persons and nations; and to maintain the former concentration camp at Dachau as a museum and international memorial. Pres. Gen. ANDRÉ DELPECH; Sec.-Gen. JEAN SAMUEL. Publ. *Bulletin Officiel du Comité International de Dachau* (2 a year).

International Federation of the Blue Cross: CP 6813, 3001 Bern, Switzerland; tel. (31) 3005860; fax (31) 3005869; e-mail ifbc.bern@bluewin.ch; internet www.eurocare.org/bluecross; f. 1877 to aid the victims of intemperance and drug addicts, and to take part in the general movement against alcoholism. Pres. Pastor RAYMOND BASSIN (Switzerland); Gen. Sec. HANS RÜTTIMAN.

International Federation of Disabled Workers and Civilian Handicapped—FIMITIC: 53173 Bonn, Beethovenallee 56–58, Germany; tel. (228) 95640; fax (228) 9564132; e-mail fimitic@tonline.de; internet www.193.189.189.10/fimitic/default.htm; f. 1953 to bring together representatives of the disabled and handicapped into an international non-political organization under the guidance of the disabled themselves; to promote greater opportunities for the disabled; to create rehabilitation centres; to act as a co-ordinating body for all similar national organizations. Mems: national groups from 27 European countries, and corresponding mems from eight countries. Pres. MARCEL ROYEZ (France); Gen. Sec. MARIJA STIGLIC (Germany). Publs *Bulletin, Nouvelles.*

International Federation of Educative Communities: Piazza S.S. Annunziale 12, 50122 Florence, Italy; tel. (055) 2469162; fax (055) 2347041; e-mail lice@lycosmail.com; f. 1948 under the auspices of UNESCO to co-ordinate the work of national associations, and to promote the international exchange of knowledge and experience in the field of childcare. Mems: national associations from 20 European countries, Israel, Canada, the USA and South Africa. Pres. ROBERT SOISSON (Luxembourg); Gen. Sec. GIANLUCA BARBONOTTI (Italy). Publ. *Bulletin* (2 a year).

International Federation of Human Rights Leagues—FIDH: 17 passage de la Main d'Or, 75011 Paris, France; tel. 1-43-55-25-28; fax 1-43-55-18-80; e-mail fidh@csi.com; internet www.fidh.imag-inet.fr; f. 1922; promotes the implementation of the Universal Declaration of Human Rights and other instruments of human rights protection; aims to raise awareness and alert public opinion to issues of human rights violations and undertakes investigation and observation missions, training and uses its consultative and observer status to lobby international authorities. Mems 105 national leagues in more than 86 countries. Pres. PATRICK BAUDOUIN. Publs *Lettre* (2 a month), mission reports.

International Federation of Social Workers—IFSW: POB 6875, Schwarztorstrasse 20, 3000 Bern, Switzerland; tel. (31) 3826015; fax (31) 3826017; e-mail secr.gen@ifsw.org; internet www.ifsw.org; f. 1928 as International Permanent Secretariat of Social Workers; present name adopted 1950; aims to promote social work as a profession through international co-operation concerning standards, training, ethics and working conditions; organizes international conferences; represents the profession at the UN and other international bodies; supports national associations of social workers. Mems: national associations in 70 countries. Pres. ELIS ENVALL (Sweden); Sec.-Gen. TOM JOHANNESEN (Switzerland).

International League against Racism and Antisemitism: CP 1754, 1211 Geneva 1, Switzerland; tel. (22) 7310633; fax (22) 7370634; e-mail licra@mnet.ch; internet www.licra.ch; f. 1927; mems in 17 countries. Pres. PIERRE AIDENBAUM (France).

International League for Human Rights: 432 Park Avenue South, 11th Floor, New York, NY 10016, USA; tel. (212) 684-1221; fax (212) 684-1696; e-mail info@ilhr.org; internet www.ilhr.org; f. 1942 to implement political, civil, social, economic and cultural rights contained in the Universal Declaration of Human Rights adopted by the United Nations and to support and protect defenders of human rights world-wide. Mems: individuals, national affiliates and correspondents throughout the world. Exec. Dir CATHERINE A. FITZPATRICK. Publs various human rights reports.

International League of Societies for Persons with Mental Handicap (European Association): Galeries de la Toison d'Or, 29 chaussée d'Ixelles, Ste 393/35, 1050 Brussels, Belgium; tel. (2) 502-28-15; fax (2) 502-80-10; e-mail secretariat@ilsmh-ea.be; internet www.ilsmh-ea.be; f. 1988 to promote the interests of people with a mental handicap without regard to nationality, race or creed; furthers co-operation between national bodies; organizes congresses, meetings and seminars. Mems: 20 societies in the 15 EU member states.

International Planned Parenthood Federation—IPPF: Regent's College, Inner Circle, Regent's Park, London, NW1 4NS, United Kingdom; tel. (20) 7487-7900; fax (20) 7487-7950; e-mail info@ippf.org; internet www.ippf.org; f. 1952; aims to promote and support sexual and reproductive health and family planning services throughout the world, with a particular focus on the needs of young people; aims to bring relevant issues to the attention of the media, Parliamentarians, academics, governmental and non-governmental orgs, and the general public; mobilizes financial resources to fund programmes and information materials; offers technical assistance and training; collaborates with other international organizations. The International Medical Panel of the IPPF, comprising leading medical experts, formulates guide-lines and statements on current medical and scientific advice and best practices. Mems: independent family planning associations in over 150 countries. Pres. ANGELA GÓMEZ; Dir-Gen. INGAR BRUEGGEMANN.

International Prisoners Aid Association: c/o Dr Ali, Department of Sociology, University of Louisville, Louisville, KY 40292, USA; tel. (502) 588-6836; fax (502) 852-7042; f. 1950; to improve prisoners' aid services for rehabilitation of the individual and protection of society. Mems: national federations in 29 countries. Pres. Dr WOLFGANG DOLEISCH (Austria); Exec. Dir Dr BADR-EL-DIN ALI Publ. *Newsletter* (3 a year).

International Scout and Guide Fellowship—ISGF: 9 rue du Champ de Mars, bte 14, 1050 Brussels, Belgium; tel. (2) 511-46-95; fax (2) 511-84-36; e-mail isgf-aisg@euronet.be; internet www.isgf.org; f. 1953 to help adult scouts and guides to keep alive the spirit of the Scout and Guide Promise and Laws in their own lives; to bring that spirit into the communities in which they live and work; to establish liaison and co-operation between national organizations for adult scouts and guides; to encourage the founding of an organization in any country where no such organization exists; to promote friendship amongst adult scouts and guides throughout the world. Mems: 90,000 in 46 member states. Chair. of Cttee NIELS ROSENBOM; Sec.-Gen. NAÏC PIRARD. Publ. *World Gazette Mondiale* (quarterly).

International Social Security Association—ISSA: CP 1, 1211 Geneva 22, Switzerland; tel. (22) 7996617; fax (22) 7998509; internet www.issa.int; f. 1927 to promote the development of social security throughout the world, mainly through the improvement of techniques and administration, in order to advance social and economic conditions on the basis of social equality. Mems: 270 institutions in 150 countries. Pres. JOHAN VERSTRAETEN (Belgium); Sec.-Gen. DALMER D. HOSKINS (USA). Publs *International Social Security Review* (quarterly in English, French, German, Spanish), *Trends in Social Security* (quarterly in English, French, German, Spanish), *Social Security Documentation* (African, Asian-Pacific and European series), *Social Security Worldwide* (CD Rom and internet), *Compendia of Conference Reports* (English, French, German, Spanish), various news bulletins.

International Social Service: 32 quai du Seujet, 1201 Geneva, Switzerland; tel. (22) 9067700; fax (22) 9067701; e-mail iss.gs@span.ch; internet www.iss-ssi.org; f. 1921 to aid families and individuals whose problems require services beyond the boundaries of the country in which they live and where the solution of these problems depends upon co-ordinated action on the part of social workers in two or more countries; to study from an international standpoint the conditions and consequences of emigration in their effect on individual, family, and social life. Operates on a non-sectarian and non-political basis. Mems: branches in 14 countries, six affiliated offices, and correspondents in some 100 other countries. Pres. Prof. Dr RAINER FRANK (Germany); Sec.-Gen. DAMIEN NGABONZIZA.

International Union of Family Organisations: 28 place Saint-Georges, 75009 Paris, France; tel. 1-48-78-07-59; fax 1-42-82-95-24; f. 1947 to bring together all organizations throughout the world which are working for family welfare; conducts permanent commissions on standards of living, housing, marriage guidance, work groups on family movements, rural families, etc.; there are six regional organizations: the Pan-African Family Organisation (Rabat, Morocco), the North America organization (Montreal, Canada), the Arab Family Organisation (Tunis, Tunisia), the Asian Union of Family Organisations (New Delhi, India), the European regional organization (Berne, Switzerland) and the Latin American Secretariat (Curitiba, Brazil). Mems: national associations, groups and governmental departments in more than 55 countries. Pres. MARIA TERESA DA COSTA MACEDO (Portugal).

International Union of Societies for the Aid of Mental Health: CSM, BP 323, 40107 Dax Cédex, France; tel. 5-58-91-48-38; fax 5-58-91-46-84; f. 1964 to group national societies and committees whose aim is to help mentally handicapped or maladjusted people. Gen. Pres Dr DEMANGEAT; Gen. Sec. Dr MINARD.

International Union of Tenants: Box 7514, 10392 Stockholm, Sweden; tel. (8) 791-02-00; fax (8) 20-43-44; e-mail magnus.hammar@hyresgasterna.se; internet www.iut.nu; f. 1955 to collaborate in safeguarding the interests of tenants; participates in activities of UNCHS (Habitat); has working groups for EC matters, eastern Europe, developing countries and for future development; holds annual council meeting and triennial congress. Mems: national tenant organizations in 24 European countries, Australia, Benin, Canada, India, Kenya, New Zealand, Tanzania and Uganda. Chair. ELISABET LÖNNGREN; Sec.-Gen. MAGNUS HAMMAR. Publ. *The Global Tenant* (quarterly).

Inter-University European Institute on Social Welfare—IEISW: 179 rue du Débarcadère, 6001 Marcinelle, Belgium; tel. (71) 44-72-67; f. 1970 to promote, carry out and publicize scientific research on social welfare and community work. Pres. JOSEPH GILLAIN; Gen. Dir SERGE MAYENCE. Publ. *COMM.*

Lions Clubs International: 300 West 22nd St, Oak Brook, IL 60523-8842, USA; tel. (630) 571-5466; fax (630) 571-8890; e-mail lions@lionsclubs.org; internet www.lionsclubs.org; f. 1917 to foster understanding among people of the world; to promote principles of good government and citizenship; and an interest in civic, cultural, social and moral welfare; to encourage service-minded people to serve their community without financial reward. Mems: 1.4m. with over 44,500 clubs in 185 countries and geographic areas. Exec. Admin. WIN HAMILTON. Publ. *The Lion* (10 a year, in 20 languages).

Médecins sans frontières—MSF: 39 rue de la Tourelle, 1040 Brussels, Belgium; tel. (2) 280-18-81; fax (2) 280-01-73; f. 1971; independent medical humanitarian org composed of physicians and other members of the medical profession; aims to provide medical assistance to victims of war and natural disasters, and longer-term programmes of nutrition, immunization, sanitation, public health, and rehabilitation of hospitals and dispensaries. Awarded the Nobel peace prize in Oct. 1999. National sections in 18 countries in Europe, Asia and North America. Dir.-Gen. Dr ERIC GOEMAERE. Publ. *Activity Report* (annually).

Pan Pacific and South East Asia Women's Association—PPSEAWA: POB 119, Nuku'alofa, Tonga; tel. 41404; e-mail nanasi @kalianet.to; internet www.ppseawa.org; ; f. 1928 to strengthen the bonds of peace by fostering better understanding and friendship among women in this region, and to promote co-operation among women for the study and improvement of social conditions; holds international conference every three years. Pres. HRH Princess NANASIPAU'U TUKU'AHO. Publ. *PPSEAWA Bulletin.*

Rotary International: 1560 Sherman Ave, Evanston, IL 60201, USA; tel. (847) 866-3000; fax (847) 328-8554; f. 1905 to carry out activities for the service of humanity, to promote high ethical standards in business and professions and to further international understanding, goodwill and peace. Mems: over 1,195,000 in 28,200 Rotary Clubs in 154 countries and 35 regions. Pres. LUIS VICENTE GIAY; Gen. Sec. GEOFFREY LARGE (USA). Publs *The Rotarian* (monthly, English), *Revista Rotaria* (bi-monthly, Spanish).

Service Civil International—SCI: St-Jacobsmarkt 82, 2000 Antwerp, Belgium; tel. (3) 266-57-27; fax (3) 232-03-44; e-mail sciint@sciint.org; internet www.sciint.org; f. 1920 to promote peace and understanding through voluntary service projects (work-camps, local groups, long-term community development projects and education). Mems: 14,000 in 36 countries; projects in 20 countries. Pres. M. RAJUDEEN. Publ. *Action* (quarterly).

Society of Saint Vincent de Paul: 5 rue du Pré-aux-Clercs, 75007 Paris, France; tel. 1-44-55-36-55; fax 1-42-61-72-56; e-mail stvincent.cgi@wanadoo.fr; internet www.cef.fr/vincenpaul; f. 1833 to conduct charitable activities such as childcare, youth work, work with immigrants, adult literacy programmes, residential care for the sick, handicapped and elderly, social counselling and work with prisoners and the unemployed—all conducted through personal contact. Mems: over 800,000 in 132 countries. Pres. JOSÉ RAMÓN DÍAZ TORREMOCHA; Sec.-Gen. YVES VERRÉ. Publ. *Vincenpaul* (quarterly, in French, English and Spanish).

SOLIDAR: 22 rue de Commerce, 1000 Brussels, Belgium; tel. (2) 500-10-20; fax (2) 500-10-30; e-mail solidar@skynet.be; internet www.solidar.org; frmly International Workers' Aid f. 1951; an association of independent development and social welfare agencies based in Europe, which are linked to the labour and democratic socialist movements; aims to contribute to the creation of radical models of economic and social development, and to advance practical solutions that enable people in all parts of the world to have increased control over their own future. Mems: agencies in 90 countries. Sec.-Gen. GIAMPIERO ALHADEFF.

World Blind Union: c/o CBC ONCE, 18 La Coruña, 28020 Madrid, Spain; tel. (91) 5713675; fax (91) 5715777; e-mail umc@once.es; internet www.once.es/wbu; f. 1984 (amalgamating the World Council for the Welfare of the Blind and the International Federation of the Blind) to work for the prevention of blindness and the welfare of blind and visually-impaired people; encourages development of braille, talking book programmes and other media for the blind; rehabilitation, training and employment; prevention and cure of blindness in co-operation with the International Agency for the Prevention of Blindness; co-ordinates aid to the blind in developing countries; conducts studies on technical, social and educational matters, maintains the Louis Braille birth-place as an international museum. Mems in 146 countries. Pres. EUCLID HERIE (Canada); Sec.-Gen. PEDRO ZURITA (Spain). Publs *World Blind* (2 a year, in English, English Braille and on cassette, in Spanish and Spanish Braille and on cassette and in French).

World Federation of the Deaf—WFD: POB 65, 00401 Helsinki, Finland; e-mail carol-lee.aquiline@wfdnews.org; internet www.wfdnews.org; f. 1951 aims to serve deaf people and their national organizations, and to represent the interests of deaf people in international forums, such as the UN system; to achieve the goal of full participation by deaf people in society; encourages deaf people to set up and run their own organizations. Priority is given to the promotion of the recognition and use of national sign languages; human rights; the education of deaf people; and deaf people in the developing world. Mems: 120 member countries. Pres. LIISA KAUPPINEN; Gen. Sec. CAROL-LEE AQUILINE. Publ. *WFD News* (3 a year).

World ORT Union: ORT House, 126 Albert St, London, NW1 7NE, United Kingdom; tel. (20) 7446-8500; fax (20) 7446-8650; e-mail wou@ort.org; f. 1880 for the development of industrial, agricultural and artisan skills among Jews; now, a highly developed educational and training organization active in over 60 countries throughout the world; conducts vocational training programmes for adolescents and adults, including instructors' and teachers' education and apprenticeship training in more than 40 countries, including technical assistance programmes in co-operation with interested governments. Mems: committees in over 40 countries. Dir-Gen. ROBERT SINGER. Publs *Annual Report, Frontline News, What in the World is ORT?*

World Veterans Federation: 17 rue Nicolo, 75116 Paris, France; tel. 1-40-72-61-00; fax 1-40-72-80-58; e-mail fmawvf@cybercable.fr; f. 1950 to maintain international peace and security by the application of the San Francisco Charter and helping to implement the Universal Declaration of Human Rights and related international conventions, to defend the spiritual and material interests of war veterans and war victims. It promotes practical international co-operation in disarmament, human rights problems, economic development, rehabilitation of the handicapped, accessibility of the man-made environment, legislation concerning war veterans and war victims, and development of international humanitarian law; in 1986 established International Socio-Medical Information Centre (United Kingdom) for psycho-medical problems resulting from

stress. Regional committees for Africa, Asia and the Pacific, and Europe and Standing Committee on Women. Mems: national organizations in 84 countries, representing about 27m. war veterans and war victims. Pres. ABDUL HAMID IBRAHIM; Sec.-Gen. MAREK HAGMAJER (Poland). Publs special studies (disarmament, human rights, rehabilitation).

Zonta International: 557 W. Randolph St, Chicago, IL 60661-2206, USA; tel. (312) 930-5848; fax (312) 930-0951; f. 1919; executive service organization; international and community service projects to promote the status of women. Mems: 36,000 in 67 countries. Pres. JOSEPHINE G. COOKE; Exec. Dir JANET HALSTEAD. Publ. *The Zontian* (quarterly).

Sport and Recreations

Arab Sports Confederation: POB 62997, Riyadh 11442, Saudi Arabia; tel. (1) 482-9427; fax (1) 482-3196; f. 1976 to encourage regional co-operation in sport. Mems: 20 national Olympic Committees, 36 Arab sports federations. Sec.-Gen. OTHMAN M. AL-SAAD. Publ. *Annual Report.*

Fédération Aéronautique Internationale (World Air Sports Federation Federation): 24 ave Mon Repos, 1005 Lausanne, Switzerland; e-mail sec@fai.org; internet www.fai.org; f. 1905 to encourage all aeronautical sports; organizes world championships and makes rules through Air Sports Commissions; endorses world aeronautical and astronautical records. Mems: in 93 countries and territories. Pres. WOLFGANG WEINREICH; Sec.-Gen. MAX BISHOP. Publ. *Air Sports International.*

General Association of International Sports Federations—GAISF: 4 blvd du Jardin Exotique, Monte Carlo, Monaco; tel. 93-50-74-13; fax 93-25-28-73; e-mail gaist@mcn.mc; f. 1967 to act as a forum for the exchange of ideas and discussion of common problems in sport; to collect and circulate information; to provide secretarial and translation services for members, organize meetings and provide technical documentation and consultancy services. Mems: 88 international sports organizations; Pres. Dr UN YONG KIM; Sec.-Gen. PETER TALLBERG (Finland). Publs *Calendar of International Sports Competitions* (2 a year), *Sportime Magazine* (quarterly, in English and French), *GAISF Calendar, Sport and Education* and *Sport and Media.*

International Amateur Athletic Federation: 17 rue Princesse Florestine, BP 359, 98007 Monte Carlo Cédex, Monaco; tel. 93-10-88-88; fax 93-15-95-15; e-mail headquarters@iaaf.org; f. 1912 to ensure co-operation and fairness among members, and to combat discrimination in athletics; to affiliate national governing bodies, to compile athletic competition rules and to organize championships at all levels; to settle disputes between members, and to conduct a programme of development for members who need coaching, judging courses, etc., and to frame regulations for the establishment of World, Olympic and other athletic records. Mems: national assens in 210 countries and territories. Gen. Sec. ISTVÁN GYULAI (Hungary). Publs *IAAF Handbook* (every 2 years), *IAAF Review* (quarterly), *IAAF Directory* (annually), *New Studies in Athletics* (quarterly).

International Amateur Boxing Association—AIBA: POB 76343, Atlanta, GA 30358, USA; tel. (770) 455-8350; fax (770) 454-6467; e-mail lbaker27@mindspring.com; internet www.aiba.net; f. 1946 as the world body controlling amateur boxing for the Olympic Games, continental, regional and inter-nation championships and tournaments in every part of the world. Mems: 191 national assens. Pres. Prof. A. CHOWDHRY (Pakistan); Sec.-Gen. LORING K. BAKER (USA). Publ. *World Amateur Boxing Magazine* (quarterly).

International Amateur Radio Union: POB 310905, Newington, CT 06131-0905, USA; tel. (860) 594-0200; fax (860) 594-0259; internet www.iaru.org; f. 1925 to link national amateur radio societies and represent the interests of two-way amateur radio communication. Mems: 150 national amateur radio societies. Pres. LARRY E. PRICE; Sec. DAVID SUMNER.

International Amateur Swimming Federation (Fédération Internationale de Natation Amateur—FINA): 9 ave de Beaumont, 1012 Lausanne, Switzerland; tel. (21) 3126602; fax (21) 3126610; internet www.fina.org; f. 1908 to promote amateur swimming and swimming sports internationally; to administer rules for swimming sports, for competitions and for establishing records; to organize world championships and FINA events; development programme to increase the popularity and quality of aquatic sports. Mems: 139 federations. Pres. MUSTAPHA LARFAOUI (Algeria); Dir CORNEL MARCULESCU. Publs *Handbook* (every 2 years), *FINA News* (monthly), *World of Swimming* (quarterly).

International Archery Federation (Fédération internationale de tir à l'arc—FITA): 135 ave de Cour, 1007 Lausanne, Switzerland; tel. (21) 6143050; fax (21) 6143055; e-mail info@archery.org; internet www.archery.org; f. 1931 to promote international archery; organizes world championships and Olympic tournaments; Biennial Congress: Beijing 2001. Mems: national amateur associations in 128 countries. Pres. JAMES L. EASTON (USA); Sec.-Gen. GIUSEPPE CINNIRELLA (Italy). Publs *Information FITA* (monthly), *The Arrow* (bulletin, quarterly), *The Target* (annually).

International Automobile Federation (Fédération Internationale de l'Automobile—FIA): 2 chemin de Blandonnet, CP 296, 1215 Geneva, Switzerland; tel. (22) 5444400; fax (22) 5444450; internet www.fia.com; f. 1904; manages world motor sport and organizes international championships. Mems: 157 national automobile clubs or asscns in 119 countries. Pres. MAX MOSLEY; Sec.-Gen. (Sport) PIERRE DE CONINCK; Sec.-Gen. (Tourism) PETER DOGGWILER.

International Badminton Federation—IBF: Manor Park Place, Rutherford Way, Cheltenham, Gloucestershire, GL51 9TU, United Kingdom; tel. (1242) 234904; fax (1242) 221030; e-mail info@intbadfed.org; internet www.intbadfed.org; f. 1934 to oversee the sport of badminton world-wide. Mems: affiliated national organizations in 147 countries and territories. Pres. LU SHENGRONG; Chief Exec. NEIL CAMERON (UK). Publs *World Badminton* (available on internet), *Statute Book* (annually).

International Basketball Federation (Fédération Internationale de Basketball): PO Box 700607, 81306 Munich, Germany; tel. (89) 7481580; fax (89) 74815833; e-mail secretariat@office.fiba.com; internet www.fiba.com; f. 1932 as International Amateur Basketball Federation (present name adopted 1989); aims to promote, supervise and direct international basketball; organizes quadrennial congress. Mems: affiliated national federations in 211 countries. Sec.-Gen. BORISLAV STANKOVIC. Publs *FIBA Assist* (monthly), *FIBA Media Guide*.

International Canoe Federation: Dozsa György ut. 1-3, 1143 Budapest, Hungary; tel. (1) 363-4832; fax (1) 221-4130; e-mail icf-hq-budapest@mail.datanet.hu; internet www.datanet.hu/icf-hq; f. 1924; administers canoeing at the Olympic Games; promotes canoe/kayak activity in general. Mems: 108 national federations. Pres. ULRICH FELDHOFF; Sec.-Gen. OTTO BONN.

International Council for Health, Physical Education, Recreation, Sport and Dance: 1900 Association Drive, Reston, VA 20191, USA; tel. (800) 213-7193; f. 1958 to encourage the development of programmes in health, physical education, recreation, sport and dance throughout the world, by linking teaching professionals in these fields.

International Cricket Council: Lord's Cricket Ground, London, NW8 8QN, United Kingdom; tel. (20) 7266-1818; fax (20) 7266-1777; f. 1909; governing body for international cricket. Annual conference. Mems: Australia, England, India, New Zealand, Pakistan, South Africa, Sri Lanka, West Indies, Zimbabwe; and 23 associate and 13 affiliate mems. Chief Exec. D. L. RICHARDS.

International Cycling Union: 37 route de Chavannes, 1007 Lausanne, Switzerland; tel. (21) 6220580; fax (21) 6220588; e-mail admin@uci.ch; internet www.uci.ch; f. 1900 to develop, regulate and control all forms of cycling as a sport. Mems: 158 federations. Pres. HEIN VERBRUGGEN (Netherlands). Publs *International Calendar* (annually), *Velo World* (6 a year).

International Equestrian Federation: CP 157, ave Mon-Repos 24, 1000 Lausanne 5, Switzerland; tel. (21) 3104747; fax (21) 3104760; e-mail info@horsesport.org; internet www.horsesport.org; f. 1921; administers equestrian events at the Olympic Games. Sec.-Gen. Dr BO HELANDER.

International Federation of Associated Wrestling Styles: 17 ave Juste-Olivier, 1006 Lausanne, Switzerland; tel. (21) 3128426; fax (21) 3236073; e-mail filalausanne@bluewin.ch; internet www.fila_wrestling.org; f. 1912 to encourage the development of amateur wrestling and promote the sport in countries where it is not yet practised; to further friendly relations between all members; to oppose any form of political, racial or religious discrimination. Mems: 142 federations. Pres. MILAN ERCEGAN; Sec.-Gen. MICHEL DUSSON. Publs *News Bulletin, Wrestling Revue*.

International Federation of Association Football (Fédération Internationale de Football Association—FIFA): Hitzigweg 11, POB 85, 8030 Zürich, Switzerland; tel. (1) 3849595; fax (1) 3849696; internet www.fifa.com; f. 1904 to promote the game of association football and foster friendly relations among players and national associations; to control football and uphold the laws of the game as laid down by the International Football Association Board; to prevent discrimination of any kind between players; and to provide arbitration in any disputes between national associations; organizes World Cup competition every four years. Mems: 204 national associations, six regional confederations. Pres. JOSEPH S. BLATTER (Switzerland); Gen. Sec. MICHEL ZEN-RUFFINEN. Publs *FIFA News* (monthly), *FIFA Magazine* (every 2 months) (both in English, French, Spanish and German).

International Federation of Park and Recreation Administration—IFPRA: Globe House, Crispin Close, Caversham, Reading, Berks, RG4 7JS, United Kingdom; tel. and fax (118) 946-1680; f. 1957 to provide a world centre where members of government departments, local authorities, and all organizations

concerned with recreational services can discuss relevant matters. Mems: 550 in over 50 countries. Gen. Sec. ALAN SMITH (UK).

International Fencing Federation: ave Mon-Repos 24, CP 128, 1000 Lausanne 5, Switzerland; tel. (21) 3203115; fax (21) 3203116; e-mail contact@fie.ch; internet www.fie.ch; f. 1913; administers fencing at the Olympic Games. Mems: 106 national federations. Pres. RENÉ ROCH.

International Gymnastic Federation: rue des Oeuches 10, CP 359, 2740 Moutier 1, Switzerland; tel. (32) 4946410; fax (32) 4946419; f. 1881 to promote the exchange of official documents and publications on gymnastics. Mems: 124 affiliated federations. Pres. BRUNO GRANDI; Gen. Sec. NORBERT BUECHE (Switzerland). Publs *Bulletin* (3 a year), *World of Gymnastics Magazine* (3 a year).

International Hockey Federation: 1 ave des Arts, Boîte 5, 1210 Brussels, Belgium; tel. (2) 219-45-37; fax (2) 219-27-61; e-mail fih@fihockey.org; internet www.fihockey.org; f. 1924 to fix the rules of outdoor and indoor hockey for all affiliated national associations; to control the game of hockey and indoor hockey; to control the organization of international tournaments, such as the Olympic Games and the World Cup. Mems: 120 national associations. Pres. JUAN ANGEL CALZADO; Sec.-Gen. ELS VAN BREDA-VRIESMAN. Publ. *World Hockey* (quarterly).

International Judo Federation: 12 rue Maamoun, 1082 Tunis, Tunisia; tel. (1) 781-057; fax (1) 801-517; e-mail dhouib@gnet.tn; internet www.ijf.org; f. 1951 to promote cordial and friendly relations between members; to protect the interests of judo throughout the world; to organize World Championships and the judo events of the Olympic Games; to develop and spread the techniques and spirit of judo throughout the world and to establish international judo regulations. Pres. YONG SUNG PARK (Republic of Korea); Gen. Sec. Dr HEDI DHOUIB (Tunisia).

International Paralympic Committee: Adenauerallee 212–214, 53113 Bonn, Germany; tel. (228) 2097200; fax (228) 2097209; e-mail info@paralympic.org; internet www.paralympic.org; f. 1989; responsible for organizing the paralympic games for sportspeople with disabilities, which are held alongside the Olympic Games; Pres. Dr ROBERT STEADWARD (Canada); Chief Operating Officer THOMAS REINECKE (Germany).

International Philatelic Federation: Zollikerstrasse 128, 8008 Zürich, Switzerland; tel. (1) 4223839; fax (1) 3831446; f. 1926 to promote philately internationally. Pres. D. N. JATIA; Sec.-Gen. M. L. HEIRI.

International Rowing Federation (Fédération internationale des Sociétés d'Aviron—FISA): 135 ave de Cour, CP 18, 1000 Lausanne 3, Switzerland; tel. (21) 6178373; fax (21) 6178375; e-mail info@fisa.org; internet www.worldrowing.com; f. 1892 to establish contacts between rowers in all countries and to draw up racing rules; world controlling body of the sport of rowing. Mems: national federations in 110 countries. Pres. DENIS OSWALD; Sec.-Gen. and Exec. Dir MATTHEW SMITH. Publs *FISA Directory* (annually), *FISA Info* (quarterly), *FISA Coach* (quarterly).

International Shooting Sport Federation: 80336 Munich, Bavariaring 21, Germany; tel. (89) 5443550; fax (89) 54435544; e-mail issfmunich@compuserve.com; internet www.issf-shooting.org; f. 1907 to promote and guide the development of the amateur shooting sports; to organize World Championships; to control the organization of continental and regional championships; to supervise the shooting events of the Olympic and Continental Games under the auspices of the International Olympic Committee. Mems: 151 federations in 146 countries. Pres. OLEGARIO VÁZQUEZ-RAÑA (Mexico); Sec.-Gen. HORST G. SCHREIBER (Germany). Publs *ISSF News, International Shooting Sport* (6 a year).

International Skating Union—ISU: chemin de Primerose 2, 1007 Lausanne, Switzerland; tel. (21) 6126666; fax (21) 6126677; e-mail info@isu.ch; internet www.isu.org; f. 1892; holds regular conferences. Mems: 73 national federations in 56 countries. Pres. OTTAVIO CINQUANTA; Gen.-Sec. FREDI SCHMID.

International Ski Federation: 3653 Oberhofen am Thunersee, Switzerland; tel. (33) 2446161; fax (33) 2435353; internet www.fis_ski.org; f. 1924 to further the sport of skiing; to prevent discrimination in skiing matters on racial, religious or political grounds; to organize World Ski Championships and regional championships and, as supreme international skiing authority, to establish the international competition calendar and rules for all ski competitions approved by the FIS, and to arbitrate in any disputes. Mems: 100 national ski associations. Pres. GIAN-FRANCO KASPER (Switzerland); Dir SARAH LEWIS (UK). Publ. *FIS Bulletin* (quarterly).

International Table Tennis Federation: ave Mon-Repos 30, 1005 Lausanne, Switzerland; tel. (21) 3407090; fax (21) 3407099; e-mail ittf@ittf.ch; internet www.ittf.com; f. 1926. Pres. ADHAM SHARARA.

International Tennis Federation: Bank Lane, Roehampton, London, SW15 5XZ, United Kingdom; tel. (20) 8878-6464; fax (20) 8878-7799; e-mail communications@itftennis.com; internet www.itftennis.com; f. 1913 to govern the game of tennis throughout the world and promote its teaching; to preserve its independence of outside authority; to produce the Rules of Tennis, to promote the Davis Cup Competition for men, the Fed. Cup for women, Olympic Games Tennis Event, wheelchair tennis, 16 cups for veterans, the ITF Sunshine Cup and ITF Continental Connelly Cup for players of 18 years old and under, the World Youth Cup for players of 16 years old and under, and the World Junior Tennis Tournament for players of 14 years old and under; to organize tournaments. Mems: 141 full and 57 associate. Pres. FRANCESCO RICCI BITTI. Publs *World of Tennis* (annually), *Davis Cup Yearbook*, *ITF World* (quarterly), *ITF This Week* (weekly).

International Volleyball Federation (Fédération Internationale de Volleyball—FIVB): ave de la Gare 12, 1001 Lausanne, Switzerland; tel. (21) 3453535; fax (21) 3453545; e-mail info@mail.fivb.ch; internet www.fivb.org; f. 1947 to encourage, organize and supervise the playing of volleyball, beach volleyball, and park volley; organizes biennial congress. Mems: 218 national federations. Pres. Dr RUBÉN ACOSTA HERNÁNDEZ; Gen. Man. JEAN-PIERRE SEPPEY. Publs *VolleyWorld* (every 2 months), *X-Press* (monthly).

International Weightlifting Federation: PF 614, 1374 Budapest, Hungary; tel. (1) 3530530; fax (1) 3530199; e-mail iwf@iwf.net; internet www.iwf.net; f. 1905 to control international weightlifting; to set up technical rules and to train referees; to supervise World Championships, Olympic Games, regional games and international contests of all kinds; to supervise the activities of national and continental federations; to register world records. Mems: 167 national organizations. Pres. Dr THOMÁS AJAN (Hungary); Gen. Sec. YANNIS SGOUROS (Greece). Publs *IWF Constitution and Rules* (every 4 years), *World Weightlifting* (quarterly).

International World Games Association: Ekeby House, Luiksestraat 23, 2587 The Hague, Netherlands; tel. (70) 3512774; fax (70) 3509911; e-mail iwga@hetnet.nl; f. 1980; organizes World Games every four years (2001: Akita, Japan), comprising 26 sports that are not included in the Olympic Games. Sec.-Gen. J. A. P. KOREN.

International Sailing Federation—ISAF: Ariadne House, Town Quay, Southampton, Hants, SO14 2AQ, United Kingdom; tel. (2380) 635111; fax (2380) 635789; e-mail sail@isaf.co.uk; internet www.sail-ing.org; f. 1907; controlling authority of sailing in all its forms throughout the world; establishes and amends international yacht racing rules, organizes the Olympic Sailing Regatta and other championships. Mems: 117 national yachting federations. Pres. PAUL HENDERSON; Sec.-Gen. ARVE SUNDHEIM.

Union of European Football Associations—UEFA: route de Genève 46, 1260 Nyon, Switzerland; tel. (22) 9944444; fax (22) 9944488; internet www.uefa.com; f. 1954. Mems: 51 national associations. Pres. LENNART JOHANSSON; CEO GERHARD AIGNER.

World Boxing Organization: c/o 100 West Randolph St, 9th Floor, Chicago, IL 60601, USA; tel. (312) 814-3145; fax (312) 814-2719; f. 1962; regulates professional boxing.

World Bridge Federation: 56 route de Vandoeuvres, 1253 Geneva, Switzerland; tel. (22) 7501541; fax (22) 7501620; f. 1958 to promote the game of contract bridge throughout the world, federate national bridge associations in all countries, conduct bridge associations in all countries, conduct world championships competitions, establish standard bridge laws. Mems: 89 countries. Pres. ERNESTO D'ORSI (Brazil). Publ. *World Bridge News* (quarterly).

World Chess Federation (Fédération Internationale des Echecs—FIDE): POB 166, 1000 Lausanne 4, Switzerland; tel. (21) 3103900; e-mail fide@fide.ch; internet www.fide.com; f. 1924; controls chess competitions of world importance and awards international chess titles. Mems: national orgs in more than 150 countries. Pres. KIRSAN ILYUMZHINOV. Publs *FIDE Forum* (every 2 months), *International Rating List* (2 a year).

World Squash Federation Ltd: 6 Havelock Rd, Hastings, East Sussex, TN34 1BP, United Kingdom; tel. (1424) 429245; fax (1424) 429250; e-mail squash@wsf.cablenet.co.uk; internet www.worldsquash.org; f. 1966. Mems: 115 national organizations. Exec. Dir EDWARD J. WALLBUTTON.

World Underwater Federation: Viale Tiziano 74, 00196 Rome, Italy; tel. (06) 36858480; fax (06) 36858490; e-mail amasmond@tin.it; internet www.cmas.org; f. 1959 to develop underwater activities; to form bodies to instruct in the techniques of underwater diving; to perfect existing equipment and encourage inventions and to experiment with newly marketed products, suggesting possible improvements; to organize international competitions. Mems: organizations in 90 countries. Pres. ACHILLE FERRERO (Italy); Sec. PIERRE DERNIER (Belgium). Publs *International Year Book of CMAS*, *Scientific Diving: A Code of Practice*, manuals.

Technology

International Union of Technical Associations and Organizations (Union Internationale des Associations et Organismes Tech-

niques—UATI): UNESCO House, 1 rue Miollis, 75015 Paris Cédex 15, France; tel. 1-45-68-27-70; fax 1-43-06-29-27; e-mail uati@unesco.org; f. 1951 (fmrly Union of International Technical Associations) under the auspices of UNESCO; aims to promote and co-ordinate activities of member organizations and represent their interests; facilitates relations with international organizations, notably UN agencies, receives proposals and makes recommendations on the establishment of new international technical associations. Mems: 25 organizations. Chair. PHILIPPE AUSSOURD (France). Publ. *Convergence* (3 a year).

MEMBER ORGANIZATIONS

Members of UATI include the following:

International Association of Hydraulic Engineering and Research—IAHR: c/o Delft Hydraulics, Rotterdamseweg 185, 2629 HD Delft, Netherlands; tel. (15) 285-88-79; fax (15) 285-84-17; e-mail iahr@iahr.nl; internet www.iahr.org; f. 1935; holds biennial congresses. Mems: 2,150 individual, 200 corporate. Sec.-Gen. H. J. OVERBEEK (Netherlands). Publs *AHR Bulletin, Journal of Hydraulic Research, Proceedings of Biennial Conferences*.

International Association of Lighthouse Authorities: 20 ter rue Schnapper, 78100 St Germain en Laye, France; tel. 1-34-51-70-01; fax 1-34-51-82-05; e-mail aismiala@easynet.fr; f. 1957; holds technical conference every four years; working groups study special problems and formulate technical recommendations, guide-lines and manuals. Mems in 80 countries. Sec.-Gen. TORSTEN KRUUSE. Publ. *Bulletin* (quarterly).

International Bridge, Tunnel and Turnpike Association: 2120 L St, NW, Suite 305, Washington, DC 20037, USA; tel. (202) 659-4620; fax (202) 659-0500; e-mail ibtta@ibtta.org; internet www.ibtta.org; f. 1932. Pres. LUIS FERREIRO; Exec. Dir. NEIL D. SCHUSTER. Publ. *Tollways* (monthly).

International Commission of Agricultural Engineering—CIGR: Institut für Landtechnik, Universität Bonn, Nassallee 5, 53 115 Bonn, Germany; tel. (228) 732389; fax (228) 739644; e-mail cigr@uni-bonn.de; internet www.ucd.ie/cigr; f. 1930. Mems: asscns from more than 50. Pres. Prof. E. H. BARTALI (Morocco); Sec.-Gen. P. SCHULZE LAMMERS (Germany). Publs *Bulletin de la CIGR, Newsletter* (quarterly), technical reports.

International Commission on Glass: Stazione Sperimentale del Vetro, Via Briati 10, 30141 Murano, Venice, Italy; tel. (041) 739422; fax (041) 739420; e-mail spevetro@ve-nettuno.it; internet www.net-tuno.it/fiera/spevetro; f. 1933 to co-ordinate research in glass and allied products, exchange information and organize conferences. Mems: 30 organizations. Pres. D. PYE; Sec.-Gen. F. NICOLETTI.

International Commission on Irrigation and Drainage: 48 Nyaya Marg, Chanakyapuri, New Delhi 110 021, India; tel. (11) 6115679; fax (11) 6115962; e-mail icid@icid.org; internet www.icid.org; f. 1950; holds triennial congresses. Mems: 70 national committees. Pres. BART SCHULTZ (Netherlands); Sec.-Gen. C. D. THATTE (India). Publs *Journal* (quarterly), *World Irrigation, Multilingual Technical Dictionary, World Flood Control*, technical books.

International Federation for the Theory of Machines and Mechanisms: PO Box 4200, Univ. of Oulu, 90014 Oulu, Finland; tel. (8) 553-2050; fax (8) 553-2026; e-mail tatu@me.oulu.fi; internet www.cim.mcgill.ca/iftomm; f. 1969; study of robots, man-machine systems, etc. Pres. K. WALDRON; Sec.-Gen. T. LEINONEN. Publ. *Mechanism and Machine Theory*.

International Federation of Automatic Control—IFAC: 2361 Laxenburg, Schlossplatz 12, Austria; tel. (2236) 71447; fax (2236) 72859; e-mail secr@ifac.co.at; internet www.ifac-control.org; f. 1957 to serve those concerned with the theory and application of automatic control and systems engineering. Mems: 48 national associations. Pres. Prof. YONG ZAI LU (China); Sec. G. HENCSEY. Publs *Automatica and Control Engineering Practice* (bi-monthly), *Newsletter* and affiliated journals.

International Gas Union: c/o N.V. Nederlandse Gasunie, POB 19, 9700 MA Groningen, Netherlands; tel. (50) 5212999; fax (50) 5255951; e-mail secr.igu@gasnie.nl; internet www.igu.org; f. 1931 to study all aspects and problems of the gas industry with a view to promoting international co-operation and the general improvement of the industry. Mems: national organizations in 59 countries. Pres. C. DÉTOURNÉ (France); Sec.-Gen. J. F. MEEDER (Netherlands).

International Institute of Welding: 90 rue des Vanesses, Z1 Paris Nord II, 93420 Villepinte, France; tel. 1-49-90-36-08; fax 1-49-90-36-80; e-mail iiw@wanadoo.fr; f. 1948. Mems: 52 societies in 40 countries. Pres. Y. FUJITA (Japan); Chief Exec. M. BRAMAT (France). Publ. *Welding in the World* (7 a year).

International Measurement Confederation: POB 457, 1371 Budapest 5, Hungary; tel. (1) 153-1562; fax (1) 156-1215; e-mail imeko.ime@mtesz.hu; internet mit.tut.fi/imeko; f. 1961; holds Congress every 3 years. Sec.-Gen. Dr TAMÁS KEMÉNY (Hungary).

International Navigation Association: Graaf de Ferraris, 11e étage, Bte 3, 156 blvd Roi Albert II, 1000 Brussels, Belgium; tel. (2)

553-71-60; fax (2) 553-71-55; e-mail navigation-aipcn-pianc@tornado.be; internet www.tornado.be/~navigation-aipcn-pianc/; f. 1885; fmrly Permanent International Assoc. of Navigation Congresses (PIANC); fosters progress in the construction, maintenance and operation of inland and maritime waterways, of inland and maritime ports and of coastal areas; publishes information in this field, undertakes studies, organizes international and national meetings. Congresses are held every four years. Mems: 40 governments, 2,780 others. Pres. Ir. R. DE PAEPE; Sec.-Gen. C. VAN BEGIN. Publs *Bulletin* (quarterly), *Illustrated Technical Dictionary* (in 6 languages), technical reports, Congress papers.

International Union for Electricity Applications: Espace Elec. CNIT, BP 10, 92053 Paris-la-Défense, France; tel. 1-41-26-56-48; fax 1-41-26-56-49; e-mail uie@uie.org; internet www.uie.org; f. 1953, present title adopted 1994. Aims to study all questions relative to electricity applications, except commercial questions; links national groups and organizes international congresses on electricity applications. Mems: national committees,corporate associated and individual members in 18 countries. Pres. RONNIE BELMANS (Belgium); Gen. Sec. Prof. MICHEL MACHIELS.

International Union of Air Pollution Prevention and Environmental Protection Associations: 44 Grand Parade, Brighton, BN2 2QA, United Kingdom; tel. (1273) 878772; fax (1273) 606626; e-mail iuappa@nsca.org.uk; f. 1963; organizes triennial World Clean Air Congress and regional conferences for developing countries (several a year). Pres. Dr W. H. PARK (Korea); Dir-Gen. R. MILLS. Publs *IUAPPA Newsletter* (quarterly), *Clean Air around the World*.

International Union of Testing and Research Laboratories for Materials and Structures: École Normale Supérieure, 61 ave du Président Wilson, 94235 Cachan Cédex, France; tel. 1-47-40-23-97; fax 1-47-40-01-13; e-mail sg@rilem.ens-cachan.fr; f. 1947 for the exchange of information and the promotion of co-operation on experimental research concerning structures and materials, for the study of research methods with a view to improvement and standardization. Mems: laboratories and individuals in 73 countries. Pres. Dr JACQUES BRESSON (France); Sec.-Gen. M. BRUSIN (France). Publ. *Materials and Structures—Testing and Research* (10 a year).

Union of the Electricity Industry—EURELECTRIC: Blvd de l'Impératrice 66, Box 2, 1000 Brussels, Belgium; tel. (2) 515-1000; fax (2) 510-1010; e-mail eurelectric@eurelectric.org; internet www.eurelectric.org; f. 1999 by merger of International Union of Producers and Distributors of Electrical Energy (UNIPEDE, f. 1925) and European Grouping of the Electricity Industry (EEIG, f. 1989); aims to study all questions relating to the production, transmission and distribution of electrical energy, to promote the image of and defend the interests of the electricity supply industry. Pres. Dr ROLF BIERHOFF; Sec.-Gen. PAUL BULTEEL. Publ. *Watt's New* (newsletter).

World Energy Council: 34 St James's St, London, SW1A 1HD, United Kingdom; tel. (20) 7930-3966; fax (20) 7925-0452; f. 1924 to link all branches of energy and resources technology and maintain liaison between world experts; holds congresses every three years. Mems: 99 committees. Pres. M. GÓMEZ DE PABLOS (Spain); Sec.-Gen. GERALD DOUCET (Canada). Publs energy supply and demand projections, resources surveys, technical assessments, reports.

World Foundrymen Organization—WFO: Konradstr. 9, POB 7190, 8023 Zürich, Switzerland; tel. (1) 2719090; fax (1) 2719292; e-mail wfo@jgp.ch; internet www.jgp.ch/wfo; Pres. J. LECETA; Gen. Sec. Dr J. GERSTER.

World Road Association (PIARC): La Grande Arche, Paroi Nord, Niveau 8, 92055 La Défense Cédex, France; tel. 1-47-96-81-21; fax 1-49-00-02-02; e-mail piarc@wanadoo.fr; internet www.piarc.org; f. 1909 as the Permanent International Association of Road Congresses; aims to promote the construction, improvement, maintenance, use and economic development of roads; organizes technical committees and study sessions. Mems: governments, public bodies, organizations and private individuals in 100 countries. Pres. O. MICHAUD (Switzerland); Sec.-Gen. J. F. COSTE (France). Publs *Bulletin, Technical Dictionary, Lexicon,* technical reports.

OTHER ORGANIZATIONS

African Organization of Cartography and Remote Sensing: 5 Route de Bedjarah, BP 102, Hussein Dey, Algiers, Algeria; tel. (2) 77-79-34; fax (2) 77-79-34; f. 1988 by amalgamation of African Association of Cartography and African Council for Remote Sensing; aims to encourage the development of cartography and of remote sensing by satellites; organizes conferences and other meetings, promotes establishment of training institutions; four regional training centres (in Burkina Faso, Kenya, Nigeria and Tunisia). Mems: national cartographic institutions of 24 African countries. Sec.-Gen. UNIS MUFTAH.

African Regional Centre for Technology: Imm. Fahd, 17th Floor, blvd Djilly Mbaye, BP 2435, Dakar, Senegal; tel. 823-77-12; fax 823-77-13; f. 1980 to encourage the development of indigenous technology and to improve the terms of access to imported tech-

nology; assists the establishment of national centres. Dep. Exec. Dir Dr OUSMANE KANE. Publs *African Technodevelopment, Alert Africa*.

AIIM International: 1100 Wayne Ave, Suite 1100, Silver Spring, USA; internet www.aiim.org; f. 1999 by merger of the Association for Information and Image Management (f. 1943) and the International Information Management Congress (f. 1962); world-wide body of the document technologies industry. Chief Exec. JOHN H. MANCINI.

Bureau International de la Recupération et du Recyclage (Bureau of International Recycling): 24 ave Franklin Roosevelt, 1050 Brussels, Belgium; tel. (2) 627-57-70; fax (2) 627-57-73; e-mail bir@bir.org; internet www.bir.org; f. 1948 as the world federation of the reclamation and recycling industries, to promote international trade in scrap iron and steel, non-ferrous metals, paper, textiles, plastics and glass. Mems: associations and individuals in 53 countries. Dir-Gen. FRANCIS VEYS.

ECMA—Standardizing Information and Communication Systems: 114 rue de Rhône, 1204 Geneva, Switzerland; tel. (22) 8496000; fax (22) 8496001; e-mail helpdesk@ecma.ch; f. 1961 to develop, in co-operation with the appropriate national, European and international organizations, as a scientific endeavour and in the general interest, standards and technical reports in order to facilitate and standardize the use of information processing and telecommunications systems; and to promulgate various standards applicable to the functional design and use of these systems. Mems: 28 ordinary and 18 associate. Sec.-Gen. JAN VAN DEN BELD. Publs *ECMA Standards, ECMA Memento*.

EUREKA: 107 rue Neerveld, Bte 5, 1200 Brussels, Belgium; tel. (2) 777-09-50; fax (2) 777-74-95; e-mail eureka.secretariat@es.eureka.be; f. 1985; aims to promote collaboration between member countries of non-military research and development activities; enables joint development of technology and supports systematic use of standardization in new technology sectors. Mems: 30 in 29 countries. Sec.-Gen. Dr HEIKKI KOTILAINEN.

European Convention for Constructional Steelwork—ECCS: 32/36 ave des Ombrages, bte 20, 1200 Brussels, Belgium; tel. (2) 762-04-29; fax (2) 762-09-35; e-mail eccs@steelconstruct.com; internet www.steelconstruct.com; f. 1955 for the consideration of problems involved in metallic construction. Member organizations in Austria, Belgium, Denmark, Croatia, Czech Republic, Estonia, Finland, France, Germany, Hungary, Italy, Japan, Republic of Korea, Luxembourg, Netherlands, Norway, Portugal, Romania, Slovenia, Spain, Sweden, Switzerland, Turkey, United Kingdom, USA. Gen. Sec. G. GENDEBEN.

European Federation of Chemical Engineering: c/o Institution of Chemical Engineers, Davis Bldg, 165–189 Railway Terrace, Rugby, Warwickshire, CV21 3HQ, United Kingdom; tel. (1788) 578214; fax (1788) 560833; internet www.icheme.org; f. 1953 to encourage co-operation in Europe between non-profit-making scientific and technical societies for the advancement of chemical engineering and its application in the process industries. Mems: 65 societies in 25 European countries; 15 corresponding societies in other countries. Chief Exec. Dr T. J. EVANS.

European Federation of Corrosion: 1 Carlton House Terrace, London, SW1Y 5DB, United Kingdom; tel. (20) 7839-4071; fax (20) 7839-1702; internet www.materials.org; f. 1955 to encourage co-operation in research on corrosion and methods of combating it. Member societies in 20 countries. Hon. Secs J. P. BERGE (France), G. KREYSA (Germany), B. A. RICKINSON (UK); Scientific Sec. P. MCINTYRE (UK).

European Federation of National Engineering Associations—FEANI: 21 rue du Beau Site, 1000 Brussels, Belgium; tel (2) 639-03-90; fax (2) 639-03-99; e-mail barbel.hakimi@feani.org; internet www.feani.org; f. 1951 to affirm the professional identity of the engineers of Europe; to strive for the unity of the engineering profession in Europe. Mems: 27 mem. countries. Pres. K. ALEXOPOULOS (Greece); Sec.-Gen. PHILIPPE WAUTERS. Publs *FEANI News, FEANI Handbook, Engineering Development International*.

European Metal Union: Einsteinbaan 1, POB 2600, 3430 GA Nieuwegein, Netherlands; tel. (30) 605-33-44; fax (30) 605-31-15; e-mail info@metaalunie.nl; f. 1954 as International Union of Metal; aims to provide liaison between national craft organizations and small and medium-sized enterprises in the metal industry; to represent members' interests at a European level; to exchange information and ideas on related subjects, such as vocational training, quality assurance, European legislation, and normalization and standardization. Mems: national federations from Austria, Belgium, Germany, Luxembourg, Netherlands and Switzerland. Pres. WILLEMIEN VAN GARDINGEN (Netherlands); Sec. HARM-JAN KEIJER (Netherlands).

European Organisation for the Exploitation of Meteorological Satellites—EUMETSAT: 64295 Darmstadt, Am Kavalleriesand 31, Germany; tel. (6151) 8077; fax (6151) 807555; e-mail ops@eumetsat.de; internet www.eumetsat.de; f. 1986; maintains and exploits European systems of meteorological satellites, including the Meteosat programme for gathering weather data. Mems: 17 European countries and three co-operating states. Chair. Dr HENRI MALCORPS (Belgium); Dir Dr TILLMANN MOHR.

European Organization for Civil Aviation Equipment— EUROCAE: 17 rue Hamelin, 75783 Paris Cédex 16, France; tel. 1-45-05-71-88; fax 1-45-05-72-30; e-mail eurocae@eurocae.com; internet www.eurocae.org; f. 1963; studies and advises on problems related to the equipment used in aeronautics and assists international bodies in the establishment of international standards. Mems: 92 manufacturers, organizations and research bodies. Pres. ALAN GARCIA; Sec.-Gen. FRANCIS GRIMAL.

Eurospace: 15-17 ave de Ségur, 75005 Paris, France; tel. 1-44-42-00-70; fax 1-44-42-00-79; e-mail letterbox@eurospace.org; internet www.eurospace.org; f. 1961; an association of European aerospace industrial companies, it is responsible for promotion of European Space activity. The Association carries out studies on the legal, economic, technical and financial aspects. It acts as an industrial adviser to the European Space Agency, in particular with regard to future space programmes and industrial policy matters. Mems: 60 in Austria, Belgium, Denmark, Finland, France, Germany, Italy, Netherlands, Norway, Spain, Sweden, Switzerland, United Kingdom. Pres. IVAN ÖFVERHOLM (Sweden); Sec.-Gen. ALAIN GAUBERT.

Inter-African Committee for Hydraulic Studies—CIEH: 01 BP 369, Ouagadougou, Burkina Faso; tel. 30-71-12; f. 1960 to ensure co-operation in hydrology, hydrogeology, climatology, urban sanitation and other water sciences, through exchange of information and co-ordination of research and other projects; administrative budget (1988/89): 110m. francs CFA; investment budget 400m. francs CFA. Mems: 13 African countries. Sec.-Gen. AMADOU DIAW. Publs *Bulletin de Liaison technique* (quarterly), research studies.

International Association for Bridge and Structural Engineering: ETH—Hönggerberg, 8093 Zürich, Switzerland; tel. (1) 6332647; fax (1) 6331241; e-mail secretariat@iabse.ethz.ch; internet www.iabse.ethz.ch; f. 1929 to exchange knowledge and advance the practice of structural engineering world-wide. Mems: 4,300 government departments, local authorities, universities, institutes, firms and individuals in 101 countries. Pres. KLAUS OSTENFELD (Denmark); Exec. Dir A. GOLAY. Publs *Structural Engineering International* (quarterly), *Congress Report, IABSE Report, Structural Engineering Documents*.

International Association for Cybernetics (Association Internationale de Cybernétique): Palais des Expositions, ave Sergent Vrithoff 2, 5000 Namur, Belgium; tel. (81) 71-71-71; fax (81) 71-71-00; e-mail cyb@info.fundp.ac.be; f. 1957 to ensure liaison between research workers engaged in various sectors of cybernetics, to promote the development of the science and of its applications and to disseminate information about it. Mems: firms and individuals in 42 countries. Chair. J. RAMAEKERS; Gen. Sec. CARINE AIGRET. Publ. *Cybernetica* (quarterly).

International Association of Technological University Libraries: c/o Helsinki University of Technology Library, POB 7000, 02015 HUT, Finland; tel. (9) 4514112; fax (9) 4514132; e-mail sinikka.koskiala@hut.fi; internet educate.lib.chalmers.se/iatul/; f. 1955 to promote co-operation between member libraries and stimulate research on library problems. Mems: 202 university libraries in 41 countries. Pres. Dr MICHAEL BREAKS (UK); Sec. Dr SINIKKA KOSKIALA (Finland). Publs *IATUL Proceedings, IATUL Newsletter* (electronic version only).

International Cargo Handling Co-ordination Association— ICHCA: 71 Bondway, London, SW8 1SH, United Kingdom; tel. (20) 7793-1022; fax (20) 7820-1703; e-mail postmaster@ichca.org.uk; internet www.ichca.org.uk; f. 1952 to foster economy and efficiency in the movement of goods from origin to destination. Mems: 2,000 in 90 countries. Pres. KEN HOGGAT; Chief Exec. GERRY ASKHAM. Publs *Cargo Today* (bimonthly), *World of Cargo Handling* (annually), *Who's Who in Cargo Handling* (annually), *Buyers' Guide to Manufacturers* (annually), safety panel briefing pamphlets.

International Colour Association: c/o Frank Rochow, LMT Lichtmesstechnik GmbH Berlin, Helmholtzstr. 9, 10587 Berlin, Germany; tel. (30) 3934028; fax (30) 3918001; f. 1967 to encourage research in colour in all its aspects, disseminate the knowledge gained from this research and promote its application to the solution of problems in the fields of science, art and industry; holds international congresses and symposia. Mems: organizations in 28 countries. Pres. PAULA ALESSI (USA); Sec. and Treasurer FRANK ROCHOW (Germany).

International Commission on Illumination—CIE: Kegelgasse 27, 1030 Vienna, Austria; tel. (1) 714-31-87-0; fax (1) 713-08-38-18; e-mail ciecb@ping.at; internet www.cie.co.at; f. 1900 as International Commission on Photometry, present name 1913; aims to provide an international forum for all matters relating to the science and art of light and lighting; to exchange information; to develop and publish international standards, and to provide guidance in their application. Mems: 40 national committees and 12 individuals. Gen. Sec. C. HERMANN. Publs standards, technical reports.

International Commission on Large Dams: 151 blvd Haussmann, 75008 Paris, France; tel. 1-40-42-68-24; fax 1-40-42-60-71; e-mail secretaire.general@icold-cigb.org; internet www.icold-cigb.org./; f. 1928; holds triennial congresses; 2000 congress: Beijing, People's Republic of China. Mems in 80 countries. Pres. C. V. J. VARMA (India); Sec.-Gen. JACQUES LECORNU. Publs *Technical Bulletin* (3/4 a year), *World Register of Dams, World Register of Mine and Industrial Wastes, Technical Dictionary on Dams*, studies.

International Committee on Aeronautical Fatigue—ICAF: c/o Prof. O. Buxbaum, Fraunhofer-Institut für Betriebsfestigkeit LBF, 64289 Darmstadt, Bartningstrasse 47, Germany; tel. (6151) 7051; fax (6151) 705214; f. 1951 for collaboration on fatigue of aeronautical structures among aeronautical bodies and laboratories by means of exchange of documents and by organizing periodical conferences. Mems: national centres in 13 countries. Sec. Prof. O. BUXBAUM (Germany).

International Council on Large High-Voltage Electric Systems—CIGRE: 21 rue d'Artois, 75008 Paris, France; tel. 1-53-89-12-90; fax 1-53-89-12-99; e-mail secretary-general@cigre.org; internet www.cigre.org; f. 1921 to facilitate and promote the exchange of technical knowledge and information between all countries in the general field of electrical generation and transmission at high voltages; holds general sessions (every 2 years), symposia. Mems: 5,000 in 79 countries. Pres. D. CROFT (Australia); Sec.-Gen. J. KOWAL (France). Publ. *Electra* (every 2 months).

International Council for Research and Innovation in Building and Construction: Postbox 1837, 3000 BV Rotterdam, Netherlands; tel. (10) 4110240; fax (10) 4334372; e-mail secretariat-@cibworld.nl; internet www.cibworld.nl; f. 1953 to encourage and facilitate co-operation in building research, studies and documentation in all aspects. Mems: governmental and industrial organizations and qualified individuals in 70 countries. Pres. Dr J. R. DUNCAN (New Zealand); Sec.-Gen. W. J. P. BAKENS. Publs *Information Bulletin* (bimonthly), conference proceedings and technical, best practice and other reports.

International Electrotechnical Commission—IEC: 3 rue de Varembé, POB 131, 1211 Geneva 20, Switzerland; tel. (22) 9190211; fax (22) 9190300; e-mail info@iec.ch; internet www.iec.ch; f. 1906 as the authority for world standards for electrical and electronic engineering: its standards are used as the basis for regional and national standards, and are used in preparing specifications for international trade. Mems: national committees representing all branches of electrical and electronic activities in some 60 countries. Gen.-Sec. A. AMIT. Publs *International Standards and Reports, IEC Bulletin, Annual Report, Catalogue of Publications*.

International Special Committee on Radio Interference: British Electrotechnical Committee, British Standards Institution, 389 Chiswick High Rd, London, W4 4AL, United Kingdom; tel. (20) 8996-9000; fax (20) 8996-7400; f. 1934; special committee of the IEC to promote international agreement on the protection of radio reception from interference by equipment other than authorized transmitters; recommends limits of such interference and specifies equipment and methods of measurement; determines requirements for immunity of sound and TV broadcasting receivers from interference and the impact of safety regulations on interference suppression. Mems: national committees of IEC and seven other international organizations. Sec. C. BECKLEY.

International Federation for Information and Documentation: POB 90402, 2509 LK The Hague, Netherlands; tel. (70) 3140671; fax (70) 3140667; e-mail fid@fid.nl; internet www.fid.nl; f. 1895; aims to promote, through international co-operation, research in and development of information science; information management and documentation; and improvement of all the processes involved in the entire life-cycle of data, information and knowledge in all fields; regional commissions for Latin America, North America and the Caribbean, Asia and Oceania, Western, Eastern and Southern Africa, North Africa and the Near East, and for Europe. Mems: 62 national, five international, 330 institutional or individual. Pres. MARTHA STONE; Exec. Dir J. STEPHEN PARKER. Publs *FID Review* (every 2 months), *FID Directory* (every 2 years).

International Federation for Information Processing: Hofstrasse 3, 2361 Laxenburg, Austria; tel. (2236) 73616; fax (2236) 736169; e-mail ifip@ifip.or.at; internet www.ifip.or.at; f. 1960 to promote information science and technology; to stimulate research, development and application of information processing in science and human activities; to further the dissemination and exchange of information on information processing; to encourage education in information processing; to advance international co-operation in the field of information processing. Mems: 45 organizations, 3 corresponding mems, 1 assoc. mem. and 11 affiliate mems. Pres. P. BOLLERSLEV (Denmark); Exec. Dir PLAMEN NEDKOV.

International Federation of Airworthiness—IFA: Suite 1A, Dralda House, Crendon Street, High Wycombe, Bucks HP13 6LS, United Kingdom; tel. (1494) 530404; fax (1494) 439984; e-mail mail@aviation-training.org; internet www.ifairworthy.org; f. 1964 to provide a forum for the exchange of international experience in maintenance, design and operations; holds annual conference; awards international aviation scholarship annually. Mems: 120, comprising 50 airlines, 17 airworthiness authorities, 23 aerospace manufacturing companies, 17 service and repair organizations, three consultancies, six professional societies, two aviation insurance companies, one aircraft leasing company, and the Flight Safety Foundation (USA). Pres. (1998–2000) ROBERT A. DAVIS (USA); Exec. Dir J. W. SAULL (UK). Publ. *IFA News* (quarterly).

International Federation of Automotive Engineering Societies—FISITA: 1 Birdcage Walk, London SW1H 9JJ, United Kingdom; tel. (20) 7973-1275; fax (20) 7973-1285; e-mail infor@fisita .com; internet www.fisita.com; f. 1947 to promote the technical and sustainable development of all forms of automotive transportation; maintains electronic job centre for automotive engineers (www.fisitajobs.com); congresses held every two years. Mems: national orgs in 32 countries. Chief Exec. IAN DICKIE. Publ. *Global Automotive Network*.

International Federation of Consulting Engineers: 13c ave du Temple, POB 86, 1000 Lausanne 12, Switzerland; tel. (21) 6544411; fax (21) 6535432; e-mail fidic@pobox.com; f. 1913 to encourage international co-operation and the setting up of standards for consulting engineers. Mems: national associations in 68 countries, comprising some 500,000 design professionals. Pres. R. WAYNE BOWES.

International Federation of Hospital Engineering: 2 Abingdon House, Cumberland Business Centre, Northumberland Rd, Portsmouth, PO5 1DS, United Kingdom; tel. (2392) 823186; fax (2392) 815927l e-mail iheem@btconnect.com; f. 1970 to promote internationally the standards of hospital engineering and to provide for the exchange of knowledge and experience in the areas of hospital and healthcare facility design, construction, engineering, commissioning, maintenance and estate management. Mems: 50 in more than 30 countries. Pres. BRUCE NOSEDA (Australia); Gen. Sec. BERNARD SHAPIRO (South Africa).

International Institute of Seismology and Earthquake Engineering: Building Research Institute, Ministry of Construction, 1 Tatehara, Tsukuba City, Ibaraki Pref., Japan; tel. (298) 79-0677; fax (298) 64-6777; e-mail iisee@kenken.go.jp; internet www.iisee .kenken.go.jp; f. 1962 to work on seismology and earthquake engineering for the purpose of reducing earthquake damage in the world; trains seismologists and earthquake engineers from the earthquake-prone countries and undertakes surveys, research, guidance and analysis of information on earthquakes and related matters. Mems: 75 countries. Dir M. MIZUNO.

International Institution for Production Engineering Research: 9 rue Mayran, 75009 Paris, France; tel. 1-45-26-21-80; fax 1-45-26-92-15; internet www.cirp.net; f. 1951 to promote by scientific research the study of the mechanical processing of all solid materials including checks on efficiency and quality of work. Mems: 510 in 40 countries. Pres. H. VAN BRUSSEL (Belgium); Sec.-Gen. M. VÉRON (France). Publ. *Annals* (2 a year).

International Iron and Steel Institute—IISI: 120 rue Col Bourg, 1140 Brussels, Belgium; tel. (2) 702-89-00; fax (2) 702-88-99; e-mail steel@iisi.be; internet www.worldsteel.org; f. 1967 to promote the welfare and interest of the world's steel industries; to undertake research in all aspects of steel industries; to serve as a forum for exchange of knowledge and discussion of problems relating to steel industries; to collect, disseminate and maintain statistics and information; to serve as a liaison body between international and national steel organizations. Mems: in over 50 countries. Sec.-Gen. IAN CHRISTMAS.

International Organization for Standardization: POB 56, 1 rue de Varembé, 1211 Geneva 20, Switzerland; tel. (22) 7490111; fax (22) 7333430; e-mail central@iso.ch; internet www.iso.ch/; f. 1947 to reach international agreement on industrial andcommercial standards. Mems: national standards bodies of 90 countries. Pres. MARIO GILBERTO CORTOPASSI (Brazil); Sec.-Gen. LAWRENCE D. EICHER. Publs *ISO International Standards, ISO Memento* (annually), *ISO 9000 and ISO 14000 News* (6 a year), *ISO Bulletin* (monthly).

International Research Group on Wood Preservation: Box 5607, 114 86 Stockholm, Sweden; tel. (8) 10-14-53; fax (8) 10-80-81; f. 1965 as Wood Preservation Group by OECD; independent since 1969; consists of five sections; holds plenary annual meeting. Mems: 315 in 51 countries. Pres. Prof. JOHN N. R. RUDDICK (Canada); Sec.-Gen. JÖRAN JERMER (Sweden). Publs technical documents and books, *Annual Report*.

International Rubber Research and Development Board—IRRDB: POB 10150, 50908 Kuala Lumpur, Malaysia; fax (3) 21620414; e-mail draziz@pop.jaring.my; internet www.irrdb.org; f. 1937. Mems: 15 research institutes. Sec. Datuk Dr A. AZIZ.

International Society for Photogrammetry and Remote Sensing: Martin Marietta Corporation, POB 8048-13A24, Philadelphia, PA 19101, USA; tel. (610) 531-3205; fax (510) 889-3296; f. 1910;

holds congress every four years, and technical symposia. Mems: 81 countries. Pres. SHUNJI MURAI (Japan); Sec.-Gen. LAWRENCE W. FRITZ (USA). Publs *International Archives of Photogrammetry and Remote Sensing, Photogrammetria*.

International Society for Soil Mechanics and Geotechnical Engineering: City University, Northampton Sq., London, EC1V 0HB, United Kingdom; tel. (20) 7477-8154; fax (20) 7477-8832; e-mail secretariat@issmge.org; internet www.issmge.org/; f. 1936 to promote international co-operation among scientists and engineers in the field of geotechnics and its engineering applications; maintains 30 technical committees; holds quadrennial international conference, regional conferences and specialist conferences. Mems: 17,000 individuals, 71 national societies, 23 corporate members. Pres. Prof. KENJI ISHIHARA; Sec.-Gen. Prof. R. NEIL TAYLOR. Publs *ISSMGE News* (quarterly), *Lexicon of Soil Mechanics Terms* (in eight languages).

International Solar Energy Society: Wiesentalstrasse 50, 79115 Freiburg, Germany; tel. (761) 459060; fax (761) 4590699; e-mail hq@ises.org; internet www.ises.org; f. 1954 to foster science and technology relating to the applications of renewable energy, to encourage research and development, to promote education and to gather, compile and disseminate information in this field; holds international conferences. Mems: approximately 4,000 in some 100 countries. Pres. Dr CESARE SILVI (Italy); Exec. Dir. BURKHARD HOLDER (Germany). Publs *Solar Energy Journal* (monthly), *Refocus Magazine* (10 a year), *Conference Proceedings*(annually) .

International Solid Wastes Association—ISWA: Overgaden Oven Vandet 48E, 1415 Copenhagen K, Denmark; tel. 32-96-15-88; fax 32-96-15-84; e-mail iswa@inet.uni2.dk; internet www.iswa.org; f. 1970; organizes conferences and establishes technical working groups. Pres. CHRISTOPH SCHARFF (Austria); Man. Dir SUZANNE ARUP VELTZÉ (Denmark) (acting).

International Tin Research Institute Ltd: Kingston Lane, Uxbridge, Middx, UB8 3PJ, United Kingdom; tel. (1895) 272406; fax (1895) 251841; internet www.itri.co.uk; f. 1932, privatized in 1995; provides technological support for the tin-producing and -consuming industries world-wide. Facilities include: soldering, electroplating, metallography, and chemical and analytical laboratories; a technical enquiry and information service; research is conducted to support existing uses of tin and to develop new applications. Dir ALAN DIBBO. Publs *Soldering Bits* (quarterly), *Tin International* (monthly).

International Union for Vacuum Science, Technique and Applications—IUVSTA: 7 Mohawk Cres., Nepean, ON K2H 7G7, Canada; tel. (613) 829-5790; fax (613) 829-3061; e-mail westwood@istar.ca; internet www.vacuum.org/iuvsta.html; f. 1958; collaborates with the International Standards Organization in defining and adopting technical standards; holds triennial International Vacuum Congress, European Vacuum Conference, triennial International Conference on Thin Films, and International Conference on Solid Surfaces; administers the Welch Foundation scholarship for postgraduate research in vacuum science and technology; scientific divisions for surface science, applied surface science, thin film, vacuum science, electronic materials, nanometer structures, plasma science and technique and vacuum metallurgy. Mems: organizations in 30 countries. Pres. Prof. D. P. WOODRUFF (UK); Sec.-Gen. Dr W. D. WESTWOOD (Canada). Publ. *News Bulletin* (quarterly).

International Water Resources Association: University of New Mexico, 1915 Roma NE, Albuquerque, NM 87131-1436, USA; tel. (505) 277-9400; fax (505) 277-9405; e-mail iwra@unm.edu; f. 1972 to promote collaboration in and support for international water resources programmes; holds conferences; conducts training in water resources management. Pres. GLENN E. STOUT (USA); Sec.-Gen. VICTOR DE KOSINSKY (Belgium). Publ. *Water International* (quarterly).

Latin-American Energy Organization (Organización Latino-americana de Energía–OLADE): Avda Mariscal Antonio José de Sucre, No N58–63 y Fernándes Salvador, Edif. OLADE, Sector San Carlos, POB 17-11-6413 CCI, Quito, Ecuador; tel. (2) 598-122; fax (2) 531-691; e-mail oladel@olade.org.ec; internet www.olade.org.ec; f. 1973 to act as an instrument of co-operation in using and conserving the energy resources of the region. Mems: 26 Latin-American and Caribbean countries. Exec. Sec. Dr JULIO HERRERA. Publ. *Energy Magazine*.

Latin-American Iron and Steel Institute: Benjamín 2944, 5°, Las Condes, Santiago, Chile; tel. (2) 233-0545; fax (2) 233-0768; e-mail ilafa@entelchile.net; internet www.ilafa.org; f. 1959 to help achieve the harmonious development of iron and steel production, manufacture and marketing in Latin America; conducts economic surveys on the steel sector; organizes technical conventions and meetings; disseminates industrial processes suited to regional conditions; prepares and maintains statistics on production, end uses, prices, etc., of raw materials and steel products within this area. Hon. mems 18; mems 63; assoc. mems 68; Chair. JULIO CÉSAR VILLARREAL; Sec.-Gen. ENRIQUE ALVAREZ. Publs *Acero Latinoamericano* (every 2 months), *Statistical Year Book, Directory of Latin American Iron and Steel Companies* (every 2 years).

Regional Centre for Services in Surveying, Mapping and Remote Sensing: POB 18118, Nairobi, Kenya; tel. (2) 803320; fax (2) 802767; e-mail rcssmrs@unep.org; f. 1975 to provide services in the professional techniques of map-making, and the application of satellite and remote sensing data in resource analysis and development planning; undertakes research and provides advisory services to African governments. Mems: 14 signatory and 10 non-signatory governments. Dir-Gen. Prof. SIMON NDYETABULA.

Regional Centre for Training in Aerospace Surveys: PMB 5545, Ile-Ife, Nigeria; tel. (36) 230050; fax (36) 230481; f. 1972 for training, research and advisory services; administered by the ECA. Mems: eight governments. Dir J. A. OGUNLAMI.

Regional Council of Co-ordination of Central and East European Engineering Organizations: c/o MTESZ, 1055 Budapest, Kossuth Lajos tér 6–8, Hungary; tel. (361) 353-4795; fax (361) 353-0317; e-mail mtesz@mtesz.hu; f. 1992. Hon. Pres. JÁNOS TÓTH.

World Association of Industrial and Technological Research Organizations—WAITRO: c/o Danish Technological Institute, POB 141, 2630 Taastrup, Denmark; tel.72-20-20-85; fax 72-20-20-80; e-mail waitro@dti.dk; internet www.waitro.org; f. 1970 by the UN Industrial Development Organization to encourage co-operation in industrial and technological research, through financial assistance for training and joint activities, arranging international seminars, and allowing the exchange of information. Mems: 200 research institutes in 80 countries. Pres. ÖMER KAYMAKCALAN (Turkey); Contact MOSES MENGU. Publs *WAITRO News* (quarterly), *WAITRO Outline*.

World Association of Nuclear Operators—WANO-CC: Kings Bldgs, 16 Smith Sq., London, SW1P 3JG, United Kingdom; tel. (20) 7828-2111; fax (20) 7828-6691; f. 1989 by operators of nuclear power plants; aims to improve the safety and operability of nuclear power plants by exchange of operating experience; four regional centres (in France, Japan, Russia and the USA) and a co-ordinating centre in the UK. Mems in 34 countries. Dir (Co-ordinating Centre) V. J. MADDEN.

World Bureau of Metal Statistics: 27A High St, Ware, Herts, SG12 9BA, United Kingdom; tel. (1920) 461274; fax (1920) 464258; f. 1949; statistics of production, consumption, stocks, prices and international trade in copper, lead, zinc, tin, nickel, aluminium and several other minor metals. Gen. Man. J. L. T. DAVIES. Publs *World Metal Statistics* (monthly), *World Tin Statistics* (monthly), *World Nickel Statistics* (monthly), *World Metal Statistics Yearbook*, *World Metal Statistics Quarterly Summary*, *World Stainless Steel Statistics* (annually), *World Wrought Copper Statistics* (annually).

World Federation of Engineering Organizations—WFEO: Maison de l'UNESCO, 1 rue Miollis, 75015 Paris, France; tel. 1-45-68-31-92; fax 1-45-68-31-14; e-mail pdeboigne@fmoi.org; internet www.unesco.org/ngo/fmoi/; f. 1968 to advance engineering as a profession in the interests of the world community; to foster co-operation between engineering organizations throughout the world; to undertake special projects through co-operation between members and in co-operation with other international bodies. Mems: 80 national, nine international. Pres. JOSÉ MEDEM SANJUAN (Spain); Exec. Dir PIERRE EDOUARD DE BOIGNE (France). Publ. *WFEO Newsletter* (2 a year).

World Petroleum Congresses: 4th floor, Suite 1, 1 Duchess St, London, W1N 3DE, United Kingdom; tel. (20) 7637-4958; e-mail pierce@world-petroleum.org; internet www.world-petroleum.org; f. 1933 to provide an international congress as a forum for petroleum science, technology, economics and management; to publish the proceedings, and to undertake related information and liaison activities; Permanent Council includes 59 member countries; 17th Congress: Rio de Janeiro, Brazil, 2002. Pres. Ir D. VAN DER MEER (Netherlands); Dir-Gen. Dr PIERCE W. F. RIEMER (UK).

Tourism

Alliance Internationale de Tourisme: 2 Chemin de Blandonnet, CP 111, 1215 Geneva 15, Switzerland; tel. (22) 5444501; fax (22) 5444550; e-mail webmaster@aitfia.ch; internet www.aitgva.ch; f. 1898, present title adopted 1919; represents motoring organizations and touring clubs around the world; aims to study all questions relating to international touring and to suggest reforms, to encourage the development of tourism and all matters concerning the motorist, traffic management, the environment, road safety, consumer protection and to defend the interests of touring associations. Mems: 140 asscns totalling 100m. members in 102 countries. Pres. F. FALCÓ (Spain); Dir Gen. P. DOGGWILER (Switzerland).

Asia Travel Marketing Association—ATMA: c/o Japan National Tourist Organization, 2-10-1 Yurakucho, Chiyoda-ku, Tokyo, Japan; tel. (3) 3216-1902; fax (3) 3216-1846; internet www.asiatravel.org; f. 1966 as East Asia Travel Association, present name adopted 1999; aims to promote tourism in the East Asian region, encourage and facilitate the flow of tourists to that region from other parts of the world, and to develop regional tourist industries by close collaboration among members. Mems: six national tourist organizations and one travel association. Pres. ICHIRO TANAKA; Sec.-Gen. JOÃO MANUEL COSTA ANTUNES.

Caribbean Tourism Organization: Sir Frank Walcott Bldg, 2nd Floor, Culloden Farm Complex, St Michael, Barbados; tel. 427-5242; fax 429-3065; e-mail ctobar@caribsurf.com; offices in New York, Canada and London; f. 1989, by merger Caribbean Tourism Association (f. 1951) and Caribbean Tourism Research and Development Centre (f. 1974); aims to encourage tourism in the Caribbean region; organizes annual Caribbean Tourism Conference, Sustainable Tourism Development Conference and Tourism Investment Conference; conducts training and other workshops on request. Mems: 33 Caribbean governments and 400 allied mems. Sec.-Gen. JEAN HOLDER. Publs *Caribbean Tourism Statistical News* (quarterly), *Caribbean Tourism Statistical Report* (annually).

European Travel Commission: 61 rue du Marché aux Herbes, 1000 Brussels, Belgium; tel. (2) 504-03-03; fax (2) 514-18-43; e-mail etc@planetinternet.be; internet www.etc-europe-travel.org; f. 1948 to promote tourism in and to Europe, to foster co-operation and the exchange of information, to organize research. Mems: national tourist organizations of 30 European countries. Exec. Dir WALTER LEU (Switzerland).

International Association of Scientific Experts in Tourism: Varnbüelstrasse 19, 9000 St Gallen, Switzerland; tel. (71) 2242530; fax (71) 2242536; e-mail aiest@unisg.ch; internet www.aiest.org; f. 1949 to encourage scientific activity by its members; to support tourist institutions of a scientific nature; to organize conventions. Mems: 400 from 40 countries. Pres. Prof. Dr PETER KELLER (Switzerland); Gen. Sec. Prof. Dr THOMAS BIEGER (Switzerland). Publ. *The Tourism Review* (quarterly).

International Congress and Convention Association: Entrada 121, 1096 EB Amsterdam, Netherlands; tel. (20) 398-19-19; fax (20) 6990781; e-mail icca@icca.nl; internet www.icca.nl; f. 1963 to establish world-wide co-operation between all involved in organizing congresses, conventions and exhibitions (including travel agents, airlines, hotels, congress centres, professional congress organizers, tourist and convention bureaux and ancillary congress services). Mems: more than 500 meeting experts from 71 countries. Pres. TUUIA LINDBERG; Exec. Dir. TOM HULTON. Publ. *International Meetings News* (6 a year).

International Hotel and Restaurant Association: 251 rue du Faubourg St Martin, 75010 Paris, France; tel. 1-44-89-94-00; fax 1-40-36-73-30; e-mail members@ih-ra.com; internet www.ihra.com; f. 1946 to act as the leader and authority on matters affecting the international hotel industry, to promote its interests and to contribute to its growth, profitability and quality of the industry world-wide; membership extended to restaurants in 1996. Mems: 120 national hospitality associations, 100 national and international hotel and restaurant chains; also independent hotels and restaurant and allied members. Dir and CEO ALAIN-PHILIPPE FEUTRÉ; Sec.-Gen. CHRISTIANE DHORNE. Publs *Hotels* (monthly), *Yearbook and Directory* (annually).

Latin-American Confederation of Tourist Organizations—COTAL: Viamonte 640, 8°, 1053 Buenos Aires, Argentina; tel. (11) 4322-4003; fax (11) 4393-5696; e-mail cotal@cscom.com.ar; f. 1957 to link Latin American national associations of travel agents and their members with other tourist bodies around the world. Mems: in 21 countries and affiliate mems in 55 countries. Pres. FERNANDO SOLER. Publ. *Revista COTAL* (every 2 months).

Pacific Asia Travel Association—PATA: Unit B1, 28th floor, Siam Tower, 989 Rama 1 Rd, Pratumwan, Bangkok 10330, Thailand; tel. (2) 658-2000; fax (2) 658-2010; e-mail patabkk@pata.th.com; internet www.pata.org; f. 1951; aims to enhance the growth, value and quality of Pacific Asia travel and tourism for the benefit of PATA members. Annual Conference held in April. Divisional offices in Monaco, Sydney, Singapore, USA. Mems: more than 2,200 governments, carriers, tour operators, travel agents and hotels. Publs *PATA Compass* (every 2 months), *Statistical Report* (quarterly), research reports, directories, newsletters.

South Pacific Tourism Organization: POB 13119, Suva, Fiji; tel. 304177; fax 301995; e-mail info@spto.org; internet www.tcsp.com; formerly the Tourism Council of the South Pacific; aims to foster regional co-operation in the development, marketing and promotion of tourism in the island nations of the South Pacific; receives EU funding and undertakes sustainable activities. Mems: American Samoa, Cook Islands, Fiji, French Polynesia, Kiribati, New Caledonia, Niue, Papua New Guinea, Samoa, Solomon Islands, Tonga, Tuvalu, Vanuatu; Chief Exec. LISIATE AKOLO.

Universal Federation of Travel Agents' Associations—UFTAA: 1 ave des Castelans, Stade Louis II-Entrée H, 98000 Monaco; tel. 92-05-28-29; fax 92-05-29-87; e-mail uftaamc@tekworld.mc; internet www.uftaa.com; f. 1966 to unite travel agents' associations, to represent the interests of travel agents at the international level, to help in international legal differences; issues literature on travel, etc. Mems: national associations of travel agencies in 112 countries. Sec.-Gen. BIRGER BÄCKMAN.

World Association of Travel Agencies: 14 rue Ferrier, 1202 Geneva, Switzerland; tel. (22) 7314760; fax (22) 7328161; e-mail wata@wata.net; internet www.wata.net; f. 1949 to foster the development of tourism, to help the rational organization of tourism in all countries, to collect and disseminate information and to participate in all commercial and financial operations which will foster the development of tourism. Individual travel agencies may use the services of the world-wide network of 200 members. Pres. ADEL ZAKI (Egypt); Sec.-Gen. MARCO AGUSTONI (Switzerland). Publ. *WATA Gazette* (quarterly).

World Tourism Organization: Calle Capitán Haya 42, 28020 Madrid, Spain; tel. (91) 5678100; fax (91) 5713733; e-mail comm@world-tourism.org; internet www.world-tourism.org; f. 1975 to promote travel and tourism; co-operates with member governments; secures financing for and carries out tourism development projects; provides training in tourism-related issues; works for sustainable and environmentally-friendly tourism development; encourages the liberalization of trade in tourism services; considers health and safety issues related to tourism; collects, analyses and disseminates data and operates a Documentation Centre. Mems: governments of 138 countries and territories, also associate members, observers and over 300 affiliated mems. Sec.-Gen. FRANCESCO FRANGIALLI. Publs *Yearbook of Tourism Statistics, Compendium of Tourism Statistics, Travel and Tourism Barometer, WTO News, Tourism Market Trends, Directory of Multilateral and Bilateral Sources of Financing for Tourism Development*, guide-lines and studies.

World Travel and Tourism Council—WTTC: 20 Grosvenor Pl., London, SW1X 7TT, United Kingdom; tel. (20) 7838-9400; fax (20) 7838-9050; e-mail enquiries@wttc.org; internet www.wttc.org; f. 1989; promotes the development of the travel/tourism industry; analyses impact of tourism on employment levels and local economies and promotes greater expenditure on tourism infrastructure; administers a 'Green Globe' certification programme to enhance environmental management throughout the industry. Pres. JEAN-CLAUDE BAUMGARTEN.

Trade and Industry

African Regional Organization for Standardization: POB 57363, Nairobi, Kenya; tel. (2) 224561; fax (2) 218792; e-mail arso@nbnet.co.ke; internet www.nbnet.co.ke/test/arso; f. 1977 to promote standardization, quality control, certification and metrology in the African region, formulate regional standards, and co-ordinate participation in international standardization activities. Mems: 24 states. Sec.-Gen. Dr ADEBAYO O. OYEJOLA. Publs *ARSO Bulletin* (2 a year), *ARSO Catalogue of Regional Standards* (annually), *ARSO Annual Report*.

Arab Iron and Steel Union—AISU: BP 4, Chéraga, Algiers, Algeria; tel. (2) 371579; fax (2) 371975; f. 1972 to develop commercial and technical aspects of Arab steel production by helping member associations to commercialize their production in Arab markets, guaranteeing them high quality materials and intermediary products, informing them of recent developments in the industry and organizing training sessions. Mems: 73 companies in 13 Arab countries. Gen. Sec. MUHAMMAD LAID LACHGAR. Publs *Arab Steel Review* (monthly), *Information Bulletin* (2 a month), *Directory* (annually).

Asian Productivity Organization: 2/F Hirakawa-cho Dai-ichi Seimei Bldg, 1-2-10, Hirakawa-cho, Chiyoda-ku, Tokyo 102–0093, Japan; tel. (3) 3408-7221; fax (3) 3408-7220; e-mail apo@gol.com; internet www.apo-tokyo.com; f. 1961 to strengthen the productivity movement in the Asian and Pacific region and disseminate technical knowledge on productivity. Mems: 18 countries. Sec.-Gen. TAKASHI TAJIMA. Publs *APO News* (monthly), *Annual Report, APO Productivity Journal* (2 a year), *Directory of National Productivity Organizations in APO member countries* (irregular) and other related studies.

Association of African Trade Promotion Organizations—AATPO: Pavillion International, BP 23, Tangier, Morocco; tel. (9) 324465; fax (9) 943779; e-mail aoapc@mtds.com; f. 1975 under the auspices of the OAU and the ECA to foster regular contact between African states in trade matters and to assist in the harmonization of their commercial policies in order to promote intra-African trade; conducts research and training; organizes meetings and trade information missions. Mems: 26 states. Sec.-Gen. Prof. ADEYINKA W. ORIMALADE. Publs *FLASH: African Trade* (monthly), *Directory of African Consultants and Experts in Trade Promotion, Directory of Trade Information Contacts in Africa, Directory of Trade Information Sources in Africa, Directory of State Trading Organizations, Directory of Importers and Exporters of Food Products in Africa, Basic Information on Africa*, studies.

Association of European Chambers of Commerce and Industry (EUROCHAMBRES): 5 rue d'Archimède, 1000 Brussels, Belgium; tel. (2) 282-08-50; fax (2) 230-00-38; e-mail eurochambres@eurochambres.be; internet www.eurochambres.be; f. 1958 to promote the exchange of experience and information among its members and to bring their joint opinions to the attention of the institutions of the European Union; conducts studies and seminars; co-ordinates EU projects. Mems: 15 full and 18 affiliated mems. Pres. JÖRG MITTELSTEN SCHEID (Germany); Sec.-Gen. ARNALDO ABRUZZINI (Italy).

Cairns Group: c/o Department of Foreign Affairs and Trade, GPO Box 12, Canberra, ACT 2601, Australia; tel. (2) 6263-2222; fax (2) 6261-3111; internet www.dfat.gov.au/trade/negotiations/cairns_group/index.html; f. 1986 by major agricultural exporting countries, aiming to bring about reforms in international agricultural trade, including reductions in export subsidies, in barriers to access and in internal support measures; represents members' interests in WTO negotiations. Mems: Argentina, Australia, Bolivia, Brazil, Canada, Chile, Colombia, Costa Rica, Fiji, Guatemala, Indonesia, Malaysia, New Zealand, Paraguay, Philippines, South Africa, Thailand, Uruguay. Chair. MARK VAILE (Australia).

Caribbean Association of Industry and Commerce—CAIC: POB 442, Trinidad Hilton, Room 351, Lady Young Rd, St Ann's, Trinidad and Tobago; tel. (868) 623-4830; fax (868) 623-6116; e-mail caic@trinidad.net; internet www.trinidad.net/caic; f. 1955; aims to encourage economic development through the private sector; undertakes research, training, assistance for small enterprises, and export promotion. Mems: chambers of commerce and enterprises in 20 countries and territories. Exec. Dir FELIPE NAGUERA. Publs *CAIC News* (2 a month), *CAIC Speaks* (monthly), *CAIC Times*(quarterly),*Business Wave* (6 a year).

Committee for European Construction Equipment—CECE: 101 rue de Stassart, 1050 Brussels, Belgium; tel. (2) 512-72-02; fax (2) 502-54-42; e-mail cece@skynet.be; f. 1959 to further contact between manufacturers, to improve market conditions and productivity and to conduct research into techniques. Mems: representatives from Belgium, Finland, France, Germany, Italy, Netherlands, Spain, Sweden, United Kingdom. Sec.-Gen. PIERRE JULIENS.

Committee of European Foundry Associations: 2 rue de Bassano, 75783 Paris Cédex 16, France; tel. 1-47-23-55-50; fax 1-47-20-44-15; f. 1953 to safeguard the common interests of European foundry industries; to collect and exchange information. Mems: associations in 14 countries. Sec.-Gen. H. CHAPOTOT.

Confederation of Asia-Pacific Chambers of Commerce and Industry: 9th Floor, 3 Sungshou Rd, Taipei 110, Taiwan; tel. (2) 27255663; fax (2) 27255665; e-mail cacci@ficnet.net; f. 1966; holds biennial conferences to examine regional co-operation; undertakes liaison with governments in the promotion of laws conducive to regional co-operation; serves as a centre for compiling and disseminating trade and business information; encourages contacts between businesses; conducts training and research. Mems: national chambers of commerce and industry of Australia, Bangladesh, Brunei, Cambodia, Hong Kong, India, Indonesia, Japan, Republic of Korea, Malaysia, Mongolia, Nepal, New Zealand, Pakistan, Papua New Guinea, Philippines, Russia, Singapore, Sri Lanka, Taiwan, Thailand, Viet Nam; also affiliate and special mems. Dir-Gen. Dr SHIN-YUAN LAI. Publs *CACCI Profile* (monthly), *CACCI Journal of Commerce and Industry* (2 a year).

Confederation of International Soft Drinks Associations—CISDA: 79 blvd St Michel, 1040 Brussels, Belgium; tel. (2) 743-40-50; fax (2) 732-51-02; e-mail mail@unesda-cisda.org; internet www.unesda-cisda.org; f. 1951 to promote co-operation among the national associations of soft drinks manufacturers on all industrial and commercial matters, to stimulate the sales and consumption of soft drinks, to deal with matters of interest to all member associations and to represent the common interests of member associations; holds a congress every year. Gen. Sec. ALAIN BEAUMONT.

Consumers International: 24 Highbury Crescent, London, N5 1RX, United Kingdom; tel. (20) 7226-6663; fax (20) 7354-0607; f. 1960 as International Organization of Consumers' Unions—IOCU; links consumer groups world-wide through information networks and international seminars; supports new consumer groups and represents consumers' interests at the international level; five regional offices. Mems: 215 associations in 93 countries. Dir-Gen. JULIAN EDWARDS. Publs *Consumer Currents* (10 a year), *World Consumer* (quarterly), *Consumidores y Desarollo* (10 a year), *Consommation-Developpement* (quarterly).

Energy Charter Secretariat: blvd de la Woluwe 56, 1200 Brussels, Belgium; tel. (2) 775-98-00; fax (2) 775-98-01; e-mail info@encharter.org; internet www.encharter.org; f. 1995 under the provisions of the Energy Charter Treaty (1991); aims to promote trade and investment in the petroleum and gas industries. Mems: 51 signatory states. Sec.-Gen. RIA KEMPER (Germany).

European Association of Advertising Agencies—EAAA: 152 blvd Brand Whitlock, 1200 Brussels, Belgium; tel. (2) 740-07-10; fax (2) 740-07-17; e-mail stig.carlson@eaaa.be; internet www.eaaa.be; f. 1960 to maintain and to raise the standards of service to advertisers of all European advertising agencies, and to strive towards uniformity in fields where this would be of benefit; to serve the interests of all agency members in Europe. Mems: 18 national advertising agency associations and 23 multinational agency groups. Pres. ALBERT WINNINGHOFF (Netherlands); Sec.-Gen. STIG CARLSON (Sweden). Publ. *Next Steps* (monthly).

European Association of Manufacturers of Radiators— EURORAD: Konradstr. 9, 8023 Zürich, Switzerland; tel. (1) 2719090; fax (1) 2719292; f. 1966 to represent the national associations of manufacturers of radiators made of steel and cast iron, intended to be attached to central heating plants and which convey heat by natural convection and radiation without the need for casing. Mems: in 15 countries. Pres. Dr H. GASSER (Belgium); Gen. Sec. K. EGLI (Switzerland).

European Association of National Productivity Centres: 60 rue de la Concorde, 1050 Brussels, Belgium; tel. (2) 511-71-00; fax (2) 511-02-97; e-mail eanpc@skynet.be; f. 1966 to enable members to pool knowledge about their policies and activities, specifically as regards the relative importance of various productivity factors, and the ensuing economic and social consequences. Mems: 19 European centres. Pres. PETER REHNSTRÖM; Sec.-Gen. A. C. HUBERT. Publs *EPI* (quarterly), *Annual Report*.

European Brewery Convention: POB 510, 2380 BB Zoeterwoude, Netherlands; tel. (71) 545-60-47; fax (71) 541-00-13; e-mail secretariat @ebc-nl.com; internet www.ebc-nl.com; f. 1947, present name adopted 1948; aims to promote scientific co-ordination in malting and brewing. Mems: national associations in Austria, Belgium, Bulgaria, Czech Republic, Denmark, Finland, France, Germany, Hungary, Ireland, Italy, Latvia, Netherlands, Norway, Portugal, Romania, Slovakia, Slovenia, Spain, Sweden, Switzerland, United Kingdom. Pres. E. PAJUNEN (Finland); Sec.-Gen. M. VAN WIJNGAARDEN (Netherlands).

European Chemical Industry Council: ave E. van Nieuwenhuyse 4, 1160 Brussels, Belgium; tel. (2) 676-72-11; fax (2) 676-73-00; e-mail mail@cefic.be; internet www.cefic.org; f. 1972; represents and defends the interests of the chemical industry relating to legal and trade policy, internal market, environmental and technical matters; liaises with intergovernmental organizations; provides secretariat for some 100 product sector groups. Mems: 16 national federations; Dir.-Gen. Dr HUGO LEVER; Sec.-Gen. JEAN-MARIE DEVOS.

European Committee for Standardization (Comité européen de normalisation—CEN): 36 rue de Stassart, 1050 Brussels, Belgium; tel. (2) 550-08-11; fax (2) 550-08-19; e-mail infodesk@cenorm.be; internet www.cenorm.be; f. 1961 to promote European standardization so as to eliminate obstacles caused by technical requirements in order to facilitate the exchange of goods and services. Mems: 19 national standards bodies, 6 associated and 14 affiliated bodies in central and eastern Europe and 4 corresponding organizations. Sec.-Gen. GEORG HONGLER.

European Committee of Associations of Manufacturers of Agricultural Machinery: 19 rue Jacques Bingen, 75017 Paris, France; tel. 1-42-12-85-90; fax 1-40-54-95-60; e-mail cema@syma.org; f. 1959 to study economic and technical problems, to protect members' interests and to disseminate information. Mems: Austria, Belgium, Denmark, Finland, France, Germany, Greece, Italy, Netherlands, Norway, Portugal, Spain, Switzerland, United Kingdom. Pres. P. SNAWWAERT (Belgium); Sec.-Gen. J. DEHOLLAIN (France).

European Committee of Textile Machinery Manufacturers: POB 190, 2700-AD Zoetermeer, Netherlands; tel. (79) 531-100; fax (79) 531-365; f. 1952; promotes general interests of the industry. Mems: organizations in Belgium, France, Germany, Italy, Netherlands, Spain, Switzerland, United Kingdom. Pres. Dr F. PAETZOLD (Germany); Gen. Sec. R. BICKER CAARTEN.

European Confederation of Iron and Steel Industries— EUROFER: 211 rue du Noyer, 1000 Brussels, Belgium; tel. (2) 738-79-20; fax (2) 736-30-01; e-mail mail@eurofer.be; f. 1976; a confederation of national federations and companies in the European steel industry which aims to foster co-operation between the member federations and companies and to represent their common interests to the EU and other international organizations. Mems: Austria, Belgium, Finland, France, Germany, Ireland, Italy, Luxembourg, Netherlands, Portugal, Spain, Sweden, United Kingdom; assoc. mems from countries of central and eastern European countries. Dir.-Gen. D. VON HÜLSEN.

European Confederation of Woodworking Industries: Allee Hof-Ter-Vleest 5, Boᵉte 4, 1070 Brussels, Belgium; tel. (2) 556-25-85; fax (2) 556-25-95; e-mail euro.wood.fed@skynet.be; internet www.cei-bois.org; f. 1952 to act as a liaison between national organizations, to undertake research and to defend the interests of the industry. Mems: national federations in 18 European countries and European sectoral organizations in woodworking. Pres. BO BORGSTRÖM (Finland); Sec.-Gen. Dr G. VAN STEERTEGEM.

European Council of Paint, Printing Ink and Artists' Colours Industry: ave E. van Nieuwenhuyse 4, 1160 Brussels, Belgium; tel.

(2) 676-7480; fax (2) 676-7490; e-mail secretariat@cepe.org; internet www.cepe.org; f. 1951 to study questions relating to paint and printing ink industries, to take or recommend measures for their development and interests, to exchange information. Mems: national associations in 17 European countries and 13 company members. Pres. F. J. RANKL; Gen. Sec. J. SCHODER.

European Federation of Associations of Insulation Enterprises: Kurfürstenstr. 129, 10785 Berlin, Germany; tel. (30) 212-86163; fax (30) 212-86160; f. 1970; groups the organizations in Europe representing insulation firms including thermal insulation, sound-proofing and fire-proofing insulation; aims to facilitate contacts between member associations, to study any problems of interest to the profession, to safeguard the interests of the profession and represent it in international forums. Mems: professional organizations in 15 European countries. Sec.-Gen. M. SCHMOLDT.

European Federation of Handling Industries: POB 179, Kirchenweg 4, 8032 Zürich, Switzerland; tel. (1) 3844844; fax (1) 3844848; f. 1953 to facilitate contact between members of the profession, conduct research, standardize methods of calculation and construction and promote standardized safety regulations. Mems: organizations in 14 European countries. Pres. PAOLO CAVANDOLI; Sec. Dr K. MEIER (Switzerland).

European Federation of Management Consultants' Associations: 3–5 ave des Arts, 1210 Brussels, Belgium; tel. (2) 250-06-50; fax (2) 250-06-51; e-mail feaco@feaco.org; internet www.feaco.org; f. 1960 to bring management consultants together and promote a high standard of professional competence in all European countries concerned, by encouraging discussions of, and research into, problems of common professional interest. Mems: 23 associations. Pres. and Chair. GIL GIDRON; Exec. Man. ELSE GROEN. Publs *Newsletter* (3 a year), *Annual Survey of the European Management Consultancy Market*.

European Federation of Plywood Industry: 33 rue de Naples, 75008 Paris, France; tel. (1) 53-42-15-57; fax (1) 53-42-15-51; f. 1957 to organize joint research between members of the industry at international level. Mems: associations in 14 European countries. Pres. PIERRE LAPEYRE.

European Federation of Tile and Brick Manufacturers: Obstgartenstrasse 28, 8035 Zürich, Switzerland; tel. (1) 3619650; fax (1) 3610205; e-mail office@tbe-euro.ch; internet www.tbe-euro.com; f. 1952 to co-ordinate research between members of the industry, improve technical knowledge, encourage professional training. Mems: associations in Austria, Belgium, Bulgaria, Czech Republic, Denmark, Finland, France, Germany, Greece, Hungary, Ireland, Italy, Netherlands, Norway, Poland, Portugal, Serbia, Slovakia, Spain, Sweden, Switzerland, Tunisia, United Kingdom. Chair. VITTORIO VITOLO; Dir Dr W. P. WELLER.

European Furniture Manufacturers Federation: 35 chaussé de Haecht, 1210 Brussels; tel. (2) 223-39-64; e-mail u.e.a.@euronet.be; internet www.u-e-a.com; f. 1950 to determine and support general interests of the European furniture industry and to facilitate contacts between members of the industry. Mems: organizations in Belgium, Denmark, Finland, France, Germany, Italy, Netherlands, Norway, Portugal, Slovenia, Spain, Sweden, Switzerland, United Kingdom. Pres. J. ENGELS; Sec.-Gen. B. DE TURCK.

European General Galvanizers Association: Croudace House, Godstone Rd, Caterham, Surrey, CR3 6RE, United Kingdom; tel. (1883) 331277; fax (1883) 331287; e-mail mail@egga.com; internet www.egga.com; f. 1955 to promote co-operation between members of the industry, especially in improving processes and finding new uses for galvanized products. Mems: associations in Austria, Belgium, Czech Republic, Denmark, Finland, France, Germany, Hungary, Iceland, Ireland, Italy, Netherlands, Norway, Portugal, Slovakia, Spain, Sweden, Switzerland, United Kingdom. Pres. E. HOFFMANN (Germany).

European Glass Container Manufacturers' Committee: Northumberland Rd, Sheffield, S10 2UA, United Kingdom; tel. (114) 268-6201; fax (114) 268-1073; e-mail l.roe@britglass.co.uk; internet www.britglass.co.uk; f. 1951 to facilitate contacts between members of the industry, inform them of legislation regarding it. Mems: representatives from 15 European countries. Sec. Dr W. G. A. COOK.

European Organization for Quality—EOQ: 3 rue de Luxembourg, 1000 Brussels, Belgium; tel. (2) 501-07-35; fax (31) 501-07-36; e-mail bjouslin@compuserve.com; internet www.eoq.org; f. 1956 to encourage the use and application of quality management with the intent to improve quality, reduce costs and increase productivity; organizes the exchange of information, documentation, etc. Member organizations in 31 European countries. Sec.-Gen. BERTRAND JOUSLIN DE NORAY. Publs *European Quality* (6 a year), *Annual Report*.

European Packaging Federation: c/o Institut Français de l'Emballage et du Conditionnement IFEC, 33 rue Louis Blanc, 93582 St-Ouen Cédex, France; tel. 1-40-11-22-12; fax 1-40-11-01-06; f. 1953 to encourage the exchange of information between national packaging institutes and to promote technical and economic progress. Mems:

organizations in Austria, Belgium, Denmark, Finland, France, Germany, Hungary, Italy, Netherlands, Poland, Spain, Switzerland, United Kingdom. Pres. J. P. POTHET (France); Sec.-Gen. A. FREIDINGER-LEGAY (France).

European Panel Federation: Hof-ter-Vleesdreef 5, 1070 Brussels, Belgium; tel. (2) 556-25-89; fax (2) 556-25-94; e-mail euro.wood .fed@skynet.be; internet www.europanels.org; f. 1958 as European Federation of Associations of Particle Board Manufacturers; present name adopted 1999; to develop and encourage international co-operation in the particle board and MDF industry. Pres. F. DE COCK; Sec.-Gen. G. VAN STEERTEGEM (Belgium). Publ. *Annual Report.*

European Patent Office—EPO: 80331 Munich, Erhardtstrasse 27, Germany; tel. (89) 2399-0; fax (89) 23994560; internet www.european-patent-office.org; f. 1977 to grant European patents according to the Munich convention of 1973; conducts searches and examination of patent applications. Mems: Austria, Belgium, Cyprus, Denmark, Finland, France, Germany, Greece, Ireland, Italy, Liechtenstein, Luxembourg, Monaco, Netherlands, Portugal, Spain, Sweden, Switzerland, United Kingdom. Pres. INGO KOBER (Germany); Chair. Admin. Council SEAN FITZPATRICK. Publs *Annual Report, Official Journal* (monthly), *European Patent Bulletin, European Patent Applications, Granted Patents.*

European Society for Opinion and Marketing Research—ESOMAR: Vondelstraat 172, 1054 GV Amsterdam, Netherlands; tel. (20) 664-21-41; fax (20) 664-29-22; e-mail email@esomar.nl; internet www.esomar.nl; f. 1948 to further professional interests and encourage high technical standards. Mems: more than 4,000 in 100 countries. Pres. JOHN KELLY (UK); Dir-Gen. JUERGEN SCHWOERER. Publs *Research World* (monthly), *ESOMAR Directory* (annually).

European Union of Coachbuilders: 46 Woluwedal, bte 14, 1200 Brussels, Belgium; tel. (2) 778-62-00; fax (2) 778-62-22; e-mail mail@ federauto.be; f. 1948 to promote research on questions affecting the industry, exchange information, and establish a common policy for the industry. Mems: national federations in Belgium, France, Germany, Italy, Luxembourg, Netherlands, Switzerland, United Kingdom. Pres. J. BLYWEERT (Belgium); Sec.-Gen. HILDE VANDER STICHELE (Belgium).

European Union of the Natural Gas Industry—EUROGAS: 4 ave Palmerston, 1000 Brussels, Belgium; tel. (2) 237-11-11; fax (2) 230-62-91; e-mail eurogas@arcadis.be. Mem. organizations in Austria, Belgium, Denmark, Finland, France, Germany, Ireland, Italy, Netherlands, Spain, Sweden, Switzerland, United Kingdom. Pres. B. BERGMANN (Germany); Gen. Sec. P. CLAUS (Belgium).

Federación de Cámaras de Comercio del Istmo Centroamericano (Federation of Central American Chambers of Commerce): Avda Cuba y Calle 33, Apdo 74, Panamá 1, Panama; tel. 227-1233; fax 227-4186; e-mail cciap@panama.phoenix.net; internet www.panacamara.com; f. 1961; for planning and co-ordinating industrial and commercial exchanges and exhibitions. Pres. EDGARDO R. CARLES; Exec. Dir JOSÉ RAMÓN VARELA C.

Federation of European Marketing Research Associations—FEMRA: Studio 38, Wimbledon Business Centre, Riverside Road, London, SW17 0BA, United Kingdom; tel. (20) 8879-0709; fax (20) 8947-2637; f. 1965 to facilitate contacts between researchers; main specialist divisions: European chemical marketing research; European technological forecasting; paper and related industries; industrial materials; automotive; textiles; methodology; information technology. Mems: 500. Pres. DAVID A. CLARK (Belgium).

General Union of Chambers of Commerce, Industry and Agriculture for Arab Countries: POB 11-2837, Beirut, Lebanon; tel. (1) 814269; fax (1) 862841; e-mail gucciaac@destination.com.lb; internet www.gucciaac.org.lb; f. 1951 to enhance Arab economic development, integration and security through the co-ordination of industrial, agricultural and trade policies and legislation. Mems: chambers of commerce, industry and agriculture in 22 Arab countries. Sec. Gen. Dr ELIAS GHANTOUS. Publs *Arab Economic Report, Al-Omran Al-Arabi* (every 2 months), economic papers, proceedings.

Global Crop Protection Federation—GCPF: ave Louise 143, 1050 Brussels, Belgium; tel. (2) 542-04-10; fax (2) 542-04-19; e-mail gcpf@pophost.eunet.be/; internet www.gcpf.org; f. 1960 as European Group of National Asscns of Pesticide Manufacturers; international body since 1967; present name adopted in 1996. Aims to harmonize national and international regulations concerning crop protection products, to support the development of the industry and to promote observation of the FAO Code of Conduct on the Distribution and Use of Pesticides. Mems: 6 regional asscns covering Africa/Middle East, Asia-Pacific, Europe, Latin America, North America and Japan. Dir-Gen. K. P. VLAHODIMOS.

Gulf Organization for Industrial Consulting: POB 5114, Doha, Qatar; tel. 858888; fax 831465; f. 1976 by the Gulf Arab states to encourage industrial co-operation among Gulf Arab states, and to pool industrial expertise and encourage joint development of projects; undertakes feasibility studies, market diagnosis, assistance in policy-making, legal consultancies, project promotion, promotion of small and medium industrial investment profiles and technical training; maintains industrial data bank. Mems: member states of Gulf Co-operation Council (q.v.). Sec.-Gen. Dr IHSAN ALI BU-HULAIGA (Saudi Arabia). Publs *GOIC Monthly Bulletin* (in Arabic), *Al Ta'awon al Sina'e* (quarterly, in Arabic and English).

Instituto Centroamericano de Administración de Empresas—INCDE (Central American Institute for Business Administration): Apdo 960, 4050 Alajuela, Costa Rica; tel. 443-0506; fax 433-9101; f. 1964; provides postgraduate programme in business administration; executive training programmes; management research and consulting; second campus in Nicaragua, libraries of 85,000 vols. Rector Dr BRIZZIO BIONDI-MORRA.

Inter-American Commercial Arbitration Commission: OAS Administration Bldg, Rm 211, 19th and Constitution Ave, NW, Washington, DC 20006, USA; tel. (202) 458-3249; fax (202) 458-3293; f. 1934 to establish an inter-American system of arbitration for the settlement of commercial disputes by means of tribunals. Mems: national committees, commercial firms and individuals in 22 countries. Dir-Gen. Dr ADRIANA POLANIA POLANIA.

International Advertising Association Inc: 521 Fifth Ave, Suite 1807, New York, NY 10175, USA; tel. (212) 557-1133; fax (212) 983-0455; e-mail iaaglobal@worldnet.att.net; internet www.iaaglobal .org; f. 1938; a global partnership of advertisers, agencies, the media and other marketing communications professionals; aims to protect freedom of commercial speech and consumer choice. Mems: more than 3,600 in 99 countries. World Congress held every 2 years, 2002: Lebanon. Pres. DAVID HANGER (UK); Dir-Gen. NORMAN VALE (USA). Publs *IAA Membership Directory and Annual Report, IAA World News.*

International Association of Buying Groups: 53119 Bonn 1, Vorgebirgsstr. 43, Germany; tel. (228) 985840; fax (228) 9858410; f. 1951 for research, documentation and compilation of statistics; holds annual conference. Mems: 300 buying groups in 13 countries. Sec.-Gen. Dr GÜNTER OLESCH.

International Association of Department Stores: 4 rue de Rome, 75008 Paris, France; tel. 1-42-94-02-02; fax 1-42-94-02-04; e-mail iads@iads.org; internet www.iads.org; f. 1928 to conduct research, exchange information and statistics on management, organization and technical problems; centre of documentation. Mems: large-scale retail enterprises in Andorra, Belgium, Czech Republic, Denmark, Finland, France, Germany, Italy, Lebanon, Netherlands, Singapore, Spain, Switzerland, United Kingdom. Pres. L. MANDAC (Germany); Gen. Sec. M. DE GROOT VAN EMBDEN (Netherlands). Publ. *Retail News Letter* (monthly).

International Association of Electrical Contractors: 5 rue Hamelin, 75116 Paris, France; tel. 1-44-05-84-20; fax 1-44-05-84-05; e-mail aie@wanadoo.fr; Pres. AAGE KJAERGAARD; Gen. Sec. DENIS HANNOTIN.

International Association of Scholarly Publishers: c/o Fred C. Bohm, Michigan State University Press, 1405 South Harrison Rd, East Lansing, MI 48823-5202, USA; tel. (517) 355-9543; fax (517) 432-2611; e-mail bohm@pilot.msu.edu; f. 1972 for the exchange of information and experience on scholarly and academic publishing by universities and others; assists in the transfer of publishing skills to developing countries. Mems: more than 140 in 38 countries. Pres. MICHAEL HUTER (Austria); Sec.-Gen. FRED C. BOHM (USA). Publs *IASP Newsletter* (every 2 months), *International Directory of Scholarly Publishers.*

International Association of the Soap, Detergent and Maintenance Products Industry: 49 sq. Marie-Louise, 1000 Brussels, Belgium; tel. (2) 230-83-71; fax (2) 230-82-88; e-mail a.i.s.e@euronet.be; f. 1967 to promote in all fields the manufacture and use of a wide range of cleaning products, polishes, bleaches, disinfectants and insecticides, to develop the exchange of statistical information and to study technical, scientific, economic and social problems of interest to its members. Mems: 31 national asscns in 25 countries. Pres. H. R. BIRCHER; Sec. P. COSTA (Belgium).

International Association of Textile Dyers and Printers: POB 518, 3900 AM Veenendaal, Netherlands; tel. (318) 564-488; fax (318) 564-487; e-mail krl@wxs.nl; f. 1967 to defend and promote the interests of members in international affairs and to provide a forum for discussion of matters of mutual interest. Mems: national trade associations representing dyers and printers in nine countries. Pres. M. TRONCONI (Italy); Sec.-Gen. C. LODIERS (Netherlands).

International Booksellers Federation—IBF: rue du Grand Hospice 34a, 1000 Belgium; tel. (2) 223-49-40; fax (2) 223-49-41; e-mail eurobooks@skynet.be; f. 1956 to promote the booktrade and the exchange of information and to protect the interests of booksellers when dealing with other international organizations; special committees deal with questions of postage, resale price maintenance, book market research, advertising, customs and tariffs, the problems of young booksellers, etc. Mems: 200 in 22 countries. Pres. YVONNE STEINBERGER; Sec.-Gen. CHRISTIANE VUIDAR. Publs *IBF-bulletin* (2 a year), *Booksellers International.*

International Bureau for the Standardization of Man-Made Fibres (BISFA): 4 ave van Nieuwenhuyse, 1160 Brussels, Belgium; tel. (2) 676-74-55; fax (2) 676-74-54; e-mail van@cirfs.org; internet www.bisfa.org; f. 1928 to examine and establish rules for the standardization, classification and naming of various categories of manmade fibres. Mems: 49. Sec.-Gen. J. SPIJKERS.

International Butchers' Confederation: 10 Bte, 4 rue Jacques de Lalaing, 1040 Brussels, Belgium; tel. (2) 230-38-76; fax (2) 230-34-51; e-mail info@cibc.be; f. 1907; aims to defend the interests of small and medium-sized enterprises in the meat trading and catering industry. Pres. ANTON KARL; Sec.-Gen. THEO WERSHOVEN.

International Confederation for Printing and Allied Industries—INTERGRAF: 18 sq. Marie-Louise, bte 25, 1040 Brussels, Belgium; tel. (2) 230-86-46; fax (2) 231-14-64; f. 1983 (formerly EUROGRAF, f. 1975) to defend the common interests of the printing and allied interests in member countries. Mems: federations in 20 countries. Pres. MARTIN HANDGRAAF; Sec.-Gen. GEOFFREY WILSON.

International Confederation of Art Dealers: 33 rue Ernest-Allard, 1000 Brussels, Belgium; tel. (2) 511-67-77; internet www .cinoa.org; f. 1936 to co-ordinate the work of associations of dealers in works of art and paintings and to contribute to artistic and economic expansion. Mems: associations in 24 countries. Pres. WALTER FEILCHENFELDT; Sec.-Gen. DORIS AMMANN.

International Co-operative Alliance—ICA: 15 route des Morillons, 1218 Grand-Saconnex, Geneva, Switzerland; tel. (22) 929-88-88; fax (22) 798-41-22; e-mail ica@coop.org; internet www.coop.org; f. 1895 for the pursuit of co-operative aims. A General Assembly and four Regional Assemblies meet every two years, on an alternating basis; a 20-member ICA Board controls the affairs of the organization between meetings of the General Assembly. Specialized bodies have been established to promote co-operative activities in the following fields: agriculture, banking, fisheries, consumer affairs, energy, tourism, communications, co-operative research, health, human resources, wholesale distribution, housing, insurance, women's participation and industrial and artisanal and service producers' co-operatives. Mems: 242 affiliated national orgs, with a total membership of more than 760m. individuals in 100 countries and four int. orgs. Pres. ROBERTO RODRIGUES (Brazil); Dir-Gen. BRUCE THORDARSON (Canada). Publs *Review of International Co-operation* (quarterly), *ICA News* (every 2 months), *Co-op Dialogue* (2 a year).

International Council of Societies of Industrial Design—ICSID: Erottajankatu 11A, 00130 Helsinki, Finland; tel. (9) 6962290; fax (9) 69622910; e-mail icsidsec@icsid.org; internet www.icsid.org; f. 1957 to encourage the development of high standards in the practice of industrial design; to improve and expand the contribution of industrial design throughout the world. Mems: 150 in 53 countries. Pres. AUGUSTO MORELLO (Italy); Sec.-Gen. KAARINA POHTO. Publs *ICSID News, World Directory of Design Schools.*

International Council of Tanners: Leather Trade House, Kings Park Rd, Moulton Park, Northampton, NN3 6JD, United Kingdom; tel. (1604) 679917; fax (1604) 679998; e-mail sec@tannerscounciliat .com; internet www.tannerscouncil.org; f. 1926 to study all questions relating to the leather industry and maintain contact with national associations. Mems: national tanners' organizations in 33 countries. Pres. TONY MOSSOP (South Africa); Sec. PAUL PEARSON (UK).

International Exhibitions Bureau: 56 ave Victor Hugo, Paris 16e, France; tel. 1-45-00-38-63; fax 1-45-00-96-15; e-mail bie@bie-paris.org; internet www.bie-paris.org; f. 1928, revised by Protocol 1972, for the authorization and registration of international exhibitions falling under the 1928 Convention. Mems: 88 states. Pres. GILLES NOGHES; Sec.-Gen. VICENTE GONZALES LOSCERTALES.

International Federation of Associations of Textile Chemists and Colourists—IFATCC: Postfach 403, 4153 Reinach 1, Switzerland; e-mail markus.krayer@cibas.com; f. 1930 for liaison on professional matters between members; and the furtherance of scientific and technical collaboration in the development of the textile finishing industry and the colouring of materials. Mems: in 22 countries. Pres. ALAIN MADOUX (France); Sec. MARKUS KRAYER (Switzerland).

International Federation of Grocers' Associations—IFGA: Vakcentrum, Woerden, Netherlands; tel. (348) 419771; fax (348) 421801; f. 1927; initiates special studies and works to further the interests of members having special regard to new conditions resulting from European integration and developments in consuming and distribution. Mems: 500,000.

International Federation of Insurance Intermediaries (Bureau International des Producteurs d'Assurances et de Réassurances—BIPAR): 40 ave Albert-Elisabeth, 1200 Brussels, Belgium; tel. (2) 735-60-48; fax (2) 732-14-18; e-mail bipar@sky-net.be; f. 1937. Mems: 43 asscns from 26 countries, representing approx. 250,000 brokers and agents. Pres. VICTOR GALCERAN; Dir HARALD KRAUSS. Publ. *BIPAR Intern* (quarterly).

International Federation of Pharmaceutical Manufacturers Associations—IFPMA: 30 rue de St Jean, POB 758, 1211 Geneva 13, Switzerland; tel. (22) 3383200; fax (22) 3383299; internet www.ifpma.org; f. 1968 for the exchange of information and international co-operation in all questions of interest to the pharmaceutical industry, particularly in the field of health legislation, science and research; development of ethical principles and practices and co-operation with national and international organizations, governmental and non-governmental. Mems: the national pharmaceutical associations of 60 countries and one regional association (representing Latin America). Pres. Prof. ROLF KREBS (Germany); Dir-Gen. Dr HARVEY E. BALE Jr (USA). Publs *IPFMA Code of Pharmaceutical Marketing Practices, Health Horizons* (3 a year), action papers, occasional publications.

International Federation of the Phonographic Industry—IFPI: 54 Regent St, London, W1R 5PJ, United Kingdom; tel. (20) 7878-7900; fax (20) 7878-7950; e-mail info@ifpi.org; internet www.ifpi.org; f. 1933; represents the interests of record producers by campaigning for the introduction, improvement and enforcement of copyright and related rights legislation and co-ordinating the recording industry's anti-piracy activities. Mems: 1,476 in 73 countries. Chair. and Chief Exec. JASON BERMAN.

International Fertilizer Industry Association: 28 rue Marbeuf, 75008 Paris, France; tel. 1-53-93-05-00; fax 1-53-93-05-45; e-mail ifa@fertilizer.org; internet www.fertilizer.org; Pres. C. E. CHILDERS; Sec.-Gen. L. M. MAENE.

International Fragrance Association—IFRA: 48 sq. Marie Louise, 1000 Brussels, Belgium; tel. (2) 2389907; fax (2) 2300265; e-mail secretariat@ifraorg.org; f. 1973 to collect and study scientific data on fragrance materials and to make recommendations on their safe use. Mems: national asscns in 14 countries. Pres. R. FENN; Exec. Dir M. WAGNER.

International Fur Trade Federation: POB 495, Weybridge, KT13 8WD, United Kingdom; internet www.iftf.com; f. 1949 to promote and organize joint action by fur trade organizations for promoting, developing and protecting trade in fur skins and/or processing thereof. Mems: 33 organizations in 27 countries. Exec. Dir J. BAILEY.

International Group of National Associations of Manufacturers of Agrochemical Products: 79A ave Albert Lancaster, 1180 Brussels, Belgium; tel. (2) 375-68-60; f. 1967 to encourage the rational use of chemicals in agriculture, the harmonization of national and international legislation, and the respect of industrial property rights; encourages research on chemical residues and toxicology. Mems: associations in 50 countries. Dir-Gen. HANS G. VAN LOEPER.

International Meat Secretariat (Office International de la Viande): 17 pl. des Vins de France, 75012 Paris, France; tel. 1-44-68-84-54; fax 1-44-68-84-53; e-mail ims@wanadoo.fr; internet www.meat-ims.org. Pres. PHILIP M. SENG; Sec.-Gen. LAURENCE WRIXON.

International Organization of Motor Manufacturers: 4 rue de Berri, 75008 Paris; tel. 1-43-59-00-13; fax 1-45-63-84-41; e-mail oica@club-internet.fr; f. 1919 to co-ordinate and further the interests of the automobile industry, to promote the study of economic and other matters affecting automobile construction; to control automobile manufacturers' participation in international exhibitions in Europe. Mems: manufacturers' associations of 16 European countries, China, Japan, the Republic of Korea and the USA; 38 assoc. mems. Gen. Sec. J. M. MULLER. Publ. *Yearbook of the World's Motor Industry.*

International Organization of the Flavour Industry—IOFI: 49 sq. Marie Louise, 1000 Brussels, Belgium; tel. (2) 2389904; fax (2) 2300265; e-mail secretariat@iofiorg.org; f. 1969 to support and promote the flavour industry; active in the fields of safety evaluation and regulation of flavouring substances. Mems: national associations in 21 countries. Pres. M. DAVIS; Exec. Dir M. WAGNER. Publs *Documentation Bulletin, Information Letters, Code of Practice.*

International Publishers' Association: 3 ave de Miremont, 1206 Geneva, Switzerland; tel. (22) 3463018; fax (22) 3475717; e-mail secretariat@ipa-uie.org; internet www.ipa-uie.org; f. 1896 to defend the freedom of publishers, promote their interests and foster international co-operation; helps the international trade in books and music, works on international copyright, and translation rights. Mems: 74 professional book publishers' organizations in 65 countries and music publishers' associations in 20 countries. Pres. ALAIN GRÜND; Sec.-Gen. J. ALEXIS KOUTCHOUMOW.

International Rayon and Synthetic Fibres Committee—CIRFS: 4 ave E. van Nieuwenhuyse, 1160 Brussels, Belgium; tel. (2) 676-74-55; fax (2) 676-74-54; e-mail info@cirfs.org; internet www.cirfs.org; f. 1950 to improve the quality and use of man-made fibres and of products made from fibres. Mems: individual producers in 24 countries. Pres. FOLKERT BLAISSE; Dir-Gen. C. PURVIS (UK). Publs *Statistical Booklet* (annually), market reports, technical test methods.

International Shopfitting Organisation: Gladbachstr. 80, 8044 Zürich, Switzerland; tel. (1) 2678100; fax (1) 2678150; e-mail petra

.isenberg@vssm.ch; internet www.shopfitting.org; f. 1959 to promote interchange of ideas between individuals and firms concerned with the common interests of shopfitting. Mems: companies in 13 countries. Pres. J. BREITENMOSER; Sec. PETRA ISENBERG.

International Textile Manufacturers Federation—ITMF: Am Schanzengraben 29, Postfach, 8039 Zürich, Switzerland; tel. (1) 2017080; fax (1) 2017134; e-mail secretariat@itmf.org; internet www.itmf.org; f. 1904, present title adopted 1978. Aims to protect and promote the interests of its members, to disseminate information, and encourage co-operation. Mems: national textile trade associations in about 50 countries. Pres. HERBERT SCHMID (Brazil); Dir-Gen. Dr HERWIG STROLZ (Austria). Publs *State of Trade Report* (quarterly), various statistics.

International Union of Marine Insurance: Gotthardstr. 3, POB 6304, Zug, Switzerland; tel. (41) 7293966; fax (41) 7293967; e-mail mail@iumi.com; internet www.iumi.com; f. 1873 to collect and distribute information on marine insurance on a world-wide basis. Mems: 54 associations. Pres. GEORG MEHL (Germany); Gen. Sec. STEFAN PELLER.

International Wool Textile Organisation: 63 Albert Drive, London, SW19 6LB, United Kingdom; tel. (20) 8788-8876; fax (20) 8788-5171; f. 1929 to link wool textile organizations in member-countries and represent their interests; holds annual International Wool Conference. Mems: in 28 countries. Pres. H. GRUNZKE (Germany); Sec.-Gen. W. H. LAKIN (UK).

International Wrought Copper Council: 6 Bathurst St, Sussex Sq., London, W2 2SD, United Kingdom; tel. (20) 7724-7465; fax (20) 7724-0308; e-mail iwcc@coppercouncil.org; internet www.copper-council.org; f. 1953 to link and represent copper fabricating industries, and to represent the views of copper consumers to raw material producers; organizes specialist activities on technical work and the development of copper. Mems: 17 national groups in Europe, Australia, Japan and Malaysia, 7 assoc. mems. Chair. SEPPO KREULA; Sec.-Gen. SIMON PAYTON.

Liaison Group of the European Mechanical, Electrical, Electronic and Metalworking Industries: Diamant Bldg, 80 blvd Reyers, 1030 Brussels, Belgium; tel. (2) 511-34-84; fax (2) 512-99-70; e-mail secretariat@orgalime.be; f. 1954 to provide a permanent liaison between the mechanical, electrical and electronic engineering, and metalworking industries of member countries. Mems: 25 trade associations in 16 European countries. Pres. ENRICO MASSIMO CARLE (Italy); Sec.-Gen. PATRICK KNOX-PEEBLES.

Union des Foires Internationales—UFI (Union of International Fairs): 35 bis, rue Jouffroy d'Abbans, 75017 Paris, France; tel. 1-42-67-99-12; fax 1-42-27-19-29; e-mail info@ufinet.org; internet www.ufinet.org; f. 1925 to increase co-operation between international trade fairs/exhibitions, safeguard their interests and extend their operations; holds annual congress and educational seminars. The Union has defined the conditions to be fulfilled to qualify as an international trade fair/exhibition, and is concerned with the standards of the events. It studies improvements which could be made in the conditions of the fairs/exhibitions and organizes educational seminars. Mems: 179 organizers with 601 approved events, 34 assoc. mems in 71 countries. Pres. Prof. MANFRED BUSCHE (Germany); Sec.-Gen. GERDA MARQUARDT (France).

Union of Industrial and Employers' Confederations of Europe—UNICE: 40 rue Joseph II, 1000 Brussels, Belgium; tel. (2) 237-65-11; fax (2) 231-14-45; e-mail main@unice.be; internet www.unice.org; f. 1958; aims to ensure that European Community policy-making takes account of the views of European business; committees and working groups work out joint positions in the various fields of interest to business and submit them to the Community institutions concerned. The Council of Presidents (of member federations) lays down general policy; the Executive Committee (of Directors-General of member federations) is the managing body; and the Committee of Permanent Delegates, consisting of federation representatives in Brussels, ensures permanent liaison with members. Mems: 20 industrial and employers' federations from the EU member states, and 14 federations from non-EU countries. Pres. GEORGES JACOBS; Sec.-Gen. (vacant). Publ. *UNICE@News* (monthly, by e-mail).

World Customs Organization—WCO: 30 rue du Marché, 1210 Brussels, Belgium; tel. (2) 209-92-11; fax (2) 209-92-92; e-mail info@wcoomd.org; internet www.wcoomd.org; f. 1952 as Customs Co-operation Council; an independent intergovernmental body that aims to enhance the effectiveness and efficiency of customs administrations in the areas of compliance with trade regulations; the protection of society; and revenue collection. Mems: governments of 153 countries or territories. Chair. Dr OBAID SAQER BUSIT (United Arab Emirates); Sec.-Gen. MICHEL DANET (France). Publ. *WCO News* (2 a year).

World Federation of Advertisers: 120 ave Louise, 1050 Brussels; tel. (2) 502-57-40; fax (2) 502-56-66; e-mail info@wfa.be; internet www.wfa.be/; f. 1953; promotes and studies advertising and its related problems; 2001 world congress: Tokyo, Japan. Mems: associations in 42 countries and 24 international companies. Pres. HANS MERKLE; Dir-Gen. BERNHARD ADRIAENSENS. Publ. *E-Monitor* (monthly).

World Packaging Organisation: 481 Carlisle Dr., Herndon, VA 20170-4823, USA; tel. (703) 318-5512; fax (703) 814-4961; e-mail wpo@pkgmatters.com; internet www.packinfo-world.org; f. 1967 to provide a forum for the exchange of knowledge of packaging technology and, in general, to create conditions for the conservation, preservation and distribution of world food production; holds annual congress and competition. Mems: Asian, North American, Latin American, European and South African packaging federations. Pres. SERGIO HABERFELD (Brazil); Gen. Sec. WILLIAM C. PFLAUM (USA).

World Trade Centers Association: One World Trade Center, Suite 7701, New York, NY 10048, USA; tel. (212) 432-2626; fax (212) 488-0064; internet www.wtca.org/; f. 1968 to promote trade through the establishment of world trade centres, including education facilities, information services and exhibition facilities; operates an electronic trading and communication system (WTC On-Line). Mems: trade centres, chambers of commerce and other organizations in 95 countries. Pres. GUY F. TOZZOLI; Chair. BRYAN MONTGOMERY. Publ. *WTCA News* (monthly).

Transport

African Airlines Association: POB 20116, Nairobi, Kenya; tel. (2) 604925; fax (2) 601173; e-mail afraa@africaonline.co.ke; internet www.afraa.org; f. 1968 to give African air companies expert advice in technical, financial, juridical and market matters; to improve air transport in Africa through inter-carrier co-operation; and to develop manpower resources. Mems: 34 national carriers.

Airports Council International—ACI: POB 16, 1215 Geneva 15-Airport, Switzerland; tel. (22) 7178585; fax (22) 7178888; e-mail aci@airports.org; internet www.airports.org; f. 1991, following merger of Airport Operators Council International and International Civil Airports Association; aims to represent and develop co-operation among airports of the world. Mems: 554 operating more than 1,400 airports in 165 countries and territories. Chair. A. GHANEM AL-HAJRI; Dir-Gen. JONATHAN HOWE; Sec.-Gen. ALEXANDER STRAHL.

Arab Air Carriers' Organization—AACO: PO Box 13-5468, Beirut, Lebanon; tel. (1) 861297; fax (1) 863168; e-mail info@aaco.org; f. 1965 to promote co-operation in the activities of Arab airline companies. Mems: 20 Arab air carriers. Pres. AKBAR AL-BAKER (Qatar); Sec.-Gen. ABDUL WAHAB TEFFAHA. Publs *bulletins, reports and research documents*.

Association of Asia Pacific Airlines: 5/F Corporate Business Centre, 151 Paseo de Roxas, 1226 Makati, Philippines; tel. (2) 8403191; fax (2) 8103518; e-mail aapahdq@aapa.org.ph; f. 1966 as Orient Airlines Asscn; present name adopted in April 1997; member carriers exchange information and plan the development of the industry within the region by means of commercial, technical and management information committees. Mems: Air New Zealand, Air Niugini, All Nippon Airways, Ansett Australia, Asiana Airlines, Cathay Pacific Airways, China Airlines, Dragonair, EVA Airways, Garuda Indonesia, Japan Airlines, Korean Air, Malaysia Airlines, Philippine Airlines, Qantas Airways, Royal Brunei Airlines, Singapore Airlines, Thai Airways International and Viet Nam Airlines. Dir.-Gen. RICHARD T. STIRLAND. Publs *AAPA Annual and Statistical Report, Orient Aviation*.

Association of European Airlines: 350 ave Louise, Bte 4, 1050 Brussels, Belgium; tel. (2) 639-89-89; fax (2) 639-89-90; e-mail aea.secretariat@aca.be; internet www.aea.be; f. 1954 to carry out research on political, commercial, economic and technical aspects of air transport; maintains statistical data bank. Mems: 29 airlines. Chair. JEAN-CYRIL SPINETTA (France); Sec.-Gen. KARL-HEINZ NEUMEISTER (Germany).

Baltic and International Maritime Council—BIMCO: Bagsvaerdvej 161, 2880 Bagsvaerd, Denmark; tel. 44-44-45-00; fax 44-44-44-50; e-mail mailbox@bimco.dk; internet www.bimco.dk; f. 1905 to unite shipowners and other persons and organizations connected with the shipping industry. Mems: in 115 countries, representing over 60% of world merchant tonnage. Pres. PHILIPPE POIRIER D'ANGE D'ORSAY (France); Sec.-Gen. FINN FRANDSEN.

Central Commission for the Navigation of the Rhine: Palais du Rhin, Place de la République, 67000 Strasbourg, France; tel. 3-88-52-20-10; fax 3-88-32-10-72; e-mail ccmr@ccr-zkr.org; f. 1815 to ensure free movement of traffic and standard river facilities to ships of all nations; draws up navigational rules, standardizes customs regulations, arbitrates in disputes involving river traffic, approves plans for river maintenance work; there is an administrative centre for social security for boatmen. Mems: Belgium, France, Germany, Netherlands, Switzerland. Sec.-Gen. JEAN-MARIE WOEHRLING (France).

Danube Commission: Benczúr utca 25, 1068 Budapest, Hungary; tel. (1) 352-1835; fax (1) 352-1839; e-mail dunacom@mail.matav.hu; internet www.dunacom.matav.hu; f. 1948; supervises implementation of the convention on the regime of navigation on the Danube; holds annual sessions; approves projects for river maintenance, supervises a uniform system of traffic regulations on the whole navigable portion of the Danube and on river inspection. Mems: Austria, Bulgaria, Croatia, Germany, Hungary, Moldova, Romania, Russia, Slovakia, Ukraine, Yugoslavia. Pres. Dr H. STRASSER; Dir-Gen. Capt. D. NEDIALKOV. Publs *Basic Regulations for Navigation on the Danube, Hydrological Yearbook, Statistical Yearbook*, proceedings of sessions.

European Civil Aviation Conference—ECAC: 3 bis Villa Emile-Bergerat, 92522 Neuilly-sur-Seine Cédex, France; tel. 1-46-41-85-44; fax 1-46-24-18-18; e-mail 101575.1313@compuserve.com; internet www.ecac-ceac.org; f. 1955; aims to promote the continued development of a safe, efficient and sustainable European air transport system. Mems: 38 European states. Pres. ALFREDO ROMA; Exec. Sec. RAYMOND BENJAMIN.

European Conference of Ministers of Transport—ECMT: 2 rue André Pascal, 75775 Paris Cédex 16, France; tel. 1-45-24-82-00; fax 1-45-24-97-42; e-mail ecmt.contact@oecd.org; internet www.oecd .org/cem; f. 1953 to achieve the maximum use and most rational development of European inland transport. Council of Ministers of Transport meets annually; Committee of Deputy Ministers meets three times a year and is assisted by Subsidiary Bodies concerned with: General Transport Policy, Railways, Roads, Inland Waterways, Investment, Road and Traffic Signs and Signals, Urban Safety, Economic Research, and other matters. Shares Secretariat staff with OECD (q.v.). Mems: 40 European countries; Associate Mems: Australia, Canada, Japan, New Zealand, USA. Sec.-Gen. G. AURBACH.

European Organisation for the Safety of Air Navigation—EUROCONTROL: 96 rue de la Fusée, 1130 Brussels, Belgium; tel. (2) 729-90-11; fax (2) 729-90-44; internet www.eurocontrol.be; f. 1963 principal objective is the development of a coherent and co-ordinated air traffic control system in Europe. A revised Convention was signed in June 1997, incorporating the following institutional structure: a General Assembly (known as the Commission in the transitional period), a Council (known as the Provisional Council) and an Agency under the supervision of the Director General; there are directorates, covering human resources and finance matters and a general secretariat. A special organizational structure covers the management of the European Air Traffic Management Programme. EUROCONTROL also operates the Experimental Centre (at Brétigny-sur-Orge, France), the Institute of Air Navigation Services (in Luxembourg), the Central Route Charges Office, the Central Flow Management Unit (both in Brussels) and the Upper Area Control Centre (in Maastricht, Netherlands). Budget (1999) €515m. Mems: Austria, Belgium, Bulgaria, Croatia, Cyprus, Czech Republic, Denmark, France, Germany, Greece, Hungary, Ireland, Italy, Luxembourg, the former Yugoslav republic of Macedonia, Malta, Monaco, Netherlands, Norway, Portugal, Romania, Slovakia, Slovenia, Spain, Sweden, Switzerland, Turkey, United Kingdom. Dir-Gen. YVES LAMBERT (France).

European Railway Wagon Pool—EUROP: SNCB/NMBS, B-Cargo 407, Section 2014, 60 rue du Trône, 1050 Brussels, Belgium; tel. (2) 525-88-55; fax (2) 525-86-91; f. 1953 for the common use of wagons put into the pool by member railways. Mems: national railway administrations of Austria, Belgium, Denmark, France, Germany, Italy, Luxembourg, Netherlands, Switzerland. Managing railway: Belgian Railways. Pres. A. MARTENS.

Forum Train Europe—FTE: Direction générale des chemins de fer fédéraux suisses, Hochschulstrasse 6, 3030 Berne, Switzerland; f. 1923 as the European Passenger Train Time-Table Conference to arrange international passenger connections by rail and water; since 1997 concerned also with rail freight. Mems: rail and steamship companies and administrations. Administered by the Directorate of the Swiss Federal Railways. Pres. P. A. URECH.

Institute of Air Transport: 103 rue la Boétie, 75008 Paris, France; tel. 1-43-59-38-68; fax 1-43-59-47-37; e-mail contac@ita-paris.com; internet www.ita-paris.com; f. 1945 as an international centre of research on economic, technical and policy aspects of air transport, and on the economy and sociology of transport and tourism; acts as economic and technical consultant in carrying out research requested by members on specific subjects; maintains a data bank, a library and a consultation and advice service; organizes training courses on air transport economics. Mems: organizations involved in air transport, production and equipment, universities, banks, insurance companies, private individuals and government agencies in 79 countries. Dir-Gen. JACQUES PAVAUX. Publs (in French and English), *ITA Press* (2 a month), *ITA Studies and Reports* (quarterly), *Aviation Industry Barometer* (quarterly).

Intergovernmental Organization for International Carriage by Rail: Gryphenhübeliweg 30, 3006 Berne, Switzerland; tel. (31) 3591010; fax (31) 3591011; e-mail otif@otif.ch; internet www.otif.ch; f. 1893 as Central Office for International Carriage by Rail, present name adopted 1985; aims to establish and develop a uniform system of law governing the international carriage of passengers, luggage and goods by rail in member states, which between them have a total of 240,000 km of railway lines. Mems: 40 states. Dir-Gen. HANS RUDOLF ISLIKER. Publ. *Bulletin des Transports Internationaux ferroviaires* (quarterly, in French and German).

International Air Transport Association—IATA: 33 route de l'Aéroport, CP 416, 1215 Geneva 15, Switzerland; tel. (22) 7992525; fax (22) 7983553; e-mail information@iata.org; internet www.iata .org; f. 1945 to represent and serve the airline industry. Aims to promote safe, reliable and secure air services; to assist the industry to attain adequate levels of profitability while developing cost-effective operational standards; to promote the importance of the industry to global social and economic development; and to identify common concerns and represent the industry in addressing these at regional and international level. Maintains regional offices in Amman, Brussels, Dakar, London, Nairobi, Santiago, Singapore and Washington, DC. Mems: 258 airline cos. Dir-Gen. PIERRE JEANNIOT; Corporate Sec. LORNE CLARK. Publ. *Airlines International* (every 2 months).

International Association for the Rhine Vessels Register—IVR: Vasteland 12E, 3011 BL Rotterdam (POB 23210, 3001 KE Rotterdam), Netherlands; tel. (10) 4116070; fax (10) 4129091; e-mail info@ivr.ne; internet www.ivr.ne; f. 1947 for the classification of Rhine ships, the organization and publication of a Rhine ships register, the unification of general average rules, and the harmonization of European inland navigation law. Mems: shipowners and associations, insurers and associations, shipbuilding engineers, average adjusters and others interested in Rhine traffic. Gen. Sec. T. K. HACKSTEINER.

International Association of Ports and Harbors: Kono Bldg, 1-23-9 Nishi-Shimbashi, Minato-ku, Tokyo 105, Japan; tel. (3) 3591-4261; fax (3) 3580-0364; e-mail iaph@msn.com; internet www .iaph.or.jp; f. 1955 to increase the efficiency of ports and harbours through the dissemination of information relative to the fields of port organization, management, administration, operation, development and promotion; to encourage the growth of water-borne commerce; holds conference every two years. Mems: 350 in 85 states. Pres. DOMINIC J. TADDEO (Canada); Sec.-Gen. SATOSHI INOUE (Japan). Publs *Ports and Harbors* (10 a year), *Membership Directory* (annually).

International Assocation of Public Transport: 17 ave Herrmann-Debroux, 1160 Brussels, Belgium; tel. (2) 673-61-00; fax (2) 660-10-72; e-mail administration@uitp.com; internet www.uitp.com; f. 1885 to study all problems connected with the urban and regional public passenger transport industry. Mems: 2,000 in 80 countries. Pres. JEAN-PAUL BAILLY (France); Sec.-Gen. HANS RAT. Publs *Public Transport International* (every 2 months), *EUExpress, Mobility News* (monthly, electronic), Statistics reports.

International Chamber of Shipping: Carthusian Court, 12 Carthusian St, London, EC1M 6EZ, United Kingdom; tel. (20) 7417-8844; fax (20) 7417-8877; e-mail ics@marisec.org; internet www.marisec.org; f. 1921 to co-ordinate the views of the international shipping industry on matters of common interest, in the policy-making, technical and legal fields of shipping operations. Mems: national associations representative of free-enterprise shipowners and operators in 39 countries, covering 50% of world merchant shipping. Sec.-Gen. J. C. S. HORROCKS.

International Container Bureau: 167 rue de Courcelles, 75017 Paris, France; tel. 1-47-66-03-90; fax 1-47-66-08-91; f. 1933 to group representatives of all means of transport and activities concerning containers, to promote combined door-to-door transport by the successive use of several means of transport; to examine and bring into effect administrative, technical and customs advances and to centralize data on behalf of its members. Mems: 800. Sec.-Gen. JEAN REY. Publ. *Container Bulletin*.

International Federation of Freight Forwarders' Associations: Baumackerstr. 24, POB 8050 Zürich, Switzerland; tel. (1) 3116511; fax (1) 3119044; e-mail info@fiata.com; internet www.fiat-a.com; f. 1926 to protect and represent its members at international level. Mems: 95 organizations and more than 2,500 associate members in 150 countries. Pres. CHRISTOPHER GILLESPIE; Dir MARCO A. SANGALETTI. Publ. *FIATA Review* (every 2 months).

International Rail Transport Committee (Comité international des transports ferroviaires—CIT): 10a Bahnhofplatz , 3000 Berne 65, Switzerland; tel. (512) 202806; fax (512) 203457; e-mail cit@sbb.ch; internet www.cit.ch; f. 1902 for the development of international law relating to railway transport on the basis of the Convention concerning International Carriage by Rail (COTIF) and its Appendices (CIV, CIM), and for the adoption of standard rules on other questions relating to international transport law. Mems: 300 transport undertakings in 37 countries. Pres. M. WEIBEL (Switzerland); Sec. M. LEIMGRUBER (Switzerland).

International Railway Congress Association: Section 10, 85 rue de France, 1060 Brussels, Belgium; tel. (2) 520-78-31; fax (2) 525-40-84; e-mail secretariat@aiccf.org; internet www.aiccf.org; f. 1885 to facilitate the progress and development of railways by holding periodical congresses and by issuing publications. Mems: governments, railway administrations and national or international organizations. Pres. E. SCHOUPPE; Sec.-Gen. A. MARTENS. Publ. *Rail International* (monthly).

International Road Federation—IRF: Washington office: 1010 Massachusetts Ave, NW, Suite 410, Washington, DC 20037, USA; tel. (202) 371-5544; fax (202) 371-5565; e-mail info@irfnet.org; internet www.irfnet.org; Geneva Office: 2 chemin de Blandonnet 1214, Vernier, Geneva, Switzerland; tel. (22) 3060260; fax (22) 3060270; f. 1948 to encourage the development and improvement of highways and highway transportation; organizes IRF world and regional meetings. Mems: 70 national road associations and 500 individual firms and industrial associations. Dir-Gen. (Washington) GERALD P. SHEA; Dir-Gen. (Geneva) M. W. WESTERHUIS. Publs *World Road Statistics* (annually), *World Highways* (8 a year).

International Road Safety (La Prevention Routière Internationale—PRI): Estrada da Luz , 90-1°, 1600-160 Lisbon, Portugal; tel. (21) 3513740; fax (21) 3582871; e-mail info@lapri.org; internet www.lapri.org; f. 1959 for exchange of ideas and material on road safety; organizes international action and congresses; assists non-member countries. Mems: 74 national organizations. Pres. JOSÉ MIGUEL TRIGOSO (Portugal); Sec.-Gen. MARTINE PETERS. Publ. *Newsletter* (6 a year).

International Road Transport Union—IRU: Centre International, 3 rue de Varembé, BP 44, 1211 Geneva, Switzerland; tel. (22) 9182700; fax (22) 9182741; e-mail iru@iru.org; internet www.iru.org; f. 1948 to study all problems of road transport, to promote unification and simplification of regulations relating to road transport, and to develop the use of road transport for passengers and goods. Represents and promotes the industry at an international level. Mems: 179 national asscns in 67 countries. Dir MARTIN MARMY.

International Shipping Federation: Carthusian Court, 12 Carthusian St, London, EC1M 6EZ, United Kingdom; tel. (20) 7417-8844; fax (20) 7417-8877; e-mail isf@marisec.org; internet www.marisec.org; f. 1909 to consider all personnel questions affecting the interests of shipowners; responsible for Shipowners' Group at conferences of the International Labour Organisation. Mems: national shipowners' organizations in 34 countries. Pres. R. WESTFAL-LARSON (Germany); Sec.-Gen. J. C. S. HORROCKS.

International Union for Inland Navigation: 7 quai du Général Koenig, 67085 Strasbourg Cédex, France; tel. 3-88-36-28-44; fax 3-88-37-04-82; f. 1952 to promote the interests of inland waterways carriers. Mems: national waterways organizations of Austria, Belgium, France, Germany, Italy, Luxembourg, Netherlands, Switzerland. Pres. PH. GRULOIS (Belgium); Sec. M. RUSCHER. Publs annual and occasional reports.

International Union of Railways (Union Internationale des Chemins de fer —UIC): 16 rue Jean-Rey, 75015 Paris, France; tel. 1-44-49-20-20; fax 1-44-49-20-29; e-mail communication@uic.asso.fr; internet www.uic.asso.fr; f. 1922 for the harmonization of railway operations and the development of international rail transport; aims to ensure international interoperability of the rail system; compiles information concerning economic, management and technical aspects of railways; co-ordinates research and collaborates with industry and the EU; organizes international conferences. Mems: 150 railways in 87 countries. Pres. MIGUEL CORSINI; Chief Exec. PHILIPPE ROUMEGUÈRE. Publs *Rail International*, jointly with the International Railway Congress Association (IRCA) (monthly, in English, French and German), *International Railway Statistics* (annually), *Activities Reports, UIC Panorama* (newsletter).

Northern Shipowners' Defence Club (Nordisk Skibsrederforening): Kristinelundv. 22, POB 3033 El., 0207 Oslo, Norway; tel. 22-13-56-00; fax 22-43-00-35; e-mail post@nordiskskibsrederforening.no; f. 1889 to assist members in disputes over charter parties, contracts, sale and purchase, taking the necessary legal steps on behalf of members and bearing the cost of such claims. Members are mainly Finnish, Swedish and Norwegian and some non-Scandinavian shipowners, representing about 1,800 ships and drilling rigs with gross tonnage of about 50 million. Man. Dir GEORG SCHEEL; Chair. MORTEN WERRING. Publ. *A Law Report of Scandinavian Maritime Cases* (annually).

Organisation for the Collaboration of Railways: Hozà 63–67, 00681 Warsaw, Poland; tel. (22) 6573600; fax (22) 6573654; e-mail osjd@osjd.org.pl; f. 1956; aims to improve standards and co-operation in railway traffic between countries of Europe and Asia; promotes co-operation on issues relating to traffic policy and economic and environmental aspects of railway traffic; ensures enforcement of the following agreements: Convention concerning international passenger traffic by railway; Regulation concerning the use of wagons in international traffic; International passenger tariff; Standard transit tariff to the convention concerning international goods traffic by rail; and contracts referring to the international transport of passengers and goods. Aims to elaborate and standardize general principles for international transport law. Conference of Ministers of member countries meets annually; Conference of Gen. Dirs of Railways meets at least once a year. Mems: ministries of transport of Albania, Azerbaijan, Belarus, Bulgaria, People's Republic of China, Cuba, Czech Republic, Estonia, Georgia, Hungary, Iran, Kazakhstan, Democratic People's Republic of Korea, Kyrgyzstan, Latvia, Lithuania, Moldova, Mongolia, Poland, Romania, Russia, Slovakia, Tajikistan, Turkmenistan, Ukraine, Uzbekistan, Viet Nam. Chair. TADEUSZ SZOZDA. Publ. *OSShD Journal* (every 2 months, in Chinese, German and Russian).

Pan American Railway Congress Association (Asociación del Congreso Panamericano de Ferrocarriles): Av. 9 de Julio 1925, 13°, 1332 Buenos Aires, Argentina; tel. (11) 4381-4625; fax (11) 4814-1823; e-mail acpf@nat.com.ar; f. 1907; present title adopted 1941; aims to promote the development and progress of railways in the American continent; holds Congresses every three years. Mems: government representatives, railway enterprises and individuals in 21 countries. Pres. JUAN CARLOS DE MARCHI (Argentina); Gen. Sec. LUIS V. DONZELLI (Argentina). Publ. *Technical Bulletin* (every 2 months).

Union of European Railway Industries—UNIFE: 221 ave Louise, 1050 Brussels, Belgium; tel. (2) 626-12-60; fax (2) 626-12-61; e-mail mail@unife.org; f. 1975 to represent companies concerned in the manufacture of railway equipment in Europe, in order to represent their collective interests towards all European and international organizations concerned. Mems: 140 companies in 14 countries; Chair. ROLF ECKRODT; Dir Gen. DREWIN NIEUWENHUIS.

World Airlines Clubs Association: c/o IATA, 800 Pl. Victoria, POB 113, Montréal, Québec, Canada H3A 2R4; tel. (514) 874-0202; fax (514) 874-1753; internet www.waca.org/; f. 1966; holds a General Assembly annually, regional meetings, international events and sports tournaments. Mems: clubs in 38 countries. Man. AUBREY WINTERBOTHAM. Publs *WACA World, WACA Contact, WACA World News,* annual report.

Youth and Students

AIESEC International: Teilingerstraat 126–128, 3032 Rotterdam, Netherlands; tel. (10) 243-06-03; fax (10) 265-13-86; e-mail info@ai.aiesec.org; internet www.aiesec.org; f. 1948 as International Association of Students in Economics and Management; develops leadership skills, and socio-economic and international understanding among young people through exchange programmes and related educational activities. Mems: 50,000 students in more than 750 higher education institutions in 87 countries and territories. Pres. MURATCAN USTUNKAYA; Vice-Pres. DAVID WHERRY. Publs *Annual Report, International Link* (magazine).

Asian Students' Association: 511 Nathan Rd, 1/F, Kowloon, Hong Kong; tel. 23880515; fax 27825535; f. 1969; aims to promote students' solidarity in struggling for democracy, self-determination, peace, justice and liberation; conducts campaigns, training of activists, and workshops on human rights and other issues of importance.There are Student Commissions for Peace, Education and Human Rights. Mems: 34 national or regional student unions, four observers. Secretariat: LINA CABAERO (Philippines), STEVEN GAN (Malaysia), CHOW WING-HANG (Hong Kong). Publs *Movement News* (monthly), *ASA News* (quarterly).

Council on International Educational Exchange: 205 East 42nd St, New York, NY 10017, USA; tel. (212) 661-1414; fax (212) 972-3231; e-mail strooboff@ciee.org; f. 1947; issues International Student Identity Card entitling holders to discounts and basic insurance; arranges overseas work and study programmes for students; co-ordinates summer work programme in the USA for foreign students; administers programmes for teachers and other professionals, sponsors conferences on educational exchange; operates a voluntary service programme. Mems: 307 colleges, universities and international educational organizations. Pres. and CEO STEVAN TROOBOFF. Publs include *Work, Study, Travel Abroad: The Whole World Handbook, Update, Volunteer!, High-School Student's Guide to Study, Travel and Adventure Abroad.*

European Law Students' Association—ELSA: 1 rue Defacqz, 1050 Brussels, Belgium; tel. (2) 534-56-79; fax (2) 534-65-86; f. 1981 to foster mutual understanding and promote social responsibility of law students and young laywers. Publs *ELSA Law Review, Legal Studies in Europe.*

European Students' Forum (Association des Etats Généraux des Etudiants de l'Europe): 15 rue Nestor de Tiere, 1040 Brussels, Belgium; tel. (2) 245-23-00; fax (2) 245-62-60; e-mail infoaegee.org; internet www. aegee.org; promotes cross-border communication and integration; holds specialized conferences. Mems: 17,000 students in 271 university cities in 40 countries.

European Youth Forum:120 rue Joseph II, 1000 Brussels, Belgium; tel. (2) 286-94-12; fax (2) 233-37-09; e-mail youthforum@youthforum.org; internet www.europeanyouthforum.com; f. 1996; promotes development of a coherent and integrated youth policy; promotes the rights of young people, as well as understanding and respect for human rights; consults with international organizations and governments on issues relevant to young people.

International Association for the Exchange of Students for Technical Experience—IAESTE: e-mail webmaster@iaeste.org; internet www.iaeste.org; f. 1948. Mems: 63 national committees. Publs *Activity Report, Annual Report.*

International Association of Dental Students: c/o FDI World Dental Federation, 7 Carlisle St, London, W1V 5RG, United Kingdom; tel. (20) 7935-7852; fax (20) 7486-0183; f. 1951 to represent dental students and their opinions internationally, to promote dental student exchanges and international congresses. Mems: 60,000 students in 45 countries (and 15,000 corresponding mems). Pres. VALENTINA STERJOVA (UK). Publ. *IADS Newsletter* (3 a year).

International Federation of Medical Students' Associations: Institute of Social Medicine, Academisch Medisch Centrum, Meibergdreef 15, 1105 Amsterdam, Netherlands; tel. (20) 5665366; fax (20) 6972316; e-mail f.w.hilhorst@amc.uva.nl; f. 1951 to promote international co-operation in professional treatment and the achievement of humanitarian ideals; provides forum for medical students; standing committees on professional exchange, electives exchange, medical education, public health, refugees and AIDS; organizes annual General Assembly. Mems: 57 associations. Sec.-Gen. MIA HILHORST. Publ. *IFMSA Newsletter* (quarterly).

International Pharmaceutical Students' Federation: POB 84200, 2508 AE The Hague, Netherlands; tel. (70) 3021992; fax (70) 3021999; e-mail ipsf@fip.nl; internet www.pharmweb.net/ipsf.html; f. 1949 to study and promote the interests of pharmaceutical students and to encourage international co-operation. Mems: 31 full mems from national organizations and 23 mems in assoc. from national or local organizations. Pres. GONÇALO SOUSA PINTO; Sec.-Gen. HELENA WESTERMARK. Publ. *IPSF News Bulletin* (3 a year).

International Union of Students: POB 58, 17th November St, 110 01 Prague 01, Czech Republic; tel. (2) 312812; fax (2) 316100; f. 1946 to defend the rights and interests of students and strive for peace, disarmament, the eradication of illiteracy and of all forms of discrimination; operates research centre, sports and cultural centre and student travel bureau; activities include conferences, meetings, solidarity campaigns, relief projects, award of 30–40 scholarships annually, travel and exchange, sports events, cultural projects. Mems: 140 organizations from 115 countries. Pres. JOSEF SKALA; Vice-Pres. MARTA HUBIČKOVÁ; Gen. Sec. GIORGOS MICHAELIDES (Cyprus). Publs *World Student News* (quarterly), *IUS Newsletter, Student Life* (quarterly), *DE—Democratization of Education* (quarterly).

International Young Christian Workers: 4 ave G. Rodenbach, 1030 Brussels, Belgium; tel. (2) 242-18-11; fax (2) 242-48-00; e-mail jociycw@skynet.be; internet www.skynet.be/sky34197; f. 1925, on the inspiration of the Priest-Cardinal Joseph Cardijn; aims to educate young workers to take on present and future responsibilities in their commitment to the working class, and to confront all the situations which prevent them from fulfilling themselves. Pres. DESROSIERS JOSÉ (Canada); Sec.-Gen. LANGWIESNER GERTRAUD (Austria). Publs *International INFO* (3 a year), *IYCW Bulletin* (quarterly).

International Youth and Student Movement for the United Nations—ISMUN: c/o Palais des Nations, 16 ave Jean-Tremblay, 1211 Geneva 10, Switzerland; tel. (22) 7985850; fax (22) 7334838; f. 1948 by the World Federation of United Nations Associations, independent since 1949; an international non-governmental organization of students and young people dedicated especially to supporting the principles embodied in the United Nations Charter and Universal Declaration of Human Rights; encourages constructive action in building economic, social and cultural equality and in working for national independence, social justice and human rights on a world-wide scale; regional offices in Austria, France, Ghana, Panama and the USA. Mems: associations in 53 countries. Sec.-Gen. JAN LÖNN. Publ. *ISMUN Newsletter* (monthly).

International Youth Hostel Federation: 1st floor, Fountain House, Parkway, Welwyn Garden City, Herts., AL8 6QW, United Kingdom; tel. (1707) 324170; fax (1707) 323980; e-mail iyhf@iyhf.demon.co.uk; f. 1932; facilitates international travel by members of the various youth hostel associations and advises and helps in the formation of youth hostel associations in all countries where no such organizations exist; records over 32m. overnight stays annually in over 4,500 youth hostels. Mems: 60 national associations with 3.7m. individual members; 17 associated national organizations. Pres. FRIEDRICH MUTH (Germany); Sec.-Gen. RAWDON LAU (Hong Kong). Publs *Annual Report, Guidebook on World Hostels* (annually), *Manual, News Bulletin.*

Junior Chamber International (JCI), Inc.: 400 University Drive (POB 140-577), Coral Gables, FL 33114-0577, USA; tel. (305) 446-7608; fax (305) 442-0041; e-mail jciwhq@ix.netcom.com; f. 1944 to encourage and advance international understanding and goodwill. Junior Chamber organizations throughout the world provide young people with opportunities for leadership training, promoting goodwill through international fellowship, solving civic problems by arousing civic consciousness and discussing social, economic and cultural questions. Mems: 400,000 in 90 countries. Pres. GEORGES A. BOUVERAT (2000/01); Sec.-Gen. BENNY ELLERBE. Publ. *JCI News* (quarterly, in English and more than six other languages).

Latin American and Caribbean Confederation of Young Men's Christian Associations (Confederación Latinoamericana y del Caribe de Asociaciones Cristianas de Jóvenes): Culpina 272, 1406 Buenos Aires, Argentina; tel. (11) 4637-4727; fax (11) 4637-4867; e-mail clacj@wamani.apc.org; f. 1914; aims to encourage the moral, spiritual, intellectual, social and physical development of young men; to strengthen the work of national Associations and to sponsor the establishment of new Associations. Mems: affiliated YMCAs in 25 countries (comprising 350,000 individuals). Pres. GERARDO VITUREIRA (Uruguay); Gen. Sec. MARCO ANTONIO HOCHSCHEIT (Brazil). Publs *Diecisiete/21* (bulletin), *Carta Abierta, Brief,* technical articles and other studies.

Pan-African Youth Movement (Mouvement pan-africain de la jeunesse): 19 rue Debbih Chérif, BP 72, Didouch Mourad, 16000 Algiers, Algeria; tel. and fax (2) 71-64-71; f. 1962; aims to mobilize and sensitize African youth to participate in socio-economic and political development and democratization; organizes conferences and seminars, youth exchanges, youth festivals. Mems: youth groups in 52 African countries and liberation movements. Publ. *MPJ News* (quarterly).

World Alliance of Young Men's Christian Associations: 12 clos Belmont, 1208 Geneva; tel. (22) 8495100; fax (22) 8495110; e-mail office@ymca.int; internet www.ymca.int; f. 1855 to unite the National Alliances of Young Men's Christian Associations throughout the world. Mems: national alliances and related associations in 128 countries. Pres. MARTIN VÖGLER (Switzerland); Sec.-Gen. NICK NIGHTINGALE (UK). Publ. *YMCA World* (quarterly).

World Assembly of Youth: International Youth Centre, Jalan Tenteram, Bandar Tun Razak, 56000 Kuala Lumpur, Malaysia; tel. 9732722; fax 9736011; internet www.jaring.my/way; f. 1949 as co-ordinating body for youth councils and organizations; organizes conferences, training courses and practical development projects. Pres. Datuk ALI RUSTAM; Sec.-Gen. HEIKKI PAKARINEN. Publs *WAY Information* (every 2 months), *Youth Roundup* (monthly), *WAY Forum* (quarterly).

World Association of Girl Guides and Girl Scouts: World Bureau, Olave Centre, 12C Lyndhurst Rd, London, NW3 5PQ, United Kingdom; tel. (20) 7794-1181; fax (20) 7431-3764; e-mail wagggs@wagggsworld.org; f. 1928 to promote unity of purpose and common understanding in the fundamental principles of the Girl Guide and Girl Scout Movement throughout the world and to encourage friendship and mutual understanding among girls and young women world-wide; World Conference meets every three years. Mems: about 9m. individuals in 136 organizations. Chair. World Board HEATHER BRANDON; Dir World Bureau LESLEY BULMAN. Publs *Triennial Report, Trefoil Round the World, Our World News.*

World Council of Service Clubs: POB 148, Wallaroo, South Australia 5556, Australia; e-mail kelly@kadina.mtx.net.au; f. 1946 to provide a means of exchange of information and news for furthering international understanding and co-operation, to facilitate the extension of service clubs, and to create in young people a sense of civic responsibility. Mems: more than 3,000 clubs in 83 countries. Sec.-Gen. SHANE KELLY.

World Federation of Democratic Youth—WFDY: POB 147, 1389 Budapest, Hungary; tel. (1) 3502202; fax (1) 3501204; e-mail wfdy@mail.matav.hu; f. 1945 to strive for peace and disarmament and joint action by democratic and progressive youth movements in support of national independence, democracy, social progress and youth rights; to support liberation struggles in Asia, Africa and Latin America; and to work for a new and more just international economic order. Mems: 152 members in 102 countries. Pres. IRAKLIS TSAVDARIDIS (Greece). Publ. *WFDY News* (every 3 months, in English, French and Spanish).

World Organization of the Scout Movement: Case Postale 241, 1211 Geneva 4, Switzerland; tel. (22) 7051010; fax (22) 7051020; e-mail worldbureau@world.scout.org; f. 1922 to promote unity and understanding of scouting throughout the world; to develop good citizenship among young people by forming their characters for service, co-operation and leadership; to provide aid and advice to members and potential member associations. The World Scout Bureau (Geneva) has regional offices in Chile, Egypt, Kenya and the Philippines (the European Region has its offices in Brussels and Geneva). Mems: over 25m. in 215 countries and territories. Sec.-Gen. Dr JACQUES MOREILLON (Switzerland). Publs *World Scouting News* (every 2 months), *Triennial Report.*

World Union of Jewish Students: Terra Sancta Compound, POB 7914, Rechavia, 91077 Jerusalem, Israel; tel. (2) 610133; fax (2) 610741; e-mail wujs@netvision.net.il; internet www.wujs.org.il; f. 1924 (by Albert Einstein); organization for national student bodies concerned with educational and political matters, where possible in co-operation with non-Jewish student organizations, UNESCO, etc.; divided into six regions; organizes Congress every two years. Mems:

52 national unions representing over 1,500,000 students. Chair. ILANIT SASSON MELCHIDE. Publs *The Student Activist Yearbook, Heritage and History, Forum, WUJS Report.*

World Young Women's Christian Association—World YWCA: 16 Ancienne Route, 1218 Grand-Saconnex, Geneva, Switzerland; tel. (22) 9296040; fax (22) 9296044; e-mail worldoffice@worldywca.org; internet www.worldywca.org; f. 1894 for the linking together of national YWCAs (now in 98 countries) for their mutual help and development and the initiation of work in countries where the Association does not yet exist; works for international understanding, for improved social and economic conditions and for basic human rights for all people. Pres. JANE WOLFE; Gen. Sec. MUSIMBI KANYORO. Publs *Annual Report, Common Concern.*

Youth for Development and Co-operation—YDC: Rijswijk-strasse 141, 1062 HN Amsterdam, Netherlands; tel. (20) 6142510; fax (20) 617-55-45; e-mail ydc@geo2.geonet.de; aims to strengthen youth structures that promote new co-operation between young people in the industrialized and developing worlds, in order to achieve development that is environmentally sustainable and socially just; seminars, conferences and campaigns on issues related to youth and development (employment, young women, structural adjustment programmes etc.) Mems: 51 organizations. Sec.-Gen. B. AUER. Publ. *FLASH Newsletter* (irregular).

PART TWO
Afghanistan–Jordan

AFGHANISTAN

Introductory Survey

Location, Climate, Language, Religion, Flag, Capital

The Islamic State of Afghanistan (or Islamic Emirate of Afghanistan, as it was unilaterally renamed by the Taliban in late 1997) is a land-locked country in south-western Asia. Its neighbours are Turkmenistan, Uzbekistan and Tajikistan to the north, Iran to the west, the People's Republic of China to the north-east and Pakistan to the east and south. The climate varies sharply between the highlands and lowlands; the temperature in the south-west in summer reaches 48.8°C (120°F), but in the winter, in the Hindu Kush mountains of the north-east, it falls to −26°C (−15°F). Of the many languages spoken in Afghanistan, the principal two are Pashtu and Dari (a dialect of Farsi or Iranian). The majority of Afghans are Muslims of the Sunni sect; there are also minority groups of Shi'ite Muslims, Hindus, Sikhs and Jews. The state flag (proportions 2 by 1) has three equal horizontal stripes from top to bottom of green, white and black, bearing in the centre in gold the state arms overlapping the three stripes. In October 1997 the Taliban administration in Kabul unilaterally decided to change the state flag: henceforth, it was to be plain white (proportions approximately 3 by 2) with, in the centre, an Arabic inscription in green lettering reading 'There is no God but Allah, and Muhammad is the Prophet of Allah'. The capital is Kabul.

Recent History

The last King of Afghanistan, Mohammad Zahir Shah, reigned from 1933 to 1973. His country was neutral during both World Wars and became a staunch advocate of non-alignment. In 1953 the King's cousin, Lt-Gen. Sardar Mohammad Daud Khan, was appointed Prime Minister and, securing aid from the USSR, initiated a series of economic plans for the modernization of the country. In 1963 Gen. Daud resigned and Dr Mohammad Yusuf became the first Prime Minister not of royal birth. Dr Yusuf introduced a new democratic Constitution in the following year, which combined Western ideas with Islamic religious and political beliefs; the King, however, did not permit political parties to operate. Afghanistan made little progress under the succeeding Prime Ministers.

In July 1973, while King Zahir was in Italy, the monarchy was overthrown by a coup, in which the main figure was the former Prime Minister, Gen. Daud. The 1964 Constitution was abolished and Afghanistan was declared a republic. Daud renounced his royal titles and took office as Head of State, Prime Minister and Minister of Foreign Affairs and Defence.

A Loya Jirgah (Supreme National Tribal Assembly), appointed from among tribal elders by provincial governors, was convened in January 1977 and adopted a new Constitution, providing for presidential government and a one-party state. Daud was elected to continue as President for six years and the Loya Jirgah was then dissolved. In March President Daud formed a new civilian Government, nominally ending military rule. However, during 1977 there was growing discontent with Daud, especially within the armed forces, and in April 1978 a coup, known (from the month) as the 'Saur Revolution', ousted the President, who was killed with several members of his family. Nur Mohammad Taraki, the imprisoned leader of the formerly banned People's Democratic Party of Afghanistan (PDPA), was released and installed as President of the Revolutionary Council and Prime Minister. The country was renamed the Democratic Republic of Afghanistan, the year-old Constitution was abolished and no political parties other than the communist PDPA were allowed to function. Afghanistan's already close relations with the USSR were further strengthened. However, opposition to the new regime led to armed insurrection, particularly by fiercely traditionalist Islamist rebel tribesmen (known, collectively, as the *mujahidin*), in almost all provinces, and the flight of thousands of refugees to Pakistan and Iran. In spite of purges of the army and civil service, Taraki's position became increasingly insecure, and in September 1979 he was ousted by Hafizullah Amin, an erstwhile Deputy Prime Minister and Minister of Foreign Affairs. Amin's imposition of rigorous communist policies proved unsuccessful and unpopular. In December he was killed in a coup, which was supported by

the entry into Afghanistan of about 80,000 combat troops from the USSR. This incursion by Soviet armed forces into a traditionally non-aligned neighbouring country aroused world-wide condemnation. Babrak Karmal, a former Deputy Prime Minister under Taraki, was installed as the new Head of State, having been flown into Kabul by a Soviet aircraft from virtual exile in eastern Europe.

Riots, strikes and inter-factional strife and purges continued into 1980 and 1981. Sultan Ali Keshtmand, hitherto a Deputy Prime Minister, replaced Karmal as Prime Minister in June 1981. In the same month the regime launched the National Fatherland Front (NFF), incorporating the PDPA and other organizations, with the aim of promoting national unity. Despite a series of government reshuffles carried out in the early 1980s, the PDPA regime continued to fail to win widespread popular support. Consequently, the Government attempted to broaden the base of its support: in April 1985 it summoned a Loya Jirgah, which ratified a new Constitution for Afghanistan, and during the second half of 1985 and the first half of 1986 elections were held for new local government organs (it was claimed that 60% of those elected were non-party members) and several non-party members were appointed to high-ranking government posts (including the chairmanship of the NFF).

In May 1986 Dr Najibullah (the former head of the state security service, KHAD) succeeded Karmal as General Secretary of the PDPA. Karmal retained the lesser post of President of the Revolutionary Council. In the same month Najibullah announced the formation of a collective leadership comprising himself, Karmal and Prime Minister Keshtmand. In November, however, Karmal was relieved of all party and government posts. Haji Muhammad Chamkani, formerly First Vice-President (and a non-PDPA member), became Acting President of the Revolutionary Council, pending the introduction of a new constitution and the establishment of a permanent legislature.

In December 1986 an extraordinary plenum of the PDPA Central Committee approved a policy of national reconciliation, involving negotiations with opposition groups, and the proposed formation of a coalition government of national unity. In early January 1987 a Supreme Extraordinary Commission for National Reconciliation, led by Abd ar-Rahim Hatif (the Chairman of the National Committee of the NFF), was formed to conduct the negotiations. The NFF was renamed the National Front (NF), and became a separate organization from the PDPA. The new policy of reconciliation won some support from former opponents, but the seven-party *mujahidin* alliance (Ittehad-i-Islami Afghan Mujahidin, Islamic Union of Afghan Mujahidin—IUAM), which was based in Peshawar, Pakistan, refused to observe the cease-fire or to participate in negotiations, while continuing to demand a complete and unconditional Soviet withdrawal from Afghanistan.

In July 1987, as part of the process of national reconciliation, several important developments occurred: a law permitting the formation of other political parties (according to certain provisions) was introduced; Najibullah announced that the PDPA would be prepared to share power with representatives of opposition groups in the event of the formation of a coalition government of national unity; and the draft of a new Constitution was approved by the Presidium of the Revolutionary Council. The main innovations incorporated in the draft Constitution were: the formation of a multi-party political system, under the auspices of the NF; the formation of a bicameral legislature, called the Meli Shura (National Assembly), composed of a Sena (Senate) and a Wolasi Jirgah (House of Representatives); the granting of a permanent constitutional status to the PDPA; the bestowal of unlimited power on the President, who was to hold office for seven years; and the reversion of the name of the country from the Democratic Republic to the Republic of Afghanistan. A Loya Jirgah ratified the new Constitution in November.

Meanwhile, a considerable proportion of the successful candidates in local elections held throughout the country in August 1987 were reported to be non-PDPA members. On 30 September Najibullah was unanimously elected as President of the Revolutionary Council, and Haji Muhammad Chamkani resumed his former post as First Vice-President. In order to strengthen his position, Najibullah ousted all the remaining supporters of former President Karmal from the Central Committee and Politburo of the PDPA in October. In the following month a Loya Jirgah unanimously elected Najibullah as President of the State.

In April 1988 elections were held to both houses of the new National Assembly, which replaced the Revolutionary Council. Although the elections were boycotted by the *mujahidin*, the Government left vacant 50 of the 234 seats in the House of Representatives, and a small number of seats in the Senate, in the hope that the guerrillas would abandon their armed struggle and present their own representatives to participate in the new administration. The PDPA itself won only 46 seats in the House of Representatives, but was guaranteed support from the NF, which gained 45, and from the various newly-recognized left-wing parties, which won a total of 24 seats. In May Dr Muhammad Hasan Sharq (a non-PDPA member and a Deputy Prime Minister since June 1987) replaced Keshtmand as Prime Minister, and in June a new Council of Ministers was appointed.

On 18 February 1989, following the completion of the withdrawal of Soviet troops from Afghanistan (see below), Najibullah implemented a government reshuffle, involving the replacement of non-communist ministers with loyal PDPA members. On the same day, Prime Minister Sharq (who had been one of the main promoters of the policy of national reconciliation) resigned from his post and was replaced by Keshtmand. Following the declaration of a state of emergency by Najibullah (citing allegations of repeated violations of the Geneva accords by Pakistan and the USA—see below) on 19 February, a PDPA-dominated 20-member Supreme Council for the Defence of the Homeland was established. The Council, which was headed by President Najibullah and was composed of ministers, members of the PDPA Politburo and high-ranking military figures, assumed full responsibility for the country's economic, political and military policies (although the Council of Ministers continued to function).

In early March 1990 the Minister of Defence, Lt-Gen. Shahnawaz Tanay, with the alleged support of the air force and some divisions of the army, led an unsuccessful coup attempt against Najibullah's Government. Najibullah subsequently enacted thorough purges of PDPA and army leaders and decided to revert rapidly to some form of constitutional civilian government. On 20 May the state of emergency was lifted; the Supreme Council for the Defence of the Homeland was disbanded; and a new Council of Ministers, under the premiership of Fazle Haq Khalikyar, was appointed. At the end of the month a Loya Jirgah was convened in Kabul, which ratified constitutional amendments, greatly reducing Afghanistan's socialist orientation; ending the PDPA's and the NF's monopoly over executive power and paving the way for fully democratic elections; introducing greater political and press freedom; encouraging the development of the private sector and further foreign investment; lessening the role of the State and affording greater prominence to Islam. The extensive powers of the presidency were, however, retained. In addition, in late June the PDPA changed its name to the Homeland Party (HP—Hizb-i Watan), and dissolved the Politburo and the Central Committee, replacing them with an Executive Board and a Central Council, respectively. The party adopted a new programme, of which the hallmark was hostility to ideology. Najibullah was unanimously elected as Chairman of the HP. An important factor in Najibullah's decision to continue with, and to extend, the process of national reconciliation was the fact that the USSR's own internal problems meant that the Soviet administration was unwilling to sustain, for much longer, the supplies of weapons, goods and credits that were helping to support the Kabul regime.

Fighting between the *mujahidin* and Afghan army units had begun in the eastern provinces after the 1978 coup and was aggravated by the implementation of unpopular social and economic reforms by the new administrations. The Afghan army relied heavily upon Soviet military aid in the form of weapons, equipment and expertise, but morale and resources were severely affected by defections to the rebels' ranks: numbers fell from around 80,000 men in 1978 to about 40,000 in 1985. During 1984–89 the guerrilla groups, which had been poorly armed at first, received ever-increasing support (both military and financial) from abroad, notably from the USA (which began to supply them with sophisticated anti-aircraft weapons in 1986), the United Kingdom and the People's Republic of China. Despite

the Government's decision to seal the border with Pakistan, announced in September 1985, and the strong presence of Soviet forces there, foreign weapons continued to reach the guerrillas via Pakistan. Many of the guerrillas established bases in the North-West Frontier Province of Pakistan (notably in the provincial capital, Peshawar). From 1985 the fighting intensified, especially in areas close to the border between Afghanistan and Pakistan. There were many violations of the border, involving shelling, bombing and incursions into neighbouring airspace. The general pattern of the war, however, remained the same: the regime held the main towns and a few strategic bases, and relied on bombing of both military and civilian targets, and occasional attacks in force, together with conciliatory measures such as the provision of funds for local development, while the rebel forces dominated rural areas and were able to cause serious disruption.

The civil war brought famine to parts of Afghanistan, and there was a mass movement of population from the countryside to Kabul, and of refugees to Pakistan and Iran. In mid-1988 a UNHCR estimate assessed the number of Afghan refugees in Pakistan at 3.15m., and the number in Iran at 2.35m. Supply convoys were often prevented from reaching the cities, owing to the repeated severing of major road links by the guerrillas. Kabul, in particular, began to suffer from severe shortages of food and fuel, which were only partially alleviated by airlifts of emergency aid supplies. As a result of the increasing danger and hardship, a number of countries temporarily closed their embassies in the capital.

From 1980 extensive international negotiations took place to try to achieve the complete withdrawal of Soviet forces from Afghanistan. Between June 1982 and September 1987 seven rounds of indirect talks took place between the Afghan and Pakistani Ministers of Foreign Affairs in Geneva, under the auspices of the UN. In October 1986 the USSR made a token withdrawal of six regiments (6,000–8,000 men) from Afghanistan. As a result of the discussions in Geneva, an agreement was finally signed on 14 April 1988. The Geneva accords consisted of five documents: detailed undertakings by Afghanistan and Pakistan, relating to non-intervention and non-interference in each other's affairs; international guarantees of Afghan neutrality (with the USA and the USSR as the principal guarantors); arrangements for the voluntary and safe return of Afghan refugees; a document linking the preceding documents with a timetable for a Soviet withdrawal; and the establishment of a UN monitoring force, which was to oversee both the Soviet troop departures and the return of the refugees. The withdrawal of Soviet troops (numbering 100,000, according to Soviet figures, or 115,000, according to Western sources) commenced on 15 May.

Neither the *mujahidin* nor Iran played any role in the formulation of the Geneva accords, and, in spite of protests by Pakistan, no agreement was incorporated regarding the composition of an interim coalition government in Afghanistan, or the 'symmetrical' cessation of Soviet aid to Najibullah's regime and US aid to the *mujahidin*. Therefore, despite the withdrawal of the Soviet troops, the supply of weapons to both sides was not halted, and the fighting continued. Pakistan repeatedly denied accusations, made by the Afghan and Soviet Governments, that it had violated the accords by continuing to harbour Afghan guerrillas and to act as a conduit for arms supplies to the latter from various sympathizers. At the end of November 1988 Soviet officials held direct talks with representatives of the *mujahidin* in Peshawar, Pakistan, the first such meeting since the start of the 10-year conflict. High-level discussions were held in early December in Saudi Arabia between Prof. Burhanuddin Rabbani, the Chairman of the IUAM, and the Soviet ambassador to Afghanistan. These discussions collapsed, however, when the *mujahidin* leaders reiterated their demand that no members of Najibullah's regime should be incorporated in any future Afghan government, while the Soviet officials continued to insist on a government role for the PDPA. In spite of the unabated violence, the USSR, adhering to the condition specified in the Geneva accords, had withdrawn all of its troops from Afghanistan by mid-February 1989.

In mid-1988 the *mujahidin* had intensified their military activities, attacking small provincial centres and launching missiles against major cities, several of which were unsuccessfully besieged. By the end of 1990, owing mainly to their lack of organization and limited experience of modern strategic warfare, the *mujahidin* had failed to achieve any significant military successes and their control was confined to rural areas (including several small provincial capitals). The guerrillas also failed to make any important advances on the political front. Talks between the IUAM and the Iranian-based Hizb-i Wahadat-i Islami (Islamic Unity Party), an alliance of eight Shi'ite Afghan resistance groups, repeatedly failed to reach any agreement as to the composition of a broadly-based interim government. Consequently, in February 1989 the IUAM convened its own Shura (Assembly) in Rawalpindi, Pakistan, at which an interim government-in-exile (known as the Afghan Interim Government, AIG) was elected. The AIG, however, was officially recognized by only four countries. It also failed to gain any substantial support or recognition from the guerrilla commanders, who were beginning to establish their own unofficial alliances inside the country. In March, however, the AIG received a form of diplomatic recognition, when it was granted membership of the Organization of the Islamic Conference (OIC). In addition, in June the US Government appointed a special envoy to the *mujahidin*, with the rank of personal ambassador. In mid-1989 the unity of the *mujahidin* forces was seriously weakened by an increase in internecine violence among the various guerrilla groups, while the AIG was riven by disputes between the moderates and the fundamentalists. The USA, Saudi Arabia and Pakistan began to reduce financial aid and military supplies to the IUAM in Peshawar, and to undertake the difficult task of delivering weapons and money directly to guerrilla commanders and tribal leaders inside Afghanistan.

Following extensive negotiations with the regional powers involved in the crisis, the UN Secretary-General made a declaration in May 1991, setting out five principles for a settlement, the main points of which were: recognition of the national sovereignty of Afghanistan; the right of the Afghan people to choose their own government and political system; the establishment of an independent and authorized mechanism to oversee free and fair elections to a broadly-based government; a UN-monitored cease-fire; and the donation of sufficient financial aid to facilitate the return of the refugees and internal reconstruction. The declaration received the approval of the Afghan and Pakistani Governments, but was rejected by the AIG.

Reflecting its disenchantment with the guerrilla cause, the US Government substantially reduced its aid to the *mujahidin* in 1991. New military campaigns had been launched by the *mujahidin* in the second half of 1990 in an attempt to impress their international supporters, disrupt the return of refugees and obstruct contacts between the Government and moderate guerillas. At the end of March 1991, following more than two weeks of heavy fighting, the south-eastern city of Khost was captured by the *mujahidin*, representing the most severe reversal sustained by the Government since the Soviet withdrawal. The *mujahidin* also carried out attacks on Gardez, Jalalabad, Ghazni, Qandahar and Herat in 1991, and communications between cities and with the Soviet border were severed.

An unexpected breakthrough towards resolving the Afghan crisis occurred in mid-September 1991, when the USA and the USSR announced that they would stop supplying arms to the warring factions, and would encourage other countries (namely Pakistan, Saudi Arabia and Iran) to do likewise. Although both the Afghan Government and the *mujahidin* welcomed this pledge, neither side showed any sign of implementing the proposed cease-fire, and, indeed, the fighting intensified around Kabul. In February 1992, however, the peace process was given a major boost when Pakistan made it clear that, rather than continuing actively to encourage the *mujahidin*, through arms supplies and training, it was urging all the guerrilla factions to support the five-point UN peace plan (see above). In doing so, Pakistan was effectively abandoning its insistence on the installation of a fundamentalist government in Kabul. There were growing fears, none the less, that the peace process might be placed in jeopardy by an increase in ethnic divisions within both the government forces and a number of *mujahidin* groups, between the majority Pashtuns and minority groups such as the Tajiks and Uzbeks. As a result of a mutiny staged by Uzbek militia forces in the Afghan army, under the command of Gen. Abdul Rashid Dostam, the northern town of Mazar-i-Sharif was captured by the *mujahidin* in March.

On 16 April 1992 events took an unexpected turn when Najibullah was forced to resign by his own ruling party, following the capture of the strategically-important Bagram air base and the nearby town of Charikar, only about 50 km north of Kabul, by the Jamiat-i Islami guerrilla group under the command of the Tajik general, Ahmad Shah Masoud. Najibullah went into hiding in the capital, under UN protection, while one of the Vice-Presidents, Abd ar-Rahim Hatif, assumed the post

of acting President. Within a few days of Najibullah's downfall, every major town in Afghanistan was under the control of different coalitions of *mujahidin* groups co-operating with disaffected army commanders. Masoud was given orders by the guerrilla leaders in Peshawar to secure Kabul. On 25 April the forces of both Masoud and of Gulbuddin Hekmatyar, the leader of a rival guerrilla group, the Pashtun-dominated Hizb-i Islami (Islamic Party), whose men were massed to the south of the capital, entered Kabul. The army surrendered its key positions, and immediately the city was riven by *mujahidin* faction-fighting. The military council that had, a few days earlier, replaced the Government relinquished power to the *mujahidin*. Having discarded the UN's proposal to form a neutral body, the guerrilla leaders in Peshawar agreed to establish a 51-member interim Islamic Jihad Council, composed of military and religious leaders, which was to assume power in Kabul. The leader of the small, moderate Jebha-i-Nejat-i-Melli (National Liberation Front), Prof. Sibghatullah Mojaddedi, was to chair the Islamic Jihad Council for two months, after which period a 10-member Leadership Council, comprising *mujahidin* chiefs and presided over by the head of the Jamiat-i Islami, Prof. Burhanuddin Rabbani, would be set up for a period of four months. Within the six months a special council was to meet to designate an interim administration which was to hold power for up to a year pending elections.

Mojaddedi arrived in Kabul on 28 April 1992 as the President of the new interim administration. The Islamic Jihad Council was not, however, supported by Hekmatyar, whose radical stance differed substantially from Mojaddedi's more tolerant outlook. At the end of the month Hekmatyar's forces lost control of their last stronghold in the centre of Kabul. Within a few weeks the Government of the newly-proclaimed Islamic State of Afghanistan had won almost universal diplomatic recognition, and by early May about one-half of the Islamic Jihad Council had arrived in the capital. An acting Council of Ministers was formed, in which Masoud was given the post of Minister of Defence and the premiership was set aside for Ustad Abdol Sabur Farid, a Tajik commander from the Hizb-i Islami (Hekmatyar declined to accept the post). As part of the process of 'Islamization', the death penalty was introduced, alcohol and narcotics were banned and the wearing of strict Islamic dress by all women was enforced. Despite Mojaddedi's repeated pleas to Hekmatyar and his followers to lay down their arms, Hekmatyar, who was particularly angered by the presence of Gen. Dostam's Uzbek forces in the capital, continued to bombard Kabul with artillery and indiscriminate rocket launches from various strongholds around the city, killing and wounding scores of citizens.

On 28 June 1992 Mojaddedi surrendered power to the Leadership Council, which immediately offered Burhanuddin Rabbani the presidency of the country and the concomitant responsibility for the interim Council of Ministers for four months, as set forth in the Peshawar Agreement (see above). In early July Farid assumed the premiership, which had been held open for him since late April. On assuming the presidency Rabbani announced the adoption of a new Islamic flag, the establishment of an economic council, which was to address the country's severe economic problems, and the appointment of a commission to draw up a new Constitution. A Deputy President was appointed in late July. In early August the withdrawal of the members of the Hizb-i Islami faction led by Maulvi Muhammad Yunus Khalis from the Leadership Council revealed serious rifts within the Government. A further problem was the continuing inter-*mujahidin* violence in Kabul. Within days the violence had escalated into a full-scale ground offensive, launched by Hekmatyar's forces against the capital. The airport was closed, hundreds of people were killed or wounded, and tens of thousands of civilians fled Kabul in fear of their lives. In response, President Rabbani expelled Hekmatyar from the Leadership Council and dismissed Prime Minister Farid. Hekmatyar demanded the expulsion of the 75,000 Uzbek militia from Kabul as a precondition to peace talks, alleging that Gen. Dostam was still closely allied to former members of the communist regime. At the end of the month a cease-fire agreement was reached between Rabbani and Hekmatyar and, after a few days of relative peacefulness, the airport was reopened. Sporadic fighting involving various *mujahidin* and militia groups (notably Gen. Dostam's Uzbek forces) continued, however, in Kabul itself and in the provinces throughout the remainder of the year. At the end of October the Leadership Council agreed to extend Rabbani's tenure of the presidency by two months. On 30

December a special advisory council, known as the Resolution and Settlement Council (Shura-e Ahl-e Hal wa Aqd), which was composed of 1,335 tribal leaders, was convened in Kabul. The Council elected Rabbani, who was the sole candidate, as President of the country for a period of a further two years. In early January 1993 200 members of the advisory council were selected to constitute the future membership of the country's legislature.

The establishment of the advisory council and the re-election of President Rabbani provoked yet further heavy fighting in Kabul and other provinces in early 1993. Owing to the worsening violence, all Western diplomats had left the capital by the end of January. In early March, however, President Rabbani, Hekmatyar, Mojaddedi and leaders of other major *mujahidin* factions held negotiations in Islamabad, at the end of which a peace accord was signed. Under the terms of the accord, an interim Government was to be established, which would hold power for 18 months; President Rabbani was to remain as Head of State, and Hekmatyar (or his nominee) was to assume the premiership of the acting Council of Ministers; a cease-fire was to be imposed with immediate effect; legislative elections were to be held within six months; a 16-member defence commission was to be formed, which would be responsible for the establishment of a national army; and all weaponry was to be seized from the warring factions in an attempt to restore peace and order. The peace accord was officially approved and signed by the Governments of Pakistan, Saudi Arabia and Iran.

Confronted with the difficult task of satisfying the demands of all the *mujahidin* groups, Hekmatyar was not able to present a new Council of Ministers until late May 1993 (it was sworn in the following month). Each *mujahidin* faction was allocated two ministerial posts, with further positions left vacant for other representatives (representatives from Gen. Dostam's group of predominantly Uzbek militiamen—known collectively as the National Islamic Movement (NIM) (Jonbesh-e Melli-e Eslami)—were offered two posts in July). One of Hekmatyar's most noteworthy decisions in the formation of the new Council of Ministers was to remove one of his most powerful rivals, Ahmad Shah Masoud, from the crucial post of Minister of Defence. The new Prime Minister promised to hold a general election by October. The temporary headquarters of the Government were situated in Charasiab, Hekmatyar's military base, about 25 km south of Kabul.

Despite the signing of the Islamabad peace accord in March 1993, the violence between the various *mujahidin* groups did not cease, and hundreds of people continued to be killed and wounded. The interim Government was beset by internal dissension and proved rather ineffectual in the administration of the war-torn country. Hekmatyar refused to co-operate with Rabbani, and frequently demanded the President's immediate and unconditional resignation. In September, however, it was reported that a new draft Constitution (known as the Basic Law) had been drawn up and approved by a special commission, in preparation for the holding of a general election. The fighting intensified in late December, when Gen. Dostam transferred his allegiance to his hitherto arch-enemy, Hekmatyar, and the supporters of the two combined to confront the forces of Rabbani and Masoud. The violence spread throughout the provinces, resulting in large numbers of military and civilian casualties and the internal displacement of thousands of people. Various unsuccessful attempts were made in 1994 by neighbouring countries and by international organizations, such as the UN and the OIC, to achieve a negotiated settlement between the main warring factions. In late June the Supreme Court ruled that Rabbani could retain the presidency for a further six months, but failed to grant a similar extension to Hekmatyar's premiership. President Rabbani's extended term in office expired at the end of December. However, he did not resign, owing to, according to various sources, the continuation of the civil war and the lack of a suitable replacement for the post.

In the latter half of 1994, a new, hitherto unknown, militant grouping emerged in Afghanistan, known as the Taliban (the plural form of 'Talib', meaning 'seeker of religious knowledge'). The movement, which at the outset comprised an estimated 25,000 fighters (the majority of whom were reported to be young Pashtun graduates of fundamentalist Islamic schools established by Afghan refugees in Pakistan), advocated the adoption of extremist practices, including the complete seclusion of women from society. Although initially claiming that they had no interest in actually assuming power in Afghanistan, the Taliban, who were led by Mola Mohammad Omar, won a major victory in October, when they captured the city of Qandahar

from the forces of Hekmatyar, which had hitherto dominated the southern provinces of the country. In February 1995 the Taliban routed Hekmatyar's men from their headquarters in Charasiab, and within a month they controlled 10 provinces, mostly in southern and south-eastern Afghanistan. However, the Taliban retreated from their advance on Kabul when Rabbani's troops launched a massive counter-offensive. By mid-1995, with both the Taliban and Hekmatyar's men held in check, President Rabbani and his supporters were enjoying an unprecedented level of authority and confidence in Kabul and its environs. This was reflected in Rabbani's reneging on his earlier promise of standing down from the presidency in late March and in the growing number of countries that were considering reopening their embassies in the Afghan capital (the Indian embassy reopened in May). In mid-1995 talks were held between Rabbani and the Taliban, but relations between the two sides remained extremely strained. In early September the Taliban achieved a notable gain when they captured the key north-western city of Herat and the surrounding province from government forces. The resurgence of the Taliban apparently provoked an attack on the Pakistani embassy in Kabul by hundreds of pro-Government demonstrators protesting against Pakistan's alleged support for the student militia; the embassy was destroyed by fire, one employee was killed and a number wounded (including the ambassador himself). In response, the Afghan ambassador to Pakistan and six other Afghan diplomats were expelled from Islamabad. In October the Taliban launched a massive ground and air assault on Kabul, but by early January 1996 had failed to breach the capital's defences. The constant bombardment of the besieged city, however, resulted in hundreds of civilian deaths, and the road blockades around the capital caused serious shortages of vital supplies.

Despite the holding of exploratory negotiations between the Rabbani Government and major opposition parties in the first quarter of 1996, the fighting in and around Kabul intensified. The President's attempts at conciliation finally proved successful, however, in late May when, in a critical development (known as the Mahipar Agreement), he persuaded Hekmatyar to rejoin the Government. Hekmatyar's forces arrived in the capital during May to defend the city against the Taliban. In late June Hekmatyar resumed the post of Prime Minister and President Rabbani appointed a new Council of Ministers in early July, which was to hold power for a period of six–12 months pending the staging of a general election. In addition, under the terms of the Mahipar Agreement, a Constitution to cover the interim period was drawn up and published.

The political situation was radically altered in late September 1996 when, as a culmination of two weeks of sweeping military advances (including the capture of the crucial eastern city of Jalalabad), the Taliban seized control of Kabul following fierce clashes with government troops, who fled northwards together with the deposed Government. One of the Taliban movement's first actions in the captured capital was the summary execution of former President Najibullah and his brother. On assuming power, the Taliban declared Afghanistan a 'complete' Islamic state and appointed an interim Council of Ministers, led by Mola Mohammad Rabbani, to administer the country (of which it now controlled about two-thirds). Pakistan, which was widely suspected of actively aiding the Islamic militia, was the first country officially to recognize the new regime. (By mid-November, however, few other countries or international organizations had followed suit—neither the UN, India, Russia nor Iran had given official recognition to the Taliban administration.) The Taliban imposed a strict and intimidatory Islamic code—women were not permitted to enter employment or be formally educated beyond the age of eight; television, non-religious music, gambling and alcohol were all banned; amputations and public stonings were enforced as forms of punishment; compulsory attendance at mosques by all men was introduced; and women were ordered into purdah.

Taliban hopes that the opposition would remain divided were thwarted following the formation in October 1996 of a powerful military and logistical alliance by Gen. Dostam, the former Minister of Defence, Ahmad Shah Masoud, and the leader of the Shi'ite Hizb-i Wahadat-i Islami, Gen. Abdol Karim Khalili. Gen. Dostam, who controlled six northern provinces, apparently decided to establish this unlikely alliance after cease-fire talks between himself and the Taliban broke down. By late October the anti-Taliban forces, whose leaders were now collectively known as the Supreme Council for the Defence of Afghanistan (the headquarters of which were situated in Gen. Dostam's stronghold of Mazar-i-Sharif), had launched a concerted offensive against Kabul in the hope of ousting the Islamic militia. Despite repeated calls for a cease-fire from various foreign governments and the UN and despite complaints by Amnesty International regarding civilian casualties and abuses of human rights, the fighting between the Taliban and the allied opposition continued into January 1997. In mid-January, following the rapid collapse of UN-sponsored talks in Islamabad, the Taliban launched an unexpected offensive, advancing north and capturing Bagram air base and the provincial capital of Charikar. By late January the Taliban had made significant military gains and had pushed the front line to about 100 km north of Kabul. There was a dramatic development in mid-May when, following the defection of the Uzbek Gen. Abdul Malik and his men to the Taliban, the latter were able to capture the strategically-important northern town of Mazar-i-Sharif with relatively little bloodshed. Gen. Dostam was reported to have fled to Turkey, and his position as leader of the NIM was assumed by Gen. Malik. The Taliban now controlled about 90% of the country, including all of the major towns and cities. Their position was also strengthened by Pakistan's decision to be the first country to accord formal recognition to the Taliban Government (closely followed by Saudi Arabia and the United Arab Emirates). Taliban control of Mazar-i-Sharif, however, was extremely brief, and within only three days of entering the town the movement was in full retreat. It appeared that Gen. Malik's tenuous alliance with the Taliban had collapsed almost immediately and his troops, together with Shi'ite militia, forced the newcomers out after ferocious fighting. The Taliban were soundly routed, and by early June their forces had retreated almost 200 km south of Mazar-i-Sharif. Taliban officials later alleged that, following the recapture of Mazar-i-Sharif, about 3,000 Taliban prisoners-of-war were summarily executed by their captors.

The regional aspect of the Afghan conflict was highlighted at the beginning of June 1997 by the Taliban decision to close down the Iranian embassy in Kabul; the Iranian Government was widely suspected of actively aiding the anti-Taliban northern alliance. The alliance was reported to have been expanded and strengthened in early June by the inclusion of the forces of Hekmatyar and of the Mahaz-i-Melli-i-Islami (National Islamic Front), led by Pir Sayed Ahmad Gailani. This new coalition, which superseded the Supreme Council for the Defence of Afghanistan, was known as the United Islamic Front for the Salvation of Afghanistan (UIFSA). Despite the arrival of thousands of reinforcements from training camps in Pakistan (many of whom, however, were inexperienced teenagers), the Taliban suffered a series of military defeats in northern Afghanistan, and by late July the UIFSA forces were within firing range of Kabul, having recaptured Charikar and the air base at Bagram. In the same month the UN Security Council demanded a cease-fire and an end to all foreign intervention in Afghanistan. In mid-1997 it was widely believed that the Taliban were supported by Pakistan and Saudi Arabia; on the opposing side, to various degrees, were ranged Iran, India, the Central Asian states (which feared the encroachment of Taliban fundamentalism) and Russia.

In mid-August 1997 it was reported that the UIFSA had appointed a new Government, based in Mazar-i-Sharif, with Rabbani continuing as President, Abdorrahim Ghafurzai as Prime Minister, Masoud as Minister of Defence and Gen. Malik as Minister of Foreign Affairs. The former Prime Minister in the anti-Taliban administration, Gulbuddin Hekmatyar, refused to recognize the new Government. Within a few days of its appointment, however, seven members of the new Government, including Prime Minister Ghafurzai, were killed in an aeroplane crash. In late August the anti-Taliban opposition alliance appointed Abdolghaffur Rawanfarhadi as new Prime Minister.

In September 1997 Gen. Dostam was reported to have returned to Mazar-i-Sharif from Turkey, and in the following month the member parties of the UIFSA re-elected him as commander of the forces of the alliance and appointed him as Vice-President of the anti-Taliban administration. However, there were reports of a bitter rivalry between Gen. Dostam and Gen. Malik and skirmishes between their respective forces. Dostam's battle for supremacy with his rival led him to make overtures to the Taliban, including offers of exchanges of prisoners of war. Gen. Dostam also accused Gen. Malik of having massacred about 3,000 Taliban prisoners earlier in the year. By late November Gen. Dostam had resumed the leadership of the NIM, ousting Gen. Malik. In late October the Taliban unilaterally decided to change the country's name to the Islamic

Emirate of Afghanistan and altered the state flag, moves that were condemned by the opposition alliance and all of Afghanistan's neighbours except Pakistan. In late 1997 the World Food Programme launched an emergency operation to help people facing starvation in the impoverished central region of Hazarajat (held by the Shi'ite Hizb-i Wahadat-i Islami), which had been blockaded by the Taliban since August. In January 1998, however, the UN was forced to suspend its airlifts of emergency supplies when Taliban aircraft bombed the area. Meanwhile, in mid-December 1997 the UN Security Council issued a communiqué expressing its concern at the alleged massacres of civilians and prisoners-of-war being perpetrated by various factions in Afghanistan. In May 1998 a UN exploratory mission visited the sites of alleged atrocities to assess the feasibility of a full-scale war-crimes investigation being carried out.

In February 1998 the political crisis in Afghanistan was temporarily overshadowed by a devastating earthquake in the northern province of Takhar, which resulted in the deaths of more than 4,500 people and left about 30,000 homeless. The international relief campaign was hampered both by poor weather conditions and by the continuing fighting. Unused aid supplies proved invaluable in May when a second severe earthquake struck north-eastern Afghanistan, killing more than 5,000 people.

In late March 1998 the UN ceased operating aid programmes in the southern province of Qandahar (where the headquarters of the Taliban were located) following attacks on staff and constant harassment by the Taliban. In the same month there were reports of factional fighting between rival members of the UIFSA in and around Mazar-i-Sharif, highlighting the fragile nature of the anti-Taliban alliance. In late April, following the launch of a major diplomatic initiative by the USA, the Taliban and the UIFSA held talks, sponsored by the UN and the OIC, in Islamabad, the first formal peace negotiations between the two opposing sides for more than a year. In early May, however, the talks broke down, and fighting resumed to the north of Kabul. One of the main reasons cited for the failure of the negotiations was the refusal of the Taliban to lift the blockade on Hazarajat, where thousands of people were reported to be at risk of imminent starvation.

Relations between the Taliban Government and the UN deteriorated in June 1998, as a result of the former's decision to close more than 100 private schools and numerous small, home-based vocational courses in Kabul, many of which were educating girls. The living conditions of the 1.2m. inhabitants of the capital were expected to worsen considerably as a result of the expulsion in July of almost all international aid agencies by the Taliban.

On 1 August 1998 the Taliban captured the northern city of Shiberghan, Gen. Dostam's new headquarters, after a number of his Uzbek commanders allegedly accepted bribes from the Taliban and switched allegiance. Gen. Dostam was reported to have fled to the Uzbek border and thence to Turkey. Following the recapture of Mazar-i-Sharif by the Taliban (who allegedly now included considerable numbers of extremist volunteers from various other Islamic countries, including Pakistan, Saudi Arabia, Algeria and Egypt) in early August 1998, 10 Iranian diplomats and one Iranian journalist who were based in the city were reported to have been captured and killed by Taliban militia. The Taliban, however, initially denied any knowledge of the whereabouts of the Iranian nationals. In early September Afghanistan and Iran appeared to be on the verge of open warfare, as 70,000 Iranian troops were deployed on the mutual border. The situation became more serious when it emerged that nine of the missing Iranian nationals had, in fact, been murdered by members of the Taliban as they stormed Mazar-i-Sharif. (It was later reported that 2,000–6,000 Shi'ite Hazara civilians had been systematically massacred by the guerrillas after recapturing the city.) Both Iran and Afghanistan massed more troops on the border; by mid-September 500,000 Iranian troops had reportedly been placed on full military alert. Tension was further heightened in early October as Iran accused the Taliban of opening fire on its troops as they continued their military exercises in the border region; the Taliban responded with similar counter-accusations. In mid-October, in an attempt to defuse the tension, the Taliban agreed to free all Iranian prisoners being held in Afghanistan and to punish those responsible for the killing of the nine Iranian diplomats (or military advisers, according to the Taliban). By the end of the year the situation appeared much calmer, with the Taliban having expressed regret for the deaths of the Iranian nationals and

Iran having scaled down its border forces and having announced that it had no intention of invading Afghanistan.

Meanwhile, on 20 August 1998 the USA launched simultaneous air-strikes against alleged terrorist bases in eastern Afghanistan and Sudan, reportedly operated by an exiled Saudi Arabian militant leader, Osama bin Laden (who was supported by the Taliban), in retaliation for the bombing of two US embassies in East Africa earlier that month. Following this action, many aid agencies (including UN agencies) withdrew their remaining expatriate staff from Afghanistan, fearing terrorist acts of vengeance. In September the Taliban suffered a considerable set-back when Saudi Arabia (one of only three countries officially to recognize the regime) withdrew its funding and political support and recalled its envoy from Kabul. The decision by the Saudi Government substantially to downgrade its relations with the Taliban appeared to have been prompted by its opposition to the reported brutality of the guerrilla authorities and to their sheltering of bin Laden. In the following month the Taliban stated that, although they were not willing to extradite the Saudi dissident, in the event of a lawsuit being filed against him, they would be prepared to place him on trial in Afghanistan. The Taliban also insisted that bin Laden (who had reportedly been resident in Afghanistan for at least two years) was under close supervision, with his activities and media access suitably restricted. In late November evidence submitted by the US Government to the Afghan Supreme Court was deemed by the latter as inadequate grounds for bin Laden's arrest.

In mid-September 1998 the Taliban captured Bamian, a Shi'ite stronghold and the last major town outside its control; this victory meant that any substantial anti-Taliban opposition was effectively restricted to Masoud's stronghold in the Panjshir Valley to the north of Kabul. Taliban advances in the north of Afghanistan alarmed Russia and the Central Asian states, which feared the unsettling potential of an extremist Islamic army along their southern borders. In December the UN Security Council threatened the Taliban with the imposition of sanctions and called on the regime to commence negotiations with the opposition. Pakistan, on the other hand, demonstrated its diplomatic isolation with regard to the Afghan situation, by defending the Taliban and urging the other members of the UN to recognize their government. In December 1998–January 1999, despite threats from local Taliban commanders, the World Food Programme delivered emergency food aid to more than 120,000 people in the beleaguered region of Hazarajat.

In January 1999 it was reported that the UIFSA had established a multi-ethnic Supreme Military Council, under the command of Masoud, the aim of which was to give fresh impetus to the anti-Taliban movement and to co-ordinate manoeuvres against Taliban forces in northern Afghanistan. Despite a certain degree of optimism being raised by the holding of UN-monitored direct peace talks between representatives of the Taliban and the UIFSA in Ashgabat, Turkmenistan, in February and March, and in Tashkent, Uzbekistan, in July, ultimately very little was achieved as a result of the negotiations. In March, however, the first UN personnel returned to Afghanistan since their evacuation in August 1998 (following the murder of three UN employees); this represented the beginning of a phased return of UN international staff to Afghanistan. In June 1999, however, the International Red Cross temporarily withdrew non-essential foreign staff from Afghanistan, following an attack on a group of the aid organization's employees by suspected Taliban guerrillas; the Red Cross demanded security guarantees for its workers before it resumed operations.

In July 1999, following reports that bin Laden was being sheltered in eastern Afghanistan, the USA imposed financial and economic sanctions on the Taliban regime in a further attempt to persuade it to hand over the terrorist leader (who the US authorities suspected of planning more atrocities) to stand trial in the USA. In response, the Taliban claimed that the sanctions would have very little impact, since the volume of direct trade between Afghanistan and the USA was minimal, and again refused to extradite bin Laden. In the following month 10 people were killed when a large bomb exploded outside the residence of the Taliban leader, Mola Mohammad Omar, in Qandahar. The Taliban initially suspected foreign involvement in the attack (which was generally believed to have been an assassination attempt), while other commentators alleged that the incident illustrated growing divisions within the Taliban movement itself and increasing opposition to Omar's perceived autocracy. In late October the Taliban leader announced an extensive reorganization of key civilian, military and diplomatic

posts, including changes in the Council of Ministers. Of especial note was the appointment of an English-speaking moderate, Wakil Ahmad Motawakkil, to the post of Minister of Foreign Affairs, in an apparent attempt to improve the international image of the Taliban.

Meanwhile, following the collapse of the peace talks in Tashkent in July 1999, the Taliban launched a massive offensive against the UIFSA in the Panjshir Valley in early August; tens of thousands of (mainly Tajik) civilians were displaced in the fighting. Masoud rapidly instigated a devastating counter-attack, and the Taliban were forced into a swift retreat towards Kabul.

The Taliban continued to campaign for international recognition, to no avail. At the 1999 session of the UN General Assembly (held in September–November) the UN again rejected the Taliban request to represent Afghanistan; the seat remained under the control of President Rabbani, the leader of the 'Islamic State of Afghanistan'. In October 1999 the UN Secretary-General's Special Envoy to Afghanistan, Lakhdar Brahimi, announced his withdrawal from his mission, owing to the lack of progress (and particularly to the alleged negative attitude of the Taliban). In February 2000 Francesc Vendrell was appointed Head of the UN Special Mission to Afghanistan and Personal Representative of the UN Secretary-General, with the rank of Assistant Secretary-General. Relations between the UN and Afghanistan, however, remained tense, culminating in the UN's temporary withdrawal of its expatriate staff from Qandahar at the end of March, following an assault on UN offices by the Taliban.

In mid-November 1999 the UN Security Council imposed an embargo on all Taliban-controlled overseas assets and a ban on the international flights of the national airline, Ariana Afghan Airlines, as a result of the Afghan regime's continuing refusal to hand over the suspected terrorist leader, bin Laden, to stand trial in the USA or in a third (possibly Islamic) country. Following the imposition of the sanctions (which, although limited and largely irrelevant in economic terms, were, nonetheless, deeply demoralizing for the already beleaguered Afghan people), there were reports of large-scale demonstrations throughout Afghanistan, and international aid organizations once again came under attack. The impact of the sanctions was expected to be alleviated, however, by the reopening of key trade routes along the Afghan–Iranian border (which had been closed for 18 months) in late November. The Taliban Government expressed hopes that the trade with Iran would compensate for the significant decrease in imports of wheat and flour from Pakistan caused by the recent imposition of stricter border controls by the new military regime in Pakistan. Although the price of basic foodstuffs in Kabul and other towns duly declined dramatically as a result of renewed trade with Iran, the general economic circumstances in Kabul worsened. In February 2000 the UN relaxed the sanctions to permit the Taliban to operate flights to Mecca, in Saudi Arabia. In October an agreement was signed to allow weekly flights from Sharjah, in the United Arab Emirates, to Qandahar, in southern Afghanistan.

In late December 1999 the Taliban attained some international standing when an Indian Airlines aircraft was hijacked by a group of Kashmiri separatists. The aeroplane, en route from Kathmandu (Nepal) to Delhi (India), eventually landed in Qandahar. Although initially the Taliban were prepared to attack the aircraft, they were deterred from doing so and eventually persuaded the hijackers to reduce their demands. Having released the passengers, the hijackers were allowed to leave Qandahar. Although the Indian Minister of External Affairs acclaimed the administration's conduct immediately after the event, two months later he accused the Taliban of participating in the hijacking. In early February 2000 an Ariana Afghan Airlines civilian passenger aircraft on a domestic flight from Kabul to Mazar-i-Sharif was hijacked by a group of Afghan nationals. The aeroplane was diverted via Central Asia and Russia to Stansted airport in the United Kingdom. The hijackers surrendered, following several days of negotiations, during which they did not repeat their initial demand for the release of Ismail Khan (the anti-Taliban rebel leader and former governor of Herat, known as the 'Lion of Herat', imprisoned by the Taliban in Afghanistan). Some of the passengers returned to Afghanistan, while more than 30 sought asylum in the United Kingdom.

During 2000 the Taliban and UIFSA suffered internal discord, with defections of senior officials occurring on both sides. In March a partial reorganization of the Taliban Interim Council of Ministers was announced. Heavy fighting, concentrated in

AFGHANISTAN

GDP in terms of purchasing power parity totalled US $19,300m. (equivalent to $800 per head).

Agriculture (including hunting, forestry and fishing), according to UN estimates, contributed 64.4% of GDP in 1993. According to the FAO, 67.3% of the economically active population were employed in the agricultural sector in 1999. Livestock plays an important role in the traditional Afghan economy and is a major source of income for the country's numerous nomadic groups. In 1999 wheat production was estimated at 2.5m. metric tons. The principal commercial products of the sector are fruit and nuts (which accounted for around 39.7% of total export earnings, according to the IMF, in 1990/91), wool and cotton, and processed hides and skins. Total cereal output declined by 16% in 1999 to an estimated 3.26m. tons, owing to a shortage of irrigation water. Afghanistan continues to depend on food imports from abroad or in the form of aid. The total cereal import requirement for the period June 1998–July 1999 was estimated by the FAO at 740,000 tons, of which about 140,000 tons was to be wheat provided by the international aid community.

According to UN estimates, the industrial sector (including mining, manufacturing, construction and power) contributed 20% of GDP in 1993, while the value of industrial output in that year decreased by 11.4%, compared with the previous year.

Mining and quarrying employed about 1.5% of the settled labour force in 1979. Natural gas is the major mineral export (accounting for about 23.6% of total export earnings, according to the IMF, in 1988/89). Salt, hard coal, copper, lapis lazuli, barytes and talc are also mined. In addition, Afghanistan has small reserves of petroleum and iron ore. In November 1998 the Taliban Government announced its intention to resume operating ruby mines in Nangarhar province. Earlier in the year the Taliban had claimed that monthly revenue from the allegedly renascent mining sector in Afghanistan totalled US $3.5m. (including revenue from the recently revived steel-smelting plant in Baghlan province).

Manufacturing employed about 10.9% of the settled labour force in 1979. Afghanistan's major manufacturing industries include food products, cotton textiles, chemical fertilizers, cement, leather and plastic goods. In 1999 only one of the four existing cement plants in Afghanistan and about 10% of the textile mills remained in operation (prior to the Soviet invasion in 1979 there were about 220 state-owned factories operating in Afghanistan). The traditional handicraft sector has better survived the devastating effects of war, however, and carpets, leather, embroidery and fur products continued to be produced. In 2000 the Board for the Promotion of Private Investment approved several projects concerning the production of items such as vegetable oil, soap and soft drinks. A plant producing Western-style soft drinks was reportedly opened in late June.

Energy is derived principally from petroleum (which is imported from Iran and republics of the former USSR, notably Turkmenistan) and coal. The Government plans to increase internal sources of energy by establishing hydro- and thermal electric power stations. In early 1996 Afghanistan signed an agreement that could eventually lead to the construction of a high-pressure natural gas pipeline across the country, which would transport gas from Turkmenistan to Pakistan. In October 1997 the US petroleum company, Unocal, established a consortium which proposed to build a US $2,000m.-pipeline across Afghanistan. In March 1998, however, Unocal announced that the project was to be indefinitely postponed, owing to the continuing civil war; the project looked unlikely ever to be carried out, following Unocal's withdrawal from the consortium in December.

The negative trend in trade was apparent throughout the 1990s. The sharpest declines in both exports and imports occurred in 1992 and 1993. During these two years the total value of exports fell to US $60m. and $62m., respectively, compared with $284m. in 1991. Similarly, the cost of imports decreased from $765m. in 1991 to $237m. in 1992 and $200m. in 1993 and continued to decline thenceforth. In 1996, following the Taliban accession to power, trade showed little sign of revival. In 1996/97, according to UN figures, total exports were estimated at $125m. and the major export commodities included fruits and nuts, hand-woven carpets, wool, cotton, hides and pelts, and precious and semi-precious gems. The most important export markets in 1997 were Pakistan, Western Europe and the USA. In 1996/97, according to UN figures, total imports were estimated at $496m. and consisted mainly of food, petroleum products and other consumer goods. The principal sources of imports in 1997 were Singapore, Japan and Western Europe. These official statistics do not, however, include illegal trade and smuggling. The trade deficit would be much lower if the illegal revenue from the export of opium were included. In the 1990s a World Bank study estimated that $2,500m. worth of goods were smuggled between Afghanistan and Pakistan each year. In late 1995 it was announced that trade tariffs were to be reduced between the member states of the Economic Cooperation Organization (ECO, see p. 175), which Afghanistan joined in late 1992.

In 1997, according to UN figures, Afghanistan received US $123.6m. in bilateral official development assistance and $155.3m. in multilateral official development assistance. The European Union (EU) was the largest single aid donor to Afghanistan.

It is extremely difficult to provide an accurate economic profile of Afghanistan, owing to the continuing civil war, population movements, communication problems and lack of reliable official statistics. Over the past 20 years or so the traditional economy has been largely replaced by a criminal economy based on drugs and smuggling. The *mujahidin* Government, which came to power in April 1992, was faced with immense economic problems, including serious food and fuel shortages, a collapsed industrial sector, a severely-damaged infrastructure, the difficulties of thousands of refugees returning to their ravaged farms and fields studded with mines, and high inflation (according to one source, inflation reached an estimated 56.7% in 1991). Urgent requests for foreign aid, however, were jeopardized to some extent by the continuing bitter infighting between rival guerrilla and militia groups and by the fact that in 1994 Afghanistan overtook Myanmar in becoming the world's leading producer of opium. According to certain Western sources, the area of land in Afghanistan under poppy cultivation increased by more than 50% in the first half of the 1990s (mainly at the expense of the traditional wheat crop). There appeared little prospect of an improvement in Afghanistan's economic situation following the Taliban seizure of power in Kabul in September 1996, particularly taking into account the subsequent introduction of a decree banning women from working (with the exception of a small number of medical staff). Levels of aid to Afghanistan fell markedly in 1997, partly in response to the Taliban regime's harsh treatment of women and other abuses of human rights. In late 1997 the World Food Programme (WFP) launched an emergency operation to help people facing starvation in the impoverished central province of Bamian. In 2000 Afghanistan suffered from the worst drought experienced by the country in 30 years. The UN pledged aid to alleviate the effect of drought. In early December 2000 the EU announced further humanitarian assistance worth $7m., thereby increasing its contribution for that year to almost $12m. Bilateral aid was also donated to Afghanistan. Heavy rain and snow in mid-December, however, were reported to have alleviated the drought over much of the country.

In 1997, according to UN estimates, about 1m. Afghans were involved in the opium trade and UN field surveys indicated that around 165,000 acres of arable land were under poppy cultivation. Despite its strict opposition to drug abuse, the main source of unofficial revenue for the Taliban is undoubtedly the drugs trade. The Taliban were reported to be levying a 20% *zakat* (a type of wealth tax) from drugs-dealers on the transport of opium out of the country. In spite of the Taliban promise to ban the crop, in the late 1990s new areas were opened up to poppy cultivation. Afghanistan's output of raw opium increased by 117% in 1999, compared with the previous year, to reach 4,581 metric tons (most of which was exported to Pakistan, Russia and Europe). A UN-sponsored drugs control programme, which is attempting to encourage Afghanistan's estimated 200,000 opium farmers to plant vegetables and cereals rather than poppies, has met with only very limited success. In July 2000 the Taliban leadership instructed the imposition of a complete ban on poppy cultivation. Although there were reports of the clearing of land and the closure of heroin-producing factories, Afghanistan remained the largest supplier of opium in the world. According to the UN International Drug Control Programme, the production of opium declined to an estimated 3,600 tons in 2000; however, this reduction was largely due to the prevailing drought.

The Taliban administration's lack of state funds was clearly illustrated by the fact that the budget for 1997/98 (excluding military expenditure) totalled a mere US $100,000. In an attempt to attract foreign investment, the Taliban offered free land to anyone willing to build a new factory in Afghanistan; but very few serious foreign investors showed any interest in this scheme. In September 1998, however, a US company, Telephone Systems International, agreed a US $415m.-contract with the Taliban to provide a telecommunications system in Kabul. It was reported in September 2000 that companies from China, Iran, the United Arab Emirates and the USA were working to supply telecommunications links to all of Afghanistan.

At the end of 1998 UNHCR estimated that about 4m. Afghan refugees had been repatriated since 1988, with around 2.6m. remaining in exile abroad (mainly in Pakistan and Iran). In addition to the refugees living abroad, it was estimated that about 1m. people were internally displaced within Afghanistan itself. In April 2000 UNHCR and Iran embarked on a joint programme for the voluntary repatriation of Afghan refugees living in Iran. By early December some 100,000 Afghans had left Iran. However, this represented only a small proportion of the estimated 1.4m.–2.0m. Afghan refugee population living in Iran.

Social Welfare

Health services available to the people of Afghanistan were scarce even before the outbreak of civil war, but have rapidly deteriorated over the past 20 years or so. There is an immense shortage of drugs and medical supplies. Qualified health personnel and medicines are provided by the international organizations and NGOs, and whatever health facilities exist now are also operated by these bodies. In view of the fact that only 29% of the population has access to health services, it is not surprising that diseases of various sorts are on the increase. The estimated average life expectancy at birth in 1998 stood at only 46 years for males and 45 for females, by far the lowest in Asia. In that year there were 150 deaths of children under 12 months old for every 1,000 live births, the highest infant mortality rate in Asia. In 1987, according to UN figures, there were 2,957 physicians (2 per 10,000 population), 329 dentists and 2,135 nursing personnel in Afghanistan. In 1988 government officials assessed the combined total of medical centres and hospitals at 196. In mid-1996 only four regional hospitals were functioning in Afghanistan.

Education

The prolonged war has resulted in a large-scale exodus of teachers, and nearly 2,000 school buildings have been destroyed. In 1996/97 it was estimated that only about 600–650 primary and secondary schools were functioning.

Primary education, which is officially compulsory, begins at seven years of age and lasts for six years. Secondary education, beginning at 13 years of age, lasts for a further six years. As a proportion of the school-age population, the total enrolment at primary and secondary schools was equivalent to 36% (males 49%; females 22%) in 1995. Primary enrolment in that year was equivalent to an estimated 49% of children in the relevant age-group (boys 64%; girls 32%), while the enrolment ratio at general secondary schools was equivalent to 22% (boys 32%; girls 11%).

Afghanistan has one of the highest levels of adult illiteracy in Asia, with an average rate (excluding the nomadic population) of 68.5% (males 52.8%; females 85.0%) in 1995, according to estimates by UNESCO.

Since 1979 higher education has been disrupted by the departure of many teaching staff from Afghanistan. In 1980 it was reported that up to 80% of university staff had fled their posts. In 1991 there were six institutions of higher education (including Kabul University, which was founded in 1932) in Afghanistan; a total of 17,000 students were enrolled in these institutions in that year.

Following their seizure of power in late September 1996, the Taliban banned education for girls over the age of eight, closed all the women's institutes of higher education and planned to draw up a new Islamic curriculum for boys' schools. In early 1998, however, there were still two co-educational universities functioning in Afghanistan (in areas not under Taliban control), one of which was situated in Bamian (with 300 students and 16 teachers). In mid-1998 the UN was angered by the Taliban decision to close more than 100 private schools and numerous small, home-based vocational courses in Kabul, many of which were educating girls. In 1999, however, the Taliban officially sanctioned the establishment of 13 schools for girls (up to the age of 12) in Kabul and its environs. According to Taliban figures, in September of that year 1,586,026 pupils were being educated by 59,792 teachers in 3,836 *madrassas* (mosque schools).

Public Holidays

According to the Hejri solar calendar, the Afghan year 1379 runs from 21 March 2000 to 20 March 2001, and the year 1380 runs from 21 March 2001 to 20 March 2002.

In March 1998 the Taliban authorities in Kabul ordered the replacement of the Hejri solar calendar with the Hejri lunar calendar.

2001: 6 March* (Id al-Adha, Feast of the Sacrifice), 21 March (Nau-roz: New Year's Day, Iranian calendar), 4 April* (Ashura, Martyrdom of Imam Husayn), 18 April (Liberation Day), 27 April (Revolution Day), 1 May (Workers' Day), 4 June * (Roze-Maulud, Birth of Prophet Muhammad), 18 August (Independence Day), 17 November* (first day of Ramadan), 17 December* (Id al-Fitr, end of Ramadan).

2002: 23 February* (Id al-Adha, Feast of the Sacrifice), 21 March (Nau-roz: New Year's Day, Iranian calendar), 24 March* (Ashura, Martyrdom of Imam Husayn), 18 April (Liberation Day), 27 April (Revolution Day), 1 May (Workers' Day), 24 May* (Roze-Maulud, Birth of Prophet Muhammad), 18 August (Independence Day), 6 November* (first day of Ramadan), 6 December* (Id al-Fitr, end of Ramadan).

* These holidays are dependent on the Islamic lunar calendar and may vary by one or two days from the dates given.

Weights and Measures

The metric system has been officially adopted but traditional weights are still used. One 'seer' equals 16 lb (7.3 kg).

Statistical Survey

Source (unless otherwise stated): Central Statistics Authority, Block 4, Macroraion, Kabul; tel. (93) 24883.

Area and Population

AREA, POPULATION AND DENSITY

Area (sq km)	652,225*
Population (census results)	
23 June 1979†	
Males	6,712,377
Females	6,338,981
Total	13,051,358
Population (official estimates at mid-year)‡	
1984	17,672,000
1985	18,136,000
1986	18,614,000
Density (per sq km) at mid-1986	28.5

* 251,773 sq miles.

† Figures exclude nomadic population, estimated to total 2,500,000. The census data also exclude an adjustment for underenumeration, estimated to have been 5% for the urban population and 10% for the rural population.

‡ These data include estimates for nomadic population (2,734,000 in 1983), but take no account of emigration by refugees. Assuming an average net outflow of 703,000 persons per year in 1980–85, the UN Population Division has estimated Afghanistan's total mid-year population (in '000) as: 14,519 in 1985; 14,529 in 1986; 14,709 in 1987 (Source: UN, *World Population Prospects: 1988*). In late 1999 it was estimated that the total Afghan refugee population numbered 2.6m., of whom 1.2m. were living in Pakistan and 1.4m. in Iran.

Population (official estimates, excluding nomads, at mid-year): 15,219,000 in 1987; 15,513,000 in 1988; 15,814,000 in 1989; 16,121,000 in 1990; 16,433,000 in 1991; 16,750,000 in 1992; 17,080,000 in 1993; 17,420,000 in 1994; 19,663,000* in 1995; 20,368,000* in 1996; 20,893,000* in 1997; 21,354,000* in 1998; 21,923,000* in 1999.

* UN estimates, including nomadic population, at mid-year (Source: UN, *World Population Prospects: The 1998 Revision*).

PROVINCES (estimates, March 1982)*

		Area (sq km)	Population	Density (per sq km)	Capital (with population)
Kabul .	.	4,585	1,517,909	331.1	Kabul (1,036,407)
Kapesa†	.	1,871	262,039	140.1	Mahmudraki (1,262)
Parvan	.	9,399	527,987	56.2	Charikar (25,117)
Wardag†	.	9,023	300,796	33.3	Maidanshar (2,153)
Loghar†	.	4,652	226,234	48.6	Baraiki Barak (1,164)‡
Ghazni	.	23,378	676,416	28.9	Ghazni (31,985)
Paktia	.	9,581	506,264	52.8	Gardiz (10,040)
Nangarhar	.	7,616	781,619	102.6	Jalalabad (57,824)
Laghman .	.	7,210	325,010	45.0	Mehterlam (4,191)
Kunar.	.	10,479	261,604	25.0	Asadabad (2,196)
Badakhshan	.	47,403	520,620	10.9	Faizabad (9,564)
Takhar	.	12,376	543,818	43.9	Taloqan (20,947)
Baghlan	.	17,109	516,921	30.2	Baghlan (41,240)
Kunduz	.	7,827	582,600	74.4	Kunduz (57,112)
Samangan.	.	15,465	273,864	17.7	Aibak (5,191)
Balkh .	.	12,593	609,590	48.4	Mazar-i-Sharif (110,367)
Jawzjan	.	25,553	615,877	24.1	Shiberghan (19,969)
Fariab	.	22,279	609,703	27.3	Maymana (40,212)
Badghis	.	21,858	244,346	11.2	Kalainow (5,614)
Herat .	.	61,315	808,224	13.2	Herat (150,497)
Farah .	.	47,788	245,474	5.1	Farah (19,761)
Neemroze .	.	41,356	108,418	2.6	Zarang (6,809)
Helmand .	.	61,829	541,508	8.8	Lashkargha (22,707)

PROVINCES (estimates, March 1982)* — continued

		Area (sq km)	Population	Density (per sq km)	Capital (with population)
Qandahar .	.	47,676	597,954	12.5	Qandahar (191,345)
Zabul .	.	17,293	187,612	10.8	Qalat (6,251)
Uruzgan	.	29,295	464,556	15.5	Terincot (3,534)
Ghor .	.	38,666	353,494	9.1	Cheghcheran (3,126)
Bamian	.	17,414	280,859	16.1	Bamian (7,732)
Paktika	.	19,336	256,470	13.3	Sheran (1,469)
Total .	.	**652,225**	**13,747,786**	**21.1**	

* Population figures refer to settled inhabitants only, excluding kuchies (nomads), estimated at 2,600,000 for the whole country.

† Formed in 1981.

‡ The capital of Loghar Province was later changed to Pul-i-Alam.

Note: Two new provinces, named Sar-e Pol and Nurestan, were formed in April 1988 and July 1988 respectively, bringing the total number of provinces in Afghanistan to 31.

PRINCIPAL TOWNS (estimated population at March 1982)

Kabul (capital) .	.	1,036,407	Kunduz	. . . .	57,112
Qandahar .	.	191,345	Baghlan	. . . .	41,240
Herat .	.	150,497	Maymana	. . .	40,212
Mazar-i-Sharif .	.	110,367	Pul-i-Khomri	. .	32,695
Jalalabad .	.	57,824	Ghazni	. . . .	31,985

Estimated population at July 1988: Kabul 1,424,400; Qandahar 225,500; Herat 177,300; Mazar-i-Sharif 130,600 (Source: UN, *Demographic Yearbook 1997*).

BIRTHS AND DEATHS (UN estimates, annual averages)

			1980–85	1985–90	1990–95
Birth rate (per 1,000).	.	.	48.9	47.1	49.7
Death rate (per 1,000)	.	.	23.0	22.7	21.7

Expectation of life (UN estimates, years at birth, 1990–95): 43.5 (males 43.0; females 44.0).

Source: UN, *World Population Prospects: The 1998 Revision*.

ECONOMICALLY ACTIVE POPULATION*
(ISIC Major Divisions, persons aged 8 years and over, 1979 census)

	Males	Females	Total
Agriculture, hunting, forestry and fishing	2,358,821	10,660	2,369,481
Mining and quarrying . .	57,492	1,847	59,339
Manufacturing	170,908	252,465	423,373
Electricity, gas and water. .	11,078	276	11,354
Construction.	50,670	416	51,086
Wholesale and retail trade . .	135,242	2,618	137,860
Transport, storage and communications	65,376	867	66,243
Other services	716,511	32,834	749,345
Total	**3,566,098**	**301,983**	**3,868,081**

* Figures refer to settled population only and exclude 77,510 persons seeking work for the first time (66,057 males; 11,453 females).

Agriculture

PRINCIPAL CROPS ('000 metric tons)

	1997	1998	1999
Wheat	2,711	2,834	2,499
Rice (paddy)	400†	450	280
Barley	250	240	216
Maize	300	330	240
Millet	22*	22*	22*
Potatoes	235*	235*	235*
Pulses	35*	35*	35*
Sesame seed	24*	24*	24*
Cottonseed	66*	66*	66*
Cotton (lint)	22*	22*	22*
Vegetables	380*	380*	380*
Watermelons	90*	90*	90*
Cantaloupes and other melons	22*	22*	22*
Grapes	330*	330*	330*
Sugar cane	38*	38*	38*
Sugar beets	1*	1*	1*
Apples	18*	18*	18*
Peaches and nectarines	14*	14*	14*
Plums	35*	35*	35*
Oranges	12*	12*	12*
Apricots	38*	38*	38*
Other fruit	168*	168*	168*

* FAO estimate(s).   † Unofficial figure.

Source: FAO.

LIVESTOCK (FAO estimates, '000 head, year ending 30 September)

	1997	1998	1999
Horses	300	300	300
Mules	23	23	23
Asses	1,160	1,160	1,160
Cattle	1,500	1,500	1,500
Camels	265	265	265
Sheep	14,300	14,300	14,300
Goats	2,200	2,200	2,200

Poultry (FAO estimates, million): 7 in 1997; 7 in 1998; 7 in 1999.

Source: FAO.

LIVESTOCK PRODUCTS (FAO estimates, '000 metric tons)

	1997	1998	1999
Beef and veal	65	65	65
Mutton and lamb	117	117	117
Goat meat	24	24	24
Poultry meat	14	14	14
Other meat	11	11	11
Cows' milk	300	300	300
Sheep's milk	201	201	201
Goats' milk	41	41	41
Cheese	16	16	16
Butter and ghee	11	11	11
Hen eggs	18	18	18
Honey	3	3	3
Wool:			
greasy	16	16	16
clean	9	9	n.a.
Cattle hides	11	11	11
Sheepskins	18	18	18
Goatskins	4	4	4

Source: FAO.

Forestry

ROUNDWOOD REMOVALS
('000 cu m, excluding bark)

	1996	1997	1998
Sawlogs, veneer logs and logs for sleepers*	856	856	856
Other industrial wood	841	862	881
Fuel wood	6,060	6,217	6,354
Total	7,757	7,935	8,091

* Assumed to be unchanged from 1976.

Source: FAO, *Yearbook of Forest Products*.

SAWNWOOD PRODUCTION (FAO estimates, '000 cu m)

	1974	1975	1976
Coniferous (softwood)	360	310	380
Broadleaved (hardwood)	50	20	20
Total	410	330	400

1977–98: Annual production as in 1976 (FAO estimates).

Source: FAO, *Yearbook of Forest Products*.

Fishing

(FAO estimates, metric tons, live weight)

	1996	1997	1998
Total catch (freshwater fishes)	1,300	1,250	1,200

Source: FAO, *Yearbook of Fishery Statistics*.

Mining

('000 metric tons, unless otherwise indicated)

	1994	1995	1996
Hard coal*†	6	5	4
Gypsum (crude)‡	3	3	3†
Natural gas (petajoules)*†	7	7	6
Salt (unrefined)*	13	13	13

* Twelve months beginning 21 March of year stated.

† Estimate(s).

‡ Data from the US Bureau of Mines.

Sources: UN, *Industrial Commodity Statistics Yearbook* and *Statistical Yearbook for Asia and the Pacific*.

Industry

SELECTED PRODUCTS
(year ending 20 March, '000 metric tons, unless otherwise indicated)

	1986/87	1987/88	1988/89
Margarine	3.5	3.3	1.8
Vegetable oil	4	n.a.	n.a.
Wheat flour*	187	203	166
Wine ('000 hectolitres)*	289	304	194
Soft drinks ('000 hectolitres)	8,500	10,300	4,700
Woven cotton fabrics (million sq metres)	58.1	52.6	32.1
Woven woollen fabrics (million sq metres)	0.4	0.3	0.3
Footwear—excl. rubber ('000 pairs)*	613	701	607
Rubber footwear ('000 pairs)*	2,200	3,200	2,200
Nitrogenous fertilizers†	56	57	55
Cement	103	104	70
Electric energy (million kWh)*‡	1,171	1,257	1,109

* Production in calendar years 1986, 1987 and 1988.
† Production in year ending 30 June.
‡ Provisional.

Wheat flour ('000 metric tons): 1,832 in 1994; 2,029 in 1995; 2,145 in 1996.
Nitrogenous fertilizers (provisional, year ending 30 June, '000 metric tons): 14 in 1994/95; 10 in 1995/96; 5 in 1996/97.
Cement (provisional, year ending 20 March, '000 metric tons): 115 in 1993/94; 115 in 1994/95; 115 in 1995/96.
Electric energy (provisional, year ending 20 March, million kWh): 687 in 1994/95; 625 in 1995/96; 593 in 1996/97.

Sources: UN, *Industrial Commodity Statistics Yearbook* and *Statistical Yearbook for Asia and the Pacific*, FAO (Rome) and US Bureau of Mines.

Finance

CURRENCY AND EXCHANGE RATES

Monetary Units
100 puls (puli) = 2 krans = 1 afghani (Af).

Sterling, Dollar and Euro Equivalents (29 December 2000)
£1 sterling = 4,476.6 afghanis;
US $1 = 3,000.0 afghanis;
€1 = 2,791.5 afghanis;
10,000 afghanis = £2.234 = $3.333 = €3.582.

Exchange Rate
The foregoing information refers to the official exchange rate. The official rate was maintained at US $1 = 1,000 afghanis between 1 May 1995 and 30 April 1996. From 1 May 1996 a rate of US $1 = 3,000 afghanis has been in operation. However, this rate is applicable to only a limited range of transactions. There is also a market-determined rate, which was US $1 = 28,700 afghanis in March 1998.

BUDGET (million afghanis, year ending 20 March)

	1983/84	1984/85
Current revenue	34,744	37,615
Taxes	13,952	17,081
Non-taxes	20,792	20,534
Current expenditure	37,760	43,177
Capital expenditure	5,433	8,000

Source: UN, *Statistical Yearbook for Asia and the Pacific*.

BANK OF AFGHANISTAN RESERVES* (US $ million at December)

	1989	1990	1991
IMF special drawing rights	10.63	9.02	6.67
Reserve position in IMF	6.41	6.97	7.01
Foreign exchange	226.65	250.41	221.22
Total	243.69	266.40	234.89

* Figures exclude gold reserves, totalling 965,000 troy ounces since 1980. Assuming a gold price of 12,850 afghanis per ounce, these reserves were officially valued at US $245.06 million in December of each year 1985–91.
1992 (US $ million at December): IMF special drawing rights 4.37; Reserve position in IMF 6.78.
1993 (US $ million at December): IMF special drawing rights 2.76; Reserve position in IMF 6.77.
1994 (US $ million at December): IMF special drawing rights 1.40; Reserve position in IMF 7.19.
1995 (US $ million at December): Reserve position in IMF 7.33.
1996 (US $ million at December): Reserve position in IMF 7.09.
1997 (US $ million at December): Reserve position in IMF 6.65.
1998 (US $ million at December): Reserve position in IMF 6.94.
Source: IMF, *International Financial Statistics*.

MONEY SUPPLY (million afghanis at 21 December)

	1989	1990	1991
Currency outside banks	222,720	311,929	454,750
Private-sector deposits at Bank of Afghanistan	12,838	13,928	19,368
Demand deposits at commercial banks	11,699	18,217	n.a.

Source: IMF, *International Financial Statistics*.

COST OF LIVING
(retail price index, excluding rent; base: 1990 = 100)

	1989	1990	1991
All items	67.9	100.0	143.8

Source: UN, *Statistical Yearbook for Asia and the Pacific*.

NATIONAL ACCOUNTS
('000 million afghanis at constant 1978 prices)
Gross Domestic Product by Economic Activity

	1991	1992	1993
Agriculture, hunting, forestry and fishing	59.9	62.7	57.3
Mining and quarrying			
Manufacturing	29.2	14.3	12.3
Electricity, gas and water			
Construction	7.0	5.8	5.5
Wholesale and retail trade, restaurants and hotels	11.1	10.5	10.1
Transport, storage and communications	4.8	4.5	2.0
Finance, insurance, real estate and business services	2.1	2.0	1.8
GDP in purchasers' values	114.1	99.8	89.0

Source: UN, *Statistical Yearbook for Asia and the Pacific*.

BALANCE OF PAYMENTS (US $ million)

	1987	1988	1989
Exports of goods f.o.b.	538.7	453.8	252.3
Imports of goods f.o.b.	−904.5	−731.8	−623.5
Trade balance	−365.8	−278.0	−371.2
Exports of services	35.6	69.6	8.2
Imports of services	−156.3	−120.0	−103.4
Balance on goods and services	−486.5	−328.4	−466.4
Other income received	19.2	23.3	20.1
Other income paid	−11.3	−11.5	−7.9
Balance on goods, services and income	−478.6	−316.6	−454.2
Current transfers received	311.7	342.8	312.1
Current transfers paid	−	−	−1.2
Current balance	−166.9	26.2	−143.3
Investment liabilities	−33.9	−4.1	−59.6
Net errors and omissions	211.6	−47.7	182.8
Overall balance	10.8	−25.6	−20.1

Source: IMF, *International Financial Statistics.*

OFFICIAL DEVELOPMENT ASSISTANCE (US $ million)

	1995	1996	1997
Bilateral	106.0	84.3	123.6
Multilateral	109.1	144.1	155.3
Total	215.1	228.4	278.9
Grants	215.2	228.5	279.0
Loans	−0.1	−0.1	−0.1
Per caput assistance (US $)	10.9	11.2	13.3

Source: UN, *Statistical Yearbook for Asia and the Pacific.*

External Trade

PRINCIPAL COMMODITIES (US $ '000, year ending 20 March)

Imports c.i.f.	1980/81	1981/82	1983/84*
Wheat	798	18,100	38,251
Sugar	40,833	50,328	25,200
Tea	28,369	n.a.	23,855
Cigarettes	5,114	7,219	12,755
Vegetable oil	17,320	26,332	30,481
Drugs	4,497	4,195	3,768
Soaps	9,991	17,256	8,039
Tyres and tubes	16,766	12,764	28,823
Textile yarn and thread	16,800	24,586	n.a.
Cotton fabrics	873	6,319	n.a.
Rayon fabrics	6,879	9,498	n.a.
Other textile goods	52,546	49,036	n.a.
Vehicles and spare parts	89,852	141,062	n.a.
Petroleum products	124,000	112,093	n.a.
Footwear (new)	2,058	5,275	5,317
Bicycles	2,042	488	1,952
Matches	1,171	1,542	1,793
Sewing machines	140	285	266
Electric and non-electric machines	2,333	765	n.a.
Chemical materials	7,464	6,636	n.a.
Agricultural tractors	1	8,280	n.a.
Fertilizers	8,325	3,300	3,904
Used clothes	2,523	1,875	5,334
Television receivers	5,391	3,241	10,139
Other items	106,662	92,307	n.a.
Total	551,748	622,416	846,022

* Figures for 1982/83 are not available.

Total imports c.i.f. (US $ million, year ending 20 March): 347 in 1994/95; 359 in 1995/96; 496 in 1996/97. Source: UN, *Statistical Yearbook for Asia and the Pacific.*

Exports f.o.b.	1988/89	1989/90	1990/91
Fruit and nuts	103,400	110,200	93,300
Karakul fur skins	6,100	3,600	3,000
Natural gas	93,200	n.a.	n.a.
Wool	30,900	5,500	9,600
Carpets	39,100	38,000	44,000
Cotton	8,000	5,300	2,500
Total (incl. others)	394,700	235,900	235,100

Source: IMF, *International Financial Statistics.*

1991/92 (million afghanis, year ending 20 March): Dried fruit and nuts 165,770; Karakul skins 4,303; Wool 19,953; Carpets and rugs 52,887.

1992/93 (million afghanis, year ending 20 March): Dried fruit and nuts 33,259; Wool 7,585; Carpets and rugs 21,920.

1995/96 (million afghanis, year ending 20 March): Dried fruit and nuts 19,282; Karakul skins 27; Wool 122; Carpets and rugs 67,083.

Total exports f.o.b. (US $ million, year ending 20 March): 102 in 1994/95; 166 in 1995/96; 125 in 1996/97.

Source: UN, *Statistical Yearbook for Asia and the Pacific.*

PRINCIPAL TRADING PARTNERS (estimates, US $ million)

Imports	1995	1996	1997
ASEAN members	50	180	148
Indonesia	3	9	18
Malaysia	15	10	11
Singapore	19	138	101
Thailand	13	23	18
SAARC members	40	43	58
Bangladesh	1	6	10
India	16	22	25
Pakistan	22	14	21
Central Asian republics	13	29	46
Kazakhstan	3	6	9
Kyrgyzstan	−	7	14
Tajikistan	−	2	3
Turkmenistan	10	14	20
Other Asian countries			
China, People's Republic	35	34	36
Hong Kong	12	7	11
Japan	92	116	97
Turkey	6	2	7
Western Europe	65	138	66
Russia	19	23	21
USA	4	8	13
Total (incl. others)	363	621	525

Exports	1995	1996	1997
ASEAN members	3	18	8
Malaysia	1	1	−
Singapore	−	5	7
Thailand	2	12	−
SAARC members	22	30	36
Bangladesh	1	1	1
India	7	4	4
Pakistan	14	25	30
Sri Lanka	−	−	1
Central Asian republics	68	6	9
Kyrgyzstan	62	−	−
Tajikistan	−	2	4
Turkmenistan	6	4	5
Other Asian countries			
China, People's Republic	15	3	1
Japan	1	2	9
Turkey	−	−	1
Western Europe	33	31	45
Russia	12	7	7
Africa	−	1	1
USA	5	16	10
Total (incl. others)	166	126	149

Source: UN, *Statistical Yearbook for Asia and the Pacific.*

Transport

ROAD TRAFFIC (estimates, '000 motor vehicles in use)

	1994	1995	1996
Passenger cars	31.0	31.0	31.0
Commercial vehicles	25.0	25.0	25.0

Source: International Road Federation, *World Road Statistics*.

CIVIL AVIATION ('000)

	1995	1996	1997
Kilometres flown	6,000	6,000	6,000
Passengers carried . . .	250	256	90
Passenger-km	276,000	286,000	158,000
Freight ton-km	38,000	40,000	50,000

Source: UN, *Statistical Yearbook*.

Tourism

	1995	1996	1997
Tourist arrivals ('000) . .	4	4	4
Tourism receipts (US $ million) .	1	1	1

Source: World Tourism Organization, *Yearbook of Tourism Statistics*.

Communications Media

	1995	1996	1997
Radio receivers ('000 in use) . .	2,400	2,550	2,750
Television receivers ('000 in use) .	200	250	270
Daily newspapers			
Number	15*	12	n.a.
Average circulation ('000			
copies)	200*	113	n.a.

* Estimate.

Source: UNESCO, *Statistical Yearbook*.

Telephones (estimates, '000 main lines in use): 29 in 1995; 29 in 1996; 29 in 1997. (Source: UN, *Statistical Yearbook*).

Education

(1995/96)

	Institutions	Teachers	Pupils
Pre-primary	88	2,110	n.a.
Primary	2,146	21,869	1,312,200
Secondary*	n.a.	19,085	512,900
Higher	n.a.	n.a.	12,800

* Figures refer to general secondary education only, excluding vocational and teacher training.

Source: UN, *Statistical Yearbook for Asia and the Pacific*.

Directory

The Constitution

Immediately after the coup of 27 April 1978 (the Saur Revolution), the 1977 Constitution was abolished. Both Nur Mohammad Taraki (Head of State from April 1978 to September 1979) and his successor, Hafizullah Amin (September–December 1979), promised to introduce new constitutions, but these leaders were removed from power before any drafts had been prepared by special commissions which they had appointed. On 21 April 1980 the Revolutionary Council ratified the Basic Principles of the Democratic Republic of Afghanistan. These were superseded by a new Constitution ratified in April 1985. Another new Constitution was ratified during a meeting of a Loya Jirgah (Supreme National Tribal Assembly), held on 29–30 November 1987. This Constitution was amended in May 1990. The following is a summary of the Constitution as it stood in May 1990.

GENERAL PROVISIONS

The fundamental duty of the State is to defend the independence, national sovereignty and territorial integrity of the Republic of Afghanistan. National sovereignty belongs to the people. The people exercise national sovereignty through the Loya Jirgah and the Meli Shura.

Foreign policy is based on the principle of peaceful co-existence and active and positive non-alignment. Friendship and co-operation are to be strengthened with all countries, particularly neighbouring and Islamic ones. Afghanistan abides by the UN Charter and the Universal Declaration of Human Rights and supports the struggle against colonialism, imperialism, Zionism, racism and fascism. Afghanistan favours disarmament and the prevention of the proliferation of nuclear and chemical weapons. War propaganda is prohibited.

Islam is the religion of Afghanistan and no law shall run counter to the principles of Islam.

Political parties are allowed to be formed, providing that their policies and activities are in accordance with the provisions of the Constitution and the laws of the country. A party that is legally formed cannot be dissolved without legal grounds. Judges and prosecutors cannot be members of a political party during their term of office.

Pashtu and Dari are the official languages.

The capital is Kabul.

The State shall follow the policy of understanding and co-operation between all nationalities, clans and tribes within the country to ensure equality and the rapid development of backward regions.

The family constitutes the basic unit of society. The State shall adopt necessary measures to ensure the health of mothers and children.

The State protects all forms of legal property, including private property. The hereditary right to property shall be guaranteed according to Islamic law.

For the growth of the national economy, the State encourages foreign investment in the Republic of Afghanistan and regulates it in accordance with the law.

RIGHTS AND DUTIES OF THE PEOPLE

All subjects of Afghanistan are equal before the law. The following rights are guaranteed: the right to life and security, to complain to the appropriate government organs, to participate in the political sphere, to freedom of speech and thought, to hold peaceful demonstrations and strikes, to work, to free education, to protection of health and social welfare, to scientific, technical and cultural activities, to freedom of movement both within Afghanistan and abroad, to observe the religious rites of Islam and of other religions, to security of residence and privacy of communication and correspondence, and to liberty and human dignity.

In criminal cases, an accused person is considered innocent until guilt is recognized by the court. Nobody may be arrested, detained or punished except in accordance with the law.

Every citizen is bound to observe the Constitution and the laws of the Republic of Afghanistan, to pay taxes and duties to the State in accordance with the provisions of the law, and to undertake military service, when and as required.

LOYA JIRGAH

This is the highest manifestation of the will of the people of Afghanistan. It is composed of: the President and Vice-Presidents, members of the Meli Shura (National Assembly), the General Prosecutor, the Council of Ministers, the Attorney-General, his deputies and members of the Attorney-General's Office, the chairman of the Constitution Council, the heads of the provincial councils, representatives from each province, according to the number of their representatives in the Wolasi Jirgah (House of Representatives), elected by the people by a general secret ballot, and a minimum of 50 people, from among prominent political, scientific, social and religious figures, appointed by the President.

The Loya Jirgah is empowered: to approve and amend the Constitution; to elect the President and to accept the resignation of the President; to consent to the declaration of war and armistice; and to adopt decisions on major questions regarding the destiny of the country. The Loya Jirgah shall be summoned, opened and chaired by the President. Sessions of the Loya Jirgah require a minimum attendance of two-thirds of the members. Decisions shall be adopted by a majority vote. In the event of the dissolution of the Wolasi Jirgah (House of Representatives), its members shall retain their membership of the Loya Jirgah until a new Wolasi Jirgah is elected. Elections to the Loya Jirgah shall be regulated by law and the procedure laid down by the Loya Jirgah itself.

THE PRESIDENT

The President is the Head of State and shall be elected by a majority vote of the Loya Jirgah for a term of seven years. No person can be elected as President for more than two terms. The President is accountable, and shall report, to the Loya Jirgah. The Loya Jirgah shall be convened to elect a new President 30 days before the end of the term of office of the outgoing President. Any Muslim citizen of the Republic of Afghanistan who is more than 40 years of age can be elected as President.

The President shall exercise the following executive powers: the supreme command of the armed forces; the ratification of the resolutions of the Meli Shura; the appointment of the Prime Minister; the approval of the appointment of ministers, judges and army officials; the granting of citizenship and the commuting of punishment; the power to call a referendum, to proclaim a state of emergency, and to declare war (with the consent of the Loya Jirgah). Should a state of emergency continue for more than three months, the consent of the Loya Jirgah is imperative for its extension.

In the event of the President being unable to perform his duties, the presidential functions and powers shall be entrusted to the first Vice-President. In the event of the death or resignation of the President, the first Vice-President shall ask the Loya Jirgah to elect a new President within one month. In the event of resignation, the President shall submit his resignation directly to the Loya Jirgah.

MELI SHURA

The Meli Shura (National Assembly) is the highest legislative organ of the Republic of Afghanistan. It consists of two houses: the Wolasi Jirgah (House of Representatives) and the Sena (Senate). Members of the Wolasi Jirgah (representatives) are elected by general secret ballot for a legislative term of five years. Members of the Sena (senators) are elected and appointed in the following manner: two people from each province are elected for a period of five years; two people from each provincial council are elected by the council for a period of three years; and the remaining one-third of senators are appointed by the President for a period of four years.

The Meli Shura is vested with the authority: to approve, amend and repeal laws and legislative decrees, and to present them to the President for his signature; to interpret laws; to ratify and annul international treaties; to approve socio-economic development plans and to endorse the Government's reports on their execution; to approve the state budget and to evaluate the Government's report on its execution; to establish and make changes to administrative units; to establish and abolish ministries; to appoint and remove Vice-Presidents, on the recommendation of the President; and to endorse the establishment of relations with foreign countries and international organizations. The Wolasi Jirgah also has the power to approve a vote of confidence or no confidence in the Council of Ministers or one of its members.

At its first session, the Wolasi Jirgah elects, from among its members, an executive committee, composed of a chairman, two deputy chairmen and two secretaries, for the whole term of the legislature. The Sena elects, from among its members, an executive committee, composed of a chairman for a term of five years, and two deputy chairmen and two secretaries for a term of one year.

Ordinary sessions of the Meli Shura are held twice a year and do not normally last longer than three months. An extraordinary session can be held at the request of the President, the chairman of either house, or one-fifth of the members of each house. The houses of the Meli Shura can hold separate or joint sessions. Sessions require a minimum attendance of two-thirds of the members of each house and decisions shall be adopted by a majority vote. Sessions are open, unless the houses decide to meet in closed sessions.

The following authorities have the right to propose the introduction, amendment or repeal of a law in either house of the Meli Shura: the President, the standing commissions of the Meli Shura, at least one-tenth of the membership of each house, the Council of Ministers, the Supreme Court, and the office of the Attorney-General.

If the decision of one house is rejected by the other, a joint committee, consisting of an equal number of members from both houses, shall be formed. A decision by the joint committee, which will be agreed by a two-thirds majority, will be considered valid after approval by the President. If the joint committee fails to resolve differences, the matter shall be discussed in a joint session of the Meli Shura, and a decision reached by a majority vote. The decisions that are made by the Meli Shura are enforced after being signed by the President.

After consulting the chairman of the Wolasi Jirgah, the chairman of the Sena, the Prime Minister, the Attorney-General and the chairman of the Constitution Council, the President can declare the dissolution of the Wolasi Jirgah, stating his justification for doing so. Re-elections shall be held within 3 months of the dissolution.

COUNCIL OF MINISTERS

The Council of Ministers is composed of: a Prime Minister, deputy Prime Ministers and Ministers. The Council of Ministers is appointed by the Prime Minister. It is empowered: to formulate and implement domestic and foreign policies; to formulate economic development plans and state budgets; and to ensure public order.

The Council of Ministers is dissolved under the following conditions: the resignation of the Prime Minister, chronic illness of the Prime Minister, the withdrawal of confidence in the Council of Ministers by the Meli Shura, the end of the legislative term, or the dissolution of the Wolasi Jirgah or the Meli Shura.

THE JUDICIARY

(See section on the Judicial System.)

THE CONSTITUTION COUNCIL

The responsibilities of this body are: to evaluate and ensure the conformity of laws, legislative decrees and international treaties with the Constitution; and to give legal advice to the President on constitutional matters. The Constitution Council is composed of a chairman, a vice-chairman and eight members, who are appointed by the President.

LOCAL ADMINISTRATIVE ORGANS

For the purposes of local administration, the Republic of Afghanistan is divided into provinces, districts, cities and wards. These administrative units are led, respectively, by governors, district administrators, mayors and heads of wards. In each province a provincial council and district councils are formed in accordance with the law. Provincial councils and district councils each elect a chairman and a secretary from among their members. The term of office of a provincial council and a district council is three years.

FINAL PROVISIONS

Amendments to the Constitution shall be made by the Loya Jirgah. Any amendment shall be on the proposal of the President, or on the proposal of one-third and the approval of two-thirds of the members of the Meli Shura. Amendment to the Constitution during a state of emergency is not allowed.

Note: Following the downfall of Najibullah's regime in April 1992, a provisional *mujahidin* Government assumed power in Kabul. In July an acting executive body, known as the Leadership Council, appointed a special commission to draw up a new and more strictly Islamic Constitution. In September 1993 it was reported that a draft Constitution had been approved by the commission, in preparation for the holding of a general election.

In May 1996, following the signing of the Mahipar Agreement between President Burhanuddin Rabbani and Gulbuddin Hekmatyar, a Constitution to cover the interim period pending the holding of a general election was drawn up and published. The main provisions of the **Constitution of the Interim Period** are as follows:

General provision: Afghanistan is an Islamic country where all aspects of the life of the people shall be conducted according to the tenets of Shari'a.

President: The President is the Head of State and exercises the highest executive power; the President is the supreme commander of the armed forces and his approval is required for the appointment of all civil and military officials; the President is authorized to declare war or peace (on the advice of the Council of Ministers or an Islamic Shura), to approve death sentences or grant pardons, to

summon and dismiss a Shura, and to sign international treaties. In the event of the President's death, the presidential functions and powers shall be entrusted to the President of the Supreme Court until a new Head of State can be appointed.

Council of Ministers: The Council of Ministers, under the leadership of the Prime Minister, shall discuss and make decisions regarding government policy (both internal and external), the annual budget and administrative regulations, all of which shall be referred to the President for his assent.

According to the Iranian news agency, IRNA, in early October 1996 the Pakistani political party, Jamiat-e-Ulema-e-Islam, had prepared a draft Constitution for Afghanistan at the request of the Taliban, who had seized control of the capital in late September.

The Government

Following the collapse of Najibullah's regime in April 1992, a provisional *mujahidin* Government was established in Kabul. For the first two months, Prof. Sibghatullah Mojaddedi held the post of acting President and headed a 51-member executive body, known as the Islamic Jihad Council, which appointed an interim Council of Ministers in early May. On 28 June Mojaddedi, in accordance with the proposals formulated in the Peshawar Agreement (see History), surrendered the presidency to Prof. Burhanuddin Rabbani, who presided over another executive body, called the Leadership Council. Rabbani held power until the end of October, when his tenure of the presidency was extended for a further two months. On 30 December a special advisory council elected Rabbani, unopposed, as President of the country for a period of a further two years. Following the signing of a peace accord by the majority of *mujahidin* groups in Islamabad in March 1993, an interim multifaction Government was established, about 25 km south of Kabul, in June. In June 1994 the Supreme Court extended Rabbani's presidency for a further six months. When this six-month period ended in early 1995, Rabbani continued to exercise power.

In late September 1996 Rabbani's Government was ousted from power by the Taliban, who captured the capital and installed a strict Islamic regime. An interim Council of Ministers was appointed, but the Taliban gave no indication of when elections would be held. The Taliban Government won little international recognition (the UN refused to recognize it) and former President Rabbani continued to be acknowledged by many as the rightful leader of Afghanistan.

HEAD OF STATE
(Islamic State of Afghanistan)

(April 2001)

President: Prof. BURHANUDDIN RABBANI.

Vice-Presidents: Gen. ABDUL RASHID DOSTAM, SAYD MANSUR NADIRI.

INTERIM COUNCIL OF MINISTERS
(Islamic State of Afghanistan)

(April 2001)

Prime Minister and Minister of Planning: Hojjat-ol Islam SAYD MOHAMMAD ALI JAWID.

First Deputy Prime Minister: Eng. QOTBODDIN HELAL.

Deputy Prime Minister: ABDOL MANAN MAKHDUM.

Minister of Defence: AHMAD SHAH MASOUD

Minister of Internal Affairs: MOHAMMAD MOHAQQEQ.

Minister of Foreign Affairs: Dr ABDOLLAH.

Minister of Security: Maj.-Gen. FAHIM.

Minister of Water and Power: Eng. AL-SAYED AHMAD MUSAVI.

Minister of Information and Culture: HEDAYATOLLAH HEDAYAT.

Minister of Agriculture: Eng. GARDIZI.

Minister of Construction Affairs: Eng. MOHAMMAD IBRAHIM ADIL.

Minister of Education: ABDOLWAKIL ABDOLWAHAB.

Minister of Finance: Eng. WAHIDOLLAH SABA'UN.

Minister of Civil Aviation: Gen. HELALODDIN.

Minister of Martyrs and the Disabled: Mawlawi SAMIOLLAH NAJEBI.

Minister of Commerce: Hojjat-ol Islam SAYD HOSAYN ALEMI BALKHI.

Minister of Labour and Social Affairs: GHULAM HUSAYN SHAHAQ.

Minister of State for Foreign Affairs: Dr NAJIBULLAH LAFRA'I.

Minister without Portfolio and Co-ordinator of International Aid: ABDOLHAI ILAHI.

Deputy Minister of Trade: MUHAMMAD AWAZ FIKRAT.

Deputy Minister of Higher Education: Mr MA'SUMYAR.

Government Adviser: SAYED ABDULHADI BALKHI.

TALIBAN HEAD OF STATE
(Islamic Emirate of Afghanistan)
(April 2001)

Emir: Mola MOHAMMAD OMAR.

TALIBAN INTERIM COUNCIL OF MINISTERS
(Islamic Emirate of Afghanistan)
(April 2001)

Chairman: (vacant).

Deputy Chairmen: Mawlawi ABDOL KABIR (Economic Issues), Alhaj Mola MOHAMMAD HASAN AKHOND (Administrative Affairs).

Minister of Foreign Affairs: Mawlawi WAKIL AHMAD MOTAWAKKIL.

Minister of Finance: Mola ABDOL WASAY AGHAJAN MOTASEM.

Minister of Civil Aviation and Tourism: Mola AKHTAR MOHAMMAD MANSUR.

Minister of Telecommunications and of Labour: Mawlawi AHMADOLLAH MOTEE.

Minister of Water and Electricity: Mola MOHAMMAD JAN AKHUND.

Minister of Internal Affairs: Mola ABDOL RAZZAQ AKHOND.

Minister of Public Works: Mawlawi MOHAMMADULLAH MOTI.

Minister of Justice: Alhaj Mola NORUDDIN TORABI.

Minister of Light Industries and Food: Mawlawi HAMDOLLAH ZAHED.

Minister of Agriculture and Animal Husbandry: Mawlawi ABDOL LATIF MANSUR.

Minister of Haj and Endowment Affairs: Alhaj SAYD GHAY-SODDIN AGHA.

Minister of Education and Training: Mola AMIR KHAN MOTAQI.

Minister of Information and Culture: Mawlawi QODRATOLLAH JAMAL.

Minister of Rural Development: Mawlawi SEDIQOLLAH.

Minister of Planning: Mola SADUDDIN SAYD.

Minister of Repatriation: Mawlawi ABDOL RAQIB.

Minister of Mines and Industries: Alhaj Mola MOHAMMAD ISA AKHUND.

Minister of National Defence: Alhaj Mola OBAIDOLLAH AKHOND.

Minister of Security (Intelligence): Qari AHMADULLAH.

Minister of Public Health: Mola ABBAS AKHUND.

Minister of Higher Education: Qari DIN MOHAMMAD HANIF.

Minister for the Promotion of Virtue and the Prevention of Vice: MOHAMMAD WALI.

Minister of Communications: Mola YAR MOHAMMAD RAHIMI.

Minister of Border and Tribal Affairs: HABIBOLLAH MANGAL.

Minister without Portfolio: Mawlawi GHIASODDIN.

Deputy Minister of Commerce: Mawlawi FAIZ MOHAMMAD FAIZAN.

MINISTRIES

Office of the Council of Ministers: Shar Rahi Sedarat, Kabul; tel. (93) 26926.

Office of the Prime Minister: Shar Rahi Sedarat, Kabul; tel. (93) 26926.

Ministry of Agriculture and Land Reform: Jamal Mina, Kabul; tel. (93) 41151.

Ministry of Border Affairs: Shah Mahmud Ghazi Ave, Kabul; tel. (93) 21793.

Ministry of Civil Aviation and Tourism: POB 165, Ansari Wat, Kabul; tel. (93) 21015.

Ministry of Commerce: Darulaman Wat, Kabul; tel. (93) 2290090; fax (93) 2290089.

Ministry of Construction Affairs: Micro-Rayon, Kabul; tel. (93) 63701.

Ministry of Defence: Darulaman Wat, Kabul; tel. (93) 41232.

Ministry of Education and Training: Mohd Jan Khan Wat, Kabul; tel. (93) 20666.

Ministry of Energy: Micro-Rayon, Kabul; tel. (93) 25109.

Ministry of Finance: Shar Rahi Pashtunistan, Kabul; tel. (93) 26041.

Ministry of Foreign Affairs: Shah Mahmud Ghazi St, Shar-i-Nau, Kabul; tel. (93) 25441.

Ministry of Higher and Vocational Education: Jamal Mina, Kabul; tel. (93) 40041; f. 1978.

Ministry of Information and Culture: Mohd Jan Khan Wat, Kabul.

Ministry of Internal Affairs: Shar-i-Nau, Kabul; tel. (93) 32441.

Ministry of Justice: Shar Rahi Pashtunistan, Kabul; tel. (93) 23404.

Ministry of Light Industries and Foodstuffs: Ansari Wat, Kabul; tel. (93) 41551.

Ministry of Mines and Industries: Shar Rahi Pashtunistan, Kabul; tel. (93) 25841.

Ministry of Planning: Shar-i-Nau, Kabul; tel. (93) 21273.

Ministry of Public Health: Micro-Rayon, Kabul; tel. (93) 40851.

Ministry of Telecommunications: Puli Bagh-i-Omomi, Kabul; tel. (93) 21341.

Ministry of Transport: Ansari Wat, Kabul; tel. (93) 25541.

Ministry of Water Resources Development and Irrigation: Darulaman Wat, Kabul; tel. (93) 40743.

Legislature

MELI SHURA*
(National Assembly)

The Meli Shura, which was established in 1987 and replaced the Revolutionary Council, was composed of two houses: the Wolasi Jirgah (House of Representatives) and the Sena (Senate). Elections were held to both houses in April 1988.

Wolasi Jirgah

Representatives were elected for five years. Of the total 234 seats, 184 were contested in the general election in April 1988. The remaining 50 seats were reserved for members of the opposition.

Sena

The Sena comprised 192 members. One-third of its members were elected for five years, one-third were elected for three years, and one-third were appointed for three years. At the general election in 1988, 115 senators were elected, while the majority of the remaining 77 seats were filled by senators appointed by the President. A small number of seats were reserved for members of the opposition.

* Following the downfall of Najibullah's regime in April 1992, an interim *mujahidin* Government took power in Kabul and both houses of the Meli Shura were dissolved. A High State Council (HSC) was formed, which was to meet regularly, under the chairmanship of the President, to discuss and make decisions regarding matters of national importance.

Political Organizations

The following were the principal *mujahidin* and militia groups operating in 2000:

The seven below were formerly members of a grand alliance, formed in 1985 and called the Ittehad-i-Islami Afghan Mujahidin (Islamic Union of Afghan Mujahidin—IUAM), based in Peshawar, Pakistan:

Three moderate/traditionalist groups:

Harakat-i-Inqilab-i-Islami (Islamic Revolutionary Movement): Pashtun; supports the Taliban; Leader Mawlawi MOHAMMAD NABI MOHAMMADI; c. 25,000 supporters (estimate). In late 1999 there were reports that the Harakat-i-Inqilab-i-Islami had been dissolved and that its former leader had joined the Taliban.

Jebha-i-Nejat-i-Melli (National Liberation Front): Pashtun; Leader Prof. Hazrat SIBGHATULLAH MOJADDEDI; Sec.-Gen. ZABIH-OLLAH MOJADDEDI; c. 15,000 supporters (estimate).

Mahaz-i-Melli-i-Islami (National Islamic Front): Pashtun; Leader Pir SAYED AHMAD GAILANI; Dep. Leader HAMED GAILANI; c. 15,000 supporters (estimate).

Four Islamic fundamentalist groups:

Hizb-i Islami Gulbuddin (Islamic Party Gulbuddin): e-mail info@hezb-e-islami.org; internet www.hezb-e-islami.org; Pashtun/Turkmen/Tajik; Leader GULBUDDIN HEKMATYAR; c. 50,000 supporters (estimate); based in Iran in 1998–99.

Hizb-i Islami Khalis (Islamic Party Khalis): Pashtun; Leader Maulvi MUHAMMAD YUNUS KHALIS; c. 40,000 supporters (estimate).

Ittehad-i-Islami (Islamic Union): Pashtun; Leader Prof. ABDUL RASUL SAYEF; Dep. Leader AHMAD SHAH AHMADZAY; c. 18,000 supporters (estimate).

Jamiat-i Islami (Islamic Society): internet www.jamiat .com; Turkmen/Uzbek/Tajik; Leaders Prof. BURHANUDDIN RABBANI, Gen. AHMAD SHAH MASOUD; Sec.-Gen. ENAYATOLLAH SHADAB; c. 60,000 supporters (estimate).

In June 1987 eight Afghan Islamic (Shi'ite) factions (based in Tehran, Iran) formed the **Hizb-i Wahadat-i Islami** (Islamic Unity Party; Hazara; Chair. of Supreme Council ALEMI BALKHI; Sec.-Gen. ABDOL KARIM KHALILI), comprising: the **Afghan Nasr Organization**

(Hazara; c. 50,000 supporters), the **Guardians of Islamic Jihad of Afghanistan,** the **United Islamic Front of Afghanistan,** the **Islamic Force of Afghanistan,** the **Dawa Party of Islamic Unity of Afghanistan,** the **Harakat-e Eslami Afghanistan** (the Islamic Movement of Afghanistan; Pashtun/Tajik/Uzbek; Leader: Ayatollah MOHAMMAD ASEF MOHSENI; Chair. of Central Council Hojjat-ol Islam SAYD MOHAMMAD ALI JAWID; c. 20,000 supporters), the **Hezbollah** (c. 4,000 supporters), and the **Islamic Struggle for Afghanistan**.

National Islamic Movement (Jonbesh-e Melli-e Eslami): f. 1992; formed mainly from troops of former Northern Command of the Afghan army; predominantly Uzbek/Tajik/Turkmen/Ismaili and Hazara Shi'ite; Leader Gen. ABDUL RASHID DOSTAM; 65,000–150,000 supporters.

Taliban: headquarters in Qandahar; internet www.taleban.com; emerged in 1994; Islamic fundamentalist; mainly Sunni Pashtuns; Leader Mola MOHAMMAD OMAR; Dep. Leader Mawlawi WAKIL AHMAD; c. 40,000 armed supporters.

Diplomatic Representation

By the end of 1992 many of the embassies listed below had been temporarily closed down and the diplomatic staff had left Kabul, owing to the continuing unrest in the capital. In early 2001 Pakistan was the only country to have a functioning embassy in Afghanistan.

EMBASSIES IN AFGHANISTAN

Austria: POB 24, Zarghouna Wat, Kabul; tel. (93) 32720; Ambassador: (vacant).

Bangladesh: Kabul; tel. (93) 25783; Chargé d'affaires a.i.: MAHMOOD HASAN.

Bulgaria: Wazir Akbar Khan Mena, Kabul; tel. (93) 20683; Ambassador: VALENTIN PETKOV GATSINSKI.

China, People's Republic: Shah Mahmud Wat, Shar-i-Nau, Kabul; tel. (93) 20446; Chargé d'affaires a.i.: ZHANG DELIANG.

Cuba: Shar Rahi Haji Yaqub, opp. Shar-i-Nau Park, Kabul; tel. (93) 30863; Ambassador: REGINO FARINAS CANTERO.

Czech Republic: Taimani Wat, Kala-i-Fatullah, Kabul; tel. (93) 32082.

France: POB 62, Shar-i-Nau, Kabul; tel. (93) 23631; Ambassador-at-large: JEAN SAINT-BACAL.

Germany: Wazir Akbar Khan Mena, POB 83, Kabul; tel. (93) 22432; Ambassador: (vacant).

Hungary: POB 830, Sin 306–308, Wazir Akbar Khan Mena, Kabul; tel. (93) 24281; Ambassador: MIHÁLY GOLUB.

India: Malalai Wat, Shar-i-Nau, Kabul; tel. (93) 30556; Chargé d'affaires a.i.: A. S. TOOR.

Indonesia: POB 532, Wazir Akbar Khan Mena, District 10, Zone 14, Road Mark Jeem House 93, Kabul; tel. (93) 20586; Ambassador: HAVID ABDUL GHANI.

Iran: Shar-i-Nau, Kabul; tel. (93) 26255; Chargé d'affaires: Mr BAHRAMI.

Iraq: POB 523, Wazir Akbar Khan Mena, Kabul; tel. (93) 24797; Ambassador: BURHAN KHALIL GHAZAL.

Italy: POB 606, Khoja Abdullah Ansari Wat, Kabul; tel. (93) 24624; Chargé d'affaires a.i.: Mr CALAMAI.

Japan: POB 80, Wazir Akbar Khan Mena, Kabul; tel. (93) 26844; Chargé d'affaires a.i.: KEIKI HIRAGA.

Korea, Democratic People's Republic: Wazir Akbar Khan Mena, House 28, Sarak 'H' House 103, Kabul; tel. (93) 22161; Ambassador: OH IN YONG.

Libya: 103 Wazir Akbar Khan Mena, Kabul; tel. (93) 25947; Ambassador: ALI AL-BARUQ AL-SHARIFI.

Mongolia: Wazir Akbar Khan Mena, Sarak 'T' House 8714, Kabul; tel. (93) 22138; Ambassador: (vacant).

Pakistan: Kabul; Ambassador: MOHAMMAD ARIF AYUB.

Poland: Gozargah St, POB 78, Kabul; tel. (93) 42461; Chargé d'affaires: Prof. ANDRZEJ WAWRZYNIAK.

Russia: Darulaman Wat, Kabul; tel. (93) 41541; Ambassador: BORIS NIKOLAYEVICH PASTUKHOV.

Saudi Arabia: Kabul; Chargé d'affaires: (vacant).

Slovakia: Taimani Wat, Kala-i-Fatullah, Kabul; tel. (93) 32082.

Sudan: Kabul.

Turkey: Shar-i-Nau, Kabul; tel. (93) 20072; Chargé d'affaires a.i.: SALEH AHSAN.

United Kingdom: Karte Parwan, Kabul; tel. (93) 30512; Ambassador: (vacant).

USA: Wazir Akbar Khan Mena, Kabul; tel. (93) 62230; Chargé d'affaires a.i.: JON D. GLASSMANN (embassy closed January 1989).

Viet Nam: 3 Nijat St, Wazir Akbar Khan Mena, Kabul; tel. (93) 26596; Ambassador: NGUYEN NGOC SINH.

Yugoslavia: POB 53, 923 Main Rd, Wazir Akbar Khan Mena, Kabul; tel. (93) 61671; Chargé d'affaires a.i.: VELIBOR DULOVIĆ.

Judicial System

The functions and structure of the judiciary are established in Articles 107–121 of the Constitution ratified by the Loya Jirgah in November 1987 and amended in May 1990.

The courts apply the provisions of the Constitution and the laws of Afghanistan, and, in cases of ambivalence, will judge in accordance with the rules of Shari'a (Islamic religious law). Trials are held in open session except when circumstances defined by law deem the trial to be held in closed session. Trials are conducted in Pashtu and Dari or in the language of the majority of the inhabitants of the locality. The right to speak in court in one's mother tongue is guaranteed to the two sides of the lawsuit.

The judiciary comprises the Supreme Court and those courts which are formed in accordance with the directives of the law. The State may establish specialized courts within the unified system of the judiciary.

The highest judicial organ is the Supreme Court, which consists of a President, Vice-President and judges, all of whom are appointed by the Head of State in accordance with the law. It supervises the judicial activities of the courts and ensures the uniformity of law enforcement and interpretation by those courts.

Death sentences are carried out after ratification by the Head of State.

President of the Supreme Court (Islamic State of Afghanistan): MOHAMMAD SHAH FAZLI.

The public prosecutor's office consists of the Attorney-General's office and those other attorneys' offices which are formed in accordance with the directives of the law. The Attorney-General supervises the activities of all the attorney offices, which are independent of local organs and answerable only to the Attorney-General himself. The Attorney-General and his deputies, who are appointed by the Head of State in accordance with the law, supervise the implementation and observance of all laws.

Attorney-General (Islamic State of Afghanistan): SAYED ABDORRAZAQ MOSAMEM (acting).

Deputy Attorney-General (Islamic State of Afghanistan): ABDUL HADY KHALILZIA.

Following the collapse of Najibullah's regime and the installation of a *mujahidin* Government in Kabul in April 1992, a judicial system fully based on the rules of Shari'a was expected to be incorporated in the *mujahidin's* new Constitution. In an apparent attempt to improve security in Kabul, special courts were established by the *mujahidin* administration to prosecute 'people who violate homes, honour, children and property'.

Following their seizure of power in the capital in September 1996, the Taliban imposed a strict Islamic code of conduct on Kabul, including the introduction of stonings, lashings, amputations and the death penalty as punishment for various crimes.

Taliban Prosecutor-General and President of the Supreme Court: Alhaj Mawlawi NUR MOHAMMAD SAQEB.

Taliban Vice-Presidents of the Supreme Court: Mawlawi SULAYMAN, Mawlawi ABDOL SATAR SEDIQI, Mawlawi RAFIOLLAH MO'AZEN, Mawlawi SHAHABODDIN DELAWAR.

Taliban Chief Justice of Military Court: ABDUL RAHMAN AGHA.

Religion

The official religion of Afghanistan is Islam. Muslims comprise 99% of the population, approximately 84% of them of the Sunni and the remainder of the Shi'ite sect. There are small minority groups of Hindus, Sikhs and Jews.

ISLAM

The High Council of Ulema and Clergy of Afghanistan: Kabul; f. 1980; 7,000 mems; Chair. Mawlawi ABDOL GHAFUR SENANI.

The Press

Some of the following newspapers and periodicals have not always appeared on a regular basis or, in a large number of cases, may have ceased publication.

PRINCIPAL DAILIES

Anis: (Friendship): Kabul; f. 1927; revived by the Taliban in 1998; evening; independent; Dari, Uzbek and Pashtu; state-owned; news and literary articles; Chief Editor MOHAMMAD S. KHARNIKASH; circ. 25,000.

Badakhshan: Faizabad; f. 1945; Dari and Pashtu; Chief Editor HADI ROSTAQI; circ. 3,000.

Dariz: Kabul.

Ettehadi-Baghlan: Baghlan; f. 1930; Dari and Pashtu; Chief Editor SHAFIQULLAH MOSHFEQ; circ. 1,200.

Hewad (Homeland): Kabul; tel. (93) 26851; f. 1959; revived by the Taliban in 1998; Pashtu; state-owned; Editor-in-Chief AMIR AFGHANPUR; circ. 12,200.

Jawzjan: Jawzjan; f. 1942; Dari and Pashtu; Chief Editor A. RAHEM HAMRO; circ. 1,500.

Kabul New Times: POB 983, Ansari Wat, Kabul; tel. (93) 61847; f. 1962 as Kabul Times, renamed 1980; English; state-owned; Editor-in-Chief M. SEDDIQ RAHPOE; circ. 5,000.

Nangarhar: Jalalabad; f. 1919; revived by the Taliban in 1998; Pashtu; state-owned; Chief Editor MORAD SANGARMAL; circ. 1,500.

Sanae: Parwan; f. 1953; Dari and Pashtu; Chief Editor G. SAKHI ESHANZADA; circ. 1,700.

Seistan: Farah; f. 1947; Dari and Pashtu; Editor-in-Chief M. ANWAR MAHAL; circ. 1,800.

Shahadat: organ of the Hizb-i Islami Gulbuddin.

Times: Kabul; English; state-owned.

Tulu-i-Afghan: Qandahar; f. 1924; Pashtu; Chief Editor TAHER SHAFEQ; circ. 1,500.

Wolanga: Paktia; f. 1943; Pashtu; Chief Editor M. ANWAR; circ. 1,500.

PERIODICALS

Afghanistan: Historical Society of Afghanistan, Kabul; tel. (93) 30370; f. 1948; quarterly; English and French; historical and cultural; Editor MALIHA ZAFAR.

Afghanistan Today: Block 106, Ansari Wat, Kabul; tel. (93) 61868; f. 1985; every 2 months; state-owned; socio-political, economics and cultural; CEO KARIM HOQOUQ; circ. 10,500.

Ahbar: Baihaki Book Publishing and Import Institute, Kabul; illustrated monthly; Dari and Pashtu; publ. by Rossiiskoye Informatsionnoye Agentstvo—Novosti.

Akhbar-e-Hafta: Kabul; f. 1989; weekly; Editor ZAHER TANIN.

Aryana: ISA Academy of Sciences, Kabul; tel. (93) 25106; f. 1943; quarterly; Pashtu and Dari; culture, history, ethnography, socioeconomics; Editor SAYED AMIN MUJAHED.

Awaz: Kabul; f. 1940; monthly; Pashtu and Dari; radio and television programmes; Editor NASIR TOHORI; circ. 20,000.

Bedar: Mazar-i-Sharif; f. 1920; weekly; Dari and Pashtu; Chief Editor ROZEQ FANI; circ, 2,500.

Erfan: Ministry of Education and Training, Mohd Jan Khan Wat, Kabul; tel. (93) 21612; f. 1923; every two months; Dari and Pashtu; education, psychology, mathematics, religion, literature and technology; Chief Editor MOHAMMAD QASEM HILAMAN; circ. 7,500.

Ershad-e-Islam (Islamic Precepts): Kabul; f. 1987; publ. by the Ministry of Islamic Affairs; Editor MUHAMMAD SALEM KHARES.

Gharjestan: Kabul; f. 1988; every two months; political and cultural; for the people of Hazara.

Gorash: Ministry of Information and Culture, Mohd Jan Khan Wat, Kabul; f. 1979; weekly; Turkmen; Chief Editor S. MISEDIQ AMINI; circ, 1,000.

Haqiqat-e-Sarbaz: Ministry of Defence, Kabul; f. 1980; 3 a week; Dari and Pashtu; Chief Editor MER JAMALUDDIN FAKHR; circ. 18,370.

Helmand: Bost; f. 1954; 2 a week; Pashtu; Editor-in-Chief M. OMER FARHAT BALEGH; circ. 1,700.

Herat: Ministry of Information and Culture, Mohd Jan Khan Wat, Kabul; f. 1923; monthly; Dari and Pashtu; Chief Editor JALIL SHABGER FOLADYON.

The Islamic Emirate: Kabul; f. 2000; monthly; English; organ of the Taliban.

Ittifak Islam: Herat; f. 1921; weekly; Dari and Pashtu; organ of Taliban; Chief Editor ABDULLAH HERAWEE.

Kabul: Afghanistan Academy of Sciences, Research Centre for Languages and Literature, Akbar Khan Mena, Kabul; f. 1931; monthly; Pashtu; literature and language research; Editor N. M. SAHEEM.

Kar: POB 756, Kabul; tel. (93) 25629; monthly; publ. by the Central Council of the National Union of Afghanistan Employees; Editor-in-Chief AZIZ AHMAD NASIR; circ. 2,500.

Kunar Periodical Journal: Asadabad; f. 1987; Pashtu; news and socio-economic issues; circ. 5,000.

Meli Jabha: Kabul; weekly.

Mojahed: Kabul; weekly; organ of the Jamiat-i Islami.

Mojala-e-Ariana (Light): Kabul; f. 1978; monthly; Dari and Pashtu; Editor-in-Chief RASHID ASHTI; circ. 1,000.

Muhasel-e-Emroz (Today's Student): Kabul; f. 1986; monthly; state-owned; juvenile; circ. 5,000.

Nengarhar: Kabul; f. 1919; weekly; Pashtu; Editor-in-Chief KARIM HASHIMI; circ. 1,500.

Palwasha: Kabul; f. 1988; fortnightly; Editor-in-Chief SHAH ZAMAN BREED.

Pamir: Micro-Rayon, Kabul; tel. (93) 20585; f. 1952; fortnightly; Dari and Pashtu; combined organ of the Kabul Cttee and Municipality; Chief Editor ENAYET POZHOHAN GURDANI; circ. 30,000.

Payam-e-Haq: Kabul; f. 1953; monthly; Dari and Pashtu; Editor-in-Chief FARAH SHAH MOHIBI; circ. 1,000.

Payam-e-Mojahed: Panjshir; weekly; organ of UIFSA.

Samangon: Aibak; f. 1978; weekly; Dari; Editor-in-Chief M. MOHSEN HASSAN; circ. 1,500.

Sawad (Literacy): Kabul; f. 1954; monthly; Dari and Pashtu; Editor-in-Chief MALEM GOL ZADRON; circ. 1,000.

Seramiasht: POB 3066, Afghan Red Crescent Society, Puli Artal, Kabul; tel. (93) 30969; f. 1958; quarterly; Dari, Pashtu and English; Editor-in-Chief SAYED ASSADULLAH STOMAN; circ. 1,000.

Shari'at: Kabul; weekly; Pashtu; central organ of the Taliban.

Sob: Kabul; tel. (93) 25240; f. 1979; weekly; Balochi; Editor-in-Chief WALIMUHAMMAD ROKHSHONI; circ. 1,000.

Takharistan: Takhar; weekly.

Talim wa Tarbia (Education): Kabul; f. 1954; monthly; publ. by Institute of Education.

Urdu (Military): Kabul; f. 1922; quarterly; Dari and Pashtu; military journal; issued by the Ministry of Defence; Chief Editor KHALILULAH AKBARI; circ. 500.

Yulduz (Star): Ministry of Information and Culture, Mohd Jan Khan Wat, Kabul; f. 1979; weekly; Uzbek and Turkmen; Chief Editor EKHAN BAYONI; circ. 2,000.

Zeray: Afghanistan Academy of Sciences, Research Centre for Languages and Literature, Akbar Khan Mena, Kabul; f. 1938; weekly; Pashtu; Pashtu folklore, literature and language; Editor MUHAMMAD NASSER; circ. 1,000.

Zhwandoon (Life): Kabul; tel. (93) 26849; f. 1944; weekly; Pashtu and Dari; illustrated; Editor ROHELA ROSEKH KHORAMI; circ. 1,400.

NEWS AGENCIES

Afghan Islamic Press: Peshawar, North-West Frontier Province, Pakistan.

Bakhtar Information Agency (BIA): Ministry of Information and Culture, Mohd Jan Khan Wat, Kabul; tel. (93) 24089; f. 1939; Head Mola ABDOL HANAN.

Foreign Bureaux

Česká tisková kancelář (ČTK) (Czech Republic): POB 673, Kabul; tel. (93) 23419.

The following foreign agencies are also represented in Kabul: Rossiiskoye Informatsionnoye Agentstvo—Novosti (RIA—Novosti) (Russia) and Tanjug (Yugoslavia).

PRESS ASSOCIATIONS

Journalists' Association: Kabul; f. 1991; Chair. AMIR AFGHANPUR; Dep. Chair. HABIB SHAMS, Lt FARUQ.

Union of Journalists of Afghanistan: Wazir Akbar Khan Mena, St 13, Kabul; f. 1980; Pres. MOHAMMAD YUSUF AYINA.

Publishers

Afghan Book: POB 206, Kabul; f. 1969; books on various subjects, translations of foreign works on Afghanistan, books in English on Afghanistan and Dari language textbooks for foreigners; Man. Dir JAMILA AHANG.

Afghanistan Today Publishers: POB 983, c/o The Kabul New Times, Ansari Wat, Kabul; tel. (93) 61847; publicity materials; answers enquiries about Afghanistan.

Balhaqi Book Publishing and Importing Institute: POB 2025, Kabul; tel. (93) 26818; f. 1971 by co-operation of the Government Printing House, Bakhtar News Agency and leading newspapers; publishers and importers of books; Pres. MUHAMMAD ANWAR NUMYALAI.

Book Publishing Institute: Herat; f. 1970 by co-operation of Government Printing House and citizens of Herat; books on literature, history and religion.

Book Publishing Institute: Qandahar; f. 1970; supervised by Government Printing House; mainly books in Pashtu language.

Educational Publications: Ministry of Education and Training, Mohd Jan Khan Wat, Kabul; tel. (93) 21716; textbooks for primary and secondary schools in the Pashtu and Dari languages; also three monthly magazines in Pashtu and in Dari.

Franklin Book Programs Inc: POB 332, Kabul.

Historical Society of Afghanistan: Kabul; tel. (93) 30370; f. 1931; mainly historical and cultural works and two quarterly magazines: *Afghanistan* (English and French), *Aryana* (Dari and Pashtu); Pres. AHMAD ALI MOTAMEDI.

Institute of Geography: Kabul University, Kabul; geographical and related works.

International Center for Pashtu Studies: Kabul; f. 1975 by the Afghan Govt with the assistance of UNESCO; research work on the Pashtu language and literature and on the history and culture of the Pashtu people; Pres. and Assoc. Chief Researcher J. K. HEKMATY; publs *Pashtu* (quarterly).

Kabul University Press: Kabul; tel. (93) 42433; f. 1950; textbooks; two quarterly scientific journals in Dari and in English, etc.

Research Center for Linguistics and Literary Studies: Afghanistan Academy of Sciences, Akbar Khan Mena, Kabul; tel. (93) 26912; f. 1978; research on Afghan languages (incl. Pashtu, Dari, Balochi and Uzbek) and Afghan folklore; Pres. Prof. MOHAMMED R. ELHAM; publs *Kabul* (Pashtu), *Zeray* (Pashtu weekly) and *Khurasan* (Dari).

Government Publishing House

Government Printing House: Kabul; tel. (93) 26851; f. 1870 under supervision of the Ministry of Information and Culture; four daily newspapers in Kabul, one in English; weekly, fortnightly and monthly magazines, one of them in English; books on Afghan history and literature, as well as textbooks for the Ministry of Education; 13 daily newspapers in 13 provincial centres and one journal and also magazines in three provincial centres; Dir MUHAMMAD AYAN AYAN.

Broadcasting and Communications

TELECOMMUNICATIONS

Afghan Wireless Communication Company (AWCC): Ministry of Communications Bldg, Mohd Jan Khan Wat, Kabul; tel. (93) 2290016; internet www.afghanwireless.com; provides national and international telephone services for Kabul and Qandahar.

BROADCASTING

Following their capture of Kabul in September 1996, the Taliban banned television and closed down the station. Radio Afghanistan was renamed Radio Voice of Shari'a; this Kabul-based station also operates Balkh Radio in Mazar-i-Sharif and Takhar Radio in Talukan.

Radio Voice of Shari'a: POB 544, Ansari Wat, Kabul; tel. (93) 20355; under the supervision of the Ministry of Information and Culture; home service in Dari and Pashtu (10 hours daily); home service in Uzbek, Turkmen, Nurestani and Pashai (50 minutes daily); foreign service in Urdu and English (30 minutes daily); Gen. Pres. Ustad Mawlawi MOHAMMED ESAQ NIZAMI; Gen. Dir of Planning and Foreign Relations Eng. ABDUL RAHMAN NASERI.

Badakhshan TV: Faizabad; operated by anti-Taliban UIFSA; broadcasts three hrs daily; Dir MOHAMMAD DIN.

Finance

(cap. = capital; auth. = authorized; p.u. = paid up; res = reserves; m. = million; brs = branches; amounts in afghanis unless otherwise stated)

BANKING

In June 1975 all banks were nationalized. There are no foreign banks operating in Afghanistan.

Da Afghanistan Bank (Central Bank of Afghanistan): Ibne Sina Wat, Kabul; tel. (93) 24075; f. 1939; main functions: banknote issue, foreign exchange regulation, credit extensions to banks and leading enterprises and companies, govt and private depository, govt fiscal agency; Head Mola Haji MOHAMMAD AHMADI; 65 brs.

Agricultural Development Bank of Afghanistan: POB 414, Cineme Pamir Bldg, Jade Maiwand, Kabul; tel. (93) 24459; f. 1959; makes available credits for farmers, co-operatives and agro-business; aid provided by IBRD and UNDP; Chair. Dr M. KABIAR; Pres. Dr ABDULLAH NAQSHBANDI.

Banke Milli Afghan (Afghan National Bank): Jana Ibn Sina, Kabul; tel. (93) 25451; f. 1932; Chair. ABDUL WAHAB ASSEFI; Pres. ELHAMUDDIN QIAM; 16 brs.

Export Promotion Bank of Afghanistan: 24 Mohd Jan Khan Wat, Kabul; tel. (93) 24447; f. 1976; provides financing for exports and export-orientated investments; Pres. MOHAMMAD YAQUB NEDA; Vice-Pres. BURHANUDDIN SHAHIM.

Industrial Development Bank of Afghanistan: POB 14, Shar-i-Nau, Kabul; tel. (93) 33336; f. 1973; provides financing for industrial development; cap. 10,500m. (1996); Pres. Haji RAHMATULLAH.

Mortgage and Construction Bank: Bldg No. 2, First Part Jade Maiwand, Kabul; tel. (93) 23341; f. 1955 to provide short- and long-term building loans; Pres. FAIZ MUHAMMAD ALOKOZI.

Pashtany Tejaraty Bank (Afghan Commercial Bank): Mohd Jan Khan Wat, Kabul; tel. (93) 26551; f. 1954 to provide short-term credits, forwarding facilities, opening letters of credit, purchase and sale of foreign exchange; Chair. Dr BASIR RANJBAR; Pres. and CEO ZIR GUL WARDAK; 14 brs.

INSURANCE

There is one national insurance company:

Afghan National Insurance Co: National Insurance Bldg, Park, Shar-i-Nau, POB 329, Kabul; tel. (93) 33531; f. 1964; mem. of Asian Reinsurance Corpn; marine, aviation, fire, motor and accident insurance; Pres. M. ABDULLAH MUDASIR; Claims Man. Eng. A. S. ALIZAI.

No foreign insurance companies are permitted to operate in Afghanistan.

Trade and Industry

GOVERNMENT AGENCIES

Board for the Promotion of Private Investment: Kabul; Head of Bd Mawlawi SHOJA'ODDIN QADAH.

Export Promotion Department: Ministry of Commerce, Darulaman Wat, Kabul; fax (93) 2290089; f. 1969; provides guidance for traders, collects and disseminates trade information, markets and performs quality control of export products.

High Commission for Combating Drugs: Kabul; Chair. Mola ABDOL HAMID AKHONZADA.

CHAMBERS OF COMMERCE AND INDUSTRY

Afghan Chamber of Commerce and Industry: Mohd Jan Khan Wat, Kabul; tel. (93) 26796; fax (93) 2290089; Head Mola MOHAMMAD DAUD ABED.

Federation of Afghan Chambers of Commerce and Industry: Darulaman Wat, Kabul; f. 1923; includes chambers of commerce and industry in Ghazni, Qandahar, Kabul, Herat, Mazar-i-Sharif, Fariab, Jawzjan, Kunduz, Jalalabad and Andkhoy.

INDUSTRIAL AND TRADE ASSOCIATIONS

Afghan Carpet Exporters' Guild: POB 3159, Darulaman Wat, Kabul; tel. (93) 41765; f. 1967; a non-profit-making, independent organization of carpet manufacturers and exporters; Pres. ZIAUDDIN ZIA; c. 1,000 mems.

Afghan Cart Company: POB 61, Zerghona Maidan, Kabul; tel. (93) 31068; f. 1988; the largest export/import company in Afghanistan; imports electrical goods, machinery, metal, cars, etc.; exports raisins, carpets, medical herbs, wood, animal hides, etc.

Afghan Fruit Processing Co: POB 261, Industrial Estate, Puli Charkhi, Kabul; tel. (93) 65186; f. 1960; exports raisins, other dried fruits and nuts.

Afghan Raisin and Other Dried Fruits Institute: POB 3034, Sharara Wat, Kabul; tel. (93) 30463; exporters of dried fruits and nuts; Pres. NAJMUDDIN MUSLEH.

Afghan Wool Enterprises: Shar-i-Nau, Kabul; tel. (93) 31963.

Afghanistan Karakul Institute: POB 506, Puli Charkhi, Kabul; tel. (93) 61852; f. 1967; exporters of furs; Pres. G. M. BAHEER.

Afghanistan Plants Enterprise: POB 122, Puli Charkhi, Kabul; tel. (93) 31962; exports medicines, plants and spices.

Handicraft Promotion and Export Centre: POB 3089, Sharara Wat, Kabul; tel. (93) 32935; MOMENA RANJBAR.

Parapamizad Co Ltd: Jadai Nader Pashtoon, Sidiq Omar Market, POB 1911, Kabul; tel. (93) 22116; export/import co; Propr PADSHAH SARBAZ.

TRADE UNIONS

National Union of Afghanistan Employees (NUAE): POB 756, Kabul; tel. (93) 23040; f. 1978, as Central Council of Afghanistan Trade Unions, to establish and develop the trade union movement, including the formation of councils and organizational cttees in the provinces; name changed in 1990; composed of seven vocational unions; 300,000 mems; Pres. A. HABIB HARDAMSHAID; Vice-Pres. ASADOLLAH POYA.

Artists' Union: Kabul; tel. (93) 23195; Chair. NASIM KHUSHGAWAR.

Balkh Council of Trade Unions: Mazar-i-Sharif; Pres. MUHAMMAD KABIR KARGAR.

Central Council of the Union of Craftsmen: Kabul; f. 1987; c. 58,000 mems.

Commerce and Transport Employees' Union: Kabul; Gen. Sec. AHMAD ZIA SIDDIQI.

Construction Employees' Union: Kabul; Gen. Sec. AMINULLAH.

Kabul Union of Furriers: Kabul; Leader ABD AL-KHALIQ.

Mines and Industries Employees' Union: Kabul; Gen. Sec. MOHAMMED AMIN.

Nangarhar Council of Trade Unions: Jalalabad; Deputy Chair. MUQREBUDDIN KARGAR.

Public Health Employees' Union: Kabul; Pres. Prof. M. RAHIM KHUSHDEL.

Public Services Employees' Union: Kabul; Gen. Sec. ABDUL MEJJER TEMORY.

Science and Culture Employees' Union: Kabul; Gen. Sec. T. HABIBZAI.

Traders' Union of Afghanistan: Kabul; Chair. REZWANQOL TAMANA.

Union of Peasant Co-operatives of the Republic of Afghanistan (UPCRA): POB 3272, Dehmazang, Kabul; tel. (93) 42683; 1,370,000 mems; Chair. FAZULLAH ALBURZ.

Weaving and Sewing Employees' Union: Kabul; Gen. Sec. A. W. KARGAR.

Writers' Union of Afghanistan: Kabul; Chair. MOHAMMAD AZAM RAHNAWARD ZARYAB; Vice-Chair. ABDOLLAH BAKHTIANI, AKBAR KARKAR.

Transport

RAILWAYS

There is no railway system currently operating in Afghanistan.

ROADS

In 1998 there were an estimated 21,000 km of roads, of which more than 18,000 km were unpaved. All-weather highways now link Kabul with Qandahar and Herat in the south and west, Jalalabad in the east and Mazar-i-Sharif and the Amu-Dar'ya river in the north.

Afghan International Transport Company: Kabul.

Afghan Container Transport Company Ltd: POB 3234, Shar-i-Nau, Kabul; tel. (93) 23088.

Afghan Transit Company: POB 530, Ghousy Market, Mohd Jan Khan Wat, Kabul; tel. (93) 22654.

AFSOTR: Kabul; resumed operations in 1998; transport co; 90 vehicles.

Land Transport Company: Khoshal Mena, Kabul; tel. (93) 20345; f. 1943; commercial transport within Afghanistan.

The Milli Bus Enterprise: Ministry of Transport, Ansari Wat, Kabul; tel. (93) 25541; state-owned and -administered; 721 buses; Pres. Eng. AZIZ NAGHABAN.

Salang-Europe International Transport and Transit: Kabul; f. 1991 as joint Afghan/Soviet co; 500 vehicles.

INLAND WATERWAYS

There are 1,200 km of navigable inland waterways, including the Amu-Dar'ya (Oxus) river, which is capable of handling vessels of up to about 500 dwt. River ports on the Amu-Dar'ya are linked by road to Kabul.

CIVIL AVIATION

There are international airports at Kabul and Qandahar, and about 40 local airports are located throughout the country.

Ministry of Civil Aviation and Tourism: POB 165, Ansari Wat, Kabul; tel. (93) 21015; Head of Civil Aviation AKHTAR MOHAMMAD MANSUR.

Ariana Afghan Airlines: POB 76, Afghan Air Authority Bldg, Ansari Wat, Kabul; tel. (93) 25541; f. 1955; merged with Bakhtar Afghan Airlines Co Ltd in 1985; govt-owned; internal services between Kabul and three provincial capitals; external services to India, Pakistan, the United Arab Emirates and Saudi Arabia; Pres. Mola HAMIDULLAH AKHUND; Operations Man. F. M. FEDAWI.

Balkh Airlines: Mazar-i-Sharif; f. 1996; passenger and cargo flights to Pakistan, Iran and Central Asian republics; Owner Gen. ABDUL RASHID DOSTAM.

Khyber Afghan Airlines: Jalalabad; Owner Haji ABDUL QADEER.

Pameer Airlines: Bagram; flights to Iran, India, Russia, Albania, Bulgaria and the UAE.

Taliban Airways Co.

Tourism

Afghanistan's potential tourism attractions include: Bamian, with its thousands of painted caves; Bandi Amir, with its suspended lakes; the Blue Mosque of Mazar; Herat, with its Grand Mosque and minarets; the towns of Qandahar and Girishk; Balkh (ancient Bactria), 'Mother of Cities', in the north; Bagram, Hadda and Surkh Kotal (of interest to archaeologists); and the high mountains of the Hindu Kush. In 1998 an estimated 4,000 tourists visited Afghanistan and receipts from tourism amounted to around US $1m.

Afghan Tour: Ansari Wat, Shar-i-Nau, Kabul; tel. (93) 30152; official travel agency supervised by ATO; Pres. MOHD KAZIM WARDAK (acting).

Afghan Tourist Organization (ATO): Ansari Wat, Shar-i-Nau, Kabul; tel. (93) 30323; f. 1958; Pres. MOHD KAZIM WARDAK (acting).

ALBANIA

Introductory Survey

Location, Climate, Language, Religion, Flag, Capital

The Republic of Albania lies in south-eastern Europe. It is bordered by Yugoslavia to the north and north-east, by the former Yugoslav republic of Macedonia to the east, by Greece to the south and by the Adriatic and Ionian Seas (parts of the Mediterranean Sea) to the west. The climate is Mediterranean throughout most of the country. The sea plays a moderating role, although frequent cyclones in the winter months make the weather unstable. The average temperature is 14°C (57°F) in the north-east and 18°C (64°F) in the south-west. The language is Albanian, the principal dialects being Gheg (north of the Shkumbini river) and Tosk (in the south). The literary language is being formed on the basis of a strong fusion of the two dialects, with the phonetic and morphological structure of Tosk prevailing. An official ban on religious worship was in effect between 1967 and 1990. Before 1946 Islam was the predominant faith, and there were small groups of Christians (mainly Roman Catholic in the north and Eastern Orthodox in the south). The national flag (proportions 7 by 5) is red, with a two-headed black eagle in the centre. The capital is Tirana (Tiranë).

Recent History

On 28 November 1912, after more than 400 years of Turkish rule, Albania declared its independence under a provisional Government. The country was occupied by Italy in 1914, but its independence was re-established in 1920. Albania was declared a republic in 1925 and Ahmet Beg Zogu was elected President. He was proclaimed King Zog in 1928 and reigned until the occupation of Albania by Italy in April 1939. Albania was united with Italy for four years, before being occupied by German forces in 1943; the Germans withdrew one year later.

The communist-led National Liberation Front (NLF), established with help from Yugoslav communists in 1941, was the most successful wartime resistance group and took power on 29 November 1944. Elections in December 1945 were based on a single list of candidates, sponsored by the communists. The new regime was led by Enver Hoxha, head of the Albanian Communist Party (ACP) since 1943. King Zog was deposed and the People's Republic of Albania was proclaimed on 11 January 1946. The ACP was renamed the Party of Labour of Albania (PLA) in 1948, the NLF having been succeeded by the Democratic Front of Albania (DFA) in 1945.

The communist regime developed close relations with Yugoslavia, including a monetary and customs union, until the latter's expulsion from the Cominform (a Soviet-sponsored body co-ordinating the activities of European Communist parties) in 1948. Albania, fearing Yugoslav expansionism, became a close ally of the USSR and joined the Moscow-based Council for Mutual Economic Assistance (CMEA) in 1949. Hoxha resigned as Head of Government in 1954, but retained effective national leadership as First Secretary of the PLA. Albania joined the Warsaw Treaty Organization (Warsaw Pact) in 1955, but relations with the USSR deteriorated when Soviet leaders attempted a *rapprochement* with Yugoslavia. The Albanian leadership declared its support for the People's Republic of China in the Sino-Soviet ideological dispute, prompting the USSR to suspend relations with Albania in 1961. Albania established increasingly close relations with China, ended participation in the CMEA in 1962 and withdrew from the Warsaw Pact in 1968. However, following the improvement of relations between China and the USA after 1972, and the death of Mao Zedong, the Chinese leader, in 1976, Sino-Albanian relations progressively deteriorated. In 1978 Albania declared its support for Viet Nam in its dispute with China, prompting the Chinese Government to suspend all economic and military co-operation with Albania.

A new Constitution was adopted in December 1976, and the country was renamed the People's Socialist Republic of Albania. In December 1981 Mehmet Shehu, Chairman of the Council of Ministers (Prime Minister) since 1954, died as a result of a shooting incident. Although officially reported to have committed suicide, there were suggestions of a leadership struggle with Hoxha, and subsequent allegations that he had been exe-

cuted. Following the death of Shehu, a new Government was formed under Adil Çarçani, hitherto the First Deputy Chairman. In November 1982 Ramiz Alia replaced Haxhi Lleshi as President of the Presidium of the People's Assembly (Head of State). A number of former state and PLA officials were reportedly executed in September 1983.

Enver Hoxha died in April 1985, and was succeeded as First Secretary of the PLA by Alia. In March 1986 Hoxha's widow, Nexhmije, was elected to the chairmanship of the General Council of the DFA. Alia was re-elected as First Secretary of the PLA and as President of the Presidium of the People's Assembly in November 1986 and February 1987, respectively. In the latter month Adil Çarçani was reappointed Chairman of the Council of Ministers.

In November 1989, on the 45th anniversary of Albania's liberation from Nazi occupation, an amnesty for certain prisoners (including some political prisoners) was declared. In December 1989 and January 1990 a number of anti-Government demonstrations were reported to have taken place, particularly in the northern town of Shkodër. In late January, while continuing to deny the reports of internal unrest, Alia announced proposals for limited political and economic reforms, including the introduction of a system of multi-candidate elections (although the leading role of the PLA was to be maintained). Extensive reforms of the judicial system were approved by the People's Assembly in May, shortly before a visit to Tirana by the UN Secretary-General, Javier Pérez de Cuéllar. The Ministry of Justice was re-established, and the number of capital offences was considerably reduced. Although Albania was to remain a secular state, the practice of religion was henceforth to be tolerated. Furthermore, Albanians were to be granted the right to foreign travel, while the penalty for attempting to flee the country illegally was reduced. In July there was renewed unrest, when anti-Government demonstrators occupied the streets of Tirana and were violently dispersed by the security forces. More than 5,000 Albanians took refuge in foreign embassies, and were subsequently granted permission to leave the country. Meanwhile, the membership of both the Council of Ministers and the Political Bureau of the PLA had been reorganized; a number of prominent anti-reformists were among those replaced.

In November 1990, in response to increasing domestic pressure, Alia announced proposals for more radical political reforms, urging that the leading role of the PLA be redefined. In December it was announced that the establishment of independent political parties was to be permitted, prior to elections to the People's Assembly, scheduled to take place in February 1991. In mid-December 1990, however, anti-Government demonstrators clashed with the security forces in several cities. Nexhmije Hoxha resigned from the chairmanship of the General Council of the DFA, and was replaced by Çarçani (who was, in turn, replaced in mid-1991).

On 20 February 1991, following widespread anti-Government demonstrations, Alia declared presidential rule. An eight-member Presidential Council was established, and a provisional Council of Ministers was appointed. Çarçani was replaced as Chairman of the Council of Ministers by Fatos Nano, a progressive economist, who had been appointed Deputy Chairman at the end of January. In late February the unrest finally ended, owing, in part, to an increased use of force by the authorities to quell the protests.

Meanwhile, following pressure from the newly established opposition parties, the elections had been postponed until the end of March 1991 to allow political organizations more time to prepare. Despite these concessions, an increasing number of ethnic Greek Albanians attempted to leave the country. In mid-March a general amnesty for all political prisoners was declared. The first stage of the multi-party elections to the People's Assembly duly took place on 31 March, and the second and third rounds of voting were held on 7 and 14 April. The PLA and affiliated organizations won 169 of the 250 seats, while the Democratic Party of Albania (DPA) secured 75 seats, and the Democratic Union of the Greek Minority (OMONIA) obtained five seats. The victory of the PLA, amid allegations of electoral malpractice, prompted dismay in some urban areas, where support for the DPA had been strong. Widespread protests ensued, and in Shkodër four people, including a local DPA leader, were killed, when the security forces opened fire on demonstrators.

In late April 1991 an interim Constitution replaced that of 1976, pending the drafting of a new constitution. The country was renamed the Republic of Albania, and the post of executive President, to be elected by two-thirds of votes cast in the People's Assembly, was created. Alia was subsequently elected to the new post, defeating the only other candidate, Namik Dokle, also of the PLA; all the opposition deputies abstained from voting. In early May Nano was reappointed Chairman of the Council of Ministers, and the Government was again reorganized. In accordance with the provisions of the interim Constitution, Alia resigned from the leadership of the PLA.

In early June 1991 the continuing general strike forced the resignation of Nano's administration. A Government of National Stability was subsequently formed, with Ylli Bufi (hitherto Minister of Food) as Chairman of the Council of Ministers. The coalition included representatives of the PLA, the DPA, the Albanian Republican Party (ARP), the Social Democratic Party (SDP) and the Agrarian Party (AP). Gramoz Pashko, a prominent member of the DPA, was appointed Deputy Chairman of the Council of Ministers and Minister of the Economy. At its 10th Congress, which took place later in June, the PLA was renamed the Socialist Party of Albania (SPA).

In August 1991, following a further seaborne exodus of migrants to Italy, the ports of Albania were placed under military control. Several vessels were refused entry by the Italian authorities, while many of the Albanians who had succeeded in disembarking were repatriated. Further opposition strikes and demonstrations were staged in subsequent weeks. In early December the Chairman of the DPA, Dr Sali Berisha, announced the withdrawal of party members from the coalition Government, despite opposition from other prominent DPA officials. The withdrawal of the seven DPA representatives, following the expulsion of three ARP ministers who had criticized the administration, forced Bufi's Government to resign. President Alia subsequently appointed an interim Government, principally composed of non-party specialists, under a new Prime Minister, Vilson Ahmeti (hitherto Minister of Food); new elections were to take place in March 1992.

A new electoral law, approved by the People's Assembly in early February 1992, reduced the number of deputies in the Assembly from 250 to 140, of whom 100 were to be elected by majority vote from single-member constituencies, while the remaining deputies were to be elected according to a system of proportional representation. Under provisions that defined legitimate political parties, OMONIA, as an organization representing an ethnic minority, was prohibited from contesting the forthcoming general election, prompting widespread protest from the Greek minority. At the general election, which was conducted in two rounds on 22 and 29 March, the DPA secured 92 of the 140 contested seats, while the SPA obtained 38 seats, the SDP seven seats, the Union for Human Rights Party (UHRP—supported by the minority Greek and Macedonian communities) two seats and the ARP one seat. According to official figures, 90% of the electorate participated. Following the defeat of the SPA, Alia resigned as President on 3 April. A few days later the new People's Assembly elected Berisha to the presidency. Berisha subsequently appointed a coalition Government, with Aleksander Meksi, a member of the DPA, as Prime Minister. In addition to the premiership, the DPA held 14 ministerial portfolios, while the SDP and ARP were allocated one portfolio each.

In July 1992 an amendment to the law on political organizations effectively banned the Albanian Communist Party. At the end of that month the DPA secured 43% of the total votes cast in the country's first multi-party local elections since the Second World War, while the SPA recovered some of the support that it had lost in the March general election, with 41% of the votes. In September divisions within the DPA resulted in the defection of a number of prominent party members, who had accused the Berisha administration of becoming increasingly right-wing and authoritarian, to form a new political grouping, the Democratic Alliance Party (DAP).

In 1992 a number of former communist officials were detained, including Nexhmije Hoxha, who was arrested on charges of corruption. In February 1993 the former Prime Minister, Vilson

Ahmeti, was placed under house arrest, following charges of corruption; further allegations concerning abuse of power resulted in the arrest of another former Prime Minister, Fatos Nano (who was now President of the SPA), in July. Nexhmije Hoxha was imprisoned for nine years in January, having been convicted of embezzling state funds. (She was released in January 1997, after her term of imprisonment was twice reduced.) In August 1993 Alia was arrested on charges of abuse of power. Later that month Ahmeti was sentenced to two years' imprisonment. The trial of Nano commenced in April 1994, despite an international campaign on his behalf, organized by the SPA, and a European Parliament resolution appealing for his release. Nano was convicted of misappropriation of state funds during his premiership in 1991, and was sentenced to 12 years' imprisonment. In July 1994 Alia, who had denied the charges against him, was sentenced to nine years' imprisonment for abuse of power and violating the rights of citizens. (In July 1995, however, under the terms of a general amnesty, Alia, and a further 30 political prisoners, were released.)

In October 1994 the draft Constitution was finally presented to Berisha, but failed to obtain the requisite two-thirds' majority approval in the People's Assembly, and was consequently submitted for endorsement at a national referendum. As a result of Berisha's personal campaign in support of the draft Constitution (which was to vest additional powers in the President, and reduce those of the legislature), the referendum was widely perceived as a vote of confidence in his leadership. At the referendum, which took place on 6 November, with the participation of 84.4% of the electorate, the draft Constitution was rejected by 53.9% of the voters, prompting demands for a general election (on the grounds that the administration lacked a popular mandate). In early December Berisha effected an extensive reorganization of the Council of Ministers. On the following day the ARP, which held only one seat in the People's Assembly, withdrew from the governing coalition. The SDP split into two factions; a new grouping, known as the Union of Social Democrats (USD—led by the Minister of Culture, Youth and Sport, Teodor Laco), remained in the coalition, while the SDP withdrew.

In March 1995 the Chairman of the DPA, Eduard Selami, was removed from his post at an extraordinary party congress, for opposing Berisha's efforts to organize a further referendum on the draft Constitution. Selami's accusations concerning Berisha's abuse of his position reinforced widespread discontent at the perceived corruption in the latter's administration. Public discontent at the slow pace of economic recovery in Albania was demonstrated by the continued flow of illegal immigrants to Italy, which, in May, deployed troops along its coast in an attempt to stem the influx.

In June 1995 Ilir Hoxha, the son of Enver Hoxha, was convicted on charges of inciting national hatred, after condemning leaders of the DPA in a newspaper interview. In September the People's Assembly adopted legislation prohibiting those in power under the former communist regime from holding public office until 2002 (thereby banning a large number of prospective candidates, including incumbent SPA deputies, from contesting legislative elections in 1996). In the same month the Minister of Justice dismissed three Supreme Court judges, owing to their alleged activities under the communist regime. The Chairman of the Supreme Court, Zef Brozi, challenged the Minister's authority to dismiss employees of the Court and refused to accept the decision. Brozi had aroused the disapproval of the Government earlier in the year, when he recommended a review of Fatos Nano's case and advocated his release. However, as a result of an amendment to the penal code, which was subsequently adopted by the Government, the Supreme Court was forced to reject Nano's appeal. Following an ensuing ruling against Brozi by the Constitutional Court, which declared his previous suspension of lower court verdicts to be illegal, he was dismissed by the People's Assembly, and replaced by his deputy. The SPA deputies boycotted the People's Assembly, in protest at Brozi's dismissal and the Government's alleged infringement of the independence of the judiciary.

In November 1995 a parliamentary commission initiated an inquiry following the discovery of a mass grave near the border town of Shkodër. Families of the deceased urged the prosecution service to initiate charges against former members of the communist regime, including Alia, who had allegedly been responsible for the killing by border guards of nationals attempting to flee the country in 1990–92. Also in November 1995 the People's Assembly approved legislation requiring senior civil servants to be investigated for their activities under the communist regime. In December 14 prominent former members of the communist regime were arrested on charges of involvement in the execution, internment and deportation of citizens for political reasons. (In May 1996 three of the former officials received death sentences, which were later commuted to terms of imprisonment, while the remaining defendants also received custodial terms in August and September.) In February Alia was detained in connection with the killing of demonstrators in Shkodër in April 1991 and the border incidents.

Following increasing division within the SPA, in March 1996 a liberal faction left the organization to form the Albanian New Socialist Party. Later that month the Government invited international representatives to observe the legislative elections, which were scheduled to take place in late May. The first round of the elections (which was preceded by SPA allegations of intimidation by the security forces) took place on 26 May; following alleged electoral irregularities, however, the principal opposition parties, including the SPA, the SDP and the DAP, withdrew from the poll and issued a statement rejecting the election results. A subsequent SPA demonstration held in protest at the alleged malpractices was violently dispersed by the security forces. The second round of the elections took place on 2 June; as a result of opposition demands for a boycott, only 59.4% of the electorate participated in the poll (compared with 89% in the first round). According to official results, the DPA secured 101 of the 115 directly elected seats (25 seats were to be allocated proportionately). However, international observers, who included representatives of the Organization for Security and Co-operation in Europe (OSCE, formerly the Conference on Security and Co-operation in Europe—CSCE, see p. 252), claimed that widespread malpractice and intimidation of voters had been perpetrated and urged the Government to conduct fresh elections, while SPA deputies initiated a hunger strike in an attempt to oblige Berisha to annul the results. Berisha rejected the allegations of government malpractice, and agreed to conduct further elections in only 17 constituencies. The principal opposition parties (which demanded that fresh elections be held, under international supervision, in all constituencies) continued their electoral boycott. Consequently, the DPA won all the seats contested in the partial elections, which took place on 16 June, thereby securing a total of 122 of the 140 seats in the People's Assembly. The SPA won 10 of the remaining seats, while the UHRP and the ARP each acquired three and the National Front two. (The SPA, however, refused to recognize the new legislature and boycotted the inaugural session of the People's Assembly.) The OSCE subsequently issued a report, stating that the elections had failed to meet international legal standards. In early July Meksi, who had been reappointed to the office of Prime Minister, formed a new Council of Ministers, principally comprising members of the DPA; the ARP, the Christian Democratic Party and the USD were also represented. Later that month a parliamentary commission was established to investigate the reported electoral violations.

In August 1996 the Government established a permanent Central Election Commission, prior to local government elections, which were scheduled to take place in October; the main opposition parties subsequently nominated a number of representatives to the Commission. Despite continued division within the SPA, Nano (who remained in prison) was re-elected as Chairman at a party congress in late August. In the local government elections, which took place in two rounds in late October, the DPA secured the highest number of votes in 58 of the 64 municipalities and in 267 of the 309 communes. Although the OSCE had withdrawn its observers, after Berisha claimed that one of its members was biased against the DPA, observers from the Council of Europe (see p. 165) declared that, despite some irregularities, the elections had been conducted fairly.

In January 1997 the collapse of several widely popular 'pyramid' financial investment schemes (which had offered high rates of interest), resulting in huge losses of individual savings, prompted violent anti-Government demonstrations, particularly in Tirana and the southern town of Vlorë. It was widely believed that members of the Government were associated with the pyramid schemes, which had allegedly financed widespread illegal activities. The People's Assembly subsequently adopted legislation prohibiting the schemes. However, the Government increased efforts to suppress the protests (which were supported by a newly established opposition alliance, Forum for Democracy): large numbers of demonstrators were arrested and prominent opposition members were publicly assaulted by the security

forces. At the end of January the People's Assembly granted Berisha emergency powers to mobilize special army units to restore order. It was reported that several people were killed in ensuing violent clashes between security forces and protesters (who continued to demand the resignation of Berisha and state reimbursement for the financial losses that they had incurred). At the end of February, however, Berisha (whose mandate was due to expire in April) was nominated as the presidential candidate for the DPA. On 3 March he was re-elected unopposed for a second five-year term (with the SPA continuing to boycott the People's Assembly).

Following an escalation in hostilities between insurgents (who seized armaments from military depots) and government troops in the south of the country, Berisha declared a national state of emergency at the beginning of March 1997, empowering security forces to shoot demonstrators and imposing total official censorship. However, insurgent groups gained control of the southern towns of Vlorë, Sarandë and Gjirokastër, while it was reported that large numbers of government forces had deserted or defected to join the rebels. Following negotiations with representatives of nine principal opposition parties, Berisha signed an agreement whereby an interim coalition government was to be installed, pending elections in June, and offered an amnesty to rebels who surrendered to the authorities. A former SPA mayor of Gjirokastër, Bashkim Fino, was appointed to the office of Prime Minister. Berisha subsequently approved the formation of a Government of National Reconciliation, which included representatives of eight opposition parties. (The DAP had withdrawn from the negotiations, after its proposal that the interior portfolio be allocated to an opposition member was rejected.) Despite these concessions, the insurgency continued, reaching the northern town of Tropojë and Tirana (where rebels seized the airport). All those detained in Tirana central prison, including Nano and Alia, were released; Nano was subsequently granted an official pardon by Berisha. The evacuation of western European and US nationals from Tirana and Durrës was impeded by the rebels, who exchanged fire with foreign troops effecting the evacuation. Extreme hardship and concern that the fighting would escalate into widespread civil conflict prompted thousands of Albanians to flee to Italy (where the Italian authorities announced they would be permitted to remain for a maximum of three months). Later in March, however, Italian naval authorities were ordered to intercept boats transporting Albanian refugees, in an effort to halt the exodus.

In late March 1997 it was reported that government forces had regained control of Tirana; the south of the country was controlled by insurgent groups opposed to the Government, while the north was largely held by paramilitary units loyal to Berisha. Following mediation by the Italian Government and an OSCE special envoy, Franz Vranitzky, southern rebel leaders, grouped in a self-designated 'national committee for public salvation', agreed to abandon hostilities in return for guarantees of amnesty. However, the rebels subsequently refused to surrender their armaments, and demanded that further legislative elections take place. The Government of National Reconciliation requested military assistance in the restoration of civil order, and in late March Fino attended a meeting of European Union (EU, see p. 181) foreign ministers in Rome, Italy, to appeal for the establishment of a multinational force to supervise humanitarian aid operations in Albania. At the end of March the UN Security Council endorsed an OSCE proposal that member states be authorized to contribute troops to the force. The 5,915-member Multinational Protection Force for Albania was established in April, with an official mission (known as Operation Alba) to facilitate the distribution of humanitarian assistance; the Italian contingent numbered 2,500, and the French 1,000, while Turkey, Greece, Spain, Romania, Austria and Denmark also contributed troops. The Multinational Protection Force (which had a mandate to remain in the country for three months) began to arrive in mid-April, and was subsequently deployed in regions under government control in northern and central Albania. After negotiations between Italian forces and insurgents at Vlorë, the leader of the 'national committee for public salvation', Ekeren Osmani, announced that he would co-operate with the Italian troops.

At the beginning of April 1997 the SPA ended its boycott of the People's Assembly, which subsequently voted to end press restrictions that had been imposed under the state of emergency in March. Later in April the National Council of the DPA endorsed Berisha's leadership of the party and removed a number of dissident members who had demanded his resignation. The son of King Zog and claimant to the throne, Leka Zogu, who returned to Albania in April, with the support of the pro-monarchist Legality Movement Party, urged that a referendum on the restoration of the monarchy take place; the principal political parties had already agreed that such a referendum be conducted. In early May the People's Assembly adopted legislation regulating the operation of the pyramid investment schemes. Following mediation by Vranitzky, the leaders of 10 major political parties agreed that further elections would take place by the end of June. However, negotiations between the parties regarding the drafting of a new electoral code ended in failure, owing to disagreement over the number of parliamentary deputies to be elected by proportional representation. Later in May the DPA submitted to the People's Assembly legislation on a new electoral system, which was approved, despite a further parliamentary boycott by SPA deputies; under the new legislation, the number of deputies in the People's Assembly was to be increased from 140 to 155, of whom 115 were to be directly elected and 40 elected on the basis of proportional representation. After further discussions between the parties, Vranitzky announced that the elections would take place on 29 June. The SPA and its allied parties agreed to participate in the elections, after Berisha complied with the stipulation that the central electoral commission be appointed by the interim Government (rather than by himself).

Election campaigning was marred by a number of violent incidents, including a number of bomb explosions in Tirana. In June 1997 the UN Security Council voted to extend the mandate of the Multinational Protection Force to mid-August. Leaders of the DPA and SPA signed an agreement in Rome pledging to abide by the results of the elections. On 29 June the first round of voting in the elections to the People's Assembly took place; a referendum on the restoration of the monarchy was conducted on the same day. Despite the presence of the Multinational Protection Force, some three people were killed in violent incidents during the voting. A further electoral ballot took place in 32 constituencies on 6 July. OSCE observers, who had monitored the voting, subsequently declared the electoral process to have been conducted satisfactorily. Later in July the central electoral commission announced that the SPA had secured 101 seats in the People's Assembly, while the DPA had won 29 seats; the SPA and its allied parties (the SDP, the Democratic Alliance Party, the AP and the UHRP) thereby secured the requisite two-thirds majority for the approval of constitutional amendments that they had proposed earlier in the month. At the referendum, 66.7% of the electorate voted in favour of retaining a republic. Only 33.3% voted in favour of the restoration of the monarchy; at the end of August the Constitutional Court upheld the result, following a legal challenge by monarchists (who had accused the central electoral commission of malpractice). On 24 July, following Berisha's resignation, the Secretary-General of the SPA, Dr Rexhep Mejdani, was elected President by the People's Assembly. Parliamentary deputies also voted to end the state of emergency, which had been imposed in March. The SPA proposed Nano to the office of Prime Minister, and a new Council of Ministers was appointed, which comprised representatives of the SPA and its allied parties, and retained Fino in the post of Deputy Prime Minister. At the end of July the new Government submitted a programme for the restoration of civil order and economic reconstruction, which received a vote of confidence in the People's Assembly. The legislature also voted in favour of auditing the existing pyramid schemes and investigating those that had been dissolved, in an effort to reimburse lost savings.

In August 1997 the Government dispatched troops to the south of the country, in an effort to restore order in major towns that were under the control of rebel forces. It was subsequently announced that Vlorë had been recaptured and a number of rebel forces arrested; the Minister of the Interior ordered that all armaments looted during the unrest be surrendered to the authorities. By mid-August the mandate of the Multinational Protection Force had officially ended and the contingent had left Albania. Foreign advisers subsequently returned to the country to assist the Government in the reorganization of the military and security services, under the terms of existing bilateral treaties. In late August a number of prominent officials and members of the armed forces, including the army Chief of Staff, the head of the security services and the Governor of the Central Bank, were replaced as part of an extensive reorganization of public services.

In early September 1997 the People's Assembly established a parliamentary commission, which was to draft a new constitution, in accordance with the amendments proposed by the SPA. Later in September an SPA member, Gafur Mazreku, shot and wounded an opposition deputy, following an acrimonious parliamentary session. Mazreku was subsequently charged with attempted murder, and the incident further exacerbated relations between the SPA and the DPA, which initiated a boycott of the People's Assembly. In October Berisha was re-elected Chairman of the DPA. In the same month Alia and a further three former senior officials were acquitted of genocide by a Tirana court (upholding a ruling of the Supreme Court), on the grounds that the charge did not exist under the penal legislation of the former communist Government.

Violent unrest continued in early 1998, with numerous minor bomb attacks, one of which, in January, destroyed SPA offices in Gjirokastër. In February tensions in Shkodër precipitated an armed revolt by civilians and rebel members of the local security forces, who seized the town's police station and released a number of prisoners from custody. Government troops subsequently restored order in Shkodër; Berisha, however, attributed responsibility for the uprising to the Nano administration, and reiterated demands that further elections be organized.

In March 1998 the DPA announced that it was to end its boycott of the People's Assembly, in order to demonstrate support for ethnic Albanians in Kosovo and Metahija, Yugoslavia (see below). Partial local government elections took place on 21 June: a government electoral coalition, Alliance for the State, secured five of the seven contested municipalities and six of the nine contested communes, while an opposition grouping, led by the DPA and known as the Union for Democracy, won the remaining polls. Despite opposition claims of irregularities, OSCE observers declared that the elections had been conducted fairly. In early July a parliamentary commission, which had been established in October 1997 to investigate the unrest earlier that year, submitted a report recommending that several senior DPA officials, including Berisha, be charged in connection with the deployment of the armed forces to suppress the protests. Later in July 1998 Nano announced that the constitutional commission had presented draft legislation, which would be submitted for approval by the People's Assembly in October; the new Constitution was subsequently to be referred for endorsement at a national referendum. In August six prominent DPA officials who had served in the previous Government were arrested in connection with alleged human rights' violations committed during the civil unrest in 1997. The DPA subsequently staged an unauthorized demonstration in Tirana to demand their release.

In early September 1998 Azem Hajdari, a prominent DPA official and close associate of Berisha, was assassinated outside the party headquarters in Tirana; Berisha accused Nano of involvement in the killing, and demanded the resignation of the Government. The incident prompted violent protests by DPA supporters, who seized government offices and occupied the state television and radio buildings. Government security forces subsequently regained control of the capital, after clashes with protesters, in which about seven people were reported to have been killed. Berisha denied government claims that the uprising constituted a coup attempt, and DPA supporters staged a demonstration in his support in Tirana. Later in September the People's Assembly voted in favour of ending Berisha's parliamentary exemption from prosecution, thereby allowing him to be charged with attempting to overthow the Government. An OSCE delegation, which mediated subsequent discussions between the political parties, condemned Berisha for inciting unrest, but also criticized Nano, owing to continued corruption within his administration. At the end of September the Minister of Public Order resigned, amid widespread criticism of the Government's failure to improve public security. Shortly afterwards Nano tended his resignation, following a meeting of the SPA leadership, having failed to reach agreement with the government coalition on the composition of a new Council of Ministers. Mejdani subsequently requested that the Secretary-General of the SPA, Pandeli Majko, who had been nominated by the party to the office of Prime Minister, form a new government. In early October a new coalition Council of Ministers, headed by Majko, was installed. Later that month the People's Assembly approved the draft Constitution; DPA members and other deputies belonging to the Union for Democracy initiated a legislative boycott. The new Constitution, which provided for the post-communist system of government, was submitted for endorsement at a national referendum, which was monitored by OSCE observers, on 22 November. The Government subsequently announced that 50.1% of the registered electorate had participated in the referendum, of whom 93.1% had voted in favour of adopting the draft Constitution. However, Berisha claimed that only 17% of the votes cast by a total of 35% of the electorate had been in favour of the new Constitution, and urged his supporters to stage further protests against the preliminary results of the referendum. The Government deployed additional security forces in Tirana in an effort to maintain public order. On 28 November Mejdani officially adopted the new Constitution. However, Berisha subsequently announced that the DPA would continue to refuse to recognize the Constitution. In July 1999 a DPA congress voted in favour of ending the boycott of the legislature, which had been initiated following the killing of Hajdari.

At an SPA party congress in September 1999 Nano (who had resigned from the party chairmanship in January) was re-elected to the post, narrowly defeating Majko. In October Majko (who, consequently, no longer had the support of the SPA deputies in the People's Assembly) resigned from the office of Prime Minister. Mejdani subsequently nominated Ilir Meta (hitherto Deputy Prime Minister), whom Nano supported, as Prime Minister. Berisha announced that the DPA would boycott a parliamentary motion to approve the new Council of Ministers formed by Meta, and that his supporters would stage mass protests following the return of Nano to the SPA leadership. In early November the new Government was formally approved in the People's Assembly (despite the opposition boycott).

In January 2000 the Union for Democracy criticized legislation governing the composition of the state electoral commission, on the grounds that the opposition coalition was not guaranteed equal representation on the body. In the same month Meta dismissed the Minister of Public Economy and Privatization, following controversy over the ministry's alleged contravention of legislation regulating the energy sector. At the same time the Minister of State to the Prime Minister was dismissed, reportedly for lack of co-operation. In late February the Deputy Foreign Minister, Ben Blushi, who had allegedly revealed details of clandestine discussions between Meta and the US Secretary of State, Madeleine Albright, was also removed from office. Disagreement between Meta and Nano over the issue subsequently emerged at a meeting of the SPA leadership, after Meta refused a request to reinstate Blushi. In March President Mejdani announced the formal abolition of the death penalty. In July both Luan Hajdaraga, the Minister of Justice, and the Minister of Defence were replaced in an extensive government reorganization. A subsequent motion in the legislature to endorse the new Council of Ministers was boycotted by the DPA, which accused the Meta Government of fostering corruption. It was, in addition, reported that Mejdani had disagreed with Meta's removal of Hajdaraga (whom the Prime Minister had several times previously attempted to dismiss).

In early September 2000 an attempted attack on Berisha, who was visiting the southern town of Fier, was repulsed by his personal security guards; it was subsequently reported that the assailant was a local DPA leader. Local government elections took place, as scheduled, in two rounds in October, following the preparation of a new voters' register, with assistance from the United Nations Development Programme (see p. 45). The first round of the elections, which took place on 1 October, was won by the SPA, with about 43% of votes cast. The DPA (which obtained about 34% of votes in the poll) claimed that widespread electoral malpractice had been perpetrated and urged the Party's supporters to boycott the second round. Nevertheless, OSCE observers, while reporting that irregularities had taken place, declared that they had not influenced the results of the poll. On 15 October about 50% of the electorate participated in the second round of voting for a number of mayoralties and local government councils where no candidates had obtained an absolute majority in the first round. Later that month the state electoral commission announced the official results, which indicated that the SPA had secured 252 seats on local government councils, while the DPA had won 118 seats. However, DPA supporters subsequently staged a series of protests at the election results, which the Party continued to refuse to recognize. In mid-November some OSCE representatives left the country, in response to threats against their personal security. At the end of that month, following continued DPA protests, anti-Government demonstrators attempted to seize the police station in the northern town of Bajram Curri; two protesters

were killed and about 20 were injured in the suppression of the attack by security forces. In December, amid the continuing dispute over the local government elections, inter-party discussions over proposed amendments to the electoral regulations were initiated, prior to elections to the People's Assembly, due to take place in mid-2001.

The gradual relaxation of Albania's isolationist policies culminated in 1990, in a declaration of its intention to establish good relations with all countries, irrespective of their social system. Until 1990 Albania remained hostile to the USSR; in July of that year, however, Albania and the USSR formally agreed to restore diplomatic relations. Diplomatic relations between Albania and the USA were re-established in March 1991 (they had been suspended since 1946), while diplomatic links between Albania and the United Kingdom were restored in May. Albania was granted observer status at the 1990 CSCE summit meeting, and became a full member of the organization in June 1991. In May 1992 the newly elected President, Berisha, made a tour of Europe. In the same month, Albania and the EC signed a 10-year agreement on trade and co-operation. In June Albania, together with 10 other countries (including six of the former Soviet republics), signed a pact to establish the Black Sea Economic Co-operation group (see p. 265), envisaging the creation of a Black Sea economic zone that would complement the EC. In December Albania was granted membership of the Organization of the Islamic Conference (OIC, see p. 266), and in the same month applied to join NATO (see p. 241), thus becoming the first former Warsaw Pact country formally to seek membership of the Western alliance. Albania joined NATO's 'Partnership for Peace' programme of military co-operation in April 1994. Albania was admitted to the Council of Europe in July 1995, having agreed to adopt a new Constitution and to take measures to fulfil the Council's requirements concerning human rights.

Albania's relations with neighbouring Greece and Yugoslavia have been strained. In August 1987 Greece formally ended the technical state of war with Albania that had been in existence since 1945. However, the status of the Greek minority in Albania, unofficially estimated to number between 200,000 and 400,000, remained a sensitive issue. Relations between Albania and Greece deteriorated in 1993, owing to Greece's deportation of some 20,000 Albanian immigrants and to the alleged mistreatment of the Greek minority in southern Albania. Relations between the two states were exacerbated further in April 1994, following a violent border incident in which two Albanian guards were killed by unidentified opponents; a series of diplomatic expulsions ensued on both sides, and the border situation remained tense, with a number of reports of minor skirmishes. In May six prominent members of the ethnic Greek organization, OMONIA, were arrested, following the alleged seizure by Albanian police of weapons and 'anti-constitutional' documents. Greece subsequently protested at the actions of the Albanian authorities by vetoing the provision of funds from the EU to Albania and by increasing the deportations of illegal Albanian immigrants. In September five of the OMONIA detainees were convicted on charges including espionage and the illegal possession of weapons, and received custodial sentences. Following the verdict, Greece and Albania recalled their mutual ambassadors. In addition, the Greek Government submitted formal protests to the UN and the EU regarding Albania's perceived maltreatment of its ethnic Greek population and closed the important Kakavija border crossing, which had hitherto been used by Albanian migrant workers. One of the OMONIA defendants was pardoned in December, following a reduction in tension between the two countries (in November Greece had withdrawn its veto on EU aid to Albania). In early February 1995 the four remaining OMONIA prisoners were released. Later that month the OSCE suspended its inquiries into the alleged persecution of the Greek minority in Albania, on the grounds that there was no case to answer. In March relations between Albania and Greece improved dramatically, following a two-day official visit to Albania by the Greek Minister of Foreign Affairs. In June the Albanian Government approved a new education bill, which recognized the right of ethnic minorities to their own language and culture. In March 1996 the Greek President, Konstantinos Stefanopoulos, visited Albania for discussions, during which a co-operation agreement was signed, apparently resolving outstanding issues of concern between the two nations. In August 1997 Albania and Greece signed an agreement whereby Albanian migrant workers in Greece would receive temporary work permits. In July 1999 the Albanian Minister of Foreign

Affairs visited Greece to discuss the increasing number of expulsions of Albanian migrants by the Greek authorities.

Relations with Yugoslavia deteriorated sharply in early 1989, when many ethnic Albanian demonstrators were killed during renewed unrest in the Yugoslav province of Kosovo and Metohija (where the population was principally composed of ethnic Albanian Muslims). In April 1993 it was reported that 10 Albanians had been killed by Yugoslav security forces while unwittingly crossing the border. As a result of increasing tension in this area, in the following month the Albanian Government requested the establishment of a UN peace-keeping mission in Kosovo to protect Albanians there. This was refused, however, and Kosovo remained a focus of political and ethnic tension. The insurgency in southern Albania in early 1997 (see above) prompted concern among western European Governments that armaments seized by the rebels might also be used to support an insurrection by ethnic Albanians in Kosovo. In November 1997, following a meeting between Prime Minister Nano and the Yugoslav President, Slobodan Milošević, it was announced that relations between Albania and Yugoslavia were to be normalized (although Milošević emphasized during the discussions that the unrest in Kosovo remained an internal issue of Yugoslavia). However, increased Serbian military activity against the ethnic Albanian majority in Kosovo in early 1998 (see chapter on Yugoslavia) was condemned by the Albanian Government; Nano urged international intervention to prevent widespread conflict in the region. In March large demonstrations were staged in Tirana in protest at Serbian violence against ethnic Albanian civilians in Kosovo. In April clashes were reported on the Albanian border with Kosovo between Serbian troops and suspected members of the paramilitary Kosovo Liberation Army (KLA—Ushtria Çlirimtare e Kosovës). The Albanian administration initiated measures to prevent the illicit transportation of armaments from northern Albania to KLA forces in Kosovo. By June, according to official figures, some 10,000 ethnic Albanian refugees had fled to northern Albania (particularly to the region of Tropojë), following continued Serbian military reprisals against the ethnic Albanian population in Kosovo. The Albanian Government adopted a programme for the resettlement of the Kosovan refugees. In mid-1998 NATO conducted a number of military exercises in Albania, in conjunction with the Albanian armed forces, in an attempt to increase pressure on the Serbian Government to end military action in Kosovo.

In late March 1999, following the failure of diplomatic efforts to persuade Milošević to accede to NATO demands (see chapter on Yugoslavia), NATO forces commenced an intensive aerial bombardment of Yugoslavia. The Albanian Government expressed support for NATO military action (and allowed Albania's air and sea facilities to be used for NATO operations), but urged the introduction of ground troops in Kosovo to prevent increasing large-scale massacres of the ethnic Albanian civilian population by Serbian forces. Further Albanian troops were deployed on the northern border with Serbia in preparation for a possible Serbian retaliatory offensive. The atrocities committed by Serbian forces in Kosovo precipitated a mass exodus of ethnic Albanian refugees from the province; by early April some 300,000 had fled to Albania. NATO troops (which later numbered about 8,000, and became known as AFOR) were dispatched to Albania to provide logistic support for humanitarian aid operations. The Government appealed for international financial assistance in providing for the Kosovo refugee population, and urged NATO to expedite Albania's admission to the Organization. It was reported that a number of ethnic Albanians had returned from abroad to join the KLA (which operated training camps in northern Albania). In early April Serbian forces bombarded Albanian border villages during heavy fighting with the KLA in Kosovo, increasing international concern that a broader regional conflict might develop. Later that month Serbian troops advanced into Albanian territory, but were repelled by members of the Albanian armed forces. By May the KLA had succeeded in establishing a supply route for the transportation of armaments from bases in northern Albania to Kosovo. Despite the further reinforcement of Albanian troops at the border with Kosovo, Serbian forces launched further attacks on KLA positions in northern Albania. Also in May Prime Minister Majko met ethnic Albanian representatives from Kosovo, in an effort to resolve differences between factions of the Kosovo Albanian leadership. In early June Milošević finally accepted a peace plan for Kosovo (see chapter on Yugoslavia). Following the subsequent withdrawal of Serbian forces from Kosovo and the deployment of an international peace-keeping force (known as KFOR) in the province, under the terms of the peace agreement, about one-half of the ethnic Albanian refugees returned to Kosovo from Albania and the former Yugoslav republic of Macedonia (FYRM) later that month. In September NATO announced that AFOR, which had been gradually withdrawing from the country, was to be replaced by a contingent, to be known as Communications Zone West (COMMZ-W), which was to be mandated to maintain civil order in Albania and to support the KFOR mission in Kosovo. At mid-2000 COMMZ-W (which was stationed in Durrës, under the command of KFOR) comprised members of the armed forces of Italy, Turkey, Greece, the USA, Germany and Denmark, while an additional Italian contingent supported COMMZ-W and Italian KFOR forces; in total, more than 1,200 troops were deployed throughout Albania. Following the repatriation to Kosovo of some 430,000 refugees during 1999, the number of refugees in Albania at mid-2000 was estimated at about 4,200 (the overwhelming majority of whom were Kosovar Albanians).

In February 1993 Albania refused to accept an application by the FYRM for membership of the CSCE, and it was only in April that Albania officially recognized the existence of the republic as an independent state. Albania was concerned at the oppression of the large ethnic Albanian minority in the FYRM, who constituted about 21% of the population and the majority of whom were Muslims. Relations between the two countries deteriorated in the course of the year, owing to a number of shooting incidents on the border. In March 1994, however, Albania urged Greece to end its economic embargo on the FYRM. Following the civil unrest in Albania in early 1997 (see above), a number of incursions into FYRM territory by armed groups of Albanian rebels were reported; in September two members of the FYRM's security forces were killed in a clash with Albanians who had entered the country illegally. In October the Ministers of Defence of Albania and the FYRM signed an agreement providing for increased security at the joint border between the two countries.

Government

Under the Constitution adopted in November 1998, legislative power is vested in the unicameral People's Assembly. The People's Assembly, which is elected for a term of four years, comprises at least 140 deputies, of whom 100 are directly elected by a simple majority and the remainder on the basis of proportional representation. The President of the Republic is Head of State, and is elected by the People's Assembly for a term of five years. Executive authority is held by the Council of Ministers, which is led by the Prime Minister as Head of Government. The Prime Minister is appointed by the President. The Prime Minister appoints a Council of Ministers, which is then presented for approval to the People's Assembly. For the purposes of local government, Albania is divided into 36 districts (*rrethe*) and one municipality, the capital. The representative organs of the basic units of local government are councils, which are elected by general direct elections for a period of three years. The Council of Ministers appoints a Prefect in every region as its representative.

Defence

In 2000 the armed forces were in the process of being reconstituted, with assistance from European Governments (particularly those of Greece and Italy). In August of that year the air force numbered 4,500 and the navy 2,500. Paramilitary forces comprised an internal security force, based in Tirana, and units in major towns, together with an estimated 500 border police. Budgetary expenditure on defence in 1998 was estimated at 10,500m. lekë. The budget proposals for 1999 allocated about 1.0% of total projected government expenditure to defence. Military service is compulsory and lasts for 12 months. From April 1999 a NATO contingent (known as AFOR), numbering about 8,000, was deployed in Albania, to assist in humanitarian aid operations, following a mass influx of refugees from Kosovo (see Recent History). In September it was announced that AFOR was to be reconstituted as a contingent to be known as Communications Zone West (COMMZ-W), which was to maintain civil order in Albania and support NATO forces in Kosovo; at mid-2000 about 1,200 troops assigned to COMMZ-W were deployed in Albania.

Economic Affairs

In 1998, according to World Bank estimates, Albania's gross national product (GNP), measured at average 1996–98 prices, was US $2,718m., equivalent to $810 per head. During 1990–98, it was estimated, GNP per head increased, in real terms, at an average annual rate of 2.7%. In 1999, according to provisional figures, GNP was estimated at $2,900m., equivalent to $870 per head (or $2,864 per head on an international purchasing-power parity basis). In 1990–98 the population increased at an average annual rate of 0.2%, according to the World Bank. Albania's gross domestic product (GDP) declined, in real terms, by an average of 0.6% per year in 1990–99, according to the IMF; however, GDP increased by an estimated 7.3% in 1999.

Agriculture (including forestry and fishing) contributed an estimated 52.6% of GDP in 1999. Some 49.5% of the labour force were engaged in the sector in 1998. In 1988 co-operatives accounted for almost 75% of agricultural output; from 1990, however, an increasing degree of private enterprise was permitted, and agricultural land was subsequently redistributed to private ownership. The principal crops are wheat, sugar beet, maize, potatoes, barley and sorghum. Agricultural GDP increased at an average annual rate of 4.6% in 1990–99. Growth in agricultural GDP was estimated at 3.7% in 1999.

Industry (comprising mining, manufacturing, construction and utilities) accounted for an estimated 25.4% of GDP in 1999 and employed 22.5% of the labour force in 1989. Principal contributors to industrial output include mining, energy generation and food-processing. Construction was the fastest-growing sector in recent years, with GDP increasing at an average annual rate of 8.6% in 1990–99 (rising by an estimated 15.0% in 1999). Industrial GDP declined at an average rate of 6.0% per year during 1990–99; however, the GDP of the sector increased by an estimated 10.8% in 1999.

Albania is one of the world's largest producers of chromite (chromium ore), possessing Europe's only significant reserves (an estimated 37m. metric tons of recoverable ore, constituting about 5% of total world deposits). The mining sector has been centred on chromite and copper since the closure of nickel and iron ore operations, together with more than one-half of the country's coal mines, in 1990. Albania has petroleum resources and its own refining facilities, and there has been considerable foreign interest in the exploration of both onshore and offshore reserves since 1991. (The acceptance of foreign capital in order to establish joint ventures was authorized in 1990.)

As in the mining sector, output in manufacturing declined sharply from 1990. The manufacturing sector is based largely on the processing of agricultural products, minerals, chemicals and building materials.

Hydroelectric generation accounted for more than 80% of total electricity production in 1988. A serious drought in 1988–90, however, led to problems in the hydroelectric sector.

Services employed 21.5% of the labour force in 1989 and provided an estimated 22.0% of GDP in 1999. In real terms, the combined GDP of the services sector increased by an average of 4.0% per year during 1990–99. The GDP of the sector increased by an estimated 12.4% in 1999.

In 1999 Albania recorded a visible trade deficit of US $663.0m., and there was a deficit of $155.4m. on the current account of the balance of payments. In 1999 the principal source of imports (an estimated 43.2%) was Italy; the other major supplier was Greece. Italy was also the principal market for exports (taking an estimated 60.0% of the total); Greece and Germany were also important purchasers. The principal exports in 1999 were miscellaneous manufactured articles (particularly clothing and accessories), basic manufactures, and crude materials. The main imports in that year were basic manufactures, food and live animals, machinery and transport equipment and miscellaneous manufactured articles.

Albania's overall budget deficit in 1998 was 47,878m. lekë (10.4% of GDP). In 1999 the deficit was 11.3% of GDP. At the end of 1998 Albania's total external debt was US $820.6m., of which $701.3m. was long-term public debt. In that year the cost of servicing the debt was equivalent to 4.5% of the value of exports of goods and services. Remittances from Albanians working abroad totalled $266m. in 1994. Foreign aid and remittances together contributed 40% of GDP in 1993. In 1992–98 the average annual rate of inflation was 28.1%; consumer prices increased by an average of 20.9% in 1998, but by an estimated average of only 0.4% in 1999. The rate of unemployment was estimated at 15.7% in late 2000. An estimated 25.1% of the Albanian labour force were working abroad in 1996.

Having reversed its long-standing policy of economic self-sufficiency, in 1991 Albania became a member of the World Bank, the IMF and the newly established European Bank for Reconstruction and Development (EBRD, see p. 176). In 1992 Albania became a founder member of the Black Sea Economic Co-operation group (known as the Organization of the Black Sea Economic Co-operation from May 1999—see p. 265).

In 1992, in response to a serious economic crisis, the newly elected Government introduced an extensive programme of reforms, providing for the transfer to private ownership of farm land, state-owned companies and housing, and the abolition of trade restrictions and price controls. A strict programme of high interest rates, reduced subsidies, banking reforms and trade liberalization, supported by the IMF, was successful in reducing the massive budget deficit, controlling inflation and stabilizing the currency. Nevertheless, illicit trade was believed to account for a high proportion of total revenue, while the country remained dependent on remittances from Albanian emigrants and foreign aid to support the current account of the balance of payments. In early 1997 the collapse of the 'pyramid' investment schemes, resulting in huge losses of individual savings, precipitated widespread civil unrest. The NATO bombardment of Kosovo in March–June 1999 prompted a mass influx of refugees (see Recent History), which placed great strain on the country's resources; however, this was partially offset by large inflows of emergency relief aid from the international community. Consequently, the rate of inflation declined sharply in 1999, while foreign-exchange reserves were strengthened to above the targeted level; progress in the privatization programme was also significant. As a result of measures implemented in late 1999, tax collection was substantially improved. In mid-2000 the IMF approved the disbursement of a loan, representing the third tranche of a three-year poverty reduction and growth facility. The Fund emphasized the importance of increasing the momentum of structural reform and recommended a further easing of monetary conditions, in view of the absence of inflationary pressures. It was stressed that a stronger commitment to financial-sector reform was essential to encourage private investment. The IMF welcomed the efforts of the Government to develop its poverty-reduction strategy, and urged it to address immediate poverty issues. GDP growth in 2001 was predicted to remain at around the 1999 level.

Social Welfare

All medical services are provided free of charge, and medicines are supplied free to infants of up to one year of age. In 1993 the number of hospitals totalled 40, and there were 10,500 beds available. In 1998 there were 129 physicians and 380 nurses for every 100,000 of the population. Kindergartens and nursery schools receive large subsidies. Women are entitled to 180 to 360 days' maternity leave, receiving 80% of their salary. There is a non-contributory state social insurance system for all workers, with 70%–100% of salary being paid during sick leave, and a pension system for the old and disabled. Retirement pensions represent 70% of the average monthly salary. Men retire between the ages of 55 and 65 years, and women between 50 and 60. Legislation relating to social assistance for the unemployed entered into force in November 1991. Municipalities and communes became responsible for social assistance in mid-1993. Of total current expenditure in the 1998 state budget, 24,329m. lekë (20.7%) was for social security, 1,621m. lekë (1.4%) for unemployment insurance, and 6,168m. lekë (5.2%) for social assistance.

Education

Education in Albania is provided free at primary and secondary level. Approximately 38% of children aged three to six years attended nursery school in 1995, compared with 59% in 1990. Children between the ages of six and 14 years attend an 'eight-year school', which is compulsory. In 1995 96% of children in the relevant age-group (boys 95%; girls 97%) were enrolled at primary schools. In 1995 secondary education was undergoing restructuring to a system comprising two alternative levels. The second level lasts for five years and qualifies students for management-level employment or higher studies. In 1995 enrolment at secondary schools was equivalent to only 35% of children in the relevant age-group, compared with 78% in 1990. In the same year there were eight universities and two institutes of higher education. In 1996/97 some 34,257 students attended institutions of higher education. Government expenditure on education amounted to 5,893m. lekë in 1994 (equivalent to 3.4% of GNP). The budget for 1999 allocated about 2.5% of projected government expenditure to education.

Public Holidays

2001: 1 January (New Year's Day), 6 March* (Great Bayram, Feast of the Sacrifice), 8 March (International Women's Day), 13–16 April (Catholic Easter), 16 April (Orthodox Easter), 28 November (Independence and Liberation Day), 17 December* (Small Bayram, end of Ramadan), 25 December (Christmas Day).

2002: 1 January (New Year's Day), 23 February* (Great Bayram, Feast of the Sacrifice), 8 March (International Women's Day), 29 March–1 April (Catholic Easter), 6 May (Orthodox Easter), 28 November (Independence and Liberation Day), 6 December* (Small Bayram, end of Ramadan), 25 December (Christmas Day).

* These holidays are dependent on the Islamic lunar calendar and may vary by one or two days from the dates given.

Weights and Measures

The metric system is in force.

Statistical Survey

Source (unless otherwise stated): Institute of Statistics (Drejtoria e Statistikës), POB 8194, Tirana; tel. (42) 22411; fax (42) 28300; e-mail root@instat.gov.al; internet www.instat.gov.al.

Area and Population

AREA, POPULATION AND DENSITY

Area (sq km)	
Land	27,398
Inland water	1,350
Total	28,748*
Population (census results)	
January 1979	2,591,000
2 April 1989	
Males	1,638,900†
Females	1,543,500†
Total	3,182,417
Population (official estimates at mid-year)	
1996	3,670,000
1997	3,731,000
1998	3,791,000†
Density (per sq km) at mid-1998	131.9

* 11,100 sq miles.   † Provisional.

Ethnic Groups (census of 2 April 1989): Albanian 3,117,601; Greek 58,758; Macedonian 4,697; Montenegrin, Serb, Croat, etc. 100; others 1,261.

DISTRICTS (estimated population at 1 January 1993)

	Population
Berat	136,939
Bulqizë	43,363
Delvinë	29,926
Devoll	37,744
Dibër	91,916
Durrës.	162,846
Elbasan	215,240
Fier	208,646
Gjirokastër	60,547
Gramsh	42,087
Has	21,271
Kavajë.	85,120
Kolonjë	25,089
Korçë	171,205
Krujë	59,997
Kuçovë	40,035
Kukës	78,061
Laç	50,712
Lezhë	65,075
Librazhd	75,300
Lushnjë	136,865
Malësi e Madhe	43,924
Mallakastër	36,287
Mat	75,436
Mirditë	49,900
Peqin	29,831
Përmet	36,979
Pogradec	72,203
Pukë	47,621
Sarandë	53,730
Shkodër	195,424
Skrapar	44,339
Tepelenë	42,365
Tiranë.	384,010
Tropojë	44,761
Vlorë	171,131
Total	**3,165,925**

PRINCIPAL TOWNS (population at mid-1990)

Tiranë (Tirana, the capital)	244,200
Durrës (Durazzo)	85,400
Elbasan	83,300
Shkodër (Scutari)	81,900
Vlorë (Vlonë or Valona)	73,800
Korçë (Koritsa)	65,400
Fier	45,200
Berat	43,800
Lushnjë	31,500
Kavajë	25,700
Gjirokastër	24,900
Kuçovë*	22,300

* This town was known as Qyteti Stalin during the period of Communist rule, but has since reverted to its former name.

Source: *Statistical Directory of Albania.*

BIRTHS, MARRIAGES AND DEATHS*

	Registered live births		Registered marriages		Registered deaths	
	Number	Rate (per 1,000)	Number	Rate (per 1,000)	Number	Rate (per 1,000)
1986 . .	76,435	25.3	25,718	8.5	17,369	5.7
1987 . .	79,696	25.9	27,370	8.9	17,119	5.6
1988 . .	80,241	25.5	28,174	9.0	17,027	5.4
1989 . .	78,862	24.7	27,655	8.6	18,168	5.7
1990 . .	82,125	25.2	28,992	8.9	18,193	5.6
1991 . .	77,361	23.8	24,853	7.6	17,743	5.4

Registered births: 60,696 (16.6 per 1,000) in 1996.

Registered marriages (provisional): 25,260 (6.8 per 1,000) in 1997.

Registered deaths: 17,238 (5.1 per 1,000) in 1992; 16,639 (4.8 per 1,000) in 1993; 17,027 (4.7 per 1,000) in 1996.

* For 1990–92 rates are based on unrevised estimates of mid-year population.

Expectation of life (years at birth, 1989/90): 72.2 (Males 69.3; Females 75.4).

Source: *Statistical Yearbook of the PSR of Albania, Statistical Yearbook of Albania* and UN, *Demographic Yearbook.*

1998: Registered live births 60,139 (birth rate 15.9 per 1,000); Registered deaths 18,250 (death rate 4.8 per 1,000) (Source: UN, *Population and Vital Statistics Report*).

ECONOMICALLY ACTIVE POPULATION
(ISIC Major Divisions, 1989 census)

	Males	Females	Total
Agriculture, hunting, forestry and fishing .	399,810	399,249	799,059
Mining and quarrying . . .			
Manufacturing	160,833	118,155	278,988
Electricity, gas and water. . .			
Construction	41,979	7,312	49,291
Trade, restaurants and hotels. .	22,171	26,447	48,618
Transport, storage and communications . . .	36,324	8,109	44,433
Financing, insurance, real estate and business services . .			
	119,279	100,905	220,184
Community, social and personal services			
Activities not adequately defined	10,293	6,798	17,091
Total employed . . .	**790,689**	**666,975**	**1,457,664**

Source: ILO, *Yearbook of Labour Statistics*.

1997 (annual averages, '000 persons): Total domestic employment 1,107 (Agricultural sector 761); Unemployed 194; Domestic labour force 1,301 (males 794, females 507). Source: IMF, *Albania: Recent Economic Developments and Statistical Appendix* (July 1999).

1998 (annual averages, '000 persons): Total domestic employment 1,085 (Agricultural sector 761); Unemployed 235; Domestic labour force 1,320 (males 803, females 517). Source: IMF, *Albania: Statistical Appendix* (July 2000).

Agriculture

PRINCIPAL CROPS (metric tons)

	1997	1998	1999
Wheat and spelt	388,391	395,067	272,000
Barley	3,738	3,248	2,900
Maize	194,818	189,130	206,000
Rye	3,029	2,901	3,400
Oats	12,067	15,400	13,200
Sorghum*	14,000	15,000	14,500
Potatoes.	126,729	144,996	161,900
Dry beans	20,546	22,683	26,000
Sunflower seed	2,177	2,652	2,700
Olives	33,347	46,816	42,012
Tomatoes	150,000	156,000	160,000
Other vegetables. . . .	250,000	260,000	260,000
Watermelons	200,000	210,000	220,000
Grapes	67,466	68,327	70,400
Sugar beet	50,947	55,740	39,900
Apples	11,300	11,500	11,800
Pears	2,200	2,400	2,400
Peaches and nectarines . .	1,800	2,000	2,000
Plums	11,000	12,000	12,100
Oranges.	3,017	2,216	2,200
Other fruits and berries . .	25,500	26,200	26,600
Tree-nuts*	3,000	3,000	3,000
Tobacco (leaves)	7,854	7,399	7,300

* FAO estimates.

Source: FAO.

LIVESTOCK ('000 head, year ending September)

	1997	1998	1999
Horses	70	65	65*
Mules*	25	25	25
Asses*	113	113	113
Cattle	771	705	720
Pigs.	97	83	81
Sheep	1,858	1,872	1,941
Goats	1,148	1,051	1,120*

* FAO estimate(s).

Poultry ('000 head): 3,358 in 1997; 3,839 in 1998; 4,000 in 1999 (unofficial figure).

Source: FAO.

LIVESTOCK PRODUCTS (metric tons)

	1997	1998	1999
Beef and veal*	32,500	32,000	33,700
Mutton and lamb* . . .	11,300	11,200	11,700
Goat meat*	4,400	5,500	6,400
Pig meat*	6,600	6,500	6,200
Poultry meat	3,700	5,100	4,700
Cows' milk	707,200	721,850	761,000
Sheep's milk. . . .	68,324	71,499	73,000
Goats' milk	74,103	67,466	73,000
Cheese†	11,200	11,200	11,400
Butter†	1,500	1,500	1,600
Poultry eggs	16,180	19,060	20,200
Wool (greasy) . . .	2,916	3,029	3,000
Cattle hides	6,600	6,688	7,040
Sheep and lamb skins . .	3,250	3,212	3,215
Goat and kid skins . . .	1,400	1,600	1,601

* Unofficial figures.   † FAO estimates.

Source: FAO.

Forestry

ROUNDWOOD REMOVALS ('000 cubic metres, excl. bark)

	1996	1997	1998
Industrial wood . . .	64	64	64
Fuel wood	346	346	346
Total	**409**	**409**	**409**

Source: FAO, *Yearbook of Forest Products*.

SAWNWOOD PRODUCTION ('000 cubic metres, incl. railway sleepers)

	1996	1997	1998
Coniferous (softwood) . . .	2	2	2
Broadleaved (hardwood) . .	3	3	3
Total	**5**	**5**	**5**

Source: FAO, *Yearbook of Forest Products*.

Fishing

(metric tons, live weight)

	1996	1997	1998
Capture	2,125	1,013	2,683
Common carp . . .	45	38	230
Silver carp . . .	52	33	104
Other cyprinids . . .	163	68	229
Salmonoids . . .	35	15	102
European hake . . .	293	185	340
Bogue	104	65	220
Surmullets . . .	64	61	143
Mullets	105	42	136
Jack and horse mackerels . .	68	18	85
European pilchard (sardine) .	196	28	28
Rays, stingrays and mantas .	23	24	86
Common squids . . .	47	34	93
Common octopus . . .	75	59	93
Aquaculture	323*	97	24
Mediterranean mussel . .	250	80	—
Total catch	**2,448**	**1,110**	**2,707**

* FAO estimate.

Note: Figures exclude Sardinia coral (metric tons): 1.2 in 1996; 0.8 in 1997; 0.5 in 1998.

Source: FAO, *Yearbook of Fishery Statistics*.

Mining

('000 metric tons, unless otherwise indicated)

	1997	1998	1999
Lignite (brown coal) . . .	40	49	33
Crude petroleum . . .	360	365	323
Natural gas (million cu metres) .	18	17	14
Copper concentrates (metric tons)*	220	3,200	900
Chromium ore (gross weight) . .	157	150	79

* Figures refer to estimated metal content.

Sources: IMF, *Albania: Statistical Appendix* (July 2000), and US Geological Survey.

Industry

SELECTED PRODUCTS
('000 metric tons, unless otherwise indicated)

	1995	1996	1997
Wheat flour	36*	89*	68
Raw sugar	3†	4	—
Wine ('000 hectolitres) . . .	170	290	—
Cigarettes (million)	685	4,830	414
Veneer sheets ('000 cubic metres)*	10	10	10
Plywood ('000 cubic metres) . .	6	6	6
Mechanical wood pulp . . .	2	2	2
Chemical wood pulp . . .	14	14	14
Paper and paperboard* . .	44	44	n.a.
Nitrogenous fertilizers (a)‡ . .	4	n.a.	n.a.
Phosphatic fertilizers (b)‡ . .	14	—	27
Soap	2	2	2
Motor spirit (petrol) . . .	74	74	15
Kerosene	74	69	11
Gas-diesel (distillate fuel) oil .	106	99	57
Residual fuel oils . . .	43	40	n.a.
Petroleum bitumen (asphalt)† . .	33	37	n.a.
Cement	238	203	100
Ferro-chromium	43	32	31
Crude steel	22	22	22
Copper (unrefined)§ . . .	3	1	—
Electric energy (million kWh) . .	4,414	5,926	5,184

* FAO estimate(s).
† Provisional or estimated production.
‡ Production in terms of (a) nitrogen or (b) phosphoric acid.
§ Data from *World Metal Statistics* (London).

Source: mainly UN, *Industrial Commodity Statistics Yearbook*.

1998 ('000 metric tons): Wine 17; Phosphatic fertilizers 12; Raw sugar 7 (FAO estimate); Motor spirit 21; Kerosene 2; Gas-diesel oil 91; Cement 84; Ferro-chromium 30; Electric energy (million kWh) 5,068.

Sources: FAO, *Production Yearbook*; IMF, *Albania: Recent Economic Developments and Statistical Appendix* (July 1999).

1999 ('000 metric tons): Phosphatic fertilizers 9; Motor spirit 20; Kerosene 1; Gas-diesel oil 65; Cement 106; Ferro-chromium 28; Electric energy (million kWh) 5,396.

Source: IMF, *Albania: Statistical Appendix* (July 2000).

Finance

CURRENCY AND EXCHANGE RATES

Monetary Units
100 qindarka (qintars) = 1 new lek.

Sterling, Dollar and Euro Equivalents (29 December 2000)
£1 sterling = 212.8 lekë;
US $1 = 142.6 lekë;
€1 = 132.7 lekë;
1,000 lekë = £4.698 = $7.011 = €7.534.

Average Exchange Rate (lekë per US $)
1998   150.63
1999   137.69
2000   143.71

STATE BUDGET (million lekë)

Revenue*	1997	1998	1999
Counterpart sales revenue . .	256	137	155
Tax revenue	46,298	72,572	83,529
Turnover tax/value-added tax	15,655	28,771	29,794
Taxes on income and profits .	3,592	6,400	10,331
Social security contributions .	13,143	15,828	18,157
Import duties and export taxes	8,960	12,615	11,450
Excise taxes	2,168	4,910	6,961
Other revenue	11,040	20,806	24,124
Profit transfer from Bank of Albania	8,067	16,400	17,591
Income from budgetary institutions	1,834	3,326	5,352
Total	57,594	93,515	107,809

* Excluding privatization receipts (million lekë): 910 in 1997; 133 in 1998; 906 in 1999.

Expenditure	1997	1998	1999
Current expenditure . . .	86,870	117,604	131,546
Wages	20,377	22,048	24,208
Social security contributions .	5,167	6,288	6,976
Interest	18,779	36,086	34,938
Operational and maintenance .	13,565	18,537	26,350
Subsidies	1,551	2,308	2,706
Social security	20,133	24,329	27,587
Unemployment insurance .	2,204	1,621	1,450
Social assistance . . .	4,274	6,168	6,360
Capital expenditure (investment)	13,751	23,789	33,614
Total	100,621	141,393	165,160

Source: IMF, *Albania: Statistical Appendix* (July 2000).

INTERNATIONAL RESERVES (US $ million at 31 December)

	1998	1999	2000
Gold*	33.70	34.50	30.40
IMF special drawing rights .	61.10	76.95	76.00
Reserve position in IMF . .	0.01	4.60	4.37
Foreign exchange . . .	287.40	287.50	271.85
Total	382.20	403.55	382.62

* Valued at market-related prices.

Source: IMF, *International Financial Statistics*.

MONEY SUPPLY (million lekë at 31 December)

	1997	1998	1999
Currency outside banks . .	72,726	68,323	81,336
Demand deposits at deposit money banks	18,941	15,405	21,668
Total money	91,667	83,728	103,004

Source: Bank of Albania.

COST OF LIVING (Consumer price index; base: 1992 = 100)

	1997	1998	1999
Food	357.8	433.2	431.9
All items (incl. others) . .	366.9	442.6	444.4

Source: ILO, *Yearbook of Labour Statistics*.

NATIONAL ACCOUNTS (million lekë at current prices)
Gross Domestic Product by Economic Activity

	1997	1998	1999*
Agriculture	191,269	250,705	266,270
Industry†	42,351	55,047	60,026
Construction	38,423	58,037	68,387
Transport	9,362	14,024	16,531
Other services . . .	60,311	82,817	94,991
GDP in purchasers' values . .	341,716	460,631	506,205
GDP at constant 1990 prices	15,325	16,548	17,748

*Figures are provisional.
† Comprising mining, manufacturing, electricity, gas and water.
Source: IMF, *Albania: Statistical Appendix* (July 2000).

BALANCE OF PAYMENTS (US $ million)

	1997	1998	1999
Exports of goods f.o.b. . . .	158.6	208.0	275.0
Imports of goods f.o.b. . . .	−693.6	−811.7	−938.0
Trade balance	−535.0	−603.6	−663.0
Exports of services . . .	63.8	86.6	269.4
Imports of services . . .	−115.2	−129.3	−163.1
Balance on goods and services	−586.4	−646.3	−556.7
Other income received . .	61.4	86.1	85.5
Other income paid . . .	−11.8	−8.7	−10.2
Balance on goods, services and income	−536.8	−569.0	−481.4
Current transfers received . .	299.8	560.8	508.9
Current transfers paid . .	−35.2	−56.9	−182.9
Current balance . . .	−272.2	−65.1	−155.4
Capital account (net) . . .	2.0	31.0	22.6
Direct investment from abroad .	47.5	45.0	41.2
Other investment assets . .	59.8	−126.9	−130.1
Other investment liabilities . .	44.1	97.3	122.6
Net errors and omissions . . .	158.4	71.1	206.2
Overall balance	39.5	52.4	107.1

Source: IMF, *International Financial Statistics*.

External Trade

PRINCIPAL COMMODITIES (US $ million)

Imports c.i.f.	1996	1997	1998
Food and live animals . . .	276.0	146.0	184.6
Meat and meat preparations . .	34.2	18.9	34.9
Fresh, chilled or frozen meat .	31.6	17.4	31.7
Poultry meat	17.8	10.8	21.4
Cereals and cereal preparations .	152.2	76.4	81.7
Wheat and meslin (unmilled) .	49.6	14.8	10.7
Meal and flour of wheat and meslin	73.0	39.8	39.4
Cereal preparations, etc. . .	18.6	15.2	23.6
Vegetables and fruit . . .	26.7	21.6	28.2
Fresh or dried fruit and nuts (excl. oil nuts) . . .	16.7	13.4	16.6
Sugar, sugar preparations and honey	37.8	14.5	22.2
Sugar and honey . . .	36.0	13.8	21.4
Raw beet and cane sugars (solid)	28.0	12.9	15.9
Beverages and tobacco . . .	19.1	5.2	13.8
Mineral fuels, lubricants, etc. (incl. electric current) . .	24.0	20.0	32.5
Petroleum, petroleum products, etc.	19.1	17.0	23.2
Refined petroleum products . .	16.0	11.6	18.7
Animal and vegetable oils, fats and waxes . . .	25.6	19.2	27.0
Fixed vegetable oils and fats .	23.4	17.2	24.2
'Soft' fixed vegetable oils .	23.2	16.2	23.5
Sunflower seed oil . .	21.8	12.7	17.3

Imports c.i.f. − *continued*	1996	1997	1998
Chemicals and related products	52.8	43.6	75.0
Medicinal and pharmaceutical products	17.9	11.6	23.0
Manufactured fertilizers . . .	5.3	5.9	16.9
Basic manufactures . . .	226.7	182.8	246.5
Leather, leather manufactures and dressed furskins . .	70.3	45.4	54.6
Leather	17.9	13.2	17.4
Manufactures of leather; saddlery and harness; parts of footwear	52.4	32.2	36.7
Parts of footwear (except metal or asbestos) . .	52.2	32.2	36.7
Textile yarn, fabrics, etc. . .	43.5	30.9	45.2
Non-metallic mineral manufactures	44.9	47.8	65.5
Lime, cement, etc. . . .	23.5	28.0	39.6
Cement	22.3	27.2	37.9
Construction materials of clay, etc.	12.3	13.6	17.8
Non-refractory ceramic bricks, tiles, pipes, etc. .	10.9	12.9	17.0
Iron and steel	20.6	21.0	30.4
Bars, rods, angles, shapes, etc. .	7.0	12.4	20.7
Machinery and transport equipment	212.4	134.2	136.8
Machinery specialized for particular industries . .	36.0	38.2	18.0
General industrial machinery, equipment and parts . .	40.7	12.7	15.5
Pumps for liquids, etc. . .	23.7	2.6	3.0
Telecommunications and sound equipment	22.3	13.3	6.9
Other electrical machinery, apparatus, etc. . .	43.2	31.2	31.8
Road vehicles and parts (excl. tyres, engines and electrical parts)	54.0	29.5	52.6
Passenger motor cars (excl. buses)	21.3	13.2	21.9
Motor vehicles for goods transport, etc. . .	21.6	11.4	20.2
Goods vehicles (lorries and trucks)	17.5	8.3	19.1
Miscellaneous manufactured articles	87.6	67.2	108.5
Clothing and accessories (excl. footwear)	35.6	28.2	51.1
Total (incl. others) . . .	938.5	629.1	840.8

Exports f.o.b.	1996	1997	1998
Food and live animals . . .	9.8	8.8	10.2
Fish, crustaceans, molluscs and preparations thereof . .	5.1	5.2	5.1
Beverages and tobacco . .	9.0	6.5	9.8
Tobacco and tobacco manufactures	8.9	6.5	9.0
Manufactured tobacco . .	7.6	5.7	7.5
Crude materials (inedible) except fuels . . .	38.1	30.2	39.9
Raw hides, skins and furskins .	4.3	3.5	1.9
Raw hides and skins (except furskins)	4.3	3.4	1.9
Cork and wood	2.1	3.2	3.3
Metalliferous ores and metal scrap	18.0	10.2	21.6
Iron ore and concentrates . .	4.3	0.2	0.1
Waste and scrap metal of iron or steel	1.0	5.2	0.1
Ores and concentrates of non-ferrous base metals . .	12.3	4.6	20.6
Chromium ores and concentrates . . .	8.9	4.6	20.5
Plants (incl. parts thereof) for use in perfumes, pharmaceuticals or pesticides	11.3	11.7	12.7
Mineral fuels, lubricants, etc.	6.4	2.4	2.5
Petroleum, petroleum products, etc.	6.2	2.2	2.4

Exports f.o.b. — *continued*	1996	1997	1998
Animal and vegetable oils, fats			
and waxes	4.7	0.1	0.5
Fixed vegetable oils and fats . .	4.7	0.1	0.5
'Soft' fixed vegetable oils .	4.6	0.1	0.4
Olive oil	4.5	0.1	0.1
Basic manufactures . .	68.1	38.3	55.7
Leather, leather manufactures			
and dressed furskins . .	42.6	25.6	40.5
Leather	3.7	3.9	4.1
Manufactures of leather;			
saddlery and harness; parts of			
footwear	39.0	21.7	36.4
Parts of footwear (except			
metal or asbestos) . . .	39.0	21.7	36.4
Iron and steel	10.9	5.3	2.0
Pig-iron, spiegeleisen, etc., and			
ferro-alloys. . . .	8.9	4.9	1.6
Ferro-alloys	5.0	4.9	1.5
Non-ferrous metals . . .	5.6	2.2	4.5
Machinery and transport			
equipment	3.6	7.9	5.9
Machinery specialized for			
particular industries . .	0.4	5.1	0.3
Civil engineering and			
contractors' plant and			
equipment	0.1	4.4	0.1
Construction and mining			
machinery . . .	0.1	4.4	0.1
Miscellaneous manufactured			
articles	68.9	42.8	82.7
Clothing and accessories (excl.			
footwear)	50.4	32.6	67.9
Men's and boys' outer garments			
of non-knitted textile fabrics	15.1	6.3	15.9
Trousers, breeches, etc. .	10.2	4.1	14.3
Women's, girls' and infants'			
outer garments of non-knitted			
textile fabrics . . .	10.0	4.6	7.4
Undergarments (excl.			
foundation garments) of non-			
knitted textile fabrics .	6.9	7.6	20.4
Men's and boys' shirts .	3.8	5.9	14.8
Shirts of cotton . .	1.4	2.3	4.9
Shirts of synthetic fibres	2.5	3.7	10.0
Women's, girls' and infants'			
undergarments . . .	1.8	1.0	5.3
Knitted or crocheted outer			
garments and accessories			
(excl. gloves, stockings, etc.),			
non-elastic	13.4	7.5	14.5
Knitted or crocheted			
undergarments (incl.			
foundation garments of non-			
knitted fabrics) . . .	5.2	6.7	9.3
Cotton undergarments, non-			
elastic	4.7	6.2	7.8
Footwear	12.0	3.3	4.4
Leather footwear . . .	11.6	3.2	4.3
Printed matter	2.3	3.3	1.9
Unused stamps, banknotes,			
share certificates, cheque			
books, etc. . . .	1.9	3.2	1.6
Total (incl. others) . . .	211.2	137.7	207.7

Source: UN, *International Trade Statistics Yearbook*.

1999 (US $ million): Total imports c.i.f. 1,140; Total exports f.o.b. 264 (Source: UN, *Monthly Bulletin of Statistics*).

PRINCIPAL TRADING PARTNERS (US $ million)*

Imports c.i.f.	1996	1997	1998
Austria	10.4	10.3	12.4
Belgium–Luxembourg . .	22.5	6.8	9.3
Bulgaria.	35.6	16.7	21.9
Croatia	13.3	2.8	5.3
France (incl. Monaco) . .	25.6	7.8	9.9
Germany	54.6	26.9	34.6
Greece	190.6	163.8	231.1
Hungary	7.2	6.5	9.2
Italy	378.2	288.4	363.6
Macedonia, former Yugoslav			
republic	18.8	12.9	n.a.
Romania	22.8	1.9	3.4
Russia	2.1	0.4	9.1
Slovenia.	11.0	9.5	12.1
Switzerland–Liechtenstein .	18.6	10.1	14.8
Turkey	39.5	27.5	27.6
United Kingdom . . .	12.7	6.5	5.4
USA	15.0	1.3	8.3
Yugoslavia	6.7	0.9	12.3
Total (incl. others) . . .	938.5	629.0	840.8

Exports f.o.b.	1996	1997	1998
Austria	2.3	2.0	3.3
Belgium–Luxembourg . .	2.8	0.7	3.1
Croatia	1.4	5.8	1.3
France (incl. Monaco) . .	4.3	2.6	2.5
Germany	14.6	9.4	11.9
Greece	27.4	28.2	41.1
Italy	122.1	68.0	124.7
Macedonia, former Yugoslav			
republic	6.5	3.6	n.a.
Netherlands	6.2	7.6	1.8
New Zealand	3.3	0.0	—
Slovenia.	2.7	1.7	2.5
Turkey	6.6	1.3	1.1
United Kingdom . . .	0.6	0.1	2.5
USA	2.5	2.0	3.5
Yugoslavia	3.1	0.5	3.7
Total (incl. others) . . .	211.1	137.7	207.7

* Imports by country of origin; exports by country of destination.

Source: UN, *International Trade Statistics Yearbook*.

Transport

RAILWAYS (traffic)

	1996	1997	1998
Passenger-km (million) . .	168	95	116
Freight ton-km (million) . .	42	23	25

Source: UN, *Statistical Yearbook*.

ROAD TRAFFIC (motor vehicles in use at 31 December)

	1996	1997	1998
Passenger cars	67,228	76,822	90,766
Buses and coaches . . .	7,612	8,747	9,227
Lorries and vans. . . .	27,774	30,105	34,378
Road tractors	2,838	3,151	2,731
Motorcycles and mopeds . .	5,541	3,645	4,109

Source: International Road Federation, *World Road Statistics*.

SHIPPING
Merchant Fleet (registered at 31 December)

	1996	1997	1998
Number of vessels . . .	33	32	25
Displacement ('000 gross registered tons)	43.4	30.4	28.7

Source: Lloyd's Register of Shipping, *World Fleet Statistics*.

International Sea-borne Freight Traffic
('000 metric tons)

	1988	1989	1990
Goods loaded	1,090	1,112	1,065
Goods unloaded	644	659	664

Source: UN, *Monthly Bulletin of Statistics*.

CIVIL AVIATION (traffic on scheduled services)

	1996	1997
Passengers carried ('000)	13	55
Passenger-km (million)	4	35
Total ton-km (million)	n.a.	3

Source: UN, *Statistical Yearbook*.

Tourism
FOREIGN TOURIST ARRIVALS BY COUNTRY OF ORIGIN*

	1996	1997	1998
Austria	1,412	751	805
Egypt	3,205	43	2,299
France	1,477	825	847
Germany	2,552	895	915
Greece	4,424	1,437	1,513
Italy	8,088	3,836	4,026
United Kingdom	1,433	1,198	1,960
USA	3,927	1,052	1,380
Yugoslavia	2,645	661	820
Total (incl. others) . . .	56,276	19,154	27,709

* Figures refer to arrivals in hotels.
Tourism receipts (US $ million): 77 in 1996; 27 in 1997.
Source: World Tourism Organization, *Yearbook of Tourism Statistics*.

Communications Media

	1995	1996	1997
Radio receivers ('000 in use) . .	700	800	810
Television receivers ('000 in use)	350	400	405
Telephones ('000 main lines in use)	42	64	87
Mobile cellular telephones (subscribers)	n.a.	2,300	3,300
Daily newspapers:			
Number	3*	5	n.a.
Average circulation ('000 copies)	130*	116	n.a.

Book production (1991): 381 titles (including 18 pamphlets).
Telefax stations (number in use, 1992): 600.
*Provisional or estimated figure.
Sources: UN, *Statistical Yearbook*, and UNESCO, *Statistical Yearbook*.

Education
(1995/96, unless otherwise indicated)

	Institutions	Teachers	Students		
			Males	Females	Total
Pre-primary . . .	2,670	4,416	42,292	42,244	84,536
Primary . . .	1,782*	31,369	288,592	269,509	558,101
Secondary					
General . . .	162†	4,147	37,392	33,999	71,391
Vocational . .	259†	2,174	12,758	5,746	18,504
Higher‡§ . .	10‖	2,348	14,880	19,377	34,257
Universities, etc.	8‖	2,304	14,841	19,121	33,962
Other . . .	2‖	44	39	256	295

* 1994/95 figure.
† 1990 figure.
‡ Figures for students include those enrolled at distance-learning institutions.
§ 1996/97 figures.
‖ 1993/94 figure.

Sources: Ministry of Education, Tirana, and UNESCO, *Statistical Yearbook*.

Directory

The Constitution

In October 1998 the People's Assembly approved a new Constitution, which had been drafted by a parliamentary commission. The Constitution was endorsed at a national referendum on 22 November, and was officially adopted on 28 November.

GENERAL PROVISIONS

Albania is a parliamentary republic. The Republic of Albania is a unitary state, with a system of government based on the separation and balancing of legislative, executive and judicial powers. Sovereignty is exercised by the people through their elected representatives. The Republic of Albania recognizes and protects the national rights of people who live outside the country's borders. Political parties are created freely, and are required to conform with democratic principles. The Republic of Albania does not have an official religion, and guarantees equality of religious communities. The economic system of the Republic of Albania is based on a market economy, and on freedom of economic activity, as well as on private and public property. The armed forces ensure the independence of the country, and protect its territorial integrity and constitutional order. Local government in the Republic of Albania is exercised according to the principle of decentralization of public power. The fundamental political, economic and social rights and freedoms of Albanian citizens are guaranteed under the Constitution.

LEGISLATURE

The People's Assembly comprises at least 140 deputies, and is elected for a term of four years. One hundred deputies are elected directly in single-member constituencies, while parties receiving more than 3% of votes cast nationally are allocated further deputies in proportion to the number of votes won. The Council of Ministers, every deputy and 20,000 voters each have the right to propose legislation. The People's Assembly makes decisions by a majority of votes, when more than one-half of the deputies are present. The 25-member Council of the Assembly is elected by the members of the People's Assembly at the beginning of the first session. The Council of the Assembly reviews preliminary draft laws, and gives opinions on specific issues.

PRESIDENT

The President of the Republic is the Head of State and represents the unity of the people. A candidate for President is proposed to the People's Assembly by a group of not less than 20 deputies. The President is elected by secret ballot by a majority of three-fifths of the members of the People's Assembly for a term of five years.

COUNCIL OF MINISTERS

The Council of Ministers comprises the Prime Minister, Deputy Prime Minister and ministers. The President of the Republic nominates as Prime Minister the candidate presented by the party or coalition of parties that has the majority of seats in the People's Assembly. The Prime Minister, within 40 days of his appointment, forms a Council of Ministers, which is presented for approval to the People's Assembly.

LOCAL GOVERNMENT

The units of local government are communes, municipalities and regions. The representative organs of the basic units of local government are councils, which are elected by general direct elections for a period of three years. The executive organ of a municipality or commune is the Chairman. The Council of Ministers appoints a Prefect in every region as its representative.

JUDICIARY

Judicial power is exercised by the High Court, as well as by the Courts of Appeal and the Courts of First Instance. The Chairman and members of the High Court are appointed by the President of the Republic, with the approval of the People's Assembly, for a term of seven years. Other judges are appointed by the President upon the proposal of a High Council of Justice. The High Council of Justice comprises the Chairman of the High Court, the Minister of Justice, three members elected by the People's Assembly for a term of five years, and nine judges who are elected by a national judicial conference. The Constitutional Court arbitrates on constitutional issues, and determines the conformity of proposed legislation with the Constitution. The Constitutional Court comprises nine members, who are appointed by the President, with the approval of the People's Assembly, for a term of nine years.

The Government

HEAD OF STATE

President of the Republic: Dr REXHEP MEJDANI (elected 24 July 1997).

COUNCIL OF MINISTERS
(May 2001)

A coalition of the Socialist Party of Albania (SPA), the Social Democratic Party of Albania (SDP), the Democratic Alliance Party (DAP), the Agrarian Party (AP), the Union for Human Rights Party (UHRP), and independents (Ind.).

Prime Minister: ILIR META (SPA).

Deputy Prime Minister and Minister of Labour and Social Affairs: MAKBULE ÇEÇO (SPA).

Minister of Foreign Affairs: PASKAL MILO (SDP).

Minister of Public Order: ILIR GJONI (Ind.).

Minister of Defence: ISMAIL LLESHI (Ind.).

Minister of Finance: ANASTAS ANGJELI (SPA).

Minister of the Public Economy and Privatization: MUSTAFA MUÇI (SPA).

Minister of Justice: ARBEN IMAMI (DAP).

Minister of Education and Science: ET'HEM RUKA (SPA).

Minister of Trade and Economic Co-operation: ERMELINDA MEKSI (SPA).

Minister of Transport: VIKTOR DODA.

Minister of Agriculture and Food: LUFTER XHUVELI (AP).

Minister of Local Government: BASHKIM FINO (SPA).

Minister of Health: LEONARD SOLIS (UHRP).

Minister of Culture, Youth and Sports: ESMERALDA URUÇI (Ind.).

Minister of Public Works: SPARTAK POÇI (SPA).

Minister of State in the Office of the Prime Minister: NDRE LEGISI (SPA).

MINISTRIES

Council of Ministers: Këshilli i Ministrave, Tirana; tel. (42) 28210; fax (42) 27888.

Ministry of Agriculture and Food: Ministria e Bujqësisë dhe Ushqimit, Bulevardi Dëshmorët e Kombit, Tirana; tel. and fax (42) 32796.

Ministry of Culture, Youth and Sports: Ministria e Kulturës, Bulevardi Dëshmorët e Kombit, Tirana; tel. (42) 32488; fax (42) 27918; e-mail kabkult@mkrs.gov.al; internet www.mkrs.gov.al.

Ministry of Defence: Ministria e Mbrojtjes, Bulevardi Dëshmorët e Kombit, Tirana; tel. (42) 22103; fax (42) 28325.

Ministry of Education and Science: Ministria e Arsimit dhe Shkences, Rruga Durrësit 23, Tirana; tel. (42) 25987; fax (42) 32002; e-mail vqano@mash.gov.al; f. 1912.

Ministry of Finance: Ministria e Financave, Bulevardi Dëshmorët e Kombit, Tirana; tel. (42) 27937; fax (42) 28494; e-mail phida@yahoo.com.

Ministry of Foreign Affairs: Ministria e Punëve të Jashtme, Bulevardi Zhan D'Ark, Tirana; tel. (42) 62055; fax (42) 32971; e-mail dshtypi@abissnet.com.al; internet www.mfa.gov.al.

Ministry of Health: Ministria e Shendetesisë, Tirana; tel. and fax (42) 64632.

Ministry of Information: Tirana; tel. and fax (42) 56269; internet www.mininf.gov.al.

Ministry of the Interior: Ministria e Brendshme, Sheshi Skënderbeu 3, Tirana; tel. (42) 28161; fax (42) 63607.

Ministry of Justice: Ministria e Drejtësisë, Bulevardi Dëshmorët e Kombit, Tirana; tel. (42) 24041; fax (42) 28359; e-mail ministidre@albaniaonline.net.

Ministry of Labour and Social Affairs: Ministria e Punës dhe Ndihmës Sociale, Rruga e Kavajes, Tirana; tel. (42) 40412; fax (42) 27779; e-mail molsa@icc-al.org; internet www.molsa.gov.al.

Ministry of Local Government: Bulevardi Dëshmorët e Kombit, Tirana; tel. (42) 33538.

Ministry of the Public Economy and Privatization: Bulevardi Dëshmorët e Kombit, Tirana; tel. (42) 25695; fax (42) 34052; e-mail postmaster@mepptirana.al; internet www.mepp.gov.al.

Ministry of Public Order: Bulevardi Dëshmorët e Kombit, Tirana; tel. and fax (42) 24364.

Ministry of Public Works and Transport: Rruga A. Toptani, Tirana; tel. and fax (42) 30919; e-mail militar@albaniaonline.net.

Ministry of State in the Office of Prime Minister: Bulevardi Dëshmorët e Kombit; tel. (42) 30846.

Ministry of Tourism: Ministria e Turizmit, Bulevardi Dëshmorët e Kombit, Tirana; tel. (42) 34668; fax (42) 34658.

Ministry of Trade and Economic Co-operation: Tirana; tel. (42) 34668; fax (42) 34658; internet www.mbet.gov.al.

Legislature

KUVENDI POPULLOR
(People's Assembly)

Tirana; e-mail mmyftiu@parliament.tirana.al; internet www .parlament.al;

President (Speaker): SKENDER GJINUSHI.

Deputy President: NAMIK DOKLE.

General Election, 29 June and 6 July 1997

Party	Seats
Socialist Party of Albania	101
Democratic Party of Albania	29
Social Democratic Party of Albania	8
Union for Human Rights Party	4
National Front Party	3
Democratic Alliance Party	2
Legality Movement Party	2
Albanian Republican Party	1
Party of National Unity	1
Agrarian Party	1
Independents	3
Total	**155**

Political Organizations

Agrarian Party (AP) (Partia Agrar Shqiptare): Rruga Budi 6, Tirana; tel. (42) 27481; fax (42) 27481; f. 1991; Chair. LUFTER XHUVELI.

Albanian Civil Party: Tirana; f. 1998; Chair. ROLAND VELKO; Sec. ETLEVA GJERMENI.

Albanian Communist Party: Tirana; f. 1991; granted legal recognition 1998; Chair. HYSNI MILLOSHI.

Albanian Conservative Party (Partia Konservatore Shqiptare): Tirana; Chair. ARMANDO RUCO.

Albanian Ecological Party (Partia Ekologjike Shqiptare): Rruga Aleksander Moissi 26, POB 135, Tirana; tel. (42) 22503; fax (42) 34413; environmental political party; Chair. Dr NAMIK VEHBI FADILE HOTI.

Albanian Green Party (Partia e Blertë Shqiptare): POB 749, Tirana; tel. and fax (42) 33309; f. 1991; campaigns on environmental issues; Chair. NEVRUZ MALUKA; Sec. SHYQRI KONDI.

Albanian Helsinki Forum (Forum Shqiptar i Helsinkit): Tirana; f. 1990; mem. International Federation of Helsinki; Chair. Prof. ARBEN PUTO.

Albanian Liberal Party (Partia Liberale Shqiptare): Tirana; f. 1991; Chair. VALTER FILE.

Albanian National Democratic Party (Partia Nacional Demokratike): Tirana; f. 1991; Chair. FATMIR ÇEKANI.

Albanian Nationalist Party: Tirana; f. 1993.

Albanian New Socialist Party: Tirana; f. 1996 by former mems of the SPA.

Albanian Republican Party (ARP) (Partia Republikane Shqiptare—PRS): Tirana; f. 1991; Gen. Council of 54 mems, Steering Commission of 21 mems; Chair. SABRI GODO; Vice-Chair. FATMIR MEDIU; Sec. CERCIZ MINGOMATAS.

Albanian Women's Federation (Forum i Grus Shqiptare): Tirana; tel. (42) 28309; f. 1991; independent organization uniting women from various religious and cultural backgrounds; Chair. DIANA ÇULI.

Albanian Workers' Movement Party (Partia Levizja e Punetoreve Shqiptare): Tirana; f. 2000; Chair. SOKOL QENDRO.

Alternative Republican Party: Tirana; f. 1993.

Çamëria Political and Patriotic Association (Shoqata Politike-Patriotike Çamëria): Tirana; supports the rights of the Çam minority

(an Albanian people) in northern Greece; f. 1991; Chair. Dr ABAZ DOJAKA.

Christian Democratic Party of Albania (CDPA): Rruga Dëshmorët e 4 Shkurtit, Tirana; tel. (42) 30042; fax (42) 33024; e-mail zbushati@albaniaonline.net; f. 1991; Pres. ZEF BUSHATI; Gen.-Sec. GASPER MOLNI.

Democratic Alliance Party (DAP): Tirana; internet www.aleanca .org; f. 1992 by former members of the DPA; Chair. NERITAN ÇEKA; Sec.-Gen. EDMOND DRAGOTI.

Democratic Alternative: Tirana; f. 1999 by breakaway faction of reformist members of the Democratic Party of Albania; Leader GENC POLLO.

Democratic Movement of the Unification of Albanians: f. 1993.

Democratic Party of Albania (DPA) (Partia Demokratike e Shqipërisë—PDSH): Rruga Punetoret e Rilindjes; Tirana; tel. (42) 28091; fax (42) 23525; e-mail profsberisha@albaniaonline.net; f. 1990; committed to centre-right democratic ideals and market economics; Chair. Prof. Dr SALI BERISHA; Sec.-Gen. RIDVAN BODE.

Democratic Prosperity Party (Partia e Prosperitetit Demokratik): Tirana; f. 1991; Chair. YZEIR FETAHU.

Democratic Party of the Right: Tirana; Leader PETRIT KALAKULA.

Democratic Union of the Greek Minority (OMONIA—Bashkimia Demokratik i Minoritet Grek): Tirana; f. 1991; Chair. JORGO LABOVITJADHI.

Democratic Unity Party (Partia e Bashkimit Demokratik): Tirana; Chair. XHEVDET LIBOHOVA.

Independent Party (Partia Indipendente): Tirana; f. 1991; Chair. EDMOND GJOKRUSHI.

Legality Movement Party (Partia Lëvizja e Legalitetit): Tirana; f. 1992; monarchist; Chair. GURI DUROLLARI.

Movement for Democracy (Levizja per Democraci): Tirana; f. 1997 by former mems of the DPA; Leader DASHAMIR SHEHI.

National Committee of the War Veterans of the Anti-Fascist National Liberation War of the Albanian People (Komiteti Kombëtar i Veteranëve të Luftës Antifashiste Nacional Çlirimtare të Popullit Shqiptar): Rruga Dëshmorët e 4 Shkurtit, Tirana; f. 1957; Chair. PIRRO DODBIBA; Gen. Sec. QAMIL PODA.

National Front (Balli Kombëtar): c/o Kuvendi Popullor, Tirana; Chair. ABAZ ERMENJI.

National Progress Party (Partia e Perparimit Kombëtar): Tirana; f. 1991; Chair. MYRTO XHAFERRI.

National Unity Party (Partia e Unitetit Kombëtar): Rruga Alqi Kondi, Tirana; tel. (42) 27498; fax (42) 23929; f. 1991; Chair. of Steering Cttee IDAJET BEQIRI.

New Party of Labour: Tirana; f. 1998; left-wing; defines itself as successor to the former communist Party of Labour of Albania.

People's Party (Partia Popullore): Tirana; f. 1991; aims to eradicate communism; Chair. BASHKIM DRIZA.

Republican Party (Partia Republika e Shqipërisë): Tirana; Chair. FATMIR MEDIU.

Right National Party: Tirana; f. 1998 by a breakaway faction of the National Front; Leader HYSEN SELFO.

Social Democratic Party of Albania (SDP) (Partia Social Demokratike e Shqipërisë—PSDS): Rruga Asim Vokshi 26, Tirana; tel. (42) 26540; fax (42) 27485; f. 1991; advocates gradual economic reforms and social justice; 100-member National Managing Council; Chair. SKENDER GJINUSHI; Gen.-Sec. DHORI KULE.

Social Justice Party (Partia e Drejtesise Shogerore): Tirana.

Social Labour Party of Albania (Partia Socialpuntore Shqiptare): Burrel; f. 1992; Pres. RAMADAN NDREKA.

Socialist Party of Albania (SPA) (Partia Socialiste e Shqipërisë—PSS): Tirana; tel. (42) 27409; fax (42) 27417; f. 1941 as Albanian Communist Party, renamed Party of Labour of Albania (PLA) in 1948, adopted present name in 1991; now rejects Marxism-Leninism and claims commitment to democratic socialism and a market economy; Managing Cttee of 81 mems, headed by Presidency of 15 mems; Chair. FATOS NANO; Sec.-Gen. GRAMOZ RUCI; 110,000 mems.

Union for Human Rights Party (UHRP) (Partia për Mbrojtjen e te Drejtave te Njeriut—PBDNj): Tirana; f. 1992; represents the Greek and Macedonian minorities; Chair. VASIL MELO; Sec.-Gen. THOMA MICO.

Union of Social Democrats (USD): Tirana; f. 1995; breakaway faction of the SDP; Leader TEODOR LACO.

Diplomatic Representation

EMBASSIES IN ALBANIA

Austria: Rruga Frederik Shiroka, Tirana; tel. (42) 33157; fax (42) 33140; e-mail austemb@adanet.com.al; Ambassador: ARNO RIEDEL.

Bulgaria: Rruga Skënderbeu 12, Tirana; tel. (42) 33155; fax (42) 32272; Ambassador: BOBI NIKOLOV BOBEV.

Canada: Rruga Brigada e Tete, Pall. 2, POB 47, Tirana; tel. (42) 57274; fax (42) 57273; Ambassador: GWYNETH KUTZ.

China, People's Republic: Rruga Skënderbeu 57, Tirana; tel. (42) 32385; fax (42) 33159; Ambassador: ZUO FURONG.

Croatia: Rruga Abdyl Frashëri, Tirana; tel. (42) 28390; fax (42) 30578; Ambassador: JOSIP JURAS.

Czech Republic: Rruga Skënderbeu 4, Tirana; tel. (42) 34004; fax (42) 34235; Chargé d'affaires a.i.: JAN POLACH.

Denmark: Rruga Nikolla Tupe 1, POB 1743, Tirana; tel. (42) 57422; fax (42) 57420; e-mail ambadan@icc.al.eu.org; internet www.ambassade-info.dk/dkalbantire.htm; Chargé d'affaires: NIELS AADAL RASMUSSEN.

Egypt: Rruga Skënderbeu 43, Tirana; tel. (42) 33022; fax (42) 32295; Ambassador: ATTIA QARAM.

France: Rruga Skënderbeu 14, Tirana; tel. (42) 34250; fax (42) 33763; Ambassador: PATRICK CHRISMANT.

Germany: Rruga Skënderbeu 8, Tirana; tel. (42) 32050; fax (42) 33497; e-mail german.embassy@icc.al.eu.org; Ambassador: PETER KIEWITT.

Greece: Rruga Frederik Shiroka 3, Tirana; tel. (42) 34290; fax (42) 34443; Ambassador: DIMITRIS ILIOLOPOULOS.

Holy See: Rruga e Durrësit 13, POB 8355, Tirana; tel. (42) 33516; fax (42) 32001; Apostolic Nuncio: Most Rev. GIOVANNI BULAITIS, Titular Archbishop of Narona.

Hungary: Rruga Skënderbeu 16, Tirana; tel. (42) 32238; fax (42) 33211; Ambassador: SÁNDOR MESZAROS.

Iran: Rruga Mustafa Matohiti 20, Tirana; tel. (42) 27869; fax (42) 30409; Ambassador: MOHAMMAD KAZEM BIGDELI SOLTANI.

Italy: Rruga Lek Dukagjini, Tirana; tel. (42) 34045; fax (42) 34276; e-mail ambittia@icc.al.eu.org; Ambassador: MARIO BOVA.

Libya: Rruga Dëshmorët e 4 Shkurtit 48, Tirana; tel. (42) 28101; fax (42) 32098; Bureau Chief: YOUSSEF ELTAEF SASSI.

Macedonia, former Yugoslav republic: Rruga Lek Dukagjini, Vila 2; tel. (42) 33036; fax (42) 32514; Ambassador: RISTO NIKOVSKI.

Norway: Rruga Dëshmorët e 4 Shkurtit 7/1; tel. and fax (42) 57035; Chargé d'affaires: TOBIAS FRAMBE.

Poland: Rruga e Durrësit 123, Tirana; tel. (42) 34190; fax (42) 33464; Ambassador: ANREZEJ CHODAKOWSKI.

Romania: Rruga Asim Zeneli, Tirana; tel. (42) 56071; fax (42) 56072; Ambassador: FILIP TEODORESCU.

Russia: Rruga Asim Zeneli 5, Tirana; tel. (42) 56040; fax (42) 56046; Ambassador: IGOR A. SAPRYKIN.

Saudi Arabia: Bulevardi Dëshmorët e Kombit; tel. (42) 48307; fax (42) 29982; Chargé d'affaires: SALEH ABDUL LATIF SIJANTAN.

Switzerland: Rruga e Elbasanit 81, Tirana; tel. (42) 34890; fax (42) 34889; e-mail swissemb@adanet.com.al; Ambassador THOMAS FELLER.

Turkey: Rruga Konferenca e Pezës 31, Tirana; tel. (42) 33399; fax (42) 32719; e-mail turkemb@interalb.al; Ambassador: AHMET MEHMET MURAT OĞUZ.

United Kingdom: Rruga Skënderbeu 12, Tirana; tel. (42) 34973; fax (42) 47697; Ambasssador: Dr PETER JANUARY.

USA: Rruga Labinoti 103, Tirana; tel. (42) 47285; fax (42) 32222; internet www.usembassy.state.gov/posts/a1/wwwhcont.html; Ambassador: JOSEPH LIMPRECHT.

Judicial System

The judicial structure comprises the High Court, the Courts of Appeal and the Courts of First Instance. The Chairman and members of the High Court are appointed by the President of the Republic, with the approval of the legislature, for a term of seven years. Other judges are appointed by the President upon the proposal of a High Council of Justice. The High Council of Justice comprises the Chairman of the High Court, the Minister of Justice, three members elected by the legislature for a term of five years, and nine judges of all levels who are elected by a national judicial conference.

The Constitutional Court: The Constitutional Court arbitrates on constitutional issues, and determines, *inter alia*, the conformity of proposed legislation with the Constitution. It is empowered to prohibit the activities of political organizations on constitutional grounds, and also formulates legislation regarding the election of the President of the Republic. The Constitutional Court comprises nine members, who are appointed by the President, with the approval of the legislature, for a term of nine years.

Chairman of the Constitutional Court: FEHMI ABDIU.

Religion

All religious institutions were closed by the Government in 1967 and the practice of religion was prohibited. In May 1990, however, the prohibition on religious activities was revoked, religious services were permitted, and, from 1991, mosques and churches began to be reopened. Under the Constitution of November 1998, Albania is a secular state which observes freedom of religious belief. On the basis of declared affiliation in 1945, it is estimated that some 70% of the population are of Muslim background (mainly Sunni or adherents of the liberal Bektashi order), 20% Eastern Orthodox Christian (mainly in the south) and some 10% Roman Catholic Christian (mainly in the north).

ISLAM

Albanian Islamic Community (Bashkesia Islame e Shqipërisë): Rruga Puntoret e Rilindjes, Tirana; f. 1991; Chair. HAFIZ H. SABRI KOÇI; Grand Mufti of Albania HAFIZ SALIH TERMAT HOXHA.

Bektashi Sect
World Council of Elders of the Bektashis: Tirana; f. 1991; Chair. RESHAT Baba BARDHI.

CHRISTIANITY
The Eastern Orthodox Church
Orthodox Autocephalous Church of Albania (Kisha Orthodhokse Autoqefale të Shqipërisë): Rruga Kavaja 151, Tirana; tel. (42) 34117; fax (42) 32109; e-mail arch-an@ocual.tirana.al; the Albanian Orthodox Church was proclaimed autocephalous at the Congress of Berat in 1922, its status was approved in 1929 and it was recognized by the Ecumenical Patriarchate in Istanbul (Constantinople), Turkey, in 1936; the Serbian, Macedonian and Greek churches do not recognize its separate existence; Archbishop ANASTAS JANULATOS.

The Roman Catholic Church
Many Roman Catholic churches have been reopened since 1990, and in September 1991 diplomatic relations were restored with the Holy See. Albania comprises two archdioceses, four dioceses and one apostolic administration. At 31 December 1997 the estimated number of adherents represented about 34.5% of the total population.

Bishops' Conference: Conferenza Episcopale dell'Albania, Rruga Labinoti, POB 1510, Tirana; tel. (42) 32082; fax (42) 30727; Pres. Most Rev. RROK K. MIRDITA, Archbishop of Durrës-Tirana.

Archbishop of Durrës-Tirana: Most Rev. RROK K. MIRDITA, Arqipeshkvia, Rruga Labinoti, Vilar e Gjermaneve 3, Tirana; tel. (42) 32082; fax (42) 30727.

Archbishop of Shkodër: Most Rev. ANGELO MASSAFRA, Kryeipeshkëvi, Sheshi Gijon Pali II, Shkodër; tel. (224) 2744.

The Press

Until 1991 the Press was controlled by the Party of Labour of Albania, now the Socialist Party of Albania (SPA), and adhered to a strongly Marxist-Leninist line. From 1991 many new periodicals and newspapers were established by the newly emerging independent political organizations. In 1994 there were some 400 newspapers and periodicals in publication.

PRINCIPAL DAILIES

Koha Jonë (Our Time): Sami Frasheri, Pallatet e Aviacionit,Tirana; tel. (42) 47004; fax (42) 47005; e-mail kohajone@albnet.net; internet www.kohajone.com; f. 1991; independent; Editor-in-Chief KICO BLUSHI; circ. 400,000.

Rilindja Demokratike (Democratic Revival): Rruga Fortuzi, Tirana; tel. (42) 29609; fax (42) 42329; f. 1991; organ of the DPA; Editor-in-Chief LORENC LIGORI; circ. 50,000.

Shekulli: Tirana; tel. (42) 51425; fax (42) 51424; independent; Editor-in-Chief ZAMIR ALUSHI.

Zëri i Popullit (The Voice of the People): Bulevardi Zhan D'Ark, Tirana; tel. (42) 22192; fax (42) 27813; e-mail zeri@zeripopullit.com; internet www.zeripopullit.com; f. 1942; daily, except Mon.; organ of the SPA; Editor-in-Chief LUAN RAMA; circ. 105,000.

PERIODICALS
Tirana
Agrovizion: Rruga d'Istria, Tirana; tel. (42) 26147; f. 1992; 2 a week; agricultural economic policies, new technology in farming, advice for farmers; circ. 3,000.

Albania: Tirana; f. 1991; weekly; organ of the Albanian Green Party; environmental issues.

Albanian Daily News: Rruga Hile Mosi, 5, Tirana; tel. and fax (42) 27639; e-mail adn@icc.al.eu.org; internet www.albaniannews.com; f. 1995; weekly English-language newspaper; Editor ARBEN LESKAJ.

Alternativa SD: Tirana; f. 1991; 2 a week; organ of the Social Democratic Party.

Arbër: Tirana; f. 1992; fortnightly; social, literary and artistic review.

The Balkans: Tirana; f. 1993; humorous review; Editor-in-Chief NIKO NIKOLLA.

Balli i Kombit (The Head of the Nation): Tirana; f. 1991.

Bashkimi Kombëtar: Bulevardi Zhan D'Ark, Tirana; tel. (42) 28110; f. 1943; Editor-in-Chief QEMAL SAKAJEVA; circ. 30,000.

Blic: Rruga Fortuzi 44, Tirana; tel. (42) 34319; e-mail blici@ juno.com; weekly; politics, information and culture; Editor ILIR YZEIRI.

Çamëria—Vatra Amtare (Çamëria—Maternal Hearth): Tirana; f. 1991; weekly; organ of the Çamëria Political and Patriotic Association.

Drita (The Light): Rruga Konferenca e Pezës 4, Tirana; tel. (42) 27036; f. 1960; weekly; publ. by Union of Writers and Artists of Albania; Editor-in-Chief BRISEIDA MEMA; circ. 31,000.

Ekonomia Botërore (World Economics): Tirana; f. 1991; monthly; independent.

Fatosi (The Valiant): Tirana; tel. (42) 23024; f. 1959; fortnightly; literary and artistic magazine for children; Editor-in-Chief XHEVAT BEQARAJ; circ. 21,200.

Filmi (The Film): Rruga 'Aleksander Moisiu' 76; tel. and fax (42) 64971; f. 1998; annual; illustrated cinema review.

Gazeta Shqiptare (Albanian Gazette): Tirana; independent; Editor CARLO BOLLINO.

Hosteni (The Goad): Tirana; f. 1945; fortnightly; political review of humour and satire; publ. by the Union of Journalists; Editor-in-Chief NIKO NIKOLLA.

The Hour of Albania: Rruga Dëshmorët e 4 Shkurtit, Tirana; tel. (42) 42042; fax (42) 34024; weekly; organ of the Christian Democratic Party of Albania; Editor-in-Chief Dr FAIK LAMA; circ. 3,000.

Kombi (The Nation): Rruga Alqi Kondi, Tirana; tel. (42) 27498; fax (42) 23929; f. 1991; 2 a week; organ of the Party of National Unity; circ. 15,000.

Kushtrim Brezash (Clarion Call of Generations): Tirana; f. 1992; weekly; organ of the National Committee of the War Veterans of the Anti-Fascist National Liberation War of the Albanian People.

Mbrojtja (The Defence): Tirana; f. 1991; monthly; publ. by the Ministry of Defence; Editor-in-Chief XHELADIN ÇELMETA.

Mësuesi (The Teacher): Tirana; f. 1961; weekly; publ. by the Ministry of Education and Science; Editor-in-Chief THOMA QENDRO.

Official Gazette of the Republic of Albania: Kuvendi Popullore, Tirana; tel. (42) 28668; fax (42) 27949; f. 1945; occasional government review.

Panorama Agroushqimore (Agro-food Panorama): Rruga d'Istria, Tirana; f. 1921, publ. under several names; monthly; specialist agricultural magazine; circ. 3,000.

Pasqyra (The Mirror): Bulevardi Zhan D'Ark, Tirana; e-mail marketingu@pasqyra.com; internet www.pasqyra.com; f. 1991 to replace *Puna* (Labour—f. 1945); 2 a week; also 4 times a year in French; organ of the Confederation of Albanian Trade Unions; Editor-in-Chief XHAFER SHATRI.

Patrioti (The Patriot): Tirana; f. 1992; organ of the Elez Isufi Patriotic Association; Editor-in-Chief VEDIP BRENSHI.

Përmbledhje Studimesh (Collection of Studies): Tirana; quarterly; summaries in French.

Progresi (Progress): Rruga Budi 6, Tirana; tel. (42) 27481; fax (42) 27481; f. 1991; 2 a week; organ of the Agrarian Party.

Republika: Rruga Sami Frasheri, Tirana; tel. and fax (42) 25988; e-mail republika@albaniaonline.net; internet www.pages .albaniaonline.net/republika; f. 1991; 2 a week; organ of the Albanian Republican Party; Editor-in-Chief YLLI RAKIPI.

Revista Pedagogjike: Naim Frashëri St 37, Tirana; fax (42) 56441; f. 1945; quarterly; organ of the Institute of Pedagogical Studies; educational development, psychology, didactic; Editor BUJAR BASKA; circ. 4,000.

Rinia e Lire (Free Youth): Tirana; f. 1992; organ of the Albanian Free Youth Federation.

Shëndeti (Health): M. Duri 2, Tirana; tel. (42) 27803; fax (42) 27803; f. 1949; monthly; publ. by the National Directorate of Health Education; issues of health and welfare, personal health care; Editors-in-Chief KORNELIA GJATA, AGIM XHUMARI.

Shqiptarja e Re (The New Albanian Woman): Tirana; f. 1943; monthly; political and socio-cultural review; Editor-in-Chief VALENTINA LESKAJ.

Sindikalisti (Trade Unionists): Tirana; f. 1991; newspaper; organ of the Union of Independent Trade Unions of Albania; Editor-in-Chief VANGJEL KOZMAI.

Skena dhe Ekrani (Stage and Screen): Tirana; quarterly; cultural review.

Spektër (The Spectre): Tirana; internet www.spekter.com.al; f. 1991; illustrated independent monthly; in Albanian and Italian.

Sporti Shquiptar: Rruga e Kavajës 23, Sheshi Ataturk, 2908 Tirana; tel. and fax (42) 20237; f. 1935; 3 a week; Editor BESNIK DIZDARI; circ. 10,000.

Tirana: Tirana; f. 1987; independent; 2 a week; publ. by Tirana District SPA.

Tregtia e Jashtme Popullore (Albanian Foreign Trade): Rruga Konferenca e Pezës 6, Tirana; tel. (42) 22934; f. 1961; 6 a year; in English and French; organ of the Albanian Chamber of Commerce; Editor AGIM KORBI.

Tribuna Demokratike (Democratic Tribune): Tirana.

Tribuna e Gazetarit (The Journalist's Tribune): Tirana; 6 a year; publ. by the Union of Journalists of Albania; Editor NAZMI QAMILI.

Ushtria dhe Koha (Army and Time): Tirana; f. 1993; monthly; publ. by the Ministry of Defence; Editor-in-Chief AGRON MANÇE.

Zeri i Atdheut (The Voice of the Country): Tirana; f. 1992; weekly.

Other Towns

Adriatiku (Adriatic): Durrës; f. 1967; independent; 2 a week.

Dibra: Dibër; f. 1991; independent; 2 a week.

Egnatia: Berat; f. 1991; independent; 2 a week.

Korçë Demokratike (Democratic Korçë): Korçë; f. 1992; organ of the Democratic Party of Albania; weekly.

Ore (The Clock): Shkodër; f. 1992; independent; 2 a week.

Universi Rinor (The Youth Universe): Korçë; f. 1991.

Zëri i Vlorës (The Voice of Vlorë): Vlorë; f. 1967; 2 a week; Editor-in-Chief DASHO METODASHAJ.

NEWS AGENCIES

Albanian Telegraphic Agency (ATA): Bulevardi Zhan D'Ark 23, Tirana; tel. (42) 22929; fax (42) 34230; e-mail hola@ata .tirana.al; internet www.ata-al.net; f. 1929; domestic and foreign news; brs in provincial towns and in Kosovo, Yugoslavia; Dir-Gen. FRROK CUPI.

Foreign Bureau

Xinhua (New China) News Agency (People's Republic of China): Rruga Zef Jubani 3, Apt 903, Tirana; tel. (42) 33139; fax (42) 48019; e-mail xinhua-tirana@china.com; Bureau Chief LI JIYU.

PRESS ASSOCIATIONS

Union of Journalists of Albania (Bashkimi i Gazetarëve të Shqipërisë): Tirana; tel. (42) 28020; f. 1949; Chair. MARASH HAJATI; Sec.-Gen. YMER MINXHOZI.

Publishers

Agjensia Qëndrore e Tregtimit të Librit Artistik dhe Shkencor (Central Agency of the Artistic and Scientific Book Trade): Tirana; tel. and fax (42) 27246.

Botime të Akademisë së Shkencave të RSH: Tirana; publishing house of the Albanian Academy of Sciences.

Botime te Universitetit Bujqësor te Tiranës: Kamzë, Tirana; publishing house of the Agricultural University of Tirana.

Botime të Shtëpisë Botuese 8 Nëntori: Tirana; tel. (42) 28064; f. 1972; books on Albania and other countries, political and social sciences, translations of Albanian works into foreign languages, technical and scientific books, illustrated albums, etc.; Dir XHEMAL DINI.

Dituria Publishing House: Rruga Dervish Hima 32, Tirana; tel. and fax (42) 25882; f. 1991; dictionaries, calendars, encyclopaedias, social sciences, biographies, fiction and non-fiction; Gen. Dir PETRIT YMERI.

Fan Noli: Tirana; tel. (42) 42739; f. 1991; Albanian and foreign literature.

Qendr e Informacionit për Bujsinë dhe Ushqimin (Information Centre for Agriculture and Food): Rruga d'Istria, Tirana; tel. (42) 26147; f. 1970; publishes various agricultural periodicals; Gen. Dir SALI ÇELA.

Shtëpia Botuese e Librit Shkollor: Tirana; tel. (42) 22331; f. 1967; educational books; Dir SHPËTIM BOZDO.

Shtëpia Botuese 'Libri Universitar': Rruga Dora d'Istria, Tirana; tel. (42) 25659; fax (42) 29268; f. 1988; publishes university textbooks

Directory

on science, medicine, engineering, geography, history, literature, foreign languages, economics, etc.; Dir MUSTAFA FEZGA.

Shtëpia Botuese e Lidhjes së Shkrimtarëve: Konferenca e Pezës 4, Tirana; tel. (42) 22691; fax (42) 25912; f. 1990; artistic and documentary literature; Dir ZIJA ÇELA.

Shtëpia Botuese Naim Frashëri: Tirana; tel. (42) 27906; f. 1947; fiction, poetry, drama, criticism, children's literature, translations; Dir GAQO BUSHAKA.

Union of Writers and Artists Publishing House: Tirana; f. 1991; fiction, poetry incl. foreign literature and works by the Albanian diaspora.

WRITERS' UNIONS

Independent Union of Writers (Bashkimi i Shkrimtarëve te Pavarur): Tirana; f. 1991; Chair. AGIM SHEHU.

Union of Writers and Artists of Albania (Lidhja e Shkrimtarëve dhe e Artistëve të Shqipërisë): Rruga Konferenca e Pezës 4, Tirana; tel. (42) 29689; f. 1945; 26 brs; 1,750 mems; Chair. BARDHYL LONDO.

Broadcasting and Communications
TELECOMMUNICATIONS

State Department of Posts and Telecommunications: Rruga Myslym Shyri 42, Tirana; tel. (42) 27204; fax (42) 33772; e-mail kote@dshpt.tirana.al; Gen. Dir HYDAJET KOPANI; Man. Dir FREDERIK KOTE.

Albanian Telecom (Telekom Shqiptar): Tirana; internet www.atnet.com.al; Dir-Gen. DHIMITRAQ RAFTI.

BROADCASTING

In 1991 state broadcasting was removed from political control and made subordinate to the Parliamentary Commission for the Media.

Radio

Radio Televizioni Shqiptare: Rruga Ismail Qemali 11, Tirana; tel. and fax (42) 22481; e-mail dushiulp@yahoo.com; internet www.rtsh.sil.al; f. 1938; two channels of domestic services (19 and five hours daily) and a third channel covering international broadcasting (two services in Albanian and seven in foreign languages); Chair. KASTRIST CAUSBI; Dir-Gen. EDUARD MAZI; Dir of Radio MARTIN LEKA.

Kontakt Radio: Rruga Muhamet Gjollesha, Kati i9, Tirana; tel. (42) 49474; fax (42) 57602; e-mail radiokontakt@albaniaonline.net; internet www.radiokontakt.com; independent radio station; commenced broadcasts Oct. 1997; Dir AGRON BALA.

Top Albania Radio: International Centre of Culture, Bulevardi Dëshmorët e Kombit, Tirana; tel. (42) 47492; fax (42) 47493; e-mail topalbaniaradio@albaniaonline.net; internet www.pages.albaniaonline.net/topalbaniaradio.

Television

Radio Televizioni Shqiptare: Rruga Ismail Qemali 11, Tirana; tel. (42) 56056; fax (42) 56058; f. 1960; broadcasts range of television programmes.

Alba Television: International Centre of Culture, Bulevardi Dëshmorët e Kombit, Tirana; tel. and fax (42) 34142; e-mail albatv@albaniaonline.net; internet www.pages.albaniaonline.net/albatv; private television station; Dir PAULIN SHKJEZI.

Shijak TV: Rruga Kavajes, Sheshi Ataturk, Tirana; tel. and fax (42) 47135; e-mail shijaktv01@albaniaonline.net; internet www.shijaktv.com; Pres. GËZIM ISMAILI.

Teutar Televizion: Tirana; e-mail teutartv@albaniaonline.net; internet www.teutartv.com.

Finance

(cap. = capital; dep. = deposits; res = reserves; m. = million; brs = branches; amounts in lekë, unless otherwise stated)

BANKING
Central Bank

Bank of Albania (Banka e Shqipërisë): Sheshi Skënderbeu 1, Tirana; tel. (42) 22752; fax (42) 23558; e-mail public@bankofalbania.org; internet www.bankofalbania.org; f. 1992; cap. US $5.5m. (Nov. 1999), res $26.4m. (Oct. 1998); Gov. SHKËLQIM CANI.

State Banks

National Commercial Bank of Albania: Bulevardi Zhan D'Ark, Tirana; tel. (42) 50955; fax (42) 50948; e-mail julian@aedp.soros.al; internet www.come.to.ncba; f. 1993, following merger of National Bank of Albania and Commercial Bank of Albania; cap. 2,700.0m.,

res 7,227.7m.,dep. 22,457.5m. (Dec. 1999); Gen. Man. SPIRO BRUMBULLI; 30 brs.

Savings Bank of Albania: Rruga Dëshmorët e 4 Shkurtit 6, Tirana; tel. (42) 24972; fax (42) 23695; e-mail name@bkursimeve.com.al; internet www.bkursimeve.com.al; f. 1991; 100% state-owned, scheduled for privatization; cap. 3.2m., res 10.5m., dep. 1,127m. (August 1999); Gen. Man. ARTAN SANTO; 25 brs.

Other Banks

American Bank of Albania (Banka Amerikanë e Shqipërisë): Rruga Ismail Qemali 27, POB 8319, Tirana; tel. (42) 48753; fax (42) 48762; e-mail americanbank@ambankalb.com; internet www.al-bambank.com; f. 1998; owned by Albanian-American Enterprise Fund (USA); cap. US $4.7m.; Chair. MICHAEL GRANOFF; Pres. and CEO LORENZO RONCARI.

Arab-Albanian Islamic Bank: Dëshmorët e Kombit 8, Tirana; tel. (42) 23873; fax (42) 28460; e-mail aaib@albaniaonline.net; f. 1994; cap. US $10m. (2000); Gen. Dir WAHEED ALAVI.

Dardania Bank: Dëshmorët e Kombit 'VEVE' Center, Tirana; tel. and fax (42) 35053; f. 1994; privately owned.

First Investment Bank: Drejtoria e Përgjithshme, Rruga e Barrikadave, Tirana; tel. (42) 33965; fax (42) 35700; e-mail biatia@adanet.com.al.

International Commercial Bank: Rruga Ded Gjo Luli 3, Tirana; tel. (42) 37567; fax (42) 37570; e-mail icba@icc.al.eu.org.

Italian-Albanian Bank: Rruga e Barrikadave, Tirana; tel. (42) 26262; fax (42) 33965; jt venture between the National Commercial Bank of Albania and Banca di Roma; 3 brs.

INSURANCE

Insurance Institute of Albania (Instituti i Sigurimeve të Shqipërisë): Rruga Dibres 91, Tirana; tel. (42) 34170; fax (42) 34180; f. 1991; all types of insurance; Gen. Dir QEMAL DISHA; 28 brs.

STOCK EXCHANGE

Albanian Stock Exchange: Sheshi Skënderbeu 1, Tirana; tel. (42) 35568; fax (42) 23558; e-mail emeka@bankofalbania.org; internet www.asc.gov.al/tiranastock.html; f. 1996; Gen. Dir ELVIN MEKA (acting).

Trade and Industry
PRIVATIZATION AGENCY

National Agency for Privatization (NAP): Tirana; tel. and fax (42) 27933; govt agency under the control of the Council of Ministers; prepares and proposes the legal framework concerning privatization procedures and implementation; Dir NIKO GLOZHENI.

SUPERVISORY ORGANIZATIONS

Albanian Securities Commission (ASC): Bulevardi Dëshmorët e Kombit, Tirana; tel. and fax (42) 28260; e-mail asc@albaniaonline.net; internet www.asc.gov.al; Chair. ELISABETA GTONI.

Albkontroll: Rruga Skënderbeu 45, Durrës; tel. (52) 23377; fax (52) 22791; f. 1962; brs throughout Albania; independent control body for inspection of goods for import and export, means of transport, etc.; Gen. Man. DILAVER MEZINI; 15 brs.

State Supreme Audit Control: Region Eurosai, Tirana; tel. and fax (42) 32491; e-mail klsh@albaniaonline.net; internet www.pages.albaniaonline.net/klsh.

DEVELOPMENT ORGANIZATIONS

Albanian Economy Development Agency (AEDA): Bulevardi Zhan D'Ark, Tirana; tel. (42) 30133; fax (42) 28439; e-mail xhepa@cpfi.tirana.al; f. 1993; govt agency to promote foreign investment in Albania and to provide practical support to foreign investors; publishes Ekonomia; Chair. SELAMI XHEPA.

Enterprise Restructuring Agency (Agjensia e Ristrukturimit te Ndermarrjeve): Rruga e Durrësit 83, Tirana; tel. (42) 27878; fax (42) 25730; govt agency established to assist state-owned enterprises to become privately owned by offering enterprise sector surveys, strategic plans and consultations; provides technical assistance; Dir ADRIATIK BANKJA.

CHAMBERS OF COMMERCE

Union of Chambers of Commerce and Industry of Albania: Rruga Kavajes 6, Tirana; tel. and fax (42) 22934; f. 1958; Pres. ANTON LEKA.

Durrës Chamber of Commerce: Durrës; f. 1988; promotes trade with southern Italy.

Gjirokastër Chamber of Commerce: Gjirokastër; f. 1988; promotes trade with Greek border area.

Korçë Chamber of Commerce and Industry: Blloku Demokracia, Korçë; tel. and fax (82) 42457; e-mail cciko@abissnet.com.al.

Shkodër Chamber of Commerce: Shkodër; promotes trade with Yugoslav border area.

There are also chambers of commerce in Kukës, Peshkopi, Pogradec, Sarandë and Vlorë.

UTILITIES
Electricity

Korporata Elektroenergjetike Shqiptare (KESH): Biloky 'Vasil Shanto', Tirana; tel. (42) 28434; fax (42) 32046; state corpn for the generation, transmission, distribution and export of electrical energy; govt-controlled; scheduled for transfer to private ownership; Chair. BASHKIM QATIPI; Gen. Dir Dr NAKO HOBDARI.

TRADE UNIONS

Until 1991 independent trade-union activities were prohibited, the official trade unions being represented in every work and production centre. During 1991, however, independent unions were established. The most important of these was the Union of Independent Trade Unions of Albania. Other unions were established for workers in various sectors of the economy.

Confederation of Albanian Trade Unions (Konfederata e Sindikatave të Shqipërise—KSSh): Bulevardi Zhan D'Ark, Tirana; f. 1991 to replace the official Central Council of Albanian Trade Unions (f. 1945); includes 17 trade union federations representing workers in different sectors of the economy; Chair. of Man. Council KASTRIOT MUÇO.

Union of Independent Trade Unions of Albania (Bashkimi i Sindikatave të Pavarura të Shqipërisë–BSPSh): Tirana; f. 1991; Chair. (vacant).

Other Trade Unions

Agricultural Trade Union Federation (Federata Sindikale e Bujqesise): Tirana; f. 1991; Leaders ALFRED GJOMO, NAZMI QOKU.

Autonomous Union of Public-Service Workers: Tirana; f. 1992; Chair. MINELLA KURETA.

Free and Independent Miners' Union (Sindikata e Lire dhe e Pavarur e Minatoreve): Tirana; f. 1991; Chair. GEZIM KALAJA.

Independent Trade Union Federation of Workers in the Artistic Articles, Handicrafts, Glassware and Ceramics Industries: Tirana; f. 1991.

Independent Trade Union Federation of the Food Industry: Tirana; f. 1991.

Independent Trade Union of Dock Workers: Durrës; f. 1992.

Independent Trade Union of Radio and Television: Tirana; f. 1991; represents interests of media workers.

Trade Union of Army and Police Civilians: Tirana; f. 1994.

Trade Union Federation of Education and Science Workers: Tirana; f. 1991; represents teachers and academics.

Trade Union Federation of Health Workers: Tirana; Chair. MINELLA MANO.

Union of Oil Industry Workers: seceded from the Confederation of Albanian Trade Unions in 1991; represents workers in the petroleum and natural gas industry; Chair. MENPOR XHEMALI.

Transport
RAILWAYS

In 1994 there were approximately 720 km of railway track, with lines linking Tirana–Vlorë–Durrës, Durrës–Kavajë–Rrogozhinë–Elbasan–Librazhd–Prenjas–Pogradec, Rrogozhinë–Lushnjë–Fier–Ballsh, Milot–Rrëshen, Vlorë–Laç–Lezhë–Shkodër and Selenicë–Vlorë. There are also standard-gauge lines between Fier and Selenicë and between Fier and Vlorë. In 2000 projects were underway to rehabilitate the Rrogozhinë–Vlorë and Fier–Ballsh railway lines. A 50-km international freight link between Shkodër and Titograd (now Podgorica), Montenegro (Yugoslavia), opened in 1986.

Albanian Railways: Durrës; tel. (52) 22311; fax (52) 22037; internet www.pages.albaniaonline.net/hsh; Gen. Dir FERDINAND XHAFERRI.

ROADS

In 1998 the road network comprised an estimated 18,000 km of classified roads, including 3,221 km of main roads and 4,278 km of secondary roads; about 30% of the total network was paved in 1995. All regions are linked by the road network, but many roads in mountainous districts are unsuitable for motor transport. A three-year public investment plan, which was initiated in 1995, included substantial funds for the rehabilitation of the road network; the principal projects were the creation of east–west (Durrës–Kapshtice) and north–south highways. In 2000 investment projects concentrated on rehabilitating the north–south corridor, in an effort to encourage more goods' transport between Italy and Croatia.

SHIPPING

At December 1998 Albania's merchant fleet had 25 vessels, with a total displacement of 28,671 grt. The chief ports are those in Durrës, Vlorë, Sarandë and Shëngjin. In 1996 the port of Himare, which was closed in 1991, was reopened. Ferry services have been established between Durrës and three Italian ports (Trieste, Bari and Ancona) and between Sarandë and the Greek island of Corfu. There is also a service between Vlorë and Brindisi (Italy). A new ferry terminal, financed by the EU, was under construction at Durrës in 2000. Furthermore, the World Bank and Italy's OPEC Fund were financing a US $23m. project to improve existing port facilities.

Adetare Shipping Agency Ltd: Durrës; tel. (52) 23883; fax (52) 23666.

Albanian State Shipping Enterprise: Porti Detar, Durrës; tel. (52) 22233; fax (52) 229111.

CIVIL AVIATION

There is a small international airport at Rinas, 25 km from Tirana. Reconstruction of the airport was undertaken in the late 1990s. Total traffic averaged 300,000 passengers and 900,000 metric tons of goods carried per year.

Albanian Airlines Mak: Rruga Minepeza 2, Tirana; tel. (42) 27606; fax (42) 28461; e-mail tiadplvasita@msmail.com; f. 1992 as Albanian Airlines, a jt venture between the Albanian state-owned air agency, Albtransport, and the Austrian airline, Tyrolean Airways; acquired in 1995 by the Kuwaiti co, Aviation World Mak, and assumed present name; scheduled services to Germany, Italy and Turkey; Commercial Man. HANS MOOK.

Tourism

In 1998 there were some 27,709 international tourist arrivals at hotels in Albania, compared with 19,154 in 1997. In 1996 receipts from tourism totalled about US $11m. The main tourist centres include Tirana, Durrës, Sarandë, Shkodër and Pogradec. The Roman amphitheatre at Durrës is one of the largest in Europe. The ancient towns of Apollonia and Butrint are important archaeological sites and there are many other towns of historic interest. However, expansion of the tourist industry has been limited by the inadequacy of Albania's infrastructure and a lack of foreign investment in the development of new facilities. Regional instability, particularly during the NATO air offensive against Yugoslavia in early 1999, also inhibited tourist activity. In August 1999 an Interministerial Council on Tourism Development Policies approved a US $258m. private-sector investment programme for the coastal towns of Durrës, Golem and Sarandë.

Albturist: Bulevardi Dëshmorët e Kombit, Hotel Dhajti, Tirana; tel. (42) 51849; fax (42) 34359; e-mail albturist.t.a.@albnet.net; brs in main towns and all tourist centres; 28 hotels throughout the country; Dir-Gen. BESNIK PELLUMBI.

Committee for Development and Tourism: Bulevardi Dëshmorët e Kombit 8, Tirana; tel. (42) 58323; fax (42) 58322; e-mail arskenderi@albaniaonline.com; govt body.

ALGERIA

Introductory Survey

Location, Climate, Language, Religion, Flag, Capital

The Democratic and People's Republic of Algeria lies in north Africa, with the Mediterranean Sea to the north, Mali and Niger to the south, Tunisia and Libya to the east, and Morocco and Mauritania to the west. The climate on the Mediterranean coast is temperate, becoming more extreme in the Atlas mountains immediately to the south. Further south is part of the Sahara, a hot and arid desert. Temperatures in Algiers, on the coast, are generally between 9°C (48°F) and 29°C (84°F), while in the interior they may exceed 50°C (122°F). Arabic is the official language, but French is widely used. There is a substantial Berber minority, whose principal language is Tamazight. Islam is the state religion, and almost all Algerians are Muslims. The national flag (proportions 3 by 2) has two equal vertical stripes, of green and white, with a red crescent moon and a five-pointed red star superimposed in the centre. The capital is Algiers (el-Djezaïr).

Recent History

Algeria was conquered by French forces in the 1830s and annexed by France in 1842. For most of the colonial period official policy was to colonize the territory with French settlers, and many French citizens became permanent residents. Unlike most of France's overseas possessions, Algeria was not formally a colony but was 'attached' to metropolitan France. However, the indigenous Muslim majority did not have equal rights, and political and economic power within Algeria was largely held by the white settler minority.

On 1 November 1954 the principal Algerian nationalist movement, the Front de libération nationale (FLN), began a war for national independence, in the course of which about 1m. Muslims were killed or wounded. Despite resistance from the Europeans in Algeria, the French Government agreed to a cease-fire in March 1962 and independence was declared on 3 July 1962. In August the Algerian provisional Government transferred its functions to the Political Bureau of the FLN, and in September a National Constituent Assembly was elected (from a single list of FLN candidates) and a Republic proclaimed. A new Government was formed, with Ahmed Ben Bella, founder of the FLN, as Prime Minister.

A draft Constitution, providing for a presidential regime with the FLN as the sole party, was adopted by the Constituent Assembly in August 1963. In September the Constitution was approved by popular referendum, and Ben Bella was elected President. Under his leadership economic reconstruction was begun and the foundation was laid for a single-party socialist state. However, the failure of the FLN to function as an active political force left real power with the bureaucracy and the army. In June 1965 the Minister of Defence, Col Houari Boumedienne, deposed Ben Bella in a bloodless coup and took control of the country as President of a Council of the Revolution, which was composed of 26 members, chiefly army officers.

Boumedienne encountered considerable opposition from left-wing members of the FLN, but from 1971 the Government was confident enough to adopt a more active social policy. French petroleum interests were nationalized, and an agrarian reform programme was initiated. In 1975 Boumedienne announced a series of measures to consolidate the regime and enhance his personal power, including the drafting of a National Charter and a new Constitution, and the holding of elections for a President and National People's Assembly. The National Charter, which enshrined both the creation of a socialist system and the maintenance of Islam as the state religion, and a new Constitution (incorporating the principles of the Charter) were approved at referendums held in June and November 1976 respectively, and in December Boumedienne was elected President unopposed, with more than 99% of the votes cast. The new formal structure of power was completed in February 1977 by the election of FLN members to the National People's Assembly.

In December 1978 President Boumedienne died, and the Council of the Revolution (now comprising only eight members) took over the Government. In January 1979 the FLN adopted a new party structure, electing a Central Committee, which was envisaged as the highest policy-making body both of the party and of the nation as a whole: this Committee was to choose a party Secretary-General, who would automatically become the sole presidential candidate. The Committee was also to elect an FLN Political Bureau (nominated by the Secretary-General). The Committee's choice of Col Ben Djedid Chadli, commander of Oran military district, as presidential candidate was endorsed by a referendum in February. Unlike Boumedienne, Chadli appointed a Prime Minister, Col Muhammad Abd al-Ghani (who retained his post as Minister of the Interior), anticipating constitutional changes that were approved by the National People's Assembly in June and which included the obligatory appointment of a premier. In mid-1980 the FLN authorized Chadli to form a smaller Political Bureau, with more limited responsibilities, thereby increasing the power of the President. Membership of the National People's Assembly was increased to 281 for the legislative elections of March 1982.

At a presidential election held in January 1984 Chadli's candidature was endorsed by 95.4% of the electorate. Chadli immediately reorganized the Government, appointing Abd al-Hamid Brahimi as Prime Minister. In 1985 Chadli initiated a public debate on Boumedienne's National Charter, resulting in the adoption of a new National Charter at a special FLN Congress in December. The revised Charter, which emphasized a state ideology based on the twin principles of socialism and Islam while encouraging the development of private enterprise, was approved by a referendum in January 1986. The number of seats in the National People's Assembly was increased to 295 for a general election in February 1987, at which all candidates were nominated by the FLN. In July of that year the Assembly adopted legislation to permit the formation of local organizations without prior government approval: a ban remained, however, on associations that were deemed to oppose the policies of the Charter or to threaten national security.

During the second half of the 1980s opposition to the Government was increasingly manifest. In 1985 22 Berber cultural and human rights activists were imprisoned after being convicted of belonging to illegal organizations, while 18 alleged supporters of the former President Ben Bella were also detained. In 1986 riots occurred at Constantine and Sétif, following student protests against inadequate facilities. In 1987 several leading activists of an Islamist group were killed by security forces, and some 200 of the group's members were given prison sentences. From mid-1988 severe unemployment, high prices, and shortages of essential supplies (resulting from economic austerity measures imposed in 1987 in response to a decline in world petroleum prices) provoked a series of strikes, and in early October rioting erupted in Algiers, spreading to Oran and Annaba: a six-day state of emergency was imposed, and (according to official sources) 159 people were killed in confrontations with the security forces, while more than 3,500 were arrested. In response to the unrest, Chadli proposed constitutional amendments that would allow non-FLN candidates to participate in elections and make the Prime Minister answerable to the National People's Assembly (rather than to the President). These reforms were approved by a referendum in November. In the same month Col Kasdi Merbah, hitherto the Minister of Health, was appointed Prime Minister, and a new Council of Ministers was formed. In December Chadli was elected President for a third term of office, obtaining 81% of the votes cast.

In February 1989 a new Constitution, signifying the end of the one-party socialist state, was approved by referendum. The formation of political associations outside the FLN was henceforth to be permitted, while the armed forces were no longer allocated a role in the development of socialism. The executive, legislative and judicial functions of the State were separated and made subject to the supervision of a Constitutional Council. In July legislation permitting the formation of political parties entered force (although they were still required to be licensed by the Government): by mid-1991 a total of 47 political parties had been registered, including a radical Islamist group, the Front islamique du salut (FIS), the Mouvement pour

la démocratie en Algérie (MDA), which had been founded by
Ben Bella in 1984, the Parti d'avant-garde socialiste (renamed
Ettahaddi in 1993), the Parti social-démocrate (PSD) and the
Berber Rassemblement pour la culture et la démocratie (RCD).
Other legislation adopted in July 1989 further reduced state
control of the economy, allowed the expansion of investment by
foreign companies, and ended the state monopoly of the press
(while leaving the principal newspapers under FLN control).
Despite these changes, strikes and riots persisted during 1989.
In September Chadli appointed a new Prime Minister, Mouloud
Hamrouche (hitherto a senior official in the presidential office),
who made extensive changes to the Council of Ministers. A
programme of economic liberalization was announced by the
new Government, and a new electoral law, adopted in March
1990, introduced a system of partial proportional representation
for local elections.

At local elections, held in June 1990 following a six-month
postponement to allow recently-registered parties time to
organize, the principal Islamist party, the FIS, received some
55% of total votes cast, while the FLN obtained about 32%. In
July, following disagreement within the FLN concerning the
pace of economic and political reform, the Prime Minister and
four other ministers resigned from the party's Political Bureau.
In the same month the Council of Ministers was reorganized
and the defence portfolio was separated from the presidency for
the first time since 1965. Also in July Chadli acceded to the
demands of the FIS for an early general election, announcing
that polling would take place in early 1991. In August 1990 a
general amnesty permitted the release of thousands of political
prisoners, and in September the former President Ben Bella
was allowed to return from exile.

In December 1990 the National People's Assembly adopted a
law whereby after 1997 Arabic would be Algeria's only official
language and the use of French and Berber in schools and in
official transactions would be punishable offences. In response,
more than 100,000 people demonstrated in Algiers against
political and religious intolerance.

In March 1991 the FLN-affiliated Union Générale des Travailleurs Algériens (UGTA) organized a two-day general strike, the
country's first since independence, in protest against recent
price rises. The Government reacted by announcing increases
in subsidies and other benefits. In April Chadli declared that
Algeria's first multi-party general election would take place in
late June. The FIS argued that a presidential election should
be held simultaneously with, or shortly after, the general election, and in May organized an indefinite general strike and
demonstrations to demand the resignation of Chadli and
changes in the electoral laws. In the wake of violent confrontations in June between Islamist activists and the security forces,
Chadli declared a state of emergency and postponed the general
election. He also announced that he had accepted the resignation
of the Prime Minister and his Government. The former Minister
of Foreign Affairs, Sid-Ahmad Ghozali, was appointed premier;
he subsequently nominated a Council of Ministers consisting
mainly of political independents. Meanwhile, following a further
week of unrest, the FLN and the FIS reached a compromise,
whereby the strike was abandoned and legislative and presidential elections were to be held before the end of 1991. In late
June, after further violent incidents between Islamists and
security forces, Chadli resigned as Chairman of the FLN. In
July army units arrested some 700 Islamists and occupied
the headquarters of the FIS. Among those arrested were the
President of the FIS, Abbasi Madani, who had threatened to
launch a *jihad* ('holy war') if the state of emergency was not
ended, and the party's Vice-President, Ali Belhadj; the two men
were charged with armed conspiracy against the State. The
state of emergency was revoked in late September.

In October 1991 Chadli formally announced that the first
round of the multi-party general election would take place on
26 December, with a second round (in those constituencies
where no candidate had secured an overall majority) scheduled
for 16 January 1992. His announcement followed approval by
the National People's Assembly of revisions to the electoral
code, including an increase in the number of seats in the
legislature from 295 to 430. In all, 231 seats were won outright
at the first round: the FIS took 188 seats (with 47.5% of the
votes cast), the Front des forces socialistes (FFS) 25, the FLN
just 15, and independents three. The FLN alleged that there
had been widespread intimidation and electoral malpractice on
the part of the FIS. On 11 January 1992 Chadli resigned as
President, announcing that he had (one week earlier) dissolved

the National People's Assembly. On the following day the High
Security Council (comprising the Prime Minister, three generals
and two senior ministers) cancelled the second round of legislative voting, at which the FIS had been expected to consolidate
its first-round victory, and on 14 January a five-member High
Council of State (HCS) was appointed to act as a collegiate
presidency until, at the latest, the expiry of Chadli's term of
office in December 1993. The HCS was to be chaired by
Muhammad Boudiaf, a veteran of the war of independence who
had been in exile since 1964, but its most influential figure was
believed to be Maj.-Gen. Khaled Nezzar, the Minister of Defence.
The other members of the HCS were Ali Haroun (the Minister
of Human Rights), Sheikh Tejini Haddam (the Rector of the
Grand Mosque in Paris) and Ali Kafi (President of the war
veterans' association, the Organisation nationale des moudjahi-
dine—ONM); Ghozali was not included, although he remained
premier. The constitutional legality of the HCS was disputed
by all the political parties, including the FLN. The 188 FIS
deputies who had been elected in December 1991 formed a
'shadow' Assembly and demanded a return to legality.

Amid sporadic outbreaks of violence, the security forces took
control of the FIS offices in February 1992. The HCS declared
a 12-month state of emergency, detention centres were opened
in the Sahara, and the FIS claimed that 150 people had been
killed, and as many as 30,000 detained, since the military-
sponsored take-over. In March the FIS was officially dissolved
by the Government. In April 1992 Boudiaf, as Chairman of the
HCS, announced the creation of a National Human Rights'
Monitoring Centre (to replace the Ministry of Human Rights)
and a 60-member National Consultative Council (NCC), which
was to meet each month in the building of the suspended
Assembly, although it was to have no legislative powers. In
June Boudiaf proposed the establishment of a National Patriotic
Rally, with committees in every village and workplace, to prepare for multi-party democracy, and promised a constitutional
review, the dissolution of the FLN and a presidential election.
Moreover, despite continuing violence, he announced the release
from detention of 2,000 FIS militants. In late June, however,
the FIS leaders, Madani and Belhadj, were brought before a
military tribunal in Blida, accused of conspiracy against the
State; the trial was adjourned until July, following the
withdrawal of the defence lawyers from the court.

On 29 June 1992 Boudiaf was assassinated while making a
speech in Annaba. The HCS ordered an immediate inquiry into
the assassination, for which the FIS denied all responsibility.
Ali Kafi succeeded Boudiaf as Chairman of the HCS, and Redha
Malek, the Chairman of the NCC, was appointed as a new
member of the HCS. (In June 1995 Lt Lembarek Boumâarafi
was sentenced to death for Boudiaf's assassination. The trial
revealed little new information, and some observers remained
sceptical about the authorities' insistence that Boumâarafi had
acted alone.) On 8 July 1992 Ghozali resigned in order to enable
Kafi to appoint his own Prime Minister. He was replaced by
Belaid Abd es-Salam, who had directed Algeria's petroleum and
gas policy for almost 20 years after independence. Abd es-Salam
appointed a new Council of Ministers later in the month.

In late July 1992 Madani and Belhadj were sentenced to 12
years' imprisonment. Violent protests erupted in Algiers and
quickly spread to other cities. Despite appeals by the Prime
Minister for a multi-party dialogue in an attempt to end civil
strife, the Government attracted widespread criticism for reinforcing its emergency powers to repress any person or organization whose activities were deemed to represent a threat to
stability. In late August a bomb explosion at Algiers airport
killed nine people and left many injured; the FIS denied any
involvement in the incident.

Political manoeuvring and attempts at reconciliation continued against a background of escalating violence throughout
the country. In February 1993 the state of emergency was
renewed for an indefinite period. Shortly afterwards an assassination attempt was made against Maj.-Gen. Nezzar, followed
by a series of attacks on other senior government officials. In
May large demonstrations were organized in Algiers, Constantine and Oran, to protest against terrorism and to demand that
there be no negotiation with its perpetrators. In June the HCS
appealed for a 'general mobilization' against terrorism, although
in the same month Abd es-Salam expressed his willingness to
open a dialogue with the militants. None the less, violence
continued unabated, with terrorist attacks increasingly targeting not only political officials but also prominent intellectual
and civilian figures.

Meanwhile, in March 1993 Kafi met representatives of the ONM and the FLN to discuss, *inter alia*, possible formulae for a transitional period and the amendment of the Constitution. In June the HCS announced that it would dissolve itself at the end of December, asserting that a modern democracy and free market economy would be created within three years of that date.

In July 1993 Liamine Zéroual (a retired general) succeeded Maj.-Gen. Nezzar as Minister of Defence, although Nezzar retained his post within the HCS. In August Redha Malek, who similarly remained a member of the HCS, was appointed to replace Abd es-Salam as Prime Minister. On the same day former Prime Minister Kasdi Merbah, now leader of the Mouvement algérien pour la justice et le développement, was assassinated, together with several of his staff. Malek, who appointed a new Council of Ministers in September, stated that the resolute stance against terrorism would be maintained, and rejected the possibility of dialogue with its perpetrators. In October the HCS appointed an eight-member National Dialogue Commission (NDC), which was charged with the preparation of a political conference to organize the transition to an elected and democratic form of government. In December it was announced that the HCS would not be disbanded until a new presidential body had been elected at the NDC conference in January 1994. However, all the main political parties (with the exception of the moderate Islamist Hamas) boycotted the conference. The HCS subsequently designated Liamine Zéroual as Head of State for a three-year term, on the apparent recommendation of senior members of the military; Zéroual, who was inaugurated as President on 31 January, retained the defence portfolio in the Council of Ministers.

In February 1994 two senior members of the FIS, Ali Djeddi and Abdelkader Boukhamkham, were released from prison, and rumours circulated that divisions had occurred within the military as a result of contacts made by high-ranking members of the regime, including Zéroual, with imprisoned Islamist leaders. Malek, who was known to be opposed to any compromise with the Islamist militants, resigned as Prime Minister in April; Mokdad Sifi, hitherto Minister of Equipment, was appointed in his place. Only 12 ministers retained their portfolios in the new Council of Ministers, and the majority of new appointees were technocrats or senior civil servants. In May the President inaugurated the National Transition Council (NTC), an interim legislature of 200 appointed members, the aim of which was to provide a forum for debate pending legislative elections. Most of the 21 parties that agreed to participate in the NTC were virtually unknown except for Hamas, and the 22 seats that were allocated to other major parties remained vacant. In the same month a group of six 'independent national figures', including former President Ben Bella, was commissioned by Zéroual to promote dialogue with Islamist militants and opposition groups.

It remained unclear whether the FIS actively supported the most prominent and radical Islamist militant group, the Groupe islamique armé (GIA) in its frequent attacks on members of the security forces, local government and the judiciary, as well as prominent public figures, intellectuals, journalists and ordinary civilians. In March 1994 an attack by Islamist militants on the high-security Tazoult prison, near Batna, resulted in the release of more than 1,000 political prisoners. Certain towns and entire neighbourhoods in some cities were virtually controlled by Islamist activists, and the deaths of a number of foreign nationals led several countries to advise their citizens to leave Algeria. In response to the rise in violence, the security forces intensified their campaign against armed Islamist groups, resorting to air attacks, punitive raids, torture and psychological warfare. Thousands of militants were killed during 1994, including the GIA leader in February and his successor in September. In mid-1994 it was reported that about 490 death sentences had been imposed, and a total of 26 official executions carried out, since the institution in February 1993 of three special courts to try suspects accused of terrorist offences. (The courts, which were frequently implicated in accusations of abuses of human rights, were abolished in February 1995.)

In August 1994 members of the FLN, the Parti du renouveau algérien (PRA), the MDA, Nahdah and Hamas engaged in what was termed a national dialogue with the Government; the meetings were boycotted, however, by Ettahaddi, the FFS and the RCD. At further negotiations, held in early September, discussion focused on two letters sent to the President by Abbasi Madani, purportedly offering a 'truce'. Madani and Belhadj were released from prison in mid-September and placed under house arrest; however, the FIS did not participate in the next round of national dialogue later that month, declaring that negotiations could take place only after the granting of a general amnesty, the rehabilitation of the FIS and the repeal of the state of emergency. The GIA threatened reprisals if the FIS entered into dialogue with the regime, and intensified its campaign of violence against secular society by targeting educational institutions. In addition to the upheaval caused by Islamist violence, the Berber RCD urged a boycott of the start of the school year, and in September a general strike was undertaken by Berber activists in the Kabyle, in protest at the exclusion of the Berber language, Tamazight, from the syllabus and at the prospect of the FIS entering the national dialogue. In May 1995 the RCD welcomed the establishment of a government body to oversee the teaching of Tamazight in schools and universities (commencing in October) and to promote its use in the official media.

In October 1994 Zéroual announced that a presidential election would be held before the end of 1995. However, the FIS and other opponents of the Algerian regime condemned the proposed organization of an election in the context of the ongoing civil conflict. In November 1994 representatives of most of the major Algerian parties, including the FIS, the FLN, the FFS and the MDA, attended a two-day conference in Rome, Italy, organized by the Sant' Egidio Roman Catholic community to foster discussion about the crisis in Algeria. The ensuing Sant' Egidio pact, endorsed by all the participants at a meeting in Rome in January 1995, rejected the use of violence to achieve or maintain power, and urged the Algerian regime to repeal the state of emergency and thereby facilitate negotiations between all parties. However, the pact was dismissed as a 'non-event' by the Government. In April Zéroual resumed discussions with the legalized opposition parties in preparation for the presidential election. Talks with the FLN and the FFS quickly collapsed, however, as both rejected the prospect of participating in an election from which the FIS was excluded. There was, none the less, speculation that the Government was still engaged in dialogue with FIS leaders. In mid-July a co-founder of the FIS and prominent opposition spokesman in France, Sheikh Sahraoui, was assassinated in a mosque in Paris. The FIS blamed the Algerian security forces for the murder, although some analysts considered it more likely to have been perpetrated by the GIA, angered by the contacts between the Government and the FIS. The incident coincided with Zéroual's announcement that dialogue with the FIS had failed.

Some 40 candidates announced their intention to contest the presidential election, the first round of which was scheduled for 16 November 1995, but in October the Constitutional Council stated that only four had succeeded in attaining the required number of signatures (an electoral decree issued by the Government in May, and promulgated by the NTC in July, stipulated that presidential candidates must obtain the endorsement of 75,000 signatures from at least 25 provinces in order to qualify): the incumbent President Liamine Zéroual; Saïd Saadi, Secretary-General of the RCD; Nourreddine Boukrouh, leader of the PRA; and Sheikh Mahfoud Nahnah, leader of Hamas. Redha Malek, who had established an anti-Islamist political party (the Alliance national républicaine—ANR) earlier in the year, notably failed to qualify as a presidential candidate. Despite an appeal by the FLN, the FFS and the FIS for voters to boycott the election, official figures showed that some 75% of the electorate participated in the poll, which was monitored by observers from the Organization of African Unity (OAU), the League of Arab States (the Arab League) and the UN. Zéroual secured an outright victory, with 61.0% of the valid votes cast, his closest rival being Sheikh Nahnah (25.6%), Saïd Saadi (9.6%) and Nourreddine Boukrouh (3.8%). Zéroual was inaugurated for a five-year term on 27 November. Shortly afterwards, despite the assassination of a high-ranking military official, the Government announced the closure of the last of seven detention centres (all of which had opened since February 1992), thereby releasing as many as 650 prisoners, many of whom were Islamist sympathizers. In late December Ahmed Ouyahia, a career diplomat, replaced Mokdad Sifi as Prime Minister. Ouyahia's Government, named in early January 1996, included two members of Hamas and a dissident leader of the FIS.

During 1995–96 the violence in Algeria continued unabated, with militant Islamist groups and the security forces appeared determined to match each other in the intensity of their offensives. The GIA launched a series of car-bomb attacks, resulting in hundreds of deaths, while the security forces claimed to have killed 1,300 Islamists in March 1995 in a week-long campaign in the Aïn-Defla, Jijel and Médéa regions. The spate of car-bomb attacks intensified from late 1995, and in February 1996 the Government imposed strict censorship measures on the media in an apparent attempt to suppress reports on the extent of the violence.

In January 1996 the FLN elected Boualem Benhamouda as its Secretary-General. On his appointment, Benhamouda strove to distance the FLN from the Sant' Egidio pact, and in February he announced that the party was prepared to enter into dialogue with the Government. In April, in an attempt to foster national reconciliation, Zéroual held bilateral discussions with more than 50 influential individuals, including leaders of trade unions and opposition groups; the FIS was not invited to participate. In the following month Zéroual announced his intention to hold legislative elections in early 1997. In addition, he proposed that a referendum be held, prior to the elections, on constitutional reform. Recommended amendments to the Constitution included measures to increase the powers of the President, while limiting his tenure to a maximum of two consecutive mandates, the creation of a Council of the Nation as a second parliamentary chamber (one-third of the members of which would be chosen by the President), the establishment of a State Council (to regulate the administrative judiciary) and a High State Court, and, significantly, a ban on political parties that were based on religion, language, gender or regional differences. It was also suggested that the electoral law be revised to allow for a system of full proportional representation. Several opposition parties reiterated their demands that the Government resume negotiations with the FIS, and argued that constitutional reform should be undertaken only after legislative elections.

Some 1,000 delegates, including representatives of the FLN, Nahdah and Hamas, attended a government-sponsored conference on national concord held in September 1996. The conference was boycotted by the FFS, the RCD, Ettahaddi and the MDA. Owing to their lack of support, Zéroual subsequently withdrew his offer to include members of opposition parties in an expanded Council of Ministers and NTC. The proposed constitutional amendments were duly approved by referendum on 28 November. According to official sources, almost 80% of the electorate participated in the referendum, of whom 85.8% voted in favour of the changes; however, a number of opposition parties disputed the results, claiming that the Government had manipulated the figures concerning the rate of participation and the votes cast in favour. The constitutional amendments were promulgated in December.

In January 1997 the Secretary-General of the UGTA, Abd al-Hak Benhamouda (who had recently announced his intention to establish a centrist political party), was shot dead in Algiers. Although an Islamist group claimed responsibility for the assassination, there was speculation that it may have been perpetrated by opponents within the regime. In February Zéroual announced that elections to the National People's Assembly would take place in late May or early June. Shortly afterwards the NTC adopted restrictive legislation concerning political parties in accordance with the amended Constitution; new electoral legislation replacing the majority system with proportional representation was also adopted. Later in February Abdelkader Bensalah, the President of the NTC, formed a centrist grouping, the Rassemblement national démocratique (RND), which was originally to have been led by Benhamouda. The RND received support from a wide range of organizations, including trade unions, anti-Islamist groups and the influential war veterans' ONM, and was closely linked with Zéroual and the Government. In the following months several more political parties emerged, while certain existing parties changed their names to comply with the new legislation. Notably, Hamas became the Mouvement de la société pour la paix (MSP).

Some 39 political parties contested the elections to the National People's Assembly, held on 5 June 1997. The FIS and Ettahaddi urged a boycott of the polls, while the MDA was banned from participating after failing to comply with the new legislation concerning political parties. (Later in June the MDA and several small political groupings were formally dissolved by the Government.) As the preliminary results of the elections began to emerge, opposition leaders complained of irregularities during the electoral process, and accused officials of manipulating the results in favour of the RND. International observers were critical of the conduct of the elections and commented that

the rate of voter participation (officially estimated at 65.5% of the electorate) seemed unrealistically high. According to the final official results, the RND won 156 of the Assembly's 380 seats, followed by the MSP (69) and the FLN (62); Nahdah took 34 seats, the FFS 20, and the RCD 19. President Zéroual asked Ahmed Ouyahia (who had tendered his resignation following the election) to form a new Government, and later in June Ouyahia announced a new Council of Ministers, comprising members of the RND, the FLN and the MSP.

In July 1997 Abdelkader Hachani, a high-ranking member of the FIS, was formally sentenced to five years' imprisonment and three years' deprivation of his civil rights; Hachani was released immediately as he had been in custody for five years. Shortly afterwards Abbasi Madani was conditionally released following a hearing at a military tribunal. The release of the two leaders was widely interpreted as a conciliatory gesture by the Government towards the Islamist opposition. In August the UN Secretary-General, Kofi Annan, angered the Algerian Government by suggesting that the UN might consider some form of intervention in Algeria in order to stem the dramatic escalation of violence. In September Madani offered in an open letter to Annan to appeal for an immediate truce. Shortly afterwards Madani was once again confined to house arrest. (Annan subsequently announced that the UN would not be considering intervention in Algeria.)

The level of violence intensified in mid-1997, with civilians increasingly becoming the target of attacks by armed Islamists. There were numerous massacres in villages to the south and west of Algiers, resulting in the deaths of hundreds of civilians and the kidnapping of many young women for 'temporary marriage'. An estimated 300 civilians were killed in August during a massacre in the Blida region; in September another 200 died during an attack on a suburb of Algiers. In late September the Armée islamique du salut (AIS, the armed wing of the FIS) declared a cease-fire, effective from October, in an attempt to expose members of the GIA as the principal perpetrators of the recent civilian massacres. The GIA admitted responsibility for the massacres, which it insisted were 'God's work'.

Elections to regional and municipal authorities took place in October 1997, at which, according to official results, the RND won more than one-half of the seats contested. All the main opposition parties, including the FLN and the MSP, accused the authorities of manipulating the results in favour of the RND, and disputed the reported high rate of voter participation (officially estimated at 66.2% of the electorate). In the following weeks several thousand people demonstrated in Algiers to protest against the alleged electoral fraud. The RND's political dominance was consolidated with appointment of the Council of the Nation in late December. Of the Council's 96 seats indirectly elected by regional and municipal authorities, 80 were won by the RND, 10 by the FLN, four by the FFS and two by the MSP; President Zéroual appointed the remaining 48 members. Abdelkader Bensalah resigned as President of the RND at the party's first congress, held in April 1998. Muhammad Tahar Benbaibeche was appointed RND Secretary-General, but the election of a successor to Bensalah was postponed. In the following month the authorities disbanded some 30 political groupings, including Ettahaddi and the PSD, for failing to satisfy the legal requirements concerning political associations.

In June 1998 there were violent protests in the Kabyle region following the assassination of Lounes Matoub, a popular Berber singer and an outspoken critic of both the Government and the fundamentalist Islamist movement. There were further protests in July when controversial legislation on the compulsory use of the Arabic language in public life (see above) came into effect. Berber activists in the Kabyle fiercely opposed the 'arabization' policy and demanded the recognition of Tamazight as an official language. In mid-September 1998 President Zéroual announced that a presidential election would be held before March 1999, nearly two years ahead of schedule. Although there were reports that Zéroual had been in ill health, most analysts suggested that the announcement had been prompted primarily by a power struggle within the regime between the faction loyal to the President (including his close adviser, Gen. Muhammad Betchine, and Prime Minister Ouyahia) and that of Lt-Gen. Muhammad Lamari, the Chief of Staff of the Army. In late October Zéroual declared that the presidential election would be postponed until April 1999 to allow political parties to prepare their campaigns. In December 1998 Ouyahia resigned; he was replaced as premier by Smail Hamdani, a widely respected senior politician and former diplomat. A new, largely unaltered Council of Ministers was subsequently appointed.

A total of 47 candidates registered to contest the presidential election; however, the Constitutional Council declared only seven eligible to stand . Abdelaziz Bouteflika, who commanded the support of the mainstream FLN and the RND, was also believed to have the support of the military establishment (he had declined a proposal by the armed forces to assume the presidency in 1994). Although the senior generals had decided not to nominate a member of the armed forces for the presidency, public support for Bouteflika by retired members of the armed forces gave rise to widespread cynicism regarding the military's assurances of its neutrality. The other candidates were: the FFS leader, Hocine Aït Ahmed; former Prime Minister Mokdad Sifi; a veteran of the war of independence, Youcef Khateb; Mouloud Hamrouche, who enjoyed the support of the reformist wing of the FLN; Ahmed Taleb Ibrahimi, a former Minister of Foreign Affairs who received support from the proscribed FIS; and Abdallah Djaballah, the leader of Nahdah, who was subsequently removed from office following the decision of senior members of the party to support Bouteflika's candidacy, and who formed a new party, the Mouvement de la réforme nationale (MRN), to promote his candidature. Following the exclusion of its leader, Sheikh Mafoud Nahnah, from the presidential election, on the grounds that he had not taken part in the war of independence (despite his candidacy in the 1995 election), the Islamist MSP eventually announced its support for Bouteflika. Bouteflika thus enjoyed the support of the four main political parties, as well as that of the UGTA and several political associations.

On the eve of the election, which took place on 15 April 1999, Bouteflika's six rivals withdrew their candidacies after Zéroual refused to postpone the poll following allegations of massive electoral fraud in favour of Bouteflika. Voting papers were, nevertheless, distributed for all seven candidates, and no official boycott of the election was organized. The credibility of the poll was, however, seriously diminished, and Bouteflika announced that he would accept the presidency only if there were both a high rate of voter participation and a large majority in his favour. According to official results, Bouteflika won 73.8% of the votes cast (his closest rival, Ibrahimi, secured 12.5%). However, this figure, together with the estimated official turn-out of more than 60%, was immediately disputed by his opponents, who maintained that only 23.3% of the registered electorate had participated, and that Bouteflika had received only 28% of the votes cast, compared with 20% for Ibrahimi. Bouteflika none the less accepted the presidency on 16 April. On the following day there were clashes between protesters and the security forces after the authorities banned a planned peaceful protest organized by the opposition parties. At his inauguration, on 27 April, Bouteflika reiterated his commitment to national reconciliation to end the civil conflict in Algeria, but pledged to continue the military campaign against terrorists and reaffirmed that the FIS would not be legalized.

Following clandestine negotiations between the Government and representatives of the FIS, in June 1999 the AIS announced the permanent cessation of its armed struggle against the Government. In July President Bouteflika announced plans for national reconciliation initiative, which some believed to be linked to the AIS truce. Bouteflika's peace plans were incorporated in a Law on Civil Concord, promulgated in July, whereby there was to be an amnesty for members of armed Islamist groups who surrendered within a six-month deadline and who were not implicated in mass killings, rape or bomb attacks on public places (perpetrators of such crimes would receive reduced sentences). The legislation was submitted for approval in a national referendum held on 16 September, when 98.6% of those who voted (85% of the electorate) indicated their support for Bouteflika's approach to restoring peace. However, critics of the Government dismissed the referendum as a device to legitimize Bouteflika's appointment to the presidency.

In his first months in office Bouteflika exhibited unprecedented candour, admitting in August 1999 that the civil conflict of the past seven years had resulted in the deaths of at least 100,000 people (hitherto the authorities had put the number of deaths at 30,000), as well as acknowledging that state monopolies were being abused by certain individuals. He replaced 22 of the 48 provincial governors (*walis*) in August, in an attempt to eradicate corruption, and dismissed a further 20 provincial (*wilayat*) general secretaries and 318 heads of administrative districts (*dairas*) in October. Furthermore, Bouteflika

announced that he would resign in January 2000 if he had failed by then to restore peace in Algeria and 'revolutionize' the country's economy. At the end of October 1999 Bouteflika pardoned 5,000 prisoners (although including only 152 condemned for offences contained within the Law on Civil Concord), bringing the total released since his installation as President to more than 14,500.

Abdelkader Hachani, the most senior member of the FIS at liberty, was assassinated in Algiers in November 1999. Hachani had favoured dialogue with all political interests, and was believed to have been involved in a secret political dialogue between the Government and the FIS. Although a member of the principal GIA faction was subsequently arrested and charged with the murder, several of Hachani's relatives claimed that the security forces, which had reportedly kept the FIS official under surveillance following his release from detention, had perpetrated the assassination.

The long delay, following Bouteflika's accession to the presidency, in appointing a new government provoked frequent media speculation that members of the military high command were consistently opposing the proposed composition of a new administration that might diminish the generals' influence on affairs of State. Such assertions were denied by the President, who finally named his Council of Ministers in December 1999. Led by Ahmed Benbitour, a former Minister of Finance, the new Government comprised members of the FLN, the MSP, Nahdah, the RCD, the ANR, the RND and the PRA, all of which had supported Bouteflika's presidential campaign.

In early January 2000, following discussions between representatives of the Government, the army and the AIS, an agreement was reached whereby the AIS pledged to disband in return for the restoration of full civil and political rights to its former members. It was estimated that some 1,500–3,000 rebels were to be granted a full pardon under the agreement, some of whom where to be temporarily enlisted in an auxiliary unit to assist the security forces in apprehending members of the GIA and of a breakaway group from the GIA, the Groupe salafiste pour la prédication et le combat (GSPC, or Da'wa wal Djihad). In mid-January, following the expiry of the amnesty period specified under the Law on Civil Concord, the Algerian Government stated that 80% of members of armed groups had surrendered. The armed forces subsequently launched a concerted assault on rebel strongholds in the north-east and south-west of the country, in an attempt to eliminate remaining anti-Government factions. Meanwhile, the Government estimated that around 600 people (many of them civilians) had been killed between July 1999 and January 2000, mostly in incidents connected to the GIA and the GSPC.

In late February 2000 President Bouteflika announced wide-ranging changes to the military high command, which included the replacement of the commanders of four of the country's six military regions. The most senior positions, however, remained unaltered. In March Cherif Rahmani, the only regional governor to hold ministerial rank, was replaced as Governor of Algiers by Abdelmalek Nourani, who (in common with the other *walis*) was to be responsible to the Ministry of the Interior and Local Authorities. In May the Government announced its refusal to grant legal recognition to al-Wafa wa al-Adl (Wafa), a new political organization formed by Ibrahimi, on the grounds that it was simply a reconstitution under another name of the outlawed FIS.

Violence persisted following the expiry of the deadline for amnesty under the Law on Civil Concord; thousands of Islamist fighters remained at large, and fears were expressed in some quarters that the conflict between militant Islamist groups and the armed forces showed signs of escalating. Indications by Bouteflika in early 2000 that an amnesty agreement with the GSPC was under consideration, on the grounds that the organization's offensives had targeted the security forces rather than civilians, were apparently refuted by the group's leader, Hassan Hattab. More than 40 people were killed in the first few days of April, and later that month the Minister of Agriculture reportedly escaped an assassination attempt while visiting a village south-west of Algiers. In July an article in the daily *Jeune Indépendant*, citing unofficial sources, claimed that some 1,100 civilians and an estimated 2,000 terrorists had been killed in Algeria since the expiry of the general amnesty in January. Later that month another newspaper stated that it had calculated the number of people killed by terrorist operations whose deaths had been reported in the press to total 777 between July 1999 and June 2000. However, both Amnesty International and the Fédération internationale des ligues des droits de l'Homme (FIDH), representatives of which visited Algeria in May and June 2000 respectively, reported that they had noted a significant decline in violence and a clear improvement in the country's human rights situation. The head of the Amnesty International delegation none the less expressed concern about the fate of an estimated 22,000 missing persons who had disappeared since 1992. Human rights organizations had been denied access to Algeria for several years; Amnesty International had notably been denounced on several occasions by the official Algerian media after issuing reports considered unbalanced in their assessments of abuses perpetrated by the armed forces and Islamist fighters. In November, at the end of a further visit to Algeria, representatives of Amnesty International expressed frustration at what they considered a lack of progress in investigating such issues as disappearances and secret detentions, stating notably that the authorities had made no response to requests for meetings with officers of the security forces.

Reports emerged in mid-August 2000 that the Algerian authorities had foiled a coup attempt; the international Arabic daily *Az-Zaman* reported that 25 officers who had deserted from the Algerian army had been arrested and detained for their part in the alleged plot.

Benbitour resigned the premiership in late August 2000. He was replaced by Ali Benflis, a former Minister of Justice who had directed Bouteflika's presidential campaign and who was subsequently appointed director of the presidential cabinet. The composition of the new Government remained largely unchanged: most senior ministers retained their posts, a notable exception being the appointment as Minister of Foreign Affairs of Abdelaziz Belkadem, a former head of the legislature who was reputedly a principal architect of the Sant' Egidio pact, in place of Youcef Yousfi, who now became Minister-delegate to the Prime Minister. Cherif Rahmani, the former Governor of Algiers, remained in government as Minister of Regional Development and the Environment. Rumours of tensions between Bouteflika and the outgoing premier were apparently confirmed when Benbitour subsequently claimed, in a letter published by the state-owned daily *El-Moudjahid*, that Bouteflika's draft presidential decree regarding financial transactions conflicted with his economic revival strategy, as approved by the Government, and maintained that Bouteflika had attempted to establish a 'parallel administration'. At the end of October, to commemorate the anniversary of the beginning of the revolution, Bouteflika pardoned 4,000 detainees. In November the Minister of State for the Interior and Local Authorities ordered the closure of all offices of the Wafa party and confiscated all its documents.

A sharp escalation in violence at the end of 2000 added weight to the arguments of those who believed that the civil conflict in Algeria, after nine years, was far from resolution. Among more than 200 deaths recorded among Islamist fighters, government forces and civilians during the first three weeks of Ramadan were those of 16 pupils and their warden at a technical college in Médéa, who in mid-December were massacred in their dormitory by armed gunmen. The first killings of foreigners for almost two years were reported in early January 2001, when four Russian expatriate workers were killed in the Annaba region. At least 125 deaths were reported as a result of continuing violence in that month. Meanwhile, there were persistent rumours of tensions between Bouteflika, the military high command and those parties opposed to any appeasement with militant fundamentalists, with some commentators suggesting that the army generals might seek to remove the President from office, regarding him as too willing to make concessions to the Islamists.

During the late 1970s and early 1980s the protracted struggle in Western Sahara embittered Algeria's relations with France, which supported the claims of Morocco. Algeria also criticized French military intervention elsewhere in Africa, while further grievances were the trade imbalance in favour of the former colonial power, and recurrent disputes over the price of Algerian exports of gas to France; the French Government's determination to reduce the number of Algerians residing in France was another source of contention. In 1986 the France co-operated with the Algerian authorities by expelling 13 members of the MDA, and in 1986–88 it suppressed three MDA newspapers that were being published in France. In 1987 the Algerian Government agreed to release the assets of former French settlers which had been 'frozen' since independence, and to allow former settlers to sell their land to the Algerian State; in

return, financial assistance was provided by France. The Algerian military take-over in January 1992 was welcomed by the French Government, and French economic and political support for the Algerian regime increased in early 1993, following the appointment of Edouard Balladur as Prime Minister of France. Alleged Islamist militants residing in France continued to be prosecuted, and in August 1994, following the killing of five French embassy employees in Algiers, 26 suspected Algerian extremists were interned in northern France; 20 of them were subsequently expelled to Burkina Faso. In September the French embassy in Algiers confirmed that entry visas would be issued to Algerians only in exceptional cases. By November the number of French nationals killed by Islamist militants in Algeria had reached 21 and the French Government urged its citizens to leave Algeria. An Air France aircraft was hijacked in Algiers in December by members of the GIA, resulting in the deaths of three passengers and, later, in the killing of the hijackers by French security forces when the aircraft landed in France. A series of arrests made in early 1995 by French police in an attempt to dismantle support networks for Islamist militants in Algeria and Tunisia did not prevent an intensification of the GIA campaign of violence in France. The GIA claimed responsibility for numerous bomb attacks across France between July and November, in which seven people were killed and more than 160 injured. The French authorities made a number of arrests and, in a widely-publicized attempted arrest, shot and killed an Algerian-born French resident whom they alleged to be a leading figure in the bombing campaign. British police also arrested two Algerian nationals suspected of involvement in the French bomb attacks. French nationals in Algeria continued to be the target of attacks by Islamist militants, and in May 1996 seven French clergymen (abducted by the GIA in March) were killed, despite apparent efforts by the French authorities to negotiate their release. In July Hervé de Charette, the French Minister of Foreign Affairs, made an official visit to Algeria, the first ministerial-level visit for three years. However, the success of the visit was marred by the assassination in August of Pierre Claverie, the French Roman Catholic Bishop of Oran, only hours after meeting de Charette. In December four people were killed and at least 45 were injured as a result of a bomb explosion on a passenger train in Paris, prompting speculation that the GIA had resumed its campaign of violence in France. The French authorities subsequently arrested numerous suspected Islamist activists. In early 1998 a French court sentenced 36 Islamist militants to terms of imprisonment of up to 10 years for providing logistical support for the bomb attacks in France in 1995. A further 138 people stood trial in France in September 1998, accused of criminal association with Algerian terrorists.

In June 1999 the French National Assembly voted unanimously to abandon the official claim that the eight-year struggle between Algerian nationalists and French troops, which began in November 1954, had been no more than 'an operation for keeping order' and thus admitted that France had indeed fought in the Algerian war of independence. Later in June the French Minister of Foreign Affairs, Hubert Védrine, visited Algeria and discussed with President Bouteflika plans to reopen the French consulates in Annaba and Oran. An apparent improvement in relations between Algeria and France was further signalled by a meeting in September between Bouteflika and the French President, Jacques Chirac, in New York (the first meeting between the leaders of the two countries since 1992). In November 1999 the President of the French Senate, Christian Poncelet, met Bouteflika in Algiers, and in January 2000 Algeria's Minister of Foreign Affairs, Youcef Yousfi, made the first official visit to France by an Algerian member of government for six years. In mid-June Bouteflika made a full state visit to France—the first of its kind by an Algerian Head of State—during which he addressed the French National Assembly and held talks with both Chirac and the French Prime Minister Lionel Jospin. Although the visit produced few tangible results, it was regarded as a success and an important step towards ending the diplomatic isolation imposed on Algeria following the military take-over in 1992. In November Gen. Jacques Massu, who had commanded French troops during the Battle of Algiers in 1957, stated in an interview with the French daily *Le Monde* that France should admit and condemn the use of torture during the conflict.

Relations with Spain were affected during the early 1980s by Spain's support for Morocco in the Western Sahara dispute, and by mutual suspicion that each country was harbouring opponents of the other's Government. In 1987 Algeria and Spain concluded an agreement allowing closer supervision of Algerian dissidents in Spain and of members of the Basque separatist movement Euskadi ta Askatasuna (ETA) in Algeria. In July 2000 the Spanish Prime Minister, José María Aznar López, became the first European head of government since 1992, to visit Algeria, where he met with Bouteflika to discuss bilateral economic co-operation.

During the 1980s Algeria attempted to achieve a closer relationship with the other countries of the Maghreb region (Libya, Mauritania, Morocco and Tunisia). In March 1983 Algeria and Tunisia signed the Maghreb Fraternity and Co-operation Treaty, establishing a basis for the creation of the long-discussed 'Great Arab Maghreb'; Mauritania signed the treaty in December. Relations with Morocco, however, continued to be affected by the dispute over Western Sahara. In May 1988 Algeria and Morocco restored diplomatic relations (severed in 1976) at ambassadorial level. Meeting in Algiers in June the five Heads of State of the Maghreb countries announced the formation of a Maghreb commission to examine areas of regional integration. In February 1989 the leaders signed a treaty establishing the Union du Maghreb arabe (UMA, see p. 310), with the aim of encouraging economic co-operation and eventually establishing a full customs union. The Algerian army's intervention in January 1992 to prevent an FIS victory in the general election provoked relief, among the Maghreb countries, in Tunisia and Morocco that the establishment of a neighbouring fundamentalist state had been pre-empted. Elsewhere in the region, Egypt particularly welcomed the military's action.

Morocco imposed entry visas on Algerian nationals in August 1994, following the murder of two Spanish tourists in Morocco, allegedly by Algerian Islamist extremists. Algeria reciprocated by closing the border between the two countries and imposing entry visas on Moroccan nationals. Tensions eased slightly in September when Algeria announced the appointment of a new ambassador to Morocco, and in early 1995 negotiations commenced on the development of bilateral co-operation. However, in December King Hassan of Morocco expressed his disapproval at Algeria's alleged continuing support for the independence of Western Sahara, and demanded that UMA activities be suspended. A UMA summit meeting, scheduled for later that month, was subsequently postponed. Indications of an improvement in relations were apparently enhanced in August 1998, when Prime Minister Ahmed Ouyahia received his Moroccan counterpart, Abd ar-Rahman el-Youssoufi, for talks. Following his accession to the presidency, Bouteflika initially attempted further to improve bilateral relations in a visit to the Moroccan capital to attend the funeral of the Moroccan King, Hassan II. However, the *rapprochement* was halted in August 1999, on the day when the imminent reopening of the common border was announced, by the massacre by the GIA of 29 civilians in the border region of Bechar. Bouteflika's public allegation that Morocco was providing sanctuary for for the perpetrators of the attack extended to accusations of drugs-trafficking and arms-dealing on the Algerian border. In September Bouteflika accused both Morocco and Tunisia of acting against the interests of the UMA by negotiating separate agreements with the European Union (EU). In February 2000 Algeria and Morocco both expressed their desire to improve bilateral relations, despite continued differences over the Western Sahara issue, and in April Bouteflika met with the new Moroccan ruler, King Muhammad, at the Africa-EU summit held in Cairo, Egypt. The two leaders agreed to establish joint committees, in an attempt to reduce the number of violent incidents on their mutual border, and joint security operations involving the two countries' armed forces began along the border in May.

In December 1996 the EU and Algeria began negotiations on Algeria's participation in a Euro-Mediterranean free-trade zone. In early 1998 EU delegations visited Algeria to express concern about the escalation of violence in the country. In October the EU agreed to commence negotiations with the Algerian Government with the aim of concluding an association agreement. In November 1999 an EU delegation visited Algiers, and negotiations on a trade partnership agreement resumed in April 2000. In January 2001 the President of the European Commission, Romano Prodi, visited Algeria, where he signed the financing protocols for a number of joint projects.

During 2000 President Bouteflika, in his capacity as Chairman of the OAU Assembly of Heads of State and Government, assumed a major role in brokering an end to the two-year territorial conflict between Ethiopia and Eritrea (qq.v.).

Representatives of the two countries concluded a cease-fire agreement in Algiers in June, and returned there in December to sign a peace accord.

Government

Under the 1976 Constitution (with modifications adopted by the National People's Assembly in June 1979 and with further amendments approved by popular referendum in November 1988, February 1989 and in November 1996), Algeria is a multi-party state, with parties subject to approval by the Ministry of the Interior. The Head of State is the President of the Republic, who is elected by universal adult suffrage for a five-year term, renewable once. The President presides over a Council of Ministers and a High Security Council. The President must appoint a Prime Minister as Head of Government, who appoints a Council of Ministers. The bicameral legislature consists of the 380-member National People's Assembly and the 144-member Council of the Nation. The members of the National People's Assembly are elected by universal, direct, secret suffrage for a five-year term. Two-thirds of the members of the Council of the Nation are elected by indirect, secret suffrage from regional and municipal authorities; the remainder are appointed by the President of the Republic. The Council's term in office is six years; one-half of its members are replaced every three years. Both the Head of Government and the parliamentary chambers may initiate legislation. Legislation must be deliberated upon respectively by the National People's Assembly and the Council of the Nation before promulgation. The country is divided into 48 departments (*wilayat*), which are, in turn, sub-divided into communes. Each *wilaya* and commune has an elected assembly.

Defence

In August 2000 the estimated strength of the armed forces was 124,000 (including 75,000 conscripts), comprising an army of 107,000, a navy of about 7,000 and an air force of 10,000. The 2000 defence budget was estimated at 138,000m. dinars. Military service is compulsory for 18 months. There are paramilitary forces of 181,200, controlled by the Ministry of Defence and the Directorate of National Security, and an estimated 100,000 self-defence militia and communal guards.

Economic Affairs

In 1998, according to estimates by the World Bank, Algeria's gross national product (GNP), measured at average 1996–98 prices, was US $46,389m., equivalent to $1,550 per head (or $4,595 on an international purchasing-power parity basis). During 1990–98, it was estimated, GNP per head declined, in real terms, at an average annual rate of 1.0%. Over the same period the population increased at an average rate of 2.6% per year. In 1999 GNP was estimated at $46,500m., equivalent to $1,550 per head. Algeria's gross domestic product (GDP) increased, in real terms, at an average annual rate of 1.6% in 1990–99. Real GDP rose by 5.1% in 1998 and by 3.3% in 1999.

Agriculture (including forestry and fishing) contributed 11.4% of GDP in 1999, and employed 24.6% of the labour force in that year. Domestic production of food crops is insufficient to meet the country's requirements. The principal crops are wheat, barley and potatoes. Dates are Algeria's principal non-hydrocarbon export; olives, citrus fruits and grapes are also grown, and wine has been an important export since the French colonial era. During 1990–99 agricultural GDP increased at an average annual rate of 3.0%. Agricultural GDP increased by 11.4% in 1998 (as the sector recovered from drought in the previous year), although the rate of growth slowed to 2.7% in 1999.

Industry (including mining, manufacturing, construction and power) contributed 50.7% of GDP in 1999, and engaged 31.2% of the employed population in 1987. During 1990–99 industrial GDP decreased at an average annual rate of 0.1%.

The mining sector engaged only 1.6% of the employed population in 1987, but provides almost all of Algeria's export earnings. Petroleum and natural gas, which together provided 30.4% of GDP in 1999, are overwhelmingly Algeria's principal exports, providing an estimated 96.6% of total export earnings in that year. Algeria's proven reserves of petroleum were 9,200m. barrels at the end of 1999, sufficient to maintain output (at that year's levels) for more than 20 years. Proven reserves of natural gas at the end of 1999 totalled 4,520,000m. cu m. Algeria currently transports natural gas through two pipelines to Spain and Italy, and feasibility studies were to be undertaken in 2001 regarding the possible construction of a further pipeline to supply other parts of Europe via Spain. Substantial reserves of iron ore, phosphates, barite (barytes), lead, zinc, mercury, salt, marble and industrial minerals are also exploited. The exploitation of gold reserves was due to commence early in 2001. The GDP of the hydrocarbons sector increased by 4.0% in 1998 and by 6.2% in 1999, while that of other mining activities expanded by 5.5% in 1998 but declined by 3.0% in 1999.

Manufacturing engaged 12.2% of the employed population in 1987, and provided 11% of GDP in 1999. In 1996 food products, beverages and tobacco accounted for 52.3% of the gross value of manufacturing output, while metals, metal products, machinery and transport equipment provided 14.7%. During 1990–98 the GDP of the manufacturing sector declined at an average annual rate of 9.0%.

Energy is derived principally from natural gas and petroleum. However, nuclear power and hydroelectricity provide additional sources of energy. Imports of energy products comprised only an estimated 1.3% of the value of merchandise imports in 1999.

Services engaged 46.0% of the employed labour force in 1987, and provided 37.9% of GDP in 1999. During 1990–99 the combined GDP of the service sectors increased at an average annual rate of 3.0%. In 1999, according to IMF estimates, Algeria recorded a visible trade surplus of US $3,400m., and the current account of the balance of payments was in balance. In 1997 the principal source of imports continued to be France (providing 23.1% of the total); other important suppliers were the USA, Italy, Spain, Canada and Germany. Italy was the principal market for exports (20.6%) in that year; other major purchasers were the USA, France, Spain, the Netherlands and Turkey. The principal exports in 1997 were mineral fuels, lubricants, etc., which accounted for 97.2% of total export revenue (petroleum and derivatives 57.2%, gas 39.9%). Other exports included vegetables, tobacco, hides and dates. The principal imports in that year were machinery and transport equipment, food and live animals, and basic manufactures.

In 1999 Algeria's overall budget deficit was 16,500m. dinars, equivalent to 0.5% of GDP. Algeria's total external debt at the end of 1998 amounted to US $30,665m., of which $28,469m. was long-term public debt. In that year the cost of debt-servicing represented 42.0% of the value of exports of goods and services. The annual rate of inflation averaged 7.8% in 1995–99. Consumer prices increased by an average of 5.0% in 1998, but inflation slowed to 2.5% in 1999. An estimated 28% of the labour force were unemployed in 1998.

Algeria is a member of the Union of the Arab Maghreb (see p. 310), which aims to promote economic integration of member states, and also of the Organization of the Petroleum Exporting Countries (OPEC, see p. 269).

The dramatic fall in international prices for petroleum during 1998 emphasized Algeria's continued over-dependence on the hydrocarbons sector and led to the erosion of foreign exchange reserves. None the less, a recovery in agricultural output, in conjunction with growth in the non-oil-related industrial sector (the first since 1991), contributed to the continued expansion of overall GDP, while a credit equivalent to some US $300m., agreed in May 1999 by the IMF under its Compensatory and Contingency Financing Facility, was intended to relieve the shortfall in export revenue arising from the oil-price crisis. By the time of Abdelaziz Bouteflika's inauguration as President in April 1999, there was a degree of optimism regarding Algeria's economic prospects, afforded by signs of a recovery in petroleum prices, together with hopes that a return of domestic political stability would attract foreign investment to both the hydrocarbons and non-oil sectors and thus enable economic reconstruction and form the basis for sustained growth. The privatization of state-owned enterprises and liberalization of the banking, energy, transport and telecommunications sectors continued during 2000, while the commencement of trading on the Algiers Stock Exchange in mid-1999 was regarded as indicative of the commitment to the participation of private investors in the Algerian economy. Owing to the sustained recovery in petroleum prices, Algeria registered a primary budget surplus in 1999,

and was expected to have done so again in 2000. Furthermore, Algeria was able both to reduce its external debt and to increase its foreign-exchange reserves. GDP growth of 5% was projected for 2000. An acceleration of the economic reform process, announced by the Algerian Government in early 2001, incorporated plans to privatize more than 180 companies by 2004; among organizations intended to be opened to private equity notably included the state hydrocarbons company, SONATRACH. None the less, the apparent failure of the Bouteflika administration to bring about a lasting civil peace remained a major deterrent to foreign investment, regarded by the country's official creditors as essential to promoting the economic diversification that would permit Algeria's chronic economic difficulties, such as unemployment (estimated at 40% of the work-force by official sources), to be addressed.

Social Welfare

Since 1974 all Algerian citizens have had the right to free medical care. In 1995, according to WHO estimates, there were 84.6 physicians per 100,000 population, 297.8 nurses per 100,000 population, and 28.2 dentists per 100,000 population. In 1999 the central Government's current budgetary expenditure included 31,200m. dinars (3.2% of total current expenditure) on hospitals, 36,200m. dinars (3.8%) on family allowances and 59,900m. dinars (6.2%) on war veterans' pensions.

Education

Education, in the national language (Arabic), is officially compulsory for nine years between six and 15 years of age. Primary education begins at the age of six and lasts for six years. Secondary education begins at 12 years of age and lasts for up to six years (comprising two cycles of three years each). In 1996 the total enrolment at primary and secondary schools was equivalent to 86% of the school-age population (90% of boys; 82% of girls). Enrolment at primary schools in that year included 94% of children in the relevant age-group (97% of boys; 91% of girls), while enrolment at secondary schools included 56% of children in the relevant age-group (58% of boys; 54% of girls). Some 12.5% of total planned expenditure in the 1997 administrative budget was allocated to education and training. Priority is being given to teacher-training, to the development of technical and scientific teaching programmes, and to adult literacy and training schemes. In addition to the 10 universities, there are seven other *centres universitaires* and a number of technical colleges. In 1995/96 a total of 347,410 students were enrolled in higher education. In 1995, according to UNESCO estimates, the average rate of adult illiteracy was 41.6% (males 28.9%; females 54.6%).

Public Holidays

2001: 1 January (New Year), 6 March* (Id al-Adha, Feast of the Sacrifice), 26 March* (Islamic New Year), 4 April* (Ashoura), 1 May (Labour Day), 4 June* (Mouloud, Birth of Muhammad), 19 June (Ben Bella's Overthrow), 5 July (Independence), 15 October* (Leilat al-Meiraj, Ascension of Muhammad), 1 November (Anniversary of the Revolution), 17 November* (Ramadan begins), 17 December* (Id al-Fitr, end of Ramadan).

2002: 1 January (New Year), 23 February* (Id al-Adha, Feast of the Sacrifice), 15 March* (Islamic New Year), 24 March* (Ashoura), 1 May (Labour Day), 24 May* (Mouloud, Birth of Muhammad), 19 June (Ben Bella's Overthrow), 5 July (Independence), 4 October* (Leilat al-Meiraj, Ascension of Muhammad), 1 November (Anniversary of the Revolution), 6 November* (Ramadan begins), 6 December* (Id al-Fitr, end of Ramadan).

* Religious holidays, which are dependent on the Islamic lunar calendar, may differ by one or two days from the dates given.

Weights and Measures

The metric system is in force.

Statistical Survey

Source (unless otherwise stated): Office National des Statistiques, 8 rue des Moussebiline, BP 55, Algiers; tel. (2) 64-77-90; e-mail ons@onssiege.ons.dz; internet www.ons.dz.

Area and Population

AREA, POPULATION AND DENSITY

Area (sq km)	2,381,741*
Population (census results)†	
20 April 1987	23,038,942
25 June 1998 (provisional)	
Males	14,471,318
Females	14,801,025
Total	29,272,343
Population (official estimates at mid-year)	
1997	29,045,000
1998	29,507,000
1999	29,950,000
Density (per sq km) at mid-1999	12.6

* 919,595 sq miles.
† Excluding Algerian nationals residing abroad, numbering an estimated 828,000 at 1 January 1978.

POPULATION BY WILAYA (ADMINISTRATIVE DISTRICT)

(provisional, 1998 census)*

	Population
Adrar	311,952
Ain Defla	659,182
Ain Témouchent	326,611
Algiers.	2,561,992
Annaba	555,485
Batna	968,820
al-Bayadh	226,528
Béchar	230,482
Béjaia	848,560
Biskra	588,648
Blida	787,069
Bordj Bou Arreridj	559,928
Bouira	626,586
Boumerdes	645,497
Chlef	884,978
Djelfa	860,981
Guelma	432,721
Ghardaia	296,926
Illizi	33,960
Jijel	574,336
Khenchela	348,122
Laghouat	327,634
Mascara	677,099
Médéa	721,861
Mila	680,815
Mostaganem	629,445
M'Sila	815,045
Naâma	165,578
Ouahran (Oran)	1,155,464
Ouargla	438,831
al-Oued	529,842
Oum al-Bouaghi	533,711
Qacentina (Constantine). . . .	815,032
Relizane	639,253
Saida	280,752
Sétif	1,315,940
Sidi-bel-Abbès	529,704
Skikda	787,118

— *continued*	Population
Souk Ahras	373,033
Tamanrasset	151,814
at-Tarf	354,213
Tébessa	550,021
Tiaret	728,513
Tindouf	32,004†
Tipaza	505,382
Tissemsilt	261,298
Tizi-Ouzou	1,101,059
Tlemcen	846,942
Total	**29,276,767**

* The provisional figure for the total population was subsequently revised to 29,272,343.
† Excluding Sahrawi refugees in camps (estimated at 170,000 in 1988).

PRINCIPAL TOWNS (provisional, population at 1998 census)

Algiers (el-Djezaïr,		Djelfa	154,265
capital) . .	1,519,570	Tébassa (Tbessa) .	153,246
Oran (Ouahran) . .	655,852	Blida (el-Boulaïda) .	153,083
Constantine (Qacen-		Skikda . . .	152,335
tina) . . .	462,187	Béjaia . . .	147,076
Batna . . .	242,514	Tiaret (Tihert) .	145,332
Annaba . . .	215,083	Chlef . . .	133,874
Sétif (Stif) . .	211,859	el-Buni . . .	133,471
Sidi-bel-Abbès . .	180,260	Béchar . . .	131,010
Biskra (Beskra) .	170,956		

BIRTHS, MARRIAGES AND DEATHS*

	Registered live births†		Registered marriages		Registered deaths†	
	Number	Rate (per 1,000)	Number	Rate (per 1,000)	Number	Rate (per 1,000)
1992 . .	799,000	30.4	159,380	6.1	160,000	6.1
1993 . .	775,000	28.2	153,137	5.7	168,000	6.3
1994 . .	776,000	28.2	147,954	5.4	180,000	6.6
1995 . .	711,000	25.3	152,786	5.5	180,000	6.4
1996 . .	654,000	22.9	156,870	5.5	172,000	6.0
1997 . .	654,000	22.5	157,831	5.4	178,000	6.1
1998 . .	620,000	21.0	158,298	5.4	172,000	5.8
1999 . .	605,000	21.2	163,126	5.5	168,000	5.6

* Figures refer to the Algerian population only. Birth registration is estimated to be at least 90% complete, but the registration of marriages and deaths is incomplete. According to UN estimates, the average annual rates per 1,000 in 1990–95 were: births 30.8; deaths 6.4.
† Excluding live-born infants dying before registration of birth.

Expectation of life (UN estimates, years at birth, 1990–95): 67.1 (males 66.0; females 68.3) (Source: UN, *World Population Prospects: The 1998 Revision*).

ECONOMICALLY ACTIVE POPULATION (1987 census)*

	Males	Females	Total
Agriculture, hunting, forestry and fishing	714,947	9,753	724,699
Mining and quarrying	64,685	3,142	67,825
Manufacturing	471,471	40,632	512,105
Electricity, gas and water.	40,196	1,579	41,775
Construction.	677,211	12,372	689,586
Trade, restaurants and hotels.	376,590	14,399	390,990
Transport, storage and communications	207,314	9,029	216,343
Financing, insurance, real estate and business services	125,426	17,751	143,178
Community, social and personal services	945,560	234,803	1,180,364
Activities not adequately defined	149,241	83,718	232,959
Total employed	3,772,641	427,183	4,199,824
Unemployed	1,076,018	65,260	1,141,278
Total labour force	4,848,659	492,443	5,341,102

* Employment data relate to persons aged 6 years and over; those for unemployment relate to persons aged 16 to 64 years. Estimates have been made independently, so the totals may not be the sum of the component parts.

1997 (sample survey, '000 persons, July–September): Agriculture, hunting, forestry and fishing 884; Mining and quarrying, manufacturing, electricity, gas and water 584; Construction 588; Trade, restaurants and hotels 838; Government services 1,317; Other services 1,496; Total employed 5,708 (males 4,819, females 889); Unemployed 2,049 (males 1,769, females 280); Total labour force 7,757 (males 6,588, females 1,169). Figures refer to males aged 15 to 60 years and females aged 15 to 55 years.

Mid-1999 (estimates in '000): Agriculture, etc. 2,499; Total labour force 10,166 (Source: FAO).

Agriculture

PRINCIPAL CROPS ('000 metric tons)

	1997	1998	1999
Wheat	662	2,280	1,100
Barley	191	700	410
Oats	17	45	29
Potatoes	948	1,100	996
Pulses	28	45	38
Rapeseed*	100	100	100
Olives	319	124	363
Tomatoes	689	752	955
Pumpkins, squash and gourds	82	82*	82*
Cucumbers and gherkins	35	42	40*
Green chillies and peppers	191	157	156
Onions (dry)	352	393	382
Carrots	125	141	135
Other vegetables	546	548*	553*
Melons and watermelons	401	502	538
Grapes	192	147	178
Dates	303	387	428
Apples	66	75	87
Pears	47	60	82
Peaches and nectarines	39	45	61
Oranges	243	280	307
Tangerines, mandarins, clementines and satsumas	90	111	115
Apricots	40	58	74
Other fruits	143	137	146
Tobacco (leaves)	8	7	6

* FAO estimate(s).

Source: FAO.

LIVESTOCK ('000 head, year ending September)

	1997	1998	1999
Sheep	16,755	17,700	18,200
Goats	3,122	3,200	3,400
Cattle	1,255	1,317	1,650
Horses	52	55*	55*
Mules	69	70*	70*
Asses	199	200*	200*
Camels	151	150*	150*

Poultry (million)*: 88 in 1997; 125 in 1998; 105 in 1999.

* FAO estimate(s).

Source: FAO.

LIVESTOCK PRODUCTS ('000 metric tons)

	1997	1998	1999
Beef and veal	102	103	117
Mutton and lamb	167	167	163
Goat meat	12	12	12
Poultry meat	205	220	200
Other meat	10	10	10
Cows' milk	850	984	1,040
Sheep's milk	175	180	220
Goats' milk	154	160	143
Poultry eggs*	100	117	120
Honey	1	2	2
Wool (greasy)	20	22	23
Cattle hides	11	11	13
Sheepskins	23	22	24
Goatskins	2	2	2

* FAO estimates.

Source: FAO.

Forestry

ROUNDWOOD REMOVALS ('000 cubic metres, excl. bark)

	1996	1997	1998
Sawlogs, veneer logs and logs for sleepers	60	68	68
Pulpwood	91	85	85
Other industrial wood	277	285	291
Fuel wood	2,187	2,239	2,291
Total	2,615	2,677	2,735

Sawnwood production ('000 cubic metres, incl. railway sleepers): 13 per year (FAO estimates) in 1980–98.

Source: FAO, *Yearbook of Forest Products*.

Fishing

('000 metric tons, live weight)

	1996	1997	1998
Capture	116.4	91.6	92.3
Bogue	1.4	1.6	3.2
Jack and horse mackerels	3.6	5.5	4.8
Sardinellas	8.2	15.7	10.0
European pilchard (sardine)	49.9	49.1	49.3
European anchovy	1.3	1.9	3.5
Crustaceans and molluscs	2.6	2.9	3.6
Aquaculture	0.3*	0.3*	0.3
Total catch	116.7*	91.9*	92.6

* FAO estimate.

Source: FAO, *Yearbook of Fishery Statistics*.

Mining

('000 metric tons, unless otherwise indicated)

	1995	1996	1997
Hard coal	22*	22	n.a.
Crude petroleum. . . .	36,152	37,469	37,656
Natural gas (petajoules) . .	2,431	2,619	2,955
Iron ore:			
gross weight*	2,200	2,250	2,260
metal content† . . .	1,100	1,100	1,100
Lead concentrates†‡ . .	1.4	1.0	1.0
Zinc concentrates†‡ . .	7.2	5.9	6.0
Mercury (metric tons)† . .	292	300	370*
Phosphate rock . . .	757	760†	n.a.

* Provisional or estimated data.
† Data from the US Bureau of Mines.
‡ Figures refer to the metal content of ores or concentrates.

Sources: UN, *Industrial Commodity Statistics Yearbook* and *Monthly Bulletin of Statistics*.

Industry

SELECTED PRODUCTS ('000 metric tons, unless otherwise indicated)

	1994	1995	1996
Olive oil (crude)	23	16	50
Refined sugar	193	198	362
Wine*	50	57	39
Beer ('000 hectolitres) . .	398	n.a.	n.a.
Soft drinks ('000 hectolitres) . .	901	n.a.	n.a.
Cigarettes (metric tons) . .	16,345	n.a.	n.a.
Footwear—excl. rubber ('000 pairs)	6,467	n.a.	n.a.
Nitrogenous fertilizers (a)† . .	62	31	8
Phosphate fertilizers (b)† . .	179	n.a.	n.a.
Naphthas	4,500‡	4,400‡	4,420
Motor spirit (petrol) . . .	2,907	2,576	2,370
Kerosene	200‡	250‡	300
Jet fuel	900‡	784‡	750
Distillate fuel oils . . .	6,896	7,189	6,432
Residual fuel oils . . .	5,810	5,535	5,733
Lubricating oils . . .	140‡	150‡	150
Petroleum bitumen (asphalt) . .	250‡	260‡	270
Liquefied petroleum gas:			
from natural gas plants .	4,510	4,384	4,423
from petroleum refineries .	520	510‡	520
Cement	6,093	6,200‡	n.a.
Pig-iron for steel-making . . .	919	940§	800§
Crude steel (ingots) . . .	772	827§	675§
Zinc—unwrought . . .	20.1	30.0§	25.0§
Refrigerators for household use			
('000)	119	n.a.	n.a.
Radio receivers ('000) . .	107	n.a.	n.a.
Television receivers ('000) . .	165	n.a.	n.a.
Buses and coaches—assembled			
(number)	468	n.a.	n.a.
Lorries—assembled (number) . .	1,230	n.a.	n.a.
Electric energy (million kWh) . .	19,888	19,714	20,654

1997 ('000 metric tons): Olive oil 49*; Wine 46*; Pig-iron for steel-making 700§; Crude steel (ingots) 427§; Zinc—unwrought 25.0§.

* Data from FAO, *Production Yearbook*.
† Production in terms of (a) nitrogen or (b) phosphoric acid.
‡ Provisional or estimated data.
§ Data from the US Bureau of Mines.

Source: mainly UN, *Industrial Commodity Statistics Yearbook*.

Finance

CURRENCY AND EXCHANGE RATES
Monetary Units
100 centimes = 1 Algerian dinar (AD).

Sterling, Dollar and Euro Equivalents (29 December 2000)
£1 sterling = 112.43 dinars;
US $1 = 75.34 dinars;
€1 = 70.11 dinars;
1,000 Algerian dinars = £8.895 = $13.273 = €14.264.

Average Exchange Rate (dinars per US $)
1998   58.739
1999   66.574
2000   75.260

BUDGET ('000 million AD)*

Revenue	1997	1998	1999
Hydrocarbon revenue. . . .	592.5	425.8	588.2
Export taxes	514.8	328.6	510.1
Domestic receipts . .	50.0	50.0	50.0
Dividends and entry rights .	27.7	47.3	28.1
Other revenue . . .	334.2	348.7	358.4
Tax revenue	314.0	329.8	314.8
Taxes on income and profits .	81.8	88.1	72.2
Taxes on goods and services .	148.1	154.9	149.7
Customs duties . . .	73.5	75.5	80.2
Non-tax revenue . . .	20.2	18.9	43.6
Total	**926.7**	**774.5**	**950.5**

Expenditure†	1997	1998	1999
Current expenditure . . .	643.6	663.9	774.7
Personnel expenditure . .	245.2	268.6	286.1
War veterans' pensions . . .	25.0	37.9	59.9
Material and supplies . .	43.6	47.5	53.6
Public services . . .	74.0	75.2	81.9
Hospitals	29.9	28.8	31.2
Current transfers . . .	146.5	123.9	166.8
Family allowances . .	44.2	42.5	36.2
Public works and social			
assistance. . . .	12.0	13.6	14.2
Food subsidies . . .	0.7	0.2	0.4
Housing	28.8	19.0	14.5
Interest payments . . .	109.4	110.8	126.4
Capital expenditure . . .	201.6	211.9	187.0
Total	**845.2**	**875.7**	**961.7**

* Figures refer to operations of the central Government, excluding special accounts. The balance (revenue less expenditure) on such accounts (in '000 million AD) was: 1.1 in 1997; –6.9 in 1998; –5.6 in 1999.
† Excluding net lending by the Treasury ('000 million AD): –1.5 in 1997; 0.1 in 1998; –0.3 in 1999. Also excluded are allocations to the Rehabilitation Fund ('000 million AD): 18.0 in 1997; 0.0 in 1998; 0.0 in 1999.

Source: IMF, *Algeria: Recent Economic Developments* (August 2000).

CENTRAL BANK RESERVES (US $ million at 31 December)

	1997	1998	1999
Gold*	264	275	268
IMF special drawing rights . .	1	2	2
Reserve position in IMF . .	—	—	117
Foreign exchange . . .	8,046	6,844	4,407
Total	**8,311**	**7,121**	**4,794**

* Valued at SDR 35 per troy ounce.

Source: IMF, *International Financial Statistics*.

MONEY SUPPLY (million AD at 31 December)*

	1997	1998	1999
Currency outside banks . .	337,620	390,780	440,260
Demand deposits at deposit money banks.	254,830	334,520	352,710
Checking deposits at post office .	71,680	81,050	87,430
Private sector demand deposits at treasury	7,430	7,330	9,380
Total money (incl. others) . .	675,960	817,260	889,780

* Figures are rounded to the nearest 10 million dinars.

Source: IMF, *International Financial Statistics*.

COST OF LIVING (Consumer Price Index for Algiers; average of monthly figures; base: 1989 = 100)

	1997	1998	1999
Foodstuffs, beverages and tobacco	539.7	570.6	577.4
Clothing and footwear . .	369.5	385.5	418.4
Housing costs . . .	541.5	580.6	597.6
All items (incl. others) . .	494.9	519.4	533.1

Source: IMF, *Algeria: Recent Economic Developments* (August 2000).

NATIONAL ACCOUNTS

National Income and Product (million AD at current prices)

	1996	1997	1998*
Compensation of employees . .	667,239.7	720,821.3	789,089.4
Operating surplus . . .	1,207,218.7	1,338,646.9	1,293,671.5
Domestic factor incomes .	1,874,458.4	2,059,468.2	2,082,760.9
Consumption of fixed capital .	195,447.6	189,513.3	211,690.5
Gross domestic product (GDP) at factor cost .	2,069,906.0	2,248,981.5	2,294,451.4
Indirect taxes, *less* subsidies .	500,122.9	522,337.3	508,686.7
GDP in purchasers' values .	2,570,028.9	2,771,318.8	2,803,138.1
Net factor income from abroad	−118,289.0	−123,730.6	−123,701.9
Gross national product . .	2,451,739.9	2,647,588.2	2,679,436.2
Less Consumption of fixed capital	195,447.6	189,513.3	211,690.5
National income in market prices	2,256,292.3	2,458,074.9	2,467,745.7
Other current transfers from abroad (net)	101,948.4	103,673.7	100,721.6
National disposable income .	2,358,240.7	2,561,748.6	2,568,467.3

* Provisional.

Expenditure on the Gross Domestic Product
('000 million AD at current prices)

	1997	1998	1999
Government final consumption expenditure	462	504	542
Private final consumption expenditure	1,410	1,525	1,635
Increase in stocks . . .	24	30	48
Gross fixed capital formation . .	681	740	825
Total domestic expenditure .	2,530	2,798	3,049
Exports of goods and services . .	846	636	881
Less Imports of goods and services .	614	653	744
GDP in purchasers' values . .	2,762	2,782	3,186

Source: IMF, *Algeria: Recent Economic Developments* (August 2000).

Gross Domestic Product by Economic Activity
('000 million AD at current prices)

	1997	1998	1999
Agriculture, forestry and fishing .	261	309	336
Hydrocarbons*	819	640	900
Mining (excl. hydrocarbons) . .			
Manufacturing (excl. hydrocarbons)	236	270	283
Electricity and water . . .			
Construction and public works .	275	299	316
Government services . . .	344	374	403
Non-government services . . .	607	662	718
Sub-total	2,542	2,554	2,956
Import taxes and duties . . .	221	226	230
GDP in purchasers' values . .	2,762	2,782	3,186

* Extraction and processing of petroleum and natural gas.

Source: IMF, *Algeria: Recent Economic Developments* (August 2000).

BALANCE OF PAYMENTS (US $ '000 million)

	1997	1998	1999*
Exports of goods f.o.b. . . .	13.8	10.1	12.3
Imports of goods f.o.b. . . .	−8.1	−8.6	−9.0
Trade balance	5.7	1.5	3.4
Exports of services . . .	1.1	0.7	0.7
Imports of services . . .	−2.2	−2.2	−2.6
Balance on goods and services.	4.6	0.0	1.5
Other income received . . .	0.3	0.4	0.2
Other income paid . . .	−2.5	−2.4	−2.5
Balance on goods, services and income	2.4	−2.0	−0.8
Transfers (net)	1.1	1.1	0.8
Current balance . . .	3.5	−0.9	0.0
Direct investment (net) . . .	0.3	0.5	0.5
Official capital (net) . . .	−2.5	−1.3	−2.0
Short-term credit (net), net errors and omissions	0.0	0.0	−0.9
Overall balance	1.2	−1.7	−2.4

* Estimates.

Source: IMF, *Algeria: Recent Economic Developments* (August 2000).

External Trade

Note: Data exclude military goods. Exports include stores and bunkers for foreign ships and aircraft.

PRINCIPAL COMMODITIES (distribution by SITC, US $ million)

Imports c.i.f.	1995	1996	1997
Food and live animals . .	2,700.9	2,501.0	2,502.4
Dairy products and birds' eggs	476.9	400.7	442.7
Milk and cream . . .	411.3	338.6	384.4
Cereals and cereal preparations .	1,252.9	1,115.4	1,270.9
Wheat and meslin (unmilled) .	726.9	495.3	730.5
Meal and flour of wheat, etc. .	335.7	416.0	318.7
Vegetables and fruit . . .	211.5	192.2	165.7
Sugar, sugar preparations and honey	324.5	267.5	216.5
Sugar and honey . . .	318.7	266.0	215.0
Crude materials (inedible) except fuels . . .	415.3	312.2	307.6
Cork and wood	218.8	139.6	169.3
Animal and vegetable oils, fats and waxes . . .	351.9	280.8	215.0
Fixed vegetable oils and fats . .	294.9	234.7	172.8
Chemicals and related products	1,200.6	771.1	853.0
Medicinal and pharmaceutical products	567.7	324.3	373.4
Medicaments (incl. veterinary) .	504.6	293.2	336.3

Imports c.i.f. — *continued*	1995	1996	1997
Basic manufactures	2,235.5	1,887.7	1,502.7
Paper, paperboard and manufactures	165.0	245.6	129.2
Non-metallic mineral manufactures	248.3	213.4	149.1
Iron and steel	899.7	742.6	547.5
Bars, rods, angles, shapes and sections	283.3	214.0	232.0
Bars and rods (excl. wire rod)	197.9	86.7	177.1
Tubes, pipes and fittings	447.7	365.3	203.4
Machinery and transport equipment	3,279.9	2,793.5	2,725.6
Power-generating machinery and equipment	299.6	306.5	216.6
Machinery specialized for particular industries	262.6	258.6	246.8
General industrial machinery, equipment and parts	1,076.1	795.6	796.7
Heating and cooling equipment	159.2	187.4	259.8
Pumps for liquids, etc.	258.0	172.3	161.4
Non-electric machine parts	432.0	214.6	202.9
Taps, cocks, valves, etc.	304.1	110.8	122.6
Office machines and automatic data-processing equipment	219.8	115.8	115.3
Telecommunications and sound equipment	323.7	165.8	187.3
Other electrical machinery, apparatus, etc.	528.1	433.8	517.8
Switchgear, etc., and parts	226.3	141.5	235.7
Road vehicles and parts*	448.5	554.4	537.1
Passenger motor cars (excl. buses)	154.2	232.7	240.5
Miscellaneous manufactured articles	387.9	399.8	407.6
Total (incl. others)	10,782.5	9,105.7	8,688.4

* Excluding tyres, engines and electrical parts.

Exports f.o.b.	1995	1996	1997
Mineral fuels, lubricants, etc.	8,909.1	10,312.7	13,504.1
Petroleum, petroleum products, etc.	6,056.0	6,719.8	7,952.8
Crude petroleum oils, etc.	4,309.8	5,329.1	5,646.5
Refined petroleum products	1,684.6	1,295.1	2,185.0
Motor spirit (petrol) and other light oils	545.1	441.9	824.2
Gas oils (distillate fuels)	522.7	378.1	627.7
Residual fuel oils	552.2	447.1	695.3
Gas (natural and manufactured)	2,840.7	3,580.9	5,548.3
Liquefied petroleum gases	1,536.2	2,336.2	3,487.1
Petroleum gases, etc., in the gaseous state	1,304.5	1,244.7	2,061.3
Chemicals and related products	114.0	284.5	152.0
Total (incl. others)	9,356.7	11,099.3	13,894.2

Source: UN, *International Trade Statistics Yearbook.*

1998 (US $ million): Total imports c.i.f. 9,416.9; Total exports f.o.b. 9,655.4.
1999 (US $ million): Total imports c.i.f. 9,168.8; Total exports f.o.b. 11,364.0.

PRINCIPAL TRADING PARTNERS (US $ million)*

Imports c.i.f.	1995	1996	1997
Argentina	66.7	91.8	52.9
Austria	219.6	120.4	90.7
Belgium-Luxembourg	247.8	215.4	228.8
Brazil	136.0	169.7	87.1
Canada	452.7	355.7	489.1
China, People's Republic	252.8	202.9	163.8
France (incl. Monaco)	2,686.9	2,227.2	2,009.5
Germany	737.3	597.2	482.6
Indonesia	116.7	86.2	76.5
Italy	1,039.1	835.1	750.7
Japan	365.8	239.8	318.5
Korea, Republic	46.8	86.3	99.2
Netherlands	144.6	149.3	204.6
Poland	43.4	32.0	94.6
Russia	75.7	62.4	110.9
Spain	923.4	1,116.0	603.7
Sweden	81.6	53.3	101.1
Syria	31.1	35.7	240.3
Tunisia	142.8	79.5	15.5
Turkey	305.0	318.4	313.9
United Kingdom	155.6	202.0	280.6
USA	1,418.0	931.3	921.0
Total (incl. others)	10,782.4	9,105.6	8,688.4

Exports f.o.b.	1995	1996	1997
Austria	116.3	159.7	185.3
Belgium-Luxembourg	367.1	328.2	504.1
Brazil	225.2	565.9	746.6
Canada	220.5	404.2	470.2
France (incl. Monaco)	1,315.6	1,457.8	2,189.1
Germany	171.5	275.8	309.5
Italy	2,098.7	2,208.8	2,866.3
Korea, Republic	121.9	116.2	44.6
Netherlands	972.4	965.6	1,170.4
Portugal	142.4	131.2	74.4
Russia	132.4	479.1	21.6
Singapore	46.0	15.0	139.6
Spain	625.1	846.2	1,247.2
Switzerland-Liechtenstein	110.1	71.2	13.2
Tunisia	108.3	101.9	59.5
Turkey	314.4	575.4	810.9
United Kingdom	204.0	258.1	252.4
USA	1,563.2	1,701.8	2,221.8
Total (incl. others)	9,356.7	11,099.2	13,894.7

* Imports by country of production; exports by country of last consignment.

Source: UN, *International Trade Statistics Yearbook.*

Transport

RAILWAYS (traffic)

	1996	1997	1998
Passengers carried ('000)	44,522	38,101	34,132
Freight carried ('000 metric tons)	8,494	7,927	8,292
Passenger-km (million)	1,826	1,360	1,163
Freight ton-km (million)	2,194	2,892	2,174

ROAD TRAFFIC ('000 motor vehicles in use at 31 December)

	1996	1997	1998
Passenger cars	1,588.0	1,615.1	1,634.4
Lorries	292.8	294.3	295.1
Vans	570.1	581.1	589.0
Buses and coaches	28.6	30.4	32.6
Motorcycles	8.9	9.0	9.0

SHIPPING

Merchant Fleet (registered at 31 December)

	1996	1997	1998
Number of vessels	151	151	148
Total displacement ('000 grt) . .	982.5	982.5	1,004.7

Source: Lloyd's Register of Shipping, *World Fleet Statistics.*

International Sea-borne Freight Traffic ('000 metric tons)

	1996	1997	1998
Goods loaded	69,000	74,300	75,500
Goods unloaded	12,800	15,200	16,000

Note: Figures are rounded to the nearest 100,000 metric tons.

CIVIL AVIATION (traffic on scheduled services)

	1995	1996	1997
Kilometres flown (million) . .	31	31	34
Passengers carried ('000) . . .	3,478	3,494	3,518
Passenger-km (million) . . .	2,855	2,863	3,130
Total ton-km (million) . . .	278	274	299

Source: UN, *Statistical Yearbook.*

Tourism

FOREIGN TOURIST ARRIVALS BY COUNTRY OF ORIGIN*

	1996	1997	1998
France	35,214	34,690	38,357
Germany	1,467	1,554	1,721
Italy	2,541	2,555	3,419
Libya	6,349	5,611	4,305
Mali	6,993	6,706	7,105
Morocco	2,067	2,470	2,399
Spain	1,826	3,664	5,818
Tunisia	19,966	17,734	20,056
Total (incl. others) . . .	93,491	94,841	107,202

* Excluding arrivals of Algerian nationals resident abroad: 511,477 in 1996; 539,920 in 1997; 571,234 in 1998.

Tourism receipts (US $ million): 24 in 1996; 20 in 1997.

Source: World Tourism Organization, *Yearbook of Tourism Statistics.*

Communications Media

	1995	1996	1997
Radio receivers ('000 in use) . .	6,700	6,870	7,100
Television receivers ('000 in use) .	2,500	3,000	3,100
Telephones ('000 main lines in use)	1,176	1,278	1,400
Telefax stations (number in use) .	5,200	6,200	7,000
Mobile cellular telephones			
(subscribers)	4,691	12,000	1,500
Book production: titles* . . .	n.a.	670	n.a.
Daily newspapers			
Number	8	5	n.a.
Average circulation ('000 copies)	1,440	1,080	n.a.

1990: Non-daily newspapers 37 (average circulation 1,409,000 copies); Other periodicals 48 (average circulation 803,000 copies).

* Excluding pamphlets.

Sources: UNESCO, *Statistical Yearbook*, and UN, *Statistical Yearbook.*

Education

(1996/97, unless otherwise indicated)

	Institutions	Teachers	Pupils
Pre-primary	n.a.	1,333	33,503
Primary	15,426	170,956	4,674,947
Secondary			
General . . . . . }	4,138 {	145,160	2,480,168
Vocational		6,788	138,074
Higher			
Universities, etc.*	n.a.	14,364	267,142
Distance-learning institutions* .	n.a.	3,213	60,095
Other*	n.a.	2,333	20,173

* 1995/96.

Sources: UNESCO, *Statistical Yearbook,* and Ministère de l'Education nationale.

Directory

The Constitution

A new Constitution for the Democratic and People's Republic of Algeria, approved by popular referendum, was promulgated on 22 November 1976. The Constitution was amended by the National People's Assembly on 30 June 1979. Further amendments were approved by referendum on 3 November 1988, on 23 February 1989, and on 28 November 1996. The main provisions of the Constitution, as amended, are summarized below:

The preamble recalls that Algeria owes its independence to a war of liberation which led to the creation of a modern sovereign state, guaranteeing social justice, equality and liberty for all. It emphasizes Algeria's Islamic, Arab and Amazigh heritage, and stresses that, as an Arab Mediterranean and African country, it forms an integral part of the Great Arab Maghreb.

FUNDAMENTAL PRINCIPLES OF THE ORGANIZATION OF ALGERIAN SOCIETY

The Republic

Algeria is a popular, democratic state. Islam is the state religion and Arabic is the official national language.

The People

National sovereignty resides in the people and is exercised through its elected representatives. The institutions of the State consolidate national unity and protect the fundamental rights of its citizens. The exploitation of one individual by another is forbidden.

The State

The State is exclusively at the service of the people. Those holding positions of responsibility must live solely on their salaries and may not, directly or by the agency of others, engage in any remunerative activity.

Fundamental Freedoms and the Rights of Man and the Citizen

Fundamental rights and freedoms are guaranteed. All discrimination on grounds of sex, race or belief is forbidden. Law cannot operate retrospectively and a person is presumed innocent until proved guilty. Victims of judicial error shall receive compensation from the State.

The State guarantees the inviolability of the home, of private life and of the person. The State also guarantees the secrecy of correspondence, the freedom of conscience and opinion, freedom of intellectual, artistic and scientific creation, and freedom of expression and assembly.

The State guarantees the right to form political associations (on condition that they are not based on differences in religion, language, race, gender or region), to join a trade union, the right to strike, the right to work, to protection, to security, to health, to leisure, to education, etc. It also guarantees the right to leave the national territory, within the limits set by law.

Duties of Citizens

Every citizen must respect the Constitution, and must protect public property and safeguard national independence. The law sanctions the duty of parents to educate and protect their children, as well as the duty of children to help and support their parents. Every citizen must contribute towards public expenditure through the payment of taxes.

The National Popular Army

The army safeguards national independence and sovereignty.

Principles of Foreign Policy

Algeria subscribes to the principles and objectives of the UN. It advocates international co-operation, the development of friendly relations between states, on the basis of equality and mutual interest, and non-interference in the internal affairs of states.

POWER AND ITS ORGANIZATION

The Executive

The President of the Republic is Head of State, Head of the Armed Forces and responsible for national defence. He must be of Algerian origin, a Muslim and more than 40 years old. He is elected by universal, secret, direct suffrage. His mandate is for five years, and is renewable once. The President embodies the unity of the nation. The President presides over meetings of the Council of Ministers. He decides and conducts foreign policy and appoints the Head of Government, who is responsible to the National People's Assembly. The Head of Government must appoint a Council of Ministers. He drafts, co-ordinates and implements his government's programme, which he must present to the Assembly for ratification. Should the Assembly reject the programme, the Head of Government and the Council of Ministers resign, and the President appoints a new Head of Government. Should the newly-appointed Head of Government's programme be rejected by the Assembly, the President dissolves the Assembly, and a general election is held. Should the President be unable to perform his functions, owing to a long and serious illness, the President of the Council of the Nation assumes the office for a maximum period of 45 days (subject to the approval of a two-thirds majority in the National People's Assembly and the Council of the Nation). If the President is still unable to perform his functions after 45 days, the Presidency is declared vacant by the Constitutional Council. Should the Presidency fall vacant, the President of the Council of the Nation temporarily assumes the office and organizes presidential elections within 60 days. He may not himself be a candidate in the election. The President presides over a High Security Council which advises on all matters affecting national security.

The Legislature

The legislature consists of the Assemblée Nationale Populaire (National People's Assembly) and the Conseil de la Nation (Council of the Nation, which was established by constitutional amendments approved by national referendum in November 1996). The members of the lower chamber, the National People's Assembly, are elected by universal, direct, secret suffrage for a five-year term. Two-thirds of the members of the upper chamber, the Council of the Nation, are elected by indirect, secret suffrage from regional and municipal authorities; the remainder are appointed by the President of the Republic. The Council's term in office is six years; one-half of its members are replaced every three years. The deputies enjoy parliamentary immunity. The legislature sits for two ordinary sessions per year, each of not less than four months' duration. The commissions of the legislature are in permanent session. The two parliamentary chambers may be summoned to meet for an extraordinary session on the request of the President of the Republic, or of the Head of Government, or of two-thirds of the members of the National People's Assembly. Both the Head of Government and the parliamentary chambers may initiate legislation. Legislation must be deliberated upon respectively by the National People's Assembly and the Council of the Nation before promulgation. Any text passed by the Assembly must be approved by three-quarters of the members of the Council in order to become legislation.

The Judiciary

Judges obey only the law. They defend society and fundamental freedoms. The right of the accused to a defence is guaranteed. The Supreme Court regulates the activities of courts and tribunals, and the State Council regulates the administrative judiciary. The Higher Court of the Magistrature is presided over by the President of the Republic; the Minister of Justice is Vice-President of the Court. All magistrates are answerable to the Higher Court for the manner in which they fulfil their functions. The High State Court is empowered to judge the President of the Republic in cases of high treason, and the Head of Government for crimes and offences.

The Constitutional Council

The Constitutional Council is responsible for ensuring that the Constitution is respected, and that referendums, the election of the President of the Republic and legislative elections are conducted in accordance with the law. The Constitutional Council comprises nine members, of whom three are appointed by the President of the Republic, two elected by the National People's Assembly, two elected by the Council of the Nation, one elected by the Supreme Court and one elected by the State Council. The Council's term in office is six years; the President of the Council is appointed for a six-year term and one-half of the remaining members are replaced every three years.

The High Islamic Council

The High Islamic Council is an advisory body on matters relating to Islam. The Council comprises 15 members and its President is appointed by the President of the Republic.

Constitutional Revision

The Constitution can be revised on the initiative of the President of the Republic (subject to approval by the National People's Assembly and by three-quarters of the members of the Council of the Nation), and must be approved by national referendum. Should the Constitutional Council decide that a draft constitutional amendment does not in any way affect the general principles governing Algerian society, it may permit the President of the Republic to promulgate the amendment directly (without submitting it to referendum) if it has been approved by three-quarters of the members of both parliamentary chambers. Three-quarters of the members of both parliamentary chambers, in a joint sitting, may propose a constitutional amendment to the President of the Republic who may submit it to referendum. The basic principles of the Constitution may not be revised.

The Government

HEAD OF STATE

President and Minister of Defence: ABDELAZIZ BOUTEFLIKA (inaugurated 27 April 1999).

COUNCIL OF MINISTERS
(April 2001)

Prime Minister: ALI BENFLIS.

Minister of State for Justice: AHMED OUYAHIA.

Minister of State for the Interior and Local Authorities: NOUREDDINE ZERHOUNI.

Minister of State for Foreign Affairs: ABDELAZIZ BELKADEM.

Minister of Finance: ABDELATIF BENACHENHOU.

Minister of Participation and Co-ordination of Reforms: HAMID TEMMAR.

Minister-delegate to the Prime Minister: YOUCEF YOUSFI.

Minister of Water Resources: SALIM SAÂDI.

Minister of Small and Medium-sized Enterprises: NOUREDDINE BOUKROUH.

Minister of Energy and Mines: CHAKIB KEHLIL.

Minister of National Education: ABOUBAKR BENBOUZID.

Minister of Communications and Culture: MAHEDIENNE AMIMOUR.

Minister of Higher Education and Scientific Research: AMMAR SAKHRI.

Minister of Youth and Sports: ABDELMALEK SELLAL.

Minister of Commerce: MOURAD MEDELCI.

Minister of Posts and Telecommunications: MUHAMMAD MAGHLAOUI.

Minister of Vocational Training: KARIM YOUNÈS.

Minister of Religious Affairs and Endowments: BOUABDELLAH GHLAMALLAH.

Minister of Housing: ABDELKADER BOUNEKRAF.

Minister of Industry and Restructuring: ABDELMADJID MENASRA.

Minister of Labour and Social Services: SOLTANI BOUGUERRA.

Minister in charge of National Solidarity: DJAMEL OULD ABBÈS.

Minister of War Veterans: MUHAMMAD CHERIF ABBAS.

Minister of Agriculture: SAÏD BERKAT.

Minister in charge of Relations with Parliament: ABDELWAHAB DERBAL.

Minister of Health and Population: MUHAMMAD-LARBI ABD AL-MOUMIN.

Minister of Public Works: AMARA BENYPUNES.

Minister of Regional Development and the Environment: CHERIF RAHMANI.

Minister of Tourism and Handicrafts: LAKHDAR DORBANI.

Minister of Transport: HAMID LOUNAOUCI.

Minister of Fisheries and Marine Resources: OMAR GHOUL.

Minister-delegate to the Minister of Higher Education and Scientific Research, in charge of Scientific Research: MUHAMMAD ALI BOUGHAZI.

Minister-delegate to the Minister of State for Foreign Affairs, with responsibility for the Algerian Expatriate Community and Regional Co-operation: ABDELAZIZ ZIARI.

Minister-delegate to the Minister of State for Foreign Affairs, responsible for African Affairs: ABDELKADER MESSAHEL.

Minister-delegate to the Minister of State for the Interior and Local Authorities, responsible for Local Authorities: ABDELMAJID TEBBOUNE.

Secretary-General of the Government: AHMED NOUI.

MINISTRIES

Office of the President: Présidence de la République, el-Mouradia, Algiers; tel. (21) 69-15-15; fax (21) 69-15-95.

Office of the Prime Minister: rue Docteur Saâdane, Algiers; tel. (21) 73-23-40; fax (21) 71-79-27.

Ministry of Agriculture: 4 route des Quatre Canons, Algiers; tel. (21) 71-17-12; fax (21) 61-57-39.

Ministry of Commerce: rue Docteur Saâdane, Algiers; tel. (21) 73-23-40; fax (21) 73-54-18.

Ministry of Communications and Culture: Palais de la Culture, Les Annassers, Kouba, Algiers; tel. (21) 69-22-01; fax (21) 68-40-41.

Ministry of Defence: Les Tagarins, el-Biar, Algiers; tel. (21) 71-15-15; fax (21) 64-67-26.

Ministry of Energy and Mines: 80 ave Ahmed Ghermoul, Algiers; tel. (21) 67-33-00; fax (21) 67-03-66; e-mail info@mem-algeria.org; internet www.mem-algeria.org.

Ministry of Finance: Immeuble Maurétania, place du Pérou, Algiers; tel. (21) 71-13-66; fax (21) 73-42-76; e-mail algeriafinance@multimania.com; internet www.multimania.com/algeriafinance.

Ministry of Fisheries and Marine Resources: Algiers.

Ministry of Foreign Affairs: place Mohamed Seddik Benyahia, el-Mouradia, Algiers; tel. (21) 69-23-33; fax (21) 69-21-61; internet www.mae.dz.

Ministry of Health and Population: 125 rue Abd ar-Rahmane Laâla, el-Madania, Algiers; tel. (21) 68-29-00; fax (21) 66-24-13; www.ands.dz.

Ministry of Higher Education and Scientific Research: 11 rue Doudou Mokhtar, Algiers; tel. (21) 91-12-56; fax (21) 91-11-97; e-mail mesrs@ist.cerist.dz; internet www.mesrs.edu.dz.

Ministry of Housing: 137 rue Didouche Mourad, Algiers; tel. (21) 74-07-22; fax (21) 74-53-83.

Ministry of Industry and Restructuring: Immeuble le Colisée, 4 rue Ahmed Bey, Algiers; tel. (21) 60-11-44; fax (21) 69-32-35; e-mail info@mir-algeria.org; internet www.mir-algeria.org.

Ministry of the Interior and Local Authorities: 18 rue Docteur Saâdane, Algiers; tel. (21) 73-23-40; fax (21) 73-43-67.

Ministry of Justice: 8 place Bir Hakem, el-Biar, Algiers; tel. (21) 92-41-83; fax (21) 92-25-60.

Ministry of Labour and Social Services: 14 blvd Mohamed Belouizdad, Algiers; tel. (21) 68-33-66; fax (21) 66-28-11.

Ministry of National Education: 8 ave de Pékin, Algiers; tel. (21) 60-67-57; fax (21) 60-57-82; e-mail men@meducation.edu.dz; internet www.meducation.edu.dz.

Ministry of National Solidarity: Palais du Government, Algiers; tel. (21) 71-91-38; fax (21) 73-59-96; e-mail info@msnf.gov.dz; internet www.msnf.gov.dz.

Ministry of Participation and Co-ordination of Reforms: Chemin Ibn Badis el-Mouiz, El-Biar, Algiers; tel. (21) 92-98-85; fax (21) 92-17-55.

Ministry of Posts and Telecommunications: 4 blvd Krim Belkacem, Algiers; tel. (21) 71-12-20; fax (21) 71-92-71; internet www.barid.dz.

Ministry of Public Works, Territorial Management, Environment and Urban Planning: Algiers.

Ministry of Religious Affairs and Endowments: 4 rue de Timgad, Hydra, Algiers; tel. (21) 60-85-55; fax (21) 60-09-36.

Ministry of Small and Medium-sized Enterprises: Immeuble le Colisée, 4 rue Ahmed Bey, Algiers; tel. (21) 60-11-44; fax (21) 59-40-50.

Ministry of Tourism and Handicrafts: 7 rue des Frères Ziata, el-Mouradia, 16000 Algiers; tel. (21) 60-33-55; fax (21) 59-13-15.

Ministry of Transport: 119 rue Didouche Mourad, Algiers; tel. (21) 74-06-99; fax (21) 74-33-95.

Ministry of Vocational Training: Algiers.

Ministry of Water Resources: BP 86, Ex Grand Séminaire, Algiers; tel. (21) 68-95-00; fax (21) 58-63-64.

Ministry of War Veterans: 2 ave du Lt. Med Benarfa, el-Biar, Algiers; tel. (21) 92-23-55; fax (21) 92-35-16.

Ministry of Youth and Sports: 3 rue Mohamed Belouizdad, Algiers; tel. (21) 66-33-50; fax (21) 68-41-71.

President and Legislature

PRESIDENT
Presidential Election, 15 April 1999

Candidate*	Votes	% of votes
ABDELAZIZ BOUTEFLIKA	7,445,045	73.76
AHMED TALEB IBRAHIMI	1,265,594	12.54
Sheikh ABDALLAH DJABALLAH	400,080	3.96
HOCINE AÏT AHMED	321,179	3.18
MOULOUD HAMROUCHE	314,160	3.11
MOKDAD SIFI	226,139	2.24
YOUCEF KHATEB	121,414	1.20
Total†	10,093,611	100.00

* Six of the seven presidential candidates withdrew prior to the election, leaving Abdelaziz Bouteflika as the only remaining official contestant.
† Excluding 559,012 invalid votes.

LEGISLATURE
Assemblée Nationale Populaire
President: ABDELKADER BENSALAH.

General Election, 5 June 1997

	Seats
Rassemblement national démocratique (RND)	156
Mouvement de la société pour la paix (MSP)	69
Front de libération nationale (FLN)	62
Nahdah	34
Front des forces socialistes (FFS)	20
Rassemblement pour la culture et la démocratie (RCD)	19
Independent	11
Parti des travailleurs (PT)	4
Parti républicain progressif (PRP)	3
Union pour la démocratie et les libertés (UDL)	1
Parti social-libéral (PSL)	1
Total	380

Conseil de la Nation
President: BACHIR BOUMAAZA.

Elections, 25 December 1997 and 30 December 2000*

	Seats*
Rassemblement national démocratique (RND)	78
Front de libération nationale (FLN)	11
Front des forces socialistes (FFS)	4
Mouvement de la société pour la paix (MSP)	3
Appointed by the President†	48
Total	144

* Deputies of the Conseil de la Nation serve a six-year term; one-half of its members are replaced every three years. Elected representatives are selected by indirect, secret suffrage from regional and municipal authorities.
† Appointed on 4 January 2001.

Political Organizations

Until 1989 the FLN was the only legal party in Algeria. The February 1989 amendments to the Constitution permitted the formation of other political associations, with some restrictions. The right to establish political parties was guaranteed by constitutional amendments in November 1996; however, political associations based on differences in religion, language, race, gender or region were proscribed. Some 39 political parties contested the legislative elections that took place in June 1997. The most important political organizations are listed below.

Alliance nationale républicaine (ANR): Algiers; f. 1995; anti-Islamist; Leader REDHA MALEK.

Congrès national algérien: Algiers; f. 1999; Leader ABDELKADER BELHAYE.

Front démocratique: Algiers; f. 1999; Leader SID-AHMED GHOZALI.

Front des forces socialistes (FFS): 56 ave Souidani Boudjemaâ, 16000 Algiers; tel. (21) 59-33-13; fax (21) 59-11-45; internet www.f-f-s.com; f. 1963; revived 1990; Leader HOCINE AÏT AHMED.

Front islamique du salut (FIS): Algiers; e-mail mail@fisalgeria.org; internet www.fisalgeria.org; f. 1989; aims to emphasize the importance of Islam in political and social life; formally dissolved by the Algiers Court of Appeal in March 1992; Leader ABBASI MADANI.

Armée islamique du salut (AIS): Algiers; military wing of the FIS; agreed a cease-fire with the Govt in Sept. 1997, which was made permanent in June 1999 in order to promote a negotiated solution to the civil conflict; voluntarily dissolved in Jan. 2000; Cmmdr MADANI MEZRAG.

Front de libération nationale (FLN): 7 rue du Stade, Hydra, Algiers; tel. (21) 59-21-49. 1954; sole legal party until 1989; socialist in outlook, the party is organized into a Secretariat, a Political Bureau, a Central Committee, Federations, Kasmas and cells; under the aegis of the FLN are various mass political organizations, including the Union Nationale de la Jeunesse Algérienne (UNJA) and the Union Nationale des Femmes Algériennes (UNFA); Sec.-Gen. BOUALEM BENHAMOUDA.

Front national algérien: Algiers; f. 1999; advocates eradication of poverty and supports the Govt's peace initiative; Pres. MOUSSA TOUATI.

Front national de renouvellement (FNR): Algiers; Leader ZINEDDINE CHERIFI.

Mouvement algérien pour la justice et le développement (MAJD): Villa Laibi, Lot. Kapiot No. 5, Bouzaréah, Algiers; tel. (21) 60-58-00; fax (21) 78-78-72; f. 1990; reformist party supporting policies of fmr Pres. Boumedienne; Leader MOULAY HABIB.

Mouvement pour la démocratie et la citoyenneté (MDC): Tizi-Ouzou; f. 1997 by dissident members of the FFS; Leader SAÏD KHELIL.

Mouvement démocratique et social (MDS): Algiers; internet www.mds.pol.dz; f. 1998 by fmr mems of Ettahadi; left-wing party; 4,000 mems; Sec.-Gen. HACHEMI CHERIF.

Mouvement pour la liberté: Algiers; f. 1999; in opposition to Pres. Bouteflika; Leader MOULOUD HAMROUCHE.

Mouvement de la réforme nationale (MRN): Algiers; f. 1998; Leader Sheikh ABDALLAH DJABALLAH.

Mouvement de la société pour la paix (MSP): 163 Hassiba Ben Bouali, Algiers; e-mail bureau@hms-algeria.net; internet www.hms-algeria.net; f. as Hamas; adopted current name in 1997; moderate Islamic party, favouring the gradual introduction of an Islamic state; Leader Sheikh MAHFOUD NAHNAH.

Nahdah: Algiers; fundamentalist Islamist group; Sec.-Gen. HABIB ADAMI.

Parti démocratique progressif (PDR): Algiers; f. 1990 as a legal party; Leader SACI MABROUK.

Parti national pour la solidarité et le développement (PNSD): Cité du 5 juillet 11, No. 22, Constantine; Leader MOHAMED CHERIF TALEB.

Parti du renouveau algérien (PRA): 29 rue des Frères Bouatik, el-Biar, Algiers; tel. (21) 56-62-78; Sec.-Gen. MUHAMMAD MENAI; Leader NOUREDDINE BOUKROUH.

Parti républicain progressif (PRP): 10 rue Ouahrani Abou-Mediêne, Cité Seddikia, Oran; tel. (41) 35-79-36; f. 1990 as a legal party; Sec.-Gen. SLIMANE CHERIF.

Parti des travailleurs (PT): Algiers; workers' party; Leader LOUISA HANOUNE.

Rassemblement pour la culture et la démocratie (RCD): 87A rue Didouche Mourad, Algiers; tel. (21) 73-62-01; fax (21) 73-62-20; internet www.rcd-dz.org; f. 1989; secular party; advocates recognition of the Berber language, Tamazight, as a national language; Pres. SAÏD SAADI.

Rassemblement national démocratique (RND): Algiers; f. 1997; centrist party; Sec.-Gen. AHMED OUYAHIA.

Union pour la démocratie et les libertés (UDL): Algiers; f. 1997; Leader ABDELKRIM SEDDIKI.

Wafa: (Fidelity) Algiers; f. 1999 by AHMED TALEB IBRAHIMI.

The following groups are in armed conflict with the Government:

Da'wa wal Djihad—Groupe salafiste pour la prédication et le combat (GSPC): f. 1998; breakaway group from the GIA; particularly active in the east of Algiers and in the Kabyle; responds to preaching by Ali Belhadj, the second most prominent member of the proscribed FIS; Leader HASSAN HATTAB.

Groupe islamique armé (GIA): the most prominent and radical Islamist militant group; Leader ANTAR ZOUABRI.

Diplomatic Representation

EMBASSIES IN ALGERIA

Angola: 14 rue Marie Curie, el-Biar, Algiers; tel. (21) 92-54-41; fax (21) 79-74-41; Ambassador: JOSÉ CÉSAR AUGUSTO.

Argentina: 26 rue Finaltieri, el-Biar, Algiers; tel. (21) 92-34-23; fax (21) 92-34-43; Ambassador: GERÓNIMO CORTES FUNES.

Austria: 17 chemin Abd al-Kader Gadouche, Hydra, Algiers; tel. (21) 69-10-86; fax (21) 56-73-52; Ambassador: BERNHARD ZIMBURG.

Belgium: 22 chemin Youcef Tayebi, el-Biar, Algiers; tel. (21) 92-24-46; fax (21) 92-50-36; Ambassador: DIRK LETTENS.

Benin: 36 Lot. du Stade, Birkhadem, Algiers; tel. (21) 56-52-71; Ambassador: LEONARD ADJIN.

Brazil: 10 chemin Laroussi Messaoud Les Glycines, BP 186, Algiers; tel. (21) 74-95-75; fax (21) 74-96-87; Ambassador: SÉRGIO THOMPSON-FLORES.

Bulgaria: 13 blvd Col Bougara, Algiers; tel. (21) 23-00-14; fax (21) 23-05-33; Ambassador: PETER GRADEV.

Burkina Faso: 20 rue des Cèdres, BP 212 Didouche Mourade, Algiers; tel. (21) 59-44-36; e-mail abf@wissal.dz.

Cameroon: 26 chemin Cheikh Bachir El-Ibrahimi, 16011 el-Biar, Algiers; tel. (21) 92-11-24; fax (21) 92-11-25; Chargé d'affaires: JEAN MISSOUP.

Canada: BP 225, 16000 Alger-Gare, 27 bis rue des Frères Benhafid, Algiers; tel. (21) 69-16-11; fax (21) 69-39-20; Ambassador: JACQUES NOISEUX.

Chad: Villa No. 18, Cité DNC, chemin Ahmed Kara, Hydra, Algiers; tel. (21) 69-26-62; fax (21) 69-26-63; Ambassador: El-Hadj MAHAMOUD ADJI.

China, People's Republic: 34 blvd des Martyrs, Algiers; tel. (21) 69-27-24; fax (21) 69-29-62; Ambassador: ZHENG AQUAN.

Congo, Democratic Republic: 5 rue Saint Georges, Kouba, Algiers; tel. (21) 59-12-27; Ambassador: IKAKI BOMELE MOLINGO.

Congo, Republic: 111 Parc Ben Omar, Kouba, Algiers; tel. (21) 58-68-00; Ambassador: PIERRE N'GAKA.

Côte d'Ivoire: Immeuble 'Le Bosquet', Le Paradou, BP 260 Hydra, Algiers; tel. (21) 69-23-78; fax (21) 69-36-83; Ambassador: GUSTAVE OUFFOUE-KOUASSI.

Cuba: 22 rue Larbi Alik, Hydra, Algiers; tel. (21) 69-21-48; fax (21) 69-32-81; Ambassador: RAFAEL POLANCO BRAHOJOS.

Czech Republic: BP 358, Villa Koudia, 3 chemin Ziryab, Algiers; tel. (21) 23-00-56; fax (21) 23-01-03; Chargé d'affaires a.i.: JOSEF BUZALKA.

Denmark: 12 ave Emile Marquis, Lot. Djenane el-Malik, 16035 Hydra, BP 384, 16000 Alger-Gare, Algiers; tel. (21) 69-27-55; fax (21) 69-28-46; Ambassador: HERLUF HANSEN.

Egypt: BP 297, 8 chemin Abdel-Kader Gadouche, 16300 Hydra, Algiers; tel. (21) 60-16-73; fax (21) 60-29-52; Ambassador: IBRAHIM YOUSSRI.

Finland: BP 256, 16035 Hydra, Algiers; tel. (21) 69-29-25; fax (21) 69-16-37; e-mail finamb@wissal.dz.

France: chemin Abd al-Kader Gadouche, Hydra, Algiers; tel. (21) 69-24-88; fax (21) 69-13-69; Ambassador: HUBERT COLIN DE VERDIÈRE.

Gabon: BP 125, Rostomia, 21 rue Hadj Ahmed Mohamed, Hydra, Algiers; tel. (21) 69-24-00; fax (21) 60-25-46; Ambassador: YVES ONGOLLO.

Germany: BP 664, Alger-Gare, 165 chemin Sfindja, Algiers; tel. (21) 74-19-56; fax (21) 74-05-21; Ambassador: STEFFEN RUDOLPH.

Ghana: 62 rue des Frères Benali Abdellah, Hydra, Algiers; tel. (21) 60-64-44; fax (21) 69-28-56; Ambassador: GEORGE A. O. KUGBLENU.

Greece: 60 blvd Col Bougara, Algiers; tel. (21) 92-34-91; fax (21) 69-16-55; Ambassador: IOANNIS DRAKOULARAKOS.

Guinea: 43 blvd Central Saïd Hamdine, Hydra, Algiers; tel. (21) 69-20-66; fax (21) 69-34-68; Ambassador: MAMADY CONDÉ.

Guinea-Bissau: 17 rue Ahmad Kara, BP 32, Colonne Volrol, Hydra, Algiers; tel. (21) 60-01-51; fax (21) 60-97-25; Ambassador: JOSÉ PEREIRA BATISTA.

Holy See: 1 rue Noureddine Mekiri, 16090 Bologhine, Algiers (Apostolic Nunciature); tel. (21) 95-45-20; fax (21) 95-40-95; Apostolic Nuncio: Most Rev. AUGUSTINE KASUJJA, Titular Archbishop of Caesarea in Numidia.

Hungary: BP 68, 18 ave des Frères Oughlis, el-Mouradia, Algiers; tel. (21) 69-79-75; fax (21) 69-81-86; Chargé d'affaires: Dr LÁSZLÓ MÁRTON.

India: BP 121, 119 Ter rue Didouche Mourad, Algiers; tel. (21) 74-71-35; fax (21) 74-85-13; e-mail eoialg@ist.cerist.dz; Ambassador: MAHESH SACHDEV.

Indonesia: BP 62, 16 chemin Abd al-Kader Gadouche, 16070 el-Mouradia, Algiers; tel. (21) 69-20-11; fax (21) 69-39-31; Ambassador: LILLAHI GRAHANA SIDHARTA.

Iraq: 4 rue Abri Arezki, Hydra, Algiers; tel. (21) 69-31-25; fax (21) 69-10-97; Ambassador: ABD AL-KARIM AL-MULLA.

Italy: 18 rue Muhammad Ouidir Amellal, el-Biar, 16030 Algiers; tel. (21) 92-23-30; fax (21) 92-59-86; e-mail ambitalgeri@ist.cerist.dz; Ambassador: ROMUALDO BETTINI.

Japan: 1 chemin el-Bakri, el-Biar, Algiers; tel. (21) 91-20-04; fax (21) 91-20-46; Ambassador: YOSHIHISA ARA.

Jordan: 6 rue du Chenoua, Algiers; tel. (21) 60-20-31; Ambassador: KHALED ABIDAT.

Korea, Democratic People's Republic: 49 rue Hamlia, Bologhine, Algiers; tel. (21) 62-39-27; Ambassador: PAK HO IL.

Korea, Republic: BP 92, 17 chemin Abdelkader Gadouche, Hydra, Algiers; tel. (21) 69-36-20; fax (21) 69-16-03; Ambassador: HEUNG-SIK CHOI.

Kuwait: chemin Abd al-Kader Gadouche, Hydra, Algiers; tel. (21) 59-31-57; Ambassador: YOUSSEFF ABDULLAH AL-AMIZI.

Lebanon: 9 rue Kaïd Ahmad, el-Biar, Algiers; tel. (21) 78-20-94; Ambassador: SALHAD NASRI.

Libya: 15 chemin Cheikh Bachir Ibrahimi, Algiers; tel. (21) 92-15-02; fax (21) 92-46-87; Ambassador: ABDEL-MOULA EL-GHADHBANE.

Madagascar: 22 rue Abd al-Kader Aouis, 16090 Bologhine, BP 65, Algiers; tel. (21) 95-03-74; fax (21) 95-17-76; Ambassador: LAURENT RADAODY-RAKOTONDRAVAO.

Mali: Villa 15, Cité DNC/ANP, chemin Ahmed Kara, Hydra, Algiers; tel. (21) 69-13-51; fax (21) 69-20-82; Ambassador: CHEICK S. DIARRA.

Mauritania: 107 Lot. Baranès, Air de France, Bouzaréah, Algiers; tel. (21) 79-21-39; fax (21) 78-42-74; Ambassador: SID AHMED OULD BABAMINE.

Mexico: BP 329, 21 rue du Commandant Amar Azzouz (ex rue Général Lapperine), el-Biar, 16030 Algiers; tel. (21) 92-40-23; fax (21) 92-34-51; e-mail mexiarl@ist.wissal.dz; Ambassador: FRANCISO CORREA VILLALOBOS.

Morocco: 8 rue des Cèdres, el-Mouradia, Algiers; tel. (21) 69-14-08; fax (21) 69-29-00; Ambassador: ABDERRAZAK DOGHMI.

Netherlands: BP 72, 23/27 chemin Cheikh Bachir Ibrahimi, el-Biar, Algiers; tel. (21) 92-28-28; fax (21) 92-37-70; e-mail nldalg@ist.cerist.dz; Ambassador: GERBEN MEIHUIZEN.

Niger: 54 rue Vercors Rostamia Bouzaréah, Algiers; tel. (21) 78-89-21; fax (21) 78-97-13; Ambassador: GOUROUZA OUMAROU.

Nigeria: BP 629, 27 bis rue Blaise Pascal, Algiers; tel. (21) 69-18-49; fax (21) 69-11-75; Ambassador: ALIYU MOHAMMED.

Oman: 53 rue Djamel Eddine, El Afghani, Bouzaréah, Algiers; tel. (21) 94-13-10; fax (21) 94-13-75; Ambassador: HELLAL AS-SIYABI.

Pakistan: BP 404, 62A Djenane el-Malik, Le Pardou, Hydra, Algiers; tel. (21) 69-37-81; fax (21) 69-22-12; e-mail parepalgiers@gwissal.dz; Ambassador: M. ASLAM RIZVI.

Poland: 37 ave Mustafa Ali Khodja, el-Biar, Algiers; tel. (21) 92-25-53; fax (21) 92-14-35; e-mail lupina@wissal.dz; Ambassador: ANDRZEJ MICHAL LUPINA.

Portugal: 7 rue Mohamed Khoudi, el-Biar, Algiers; tel. (21) 78-48-20; fax (21) 92-54-14; Ambassador: EDUARDO MANUEL FERNANDES.

Qatar: BP 118, 7 chemin Doudou Mokhtar, Algiers; tel. (21) 92-28-56; fax (21) 92-24-15; Ambassador: HOCINE ALI EDDOUSRI.

Romania: 24 rue Abri Arezki, Hydra, Algiers; tel. (21) 60-08-71; fax (21) 69-36-42; Ambassador: DUMITRU OLARU.

Russia: 7 chemin du Prince d'Annam, el-Biar, Algiers; tel. (21) 92-31-39; fax (21) 92-28-82; Ambassador: ALEKSANDR ADSENYONOK.

Saudi Arabia: 62 rue Med. Drafini, chemin de la Madeleine, Hydra, Algiers; tel. (21) 60-35-18; Ambassador: HASAN FAQQI.

Senegal: BP 379, Alger-Gare, 1 chemin Mahmoud Drarnine, Hydra, Algiers; tel. (21) 69-16-27; fax (21) 69-26-84; Ambassador: SAÏDOU NOUROU.

Slovakia: BP 84, 7 chemin du Ziryab, Didouche Mourad, 16006 Algiers; tel. (21) 22-01-31; fax (21) 23-00-51; Chargé d'affaires a.i.: TOMÁŠ FELIX.

South Africa: Sofitel Hotel, 172 rue Hassuba Ben Bouali, Algiers; tel. (21) 68-52-10; fax (21) 66-21-04.

Spain: 46 bis rue Mohamed Chabane, el-Biar, Algiers; tel. (21) 92-27-13; fax (21) 92-27-19; Ambassador: RICARDO ZALACAIN.

Sudan: 8 Shara Baski Brond, el-Yanabia, Bir Mourad Rais, Algiers; tel. (21) 56-66-23; fax (21) 69-30-19; Ambassador: YOUCEF FADUL AHMED.

Sweden: rue Olof Palme, Nouveau Paradou, Hydra, Algiers; tel. (21) 69-23-00; fax (21) 69-19-17; Ambassador: KRISTEL GORANSSON.

Switzerland: BP 443, 2 rue Numéro 3, 16035 Hydra, Algiers; tel. (21) 60-04-22; fax (21) 60-98-54; Ambassador: ANDRÉ VON GRAFFENINED.

Syria: Domaine Tamzali, 11 chemin Abd al-Kader Gadouche, Hydra, Algiers; tel. (21) 91-20-26; fax (21) 91-20-30; Ambassador: ABELJABER ALDAHAK.

Tunisia: 11 rue du Bois de Boulogne, el-Mouradia, Algiers; tel. (21) 60-13-88; fax (21) 69-23-16; Ambassador: MOHAMED EL FADHAL KHALIL.

Turkey: Villa dar el Ouard, chemin de la Rochelle, blvd Col Bougara, Algiers; tel. (21) 23-00-04; fax (21) 23-01-12; Ambassador: ATTILA UZER.

United Arab Emirates: BP 165, Alger-Gare, 14 rue Muhammad Drarini, Hydra, Algiers; tel. (21) 69-25-74; fax (21) 69-37-70; Ambassador: HAMAD SAÏD AZ-ZAABI.

United Kingdom: BP 08, Alger-Gare, 16000 Algiers, Résidence Cassiopée, Bâtiment B, 7 chemin des Glycines, Algiers; tel. (21) 23-00-92; fax (21) 23-00-69; Ambassador: WILLIAM B. SINTON.

USA: BP 549, 4 chemin Cheikh Bachir Ibrahimi, 16000 Alger-Gare, Algiers; tel. (21) 60-11-86; fax (21) 60-39-79; e-mail amembalg@ist .cerist.dz; Ambassador: JANET SANDERSON.

Venezuela: BP 297, 3 impasse Ahmed Kara, Algiers; tel. (21) 69-38-46; fax (21) 69-35-55; Ambassador: EDUARDO SOTO ALVAREZ.

Viet Nam: 30 rue de Chenoua, Hydra, Algiers; tel. (21) 69-27-52; fax (21) 69-37-78; Ambassador: TRAN XUAN MAN.

Yemen: Villa 19, Cité DNC, rue Ahmed Kara, Hydra, Algiers; tel. (21) 69-30-85; fax (21) 69-17-58; Ambassador: GASSEM ASKAR DJEBRANE.

Yugoslavia: BP 366, 7 rue des Frères Benhafid, Hydra, Algiers; tel. (21) 69-12-18; fax (21) 69-34-72; Chargé d'affaires a.i.: DIMITRIJE BABIĆ.

Judicial System

The highest court of justice is the Supreme Court (Cour suprême) in Algiers. Justice is exercised through 183 courts (tribunaux) and 31 appeal courts (cours d'appel), grouped on a regional basis. New legislation, promulgated in March 1997, provided for the eventual establishment of 214 courts and 48 appeal courts. The Cour des comptes was established in 1979. Algeria adopted a penal code in 1966, retaining the death penalty. In February 1993 three special courts were established to try suspects accused of terrorist offences; however, the courts were abolished in February 1995. Constitutional amendments, introduced in November 1996, provided for the establishment of a High State Court (empowered to judge the President of the Republic in cases of high treason, and the Head of Government for crimes and offences), and a State Council to regulate the administrative judiciary. In addition, a Conflicts Tribunal is to be established to adjudicate in disputes between the Supreme Court and the State Council.

Supreme Court: ave du 11 décembre 1960, Ben Aknoun, Algiers; tel. and fax (21) 92-44-89.

President of Supreme Court: A. NASRI.

Procurator-General: M. DAHMANI.

Religion

ISLAM

Islam is the official religion, and the whole Algerian population, with a few rare exceptions, is Muslim.

High Islamic Council: place Cheikh Abd al-Hamid ibn Badis, Algiers.

President of the High Islamic Council: (vacant).

CHRISTIANITY

The European inhabitants, and a few Arabs, are generally Christians, mostly Roman Catholics.

The Roman Catholic Church

Algeria comprises one archdiocese and three dioceses (including one directly responsible to the Holy See). In December 1998 there were an estimated 2,750 adherents in the country.

Bishops' Conference: Conférence des Evêques de la Région Nord de l'Afrique (CERNA), 13 rue Khélifa-Boukhalfa, 16000 Alger-Gare, Algiers; tel. (21) 74-41-22; fax (21) 72-86-09; f. 1985; Pres. Most Rev. HENRI TEISSIER, Archbishop of Algiers; Sec.-Gen. Fr ROMAN STÄGER.

Archbishop of Algiers: Most Rev. HENRI TEISSIER, 22 Chemin d'Hydra, 16030 El Biar, Algiers; tel. (21) 92-56-67; fax (21) 92-55-76.

Protestant Church

Protestant Church of Algeria: 31 rue Reda Houhou, 16000 Alger-Gare, Algiers; tel. and fax (21) 71-62-38; three parishes; 1,500 mems; Pastor Dr HUGH G. JOHNSON.

The Press

DAILIES

L'Authentique: Algiers; internet www.authentique-dz.com; French.

Al-Badil: Algiers; relaunched 1990; MDA journal in French and Arabic; circ. 130,000.

Ach-Cha'ab (The People): 1 place Maurice Audin, Algiers; e-mail ech-chaab@ech-chaab.com; internet www.ech-chaab.com; f. 1962; FLN journal in Arabic; Dir KAMEL AVACHE; circ. 24,000.

Al-Djeza'ir El-Ghad (Algeria of Tomorrow): Algiers; f. 1999; Arabic; Editor MUSTAPHA HACINI.

Al-Djeza'ir El-Youm: Algiers; Arabic; circ. 54,000.

Echourouk El Yaoumi: Algiers; f. 2000; Arabic.

L'Expression: Algiers; f. 2000; French; Editor AHMED FATTANI.

El Fedjr: Algiers; f. 2000; Arabic.

Horizons: 20 rue de la Liberté, Algiers; tel. (21) 73-47-25; fax (21) 73-61-34; e-mail admin@horizons-dz.com; internet www .horizons-dz.com; f. 1985; evening; French; circ. 35,000.

Le Jeune Indépendant: Algiers; tel. (21) 67-07-48; fax (21) 67-07-46; e-mail info@ji-algeria.com; internet www.ji-algeria.com; f. 1997; French; circ. 60,000.

Al-Joumhouria (The Republic): 6 rue Bensenouci Hamida, Oran; f. 1963; Arabic; Editor BOUKHALFA BENAMEUR; circ. 20,000.

Le Journal: Algiers; f. 1992; French.

El Khabar: Maison de la Presse 'Tahar Djaout', 1 rue Bachir Attar, place du 1er mai, Algiers; tel. (21) 67-07-05; fax (21) 67-07-10; e-mail admin@elkhabar.com; internet www.elkhabar.com; f. 1990; Arabic; Gen. Man. CHERIF REZKI; circ. 400,000.

Liberté: 37 rue Larbi Ben M'Hidi, BP 178, Alger-Gare, Algiers; tel. (21) 69-25-88; fax (21) 69-35-46; e-mail webmaster@liberte-algeria .com; internet www.liberte-algerie.com; French; independent; Dir-Gen. ABROUS OUTOUDERT; circ. 20,000.

Al-Massa: Maison de la Presse, Abd al-Kader Safir, Kouba, Algiers; tel. (21) 59-54-19; fax (21) 59-64-57; f. 1977; evening; Arabic; circ. 45,000.

Le Matin: Maison de la Presse, 1 rue Bachir Attar, 16016 Algiers; tel. (21) 66-07-08; fax (21) 66-20-97; e-mail info@lematin-dz.com; internet www.lematin-dz.com; French; Dir MUHAMMAD BENCHICOU.

El-Moudjahid (The Fighter): 20 rue de la Liberté, Algiers; tel. (21) 637030; internet www.elmoudjahid-dz.com; f. 1965; govt journal in French and Arabic; Dir ZOUBIR ZEMZOUM; circ. 392,000.

An-Nasr (The Victory): BP 388, Zone Industrielle, La Palma, Constantine; tel. (31) 93-92-16; f. 1963; Arabic; Editor ABDALLAH GUETTAT; circ. 340,000.

La Nouvelle République: Algiers; French.

Onest Tribune: Oran; e-mail redact@ouest-tribune.com; internet www.ouest-tribune.com; French.

Le Quotidien d'Oran: 63 ave de l'ANP, BP 110, Oran; (41) 32-63-09; fax (41) 32-51-36; www.quotidien-oran.com; French.

Le Soir d'Algérie: Algiers; e-mail info@lesoirdalgerie.com; internet www.lesoirdalgerie.com; f. 1990; evening; independent information journal in French; Editors ZOUBIR SOUISSI, MAAMAR FARRAH; circ. 80,000.

La Tribune: Algiers; e-mail latribune@latribune-online.com; internet www.latribune-online.com; f. 1994; current affairs journal in French; Editor BAYA GACEMI.

El Watan: Maison de la Presse, 1 rue Bachir Attar, 16016 Algiers; tel. (21) 68-21-83; fax (21) 68-21-87; e-mail infos@elwatan.com; internet www.elwatan.com; French; Dir OMAR BELHOUCHET.

WEEKLIES

Algérie Actualité: 2 rue Jacques Cartier, 16000 Algiers; tel. (21) 63-54-20. 1965; French; Dir KAMEL BELKACEM; circ. 250,000.

Al-Hadef (The Goal): Algiers; tel. (21) 93-92-16; f. 1972; sports; French; Editor-in-Chief LARBI MOHAMED ABBOUD; circ. 110,000.

Libre Algérie: Algiers; French; organ of the FFS.

La Nation: Algiers; French; Editor SALIMA GHEZALI; circ. 35,000.

Révolution Africaine: Maison de la Presse, Kouba, Algiers; tel. (21) 59-77-91; fax (21) 59-77-92; current affairs journal in French; socialist; Dir FERRAH ABDELLALI; circ. 50,000.

El Wadjh al-Akhar (The Other Face): Algiers; Arabic.

OTHER PERIODICALS

Al-Acala: 4 rue Timgad, Hydra, Algiers; tel. (21) 60-85-55; fax (21) 60-09-36; f. 1970; published by the Ministry of Religious Affairs; fortnightly; Editor MUHAMMAD AL-MAHDI.

Algérie Médicale: Algiers; f. 1964; publ. of Union médicale algérienne; 2 a year; circ. 3,000.

Alouan (Colours): 119 rue Didouche Mourad, Algiers; f. 1973; cultural review; monthly; Arabic.

Bibliographie de l'Algérie: Bibliothèque Nationale d'Algérie, BP 127, Hamma el-Annasser, 16000 Algiers; tel. (21) 67-18-67; fax (21) 67-29-99; f. 1963; lists books, theses, pamphlets and periodicals published in Algeria; 2 a year; Arabic and French; Dir-Gen. MOHAMED AÏSSA OUMOUSSA.

Ach-Cha'ab ath-Thakafi (Cultural People): Algiers; f. 1972; cultural monthly; Arabic.

Ach-Chabab (Youth): Algiers; journal of the UNJA; bi-monthly; French and Arabic.

Al-Djeich (The Army): Office de l'Armée Nationale Populaire, Algiers; f. 1963; monthly; Algerian army review; Arabic and French; circ. 10,000.

Journal Officiel de la République Algérienne Démocratique et Populaire: BP 376, Saint-Charles, Les Vergers, Bir Mourad Rais, Algiers; tel. (21) 54-35-06; fax (21) 54-35-12; f. 1962; French and Arabic.

Nouvelles Economiques: 6 blvd Amilcar Cabral, Algiers; f. 1969; publ. of Institut Algérien du Commerce Extérieur; monthly; French and Arabic.

Révolution et Travail: Maison du Peuple, 1 rue Abdelkader Benbarek, place du 1er mai, Algiers; tel. (21) 66-73-53; journal of UGTA (central trade union) with Arabic and French editions; monthly; Editor-in-Chief RACHIB AÏT ALI.

Revue Algérienne du Travail: Algiers; f. 1964; labour publication; quarterly; French.

Ath-Thakafa (Culture): 2 place Cheikh ben Badis, Algiers; tel. (21) 62-20-73; f. 1971; every 2 months; cultural review; Editor-in-Chief CHEBOUB OTHMANE; circ. 10,000.

NEWS AGENCIES

Agence Algérienne d'Information: Maison de la Presse Tahar Djaout, Place de 1er Mai, Algiers; tel. and fax (21) 67-07-32; e-mail aai@aai-online.com; internet www.aai-online.com; f. 1999.

Algérie Presse Service (APS): 2 rue Farid Zouieche, Kouba, 16050 Algiers; tel. (21) 68-94-43; fax (21) 68-91-45; e-mail aps@wissal.dz; internet www.aps.dz; f. 1962.

Foreign Bureaux

Agence France-Presse (AFP): 6 rue Abd al-Karim el-Khettabi, Algiers; tel. (21) 72-16-54; fax (21) 72-14-89; Chief MARC PONDAVEN.

Agencia EFE (Spain): 4 ave Pasteur, 15000 Algiers; tel. (21) 71-85-59; fax (21) 73-77-62; Chief MANUEL OSTOS LÓPEZ.

Agenzia Nazionale Stampa Associata (ANSA) (Italy): 4 ave Pasteur, Algiers; tel. (21) 63-73-14; fax (21) 61-25-84; Rep. CARLO DI RENZO.

Associated Press (AP) (USA): BP 769, 4 ave Pasteur, Algiers; tel. (21) 63-59-41; fax (21) 63-59-42; Rep. RACHID KHIARI.

Informatsionnoye Telegrafnoye Agentstvo Rossii—Telegrafnoye Agentstvo Suverennykh Stran (ITAR—TASS) (Russia): 21 rue de Boulogne, Algiers; Chief KONSTANTIN DUDAREV.

Reuters (UK): Algiers; tel. (21) 74-70-53; fax (21) 74-53-75.

Rossiiskoye Informatsionnoye Agentstvo—Novosti (RIA-Novosti) (Russia): Algiers; Chief Officer YURII S. BAGDASAROV.

Xinhua (New China) News Agency (People's Republic of China): 32 rue de Carthage, Hydra, Algiers; tel. and fax (21) 69-27-12; Chief WANG LIANZHI.

Wikalat al-Maghreb al-Arabi (Morocco) and the Middle East News Agency (Egypt) are also represented.

Publishers

Entreprise Nationale du Livre (ENAL): 3 blvd Zirout Youcef, BP 49, Algiers; tel. and fax (21) 73-58-41. 1966 as Société Nationale d'Edition et de Diffusion, name changed 1983; publishes books of all types, and imports, exports and distributes printed material, stationery, school and office supplies; Pres. and Dir-Gen. HASSEN BENDIF.

Office des Publications Universitaires: 1 place Centrale de Ben Aknoun, Algiers; tel. (21) 78-87-18; publishes university textbooks.

Broadcasting and Communications

TELECOMMUNICATIONS

Entreprise Nationale des Télécommunications (ENTC): 1 ave du 1er novembre, Tlemcen; tel. (43) 20-76-71; fax (43) 26-39-51; f. 1978; national telecommunications org; jt venture with Sweden: Dir-Gen. SIBAWAGHI SAKER.

BROADCASTING

Radio

Arabic Network: transmitters at Adrar, Aïn Beïda, Algiers, Béchar, Béni Abbès, Djanet, El Goléa, Ghardaia, Hassi Messaoud, In Aménas, In Salah, Laghouat, Les Trembles, Ouargla, Reggane, Tamanrasset, Timimoun, Tindouf.

French Network: transmitters at Algiers, Constantine, Oran and Tipaza.

Kabyle Network: transmitter at Algiers.

Radiodiffusion Algérienne: 21 blvd des Martyrs, Algiers; tel. (21) 69-34-04; fax (21) 60-58-14; e-mail radioalg@ist.cerist.dz; govt-controlled; Dir-Gen. ABDELKADER LALMI.

Television

The principal transmitters are at Algiers, Batna, Sidi-Bel-Abbès, Constantine, Souk-Ahras and Tlemcen. Television plays a major role in the national education programme.

Télévision Algérienne (ENTV): 21 blvd des Martyrs, Algiers; tel. (21) 60-23-00; fax (21) 60-19-22; internet www.entv.dz; Dir-Gen. HAMRAOUI HABIB CHAWKI.

Finance

(cap. = capital; res = reserves; dep. = deposits; brs = branches; m. = million; amounts in Algerian dinars)

BANKING

Central Bank

Banque d'Algérie: 38 ave Franklin Roosevelt, 16000 Algiers; tel. (21) 23-02-32; fax (21) 23-01-50; e-mail bacom@ist.cerist.dz; internet bank-of-algeria.cerist.dz; f. 1963 as Banque Centrale d'Algérie; present name adopted 1990; cap. 40m.; bank of issue; Gov. ABDELOUAHAB KERAMANE; 50 brs.

Nationalized Banks

Banque Al-Baraka d'Algérie: Haï Bouteldja Houidef, Villa n°1 Rocades Sud, Ben Aknoun, Algiers; tel. (21) 91-64-50; fax (21) 91-64-57; e-mail info@albaraka-bank.com; internet www.albaraka-bank.com; f. 1991; cap. 500m., total assets 9,932m. (Dec. 1998); Algeria's first Islamic financial institution; owned by the Jeddah-based Al-Baraka Investment and Development Co (50%) and the local Banque de l'Agriculture et du Développement Rural (BADR) (50%); Chair. MUHAMMAD TEWFIK AL-MAGHARIBI; Gen. Man. MUHAMMAD SEDDIK HAFID.

Banque Extérieure d'Algérie (BEA): 11 Boulevard Col Amirouche, 16000, Algiers; tel. (21) 23-93-30; fax (21) 23-90-99; e-mail bea@algerianetwork.net; internet www.bea.algerianetwork.net; f. 1967; cap. 5,600m., res 31,269m., total assets 405,481m. (Dec. 1996); chiefly concerned with energy and maritime transport sectors; Chair. MUHAMMAD BENHALIMA; Dir-Gen. HOCINE HANNACHI; 80 brs.

Banque du Maghreb Arabe pour l'Investissement et le Commerce: 7 rue de Bois, Hydra, Algiers; tel. (21) 59-07-60; fax (21) 59-02-30; owned by the Algerian Govt (50%) and the Libyan Govt (50%); Pres. M. HAKIKI; Dir-Gen. IBRAHIM ALBISHARY.

Banque Nationale d'Algérie (BNA): 8 blvd Ernesto Ché Guévara, 16000 Algiers; tel. (21) 71-55-64; fax (21) 71-47-59; e-mail dg-bna@bna.com.dz; internet www.bna.com.dz; f. 1966; cap. 8,000m., res 10,227m., dep. 68,920m. (Dec. 1995); specializes in industry, transport and trade sectors; Chair. and Man. Dir MUHAMMAD TERBECHE; 163 brs.

Crédit Populaire d'Algérie (CPA): BP 1031, 2 blvd Col Amirouche, 16000 Algiers; tel. (21) 64-13-34; fax (21) 64-11-79; f. 1966; cap. 13,600m., total assets 353,863m. (Dec. 1996); specializes in light industry, construction and tourism; Chair. EL HACHEMI MEGHAOUI; 117 brs.

Development Banks

Banque de l'Agriculture et du Développement Rural (BADR): 17 blvd Col Amirouche, 16000 Algiers; tel. (21) 74-61-30; fax (21) 74-57-68; f. 1982; cap. 33,000m., res 1,296m., dep. 354,262m. (Dec. 1998); finance for the agricultural sector; Chair. and Man. Dir MOURAD DAMARDJI; 270 brs.

Banque Algérienne de Développement (BAD): Lot Mont-Froid, Zonka, Birkhadem, BP 36, 13336 Algiers; tel. (21) 55-22-89; fax (21) 55-48-63; e-mail bad@ist.cerist.dz; f. 1963; cap. 100m., total assets 166,459.8m. (Dec. 1997); a public establishment with fiscal sovereignty; aims to contribute to Algerian economic devt through long-term investment programmes; Chair. and Dir-Gen. MUHAMMAD KERKEBANE; 4 brs.

Banque de Développement Local (BDL): 5 rue Gaci Amar, Staouéli, Grand Governorat d'Alger; tel. (21) 39-28-01; fax (21) 39-37-90; f. 1985; regional devt bank; scheduled for partial privatization in 1999; cap. and res 6,555.4m. (1996); Pres. and Dir-Gen. ABD AL-MAJID NASSOU; 14 brs.

Caisse Nationale d'Epargne et de Prévoyance (CNEP): 42 blvd Khélifa Boukhalfa, Algiers; tel. (21) 71-33-53; fax (21) 71-41-31; f. 1964; 206,915.8m. (Dec. 1992); savings and housing bank; Dir-Gen. MUHAMMAD LOUHAB.

Private Banks

EFG Hermes SPA: Algiers; f. 2000.

Mouna Bank: Oran; f. 1998; cap. 260m.; Pres. AHMED BENSADOUN.

Union Bank: 5 bis, chemin Mackley, el-Biar, 16030 Algiers; tel. (21) 91-45-49; fax (21) 91-45-48; internet www.ub-alger.com; f. 1995; cap. 250m., total assets 1,591m. (Dec. 1997); principal shareholder Brahim Hadjas; Pres. SELIM BENATA.

Foreign Banks

Arab Banking Corpn (Bahrain): 54 ave des Trois Frères Bouaddou, BP 367, Bir Mourad Rais, Algiers; tel. (21) 54-15-15; fax (21) 54-16-04; e-mail abcbank@ist.cerist.dz; total assets US $1,477.2m.

Natexis Al-Amana Banque (France): Algiers; f. 1999; owned by Natexis Banques Populaires; Man. Dir HOCINE MOUFFOK.

STOCK EXCHANGE

The Algiers Stock Exchange began trading in July 1999.

Commission d'Organisation et de Surveillance des Opérations de Bourse (COSOB): Algiers; tel. (21) 71-27-25; fax (21) 71-21-98; internet www.cosob.com.dz; Chair. BELKACEM IRATNI; Gen. Sec. ABDELHAKIM BERRAH.

INSURANCE

Insurance is a state monopoly; however, in 1997 regulations were drafted to permit private companies to enter the Algerian insurance market.

Caisse Nationale de Mutualité Agricole: 24 blvd Victor Hugo, Algiers; tel. (21) 73-46-31; fax (21) 73-34-79; f. 1972; Dir-Gen. YAHIA CHERIF BRAHIM; 47 brs.

Cie Algérienne d'Assurance et de Réassurance (CAAR): 48 rue Didouche Mourad, 16000 Algiers; tel. (21) 72-71-90; fax (21) 72-71-97; f. 1963 as a public corpn; Pres. ALI DJENDI.

Cie Centrale de Réassurance (CCR): Lot No 1, Saïd-Hamdine-Bmr, Algiers; tel. (21) 64-47-37; fax (21) 69-47-78; f. 1973; general; Chair. DJAMEL-EDDINE CHOUAÏB CHOUITER.

Société Nationale d'Assurances (SNA): 5 blvd Ernesto Ché Guévara, Algiers; tel. (21) 71-47-60; fax (21) 71-22-16; f. 1963; state-sponsored co; Pres. KACI AISSA SLIMANE; Chair. and Gen. Man. LATROUS AMARQ.

Trust Algeria: Algiers; tel. (21) 60-56-15; fax (21) 60-95-12; e-mail trust@algeriainfo.com; internet www.trust-algeria.algeriainfo.com; f. 1997; 65% owned by Trust Insurance Co (Bahrain) and Qatar General Insurance and Reinsurance Co, 35% owned by Compagnie Algérienne d'Assurance.

Trade and Industry

GOVERNMENT AGENCIES

Centre Algérien pour la Promotion des Investissements (CALPI): Algiers; f. 1994 to promote investment; offices in the 48 administrative districts.

Conseil National des Participations de L'Etat (CNPE): Algiers; supervises state holdings; participants include the Prime Minister and reps of 16 govt ministries; Sec.-Gen. AHMED EL-ANTRI TIBAOUI.

DEVELOPMENT ORGANIZATIONS

Agence Nationale pour l'Aménagement du Territoire (ANAT): 30 ave Muhammad Fellah, Algiers; tel. (21) 58-48-12; fax (21) 68-85-03; f. 1980; Pres. and Dir-Gen. KOUIDER DJEBLI.

Engineering Environment Consult (EEC): BP 395, Alger-Gare, 50 rue Khélifa Boukhalfa, Algiers; tel. (21) 73-33-90; fax (21) 73-24-81; e-mail eec@wissal.dz; internet eldjazair.net.dz/economie/eec/eec.htm; f. 1982; Dir-Gen. MUHAMMAD BENTIR.

Institut National de la Production et du Développement Industriel (INPED): 126 rue Didouche Mourad, Boumerdès; tel. (21) 41-52-50.

CHAMBERS OF COMMERCE

Chambre Française de Commerce et d'Industrie en Algérie (CFCIA): 1 rue Lt Mohamed Touileb, Algiers; tel. (21) 73-28-28; fax (21) 63-75-33; f. 1965; Pres. JEAN-PIERRE DEQUEKER; Dir JEAN-FRANÇOIS HEUGAS.

Chambre Algérienne de Commerce et d'Industrie (CACI): BP 100, Palais Consulaire, rue Amilcar Cabral, Algiers; tel. (21) 57-55-55; fax (21) 57-70-25; f. 1980; Dir-Gen. MUHAMMAD CHAMI.

INDUSTRIAL AND TRADE ASSOCIATIONS

Association Nationale des Fabrications et Utilisateurs d'Emballages Métalliques: BP 245, rue de Constantine, Algiers; Pres. OTHMANI.

Centre National des Textiles et Cuirs (CNTC): BP 65, route du Marché, Boumerdes; tel. (21) 81-13-23; fax (21) 81-13-57.

Entreprise Nationale de Développement des Industries Alimentaires (ENIAL): 2 rue Ahmed Aït Muhammad, Algiers; tel. (21) 76-51-42; Dir-Gen. MOKRAOUI.

Entreprise Nationale de Développement des Industries Manufacturières (ENEDIM): 22 rue des Fusillés, El Anasser, Algiers; tel. (21) 68-13-43; fax (21) 67-55-26; f. 1983; Dir-Gen. FODIL.

Entreprise Nationale de Développement et de Recherche Industriels des Matériaux de Construction (ENDMC): BP 78, 35000 Algiers; tel. (21) 41-50-70. 1982; Dir-Gen. A. TOBBAL.

Groupement pour l'Industrialisation du Bâtiment (GIBAT): BP 51, 3 ave Colonel Driant, 55102 Verdun, France; tel. 29-86-09-76; fax 29-86-20-51; Dir JEAN MOULET.

Institut Algérien de la Propriété Industrielle (INAPI): 40–42 rue Larbi Ben M'hidi, 16000 Algiers; tel. (21) 73-60-84; fax (21) 73-55-81; f. 1973; Dir-Gen. M. BOUHNIK AMOR.

Institut National Algérien du Commerce Extérieur (COMEX): 6 blvd Anatole-France, Algiers; tel. (21) 62-70-44; Dir-Gen. SAAD ZERHOUNI.

Institut National des Industries Manufacturières (INIM): 35000 Boumerdès; tel. (21) 81-62-71; fax (21) 82-56-62; f. 1973; Dir-Gen. HOCINE HASSISSI.

State Trading Organizations

Since 1970 all international trading has been carried out by state organizations, of which the following are the most important:

Entreprise Nationale d'Approvisionnement en Bois et Dérivés (ENAB): BP 166, Alger-Gare, 2 blvd Muhammad V, Algiers; tel. (21) 63-75-02; fax (21) 61-10-89; import and distribution of wood and derivatives and other building materials; Dir-Gen. El-Hadj REKHROUKH.

Entreprise Nationale d'Approvisionnement en Outillage et Produits de Quincaillerie Générale (ENAOQ): 5 rue Amar Semaous, Hussein-Dey, Algiers; tel. (21) 23-31-83; fax (21) 59-84-54; tools and general hardware; Dir-Gen. SMATI BAHIDJ FARID.

Entreprise Nationale d'Approvisionnements en Produits Alimentaires (ENAPAL): Algiers; tel. (21) 76-10-11. 1983; monopoly of import, export and bulk trade in basic foodstuffs; brs in more than 40 towns; Chair. LAID SABRI; Man. Dir BRAHIM DOUAOURI.

Entreprise Nationale d'Approvisionnement et de Régulation en Fruits et Légumes (ENAFLA): BP 42, 12 ave des Trois Frères Bouadou, Bir Mourad Rais, Algiers; tel. (21) 54-10-10; fax (21) 56-79-59; f. 1983; division of the Ministry of Commerce; fruit and vegetable marketing, production and export; Man. Dir RÉDHA KHELEF.

Entreprise Nationale de Commerce: 6–9 rue Belhaffat-Ghazali, Hussein Dey, Algiers; tel. (21) 77-43-20; monopoly of imports and distribution of materials and equipment; Dir-Gen. MUHAMMAD LAÏD BELARBIA.

Office Algérien Interprofessionel des Céréales (OAIC): 5 rue Ferhat-Boussaad, Algiers; tel. (21) 73-26-01; fax (21) 73-22-11; f. 1962; monopoly of trade in wheat, rice, maize, barley and products derived from these cereals; Gen. Man. LAÏD TALAMALI.

Office National de la Commercialisation des Produits Viti-Vinicoles (ONCV): 112 Quai-Sud, Algiers; tel. (21) 73-72-75; fax (21) 73-72-97; f. 1968; monopoly of importing and exporting products of the wine industry; Man. Dir SAÏD MEBARKI.

UTILITIES

Société Nationale de l'Electricité et du Gaz (SONELGAZ): 2 blvd Colonel Krim Belkacem, Algiers; tel. (21) 74-82-60; fax (21) 61-54-77; monopoly of production, distribution and transportation of electricity and transportation and distribution of natural gas; Gen. Man. AÏSSA ABDELKRIM BENGHANEM.

Electricity

Entreprise de Travaux d'Electrification (KAHRIF): Villa Malwall, Ain d'Heb, Médéa; tel. (25) 50-26-96; f. 1982; study of electrical infrastructure; Dir-Gen. A. AL-BAKI BELABDOUN.

Gas

Entreprise Nationale des Gaz Industriels (ENGI): BP 247, route de Baraki, Gué de Constantine, Algiers; tel. (21) 77-85-81; fax (21) 77-11-94; production and distribution of gas; Gen. Man. LAHOCINE BOUCHERIT.

Water

Agence Nationale de l'Eau Potable et Industrielle et de l'Assainissement (AGEP): Algiers; state water co.

STATE HYDROCARBONS COMPANIES

Société Nationale pour la Recherche, la Production, le Transport, la Transformation et la Commercialisation des Hydrocarbures (SONATRACH): 10 rue du Sahara, Hydra, Algiers; tel. (21) 60-60-28; fax (21) 71-52-75; e-mail sonatrach@sonatrach.dz; internet www.sonatrach.dz; f. 1963; exploration, exploitation, transport and marketing of petroleum, natural gas and their products; Chair. ABDELHAK BOUHAFS; Vice-Pres ALI HACHED (Marketing), ABDELHADI ZERGUINE (Transport), BACHIR ACHOUR (Liquefaction), DJAMEL EDINE KHENE (Exloration and Production).

Since 1980 the following associated companies have shared SONATRACH's functions:

Entreprise Nationale de Canalisation (ENAC): Muhammadia, rue Benyoucef Khattab, El Harrach, Algiers; tel. (21) 53-85-49; fax (21) 53-85-53; piping; Dir-Gen. RACHID HAMADOU.

Entreprise Nationale d'Engineering Pétrolier (ENEP): 2 blvd Muhammad V, Algiers; tel. (21) 64-08-37; fax (21) 63-71-83; design and construction for petroleum-processing industry; Gen. Man. MUSTAPHA MEKIDECHE.

Entreprise Nationale de Forage (ENAFOR): BP 211, 30500 Hassi Messaoud, Algiers; tel. (21) 73-71-35; fax (21) 73-22-60; drilling; Dir-Gen. ABD AR-RACHID ROUABAH.

Entreprise Nationale de Génie Civil et Bâtiments (GCB): BP 23, route de Corso, Boudouaou, Algiers; tel. (21) 84-65-26; fax (21) 84-60-09; civil engineering; Dir-Gen. ABD EL-HAMID ZERGUINE.

Entreprise Nationale de Géophysique (ENAGEO): BP 140, 30500 Hassi Messaoud, Ouargla; tel. (29) 73-77-00; fax (29) 73-72-12; e-mail enageodg@ist.cerist.dz; geophysics; Dir-Gen. RABAH DJEDDI.

Entreprise Nationale des Grands Travaux Pétroliers (ENGTP): BP 09, Zone Industrielle, Reghaïa, Boumerdes; tel. (21) 80-06-80; fax (21) 85-14-70; f. 1980; major industrial projects; Dir-Gen. B. DRIAD.

Entreprise Nationale des Plastiques & Caoutchoucs (ENPC): BP 452–453, Zone industrielle, Sétif; tel. (36) 90-64-99; fax (36) 90-05-65; production and marketing of rubber and plastics products; Dir-Gen. MAHIEDDINE ECHIKH.

Entreprise Nationale des Services Pétroliers (ENSP): BP 83, Hassi Messaoud, Ouargla; tel. (29) 73-73-33; fax (29) 73-82-01; internet www.enspgroup.com; oil-well services; Dir-Gen. A. GASMI.

Entreprise Nationale des Travaux aux Puits (ENTP): BP 71, In-Amenas, Illizi; oil-well construction; Dir-Gen. ABD AL-AZIZ KRISSAT.

Société Nationale de Commercialisation et de Distribution des Produits Pétroliers (NAFTAL, SpA): BP 73, route des Dunes, Cheraga, Algiers; tel. (21) 36-09-69; fax (21) 37-57-11; f. 1987; international marketing and distribution of petroleum products; Gen. Man. NOREDINE CHEROUATI.

TRADE UNIONS

Union Générale des Travailleurs Algériens (UGTA): Maison du Peuple, place du 1er mai, Algiers; tel. (21) 66-89-47. 1956; 800,000 mems; Sec.-Gen. ABDELMADJID SIDI SAID .

There are 10 national 'professional sectors' affiliated to UGTA. These are:

Secteur Alimentation, Commerce et Tourisme (Food, Commerce and Tourist Industry Workers): Gen. Sec. ABD AL-KADER GHRIBLI.

Secteur Bois, Bâtiments et Travaux Publics (Building Trades Workers): Gen. Sec. LAIFA LATRECHE.

Secteur Education et Formation Professionnelle (Teachers): Gen. Sec. SAÏDI BEN GANA.

Secteur Energie et Pétrochimie (Energy and Petrochemical Workers): Gen. Sec. ALI BELHOUCHET.

Secteur Finances (Financial Workers): Gen. Sec. MUHAMMAD ZAAF.

Secteur Information, Formation et Culture (Information, Training and Culture).

Secteur Industries Légères (Light Industry): Gen. Sec. ABD AL-KADER MALKI.

Secteur Industries Lourdes (Heavy Industry).

Secteur Santé et Sécurité Sociale (Health and Social Security Workers): Gen. Sec. ABD AL-AZIZ DJEFFAL.

Secteur Transports et Télécommunications (Transport and Telecommunications Workers): Gen. Sec. EL-HACHEMI BEN MOUHOUB.

Al-Haraka al-Islamiyah lil-Ummal al-Jazarivia (Islamic Movement for Algerian Workers): Tlemcen; f. 1990; based on teachings of Islamic faith and affiliated to the FIS.

Union Nationale des Paysans Algériens (UNPA): f. 1973; 700,000 mems; Sec.-Gen. AÏSSA NEDJEM.

Transport

RAILWAYS

A new authority, Infrafer (Entreprise Publique Economique de Réalisation des Infrastructures Ferroviaires), was established in 1987 to take responsibility for the construction of new track. In the following year a project to build an underground railway network in Algiers was revived in a modified form.

Entreprise Métro d'Alger: 4 chemin de Wilaya 13, Kouba, Algiers; tel. (21) 58-67-68; fax (21) 68-97-05; construction of a 26.5-km metro railway line began in 1989; initial 12.5-km section (16 stations) scheduled to open in two stages, starting in 2000; Dir-Gen. H. BELLIL.

Infrafer (Entreprise Publique Economique de Réalisation des Infrastructures Ferroviaires): BP 208, 35300 Rouiba; tel. (21) 85-27-47; fax (21) 85-17-55; f. 1987; Pres. and Dir-Gen. K. BENMAMI.

Société Nationale des Transports Ferroviaires (SNTF): 21–23 blvd Muhammad V, Algiers; tel. (21) 71-15-10; fax (21) 74-81-90; f. 1976 to replace Société Nationale des Chemins de Fer Algériens; 4,820 km of track, of which 304 km are electrified and 1,156 km are narrow gauge; daily passenger services from Algiers to the principal provincial cities and services to Tunisia and Morocco; Dir-Gen. ABD AL-ADIM BENALLEGUE.

ROADS

In 1996 there were an estimated 104,000 km of roads and tracks, of which 640 km were motorways, 25,200 km were main roads and 23,900 km were secondary roads. The French administration built a good road system (partly for military purposes), which, since independence, has been allowed to deteriorate in parts. New roads have been built linking the Sahara oil fields with the coast, and the Trans-Sahara highway is a major project. In 1996 it was estimated that the cost of renovating the national road system would total US $4,124m.

Société Nationale des Transports Routiers (SNTR): 27 rue des Trois Frères Bouadou, Bir Mourad Rais, Algiers; tel. (21) 54-06-00; fax (21) 54-05-35; e-mail dg-sntr@sntr-dz.com; internet www.groupe-sntr.com; f. 1967; holds a monopoly of goods transport by road; Chair. and Dir-Gen. ABDALLAH BENMAAROUF.

Société Nationale des Transports des Voyageurs (SNTV): Algiers; tel. (21) 66-00-52. 1967; holds monopoly of long-distance passenger transport by road; Man. Dir M. DIB.

SHIPPING

Algiers is the main port, with anchorage of between 23 m and 29 m in the Bay of Algiers, and anchorage for the largest vessels in Agha Bay. The port has a total quay length of 8,380 m. and is expected to be able to handle 250,000 containers per year by 2005. There are also important ports at Annaba, Arzew, Béjaia, Djidjelli, Ghazaouet, Mostaganem, Oran, Skikda and Ténés. Petroleum and liquefied gas are exported through Arzew, Béjaia and Skikda. Algerian crude petroleum is also exported through the Tunisian port of La Skhirra. In December 1999 Algeria's merchant fleet totalled 144 vessels, amounting to 964,186 grt.

Cie Algéro-Libyenne de Transports Maritimes (CALTRAM): 19 rue des Trois Frères Bouadou, Bir Mourad Rais, Algiers; tel. (21) 57-17-00; fax (21) 54-21-04; Man. Dir A. HASMIM.

Entreprise Nationale de Réparations Navales (ERENAV): quai no. 12, Algiers; tel. (21) 42-04-00; fax (21) 71-31-72; f. 1987; ship repairs; Dir-Gen. MUHAMMAD FARES.

Entreprise Nationale de Transport Maritime de Voyageurs—Algérie Ferries (ENTMV): BP 467, 5,6 Jawharlal Nehru, Algiers; tel. (21) 74-04-85; fax (21) 64-88-76; f. 1987 as part of restructuring of SNTM-CNAN; responsible for passenger transport; operates car ferry services between Algiers, Annaba, Skikda, Alicante, Marseilles and Oran; Dir-Gen. A. CHERIET.

Entreprise Portuaire d'Alger (EPAL): BP 16, 2 rue d'Angkor, Alger-Gare, Algiers; tel. (21) 71-54-39; fax (21) 71-54-52; e-mail portalg@ist.cerist.dz; f. 1982; responsible for management and growth of port facilities and sea pilotage; Dir-Gen. ALI FERRAH.

Entreprise Portuaire d'Annaba (EPAN): BP 1232, Môle Cigogne-Quai nord, Annaba; tel. (38) 86-31-31; fax (38) 86-54-15; e-mail epan@annaba-port.com; internet www.annaba.port.com; Man. Dir DJILANI SALHI.

Entreprise Portuaire d'Arzew (EPA): BP 46, 7 rue Larbi Tebessi, Arzew; tel. (41) 37-24-91; fax (41) 47-49-90; Man. Dir CHAIB OUMER.

Entreprise Portuaire de Béjaia (EPB): BP 94, Môle de la Casbah, Béjaia; tel. (34) 21-18-07; fax (34) 22-25-79; Man. Dir M. BOUMSILA.

Entreprise Portuaire de Djen-Djen (EPDJ): BP 87, El Achouat, Djen-Djen, Djidjelli; tel. (5) 45-00-36; fax (5) 44-02-72; f. 1984; Man. Dir MUHAMMAD ATMANE.

Entreprise Portuaire de Ghazaouet (EPG): BP 217, Route du Phare, 13400 Ghazaouet; tel. (7) 32-33-45; fax (7) 32-31-75; Man. Dir B. ABDELMALEK.

Entreprise Portuaire de Mostaganem (EPM): BP 131, quai du Port, Mostaganem; tel. (45) 21-14-11; fax (45) 21-78-05; Dir-Gen. M. LAKEHAL.

Entreprise Portuaire d'Oran (EPO): BP 106, 6 blvd Mimouni Lahcène, Oran; tel. (41) 39-26-25; fax (41) 39-53-52; Man. Dir M. S. LOUHIBI.

Entreprise Portuaire de Skikda (EPS): BP 65, 46 ave Rezki Rahal, Skikda; tel. (38) 75-68-27; fax (38) 75-20-15; Man. Dir M. LEMRABET.

Entreprise Portuaire de Ténès (EPT): BP 18, 02200 Ténès; tel. (3) 76-72-76; fax (3) 76-61-77; Man. Dir K. EL-HAMRI.

NAFTAL Division Aviation Marine: BP 70, Aéroport Houari Boumedienne, Dar-el-Beïda, Algiers; tel. (21) 50-95-50; fax (21) 50-67-09; Dir HAMZA BELAIDI.

Société Générale Maritime (GEMA): 2 rue J. Nehru, Algiers; tel. (21) 74-73-00; fax (21) 74-76-73; f. 1987 as part of restructuring of SNTM-CNAN; responsible for merchant traffic; Dir-Gen. MUHAMMAD GUENOUN.

Société Nationale de Transport Maritime et Cie Nationale Algérienne de Navigation (SNTM-CNAN): BP 280, 2 quai no. 9, Nouvelle Gare Maritime, Algiers; tel. (21) 71-14-78; fax (21) 73-02-33; f. 1963; state-owned co which owns and operates fleet of freight ships; rep. office in Marseilles (France) and rep. agencies in Antwerp (Belgium), Valencia (Spain) and the principal ports in many other countries; Gen. Man. ABDELHAMID KARA.

Société Nationale de Transports Maritimes des Hydrocarbures et des Produits Chimiques (SNTM-HYPROC): BP 60, Arzew, 31200 Oran; tel. (41) 47-48-55; fax (41) 37-62-45; e-mail hyproc@hyproc.com; internet www.hyproc.com; f. 1982; Pres. and Dir-Gen. MUSTAPHA ZENASNI.

CIVIL AVIATION

Algeria's principal international airport, Houari Boumedienne, is situated 20 km from Algiers. At Constantine, Annaba, Tlemcen and Oran there are also airports that meet international requirements. There are, in addition, 65 aerodromes, of which 20 are public, and a further 135 airstrips connected with the petroleum industry.

Air Algérie (Entreprise Nationale d'Exploitation des Services Aériens): BP 858, 1 place Maurice Audin, Immeuble el-Djazair, Algiers; tel. (21) 74-24-28; fax (21) 61-05-53; e-mail contact@airalgerie.dz; internet www.airalgerie.dz; f. 1953 by merger; state-owned from 1972; internal services and extensive services to Europe, North and West Africa, and the Middle East; Chair. and Dir-Gen. TAYEB BENOUIS; Sec.-Gen. NOUREDDINE MERROUCHE.

Air Maghreb: planned consortium of the national airlines of Algeria, Libya, Mauritania, Morocco and Tunisia; the merger of the airlines has been delayed indefinitely.

Antinea Airlines: Algiers; domestic and international cargo and passenger services.

Desert Aviation Co: Touggourt; f. 1999; private co; internal flights; Exec. Dir CHOKRI MIAADI.

Ecoair International: 12 rue Branly, El Mouradia, Algiers; f. 1998; private co operating domestic and international passenger flights.

Khalifa Airways: Lotissement Ben Haddadi No. 61, Cheraga, Algiers; f. 1999; private co operating domestic and international passenger flights.

Saharan Airlines: Touggourt; f. 1999; domestic passenger services.

Tassili Airlines: blvd Mustapha Ben Boulaid, 301 Hassi Messaoud; tel. (9) 73-84-25; fax (9) 73-84-24; f. 1997; jt venture between SONATRACH and Air Algérie; domestic passenger services.

Tourism

Algeria's tourist attractions include the Mediterranean coast, the Atlas mountains and the desert. In 1998 a total of 678,436 tourists visited Algeria, compared with 722,682 in 1991. Receipts from tourism totalled US $24m. in 1996. In that year there were 737 hotels, with a total of 64,695 beds.

Agence Nationale de Développement Touristique (ANDT): BP 151, Sidi Fredj Staoueli, Algiers; tourism promotion; Dir-Gen. ABDELKRIM BOUCETTA.

Office National du Tourisme (ONT): 2 rue Ismail Kerrar, Algiers; tel. (21) 71-29-82; fax (21) 71-29-85; e-mail info@algeria-tourism.org; internet www.algeria-tourism.org; f. 1990; state institution; oversees tourism promotion policy; Dir-Gen. ABDELKADER GOUTI (acting).

ONAT-TOUR (Opérateur National Algérien de Tourisme): 126 bis A, rue Didouche Mourod, 16000 Algiers; tel. (21) 74-33-76; fax (21) 74-32-14; f. 1962; Dir-Gen. BELKACEMI HAMMOUCHE.

Société de Développement de l'Industrie Touristique en Algérie (SODITAL): 72 rue Asselah Hocine, Algiers; f. 1989; Dir-Gen. NOUREDDINE SALHI.

TCA-TOUR (Touring Club d'Algérie): BP 18, Birkhamden; rue Hacéne Benaamane, quartier les vergers, Algiers; tel. (21) 56-90-16; fax (21) 54-19-39; Dir-Gen. ABDERAHMANE ABD-EDDAIM.

ANDORRA

Introductory Survey

Location, Climate, Language, Religion, Flag, Capital

The Principality of Andorra lies in the eastern Pyrenees, bounded by France and Spain, and is situated roughly midway between Barcelona and Toulouse. The climate is alpine, with much snow in winter and a warm summer. The official language is Catalan, but French and Spanish are also widely spoken. Most of the inhabitants profess Christianity, and about 94% are Roman Catholics. The civil flag (proportions 3 by 2) has three equal vertical stripes, of blue, yellow and red. The state flag has, in addition, the state coat of arms (a quartered shield above the motto *Virtus unita fortior*) in the centre of the yellow stripe. The capital is Andorra la Vella.

Recent History

Owing to the lack of distinction between the authority of the General Council (Consell General) of Andorra and the Co-Princes (Coprínceps—the President of France and the Spanish Bishop of Urgel) who have ruled the country since 1278, the Andorrans encountered many difficulties in their attempts to gain international status for their country and control over its essential services.

Until 1970 the franchise was granted only to third-generation Andorran males who were more than 25 years of age. Thereafter, women, persons aged between 21 and 25, and second-generation Andorrans were allowed to vote in elections to the General Council. In 1977 the franchise was extended to include all first-generation Andorrans of foreign parentage who were aged 28 and over. The electorate remained small, however, when compared with the size of the population, and Andorra's foreign residents (who comprised 66.8% of the total population at December 1998) increased their demands for political and nationality rights. Immigration is on a quota system, being restricted primarily to French and Spanish nationals intending to work in Andorra.

Prior to 1993, political parties were not directly represented in the General Council, but there were loose groupings with liberal and conservative sympathies. The country's only political organization, the Partit Democràtic d'Andorra (PDA), was technically illegal, and in the 1981 elections to the General Council the party urged its supporters to cast blank votes.

In 1980, during discussions on institutional reform, representatives of the Co-Princes and the General Council agreed that an executive council should be formed, and that a referendum should be held on changes to the electoral system. In early 1981 the Co-Princes formally requested the General Council to prepare plans for reform, in accordance with these proposals. Following the December elections to the General Council, in January 1982 the new legislature elected Oscar Ribas Reig as Head of Government (Cap de Govern). Ribas Reig appointed an executive of six ministers, who expressed their determination to provide Andorra with a written constitution. The formation of the executive body, known as the Govern, constituted the separation of powers between an executive and a legislature, and represented an important step towards institutional reform.

Severe storm damage in November 1982, and the general effects of the world-wide economic recession, led to a controversial vote by the General Council, in August 1983, in favour of the introduction of income tax, in an effort to alleviate Andorra's budgetary deficit and to provide the Government with extra revenue for development projects. Subsequent government proposals for an indirect tax on bank deposits, hotel rooms and property sales encountered strong opposition from financial and tourism concerns, and prompted the resignation of the Government in April 1984. Josep Pintat Solans, a local business executive, was elected unopposed by the General Council as Head of Government in May. In August, however, the Ministers of Finance and of Industry, Commerce and Agriculture resigned, following disagreements concerning the failure to implement economic reforms (including the introduction of income tax).

At the December 1985 elections to the General Council the electorate was increased by about 27%, as a result of the newly-introduced lower minimum voting age of 18 years. The Council

re-elected Pintat Solans as Head of Government in January 1986, when he won the support of 27 of its 28 members.

In September 1986 President François Mitterrand of France and the Bishop of Urgel, Dr Joan Martí Alanis (respectively the French and Spanish Co-Princes), met in Andorra to discuss the principality's status in relation to the European Community (EC, now European Union—EU—see p. 181), as well as the question of free exchange of goods between the members of the EC and Andorra, following Spain's admission to the Community in January of that year.

In April 1987 the Consejo Sindical Interregional Pirineos-Mediterráneo, a collective of French and Spanish trade unions, in conjunction with the Andorran Asociación de Residentes Andorranos, began to claim rights, including those of freedom of expression and association and the right to strike, on behalf of 20,000 of its members who were employed as immigrant workers in Andorra.

Further proposals for institutional reforms were approved by the General Council in October 1987. The transfer to the Andorran Government of responsibility for such matters as public order was proposed, while the authority of the Co-Princes in the administration of justice was recognized. The drafting of a constitution for Andorra was also envisaged. The implementation of the reforms was, however, dependent on the agreement of the Co-Princes.

Municipal elections were held in December 1987, at which 80% of the electorate voted; however, the number of citizens eligible to vote represented only 13% of Andorra's total population. For the first time, the election campaign involved the convening of meetings and the use of the media, in addition to traditional canvassing. Although Andorra then had no political parties as such, four of the seven seats were won by candidates promoting a conservative stance.

In April 1988 Andorra enacted legislation recognizing the Universal Declaration of Human Rights, adopted by the UN General Assembly in 1948. In June 1988 the first Andorran trade union was established by two French union confederations and by the Spanish Unión General de Trabajadores. (There were about 26,000 salaried workers in Andorra at this time, 90% of whom were of French or Spanish origin.) In the following month, however, the General Council rejected the formation of the union, as it did not recognize workers' right of association and prohibited the existence of any union.

Elections to the General Council took place in December 1989, at which more than 80% of the electorate participated. In January 1990 the new Council elected the reformist Ribas Reig as Head of Government, with the support of 22 members. In June the Council voted unanimously to establish a special commission to draft a constitution. The proposed document was to promulgate popular sovereignty and to constitutionalize the Co-Princes. In April 1991 representatives of the Co-Princes agreed to recognize popular sovereignty in Andorra and to permit the drafting of a constitution, which would be subject to approval by referendum. In September, however, Ribas Reig was threatened with a vote of 'no confidence' by traditionalist members of the Council. There followed a period of political impasse, during which no official budget was authorized for the principality. In January 1992, following small, but unprecedented, public demonstrations in protest against the political deadlock, Ribas Reig and the General Council resigned. A general election took place in April, at which 82% of the electorate (of 8,592 voters) voted. However, the result was inconclusive, necessitating a second round of voting one week later, following which supporters of Ribas Reig controlled 17 of the 28 seats. Accordingly, Ribas Reig was re-elected as Head of Government.

At a referendum held in March 1993, in which 75.7% of the electorate participated, 74.2% of those who voted approved the draft Constitution. The document was signed by the Co-Princes in April, and was promulgated on 4 May. Under its provisions, the Co-Princes remained as Heads of State, but with greatly reduced powers, while Andorran nationals were afforded full sovereignty and (together with foreigners who had lived in

Andorra for at least 20 years) were authorized to form and to join political parties and trade unions. The Constitution provided for the establishment of an independent judiciary, and permitted the principality to formulate its own foreign policy and to join international organizations. The Co-Princes were to retain a right of veto over treaties with France and Spain that affected Andorra's borders or security.

The first general election under the terms of the new Constitution took place on 12 December 1993. One-half of the General Council's 28 members were directly elected from the single national constituency, the remainder being elected by Andorra's seven parishes (two for each parish). No party won an overall majority of seats, the largest number (eight) being secured by Ribas Reig's Agrupament Nacional Democràtic (AND—the successor to the PDA); Nova Democràcia (ND) and the Unió Liberal (UL) each won five seats. Some 80.8% of the electorate participated in the election. In January 1994 Ribas Reig was re-elected Head of Government, supported by the AND and the ND, together with the two representatives of the Iniciatíva Democràtica Nacional (IDN). He announced that it would be a priority of his administration to restore economic growth by means of financial reforms and infrastructural development. Opposition to Ribas Reig's proposed budget and tax legislation, however, led in November to the adoption by the General Council of a motion expressing 'no confidence' in the Government. Ribas Reig immediately submitted his resignation; Marc Forné Molné, the leader of the UL, was subsequently elected Head of Government, and was inaugurated in late December.

Forné Molné's Government lacked an overall majority in the General Council; however, the support of councillors from regional political organizations enabled the Government to adopt more than 30 acts (between December 1994 and July 1996), including controversial legislation regarding foreign nationals (see Economic Affairs). Municipal elections, at which some 77.7% of the electorate voted, took place in December 1995. Bibiana Rossa (a former Minister of Health) became the first woman in Andorra to be elected to the office of mayor (of Canillo). After being censured twice in one year by the General Council, Forné Molné was obliged to announce that a general election would be held in early 1997. Elections to the Council took place on 16 February 1997, at which 81.6% of the registered electorate (of 10,837 voters) participated. The UL won an overall majority of seats (16 of 28); six seats were secured by the AND, while the ND, the IDN and the Unió Parroquiai d'Ordino (UPO) took two each. In April Forné Molné announced the formation of a new, expanded Government. The UL was subsequently renamed the Partit Liberal d'Andorra (PLA). On 17 June 1998 Càndid Naudi Mora was appointed to the newly-created position of Minister of Territorial Development. In 2000 the AND split into two parties, the Partit Socialdemòcrata (PS) and the Partit Demòcrata (PD).

Elections to the General Council took place on 4 March 2001, at which 81.6% of the registered electorate (of some 13,342 voters) participated; however, the number of citizens eligible to vote represented only 20.7% of Andorra's total population. The PLA won an overall majority of seats (15 of 28); six seats were secured by the PS, while the PD took five seats and the two final seats went to independent candidates. Forné Molné was re-elected Head of Government. He announced that it would be a priority of his administration to construct an overhead train system to ease traffic problems, and to make a bid to host the Winter Olympic Games. On 9 April Forné Molné announced his new Government, which comprised few changes. In a slightly controversial move, he abolished the position of Minister of the Presidency.

Following the referendum of March 1993, Andorra formally applied for membership of the Council of Europe (see p. 165), gaining entry in October 1994. In June 1993 the Andorran Government signed a treaty of co-operation with France and Spain, which explicitly recognized the sovereignty of Andorra. In the following month Andorra became the 184th member of the UN. In late 1993 France and Spain established embassies in Andorra, and Andorra subsequently opened embassies in Paris and Madrid. In September 1997 Jacques Chirac made his first official visit to Andorra in his capacity as President of France.

Government

Andorra is a co-principality, under the suzerainty of the President of France and the Spanish Bishop of Urgel. However, since May 1993, when the Constitution of the Principality of Andorra was promulgated, these positions have been almost purely honorary.

The General Council comprises 28 councillors, who are elected by universal suffrage for a four-year period. Two councillors are directly elected by each of the seven parishes of Andorra, and the remainder by a single national constituency. At its opening session the Council elects as its head the Speaker (Síndic General) and the Deputy Speaker (Subsíndic General), who cease to be members of the Council on their election. The General Council elects the Head of Government, who appoints ministers to the Govern.

Andorra is divided into seven parishes, each of which is administered by a Communal Council. Communal councillors are elected for a four-year term by direct universal suffrage. At its opening session each Communal Council elects two consuls, who preside over it.

Defence

Andorra has no defence budget.

Economic Affairs

In 1996 Andorra's national revenue totalled an estimated US 1,194m., equivalent to $18,514 per head. Traditionally an agricultural country, Andorra's principal crops are tobacco and potatoes; livestock-rearing is also of importance. However, the agricultural sector accounted for only 0.5% of total employment in 2000, and Andorra is dependent on imports of foodstuffs to satisfy domestic requirements.

Industry in Andorra includes the manufacture of cigars and cigarettes, together with the production of textiles, leather goods, wood products and processed foodstuffs. Iron, lead, alum and stone are also produced. Including construction, industry provided 20.2% of total employment in 2000.

The country's hydroelectric power plant supplies only about one-quarter of domestic needs, and Andorra is dependent on imports of electricity and other fuels from France and Spain. Andorra's total electricity consumption in 1999 amounted to 392.5m. kWh.

After 1945 Andorra's economy expanded rapidly, as a result of the co-principality's development as a market for numerous European and overseas goods, owing to favourable excise conditions. The trade in low-duty consumer items and tourism are therefore the most important sources of revenue. An estimated 2.3m. tourists visited Andorra in 1999. The absence of income tax and other forms of direct taxation favoured the development of Andorra as a 'tax haven'. The banking sector makes a significant contribution to the economy.

Andorra's external trade is dominated by the import of consumer goods destined for sale to visitors. In 1999 imports were valued at 171,262m. pesetas and exports at 6,691m. pesetas. Spain and France are Andorra's principal trading partners, respectively providing 44.8% and 29.2% of imports and taking 60.0% and 30.7% of exports in 1999.

In 1998 Andorra recorded a budgetary deficit of 2,013m. pesetas. For 2000 expenditure was projected at 38,280m. pesetas and revenue at 36,267m. pesetas. In the absence of direct taxation, the Government derives its revenue from levies on imports and on financial institutions, indirect taxes on petrol and other items, stamp duty and the sale of postage stamps. There is reportedly no unemployment in Andorra: the restricted size of the indigenous labour force necessitates high levels of immigration.

In March 1990 Andorra approved a trade agreement with the European Community (EC, now European Union, EU, see p. 181), which was effective from July 1991, allowing for the establishment of a customs union with the EC and enabling Andorran companies to sell non-agricultural goods to the EU market without being subject to the external tariffs levied on third countries. Andorra benefits from duty-free transit for goods imported via EU countries. Notable impediments to growth in Andorra include the narrow economic base and the inability of the agricultural and manufacturing sectors to fulfil domestic needs. As part of initiatives to establish Andorra as a major financial centre, a law regulating financial services was approved in late 1993. In mid-1994 legislation was approved requiring banks to invest as much as 4% of their clients' deposits in a fund intended to alleviate the public debt. Controversial legislation was adopted in 1996 to allow certain foreign nationals to become 'nominal residents' (individuals who, for the purposes of avoiding taxation, establish their financial base in Andorra), on condition that they pay an annual levy of some 1m. pesetas, in addition to a deposit. The practice of granting this status (without the levy) had been suspended in 1992; however, in the mid-1990s those already accorded nominal residency were estimated to contribute 90% of Andorra's bank deposits. Plans were announced in 1997 to remove restrictions on foreign investment in the country, which currently limit investors to holding a maximum of one-third of the capital of any Andorran business. In October Andorra's request to commence negotiations for membership of the World Trade Organization (WTO, see p. 292) was approved by the WTO General Council. In late 1999 it was reported that the Government was considering the introduction of value-added tax and a duty on the sale of property.

Social Welfare

In 1996 there was one hospital in Andorra, providing 2.2 beds per 1,000 inhabitants, and in 1998 there were an estimated 253.0 physicians per 100,000 inhabitants and 283.0 nurses per 100,000 inhabitants. The 2000 budget allocated 1,828m. pesetas (4.8% of total expenditure) to welfare and health services. A formal system of social security was established in 1966–68, and provides for sickness benefits, old-age pensions and workers' insurance. Contributions are made both by employers and workers.

Education

Education is compulsory for children of between six and 16 years of age, and is provided free of charge by Catalan-, French- and Spanish-language schools. Six years of primary education are followed by four years of secondary schooling. University education is undertaken abroad, although there are two centres for vocational training in Andorra. In 1998/99 there were a total of 9,278 pupils attending Andorra's 33 schools, while 1,644 students were in higher education. The 2000 budget allocated 6,174m. pesetas (16.1% of total expenditure) to education, youth and sports.

Public Holidays

2001: 1 January (New Year's Day), 6 January (Epiphany), 14 March (Constitution Day), 13 April (Good Friday), 16 April (Easter Monday), 1 May (Labour Day), 4 June (Whit Monday), 15 August (Assumption), 8 September (National Holiday), 1 November (All Saints' Day), 8 December (Immaculate Conception), 25 December (Christmas), 26 December (St Stephen's Day).

2002: 1 January (New Year's Day), 6 January (Epiphany), 14 March (Constitution Day), 29 March (Good Friday), 1 April (Easter Monday), 1 May (Labour Day), 20 May (Whit Monday), 15 August (Assumption), 8 September (National Holiday), 1 November (All Saints' Day), 8 December (Immaculate Conception), 25 December (Christmas), 26 December (St Stephen's Day).

Each Parish also holds its own annual festival, which is taken as a public holiday, usually lasting for three days, in July, August or September.

Weights and Measures

The metric system is in force.

Statistical Survey

Source (unless otherwise stated): Servei d'Estudis i d'Estadística, Ministeri de Finances i Interior, Carrer Dr Vilanova, 13 Edif. Davi, Esc. C5è, Andorra la Vella; tel. 865345; fax 867898; e-mail servest@andorra.ad; internet estudis-estadistica.finances.ad.

AREA AND POPULATION

Area: 467.76 sq km (180.6 sq miles).

Population (December 1999): 65,971 (males 34,433; females 31,538); comprising 22,743 Andorrans, 27,588 Spanish, 6,894 Portuguese, 4,384 French and 4,362 others. *Capital:* Andorra la Vella, population 21,189.

Births, Marriages and Deaths (1999): Registered live births 833; Registered marriages 178; Registered deaths 207.

Employment (August 2000): Agriculture, forestry and fishing 167; Industry (incl. construction) 6,876; Services 24,925; Other 1,992; Total 33,962.

AGRICULTURE

Principal Crop (metric tons, 1998): Tobacco 654.6.

Livestock (1998/99): Cattle 1,296; Sheep 2,011; Horses 1,109; Goats 717.

FINANCE

Currency and Exchange Rates: French and Spanish currencies are both in use. *French currency:* 100 centimes = 1 franc. *Sterling, Dollar and Euro Equivalents* (29 December 2000): £1 sterling = 10.5193 francs; US $1 = 7.0495 francs; €1 = 6.5596 francs; 1,000 French francs = £95.06 = $141.85 = €152.45. *Average Exchange Rate* (francs per US dollar): 5.8995 in 1998; 6.1570 in 1999; 7.1198 in 2000. *Spanish currency:* 100 céntimos = 1 peseta. *Sterling, Dollar and Euro Equivalents* (29 December 2000): £1 sterling = 266.83 pesetas; US $1 = 178.81 pesetas; €1 = 166.39 pesetas; 1,000 Spanish pesetas = £3.748 = $5.592 = €6.010. *Average Exchange Rate* (pesetas per US dollar): 149.40 in 1998; 156.17 in 1999; 180.60 in 2000. Note: Since the introduction of the euro, with French and Spanish participation, on 1 January 1999, fixed exchange rates of €1 = 6.55957 francs and €1 = 166.386 pesetas have been in operation.

Budget (million pesetas, 2000): *Expenditure:* Ministry of the Presidency and the Interior 5,076, Ministry of Agriculture and the Environment 973, Ministry of Foreign Affairs 757, Ministry of Finance 936, Ministry of Territorial Development 14,514, Ministry of Education, Youth and Sports 5,483, Ministry of the Economy 407, Ministry of Welfare and Public Health 1,828, Ministry of Tourism and Culture 2,130, Transfers to local authorities 6,174, Total (incl. others) 38,280; *Revenue:* Indirect taxes on commodities 26,940, Other taxes 955, Administrative fees and charges, sales and other receipts 1,334, Property income 7,038, Total (incl. others) 36,267.

EXTERNAL TRADE

Principal Commodities (million pesetas, 1998): *Imports:* Live animals and animal products 9,680 (Milk and dairy products; eggs; natural honey 4,992); Prepared foodstuffs; beverages, spirits and vinegar; tobacco and manufactured substitutes 27,139 (Alcoholic and non-alcoholic beverages 9,366; Tobacco 6,205); Mineral products 6,976 (Mineral fuels and oils, etc. 5,689); Products of chemical or allied industries 15,666 (Perfumery products and toiletries 11,205); Wood pulp, etc.; paper and paperboard and articles thereof 4,879; Textiles and textile articles 17,043 (Non-knitted clothing and accessories 6,448); Base metals and articles thereof 5,475; Machinery and mechanical appliances; electrical equipment; sound and television apparatus 27,057 (Boilers, non-electric machinery and mechanical appliances 9,614; Electrical machinery and appliances; sound and television apparatus 17,443); Vehicles, aircraft, vessels and associated transport equipment 14,625 (Passenger motor cars, tractors and other road vehicles 14,190); Optical, photographic, cinematographic, precision and medical instruments, etc.; clocks and watches; musical instruments 8,714; Total (incl. others) 161,426. *Exports:* Prepared foodstuffs; beverages, spirits and vinegar; tobacco and manufactured substitutes 872 (Alcoholic and non-alcoholic beverages 418; Tobacco 432); Products of chemical or allied industries 405 (Perfumery products and toiletries 336); Raw hides and skins, leather, furskins and articles thereof; saddlery and harness; travel goods, handbags, etc. 1,117 (Leather objects 1,107); Wood pulp, etc.; paper and paperboard and articles thereof 1,094 (Printed matter 1,048); Textiles and textile articles 695 (Non-knitted clothing and accessories 391); Machinery and mechanical appliances; electrical equipment; sound and television apparatus 1,422 (Boilers, non-electric machinery and mechanical appliances 306; Electrical machinery and appliances; sound and television apparatus 1,116); Vehicles, aircraft, vessels and associated transport equipment 1,228 (Passenger motor cars, tractors and other road vehicles 1,143); Furniture, bed linen, etc.; lighting devices 326; Total (incl. others) 8,637.

Principal Trading Partners (million pesetas, 1999): *Imports:* China, People's Republic 2,063; France 50,059; Germany 7,127; Italy 6,994; Japan 5,773; Netherlands 1,998; Spain 76,676; Switzerland 3,066; United Kingdom 4,151; USA 3,611; Total (incl. others) 171,262. *Exports:* France 2,052; Spain 4,016; Russia 94; Total (incl. others) 6,691.

TRANSPORT

Road Traffic (registered motor vehicles, 1999): Total 58,130. *1996:* Passenger cars 35,358; Commercial vehicles 4,238.

TOURISM

Tourist Arrivals (1999): Spanish 1,585,865; French 621,216; Other 139,920; Total 2,347,001.

COMMUNICATIONS MEDIA

Radio Receivers (1997): 16,000 in use.

Television Receivers (1997): 27,000 in use.
Source: UNESCO, *Statistical Yearbook*.

Daily Newspapers (1999): 2 titles published.

Telephones (main lines in use, September 2000): 33,856.

Telefax Stations (number in use, 1996): 1,450.

Mobile Cellular Telephones (subscribers, September 2000): 22,980.

EDUCATION*

School enrolment (1998/99): 9,278.

University (1998/99): 1,390.

Other students (1998/99): 254.

* Part of the educational systems is undertaken by Spain and France.

Directory

The Constitution

The Constitution of the Principality of Andorra came into force on 4 May 1993, having been approved by the Andorran people in a referendum on 14 March. The official name of the independent state is Principat d'Andorra. The Constitution asserts that Andorra is 'a Democratic and Social independent state abiding by the Rule of Law', and defines the fundamental rights, freedoms and obligations of Andorran citizens and delineates the functions and competences of the organs of state.

In accordance with Andorran tradition, the Co-Princes (Coprínceps), respectively the Bishop of Urgel and the President of the French Republic, are titular Heads of State.

The legislature is the General Council (Consell General), one-half of whose members are elected from a single national constituency, the remainder being elected to represent Andorra's seven parishes (Parròquies); members are elected to the General Council for four years. Elections are on the basis of direct universal adult suffrage. The ruling organ of the General Council is the Sindicatura, headed by a Speaker (Síndic General).

The Govern (the executive organ of state) is directed by the Head of Government (Cap de Govern), who is elected by the General Council (and formally appointed by the Co-Princes) and who must command the support of the majority of the legislature's members. The Head of Government nominates government ministers, who may not at the same time be members of the General Council. The Head of Government is restricted to two consecutive full terms of office.

The Constitution defines the composition and powers of the judiciary, the highest organ of which is the Higher Court of Justice.

The Constitution defines the functions of the communal councils (Comuns), which are the organs of representation and administration of the parishes.

Revision of the Constitution shall require the approval of two-thirds of the members of the General Council and ratification by a referendum.

The Constitutional Court is the supreme interpreter of the Constitution. Its decisions are binding for public authorities and for individuals.

The Government

HEADS OF STATE

Episcopal Co-Prince: Dr JOAN MARTÍ ALANIS, Bishop of Urgel.
French Co-Prince: JACQUES CHIRAC.

GOVERNMENT
(April 2001)

Head of Government: MARC FORNÉ MOLNÉ.
Minister of Finance: MIREIA MAESTRE CORTADELLA.
Minister of Foreign Affairs: JULI MINOVES TRIQUELL.
Minister of the Economy: MIQUEL ALVAREZ MARFANY.
Minister of Territorial Development: JORDI SERRA MALLEU.
Minister of Welfare and Public Health: MÒNICA CODINA TORT.
Minister of Education, Youth and Sports: PERE CERVÓS CARDONA.
Minister of Tourism and Culture: ENRIC PUJAL ARENY.
Minister of Agriculture and the Environment: OLGA ADELLACH COMA.
Minister of Justice and the Interior: JORDI VISENT GUITART.

MINISTRIES

Office of the Head of Government: Govern d'Andorra, Carrer Prat de la Creu 62–64, Andorra la Vella; tel. 875700; fax 822882; internet www.andorra.ad/govern/.

Ministry of Agriculture and the Environment: Carrer Prat de la Creu 62–64, Andorra la Vella; tel. 875700; fax 828906.

Ministry of the Economy: Govern d'Andorra, Edif. Administratiu, Carrer Prat de la Creu 62–64, Andorra la Vella; tel. 875700; fax 861519.

Ministry of Education, Youth and Sports: Carrer Bonaventura Armengol 6, Edif. Crèdit Centre, Andorra la Vella; tel. 866585; fax 861229.

Ministry of Finance: Carrer Prat de la Creu 62–64, Andorra la Vella; tel. 875700; fax 860962.

Ministry of Foreign Affairs: Carrer Prat de la Creu 62–64, Andorra la Vella; tel. 875700; fax 869559.

Ministry of Justice and the Interior: Carrer Ciutat de Sabadell, Escaldes-Engordany; tel. 872080; fax 869250; internet www .finances.ad.

Ministry of Territorial Development: Carrer Prat de la Creu 62–64, Andorra la Vella; tel. 875700; fax 861313.

Ministry of Tourism and Culture: Carrer Prat de la Creu 62–64, Andorra la Vella; tel. 875700; fax 860184; e-mail turisme@ andorra.ad; internet www.turisme.ad.

Ministry of Welfare and Public Health: Avinguda Príncep Benlloch 26, Andorra la Vella; tel. 860345; fax 861933; internet www.salutibenestar.ad.

Legislature

CONSELL GENERAL
(General Council)

Síndic General (Speaker): FRANCESC ARENY CASAL (PLA).
Subsíndic General (Deputy Speaker): MIQUEL ÁLVAREZ MARFANY (PLA).

General Election, 4 March 2001

Party	Votes cast	Seats
Partit Liberal d'Andorra	4,309	15
Partit Socialdemòcrata	2,683	6
Partit Demòcrata	2,198	5
Independent candidates	1,702	2
Total	**10,892**	**28**

Political Organizations

The establishment of political parties was sanctioned under the Constitution that was promulgated in May 1993.

Iniciatíva Democratica Nacional (IDN): Plaça Rebés 1, 2°, Andorra la Vella; tel. 866406; fax 866306; e-mail idn@andorra.ad; f. 1993; Leader VICENÇ MATEU ZAMORA.

Nova Democràcia (ND): Andorra la Vella; f. 1993; Leader JAUME BARTOMEU CASSANY.

Partit Demòcrata: Avda del Fener 15-17, 1r C, Andorra la Vella; tel. 805777; fax 805779; e-mail partitdemocrata@andorra.ad; internet www.partitdemocrata.ad; f. 2000 after Agrupament Nacional Democràtic split into two parties; Leader JORDI MAS TORRES.

Partit Liberal d'Andorra: Edif. Eland, 4°, Carrer del Fener 11, Andorra la Vella; tel. 869708; fax 869728; e-mail pla@andorra.ad; internet www.partitliberal.ad; f. 1992 as Unió Liberal; Leader MARC FORNÉ MOLNÉ.

Partit Socialdemòcrata (PS): Carrer Verge del Pilar 5, 3°, Andorra la Vella; tel. 805260; fax 821746; e-mail partitsocialdemocrat@ andorra.ad; internet www.psa.ad; f. 2000 after the Agrupament Nacional Democràtic split into two parties; Leader JAUME BARTUMEU CASSANY.

Unió Parroquiai d'Ordino (UPO): Leader SIMÓ DURÓ COMA.

Diplomatic Representation

EMBASSIES IN ANDORRA

France: Carrer-les-Canals 38–40, POB 155, Andorra la Vella; tel. 820809; Ambassador: HENRI LECLERCQ.

Spain: Carrer Prat de la Creu 34, Andorra la Vella; tel. 800030; fax 868500; Ambassador: JUAN MARÍA LÓPEZ-AGUILAR.

Judicial System

The 1993 Constitution guarantees the independence of the judiciary.

Judicial power is vested, in the first instance, in the Magistrates' Courts (Batllia) and in the Judges' Tribunal (Tribunal de Batlles), the criminal-law courts (Tribunal de Corts) and the Higher Court of Justice (Tribunal Superior de la Justícia). The judiciary is represented, directed and administered by the Higher Council of Justice (Consell Superior de la Justícia), whose five members are appointed for single terms of six years. Final jurisdiction, in constitutional matters, is vested in the Constitutional Court (Tribunal Constitucional), whose four members hold office for no more than two consecutive eight-year terms.

The Press

In 1996 the average weekly circulation of the local press totalled 10,000.

7 DIES: Avinguda Riberaygua 39, Andorra la Vella; tel. 863700; fax 863800; weekly; local issues; Catalan; Pres. MARC VILA AMIGÓ; Dir ROSA MARI SORRIBES.

Butlletí Oficial de Principat d'Andorra: Andorra la Vella; official govt gazette; tel. 861400; fax 864300.

Diari d'Andorra: Avinguda Riberaygua 39, Andorra la Vella; tel. 863700; fax 863800; internet www.diariandorra.ad; f. 1991; daily; local issues; Catalan; Pres. MARC VILA AMIGÓ; Dir IGNASI PLANELL; circ. 3,000.

El Periòdic d'Andorra: Parc de la Mola 10, Torre Caldea, Escaldes-Engordany; tel. 736200; fax 736210; internet www.elperiodico.es/andorra; daily; local issues; Catalan; Dir JOSEP ANTON ROSSELL PUJOL.

Broadcasting and Communications

TELECOMMUNICATIONS

Servei de Telecomunicacions d'Andorra (STA): Avinguda Meritxell 112, Andorra la Vella; tel. 875000; fax 860600; e-mail sta@sta.ad; internet www.sta.ad/; provides national and international telecommunications services; Dir RAMON PLA.

BROADCASTING
Radio

Ràdio Andorra: Baixada del Molí, Andorra la Vella; tel. 873777; fax 864999; e-mail rtvasa@andorra.ad; internet www.andorra.ad/orta; f. 1991 as an Andorran-owned commercial public broadcasting service, to replace two stations which closed in 1981, following the expiry of their contracts with French and Spanish companies; Dir ENRIC CASTELLET.

Ràdio Valira: Avinguda Meritxell 9, 1st Floor, Andorra la Vella; tel. 829600; fax 828273; e-mail radiovalira@radiovalira.ad; internet www.radiovalira.com; f. 1985; public commercial broadcasting service; Dirs GUALBERTO OSSORIO, JOSÉ RABADA.

Television

In 1996 Andorra was able to receive broadcasts from seven television stations (excluding channels received by satellite or cable).

Andorra Televisió: Baixada del Molí, Andorra la Vella; tel. 873777; fax 864999; e-mail rtvasa@andorra.ad; internet www.andorra.ad/orta; f. 1995 as an Andorran-owned commercial public broadcasting service; Dir ENRIC CASTELLET.

Antena 7: Avinguda les Escoles 16, Escaldes-Engordany; tel. 824433; fax 826088; private co; in 1987 began to transmit one hour of Andorran-interest programmes from the Spanish side of the border.

Finance

(cap. = capital; res = reserves; dep. = deposits; m. = million; brs = branches; amounts in Spanish pesetas)

PRINCIPAL BANKS

Banc Agricol i Comercial d'Andorra SA: POB 49, Avinguda Fiter i Rossell, 4 bis, Escaldes-Engordany; tel. 873345; fax 873350; e-mail internacional@banc-agricol.ad; internet www.banc-agricol.ad; f. 1930; cap. 6,000m., res 22,934m., dep. 201,593m. (Dec. 1999);

Pres. MANUEL CERQUEDA-DONADEU; Gen. Man. JAUME SABATER ROVIRA; 9 brs.

Banc Internacional d'Andorra SA: POB 8, Avinguda Meritxell 32, Andorra la Vella; tel. 884488; fax 884499; e-mail bibm@bibm.ad; internet www.bibm.ad; f. 1958; affiliated to Banco Bilbao Vizcaya, Spain; cap. 7,056m., res 20,467m., dep. 303,641m. (Dec. 1999); Hon. Chair. JOAN MORA FONT; Chair. of Bd of Dirs JORDI ARISTOT MORA; 4 brs.

Banca Mora SA: POB 8, Plaça Coprínceps 2, Escaldes-Engordany; tel. 884488; fax 884499; e-mail bibm@bibm.ad; internet www.bibm.ad; f. 1952; subsidiary of Banc Internacional d'Andorra SA; cap. 5,000m., res 6,456m., dep. 135,469m. (Dec. 1999); Chair. FRANCESC MORA FONT; CEO JORDI ARISTOT MORA; 7 brs.

Banca Privada d'Andorra SA: POB 25, Avinguda Carlemany 119, Escaldes-Engordany; tel. 873500; fax 873517; e-mail bpa@bpa.ad; internet www.bpa.ad; f. 1958; fmrly Banca Cassany SA; cap. 5,250m., res 345m., dep. 80,737m. (Dec. 1999); Pres. HIGINI CIERCO I GARCÍA; Gen. Man. JOAN PAU MIQUEL PRATS; 4 brs.

Banca Reig SA: Avinguda Meritxell 79, Andorra la Vella; tel. 872872; fax 872875; e-mail reigbank@andorra.ad; f. 1956; cap. 5,000m., res 10,444m., dep. 154,919m. (Dec. 2000); Pres. OSCAR RIBAS REIG; CEO ORIOL RIBAS DURÓ; 4 brs.

Crèdit Andorrà: Avinguda Meritxell 80, Andorra la Vella; tel. 888035; fax 888881; internet www.creditandorra.ad; f. 1955; cap. 10,000m., res 43,194m., dep. 520,374m. (Dec. 1999); Chair. J. CASAL; Gen. Man. J. PERALBA; 14 brs.

CHAMBER OF COMMERCE

Cambra de Comerç, Indústria i Serveis d'Andorra: Carrer Prat de la Creu 8, Edif. Le Mans, Despatx 204-205, Andorra la Vella; tel. 863232; fax 863233; e-mail ccis@andorra.ad; internet www.andorra.ad/ccis/; Pres. JORDI MARQUET MANDICÓ.

Transport
RAILWAYS

There are no railways in Andorra, but the nearest stations are Ax-les-Thermes, L'Hospitalet and La Tour de Carol, in France (with trains from Toulouse and Perpignan), and Puigcerdá, in Spain, on the line from Barcelona. There is a connecting bus service from all four stations to Andorra. In 2001 the Government announced a ptas 40,000m. plan to construct an overhead train system to alleviate traffic problems in Andorra la Vella.

ROADS

A good road connects the Spanish and French frontiers, passing through Andorra la Vella. In 1996 there were 279 national roads, 198 of which were tarmacked.

CIVIL AVIATION

There is an airport at Seo de Urgel in Spain, 20 km from Andorra la Vella. In early 2001 plans were announced to redevelop the airport as a one-runway international airport for Andorra, at a cost of ptas 2,000m.

Tourism

Andorra has attractive mountain scenery, and winter sports facilities are available at six skiing centres. Tourists are also attracted by Andorra's duty-free shopping facilities. In 1999 there were 267 hotels and hostels in Andorra. An estimated 2.3m. tourists visited Andorra in 1999.

Andorra Department of Tourism: Carrer Prat de la Creu 62, Andorra la Vella; tel. 875700; fax 860184; e-mail turisme@andorra.ad; internet www.turisme.ad.

Andorra Hotel Association: Antic Carrer Major 18, Andorra la Vella; tel. 820602; fax 861539; e-mail uhotelera@internet.ad; internet www.uha.ad; Pres. MARC ALEIX.

Sindicat d'Iniciativa Oficina de Turisme: Carrer Dr Vilanova, Andorra la Vella; tel. 820214; fax 825823.

ANGOLA

Introductory Survey

Location, Climate, Language, Religion, Flag, Capital

The Republic of Angola lies on the west coast of Africa. The Cabinda district is separated from the rest of the country by the estuary of the River Congo and territory of the Democratic Republic of the Congo (DRC—formerly Zaire), with the Republic of the Congo lying to its north. Angola is bordered by the DRC to the north, Zambia to the east and Namibia to the south. The climate is tropical, locally tempered by altitude. There are two distinct seasons (wet and dry) but little seasonal variation in temperature. It is very hot and rainy in the coastal lowlands but temperatures are lower inland. The official language is Portuguese, but African languages (mainly Umbundo, Kimbundo, Kikongo, Chokwe and Ganguela) are also in common use. Much of the population follows traditional African beliefs, although a majority profess to be Christians, mainly Roman Catholics. The flag (proportions 3 by 2) has two equal horizontal stripes, of red and black; superimposed in the centre, in gold, are a five-pointed star, half a cog-wheel and a machete. The capital is Luanda.

Recent History

Formerly a Portuguese colony, Angola became an overseas province in 1951. African nationalist groups began to form in the 1950s and 1960s, including the Movimento Popular de Libertação de Angola (MPLA) in 1956, the Frente Nacional de Libertação de Angola (FNLA) in 1962 and the União Nacional para a Independência Total de Angola (UNITA) in 1966. Severe repression followed an unsuccessful nationalist rebellion in 1961, but after a new wave of fighting in 1966, nationalist guerrilla groups were able to establish military and political control in large parts of eastern Angola and to press westward. Following the April 1974 *coup d'état* in Portugal, Angola's right to independence was recognized, and negotiations between the Portuguese Government and the nationalist groups began in September. After the formation of a common front by these groups, it was agreed that Angola would become independent in November 1975.

In January 1975 a transitional Government was established, comprising representatives of the MPLA, the FNLA, UNITA and the Portuguese Government. However, violent clashes between the MPLA and the FNLA occurred in March, as a result of the groups' political differences, and continued throughout the country. By the second half of 1975 control of Angola was effectively divided between the three major nationalist groups, each aided by foreign powers. The MPLA (which held the capital) was supported by the USSR and Cuba, the FNLA by Zaire and Western powers (including the USA), while UNITA was backed by South African forces. The FNLA and UNITA formed a united front to fight the MPLA.

The Portuguese Government proclaimed Angola independent from 11 November 1975, transferring sovereignty to 'the Angolan people' rather than to any of the liberation movements. The MPLA proclaimed the People's Republic of Angola and the establishment of a government in Luanda under the presidency of the movement's leader, Dr Agostinho Neto. The FNLA and UNITA proclaimed the Democratic People's Republic of Angola and a coalition government, based in Nova Lisboa (renamed Huambo). By the end of February 1976, however, the MPLA, aided by Cuban technical and military expertise, had effectively gained control of the whole country. South African troops were withdrawn from Angola in March, but Cuban troops remained to assist the MPLA regime in countering guerrilla activity by the remnants of the defeated UNITA forces.

In May 1977 an abortive coup, led by Nito Alves (a former minister), resulted in a purge of state and party officials. In December the MPLA was renamed the Movimento Popular de Libertação de Angola—Partido do Trabalho (MPLA—PT), but further divisions became evident in December 1978, when President Neto abolished the post of Prime Minister and ousted several other ministers.

Neto died in September 1979, and José Eduardo dos Santos, hitherto the Minister of Planning, was unanimously elected party leader and President by the MPLA—PT Central Committee. Dos Santos continued to encourage strong links with the Soviet bloc, and led campaigns to eliminate corruption and inefficiency. Elections to the National People's Assembly, which replaced the Council of the Revolution, were first held in 1980. Fresh elections, due to be held in 1983, were postponed until 1986, owing to political and military problems.

The MPLA—PT Government's recovery programme was continually hindered by security problems. Although the FNLA rebel movement reportedly surrendered to the Government in 1984, UNITA conducted sustained and disruptive guerrilla activities, mainly in southern and central Angola, throughout the 1980s. In addition, forces from South Africa, which was providing UNITA with considerable military aid, made numerous armed incursions over the Angolan border with Namibia, ostensibly in pursuit of guerrilla forces belonging to the South West Africa People's Organisation (SWAPO), which was supported by the Angolan Government. In 1983 regional military councils were established in the provinces affected by the fighting. Although the Government's military campaign against UNITA appeared to be increasingly successful during 1985, the rebels' position was strengthened in 1986, when US military aid began to arrive. (The US Government continued to provide covert military aid to UNITA until 1990.) Nevertheless, UNITA was excluded from a series of major peace negotiations, between Angola, Cuba and South Africa (with the unofficial mediation of the USA), which commenced in May 1988. By mid-July the participants had agreed to a document containing the principles for a peace settlement that provided for independence for Namibia, the discontinuation of South African military support for UNITA and the withdrawal of Cuban troops from Angola. In July and August Dr Jonas Savimbi, the President of UNITA, travelled to the USA and to several European and African capitals to seek support for UNITA's demands to be included in the negotiations. Although movement for a negotiated settlement between the MPLA—PT Government and UNITA then gathered momentum, UNITA's position became vulnerable in August, when a cease-fire between Angola and South Africa was declared and South African troops were withdrawn from Angola. UNITA refused to adhere to the cease-fire. Following the conclusion of the New York accords on Angola and Namibia in December, the US Government renewed its commitment to the rebels.

During late 1988 peace initiatives emerged from within Africa with regard to the Angolan civil war. Several African states (including Zaire) were involved in efforts, supported by the USA, to pressurize the Angolan Government into negotiating an internal settlement with UNITA. In December the UN Security Council established the UN Angola Verification Mission (UNAVEM) to verify the phased withdrawal of Cuban troops from Angola, which was completed in May 1991.

In February 1989 the Angolan Government offered a 12-month amnesty to members of the rebel organization; UNITA, restating its aim of entering into a transitional coalition government with the MPLA—PT as a prelude to multi-party elections, responded to the amnesty by launching a major offensive against government targets. This was abandoned shortly afterwards, following the intercession of President Houphouët-Boigny of Côte d'Ivoire. In March dos Santos announced that he was willing to attend a regional summit conference on the Angolan civil war; Savimbi, in turn, announced that he would honour a unilateral moratorium on offensive military operations until mid-July. In May, at a conference in Luanda, dos Santos presented a peace plan that envisaged the cessation of US aid to UNITA and offered the rebels reintegration into society; this was rejected by UNITA. Nevertheless, in June both dos Santos and Savimbi attended a conference at Gbadolite, in Zaire, convened by the Zairean President, Mobutu Sese Seko. Mobutu succeeded in mediating a peace agreement between the Angolan Government and UNITA, in accordance with which a cease-fire came into effect on 24 June. The full terms of the accord were not, however, made public at that time, and it subsequently became apparent that these were interpreted differently by each party. Within one week, each side had accused the other of violating the cease-fire, and in August Savimbi announced a resumption of hostilities.

In September 1989, after boycotting a conference of African Heads of State in Kinshasa, Zaire, at which the June peace accord had been redrafted, Savimbi announced a series of counter-proposals, envisaging the creation of an African peace-keeping force, to supervise a renewed cease-fire, and the commencement of negotiations between UNITA and the Angolan Government towards a settlement providing the foundation of a multi-party democracy in Angola. In October, following a meeting with President Bush of the USA, Savimbi agreed to resume peace talks with the Angolan Government, with Mobutu acting as mediator. In December dos Santos proposed a peace plan that envisaged some political reform, but did not include provisions for a multi-party political system; the plan was rejected by UNITA.

In July 1990 the Central Committee of the MPLA—PT announced that the Government would allow Angola to 'evolve towards a multi-party system'. In October the Central Committee proposed a general programme of reform, including the replacement of the party's official Marxist-Leninist ideology with a commitment to 'democratic socialism', the legalization of political parties, the transformation of the army from a party institution to a state institution, the introduction of a market economy, a revision of the Constitution and the holding of multi-party elections in 1994, following a population census. These proposals were formally approved by the MPLA—PT in December. However, the Government and UNITA continued to disagree over the timing of elections and the status of UNITA pending the elections. UNITA insisted on immediate political recognition as a precondition for a cease-fire and the holding of elections by the end of 1991.

In March 1991 the People's Assembly approved legislation permitting the formation of political parties. On 1 May the Government and UNITA concluded a peace agreement in Estoril, Portugal. The agreement provided for a cease-fire from 15 May, which was to be monitored by a joint political and military commission, comprising representatives from the MPLA—PT, UNITA, the UN, Portugal, the USA and the USSR. A new national army of 50,000 men was to be established, comprising equal numbers of government and UNITA soldiers. Free and democratic elections were to be held by the end of 1992. In May 1991 the Government approved legislation allowing all exiles one year in which to return to Angola. The cease-fire took effect, according to plan, on 15 May, despite an intensification of hostilities prior to that date. On 31 May the Government and UNITA signed a formal agreement in Lisbon, Portugal, ratifying the Estoril agreement. Meanwhile, all Cuban troops had been withdrawn from Angola, but the UN Security Council agreed to prolong the presence of the UN Angola Verification Mission (as UNAVEM II), with a mandate to ensure implementation of the peace accords. In July the Standing Commission of the People's Assembly approved a new amnesty law, under the terms of which amnesty would be granted for all crimes against state security as well as for military and common law offences committed before 31 May 1991.

A reshuffle of the Council of Ministers in July 1991 included the appointment of Fernando José França van-Dúnem to the post of Prime Minister, thus reintroducing the premiership to the Government. Supreme executive power remained, however, with the President.

In September 1991 Savimbi returned to Luanda for the first time since the civil war began in 1975, and UNITA headquarters were transferred to the capital from Jamba in October. In the following month dos Santos announced that legislative and presidential elections were to take place in September 1992, subject to the extension of state administration to areas still under UNITA control and the confinement of all UNITA forces to assembly points by mid-December 1991. In January 1992, on the recommendation of the joint political and military commission, a monitoring task group was established to oversee the implementation of the peace agreement. The creation of the group, which included members of the Government, UNITA and UNAVEM II, followed growing concern over the reported decline in the number of government and UNITA troops in confinement areas and the reoccupation of territory by UNITA forces.

Representatives of the Government and 26 political parties met in Luanda in January 1992 to discuss the transition to multi-party democracy. UNITA boycotted the meeting, but in February it held talks with the Government, at which it was agreed that the elections would be conducted on the basis of

proportional representation, with the President elected for a five-year term, renewable for a maximum of three terms. The legislature would be a national assembly, elected for a four-year term. In April the People's Assembly adopted electoral legislation incorporating these decisions and providing for the creation of a national assembly of 223 members (90 to be elected in 18 provincial constituencies and the remainder from national lists).

In April 1992 the Supreme Court approved UNITA's registration as a political party. In May the MPLA—PT held an extraordinary congress to prepare for the forthcoming elections. The delegates voted to enlarge the membership of the Central Committee to allow the inclusion of prominent dissidents who had returned to the party. The Central Committee recommended that the Political Bureau further expand its membership with a view to broadening the base of the party's support. During the congress the delegates also voted to remove the suffix Partido do Trabalho (Party of Labour or Workers' Party) from the organization's official name. In August the legislature approved a further revision of the Constitution, removing the remnants of the country's former Marxist ideology, and deleting the words 'People's' and 'Popular' from the Constitution and from the names of official institutions. The name of the country was changed from the People's Republic of Angola to the Republic of Angola.

Increased tension and outbreaks of violence in the period preceding the general election, which was due to be held on 29 and 30 September 1992, seriously threatened to disrupt the electoral process. In early September in Cabinda province, the enclave that provides most of Angola's petroleum revenue, secessionist groups, notably the Frente de Libertação do Enclave de Cabinda (FLEC), intensified attacks on government troops. Also in that month, clashes took place between UNITA and government forces in Bié province.

On 27 September 1992 the government Forças Armadas Populares de Libertação de Angola (FAPLA) and the UNITA forces were formally disbanded, and the new national army, the Forças Armadas de Angola (FAA), was officially established. However, the process of training and incorporating FAPLA and UNITA troops into the new 50,000-strong national army had been hindered by delays in the demobilization programme. By 28 September fewer than 10,000 soldiers were ready to be sworn in as members of the FAA. Tens of thousands of government troops were reported to be awaiting demobilization or to have abandoned confinement areas, owing to poor conditions and non-payment of wages. Military observers reported that only a small percentage of UNITA soldiers had been demobilized, and that UNITA retained a heavily armed and disciplined force.

Presidential and legislative elections were held, as scheduled, on 29 and 30 September 1992. When preliminary results indicated victory for the MPLA in the elections to the new National Assembly, Savimbi accused the Government of electoral fraud, withdrew his troops from the FAA, and demanded the suspension of the official announcement of the election results until an inquiry into the alleged electoral irregularities had been conducted. According to the provisions of the electoral law, a second round of the presidential election was required to be held between dos Santos and Savimbi, as neither candidate had secured 50% of the votes cast in the first round. Savimbi, who had retreated to the UNITA-dominated province of Huambo, agreed to participate in this second round on the condition that it be conducted by the UN, while the Government insisted that the election should not take place until UNITA had satisfied the conditions of the Estoril peace agreement by transferring its troops to assembly points or to the FAA.

Following the announcement, on 17 October 1992, of the official results of the elections, which the UN had declared to have been free and fair, violence broke out between MPLA and UNITA supporters in the cities of Luanda and Huambo. By the end of October hostilities had spread throughout Angola, with the majority of UNITA's demobilized soldiers returning to arms. On 20 November, following negotiations with UN diplomats, Savimbi issued a statement in which he agreed to abide by the results of the September elections, although he maintained that the ballot had been fraudulent. Subsequently dos Santos announced that the new National Assembly, which was to be formed in accordance with the results of the September elections, would be inaugurated on 26 November. On that day delegations from the Government and UNITA met in Namibe in an effort to resolve the crisis. A joint communiqué was issued, declaring full acceptance of the validity of the May 1991 Estoril peace agreement and the intention to implement immediately a nation-wide cease-fire. However, UNITA's 70 elected deputies failed to attend the inauguration of the National Assembly. On 27 November dos Santos announced the appointment of Marcolino José Carlos Moco, the Secretary-General of the MPLA, as Prime Minister. At the end of November, in violation of the recently signed Namibe accord, hostilities broke out in the north of the country. On 2 December a new Council of Ministers was announced, including minor ministerial positions for members of the FNLA, the Fórum Democrático Angolano, the Partido Renovador Social and the Partido de Aliança de Juventude, Operários e Camponêses de Angola. In addition, one full and four deputy ministerial posts were reserved for UNITA, which was allowed one week to join the Government. UNITA subsequently nominated a number of its officials to the reserved posts. According to a statement by the Prime Minister, however, the appointment of UNITA officials to the Government was entirely dependent upon the implementation of the Estoril peace agreement.

The situation in Angola throughout 1993 and 1994 was characterized by continuous efforts by the UN to negotiate a permanent peace accord between the Government and UNITA. Meanwhile, civil war, in which both sides claimed military gains and suffered heavy losses, continued. In early 1993 some 10,000 people died during two months of heavy fighting for control of the second largest city, Huambo. Diplomatic moves to end the hostilities included unsuccessful talks in Addis Ababa, Ethiopia, convened by the UN in January 1993, abortive talks in Abidjan, Côte d'Ivoire, in April–May, and lengthy negotiations in Lusaka, Zambia, which commenced in late 1993. In May 1993 the US President, Bill Clinton, announced that the USA was to recognize the Angolan Government. In September 1993, following reports of an intensification of UNITA activity, the UN imposed an arms and petroleum embargo against the rebels, including an embargo, the 'freezing' of UNITA's foreign assets, and the expulsion of its representatives from Western capitals. However, in November, UNITA agreed to withdraw its forces to UN-monitored confinement areas. In response, the UN agreed to delay the imposition of further sanctions against UNITA.

As a consequence of the Lusaka talks, by 10 December an agreement had reportedly been reached between UNITA and the Government on issues concerning the demobilization and confinement of UNITA troops, the surrender of UNITA weapons to the UN, and the integration of UNITA generals into the FAA, prompting the UN again to postpone additional sanctions against the rebels. The Lusaka talks resumed in January 1994, and agreement was reached on the formation, under UN supervision, of a national police force of 26,700 members, of which UNITA was to provide 5,500. Further talks culminated in the signing, on 17 February, of a document on national reconciliation. Acceptance of the September 1992 election results by both sides was also reaffirmed. However, progress at the Lusaka peace talks slowed as discussions advanced to the issue of the participation of UNITA in central and local government. Negotiations on the distribution of ministerial posts appeared to have reached an impasse in March, and negotiations instead moved on to discuss the conclusion of the electoral process: the second round of presidential elections between dos Santos and Savimbi. In May agreement was officially confirmed regarding these elections, although some related issues remained to be discussed, including the role of the independent observers. Further talks, concerning UNITA's representation in the Council of Ministers and the status of Savimbi, reached a stalemate in May. Talks continued in Lusaka in late June, culminating in the signing of an 18-point document on national reconciliation.

In July 1994 President Mandela of South Africa hosted talks in Pretoria between the Presidents of Angola, Mozambique and Zaire. The discussions concentrated on allegations of Zairean support for UNITA and resulted in the re-establishment of a joint defence and security commission between Angola and Zaire, with the aim of curbing the supply of armaments to the rebels. In August UNITA acceded to government insistence that its officials be permitted to participate in government institutions only after the total demilitarization of the movement, and an 11-point procedural accord, enabling discussions on full reconciliation, was signed.

Throughout July and August 1994 the question of the governorship of Huambo continued to constitute the main obstacle to the furtherance of the peace talks. On 8 September UNITA reportedly accepted a proposal by mediators for the allocation to UNITA of government positions that included some 170 posts in central and local administration, but excluded the governorship of Huambo. In mid-September the Government and UNITA agreed on the general principles governing the mandate of a new UN Angola Verification Mission—UNAVEM III. At the end of that month, following successive extensions, the UN Security Council further extended the mandate of UNAVEM II until 31 October and urged both sides to sign a peace accord by 15 October. However, talks continued throughout October, concentrating on the issue of Savimbi's security and the replacement of the joint political and military commission with a new joint commission, which was to be chaired by the UN Secretary-General's special representative, Alioune Blondin Beye, and was to comprise representatives of the Government and UNITA and observers from the USA, Russia and Portugal. A peace accord was finally initialled on 31 October and formally signed on 20 November. However, hostilities continued beyond 22 November, when a permanent cease-fire was to have come into force, notably in Huambo and in Bié province.

In December 1994 the UN Security Council extended the mandate of UNAVEM II until 8 February 1995, when it was to be superseded by UNAVEM III, on condition that the cease-fire was observed. In January 1995 a meeting took place at Chipipa, in Huambo province, between the Chief of General Staff of the FAA and his UNITA counterpart, at which agreement was reached on an immediate cessation of hostilities nation-wide. Despite this undertaking, however, the fighting continued. In February 1995 the UN Security Council adopted a resolution creating UNAVEM III. However, the deployment of the new peace-keeping mission remained conditional on the cessation of hostilities and the disengagement of government and UNITA forces.

In March 1995 both the Government and UNITA were criticized in a report made to the UN Security Council by the UN Secretary-General, Dr Boutros Boutros-Ghali, who accused the two sides of a lack of goodwill in implementing the peace process. The report, which followed continued and widespread violations of the truce, set a deadline of 25 March for the two sides to demonstrate a genuine commitment to the peace process. It also appealed for preparations to be expedited to enable the prompt transfer of UNITA troops into the FAA. Following a meeting of the joint commission, Beye confirmed that the majority of UNAVEM III personnel would begin arriving in early May. In April the joint commission reported a significant reduction in violations of the cease-fire. However, at the same time Boutros-Ghali indicated that reports of military preparations, including the acquisition of arms from abroad, remained a serious cause of concern.

In early May 1995, in what represented an important development in the peace process, dos Santos and Savimbi met in Lusaka for direct talks. The meeting concluded with the ratification of the Lusaka peace accord. Notably, Savimbi recognized the status of dos Santos as President of Angola and pledged his full co-operation in the reconstruction of the nation. The two leaders agreed to accelerate the consolidation of the cease-fire, to create conditions for the deployment of UNAVEM III, to expedite the integration of UNITA troops into the FAA, and to establish a government of unity based on the provisions of the Lusaka accord (subsequent to the demobilization of the UNITA forces). Dos Santos requested that Savimbi nominate immediately the UNITA appointees to the new government.

In June 1995 the MPLA announced its decision to propose a revision of the Constitution to create two new posts of Vice-President, of which one was to be offered to Savimbi, conditional upon the prior disbanding of UNITA forces. The other vice-presidency was to be assumed by the then President of the National Assembly, Fernando José França van-Dúnem. Later that month Savimbi, who had publicly expressed his intention to accept the vice-presidency, declared the war in Angola to be at an end and appealed to neighbouring nations to prevent the traffic of arms to the country. In July the National Assembly approved the proposed constitutional amendment to create the two new vice-presidential positions, and Boutros-Ghali announced that the deployment of UNAVEM III personnel would be completed by the end of August.

In September 1995 the joint commission expressed concern at continuing violations of the cease-fire. However, in the following month, figures issued by UNAVEM III revealed that recorded cease-fire violations had decreased by approximately 50% between July and September. In late September the Government signed a four-month cease-fire agreement with FLEC—

Renovada, a faction of FLEC. It was anticipated that the agreement, which followed an offensive by FLEC—Renovada on Cabinda City in the previous month, would facilitate the negotiation, between the Government and all factions of FLEC, of a pact aimed at national reconciliation.

In late September 1995 dos Santos and Savimbi met for direct talks in Brussels, Belgium, immediately prior to the convention there of an international donors' conference on Angola. At the conference donors pledged a total of US $997.5m. towards Angola's national rehabilitation and reconciliation programme, of which $200m. was to be allocated to emergency humanitarian assistance. The cantonment of UNITA forces began officially in late November. However, continued hostilities were reported that month, including confrontations in the diamond-producing areas of the north-east and in the Cabinda enclave. In December, following concerted military operations by government forces aimed at occupying UNITA-controlled territory in Zaire province, UNITA suspended the confinement of its troops. In an effort to promote confidence in the peace process in advance of discussions to be conducted that month with US President Clinton, dos Santos promptly introduced a number of conciliatory measures, including the withdrawal of government troops from positions seized in Zaire province, and the confinement, which began the following month, of the paramilitary Rapid Intervention Force. In January 1996 UNITA resumed the process of confining its troops. By early February, however, UNITA had succeeded in confining only some 8,200 troops, prompting the UN Security Council to renew the mandate of UNAVEM III. In January, following discussions conducted in Brazzaville, Republic of the Congo, the Government and FLEC—Renovada agreed to extend the cease-fire accord secured in September 1995.

In March 1996 discussions between dos Santos and Savimbi, conducted in Libreville, Gabon, resulted in agreement on the establishment of a government of national unity, in accordance with the provisions of the Lusaka accord, by the end of July. Savimbi presented a proposal listing the UNITA governmental nominees, while dos Santos formally invited Savimbi to assume the vice-presidency. (Later in March, however, Savimbi demanded the inclusion of other opposition parties in the government of national unity, presenting as a condition to his own participation the inclusion in the new administration of the President of the FNLA, Holden Roberto.) Agreement was also reached in Libreville on the formation of the unified national army, which, it was envisaged, would be concluded in June. In subsequent talks between representatives of the Government and UNITA it was agreed that 18 UNITA generals would be appointed to command posts in the new unified FAA. It was also established that 26,300 of UNITA's total force of some 62,000 would be integrated into the FAA. In late May, following negotiations between the Government and UNITA, agreement was reached on a programme to integrate UNITA troops into the FAA. Selection of UNITA personnel was to begin on 1 June. During May Savimbi introduced further conditions for his acceptance of the vice-presidency and expressed his intention to retain control of diamond-producing areas in north-eastern Angola. In mid-May the Government and a Cabinda secessionist faction, FLEC—Forças Armadas Cabindesas (FLEC—FAC), signed an agreement outlining the principles of a cease-fire. However, following renewed fighting later that month between government troops and the secessionists, the leader of FLEC—FAC, Henrique N'zita Tiago, declared that a definitive cease-fire would only follow the withdrawal of the FAA from Cabinda.

In mid-1996 public protest at deteriorating economic conditions and the high level of corruption within the state apparatus placed increasing political pressure on dos Santos, who responded in early June with the dismissal of the Moco administration. Moco was succeeded as Prime Minister by the President of the National Assembly (and former Prime Minister), Fernando José França van-Dúnem. A new Government was sworn in on 8 June, with only limited changes to the previous administration. In late August, following its party congress, UNITA issued a communiqué declining the appointment of Savimbi to the position of national Vice-President. UNITA did not propose the appointment of another of its officials to the post, and in September Beye confirmed that the offer of the vice-presidency had become void.

In October 1996 delays in the implementation of the provisions of the Lusaka accord prompted the UN Security Council to threaten the imposition of sanctions against UNITA unless it met certain requirements by 20 November, including the

surrender of weapons and the designation of those UNITA troops to be integrated into the FAA. In the following month the National Assembly adopted a constitutional revision extending its mandate, which was due to expire that month, for a period of between two and four years, pending the establishment of suitable conditions for the conduct of free and fair elections. Despite assertions by UNITA that it had fully disarmed in accordance with the terms of the Lusaka accord, UNAVEM III expressed concern in December 1996 that some 15,705 UNITA troops had deserted confinement areas. At the same time UN sources reported the existence of a residual UNITA force of some 15,000 well-armed troops in central and north-eastern Angola. Despite these apparent obstacles to the further implementation of the peace accord, the Government announced in the same month that the UNITA deputies who had been elected in 1992 would join the National Assembly in mid-January 1997, and that the new government of national unity and reconciliation would be inaugurated on 25 January. However, following the failure of the UNITA deputies to join the National Assembly, the Government postponed the inauguration of the new administration. In February UNITA asserted that it would only send its deputies and government nominees to the capital if the Government first agreed to negotiate a draft programme for the government of national unity and reconciliation. In March the Government conceded to UNITA's demand and a basic programme was formulated. In April an agreement was reached to accord Savimbi the special status of official 'leader of the opposition'. Subsequent to the arrival of the full contingent of UNITA deputies and government nominees in Luanda, on 11 April the new Government of National Unity and Reconciliation was inaugurated, although the ceremony was not attended by Savimbi, who maintained that his personal security could not be guaranteed. As envisaged, UNITA assumed the ministerial portfolios of geology and mines, trade, health, and hotels and tourism, and a further seven deputy ministerial posts. Ten minor political parties were also represented in the 87-member Government.

In May 1997 the Angolan Government officially recognized the new Government of Laurent-Désiré Kabila in the Democratic Republic of the Congo (DRC, formerly Zaire). The Angolan Government had actively supported Kabila's rebels during the civil war in Zaire, while UNITA, which relied on Zaire as a conduit for exporting diamonds and importing arms, had reportedly sent some 2,000 troops to support President Mobutu. In the light of the defeat of UNITA's main ally, the Government subsequently launched a military offensive on UNITA strongholds in the north-eastern provinces of Lunda-Sul and Lunda-Norte in what appeared to be an attempt to eradicate UNITA as a military force.

On 30 June 1997 the UN Security Council unanimously approved the UN Secretary-General's recommendations that UNAVEM III be discontinued, following numerous extensions to its mandate, and replaced by a scaled-down observer mission, the United Nations Observer Mission in Angola (MONUA), with a seven-month mandate to oversee the implementation of the remaining provisions of the Lusaka accord, including the reinstatement of state administration throughout the country. MONUA began operating on 1 July. In late July the UN again condemned UNITA's failure to adhere to the Lusaka accord and threatened to impose further sanctions on the movement, including travel restrictions, if it did not take irreversible steps towards fulfilling its obligations. A deadline of 15 August was set by which date UNITA was to give a full account of its military strength and to allow for the disarmament of its troops and the extension of state administration into those areas under its control. UNITA , however, failed to meet the requirements stipulated by the UN, which on 28 August unanimously adopted new sanctions. However, the implementation of the resolution was delayed until 30 September, affording UNITA a further opportunity to resume the peace process. At the end of August UNITA announced that it intended to comply with the demands of the UN in order to avoid the imposition of new sanctions. In September 1997 the restoration of state administration proceeded in several districts, and, despite unsatisfactory progress in the demobilization of UNITA's residual force, was sufficient to prompt the UN Security Council, at the end of that month, to postpone the implementation of the sanctions for a further 30 days. In October UNITA ceded control of one of the country's principal diamond mines, at Luzamba in Lunda-Norte, to the Government.

In July 1997 government delegations from Angola and the Republic of the Congo met in Cabinda to discuss the security situation along the border between the Angolan exclave and the Congo, following armed clashes between Angolan soldiers and FLEC separatists apparently operating from Congolese territory. The talks resulted in proposals to strengthen border security, including the establishment of a joint police force, comprising representatives from both countries and UNHCR. However, in October it became evident that FAA troops were actively supporting the former Marxist ruler of the Congo, Gen. Denis Sassou-Nguesso, in his attempts to overthrow the Government of President Pascal Lissouba. Angola's involvement had been prompted by attacks on Cabinda by FLEC and UNITA forces operating from bases in the Congo provided by Lissouba. In mid-October Sassou-Nguesso's Cobra militia, with Angolan assistance, succeeded in securing his return to power in the Congo.

On 31 October 1997, as a result of UNITA's continued failure to meet its obligations under the peace accord, the UN Security Council finally ordered the implementation of additional sanctions against the movement, including a ban on international travel for UNITA officials and the closure of UNITA offices abroad. In late November UNITA expressed its intention to continue to pursue a peaceful settlement, and during the ensuing months ceded further territory to state administration, including the important Cuango valley diamond mines in Lunda-Norte province.

In January 1998 a new schedule was agreed for the implementation of the Lusaka protocol, which stipulated a deadline of 28 February for its terms to be met. This schedule was subsequently revised, allowing UNITA until 16 March to complete its demobilization. In early March UNITA issued a declaration announcing the disbandment of its remaining forces, following which it received official recognition as a legally constituted party. Later that month the Government implemented the special status agreed for Savimbi, and legislation was adopted allowing him to retain a 400-strong personal guard. However, despite these developments, allegations persisted of preparations by UNITA for a resumption of hostilities. During May there were reports of escalating conflict in Lunda-Norte and Benguela provinces. By June fighting had spread to 14 of the country's 18 provinces resulting in the displacement of some 150,000 people. In July many members of UNITA were reported to have left Luanda and a meeting of the joint commission had to be postponed owing to the absence of UNITA's chief representative, Isaias Samakuva. Later that month the Southern African Development Community (SADC) issued a communiqué urging UNITA to resume negotiations with the Government. In early August Samakuva returned to Luanda and Issa Diallo was appointed by the UN Secretary-General to replace Beye (who had died in June). In mid-August the Government threatened to suspend UNITA's representatives in the Government and the legislature unless it had disarmed fully and ceded all remaining territory under its control by 28 August. In late August UNITA accused the observer countries in the joint commission (Portugal, Russia and the USA) of bias in the Government's favour and declared that it would no longer negotiate with them. On 31 August the Government suspended UNITA's government and parliamentary representatives from office.

On 2 September 1998 a group of five UNITA moderates, who were based in the capital and led by the suspended Minister of Hotels and Tourism, Jorge Alicerces Valentim, issued a manifesto declaring the suspension of Savimbi and the introduction of an interim UNITA leadership, pending a general congress of the party. However, the group, which styled itself UNITA—Renovada (UNITA—R), commanded very limited support among UNITA's leaders in Luanda, while UNITA's Secretary-General dismissed the group as irrelevant. Conversely, the Government welcomed the development, recognizing UNITA—R as the sole and legitimate representative of UNITA in negotiations concerning the implementation of the Lusaka peace process. Dos Santos was supported in this decision by the SADC, which passed a resolution denouncing Savimbi and recognizing the new group. The UN Security Council continued to seek a dialogue between dos Santos and Savimbi as the only solution to the conflict. In late September the Government revoked the suspension of UNITA's representatives in the Government and legislature, but dismissed UNITA's Minister of Geology and Mines, Marcos Samondo. In October 1998 the National Assembly revoked Savimbi's special status. In that month UNITA—R failed to impose its candidate to lead the UNITA

parliamentary group when Abel Chivukuvuku was overwhelmingly re-elected as its Chairman. Chivukuvuku, who, while no longer claiming allegiance to Savimbi, was opposed to UNITA—R, subsequently announced the formation of his own wing of UNITA.

In November 1998, following increasingly frequent outbreaks of fighting in a number of regions, the UN Security Council demanded that UNITA withdraw immediately from territories that it had reoccupied through military action and complete the demilitarization of its troops. At the fourth congress of the MPLA, conducted in December, dos Santos asserted that military action was the only way to subdue UNITA and bring peace to Angola. João Manuel Gonçalves Lourenço was elected Secretary-General of the MPLA, while dos Santos was re-elected unopposed as party President.

In December 1998 the military situation deteriorated considerably prompting the Government to approve the introduction of compulsory military service. In a report made to the UN Security Council that month the UN Secretary-General, Kofi Annan, declared that Angola was once again at war and questioned whether the UN still had a role to play in the country. The UN also warned of a major humanitarian crisis in the country where more than 400,000 people were reported to have abandoned their homes to escape the fighting. However, in late December the UN World Food Programme was forced to suspend its flights in Angola following the shooting down by UNITA of a UN aircraft. In January 1999 a further UN aircraft was shot down by the rebels.

In late January 1999 dos Santos reorganized the Council of Ministers in an effort to address the prevailing military and economic crisis. Notably, the premiership was assumed by dos Santos himself. In that month UNITA—R conducted its first congress in Luanda, at which Eugénio N'Golo 'Manuvakola' was elected leader of the breakaway faction. In a report to the UN Security Council issued in mid-January, Annan recommended the withdrawal of MONUA from Angola (after successive extensions to its mandate), declaring that, despite expenditure of US $1,500m. over the previous four years, conditions had deteriorated to such an extent that UN personnel were no longer able to function. Both the Government and UNITA had indicated that they favoured the withdrawal of the UN; dos Santos openly criticized the UN for having lost control of the peace process. In February the UN Security Council voted unanimously to end MONUA's mandate and withdraw its operatives by 20 March, although the UN expressed its intention to seek the Government's approval to maintain a presence in the country in the form of a 'follow-up' mission, intended to focus on issues concerning humanitarian assistance and human rights.

In the wake of the renewed hostilities, some 780,000 people were reported to have fled to government-occupied towns by late April 1999. The cities of Huambo, Kuito and Malanje were under siege by UNITA forces, and, with access to the cities impeded and food stocks declining, a major humanitarian crisis was developing. Some 10,000 people, including 4,000 civilians, were estimated to have died in the four months since the resumption of the war. In May the Government rejected an offer made by Savimbi for peace talks and announced that the FAA was preparing to mount an offensive against the UNITA strongholds of Andulo and Bailundo. In June the Government agreed in principle to the presence of a small 'follow-up' mission of UN observers in Angola. (In October it was agreed that the mission would comprise some 30 UN officials.)

In October 1999, following a large-scale offensive by the FAA in northern, eastern and central Angola, the Government claimed to have made considerable gains, including, most notably, the capture of UNITA's headquarters in Andulo and Bailundo. While UNITA denied that the towns had fallen to the Government, there were reports that Savimbi had fled the area. In a letter to the Government received in late October, Savimbi warned that UNITA troops were approaching the capital and called for dialogue towards a 'national pact'. The Government, however, dismissed the possibility of further talks, demanding instead the full implementation of the Lusaka protocol. Also that month four UNITA members of the legislature, who had been detained by the security forces in January and charged with committing crimes against the security of the state, were released by order of the Supreme Court owing to insufficient evidence. The arrests had occurred following the refusal of the four deputies to join UNITA—R. In September a UNITA parliamentarian was found shot dead on the outskirts of Luanda.

During 1999 the UN increased its efforts to impose sanctions on UNITA, with the appointment of Canada's ambassador to the UN, Robert Fowler, as Chairman of the UN Sanctions Committee. In July the UN allocated US $1m. for a six-month investigation into UNITA's funding of its war effort, the source of its armaments and the inefficacy of the sanctions imposed against it. A UN report, prepared by Fowler and published in June, disclosed the contravention of UN sanctions by a number of African heads of state, including the Presidents of Togo and Burkina Faso, who were apparently involved in the trading of arms for UNITA-mined diamonds. (Angola threatened to boycott the Organization of African Unity summit, due to be held in Togo in June 2000, because of Togo's alleged involvement in the contravention of UN sanctions; Togo subsequently banned all sales of Angolan diamonds, except those bearing a certificate of origin.) In October, following discussions with Fowler, the South African diamond company De Beers, which controls the majority of the international trade in diamonds, announced that it had placed a worldwide embargo on the purchase of all diamonds from Angola, except those whose acquisition was already under contract. The Angolan Government also attempted to stem the flow of illegal diamonds by introducing a strict regime of stone certification.

Fighting between UNITA and government troops continued throughout early 2000, and in January dos Santos announced a minor cabinet reshuffle. Manuel António Africano replaced Manuel Gunjo as Minister of Geology and Mines, following Gunjo's death in October 1999, while Albertina Júlia Hamukuya replaced Adelino Manacas as Minister of Health.

In March 2000 a number of African leaders, as well as individuals in Belgium and Bulgaria, were criticized in a UN report for allegedly violating sanctions that had been imposed on UNITA following the discovery of the trade in illegally-mined diamonds. In response, the Angolan Government announced the establishment of a state-owned company, Ascorp, which was to be responsible for centralizing and regulating the country's diamond trade. Furthermore, in April, the UN Security Council adopted a resolution calling for an investigation into the violation of sanctions; a report was expected to be presented to the Council in November.

At the end of June 2000 the Angolan Government and UNITA representatives were reported to have held secret talks, apparently prompted by a conference on the possible means of achieving peace in Angola, which had been organized by the Mozambican Higher Institute of International Relations in Maputo. The conference was attended by the Angolan Deputy Minister of Foreign Affairs, George Chicoti, by Eugénio N'Golo 'Manuvakola' from UNITA—R and by Abel Chivukuvuku from UNITA. At a peace congress held by the Episcopal Conference of Angola and São Tomé in Luanda in July, delegates appealed for a cease-fire.

In August 2000 the Angolan Chief of Staff of the Armed Forces, Gen. João de Matos, announced that Savimbi would no longer be prosecuted for his failure to uphold the cease-fire imposed after the 1992 elections. However, he also stated that, although a position would be made available in the National Assembly for Savimbi, he would not be offered the vice-presidency.

In early October 2000 a minor cabinet reshuffle was effected, at which Julio Bessa was nominated Minister of Finance, and Joaquim Duarte da Costa David became Minister of Industry. Later that month UNITA put forward a 12-point peace plan, which proposed the formation of a 'broad consensus government', the depoliticization of the armed forces, the police and public administration, and the establishment of a national commission to monitor the use of public funds. However, the proposal was rejected by the Minister of Foreign Affairs, João Bernardo de Miranda. Nevertheless, UNITA reiterated its desire to negotiate with the Angolan Government, on condition that the current Portuguese, US and Russian observers be replaced by Angolans, that the sanctions imposed on UNITA in 1993 be revoked, and that the second round of the 1992 presidential elections be held. In November, however, UNITA admitted responsibility for shooting down an aircraft, allegedly carrying diamonds stolen from UNITA territory, killing all 48 passengers on board. Moreover, UNITA rejected an amnesty for all perpetrators of war crimes, which was declared by dos Santos in a speech marking the 25th anniversary of Angola's independence.

Following the internal uprising in August 1998 against the Kabila regime in the DRC, the Angolan Government moved swiftly to provide Kabila with military support against the rebels. In September the number of FAA troops in the DRC was estimated at 5,000. In October, as the conflict escalated in the east of the DRC, Angola, in alliance with Namibia and Zimbabwe, announced its intention to continue supporting Kabila until the rebels were defeated.

Relations with Zambia became tense during 1999 following persistent allegations that it was actively supporting UNITA and allowing its territory to be used as a transit point for the provision of arms and supplies to the rebels. It was further alleged that senior ministers in the Zambian Government had been personally involved in contravening sanctions. It was claimed that several explosions in the Zambian capital, Lusaka, in February, including one at the Angolan embassy, were linked to this tension, and an Angolan national was arrested in connection with the incidents. In June, following co-operation talks between the respective governments, an agreement was signed putting aside past disputes. However, in May 2000 the Zambian Minister of Defence, Chitalu Sampa, accused the FAA of carrying out raids in Zambian territory and killing a Zambian soldier; the allegations were denied by Angola. However, both countries subsequently agreed to increase cross-border co-operation, and Zambian government officials confirmed that UNITA rebels would not be allowed to undertake any military incursions into Angola from Zambian territory. Meanwhile, clashes reportedly took place along the Namibian border with Angola, during which UNITA rebels were killed or arrested by the Namibian security forces.

In July 1996 Angola was among the five lusophone African countries that, together with Portugal and Brazil, formed the Comunidade dos Países de Língua Portuguesa (CPLP, see p. 317), a Portuguese-speaking commonwealth seeking to achieve collective benefits from co-operation in technical, cultural and social matters.

Government

In March 1991 and in the first half of 1992 the Government of the Movimento Popular de Libertação de Angola—Partido do Trabalho (MPLA—PT) introduced a series of far-reaching amendments to the 1975 Constitution, providing for the establishment of a multi-party democracy (hitherto, no other political parties, apart from the ruling MPLA—PT, had been permitted). According to the amendments, legislative power was to be vested in the National Assembly, with 223 members elected for four years on the basis of proportional representation. Executive power was to be held by the President, who was to be directly elected for a term of five years (renewable for a maximum of three terms). As Head of State and Commander-in-Chief of the armed forces, the President was to govern with the assistance of an appointed Council of Ministers.

For the purposes of local government, the country is divided into 18 provinces, each administered by an appointed Governor.

Legislative elections, held in September 1992, resulted in victory for the MPLA. However, in the presidential election, which was held at the same time, the MPLA's candidate and incumbent President, José Eduardo dos Santos, narrowly failed to secure the 50% of the votes necessary to be elected President. Following a resumption of hostilities between UNITA and government forces, the conduct of a second round of presidential elections was held in abeyance, with dos Santos remaining in the presidency. The inauguration of the National Assembly took place, in the absence of UNITA's 70 elected delegates, in late November 1992. In accordance with the terms of the Lusaka peace accord of November 1994, in April 1997 a new Government of National Unity and Reconciliation was inaugurated in which UNITA held four portfolios. The second round of presidential elections having been abandoned, Savimbi was accorded the official title of 'leader of the opposition'. Meanwhile, in November 1996 the National Assembly had adopted a constitutional revision extending the parliamentary mandate, which was due to expire that month, for a period of between two and four years in order to allow for the establishment of suitable conditions for the conduct of elections. In November 1998 Savimbi's 'special status' as 'leader of the opposition' was revoked.

Defence

In December 1990 the governing party, the Movimento Popular de Libertação de Angola—Partido do Trabalho (MPLA—PT), agreed to terminate the party's direct link with the armed forces. In accordance with the peace agreement concluded by the Government and the União Nacional para a Independência Total de Angola (UNITA) in May 1991 (see Recent History), a new 50,000-strong national army, the Forças Armadas de

Angola (FAA), was to be established, comprising equal numbers of government forces, the Forças Armadas Populares de Libertação de Angola (FAPLA), and UNITA soldiers. The formation of the FAA was to coincide with the holding of a general election in late September 1992. Pending the general election, a cease-fire between FAPLA and UNITA forces, which commenced in mid-May 1991, was monitored by a joint political and military commission, comprising representatives of the MPLA—PT, UNITA, the UN, Portugal, the USA and the USSR. This commission was to oversee the withdrawal of FAPLA and UNITA forces to specific confinement areas, to await demobilization. Although not all troops had entered the confinement areas, demobilization began in late March 1992. Military advisers from Portugal, France and the United Kingdom were to assist with the formation of the new national army. However, the demobilization process and the formation of the FAA fell behind schedule and were only partially completed by the end of September and the holding of the general election. Following the election, UNITA withdrew its troops from the FAA, alleging electoral fraud on the part of the MPLA, and hostilities resumed. Following the signing of the Lusaka peace accord in November 1994, preparations for the confinement and demobilization of troops, and the integration of the UNITA contingent into the FAA, resumed. In mid-1995 agreement was reached between the Government and UNITA on the enlargement of the FAA to comprise a total of 90,000 troops, and discussions began concerning the potential formation of a fourth, non-combatant branch of the FAA, which would engage in public works projects. The internment of UNITA forces began in November 1995. In March 1996 agreement was reached that the unified FAA would include 26,300 UNITA troops. The process of selecting UNITA troops for integration into the FAA began in June. In December the UN Angola Verification Mission (UNAVEM III) expressed concern that, of a total of 70,336 UNITA troops registered at confinement areas, some 15,705 had deserted. At that time UN sources reported the existence of a residual UNITA force estimated at 15,000 well-armed troops operating in central and north-eastern Angola. In mid-1997 the Government estimated that UNITA's residual force numbered some 25,000–30,000 troops, while UNITA claimed to have retained a force of only 2,963 'police'. In March 1998 UNITA issued a declaration announcing the complete demobilization of its forces. However, military sources believed that, despite this declaration, UNITA retained a force of some 15,000 troops and substantial quantities of heavy weaponry. Evidence of the existence of a large UNITA force became apparent with the escalation of widespread hostilities in Angola from mid-1998. In August 2000 it was estimated that UNITA retained a force of some 20,000 troops.

In August 2000 the FAA had an estimated total strength of 107,500: army 100,000, navy 1,500 and air force 6,000. In addition, there was a paramilitary force numbering an estimated 10,000.

The defence budget for 2000 was US $542m.

Economic Affairs

In 1998, according to estimates by the World Bank, Angola's gross national product (GNP), measured at average 1996–98 prices, was US $4,578m., equivalent to $380 per head (or $999 per head on an international purchasing-power parity basis). During 1990–98 GNP per head declined, in real terms, by an estimated average annual rate of 8.2%. Over the same period, Angola's population increased at an average annual rate of 3.8%. In 1999 GNP was estimated at $2,700m. ($220 per head). Angola's gross domestic product (GDP) declined, in real terms, by an average of 0.8% per year in 1990–99. However, according to the IMF, real GDP rose by 6.2% in 1997, 3.2% in 1998 and by 2.7% in 1999.

Agriculture, forestry and fishing contributed 6.9% of GDP in 1999. An estimated 72.4% of the total working population were employed in the agricultural sector in 1998. Coffee is the principal cash crop. The main subsistence crops are cassava, maize, sugar cane, bananas and sweet potatoes. During 1990–99 agricultural GDP declined at an average rate of 3.1% per year.

Industry (including mining, manufacturing, construction and power) provided 77.3% of GDP in 1999. Industrial GDP increased, in real terms, at an average rate of 4.2% per year in 1990–99. Industry employed an estimated 10.5% of the labour force in 1991.

Mining contributed 70.3% of GDP in 1999. Petroleum production (including liquefied petroleum gas) accounted for 61.5% of GDP in that year. Angola's principal mineral exports are petroleum and diamonds. In addition, there are reserves of iron ore, copper, lead, zinc, gold, manganese, phosphates, salt and uranium.

The manufacturing sector provided 3.6% of GDP in 1999. According to the World Bank, during 1990–98 the GDP of the sector declined at an average annual rate of 2.7%; according to the IMF, it increased by 9.3% in 1997, by 4.9% in 1998 and by 7.1% in 1999. The principal branch of manufacturing is petroleum refining. Other manufacturing activities include food-processing, brewing, textiles and construction materials.

Energy is derived mainly from hydroelectric power. Angola's power potential exceeds its requirements.

Services accounted for 15.8% of GDP in 1999. In real terms, the combined GDP of the service sectors declined at an average rate of 3.4% per year in 1990–99. The service sectors employed an estimated 20.1% of the labour force in 1991.

In 1999 Angola recorded an estimated visible trade surplus of US $2,077m., while there was an estimated deficit of $1,797m. on the current account of the balance of payments. In 1999 the principal source of imports (18.8%) was Portugal; other major suppliers were the USA, South Africa and France. In that year the principal market for exports (59.5%) was the USA; other notable purchasers were the People's Republic of China and Taiwan. The principal exports in 1999 were petroleum and petroleum products, accounting for 87.6% of total export earnings. The principal imports in 1985 were foodstuffs, transport equipment, electrical equipment and base metals.

In 1999 Angola recorded a budget surplus of 172m. kwanza (equivalent to 1.1% of GDP). Angola's total external debt at the end of 1998 was US $12,173m., of which $10,616m. was long-term public debt. In that year the cost of debt-servicing was equivalent to 34.4% of the value of exports of goods and services. The rate of inflation in the year to December was 135% in 1998 and 329% in 1999.

Angola is a member of both the Common Market for Eastern and Southern Africa (COMESA, see p. 148) and the Southern African Development Community (SADC, see p. 280), which was formed with the aim of reducing the economic dependence of southern African states on South Africa.

Since independence, exploitation of Angola's extensive mineral reserves, hydroelectric potential and abundant fertile land has been severely impaired by internal conflict, as well as an acute shortage of skilled personnel. Angola's prospects depend greatly on a definitive resolution of the civil strife, the successful reintegration of the displaced population and the rehabilitation of the country's devastated infrastructure. In the late 1990s the development of the petroleum sector continued apace. In mid-1997 the French company Elf Aquitaine announced the discovery of one of Africa's largest ever petroleum fields, with estimated reserves of 3,500m. barrels. Further significant discoveries were made in 1998–99. However, in 1999 the vast majority of petroleum revenue was being used to service loans, many of which had been put towards financing the Government's military expenditure following the resumption of full-scale hostilities in late 1998. Nevertheless, national output of crude petroleum was projected to increase to 1.4m. b/d in 2003 (compared with 800,000 b/d in 1998). In December 1999 a new currency, the kwanza, replaced the readjusted kwanza at a rate of 1 kwanza = 1,000,000 readjusted kwanza. The state budget for 2000, approved in January of that year, projected total revenue at 19,900m. kwanza, while expenditure was increased in areas such as defence and security, health, and education. In mid-2000, however, following a rise in oil revenue, state expenditure was increased by some 30% to 41,400m. kwanza. Furthermore, in April, an agreement was signed with the IMF, which, it was hoped, would encourage greater economic stability, principally by reducing inflation and encouraging growth in sectors other than the petroleum industry, and eventually lead to a long-term loan from the IMF, in the form of a Poverty Reduction and Growth Facility, in early 2001. However, it was announced in August that inflation had risen dramatically (to 125.6%) in the first seven months of 2000.

Social Welfare

Medical care is provided free of charge, but its availability is limited by a shortage of trained personnel and medicines. In 1993 Angola had 31 hospitals, 246 health centres and 1,288 health posts, with a total of 12,297 beds. There were 630 doctors and 5,780 paramedics working in the country. The 1999 budget allocated an estimated 250m. kwanza (2.8% of total expenditure) to health. War veterans receive support from the Ministry of Defence.

Education

Education is officially compulsory for eight years, between seven and 15 years of age, and is provided free of charge by the Government. Primary education begins at six years of age and lasts for four years. Secondary education, beginning at the age of 10, lasts for up to seven years, comprising a first cycle of four years and a second of three years. In 1973, under Portuguese rule, primary school pupils numbered only 300,000, but by 1991/92 there were 989,443 pupils. Enrolment at secondary schools (including students receiving vocational instruction and teacher-training) increased from 57,829 in 1970 to 218,987 in 1991/92. As a proportion of the school-age population, the total enrolment at primary and secondary schools was 45% in 1991. Higher education is being encouraged. The only university, Agostinho Neto University in Luanda, had 5,736 students in 1986/87. The number of students attending courses at the university and other equivalent institutions in 1991/92 was 6,331. Much education is now conducted in vernacular languages rather than Portuguese. In 1991 the People's Assembly approved legislation permitting the foundation of private educational establishments. At independence the estimated rate of adult illiteracy was more than 85%. A national literacy campaign was launched in 1976, and the average rate of adult illiteracy in 1990 was estimated by UNESCO to be 58.3% (males 44.4%, females 71.5%). The 1999 budget allocated an estimated 430m. kwanza (4.8% of total expenditure) to education.

Public Holidays

2001: 1 January (New Year's Day), 4 February (Anniversary of the outbreak of the armed struggle against Portuguese colonialism), 27 March (Victory Day)*, 13 April (Good Friday), 14 April (Youth Day)*, 16 April (Easter Monday), 1 May (Workers' Day), 1 August (Armed Forces' Day)*, 17 September (National Hero's Day, birthday of Dr Agostinho Neto), 11 November (Independence Day), 1 December (Pioneers' Day)*, 10 December (Anniversary of the Foundation of the MPLA), 25 December (Christmas Day and Family Day).

2002: 1 January (New Year's Day), 4 February (Anniversary of the outbreak of the armed struggle against Portuguese colonialism), 27 March (Victory Day)*, 29 March (Good Friday), 1 April (Easter Monday), 14 April (Youth Day)*, 1 May (Workers' Day), 1 August (Armed Forces' Day)*, 17 September (National Hero's Day, birthday of Dr Agostinho Neto), 11 November (Independence Day), 1 December (Pioneers' Day)*, 10 December (Anniversary of the Foundation of the MPLA), 25 December (Christmas Day and Family Day).

* Although not officially recognized as public holidays, these days are popularly treated as such.

Weights and Measures

The metric system is in force.

Statistical Survey

Source (unless otherwise stated): Instituto Nacional de Estatística, Luanda.

Area and Population

AREA, POPULATION AND DENSITY

Area (sq km)	1,246,700*
Population (census results)	
30 December 1960	4,480,719
15 December 1970	
Males	2,943,974
Females	2,702,192
Total	5,646,166
Population (official estimates at mid-year)†	
1997	12,240,000
1998	12,595,000
1999	12,960,000
Density (per sq km) at mid-1999	10.4

* 481,354 sq miles.
† Population figures are projected from the 1970 census. In mid-1996, according to a nation-wide survey, the population was an estimated 15,300,000.

DISTRIBUTION OF POPULATION BY PROVINCE
(provisional estimates, mid-1995)

	Area (sq km)	Population	Density (per sq km)
Luanda	2,418	2,002,000	828.0
Huambo	34,274	1,687,000	49.2
Bié	70,314	1,246,000	17.7
Malanje	87,246	975,000	11.2
Huíla	75,002	948,000	12.6
Uíge	58,698	948,000	16.2
Benguela	31,788	702,000	22.1
Cuanza-Sul . . .	55,660	688,000	12.4
Cuanza-Norte . . .	24,110	412,000	17.1
Moxico	223,023	349,000	1.6
Lunda-Norte . . .	102,783	311,000	3.0
Zaire	40,130	247,000	6.2
Cunene	88,342	245,000	2.8
Cabinda	7,270	185,000	25.4
Bengo	31,371	184,000	5.9
Lunda-Sul . . .	56,985	160,000	2.8
Cuando-Cubango . .	199,049	137,000	0.7
Namibe	58,137	135,000	2.3
Total	1,246,600	11,561,000	9.3

PRINCIPAL TOWNS (population at 1970 census)

Luanda (capital) .	480,613*	Benguela . .	40,996
Huambo (Nova		Lubango (Sá da	
Lisboa) . .	61,885	Bandeira) . .	31,674
Lobito . . .	59,258	Malanje . . .	31,559

* 1982 estimate: 1,200,000.

Source: Direcção dos Serviços de Estatística.

BIRTHS AND DEATHS (UN estimates, annual averages)

	1980–85	1985–90	1990–95
Birth rate (per 1,000) . . .	50.8	51.3	50.8
Death rate (per 1,000) . . .	22.8	21.3	19.2

Expectation of life (UN estimates, years at birth, 1990–95): 46.5 (males 44.9; females 48.1).

Source: UN, *World Population Prospects: The 1998 Revision*.

ECONOMICALLY ACTIVE POPULATION
(estimates, '000 persons, 1991)

	Males	Females	Total
Agriculture, etc.	1,518	1,374	2,892
Industry	405	33	438
Services	644	192	836
Total labour force . . .	2,567	1,599	4,166

Source: UN Economic Commission for Africa, *African Statistical Yearbook*.

Mid-1999 (estimates in '000): Agriculture, etc. 4,132; Total (incl. others) 5,729. Source: FAO.

Agriculture

PRINCIPAL CROPS ('000 metric tons)

	1997	1998	1999
Wheat*	5	6	4
Rice (paddy)*	21	21	16
Maize†	370	505	428
Millet†	62	89	102
Potatoes	24*	25*	19†
Sweet potatoes	189*	190*	182†
Cassava (Manioc)† . . .	2,326	3,211	3,130
Dry beans†	66	86	68
Groundnuts (in shell) . . .	17*	18*	11†
Sunflower seed*	10	11	9
Cottonseed	12†	12†	3*
Cotton (lint)	4†	4†	1*
Palm kernels*	16	16	15
Palm oil*	53	54	50
Vegetables*	256	263	240
Citrus fruit*	80	82	75
Pineapples*	36	38	32
Bananas*	300	310	290
Other fruits*	30	31	26
Sugar cane*	310	340	340
Coffee (green)†	4	5	4
Tobacco (leaves)	4†	4*	3*
Sisal*	1	1	1

* FAO estimate(s).   † Unofficial figure(s).

Source: FAO.

LIVESTOCK ('000 head, year ending September)

	1997	1998	1999
Cattle†	3,556	3,898	3,900
Pigs*	820	810	800
Sheep†	280	305	336
Goats*	1,720	1,861	2,000

Poultry (million)*: 7 in 1997; 7 in 1998; 7 in 1999.

* FAO estimates.   † Unofficial figures.

Source: FAO.

LIVESTOCK PRODUCTS ('000 metric tons)

	1997	1998	1999
Beef and veal*	77	85	85
Goat meat	7	8	9
Pig meat*	29	29	29
Poultry meat	7	7	8
Other meat	8	9	9
Cows' milk*	175	190	191
Cheese	1	1	1
Poultry eggs	4	4	4
Honey	23	22	22
Cattle hides	11	13	13

* FAO estimates.

Source: FAO.

Forestry

ROUNDWOOD REMOVALS
('000 cubic metres, excluding bark)

	1996	1997	1998
Sawlogs, veneer logs and logs for sleepers*	66	66	66
Other industrial wood	954	986	1,018
Fuel wood	5,053	5,220	5,388
Total	6,073	6,272	6,472

* Annual output assumed to be unchanged since 1990.

Source: FAO, *Yearbook of Forest Products.*

SAWNWOOD PRODUCTION
('000 cubic metres, including railway sleepers)

	1996	1997	1998
Total	5	5	5

Source: FAO, *Yearbook of Forest Products.*

Fishing

('000 metric tons, live weight)

	1996	1997	1998
Freshwater fishes	6.0	6.0	6.0
West African croakers	4.0	1.6	7.1
Dentex	2.6	1.6	8.7
Cunene horse mackerel	19.8	35.8	39.7
Sardinellas	17.5	21.0	45.5
Total catch (incl. others)	137.8	136.1	145.8

Source: FAO, *Yearbook of Fishery Statistics.*

Mining

('000 metric tons, unless otherwise indicated)

	1997	1998	1999
Crude petroleum*	36,500	36,000	38,500
Natural gas (million cu metres)†	20,000	n.a.	n.a.
Salt (unrefined)	30	30†	n.a.
Diamonds ('000 carats):			
Industrial	124	364	120
Gem	1,110	2,400	1,080

* Data from BP Amoco, *Statistical Review of World Energy 2000.*
† Estimate(s).

Source: mainly US Geological Survey.

Industry

SELECTED PRODUCTS
('000 metric tons, unless otherwise indicated)

	1997	1998	1999
Frozen fish	27.2	56.8	57.7
Wheat flour	52.0	46.0	57.5
Maize flour	134.1	113.5	n.a.
Yam flour	260.0	260.0	n.a.
Bread	150.1	70.0	87.5
Beer ('000 litres)	115.0	128.8	160.9
Jet fuels	292.3	285.0	338.5
Motor spirit (petrol)	114.6	101.7	128.1
Kerosene	19.7	28.3	30.4
Distillate fuel oils	466.3	485.7	493.0
Residual fuel oils	680.6	591.0	646.8
Butane gas	32.6	28.5	30.5
Cement	219.0	n.a.	n.a.

Source: IMF, *Angola: Recent Economic Developments* (August 2000).

Finance

CURRENCY AND EXCHANGE RATES

Monetary Units
100 lwei = 1 kwanza.

Sterling, Dollar and Euro Equivalents (29 December 2000)
£1 sterling = 25.10 kwanza;
US $1 = 16.82 kwanza;
€1 = 15.65 kwanza;
1,000 kwanza = £39.85 = $59.46 = €63.90.

Average Exchange Rate (kwanza per US $)

1998	0.393
1999	2.791
2000	10.041

Note: An official exchange rate of US $1 = 29.62 kwanza was introduced in 1976 and remained in force until September 1990. In that month the kwanza was replaced, at par, by the new kwanza. At the same time, it was announced that the currency was to be devalued by more than 50%, with the exchange rate adjusted to US $1 = 60 new kwanza, with effect from 1 October 1990. This rate remained in force until 18 November 1991, when a basic rate of US $1 = 90 new kwanza was established. The currency underwent further devaluation, by 50% in December 1991, and by more than 67% on 15 April 1992, when a basic rate of US $1 = 550 new kwanza was established. In February 1993 the currency was again devalued, when a basic rate of US $1 = 7,000 new kwanza was established. In April 1993 this was adjusted to US $1 = 4,000 new kwanza, and in October to US $1 = 6,500 new kwanza, a devaluation of 38.5%. Following a series of four devaluations in February and March 1994, a rate of US $1 = 35,000 new kwanza was established in late March. In April 1994 the introduction of a new method of setting exchange rates resulted in an effective devaluation, to US $1 = 68,297 new kwanza, and provided for an end to the system of multiple exchange rates. Further substantial devaluations followed, and in July 1995 a 'readjusted' kwanza, equivalent to 1,000 new kwanza, was introduced. The currency, however, continued to depreciate. Between July 1997 and June 1998 a fixed official rate of US $1 = 262,376 readjusted kwanza was in operation. In May 1999 the Central Bank announced its decision to abolish the existing dual currency exchange rate system. In December 1999 the readjusted kwanza was replaced by a new currency, the kwanza, equivalent to 1m. readjusted kwanza. The former currency was to remain in circulation for a transitional period. Some of the figures in this Survey are still in terms of the readjusted kwanza.

BUDGET (million kwanza)

Revenue	1997	1998	1999
Tax revenue .	670	674	7,495
Income tax	445	360	5,676
Petroleum corporate tax .	369	303	5,363
Petroleum transaction tax	52	4	50
Tax on goods and services .	171	231	1,549
Petroleum sector .	144	170	1,221
Diamond sector .	—	1	74
Taxes on foreign trade	34	56	224
Other taxes	20	27	46
Stamp tax	14	17	39
Non-tax revenue .	9	11	45
Total	679	685	7,540

Expenditure*	1997	1998	1999
General public services	174	194	1,440
Defence and public order .	391	288	3,670
Peace process	6	—	10
Education	48	66	430
Health	31	35	250
Economic affairs and services .	182	142	920
Interest payments	98	175	960
Total (incl. others)	977	1,056	8,940

* Including adjustments for unrecorded transactions. The data include lending minus repayments.

Source: IMF, *Angola: Recent Economic Developments* (August 2000).

INTERNATIONAL RESERVES (US $ million at 31 December)

	1997	1998	1999
IMF special drawing rights	0.16	0.17	0.18
Foreign exchange	396.27	203.29	495.93
Total	396.43	203.46	496.10

Source: IMF, *International Financial Statistics*.

MONEY SUPPLY ('000 million readjusted kwanza at 31 December)

	1997	1998	1999
Currency outside banks .	101,619	165,686	650,450
Demand deposits at banking institutions	93,292	106,583	510,630
Total (incl. others)	194,910	272,432	1,161,080

Source: IMF, *International Financial Statistics*.

COST OF LIVING

(Consumer Price Index for Luanda at December; base: 1994 average = 100)

	1997	1998	1999
Food	318,800	687,938	3,551,169
Clothing	420,563	1,250,460	5,808,275
Rent, fuel and light	4,572,243	5,647,634	12,901,550
All items (incl. others)	504,843	1,185,134	5,083,923

Source: IMF, *Angola: Recent Economic Developments* (August 2000).

NATIONAL ACCOUNTS
Composition of the Gross National Product (US $ million)

	1987	1988	1989
Gross domestic product (GDP) at factor cost .	6,482	6,877	7,682
Indirect taxes	94	95	117
Less Subsidies	189	122	93
GDP in purchasers' values	6,386	6,850	7,706
Net factor income from abroad	−402	−938	−1,079
Gross national product	5,984	5,912	6,627

Gross Domestic Product by Economic Activity
(million kwanza at current prices)

	1997	1998	1999
Agriculture, forestry and fishing	158	330	1,076
Mining	918	1,093	10,968
Manufacturing .	77	160	554
Electricity and water	1	2	6
Construction	71	156	529
Trade .	283	489	1,370
Other services .	206	267	1,102
Sub-total .	1,714	2,497	15,605
Import duties .	41	35	37
GDP in purchasers' values	1,755	2,533	15,644

Source: IMF, *Angola: Recent Economic Developments* (August 2000).

BALANCE OF PAYMENTS (US $ million)

	1997	1998	1999
Exports of goods f.o.b.	5,007	3,543	5,344
Imports of goods f.o.b.	−2,477	−2,079	−3,267
Trade balance .	2,529	1,464	2,077
Services (net)			
Interest payments (net) .	−3,399	−3,487	−3,874
Unrequited transfers (net)			
Current balance	−869	−2,023	−1,797
Direct investment (net) .	492	1,115	2,520
Other long-term capital (net) .	267	−965	−705
Short-term capital (net) .	−668	−172	−263
Net errors and omissions .	−32	673	4
Overall balance .	−810	−1,372	−240

Source: IMF, *Angola: Recent Economic Developments* (August 2000).

External Trade

SELECTED COMMODITIES

Imports (million kwanza)	1983	1984	1985
Animal products .	1,315	1,226	1,084
Vegetable products	2,158	3,099	2,284
Fats and oils	946	1,006	1,196
Food and beverages	2,400	1,949	1,892
Industrial chemical products .	1,859	1,419	1,702
Plastic materials	431	704	454
Paper products	376	380	411
Textiles .	1,612	1,816	1,451
Base metals .	1,985	3,730	2,385
Electrical equipment .	3,296	2,879	2,571
Transport equipment	2,762	2,240	3,123
Total (incl. others)	20,197	21,370	19,694

Total Imports (US $ million): 2,477 in 1997; 2,079 in 1998; 3,267 in 1999 (Source: IMF, *Angola: Recent Economic Developments* (August 2000)).

Exports (US $ million)	1997	1998	1999
Crude petroleum .	4,506	3,018	4,609
Refined petroleum products .	101	62	75
Diamonds .	348	432	629
Total (incl. others) .	5,007	3,543	5,344

Source: IMF, *Angola: Recent Economic Developments* (August 2000).

PRINCIPAL TRADING PARTNERS (percentage of total trade)*

Imports c.i.f.	1997	1998	1999
Brazil	4.0	6.0	5.1
China, People's Repub.	1.4	1.8	1.3
France	5.8	5.8	8.2
Germany	2.3	2.4	1.7
Italy	2.7	3.7	4.5
Netherlands	4.6	5.1	3.6
Portugal	22.4	20.3	18.8
South Africa	9.2	9.7	11.9
Spain	8.5	4.9	5.9
United Kingdom	6.4	3.4	6.2
USA	13.6	17.6	14.6

Exports f.o.b.	1997	1998	1999
China, People's Repub.	13.2	4.0	8.2
France	3.9	2.9	2.1
Germany	0.7	1.7	2.4
Italy	0.4	1.4	1.4
Portugal	1.0	0.6	0.5
Spain	1.9	0.8	0.6
Taiwan	1.7	8.2	7.7
USA	64.9	63.8	59.5

* Data are compiled on the basis of reporting by Angola's trading partners.
Source: IMF, *Direction of Trade Statistics* in *Angola: Recent Economic Developments* (August 2000).

Transport

GOODS TRANSPORT ('000 metric tons)

	1988	1989	1990
Road	1,056.7	690.1	867.3
Railway	580.9	510.3	443.2
Water	780.8	608.6	812.1
Air	24.6	10.5	28.3
Total	2,443.0	1,819.5	2,150.9

Sources: Instituto Nacional de Estatística; Ministério de Transporte e Comunicações.

PASSENGER TRANSPORT ('000 journeys)

	1988	1989	1990
Road	12,699.2	32,658.7	48,796.1
Railway	6,659.7	6,951.2	6,455.8
Water	151.8	163.2	223.8
Air	608.9	618.4	615.9
Total	20,119.6	40,391.5	56,091.6

Sources: Instituto Nacional de Estatística; Ministério de Transporte e Comunicações.

ROAD TRAFFIC (estimates, motor vehicles in use at 31 December)

	1994	1995	1996
Passenger cars	180,000	197,000	207,000
Lorries and vans	32,340	26,000	25,000
Total	212,340	223,000	232,000

Source: IRF, *World Road Statistics*.

SHIPPING

Merchant Fleet (registered at 31 December)

	1996	1997	1998
Number of vessels	113	109	123
Total displacement (grt)	81,856	68,031	73,907

Source: Lloyd's Register of Shipping, *World Fleet Statistics*.

International Sea-borne Freight Traffic
(estimates, '000 metric tons)

	1989	1990	1991
Goods loaded	19,980	21,102	23,288
Goods unloaded	1,235	1,242	1,261

Source: UN Economic Commission for Africa, *African Statistical Yearbook*.

CIVIL AVIATION (traffic on scheduled services)

	1995	1996	1997
Kilometres flown (million)	8	8	8
Passengers carried ('000)	553	585	555
Passenger-km (million)	833	880	620
Total ton-km (million)	133	141	97

Source: UN, *Statistical Yearbook*.

Tourism

FOREIGN TOURIST ARRIVALS

Country of origin	1996	1997	1998
Belgium	943	4,151	473
Brazil	1,732	2,175	2,835
Congo, Republic	467	1,054	844
France	1,726	5,553	4,335
Italy	425	1,839	891
Namibia	356	1,703	175
Portugal	6,927	14,282	19,412
South Africa	1,545	8,067	2,728
Total (incl. others)	20,978	45,139	52,011

Tourism receipts (US $ million): 10 in 1995; 9 in 1996; 9 in 1997.
Source: World Tourism Organization, *Yearbook of Tourism Statistics*.

Communications Media

	1995	1996	1997
Radio receivers ('000 in use) . .	370	600	630
Television receivers ('000 in use) .	80	100	150
Telephones ('000 main lines in use)	53	53	62
Mobile cellular telephones			
(subscribers)	1,994	3,298	7,052
Daily newspapers			
Number	5	5	n.a.
Average circulation ('000 copies)	122	128	n.a.

Book production: 47 titles (books 35, pamphlets 12) and 419,000 copies (books 338,000, pamphlets 81,000) in 1985; 14 titles (all books) and 130,000 copies in 1986; 22 titles (all books) in 1995.

Sources: UNESCO, *Statistical Yearbook*; UN, *Statistical Yearbook*.

Education

(1991/92)

	Teachers	Pupils
Pre-primary	n.a.	214,867
Primary	31,062*	989,443
Secondary:		
general	5,138†	196,099
teacher training	280‡	10,772
vocational	286†	12,116
Higher	787	6,331

* Figure for school year 1990/91.
† Figure for school year 1989/90.
‡ Figure for school year 1987/88.

Source: mainly UNESCO, *Statistical Yearbook*.

Directory

The Constitution

The MPLA regime adopted an independence Constitution for Angola in November 1975. It was amended in October 1976, September 1980, March 1991, April and August 1992, and November 1996. The main provisions of the Constitution, as amended, are summarized below:

BASIC PRINCIPLES

The Republic of Angola shall be a sovereign and independent state whose prime objective shall be to build a free and democratic society of peace, justice and social progress. It shall be a democratic state based on the rule of law, founded on national unity, the dignity of human beings, pluralism of expression and political organization, respecting and guaranteeing the basic rights and freedoms of persons, whether as individuals or as members of organized social groups. Sovereignty shall be vested in the people, which shall exercise political power through periodic universal suffrage.

The Republic of Angola shall be a unitary and indivisible state. Economic, social and cultural solidarity shall be promoted between all the Republic's regions for the common development of the entire nation and the elimination of regionalism and tribalism.

Religion

The Republic shall be a secular state and there shall be complete separation of the State and religious institutions. All religions shall be respected.

The Economy

The economic system shall be based on the coexistence of diverse forms of property—public, private, mixed, co-operative and family—and all shall enjoy equal protection. The State shall protect foreign investment and foreign property, in accordance with the law. The fiscal system shall aim to satisfy the economic, social and administrative needs of the State and to ensure a fair distribution of income and wealth. Taxes may be created and abolished only by law, which shall determine applicability, rates, tax benefits and guarantees for taxpayers.

Education

The Republic shall vigorously combat illiteracy and obscurantism and shall promote the development of education and of a true national culture.

FUNDAMENTAL RIGHTS AND DUTIES

The State shall respect and protect the human person and human dignity. All citizens shall be equal before the law. They shall be subject to the same duties, without any distinction based on colour, race, ethnic group, sex, place of birth, religion, level of education, or economic or social status.

All citizens aged 18 years and over, other than those legally deprived of political and civil rights, shall have the right and duty to take an active part in public life, to vote and be elected to any state organ, and to discharge their mandates with full dedication to the cause of the Angolan nation. The law shall establish limitations in respect of non-political allegiance of soldiers on active service, judges and police forces, as well as the electoral incapacity of soldiers on active service and police forces.

Freedom of expression, of assembly, of demonstration, of association and of all other forms of expression shall be guaranteed. Groupings whose aims or activities are contrary to the constitutional order and penal laws, or that, even indirectly, pursue political objectives through organizations of a military, paramilitary or militarized nature shall be forbidden. Every citizen has the right to a defence if accused of a crime. Individual freedoms are guaranteed. Freedom of conscience and belief shall be inviolable. Work shall be the right and duty of all citizens. The State shall promote measures necessary to ensure the right of citizens to medical and health care, as well as assistance in childhood, motherhood, disability, old age, etc. It shall also promote access to education, culture and sports for all citizens.

STATE ORGANS

President of the Republic

The President of the Republic shall be the Head of State, Head of Government and Commander-in-Chief of the Angolan armed forces. The President of the Republic shall be elected directly by a secret universal ballot and shall have the following powers:

to appoint and dismiss the Prime Minister, Ministers and other government officials determined by law;

to appoint the judges of the Supreme Court;

to preside over the Council of Ministers;

to declare war and make peace, following authorization by the National Assembly;

to sign, promulgate and publish the laws of the National Assembly, government decrees and statutory decrees;

to preside over the National Defence Council;

to decree a state of siege or state of emergency;

to announce the holding of general elections;

to issue pardons and commute sentences;

to perform all other duties provided for in the Constitution.

National Assembly

The National Assembly is the supreme state legislative body, to which the Government is responsible. The National Assembly shall be composed of 223 deputies, elected for a term of four years. The National Assembly shall convene in ordinary session twice yearly and in special session on the initiative of the President of the National Assembly, the Standing Commission of the National Assembly or of no less than one-third of its deputies. The Standing Commission shall be the organ of the National Assembly that represents and assumes its powers between sessions.

Government

The Government shall comprise the President of the Republic, the ministers and the secretaries of state, and other members whom the law shall indicate, and shall have the following functions:

to organize and direct the implementation of state domestic and foreign policy, in accordance with decision of the National Assembly and its Standing Commission;

to ensure national defence, the maintenance of internal order and security, and the protection of the rights of citizens;

to prepare the draft National Plan and General State Budget for approval by the National Assembly, and to organize, direct and control their execution;

The Council of Ministers shall be answerable to the National Assembly. In the exercise of its powers, the Council of Ministers shall issue decrees and resolutions.

Judiciary

The organization, composition and competence of the courts shall be established by law. Judges shall be independent in the discharge of their functions.

Local State Organs

The organs of state power at provincial level shall be the Provincial Assemblies and their executive bodies. The Provincial Assemblies shall work in close co-operation with social organizations and rely on the initiative and broad participation of citizens. The Provincial Assemblies shall elect commissions of deputies to perform permanent or specific tasks. The executive organs of Provincial Assemblies shall be the Provincial Governments, which shall be led by the Provincial Governors. The Provincial Governors shall be answerable to the President of the Republic, the Council of Ministers and the Provincial Assemblies.

National Defence

The State shall ensure national defence. The National Defence Council shall be presided over by the President of the Republic, and its composition shall be determined by law. The Angolan armed forces, as a state institution, shall be permanent, regular and non-partisan. Defence of the country shall be the right and the highest indeclinable duty of every citizen. Military service shall be compulsory. The forms in which it is fulfilled shall be defined by the law.

Note: In accordance with the terms of the Lusaka peace accord of November 1994, in April 1997 a new Government of National Unity and Reconciliation was inaugurated in which UNITA held four portfolios. In November 1996 the National Assembly adopted a constitutional revision extending the parliamentary mandate, which was due to expire that month, for a period of between two and four years in order to allow for the establishment of suitable conditions for the conduct of elections.

The Government

HEAD OF STATE

President: José Eduardo dos Santos (assumed office 21 September 1979).

COUNCIL OF MINISTERS
(April 2001)

Prime Minister: JOSÉ EDUARDO DOS SANTOS.

Minister of Defence: Gen. KUNDI PAIHAMA.

Minister of the Interior: FERNANDO DA PIEDADE DIAS DOS SANTOS.

Minister of Foreign Affairs: JOÃO BERNARDO DE MIRANDA.

Minister of Territorial Administration: FERNANDO FAUSTINO MUTEKA.

Minister of Finance: JÚLIO BESSA.

Minister of Economic Planning: ANA DIAS LOURENÇO.

Minister of Petroleum: JOSÉ BOTELHO DE VASCONCELOS.

Minister of Industry: JOAQUIM DUARTE DA COSTA DAVID.

Minister of Agriculture and Rural Development: GILBERTO BUTA LUTUKUTA.

Minister of Fisheries and Environment: MARIA DE FÁTIMA MONTEIRO JARDIM.

Minister of Geology and Mines: MANUEL ANTÓNIO AFRICANO.

Minister of Public Works and Housing: ANTÓNIO HENRIQUES DA SILVA.

Minister of Transport: ANDRÉ LUÍS BRANDÃO.

Minister of Trade: VICTORINO DOMINGOS HOSSI.

Minister of Health: ALBERTINA JÚLIA HAMUKUAYA.

Minister of Education and Culture: ANTÓNIO BURITY DA SILVA NETO.

Minister of Social Welfare: ALBINO MALUNGO.

Minister of Youth and Sports: JOSÉ MARCOS BARRICA.

Minister of Justice: Dr PAULO TCHIPILICA.

Minister of Public Administration, Employment and Social Security: Dr ANTÓNIO DOMINGOS PITRA COSTA NETO.

Minister of Social Communication: Dr PEDRO HENDRIK VAAL NETO.

Minister of Science and Technology: JOÃO BAPTISTA NGANDA GINA.

Minister of Post and Telecommunications: LICÍNIO TAVARES RIBEIRO.

Minister of Family and the Promotion of Women: CÂNDIDA CELESTE DA SILVA.

Minister of War Veterans: PEDRO JOSÉ VAN-DÚNEM.

Minister of Hotels and Tourism: JORGE ALICERCES VALENTIM.

Minister of Energy and Water: LUIS FILIPE DA SILVA.

Secretaries of State with Independent Charge

Secretary of State for Coffee: GILBERTO BUTA LUTUKUTA.

Secretary of State for Environment: MANUEL DAVID MENDES.

MINISTRIES

All Ministries are located in Luanda.

Ministry of Agriculture and Rural Development: Avda Norton de Matos 2, Luanda.

Ministry of Defence: Rua Silva Carvalho ex Quartel General, Luanda.

Ministry of Education and Culture: Avda Comandante Jika, CP 1281, Luanda; tel. (2) 321592; fax (2) 321592.

Ministry of Finance: Avda 4 de Fevereiro, Luanda; tel. (2) 344628.

Ministry of Fisheries and Environment: Avda 4 de Fevereiro 25, Predio Atlântico, Luanda; tel. (2) 392782.

Ministry of Foreign Affairs: Avda Comandante Jika, Luanda.

Ministry of Geology and Mines: CP 1260, Luanda; tel. (2) 322766; fax (2) 321655.

Ministry of Health: Rua Diogo Cão, Luanda.

Ministry of the Interior: Avda 4 de Fevereiro, Luanda.

Ministry of Justice: Largo do Palácio, Luanda.

Ministry of Petroleum: Avda 4 de Fevereiro 105, CP 1279, Luanda; tel. (2) 337448.

Ministry of Public Administration, Employment and Social Security: Rua 17 de Setembro 32, CP 1986, Luanda; tel. (2) 339656; fax (2) 339054.

Ministry of Social Communication: Avda Comandante Válodia, CP 2608, Luanda; tel. (2) 343495.

Ministry of Trade: Largo Kinaxixi 14, Luanda; tel. (2) 344525.

Ministry of Transport and Communications: Avda 4 de Fevereiro 42, CP 1250-C, Luanda; tel. (2) 370061.

PROVINCIAL GOVERNORS*

Bengo: EZELINO MENDES.

Benguela: DUMILDE DAS CHAGAS SIMÕES RANGEL.

Bié: LUÍS PAULINO DOS SANTOS.

Cabinda: JOSÉ AMARO TATI.

Cuando-Cubango: MANUEL GAMA.

Cuanza-Norte: MANUEL PEDRO PACAVIRA.

Cuanza-Sul: FRANCISCO HIGINO LOPES CARNEIRO.

Cunene: PEDRO MUTINDE.

Huambo: PAULO KASSOMA.

Huíla: FRANCISCO JOSÉ RAMOS DA CRUZ.

Luanda: JOSÉ ANÍBAL LOPES ROCHA.

Lunda-Norte: MANUEL FRANCISCO GOMES MAIATO.

Lunda-Sul: FRANCISCO SOZINHO CHIUBSA.

Malanje: FLAVIO FERNANDES.

Moxico: JOÃO ERNESTO DOS SANTOS (LIBERDADE).

Namibe: SALOMEO JOSÉ LUETO SIRIMBIMBE.

Uíge: CORDERO ERNESTO ZACUNDOMBA.

Zaire: LUDI KISSASSUNDA.

*All Governors are ex-officio members of the Government.

President and Legislature

PRESIDENT*
Presidential Election, 29 and 30 September 1992

	Votes	% of votes
JOSÉ EDUARDO DOS SANTOS (MPLA)	1,953,335	49.57
Dr JONAS MALHEIRO SAVIMBI (UNITA)	1,579,298	40.07
ANTÓNIO ALBERTO NETO (PDA)	85,249	2.16
HOLDEN ROBERTO (FNLA)	83,135	2.11
HONORATO LANDO (PDLA)	75,789	1.92
LUÍS DOS PASSOS (PRD)	59,121	1.47
BENGUI PEDRO JOÃO (PSD)	38,243	0.97
SIMÃO CACETE (FPD)	26,385	0.67
DANIEL JÚLIO CHIPENDA (Independent)	20,646	0.52
ANÁLIA DE VICTÓRIA PEREIRA (PLD)	11,475	0.29
RUI DE VICTÓRIA PEREIRA (PRA)	9,208	0.23
Total	**3,940,884**	**100.00**

NATIONAL ASSEMBLY

President: ROBERTO DE ALMEIDA.

Legislative Election, 29 and 30 September 1992

	Votes	% of votes	Seats†
MPLA	2,124,126	53.74	129
UNITA	1,347,636	34.10	70
FNLA	94,742	2.40	5
PLD	94,269	2.39	3
PRS	89,875	2.27	6
PRD	35,293	0.89	1
AD Coalition	34,166	0.86	1
PSD	33,088	0.84	1
PAJOCA	13,924	0.35	1
FDA	12,038	0.30	1
PDP—ANA	10,620	0.27	1
PNDA	10,281	0.26	1
CNDA	10,237	0.26	—
PSDA	19,217	0.26	—
PAI	9,007	0.23	—
PDLA	8,025	0.20	—
PDA	8,014	0.20	—
PRA	6,719	0.17	—
Total	**3,952,277**	**100.00**	**220**

* Under the terms of the electoral law, a second round of presidential elections was required to take place in order to determine which of the two leading candidates from the first round would be elected. However, a resumption of hostilities between UNITA and government forces prevented a second round of presidential elections from taking place. The electoral process was to resume only when the provisions of the Estoril peace agreement, concluded in May 1991, had been fulfilled. However, provision in the Lusaka peace accord of November 1994 for the second round of presidential elections was not pursued.

† According to the Constitution, the total number of seats in the National Assembly is 223. On the decision of the National Electoral Council, however, elections to fill three seats reserved for Angolans resident abroad were abandoned.

Political Organizations

Aliança Democrática de Angola: Leader SIMBA DA COSTA.

Angolan Alliance and Hamista Party.

Angolan Democratic Coalition (AD Coalition): Pres. EVIDOR QUIELA (acting).

Angolan Democratic Confederation: f. 1994; Chair. GASPAR NETO.

Angolan Democratic Unification: Leader EDUARDO MILTON SIVI.

Associação Cívica Angolana (ACA): f. 1990; Leader JOAQUIM PINTO DE ANDRADE.

Centro Democrático Social (CDS): Pres. MATEUS JOSÉ; Sec.-Gen. DELFINA FRANCISCO CAPCIEL.

Christian Democratic Convention: Leader GASPAR NETO.

Democratic Civilian Opposition: f. 1994; opposition alliance including:

> **Convenção Nacional Democrata de Angola (CNDA):** Leader PAULINO PINTO JOÃO.
>
> **Frente Nacional de Libertação de Angola (FNLA):** internet www.fnla.org; f. 1962; Pres. LUCAS NGONDA.
>
> **Frente para a Democracia (FPD):** Leader NELSO PESTANA; Sec.-Gen. FILOMENO VIEIRA LOPES.
>
> **Movimento de Defesa dos Interesses de Angola—Partido de Consciência Nacional:** Leader ISIDORO KLALA.
>
> **National Ecological Party of Angola:** Leader SUKAWA DIZI-ZEKO RICARDO.
>
> **National Union for Democracy:** Leader SEBASTIÃO ROGERIO SUZAMA.
>
> **Partido Renovador Social (PRS):** Pres. EDUARDO KWANGANA.
>
> **Party of Solidarity and the Conscience of Angola:** Leader FERNANDO DOMBASSI QUIESSE.

Fórum Democrático Angolano (FDA): Leader JORGE REBELO PINTO CHICOTI.

Frente de Libertação do Enclave de Cabinda (FLEC): f. 1963; comprises several factions, claiming total forces of c. 5,000 guerrillas, seeking the secession of Cabinda province; mem. groups include:

> **Frente Democrática de Cabinda (FDC):** Leader FRANCISCO XAVIER LUBOTA.
>
> **Frente de Libertação do Enclave de Cabinda—Forças Armadas Cabindesas (FLEC—FAC):** Chair. HENRIQUE TIAGO N'ZITA; Chief-of-Staff (FAC) Commdr ESTANISLAU MIGUEL BOMBA.
>
> **Frente de Libertação do Enclave de Cabinda—Renovada (FLEC—R):** Pres. ANTÓNIO BENTO BEMBE; Sec.-Gen. ARTURO CHIBASA.

Movimento Amplo para a Democracia: Leader FRANCISCO VIANA.

Movimento Popular de Libertação de Angola (MPLA) (People's Movement for the Liberation of Angola): Luanda; f. 1956; in 1961–74 conducted guerrilla operations against Portuguese rule; governing party since 1975; known as Movimento Popular de Libertação de Angola—Partido do Trabalho (MPLA—PT) (People's Movement for the Liberation of Angola—Workers' Party) 1977–92; in Dec. 1990 replaced Marxist-Leninist ideology with commitment to 'democratic socialism'; Chair. JOSÉ EDUARDO DOS SANTOS; Sec.-Gen. JOÃO MANUEL GONÇALVES LOURENÇO.

Movimento de Unidade Democrática para a Reconstrução (Mudar): Leader MANUEL DOS SANTOS LIMA.

National Union for the Light of Democracy and Development of Angola: Pres. MIGUEL MUENDO; Sec.-Gen. DOMINGOS CHIZELA.

Partido de Aliança de Juventude, Operários e Camponêses de Angola (PAJOCA) (Angolan Youth, Workers' and Peasants' Alliance Party): Leader MIGUEL JOÃO SEBASTIÃO.

Partido para a Aliança Popular: Leader CAMPOS NETO.

Partido Angolano Independente (PAI): Leader ADRIANO PARREIRA.

Partido Democrático Angolano (PDA): Leader ANTÓNIO ALBERTO NETO.

Partido Liberal Democrata (PLD): Leader ANÁLIA DE VICTÓRIA PEREIRA.

Partido Nacional Democrata de Angola (PNDA): Sec.-Gen. PEDRO JOÃO ANTÓNIO.

Partido Reformador de Angola (PRA): Leader RUI DE VICTÓRIA PEREIRA.

Partido Renovador Democrático (PRD): Leader LUÍS DOS PASSOS.

Partido Republicano Conservador de Angola (PRCA): Leader MARTINHO MATEUS.

Partido Social Democrata (PSD): Leader BENGUI PEDRO JOÃO.

Partido do Trabalho de Angola (PTA): Leader AGOSTINHO PALDO.

Patriotic Front: f. 1995; opposition alliance including:

> **Partido Angolano Liberal (PAL):** Leader MANUEL FRANCISCO LULO (acting).
>
> **Partido Democrático Liberal de Angola (PDLA):** Leader HONORATO LANDO.
>
> **Partido Democrático para o Progresso—Aliança Nacional de Angola (PDP—ANA):** Leader MFUFUMPINGA NLANDU VICTOR.
>
> **Partido Social Democrata de Angola (PSDA):** Leader ANDRÉ MILTON KILANDONOCO.

Peaceful Democratic Party of Angola: Leader ANTÓNIO KUNZOLAKO.

Unangola: Leader ANDRÉ FRANCO DE SOUSA.

União Nacional para a Independência Total de Angola (UNITA): internet www.kwacha.org; f. 1966 to secure independence from Portugal; later received Portuguese support to oppose the MPLA; UNITA and the Frente Nacional de Libertação de Angola conducted guerrilla campaign against the MPLA Govt with aid from some Western countries, 1975–76; supported by South Africa until 1984 and in 1987–88, and by USA after 1986; obtained legal status in March 1998; support drawn mainly from Ovimbundu ethnic group; Pres. Dr JONAS MALHEIRO SAVIMBI; Sec.-Gen. PAULO LUKAMBA 'GATO'.

> **UNITA—Renovada:** Rua Comandante Bula 71–73, São Paulo, Luanda; internet www.unita.org; f. 1998; splinter group claiming to be legitimate leadership of UNITA and recognized as such by MPLA, although commanding minority support among UNITA mems; Pres. of Political Commission EUGÉNIO ANTONINO N'GOLO 'MANUVAKOLA'.

United Front for the Salvation of Angola: Leader JOSÉ AUGUSTO DA SILVA COELHO.

Vofangola: Leader LOMBY ZUENDOKI.

Diplomatic Representation

EMBASSIES IN ANGOLA

Algeria: Luanda; Ambassador: HANAFI OUSSEDIK.

Belgium: Avda 4 de Fevereiro 93, CP 1203, Luanda; tel. (2) 336437; fax (2) 336438; e-mail luanda@diplobel.org; Ambassador: MICHEL VANTROYEN.

Brazil: Rua Houari Boumedienne 132, CP 5428, Luanda; tel. (2) 344848; Ambassador: PAULO DYRCEU PINHEIRO.

Bulgaria: Rua Fernão Mendes Pinto 35, CP 2260, Luanda; tel. (2) 321010; Chargé d'affaires a.i.: LILO TOCHEV.

Cape Verde: Rua Alexandre Peres 29, Luanda; tel. (2) 333211; Ambassador: JOSÉ LUÍS JESUS.

China, People's Republic: Rua Houari Boumedienne 196, Luanda; tel. (2) 344185; Ambassador: JIANG YUANDE.

Congo, Democratic Republic: Rua Cesario Verde 24, Luanda; tel. (2) 361953; Ambassador: MUNDINDI DIDI KILENGO.

Congo, Republic: Rua 4 de Fevereiro 3, Luanda; Ambassador: ANATOLE KHONDO.

Côte d'Ivoire: Rua Riyad 41-43, Luanda; tel. (2) 390150; fax (2) 333997; Ambassador: ETIENNE MIEZAN EZO.

Cuba: Rua Che Guevara 42, Bairro Ingombotas, Luanda; tel. (2) 339165; Ambassador: JUAN B. PUJOL-SÁNCHEZ.

Egypt: Rua Comandante Stona 247, Luanda; tel. (2) 321590; Ambassador: ANWAR DAKROURY.

France: Rua Reverendo Pedro Agostinho Neto 31–33, Luanda; tel. (2) 334335; fax (2) 391949; Ambassador: ALAIN RICHARD.

Gabon: Avda 4 de Fevereiro 95, Luanda; tel. (2) 372614; Ambassador: RAPHAËL NKASSA-NZOGHO.

Germany: Avda 4 de Fevereiro 120, CP 1295, Luanda; tel. (2) 334516; fax (2) 334516; Ambassador: Dr HENDRIK DANE.

Ghana: Rua Cirilo da Conceição e Silva 5, CP 1012, Luanda; tel. (2) 339222; fax (2) 338235; Ambassador: SIMON S. PULI.

Guinea: Luanda.

Holy See: Rua Luther King 123, CP 1030, Luanda (Apostolic Nunciature); tel. (2) 336289; fax (2) 332378; e-mail nunc.nuncio@ebonet.net; Apostolic Nuncio: Most Rev. ALDO CAVALLI, Titular Archbishop of Vibo Valentia.

Hungary: Rua Comandante Stona 226-228, Luanda; tel. (2) 32313; fax (2) 322448; Ambassador: Dr GÁBOR TÓTH.

India: Prédio dos Armazens Carrapas 81, 1°, D, CP 6040, Luanda; tel. (2) 345398; fax (2) 342061; Ambassador: BALDEV RAJ GHULIANI.

Israel: Rua Rainha Ginga 34, 11° andar, Luanda; tel. (2) 397901; fax (2) 396366; internet www.israel.org.br/luanda; Ambassador: TAMAR GOLA.

Italy: Edif. Rua dos Enganos 1, CP 6220, Luanda; tel. (2) 393533; fax (2) 333743; e-mail embitaly@ebonet.net; Ambassador: ALFREDO BASTIANELLY.

Korea, Democratic People's Republic: Rua Cabral Moncada 116–120, CP 599, Luanda; tel. (2) 395575; fax (2) 332813; Ambassador: HYON SOK.

Morocco: Largo 4 de Fevereiro 3, Luanda; tel. (2) 338847.

Mozambique: Luanda; tel. (2) 330811; Ambassador: M. SALESSIO.

Namibia: Rua dos Cocqueiros, CP 953, Luanda; tel. (2) 395483; fax (2) 339234; e-mail embnam@netangola.com.

Netherlands: Edif. Secil, Avda 4 de Fevereiro 42, CP 3624, Luanda; tel. (2) 333540; fax (2) 333699; e-mail lua@gg.lua.minbuza.nl; Ambassador: H. KROON.

Nigeria: Rua Houari Boumedienne 120, CP 479, Luanda; tel. (2) 340084; Ambassador: AGWOM GOKIR GOTIP.

Poland: Rua Comandante N'zaji 21–23, CP 1340, Luanda; tel. (2) 323086; Ambassador: JAN BOJKO.

Portugal: Rua Karl Marx 50, CP 1346, Luanda; tel. (2) 333027; Ambassador: RAMALHO ORTIGÃO.

Romania: Ramalho Ortigão 30, Alvalade, Luanda; tel. and fax (2) 321076; Ambassador: MARIN ILIESCU.

Russia: Rua Houari Boumedienne 170, CP 3141, Luanda; tel. (2) 345028; Ambassador: YURII KAPRALOV.

São Tomé and Príncipe: Rua Armindo de Andrade 173–175, Luanda; tel. (2) 345677; Ambassador: ARIOSTO CASTELO DAVID.

Slovakia: Rua Amílcar Cabral 5, CP 2691, Luanda; tel. (2) 334456.

South Africa: Rua Manuel Fernandes Caldeira 6B, CP 6212 Luanda; tel. (2) 397391; fax (2) 339126; Ambassador: R. J. M. MAMPANE.

Spain: Avda 4 de Fevereiro 95, 1°, CP 3061, Luanda; tel. (2) 391187; fax (2) 332884; e-mail embespao@mail.mae.es; Ambassador: ALVARO IRANZO.

Sweden: Rua Garcia Neto 9, Luanda; tel. (2) 340424; Ambassador: LENA SUND.

Switzerland: Avda 4 de Fevereiro 129, 2°, CP 3163, Luanda; tel. (2) 338314; fax (2) 336878; Chargé d'affaires a.i.: ARNOLDO LARDI.

Tanzania: Rua Joaquim Kapango 57–63, Luanda; tel. (2) 330536.

United Kingdom: Rua Diogo Cão 4, CP 1244, Luanda; tel. (2) 334583; fax (2) 333331; e-mail britemb.ang@ebonet.net; Ambassador: CAROLINE M. T. ELMES.

USA: Rua Houari Boumedienne 32, Miramar, CP 6468, Luanda; tel. (2) 347028; fax (2) 346924; Ambassador: JOSEPH SULLIVAN.

Viet Nam: Rua Comandante N'zaji 66–68, CP 75, Luanda; tel. (2) 323388; Ambassador: NGUYEN HUY LOI.

Yugoslavia: Rua Comandante N'zaji 25–27, Luanda; tel. (2) 321421; fax (2) 321724; Chargé d'affaires a.i.: BRANKO MARKOVIĆ.

Zambia: Rua Rei Katyavala 106–108, CP 1496, Luanda; tel. (2) 331145; Ambassador: BONIFACE ZULU.

Zimbabwe: Edif. do Ministério de Transportes e Comunicações, Avda 4 de Fevereiro 42, CP 428, Luanda; tel. (2) 310125; fax (2) 311528; Ambassador: B. G. CHIDYAUSIKU.

Judicial System

There is a Supreme Court and Court of Appeal in Luanda. There are also civil, criminal and military courts.

Chief Justice of the Supreme Court: JOÃO FELIZARDO.

Religion

Much of the population follows traditional African beliefs, although a majority profess to be Christians, mainly Roman Catholics.

CHRISTIANITY

Conselho de Igrejas Cristãs em Angola (Council of Christian Churches in Angola): Rua Amílcar Cabral 182, 1° andar, CP 1659, Luanda; tel. (2) 330415; fax (2) 393746; f. 1977; 14 mem. churches; five assoc. mems; one observer; Pres. Rev. ALVARO RODRIGUES; Gen. Sec. Rev. AUGUSTO CHIPESSE.

Protestant Churches

Evangelical Congregational Church in Angola (Igreja Evangélica Congregacional em Angola): CP 551, Huambo; tel. 3087; 100,000 mems; Gen. Sec. Rev. JÚLIO FRANCISCO.

Evangelical Pentecostal Church of Angola (Missão Evangélica Pentecostal de Angola): CP 219, Porto Amboim; 13,600 mems; Sec. Rev. JOSÉ DOMINGOS CAETANO.

United Evangelical Church of Angola (Igreja Evangélica Unida de Angola): CP 122, Uíge; 11,000 mems; Gen. Sec. Rev. A. L. DOMINGOS.

Other active denominations include the African Apostolic Church, the Church of Apostolic Faith in Angola, the Church of Our Lord Jesus Christ in the World, the Evangelical Baptist Church, the Evangelical Church in Angola, the Evangelical Church of the Apostles of Jerusalem, the Evangelical Reformed Church of Angola, the Kimbanguist Church in Angola and the United Methodist Church.

The Roman Catholic Church

Angola comprises three archdioceses and 12 dioceses. At 31 December 1998 an estimated 43.5% of the total population were adherents.

Bishops' Conference: Conferência Episcopal de Angola e São Tomé, CP 87, Luanda; tel. (2) 343686; fax (2) 345504; f. 1967; Pres. Most Rev. ZACARIAS KAMWENHO, Archbishop of Lubango.

Archbishop of Huambo: Most Rev. FRANCISCO VITI, Arcebispado, CP 10, Huambo; tel. 20130.

Archbishop of Luanda: Cardinal ALEXANDRE DO NASCIMENTO, Arcebispado, Largo do Palácio, CP 87, 1230-C, Luanda; tel. (2) 331481; fax (2) 334433; e-mail arquidiocese@snet.co.ao.

Archbishop of Lubango: Most Rev. ZACARIAS KAMWENHO, Arcebispado, CP 231, Lubango; tel. 20405; fax 23547.

The Press

The press was nationalized in 1976.

DAILIES

Diário da República: CP 1306, Luanda; official govt bulletin.

O Jornal de Angola: Rua Rainha Ginga 18–24, CP 1312, Luanda; tel. (2) 338947; fax (2) 333342; f. 1923; Dir-Gen. LUÍS FERNANDO; mornings and Sun.; circ. 41,000.

Newspapers are also published in several regional towns.

PERIODICALS

Actual: Luanda; weekly; Editor JOAQUIM ALVES.

Agora: Luanda; weekly; Dir ANGUEAR DOS SANTOS.

Angola Norte: CP 97, Malanje; weekly.

A Célula: Luanda; political journal of MPLA; monthly.

Comércio Externo: Rua da Missão 81, CP 6375, Luanda; tel. (2) 334060; fax (2) 392216; f. 1993 as *Comércio Actualidade*; Editor VICTOR ALEIXO.

Correio da Semana: Rua Rainha Ginga 18–24, CP 1213, Luanda; tel. (2) 331623; fax (2) 333342; f. 1992; owned by *O Jornal de Angola*; weekly; Editor-in-Chief MANUEL DIONISIO.

Eme: Rua Ho Chi Minh, Luanda; tel. (2) 321130; f. 1996; MPLA publ.

Folha 8: Rua Conselheiro Julio de Vilhena 24, 5° andar, Luanda; tel. (2) 391943; fax (2) 392289; two a week; Dir WILLIAM TONET.

Horizonte: Rua da Samba 144, 1° andar, Luanda.

Jornal de Benguela: CP 17, Benguela; two a week.

Lavra & Oficina: CP 2767-C, Luanda; tel. (2) 322155; f. 1975; journal of the Union of Angolan Writers; monthly; circ. 5,000.

Militar: Luanda; f. 1993; Editor-in-Chief CARMO NETO.

Noticias de Angola: Calçada G. Ferreira, Luanda; weekly.

Novembro: CP 3947, Luanda; tel. (2) 331660; monthly; Dir ROBERTO DE ALMEIDA.

O Planalto: CP 96, Huambo; two a week.

Tempos Novos: Avda Combatentes 244, 2° andar, CP 16088, Luanda; tel. (2) 349534; fax (2) 349534.

A Voz do Povo: Rua João de Deus 99-103, Vila Alice, Luanda.

A Voz do Trabalhador: Avda 4 de Fevereiro 210, CP 28, Luanda; journal of União Nacional de Trabalhadores Angolanos (National Union of Angolan Workers); monthly.

NEWS AGENCIES

ANGOP: Rua Rei Katiavala 120, CP 2181, Luanda; tel. (2) 391525; fax (2) 391537; Dir-Gen. and Editor-in-Chief AVELINO MIGUEL.

Foreign Bureaux

Agence France-Presse (AFP): Prédio Mutamba, CP 2357, Luanda; tel. (2) 334939; Bureau Chief MANUELA TEIXEIRA.

Allgemeiner Deutscher Nachrichtendienst (ADN) (Germany): CP 3193, Luanda; Correspondent GUDRUN GROSS.

Informatsionnoye Telegrafnoye Agentstvo Rossii – Telegrafnoye Agentstvo Suverennykh Stran (ITAR–TASS) (Russia):

Rua Marechal Tito 75, CP 3209, Luanda; tel. (2) 342524; Correspondent VLADIMIR BORISOVICH BUYANOV.

Inter Press Service (IPS) (Italy): c/o Centro de Imprensa Anibal de Melo, Rua Cequeira Lukoki 124, Luanda; tel. (2) 334895; fax: (2) 393445; Correspondent CHRIS SIMPSON.

Prensa Latina (Cuba): Rua D. Miguel de Melo 92-2, Luanda; tel. (2) 336804; Chief Correspondent LUÍS MANUEL SÁEZ.

Reuters (UK): c/o Centro de Imprensa Anibal de Melo, Rua Cequeira Lukoki 124, Luanda; tel. (2) 334895; fax (2) 393445; Correspondent CRISTINA MULLER.

Rossiyskoye Informatsionnoye Agentstvo—Novosti (RIA—Novosti) (Russia): Luanda; Chief Officer VLADISLAV Z. KOMAROV.

Xinhua (New China) News Agency (People's Republic of China): Rua Karl Marx 57-3, andar E, Bairro das Ingombotas, Zona 4, Luanda; tel. (2) 332415; Correspondent ZHAO XIAOZHONG.

Publishers

Empresa Distribuidora Livreira (EDIL), UEE: Rua da Missão 107, CP 1245, Luanda; tel. (2) 334034.

Neográfica, SARL: CP 6518, Luanda; publrs of *Novembro*.

Nova Editorial Angolana, SARL: CP 1225, Luanda; f. 1935; general and educational; Man. Dir POMBO FERNANDES.

Offsetográfica Gráfica Industrial Lda: CP 911, Benguela; tel. 32568; f. 1966; Man. FERNANDO MARTINS.

Government Publishing House

Imprensa Nacional, UEE: CP 1306, Luanda; f. 1845; Gen. Man. Dr ANTÓNIO DUARTE DE ALMEIDA E CARMO.

Broadcasting and Communications

TELECOMMUNICATIONS

Angola Telecom: Rua I Congresso 26, CP 625, Luanda; tel. (2) 331032; fax (2) 395446; international telecommunications.

BROADCASTING

Radio

Rádio Nacional de Angola: Rua Comandante Jika, CP 1329, Luanda; tel. (2) 323172; fax (2) 324647; broadcasts in Portuguese, English, French, Spanish and vernacular languages (Chokwe, Kikongo, Kimbundu, Kwanyama, Fiote, Ngangela, Luvale, Songu, Umbundu); Dir-Gen. MANUEL RABELAIS.

Luanda Antena Comercial (LAC): Praceta Luther King 5, Luanda; tel. (2) 396229; e-mail lac@ebonet.net.

Rádio Eclésia: Rua Comandante Bula 118, CP 3579, Luanda; tel. (2) 343041; fax (2) 343093; e-mail reclesia@ebonet.net; Dir-Gen. D. BENEDITO ROBERTO.

Television

Televisão Popular de Angola (TPA): Rua Ho Chi Minh, CP 2604, Luanda; tel. (2) 320025; fax (2) 391091; f. 1975; state-controlled; Man. Dir CARLOS CUNHA.

Finance

(cap. = capital; res = reserves; dep. = deposits; m. = million; brs = branches; amounts in kwanza (equivalent to 1m. readjusted kwanza), unless otherwise indicated)

BANKING

All banks were nationalized in 1975. In 1995 the Government authorized the formation of private banks.

Central Bank

Banco Nacional de Angola: Avda 4 de Fevereiro 151, CP 1298, Luanda; tel. (2) 332633; fax (2) 390579; e-mail bnagab@ ebonet; internet www.ebonet.net/bna; f. 1976; bank of issue; cap. 5m., res 1m., dep. 63.8m. (1997); Gov. AGUINALDO JAIME.

Commercial Banks

Banco de Poupança e Crédito (BPC): Largo Saydi Mingas, CP 1343, Luanda; tel. (2) 393790; fax (2) 393790; 100% state-owned; cap. 10,000m. old kwanza (Dec. 1992); Chair. AMILCAR S. AZEVEDO SILVA; brs throughout Angola.

Caixa de Crédito Agro-Pecuario e Pescas (CCAPP): Rua Rainha Ginga 83; tel. (2) 392749; fax (2) 392225; f. 1991; assumed commercial operations of Banco Nacional de Angola in 1996.

Development Bank

Banco de Comércio e Indústria SARL: Avda 4 de Fevereiro 85, CP 1395, Luanda; tel. (2) 333684; fax (2) 334924; e-mail oscarn@ ebonet.net; f. 1991; 91% state-owned; provides loans to businesses in all sectors; cap. 3.5m., res 7.3m., dep. 131.9m. (1998); Chair. PEDRO MAIANGALA PUNA; 2 brs.

Investment Bank

Banco Africano de Investimentos SARL (BAI): Rua Major Kanhangulo, Luanda; tel. (2) 337639; fax (2) 335486; e-mail rabreu@ bainet.ebonet.net; f. 1997; 37.5% interest owned by Angolan shareholders; Pres. Dr MÁRIO A. PALHARES.

Foreign Banks

Banco Espírito Santo e Comercial de Lisboa SA: 5-3°, Rua Cirilo da Conceição Silva, CP 1471, Luanda; tel. (2) 392287; fax (2) 391484; Rep. JOSÉ RIBEIRO DA SILVA.

Banco de Fomento e Exterior SA: Agrencia da Missão, Luanda; tel. (2) 394275; fax (2) 397090; Man. TERESA MATEUS.

Banco Português do Atlântico: Largo Rainha Ginga 6–8, CP 5726, Luanda; tel. (2) 397946; fax (2) 397397.

Banco Totta e Açores SA: Avda 4 de Fevereiro 99, CP 1231, Luanda; tel. (2) 336440; fax (2) 333233; e-mail totta-ang@edonet.net; Gen. Man. Dr MÁRIO NELSON MAXIMINO.

INSURANCE

Empresa Nacional de Seguros e Resseguros de Angola (ENSA), UEE: Avda 4 de Fevereiro 93, CP 5778, Luanda; tel. (2) 332991; fax (2) 332946; f. 1978.

Trade and Industry

SUPERVISORY BODY

National Supplies Commission: Luanda; f. 1977 to combat sabotage and negligence.

CHAMBERS OF COMMERCE

Angolan Chamber of Commerce and Industry: Largo do Kinaxixi 14, 1° andar, CP 92, Luanda; tel. (2) 344506; fax (2) 344629; Pres. ANTÓNIO JOÃO DOS SANTOS.

Associação Comercial de Luanda: Edifício Palácio de Comércio, 1° andar, CP 1275, Luanda; tel. (2) 322453.

STATE TRADING ORGANIZATIONS

Angomédica, UEE: Rua do Sanatório, Bairro Palanca, CP 2698, Luanda; tel. (2) 363765; fax (2) 362336; f. 1981 to import pharmaceutical goods; Gen. Dir Dr FÁTIMA SAIUNDO.

Ascorp: Luanda; state-owned diamond trading co; Pres. NOE BALTAZAR.

Direcção dos Serviços de Comércio (Dept of Trade): Largo Diogo Cão, CP 1337, Luanda; f. 1970; brs throughout Angola.

Epmel, UEE: Rua Karl Marx 35–37, Luanda; tel. (2) 330943; industrial agricultural machinery.

Exportang, UEE: Rua dos Enganos 1A, CP 1000, Luanda; tel. (2) 332363; co-ordinates exports.

Importang, UEE: Calçada do Município 10, CP 1003, Luanda; tel. (2) 337994; f. 1977; co-ordinates majority of imports; Dir-Gen. SIMÃO DIOGO DA CRUZ.

Maquimport, UEE: Rua Rainha Ginga 152, CP 2975, Luanda; tel. (2) 339044; f. 1981 to import office equipment.

Mecanang, UEE: Rua dos Enganos, 1°–7° andar, CP 1347, Luanda; tel. (2) 390644; f. 1981 to import agricultural and construction machinery, tools and spare parts.

STATE INDUSTRIAL ENTERPRISES

Companhia do Açúcar de Angola: Rua Direita 77, Luanda; production of sugar.

Companhia Geral dos Algodões de Angola (COTONANG): Avda da Boavista, Luanda; production of cotton textiles.

Empresa Abastecimento Técnico Material (EMATEC), UEE: Largo Rainha Ginga 3, CP 2952, Luanda; tel. (2) 338891; technical and material suppliers to the Ministry of Defence.

Empresa Açucareira Centro (OSUKA), UEE: Estrada Principal do Lobito, CP 37, Catumbela; tel. 24681; sugar industry.

Empresa Açucareira Norte (ACUNOR), UEE: Rua Robert Shilds, Caxito, Bengo; tel. 71720; sugar production.

Empresa Angolana de Embalagens (METANGOL), UEE: Rua Estrada do Cacuaco, CP 151, Luanda; tel. (2) 370680; production of non-specified metal goods.

ANGOLA

Directory

Empresa de Cimento de Angola (CIMANGOLA), UEE: Avda 4 de Fevereiro 42, Luanda; tel. (2) 371190; f. 1954; 69% state-owned; cement production; exports to several African countries.

Empresa de Construção de Edificações (CONSTROI), UEE: Rua Alexandre Peres, CP 2566, Luanda; tel. (2) 333930; construction.

Empresa de Pesca de Angola (PESCANGOLA), UEE: Luanda; f. 1981; state fishing enterprise, responsible to Ministry of Fisheries and Environment.

Empresa de Rebenefício e Exportação do Café de Angola (CAFANGOL), UEE: Rua Robert Shields 4/6, CP 342, Luanda; tel. (2) 337916; fax (2) 334742; e-mail cafango@arrobasnet.co.ao; f. 1983; nat. coffee-processing and trade org; proposed transfer to private sector announced in 1991; Dir-Gen. ALVARO FARIA.

Empresa de Tecidos de Angola (TEXTANG), UEE: Rua N'gola Kiluanji-Kazenga, CP 5404, Luanda; tel. (2) 381134; production of textiles.

Empresa Nacional de Cimento (ENCIME), UEE: CP 157, Lobito; tel. (711) 2325; cement production.

Empresa Nacional de Comercialização e Distribuição de Produtos Agrícolas (ENCODIPA): Luanda; central marketing agency for agricultural produce; numerous brs throughout Angola.

Empresa Nacional de Diamantes de Angola (ENDIAMA), UEE: Rua Major Kanhangulo 100, CP 1247, Luanda; tel. (2) 392336; fax (2) 337276; f. 1981 as the sole diamond-mining concession; commenced operations 1986; Dir-Gen. AUGUSTO PAULINO ALMEIDA NETO.

Empresa Nacional de Ferro de Angola (FERRANGOL): Rua João de Barros 26, CP 2692, Luanda; tel. (2) 373800; iron production; Dir ARMANDO DE SOUSA (MACHADINHO).

Empresa Nacional de Manutenção (MANUTECNICA), UEE: Rua 7, Avda do Cazenga 10, CP 3508, Luanda; tel. (2) 383646; assembly of machines and specialized equipment for industry.

Empresa Texteis de Angola (ENTEX), UEE: Avda Comandante Kima Kienda, CP 5720, Luanda; tel. (2) 336182; weaving and tissue finishing.

Geotécnica Unidad Económica Estatal: Rua Angola Kilmanse 389/393, Luanda; tel. (2) 381795; fax (2) 382730; f. 1978 for surveying and excavation; Man. P. M. M. ELVINO Jnr; 500 employees.

Siderurgia Nacional, UEE: CP Zona Industrial do Forel das Lagostas, Luanda; tel. (2) 373028; f. 1963, nationalized 1980; steelworks and rolling mill plant.

Sociedade Nacional de Combustíveis de Angola (SONANGOL): Rua I Congresso do MPLA, CP 1318, Luanda; tel. (2) 331690; fax (2) 391782; f. 1976 for exploration, production and refining of crude petroleum, and marketing and distribution of petroleum products; sole concessionary in Angola, supervises on- and offshore operations of foreign petroleum cos; holds majority interest in jt ventures with Cabinda Gulf Oil Co (Cabgoc), Fina Petróleos de Angola and Texaco Petróleos de Angola; Man. Dir JOAQUIM DAVID.

Sociedade Unificada de Tabacos de Angola, Lda (SUT): Rua Deolinda Rodrigues 530/537, CP 1263, Luanda; tel. (2) 391630; fax (2) 362138; f. 1919; tobacco products; Gen. Man. Dr MANUEL LAMAS.

UTILITIES

Electricity

Empresa Nacional de Construções Eléctricas (ENCEL), UEE: Rua Comandante Che Guevara 185/7, Luanda; tel. (2) 391630; fax (2) 331411; e-mail encel.dg@netangola.com; f. 1982.

Empresa Nacional de Electricidade (ENE), UEE: Edifício Geominas, 6°–7° andar, CP 772, Luanda; tel. (2) 321529; fax (2) 323382; e-mail enedg@netangola.com; f. 1980; production and distribution of electricity; Dir-Gen. Eng. MARIO FERNANDO PONTES MOREIRA FONTES.

TRADE UNIONS

Angolan General Independent and Free Trade Union Confederation: Chair. MANUEL DIFUILA.

União Nacional de Trabalhadores Angolanos (UNTA) (National Union of Angolan Workers): Avda 4 de Fevereiro 210, CP 28, Luanda; tel. (2) 334670; fax (2) 393590; f. 1960; Pres. MANUEL DIOGO DA SILVA NETO; Gen. Sec. MANUEL AUGUSTO VIAGE; 600,000 mems.

Transport

The transport infrastructure has been severely dislocated by the civil war.

RAILWAYS

The total length of track operated was 2,952 km in 1987. There are plans to extend the Namibe line beyond Menongue and to construct north–south rail links.

Caminhos de Ferro de Angola: Avda 4 de Fevereiro 42, CP 1250-C, Luanda; tel. (2) 339794; fax (2) 339976; f. 1975; nat. network operating four fmrly independent systems covering 2,952 track-km; Nat. Dir R. M. DA CONCEIÇÃO JUNIOR.

Amboim Railway: Porto Amboim; f. 1922; 123 track-km; Dir A. GUIA.

Benguela Railway (Companhia do Caminho de Ferro de Benguela): Rua Praça 11 Novembro 3, CP 32, Lobito; tel. (711) 22645; fax (711) 22865; f. 1903, line completed 1928; owned 90% by Tank Consolidated Investments (a subsidiary of Société Générale de Belgique), 10% by Govt of Angola; line carrying passenger and freight traffic from the port of Lobito across Angola, via Huambo and Luena, to the border of the Democratic Republic of the Congo (fmrly Zaire), where it connects with that country's railway system, which, in turn, links with Zambia Railways, thus providing the shortest west coast route for central African trade; 1,394 track-km; guerrilla operations by UNITA suspended all international traffic from 1975, with only irregular services from Lobito to Huambo being operated; a declaration of intent to reopen the cross-border lines was signed in 1987 by Angola, Zambia and Zaire, and the rehabilitation of the railway was a priority of a 10-year programme, planned by the SADCC (now SADC), to develop the 'Lobito corridor'; in 1997 an Italian company, Tor di Vale, began a US $450m.-programme of repairs to the railway; minimum repairs allowing the resumption of freight traffic were expected to take three years to complete, to be followed by further modernization, including the reconstruction of 22 passenger stations; Dir-Gen. DANIEL QUIPAXE.

Luanda Railway (Empresa de Caminho de Ferro de Luanda, UEE): CP 1250-C, Luanda; tel. (2) 370061; f. 1886; serves an iron, cotton and sisal-producing region between Luanda and Malanje; reconstruction of Luanda–Dondo rail link completed 1997, rehabilitation of Dondo–Malanje section proceeding in 1999; 536 track-km; Man. A. ALVARO AGANTE.

Namibe Railway: CP 130, Lubango; f. 1905; main line from Namibe to Menongue, via Lubango; br. lines to Chibia and iron ore mines at Cassinga; 899 track-km; Gen. Man. J. SALVADOR.

ROADS

In 1996 Angola had 72,626 km of roads, of which 7,955 km were main roads and 15,571 km were secondary roads. About 25% of roads were paved. In 1997 the state-owned road construction and maintenance company, the Instituto de Estradas de Angola, reported that 80% of the country's road network was in disrepair and that the cost of rebuilding the roads and bridges damaged during the civil conflict would total some US $4,000m.

SHIPPING

The main harbours are at Lobito, Luanda and Namibe; the commercial port of Porto Amboim, in Cuanza-Sul province, has been closed for repairs since 1984. The expansion of port facilities in Cabinda was due to begin in late 1995 and was expected to be completed within two years. In 1983 a regular shipping service began to operate between Luanda and Maputo (Mozambique). Under the emergency transport programme launched in 1988, refurbishment work was to be undertaken on the ports of Luanda and Namibe. The first phase of a 10-year SADCC (now SADC) programme to develop the 'Lobito corridor', for which funds were pledged in January 1989, was to include the rehabilitation of the ports of Lobito and Benguela.

Angonave—Linhas Marítimas de Angola, UEE: Rua Serqueira 31, CP 5953, Luanda; tel. (2) 330144; shipping line; Dir-Gen. FRANCISCO VENÂNCIO.

Cabotang—Cabotagem Nacional Angolana, UEE: Avda 4 de Fevereiro 83A, Luanda; tel. (2) 373133; operates off the coasts of Angola and Mozambique; Dir-Gen. JOÃO OCTAVIO VAN-DÚNEM.

Empresa Portuária do Lobito, UEE: Avda da Independência, CP 16, Lobito; tel. (711) 2710; long-distance sea transport; Gen. Man. JOSÉ CARLOS GOMES.

Empresa Portuária de Moçâmedes—Namibe, UEE: Rua Pedro Benje 10A and 10C, CP 49, Namibe; tel. (64) 60643; long-distance sea transport; Dir HUMBERTO DE ATAIDE DIAS.

Secil Marítima SARL, UEE: Avda 4 de Fevereiro 42, 1° andar, CP 5910, Luanda; tel. (2) 335230.

453

CIVIL AVIATION

Air Nacoia: Rua Comandante Che Guevara 67, 1° andar, Luanda; tel. and fax (2) 395477; f. 1993; Pres. SALVADOR SILVA.

TAAG—Linhas Aéreas de Angola: Rua da Missão 123, CP 79, Luanda; tel. (2) 332485; fax (2) 393548; f. 1939; internal scheduled passenger and cargo services, and services from Luanda to destinations within Africa and to Europe, South America and the Caribbean; Chair. JÚLIO SAMPAIO ALMEIDA; Dir-Gen. ABEL ANTÓNIO LOPES.

Angola Air Charter: Aeroporto Internacional 4 de Fevereiro, CP 3010, Luanda; tel. (2) 330994; fax (2) 392229; f. 1992; subsidiary of TAAG; CEO A. DE MATOS.

Transafrik International: Rua Joaquim Kapango, CP 2839, Luanda; tel. (2) 352141; fax (2) 354183; f. 1986; operates contract cargo services mainly within Africa; Man. Dir ERICH F. KOCH; Gen. Man. PIMENTAL ARAUJO.

Tourism

National Tourist Agency: Palácio de Vidro, CP 1240, Luanda; tel. (2) 372750.

ANTARCTICA

Source: Scientific Committee on Antarctic Research, Scott Polar Research Institute, Lensfield Rd, Cambridge, CB2 1ER, United Kingdom; tel. (1223) 362061; fax (1223) 336550; e-mail execsec@scar.demon.co.uk; internet www.scar.org.

The Continent of Antarctica is estimated to cover 13,661,000 sq km. There are no indigenous inhabitants, but a number of permanent research stations have been established. W. S. Bruce, of the Scottish National Antarctic Expedition (1902–04), established a meteorological station on Laurie Island, South Orkney Islands, on 1 April 1903. After the expedition, this was transferred to the Argentine authorities (the British Government having declined to operate the station), who have maintained the observatory since 22 February 1904 (see Orcadas, below). The next permanent stations were established in 1944 by the United Kingdom, and then subsequently by other countries.

Wintering Stations

(The following list includes wintering stations south of latitude 60° occupied during austral winter 2000)

	Latitude	Longitude
ARGENTINA		
General Belgrano II, Bertrab Nunatak, Luitpold Coast	77° 52′ S	34° 38′ W
Esperanza, Hope Bay	63° 24′ S	57° 00′ W
Teniente Jubany, King George Island	62° 14′ S	58° 40′ W
Vicecomodoro Marambio, Seymour Island	64° 15′ S	56° 39′ W
Orcadas, Laurie Island	60° 44′ S	44° 44′ W
General San Martín, Barry Island	68° 08′ S	67° 06′ W
AUSTRALIA		
Casey, Vincennes Bay, Budd Coast	66° 17′ S	110° 31′ E
Davis, Ingrid Christensen Coast	68° 35′ S	77° 58′ E
Mawson, Mac. Robertson Land	67° 36′ S	62° 52′ E

In a report published in 1997 the Australian Government's advisory body on the Antarctic proposed that future research work might be concentrated at the Davis station, thus enabling Casey and Mawson to be leased to other countries or to strictly regulated tour operators. (In 1998/99 the total number of tourists visiting Antarctica—mainly on special 'eco-cruises'—amounted to about 10,000.)

BRAZIL		
Comandante Ferraz, King George Island	62° 05′ S	58° 23′ W
CHILE		
Capitán Arturo Prat, Greenwich Island	62° 30′ S	59° 41′ W
General Bernardo O'Higgins, Cape Legoupil	63° 19′ S	57° 54′ W
Presidente Eduardo Frei, King George Island	62° 12′ S	58° 58′ W
Professor Julio Escudero, King George Island	62° 12′ S	58° 59′ W
PEOPLE'S REPUBLIC OF CHINA		
Chang Cheng (Great Wall), King George Island	62° 13′ S	58° 58′ W
Zhongshan, Princess Elizabeth Land	69° 22′ S	76° 23′ E
FRANCE		
Dumont d'Urville, Terre Adélie	66° 40′ S	140° 00′ E

A new research station, Concorde (at Dome C—75° 06′ S 123° 23′ E), was officially open for summer routine operations in December 1997 as a joint venture with Italy; the station was expected to be opened year round from 2003.

GERMANY		
Neumayer, Ekstrømisen	70° 38′ S	8° 16′ W
INDIA		
Maitri, Schirmacheroasen	70° 46′ S	11° 44′ E
JAPAN		
Syowa, Ongul	69° 00′ S	39° 35′ E

REPUBLIC OF KOREA		
King Sejong, King George Island	62° 13′ S	58° 47′ W
NEW ZEALAND		
Scott Base, Ross Island	77° 51′ S	166° 46′ E
POLAND		
Henryk Arctowski, King George Island	62° 10′ S	58° 28′ W
RUSSIA		
Bellingshausen, King George Island	62° 12′ S	58° 58′ W
Mirnyy, Queen Mary Land	66° 33′ S	93° 01′ E
Molodezhnaya, Enderby Land	67° 40′ S	45° 51′ E
Novolazarevskaya, Prinsesse Astrid Kyst	70° 46′ S	11° 50′ E
Progress, Princess Elizabeth Land	69° 23′ S	76° 23′ E
Vostok, East Antarctica	78° 28′ S	106° 48′ E
SOUTH AFRICA		
SANAE, Vesleskarvet	71° 41′ S	2° 50′ W
UKRAINE		
Vernadsky, Argentine Islands	65° 15′ S	64° 15′ W
UNITED KINGDOM		
Halley, Brunt Ice Shelf, Caird Coast	75° 36′ S	26° 32′ W
Rothera, Adelaide Island	67° 34′ S	68° 07′ W

In May 1990 the UK built an airstrip at the Rothera scientific station.

USA		
McMurdo, Ross Island	77° 51′ S	166° 40′ E
Palmer, Anvers Island	64° 47′ S	64° 03′ W
Amundsen-Scott		South Pole*

* The precise co-ordinates of the location of this station are: 89° 59′ 51″ S, 139° 16′ 23″ E.

URUGUAY		
Artigas, King George Island	62° 11′ S	58° 54′ W

Territorial Claims

Territory	Claimant State
Antártida Argentina	Argentina
Australian Antarctic Territory	Australia
British Antarctic Territory	United Kingdom
Dronning Maud Land	Norway
Ross Dependency	New Zealand
Terre Adélie	France
Territorio Chileno Antártico	Chile

These claims are not recognized by the USA or Russia. No formal claims have been made in the sector of Antarctica between 90° W and 150° W.

See also Article 4 of the Antarctic Treaty, below.

Research

Scientific Committee on Antarctic Research (SCAR) of the **International Council for Science (ICSU):** Secretariat: Scott Polar Research Institute, Lensfield Rd, Cambridge, CB2 1ER, England; tel. (1223) 362061; fax (1223) 336550; e-mail execsec@scar .demon.co.uk; internet www.scar.org; f. 1958 to initiate, promote and co-ordinate scientific research in the Antarctic, and to provide scientific advice to the Antarctic Treaty System; 26 full mems; six assoc. mems.

President: Dr R. H. Rutford (USA).

Vice-Presidents: Dr R. Schlich (France), Dr J. Valencia (Chile), Prof. A. D. M. Walker (South Africa), Prof. C. G. Rapley (United Kingdom).

Executive Secretary: Dr P. D. Clarkson.

The Antarctic Treaty

The Treaty (summarized below) was signed in Washington, DC, on 1 December 1959 by the 12 nations co-operating in the Antarctic during the International Geophysical Year, and entered into force on 23 June 1961. The Treaty made provision for a review of its terms, 30 years after ratification; however, no signatory to the Treaty has requested such a review.

Article 1. Antarctica shall be used for peaceful purposes only.

Article 2. On freedom of scientific investigation and co-operation.

Article 3. On exchange of information and personnel.

Article 4. i. Nothing contained in the present Treaty shall be interpreted as:

(a) a renunciation by any Contracting Party of previously asserted rights of or claims to territorial sovereignty in Antarctica;

(b) a renunciation or diminution by any Contracting Party of any basis of claim to territorial sovereignty in Antarctica which it may have whether as a result of its activities or those of its nationals in Antarctica, or otherwise;

(c) prejudicing the position of any Contracting Party as regards its recognition or non-recognition of any other State's right of or claim or basis of claim to territorial sovereignty in Antarctica.

ii. No acts or activities taking place while the present Treaty is in force shall constitute a basis for asserting, supporting or denying a claim to territorial sovereignty in Antarctica or create any rights of sovereignty in Antarctica. No new claim, or enlargement of an existing claim, to territorial sovereignty in Antarctica shall be asserted while the present Treaty is in force.

Article 5. Any nuclear explosions in Antarctica and the disposal there of radioactive waste material shall be prohibited.

Article 6. On geographical limits and rights on high seas.

Article 7. On designation of observers and notification of stations and expeditions.

Article 8. On jurisdiction over observers and scientists.

Article 9. On consultative meetings.

Articles 10–14. On upholding, interpreting, amending, notifying and depositing the Treaty.

ORIGINAL SIGNATORIES

Argentina	France	South Africa
Australia	Japan	USSR (former)
Belgium	New Zealand	United Kingdom
Chile	Norway	USA

ACCEDING STATES

Austria, Brazil, Bulgaria, Canada, the People's Republic of China, Colombia, Cuba, the Czech Republic, Denmark, Ecuador, Finland, Germany, Greece, Guatemala, Hungary, India, Italy, the Democratic People's Republic of Korea, the Republic of Korea, the Netherlands, Papua New Guinea, Peru, Poland, Romania, Slovakia, Spain, Sweden, Switzerland, Turkey, Ukraine, Uruguay, Venezuela.

Brazil, Bulgaria, the People's Republic of China, Ecuador, Finland, Germany, India, Italy, the Republic of Korea, the Netherlands, Peru, Poland, Spain, Sweden and Uruguay have achieved consultative status under the Treaty, by virtue of their scientific activity in Antarctica.

ANTARCTIC TREATY CONSULTATIVE MEETINGS

Meetings of representatives from all the original signatory nations of the Antarctic Treaty and acceding nations accorded consultative status (27 in 2000), are held every one to two years to discuss scientific, environmental and political matters. The 23nd meeting was held in Lima, Peru, in May–June 1999. The representatives elect a Chairman and Secretary. Committees and Working Groups are established as required.

Among the numerous measures that have been agreed and implemented by the Consultative Parties are several designed to protect the Antarctic environment and wildlife. These include Agreed Measures for the Conservation of Antarctic Flora and Fauna, the designation of Specially Protected Areas and Sites of Special Scientific Interest, a Convention for the Conservation of Antarctic Seals, and a Convention on the Conservation of Antarctic Marine Living Resources.

A Convention on the Regulation of Antarctic Mineral Resource Activities (the Wellington Convention) was adopted in June 1988 and was opened for signature in November. To enter into force, the Wellington Convention required the ratification of 16 of the Consultative Parties (then numbering 22). However, France and Australia opposed the Convention, which would permit mineral exploitation (under stringent international controls) in Antarctica, and proposed the creation of an Antarctic wilderness reserve. An agreement was reached at the October 1989 Consultative Meeting, whereby two extraordinary meetings were to be convened in 1990, one to discuss the protection of the environment and the other to discuss the issue of liability for environmental damage within the framework of the Wellington Convention. In September 1990 the Government of New Zealand, which played a major role in drafting the Wellington Convention, reversed its policy, stating that it was no longer willing to ratify the Convention. At the same time, it introduced legislation in the New Zealand House of Representatives to ban all mining and prospecting activities from its territories in Antarctica. At the special meeting held in Chile in November–December 1990, the Consultative Parties failed to reach an agreement regarding the protection of Antarctica's environment, although a draft protocol was approved that included provisions for elaborating the issue of liability for environmental damage. This formed the basis for a further meeting in Madrid, Spain, in April 1991. France, Australia and 16 other countries supported a permanent ban on mining, whereas the USA, the United Kingdom, Japan, Germany and four others were in favour of a moratorium. Subsequently, however, Japan and Germany transferred their allegiance to the Australian-French initiative, exerting considerable pressure on the USA and the United Kingdom, whose position became increasingly isolated. Agreement was eventually reached on a ban on mining activity for 50 years, and mechanisms for a review of the ban after 50 years, or before if all Parties agree. This agreement is embodied in Article 7 of the Protocol on Environmental Protection to the Antarctic Treaty, which was adopted by the original signatory nations in October 1991 immediately prior to the 16th Consultative Meeting. By late 1997 the Protocol had been ratified by all of the Consultative Parties (then numbering 26), and it entered into force on 14 January 1998. Thus there can be mining in the Antarctic only with the consent of all the present Consultative Parties, and even then only when a regulatory regime is in place. The first four annexes to the Protocol, providing for environmental impact assessment, conservation of fauna and flora, waste disposal, and monitoring of marine pollution, entered into force with the Protocol, but the fifth annex, on area protection, agreed after the adoption of the Protocol, has yet to take effect. A sixth annex on environmental liability is currently being negotiated. At the 22nd Consultative Meeting, held in mid-1998, the Committee for Environmental Protection (CEP) was established, under the provisions of the Protocol on Environmental Protection, and held its first meeting. In January 1999 the first ever political meeting held in Antarctica took place at the US McMurdo Station on Ross Island, attended by representatives of 24 of the then 43 countries acceding to the Antarctic Treaty; all of the participants reaffirmed their commitment to the protection of the Antarctic environment under the terms of the Treaty. No Consultative Meeting took place in 2000, although the Netherlands hosted a meeting of the CEP, followed by a half-day meeting at which parties to the Treaty adopted the CEP's recommendations.

At a meeting of the International Whaling Commission (see p. 300), held in Mexico in May 1994, it was agreed to establish a whale sanctuary around Antarctica below 40° S. The sanctuary, which was expected to protect about 80% of the world's remaining whales from commercial hunting, came into effect in December.

In May 1997 the World Meteorological Organization (see p. 000) suggested that long-term prospects for the rate of depletion of the ozone layer over Antarctica might be improving, but that strong statistical evidence of such a trend might not become apparent for at least five years. In late 1998 the New Zealand Government reported that the largest ozone hole on record, covering more than 27m. sq km, had formed over Antarctica. In late 1999, however, the US National Aeronautics and Space Administration (NASA) reported that the ozone hole had decreased in size to 25.4m. sq km.

There has been speculation that the calving of a 1,300-sq km iceberg from the Larsen A ice-shelf at the northern Antarctic Peninsula in early 1995 may have been attributable to the normal cycle of loss by calving; however, there is stronger evidence that the disintegration of a further considerable area of the ice shelf during the past 50 years was the result of climate warming. Research published by British scientists in October 1998, based on measurements of the Antarctic ice taken by satellite between 1992 and 1996, indicated, however, that the Antarctic ice sheet was not melting to any significant extent, as had been feared. Despite this, it was anticipated that average sea levels throughout the world would rise in the 21st century by more than had previously been predicted, as a result of other factors including the thermal expansion of the oceans. According to the results of joint research by British and American scientists announced in early 1999, the Larsen B and Wilkins ice-shelves were reported to have lost nearly 3,000 sq km of their total area during the preceding year. This calving constituted a rate of loss much greater than predicted and was offered by some experts as evidence of climate warming on a global scale.

ANTIGUA AND BARBUDA

Introductory Survey

Location, Climate, Language, Religion, Flag, Capital

The country comprises three islands: Antigua (280 sq km—108 sq miles), Barbuda (161 sq km—62 sq miles) and the uninhabited rocky islet of Redonda (1.6 sq km—0.6 sq mile). They lie along the outer edge of the Leeward Islands chain in the West Indies. Barbuda is the most northerly (40 km—25 miles north of Antigua), and Redonda is 40 km south-west of Antigua. The French island of Guadeloupe lies to the south of the country, the United Kingdom Overseas Territory of Montserrat to the south-west and Saint Christopher and Nevis to the west. The climate is tropical, although tempered by constant sea breezes and the trade winds, and the mean annual rainfall of 1,000 mm (40 ins) is slight for the region. The temperature averages 27°C (81°F), but can rise to 33°C (93°F) during the hot season between May and October. English is the official language, but an English patois is commonly used. The majority of the inhabitants profess Christianity, and are mainly adherents of the Anglican Communion. The national flag consists of an inverted triangle centred on a red field; the triangle is divided horizontally into three unequal bands, of black, blue and white, with the black stripe bearing a symbol of the rising sun in gold. The capital is St John's, on Antigua.

Recent History

Antigua was colonized by the British in the 17th century. The island of Barbuda, formerly a slave stud farm for the Codrington family, was annexed to the territory in 1860. Until December 1959 Antigua and other nearby British territories were administered, under a federal system, as the Leeward Islands. The first elections under universal adult suffrage were held in 1951. The colony participated in the West Indies Federation, which was formed in January 1958 but dissolved in May 1962.

Attempts to form a smaller East Caribbean Federation failed, and most of the eligible colonies subsequently became Associated States in an arrangement that gave them full internal self-government while the United Kingdom retained responsibility for defence and foreign affairs. Antigua attained associated status in February 1967. The Legislative Council was replaced by a House of Representatives, the Administrator became Governor and the Chief Minister was restyled Premier.

In the first general election under associated status, held in February 1971, the Progressive Labour Movement (PLM) ousted the Antigua Labour Party (ALP), which had held power since 1946, by winning 13 of the 17 seats in the House of Representatives. George Walter, leader of the PLM, replaced Vere C. Bird, Sr, as Premier. However, a general election in February 1976 was won by the ALP, with 11 seats, while the seat representing Barbuda was won by an independent. Vere Bird, the ALP's leader, again became Premier, while Lester Bird, one of his sons, became Deputy Premier.

In 1975 the Associated States agreed to seek independence separately. In the 1976 elections the PLM campaigned for early independence while the ALP opposed it. In September 1978, however, the ALP Government declared that the economic foundation for independence had been laid, and a premature general election was held in April 1980, when the ALP won 13 of the 17 seats. There was strong opposition in Barbuda to gaining independence as part of Antigua, and at local elections in March 1981 the Barbuda People's Movement (BPM), which continued to campaign for secession from Antigua, won all the seats on the Barbuda Council. However, the territory finally became independent, as Antigua and Barbuda, on 1 November 1981, remaining within the Commonwealth. The grievances of the Barbudans concerning control of land and devolution of power were unresolved, although the ALP Government had conceded a certain degree of internal autonomy to the Barbuda Council. The Governor, Sir Wilfred Jacobs, became Governor-General, while the Premier, Vere Bird, Sr, became the country's first Prime Minister.

Following disagreements within the opposition PLM, George Walter formed his own political party, the United People's Movement (UPM), in 1982. In April 1984, at the first general election since independence, divisions within the opposition allowed the ALP to win all of the 16 seats that it contested. The remaining seat, representing Barbuda, was retained by an unopposed independent (who subsequently formed the Barbuda National Party—BNP). A new opposition party, the National Democratic Party (NDP), was formed in Antigua in 1985. In April 1986 it merged with the UPM to form the United National Democratic Party (UNDP). Dr Ivor Heath, who had led the NDP, was elected leader of the new party.

In November 1986 controversy surrounding a rehabilitation scheme at the international airport on Antigua led to an official inquiry, which concluded that Vere Bird, Jr (a senior minister and the eldest son of the Prime Minister), had acted inappropriately by awarding part of the contract to a company with which he was personally involved. The affair divided the ALP, with eight ministers (including Lester Bird, the Deputy Prime Minister) demanding the resignation of Vere Bird, Jr, and Prime Minister Bird refusing to dismiss him. The rifts within the ALP and the Bird family continued into 1988, when new allegations of corruption implicated Lester Bird. At a general election in March 1989 the ALP remained the ruling party by retaining 15 of the 16 seats that it had held previously. The UNDP won more than 30% of the total votes, but only one seat. The Barbuda seat was won by the BPM.

In April 1990 the Government of Antigua and Barbuda received a diplomatic note of protest from the Government of Colombia regarding the sale of weapons to the Medellín cartel of drugs-traffickers in Colombia. The weapons had originally been sold by Israel to Antigua and Barbuda but, contrary to regulation, were then immediately shipped on to Colombia in April 1989. The communication from the Colombian Government implicated Vere Bird, Jr, and the Prime Minister eventually agreed to establish a judicial inquiry. In October 1990 the Chamber of Commerce recommended the resignation of the Government. In the following month a news agency obtained a copy of the unpublished report of the inquiry, which accused Antigua and Barbuda of having become 'engulfed in corruption'. In addition, the report revealed the activities of a number of British mercenaries on Antigua, involved in the training of paramilitary forces employed by Colombian drugs-trafficking organizations. Also in November, acting upon the recommendations of the report, the Government of Antigua and Barbuda dismissed Vere Bird, Jr, and banned him for life from holding office in the Government. The head of the defence force, Col Clyde Walker, was also dismissed.

Discontent within the ALP (including dissatisfaction with the leadership of Vere Bird, Sr), provoked a serious political crisis in early 1991. The Minister of Finance, John St Luce, resigned in February, after claiming that his proposals for a restructuring of government were ignored by the Prime Minister. A subsequent cabinet reshuffle (in which Lester Bird lost his deputy premiership) provoked the immediate resignation of three ministers. In September, however, Lester Bird and John St Luce accepted invitations from the Prime Minister to rejoin the Cabinet.

In early 1992 further reports of corruption involving Vere Bird, Sr, provoked public unrest and demands for his resignation. In April the Antigua Caribbean Liberation Movement (ACLM), the PLM and the UNDP consolidated their opposition to the Government by merging to form the United Progressive Party (UPP). In response to mounting public pressure, the ALP convened in May to elect a new leader. However, Vere Bird, Sr, retained the post, following an inconclusive result after the two candidates, Lester Bird and John St Luce, received an equal number of votes. In August further controversy arose when proposed anti-corruption legislation (which had been recommended following the Colombian arms scandal in 1991) was withdrawn as a result of legal intervention by the Prime Minister.

On 10 June 1993 James (later Sir James) Carlisle took office as Governor-General, replacing Sir Wilfred Jacobs. In September the ALP convened in order to hold further leadership elections. As a result of the vote, Lester Bird became leader of the party, while Vere Bird, Jr, was elected as Chairman.

At a general election in March 1994 the ALP remained the ruling party, although with a reduced majority, having secured 11 seats; the UPP won five and the BPM retained the Barbuda seat. Following the election, Lester Bird assumed the premiership. Despite some criticism, the election was generally thought to have been free and fair.

Controversy continued to surround the Government in 1995. In February of that year an ALP activist, Leonard Aaron, was charged with threatening to murder Tim Hector, editor of an opposition newspaper, *The Outlet*. It was reported that Hector's house had been burgled on several occasions, when material containing allegedly incriminating information relating to members of the Government had been stolen. Aaron was subsequently released, following the intervention of the Prime Minister. Furthermore, in May the Prime Minister's brother, Ivor Bird, was arrested following an incident in which he collected luggage at V. C. Bird International Airport from a Barbadian citizen from Venezuela, which contained 12 kg of cocaine. *The Outlet* claimed that such an exchange had occurred on at least three previous occasions. Ivor Bird's subsequent release from police custody, upon payment of a fine of EC $200,000, attracted considerable criticism. In an attempt to improve the country's worsening reputation as a centre for drugs-trafficking, the Government proposed legislation in early 1996 which aimed to curb the illegal drugs trade. Moreover, later that year Wrenford Ferrance, a former financial controller at the Organisation of Eastern Caribbean States (OECS—see p. 309), was appointed to the newly-created position of Special Adviser to the Government on money-laundering and on the control of illicit drugs. However, a report published by the US Government in early 1998 found Antigua and Barbuda to be 'of primary concern' with regard to both of these illegal activities.

Meanwhile, in September 1995 Antigua and Barbuda suffered extensive damage when the islands were struck by 'Hurricane Luis'. The storm, which caused damage estimated at US $300m., seriously affected some 75% of buildings and left almost one-half of the population homeless. Discussions between the Government and the World Bank, the International Monetary Fund (IMF) and other financial institutions took place in late 1995, in an attempt to resolve some of the economic problems caused by the hurricane.

A major cabinet reorganization, effected in May 1996, was controversial because of the appointment to the post of Special Adviser to the Prime Minister of Vere Bird, Jr, who had been declared unfit for public office following a judicial inquiry in 1990 (see above). In September 1996 Molwyn Joseph resigned as Minister of Finance over allegations that he had used his position in order to evade the payment of customs duties on the import of a vintage motor car. His resignation followed an opposition protest, at which the UPP leader, Baldwin Spencer, and seven other party members, including Tim Hector, were arrested (charges brought against them were later dismissed). A further demonstration took place at the end of the month, when some 10,000 people demanded a full inquiry into the affair and an early general election. In early December 1997, however, Joseph was reinstated in the Cabinet, assuming the new post of Minister of Planning, Implementation and the Environment; the appointment was vehemently condemned by the opposition.

In March 1997 the opposition BPM defeated the ALP's ally, the New Barbuda Development Movement, in elections to the Barbuda Council, winning all five of the contested seats and thus gaining control of all the seats in the nine-member Council. In the same month the High Court upheld a constitutional motion presented by Baldwin Spencer seeking the right of expression for the opposition on state-owned radio and television (denied during the electoral campaign in March 1994). In May and June the UPP boycotted sittings of the House of Representatives (the first legislative boycotts in the country's history) during a parliamentary debate on a proposed US $300m.-tourism development on Guiana Island, which was to be constructed by a Malaysian company. The opposition claimed that the Prime Minister had failed to publish the proposals for public discussion prior to the parliamentary debate and that the 2,000-room hotel project would have adverse effects on the island's ecology. The project was, none the less, endorsed by the legislature. In September Spencer applied to the High Court to have the hotel project agreement declared illegal and unconstitutional. However, his objections were overruled by the High Court in November, and a subsequent appeal, made to the Eastern Caribbean Court of Appeal, was also dismissed in April 1998. (The Prime Minister had rejected demands for

a referendum on the controversial scheme in October 1997.) However, the Guiana Island project continued to provoke controversy. In December 1997 Vere Bird, Jr, was slightly wounded in a shooting incident on the same day as the Government agreed terms for the compulsory resettlement of the island's sole occupants, Cyril 'Taffy' Bufton and his wife. Bufton was subsequently charged with attempted murder, but was acquitted in October 1998. The UPP denied government allegations of its involvement in the attack.

Meanwhile, in August 1997 *The Outlet* published further allegations regarding government-supported drugs-trafficking, including a claim that a Colombian drug cartel had contributed US $1m. to the ALP's election campaign in 1994. In response, Prime Minister Lester Bird obtained a High Court injunction in early September prohibiting the newspaper from publishing further material relating to the allegations. In November the printing presses of *The Outlet* were destroyed by fire, two days after the newspaper's editor, Tim Hector, had publicly alleged that a large consignment of 'sophisticated' weaponry had entered Antigua. The Government denied allegations that it was responsible for the fire, and stated that a shipment of 'basic' arms had been imported for police use.

In February 1997 the Government announced that four Russian and one Ukrainian 'offshore' banks were to be closed down, amid suspicions of money-laundering for the Russian mafia. Wrenford Ferrance, the government Special Adviser, stated that, since the country's 'offshore' banking system lacked adequate regulation, no new 'offshore' banking applications would be accepted until new legislation was passed. In April Ferrance was appointed to the post of superintendent of 'offshore' banks and insurance companies and director of international business corporations. Following the collapse, under suspicious circumstances, of the Antigua-based European Union Bank in August, the 51 remaining 'offshore' banks in Antigua and Barbuda were requested to submit full details of their operations in an attempt to combat further fraud. However, in May 1998 two more 'offshore' banks were implicated in a money-laundering case. In October the Government introduced legislation aimed at preventing such irregularities, while simultaneously promoting the development of the 'offshore' financial sector. However, in March 1999 the US Government published a report which claimed that the recent Antiguan legislation had weakened regulations concerning money-laundering and increased the secrecy surrounding 'offshore' banks. It also advised US banks to scrutinize all financial dealings with Antigua and Barbuda, which was described as a potential 'haven for money-laundering activities'. In April the United Kingdom issued a similar financial advisory to its banks. In response, in July Antigua became the first Eastern Caribbean country to bring into force a treaty with the USA on extradition and mutual legal assistance. Furthermore, in September the Government announced the establishment of an independent body to regulate 'offshore' banking, and promised to make existing controls more stringent. In November the authorities uncovered a significant money-laundering operation, run by a former Ukrainian prime minister. Nevertheless, in 2000 Antigua and Barbuda's financial system was criticized by the Organisation for Economic Co-operation and Development (OECD) and the OECD's Financial Action Task Force (FATF).

In November 2000 the Government introduced a controversial 2% turnover tax, prompting businesses to close for three days in protest. In the same month Prime Minister Bird requested that the IMF send a team of tax specialists to the islands to consult with the Government, the private sector and trade unions on the development of a 'new, efficient and modern' tax system. The Government forecast that the review and adoption of the new arrangements could take between 18 months and two years. In August 1998 the House of Representatives approved an amendment to voting regulations, granting the right to vote to all citizens who had been born abroad (including non-Commonwealth citizens) but who had been resident in Antigua and Barbuda for more than three years. Opposition members accused the Government of enlarging the electoral register for political advantage; these allegations were strenuously denied.

At a general election held on 9 March 1999, the ALP increased its representation in the 17-seat House of Representatives from 11 to 12, at the expense of the UPP, which secured four seats; the BPM retained its single seat. Following the election, Lester Bird was reappointed Prime Minister, and a new Cabinet was duly appointed, which controversially included Vere Bird, Jr, as Minister of Agriculture, Lands and Fisheries (despite the

1990 ruling declaring him unfit to hold public office). The UPP subsequently filed electoral petitions alleging breaches of electoral law in six constituencies (all of which were either dismissed or withdrawn in July). Independent observers, meanwhile, declared the election to have been free, although they expressed reservations concerning its fairness, owing to the ALP's large-scale expenditure and use of the media during its electoral campaign.

In June 1999 Vere Bird, Sr, Antigua's first premier and the founder of the ALP, died in St John's. At the fourth convention of the UPP, held in November, Vincent Derrick was re-elected as Chairman of the party, while Charlesworth Samuel was named deputy leader.

In January 2000 the Government established a commission, chaired by Sir Fred Philips, a former governor of Saint Christopher and Nevis, to review the Constitution. The commission was to examine the role of the Government, political parties and non-governmental organizations, and was to focus on the maintenance of democracy and accountability.

In elections to the Barbuda Council in March 2001 the BPM retained control of all nine seats.

In foreign relations the ALP Government follows a policy of non-alignment, although the country has strong links with the USA, and actively assisted in the US military intervention in Grenada in October 1983 as a member of the OECS. Antigua and Barbuda is also a member of the Caribbean Community and Common Market (CARICOM—see p. 142), but in 1988 proved to be a leading opponent of closer political federation within either organization. The Government did, however, agree to the reduction of travel restrictions between OECS members (which took effect in January 1990).

Government

Antigua and Barbuda is a constitutional monarchy. Executive power is vested in the British sovereign, as Head of State, and exercised by the Governor-General, who represents the sovereign locally and is appointed on the advice of the Antiguan Prime Minister. Legislative power is vested in Parliament, comprising the sovereign, a 17-member Senate and a 17-member House of Representatives. Members of the House are elected from single-member constituencies for up to five years by universal adult suffrage. The Senate is composed of 11 members (of whom one must be an inhabitant of Barbuda) appointed on the advice of the Prime Minister, four appointed on the advice of the Leader of the Opposition, one appointed at the discretion of the Governor-General and one appointed on the advice of the Barbuda Council. Government is effectively by the Cabinet. The Governor-General appoints the Prime Minister and, on the latter's recommendation, selects the other ministers. The Prime Minister must be able to command the support of a majority of the House, to which the Cabinet is responsible. The Barbuda Council has nine seats, with partial elections held every two years.

In July 2000 it was announced that there was to be public consultation on electoral reform, and in December a Commonwealth review of the administration of Barbuda recommended the maintenance of the existing constitutional relationship between Barbuda and Antigua.

Defence

There is a small defence force of 150 men (army 125, navy 25). The US Government leases two military bases on Antigua. Antigua and Barbuda participates in the US-sponsored Regional Security System. The defence budget in 2000 was estimated at EC $12.0m.

Economic Affairs

In 1998, according to estimates by the World Bank, Antigua and Barbuda's gross national product (GNP), measured at average 1996–98 prices, was US $565m., equivalent to US $8,450 per head (or $8,890 per head on an international purchasing-power parity basis). During 1990–98, it was estimated, GNP per head increased, in real terms, at an average annual rate of 3.4%. Over the same period, the population increased at an average rate of 0.6% per year. Measured at factor cost, the country's gross domestic product (GDP) increased, in real terms, at an average annual rate of 2.9% in 1990–98. According to the Eastern Caribbean Central Bank, real GDP increased by 5.6% in 1997, by 3.9% in 1998 and by an estimated 4.0% in 1999.

Agriculture (including forestry and fishing) engaged 3.9% of the labour force in 1991. The sector contributed 3.6% of GDP in 1999. Agricultural GDP increased, in real terms, between 1990

and 1998 at an average rate of 1.1% per year. It rose by 4.8% in 1997, by 4.2% in 1998 and by 3.2% in 1999. The principal crops are cucumbers, pumpkins, sweet potatoes, mangoes, coconuts, limes, melons and the speciality 'Antigua Black' pineapple. In 2000 the Ministry of Agriculture, Lands and Fisheries announced a programme to encourage farmers to increase production. Lobster, shrimp and crab farms are in operation, and further projects to develop the fishing industry were undertaken in the 1990s.

Industry (comprising mining, manufacturing, construction and utilities) employed 18.9% of the labour force in 1991 and provided 17.7% of GDP in 1999. The principal industrial activity is construction, accounting for 11.6% of total employment in 1991. Industrial GDP increased, in real terms, at an average rate of 3.4% per year during 1990–98. It rose by 8.3% in 1997, by 3.1% in 1998 and by 8.5% in 1999.

Mining and quarrying employed only 0.2% of the labour force in 1991 and contributed 1.6% of GDP in 1999. The real GDP of the mining sector increased at an average rate of 2.7% per year during 1990–98. It rose by 6.1% in 1996, by 5.0% in 1997 and by an estimated 8.0% in 1998.

The manufacturing sector consists of some light industries producing garments, paper, paint, furniture, food and beverage products, and the assembly of household appliances and electrical components for export. Manufacturing contributed 2.1% of GDP in 1999, when construction provided 11.3%. In real terms, the GDP of the manufacturing sector declined at an average rate of 0.6% per year during 1990–98. Real GDP in manufacturing increased by 4.0% in 1996, while construction activity increased by 12.0% (mainly owing to ongoing rehabilitation projects necessitated by 'Hurricane Luis'). In 1997 real GDP growth in the manufacturing and construction sectors was estimated to be, respectively, 6.0% and 8.0%. Manufacturing GDP increased by an estimated 5.5% in 1998, when construction growth was 10.0%.

Most of the country's energy production is derived from imported fuel. Imports of mineral fuels, lubricants and related materials accounted for 8.4% of total imports in 1998.

Services provided 70.2% of employment in 1991 and 78.7% of GDP in 1999. The combined GDP of the service sectors increased, in real terms, at an average rate of 3.0% per year during 1990–98. It rose by 5.2% in 1997, by 6.8% in 1998 and by 6.5% in 1999. Tourism is the main economic activity, providing approximately 35% of employment in 1991, and accounted (directly and indirectly) for some 60% of GDP in the mid-1990s. By 1998 the industry showed significant signs of recovery, following the severe effects of 'Hurricane Luis' (despite suffering a minor set-back in September 1998, when 'Hurricane Georges' resulted in the closure of several hotels). Tourist arrivals increased from 470,975 in 1995 to 577,024 in 1998, and to 588,866 in 1999; expenditure by tourists rose from EC $749.3m. in 1997 to EC $759.6m. in 1998 and to EC $782.9m. in 1999. The real GDP of the hotels and restaurants sector increased by 5.6% in 1996 and by an estimated 5.7% in 1997; however, it fell by 2.2% in 1998. Most tourists are from the USA (31% in 1998), the United Kingdom (27%), Canada (7%) and other Caribbean countries (11%).

Antigua and Barbuda recorded a visible trade deficit in 1999 of EC $819.0m. and a deficit of EC $168.5m. on the current account of the balance of payments. The country's principal trading partners are the other members of CARICOM (see p. 142), the USA, the United Kingdom and Canada. In 1998 the USA provided 26.6% of total imports and was also one of the main markets for exports (mainly re-exports).

In 1999 there was an estimated budgetary deficit of EC $78.29m. Budget proposals for the fiscal year ending 31 December 2000 envisaged total expenditure of EC 476.1m., compared with revenue of EC $465.1m., resulting in a deficit of EC $11.0m. In that year debt-servicing costs were expected to account for EC $102.5m. By the end of 1998 total external debt amounted to US $357.0m. The estimated annual average rate of inflation was 3.0% in 1996, 0.3% in 1997 and 3.4% in 1998. Central government sources predicted a 2.0% rise in consumer prices in 2000. The rate of unemployment at the end of 1998 was reported to be 5% of the labour force.

Antigua and Barbuda is a member of CARICOM, the OECS, the Organization of American States (see p. 261), and is a signatory of the Lomé Conventions and its successor agreement with the EU (see p. 208).

In the late 20th century the Government sought to diversify the economy, which is dominated by tourism. In May 1993 the

Senate approved legislation to allow the establishment of a free-trade zone, to encourage the manufacture of goods for export, in the north-east of Antigua. Consumption taxes were introduced in January 1995 (to coincide with the implementation of the CARICOM common external tariff) and provoked widespread public unrest. In April 1996 the Government introduced a programme of economic austerity, which included a public-sector pay 'freeze'. By 1997 the country was experiencing a degree of economic recovery, and in July 1998 it joined fellow members of the OECS in applying for group membership of the Inter-American Development Bank (IBD, see p. 212). Despite a deceleration in economic growth in 1998 (largely as a result of infrastructural damage caused by 'Hurricane Georges'), the economy was reported to have grown by 3.5% in 1999, as a result of continued buoyancy in the construction sector and increased tourist arrivals. In September 1999 the Government announced plans to transfer the state broadcasting service to private ownership. In the following month it was reported that all but two of the country's external debts had been rescheduled and in August 2000 the United Kingdom agreed to cancel US $9m. in debt and to reschedule a further $6m. over 10 years. In the late 1990s the Government's attempts to develop the 'offshore' financial sector were restricted, following several cases of money-laundering (see History).

Social Welfare

There are two state welfare schemes, both funded by contributions from employers and employees. The Social Security Scheme provides pensions and benefits for maternity, disability and sickness, while the Medical Benefits Scheme awards grants for the treatment of specific chronic diseases. Antigua has a 220-bed general hospital and 25 health centres and clinics. In 1997 work began on the construction of a new hospital, the Mount St John's Medical Complex, near the capital; the project, estimated to cost EC $80m., was to be financed by a US company and was nearing completion in 2000. In 1993 there was one physician for every 1,316 inhabitants.

Education

Education is compulsory for 11 years between five and 16 years of age. Primary education begins at the age of five and normally lasts for seven years. Secondary education, beginning at 12 years of age, lasts for five years, comprising a first cycle of three years and a second cycle of two years. In 1987/88 there were 43 primary and 15 secondary schools; the majority of schools are administered by the Government. In 1991/92 some 9,298 primary school pupils and 5,845 secondary school pupils were enrolled. Teacher-training and technical training are available at the Antigua State College in St John's. An extra-mural department of the University of the West Indies offers several foundation courses leading to higher study at branches elsewhere. The adult literacy rate in Antigua and Barbuda is more than 90%, one of the highest rates in the Eastern Caribbean. Current government expenditure on education in 1993/94 was projected at EC $37.1m., equivalent to 12.8% of total budgetary expenditure.

Public Holidays

2001: 1 January (New Year's Day), 13 April (Good Friday), 16 April (Easter Monday), 7 May (Labour Day), 4 June (Whit Monday), 9 June (Queen's Official Birthday), 2 July (Vere C. Bird, Sr Day), 6–7 August (Carnival), 1 November (Independence Day), 25–26 December (Christmas).

2002: 1 January (New Year's Day), 29 March (Good Friday), 1 April (Easter Monday), 6 May (Labour Day), 20 May (Whit Monday), 8 June (Queen's Official Birthday), 1 July (Vere C. Bird, Sr Day), 5–6 August (Carnival), 1 November (Independence Day), 25–26 December (Christmas).

Weights and Measures

The imperial system is in use, but a metrication programme is being introduced.

Statistical Survey

Source (unless otherwise stated): Ministry of Finance, High St, St John's; tel. 462-4860; fax 462-1622.

AREA AND POPULATION

Area: 441.6 sq km (170.5 sq miles).

Population: 65,525 (males 31,054, females 34,471) at census of 7 April 1970; 62,922 (provisional result) at census of 28 May 1991; 69,866 (official estimate) at mid-1998.

Density (estimate, mid-1998): 158.1 per sq km.

Principal Town: St John's (capital), population 22,342 at 1991 census.

Births, Marriages and Deaths (registrations): Live births (provisional, 1997) 1,448 (birth rate 21.6 per 1,000); Marriages (1987) 343 (marriage rate 5.4 per 1,000); Deaths (1995) 434 (death rate 6.4 per 1,000). Source: UN, *Demographic Yearbook*.

Expectation of Life (World Bank estimate, years at birth, 1998): 75.

Employment (persons aged 15 years and over, census of 28 May 1991): Agriculture, forestry and fishing 1,040; Mining and quarrying 64; Manufacturing 1,444; Electricity, gas and water 435; Construction 3,109; Trade, restaurants and hotels 8,524; Transport, storage and communications 2,395; Finance, insurance, real estate and business services 1,454; Community, social and personal services 6,406; Activities not adequately defined 1,882; Total employed 26,753 (males 14,564, females 12,189). Source: ILO, *Yearbook of Labour Statistics*.

1998: Total active labour force (estimate) 30,000. Source: IMF *Antigua and Barbuda: Statistical Annex* (December 1999).

AGRICULTURE, ETC.

Principal Crops (FAO estimates, '000 metric tons, 1999): Vegetables 1.6; Melons 0.7; Mangoes 1.3; Other fruits 7.0. Source: FAO.

Livestock (FAO estimates, '000 head, year ending September 1999): Asses 1; Cattle 16; Pigs 2; Sheep 12; Goats 12; Poultry 90. Source: FAO.

Livestock Products (FAO estimates, '000 metric tons, 1999): Beef and veal 1; Cows' milk 6. Source: FAO.

Fishing (FAO estimates, metric tons, live weight, 1998): Total catch 500 (Marine fishes 380, Caribbean spiny lobster 65, Stromboid conchs 55). Source: FAO, *Yearbook of Fishery Statistics*.

INDUSTRY

Production (estimates, 1988): Rum 4,000 hectolitres; Wines and vodka 2,000 hectolitres; Electric energy (1995) 98m. kWh. Source: UN, *Industrial Commodity Statistics Yearbook*.

FINANCE

Currency and Exchange Rates: 100 cents = 1 Eastern Caribbean dollar (EC $). *Sterling, US Dollar and Euro Equivalents* (29 December 2000): £1 sterling = EC $4.029; US $1 = EC $2.700; €1 = EC $2.512; EC $100 = £24.82 = US $37.04 = €39.80. *Exchange rate:* Fixed at US $1 = EC $2.700 since July 1976.

Budget (EC $ million, preliminary, 1999): *Revenue:* Tax revenue 302.4 (Taxes on income and profits 35.1, Taxes on domestic goods and services 63.3, Taxes on international transactions 199.8); Other current revenue 44.7; Capital revenue 4.0; Total 351.1, excluding grants received (6.8). *Expenditure:* Current expenditure 388.6 (Personal emoluments 220.0, Other goods and services 98.5, Interest payments 31.8, Transfers and subsidies 38.4); Capital expenditure 47.5; Total 436.1. Source: Eastern Caribbean Central Bank, *Report and Statement of Accounts*.

International Reserves (US $ million at 31 December 1999): IMF special drawing rights 0.01; Foreign exchange 69.72; Total 69.73. Source: IMF, *International Financial Statistics*.

Money Supply (EC $ million at 31 December 1999): Currency outside banks 85.01; Demand deposits at deposit money banks 241.08; Total money (incl. others) 326.13. Source: IMF, *International Financial Statistics*.

Cost of Living (Consumer Price Index; base: 1990 = 100): 93.5 in 1989; 100.0 in 1990; 105.7 in 1991. Source: ILO, *Yearbook of Labour Statistics*.

Expenditure on the Gross Domestic Product (EC $ million at current prices, 1999): Government final consumption expenditure 401.4; Private final consumption expenditure 897.3; Gross capital formation 807.1; *Total domestic expenditure* 2,105.8; Exports of goods and services 1,159.5; *Less* Imports of goods and services

1,506.3; *GDP in purchasers' values* 1,759.0. Source: IMF, *International Financial Statistics*.

Gross Domestic Product by Economic Activity (EC $ million at current prices, 1999): Agriculture, hunting, forestry and fishing 59.12; Mining and quarrying 25.74; Manufacturing 33.64; Electricity and water 44.71; Construction 183.38; Trade 162.36; Restaurants and hotels 179.64; Transport and communications 310.69; Finance, insurance, real estate and business services 254.83; Government services 260.85; Other community, social and personal services 110.75; *Sub-total* 1,625.70; *Less* Imputed bank service charges 128.59; *GDP at factor cost* 1,497.11. Source: Eastern Caribbean Central Bank, *National Accounts*.

Balance of Payments (EC $ million, 1999): Exports of goods f.o.b. 96.89; Imports of goods f.o.b. –915.86; *Trade balance* –818.97; Exports of services 1,162.91; Imports of services –487.40; *Balance on goods and services* –143.46; Other income received 9.73; Other income paid –90.48; *Balance on goods, services and income* –224.21; Current transfers received 66.19; Current transfers paid –10.47; *Current balance* –168.49; Capital account (net) 22.78; Direct investment (net) 71.63; Portfolio investment (net) 7.25; Other investment (net) 32.28; Net errors and omissions 62.53; *Overall balance* 27.98. Source: Eastern Caribbean Central Bank, *Balance of Payments*.

EXTERNAL TRADE

Total Trade (EC $ million): *Imports c.i.f.:* 999.7 in 1997; 1,056.5 in 1998; 1,040.8 in 1999. *Exports f.o.b.:* 104.8 in 1997; 100.9 in 1998; 96.9 in 1999. Source: Eastern Caribbean Central Bank, *Balance of Payments*.

Principal Commodities (EC $ million, estimates 1998): *Imports:* Food and live animals 89.2; Beverages and tobacco 27.1; Mineral fuels, lubricants, etc. 72.1; Chemicals and related products 50.0; Basic manufactures 252.1; Machinery and transport equipment 232.8; Miscellaneous manufactured articles 113.6. Total (incl. others) 854.6. *Exports:* Food and live animals 2.4; Mineral fuels, lubricants, etc. 13.7; Chemicals and related products 6.2; Basic manufactures 6.6; Machinery and transport equipment 22.6; Miscellaneous manufactured articles 25.1; Total (incl. others) 78.3. Source: OECS, *External Merchandise Trade Annual Report*.

Principal Trading Partners (EC $ million, estimates, 1998): *Imports:* Barbados 14.7; Canada 26.0; Trinidad and Tobago 26.6; United Kingdom 86.3; USA 227.5; Total (incl. others) 854.6. *Exports:* Barbados 7.4; Canada 1.4; French West Indies 1.3; Italy 1.8; Jamaica 1.6; Montserrat 2.5; Saint Christopher and Nevis 3.6; Saint Lucia 5.7; Trinidad and Tobago 5.7; United Kingdom 4.8, USA 1.4; Total (incl. others) 78.3. Source: OECS, *Digest of Trade Statistics*.

TRANSPORT

Road Traffic (registered vehicles, 1995): Passenger motor cars 15,100; Commercial vehicles 4,800. Source: UN, *Statistical Yearbook*.

Shipping (international freight traffic, '000 metric tons, 1990): Goods loaded 28; Goods unloaded 113 (Source: UN, *Monthly Bulletin of Statistics*). Arrivals (vessels, 1987): 3,940. *Merchant Fleet* (registered at 31 December): 575 vessels (total displacement 2,787,829 grt) in 1998. (Source: Lloyd's Register of Shipping, *World Fleet Statistics*).

Civil Aviation (traffic on scheduled services, 1997): Kilometres flown (million) 12; Passengers carried ('000) 1,250; Passenger-km (million) 250; Total ton-km (million) 23. Source: UN, *Statistical Yearbook*.

TOURISM

Visitor Arrivals: 540,773 in 1997; 577,024 in 1998; 588,866 (231,714 stop-overs, 328,038 cruise-ship passengers, 17,358 yacht passengers, 11,756 excursionists) in 1999.

Tourism Receipts (EC $ million): 749.3 in 1997; 759.6 in 1998; 782.9 in 1999.

Source: Eastern Caribbean Central Bank, *Statistical Digest, Balance of Payments* and *Report and Statement of Accounts*.

COMMUNICATIONS MEDIA

Daily Newspaper (1996): 1 (estimated circulation 6,000)*.

Non-Daily Newspapers (1996): 4*.

Radio Receivers (1997): 36,000 in use*.

Television Receivers (1997): 31,000 in use*.

Telephones (1996): 27,556 in use.

Telefax Stations (year ending 31 March 1997): 850 in use†.

Mobile Telephones (year ending 31 March 1997): 1,300 subscribers†.

* Source: UNESCO, *Statistical Yearbook*.

† Source: UN, *Statistical Yearbook*.

EDUCATION

Pre-primary (1983): 21 schools; 23 teachers; 677 pupils.

Primary (1987/88): 43 schools; 446 teachers; 9,298 students (1991/92).

Secondary (1991/92): 15 schools (1987/88); 400 teachers (estimate); 5,845 students.

Tertiary (1986): 2 colleges; 631 students.

Directory

The Constitution

The Constitution, which came into force at the independence of Antigua and Barbuda on 1 November 1981, states that Antigua and Barbuda is a 'unitary sovereign democratic state'. The main provisions of the Constitution are summarized below:

FUNDAMENTAL RIGHTS AND FREEDOMS

Regardless of race, place of origin, political opinion, colour, creed or sex, but subject to respect for the rights and freedoms of others and for the public interest, every person in Antigua and Barbuda is entitled to the rights of life, liberty, security of the person, the enjoyment of property and the protection of the law. Freedom of movement, of conscience, of expression (including freedom of the press), of peaceful assembly and association is guaranteed and the inviolability of family life, personal privacy, home and other property is maintained. Protection is afforded from discrimination on the grounds of race, sex, etc., and from slavery, forced labour, torture and inhuman treatment.

THE GOVERNOR-GENERAL

The British sovereign, as Monarch of Antigua and Barbuda, is the Head of State and is represented by a Governor-General of local citizenship.

PARLIAMENT

Parliament consists of the Monarch, a 17-member Senate and the House of Representatives composed of 17 elected members. Senators are appointed by the Governor-General: 11 on the advice of the Prime Minister (one of whom must be an inhabitant of Barbuda), four on the advice of the Leader of the Opposition, one at his own discretion and one on the advice of the Barbuda Council. The Barbuda Council is the principal organ of local government in that island, whose membership and functions are determined by Parliament. The life of Parliament is five years.

Each constituency returns one Representative to the House who is directly elected in accordance with the Constitution.

The Attorney-General, if not otherwise a member of the House, is an ex-officio member but does not have the right to vote.

Every citizen over the age of 18 is eligible to vote.

Parliament may alter any of the provisions of the Constitution.

THE EXECUTIVE

Executive authority is vested in the Monarch and exercisable by the Governor-General. The Governor-General appoints as Prime Minister that member of the House who, in the Governor-General's view, is best able to command the support of the majority of the members of the House, and other ministers on the advice of the Prime Minister. The Governor-General may remove the Prime Minister from office if a resolution of no confidence is passed by the House and the Prime Minister does not either resign or advise the Governor-General to dissolve Parliament within seven days.

The Cabinet consists of the Prime Minister and other ministers and the Attorney-General.

The Leader of the Opposition is appointed by the Governor-General as that member of the House who, in the Governor-General's view, is best able to command the support of a majority of members of the House who do not support the Government.

CITIZENSHIP

All persons born in Antigua and Barbuda before independence who, immediately prior to independence, were citizens of the United Kingdom and Colonies automatically become citizens of Antigua and Barbuda. All persons born outside the country with a parent or grandparent possessing citizenship of Antigua and Barbuda automatically acquire citizenship as do those born in the country after independence. Provision is made for the acquisition of citizenship by those to whom it would not automatically be granted.

The Government

Head of State: HM Queen ELIZABETH II (succeeded to the throne 6 February 1952).

Governor-General: Sir JAMES CARLISLE (took office 10 June 1993).

CABINET
(April 2001)

Prime Minister and Minister of Foreign Affairs, Caribbean Community Affairs, Defence and Security, Finance and Merchant Shipping: LESTER BIRD.

Minister of Justice and Legal Affairs, and Attorney-General: Dr ERROL CORT.

Minister of Public Utilities, Aviation, Transport and Housing: ROBIN YEARWOOD.

Minister of Home Affairs, Urban Development and Renewal and Social Improvement: JOHN ST LUCE.

Minister of Tourism and the Environment: MOLWYN JOSEPH.

Minister of Health: (vacant).

Minister of Education, Culture and Technology: Dr RODNEY WILLIAMS.

Minister of Agriculture, Lands and Fisheries: VERE BIRD, Jr.

Minister of Trade, Industry and Business Development: HILROY HUMPHREYS.

Minister of Labour, Co-operatives and Public Safety: STEADROY BENJAMIN.

Minister of Planning, Implementation and Public Service Affairs: GASTON BROWN.

Minister of Youth Affairs and Sports: Sen. GUY YEARWOOD.

Minister of State in the Office of the Prime Minister with responsibility for Finance: Sen. ASOT MICHAEL.

Minister of State in the Ministry of Trade with responsibility for Industrial Development and Manufacturing: JEREMY LONGFORD.

Minister of State in the Ministry of Public Works, Communications and Insurance with responsibility for Development Control Authority and Youth Empowerment: Sen. BERNARD GEORGE WALKER.

Minister of State in the Office of the Prime Minister with responsibility for Information and Broadcasting: Sen. GUY YEARWOOD.

MINISTRIES

Office of the Prime Minister: Queen Elizabeth Highway, St John's; tel. 462-4956; fax 462-3225; e-mail pmo@candw.ag; internet www.antiguabarbuda.net/pmo.

Ministry of Agriculture, Lands and Fisheries: Queen Elizabeth Highway, St John's; tel. 462-1543; fax 462-6104.

Ministry of Education, Culture and Technology: Church St, St John's; tel. 462-4959; fax 462-4970.

Ministry of Finance: High St, St John's; tel. 462-4860; fax 462-1622.

Ministry of Foreign Affairs: Queen Elizabeth Highway, St John's; tel. 462-1052; fax 462-2482; e-mail minforeign@candw.ag; internet www.antiguabarbuda.net/external.

Ministry of Health: St John's St, St John's; tel. 462-1600; fax 462-5003.

Ministry of Home Affairs, Urban Development and Renewal and Social Improvement: St John's.

Ministry of Justice and Legal Affairs, and Office of the Attorney-General: Hadeed Bldg, Redcliffe St, St John's; tel. 462-6037; fax 562-1879; e-mail legalaffairs@candw.ag; internet www.antiguabarbuda.net/ag.

Ministry of Labour, Co-operatives and Public Safety: Redcliffe St, St John's; tel. 462-0011; fax 462-1595.

Ministry of Planning, Implementation and Public Service Affairs: St John's.

Ministry of Public Safety: St John's.

Ministry of Public Utilities, Aviation, Transport and Housing: St John's St, St John's; tel. 462-0894; fax 462-1529.

Ministry of Public Works, Communications and Insurance: St John's.

Ministry of Tourism and the Environment: Queen Elizabeth Highway, St John's; tel. 462-4625; fax 462-2836; e-mail mintourenv@candw.ag.

Ministry of Trade, Industry and Business Development: Redcliffe St, St John's; tel. 462-1543; fax 462-5003.

Ministry of Youth Affairs and Sports: St John's.

Legislature

PARLIAMENT
Senate

President: MILLICENT PERCIVAL.

There are 17 nominated members.

House of Representatives

Speaker: BRIDGETTE HARRIS.

Ex-Officio Member: The Attorney-General.

Clerk: L. DOWE.

General Election, 9 March 1999

Party			Votes cast	%	Seats
Antigua Labour Party	.	.	17,417	52.6	12
United Progressive Party	.	.	14,817	44.8	4
Barbuda People's Movement	.		418	1.3	1
Independents and others	.	.	439	1.3	—
Total	.	.	33,091	100.0	17

Political Organizations

Antigua Labour Party (ALP): St Mary's St, POB 948, St John's; tel. 462-2235; f. 1968; Leader LESTER BIRD; Chair. VERE BIRD, Jr.

Barbuda Independence Movement: Codrington; f. 1983 as Organisation for National Reconstruction, re-formed 1988; advocates self-government for Barbuda; Pres. ARTHUR SHABAZZ-NIBBS.

Barbuda National Party: Codrington; Leader ERIC BURTON.

Barbuda People's Movement (BPM): Codrington; campaigns for separate status for Barbuda; Parliamentary Leader THOMAS HILBOURNE FRANK; Chair. FABIAN JONES.

National Reform Movement (NRM): POB 1318, St John's.

New Barbuda Development Movement: Codrington; linked with the Antigua Labour Party.

United Progressive Party (UPP): Nevis Street, St John's; tel. 462-1818; fax 462-5937; e-mail upp@candw.ag; f. 1992 by merger of the Antigua Caribbean Liberation Movement (f. 1979), the Progressive Labour Movement (f. 1970) and the United National Democratic Party (f. 1986); Leader BALDWIN SPENCER; Dep. Leader CHARLESWORTH SAMUEL; Chair. VINCENT DERRICK.

Diplomatic Representation

EMBASSIES AND HIGH COMMISSION IN ANTIGUA AND BARBUDA

China, People's Republic: Cedar Valley, POB 1446, St John's; tel. 462-1125; (Ambassador resident in Barbados).

United Kingdom: British High Commission, Price Waterhouse Centre, 11 Old Parham Rd, POB 483, St John's; tel. 562-2124; fax 462-2806; e-mail britishh@candw.ag; (High Commissioner resident in Barbados).

Venezuela: Cross and Redcliffe Sts, POB 1201, St John's; tel. 462-1574; fax 462-1570; e-mail venezuela@mail.candw.ag; Ambassador: ALBERTO GARANTÓN.

Judicial System

Justice is administered by the Eastern Caribbean Supreme Court, based in Saint Lucia, which consists of a High Court of Justice and a Court of Appeal. One of the Court's Puisne Judges is resident in and responsible for Antigua and Barbuda, and presides over the Court of Summary Jurisdiction on the islands. There are also Magistrates' Courts for lesser cases.

Chief Justice: DENNIS BYRON.

Solicitor-General: LEBRECHT HESSE.

Attorney-General: Dr ERROL CORT.

Religion

The majority of the inhabitants profess Christianity, and the largest denomination is the Church in the Province of the West Indies (Anglican Communion).

CHRISTIANITY

Antigua Christian Council: POB 863, St John's; tel. 462-0261; f. 1964; five mem. churches; Pres. Rt Rev. DONALD J. REECE (Roman Catholic Bishop of St John's—Basseterre); Exec. Sec. EDRIS ROBERTS.

The Anglican Communion

Anglicans in Antigua and Barbuda are adherents of the Church in the Province of the West Indies. The diocese of the North Eastern Caribbean and Aruba comprises 12 islands: Antigua, Saint Christopher (St Kitts), Nevis, Anguilla, Barbuda, Montserrat, Dominica, Saba, St Maarten/St Martin, Aruba, St Bartholomew and St Eustatius; the total number of Anglicans is about 60,000. The See City is St John's, Antigua.

Bishop of the North Eastern Caribbean and Aruba: Rt Rev. LEROY ERROL BROOKS, Bishop's Lodge, POB 23, St John's; tel. 462-0151; fax 462-2090; e-mail dioceseneca@candw.ag.

The Roman Catholic Church

The diocese of St John's-Basseterre, suffragan to the archdiocese of Castries (Saint Lucia), includes Anguilla, Antigua and Barbuda, the British Virgin Islands, Montserrat and Saint Christopher and Nevis. At 31 December 1998 there were an estimated 14,313 adherents in the diocese. The Bishop participates in the Antilles Episcopal Conference (whose Secretariat is based in Port of Spain, Trinidad).

Bishop of St John's-Basseterre: Rt Rev. DONALD JAMES REECE, Chancery Offices, POB 836, St John's; tel. 461-1135; fax 462-2383; e-mail djr@candw.ag.

Other Christian Churches

Antigua Baptist Association: POB 277, St John's; tel. 462-1254; Pres. IVOR CHARLES.

Methodist Church: c/o POB 863, St John's; Superintendent Rev. ELOY CHRISTOPHER.

St John's Evangelical Lutheran Church: Woods Centre, POB W77, St John's; tel. 462-2896; e-mail lutheran@candw.ag; Pastors M. HENRICH, J. STERNHAGEN, T. SATORIUS.

There are also Pentecostal, Seventh-day Adventist, Moravian, Nazarene, Salvation Army and Wesleyan Holiness places of worship.

The Press

Antigua Sun: Woods Mall, POB W263, Friar's Hill Rd, St John's; tel. 480-5960; fax 480-5968; e-mail antiguasun@stanfordeagle.com; internet www.antiguanice.com/thesun; twice weekly; Publr ALLEN STANFORD.

Business Expressions: POB 774, St John's; tel. 462-0743; fax 462-4575; e-mail chamcom@candw.ag; monthly; organ of the Antigua and Barbuda Chamber of Commerce and Industry.

Daily Observer: Fort Rd, POB 1318, St John's; fax 462-5561; internet www.antiguaobserver.com; Publr SAMUEL DERRICK; Editor WINSTON A. DERRICK.

The Nation's Voice: Public Information Division, Church St and Independence Ave, POB 590, St John's; tel. 462-0090; weekly.

National Informer: St John's; weekly.

The Outlet: Marble Hill Rd, McKinnons, POB 493, St John's; tel. 462-4410; fax 462-0438; e-mail outletpub@candw.ag; f. 1975; weekly; publ. by the Antigua Caribbean Liberation Movement (founder member of the United Progressive Party in 1992); Editor TIM HECTOR; circ. 5,000.

The Worker's Voice: Emancipation Hall, 46 North St, POB 3, St John's; tel. 462-0090; f. 1943; twice weekly; official organ of the Antigua Labour Party and the Antigua Trades and Labour Union; Editor NOEL THOMAS; circ. 6,000.

FOREIGN NEWS AGENCY

Inter Press Service (IPS) (Italy): Old Parham Rd, St John's; tel. 462-3602; Correspondent LOUIS DANIEL.

Publishers

Antigua Printing and Publishing Ltd: POB 670, St John's; tel. 462-1265; fax 462-6200.

Wadadli Productions Ltd: POB 571, St John's; tel. 462-4489.

Broadcasting and Communications

TELECOMMUNICATIONS

Most telephone services are provided by the Antigua Public Utilities Authority (see Trade and Industry).

Cable & Wireless (Antigua and Barbuda) Ltd: 42–44 St Mary's St, St John's; internet www.cwantigua.com; owned by Cable & Wireless PLC (United Kingdom).

RADIO

ABS Radio: POB 590, St John's; tel. 462-3602; internet www.cmattcomm.com/abs.htm; f. 1956; subsidiary of Antigua and Barbuda Broadcasting Service (see Television, below); Programme Man. D. L. PAYNE.

Caribbean Radio Lighthouse: POB 1057, St John's; tel. 462-1454; e-mail cradiolight@candw.ag; internet www.mannelli.com/lighthouse; f. 1975; religious broadcasts; operated by Baptist Int. Mission Inc. (USA); Dir Curtis L. Waite.

Caribbean Relay Co Ltd: POB 1203, St John's; tel. 462-0994; fax 462-0487; e-mail cm-crc@candw.ag; jtly-operated by British Broadcasting Corpn and Deutsche Welle.

Radio ZDK: Grenville Radio Ltd, POB 1100, St John's; tel. 462-1100; f. 1970; commercial; Programme Dir Ivor Bird; CEO E. Philip.

Sun FM Radio: St John's; commercial.

TELEVISION

Antigua and Barbuda Broadcasting Service (ABS): Directorate of Broadcasting and Public Information, POB 590, St John's; tel. 462-0010; fax 462-4442; scheduled for privatization; Dir-Gen. Hollis Henry; CEO Denis Leandro; subsidiary:

ABS Television: POB 1280, St John's; tel. 462-0010; fax 462-1622; f. 1964; Programme Man. James Tanny Rose.

CTV Entertainment Systems: 25 Long St, St John's; tel. 462-0346; fax 462-4211; cable television co; transmits 13 channels of US television 24 hours per day to subscribers; Programme Dir J. Cox.

Finance

(cap. = capital; res = reserves; dep. = deposits; brs = branches)

BANKING

The Eastern Caribbean Central Bank (see p. 310), based in Saint Christopher, is the central issuing and monetary authority for Antigua and Barbuda.

Antigua Barbuda Investment Bank Ltd: High St and Corn Alley, POB 1679, St John's; tel. 480-2700; fax 480-2750; e-mail aob@candw.ag; f. 1990; cap. EC $6.3m., res EC $2.3m., dep. EC $107.5m. (Sept. 1997); three subsidiaries: Antigua Overseas Bank Ltd, ABI Trust Ltd and AOB Holdings Ltd; Chair. Eustace Francis; Man. Dir McAlister Abbott; 2 brs.

Antigua Commercial Bank: St Mary's and Thames Sts, POB 95, St John's; tel. 462-1217; fax 462-1220; internet www.actionline.com; f. 1955; auth. cap. EC $5m.; Man. John Benjamin; 2 brs.

Antigua and Barbuda Development Bank: 27 St Mary's St, POB 1279, St John's; tel. 462-0838; fax 462-0839; f. 1974; Man. S. Alex Osborne.

Bank of Antigua: 1000 Airport Blvd, Coolidge, POB 315, St John's; tel. 462-4282; fax 462-4718; internet www.bankofantigua.com; Chair. Allen Stanford; 1 br.

Foreign Banks

Bank of Nova Scotia (Canada): High St, POB 342, St John's; tel. 480-1500; fax 480-1554; Man. Len Wright.

Barclays Bank PLC (UK): High St, POB 225, St John's; tel. 480-5000; fax 462-4910; Man. Winston St Agathe.

Canadian Imperial Bank of Commerce: High St and Corn Alley, POB 28, St John's; tel. 462-0836; fax 462-4439; Man. G. R. Hilts.

Caribbean Banking Corporation Ltd (Trinidad and Tobago): 45 High St, POB 1324, St John's; tel. 462-4217; fax 462-5040; Man. B. P. de Castro.

Royal Bank of Canada: High and Market Sts, POB 252, St John's; tel. 480-1151; offers a trustee service.

Swiss American National Bank of Antigua Ltd: High St, POB 1302, St John's; tel. 462-4460; fax 462-0274; f. 1983; cap. US $1.0m., res US $2.1m., dep. US $31.9m. (Dec. 1993); Gen. Man. John Greaves; 3 brs.

In mid-1997 there were 51 registered 'offshore' banks in Antigua and Barbuda.

INSURANCE

Several foreign companies have offices in Antigua. Local insurance companies include the following:

General Insurance Co Ltd: Upper Redcliffe St, POB 340, St John's; tel. 462-2346; fax 462-4482.

Sentinel Insurance Co Ltd: Coolidge, POB 207, St John's; tel. 462-4603.

State Insurance Corpn: Redcliffe St, POB 290, St John's; tel. 462-0110; fax 462-2649; f. 1977; Chair. Dr Vincent Richards; Gen. Man. Rolston Barthley.

Trade and Industry

DEVELOPMENT ORGANIZATIONS

Barbuda Development Agency: St John's; economic development projects for Barbuda.

Development Control Authority: St John's; internet www.antiguagov.com/dca.

Industrial Development Board: Newgate St, St John's; tel. 462-1038; fax 462-1033; f. 1984 to stimulate investment in local industries.

St John's Development Corporation: Heritage Quay, POB 1473, St John's; tel. 462-2776; fax 462-3931; e-mail stjohnsdevcorp@candw.ag; internet www.firstyellow.com/stjohnsdev; f. 1986; manages the Heritage Quay Duty Free Shopping Complex, Vendors' Mall, Public Market and Cultural and Exhibition Complex.

CHAMBER OF COMMERCE

Antigua and Barbuda Chamber of Commerce and Industry Ltd: Redcliffe St, POB 774, St John's; tel. 462-0743; fax 462-4575; e-mail chamcom@candw.ag; f. 1944 as Antigua Chamber of Commerce Ltd; name changed as above in 1991, following the collapse of the Antigua and Barbuda Manufacturers' Asscn; Pres. Clarvis Joseph.

INDUSTRIAL AND TRADE ASSOCIATIONS

Antigua Cotton Growers' Association: Dunbars, St John's; tel. 462-4962; Chair. Francis Henry; Sec. Peter Blanchette.

Antigua Fisheries Corpn: St John's; e-mail fisheries@candw.ag; partly funded by the Antigua and Barbuda Development Bank; aims to help local fishermen.

Antigua Sugar Industry Corpn: Gunthorpes, POB 899, St George's; tel. 462-0653.

Private Sector Organization of Antigua and Barbuda: St John's.

EMPLOYERS' ORGANIZATION

Antigua Employers' Federation: Upper High Street, POB 298, St John's; tel. 462-0449; fax 462-0449; e-mail aempfed@candw.ag; f. 1950; 120 mems; Chair. Joan Underwood; Exec. Sec. Henderson Bass.

UTILITIES

Antigua Public Utilities Authority (APUA): St Mary's St, POB 416, St John's; tel. 480-7000; fax 462-2782; generation, transmission and distribution of electricity; internal telecommunications; collection, treatment, storage and distribution of water; Gen. Man. Peter Benjamin.

TRADE UNIONS

Antigua and Barbuda Meteorological Officers Association: c/o V. C. Bird International Airport, Gabatco, POB 1051, St John's; tel. and fax 462-4606; Pres. Leonard Josiah.

Antigua and Barbuda Public Service Association (ABPSA): POB 1285, St John's; tel. 463-6427; fax 461-5821; e-mail abpsa@candw.ag; Pres. James Spencer; Gen. Sec. Elloy de Freitas; 550 mems.

Antigua and Barbuda Union of Teachers: c/o Ministry of Education, Culture and Technology, Church St, St John's; tel. 462-2692; Pres. Colin Greene; Sec. Foster Roberts.

Antigua Trades and Labour Union (ATLU): 46 North St, POB 3, St John's; tel. 462-0090; fax 462-4056; e-mail atandlu@candw.ag; f. 1939; affiliated to the Antigua Labour Party; Pres. Wigley George; Gen. Sec. Natalie Payne; about 10,000 mems.

Antigua Workers' Union (AWU): Freedom Hall, Newgate St, POB 940, St John's; tel. 462-2005; fax 462-5220; e-mail awu@candw.ag; f. 1967 following split with ATLU; not affiliated to any party; Pres. Maurice Christian; Gen. Sec. Keithlyn Smith; 10,000 mems.

Transport

ROADS

There are 384 km (239 miles) of main roads and 781 km (485 miles) of secondary dry-weather roads.

SHIPPING

The main harbour is the St John's Deep Water Harbour. It is used by cruise ships and a number of foreign shipping lines. There are regular cargo and passenger services internationally and regionally. At Falmouth, on the south side of Antigua, is a former Royal Navy dockyard in English Harbour. The harbour is now used by yachts and private pleasure craft.

Antigua and Barbuda Port Authority: Deep Water Harbour, POB 1052, St John's; tel. 462-4243; fax 462-2510; f. 1968; responsible to Ministry of Finance; Chair. Llewellyn Smith; Port Man. Leroy Adams.

Directory

Joseph, Vernon, Toy Contractors Ltd: Nut Grove St, St John's.

Parenzio Shipping Co Ltd: Nevis St, St John's.

Vernon Edwards Shipping Co: Thames St, POB 82, St John's; tel. 462-2034; fax 462-2035; e-mail vedwards@candw.ag; cargo service to and from San Juan, Puerto Rico.

The West Indies Oil Co Ltd: Friars Hill Rd, POB 230, St John's; tel. 462-0140; fax 462-0543.

CIVIL AVIATION

Antigua's V.C. Bird (formerly Coolidge) International Airport, 9 km (5.6 miles) north-east of St John's, is modern and accommodates jet-engined aircraft. There is a small airstrip at Codrington on Barbuda. Antigua and Barbuda Airlines, a nominal company, controls international routes, but services to Europe and North America are operated by American Airlines (USA), Continental Airlines (USA), Lufthansa (Germany) and Air Canada. Antigua and Barbuda is a shareholder in, and the headquarters of, the regional airline, LIAT. Other regional services are operated by BWIA (Trinidad and Tobago) and Air BVI (British Virgin Islands).

LIAT (1974) Ltd: POB 819, V.C. Bird Int. Airport, St John's; tel. 480-5600; fax 480-5625; e-mail li.sales.mrkting@candw.ag; internet www.liatairline.com; f. 1956 as Leeward Islands Air Transport Services, jointly-owned by 11 regional Govts; privatized in 1995; shares are held by the Govts of Antigua and Barbuda, Montserrat, Grenada, Barbados, Trinidad and Tobago, Jamaica, Guyana, Dominica, Saint Lucia, Saint Vincent and the Grenadines and Saint Christopher and Nevis (30.8%), BWIA (29.2%), LIAT employees (13.3%) and private investors (26.7%); scheduled passenger and cargo services to 19 destinations in the Caribbean; charter flights are also undertaken; Chair. AZIZ HADEED; Exec. Dir DAVID JARDINE.

Carib Aviation Ltd: V.C. Bird Int. Airport; tel. 462-3147; fax 462-3125; e-mail caribav@candw.ag; charter co; operates regional services.

Tourism

Tourism is the country's main industry. Antigua offers a reputed 365 beaches, an annual international sailing regatta and Carnival week, and the historic Nelson's Dockyard in English Harbour (a national park since 1985). Barbuda is less developed but is noted for its beauty, wildlife and beaches of pink sand. In 1986 the Government established the St John's Development Corporation to oversee the redevelopment of the capital as a commercial duty-free centre, with extra cruise-ship facilities. In 1999 there were 588,866 tourist arrivals, including 328,038 cruise-ship passengers. In 1998 some 31% of stop-over visitors came from the USA, 27% from the United Kingdom, 19% from other Caribbean countries and 7% from Canada. There were an estimated 3,225 hotel rooms in 1996.

Antigua and Barbuda Department of Tourism: Nevis St and Friendly Alley, POB 363, St John's; tel. 462-0029; fax 462-2483; e-mail info@antigua-barbuda.org; internet www.antigua-barbuda .org; Dir-Gen. SHIRLENE NIBBS; Asst Man. IRMA TOMLINSON.

Antigua Hotels and Tourist Association (AHTA): Island House, Newgate St, POB 454, St John's; tel. 462-3703; fax 462-3702; e-mail ahta@candw.ag; internet www.antiguahotels.org; Chair. ROBERT S. SHERMAN; Exec. Dir CYNTHIA G. SIMON.

ARGENTINA

Introductory Survey

Location, Climate, Language, Religion, Flag, Capital

The Argentine Republic occupies almost the whole of South America south of the Tropic of Capricorn and east of the Andes. It has a long Atlantic coastline stretching from Uruguay and the River Plate to Tierra del Fuego. To the west lie Chile and the Andes mountains, while to the north are Bolivia, Paraguay and Brazil. Argentina also claims the Falkland Islands (known in Argentina as the Islas Malvinas), South Georgia, the South Sandwich Islands and part of Antarctica. The climate varies from sub-tropical in the Chaco region of the north to sub-arctic in Patagonia, generally with moderate summer rainfall. Temperatures in Buenos Aires are usually between 5°C (41°F) and 29°C (84°F). The language is Spanish. The great majority of the population profess Christianity: more than 90% are Roman Catholics and about 2% Protestants. The national flag (proportions 14 by 9) has three equal horizontal stripes, of light blue (celeste), above white, above light blue. The state flag (proportions 2 by 1) has the same design with, in addition, a gold 'Sun of May' in the centre of the white stripe. The capital is Buenos Aires.

Recent History

During the greater part of the 20th century, government in Argentina tended to alternate between military and civilian rule. In 1930 Hipólito Yrigoyen, a member of the reformist Unión Cívica Radical (UCR), who in 1916 had become Argentina's first President to be freely elected by popular vote, was overthrown by an army coup, and the country's first military regime was established. Civilian rule was restored in 1932, only to be supplanted by further military intervention in 1943. A leading figure in the new military regime, Col (later Lt-Gen.) Juan Domingo Perón Sosa, won a presidential election in 1946. As President, he established the Peronista party in 1948 and pursued a policy of extreme nationalism and social improvement, aided by his second wife, Eva ('Evita') Duarte de Perón, whose popularity (particularly among industrial workers and their families) greatly enhanced his position and contributed to his re-election as President in 1951. In 1954, however, his promotion of secularization and the legalization of divorce brought him into conflict with the Roman Catholic Church. In September 1955 President Perón was deposed by a revolt of the armed forces. He went into exile, eventually settling in Spain, from where he continued to direct the Peronist movement.

Following the overthrow of Perón, Argentina entered another lengthy period of political instability. Political control continued to pass between civilian (mainly Radical) and military regimes during the late 1950s and the 1960s. This period was also characterized by increasing guerrilla activity, particularly by the Montoneros, a group of left-wing Peronist sympathizers, and urban guerrilla groups intensified their activities in 1971 and 1972.

Congressional and presidential elections were conducted in March 1973. The Frente Justicialista de Liberación, a Peronist coalition, won control of the National Congress (Congreso Nacional), while the presidential election was won by the party's candidate, Dr Héctor Cámpora, who assumed the office in May. However, Cámpora resigned in July, to enable Gen. Perón, who had returned to Argentina in June, to contest a fresh presidential election. In September Perón was returned to power, with more than 60% of the votes. He took office in October, with his third wife, María Estela ('Isabelita') Martínez de Perón, as Vice-President.

Gen. Perón died in July 1974 and was succeeded as President by his widow. The Government's economic austerity programme and the soaring rate of inflation caused widespread strike action, prompted dissension among industrial workers, and led to demands for the resignation of 'Isabelita' Perón. In March 1976 the armed forces, led by Gen. Jorge Videla (Commander of the Army), overthrew the President and installed a three-man junta: Gen. Videla was sworn in as President. The junta made substantial alterations to the Constitution, dissolved Congress, suspended all political and trade union activity and removed most government officials from their posts. Several hundred people

were arrested, while 'Isabelita' Perón was detained and later went into exile.

The military regime launched a successful, although ferocious, offensive against left-wing guerrillas and opposition forces. The imprisonment, torture and murder of suspected left-wing activists by the armed forces provoked domestic and international protests against violations of human rights. Repression eased in 1978, after all armed opposition had been eliminated.

In March 1981 Gen. Roberto Viola, a former member of the junta, succeeded President Videla and made known his intention to extend dialogue with political parties as a prelude to an eventual return to democracy. Owing to ill health, he was replaced in December by Lt-Gen. Leopoldo Galtieri, the Commander-in-Chief of the Army, who attempted to cultivate popular support by continuing the process of political liberalization initiated by his predecessor.

In April 1982, in order to distract attention from an increasingly unstable domestic situation, and following unsuccessful negotiations with the United Kingdom in February over Argentina's long-standing sovereignty claim, President Galtieri ordered the invasion of the Falkland Islands (Islas Malvinas) (see chapter on the Falkland Islands, Vol. II). The United Kingdom recovered the islands after a short conflict, in the course of which about 750 Argentine lives were lost. Argentine forces surrendered in June 1982, but no formal cessation of hostilities was declared until October 1989. Humiliated by the defeat, Galtieri was forced to resign, and the members of the junta were replaced. The army, under the control of Lt-Gen. Cristino Nicolaides, installed a retired general, Reynaldo Bignone, as President in July 1982. The armed forces were held responsible for the disastrous economic situation, and the transfer of power to a civilian government was accelerated. Moreover, in 1983 a Military Commission of Inquiry into the Falklands conflict concluded in its report that the main responsibility for Argentina's defeat lay with members of the former junta, who were recommended for trial. Galtieri was sentenced to imprisonment, while several other officers were put on trial for corruption, murder and insulting the honour of the armed forces. Meanwhile, in August 1983 the regime approved the Ley de Pacificación Nacional, an amnesty law which granted retrospective immunity to the police, the armed forces and others for political crimes that had been committed over the previous 10 years.

In February 1983 the Government announced that general and presidential elections would be held on 30 October. At the elections, the UCR defeated the Peronist Partido Justicialista (PJ), attracting the votes of many former Peronist supporters. The UCR won 317 of the 600 seats in the presidential electoral college, and 129 of the 254 seats in the Chamber of Deputies (Cámara de Diputados), although the PJ won a narrow majority of provincial governorships. Dr Raúl Alfonsín, the UCR candidate, took office as President on 10 December. President Alfonsín promptly announced a radical reform of the armed forces, which led to the immediate retirement of more than one-half of the military high command. In addition, he repealed the Ley de Pacificación Nacional and ordered the court martial of the first three military juntas to rule Argentina after the 1976 coup, for offences including abduction, torture and murder. Public opposition to the former military regime was reinforced by the discovery and exhumation of hundreds of bodies from unmarked graves throughout the country. (It was believed that 15,000–30,000 people 'disappeared' during the so-called 'dirty war' between the former military regime and its opponents in 1976–83.) In December the Government announced the formation of the National Commission on the Disappearance of Persons to investigate the events of the 'dirty war'. The trial of the former leaders began in April 1985. Several hundred prosecution witnesses gave testimonies which revealed the systematic atrocities and the campaign of terror perpetrated by the former military leaders. In December four of the accused were acquitted, but sentences were imposed on the remaining five, including sentences of life imprisonment for Gen. Videla and Adm. Eduardo Massera. The court martial of the members of the junta that had held power during the Falklands conflict was conducted concurrently with the trial of the former military leaders. In May 1986 all three members of the junta were found guilty of negligence and received prison sentences, including a term of 12 years for Galtieri.

In late 1986 the Government sought approval for the Punto Final ('Full Stop') Law, whereby civil and military courts were to begin new judicial proceedings against members of the armed forces accused of violations of human rights, within a 60-day period ending on 22 February 1987. The pre-emptive nature of the legislation provoked widespread popular opposition but was, nevertheless, approved by Congress in December 1986. However, in May 1987, following a series of minor rebellions at army garrisons throughout the country, the Government announced new legislation, known as the Obediencia Debida ('Due Obedience') law, whereby an amnesty was to be declared for all but senior ranks of the police and armed forces. Therefore, under the new law, of the 350–370 officers hitherto due to be prosecuted for alleged violations of human rights, only 30–50 senior officers were now to be tried. The legislation provoked great controversy, and was considered to be a decisive factor in the significant gains made by the PJ at gubernatorial and legislative elections conducted in September. The UCR's defeat was also attributed to its imposition, in July, of an unpopular economic programme of strict austerity measures.

Two swiftly-suppressed army rebellions in January and December 1988 (led by Lt-Col Aldo Rico and Col Mohamed Ali Seineldín, respectively) demonstrated continuing military disaffection. In both incidents, the rebel military factions demanded higher salaries for soldiers, an increase in the military budget and some form of amnesty for officers awaiting trial for violations of human rights during the 'dirty war'.

In January 1989 the army quickly repelled an attack by 40 left-wing activists on a military base at La Tablada, in which 39 lives were lost. Many of the guerrilla band were identified as members of the Movimiento Todos por la Patria.

In the campaign for the May 1989 elections, Carlos Saúl Menem headed the Frente Justicialista de Unidad Popular (FREJUPO) electoral alliance, comprising his own PJ grouping, the Partido Demócrata Cristiano (PDC) and the Partido Intransigente (PI). On 14 May the Peronists were guaranteed a return to power, having secured, together with the two other members of the FREJUPO alliance, 48.5% of the votes cast in the presidential election and 310 of the 600 seats in the electoral college. The Peronists were also victorious in the election for 127 seats (one-half of the total) in the Chamber of Deputies, winning 45% of the votes and 66 seats, in contrast to the 29% (41 seats) obtained by the UCR. The failure of attempts by the retiring and incoming administrations to collaborate, and the reluctance of the Alfonsín administration to continue in office with the prospect of further economic embarrassment, left the nation in a political vacuum. Menem was due to take office as President on 10 December 1989, but the worsening economic situation compelled Alfonsín to resign five months earlier than scheduled. Menem took office on 8 July.

Rumours of a possible amnesty, agreed between the newly-elected Government and military leaders, prompted the organization of a massive demonstration in support of human rights in Buenos Aires in September 1989. In October, however, the Government issued decrees whereby 210 officers, NCOs and soldiers who had been involved in the 'dirty war', the governing junta during the Falklands conflict (including Gen. Galtieri) and leaders of three recent military uprisings (including Lt-Col Rico and Col Seineldín) were pardoned.

Economic affairs dominated the latter half of 1989 and much of 1990. The Minister of the Economy, Néstor Rapanelli, introduced several measures, including the devaluation of the austral, but these failed to reverse the trend towards hyperinflation, and Rapanelli resigned in December 1989. His successor, Antonio Erman González, introduced a comprehensive plan for economic readjustment, incorporating the expansion of existing plans for the transfer to private ownership of many state-owned companies, the rationalization of government-controlled bodies, and the restructuring of the nation's financial systems. In August 1990 Erman González appointed himself head of the Central Bank and assumed almost total control of the country's financial structure. Public disaffection with the Government's economic policy was widespread. Failure to contain the threat of hyperinflation led to a loss in purchasing power, and small-scale food riots and looting became more frequent. The Government's rationalization programme proved unpopular with public-sector employees, and resulted in industrial action and

demonstrations, organized from within the sector with the support of trade unions, political opposition parties and human-rights groups.

Widespread public concern at the apparent impunity of military personnel increased following President Menem's suggestion that a further military amnesty would be granted before the end of 1990, and was exacerbated by rumours of escalating military unrest (which were realized in December 1990 when 200–300 rebel soldiers staged a swiftly-suppressed uprising at the Patricios infantry garrison in Buenos Aires). A second round of presidential pardons was announced in late December. More than 40,000 demonstrators gathered in Buenos Aires to protest against the release of former military leaders, including Gen. Videla, Gen. Viola and Adm. Massera. Critics and political opponents dismissed Menem's claims that such action was essential for the effective 'reconciliation' of the Argentine people. In mid-1991 it was announced that the number of armed forces personnel was to be reduced by some 20,000 men; military spending was also to be restricted.

During 1991 the popularity and the political reputation of President Menem were dramatically undermined by the highly-publicized deterioration in marital relations between the President and his wife, Zulema Yoma, and by a succession of corruption scandals in which members of the Yoma family were implicated. In January 1991 Menem was obliged to reorganize the Cabinet, following allegations that government ministers and officials had requested bribes from US businessmen during the course of commercial negotiations. Later in the month, the President was forced to implement a second cabinet reshuffle when his economic team, led by Erman González, resigned following a sudden spectacular decline in the value of the austral in relation to the US dollar.

In mid-1991, following congressional approval of an amendment to the electoral law, it was announced that gubernatorial and congressional elections would take place later in the year. In the first two rounds of voting, the Peronists were unexpectedly successful, wresting the governorship of San Juan from the provincial Bloquista party in August, and securing control of nine of the 12 contested provinces (including the crucial province of Buenos Aires) in September. The third and fourth rounds of voting, in October and December, respectively, proved less successful for the PJ. Overall, however, the Peronists secured control of 14 of the 24 contested territories and increased their congressional representation by seven seats, compared with a five-seat reduction in the congressional representation of the UCR.

The success of the Peronist campaign was widely attributed to the popularity of the Minister of the Economy, Domingo Cavallo, and the success of the economic policies that he had implemented since succeeding Erman González. New economic measures included the abolition of index-linked wage increases and, most dramatically, the announcement that the austral would become freely convertible from April. This new initiative soon achieved considerable success in reducing inflation, and impressed international finance organizations sufficiently to secure the negotiation of substantial loan agreements. In October 1991 the President issued a comprehensive decree ordering the removal of almost all of the remaining bureaucratic apparatus of state regulation of the economy, and in November the Government announced plans to accelerate the transfer to private ownership of the remaining public-sector concerns. Continuing economic success in 1992 helped to secure agreements for the renegotiation of repayment of outstanding debts with the Government's leading creditor banks and with the 'Paris Club' of Western creditor governments.

However, in November 1992 the Confederación General del Trabajo (CGT—General Confederation of Labour) organized a one-day general strike, in protest at the Government's continuing programme of economic austerity. The strike, which was well-supported in the provinces but only partially observed in the capital, was precipitated by revelations that senior government officials were to receive pay increases of as much as 200%.

Meanwhile, President Menem sought to consolidate his own position and to increase the popularity of his party in the months preceding legislative elections scheduled for 3 October 1993, at which the Peronists hoped to make significant gains in order to facilitate Menem's wish to effect a constitutional amendment that would allow him to pursue a second, consecutive presidential term. The elections to renew 127 seats in the Chamber of

Deputies were won convincingly by the ruling PJ party, with 42.3% of the votes, while the UCR obtained 30% of the votes.

An unexpected development in November 1993 was the return to political prominence of former President Alfonsín. While UCR opposition to Menem's presidential ambitions had remained vociferous, several opposition leaders, notably Alfonsín, feared that the UCR would be excluded from negotiations on constitutional reform, should the unorthodox political manoeuvring of the Peronists, largely orchestrated by the President of the Senate, Menem's brother Eduardo, succeed in propelling the reform proposal through the legislature. Alfonsín, also anxious to avoid another humiliating defeat for the UCR at a national referendum which Menem had elected to organize in late 1993 on the question of constitutional reform, entered into a dialogue with the President, which resulted in a declaration, in early November, that a framework for constitutional reform had been negotiated, apparently in return for Menem's postponement of the referendum and acceptance of modified reform proposals. Hopes for the successful conclusion of a bilateral agreement on constitutional reform were further encouraged, later in November, by the election of Alfonsín to the presidency of the UCR. The terms of the agreement, detailing the central reform issues of the possibility of re-election of the President for one consecutive term, a reduction in the presidential term, to four years, the abolition of the presidential electoral college, the delegation of some presidential powers to a Chief of Cabinet, an increase in the number of seats in the Senate and a reduction in the length of the mandate of all senators, a reform of the procedure for judicial appointments, the removal of religious stipulations from the terms of eligibility for presidential candidates, and the abolition of the President's power to appoint the mayor of the federal capital, were endorsed by the UCR national convention in early December, and the need for constitutional reform was approved by Congress later in the month. Elections to a 305-member constituent assembly were to be conducted in early 1994. Menem immediately declared his intention to seek re-election in 1995.

Elections to the Constituent Assembly took place in April 1994. While the Peronists won the largest share of the vote (37.8%—136 seats), they failed to secure an absolute majority in the Assembly. The UCR won only 19.9% of the votes, equivalent to 75 seats in the Assembly, while a centre-left coalition, Frente Grande, emerged unexpectedly as the third political force (with 12.5% of the votes and 31 seats), having campaigned against institutionalized corruption. The Assembly was inaugurated in May 1994, and by mid-August it had successfully incorporated the crucial recommendations of the December 1993 constitutional reform pact between the PJ and the UCR (see above) into the 1853 Constitution. On 24 August 1994 a new Constitution, containing 19 new articles, 40 amendments to existing articles and a new chapter on civil rights and guarantees, was duly promulgated. An electoral timetable was also established by the Assembly, with presidential, legislative and provincial elections all scheduled for May 1995. In December 1994 the Senate approved the new electoral code providing for the direct election of a president and a vice-president and for a second round of voting for the first- and second-placed candidates in the event of a closely contested election.

In January 1995 Carlos Ruckauf, the Minister of the Interior, was named as President Menem's running mate for the new post of vice-president. Menem's campaign for re-election concentrated on the economic success of his previous administration and, despite the increasingly precarious condition of the economy during 1995 (see below), was sufficiently successful to secure 49.9% of the votes at the presidential election conducted on 14 May, thereby avoiding a second ballot. José Octavio Bordón, the candidate of the Frente del País Solidario (Frepaso—a centre-left alliance of socialist, communist, Christian Democrat and dissident Peronist groups formed in late 1994) was second with 29.3% of the votes, ahead of the UCR candidate, Horacio Massaccesi, who received 17.0% of the votes. The Peronists were also successful in nine of the 14 gubernatorial contests; however, Frepaso, with almost 35% of the votes, won the largest share of the 130 contested seats in the Chamber of Deputies at legislative elections conducted concurrently, and significantly increased its representation in the Senate (as did the Peronists) largely at the expense of the UCR. (In September 1995 Alfonsín resigned as UCR party leader in response to dwindling popular support for the party's policies; Rodolfo Terragno was elected as his successor in November.) Menem was inaugurated as President for a four-year term on 8 July 1995. The composition

of a largely unaltered Cabinet was announced simultaneously, led by Eduardo Bauzá, in the new post of Cabinet Chief. The Peronists performed well at gubernatorial elections conducted in late 1995, but suffered an unexpected defeat at senatorial elections in the capital in October at which the Peronist candidate was beaten into third place by the Frepaso and UCR candidates respectively. Menem's executive power was increased in February 1996 when Congress endorsed the Administrative Reform Act, enabling the Government to merge certain state agencies and reduce public expenditure considerably.

Meanwhile, the Government's ongoing programme of economic austerity continued to provoke violent opposition, particularly from the public sector, where redundancies and a 'freeze' on salaries had been imposed in many provinces. A protest march in the capital in July 1994 and a general strike in August were organized by two of Argentina's dissident trade-union confederations, the Congreso de los Trabajadores Argentinos (CTA) and the Movimiento de Trabajadores Argentinos (MTA), and were well supported, despite opposition from the country's largest trade-union confederation, the CGT. However, in August a 12-month moratorium on appointments in the public sector was announced, as were plans to privatize several more state enterprises. In March 1995 the Government presented an economic consolidation programme aimed at protecting the Argentine currency against devaluation and supporting the ailing banking sector, which had been adversely affected by the financial crisis in Mexico in late 1994. Subsequent austerity measures adopted by provincial governments, together with a dramatic increase in the rate of unemployment, provoked widespread social unrest in the city of Córdoba in mid-1995 (prompting the resignation of the incumbent Governor six months before the scheduled inauguration of the Governor-elect) and in the province of Río Negro in September. The publication of official unemployment figures for July of 18.6% led Menem to announce, in August, a series of employment initiatives. General strikes organized in April and September were only partially observed, principally in those provinces already experiencing social unrest.

In February 1996 it was revealed that Domingo Cavallo, the Minister of the Economy, had paid a minimal amount of income tax in 1994. Cavallo, whose economic reform programme had concentrated on combating tax evasion and corruption, denounced the claims and insisted that he was the victim of a campaign to discredit him. Cavallo's position was undermined further in March 1996, when President Menem dismissed one of Cavallo's close associates, Haroldo Grisanti, the Postmaster-General (indicted on charges of fraudulent actions against the public administration), and when responsibility for telecommunications was transferred from the Ministry of the Economy to the Secretary-General of the Presidency. Later in the month Jorge Rodríguez, hitherto Minister of Education and Culture, was appointed Cabinet Chief in place of Bauzá, who had resigned citing ill health.

In June 1996 the Government suffered a serious political defeat when a UCR candidate, Fernando de la Rúa, won almost 40% of the votes cast in the first direct elections for the Mayor of the Federal District of Buenos Aires; a Frepaso candidate secured 26.5% of the votes, while the incumbent Peronist Mayor, Jorge Domínguez, received only 18% of the ballot. In concurrent elections to the 60-member Constituent Assembly (which was charged with drafting a constitution for the newly-autonomous Federal District of Buenos Aires), Frepaso candidates secured 25 seats, the UCR 19, the PJ 11 and the recently-formed Nueva Dirigencia (ND, led by a former Peronist, Gustavo Béliz) five. The results were widely believed to reflect growing discontent with the Government's inability to redress the problems of recession and high levels of unemployment. In July the Government was again undermined by the resignations of Rodolfo Barra, the Minister of Justice (who had been criticized for the slow progress made in resolving anti-semitic attacks and who had subsequently conceded that he had belonged to a fascist group in his youth), and that of Oscar Camilión, the Minister of Defence, whose parliamentary immunity was to be removed to allow investigations in connection with the illegal sale of armaments to Ecuador and Croatia. More significant, however, was the dismissal of Cavallo from the post of Minister of the Economy, following months of bitter dispute with the President and other cabinet members. Roque Fernández, hitherto President of the Central Bank, assumed the economy portfolio. Cavallo became increasingly vociferous in his attacks against the integrity of certain cabinet members, and, in October, as Menem launched a well-publicized campaign against corruption after the discovery of wide-scale malpractice within the customs service, he accused the Government of having links with organized crime.

Industrial unrest continued during 1996, and in August a 24-hour general strike, organized by the CGT, the MTA and the CTA, received widespread support. A 36-hour strike in September was also widely observed, and was supported by Frepaso, the UCR and several Peronist deputies and senators. None the less, in that month taxation and austerity measures secured congressional approval, albeit with significant amendments. In October relations between the Government and the trade unions deteriorated, following the submission to Congress of controversial labour reform legislation. In December, owing to the slow pace at which debate on the bill was progressing in Congress, President Menem introduced part of the reforms by decree. Although three decrees were signed, radically altering labour contracts, in January 1997 a court declared that they were unconstitutional.

In January 1997 there was public outcry at the mafia-style murder of an investigative news photographer who had been examining alleged links between drugs-traffickers and policemen in the province of Buenos Aires, as well as between certain provincial officials and Alfredo Yabrán, a controversial businessman whom Cavallo had accused of corruption. Policemen from the province of Buenos Aires and Yabrán's chief of security were subsequently implicated in the murder. (In May 1998, shortly after a warrant had been issued for his arrest in connection with the murder, Yabrán committed suicide.) In March 1997 Eduardo Duhalde, the Peronist Governor of the province of Buenos Aires, initiated a radical reorganization of the provincial police in an attempt to avert attention from the politically sensitive issue of corruption, with which the PJ was increasingly associated. Nevertheless, in June Elías Jassan, the Minister of Justice, tendered his resignation after admitting maintaining links with Yabrán, having previously denied that he had ever met him.

The popularity of the PJ was undermined further by an upsurge in social and industrial unrest during 1997, which was primarily the result of widespread discontent with proposed labour reforms, reductions in public expenditure and the high level of unemployment. In May violent protests erupted across Argentina as police clashed with thousands of demonstrators who had occupied government buildings and blockaded roads and bridges. In July some 30,000 people demonstrated in the capital to protest at the high level of unemployment, which was estimated at more than 17%. However, a general strike in August, organized by the MTA and the CTA, was only partially observed and was not supported by the CGT, which in May was reported to have reached a compromise agreement with the Government concerning labour reforms.

In March 1997 Cavallo founded his own political party, Acción por la República (AR), and in July he and Béliz of the ND formed an alliance to contest the forthcoming congressional elections. In the following month the leaders of Frepaso and the UCR confirmed that they had agreed to an electoral pact, known as the Alianza por el Trabajo, la Justicia y la Educación (ATJE), in order to present joint lists in certain constituencies, notably in the province of Buenos Aires, and to remain in alliance subsequently.

At the mid-term congressional elections, held on 26 October 1997, the UCR and Frepaso (in both separate and joint lists) won 45.6% of the votes and 61 of the 127 seats contested, in contrast to the 36.3% (51 seats) obtained by the PJ; of the remaining 15 seats, three were secured by AR–ND. The PJ thus lost its overall majority in the Chamber of Deputies (its total number of seats in the Chamber being reduced to 118), while the UCR and Frepaso together increased their representation to 110 seats. More significant was the PJ's poor performance in the critical constituency of the province of Buenos Aires, where it received only 41.3% of the votes, compared with the ATJE's 48.3%.

In December 1997 President Menem appointed Erman González as Minister of Labour and Social Security, following the resignation of Armando Caro Figueroa, who had been criticized for failing to introduce labour reforms. Legislation concerning labour reforms, including the elimination of short-term contracts and a reduction in redundancy payments, was finally approved by Congress in September 1998.

Preparations for the 1999 presidential election gained momentum in April 1998 with the UCR's selection of Fernando

de la Rúa as the party's candidate. In a nation-wide primary in November, de la Rúa was elected as the ATJE presidential candidate, defeating Graciela Fernández Meijide, the highly-regarded Frepaso nominee. In December Carlos 'Chacho' Alvarez of Frepaso was formally nominated as de la Rúa's running mate, while Fernández Meijide was to contest the governorship of Buenos Aires. In July President Menem abandoned a controversial campaign to amend the Constitution in order to allow him to contest the presidency for a third consecutive term of office. The campaign was vociferously opposed by the leading PJ contender, Eduardo Duhalde, who had threatened to hold a provincial plebiscite on the issue. Duhalde's main rival for the PJ presidential nomination was Ramón 'Palito' Ortega, a former Governor of Tucumán, who had been appointed Secretary of Social Development in April. The popularity of the PJ remained low, not least because of the corruption scandals that had beset the Menem administration, and in November the President was accused of seeking to undermine the independence of the judiciary when he demanded the investigation of a prosecutor probing allegations of government involvement in the sale of armaments to Ecuador and Croatia. In September a judge had ordered that Erman González, who had held the defence portfolio at the time of the alleged incidents, be summoned to testify in the investigation. Guido di Tella, the Minister of Foreign Affairs, and Menem's brother-in-law, Emir Yoma, a former presidential adviser, were also implicated in the case. An agreement reached by Duhalde and Ortega to run jointly in the PJ presidential primary seemed to restore some unity to the party, although it was apparent that Menem had not entirely abandoned the idea of a re-election bid. In March 1999, however, the Supreme Court rejected appeals for Menem to be allowed to stand in the October elections.

In May 1999 a decision to reduce substantially the education budget by presidential decree prompted Susana Decibe, the Minister of Culture and Education, to resign in protest. The Government was subsequently forced to reverse the cuts, in response to widespread political and public discontent. Later that month the ruling administration was further undermined by the scandal surrounding the resignation of Erman González, the Minister of Labour and Social Security, following revelations that he was being paid a generous special pension (granted by Menem in recognition of his years of service), in addition to his ministerial salary.

In June 1999 Duhalde officially received the PJ presidential nomination after the only other contender, Adolfo Rodríguez Saa, the Governor of San Luis, withdrew from the contest. Moreover, in August Duhalde's candidacy was publicly endorsed by Menem, who pledged to campaign for his former rival. Meanwhile, however, social unrest escalated in several provinces, as economic recession led to rising levels of unemployment and non-payment of public-sector salaries.

At the presidential election, conducted on 24 October 1999, de la Rúa (with 48.50% of the votes) defeated Duhalde (who secured 38.09%), thereby ending 10 years of Menem's Peronist rule. The ATJE also performed well in concurrent elections to renew 130 of the 257 seats in the Chamber of Deputies, winning 63 seats, while the PJ secured 50 seats and Cavallo's AR won nine. The ATJE's total number of seats in the Chamber increased to 127—only two short of an absolute majority—in contrast to the PJ, whose representation was reduced to 101 seats. However, in gubernatorial elections held on the same day, the ATJE candidate, Graciela Fernández Meijide, failed to secure the critical province of Buenos Aires, where Carlos Ruckauf, the outgoing Vice-President, was elected. As a result of the elections the PJ controlled 14 of the 24 provincial administrations, while the ATJE held only six. On 24 November de la Rúa formally announced the composition of his new Cabinet, which significantly comprised a large number of economists. De la Rúa took office as President on 10 December, with Alvarez as his Vice-President. Later that month the new Congress approved an austerity budget that reduced public expenditure by US $1,400m., as well as a major tax-reform programme and a federal revenue-sharing scheme.

In April 2000 the Senate approved a controversial major revision of employment law. The legislation met with public criticism and led to mass demonstrations by public-sector workers and, subsequently, to two 24-hour national strikes organized by the CGT. In May the ruling ATJE candidate, Aníbal Ibarra, was elected Mayor of the Federal District of Buenos Aires. Later that year the Government came under intense pressure after it was alleged that some senators had received bribes from government officials to pass the employment legislation. In September the Senate voted to end the immunity that protected law-makers, judges and government ministers from criminal investigation in order to allow an inquiry into the corruption allegations. The political crisis intensified on 6 October when Carlos Alvarez resigned as Vice-President, one day after a cabinet reorganization, in which two ministers implicated in the bribery scandal were not removed. One of these, former labour minister Alberto Flamarique, who was appointed Presidential Chief of Staff in the reshuffle, resigned later the same day and was replaced by Chrystian Colombo. The other, Fernando de Santibáñez, head of the state intelligence service (SIDE), resigned from the Government in late October. Earlier that month the Senate President, José Genoud, also resigned after he too was implicated in the bribery allegations.

The economic situation continued to deteriorate in 2000. In November thousands of unemployed workers blocked roads throughout the country to demand jobs, welfare programmes and improvements in standards of living. In the same month the country was paralysed by a 36-hour national strike, organized in response to the Government's proposed introduction of an International Monetary Fund (IMF)-backed economic recovery package that included a five-year freeze on federal and provincial spending. Additional measures included a reform of the pension system and an increase in the female retirement age. In early December Congress approved the reforms and in mid-December the IMF approved a package, worth an estimated US $20,000m., necessary to meet Argentina's external financing requirement for 2001.

The resignation of the Minister of the Economy, José Luis Machinea, precipitated another political crisis in early March 2001. The announcement by his successor, Ricardo López Murphy, of major reductions in public expenditure, resulted in several ministerial resignations. As a consequence, in late March a second reshuffle occurred, in which the most notable appointee was Domingo Cavallo as the new Minister of the Economy.

Despite the public expressions of regret (in 1995) by the heads of the navy, the army and the air force for crimes committed by the armed forces during 1976–83, issues concerning the 'dirty war' remained politically sensitive at the end of the 20th century. Plans announced in January 1998 by President Menem to demolish the Naval Mechanics School (formerly the principal torture centre used by the military) and replace it with a monument to national reconciliation had to be suspended after protesters demanded that the premises be converted into a museum, as a reminder to future generations of the atrocities committed. Later in January Alfredo Astiz, a notorious former naval captain, was deprived of his rank and pension after he defended the elimination of political opponents during the dictatorship. In the following month the Swiss authorities revealed that they had discovered a number of Swiss bank accounts belonging to former Argentine military officials, including Astiz and Antonio Domingo Bussi, then Governor of Tucumán. It was rumoured that the accounts contained funds stolen by the military regime from Argentines who had been detained or 'disappeared'. In March Congress approved legislation repealing the Punto Final and Obediencia Debida laws (adopted in 1986 and 1987, respectively); however, the new legislation was not retrospective and would not affect those who had already received an amnesty. In June Gen. Videla was arrested in connection with the abduction and illegal adoption of children whose parents had 'disappeared' during the dictatorship, and in November Adm. Massera was summoned to give evidence. As many as 300 infants born in special holding centres during the 'dirty war' were believed to have been abducted by the military. In the following months further arrests were made in connection with the alleged kidnappings, including that of former President Reynaldo Bignone, former army chief Lt-Gen. Cristino Nicolaides and former navy chief Vice-Adm. Rubén Oscar Franco. In April 2000 a mass grave was discovered in Lomas de Zamora, containing the remains of about 90 victims of the 'dirty war'.

In May 1985 a treaty was formally ratified by representatives of the Argentine and Chilean Governments, concluding the territorial dispute over three small islands in the Beagle Channel, south of Tierra del Fuego. The islands were awarded to Chile, while Argentine rights to petroleum and other minerals in the disputed waters were guaranteed. In August 1991 Argentina and Chile reached a settlement regarding disputed claims to territory in the Antarctic region; however, the sovereignty of the territory remained under dispute, necessitating the signing of an additional protocol in late 1996. In December 1998 the Presidents of the two countries signed a new agreement on the border demarcation of the contested 'continental glaciers' territory in the Antarctic region (despite the 1991 treaty); the accord became effective in June 1999 following ratification by the Argentine and Chilean legislatures. Meanwhile, the two countries' navies held joint exercises for the first time in August 1998. In February 1999, during a meeting held in Ushuaia, southern Argentina, President Menem and the Chilean President, Eduardo Frei Ruiz-Tagle, signed a significant defence agreement and issued a joint declaration on both countries' commitment to the consolidation of their friendship.

Full diplomatic relations were restored with the United Kingdom in February 1990, following senior-level negotiations in Madrid, Spain. The improvement in relations between Argentina and the United Kingdom prompted the European Community (now European Union) to sign a new five-year trade and co-operation agreement with Argentina in April. In November Argentina and the United Kingdom concluded an agreement for the joint administration of a comprehensive protection programme for the lucrative South Atlantic fishing region. Subsequent agreements to regulate fishing in the area were concluded in 1992 and 1993. A diplomatic accord, signed in September 1991, significantly reduced military restrictions in the region, which the United Kingdom had imposed on Argentina following the Falklands conflict. The question of sovereignty over the disputed islands was not resolved. The results of preliminary seismic investigations (published in late 1993), which indicated rich petroleum deposits in the region, were expected to further complicate future negotiations. Although a comprehensive agreement on exploration was signed by both countries in New York in September 1995, negotiations on fishing rights in the region remained tense. In late 1996 the Argentine Government suggested, for the first time, that it might consider shared sovereignty of the Falkland Islands with the United Kingdom. The proposal was firmly rejected by the British Government and by the Falkland Islanders, who reiterated their commitment to persuading the UN Special Political and Decolonization Committee to adopt a clause allowing the Islanders the right to self-determination. Anglo-Argentine relations improved in November 1996 when Lt-Gen. Martín Balza, the Chief of Staff of the Argentine Army, became the first high-ranking Argentine military official to visit the United Kingdom since 1982. Relations between Argentina and the United Kingdom were consolidated further in January 1997 when the two countries agreed to resume negotiations on a long-term fisheries accord. Moreover, in October 1998 President Menem made an official visit to the United Kingdom, during which he held talks with the British Prime Minister, Tony Blair, on issues including the arms embargo, defence, trade and investment. Notably, Menem paid tribute to the British servicemen who died during the 1982 conflict, while he also appealed for an 'imaginative' solution to the Falkland Islands sovereignty issue. Earlier in 1998 relations with the United Kingdom had been strained by the presentation of draft legislation to the Argentine Congress on the imposition of sanctions on petroleum companies and fishing vessels operating in Falkland Island waters without Argentine authorization. In late 1998 the United Kingdom announced the partial lifting of its arms embargo against Argentina. There were also reports that Argentina and the United Kingdom were considering the establishment of an advisory council, based in the Falkland Islands, as part of negotiations on a new status for the territory. In March 1999, during an official visit to Argentina, Prince Charles, heir to the British throne, paid tribute to the Argentine soldiers who died in the Falklands conflict, although his apparent support for the Islanders' right to self-determination provoked some controversy. In May formal negotiations were held in London between the British and Argentine Governments and members of the Falkland Islands legislature. Following further talks in July, an agreement was reached providing for an end to the ban on Argentine citizens visiting the Falkland Islands and for the restoration of air links between the islands and South America, with stopovers in Argentina to be introduced from mid-October. In September 1999 Argentine and British government officials reached an understanding on co-operation against illegal fishing in the South Atlantic, and naval forces from both countries held joint exercises in the region in November.

In March 1991 the Presidents of Argentina, Brazil, Paraguay and Uruguay signed the Asunción treaty in Paraguay, thereby confirming their commitment to the creation of a Southern Common Market, Mercosur (Mercado Común del Sur). Mercosur duly came into effect on 1 January 1995. While a complete common external tariff was not expected until 2006, customs barriers on 80%–85% of mutually exchanged goods were removed immediately. The effects of economic recession and the devaluation of the Brazilian currency in January 1999 provoked a series of trade disputes within Mercosur during that year, particularly between Argentina and Brazil, the two largest members. Meanwhile, relations with Paraguay were strained by Argentina's refusal, in September 1999, to extradite Gen. Lino César Oviedo Silvo, who had been granted asylum in March following the assassination of the Paraguayan Vice-President Luis María Argaña. Relations improved to some extent at the end of September as a result of Oviedo's relocation to the remote territory of Tierra del Fuego. Oviedo disappeared on 9 December, the day before de la Rúa took office. He was subsequently arrested in Brazil.

In late 1997, following a visit to Argentina by the US President, Bill Clinton, the US Congress declared Argentina a 'special non-NATO ally', affording the country privileged access to US surplus defence supplies and certain military funding. Chile and Brazil criticized the granting of the special status, claiming it would lead to a regional imbalance. In January 1999, during a visit by President Menem to Washington, DC, a number of US-Argentine defence agreements were signed, which aimed to enhance military co-operation between the two countries.

In late 1996 a criminal investigation was begun in Spain regarding the torture, disappearance and killing of several hundred Spanish citizens in Argentina during 1976–83. A parallel investigation was instigated into the abduction of 54 children of Spanish victims during this period. In October 1997 Adolfo Scilingo, a former Argentine military official, was arrested in Madrid, Spain, after admitting to his involvement in the 'dirty war'. During that year a Spanish High Court judge issued international arrest warrants for several other Argentine officers, including Adm. Massera and Gen. Galtieri. The investigations continued in 1998–99, and by October 1999 a reported 192 Argentines had been indicted on charges of genocide, terrorism and torture. In November international arrest warrants were issued for 98 of those accused, although any request for extradition was likely to be refused by the Argentine Government. Shortly afterwards Adolfo Scilingo, now on bail in Spain awaiting trial, was reported to have retracted his earlier confession, claiming that he had been pressured to lie under oath. On 30 December the Spanish magistrate Baltasar Garzón issued international arrest warrants for 49 people, including former military presidents Videla and Galtieri, effectively confining them to Argentine territory. However, in January 2000 a federal judge refused to extradite them.

In May 1998 diplomatic relations with Iran were reduced to a 'minimum level' after evidence emerged of Iranian involvement in a bomb attack on a Jewish social centre in Buenos Aires in 1994, which resulted in 86 fatalities. In September 1999 the Argentine Supreme Court issued an arrest warrant for Imad Mughniyah, a leader of the fundamentalist Shi'ite Hezbollah, who was suspected of involvement in a bomb attack on the Israeli embassy in Buenos Aires in 1992.

Government

For administrative purposes Argentina comprises 1,617 municipalities located in 22 provinces, the Federal District of Buenos Aires, and the National Territory of Tierra del Fuego.

Legislative power is vested in the bicameral Congress (Congreso): the Chamber of Deputies (Cámara de Diputados) has 257 members, elected by universal adult suffrage for a term of four years (with approximately one-half of the seats renewable every two years). In accordance with the amended Constitution, promulgated in August 1994, from 1995 legislative elections provided for an expanded Senate (Senado), which was eventually to have 72 members, with three members drawn from each of the 22 provinces, the Federal District of Buenos Aires and the National Territory of Tierra del Fuego. A reduced, six-year term of office was to be in place by 2001, with one-third of the Senate elected every three years. The President is directly elected for a four-year term, renewable once. Each province has its own elected Governor and legislature, concerned with all matters not delegated to the Federal Government.

Defence

Conscription was ended on 1 April 1995. The total strength of the regular armed forces in August 2000 was 71,100, comprising a 41,400-strong army, a 17,200-strong navy and an air force of 12,500 men. There were also paramilitary forces numbering 31,240 men. The defence budget for 2000 put defence expenditure at 3,800m. new pesos.

Economic Affairs

In 1998, according to estimates by the World Bank, Argentina's gross national product (GNP), measured at average 1996–98 prices, was US $290,261m., equivalent to $8,030 per head (or $11,728 on an international purchasing-power parity basis). During 1990–98, it was estimated, GNP per head increased, in real terms, at an average annual rate of 4.2%. Over the same period, Argentina's population increased at an average rate of 1.5% per year. In 1999 GNP was $277,900m., equivalent to $7,600 per head. The country's gross domestic product (GDP) increased, in real terms, at an average annual rate of 4.9% during 1990–99. Real GDP increased by 8.1% in 1997 and by 3.9% in 1998, but declined by 3.0% in 1999.

Agriculture (including forestry and fishing) contributed 6% of GDP in 1999 and employed an estimated 10.2% of the labour force in mid-1998. The principal cash crops are wheat, maize, sorghum and soybeans. Beef production is also important. During 1990–99 agricultural GDP increased at an average annual rate of 3.1%. The GDP of the sector increased by 10.3% in 1998.

Industry (including mining, manufacturing, construction and power) engaged 25.3% of the employed labour force in 1991 and provided 32% of GDP in 1999. During 1990–99 industrial GDP increased, in real terms, at an estimated average annual rate of 4.8%.

Mining contributed 1.5% of GDP in 1998, and employed 0.4% of the working population in 1991. Argentina has substantial deposits of petroleum and natural gas, as well as steam coal and lignite. In late 1997 the Bajo de la Alumbrera open-pit gold and copper mine became operational, leading to forecasts of a substantial rise in mineral output in the late 1990s. The GDP of the mining sector increased, in real terms, at an average rate of 7.3% per year during 1993–98; growth of 2.3% was recorded in 1998.

Manufacturing contributed 22% of GDP in 1999, and employed 17.3% of the working population in 1991. In 1993 the most important branches of manufacturing, measured by gross value of output, were food products and beverages (accounting for 26.4% of the total), chemical products (10.5%), transport equipment (9.9%) and petroleum refineries. During 1993–98 manufacturing GDP increased, in real terms, at an estimated average annual rate of 2.8%. Manufacturing GDP increased by 9.2% in 1997, and by 1.6% in 1998.

Energy is derived principally from hydroelectric power (responsible for the production of 38.5% of total electricity in 1998) and coal. In 1998 9.8% of Argentina's total energy requirements were produced by its two nuclear power stations. In that year imports of mineral fuels comprised 10.5% of the country's total energy requirements.

Services engaged 62.7% of the employed labour force in 1991 and accounted for 61% of GDP in 1999. The combined GDP of the service sectors increased, in real terms, at an estimated average rate of 4.8% per year during 1990–99; growth of 4.7% was recorded in 1998.

In 1999 Argentina recorded a visible trade deficit of US $829m., and there was a deficit of $12,152m. on the current account of the balance of payments. In 1999 (according to provisional figures) the principal source of imports (21.9%) was Brazil, just ahead of the USA (19.6%). Brazil also accounted for 24.4% of exports. Other major trading partners in 1999 were Italy, Chile and Germany. The principal exports in that year were food and live animals, machinery and transport equipment, basic manufactures and animal and vegetable oils and fats. The principal imports were machinery and transport equipment, chemical and mineral products, and basic manufactures.

In 1997 there was a budget deficit of 4,281.7m. new Argentine pesos, equivalent to 1.5% of GDP. Argentina's total external debt was US $144,050m. at the end of 1998, of which $76,799m. was long-term public debt. In that year the total cost of debt-servicing was equivalent to 58.2% of revenue from exports of goods and services. The annual rate of inflation averaged 19.3% in 1990–98, although consumer prices increased by an annual average of only 0.5% and 0.9% in 1997 and 1998, respectively, and declined by 1.2% in 1999. Record national unemployment of 18.6% (equivalent to 2.2m. workers) was reported in May 1995; by May 1999, however, the level had declined to 14.5%.

During 1986–90 Argentina signed a series of integration treaties with neighbouring Latin American countries, aimed at increasing bilateral trade and establishing the basis for a Latin American economic community. Argentina is a member of ALADI (see p. 230) and of Mercosur (see p. 284).

Economic growth in Argentina in the 1980s was hampered primarily by massive external debt obligations, limited access to financial aid and a scarcity of raw materials. In 1989, however, the IMF approved a stand-by loan of US $1,400m. in recognition of the austerity measures adopted under the Menem administration. Further deregulation of the economy, and the success of new economic measures introduced by the Government in the early 1990s (including a programme of privatization), drastically reduced inflation and helped to secure agreements to reschedule debt repayments and the disbursement of loans from international financial organizations. Attempts to support the Argentine peso in the aftermath of the collapse of the Mexican currency in early 1995 imposed severe restrictions on public expenditure, which, together with a dramatic rise in the rate of unemployment, led to widespread social unrest. Real GDP declined by 2.8% in 1995, but it subsequently recovered, and economic growth of 8.1% was recorded in 1997. From mid-1998, however, the economy began to contract, with both trade and budget deficits widening, as international prices for certain commodities fell, adversely affecting exports. Exports declined further in 1999 following the devaluation of the Brazilian currency in January, and the economy entered recession; annual GDP declined by 3% in 1999. In August Congress approved fiscal convertibility legislation, which imposed limitations on public expenditure, with the aim of achieving a balanced budget by 2003. However, the economy continued to experience problems in 2000, owing to further decreases in the price of commodity exports, as well as an uncompetitive US dollar (to which the peso is tied), and increased international interest rates, which increased the debt burden. In order to obtain IMF funds to meet Argentina's external financing requirements for 2001, an agreement to 'freeze' public spending until 2005 was reached between the Federal Government and provincial governments in 2000. Growth of 1% was forecast for 2000 and the budget approved by Congress in December of that year was based on growth of 2.5% in 2001.

Social Welfare

Social welfare benefits comprise three categories: retirement, disability and survivors' pensions; family allowances; and health insurance. The first is administered by the Administración Nacional de Seguridad Social (part of the Ministry of Labour and Social Security) and funded by compulsory contributions from all workers, employed and self-employed, over 18 years of age. The second is supervised by the Administración Nacional de Seguridad Social and funded by employers. The third is administered by the Administración Nacional del Seguro de Salud, by means of public funds, and may be provided only by authorized public institutions. Work insurance is the responsibility of the employer. In 1993 the Government approved reforms to the pension system, which offered contributors a choice between privately-managed and state-operated schemes. In the case of privately-managed pension funds (Administradoras de Fondos de Jubilación y Pensión—AFJPs), employees set aside 11% of their monthly salaries, 7.5% of which goes toward retirement. On retirement (at 65 years of age for men and 60 years of age for women), employees can use these funds to purchase an annuity from an insurance company or begin to withdraw funds at a specified monthly rate. Pension managers are required to maintain sufficient reserves to honour a minimum pension guaranteed by the Government. AFJPs are monitored by a government supervisory body. There is considerable foreign participation in the management of the AFJPs and the country's three most successful funds, Consolidar, Máxima, SA and Siembra, have strong links with Dresdner Bank AG, Deutsche Bank AG and Citibank NA, respectively. In November 2000 the Government announced plans to eliminate state pensions from 2002, limiting the state's participation to providing for those pensioners who were unable to capitalize their accounts sufficiently. As part of the reforms, the retirement age for women was to be increased to 65 years of age. Of total government expenditure in 1997, 1,049.3m. new pesos (2.3%) was for health, and a further 23,392.4m. new pesos (52.3%) was for social security and welfare.

In the early 1990s there were 268 physicians for every 100,000 inhabitants in Argentina (one of the best doctor–patient ratios of any country in Latin America) and 54 nurses per 100,000 inhabitants. In 1995 there were 155,822 hospital beds in Argentina.

Education

Education from pre-school to university level is available free of charge. Education is officially compulsory for all children at primary level, between the ages of six and 14 years. Secondary education lasts for between five and seven years, depending on the type of course: the normal certificate of education (bachillerato) course lasts for five years, whereas a course leading to a technical or agricultural bachillerato lasts for six years. Technical education is supervised by the Consejo Nacional de Educación Técnica. The total enrolment at primary and secondary schools in 1996 was estimated at 99.4% and 67.2% of the school-age population, respectively. Non-university higher education, usually leading to a teaching qualification, is for three or four years, while university courses last for four years or more. There are 36 state universities and 48 private universities. Central government expenditure on education in 1997 was 2,561.0m. new pesos (5.7% of total public expenditure).

According to official estimates, the average rate of adult illiteracy in 1997 was 4.0%.

Public Holidays

2001: 1 January (New Year's Day), 13 April (Good Friday), 1 May (Labour Day), 25 May (Anniversary of the 1810 Revolution), 14 June (for Occupation of the Islas Malvinas), 20 June (for Flag Day), 9 July (Independence Day), 17 August (for Death of Gen. José de San Martín), 12 October (for Columbus Day), 25 December (Christmas).

2002: 1 January (New Year's Day), 29 March (Good Friday), 1 May (Labour Day), 25 May (Anniversary of the 1810 Revolution), 10 June (Occupation of the Islas Malvinas), 24 June (for Flag Day), 9 July (Independence Day), 19 August (for Death of Gen. José de San Martín), 14 October (for Columbus Day), 25 December (Christmas).

Weights and Measures

The metric system is in force.

Statistical Survey

Sources (unless otherwise stated): Instituto Nacional de Estadística y Censos, Avda Julio A. Roca 609, 1067 Buenos Aires; tel. (11) 4349-9652; fax (11) 4349-9621; e-mail ces@indec.mecon.ar; internet www.indec.mecon.ar; and Banco Central de la República Argentina, Reconquista 266, 1003 Buenos Aires; tel. (11) 4394-8111; fax (11) 4334-5712.

Area and Population

AREA, POPULATION AND DENSITY

Area (sq km)	2,780,400*
Population (census results)†	
22 October 1980	27,949,480
15 May 1991	
Males	15,937,980
Females	16,677,548
Total	32,615,528
Population (official estimates at mid-year)	
1998	36,124,933
1999	36,578,358
2000	37,031,802
Density (per sq km) at mid-2000	13.3

* 1,073,518 sq miles. The figure excludes the Falkland Islands (Islas Malvinas) and Antarctic territory claimed by Argentina.
† Figures exclude adjustment for underenumeration, estimated to have been 1% at the 1980 census and 0.9% at the 1991 census.

PROVINCES (mid-2000)

	Area (sq km)	Estimated population*	Density (per sq km)	Capital
Buenos Aires—				
Federal District .	200	3,046,663	15,233.3	
Buenos Aires—				
Province . .	307,571	14,214,701	46.2	La Plata
Catamarca . .	102,602	318,147	3.1	San Fernando del Valle de Catamarca
Chaco . . .	99,633	951,795	9.6	Resistencia
Chubut . . .	224,686	448,028	2.0	Rawson
Córdoba . .	165,321	3,090,803	18.7	Córdoba
Corrientes . .	88,199	921,933	10.5	Corrientes
Entre Ríos . .	78,781	1,113,438	14.1	Paraná
Formosa . .	72,066	504,185	7.0	Formosa
Jujuy . . .	53,219	604,002	11.3	San Salvador de Jujuy
La Pampa . .	143,440	306,113	2.1	Santa Rosa
La Rioja . .	89,680	280,198	3.1	La Rioja
Mendoza . .	148,827	1,607,618	10.8	Mendoza
Misiones . .	29,801	995,326	33.4	Posadas
Neuquén . .	94,078	560,726	6.0	Neuquén
Río Negro . .	203,013	618,486	3.0	Viedma
Salta . . .	155,488	1,067,347	6.9	Salta
San Juan . .	89,651	578,504	6.5	San Juan
San Luis . .	76,748	363,345	4.7	San Luis
Santa Cruz . .	243,943	206,897	0.8	Río Gallegos
Santa Fe . .	133,007	3,098,661	23.3	Santa Fe
Santiago del Estero	136,351	725,993	5.3	Santiago del Estero
Tucumán . .	22,524	1,293,349	57.4	San Miguel de Tucumán
Territory				
Tierra del Fuego .	21,571	115,538	5.4	Ushuaia
Total . . .	2,780,400	37,031,802	13.3	Buenos Aires

* Figures have been estimated independently, so the total may not be the sum of the component parts.

PRINCIPAL TOWNS (population at 1991 census)*

Buenos Aires		San Isidro . . .	299,023
(capital) . . .	2,965,403	Vicente López . .	289,505
Córdoba . .	1,157,507	Moreno . .	287,715
San Justo		Esteban Echeverría	275,793
(La Matanza) .	1,121,298	Bahía Blanca . .	260,096
Rosario . .	907,718	Corrientes . . .	258,103
General Sarmiento .	652,969	Tigre . . .	257,922
Morón . .	643,553	Florencio Varela .	254,997
Lomas de		Berazategui . .	244,929
Zamora . .	574,330	Resistencia . .	229,212
La Plata . .	521,936	Paraná . .	207,041
Mar del Plata . .	512,880	Posadas . .	201,273
Quilmes . .	511,234	Villa Nueva	
San Miguel de		(Guaymallén) .	200,595
Tucumán . .	470,809	Santiago del Estero	189,947
Lanús . .	468,561	Godoy Cruz . .	179,588
Almirante Brown .	450,698	San Salvador de	
General San		Jujuy . . .	178,748
Martín . .	406,809	Neuquén . .	167,296
Merlo . . .	390,858	Formosa . .	147,636
Salta . . .	367,550	Las Heras . .	145,823
Santa Fe . .	353,063	San Fernando . .	141,063
Caseros . .	349,376	Río Cuarto . .	134,355
Avellaneda . .	344,991		

* In each case the figures refer to the city proper. At the 1991 census the population of the Buenos Aires agglomeration was 11,298,030.

BIRTHS AND DEATHS

	Registered live births		Registered deaths	
	Number	Rate (per 1,000)	Number	Rate (per 1,000)
1991 . . .	694,776	21.1	255,609	7.8
1992 . . .	678,761	20.3	262,287	7.9
1993 . . .	667,518	19.8	267,286	7.9
1994 . . .	707,869	20.7	260,245	7.6
1995 . . .	658,735	18.9	268,997	7.7
1996 . . .	675,437	19.2	268,715	7.6
1997 . . .	692,357	19.4	270,910	7.6
1998 . . .	683,301	18.9	280,180	7.8

Marriages: 158,805 (marriage rate 4.6 per 1,000) in 1995; 148,721 (4.2 per 1,000) in 1996.

Source: mainly UN, *Demographic Yearbook* and *Population and Vital Statistics Report*.

Expectation of life (UN estimates, years at birth, 1990–95): 71.9 (males 68.6; females 75.7). Source: UN, *World Population Prospects: The 1998 Revision*.

ECONOMICALLY ACTIVE POPULATION
(persons aged 14 years and over, census of 15 May 1991)

	Males	Females	Total
Agriculture, hunting, forestry and fishing	1,142,674	222,196	1,364,870
Mining and quarrying	43,905	3,525	47,430
Manufacturing	1,590,713	546,090	2,136,803
Electricity, gas and water	92,469	11,318	103,787
Construction	818,831	17,617	836,448
Wholesale and retail trade, restaurants and hotels	1,730,600	808,702	2,539,302
Transport, storage and communication	583,938	54,024	637,962
Finance, insurance, real estate and business services	432,264	222,757	655,021
Community, social and personal services	1,459,492	2,464,552	3,924,044
Activities not adequately described	81,013	41,648	122,661
Total employed	7,975,899	4,392,429	12,368,328
Unemployed	447,488	386,384	833,872
Total labour force	8,423,387	4,778,813	13,202,200

1995 (provisional figures, sample survey, persons aged 15 years and over): Total active population 14,345,171 (males 9,087,075; females 5,258,096) (Source: ILO, *Yearbook of Labour Statistics*).

Mid-1999 (estimates in '000): Agriculture, etc. 1,466; Total labour force 14,692 (Source: FAO).

Agriculture

PRINCIPAL CROPS ('000 metric tons)

	1997	1998	1999
Wheat	15,000	12,200	14,200
Rice (paddy)	1,205	1,036	1,658
Barley	926	539	400
Maize	15,536	19,360	13,500
Rye	62	66	104
Oats	517	383	507
Millet	44	47	45
Sorghum	2,499	3,762	3,222
Potatoes	3,080	3,412	3,450*
Sweet potatoes	242	312	315*
Cassava (Manioc)*	160	160	165
Dry beans	269	303	310*
Other pulses	59	61	65*
Soybeans	11,000	18,732	19,500
Groundnuts (in shell)	401	896	468
Sunflower seed	5,450	5,600	7,100
Linseed	72	75	85
Olives*	92	88	85
Tomatoes	711	647	650*
Pumpkins, squash and gourds*	428	428	430
Onions (dry)	626	798	800*
Carrots	241	210*	210*
Watermelons*	130	130	125
Grapes	2,482	2,075*	2,500*
Sugar cane*	19,450	19,400	19,400
Apples	1,118	1,034	1,056*
Pears	533	537	540*
Peaches and nectarines	226	257	250*
Oranges	919	984	780†
Tangerines, mandarins, clementines and satsumas	400	394	340†
Lemons and limes	970	1,021	1,050†
Grapefruit and pomelos	241	216	210†
Bananas*	170	170	175
Tea (made)	54	57	49
Tobacco (leaves)	123	116	113†
Cotton (lint)	300†	316	198*

* FAO estimate(s).   † Unofficial figure.

Source: FAO.

LIVESTOCK ('000 head, year ending September)

	1997	1998	1999
Horses*	3,300	3,300	3,300
Mules*	175	175	175
Asses*	90	90	90
Cattle	54,500	54,600	55,000*
Pigs	3,200	3,200*	3,200*
Sheep†	17,295	15,232	14,000
Goats	3,428	3,428*	3,428*
Chickens*	55,000	60,000	60,000
Ducks*	2,200	2,200	2,200
Geese*	120	120	120
Turkeys	2,700	2,700	2,700

* FAO estimate(s).   † Unofficial figures.

Source: FAO.

LIVESTOCK PRODUCTS ('000 metric tons)

	1997	1998	1999
Beef and veal	2,705	2,656	2,650*
Mutton and lamb*	58	48	45
Goat meat	7	7	7
Pig meat	137	156	156†
Horse meat†	50	50	50
Poultry meat	792	896	951
Cows' milk	9,372	9,743	9,750†
Butter*	49	52	55
Cheese	445	420	425*
Hen eggs	256*	236*	236†
Wool (greasy)	64	65	65†
Cattle hides (fresh)	384	369	381

* Unofficial figure(s).   †FAO estimate(s).

Source: FAO.

Forestry

ROUNDWOOD REMOVALS ('000 cubic metres, excl. bark)

	1996	1997	1998
Sawlogs, veneer logs and logs for sleepers	3,575	3,575	3,575
Pulpwood	3,685	3,685	3,685
Other industrial wood	427	427	427
Fuel wood	3,741	3,741	3,741
Total	11,428	11,428	11,428

Source: FAO, *Yearbook of Forest Products*.

SAWNWOOD PRODUCTION
('000 cubic metres, incl. railway sleepers)

	1996	1997	1998
Coniferous (softwood)	594	594	594
Broadleaved (hardwood)	1,117	1,117	1,117
Total	1,711	1,711	1,711

Source: FAO, *Yearbook of Forest Products*.

Fishing

('000 metric tons, live weight)

	1996	1997	1998
Capture .	1,248.7	1,351.1	1,128.8
Southern blue whiting .	85.0	79.9	71.6
Argentine hake	597.6	584.0	458.4
Patagonian grenadier .	44.1	41.8	96.2
Argentine shortfin squid	292.6	412.0	291.2
Aquaculture .	1.3	1.3	1.3*
Total catch	1,250.1	1,352.4	1,130.2

*FAO estimate.

Note: The data exclude aquatic plants (FAO estimates, '000 metric tons, capture only): 2.3 in 1996; 2.3 in 1997; 2.3 in 1998. Also excluded are aquatic mammals, recorded by number rather than by weight. The number of toothed whales caught was 15 in 1998.

Source: FAO, *Yearbook of Fishery Statistics.*

Mining

('000 metric tons, unless otherwise indicated)

	1996	1997	1998
Crude petroleum ('000 cu metres) .	45,570	48,403	49,147*
Natural gas (million cu metres) .	34,650	37,073	38,631*
Lead ore† .	11.3	13.8	15.0
Zinc ore† .	31.1	33.4	35.6
Silver ore (metric tons) .	50.4	52.6	35.8
Uranium ore (metric tons)† .	27	41	9
Gold ore (kilograms)† .	723	2,289	20,400

* Estimate.
† Figures refer to the metal content of ores and concentrates.

1999 (estimates): Crude petroleum 46,508,000 cu m; Natural gas 42,425m. cu m.

Industry

SELECTED PRODUCTS ('000 metric tons, unless otherwise indicated)

	1997	1998	1999
Wheat flour* .	3,640	3,739	3,563
Beer (sales,'000 hectolitres) .	12,687	12,395*	12,503†
Cigarettes (million units) .	1,940	1,967	1,996
Paper and paper products .	1,143	1,159	1,130
Rubber tyres for motor vehicles ('000) .	8,138	9,190	8,085
Portland cement .	6,769	7,092	7,187*
Distillate fuel oils .	10,490	10,709	11,070
Residual fuel oils .	1,702	1,740	1,817
Motor spirit (petrol)('000 cu metres) .	7,094	7,736	7,864
Kerosene ('000 cu metres) .	203	181	171
Passenger motor vehicles ('000 units) .	366	353	225
Refrigerators ('000 units) .	410	424	403
Washing machines ('000 units)	603*	624	413
Television receivers ('000) .	1,630	1,592	1,335
Electric energy (million kWh) .	73,240	76,200	78,493*

* Provisional figure(s).
† Estimate.

Finance

CURRENCY AND EXCHANGE RATES

Monetary Units:
100 centavos = 1 nuevo peso argentino (new Argentine peso).

Sterling, Dollar and Euro Equivalents (29 December 2000)
£1 sterling = 1.4915 nuevos pesos;
US $1 = 99.95 centavos;
€1 = 93.00 centavos;
100 nuevos pesos = £67.05 = $100.05 = €107.52.

Note: The nuevo peso argentino was introduced on 1 January 1992, replacing the austral at a rate of 1 nuevo peso = 10,000 australes. The austral had been introduced on 15 June 1985, replacing the peso argentino at the rate of 1 austral = 1,000 pesos argentinos. The peso argentino, equal to 10,000 former pesos, had itself been introduced on 1 June 1983. The official exchange rate has been fixed at US $1 = 99.95 centavos since April 1996.

BUDGET (million new pesos)*

Revenue	1998	1999
Taxation .	50,785.5	51,200.7
Taxes on income, profits, etc. .	9,654.0	9,401.0
Social security contributions .	10,857.0	9,910.0
Domestic taxes on goods and services .	27,390.0	26,038.0
Value-added tax .	20,857.0	18,771.0
Excises .	1,942.0	1,830.0
Taxes on international trade and transactions	2,875.0	2,364.0
Import duties .	2,694.0	2,227.0
Export duties .	28.0	25.0
Other current revenue .	3,530.5	4,422.2
Capital revenue .	428.6	998.4
Total revenue .	54,744.6	56,621.3

Expenditure	1998	1999
General public services .	4,602.7	5,375.3
Defence .	1,994.3	2,076.5
Public order and safety .	1,414.8	1,496.4
Education and culture .	2,847.3	3,192. 8
Health .	3,109.5	3,180.0
Social security and welfare .	22,525.9	22,464.5
Housing and community amenities .	1,079.7	878.0
Other social services .	1,180.4	1,086.2
Economic affairs and services .	2,867.7	2,495.5
Agriculture .	386.1	361.4
Fuel, energy and mining .	348.7	373.1
Transportation and communication .	1,914.8	1,587.3
Industry .	98.4	99.2
Other purposes .	162.0	114.0
Interest payments .	6,991.7	8,680.9
Sub-total .	48,776.0	51,040.0
Adjustment to cash basis .	11,236.9	12,622.0
Total expenditure .	60,012.9	63,662.0
Current .	55,975.0	59,548.1
Capital .	4,037.9	4,113.9

2000 (forecasts, million new pesos): *Revenue:* Taxation 52,023.2; Other current revenue 3,730.8; Capital revenue 878.6; Total 56,632.6; *Expenditure:* Current expenditure 57,712.8; Capital expenditure 3,388.1; Total 61,100.9.

* Budget figures refer to the consolidated accounts of the public sector, comprising the central Government, provincial and municipal governments, and publicly-owned enterprises.

INTERNATIONAL RESERVES (US $ million at 31 December)

	1997	1998	1999
Gold* .	120	124	121
IMF special drawing rights .	167	264	138
Foreign exchange .	22,153	24,488	26,114
Total .	22,440	24,876	26,373

* Valued at US $332 per troy ounce in 1997, at $344 per ounce in 1998 and at $358 per ounce in 1999.

Source: IMF, *International Financial Statistics.*

MONEY SUPPLY (million new pesos at 31 December)

	1997	1998	1999
Currency outside banks . . .	13,331	13,503	13,736
Demand deposits at commercial banks.	8,151	7,986	8,106
Total money	21,482	21,489	21,842

Source: IMF, *International Financial Statistics.*

COST OF LIVING (Consumer Price Index for Buenos Aires metropolitan area; annual averages; base: 1988 = 100)

	1997	1998	1999
Food	274,621	279,216	268,980
Clothing.	176,184	171,767	165,508
Housing.	323,543	320,884	325,006
All items (incl. others) . .	323,668	326,661	322,849

NATIONAL ACCOUNTS (million new pesos at current prices)
Expenditure on the Gross Domestic Product

	1997	1998	1999
Government final consumption expenditure	35,325	35,474	36,352
Private final consumption expenditure	207,108	210,857	197,195
Gross fixed capital formation . .	56,727	59,276	53,909
Total domestic expenditure .	299,160	305,534*	287,456
Exports of goods and services . .	30,939	31,088	27,827
Less Imports of goods and services . .	37,240	38,491	32,515
GDP in purchasers' values .	292,859	298,131	282,769
GDP at constant 1993 prices .	277,441	288,195	279,511

*Including adjustment.

Source: IMF, *International Financial Statistics.*

Gross Domestic Product by Economic Activity

	1997	1998*	1999*
Agriculture, hunting and forestry .	14,625	15,275	11,636
Fishing	668	647	693
Mining and quarrying . . .	5,633	4,291	4,821
Manufacturing	53,382	53,266	48,471
Electricity, gas and water supply	5,502	5,749	6,041
Construction	15,080	16,635	15,970
Wholesale and retail trade . .	41,477	42,385	37,849
Hotels and restaurants . .	7,644	8,110	7,957
Transport, storage and communications	22,952	23,952	22,614
Financial intermediation . .	10,116	10,393	10,955
Real estate, renting and business activities .	44,567	45,522	45,511
Public administration and defence†	15,860	15,463	16,820
Education, health and social work	21,366	22,155	22,730
Other community, social and personal service activities‡ .	14,221	14,111	14,059
Sub-total	273,093	278,632	266,127
Value-added tax	20,474	20,857	18,771
Import duties	2,827	2,741	2,278
Less Imputed bank service charge	3,534	4,099	4,406
GDP in purchasers' values .	292,859	298,131	282,769

*Provisional figures.
† Including extra-territorial organizations and bodies.
‡ Including private households with employed persons.

BALANCE OF PAYMENTS (US $ million)

	1997	1998	1999
Exports of goods f.o.b. . . .	26,431	26,441	23,316
Imports of goods f.o.b. . . .	−28,554	−29,558	−24,145
Trade balance	−2,123	−3,117	−829
Exports of services . . .	4,509	4,684	4,448
Imports of services . . .	−8,687	−9,015	−8,416
Balance on goods and services .	−6,301	−7,448	−4,797
Other income received . .	5,501	6,183	6,137
Other income paid . . .	−11,590	−13,518	−13,984
Balance on goods, services and income	−12,390	−14,783	−12,644
Current transfers received . .	542	615	575
Current transfers paid . . .	−106	−106	−83
Current balance . . .	−11,954	−14,274	−12,152
Direct investment abroad. . .	−3,656	−2,166	−1,195
Direct investment from abroad .	8,755	6,526	23,152
Portfolio investment assets . .	−1,320	−2,176	−1,977
Portfolio investment liabilities .	12,407	10,515	−4,641
Other investment assets . . .	−7,131	210	−2,213
Other investment liabilities . .	7,771	4,909	2,020
Net errors and omissions . .	−1,498	574	−1,049
Overall balance . . .	3,374	4,118	1,945

Source: IMF, *International Financial Statistics.*

External Trade

PRINCIPAL COMMODITIES (distribution by SITC, US $ million)

Imports c.i.f.	1996	1997	1998
Food and live animals . .	1,025.7	1,212.0	1,221.3
Crude materials (inedible) except fuels	787.4	1,023.4	912.8
Mineral fuels, lubricants, etc. .	885.8	927.1	818.0
Petroleum, petroleum products, etc. .	616.7	617.7	490.4
Chemicals and related products	4,264.1	4,724.3	4,799.5
Organic chemicals . . .	1,226.9	1,397.6	1,362.6
Medicinal and pharmaceutical products . . .	582.6	663.6	781.1
Artificial resins, plastic materials, etc.	770.9	961.2	941.5
Products of polymerization, etc.	479.6	632.8	591.5
Basic manufactures . .	3,544.8	4,615.4	4,686.5
Paper, paperboard and manufactures . . .	721.8	865.8	916.0
Paper and paperboard (not cut to size or shape) . .	583.1	693.3	761.4
Textile yarn, fabrics, etc. . .	609.7	792.5	794.7
Iron and steel	525.0	845.0	797.4
Machinery and transport equipment . .	10,902.0	14,794.2	15,449.0
Power-generating machinery and equipment	887.5	1,115.4	1,494.8
Internal combustion piston engines and parts . .	506.9	719.8	654.0
Machinery specialized for particular industries . .	1,091.0	1,435.0	1,354.3
General industrial machinery, equipment and parts . .	1,867.0	2,247.4	2,179.8
Office machines and automatic data-processing equipment .	815.3	1,125.0	1,249.4
Automatic data-processing machines, etc. . .	543.1	746.2	806.3
Telecommunications and sound equipment . . .	1,083.1	1,720.7	1,685.2
Television and radio-broadcasting transmitters, etc.	281.4	653.4	682.3
Other electrical machinery, apparatus, etc. . . .	1,604.3	2,112.6	2,074.8

Imports c.i.f. — *continued*	1996	1997	1998
Road vehicles and parts*	2,983.7	4,383.9	4,874.4
Passenger motor cars (excl. buses)	1,198.4	1,561.3	1,623.1
Motor vehicles for goods transport, etc.	532.9	866.5	1,169.9
Goods vehicles (lorries and trucks)	509.4	839.8	1,129.8
Parts and accessories for cars, buses, lorries, etc.*	1,061.4	1,620.3	1,686.0
Miscellaneous manufactured articles	2,209.7	2,779.2	2,883.2
Total (incl. others)	23,761.6	30,349.5	31,029.7

Exports f.o.b.	1996	1997	1998
Food and live animals	9,241.6	9,899.2	9,042.4
Meat and meat preparations	1,073.9	1,024.3	817.4
Fresh, chilled or frozen meat	781.0	763.5	590.7
Meat of bovine animals	627.1	622.8	474.1
Fish, crustaceans, molluscs and preparations	1,003.9	1,028.4	861.8
Fish, fresh (live or dead), chilled or frozen	494.9	535.9	452.0
Cereals and cereal preparations	2,802.9	3,293.6	3,254.5
Wheat (including spelt) and meslin, unmilled	1,065.7	1,343.1	1,298.4
Maize (corn), unmilled	1,239.4	1,346.8	1,335.2
Vegetables and fruit	1,180.5	1,273.8	1,264.6
Fresh or dried fruit and nuts (excl. oil nuts)	508.7	534.7	512.8
Feeding-stuff for animals (excl. unmilled cereals)	2,367.0	2,399.3	1,945.9
Oilcake and other residues	2,293.4	2,313.6	1,867.5
Cake, etc., of soya beans	1,984.1	2,039.7	1,691.7
Crude materials (inedible) except fuels	1,869.2	1,137.0	1,987.2
Oil seeds and oleaginous fruit	955.1	326.8	1,030.9
Soya beans	588.2	144.4	643.1
Textile fibres and waste	625.5	451.7	296.0
Cotton	500.8	335.9	226.3
Mineral fuels, lubricants, etc.	3,096.2	3,073.8	1,937.7
Petroleum, petroleum products, etc.	2,973.3	2,933.5	1,790.4
Crude petroleum oils, etc.	2,320.0	2,176.0	1,227.9
Refined petroleum products	584.9	701.0	514.0
Animal and vegetable oils, fats and waxes	1,882.6	2,203.5	2,580.2
Fixed vegetable oils and fats	1,857.2	2,179.0	2,556.8
Soya bean oil	900.8	1,043.0	1,383.6
Sunflower seed oil	832.1	1,000.1	1,029.5
Chemicals and related products	1,320.1	1,499.5	1,679.3
Basic manufactures	2,852.0	3,172.6	2,806.1
Leather, leather manufactures and dressed furskins	926.5	1,016.1	835.0
Leather	823.8	932.3	767.3
Iron and steel	797.8	865.3	827.2
Tubes, pipes and fittings	457.9	530.1	515.7
Machinery and transport equipment	2,592.5	3,944.5	4,060.0
Road vehicles and parts*	1,514.6	2,620.4	2,943.7
Passenger motor cars (excl. buses)	803.9	1,509.1	1,605.4
Motor vehicles for goods transport, etc.	253.1	606.5	793.0
Goods vehicles (lorries and trucks)	250.6	597.9	775.2
Miscellaneous manufactured articles	667.0	702.1	647.3
Total (incl. others)	23,809.7	26,264.4	25,322.6

* Excluding tyres, engines and electrical parts.

Source: UN, *International Trade Statistics Yearbook*.

1999 (US $ million): Imports c.i.f. 25,508; Exports f.o.b. 23,333.

PRINCIPAL TRADING PARTNERS (US $ million)

Imports c.i.f.	1997	1998	1999*
Belgium	291	289	259
Brazil	6,914	7,005	5,596
Canada	450	385	290
Chile	688	708	639
China, People's Republic	1,006	1,167	992
France (incl. Monaco)	1,375	1,584	1,504
Germany	1,655	1,876	1,409
Italy	1,747	1,605	1,355
Japan	1,150	1,453	1,608
Mexico	610	603	491
Paraguay	320	348	304
Spain	1,256	1,285	1,000
United Kingdom	802	797	543
USA	6,095	6,227	4,996
Uruguay	371	528	389
Total (incl. others)	30,450	31,378	25,508

Exports f.o.b.	1997	1998	1999*
Belgium	304	278	310
Bolivia	464	431	321
Brazil	8,133	7,949	5,690
Canada	135	227	239
Chile	1,932	1,857	1,869
China, People's Republic	871	682	508
France (incl. Monaco)	310	315	349
Germany	503	564	629
Iran	659	476	155
Italy	730	753	689
Japan	554	657	528
Mexico	216	261	282
Netherlands	880	1,100	1,013
Paraguay	624	622	563
Peru	306	326	213
South Africa	304	253	308
Spain	623	842	962
United Kingdom	320	256	263
USA	2,204	2,212	2,653
Uruguay	840	843	812
Venezuela	315	364	247
Total (incl. others)	26,431	26,434	23,333

* Provisional.

Transport

RAILWAYS (traffic)

	1997	1998	1999
Passengers carried (million)	459	480	481
Freight carried ('000 tons)	18,904	18,828	17,489
Passenger-km (million)	9,324	9,652	9,102
Freight ton-km (million)	9,835	9,824	9,102

ROAD TRAFFIC (motor vehicles in use)

	1995	1996	1997
Passenger cars	4,665,329	4,783,908	4,901,608
Buses and coaches	37,568	38,434	40,639
Lorries and vans	1,200,569	1,248,527	1,338,405
Motorcycles and mopeds	35,000	35,640	n.a.

Source: International Road Federation, *World Road Statistics*.

SHIPPING
Merchant Fleet (registered at 31 December)

	1996	1997	1998
Number of vessels	480	513	501
Total displacement ('000 grt)	586.3	579.4	498.7

Source: Lloyd's Register of Shipping, *World Fleet Statistics*.

International Sea-borne Freight Traffic ('000 metric tons)

	1996	1997	1998
Goods loaded . . .	52,068	58,512	69,372
Goods unloaded . .	16,728	19,116	19,536

Source: UN, *Monthly Bulletin of Statistics*.

CIVIL AVIATION (traffic on scheduled services)

	1995	1996	1997
Kilometres flown (million) . .	108	133	155
Passengers carried ('000) . .	6,642	7,193	8,600
Passenger-km (million) . .	11,892	13,360	14,338
Total ton-km (million) . .	1,338	1,447	1,600

Source: UN, *Statistical Yearbook*.

Tourism

	1996	1997	1998
Tourist arrivals ('000) . .	4,286	4,540	4,860
Tourist receipts (US $ million) .	4,572	4,069	5,363

Communications Media

	1995	1996	1997
Radio receivers ('000 in use) . .	23,500	23,850	24,300
Television receivers ('000 in use)	7,600	7,800	7,950
Telephones* ('000 main lines in use)	5,532	6,120	6,824
Telefax stations*† ('000 in use)	50	60	70
Mobile cellular telephones* ('000 subscribers) . . .	340.7	667.0	2,009.1
Daily newspapers	190†	181	n.a
Books (number of titles) . .	9,113	9,850	11,919

* Year ending September.
† Estimate(s).
1998: Telephones ('000 main lines in use) 7,095; Books (number of titles) 13,156
Sources: mainly UNESCO, *Statistical Yearbook*, and UN, *Statistical Yearbook*.

Education

(1998)

	Institutions	Students	Teachers*
Pre-primary	15,723	1,167,943	65,708
Primary	22,395	5,262,066	295,488
Secondary	6,373	2,539,749	238,791
Universities†	36	958,405	n.a.
Colleges of higher education . .	1,664	384,160	43,921

* 1994 figures.
† State universities only.
Source: Ministerio de Cultura y Educación.

Directory

The Constitution

The return to civilian rule in 1983 represented a return to the principles of the 1853 Constitution, with some changes in electoral details. In August 1994 a new Constitution was approved, which contained 19 new articles, 40 amendments to existing articles and the addition of a chapter on New Rights and Guarantees. The Constitution is summarized below:

DECLARATIONS, RIGHTS AND GUARANTEES

Each province has the right to exercise its own administration of justice, municipal system and primary education. The Roman Catholic religion, being the faith of the majority of the nation, shall enjoy state protection; freedom of religious belief is guaranteed to all other denominations. The prior ethnical existence of indigenous peoples and their rights, as well as the common ownership of lands they traditionally occupy, are recognized. All inhabitants of the country have the right to work and exercise any legal trade; to petition the authorities; to leave or enter the Argentine territory; to use or dispose of their properties; to associate for a peaceable or useful purpose; to teach and acquire education, and to express freely their opinion in the press without censorship. The State does not admit any prerogative of blood, birth, privilege or titles of nobility. Equality is the basis of all duties and public offices. No citizens may be detained, except for reasons and in the manner prescribed by the law; or sentenced other than by virtue of a law existing prior to the offence and by decision of the competent tribunal after the hearing and defence of the person concerned. Private residence, property and correspondence are inviolable. No one may enter the home of a citizen or carry out any search in it without his consent, unless by a warrant from the competent authority; no one may suffer expropriation, except in case of public necessity and provided that the appropriate compensation has been paid in accordance with the provisions of the laws. In no case may the penalty of confiscation of property be imposed.

LEGISLATIVE POWER

Legislative power is vested in the bicameral Congreso (Congress), comprising the Cámara de Diputados (Chamber of Deputies) and the Senado (Senate). The Chamber of Deputies has 257 directly-elected members, chosen for four years and eligible for re-election; approximately one-half of the membership of the Chamber shall be renewed every two years. Until October 1995 the Senate had 48 members, chosen by provincial legislatures for a nine-year term, with one-third of the seats renewable every three years. Since October 1995 elections have provided for a third senator, elected by provincial legislatures. From 2001 the members of the expanded Senate will serve a six-year term.

The powers of Congress include regulating foreign trade; fixing import and export duties; levying taxes for a specified time whenever the defence, common safety or general welfare of the State so requires; contracting loans on the nation's credit; regulating the internal and external debt and the currency system of the country; fixing the budget and facilitating the prosperity and welfare of the nation. Congress must approve required and urgent decrees and delegated legislation. Congress also approves or rejects treaties, authorizes the Executive to declare war or make peace, and establishes the strength of the Armed Forces in peace and war.

EXECUTIVE POWER

Executive power is vested in the President, who is the supreme head of the nation and controls the general administration of the country. The President issues the instructions and rulings necessary for the execution of the laws of the country, and himself takes part in drawing up and promulgating those laws. The President appoints, with the approval of the Senate, the judges of the Supreme Court and all other competent tribunals, ambassadors, civil servants, members of the judiciary and senior officers of the Armed Forces and bishops. The President may also appoint and remove, without reference to another body, his cabinet ministers. The President is Commander-in-Chief of all the Armed Forces. The President and Vice-President are elected directly for a four-year term, renewable only once.

JUDICIAL POWER

Judicial power is exercised by the Supreme Court and all other competent tribunals. The Supreme Court is responsible for the internal administration of all tribunals. In April 1990 the number of Supreme Court judges was increased from five to nine.

PROVINCIAL GOVERNMENT

The 22 provinces, the Federal District of Buenos Aires and the National Territory of Tierra del Fuego retain all the power not delegated to the Federal Government. They are governed by their own institutions and elect their own governors, legislators and officials.

The Government

HEAD OF STATE

President of the Republic: FERNANDO DE LA RÚA (took office 10 December 1999).

Vice-President of the Republic: (vacant).

CABINET
(April 2001)

Cabinet Chief: CHRYSTIAN COLOMBO.

Minister of the Interior: RAMÓN MESTRE.

Minister of Foreign Affairs: ADALBERTO RODRÍGUEZ GIAVARINI.

Minister of Education: ANDRÉS DELICH.

Minister of Defence: HORACIO JAUNARENA.

Minister of the Economy: DOMINGO CAVALLO.

Minister of Infrastructure and Housing: CARLOS BASTOS.

Minister of Labour: PATRICIA BULLRICH.

Minister of Health and Social Development: HÉCTOR LOMBARDO.

Minister of Justice: JORGE DE LA RÚA.

MINISTRIES

General Secretariat to the Presidency: Balcarce 50, 1064 Buenos Aires; tel. (11) 4344-3662; fax (11) 4344-3789; e-mail secgral @presidencia.net.ar.

Ministry of Defence: Avda Paseo Colón 255, 9°, 1063 Buenos Aires; tel. (11) 4343-1560; fax (11) 4331-7745; internet www.mindef.gov.ar.

Ministry of the Economy: Hipólito Yrigoyen 250, 1310 Buenos Aires; tel. (11) 4342-6411; fax (11) 4331-7426; internet www.mecon .gov.ar.

Ministry of Education: Pizzurno 935, 1020 Buenos Aires; tel. (11) 442-4551; fax (11) 4812-8905; internet www.me.gov.ar/index1.html.

Ministry of Foreign Affairs: Reconquista 1088, 1003 Buenos Aires; tel. (11) 4311-0071; fax (11) 4311-5730; internet www.mrecic .gov.ar.

Ministry of Health: 9 de Julio 1925, 1332 Buenos Aires; tel. (11) 4381-8911; fax (11) 4381-2182; internet www.msal.gov.ar.

Ministry of Infrastructure and Housing: Buenos Aires.

Ministry of the Interior: Balcarce 50, 1064 Buenos Aires; tel. (11) 446-9841; fax (11) 4331-6376; internet www.mininterior.gov.ar.

Ministry of Justice: Talcahuano 550, 1013 Buenos Aires; tel. (11) 4803-4051; fax (11) 4803-3955; internet www.jus.gov.ar.

Ministry of Labour: Leandro N. Alem 650, 1001 Buenos Aires; tel. (11) 4311-2913; fax (11) 4312-7860; internet www.trabajo.gov.ar.

Ministry of Social Development: Avda 9 de Julio 1925, 14°, 1332 Buenos Aires; e-mail desarrollosocial@viaetworks.net.ar; internet www.desarrollosocial.gov.ar/Home.jsp.

President and Legislature

PRESIDENT

Election, 24 October 1999

Candidates	Votes	% votes cast
FERNANDO DE LA RÚA (ATJE)	9,039,892	48.50
EDUARDO DUHALDE (PJ)	7,100,678	38.09
DOMINGO CAVALLO (AR)	1,881,417	10.09
Others	618,846	3.32
Total	**18,640,833**	**100.00**

CONGRESO
Cámara de Diputados
(Chamber of Deputies)

President: RAFAEL MANUEL PASCUAL.

The Chamber has 257 members, who hold office for a four-year term, with approximately one-half of the seats renewable every two years.

Legislative Elections, 24 October 1999*

	Seats
Alianza para el Trabajo, la Justicia y la Educación (ATJE)†	127
Partido Justicialista (PJ).	101
Acción por la República (AR).	12
Others	17
Total	**257**

* The table indicates the distribution of the total number of seats, following the elections for 130 seats.

† Alliance comprising Frente del País Solidario and the Unión Cívica Radical.

Senado
(Senate)

President: MARIO LOSADA.

Distribution of Seats, November 1997*

	Seats
Partido Justicialista (PJ)	36
Unión Cívica Radical (UCR)	15
Frente del País Solidario (Frepaso)	2
Provincial parties	10
Total	**63**

* Until October 1995 the Senate comprised 48 members, who were nominated by the legislative bodies of the Federal District, the National Territory, and each province (two Senators for each), with the exception of Buenos Aires, which elected its Senators by means of a special Electoral College. The Senate's term of office was nine years, with one-third of the seats renewable every three years. Since October 1995 elections have provided for an expanded Senate (three members from each region) with a six-year term of office (one-third of the seats being renewable every three years).

PROVINCIAL ADMINISTRATORS
(March 2001)

Mayor of the Federal District of Buenos Aires: ANÍBAL IBARRA.

Governor of the Province of Buenos Aires: CARLOS RUCKAUF.

Governor of the Province of Catamarca: OSCAR CASTILLO.

Governor of the Province of Chaco: ANGEL ROZAS.

Governor of the Province of Chubut: JOSÉ LUIS LIZURUME.

Governor of the Province of Córdoba: JOSÉ MANUEL DE LA SOTA.

Governor of the Province of Corrientes: (vacant)*.

Governor of the Province of Entre Ríos: SERGIO MONTIEL.

Governor of the Province of Formosa: GILDO INSFRÁN.

Governor of the Province of Jujuy: EDUARDO FELLNER.

Governor of the Province of La Pampa: RUBÉN HUGO MARÍN.

Governor of the Province of La Rioja: ANGEL EDUARDO MAZA.

Governor of the Province of Mendoza: ROBERTO IGLESIAS.

Governor of the Province of Misiones: CARLOS ROVIRA.

Governor of the Province of Neuquén: JORGE SOBISCH.

Governor of the Province of Río Negro: PABLO VERANI.

Governor of the Province of Salta: JUAN CARLOS ROMERO.

Governor of the Province of San Juan: ALFREDO AVELÍN.

Governor of the Province of San Luis: ADOLFO RODRÍGUEZ SAA.

Governor of the Province of Santa Cruz: NÉSTOR KIRSCHNER.

Governor of the Province of Santa Fe: CARLOS REUTEMANN.

Governor of the Province of Santiago del Estero: CARLOS JUÁREZ.

Governor of the Province of Tucumán: JULIO MIRANDA.

Governor of the Territory of Tierra del Fuego: CARLOS MANFRE-DOTTI.

* Ramón Mestre was appointed as mediator of Corrientes in December 1999.

Political Organizations

Acción por la República—Nueva Dirigencia (AR—ND): Buenos Aires; f. 1997; electoral alliance; Leaders DOMINGO CAVALLO, GUSTAVO BÉLIZ.

Acción por la República (AR): Buenos Aires; e-mail accionrepublic@geocities.com; f. 1997; right-wing; Leader DOMINGO CAVALLO.

Nueva Dirigencia (ND): Buenos Aires; f. 1996; centre-right; Leader GUSTAVO BÉLIZ.

Alianza para el Trabajo, la Justicia y la Educación (ATJE): Buenos Aires; f. 1997; electoral alliance comprising the UCR and Frepaso.

Frente del País Solidario (Frepaso): Buenos Aires; internet www.visit-ar.com/nuevoespacio/frepaso.htm; f. 1994; centre-left coalition of socialist, communist and Christian Democrat groups; Leader CARLOS ALVAREZ.

Unión Cívica Radical (UCR): Alsina 1786, 1088 Buenos Aires; tel. and fax (11) 4375-2000; e-mail info@ucr.org.ar; internet www.ucr.org.ar; moderate; f. 1890; Pres. RAÚL ALFONSÍN; 2,920,650 mems.

Movimiento por la Dignidad y la Independencia (Modin): Buenos Aires; f. 1991; right-wing; Leader Col ALDO RICO.

Movimiento de Integración y Desarrollo (MID): Buenos Aires; f. 1963; Leader ARTURO FRONDIZI; 145,000 mems.

Movimiento al Socialismo (MAS): Chile 1362, 1098 Buenos Aires; tel. (11) 4381-2718; fax (11) 4381-2976; e-mail mas@giga.com.ar; internet www.wp.com/mas; Leaders RUBÉN VISCONTI, LUIS ZAMORA; 55,000 mems.

Partido Comunista de Argentina: Buenos Aires; f. 1918; Leader PATRICIO ECHEGARAY; Sec.-Gen. ATHOS FAVA; 76,000 mems.

Partido Demócrata Cristiano (PDC): Combate de los Pozos 1055, 1222 Buenos Aires; fax (11) 426-3413; f. 1954; Leader ESIO ARIEL SILVEIRA; 85,000 mems.

Partido Demócrata Progresista (PDP): Chile 1934, 1227 Buenos Aires; Leader RAFAEL MARTÍNEZ RAYMONDA; 97,000 mems.

Partido Intransigente: Buenos Aires; f. 1957; left-wing; Leaders Dr OSCAR ALENDE, LISANDRO VIALE; Sec. MARIANO LORENCES; 90,000 mems.

Partido Justicialista (PJ): Buenos Aires; Peronist party; f. 1945; Pres. CARLOS SAÚL MENEM; 3m. mems; three factions within party:

Frente Renovador, Justicia, Democracia y Participación—Frejudepa: f. 1985; reformist wing; Leaders CARLOS SAÚL MENEM, ANTONIO CAFIERO, CARLOS GROSSO.

Movimiento Nacional 17 de Octubre: Leader HERMINIO IGLESIAS.

Oficialistas: Leaders JOSÉ MARÍA VERNET, LORENZO MIGUEL.

Partido Nacional de Centro: Buenos Aires; f. 1980; conservative; Leader RAÚL RIVANERA CARLES.

Partido Nacionalista de los Trabajadores (PNT): Buenos Aires; f. 1990; extreme right-wing; Leader ALEJANDRO BIONDINI.

Partido Obrero: Ayacucho 444, Buenos Aires; tel. (11) 4953-3824; fax (11) 4953-7164; internet www.po.org.ar; f. 1982; Trotskyist; Leaders JORGE ALTAMIRA, CHRISTIAN RATH; 61,000 mems.

Partido Popular Cristiano: Leader JOSÉ ANTONIO ALLENDE.

Partido Socialista Democrático: Rivadavia 2307, 1034 Buenos Aires; Leader AMÉRICO GHIOLDI; 39,000 mems.

Partido Socialista Popular: f. 1982; Leaders GUILLERMO ESTÉVEZ BOERO, EDGARDO ROSSI; 60,500 mems.

Política Abierta para la Integridad Social (PAIS): Buenos Aires; f. 1994 following split with the PJ.

Unión del Centro Democrático (UCeDé): Buenos Aires; f. 1980 as coalition of eight minor political organizations to challenge the 'domestic monopoly' of the populist movements; Leader ÁLVARO ALSOGARAY.

Unión para la Nueva Mayoría: Buenos Aires; f. 1986; centre-right; Leader JOSÉ ANTONIO ROMERO FERIS.

The following political parties and groupings contested the 1999 presidential elections: Alianza Cristiana Social, Frente para la Resistencia Social, Izquierda Unida, Partido Humanista, Partido Obrero, Partido Socialista Auténtico and the Partido de Trabajadores Socialistas.

Other parties and groupings include: Afirmación Peronista, Alianza Socialista, Confederación Socialista Argentina, Cruzada Renovadora (San Juan), Frente Cívica y Socialista (Catamarca), Fuerza Republicana (Tucumán), Movimiento Línea Popular, Movimiento Patriótico de Liberación, Movimiento Peronista, Movimiento Popular Neuquino, Movimiento Popular (Tierra del Fuego), Partido Autonomista (Corrientes), Partido Bloquista de San Juan, Partido Conservador Popular, Partido Izquierda Nacional, Partido Liberal (Corrientes), Partido Obrero Comunista Marxista-Leninista, Partido Socialista Unificado and Renovador de Salta.

The following political parties and guerrilla groups are illegal:

Intransigencia y Movilización Peronista: Peronist faction; Leader NILDA GARRES.

Movimiento Todos por la Patria (MTP): left-wing movement.

Partido Peronista Auténtico (PPA): f. 1975; Peronist faction; Leaders MARIO FIRMENICH, OSCAR BIDEGAIN, RICARDO OBREGÓN CANO.

Partido Revolucionario de Trabajadores: political wing of the **Ejército Revolucionario del Pueblo (ERP)**; Leader LUIS MATTINI.

Triple A—Alianza Anticomunista Argentina: extreme right-wing; Leader ANÍBAL GORDON (in prison).

Diplomatic Representation

EMBASSIES IN ARGENTINA

Albania: Avda del Libertador 946, 4°, 1001 Buenos Aires; tel. (11) 4812-8366; fax (11) 4815-2512; e-mail ambasada.bue@netsat.com.ar; Ambassador: EDMOND TRAKO.

Algeria: Montevideo 1889, 1021 Buenos Aires; tel. (11) 4815-1271; fax (11) 4815-8837; e-mail argelia@peoples.com.ar; Ambassador: NOURREDINE AYADI.

Armenia: Avda Roque S. Peña 570, 3°, 1035 Buenos Aires; tel. (11) 4345-2051; fax (11) 4343-2467; e-mail armenia@teletel.com.ar; Ambassador: ARA AIVASYAN.

Australia: Villanueva 1400, 1426 Buenos Aires; tel. (11) 4777-6580; fax (11) 4776-3349; e-mail dima-buenos_aires@dfait.gov.au; internet www.australia.org.ar; Ambassador: SHARYN MINAHAN.

Austria: French 3671, 1425 Buenos Aires; tel. (11) 4802-7195; fax (11) 4805-4016; Ambassador: STANDENAT YURI.

Belarus: Cazadores 2166, 1428 Buenos Aires; tel. (11) 4788-9394; fax (11) 4788-2322; Ambassador: VADIM LAZERKO.

Belgium: Defensa 113, 8°, 1065 Buenos Aires; tel. (11) 4331-0066; fax (11) 4311-0814; e-mail buenosaires@diplobel.org; internet www.diplobel.org/argentina/default.htm; Ambassador: RONALD DE LANGHE.

Bolivia: Avda Corrientes 545, 2°, 1043 Buenos Aires; tel. (11) 4394-6042; Ambassador: FERNANDO B. BALLIVIAN.

Bosnia and Herzegovina: Miñones 2445, Buenos Aires; tel. (11) 4896-0284; fax (11) 4896-0351; Ambassador: DUSKO LADAN.

Brazil: Arroyo 1142, 1007 Buenos Aires; tel. (11) 444-0035; fax (11) 4814-4085; e-mail embras@embrasil.org.ar; internet www.brasil.org.ar; Ambassador: SEBASTIÃO DO REGO BARROS NETTO.

Bulgaria: Mariscal A. J. de Sucre 1568, 1428 Buenos Aires; tel. (11) 4781-8644; fax (11) 4786-6273; e-mail embular@sinectis.com.ar; internet www.sinectis.com.ar/u/embular; Ambassador: ATRANAS I. BUDEV.

Canada: Tagle 2828, 1425 Buenos Aires; tel. (11) 4805-3032; fax (11) 4806-1209; internet www.dfait-maeci.gc.ca/bairs; Ambassador: JEAN-PAUL HUBERT.

Central African Republic: Marcelo T. de Alvear 776, Edif. Charcas, Buenos Aires; tel. (11) 4312-2051.

Chile: Tagle 2762, 1425 Buenos Aires; tel. (11) 4802-7020; Ambassador: JORGE ARRATE MACNIVEN.

China, People's Republic: Avda Crisólogo Larralde 5349, 1431 Buenos Aires; tel. (11) 4543-8862; Ambassador: XU YICONG.

Colombia: Carlos Pellegrini 1363, 3°, 1011 Buenos Aires; tel. (11) 4325-0494; fax (11) 4322-9370; e-mail emargent@internet.siscotel.com; Ambassador: NELSON P. HERNÁNDEZ.

Congo, Democratic Republic: Callao 322, 2°, Buenos Aires; tel. (11) 4373-7565; fax (11) 4374-9865; Ambassador: BADASSA-BAHADUKA.

Costa Rica: Avda Callao 1103, 9°I, 1023 Buenos Aires; tel. (11) 4815-8160; fax (11) 4815-8159; Ambassador: EDUARDO F. OTOYA BOULANG.

Croatia: Gorostiaga 2104, 1426 Buenos Aires; tel. (11) 4777-6409; fax (11) 4777-9159; Ambassador: MATKO MEDO.

Cuba: Virrey del Pino 1810, 1426 Buenos Aires; tel. (11) 4782-9049; fax (11) 4786-7713; e-mail embcuba@teletel.com.ar; Ambassador: ALEJANDRO J. GONZÁLEZ.

Czech Republic: Avda Figueroa Alcorta 3240, 1425 Buenos Aires; tel. (11) 4801-3804; e-mail buenosaires@embassy.mzv.cz; Ambassador: EDITA HRDA.

Denmark: Avda Leandro N. Alem 1074, 9°, 1001 Buenos Aires; tel. (11) 4312-6901; fax (11) 4312-7857; e-mail ambadane@ambadane.org.ar; Ambassador: JENS PETER LARSEN.

Dominican Republic: Avda Santa Fe 1206, 2°C, 1059 Buenos Aires; tel. (11) 4811-4669; fax (11) 4804-3902; Ambassador: CIRILO J. CASTELLANOS ARAÚJO.

Ecuador: Quintana 585, 9° y 10°, 1129 Buenos Aires; tel. (11) 4804-0073; fax (11) 4804-0074; Ambassador: EDUARDO R. MORA ANDA.

Egypt: Olleros 2140, 1425 Buenos Aires; tel. (11) 4899-0300; fax (11) 4899-0803; Ambassador: MOHAMED DAGHASH.

El Salvador: Avda Santa Fe 882, 12°A, 1059 Buenos Aires; tel. (11) 4311-1864; fax (11) 4314-7628; Ambassador: ALFONSO QUIÑÓNEZ MEZA.

Finland: Avda Santa Fe 846, 5°, 1059 Buenos Aires; tel. (11) 4312-0600; fax (11) 4312-0670; e-mail finembue@sinectis.com.ar; internet www.finlandia.org.ar; Ambassador: ERKKI KIVIMÄKI.

France: Cerrito 1399, 1010 Buenos Aires; tel. (11) 4819-2930; fax (11) 4393-1235; e-mail ambafr@impsat1.com.ar; internet www.embafrancia-argentina.org; Ambassador: PAUL DIJOUD.

Gabon: Avda Figueroa Alcorta 3221, 1425 Buenos Aires; tel. (11) 4801-9840; Ambassador: J.-B. EYI-NKOUMOU.

Germany: Villanueva 1055, 1426 Buenos Aires; tel. (11) 4778-2500; fax (11) 4778-2550; e-mail embalem@infovia.com.ar; internet www.embalemana.com.ar; Ambassador: HANS ULRICH D. SPOHN.

Greece: Avda Roque S. Peña 547, 4°, 1035 Buenos Aires; tel. (11) 4342-4598; fax (11) 4342-2838; Ambassador: GEORGES GEORGIOU.

Guatemala: Avda Santa Fe 830, 5°, 1059 Buenos Aires; tel. (11) 4313-9160; fax (11) 4313-9181; e-mail embagua@peoples.com.ar; Ambassador: ERNESTO GÁLVEZ CORONADO.

Haiti: Avda Figueroa Alcorta 3297, 1425 Buenos Aires; tel. (11) 4802-0211; fax (11) 4802-3984; e-mail embahaiti@interar.com.ar; Ambassador: EDRIS SAINT-AMAND.

Holy See: Avda Alvear 1605, 1014 Buenos Aires; tel. (11) 4813-9697; fax (11) 4815-4097; Apostolic Nuncio: Most Rev. SANTOS ABRIL Y CASTELLÓ, Titular Archbishop of Tamada.

Honduras: Avda Libertador 1146, 1112 Buenos Aires; tel. (11) 4804-6181; fax (11) 4804-3222; Ambassador: NAPOLEÓN ALVAREZ ALVARADO.

Hungary: Coronel Díaz 1874, 1425 Buenos Aires; tel. (11) 4822-0767; fax (11) 4805-3918; e-mail hungria@escape.com.ar; Ambassador: BELA BARDOCZ.

India: Córdoba 950, 4°, 1054 Buenos Aires; tel. (11) 4393-4001; fax (11) 4393-4063; e-mail indembarg@infomatic.com.ar; internet www.indembarg.org.ar; Ambassador: NIGAM PRAKASH.

Indonesia: Mariscal Ramón Castilla 2901, 1425 Buenos Aires; tel. (11) 4807-2211; fax (11) 4802-4448; e-mail emindo@tournet.com.ar; Ambassador: ACHMAD SURYADI.

Iran: Avda Figueroa Alcorta 3229, 1425 Buenos Aires; tel. (11) 4802-1470; fax (11) 4805-4409; Chargé d'affaires a.i.: ABDOLRA SADATIFAR.

Ireland: Suipacha 1380, 2°, 1011 Buenos Aires; tel. (11) 4325-8588; fax (11) 4325-7572; e-mail embirl@tournet.com.ar; internet irlgov.ie/iveagh; Ambassador: PAULA SLATTERY.

Israel: Avda. de Mayo 701, 10°, 1084 Buenos Aires; tel. (11) 4338-2500; internet www.israel-embassy.org.ar/embajada.html; Ambassador: BENJAMIN ORON.

Italy: Billinghurst 2577, 1425 Buenos Aires; tel. (11) 4802-0071; fax (11) 4804-4914; e-mail stampa@ambitalia-bsas.org.ar; internet www.ambitalia-bsas.org.ar; Ambassador: GIOVANNI JANNUZZI.

Japan: Bouchard 547, 17°, Buenos Aires; tel. (11) 4318-8200; fax (11) 4318-8210; Ambassador: TERUO KIJIMA.

Korea, Republic: Avda del Libertador 2395, 1425 Buenos Aires; tel. (11) 4802-8062; fax (11) 4803-6993; e-mail embcorea@cscom.com.ar; internet www.mofat.go.kr/argentina.htm; Ambassador: SEUNG-YOUNG KIM.

Kuwait: Uruguay 739, 1015 Buenos Aires; tel. (11) 4374-7202; fax (11) 4374-8718; e-mail kuwait@microstar.com.ar; internet www.kuwait.com.ar; Ambassador: SALEM G. AZ-ZAMANAN.

Lebanon: Avda del Libertador 2354, 1425 Buenos Aires; tel. (11) 4802-4492; fax (11) 4802-2909; Ambassador: HICHAM SALIM HAMDAN.

Libya: 3 de Febrero 1358, 1426 Buenos Aires; tel. (11) 4788-3760; fax (11) 4788-9394; Chargé d'affaires a.i.: ASSED MOHAMED ALMUTAA.

Malaysia: Villanueva 1040-1048, 1062 Buenos Aires; tel. (11) 4776-0504; e-mail malasia@fibertel.com.ar; Ambassador: Dato M. SAN-THANANABAN.

Malta: Avda de Mayo 633, 7°, 1084 Buenos Aires; tel. (11) 4312-7704; fax (11) 4312-7687; Ambassador: PEDRO DE OCAMPO.

Mexico: Larrea 1230, 1117 Buenos Aires; tel. (11) 4821-7172; fax (11) 4821-7251; e-mail embamexarg@intlink.com.ar; Ambassador: JAIME G. FIGUEROA ZAMUDIO.

Morocco: Mariscal Ramón Castilla 2952, 1425 Buenos Aires; tel. (11) 4801-8154; fax (11) 4802-0136; e-mail sifamabueno@tournet.com.ar; internet www.embajadamarruecos.com.ar; Ambassador: MOHAMED MAA EL-AININ.

Netherlands: Avda de Mayo 701, 19°, 1084 Buenos Aires; tel. (11) 4334-4000; fax (11) 4334-2717; e-mail nlgovbue@informatic.com.ar; Ambassador: J. E. CRAANEN.

New Zealand: Buenos Aires; tel. (11) 4328-0747; fax (11) 4328-0757; Ambassador: CAROLINE FORSYTH.

Nicaragua: Avda Corrientes 2548, 4°I, 1426 Buenos Aires; tel. (11) 4951-3463; fax (11) 4952-7557; e-mail embanic@overnet.com.ar; Ambassador: ARIEL RAMÓN GRANERA SACASA.

Nigeria: Rosales 2674, 1636 Olivos, Buenos Aires; tel. (11) 4771-6541; fax (11) 4790-7564; Ambassador: MOHAMMAD A. WALI.

Norway: Esmeralda 909, 3°B, 1007 Buenos Aires; tel. (11) 4312-2204; fax (11) 4315-2831; e-mail embajada.noruega@way.net.ar; Ambassador: SISSEL BREIE.

Pakistan: Gorostiaga 2176, 1426 Buenos Aires; tel. (11) 4782-7663; fax (11) 4776-1186; e-mail parepbaires@sinectis.com.ar; Ambassador: SAEED KHALID.

Panama: Avda Santa Fe 1461, 5°, 1060 Buenos Aires; tel. (11) 4811-1254; fax (11) 4814-0450; e-mail epar@ba.net; Ambassador: MERCEDES ALFARO DE LÓPEZ.

Paraguay: Avda Las Heras 2545, 1425 Buenos Aires; tel. (11) 4802-3826; fax (11) 4801-0657; Ambassador: OSCAR FACUNDO YNSFRÁN.

Peru: Avda del Libertador 1720, 1425 Buenos Aires; tel. (11) 4802-2000; fax (11) 4802-5887; Ambassador: HUGO DE ZELA MARTÍNEZ.

Philippines: Juramento 1945, 1428 Buenos Aires; tel. (11) 4781-4173; fax (11) 4783-8171; e-mail phba@peoples.com.ar; Ambassador: CARLOS A. VILLA ABRILLE.

Poland: Alejandro M. de Aguado 2870, 1425 Buenos Aires; tel. (11) 4802-9681; fax (11) 4802-9683; e-mail polemb@datamarkets.com.ar; Ambassador: EUGENIUSZ NOWORYTA.

Portugal: Córdoba 315, 3°, 1054 Buenos Aires; tel. (11) 4311-2586; fax (11) 4311-2586; Ambassador: MARCELLO DE ZAFFIRI D. MATHIAS.

Romania: Arroyo 962-970, 1007 Buenos Aires; tel. and fax (11) 4322-2630; e-mail embarombue@fibertel.com.ar; Ambassador: CRISTIAN LAZARESCU.

Russia: Rodríguez Peña 1741, 1021 Buenos Aires; tel. (11) 4813-1552; fax (11) 4812-1794; Ambassador: IAN A. BURLIAY.

Saudi Arabia: Alejandro M. de Aguado 2881, 1425 Buenos Aires; tel. (11) 4802-4735; Ambassador: ADNAN B. BAGHDADI.

Slovakia: Avda Figueroa Alcorta 3240, 1425 Buenos Aires; tel. (11) 4786-0692; fax (11) 4786-0938; Ambassador: JAN JURISTA.

Slovenia: Suipacha 1380, 3°, 1001 Buenos Aires; tel. (11) 4393-2067; fax (11) 4326-0829; Ambassador: JANEZ ZGAJNAR.

South Africa: Marcelo T. de Alvear 590, 8°, 1058 Buenos Aires; tel. (11) 4317-2900; fax (11) 4317-2951; e-mail saemba@sicoar.com; Ambassador: AUBREY X. NKOMO.

Spain: Mariscal Ramón Castilla 2720, 1425 Buenos Aires; tel. (11) 4802-6031; fax (11) 4802-0719; Ambassador: MANUEL ALABART.

Sweden: Casilla 3599, Correo Central 1000, Buenos Aires; tel. (11) 4311-3088; fax (11) 4311-8052; e-mail swedemb@infovia.com.ar; Ambassador: PETER LANDELIUS.

Switzerland: Avda Santa Fe 846, 10°, 1059 Buenos Aires; tel. (11) 4311-6491; fax (11) 4313-2998; e-mail vertretung@bue.rep.admin.ch; Ambassador: ARMIN RITZ.

Syria: Calloa 956, 1023 Buenos Aires; tel. (11) 4813-2113; fax (11) 4814-3211; Ambassador: ABD AL-HASSIB ITSWANI.

Thailand: Virrey del Pino 2458, 6°, 1426 Buenos Aires; tel. (11) 4785-6504; fax (11) 4785-6548; e-mail thbsemb@tournet.com.ar; Ambassador: PONGSAK DISYATAT.

Tunisia: Ciudad de la Paz 3086, 1429 Buenos Aires; tel. (11) 4544-2618; fax (11) 4545-6369; e-mail embtun@peoples.com.ar; Ambassador: GHAZI JOMAA.

Turkey: 11 de Setiembre 1382, 1426 Buenos Aires; tel. (11) 4788-3239; fax (11) 4784-9179; e-mail iyihava@ba.net; Ambassador: ERHAN YIGITBASIOGLU.

Ukraine: Lafinur 3057, 1425 Buenos Aires; tel. (11) 4802-7316; fax (11) 4802-3864; Chargé d'affaires a.i.: IHOR IUMASSOV.

United Kingdom: Dr Luis Agote 2412/52, 1425 Buenos Aires; tel. (11) 4803-7070; fax (11) 4806-5713; e-mail ukembarg@starnet .net.ar; internet www.britain.org.ar; Ambassador: Sir ROBIN CHRISTOPHER.

USA: Avda Colombia 4300, 1425 Buenos Aires; tel. (11) 4774-7611; fax (11) 4775-4205; internet usembassy.state.gov/baires_embassy; Ambassador: JAMES D. WALSH.

Uruguay: Avda Las Heras 1907, 1127 Buenos Aires; tel. (11) 4803-6030; fax (11) 4807-3050; e-mail embarou@impsat1.com.ar; Ambassador: ALBERTO C. VOLONTE BERRO.

Venezuela: Virrey Loreto 2035, 1428 Buenos Aires; tel. (11) 4788-4944; fax (11) 4784-4311; e-mail venargs@peoples.com.ar; internet www.la.embajada.com.ar; Ambassador: EDMUNDO GONZÁLEZ URRUTIA.

Viet Nam: 11 de Septiembre 1442, 1426 Buenos Aires; tel. (11) 4783-1802; fax (11) 4782-0078; e-mail sqvnartn@teletel.com.ar; Ambassador: TRAN-QUANG HOAN.

Yugoslavia: Marcelo T. de Alvear 1705, 1060 Buenos Aires; tel. (11) 4811-2860; fax (11) 4812-1070; e-mail snovak@ipm.net; Ambassador: GOJKO CELEBIC.

Judicial System

SUPREME COURT

Corte Suprema: Talcahuano 550, 4°, 1013 Buenos Aires; tel. (11) 440-0837; fax (11) 440-2270; internet www.pjn.gov.ar/corte.htm.

The nine members of the Supreme Court are appointed by the President, with the agreement of at least two-thirds of the Senate. Members are dismissed by impeachment.

President: JULIO SALVADOR NAZARENO.

Vice-President: EDUARDO MOLINÉ O'CONNOR.

Justices: CARLOS SANTIAGO FAYT, AUGUSTO CÉSAR BELLUSCIO, ENRIQUE SANTIAGO PETRACCHI, ADOLFO VÁZQUEZ, ANTONIO BOGGIANO, GUILLERMO A. F. LÓPEZ, GUSTAVO A. BOSSERT.

OTHER COURTS

Judges of the lower, national or further lower courts are appointed by the President, with the agreement of the Senate, and are dismissed by impeachment. From 1999, however, judges were to retire on reaching 75 years of age.

The Federal Court of Appeal in Buenos Aires has three courts: civil and commercial, criminal, and administrative. There are six other courts of appeal in Buenos Aires: civil, commercial, criminal, peace, labour, and penal-economic. There are also federal appeal courts in: La Plata, Bahía Blanca, Paraná, Rosario, Córdoba, Mendoza, Tucumán and Resistencia. In August 1994, following constitutional amendments, the Office of the Attorney-General was established as an independent entity and a Council of Magistrates was envisaged. In December 1997 the Senate adopted legislation to create the Council.

The provincial courts each have their own Supreme Court and a system of subsidiary courts. They deal with cases originating within and confined to the provinces.

Attorney-General: OSCAR LUJÁN FAPPIANO.

Religion

CHRISTIANITY

More than 90% of the population are Roman Catholics and about 2% are Protestants.

Federación Argentina de Iglesias Evangélicas (Argentine Federation of Evangelical Churches): José María Moreno 873, 1424 Buenos Aires; tel. and fax (11) 4922-5356; e-mail faie@faie.com.ar; f. 1938; 29 mem. churches; Pres. Rev. RODOLFO B. REINICH (Río de la Plata Evangelical Church); Exec. Sec. Rev. FLORENCIA HIMITIAN.

The Roman Catholic Church

Argentina comprises 14 archdioceses, 49 dioceses (including one each for Uniate Catholics of the Ukrainian rite, of the Maronite rite and of the Armenian rite) and three territorial prelatures. The Archbishop of Buenos Aires is also the Ordinary for Catholics of Oriental rites, and the Bishop of San Gregorio de Narek en Buenos Aires is also the Apostolic Exarch of Latin America and Mexico for Catholics of the Armenian rite.

Bishops' Conference: Conferencia Episcopal Argentina, Suipacha 1034, 1008 Buenos Aires; tel. (11) 4328-0993; fax (11) 4328-9570; e-mail seccea@satlink.com.ar; f. 1959; Pres. Mgr ESTANISLAO ESTEBAN KARLIC, Archbishop of Paraná.

Armenian Rite

Bishop of San Gregorio de Narek en Buenos Aires: VARTAN WALDIR BOGHOSSIAN, Charcas 3529, 1425 Buenos Aires; tel. (11) 4824-1613; fax (11) 4827-1975; e-mail exarmal@usa.net; internet www.fast.to/exarcado.

Latin Rite

Archbishop of Bahía Blanca: RÓMULO GARCÍA, Avda Colón 164, 8000 Bahía Blanca; tel. (291) 455-0707; fax (291) 452-2070; e-mail arzobispado@bblanca.com.ar.

Archbishop of Buenos Aires: Cardinal JORGE BERGOGLIO, Arzobispado, Rivadavia 415, 1002 Buenos Aires; tel. (11) 4343-3925; fax (11) 4334-8373; e-mail arzobispado@arzbaires.org.ar.

Archbishop of Córdoba: CARLOS JOSÉ NÁÑEZ, Hipólito Yrigoyen 98, 5000 Córdoba; tel. (351) 422-1015; fax (351) 425-5082.

Archbishop of Corrientes: DOMINGO SALVADOR CASTAGNA, 9 de Julio 1543, 3400 Corrientes; tel. and fax (3783) 422436; e-mail arzctes@ arnet.com.ar.

Archbishop of La Plata: CARLOS GALÁN, Arzobispado, Calle 14, 1009, 1900 La Plata; tel. (221) 425-1656; fax (221) 425-8269; e-mail arzolap@satlink.com.

Archbishop of Mendoza: JOSÉ MARÍA ARANCIBIA, Catamarca 98, 5500 Mendoza; tel. (261) 423-3862; fax (261) 429-5415; e-mail arzobispadomza@supernet.com.ar.

Archbishop of Mercedes-Luján: EMILIO OGNÉNOVICH, Calle 22, No 745, 6600 Mercedes, Buenos Aires; tel. (2324) 432-412; fax (2324) 432-104.

Archbishop of Paraná: Mgr ESTANISLAO ESTEBAN KARLIC, Monte Caseros 77, 3100 Paraná; tel. (343) 431-1440; fax (343) 423-0372; e-mail arzparan@satlink.com.ar.

Archbishop of Resistencia: CARMELO JUAN GIAQUINTA, Bartolomé Mitre 363, Casilla 35, 3500 Resistencia; tel. and fax (3722) 434573; e-mail arzobrcia@lareel.com.ar.

Archbishop of Rosario: EDUARDO VICENTE MIRÁS, Córdoba 1677, 2000 Rosario; tel. (341) 425-1298; fax (341) 425-1207; e-mail arzobros@lidernet.co.ar; internet www.lidernet.com.ar/arzobros.

Archbishop of Salta: MARIO ANTONIO CARGNELLO, España 596, 4400 Salta; tel. (387) 421-4306; fax (387) 421-3101.

Archbishop of San Juan de Cuyo: ITALO SEVERINO DI STÉFANO, Bartolomé Mitre 250 Oeste, 5400 San Juan de Cuyo; tel. (264) 422-2578; fax (264) 427-3530.

Archbishop of Santa Fe de la Vera Cruz: EDGARDO GABRIEL STORNI, Avda General López 2720, 3000 Santa Fe; tel. (342) 459-5791; fax (342) 459-4491; e-mail arzobsfe@infovia.com.ar.

Archbishop of Tucumán: LUIS HÉCTOR VILLALBA, Avda Sarmiento 895, 4000 San Miguel de Tucumán; tel. (381) 422-6345; fax (381) 431-0617; e-mail arztuc@arnet.com.ar.

Maronite Rite

Bishop of San Charbel en Buenos Aires: CHARBEL MERHI, Eparquía Maronita, Paraguay 834, 1057 Buenos Aires; tel. (11) 4311-7299; fax (11) 4312-8348; e-mail mcharbel@hotmail.com.

Ukrainian Rite

Bishop of Santa María del Patrocinio en Buenos Aires: (vacant); Apostolic Administrator: Rt Rev. MIGUEL MYKYCEJ (Titular Bishop of Nazianzus), Ramón L. Falcón 3950, Casilla 28, 1407 Buenos Aires; tel. (11) 4671-4192.

The Anglican Communion

The Iglesia Anglicana del Cono Sur de América (Anglican Church of the Southern Cone of America) was formally inaugurated in Buenos Aires in April 1983. The Church comprises seven dioceses: Argentina, Northern Argentina, Chile, Paraguay, Peru, Bolivia and Uruguay. The Primate is the Bishop of Northern Argentina.

Bishop of Argentina: Rt Rev. DAVID LEAKE, 25 de Mayo 282, 1002 Buenos Aires; Casilla 4293, Correo Central 1000, Buenos Aires; tel. (11) 4342-4618; fax (11) 4331-0234; e-mail diocesisanglibue@arnet.com.ar.

Bishop of Northern Argentina: Rt Rev. MAURICE SINCLAIR, Casilla 187, 4400 Salta; jurisdiction extends to Jujuy, Salta, Tucumán, Catamarca, Santiago del Estero, Formosa and Chaco; tel. (387) 431-1718; fax (387) 431-2622; e-mail sinclair@salnet.com.ar.

Protestant Churches

Convención Evangélica Bautista Argentina (Baptist Evangelical Convention): Virrey Liniers 42, 1174 Buenos Aires; tel. and fax (11) 4864-2711; e-mail ceba@sion.com; f. 1909; Pres. CARLOS A. CARAMUTTI.

Iglesia Evangélica Congregacionalista (Evangelical Congregational Church): Perón 525, 3100 Paraná; tel. (43) 21-6172; f. 1924; 100 congregations, 8,000 mems, 24,000 adherents; Supt Rev. REYNOLDO HORSTT.

Iglesia Evangélica Luterana Argentina (Evangelical Lutheran Church of Argentina): Ing. Silveyra 1639-41, 1607 Villa Adelina, Buenos Aires; tel. (11) 4766-7948; fax (11) 4766-7948; f. 1905; 30,000 mems; Pres. WALDOMIRO MAILI.

Iglesia Evangélica del Río de la Plata (Evangelical Church of the River Plate): Mariscal Sucre 2855, 1428 Buenos Aires; tel. (11) 4787-0436; fax (11) 4787-0335; e-mail ierp@ierp.org.ar; f. 1899; 40,000 mems; Pres. JUAN PEDRO SCHAAD.

Iglesia Evangélica Metodista Argentina (Methodist Church of Argentina): Rivadavia 4044, 3°, 1205 Buenos Aires; tel. (11) 4982-3712; fax (11) 4981-0885; e-mail iema@iema.com.ar; internet www.iema.com.ar; f. 1836; 6,040 mems, 9,000 adherents, seven regional superintendents; Bishop ALDO M. ETCHEGOYEN; Exec. Sec.-Gen. Bd DANIEL A. FAVARO.

JUDAISM

Delegación de Asociaciones Israelitas Argentinas—DAIA (Delegation of Argentine Jewish Associations): Pasteur 633, 7°, 1028 Buenos Aires; tel. and fax (11) 4953-1785; e-mail daia@infovia.com.ar; f. 1935; there are about 250,000 Jews in Argentina, mostly in Buenos Aires; Pres. Dr RUBÉN E. BERAJA; Sec.-Gen. Dr JOSÉ KESTELMAN.

The Press

PRINCIPAL DAILIES

Buenos Aires

Ambito Financiero: Avda Paseo Colón 1196, 1063 Buenos Aires; tel. (11) 4349-1500; fax (11) 4349-1505; e-mail correo@afinanciero.com; internet www.afinanciero.com; f. 1976; morning (Mon.–Fri.); business; Dir JULIO A. RAMOS; circ. 115,000.

Buenos Aires Herald: Azopardo 455, 1107 Buenos Aires; tel. (11) 4342-1535; fax (11) 4334-7917; e-mail info@buenosairesherald.com; internet www.buenosairesherald.com; f. 1876; English; morning; independent; Editor-in-Chief ANDREW GRAHAM YOOLL; circ. 20,000.

Boletín Oficial de la República Argentina: Suipacha 767, 1008 Buenos Aires; tel. (11) 4322-3982; fax (11) 4322-3982; f. 1893; morning (Mon.–Fri.); official records publication; Dir RUBÉN ANTONIO SOSA; circ. 15,000.

Clarín: Piedras 1743, 1140 Buenos Aires; tel. (11) 4309-7500; fax (11) 4309-7559; e-mail lectores@www.clarin.com; internet www.clarin.com; f. 1945; morning; independent; Dir ERNESTINA L. HERRERA DE NOBLE; circ. 616,000 (daily), 1.0m. (Sunday).

Crónica: Avda Juan de Garay 40, 1063 Buenos Aires; tel. (11) 4361-1001; fax (11) 4361-4237; f. 1963; morning and evening; Dir MARIO ALBERTO FERNÁNDEZ (morning), RICARDO GANGEME (evening); circ. 330,000 (morning), 190,000 (evening), 450,000 (Sunday).

El Cronista: Honduras 5663, 1414 Buenos Aires; tel. (11) 4778-6789; fax (11) 4778-6727; e-mail cronista@sadei.org.ar; f. 1908; morning; Dir NÉSTOR SCIBONA; circ. 65,000.

Diario Popular: Beguiristain 142, 1872 Sarandí, Avellaneda, Buenos Aires; tel. (11) 4204-2778; fax (11) 4205-2376; e-mail redacpop@inea.net.ar; f. 1974; morning; Dir ALBERTO ALBERTENGO; circ. 145,000.

La Gaceta: Beguiristain 182, 1870 Avellaneda, Buenos Aires; Dir RICARDO WEST OCAMPO; circ. 35,000.

La Nación: Bouchard 551, 1106 Buenos Aires; tel. (11) 4319-1600; fax (11) 4319-1969; e-mail cescribano@lanacion.com.ar; internet www.lanacion.com.ar; f. 1870; morning; independent; Dir BARTOLOMÉ MITRE; circ. 184,000.

Página 12: Avda Belgrano 671, 1092 Buenos Aires; tel. (11) 4334-2334; fax (11) 4334-2335; e-mail lectores@pagina12.com.ar; internet www.pagina12.com.ar; f. 1987; morning; independent; Dir ERNESTO TIFFEMBERG; Editor FERNANDO SOKOLOWICZ; circ. 280,000.

La Prensa: Azopardo 715, 1107 Buenos Aires; tel. (11) 4349-1000; fax (11) 4349-1025; e-mail laprensa@interlink.com; internet www.interlink.com.ar/laprensa; f. 1869; morning; independent; Dir FLORENCIO ALDREY IGLESIAS; circ. 100,000.

La Razón: Río Cuarto 1242, 1168 Buenos Aires; tel. and fax (11) 4309-6000; e-mail larazon@arnet.com.ar; internet www.larazon.com.ar; f. 1992; evening; Dir OSCAR MAGDALENA; circ. 62,000.

El Sol: Hipólito Yrigoyen 122, Quilmes, 1878 Buenos Aires; tel. and fax (11) 4257-6325; e-mail elsol@elsolquilmes.com.ar; internet www.elsolquilmes.com.ar; f. 1927; Dir RODRIGO GHISANI; circ. 25,000.

Tiempo Argentino: Buenos Aires; tel. (11) 428-1929; Editor Dr TOMÁS LEONA; circ. 75,000.

PRINCIPAL PROVINCIAL DAILIES

Catamarca

El Ancasti: Sarmiento 526, 1°, 4700 Catamarca; tel. and fax (3833) 431385; e-mail ancasti@satlink.com; f. 1988; morning; Dir ROQUE EDUARDO MOLAS; circ. 8,000.

Chaco

Norte: Carlos Pellegrini 744, 3500 Resistencia; tel. (3722) 428204; fax (3722) 426047; e-mail prensanorte@diarionorte.com.ar; f. 1968; Dir MIGUEL A. FERNÁNDEZ; circ. 14,000.

Chubut

Crónica: Impresora Patagónica, Namuncurá 122, 9000 Comodoro Rivadavia; tel. (297) 447-1200; fax (297) 447-1780; e-mail cronica@arnet.com.ar; f. 1962; morning; Dir Dr DIEGO JOAQUÍN ZAMIT; circ. 15,000.

Córdoba

Comercio y Justicia: Mariano Moreno 378, 5000 Córdoba; tel. and fax (351) 422-0202; e-mail sistemas@powernet.com.ar; internet www.powernet.com.ar/cyj; f. 1939; morning; economic and legal news; Editor PABLO EGUÍA; circ. 5,800.

La Voz del Interior: Avellaneda 1661, 5000 Córdoba; tel. (351) 4757200; fax (351) 4757201; e-mail lavoz@satlink.com; internet www.intervoz.com.ar; f. 1904; morning; independent; Dir Dr CARLOS HUGO JORNET; circ. 68,000.

Corrientes

El Litoral: Hipólito Yrigoyen 990, 3400 Corrientes; tel. and fax (3783) 422227; e-mail el-litoral@compunort.com.ar; internet www.corrientes.com.ar/el-litoral/; f. 1960; morning; Dir CARLOS A. ROMERO FERIS; circ. 25,000.

El Territorio: Avda Quaranta 4307, 3300 Posadas; tel. and fax (3752) 452100; e-mail elterritorio@elterritorio.com.ar; internet www.elterritorio.com.ar; f. 1925; Dir GONZALO PELTZER; circ. 22,000 (Mon.–Fri.), 28,000 (Sunday).

Entre Ríos

El Diario: Buenos Aires y Urquiza, 3100 Paraná; tel. (343) 423-1000; fax (343) 431-9104; e-mail saer@satlink.com; internet www .eldiario.com.ar; f. 1914; morning; democratic; Dir Dr LUIS F. ETCHEVEHERE; circ. 25,000.

El Heraldo: Quintana 42, 3200 Concordia; tel. (345) 421-5304; fax (345) 421-1397; e-mail heraldo@infovia.com.ar; internet www .elheraldo.com.ar; f. 1915; evening; Editor Dr CARLOS LIEBERMANN; circ. 10,000.

Mendoza

Los Andes: Avda San Martín 1049, 5500 Mendoza; tel. (261) 4491200; fax (261) 4202011; e-mail amartinez@losandes.com.ar; internet www.losandes.net; f. 1982; morning; Dir JORGE ENRIQUE OVIEDO; circ. 107,000.

Provincia de Buenos Aires

El Atlántico: Bolívar 2975, 7600 Mar del Plata; tel. (223) 435462; f. 1938; morning; Dir OSCAR ALBERTO GASTIARENA; circ. 20,000.

La Capital: Avda Champagnat 2551, 7600 Mar del Plata; tel. (223) 478-8490; fax (223) 478-1038; e-mail diario@lacapitalnet.com.ar; internet www.lacapitalnet.com.ar; f. 1905; Dir FLORENCIO ALDREY IGLESIAS; circ. 32,000.

El Día: Avda A. Diagonal 80, 817-21, 1900 La Plata; tel. (221) 425-0101; fax (221) 423-2996; e-mail redaccion@eldia.com; f. 1884; morning; independent; Dir RAÚL E. KRAISELBURD; circ. 54,868.

Ecos Diarios: Calle 62, No 2486, 7630 Necochea; tel. (2262) 430754; fax (2262) 420485; e-mail ecosdiar@satlink.com; internet www .ecosdiarios.com.ar; f. 1921; morning; independent; Dir GUILLERMO IGNACIO; circ. 6,000.

La Nueva Provincia: Sarmiento 54–64, 8000 Bahía Blanca; tel. (291) 459-0000; fax (291) 459-0001; e-mail nprovin@relay.startel; internet www.lanueva.com.ar; f. 1898; morning; independent; Dir DIANA JULIO DE MASSOT; circ. 36,000 (Mon.–Fri.), 55,000 (Sunday).

La Voz del Pueblo: Avda San Martín 991, 7500 Tres Arroyos; tel. (2983) 430680; fax (2938) 430682; e-mail redaccion@lavozdelpueblo .com.ar; f. 1902; morning; independent; Dir ALBERTO JORGE MACIEL; circ. 8,500.

Río Negro

Río Negro: 9 de Julio 733, 8332, Gen. Roca, Río Negro; tel. (2941) 439300; fax (2941) 430517; e-mail rnredaccion@rionet.rionegro .com.ar; internet www.rionegro.com.ar; f. 1912; morning; Editor NÉLIDA RAJNERI DE GAMBA.

Salta

El Tribuno: Avda Ex Combatientes de Malvinas 3890, 4400 Salta; tel. (387) 424-0000; fax (387) 424-1382; e-mail tribuno@salnet .com.ar; internet www.eltribuno.com.ar; f. 1949; morning; Dir ROBERTO EDUARDO ROMERO; circ. 25,000.

San Juan

Diario de Cuyo: Mendoza 380 Sur, 5400 San Juan; tel. (264) 429-0016; fax (264) 429-0004; e-mail diarcuyo@esternet.net.ar; f. 1947; morning; independent; Dir FRANCISCO MONTES; circ. 25,000.

San Luis

El Diario de La República: Junín 741, 5700 San Luis; tel. (2623) 422037; fax (2623) 428770; e-mail paynesa@infovia.com.ar; f. 1966; Dir ZULEMA A. RODRÍGUEZ SAA DE DIVIZIA; circ. 12,000.

Santa Fe

La Capital: Sarmiento 763, 2000 Rosario; tel. (341) 420-1100; fax (341) 420-1114; e-mail elagos@lacapital.com.ar; f. 1867; morning; independent; Dir CARLOS MARÍA LAGOS; circ. 65,000.

El Litoral: Avda 25 de Mayo 3536, 3000 Santa Fe; tel. (342) 450-2500; fax (342) 450-2530; e-mail litoral@litoral.com.ar; internet www.litoral.com.ar; f. 1918; morning; independent; Dir GUSTAVO VÍTTORI; circ. 37,000.

Santiago del Estero

El Liberal: Libertad 263, 4200 Santiago del Estero; tel. (385) 422-4400; fax (385) 422-4538; e-mail liberal@teletel.com.ar; internet www.sdnet.com.ar; f. 1898; morning; Exec. Dir JOSÉ LUIS CASTIGLIONE; Editorial Dir Dr JULIO CÉSAR CASTIGLIONE; circ. 20,000.

Tucumán

La Gaceta: Mendoza 654, 4000 San Miguel de Tucumán; tel. (381) 431-1111; fax (381) 431-1597; e-mail redaccion@lagaceta.com.ar; internet www.lagaceta.com.ar; f. 1912; morning; independent; Dir ALBERTO GARCÍA HAMILTON; circ. 70,000.

WEEKLY NEWSPAPER

El Informador Público: Uruguay 252, 3°F, 1015 Buenos Aires; tel. (11) 4476-3551; fax (11) 4342-2628; f. 1986.

PERIODICALS

Aeroespacio: Casilla 37, Sucursal 12B, 1412 Buenos Aires; tel. and fax (11) 4514-1562; e-mail info@aeroespacio.com.ar; internet www.aeroespacio.com.ar; f. 1940; every 2 months, aeronautics; Dir JORGE A. CUADROS; circ. 24,000.

Billiken: Azopardo 579, 1307 Buenos Aires; tel. (11) 4342-7071; fax (11) 4343-7040; e-mail artebilliken@atlantida.com.ar; f. 1919; weekly; children's magazine; Dir JUAN CARLOS PORRAS. circ. 240,000.

Casas y Jardines: Sarmiento 643, 1382 Buenos Aires; tel. (11) 445-1793; f. 1932; every 2 months; houses and gardens; publ. by Editorial Contémpora SRL; Dir NORBERTO M. MUZIO.

Chacra y Campo Moderno: Editorial Atlántida, SA, Azopardo 579, 1307 Buenos Aires; tel. (11) 4331-4591; fax (11) 4331-3272; f. 1930; monthly; farm and country magazine; Dir CONSTANCIO C. VIGIL; circ. 35,000.

Claudia: Avda Córdoba 1345, 12°, Buenos Aires; tel. (11) 442-3275; fax (11) 4814-3948; f. 1957; monthly; women's magazine; Dir ANA TORREJÓN; circ. 150,000.

El Economista: Avda Córdoba 632, 2°, 1054 Buenos Aires; tel. (11) 4322-7360; fax (11) 4322-8157; f. 1951; weekly; financial; Dir Dr D. RADONJIC; circ. 37,800.

Fotografía Universal: Buenos Aires; monthly; circ. 39,500.

Gente: Azopardo 579, 3°, 1307 Buenos Aires; tel. (11) 433-4591; f. 1965; weekly; general; Dir JORGE DE LUJÁN GUTIÉRREZ; circ. 133,000.

El Gráfico: Paseo Colón 505, 2°, 1063 Buenos Aires; tel. (11) 4341-5100; fax (11) 4341-5137; f. 1919; weekly; sport; Dir ALDO PROIETTO; circ. 127,000.

Guía Latinoamericana de Transportes: Florida 8287 esq. Portinari, 1669 Del Viso (Ptdo de Pilar), Provincia de Buenos Aires; tel. (11) 4320-7004; fax (11) 4307-1956; f. 1968; every 2 months; travel information and timetables; Editor Dr ARMANDO SCHLECKER HIRSCH; circ. 7,500.

Humor: Venezuela 842, 1095 Buenos Aires; tel. (11) 4334-5400; fax (11) 411-2700; f. 1978; every 2 weeks; satirical revue; Editor ANDRÉS CASCIOLI; circ. 180,000.

Legislación Argentina: Talcahuano 650, 1013 Buenos Aires; tel. (11) 4371-0528; e-mail jurispru@lvd.com.ar; f. 1958; weekly; law; Dir RICARDO ESTÉVEZ BOERO; circ. 15,000.

Mercado: Rivadavia 877, 2°, 1002 Buenos Aires; tel. (11) 4346-9400; fax (11) 4343-7880; e-mail mdiez@mercado.com.ar; internet www.mercado.com.ar; f. 1969; monthly; business; Dir MIGUEL ANGEL DIEZ; circ. 28,000.

Mundo Israelita: Pueyrredón 538, 1°B, 1032 Buenos Aires; tel. (11) 4961-7999; fax (11) 4961-0763; f. 1923; weekly; Editor Dr JOSÉ KESTELMAN; circ. 15,000.

Nuestra Arquitectura: Sarmiento 643, 5°, 1382 Buenos Aires; tel. (11) 445-1793; f. 1929; every 2 months; architecture; publ. by Editorial Contémpora SRL; Dir NORBERTO M. MUZIO.

Para Ti: Azopardo 579, 1307 Buenos Aires; tel. (11) 4331-4591; fax (11) 4331-3272; f. 1922; weekly; women's interest; Dir ANÍBAL C. VIGIL; circ. 104,000.

Pensamiento Económico: Avda Leandro N. Alem 36, 1003 Buenos Aires; tel. (11) 4331-8051; fax (11) 4331-8055; e-mail cac@cac.com.ar; internet www.cac.com.ar; f. 1925; quarterly; review of Cámara Argentina de Comercio; Dir Dr CARLOS L. P. ANTONUCCI.

La Prensa Médica Argentina: Junín 845, 1113 Buenos Aires; tel. (11) 4961-9793; fax (11) 4961-9494; e-mail presmedarg@hotmail.com; f. 1914; monthly; medical; Editor Dr P. A. LÓPEZ; circ. 8,000.

Prensa Obrera: Ayacucho 444, Buenos Aires; tel. (11) 4953-3824; fax (11) 4953-7164; f. 1982; weekly; publication of Partido Obrero; circ. 16,000.

La Semana: Sarmiento 1113, 1041 Buenos Aires; tel. (11) 435-2552; general; Editor DANIEL PLINER.

La Semana Médica: Arenales 3574, 1425 Buenos Aires; tel. (11) 4824-5673; f. 1894; monthly; Dir Dr EDUARDO F. MELE; circ. 7,000.

Siete Días Ilustrados: Avda Leandro N. Alem 896, 1001 Buenos Aires; tel. (11) 432-6010; f. 1967; weekly; general; Dir RICARDO CÁMARA; circ. 110,000.

Técnica e Industria: Buenos Aires; tel. (11) 446-3193; f. 1922; monthly; technology and industry; Dir E. R. FEDELE; circ. 5,000.

Visión: French 2820, 2°A, 1425 Buenos Aires; tel. (11) 4825-1258; fax (11) 4827-1004; e-mail edlatin@visionmag.com.ar; f. 1950; fortnightly; Latin American affairs, politics; Editor LUIS VIDAL RUCABADO.

Vosotras: Avda Leandro N. Alem 896, 3°, 1001 Buenos Aires; tel. (11) 432-6010; f. 1935; women's weekly; Dir ABEL ZANOTTO; circ. 33,000. Monthly supplements: **Labores:** circ. 130,000; **Modas:** circ. 70,000.

NEWS AGENCIES

Agencia TELAM, SA: Bolívar 531, 1066 Buenos Aires; tel. (11) 4342-2161; fax (11) 4339-0353; Dir OMAR CERIGLIANO.

Diarios y Noticias (DYN): Avda Julio A. Roca 636, 8°, 1067 Buenos Aires; tel. (11) 4342-3040; fax (11) 4342-3043; e-mail info@dyn.com.ar; internet www.dyn.com.ar; Editor SANTIAGO GONZÁLEZ.

Noticias Argentinas, SA (NA): Suipacha 570, 3°B, 1008 Buenos Aires; tel. (11) 4394-7522; fax (11) 4394-7648; f. 1973; Dir LUIS FERNANDO TORRES.

Foreign Bureaux

Agence France-Presse (AFP): Avda Corrientes 456, 3°, Of. 34/37, 1366 Buenos Aires; tel. (11) 4394-8169; fax (11) 4393-9912; e-mail afp-baires@tournet.com.ar; internet www.afp.com; Bureau Chief JEAN VIREBAYRE.

Agencia EFE (Spain): Guido 1770, 1016 Buenos Aires; tel. (11) 4812-9596; fax (11) 4815-8691; Bureau Chief AGUSTÍN DE GRACIA.

Agenzia Nazionale Stampa Associata (ANSA) (Italy): San Martín 320, 6°, 1004 Buenos Aires; tel. (11) 4394-7568; fax (11) 4394-5214; e-mail ansabairestec@infovia.com.ar; Bureau Chief ANTONIO CAVALLARI.

Associated Press (AP) (USA): Bouchard 551, 5°, Casilla 1296, 1106 Buenos Aires; tel. (11) 4311-0081; fax (11) 4311-0082; Bureau Chief WILLIAM H. HEATH.

Deutsche Presse-Agentur (dpa) (Germany): Buenos Aires; tel. (11) 4311-5311; e-mail msvgroth@ba.net; Bureau Chief Dr HENDRIK GROTH.

Informatsionnoye Telegrafnoye Agentstvo Rossii-Telegrafnoye Agentstvo Suverennykh Stran (ITAR-TASS) (Russia): Avda Córdoba 652, 11°E, 1054 Buenos Aires; tel. (11) 4392-2044; Dir ISIDORO GILBERT.

Inter Press Service (IPS) (Italy): Buenos Aires; tel. (11) 4394-0829; Bureau Chief RAMÓN M. GORRIARÁN; Correspondent GUSTAVO CAPDEVILLA.

Magyar Távirati Iroda (MTI) (Hungary): Marcelo T. de Alvear 624, 3° 16, 1058 Buenos Aires; tel. (11) 4312-9596; Correspondent ENDRE SIMÓ.

Prensa Latina (Cuba): Buenos Aires; tel. (11) 4394-0565; Correspondent MARIO HERNÁNDEZ DEL LLANO.

Reuters (United Kingdom): Avda Eduardo Madero 940, 25°, 1106 Buenos Aires; tel. (11) 4318-0600; fax (11) 4318-0698; Dir CARLOS PÍA MANGIONE.

United Press International (UPI) (USA): Avda Belgrano 271, Casilla 796, Correo Central 1000, 1092 Buenos Aires; tel. (11) 434-5501; fax (11) 4334-1818; Dir ALBERTO J. SCHAZÍN.

Xinhua (New China) News Agency (People's Republic of China): Tucumán 540, 14°, Apto D, 1049 Buenos Aires; tel. (11) 4313-9755; Bureau Chief JU QINGDONG.

The following are also represented: Central News Agency (Taiwan), Interpress (Poland), Jiji Press (Japan).

PRESS ASSOCIATION

Asociación de Entidades Periodísticas Argentinas (ADEPA): Chacabuco 314, 3°, 1069 Buenos Aires; tel. and fax (11) 4331-1500; e-mail adepa@ciudad.com.ar; internet www.adepa.com.ar; f. 1962; Pres. GUILLERMO IGNACIO.

Publishers

Editorial Abril, SA: Suipacha 664, 1093 Buenos Aires; tel. (11) 4331-0112; f. 1961; fiction, non-fiction, children's books, textbooks; Dir ROBERTO M. ARES.

Editorial Acme, SA: Santa Magdalena 635, 1277 Buenos Aires; tel. (11) 428-2014; f. 1949; general fiction, children's books, agriculture, textbooks; Man. Dir EMILIO I. GONZÁLEZ.

Aguilar, Altea, Taurus, Alfaguara, SA de Ediciones: Beazley 3860, 1437 Buenos Aires; tel. (11) 4912-7220; fax (11) 4912-7440; internet www.santillana.com.ar; f. 1946; general, literature, children's books; Gen. Man. CARLOS CALVO.

Editorial Albatros, SACI: Hipólito Yrigoyen 3920, 1208 Buenos Aires; tel. (11) 4982-5439; fax (11) 4981-1161; f. 1967; technical, non-fiction, social sciences, sport, children's books, medicine and agriculture; Pres. ANDREA INÉS CANEVARO.

Amorrortu Editores, SA: Paraguay 1225, 7°, 1057 Buenos Aires; tel. (11) 4393-8812; fax (11) 4325-6307; f. 1967; anthropology, religion, economics, sociology, philosophy, psychology, psychoanalysis, current affairs; Man. Dir HORACIO DE AMORRORTU.

Angel Estrada y Cía, SA: Bolívar 462-66, 1066 Buenos Aires; tel. (11) 4331-6521; fax (11) 4331-6527; f. 1869; textbooks, children's books; Gen. Man. OSCAR DOMECQ.

Editorial El Ateneo, Librerías Yenny, SA: Patagones 2463, 1282 Buenos Aires; tel. (11) 4942-9002; fax (11) 4942-9162; e-mail librerías@yenny.com.ar; f. 1912; medicine, engineering, economics and general; Pres. EDUARDO CARLOS GRUNEISEN; Commercial Dir JORGE GONZÁLEZ.

Editorial Atlántida, SA: Azopardo 579, 1307 Buenos Aires; tel. (11) 4346-0100; fax (11) 4331-3272; internet www.atlantida.com; f. 1918; fiction and non-fiction, children's books; Chair. JORGE CONSTANCIO TERRA.

Ediciones La Aurora: Buenos Aires; tel. and fax (11) 4941-8940; f. 1925; general, religion, spirituality, theology, philosophy, psychology, history, semiology, linguistics; Dir Dr HUGO O. ORTEGA.

Az Editora, SA: Paraguay 2351, 1121 Buenos Aires; tel. (11) 961-4036; fax (11) 961-0089; f. 1976; social sciences and medicine; Pres. DANTE OMAR VILLALBA.

Biblioteca Nacional de Maestros: c/o Ministry of Education, Pizzurno 935, planta baja, 1020 Buenos Aires; tel. (11) 4811-0275; e-mail gperrone@me.gov.ar; internet www.bnm.me.gov.ar; f. 1884; Dir GRACIELA PERRONE.

Centro Editor de América Latina, SA: Salta 38, 3°, 1074 Buenos Aires; tel. (11) 435-9449; f. 1967; literature, history; Man. Dir JOSÉ B. SPIVACOW.

Editorial Claretiana: Lima 1360, 1138 Buenos Aires; tel. (11) 427-9250; fax (11) 427-4015; e-mail editorial@editorialclaretiana.com.ar; internet www.editorialclaretiana.com.ar; f. 1956; Catholicism; Dir GUSTAVO LARRAZÁBAL.

Editorial Claridad, SA: Viamonte 1730, 1°, 1055 Buenos Aires; tel. (11) 4371-6402; fax (11) 4375-1659; e-mail editorial@heliasta.com.ar; internet www.heliasta.com.ar; f. 1922; literature, biographies, social science, politics, reference, dictionaries; Pres. Dra ANA MARÍA CABANELLAS.

Club de Lectores: Avda de Mayo 624, 1084 Buenos Aires; tel. (11) 434-6251; f. 1938; non-fiction; Dir JUAN MANUEL FONTENLA.

Club de Poetas: Casilla 189, 1401 Buenos Aires; f. 1975; poetry and literature; Exec. Dir JUAN MANUEL FONTENLA.

Editorial Columba, SA: Sarmiento 1889, 5°, 1044 Buenos Aires; tel. (11) 445-4297; f. 1953; classics in translation, 20th century; Man. Dir CLAUDIO A. COLUMBA.

Editorial Contémpora, SRL: Sarmiento 643, 5°, 1382 Buenos Aires; tel. (11) 445-1793; architecture, town-planning, interior decoration and gardening; Dir NORBERTO C. MUZIO.

Cosmopolita, SRL: Piedras 744, 1070 Buenos Aires; tel. and fax (11) 4361-8049; f. 1940; science and technology; Man. Dir RUTH F. DE RAPP.

Depalma, SA: Talcahuano 494, 1013 Buenos Aires; tel. (11) 4371-7306; fax (11) 4371-6913; e-mail info@ed-depalma.com; internet www.ed-depalma.com; f. 1944; periodicals and books covering law, politics, sociology, philosophy, history and economics; CEO ALBERTO O. ERMILIO; Dir NICOLAS VON DER PAHLEN.

Editorial Difusión, SA: Sarandi 1065–67, 1307 Buenos Aires; tel. (11) 4941-0088; f. 1937; literature, philosophy, religion, education, textbooks, children's books; Dir DOMINGO PALOMBELLA.

Edicial, SA: Rivadavia 739, 1002 Buenos Aires; tel. (11) 4342-8481; fax (11) 4343-1151; e-mail edicial@ssdnet.com.ar; internet www.ssdnet.com.ar/edicial; f. 1931; education; Man. Dir J. A. MUSSET.

Emecé Editores, SA: Alsina 2062, 1090 Buenos Aires; tel. (11) 4954-0105; fax (11) 4953-4200; e-mail editorial@emece.com.ar; internet www.emece.com.ar; f. 1939; fiction, non-fiction, biographies, history, art, essays; Pres. ALFREDO DEL CARRIL.

Espasa Calpe Argentina, SA: Buenos Aires; tel. (11) 4342-0073; fax (11) 4345-1776; f. 1937; literature, science, dictionaries; publ. *Colección Austral*; Dir GUILLERMO SCHAUELZON.

Angel Estrada y Cía, SA: Bolívar 462-466, 1066 Buenos Aires; tel. (11) 331-6521; f. 1869; education; Gen. Man. ZSOLT ARÁRDY.

EUDEBA—Editorial Universitaria de Buenos Aires: Rivadavia 1573, 1033 Buenos Aires; tel. (11) 4383-8025; fax (11) 4383-2202;

e-mail eudeba@eudeba.com.ar; internet www.eudeba.com.ar; f. 1958; university text books and general interest publications; Pres. Dr LUIS YANES.

Fabril Editora, SA: Buenos Aires; tel. (11) 421-3601; f. 1958; non-fiction, science, arts, education and reference; Editorial Man. ANDRÉS ALFONSO BRAVO; Business Man. RÓMULO AYERZA.

Editorial Glem, SACIF: Avda Caseros 2056, 1264 Buenos Aires; tel. (11) 426-6641; f. 1933; psychology, technology; Pres. JOSÉ ALFREDO TUCCI.

Editorial Guadalupe: Mansilla 3865, 1425 Buenos Aires; tel. (11) 4826-8587; fax (11) 4805-4112; e-mail ventas@editorialguadalupe.com.ar; f. 1895; social sciences, religion, anthropology, children's books, and pedagogy; Dir P. LORENZO GOYENECHE.

Editorial Heliasta, SRL: Viamonte 1730, 1°, 1055 Buenos Aires; tel. (11) 4371-6402; fax (11) 4375-1659; e-mail editorial@heliasta.com.ar; internet www.heliasta.com.ar; f. 1944; literature, biography, dictionaries, legal; Pres. Dra ANA MARÍA CABANELLAS.

Editorial Hemisferio Sur, SA: Pasteur 743, 1028 Buenos Aires; tel. (11) 4952-9825; fax (11) 4952-8454; e-mail informe@hemisferiosur.com.ar; internet www.hemisferiosur.com.ar; f.1966; agriculture, veterinary and food science; Man. Dir ADOLFO JULIÁN PEÑA.

Editorial Hispano-Americana, SA (HASA): Alsina 731, 1087 Buenos Aires; tel. (11) 4331-5051; f. 1934; science and technology; Pres. Prof. HÉCTOR OSCAR ALGARRA.

Editorial Inter-Médica, SAICI: Junín 917, 1°, Casilla 4625, 1113 Buenos Aires; tel. (11) 4961-9234; fax (11) 4961-5572; e-mail info@inter-medica.com.ar; internet www.inter-medica.com.ar; f. 1959; medicine, dentistry, psychology, psychiatry, veterinary; Pres. JORGE MODYEIEVSKY.

Editorial Inter-Vet, SA: Avda de los Constituyentes 3141, Buenos Aires; tel. (11) 451-2382; f. 1987; veterinary; Pres. JORGE MODYEIEVSKY.

Kapelusz Editora, SA: San José 831, 1076 Buenos Aires; tel. (11) 4342-7400; fax (11) 4331-8020; e-mail pedidos@kapelusz.com.ar; internet www.kapelusz.com.ar; f. 1905; textbooks, psychology, pedagogy, children's books; Gen. Man. TOMÁS CASTILLO.

Editorial Kier, SACIFI: Avda Santa Fe 1260, 1059 Buenos Aires; tel. (11) 4811-0507; fax (11) 4811-3395; e-mail info@kier.com.ar; internet www.kier.com.ar; f. 1907; Eastern doctrines and religions, astrology, parapsychology, tarot, I Ching, occultism, cabbala, freemasonry and natural medicine; Pres. HÉCTOR S. PIBERNUS; Mans SERGIO PIBERNUS, OSVALDO PIBERNUS, CRISTÍNA GRIGNA.

Ediciones Librerías Fausto: Avda Corrientes 1316, 1043 Buenos Aires; tel. (11) 4476-4919; fax (11) 4476-3914; f. 1943; fiction and non-fiction; Man. RAFAEL ZORRILLA.

Carlos Lohlé, SA: Tacuarí 1516, 1139 Buenos Aires; tel. (11) 427-9969; f. 1953; philosophy, religion, belles-lettres; Dir FRANCISCO M. LOHLÉ.

Editorial Losada, SA: Moreno 3362/64, 1209 Buenos Aires; tel. (11) 4863-8608; fax (11) 4864-0434; f. 1938; general; Pres. JOSÉ JUAN FERNÁNDEZ REGUERA.

Ediciones Macchi, SA: Alsina 1535/37, 1088 Buenos Aires; tel. (11) 446-2506; fax (11) 446-0594; f. 1947; economic sciences; Pres. RAÚL LUIS MACCHI; Dir JULIO ALBERTO MENDONÇA.

Editorial Médica Panamericana, SA: Marcelo T. de Alvear 2145, 1122 Buenos Aires; tel. (11) 4821-5520; fax (11) 4825-5006; e-mail info@medicapanamericana.com.ar; internet www.medicapanamericana.com.ar; f. 1962; medicine and health sciences; Pres. HUGO BRIK.

Ediciones Nueva Visión, SAIC: Tucumán 3748, 1189 Buenos Aires; tel. (11) 4864-5050; fax (11) 4863-5980; e-mail ednuevavision@ciudad.com.ar; f. 1954; psychology, education, social sciences, linguistics; Man. Dir HAYDÉE P. DE GIACONE.

Editorial Paidós: Defensa 599, 1°, 1065 Buenos Aires; tel. (11) 4331-2275; fax (11) 4345-6769; f. 1945; social sciences, medicine, philosophy, religion, history, literature, textbooks; Man. Dir MARITA GOTTHEIL.

Plaza y Janés, SA: Buenos Aires; tel. (11) 486-6769; popular fiction and non-fiction; Man. Dir JORGE PÉREZ.

Editorial Plus Ultra, SA: Callao 575, 1022 Buenos Aires; tel. (11) 4374-2953; f. 1964; literature, history, textbooks, law, economics, politics, sociology, pedagogy, children's books; Man. Editors RAFAEL ROMÁN, LORENZO MARENGO.

Editorial Santillana: Buenos Aires; f. 1960; education; Pres. JESÚS DE POLANCO GUTÉRREZ.

Schapire Editor, SRL: Uruguay 1249, 1016 Buenos Aires; tel. (11) 4812-0765; fax (11) 4815-0369; f. 1941; music, art, theatre, sociology, history, fiction; Dir MIGUEL SCHAPIRE DALMAT.

Editorial Sigmar, SACI: Belgrano 1580, 7°, 1093 Buenos Aires; tel. (11) 4383-3045; fax (11) 4383-5633; e-mail editorial@sigmar.com.ar; f. 1941; children's books; Man. Dir ROBERTO CHWAT.

Editorial Sopena Argentina, SACI e I: Buenos Aires; tel. (11) 438-7182; f. 1918; dictionaries, classics, chess, health, politics, history, children's books; Exec. Pres. DANIEL CARLOS OLSEN.

Editorial Stella: Viamonte 1984, 1056 Buenos Aires; tel. (11) 446-0346; general non-fiction and textbooks; owned by Asociación Educacionista Argentina.

Editorial Sudamericana, SA: Humberto 545, 1°, 1103 Buenos Aires; tel. (11) 4300-5400; fax (11) 4362-7364; e-mail edsudame@satlink.com; f. 1939; general fiction and non-fiction; Gen. Man. OLAF HANTEL.

Editorial Troquel, SA: Dr E. Finochietto 473, 1143 Buenos Aires; tel. (11) 427-1116; fax (11) 423-9350; f. 1954; general literature, and textbooks; Pres. GUSTAVO A. RESSIA.

PUBLISHERS' ASSOCIATION

Cámara Argentina de Publicaciones: Reconquista 1011, 6°, 1003 Buenos Aires; tel. (11) 4311-6855; f. 1970; Pres. AGUSTÍN DOS SANTOS; Man. LUIS FRANCISCO HOULIN.

Broadcasting and Communications

Secretaría de Comunicaciones: Sarmiento 151, 4°, 1000 Buenos Aires; tel. (11) 4318-9410; fax (11) 4318-9432; co-ordinates 30 stations and the international service; Sec. Dr GERMÁN KAMMERATH.

> **Subsecretaría de Planificación y Gestión Tecnológica:** Sarmiento 151, 4°, 1000 Buenos Aires; tel. (11) 4311-5909; Under-Sec. Ing. LEONARDO JOSÉ LEIBSON.

> **Subsecretaría de Radiocomunicaciones:** Sarmiento 151, 4°, 1000 Buenos Aires; tel. (11) 4311-5909; Under-Sec. Ing. ALFREDO R. PARODI.

> **Subsecretaría de Telecomunicaciones:** Sarmiento 151, 4°, 1000 Buenos Aires; tel. (11) 4311-5909; Under-Sec. JULIO I. GUILLÁN.

Comité Federal de Radiodifusión (COMFER): Suipacha 765, 9°, 1008 Buenos Aires; tel. (11) 4320-4900; fax (11) 4394-6866; f. 1972; controls various technical aspects of broadcasting and transmission of programmes; Head JOSÉ AIELLO.

TELECOMMUNICATIONS

Cámara de Informática y Comunicaciones de la República Argentina (CICOMRA): Avda Córdoba 744, 2°, 1054 Buenos Aires; tel. (11) 4325-8839; fax (11) 4325-9604; e-mail cicomra@starnet.net.ar.

Comisión Nacional de Comunicaciones (CNC): Perú 103, 9°, 1067 Buenos Aires; tel. (11) 4347-9242; fax (11) 4347-9244; Pres. Dr ROBERTO CATALÁN.

Cía Ericsson SACI: Avda Madero, 1020 Buenos Aires; tel. (11) 4319-5500; fax (11) 4315-0629; Dir-Gen. Ing. ROLANDO ZUBIRÁN.

Cía de Radiocomunicaciones Móviles SA: Tucumán 744, 9°, 1049 Buenos Aires; tel. (11) 4325-5006; fax (11) 4325-5334; mobile telecommunications co; Pres. Lic. MAURICIO E. WIOR.

Movicom: Tucumán 744, 2°, 1049 Buenos Aires; tel. (11) 4978-4773; fax (11) 4978-7373; e-mail rree@movi.com.ar; internet www.movi.com.ar; telecommunications services, including cellular phones, trunking, paging and wireless access to the internet; Pres. Lic. MAURICIO WIOR.

Telecom Argentina: Alicia Moreau de Justo 50, 1107 Buenos Aires; tel. (11) 4968-4000; fax (11) 4968-1420; e-mail inversores@intersrv.telecom.com.ar; internet www.telecom.com.ar; provision of telecommunication services in the north of Argentina; Pres. JUAN CARLOS MASJOAN.

Telecomunicaciones Internacionales de Argentina TELINTAR SA: 25 de Mayo 457, 7°, 1002 Buenos Aires; tel. (11) 4318-0500; fax (11) 4313-4924; e-mail mlamas@telintar.com.ar; internet www.telintar.com.ar; Sec.-Gen. Dr MARCELO MIGUEL LAMAS.

Telefónica de Argentina SA (TASA): Tucumán 1, 17°, 1049 Buenos Aires; tel. (11) 4345-5772; fax (11) 4345-5771; e-mail gabello@telefonica.com.ar; internet www.telefonica.com.ar; provision of telecommunication services in the south of Argentina; Pres. CARLOS FERNÁNDEZ PRIDA.

RADIO

There are three privately-owned stations in Buenos Aires and 72 in the interior. There are also 37 state-controlled stations, four provincial, three municipal and three university stations. The principal ones are Radio Antártida, Radio Argentina, Radio Belgrano, Radio Ciudad de Buenos Aires, Radio Excelsior, Radio Mitre, Radio El Mundo, Radio Nacional, Radio del Plata, Radio Rivadavia and Radio Splendid, all in Buenos Aires.

Servicio Oficial de Radiodifusión (SOR): Maipú 555, 1006 Buenos Aires; tel. (11) 4325-1969; fax (11) 4325-9433; e-mail rna@mecon.ar; Dir PATRICIA IVONE BARRAL; controls:

Cadena Argentina de Radiodifusión (CAR): Avda Entre Ríos 149, 3°, 1079 Buenos Aires; tel. (11) 4325-9100; fax (11) 4325-9433; groups all national state-owned commercial stations which are operated directly by the Subsecretaría Operativa.

LRA Radio Nacional de Buenos Aires: Maipú 555, 1006 Buenos Aires; tel. and fax (11) 4325-9433; e-mail rna@mecon.ar; f. 1937; Dir PATRICIA IVONE BARRAL.

Radiodifusión Argentina al Exterior (RAE): Maipú 555, 1006 Buenos Aires; tel. (11) 4325-6368; fax (11) 4325-9433; e-mail rna@mecon.ar; f. 1958; broadcasts in eight languages to all areas of the world; Dir-Gen. PERLA DAMURI.

Asociación de Radiodifusoras Privadas Argentinas (ARPA): Juan D. Perón 1561, 8°, 1037 Buenos Aires; tel. (11) 4382-4412; f. 1958; an association of all but three of the privately-owned commercial stations; Pres. DOMINGO F. L. ELÍAS.

TELEVISION

There are 44 television channels, of which 29 are privately-owned and 15 are owned by provincial and national authorities. The national television network is regulated by the Comité Federal de Radiodifusión (see above).

The following are some of the more important television stations in Argentina: Argentina Televisora Color LS82 Canal 7, LS83 (Canal 9 Libertad), LS84 (Canal 11 Telefé), LS85 Canal 13 ArTeAr SA, LV80 Telenueva, LU81 Teledifusora Bahiense SA, LV81 Canal 12 Telecor SACI, Dicor Difusión Córdoba, LV80 TV Canal 10 Universidad Nacional Córdoba, and LU82 TV Mar del Plata SA.

Asociación de Teleradiodifusoras Argentinas (ATA): Avda Córdoba 323, 6°, 1054 Buenos Aires; tel. (11) 4312-4208; fax (11) 4315-4681; e-mail info@ata.org.ar; internet www.ata.org.ar; f. 1959; asscn of 22 private television channels; Pres. CARLOS FONTAN BALESTRA.

ATC—Argentina Televisora Color LS82 TV Canal 7: Avda Figueroa Alcorta 2977, 1425 Buenos Aires; tel. (11) 4802-6001; fax (11) 4802-9878; state-controlled channel; Dir RENÉ JOLIVET.

Azul Televisión—LS83 (Canal 9 Libertad): Dorrego 1708, Buenos Aires; tel. (11) 777-2321; fax (11) 777-9620; e-mail noticias@azultv.com; internet www.azultv.com; private channel; Dir ALEJANDRO RAMAY.

LS84 (Canal 11 Telefé): Pavón 2444, 1248 Buenos Aires; tel. (11) 4941-9549; fax (11) 4942-6773; leased to a private concession in 1992; Pres. PEDRO SIMONCINI.

LS85: Canal 13 (ArTeAr SA): Avda San Juan 1170, 1147 Buenos Aires; tel. (11) 4305-0013; fax (11) 4307-0315; e-mail webmaster@webtv.artear.com; internet www.webtv.artear.com.ar; f. 1989; leased to a private concession in 1992; Dir-Gen. LUCIO PAGLIARO.

Finance

(cap. = capital; res = reserves; dep. = deposits; m. = million; amounts in nuevos pesos argentinos—$, unless otherwise stated)

BANKING

At the end of 1998 there were three public banks, 14 municipal banks, 44 domestic private banks, 39 foreign private banks and four co-operative banks.

Central Bank

Banco Central de la República Argentina: Reconquista 266, 1003 Buenos Aires; tel. (11) 4348-3500; fax (11) 4348-3955; e-mail sistema@bcra.gov.ar; internet www.bcra.gov.ar; f. 1935 as a central reserve bank; it has the right of note issue; all capital is held by the State; cap. $1,921m., res $1,074m., dep. $1,477m. (Dec. 1998); Gov. ROQUE BENJAMIN FERNÁNDEZ; Pres. PEDRO POU.

Government-owned Commercial Banks

Banco de la Ciudad de Buenos Aires: Florida 302, 1313 Buenos Aires; tel. (11) 4329-8600; fax (11) 4112-098; e-mail bciudad5@bancociudad.com.ar; internet www.bancociudad.com.ar; municipal bank; f. 1878; cap. and res $200.0m., dep. $2,836.3m. (Oct. 1998); Chair. HORACIO CHIGHIZOLA; 31 brs.

Banco de Inversión y Commercio Exterior, SA (BICE): 25 de Mayo 526, 1002 Buenos Aires; tel. (11) 4317-6900; fax (11) 4311-5596; e-mail presidencia@bice.com.ar; internet www.bice.com.ar; f. 1991; dep. $237.1m. (Dec. 1998); Pres. DIEGO YOFRE.

Banco de la Nación Argentina: Bartolomé Mitre 326, 1036 Buenos Aires; tel. (11) 4347-6000; fax (11) 4347-8078; internet www.bna.com.ar; f. 1891; national bank; cap. $381.0m., res $1,717.5m., dep. $15,422.7m. (Dec. 1998); Pres. ENRIQUE OLIVERA; 541 brs.

Banco de la Pampa: Carlos Pellegrini 255, 6300 Santa Rosa; tel. (2954) 433008; fax (2954) 433196; f. 1958; cap. $6.9m., res $136.2m., dep. $873.6m. (June 1999); Pres. LUIS E. ROLDÁN; 112 brs.

Banco de la Provincia de Buenos Aires: Avda San Martín 137, 1004 Buenos Aires; tel. (11) 4331-2561; fax (11) 4331-5154; e-mail baprocri@internet.siscotel.com; internet www.bpba.com; f. 1822; provincial bank; cap. $750.0m., res $472.4m., dep. $12,452.9m. (Dec. 1998); Pres. RICARDO GUTIÉRREZ; 313 brs.

Banco de la Provincia del Chubut: Rivadavia 615, 9103 Rawson; tel. (2965) 482506; dep. $170.0m., total assets $456.8m. (May 1995); Principal Officer FREDERICO G. POLAK.

Banco de la Provincia de Córdoba: San Jerónimo 166, 5000 Córdoba; tel. (351) 420-7200; fax (351) 422-9718; e-mail gcomexterior@bancocordoba.com; internet www.bancocordoba.com; f. 1873; provincial bank; cap. $47.6m., res $142.8m., dep. $1,036.1 (Dec. 1994); Pres. JUAN A. ÓMEDO GUERRA; 152 brs.

Banco de la Provincia de Jujuy: Alvear 999, 4600 San Salvador de Jujuy; tel. (3882) 423003; f. 1933; dep. $87.9m., total assets $134.8m. (May 1995); Pres. Dr ARMANDO EDUARDO FERNÁNDEZ.

Banco de la Provincia del Neuquén: Avda Argentina 41/45, 8300 Neuquén; tel. (299) 434221; fax (299) 4480439; internet www.bpn.com.ar; f. 1960; dep. $232.8m., total assets $388.6m. (March 1995); Pres. OMAR SANTIAGO NEGRETTI; 22 brs.

Banco de la Provincia de San Luis: Rivadavia 602, 5700 San Luis; tel. (2623) 425013; fax (2623) 424943; dep. $88.8m., total assets $107.8m. (May 1995); Principal Officer SALVADOR OMAR CAMPO.

Banco de la Provincia de Santa Cruz: Avda General Roca 802, 9400 Río Gallegos; tel. (2966) 420845; dep. $211.7m., total assets $382.1m. (June 1995); Govt Admin. EDUARDO LABOLIDA.

Banco de la Provincia de Santiago del Estero: Avda Belgrano 529 Sur, 4200 Santiago del Estero; tel. (385) 422-2300; dep. $69.9m., total assets $101.6m. (Jan. 1995); Pres. AMÉRICO DAHER.

Banco de la Provincia de Tucumán: San Martín 362, 4000 San Miguel de Tucumán; tel. (381) 431-1709; dep. $164.7m., total assets $359.5m. (March 1995); Govt Admin. EMILIO APAZA.

Banco Provincial de Salta: España 550, 4400 Salta; tel. (387) 422-1300; fax (387) 431-0020; f. 1887; dep. $40.7m., total assets $125.0m. (June 1995); Pres. Dr REYNALDO ALFREDO NOGUEIRA; 19 brs.

Banco Social de Córdoba: 27 de Abril 185, 1°, 5000 Córdoba; tel. (351) 422-3367; dep. $187.3m., total assets $677.3m. (June 1995); Pres. Dr JAIME POMPAS.

Banco del Territorio Nacional de Tierra del Fuego, Antártida e Islas del Atlántico Sur: San Martín, esq. Roca, 9410 Ushuaia; tel. (2901) 424087; national bank; cap. and res $21.8m., dep. $54.2m. (June 1992); Pres. OSVALDO MANUEL RODRÍGUEZ.

Nuevo Banco de Santa Fé, SA: Tucumán 2545, 2°, 3000 Santa Fe; tel. (341) 452-2225; fax (341) 452-1037; e-mail nbsdirsf@infovia .com.ar; f. 1847 as Banco Provincial de Santa Fe, adopted current name in 1998; provincial bank; cap. $60.0m., res $31.1m., dep. $643.5m.; Chair. JOSÉ ENRIQUE ROHM; 105 brs.

Private Commercial Banks

Banco BI Creditanstalt, SA: Bouchard 547, 24°, 1106 Buenos Aires; tel. (11) 4319-8400; fax (11) 4319-8230; e-mail bi_credit@impsat1.com.ar; f. 1971; fmrly Banco Interfinanzas; cap. $38.3m., res $8.0m., dep. $367.8m. (Dec. 1999); Pres. Dr MIGUEL ANGEL ANGELINO.

Banco Baires, SA: Buenos Aires; tel. (11) 4394-5851; fax (11) 4325-8548; f. 1956 as Baires Exchange House, adopted current name in 1992 following merger with Banco Mediterráneo, SA; cap. $11.6m., res $1.3m., dep. $56.5m. (Dec. 1994); Pres. G. ANÍBAL MENÉNDEZ.

Banco Bansud, SA: Sarmiento 447, 1041 Buenos Aires; tel. (11) 4348-6500; fax (11) 4325-5641; internet www.bansud.com; f. 1995 after merger of Banesto Banco Shaw, SA and Banco del Sud, SA; cap. $44.4m., res $302.2m., dep. $1,432.7m. (June 1997); Pres. LEONARDO ANIDJAR; 39 brs.

Banco Caja de Ahorro, SA: Avda Corrientes 629, 1324 Buenos Aires; tel. (11) 4323-5000; fax (11) 4323-5073; internet www.lacaja .com.ar; f. 1923 as Banco Mercantil Argentino, SA, adopted current name in 1999 following merger with Banco Caja de Ahorro, SA; cap. $0.1m., res $61.5m., dep. $587.3m. (Dec. 1997); Pres. NOEL WERTHEIN.

Banco CMF, SA: Macacha Güemes 555, Puerto Madero, 1107 Buenos Aires; tel. (11) 4318-6800; fax (11) 4318-6859; f. 1978 as Corporación Metropolitana de Finanzas, SA, adopted current name in 1999; cap. $41.0m., res $4.7m., dep. $433.7m. (Dec. 1998); Pres. JOSÉ P. BENEGAS LYNCH.

Banco Comercial Israelita, SA: Bartolomé Mitre 702, 2000 Rosario; tel. (341) 420-0557; fax (341) 420-0517; f. 1921; cap. $4.3m., res $20.5m., dep. $232.0m. (June 1998); Pres. Ing. DAVID ZCARNY; 4 brs.

Banco de Corrientes: 9 de Julio 1099, esq. San Juan, 3400 Corrientes; tel. (3783) 479200; fax (3783) 479283; f. 1951 as Banco de la República de Corrientes; adopted current name in 1993, after transfer to private ownership; cap. and res $38.5m., dep. $126.7m. (June 1995); Pres. JUAN RAMÓN BRANCHI; 33 brs.

Banco Crédito Provincial SA: Calle 7, esq. 50, Casilla 54, 1900 La Plata; tel. and fax (221) 429-2000; f. 1911; cap. $2.5m., res $40.5m., dep. $160.5m. (June 1995); Pres. ANTONIO R. FALABELLA; 47 brs.

Banco de Entre Ríos SA: Monte Caseros 128, 3100 Paraná; tel. (343) 423-1200; fax (343) 421-1221; e-mail bersaext@satlink.com; f. 1935; provincial bank; transferred to private ownership in 1995; cap. $55.2m., res $3.2m., dep. $715.5m. (June 1999); Pres. CARLOS ALBERTO CELAÁ; 29 brs.

Banco Florencia, SA: Reconquista 353, 1003 Buenos Aires; tel. (11) 4325-5949; fax (11) 4325-5849; f. 1984; cap. and res $8.8m., dep. $11.8m. (Dec. 1993); Chair. ALBERTO BRUNET; Vice-Chair. JORGE GONZÁLEZ.

Banco Francés, SA: Reconquista 199, 1003 Buenos Aires; tel. (11) 4346-4000; fax (11) 4346-4320; internet www.bancofrances.com; f. 1886 as Banco Francés del Río de la Plata, SA; adopted current name in 1998 following merger with Banco de Crédito Argentino; dep. US $5,883.6m., total assets US $9,447.4m. (March 1999); Chair. GERVÁSIO COLLAR ZAVALETA; 75 brs.

Banco de Galicia y Buenos Aires SA: Juan D. Perón 407, Casilla 86, 1038 Buenos Aires; tel. (11) 4394-7080; fax (11) 4393-1603; internet www.bancogalicia.com.ar; f. 1905; cap. $405.4m., res $516.0m., dep. $11,640.3m. (June 1999); Chair. EDUARDO J. ESCASANY; 165 brs.

Banco General de Negocios, SA: Esmeralda 120/38, 1035 Buenos Aires; tel. (11) 4320-6100; fax (11) 4334-6422; f. 1978; dep. $591.2m. (Dec. 1998); Chair. JOSÉ E. ROHM.

Banco Israelita de Córdoba, SA: Ituzaingó 60, 5000 Córdoba; tel. (351) 420-3200; fax (351) 424-3616; f. 1942; cap. $9.0m., res $18.3m., dep. $160.5m. (June 1995); Pres. JUAN MACHTEY; 20 brs.

Banco Macro, SA: Sarmiento 735, 1041 Buenos Aires; tel. (11) 4323-6300; fax (11) 4325-6935; e-mail bmmholding@inea.com.ar; f. 1997 by merger of Banco Macro, SA (f. 1988) and Banco de Misiones, SA; adopted current name in 1991 following merger with Banco de Salta, SA; cap. and res $96.7m., dep. $668.8m. (Dec. 1999); Pres. JORGE HORACIO BRITO.

Banco Mariva, SA: Sarmiento 500, 1041 Buenos Aires; tel. (11) 4331-7571; fax (11) 4321-2222; f. 1980; cap. $30.0m., res $10.0m., dep. $206.3m. (Dec.1994); Pres. RICARDO MAY.

Banco Popular Financiero: Sobremonte 801, Casilla 5800, Río Cuarto, Córdoba; tel. (3586) 430001; f. 1964; cap. and res $8.8m., dep. $41.2m. (June 1992); Pres. JOSÉ OSVALDO TRAVAGLIA; Vice-Pres. HUGO RICARDO LARDONE.

Banco Río de la Plata, SA: Bartolomé Mitre 480, 1036 Buenos Aires; tel. (11) 4341-1000; fax (11) 4341-1554; internet www .bancorio.com.ar; f. 1908; cap. $150.0m., res $269.1m., dep. $5,372.6m. (Dec. 1996); Pres. JORGE GREGORIO PÉREZ COMPAÑO; 169 brs.

Banco Suquía, SA: 25 de Mayo 160, 5000 Córdoba; tel. (351) 420-0200; fax (351) 420-0443; internet www.bancosuquia.com.ar; f. 1961 as Banco del Suquía, SA; adopted current name in 1998; cap. $80.6m., res $66.1m., dep. $1,481.5m. (June 1998); Pres. ALDO BENITO ROGGIO; Gen. Man. RAÚL FERNÁNDEZ; 98 brs.

Banco de Valores, SA: Sarmiento 310, 1041 Buenos Aires; tel. (11) 4323-6900; fax (11) 4334-1731; e-mail bcoval@internet.siscotel.com; internet www.bancodevalores.com; f. 1978; cap. $10.0m., res $5.9m., dep. $201.8m. (Dec. 1998); Pres. MIGUEL A. AMORETTI; 1 br.

Banco Velox, SA: San Martín 298, 1004 Buenos Aires; tel. (11) 4320-0200; fax (11) 4393-7672; f. 1983; cap. and res $97.4m., dep. $261.0m. (June 1999); Pres. JUAN PEIRANO; 8 brs.

Banex: San Martín 136, 1004 Buenos Aires; tel. (11) 4340-3000; fax (11) 4334-4402; internet www.banex.com.ar; f. 1998 by merger of Exprinter Banco with Banco San Luis, SA; cap. $29.1m., res $15.8m., dep. $188.4m. (Dec. 1998); Pres. MARÍA DEL CARMEN ALGORTA DE SUPERVIELLE.

HSBC Banco Roberts, SA: 25 de Mayo 701, 26°, 1084 Buenos Aires; tel. (11) 4344-3333; fax (11) 4334-6404; f. 1978 as Banco Roberts, SA; adopted current name in 1998; cap. $219.7m., res $100.2m., dep. $4,473.8m. (June 1999); Chair. and CEO MICHAEL SMITH; 68 brs.

Nuevo Banco del Chaco, SA: Güemes 40, 3500 Resistencia; tel. (3722) 424888; f. 1958 as Banco del Chaco; transferred to private ownership and adopted current name in 1994; cap. $10.5m., dep. $45.4m. (June 1995); 28 brs.

Nuevo Banco de Formosa: 25 de Mayo 102, 3600 Formosa; tel. (3717) 426030; transferred to private ownership in 1995; dep. $145.3m., total assets $235.7m. (May 1995); Pres. JOSÉ MANUEL PABLO VIUDES.

Co-operative Banks

Banco Almafuerte Cooperativo Ltdo: Corrales Viejos 64, 1437 Buenos Aires; tel. (11) 4911-5153; fax (11) 4911-6887; f. 1978; cap. $18.3m., res $38.1m., dep. $378.4m. (Dec. 1997); Pres. Dr ELIAS FARAH; 27 brs.

Banco Credicoop Cooperativo Ltdo: Reconquista 484, 1003 Buenos Aires; tel. (11) 4320-5000; fax (11) 4324-5891; e-mail credicoop@rcc.com.ar; internet www.credicoop.com.ar; f. 1979; cap. $0.4m., res $210.5m., dep. $1,870.1m. (June 1999); Pres. RAÚL GUELMAN.

Banco Mayo Cooperativo Ltdo: Sarmiento 706, 1041 Buenos Aires; tel. (11) 4329-2400; fax (11) 4326-8080; f. 1978; cap. $83.4m., res $32.4m., dep. $904.2m. (June 1997); Chair. RUBÉN E. BERAJA; 106 brs.

Banco Patricios: Florida 101, 1005 Buenos Aires; tel. (11) 4331-1786; fax (11) 4331-6887; f. 1927; cap. and res $19.1m., dep. $144.0m. (Dec. 1993); Pres. Dr ALBERTO SPOLSKI.

Banco Roco Cooperativo Ltdo: 25 de Mayo 122, 1002 Buenos Aires; tel. (11) 4342-0051; fax (11) 4331-6596; f. 1961; cap. and res $10.8m., dep. $58.1m. (Dec. 1992); Pres. ALFREDO B. ARREGUI.

Other National Bank

Banco Hipotecario Nacional: Alsina 353, 1087 Buenos Aires; tel. (11) 4347-5470; fax (11) 4347-5416; f. 1886; partially privatized in Jan. 1999; mortgage bank; cap. and res $322.4m., dep. $83.6m. (April 1992); Govt Admin. HORACIO JOSÉ AGUSTÍN ALVAREZ RIVERO; 23 brs.

Foreign Banks

ABN Amro Bank N.V. (Netherlands): Florida 361, Casilla 171, 1005 Buenos Aires; tel. (11) 4320-0600; fax (11) 4322-0839; f. 1914; cap. and res $37.7m., dep. $94.5m. (June 1992); Gen. Man. CÉSAR A. DEYMONNAZ.

Banca Nazionale del Lavoro, SA—BNL (Italy): Florida 40, 1005 Buenos Aires; tel. (11) 4323-4400; fax (11) 4323-4689; internet www.bnl.com.ar; cap. $272m., dep. $2,306m. (June 1999); took over Banco de Italia y Río de la Plata in 1987; Pres. ADEMARO LANZARA; Gen. Man. NICCOLO PANDOLFIU; 136 brs.

Banco do Brasil, SA (Brazil): Sarmiento 487, Casilla 2684, 1041 Buenos Aires; tel. (11) 4394-0939; fax (11) 4394-9577; f. 1960; cap. and res $33.9m., dep. $2.0m. (June 1992); Gen. Man. HÉLIO TESTONI.

Banco do Estado de São Paulo (Brazil): Tucumán 821, Casilla 2177, 1049 Buenos Aires; tel. (11) 4325-9533; fax (11) 4325-9527; cap. and res $11.7m., dep. $6.7m. (June 1992); Gen. Man. CARLOS ALBERTO BERGAMASCO.

Banco Europeo para América Latina (BEAL), SA: Juan D. Perón 338, 1038 Buenos Aires; tel. (11) 4331-6544; fax (11) 4331-2010; e-mail bealbsa@inter.prov.com; f. 1914; cap. and res $60m., dep. $121m. (Nov. 1996); Gen. Mans JEAN PIERRE SMERD, KLAUS KRSGER.

Banco Itaú Buen Ayre, SA (Brazil): 25 de Mayo 476, 2°, 1002 Buenos Aires; tel. (11) 4325-6698; fax (11) 4394-1057; internet www.itau.com.ar; fmrly Banco Itaú Argentina, SA, renamed as above following purchase of Banco del Buen Ayre, SA, in May 1998; cap. and res $20.2m., dep. $1.2m. (June 1992); Dir-Gen. ANTONIO CARLOS B. DE OLIVEIRA; 94 brs.

Banco Sudameris Argentina, SA: Juan D. Perón 500, 1038 Buenos Aires; tel. (11) 4329-5200; fax (11) 4331-2793; e-mail marketing@sudameris.com.ar; internet www.sudameris.com.ar; f. 1912; cap. $89.0m., res $11.5m., dep. $977.2m. (Dec. 1998); Exec. Dir CARLOS GONZÁLEZ TABOADA.

Banco Supervielle-Société Générale, SA: Reconquista 330, 1003 Buenos Aires; tel. (11) 4329-8000; fax (11) 4329-8080; e-mail info@ ar.socgen.com; internet www.supervielle.com.ar; f. 1887 as Banco Supervielle de Buenos Aires, SA, adopted current name in 1979; cap. $50.5m., res $25.7m., dep. $649.7m. (Dec. 1997); Chair. and Gen. Man. MARC-EMMANUEL VIVES; 40 brs.

Bank of Tokyo-Mitsubishi, Ltd (Japan): Avda Corrientes 420, 1043 Buenos Aires; tel. (11) 4348-2001; fax (11) 4322-6607; f. 1956; cap. and res $20m., dep. $81m. (Sept. 1994); Gen. Man. KAZUO OMI.

BankBoston NA (USA): Florida 99, 1005 Buenos Aires; tel. (11) 4346-2000; fax (11) 4346-3200; f. 1784; cap. $456.8m., dep. $4,012m.; total assets $8,677m. (Sept. 1998); Pres. Ing. MANUEL SACERDOTE; 139 brs.

Banque Nationale de Paris, SA (France): 25 de Mayo 471, 1002 Buenos Aires; tel. (11) 4318-0318; fax (11) 4311-1368; f. 1981; cap. and res $29.4m., dep. $86.7m. (June 1992); Gen. Man. CHISLAIN DE BEAUCÉ.

Chase Manhattan Bank (USA): Arenales 707, 5°, 1061 Buenos Aires; tel. (11) 4319-2400; fax (11) 4319-2416; f. 1904; cap. and res $46.3m., dep. $12,387m. (Sept. 1992); Gen. Man. MARCELO PODESTÁ.

Citibank, NA (USA): Colón 58, Bahía Blanca, 8000 Buenos Aires; tel. (11) 4331-8281; f. 1914; cap. and res $172.8m., dep. $660.8m. (June 1992); Pres. RICARDO ANGLES; Vice-Pres. GUILLERMO STANLEY; 16 brs.

Deutsche Bank Argentina, SA (Germany): Bartolomé Mitre 401, Casilla 995, 1036 Buenos Aires; tel. (11) 4343-2510; fax (11) 4343-

3536; f. 1960; cap. and res \$123.6m., dep. \$801.0m. (June 1994); Gen. Man. GERARDO GREISER; 47 brs.

Lloyds Bank (Bank of London and South America) Ltd (United Kingdom): Tronador 4890, 13°, Casilla 128, 1003 Buenos Aires; tel. (11) 4335-3551; fax (11) 4342-7487; f. 1862; subsidiary of Lloyds Bank TSB Group; cap. and res \$108.1m., dep \$583.4m. (Sept. 1997); Gen. Man. for Argentina COLIN J. MITCHELL; 31 brs.

Morgan Guaranty Trust Co of New York (USA): Avda Corrientes 411, 1043 Buenos Aires; tel. and fax (11) 4325-8046; cap. and res \$29.1m., dep. \$11.6m. (June 1992); Gen. Man. JOSÉ MCLOUGHLIN.

Republic National Bank of New York (USA): Bartolomé Mitre 343, 1036 Buenos Aires; tel. (11) 4343-0161; fax (11) 4331-6064; cap. and res \$17.2m., dep. \$13.6m. (March 1994); Gen. Man. ALBERTO MUCHNICK.

Scotiabank Quilmes, SA (Canada): Juan D. Perón 564, 1038 Buenos Aires; tel. (11) 1338-8000; fax (11) 4338-8511; e-mail bqcorp@infovia.com.ar; internet www.scotiabankquilmes.co.ar; f. 1907 as Banco Popular de Quilmes, SA, adopted current name in 1999 following merger with the Bank of Nova Scotia; cap. \$133.0m., res \$5.0m., dep. \$2,107.2m.; Pres. WILLIAM PETER SUTTON; 88 brs.

Bankers' Associations

Asociación de Bancos de la Argentina (ABA): San Martín 229, 10°, 1004 Buenos Aires; tel. (11) 4394-1430; fax (11) 4394-6340; e-mail webmaster@aba-argentina.com; internet www.aba-argentina.com; f. 1999 by merger of Asociación de Bancos de la República Argentina (f. 1919) and Asociación de Bancos Argentinos (f. 1972); Pres. Lic. EDUARDO J. ESCASANY; Exec. Dir Dr NORBERTO CARLOS PERUZZOTTI.

Asociación de Bancos del Interior de la República Argentina (ABIRA): Avda Corrientes 538, 4°, 1043 Buenos Aires; tel. (11) 4394-3439; fax (11) 4394-5682; f. 1956; Pres. Dr JORGE FEDERICO CHRISTENSEN; Dir RAÚL PASSANO; 30 mems.

Asociación de Bancos de Provincia de la República Argentina (ABAPRA): Florida 470, 1°, 1005 Buenos Aires; tel. (11) 4322-6321; fax (11) 4322-6721; f. 1959; Pres. JOSÉ MANUEL PABLO VIUDES; Man. LUIS B. BUCAFUSCO; 31 mems.

Federación de Bancos Cooperativos de la República Argentina (FEBANCOOP): Maipú 374, 9°/10°, 1006 Buenos Aires; tel. (11) 4394-9949; f. 1973; Pres. OMAR C. TRILLO; Exec. Sec. JUAN CARLOS ROMANO; 32 mems.

STOCK EXCHANGES

Mercado de Valores de Buenos Aires, SA: 25 de Mayo 367, 8°–10°, 1002 Buenos Aires; tel. (11) 4313-6021; fax (11) 4313-4472; internet www.merval.sba.com.ar; Pres. EUGENIO DE BARY.

There are also stock exchanges at Córdoba, Rosario, Mendoza and La Plata.

Supervisory Authority

Comisión Nacional de Valores (CNV): 25 de Mayo 175, 1002 Buenos Aires; tel. (11) 4342-4607; fax (11) 4331-0639; e-mail gharte@mecon.ar; internet www.cnv.gob.ar; monitors capital markets; Pres. GUILLERMO HARTENECK.

INSURANCE

Superintendencia de Seguros de la Nación: Avda Julio A. Roca 721, 5°, 1067 Buenos Aires; tel. (11) 4331-9821; fax (11) 4331-8733; f. 1938; Superintendent Dr IGNACIO WARNES.

In December 1993 there were 249 insurance companies operating in Argentina, of which 11 were foreign. The following is a list of those offering all classes or a specialized service.

La Agrícola, SA: Buenos Aires; tel. (11) 4394-5031; f. 1905; associated co La Regional; all classes; Pres. LUIS R. MARCO; First Vice-Pres. JUSTO J. DE CORRAL.

Aseguradora de Créditos y Garantías, SA: Avda Corrientes 415, 4°, 1043 Buenos Aires; tel. (11) 4394-4037; fax (11) 4394-0320; e-mail acgtias@infovia.com.ar; internet www.acg.com.ar; f. 1965; Pres. Lic. HORACIO SCAPPARONE; Exec. Vice-Pres. Dr ANÍBAL E. LÓPEZ.

Aseguradora de Río Negro y Neuquén: Avda Alem 503, Cipolletti, Río Negro; tel. (299) 477-2725; fax (299) 477-0321; f. 1960; all classes; Gen. Man. ERNESTO LÓPEZ.

Aseguradores de Cauciones, SA: Paraguay 580, 1057 Buenos Aires; tel. (11) 4318-3700; fax (11) 4318-3799; e-mail directorio@caucion.com.ar; internet www.caucion.com.ar; f. 1968; all classes; Pres. JOSÉ DE VEDIA.

Aseguradores Industriales, SA: Juan D. Perón 650, 6°, 1038 Buenos Aires; tel. (11) 4326-8881; fax (11) 4326-3742; f. 1961; all classes; Exec. Pres. Dir LUIS ESTEBAN LOFORTE.

La Austral: Buenos Aires; tel. (11) 442-9881; fax (11) 4953-4459; f. 1942; all classes; Pres. RODOLFO H. TAYLOR.

Colón, Cía de Seguros Generales, SA: San Martín 548–550, 1004 Buenos Aires; tel. (11) 4320-3800; fax (11) 4320-3802; f. 1962; all classes; Gen. Man. L. D. STSCK.

Columbia, SA de Seguros: Juan D. Perón 690, 1038 Buenos Aires; tel. (11) 4325-0208; fax (11) 4326-1392; f. 1918; all classes; Pres. MARTA BLANCO; Gen. Man. HORACIO H. PETRILLO.

El Comercio, Cía de Seguros a Prima Fija, SA: Avda Corrientes 415, 3° y 5°, 1043 Buenos Aires; tel. (11) 4394-9111; fax (11) 4393-1207; f. 1889; all classes; Pres. DONALD JOSÉ SMITH BALMACEDA; Man. PABLO DOMINGO F. LONGO.

Cía Argentina de Seguros de Créditos a la Exportación, SA: Corrientes 345, 7°, 1043 Buenos Aires; tel. (11) 4313-3048; fax (11) 4313-2919; f. 1967; covers credit and extraordinary and political risks for Argentine exports; Pres. LUIS ORCOYEN; Gen. Man. Dr MARIANO A. GARCÍA GALISTEO.

Cía Aseguradora Argentina, SA: Avda Roque S. Peña 555, 1035 Buenos Aires; tel. (11) 430-1571; fax (11) 430-5973; f. 1918; all classes; Man. GUIDO LUTTINI; Vice-Pres. ALBERTO FRAGUIO.

La Continental, Cía de Seguros Generales SA: Avda Corrientes 655, 1043 Buenos Aires; tel. (11) 4393-8051; fax (11) 4325-7101; f. 1912; all classes; Pres. RAÚL MASCARENHAS.

La Franco-Argentina, SA: Buenos Aires; tel. (11) 430-3091; f. 1896; all classes; Pres. Dr GUILLERMO MORENO HUEYO; Gen. Man. Dra HAYDÉE GUZIAN DE RAMÍREZ.

Hermes, SA: Edif. Hermes, Bartolomé Mitre 754/60, 1036 Buenos Aires; tel. (11) 4331-4506; fax (11) 4343-5552; e-mail hermes@mbox.servicenet.com.ar; f. 1926; all classes; Pres. DIONISIO KATOPODIS; Gen. Man. FRANCISCO MARTÍN ZABALO.

India, Cía de Seguros Generales SA: Avda Roque S. Peña 728/36, 1035 Buenos Aires; tel. (11) 4328-6001; fax (11) 4328-5602; f. 1950; all classes; Pres. ALFREDO JUAN PRIESSE; Vice-Pres. Dr RAÚL ALBERTO GUARDIA.

Instituto Italo-Argentino de Seguros Generales, SA: Avda Roque S. Peña 890, 1035 Buenos Aires; tel. (11) 4320-9200; fax (11) 4320-9229; f. 1920; all classes; Pres. ALEJANDRO A. SOLDATI.

La Meridional, Cía Argentina de Seguros SA: Juan D. Perón 646, 1038 Buenos Aires; tel. (11) 4909-7000; fax (11) 4909-7274; e-mail meridi@starnet.net.ar; f. 1949; life and general; Pres. GUILLERMO V. LASCANO QUINTANA; Gen. Man. PETER HAMMER.

Plus Ultra, Cía Argentina de Seguros, SA: San Martín 548–50, 1004 Buenos Aires; tel. (11) 4393-5069; f. 1956; all classes; Gen. Man. L. D. STSCK.

La Primera, SA: Blvd Villegas y Oro, Trenque Lauquén, Prov. Buenos Aires; tel. (11) 4393-8125; all classes; Pres. ENRIQUE RAÚL U. BOTTINI; Man. Dr RODOLFO RAÚL D'ONOFRIO.

La Rectora, SA: Avda Corrientes 848, 1043 Buenos Aires; tel. (11) 4394-6081; fax (11) 4394-2071; f. 1951; all classes; Pres. PEDRO PASCUAL MEGNA; Gen. Man. ANTONIO LÓPEZ BUENO.

La República Cía Argentina de Seguros Generales, SA: San Martín 627/29, 1374 Buenos Aires; tel. (11) 4314-1000; fax (11) 4318-8778; f. 1928; group life and general; Pres. JUAN E. CAMBIASO; Gen. Man. EDUARDO ESCAFFI.

Sud América Terrestre y Marítima Cía de Seguros Generales, SA: Florida 15, 2°, Galería Florida 1, 1005 Buenos Aires; tel. (11) 4340-5100; fax (11) 4340-5380; f. 1919; all classes; Pres. EMA SÁNCHEZ DE LARRAGOITI; Vice-Pres. ALAIN HOMBREUX.

La Unión Gremial, SA: Mitre 665/99, 2000 Rosario, Santa Fe; tel. (341) 426-2900; fax (341) 425-9802; f. 1908; general; Gen. Man. EDUARDO IGNACIO LLOBET.

La Universal: Buenos Aires; tel. (11) 442-9881; fax (11) 4953-4459; f. 1905; all classes; Pres. RODOLFO H. TAYLOR.

Zurich-Iguazú Cía de Seguros, SA: San Martín 442, 1004 Buenos Aires; tel. (11) 4329-0400; fax (11) 4322-4688; f. 1947; all classes; Pres. RAMÓN SANTAMARINA.

Reinsurance

Instituto Nacional de Reaseguros: Avda Julio A. Roca 694, 1067 Buenos Aires; tel. (11) 4334-0084; fax (11) 4334-5588; f. 1947; reinsurance in all branches; Pres. and Man. REINALDO A. CASTRO.

Insurance Associations

Asociación Argentina de Cías de Seguros (AACS): 25 de Mayo 565, 2°, 1002 Buenos Aires; tel. (11) 4312-7790; fax (11) 4312-6300; e-mail secret@aacsra.org.ar; f. 1894; 60 mems; Pres. ROBERTO F. E. SOLLITTO.

Asociación de Entidades Aseguradoras Privadas de la República Argentina (EAPRA): Esmeralda 684, 4°, 1007 Buenos Aires; tel. (11) 4393-2268; fax (11) 4393-2283; f. 1875; asscn of 12 foreign insurance cos operating in Argentina; Pres. Dr PIERO ZUPPELLI; Sec. BERNARDO VON DER GOLTZ.

Trade and Industry

GOVERNMENT AGENCIES

Cámara de Exportadores de la República Argentina: Avda Roque S. Peña 740, 1°, 1035 Buenos Aires; tel. (11) 4394-4351; fax (11) 4328-1003; e-mail contacto@cera.org.ar; internet www.cera.org.ar; f. 1943 to promote exports; 700 mems.

Consejo Federal de Inversiones: San Martín 871, 1004 Buenos Aires; tel. (11) 4313-5557; fax (11) 4313-4486; federal board to co-ordinate domestic and foreign investment and provide technological aid for the provinces; Sec.-Gen. Ing. JUAN JOSÉ CIÁCERA.

Dirección de Forestación (DF): Avda Paseo Colón 982, anexo jardin, 1063 Buenos Aires; tel. (11) 4349-2124; fax (11) 4349-2102; e-mail fsanti@sagyp.mecon.ar; assumed the responsibilities of the national forestry commission (Instituto Forestal Nacional—IFONA) in 1991, following its dissolution; supervised by the Secretaría de Agricultura, Ganadería y Pesca; maintains the Centro de Documen-tación e Información Forestal; Library Man. NILDA E. FERNÁNDEZ.

Instituto de Desarrollo Económico y Social (IDES): Araoz 2838, 1425 Buenos Aires; tel. (11) 4804-4949; fax (11) 4804-5856; e-mail ides@clasco.edu.ar; internet www.clacso.edu.ar/~ides; f. 1960; investigation into social sciences and promotion of social and econ-omic devt; 700 mems; Pres. BERNARDO KOSACOFF; Sec. ADRIANA MARSHALL.

Junta Nacional de Granos: Avda Paseo Colón 359, 1063 Buenos Aires; tel. (11) 430-0641; national grain board; supervises commer-cial practices and organizes the construction of farm silos and port elevators; Pres. JORGE CORT.

Secretaría de Agricultura, Ganadería, Pesca y Alimentación: Avda Paseo Colón 922/982, 1°, Of. 146, 1063 Buenos Aires; tel. (11) 4349-2291; fax (11) 4349-2292; e-mail mpelle@sagyp.mecon.ar; internet www.siiap.sagyp.mecon.ar; f. 1871; undertakes regulatory, promotional, advisory and administrative responsibilities on behalf of the meat, livestock and fisheries industries; Sec. FELIPE C. SOLA.

Sindicatura General de Empresas Públicas: Lavalle 1429, 1048 Buenos Aires; tel. (11) 449-5415; fax (11) 4476-4054; f. 1978; to exercise external control over wholly- or partly-owned public enter-prises; Pres. ALBERTO R. ABAD.

DEVELOPMENT ORGANIZATIONS

Instituto Argentino del Petróleo y Gas: Maipú 645, 3°, 1006 Buenos Aires; tel. (11) 4325-8008; fax (11) 4393-5494; e-mail informa@iapg.org.ar; internet www.iapg.org.ar; f. 1958; established to promote the devt of petroleum exploration and exploitation; Pres. Ing. E. J. ROCCHI.

Secretario de Programación Económica: Hipólito Yrigoyen 250, 8°, Of. 819, Buenos Aires; tel. (11) 4349-5710; fax (11) 4349-5714; f. 1961 to formulate national long-term devt plans; Sec. Dr JUAN JOSÉ LACH.

Sociedad Rural Argentina: Florida 460, 1005 Buenos Aires; tel. (11) 4324-4700; fax (11) 4324-4774; f. 1866; private org. to promote the devt of agriculture; Pres. ENRIQUE C. CROTTO; 9,400 mems.

CHAMBERS OF COMMERCE

Cámara Argentina de Comercio: Avda Leandro N. Alem 36, 1003 Buenos Aires; tel. (11) 4331-8051; fax (11) 4331-8055; e-mail gerencia@cac.com.ar; f. 1924; Pres. JORGE LUIS DI FIORI.

Cámara de Comercio, Industria y Producción de la República Argentina: Florida 1, 4°, 1005 Buenos Aires; tel. (11) 4331-0813; fax (11) 4331-9116; f. 1913; Pres. JOSÉ CHEDIEK; Vice-Pres. Dr FAUSTINO S. DIÉGUEZ, Dr JORGE M. MAZALAN; 1,500 mems.

Cámara de Comercio Exterior de Rosario: Avda Córdoba 1868, 2000 Rosario, Santa Fe; tel. and fax (341) 425-7147; e-mail ccer@commerce.com.ar; internet www.commerce.com.ar; f. 1958; deals with imports and exports; Pres. JUAN CARLOS RETAMERO; Vice-Pres. EDUARDO C. SALVATIERRA; 150 mems.

Similar chambers are located in most of the larger centres and there are many foreign chambers of commerce.

INDUSTRIAL AND TRADE ASSOCIATIONS

Asociación de Importadores y Exportadores de la República Argentina: Avda Belgrano 124, 1°, 1092 Buenos Aires; tel. (11) 4342-0010; fax (11) 4342-1312; e-mail aiera@aiera.org.ar; internet www.aiera.org.ar; f. 1966; Pres. HÉCTOR MARCELLO VIDAL; Man. ADRIANO DE FINA.

Asociación de Industriales Textiles Argentinos: Buenos Aires; tel. (11) 4373-2256; fax (11) 4373-2351; f. 1945; textile industry; Pres. BERNARDO ABRAMOVICH; 250 mems.

Asociación de Industrias Argentinas de Carnes: Buenos Aires; tel. (11) 4322-5244; meat industry; refrigerated and canned beef and mutton; Pres. JORGE BORSELLA.

Asociación Vitivinícola Argentina: Güemes 4464, 1425 Buenos Aires; tel. (11) 4774-3370; f. 1904; wine industry; Pres. LUCIANO COTUMACCIO; Man. Lic. MARIO J. GIORDANO.

Cámara de Sociedades Anónimas: Florida 1, 3°, 1005 Buenos Aires; tel. (11) 4342-9013; fax (11) 4342-9225; Pres. Dr ALFONSO DE LA FERRERE; Man. CARLOS ALBERTO PERRONE.

Centro de Exportadores de Cereales: Bouchard 454, 7°, 1106 Buenos Aires; tel. (11) 4311-1697; fax (11) 4312-6924; f. 1943; grain exporters; Pres. RAUL S. LOEH.

Confederaciones Rurales Argentinas: México 628, 2°, 1097 Buenos Aires; tel. (11) 4261-1501; Pres. ARTURO J. NAVARRO.

Coordinadora de Actividades Mercantiles Empresarias: Buenos Aires; Pres. OSVALDO CORNIDE.

Federación Lanera Argentina: Avda Paseo Colón 823, 5°, 1063 Buenos Aires; tel. (11) 4300-7661; fax (11) 4361-6517; f. 1929; wool industry; Pres. JULIO AISENSTEIN; Sec. RICHARD VON GERSTENBERG; 80 mems.

EMPLOYERS' ORGANIZATION

Unión Industrial Argentina (UIA): Avda Leandro N. Alem 1067, 11°, 1001 Buenos Aires; tel. (11) 4313-4474; fax (11) 4313-2413; e-mail uia01@act.net.ar; f. 1887; re-established in 1974 with the fusion of the Confederación Industrial Argentina (CINA) and the Confederación General de la Industria; following the dissolution of the CINA in 1977, the UIA was formed in 1979; asscn of manufactu-rers, representing industrial corpns; Pres. OSVALDO RIAL; Sec.-Gen. Dr JOSÉ I. DE MENDIGUREN.

UTILITIES

Regulatory Authorities

Ente Nacional Regulador de la Electricidad (ENRE): Avda Eduardo Madero 1020, 10°, 1106 Buenos Aires; tel. (11) 4314-5805; fax (11) 4314-5416; internet www.enre.gov.ar.

Ente Nacional Regulador del Gas (ENARGAS): Suipacha 636, 10°, 1008 Buenos Aires; tel. (11) 4325-9292; fax (11) 4348-0550; internet www.enargas.gov.ar.

Electricity

Central Costanera, SA (CECCO): Avda España 3301, 1107 Buenos Aires; tel. (11) 4307-3040; fax (11) 4307-1706; generation, transmission, distribution and sale of thermal electric energy; Chair. JAIME BAUZÁ BAUZÁ.

Central Puerto, SA (CEPU): Avda Tomás Edison 2701, 1104 Buenos Aires; tel. (11) 4317-5000; fax (11) 4317-5099; electricity generating co; CEO ANTONIO BÜCHI BUĆ.

Comisión Nacional de Energía Atómica (CNEA): Avda del Libertador 8250, 1429 Buenos Aires; tel. (11) 4704-1384; fax (11) 4704-1176; e-mail freijo@cnea.edu.ar; internet www.cnea .gov.ar; f. 1950; scheduled for transfer to private ownership; nuclear energy science and technology; Pres. JACOBO DAN BENINSON.

Comisión Técnica Mixta de Salto Grande (CTMSG): Avda Leandro N. Alem 449, 1003 Buenos Aires; operates Salto Grande hydroelectric station, which has an installed capacity of 650 MW; joint Argentine-Uruguayan project.

Dirección de Energía de la Provincia de Buenos Aires: Calle 55, No. 570, La Reja, 1900 Buenos Aires; tel. (11) 4415-000; fax (11) 4216-124; f. 1957; electricity co for province of Buenos Aires; Dir AGUSTÍN NÚÑEZ.

Empresa Distribuidora y Comercializadora Norte, SA (EDENOR): Azopardo 1025, 1107 Buenos Aires; tel. (11) 4348-2121; fax (11) 4334-0805; e-mail ofitel@edenor.com.ar; internet www .edenor.com.ar; distribution of electricity.

Empresa Distribuidora Sur, SA (EDESUR): San José, 140, 1076 Buenos Aires; tel. (11) 4381-8981; fax (11) 4383-3699; internet www.edesur.com.ar; f. 1992; distribution of electricity; Gen. Man. Ing. JOSÉ MARÍA ROVIRA.

Entidad Binacional Yacyretá: Avda Eduardo Madero 942, 21°–22°, 1106 Buenos Aires; tel. (11) 4510-7500; e-mail rrpp@eby.org.ar; internet www.yacyreta.org.ar; operates the hydroelectic dam at Yacyretá on the Paraná river, owned jointly by Argentina and Paraguay. Completed in 1998, it is one of the world's largest hydroelectric complexes, consisting of 20 generators with a total generating capacity of 2,700 MW.

Hidronor Ingenieria y Servicios, SA (HISSA): Hipólito Yrigoyen 1530, 6°, 1089 Buenos Aires; tel. and fax (11) 4382-6316; e-mail info@hidronor.com; formerly HIDRONOR, SA, the largest producer of electricity in Argentina; responsible for developing the hydroelec-tric potential of the Limay and neighbouring rivers; transferred to private ownership in 1992 and divided into the following companies:

Central Hidroeléctrica Alicurá, SA: Avda Leandro N. Alem 712, 7°, 1001 Buenos Aires.

Central Hidroeléctrica Cerros Colorados, SA: Avda Leandro N. Alem 690, 12°, 1001 Buenos Aires.

Central Hidroeléctrica El Chocón, SA: Suipacha 268, 9°, Of. A, Buenos Aires.

Hidroeléctrica Piedra del Aguila, SA: Avda Tomás Edison 1251, 1104 Buenos Aires; tel. (11) 4315-2586; fax (11) 4317-5174; Pres. Dr URIEL FEDERICO O'FARRELL; Gen. Man. IGNACIO J. ROSNER.

Transener, SA: Avda Paseo Colón 728, 6°, 1063 Buenos Aires; tel. (11) 4342-6925; fax (11) 4342-7147; energy transmission co.

Pérez Companc, SA: Maipú 1, 1084 Buenos Aires; tel. (11) 4331-8393; fax (11) 4331-8369; internet www.pecom.com.ar; operates the hydroelectric dam at Pichi Picún Leufu; Chair. JORGE GREGORIO PÉREZ COMPANC.

Servicios Eléctricos del Gran Buenos Aires, SA (SEGBA): Balcarce 184, 1002 Buenos Aires; tel. (11) 4331-1901; Principal Officer CARLOS A. MATTAUSCH.

Gas

Distribuidora de Gas del Centro, SA: Avda Hipólito Yrigoyen 475, 5000 Córdoba; tel. (351) 4688-100; fax (351) 4681-568; state-owned co, distributes natural gas.

Metrogás, SA: Avda Montes de Oca 1120, 1271 Buenos Aires; tel. (11) 4309-1000; fax (11) 4309-1366; internet www.metrogas.com; gas distribution; Dir-Gen. WILLIAM ADAMSON.

Transportadora de Gas del Norte, SA: Don Bosco 3672, 3°, 1206 Buenos Aires; tel. (11) 4959-2000; fax (11) 4959-2253; state-owned co, distributes natural gas; Gen. Man. FREDDY CAMEO.

Transportadora de Gas del Sur, SA (TGS): Don Bosco 3672, 5°, 1206 Buenos Aires; tel. (11) 4865-9050; fax (11) 4865-9059; e-mail totgs@tgs.com.ar; internet www.tgs.com.ar; processing and transport of natural gas; Gen. Dir EDUARDO OJEA QUINTANA

Water

Aguas Argentinas: Buenos Aires; distribution of water in Buenos Aires; privatized in 1993; Dir-Gen. JEAN-LOUIS CHAUSSADE.

TRADE UNIONS

Congreso de los Trabajadores Argentinos (CTA): Buenos Aires; dissident trade union confederation; Leader VÍCTOR DE GENARO.

Confederación General del Trabajo—CGT (General Confederation of Labour): Buenos Aires; f. 1984; Peronist; represents approx. 90% of Argentina's 1,100 trade unions; Sec.-Gen. HUGO MOYANO.

Movimiento de Trabajadores Argentinos (MTA): Buenos Aires; dissident trade union confederation.

Transport

Comisión Nacional de Regulación del Transporte (CNRT): Maipú 88, 1084, Buenos Aires; tel. (11) 4819-3000; e-mail msenet@mecon.gov.ar; internet www.cnrt.gov.ar; regulates domestic and international transport services; part of Ministry of Infrastructure and Housing.

Secretaría de Obras Públicas y Transporte: Hipólito Yrigoyen 250, 12°, 1310 Buenos Aires; tel. (11) 4349-7254; fax (11) 4349-7201; Sec. Ing. ARMANDO GUIBERT.

Secretaría de Transporte Metropolitano y de Larga Distancia: Hipólito Yrigoyen 250, 12°, 1310 Buenos Aires; tel. (11) 4349-7162; fax (11) 4349-7146; Under-Sec. Dr ARMANDO CANOSA.

Secretaría de Transporte Aero-Comercial: Hipólito Yrigoyen 250, 12°, 1310 Buenos Aires; tel. (11) 4349-7203; fax (11) 4349-7206; Under-Sec. Arq. FERMÍN ALARCIA.

Dirección de Estudios y Proyectos: Hipólito Yrigoyen 250, 12°, 1310 Buenos Aires; tel. (11) 4349-7127; fax (11) 4349-7128; Dir Ing. JOSÉ LUIS JAGODNIK.

RAILWAYS

Lines: General Belgrano (narrow-gauge), General Roca, General Bartolomé Mitre, General San Martín, Domingo Faustino Sarmiento (all wide-gauge), General Urquiza (medium-gauge) and Línea Metropolitana, which controls the railways of Buenos Aires and its suburbs. There are direct rail links with the Bolivian Railways network to Santa Cruz de la Sierra and La Paz; with Chile, through the Las Cuevas–Caracoles tunnel (across the Andes) and between Salta and Antofagasta; with Brazil, across the Paso de los Libres and Uruguayana bridge; with Paraguay (between Posadas and Encarnación by ferry-boat); and with Uruguay (between Concordia and Salto). In 1995 there were 33,000 km of tracks. In the Buenos Aires commuter area 270.4 km of wide-gauge track and 52 km of medium gauge track are electrified.

Plans for the eventual total privatization of Ferrocarriles Argentinos (FA) were initiated in 1991, with the transfer to private

ownership of the Rosario–Bahía Blanca grain line and with the reallocation of responsibility for services in Buenos Aires to the newly-created Ferrocarriles Metropolitanos, prior to its privatization.

In early 1993 central government funding for the FA was suspended and responsibility for existing inter-city passenger routes was devolved to respective provincial governments. However, owing to lack of resources, few provinces have successfully assumed the operation of services, and many trains have been suspended. At the same time, long-distance freight services were sold as six separate 30-year concessions (including lines and rolling stock) to private operators. By late 1996 all freight services had been transferred to private management, with the exception of Ferrocarril Belgrano, SA, which was in the process of undergoing privatization. The Buenos Aires commuter system was divided into eight concerns (one of which incorporates the underground railway system) and was offered for sale to private operators as 10- or 20-year (subsidized) concessions. The railway network is currently regulated by the National Commission for Transport Regulation (CNRT—see above).

Ferrocarriles Argentinos (FA): Salta 1929, 1137 Buenos Aires; tel. (11) 4304-1557; fax (11) 4313-3129; f. 1948 with the nationalization of all foreign property; autonomous body but policies established by the Secretaría de Obras Públicas y Transporte; dismantled and responsibilities transferred in 1993 (see above); Trustee DANIEL OSCAR HALPERIN; Gen. Man. P. SUÁREZ.

Ferrocarriles Metropolitanos, SA (FEMESA): Bartolomé Mitre 2815, Buenos Aires; tel. (11) 4865-4135; fax (11) 4861-8757; f. 1991 to assume responsibility for services in the capital; 820 km of track; Pres. MATÍAS ORDÓÑEZ; concessions to operate services have been awarded to:

Ferrovías.

Metropolitano: f. 1993; operates three commuter lines.

Metrovías: Bartolomé Mitre 3342, 1201 Buenos Aires; tel. (11) 4959-6800; fax (11) 4866-3037; e-mail info@metrovias.com.ar; internet www.metrovias.com; f. 1994; operates subway (Subterráneos de Buenos Aires—see below) and two commuter lines.

Trainmet.

Trenes de Buenos Aires: took over operations of two commuter lines from state in 1995.

Cámara de Industriales Ferroviarios: Alsina 1609, 1°, Buenos Aires; tel. (11) 4371-5571; private org. to promote the devt of Argentine railway industries; Pres. Ing. ANA MARÍA GUIBAUDI.

The following consortia were awarded 30-year concessions to operate rail services, during 1991–94:

Consorcio Nuevo Central Argentino (CNCA): Buenos Aires; operates freight services on the Bartolomé Mitre lines; 5,011 km of track; Pres. H. URQUIA.

Ferrocarril Buenos Aires al Pacífico/San Martín (BAP): Avda Santa Fe 4636, 3°, Buenos Aires; tel. (11) 4778-2486; fax (11) 4778-2493; operates services on much of the San Martín line, and on 706 km of the Sarmiento line; 6,106 km of track; Pres. and Gen. Man. E. GLEZER.

Ferrocarril General Belgrano, SA (FGB): Maipú 88, 1084 Buenos Aires; tel. and fax (11) 4343-7220; fax (11) 4343-7229; f. 1993; operates freight services; Pres. Dr IGNACIO A. LUDVEÑA.

Ferrocarril Mesopotámico General Urquiza (FMGU): Avda Santa Fe 4636, 3°, 1425 Buenos Aires; tel. (11) 4778-2425; fax (11) 4778-2493; operates freight services on the Urquiza lines; 2,272 km of track; Pres. and Gen. Man. E. GLEZER.

Ferroexpreso Pampeano (FEPSA): Bouchard 680, 9°, 1106 Buenos Aires; tel. (11) 4318-4900; fax (11) 4510-4945; operates services on the Rosario–Bahía Blanca grain lines; 5,193 km of track; Pres. H. MASOERO.

Ferrosur Roca (FR): Bouchard 680, 8°, 1106 Buenos Aires; tel. (11) 4319-3900; fax (11) 4319-3901; e-mail ferrosur@impsat1.com.ar; operator of freight services on the Roca lines since 1993; 3,000 km of track; Pres. AMELIA LACROZE DE FORTABAT; Gen. Man. SERGIO DO REGO.

Buenos Aires also has an underground railway system:

Subterráneos de Buenos Aires: Bartolomé Mitre 3342, 1201 Buenos Aires; tel. (11) 4862-6844; fax (11) 4864-0633; f. 1913; became completely state-owned in 1951; fmrly controlled by the Municipalidad de la Ciudad de Buenos Aires; responsibility for operations was transferred, in 1993, to a private consortium (Metrovías) with a 20-year concession; five underground lines totalling 36.5 km, 63 stations, and a 7.4 km light rail line with 13 stations, which was inaugurated in 1987; Pres. A.VERRA.

ROADS

In 1998 there were 215,434 km of roads, of which 29.5% were paved. Four branches of the Pan-American highway run from Buenos Aires to the borders of Chile, Bolivia, Paraguay and Brazil. In 1996 9,932 km of main roads were under private management. Construction work on a 41-km bridge across the River Plate (linking Punta Lara in Argentina with Colonia del Sacramento in Uruguay) was scheduled to begin in the late 1990s.

Dirección Nacional de Vialidad: Avda Julio A. Roca 378, Buenos Aires; tel. (11) 4343-2838; fax (11) 4343-7292; controlled by the Secretaría de Transportes; Gen. Man. Ing. ELIO VERGARA.

Asociación Argentina de Empresarios Transporte Automotor (AAETA): Bernardo de Irigoyen 330, 6°, 1072 Buenos Aires; e-mail aaeta@sei.com.ar; internet www.aaeta.org.ar; Gen. Man. Ing. MARCELO GONZÁLEZ.

Federación Argentina de Entidades Empresarias de Auto-transporte de Cargas (FADEAC): Avda 25 de Mayo 1370, 3°, 1372 Buenos Aires; tel. (11) 4383-3635; Pres. ROGELIO CAVALIERI IRIBARNE.

There are several international passenger and freight services including:

Autobuses Sudamericanos, SA: Buenos Aires; tel. (11) 4307-1956; fax (11) 4307-1956; f. 1928; international bus services; car and bus rentals; charter bus services; Pres. ARMANDO SCHLECKER HIRSCH; Gen. Man. MIGUEL ANGEL RUGGIERO.

INLAND WATERWAYS

There is considerable traffic in coastal and river shipping, mainly carrying petroleum and its derivatives.

Dirección Nacional de Construcciones Portuarias y Vías Navegables: Avda España 221, 4°, Buenos Aires; tel. (11) 4361-5964; responsible for the maintenance and improvement of waterways and dredging operations; Dir Ing. ENRIQUE CASALS DE ALBA.

SHIPPING

There are more than 100 ports, of which the most important are Buenos Aires, Quequén and Bahía Blanca. There are specialized terminals at Ensenada, Comodoro Rivadavia, San Lorenzo and Campana (petroleum); Bahía Blanca, Rosario, Santa Fe, Villa Concepción, Mar del Plata and Quequén cereals); and San Nicolas and San Fernando (raw and construction materials). In 1998 Argentina's merchant fleet totalled 501 vessels amounting to 498,715 grt.

Administración General de Puertos: Avda Ing. Huergo 431, 1°, Buenos Aires; tel. (11) 4343-2425; fax (11) 4331-0298; e-mail comercial@bairesport.gov.ar; internet www.bairesport.gov.ar; f. 1956; state enterprise for direction, administration and exploitation of all national sea- and river-ports; scheduled for transfer to private ownership; Pres. LUIS A. ROURA.

Capitanía General del Puerto: Avda Julio A. Roca 734, 2°, 1067 Buenos Aires; tel. (11) 434-9784; f. 1967; co-ordination of port operations; Port Captain Capt. PEDRO TARAMASCO.

Administración General de Puertos (Santa Fe): Duque 1 Cabacera, Santa Fe; tel. (42) 41732.

Consorcio de Gestión del Puerto de Bahía Blanca: Avda Dr Mario M. Guido s/n, 8103 Provincia de Buenos Aires; tel. (91) 57-3213; Pres. JOSÉ E. CONTE; Sec.-Gen. CLAUDIO MARCELO CONTE.

Terminales Portuarias Argentinas: Buenos Aires; operates one of five recently privatized cargo and container terminals in the port of Buenos Aires.

Terminales Río de la Plata: Buenos Aires; operates one of five recently privatized cargo and container terminals in the port of Buenos Aires.

Empresa Líneas Marítimas Argentinas, SA (ELMA): Avda Corrientes 389, 1327 Buenos Aires; tel. (11) 4312-9245; fax (11) 4311-7954; f. 1941 as state-owned org.; transferred to private ownership in 1994; operates vessels to northern Europe, the Mediterranean, west and east coasts of Canada and the USA, Gulf of Mexico, Caribbean ports, Brazil, Pacific ports of Central and South America, Far East, northern and southern Africa and the Near East; Pres. PABLO DOMINGO DE ZORZI.

Other private shipping companies operating on coastal and overseas routes include:

Antártida Pesquera Industrial: Moreno 1270, 5°, 1091 Buenos Aires; tel. (11) 4381-0167; fax (11) 4381-0519; Pres. J. M. S. MIRANDA; Man. Dir J. R. S. MIRANDA.

Astramar Cía Argentina de Navegación, SAC: Buenos Aires; tel. (11) 4311-3678; fax (11) 4311-7534; Pres. ENRIQUE W. REDDIG.

Bottacchi SA de Navegación: Maipú 509, 2°, 1006 Buenos Aires; tel. (11) 4392-7411; fax (11) 411-1280; Pres. ANGEL L. M. BOTTACCHI.

Maruba S. en C. por Argentina: Maipú 535, 7°, 1006 Buenos Aires; tel. (11) 4322-7173; fax (11) 4322-3353; Chartering Man. R. J. DICKIN.

Yacimientos Petrolíferos Fiscales (YPF): Avda Roque S. Peña 777, 1364 Buenos Aires; tel. (11) 446-7271; privatization finalized in 1993; Pres. NELLS LEÓN.

CIVIL AVIATION

Argentina has 10 international airports (Aeroparque Jorge Newbery, Córdoba, Corrientes, El Plumerillo, Ezeiza, Jujuy, Resistencia, Río Gallegos, Salta and San Carlos de Bariloche). Ezeiza, 35 km from Buenos Aires, is one of the most important air terminals in Latin America. More than 30 airports were scheduled for transfer to private ownership in the late 1990s.

Aerolíneas Argentinas: Bouchard 547, 9°, 1106 Buenos Aires; tel. (11) 4317-3000; fax (11) 4317-3593; internet www.aerolineas .com.ar; f. 1950; transfer to private ownership initiated in 1990; services to North and Central America, Europe, the Far East, New Zealand, South Africa and destinations throughout South America; the internal network covers the whole country; passengers, mail and freight are carried; Pres. MANUEL MORÁN.

Austral Líneas Aéreas (ALA): Avda Leandro N. Alem 1134, 1001 Buenos Aires; tel. (11) 4317-3600; fax (11) 4317-3777; internet www.austral.com.ar; f. 1971; domestic flights linking 27 cities in Argentina; Pres. MANUEL MORÁN.

CATA Líneas Aéreas S.A.C.I.F.I.: Cerrito 1320, 3°, 1010 Buenos Aires; tel. (11) 4812-3390; fax (11) 4627-3721; e-mail cataaer@ satlink.com; internet www.webs.satlink.com/usuarios/c/cataaer; f. 1978; domestic passenger flights; Pres. ROQUE PUGLIESE.

Líneas Aéreas Entre Ríos: Salvador Caputo, Paraná , Entre Ríos; tel. (343) 436-2013; fax (343) 436-2177; e-mail contable@laer.com.ar; internet www.laer.com.ar; f. 1988; scheduled domestic passenger services; Gen. Man. LUIS VARISCO.

Líneas Aéreas del Estado (LADE): Perú 710, 1068 Buenos Aires; tel. (11) 4362-1853; fax (11) 4300-0031; e-mail director@lade.com.ar; Dir GUILLERMO JOSÉ TESTONI.

Líneas Aéreas Privadas Argentinas (LAPA): Avda Santa Fe 1970, 2°, 1123 Buenos Aires; tel. (11) 4812-0953; fax (11) 4814-2100; e-mail gcaputi@lapa.com.ar; f. 1976; domestic scheduled passenger services, and international routes to Uruguay; Pres. GUSTAVO ANDRÉS DEUTSCH.

Transporte Aéreo Costa Atlántica (TACA): Bernardo de Yrigoyen 1370, 1°, Ofs 25–26, 1138 Buenos Aires; tel. (11) 4307-1956; fax (11) 4307-8899; f. 1956; domestic and international passenger and freight services between Argentina and Bolivia, Brazil and the USA; Pres. Dr ARMANDO SCHLECKER HIRSCH.

Transportes Aéreos Neuquén: Diagonal 25 de Mayo 180, 8300 Neuquén; tel. (299) 4423076; fax (299) 4488926; e-mail tancentr@satlink.com.ar; domestic routes; Pres. JOSÉ CHALÉN; Gen. Man. PATROCINIO VALVERDE MORAIS.

Valls Líneas Aéreas: Río Grande, Tierra del Fuego; f. 1995; operates three routes between destinations in southern Argentina, Chile and the South Atlantic islands.

Tourism

Argentina's superb tourist attractions include the Andes mountains, the lake district centred on Bariloche (where there is a National Park), Patagonia, the Atlantic beaches and Mar del Plata, the Iguazú falls, the Pampas and Tierra del Fuego. Tourist arrivals in Argentina in 1998 totalled 4,859,867. In the same year tourist receipts were US $5,363m.

Secretaría de Turismo de la Nación: Suipacha 1111, 20°, 1368 Buenos Aires; tel. (11) 4312-5611; fax (11) 4313-6834; internet www.turismo.gov.ar; Sec. FRANCISCO MAYORGA.

Asociación Argentina de Agencias de Viajes y Turismo (AAAVYT): Viamonte 640, 10°, 1053 Buenos Aires; tel. (11) 4325-4691; fax (11) 4322-9641; e-mail secretaria@aaavyt.org.ar; f. 1951; Pres. MARCOS A. PALACIOS; Gen. Man. GERARDO BELO.

ARMENIA

Introductory Survey

Location, Climate, Language, Religion, Flag, Capital

The Republic of Armenia is situated in south-west Transcaucasia, on the north-eastern border of Turkey. Its other borders are with Iran to the south, Azerbaijan to the east, and Georgia to the north. The Nakhichevan Autonomous Republic, an Azerbaijani territory, is situated to the south, separated from the remainder of Azerbaijan by Armenian territory. The climate is typically continental: dry, with wide temperature variations. Winters are cold, the average January temperature in Yerevan being –3°C (26°F), but summers can be very warm, with August temperatures averaging 25°C (77°F), although high altitude moderates the heat in much of the country. Precipitation is low in the Yerevan area (annual average 322 mm), but much higher in the mountains. The official language is Armenian, the sole member of a distinct Indo-European language group. It is written in the Armenian script. Kurdish is used in broadcasting and publishing for some 56,000 Kurds inhabiting Armenia. Most of the population are adherents of Christianity, the largest denomination being the Armenian Apostolic Church. There are also Russian Orthodox, Protestant, Islamic and Yazidi communities. The national flag (approximate proportions 3 by 2) consists of three equal horizontal stripes, of red, blue and orange. The capital is Yerevan.

Recent History

Although Armenia was an important power in ancient times, for much of its history it has been ruled by foreign states. In 1639 Armenia was partitioned, with the larger, western part being annexed by Turkey and the eastern region becoming part of the Persian Empire. In 1828, after a period of Russo–Persian conflict, eastern Armenia was ceded to the Russian Empire by the Treaty of Turkmanchai, and subsequently became a province of the Empire. At the beginning of the 20th century Armenians living in western, or Anatolian, Armenia, under Ottoman rule, were subject to increasing persecution by the Turks. As a result of brutal massacres and deportations (particularly in 1915), the Anatolian lands were largely emptied of their Armenian population, and it was estimated that during 1915–22 some 1.5m. Armenians perished. After the collapse of Russian imperial power in 1917, Russian Armenia joined the anti-Bolshevik Transcaucasian Federation, which included Georgia and Azerbaijan. This collapsed when threatened by Turkish forces, and on 28 May 1918 Armenia was proclaimed an independent state. Without Russian protection, however, the newly formed republic was almost defenceless against Turkish expansionism and was forced to cede the province of Kars and other Armenian lands to Turkey. Armenia was recognized as an independent state by the Allied Powers and by Turkey in the Treaty of Sèvres, signed on 10 August 1920. However, the rejection of the Treaty by the new Turkish ruler, Mustafa Kemal, left Armenia vulnerable to renewed Turkish threats. In September Turkish troops attacked Armenia, but they were prevented from establishing full control over the country by the invasion of Armenia, from the east, by Russian Bolshevik troops, and the founding, on 29 November 1920, of a Soviet Republic of Armenia. In December 1922 the republic became a member, together with Georgia and Azerbaijan, of the Transcaucasian Soviet Federative Socialist Republic (TSFSR), which, in turn, became a constituent republic of the USSR. In 1936 the TSFSR was dissolved and Armenia became a full union republic of the USSR.

Although many Armenians suffered under Communist rule, advances were made in economic and social development. During the period of tsarist rule Russian Armenia had been an underdeveloped region of the empire, with very little infrastructure; however, in the Armenian Soviet Socialist Republic (SSR), the authorities implemented a policy of forced modernization, which expanded communications and introduced industrial plants. Literacy and education were also improved. A programme to collectivize agriculture, initiated on a voluntary basis in 1928, engendered little enthusiasm; collectivization was enforced in 1930, and many thousands of peasants who opposed it were deported. Armenians experienced further suffering during the Stalinist purges of the late 1930s, in which thousands

of people were executed or imprisoned. During the Second World War (1939–45), Armenia avoided occupation by German forces, despite their invasion of the USSR in June 1941. Consequently, the republic provided an essential source of labour for the Soviet economy, and as many as 600,000 Armenians served in the Soviet armies (of whom an estimated 350,000 were killed). In the immediate post-war period the Soviet Government gave priority to developing the industrial sector in Armenia, while expanding the agricultural collectivization programme. In the late 1940s an estimated 150,000 Armenians of the 'diaspora' returned to the republic.

The Soviet leader Mikhail Gorbachev's policies of *perestroika* (restructuring) and *glasnost* (openness), introduced following his accession to power in 1985, had little initial impact in Armenia. The first manifestations of the new policies were campaigns against corruption in the higher echelons of the Communist Party of Armenia (CPA). On a more public level, environmental problems became a focus for popular protest. The first demonstrations against ecological degradation took place in September 1987, but the demands of protesters soon began to include the redress of historical and political grievances.

Of the historical and ethnic issues discussed in late 1987 and early 1988, the most significant was the status of Nagornyi Karabakh, an autonomous oblast (region) within neighbouring Azerbaijan, largely populated by (non-Muslim) Armenians, control of which had been ceded to Azerbaijan in 1921 (see chapter on Azerbaijan). Demands for the incorporation of Nagornyi Karabakh into the Armenian SSR began within the enclave in early 1988. In February as many as 1m. people took part in demonstrations in Yerevan, the Armenian capital, in support of these demands. The demonstrations were organized by Yerevan intellectuals, who formed a group known as the Karabakh Committee. In response to increased unrest within Armenia, many Azerbaijanis began to leave the republic. Rumours of ill-treatment of the refugees led to anti-Armenian riots in Sumgait (Azerbaijan) in late February, in which 26 Armenians died. This event provoked further Armenian anger, which was compounded by the decision of the Presidium of the USSR's Supreme Soviet (legislature) not to transfer Nagornyi Karabakh to Armenia. Strikes and rallies continued under the leadership of the officially outlawed Karabakh Committee, and the inability of the local authorities to control the unrest led to the dismissal, in May, of the First Secretary (leader) of the CPA. In December, however, the issue of Nagornyi Karabakh was temporarily subordinated to the problems of overcoming the effects of a severe earthquake, which had struck northern Armenia. Some 25,000 people were reported to have been killed and many thousands more were made homeless. In the chaos following the earthquake the members of the Karabakh Committee were arrested, ostensibly for interfering in relief work. They were released only in May 1989, after huge demonstrations took place, protesting against their continued internment. Meanwhile, in January 1989, the Soviet Government had formed a Special Administration Committee of the Council of Ministers to preside over Nagornyi Karabakh, although the enclave remained under formal Azerbaijani jurisdiction.

Throughout 1989 *glasnost* allowed a much fuller examination of Armenian history and culture, and several unofficial groups, concerned with both cultural and political issues, were formed. In May the *yerakuyn*, the national flag of independent Armenia, was flown again, and 28 May, the anniversary of the establishment of independent Armenia, was declared a national day. However, internal politics continued to be dominated by events in Nagornyi Karabakh, and unrest continued both in Armenia and within the enclave. In September Azerbaijan implemented an economic blockade against Armenia, seriously affecting the reconstruction programme required after the 1988 earthquake. In November 1989 the Special Administration Committee was disbanded, and Azerbaijan resumed control over Nagornyi Karabakh. This prompted the Armenian Supreme Soviet to declare the enclave part of a 'unified Armenian Republic'. In January 1990 this was declared unconstitutional by the USSR's Supreme

Soviet. The Armenian Supreme Soviet responded by granting itself the power to veto any legislation approved by the central authorities.

The increasing disillusionment with the Soviet Government was apparently responsible for the low level of participation in the elections to the Armenian Supreme Soviet, which took place in May–July 1990. No party achieved an overall majority, but the Armenian Pan-National Movement (APNM), the successor to the Karabakh Committee, was the largest single party, with some 35% of the seats in the legislature. Supported by other non-communist groups, Levon Ter-Petrossian, a leader of the APNM, defeated Vladimir Movsissian, the First Secretary of the CPA, in elections to the chairmanship of the Supreme Soviet. Vazgen Manukian, also a leader of the APNM, was appointed Prime Minister. On 23 August the legislature adopted a declaration of sovereignty, including a claim to the right to maintain armed forces and a demand for international recognition that the Turkish massacres of Armenians in 1915 constituted genocide. The Armenian SSR was renamed the Republic of Armenia. The new Government began to establish political and commercial links with the Armenian diaspora, and several prominent exiles returned to the republic. In late November 1990 the CPA, after heated debate, voted to become an independent organization within the Communist Party of the Soviet Union (CPSU).

The Armenian Government refused to enter into the negotiations between Soviet republics on a new treaty of union, which took place in late 1990 and early 1991, and officially boycotted the referendum on the renewal of the USSR, which was held in March 1991 in nine republics. Instead, the legislature decided to conduct a referendum on Armenian secession from the USSR, to be held in September. Initially, it was planned that the referendum would be conducted within the provisions of the Soviet law on secession, adopted in April by the all-Union Supreme Soviet. This entailed a transitional period of at least five years before full independence could be achieved.

In late April 1991 there was an escalation of tension in the Nagornyi Karabakh region. The Armenian Government continued to deny any direct involvement in the violence, claiming that the attacks were outside its control, being organized by units of the ethnic Armenian 'Nagornyi Karabakh self-defence forces'. However, Azerbaijan countered that Armenia was, in fact, playing an aggressive role in the conflict, and made reference to 'Armenian expeditionary forces'. In a further complication, Armenia suggested that the Soviet leadership was supporting Azerbaijan, following the latter's agreement to sign the new union treaty, and punishing Armenia for its moves towards independence, for its refusal to take part in discussions on the union treaty and for its nationalization of CPA property.

The moderate policies of the new APNM-led Government, especially in developing relations with Turkey, attracted criticism from more extreme nationalist groups, notably the Union for National Self-Determination (UNS), which continued to seek the recovery of lands lost to Turkey after the First World War. The CPA attacked the Government for its willingness to promote relations with Turkey, as did the Armenian Revolutionary Federation (ARF, or Dashnaktsutyun, which had formed the Government of independent Armenia during 1918–20). The CPA also strongly opposed the idea of secession, while the ARF advocated a more gradual process towards independence. The UNS campaigned for immediate secession, which was in breach of the constitutional procedure.

The attempted coup in Moscow, and subsequent events of August 1991, forced the Government to accelerate the moves towards secession, and provided further support for those advocating complete independence for Armenia. The referendum on independence took place, as scheduled, on 21 September. According to official returns, 94.4% of the electorate took part, and 99.3% of voters supported Armenia's becoming 'an independent, democratic state outside the Union'. On 23 September, instead of conforming to the Soviet law on secession, the Supreme Soviet declared Armenia to be thenceforth a fully independent state. Meanwhile, in early September, a congress of the CPA voted to dissolve the party.

The independence declaration was followed, on 16 October 1991, by an election to the post of President of the Republic. Six candidates participated in the poll, but it was won overwhelmingly by the incumbent, Ter-Petrossian (with some 87% of the total votes). The President continued to demand international recognition of Armenia, but on 18 October, with the leaders of seven other Soviet republics, he signed a treaty to establish an economic community, stressing, however, that it did not encroach on Armenia's political independence, and refusing to sign a new treaty on political union. The Armenian leadership did, nevertheless, join the Commonwealth of Independent States (CIS, see p. 157), and signed the founding Alma-Ata (Almaty) Declaration, on 21 December. In early 1992 Armenia was admitted to the Conference on Security and Co-operation in Europe (CSCE, which was renamed the Organization for Security and Co-operation in Europe—OSCE—in December 1994, see p. 252) and the UN.

Economic conditions in Armenia deteriorated alarmingly during 1992, and there were widespread shortages of foodstuffs and fuel. The situation was exacerbated not only by the continuing conflict in Nagornyi Karabakh (see below), but also by the fighting in neighbouring Georgia (impeding supplies to Armenia), and the ongoing economic blockade by Azerbaijan (and its ally, Turkey). Compounding the economic crisis was the enormous influx of refugees from Nagornyi Karabakh and Azerbaijan. There were also growing signs of public dissatisfaction with the Ter-Petrossian administration, and in mid-August mass rallies were staged in Yerevan to demand the President's resignation. In February 1993 there were further large-scale rallies in Yerevan, at which demonstrators protested at the continuing energy crisis and reiterated demands for Ter-Petrossian to resign. Earlier in the month Ter-Petrossian had dismissed the Prime Minister, Khosrov Haroutunian, following disagreements over economic and social policy. A new Council of Ministers was subsequently announced; it was headed by Hrant Bagratian, who was widely known as an economic reformist.

Armenia's economic crisis intensified during 1993. Popular resentment against Ter-Petrossian's leadership increased, and hundreds of thousands of Armenians were reported to have emigrated, owing to the level of economic hardship. In the latter half of 1994 thousands of people participated in anti-Government protests, which were organized at regular intervals by the Union of Civic Accord (UCA), an association of opposition groups.

The assassination in December 1994 of a former mayor of Yerevan prompted the Government to effect a number of measures aimed at eliminating terrorism. By far the most radical of these was the suspension in late December of the leading opposition party, the ARF. The party was officially charged with having engaged in 'terrorist activities, political murders and drugs-trafficking'. Anti-Government forces condemned these measures and monthly rallies were organized by the UCA in early 1995 in protest at official harassment of opposition activists.

Armenia's first post-Soviet legislative elections were held in July 1995. Thirteen parties and organizations contested the 190 seats of the new National Assembly under a mixed system of voting (150 seats to be filled by majority vote and the remaining 40 by proportional representation on the basis of party lists). Nine parties, including the ARF, were barred from participation. The Republican bloc (an alliance of six groups, led by the APNM) won an overwhelming majority of the seats in the Assembly (119). Eight seats were won by the Shamiram Women's Party, while the revived CPA achieved seven. The UNS took three seats and the ARF, despite the official ban, succeeded in winning one seat. Forty-five independent candidates won representation in the Assembly. Some irregularities were reported by OSCE observers, and opposition parties contested the authenticity of the election results. In late July President Ter-Petrossian appointed the new Government, in which Hrant Bagratian remained as Prime Minister. A referendum on the new Armenian Constitution (under discussion from late 1992) was held simultaneously with the general election. Of the 56% of the electorate who participated in the plebiscite, some 68% voted in favour of the Constitution, which granted wide-ranging executive authority to the President. Under the existing electoral law, the National Assembly comprised 190 deputies; however, the new Constitution provided for an Assembly of 131 deputies (effective from the next general election).

The presidential election was held on 22 September 1996. Ter-Petrossian was the candidate of the Republican bloc, while five opposition parties united to support Vazgen Manukian, the Chairman of the National Democratic Union (NDU). Preliminary results indicated that Ter-Petrossian had been re-elected; however, the opposition alleged that widespread electoral malpractice had been perpetrated, and thousands of opposition supporters staged protest rallies in Yerevan, demanding the

President's resignation. International observers reported serious irregularities in the electoral proceedings, which cast doubt on the validity of the result. On 25 September supporters of Manukian stormed the National Assembly building, injuring, among others, the Chairman and his deputy. A temporary ban on rallies was imposed, and large numbers of opposition supporters, including parliamentary deputies, were arrested. According to the final election results, Ter-Petrossian received 51.8% of votes cast, while Manukian secured 41.3% (although he achieved a significantly higher percentage than Ter-Petrossian in Yerevan). Opposition parties maintained their demand for fresh elections and a number of them also boycotted the elections to the new bodies of local government, established by the Constitution in 1995, which were held in November. The resignation of Bagratian as Prime Minister, allegedly in response to opposition to his programme of economic reforms, was announced in November 1996; he was replaced by Armen Sarkissian. The latter resigned in March 1997 on grounds of ill health, and was replaced by Robert Kocharian, hitherto the President of Nagornyi Karabakh, in what was regarded as an attempt by Ter-Petrossian to reduce the pressure from opposition parties to hold fresh presidential elections.

Following the unexpected resignation of Ter-Petrossian on 3 February 1998, as a result of government disputes over his support of the OSCE plan for a peaceful, step-by-step settlement in Nagornyi Karabakh (see below), a presidential election was held on 16 March. In a second round of voting, the acting President and incumbent Prime Minister, Robert Kocharian, achieved victory over the former Soviet-era CPA leader, Karen Demirchian, with 59.5% of the votes cast. The results were declared valid, despite some OSCE-reported electoral irregularities, and Kocharian was inaugurated as President on 9 April. On the following day Kocharian appointed Armen Darbinian, the erstwhile Minister of Finance and the Economy, as Prime Minister.

In early May 1998 Kocharian relegalized the ARF, and appointed two more members of the party, including its leader, Vahan Hovhanissian, to positions in the Government (one member of the ARF had been included in the Government on its appointment the previous month). Later in May the President announced the formation of a commission to formulate constitutional amendments. In March 1999 the President approved six amendments, including proposals to reduce the size of the National Assembly by a further 30 deputies. If passed by the National Assembly, the proposed amendments were to be subject to a national referendum. Meanwhile, in early July 1998 it was announced that, as part of a major reform to the judicial and legal system, the Supreme Court was to be replaced by a Court of Cassation.

A controversial new law on electoral procedure, approved by the National Assembly in November 1998 (despite fierce opposition from a number of deputies), which provided for a 131-member legislature, composed of 75 deputies elected by majority vote through single-mandate constituencies and the remaining 56 chosen under a system of proportional representation on the basis of party lists, was fully adopted in February 1999; shortly afterwards it was announced that legislative elections were to be held on 30 May. In April the Republican Party of Armenia (RPA) and the People's Party of Armenia (PPA) formed an electoral alliance, the Unity bloc (Miasnutiun), which was to campaign as a single party. The Unity bloc proved highly successful, winning a total of 55 seats in the National Assembly. The CPA secured 11 seats and the ARF obtained nine, while the Law and Unity bloc, the Law-governed Country Party and the NDU won six seats each; the APNM, the Armenian Democratic Party, the Mission Party and the National Concord Party each secured one seat, and independents accounted for the remaining 32. In July independents won the two remaining seats in the by-elections held in two constituencies where the results had been annulled. Meanwhile, in early June Darbinian was replaced as Prime Minister by Vazgen Sarkissian, the unofficial leader of the RPA and hitherto Minister of Defence; Darbinian was demoted to the post of Minister of the Economy. At the first session of the new National Assembly, which was held several days later, Karen Demirchian, a former Communist leader, but now head of the PPA, was elected Chairman of the legislature. Later in June a government reorganization was conducted, including the division of a number of ministries.

In January 1999 the Prosecutor-General petitioned the National Assembly for permission to arrest the Chairman of the APNM and former Minister of the Interior, Vano Siradeghian,

thereby removing his parliamentary immunity, for his alleged participation in a number of political murders in the mid-1990s. The petition was rejected, and Siradeghian left the country, reportedly for medical treatment, shortly afterwards. In February, however, the legislature, under threat of dissolution, endorsed the petition, and on his return to Armenia in May, Siradeghian (who had been re-elected Chairman of the APNM *in absentia*) was placed under arrest; his trial commenced in Yerevan in January 2000.

Politically-motivated attacks and murders were rife in Armenia during late 1998 and 1999. In February 1999 the Deputy Minister of the Interior and National Security and commander of Armenia's internal troops, Maj.-Gen. Artsrun Makarian, was found shot dead; Makarian's bodyguards were subsequently charged with the murder, amid speculation that he had been killed to prevent him from giving evidence against Siradeghian.

On 27 October 1999 Armenia was thrown into political turmoil when five gunmen besieged the National Assembly debating chamber. Eight people were killed during the attack, including Prime Minister Sarkissian, the Chairman of the legislature, Karen Demirchian, and his two deputies, and the Minister for Urgent Issues, Leonard Petrossian. The gunmen (who claimed no political affiliation) held some 50 hostages for several hours; their stated aim was to seek revenge against the 'corrupt political elite'. Having voluntarily surrendered, following overnight negotiations with President Kocharian, the assailants were charged with terrorist offences and with murder. In the aftermath of the attack, the Minister of the Interior and the Minister of National Security both tendered their resignations (which were accepted, following the appointment of a new Prime Minister). At the beginning of November the National Assembly held an extraordinary sitting, at which Armen Khachatrian, of the PPA, was elected Chairman of the legislature. On the following day President Kocharian appointed Aram Sarkissian, the younger brother of Vazgen and a political novice, as the new Prime Minister, on the recommendation of members of the Unity bloc. A number of new ministers were appointed in mid-November; at the same time the post of Minister for Urgent Issues was abolished. In February 2000 further cabinet changes were made.

In April 2000 the majority Unity bloc initiated impeachment proceedings against President Kocharian, as a result of his decision not to allow the Military Prosecutor-General, Gagik Jahangirian, to testify in a parliamentary hearing concerning the shootings of October 1999. Three days later, however, a majority in the National Assembly voted to cancel the proceedings, on the grounds that the President had not acted in contravention of the Constitution. In early May the Prime Minister was dismissed by Kocharian, who cited his inability to work with the Sarkissian Government. Andranik Markarian, the leader of the RPA, was appointed premier on 12 May and a cabinet reshuffle took place later that month. Both the President and the new Prime Minister pledged to end the conflict that had hitherto existed between their respective posts and the legislature.

In late September 2000 Armen Khachatrian stood down as Chairman of the legislature, as the result of dissension between the two constituent factions of the Unity bloc, led by Khachatrian and Prime Minister Markarian. However, following an inquiry, initiated at the request of the President, the Constitutional Court declared Khachatrian's resignation to have contravened the Constitution, and he was reinstated. In November the Minister of Finance and the Economy, Levon Barkhoudarian, was dismissed by the President, reportedly owing to the accumulation of wages' and pensions' arrears; he was replaced by Vardan Khachatrian. In the same month the Minister for State Revenues resigned, to be replaced by Andranik Manukian.

In late October 2000, while President Kocharian was absent owing to medical reasons, the opposition demanded his resignation, amid claims that he had taken steps of detriment to the country, with regard to Nagornyi Karabakh. At the end of October a protest rally was held, attended by some 15,000 people. One of the organizers of the demonstration, Arkadii Vardanian, was subsequently arrested and charged with attempting to overthrow the Government.

The proclamation of Armenia's independence in September 1991 led to an escalation of hostilities in the disputed enclave of Nagornyi Karabakh. In that month the territory declared itself an independent republic, and the violence intensified following the dissolution of the USSR in December. In January

1992 the President of Azerbaijan, Ayaz Mutalibov, placed the region under direct presidential rule; in the same month Azerbaijani forces surrounded and attacked Stepanakert, the capital of Nagornyi Karabakh, while the Armenians laid siege to Shusha, a town with a mainly Azerbaijani population. In May the Nagornyi Karabakh self-defence forces (which the Armenian Government continued to claim to be operating without its military support) captured Shusha, thereby gaining complete control of the enclave and ending the bombardment of Stepanakert. With the capture of the strategically-important Lachin valley, the Armenian militia succeeded in opening a 'corridor' inside Azerbaijan, linking Nagornyi Karabakh with Armenia proper.

In June 1992 Azerbaijani forces launched a sustained counter-offensive in Nagornyi Karabakh, recapturing villages both inside and around the enclave, and expelling several thousand inhabitants, thus exacerbating the already urgent refugee crisis. In early August Azerbaijani forces resumed the bombardment of Stepanakert. In response to the escalation of attacks and ensuing military gains by Azeri forces, the Nagornyi Karabakh legislature declared a state of martial law, and a state defence committee, in close alignment with the Ter-Petrossian administration, replaced the enclave's government.

In early 1993 the military situation in Nagornyi Karabakh was reversed, as Armenian forces undertook a series of successful offensives, regaining territory that they had lost in 1992 and also taking control of large areas of Azerbaijan surrounding the enclave. With the capture of the Kelbajar district of Azerbaijan in April 1993, the Armenians succeeded in creating a second corridor linking the enclave with Armenia and effectively securing the whole swath of Azerbaijani territory extending south to the Lachin corridor. Many thousands of Azeris fled or were expelled from their homes. The Armenian position was only strengthened by the growing political turmoil in Azerbaijan in mid-1993 (q.v.), and by late June Armenian forces had secured full control of Nagornyi Karabakh.

The Armenian seizure of Azerbaijani territory prompted widespread international condemnation, particularly by neighbouring Turkey and Iran, the latter fearing a massive influx of refugees from south-western Azerbaijan. Resolutions adopted by the UN Security Council, demanding the withdrawal of Armenian forces from Azerbaijan, went unheeded; by late August 1993 as much as 20% of Azerbaijan's total territory was reported to have been captured by the Nagornyi Karabakh Armenian forces. In late October the Turkish leadership stated that no normalization of relations between Turkey and Armenia could occur until Armenian aggression in Azerbaijan had ceased. Nevertheless, hostilities reintensified: yet more Azerbaijani territory came under the control of the Armenians, who had extended their operations as far south as the Azerbaijan-Iran border. Azeri forces launched a major new counter-offensive in December, recapturing some of the territory that they had lost to the Armenians during the year. A series of cease-fire agreements was reached in the first half of 1994, but none was lasting. In February it was reported that as many as 18,000 people had been killed since 1988, with a further 25,000 wounded. The number of displaced Azeris was believed to have exceeded 1m.

However, in early May 1994, following protracted mediation by the CSCE and Russia, a new cease-fire agreement was signed by the Ministers of Defence of Armenia and Azerbaijan and representatives of Nagornyi Karabakh. Although some violations of the cease-fire were subsequently reported, the agreement was formalized in late July. Ter-Petrossian held talks with the President of Azerbaijan, Heydar Aliyev, in Moscow, in early September. Although agreement was reached on some key provisions of a future peace treaty, Aliyev stated that his willingness to negotiate such an accord depended on the unconditional withdrawal of Armenian forces from occupied Azerbaijani territory. Negotiations were held at regular intervals throughout 1995 under the aegis of the 'Minsk Group' of the OSCE. However, progress towards reaching a political settlement was hampered by Azerbaijan's demand for the return of Lachin and Shusha regions, as well as by its apparent unwillingness to recognize the Nagornyi Karabakh leadership as an equal party in the negotiations. Nevertheless, the cease-fire continued to be observed, with only sporadic violations reported, and in May the three sides carried out a large-scale exchange of prisoners of war. Direct discussions between Armenia and Azerbaijan, which were held in conjunction with the OSCE negotiations, were initiated in December.

Ter-Petrossian and Aliyev met, together with President Shevardnadze of Georgia, in April 1996 in Luxembourg, where they signed an agreement on partnership and co-operation with the European Union (EU, see p. 181) and affirmed their commitment to the 1994 cease-fire. A further exchange of prisoners of war occurred in May 1996. Little progress was made in the negotiations in the following months, and elections to the post of President of Nagornyi Karabakh, held in November, were condemned by Azerbaijan and criticized by the Minsk Group as a hindrance to the peace process. Robert Kocharian, the incumbent President, was re-elected with some 86% of the votes cast. He subsequently appointed Leonard Petrossian as Prime Minister.

In December 1996 Ter-Petrossian and Aliyev attended an OSCE summit meeting in Lisbon, Portugal. Following demands by Azerbaijan, the OSCE Chairman issued a statement recommending three principles that would form the basis of a future political settlement in the enclave: the territorial integrity of Armenia and Azerbaijan; the legal status of Nagornyi Karabakh, which would be granted broad autonomy within Azerbaijan; and security guarantees for the population of Nagornyi Karabakh. Armenia, however, refused to accept the terms of the statement.

Relations between the two countries deteriorated in early 1997, with mutual accusations of the stockpiling of weapons in preparation for the renewal of military conflict in Nagornyi Karabakh. In April Armenia temporarily withdrew from the direct negotiations that were being held in conjunction with the OSCE talks, and this was followed by a series of clashes on the Armenian-Azerbaijani border, which left many people killed and wounded. Negotiations under the auspices of the OSCE continued, however, and it was reported in late May that new proposals for a settlement to the conflict had been offered to the participants. Fresh elections to the post of President of Nagornyi Karabakh in early September, which were called following the appointment of Kocharian as Prime Minister of Armenia, were won by Arkadii Gukassian, with some 90% of the votes, but were criticized by the international community. Gukassian reportedly rejected the OSCE peace settlement on the grounds that the proposals presupposed Azerbaijan's sovereignty over the enclave. However, in late September it was reported that Armenia had accepted, in principle, the OSCE's plan for a stage-by-stage settlement of the conflict, which entailed the withdrawal of Armenian forces from six districts around Nagornyi Karabakh, to be followed by a decision on the status of the Shusha and Lachin corridors, and on the status of Nagornyi Karabakh itself. A statement by President Ter-Petrossian that Nagornyi Karabakh could hope neither to gain full independence, nor be united with Armenia, was severely condemned by opposition parties, and appeared to indicate a significant change in policy on the part of the President. Ter-Petrossian's cautious and moderate approach to the Nagornyi Karabakh crisis provoked much government disapproval and led to the President's resignation in early February 1998. His replacement, Kocharian, who was born in Nagornyi Karabakh, was expected to adopt a more belligerent and nationalistic stance towards resolving the situation in the disputed enclave. In June Leonard Petrossian resigned as Prime Minister of Nagornyi Karabakh, following a rift with his Minister of Defence; the erstwhile Deputy Prime Minister, Zhirayr Pogossian, replaced him in the premiership and a government reorganization was carried out. In late November the Armenian Government announced that, despite some reservations, it officially accepted the latest proposals put forward by the Minsk Group regarding a settlement of the conflict in Nagornyi Karabakh, which were based on the principle of a 'common state'; Azerbaijan, however, rejected the proposals. Minor cease-fire violations were committed by both sides during late 1998. Following an escalation in hostilities in mid-1999, both sides accused the other of attempting to destroy the 1994 cease-fire agreement. Despite a series of meetings between Presidents Kocharian and Aliyev in the second half of 1999, no substantive progress was made regarding the conflict. Meanwhile, in June President Gukassian dismissed Prime Minister Pogossian and the Government of Nagornyi Karabakh owing to their failure to resolve the enclave's economic problems. At the end of that month Anushavan Danielian was appointed to head a new administration. In July Pogossian was arrested and charged with illegally possessing arms and ammunition, and with losing a state document. In March 2000 President Gukassian sustained serious injuries following an attack by gunmen in Stepanakert. Among those arrested in connection with the assassination attempt was the former Minister of Defence of Nagornyi Karabakh, Samuel Babaian.

Armenia's relations with Russia in 1997 focused on the ratification by the Armenian legislature in April of a treaty allowing Russia to maintain military bases in Armenia for a period of 25 years. The ties between Russia and Armenia were reinforced by a declaration of alliance and co-operation and a number of bilateral agreements, concluded in September 2000. Armenia's close diplomatic and military links with Russia during the late 1990s (including reports of large supplies of Russian armaments to Armenia) were met with disapproval and suspicion on the part of the Azerbaijani Government. Armenia's relations with Georgia were furthered by the visit of the Georgian President, Eduard Shevardnadze, in May 1997, during which several co-operation agreements were signed. Relations were somewhat strained from late 1998, owing to the sporadic nature of Armenia's supply of electricity to Georgia (initiated only in September 1998), as a result of the latter's non-payment of bills. In September 1999, however, the two countries signed a declaration on the basic principles of co-operation and in March 2000 agreement was reached on the restructuring of arrears. Relations with Turkey remained uneasy, and in June an Armenian delegation invited to Turkey to attend a peace forum for the Caucasus was expelled. In October Turkey also co-operated with Azerbaijan to prevent Armenia from becoming a full member of the European Conference of Transport Ministers, thereby preventing the transit of Armenian vehicles through Azerbaijani territory. In the same month legislation that was to have recognized as genocide the massacre of Armenians by the Turks in 1915 was withdrawn from the US Congress, following the intervention of President Bill Clinton. In November, however, Italy expressed solidarity with Armenia by claiming the actions of 1915 to be genocide. In January 2001 the French parliament also adopted legislation recognizing as genocide the massacre of the Armenians. In August 2000 Armenia was the last of the countries bordering Iran to sign a treaty with the USA on the non-proliferation of nuclear weapons; the latter country also made clear its disapproval of plans for the construction of a natural-gas pipeline between Iran and Armenia.

In June 2000 the Parliamentary Assembly of the Council of Europe (PACE, see. p. 165) voted to admit both Armenia and Azerbaijan to that organization; both countries became full members in January 2001.

Government

Under the Constitution of 1995, the President of the Republic is Head of State and Supreme Commander-in-Chief of the armed forces, but also holds broad executive powers. The President is directly elected for a term of five years (and for no more than two consecutive terms of office). The President appoints the Prime Minister and, on the latter's recommendation, the members of the Government. Legislative power is vested in the 131-member National Assembly, which is elected for a four-year term by universal adult suffrage. For administrative purposes, Armenia is divided into 11 regions (*marz*), including the capital, Yerevan. The regions are subdivided into communities (*hamaynk*).

Defence

Following the dissolution of the USSR in December 1991, Armenia became a member of the Commonwealth of Independent States and its collective security system. The country also began to establish its own armed forces (estimated to number some 41,300 in August 2000). Military service is compulsory and lasts for 18 months (a law was passed in 2000, however, allowing for the exemption from military service, of university graduates and those engaged in certain professions). Some mobilization of reserves by conscription was reported. There is also a paramilitary force of an estimated 1,000, attached to the Ministry of National Security. In August 2000 there were approximately 3,100 Russian troops stationed on Armenian territory. The budget for 2000 allocated an estimated US $96m. to defence. In October 1994 Armenia joined NATO's 'Partnership for Peace' programme of military co-operation (see p. 243).

Economic Affairs

In 1998, according to estimates by the World Bank, Armenia's gross national product (GNP), measured at average 1996–98 prices, was US $1,728m., equivalent to $460 per head (or $2,074 on an international purchasing-power parity basis). During 1990–98, it was estimated, GNP per head declined at an average

annual rate of 4.7% in real terms, while the population increased at an average rate of 1.0% per year. It was estimated that, during 1990–98, Armenia's gross domestic product (GDP) decreased, in real terms, by an average of 4.7% annually. However, GDP increased by 3.3% in 1997, by 7.2% in 1998 and by 3.1% in 1999.

According to government figures, in 1998 agriculture and forestry contributed 31.1% of GDP and employed 42.5% of the working population. The FAO estimated the proportion of the working population employed in agriculture at 13.6% in 1998. The principal crops are potatoes and other vegetables, cereals and fruit. By late 1996 privatization of arable land was near to completion. Private farms accounted for some 98% of agricultural production in 1998. During 1990–99, according to estimates by the World Bank, agricultural GDP decreased, in real terms, at an average annual rate of 0.3%. The GDP of the sector increased by 4.0% in 1995 and by 1.7% in 1996.

According to government figures, in 1998 industry (including mining, manufacturing, construction and power) contributed 30.3% of GDP. In 1998 the sector employed 19.9% of the working population. According to the World Bank, industrial GDP increased at an average annual rate of 5.1% during 1980–90. However, during 1990–99 industrial GDP declined by an average of 9.0% annually. The GDP of the sector increased by 1.0% in 1995 and by 5.4% in 1996. According to government figures, industrial GDP grew by 2.5% in 1998, compared with 1997.

Armenia's mining sector has not yet been extensively developed. Copper, molybdenum, gold, silver and iron are extracted on a small scale, and there are reserves of lead and zinc. There are also substantial, although largely unexploited, reserves of mineral salt, calcium oxide and carbon, although, at the beginning of 2001, there were plans for a British company to commence mineral production in Armenia, within the framework of the EU's programme of Technical Assistance to the Commonwealth of Independent States (TACIS). Production of gold decreased significantly in the 1990s, but the Government hoped to encourage a recovery in the industry, following the conclusion of an agreement with a Canadian company to develop new extraction facilities, which went into production in 1998.

In 1999, according to the World Bank, the manufacturing sector provided 23% of Armenia's GDP. In 1995 the principal branches of manufacturing, measured by gross value of output, were food-processing and beverages (accounting for 40.5% of the total), machinery and metal products (13.0%), textiles and clothing (8.0%), chemicals (5.2%), and non-metallic mineral products (5.5%). Shortages of energy and raw materials in the mid-1990s resulted in a change of emphasis in industrial production, with the production of textiles and jewellery, for example, increasing, while traditional industries declined. During 1990–99 the GDP of the manufacturing sector declined at an average annual rate of 9.8%.

Armenia is heavily dependent on imported energy. The two principal suppliers of energy products are Russia (petroleum and derivatives) and Turkmenistan (natural gas); there are also plans to build a natural-gas pipeline to Armenia from Iran. It is, however, thought probable that Armenia has significant reserves of petroleum and natural gas. Hydroelectricity was the only significant domestic source of energy in 1994, providing 63.1% of Armenia's electricity supply. The country's sole nuclear power station, at Medzamor, was closed following the earthquake of 1988. However, in late 1995, in view of Armenia's worsening energy crisis, the station's second generating unit resumed operations, following restoration work. By 1995, with the recommissioning of the Medzamor power station, hydroelectricity provided only 35% of the country's electricity supply, and nuclear power contributed 5.5%. The nuclear share increased to 40.5% in the first six months of 1999. In 1996 proposals were made for the construction of a new nuclear power plant, scheduled for completion in 2010. By July 1999 Armenia had a surplus of electricity, some of which was exported to Georgia; a new high-voltage electricity line opened between the two countries in December 2000, despite a lack of consensus on the terms of its operation. In September 1999 Armenia signed an agreement with the EU Department for Relations with the CIS on shutting down the Medzamor power station by 2004. The agreement was, however, dependent on the construction of adequate alternative energy facilities. Imports of energy products comprised 31.3% of the value of merchandise imports in 1995.

The services sector contributed 38.6% of GDP in 1998 and an estimated 38.7% in 1999, and engaged 36.7% of the employed labour force in 1996. During 1980–90 the GDP of the sector increased by an annual average of 4.6%. However, services GDP declined by an average of 6.2% annually during 1990–99. The GDP of the sector increased by 23.2% in 1995 and by 13.6% in 1996. According to official statistics, growth of sectoral GDP was 8.5% in 1998, compared with 1997.

In 1998 Armenia recorded a visible trade deficit of US $577.4m., while the deficit on the current account of the balance of payments was $418.0m. In 1998 the principal source of imports, according to official statistics, was Russia, which provided 21.2% of the total; other main sources were the USA and the United Kingdom. In that year the major market for exports was Russia. Other important purchasers were Belgium, Iran and Turkmenistan. The principal exports in 1995 were pearls, precious and semi-precious stones, precious metals, imitation jewellery and coins; machinery and electrical equipment; and base metals. The principal imports in that year were mineral products, vegetable products, and live animals and animal products.

In 1998, according to official sources, there was a budgetary deficit of 40,690m. drams (equivalent to 4.3% of GDP). At the end of 1998 Armenia's total external debt was US $799.7m. (equivalent to 29% of GNP), of which $564m. was long-term public debt. In that year the cost of debt-servicing was equivalent to 8.9% of the value of exports of goods and services. The average annual rate of inflation was 176.0% in 1995, 18.7% in 1996, 13.9% in 1997, 8.7% in 1998 and 0.6% in 1999. At 1 April 1999 some 159,721 people were officially registered as unemployed, giving an unemployment rate of 10.5%.

Armenia is a member of the IMF, the World Bank and the European Bank for Reconstruction and Development (EBRD, see p. 176). It is also a member of the Organization of the Black Sea Economic Co-operation (BSEC, see p. 265), and attained membership of the World Trade Organization (WTO, see p. 292) in November 2000.

The collapse of the Soviet central planning system and internal trading structures exacerbated an already critical economic situation in Armenia. The decline was compounded by the severe effects of the earthquake in 1988 and of the conflict in Nagornyi Karabakh, which resulted in a massive influx of refugees from the enclave and from Azerbaijan. The economic blockade of Armenia by Azerbaijan and, subsequently, Turkey, as well as the civil war in Georgia, resulted in widespread shortages of food and fuel, and a concomitant decline in industrial production, owing to a lack of essential raw materials. A wide-ranging programme of economic reforms was initiated in the early 1990s, which included price liberalization, the promotion of privatization and a rationalization of the taxation system. By 1994 the first signs of economic recovery were observed, with growth in GDP and a decrease in the rate of inflation. The Government expanded its reform programme in the mid-1990s, to include a review of public-sector administration and expenditure, and reform of the energy sector. New agreements, which provided for the supply to Armenia of nuclear fuel and electricity, were concluded with Russia and Iran, respectively, in 1997, and a further agreement was reached with a Russian company, Gazprom, and an international energy corporation, concerning deliveries of natural gas and the upgrading of Armenia's gas infrastructure. The privatization programme was well advanced by late 1998 and the privatization of the country's four energy-distribution networks was scheduled to be completed in March 2000. In July 1999, however, the Minister of Finance announced that the Armenian economy was in recession, having been affected by the ongoing Russian economic crisis to a much greater extent than had been anticipated. This problem was compounded by the political crisis that followed the assassination in October of the Prime Minister and seven other government officials. The state budget for 2000, which was passed in March, envisaged a budgetary deficit of less than 5% of GDP, growth in GDP of 6% and consumer-price inflation of 5%. In September 1999 an agreement was reached with the World Bank that preferential credits worth US $238m. would be allocated to Armenia in 2000–03, which were to be used for medium-term economic programmes. Although progress was made during 2000 in restructuring the financial and energy sectors and providing increased spending on the health and education systems, in October international donor organizations criticized the pace of reform, and urged the Government to take action to encourage private-sector development and accelerate the privatization process. However, in the same month donor organizations agreed to supply aid and loans to Armenia, amounting to some US $350m. by the end of 2001; of this total, the World Bank was to provide some $75m. In December 2000, under the terms of a memorandum on assistance signed between Armenia and the Netherlands in 1998, over $4m. was allocated to develop agriculture, power engineering and ecology in Armenia.

Social Welfare

Much of Armenia's expenditure on health and welfare services during the 1990s was directed towards the victims of the 1988 earthquake, which caused an estimated 25,000 deaths and 8,500m. roubles' worth of damage. However, the collapse of the USSR and the escalation of the conflict in Nagornyi Karabakh encouraged a large number of refugees to flee to Armenia, creating new demands on social expenditure at a time of restricted government revenue. Furthermore, the adaptation to a market economy and the economic blockade on the country also exacerbated the situation. In 1992 it was estimated that about one-seventh of the population was 'in need' (excluding refugees—estimated at some 350,000). The Government sought to control social expenditure by targeting resources, as well as encouraging private and voluntary involvement.

A Pension Fund was created in 1991, and was subsequently merged with the Employment Fund, to create the Pension and Employment Fund, which, in 1992, was the only extrabudgetary fund remaining in Armenia. In September 1997 607,111 people were in receipt of state pensions, of which 71.7% were provided on account of old age. In 1993 there was one physician for every 261 people. In 1995 there were 90 hospital beds per 10,000 inhabitants. Current expenditure on health by all levels of government in 1996 was 6,306.4m. drams.

Education

Education is compulsory for nine years, to be undertaken between the ages of six and 17 years. Until the early 1990s the general education system conformed to that of the centralized Soviet system, but extensive changes were then introduced, with greater emphasis placed on Armenian history and culture. Primary education usually begins at seven years of age and lasts for four years. Secondary education, beginning at 11 years of age, comprises a first cycle of four years and a second of two years. In 1996 total enrolment at primary and secondary schools was equivalent to 87% of the school-age population. Primary enrolment in that year was equivalent to 86% of children in the relevant age-group, while the comparable ratio for secondary enrolment was 88%. Most instruction in higher institutions is in Armenian, although Russian is widely taught as a second language. In addition to Yerevan State University and the State Engineering University, higher education is provided at 13 institutes of higher education, with a total enrolment, in the 1996/97 academic year, of 35,517 students. Current expenditure on education by all levels of government in 1996 was 3,418.6m. drams. In 1989, according to census results, the rate of adult illiteracy in Armenia was 1.2% (males 0.6%; females 1.9%).

Public Holidays

2001: 1–2 January (New Year), 6 January (Christmas), 14–15 April (Easter), 24 April (Armenian Genocide Commemoration Day), 9 May (Victory Day), 28 May (Declaration of the First Armenian Republic Day), 21 September (Independence Day), 7 December (Day of Remembrance of the 1988 Earthquake), 31 December (New Year's Eve).

2002: 1–2 January (New Year), 6 January (Christmas), 24 April (Armenian Genocide Commemoration Day), 4–5 May (Easter), 9 May (Victory Day), 28 May (Declaration of the First Armenian Republic Day), 21 September (Independence Day), 7 December (Day of Remembrance of the 1988 Earthquake), 31 December (New Year's Eve).

Weights and Measures

The metric system is in force.

Statistical Survey

Principal sources: National Statistical Service of the Republic of Armenia, 375010 Yerevan, Republic Sq., Government House 3; tel. (1) 52-42-13; fax (1) 52-19-21; e-mail armstat@sci.am; internet www.armstat.am; IMF, *Armenia, Economic Review, Recent Economic Developments* and *International Financial Statistics: Supplement on Countries of the Former Soviet Union*; World Bank, *Statistical Handbook: States of the Former USSR* and *World Tables*.

Area and Population

AREA, POPULATION AND DENSITY

Area (sq km)	29,743*
Population (census results)†	
17 January 1979	3,037,259
12 January 1989	
Males	1,619,308
Females	1,685,468
Total	3,304,776
Population (official estimates at 1 January)‡	
1998	3,791,200
1999	3,798,200
2000	3,803,400
Density (per sq km) at 1 January 2000	127.9

* 11,484 sq miles.
† Figures refer to *de jure* population. The *de facto* total at the 1989 census was 3,287,677.
‡ Including persons temporarily absent (475,200 at 1 January 1999).

POPULATION BY NATIONALITY
(permanent inhabitants, 1989 census)

	%
Armenian	93.3
Azerbaijani	2.6
Kurdish	1.7
Russian	1.5
Others	0.9
Total	100.0

POPULATION BY MARZER (PROVINCES)
(estimates, 1 January 2000)

Marz (Province)	Population
Yerevan	1,248,200
Aragatsotn	167,500
Ararat	310,800
Armavir	322,300
Gegharkunik	278,600
Lori	394,400
Kotaik	329,400
Shirak	362,300
Syunik	163,900
Vayots Dzor	69,200
Tavush	156,800
Total	3,803,400

PRINCIPAL TOWNS (estimated population at 1 January 1999)

Yerevan (capital)	1,248,700	Vagarshapat (Echmiadzin)	65,500
Gyumri*	211,700	Razdan	63,900
Vanadzor†	172,700	Abovian	61,100

* Formerly Leninakan.
† Formerly Kirovakan.

BIRTHS, MARRIAGES AND DEATHS

	Registered live births		Registered marriages		Registered deaths	
	Number	Rate (per 1,000)	Number	Rate (per 1,000)	Number	Rate (per 1,000)
1992	70,581	19.2	22,955	6.2	25,824	7.0
1993	59,041	15.8	21,514	5.8	27,500	7.4
1994	51,143	13.7	17,118	4.6	24,652	6.6
1995	48,960	13.0	15,911	4.2	24,842	6.6
1996	48,134	12.8	14,234	3.8	24,936	6.6
1997	43,929	11.6	12,521	3.3	23,985	6.3
1998	39,366	10.4	11,365	3.0	23,210	6.1
1999	36,558	9.6	12,485	3.3	24,091	6.3

Expectation of life (years at birth, 1998): 74.7 (males 70.8; females 78.1).

ECONOMICALLY ACTIVE POPULATION
(annual averages, '000 persons)

	1996	1997	1998
Material sphere	1,060.2	1,012	989
Agriculture	583.5	564	566
Forestry	2.5	2	2
Industry*	255.0	229	209
Construction	68.0	60	57
Transport and communications	26.7	28	28
Trade and catering	110.2	116	113
Other activities	14.3	13	14
Non-material sphere	375.4	359	348
Education, culture and art	173.8	161	155
Science	13.0	14	16
Health, physical culture and social welfare	81.7	81	79
Housing and personal services	50.6	47	43
General administration	28.6	30	29
Other activities	27.7	26	27
Total employed	1,435.6	1,371	1,337
Registered unemployed	147.9	166	139
Total labour force	1,583.5	1,538	1,476

* Principally mining, manufacturing, electricity, gas and water.

Agriculture

PRINCIPAL CROPS ('000 metric tons)

	1997	1998	1999
Wheat	184	244	214
Barley	59	71	65
Maize	10	6	13†
Other cereals	2	2	9
Potatoes	360	425	414
Pulses	4	3	1*
Cabbages	88†	90†	95*
Tomatoes	141	145†	146*
Cauliflowers	4†	5†	5*
Cucumbers and gherkins	35†	40†	27*
Onions (dry)	32†	36†	36*
Garlic	12†	14†	13*
Peas (green)	6†	5†	4*
Carrots	10†	12†	11*
Other vegetables	42	48	56*
Watermelons‡	62	60	65*
Grapes	108	106	115
Apples	49	56†	56*
Pears	10†	16†	16*
Peaches and nectarines	20†	21†	22*
Plums	14†	14†	13*
Apricots	16†	19†	16*
Almonds*	2	1	1

* FAO estimate(s).   † Unofficial figure.
‡ Including melons, pumpkins and squash.
Source: FAO.

LIVESTOCK ('000 head, year ending September)

	1997	1998	1999
Horses	13	13	12
Asses*	3	3	3
Cattle	510	466	469
Pigs	54	57	68
Sheep†	566	510	534
Goats†	13	12	12
Rabbits*	5	5	5
Chickens	2,901	2,900	3,190
Turkeys*	200	180	180

* FAO estimate(s).   † Unofficial figures.
Source: FAO.

LIVESTOCK PRODUCTS ('000 metric tons)

	1997	1998	1999
Beef and veal	35	36	35†
Mutton and lamb	5	5	5†
Pig meat	5	6	6†
Poultry meat	4	5	5†
Cows' milk	425	445	452†
Sheep's milk†	10	13	14
Cheese	9	10	10
Hen eggs†	12	12	18
Wool (greasy)	1	1*	1*

* FAO estimate.   † Unofficial figure(s).
Source: FAO.

Forestry

ROUNDWOOD REMOVALS ('000 cubic metres, excluding bark)

	1997	1998
Total (all fuel wood)	62	36

Source: FAO, *Yearbook of Forest Products.*

Fishing

(metric tons, live weight)

	1996	1997	1998
Capture	580	580	698
Common carp	91	32	14
Crucian carp	28	23	42
Other cyprinids	33	7	37
Whitefishes	428	512	605
Aquaculture	650	670	437
Common carp	301	290	101
Silver carp	46	39	19
Rainbow trout	296	305	308
Total catch	1,230	1,250	1,135

Source: FAO, *Yearbook of Fishery Statistics.*

Mining

	1996	1997	1998
Copper concentrates (metric tons)*†	9,100	9,000	9,200
Molybdenum concentrates (metric tons)*	1,800	1,800†	1,800†
Silver ores (kg)*	626	1,000†	n.a.
Gold ores (kg)*	244	500†	350†
Salt ('000 metric tons)	26	26†	26†

* Figures refer to the metal content of ores and concentrates.
† Estimated production.
1999: Gold ores 400 kg (estimated metal content).
Source: US Geological Survey.

Industry

SELECTED PRODUCTS ('000 metric tons, unless otherwise indicated)

	1994	1995	1996
Margarine	n.a.	0.1	0.1
Wheat flour	290	265	156
Ethyl alcohol ('000 hectolitres)	7	2	0
Wine ('000 hectolitres)	227	102	48
Beer ('000 hectolitres)	70	53	29
Mineral water ('000 hectolitres)	48	78	119
Soft drinks ('000 hectolitres)	13	12	59
Cigarettes (million)	2,014	1,043	152
Wool yarn—pure and mixed (metric tons)	200	200	200
Cotton yarn—pure and mixed (metric tons)	400	200	300
Woven cotton fabrics ('000 metres)	200	100	600
Silk fabrics ('000 sq metres)	653	370	143
Woven woollen fabrics ('000 sq metres)	300	100	200
Carpets ('000 sq metres)	35	29	23
Leather footwear ('000 pairs)	1,612	656	305
Caustic soda (Sodium hydroxide)	4	4	4
Synthetic rubber	2.1	1.5	2.8
Non-cellulosic continuous fibres (metric tons)	200	300	400
Rubber tyres ('000)*	104	90	54
Rubber footwear ('000 pairs)	205	79	56
Quicklime	3	3	2
Cement	122	228	281
Aluminium plates, sheets, strip and foil	1.1	1.4	0.4
Domestic washing machines ('000)	n.a.	1	n.a.
Lorries (number)	446	232	114
Bicycles ('000)	12	8	7
Watches ('000)	3	1	2
Clocks ('000)†	362	392	216
Electric energy (million kWh)	5,658	5,561	6,214

* For road motor vehicles.
† Including electric clocks.

Source: UN, *Industrial Commodity Statistics Yearbook*.

1997 ('000 metric tons, unless otherwise indicated): Wine ('000 hectolitres) 33.7; Carpets ('000 sq metres) 14; Cement 293; Lorries (number) 27; Electric energy (million kWh) 6,030.
1998 ('000 metric tons, unless otherwise indicated): Wine ('000 hectolitres) 14.9; Wheat flour 103.7; Mineral water ('000 hectolitres) 109.9; Cigarettes (million) 2,488.1; Wool yarn—pure and mixed (metric tons) 79.2; Cotton yarn—pure and mixed (metric tons) 144.9; Woven cotton fabrics ('000 sq metres) 285.7; Woven woollen fabrics ('000 sq metres) 77.6; Carpets ('000 sq metres) 19.1; Quicklime 2.2; Cement 314.3; Electric energy (million kWh) 5,684.
1999 ('000 metric tons, unless otherwise indicated): Wheat flour 148.0; Mineral water ('000 hectolitres) 112.7; Cigarettes (million) 3,495.2; Wool yarn—pure and mixed (metric tons) 28.4; Cotton yarn—pure and mixed (metric tons) 60.3; Woven cotton fabrics ('000 sq metres) 117.0; Woven woollen fabrics ('000 sq metres) 5.4; Carpets ('000 sq metres) 18.4; Quicklime 3.8; Cement 286.9; Electric energy (million kWh) 5,716.0.

(Source: partly IMF, *Republic of Armenia: Recent Economic Developments*, November 1999).

Finance

CURRENCY AND EXCHANGE RATES

Monetary Units
100 louma = 1 dram.

Sterling, Dollar and Euro Equivalents (29 December 2000)
£1 sterling = 824.0 drams;
US $1 = 552.2 drams;
€1 = 513.8 drams;
1,000 drams = £1.214 = $1.811 = €1.946.

Average Exchange Rate (drams per US $)
1998   504.92
1999   535.06
2000   539.53

Note: The dram was introduced on 22 November 1993, replacing the Russian (formerly Soviet) rouble at a conversion rate of 1 dram = 200 roubles. The initial exchange rate was set at US $1 = 14.3 drams, but by the end of the year the rate was $1 = 75 drams. After the introduction of the dram, Russian currency continued to circulate in Armenia. The rouble had been withdrawn from circulation by March 1994.

STATE BUDGET (million drams)*

Revenue	1996	1997	1998
Tax revenue	85,051	130,714	162,337
Value-added tax	21,520	39,323	59,844
Excises	11,323	18,679	19,397
Enterprise profits tax	16,761	16,070	12,294
Personal income tax	8,795	14,712	15,246
Land tax	1,940	2,676	1,393
Customs duties	5,875	10,597	10,625
Payroll taxes	14,717	22,050	25,699
Other taxes	4,120	6,607	17,840
Other revenue	21,884	16,094	26,280
Grants	9,671	11,618	9,058
Total	**116,606**	**158,426**	**197,674**

Expenditure	1996	1997	1998
Current expenditure	129,740	172,086	183,100
Wages	18,983	24,774	29,632
Subsidies	815	4,451	1,051
Interest	17,273	21,702	17,808
Transfers	32,009	43,214	52,460
Pensions and social protection	28,840	34,898	47,342
Goods and services	60,660	77,945	82,142
Health and education	9,725	11,954	19,416
Other	50,935	65,991	62,726
Capital expenditure	26,794	27,940	46,424
Net lending	15,962	5,356	8,840
Restructuring expenses	855	—	—
Total	**173,351**	**205,382**	**238,364**

* Figures refer to the consolidated accounts of republican and local authorities, including the operations of the Pension and Employment Fund.

INTERNATIONAL RESERVES (US $ million at 31 December)

	1997	1998	1999
Gold*	10.72	12.37	12.69
IMF special drawing rights	37.28	28.00	40.68
Reserve position in IMF	0.01	0.01	—
Foreign exchange	191.46	287.28	277.88
Total	**239.47**	**327.66**	**331.25**

* National valuation.

Source: IMF, *International Financial Statistics*.

MONEY SUPPLY (million drams at 31 December)

	1997	1998	1999
Currency outside banks	37,596	41,370	42,610
Demand deposits at commercial banks	6,372	11,216	9,553
Total money (incl. others)	**44,055**	**52,678**	**52,227**

Source: IMF, *International Financial Statistics*.

COST OF LIVING (Consumer Price Index; base: 1994 = 100)

	1997	1998	1999
Food (incl. non-alcoholic beverages)	361.6	384.0	362.4
Electricity, gas and other fuels	677.7	745.5	884.9
Clothing (incl. footwear) . . .	220.2	229.9	231.5
Rent	7,603.6	12,873	12,899
All items (incl. others) . . .	373.2	405.6	408.2

Source: ILO, *Yearbook of Labour Statistics.*

NATIONAL ACCOUNTS (million drams at current prices)
Expenditure on the Gross Domestic Product

	1997	1998	1999
Government final consumption expenditure	90,220	105,589	105,974
Private final consumption expenditure . . .	832,638	956,322	944,652
Increase in stocks . . .	23,015	27,900	29,586
Gross fixed capital formation .	130,336	154,925	162,630
Total domestic expenditure	1,076,209	1,244,736	1,242,842
Exports of goods and services . .	163,065	181,552	206,864
Less Imports of goods and services	468,722	504,820	490,722
Sub-total	623,853	921,468	958,985
Statistical discrepancy* . . .	33,783	33,917	28,132
GDP in purchasers' values . .	804,336	955,385	987,117

* Referring to the difference between the sum of the expenditure components and official estimates of GDP, compiled from the production approach.
Source: IMF, *International Financial Statistics.*

Gross Domestic Product by Economic Activity*

	1996	1997	1998
Agriculture and forestry . . .	217,594	244,287	295,628
Industry†	156,980	192,056	207,452
Construction.	63,124	64,242	80,936
Transport and communications .	31,023	43,330	48,528
Trade and catering . . .	63,262	72,992	82,401
Other services	128,328	181,648	236,957
Total	660,311	798,555	951,901

* Figures are provisional. The revised totals (in million drams) are: 661,209 in 1996; 804,336 in 1997; 955,385 in 1998.
† Principally mining, manufacturing, electricity, gas and water.

BALANCE OF PAYMENTS (US $ million)

	1997	1998	1999
Exports of goods f.o.b. . . .	233.6	228.9	247.3
Imports of goods f.o.b. . . .	−793.1	−806.3	−721.3
Trade balance	−559.5	−577.4	−474.0
Exports of services . . .	96.6	130.3	135.8
Imports of services . . .	−159.4	−208.7	−197.9
Balance on goods and services	−622.2	−655.8	−536.1
Other income received . . .	139.0	103.9	93.6
Other income paid . . .	−40.4	−43.5	−38.6
Balance on goods, services and income	−523.7	−595.4	−481.2
Current transfers received . .	252.4	203.0	200.6
Current transfers paid . .	−35.2	−25.6	−26.5
Current balance	−306.5	−418.0	−307.1
Capital account (net) . . .	10.9	9.7	12.6
Direct investment from abroad .	51.9	220.8	122.0
Portfolio investment assets . .	−0.1	0.6	0.1
Portfolio investment liabilities .	15.9	−16.6	1.6
Other investment assets . .	40.8	20.0	3.0
Other investment liabilities . .	226.4	165.6	159.5
Net errors and omissions . . .	10.8	18.4	13.1
Overall balance	50.0	0.6	4.8

Source: IMF, *International Financial Statistics.*

External Trade

PRINCIPAL COMMODITIES (US $ '000)

Imports c.i.f.	1997	1998	1999
Live animals and animal products	58,530	46,973	41,639
Vegetable products . . .	105,310	117,806	75,941
Animal or vegetable fats and oils; prepared edible fats; animal or vegetable waxes . . .	24,572	19,333	18,092
Prepared foodstuffs; beverages, spirits and vinegar; tobacco and manufactured substitutes . .	86,066	110,049	77,037
Mineral products. . . .	209,779	206,066	171,619
Products of chemical or allied industries	85,195	73,692	70,839
Plastics, rubber and articles thereof	23,520	27,309	17,361
Paper-making materials; paper and paperboard and articles thereof	16,090	26,905	18,596
Textiles and textile articles .	33,713	31,697	30,201
Natural or cultured pearls, precious and semi-precious stones, precious metals and articles thereof; imitation jewellery; coin	47,473	45,541	86,740
Base metals and articles thereof	24,619	20,101	23,877
Machinery and mechanical appliances; electrical equipment; sound and television apparatus.	102,178	78,922	86,993
Vehicles, aircraft, vessels and associated transport equipment	15,754	47,281	33,086
Total (incl. others) . . .	892,322	902,389	801,676

Exports f.o.b.	1997	1998	1999
Prepared foodstuffs; beverages, spirits and vinegar; tobacco and manufactured substitutes . .	24,621	16,778	16,149
Mineral products. . . .	17,873	30,757	39,157
Plastics, rubber and articles thereof	9,198	8,050	9,093
Textiles and textile articles .	10,566	13,574	13,711
Natural or cultured pearls, precious and semi-precious stones, precious metals and articles thereof; imitation jewellery; coin	55,215	53,062	99,911
Base metals and articles thereof	57,679	40,338	24,999
Machinery and mechanical appliances; electrical equipment; sound and television apparatus	32,175	40,849	17,544
Optical, photographic, measuring, precision and medical apparatus; clocks and watches; musical instruments . .	4,816	3,745	1,622
Miscellaneous manufactured articles	4,921	2,474	317
Total (incl. others) . . .	232,495	220,516	233,540

PRINCIPAL TRADING PARTNERS (US $ '000)

Imports c.i.f.	1997	1998	1999
Belgium	49,673	54,631	85,218
Bulgaria	25,443	16,186	12,097
China, People's Repub.	7,296	9,960	n.a.
France	19,461	27,414	12,326
Georgia	38,248	26,830	26,872
Germany	26,222	34,037	34,588
Greece	10,223	9,131	13,139
Iran	88,671	63,913	78,496
Italy	36,244	34,584	23,739
Netherlands	15,438	9,648	5,123
Panama	3,026	22,083	n.a.
Russia	215,862	191,403	138,271
Switzerland	22,636	25,635	16,416
Turkey	38,396	56,780	40,194
Turkmenistan	27,671	554	777
Ukraine	11,560	8,932	7,930
United Arab Emirates	71,732	54,481	40,356
United Kingdom	10,451	69,136	67,046
USA	116,087	96,301	85,689
Total (incl. others)	892,322	902,389	801,676

Exports f.o.b.	1997	1998	1999
Belgium	46,966	49,839	84,253
Georgia	10,727	9,573	11,244
Germany	9,282	9,303	10,206
Iran	42,584	31,392	34,214
Lebanon	4,219	1,345	n.a.
Netherlands	6,236	7,912	438
Russia	62,899	39,986	33,830
Switzerland	1,572	2,482	3,749
Syria	2,754	1,296	n.a.
Turkey	7,153	2,988	1,129
Turkmenistan	13,752	22,726	6,156
Ukraine	3,492	3,972	2,096
United Arab Emirates	2,938	3,696	2,636
United Kingdom	1,161	8,098	9,448
USA	7,110	11,567	16,222
Total (incl. others)	232,495	220,516	233,540

Transport

RAILWAYS (traffic)

	1997	1998	1999
Passenger journeys ('000)	1,924.2	1,612.4	1,323.5
Passenger-km (million)	84.0	52.3	46.4
Freight carried ('000 metric tons)	1,471.2	1,730.8	1,389.3
Freight ton-km (million)	381.1	420.5	323.9

CIVIL AVIATION (traffic on scheduled services)

	1996	1997
Kilometres flown (million)	9	8
Passengers carried ('000)	358	368
Passengers-km (million)	747	767
Total ton-km (million)	79	80

Source: UN, *Statistical Yearbook*.

Tourism

ARRIVALS BY NATIONALITY

	1996	1997	1998
France	520	2,266	2,280
Germany	634	890	1,025
Greece	287	558	768
Iran	531	2,056	1,104
Japan	91	272	627
Lebanon	108	726	894
Netherlands	130	221	591
Turkey	147	1,101	714
United Kingdom	546	940	1,636
USA	778	2,601	3,804
Total (incl. others)	13,388	23,430	31,837

Tourism receipts (US $ million): 5 in 1996; 7 in 1997; 10 in 1998.

Sources: World Tourism Organization, *Yearbook of Tourism Statistics*, and World Bank, *World Development Indicators*.

Communications Media

	1994	1995	1996
Television receivers ('000 in use)	800	815	820
Book production†:			
Titles	224	n.a.	396
Copies ('000)	1,739	n.a.	20,212
Daily newspapers:			
Titles	7	7	11
Average circulation ('000 copies)	84*	85*	n.a.
Non-daily newspapers:			
Titles	n.a.	83	112
Average circulation ('000 copies)	n.a.	268	304*
Other periodicals:			
Titles	n.a.	n.a.	44
Average circulation ('000 copies)	n.a.	n.a.	541

* Provisional.
† Figures refer to first editions only, including pamphlets (27 titles and 83,000 copies in 1994).

Television receivers ('000 in use): 825 in 1997.

Source: UNESCO, *Statistical Yearbook*.

Telephones ('000 main lines in use): 583 in 1995; 580 in 1996; 568 in 1997 (Source: UN, *Statistical Yearbook*).
Telefax stations (number in use): 300 in 1994; 350 in 1996; 70 in 1997 (Source: UN, *Statistical Yearbook*).
Mobile cellular telephones (subscribers): 300 in 1996; 6,220 in 1997 (Source: UN, *Statistical Yearbook*).

Education

(1996/97)

	Institutions	Teachers	Students
Pre-primary	978	9,981	68,426
Primary	1,404	13,620	256,475
Secondary:			
General	1,467	61,800	594,200
Vocational	72	n.a.	24,200
Higher schools (incl. universities)	15	4,065	35,517

Sources: Ministry of Education and Science; UNESCO, *Statistical Yearbook*.

Directory

The Constitution

The Constitution was approved by some 68% of the electorate in a national referendum, held on 5 July 1995. It replaced the amended Soviet Constitution of 1978. The following is a summary of the new Constitution's main provisions:

GENERAL PROVISIONS OF CONSTITUTIONAL ORDER

The Republic of Armenia is an independent democratic state; its sovereignty is vested in the people, who execute their authority through free elections, referendums and local self-government institutions and officials, as defined by the Constitution. Referendums, as well as elections of the President of the Republic, the National Assembly and local self-government bodies, are carried out on the basis of universal, equal, direct suffrage by secret ballot. Through the Constitution and legislation, the State ensures the protection of human rights and freedoms, in accordance with the principles and norms of international law. A multi-party political system is guaranteed. The establishment of political parties is a free process, but the activities of political parties must not contravene the Constitution and the law. The right to property is recognized and protected. Armenia conducts its foreign policy based on the norms of international law, seeking to establish neighbourly and mutually beneficial relations with all countries. The State ensures the protection of the environment, historical and cultural monuments, as well as cultural values. The official language is Armenian.

FUNDAMENTAL HUMAN AND CIVIL RIGHTS AND FREEDOMS

The acquisition and loss of citizenship are prescribed by law. A citizen of the Republic of Armenia may not be simultaneously a citizen of another country. The rights, liberties and duties of citizens of Armenia, regardless of nationality, race, sex, language, creed, political or other convictions, social origin, property and other status, are guaranteed. No one shall be subject to torture or cruel treatment. Every citizen has the right to freedom of movement and residence within the republic, as well as the right to leave the republic. Every citizen has the right to freedom of thought, speech, conscience and religion. The right to establish or join associations, trade unions, political organizations, etc., is guaranteed, as is the right to strike for protection of economic, social and labour interests. Citizens of the republic who have attained 18 years of age are entitled to participate in state government through their directly elected representatives or by expression of free will.

Every citizen has the right to social insurance in the event of old age, disability, sickness, widowhood, unemployment, etc. Every citizen has the right to education. Education is provided free at elementary and secondary state educational institutions. Citizens belonging to national minorities have the right to preserve their traditions and to develop their language and culture. Everyone charged with a penal offence has the right to be presumed innocent until proved guilty. The advocacy of national, racial and religious hatred, and the propagation of violence and war, are prohibited.

THE PRESIDENT OF THE REPUBLIC

The President of the Republic of Armenia ensures the observance of the Constitution and the effective operation of the legislative, executive and juridical authorities. The President is the guarantor of the independence, territorial integrity and security of the republic. He/she is elected by citizens of the republic for a period of five years. Any person who has the right to participate in elections, has attained the age of 35 years, and has been a resident citizen of Armenia for the preceding 10 years is eligible for election to the office of President. No person may be elected to the office for more than two successive terms.

The President signs and promulgates laws adopted by the National Assembly, or returns draft legislation to the National Assembly for reconsideration; may dismiss the National Assembly and declare special elections to it, after consultation with the Prime Minister and the Chairman of the National Assembly; appoints and dismisses the Prime Minister; appoints and dismisses the members of the Government, upon the recommendation of the Prime Minister; appoints civil service officials; establishes deliberation bodies; represents Armenia in international relations, co-ordinates foreign policy, concludes international treaties, signs international treaties ratified by the National Assembly, and ratifies agreements between governments; appoints and recalls diplomatic representatives of Armenia to foreign countries and international organizations, and receives the credentials of diplomatic representatives of foreign countries; appoints the Procurator-General, as nominated by the Prime Minister; appoints members and the Chairman of the Constitutional Court; is the Supreme Commander-in-Chief of the armed forces; takes decisions on the use of the armed forces; grants titles of honour; and grants amnesties to convicts.

THE NATIONAL ASSEMBLY

Legislative power in the Republic of Armenia is executed by the National Assembly. The Assembly comprises 131 deputies, elected for a four-year term. Any person who has attained the age of 25 years and has been a permanent resident and citizen of Armenia for the preceding five years is eligible to be elected a deputy.

The National Assembly deliberates and enacts laws; has the power to express a vote of 'no confidence' in the Government; confirms the state budget, as proposed by the Government; supervises the implementation of the state budget; elects its Chairman (Speaker) and two Deputy Chairmen; appoints the Chairman and Deputy Chairman of the Central Bank, upon the nomination of the President; and appoints members of the Constitutional Court.

At the suggestion of the President of the Republic, the National Assembly declares amnesties; ratifies or declares invalid international treaties; and declares war. Upon the recommendation of the Government, the National Assembly confirms the territorial and administrative divisions of the republic.

THE GOVERNMENT

Executive power is realized by the Government of the Republic of Armenia, which is composed of the Prime Minister and the Ministers. The Prime Minister is appointed by the President; upon the recommendation of the Prime Minister, the President appoints the remaining Ministers. The Prime Minister directs the current activities of the Government and co-ordinates the activities of the Ministers.

The Government presents the programme of its activities to the National Assembly for approval; presents the draft state budget to the National Assembly for confirmation, ensures implementation of the budget and presents a report on its implementation to the National Assembly; manages state property; ensures the implementation of state fiscal, loan and tax policies; ensures the implementation of state policy in the spheres of science, education, culture, health care, social security and environmental protection; ensures the implementation of defence, national security and foreign policies; and takes measures to strengthen adherence to the laws, to ensure the rights and freedoms of citizens, and to protect public order and the property of citizens.

JUDICIAL POWER*

In the Republic of Armenia the courts of general competence are the tribunal courts of first instance, the review courts and the courts of appeal. There are also economic, military and other courts. The guarantor of the independence of judicial bodies is the President of the Republic. He/she is the Head of the Council of Justice. The Minister of Justice and the Procurator-General are the Deputy Heads of the Council of Justice. Fourteen members appointed by the President of the Republic for a period of five years are included in the Council. The Constitutional Court is composed of nine members, of whom the National Assembly appoints five and the President of the Republic appoints four. The Constitutional Court, *inter alia*, determines whether decisions of the National Assembly, decrees and orders of the President, and resolutions of the Government correspond to the Constitution; decides, prior to ratification of an international treaty, whether the obligations created in it correspond to the Constitution; resolves disputes relating to referendums and results of presidential and legislative elections; and decides on the suspension or prohibition of the activity of a political party.

TERRITORIAL ADMINISTRATION AND LOCAL SELF-GOVERNMENT

The administrative territorial units of the Republic of Armenia are regions and communities. Regions are comprised of rural and urban communities. Local self-government takes place in the communities. Bodies of local self-government, community elders and the community head (city mayor or head of village) are elected for a three-year period to administer community property and solve issues of community significance. State government is exercised in the regions. The Government appoints and dismisses regional governors, who carry out the Government's regional policy and co-ordinate the performance of regional services by state executive bodies. The city of Yerevan has the status of a region.

* The new judicial system came into force in January 1999. The Supreme Court was replaced by the Court of Cassation, and Appel-

late Courts were to operate in the place of People's Courts. Members of the Court of Cassation were to be appointed by the President, for life.

The Government

HEAD OF STATE

President: ROBERT KOCHARIAN (acting from 3 February 1998, elected 30 March, inaugurated 9 April).

GOVERNMENT

(March 2001)

Prime Minister: ANDRANIK MARKARIAN.

Minister of Foreign Affairs: VARTAN OSKANIAN.

Minister of Internal Affairs: Lt-Gen. HAIK HAROUTUNIAN.

Minister of National Security: Lt-Gen. KARLOS PETROSSIAN.

Minister of Defence: SERGE SARKISSIAN.

Minister of Finance and the Economy: HAIK KHACHATRIAN.

Minister of Justice: DAVID HAROUTUNIAN.

Minister of Industrial Infrastructure: DAVID ZADOIAN.

Minister of Energy: KAREN GALUSTIAN.

Minister of Territorial Administration: HOVIK ABRAMIAN.

Minister of Town Planning: DAVID LOKIAN.

Minister of Social Security: RAZMIK MARTIROSSIAN.

Minister of Health: ARARAT MKRTCHIAN.

Minister of Agriculture: ZAVEN GEVORKIAN.

Minister of Environmental Protection: MURAD MURADIAN.

Minister of Industry and Trade: KAREN CHSHMARITIAN.

Minister of Education and Science: EDUARD GHAZARIAN.

Minister of Culture, Youth Affairs and Sports: ROLAND SHAROIAN.

Minister of Transport and of Communications: YERVAND ZAKHARIAN.

Minister of State Property: DAVID VARDANIAN.

Minister of State Revenues: ANDRANIK MANUKIAN.

Mayor of Yerevan: RUBEN NAZARIAN.

MINISTRIES

Office of the President: 375077 Yerevan, Marshal Baghramian St 26; tel. (1) 52-02-04; fax (1) 52-15-51; internet www.president.am.

Office of the Prime Minister: 375010 Yerevan, Republic Sq. 1, Govt House; tel. (1) 52-03-60; fax (1) 15-10-35.

Ministry of Agriculture: 375010 Yerevan, Nalbandian St 48; tel. (1) 52-46-41; fax (1) 15-10-86.

Ministry of Communications: 375010 Yerevan, Nalbandian St 28; tel. (1) 52-66-32; fax (1) 15-15-55; e-mail armoc@mbox.amilink.net.

Ministry of Culture, Youth Affairs and Sports: 375010 Yerevan, Tumanian St 5; tel. (1) 52-93-49; fax (1) 52-39-22.

Ministry of Defence: Yerevan, Proshian Settlement, G. Shaush St 60G; tel. (1) 38-94-52; fax (1) 15-14-45.

Ministry of Education and Science: 375010 Yerevan, Movses Khorenatsi St 13; tel. (1) 52-66-02; fax (1) 58-04-03.

Ministry of Energy: 375010 Yerevan, Republic Sq. 2, Govt House 2; tel. (1) 52-19-64; fax (1) 15-16-87.

Ministry of Environmental Protection: 375002 Yerevan, Moskovian St 35; tel. (1) 52-10-99; fax (1) 53-18-61; e-mail interdept@freenet.am.

Ministry of Finance and the Economy: 375010 Yerevan, Melik-Adamian St 1; tel. (1) 52-70-82; fax (1) 52-37-45; e-mail staff@mf.gov.am.

Ministry of Foreign Affairs: 375010 Yerevan, Republic Sq. 1, Govt House 2; tel. (1) 52-35-31; fax (1) 15-10-42; internet www.armeniaforeignministry.com.

Ministry of Health: 375001 Yerevan, Tumanian St 8; tel. (1) 58-24-13; fax (1) 15-10-97.

Ministry of Industrial Infrastructure: 375010 Yerevan, Republic Sq., Govt House; fax (1) 52-32-00.

Ministry of Industry and Trade: 375008 Yerevan, Hanrapetoutian St 5; tel. (1) 52-61-34; fax (1) 15-16-75.

Ministry of Internal Affairs and National Security: 375025 Yerevan, Nalbandian St 104; tel. (1) 56-09-08; fax (1) 57-84-40.

Ministry of Justice: 375010 Yerevan, Khorhrdaranayin St 8; tel. (1) 58-21-57; fax (1) 58-24-49.

Ministry of Local Government and Urban Development: 375010 Yerevan, Republic Sq., Govt House; tel. (1) 58-90-80; fax (1) 52-32-00.

Ministry of Social Security: 375025 Yerevan, Terian St 69; tel. (1) 52-68-31; fax (1) 15-19-20.

Ministry of State Property: 375010 Yerevan, Republic Sq. 2, Govt House; tel. (1) 52-42-13; fax (1) 52-65-57; internet www.privatization.am.

Ministry of State Revenues: 375015 Yerevan, Movses Khorenatsi St 3; tel. (1) 53-91-95; fax (1) 53-82-26.

Ministry of Transport: 375015 Yerevan, Zakian St 10; tel. (1) 56-33-91; fax (1) 56-05-28.

Office of the Mayor of Yerevan: Yerevan, Grigor Lusavorichi St; tel. (1) 52-58-47.

Office of the State Department for Emergency Situations: 375010 Yerevan, Republic Sq., Govt House; tel. (1) 53-16-12; fax (1) 15-10-36.

President and Legislature

PRESIDENT

Presidential Election, First Ballot, 16 March 1998

Candidates	% of votes
ROBERT KOCHARIAN	38.76
KAREN DEMIRCHIAN	30.67
VAZGEN MANUKIAN (National Democratic Union)	12.24
SERGEI BADALIAN (Communist Party of Armenia)	11.01
PARUIR HAIRIKIAN (Union for National Self-Determination)	5.41
Others	1.91
Total	100.00

Second Ballot, 30 March 1998

Candidates	% of votes
ROBERT KOCHARIAN	59.49
KAREN DEMIRCHIAN	40.51
Total	100.00

NATIONAL ASSEMBLY

375095 Yerevan, Marshal Baghramian St 19; tel. (1) 58-82-25; fax (1) 52-98-26.

Chairman: ARMEN KHACHATRIAN.

Deputy Chairmen: TIGRAN TOROSSIAN, GAGIK ASLANIAN.

General Election, 30 May 1999

Parties and blocs	% of vote for seats by proportional representation	Total seats
Unity bloc*	41.2	55
Communist Party of Armenia	12.1	11
Armenian Revolutionary Federation	7.7	9
Law and Unity bloc	8.0	6
Law-governed Country Party of Armenia	5.3	6
National Democratic Union	5.2	6
Armenian Pan-National Movement	1.2	1
Armenian Democratic Party	1.0	1
Mission Party	0.8	1
National Concord Party	—	1
Independents	—	32
Total (incl. others)	100.0	131†

* A coalition of the Republican Party of Armenia and the People's Party of Armenia.

† Results were annulled in two constituencies; the subsequent by-elections, which were held in July, were won by independents.

Political Organizations

At mid-July 2000 there were 92 political parties registered with the Ministry of Justice.

Armenian Christian Democratic Union: Yerevan, Nubarashen St 16; tel. (1) 47-68-68; Chair. AZAD ARSHAKIAN.

Armenian Democratic Agricultural Party: Yerevan, Kutuzov St 1/7; tel. (1) 26-40-03; Chair. TELMAN DILANIAN.

Armenian Democratic Party: Yerevan, Koriun St 14; tel. (1) 52-52-73; f. 1992 by elements of Communist Party of Armenia; Chair. ARAM SARKISSIAN.

Armenian Monarchists Party: Aparan, Garegin Nejdeh St 13/11; tel. (520) 85-20; Chair. TIGRAN PETROSSIAN.

Armenian National Democratic Party—21st Century: Yerevan; f. 1998; Chair. DAVID SHAKHNAZARIAN; Pres. ARKADII VARDANIAN.

Armenian National Party: Yerevan; f. 1996.

Armenian Pan-National Movement (APNM) (Haiots Hamazgaien Sharjoum): 375019 Yerevan, Khanjian St 27; tel. (1) 57-04-70; f. 1989; Pres. LEVON TER-PETROSSIAN; Chair. ALEKSANDR ARZUMANIAN.

Armenian Revolutionary Federation (ARF) (Hai Heghapokhakan Dashnaktsutyun): 375025 Yerevan, Miasniak Ave 2; internet www.arf.am; f. 1890; formed the ruling party in independent Armenia, 1918–20; prohibited under Soviet rule, but continued its activities in other countries; permitted to operate legally in Armenia from 1991; suspended in December 1994; legally reinstated 1998; 40,000 mems; Chair. RUBEN HAGOBIAN, VAHAN HOVHANISSIAN.

Ayastan: Yerevan; Chair. MIASNIK ALKHASIAN.

Ayots Tun (Armenian Home, Armianskii Dom): Yerevan; Chair. VARDAN PETROSSIAN.

Azatutyun (Freedom): Yerevan; f. 1997; liberal, right-wing; Leader HRANT BAGRATIAN.

Communist Party of Armenia (CPA): Yerevan, Marshal Baghramian St 10; tel. (1) 56-79-33; fax (1) 53-38-55; f. 1920; dissolved 1991, relegalized 1992; c. 50,000 mems; Chair. VLADIMIR DARBINIAN.

Haykandoukht Women's Party: Yerevan; Leader ARMENOUHI KAZARIAN.

Armenian Social Democratic Party (Hunchakian): Yerevan, Aghbiur Serob St 7; tel. (1) 27-33-15; internet www.hunchak.org.am; Chair. ERNEST SOGOMONIAN.

Law-Governed Country Party of Armenia (Orinats Yerkir): Yerevan; f. 1998; centrist; 1,100 mems; Head ARTUR BAGDASARIAN.

Liberal Democratic Party (Ramgavar Azadagan): 375009 Yerevan, Koriun St 19A; tel. (1) 52-64-03; fax (1) 52-53-23; f. 1991; Leader VIGEN KHACHATRIAN.

Mission Party (Arakelutun): c/o National Assembly, 375095 Yerevan, Marshal Baghramian St 19.

National Concord Party: c/o National Assembly, 375095 Yerevan, Marshal Baghramian St 19; f. 1998; Leaders GARNIK ISAGULIAN, IGOR MURADIAN, GRANT KHACHATRIAN.

National Democratic Union: Yerevan, Abovian St 12; tel. and fax (1) 56-31-88; e-mail adjm@arminco.com; f. 1991 as a splinter party of the APNM (see above); Leader DAVIT VARDANIAN; Chair. VAZGEN MANUKIAN.

New Way Party (Nor Ugi): Yerevan; f. 1998; Leader ASHOT BLEYAN.

People's Party of Armenia (PPA): Yerevan; f. 1998; Chair. STEPAN DEMIRCHIAN; Sec. AMAYAK OVANESIAN.

Republican Party of Armenia (RPA): Yerevan, Tumanian St 23; tel. (1) 58-00-31; fax (1) 56-60-34; f. 1990 following a split in the UNS (see below); merged with Yerkrapah Union of Volunteers in 1999; 13 territorial orgs; 5,500 mems; Chair. ANDRANIK MARKARIAN.

Shamiram Women's Party: Yerevan; f. 1995.

Stability Party: Yerevan; f. 2000; Leader VARDAN AYVAZIAN.

Union for National Self-Determination (UNS): 375013 Yerevan, Grigor Lusavorichi St 15; tel. (1) 52-55-38; Chair. PARUIR HAIRIKIAN.

Union of Right Forces: Yerevan; f. 2000 as an alliance of a number of right-wing parties.

Union of Social Democratic Forces: Yerevan; f. 2000.

Union of Socialist Forces: Yerevan; f. 1997 as an alliance of several left-wing parties; Leader ASHOT MANUCHARIAN.

Diplomatic Representation

EMBASSIES IN ARMENIA

Bulgaria: Yerevan, Nor Aresh 11 St 85; Ambassador: IVAN IVANSHEV.

China, People's Republic: Yerevan, Marshal Baghramian St 12; tel. (1) 56-00-67; fax (1) 15-11-43; Ambassador: PAK U. CHUN.

Egypt: Yerevan, Dzorapi St 72, Hotel Hrazdan, 10th Floor; tel. (1) 53-73-04; fax (1) 15-11-60; e-mail egyemb@arminco.com; Ambassador: SAID IMAM MAHMOUD SAID.

France: 375015 Yerevan, Grigor Lusavorichi St 8; tel. (1) 56-11-03; fax (1) 15-11-05; e-mail secretar@ambafran.arminco.com; Ambassador: MICHEL LEGRAS.

Georgia: Yerevan, Arami St 42; tel. (1) 56-43-57; fax (1) 56-41-83; e-mail georgia@arminco.com; Ambassador: NIKOLOZ NIKOLOZISHVILI.

Germany: Yerevan, Charents St 29; tel. (1) 52-32-79; fax (1) 15-11-12; e-mail germemb@arminco.com; Ambassador: VOLKER SEITZ.

Greece: Yerevan, Dzorapi St 72, Hotel Hrazdan, 5th Floor; tel. (1) 53-00-51; fax (1) 15-11-70; e-mail grembarm@arminco.com; Ambassador: PANAYOTIS ZOGRAFOS.

India: Yerevan, Dzorapi St 72, Hotel Hrazdan; tel. (1) 53-50-27; fax (1) 53-78-33; e-mail inemyr@arminco.com; Ambassador: RAJENDER PRAKASH.

Iran: Yerevan, Budaghian St 1; tel. (1) 52-98-30; fax (1) 15-13-85; e-mail emiranar@arminco.com; internet www.iranembassy.r.am/home.htm; Ambassador: MOHAMMED FARHAD KOLEINI.

Lebanon: Yerevan, Vardanants St 7; tel (1) 52-65-40; fax (1) 15-11-28; Chargé d'affaires a.i.: SAAD ZAKHIA.

Malta: Yerevan, Tigran Mets St 13; tel. and fax (1) 52-71-27; Ambassador: ANDRÉ GUTZWILLER.

Romania: Yerevan, Amirian St 1, Rm 802, Hotel Armenia; tel. (1) 59-98-02; Ambassador: PAVEL PLATONA.

Russian Federation: Yerevan, Grigor Lusavorichi St 13A; tel. (1) 56-74-27; fax (1) 50-52-37; Ambassador: ANATOLII DRYUKOV.

Syria: Yerevan, Marshal Baghramian St 4; tel. (1) 52-40-28; fax (1) 52-40-58; Chargé d'Affaires a. i.: HAMED HASAN.

Ukraine: Yerevan, Erznkian St 58; tel. and fax (1) 56-24-36; Ambassador: OLEKSANDER BOZHKO.

United Arab Emirates: Yerevan.

United Kingdom: Yerevan, Charents St 28; tel. (1) 15-18-41; fax (1) 15-18-07; e-mail britemb@arminco.com; Ambassador: TIMOTHY JONES.

USA: Yerevan, Marshal Baghramian St 18; tel. (1) 15-15-51; fax (1) 15-15-50; e-mail lemmonmc@wo_state.gov; internet www.arminco.com/embusa/index.htm; Ambassador: MICHAEL C. LEMMON.

Judicial System

A new judicial and legal system came into force in January 1999. The Supreme Court was replaced by the Court of Cassation, and Appellate Courts were to operate in the place of People's Courts. Members of the Court of Cassation were to be appointed by the President, for life.

Constitutional Court: 375019 Yerevan, Marshal Baghramian St 10; e-mail armlaw@concourt.am; internet www.concourt.am; Chair. GAGIK HAROUTUNIAN.

Chairman of the Court of Cassation: TARIEL K. BARSEGIAN.

Prosecutor-General: AGHVAN HOVSEPIAN.

Religion

The major religion is Christianity. The Armenian Apostolic Church is the leading denomination and was widely identified with the movement for national independence. There are also Russian Orthodox and Islamic communities, although the latter lost adherents as a result of the departure of large numbers of Muslim Azeris from the republic. Most Kurds are also adherents of Islam, although some are Yazidis.

GOVERNMENT AGENCY

Council for the Affairs of the Armenian Church: 375001 Yerevan, Abovian St 3; tel. (1) 56-46-34; fax (1) 56-41-81.

CHRISTIANITY

Armenian Apostolic Church: Etchmiadzin, Vagharshapat City; tel. (1) 15-11-98; fax (1) 15-10-77; e-mail mairator@arminco.com; nine dioceses in Armenia, four in other ex-Soviet republics and 25 dioceses and bishoprics in the rest of the world; 7m. members worldwide (some 4m. in Armenia); 15 monasteries and three theological seminaries in Armenia; Supreme Patriarch GAREGIN II, Catholicos of All Armenians.

The Roman Catholic Church

Armenian Rite

Armenian Catholics in Eastern Europe are under the jurisdiction of an Ordinary (equivalent to a bishop with direct authority). At 31 December 1997 there were an estimated 220,000 adherents within this jurisdiction, including about 30,000 in Armenia itself.

Ordinary: Most Rev. NERSES DER-NERSESSIAN (Titular Archbishop of Sebaste), Gyumri, Atarbekian St 82; tel. (41) 22-115; fax (41) 3-49-59; e-mail armorda@shirak.am.

Latin Rite

The Apostolic Administrator of the Caucasus is the Apostolic Nuncio

(Ambassador of the Holy See) to Georgia, Armenia and Azerbaijan, who is resident in Tbilisi, Georgia.

The Press

PRINCIPAL NEWSPAPERS

In Armenian except where otherwise stated.

Ankakhutiun (Independence): 375013 Yerevan, Grigor Lusavorichi St 15; tel. (1) 58-18-64; daily; organ of the Union for National Self-Determination; Editor PARUIR HAIRIKIAN.

Aravot: 375023 Yerevan, Arshakunyats Ave 2, 10th Floor; tel. (1) 52-87-52; fax (1) 52-87-52; e-mail root@aravot.arminco.com; internet www.aravot.am; Editor A. ABRAMIAN.

Avangard: 375023 Yerevan, Arshakunyats Ave 2; f. 1923; 3 a week; organ of the Youth League of Armenia; Editor M. K. ZOHRABIAN.

Azg (The Nation): 375010 Yerevan, Hanrapetoutian St 47; tel. (1) 52-16-35; e-mail azg2@arminco.com; f. 1990; Editor S. SARKISSIAN.

Bravo: Yerevan, Abovian St 12, Hotel Yerevan; tel. (1) 55-44-05; weekly; Editor K. KAZARIAN.

Delovoi Express: Yerevan, Zarian St 22, 2nd Floor; tel. (1) 25-26-83; fax (1) 25-90-23; e-mail eis@arminco.com; f. 1992; weekly; Editor E. NAGDALIAN.

Epokha (Epoch): 375023 Yerevan, Arshakunyats Ave 2; f. 1938; fmrly *Komsomolets*; weekly; Russian; organ of the Youth League of Armenia; Editor V. S. GRIGORIAN.

Golos Armenii (The Voice of Armenia): 375023 Yerevan, Arshakunyats Ave 2, 7th Floor; tel. (1) 52-77-23; e-mail root@goloss.arminco.com; f. 1934 as *Kommunist*; 3 a week; in Russian; Editor F. NASHKARIAN.

Grakan Tert (Literary Paper): 375019 Yerevan, Marshal Baghramian St 3; tel. (1) 52-05-94; f. 1932; weekly; organ of the Union of Writers; Editor F. H. MELOIAN.

Hanrapetakan: Yerevan, Tumanian St 23; tel. (1) 58-00-31; fax (1) 56-60-34; organ of the Republican Party of Armenia.

Hayastan (Armenia): 375023 Yerevan, Arshakunyats Ave 2; tel. (1) 52-84-50; f. 1920; 6 a week; in Russian; Editor G. ABRAMIAN.

Hayk (Armenia): 375023 Yerevan, Arshakunyats Ave 2, 11th Floor; tel. (1) 52-77-01; e-mail root@hayk.arminco.com; weekly; organ of the Armenian Pan-National Movement; Editor V. DAVTIAN; circ. 30,000.

Hayots Ashkhar: Yerevan, Tumanian St 38; tel. (1) 53-88-65; Editor G. MKRTCHIAN.

Hazatamart (The Battle for Freedom): 375070 Yerevan, Atarbekian 181; organ of the Armenian Revolutionary Federation (ARF); Editor M. MIKAYELIAN.

Hnchak Hayastani (The Bell of Armenia): 375019 Yerevan, Lord Byron St 12; weekly.

Marzakan Hayastan: 375023 Yerevan, Arshakunyats Ave 5; tel. (1) 52-62-41; weekly; Editor S. MOURADIAN.

Molorak: 375023 Yerevan, Arshakunyats Ave 5; tel. (1) 52-62-12; daily; Editor H. GHAGHRINIAN.

Respublika Armenia: 375023 Yerevan, Arshakunyats Ave 2, 9th Floor; tel. (1) 52-69-69; e-mail root@ra.arminco.com; Editor A. KHANBABIAN.

Ria Taze (New Way): Yerevan; 2 a week; Kurdish.

Vozny (Hedgehog): 375023 Yerevan, Arshakunyats Ave 2, 12th Floor; tel. (1) 52-63-83; f. 1954; Editor A. SAHAKIAN.

Yerevanyan Orer (Yerevan Days): Yerevan; Editor M. AIRAPETIAN.

Yerkir (Country): 70 Yerevan, Zavarian St 181; tel. (1) 57-10-95; e-mail erkir@arminco.com; internet www.spyur.am/eng/2250.htm; f. 1991; daily; organ of the ARF.

Yerokoyan Yerevan (Evening Yerevan): 375023 Yerevan, Arshakunyats Ave 2, 10th Floor; tel. (1) 52-97-52; weekly; organ of Yerevan City Council; Editor N. YENGIBARIAN.

Yeter: Yerevan, Manukian St 5; tel. (1) 55-34-13; weekly; Editor G. KAZARIAN.

Zroutsakits: 375023 Yerevan, Arshakunyats Ave 2, 2nd Floor; tel. (1) 52-84-30; weekly; Editor M. MIRIDJANIAN.

PRINCIPAL PERIODICALS

Aghbiur (Source): Yerevan; f. 1923, fmrly *Pioner*; monthly; for teenagers; Editor T. V. TONOIAN.

Armenian Kommersant: Yerevan, Koriuni St 19A; tel. (1) 52-79-77; monthly; Editor M. VARTANIAN.

Aroghchapautyun (Health): 376001 Yerevan, Tumanian St 8; tel. (1) 52-35-73; e-mail mharut@dmc.am; f. 1956; quarterly; journal of the Ministry of Health; Editor M. A. MURADIAN; circ. 2,000–5,000.

Arvest (Art): 375001 Yerevan, Tumanian St 5; f. 1932, fmrly *Sovetakan Arvest* (Soviet Art); monthly; publ. by the Ministry of Culture, Youth Affairs and Sports; Editor G. A. AZAKELIAN.

Chetvertaya Vlast: Yerevan, Abovian St 12, Hotel Yerevan, Room 105; tel. (1) 59-73-81; monthly; Editor A. GEVORKIAN.

Ekonomika (Economics): Yerevan, Vardanants St 2; tel. (1) 52-27-95; f. 1957; monthly; organ of the Ministry of the Economy; Editor R. H. SHAKHKULIAN; circ. 1,500–2,000.

Garun (Spring): 375015 Yerevan, Karmir Banaki St 15; tel. (1) 56-29-56; f. 1967; monthly; independent; fiction and socio-political issues; Editor L. Z. ANANIAN.

Gitutyun ev Tekhnika (Science and Technology): 375048 Yerevan, pr. Komitasa 49/3; tel. (1) 23-37-27; f. 1963; quarterly; journal of the Research Institute of Scientific-Technical Information and of Technological and Economic Research; Dir M. B. YEDILIAN; Editor M. A. CHUGURIAN; circ. 1,000.

Hayastani Ashkhatavoruhi (Working Women of Armenia): Yerevan; f. 1924; monthly; Editor A. G. CHILINGARIAN.

Hayreniky Dzayn (Voice of the Motherland): Yerevan; f. 1965; weekly; organ of the Armenian Committee for Cultural Relations with Compatriots Abroad; Editor L. H. ZAKARIAN.

Iravounk: 375002 Yerevan, Yeznik Koghbatsu St 50A; tel. (1) 53-27-30; fax (1) 53-26-76; e-mail iravunk@sim.arminco.com; f. 1989; monthly; Editor H. BABUKHANIAN; circ. 18,000.

Literaturnaya Armeniya (Literature of Armenia): 375019 Yerevan, Marshal Baghramian St 3; tel. (1) 56-36-57; f. 1958; monthly; journal of the Union of Writers; fiction; Russian; Editor A. M. NALBANDIAN.

Nork: Yerevan; f. 1934; fmrly *Sovetakan Grakanutyun* (Soviet Literature); monthly; journal of the Union of Writers; fiction; Russian; Editor R. G. OVSEPIAN.

Novoye Vremya: 375023 Yerevan, Arshakunyats Ave 2, 3rd Floor; tel. (1) 52-29-61; 2 a week; Editor R. SATIAN.

Veratsnvats Hayastan (Reborn Armenia): Yerevan; f. 1945 as *Sovetakan Hayastan* (Soviet Armenia); monthly; journal of the Armenian Committee for Cultural Relations with Compatriots Abroad; fiction; Editor V. A. DAVITIAN.

Yerevan Times: 375009 Yerevan, Isaahakian St 28, 3rd Floor; tel. (1) 52-82-70; fax (1) 15-17-38; e-mail yertime@armpress.arminco.com; weekly; English; Editor T. HAKOBIAN.

NEWS AGENCIES

Armenpress (Armenian Press Agency): 375009 Yerevan, Isaahakian St 28, 4th Floor; tel. (1) 52-67-02; fax (1) 15-17-38; e-mail root@armpress.arminco.com; internet www.armenpress.am; state information agency, transformed into state joint-stock company in 1997; Dir T. HAKOBIAN.

Noyan Tapan (Noah's Ark): 375009 Yerevan, Isaahakian St 28, 3rd Floor; tel. and fax (1) 52-42-18; e-mail nt@nt.arminco.com; Dir TIGRAN HAROUTUNIAN.

Past: 375023 Yerevan, Arshakunyats Ave 2, 15th Floor; tel. (1) 53-86-18; Dir T. NAGDALIAN.

Snark: 375009 Yerevan, Isaahakian St 28, 2nd Floor; tel. (1) 52-99-42; fax (1) 56-04-92; e-mail snark@arminco.com; internet www.snark.am; f. 1991; Dir EMMANUIL MKRTCHIAN.

Publishers

Academy of Sciences Publishing House: 375019 Yerevan, Marshal Baghramian St 24G; Dir KH. H. BARSEGHIAN.

Anait: Yerevan; art publishing.

Arevik (Sun Publishing House): 375009 Yerevan, Terian St 91; tel. (1) 52-45-61; f. 1986; political, scientific, fiction for children; Dir V. S. KALANTARIAN.

Hayastan (Armenia Publishing House): 375009 Yerevan, Isaahakian St 91; tel. (1) 52-85-20; f. 1921; political and fiction; Dir DAVID SARKISSIAN.

Haykakan Hanragitaran (Armenian Encyclopaedia): 375001 Yerevan 1, Tumanian St 17; tel. (1) 52-43-41; fax (1) 52-06-67; f. 1967; encyclopaedias and other reference books; Editor H. M. HIRAZIAN.

Luys (Enlightenment Publishing House): Yerevan, Kirov St 19A; textbooks; Dir S. M. MOVSISSIAN.

Nairi: Yerevan, Terian St 91; fiction; Dir H. H. FELEKHIAN.

Broadcasting and Communications

TELECOMMUNICATIONS

ArmenTel: Yerevan; internet www.armentel.com; transferred to private ownership in 1998; 10% state-owned, 90% owned by Hellenic Telecommunications Organization (Greece); Exec. Dir GAREGIN MOVSESSIAN; Dep. Exec. Dir ANDRANIK POGOSSIAN.

BROADCASTING
Radio
Armenian Radio: 375070 Yerevan, Vardanants 28, apt 34; tel. (1) 55-11-43; fax (1) 15-16-00; e-mail armen@armradio.am; 3 programmes; broadcasts inside the republic in Armenian, Russian and Kurdish; external broadcasts in Armenian, Russian, Kurdish, Azeri, Arabic, English, French, Spanish and Farsi; transformed into state joint-stock company in 1997; Dir-Gen. ARMEN AMIRIAN.

Television
National Television of Armenia: 375025 Yerevan, A. Manukian St 5; tel. (1) 55-25-02; fax (1) 55-15-13; internet www.armtv.am; broadcasts in Armenian and occasionally in Russian; transformed into state joint-stock company in 1997; Dir ROBERT HAROUTUNIAM (acting).

Finance

(cap. = capital; res = reserves; dep. = deposits; m. = million; brs = branches; amounts in drams, unless otherwise stated)

BANKING
Central Bank
Central Bank of the Republic of Armenia: 375010 Yerevan, Nalbandian St 6; tel. (1) 58-38-41; fax (1) 15-11-07; e-mail cba@mbox .amilink.net; internet www.cba.am; f. 1991; cap. 100m., res 162.2m. (Nov. 1998); Chair. TIGRAN SARKISSIAN.

Commercial Banks
In November 1999 there were 31 commercial banks in operation in Armenia. Some of the most influential of these are listed below:

Ardshinbank (ASHB): 375010 Yerevan, Deghatan St 3; tel. and fax (1) 15-11-55; e-mail international@ardshin.bank.am; f. 1922, reorganized as joint-stock commercial bank for industry and construction in 1992; restructured 1997; largest bank in Armenia; cap. 500.0m., res 713.8m., dep. 11,522.9m. (Dec. 1998); Chair. ARAM VARDANIAN; Gen. Man. LEVON FARMANIAN; 33 brs.

Armagrobank Open Joint-Stock Company: 375015 Yerevan, M. Khorenatsi St 7A; tel. (1) 53-43-42; fax (1) 60-71-23; e-mail agrobank@agrobank.am; internet www.agrobank.am; f. 1991, incorporated as joint-stock co in 1992; cap. 279m.; Chair. GRIGOR GHONJEIAN; 36 brs.

Armaviabank: 375014 Yerevan, Sevaki St 1; tel. (1) 28-88-57; fax (1) 28-19-40.

Armenian Development Bank: 375015 Yerevan, Paronian St 21/7; tel. (1) 53-00-94; fax (1) 53-32-33; e-mail root@adb.infocom .amilink; f. 1990; cap. 628.3m., res 383.5m., dep. 2,293.4m. (Nov. 1999); Chair. ALEKSANDR GRIGORIAN.

Armenian Economy Development Bank (Armeconombank): 375002 Yerevan, Amirian St 23/1; tel. (1) 53-88-00; fax (1) 15-11-49; e-mail bank@aeb.am; internet www.aeb.am; incorporated as joint-stock co in 1992; corporate banking; cap. 1,000m., res 52.8m., dep. 1,462.9m. (Nov. 1998); Chair. of Bd SARIBEK SUKIASSIAN; 22 brs.

Armenian Import-Export Bank CjSC (Armimpexbank): 375010 Yerevan, Nalbandian St 2; tel. (1) 58-99-06; fax (1) 56-48-87; e-mail jav@impex.infocom.amilink.net; f. 1992 by reorganization of Armenian br. of the Vneshekonombank of the former USSR; joint-stock co with foreign shareholding; cap. US $3.1m., dep. US $14m. (Sept. 1999); Chair. of Bd B. ASATRIAN; 8 brs.

Arminvestbank: 375010 Yerevan, Vardanants St 13; tel. (1) 52-37-18; fax (1) 90-72-10; e-mail ibank@dolphin.am; f. 1992; cap. US $1.1m., res US $0.2m., dep. US $2.3m.; Chair. of Bd VAROUZHAN AMIRAGIAN.

Bank Mellat CjSC: 375010 Yerevan, Amirian St 6; tel. (1) 58-13-54; fax (1) 15-18-11; e-mail mellat_y@hotmail.com; cap. and res 405.6m., dep. 4,446.2m. (Dec. 1998); Chair. ESSA GHAREMANI CHABOCK.

Converse Bank Corpn: 375051 Yerevan, Komitas Ave 49; tel. (1) 56-28-66; fax (1) 90-60-72; e-mail post@converse.r.am; internet www.converse.r.am; f. 1994; cap. 66.7m., res 999.3m., dep. 9.8m. (Dec. 1998); Pres. KHOURI MODALAL; Chief Exec. SMBAT NASIBIAN.

Credit-Yerevan Joint-Stock Commercial Bank: 375010 Yerevan, Amirian St 2/8; tel. (1) 58-90-65; fax (1) 15-18-20; e-mail garik@mail.creyer.am; f. 1993; cap. US $2.1m. (Nov. 1998); Pres. MARTIN HOVHANNISIAN.

HSBC Bank of Armenia: 375010 Yerevan, Amirian St 1; tel. (1) 56-32-29; fax (1) 15-18-58; e-mail hsbc@arminco.com; f. 1996; cap. 2,438m., res 858.7m., dep. 11,423m. (Nov. 1998); Chief Exec. J. A. J. HUNT; 1 br.

Shirakinvestbank: 377500 Gyumri, G. Njdeh St 7; tel. (41) 23-86-5; fax (41) 34-88-3; e-mail shib@shirak.am; internet www.shirak.am/bus/shib/shib.html; f. 1996; cap. and res 338.3m., dep. 943.6m. (Dec. 1997); Chair. GRIGOR KONJEIAN; Pres. MESROP KARAPETIAN.

United Bank: 375004 Yerevan, Spendiarov St 4; tel. (1) 53-69-05; fax (1) 06-955; e-mail ubank@arm.r.am; internet www.ubank.am; f. 1996; cap. 1.5m., dep. 19.7m. (Dec. 1998); Chair. BENIK HAROUTUNIAN.

Savings Bank
Armsavingbank: 375010 Yerevan, Nalbandian St 46; tel. (1) 58-04-51; fax (1) 56-55-78; e-mail root@sberbank.armenia.su; reorganized 1996; cap. 444.4m., res 138.6m., dep. 3,320.1m. (Nov. 1998); Chair. HOVHANNES MANDAKUNI; 35 regional brs.

Banking Association
Association of Banks of Armenia: Yerevan; Pres. TIGRAN SARKISSIAN.

COMMODITY AND STOCK EXCHANGES
Adamand Stock and Commodity Exchange: Yerevan, Hanrapetoutian St 5; tel. (1) 27-19-36; fax (1) 27-69-21; Dir SUREN KAPLANIAN.

Gyumri Stock Exchange: 375504 Gyumri, Abovian St 244; tel. (41) 2-31-09; fax (41) 2-10-23; f. 1995; Dir SISAK MCHITARIAN.

Yerevan Commodity and Raw Materials Exchange: Yerevan; f. 1991; authorized cap. 5m.; Gen. Man. ARA ARZUMANAIAN.

Yerevan Stock Exchange: 375010 Yerevan, Hanrapetoutian St 5; tel. (1) 52-32-01; fax (1) 15-15-48; f. 1993; Pres. Dr SEDRAK SEDRAKIAN.

INSURANCE
Iran-Armenian Insurance Co: Yerevan; f. 1997.

Armenian Financial Insurance Co (AFIC): 375010 Yerevan, Hanrapetoutian St 5; tel. (1) 52-77-93; fax (1) 15-15-48; e-mail imamik@yse.armenia.su; f. 1996; Exec. Man. LEVON MAMIKONIAN.

Trade and Industry

CHAMBER OF COMMERCE
Chamber of Commerce and Industry of the Republic of Armenia: 375033 Yerevan, Hanrapetoutian St 39; tel. (1) 56-54-38; fax (1) 56-50-71; Chair. ASHOT SARKISSIAN.

INDUSTRIAL AND TRADE ASSOCIATION
Armenintorg—Armenian State Foreign Economic and Trade Association: 375012 Yerevan, Hr. Kochar St 25; tel. (1) 22-43-10; fax (1) 22-00-34; f. 1987; import and export of all types of goods, marketing, consultancy, auditing and other services, conducts training programmes, arranges international exhibitions and trade fairs; Gen. Dir Dr ARMEN R. DARBINIAN; 20 employees.

EMPLOYERS' ORGANIZATIONS
Armenian Business Forum: Yerevan; tel. (1) 52-75-43; fax (1) 52-43-32; f. 1991; promotes joint ventures, foreign capital investments; Pres. VAHE JAZMADARIAN.

Armenian Union of Industrialists and Entrepreneurs: Yerevan; Chair. ARAM VARDANIAN.

UTILITIES
Armenian Energy Commission: Yerevan; Chair. VARDAN MOVSISIAN.

Electricity
Medzamor Nuclear Plant: Medzamor; VVER-440 pressurized water-reactor, with a 410 MW operating capacity.

Gas
Armgazprom: Yerevan, Tbilisskoe St 43; tel. (1) 28-60-70; fax (1) 28-65-31; state gas company; Dir ROLAND ADONTS.

Armrosgazprom: Yerevan; f. 1997; Armenian-Russian joint-stock co; Exec. Chair. ROLAND ADONTS; Dep. Exec. Chair. VIKTOR BRLYANSKIKH.

TRADE UNIONS
General Confederation of Armenian Trade Unions: 375010 Yerevan, Hanrapetoutian St; tel. (1) 58-36-82; fax (1) 56-60-33; Chair. MARTIN HAROUTUNIAN.

Transport

RAILWAYS
In 1995 there were 806 km of railway track. There are international lines to Iran and Georgia; lines to Azerbaijan and Turkey remained closed in 2001, as a result of those countries' continuing economic blockade of Armenia.

Armenia Railways: 375005 Yerevan, Tigran the Great St 50; tel. (1) 54-42-28; f. 1992 following the dissolution of the former Soviet Railways; Pres. G. G. BERIAN.

Metropolitan Railway

An initial 10-km route, with nine stations, opened in 1981, and a 10-km extension, with two stations, was under construction. A second line was planned, and proposals envisaged the installation of a 47-km network.

Yerevan Metro: 375033 Yerevan, Marshal Baghramian St 76; tel. (1) 27-45-43; fax (1) 15-13-95; f. 1981; Gen. Man. H. BEGLARIAN.

ROADS

In 1998 there were an estimated 15,998 km of roads in Armenia (including 7,567 km of motorways, 3,361 km of highways and 4,206 km of secondary roads). In the mid-1990s some 40% of the network was estimated to be in poor condition and in need of repair. In 1996 plans were made to upgrade existing roads, and to construct some 1,400 km of new roads over the next four years, with financial assistance from various international organizations. As a result of the economic blockade imposed in 1989 by Azerbaijan (and subsequently reinforced by Turkey), the Kajaran highway linking Armenia with Iran emerged as Armenia's most important international road connection; in December 1995 a permanent road bridge over the Araks (Aras) river was opened, strengthening this link. In mid-1997 a bus route to Syria was opened—the first overland route between the two countries.

CIVIL AVIATION

Armenian Airlines: 375042 Yerevan, Zvarnots Airport; tel. (1) 28-28-60; fax (1) 15-13-93; f. 1993; operates scheduled and charter passenger services to countries of the CIS, Europe and the Middle East; Man. Dir VYACHESLAV YARALOV.

Tourism

Prior to secession from the USSR in 1991, Armenia attracted a number of tourists from the other Soviet republics. Following its independence, however, tourism severely declined, although in the late 1990s some European firms were beginning to introduce tours to the country. According to the World Tourism Organization, tourism receipts increased from about US $5m. in 1995 to $7m. in 1997. Receipts, according to the World Bank, increased further, to $10m., in 1998. The major tourist attractions were the capital, Yerevan; Artashat, an early trading centre on the 'Silk Road'; and medieval monasteries. There was, however, little accommodation available outside the capital.

Directorate of Trade, Tourism and Services: Ministry of Industry and Trade, 375010 Yerevan, Hanrapetoutian St 5; tel. (1) 58-94-94; fax (1) 56-61-23; e-mail garnikn@yahoo.com; Dir ARTAK DAVTIAN.

Armenia Association of Tourism: Yerevan, Amirian St 27; tel. (1) 53-45-01; fax (1) 56-39-27; e-mail nta@freenet.am; Chair. ARTHUR VOSKANIAN.

Tourism Armenia: 375010 Yerevan, 15 Khanjian St 15; tel. (1) 57-80-01; fax (1) 57-83-51.

AUSTRALIA

Introductory Survey

Location, Climate, Language, Religion, Flag, Capital

The Commonwealth of Australia occupies the whole of the island continent of Australia, lying between the Indian and Pacific Oceans, and its offshore islands, principally Tasmania to the south-east. Australia's nearest neighbour is Papua New Guinea, to the north. In the summer (November–February) there are tropical monsoons in the northern part of the continent (except for the Queensland coast), but the winters (July–August) are dry. Both the north-west and north-east coasts are liable to experience tropical cyclones between December and April. In the southern half of the country, winter is the wet season; rainfall decreases rapidly inland. Very high temperatures, sometimes exceeding 50°C (122°F), are experienced during the summer months over the arid interior and for some distance to the south, as well as during the pre-monsoon months in the north. The official language is English; 170 indigenous languages are spoken by Aboriginal and Torres Strait Islander peoples. At the census of 1996 70.9% of the population professed Christianity (of whom 27.0% were Roman Catholic and 22.0% Anglican). The national flag (proportions 2 by 1) is blue, with a representation of the United Kingdom flag in the upper hoist, a large seven-pointed white star in the lower hoist and five smaller white stars, in the form of the Southern Cross constellation, in the fly. The capital, Canberra, lies in one of two enclaves of federal territory known as the Australian Capital Territory (ACT).

Recent History

Since the Second World War, Australia has played an important role in Asian affairs, and has strengthened its political and economic ties with Indonesia, and the other countries of South-East Asia, and with Japan. The country co-operates more closely than formerly with the USA (see ANZUS, p. 316), and has given much aid to Asian and Pacific countries.

At the election of December 1949 the ruling Australian Labor Party (ALP) was defeated by the Liberal Party, in coalition with the Country Party. In January 1966 Sir Robert Menzies resigned after 16 years as Prime Minister, and was succeeded by Harold Holt, who was returned to office at elections in December of that year. However, Holt died in December 1967. His successor, Senator John Gorton, took office in January 1968 but resigned, after losing a vote of confidence, in March 1971. William McMahon was Prime Minister from March 1971 until December 1972, when, after 23 years in office, the Liberal-Country Party coalition was defeated at a general election for the House of Representatives. The ALP, led by Gough Whitlam, won 67 of the 125 seats in the House. Following a conflict between the Whitlam Government and the Senate, both Houses of Parliament were dissolved in April 1974, and a general election was held in May. The ALP was returned to power, although with a reduced majority in the House of Representatives. However, the Government failed to gain a majority in the Senate, and in October 1975 the Opposition in the Senate obstructed legislative approval of budget proposals. The Government was not willing to consent to a general election over the issue, but in November the Governor-General, Sir John Kerr, intervened and took the unprecedented step of dismissing the Government. A caretaker Ministry was installed under Malcolm Fraser, the Liberal leader, who formed a coalition Government with the Country Party. This coalition gained large majorities in both Houses of Parliament at a general election in December 1975, but the majorities were progressively reduced at general elections in December 1977 and October 1980.

Fraser's coalition Government was defeated by the ALP at a general election in March 1983. Robert (Bob) Hawke, who had replaced William (Bill) Hayden as Labor leader in the previous month, became the new Prime Minister and immediately organized a meeting of representatives of government, employers and trade unions to reach agreement on a prices and incomes policy (the 'Accord') that would allow economic recovery. Hawke called a general election for December 1984, 15 months earlier than necessary, and the ALP was returned to power with a reduced majority in the House of Representatives. The opposition coali-

tion between the Liberal Party and the National Party (formerly known as the Country Party) collapsed in April 1987, when 12 National Party MPs withdrew from the agreement and formed the New National Party (led by the right-wing Sir Johannes Bjelke-Petersen, the Premier of Queensland), while the remaining 14 National Party MPs continued to support their leader, Ian Sinclair, who wished to remain within the alliance. Parliament was dissolved in June, in preparation for an early general election in July. The election campaign was dominated by economic issues. The ALP was returned to office with an increased majority, securing 86 of the 148 seats in the House of Representatives. The Liberal and National Parties announced the renewal of the opposition alliance in August. Four months later, Bjelke-Petersen was forced to resign as Premier of Queensland, under pressure from National Party officials.

During 1988 the Hawke Government suffered several defeats at by-elections, seemingly as a result of a decline in living standards and an unpopular policy of wage restraint. The ALP narrowly retained power at state elections in Victoria, but was defeated in New South Wales, where it had held power for 12 years. In May 1989 the leader of the Liberal Party, John Howard, was replaced by Andrew Peacock, and Charles Blunt succeeded Ian Sinclair as leader of the National Party. In July a commission of inquiry into alleged corruption in Queensland published its report. The Fitzgerald report documented several instances of official corruption and electoral malpractice by the Queensland Government, particularly during the administration of Bjelke-Petersen. Following the publication of the report, support for the National Party within Queensland declined once more, and in December the ALP defeated the National Party in the state election (the first time that it had defeated the National Party in Queensland since 1957). By the end of 1991 four former members of the Queensland Cabinet and the former chief of the state's police force had received custodial sentences. The trial of Bjelke-Petersen, initially on charges of perjury and corruption but subsequently of perjury alone, resulted in dismissal of the case, when the jury failed to reach a verdict.

In February 1990 Hawke announced that a general election for the House of Representatives and for 40 of the 76 seats in the Senate was to be held on 24 March. The Government's position in the period preceding the election had been strengthened by the ALP's victory in Queensland in December 1989, the removal of an unpopular Labor leadership in Western Australia and its replacement by the first female Premier, Dr Carmen Lawrence, and by the support that it secured from environmental groups as a result of its espousal of 'green' issues. Although the opposition parties won the majority of the first-preference votes in the election for the House of Representatives, the endorsement of the environmental groups delivered a block of second-preference votes to the ALP, which was consequently returned to power, albeit with a reduced majority, securing 78 of the 148 seats. Following its defeat, Peacock immediately resigned as leader of the Liberal Party and was replaced by Dr John Hewson, a former professor of economics. Blunt lost his seat in the election and was succeeded as leader of the National Party by Timothy Fischer.

In September 1990, at a meeting of senior ALP members, government proposals to initiate a controversial programme of privatization were endorsed, effectively ending almost 100 years of the ALP's stance against private ownership. In October plans for constitutional and structural reform were approved in principle by the leaders of the six state and two territory governments. The proposed reforms envisaged the creation of national standards in regulations and services. They also aimed to alleviate the financial dependence of the states and territories on the Federal Government. These suggested reforms, however, encountered strong opposition from sections of the public services, the trade unions and the business community. In July 1991 the leaders of the federal and state Governments finally agreed to reforms in the country's systems of marketing, transport, trade and taxation, with the aim of creating a single national economy from 1992.

In April 1991, as a result of preliminary investigations by a Royal Commission into the financial dealings of the Labor Government of Western Australia in the 1980s, Brian Burke, the former state Premier, resigned as Australia's ambassador to Ireland and the Holy See. Owing to the alleged irregularities, more than $A1,000m. of public funds were believed to have been lost. In May the Premier of New South Wales called a state election, 10 months earlier than was necessary, in an attempt to take advantage of the problems of Labor administrations at federal and state level. However, the Liberal-National Party Government lost its overall majority and was able to retain power only with the support of independent members of the state legislature.

In June 1991, following months of divisions within the ALP, Hawke narrowly defeated a challenge to his leadership from Paul Keating, the Deputy Prime Minister and Treasurer, who accused the Prime Minister of reneging on a promise to resign in his favour before the next general election. This cast doubt on Hawke's credibility, as he had assured Parliament and the public in 1990 that he would continue as leader for the whole of the parliamentary term. Following his defeat, Keating resigned. In December Hawke dismissed John Kerin, Keating's replacement as Treasurer, following a series of political and economic crises. Hawke called another leadership election, but, on this occasion, he was defeated by Keating, who accordingly became Prime Minister. A major reorganization of the Cabinet followed. John Dawkins, a staunch supporter of Keating, was appointed Treasurer.

Following the ALP's recent defeat in state elections in Tasmania, the party encountered further embarrassment in April 1992, when a by-election in Melbourne to fill the parliamentary seat vacated by Bob Hawke was won by a local football club coach, standing as an independent candidate. In May the Prime Minister suffered another set-back, when Graham Richardson, the Minister for Transport and Communications, resigned, owing to his implication in a scandal involving a relative who was alleged to have participated in an illegal scheme whereby Taiwanese investors were able to secure US residency rights via the Marshall Islands. Meanwhile, Brian Burke, the former Premier of Western Australia, had been arrested. It was alleged that, during his term of office, he had misappropriated more than $A17,000 from a parliamentary expense account. In October 1992 the conclusions of the inquiry into the ALP's alleged involvement in corrupt practices in Western Australia were released. The Royal Commission was highly critical of the improper transactions between successive governments of Western Australia and business entrepreneurs. The conduct of Brian Burke drew particular criticism. (In July 1994 Burke received a prison sentence of two years upon conviction on four charges of fraud; he was released in February 1995, but was sentenced to three years' imprisonment in February 1997 for the theft of $A122,000 from ALP funds.) Furthermore, in February 1995 Ray O'Connor, Premier of Western Australia between 1982 and 1983, received a prison sentence of 18 months, having been found guilty of the theft in 1984 of $A25,000, intended as a donation to the Liberal Party. He was released in August 1995.

In September 1992 John Bannon became the seventh state Premier since 1982 to leave office in disgrace. The resignation of the ALP Premier of South Australia was due to a scandal relating to attempts to offset the heavy financial losses incurred by the State Bank of South Australia. At state elections in Queensland in mid-September, the ALP administration of Wayne Goss was returned to power. In the following month, however, the ruling ALP was defeated in state elections in Victoria. Furthermore, in November a new financial scandal emerged: the federal Treasurer was alleged to have suppressed information pertaining to the former ALP Government of Victoria which, in a clandestine manner prior to the state elections, was believed to have exceeded its borrowing limits.

By late 1992, therefore, the ALP's prospects of being returned to office at the forthcoming general election appeared to have been seriously damaged. Proposals for radical tax and economic reforms that were advocated by the federal opposition leader, Dr John Hewson, attracted much attention. At state elections in Western Australia in February 1993, the incumbent Labor Government was defeated. Dr Carmen Lawrence was replaced as Premier by Richard Court of the Liberal-National coalition.

Nevertheless, at the general election, held on 13 March 1993, the ALP was unexpectedly returned to office, for a fifth consecutive term, having secured 80 of the 147 seats in the House of

Representatives. In January 1994 the Government was embarrassed by the resignation of the Minister of Industry, Technology and Regional Development, Alan Griffiths, as a result of allegations that public funds and ALP resources had been misappropriated in order to meet the private business debts incurred by his Melbourne sandwich shop. In the following month Ros Kelly, the Minister for Environment, Sport and Territories and close associate of the Prime Minister, yielded to pressure to resign, owing to a scandal relating to the alleged use of community sports grants to attempt to influence voters in vulnerable ALP-held constituencies prior to the 1993 general election. In May 1994 Dr John Hewson was replaced as leader of the Liberal Party by Alexander Downer, a supporter of the monarchy. Downer was therefore expected to lead the campaign against Paul Keating's proposal that Australia become a republic (see below). In January 1995, however, Downer resigned. The party leadership was resumed by John Howard, also a monarchist.

At state elections in New South Wales in March 1995 the ALP defeated the ruling Liberal-National coalition. Robert (Bob) Carr was appointed Premier. At a federal by-election in Canberra, however, the ALP suffered a serious reverse when, for the first time in 15 years, the seat fell to the Liberal Party. In July, at state elections in Queensland, the ALP Government of Wayne Goss was narrowly returned to office, only to be ousted following a by-election defeat in February 1996. In June 1995, meanwhile, the Deputy Prime Minister, Brian Howe, who intended to retire at the next general election, announced his resignation from the Cabinet. He was replaced by the Minister for Finance, Kim Beazley.

At the general election held on 2 March 1996 the Liberal-National coalition achieved a decisive victory, securing a total of 94 of the 148 seats in the House of Representatives. The ALP won only 49 seats. In the Senate the minor parties and independent members retained the balance of power. John Howard of the Liberal Party became Prime Minister, and immediately promised to give priority to the issues of industrial relations, the transfer to partial private ownership of the state telecommunications company, Telstra, and to expanding relations with Asia. The leader of the National Party, Tim Fischer, was appointed Deputy Prime Minister and Minister for Trade. Paul Keating was replaced as leader of the ALP by Kim Beazley.

In August 1996, in an unprecedented display of violence, demonstrators protesting against proposed budget cuts stormed the Parliament building in Canberra. Clashes between the police and the protesters resulted in many injuries. Meanwhile, fears for Australia's tradition of racial tolerance continued to grow. In October Pauline Hanson, a newly-elected independent member of the House of Representatives, aroused much controversy when, in a speech envisaging 'civil war', she reiterated her demands for the ending of immigration from Asia and for the elimination of special funding for Aboriginal people. The Prime Minister attracted criticism for his failure to issue a direct denunciation of the views of Pauline Hanson, a former member of the Liberal Party. The increasingly bitter debate also damaged Australia's image in the countries of Asia, a vital source of investment and of tourist revenue. In March 1997, moreover, the One Nation Party was established by Pauline Hanson and rapidly attracted support. In May, while attending a fund-raising rally in Perth, Pauline Hanson was besieged by more than 1,000 opponents. Larger protests against her policies followed in Melbourne and Canberra. Meanwhile, after his initial weak response, the Prime Minister condemned the views of the founder of the One Nation Party. In August, as fears for Australian revenue from Asian investment, trade and tourism grew, the Government issued a document on foreign policy, in which Pauline Hanson's views were strongly repudiated and in which Australia's commitment to racial equality was reiterated. In order to counter the negative impact of the activities of the One Nation Party, a special diplomatic unit was established. In November 1997, furthermore, former Prime Ministers Keating, Hawke and Whitlam published a statement denouncing Pauline Hanson.

During 1997 a scandal arising from apparently illicit claims for parliamentary travel allowances led to a number of resignations, and in October the Prime Minister announced major changes in the composition of his Government. . In the same month Senator Cheryl Kernot, leader of the Australian Democrats Party, announced her defection to the ALP, from where she hoped better to oppose the Liberal-National Government.

In early 1998 the long-standing tension between the National Farmers' Federation and the powerful Maritime Union of Australia (MUA) developed into a bitter dispute over trade unionists' rights when farmers established their own non-unionized stevedoring operation in Melbourne to handle their exports, in protest at high dockside costs and alleged inefficiency. The confrontation escalated in April, when Patrick Stevedores, a major cargo-handling company based in Sydney, dismissed its entire union-ized work-force of 1,400 dockers, with the intention of replacing them with secretly-trained contract workers. As part of its campaign to break the MUA monopoly (the offensive being supported by the Government), Patrick Stevedores drafted in hundreds of security guards to its 14 terminals around Australia, in an operation to lock out the dockers. The Federal Court, however, subsequently ruled that Patrick Stevedores had acted illegally and ordered the company to reinstate the 1,400 trade unionists. Following the rejection of an appeal to the High Court by Patrick Stevedores and the return to work of the dockers in May, the Prime Minister nevertheless pledged to press ahead with waterfront reform. Although the majority of Australians appeared to support the reform of labour practices in the country's ports, the Government's handling of the dispute had attracted much criticism.

In December 1997 the New One Nation Party was established by former supporters of Pauline Hanson, who had apparently become disillusioned with her autocratic style of leadership. In June 1998, at state elections in Queensland, the One Nation Party won 23% of first-preference votes, thus unexpectedly securing 11 of the 89 seats in the legislature and leading to renewed concern among tourism and business leaders. In August it was announced that an early general election was to be held in October. As the campaign commenced, former Prime Ministers Whitlam, Fraser, Hawke and Keating signed an open letter urging citizens not to support racist candidates at the forthcoming election.

At the election, conducted on 3 October 1998, the Liberal-National coalition was narrowly returned to office, winning a total of 80 of the 148 seats in the House of Representatives. The ALP increased its representation to 67 seats. Contrary to expectations, the One Nation Party failed to win any representation in the lower house, the controversial Pauline Hanson losing her Queensland seat. (The one seat secured by the One Nation Party in the Senate was subsequently subjected to a legal challenge, owing to the candidate's apparent failure to meet citizenship requirements—see below.) In a referendum held on the same day, the electorate of the Northern Territory unexpect-edly rejected a proposal for the territory's elevation to full statehood. In mid-October the Prime Minister announced the composition of his new Cabinet; most senior ministers retained their portfolios. Changes included the establishment of a special portfolio (transport and regional services) to focus on rural issues, in response to the ruling coalition's poor electoral per-formance in rural areas. John Howard also created a new Ministry of Financial Services and Regulation. The incoming Government's programme incorporated the implementation of a controversial 10% goods-and-services tax (GST) and the transfer to the private sector of the remaining two-thirds of the assets of Telstra.

In February 1999 Pauline Hanson was re-elected leader of the One Nation Party, despite a series of defections, including the departure from the party of several of the 11 One Nation members of the Queensland legislature. At state elections in New South Wales in March, at which the ALP was returned to power, the One Nation Party won two seats in the 42-member upper chamber. In June a court ruled that the One Nation Senator was ineligible to occupy her seat in the federal upper house, owing to her failure to renounce her British citizenship prior to the general election. She was subsequently replaced by another member of the One Nation Party.

In January 2000 police officers in Queensland and New South Wales raided premises belonging to the One Nation Party, seizing hundreds of documents relating to the party's member-ship and its financial structure. In April the Queensland Elec-toral Commission ruled that the party had been fraudulently registered by the falsification of significant sections of its 200-name membership list, in order to qualify for public funding in Queensland. Consequently, the party was ordered to repay some $A0.5m. of state funds which it had received. Moreover, as the sole signatory on the registration papers, Pauline Hanson found herself personally responsible for the repayment. In August it was reported that Hanson was attempting to re-register the party.

Following a protracted debate, in June 1999 the Senate nar-rowly approved the Government's proposal to dispose of a fur-ther 16.6% of the assets of Telstra (to bring the total transferred to the private sector to 49.9%). Two independent Senators, including the veteran Brian Harradine of Tasmania, had ini-tially opposed the plan, but reversed their stance in exchange for commitments of additional funding for their respective regions. Kim Beazley, leader of the opposition ALP, denounced the arrangement as 'shameful'. The Treasurer, however, main-tained that the sale of a further tranche of the telecommunica-tions corporation would permit the Government drastically to reduce public debt. The Senate subsequently approved proposals to introduce the GST (which became effective on 1 July 2000).

In June 1999 Tim Fischer, Deputy Prime Minister and Min-ister for Trade and leader of the National Party, unexpectedly announced his resignation. He was replaced as leader of the National Party by John Anderson, hitherto Minister for Trans-port and Regional Services, those portfolios being retained upon his subsequent appointment as Deputy Prime Minister. Mark Vaile, hitherto Minister for Agriculture, Forestry and Fisheries, became Minister for Trade.

Following state elections in Victoria in September 1999, the Liberal-National Premier, Jeffrey Kennett, was replaced by Stephen Bracks of the ALP. The defeat of the Liberal-National coalition was regarded as a set-back to the Federal Gov-ernment's programme of economic reform, the transfer of public utilities to the private sector having been particularly unpopular among the voters of Victoria.

In September 2000 Australia hosted the Olympic Games in Sydney. The event was widely perceived as having been suc-cessful and of particular benefit to the local economy. However, the fact that security forces were given emergency powers to shoot on sight anyone thought likely to pose a threat to security at the Games caused some controversy, with civil rights groups expressing concern that the draconian anti-terrorist measures might persist after the conclusion of the event. In the same month a series of violent confrontations occurred between demonstrators and security personnel in Melbourne at a three-day summit meeting of the World Economic Forum. The demon-strators, several of whom were injured in the clashes, were protesting against capitalism and economic globalization.

A marked increase in illegal immigration during 1999 and 2000 prompted the introduction of new legislation empowering Australian police to board vessels in international waters. In 1999 almost 2,000 illegal immigrants were intercepted by the authorities and transferred to detention centres in Australia, while many others were believed to have died in the attempt to enter the country. In April 2000 more than 250 people, mostly from Iran and Iraq, died when their three boats sank in rough seas while trying to enter Australia illegally. The issue of alleged maltreatment of illegal immigrants captured in Australia was highlighted by events at a privately-run detention centre in Woomera, South Australia. Inmates at the centre, which was situated in a remote location near a former missile-testing range, had staged a riot in June 2000 and a break-out in August, in protest at conditions at the facility. Moreover, in November the Government ordered an inquiry into allegations that chil-dren at the centre had been subjected to systematic sexual abuse. Campaigners, who had repeatedly appealed for more humane treatment of illegal immigrants, claimed that the Gov-ernment had suppressed evidence of abuse at Woomera and other detention centres.

A state election in Western Australia in February 2001 res-ulted in defeat for the governing Liberal-National coalition and the replacement of Premier Richard Court by the state's Labor leader, Geoffrey Gallop. Ongoing anxieties regarding illegal immigration were reflected in the unexpected success of the One Nation Party, which secured almost 10% of votes at the poll. At the state election in Queensland in the same month, the ALP Government, led by Peter Beattie, was decisively re-elected. The One Nation Party garnered 9% of the total votes. The next federal election was scheduled to be held by Nov-ember 2001.

In March 1986, meanwhile, Australia's constitutional links with the United Kingdom (UK) were reduced by the Australia Act, which abolished the British Parliament's residual legisla-tive, executive and judicial controls over Australian state law. In February 1992, shortly after a visit by Queen Elizabeth, Paul Keating caused a furore by accusing the UK of abandoning Australia to the Japanese threat during the Second World War. Following a visit to the UK in September 1993, Keating announced that Australia was to become a republic by the year 2001, subject to approval by referendum. Sir William Deane succeeded William Hayden as Governor-General in February 1996, the former's term of office being scheduled to expire at the end of the year 2000. Although John Howard personally favoured the retention of the monarchy, in 1996 the new Prime Minister announced plans for a constitutional convention, prior to the holding of a referendum on the issue if necessary. In an unexpected development in January 1997, the Deputy Prime Minister put forward proposals for the removal from the Constitution of all references to the monarch and for the transfer of the Queen's functions to Australia's Chief Justice.

Voluntary postal voting to select, from among 609 candidates, 76 delegates who were to attend the constitutional convention (scheduled for February 1998) commenced in November 1997. The complex system of preferential voting, however, appeared to give rise to much confusion, particularly in New South Wales where a total of 174 candidates were contesting 20 places at the forthcoming convention. In addition to the official groupings, the Australian Republican Movement (ARM) and Australians for a Constitutional Monarchy (ACM), numerous other republican and monarchist, as well as individual, candidates were standing for election. Only 42.6% of registered voters were reported to have returned their ballot papers, the participation rate in New South Wales being only 39.9%. In February 1998, following nine days of debate, a majority of the 152 delegates (a further 76 having been appointed by the Government) endorsed proposals to adopt a republican system and to replace the British monarch as Head of State. Although the Constitutional Convention was dominated by Republicans, delegates were divided over the method of election of a future head of state.

In December 1998 it was confirmed that a referendum on the republican issue would be held in late 1999. In August 1999 the Federal Parliament gave approval to the wording of the question to be posed to the electorate, which was to be asked if support was forthcoming for an 'act to alter the Constitution to establish the Commonwealth of Australia as a republic with the Queen and Governor-General being replaced by a President appointed by a two-thirds majority of the members of the Commonwealth Parliament'. At the referendum, conducted on 6 November 1999, 55% of voters favoured the retention of the monarchy. Moreover, some 61% of voters expressed opposition to a proposal to include a preamble to the Constitution, recognizing Aborigines as 'the nation's first people'. Although the result was regarded as a victory for Howard, who had campaigned for the retention of the monarchy, many observers interpreted the result as a rejection of the particular republican system offered, opinion polls having indicated that more than two-thirds of Australians would support the introduction of a republican system of government if the President were to be directly elected.

In May 1987 Australia and the UK began a joint operation to ascertain the extent of plutonium contamination resulting from British nuclear weapons testing at Maralinga in South Australia between 1956 and 1963. Many Australians were highly critical of the UK's apparent disregard for the environmental consequences of the tests and of the British authorities' failure to make adequate arrangements to protect the local Aboriginal people, who were now campaigning for a thorough decontamination of their traditional lands. In June 1993 Australia announced its acceptance of $A45m. in compensation from the British Government for the cost of the decontamination. In December 1994 the displaced Aboriginal people and the federal Government reached agreement on a compensation settlement of $A13.5m., to be spent on health, employment and infrastructural projects. In January 1999, furthermore, it was announced that the Australian and British Governments were to conduct separate inquiries into research linking the nuclear tests to the numerous cases of a rare form of cancer in servicemen who had witnessed the explosions. In March 2000 it was announced that a joint decontamination programme effected by the British and Australian Governments had been completed. However, it was reported that despite the removal of 300,000 cu m of plutonium-contaminated topsoil during the operation, some 120 sq km of the territory was still considered too contaminated for continual habitation.

The sensitive issue of Aboriginal land rights was addressed by the Government in August 1985, when it formulated proposals for legislation that would give Aboriginal people inalienable freehold title to national parks, vacant Crown land and former Aboriginal reserves, in spite of widespread opposition from state governments (which had previously been responsible for their

own land policies), from mining companies and from the Aboriginal people themselves, who were angered by the Government's withdrawal of its earlier support for the Aboriginal right to veto mineral exploitation. In October 1985 Ayers Rock, in the Northern Territory, was officially transferred to the Mutijulu Aboriginal community, on condition that continuing access to the rock (the main inland tourist attraction) be guaranteed. In 1986, however, the Government abandoned its pledge to impose such federal legislation on unwilling state governments, and this led to further protests from Aboriginal leaders. In June 1991 the Government imposed a permanent ban on mining at an historical Aboriginal site in the Northern Territory.

An important precedent was established in June 1992, when the High Court overruled the concept of *terra nullius* (unoccupied land) by recognizing the existence of land titles that predated European settlement in 1788 in cases where a close association with the land in question had been continued; however, land titles legally acquired since 1788 were to remain intact. As a result of the 'Mabo' decision of 1992 (named after the Aboriginal claimant, Eddie Mabo), in December 1993 Parliament approved the Native Title Act, historic legislation granting Aboriginal people the right to claim title to their traditional lands. Despite the Prime Minister's personal involvement in the issue, the legislation aroused much controversy, particularly in Western Australia (vast areas of the state being vacant Crown land) where rival legislation to replace native title rights with lesser rights to traditional land usage, such as access for ceremonial purposes only, had been enacted. In March 1995 the High Court declared the Native Title Act to be valid, rejecting as unconstitutional Western Australia's own legislation. The ruling was expected to have widespread implications for the mining industry.

In October 1996, following protracted delays in the development of a valuable zinc mine in Queensland owing to Aboriginal land claims, the Howard Government announced proposals to amend the Native Title Act to permit federal ministers to overrule Aboriginal concerns if a project of 'major economic benefit' to Australia were threatened. Other proposed amendments included the simplification of the process of negotiation between potential developers and Aboriginal claimants. In December the Larrakia people of the Northern Territory presented a claim under the Native Title Act. The area in question incorporated the city of Darwin and was thus the first such claim to encompass a provincial capital. In the same month the federal High Court upheld an appeal by two Aboriginal communities in Queensland (including the Wik people of Cape York) against an earlier ruling that prevented them from submitting a claim to land leased by the state Government to cattle and sheep farmers. The Court's decision, known as the Wik judgment, was expected to encourage similar challenges to 'pastoral' leases, which covered 40% of Australia. Vociferous protests from farmers, who were strongly opposed to the co-existence of native title and pastoral leases, followed.

In April 1997 the first native title deed to be granted on mainland Australia was awarded to the Dunghutti people of New South Wales. In the same month the Prime Minister announced the introduction of legislation to clarify the issue of land tenure; a 10-point plan was to be drawn up in consultation with state governments and with representatives of the Aboriginal community. In September the Government introduced the Wik Native Title Bill, which was subsequently passed by the House of Representatives. In November, however, the Senate questioned the constitutional validity of the proposed legislation, whereby pastoralists' rights and activities would prevail over, but not extinguish (as had been assumed), the Aboriginal people's rights to Native Title. In December the Government refused to accept the Senate's proposed amendments to the legislation, thus raising the possibility of an early general election dominated by Aboriginal issues. In April 1998 the Senate rejected the legislation for a second time. Finally, in July, following a protracted and acrimonious debate, the Senate narrowly approved the Native Title Amendment Bill, thereby restricting the Aboriginal people's rights to claim access to Crown land leased to farmers. The passage of the controversial legislation was immediately denounced by Aboriginal leaders, who threatened to enlist international support for their cause. In the same month, however, the federal court of Darwin granted communal (but not exclusive) native title to the waters and seabed around Croker Island in the Northern Territory to five Aboriginal groups. With about 140 similar claims over Australian waters pending, the historic ruling represented the first recognition of native title rights over the sea. In March 1999, in a conciliatory gesture that settled a land claim case outstanding since 1845, the Tasmanian Government relinquished the site of a mission station at Wybellena, where 200 Aboriginal people had been forcibly resettled; most had subsequently died of disease and maltreatment.

In November 1987 an official commission of inquiry into the cause of the high death rate among Aboriginal prisoners recommended immediate government action, and in July 1988 it was announced that 108 cases remained to be investigated. In August 1988 a UN report accused Australia of violating international human rights in its treatment of the Aboriginal people. In November the Government announced an inquiry into its Aboriginal Affairs Department, following accusations, made by the opposition coalition, of nepotism and misuse of funds. The commission of inquiry published its first official report in February 1989. Following the report's recommendations, the Government announced the creation of a $A10m. programme to combat the high death rate among Aboriginal prisoners. In October an unofficial study indicated that Aboriginal people, although accounting for only 1% of the total population of Australia, comprised more than 20% of persons in prison. In May 1991 the report of the Royal Commission into Aboriginal Deaths in Custody was published, after three years of investigation. The report outlined evidence of racial prejudice in the police force and included more than 300 recommendations for changes in policies relating to Aboriginal people, aimed at improving relations between the racial groups of Australia and granting Aboriginal people greater self-determination and access to land ownership. In June Parliament established a Council for Aboriginal Reconciliation. In March 1992, Aboriginal deaths in custody having continued, radical plans for judicial, economic and social reforms, aimed at improving the lives of Aboriginal people, were announced. The Government made an immediate allocation of $A150m.; a total of $A500m. was to be made available over the next 10 years. In February 1993 the human rights organization, Amnesty International, issued a highly critical report on the prison conditions of Aboriginal people. In March 1996 Amnesty International claimed that Australia had made little progress with regard to its treatment of Aboriginal prisoners. In March 2000 the UN Committee on Elimination of Racial Discrimination issued a report denouncing Australia's treatment of its indigenous people. The report was particularly critical of the mandatory prison sentences for minor property offences in force in the Northern Territory and Western Australia, which appeared to target juvenile Aborigines. In July a legal case was initiated against the Australian Government accusing it of breaching the human rights of Aboriginal people with these harsh mandatory sentencing laws.

In July 1996 the Roman Catholic Church issued an apology for its role in the forcible removal from their parents of tens of thousands of Aboriginal children, in a controversial practice of placement in white foster homes, where many were abused. This policy of assimilation had continued until the late 1960s. In August 1996 the new Governor-General, Sir William Deane, urged all state parliaments to affirm their support for reconciliation with the Aboriginal people. The legislature of South Australia was the first to do so, in November. In May 1997 the publication of the findings of a two-year inquiry into the removal of as many as 100,000 Aboriginal children from their families had profound political repercussions. The author of the report, a distinguished former judge and President of the Human Rights and Equal Opportunities Commission, urged the Government to issue a formal apology to the 'stolen generation'. At a conference on reconciliation at the end of the month, the Prime Minister made an unexpected personal apology. The Government, however, repudiated the commission's assertion that the policy of assimilation had been tantamount to genocide and rejected recommendations that compensation be paid to victims. In December the Government reaffirmed that it would not issue a formal apology to the 'stolen generation'. A $A63m. programme to help reunite divided Aboriginal families was nevertheless announced. In February 1998 the Anglican Church apologized unreservedly for its part in the removal of Aboriginal children from their families. In May 2000, when 250,000 citizens took part in a march across Sydney Harbour Bridge, the Prime Minister refused to involve himself fully in the campaign for reconciliation between White and Aboriginal Australia, and ruled out any notion of a treaty. Two separate UN reports, released in March and July 2000, were highly critical of Australia's treatment of the Aboriginal population. The findings of the

UN Committee on Elimination of Racial Discrimination (see above), and subsequently of the UN Human Rights Committee, were strongly rejected by the Australian Government. In August 2000, at the conclusion of a test case brought in the Northern Territory by two members of the 'stolen generation', who hoped to win compensation for the trauma occasioned by their removal from their families, the Federal Court ruled that the Government was not obliged to pay punitive damages to the two Aboriginal claimants, on the grounds of insufficient evidence. As many as 30,000 similar cases had been pending. In December some 300,000 people took part in demonstrations in Melbourne and Perth in support of reconciliation between the white and indigenous communities, and the Prime Minister was subject to renewed pressure to apologize for the treatment of Aboriginal people by white settlers. A Senate committee recommended issuing an apology to the 'stolen generation' and establishing a reparations tribunal to deal with compensation claims. However, the Government strongly rejected the recommendations.

In foreign affairs, the Hawke and Keating Governments placed greater emphasis on links with South-East Asia. This policy was continued by John Howard, who pledged to expand relations with Asia. In January 1989 Hawke proposed the creation of an Asia-Pacific Economic Co-operation forum (APEC, see p. 128) to facilitate the exchange of services, tourism and direct foreign investment in the region. The inaugural APEC conference took place in Canberra in November 1989.

Australian relations with Indonesia, which had been strained since the Indonesian annexation of the former Portuguese colony of East Timor in 1976, improved in August 1985, when Hawke made a statement recognizing Indonesian sovereignty over the territory, but subsequently deteriorated, following the publication in a Sydney newspaper, in April 1986, of an article containing allegations of corruption against the Indonesian President, Gen. Suharto. Relations between Australia and Indonesia improved in December 1989, when they signed an accord regarding joint exploration for petroleum and gas reserves in the Timor Gap, an area of sea forming a disputed boundary between the two countries. Portugal, however, withdrew its ambassador from Canberra in protest, and in February 1991 instituted proceedings against Australia at the International Court of Justice. In June 1995 the Court refused to invalidate the exploration treaty. In April 1992 Paul Keating's visit to Indonesia, the new Prime Minister's first official overseas trip, aroused controversy, owing to the repercussions of the massacre of unarmed civilians in East Timor by Indonesian troops in November 1991. In July 1995, owing to strong opposition in Australia, Indonesia was obliged to withdraw the appointment as ambassador to Canberra of Lt-Gen. (retd) Herman Mantiri, a former Chief of the General Staff of the Armed Forces and an apparent supporter of the November 1991 Dili massacre. Nevertheless, in December 1995 Australia and Indonesia unexpectedly signed a joint security treaty. In March 1996 a new Indonesian ambassador took up his appointment in Canberra, and in September, following a visit to Jakarta by John Howard, Indonesia accepted Australia's ambassador-designate.

Meanwhile, the investigation into the deaths of six Australia-based journalists (including two Britons) in East Timor in 1975 had been reopened, and in June 1996 a government report concluded that they had been murdered by Indonesian soldiers. In October 1996, as Canberra continued to fail to denounce the Suharto Government's violations of human rights, Australian senators from all parties urged the Government to withdraw its recognition of Indonesian sovereignty over East Timor. In March 1997 Australia and Indonesia signed a treaty defining their seabed and 'economic zone' boundaries. The political unrest in Indonesia in early 1998, culminating in President Suharto's replacement in May, caused deep concern in Australia. In August the International Commission of Jurists, the Geneva-based human-rights organization, reported that five of the six journalists had been murdered in an East Timorese village in October 1975 in an attempt to conceal the invasion of the territory, while the sixth man was killed in Dili in December of that year. Furthermore, it was claimed that the Australian embassy in Jakarta had been aware of the forthcoming invasion of East Timor but had failed to give adequate warning to the journalists. In October 1998, as newly-emerging evidence continued to suggest that the truth had been suppressed and as interest in the matter was renewed in the United Kingdom, the Indonesian Government declared that it would not open an inquiry into the deaths of the two British journalists, maintaining that they and their colleagues had been killed in crossfire. Australia, however, announced that its judicial inquiry was to be reopened. Government documents declassified in late 2000 proved conclusively that Australian officials had prior knowledge of Indonesia's plans to invade East Timor.

In January 1999, in a significant shift in its policy, Australia announced that henceforth it would support eventual self-determination for East Timor. (Australia had been the only developed nation to recognize Indonesia's annexation of the territory.) In late January, furthermore, Australia welcomed the Indonesian Government's declaration of its willingness to consider the possibility of full independence, if proposals for autonomy were rejected by the East Timorese people. During 1999, however, Australia became increasingly concerned at the deteriorating security situation in East Timor. The announcement of the result of the referendum on the future of East Timor, held in late August, at which the territory's people voted overwhelmingly in favour of independence (see chapter on Indonesia) led to a rapid escalation of the violence. As pro-Jakarta militias embarked upon a campaign of murder and arson against innocent civilians, most of whom were forced to flee their homes, thousands of refugees were airlifted to safety in northern Australia. With a commitment of 4,500 troops in its largest operation since the Viet Nam War, Australia took a leading role in the deployment of a multinational peace-keeping force, the first contingent of which landed in East Timor on 20 September 1999. Several Asian countries, however, in particular Malaysia and Thailand, along with Indonesia itself (which earlier in the month had suspended its security pact with Australia), were critical of Australia's bias towards pro-independence groups and of the country's apparent aggressive approach to its role in the operation, which some observers considered would have been more appropriately led by the Association of South East Asian Nations (ASEAN). A deterioration in relations between the two countries led Abdurrahman Wahid, who replaced Habibie as President of Indonesia, to postpone an official visit to Australia in mid-2000. A series of postponements or cancellations of ministerial meetings followed. In a further demonstration of anti-Australian feeling, the Canberra's ambassador to Indonesia was assaulted by a pro-Jakarta mob in Makassar, Sulawesi, in November 2000. In the same month the Australian Government agreed to help create an East Timor defence force, contributing some US $26m. over five years and providing training for police officers and border guards.

A crisis in Australia's relations with Malaysia arose in late 1993, when Keating described the Malaysian Prime Minister as a 'recalcitrant' for his failure to attend the APEC summit meeting in Seattle, USA, in November. Relations subsequently improved, however, and in January 1996 Keating paid the first official visit to Malaysia by an Australian Prime Minister since 1984. During 1999 Australia was critical of the continued detention and the trials of Anwar Ibrahim, the former Deputy Prime Minister and Minister of Finance (see chapter on Malaysia).

Australia's relations with the People's Republic of China, meanwhile, continued to be strained by the issue of China's nuclear-testing programme, and deteriorated further in September 1996 when the Dalai Lama, the exiled spiritual leader of Tibet, was received in Sydney by the Prime Minister. In March 1997, however, the Australian Prime Minister began a six-day official visit to China, where he had discussions with Premier Li Peng. In July 1999, during a visit to Beijing by the Australian Minister of Foreign Affairs, Australia endorsed China's bid for membership of the World Trade Organization (WTO). The two countries also signed a bilateral trade pact. In September, however, President Jiang Zemin's visit to Australia was disrupted by pro-Tibet and Taiwan activists. Australia's relations with Japan were strained in the late 1990s by a fishing dispute relating to the latter's failure to curb its catches of the endangered southern bluefin tuna, as agreed in a treaty of 1993, of which New Zealand was also a signatory. In August 1999, however, an international tribunal ruled in favour of Australia and New Zealand.

In May 2000 diplomatic relations between Australia and the Democratic People's Republic of Korea, which had been severed in 1975, were restored. Discussions between the two nations, initiated by the North Korean Government in April 1999, had been dominated by the International Atomic Energy Agency's concerns over nuclear facilities and long-range missile testing. The Australian Minister of Foreign Affairs paid an official two-day visit to Pyongyang in November 2000.

The viability of the ANZUS military pact, which was signed in 1951, linking Australia, New Zealand and the USA, was disputed by the US Government following the New Zealand Government's declaration, in July 1984, that vessels which were believed to be powered by nuclear energy, or to be carrying nuclear weapons, would be barred from the country's ports. Hawke did not support the New Zealand initiative, and Australia continued to participate with the USA in joint military exercises from which New Zealand had been excluded. However, the Hawke Government declined directly to endorse US retaliation against New Zealand, and in 1986 stated that Australia regarded its 'obligations to New Zealand as constant and undiminishing'. In March 1987 proposals for an ambitious new defence strategy were published, following the recommendations of a government commissioned report advocating a comprehensive restructuring of the country's military forces, on the basis of greater self-reliance. The cost of the plan, however, was estimated at $A25,000m. over 15 years. In September 1990 Australia and New Zealand signed an agreement to establish a joint venture to construct as many as 12 naval frigates to patrol the South Pacific. In February 1994 the USA announced its decision to resume senior-level contacts with New Zealand. In July 1996 Australia and the USA upgraded their defence alliance. In 1999 Australia's trading relations with the USA were strained by the latter's imposition of tariffs on imports of Australian lamb. In October Australia urged that the dispute be settled by means of a WTO panel.

Owing to Australian opposition to French test explosions of nuclear weapons at Mururoa Atoll (French Polynesia) in the South Pacific Ocean, a ban on uranium sales to France was introduced in 1983. However, in August 1986 the Government announced its decision to resume uranium exports. In December Australia ratified a treaty declaring the South Pacific area a nuclear-free zone. France's decision, in April 1992, to suspend its nuclear-testing programme was welcomed by Australia. In June 1995, however, the French President's announcement that the programme was to be resumed provoked outrage throughout the Pacific region. The Australian ambassador to France was recalled, and the French consulate in Perth was destroyed in an arson attack. Further widespread protests followed the first of the new series of tests in September. Australia's relations with the UK were strained by the British Government's refusal to join the condemnation of France's policy. The final test was conducted in January 1996. On an official visit to Paris in September, the Australian Minister for Foreign Affairs adopted a conciliatory stance (which drew much criticism from anti-nuclear groups). A ban on new contracts for the supply of uranium to France, imposed in September 1995, was removed in October 1996. Meanwhile, Australia remained committed to achieving the elimination of all nuclear testing. In August, following a veto of the draft text by India and Iran at the UN Conference on Disarmament in Geneva, Australia took the initiative in leading an international effort to secure the passage of the Comprehensive Test Ban Treaty. In an unusual procedure, the Treaty was referred to the UN General Assembly, which voted overwhelmingly in its favour in September.

Relations with neighbouring Pacific island states were strained in mid-1997. In July Australia was embarrassed by the unauthorized publication of a secret official document in which certain regional politicians were described as corrupt and incompetent. At a meeting of the South Pacific Forum in September, the member countries failed to reach agreement on a common policy regarding mandatory targets for the reduction of emissions of the so-called 'greenhouse gases'. The low-lying nation of Tuvalu was particularly critical of Australia's refusal to compromise, the Australian Prime Minister declaring that the Pacific islands' concerns over rising sea levels were exaggerated.

Australia's relations with Papua New Guinea were strained in early 1997 as a result of the latter's decision to engage the services of a group of mercenaries in the Government's operations against secessionists on the island of Bougainville. Fearing for the stability of the South Pacific region, the Australian Prime Minister denounced the use of foreign forces as unacceptable. In January 1998 a permanent ceasefire agreement between the Papua New Guinea Government and the Bougainville secessionists, which was to take effect in April, was signed in New Zealand. Australia reaffirmed its commitment to the provision of a peace-monitoring force. In July Australian forces responded promptly to an appeal for assistance following a series of tsunami, which killed thousands of villagers on the north-west coast of Papua New Guinea. Australia subsequently provided substantial relief aid.

Australia played a leading role in the events following a coup in Solomon Islands, which took place in June 2000. The Australian Navy dispatched a warship to assist in the evacuation of Australian and other nationals from the islands, while a similar ship anchored offshore served as a venue for negotiations between the two warring ethnic militias. The Australian Minister for Foreign Affairs led an international delegation with the aim of facilitating discussions between the factions. In October a peace agreement was signed in Townsville, Queensland, which ended the two-year conflict. The Australian Government subsequently offered to contribute to a group of international peace monitors, in an attempt to ensure continued stability in the islands.

Government

Australia comprises six states and three territories. Executive power is vested in the British monarch and exercised by the monarch's appointed representative, the Governor-General, who normally acts on the advice of the Federal Executive Council (the Ministry), led by the Prime Minister. The Governor-General appoints the Prime Minister and, on the latter's recommendation, other Ministers.

Legislative power is vested in the Federal Parliament. This consists of the monarch, represented by the Governor-General, and two chambers elected by universal adult suffrage (voting is compulsory). The Senate has 76 members (12 from each state and two each from the Northern Territory and the Australian Capital Territory), who are elected by a system of proportional representation for six years when representing a state, with half the seats renewable every three years, and for a term of three years when representing a territory. The House of Representatives has 148 members, elected for three years (subject to dissolution) from single-member constituencies. The Federal Executive Council is responsible to Parliament.

Each state has a Governor, representing the monarch, and its own legislative, executive and judicial system. The state governments are essentially autonomous, but certain powers are placed under the jurisdiction of the Federal Government. All states except Queensland have an Upper House (the Legislative Council) and a Lower House (the Legislative Assembly or House of Assembly). The chief ministers of the states are known as Premiers, as distinct from the Federal Prime Minister. The Northern Territory (self-governing since 1978) and the Australian Capital Territory (self-governing since 1988) have unicameral legislatures, and each has a government led by a Chief Minister. The Jervis Bay Territory is not self-governing.

Defence

Australia's defence policy is based on collective security, and it is a member of the British Commonwealth Strategic Reserve and of ANZUS, with New Zealand and the USA. Australia also participates in the Five-Power Defence Arrangements, with New Zealand, Malaysia, Singapore and the United Kingdom. In August 2000 Australia's armed forces numbered 50,600 (army 24,150, navy 12,500, air force 13,950). Defence expenditure for 2001 was budgeted at $A12,200m. Service in the armed forces is voluntary. In September 1999 Australia committed 4,500 troops to the peace-keeping operation in East Timor, where 1,620 remained in August 2000. In December 2000 the Government announced an increase in defence expenditure of some $A 13,000m. over the next decade.

Economic Affairs

In 1998, according to estimates by the World Bank, Australia's gross national product (GNP), measured at average 1996–98 prices, was US $387,006m., equivalent to US $20,640 per head (or US $21,795 per head on an international purchasing-power parity basis). It was estimated that Australia's GNP per head increased, in real terms, at an average rate of 2.8% per year between 1990 and 1998. Over the same period, the population increased at an average annual rate of 1.3%. In 1999 GNP totalled an estimated US $380,800m. (US $20,050 per head). The country's gross domestic product (GDP) increased, in real terms, by an annual average of 3.8% in 1990–99. GDP expanded by 4.4% in 1999. Total GDP was valued at US $392,600m. (US $20,700 per head) in 1999.

Agriculture (including forestry, hunting and fishing) contributed 3.2% of GDP in 1997/98, and engaged 4.9% of the employed labour force in 1999. The principal crops are wheat, fruit, sugar and cotton. Australia is the world's leading producer of wool. Export earnings from greasy wool, however, declined from $A1,715m. in 1998 to $A1,494m. in 1999. The export of wine is of increasing importance, rising from 10m. litres in 1986 to 258m. litres in 1999. The value of wine exports totalled $A1,195m. in 1999. Beef production is also important, contributing an estimated 15.4% of the value of gross farm output in 1998/99. Between 1989/90 and 1996/97 agricultural GDP increased at an average annual rate of 3.0%, but it declined by 1.4%, compared with the previous year, in 1997/98.

Industry (comprising mining, manufacturing, construction and utilities) employed 21.5% of the working population in 1999, and provided 26.0% of GDP in 1997/98. Industrial GDP increased at an average rate of 1.4% per year between 1989/90 and 1996/97 and grew by 4.5% in 1997/98.

The mining sector employed 0.9% of the working population in 1999, and contributed 4.6% of GDP in 1997/98. Australia is one of the world's leading exporters of coal. Earnings from coal and related products in 1998/99 reached $A9,302m., more than 10.8% of total export receipts in that year. The other principal minerals extracted are iron ore, gold, silver, petroleum and natural gas. Bauxite, zinc, copper, titanium, nickel, tin, lead, zirconium and diamonds are also mined. Between 1989/90 and 1996/97 the GDP of the mining sector increased at an average annual rate of 2.9%, and GDP rose by 5.3% in 1997/98.

Manufacturing contributed 12.8% of GDP in 1997/98. The sector employed 12.3% of the working population in 1999. Measured by the value of sales, the principal branches of manufacturing in 1998/99 were food, beverages and tobacco (20.2%), equipment and machinery (20.3%), metal products (16.4%), petroleum, coal and chemical products (14.0%), printing, publishing and recording (9.8%) and wood and paper products (6.2%). The manufacturing sector's GDP grew at an average annual rate of 1.2% between 1989/90 and 1996/97, increasing by 1.5% in 1997/98.

Energy is derived principally from petroleum, natural gas and coal. Production of petroleum declined from 30,763m. litres in 1995/96 to 29,130m. litres in 1996/97, while that of black coal increased from 194.5m. tons in 1995/96 to 205.4m. tons in 1996/97.

The services sector provided 70.7% of GDP in 1997/98, and engaged 73.6% of the employed labour force in 1999. The tourism industry is of growing significance. The number of visitor arrivals increased from 4.2m. in 1998 to 4.5m. in 1999, when tourist receipts reached $A17,000m. It was estimated that in 1995/96 the tourism sector contributed 7.4% of GDP and accounted for 8.4% of total employment. The GDP of the services sector increased at an average annual rate of 4.2% between 1989/90 and 1996/97 and rose by 4.8% in 1997/98.

In 1999 Australia recorded a visible trade deficit of US $9,780m., and there was a deficit of US $22,861m. on the current account of the balance of payments. In the year ending 30 June 1999 the principal source of imports was the USA (21.4%), followed by Japan (13.9%). Japan was the principal market for exports in that year (19.3%), followed by the USA(9.3%) and the Republic of Korea (7.4%). Other major trading partners are New Zealand, the United Kingdom, Singapore, Taiwan and the People's Republic of China. The principal exports were metalliferous ores (sales of gold being of increasing significance), coal, machinery, non-ferrous metals, textile fibres (mainly wool), and meat (mainly beef). The principal imports were machinery and transport equipment, basic manufactures, and chemicals and related products.

In the 1999/2000 financial year a budgetary surplus of $A9,514m. was recorded. A surplus of $A2,800m. was forecast for 2000/01. In mid-1998 Australia's net external debt stood at $A227,033m. (equivalent to 39.5% of annual GDP). An estimated 7.2% of the labour force were unemployed in 1999 and the rate stood at 6.6% in January 2001. The annual rate of inflation averaged 2.0% in 1991–2000. Consumer prices rose by 1.5% in 1999.

Australia is a member of the Asian Development Bank (see p. 131), the Pacific Islands Forum (formerly the South Pacific Forum, see p. 276) and the Pacific Community (formerly the South Pacific Commission—see p. 275). In 1989 Australia played a major role in the creation of the Asia-Pacific Economic Co-operation group (APEC, see p. 128), which aimed to stimulate economic development in the region. Australia is also a member of the OECD (see p. 247), of the Cairns Group (see p. 354) and of the International Grains Council (see p. 304).

Upon taking office in March 1996, the Howard Government confirmed its determination to achieve fiscal balance. One of the principal aims of the administration's programme was the transfer to the private sector of Telstra, the state-owned telecommunications company. The sale of one-third of the company's assets took place in November 1997, raising revenue of $A14,300m. and representing the most successful Australian flotation to date. In late 1999 a further 16.6% of Telstra's assets were sold. The Government also remained committed to the deregulation of the labour market. The 1997/98 budget resulted in the first surplus for many years. The 1998/99 budget aimed to prepare the way for radical tax reforms, including the introduction of a controversial 10% goods-and-services tax (GST) from mid-2000. The 1999/2000 budget allocated additional funding (of $A800m.) to the biotechnology industry, the sector being regarded as a significant source of future economic growth. The 2000/01 budget, presented in May 2000, provided for additional funding for rural communities. A total of $A1,800m. (of which $A562m. was to be allocated to regional health programmes) was to be released over the next four years. The Government envisaged a GDP growth rate of 3.75% in 2000/01. During 2000 Australia experienced a sharp increase in earnings from its commodity exports owing to a decline in the Australian dollar, which fell to its lowest level against the US dollar since its flotation in 1983. The value of mineral exports increased by some 13% (to US $43,800m.) in that year with exports of crude petroleum alone earning revenue some 180% higher than in 1999. The economic benefits of this situation, however, were tempered by extensive damage to crops (most significantly the wheat crop) caused by drought in late 2000, followed by heavy rains and severe flooding. The weakness of the Australian dollar led to increased support for the idea of a common currency with New Zealand (the latter having experienced a similar decline in the value of its currency against the US dollar).

Social Welfare

Australia provides old-age, invalid and widows' pensions, unemployment, sickness and supporting parents' benefits, family allowances and other welfare benefits and allowances. In 1998/99 Australia had 1,257 hospitals (755 public and 502 private), with a total of 77,631 beds (53,885 public and 23,746 private). In 1999/2000 there were some 38,000 general practitioners and 17,200 specialist practitioners. There were 151,200 nurses registered in the country in that year. The desert interior is served by the Royal Flying Doctor Service. Expenditure on health by both the public and private sectors in 1998/99 was estimated at $A50,346m. (equivalent to 8.5% of GDP). In 1999/2000 public expenditure on health totalled $A23,540m., while social security and welfare were allocated $A57,129m.

In 1984 the Government introduced a system of universal health insurance, known as Medicare, whereby every Australian is protected against the costs of medical and hospital care. Where medical expenses are incurred, Medicare covers patients for 85% of the government-approved Schedule Fee for services. For private in-patients in hospitals, 75% of the Schedule Fee for services is payable. The Medicare scheme is financed in part by a levy, normally of 1.5%, on taxable incomes above a certain level.

Education

Education is the responsibility of each of the states and the Federal Government. It is compulsory, and available free of charge, for all children from the ages of six to 15 years (16 in Tasmania). Primary education generally begins at six years of age and lasts for six years. Secondary education, beginning at the age of 12, usually lasts for five years. As a proportion of children in the relevant age-groups, the enrolment ratios in 1997 were 95% in primary schools and 89% in 1996 in secondary schools. In 1999 there were 1,378,200 children enrolled in government primary schools and 869,200 in secondary schools, while 979,300 children were attending private schools (507,200 primary and 472,100 secondary). Special services have been developed to fulfil the requirements of children living in the remote 'outback' areas, notably Schools of the Air, using two-way receiver sets. A system of one-teacher schools and correspondence schools also helps to satisfy these needs. Under a major reform programme initiated in 1988, the binary system of universities and colleges of advanced education was replaced by a unified national system of fewer and larger institutions. In 1999 there were 42 publicly-funded institutions of higher education. In the same year students totalled 686,300. Most courses last from three to six years. Public expenditure on education in the financial year 1999/2000 was $A10,587m.

Public Holidays*

2001: 1 January (New Year's Day), 26 January (Australia Day), 13–16 April (Easter), 25 April (Anzac Day), 11 June (Queen's Official Birthday, except Western Australia), 25–26 December (Christmas Day, Boxing Day).

2002 (provisional): 1 January (New Year's Day), 26 January (Australia Day), 29 March–1 April (Easter), 25 April (Anzac Day), 10 June (Queen's Official Birthday, except Western Australia), 25–26 December (Christmas Day, Boxing Day).

* National holidays only. Some states observe these holidays on different days. There are also numerous individual state holidays.

Weights and Measures

The metric system is in force.

Statistical Survey

Source (unless otherwise stated): Australian Bureau of Statistics, POB 10, Belconnen, ACT 2616; tel. (2) 6252-7911; fax (2) 6251-6009; internet www.abs.gov.au.

Area and Population

AREA, POPULATION AND DENSITY

Area (sq km)	7,692,030*
Population (census results)†	
6 August 1991	
Total	16,847,310
6 August 1996	
Males	8,849,224
Females	9,043,199
Total	17,892,423
Population (official estimates at mid-year)†	
1997	18,524,200
1998	18,730,000
1999 (provisional)	18,967,000
Density (per sq km) at mid-1999	2.5

* 2,969,909 sq miles.
† Census results exclude, and estimates include, an adjustment for under-enumeration, estimated to have been 1.9% in 1991. Estimates also exclude overseas visitors in Australia and include Australian residents temporarily overseas. On this basis, the adjusted census total was 17,317,800 (provisional) in 1991.

STATES AND TERRITORIES (30 June 1998)

	Area (sq km)	Estimated Population	Density (per sq km)
New South Wales (NSW) .	800,640	6,341,600	7.9
Victoria	227,420	4,660,900	20.5
Queensland . . .	1,730,650	3,456,300	2.0
South Australia. . .	983,480	1,487,300	1.5
Western Australia . .	2,529,880	1,831,400	0.7
Tasmania	68,400	471,900	6.9
Northern Territory . .	1,349,130	190,000	0.1
Australian Capital Territory			
(ACT)	2,360	308,400	130.7
Jervis Bay Territory . .	70	n.a.	n.a.
Total	7,692,030	18,750,100*	2.4

* Includes populations of Jervis Bay Territory, Christmas Island and the Cocos (Keeling) Islands.

PRINCIPAL TOWNS (estimated population at 30 June 1998)*

Canberra (national capital)	308,100
Sydney (capital of NSW)	3,986,700
Melbourne (capital of Victoria). . . .	3,371,300
Brisbane (capital of Queensland) . . .	1,574,600
Perth (capital of W Australia)	1,341,900
Adelaide (capital of S Australia) . . .	1,088,400
Newcastle	473,900
Gold Coast-Tweed	379,200
Wollongong	260,100
Hobart (capital of Tasmania)	195,000
Sunshine Coast	167,800
Geelong	154,100
Townsville	124,900
Cairns	112,000

* Figures refer to metropolitan areas, each of which normally comprises a municipality and contiguous urban areas.

BIRTHS, MARRIAGES AND DEATHS*

	Registered live births		Registered marriages		Registered deaths	
	Number	Rate (per 1,000)	Number	Rate (per 1,000)	Number	Rate (per 1,000)
1991 . .	257,247	14.9	113,869	6.6	119,146	6.9
1992 . .	264,151	15.1	114,752	6.6	123,660	7.1
1993 . .	260,229	14.7	113,255	6.4	121,599	6.9
1994 . .	258,051	14.5	111,174	6.2	126,692	7.1
1995 . .	256,190	14.2	109,386	6.1	125,133	6.9
1996 . .	253,834	13.9	106,103	5.8	128,719	7.0
1997 . .	251,842	13.5	106,735	5.8	129,350	6.9
1998 . .	249,283†	13.3	110,598	5.9	127,952†	6.8

* Data are tabulated by year of registration rather than by year of occurrence.
† Data are tabulated by year of occurrence.

Expectation of life (years at birth, 1997): males 75.57, females 81.27.

ECONOMICALLY ACTIVE POPULATION (annual averages, '000 persons aged 15 years and over, excluding armed forces)

	1997	1998	1999
Agriculture, forestry and fishing .	428.4	422.2	431.9
Mining	82.3	83.7	76.4
Manufacturing	1,134.5	1,099.6	1,073.0
Electricity, gas and water supply .	65.3	64.9	64.6
Construction.	579.8	620.3	663.1
Wholesale trade	489.9	509.6	522.1
Retail trade	1,229.6	1,266.6	1,322.5
Accommodation, cafés and			
restaurants	402.3	408.6	417.6
Transport and storage . .	395.3	396.0	414.3
Communication services . .	156.1	149.0	154.6
Finance and insurance . .	314.7	321.4	315.3
Property and business services .	859.8	926.0	961.5
Government administration and			
defence	353.6	335.4	349.5
Education	578.5	593.4	612.2
Health and community services .	779.1	813.3	814.5
Cultural and recreational services.	201.3	205.0	212.5
Personal and other services . .	333.2	341.8	341.9
Total employed . . .	8,383.6	8,556.7	8,747.4
Unemployed	785.7	746.4	684.4
Total labour force (incl. others)	9,204.7	9,343.5	9,467.1
Males	5,234.2	5,300.1	5,359.6
Females	3,970.5	4,043.4	4,107.5

Source: *ABS Labour Force Australia.*

Agriculture

PRINCIPAL CROPS ('000 metric tons)

	1997	1998	1999
Wheat	19,224	21,122	24,058
Rice (paddy)	1,255	1,390	1,084
Barley	6,482	5,680	4,280
Maize	398	271	322
Oats	1,583	1,874	1,473
Sorghum	1,425	1,081	1,664
Potatoes	1,286	1,372	1,372*
Dry peas	316	298	357
Other pulses	2,005	2,116	2,106
Soybeans (Soya beans)	74	109	105
Sunflower seed	143	209	147
Rapeseed	855	1,761	2,400
Cottonseed	860	941	n.a.
Cotton (lint)	608	666	716
Cabbages	66	58	58*
Tomatoes	380	394*	394
Cauliflower	105	110*	110*
Pumpkins, squash and gourds	101	105*	105*
Onions (dry)	200*	219	219*
Green peas	95	76	76*
Carrots	257	267	267*
Watermelons	100	100*	100*
Grapes	943	1,097	1,198
Sugar cane	38,463	39,531	36,922
Apples	353	309	334
Pears	168	153	165†
Peaches and nectarines	88	90*	90*
Oranges	500	443	470*
Pineapples	123	123*	123*
Bananas	223	230*	230*

* FAO estimate.
† Unofficial figure.
Source: FAO.

LIVESTOCK ('000 head at 31 March)

	1997	1998	1999
Horses*	230	220	220
Cattle	26,780	26,710	25,833
Pigs	2,555	2,768	2,604
Sheep	120,228	117,494	117,176
Goats	230*	220	180*
Chickens	81,000	83,000*	92,000*

* FAO estimate(s).
Source: mainly FAO.

LIVESTOCK PRODUCTS ('000 metric tons)

	1997	1998	1999
Beef and veal	1,810	1,955	2,011
Mutton and lamb	566	616	614
Goat meat	9	4	4
Pig meat	336	358	370
Horse meat	22	21	21
Poultry meat	516	573	593
Cows' milk	9,304	9,731	10,490
Butter	147	161	161*
Cheese	285	295	308
Hen eggs*	195	200	200
Honey	27	22	22*
Wool:			
greasy*	728	704	673
clean*	473	473	n.a.
Cattle hides*	211	230	230
Sheepskins	130	141	137

* FAO estimate(s).
Note: Figures for meat and milk refer to the 12 months ending 30 June of the year stated.
Source: FAO.

Forestry

ROUNDWOOD REMOVALS ('000 cubic metres, excl. bark)

	1996	1997	1998
Sawlogs, veneer logs and logs for sleepers	9,675	9,954	10,100
Pulpwood	9,065	9,414	9,578
Other industrial wood	600	540	557
Fuel wood	2,700	2,700	2,700
Total	22,040	22,608	22,935

Source: FAO, *Yearbook of Forest Products*.

SAWNWOOD PRODUCTION ('000 cubic metres, incl. sleepers)

	1996	1997	1998
Coniferous (softwood)	2,053	2,063	2,327
Broadleaved (hardwood)	1,477	1,418	1,322
Total	3,530	3,481	3,649

Source: FAO, *Yearbook of Forest Products*.

Fishing

('000 metric tons, live weight, year ending 30 June)

	1995/96	1996/97	1997/98
Capture	203.3	198.3	201.2
Silver gemfish*	6.5	7.0	8.0
Sharks, rays, skates, etc.	8.7	12.6	10.5
Australian spiny lobster	9.9	9.9	10.4
Penaeus shrimps	25.3	23.7	24.5
Scallops	12.3	8.6	9.9
Aquaculture	25.3	26.6	27.8
Atlantic salmon	7.6	7.6	7.1
Total catch	228.6	225.0	229.0

* FAO estimates.

Note: Figures exclude aquatic plants ('000 metric tons, capture only): 18.6 in 1996; 21.2 in 1997; 20.8 in 1998. Also excluded are crocodiles, recorded by number rather than by weight. The number of Estuarine crocodiles caught was: 9,054 in 1996; 8,777 in 1997; 9,896 in 1998. The number of Austalian crocodiles caught was: 1,641 in 1996; 194 in 1997; 309 in 1998. Also excluded are pearl oyster shells (estimates, metric tons): 240 in 1996; 250 in 1997; 250 in 1998.

Source: FAO, *Yearbook of Fishery Statistics*.

Mining*

(year ending 30 June, '000 metric tons, unless otherwise indicated)

	1994/95	1995/96	1996/97
Coal (black)	191,903	194,492	205,442
Coal, brown (lignite) . .	50,679	54,281	58,886
Bauxite	45,384	50,724	46,874
Mineral sands†	2,375	2,491	3,044
Iron ore (incl. pellets) . .	137,525	137,267	162,480
Lead concentrate . . .	766	774	774
Zinc concentrate‡ . . .	1,699	1,295	2,007
Copper concentrate and precipitate§ . . .	9,423	1,316	1,787
Antimony (metric tons)‖ .	900¶	1,300**	1,300††
Cadmium (refined, metric tons)‡‡	838¶	639**	632††
Cobalt (metric tons)‡‡§§ .	2,500¶	2,800**	3,000††
Manganese ore†† . . .	1,066.0¶§§	1,023.0**	1,024.0
Ilmenite	1,808.0¶§§	2,028.0**‡‡	2,233.0††
Tin (metric tons)‖‖ . .	9,057	11,568	10,164
Crude petroleum (incl. condensate, million litres)	31,301	30,763	29,130
Natural gas (petajoules) . .	1,163	1,194	1,189
Gold (kg)‡‡ . . .	253,504¶	289,530**	311,360††
Silver (metric tons)‖ . .	920¶	1,020**	1,106††
Nickel‡‡	77¶	74**	74††
Uranium concentrate (metric tons).	3,712	4,975	n.a.
Diamonds—industrial ('000 carats)	22,381¶	23,096**††	22,100††‡‡
Diamonds—gem ('000 carats)‡‡	18,300¶	18,897**	18,100††

* Figures for metallic minerals represent metal contents based on chemical assay, except figures for bauxite, iron and manganese, which are in terms of gross quantities produced.
† Includes ilmenite, beneficiated ilmenite, leucoxene, monazite, rutile and zircon.
‡ Includes zinc-lead concentrate.
§ Excluding copper concentrate of South Australia.
‖ Data from *World Metal Statistics* (London). (Source: UN, *Industrial Commodity Statistics Yearbook*.)
¶ January–December 1995.
** January–December 1996.
†† January–December 1997.
‡‡ Estimated by US Bureau of Mines (Source: UN, *Industrial Commodity Statistics Yearbook*).
§§ Provisional figure(s).
‖‖ Source: UN, *Industrial Commodity Statistics Yearbook*.

Industry

SELECTED PRODUCTS
(year ending 30 June, '000 metric tons, unless otherwise indicated)

	1994/95	1995/96	1996/97
Pig-iron	7,449	7,553	7,346
Blooms and slabs from continuous casting	7,807	7,951	7,775
Aluminium—unwrought* . .	1,285†	1,331	n.a.
Copper—unwrought . . .	281†	282	305
Lead—unwrought* . . .	205†	223	202
Zinc—unwrought* . . .	312†	330	319
Tin—unwrought (metric tons)* .	455†	550	570
Motor spirit (petrol—million litres)	17,911†	18,358	18,084
Fuel oil (million litres) . .	2,431†	1,998	1,795
Diesel-automotive oil (million litres).	11,365†	12,202	12,968
Aviation turbine fuel (million litres)	n.a.	4,882	5,284
Electric motors ('000). . .	3,099	2,850	2,669
Clay bricks (million) . . .	1,860	1,455	1,468
Superphosphate†	1,590	1,697	n.a.
Refrigerators ('000) . . .	408	414	398
Woven man-made fibres ('000 sq metres)	185,171	149,066	142,194
Woven cotton fabrics (incl. towelling, '000 sq metres) . .	51,938	63,886	60,616
Woven woollen fabrics (incl. blanketing, '000 sq metres) . .	8,189	6,523	6,300
Cotton yarn (metric tons) . .	37,643	36,955	39,853
Wool yarn (metric tons) . .	23,093	20,063	18,284
Textile floor coverings ('000 sq metres)	47,258	42,683	44,681
Electricity (million kWh) . . .	165,063	167,544	168,415
Cement	7,124	6,397	6,701
Concrete—ready-mixed ('000 cu m)	15,892	14,556	15,544
Newsprint	423	446	422
Motor vehicles ('000) . . .	328	328	331
Wheat flour‡	1,355	1,414	1,556
Plastics in primary forms . .	1,240	1,222	1,235
Non-laminated particle board ('000 sq metres) . . .	846	804	774
Domestic washing machines ('000)	305	297	268
Confectionery	182.4	187.0	181.1
Beer (million litres) . . .	1,788	1,743	1,735
Tobacco and cigarettes (metric tons)	23,083	20,390	22,193

* Primary refined metal only.
† Source: Australian Bureau of Agricultural and Resource Economics (ABARE), ACT.
‡ Source: UN, *Industrial Commodity Statistics Yearbook*.

1997/98 ('000 metric tons, unless otherwise indicated): Pig-iron 7,928; Blooms and slabs from continuous casting 8,356; Copper (unwrought) 286; Lead (unwrought) 185; Zinc (unwrought) 304; Tin (unwrought, metric tons) 650; Motor spirit (million litres) 18,592; Fuel oil (million litres) 1,673; Diesel-automotive fuel (million litres) 13,183; Aviation turbine fuel (million litres) 5,423; Clay bricks (million) 1,532; Electricity (million kWh) 176,212; Cement 7,236; Concrete (ready-mixed, '000 cu m) 17,412; Newsprint 402; Beer (million litres) 1,757; Tobacco and cigarettes (metric tons) 21,257.

1998/99: Wine (million litres) 793.4. Source: Australian Wine and Brandy Corporation.

Finance

CURRENCY AND EXCHANGE RATES

Monetary Units
100 cents = 1 Australian dollar ($A).

Sterling, US Dollar and Euro Equivalents (29 December 2000)
£1 sterling = $A2.6935;
US $1 = $A1.8051;
€1 = $A1.6796;
$A100 = £37.13 = US $55.40 = €59.54.

Average Exchange Rate (US $ per Australian dollar)
1998	0.6294
1999	0.6453
2000	0.5823

COMMONWEALTH GOVERNMENT BUDGET
($A million, year ending 30 June)

Revenue	1997/98	1998/99	1999/2000
Tax revenue .	132,219	141,104	152,457
Direct taxes	95,366	103,017	113,687
Individuals	70,822	76,729	83,161
Companies .	19,406	20,734	23,982
Indirect taxes, etc. .	31,296	32,415	33,534
Non-tax revenue .	4,749	5,341	17,465
Total	136,969	146,444	169,921

Expenditure	1997/98	1998/99	1999/2000
Defence .	10,473	11,202	9,956
Education .	10,756	9,736	10,587
Health .	20,658	23,343	23,540
Social security and welfare	50,187	52,779	57,129
Economic services	7,720	7,666	7,924
General public services	7,532	8,142	19,131
Public-debt interest	8,401	7,508	9,493
Total (incl. others)	135,784	140,814	160,408

Source: Reserve Bank of Australia, *Bulletin.*

OFFICIAL RESERVES (US $ million at 31 December)

	1997	1998	1999
Gold*	740	737	743
IMF special drawing rights	19	18	72
Reserve position in IMF .	727	1,256	1,633
Foreign exchange	16,099	13,366	19,507
Total	17,585	15,377	21,955

* Valued at market-related prices.

Source: IMF, *International Financial Statistics.*

MONEY SUPPLY ($A million at 31 December)

	1997	1998	1999
Currency outside banks	21,098	22,784	24,602
Demand deposits at trading and savings banks .	86,965	91,864	101,179
Total money (incl. others)	108,352	114,794	125,943

Source: IMF, *International Financial Statistics.*

COST OF LIVING (Consumer Price Index*; base: 1990 = 100)

	1997	1998	1999
Food	119.0	122.3	126.4
Electricity, gas and other fuels†	120.4	120.1	120.0
Clothing.	104.9	104.8	103.7
Rent‡	93.9	91.7	94.7
All items (incl. others)	116.4	117.3	119.1

* Weighted average of eight capital cities.
† From September 1998 including water and sewerage.
‡ Including expenditure on maintenance and repairs of dwellings; from September 1998 excluding mortgage interest charges and including house purchase and utilities.

Source: ILO, *Yearbook of Labour Statistics.*

NATIONAL ACCOUNTS ($A million, year ending 30 June)
National Income and Product (at current prices)

	1995/96	1996/97	1997/98
Compensation of employees	242,231	258,759	270,084
Operating surplus	126,761	129,324	140,079
Domestic factor incomes	368,992	388,083	410,163
Consumption of fixed capital .	80,611	82,372	88,016
Gross domestic product (GDP) at factor cost.	449,603	470,455	498,179
Indirect taxes } *Less* Subsidies }	59,203	61,749	64,966
GDP in purchasers' values .	508,806	532,204	563,145
Net factor income from abroad	−19,874	−19,296	−18,794
Gross national product	488,932	512,908	544,351
Less Consumption of fixed capital .	80,611	82,372	88,016
National income in market prices	408,321	430,536	456,335

Expenditure on the Gross Domestic Product (at current prices)

	1996/97	1997/98	1998/99
Government final consumption expenditure	97,481	103,045	107,945
Private final consumption expenditure	313,575	333,407	352,650
Increase in stocks	−164	960	4,844
Gross fixed capital formation .	121,170	133,215	141,126
Statistical discrepancy	—	—	1,679
Total domestic expenditure	532,062	570,627	608,244
Exports of goods and services	105,160	113,829	111,603
Less Imports of goods and services	103,590	118,575	126,536
GDP in purchasers' values .	533,632	565,881	593,311

Gross Domestic Product by Economic Activity
(provisional, at constant 1989/90 prices)

	1995/96	1996/97	1997/98*
Agriculture, hunting, forestry and fishing	15,873	18,218	16,668
Mining and quarrying	18,668	19,307	23,769
Manufacturing	59,184	61,138	65,878
Electricity, gas and water.	13,707	14,271	14,292
Construction.	27,147	28,177	30,003
Wholesale and retail trade	74,547	77,612	61,519
Transport, storage and communications	40,642	42,959	49,129
Finance, insurance, real estate and business services	51,878	63,054	92,060
Ownership of dwellings	41,905	44,124	49,169
Public administration and defence	15,393	15,471	23,185
Other community, recreational and personal services (incl. restaurants and hotels)	67,268	68,305	88,849
Sub-total	426,212	452,636	514,522
Import duties	5,439	5,935 }	42,734†
Less Imputed bank service charge	8,259	9,844 }	
Statistical discrepancy	10,500	1,848	−333
GDP in purchasers' values .	433,892‡	450,575	556,923

* At constant 1996/97 prices.
† Referring to taxes, less subsidies, on products.
‡ Revised total is $A437,264 million.

BALANCE OF PAYMENTS (US $ million)

	1997	1998	1999
Exports of goods f.o.b. . . .	64,893	55,848	56,048
Imports of goods f.o.b. . . .	−63,044	−61,215	−65,828
Trade balance	1,849	−5,367	−9,780
Exports of services . . .	18,488	16,156	17,356
Imports of services . . .	−18,844	−17,222	−18,395
Balance on goods and services.	−1,493	−6,483	−10,820
Other income received . .	7,162	6,377	6,848
Other income paid . . .	−21,055	−17,837	−18,853
Balance on goods, services and			
income	−12,400	−17,943	−22,825
Current transfers received . .	2,742	2,676	3,054
Current transfers paid . .	−2,972	−2,991	−3,089
Current balance . . .	−12,631	−18,258	−22,861
Capital account (net). . .	903	670	860
Direct investment abroad. .	−6,424	−2,329	2,876
Direct investment from abroad .	7,717	6,176	5,655
Portfolio investment assets .	−19	−1,605	−6,329
Portfolio investment liabilities .	10,741	4,458	19,708
Financial derivatives assets .	206	78	−130
Financial derivatives liabilities .	1,038	−385	534
Other investment assets . .	−6,022	−107	−2,858
Other investment liabilities .	8,372	9,498	9,958
Net errors and omissions . .	−1,007	−238	−708
Overall balance	2,873	−2,040	6,705

Source: IMF, *International Financial Statistics.*

External Trade

PRINCIPAL COMMODITIES ($A million, year ending 30 June)

Imports f.o.b.	1996/97	1997/98	1998/99
Food and live animals . . .	2,985	3,460	3,760
Beverages and tobacco. . .	502	575	622
Crude materials (inedible)			
except fuels	1,487	1,605	1,611
Mineral fuels, lubricants, etc. .	5,164	4,437	4,620
Petroleum, petroleum products, etc.	5,055	4,338	4,524
Animal and vegetable oils, fats			
and waxes	266	258	296
Chemicals and related products	9,028	10,276	11,434
Organic chemicals . . .	2,040	2,135	2,388
Medicinal and pharmaceutical			
products	1,998	2,544	3,041
Basic manufactures . . .	10,724	12,531	12,859
Paper, paperboard and			
manufactures	1,769	1,990	2,082
Textile yarn, fabrics, etc. . .	2,284	2,521	2,589
Machinery and transport			
equipment	36,782	41,908	45,425
Power-generating machinery and			
equipment	1,895	2,040	2,265
Machinery specialized for			
particular industries . .	4,043	4,244	4,234
General industrial machinery and			
equipment and parts . .	4,649	5,439	5,772
Office machines and automatic			
data-processing machines .	5,984	6,961	7,103
Telecommunications and sound-			
recording and reproducing			
apparatus and equipment . .	3,669	3,980	4,927
Other electrical machinery,			
apparatus, appliances and parts	4,912	5,426	5,874
Road vehicles	8,579	11,300	11,904
Other transport equipment .	2,443	1,936	2,848
Miscellaneous manufactured			
articles	11,349	13,458	14,466
Clothing and accessories . .	1,841	2,278	2,459
Professional, scientific and			
controlling instruments and			
apparatus.	1,944	2,295	2,533
Other commodities and			
transactions	712	2,177	2,531
Non-monetary gold (excl. gold ores			
and concentrates) . . .	590	2,006	2,351
Total	78,998	90,684	97,623

Imports f.o.b. — *continued*	1996/97	1997/98	1998/99

Exports f.o.b.	1996/97	1997/98	1998/99
Food and live animals . . .	16,311	16,045	15,453
Meat and meat preparations . .	2,958	3,731	4,000
Dairy products and birds' eggs .	1,759	1,907	2,225
Cereals and cereal preparations .	5,954	5,098	5,041
Sugars, sugar preparations and			
honey.	1,695	1,341	150
Beverages and tobacco. . .	782	1,059	1,238
Crude materials (inedible)			
except fuels	15,615	17,878	17,219
Textile fibres and waste* . . .	4,619	5,105	4,070
Metalliferous ores and metal scrap	9,051	10,422	10,665
Mineral fuels, lubricants, etc. .	13,705	15,401	14,162
Coal, coke and briquettes. . .	8,005	9,587	9,302
Petroleum, petroleum products, etc.	3,805	3,846	3,133
Gas (natural and manufactured) .	1,895	1,968	1,727
Animal and vegetable oils, fats			
and waxes	232	333	377
Chemicals and related products	3,045	3,298	3,575
Basic manufactures . . .	9,257	10,544	10,117
Iron and steel	1,623	1,858	1,540
Non-ferrous metals . . .	4,434	5,319	5,399
Machinery and transport			
equipment	10,683	11,111	10,324
Office machines and automatic			
data-processing machines . .	1,627	1,725	1,455
Other machinery. . . .	5,402	5,831	5,373
Transport equipment. . .	3,637	3,555	3,496
Miscellaneous manufactured			
articles	2,827	3,192	3,447
Other commodities and			
transactions	6,476	8,909	2,531
Non-monetary gold (excl. gold ores			
and concentrates) . . .	4,717	6,263	6,335
Total	78,932	87,769	86,000

* Excluding wool tops.

PRINCIPAL TRADING PARTNERS ($A million, year ending 30 June)

Imports f.o.b.	1996/97	1997/98	1998/99
Canada	1,265	1,436	1,547
China, People's Republic . . .	4,203	5,303	6,106
France	1,980	2,029	2,203
Germany	4,558	5,207	6,082
Hong Kong	900	1,031	1,229
Indonesia	1,864	2,868	3,272
Italy	2,304	2,614	2,916
Japan	10,241	12,660	13,586
Korea, Republic	2,550	3,767	3,895
Malaysia	1,891	2,404	2,845
Netherlands	817	847	918
New Zealand	3,685	3,723	3,950
Papua New Guinea . . .	1,091	768	781
Saudi Arabia	858	648	532
Singapore	2,620	2,643	2,947
Sweden	1,497	1,557	1,576
Switzerland	895	950	1,092
Taiwan	2,522	2,809	2,979
Thailand	1,201	1,480	1,902
United Arab Emirates . . .	800	492	201
United Kingdom	5,182	5,593	5,548
USA	17,642	19,834	20,893
Total (incl. others)	78,998	90,684	97,623

Exports f.o.b.			1996/97	1997/98	1998/99
Belgium-Luxembourg	.	.	923	1,154	1,082
Canada	.	.	1,178	1,276	1,274
China, People's Republic	.	.	3,584	3,872	3,945
France	.	.	799	856	914
Germany	.	.	1,058	1,243	1,415
Hong Kong	.	.	3,105	4,138	3,068
India	.	.	1,493	1,852	1,858
Indonesia	.	.	3,305	2,751	2,200
Italy	.	.	1,354	1,752	1,562
Japan	.	.	15,377	17,582	16,587
Korea, Republic	.	.	7,134	6,397	6,324
Malaysia	.	.	2,332	2,097	1,857
Netherlands	.	.	584	829	863
New Zealand	.	.	6,214	5,663	5,820
Papua New Guinea	.	.	1,272	1,152	1,012
Philippines	.	.	1,226	1,163	1,208
Singapore	.	.	3,410	3,697	3,421
South Africa	.	.	1,014	1,093	943
Switzerland	.	.	237	1,097	443
Taiwan	.	.	3,620	4,180	4,198
Thailand	.	.	1,693	1,390	1,306
United Arab Emirates	.	.	665	1,066	835
United Kingdom	.	.	2,357	3,040	4,419
USA	.	.	5,526	7,794	7,982
Total (incl. others)	.	.	78,932	87,769	86,000

Transport

RAILWAYS (traffic)

	1996/97*	1997/98	1998/99
Passengers carried (million) . .	584.0	587.7	595.2
Freight carried (millon metric tons)	470.1	487.5	492.0
Freight ton-km (million) . .	68,176	n.a.	n.a.

* Traffic on government railways only.

ROAD TRAFFIC ('000 vehicles registered at 31 October)

	1997	1998	1999
Passenger vehicles . .	9,206.2	9,526.7	9,719.9
Light commercial vehicles . .	1,632.2	1,686.4	1,721.2
Trucks	418.4	426.9	427.8
Buses	61.1	64.0	65.9
Motor cycles . . .	313.1	328.8	333.8

SHIPPING
Merchant Fleet (registered at 31 December)

	1996	1997	1998
Number of vessels . .	625	617	617
Total displacement ('000 grt) .	2,717.9	2,606.6	2,188.1

Source: Lloyd's Register of Shipping, *World Fleet Statistics*.

INTERNATIONAL SEA-BORNE TRAFFIC
('000 metric tons, year ending 30 June)

	1995/96	1996/97	1997/98
Goods loaded . . .	373,788	405,084	427,968
Goods unloaded . . .	47,208	49,980	52,032

Source: UN, *Monthly Bulletin of Statistics*.

CIVIL AVIATION (traffic)*

	1997	1998	1999
International services:			
Passenger arrivals . . .	7,090,979	7,153,514	7,540,535
Passenger departures . .	7,010,931	7,084,655	7,442,226
Freight carried (metric tons)	649,371	631,908	680,458
Mail carried (metric tons) .	21,975	23,437	25,316
Domestic services†:			
Passengers carried . .	23,375,317	23,574,788	24,375,906
Passenger-km ('000) . .	26,357,069	26,774,140	27,842,795
Freight and mail carried (metric tons)	190,680	192,770	192,326

* Includes Christmas Island and Norfolk Island.
† Year ending 30 June.

Tourism

VISITOR ARRIVALS BY COUNTRY OF ORIGIN*

	1997	1998	1999
Canada	64,752	71,690	78,393
China, People's Republic . .	65,843	76,543	97,996
Germany	128,874	127,381	144,509
Hong Kong . . .	151,737	143,428	134,158
Indonesia	160,366	93,032	90,992
Japan	813,892	751,107	707,463
Korea, Republic . . .	233,815	66,635	108,634
Malaysia	143,683	112,074	139,793
New Zealand . . .	685,655	709,390	728,798
Papua New Guinea . .	43,957	44,924	50,429
Singapore	239,306	247,079	266,966
Taiwan	153,247	149,958	147,495
Thailand	68,569	49,124	61,849
United Kingdom . . .	410,620	528,431	528,431
USA	329,586	373,911	417,046
Total (incl. others) . . .	4,317,870	4,167,206	4,459,503

* Visitors intending to stay for less than one year.

Receipts from tourism ($A million): 16,452 in 1997; 16,300 in 1998; 17,000 in 1999.

Source: Australian Tourist Commission, Sydney.

Communications Media
('000 at 30 June)

	1995	1996	1997
Radio receivers in use . . .	23,300	25,000	25,500
Television receivers in use . .	8,850	10,000	10,150
Telephone services in operation .	8,900	9,170	9,350
Telefax stations in use . .	700	800	900
Mobile telephones (subscribers) .	2,305	3,815	4,893

Book production (1994): 10,835 titles.
Newspapers (1996): 65 dailies (estimated combined circulation 5,370,000); 98 non-dailies (circulation 383,000).

Source: mainly UNESCO, *Statistical Yearbook*.

Education
(1999)

	Institutions	Teaching staff	Students ('000)
Government schools . .	7,008	150,500*	2,247.7†
Non-government schools . .	2,592	65,200*	979.0‡
Higher educational institutions	42§	32,406	686.3

* Full-time teaching staff and full-time equivalent of part-time teaching staff.
† Comprising 1,378.2 primary and 869.2 secondary students.
‡ Comprising 507.2 primary and 472.1 secondary students.
§ Public institutions only.

Directory

The Constitution

The Federal Constitution was adopted on 9 July 1900 and came into force on 1 January 1901. Its main provisions are summarized below:

PARLIAMENT

The legislative power of the Commonwealth of Australia is vested in a Federal Parliament, consisting of HM the Queen (represented by the Governor-General), a Senate, and a House of Representatives. The Governor-General may appoint such times for holding the sessions of the Parliament as he or she thinks fit, and may also from time to time, by proclamation or otherwise, prorogue the Parliament, and may in like manner dissolve the House of Representatives. By convention, these powers are exercised on the advice of the Prime Minister. After any general election Parliament must be summoned to meet not later than 30 days after the day appointed for the return of the writs.

THE SENATE

The Senate is composed of 12 senators from each state, two senators representing the Australian Capital Territory and two representing the Northern Territory. The senators are directly chosen by the people of the state or territory, voting in each case as one electorate, and are elected by proportional representation. Senators representing a state have a six-year term and retire by rotation, one-half from each state on 30 June of each third year. The term of a senator representing a territory is limited to three years. In the case of a state, if a senator vacates his or her seat before the expiration of the term of service, the houses of parliament of the state for which the senator was chosen shall, in joint session, choose a person to hold the place until the expiration of the term or until the election of a successor. If the state parliament is not in session, the Governor of the state, acting on the advice of the state's executive council, may appoint a senator to hold office until parliament reassembles, or until a new senator is elected.

The Senate may proceed to the dispatch of business notwithstanding the failure of any state to provide for its representation in the Senate.

THE HOUSE OF REPRESENTATIVES

In accordance with the Australian Constitution, the total number of members of the House of Representatives must be as nearly as practicable double that of the Senate. The number in each state is in proportion to population, but under the Constitution must be at least five. The House of Representatives is composed of 148 members, including two members for the Australian Capital Territory and one member for the Northern Territory.

Members are elected by universal adult suffrage and voting is compulsory. Only Australian citizens are eligible to vote in Australian elections. British subjects, if they are not Australian citizens or already on the rolls, have to take out Australian citizenship before they can enrol and before they can vote.

Members are chosen by the electors of their respective electorates by the preferential voting system.

The duration of the Parliament is limited to three years.

To be nominated for election to the House of Representatives, a candidate must be 18 years of age or over, an Australian citizen, and entitled to vote at the election or qualified to become an elector.

THE EXECUTIVE GOVERNMENT

The executive power of the Federal Government is vested in the Queen, and is exercisable by the Governor-General, advised by an Executive Council of Ministers of State, known as the Federal Executive Council. These ministers are, or must become within three months, members of the Federal Parliament.

The Australian Constitution is construed as subject to the principles of responsible government and the Governor-General acts on the advice of the ministers in relation to most matters.

THE JUDICIAL POWER

See Judicial System, p. 529.

THE STATES

The Australian Constitution safeguards the Constitution of each state by providing that it shall continue as at the establishment of the Commonwealth, except as altered in accordance with its own provisions. The legislative power of the Federal Parliament is limited in the main to those matters that are listed in section 51 of the Constitution, while the states possess, as well as concurrent powers in those matters, residual legislative powers enabling them to legislate in any way for 'the peace, order and good Government' of their respective territories. When a state law is inconsistent with a law of the Commonwealth, the latter prevails, and the former is invalid to the extent of the inconsistency.

The states may not, without the consent of the Commonwealth, raise or maintain naval or military forces, or impose taxes on any property belonging to the Commonwealth of Australia, nor may the Commonwealth tax state property. The states may not coin money.

The Federal Parliament may not enact any law for establishing any religion or for prohibiting the exercise of any religion, and no religious test may be imposed as a qualification for any office under the Commonwealth.

The Commonwealth of Australia is charged with protecting every state against invasion, and, on the application of a state executive government, against domestic violence.

Provision is made under the Constitution for the admission of new states and for the establishment of new states within the Commonwealth of Australia.

ALTERATION OF THE CONSTITUTION

Proposed laws for the amendment of the Constitution must be passed by an absolute majority in both Houses of the Federal Parliament, and not less than two or more than six months after its passage through both Houses the proposed law must be submitted in each state to the qualified electors.

In the event of one House twice refusing to pass a proposed amendment that has already received an absolute majority in the other House, the Governor-General may, notwithstanding such refusal, submit the proposed amendment to the electors. By convention, the Governor-General acts on the advice of the Prime Minister. If in a majority of the states a majority of the electors voting approve the proposed law and if a majority of all the electors voting also approve, it shall be presented to the Governor-General for Royal Assent.

No alteration diminishing the proportionate representation of any state in either House of the Federal Parliament, or the minimum number of representatives of a state in the House of Representatives, or increasing, diminishing or altering the limits of the state, or in any way affecting the provisions of the Constitution in relation thereto, shall become law unless the majority of the electors voting in that state approve the proposed law.

STATES AND TERRITORIES

New South Wales

The state's executive power is vested in the Governor, appointed by the Crown, who is assisted by an Executive Council composed of cabinet ministers.

The state's legislative power is vested in a bicameral Parliament, composed of the Legislative Council and the Legislative Assembly. The Legislative Council consists of 42 members directly elected for the duration of two parliaments (i.e. eight years), 21 members retiring every four years. The Legislative Assembly consists of 93 members and sits for four years.

Victoria

The state's legislative power is vested in a bicameral Parliament: the Upper House, or Legislative Council, of 44 members, elected for two terms of the Legislative Assembly; and the Lower House, or Legislative Assembly, of 88 members, elected for a minimum of three and maximum of four years. One-half of the members of the Council retires every three–four years.

In the exercise of the executive power the Governor is assisted by a cabinet of responsible ministers. Not more than six members of the Council and not more than 17 members of the Assembly may occupy salaried office at any one time.

The state has 88 electoral districts, each returning one member, and 22 electoral provinces, each returning two Council members.

Queensland

The state's executive power is vested in the Governor, appointed by the Crown, who is assisted by an Executive Council composed of Ministers. The state's legislative power is vested in the Parliament comprising the Legislative Assembly (composed of 89 members who are elected at least every three years to represent 89 electoral districts) and the Governor, who assents to bills passed by the Assembly. The state's Constitution anticipates that Ministers are also members of the Legislative Assembly and provides that up to 18 members of the Assembly can be appointed Ministers.

South Australia

The state's Constitution vests the legislative power in a Parliament elected by the people and consisting of a Legislative Council and a House of Assembly. The Council is composed of 22 members, one-half of whom retires every three years. Their places are filled by new members elected under a system of proportional representation, with the whole state as a single electorate. The executive has no authority to dissolve this body, except in circumstances warranting a double dissolution.

The 47 members of the House of Assembly are elected for four years from 45 electoral districts.

The executive power is vested in a Governor, appointed by the Crown, and an Executive Council consisting of 10 responsible ministers.

Western Australia

The state's administration is vested in the Governor, a Legislative Council and a Legislative Assembly.

The Legislative Council consists of 34 members, two of the six electoral regions returning seven members on a proportional representation basis, and four regions returning five members. Election is for a term of four years.

The Legislative Assembly consists of 57 members, elected for four years, each representing one electorate.

Tasmania

The state's executive authority is vested in a Governor, appointed by the Crown, who acts upon the advice of his premier and ministers, who are elected members of either the Legislative Council or the House of Assembly. The Council consists of 15 members who sit for six years, retiring in rotation. The House of Assembly has 25 members elected for four years.

Northern Territory

On 1 July 1978, the Northern Territory was established as a body politic with executive authority for specified functions of government. Most functions of the Federal Government were transferred to the Territory Government in 1978 and 1979, major exceptions being Aboriginal affairs and uranium mining.

The Territory Parliament consists of a single house, the Legislative Assembly, with 25 members. The first Parliament stayed in office for three years. As from the election held in August 1980, members are elected for a term of four years.

The office of Administrator continues. The Northern Territory (Self-Government) Act provides for the appointment of an Administrator by the Governor-General charged with the duty of administering the Territory. In respect of matters transferred to the Territory Government, the Administrator acts with the advice of the Territory Executive Council; in respect of matters retained by the Commonwealth, the Administrator acts on Commonwealth advice.

Australian Capital Territory

On 29 November 1988 the Australian Capital Territory (ACT) was established as a body politic. The ACT Government has executive authority for specified functions, although a number of these were to be retained by the Federal Government for a brief period during which transfer arrangements were to be finalized.

The ACT Parliament consists of a single house, the Legislative Assembly, with 17 members. The first election was held in March 1989. Members are elected for a term of three years.

The Federal Government retains control of some of the land in the ACT for the purpose of maintaining the Seat of Government and the national capital plan.

Jervis Bay Territory

Following the attainment of self-government by the ACT (see above), the Jervis Bay Territory, which had formed part of the ACT since 1915, remained a separate Commonwealth Territory, administered by the then Department of the Arts, Sport, the Environment and Territories. The area is governed in accordance with the Jervis Bay Territory Administration Ordinance, issued by the Governor-General on 17 December 1990.

The Government

Head of State: HM Queen Elizabeth II (succeeded to the throne 6 February 1952).
Governor-General-designate: Most Rev. Peter J. Hollingworth (to assume office 29 June 2001).

THE MINISTRY
(May 2001)
Cabinet Ministers

Prime Minister: John Howard.
Deputy Prime Minister and Minister for Transport and Regional Services: John Anderson.

Minister for Foreign Affairs: Alexander Downer.
Treasurer: Peter Costello.
Minister for Trade: Mark Vaile.
Minister for the Environment and Heritage, Leader of the Government in the Senate: Senator Robert Hill.
Minister for Communications, Information Technology and the Arts, Deputy Leader of the Government in the Senate: Senator Richard Alston.
Minister for Employment, Workplace Relations and Small Business, Leader of the House: Peter Reith.
Minister for Family and Community Services: Senator Jocelyn Newman.
Minister for Defence: John Moore.
Minister for Health and Aged Care: Dr Michael Wooldridge.
Minister for Finance and Administration: John Fahey.
Minister for Education, Training and Youth Affairs: Dr David Kemp.
Minister for Industry, Science and Resources: Senator Nick Minchin.
Attorney-General: Daryl Williams.
Minister for Agriculture, Forestry and Fisheries: Warren Truss.
Minister for Immigration and Multicultural Affairs: Phillip Ruddock.

Other Ministers

Minister of Aboriginal Affairs and Torres Strait Islander Affairs: John Herron.
Minister Assisting the Prime Minister and Minister for Forestry and Conservation: Wilson Tuckey.
Assistant Treasurer: Senator Rod Kemp.
Minister for Financial Services and Regulation: Joe Hockey.
Minister for Regional Services, Territories and Local Government: Senator Ian MacDonald.
Minister for the Arts and the Centenary of Federation, Deputy Leader of the House: Peter McGauran.
Minister for Employment Services: Anthony Abbott.
Minister for Community Services: Lawrence Anthony.
Minister Assisting the Prime Minister for Defence and Minister for Veterans' Affairs: Bruce Scott.
Minister for Aged Care: Bronwyn Bishop.
Special Minister of State: Senator Chris Ellison.
Minister Assisting the Prime Minister for the Public Service: Trish Worth.
Minister for Sport and Tourism: Jacqueline Kelly.
Minister Assisting the Prime Minister for the Sydney 2000 Games: Warren Entsch.
Minister for Justice and Customs: Senator Amanda Vanstone.
Minister Assisting the Prime Minister for Reconciliation: Senator Kay Patterson.

DEPARTMENTS

Department of the Prime Minister and Cabinet: 3–5 National Circuit, Barton, ACT 2600; tel. (2) 6271-5111; fax (2) 6271-5414; internet www.dpmc.gov.au.

Aboriginal and Torres Strait Islander Commission: Lovett Tower, Woden Town Centre, Phillip, ACT 2606; tel. (2) 6121-4000; fax (2) 6121-4621; internet www.atsic.gov.au.

Department of Agriculture, Fisheries and Forestry: GPOB 858, Canberra, ACT 2601; tel. (2) 6272-3933; fax (2) 6272-5161; internet www.affa.gov.au/home.html.

Attorney-General's Department: Robert Garran Offices, Barton, ACT 2600; tel. (2) 6250-6666; fax (2) 6250-5900; internet www.law.gov.au.

Department of Communications, Information Technology and the Arts: GPOB 2154, Canberra, ACT 2601; tel. (2) 6271-1000; fax (2) 6271-1901; internet www.dcita.gov.au.

Department of Defence: Russell Offices, Canberra, ACT 2600; tel. (2) 6265-9111; e-mail webmaster@cbr.defence.gov.au; internet www.defence.gov.au.

Department of Education, Training and Youth Affairs: GPOB 9880, Canberra, ACT 2601; tel. (2) 6240-9539; fax (2) 6240-8571; e-mail library@detya.gov.au; internet www.detya.gov.au.

Department of Employment, Workplace Relations and Small Business: GPO Box 9879, Canberra, ACT 2601; tel. (2) 6121-7547; fax (2) 6121-7542; e-mail webmaster@dewrsb.gov.au; internet www.dewrsb.gov.au.

Department of the Environment and Heritage: GPOB 787, Canberra, ACT 2601; tel. (2) 6274-1111; fax (2) 6274-1123; internet www.environment.gov.au.

Department of Family and Community Services: Box 7788, Canberra Mail Centre, ACT 2610; tel. (2) 6244-7788; fax (2) 6244-5540; internet www.facs.gov.au.

Department of Finance and Administration: King Edward Tce, Parkes, ACT 2600; tel. (2) 6263-2222; fax (2) 6273-3021; internet www.dofa.gov.au.

Department of Foreign Affairs and Trade: GPO Box 12, Canberra City, ACT 2601; tel. (2) 6261-1111; fax (2) 6261-3959; internet www.dfat.gov.au.

Department of Health and Aged Care: GPOB 9848, Canberra, ACT 2601; tel. (2) 6289-1555; fax (2) 6281-6946; internet www.health.gov.au.

Department of Immigration and Multicultural Affairs: Benjamin Offices, Chan St, Belconnen, ACT 2617; tel. (2) 6264-1111; fax (2) 6264-2670; internet www.immi.gov.au.

Department of Industry, Science and Resources: 20 Allara St, Canberra, ACT 2601; tel. (2) 6213-6000; fax (2) 6213-7000; e-mail distpubs@isr.gov.au; internet www.isr.gov.au.

Department of Transport and Regional Services: GPOB 594, Canberra, ACT 2601; tel. (2) 6274-7111; fax (2) 6257-2505; e-mail publicaffairs@dotrs.gov.au; internet www.dotrs.gov.au.

Department of the Treasury: Langton Crescent, Parkes, ACT 2600; tel. (2) 6263-2111; fax (2) 6273-2614; internet www.treasury .gov.au.

Department of Veterans' Affairs: POB 21, Woden, ACT 2606; tel. (2) 6289-1111; fax (2) 6289-6025; internet www.dva.gov.au.

Legislature

FEDERAL PARLIAMENT
Senate
President: Senator MARGARET REID.

Election, 3 October 1998

Party	Seats*
Liberal Party of Australia	31
Australian Labor Party	29
Australian Democrats Party	9
National Party of Australia	4
Greens	1
Independent	1
One Nation	1
Total	**76**

* Party representation from 1 July 1999. The election was for 36 of the 72 seats held by state senators and for all four senators representing the Northern Territory and the Australian Capital Territory (the terms of the latter being limited to three years). The figures for seats refer to the totals held after the election.

House of Representatives
Speaker: NEIL ANDREW.

Election, 3 October 1998

Party	Seats
Australian Labor Party	67*
Liberal Party of Australia	64
National Party of Australia	16
Independent	1
Total	**148**

* Owing to the death of a candidate shortly before the election, polling for one seat was postponed until 21 November.

State and Territory Governments
(May 2001)

NEW SOUTH WALES
Governor: GORDON SAMUELS, Level 3, Chief Secretary's Bldg, 121 Macquarie St, Sydney, NSW 2000; tel. (2) 9242-4200; fax (2) 9242-4266; e-mail ersm1@waratah.www.nsw.gov.au; internet www.nsw .gov.au.

Premier: ROBERT (BOB) J. CARR (Labor), Level 40, Governor Macquarie Tower, 1 Farrer Place, Sydney, NSW 2000; tel. (2) 9228-5239; fax (2) 9228-3935; e-mail bob.carr@www.nsw.gov.au.

VICTORIA
Governor: JOHN LANDY, Government House, Melbourne, Vic 3004; tel. (3) 9655-4211; fax (3) 9650-9050; internet www.vic.gov.au.

Premier: STEPHEN P. BRACKS (Labor); internet www.premier.vic .gov.au.

QUEENSLAND
Governor: Maj.-Gen. PETER M. ARNISON, Government House, Brisbane, Qld 4001; tel. (7) 3858-5700; fax (7) 3858-5701; e-mail govhouse@govhouse.qld.gov.au; internet www.govhouse.qld.gov.au.

Premier: PETER D. BEATTIE (Labor), Executive Bldg, 100 George St, Brisbane, Qld 4002; tel. (7) 3224-2111; fax (7) 3229-2990; internet www.premiers.qld.gov.au.

SOUTH AUSTRALIA
Governor: Sir ERIC JAMES NEAL, Government House, North Terrace, Adelaide, SA 5000; tel. (8) 8203-9800; fax (8) 8203-9899; e-mail govthsesa@saugov.sa.gov.au; internet www.sa.gov.au.

Premier: JOHN W. OLSEN (Liberal-National), 178 North Terrace, Adelaide, SA 5000; tel. (8) 8303-2290; fax (8) 8303-2283; e-mail premier@saugov.sa.gov.au; internet www.ministers.sa.gov.au/premier/welcome/welcome.html.

WESTERN AUSTRALIA
Governor: Lt-Gen. JOHN MURRAY SANDERSON, Government House, Perth, WA 6000; tel. (8) 9429-9199; fax (8) 9325-4476; e-mail govhouse@govhouse.wa.gov.au; internet www.wa.gov.au.

Premier: GEOFF REY GALLOP (Labor), 24th Floor, 197 St George's Terrace, Perth, WA 6000; tel. (8) 9222-9888; fax (8) 9322-1213; e-mail wa-government@mpc.wa.gov.au; internet www .premier.wa.gov.au.

TASMANIA
Governor: Sir GUY STEPHEN MONTAGUE GREEN, Government House, Hobart, Tas 7000; tel. (3) 6234-2611; fax (3) 6234-2556; internet www.tas.gov.au.

Premier: JAMES A. BACON (Labor), GPOB 123B, Hobart, Tas 7001; tel. (3) 6233-3464; fax (3) 6234-1572; e-mail premier@dpac.tas .gov.au; internet www.premier.tas.gov.au.

NORTHERN TERRITORY
Administrator: Dr NEIL RAYMOND CONN, Government House, The Esplanade, Darwin, NT 0800; tel. (8) 8999-7103; fax (8) 8981-9379; internet www.nt.gov.au/administrator.

Chief Minister: DENIS G. BURKE (Liberal-National); GPOB 3146, Darwin, NT 0801; tel. (8) 8999-6222; fax (8) 8999-6670; internet www.nt.gov.au/ministers/.

AUSTRALIAN CAPITAL TERRITORY
Chief Minister: GARY HUMPHRIES (Liberal-National); Legislative Assembly Bldg, Civic Square, London Circuit, Canberra, ACT 2601; tel. (2) 6205-0101; fax (2) 6205-0399; e-mail canberraconnect@ .act.gov.au; internet www.act.gov.au.

Political Organizations

Australians for Constitutional Monarchy (ACM): GPOB 9841, Sydney, NSW 2001; tel. (2) 9231-2200; fax (2) 9231-2359; e-mail acmhq@norepublic.com.au; internet www.norepublic.com.au; f. 1992; also known as No Republic; Exec. Dir KERRY JONES.

Australian Democrats Party: Victorian Division, G1/Eastbourne House, 62 Wellington Pde, East Melbourne, Vic 3002; tel. (3) 9419-5808; fax (3) 9419-5697; e-mail senator.lees@democrats.org.au; internet www.democrats.org.au/; f. 1971; comprises the fmr Liberal Movement and the Australia Party; Leader Senator MEG LEES.

Australian Labor Party (ALP): Centenary House, 19 National Circuit, Barton, ACT 2600; tel. (2) 6273-3133; fax (2) 6273-2031; e-mail natsect@alp.org.au; internet www.alp.org.au/; f. 1891; advocates social democracy; trade unions form part of its structure; Fed. Parl. Leader KIM BEAZLEY; Nat. Pres. BARRY O. JONES; Nat. Sec. GEOFF WALSH.

Australian Republican Movement (ARM): POB A870, Sydney South, NSW 1235; tel. (2) 9267-8022; fax (2) 9267-8155; e-mail republic@ozemail.com.au; internet www.republic.org.au; Chair. GREG BARNS; Nat. Dir JAMES TERRIE.

Communist Party of Australia: 65 Campbell St, Surry Hills, NSW 2010; tel. (2) 9212-6855; fax (2) 9281-5795; e-mail cpa@cpa .org.au; internet www.cpa.org.au; f. 1971; fmrly Socialist Party; advocates public ownership of the means of production, working-class political power; Pres. Dr H. MIDDLETON; Gen. Sec. P. SYMON.

Liberal Party of Australia: Federal Secretariat, Cnr Blackall and Macquarie Sts, Barton, ACT 2600; tel. (2) 6273-2564; fax (2) 6273-1534; e-mail libadm@liberal.org.au; internet www.liberal.org.au; f. 1944; advocates private enterprise, social justice, individual liberty and initiative; committed to national development, prosperity and security; Fed. Dir LYNTON CROSBY; Fed. Parl. Leader JOHN HOWARD.

National Party of Australia: John McEwen House, National Circuit, Barton, ACT 2600; tel. (2) 6273-3822; fax (2) 6273-1745; e-mail npafed@ozemail.com.au; internet www.ozemail.com.au/~npafed/; f. 1916 as the Country Party of Australia; adopted present name in 1982; advocates balanced national development based on free enterprise, with special emphasis on the needs of people outside the major metropolitan areas; Fed. Pres. HELEN DICKIE; Fed. Parl. Leader JOHN ANDERSON; Fed. Dir PAUL DAVEY.

One Nation Party: c/o The Senate, Canberra; e-mail senator .harris@aph.gov.au; internet www.aph.gov.au/senate/senators/homepages/web/s-8hc.htm; f. 1997; opposes globalization, high immigration and special funding for Aboriginal people, advocates public ownership of major services; Leader PAULINE HANSON; Vice-Pres. JOHN FISHER.

Other political organizations include the Green Party.

Diplomatic Representation

EMBASSIES AND HIGH COMMISSIONS IN AUSTRALIA

Argentina: POB 4835, Kingston, ACT 2604; tel. (2) 6273-9111; fax (2) 6273-0500; e-mail eaust@canberra.teknet.net.au; Ambassador: NÉSTOR E. STANCANELLI.

Austria: POB 3375, Manuka, ACT 2603; tel. (2) 6295-1533; fax (2) 6239-6751; e-mail austria@dynamite.com.au; internet www.austriaemb.org.au/; Ambassador: Dr OTMAR KOLER.

Bangladesh: POB 5, Red Hill, ACT 2603; tel. (2) 6295-3328; fax (2) 6295-3351; e-mail bdoot.canberra@cyberone.com.au; High Commissioner: MIRZA SHAMSUZZAMAN.

Belgium: 19 Arkana St, Yarralumla, ACT 2600; tel. (2) 6273-2501; fax (2) 6273-3392; e-mail canberra@diplobel.org; Ambassador: BERNARD LAUWAERT.

Bosnia and Herzegovina: 5 Beale Crescent, Deakin, ACT 2600; tel. (2) 6232-4646; fax (2) 6232-5554; e-mail bihembcbr@webone .com.au; internet www.bosnia.webone.com.au; Ambassador: Dr RADOMIR DAVIDOVIĆ.

Brazil: GPOB 1540, Canberra, ACT 2601; tel. (2) 6273-2372; fax (2) 6273-2375; e-mail brazil@connect.net.au; internet brazil.org.au; Ambassador: ANTÔNIO AUGUSTO DAYRELL DE LIMA.

Brunei: 16 Bulwarra Close, O'Malley, ACT 2606; tel. (2) 6290-1801; fax (2) 6286-1554; High Commissioner: Pehin Dato' Haji HUSIN AHMAD.

Cambodia: 5 Canterbury Crescent, Deakin, ACT 2600; tel. (2) 6273-1259; fax (2) 6273-1053; e-mail cambodianembassy@interact.net.au; internet www.embassy of cambodian.org.nz/au.htm; Ambassador: HOR NAMBORA.

Canada: Commonwealth Ave, Canberra, ACT 2600; tel. (2) 6270-4000; fax (2) 6273-3285; internet www.canada.org.au; High Commissioner: (vacant).

Chile: POB 69, Red Hill, ACT 2603; tel. (2) 6286-2430; fax (2) 6286-1289; e-mail chilemb@embachileaustralia.com; internet www .embachile-australia.com; Ambassador: CRISTÓBAL VALDÉS.

China, People's Republic: 15 Coronation Drive, Yarralumla, ACT 2600; tel. (2) 6273-4780; fax (2) 6273-4235; Ambassador: ZHOU WENZHONG.

Colombia: GPOB 2892, Canberra City, ACT 2601; tel. (2) 6257-2027; fax (2) 6257-1448; e-mail emaustralia@dynamite.com.au; Ambassador: JUAN SANTIAGO URIBE.

Croatia: 14 Jindalee Crescent, O'Malley, ACT 2606; tel. (2) 6286-6988; fax (2) 6286-3544; e-mail croemb@bigpond.com; Ambassador: Dr MLADEN IBLER.

Cyprus: 30 Beale Crescent, Deakin, ACT 2600; tel. (2) 6281-0832; fax (2) 6281-0860; e-mail cyphicom@dynamite.com.au; High Commissioner: ANDREAS GEORGIADES.

Czech Republic: 8 Culgoa Circuit, O'Malley, ACT 2606; tel. (2) 6290-1386; fax (2) 6290-0006; e-mail canberra@embassy.mzv.cz; Ambassador: JOSEF SLÁDEK.

Denmark: 15 Hunter St, Yarralumla, ACT 2600; tel. (2) 6273-2195; fax (2) 6273-3864; e-mail dkembact@dynamite.com.au; Ambassador: JENS OSTENFELD.

Ecuador: 1st Floor, Law Society Bldg of Canberra, 11 London Circuit, ACT 2601; tel. (2) 6262-5282; fax (2) 6262-5285; e-mail embecu@hotkey.net.au; Ambassador: ABELARDO POSSO-SERRANO.

Egypt: 1 Darwin Ave, Yarralumla, ACT 2600; tel. (2) 6273-4437; fax (2) 6273-4279; Ambassador: GILLANE ALLAM.

Fiji: POB 159, Deakin West, ACT 2600; tel. (2) 6260-5115; fax (2) 6260-5105; e-mail fhc@cyberone.com.au; High Commissioner: Ratu ISOA GAVIDI.

Finland: 10 Darwin Ave, Yarralumla, ACT 2600; tel. (2) 6273-3800; fax (2) 6273-3603; e-mail finland@dynamite.com.au; internet www.finland.org.au; Ambassador: ESKO HAMILO.

France: 6 Perth Ave, Yarralumla, ACT 2600; tel. (2) 6216-0100; fax (2) 6216-0127; e-mail embassy@france.net.au; internet www.france.net.au; Ambassador: PIERRE VIAUX.

Germany: 119 Empire Circuit, Yarralumla, ACT 2600; tel. (2) 6270-1911; fax (2) 6270-1951; e-mail embgerma@bigpond.net.au; internet www.germanembassy.org.au; Ambassador: Dr HORST BÄCHMANN.

Greece: 9 Turrana St, Yarralumla, ACT 2600; tel. (2) 6273-3011; fax (2) 6273-2620; e-mail greekemb@dynamite.com.au; Ambassador: IOANNIS BEVERATOS.

Holy See: POB 3633, Manuka, ACT 2603 (Apostolic Nunciature); tel. (2) 6295-3876; Apostolic Nuncio: Most Rev. FRANCESCO CANALINI, Titular Archbishop of Valeria.

Hungary: 17 Beale Crescent, Deakin, ACT 2600; tel. (2) 6282-3226; fax (2) 6285-3012; e-mail hungcbr@spirit.com.au; Ambassador: Dr ISTVÁN GYÜRK.

India: 3–5 Moonah Place, Yarralumla, ACT 2600; tel. (2) 6273-3999; fax (2) 6273-3328; e-mail hciisi@cyberone.com.au; High Commissioner: C. P. RAVINDRANATHAN.

Indonesia: 8 Darwin Ave, Yarralumla, ACT 2600; tel. (2) 6273-3222; fax (2) 6250-8600; e-mail kbricbr@dynamite.com.au; Ambassador: ARIZAL EFFENDI.

Iran: POB 3219, Manuka, ACT 2603; tel. (2) 6290-2421; fax (2) 6290-2431; internet www.mfa.gov.ir; Ambassador: Dr GHOLAMALI KHOSHROO.

Iraq: 48 Culgoa Circuit, O'Malley, ACT 2606; tel. (2) 6286-1333; fax (2) 6290-1788; Chargé d'affaires: NATIK A. RADHI.

Ireland: 20 Arkana St, Yarralumla, ACT 2600; tel. (2) 6273-3022; fax (2) 6273-3741; e-mail irishemb@computech.com.au; Ambassador: RICHARD A. O'BRIEN.

Israel: 6 Turrana St, Yarralumla, ACT 2600; tel. (2) 6273-1309; telex 62224; fax (2) 6273-4273; e-mail israel.aust@embassy.net.au; internet www.mfa.gov.il; Ambassador: GABBY LEVY.

Italy: 12 Grey St, Deakin, ACT 2600; tel. (2) 6273-3333; fax (2) 6273-4223; e-mail embassy@ambitalia.org.au; internet www .ambitalia.org.au; Ambassador: GIOVANNI CASTELLANETA.

Japan: 112 Empire Circuit, Yarralumla, ACT 2600; tel. (2) 6273-3244; fax (2) 6273-1848; e-mail embofjpn@ozemail.com.au; internet www.japan.org.au; Ambassador: MASAJI TAKAHASHI.

Jordan: 20 Roebuck St, Red Hill, ACT 2603; tel. (2) 6295-9951; fax (2) 6239-7236; Ambassador: Dr KHALDOUN THARWAT TALHOUNI.

Kenya: GPOB 1990, Canberra, ACT 2601; tel. (2) 6247-4788; fax (2) 6257-6613; e-mail kenrep@dynamite.com.au; High Commissioner: STEVEN A. LOYATUM.

Korea, Democratic People's Republic: Canberra.

Korea, Republic: 113 Empire Circuit, Yarralumla, ACT 2600; tel. (2) 6270-4100; fax (2) 6273-4839; e-mail pol@embrok-canberra .org.au; internet www.mofat.go.kr/en–australia.htm; Ambassador: SHIN HYO-HUN.

Laos: 1 Dalman Crescent, O'Malley, ACT 2606; tel. (2) 6286-4595; fax (2) 6290-1910; Ambassador: SOUTSAKHONE PATHAMMAVONG.

Lebanon: 27 Endeavour St, Red Hill, ACT 2603; tel. (2) 6295-7378; fax (2) 6239-7024; Ambassador: MICHEL BITAR.

Malaysia: 7 Perth Ave, Yarralumla, ACT 2600; tel. (2) 6273-1543; fax (2) 6273-2496; e-mail malaysia@aucom.com.au; High Commissioner: Dato' ADNAN OTHMAN.

Malta: 38 Culgoa Circuit, O'Malley, ACT 2606; tel. (2) 6290-1724; fax (2) 6290-2453; e-mail maltahc@dynamite.com.au; High Commissioner: IVES DE BARRO.

Mauritius: 2 Beale Crescent, Deakin, ACT 2600; tel. (2) 6281-1203; fax (2) 6282-3235; e-mail Mauritius@caber.net; High Commissioner: PATRICE CURÉ.

Mexico: 14 Perth Ave, Yarralumla, ACT 2600; tel. (2) 6273-3905; fax (2) 6273-1190; e-mail embamex@mexico.org.au; internet www.embassyofmexicoinaustralia.org; Ambassador: RAPHAEL STEGER-CATAÑO.

Myanmar: 22 Arkana St, Yarralumla, ACT 2600; tel. (2) 6273-3811; fax (2) 6273-4357; Ambassador: U MAUNG MAUNG LAY.

Netherlands: 120 Empire Circuit, Yarralumla, ACT 2600; tel. (2) 6273-3111; fax (2) 6273-3206; e-mail nlgovcan@ozemail.com.au; Ambassador: ALBERTUS J. A. M. NOOIJ.

New Zealand: Commonwealth Ave, Canberra, ACT 2600; tel. (2) 6270-4211; fax (2) 6273-3194; e-mail nzhccba@dynamite.com.au; High Commissioner: SIMON MURDOCH.

Nigeria: POB 241, Civic Square, ACT 2608; tel. (2) 6286-1322; fax (2) 6286-5332; e-mail nigeria@dynamite.com.au; High Commissioner: Dr Rufai A. O. Soule.

Norway: 17 Hunter St, Yarralumla, ACT 2600; tel. (2) 6273-3444; fax (2) 6273-3669; e-mail emb.canberra@mfa.no; Ambassador: Ove Thorsheim.

Pakistan: POB 684, Mawson, ACT 2607; tel. (2) 6290-1676; fax (2) 6290-1073; e-mail parepcanberra@actonline.com.au; High Commissioner: Kmizar Hayat Khan Niazi.

Papua New Guinea: POB E432, Queen Victoria Terrace, Kingston, ACT 2600; tel. (2) 6273-3322; fax (2) 6273-3732; High Commissioner: Renagi R. Lohia.

Peru: POB 106, Red Hill, ACT 2603; tel. (2) 6273-8752; fax (2) 6273-8754; e-mail emperuau@dynamite.com.au; internet www .users.netinfo.com.au/~embaperuaussie; Ambassador: José Luis Garaycochea.

Philippines: POB 3297, Manuka, ACT 2603; tel. (2) 6273-2536; fax (2) 6273-3984; e-mail embaphil@iaccess.com.au; Ambassador: Delia Domingo-Albert.

Poland: 7 Turrana St, Yarralumla, ACT 2600; tel. (2) 6273-1208; fax (2) 6273-3184; e-mail ambpol@clover.com.au; Ambassador: Dr Tadeusz Szumowski.

Portugal: 23 Culgoa Circuit, O'Malley, ACT 2606; tel. (2) 6290-1733; fax (2) 6290-1957; e-mail embport@dynamite.com.au; Ambassador: Dr Zózimo Justo da Silva.

Romania: 4 Dalman Crescent, O'Malley, ACT 2606; tel. (2) 6286-2343; fax (2) 6286-2433; e-mail roembcbr@cyberone.com.au; Ambassador: Manuela Vulpe.

Russia: 78 Canberra Ave, Griffith, ACT 2603; tel. (2) 6295-9033; fax (2) 6295-1847; e-mail rusemb@dynamite.com.au; Ambassador: Rashit Khamidulin.

Samoa: POB 3274, Manuka, ACT 2603; tel. (2) 6286-5505; fax (2) 6286-5678; e-mail samoahcaussi@netspeed.com.au; High Commissioner: Leiataua Dr Kilifoti S. Eteuati.

Saudi Arabia: POB 63, Garran, ACT 2605; tel. (2) 6282-6999; fax (2) 6282-8911; e-mail saudiemb@hotmail.com; Ambassador: Mohamad I. al-Hejailan.

Singapore: 17 Forster Crescent, Yarralumla, ACT 2600; tel. (2) 6273-3944; fax (2) 6273-3260; e-mail shc.cbr@u030.aone.net.au; High Commissioner: Ashok Kumar Mirpuri.

Slovakia: 47 Culgoa Circuit, O'Malley, ACT 2606; tel. (2) 6290-1516; fax (2) 6290-1755; e-mail slovak@cyberone.com.au; Ambassador: Dr Anna Tureničová.

Slovenia: POB 284, Civic Square, Canberra, ACT 2608; tel. (2) 6243-4830; fax (2) 6243-4827; e-mail vca@mzz-dkp.sigov.si; internet slovenia.webone.com.au; Chargé d'affaires: Helena Drnovšek Zorko.

Solomon Islands: POB 256, Deakin West, ACT 2600; tel. (2) 6282-7030; fax (2) 6282-7040; e-mail info@solomon.emb.gov.au; High Commissioner: Milner Tozaka.

South Africa: cnr State Circle and Rhodes Place, Yarralumla, ACT 2600; tel. (2) 6273-2424; fax (2) 6273-3543; e-mail info@rsa .emb.gov.au; internet www.rsa.emb.gov.au; High Commissioner: Zolile Magugu.

Spain: POB 9076, Deakin, ACT 2600; tel. (2) 6273-3555; fax (2) 6273-3918; e-mail embespau@mail.mae.es; Ambassador: Emilio Fernández Castaño.

Sri Lanka: 35 Empire Circuit, Forrest, ACT 2603; tel. (2) 6239-7041; fax (2) 6239-6166; e-mail slhc@atrax.net.au; internet slhccanberra.wejump.com; High Commissioner: H. K. J. R. Bandara.

Sweden: 5 Turrana St, Yarralumla, ACT 2600; tel. (2) 6270-2700; fax (2) 6270-2755; e-mail sweden@netinfo.com.au; Ambassador: Lars-Erik Wingren.

Switzerland: 7 Melbourne Ave, Forrest, ACT 2603; tel. (2) 6273-3977; fax (2) 6273-3428; e-mail vertretung@can.rep.admin.ch; Ambassador: André Faivet.

Thailand: 111 Empire Circuit, Yarralumla, ACT 2600; tel. (2) 6273-1149; fax (2) 6273-1518; e-mail thai@csccs.com.au; Ambassador: Sawanit Kongsiri.

Turkey: 60 Mugga Way, Red Hill, ACT 2603; tel. (2) 6295-0227; fax (2) 6239-6592; e-mail turkembs@ozemail.com.au; internet www.ozemail.com.au/~turkembs; Ambassador: Umut Arik.

United Arab Emirates: 36 Culgoa Circuit, O'Malley, ACT 2606; tel. (2) 6286-8802; fax (2) 6286-8804; e-mail UAEAUS@interact.net.au; internet www.users.bigpond.com/UAEAUS; Ambassador: Khalifa Mohammed Bakhit al-Falasi.

United Kingdom: Commonwealth Ave, Canberra, ACT 2600; tel. (2) 6270-6666; fax (2) 6273-3236; e-mail BHC.Canberra@uk.emb .gov.au; internet www.uk.emb.gov.au; High Commissioner: Sir Alastair Goodlad.

USA: Moonah Place, Yarralumla, ACT 2600; tel. (2) 6270-5000; fax (2) 6270-5970; Ambassador: Edward W. Gnehm.

Uruguay: POB 5058, Kingston, ACT 2604; tel. (2) 6273-9100; fax (2) 6273-9099; e-mail urucan@dynamite.com.au; Ambassador: Pablo Sader.

Venezuela: 5 Culgoa Circuit, O'Malley, ACT 2606; tel. (2) 6290-2968; fax (2) 6290-2911; e-mail embaustralia@venezuela-emb -org.au; internet www.venezuela-emb.org.au; Chargé d'affaires: Ivan Suros-Escalona.

Viet Nam: 6 Timbarra Crescent, O'Malley, ACT 2606; tel. (2) 6286-6059; fax (2) 6286-4534; e-mail vemembassy@webone.com.au; Ambassador: Vu Chi Cong.

Yugoslavia: POB 728, Mawson, ACT 2607; tel. (2) 6290-2630; fax (2) 6290-2631; Ambassador: Dragan Dragojlović.

Zimbabwe: 11 Culgoa Circuit, O'Malley, ACT 2606; tel. (2) 6286-2700; fax (2) 6290-1680; e-mail zimbabwe@dynamite.com.au; High Commissioner: Prof. Florence L. Chitauro.

Judicial System

The judicial power of the Commonwealth of Australia is vested in the High Court of Australia, in such other Federal Courts as the Federal Parliament creates, and in such other courts as it invests with Federal jurisdiction.

The High Court consists of a Chief Justice and six other Justices, each of whom is appointed by the Governor-General in Council, and has both original and appellate jurisdiction.

The High Court's original jurisdiction extends to all matters arising under any treaty, affecting representatives of other countries, in which the Commonwealth of Australia or its representative is a party, between states or between residents of different states or between a state and a resident of another state, and in which a writ of mandamus, or prohibition, or an injunction is sought against an officer of the Commonwealth of Australia. It also extends to matters arising under the Australian Constitution or involving its interpretation, and to many matters arising under Commonwealth laws.

The High Court's appellate jurisdiction has, since June 1984, been discretionary. Appeals from the Federal Court, the Family Court and the Supreme Courts of the states and of the territories may now be brought only if special leave is granted, in the event of a legal question that is of general public importance being involved, or of there being differences of opinion between intermediate appellate courts as to the state of the law.

Legislation enacted by the Federal Parliament in 1976 substantially changed the exercise of Federal and Territory judicial power, and, by creating the Federal Court of Australia in February 1977, enabled the High Court of Australia to give greater attention to its primary function as interpreter of the Australian Constitution. The Federal Court of Australia has assumed, in two divisions, the jurisdiction previously exercised by the Australian Industrial Court and the Federal Court of Bankruptcy and was additionally given jurisdiction in trade practices and in the developing field of administrative law. In 1987 the Federal Court of Australia acquired jurisdiction in federal taxation matters and certain intellectual property matters. In 1991 the Court's jurisdiction was expanded to include civil proceedings arising under Corporations Law. Jurisdiction has also been conferred on the Federal Court of Australia, subject to a number of exceptions, in matters in which a writ of mandamus, or prohibition, or an injunction is sought against an officer of the Commonwealth of Australia. The Court also hears appeals from the Court constituted by a single Judge, from the Supreme Courts of the territories, and in certain specific matters from State Courts, other than a Full Court of the Supreme Court of a state, exercising Federal jurisdiction.

In March 1986 all remaining categories of appeal from Australian courts to the Queen's Privy Council in the UK were abolished by the Australia Act.

FEDERAL COURTS

High Court of Australia

POB E435, Kingston, Canberra, ACT 2604; tel. (2) 6270-6811; fax (2) 6270-6868; internet www.hcourt.gov.au.

Chief Justice: Anthony Murray Gleeson.

Justices: Mary Gaudron, Michael McHugh, William Gummow, Michael Donald Kirby, Kenneth Madison Hayne, Ian David Francis Callinan.

Federal Court of Australia

Chief Justice: Michael Eric John Black.

In 1999 there were 49 other judges.

Family Court of Australia

Chief Justice: Alistair Bothwick Nicholson.

In 1999 there were more than 50 other judges.

NEW SOUTH WALES
Supreme Court
Chief Justice: JAMES JACOB SPIGELMAN.
President: KEITH MASON.
Chief Judge in Equity: DAVID HARGRAVES HODGSON.
Chief Judge at Common Law: JAMES ROLAND TOMSON WOOD.

VICTORIA
Supreme Court
Chief Justice: JOHN HARBER PHILLIPS.
President of the Court of Appeal: JOHN SPENCE WINNEKE.

QUEENSLAND
Supreme Court
Chief Justice: PAUL DE JERSEY.
President of the Court of Appeal: MARGARET MCMURDO.
Senior Judge Administrator, Trial Division: MARTIN PATRICK MOYNIHAN.

Central District (Rockhampton)
Resident Judge: PETER RICHARD DUTNEY.

Northern District (Townsville)
Resident Judge: KEIRAN ANTHONY CULLINANE.

Far Northern District (Cairns)
Resident Judge: STANLEY GRAHAM JONES.

SOUTH AUSTRALIA
Supreme Court
Chief Justice: JOHN JEREMY DOYLE.

WESTERN AUSTRALIA
Supreme Court
Chief Justice: DAVID KINGSLEY MALCOLM.

TASMANIA
Supreme Court
Chief Justice: WILLIAM JOHN ELLIS COX.

AUSTRALIAN CAPITAL TERRITORY
Supreme Court
Chief Justice: JEFFREY ALLAN MILES.

NORTHERN TERRITORY
Supreme Court
Chief Justice: BRIAN FRANK MARTIN.

Religion

CHRISTIANITY
According to the population census of August 1996, Christians numbered an estimated 12,582,764.

National Council of Churches in Australia: Private Bag 199, QVB PO, Sydney, NSW 1230; tel. (2) 9299-2215; fax (2) 9262-4514; e-mail christianworldservice@ncca.org.au; internet www.ncca.org.au; f. 1946; 14 mem. churches; Pres. Archbishop JOHN BATHERSBY; Gen. Sec. Rev. DAVID GILL.

The Anglican Communion
The constitution of the Church of England in Australia, which rendered the church an autonomous member of the Anglican Communion, came into force in January 1962. The body was renamed the Anglican Church of Australia in August 1981. The Church comprises five provinces (together containing 22 dioceses) and the extra-provincial diocese of Tasmania. At the 1996 population census there were 3,903,324 adherents.

National Office of the Anglican Church: General Synod Office, Box Q190, QVB PO, Sydney, NSW 1230; tel. (2) 9265-1525; fax (2) 9264-6552; e-mail gensec@anglican.org.au; internet www.anglican.org.au; Gen. Sec. Rev. Dr B. N. KAYE.

Archbishop of Adelaide and Metropolitan of South Australia: Most Rev. IAN G. C. GEORGE, Bishop's Court, 45 Palmer Place, North Adelaide, SA 5006; fax (8) 8305-9399; e-mail Igeorge.churchoffice@anglicare-sa.org.au.

Archbishop of Brisbane and Metropolitan of Queensland: (until June 2001) Most Rev. PETER J. HOLLINGWORTH, Bishopsbourne, Box 421, GPO, Brisbane, Qld 4001; tel. (7) 3835-2218; fax (7) 3832-

5030; e-mail relliott@anglicanbrisbane.org.au; internet www.anglicanbrisbane.gil.com.au.

Archbishop of Melbourne and Metropolitan of Victoria: Most Rev. PETER R. WATSON, Bishopscourt, 120 Clarendon St, East Melbourne, Vic 3002; tel. (3) 9653-4220; fax (3) 9650-2184; e-mail archbishop@melbourne.anglican.com.au.

Archbishop of Perth and Metropolitan of Western Australia, Primate of Australia: Most Rev. Dr PETER F. CARNLEY, GPOB W2067, Perth, WA 6846; tel. (8) 9325-7455; fax (8) 9325-6741; e-mail abcsuite@perth.anglican.org; internet www.perth.anglican.org; also has jurisdiction over Christmas Island and the Cocos (Keeling) Islands.

Archbishop of Sydney and Metropolitan of New South Wales: (until June 2001) Most Rev. R. H. GOODHEW, POB Q190, QVB Post Office, Sydney, NSW 1230; tel. (2) 9265-1521; fax (2) 9265-1504; e-mail archbishop@sydney.anglican.asn.au; internet www.anglican-mediasydney.asn.au.

The Roman Catholic Church
Australia comprises five metropolitan archdioceses, two archdioceses directly responsible to the Holy See and 25 dioceses, including one diocese each for Catholics of the Maronite, Melkite and Ukrainian rites, and one military ordinariate. At the census of 1996 there were 4.8m. adherents in the country.

Australian Catholic Bishops' Conference: GPO Box 368, Canberra, ACT 2601; tel. (2) 6201-9845; fax (2) 6247-6083; e-mail gensec@catholic.org.au; internet www.catholic.org.au; f. 1979; Pres. Most Rev. FRANCIS PATRICK CARROLL, Archbishop of Canberra and Goulburn; Sec. Very Rev. BRIAN V. FINNIGAN.

Archbishop of Adelaide: Most Rev. LEONARD A. FAULKNER, GPO Box 1364, Adelaide, South Australia 5001; tel. (8) 8210-8108; fax (8) 8223-2307.

Archbishop of Brisbane: Most Rev. JOHN A. BATHERSBY, Archbishop's House, 790 Brunswick St, New Farm, Brisbane, Qld 4005; tel. (7) 3224-3364; fax (7) 3358-1357; e-mail archbishop@bne.catholic.net.au.

Archbishop of Canberra and Goulburn: Most Rev. FRANCIS PATRICK CARROLL, GPOB 89, Canberra, ACT 2601; tel. (2) 6248-6411; fax (2) 6247-9636.

Archbishop of Hobart: Most Rev. ADRIAN DOYLE, GPOB 62, Hobart, Tas 7001; tel. (3) 6225-1920; fax (3) 6225-3865; e-mail archbishop.hobart@cdftas.com; internet www.busker.trumpet.com.au/cathtas/.

Archbishop of Melbourne: Most Rev. GEORGE PELL, GPOB 146, East Melbourne, Vic 3002; tel. (3) 9926-5677; fax (3) 9926-5617.

Archbishop of Perth: Most Rev. BARRY J. HICKEY, St Mary's Cathedral, 12 Victoria Sq., Perth, WA 6000; tel. (8) 9223-1350; fax (8) 9221-1716; e-mail archsec@perth.catholic.org.au; internet www.perth.catholic.org.au.

Archbishop of Sydney: Cardinal EDWARD BEDE CLANCY, Archdiocesan Chancery, Polding House, 13th Floor, 276 Pitt St, Sydney, NSW 2000; tel. (2) 9390-5100; fax (2) 9261-8312.

Orthodox Churches
Greek Orthodox Archdiocese of Australia: 242 Cleveland St, Redfern, Sydney, NSW 2016; tel. (2) 9698-5066; fax (2) 9698-5368; f. 1924; 700,000 mems; Primate His Eminence Archbishop STYLIANOS.

The Antiochian, Coptic, Romanian, Serbian and Syrian Orthodox Churches are also represented.

Other Christian Churches
Baptist Union of Australia: POB 377, Hawthorn, Vic 3122; tel. (3) 9818-0341; fax (3) 9818-1041; e-mail bua@baptistvic.asn.au; f. 1926; 64,159 mems; 883 churches; Nat. Pres. Rev. TIM COSTELLO; Nat. Sec. C. K. MOSS.

Churches of Christ in Australia: POB 55, Helensburgh, NSW 2508; tel. (2) 4294-1913; fax (2) 4294-1914; e-mail bobsmit@ozemail.com.au; internet www.churchesofchrist.org.au; 36,000 mems; Pres. Rev. PETER OVERTON; Co-ordinator Rev. ROBERT SMITH.

Lutheran Church of Australia: National Office, 197 Archer St, North Adelaide, SA 5006; tel. (8) 8267-7300; fax (8) 8267-7310; e-mail president@lca.org.au; internet www.lca.org.au; f. 1966; 98,191 mems; Pres. Rev. M. P. SEMMLER.

Uniting Church in Australia: POB A2266, Sydney South, NSW 1235; tel. (2) 8267-4200; fax (2) 8267-4222; e-mail assysec@nat.uca.org.au; internet www.nat.uca.org.au; f. 1977 with the union of Methodist, Presbyterian and Congregational Churches; 1.4m. mems; Pres. Rev. Prof. JAMES HAIRE; Sec. Rev. GREGOR HENDERSON.

Other active denominations include the Pentecostal Church (174,720 adherents in 1996), the Armenian Apostolic Church, the Assyrian Church of the East and the Society of Friends (Quakers).

JUDAISM

Great Synagogue: 166 Castlereagh St, Sydney, NSW; tel. (2) 9267-2477; fax (2) 9264-8871; e-mail admin@greatsynagogue.com.au; internet www.greatsynagogue.com.au; f. 1828; Sr Minister Rabbi RAYMOND APPLE.

OTHER FAITHS

According to the provisional results of the August 1996 census, Muslims numbered 200,185, Buddhists 199,812 and Hindus 67,279.

The Press

The total circulation of Australia's daily newspapers is very high, but in the remoter parts of the country weekly papers are even more popular. Most of Australia's newspapers are published in sparsely populated rural areas where the demand for local news is strong. The only newspapers that may fairly claim a national circulation are the dailies *The Australian* and *Australian Financial Review*, and the weekly magazines *The Bulletin, Time Australia* and *Business Review Weekly*, the circulation of most newspapers being almost entirely confined to the state in which each is produced.

ACP Publishing Pty Ltd: 54–58 Park St, Sydney, NSW 2000; tel. (2) 9282-8000; fax (2) 9267-4371; fmrly Australian Consolidated Press Ltd; publishes *Australian Women's Weekly, The Bulletin with Newsweek, Cleo, Cosmopolitan, Woman's Day, Dolly, Belle, Street Machine* and more than 70 other magazines.

APN News and Media Ltd: 10th Floor, 300 Ann St, Brisbane, Qld 4000; tel. (7) 3307-0300; fax (7) 3307-0307; Chair. L. P. HEALY; Chief Exec. VINCENT CROWLEY.

John Fairfax Holdings Ltd: POB 506, Sydney, NSW 2001; tel. (2) 9282-2833; fax (2) 9282-3133; internet www.faxj.com.au; f. 1987; Chair. BRIAN POWERS; Chief Exec. FREDERICK G. HILMER; publs include *The Sydney Morning Herald, The Australian Financial Review* and *Sun-Herald* (Sydney), *The Age* and BRW Publications (Melbourne); also provides online and interactive services.

The Herald and Weekly Times Ltd: POB 14999, Melbourne MC, Vic 8001; tel. (3) 9292-2000; fax (3) 9292-2002; e-mail newspapers @hwt.newsltd.com.au; acquired by News Ltd in 1987; Chair. JANET CALVERT-JONES; Man. Dir JULIAN CLARKE; publs include *Herald Sun, Sunday Herald Sun, The Weekly Times*.

The News Corporation: 2 Holt St, Surry Hills, Sydney, NSW 2010; tel. (2) 9288-3000; fax (2) 9288-2300; internet www.newscorp.com; Chair. and CEO K. RUPERT MURDOCH; controls *The Australian* and *The Weekend Australian* (national), *Daily Telegraph, Sunday Telegraph* (Sydney), *The Herald Sun* and *Sunday Herald Sun* (Victoria), *Northern Territory News* (Darwin), *Sunday Times* (Perth), *Townsville Bulletin, Courier Mail, Sunday Mail* (Queensland), *The Mercury* (Tasmania), *The Advertiser, Sunday Mail* (South Australia).

Rural Press Ltd: 159 Bells Line of Road, North Richmond, NSW 2754; tel. (2) 4570-4444; fax (2) 4570-4663; e-mail cosec@rpl.com.au; internet www.rpl.com.au; Chair. JOHN B. FAIRFAX; Man. Dir B. K. MCCARTHY.

West Australian Newspapers Holdings Ltd: Newspaper House, 50 Hasler Rd, Osborne Park, WA 6017; tel. (8) 9482-3111; fax (8) 9482-9080; Chair. T. R. EASTWOOD; Man. Dir D. W. THOMPSON.

Other newspaper publishers include Federal Capital Press (K. Stokes).

NEWSPAPERS
Australian Capital Territory
The Canberra Times: 9 Pirie St, Fyshwick, ACT 2609; POB 7155, Canberra Mail Centre, ACT 2610; tel. (2) 6280-2122; fax (2) 6280-2282; f. 1926; daily and Sun.; morning; Editor JACK WATERFORD; circ. 42,444 (Mon.–Fri.), 72,008 (Sat.), 40,488 (Sun.).

New South Wales
Dailies
The Australian: News Ltd, 2 Holt St, Surry Hills, NSW 2010, POB 4245; tel. (2) 9288-3000; fax (2) 9288-3077; f. 1964; edited in Sydney, simultaneous edns in Sydney, Melbourne, Perth, Townsville, Adelaide and Brisbane; Editor-in-Chief DAVID ARMSTRONG; Editor CAMPBELL REID; circ. 122,500 (Mon.–Fri.); *The Weekend Australian* (Sat.) 311,000.

Australian Financial Review: 201 Sussex St, GPOB 506, Sydney, NSW 2000; tel. (2) 9282-2512; fax (2) 9282-3137; f. 1951; Mon.–Fri.; distributed nationally; Publr/Editor-in-Chief MICHAEL GILL; Editor COLLEEN RYAN; circ. 92,500 (Mon.–Fri.), 86,500 (Sat.).

The Daily Telegraph: 2 Holt St, Surry Hills, NSW 2010; tel. (2) 9288-3000; fax (2) 9288-2300; f. 1879, merged in 1990 with Daily Mirror (f. 1941); 24-hour tabloid; CEO LACHLAN MURDOCH; circ. 442,000.

The Manly Daily: 26 Sydney Rd, Manly, NSW 2095; tel. (2) 9977-3333; fax (2) 9977-2831; e-mail manlydailynews@cng .newsltd.com.au; f. 1906; Tue.–Sat.; Editor STEVE STICKNEY; circ. 89,326.

The Newcastle Herald: 28–30 Bolton St, Newcastle, NSW 2300; tel. (2) 4979-5000; fax (2) 4979-5888; f. 1858; morning; 6 a week; Editor-in-Chief ALAN OAKLEY; circ. 51,500.

The Sydney Morning Herald: 201 Sussex St, GPOB 506, Sydney, NSW 2001; tel. (2) 9282-2822; fax (2) 9282-3253; internet www.smh.com.au; f. 1831; morning; Editor-in-Chief and Publr ALAN REVELL; circ. 231,508 (Mon.–Fri.), 400,000 (Sat.).

Weeklies
Bankstown Canterbury Torch: Nabberly House, Cnr Marion St and Airport Ave, Bankstown, NSW 2200; tel. (2) 9795-0000; fax (2) 9795-0096; f. 1920; Wed.; Editor CHARLES ELIAS; circ. 86,577.

Northern District Times: 79 Rowe St, Eastwood, NSW 2122; tel. (2) 9858-1766; fax (2) 9804-6901; f. 1921; Wed.; Editor D. BARTOK; circ. 55,302.

The Parramatta Advertiser: 142 Macquarie St, Parramatta, NSW 2150; tel. (2) 9689-5370; fax (2) 9689-5353; Wed.; Editor LES POBJIE; circ. 96,809.

St George and Sutherland Shire Leader: 182 Forest Rd, Hurstville, NSW 2220; tel. (2) 9598-3999; fax (2) 9598-3987; f. 1960; Tue. and Thur.; Editor PETER ALLEN; circ. 143,595.

Sun-Herald: 201 Sussex St, GPOB 506, Sydney, NSW 2001; tel. (2) 9282-2822; fax (2) 9282-2151; e-mail shmedia@mail.fairfax.com.au; internet www.smh.com.au; f. 1953; Sun.; Editor-in-Chief and Publr ALAN REVELL; circ. 580,000.

Sunday Telegraph: 2 Holt St, Surry Hills, NSW 2010; tel. (2) 9288-3000; fax (2) 9288-2300; f. 1938; Editor ROY MILLER; circ. 718,000.

Northern Territory
Daily
Northern Territory News: Printers Place, POB 1300, Darwin, NT 0801; tel. (8) 8944-9900; fax (8) 8981-6045; f. 1952; Mon.–Sat.; Gen. Man. D. KENNEDY; circ. 24,470.

Weekly
Sunday Territorian: Printers Place, GPOB 1300, Darwin, NT 0801; tel. (8) 8944-9900; fax (8) 8981-6045; Sun.; Editor DAVID COREN; circ. 26,437.

Queensland
Daily
Courier-Mail: 41 Campbell St, Bowen Hills, Brisbane, Qld 4006; tel. (7) 3252-6011; fax (7) 3252-6696; f. 1933; morning; Editor-in-Chief C. MITCHELL; circ. 250,875.

Weekly
Sunday Mail: Campbell St, Bowen Hills, Brisbane, Qld 4006; tel. (7) 3666-8000; fax (7) 3666-6692; e-mail smletters@qnp.newsltd.com.au; f. 1923; Editor MICHAEL PRAIN; circ. 598,065.

South Australia
Daily
The Advertiser: 121 King William St, Adelaide, SA 5001; tel. (8) 8206-2220; fax (8) 8206-3669; e-mail tiser@adv.newsltd.com.au; f. 1858; morning; Editor MELVIN MANSELL; circ. 203,440 (Mon.–Fri.), 274,045 (Sat.).

Weekly
Sunday Mail: 9th Floor, 121 King William St, Adelaide, SA 5000; tel. (8) 8206-2000; fax (8) 8206-3646; e-mail sullivank@adv .newsltd.com.au; f. 1912; Editor KERRY SULLIVAN; circ. 345,200.

Tasmania
Dailies
The Advocate: POB 63, Burnie 7320; tel. (3) 6440-7405; fax (3) 6440-7461; e-mail letters.advocate@harrisgroup.com.au; f. 1890; morning; Editor PETER DWYER; circ. 25,623.

Examiner: 71–75 Paterson St, POB 99A, Launceston, Tas 7250; tel. (3) 6331-5111; fax (3) 6334-7328; e-mail mail@examiner.com.au; internet www.examiner.com.au/examiner/; f. 1842; morning; independent; Editor R. J. SCOTT; circ. 38,721.

Mercury: 91–93 Macquarie St, Hobart, Tas 7000; tel. (3) 6230-0622; fax (3) 6230-0711; e-mail mercuryedletter@dbl .newsltd.com.au; internet www.news.com.au; f. 1854; morning; Man. Dir REX GARDNER; Editor I. MCCAUSLAND; circ. 52,136.

Weeklies
Sunday Examiner: 71–75 Paterson St, Launceston, Tas 7250; tel. (3) 6315-111; fax (3) 6347-328; e-mail mail@examiner.com.au; f. 1924; Editor R. J. SCOTT; circ. 42,000.

Sunday Tasmanian: 91–93 Macquarie St, Hobart, Tas 7000; tel. (3) 6230-0622; fax (3) 6230-0711; e-mail mercuryedletter@ trump.net.au; f. 1984; morning; Man. Dir REX GARDNER; Editor IAN MCCAUSLAND; circ. 53,449.

Victoria
Dailies

The Age: 250 Spencer St (cnr Lonsdale St), Melbourne, Vic 3000; tel. (3) 9600-4211; fax (3) 9601-2598; e-mail Ntlenham@ theage.fairfax.com.au; internet www.theage.com.au; f. 1854; independent; morning, incl. Sun.; Publr and Editor-in-Chief STEVE HARRIS; Editor MICHAEL GAWENDA; circ. 196,000 (Mon.–Fri.), 330,000 (Sat.).

Herald Sun: HWT Tower, 40 City Rd, Southbank, Vic 3006; tel. (3) 9292-2000; fax (3) 9292-2112; e-mail hldsun@hwt.newsltd.com.au; internet www.heraldsun.com.au; f. 1840; 24-hour tabloid; Editor PETER BLUNDEN; circ. 547,965.

Weeklies

Progress Press: 360 Burwood Rd, Hawthorn, Vic 3122; tel. (3) 9818-0555; fax (3) 9818-0029; e-mail editor@ldr.newsltd.com.au; f. 1960; Tue.; Editor LYNNE KINSEY; circ. 74,829.

Sunday Herald Sun: HWT Tower, 40 City Rd, Southbank, Vic 3006; tel. (3) 9292-2000; fax (3) 9292-2080; e-mail sundayhs@hwt.newsltd.com.au; f. 1991; Editor ALAN HOWE; circ. 510,000.

Western Australia
Daily

The West Australian: POB D162, Perth, WA 6001; tel. (8) 9482-3111; fax (8) 9482-3399; e-mail editor@wanews.com.au; f. 1833; morning; Editor BRIAN ROGERS; circ. 214,000 (Mon.–Fri.), 386,000 (Sat.).

Weekly

Sunday Times: 34–42 Stirling St, Perth, WA 6000; tel. (8) 9326-8326; fax (8) 9221-1121; f. 1897; Gen. Man. BILL REPARD; Man. Editor DON SMITH; circ. 346,014.

PRINCIPAL PERIODICALS
Weeklies and Fortnightlies

Australasian Post: 35-51 Mitchell St, McMahon's Point, NSW 2060; tel. (2) 9464-3129; fax (2) 9464-3169; e-mail aussiepost@ pacpubs.com.au; f. 1864; factual, general interest, Australiana; Mon.; Editor GILL CHALMERS; circ. 81,640.

The Bulletin: 54 Park St, Sydney, NSW 2000; tel. (2) 9282-8227; fax (2) 9267-4359; f. 1880; Wed.; Editor-in-Chief GERALD STONE; circ. 91,771.

Business Review Weekly: Level 2, 469 La Trobe St, Melbourne, Vic 3000; tel. (3) 9603-3888; fax (3) 9670-4328; f. 1981; Chair. and Editorial Dir ROBERT GOTTLIEBSEN; Editor ROSS GREENWOOD; circ. 75,166.

The Countryman: 219 St George's Terrace, Perth, WA 6000; GPO Box D162, Perth 6001; tel. (8) 9482-3322; fax (8) 9482-3324; e-mail countryman@wanews.com.au; f. 1885; Thur.; farming; Editor GARY MCGAY; circ. 13,444.

The Medical Journal of Australia: Private Bag 901, North Sydney, NSW 2059; tel. (2) 9954-8666; fax (2) 9954-8699; e-mail mja@ampco.com.au; internet www.mja.com.au; f. 1914; fortnightly; Editor Dr MARTIN VAN DER WEYDEN; circ. 27,318.

New Idea: 35–51 Mitchell St, McMahons Point, NSW 2060; tel. (2) 9464-3200; fax (2) 9464-3203; e-mail newidea@pacpubs.com.au; weekly; women's; Editorial Dir BUNTY AVIESON; circ. 471,000.

News Weekly: POB 186, North Melbourne, Vic 3051; tel. (3) 9326-5757; fax (3) 9328-2877; e-mail freedom@connexus.net.au; f. 1943; publ. by National Civic Council; fortnightly; Sat.; political, social, educational and trade union affairs; Editor PETER WESTMORE; circ. 12,000.

People: 54 Park St, Sydney, NSW 2000; tel. (2) 9282-8743; fax (2) 9267-4365; e-mail sbutler-white@acp.com.au; weekly; Editor SIMON BUTLER-WHITE; circ. 70,000.

Picture: GPOB 5201, Sydney, NSW 1028; tel. (2) 9282-8367; fax (2) 9267-4372; e-mail picture@acp.com.au; weekly; men's; Editor TIM SCOTT; circ. 162,864.

Queensland Country Life: POB 586, Cleveland, Qld 4163; tel. (7) 3826-8200; fax (7) 3821-1236; f. 1935; Thur.; Editor CHRIS GRIFFITH; circ. 33,900.

Stock and Land: 10 Sydenham St, Moonee Ponds, Vic 3039; tel. (3) 9287-0900; fax (3) 9287-5622; e-mail stockland@ruralpress.com; internet www.stockandland.com; f. 1914; weekly; agricultural and rural news; Editor JOHN CARSON; circ. 12,608.

That's Life!: 35–51 Mitchell St, McMahons Point, NSW 2060; tel. (2) 9464-3300; fax (2) 9464-3480; f. 1994; weekly; features; Editor BEV HADGRAFT; circ. 465,500 (incl. New Zealand).

Time Australia Magazine: GPOB 3873, Sydney, NSW 2001; tel. (2) 9925-2646; fax (2) 9954-0828; e-mail time.letters@time.com.au; internet www.time.com.au; Editor STEVE WATERSON; circ. 111,000.

TV Week: 35–51 Mitchell St, McMahons Point, NSW 2060; tel. (2) 9464-3306; fax (2) 9464-3571; e-mail tvweek@pacpubs.com.au; internet www.tvweek.com.au; f. 1957; Wed.; colour national; Editor KATIE EKBERG; circ. 364,044.

The Weekly Times: POB 14999, Melbourne City MC, Vic 8001; tel. (3) 9292-2000; fax (3) 9292-2697; e-mail wtimes@hwt .newsltd.com.au; internet www.news.com.au; f. 1869; farming, regional issues, country life; Wed.; Editor PETER FLAHERTY; circ. 78,900.

Woman's Day: 54–58 Park St, POB 5245, Sydney, NSW 1028; tel. (2) 9282-8000; fax (2) 9267-4360; e-mail Womansday@ publishing.acp.com.au; weekly; circulates throughout Australia and NZ; Editor MICHELE CRAWSHAW; circ. 765,170.

Monthlies and Others

Architectural Product News: Architecture Media Pty Ltd, Level 3, 4 Princes St, Port Melbourne, Vic 3207; tel. (3) 9646-4760; fax (3) 9646-4918; e-mail apn@archmedia.com.au; internet www.arhmedia .com.au; 6 a year; Editor SUE HARRIS; circ. 24,884.

Architecture Australia: Architecture Media Pty Ltd, Level 3, 4 Princes St, Port Melbourne, Vic 3207; tel. (3) 9646-4760; fax (3) 9646-4918; e-mail aa@archmedia.com.au; internet www.arch media.com.au; f. 1904; 6 a year; Editor IAN CLOSE; circ. 14,093.

Australian Hi-Fi: POB 5555, St Leonards, NSW 1590; tel. (2) 9901-6100; fax (2) 9901-6198; e-mail hifi@horwitz.com.au; f. 1970; every 2 months; consumer tests on hi-fi and home theatre equipment; Editor GREG BORROWMAN; circ. 11,800.

Australian Home Beautiful: 35–51 Mitchell St, McMahons Point, NSW 2059; tel. (2) 9464-3300; fax (2) 9464-3263; e-mail homebeaut@ pacpubs.com.au; f. 1925; monthly; Editor ANDREA JONES; circ. 81,496.

Australian House and Garden: 54 Park St, Sydney, NSW 2000; tel. (2) 9282-8456; fax (2) 9267-4912; e-mail h&g@acp.com.au; f. 1948; monthly; design, decorating, renovating, gardens, food and travel; Editor ANNY FRIIS; circ. 110,000.

Australian Journal of Mining: Informa Australia Pty Ltd, Level 2, 120 Sussex St, Sydney, NSW 2000; e-mail charles.macdonald@ informa.com.au; f. 1986; monthly; mining and exploration throughout Australia and South Pacific; Editor CHARLES MCDONALD; circ. 6,771.

Australian Journal of Pharmacy: 100 Harris St, Pyrmont, NSW 2009; tel. (2) 8587-7000; fax (2) 8587-7100; f. 1886; monthly; journal of the associated pharmaceutical orgs; Man. Editor DAVID WESTON; circ. 6,443.

Australian Law Journal: 100 Harris St, Pyrmont, NSW 2009; tel. (2) 8587-7000; fax (2) 8587-7104; f. 1927; monthly; Editor Justice P. W. YOUNG; circ 4,500.

Australian Photography: POB 606, Sydney, NSW 1041; tel. (2) 9281-2333; fax (2) 9281-2750; e-mail robertkeeley@gaffa.com.au; monthly; Editor ROBERT KEELEY; circ. 9,010.

The Australian Women's Weekly: 54–58 Park St, Sydney, NSW 2000; tel. (2) 9282-8000; fax (2) 9267-4459; e-mail FDaniele@ acp.com.au; f. 1933; monthly; Editor DEBORAH THOMAS; circ. 800,000.

Belle: 54 Park St, Sydney, NSW 2000; tel. (2) 9282-8000; fax (2) 9267-8037; e-mail belle@acp.com.au; f. 1975; every 2 months; Editor ERIC MATTHEWS; circ. 44,663.

Better Homes and Gardens: 45 Jones St, Ultimo, NSW 2007; tel. (2) 9692-2000; fax (2) 9692-2264; e-mail philippah@mm.com.au; f. 1978; 13 a year; Editor TONI EATTS; circ. 340,133.

Cleo: 54 Park St, Sydney, NSW 2000; POB 4088, Sydney, NSW 2001; tel. (2) 9282-8617; fax (2) 9267-4368; f. 1972; women's monthly; Editor DEBORAH THOMAS; circ. 263,353.

Commercial Photography: GPOB 606, Sydney, NSW 1041; tel. (2) 9281-2333; fax (2) 9281-2750; e-mail yaffa@flex.com.au; every 2 months; journal of the Professional Photographers Asscn of Australia and Photographic Industry Marketing Asscn of Australia; Editor SAIMA MOREL; circ. 3,835.

Cosmopolitan: 54 Park St, Sydney, NSW 2000; tel. (2) 9282-8039; fax (2) 9267-4457; e-mail cosmo@acp.com.au; f. 1973; monthly; Editor MIA FREEDMAN; circ. 203,058.

Dolly: 54–58 Park St, Sydney, NSW 1028; tel. (2) 9282-8437; fax (2) 9267-4911; e-mail dolly@ninemsn.com.au; internet www.ni-nemsn.com.au/dolly; f. 1970; monthly; for young women; Editor VIRG-INIA KNIGHT; circ. 177,268.

Ecos: CSIRO, POB 1139, Collingwood, Vic 3066; tel. (3) 9662-7500; fax (3) 9662-7555; internet www.publish.csiro.au; f. 1974; quarterly; reports of CSIRO environmental research findings for the nonspecialist reader; Editor BRYONY BENNETT; circ. 8,000.

Electronics Australia: POB 199, Alexandria, NSW 1435; tel. (2) 9353-0620; fax (2) 9353-0613; e-mail electaus@fpc.com.au; internet www.electronicsaustralia.com.au; f. 1922; monthly; technical, radio, television, microcomputers, hi-fi and electronics; Editor GRAHAM CATTLEY; circ. 20,900.

Elle: 54 Park St, Sydney, NSW 2000; tel. (2) 9282-8790; fax (2) 9267-4375; f. 1990; monthly; Editor MARINA GO; circ. 68,154.

Family Circle: Pier 8/9, 23 Hickson Rd, Millers Point, NSW 2000; tel. (2) 8220-2000; fax (2) 8220-2111; e-mail family_circle@mm.com.au; 13 a year; circ. 235,860.

Gardening Australia: POB 199, Alexandria, NSW 1435; tel. (2) 9353-6666; fax (2) 9317-4615; f. 1991; monthly; Editor ANNE LAWTON; circ. 93,000.

Houses: Architecture Media Pty Ltd, Level 3, 4 Princes St, Port Melbourne, Vic 3207; tel. (3) 9646-4760; fax (3) 9646-4918; e-mail houses@archmedia.com.au; internet www.archmedia.com.au; f. 1989; 4 a year; Editor SUE HARRIS; circ. 20,030.

HQ: 54 Park St, Sydney, NSW 1028; tel. (2) 9282-8260; fax (2) 9267-3616; e-mail hq@publishing.acp.com.au; internet www.hq.ninemsn.com.au; f. 1989; every 2 months; Publr JOHN ALEXANDER; Editor KATHY BAIL; circ. 32,837.

Manufacturers' Monthly: Level 1/28 Riddell Parade, Elsternwick, Vic 3185; tel. (3) 9245-7777; fax (3) 9245-7750; f. 1961; Editor GREG VIDEON; circ. 15,188.

Modern Boating: The Federal Publishing Co Pty Ltd, 180 Bourke Rd, Alexandria, NSW 2015; tel. (2) 9353-6666; fax (2) 9353-0613; f. 1965; every 2 months; Editor MARK ROTHFIELD; circ. 9,007.

Motor: Locked Bag 12, Oakleigh, Vic 3166; tel (3) 9567-4200; fax (3) 9563-4554; e-mail motor@acpaction.com.au; f. 1954; monthly; Editor GED BULMER; circ. 41,414.

New Woman: Murdoch Magazines, 45 Jones St, Ultimo, NSW 2007; tel. (2) 9692-2000; fax (2) 9692-2488; monthly; Editor-in-Chief GAY BRYANT; circ. 108,444.

The Open Road: L27, 388 George St, Sydney, NSW 2000; tel. (2) 9292-9275; fax (2) 9292-9069; f. 1927; every 2 months; journal of National Roads and Motorists' Asscn (NRMA); Editor LEE ATKINSON; circ. 1,555,917.

Personal Investor: Level 2, 469 La Trobe St, Melbourne, Vic 3000; tel. (3) 9603-3888; fax (3) 9670-4328; e-mail pieditor@brw.fairfax.com.au; internet www.personalinvestor.com.au; monthly; Editor ROBIN BOWERMAN; circ. 66,097.

Reader's Digest: 26–32 Waterloo St, Surry Hills, NSW 2010; tel. (2) 9690-6111; fax (2) 9690-6211; monthly; Editor-in-Chief BRUCE HEILBUTH; circ. 508,142.

Street Machine: Locked Bag 756, Epping, NSW 2121; tel. (2) 9868-4832; fax (2) 9869-7390; e-mail streetmachine@acpaction.com.au; Editor MARK OASTLER; circ. 55,000.

TV Hits: Private Bag 9900, North Sydney, NSW 2059; tel. (2) 9464-3300; fax (2) 9464-3508; f. 1988; monthly; circ. 114,509.

TV Soap: 55 Chandos St, St Leonards, NSW 2065; tel. (2) 9901-6100; fax (2) 9901-6166; f. 1983; monthly; Editor BEN MITCHELL; circ. 103,000.

Vogue Australia: Level 2, 170 Pacific Highway, Greenwich, NSW 2065; tel. (2) 9964-3888; fax (2) 9964-3879; f. 1959; monthly; fashion; Editor JULIET ASHWORTH; circ. 54,705.

Wheels: GPOB 4088, Sydney, NSW 2001; tel. (2) 9263-9734; fax (2) 9263-9702; internet www.wheelsmag.com.au; f. 1953; monthly; international motoring magazine; circ. 60,286.

Wildlife Research: CSIRO Publishing, 150 Oxford St, POB 1139, Collingwood, Vic 3066; tel. (3) 9662-7622; fax (3) 9662-7611; e-mail wr@publish.csiro.au; internet www.publish.csiro.au/journals/wr; f. 1974; 6 a year; Man. Editor D. W. MORTON; circ. 1,000.

Your Garden: 35–51 Mitchell St, McMahons Point, NSW 2060; tel. (2) 9464-3586; fax (2) 9464-3487; e-mail yg@pacpubs.com.au; monthly; Editor KANDY SHEPHERD; circ. 60,246.

NEWS AGENCIES

AAP Information Services: Locked Bag 21, Grosvenor Place, Sydney, NSW 2000; tel. (2) 9322-8000; fax (2) 9322-8888; f. 1983; owned by major daily newspapers of Australia; Chair. and CEO C. L. CASEY.

Foreign Bureaux

Agence France-Presse (AFP): 7th Floor, 259 George St, Sydney, NSW 2000; tel. (2) 9251-1544; fax (2) 9251-5230; e-mail afpsydney@compuserve.com; internet www.afp.com; Bureau Chief RON WALL.

Agenzia Nazionale Stampa Associata (ANSA) (Italy): Suite 4, 2 Grosvenor St, Bondi Junction, NSW 2022; tel. (2) 9369-1427; fax (2) 9369-4351; e-mail ansasyd@ozemail.com.au; Bureau Chief CLAUDIO MARCELLO.

Deutsche Presse-Agentur (dpa) (Germany): 36 Heath St, Mona Vale, NSW 2103; tel. (2) 9979-8253; fax (2) 9997-3154; e-mail hofman@zip.com.au; Correspondent ALEXANDER HOFMAN.

Jiji Press (Australia) Pty Ltd (Japan): GPOB 2584, Sydney, NSW 2001; tel. (2) 9299-5404; fax (2) 9299-5405; e-mail jijiaust@bigpond.com; Bureau Chief SATOSHI MIYAUCHI.

Kyodo News Service (Japan): Level 7, 9 Lang St, Sydney, NSW 2000; tel. (2) 9251-5240; fax (2) 9251-4980; Bureau Chief MICHITAKA YAMADA.

Reuters Australia Pty Ltd: Level 30, 60 Margaret St, Sydney, NSW 2000; Bureau Chief RUTH PITCHFORD.

Xinhua (New China) News Agency (People's Republic of China): 50 Russell St, Hackett, Canberra, ACT 2602; tel. (2) 6248-6369; fax (2) 6257-4706; Chief Correspondent LIN ZHENXI.

The Central News Agency (Taiwan) and the New Zealand Press Association are represented in Sydney, and Antara (Indonesia) is represented in Canberra.

PRESS ASSOCIATIONS

Australian Press Council: Suite 303, 149 Castlereagh St, Sydney, NSW 2000; tel. (2) 9261-1930; fax (2) 9267-6826; e-mail info@presscouncil.org.au; internet www.presscouncil.org.au; Chair. Prof. KEN MCKINNON.

Australian Suburban Newspapers Association: POB Q1527, QVB, NSW 1230; tel. (2) 9248-7381; fax (2) 9299-0087; e-mail rebecca@printnet.com.au; Sec. REBECCA LASKA.

Country Press Association of New South Wales Inc: POB Q182, Queen Victoria Bldg, Sydney, NSW 2000; tel. (2) 9299-4658; fax (2) 9299-1892; f. 1900; Exec. Dir D. J. SOMMERLAD; 120 mems.

Country Press Association of SA Incorporated: 198 Greenhill Rd, Eastwood, SA 5063; tel. (8) 8373-6533; fax (8) 8373-6544; f. 1912; represents South Australian country newspapers; Pres. B. PRICE; Exec. Dir M. R. TOWNSEND.

Country Press Australia: POB Q182, Queen Victoria Bldg, Sydney, NSW 2000; tel. (2) 9299-4658; fax (2) 9299-1892; f. 1906; Exec. Dir D. J. SOMMERLAD; 420 mems.

Queensland Country Press Association: POB 103, Paddington, Qld 4064; tel. (7) 3356-0033; Pres. M. HODGSON; Sec. N. D. MCLARY.

Tasmanian Press Association Pty Ltd: 71–75 Paterson St, Launceston, Tas 7250; tel. (3) 6320-255; Sec. L. WHISH-WILSON.

Victorian Country Press Association Ltd: 33 Rathdowne St, Carlton, Vic 3053; tel. (3) 9662-3244; fax (3) 9663-7433; e-mail vcpa@vcpa.com.au; f. 1910; Pres. G. KELLY; Exec. Dir J. E. RAY; 114 mems.

Publishers

Allen and Unwin Pty Ltd: 9 Atchison St, St Leonards, NSW 2065; tel. (2) 8425-0100; fax (2) 9906-2218; e-mail frontdesk@allen-unwin.com.au; internet www.allen-unwin.com.au; fiction, trade, academic, children's; Man. Dir PATRICK A. GALLAGHER.

Australasian Medical Publishing Co Pty Ltd: Level 1, 76 Berry St, North Sydney, NSW 2060; tel. (2) 9954-8666; fax (2) 9956-7644; e-mail ampco@ampco.com.au; internet www.ampco.com.au; f. 1913; scientific, medical and educational; CEO Dr MARTIN VAN DER WEYDEN.

Britannica.com.au: Locked Bag 927, North Sydney, NSW 2060; tel. (2) 9923-5600; fax (2) 9929-3753; e-mail ebsales@eba.com.au; internet www.britannica.com; reference, education, art, science and commerce; Man. Dir COOMA CHELLIAH.

Butterworths: Tower 2, 475 Victoria Ave, Chatswood, NSW 2067; tel. (2) 9422-2222; fax (2) 9422-2444; internet www.butterworths.com.au; f. 1910; div. of Reed International Books Australia Pty Ltd; legal and commercial; Man. Dir ANTHONY KINNEAR.

Cambridge University Press (Australia): 10 Stamford Road, Oakleigh, Melbourne, Vic 3166; tel. (3) 9568-0322; fax (3) 9569-9292; e-mail info@cup.edu.au; internet www.cup.edu.au; scholarly and educational; Dir SANDRA MCCOMB.

Commonwealth Scientific and Industrial Research Organisation (CSIRO Publishing): 150 Oxford St, POB 1139, Collingwood, Vic 3066; tel. (3) 9662-7500; fax (3) 9662-7555; e-mail info@publish.csiro.au; internet www.publish.csiro.au; f. 1926; scientific and technical journals, books, magazines, videos, CD-ROMs; Gen. Man. P. W. REEKIE.

Doubleday Australia Pty Ltd: 91 Mars Rd, Lane Cove, NSW 2066; tel. (2) 9427-0377; fax (2) 9427-6973; educational, trade, non-fiction, Australiana; Man. Dir DAVID HARLEY.

Gordon and Gotch Ltd: 25–37 Huntingdale Rd, Private Bag 290, Burwood, Vic 3125; tel. (3) 9805-1700; fax (3) 9808-0714; general; Chair. and Man. Dir I. D. GOLDING.

Harcourt Australia Pty Ltd: 30–52 Smidmore St, Marrickville, NSW 2204; tel. (2) 9517-8999; fax (2) 9517-2249; e-mail service@harcourt.com.au; internet www.harcourt.com.au; business, science, humanities, social science, engineering, medicine, etc.; Man. Dir BRIAN M. BRENNAN.

Harlequin Enterprises (Australia) Pty Ltd: Unit 2, 3 Gibbes St, Chatswood, NSW 2067; tel. (2) 9417-7333; fax (2) 9415-9292; e-mail harlequin@romance.net.au; internet www.romance.net.au; romantic fiction; Man. Dir NANCY PETERS.

Hodder Headline Australia Pty Ltd: Level 22, 201 Kent, Sydney, NSW 2000; tel. (2) 8248-0800; fax (2) 8248-0810; e-mail auspub @hha.com.au; internet www.hha.com.au; fiction, general, technical, children's; Man. Dir MALCOLM EDWARDS.

Hyland House Publishing Pty Ltd: POB 122, Flemington, Vic 3031; tel. and fax (3) 9376-4461; e-mail hyland3@netspace.net.au; f. 1976; trade, general, gardening, pet care, Aboriginal, Asian-Pacific public policy, fiction; Rep. MICHAEL SCHOO.

Lansdowne Publishing: Level 1, 18 Argyle St, The Rocks, NSW 2000; tel. (2) 9240-9222; fax (2) 9241-4818; e-mail valerie@ lanspub.com.au; cookery, gardening, health, history, pet care; Chief Exec. STEVEN MORRIS.

LBC Information Services: 100 Harris St, Pyrmont, NSW 2009; tel. (2) 8587-7000; fax (2) 8587-7100; e-mail lbccustomer@thomson .com.au; legal and professional; Man. Dir E. J. COSTIGAN.

Lothian Books: 11 Munro St, Port Melbourne, Vic 3207; tel. (3) 9645-1544; fax (3) 9646-4882; e-mail books@lothian.com.au; internet www.lothian.com.au; f. 1888; gardening, health, craft, business, New Age, self-help, general non-fiction and children's picture books; Man. Dir PETER LOTHIAN.

McGraw-Hill Book Publishing Co Australia Pty Ltd: 4 Barcoo St, Roseville, Sydney, NSW 2069; tel. (2) 9415-9899; fax (2) 9417-8872; e-mail sydney.reception@mcgraw-hill.com; internet www.mcgraw-hill.com.au; educational, professional and technical; Man. Dir FIRGAL ADAMS.

Melbourne University Press: 268 Drummond St, Carlton South, Vic 3053; tel. (3) 9347-3455; fax (3) 9349-2527; e-mail info@ mup.unimelb.edu.au; internet www.mup.com.au; f. 1922; scholarly non-fiction, Australian history and biography; Chair. Prof. BARRY SHEEHAN; Dir JOHN MECKAN.

Murdoch Books: Pier 8/9, 23 Hickson Rd, Millers Point, NSW 2000; tel. (2) 8220-2000; fax (2) 8220-2558; e-mail georinas@m.m.com.au; general non-fiction; Publr KAY SCARLETT.

National Library of Australia: Parkes Place, Canberra, ACT 2600; tel. (2) 6262-1111; fax (2) 6262-5081; e-mail infoserv@nla.gov.au; internet www.nla.gov.au; f. 1960; national bibliographic service, etc.; Publications Dir PAUL HETHERINGTON.

Nelson Thomson Learning: 102 Dodds St, South Melbourne, Vic 3205; tel. (3) 9685-4111; fax (3) 9685-4199; e-mail customerservice @nelson.com.au; internet www.nelsonitp.com; educational; Man. Dir G. J. BROWNE.

Oxford University Press: 253 Normanby Rd, South Melbourne, Vic 3205; tel. (3) 9934-9123; fax (3) 9934-9100; f. 1908; general non-fiction and educational; Man. Dir MAREK PALKA.

Pan Macmillan Australia Pty Ltd: Level 18, St Martin's Tower, 31 Market St, Sydney, NSW 2000; tel. (2) 9261-5611; fax (2) 9261-5047; e-mail publicity@macmillan.wm.au; general, reference, children's, fiction, non-fiction; Chair. R. GIBB.

Pearson Education Australia Pty Ltd: 95 Coventry St, South Melbourne, Vic 3205; tel. (3) 9697-0666; fax (3) 9699-2041; e-mail longman.sales@pearsoned.com.au.; internet www.pearsoned.com .au; f. 1957; mainly educational, academic, computer, some general; Man. Dir PAT EVANS.

Penguin Books Australia Ltd: 487/493 Maroondah Highway, POB 257, Ringwood, Vic 3134; tel. (3) 9871-2400; fax (3) 9870-9618; internet www.penguin.com.au; f. 1946; general; Man. Dir PETER FIELD; Publishing Dir ROBERT SESSIONS.

Random House Australia Pty Ltd: 20 Alfred St, Milsons Point, NSW 2061; tel. (2) 9954-9966; fax (2) 9954-4562; e-mail random@ randomhouse.com.au; internet www.randomhouse.com.au; fiction, non-fiction, children's and illustrated; Man. Dir JULIET ROGERS; Deputy Man. Dir MARGARET SEALE.

Reader's Digest (Australia) Pty Ltd: POB 4353, Sydney, NSW 2000; tel. (2) 9690-6111; fax (2) 9699-8165; general; Man. Dir WILLIAM B. TOOHEY.

Reed Educational & Professional Publishing: POB 460, Port Melbourne, Vic 3207; tel. (3) 9245-7111; fax (3) 9245-7333; e-mail admin@reededucation.com.au; primary, secondary and tertiary educational, incl. electronic; division of Reed International; Man. Dir DAVID O'BRIEN.

Scholastic Australia Pty Ltd: Railway Crescent, Lisarow, POB 579, Gosford, NSW 2250; tel. (2) 4328-3555; fax (2) 4323-3827; internet www.scholastic.com.au; f. 1968; educational and children's; Man. Dir KEN JOLLY.

Schwartz Publishing (Victoria) Pty Ltd: 45 Flinders Lane, Melbourne, Vic 3000; tel. (3) 9654-2000; fax (3) 9650-5418; fiction, non-fiction; Dir MORRY SCHWARTZ.

Simon and Schuster Australia: 20 Barcoo St, POB 507, East Roseville, NSW 2069; tel. (2) 9415-9900; fax (2) 9417-4292; general fiction, non-fiction, cooking, gardening, craft, parenting, health, history, travel and biography; Man. Dir JON ATTENBOROUGH.

Thames and Hudson (Australia) Pty Ltd: 11 Central Boulevard, Portside Business Park, Fishermans Bend, Vic 3207; tel. (3) 9646-7788; fax (3) 9646-8790; e-mail thaust@thaust.com.au; art, history, archaeology, architecture, photography, design, fashion, textiles, lifestyle; Man. Dir PETER SHAW.

D. W. Thorpe: 18 Salmon St, Locked Bag 20, Port Melbourne, Vic 3207; tel. (3) 9245-7370; fax (3) 9245-7395; e-mail customer.service@ thorpe.com.au; bibliographic, library and book trade reference; Publishing Man. PAULENE MOREY.

Time Life Australia Pty Ltd: Level 12, 33 Berry St, North Sydney, NSW 2060; tel. (2) 8925-3800; fax (2) 9957-4227; general and educational; Man. Dir ROBERT HARDY.

UNSW Press Ltd: UNSW, Sydney, NSW 2052; tel. (2) 9664-0999; fax (2) 9664-5420; e-mail info.press@unsw.edu.au; f. 1961; scholarly, general and tertiary texts; Man. Dir Dr ROBIN DERRICOURT.

University of Queensland Press: POB 6042, St Lucia, Qld 4067; tel. (7) 3365-2127; fax (7) 3365-7579; e-mail uqp@uqp.uq.edu.au; internet www.uqp.uq.edu.au; f. 1948; scholarly and general cultural interest, incl. Black Australian writers, adult and children's fiction; Gen. Man. LAURIE MULLER.

University of Western Australia Press: c/o University of Western Australia, Nedlands, WA 6907; tel. (8) 9380-3670; fax (8) 9380-1027; e-mail uwap@cyllene.uwa.edu.au; internet www.uwapress.uwa .edu.au; f. 1954; natural history, history, literary studies, Australiana, children's, general non-fiction; Dir Dr JENNY GREGORY.

John Wiley & Sons Australia, Ltd: POB 1226, Milton, Qld 4064; tel. (7) 3859-9755; fax (7) 3859-9715; e-mail brisbane@johnwiley .com.au; internet www.johnwiley.com.au; f. 1954; educational, reference and trade; Man. Dir PETER DONOUGHUE.

Government Publishing House

AusInfo: GPOB 1920, Canberra, ACT 2601; tel. (2) 6275-3442; fax (2) 6275-3682; internet www.ausinfo.gov.au; f. 1970; fmrly Australian Govt Publishing Service; Assistant Sec. MICHELLE KINNANE.

PUBLISHERS' ASSOCIATION

Australian Publishers Association Ltd: Suite 59, Level 3, 89 Jones St, Ultimo, NSW 2007; tel. (2) 9281-9788; fax (2) 9281-1073; e-mail apa@magna.com.au; internet www.publishers.asn.au; f. 1949; c. 150 mems; Pres. SANDY GRANT; Dir SUSAN BLACKWELL.

Broadcasting and Communications

TELECOMMUNICATIONS

By mid-2000 more than 40 licensed telecommunication carriers were in operation.

AAPT Ltd: AAPT Centre, 9 Lang St, Sydney, NSW 2000; tel. (2) 9377-7000; fax (2) 9377-7133; internet www.aapt.com.au; f. 1991; long-distance telecommunications carrier; Chair C. L. CASEY; CEO and Man. Dir L. WILLIAMS.

Cable & Wireless Optus Ltd: POB 1, North Sydney, NSW 2059; tel. (2) 9342-7800; fax (2) 9342-7100; internet www.cwo.net .au; f. 1991; general and mobile telecommunications, data and internet services, pay-TV; Chair. Sir RALPH ROBINS; Chief Exec. CHRIS ANDERSON.

Matrix Telecommunications Services: 1st Floor, 24 Artamon Rd, Willoughby, NSW 2068; tel. (2) 9290-4111; fax (2) 9262-2574; f. 1985; mobile communication services; Chair. MARK CARNEGIE; Pres. and CEO JOSEPH YANG.

One.Tel Ltd: Level 28, 9 Castlereagh St, Sydney, NSW 2000; tel. (2) 9777-8111; fax (2) 9777-8199; internet www.onetel.com.au; telecommunication services; Chair. JOHN GREAVES.

Telstra Corpn Ltd: Level 14, 231 Elizabeth St, Sydney, NSW 2000; tel. (2) 9287-4677; fax (2) 9287-5869; internet www.telstra.com.au; general and mobile telecommunication services; Man. Dir and Chief Exec. ZIGGY SWITKOWSKI.

Vodafone Pacific Pty Ltd: Tower A, 799 Pacific Highway, Chatswood, NSW 2067; tel. (2) 9878-7000; fax (2) 9878-7788; internet www.vodafone.com.au; mobile telecommunication services.

Regulatory Authority

Australian Communications Authority (ACA): POB 13112, Law Courts, Melbourne, Vic 8010; tel. (3) 9963-6800; fax (3) 9963-6899; e-mail candinfo@aca.gov.au; internet www.aca.gov.au; f. 1997 through merger of Australian Telecommunications Authority and Spectrum Management Agency; regulator for telecommunications and radiocommunications; Chair. TONY SHAW.

BROADCASTING

Many programmes are provided by the non-commercial statutory corporation, the Australian Broadcasting Corporation (ABC). Commercial radio and television services are provided by stations operated by companies under licences granted and renewed by the Australian Broadcasting Authority (ABA). They rely for their income on the broadcasting of advertisements. In mid-1993 there were 166 commercial radio stations in operation, and 44 commercial television stations.

In 1997 there were an estimated 25.5m. radio receivers and 10.2m. television receivers in use.

Australian Broadcasting Corporation (ABC): 700 Harris St, Ultimo, POB 9994, Sydney, NSW 2001; tel. (2) 9333-1500 (radio), telex 176464 (radio), 120432 (television); fax (2) 9333-2603 (radio), (2) 9950-3050 (television); e-mail comments@your.abc.net.au; internet www.abc.net.au; f. 1932 as Australian Broadcasting Commission; one national television network operating on about 600 transmitters and six radio networks operating on more than 6,000 transmitters; Chair. DONALD MCDONALD; Man. Dir JONATHAN SHIER.

Radio Australia: international service broadcast by short wave and satellite in English, Indonesian, Standard Chinese, Khmer, Tok Pisin and Vietnamese.

Radio

Federation of Australian Radio Broadcasters Ltd: POB 299, St Leonards, NSW 1590; tel. (2) 9906-5944; fax (2) 9906-5128; e-mail mail@commercialradio.com.au; internet www.commercialradio.com; asscn of privately-owned commercial stations; CEO D. BACON.

Major Commercial Broadcasting Station Licensees

5AD Broadcasting Co Pty Ltd: 201 Tynte St, Nth Adelaide, SA 5006; tel. (8) 8300-1000; fax (8) 8300-1020; internet www.5adfm.com.au; also operates 5DN; Gen. Man. GRAEME TUCKER.

Associated Communications Enterprises (ACE) Radio Broadcasters Pty Ltd: POB 7515, Melbourne, Vic 3004; tel. (3) 9645-9877; fax (3) 9645-9886; operates six stations; Man. Dir S. EVERETT.

Austereo Pty Ltd: Ground Level, 180 St Kilda Rd, St Kilda, Vic 3182; tel. (3) 9230-1051; fax (3) 9593-9007; e-mail pharvie@austereo.com.au; internet www.austereo.com.au; operates 14 stations; Exec. Chair. PETER HARVIE.

Australian Radio Network Pty Ltd: Level 8, 99 Mount St, North Sydney, NSW 2060; tel. (2) 9464-1000; fax (2) 9464-1010; operates nine stations; CEO NEIL MOUNT.

Australian Regional Broadcasters: 1 June Rd, Gooseberry Hill, WA 6076; tel. (8) 9472-8900; fax (8) 9472-8911; operates three stations; Man. Dir NICK RINGROSE.

Bass Radio: 109 York St, Launceston, Tas 7250; tel. (3) 6331-4844; fax (3) 6334-5858; operates five radio stations and part of RG Capital Radio; Man. DAVE HILL.

Capital Radio: 28 Sharp St, Cooma, NSW 2630; tel. (2) 6452-1521; fax (2) 6452-1006; operates four stations; Man. Dir KEVIN BLYTON.

DMG Regional Radio Pty Ltd: Level 9, 2 Bridge St, Sydney, NSW 2000; tel. (2) 9258-4999; fax (2) 9241-2224; e-mail sydoff@dmgradio.com.au; internet www.dmgradio.com.au; operates 59 stations; Gen. Mans KEN GANNAWAY (Western Group), DAVID SCOPELLITI (Northern Group); Chair. PAUL THOMPSON.

Grant Broadcasting: 63 Minimbah Rd, Northbridge, NSW 2063; tel. (2) 9958-7301; fax (2) 9958-6906; operates seven stations; Gen. Man. JANET CAMERON.

Greater Cairns Radio Ltd: Virginia House, Abbott St, Cairns, Qld 4870; tel. (7) 4050-0846; fax (7) 4051-8060; Gen. Man. J. ELLER.

Macquarie Radio Network Pty Ltd: POB 4290, Sydney, NSW 2001; tel. (2) 9269-0646; fax (2) 9287-2772; operates 2GB and 2CH; CEO GEORGE BUSCHMAN.

Moree Broadcasting and Development Company Ltd: 87–89 Balo St, Moree, NSW 2400; tel. (2) 6752-1155; fax (2) 6752-2601; operates two stations; Man. KEN BIRCH.

Radio 2SM Gold 1269: 186 Blues Point Rd, North Sydney, NSW 2060; tel. (2) 9922-1269; fax (2) 9954-3117; f. 1931; CEO and Chair. C. M. MURPHY.

RadioWest Hot FM: POB 10067, Kalgoorlie, WA 6430; tel. (8) 9021-2666; fax (8) 9091-2209; e-mail radio6KG@gold.net.au; f. 1931.

Regional Broadcasters (Australia) Pty: McDowal St, Roma, Qld 4455; tel. (7) 4622-1800; fax (7) 4622-3697; Chair. G. MCVEAN.

RG Capital Radio Pty Ltd: Level 2, Seabank Bldg, 12–14 Marine Parade, Southport, Qld 4215; tel. (7) 5591-5000; fax (7) 5591-2869; operates 14 stations; Man. Dir RHYS HOLLERAN.

Rural Press Ltd: Cnr Pine Mt Rd and Hill St, Raymonds Hill, Qld 4305; tel. (7) 3201-6000; fax (7) 3812-3060; internet www.rpl.com.au; f. 1911; operates five stations; Gen. Man. RICHARD BURNS.

SEA FM Pty Ltd: POB 5910, Gold Coast Mail Centre, Bundall, Qld 4217; tel. (7) 5591-5000; fax (7) 5591-6080; operates 28 stations; Man. Dir RHYS HOLLERAN.

Southern Cross Broadcasting (Australia) Ltd: see under Television.

Supernetwork Radio Pty Ltd: POB 97, Coolangatta, Qld 4225; tel. (7) 5524-4497; fax (7) 5554-3970; operates 15 stations; Chair. W. CARALIS.

Tamworth Radio Development Company Pty Ltd: POB 497, Tamworth, NSW 2340; tel. (2) 6765-7055; fax (2) 6765-2762; operates five stations; Man. W. A. MORRISON.

Tasmanian Broadcasting Network (TBN): POB 665G, Launceston, Tas 7250; tel. (3) 6431-2555; fax (3) 6431-3188; operates three stations; Chair. K. FINDLAY.

Wesgo Ltd: POB 234, Seven Hills, NSW 2147; tel. (2) 9831-7611; fax (2) 9831-2001; operates eight stations; CEO G. W. RICE.

Television

Federation of Australian Commercial Television Stations (FACTS): 44 Avenue Rd, Mosman, NSW 2088; tel. (2) 9960-2622; fax (2) 9969-3520; f. 1960; represents all commercial television stations; Chair. JOHN MCALPINE; Gen. Man. TONY BRANIGAN.

Commercial Television Station Licensees

Amalgamated Television Services Pty Ltd: Mobbs Lane, Epping, NSW 2121; tel. (2) 9877-7777; fax (2) 9877-7888; f. 1956; originating station for Seven Network TV programming; Exec. Chair. KERRY STOKES.

Australian Capital Television Pty Ltd (Ten Capital): Private Bag 10, Dickson, ACT 2602; tel. (2) 6242-2400; fax (2) 6241-7230; f. 1962; Gen. Man. ERIC PASCOE.

Brisbane TV Ltd: GPOB 604, Brisbane, Qld 4001; tel. (7) 3369-7777; fax (7) 3368-2970; f. 1959; operates one station; mem. of Seven Network; Man. Dir L. M. RILEY.

Broken Hill Television Ltd: POB 472, Rocky Hill, Broken Hill, NSW 2880; tel. (8) 8087-6013; fax (8) 8087-8492; f. 1968; operates one station; Chair. PETER STORROCK; Chief Exec. D. WESTON.

Channel 9 South Australia Pty Ltd: 202 Tynte St, North Adelaide 5006; tel. (8) 8267-0111; fax (8) 8267-3996; f. 1959; Gen. Man. M. COLSON.

Channel Seven Adelaide Pty Ltd: 45–49 Park Terrace, Gilberton, SA 5081; tel. (8) 8342-7777; fax (8) 8342-7717; f. 1965; operates SAS Channel 7; mem. of Seven Network; Man. Dir MAX WALTERS.

Channel Seven Melbourne Pty Ltd: 119 Wells St, Southbank, Vic 3006; tel. (3) 9697-7777; fax (3) 9697-7888; e-mail daspinall@seven.com.auf. 1956; operates one station; Chair. KERRY STOKES; Man. Dir DAVID ASPINALL.

Channel Seven Perth Pty Ltd: POB 77, Tuart Hill, WA 6060; tel. (8) 9344-0777; fax (8) 9344-0670; f. 1959; Chair. C. S. WHARTON.

General Television Corporation Pty Ltd: 22–46 Bendigo St, POB 100, Richmond, Vic 3121; tel. (3) 9429-0201; fax (3) 9429-3670; internet www.nine.msn.com.au; f. 1957; operates one station; Man. Dir GRAEME YARWOOD.

Golden West Network: POB 5090, Geraldton, WA 6531; tel. (8) 9921-4422; fax (8) 9921-8096.

Golden West Network Pty Ltd: POB 1062, West Perth, WA 6872; tel. (8) 9481-0050; fax (8) 9321-2470; f. 1967; operates three stations (SSW10, VEW and WAW); Gen. Man. W. FENWICK.

Imparja Television Pty Ltd: POB 52, Alice Springs, NT 0871; tel. (8) 8950-1411; fax (8) 8953-0322; e-mail imparja@ozemail.com.au; internet www.imparja.com.au; CEO CORALLIE FERGUSON.

Independent Broadcasters of Australia Pty Ltd: POB 285, Sydney, NSW 2001; tel. (2) 9264-9144; fax (2) 9264-6334; fmrly Regional Television Australia Pty Ltd; Chair. GRAEME J. GILBERTSON; Sec. JEFF EATHER.

Mt Isa Television Pty Ltd: 110 Canooweal St, Mt Isa, Qld 4825; tel. (7) 4743-8888; fax (7) 4743-9803; f. 1971; operates one station; Station Man. LYALL GREY.

NBN Ltd: Mosbri Crescent, POB 750L, Newcastle, NSW 2300; tel. (2) 4929-2933; fax (2) 4926-2936; f. 1962; operates one station; Man. Dir DENIS LEDBURY.

Network Ten Ltd: GPOB 10, Sydney, NSW 2001; tel. (2) 9650-1010; fax (2) 9650-1170; operates Australian TV network and commercial stations in Sydney, Melbourne, Brisbane, Perth and Adelaide; CEO JOHN MCALPINE.

Nine Network Australia Pty Ltd: POB 27, Willoughby, NSW 2068; tel. (2) 9906-9999; fax (2) 9958-2279; internet www.ninemsn.com.au; f. 1956; division of Publishing and Broadcasting Ltd; operates three stations: TCN Channel Nine Pty Ltd (Sydney), Queensland Television Ltd (Brisbane) and General Television Corporation Ltd (Melbourne); CEO DAVID LECKIE.

Northern Rivers Television Pty Ltd: Peterson Rd, Locked Bag 1000, Coffs Harbour, NSW 2450; tel. (2) 6652-2777; fax (2) 6652-3034; f. 1965; CEO GARRY DRAFFIN.

Prime Television Group: Level 6, 1 Pacific Highway, North Sydney, NSW 2060; tel. (2) 9965-7700; fax (2) 9965-7729; e-mail primetv@primetv.com.au; internet www.primetv.com.au; Chair. PAUL RAMSAY; CEO BRENT HARMAN.

Prime Television (Northern) Pty Ltd: POB 2077, Elermore Vale, NSW 2287; tel. (2) 4952-0500; fax (2) 4952-0502; internet www.primetv.com.au; Gen. Man. BRAD JONES.

Prime Television (Southern) Pty Ltd: POB 465, Orange, NSW 2800; tel. (2) 6361-6888; fax (2) 6363-1889; Gen. Man. D. THISTLETHWAITE.

Prime Television (Victoria) Pty Ltd: Sunraysia Highway, Ballarat, Vic 3350; tel. (3) 5337-1777; fax (3) 5337-1700; Gen. Man. WARWICK FENWICK.

Queensland Television Ltd: POB 72, GPO Brisbane, Qld 4001; tel. (7) 3214-9999; fax (7) 3369-3512; f. 1959; operates one station; Gen. Man. IAN R. MÜLLER.

Seven Network Ltd: Level 13, 1 Pacific Highway, North Sydney, NSW 2060; tel. (2) 9967-7903; fax (2) 9967-7972; internet www.seven.com.au; owns Amalgamated Television Services Pty Ltd (Sydney), Brisbane TV Ltd (Brisbane), HSV Channel 7 Pty Ltd (Melbourne), South Australian Telecasters Ltd (Adelaide) and TVW Enterprises Ltd (Perth); Exec. Chair. KERRY STOKES.

   Australia Television: international satellite service; broadcasts to more than 30 countries and territories in Asia and the Pacific.

Seven Queensland: 140–142 Horton Parade, Maroochydore, Qld 4558; tel. (7) 5430-1777; fax (7) 5430-1767; f. 1965; fmrly Sunshine Television Network Ltd; Man. Dir LES RILEY.

Southern Cross Broadcasting (Australia) Ltd: 41–49 Bank St, South Melbourne, Vic 3205; tel. (3) 9243-2100; fax (3) 9690-0937; internet www.scbnetwork.com.au; f. 1932; operates four TV and four radio stations; Man. Dir A. E. BELL.

Southern Cross Television (TNT9) Pty Ltd: Watchorn St, Launceston, Tas 7250; tel. (3) 6344-0202; fax (3) 6343-0340; f. 1962; operates one station; Gen. Man. BRUCE ABRAHAM.

Special Broadcasting Service (SBS): Locked Bag 028, Crows Nest, NSW 1585; tel. (2) 9430-2828; fax (2) 9430-3700; e-mail sbs.com.au; internet www.sbs.com.au; f. 1980; national multi-cultural broadcaster of TV and radio; Man. Dir NIGEL MILAN.

Spencer Gulf Telecasters Ltd: POB 305, Port Pirie, SA 5540; tel. (8) 8632-2555; fax (8) 8633-0984; e-mail dweston@centralonline .com.au; internet www.centralonline.com.au; f. 1968; operates two stations; Chair. P. M. STURROCK; Chief Exec. D. WESTON.

Swan Television & Radio Broadcasters Pty Ltd: POB 99, Tuart Hill, WA 6939; tel. (8) 9449-9999; fax (8) 9449-9900; Gen. Man. P. BOWEN.

Telecasters Australia Ltd: Level 8, 1 Elizabeth Plaza, North Sydney, NSW 2060; tel. (2) 9922-1011; fax (2) 9922-1033; internet www.telecasters.com.au; operates commercial TV services of TEN Queensland, TEN Northern NSW, Seven Central and Seven Darwin.

Territory Television Pty Ltd: POB 1764, Darwin, NT 0801; tel. (8) 8981-8888; fax (8) 8981-6802; f. 1971; operates one station; Gen. Man. A. G. BRUYN.

WIN Television Griffith Pty Ltd: 161 Remembrance Driveway, Griffith, NSW 2680; tel. (2) 6962-4500; fax (2) 6962-0979; e-mail mtntv@ozemail.com.au; fmrly MTN Television; Man. Dir RAY GAMBLE.

WIN Television Loxton Pty Ltd: Murray Bridge Rd, POB 471, Loxton, SA 5333; tel. (8) 8584-6891; fax (8) 8584-5062; f. 1976; operates one station; Exec. Chair. E. H. URLWIN; Gen. Man. W. L. MUDGE.

WIN Television Mildura Pty Ltd: 18 Deakin Ave, Mildura, Vic 3500; tel. (3) 5023-0204; fax (3) 5022-1179; f. 1965; Chair. JOHN RUSHTON; Man. NOEL W. HISCOCK.

WIN Television NSW Network: Television Ave, Mt St Thomas, Locked Bag 8800, South Coast Mail Centre, NSW 2521; tel. (2) 4223-4199; fax (2) 4227-3682; internet www.wintv.com.au; f. 1962; Man. Dir K. KINGSTON; CEO JOHN RUSHTON.

WIN Television Qld Pty Ltd: POB 568 Rockhampton, Qld 4700; tel. (7) 4930-4499; fax (7) 4930-4490; Station Man. R. HOCKEY.

WIN Television Tas Pty Ltd: 52 New Town Rd, Hobart, Tas 7008; tel. (3) 6228-8999; fax (3) 6228-8991; e-mail wintas.com.au; internet www.wintv.com.au; f. 1959; Gen. Man. GREG RAYMENT.

WIN Television Vic Pty Ltd: POB 464, Ballarat, Vic 3353; tel. (3) 5320-1366; fax (3) 5333-1598; internet www.winnet.com.au; f. 1961; operates five stations; Gen. Man. DAVID LANGSFORD.

Satellite, Cable and Digital Television

Digital television was to become available in metropolitan areas from January 2001.

Austar United Communications: Level 29, AAP Centre, 259 George St, Sydney NSW 2000, tel. (2) 9251-6999; fax (2) 9251-6136; internet www.austarunited.com.au; began operations in 1995; 427,000 subscribers (Aug. 2000); CEO JOHN C. PORTER.

Foxtel: Foxtel Television Centre, Pyrmont, Sydney; internet www.foxtel.com.au; owned by the News Corpn, Telstra Corpn and PBL; 534,000 subscribers (Sept. 1999).

Optus Vision: Tower B, Level 15, 16 Zenith Centre, 821–841 Pacific Highway, Chatswood, NSW 2067; commenced cable services on 11 channels in 1995; 210,000 subscribers (March 1999).

Regulatory Authority

Australian Broadcasting Authority: POB Q500, QVB Post Office, NSW 1230; tel. (2) 9334-7700; fax (2) 9334-7799; e-mail info@aba.gov.au; internet www.aba.gov.au; regulates radio and TV broadcasting; Chair. Prof. DAVID FLINT.

Finance

Radical reforms of the financial sector, to be introduced from 1998, were announced in September 1997. The banking system was to be opened up to greater competition. The licensing and regulation of deposit-taking institutions was to be supervised by the new Australian Prudential Regulation Authority, while consumer protection was to be the responsibility of the Australian Corporations and Financial Services Commission.

(cap. = capital; p.u. = paid up; res = reserves; dep. = deposits; m. = million; brs = branches; amounts in Australian dollars)

Australian Prudential Regulation Authority (APRA): GPOB 9836, Sydney, NSW 2000; tel. (2) 9210-3000; fax (2) 9210-3411; e-mail APRAinfo@apra.gov.au; internet www.apra.gov.au; responsible for regulation of banks, insurance cos, superannuation funds, credit unions, building societies and friendly societies; CEO GRAEME THOMPSON.

BANKING
Central Bank

Reserve Bank of Australia: GPOB 3947, Sydney, NSW 2001; tel. (2) 9551-8111; fax (2) 9551-8000; e-mail rbainfo.@rba .gov.au; internet www.rba.gov.au; f. 1911; responsible for monetary policy, financial system stability, payment system development; cap. and res 7,237m., dep. 10,383m., total assets 49,073m., notes on issue 23,552m. (June 1999); Gov. IAN MACFARLANE.

Development Bank

Primary Industry Bank of Australia Ltd: GPOB 4577, Sydney, NSW 1042; tel. (2) 9234-4200; fax (2) 9221-6218; internet www.piba .com.au; f. 1978; cap. 123.2m., res 2.5m.; Chair. H. G. GENTIS; 21 brs.

Trading Banks

ABN AMRO Australia Ltd: NAB House, 255 George St, Sydney, NSW 2000; tel. (2) 9259-5711; fax (2) 9259-5444; f. 1983; cap. 70m., res 65m. (Dec. 1997); CEO STEVE CRANE.

Arab Bank Australia Ltd: GPOB N645, Grosvenor Place, Sydney, NSW 1220; tel. (2) 9377-8900; fax (2) 9221-5428; internet www.arab-bank.co.au; cap. 55.0m., dep. 365.7m. (Dec. 1999); Chair. KHALID SHOMAN; Man. Dir JACK BEIGHTON.

Australia and New Zealand Banking Group Ltd: 100 Queen St, Melbourne, Vic 3000; POB 537 E, Melbourne, Vic 3001; tel. (3) 9273-5555; fax (3) 9273-4909; internet www.anz.com; f. 1835; present name adopted in 1970; cap. 8,893.0m., res 536.0m., dep. 105,560.0m. (1999); 807 brs; Chair. C. B. GOODE; CEO JOHN McFARLANE.

BA Australia Ltd: Level 63, MLC Centre, 19–29 Martin Place, Sydney, NSW 2000; tel. (2) 9931-4200; fax (2) 9221-1023; f. 1964; cap. 150.3m. (Dec. 1998); Man. Dir TERRY FRANCIS.

Bank of Melbourne: 360 Collins St, Melbourne, Vic 3000; tel. (3) 9608-3222; fax (3) 9608-3700; division of Westpac Banking Corpn; f. 1989; cap. 752m., dep. 8,706m. (1997); Chair. CHRIS STEWART; CEO MATTHEW SLATTER; 129 brs.

Bank of Queensland Ltd: 229 Elizabeth St, POB 898, Brisbane, Qld 4001; tel. (7) 3212-3333; fax (7) 3212-3399; internet www.boq.com.au; f. 1874; cap. 139.9m., res 2.4m., dep. 2,631.0m. (Aug. 1999); Chair. NEIL ROBERTS; Chief Exec. JOHN K. DAWSON; 96 brs.

Bank of Tokyo-Mitsubishi (Australia) Ltd: Level 26, Gateway, 1 Macquarie Place, Sydney, NSW 2000; tel. (2) 9255-1111; fax (2) 9247-4266; e-mail btmacorp@mt.net.au; cap. 152.9m., res 34,000m., dep. 1,603.5m. (Dec. 1999); f. 1985; Chair. R. NICOLSON; Man. Dir H. YOKOYAMA.

Bank of Western Australia Ltd (BankWest): Level 7, BankWest Tower, 108 St George's Terrace, POB E237, Perth, WA 6001; tel. (8) 9449-7000; fax (8) 9449-7050; e-mail finmkts@bankwest.com.au.;

internet www.bankwest.com.au; f. 1895 as Agricultural Bank of Western Australia, 1945 as Rural and Industries Bank of Western Australia; present name adopted in 1994; cap. 575.3m., res 2.3m., dep. 9,753.5m. (Feb. 1999); Chair. IAN C. R. MACKENZIE; Man. Dir TERRY C. BUDGE; 109 brs.

Bankers' Trust Australia Ltd: GPOB H4, Australia Sq., Sydney, NSW 2000; tel. (2) 9259-3555; fax (2) 9259-9800; internet www.btal .com.au; f. 1986; cap. 273.3m., dep. 6,266.8m. (Dec. 1997); Man. Dir R. A. FERGUSON; 5 brs.

The Chase Manhattan Bank: GPOB 9816, NSW 2001; tel. (2) 9250-4111; fax (2) 9250-4554; internet www.chase.com; Man. Dir W. SCOTT REID.

Citibank Ltd: GPOB 40, Sydney, NSW 1027; tel. (2) 9239-9100; fax (2) 9239-9110; internet www.citibank.com.au; f. 1954; cap. 457m., res 1m., dep. 5,619m. (Dec. 1998); Country Corporate Officer WILLIAM W. FERGUSON.

Commonwealth Bank of Australia: Level 1, 48 Martin Place, Sydney, NSW 1155; tel. (2) 9378-2000; fax (2) 9378-3317; internet www.commbank.com.au; f. 1912; cap. 3,526.0m., res 1,511.0m., dep. 96,677m. (June 1999); Chair. J. T. RALPH; CEO Dir D. V. MURRAY; more than 1,500 brs world-wide; merged with Colonial Ltd in 2000.

HSBC Bank Australia Ltd: Level 8, 1 O'Connell Street, Sydney, NSW 2000; tel. (2) 9255-2888; fax (2) 9255-2332; internet www.hsbc.com.au; f. 1985; fmrly HongkongBank of Australia; cap. 500.0m., res 60.1m., dep. 4,237.6m. (Dec. 1997); CEO CHRIS CROOK; 18 brs.

IBJ Australia Bank Ltd: 21st Level, Colonial Centre, 52 Martin Place, Sydney, NSW 2000; tel. (2) 9377-8888; fax (2) 9377-8884; internet www.ibj.com.au; f. 1985; subsidiary of Mizuho Holdings Inc; cap. 104.0m., res 40.0m., dep. 1,336.0m. (Dec. 2000); Chair. M. J. PHILLIPS; Man. Dir T. INOSE.

ING Bank (Australia) Ltd: Level 1, 347 Kent St, Sydney, NSW 2000; tel. (2) 9234-8444; fax (2) 9290-3683; cap. 60m., res 1.3m., dep. 1,015.4m. (Dec. 1998); Gen. Man. JULIE BROWN.

Macquarie Bank Ltd: 1 Martin Place, Sydney, NSW 2000; tel. (2) 8232-3333; fax (2) 8232-3350; internet www.macquarie .com.au; f. 1969 as Hill Samuel Australia Ltd; present name adopted in 1985; cap. 372.8m., res 390.1m., dep. 12,710.5m. (March 2000); Chair. DAVID S. CLARKE; Man. Dir ALLAN E. MOSS; 5 brs.

National Australia Bank Ltd: 500 Bourke St, Melbourne, Vic 3000; tel. (3) 8641-3500; fax (3) 8641-4916; internet www .national.com.au/; f. 1858; cap. 9,286m., res 802m., dep. 162,468m. (Sept. 1999); Chair. M. R. RAYNER; Exec. Dir FRANK CICUTTO; 2,349 brs.

N. M. Rothschild & Sons (Australia) Ltd: Level 16, 1 O'Connell St, Sydney, NSW 2000; tel. (2) 9323-2000; fax (2) 9323-2323; internet www.rothschild.com.au; f. 1967 as International Pacific Corpn; cap. 130.0m., dep. 851.8m. (March 1999); Chair. PHILIP BRASS; Chief Exec. RICHARD LEE.

SG Australia Ltd: Level 21, 400 George St, Sydney, NSW 2000; tel. (2) 9210-8000; fax (2) 9231-2196; internet www.sgal@zip.com.au; f. 1981; fmrly Société Générale; cap. 21.5m., res 208m., dep. 5,656m. (Dec. 1999); CEO MICHEL L. MACAGNO.

St George Bank Ltd: Locked Bag 1, PO, Kogarah, NSW 1485; tel. (2) 9236-1111; fax (2) 9952-1066; e-mail stgeorge@stgeorge.com.au; internet www.stgeorge.com.au; f. 1937 as building society; cap. 3,174m., res 130m., dep. 35,047m. (Sept. 2000); Chair. F. J. CONROY; CEO and Man. Dir EDWARD O'NEAL; 421 brs.

Standard Chartered Bank Australia Ltd: Level 11, 345 George St, Sydney, NSW; tel. (2) 9232-6599; fax (2) 9232-9345; f. 1986; cap. 226.2m., dep. 667.8m. (Dec. 1999); Chair. Sir BRUCE MACKLIN; CEO DAVID MANSON.

Toronto Dominion Australia Ltd: Level 34, Rialto South Tower, 525 Collins St, Melbourne, Vic 3000; tel. (3) 1993-1344; fax (3) 9614-0083; internet www.tdbank.ca; f. 1970; cap. 191.5m., res 6.0m., dep. 3,435.4m. (Oct. 1997); Man. Dir W. C. JACOBSON.

Westpac Banking Corporation: 60 Martin Place, Sydney, NSW 2000; tel. (2) 9226-3311; fax (2) 9226-4128; e-mail westpac@westpac .com.au; internet www.westpac.com.au; f. 1817; cap. 1,853m., res 3,888m., dep. 79,687m. (Sept. 1999); Chair. JOHN UHRIG; Man. Dir D. R. MORGAN.

Foreign Banks

Bank of China (People's Republic of China): 39–41 York St, Sydney, NSW 2000; tel. (2) 9267-5188; fax (2) 9262-1794; e-mail bocsyd@ bigpond.com.au; Gen. Man. GAO JI LU.

Bank of New Zealand: 9th Floor, BNZ House, 333–339 George St, Sydney, NSW 2000; tel. (2) 9290-6666; fax (2) 9290-3414; Chief Operating Officer G. ARMBRUSTER.

BNP Paribas (France): 60 Castlereagh St, Sydney, NSW 2000; POB 269, Sydney, NSW 2001; tel. (2) 9232-8733; fax (2) 9221-3026; e-mail bnp@bnp.com.au; internet www.bnp.com.au; Gen. Man. ROLAND GIRAULT; 4 brs.

Deutsche Bank AG (Germany): GPOB 7033, Sydney, NSW 2001; tel. (2) 9258-3666; fax (2) 9241-2565; Man. Dir KENNETH C. BORDA.

STOCK EXCHANGE

Australian Stock Exchange Ltd (ASX): Level 9, 20 Bridge St, Sydney, NSW 2000; tel. (2) 9227-0000; fax (2) 9227-0885; e-mail info@asx.com.au; internet www.asx. com; f. 1987 by merger of the stock exchanges in Sydney, Adelaide, Brisbane, Hobart, Melbourne and Perth, to replace the fmr Australian Associated Stock Exchanges; demutualized and listed Oct. 1998; Chair. MAURICE NEWMAN; Man. Dir and CEO RICHARD HUMPHRY.

Supervisory Body

Australian Securities and Investments Commission: GPOB 4866, Sydney, NSW 1042; tel. (2) 9911-2000; fax (2) 9911-2030; e-mail infoline@asic.gov.au; internet www.asic.gov.au; f. 1990; corporations and financial products regulator; Chair. ALAN CAMERON.

PRINCIPAL INSURANCE COMPANIES

Allianz Australia Ltd: 2 Market St, Sydney, NSW 2000; tel. (2) 9390-6222; fax (2) 9390-6425; internet www.allianz.com.au; f. 1914; workers' compensation; fire, general accident, motor and marine; Chair. J. S. CURTIS; Man. Dir T. TOWELL.

AMP Ltd: AMP Bldg, 33 Alfred St, Sydney, NSW 2000; tel. (2) 9257-5000; fax (2) 9257-7886; internet www.amplimited.com.au; f. 1849; fmrly Australian Mutual Provident Society; life insurance; Chair. STAN WALLIS; Man. Dir PAUL BATCHELOR.

AMP General Insurance Ltd: 10 Loftus St, Sydney Cove, NSW 2000; tel. (2) 9257-2500; fax (2) 9257-2199; internet www.amp.com.au; f. 1958; Chair. GREG COX; Man. Dir GAVIN PEACE.

Australian Guarantee Corpn Ltd: 130 Phillip St, Sydney, NSW 2000; tel. (2) 9234-1122; fax (2) 9234-1225; f. 1925; Chair. J. A. UHRIG; Man. Dir R. THOMAS.

Australian Unity General Insurance Ltd: 114 Albert Rd, South Melbourne, Vic 3205; tel. (3) 9697-0219; fax (3) 9690-5556; e-mail webmaster@austunity.com.au; internet www.austunity.com.au; f. 1948; Chair. LEON HICKEY; Chief Exec. M. W. SIBREE.

Catholic Church Insurances Ltd: 324 St Kilda Rd, Melbourne, Vic 3004; tel. (3) 9934-3000; fax (3) 9934-3460; f. 1911; Chair. Most Rev. KEVIN MANNING, Bishop of Parramatta; Gen. Man. PETER RUSH.

CGU Insurance Ltd: CGU Centre, 485 La Trobe St, Melbourne, Vic 3000; tel. (3) 9601-8222; fax (3) 9601-8366; f. 1960; fire, accident, marine; Chair. HUGH FLETCHER; Man. Dir I. M. BALFE.

Colonial Ltd: 330 Collins St, Melbourne, Vic 3000; tel. (3) 9200-6111; fax (3) 9200-6294; internet www.colonial.com.au; f. 1873; Chair. D. S. ADAM; Group Man. Dir and CEO PETER SMEDLEY; group merged with Commonwealth Bank of Australia in 2000.

The Copenhagen Reinsurance Co Ltd: 60 Margaret St, Sydney, NSW 2000; tel. (2) 9247-7266; fax (2) 9235-3320; internet www .copre.com; reinsurance; Gen. Man. ANDREW ALLISON.

FAI Insurances Ltd: FAI Insurance Group, 333 Kent St, Sydney, NSW 1026; tel. (2) 9274-9000; fax (2) 9274-9000; internet www.fai .com.au; f. 1953; Chair. JOHN LANDERER; CEO RODNEY ADLER.

Fortis Australia Ltd: 464 St Kilda Rd, Melbourne, Vic 3004; tel. (3) 9869-0300; fax (3) 9820-8537; CEO R. B. WILLING..

General and Cologne Reinsurance Australasia Ltd: Level 13, 225 George St, Sydney, NSW 2000; tel. (2) 9336-8100; fax (2) 9251-1665; f. 1961; reinsurance, fire, accident, marine; Chair. F. A. McDONALD; Man. Dir G. C. BARNUM.

GIO Australia Holdings Ltd: Level 39, Governor Phillip Tower, 1 Farrer Place, Sydney, NSW 2000; tel. (2) 9255-8090; fax (2) 9251-2079; e-mail emailus@gio.com.au; internet www.gio.com.au; f. 1926; CEO PETER CORRIGAN.

Guild Insurance Ltd: Guild House, 40 Burwood Rd, Hawthorn, Vic 3122; tel. (3) 9810-9820; fax (3) 9819-5670; f. 1963; Man. Dir W. K. BASTIAN.

HIH Insurance Ltd: AMP Centre, 50 Bridge St, Sydney, NSW 2000; tel. (2) 9650-2000; fax (2) 9650-2030; internet www.hih.com.au; f. 1968; Chair. G. A. COHEN; CEO R. R. WILLIAMS.

Lumley General Insurance Ltd: Lumley House, 309 Kent St, Sydney, NSW 1230; tel. (2) 9248-1111; fax (2) 9248-1122; e-mail general@lumley.com.au; Man. Dir D. M. MATCHAM.

Mercantile Mutual Holdings Ltd: 347 Kent St, Sydney, NSW; tel. (2) 9234-8111; fax (2) 9299-3979; internet www.mercantile mutual.com.au; f. 1878; Chair. A. R. BERG; Man. Dir R. J. ATFIELD.

The National Mutual Life Association of Australasia Ltd: 447 Collins St, Melbourne, Vic 3000; tel. (3) 9618-4920; fax (3) 9616-3445; e-mail investor.relations@axa.com.au; internet www.axa .com.au; f. 1869; life insurance, superannuation, income protection; Chair. R. H. ALLERT; Group CEO A. L. OWEN.

NRMA Insurance Ltd: 151 Clarence St, Sydney, NSW 2000; tel. (2) 9292-9222; fax (2) 9292-8472; f. 1926; CEO MALCOLM JONES.

NZI Insurance Australia Ltd: 9th Floor, 10 Spring St, Sydney, NSW 2000; tel. (2) 9551-5000; fax (2) 9551-5865; Man. Dir H. D. SMITH.

QBE Insurance Group Ltd: 82 Pitt St, Sydney, NSW 2000; tel. (2) 9375-4444; fax (2) 9235-3166; internet www.qbe.com; f. 1886; general insurance; Chair. E. J. CLONEY; Man. Dir F. M. O'HALLORAN.

RAC Insurance Pty Ltd: 228 Adelaide Terrace, Perth, WA 6000; tel. (8) 9421-4444; fax (8) 9421-4593; f. 1947; Gen. Man. TONY CARTER.

RACQ Insurance: POB 4, Springwood, Qld 4127; tel. (7) 3361-2444; fax (7) 3361-2199; e-mail inorris@gio.com.au; internet www.racqinsurance.com.au; f. 1995; CEO I. W. NORRIS.

RACV: 550 Princes Highway, Noble Park, Vic 3174; tel. (3) 9790-2211; fax (3) 9790-3091.

RSA Insurance Australia Ltd: 465 Victoria Ave, Chatswood, NSW 2067; tel. (2) 9978-9000; fax (2) 9978-9807; fire, accident and marine insurance; Gen. Man. E. KULK.

Suncorp Metway: 36 Wickham Tce, Brisbane, Queensland 4001; tel. (7) 3835-5355; fax (7) 3362-2890; internet www.suncorpmetway .com.au; f. c. 1916; Chair. JOHN LAMBLE; CEO STEVE JONES.

Swiss Re Australia Ltd: 31 Queen St, Melbourne, Vic 3000; tel. (3) 9616-9200; fax (3) 9621-2446; f. 1962; fmrly Australian Reinsurance Co Ltd; reinsurance; Chair. R. H. SYME; Man. Dir R. G. WATTS.

Transport Industries Insurance Co Ltd: 310 Queen St, Melbourne, Vic 3000; tel. (3) 9623-3355; fax (3) 9623-2624; f. 1960; Chair. R. H. Y. SYME; Man. Dir R. G. WATTS.

Wesfarmers Federation Insurance Ltd: 184 Railway Parade, Bassendean, WA 6054; tel. (8) 9273-5333; fax (8) 9273-5290; e-mail mel.rom@wfi.wesfarmers.com.au; internet www.wfi.com.au; Gen. Man. R. J. BUCKLEY.

Westpac Life Ltd: 35 Pitt St, Sydney, NSW 2000; tel. (2) 9220-4768; f. 1986; CEO DAVID WHITE.

World Marine & General Insurances Ltd: 600 Bourke St, Melbourne, Vic 3000; tel. (3) 9609-3333; fax (3) 9609-3634; f. 1961; Chair. G. W. MCGREGOR; Man. Dir A. E. REYNOLDS.

Zurich Financial Services Australia Ltd: 5 Blue St, North Sydney, NSW 2060; tel. (2) 9391-1111; fax (2) 9922-4630; CEO MALCOLM M. JONES.

Insurance Associations

Australian Insurance Association: GPOB 369, Canberra, ACT 2601; tel. (2) 6274-0609; fax (2) 6274-0666; f. 1968; Pres. RAYMOND JONES; Exec. Sec. P. M. MURPHY.

Australian Insurance Institute: Level 17, 31 Queen St, Melbourne, Vic 3000; tel. (3) 9629-4021; fax (3) 9629-4024; e-mail ceo@aii.com.au; internet www.aii.com.au; f. 1919; Pres. DAVID SANDOE; CEO JOAN FITZPATRICK; 11,984 mems.

Insurance Council of Australia Ltd: Level 3, 56 Pitt St, Sydney, NSW 2000; tel. (2) 9253-5100; fax (2) 9253-5111; internet www.ica .com.au; f. 1975; CEO ALAN MASON.

Investment and Financial Services Ltd (IFSA): Level 24, 44 Market St, Sydney, NSW 2000; tel. (2) 9299-3022; fax (2) 9299-3198; e-mail ifsa@ifsa.com.au; f. 1996; fmrly Life, Investment and Superannuation Asscn of Australia Inc; Chair. IAN MARTIN; CEO LYNN RALPH.

Trade and Industry

CHAMBERS OF COMMERCE

International Chamber of Commerce: POB E118, Kingston, Canberra, ACT 2604; tel. (2) 6295-1961; fax (2) 6295-0170; f. 1927; 65 mems; Chair. C. S. CULLEN; Sec.-Gen. H. C. GRANT.

Australian Chamber of Commerce and Industry (ACCI): POB E14, Kingston, ACT 2604; tel. (2) 6273-2311; fax (2) 6273-3286; e-mail acci@acci.asn.au; internet www.acci.asn.au; Pres. Dr JOHN KENIRY; CEO MARK PATERSON.

Chamber of Commerce and Industry of Western Australia (CCIWA): POB 6209, East Perth, WA 6892; tel. (8) 9365-7555; fax (8) 9365-7616; e-mail whitaker@cciwa.com; internet www.cciwa .com.au; f. 1890; 6,000 mems; Chief Exec. LYNDON ROWE; Pres. TONY HOWARTH.

Queensland Chamber of Commerce and Industry: Industry House, 375 Wickham Terrace, Brisbane, Qld 4000; tel. (7) 3842-2244; fax (7) 3832-3195; e-mail qcci@qcci.com.au; internet www.qcci.com.au; f. 1868; operates World Trade Centre, Brisbane; 3,800 mems; CEO CLIVE BUBB.

South Australian Employers' Chamber of Commerce and Industry Inc: Enterprise House, 136 Greenhill Road, Unley, SA 5061; tel. (8) 8300-0000; fax (8) 8300-0001; e-mail enquiries@ business-sa.com; internet www.business-sa.com; f. 1839; 4,700 mems; CEO P. VAUGHAN.

State Chamber of Commerce (New South Wales): Level 12, 83 Clarence St, GPO 4280, Sydney, NSW 2001; tel. (2) 9350-8100; fax (2) 9350-8199; operates World Trade Centre, Sydney; Deputy Gen. Man. DIANE HACKING.

Tasmanian Chamber of Commerce and Industry: GPOB 793H, Hobart, Tas 7001; tel. (3) 6234-5933; fax (3) 6231-1278; CEO TIM ABEY.

Victorian Employers' Chamber of Commerce and Industry: Employers' House, 50 Burwood Rd, Hawthorn, Vic 3122; tel. (3) 9251-4333; fax (3) 9819-3826; e-mail itd@vecci.org.au; f. 1885; CEO N. FEELY.

AGRICULTURAL, INDUSTRIAL AND TRADE ASSOCIATIONS

The Agriculture and Resource Management Council of Australia and New Zealand: Dept of Agriculture, Fisheries and Forestry—Australia, Barton, Canberra, ACT 2600; tel. (2) 6272-5216; fax (2) 6272-4772; e-mail armcanz.contact@affa.gov.au; internet www.affa.gov.au/armcanz; f. 1992 to develop integrated and sustainable agricultural and land and water management policies, strategies and practices; mems comprising the Commonwealth/state/territory and New Zealand ministers responsible for agriculture, soil conservation, water resources and rural adjustment matters; Sec. J. W. GRAHAM.

 Standing Committee on Agriculture and Resource Management: f. 1992; an advisory body to the Agriculture and Resource Management Council of Australia and New Zealand; comprises the heads of Commonwealth/state/territory and New Zealand agencies responsible for agriculture, soil conservation and water resources and representatives from CSIRO, Bureau of Meteorology and rural adjustment authorities; Sec. J. W. GRAHAM.

Australian Business Ltd: Private Bag 938, North Sydney, NSW 2059; tel. (2) 9927-7500; fax (2) 9923-1166; e-mail chamber@abol.net; internet www.australianbusiness.com.au; f. 1885; fmrly Chamber of Manufactures of NSW; CEO P. M. HOLT.

Australian Dairy Corporation: Locked Bag 104, Flinders Lane, Vic 8009; tel. (3) 9694-3777; fax (3) 9694-3888; internet www .dairycorp.com.au; provides services to industry in areas of trade policy and market access, domestic and export market devt, and export agency; Chair. DES NICHOLL; Man. Dir ALEXANDER MURDOCH.

Australian Manufacturers' Export Council: POB E14, Queen Victoria Terrace, Canberra, ACT 2600; tel. (2) 6273-2311; fax (2) 6273-3196; f. 1955; Exec. Dir G. CHALKER.

Australian Wool Services Ltd: Wool House, 369 Royal Parade, Parkville, Vic 3052; tel. (3) 9341-9111; fax (3) 9341-9273; internet www.wool.com.au; f. 2001 following the privatization of the Australian Wool Research and Promotion Organisation; operates two subsidiaries, Australian Wool Innovation which manages wool levy funds and invests in research and development, and The Woolmark Company responsible for commercial development; Chair. RODNEY PRICE.

AWB Ltd: Ceres House, 528 Lonsdale St, Melbourne, Vic 3000; tel. (3) 9209-2000; fax (3) 9670-2782; e-mail awb@awb.com.au; internet www.awb.com.au; f. 1939; fmrly Australian Wheat Board; national and international marketing of grain, financing and marketing of wheat and other grains for growers; 12 mems; Chair. TREVOR FLUGGE; CEO ANDREW LINDBERG.

Business Council of Australia: 15th Floor, 10 Queens Rd, Melbourne, Vic 3004; tel. (3) 9274-7777; fax (3) 9274-7744; public policy research and advocacy; governing council comprises chief execs of Australia's major cos; Pres. STAN WALLIS; Exec. Dir DAVID BUCKINGHAM.

Cotton Australia: Level 2, 490 Crown St, Surry Hills, NSW 2010; tel. (2) 9360-8500; fax (2) 9360-8555; e-mail talktous@ cottonaustralia.com.au; internet www.cottonaustralia.com.au; Chair. CHARLES WILSON.

Meat and Livestock Australia: 165 Walker St, North Sydney, NSW 2060; tel. 1800-023-100; fax (2) 9463-9230; internet www.mla .com.au; producer-owned co; represents, promotes, protects and furthers interests of industry in both the marketing of meat and livestock and devt of industry-based research and devt activities; Chair. DAVID CROMBIE.

National Farmers' Federation: POB E10, Kingston, ACT 2604; tel. (2) 6273-3855; fax (2) 6273-2331; e-mail nff@nff.org.au; internet www.nff.org.au; Pres. IAN DONGES; Exec. Dir ANNA CRONIN.

Trade Policy Advisory Council (TPAC): c/o Dept of Foreign Affairs and Trade, R. G. Casey Bldg, John McEwen Cres., Barton, ACT 2600; tel. (2) 6262-2125; fax (2) 6261-2465; f. 1958; advises the Minister for Trade on policy issues; Chair. GEOFF ALLEN.

Wool Council Australia: POB E10, Kingston, Canberra, ACT 2604; tel. (2) 6273-2531; fax (2) 6273-1120; e-mail woolcouncil @nff.org.au; internet www.farmwide.com.au/nff/wool/wool/htm;

comprises 20 mems; represents wool-growers in dealings with the Federal Govt and industry; Pres. DAVID WOLFENDEN.

EMPLOYERS' ORGANIZATIONS

Australian Co-operative Foods Ltd: Level 12, 168 Walker St, North Sydney, NSW 2060; tel. (2) 9903-5222; fax (2) 9957-3530; e-mail exports@dairyfarmers.com.au; f. 1900; Man. Dir A. R. TOOTH.

Australian Industry Group: 51 Walker St, North Sydney, NSW 2060; tel. (2) 9466-5566; fax (2) 9466-5599; e-mail louisep@aignsw.aigroup.asn.au; internet www.aigroup.asn.au; f. 1998 through merger of MTIA and ACM; 11,500 mems; Nat. Pres. G. J. ASHTON; CEO ROBERT N. HERBERT; 11,500 mems.

National Meat Association: 25–27 Albany St, Crows Nest, NSW 2065; POB 1208, Crows Nest, NSW 1585; tel. (2) 9906-7767; fax (2) 9906-8022; e-mail meat@magna.com.au; internet www.nmaa.org.au; f. 1928; Pres. GARY HARDWICK; CEO G. JUREIDINI.

NSW Farmers' Association: GPOB 1068, Sydney, NSW 1041; tel. (2) 9251-1700; fax (2) 9231-5249; e-mail emailus@nswfarmers.org.au; internet www.nswfarmers.org.au; f. 1978; CEO JONATHAN MCKEOWN.

UTILITIES

Australian Gas Association (AGA): GPOB 323, Canberra, ACT 2601; tel. (2) 6272-1555; fax (2) 6272-1566; e-mail canberra@gas.asn.au; internet www.gas.asn.au; 1,000 mems, incl. more than 300 corporate mems; Chair. PHIL HARVEY; Chief Exec. BILL NAGLE.

Australian Institute of Energy: POB 268, Toukley, NSW 2263; tel. 1800-629-945; fax (2) 4393-1114; e-mail aie@tpgi.com.au; internet www.aie.org.au.

Electricity Supply Association of Australia: POB A2492, Sydney South, NSW 1235; tel. (2) 9233-7222; fax (2) 9233-7244; internet www.esaa.com.au; CEO KEITH ORCHISON.

Electricity Companies

Actew AGL: GPOB 366, Canberra City, ACT 2601; tel. (2) 6248-3111; e-mail webmaster@actewagl.com.au; internet www.actewagl.com.au; f. 2000 by amalgamation of ACTEW Corpn Ltd and AGL; supplier of electricity, gas, water and wastewater services.

Delta Electricity: POB Q863, QVB, NSW 1230; tel. (2) 9285-2700; fax (2) 9285-2777; internet www.de.com.au; f. 1996; Chief Exec. JIM HENNESS.

ENERGEX: GPOB 1461, Brisbane, Qld 4001; tel. (7) 3407-4000; fax (7) 3407-4609; e-mail enquiries@energex.com.au; internet www.energex.com.au; largest electricity distribution corpn in Queensland; CEO GREG MADDOCK.

EnergyAustralia: 145 Newcastle Rd, Wallsend, NSW 2287; tel. (2) 4951-9346; fax (2) 4951-9351; e-mail energy@energy.com.au; internet www.energy.com.au; supplies customers in NSW; CEO PETER HEADLEY; Man. Dir PAUL BROAD.

Ergon Energy: POB 107, Albert St, Brisbane, Qld 4002; tel. (7) 3228-8222; fax (7) 3228-8118; internet www.ergon.com.au; national retailer of electricity.

Generation Victoria Corpn—Ecogen Energy: 5th Floor, 416 Collins St, Melbourne, Vic 3000; tel. (3) 9679-4600; fax (3) 9679-4619; internet www.ecogen-energy.com.au/; f. 1994; CEO GERRY BASTEN.

Great Southern Energy: Level 1, Citilink Plaza, Morriset St, Queanbeyan, NSW 2620; tel. (2) 6214-9600; fax (2) 6214-9860; e-mail mail@gsenergy.com.au; internet www.gsenergy.com.au; state-owned electricity and gas distributor; Chair. BRUCE RODELY.

Powercor Australia Ltd: 40 Market St, Melbourne, Vic 3000; tel. (3) 9683-4444; fax (3) 9683-4499; e-mail info@powercor.com.au; internet www.powercor.com.au; Chair JACK KELLY; CEO PAUL LORENZINI.

Snowy Mountains Hydro-electric Authority: POB 332, Cooma, NSW 2630; tel. (2) 6452-1777; fax (2) 6452-3794; e-mail info@snowyhydro.com.au; internet www.snowyhydro.com.au.

United Energy Ltd: Level 13, 101 Collins St, Melbourne, Vic 3000; fax (3) 9222-8588; e-mail info@mail.ue.com.au; internet www.ue.com.au; f. 1994, following division of State Electricity Commission of Victoria; transferred to private sector; distributor of electricity and gas.

Western Power Corpn: GPOB L921, Perth, WA 6842; tel. (8) 9326-4911; fax (8) 9326-4595; e-mail info@wpcorp.com.au; internet www.wpcorp.com.au; f. 1995; principal supplier of electricity in WA; Chair. HECTOR STEBBINS (acting); Man. Dir DAVID EISZELE.

Gas Companies

AlintaGas: GPOB W2030, Perth, WA 6846; e-mail david.sweet@alintagas.com.au; internet www.alintagas.com.au; f. 1995; CEO PHIL HARVEY.

Allgas Energy Ltd: 150 Charlotte St, Brisbane, Qld 4000; tel. (7) 3404-1822; fax (7) 3404-1821; e-mail ael@allgas.com.au; internet www.allgas.com.au; f. 1885; Gen. Man. G. J. DRUMMOND.

Australian Gas Light Co: AGL Centre, Corner Pacific Highway and Walker St, North Sydney, NSW 2060; tel. (2) 9922-0101; fax (2) 9957-3671; e-mail aglmail@agl.com.au; internet www.agl.com.au; f. 1837; Chair. M. J. PHILLIPS; Man. Dir. L. F. BLEASEL.

Envestra: 10th Floor, 81 Flinders St, Adelaide, SA 5000; tel. (8) 8227-1500; fax (8) 8277-1511; e-mail des.petherick@envestra.com.au; internet www.envestra.com.au; f. 1997 by merger of South Australian Gas Co, Gas Corpn of Queensland and Centre Gas Pty Ltd; Chair. R. W. PIPER; Man. Dir O. G. CLARK.

Epic Energy: GPOB 657, Brisbane, Qld 4001; tel. (7) 3218-1600; fax (7) 3218-1650; internet www.epicenergy.com.au; Australia's largest gas transmission co; privately owned.

TRADE UNIONS

Australian Council of Trade Unions (ACTU): North Wing, Trades Hall, 54 Victoria St, Carlton South, Vic 3053; tel. (3) 9663-5266; fax (3) 9663-4051; e-mail mailbox@actu.asn.au; internet www.worksite.actu.asn.au; f. 1927; br. in each state, generally known as a Trades and Labour Council; 51 affiliated trade unions; Pres. SHARAN BURROW; Sec. GREGORY COMBET.

Principal Affiliated Unions

Association of Professional Engineers, Scientists & Managers, Australia (APESMA): POB 1272L, Melbourne, Vic 3001; tel. (3) 9695-8800; fax (3) 9696-9312; e-mail info@apesma.asn.au; internet www.apesma.asn.au; Pres. ROB J. ALLEN; Sec. GREG SUTHERLAND; 24,000 mems.

Australasian Meat Industry Employees' Union (AMIEU): 377 Sussex St, Sydney, NSW 2000; tel. (2) 9264-2279; fax (2) 9261-1970; e-mail amieu_fed@bigpond.com; Fed. Pres. JOHN PYSING; Fed. Sec. T. R. HANNAN; 24,400 mems.

Australian Education Union: POB 1158, South Melbourne, Vic 3205; tel. (3) 9254-1800; fax (3) 9254-1805; e-mail aeu@edunions.labor.net.au; internet www.edunions.labor.net.au/aeu/; f. 1984; Fed. Pres. DENIS FITZGERALD; Fed. Sec. ROBERT DURBRIDGE; 151,000 mems.

Australian Liquor, Hospitality and Miscellaneous Workers Union (LHMU): Locked Bag 9, Haymarket, NSW 1240; tel. (2) 9281-9511; fax (2) 9281-4480; e-mail lhmu@lhmu.org.au; internet www.lhmu.org.au; f. 1992; Nat. Pres. HELEN CREED; Nat. Sec. JEFF LAWRENCE; 150,000 mems.

Australian Manufacturing Workers' Union/AMWU: POB 160, Granville, NSW 2142; tel. (2) 9897-9133; fax (2) 9897-9274; e-mail amwu2@amwu.asn.au; internet www.amwu.asn.au; Nat. Pres. JULIUS ROE; Nat. Sec. DOUG CAMERON; 170,000 mems.

Australian Services Union (ASU): Ground Floor, 116 Queensberry St, Carlton South, Vic 3053; tel. (3) 9342-1400; fax (3) 9342-1499; e-mail asunatm@asu.asn.au; internet www.asu.asn.au; f. 1885 amalgamated, in present form in 1993; Nat. Sec. PAUL SLAPE; 165,000 mems.

Australian Workers' Union (AWU): Suite 15, 245 Chalmers St, Redfern, NSW 2016; tel. (2) 9690-1022; fax (2) 9690-1020; e-mail nat.office@awu.net.au; internet www.awu.net.au; f. 1886; Nat. Pres. GRAHAM ROBERTS; Nat. Sec. TERRY MUSCAT; 160,000 mems.

Communications, Electrical, Electronic, Energy, Information, Postal, Plumbing and Allied Services Union of Australia (CEPU): POB 812, Rockdale, NSW 2216; tel. (2) 9597-4499; fax (2) 9597-6354; e-mail edno@cepu.mpx.com.au; internet www.cepu.asn.au; Nat. Sec. PETER TIGHE; 180,000 mems.

Community and Public Sector Union (CPSU): Level 5, 191–199 Thomas St, Haymarket, NSW 2000; tel. (2) 9334-9200; fax (2) 9334-9250; e-mail cpsu@cpsu.org; internet www.cpsu.org; Nat. Pres. MATTHEW REYNOLDS; Nat. Sec. WENDY CAIRD; 200,000 mems.

Construction, Forestry, Mining and Energy Union (CFMEU): Box Q235, Queen Victoria Bldg PO, Sydney, NSW 2000; tel. (2) 9267-3393; fax (2) 9267-2460; internet www.cfmeu.asn.au; f. 1992 by amalgamation; Pres. T. SMITH; Sec. J. MAITLAND; 120,000 mems.

Finance Sector Union of Australia (FSU): 341 Queen St, Melbourne, Vic 3000; tel. (3) 9261-5300; fax (3) 9670-2940; e-mail fsuinfo@fsunion.org.au; internet www.fsunion.org.au; f. 1991; Nat. Pres. JOY MCSHANE; Nat. Sec. TONY BECK; 85,000 mems.

Health Services Union of Australia (HSUA): POB 560, Flemington, Vic 3031; tel. (3) 9376-8242; fax (3) 9376-8243; e-mail union@hsua.asn.au; internet www.hsua.asn.au; Nat. Pres. MICHAEL WILLIAMSON; Nat. Sec. ROBERT ELLIOTT; 90,000 mems.

Independent Education Union of Australia (IEU): POB 1301, South Melbourne, Vic 3205; tel. (3) 9254-1830; fax (3) 9254-1835; e-mail ieu@ieu.org.au; internet www.ieu.org.au; Fed. Sec. LYNNE ROLLEY; Fed. Pres. RICHARD SHEARMAN; 45,000 mems.

Maritime Union of Australia (MUA): 365 Sussex St, Sydney, NSW 2000; tel. (2) 9267-9134; fax (2) 9261-3481; e-mail muano@mua.org.au; internet www.mua.tcp.net.au; f. 1993; Nat. Sec. PADDY CRUMLIN; 10,619 mems.

Media, Entertainment & Arts Alliance (MEAA): POB 723, Strawberry Hills, NSW 2012; tel. (2) 9333-0999; fax (2) 9333-0933; e-mail mail@meaa.aust.com; internet www.alliance.aust.com; Fed. Sec. CHRISTOPHER WARREN; 30,000 mems.

National Union of Workers (NUW): POB 343, North Melbourne, Vic 3051; tel. (3) 9287-1850; fax (3) 9287-1818; e-mail nuwnat@nuw.org.au; internet www.nuw.org.au; Gen. Sec. GREG SWORD; Gen. Pres. PAUL STAFFORD; 100,000 mems.

Rail, Tram and Bus Union (RTBU): 83–89 Renwick St, Redfern, NSW 2016; tel. (2) 9310-3966; fax (2) 9319-2096; e-mail publictu@magna.com.au; internet www.vtown.com.au/vunions.rtbu; Nat. Pres. R. PLAIN; Nat. Sec. R. G. JOWETT; 35,000 mems.

Shop, Distributive & Allied Employees Association (SDA): 5th Floor, 53 Queen St, Melbourne, Vic 3000; tel. (3) 9629-2299; fax (3) 9629-2646; e-mail sdanat@c031.aone.net.au; internet www.sda.org.au; f. 1908; Nat. Pres. DON FARRELL; Nat. Sec. JOE DE BRUYN; 230,000 mems.

Textile, Clothing and Footwear Union of Australia (TCFUA): Ground Floor, 28 Anglo Rd, Campsie, NSW 2194; tel. (2) 9789-4188; fax (2) 9789-6510; e-mail tcfua@tcfua.org.au; f. 1919; Pres. BARRY TUBNER; 21,354 mems.

Transport Workers' Union of Australia (TWU): Level 3, 18–20 Lincoln Sq., North Carlton, Vic 3053; tel. (3) 9347-0099; fax (3) 9347-2502; e-mail twu@twu.com.au; internet www.twu-federal.asn.au; Fed. Pres. HUGHIE WILLIAMS; Fed. Sec. JOHN ALLAN; 71,000 mems.

United Firefighters' Union of Australia (UFU of A): POB 289, Torrensville, SA 5031; tel. (8) 8352-7211; fax (8) 8234-1031; e-mail ufua@senet.com.au; Nat. Pres. SIMON FLYNN; Nat. Sec. PAUL CAICA; 11,000 mems.

Transport

Australian Transport Council: POB 594, Canberra, ACT 2601; tel. (2) 6274-7851; fax (2) 6274-7703; internet www.atcouncil.gov.au; f. 1993; mems include: Federal Minister for Transport and Regional Services, State, Territory and New Zealand Ministers responsible for transport, roads and marine and ports; initiates discussion, and reports as necessary, on any matter relating to better co-ordination of transport development, while encouraging modernization and innovation; promotes research; Sec. D. JONES.

State Transit Authority of New South Wales: 100 Miller St, North Sydney, NSW 2060; tel. (2) 9245-5777; fax (2) 9245-5710; internet www.sta.nsw.gov.au; operates government buses and ferries in Sydney and Newcastle metropolitan areas; Chair. DAVID HERLIHY; CEO JOHN STOTT.

TransAdelaide (South Australia): GPOB 2351, Adelaide, SA 5001; tel. (8) 8218-2200; fax (8) 8218-4399; e-mail info@transadelaide.sa.gov.au; internet www.transadelaide.com.au; f. 1994; fmrly State Transport Authority; operates metropolitan train, bus, tram and Busway services; Gen. Man. SUE FILBY.

RAILWAYS

In 1999 there were 39,930 km of railways in Australia (including tram and light rail track).

National Rail Corporation Ltd: 85 George St, Parramatta, NSW 2150; tel. (2) 9685-2555; fax (2) 9687-1808; e-mail information@nrc.com.au; internet www.nationalrail.com.au; freight; Chair. P. YOUNG; Man. Dir V. J. GRAHAM.

Public Transport Corporation (Victoria): Level 15, 589 Collins St, Melbourne, Vic 3000; tel. (3) 9619-4222; fax (3) 9619-4911; e-mail j.barry@ptc.vic.gov.au; f. 1989; Exec. Dir JOHN R. BARRY.

QR (Queensland Rail): POB 1429, Brisbane, Qld 4001; tel. (7) 3235-2222; fax (7) 3235-1799; Chief Exec. VINCE O'ROURKE.

State Rail Authority of New South Wales: POB K349, Haymarket, NSW 1238; tel. (2) 9379-3000; fax (2) 9379-2090; internet www.staterail.nsw.gov.au; f. 1980; responsible for passenger rail and associated coach services in NSW; Chief Exec. SIMON LANE.

Western Australian Government Railways (Westrail): Westrail Centre, POB S1422, Perth 6845, WA; tel. (8) 9326-2222; fax (8) 9326-2589; internet www.westrail.wa.gov.au; statutory authority competing in the freight, passenger and related transport markets in southern WA; operates 5,369 main line route-km of track; Commr WAYNE JAMES (acting).

ROADS

In June 2000 there were 805,835 km of roads open for general traffic. In 1996 this included 1,000 km of freeways, a further 103 km of toll roads, 45,889 km of highways, 77,045km of arterial and major roads and 30,596 of secondary tourist and other roads. Local roads in urban areas account for 93,677 km of the network and those in rural localities for 537,278 km.

Austroads Inc: POB K659, Haymarket, NSW 2000; tel. (2) 9264-7088; fax (2) 9264-1657; e-mail austroads@austroads.com.au; internet www.austroads.com.au; f. 1989; asscn of road transport and traffic authorities.

SHIPPING

In December 1998 the Australian merchant fleet comprised 617 vessels, with a total displacement of 2,188,146 grt.

Adsteam Marine Ltd: Level 22, 6 O'Connell St, Sydney, NSW 2000; tel. (2) 9232-3955; fax (2) 9232-3988; e-mail info@adsteam.com.au; f. 1875; fmrly Adelaide Steamship Co; Man. Dir DAVID RYAN; Chief Exec. CLAY FREDERICK.

ANL Ltd (Australian National Line): POB 2238T, Melbourne, Vic 3001; tel. (3) 9257-0555; fax (3) 9257-0619; e-mail anl@anl.com.au; f. 1956; shipping agents; coastal and overseas container shipping and coastal bulk shipping; container management services; overseas container services to Hong Kong, Taiwan, the Philippines, Korea, Singapore, Malaysia, Thailand, Indonesia and Japan; extensive transhipment services; Chair. E. G. ANSON; CEO R. B. PERKINS.

BHP Transport Pty Ltd: 27th Level, 600 Bourke St, POB 86A, Melbourne, Vic 3000; tel. (3) 9609-3333; fax (3) 9609-2400; Chair. JEREMY ELLIS; Man. Dir JOHN B. PRESCOTT.

William Holyman and Sons Pty Ltd: No. 3 Berth, Bell Bay, Tas 7253; tel. (3) 6382-2383; fax (3) 6382-3391; coastal services; Chair. R. J. HOY.

Howard Smith Ltd: POB N364, Grosvenor Place, Sydney, NSW 2000; tel. (2) 9230-1777; fax (2) 9251-1190; e-mail info@hst.com.au; internet www.howardsmith.com.au; harbour towage and other services; Chair. FRANCIS JOHN CONROY; CEO KENNETH JOHN MOSS.

CIVIL AVIATION

Ansett Australia (Ansett Australia Holdings Ltd): 501 Swanston St, Melbourne, Vic 3000; tel. (3) 9623-3333; e-mail tracy-Barrie@ansett.com.au; internet www.ansett.com.au; f. 1936; domestic and international passenger and cargo services; Exec. Chair. CRAIG WALLACE (acting).

Eastern Australia Airlines: POB 538, Mascot, Sydney, NSW 2020; tel. (2) 9691-2333; fax (2) 9693-2715; internet www.qantas.com.au; subsidiary of Qantas; domestic flights; Gen. Man. BEVAN J. COOTE.

Impulse Airlines: Eleventh St, Sydney Kingsford-Smith Airport, Mascot, NSW 2020; tel. (2) 9317-5400; fax (2) 9317-3440; e-mail info@ImpulseAirlines.com.au; internet www.impulseairlines.com.au; f. 1992; domestic services; Chief Exec./Chair. GERRY MCGOWAN; Exec. Dir SUE MCGOWAN.

National Jet Systems: Level 9, Southgate House, 435 King William St, Adelaide, SA 5000; tel. (8) 8304-5600; fax (8) 8304-5650; internet www.natjet.com.au; f. 1989; domestic services; Man. Dir DANIELA MARSILLI.

Qantas Airways Ltd: Qantas Centre, 203 Coward St, Mascot, NSW 2020; tel. (2) 9691-3636; fax (2) 9691-3339; internet www.qantas.com.au; f. 1920 as Queensland and Northern Territory Aerial Services; Australian Govt became sole owner in 1947; merged with Australian Airlines in Sept. 1992; British Airways purchased 25% in March 1993; remaining 75% transferred to private sector in 1995; services throughout Australia and to 36 countries, including destinations in Europe, Africa, the USA, Canada, South America, Asia, the Pacific and New Zealand; Chair. MARGARET JACKSON; CEO JAMES STRONG.

Spirit Airlines: Level 9, 580 St Kilda Rd, Melbourne, Vic 3004; fax (3) 9510-4095; e-mail info@spiritairlines.com.au; internet www.spiritairlines.com.au/; f. 1998; domestic services; CEO MIKE DIXON.

Sunstate Airlines: Lobby 3, Level 2, 153 Campbell St, Bowen Hills, Qld 4006; tel. (7) 3308-9022; fax (7) 3308-9088; e-mail akilroy@qantas.com.au; f. 1982; wholly owned by Qantas; operates passenger services within Queensland and to Newcastle (NSW) and Lord Howe Island; Gen. Man. ASHLEY KILROY.

Virgin Blue: Centenary Place, Level 7, 100 Wickham St, Brisbane, Qld; tel. (7) 3295-3000; e-mail customercare@virginblue.com.au; internet www.virginblue.com.au; domestic services; CEO BRETT GODFREY.

Tourism

The main attractions are the cosmopolitan cities, the Great Barrier Reef, the Blue Mountains, water sports and also winter sports in the Australian Alps, notably the Snowy Mountains. The town of Alice Springs, the Aboriginal culture and the sandstone monolith of Ayers Rock (Uluru) are among the attractions of the desert interior. Much of Australia's wildlife is unique to the country. Australia received 4,459,503 foreign visitors in 1999. The majority of visitors came from New Zealand, Japan, the United Kingdom and the USA. Receipts totalled \$A16,300m. in 1998. The 2000 Olympic Games were held in Sydney in September.

Australian Tourist Commission: GPOB 2721, Sydney, NSW 1006; Level 4, 80 William St, Woolloomooloo, Sydney, NSW 2011; tel. (2) 9360-1111; fax (2) 9331-6469; internet www.atc.net.au; f. 1967 for promotion of international inbound tourism; 13 offices overseas; Chair. NICK EVERS; Man. Dir JOHN MORSE.

AUSTRALIAN EXTERNAL TERRITORIES
CHRISTMAS ISLAND

Introduction

Christmas Island lies 360 km south of Java Head (Indonesia) in the Indian Ocean. The nearest point on the Australian coast is North West Cape, 1,408 km to the south-east. Christmas Island has no indigenous population. The population was 1,906 at the 1996 census (compared with 1,275 in 1991), comprising mainly ethnic Chinese (some 70%), but there were large minorities of Malays (about 10%) and Europeans (about 20%). A variety of languages are spoken, but English is the official language. The predominant religious affiliation is Buddhist (55% in 1991). The principal settlement and only anchorage is Flying Fish Cove.

Following annexation by the United Kingdom in 1888, Christmas Island was incorporated for administrative purposes with the Straits Settlements (now Singapore and part of Malaysia) in 1900. Japanese forces occupied the island from March 1942 until the end of the Second World War, and in 1946 Christmas Island became a dependency of Singapore. Administration was transferred to the United Kingdom on 1 January 1958, pending final transfer to Australia, effected on 1 October 1958. The Australian Government appointed Official Representatives to the Territory until 1968, when new legislation provided for an Administrator, appointed by the Governor-General. Responsibility for administration lies with the Minister for Regional Services, Territories and Local Government. In 1980 an Advisory Council was established for the Administrator to consult. In 1984 the Christmas Island Services Corporation was created to perform those functions which are normally the responsibility of municipal government. This body was placed under the direction of the Christmas Island Assembly, the first elections to which took place in September 1985. Nine members were elected for one-year terms. In November 1987 the Assembly was dissolved, and the Administrator empowered to perform its functions. The Corporation was superseded by the Christmas Island Shire Council in 1992.

In May 1994 an unofficial referendum on the island's status was held concurrently with local government elections. At the poll, sponsored by the Union of Christmas Island Workers, the islanders rejected an option to secede from Australia, but more than 85% of voters favoured increased local government control. The referendum was prompted, in part, by the Australian Government's plans to abolish the island's duty-free status (which had become a considerable source of revenue).

Since 1981 all residents of the island have been eligible to acquire Australian citizenship. In 1984 the Australian Government extended social security, health and education benefits to the island, and enfranchised Australian citizens resident there. Full income-tax liability was introduced in the late 1980s.

During the late 1990s an increasing number of illegal immigrants travelling to Australia landed on Christmas Island. In January 2001 Australian government officials denied claims by Christmas Islanders that some 86 illegal immigrants who had arrived at the island from the Middle East via Indonesia were being detained in inhumane conditions. Local people claimed that the detainees were sleeping on concrete floors and were being denied adequate food and medical care.

The economy has been based on the recovery of phosphates. During the year ending 30 June 1984 about 463,000 metric tons were exported to Australia, 332,000 tons to New Zealand and 341,000 tons to other countries. Reserves were estimated to be sufficient to enable production to be maintained until the mid-1990s. In November 1987 the Australian Government announced the closure of the phosphate mine, owing to industrial unrest, and mining activity ceased in December. In 1990, however, the Government allowed private operators to recommence phosphate extraction, subject to certain conditions such as the preservation of the rainforest. A total of 220,000 metric tons of phosphates were produced in 1995. In that year an estimated 100 people were employed in the phosphate industry (whose activities consisted largely of the removal of stockpiles). A new 21-year lease, drawn up by the Government and Phosphate Resources Ltd, took effect in February 1998. The agreement incorporated environmental safeguards and provided for a conservation levy, based on the tonnage of phosphate shipped, which was to finance a programme of rainforest rehabilitation.

Efforts have been made to develop the island's considerable potential for tourism. In 1989, in an attempt to protect the natural environment and many rare species of flora and fauna (including the Abbott's Booby and the Christmas frigate bird), the National Park was extended to cover some 70% of the island. A hotel and casino complex, covering 47 ha of land, was opened in November 1993. In 1994 revenue from the development totalled $A500m. A 50-room extension to the complex was constructed in 1995. In early 1997, however, fears for the nascent industry were expressed, following the decision by Ansett Australia to discontinue its twice-weekly air service to the island from September of that year. Despite the subsequent commencement of a weekly flight from Perth, Australia, operated by National Jet Systems, the complex was closed down in April 1998 and some 350 employees were made redundant. In July the resort's casino licence was cancelled and a liquidator was appointed to realize the complex's assets. The closure of the resort had serious economic and social repercussions for the island.

Proposals for the development of a communications satellite launching facility on the island were under consideration in 1998. An assessment of the environmental impact of the proposed scheme was scheduled for completion by 1999.

Between 1992 and 1999 the Australian Government invested an estimated $A110m. in the development of Christmas Island's infrastructure as part of the Christmas Island Rebuilding Programme. The main areas of expenditure under this programme have been a new hospital, the upgrading of ports facilities, school extensions, the construction of housing, power, water supply and sewerage, and the repair and construction of roads. In 2000 further improvements to marine facilities and water supply were to be carried out, in addition to the construction of new housing to relocate islanders away from a major rockfall risk area. The cost of the island's imports from Australia declined from $A15m. in 1997/98 to $A13m. in 1998/99 when the Territory's exports to that country earned $A9m. In 1998/99 imports from New Zealand cost $NZ9m. An estimated 7.5% of the island's population were unemployed in 1996.

Statistical Survey

AREA AND POPULATION

Area: 135 sq km (52 sq miles).

Population: 2,871 (males 1,918, females 953) at census of 30 June 1981; 1,275 at August 1991 census; 1,906 (males 1,023, females 883) at 1996 census. *Ethnic Groups* (1981): Chinese 1,587; Malay 693; European 336; Total (incl. others) 2,871. Source: mainly UN, *Demographic Yearbook*.

1998: 1,700 (estimate). Source: *The Commonwealth Yearbook*.

Density (1996): 14.1 per sq km.

Births and Deaths (1985): Registered live births 36 (birth rate 15.8 per 1,000); Registered deaths 2.

Labour Force (1996): 971 (employed 898, unemployed 73).

MINING

Natural Phosphates (official estimates, '000 metric tons): 285 in 1994; 220 in 1995.

FINANCE

Currency and Exchange Rates: Australian currency is used (see p. 521).

EXTERNAL TRADE

Principal Trading Partners (phosphate exports, '000 metric tons, year ending 30 June 1984): Australia 463; New Zealand 332; Total (incl. others) 1,136.

1998/99 ($A million): *Imports:* Australia 13. *Exports:* Australia 9. Source: Australian Bureau of Statistics, *Year Book Australia*.

1998/99 ($NZ million): *Imports:* New Zealand 9. Source: Statistics New Zealand, *New Zealand Official Yearbook*.

TRANSPORT

International Sea-borne Shipping (estimated freight traffic, '000 metric tons, 1990): Goods loaded 1,290; Goods unloaded 68. Source: UN, *Monthly Bulletin of Statistics.*

TOURISM

Visitor Arrivals and Departures by Air: 27,479 in 1995; 14,513 in 1996; 3,895 in 1997. Source: *Year Book Australia.*

COMMUNICATIONS MEDIA

Radio Receivers (1997): 1,000 in use.
Television Receivers (1997): 600 in use.

EDUCATION

Pre-primary (1992): 53 pupils.
Primary (1992): 253 pupils.
Secondary (1992): 53 pupils.
Source: *The Commonwealth Yearbook.*

Directory

The Government

The Administrator, appointed by the Governor-General of Australia and responsible to the Minister for Regional Services, Territories and Local Government, is the senior government representative on the island.

Administrator: WILLIAM TAYLOR.

Administration Headquarters: POB AAA, Christmas Island 6798, Indian Ocean; tel. (8) 9164-7901; fax (8) 9164-8524.

Shire of Christmas Island: George Fam Centre, POB 863, Christmas Island 6798, Indian Ocean; tel.(8) 9164-8300; fax (8) 9164-8304; e-mail soci@iocomm.com.au.

Judicial System

The judicial system comprises the Supreme Court, District Court, Magistrate's Court and Children's Court.

Supreme Court: c/o Govt Offices, Christmas Island 6798, Indian Ocean; tel. (8) 9164-7911; fax (8) 9164-8530; Judges (non-resident): ROBERT SHERATON FRENCH, MALCOLM CAMERON LEE.

Managing Registrar: JEFFERY LOW, Govt Offices, Christmas Island 6798, Indian Ocean; tel. (8) 9164-7911; fax (8) 9164-8530.

Religion

According to the census of 1991, of the 1,275 residents of Christmas Island, some 55% were Buddhists, 10% were Muslims, and 15% were Christians. Within the Christian churches, Christmas Island lies in the jurisdiction of both the Anglican and Roman Catholic Archbishops of Perth, in Western Australia.

The Press

The Islander: Shire of Christmas Island, George Fam Centre, POB 863, Christmas Island 6798, Indian Ocean; tel. (8) 9164-8300; fax (8) 9164-8304; newsletter; fortnightly; Editor TENG BOON EIANG.

Broadcasting and Communications

BROADCASTING

Radio

Christmas Island Community Radio Service: POB AAA, Christmas Island 6798, Indian Ocean; tel. (8) 9164-8316; fax (8) 9164-8315; f. 1967; operated by the Administration since 1991; daily broadcasting service by Radio VLU-2 on 1422 KHz and 102 MHz FM, in English, Malay, Cantonese and Mandarin; Station Man. The Administrator.

Christmas Island Tropical Radio VLU2: POB AAA, Christmas Island 6798, Indian Ocean; tel. (8) 9164-8316; fax (8) 9164-8315; Chair. DAVID MASTERS; Station Man. The Administrator.

Television

Christmas Island Television: POB AAA, Christmas Island 6798, Indian Ocean.

Finance

BANKING

Commercial Bank

Westpac Banking Corpn (Australia): Flying Fish Cove, Christmas Island, Indian Ocean; tel. (8) 9164-8221; fax (8) 9164-8241.

Trade and Industry

Shire of Christmas Island: George Fam Centre, POB 863, Christmas Island 6798, Indian Ocean; tel. (8) 9164-8300; fax (8) 9164-8304; e-mail soci@iocomm.com.au; f. 1992 by Territories Law Reform Act to replace Christmas Island Services Corpn; provides local govt services; manages tourism and economic development; Pres. DAVID MCLANE; CEO DAVID PRICE.

Christmas Island Chamber of Commerce: Christmas Island 6798, Indian Ocean; tel. (8) 9164-8249.

Christmas Island Utilities: Christmas Island 6798, Indian Ocean; tel. (8) 9164-8504; operates power, port and airport facilities; Gen. Man. BRYN MARTIN.

Union of Christmas Island Workers—UCIW: Poon Saan Rd, POB 84, Christmas Island 6798, Indian Ocean; tel. (8) 9164-8471; fax (8) 9164-8470; fmrly represented phosphate workers; Pres. CHAN BOO HWA; Gen. Sec. GORDON THOMSON; 800 mems.

Transport

There are good roads in the developed areas. National Jet Systems operate a weekly flight from Perth, via the Cocos (Keeling) Islands, and a private Christmas Island-based charter company operates services to Jakarta, Indonesia. In 1997 arrivals and departures by air in Christmas Island totalled 3,895 (compared with 14,513 in the previous year). The Australian National Line (ANL) operates ships to the Australian mainland. Cargo vessels from Fremantle deliver supplies to the island every four to six weeks. The Joint Island Supply System, established in 1989, provides a shipping service for Christmas Island and the Cocos Islands. The only anchorage is at Flying Fish Cove.

Tourism

Tourism is a growing sector of the island's economy. Visitors are attracted by the unique flora and fauna, as well as the excellent conditions for scuba-diving and game-fishing. In 2000 there were approximately 90 hotel rooms on the island.

Christmas Island Tourism Association/Christmas Island Visitor Information Centre: POB 63, Christmas Island 6798, Indian Ocean; tel. (8) 9164-8382; fax (8) 9164-8080; e-mail cita@christmas.net.au; internet www.christmas.net.au.

Christmas Island Tours and Travel: Christmas Island 6798, Indian Ocean; tel. (8) 9164-7168; Dir TAN SIM KIAT.

Parks Australia: POB ZZZ, Christmas Island 6798, Indian Ocean; tel. (8) 9164-8700; fax (8) 9164-8755.

COCOS (KEELING) ISLANDS

Introduction

The Cocos (Keeling) Islands are 27 in number and lie 2,768 km north-west of Perth, in the Indian Ocean. The islands form two low-lying coral atolls, densely covered with coconut palms. The climate is equable, with temperatures varying from 21°C (69°F) to 32°C (88°F), and rainfall of 2,000 mm per year. In 1981 some 58% of the population were of the Cocos Malay community, and 26% were Europeans. The Cocos Malays are descendants of the people brought to the islands by Alexander Hare and of labourers who were subsequently introduced by the Clunies-Ross family (see below). English is the official language, but Cocos Malay and Malay are also widely spoken. Most of the inhabitants are Muslims (56.8% in 1981). Home Island, which had a population of 446 in mid-1992, is where the Cocos Malay community is based. The only other inhabited island is West Island, with a population of 147 in mid-1992, and where most of the European community lives, the administration is based and the airport is located. The total population of the islands was 621 at the 1998 census.

The islands were uninhabited when discovered by Capt. William Keeling, of the British East India Company, in 1609, and the first settlement was not established until 1826, by Alexander Hare. The islands were declared a British possession in 1857 and came successively under the authority of the Governors of Ceylon (now Sri Lanka), from 1878, and the Straits Settlements (now Singapore and part of Malaysia), from 1886. Also in 1886 the British Crown granted all land on the islands above the high-water mark to John Clunies-Ross and his heirs and successors in perpetuity. In 1946, when the islands became a dependency of the Colony of Singapore, a resident administrator, responsible to the Governor of Singapore, was appointed. Administration of the islands was transferred to the Commonwealth of Australia on 23 November 1955. The agent of the Australian Government was known as the Official Representative until 1975, when an Administrator was appointed. The Minister for Regional Services, Territories and Local Government is responsible for the governance of the islands. The Territory is part of the Northern Territory Electoral District.

In June 1977 the Australian Government announced new policies concerning the islands, which resulted in its purchase from John Clunies-Ross of the whole of his interests in the islands, with the exception of his residence and associated buildings. The purchase for $A6.5m. took effect on 1 September 1978. An attempt by the Australian Government to acquire Clunies-Ross' remaining property was deemed by the Australian High Court in October 1984 to be unconstitutional.

In July 1979 the Cocos (Keeling) Islands Council was established, with a wide range of functions in the Home Island village area (which the Government transferred to the Council on trust for the benefit of the Cocos Malay community) and, from September 1984, in the greater part of the rest of the Territory.

On 6 April 1984 a referendum to decide the future political status of the islands was held by the Australian Government, with UN observers present. A large majority voted in favour of integration with Australia. As a result, the islanders were to acquire the rights, privileges and obligations of all Australian citizens. In July 1992 the Cocos (Keeling) Islands Council was replaced by the Cocos (Keeling) Islands Shire Council, modelled on the local government and state law of Western Australia.

Following unsuccessful investment in a shipping venture, the Clunies-Ross family was declared bankrupt in mid-1993, and the Australian Government took possession of its property.

Although local fishing is good, some livestock is kept and domestic gardens provide vegetables, bananas and papayas (pawpaws), the islands are not self-sufficient, and other foodstuffs, fuels and consumer items are imported from mainland Australia. A Cocos postal service (including a philatelic bureau) came into operation in September 1979, and revenue from the service is used for the benefit of the community.

Coconuts, grown throughout the islands, are the sole cash crop: total output was an estimated 6,100 metric tons in 1999. Total exports of coconuts in 1984/85 were 202 metric tons. The cost of the islands' imports from Australia decreased from $A5m. in 1997/98 to $A4m. in 1998/99. Exports to Australia totalled

$A2m. in 1996/97. Some 8% of the population were unemployed in 1996.

It was hoped that a tourist industry could be developed to provide an additional source of revenue for the islands by the late 1990s.

Primary education is provided at the schools on Home and West Islands. Secondary education is provided to the age of 16 years on West Island. A bursary scheme enables Cocos Malay children to continue their education on the Australian mainland.

Statistical Survey

AREA AND POPULATION

Area: 14.2 sq km (5.5 sq miles).

Population: 555 (males 298, females 257) at census of 30 June 1981; 647 at census of 1991; 593 (Home Island residents 446, West Island residents 147) at mid-1992; 655 (males 338, females 317) at census of 1996; 621 at census of 1998. *Ethnic Groups* (1981): Cocos Malay 320; European 143; Total (incl. others) 555. Source: mainly UN, *Demographic Yearbook*.

Density (1998): 43.7 per sq km.

Births and Deaths (1986): Registered live births 12 (birth rate 19.8 per 1,000); Registered deaths 2.

Labour Force (1996): 253 (employed 233, unemployed 20).

AGRICULTURE

Production (FAO estimates, metric tons, 1999): Coconuts 6,100; Copra 1,000 (1998). Source: FAO.

FINANCE

Currency and Exchange Rates: Australian currency is used (see p. 521).

COMMUNICATIONS MEDIA

Radio Receivers (1992): 300 in use.

EXTERNAL TRADE

Principal Commodities (metric tons, year ending 30 June 1985): *Exports*: Coconuts 202. *Imports*: Most requirements come from Australia. The trade deficit is offset by philatelic sales and Australian federal grants and subsidies.

1998/99 ($A '000): *Imports*: Australia 4,000. *Exports:* Australia n.a. Source: *Year Book Australia*.

Directory

The Government

The Administrator, appointed by the Governor-General of Australia and responsible to the Minister for Regional Services, Territories and Local Government, is the senior government representative in the islands.

Administrator: WILLIAM TAYLOR (non-resident).

Administrative Headquarters: POB 1093, West Island, Cocos (Keeling) Islands 6799, Indian Ocean; tel. (8) 9162-6769; fax (8) 9162-6697.

Cocos (Keeling) Islands Shire Council: POB 94, Home Island, Cocos (Keeling) Islands 6799, Indian Ocean; tel. (8) 9162-6649; fax (8) 9162-6668; e-mail info@shire.cc; f. 1992 by Territories Law Reform Act; Pres. MOHAMMED SAID CHONGKIN; CEO BOB JARVIS.

Judicial System

Supreme Court, Cocos (Keeling) Islands: West Island Police Station, Cocos (Keeling) Islands 6799, Indian Ocean; tel. (8) 9162-6615; fax (8) 9162-6697; Judge: ROBERT SHERATON FRENCH; Additional Judge: MALCOLM CAMERON LEE.

Magistrates' Court, Cocos (Keeling) Islands: Special Magistrate: (vacant).

Managing Registrar: BOB HOLLAND; Cocos (Keeling) Islands 6799, Indian Ocean; tel. (8) 9162-6615; fax (8) 9162-6697.

Religion

According to the census of 1981, of the 555 residents, 314 (some 57%) were Muslims and 124 (22%) Christians. The majority of Muslims live on Home Island, while most Christians are West Island residents. The Cocos Islands lie within both the Anglican and the Roman Catholic archdioceses of Perth (Western Australia).

Broadcasting and Communications

BROADCASTING

Radio

Radio VKW Cocos: POB 33, Cocos (Keeling) Islands 6799, Indian Ocean; tel. (8) 9162-6666; e-mail vkw@kampong.cc; non-commercial; daily broadcasting service in Cocos Malay and English; Station Man. CATHERINE CLUNIES-ROSS.

Television

A television service, broadcasting Indonesian, Malaysian and Australian satellite television programmes and videotapes of Australian television programmes, began operating on an intermittent basis in September 1992.

Industry

Cocos (Keeling) Islands Co-operative Society Ltd: Home Island, Cocos (Keeling) Islands 6799, Indian Ocean; tel. (8) 9162-6702; fax (8) 9162-6764; f. 1979; conducts the business enterprises of the Cocos Islanders; activities include boat construction and repairs, copra and coconut production, sail-making, stevedoring and airport operation; owns and operates a supermarket and tourist accommodation; Chair. MOHAMMED SAID BIN CHONGKIN; Gen. Man. RONALD TAYLOR.

Transport

National Jet Systems operate a weekly service from Perth, via Christmas Island, for passengers, supplies and mail to and from the airport on West Island. Cargo vessels from Singapore and Perth deliver supplies, at intervals of four to six weeks.

Cocos Trader: Cocos (Keeling) Islands 6799, Indian Ocean; tel. (8) 9162-6612; shipping agent.

Tourism

Cocos Island Tourism Association: POB 30, Cocos (Keeling) Islands 6799, Indian Ocean; tel. (8) 9162-6790; fax (8) 9162-6696; e-mail info@cocos-tourism.cc.

NORFOLK ISLAND

Introductory Survey

Location, Climate, Language, Religion, Capital

Norfolk Island lies off the eastern coast of Australia, about 1,400 km east of Brisbane, to the south of New Caledonia and 640 km north of New Zealand. The Territory also comprises uninhabited Phillip Island and Nepean Island, 7 km and 1 km south of the main island respectively. Norfolk Island is hilly and fertile, with a coastline of cliffs and an area of 34.6 sq km (13.3 sq miles). It is about 8 km long and 4.8 km wide. The climate is mild and subtropical, and the average annual rainfall is 1,350 mm, most of which occurs between May and August. The resident population, which numbered 1,772 in August 1996, consists of 'islanders' (descendants of the mutineers from HMS *Bounty*, evacuated from Pitcairn Island, who numbered 683 in 1996) and 'mainlanders' (originally from Australia, New Zealand or the United Kingdom). English is the official language, but a local Polynesian dialect (related to Pitcairnese) is also spoken. Most of the population (70.4% at the 1996 census) adhere to the Christian religion. The capital of the Territory is Kingston.

Recent History and Economic Affairs

The island was uninhabited when discovered in 1774 by a British expedition, led by Capt. James Cook. Norfolk Island was used as a penal settlement from 1788 to 1814 and again from 1825 to 1855, when it was abandoned. In 1856 it was resettled by 194 emigrants from Pitcairn Island, which had become over-populated. Norfolk Island was administered as a separate colony until 1897, when it became a dependency of New South Wales. In 1913 control was transferred to the Australian Government. Norfolk Island has a continuing dispute with the Australian Government concerning the island's status as a territory of the Commonwealth of Australia. There have been successive assertions of Norfolk Island's right to self-determination, as a distinct colony.

Under the Norfolk Island Act 1979, Norfolk Island is progressing to responsible legislative and executive government, enabling the Territory to administer its own affairs to the greatest practicable extent. Wide powers are exercised by the nine-member Legislative Assembly and by the Executive Council, comprising the executive members of the Legislative Assembly who have ministerial-type responsibilities. The Act preserves the Australian Government's responsibility for Norfolk Island as a territory under its authority, with the Minister for Regional Services, Territories and Local Government as the responsible minister. The Act indicated that consideration would be given within five years to an extension of the powers of the Legislative Assembly and the political and administrative institutions of Norfolk Island. In 1985 legislative and executive responsibility was assumed by the Norfolk Island government for public works and services, civil defence, betting and gaming, territorial archives and matters relating to the exercise of executive authority. In 1988 further amendments empowered the Legislative Assembly to select a Norfolk Island government auditor (territorial accounts were previously audited by the Commonwealth Auditor-General). The office of Chief Minister was replaced by that of the President of the Legislative Assembly. David Ernest Buffett was reappointed to this post following the May 1992 general election. A lack of consensus among members of the Executive Council on several major issues prompted early legislative elections in April 1994. The newly-elected seventh Legislative Assembly was significant in having three female members. Following elections in April 1997, in which 22 candidates contested the nine seats, George Smith was appointed President (subsequently reverting to the title of Chief Minister) of the eighth Legislative Assembly. At legislative elections in February 2000 three new members were elected to the Assembly, and Ronald Nobbs was subsequently appointed Chief Minister.

In December 1991 the population of Norfolk Island overwhelmingly rejected a proposal, made by the Australian Government, to include the island in the Australian federal electorate. The outcome of the poll led the Australian Government, in June 1992, to announce that it had abandoned the plan. Similarly, in late 1996 a proposal by the Australian Government to combine Norfolk Island's population with that of Canberra for record-keeping purposes was strongly opposed by the islanders.

In late 1997 the Legislative Assembly debated the issue of increased self-determination for the island. Pro-independence supporters argued that the Territory could generate sufficient income by exploiting gas- and oilfields in the island's exclusive economic zone.

In August 1998 a referendum proposing that the Norfolk Island electoral system be integrated more closely with that of mainland Australia (initiated in Canberra by the Minister for Regional Development, Territories and Local Government) was rejected by 78% of the Territory's electorate. A similar referendum in May 1999 was opposed by 73% of voters. Frustration with the Australian Government's perceived reluctance to facilitate the transfer of greater powers to the Territory (as outlined in the Norfolk Island Act of 1979, see above) led the island's Legislative Assembly in mid-1999 to vote by seven members to one in favour of full internal self-government. Negotiations regarding the administration of crown land on the island, which continued in 2000, were seen as indicative of the islanders' determination to pursue greater independence from Australia.

Despite the island's natural fertility, agriculture is no longer the principal economic activity. About 400 ha of land are arable. The main crops are Kentia palm seed, cereals, vegetables and fruit. Cattle and pigs are farmed for domestic consumption. Development of a fisheries industry is restricted by the lack of a harbour. Some flowers and plants are grown commercially. The administration is increasing the area devoted to Norfolk Island pine and hardwoods. Seed of the Norfolk Island pine is exported. Potential oil- and gas-bearing sites in the island's waters may provide a possible future source of revenue. A re-export industry has been developed to serve the island's tourist industry. In early 1999 the Norfolk Island Legislative Assembly announced plans to seek assistance from the Australian Government to establish an offshore financial centre on the island.

In 1999/2000 imports from Australia cost $A22.7m. (compared with $17.6m. in the previous year). In 1998/99 exports to Australia earned $A1m. In 1999/2000 imports from New Zealand totalled $A9.3m. (compared with $A9.0m. in the previous year). In 1999/2000 the cost of imports totalled $A59.1m., while revenue from exports amounted to $A2.8m. The authorities receive revenue from customs duties (some $A3.2m., equivalent to 30.8% of total revenue in 1999/2000) and the sale of postage stamps, but tourism is the island's main industry. In 1999/2000 there were 38,298 tourist arrivals on the island. In 1985 and 1986 the Governments of Australia and Norfolk Island jointly established the 465-ha Norfolk Island National Park. This was to protect the remaining native forest, which is the habitat of several unique species of flora (including the largest fern in the world) and fauna (such as the Norfolk Island green parrot, the guavabird and the boobook owl). Conservation efforts include the development of Phillip Island as a nature reserve.

Education

Education is free and compulsory for all children between the ages of six and 15. Pupils attend the government school from infant to secondary level. A total of 314 pupils were enrolled at infant, primary and secondary levels in 1999/2000. Students wishing to follow higher education in Australia are eligible for bursaries and scholarships. The budgetary allocation for education was $A1,629,400 in 1999/2000 (equivalent to 15.8% of total expenditure).

Weights and Measures

The metric system is in force.

Statistical Survey

Source: The Administration of Norfolk Island, Administration Offices, Kingston, Norfolk Island 2899; tel. 22001; fax 23177.

AREA AND POPULATION

Area: 34.6 sq km (13.3 sq miles).

Population: 2,285 (males 1,111, females 1,174), including 373 visitors, at census of 6 August 1991; 1,896 (resident population) at

30 June 1993; 2,181 (males 1,039, females 1,142), including 409 visitors, at census of 6 August 1996.

Density (resident population, 1996): 51.2 per sq km.

Births, Marriages and Deaths (1999/2000): Live births 24; Marriages 32; Deaths 20.

Economically Active Population (persons aged 10 years and over, 1996 census): 1,273 (males 629, females 644).

FINANCE

Currency and Exchange Rates: Australian currency is used (see p. 521).

Budget (year ending 30 June 2000): Revenue $A10,382,800 (Customs duties $A3,200,000); Expenditure $A10,319,900 (Education $A1,629,400).

EXTERNAL TRADE

1999/2000 (year ending 30 June): *Imports*: $A59,110,044, mainly from Australia and New Zealand. *Exports*: $A2,773,442.

Trade with Australia ($A million, 1999/2000): *Imports* 22.7.

Trade with New Zealand ($A million, 1999/2000): *Imports* 9.3.

TOURISM

Visitors (year ending 30 June): 35,626 in 1997/98; 36,514 in 1998/99; 38,298 in 1999/2000.

COMMUNICATIONS MEDIA

Radio Receivers (1996): 2,500 in use.

Television Receivers (1996): 1,200 in use.

Non-daily Newspaper (1996): 1 (estimated circulation 1,000).

EDUCATION

Institution (1997): 1 state school incorporating infant, primary and secondary levels.

Teachers (1999/2000): Full-time 23; Part-time 2.

Students (1999/2000): Infants 79; Primary 116; Secondary 119.

Directory
The Constitution

The Norfolk Island Act 1979 constitutes the administration of the Territory as a body politic and provides for a responsible legislative and executive system, enabling it to administer its own affairs to the greatest practicable extent. The preamble of the Act states that it is the intention of the Australian Parliament to consider the further extension of powers.

The Act provides for an Administrator, appointed by the Australian Government, who shall administer the government of Norfolk Island as a territory under the authority of the Commonwealth of Australia. The Administrator is required to act on the advice of the Executive Council or the responsible Commonwealth Minister in those matters specified as within their competence. Every proposed law passed by the Legislative Assembly must be effected by the assent of the Administrator, who may grant or withhold that assent, reserve the proposed law for the Governor-General's pleasure or recommend amendments.

The Act provides for the Legislative Assembly and the Executive Council, comprising the executive members of the Assembly who have ministerial-type responsibilities. The nine members of the Legislative Assembly are elected for a term of not more than three years under a cumulative method of voting: each elector is entitled to as many votes (all of equal value) as there are vacancies, but may not give more than four votes to any one candidate. The nine candidates who receive the most votes are declared elected.

The Government

The Administrator, who is the senior representative of the Commonwealth Government, is appointed by the Governor-General of Australia and is responsible to the Minister for Regional Services, Territories and Local Government. A form of responsible legislative and executive government was extended to the island in 1979, as outlined above.

Administrator: TONY MESSNER (assumed office on 4 August 1997).

EXECUTIVE COUNCIL
(April 2001)

Chief Minister and Minister for Finance and Government Services: RONALD C. NOBBS.

Minister for Immigration and Community Services: ADRIAN COOK.

Minister for Tourism and Commerce: GEORGE SMITH.

Minister for Health: GEOFFERY R. GARDNER.

MINISTRIES

All Ministries are located at: Old Military Barracks, Kingston, Norfolk Island 2899.

GOVERNMENT OFFICES

Office of the Administrator: New Military Barracks, Norfolk Island 2899; tel. 22152; fax 22681.

Administration of Norfolk Island: Administration Offices, Kingston, Norfolk Island 2899; tel. 22001; fax 23177; all govt depts; Chief Administrative Officer: IVENS F. BUFFETT.

Legislature
LEGISLATIVE ASSEMBLY

Nine candidates are elected for not more than three years. The most recent general election was held on 23 February 2000.

Speaker: DAVID ERNEST BUFFETT.

Deputy Speaker: JOHN MCCOY.

Other Members: RONALD C. NOBBS, GEOFFERY R. GARDNER, GEORGE SMITH, ADRIAN COOK, BRIAN G. BATES, JOHN T. BROWN, BRUCE WALKER.

Judicial System

Supreme Court of Norfolk Island: Kingston; appeals lie to the Federal Court of Australia.

Judges: BRYAN ALAN BEAUMONT (Chief Justice), MURRAY RUTLEDGE WILCOX.

Religion

The majority of the population professes Christianity (70.4%, according to the census of 1996), with the principal denominations being the Church of England (38%), the Uniting Church (14%) and the Catholic Church (11%).

The Press

Norfolk Island Government Gazette: Kingston, Norfolk Island 2899; tel. 22001; fax 23177; weekly.

Norfolk Islander: Greenways Press, POB 150, Norfolk Island 2899; tel. 22159; fax 22948; f. 1965; weekly; Co-Editors TOM LLOYD, TIM LLOYD; circ. 1,000.

Broadcasting and Communications
BROADCASTING
Radio

Norfolk Island Broadcasting Service: New Cascade Rd, POB 456, Norfolk Island 2899; tel. 22137; fax 23298; e-mail 2niradio@ni.net.nf; internet www.users.nf/nfradio/; govt-owned; non-commercial; broadcasts 112 hours per week; relays television and radio programmes from Australia; Broadcast Man. MARGARET MEADOWS.

Radio VL2NI: New Cascade Rd, POB 456, Norfolk Island 2899; tel. 22137; fax 23298; e-mail 2niradio@ni.net.nf; internet www.users.nf/nfradio/.

Television

Norfolk Island Broadcasting Service: (see Radio).

Norfolk Island Television Service: f. 1987; govt-owned; relays programmes of Australian Broadcasting Corpn, Special Broadcasting Service Corpn and Central Seven TV by satellite.

TV Norfolk (TVN): locally-operated service featuring programmes of local events and information for tourists.

Finance
BANKING

Commonwealth Bank of Australia (Australia): Taylors Rd, Norfolk Island 2899; tel. 22144; fax 22805.

Westpac Banking Corpn Savings Bank Ltd (Australia): Burnt Pine, Norfolk Island 2899; tel. 22120; fax 22808.

Trade

Norfolk Island Chamber of Commerce: POB 370, Norfolk Island 2899; tel. 22018; fax 23106; e-mail monica@worldtraders.nf; f. 1966; affiliated to the Australian Chamber of Commerce; 60 mems; Pres. Bruce Walker; Sec. Monica Anderson.

Transport

ROADS

There are about 100 km of roads, including 85 km of sealed road.

SHIPPING

Norfolk Island is served by the three shipping lines, Neptune Shipping, Pacific Direct Line and Roslyndale Shipping Company Pty Ltd. A small tanker from Nouméa (New Caledonia) delivers petroleum products to the island and another from Australia delivers liquid propane gas.

CIVIL AVIATION

Norfolk Island has one airport, with two runways (of 1,900 m and 1,550 m), capable of taking medium-sized jet-engined aircraft. Air New Zealand operates a twice-weekly direct service between Christchurch and Norfolk Island (via Auckland). Charter flights from Lord Howe Island and occasionally from New Caledonia also serve the island. The cessation of scheduled services from Australia by Ansett Australia in 1997 had an adverse effect on the island's important tourist industry. As a consequence, Norfolk Jet Express was established to provide a weekly service to Australia, and Flight West Airlines began to operate a twice-weekly flight from Brisbane and Sydney (Australia) to the island. In February 1999 Air Nauru began to operate a weekly charter flight service to Norfolk Island from Sydney, under contract with Norfolk Jet Express.

Tourism

Visitor arrivals totalled 36,514 in 1998/99.

Norfolk Island Visitors Information Centre: Taylors Rd, Burnt Pine, POB 211, Norfolk Island 2899; tel. 22147; fax 23109; e-mail info@nigtb.gov.nf; internet www.norfolkisland.nf; Gen. Man. Joanne Libline.

OTHER TERRITORIES

Territory of Ashmore and Cartier Islands

The Ashmore Islands (known as West, Middle and East Islands) and Cartier Island are situated in the Timor Sea, about 850 km and 790 km west of Darwin respectively. The Ashmore Islands cover some 93 ha of land and Cartier Island covers 0.4 ha. The islands are small and uninhabited, consisting of sand and coral, surrounded by shoals and reefs. Grass is the main vegetation. Maximum elevation is about 2.5 m above sea-level. The islands abound in birdlife, sea-cucumbers (*bêches-de-mer*) and, seasonally, turtles.

The United Kingdom took formal possession of the Ashmore Islands in 1878, and Cartier Island was annexed in 1909. The islands were placed under the authority of the Commonwealth of Australia in 1931. They were annexed to, and deemed to form part of, the Northern Territory of Australia in 1938. On 1 July 1978 the Australian Government assumed direct responsibility for the administration of the islands, which rests with a parliamentary secretary appointed by the Minister for Regional Services, Territories and Local Government. Periodic visits are made to the islands by the Royal Australian Navy and aircraft of the Royal Australian Air Force, and the Civil Coastal Surveillance Service makes aerial surveys of the islands and neighbouring waters. The oilfields of Jabiru and Challis are located in waters adjacent to the Territory.

In August 1983 Ashmore Reef was declared a national nature reserve. An agreement between Australia and Indonesia permits Indonesian traditional fishermen to continue fishing in the territorial waters and to land on West Island to obtain supplies of fresh water. In 1985 the Australian Government extended the laws of the Northern Territory to apply in Ashmore and Cartier, and decided to contract a vessel to be stationed at Ashmore Reef during the Indonesian fishing season (March–November) to monitor the fishermen.

In October 2000 a boat containing 33 suspected illegal immigrants believed to be heading for Australia from the Middle East via Indonesia landed at Ashmore Reef. The immigrants, who were transferred to a detention centre on the Australian mainland, were typical of the increasing numbers of refugees and asylum-seekers hoping to gain residency in Australia.

Australian Antarctic Territory

The Australian Antarctic Territory was established by Order in Council in February 1933 and proclaimed in August 1936, subsequent to the Australian Antarctic Territory Acceptance Act (1933). It consists of the portion of Antarctica (divided by the French territory of Terre Adélie) lying between 45°E and 136°E, and between 142°E and 160°E. The Antarctic Division of the Department of the Environment, Sport and Territories (subsequently renamed the Department of the Environment and Heritage) was established in 1948 as a permanent agency, and to administer and provide support for the Australian National Antarctic Research Expeditions (ANARE), which maintains three permanent scientific stations (Mawson, Davis and Casey) in the Territory. The area of the Territory is estimated to be 5,896,500 sq km (2,276,650 sq miles), and there are no permanent inhabitants, although there is a permanent presence of scientific personnel. In late 1997 the Antarctic Science Advisory Committee suggested closing two of Australia's three research stations (Mawson and Casey), partly as a result of the increasing automation of data-gathering, and the establishment of an airline service and a base for adventure tourism. Environmentalists expressed alarm at proposals in the late 1990s to encourage tourism in the Territory, which, they claimed, could damage the area's sensitive ecology. The Territory is administered by the Antarctic Division of the Department of the Environment and Heritage. Australia is a signatory to the Antarctic Treaty (see p. 456).

Coral Sea Islands Territory

The Coral Sea Islands became a Territory of the Commonwealth of Australia under the Coral Sea Islands Act of 1969. The Territory lies east of Queensland, between the Great Barrier Reef and longitude 156° 06′E, and between latitude 12°S and 24°S, and comprises several islands and reefs. The islands are composed largely of sand and coral, and have no permanent fresh water supply, but some have a cover of grass and scrub. The area has been known as a notorious hazard to shipping since the 19th century, the danger of the reefs being compounded by shifting sand cays and occasional tropical cyclones. The Coral Sea Islands have been acquired by Australia by numerous acts of sovereignty since the early years of the 20th century.

Spread over a sea area of approximately 780,000 sq km (300,000 sq miles), all the islands and reefs in the Territory are very small, totalling only a few sq km of land area. They include Cato Island, Chilcott Islet in the Coringa Group, and the Willis Group. In 1997 the Coral Sea Islands Act was amended to include Elizabeth and Middleton Reefs. A meteorological station, operated by the Commonwealth Bureau of Meteorology and with a staff of four, has provided a service on one of the Willis Group since 1921. The other islands are uninhabited. There are eight automatic weather stations (on Cato Island, Flinders Reef, Frederick Reef, Holmes Reef, Lihou Reef, Creal Reef, Marion Reef and Gannet Cay) and several navigation aids distributed throughout the Territory.

The Act constituting the Territory did not establish an administration on the islands, but provides means of controlling the activities of those who visit them. The Lihou Reef and Coringa-Herald National Nature Reserves were established in 1982 to provide protection for the wide variety of terrestrial and marine wildlife, which include rare species of birds and sea turtles (one of which is the largest, and among the most endangered, of the world's species of sea turtle). The Australian Government has concluded agreements for the protection of endangered and migratory birds with Japan and the People's Republic of China. The Governor-General of Australia is empowered to make ordinances for the peace, order and good government of the Territory and, by ordinance, the laws of the Australian Capital Territory apply. The Supreme Court and Court of Petty Sessions of Norfolk Island have jurisdiction in the Territory. The Territory is administered by a parliamentary secretary appointed by the Minister for Regional Services, Territories and Local Government, and the area is visited regularly by the Royal Australian Navy.

Territory of Heard Island and the McDonald Islands

These islands are situated about 4,000 km (2,500 miles) southwest of Perth, Western Australia. The Territory, consisting of Heard Island, Shag Island (8 km north of Heard) and the McDonald Islands, is almost entirely covered in ice and has a total area of 369 sq km (142 sq miles). The Territory has been administered by the Australian Government since December 1947, when it established a scientific research station on Heard Island (which functioned until 1955) and the United Kingdom ceded its claim to sovereignty. There are no permanent inhabitants, but Australian expeditions visit occasionally. The island is of considerable scientific interest, as it is believed to be one of the few Antarctic habitats uncontaminated by introduced organisms. Heard Island is about 44 km long and 20 km wide and possesses an active volcano, named Big Ben. In January 1991 an international team of scientists travelled to Heard Island to conduct research involving the transmission of sound waves, beneath the surface of the ocean, in order to monitor any evidence of the 'greenhouse effect' (melting of polar ice and the rise in sea-level as a consequence of pollution). The pulses of sound, which travel at a speed largely influenced by temperature, were to be received at various places around the world, with international co-operation. Heard Island was chosen for the experiment because of its unique location, from which direct paths to the five principal oceans extend. The McDonald Islands, with an area of about 1 sq km (0.4 sq miles), lie some 42 km west of Heard Island. In late 1997 Heard Island and the

McDonald Islands were accorded World Heritage status by UNESCO in recognition of their outstanding universal significance as a natural landmark. In mid-1999 concern was expressed that stocks of the Patagonian toothfish in the waters around the islands were becoming depleted as a result of over-exploitation, mainly by illegal operators. The islands are administered by the Antarctic Division of the Department of the Environment and Heritage.

AUSTRIA

Introductory Survey

Location, Climate, Language, Religion, Flag, Capital

The Republic of Austria lies in central Europe, bordered by Switzerland and Liechtenstein to the west, by Germany and the Czech Republic to the north, by Hungary and Slovakia to the east, and by Italy and Slovenia to the south. The climate varies sharply, owing to great differences in elevation. The mean annual temperature lies between 7°C and 9°C (45°F and 48°F). The population is 99% German-speaking, with small Croat and Slovene-speaking minorities. The majority of the inhabitants profess Christianity: about 70% are Roman Catholics and about 5% are Protestants. The national flag (proportions 3 by 2) consists of three equal horizontal stripes, of red, white and red. The state flag has, in addition, the coat of arms (a small shield, with horizontal stripes of red separated by a white stripe, superimposed on a black eagle, wearing a golden crown and holding a sickle and a hammer in its feet, with a broken chain between the legs) in the centre. The capital is Vienna (Wien).

Recent History

Austria was formerly the centre of the Austrian (later Austro-Hungarian) Empire, which comprised a large part of central Europe. The Empire, under the Habsburg dynasty, was dissolved in 1918, at the end of the First World War, and Austria proper became a republic. The first post-war Council of Ministers was a coalition led by Dr Karl Renner, who remained Chancellor until 1920, when a new Constitution introduced a federal form of government. Many of Austria's inhabitants favoured union with Germany but this was forbidden by the post-war peace treaties. In March 1938, however, Austria was occupied by Nazi Germany's armed forces and incorporated into the German Reich, led by the Austrian-born Adolf Hitler.

After Hitler's defeat in Austria, a provisional Government, under Dr Renner, was established in April 1945. In July, following Germany's surrender to the Allied forces, Austria was divided into four zones, occupied by forces of the USA, the USSR, the United Kingdom and France. At the first post-war elections to the 165-seat Nationalrat (National Council), held in November 1945, the conservative Österreichische Volkspartei (ÖVP, Austrian People's Party) won 85 seats and the Sozialistische Partei Österreichs (SPÖ, Socialist Party of Austria) secured 76. The two parties formed a coalition Government. In December Dr Renner became the first Federal President of the second Austrian Republic, holding office until his death in December 1950. However, it was not until May 1955 that the four powers signed a State Treaty with Austria, ending the occupation and recognizing Austrian independence, effective from 27 July; occupation forces left in October.

More than 20 years of coalition government came to an end in April 1966 with the formation of a Council of Ministers by the ÖVP alone. Dr Josef Klaus, the Federal Chancellor since April 1964, remained in office. The SPÖ achieved a relative majority in the March 1970 general election and formed a minority Government, with Dr Bruno Kreisky (a former Minister of Foreign Affairs, who had been party leader since 1967) as Chancellor. In April 1971 the incumbent President, Franz Jonas of the SPÖ, was re-elected, defeating the ÖVP candidate, Dr Kurt Waldheim, a former Minister of Foreign Affairs (who subsequently served two five-year terms as UN Secretary-General, beginning in January 1972). The SPÖ won an absolute majority of seats in the Nationalrat at general elections in October 1971 (when the number of seats was increased from 165 to 183) and October 1975. President Jonas died in April 1974, and the subsequent presidential election, held in June, was won by Dr Rudolf Kirchschläger, who had been the Minister of Foreign Affairs since 1970. He was re-elected for a second six-year term in 1980.

In November 1978 a government proposal to commission Austria's first nuclear power plant was defeated in a national referendum. Despite expectations that Chancellor Kreisky would resign, he received the full support of the SPÖ and emerged in an apparently even stronger position. At the general election in May 1979 the SPÖ increased its majority in the Nationalrat. The general election of April 1983, however, marked the end of the 13-year era of one-party government: the SPÖ lost its absolute majority in the Nationalrat and Kreisky, unwilling to participate in a coalition, resigned as Chancellor. The reduction in the SPÖ's representation was partly attributed to the emergence of two environmentalist 'Green' parties, both founded in 1982. The two parties together received more than 3% of the total votes, but failed to win any seats. Kreisky's successor, Dr Fred Sinowatz (the former Vice-Chancellor and Minister of Education), took office in May, leading a coalition of the SPÖ and the right-of-centre Freiheitliche Partei Österreichs (FPÖ, Freedom Party of Austria). The new Government continued the social welfare policy that had been pursued by its predecessor, in addition to maintaining Austria's foreign policy of 'active neutrality'.

A presidential election was held in May 1986 to choose a successor to Kirchschläger. The SPÖ candidate was Dr Kurt Steyrer (the Minister of Health and Environment), while Dr Waldheim, the former UN Secretary-General, stood as an independent candidate, although with the support of the ÖVP. The campaign was dominated by allegations that Waldheim, a former officer in the army of Nazi Germany, had been implicated in atrocities committed by the Nazis in the Balkans during 1942–45; the ensuing controversy divided the country and brought unexpected international attention to the election. Waldheim won a run-off ballot in June 1986, with 54% of the votes cast. The defeat of the SPÖ presidential candidate led Chancellor Sinowatz and four of his ministers to resign. Dr Franz Vranitzky, hitherto the Minister of Finance, became the new Chancellor. In September the FPÖ elected a controversial new leader, Dr Jörg Haider, who represented the far right wing of his party. This precipitated the end of the partnership between the SPÖ and the FPÖ, and the general election for the Nationalrat, scheduled for April 1987, was brought forward to November 1986. No party won an absolute majority: the SPÖ took 80 seats, the ÖVP 77, the FPÖ 18 and an alliance of three 'Green' parties eight. Following several weeks of negotiations, a 'grand coalition' of the SPÖ and the ÖVP, with Vranitzky as Chancellor, was formed in January 1987.

Waldheim's election to the presidency was controversial both domestically and internationally, and Austria's relations with Israel and the USA, in particular, were severely strained. In February 1988 a specially-appointed international commission of historians concluded that Waldheim must have been aware of the atrocities that had been committed. Waldheim refused to resign, but in June 1991 he announced that he would not seek a second presidential term.

At the general election held in October 1990 the SPÖ retained its position as the largest single party, increasing its number of seats in the Nationalrat by one, to 81, while the ÖVP obtained only 60 seats, a decline of 17; the FPÖ increased its representation by 15 seats, to 33. The FPÖ's success was attributed, in large part, to its support for restrictions on immigration, especially from eastern Europe. The Grüne Alternative Liste (GAL, Green Alternative List), an informal electoral alliance comprising Die Grüne Alternative (The Green Alternative) and the Vereinte Grüne Österreichs (United Green Party of Austria), increased 'Green' representation by one seat, to nine. In December, following several weeks of negotiations, the SPÖ and the ÖVP formed a new coalition Government, again led by Vranitzky.

A congress of the SPÖ held in June 1991 voted to revert to the party's original name, the Sozialdemokratische Partei Österreichs (SPÖ, Social-Democratic Party of Austria). In the same month the FPÖ leader, Dr Haider, was dismissed as Governor of Carinthia (Kärnten) after publicly praising Hitler's employment policies. In December the Nationalrat approved government legislation whereby Austria became the only country in Europe able to reject asylum requests from individuals without identity papers. Following the imprisonment, in January 1992, of a prominent right-wing activist for demanding the restoration of the Nazi party, and the subsequent fire-bombing of a refugee hostel by neo-Nazis in northern Austria, the Nationalrat voted unanimously in February to amend anti-Nazi legislation. The minimum prison sentence for Nazi agitation was reduced from five years to one year (in order to increase the number of successful prosecutions) and denial of the Nazi Holocaust was made a criminal offence.

At the presidential election held in April 1992 the two main candidates were Dr Rudolf Streicher (hitherto the Minister of Public Economy and Transport), for the SPÖ, and Dr Thomas Klestil (a former ambassador to the USA), representing the ÖVP. No candidate achieved the required 50% of the vote at the first ballot, but in the second 'run-off' ballot, held in May, Klestil received almost 57% of the votes cast; he assumed the presidency in July.

In June 1992 a 32-year-old dispute between Austria and Italy was resolved when Austria formally accepted autonomy proposals for Italy's German-speaking Trentino-Alto Adige (South Tyrol) region. In January 1993 the FPÖ organized a national petition seeking to require the Nationalrat to debate the introduction of legislation that would halt immigration into Austria and impose stricter controls on foreign residents in the country (the estimated number of whom had increased from 350,000 to 600,000 since 1989). Although the petition was signed by 7.4% of the electorate (417,000 signatures, compared with the constitutional requirement of 100,000 to force parliamentary debate), the result was considered disappointing by the FPÖ. The initiative was strongly opposed by a broad coalition of politicians, church leaders and intellectuals. In February 1993 five FPÖ deputies in the Nationalrat left the party, partly in protest at the petition on immigration, and formed a new political organization, the Liberales Forum (LiF, Liberal Forum), under the leadership of Dr Heide Schmidt, hitherto the Vice-President of the FPÖ. In December four campaigners for tolerance towards immigrant and refugee communities, including the Mayor of Vienna, were injured by letter bombs. (In March 1999 a lone right-wing extremist was sentenced to life imprisonment, having been found guilty of perpetrating these and other bomb attacks during the 1990s against members and supporters of ethnic minorities, including an assault in February 1995 which killed four gypsies.)

In late 1993 an ongoing debate over Austria's future in Europe intensified when the European Union (EU, see p. 181) set a deadline of 1 March 1994 by which time the conditions of Austria's entry into the Union (pending a national referendum) were to be agreed. Austria strongly defended its right to preserve its neutrality, to uphold higher environmental standards and to impose restrictions on the transit of road-freight traffic through the Austrian Alps. Eventually a number of compromises were reached, including an extension of the existing limit on lorry transit traffic until 2001. At the ensuing national referendum on the terms of Austria's membership of the EU, held in June 1994, some two-thirds of voters (66.4%) supported Austria's entry into the Union. Following the referendum Austria announced plans to sign NATO's Partnership for Peace programme (see p. 243). Austria was formally admitted to the EU on 1 January 1995. Observer status at Western European Union (see p. 286) was subsequently granted.

At the general election held in October 1994 the ruling coalition lost its two-thirds' majority in the Nationalrat. The SPÖ obtained 66 seats (winning 35% of the votes cast), the ÖVP took 52 seats (with 28% of the votes cast), and the FPÖ (which had campaigned against Austria's accession to the EU) increased its share of the votes cast by 6%, to 23%, securing 42 seats. The GAL and the LiF also made gains, winning 13 and 10 seats respectively. The success of the FPÖ's populist campaign, which had concentrated on countering corruption and immigration and had advocated referendum- rather than parliamentary-based governance, unsettled the Austrian political establishment after years of relative consensus. At the end of November, following protracted negotiations, the SPÖ and ÖVP finally agreed to form a new coalition Government, with Vranitzky remaining as Chancellor.

The new SPÖ-ÖVP coalition was beleaguered by disagreements, mainly concerning differences in approach to the urgent need to reduce the annual budgetary deficit in compliance with Austria's commitment, as a member of the EU, to future economic and monetary union (EMU). In March 1995 four ministers resigned from the Government, including the Minister of Finance, Ferdinand Lacina, whose draft 1995 budget, containing several economic austerity measures, had generated widespread adverse criticism. In April Dr Erhard Busek, the Vice-Chancellor and Minister of Education and Culture,

resigned from both posts and was replaced as Chairman of the ÖVP by Dr Wolfgang Schüssel; Busek had been widely blamed for the ruling coalition's poor performance at the October 1994 election. A reorganization of ministerial posts was undertaken at the end of April 1995. In October a deepening rift between the SPÖ and ÖVP regarding the means of curtailing the 1996 budgetary deficit (with the former advocating increased taxation measures and the latter proposing to restrain public expenditure) proved irreconcilable, culminating in the collapse of the coalition. Consequently a new general election was held in December 1995. The SPÖ improved upon its disappointing performance at the previous election, receiving 38.1% of the votes cast and winning 71 of the 183 seats in the Nationalrat. The ÖVP secured 28.3% of the votes cast (obtaining 53 seats), the FPÖ (which had been popularly restyled the Freiheitlichen in January 1995) 21.9% (40 seats), the LiF 5.5% (10 seats) and the GAL 4.8% (nine seats). In early March 1996, following lengthy negotiations, the SPÖ and ÖVP agreed an economic programme and formed a new coalition Government, with Vranitzky remaining as Chancellor. In June the Minister of Economic Affairs, Johannes Ditz of the ÖVP, resigned, reportedly following disagreements within his party over the pace of economic reform. In mid-January 1997 Vranitzky unexpectedly resigned as Chancellor. Viktor Klima, the Minister of Finance, was appointed as his successor, both as Chancellor and as Chairman of the SPÖ, and the Council of Ministers was reorganized.

Meanwhile, mounting popular disillusionment with Austria's membership of the EU was reflected in the results of the first national elections to the European Parliament, which took place in October 1996. The FPÖ, which continued to oppose EU membership, won an unprecedented 27.6% of the votes cast, at the expense of the SPÖ, which registered its worst ever election performance, with 29.1% of the votes cast. The ÖVP secured 29.6% of the votes cast. At concurrent elections to the Vienna city administration the SPÖ lost the absolute majority of seats that it had held since the end of the Second World War, while the FPÖ increased their representation. The election results were regarded as a protest against the ruling coalition's alleged misrepresentation, prior to the June 1994 referendum, of the immediate effects of admission to the EU; the Government's programme of economic austerity measures was particularly unpopular, while demands by the EU that Austria abolish anonymously-held bank accounts were also resented. Austria assumed the EU presidency for the first time in July 1998.

In March 1998, following months of debate, the Government announced that Austria would not apply to join NATO, and would thereby preserve its traditional neutrality (as favoured by the SPÖ, but opposed by the ÖVP). Nevertheless, in early April 1999 Austria, in conjunction with the three other officially neutral EU member states, signed an EU declaration stating that the ongoing bombing of Serbia by NATO forces was 'both necessary and warranted'.

At the presidential election held in April 1998 Klestil was re-elected emphatically, winning 63.5% of the votes cast. The FPÖ made significant gains at regional elections in early March 1999, becoming the dominant party in Dr Haider's home province of Carinthia; Haider was subsequently elected Governor of Carinthia (having previously been dismissed from that post in 1991—see above). At elections to the European Parliament, which took place in June 1999, the SPÖ and ÖVP showed improved performances, securing 31.7% and 30.6% of the votes cast respectively. The FPÖ took 23.5% of the votes cast. The participation rate was, however, relatively low (49.0%). The general election held in early October resulted in unprecedented success for the FPÖ, which, by a narrow margin of 415 votes, took second place ahead of the ÖVP. The SPÖ won 65 of the 183 seats in the Nationalrat (with 33.2% of the votes cast), while the FPÖ and ÖVP both secured 52 seats (each with 26.9% of the votes cast). The GAL took 14 seats (7.4%). The FPÖ had campaigned on a programme which included a halt to immigration, the obstruction of the projected eastwards expansion of the EU, the radical deregulation of the business sector and the introduction of a uniform low rate of income tax and of hugely increased child allowances for Austrian citizens. Dr Haider appeared to have inflamed popular fears that the planned admission to the EU of Austria's eastern neighbours would flood the domestic market with cheap labour, thereby causing the level of unemployment to rise. During the FPÖ campaign Haider allegedly revived nationalist terminology previously employed by the Nazi regime; nevertheless, he consistently denied embracing neo-Nazi ideology. The election result was most widely regarded as a protest against the 12-year old 'grand' SPÖ-ÖVP coalition, which had acquired a reputation for unwieldy bureaucracy and for sanctioning politically-motivated appointments to public companies.

Following the election, protracted negotiations took place with a view to forming a new administration. In late January 2000, following a failed attempt to reconstruct the SPÖ-ÖVP coalition, the SPÖ announced that it would not attempt to form a minority government. At the beginning of February President Klestil reluctantly presided over the inauguration of an ÖVP-FPÖ coalition Government, with the ÖVP leader, Dr Schüssel, as Chancellor. Dr Haider elected not to participate directly in the new administration, which comprised an FPÖ Vice-Chancellor, Dr Susanne Riess-Passer, and five FPÖ ministers (including those responsible for finance, justice and defence). Although the new coalition had committed itself to respecting human rights and had adopted a relatively moderate political programme, the participation in government of the FPÖ provoked strong opposition both within Austria (where numerous demonstrations were organized) and abroad. Israel and the USA immediately recalled their ambassadors from Vienna, pending a reassessment of bilateral relations, while Austria's 14 fellow EU member states each suspended bilateral political co-operation, maintaining diplomatic relations at a 'technical' level, pending the removal of the FPÖ from the coalition. In late February Dr Haider announced that he was to resign as leader of the FPÖ, stating that he would concentrate instead on his job as Governor of Carinthia; few people, however, doubted that he would remain the *de facto* leader of the party.

In April 2000 the SPÖ party Chairman, Alfred Gusenbauer, apologized for decades of political opportunism and acknowledged that the SPÖ had erred in embracing and promoting former Nazis after the Second World War in its efforts to become Austria's most powerful political force. He later established a commission of independent historians to look into the matter. His initiative was expected to put pressure on the coalition Government to launch similar projects, but officials from both parties claimed they had already dealt with the issue and had no plans to follow suit. However, in June Ernest Windholz, the newly-elected head of the FPÖ in Lower Austria, provoked controversy by using a Nazi-era slogan to honour long-serving members of his party. The slogan ('unsere ehre heisst treue'— 'our honour is called loyalty') was a motto of the armed SS wing of Hitler's Nazi party. The incident was thought to have harmed Austria's chances of having sanctions lifted at a forthcoming EU summit meeting, the last such meeting before the rotating EU presidency was to be assumed by France, which had pressed for the introduction of the sanctions. Prospects improved, however, by the end of that month when Chancellor Schüssel agreed to the nomination by the President of the Court of Human Rights of a three-person delegation to examine the Austrian Government's commitment to common European values (with particular regard to the rights of minority groups, immigrants and refugees and to the political philosophy of the FPÖ). Following the delegation's report, the 14 members of the EU would reassess the necessity for sanctions. Schüssel, however, declined to abandon a referendum, which he had announced in May, and which was scheduled to take place in October/November, in which Austrian voters would be invited to express their views on sanctions and future policy towards the EU. The Austrian Government also warned that the continuation of sanctions could affect EU decisions on constitutional reform and the accession of new member states. The delegation (Martti Ahtisaari, the former Finnish President; Jochen Frowein, Director of the Max-Planck Institute in Heidelberg; and Marcelino Oreja, the former Spanish Minister of Foreign Affairs) visited Austria in late July, and issued its report in September. A report by the European Commission against Racism and Intolerance (ECRI), which expressed deep concern about the racist propaganda in Austria and criticized the FPÖ, was leaked to the press shortly before the EU delegation was due to make its decision. The delegation recommended, however, that the sanctions against Austria be lifted on the grounds that they were counter-productive and tended to generate increased nationalist sentiment. Although the report did criticize the xenophobic tendencies of the FPÖ, it confirmed that Austria's treatment of minorities was superior to that of many EU member states and that incidences of violence against foreigners were less frequent in Austria than in other EU countries. The report also criticized the FPÖ for trivializing Nazism and threatening press freedom by using libel suits to silence criticism. Concurrently, economic

analysts reported that continuing the sanctions against Austria could adversely affect the euro, which had reached a record low against the dollar (EU ministers responsible for finance were meeting in the same week to discuss the euro's future). As a result, the EU lifted its sanctions in September, but at the same time warned that it would continue to monitor closely the influence of the FPÖ, and Dr Haider, upon government policies. The decision represented a defeat for France, which had strongly supported the retention of sanctions, and was condemned by the Israeli Government.

Shortly after the lifting of EU sanctions in September 2000, Dr Haider attended a reunion of veterans of the Third Reich where he made a speech in which he praised those gathered as good citizens and reiterated comments that survivors of the war had been maligned. He also demanded justice for German and Austrian citizens who had lost property after the war. He provoked further criticism when he spent over 1m. Schilling on the restoration of Nazi frescoes, previously housed in the Carinthian parliament building, for display in a museum. Dr Haider visited the Vatican in mid-December; his meeting with the Pope aroused strong protests.

The end of 2000 was a troubled time for the FPÖ, whose influence and popularity, which had benefited from the imposition of EU sanctions, was beginning to wane. They fared badly in a regional election in Styria (Steiermark) in October, slipping into third position with just 12.4% of the votes cast (compared with 17.1% in the previous regional election) and also performed poorly in a regional election in the eastern province of Burgenland in December; the decline in support was widely attributed to the FPÖ losing their appeal as a 'protest party' upon entering into government. In November 2000 the Minister of Science and Transport, Michael Schmid, resigned from the coalition Government, citing the party's poor electoral performance in Styria. He was the third FPÖ minister to resign since the formation of the Government in February, provoking accusations that the party was unfit to govern. Schmid subsequently resigned from the FPÖ after refusing to pay one-half of his government pension into a party fund. Poor electoral results, instability and repeated indiscretions linking the party with Nazism were, however, overshadowed by the emergence of a major political scandal. In October the FPÖ were accused of illicitly obtaining police files to discredit opponents, including the former Minister of Finance, Caspar Einem. The allegations surfaced as a result of a book published by a former police officer, Josef Kleindienst, in which he confessed to securing such documents and testified that many other police officers had done so for financial reward. A formal investigation was launched into 18 members of the FPÖ, including Haider and the Minister of Justice, Dieter Böhmdorfer, who for many years had been Dr Haider's lawyer. Böhmdorfer, who had been deemed unfit for office by the EU delegation in September, was accused of using illegally obtained police documents when representing Haider in court. He rejected calls from the opposition and the judges' union to resign, and in October survived a vote of 'no confidence', the third such vote in his short ministerial career. By November the number of FPÖ members under investigation had risen to 67. Officials from the prosecutor's office raided the homes of FPÖ officials, including the party leader in Vienna, Hilmar Kabas, and Dr Haider's bodyguard, a police officer named Horst Binder. Kabas had already been damaged by reports that he had visited a brothel in Vienna allegedly operated by Russian immigrants; Kabas claimed he was investigating the premises. The raid on Binder's home uncovered a note, allegedly from him to Dr Haider, which suggested that Binder had sent confidential police files to Dr Haider following requests for information from several senior FPÖ members. Both parties claimed the note was a forgery. Eleven police officers were suspended in connection with the scandal.

During the late 1990s a number of lawsuits were filed by US interests against several Austrian banks, which were accused of having profited during the Second World War from handling stolen Jewish assets. In November 1999 Bank Austria AG agreed to pay US $33m. as compensation to Holocaust survivors and, furthermore, to establish a humanitarian fund to assist survivors resident in Austria. Similar lawsuits were also filed against the Government, and in February 2000 Chancellor Schüssel appointed a former President of Bank Austria AG, Maria Schaumayer, as the co-ordinator in charge of Nazi-era compensation claims. In July the legislature approved the establishment of a €438m. fund, which was to be financed by unspecified contributions from the Government and from Austrian businesses (which had profited from slave labour), to compensate an estimated 150,000 concentration camp inmates, who had been forced into slave labour by the Nazis. However, doubts subsequently surfaced as to whether Austrian businesses would agree to pay for their share of the compensation fund. Another potential problem facing the settlement of the slave-labourers' claims was that class-action lawyers were threatening not to drop their claims unless the agreement contained a firm commitment to a similarly extensive solution for the restitution of Jewish property. In January 2001, however, Austria signed an agreement with the USA to pay US \$500m. to compensate Jews for property lost when the Nazis took power, in return for the dismissal of survivors' lawsuits. The agreement, which allowed for the first payments to take place in March/April, was strongly criticized by Haider.

In August 2000 survivors of the Nazi child-euthanasia programme, which promoted the extermination of people considered to be sub-standard, appealed to the EU for help in bringing a distinguished psychiatrist, Dr Heinrich Gross, to justice. He was accused of murdering 772 children during the Second World War as part of the programme, but had been declared unfit to stand trial in the Austrian courts in March due to the onset of dementia. Gross had undergone a trial in 1950, following which a guilty verdict had been overturned owing to alleged irregularities in the evidence. Since 1953, however, when he joined the SPÖ, the Austrian authorities had failed to take action against him. A Vienna court ordered the state broadcasting corporation to pay Gross 30,000 Schilling for undermining the presumption of his innocence.

The Heads of Government of Austria, Hungary and Slovakia met on several occasions during the late 1990s in order to pursue co-operation on security and economic issues. In September 1999, however, Austria threatened to hinder Slovakia's entry into the EU, in protest at the alleged inadequacy of that country's nuclear safety standards. There were protests throughout 2000 against the proposed activation of a Soviet-designed nuclear reactor in Temelin in the Czech Republic, 48 km from the border with Austria; both Austria and Germany claimed the reactor was dangerously flawed. An agreement was signed in December under which the reactor would not operate until a full evaluation of the plant's safety and environmental impact was completed. The report was due to be published in May or June of 2001. Demonstrations against the activation of the plant, however, continued into 2001.

Government

Austria is a federal republic, divided into nine provinces, each with its own provincial assembly and government. Legislative power is held by the bicameral Federal Assembly. The first chamber, the Nationalrat (National Council), has 183 members, elected by universal adult suffrage for four years (subject to dissolution) on the basis of proportional representation. The second chamber, the Bundesrat (Federal Council), has 64 members, elected for varying terms by the provincial assemblies. The Federal President, elected by popular vote for six years, is the Head of State, and normally acts on the advice of the Council of Ministers, which is led by the Federal Chancellor, and which is responsible to the Nationalrat.

Defence

After the ratification of the State Treaty in 1955, Austria declared its permanent neutrality. To protect its independence, the armed forces were instituted. Austria reaffirmed its neutrality in March 1998, having evaluated the possibility of joining NATO. Military service is compulsory and normally consists of seven months' initial training, followed by a maximum of 30 days' reservist training over 10 years (officers, non-commissioned officers and specialists undergo 60–90 days' reservist training). In August 2000 the total armed forces numbered 35,500 (including 17,500 conscripts). The air force (numbering 6,500, of whom 3,400 were conscripts) is an integral part of the army. Total reserves numbered 75,000, compared with 100,700 in August 1999 and 200,000 in June 1992. The estimated defence budget for 2001 amounted to 22,500m. Schilling.

Economic Affairs

In 1998, according to estimates by the World Bank, Austria's gross national product (GNP), measured at average 1996–98 prices, was US \$216,697m., equivalent to \$26,830 per head (or \$23,145 per head on an international purchasing-power parity basis). During 1990–98, it was estimated, GNP per head increased, in real terms, by an average annual rate of 1.5%. Over

the same period, the population increased at an average rate of only 0.6% per year. Austria's gross domestic product (GDP) grew, in real terms, at an average annual rate of 2.2% in 1990–99. Real GDP grew by 3.3% in 1998 and by 2.8% in 1999.

The contribution of agriculture (including hunting, forestry and fishing) to GDP was 2.1% in 1999. In that year some 6.1% of the economically active population were engaged in the agricultural sector. Austrian farms produce more than 90% of the country's food requirements, and surplus dairy products are exported. The principal crops are wheat, barley, maize and sugar beet. The GDP of the agricultural sector increased, in real terms, at an average annual rate of 2.8% in 1990–99; it increased by 2.5% in 1998 but declined by 3.1% in 1999.

Industry (including mining and quarrying, manufacturing, construction and power) contributed 31.4% of GDP in 1999, and engaged 30.4% of the economically active population in that year. Industrial GDP increased, in real terms, at an average annual rate of 2.5% in 1990–99; it increased by 3.7% in 1998 and by 2.5% in 1999.

In 1999 mining and quarrying contributed 0.4% of GDP and employed 0.3% of the economically active population. The most important indigenous mineral resource is iron ore (1.8m. metric tons, with an iron content of 31%, were mined in 1998). Austria also has deposits of petroleum, lignite, magnesite, lead and some copper. The GDP of the mining sector declined, in real terms, at an average rate of 2.6% per year during 1990–99; it declined by 2.7% in 1998 but increased by 4.4% in 1999.

Manufacturing contributed 20.1% of GDP and engaged 20.3% of the economically active population in 1999. Measured by the value of output, the principal branches of manufacturing in 1995 were metals and metal products (accounting for 15.1% of the total), food products (11.7%), wood and paper products (10.1%), non-electric machinery (9.9%) and electrical machinery and telecommunications equipment (9.8%). The production of chemicals and road vehicles are also important activities. The GDP of the manufacturing sector increased, in real terms, at an average annual rate of 2.8% during 1990–99; it increased by 4.5% in 1998 and 2.4% in 1999.

Hydroelectric power resources provide the major domestic source of energy, accounting for 64.8% of total electricity production in 1997, followed by gas (15.5%), coal (11.8%) and oil (5.0%). Austria is heavily dependent on imports of energy, mainly from eastern Europe. Net imports of energy for commercial use were equivalent to 71% of the total in 1997. Imports of mineral fuels accounted for 4.4% of the total cost of imports in 1999.

The services sector contributed 66.5% of GDP and employed 63.5% of the economically active population in 1999. Tourism has traditionally been a leading source of revenue, providing receipts of about 142,000m. Schilling in 1999. In June 2000 the Government introduced legislation which would end the right to open secret bank accounts from November and phase out existing anonymous accounts by June 2002. The GDP of the services sector increased, in real terms, at an average annual rate of 2.1%; it increased by 3.1% in 1998 and 1.6% in 1999.

In 1999 Austria recorded a visible trade deficit of US \$3,560m., and the current account of the balance of payments showed a deficit of \$5,701m. Much of Austria's trade is conducted with other member countries of the European Union (EU, see p. 181), which accounted for 68.8% of Austria's imports and 62.8% of exports in 1999. In that year the principal source of imports (41.9%) was Germany; other major sources were Italy (7.6%), the USA (5.3%) and France (5.0%). Germany was also the principal market for exports (34.9%); other significant markets were Italy (8.4%), Switzerland (6.0%) and Hungary (4.9%). The principal exports in 1999 were machinery and transport equipment and basic manufactures. The principal imports were also machinery and transport equipment (particularly road vehicles and electrical machinery) and basic manufactures.

The federal budget for 1999 produced a deficit of 82,100m. Schilling, equivalent to 2.5% of GDP. The central Government's debt was 1,623,361m. Schilling at 31 December 1999, equivalent to 59.9% of annual GDP. The average annual rate of inflation was 2.3% in 1990–99. Consumer prices increased by 0.9% in 1998 and 0.6% in 1999. In November 1999 some 4.4% of the labour force were unemployed.

Austria joined the European Union (EU, see p. 181) on 1 January 1995, having resigned its membership of the European Free Trade Association at the end of 1994. The country is also a member of the Organisation for Economic Co-operation and Development (OECD—see p. 247).

The new right-wing coalition Government, which assumed power in February 2000, began the implementation of reforms not undertaken under previous Social Democratic coalitions and challenged powerful institutional interests. Despite the imposition of EU sanctions in protest at the inclusion of the right-wing FPÖ in the Government, total exports increased by 16.7% in the first six months of 2000, aided by a surge in demand from Austria's main trading partners. Although Austria lost four small projects as a result of the sanctions (which were lifted in September), it continued to attract substantial inward investment (new investment totalled 8,000m. Schilling in the first 10 months of the year, creating 6,000 new jobs). Although the IMF praised Austria's GDP growth and its low inflation and unemployment, it criticized the country's fiscal consolidation which had stalled in 1998 and the slow implementation of structural reforms. The Government responded by announcing in July that it would accelerate its planned reduction of the budget deficit from its original target of 1.3% of GDP by 2003 to zero in 2002. Concerns were, however, expressed that the plans were two-thirds dependent on tax increases and only one-third on spending reductions. The Government did, however, show a commitment to reducing Austria's public expenditure, which was very high by EU standards, in its plans to cut 14,000 jobs (8% of the public-sector labour force) over the subsequent three years. This measure demonstrated the Government's willingness to disregard the objections of interest groups like the Social Partnership (a network of formal and informal consultations between government, industry and the unions), which although instrumental in preserving Austria's enviable strike-free record, had also hindered vital reforms. The Government introduced reforms in areas such as education and pensions and announced the liberalization and deregulation of the energy sector. The Government also emphasized its commitment to abolishing the traditional *proporz* system under which public-sector jobs were allocated to party supporters. The state holding company, the Österreichische Industrieholding AG (ÖIAG) was transformed by the replacement of party appointees with professional business executives, who accelerated the privatization programme (which had proceeded lamentably slowly under previous regimes) and were prepared to consider the benefits of divesting core shareholdings to bring in strategic partners. This new attitude in government was reflected in the private sector through the merger of Bank Austria AG with the German HypoVereinsbank in July, demonstrating that national ownership was no longer the prime consideration. By the end of 2000 the ÖIAG had already sold 100% of the postal savings bank and was seeking buyers of its stakes in the former Austrian tobacco monopoly, Austria Tabak, Vienna Airport, the state-owned printing company and Vienna's most famous auction house. Despite EU sanctions, Austria, which was one of the 11 participants of the third stage of economic and monetary union of the EU (the launch of the euro in January 1999), remained committed to the EU. One of the Government's main challenges was the impending enlargement of the EU to include eastern European countries. While Austria already invested widely in these neighbouring economies and was expected to benefit from their inclusion in the EU, it was also concerned with regard to the issues of free movement of labour, nuclear safety and agriculture (which had already been affected by the removal of protective trade barriers on Austria's accession to the EU in January 1995).

Social Welfare

The social insurance system covers all wage-earners and salaried employees, agricultural and non-agricultural self-employed and dependants, regardless of nationality. The coverage is compulsory and provides earnings-related benefits in the event of old age, invalidity, death, sickness, maternity and injuries at work. About 99% of the population are protected. There are separate programmes that provide unemployment insurance, family allowance, long-term care allowances, benefits for war victims, etc. In 1998 Austria had 330 hospitals with 74,810 beds (one for every 105 inhabitants), and in December 1999 there were 33,521 physicians working in the country. Of total expenditure by the central Government in 1996, 130,800m. Schilling (13.0%) was for health services, while a further 416,070m. Schilling (41.2%) was for social security and welfare. In 1997 total expenditure by the central Government on social welfare amounted to some 725,000m. Schilling.

Education

The central controlling body is the Federal Ministry of Education, Science and Cultural Affairs. Provincial boards (Landesschulräte) supervise school education in each of the nine federal provinces. Expenditure on education by all levels of government in 1997 was 161,308m. Schilling (equivalent to 6.4% of GDP).

Education is free and compulsory between the ages of six and 15 years. In 1996 enrolment at pre-primary level was equivalent to 80% of those in the relevant age-group (males 80%; females 81%). In 1996 enrolment at primary level included 87% of children in the relevant age-group. Enrolment at secondary level in that year included 88% of children in the relevant age-group (males 88%; females 89%). Children undergo four years' primary education at a Volksschule, after which they choose between two principal forms of secondary education. This may be a Hauptschule which, after four years, may be followed by one of a variety of schools offering technical, vocational and other specialized training, some of which provide a qualification for university. Alternatively, secondary education may be obtained in an Allgemeinbildende höhere Schule, which provides an eight-year general education covering a wide range of subjects, culminating in the Reifeprüfung or Matura. This gives access to all Austrian universities. In addition, all Austrian citizens over the age of 24, and with professional experience, may attend certain university courses in connection with their professional career or trade.

Opportunities for further education exist at 18 universities as well as 13 colleges of technology, all of which have university status, and schools of art and music. Institutes of adult education (Volkshochschulen) are found in all provinces, as are other centres operated by public authorities, church organizations and the Austrian Trade Union Federation. In 1996 enrolment at tertiary level was equivalent to 48% of those in the relevant age-group (males 48%; females 49%).

Public Holidays

2001: 1 January (New Year's Day), 6 January (Epiphany), 16 April (Easter Monday), 1 May (Labour Day), 24 May (Ascension Day), 4 June (Whit Monday), 14 June (Corpus Christi), 15 August (Assumption), 26 October (National Holiday), 1 November (All Saints' Day), 8 December (Immaculate Conception), 25 December (Christmas Day), 26 December (St Stephen's Day).

2002: 1 January (New Year's Day), 6 January (Epiphany), 1 April (Easter Monday), 1 May (Labour Day), 9 May (Ascension Day), 20 May (Whit Monday), 30 May (Corpus Christi), 15 August (Assumption), 26 October (National Holiday), 1 November (All Saints' Day), 8 December (Immaculate Conception), 25 December (Christmas Day), 26 December (St Stephen's Day).

Weights and Measures

The metric system is in force.

Statistical Survey

Source (unless otherwise stated): Austrian Central Statistical Office, Hintere Zollamtsstr. 2B, 1033 Vienna;
tel. (222) 711-28-76-55; fax (222) 715-68-28; e-mail info@oestat.gv.at; internet www.oestat.gv.at.

Area and Population

AREA, POPULATION AND DENSITY

Area (sq km)	83,858*
Population (census results)†	
12 May 1981	7,555,338
15 May 1991	
Males	3,753,989
Females	4,041,797
Total	7,795,786
Population (official estimates at mid-year)	
1997	8,072,182
1998	8,078,449
1999	8,092,254
Density (per sq km) at mid-1999	96.5

* 32,378 sq miles.
† Figures include all foreign workers.

PROVINCES (31 December 1999)

	Area (sq km)	Population ('000)	Density (per sq km)	Capital (with population)
Burgenland . . .	3,965.4	278.8	70.3	Eisenstadt (11,688)
Kärnten (Carinthia) .	9,533.0	563.9	59.1	Klagenfurt (91,141)
Niederösterreich (Lower Austria) .	19,173.3	1,541.0	80.4	Sankt Pölten (49,352)
Oberösterreich (Upper Austria).	11,979.6	1,378.9	115.1	Linz (188,022)
Salzburg . . .	7,154.2	516.4	72.2	Salzburg (144,247)
Steiermark (Styria) .	16,388.1	1,202.8	73.4	Graz (240,967)
Tirol (Tyrol) . .	12,647.8	668.3	54.4	Innsbruck (111,752)
Vorarlberg . .	2,601.4	348.6	134.0	Bregenz (26,571)
Wien (Vienna). .	415.0	1,608.1	3,874.9	
Total. . .	83,858.1	8,107.0	96.7	

PRINCIPAL TOWNS
(population at 31 December 1999)

Vienna (capital) .	1,608,144	Klagenfurt . .	91,141
Graz . . .	240,967	Villach . .	57,422
Linz . . .	188,022	Wels . .	56,894
Salzburg . .	144,247	Sankt Pölten .	49,352
Innsbruck . .	111,752	Dornbirn . .	41,811

BIRTHS, MARRIAGES AND DEATHS

	Registered live births		Registered marriages		Registered deaths	
	Number	Rate (per 1,000)	Number	Rate (per 1,000)	Number	Rate (per 1,000)
1992 . .	95,302	12.1	45,701	5.8	83,162	10.5
1993 . .	95,227	11.9	45,014	5.6	82,517	10.3
1994 . .	92,415	11.5	43,284	5.4	80,684	10.0
1995 . .	88,669	11.0	42,946	5.3	81,171	10.1
1996 . .	88,809	10.9	42,298	5.2	80,790	9.9
1997 . .	84,045	10.4	41,394	5.1	79,432	9.8
1998 . .	81,233	10.1	39,143	4.8	78,339	9.7
1999 . .	78,138	9.7	39,485	4.9	78,200	9.7

Expectation of life (years at birth, 1999): Males 75.0; Females 80.9.

ECONOMICALLY ACTIVE POPULATION*
('000 persons aged 15 years and over)

	1997	1998	1999
Agriculture, hunting and forestry	249.8	241.7	230.3
Fishing	0.3	0.3	0.3
Mining and quarrying . .	9.0	11.6	11.2
Manufacturing . . .	758.1	757.0	763.3
Electricity, gas and water supply .	38.3	35.8	31.2
Construction. . . .	312.5	318.3	336.4
Wholesale and retail trade; repair of motor vehicles, motorcycles and personal and household goods	580.4	581.7	592.8
Hotels and restaurants . .	215.5	216.0	212.2
Transport, storage and communications . . .	232.4	241.9	254.4
Financial intermediation . .	142.3	138.9	141.8
Real estate, renting and business activities	239.0	232.9	240.6
Public administration and defence; compulsory social security	263.1	252.4	247.7
Education	210.9	217.8	220.2
Health and social work . .	293.6	298.7	301.3
Other community, social and personal service activities . .	154.9	158.4	161.6
Private households with employed persons	14.0	14.0	12.3
Extra-territorial organizations and bodies.	5.2	5.9	4.8
Total employed . . .	3,719.4	3,723.3	3,762.3
Unemployed	164.8	165.0	146.7
Total labour force . .	3,884.2	3,888.2	3,909.0
Males	2,216.3	2,214.1	2,221.4
Females.	1,667.8	1,674.1	1,687.7

* Yearly averages, based on the results of quarterly sample surveys. The figures include members of the armed forces, except conscripts not employed before their military service.

Source: ILO, *Yearbook of Labour Statistics*.

Agriculture

PRINCIPAL CROPS ('000 metric tons)

	1997	1998	1999
Wheat	1,352.3	1,341.8	1,416.2
Barley	1,257.8	1,211.6	1,152.8
Maize	1,841.7	1,646.3	1,699.6
Rye	207.2	236.4	218.2
Oats	196.7	164.2	152.4
Triticale (wheat-rye hybrid) .	105.8	127.8	120.0
Mixed grain . . .	47.2	48.2	47.0
Potatoes. . . .	676.9	646.9	711.7
Soybeans (soya beans) . .	33.5	50.5	50.0*
Sunflower seed . . .	43.9	56.9	64.1
Rapeseed . . .	129.1	128.4	194.3
Cabbages . . .	63.0	87.0	78.4
Lettuce	52.4	50.3	53.9
Cucumbers and gherkins . .	39.8	39.0	44.5
Onions (dry). . .	92.5	102.1	134.6
Carrots	47.3	35.7	75.9
Grapes	234.3	351.4	364.4
Sugar beet . . .	3,011.9	3,314.1	3,216.7
Apples	477.3	416.5	409.7
Pears	69.9	132.4	114.0
Plums	76.7	49.5	44.9
Cherries (incl. sour) . .	25.5	35.8	29.5

* Unofficial figure.

Source: partly FAO.

LIVESTOCK ('000 head at December)

					1997	1998	1999
Horses	.	.	.	.	74.2	75.3	81.6
Cattle	.	.	.	.	2,197.9	2,171.7	2,152.8
Pigs.	.	.	.	.	3,679.9	3,810.3	3,433.0
Sheep	.	.	.	.	383.7	360.8	352.3
Goats	.	.	.	.	58.3	54.2	58.0
Chickens	.	.	.	.	13,949.6	13,539.7	13,797.8
Ducks	.	.	.	.	95.3	95.5	
Geese	.	.	.	.	22.0	26.4	700.3
Turkeys .	.	.	.	.	693	645.3	

LIVESTOCK PRODUCTS ('000 metric tons)

					1997	1998	1999
Beef and veal	.	.	.	.	206.0	196.9	203.3
Mutton and lamb	.	.	.	.	6.7	6.7	6.3*
Pig meat†	.	.	.	.	556.1	592.2	499.0
Poultry meat	.	.	.	.	102.5	106.0	101.7
Cows' milk	.	.	.	.	3,089.8	3,255.5	3,349.9
Sheep's milk.	.	.	.	.	6.6	7.9	7.5†
Goats' milk	.	.	.	.	15.7	15.9	16.1
Cheese	.	.	.	.	127.0	134.8	136.8
Butter	.	.	.	.	41.8	42.4	36.8
Hen eggs	.	.	.	.	100.1	99.4	92.1
Honey	.	.	.	.	6.0	7.5	6.5*
Cattle hides (fresh)*	.	.	.	25.0	22.0	22.0

* FAO estimate(s).
† Unofficial figure(s).

Source: FAO.

Forestry

ROUNDWOOD REMOVALS ('000 cubic metres, excl. bark)

	1996	1997	1998
Sawlogs, veneer logs and logs for sleepers	8,195	8,530	8,165
Pitprops (mine timber), pulpwood, and other industrial wood .	3,018	2,772	2,693
Fuel wood	3,797	3,423	3,176
Total	15,010	14,726	14,033

1999 ('000 cubic metres): Total removals 14,084.

SAWNWOOD PRODUCTION ('000 cubic metres, incl. railway sleepers)

	1996	1997	1998
Coniferous (softwood). . .	7,950	8,254	8,534
Broadleaved (hardwood) . .	250	196	203
Total	8,200	8,450	8,737

Source: FAO, *Yearbook of Forest Products*.

Fishing

(metric tons, live weight)

					1996	1997	1998
Capture .	.	.	.	.	450	465	451
Common carp	.	.	.		450	465	451
Aquaculture .	.	.	.		2,952	3,021	2,911
Common carp	.	.	.		810	540	565
Sea trout	.	.	.		—	70	104
Rainbow trout .	.	.	.		2,139	2,160	1,997
Brook trout	.	.	.		—	170	195
Total catch .	.	.	.		3,402	3,486	3,362

Source: FAO, *Yearbook of Fishery Statistics*.

Mining

('000 metric tons, unless otherwise indicated)

			1997	1998	1999
Brown coal (incl. lignite) .	.	.	1,130.3	1,140.2	1,137.4
Crude petroleum.	.	.	972.3	1,014.5	1,063.5
Iron ore:					
gross weight	.	.	1,794.1	1,792.0	1,747.0
metal content*†	.	.	490	500	500
Magnesite (crude)	.	.	790.3	722.9	748.6
Tungsten, concentrate (metric tons)†‡	.		1,400*	1,423	1,610
Graphite (natural)	.	.	12.6	10.7	2.6
Gypsum and anhydrite (crude)	.	975.7	961.4	999.2
Kaolin	.	.	266.1	298.1	152.5
Natural gas (million cu metres)	.	1,427.9	1,567.8	1,740.7

* Estimated production.
† Data from the US Geological Survey.
‡ Figures refer to metal content.

Industry

SELECTED PRODUCTS
('000 metric tons, unless otherwise indicated)

					1996	1997	1998*
Wheat flour	.	.	.	.	297	272	274
Raw sugar	.	.	.	.	535	529	533
Wine ('000 hectolitres)	.	.	2,110	1,801	2,703
Beer ('000 hectolitres)	.	.	9,427	9,304	8,948
Cotton yarn—pure and mixed (metric tons)	.		19,639	21,849	24,829
Woven cotton fabrics—pure and mixed ('000 sq metres) . . .		97,726	100,076	101,133
Wool yarn—pure and mixed (metric tons)	.	.		2,537	2,692	n.a.
Woven woollen fabrics—pure and mixed ('000 sq metres) . .		17,515	22,279	26,594
Mechanical wood pulp	.	.	344	378	376
Chemical and semi-chemical wood pulp	.	.	.	1,051	1,097	1,116
Newsprint	.	.	.	.	361	397	376
Other printing and writing paper .		1,787	1,826	2,003
Other paper and paperboard .	.	1,505	1,593	1,630
Plastics and resins	.	.	.	993	1,035	1,074
Motor spirit (petrol) .	.	.	2,298	2,410	2,158
Jet fuel .	.	.	.	.	478	505	n.a.
Distillate fuel oils	.	.	.	3,604	3,916	3,892
Residual fuel oils	.	.	.	1,421	1,540	1,347
Cement .	.	.	.	.	3,900	3,944	3,958
Crude steel† .	.	.	.	4,442	5,196	5,298
Refined copper—unwrought (metric tons): secondary†	.	.	57,000	65,000	76,000
Refined lead—unwrought (metric tons): secondary†	.	.	22,000	22,000	22,000
Passenger motor cars (number)	.	97,386	97,774	n.a.
Motorcycles, etc. (number)	.	.	18,618	17,007	19,832
Construction: new dwellings completed (number)	.	.	57,984	58,029	57,450
Electric energy (million kWh) .	.	54,835	56,851	57,394
Manufactured gas (terajoules)‡	.	27,730	30,132	30,076

* Provisional figures.
† Data from the US Geological Survey.
‡ Production of blast-furnace gas and coke-oven gas.

Sources: mainly Austrian Central Statistical Office, Vienna; FAO, *Yearbook of Forest Products*; UN, *Industrial Commodity Statistics Yearbook* and *Monthly Bulletin of Statistics*; International Road Federation, *World Road Statistics*.

Finance

CURRENCY AND EXCHANGE RATES

Monetary Units
100 Groschen = 1 Schilling.

Sterling, Dollar and Euro Equivalents (29 December 2000)
£1 sterling = 22.067 Schilling;
US $1 = 14.788 Schilling;
€1 = 13.760 Schilling;
1,000 Schilling = £45.32 = $67.62 = €72.67.

Average Exchange Rate (Schilling per US $)
1998   12.379
1999   12.916
2000   14.935

Note: Since the introduction of the euro, with Austrian participation, on 1 January 1999, a fixed exchange rate of €1 = 13.7603 Schilling has been in operation.

FEDERAL BUDGET (million Schilling)*

Revenue	1996	1997	1998
Direct taxes on income and wealth	235,141	258,700	272,442
Social security contributions— unemployment insurance	45,300	45,926	47,709
Indirect taxes	204,257	211,454	245,613
Current transfers	61,935	72,685	72,646
Sales and charges	18,777	14,770	16,293
Interest, shares of profit and other income	37,092	118,594	35,243
Sales of assets	10,523	18,681	7,483
Repayments of loans granted	634	395	701
Capital transfers	386	285	391
Borrowing	219,596	234,553	401,967
Other revenue	7,869	3,936	4,076
Total	841,510	979,979	1,104,564

Expenditure	1997	1998	1999
Public services	3,820	4,332	4,678
National defence	21,402	21,669	22,323
National security	27,622	28,944	30,194
Education	68,236	72,003	75,127
Health	20,115	25,257	25,590
Social welfare	214,777	216,967	222,739
Housing	25,257	25,131	25,082
Culture	587	596	606
Art	8,502	8,752	8,694
Science and research	29,149	31,212	32,845
Economic affairs and services	217,006	133,920	124,383
Energy	78	43	26
Agriculture and forestry	24,748	23,298	22,054
Trade and industry	12,479	12,269	11,462
Roads	93,364	7,585	7,299
Other transportation	81,853	87,614	79,978
Services	4,484	3,111	3,564
Other expenditures	363,697	551,265	637,169
Interest payments	184,800	237,358	250,446
Total	1,000,170	1,120,048	1,209,429

* Figures refer to federal government units covered by the general budget. The data exclude the operations of social insurance institutions and other units with their own budgets.

Revenue (revised figures, million Schilling): 1,000,170 (Borrowing 234,553) in 1997; 1,120,048 (Borrowing 408,475) in 1998; 1,209,429 (Borrowing 409,014) in 1999.

NATIONAL BANK RESERVES (US $ million at 31 December)

	1997	1998	1999
Gold*	1,168	2,795	3,810
IMF special drawing rights	168	149	145
Reserve position in IMF	963	1,365	959
Foreign exchange	18,605	20,918	14,016
Total	20,904	25,227	18,930

* Valued at 60,000 Schilling per kilogram.

Source: IMF, *International Financial Statistics*.

MONEY SUPPLY ('000 million Schilling at 31 December)

	1997	1998	1999*
Currency outside banks	178.8	n.a.	13.92
Demand deposits at deposit money banks	273.5	n.a.	42.15
Total money	452.3	n.a.	56.07

* Figures in '000 million euros.

Source: IMF, *International Financial Statistics*.

COST OF LIVING (Consumer Price Index; base: 1996 = 100)

	1997	1998	1999
Food and beverages	101.7	103.5	103.4
Rent (incl. maintenance and repairs)	102.3	105.1	106.9
Fuel and light	103.2	101.3	101.0
Clothing	100.3	100.3	99.9
Total (incl. others)	101.3	102.2	102.8

NATIONAL ACCOUNTS ('000 million Schilling at current prices)

National Income and Product

	1997	1998	1999
Compensation of employees	1,315.46	1,367.52	1,418.19
Operating surplus	512.02	544.62	557.02
Domestic factor incomes	1,827.48	1,912.14	1,975.21
Consumption of fixed capital	359.23	373.70	388.32
Gross domestic product at factor cost	2,186.71	2,285.84	2,363.53
Indirect taxes } *Less* Subsidies }	326.76	328.82	348.51
GDP in purchasers' values	2,513.48	2,614.66	2,712.03
Factor income received from abroad } *Less* Factor income paid abroad }	−26.84	−28.67	−47.41
Gross national product	2,486.64	2,585.99	2,664.62
Less Consumption of fixed capital	359.23	373.70	388.32
National income in market prices	2,127.41	2,212.29	2,276.31
Other current transfers from abroad } *Less* Other current transfers paid abroad }	−10.24	−16.59	−13.99
National disposable income	2,117.18	2,195.70	2,262.32

Expenditure on the Gross Domestic Product

	1997	1998	1999
Government final consumption expenditure	494.52	513.36	538.22
Private final consumption expenditure	1,440.93	1,490.16	1,535.54
Increase in stocks } Gross fixed capital formation }	607.76	631.71	651.31
Total domestic expenditure	2,543.21	2,635.23	2,725.07
Exports of goods and services	1,074.26	1,137.71	1,222.77
Less Imports of goods and services	1,113.09	1,153.33	1,236.06
Statistical discrepancy	9.12	−4.95	0.25
GDP in purchasers' values	2,513.48	2,614.66	2,712.03
GDP at constant 1995 prices	2,450.40	2,530.20	2,601.60

Gross Domestic Product by Economic Activity

	1997	1998	1999
Agriculture, hunting, forestry and fishing	57.26	57.39	53.92
Mining and quarrying	8.78	8.41	9.17
Manufacturing	472.59	496.93	508.91
Electricity, gas and water.	62.36	64.45	63.43
Construction.	189.99	201.03	212.83
Wholesale and retail trade	302.77	312.54	323.72
Restaurants and hotels	90.14	95.80	101.20
Transport, storage and communications	171.91	178.58	179.26
Finance and insurance	167.64	168.02	162.24
Real estate and business services*	359.37	376.84	398.22
Public administration and defence	157.27	162.03	168.17
Other services	327.21	339.17	349.24
Sub-total	2,367.30	2,461.19	2,530.31
Less Imputed bank service charges	125.46	124.59	116.14
GDP at basic prices	2,241.84	2,336.60	2,414.17
Taxes on products *Less* Subsidies on products	} 271.64	278.07	297.87
GDP in purchasers' values .	2,513.48	2,614.66	2,712.03

* Including imputed rents of owner-occupied dwellings.

BALANCE OF PAYMENTS (US $ million)

	1997	1998	1999
Exports of goods f.o.b.	58,662	62,826	63,695
Imports of goods f.o.b.	−62,936	−66,480	−67,255
Trade balance	−4,274	−3,654	−3,560
Exports of services	29,605	32,347	30,947
Imports of services	−28,569	−30,161	−28,390
Balance on goods and services.	−3,239	−1,468	−1,003
Other income received	10,393	10,784	10,474
Other income paid	−10,682	−12,011	−13,186
Balance on goods, services and income	−3,527	−2,695	−3,715
Current transfers received	2,912	2,920	2,905
Current transfers paid	−4,605	−4,834	−4,890
Current balance	−5,221	−4,609	−5,701
Capital account (net)	26	−206	−145
Direct investment abroad	−1,984	−2,759	−2,712
Direct investment from abroad	2,624	6,034	2,979
Portfolio investment assets	−10,157	−11,341	−27,664
Portfolio investment liabilities	10,956	16,570	26,313
Financial derivatives assets	−191	−407	−266
Financial derivatives liabilities	223	−100	101
Other investment assets	−5,208	−810	−12,401
Other investment liabilities	5,403	1,381	18,564
Net errors and omissions.	476	−250	−1,066
Overall balance	−3,053	3,503	−1,999

Source: IMF, *International Financial Statistics*.

External Trade

Note: Austria's customs territory excludes Mittelberg im Kleinen Walsertal (in Vorarlberg) and Jungholz (in Tyrol). The figures also exclude trade in silver specie and monetary gold.

PRINCIPAL COMMODITIES
(distribution by SITC, million Schilling)

Imports c.i.f.	1997	1998	1999
Food and live animals .	44,285.8	45,556.4	47,163.3
Crude materials (inedible) except fuels	32,417.3	32,716.9	34,219.6
Mineral fuels, lubricants, etc. (incl. electric current)	41,691.1	35,292.8	39,643.2
Petroleum, petroleum products, etc.	26,429.8	21,052.0	26,844.0
Chemicals and related products	83,792.2	90,081.5	92,871.3
Medicinal and pharmaceutical products	23,334.6	27,460.3	30,660.2
Medicaments (incl. veterinary medicaments)	n.a.	n.a.	18,837.0
Basic manufactures	144,583.1	152,127.4	153,219.0
Paper, paperboard and manufactures	16,580.4	17,655.0	19,195.7
Textile yarn, fabrics, etc..	21,725.8	21,615.6	21,950.5
Iron and steel	19,270.6	22,032.7	19,061.4
Non-ferrous metals	19,733.7	20,276.5	18,417.1
Other metal manufactures	32,042.0	34,560.0	37,439.5
Machinery and transport equipment	301,564.2	334,650.8	370,801.0
Power-generating machinery and equipment	20,532.7	23,270.3	24,845.6
Machinery specialized for particular industries	26,299.2	26,697.6	27,209.1
General industrial machinery, equipment and parts	43,720.4	45,361.1	46,924.7
Office machines and automatic data-processing machines	24,681.9	27,149.5	32,588.8
Automatic data-processing machines and units	n.a.	n.a.	20,914.5
Telecommunications and sound equipment.	22,096.0	29,912.0	35,749.1
Other electrical machinery, apparatus, etc..	57,297.4	63,774.7	67,823.1
Road vehicles and parts (excl. tyres, engines and electrical parts).	86,793.4	97,016.5	108,882.8
Passenger motor cars (excl. buses)	n.a.	n.a.	52,908.9
Parts for cars, buses, lorries, etc.	n.a.	n.a.	32,231.6
Other transport equipment	n.a.	n.a.	19,085.8
Miscellaneous manufactured articles	133,825.0	140,751.5	151,974.6
Furniture and parts	16,503.1	17,064.2	18,932.8
Clothing and accessories (excl. footwear)	35,497.9	36,636.5	39,300.4
Total (incl. others)	790,250.8	842,128.0	898,760.9

Exports f.o.b.	1997	1998	1999
Food and live animals .	27,082.1	29,010.0	31,776.8
Crude materials (inedible) except fuels	25,712.7	26,190.0	29,475.9
Cork and wood.	n.a.	n.a.	16,989.0
Chemicals and related products	69,319.5	72,128.0	77,820.6
Medicinal and pharmaceutical products	18,752.0	19,117.1	22,868.1
Basic manufactures	185,320.9	204,586.3	198,687.6
Paper, paperboard and manufactures	36,290.8	38,416.3	39,066.3
Paper and paperboard (not cut to size or shape)	n.a.	n.a.	27,815.9
Textile yarn, fabrics, etc..	23,647.5	24,751.9	24,369.9
Non-metallic mineral manufactures	18,717.6	17,828.8	18,036.2
Iron and steel	33,039.1	45,276.3	35,068.3
Non-ferrous metals	16,008.0	16,863.1	16,635.7
Other metal manufactures	34,848.2	37,091.9	40,279.9

Exports f.o.b. — *continued*	1997	1998	1999
Machinery and transport equipment	293,110.2	321,215.4	357,518.7
Power-generating machinery and equipment	39,107.6	41,033.4	46,387.4
Internal combustion piston engines and parts	n.a.	n.a.	33,567.4
Machinery specialized for particular industries	39,511.6	42,723.1	44,847.9
General industrial machinery, equipment and parts	44,074.6	47,441.2	49,788.5
Telecommunications and sound equipment	25,993.7	28,624.8	28,099.9
Other electrical machinery, apparatus, etc.	54,854.6	61,503.2	67,186.7
Road vehicles and parts (excl. tyres, engines and electrical parts)	61,530.3	68,490.7	82,688.1
Passenger motor cars (excl. buses)	n.a.	n.a.	38,354.8
Parts for cars, buses, lorries, etc.	n.a.	n.a.	26,359.0
Other transport equipment	n.a.	n.a.	18,938.4
Miscellaneous manufactured articles	99,379.3	106,256.9	114,727.5
Clothing and accessories (excl. footwear)	16,557.3	17,003.0	17,956.4
Musical instruments, parts and accessories	n.a.	n.a.	16,939.0
Total (incl. others)	715,016.2	774,738.0	829,276.5

PRINCIPAL TRADING PARTNERS (million Schilling)*

Imports c.i.f.	1997	1998	1999
Belgium-Luxembourg	18,970.8	20,171.2	19,345.5
China, People's Republic	10,784.6	11,099.6	12,611.1
Czech Republic	17,581.4	19,934.9	22,358.0
France	36,980.1	41,317.3	45,285.9
Germany	329,322.7	351,881.7	376,754.3
Hungary	24,412.3	27,629.2	29,927.6
Italy	66,803.5	67,511.9	68,232.5
Japan	17,345.5	19,708.9	22,477.8
Netherlands	26,229.3	28,978.3	28,640.0
Poland	7,049.0	8,072.5	8,178.7
Russia	11,888.0	10,556.9	9,714.3
Slovakia	8,097.0	9,043.9	10,517.3
Spain	11,842.0	12,898.5	13,220.4
Sweden	10,543.1	12,139.4	12,037.2
Switzerland-Liechtenstein	26,269.3	29,997.0	31,782.8
United Kingdom	24,050.6	25,657.7	27,871.6
USA	42,308.4	40,643.7	48,022.2
Total (incl. others)	790,250.8	842,128.0	898,711.2

Exports f.o.b.	1997	1998	1999
Belgium-Luxembourg	12,318.3	13,786.7	13,587.4
Croatia	10,224.0	8,407.6	7,957.2
Czech Republic	21,005.6	21,816.6	23,365.6
France	29,479.8	34,756.3	36,757.1
Germany	250,854.6	278,550.8	289,720.5
Hungary	34,978.4	38,251.3	40,817.1
Italy	59,316.9	66,574.1	69,692.7
Japan	8,976.0	7,172.8	10,048.8
Netherlands	19,292.0	18,723.2	19,158.7
Poland	11,823.1	12,395.6	13,115.9
Russia	9,974.6	7,380.1	6,441.6
Slovakia	9,642.0	9,493.3	9,247.0
Slovenia	12,904.8	12,962.0	14,462.2
Spain	16,139.4	20,859.3	24,082.5
Sweden	9,027.4	9,310.5	9,600.6
Switzerland-Liechtenstein	34,822.9	41,972.9	53,425.7
United Kingdom	29,640.3	32,464.8	36,472.2
USA	26,210.2	31,365.0	37,846.1
Total (incl. others)	715,016.2	774,738.0	829,278.2

* Imports by country of production; exports by country of consumption.

Transport

RAILWAYS (Federal Railways only)

	1996	1997	1998
Passenger-km (millions)	9,689	8,647.3	n.a.
Freight net ton-km (millions)	13,909.0	14,791.1	15,347.8
Freight tons carried ('000)	69,948.0	74,346.6	76,508.4

1999: Freight tons carried ('000) 78,018.

ROAD TRAFFIC (motor vehicles in use at 31 December)

	1997	1998	1999
Private cars	3,782,544	3,887,174	4,009,604
Buses and coaches	9,718	9,675	9,834
Goods vehicles	300,726	309,630	318,757
Motorcycles and scooters	212,791	237,767	263,297
Mopeds	362,953	362,864	359,630

SHIPPING

Merchant Fleet (registered at 31 December)

	1996	1997	1998
Number of vessels	29	13	22
Total displacement ('000 grt)	94.7	83.4	68.0

Source: Lloyd's Register of Shipping, *World Fleet Statistics*.

Freight Traffic ('000 metric tons)

	1995	1996	1997
Goods loaded	1,311	1,352	1,479
Goods unloaded	5,122	5,830	5,766

CIVIL AVIATION (Austrian Airlines, '000)

	1997	1998	1999
Kilometres flown	59,735	64,595	69,769
Passenger ton-km	597,875	695,046	817,454
Cargo ton-km	158,726	160,319	214,030
Mail ton-km	7,308	9,535	14,257

Tourism

FOREIGN TOURIST ARRIVALS (by country of origin)*

	1996	1997	1998
Belgium-Luxembourg	415,844	391,336	339,734
France-Monaco	536,819	486,862	505,454
Germany	9,877,394	9,391,361	9,667,328
Italy	856,354	896,158	950,632
Netherlands	1,073,008	1,031,979	1,045,377
Switzerland-Liechtenstein	746,106	699,543	700,643
United Kingdom	512,578	531,926	562,407
USA	575,178	578,581	662,837
Total (incl. others)	17,089,973	16,642,400	17,269,097

* Arrivals at accommodation establishments.

Receipts from tourism (US $ million): 13,990 in 1996; 12,393 in 1997 (Source: World Tourism Organization, *Yearbook of Tourism Statistics*).

Communications Media

	1997	1998	1999
Telephones (individual lines in use)	3,726,000	3,570,000	3,202,000
Radio licences issued	2,769,705	2,778,912	2,766,612
Television licences issued . . .	2,636,677	2,673,765	2,670,743
Book titles produced	20,942	21,428	18,719
Daily newspapers	17	17	17
Weekly newspapers	151	155	159
Other periodicals	2,637	2,685	2,774

Telefax stations ('000 in use): 210.0 in 1993; 240.0 in 1994; 284.7 in 1995 (Source: UN, *Statistical Yearbook*).

Mobile cellular telephones ('000 subscribers): 383.5 in 1995; 598.7 in 1996; 1,159.7 in 1997 (Source: UN, *Statistical Yearbook*).

Education

(1998/99)

	Institutions	Staff	Students
Primary	3,720	35,923	396,245
General secondary and upper			
primary	1,711	59,147	480,137
Compulsory vocational . . .	189	4,558	131,196
Technical and vocational . . .	718	19,864	189,117
Teacher training:			
second level	39	1,401	13,137
third level	33	2,460	11,578
Universities	18	17,378	222,163
Tertiary vocational	46	1,216*	7,867

* 1997/98 figure.

Directory

The Constitution

The Austrian Constitution of 1920, as amended in 1929, was restored on 1 May 1945. Its main provisions, with subsequent amendments, are summarized below:

Austria is a democratic republic, having a Federal President (Bundespräsident), elected directly by the people, and a bicameral legislature, the Federal Assembly (Bundesversammlung), consisting of the National Council (Nationalrat) and the Federal Council (Bundesrat). The republic is organized on the federal system, comprising the nine federal provinces (Bundesländer) of Burgenland, Carinthia (Kärnten), Lower Austria (Niederösterreich), Upper Austria (Oberösterreich), Salzburg, Styria (Steiermark), Tyrol (Tirol), Vorarlberg and Vienna (Wien). There is universal suffrage for men and women who are more than 18 years of age.

The Nationalrat consists of 183 members, elected by universal direct suffrage, according to a system of proportional representation. It functions for a maximum period of four years.

The Bundesrat represents the Bundesländer. Lower Austria sends 12 members, Vienna and Upper Austria 11 each, Styria 10, Carinthia and Tyrol five each, Salzburg four, and Burgenland and Vorarlberg three each, making 64 in all. The seats are divided between the parties according to the number of seats that they control in each Provincial Assembly (Landtag) and are held during the life of the provincial government (Landesregierung) that they represent. Each Länder, in turn, provides the Chairman for six months.

The Bundesversammlung meets for certain matters of special importance, for example to witness the swearing-in of the President. It can also be convened to declare war or to demand a referendum on the deposition of the President, if demanded by the Nationalrat.

The Federal President, elected by popular vote, is the head of state and holds office for a term of six years. The President is eligible for re-election only once in succession. Although invested with special emergency powers, the President normally acts on the authority of the Council of Ministers, which is responsible to the Nationalrat for governmental policy.

The Government consists of the Federal Chancellor, the Vice-Chancellor and the other ministers and state secretaries, who may vary in number. The Chancellor is chosen by the President, usually from the party with the strongest representation in the newly elected Nationalrat, and the other ministers are then chosen by the President on the advice of the Chancellor.

If the Nationalrat adopts an explicit motion expressing 'no confidence' in the Federal Government or individual members thereof, the Federal Government or the federal minister concerned is removed from office.

All new legislative proposals must be read and submitted to a vote in both chambers of the Bundesversammlung. A new draft law is presented first to the Nationalrat, where it usually has three readings, and secondly to the Bundesrat, where it can be delayed, but not vetoed.

The Constitution also provides for appeals by the Government to the electorate on specific points by means of referendum. If a petition supported by 100,000 electors or more is presented to the Government, the Government must submit it to the Nationalrat.

The Landtag exercises the same functions in each province as the Nationalrat does in the State. The members of the Landestag elect the Landesregierung consisting of a provincial governor (Landeshauptmann) and his or her councillors (Landesräte). They are responsible to the Landtag.

The spheres of legal and administrative competence of both national and provincial governments are clearly defined. The Constitution distinguishes four groups:

1. Law-making and administration are the responsibility of the State: e.g. foreign affairs, justice and finance.

2. Law-making is the responsibility of the State, administration is the responsibility of the provinces: e.g. elections, population matters and road traffic.

3. The State formulates the rudiments of the law, the provinces enact the law and administer it: e.g. charity, rights of agricultural workers, land reform.

4. Law-making and administration are the responsibility of the provinces in all matters not expressly assigned to the State: e.g. municipal affairs.

The Government

HEAD OF STATE

Federal President: Dr THOMAS KLESTIL (sworn in 8 July 1992; re-elected 19 April 1998).

COUNCIL OF MINISTERS
(April 2001)

A coalition of the Freiheitliche Partei Österreichs (FPÖ) and the Österreichische Volkspartei (ÖVP).

Federal Chancellor: Dr WOLFGANG SCHÜSSEL (ÖVP).

Vice-Chancellor and Minister for Public Affairs and Sports: Dr SUSANNE RIESS-PASSER (FPÖ).

Minister of Foreign Affairs: Dr BENITA FERRERO-WALDNER (ÖVP).

Minister of Economic Affairs and Labour: Dr MARTIN BARTENSTEIN (ÖVP).

Minister of Social Affairs and Generations: HERBERT HAUPT (FPÖ).

Minister of Finance: KARL-HEINZ GRASSER (FPÖ).

Minister of the Interior: Dr ERNST STRASSER (ÖVP).

Minister of Justice: Dr DIETER BÖHMDORFER (FPÖ).

Minister of Defence: HERBERT SCHEIBNER (FPÖ).

Minister of Agriculture, Forestry, Prevention of Water Pollution and Environmental Affairs: WILHELM MOLTERER (ÖVP).

Minister of Education, Science and Cultural Affairs: ELISABETH GEHRER (ÖVP).

Minister of Innovation and Future: Dr MONICA FORSTINGER (FPÖ).

Secretary of State in the Federal Chancellery: FRANZ MORAK (ÖVP).

Secretary of State for Tourism in the Ministry of Economic Affairs and Labour: MARES ROSSMANN (FPÖ).

Secretary of State for Health in the Ministry of Social Affairs and Generations: Prof. Dr REINHART WANECK (FPÖ).

Secretary of State in the Ministry of Finance: Dr ALFRED FINZ (ÖVP).

MINISTRIES

Office of the Federal President: Hofburg, 1010 Vienna; tel. (1) 534-22-0; fax (1) 535-65-12; internet hofburg.at.

Office of the Federal Chancellor: Ballhausplatz 2, 1014 Vienna; tel. (1) 531-15-0; fax (1) 535-03-380; internet www.austria.gv.at.

Office of the Vice-Chancellor and Minister for Public Affairs and Sports: Minoritenplatz 3, 1014 Vienna; tel. (1) 531-15-0.

Ministry of Agriculture, Forestry, Prevention of Water Pollution and Environmental Affairs: Stubenring 1, 1010 Vienna; tel. (1) 711-00-0; fax (1) 710-32-54; internet www.bmlf.gv.at.

Ministry of Defence: Dampfschiffstr. 2, 1030 Vienna; tel. (1) 515-95-0; fax (1) 515-95-17033; e-mail pid1@bmlv.gv.at; internet www.bundesheer.gv.at.

Ministry of Economic Affairs and Labour: Stubenring 1, 1010 Vienna; tel. (1) 711-00-0; fax (1) 713-79-95; e-mail post@bmwa.gv.at; internet www.bmwa.gv.at.

Ministry of Education, Science and Cultural Affairs: Minoritenplatz 5, 1014 Vienna; tel. (1) 531-20-00; fax (1) 531-20-00; internet www.bmuk.gv.at.

Ministry of the Environment, Youth and Family Affairs: Cobdengasse 2, 1010 Vienna; tel. (1) 515-22-0; fax (1) 515-22-72-32; internet www.bmu.gv.at.

Ministry of Finance: Himmelpfortgasse 4–8B, 1010 Vienna; tel. (1) 514-33-0; fax (1) 512-78-69; internet www.bmf.gov.at.

Ministry of Foreign Affairs: Ballhausplatz 2, 1014 Vienna; tel. (1) 531-15-0; fax (1) 535-45-30; internet www.bmaa.gv.at.

Ministry of Innovation and Future: Radetzkystr. 2, 1030 Vienna; tel. (1) 711-62-0; fax (1) 531-20-4499; internet www.bmwv.gv.at.

Ministry of the Interior: Herrengasse 7, 1014 Vienna; tel. (1) 531-26-0; fax (1) 531-26-39-10; internet www.bmi.gv.at.

Ministry of Justice: Museumstr. 7, 1016 Vienna; tel. (1) 521-52-0; fax (1) 521-52-72-7.

Ministry of Social Affairs and Generations: Stubenring 1, 1010 Vienna; tel. (1) 711-00; fax (1) 711-00-64-69; e-mail einlaufstelle@bmsg.gv.at; internet www.bmsg.gv.at.

President and Legislature

PRESIDENT

Presidential Election, 19 April 1998

Candidates	Votes	%
Dr Thomas Klestil (ÖVP)	2,626,860	63.5
Gertraud Knoll (Independent) . .	559,943	13.5
Dr Heide Schmidt (FPÖ) . . .	458,491	11.1
Richard Lugner (Independent) . .	411,378	9.9
Karl Walter Novak (Independent) . .	80,741	2.0
Total	**4,137,413**	**100.0**

FEDERAL ASSEMBLY

Nationalrat
(National Council)

President of the Nationalrat: Dr Heinz Fischer.

General Election, 3 October 1999

	Votes	% of Total	Seats
Social-Democratic Party (SPÖ)	1,532,448	33.15	65
Freedom Party (FPÖ) . .	1,244,087	26.91	52
People's Party (ÖVP) . .	1,243,672	26.91	52
Green Alternative List (GAL)*	342,260	7.40	14
Liberal Forum (LiF) . .	168,612	3.65	—
The Independents (DU) .	46,943	1.02	—
Others . . .	44,332	0.96	—
Total	**4,622,354**	**100.00**	**183**

* An informal electoral alliance comprising Die Grüne Alternative (Green Alternative) and Vereinte Grüne Österreichs (United Green Party of Austria).

Bundesrat
(Federal Council)
(January 2001)

Chairman of the Bundesrat: Gerd Klamt (Jan. 2001–June 2001).

Provinces	Total seats	SPÖ	ÖVP	FPÖ
Burgenland	3	2	1	—
Carinthia (Kärnten) . .	5	1	1	3
Lower Austria (Niederösterreich)	12	5	6	1
Upper Austria (Oberösterreich)	11	4	5	2
Salzburg	4	—	3	1
Styria (Steiermark) . .	10	4	4	2
Tyrol (Tirol)	5	1	3	1
Vorarlberg	3	—	2	1
Vienna (Wien) . . .	11	5	2	4
Total	**64**	**22**	**27**	**15**

Political Organizations

Freiheitliche Partei Österreichs (FPÖ/Die Freiheitlichen) (Freedom Party): Kärntnerstr. 28, 1010 Vienna; tel. (1) 512-35-35; fax (1) 513-88-58; internet www.fpoe.at; f. 1955, partially succeeding the Verband der Unabhängigen (League of Independents, f. 1949); popularly known as Die Freiheitlichen; populist right-wing party advocating the participation of workers in management, stricter immigration controls and deregulation in the business sector; opposes Austria's membership of the EU; Chair. Dr Susanne Riess-Passer; Gen. Sec. Peter Westentheler.

Die Grünen–Die Grüne Alternative (Greens–Green Alternative): Lindengasse 40, 1070 Vienna; tel. (1) 521-25-0; fax (1) 526-91-10; e-mail bundesbuero@gruene.at; internet www.gruene.at; f. 1986; campaigns for environmental protection, peace and social justice; Chair. and Leader of Parliamentary Group Prof. Dr Alexander Van der Bellen.

Kommunistische Partei Österreichs (KPÖ) (Communist Party of Austria): Weyringergasse 33/5, 1040 Vienna; tel. (1) 503-65-80; fax (1) 503-65-80-411; e-mail kpoe@magnet.at; internet www.kpoenet.at; f. 1918; strongest in the industrial centres and trade unions; advocates a policy of strict neutrality and opposes Austria's membership of the EU; Chair. Walter Baier.

Liberales Forum (LiF) (Liberal Forum): Doblhoffgasse 4, 1010 Vienna; tel. (1) 403-13-00; e-mail bund@lif.at; internet www.lif.at; f. 1993 by fmr mems of Freiheitliche Partei Österreichs; Leader Dr Friedhelm Frischenschlager.

Österreichische Volkspartei (ÖVP) (Austrian People's Party): Lichtenfelsgasse 7, 1010 Vienna; tel. (1) 401-26; fax (1) 401-26-32-9; internet www.oevp.or.at; f. 1945; Christian-Democratic party; advocates an ecologically-orientated social market economy; 760,000 mems; Chair. Dr Wolfgang Schüssel; Sec.-Gen. Maria Rauch-Kallat.

Sozialdemokratische Partei Österreichs (SPÖ) (Social-Democratic Party of Austria): Löwelstr. 18, 1014 Vienna; tel. (1) 534-27-0; fax (1) 535-96-83; e-mail spoe@spoe.at; internet www.spoe.at; f. as the Social-Democratic Party in 1889, subsequently renamed the Socialist Party, reverted to its original name in 1991; advocates democratic socialism and Austria's permanent neutrality; 500,000 mems; Chair. Dr Alfred Gusenbauer; Secs Andrea Kuntzl, Doris Bures.

Die Unabhängigen (DU) (Independents): Gablenzgasse 11, 1015 Vienna; tel. (1) 981-40-202; fax (1) 981-40-99; e-mail service@ldu.at; f. 1999; Chair. Richard Lugner.

Vereinte Grüne Österreichs (VGÖ) (United Green Party of Austria): Linz; tel. (732) 66-83-91; fax (732) 65-06-68; f. 1982; ecologist party; Chair. Adi Pinter; Gen. Secs Wolfgang Pelikan, Günter Ofner.

Diplomatic Representation

EMBASSIES IN AUSTRIA

Afghanistan: Kaiserstr. 84/1/3, 1070 Vienna; tel. (1) 524-78-06; fax (1) 524-78-07; Chargé d'affaires: Farid A. Amin.

Albania: An den langen Lüssen 1, 1190 Vienna; tel. (1) 328-86-56; fax (1) 328-86-58; Ambassador: Albert Sejdiaj.

Algeria: Rudolfinergasse 16–18, 1190 Vienna; tel. (1) 369-88-53; fax (1) 369-88-56; Ambassador: Mokhtar Reguieg.

Angola: Strohgasse 45, 1030 Vienna; tel. (1) 718-74-88; fax (1) 718-74-86; e-mail embangola.vienna@magnet.at; Ambassador: Dr Fidelino Loy de Jesus Figueiredo.

Argentina: Goldschmiedgasse 2/1, 1010 Vienna; tel. (1) 533-85-77; fax (1) 533-87-97; Ambassador: (vacant).

Armenia: Neubaugasse 12–14/1/16, 1070 Vienna; tel. (1) 522-74-79; fax (1) 522-74-81; Chargé d'affaires: Samuel Mkrtchian.

Australia: Mattiellistr. 2–4/III, 1040 Vienna; tel. (1) 512-85-80; fax (1) 504-11-78; Ambassador: Lance Louis Joseph.

Azerbaijan: Strozzigasse 10, 1080 Vienna; tel. (1) 403-13-22; fax (1) 403-13-23; e-mail azerbembvienna@compuserve.com; Ambassador: Vagif Sadykhov.

Belarus: Hüttelbergstr. 6, 1140 Vienna; tel. (1) 419-96-30; fax (1) 416-96-30-30; Ambassador: Viktor Gaisenak.

Belgium: Wohllebengasse 6, 1040 Vienna; tel. (1) 502-07; fax (1) 502-07-11; Ambassador: Michel Adam.

Bolivia: Waaggasse 10/4, 1040 Vienna; tel. (1) 587-46-75; fax (1) 586-68-80; e-mail embol.austria@chello.at; Ambassador: Jaime Niño de Guzmán Quiroz.

Bosnia and Herzegovina: Tivoligasse 54, 1120 Vienna; tel. (1) 811-85-55; fax (1) 811-85-69; Ambassador: Prof. Dr Emina Kečo-Isaković.

Brazil: Lugeck 1/V/15, 1010 Vienna; tel. (1) 512-06-31; fax (1) 513-50-56; e-mail ausbrem@xpoint.at; Ambassador: Affonso Celso de Ouro-Preto.

Bulgaria: Schwindgasse 8, 1040 Vienna; tel. (1) 505-64-44; fax (1) 505-14-23; e-mail bulgamb@eunet.at; Ambassador: Dr Kiril Kalev.

Burkina Faso: Prinz-Eugen-Str. 18, 1040 Vienna; tel. (1) 503-82-64; fax (1) 503-82-64-20; Ambassador: Thomas Sanon.

Canada: Laurenzerberg 2, 1010 Vienna; tel. (1) 531-38-30-00; fax (1) 531-38-33-21; internet www.kanada.at; Ambassador: Paul Dubois.

Cape Verde: Schwindgasse 20, 1040 Vienna; tel. (1) 503-87-27; fax (1) 503-87-29; Ambassador: Luís de Matos Monteiro da Fonseca.

Chile: Lugeck 1/III/10, 1010 Vienna; tel. (1) 512-23-53; fax (1) 512-92-08-33; e-mail echileat@netway.at; Ambassador: Osvaldo Puccio Huidobro.

China, People's Republic: Metternichgasse 4, 1030 Vienna; tel. (1) 714-31-49-48; fax (1) 713-68-16; Ambassador: Liu Changye.

Colombia: Stadiongasse 6–8, 1010 Vienna; tel. (1) 406-44-46; fax (1) 408-83-03; e-mail embcol@atnet.at; Ambassador: Héctor Charry Samper.

Costa Rica: Schlöglgasse 10, 1120 Vienna; tel. (1) 804-05-37; fax (1) 804-90-71; e-mail aviram@aktiv.co.at; Chargé d'affaires: Stella Aviram Neuman.

Croatia: Heuberggasse 10, 1170 Vienna; tel. (1) 480-20-83; fax (1) 480-29-42; e-mail vlprhbec@reinprecht.at; Ambassador: Prof. DRAZEN VUKOV COLIĆ.

Cuba: Postfach 36; Himmelhofgasse 40 a-c, 1130 Vienna; tel. (1) 877-81-98; fax (1) 877-81-98-30; e-mail embcubvie@magnet.at; Ambassador: LUIS GARCÍA PERAZA.

Cyprus: Parkring 20, 1010 Vienna; tel. (1) 513-06-30; fax (1) 513-06-32; e-mail embassy2@cyprus.vienna.at; Ambassador: NICOLAS D. MACRIS.

Czech Republic: Penzingerstr. 11–13, 1140 Vienna; tel. (1) 894-21-25; fax (1) 894-12-00; Ambassador: JIŘÍ GRUSA.

Denmark: Postfach 298, Führichgasse 6, 1015 Vienna; tel. (1) 512-79-04-0; fax (1) 513-81-20; Ambassador: HENRIK WÖHLK.

Ecuador: Goldschmiedgasse 10/2/24, 1010 Vienna; tel. (1) 535-32-08; fax (1) 535-08-97; e-mail embaustria@council.net; Ambassador: PATRICIO PALACIOS.

Egypt: Hohe Warte 52, 1190 Vienna; tel. and fax (1) 370-81-04; Ambassador: Dr MOSTAFA M. EL-FEKI.

Estonia: Wohllebengasse 9/13, 1040 Vienna; tel. (1) 503-77-61; fax (1) 503-77-62; Ambassador: TOIVO TASA.

Ethiopia: Zaunergasse 1–3, 1030 Vienna; tel. (1) 710-21-68; fax (1) 710-21-71; e-mail ethiopia@eunet.at; Ambassador: MENBERE ALE-MAYEHU.

Finland: Gonzagagasse 16, 1010 Vienna; tel. (1) 531-59-0; fax (1) 535-57-03; Ambassador: TOM CARL ERNST GRÖNBERG.

France: Technikerstr. 2, 1040 Vienna, tel. (1) 505-47-47; fax (1) 505-63-92-68; Ambassador: JEAN CADET.

Georgia: Marokkanergasse 16, 1030 Vienna; tel. (1) 710-36-11; fax (1) 710-36-10; Ambassador: LEVAN MIKELADZE.

Germany: Metternichgasse 3, 1030 Vienna; tel. (1) 711-54; fax (1) 713-83-66; internet www.deubowien.magnet.at; Ambassador: URSULA SEILER-ALBRING.

Greece: Argentinierstr. 14, 1040 Vienna; tel. (1) 505-57-91; fax (1) 505-62-17; Ambassador: JEAN YENNIMATAS.

Guatemala: Salesianergasse 25/1/5, 1030 Vienna; tel. (1) 714-35-70; fax (1) 714-35-70-15; Ambassador: FEDERICO ADOLFO URRUELA PRADO.

Guinea-Bissau: Kaasgrabengasse 61, 1190 Vienna; tel. (1) 328-80-62; fax (1) 328-80-63; Chargé d'affaires: EDUARD W. BURGE.

Holy See: Theresianumgasse 31, 1040 Vienna; tel. (1) 505-13-27; fax (1) 505-61-40; Apostolic Nuncio: Most Rev. DONATO SQUICCIARINI, Titular Archbishop of Tiburnia.

Hungary: Bankgasse 4–6, 1010 Vienna; tel. (1) 533-26-31; fax (1) 535-99-40; e-mail ungboa@eunet.at; Ambassador: Dr SÁNDOR PEISCH.

India: Kärntner Ring 2A, 1015 Vienna; tel. (1) 505-86-66-69; fax (1) 505-92-19; Ambassador: YOGESH MOHAN TIWARI.

Indonesia: Gustav-Tschermak-Gasse 5–7, 1180 Vienna; tel. (1) 479-05-37; fax (1) 479-05-57; Ambassador: RHOUSDY SOERIATMADJA.

Iran: Jaurèsgasse 9, 1030 Vienna; tel. (1) 712-26-57; fax (1) 713-46-94; e-mail botschaft.d.islam.rep.iran@acv.at; Ambassador: EBRAHIM RAHIM POUR.

Iraq: Johannesgasse 26, 1010 Vienna; tel. (1) 713-81-95-96; fax (1) 713-67-20; Chargé d'affaires: KHALID A. NASIR.

Ireland: Hilton Centre, 16th Floor, 1030 Vienna; tel. (1) 715-42-46; fax (1) 713-60-04; Ambassador: THELMA MARIA DORAN.

Israel: Anton-Frank-Gasse 20, 1180 Vienna; tel. (1) 470-47-41; fax (1) 470-47-46; Ambassador: (withdrawn in Feb. 2000).

Italy: Rennweg 27, 1030 Vienna; tel. (1) 712-51-21; fax (1) 713-97-19; e-mail ambitalviepress@via.at; Ambassador: Dr PIER LUIGI RACHELE.

Japan: Heßgasse 6, 1010 Vienna; tel. (1) 531-92-0; fax (1) 532-05-90; internet www.embjapan.at; Ambassador: YUSHU TAKASHIMA.

Jordan: Doblhoffgasse 3/2, 1010 Vienna; tel. (1) 405-10-25; fax (1) 405-10-31; Ambassador: Dr MAZEN ARMOUTI.

Kazakhstan: Billrothstr. 2/23, 1190 Vienna; tel. (1) 367-91-75; fax (1) 367-91-74; Ambassador Dr SAGYNBEK T. TURSYNOV.

Kenya: Neulingasse 29/8, 1030 Vienna; tel. (1) 712-39-19; fax (1) 712-39-22.

Korea, Democratic People's Republic: Beckmanngasse 10–12, 1140 Vienna; tel. (1) 894-23-11; fax (1) 894-31-74; Ambassador: KIM KWANG SOP.

Korea, Republic: Gregor-Mendel-Str. 25, 1180 Vienna; tel. (1) 478-19-91; fax (1) 478-10-13; Ambassador: BAN KI-MOON.

Kuwait: Universitätsstr. 5, 1010 Vienna; tel. (1) 405-56-46; fax (1) 408-56-00; Ambassador: FAISAL R. AL-GHAIS.

Kyrgyzstan: Naglergasse 25/5, 1010 Vienna; tel. (1) 535-03-78; fax (1) 535-03-79-131; e-mail kyrbot@kyrbotwien.or.at; Ambassador: KAMIL BAIALINOV.

Latvia: Währingerstr. 3/8, 1090 Vienna; tel. (1) 403-31-12; fax (1) 403-31-12/27; e-mail lettbox@netway.at; Ambassador: Dr MĀRTIŅŠ VIRSIS.

Lebanon: Oppolzergasse 6/3, 1010 Vienna; tel. (1) 533-88-21; fax (1) 533-49-84; e-mail ambassade.liban@vienna.telecom.at; Ambassador: SAMIR CHAMMA.

Libya: Blaasstr. 33, 1190 Vienna; tel. (1) 367-76-39; fax (1) 367-76-01; Secretary of People's Bureau: Dr SAID ABDULAATI MOHAMED.

Liechtenstein: Löwelstr. 8/7, 1010 Vienna; tel. (1) 535-92-11; fax (1) 535-92-114; e-mail liechtenstein.embassy.vienna@buie.li; Ambassador: Princess MARIA-PIA KOTHBAUER OF LIECHTENSTEIN.

Lithuania: Löwengasse 47, 1030 Vienna; tel. (1) 718-54-67; fax (1) 718-54-69; e-mail chancery@mail.austria.eu.net; Ambassador: GINTÉ DAMUSIS.

Luxembourg: Sternwartestr. 81, 1180 Vienna; tel. (1) 478-21-42; fax (1) 478-21-44; Ambassador: GEORGES SANTER.

Macedonia, former Yugoslav republic: Kaiserstr. 84/1/5, 1070 Vienna; tel. (1) 524-87-56; fax (1) 524-87-53; e-mail macembassy@aon.at; Ambassador: OGNEN MALESKI.

Malaysia: Prinz-Eugen-Str. 18, 1040 Vienna; tel. (1) 505-10-42-0; fax (1) 505-79-42; e-mail mwvienna@netway.at; Ambassador: HUSSEIN HANIFF.

Malta: Opernring 5/1, 1010 Vienna; tel. (1) 586-50-10; fax (1) 586-50-109; e-mail moboso@aon.at; Ambassador: Dr NOEL BUTTIGIEG-SCICLUNA.

Mexico: Türkenstr. 15, 1090 Vienna; tel. (1) 310-73-83; fax (1) 310-73-87; e-mail embamex@embamex.or.at; Ambassador: ROBERTA LAJOUS.

Moldova: Taborstr. 24A, 1020 Vienna; tel. (1) 216-60-03; fax (1) 214-19-97; e-mail amda@netway.at; Ambassador: Dr VALENTIN CIUMAC.

Morocco: Opernring 3–5/I/4, 1010 Vienna; tel. (1) 586-66-50; fax (1) 586-76-67; Ambassador: ABDERRAHIM BENMOUSSA.

Namibia: Strozigasse 10/15, 1080 Vienna; tel. (1) 402-93-74; fax (1) 402-93-70; Ambassador: HINYANGERWA P. ASHEEKE.

Netherlands: Postfach 190, 1010 Vienna; tel. (1) 589-39; fax (1) 589-39-265; e-mail nlgovwen@eunet.at; internet www.netherlands-embassy.at; Ambassador: JAAP RAMAKER.

Nicaragua: Ebendorferstr. 10/3/12, 1010 Vienna; tel. (1) 403-18-38; fax (1) 403-27-52; e-mail 113350.2341@compuserve.com; Ambassador: SUYAPA INDIANA PADILLA TERCERO.

Nigeria: Postfach 183, Rennweg 25, 1030 Vienna; tel. (1) 712-66-85; fax (1) 714-14-02; Ambassador: ALBERT AZUBOGU ANOPUECHI.

Norway: Bayerngasse 3, 1030 Vienna; tel. (1) 715-66-92; fax (1) 712-65-52; e-mail ambvie@chello.at; Ambassador: HELGA HERNES.

Oman: Währingerstr. 2–4/24–25, 1090 Vienna; tel. (1) 310-86-43; fax (1) 310-72-68; Ambassador: SALIM M. AR-RIYAMI.

Pakistan: Hofzeile 13, 1190 Vienna; tel. (1) 368-73-81; fax (1) 368-73-76; e-mail parep.vienna@telecom.at; Ambassador: (vacant).

Panama: Elisabethstr. 4–5/4/10, 1010 Vienna; tel. (1) 587-23-47; fax (1) 586-30-80; e-mail mail@empanvienna.co.at; Ambassador: Dr JORGE ENRIQUE HALPHEN PÉREZ.

Paraguay: Strohgasse 16/6, 1030 Vienna; tel. (1) 715-56-08; fax (1) 715-56-09; e-mail embapar@abacus.at; Chargé d'affaires: MARÍA CRISTINA ACOSTA-ALVAREZ.

Peru: Gottfried-Keller-Gasse 2/8, 1030 Vienna; tel. (1) 713-43-77; fax (1) 712-77-04; e-mail peru.emb@xpoint.at; Ambassador: GILBERT CHAUNY DE PORTURAS-HOYLE.

Philippines: Laurenzerberg 2, 1010 Vienna; tel. (1) 533-24-01; fax (1) 533-24-01-24; e-mail phat@ping.at; Ambassador: JOSÉ A. ZAIDE.

Poland: Hietzinger Hauptstr. 42C, 1130 Vienna; tel. (1) 870-15; fax (1) 870-15-22-2; Ambassador: Prof. Dr JAN BARCZ.

Portugal: Opernring 3/1, 1010 Vienna; tel. (1) 586-75-36; fax (1) 586-75-36-99; e-mail portugal@portembassy.at; Ambassador: ÁLVARO DE MENDONÇA E MOURA.

Qatar: Richard-Kralik-Platz 1, 1180 Vienna; tel. (1) 479-98-03; fax (1) 478-49-66; Chargé d'affaires: SALEH ABDULLAH AL-BOUANIN.

Romania: Prinz-Eugen-Str. 60, 1040 Vienna; tel. (1) 505-32-27; fax (1) 504-14-62; Chargé d'affaires: STEFANA GREAVU.

Russia: Reisnerstr. 45–47, 1030 Vienna; tel. (1) 712-12-29; fax (1) 712-33-88; e-mail russia@embassy.vienna.at; Ambassador: VLADIMIR M. GRININ.

San Marino: Getreidemarkt 12, 1010 Vienna; tel. (1) 586-21-80; fax (1) 586-22-35; Ambassador: GIOVANNI VITO MARCUCCI.

Saudi Arabia: Parkring 10, 5. Stock, 1010 Vienna; tel. (1) 368-23-16; fax (1) 368-25-60; Ambassador: OMER MUHAMMED KURDI.

Slovakia: Armbrustergasse 24, 1190 Vienna; tel. (1) 318-90-55-201; fax (1) 318-90-55-208; e-mail zuwien.pol@aon.at; internet www.slovak-trade.at; Ambassador: ĽUBOR BYSTRICKÝ.

Slovenia: Nibelungengasse 13/3, 1010 Vienna; tel. (1) 586-13-09; fax (1) 586-12-65; Ambassador: IVO VAJGL.

South Africa: Sandgasse 33, 1190 Vienna; tel. (1) 320-64-93; fax (1) 320-64-93-51; e-mail saembvie@ins.at; internet www.saembvie.ins.at; Ambassador: N. J. MXAKATO-DISEKO.

Spain: Argentinierstr. 34, 1040 Vienna; tel. (1) 505-57-80; fax (1) 505-57-88-25; Ambassador: RICARDO DÍEZ-HOCHLEITNER RODRÍGUEZ.

Sri Lanka: Rainergasse 1/2/5, 1040 Vienna; tel. (1) 503-79-88; fax (1) 503-79-93; e-mail embassy@srilanka.at; internet www .embassy.srilanka.at; Ambassador: ANIL MOONESINGHE.

Sudan: Reisnerstr. 29/5, 1030 Vienna; tel. (1) 710-23-43; fax (1) 710-23-46; e-mail sudan-embassy-vienna@aon.at; internet www .members.aon.at/sudanivienna; Ambassador: ABD EL-GHAFFAR ABD ER-RAHMAN HASSAN.

Sweden: Obere Donaustr. 49–51, 1025 Vienna; tel. (1) 217-53-200; fax (1) 217-53-370; e-mail ambassaden.wien@foreign.ministry.se; Ambassador: BJÖRN SKALA.

Switzerland: Prinz-Eugen-Str. 7, 1030 Vienna; tel. (1) 795-05; fax (1) 795-05-21; Chargé d'affaires: MARKUS PETER.

Syria: Wallnerstr. 8, 1010 Vienna; tel. (1) 533-46-33; fax (1) 533-46-32; Ambassador: Dr RIAD SIAGE.

Tajikistan: Wallnergasse 8, 1090 Vienna; tel. and fax (1) 409-82-66; Ambassador: KHAMROKHON ZARIPOV.

Thailand: Cottagegasse 48, 1180 Vienna; tel. (1) 478-27-97; fax (1) 478-29-07; e-mail thai.vn@embthai.telecom.at; Ambassador: SORAY-OUTH PROMPOJ.

Tunisia: Opernring 5/3, 1010 Vienna; tel. (1) 581-52-81; fax (1) 581-55-92; Ambassador: ABDELAZIZ CHAABANE.

Turkey: Prinz-Eugen-Str. 40, 1040 Vienna; tel. (1) 505-73-38-0; fax (1) 505-36-60; Ambassador: ÖMER ERSAN.

Turkmenistan: Argentinierstr. 22/11/EG, 1040 Vienna; tel. (1) 503-64-70; fax (1) 503-64-73; e-mail turkmen.dec.osce@chello.at; Ambassador: VLADIMIR KAOYROV.

Ukraine: Naaffgasse 23, 1180 Vienna; tel. (1) 479-71-72; fax (1) 479-71-72-47; e-mail ukremb@netway.at; Ambassador: MYKOLA P. MAKAREVYCH.

United Arab Emirates: Peter-Jordan-Str. 66, 1190 Vienna; tel. (1) 368-14-55; fax (1) 368-44-85; Chargé d'affaires: AHMED RASHED AD-DOSARI.

United Kingdom: Jaurèsgasse 12, 1030 Vienna; tel. (1) 716-13-0; fax (1) 716-13-69-00; e-mail press@britishembassy.at; internet www .britishembassy.at; Ambassador: ANTONY FORD.

USA: Boltzmanngasse 16, 1090 Vienna; tel. (1) 313-39; fax (1) 310-06-82; Ambassador: (withdrawn in Feb. 2000).

Uruguay: Palais Esterhazy, Wallnerstr. 4/3/17, 1010 Vienna; tel. (1) 535-66-36; fax (1) 535-66-18; e-mail uruvien@embuy.or.at; Ambassador: FRUCTUOSO PITTALUGA.

Uzbekistan: Porzellangasse 32/5, 1090 Vienna; tel. (1) 315-39-94; fax (1) 315-39-93; e-mail botschaft.usbekistan@aon.at; Chargé d'affaires: SHUKRAT KHAKIMOV.

Venezuela: Marokkanergasse 22, 1030 Vienna; tel. (1) 712-26-38; fax (1) 715-32-19; Ambassador: Prof. Dr DEMETRIO BOERSNER.

Viet Nam: Félix-Mottl-Str. 20, 1190 Vienna; tel. (1) 368-07-55; fax (1) 368-07-54; e-mail embassyofvietnam@netway.at; Ambassador: NGUYEN XUAN HONG.

Yemen: Karolinengasse 5/7, 1040 Vienna; tel. (1) 503-29-30; fax (1) 505-31-59; e-mail vienna@yemen-embassy.at; Ambassador: Dr HASSAN MOHAMED MAKKI.

Yugoslavia: Rennweg 3, 1030 Vienna; tel. (1) 713-25-95; fax (1) 713-25-97; e-mail yuambaus@ins.at; Ambassador: Dr RADOS SMILJKOVIĆ.

Zimbabwe: Strozzigasse 10/15, 1080 Vienna; tel. (1) 407-92-36; fax (1) 407-92-38; Ambassador: EVELYN LILLIAN KAWONZA.

Judicial System

The Austrian legal system is based on the principle of a division between legislative, administrative and judicial power. There are three supreme courts (Verfassungsgerichtshof, Verwaltungsgerichtshof and Oberster Gerichtshof). The judicial courts are organized into about 200 local courts (Bezirksgerichte), 17 provincial and district courts (Landes- und Kreisgerichte), and four higher provincial courts (Oberlandesgerichte) in Vienna, Graz, Innsbruck and Linz.

SUPREME ADMINISTRATIVE COURTS

Verfassungsgerichtshof (Constitutional Court): Judenplatz 11, 1010 Vienna; tel. (1) 531-22-0; fax (1) 531-22-499; e-mail vfgh@vfgh.gv.at; internet www.vfgh.gv.at; f. 1919; deals with matters affecting the Constitution, examines the legality of legislation and administration; Pres. Prof. Dr LUDWIG ADAMOVICH; Vice-Pres. Prof. Dr KARL KORINEK.

Verwaltungsgerichtshof (Administrative Court): Judenplatz 11, 1010 Vienna; tel. (1) 531-11; fax (1) 531-11-135; deals with matters affecting the legality of administration; Pres. Prof. Dr CLEMENS JABLONER; Vice-Pres. Prof. Dr WOLFGANG PESENDORFER.

SUPREME JUDICIAL COURT

Oberster Gerichtshof: Schmerlingplatz 10–11, 1016 Vienna; tel. (1) 521-52-0; fax (1) 521-52-37-10; Pres. Dr ERWIN FELZMANN; Vice-Pres Dr HORST SCHLOSSER, Hon. Prof. Dr KONRAD BRUSTBAUER.

Religion

CHRISTIANITY

Ökumenischer Rat der Kirchen in Österreich (Ecumenical Council of Churches in Austria): Fleischmarkt 13, 1010 Vienna; tel. (1) 533-29-65; fax (1) 533-38-89; f. 1958; 14 mem. Churches, 11 observers; Hon. Pres. Bishop MICHAEL STAIKOS (Greek Orthodox Church); Vice-Pres Dr JOHANNES DANTINE (Protestant Church of the Augsburgian Confession), Mother Superior CHRISTINE GLEIXNER (Roman Catholic Church); Sec. Superintendent HELMUT NAUSNER (United Methodist Church).

The Roman Catholic Church

Austria comprises two archdioceses, seven dioceses and the territorial abbacy of Wettingen-Mehrerau (directly responsible to the Holy See). The Archbishop of Vienna is also the Ordinary for Catholics of the Byzantine rite in Austria (totalling an estimated 5,000 at 31 December 1997). At 31 December 1999 there were an estimated 5,671,064 adherents (about 68.5% of the population).

Bishops' Conference: Österreichische Bischofskonferenz, Wollzeile 2, 1010 Vienna; tel. (1) 516-11-32-80; fax (1) 516-11-34-36; e-mail sekretariat@bischofskonferenz.at; internet www .bischofskonferenz.at; f. 1849; Pres. Cardinal Dr CHRISTOPH SCHÖNBORN, Archbishop of Vienna; Sec. Mgr Dr ÄGIDIUS ZSIFKOVICS.

Archbishop of Salzburg: Most Rev. Dr GEORG EDER, Postfach 62, 5020 Salzburg, Kapitelplatz 2; 5010 Salzburg; tel. (662) 80-47-100; fax (662) 80-47-75; e-mail erzbischof-eder@kirchen.net; internet www.kirchen.net.

Archbishop of Vienna: Cardinal Dr CHRISTOPH SCHÖNBORN, Wollzeile 2, 1010 Vienna; tel. (1) 515-52-32-20; fax (1) 515-52-37-60.

Orthodox Churches

The Armenian Apostolic Church and the Bulgarian, Coptic, Greek, Romanian, Russian, Serbian and Syrian Orthodox Churches are active in Austria.

The Anglican Communion

Within the Church of England, Austria forms part of the diocese of Gibraltar in Europe. The Bishop is resident in London.

Archdeacon of the Eastern Archdeaconry: Ven. JEREMY PEAKE, Thugutstr. 2/12, 1020 Vienna; tel. and fax (1) 663-92-09-264.

Protestant Churches

Bund der Baptistengemeinden in Österreich (Fed. of Baptist Communities): Krummgasse 7/4, 1030 Vienna; tel. (1) 713-68-28; fax (1) 713-68-28-4; Pres. Rev. HORST FISCHER.

Evangelische Kirche Augsburgischen Bekenntnisses in Österreich (Protestant Church of the Augsburgian Confession): Severin-Schreiber-Gasse 3, 1180 Vienna; tel. (1) 479-15-23; fax (1) 479-15-23-110; e-mail bischof@okr-evang.at; internet www.evang .at; 340,422 mems; Bishop Mag. HERWIG STURM.

Evangelische Kirche HB (Helvetischen Bekenntnisses) (Protestant Church of the Helvetic Confession): Dorotheergasse 16, 1010 Vienna; tel. (1) 513-65-64; fax (1) 512-44-90; e-mail kirche-hb@ evang.at; 15,863 mems; Landessuperintendent Pfr. PETER KARNER.

Evangelisch-methodistische Kirche (United Methodist Church): Landgutgasse 39/7, 1100 Vienna; tel. (1) 604-53-47; fax (1) 606-67-17; Superintendent HELMUT NAUSNER.

Other Christian Churches

Altkatholische Kirche Österreichs (Old Catholic Church in Austria): Schottenring 17, 1010 Vienna; tel. (1) 317-83-94; fax (1) 317-83-95-9; c. 18,000 mems; Bishop BERNHARD HEITZ.

JUDAISM

There are about 10,000 Jews in Austria.

Israelitische Kultusgemeinde (Jewish Community): Seitenstettengasse 4, 1010 Vienna; tel. (1) 531-04-0; fax (1) 533-15-77; Pres. Dr ARIEL MUZICANT.

The Press

Austria's first newspaper was published in 1605. The *Wiener Zeitung*, founded in 1703, is the world's oldest daily paper. Restrictions on press freedom are permissible only within the framework of Article 10 (2) of the European Convention of Human Rights.

The Austrian Press Council (Presserat), founded in 1961, supervises the activities of the press. Vienna is the focus of newspaper and periodical publishing, although there is also a strong press in some provinces. The three highest circulation dailies are the *Neue Kronen-Zeitung,* the *Kurier,* and the *Kleine Zeitung* (Graz).

PRINCIPAL DAILIES

Bregenz

Neue Vorarlberger Tageszeitung: Arlbergstr. 117, 6901 Bregenz; tel. (5574) 40-90; fax (5574) 40-93-00; f. 1972; morning; independent; Editor (vacant); circ. 20,136.

Vorarlberger Nachrichten: Kirchstr. 35, 6901 Bregenz; tel. (5574) 51-22-27; fax (5574) 51-22-30; internet www.vol.at; morning; Editor EUGEN A. RUSS; circ. 74,948.

Graz

Kleine Zeitung: Schönaugasse 64, 8011 Graz; tel. (316) 87-50; fax (316) 87-54-03-4; internet www.kleine.co.at; f. 1904; independent; Chief Editor Dr ERWIN ZANKEL; circ. 177,050.

Neue Zeit: Ankerstr. 4, 8054 Graz; tel. (316) 28-08-0; fax (316) 28-08-32-5; f. 1945; morning; Editor JOSEF RIEDLER.

Innsbruck

Tiroler Tageszeitung: Ing.-Etzel-Str. 30, 6020 Innsbruck; tel. (512) 53-54-0; fax (512) 57-59-24; e-mail redaktion@tt.com; internet www.tirol.com/tt; morning; independent; Chief Editor CLAUS REITAN; circ. 112,690.

Klagenfurt

Kärntner Tageszeitung: Viktringer Ring 28, 9020 Klagenfurt; tel. (463) 58-66-0; fax (463) 58-66-32-1; f. 1946; morning except Monday; Socialist; Chief Editor Dr HELLWIG VALENTIN.

Kleine Zeitung: Funderstr. 1A, 9020 Klagenfurt; tel. (463) 200-58-00; fax (463) 56-50-0; independent; Editor Dr HORST PIRKER; circ. 99,380.

Linz

Neues Volksblatt: Hafenstr. 1–3, 4010 Linz; tel. (732) 76-06-0; fax (732) 77-92-42; e-mail volksblatt@volksblatt.at; internet www.volksblatt.at; f. 1869; Austrian People's Party; Chief Editor Dr FRANZ ROHRHOFER.

Oberösterreichische Nachrichten: Promenade 23, 4010 Linz; tel. (732) 78-05-41-0; fax (732) 78-05-21-7; internet www.oon.at; f. 1865; morning; independent; Chief Editor Dr HANS KÖPPL; circ. 123,470.

Salzburg

*Salzburger Nachrichten: Karolingerstr. 40, 5021 Salzburg; tel. (662) 83-73-0; fax (662) 83-73-39-9; e-mail service@salzburg.com; internet www.salzburg.com; f. 1945; morning; independent; Editor-in-Chief RONALD ARAZON; circ. 99,123.

Salzburger Volkszeitung: Bergstr. 12, 5020 Salzburg; tel. (662) 87-94-91; fax (662) 87-94-91-13; e-mail suz-redaktion@sbg.at; Austrian People's Party; Editor HELMUT MÖDLHAMMER; circ. weekdays 12,030.

Vienna

*Kurier: Seidengasse 11, 1072 Vienna; tel. (1) 521-00; fax (1) 521-00-22-63; e-mail leser@kurier.at; internet www2.kurier.at; f. 1954; independent; Chief Editor PETER RABL; circ. weekdays 334,204, Sunday 545,700.

*Neue Kronen-Zeitung: Muthgasse 2, 1190 Vienna; tel. (1) 360-10; fax (1) 369-83-85; internet www.krone.at; f. 1900; independent; Editor HANS DICHAND; circ. weekdays 510,226, Sunday 751,296.

*Die Presse: Parkring 12a, 1015 Vienna; tel. (1) 514-14; fax (1) 514-14-400; e-mail chefredaktion@presse-wien.at; internet www.diepresse.at; f. 1848; morning; independent; Editors JULIUS KAINZ, Dr THOMAS CHORHERR; circ. Mon.–Wed. 96,000, Thur.–Fri. 105,000; Sat. 156,000.

*Der Standard: Herrengasse 19–21, 1014 Vienna; tel. (1) 531-70; fax (1) 531-70-13-1; e-mail documentation@derstandard.at; internet www.derstandard.at; f. 1988; independent; Editors-in-Chief OSCAR BRONNER, Dr GERFRIED SPERL; circ. 104,050.

*Wiener Zeitung: Rennweg 16, 1037 Vienna; tel. (1) 797-89; fax (1) 797-89-43-3; internet www.wienerzeitung.at; f. 1703; morning; official govt paper; Editor HORST TRAXLER; circ. 20,020.

* National newspapers.

PRINCIPAL WEEKLIES

Blickpunkt: E.-Bodem-Gasse 6, 6020 Innsbruck; tel. (512) 32-00; fax (512) 32-01-20; Editor OTTO STEIXNER.

Die Furche: Lobkowitzplatz 1, Singerstr. 7, 1010 Vienna; tel. (1) 512-52-61; fax (1) 512-82-15; f. 1945; Catholic; Editor Dr GOTTFRIED MOIK.

Die ganze Woche: Ignaz-Köck-Str. 17, 1210 Vienna; tel. (1) 391-60-0; fax (1) 391-60-06-4; circ. 582,060.

industrie: Reisnerstr. 40/2, 1030 Vienna; tel. (1) 711-95-0; fax (1) 711-95-52-99; Editor MILAN FRÜHBAUER; circ. 14,330.

IW-Internationale Wirtschaft: Nikolsdorfer Gasse 7–11, 1051 Vienna; tel. (1) 546-64-346; fax (1) 546-64-342; economics; Editor NIKOLAUS GERSTMAYER; circ. 13,430.

Kärntner Nachrichten: Waagplatz 7, 9010 Klagenfurt; tel. (463) 51-14-17-22; fax (463) 50-41-85; f. 1954; Editor HANS RIEPAN.

Die neue Wirtschaft: Nikolsdorfer Gasse 7–11, 1051 Vienna; tel. (1) 546-64-24-7; fax (1) 546-64-34-7; economics; circ. 25,650.

Neue Wochenschau: J. N. Bergerstr. 2, 7210 Mattersburg; tel. and fax (2622) 67-47-3; f. 1908; Editor HELMUT WALTER; circ. 128,500.

NFZ—Neue Freie Zeitung: Postfach 81, 1013 Vienna; Esslinggasse 14–16, 1010 Vienna; tel. (1) 512-35-35-311; fax (1) 512-35-35-412; e-mail redaktion.nfz@fpoe.at; organ of Freedom Party; Chief Editor MICHAEL A. RICHTER; circ. 70,000.

Niederösterreichische Nachrichten: Gutenbergstr. 12, 3100 St Pölten; tel. (2742) 80-20; fax (2742) 80-21-48-0; e-mail chefredaktion@noen.at; internet www.noen.at; Editor HARALD KNABL; circ. 158,972.

Oberösterreichische Rundschau: Hafenstr. 1–3, 4010 Linz; tel. (732) 76-16-0; fax (732) 76-16-30-7; Editor-in-Chief RUDOLF CHMELIR; circ. 284,650.

Der Österreichische Bauernbündler: Schenkenstr. 2, 1014 Vienna; tel. (1) 533-16-76-16; fax (1) 533-16-76-45; Editor Prof. PAUL GRUBER; circ. 70,000.

Präsent: Exlgasse 20, 6020 Innsbruck; tel. (512) 22-33; fax (512) 22-33-50-1; f. 1892; independent Catholic; Chief Editor PAUL MVIGG.

Samstag: Faradaygasse 6, 1081 Vienna; tel. (1) 795-94-13-5; e-mail samstag@heroldwien.at; f. 1951; weekly; independent; Chief Editor GERLINDE KOLANDA; circ. 41,000.

Tiroler Bauernzeitung: Brixner Str. 1, 6021 Innsbruck; tel. (512) 59-90-00; fax (1) 59-90-03-1; publ. by Tiroler Bauernbund; Chief Dir GEORG KEUSCHNIGG; circ. 23,000.

Volksstimme: Weyringergasse 35/DG, 1040 Vienna; tel. (1) 503-68-28; fax (1) 503-66-38; e-mail redaktion@volksstimme.at; f. 1994; Chief Editor WALTER BAIER.

POPULAR PERIODICALS

Agrar Post: Schulstr. 64, 2103 Langenzersdorf; tel. (2244) 46-47; f. 1924; monthly; agriculture.

Austria-Ski: Olympiastr. 10, 6020 Innsbruck; tel. (512) 335-01-0; fax (512) 367-99-8; 6 a year; official journal of Austrian Skiing Asscn; Editor Mag. JOSEF SCHMID.

auto touring: Tauchnergasse 5, 3400 Klosterneuburg; tel. (2243) 40-40; fax (2243) 40-43-72-1; e-mail ottoburghart@oeamtc.at; monthly; official journal of the Austrian Automobile Organizations; Editor-in-Chief OTTO BURGHART; circ. 1,180,000.

Bunte Österreich: Karl-Luegel-Platz 2, 1010 Vienna; tel. (1) 513-88-33; fax (1) 513-88-38; illustrated weekly.

Frauenblatt: Faradaygasse 6, 1032 Vienna; tel. (1) 795-94-13-5; e-mail samstag@heroldwien.at; women's weekly; Editor GERLINDE KOLANDA; circ. 22,300.

Die Neue Sportzeitung: Piaristengasse 16, 1080 Vienna; tel. (1) 405-55-88; fax (1) 402-49-60; e-mail redaktion@sportzeitung.at; internet www.sportzeitung.at; f. 1949; weekly sports illustrated; Editor HORST HÖTSCH; circ. 28,330.

News: Praterstr. 31, 1020 Vienna; tel. (1) 213-12-0; fax (1) 213-12-30-0; weekly; illustrated; Editor WOLFGANG FELLNER; circ. 342,244.

Profil: Lindengasse 52, 1070 Vienna; tel. (1) 534-70-0; fax (1) 535-32-50; e-mail redaktion@profil.at; internet www.profil.at; f. 1970; weekly; political, general; independent; circ. 100,000.

RZ—Wochenschau: Vienna; tel. (1) 523-56-46; fax (1) 523-56-46-22; f. 1936; weekly illustrated; Chief Editor PAUL WEISS.

Trend: Marc-Aurel-Str. 10–12, 1010 Vienna; tel. (1) 534-70; monthly; economics.

TV Media: Taborstr. 1–3, 1020 Vienna; tel. (1) 213-120; weekly; illustrated; Editor WOLFGANG FELLNER; circ. 210,150.

Vídeňské svobodné listy: Margaretenplatz 7/2, 1050 Vienna; tel. (1) 587-83-08; fortnightly for Czech and Slovak communities in Austria; Editor HEINRICH DRAZDIL.

Welt der Frau: Lustenauerstr. 21, 4020 Linz; tel. (732) 77-00-01-11; fax (732) 77-00-01-24; women's monthly magazine; circ. 73,530.

Wiener: Büropark Donau, Donaustr. 102, 3400 Klosterneuburg; tel. (1) 88-60-0; fax (1) 88-60-01-99; monthly; Chief Editor HANS SCHMID; circ. 130,530.

SPECIALIST PERIODICALS

Eurocity: Leberstr. 122, 1110 Vienna; tel. (1) 740-95-46-4; fax (1) 740-95-49-1; e-mail eurocity.zv@bohmann.co.at; internet www.eurocity.at; f. 1928; every 2 months; Editor-in-Chief GEORG KARP; circ. 70,000.

Forum: Museumstr. 5, 1070 Vienna; tel. (1) 932-73-3; fax (1) 938-36-8; f. 1954; every 2 months; international magazine for cultural freedom, political equality and labour solidarity; Editor-in-Chief GERHARD OBERSCHLICK.

itm praktiker: ZB-Verlag, Marochallplatz 23/1/21, 1125 Vienna; tel. (1) 804-04-74; fax (1) 804-44-39; technical hobbies; Chief Editor GERHARD K. BUCHBERGER; circ. 18,800.

Juristische Blätter (mit Beilage 'Wirtschaftsrechtliche Blätter'): Springer Verlag, Sachsenplatz 4, 1201 Vienna; tel. (1) 330-24-15-0; fax (1) 330-24-26; internet www.springer.at/jbl; f. 1872; monthly; Editors F. BYDLINSKI, M. BURGSTALLER.

Die Landwirtschaft: Löwelstr. 16, 1010 Vienna; tel. (1) 534-41; fax (1) 534-41-45-0; f. 1923; monthly; agriculture and forestry; owned and publ. by Österreichischer Agrarverlag; Editor GERD RITTENAUER.

Liberal Konkret: Reichsratstr. 7/10, 1010 Vienna; tel. (1) 402-78-81; fax (1) 402-78-89; e-mail bund@lif.or.at; internet www.lif.or.at; 10 a year; organ of Liberal Forum.

Literatur und Kritik: Otto-Müller-Verlag, Ernest-Thun-Str. 11, 5020 Salzburg; tel. (662) 88-19-74; fax (662) 87-23-87; f. 1966; 5 a year; Austrian and European literature and criticism; Editor KARL-MARKUS GAUSS.

Monatshefte für Chemie: Sachsenplatz 4–6, 1201 Vienna; tel. (1) 330-24-15-0; f. 1880; monthly; chemistry; Man. Editor K. SCHLÖGL.

Österreichische Ärztezeitung: Weihburggasse 9, 1010 Vienna; tel. (1) 512-44-86; fax (1) 512-44-86-24; e-mail presse.verlags@oak.at; f. 1945; 21 a year; organ of the Austrian Medical Board; Editor MARTIN STICKLER.

Österreichische Ingenieur- und Architekten-Zeitschrift (ÖIAZ): Eschenbachgasse 9, 1010 Vienna; tel. (1) 587-35-36-28; fax (1) 587-35-36; e-mail office@oiav.at; internet www.members.eunct.at/oiavi; f. 1849; 6 a year; Editor Dr GEORG WIDTMANN; circ. 3,000.

Österreichische Monatshefte: Lichtenfelsgasse 7, 1010 Vienna; tel. (1) 401-26-53-2. 1945; monthly; organ of Austrian People's Party; Editor GERHARD WILFLINGER.

Österreichische Musikzeitschrift: Hegelgasse 13, 1010 Vienna; tel. (1) 512-68-69; fax (1) 512-46-29; f. 1946; monthly; Editor Dr M. DIEDERICHS-LAFITE; circ. 5,000.

Reichsbund-Aktuell mit SPORT: Laudongasse 16/3/2a, 1080 Vienna; tel. and fax (1) 405-54-06; f. 1917; monthly; Catholic; organ of Reichsbund, Bewegung für christliche Gesellschaftspolitik und Sport; Editor WALTER RAMING; circ. 12,000.

Welt der Arbeit: Altmannsdorferstr. 154–156, 1230 Vienna; tel. (1) 662-32-96; socialist industrial journal; Editor WALTER KRATZER; circ 64,350.

Wiener klinische Wochenschrift: Sachsenplatz 4–6, 1201 Vienna; tel. (1) 330-24-15; fax (1) 330-24-26; f. 1888; medical bi-weekly; Editors O. KRAUPP, H. SINZINGER.

Die Zukunft: Löwelstr. 18, 1014 Vienna; tel. (1) 534-27-20-6; fax (1) 535-96-83; monthly; organ of Social-Democratic Party of Austria; Editor ALBRECHT K. KONECNY; circ. 15,000.

NEWS AGENCIES

APA (Austria Presse-Agentur): Internationales Pressezentrum (IPZ), Gunoldstr. 14, 1199 Vienna; tel. (1) 360-60-0; fax (1) 360-60-30-99; e-mail marketing@apa.at; internet www.apa.at; f. 1946; co-operative agency of the Austrian Newspapers and Broadcasting Co (private co); 37 mems; Man. Dir Dr WOLFGANG VYSLOZIL; Chief Editor WOLFGANG MAYR.

Foreign Bureaux

Agence France-Presse (AFP) (France): IPZ, Gunoldstr. 14, 1199 Vienna; tel. (1) 368-31-87; fax (1) 368-31-88-20; e-mail afpvie@afp.com; Bureau Chief PATRICK RAHIR.

Agenzia Nazionale Stampa Associata (ANSA) (Italy): IPZ, Gunoldstr. 14, 1199 Vienna; tel. (1) 368-13-00; fax (1) 368-79-35; Bureau Chief ROBERTO PAPI.

Associated Press (AP) (USA): IPZ, Gunoldstr. 14, 1199 Vienna; tel. (1) 368-41-56; fax (1) 369-15-58; Bureau Chief ROBERT REID.

Central News Agency (CNA) (Taiwan): Trubelgasse 17-4-40, 1030 Vienna; tel. (1) 799-17-02; fax (1) 798-45-98; Bureau Chief OU CHUN-LIN.

Česká tisková kancelář (ČTK) (Czech Republic): Vienna; tel. and fax (1) 439-21-8.

Deutsche Presse-Agentur (dpa) (Germany): IPZ, Gunoldstr. 14, 1199 Vienna; tel. (1) 368-21-58; fax (1) 369-85-49.

Informatsionnoye Telegrafnoye Agentstvo Rossii—Telegrafnoye Agentstvo Suverennykh Stran (ITAR—TASS) (Russia): Grosse Neugasse 28, 1040 Vienna; tel. (1) 810-43-1; fax (1) 566-53-6; Correspondent ALEKSANDR S. KUZMIN.

Jiji Tsushin-Sha (Japan): IPZ, Gunoldstr. 14, 1199 Vienna; tel. (1) 369-17-97; fax (1) 369-10-52; Bureau Chief SATO NOBUYUKI.

Kyodo Tsushin (Japan): IPZ, Gunoldstr. 14/130, 1199 Vienna; tel. (1) 368-15-20; fax (1) 369-92-52-2; e-mail kyodowien@apanet.at; internet www.kyodo.co.jp; Bureau Chief MASATOSHI NAGATA.

Magyar Távirati Iroda (MTI) (Hungary): Premreinergasse, Vienna; tel. and fax (1) 876-69-94; Correspondent ZSÓFIA FÜLEP.

Novinska Agencija Tanjug (Tanjug) (Yugoslavia): Vienna; tel. (1) 37-60-82; fax (1) 368-11-80.

Reuters (UK): Börsegasse 11, 1010 Vienna; tel. (1) 531-12-0; fax (1) 531-12-5; Bureau Chief DAVID T. CROUCH.

Xinhua (New China) News Agency (People's Republic of China): Reisnerstr. 15/8, 1030 Vienna; tel. (1) 713-41-40; fax (1) 714-14-57; Chief Correspondent YANG HUANQIN.

PRESS ASSOCIATIONS

Österreichischer Zeitschriften- und Fachmedien-Verband (Asscn of Periodical Publrs): Hörlgasse 18/5, 1090 Vienna; tel. and fax (1) 319-70-01; e-mail oezv@chello.at; internet www.oezv.or.at; f. 1946; 176 mems; Pres. Dr RUDOLF BOHMANN; Man. Dir Dr WOLFGANG BRANDSTETTER.

Verband Österreichischer Zeitungen (Newspaper Asscn of Austria): Renngasse 12, 1010 Vienna; tel. (1) 533-79-79-0; fax (1) 533-79-79-22; e-mail gs@voez.co.at; internet www.voez.at; f. 1946; 14 daily and most weekly papers are mems; Pres. Dr MAX DASCH; Sec.-Gen. Dr WALTER SCHAFFELHOFER.

Publishers

Akademische Druck- und Verlagsanstalt: Postfach 598, Auersperggasse 12, 8010 Graz; tel. (316) 36-44; fax (316) 36-44-24; e-mail info@adeva.com; internet www.adeva.com; f. 1949; scholarly reprints and new works, facsimile editions of Codices; Dir Dr URSULA STRUZL.

Alekto Verlag GmbH: Radetzkystr. 10, 9020 Klagenfurt; tel. (463) 515230; fax (463) 503351; e-mail bali@bali.co.at; literature; Man. Dir STEFAN ZEFFERER.

Betz, Annette, Verlag GmbH: Alser Str. 24, 1091 Vienna; tel. (1) 404-44-0; fax (1) 404-44-5; internet www.annettebetz.com; f. 1962; Man. Dir Dr JOHANNA RACHINGER.

Blackwell Wissenschafts-Verlag GmbH: Firmiangasse 7, 1130 Vienna; tel. (1) 877-93-51-0; fax (1) 877-93-51-24; e-mail verlag@blackwis.at; internet www.blackwis.de; f. 1989; medicine, medical journals; Dir MARTIN WILKINSON.

Böhlau Verlag GmbH & Co KG: Sachsenplatz 4–6, 1201 Vienna; tel. (1) 330-24-27; fax (1) 330-24-32; e-mail boehlau@boehlau.at; internet www.boehlau.at; f. 1947; history, law, philology, the arts, sociology; Dirs Dr PETER RAUCH, RUDOLF SIEGLE.

Bohmann Druck und Verlag GmbH & Co KG: Universitätsstr. 11, 1010 Vienna; tel. (1) 407-27-08; fax (1) 407-27-08-88; e-mail buchverlag@bohmann.co.at; internet www.bohmann-buch.co.at; f. 1936; trade, technical and educational books and periodicals.

Christian Brandstätter, Verlag und Edition: Schwarzenbergstr. 5, 1070 Vienna; tel. (1) 514-05-233; fax (1) 514-05-231; e-mail books@cbv.co.at; f. 1982; art books; Chair. Dr CHRISTIAN BRAND-STÄTTER.

Wilhelm Braumüller Universitätsverlagsbuchhandlung, GmbH: Servitengasse 5, 1092 Vienna; tel. (1) 319-14-82; fax (1) 310-28-05; e-mail office@braumueller.at; internet www.braumueller.at; f. 1783; sociology, politics, history, law, ethnology, linguistics, journalism, communications, psychology, philosophy, literature and theatre; university publrs; Dir BRIGITTE PFEIFER.

Czernin Verlag GmbH: Stallburggasse 2, 1010 Vienna; tel. (1) 512-01-32; fax (1) 512-01-32-15; e-mail office@czernin-verlag.com; internet www.czernin-verlag.com.

Franz Deuticke Verlagsgesellschaft mbH: Hegelgasse 21, 1010 Vienna; tel. (1) 514-05-281; fax (1) 514-05-289; e-mail schmidt@oebv.co.at; f. 1878; culture, literature, travel guides; Dirs WALTER AMON, Dr MARTINA SCHMIDT.

Ludwig Doblinger Musikhaus-Musikverlag: Dorotheergasse 10, 1010 Vienna; tel. (1) 515-03-0; fax (1) 515-03-51; e-mail music@doblinger.co.at; f. 1876; music; Dir HELMUTH PANY.

Edition Ergo Sum: Berggasse 31, 2391 Kaltenleutgeben, f. as Anna Pichler Verlag GmbH; present name adopted 2000.

Freytag-Berndt und Artaria KG Kartographische Anstalt: Brunnerstr. 69, 1231 Vienna; tel. (1) 869-90-90; fax (1) 869-88-55; e-mail sales@freytag-berndt.at; interent www.freytag-berndt.at;

f. 1879 (1770–Artaria); geography, maps and atlases; Chair. Dr CHRISTIAN HALBWACHE.

Gerold & Co: Graben 31, 1011 Vienna; tel. (1) 533-50-14; fax (1) 533-50-14-18; f. 1867; philology, literature, eastern Europe, sociology and philosophy; Dir PETER NEUSSER.

Jugend and Volk GmbH: Universitätsstr. 11, 1016 Vienna; tel. (1) 407-27-07; fax (1) 407-27-07-22; e-mail verlag@jugendvolk.at; internet www.jugendvolk.at; f. 1921; pedagogics, art, literature, children's books.

Kunstverlag Wolfrum: Augustinerstr. 10, 1010 Vienna; tel. (1) 512-53-98-0; fax (1) 512-53-98-57; f. 1919; art; Dir HUBERT WOLFRUM.

Leykam Verlag: Stempfergasse 3, 8011 Graz; tel. (316) 80-76; fax (316) 80-76-39; f. 1585; art, literature, academic, law; Dir Dr KLAUS BRUNNER.

Linde Verlag Wien: Scheydgasse 24, 1211 Vienna; tel. (1) 278-05-26; fax (1) 278-05-26-23; e-mail office@linde-verlag.at; f. 1925; business; Man. Dir HEIDELINDE LANGMAYR.

Manz'sche Verlags- und Universitätsbuchhandlung GmbH: Kohlmarkt 16, 1014 Vienna; tel. (1) 531-61-0; fax (1) 531-61-181; e-mail verlag@manz.at; f. 1849; law, political and economic sciences; textbooks and schoolbooks; Man. Dir Dr WOLFGANG PICHLER.

Wilhelm Maudrich: Spitalgasse 21a, 1096 Vienna; tel. (1) 408-58-92; fax (1) 408-50-80; e-mail medbook@maudrich.com; internet www.maudrich.com; f. 1909; medical; Man. Dir GERHARD GROIS.

Molden Verlag GmbH: Stadiongasse 6–8, 1010 Vienna; tel. (1) 403-94-09; fax (1) 402-17-55.

Otto Müller Verlag: Ernest-Thun-Str. 11, 5021 Salzburg; tel. (662) 88-19-74; fax (662) 87-23-87; f. 1937; general; Man. ARNO KLEIBEL.

öbv & hpt Verlagsgesellschaft mbH: Frankgasse 4, 1090 Vienna; tel. (1) 401-36; fax (1) 401-36-185; e-mail office@oebvhpt.at.

Pinguin Verlag Pawlowski GmbH: Lindenbühelweg 2, 6021 Innsbruck; tel. (512) 28-11-83; fax (512) 29-32-43; f. 1945; illustrated books; Dirs OLAF PAWLOWSKI, HELLA PFLANZER.

Residenz Verlag GmbH: Gaisbergstr. 6, 5020 Salzburg; tel. (662) 64-19-86; fax (662) 64-35-48; e-mail residenz@oebv.co.at; f. 1956; Dir Dr MARTINA SCHMIDT.

Anton Schroll & Co: Spengergasse 37, 1051 Vienna; tel. (1) 544-56-41; fax (1) 544-56-41-66; f. 1884; also in Munich; art books; Man. F. GEYER.

Springer-Verlag KG: Sachsenplatz 4–6, 1201 Vienna; tel. (1) 330-24-15; fax (1) 330-24-26; f. 1924; medicine, science, technology, law, sociology, economics, periodicals; Man. Dir RUDOLF SIEGLE.

Leopold Stocker Verlag: Hofgasse 5, 8011 Graz; tel. (316) 82-16-36; fax (316) 83-56-12; f. 1917; history, nature, hunting, fiction, agriculture, textbooks; Dir WOLFGANG DVORAK-STOCKER.

Verlag Kerle im Verlag Herder & Co: Wollzeile 33, 1010 Vienna; tel. (1) 512-14-13; fax (1) 512-14-13-60; f. 1886; children's books, juvenile.

Verlag Kremayr & Scheriau: Niederhofstr. 37, 1121 Vienna; tel. (1) 811-02; fax (1) 811-02-616; f. 1951; non-fiction, history.

Verlag Oldenbourg: Neulinggasse 26/12, 1030 Vienna; tel. (1) 712-62-58; fax (1) 712-62-58-19; e-mail gala@oldenbourg.co.at; f. 1959; Dir Dr THOMAS CORNIDES.

Verlag Orac: Graben 17, 1010 Vienna; tel. (1) 534-52; fax (1) 534-52-14-1; e-mail bestellung@orac.at; internet www.orac.at; f. 1946; Dir Dr DIETRICH SCHERF.

Verlag Styria: Schönaugasse 64, 8011 Graz; tel. (316) 80-63-0; fax (316) 80-63-70-04; e-mail skaiser@styria.co.at; f. 1869; literature, history, theology, philosophy; Chair. Dr REINHARD HABER-FELLNER.

Verlagsanstalt Tyrolia GmbH: Postfach 220, Exlgasse 20, 6020 Innsbruck; tel. (512) 22-33; fax (512) 22-33-50-1; e-mail tyrolia @tyrolia-verlagsanstalt.co.at; f. 1888; geography, history, science, children's, religion, fiction; Chair. Dr RAIMUND TISCHLER.

Verlagsbuchhandlung Brüder Hollinek und Co GmbH: Luisenstr. 20, 3002 Purkersdorf; tel. and fax (2231) 673-65; f. 1872; science, law and administration, printing, reference works, dictionaries; Dir RICHARD HOLLINEK.

Carl Ueberreuter Verlag: Alserstr. 24, 1091 Vienna; tel. (1) 404-44-0; fax (1) 404-44-5; e-mail office@vcu.ueberreuter.com; internet www.ueberreuter.at; non-fiction, children's; CEO JOHANNA RACHINGER.

Universal Edition: Brucknerstr. 6, 1040 Vienna; tel. (1) 337-23-0; fax (1) 337-23-40-0; e-mail office@universaledition.com; internet www.universaledition.com; f. 1901; music; Dir Dr J. JURANEK; Dir. MARION VON HARTLIEB.

Urban & Schwarzenberg GmbH: Frankgasse 4, 1096 Vienna; tel. (1) 405-27-31; fax (1) 405-27-24-41; f. 1866; science, medicine; Dir GUNTER ROYER.

Paul Zsolnay Verlag GmbH: Prinz-Eugen-Str. 30, 1041 Vienna; tel. (1) 505-76-61; fax (1) 505-76-61-10; e-mail info@zsolnay.at; f. 1923; fiction, non-fiction; Dirs MICHAEL KRÜGER, STEPHAN D. JOSS.

Government Publishing House

Verlag Österreich (Austrian Publishing House): Rennweg 16, 1037 Vienna; tel. (1) 797-89-407; fax (1) 797-89-419; e-mail verlag-oesterreich@verlag.oesd.co.at; f. 1804; law, CD-ROMs.

PUBLISHERS' ASSOCIATION

Hauptverband des Österreichischen Buchhandels (Ascn of Austrian Publrs and Booksellers): Grünangergasse 4, 1010 Vienna; tel. (1) 512-15-35; fax (1) 512-84-82; e-mail sekretariat@hvb.at; internet www.buecher.at; f. 1859; Pres. Dr ANTON C. HILSCHER; 605 mems.

Broadcasting and Communications

TELECOMMUNICATIONS

Telekom-Control Österreichische Gesellschaft für Telekommunikationsregulierung GmbH: Mariahilferstr. 77–79, 1060 Vienna; tel. (1) 580-58-0; fax (1) 580-58-9-191; e-mail tkc@tkc.at; internet www.tkc.at; f. 1997; regulatory body for the telecommunications sector.

Telekom Austria AG: Schwarzenbergplatz 3, 1010 Vienna; tel. and fax (1) 590-59-1; e-mail kundenservice@telekom.at; internet www.telekom.at; f. 1998; Dir-Gen. HEINZ SUNDT.

Connect Austria Gesellschaft für Telekommunikation GmbH: Brunnerstr. 52, 1210 Vienna; tel. (1) 277-28-0; internet www .connectaustria.at; Chair. FRANZ GEIGER.

max.mobil Telekommunikation Service GmbH: Kelsenstr. 5–7, 1030 Vienna; tel. (1) 795-85-0; fax (1) 795-85-53-2; internet www.maxmobil.at; Chair. Dr STEPHAN HUXOLD.

mobilkom Austria AG: Treustr. 43, 1200 Vienna; tel. (1) 331-61-0; internet www.mobilkom.at.

tele.ring Telekom Service GmbH & Co KG: Hainburgerstr. 33, 1030 Vienna; tel. (1) 931-01-20; e-mail info@telering.co.at; internet www.telering.at; 54%-owned by Mannesmann AG (Germany).

RADIO AND TELEVISION

The state-owned Österreichischer Rundfunk (ORF) provides three national and nine regional radio channels, as well as an overseas service. The ORF also has two terrestrial television channels, and operates a satellite station in conjunction with German and Swiss companies. While the ORF retains a monopoly over television broadcasting in Austria, the provision of radio services was liberalized in 1998, when a number of commercial radio stations were launched.

Österreichischer Rundfunk (ORF) (Austrian Broadcasting Company): Würzburggasse 30, 1136 Vienna; tel. (1) 878-78-0; fax (1) 878-78-22-50; e-mail anfrage@orf.at; internet www.orf.at; f. 1924; state-owned; Dir-Gen. GERHARD WEIS; Dirs Dr HANNES LEOPOLDSEDER, KATHRIN ZECHNER (Television), Dr MANFRED JOCHUM (Radio).

Finance

(cap. = capital; res = reserves; dep. = deposits; m. = million; brs = branches; amounts in Schilling)

BANKS

Banks in Austria, apart from the National Bank, belong to one of five categories. The first category comprises banks that are organized as corporations (i.e. joint-stock and private banks), and special-purpose credit institutions; the second category comprises savings banks; the third category comprises co-operative banks. Co-operative banks include rural credit co-operatives (Raiffeisenbanken) and industrial credit co-operatives (Volksbanken). The remaining two categories comprise the mortgage banks of the various Austrian Länder, and the building societies. The majority of Austrian banks (with the exception of the building societies) operate on the basis of universal banking, although certain categories have specialized. Banking operations are governed by the Banking Act of 1993 (Bankwesengesetz–BWG).

Central Bank

Oesterreichische Nationalbank (Austrian National Bank): Postfach 61, Otto-Wagner-Platz 3, 1090 Vienna; tel. (1) 404-20-0; fax (1) 404-66-96; internet www.oenb.at; f. 1922; cap. 150m. (Dec. 1997), res 126,216m., dep. 224,009m. (Dec. 1998); Pres. ADOLF WALA; Gov. Dr KLAUS LIEBSCHER; 8 brs.

Commercial Banks

Adria Bank AG: Tegetthoffstr. 1, 1010 Vienna; tel. (1) 514-09; fax (1) 514-09-43; f. 1980; cap. 170m., res 238m., dep. 2,558m. (Dec. 1999); Mans CIRIL KRPAC, Dr ALFRED SCHERHAMMER.

Anglo Irish Corporate Bank (Austria) AG: Postfach 306, Rathaustr. 20, 1010 Vienna; tel. (1) 406-61-61; fax (1) 405-81-42; e-yymail pb@angloirishbank.at; f. 1998; cap. 190m., res 104m., dep. 3,035m. (Dec. 1998); Chair. and CEO T. CARROLL.

Bank Austria AG: Vordere Zollamtsstr. 13, 1030 Vienna; tel. (1) 711-91-0; fax (1) 711-91-28-72; internet www.bankaustria.com; f. 1991 by merger of Österreichische Länderbank and Zentralsparkasse und Kommerzialbank; due to merge with HypoVereinsbank AG of Germany in mid-2001; cap. 17,980m., res 42,615m., dep. 1,446,030m. (Dec. 1998); Chair. Bd of Man. Dir GERHARD RANDA; 529 brs.

Bank Austria Creditanstalt International AG: Am Hof 2, 1010 Vienna; tel. (1) 536-36-0; fax (1) 536-36-61-0; e-mail info@at .bacai.com; f. 1998 through merger of international business of Bank Austria AG (see above) with Creditanstalt AG (f. 1855); wholly owned by Bank Austria AG.

Bank Austria Handelsbank AG: Postfach 83, Operngasse 6, 1015 Vienna; tel. (1) 514-40-0; fax (1) 512-66-01; f. 1935, present name adopted 1994; cap. 331m., res 160m., dep. 5,192m. (Dec. 1999); Chair. KARL SAMSTAG.

Bank für Arbeit und Wirtschaft AG (BAWAG): Seitzergasse 2–4, 1010 Vienna; tel. (1) 534-53-0; fax (1) 534-53-2840; e-mail bawag@bawag.com; internet www.bawag.com; f. 1947; present name adopted 1963; purchased PSK, the state-owned postal bank in Aug. 2000; cap. 8,157m., res 9,700m., dep. 244,583m. (Dec. 1998); Chair. and CEO HELMUT ELSNER; 154 brs.

Bank Winter und Co AG: Singerstr. 10, 1011 Vienna; tel. (1) 515-04-0; fax (1) 515-04-21-3; f. 1959; cap. 650m., res 1,244m., dep. 22,975m. (June 1999); Chair. THOMAS MOSKOVICS; 1 br.

Bankhaus Schelhammer und Schattera AG: Postfach 618, 1011 Vienna; Goldschmiedgasse 3, 1010 Vienna; tel. (1) 534-34; fax (1) 534-34-64; e-mail foreign-dept@schelhammer.at; internet www .schelhammer.at; f. 1832; cap. 410m., res 355m., dep. 4,493m. (Dec. 1999); Chair. Dr HEINZ BURGMANN; 1 br.

Centro Internationale Handelsbank AG: Postfach 272, Tegetthoffstr. 1, 1015 Vienna; tel. (1) 515-20-0; fax (1) 513-43-96; e-mail general@centrobank.com; internet www.centrobank.com; f. 1973; cap. 655m., res 227m., dep. 4,616m. (Dec. 1998); Exec. Bd Dr GERHARD VOGT (Chair.), JERZY PLUSA, CHRISTIAN SPERK.

Citibank International Plc (Austria): Schwarzenbergplatz 3, 1010 Vienna; tel. (1) 717-17-0; fax (1) 713-92-06; f. 1959 as Internationale Investitions- und Finanzierungs Bank AG; present name adopted 1978; wholly-owned subsidiary of Citibank Overseas Investment Corpn; Gen. Man. ALBRECHT STAERKER.

Deutsche Bank (Austria) AG: Hohenstaufengasse 4, 1010 Vienna; tel. (1) 531-81-0; fax (1) 533-94-59; f. 1989; cap. 250m., res 386m., dep. 10,200m. (Dec. 1994); Man. Dirs Dr WILFRIED AMANSHAUSER, KARL-FRIEDRICH SCHALLER, CHRISTOPH BREWKA.

Donau-Bank AG: Postfach 1451, Parkring 6, 1011 Vienna; tel. (1) 515-35; fax (1) 515-35-29-7; e-mail donau-bank.allgem@telecom .at; f. 1974; cap. 1,105m., res 839m., dep. 10,978m. (Dec. 1998); Chair. ANDREI E. TCHETYRKIN.

Kathrein und Co Privatgeschäftsbank AG: Postfach 174, Wipplingerstr. 25, 1013 Vienna; tel. (1) 534-51-0; fax (1) 534-51-221; e-mail privatgeschaeftsbank.ag@kathrein.at; internet www .kathrein.at; f. 1924; cap. 440m., res 76m., dep. 1,844m. (Dec. 1998); Chair. Dr CHRISTOPH KRAUS.

Meinl Bank AG: Postfach 99, Bauernmarkt 2, 1015 Vienna; tel. (1) 531-88, fax (1) 531-88-44; f. 1922; cap. 328m., res 447m., dep. 3,876m. (Dec. 1999); Chair. Dr ANTON OSOND; 2 brs.

SKWB Schoellerbank AG: Renngasse 1–3, 1010 Vienna; tel. (1) 534-71-0; fax (1) 534-71-635; internet www.skwbschoellerbank .at; f. 1998 by merger of Schoellerbank AG (f. 1833) and Salzburger Kredit-und Wechsel-Bank AG (f. 1922); Chair. Dr STEPHAN SCHÜLLER.

Regional Banks

Allgemeine Sparkasse Oberösterreich Bank AG: Postfach 92, Promenade 11–13, 4041 Linz; tel. (732) 73-91-0; fax (732) 73-91-28-01; internet www.ask.co.at; f. 1849; cap. 170m., res 692m., dep. 79,013m. (Dec. 1998); Chair. HORST ALEXANDER SPITZKOPF; 121 brs.

Bank für Kärnten und Steiermark AG: St. Veiter Ring 43, 9020 Klagenfurt; tel. (463) 58-58; fax (463) 58-58-94-3; e-mail bks@bks.at; internet www.bks.at; f. 1922; cap. 1,342m., res 1,759m., dep. 34,957m. (Dec. 1998); Pres. Dr HEINRICH TREICHL; 6 brs.

Bank für Tirol und Vorarlberg AG: Erlerstr. 5–9, 6020 Innsbruck; tel. (512) 53-33-0; fax (512) 533-31-33; e-mail btv@btv.at; internet www.btv.at; f. 1904; cap. 2,139m., res 2,080m., dep. 54,884m. (Dec. 1999); Chair. PETER GAUGG; 35 brs.

Bankhaus Carl Spängler und Co AG: Postfach 41, 5024 Salzburg; Schwarzstr. 1, 5020 Salzburg; tel. (662) 86-86; fax (662) 86-86-15-8; e-mail bankhaus@spaengler.co.at internet www.spaengler .co.at; f. 1828; cap. 144m., res 205m., dep. 4,748m. (Dec. 1998); Gen. Man. HEINRICH SPANGLER; 12 brs.

Bankhaus Krentschker und Co AG: Am Eisernen Tor 3, 8010 Graz; tel. (316) 80-30-0; fax (316) 80-30-94-9; e-mail mail@ krentschker.at; internet www.krentschker.at; f. 1924; cap. 365m., res 351m., dep. 9,599m. (Dec. 1998); Chair. Dr JÖRG BRUCKBAUER; 3 brs.

HYPO Alpe-Adria-Bank AG: Postfach 517, Alpe-Adria-Platz 1, 9020 Klagenfurt; tel. (463) 58-60; fax (463) 58-60-50; internet www.hypo-alpe-adria.com; f. 1896 as Kärntner Landes- und Hypothekenbank AG; present name adopted 1999; cap. 460m., res 1,569m., dep. 47,242m. (Dec. 1998); Man. Dirs Dr WOLFGANG KULTERER, Dr JÖRG SCHUSTER; 10 brs.

Landes-Hypothekenbank Tirol AG: Postfach 524, Meranerstr. 8, 6020 Innsbruck; tel. (512) 59-11-0; fax (512) 59-11-21-21; e-mail office@hypotirol.at; internet www.hypotirol.at; f. 1901; cap. 538m., res 2,141m., dep. 56,238m. (Dec. 1998); Pres. Dr JOSEF PRADER; 23 brs.

Niederösterreichische Landesbank-Hypothekenbank AG: Kremsergasse 20, 3100 St Pölten; tel. (2742) 49-20; fax (2742) 49-20-14-44; e-mail hypobank@hypobank.co.at; internet www.hypobank.co.at; f. 1889; cap. 657m., res 1,606m., dep. 50,981m. (Dec. 1999); Chair. PETER REINBACHER; Gen. Man. WERNER SCHMITZER; 27 brs.

Oberbank AG: Hauptplatz 10–11, 4020 Linz; tel. (732) 78-02-0; fax (732) 78-58-04; e-mail tre@oberbank.at; internet www.oberbank.at; f. 1869 as Bank für Oberösterreich und Salzburg AG; present name adopted 1998; cap. 3,337m., res 4,167m., dep. 97,798m. (Dec. 1999); Chair. Dr HERMANN BELL; 96 brs and sub-brs.

Oberösterreichische Landesbank AG: Landstr. 38, 4020 Linz; tel. (70) 76-39-0; fax (70) 76-39-20-5; e-mail innovationsservice@hypo-ooe.at; internet www.hypo.at; f. 1891; cap. 651m., res 1,302m., dep. 39,895m. (Dec. 1998); Pres. Dr WOLFGANG STAMPFL; Gen. Man. Dr WOLFGANG LANGBAUER; 14 brs.

Privatinvest Bank AG: Postfach 16, Griesgasse 11, 5010 Salzburg; tel. (662) 80-48-0; fax (662) 80-48-33-3; e-mail piag@piag.at; internet www.privatinvestbank.com; f. 1885 as Bankhaus Daghofer & Co; present name adopted 1990; cap. 80m., res 72m., dep. 2,398m. (Dec. 1999); Chair. HANS-WERNER ZESCHKY.

Quelle Bank C. A. Steinhäusser AG: Kornstr. 4, 4060 Linz; tel. (732) 68-67-0; fax (732) 68-67-15-0; f. 1856 as Bankhaus C. A. Steinhäusser AG; present name adopted 1991; cap. 130m. (1994); Mans BERND SCHADRACK, ERNST DEMUTH.

Salzburger Landes-Hypothekenbank AG: Postfach 136, Residenzplatz 7, 5010 Salzburg; tel. (662) 804-60; fax (662) 804-65-69-2; cap. 866m., res 852m., dep. 33,569m. (Dec. 1998); Gen. Man. Dr KURT ADELSBURG.

Steiermärkische Bank und Sparkassen AG: Postfach 844, Sparkassenplatz 4, Landhausgasse 16, 8011 Graz; tel. (316) 80-33-0; fax (316) 80-33-30; internet www.sparkasse.at/steiermaerkische; f. 1825 as Steiermärkischer Sparkasse Graz; present name adopted 1992; cap. 1,384m., res 2,999m., dep. 56,785m. (Dec. 1998); Chair. JOSEPH KASSLER; 95 brs.

Tiroler Sparkasse-Bankaktiengesellschaft Innsbruck: Sparkassenplatz 1, 6020 Innsbruck; tel. (512) 59-05; fax (512) 59-10-50-0; f. 1822 as Sparkasse der Stadt Innsbruck; present name adopted 1990, following merger in 1975; cap. 2,100m., res 1,796m., dep. 35,587m. (Dec. 1998); Chair. and Gen. Man. Dr E. WUNDERBALDINGER; 49 brs.

Volkskreditbank AG: Postfach 116, Rudigierstr. 5–7, 4010 Linz; tel. (70) 76-37-0; fax (70) 76-37-60-0; e-mail international@vkb -bank.at; internet www.vkb-bank.at; f. 1872; cap. 260m., res 1,422m., dep. 18,864m. (Dec. 1998); Gen. Man. Dr GERNOT KRENNER; 45 brs.

Vorarlberger Landes- und Hypothekenbank AG: Hypo-Passage 1, 6900 Bregenz; tel. (5574) 414-0; fax (5574) 414-35-7; e-mail info@hypovbg.at; internet www.hypovbg.at; f. 1899; cap. 1,745m., res 2,892m., dep. 46,027m. (Dec. 1998); Chair. Dr KURT RUPP; 22 brs.

Specialized Banks

CAIB Investment Bank AG: Nibelungengasse 15, 1011 Vienna; tel. (1) 588-84-0; fax (1) 585-42-42; e-mail vienna@ca-ib.com; internet www.ca-ib.com; f. 1997; wholly owned by Bank Austria Creditanstalt International AG; cap. 400m., res 227m., dep. 3,117m. (Dec. 1997); Chair. WILHELM HEMETSBERGER.

Internationale Bank für Aussenhandel AG: Neuer Markt 1, 1011 Vienna; tel. (1) 515-56-0; fax (1) 515-56-50; f. 1970; cap. 75m., res 123m., dep. 5,229m. (Dec. 1994); Mans Dr WALTER BEYER, ILSE SMEYKAL.

Oesterreichische Kontrollbank AG: Postfach 70, Am Hof 4, 1010 Vienna; tel. (1) 531-27-0; fax (1) 531-27-698; e-mail oeffentlichkeitsarbeit@oekb.co.at; internet www.oekb.co.at; f. 1946; export financing, stock exchange clearing, money market operations; cap. 440m., res 2,160m., dep. 4,390m. (Dec. 1998); Mans Dr JOHANNES ATTEMS, Dr RUDOLF SCHOLTEN.

Österreichische Investitionskredit AG: Renngasse 10, 1013 Vienna; tel. (1) 531-35-0; fax (1) 531-35-99-3; cap. 3,007m. (1994); Gen. Man. Dkfm. ALFRED REITER.

Österreichische Kommunalkredit AG: Türkenstr. 9, 1092 Vienna; tel. (1) 316-31-0; fax (1) 316-31-10-5; e-mail kommunal@kommunalkredit.at; internet www.kommunalkredit.at; f. 1958; cap. 374m., dep. 5,727m. (1994); Mans Dr REINHARD PLATZER, GERHARD GANGL.

Österreichischer Exportfonds GmbH: Neulinggasse 29, 1031 Vienna; tel. (1) 712-61-51-0; fax (1) 712-61-51-30; cap. 122m. (1994); Mans HERBERT NIEMETZ, BRIGITTE BRUCK.

Savings Banks

Dornbirner Sparkasse: Postfach 199, Bahnhofstr. 2, 6850 Dornbirn; tel. (5572) 381-10; fax (5572) 381-14; e-mail spk.dornbirn@telecom.at; internet www.dornbirn.sparkasse.at; cap. 150m., res 1,394m., dep. 16,186m. (Dec. 1998); Chair. WOLFGANG RÜMMELE; 15 brs.

Erste Bank der österreichischen Sparkassen AG (Erste Bank) (First Austrian Savings Bank): Postfach 162, Graben 21, 1010 Vienna; tel. (1) 531-00-0; fax (1) 531-00-22-72; e-mail servicecenter@erstebank.at; internet www.erstebank.at; f. 1819; present name adopted 1997; cap. 11,855m., res 19,850m., dep. 532,037m. (Dec. 1998); Chair. and CEO ANDREAS TREICHL; 357 brs.

Kärntner Sparkasse: Neuerplatz 14, 9020 Klagenfurt; tel. (463) 588-80; fax (463) 588-82-91; e-mail info@kaerntnersparkasse.co.at; internet www.kaerntnersparkasse.at; f. 1835; cap. 1,166m., res 1,144m., dep. 25,604m. (Dec. 1998); Pres. HANS LETTNER; Chair. and Gen. Man. Mag ALOLS HOCHEGGER; 57 brs.

Österreichische Postsparkasse AG (PSK): Georg-Coch Platz 2, 1018 Vienna; tel. (1) 51-40-00; fax (1) 514-00-17-00; internet www.psk.co.at/psk; f. 1883; sold to BAWAG in Aug. 2000; cap. 2,596m., res 7,018m., dep. 257,772m. (Dec. 1998); CEO MAX KOTHBAUER.

Salzburger Sparkasse Bank AG: Postfach 5000, Alter Markt 3, 5021 Salzburg; tel. (662) 80-40-0; fax (662) 80-40-81; internet www.salzburger-sparkasse.co.at; f. 1855; cap. 1,383m., res 1,899m., dep. 43,756m. (Dec. 1999); Gen. Man. WALTER SCHWIMBERSKY; 79 brs.

Co-operative Banks

Österreichische Volksbanken-AG: Peregringasse 3, 1090 Vienna; tel. (1) 313-40-37-89; fax (1) 313-40-31-70; e-mail infomail@oevag.volksbank.at; internet www.oevag.volksbank.at; f. 1922; cap. 2,701m., res 3,124m., dep. 82,387m. (Dec. 1998); Chair. and CEO Dr KLAUS THALHAMMER.

Raiffeisenlandesbank Kärnten rGmbH: St. Veiter Ring 53, 9020 Klagenfurt; tel. (463) 581-52-7-0; fax (463) 581-53-6; internet www.raiffeisen.at; cap. 142m., res 645m., dep. 14,727m. (Dec. 1998); Chair. Dr KLAUS PEKAREK.

Raiffeisenlandesbank Niederösterreich-Wien rGmbH: Freidrich-Wilhelm-Raiffeisen-Platz 1, Raiffeisenhaus, 1020 Vienna; tel. (1) 21-13-60; fax (1) 21-13-62-22-3; internet www.rlbnoew.at; f. 1898; cap. 2,265m., res 3,964m., dep. 110,577m. (Dec. 1996); Chair. Dr CHRISTIAN KONRAD.

Raiffeisenlandesbank Oberösterreich rGmbH: Postfach 455, Raiffeisenplatz 1, 4021 Linz; tel. (732) 65-96-0; fax (732) 65-96-35-29; e-mail rlbl@rlb.linz.raffeisen.at; internet www.rlbooe.at; f. 1900; cap. 2,811m., res 3,447m., dep. 86,070m. (Dec. 1997); Chair. Dr LUDWIG SCHARINGER.

Raiffeisenlandesbank Steiermark rGmbH: Kaiserfeldgasse 5–7, 8010 Graz; tel. (316) 80-36-0; fax (316) 80-36-17-11-3; internet www.raiffeisen.at; f. 1927; cap. 1,330m., res 2,301m., dep. 43,312m. (Dec. 1998); Chair. JOSEF RIEGLER.

Raffeisenlandesbank Vorarlberg Waren-und Revisions Verbank rGmbH: Rheinstr. 11, 6901 Bregenz; tel. (5574) 4050; fax (5574) 405-333; internet www.vol.at; cap. 199m., res 849m., dep. 21,249m. (Dec. 1998); Chair. VIKTOR RINDERER.

Raffeisenverband Salzburg reg Gen mbH: Schwarzstr. 13–15, 5024 Salzburg; tel. (662) 88860; fax (662) 888-65-24; f. 1905; present name adopted 1949; cap. 408m., res 1,858m., dep. 38,395m. (Dec. 1998); Chair. MANFRED HOLZTRATTNER.

Raiffeisen Zentralbank Österreich AG (RZB-Austria): Am Stadtpark 9, 1030 Vienna; tel. (1) 717-07-0; fax (1) 717-07-17-15; internet www.rzb.at; f. 1927; cap. 4,995m., res 8,499m., dep. 266,689m. (Dec. 1998); central institute of the Austrian Raiffeisen banking group; Chair. Supervisory Bd Dr CHRISTIAN KONRAD; Chair. Bd of Management Dr WALTER ROTHENSTEINER.

Bankers' Organization

Verband österreichischer Banken und Bankiers (Asscn of Austrian Banks and Bankers): Postfach 132, Börsegasse 11, 1013 Vienna; tel. (1) 535-17-71; fax (1) 535-17-71/38; e-mail voebb@voebb.at; internet www.voebb.at; f. 1945; Pres. HELMUT ELSNER; Gen. Sec. FRANZ OVESNY; 54 mems.

STOCK EXCHANGES

Wiener Börse (Vienna Stock Exchange): Postfach 192, Strauchagasse 1-3, 1014 Vienna; tel. (1) 531-65-0; fax (1) 532-97-40; e-mail communications@vienna-stock-exchange.at; internet www.wbag.at; f. 1771; 50% state-owned; two sections: Stock Exchange, Commodity Exchange; Pres. GERHARD REIDLINGER; Gen. Sec. Dr ULRICH KAMP.

Österreichische Termin- und Optionenbörse (Austrian Futures and Options Exchange): Postfach 192, Strauchgasse 1-3, 1014 Vienna; tel. (1) 531-65-0; fax (1) 532-97-40; f. 1991; by appointment to the Vienna Stock Exchange, provides a fully automated screen-based trading system, the Austrian Traded Index (ATX), and acts as clearing house for options and futures; trades futures on the Austrian Govt Bond (Bond-Futures) and options on six Austrian stocks listed on the Vienna Stock Exchange; CEO Dr CHRISTIAN IMO.

INSURANCE COMPANIES

A selection of companies is given below.

Allianz Elementar Versicherungs-AG: Hietzinger Kai 101–105; 1130 Vienna; tel. (1) 878-07-0; fax (1) 878-07-53-90; e-mail 106534.1555@compuserv.com; internet www.allianz.co.at; f. 1860; all classes except life insurance; Gen. Man. Dr ALEXANDER HOYOS.

Allianz Elementar Lebensversicherung-AG: Hietzinger Kai 101–105, 1130 Vienna; tel. (1) 878-07-0; fax (1) 878-07-27-03; e-mail office@allianz.at; internet www.allianz.at; life insurance; Gen. Man. Dr ALEXANDER HOYOS.

Allgemeine Pechtsschutz Versicherungs-AG (ARAG): Heinrichsgasse 4, 1013 Vienna; tel. (1) 531-02-0; fax (1) 531-02-923; e-mail info@arag.at; internet info@arag.at; Man. Dr HERBERT KITTINGER.

AXA Nordstern Colonia Versicherungs-AG: Uraniastr. 2, 1010 Vienna; tel. (1) 711-50-0; fax (1) 711-50-212; e-mail kundendienst@axa-versicherung.at; internet www.axa-versicherung.at; Gen. Man. DAVID FURTWÄNGLER.

Donau Allgemeine Versicherungs-AG: Schottenring 15, 1010 Vienna; tel. (1) 313-11; fax (1) 310-77-51; e-mail donau@donauversicherung.at; internet www.donauversicherung.at; f. 1867; all classes; Gen. Man. Dr GÜNTER GEYER.

Generali Versicherung AG: Landskrongasse 1–3, 1011 Vienna; tel. (1) 534-01; fax (1) 534-01/12-26; e-mail headoffice@generali.at; internet www.generali.co.at; f. 1882 as Erste Österreichische Allgemeine Unfall-Versicherungs-Gesellschaft; Gen. Man. Dr HANS PEER.

Grazer Wechselseitige Versicherung: Herrengasse 18–20, 8011 Graz; tel. (316) 80-37-0; fax (316) 80-37-41-4; f. 1828; all classes; Gen. Man. Dr OTHMAR EDERER.

Interunfall Versicherungs-AG: Tegetthoffstr. 7, 1011 Vienna; tel. (1) 514-03-0; fax (1) 514-03-4590; e-mail z-v@interunfall.at; internet www.interunfall.at; all classes of insurance (including reinsurance); Man. Dr HANS PEER.

Raffeisen-Versicherung AG: Untere Donaustr. 25, 1021 Vienna; tel. (1) 211-19-0; fax (1) 211-19-11-34; e-mail kommunikation@raiffeisen-versicherung.at; internet www.raiffeisen-versicherung.at; Dir Dr PETER EICHLER.

Salzburger Landes-Versicherung AG: Auersperstr. 9, 5021 Salzburg; tel. (662) 899-98-0; fax (662) 889-98-109; e-mail sekretariat@slv.co.at; internet www.slv.co.at; Gen. Man. Dr JOSEF GLASER.

Sparkassen Versicherung AG: Wipplingerstr. 36–38, 1011 Vienna; tel. (1) 313-81-0; fax (1) 313-81-300; e-mail sag@s-versicherung.co.at; internet www.s-versicherung.co.at; Gen. Man. Dr MICHAEL HARRER.

Uniqa Versicherungen AG: Praterstr. 1–7, 1021 Vienna; tel. (1) 211-11-0; fax (1) 214-33-36; e-mail kommunikation@uniqa.at; internet www.uniqa.at; present name adopted 1999, fmrly Versicherungsanstalt der österreichischen Bundesländer Versicherungs-AG; Chair. HERBERT SCHIMETSCHEK.

Wiener Städtische Allgemeine Versicherung AG: Schottenring 30, Ringturm, 1010 Vienna; tel. (1) 531-39-0; fax (1) 535-34-37; e-mail mail-us@wr.staedtische.co.at; internet www.staedtische.co.at; f. 1824; all classes; CEO Dr SIEGFRIED SELLITSCH.

Wüstenrot Versicherungs-AG: Alpenstr. 61, 5033 Salzburg; tel. (662) 638-60; fax (662) 638-66-52; e-mail versicherung@wuestenrot.co.at; internet www.wuestenrot.co.at; Gen. Man. HELMUT GEIER.

Zürich Kosmos Versicherungen AG: Schwarzenbergplatz 15, 1015 Vienna I; tel. (1) 501-25-0; fax (1) 505-04-85; internet www.zuerichkosmos.at; f. 1910; all classes; Gen. Man. FRANZ WIPFLI.

Insurance Organization

Verband der Versicherungsunternehmen Österreichs (Asscn of Austrian Insurance Cos): Schwarzenbergplatz 7, 1030 Vienna; tel. (1) 711-56-0; fax (1) 711-56-27-0; e-mail versver@ibm.net; internet www.vvo.at; f. 1945; Pres. Dr ALEXANDER HOYOS; Gen. Sec. HERBERT RETTER; 86 mems.

AUSTRIA

Trade and Industry

GOVERNMENT AGENCIES

Austrian Business Agency (ABA): Opernring 3, 1010 Vienna; fax (1) 586-86-59; e-mail austrian.business@telecom.at; internet www.aba.gv.at; Man. Dir RENÉ SIEGL.

Österreichische Industrieholding AG (ÖIAG): Postfach 99, Kantgasse 1, 1015 Vienna; tel. (1) 711-14-0; fax (1) 711-14-37-8; f. 1970; Mans. KARL HOLLWEGER, Dr ERICH BECKER.

CHAMBERS OF COMMERCE

All Austrian enterprises must by law be members of the Economic Chambers. The Federal Economic Chamber promotes international contacts and represents the economic interests of trade and industry on a federal level. Its Foreign Trade Organization includes about 90 offices abroad.

Wirtschaftskammer Österreich (Austrian Federal Economic Chamber): Wiedner Hauptstr. 63, 1045 Vienna; tel. (1) 501-05; fax (1) 502-06-25-0; e-mail mservice@wkoe.wk.or.at; f. 1946; six depts: Commerce, Industry, Small-scale Production, Banking and Insurance, Transport and Tourism; these divisions are subdivided into branch asscns; Local Economic Chambers with divisions and branch asscns in each of the nine Austrian provinces; Pres. CHRISTOPH LEITL; Sec.-Gen. GÜNTER STUMMVOLL; c. 300,000 mems.

INDUSTRIAL AND TRADE ASSOCIATIONS

Wirtschaftskammer Österreich—Bundessektion Industrie: Wiedner Hauptstr. 63, 1045 Vienna; tel. (1) 501-05-34-57; fax (1) 501-05-27-3; e-mail bsi@wkoesk.wk.or.at; internet www.wk.or.at/bsi; f. 1896 as Zentralverband der Industrie Österreichs (Central Fed. of Austrian Industry), merged into present org. 1947; Chair. HEINZ KESSLER; Dir JOACHIM LAMEL; comprises the following industrial feds:

Fachverband der Audiovisions-und Filmindustrie Österreichs (Film): Postfach 327, Wiedner Hauptstr. 63, 1045 Vienna; tel. (1) 501-05-30-10; fax (1) 501-05-27-6; e-mail film@fafo.at; Chair. MICHAEL WOLKENSTEIN, Prof. Dr ELMAR A. PETERLUNGER; 1,700 mems.

Fachverband der Bauindustrie (Building): Karlsgasse 5, 1040 Vienna; tel. (1) 504-15-51; fax (1) 504-15-55; e-mail sekretariat@bauindustrie.at; internet www.bauindustrie.at; Chair. Ing. ERNST NUSSBAUMER; Dir Dr JOHANNES SCHENK; 150 mems.

Fachverband der Bekleidungsindustrie (Clothing): Schwarzenbergplatz 4, 1037 Vienna; tel. (1) 712-12-96; fax (1) 713-92-04; e-mail office@fashion-industry.at; internet www.fashion-industry.at; Chair. WILHELM EHRLICH; Dir CHRISTOPH HAIDINGER; 280 mems.

Fachverband der Bergwerke und Eisenerzeugenden Industrie (Mining and Steel Production): Postfach 300, Goethegasse 3, 1015 Vienna; tel. (1) 512-46-01; fax (1) 512-46-01-20; e-mail fvil@wkoesk.wk.or.at; internet www.wk-or.at/bergbau-stahl; Chair. Gen. Dir Dr PETER STRAHAMMER; Sec. Ing. Mag. HERMANN PRINZ; 51 mems.

Fachverband der Chemischen Industrie (Chemicals): Postfach 325, Wiedner Hauptstr. 63, 1045 Vienna; tel. (1) 501-05-280; fax (1) 502-06-28-0; e-mail office@fcio.wko.at; internet www.fcio.at; Pres. Dr WOLFGANG FRANK; Gen. Dir Dr WOLFGANG EICKHOFF; 530 mems.

Fachverband der Eisen- und Metallwarenindustrie Österreichs (Iron and Metal Goods): Postfach 335, Wiedner Hauptstr. 63, 1045 Vienna; tel. (1) 501-05; fax (1) 505-09-28; internet www.fmwi.at; f. 1908; Chair. REINHARD JORDAN; Gen. Man. Dr WOLFGANG LOCKER; 800 mems.

Fachverband der Elektro- und Elektronikindustrie (Electrical): Mariahilferstr. 37–39, 1060 Vienna; tel. (1) 588-39-0; fax (1) 586-69-71; Chair. Dr WALTER WOLFSBERGER; Dir Dr HEINZ RASCHKA; 558 mems.

Fachverband der Fahrzeugindustrie (Vehicles): Wiedner Hauptstr. 63, 1045 Vienna; tel. (1) 501-05; fax (1) 502-06-28-9; Pres. Dr RICHARD DAIMER; Gen. Sec. ERIK BAIER; 160 mems.

Fachverband der Gas- und Wärmeversorgungsunternehmungen (Gas and Heating): Schubertring 14, 1010 Vienna; tel. (1) 513-15-88; fax (1) 513-15-88-25; e-mail info@fv.ovgw.or.at; Gen. Dir Dr KARL SKYBA; 190 mems.

Fachverband der Giessereiindustrie (Foundries): Postfach 339, Wiedner Hauptstr. 63, 1045 Vienna; tel. (1) 501-05-34-63; fax (1) 502-06-27-9; e-mail giesserei@wko.at; Chair. MICHAEL ZIMMERMANN; Dir Dipl. Ing. Dr HANSJÖRG DICHTL; 60 mems.

Fachverband der Glasindustrie (Glass): Wiedner Hauptstr. 63, 1045 Vienna; tel. (1) 501-05/3428; fax (1) 501-05/281; e-mail office@fvglas.at; Chair. RUDOLF SCHRAML; Dir ALEXANDER KRISSMANEK; 65 mems.

Fachverband der Holzindustrie Österreichs (Wood): Postfach 123, Schwarzenbergplatz 4, 1037 Vienna; tel. (1) 712-26-01-0; fax (1) 712-26-01-19; e-mail office@saege.at; internet www.holzindustrie.at; f. 1947 as Fachverband der Sägeindustrie Österreichs; present name adopted 2000; Chair. Dr ERICH WIESNER; Dir Dr GERHARD ALTRICHTER; 1,800 mems.

Fachverband der Holzverarbeitenden Industrie (Wood Processing): Postfach 123, Schwarzenbergplatz 4, 1037 Vienna; tel. (1) 712-26-01; fax (1) 713-03-09; e-mail office@holzindustrie.at; f. 1946; Chair. Dr ERICH WIESNER; Dir Dr CLAUDIUS KOLLMANN; 360 mems.

Fachverband der Ledererzeugenden Industrie (Leather Production): Postfach 312, Wiedner Hauptstr. 63, 1045 Vienna 4; tel. (1) 501-05-34-53; fax (1) 501-05-278; e-mail fvleder@wko.at; f. 1945; Chair. HELMUT SCHMIDT; Dir PETER KOVACS; 8 mems.

Fachverband der Lederverarbeitenden Industrie (Leather Processing): Postfach 313, Wiedner Hauptstr. 63, 1045 Vienna; tel. (1) 501-05; fax (1) 501-05-278; e-mail fvleder@wko.at; f. 1945; Chair. JOSEPH LORENZ; Dir PETER KOVACS; 45 mems.

Fachverband der Maschinen- und Stahlbauindustrie (Machinery and Steel Construction): Wiedner Hauptstr. 63, 1045 Vienna; tel. (1) 502-25; fax (1) 505-10-20; Pres. Dr JOSEF BERTSCH; Dir RUDOLF TUPPA; 850 mems.

Fachverband der NE-Metallindustrie (Metals): Postfach 338, Wiedner Hauptstr. 63, 1045 Vienna; tel. (1) 501-05-33-09; fax (1) 501-05-33-78; e-mail nemetall@wko.at; f. 1946; Chair. Dr OTHMAR RANKL; Dir Dr GÜNTER GREIL; 69 mems.

Fachverband der Mineralölindustrie (Oil): Erdbergstr. 72, 1031 Vienna; tel. (1) 713-23-48; fax (1) 713-05-10; e-mail office@oil-gas.at; internet www.oil-gas.at; f. 1947; Gen. Dirs Dr RICHARD SCHENZ, Dr RUDOLF MERTEN; 20 mems.

Fachverband der Nahrungs- und Genussmittelindustrie (Provisions): Zaunergasse 1-3, Vienna; tel. (1) 712-21-21; fax (1) 713-18-02; Chair. Dr ERWIN BUNDSCHUH; Dir Dr MICHAEL BLASS; 674 mems.

Fachverband der Papier und Pappe verarbeitenden Industrie (Paper and Board Processing): Brucknerstr. 8, 1041 Vienna; tel. (1) 505-53-82-0; fax (1) 505-90-18; e-mail ppv@ppv.at; Chair. GUSTAV GLÖCKLER; 134 mems.

Fachverband der Papierindustrie (Paper): Gumpendorferstr. 6, 1061 Vienna; tel. (1) 588-86-0; fax (1) 588-86-22-2; e-mail fvpapier@cafvpapier.wk.or.at; Chair. Dr ROBERT LAUNSKY-TIEFFENTHAL; Dir Dr GEROLF OTTAWA; 30 mems.

Fachverband der Stein- und keramischen Industrie (Stone and Ceramics): Postfach 329, Wiedner Hauptstr. 63, 1045 Vienna; tel (1) 501-05-35-31; fax (1) 505-62-40; e-mail steine@wkoesk.wk.or.at; internet www.baustaffindustrie.at; f. 1946; Chair. Dr CARL HENNRICH; Pres. ERHARD SCHASCHL; 400 mems.

Fachverband der Textilindustrie (Textiles): Rudolfsplatz 12, 1013 Vienna; tel. (1) 533-37-26-0; fax (1) 533-37-26-40; e-mail fvtextil@fvtextil.wk.or.at; internet www.textilindustrie.at; Pres. Dr PETER PFNEISL; Dir Dr WOLFGANG ZEYRINGER; 265 mems.

UTILITIES
Electricity

Energie-Versorgung-Niederösterreich AG (EVN): Johann-Steinboeck-Str. 1, 2344 Maria Enzersdorf; tel. (2742) 80-00; fax (2742) 80-03-60; Chair. Dr RUDOLF GRUBER.

Burgenländische Elektrizitätswirtschafts-AG: Kasemenstr. 9, 7001 Eisenstadt; tel. (2682) 900-01-02-1; fax (2682) 900-01-91-0; e-mail guenther.ofner@bewag.co.at; Chair. Dr GÜNTHER OFNER.

Kärntner Elektrizitäts-AG: Arnulfplatz 2, 9020 Klagenfurt; tel. (463) 52-50; fax (463) 52-51-59-6; Chair. Dr GÜNTHER BRESITZ.

Oberösterreichische Kraftwerke AG: Böhmerwaldstr. 3, 4020 Linz; tel. (732) 65-93-0; fax (732) 65-93-36-00; Chair. Dr LEOPOLD WINDTNER.

Österreichische Elektrizitätswirtschafts-AG: Am Hof 6A, 1010 Vienna; tel. (1) 531-13-0; fax (1) 531-13-41-91; e-mail info@pol.verbund.co.at; internet www.verbund.co.at/verbund; federal electricity authority; operates national grid, wholesales electricity to the nine regional operators; Dir HANS HAIDER.

Salzburg AG für Energie, Verkehr und Telekommunikation: Bayerhamerstr. 16, 5021 Salzburg; tel. (662) 88-84-0; fax (662) 88-84-17-0; e-mail offic@salzburg-ag.at; internet www.salzburg-ag.at; Chair. Dr JOHANN OBERHAMBERGER.

Steirische Wasserkraft- und Elektrizitäts-AG: Leonhardgurtel 10, 8011 Graz; tel. (316) 3870; fax (316) 387290; Chair. Dr OSWIN KOIS.

Tiroler Wasserkraftwerke AG: Landhausplatz, 6010 Innsbruck; tel. (512) 50-60; fax (512) 50-62-12-6; Chair. Dr HELMUT MAYR.

Vorarlberger Kraftwerke AG: Weidachstr. 6, 6900 Bregenz; tel. (5574) 601-0; fax (5574) 60-15-00; e-mail energie@vkw.at; internet www.vkw.at; Chair. Dr LEO WAGNER, Dr OTTO WAIBEL.

WienStrom GmbH: Mariannegasse 4, 1095 Vienna; tel. (1) 400-43-00-00; fax (1) 400-43-00-99; e-mail vavra@wienstrom.co.at; internet www.wienstrom.co.at; f. 1902; Chair. HELMUT KASTL.

Gas

BEGAS-Burgenländische Erdgasversorgungs-AG: Kasernenstr. 10, 7000 Eisenstadt; tel. (2682) 70-9; fax (2682) 70-91-74; Chair. HERIBERT ARTINGER.

Oberösterreichische Ferngas-AG: Neubauzeile 99, 4030 Linz; tel. (732) 38-83; fax (732) 37-72-19; Chair. MAX DOBRUCKT.

Steirische Ferngas-AG: Gaslaternenweg 4, 8041 Graz; tel. (316) 476-0; fax (316) 476-30; e-mail office@steirische-ferngas.at; internet www.steirische.ferngas; Chair. BERNARD ALRAN, PETER KOBERL, MAX POLZL.

Water

Österreichischer Wasser- und Abfallwirtschaftsverband (ÖWAV) (Austrian Water and Refuse Board): Marc-Awel-Str. 5, 1010 Vienna; tel. (1) 535-5-70; fax (1) 535-40-64; e-mail randl@oewav.at; internet www.oewav.at.

TRADE UNIONS

Österreichischer Gewerkschaftsbund (ÖGB) (Austrian Trade Union Fed.): Hohenstaufengasse 10–12, 1010 Vienna; tel. (1) 534-44; fax (1) 534-44-20-4; e-mail oegb@oegb.or.at; internet www.oegb.or.at; non-party union org. with voluntary membership; f. 1945; org. affiliated with ICFTU and the European Trade Union Confederation (ETUC); Pres. FRIEDRICH VERZETNITSCH; Exec. Secs KARL DROCHTER, Dr RICHARD LEUTNER; 1,497,584 mems (Dec. 1997); comprises the following 14 trade unions:

Gewerkschaft Agrar-Nahrung-Genuss (Agricultural, Food, Beverage and Tobacco Workers): Albertgasse 35, 1081 Vienna; tel. (1) 401-49; fax (1) 401-49-20; e-mail ang@ang.oegb.or.at; Chair. Dr LEOPOLD SIMPERL; 40,113 mems (1989).

Gewerkschaft Bau-Holz (Building Workers and Woodworkers): Ebendorferstr. 7, 1010 Vienna; tel. (1) 401-47; fax (1) 401-47-25-8; e-mail johann-driemer@gbh.oegb.or.at; Chair. JOHANN DRIEMER; 171,000 mems (1997).

Gewerkschaft der Chemiearbeiter (Chemical Workers): Stumpergasse 60, 1060 Vienna; tel. (1) 597-15-01; fax (1) 597-21-01-23; Chair. GERHARD LINNER; 51,172 mems (1993).

Gewerkschaft Druck und Papier (Printing and Paper Trade Workers): Postfach 91, Seidengasse 15–17, 1070 Vienna; tel. (1) 523-82-31; fax (1) 523-81-32-28; e-mail gewdu@netway.at; f. 1842; Chair. FRANZ BITTNER; 18,023 mems (1999).

Gewerkschaft der Eisenbahner (Railwaymen): Margaretenstr. 166, 1051 Vienna; tel. (1) 546-41-50-0; fax (1) 546-41-50-4; e-mail gde@gde.oegb.or.at; Chair. WILHELM HABERZETTL; 100,000 mems (2000).

Gewerkschaft der Gemeindebediensteten (Municipal Employees): Maria-Theresien-Str. 11, 1090 Vienna; tel. (1) 313-16-83-00; fax (1) 313-16-7701; e-mail gdg@gdg.oegb.or.at; internet www.oegb.or.at/gdg; Chair. GÜNTER WENINGER; 176,623 mems (1998).

Gewerkschaft Handel, Transport, Verkehr (Workers in Commerce and Transport): Teinfaltstr. 7, 1010 Vienna; tel. (1) 534-54; fax (1) 534-54-32-5; f. 1904; Chair. PETER SCHNEIDER; 37,846 mems (1989).

Gewerkschaft Hotel, Gastgewerbe, Persönlicher Dienst (Hotel and Restaurant Workers): Hohenstaufengasse 10, 1013 Vienna; tel. (1) 534-44; fax (1) 534-44-50-5; e-mail hgpd@cahgpd.oegb.or.at; f. 1906; Chair. RUDOLF KASKE; 50,977 mems (1997).

Gewerkschaft Kunst, Medien, Sport, freie Berufe (Musicians, Actors, Artists, Journalists, etc.): Maria-Theresien-Str. 11, 1090 Vienna; tel. (1) 313-16; fax (1) 313-16-77-00; e-mail sekretariat@kmsfb.oegb.or.at; f. 1945; Chair. ERNST KÖRMER; Sec.-Gen. THOMAS LINZBAUER; 15,700 mems (2000).

Gewerkschaft Metall-Bergbau-Energie (Metal Workers, Miners and Power Supply Workers): Plösslgasse 15, 1041 Vienna; tel. (1) 501-46-0; fax (1) 501-46-13-30-0; e-mail gmbe@gmbe.oegb.or.at; f. 1890; Chair. RUDOLF NÜRNBERGER; 206,241 mems (1997).

Gewerkschaft Öffentlicher Dienst (Public Employees): Teinfaltstr. 7, 1010 Vienna; tel. (1) 534-54-0; fax (1) 534-54-20-7; e-mail goed@goed.or.at; internet www.goed.or.at; f. 1945; Chair. FRITZ NEUGEBAUER; Gen. Secs Dr MANFRED MÖGELE, GERHARD NEUGEBAUER, Dr ANDRÉ ALVARADO-DUPUY; 228,000 mems (1993).

Gewerkschaft der Post- und Fernmeldebediensteten (Postal and Telegraph Workers): Postfach 343, Biberstr. 5, 1010 Vienna; tel. (1) 512-55-11; fax (1) 512-55-11/52; e-mail gpf@gpf.oegb.or.at; Chair. HANS-GEORG DÖRFLER; 77,227 mems (1999).

Gewerkschaft der Privatangestellten (Commercial, Clerical and Technical Employees): Deutschmeisterplatz 2, 1013 Vienna;

tel. and fax (1) 313-93; Chair. HANS SALLMUTTER; 301,046 mems (1997).

Gewerkschaft Textil, Bekleidung, Leder (Textile, Garment and Leather Workers): Hohenstaufengasse 10, 1010 Vienna; tel. (1) 534-44; fax (1) 534-44-49-8; e-mail tbl@tbl.oegb.or.at; f. 1945; Chair. HARALD ETTL; 38,580 mems (1989).

Bundesfraktion Christlicher Gewerkschafter im Österreichischen Gewerkschaftsbund (Christian Trade Unionists' Section of the Austrian Trade Union Fed.): Hohenstaufengasse 12, 1010 Vienna; tel. (1) 534-44; organized in Christian Trade Unionists' Sections of the above 14 trade unions; affiliated with WCL; Sec.-Gen. KARL KLEIN.

Transport
RAILWAYS

Austrian Federal Railways operates more than 90% of all the railway routes in Austria. There are 5,600 km of track and all main lines are electrified.

Österreichische Bundesbahnen (ÖBB) (Austrian Federal Railways): Head Office: Elisabethstr. 9, 1010 Vienna; tel. (1) 58-00-0; fax (1) 58-00/25-00-1; Gen. Dir Dr HELMUT DRAXLER.

Innsbruck Divisional Management: Claudiastr. 2, 6020 Innsbruck; tel. (512) 50-33-00-0; fax (512) 50-35-00-5; Dir JOHANN LINDENBERGER.

Linz Divisional Management: Bahnhofstr. 3, 4021 Linz; tel. (732) 69-09-0; fax (732) 69-09-18-33; Dir HELMUTH AFLENZER; Vice-Dir KLAUS SEEBACHER.

Vienna Divisional Management: Nordbahnstr. 50, 1020 Vienna; fax (1) 580-05-00-00; fax (1) 580-02-56-01; Dir FRANZ POLZER.

Villach Divisional Management: 10-Oktober-Str. 20, 9501 Villach; tel. (4242) 20-20-32-00; fax (4242) 20-20-32-29; e-mail willibald.schicho@gv.oebb.at; internet www.railcargo.at; Dir WILIBALD SCHICHO.

Other railway companies include: Achenseebahn AG, AG der Wiener Lokalbahnen, Graz-Köflacher Eisenbahn- und Bergbau GmbH, Lokalbahn, Montafonerbahn AG, Raab-Oedenburg-Ebenfurter Eisenbahn, Salzburger Stadtwerke AG-Verkehrsbetriebe, Steiermärkische Lokalbahnen, Stern & Hafferl Verkehrs GmbH, Zillertaler Verkehrsbetriebe AG.

ROADS

At 31 December 1997 Austria had about 200,000 km of classified roads, of which 1,613 km were modern motorways, 9,970 km main roads, 19,822 km secondary roads and 98,000 km other roads.

INLAND WATERWAYS

The Danube (Donau) is Austria's only navigable river. It enters Austria from Germany at Passau and flows into Slovakia near Hainburg. The length of the Austrian section of the river is 351 km. Danube barges carry up to 1,800 metric tons, but loading depends on the water level, which varies considerably throughout the year. Cargoes are chiefly petroleum and derivatives, coal, coke, iron ore, iron, steel, timber and grain. Transport on the Danube was severely disrupted by the NATO bombing of Serbian bridges in early 1999. The Rhine-Main-Danube Canal opened in 1992. A passenger service is maintained on the Upper Danube and between Vienna and the Black Sea. Passenger services are also provided on Bodensee (Lake Constance) and Wolfgangsee by Austrian Federal Railways, and on all the larger Austrian lakes.

CIVIL AVIATION

The main international airport is located at Schwechat, near Vienna. There are also international flights from Graz, Innsbruck, Klagenfurt, Linz and Salzburg, and internal flights between these cities.

Principal Airlines

Austrian Airlines (Österreichische Luftverkehrs AG): Fontanastr. 1, 1107 Vienna; tel. (1) 176-6; fax (1) 688-55-05; e-mail public.relations@aua.com; internet www.aua.com; f. 1957; 39.7% state-owned; serves 123 cities in 67 countries world-wide; Chair. Dr RUDOLF STREICHER; Pres Dr HERBERT BAMMER, MARIO REHULKA.

Austrian Airtransport (AAT): Postfach 50, Fontanastr. 1, 1107 Vienna; tel. (1) 688-16-91; fax (1) 688-11-91; f. 1964; 80% owned by Austrian Airlines, from which it leases most of its aircraft; operates scheduled and charter flights for passengers and cargo, and tour services; Man Dir Dr HERBERT KOSCHIER.

Lauda Air Luftfahrt AG: Postfach 56, Lauda Air Bldg, 1300 Vienna-Schwechat; tel. (1) 7000-0; fax (1) 7000-790-15; e-mail office@laudaair.com; internet www.laudaair.com; f. 1979; became a scheduled carrier 1987; 47% owned by Austrian Airlines; operates scheduled passenger services and charter flights to Europe, Australia, the Far East and the USA; Chair. FERDINAND SCHMIDT.

Tiroler Luftfahrt AG (Tyrolean Airways): Postfach 98, Fürstenweg 176, 6026 Innsbruck; tel. (512) 22-2-0; fax (512) 22-22-90-05; internet www.telecom.at/tyrolean; f. 1958 as Aircraft Innsbruck; adopted present name 1980; operates scheduled services and charter flights within Austria and to other European countries; Pres. and CEO FRITZ FEITL.

Tourism

Tourism plays an important part in the Austrian economy. However, receipts from the sector, estimated at 161,000m. Schilling in 1991,

declined during the 1990s, and stood at 134,100m. Schilling in 1997 and an estimated 139,200m. Schilling in 1998. In 1998 Austria received 17.3m. foreign visitors at accommodation establishments (compared with 19.1m. visitors in 1992). The country's mountain scenery attracts visitors in both summer and winter, while Vienna and Salzburg, hosts to a number of internationally-renowned art festivals, are important cultural centres.

Österreich Werbung (Austrian National Tourist Office): Margaretenstr. 1, 1040 Vienna; tel. (1) 588-66-0; fax (1) 588-66-20; internet www.austria-tourism.at; f. 1955.

AZERBAIJAN

Introductory Survey

Location, Climate, Language, Religion, Flag, Capital

The Azerbaijan Republic is situated in eastern Transcaucasia, on the western coast of the Caspian Sea. To the south it borders Iran, to the west Armenia, to the north-west Georgia, and to the north the Republic of Dagestan, in Russia. The Nakhichevan Autonomous Republic is part of Azerbaijan, although it is separated from the rest of Azerbaijan by Armenian territory. Azerbaijan also includes the Nagorno-Karabakh Autonomous Oblast (Nagornyi Karabakh), which is largely populated by Armenians but does not legally constitute part of Armenia. The Kura plain has a dry, temperate climate with an average July temperature of 27°C (80°F) and an average January temperature of 1°C (34°F). Average annual rainfall on the lowlands is 200 mm–300 mm, but the Lenkoran plain normally receives between 1,000 mm and 1,750 mm. The official language is Azerbaijani (Azeri), one of the South Turkic group of languages; in 1992 the Turkish version of the Latin script replaced the Cyrillic alphabet (which had been in use since 1939). Religious adherence corresponds largely to ethnic origins: almost all ethnic Azerbaijanis are Muslims, some 70% being Shi'ite and 30% Sunni. There are also Christian communities, mainly representatives of the Russian Orthodox and Armenian Apostolic denominations. The national flag (proportions 2 by 1) consists of three equal horizontal stripes, of pale blue, red and green, with a white crescent moon framing a white eight-pointed star on the central red stripe. The capital is Baku.

Recent History

An independent state in ancient times, Azerbaijan was dominated for much of its subsequent history by foreign powers. Under the Treaty of Turkmanchai of 1828, Azerbaijan was divided between Persia (now Iran, which was granted southern Azerbaijan) and Russia (northern Azerbaijan). During the latter half of the 19th century petroleum was discovered in Azerbaijan, and by 1900 the region had become one of the world's leading petroleum producers. Immigrant Slavs began to dominate Baku and other urban areas.

After the October Revolution of 1917 in Russia, there was a short period of pro-Bolshevik rule in Baku before a nationalist Government took power and established an independent state on 28 May 1918, with Gyanja (formerly Elisavetpol, but renamed Kirovabad in 1935) as the capital. Independent Azerbaijan was occupied by troops of both the Allied and Central Powers; after their withdrawal, it was invaded by the Red Army in April 1920, and on 28 April a Soviet Republic of Azerbaijan was established. In December 1922 the republic became a member of the Transcaucasian Soviet Federative Socialist Republic (TSFSR), which entered the USSR as a constituent republic on 31 December. The TSFSR was disbanded in 1936, and Azerbaijan became a full union republic, the Azerbaijan Soviet Socialist Republic (SSR).

Following the Soviet seizure of power in 1920, many nationalist and religious leaders and their followers were persecuted or killed. Religious intolerance was particularly severe in the 1930s, and many mosques and religious sites were destroyed. In 1930–31 forced collectivization of agriculture led to peasant uprisings, which were suppressed by Soviet troops. The Stalinist purges of 1937–38 involved the execution or imprisonment of many members of the Communist Party of Azerbaijan (CPA), including Sultan Mejit Efendiyev, the republic's leader, and two republican premiers. In 1945 the Soviet Government attempted to unite the Azerbaijani population of northern Iran with the Azerbaijan SSR, by providing military support for a local 'puppet' government in Iran; Soviet troops were forced to withdraw from northern Iran in the following year by US-British opposition.

The most influential of Azerbaijan's Communist leaders in the period following the Second World War was Heydar Aliyev, who was installed as First Secretary of the CPA in 1969. He greatly increased the all-Union sector of the economy at the expense of republican industry, while retaining popularity with his liberal attitude to local corruption. Attempts to address corruption in the CPA followed the accession to power of Mikhail

Gorbachev, who became leader of the USSR in 1985. Aliyev was dismissed in October 1987, but popular dissatisfaction with the poor state of the economy and the party élite became more vocal. Unlike most Soviet republics, Azerbaijan had an annual trade surplus with the rest of the USSR, and yet its income per head was the lowest outside Central Asia. Public grievances over economic mismanagement and the privileges enjoyed by the party leadership were expressed at demonstrations in November 1988. Protesters occupied the main square in Baku, the capital, for 10 days, before being dispersed by troops, who arrested the leaders of the demonstrations.

The initial impetus, however, for the demonstrations was the debate on the status of Nagornyi Karabakh (an autonomous region within Azerbaijan) and Nakhichevan (an autonomous republic of Azerbaijan, separated from it by Armenian land). Both territories were claimed by Armenia, on historical grounds, and Nagornyi Karabakh had an overwhelming majority of (non-Muslim) Armenians in its population. Nakhichevan, despite an apparent surrender of Azerbaijan's claims to the territory in 1920, never became part of Soviet Armenia. The Soviet-Turkish Treaty of March 1921 included a clause guaranteeing Azerbaijani jurisdiction over Nakhichevan. The 45%–50% of the republic's population that had been ethnically Armenian in 1919 was reduced to less than 5% by 1989. Nagornyi Karabakh had been a disputed territory during the period of Armenian and Azerbaijani independence (1918–20), but in June 1921 the Bureau for Caucasian Affairs (the Kavburo) voted to unite Nagornyi Karabakh with Armenia. However, some days after the Kavburo vote, following an intervention by Stalin, the decision was reversed. In 1923 the territory was declared an autonomous oblast (region) within the Azerbaijan SSR. There were attempts to challenge Azerbaijan's jurisdiction over the region, including two petitions by the inhabitants of Nagornyi Karabakh in the 1960s, but they were strongly opposed by the Soviet and Azerbaijani authorities.

Conflict over the territory re-emerged in February 1988, when the Nagornyi Karabakh regional soviet (council) requested the Armenian and Azerbaijani Supreme Soviets to agree to the transfer of the territory to Armenia. The Soviet and Azerbaijani authorities rejected the request, thus provoking huge demonstrations by Armenians, not only in Nagornyi Karabakh, but also in the Armenian capital, Yerevan. Azerbaijanis began leaving Armenia, and reports that refugees had been attacked led to three days of anti-Armenian violence in the Azerbaijani town of Sumgait. According to official figures, 32 people died, 26 of whom were Armenians. Disturbances over the issue of Nagornyi Karabakh continued throughout 1988, leading to a large-scale exodus of refugees from both Armenia and Azerbaijan.

In January 1989, in an attempt to end the tension, the Soviet Government suspended the activities of the local authorities in Nagornyi Karabakh and established a Special Administration Committee (SAC), responsible to the USSR Council of Ministers. Although it was stressed that the region would formally retain its status as an autonomous oblast within Azerbaijan, the decision was widely viewed by Azerbaijanis as an infringement of the country's territorial integrity. This imposition of 'direct rule' from Moscow and the dispatch of some 5,000 Soviet troops did little to reduce tensions within Nagornyi Karabakh, where Armenians went on strike from May until September.

In mid-1989 the nationalist Popular Front of Azerbaijan (PFA) was established. Following sporadic strikes and demonstrations throughout August, the PFA organized a national strike in early September and demanded discussion on the issue of sovereignty, the situation in Nagornyi Karabakh, the release of political prisoners and official recognition of the PFA. After one week, the Azerbaijan Supreme Soviet agreed to concessions to the PFA, including official recognition. In addition, draft laws on economic and political sovereignty were published, and on 23 September the Supreme Soviet adopted the 'Constitutional Law on the Sovereignty of the Azerbaijan SSR', effectively a declaration of sovereignty. The conflict with Armenia continued, with the imposition by Azerbaijan of an economic blockade of Armenia.

In November 1989 the Soviet Government transferred control of Nagornyi Karabakh from the SAC to an Organizing Committee, dominated by ethnic Azerbaijanis. This decision was denounced by the Armenian Supreme Soviet, which declared Nagornyi Karabakh to be part of a 'unified Armenian republic', prompting further outbreaks of violence in Nagornyi Karabakh and along the Armenian–Azerbaijani border. Growing unrest within Azerbaijan, exacerbated by the return of refugees from Armenia to Baku, was directed both at the local communist regime and at ethnic Armenians.

In January 1990 radical members of the PFA led assaults on CPA and government buildings in Baku and other towns. Border posts were attacked on the Soviet–Iranian border, and nationalist activists seized CPA buildings in Nakhichevan and declared its secession from the USSR. In addition, renewed violence against Armenians, with some 60 people killed in rioting in Baku, led to a hasty evacuation of the remaining non-Azerbaijanis, including ethnic Russians, from the city. On 19 January a state of emergency was declared in Azerbaijan, and Soviet troops were ordered into Baku, where the PFA was in control. According to official reports, 131 people were killed, and some 700 wounded, during the Soviet intervention. The inability of the CPA to ensure stability in the republic led to the dismissal of Abdul Vezirov as First Secretary of the Party; he was replaced by Ayaz Mutalibov.

Despite the arrest of leading members of the PFA and the outlawing of other radical nationalist organizations, continuing unrest caused the election to the republic's Supreme Soviet (held in most of the other Soviet republics in February 1990) to be postponed. When the election did take place, in September–October 1990, the CPA won an overall majority. The opposition Democratic Alliance (which included the PFA), however, questioned the validity of the election. In addition, the continuing state of emergency, which prohibited large public meetings, severely disrupted campaigning by the opposition. When the new Supreme Soviet convened in February 1991, some 80% of the deputies were members of the CPA. The small group of opposition deputies united as the Democratic Bloc of Azerbaijan.

Unlike the other Caucasian republics (Armenia and Georgia), Azerbaijan declared a willingness to sign a new Union Treaty and participated in the all-Union referendum on the preservation of the USSR, which took place in March 1991. Official results of the referendum demonstrated a qualified support for the preservation of the USSR, with 75.1% of the electorate participating, of whom 93.3% voted for a 'renewed federation'. In Nakhichevan, however, only some 20% of eligible voters approved President Gorbachev's proposal. Opposition politicians also contested the results of the referendum, claiming that only 15%–20% of the electorate had actually participated.

In August 1991, when the State Committee for the State of Emergency seized power in Moscow, Mutalibov issued a statement that appeared to demonstrate support for the coup. Despite denials that he had supported the coup leaders, large demonstrations took place, demanding his resignation, the declaration of Azerbaijan's independence, the repeal of the state of emergency, and the postponement of the presidential election, scheduled for 8 September. The opposition was supported by Heydar Aliyev, now the Chairman of the Supreme Majlis (legislature) of Nakhichevan, who had become increasingly critical of Mutalibov's leadership. Mutalibov responded by ending the state of emergency and resigning as First Secretary of the CPA; on 30 August the Azerbaijani Supreme Soviet voted to 'restore the independent status of Azerbaijan'.

The election to the presidency proceeded, although it was boycotted by the opposition, with the result that Mutalibov was the only candidate. According to official results, he won 84% of the total votes cast. At a congress of the CPA, held later in September 1991, it was agreed to dissolve the party.

Independence was formally restored on 18 October 1991. The Supreme Soviet voted not to sign the treaty to establish an economic community, which was signed by the leaders of eight other Soviet republics on the same day. In a further move towards full independence, the Supreme Soviet adopted legislation allowing for the creation of national armed forces, and Azerbaijani units began to take control of the Soviet Army's military facilities in the republic. However, Azerbaijan did join the Commonwealth of Independent States (CIS, see p. 157), signing the Almaty (Alma-Ata) Declaration on 21 December.

Following the dissolution of the USSR, hostilities intensified in Nagornyi Karabakh. In March 1992 President Mutalibov resigned, owing to military reverses suffered by Azeri forces. He was replaced, on an interim basis, by Yagub Mamedov, the Chairman of the Milli Majlis, or National Assembly (which had replaced the Supreme Soviet following its suspension in late 1991), pending a presidential election in June. However, further military reverses prompted the Majlis to reinstate Mutalibov as President in mid-May. His immediate declaration of a state of emergency and the cancellation of the forthcoming presidential election outraged the opposition PFA, which organized a large-scale protest rally in Baku. The demonstrators occupied both the Majlis building and the presidential palace, and succeeded in deposing Mutalibov, who had held office for only one day. (He subsequently took refuge in Russia.) The PFA's effective takeover was consolidated in the following month, when the party's leader, Abulfaz Elchibey, was elected President of Azerbaijan by direct popular vote, defeating four other candidates by a substantial margin.

During 1992 the Government had to contend with a steadily deteriorating economic situation, largely the result of the continuing conflict in Nagornyi Karabakh and the collapse of the former Soviet economic system. Severe shortages of food and fuel were reported throughout the country, and the Government's failure to provide adequate support for an estimated 500,000 refugees from Nagornyi Karabakh and from Armenia prompted protest actions in Baku from mid-1992.

The background of military defeats and continuing economic decline severely undermined the Government and led to divisions within the PFA in early 1993. In June a rebel army, led by Col Surat Husseinov (the former Azerbaijani military commander in Nagornyi Karabakh), seized the city of Gyanja and advanced towards the capital, with the apparent intention of deposing Elchibey. In an attempt to bolster his leadership, Elchibey summoned Heydar Aliyev to Baku; in mid-June Aliyev was elected Chairman of the legislature. Following Elchibey's subsequent flight from the capital, Aliyev announced that he had assumed the powers of the presidency. There ensued what appeared to be a power struggle between Aliyev and Husseinov, following the bloodless capture of Baku by the rebel forces. However, in late June virtually all presidential powers were transferred, on an acting basis, to Aliyev by the Milli Majlis (which had voted to impeach Elchibey), and Husseinov was appointed Prime Minister, with control over all security services.

A referendum of confidence in Elchibey (who had taken refuge in Nakhichevan and still laid claim to the presidency) was held in late August 1993; of the 92% of the electorate that participated, 97.5% voted against him. The Milli Majlis endorsed the result and announced the holding of a direct presidential election. This took place on 3 October: Aliyev was elected President of Azerbaijan, defeating two other candidates, with 98.8% of the votes cast. In the months preceding the election there had been an escalation of harassment of opposition members, particularly the PFA. Several leading supporters of Elchibey were arrested, and PFA rallies were violently dispersed. The PFA boycotted the election in protest.

The domestic political situation remained tense during 1994. There was a noticeable increase in organized crime (drugs-trafficking, in particular) as well as political violence. Opponents of President Aliyev and his New Azerbaijan Party (NAP) were subject to increasing harassment, and their media activities were severely restricted. In February more than 40 members of the PFA were arrested at a regional conference of the party. In the following month police raided the PFA headquarters in Baku, arresting more than 100 people; the PFA, it was claimed, had been planning to overthrow the Government. The signature, in May, of a cease-fire in Nagornyi Karabakh (see below) led to further unrest in Azerbaijan. Nationalist opposition leaders claimed that the cease-fire would result in humiliating concessions by Azerbaijan and would be followed by the deployment of Russian troops as peace-keepers in Azerbaijan. Large-scale, anti-Government demonstrations were organized by the PFA in Baku in May and September.

A new political crisis arose in late September 1994 when the Deputy Chairman of the Milli Majlis and Aliyev's security chief were assassinated; three members of the special militia (known as OPON) attached to the Ministry of Internal Affairs were subsequently arrested. In early October some 100 OPON troops, led by Rovshan Javadov (a Deputy Minister of Internal Affairs), stormed the office of the Procurator-General, taking him and his officials hostage and securing the release of the three OPON members in custody. President Aliyev described the incident as an attempted coup and declared a state of emergency in Baku and Gyanja.

In the immediate aftermath of these events, other forces mutinied in Baku and elsewhere in Azerbaijan. In Gyanja, rebel forces, reportedly led by a relative of Surat Husseinov, occupied government and strategic buildings, although troops loyal to Aliyev quickly re-established control. Despite Husseinov's assurances of allegiance to Aliyev, the President dismissed him as Prime Minister, replacing him, on an acting basis, with Fuad Kuliyev. However, Aliyev stated that he himself would head the Government for the immediate future. The President then initiated a series of purges of senior members of the Government and the armed forces. In mid-October 1994 the Milli Majlis voted unanimously to remove Husseinov's parliamentary immunity from prosecution, in order that he could be arrested on charges of treason. However, Husseinov was believed to have fled to Russia.

Azerbaijan experienced only a short period of calm before political turmoil occurred again. In March 1995, following a decree by the Government to disband the OPON militia (which had remained under the control of Javadov), OPON forces seized government and police buildings in Baku and in north-western Azerbaijan. Many casualties were reported as government forces clashed with the OPON units, but the rebellion was crushed when government troops stormed the OPON headquarters near Baku; Javadov and many of his men were killed, and some 160 rebels were arrested. Aliyev accused former President Elchibey and Surat Husseinov of collusion in the attempted coup. In the aftermath of the unrest the PFA was also accused of involvement, and the party was banned. In early April Aliyev extended the state of emergency in Baku (introduced in October 1994) until June. However, the state of emergency in Gyanja was lifted. In May Fuad Kuliyev was confirmed as Prime Minister.

Political life in the latter half of 1995 was dominated by preparations for Azerbaijan's first post-Soviet legislative election. However, unrest continued: in late July a new plot to overthrow Aliyev was allegedly uncovered. This was again linked to Elchibey, Husseinov and other anti-Aliyev forces based in exile in Moscow. The harassment of opposition parties in Azerbaijan intensified, and in August–October a number of parties, as well as independent candidates, were refused permission to participate in the forthcoming election. In response, opposition parties staged protest actions in Baku.

The election of the new, 125-member Milli Majlis took place, as scheduled, on 12 November 1995. Of Azerbaijan's 31 officially-registered parties, as few as eight were, in the event, permitted to participate; of these, only two were opposition parties—the PFA (recently relegalized) and the National Independence Party (NIP). Almost 600 independent candidates were barred from participation. The election was held under a mixed system of voting: 25 seats were to be filled by proportional representation and the remaining 100 by majority vote in single-member constituencies. These included the constituencies of Nagornyi Karabakh and of the other Armenian-occupied territories (refugees from those regions voted in areas under Azerbaijani control, in anticipation of the eventual restoration of the country's territorial integrity). The result demonstrated widespread support for President Aliyev and his NAP, which won 19 of the 25 party seats (with the PFA and the NIP receiving three seats each). The NAP and independent candidates supporting Aliyev won an overwhelming majority of single-constituency seats. Of the remaining 28 seats in the Majlis, 27 were filled at 'run-off' elections held in late November 1995 and in February 1996, while one seat remained vacant. Some international observers monitoring the election declared that it had not been conducted in a free and fair manner and that 'serious electoral violations' had occurred. The Round Table bloc (a loose association of 21 opposition parties) claimed that the new legislature was 'illegal' and demanded that a fresh election be held.

On the same occasion as the election of the Milli Majlis, Azerbaijan's new Constitution was approved by an overwhelming majority of the electorate (officially, 91.9%) in a national referendum. The Constitution, which replaced the 1978 Soviet version, provided for a secular state, headed by the President, who was accorded wide-ranging executive powers.

In early 1996 supporters of Surat Husseinov and former President Elchibey received lengthy custodial sentences for their involvement in the alleged coup attempts of October 1994 and March 1995. In February 1996 two former members of the Government were sentenced to death on charges of treason and

several other former government members were sentenced to death on charges of conspiracy in the following months. Former President Mutalibov, whom Aliyev had accused of conspiring with Javadov, was arrested in Russia in April. He remained in Moscow, however, for medical treatment. The Russian authorities later refused to extradite Mutalibov, on the grounds that there was insufficient evidence against him.

Repressive measures against the opposition continued, with the seizure by the police of the PFA headquarters in April 1996. Several members of the party were later arrested, one for an alleged attempt to assassinate Aliyev in 1993, and the others on charges of establishing illegal armed groups. In July 1996 Aliyev criticized the Cabinet of Ministers for failing to implement economic-reform proposals, and dismissed several senior government officials for corruption. Fuad Kuliyev resigned from the office of Prime Minister, officially on grounds of ill health, after he was accused by Aliyev of hindering the process of reform; Artur Rasizade, hitherto first Deputy Prime Minister, was appointed acting Prime Minister. (His appointment as Prime Minister was confirmed in November.) This was followed, in September, by the resignation, also allegedly on grounds of ill health, of the Chairman of the Milli Majlis, Rasul Kuliyev, who had been criticized by the NAP. Murtuz Aleskerov, a staunch supporter of Aliyev, was elected in his place.

In January 1997 the Azerbaijani authorities released details of an abortive coup in October 1996, which had reportedly been organized by, among others, Mutalibov and Surat Husseinov. Charges were subsequently brought against some 40 alleged conspirators; in early 1997 many people, including 31 former members of the Baku police force, received prison sentences for their part in the attempted coups of October 1994 and March 1995. Husseinov was extradited from Russia to Azerbaijan in March 1997, and his trial, on charges of treason, began in July 1998. (In February 1999 he was sentenced to life imprisonment.) Meanwhile, in February 1997 four leading members of the opposition Islamic Party of Azerbaijan, including its Chairman, Ali Akram Aliyev, went on trial on charges of espionage on behalf of Iran (which denied any involvement). The trial concluded in April, and the four men received lengthy terms of imprisonment.

In April 1997 President Aliyev established a Security Council, the creation of which was stipulated in the 1995 Constitution. The formation in that month of an informal alliance of 10 parties (including the ruling NAP) to support Aliyev's policies and his candidacy in the 1998 presidential election, was criticized as unrepresentative by the opposition PFA; nevertheless, in May 1997, following a renewed outbreak of hostilities on the Armenian–Azerbaijani border (see below), many opposition parties issued a statement expressing their intention to support the Government, should war be declared on Armenia. Meanwhile, former President Elchibey was elected Chairman of the Democratic Congress, an opposition alliance.

In January 1998 the Azerbaijani authorities accused the former Chairman of the Milli Majlis, Rasul Kuliyev (who was resident in the USA), of organizing a conspiracy to depose President Aliyev. In April Kuliyev, who denied the accusations, was charged *in absentia* with alleged abuses of power while in office. In May legislation was passed creating a 24-member Central Electoral Commission, 12 members of which were to be directly appointed by the President, and 12 by the legislature. Opposition parties that had demanded that 17 of the 24 members should be representatives of political parties protested against the passage of the controversial legislation. A law regarding presidential elections was approved in June, requiring candidates to collect 50,000 signatures to stand, and setting a minimum level of voter participation of 50%. This was reduced to 25% when the bill was amended in July, and each voter was allowed to endorse more than one candidate. The opposition protested that the law favoured Aliyev's re-election, and launched a series of rallies and demonstrations demanding the cancellation of the presidential election, which was scheduled to be held in October. On 12 September police and demonstrators clashed violently in Baku, resulting in some 70–100 injuries and a number of arrests. Subsequent demonstrations were conducted peacefully following the imposition of new restrictions on public protests. Meanwhile, in August, Aliyev issued a decree dismantling the General Directorate of State Secrets, thereby effectively abolishing media censorship. Harassment of the independent media continued, however. In November a number of employees of independent newspapers staged a hunger strike in the capital to protest at alleged police brutality towards journalists and the instigation of libel proceedings against the opposition media.

The presidential election was held, as planned, on 11 October 1998, despite continuing opposition; according to official results, Heydar Aliyev was re-elected, with 77.6% of the total votes cast. Five other candidates contested the election. The polls were criticized by the Organization for Security and Co-operation in Europe (OSCE, known as the Conference on Security and Co-operation in Europe—CSCE, until December 1994—see p. 252) and the Council of Europe (see p. 165) for failing to meet international standards. Unrest continued, owing to the opposition's dissatisfaction with the validity of the results, and in November the Prosecutor-General announced that criminal proceedings would be instigated against a number of opposition leaders for sedition. The Cabinet of Ministers resigned shortly after the presidential election, as required by the Constitution. In late October the majority of ministers, including Prime Minister Rasizade, were reconfirmed in their positions by President Aliyev. In late December the Milli Majlis approved a revised Constitution for Nakhichevan, which defined the enclave as 'an autonomous state' within Azerbaijan. The amended Constitution had earlier been endorsed by the Nakhichevan legislature. The revisions were opposed by a number of deputies, on the grounds that the enclave's redefined status as a state within a state could set an undesirable precedent. In the same month the opposition Round Table bloc announced its dissolution; the erstwhile component parties of the alliance stated that they intended to work with a new coalition, the Movement for Democratic Elections and Electoral Reform, which was established in November and was composed of 23 opposition groups. It was reported that the new movement's primary aim was to campaign for the annulment of the recent presidential election.

In the first half of 1999 President Aliyev's poor health caused fears of instability and reports circulated that Aliyev was grooming his son Ilham (the Vice-Chairman of the State Oil Company of the Azerbaijan Republic) to assume the presidency. Following medical treatment in the USA in April, however, the President's health improved and in the following months he made a number of cabinet changes and announced, in September, that he was prepared to stand for a third term; none the less, Ilham Aliyev's political profile continued to be raised, and he was elected Chairman of the pro-Aliyev NAP in December. Meanwhile, in April a newly-founded grouping in the legislature, the Democratic Congress, which comprised, among other parties, the PFA and the Civic Solidarity Party (CSP—some 17 deputies in total), began a boycott of the Milli Majlis, on the grounds that the Government had violated the rights of opposition deputies by refusing to discuss draft laws on municipal elections. The boycott was ended in late June following negotiations with the Government.

Azerbaijan's first municipal elections since independence were held in December 1999, thereby fulfilling a prerequisite for membership of the Council of Europe. However, mass electoral violations were observed and in March 2000 repeat elections were held to 75 municipal councils where the vote had been deemed invalid. Although there were reports of numerous infringements of press freedoms in 2000, including the suspension of several publications and the arrest of a number of journalists, among them a prominent newspaper editor, President Aliyev made continued concessions towards Council of Europe membership, such as the granting of amnesties to political prisoners.

In April 2000 a demonstration was organized by the Democratic Congress, which demanded the introduction of measures to ensure that the legislative election due to be held in November would be free and fair. Following the demonstration, which was attended by up to 20,000 people, many arrests were made, and the security forces were accused of having used excessive force. In mid-May the Milli Majlis passed a draft law on the composition of the Central Electoral Commission, which was endorsed by the Government and rejected by opposition parties.

The death, in August 2000, of former President Abulfaz Elchibey, prompted divisions to emerge within both the PFA and the Democratic Congress. The PFA divided into traditionalist and reformist factions, with separate Supreme Councils; the Central Electoral Commission recognized only the reformist wing, led by Ali Kerimov. The Democratic Congress was forced to restructure when five parties, including the reformist branch of the PFA, left in October. Shortly afterwards the traditionalist faction of the PFA, led by Murmahmud Fattayev, reached agreement with Musavat to co-operate for the duration of the election. Meanwhile, in September the Central Electoral Commission

refused to register eight opposition parties for the legislative election. Although the Commission's decision was revoked at the request of President Aliyev, following strong criticism from the US Government, a number of political parties (largely those that had initially been prevented from registering) decided to boycott the election, condemning it as 'undemocratic'. In October a warrant was issued for the arrest of Rasul Kuliyev (who remained in exile in the USA), on charges of having attempted to organize a coup in March. However, allegations circulated that the warrant was politically motivated, in order to prevent Kuliyev's participation in the legislative election; in January 2001 seven people were convicted of having collaborated with Kuliyev in the coup attempt.

The legislative election, held, as scheduled, on 5 November 2000, was condemned by the OSCE for falsification of results and intimidatory practices. Country-wide protests followed, which appeared likely to threaten Azerbaijan's membership of the Council of Europe. Of the 25 seats filled by proportional representation, 17 were obtained by the NAP and four by the PFA, while the CPA and the CSP each secured two seats in the legislature. Of the 99 seats contested in single-mandate constituencies, 62 were gained by the NAP and 26 by independent candidates; the election results were declared invalid in 11 constituencies and repeat elections were held on 7 January 2001, despite rallies, demands that a fresh legislative election be held and a request that the Court of Appeal declare the election to have been invalid. Several parties chose, once again, to boycott the repeat elections. Ultimately, the reformist faction of the PFA reversed an earlier decision to reject the legitimacy of the legislature and took up its seats in the Milli Majlis, as did the CSP, although both parties pledged to continue to campaign for new elections to be held. The traditionalist faction of the PFA continued its boycott of parliament, as did Musavat and two other opposition parties.

At the time of the disintegration of the USSR in late 1991, the leadership of Nagornyi Karabakh declared the enclave to be an independent republic. Azerbaijan refused to accept the territory's attempts to secede, and in January 1992 Nagornyi Karabakh was placed under direct presidential rule. International efforts to negotiate a peace settlement foundered, owing to Azerbaijan's insistence that the conflict was a domestic problem. Military successes by the ethnic Armenian forces of Nagornyi Karabakh in early 1992 culminated in the creation, in May, of a 'corridor' through Azerbaijani territory to link Nagornyi Karabakh with Armenia proper. Despite a successful Azerbaijani counter-offensive in late 1992, ethnic Armenian forces were able to open a second corridor in early 1993, following which they extended their operations into Azerbaijan itself, apparently in an attempt to create a secure zone around Nagornyi Karabakh. By August some 20% of Azerbaijan's territory had been seized by Armenian units, while all of Nagornyi Karabakh had already come under their control. The Armenian military gains prompted mounting alarm among the Azeri population, and there was a massive new movement of refugees fleeing from Armenian-occupied territory. The Armenian offensive in Azerbaijan continued, despite widespread international condemnation. Although it did not directly accuse Armenia itself of aggression, the UN Security Council adopted a series of resolutions demanding an immediate cease-fire and the withdrawal of all Armenian units from Azerbaijan. There were also strong protests by Turkey and Iran, both of which mobilized troops in regions bordering Armenia and Azerbaijan in September. In December Azeri forces launched a new counter-offensive in Nagornyi Karabakh, recapturing some areas that they had lost to Armenian control, although suffering heavy casualties. Meanwhile, international efforts to halt the conflict continued. These were led by the 'Minsk Group', which had been established by the CSCE in 1992 to provide a framework for peace negotiations between the parties. However, all cease-fire agreements were quickly violated. In early 1994 it was estimated that, since the conflict began in 1988, some 18,000 people had been killed and a further 25,000 had been wounded. The number of Azeri refugees was believed to have exceeded 1m.

However, in early May 1994 a major breakthrough was achieved with Azerbaijan's signature of the so-called Bishkek Protocol, which had been adopted several days previously at a meeting of the CIS Inter-Parliamentary Assembly, with the approval of representatives of both Armenia and Nagornyi Karabakh. The protocol, although not legally binding, was regarded as an expression of willingness by the warring factions to negotiate a lasting peace accord. On 8 May the Nagornyi Karabakh leadership ordered its forces to cease hostilities, in accordance with the protocol. Although isolated violations were subsequently reported, the cease-fire remained in force. In the latter half of the year efforts were made to co-ordinate the separate peace proposals of the CSCE 'Minsk Group' and Russia. However, Azerbaijan refused either to negotiate a peace settlement or to discuss the future status of Nagornyi Karabakh until Armenian forces were withdrawn entirely from occupied Azerbaijani territory and Azerbaijani refugees had returned to their homes. Azerbaijan also insisted that international peacekeeping forces be deployed in Nagornyi Karabakh (as opposed to the Russian- and CIS-led force favoured by Armenia). In December, at a summit meeting of the CSCE (subsequently known as the OSCE), delegates agreed in principle to deploy a 3,000-strong multinational peace-keeping force in Nagornyi Karabakh; Russia was to contribute not more than 30% of the peacekeepers.

In 1995, although negotiations continued to be held under the aegis of the OSCE and only minor violations of the cease-fire were reported, no real progress towards a full political settlement was achieved. Nevertheless, in May the exchange of prisoners of war and other hostages was commenced. In April–June a new 33-seat republican legislature was elected in Nagornyi Karabakh (replacing the former 81-member Supreme Soviet). Robert Kocharian, hitherto Chairman of the State Defence Committee, was appointed to the new office of an executive presidency. In August the new legislature extended martial law in Nagornyi Karabakh until January 1996 (subsequently extended until December 1997).

Negotiations to reach a political settlement continued throughout 1996. Aliyev, who met President Ter-Petrossian of Armenia on several occasions, continued to affirm his commitment to Azerbaijan's territorial integrity, reiterating that Nagornyi Karabakh could be granted autonomy within Azerbaijan, but not full independence. The cease-fire remained in force and a further exchange of prisoners of war was carried out in May. The election to the office of President of Nagornyi Karabakh was held in November, despite earlier criticism from the OSCE and condemnation by Azerbaijan, and Kocharian, the incumbent President, was re-elected with more than 85% of votes cast. Azerbaijani refugees from the enclave staged protests in Baku, while Azerbaijan declared that it would not recognize the election results. Kocharian subsequently appointed Leonard Petrossian as Prime Minister of Nagornyi Karabakh.

In December 1996 Aliyev and Ter-Petrossian attended a summit meeting of the OSCE, in Lisbon, Portugal. Following demands by Azerbaijan, a statement was released by the OSCE Chairman, recommending three principles that would form the basis of a political settlement to the conflict: the territorial integrity of Armenia and Azerbaijan; legal status for Nagornyi Karabakh, which would be granted self-determination within Azerbaijan; and security guarantees for the population of Nagornyi Karabakh. However, Armenia refused to accept the terms of the statement.

Relations between Azerbaijan and Armenia deteriorated in February 1997, when Azerbaijan expressed concern at the provision of weapons to Armenia by several countries, including Russia, and condemned it as a violation of the Conventional Forces in Europe (CFE) Treaty. Armenia retaliated by accusing Azerbaijan of preparing for a military offensive against Nagornyi Karabakh to regain the territory. The admission by the Russian Minister of Defence that weapons had been delivered to Armenia in 1994–96 without the authorization, or knowledge, of the Russian Government, resulted in a deterioration in relations between Russia and Azerbaijan, particularly since Russia, as a participant in the 'Minsk Group', was expected to act as an impartial mediator. Azerbaijan demanded that the issue be investigated by the signatories to the CFE Treaty. Negotiations under the auspices of the OSCE resumed in Moscow in April, but little progress was made, and later in that month a series of clashes, which left many people killed or wounded, occurred on the Armenian–Azerbaijani border, with each side accusing the other of initiating the hostilities.

In late May 1997 a draft peace settlement for the disputed enclave was presented by the 'Minsk Group' to Armenia and Azerbaijan. Although the proposals were initially rejected, a revised plan, issued in July, received the qualified support of President Aliyev. The proposals provided for a stage-by-stage settlement of the conflict: Nagornyi Karabakh would receive autonomous status within Azerbaijan, and the withdrawal of Armenian forces from the enclave was to be followed by the deployment of OSCE peace-keeping troops, which would guarantee freedom of movement through the Lachin corridor linking Armenia with Nagornyi Karabakh. The appointment of Robert Kocharian as Prime Minister of Armenia in March 1997 and the proposed presidential election in Nagornyi Karabakh, scheduled for September, were severely criticized by Aliyev; the Azerbaijani authorities also expressed concern at the conclusion of a partnership treaty between Armenia and Russia, fearing that a strengthening of relations between the two countries was a hindrance to the peace process.

The election of Arkadii Gukassian to the post of President of Nagornyi Karabakh, in September 1997, was not recognized by the international community and threatened to hamper further progress on reaching a settlement, owing to his outright dismissal of the OSCE proposals; it was reported later in that month, however, that both Azerbaijan and Armenia had accepted the revised plan drawn up by the 'Minsk Group'. In addition, in an apparently significant change in policy, President Ter-Petrossian of Armenia publicly admitted that Nagornyi Karabakh could expect neither to gain full independence, nor to be united with Armenia. Moreover, the Azerbaijani authorities indicated that they would be willing to discuss with the leadership of Nagornyi Karabakh the level of autonomy to be granted to the enclave, providing that the principles of the Lisbon statement were accepted, having previously refused to recognize the Nagornyi Karabakh administration as an equal party in the negotiations.

Ter-Petrossian's cautious and moderate approach to the Nagornyi Karabakh crisis provoked much governmental disapproval and led to the President's resignation in early February 1998. His replacement, Kocharian, who was born in Nagornyi Karabakh, was expected to adopt a more belligerent and nationalistic stance towards resolving the situation in the disputed enclave. In June Leonard Petrossian resigned as Prime Minister of Nagornyi Karabakh, following a rift with his Minister of Defence; the erstwhile Deputy Prime Minister, Zhirayr Pogossian, replaced him in the premiership and a government reorganization was carried out. In late November the Armenian Government announced that, despite some reservations, it officially accepted the latest proposals put forward by the 'Minsk Group' regarding a settlement of the conflict in Nagornyi Karabakh, which were based on the principle of a 'common state' (comprising Azerbaijan and Nagornyi Karabakh). The Azerbaijani Government, however, rejected the proposals, claiming that they threatened the territorial integrity of Azerbaijan. Minor cease-fire violations were committed by both sides in late 1998.

An escalation in hostilities in mid-1999 prompted mutual accusations by Azerbaijan and Armenia that the other was attempting to destroy the 1994 cease-fire agreement. Presidents Kocharian and Aliyev met on several occasions in the latter half of 1999, but no substantive progress was made towards resolving the crisis. Meanwhile, in June President Gukassian dismissed the Government of Nagornyi Karabakh for failing to remedy the enclave's economic problems; at the end of that month Anushavan Danielian was appointed to head a new administration. In July former Prime Minister Zhirayr Pogossian was arrested and charged with the illegal possession of arms and ammunition, and with having been responsible for losing a state document. Samuel Babaian, Minister of Defence until June and an ally of Pogossian, who opposed Gukassian's political stance, was subsequently dismissed as army commander. Following an assassination attempt on President Gukassian in late March 2000, Babaian was arrested and charged with organizing the attack, as part of a purported coup. A legislative election was held in Nagornyi Karabakh on 18 June. Five parties contested the election to the 33-seat legislature; the pro-Presidential Democratic Artsakh Party attained the most seats, with 13. Direct talks between the Armenian and Azerbaijani Governments continued in 2000, but little progress was made towards reaching a final solution to the crisis.

Although it signed the Almaty Declaration in December 1991, Azerbaijan's subsequent attitude towards its membership of the CIS was equivocal. Indeed, the Milli Majlis failed to ratify the Commonwealth's founding treaty, and in October 1992 it voted overwhelmingly against further participation in the CIS. However, with the overthrow of the nationalist PFA Government and the accession to power of Heydar Aliyev, the country's position regarding the CIS was reversed, and in September 1993 Azerbaijan was formally admitted to full membership of the body. In February 1999, however, it was reported that Azerbaijan would not renew its membership of the CIS collective security treaty because of the continued occupation of Nagornyi Karabakh by Armenian troops, and in protest against Russia's continuing supply of armaments to Armenia. Negotiations concerning the repair and reopening of an existing oil pipeline from Azerbaijan, via Chechnya, to Novorossiisk on Russia's Black Sea coast, were the focus of Azerbaijani-Russian relations in 1997. Security guarantees for personnel working on the pipeline were an essential part of the discussions (owing to the ongoing conflict in Chechnya), and Azerbaijan actively pursued the development of alternative, new pipelines, primarily through Georgia and Turkey (see Economic Affairs). The refurbished pipeline to Novorossiisk became operational in November; by April 1999, however, a new pipeline carrying crude petroleum from Baku to the Georgian port of Supsa was fully operational. In October of that year relations between Russia and Azerbaijan became further strained, when it was reported that a Russian military aircraft had accidentally bombed a village in northern Azerbaijan. However, a visit to Azerbaijan by the Russian President, Vladimir Putin, in January 2001, and the signature of a number of co-operation agreements appeared to signal a new phase in relations between the two countries. Meanwhile, in 1997 a dispute with Turkmenistan concerning ownership of the Kyapaz (known as Serdar by Turkmenistan) offshore oilfield (the legal status of the Caspian Sea has yet to be established by the littoral states, following the dissolution of the USSR) threatened the conclusion of a contract with Russia to develop the area. In February 1998 Azerbaijan and Turkmenistan held talks regarding the delineation of their disputed border in the Caspian Sea.

The strengthening of relations with Turkey, which had been cultivated by successive leaderships following independence in 1991, continued under Aliyev. Throughout the conflict over Nagornyi Karabakh, Azerbaijan was supported by Turkey, which provided humanitarian and other aid, and reinforced Azerbaijan's economic blockade of Armenia. An intergovernmental agreement in support of the construction of a petroleum pipeline from the Azerbaijani oilfields to the Turkish port of Ceyhan via Tbilisi, Georgia, was signed in October 1998; a further agreement was signed by the Azerbaijani Government with the State Oil Company of the Azerbaijan Republic (SOCAR) and a number of petroleum companies in October 2000. Concerning relations with neighbouring Iran, it was believed that the large Azeri minority there (numbering an estimated 20m.) might prove to be a potential source of tension. In early 1995 it was reported that ethnic Azeri organizations in northern areas of Iran had established a 'national independence front' in order to achieve unification with Azerbaijan. Nevertheless, official relations between Iran and Azerbaijan remained amicable, and bilateral trade increased significantly in the 1990s, with Iran becoming one of Azerbaijan's largest trading partners by 1997. Relations deteriorated in 1999, however, following Azerbaijani allegations, which were denied by Iran, that Iranian spies had been operating in Azerbaijan to supply Armenia with military intelligence and that Islamist guerrillas had been trained in Iran as part of a plot against the Azerbaijani Government.

Relations with the USA expanded significantly in the mid-1990s, and in July 1997 President Aliyev visited the USA, the first visit by an Azerbaijani Head of State since the country regained its independence. An agreement was signed on military co-operation between the two countries, and four contracts between SOCAR and US petroleum companies to develop off-shore oilfields in the Caspian Sea were also concluded. The USA assumed co-chairmanship of the 'Minsk Group' in early 1997, together with Russia and France. US-Azerbaijani relations were strengthened in 1999 and 2000. New contracts for the development of the petroleum industry, worth US $10m., were signed during a visit to Washington, DC, by Aliyev in April 1999. The USA also expressed its support for the proposed Baku–Ceyhan pipeline (see above), and a financial agreement on its construction was signed in Washington in April 2000.

In March 1992 Azerbaijan was admitted to the UN; it subsequently became a member of the CSCE. In April 1996, together with Armenia and Georgia, Azerbaijan signed a co-operation agreement with the European Union (see p. 181). Azerbaijan was awarded observer status at NATO in June 1999, and in the following month it sent 30 troops to form part of the NATO peace-keeping force in the province of Kosovo and Metahija, the Federal Republic of Yugoslavia. Azerbaijan was finally inaugurated as a full member of the Council of Europe on 25 January 2001 (as was Armenia).

Government

Under the Constitution of November 1995, the President of the Azerbaijan Republic is Head of State and Commander-in-Chief of the armed forces. The President, who is directly elected for a five-year term of office, holds supreme executive authority in conjunction with the Cabinet of Ministers, which is appointed by the President and is headed by the Prime Minister. Supreme legislative power is vested in the 125-member Milli Majlis (National Assembly), which is directly elected (under a mixed system of voting) for a five-year term.

Defence

After gaining independence in 1991, Azerbaijan began the formation of national armed forces. In August 2000 these numbered 72,100: an army of 61,800, a navy of 2,200 and an air force of 8,100. Military service is for 17 months (but may be extended for ground forces). The Ministry of Internal Affairs controls a militia of an estimated 10,000 and a border guard of some 5,000. As a member of the CIS, Azerbaijan's naval forces operate under CIS (Russian) control. In May 1994 Azerbaijan became the 15th country to join NATO's 'Partnership for Peace' (see p. 243) programme of military co-operation. The 2000 budget allocated an estimated US $119m. to defence.

Economic Affairs

In 1998, according to World Bank estimates, Azerbaijan's gross national product (GNP), measured at average 1996–98 prices, was US $3,821m., equivalent to $480 per head (or $2,168 per head on an international purchasing-power parity basis). During 1990–98, it was estimated, GNP per head declined at an average annual rate of 12.5% in real terms. Over the same period the population increased at an average rate of 1.4% per year. During 1990–98 Azerbaijan's gross domestic product (GDP) decreased, in real terms, at an average rate of 11.5% annually. Real GDP increased by 1.2% in 1996, by 5.8% in 1997, by 10.0% in 1998 and by 7.4% in 1999.

Agriculture (including forestry) contributed 21.7% of GDP in 1998 and 23.3% in 1999, owing to a good grain harvest. In 1999 some 42.3% of the working population were employed in the sector. The principal crops are grain, watermelons and other fruit, vegetables and cotton. By mid-1999 some 80% of state-owned agriculture had passed into private ownership, and land reform was expected to be complete by the end of that year. More than 80% of the production of vegetables, fruit, livestock and animal products was generated by private farms by the end of 1997. During 1990–98 Azerbaijan's gross agricultural output decreased at an average annual rate of 1.4%. According to the IMF, agricultural GDP decreased by 6.9% in 1997, but increased by 3.9% in 1998 and by 7.1% in 1999.

Industry (including mining, manufacturing, construction and power) contributed 35.4% of GDP in 1999, according to the World Bank. In that year, according to official sources, 11.7% of the working population were employed in industry. The real GDP of the industrial sector increased by 16.8% in 1997 and by 19.9% in 1998. Those sectors associated with the petroleum industry, such as construction, have experienced steady growth, whereas non-petroleum-based industries have demonstrated a significant decline.

Azerbaijan is richly endowed with mineral resources, the most important of which is petroleum. The country's known reserves of petroleum were estimated to total 1,300m.–1,500m. metric tons in December 1996, of which more than 95% was located in offshore fields in the Caspian Sea. Production of crude petroleum declined by 1% in 1996 (compared with the previous year), and also decreased in 1997 and 1998, owing mainly to inefficient technology and poor maintenance of the oilfields. However, production increased by 20.9% in 1999 and was projected to increase further in 2000–2002. In September 1994 the Azerbaijani Government and a consortium of international petroleum companies, the Azerbaijan International Operating Company (AIOC), concluded an agreement to develop these offshore oilfields. By mid-2000 the State Oil Company of the Azerbaijan Republic (SOCAR) had signed 20 production-sharing agreements with international partners, largely for the exploration of new fields. Production of 'early' oil began in October 1997 and accounted for a 50% increase in overall petroleum extraction over the following two years. The petroleum was transported to the Russian Black Sea port of Novorossiisk, via Chechnya, and the first shipment of petroleum from AIOC-operated fields was made in November. During 1999, however, technical problems with the pipeline and the conflict in Chechnya caused regular closures; a new section of the pipeline, avoiding Chechnya, was completed in March 2000. A further pipeline, transporting petroleum from Baku to the Georgian port of Supsa, opened April 1999. However, projected exports of petroleum demanded greater capacity and other possible pipeline routes were discussed; in October 2000 the Government of Azerbaijan signed an agreement with SOCAR and a consortium of petroleum companies on the construction of a pipeline from Baku to Ceyhan in Turkey. It was envisaged that production of crude petroleum would exceed 1m. barrels per day when all the fields were developed. Azerbaijan also has substantial reserves of natural gas, most of which are located off shore. In July 1999 a massive gasfield was discovered at Shah Deniz in the Caspian Sea, with sufficient reserves (estimated to be in excess of 400,000m. cu m) for eventual major exports to Turkey. Other minerals extracted include gold, silver, iron ore, alunite (alum-stone), iron pyrites, barytes, cobalt and molybdenum.

Production in the manufacturing sector has declined significantly since 1991, owing to the collapse of the Soviet internal trading systems and the increasing cost of energy products. In 1996 the principal branches of manufacturing, measured by gross value of output, were petroleum refineries (accounting for 47.6% of the total), textiles (13.0%), chemicals (3.2%) and food products and beverages (1.3%). According to the World Bank, manufacturing contributed 10.4% of GDP in 1998 and 5.5% in 1999. The sector declined by an annual average of 30.2% in 1989–99.

In 1992 Azerbaijan's supply of primary energy was provided by natural gas (58%), nuclear power (31%), petroleum and petroleum products (6%) and hydroelectric and other sources (5%). In 1997 some 85% of electricity generation was provided by thermal power stations (with two-thirds of these powered by mazout, residual fuel oil), while the remaining 15% was provided by hydroelectric stations. In 1999 Azerbaijan imported power from and participated in energy exchanges with Georgia, Iran, Russia and Turkey.

The services sector has expanded since 1991, with retail trade, restaurants and hotels gaining in importance, concomitantly with the petroleum industry, in the mid-1990s. In 1999, according to official sources, services accounted for 46.0% of employment and provided 41.3% of GDP. According to the World Bank, the real GDP of the services sector increased by 8.9% in 1997 and by 0.9% in 1998.

In 1999 Azerbaijan recorded a visible trade deficit of US $408m., which was greatly reduced from that of 1998, as was the deficit of $600m. on the current account of the balance of payments. In 1999 the principal source of imports was Russia (21.9%). Other major sources of imports were Turkey, the United Kingdom and the USA. The main market for exports in that year was Italy (33.7%). Other important purchasers were Russia, Georgia, and Turkey. The major exports in 1999 were petroleum products (accounting for 78.7% of the total) and food. The principal imports in that year were machinery and transport equipment (45.4%) and food.

Azerbaijan's overall budget deficit for 1999 was estimated at some 479,463m. manats. At the end of 1998 the country's total external debt was estimated to be US $693.4m., of which $307.7m. was long-term public debt. The cost of debt-servicing in that year was equivalent to only 2.3% of the value of exports of goods and services. The annual rate of inflation averaged 260.6% during 1990–98. Consumer prices increased by an average of 1,664% in 1994 and by 412% in 1995. However, the average inflation rate declined to 19.8% in 1996, to 3.7% in 1997, and to -0.8% in 1998; in 1999 deflation of 8.5% was recorded. In November 1999, according to government figures, some 1.8m. people (42.4% of the labour force) were unemployed or underemployed; however, only 45,211 were actually registered as unemployed at the end of 1999.

Azerbaijan became a member of the IMF and the World Bank in 1992. It also joined the Islamic Development Bank (see p. 229), the European Bank for Reconstruction and Development (EBRD, see p. 176), the Economic Co-operation Organization (ECO, see p. 175) and the Black Sea Economic Co-operation group (known as the Organization of the Black Sea Economic Co-operation from May 1999—see p. 265). In February 2000 Azerbaijan also became a member of the Asian Development Bank (see p. 131).

The dissolution of the USSR in 1991, the conflict in Nagornyi Karabakh and the disruption of trade routes through Georgia and Chechnya have all caused significant economic problems for Azerbaijan. However, owing to its enormous mineral wealth,

Azerbaijan's prospects for eventual economic prosperity are considered to be favourable, although major investment and foreign technological expertise are required for the full potential of the country's unexploited mineral reserves to be realized. The agreements that have been concluded with international consortia to develop these reserves were expected greatly to improve Azerbaijan's economic situation, as was the endorsement of the TRACECA (Transport Corridor Europe–Caucasus–Asia) project by the 12 countries along the route of the ancient 'Silk Road', which was signed in Baku in September 1998. The Government's stabilization and reform programme, adopted in early 1995, had achieved considerable success by 1998, when Azerbaijan enjoyed negative growth in the rate of inflation and strong GDP expansion. However, there was a sharp decline in net foreign investment in 1999, largely owing to a decline in activity in the petroleum industry, pending a final decision on routes for the construction of new export pipelines, with the capacity to meet the projected demand for petroleum exports from 2004. None the less, both private and public savings increased in 1999, reflecting the growth in petroleum and overall export prices. Moreover, the easing of monetary and exchange-rate policies in the latter half of 1999 helped to restore confidence in the manat, after the adverse impact of the Russian financial crisis of 1998, and led to a gradual increase in consumer-price inflation in 2000 (it had been negative in 1999). The budget for 2001 envisaged a budget deficit of 2.0% of GDP, compared with the 2.6% predicted for 2000. Despite these positive indicators, in February 2000 the IMF briefly suspended the disbursement of the final US $21m. tranche of an Enhanced Structural Adjustment Facility (ESAF) loan, in response to Azerbaijan's failure to fulfil all of its obligations under the Fund's economic programme. However, by the end of 2000 Azerbaijan had increased fiscal revenues (reflecting improvements to the tax administration), reduced wages', pensions' and benefits' arrears in the public sector, attained its budgetary targets and finally established a State Oil Fund, after a delay of one year. The country's privatization programme had also entered its second phase, after a period of stagnation. A new IMF loan agreement for 2001–03 was expected to be agreed in December 2001, although it was to be dependent on Azerbaijan's compliance with new programmes of structural reform and poverty reduction. In addition, the World Bank agreed to provide loans of US $50m.–$100m. in 2001, to support financial, health-care and social reforms towards poverty eradication.

Social Welfare

Azerbaijan has a comprehensive social security system, which aims to ensure that no citizen receives less than a subsistence income and that health care and education are freely available to all. However, in the late 1990s Azerbaijan's social-welfare system was under enormous strain, owing to the conflict in Nagornyi Karabakh (see Recent History) and the massive influx of refugees into the republic, as well as the effects of comprehensive economic reforms. Among the most important provisions of the system are: old-age, disability, and survivor pensions; birth, child, and family allowances, as well as benefits for sick leave, maternity leave, temporary disability, and burial; unemployment compensation; price subsidies; and tax exemptions for specific social groups. The above social benefits are financed by three extrabudgetary funds, the Social Protection Fund, the Employment Fund and the Disabled Persons' Fund. The Social Protection Fund receives transfers from the republican budget, as well as contributions from employers and employees, and the Employment Fund is financed by social-insurance contributions from employers. In 1999 government expenditure on health care, at 186,162m. manats, amounted to 1.0% of GDP. Transfers to households by the Social Protection Fund in 1999 totalled 1,335,000m. manats (8.1% of GDP), including 695,000m. manats in pensions. At the end of 1999, according to official figures, some 1.2m. people were receiving pensions, 728,000 of whom were old-age pensioners. Since the late 1990s the retirement age has been increasing by six months annually, from 54 to 57 years for women and from 59 to 62 years for men; at the beginning of 2000 the retirement ages stood at 56.5 years and 61.5 years, respectively.

Azerbaijan's first private hospital was opened, in the Nakhichevan Autonomous Republic, in May 1998. In 1998, according to the IMF, there were 8.5 hospital beds per 1,000 people. There were 3.9 physicians per 1,000 inhabitants in 1999.

Education

Before 1918 Azerbaijan was an important centre of learning among Muslims of the Russian Empire. Under Soviet rule, a much more extensive education system was introduced. In the early 1990s this was reorganized, as part of overall economic and political reforms. Education is officially compulsory between the ages of six and 17 years. Primary education begins at six years of age and lasts for four years. Secondary education, beginning at 10, comprises a first cycle of five years and a second cycle of two years. In 1996 total enrolment at primary and secondary schools was equivalent to 89% of the school-age population (males 87%; females 91%). Approximately 85% of secondary schools use Azerbaijani as the medium of instruction, while some 13% use Russian. Since 1992 a Turkic version of the Latin alphabet has been used in Azerbaijani-language schools (replacing the Cyrillic script). There were 17 institutions of higher education in 1992; courses of study for full-time students last between four and five years. Higher education institutes include Baku State University, which specializes in the sciences, and the State Petroleum Academy, which trains engineers for the petroleum industry. In 1995 it was estimated that the rate of adult illiteracy in Azerbaijan was only 0.4% (males 0.3%; females 0.5%). Government expenditure on education was estimated to total 3.6% of GDP in 1998 and in 1999 it totalled 795,060m. manats (representing 21.8% of total government expenditure).

Public Holidays

2001: 1 January (New Year), 20 January (Day of Sorrow), 6 March* (Kurban Bayramy, Sacrifice Day), 8 March (International Women's Day), 22 March (Noruz Bayrami, Festival of Spring), 1 May (Labour Day), 9 May (Victory Day), 28 May (Republic Day), 15 June (Day of Liberation of the Azerbaijani People), 9 October (Day of the Armed Services), 18 October (Day of Statehood), 12 November (Constitution Day), 17 November (Day of National Survival), 17 December* (Ramazan Bayramy, end of Ramadan), 31 December (Day of Azerbaijani Solidarity World-wide).

2002: 1 January (New Year), 20 January (Day of Sorrow), 23 February* (Kurban Bayramy, Sacrifice Day), 8 March (International Women's Day), 22 March (Noruz Bayrami, Festival of Spring), 1 May (Labour Day), 9 May (Victory Day), 28 May (Republic Day), 15 June (Day of Liberation of the Azerbaijani People), 9 October (Day of the Armed Services), 18 October (Day of Statehood), 12 November (Constitution Day), 17 November (Day of National Survival), 6 December* (Ramazan Bayramy, end of Ramadan), 31 December (Day of Azerbaijani Solidarity World-wide).

* These holidays are dependent on the Islamic lunar calendar and may vary by one or two days from the dates given.

Weights and Measures

The metric system is in force.

Statistical Survey

Source (unless otherwise stated): State Statistical Committee of Azerbaijan Republic, 370136 Baku, Inshatchilar St; tel. (12) 38-64-98; fax (12) 38-24-42; e-mail gks@baku-az.net; internet www.statcom.baku-az.com.

Area and Population

AREA, POPULATION AND DENSITY

Area (sq km)	86,600*
Population (census results)†	
12 January 1989	7,021,178
27 January 1999 (provisional)	
Males	4,119,000
Females	3,834,000
Total	7,953,000
Population (official estimates at 31 December)	
1997	7,876,700
1998	7,949,300
1999	8,016,200
Density (per sq km) at 31 December 1999 . . .	92.6

* 33,400 sq miles.
† Figures refer to *de jure* population. The *de facto* total at the 1989 census was 7,037,867.

ETHNIC GROUPS (permanent inhabitants, 1989 census)

	Number ('000)	%
Azeri	5,805.0	82.7
Russian	392.3	5.6
Armenian	390.5	5.6
Lezghi	171.4	2.4
Avar	44.1	0.6
Ukrainian	32.3	0.5
Jewish	30.8	0.4
Tatar	28.6	0.4
Georgian	14.2	0.2
Others	112.0	1.6
Total	7,021.2	100.0

PRINCIPAL TOWNS (estimated population at 31 December 1996)

Baki		Nakhichevan	. .	63,100
(Baku, the capital)	1,066,800*	Seki (Sheki)	. .	61,500
Gyanja† . . .	291,900	Garachukhur	. .	60,000
Sumgait . . .	248,500	Khankendi		
Mingachevir		(Stepanakert)	.	55,300
(Mingechaur) .	97,200	Yevlakh .	. .	50,400
Ali Bayramli .	68,900	Lenkoran .	. .	47,000
Bakikhanov .	63,300	Mastaga (Mashtagi)	.	43,100

* The population of the Baku agglomeration (including Bakikhanov, Garachukhur and Mastaga) was 1,727,200.
† Known as Kirovabad between 1935 and 1989.

BIRTHS, MARRIAGES AND DEATHS

	Registered live births		Registered marriages		Registered deaths	
	Number	Rate (per 1,000)	Number	Rate (per 1,000)	Number	Rate (per 1,000)
1994 . .	159,761	n.a.	47,147	n.a.	54,921	n.a.
1995 . .	143,315	18.9	43,130	5.7	50,828	6.7
1996 . .	129,247	16.9	38,572	5.1	48,242	6.3
1997 . .	132,052	17.1	46,999	6.1	46,962	6.1
1998 . .	123,996	15.9	40,900*	5.2	46,299	5.9
1999 . .	117,500*	14.9	37,400*	4.8	46,300*	5.9

* Figures are rounded to the nearest 100.
Expectation of life (years at birth, 1999): 71.6 (males 67.7; females 75.0).

ECONOMICALLY ACTIVE POPULATION*
(ISIC Major Divisions, annual average, '000 persons)

	1998	1999
Agriculture, hunting, forestry and fishing . .	1,565.8	1,566.8
Mining and quarrying	58.4	58.8
Manufacturing	143.0	143.2
Electricity, gas and water. . . .	55.0	55.1
Construction.	174.0	174.2
Trade, restaurants and hotels. . . .	734.4	732.0
Transport, storage and communications . .	169.0	169.9
Financing, insurance, real estate and business		
services	66.5	67.1
Community, social and personal services .	735.1	734.5
Activities not adequately defined . . .	0.3	0.3
Total employed.	3,701.5	3,701.9
Unemployed	42.3	45.2
Total labour force	3,743.8	3,747.1
Males	1,954.1	1,955.7
Females	1,789.1	1,791.4

* Figures refer to males aged 16 to 59 years and females aged 16 to 54 years.
Source: ILO, *Yearbook of Labour Statistics*.

Agriculture

PRINCIPAL CROPS ('000 metric tons)

	1997	1998	1999
Wheat	935	820	816
Barley	153	79	74
Maize	19	29	100
Potatoes.	223	313	334
Seed cotton	125	113	97
Cabbages	44	33	46
Tomatoes	206	210	317
Cucumbers and gherkins .	49	53	71
Onions (dry)	40	62	79
Other vegetables . . .	157	145	155
Watermelons† ‡ . . .	57	79	148
Grapes	145	108	140
Apples	214*	248*	126
Pears	15*	18*	20†
Peaches and nectarines . .	28*	33*	35†
Plums	25*	29*	17
Citrus fruits	24*	32*	33†
Apricots	18*	22*	16
Tea (made)	2	1	1†
Tobacco (leaves) . . .	15	15	9
Cotton (lint)	37*	34*	39

* Unofficial figure.   † FAO estimate(s).
‡ Including melons, pumpkins and squash.
Source: FAO.

LIVESTOCK ('000 head, year ending September)

	1997	1998	1999
Horses	49	53	56
Asses	28	31	33
Cattle	1,780	1,843	1,910
Buffaloes	303	293	290*
Pigs	23	21	26
Sheep	4,648	4,896	5,132
Goats	274	371	381
Chickens†	11,500	12,800	13,443
Turkeys†	531	434	431

* FAO estimate.   † Unofficial figures.

Source: FAO.

LIVESTOCK PRODUCTS ('000 metric tons)

	1997	1998	1999
Beef and veal	48	50	52
Mutton and lamb . . .	26	32	33
Pig meat	2	1	1
Poultry meat	15	17	17
Cows' milk	882	947	991
Cheese	1	1	1
Hen eggs*	28	29	28
Wool: greasy	10	10	11
Cattle hides (fresh) . .	8	8	9
Sheepskins (fresh) . .	3	4	4

* Unofficial figures.

Source: FAO.

Fishing

(metric tons, live weight)

	1996	1997	1998
Capture	6,627	5,119	4,678
Freshwater bream . .	402	346	314
Azov sea sprat . . .	5,828	4,420	4,043
Aquaculture	419	364	211
Common carp . . .	222	163	80
Silver carp . . .	185	185	119
Total catch	7,046	5,483	4,889

Source: FAO, *Yearbook of Fishery Statistics.*

Mining

	1997	1998	1999
Crude petroleum ('000 metric tons)	9,100	11,400	13,800
Natural gas (million cu metres) .	6,000	5,600	6,000

Source: IMF, *Azerbaijan Republic: Recent Economic Developments and Selected Issues* (September 2000).

Industry

SELECTED PRODUCTS ('000 metric tons, unless otherwise indicated)

	1995	1996	1997
Steel	39	3	25
Cement	196	223	315
Potassic fertilizers* . . .	0	2	5
Sulphuric acid	24	31	53
Caustic soda	36	33	23
Concrete (reinforced, million cu m)	91	n.a.	n.a.
Bricks (million)	26	11	15
Television receivers ('000) .	4	1	1
Bicycles ('000)	4	2	0
Electric motors ('000) . . .	512	n.a.	n.a.
Electric energy (million kWh) . .	17,040	17,088	n.a.
Jet fuels	504	527	n.a.
Motor spirit (petrol) . . .	1,128	737	n.a.
Kerosene	600	500	n.a.
Gas-diesel (distillate fuel) oil . .	2,213	2,111	n.a.
Lubricants	127	128	n.a.
Residual fuel oil (Mazout) . .	4,220	3,995	n.a.

* Production in terms of potassium oxide.

Source: partly UN, *Industrial Commodity Statistics Yearbook.*

Finance

CURRENCY AND EXCHANGE RATES

Monetary Units

100 gopik = 1 Azerbaijani manat.

Sterling, Dollar and Euro Equivalents (29 December 2000)

£1 sterling = 6,811.9 manats;
US $1 = 4,565.0 manats;
€1 = 4,247.7 manats;
10,000 manats = £1.468 = $2.191 = €2.354.

Average Exchange Rate (Azerbaijani manats per US $)

1998   3,869.0
1999   4,120.2
2000   4,474.2

Note: The Azerbaijani manat was introduced in August 1992, initially to circulate alongside the Russian (formerly Soviet) rouble, with an exchange rate of 1 manat = 10 roubles. In December 1993 Azerbaijan left the rouble zone, and the manat became the country's sole currency.

STATE BUDGET ('000 million manats)

Revenue*	1997	1998	1999†
Taxation	2,237.5	2,905.2	3,136.5
Taxes on income, profits and			
capital gains . . .	479.9	645.5	725.4
Social security contributions .	548.8	723.9	733.0
Taxes on property . . .	35.6	72.8	59.7
Domestic taxes on goods and			
services	967.6	1,172.7	1,323.8
General sales, turnover or			
value-added taxes . .	479.1	603.2	692.6
Excises	177.0	238.0	377.2
Taxes on international trade and			
transactions	196.7	280.0	283.0
Other current revenue . .	112.5	170.9	180.5
Total	2,350.0	3,076.0	3,317.0

Expenditure‡	1997	1998	1999†
General public services	356.3	250.0	255.3
Defence	357.9	463.1	472.1
Public order and safety	256.4	380.2	482.9
Education	117.0	140.8	136.3
Health	149.4	45.1	34.7
Social security and welfare	965.0	1,227.3	1,412.1
Housing and community amenities	1.5	1.7	1.5
Recreational, cultural and religious affairs and services	52.4	61.4	54.7
Economic affairs and services	358.4	418.4	362.4
Agriculture, forestry, fishing and hunting	151.7	160.5	169.7
Mining and mineral resources, manufacturing and construction	121.9	177.5	125.5
Other purposes	466.9	1,083.4	1,122.0
Sub-total	3,080.9	4,071.2	4,333.9
Adjustment	−52.4	−78.1	−73.0
Total	3,028.6	3,993.1	4,260.9
Current	2,518.1	3,148.4	3,526.7
Capital	510.5	844.8	734.2

* Excluding grants received from abroad ('000 million manats): 52.0 in 1997; 67.0 in 1998; 63.2 (forecast) in 1999.
† Forecasts.
‡ Excluding lending minus repayments ('000 million manats): −284.7 in 1997; −227.1 in 1998; −401.3 in 1999.

Source: IMF, *Government Finance Statistics Yearbook*.

INTERNATIONAL RESERVES (US $ million at 31 December)

	1998	1999	2000
Gold*	1.37	—	—
IMF special drawing rights	0.11	7.07	6.60
Reserve position in IMF	0.01	0.01	0.01
Foreign exchange	447.20	665.50	672.99
Total	448.69	672.59	679.61

* National valuation.
Source: IMF, *International Financial Statistics*.

MONEY SUPPLY ('000 million manats at 31 December)

	1997	1998	1999
Currency outside banks	1,170.5	926.0	1,135.8
Demand deposits at commercial banks	323.8	203.0	215.8
Total money (incl. others)	1,524.1	1,134.5	1,357.4

Source: IMF, *International Financial Statistics*.

COST OF LIVING (Consumer Price Index; base: 1993 = 100)

	1997	1998	1999
Food	10,964.0	10,816.9	9,630.3
All items (incl. others)	11,217.7	11,131.0	10,182.1

Source: UN, *Monthly Bulletin of Statistics*.

NATIONAL ACCOUNTS

Expenditure on the Gross Domestic Product
('000 million manats at current prices)

	1997	1998	1999
Government final consumption expenditure	1,932.2	1,973.6	2,019.8
Private final consumption expenditure	12,524.2	13,410.0	12,750.9
Gross fixed capital formation	5,121.4	6,268.1	4,341.9
Total domestic expenditure	19,577.8	21,651.7	19,112.6
Exports of goods and services	4,579.5	3,907.7	5,285.4
Less Imports of goods and services	8,365.9	9,382.3	7,909.5
GDP in purchasers' values	15,791.4	16,177.0	16,488.5

Source: IMF, *Azerbaijan Republic: Recent Economic Developments and Selected Issues* (September 2000).

Gross Domestic Product by Economic Activity
(million manats at current prices)

	1993	1994	1995
Agriculture and forestry	42,562	605,996	2,837,056
Industry*	39,127	309,639	2,306,855
Construction	11,759	138,755	274,172
Trade and catering†	8,451	117,419	735,534
Transport and communications‡	12,532	230,046	2,659,713
Other activities of the material sphere	732	4,371	32,276
Finance and insurance	11,277	104,951	432,693
Housing	1,109	19,416	71,508
General administration and defence	9,415	96,018	392,271
Other community, social and personal services	22,260	228,460	894,859
Private non-profit institutions serving households	220	515	2,400
Sub-total	159,445	1,855,586	10,639,337
Less Imputed bank service charge	10,045	91,383	375,211
GDP at factor cost	149,400	1,764,203	10,264,126
Indirect taxes	20,468	105,223	604,074
Less Subsidies	12,786	68,622	299,967
GDP in purchasers' values	157,082	1,800,804	10,568,233

* Comprising manufacturing (except printing and publishing), mining and quarrying, electricity, gas, water, logging and fishing.
† Including material supply and procurement.
‡ Including road maintenance.

BALANCE OF PAYMENTS (US $ million)

	1997	1998	1999
Exports of goods f.o.b.	808.3	677.8	1,025.2
Imports of goods f.o.b.	−1,375.2	−1,723.9	−1,433.4
Trade balance	−566.9	−1,046.2	−408.2
Exports of services	341.8	331.7	256.8
Imports of services	−726.0	−700.8	−485.1
Balance on goods and services	−951.1	−1,415.2	−636.5
Other income received	22.8	38.3	11.0
Other income paid	−32.3	−51.6	−56.0
Balance on goods, services and income	−960.6	−1,428.5	−681.5
Current transfers received	95.7	145.0	134.5
Current transfers paid	−50.9	−80.9	−52.8
Current balance	−915.8	−1,364.5	−599.7
Capital account (net)	−10.2	−0.7	n.a.
Direct investment from abroad	1,114.8	1,023.0	510.3
Portfolio investment assets	1.1	—	n.a.
Portfolio investment liabilities	—	0.4	n.a.
Other investment assets	−102.6	22.3	−81.0
Other investment liabilities	78.8	280.4	260.9
Net errors and omissions	−27.0	−20.1	42.4
Overall balance	139.2	−59.2	132.9

Source: IMF, *International Financial Statistics*.

External Trade

PRINCIPAL COMMODITIES (US $ million)

Imports c.i.f.*	1997	1998	1999
Food	181	175	185
Metals and metal products	109	127	112
Chemicals and petrochemicals†	50	79	58
Machinery and transport equipment	219	458	470
Total (incl. others)	794	1,077	1,036

Exports f.o.b.	1997	1998	1999
Food	55	47	60
Cotton	123	49	22
Petroleum products	452	418	731
Metals and metal products	15	13	25
Chemicals and petrochemicals†	13	11	23
Machinery and transport equipment	41	41	48
Total (incl. others)	781	606	929

* Excluding shuttle trade.
† Including pharmaceutical products.

Source: IMF, *Azerbaijan Republic: Economic Developments and Selected Issues* (September 2000).

PRINCIPAL TRADING PARTNERS (US $ million)

Imports c.i.f.	1997	1998	1999
Belarus	n.a.	14.8	n.a.
Belgium-Luxembourg	n.a.	27.1	n.a.
France	n.a.	19.1	24.9
Georgia	37*	25.2	9.5
Germany	n.a.	46.7	46.3
Iran	49	42.6	47.4
Japan	n.a.	n.a.	55.5
Kazakhstan	30	44.4	24.9
Netherlands	n.a.	16.7	n.a.
Norway	n.a.	n.a.	37.0
Russia	152	193.8	226.5
Singapore	n.a.	n.a.	41.3
Switzerland	n.a.	12.8	3.5
Turkey	180	220.1	143.0
Turkmenistan	25	26.4	12.9
Ukraine	86	93.0	38.5
United Arab Emirates	42*	45.6	12.0*
United Kingdom	14*	69.9	67.1
USA	n.a.	39.8	83.0
Total (incl. others)	794	1,077.2	1,035.7

* Source: IMF, *Azerbaijan Republic: Recent Economic Developments and Selected Issues* (September 2000).

Exports f.o.b.	1997	1998	1999
Bulgaria	n.a.	10.8	n.a.
France	n.a.	11.7	58.1
Georgia	133	76.9	71.7
Greece	n.a.	12.4	n.a.
Iran	190	44.5	22.7
Israel	n.a.	n.a.	56.9
Italy	n.a.	45.1	313.1
Kazakhstan	9	10.6	4.1
Russia	181	105.8	83.1
Switzerland	n.a.	17.1	36.8
Turkey	41	135.8	69.1
Turkmenistan	n.a.	13.9	8.9
Ukraine	32	12.0	24.0
United Kingdom	1	40.4	11.0
USA	n.a.	13.9	29.8
Total (incl. others)	781	606.2	929.2

Source: partly State Statistical Committee of Azerbaijan Republic.

Transport

RAILWAYS

	1997	1998	1999
Passenger-kilometres (million)	491	533	422
Freight carried (million metric tons)	11.3	13.5	11.7
Freight ton-kilometres (million)	3,515	4,702	5,052

ROAD TRAFFIC (vehicles in use at 31 December)

	1996	1997	1998
Passenger cars	273,656	271,265	281,320
Buses	12,925	12,053	13,666
Lorries and vans	77,710	71,938	79,934

Source: International Road Federation, *World Road Statistics*.

SHIPPING
Merchant Fleet (registered at 31 December)

	1996	1997	1998
Number of vessels	289	288	287
Total displacement ('000 grt)	636.1	632.7	650.9

Source: Lloyd's Register of Shipping, *World Fleet Statistics*.

CIVIL AVIATION (traffic on scheduled services)

	1995	1996	1997
Kilometres flown (million)	21	21	16
Passengers carried ('000)	1,156	1,233	982
Passenger-km (million)	1,650	1,743	1,283
Total ton-km (million)	183	183	144

Source: UN, *Statistical Yearbook*.

Passenger-km (estimates, million): 843 in 1998; 614 in 1999 (Source: International Civil Aviation Organization).

Tourism

TOURIST ARRIVALS BY COUNTRY OF ORIGIN

	1997	1998
CIS countries*	132,151	301,287
Iran	103,724	139,300
Israel	8,157	1,898
Turkey	28,709	19,103
United Kingdom	8,636	5,197
Total (incl. others)	305,830	483,163

* Comprising Armenia, Belarus, Georgia, Kazakhstan, Kyrgyzstan, Moldova, Russia, Tajikistan, Turkmenistan, Ukraine and Uzbekistan.

1999: Total tourist arrivals 602,047.

Tourism receipts (US $ million): 146 in 1995; 158 in 1996; 159 in 1997 (Source: World Tourism Organization, *Yearbook of Tourism Statistics*).

Communications Media

	1995	1996	1997
Radio receivers ('000 in use) . .	160	170	175
Television receivers ('000 in use) .	156	167	170
Telephones ('000 main lines in use)	640	645	663
Mobile cellular telephones			
(subscribers)	6,000	17,000	40,000
Book production:*			
Titles	498	542	496
Copies ('000) . . .	3,592	2,643	n.a.
Daily newspapers:			
Number	3	6	n.a.
Average circulation ('000) . .	210†	n.a.	n.a.
Non-daily newspapers:			
Number	238	251	n.a.

Telefax stations (1994): 2,500 in use.

* Figures include pamphlets.
† Provisional figure.

Sources: UN, *Statistical Yearbook*, and UNESCO, *Statistical Yearbook*.

Book production (titles): 444 in 1998; 400 in 1999.

Education

(1996/97, unless otherwise indicated)

	Institutions	Teachers	Students
Pre-primary	1,867	13,033	96,318
Primary	4,454	35,514	719,013
Secondary	n.a.	105,656*	819,625
General	n.a.	85,001	802,338
Teacher-training . . .	n.a.	n.a.	721†
Vocational	167‡	n.a.	17,287
Higher	17§	15,929**	115,116

* 1995/96. † 1993/94. ‡ 1991. § 1992. ** provisional.

Source: mainly UNESCO, *Statistical Yearbook*.

Directory

The Constitution

The new Constitution was endorsed by 91.9% of the registered electorate in a national referendum, held on 12 November 1995. It replaced the amended Soviet Constitution of 1978. The following is a summary of the 1995 Constitution's main provisions:

GENERAL PROVISIONS

The Azerbaijan Republic is a democratic, secular and unitary state. State power is vested in the people, who implement their sovereign right through referendums and their directly elected representatives. No individual or organization has the right to usurp the power of the people. State power is exercised on the principle of the division of powers between the legislature, the executive and the judiciary. The supreme aim of the state is to ensure human and civil rights and freedoms. The territory of the Azerbaijan Republic is inviolable and indivisible. Azerbaijan conducts its foreign policy on the basis of universally accepted international law. The state is committed to a market economic system and to freedom of entrepreneurial activity. Three types of ownership—state, private and municipal—are recognized; natural resources belong to the Azerbaijan Republic. The state promotes the development of art, culture, education, medical care and science, and defends historical, material and spiritual values. All religions are equal by law; the spread of religions that contradict the principles of humanity is prohibited. The state language is Azerbaijani, although the republic guarantees the free use of other languages. The capital is Baku.

MAJOR RIGHTS, FREEDOMS AND RESPONSIBILITIES

Every citizen has inviolable, undeniable and inalienable rights and freedoms. Every person is equal before the law and the courts, regardless of sex, race, nationality, religion, origin, property and other status, and political or other convictions. Every person has the right to life. Any person charged with a penal offence is considered innocent until proven guilty. Capital punishment as an extreme measure of punishment, while still in force, can be applied for grave crimes. Every person has the right to freedom of thought, speech, conscience and religion. Everyone has the right to protect their national and ethnic affiliation. No-one is to be subject to torture, torment or the humiliation of human dignity. The mass media are free, and censorship is prohibited. Every person has the right to freedom of movement and residence within the republic, and the right to leave the republic. The right to assemble publicly is guaranteed, and every person has the right to establish a political party, trade union or other organization; the activity of unions that seek to overthrow state power is prohibited. Citizens of the Azerbaijan Republic have the right to participate in the political life of society and the state, and the right to elect and to be elected to government bodies, and to participate in referendums. Every person has the right to health protection and medical aid, and the right to social security in old age, sickness, disability, unemployment, etc. The state guarantees the right to free secondary education.

THE LEGISLATIVE

The supreme legislative body is the 125-member Milli Majlis (National Assembly). Deputies are elected by universal, equal, free, direct suffrage, and by secret ballot, for a five-year term. Any citizen who has reached the age of 25 years is eligible for election, with the exception of those possessing dual citizenship, those performing state service, and those otherwise engaged in paid work, unless employed in the creative, scientific and education sectors. The instigation of criminal proceedings against a deputy, and his or her detention or arrest, are only permitted on the decision of the Milli Majlis, on the basis of a recommendation by the Prosecutor-General. The Milli Majlis passes legislation, constitutional laws and resolutions; ratifies or denunciates treaties, agreements and conventions; ratifies the state budget; gives consent to declare war, on the recommendation of the President of the Republic; confirms administrative and territorial divisions; and declares amnesties. Upon the nomination of the President, the Milli Majlis is authorized to approve the appointment of the Prime Minister and the Prosecutor-General; appoint and dismiss members of the Constitutional Court and Supreme Court; and appoint and dismiss the Chairperson of the National Bank. It also has the power to express a vote of 'no confidence' in the Government; to call a referendum; to initiate impeachment proceedings against the President, on the recommendation of the Constitutional Court; and to introduce draft legislation and other issues for parliamentary discussion.

EXECUTIVE POWER

The President, who is directly elected for a term of five years, is Head of State and Commander-in-Chief of the Armed Forces. Executive power is held by the President, who acts as guarantor of the independence and territorial integrity of the republic. Any university graduate aged 35 years or over, who has the right to vote, has been a resident of the republic for the preceding 10 years, has never been tried for a major crime, and who is exclusively a citizen of the Azerbaijan Republic, is eligible for election to the office of President. The President appoints and dismisses the Cabinet of Ministers, headed by the Prime Minister, which is the highest executive body.

The President calls legislative elections; concludes international treaties and agreements, and submits them to the Milli Majlis for ratification; signs laws or returns draft legislation to the Milli Majlis for reconsideration; proposes candidates for the Constitutional Court, the Supreme Court and the Economic Court, and nominates the Prosecutor-General and the Chairman of the National Bank; appoints and recalls diplomatic representatives of Azerbaijan to foreign countries and international organizations, and receives the credentials of diplomatic representatives; may declare a state of emergency or martial law; and grants titles of honour.

The President enjoys immunity from prosecution during his or her period in office. In the event that the President commits a grave crime, he may be removed from office on the recommendation of the Supreme Court and the Constitutional Court, and with the approval of the Milli Majlis.

THE JUDICIARY

Judicial power is implemented only by the courts. Judges are independent and are subordinate only to the Constitution and the law; they are immune from prosecution. Trials are held in public, except in specialized circumstances.

The Constitutional Court is composed of nine members, appointed by the Milli Majlis on the recommendation of the President. It determines, among other things, whether presidential decrees, resolutions of the Milli Majlis and of the Cabinet of Ministers, laws of the Nakhichevan Autonomous Republic, and international treaties correspond to the Constitution; and decides on the prohibition of the activities of political parties. The Supreme Court is the highest judicial body in administrative, civil and criminal cases; the Economic Court is the highest legal body in considering economic disputes.

AUTONOMOUS REPUBLIC OF NAKHICHEVAN*

The Nakhichevan Autonomous Republic is an autonomous republic forming an inalienable part of the Azerbaijan Republic. It has its own Constitution, which must not contravene the Constitution and laws of Azerbaijan. Legislative power in Nakhichevan is vested in the 45-member Ali Majlis (Supreme Assembly), which serves a five-year term, and executive power is vested in the Cabinet of Ministers. The Ali Majlis elects a Chairman from among its members, as the highest official in the Republic of Nakhichevan. The Ali Majlis is responsible for the budget, the approval of economic and social programmes; and the approval of the Cabinet of Ministers. The Ali Majlis may dismiss its Chairman and express 'no confidence' in the Cabinet of Ministers, which is appointed by the Ali Majlis on the recommendation of the Prime Minister of Nakhichevan (the Chairman of the Cabinet of Ministers). The Prime Minister of Nakhichevan is, likewise, appointed by the Ali Majlis on the nomination of the President of Azerbaijan. Heads of local executive power in Nakhichevan are appointed by the President of Azerbaijan, after consultation with the Chairman of the Ali Majlis and the Prime Minister of Nakhichevan. Justice is administered by the courts of the Republic of Nakhichevan.

*In December 1998 the Milli Majlis approved a revised Constitution for Nakhichevan, which defined the enclave as an 'autonomous state' within Azerbaijan.

LOCAL SELF-GOVERNMENT

Local government in rural areas and towns, villages and settlements is exercised by elected municipalities.

RIGHTS AND LAW

The Constitution has supreme legal force. Amendments and additions may only be introduced following a referendum.

The Government

HEAD OF STATE

President: HEYDAR ALIRZA OGLU ALIYEV (elected by direct popular vote, 3 October 1993; inaugurated on 10 October 1993; re-elected 11 October 1998; inaugurated on 18 October 1998).

CABINET OF MINISTERS
(May 2001)

Prime Minister: ARTUR TAHIR OGLU RASIZADE.

First Deputy Prime Minister: ABBAS A. ABBASSOV.

Deputy Prime Ministers: ELCHIN ILYAS OGLU EFENDIYEV, ABID QOCA OGLU SHARIFOV, ALI SAMIL OGLU HASANOV, YAQUB ABDULLA OGLU AYYUBOV, HACIBALA IBRAHIM OGLU ABUTALIBOV.

Minister of Public Health: ALI BINNET OGLU INSANOV.

Minister of Foreign Affairs: VILAYAT MUKHTAR OGLU KULIYEV.

Minister of Agriculture and Produce: IRSHAD NADIR OGLU ALIYEV.

Minister of Internal Affairs: Col RAMIL IDRIS OGLU USUBOV.

Minister of Culture: POLAD BYUL-BYUL OGLU.

Minister of Education: MISIR CUMAYIL OGLU MARDANOV.

Minister of Communications: NADIR ALI OGLU AKHMEDOV.

Minister of Finance: AVAZ AKBAR OGLU ALEKPEROV.

Minister of Justice: FIKRET FARRUKH OGLU MAMMADOV.

Minister of Labour and Social Protection: ALI TEYMUR OGLU NAGIYEV.

Minister of National Security: Lt-Gen. NAMIG RASID OGLU ABBASOV.

Minister of Defence: Col-Gen. SAFAR AKHUNDBALA OGLU ABIYEV.

Minister of Information and the Press: SIRUS KHUDADAT OGLU TEBRIZLI.

Minister of Youth and Sport: ABULFAZ MURSAL OGLU KARAYEV.

Minister of Economic Development: FARKHAD SOKHRAT OGLU ALIYEV.

Chairmen of State Committees

Chairman of the State Tax Inspection Committee: FAZIL MAMMADOV.

Chairman of the State Committee for Securities: HEYDAR BABAYEV.

Chairman of the State Committee for Inter-ethnic Relations: ABBAS ABBASSOV.

Chairman of the State Committee for Construction and Architectural Affairs: ABID G. SHARIFOV.

Chairman of the State Committee for Anti-monopoly Policy and Enterprise Support: RAHIB GULIYEV.

Chairman of the State Committee for Statistics: ARIF A. VELIYEV.

Chairman of the State Committee for Geology and Mineral Resources: ISLAM TAGIYEV.

Chairman of the State Committee for Ecology and Environmental Protection: ALI HASANOV.

Chairman of the State Committee for Supervision of Safety at Work in Industry and Mining: YAGUB EYYUBOV.

Chairman of the State Committee for Geodesy and Cartography: ADIL SULTANOV.

Chairman of the State Committee for Material Resources: HULMAMMAD JAVADOV.

Chairman of the State Committee for Specialized Machinery: SABIR ALEKPEROV.

Chairman of the State Committee for Science and Technology: AZAD MIRZAJANZADE.

Chairman of the State Land Committee: HARIB MAMMADOV.

Chairman of the State Customs Committee: KAMALEDDIN HEYDAROV.

Chairman of the State Committee for Veterinary Affairs: MIRSALEH HUSEYNOV.

Chairman of the State Committee for Hydrometeorology: ZULFUGAR MUSAYEV.

Chairman of the State Committee for the Protection and Refurbishment of Historical and Cultural Monuments: FAKHREDDIN MIRALIYEV.

Chairman of the State Committee for Refugees and Involuntary Migrants: ALI HASANOV.

Chairman of the State Committee for Improvements of Soil and Water Economy: AHMED AHMEDZADE.

Chairman of the State Committee for Women's Issues: ZAHRA GULIYEVA.

Chairman of the State Insurance Inspectorate of the Cabinet of Ministers: AZER JAFAROV.

MINISTRIES

Office of the President: 370066 Baku, Istiklal St 19; tel. (12) 92-77-38; fax (12) 98-31-54; e-mail root@lider.baku.az; internet www.president.gov.az.

Office of the Prime Minister: 370066 Baku, Lermontov St 63; tel. (12) 92-66-23; fax (12) 92-91-79.

Ministry of Agriculture and Produce: 370016 Baku, Azadlyg Sq. 1, Govt House; tel. (12) 93-53-55.

Ministry of Communications: 370139 Baku, Azerbaijan Ave 33; tel. (12) 93-00-04; fax (12) 98-42-85; e-mail behm@azerin.com.

Ministry of Culture: 370016 Baku, Azadlyg Sq. 1, Govt House; tel. (12) 93-43-98; fax (12) 93-56-05; internet www.culture.az/minist_e.htm.

Ministry of Defence: 370139 Baku, Azerbaijan Ave; tel. (12) 39-41-89; fax (12) 92-92-50.

Ministry of Economic Development: 370016 Baku, Azadlyg Sq. 1, Govt House; tel. (12) 93-61-62; fax (12) 93-20-25.

Ministry of Education: 370016 Baku, Azadlyg Sq. 1, Govt House; tel. (12) 93-72-66; fax (12) 98-75-69; internet www.edu.gov.az.

Ministry of Finance: 370022 Baku, Samed Vurghun St 83; tel. (12) 93-30-12; fax (12) 98-71-84; e-mail adalet-ferd@artel.net.az.

Ministry of Foreign Affairs: 370004 Baku, Ghanjlar meydani 3; tel. (12) 92-68-56; fax (12) 92-56-06.

Ministry of Information and the Press: 370001 Baku, A. Karayev St 12; tel. (12) 92-63-57; fax (12) 92-93-33.

Ministry of Internal Affairs: 370005 Baku, Gusi Hajiyev St 7; tel. (12) 92-57-54; fax (12) 98-22-85; internet www.mia.gov.az.

Ministry of Justice: 370601 Baku, Bul-Bul Ave 13; tel. (12) 93-97-85; fax (12) 98-49-41.

Ministry of Labour and Social Protection: 370016 Baku, Azadlyg Sq. 1, Govt House; tel. (12) 93-05-42; fax (12) 93-94-72.

Ministry of National Security: 370602 Baku, Parliament Ave 2; tel. (12) 95-01-63; fax (12) 95-04-91.

Ministry of Public Health: 370014 Baku, Malaya Morskaya St 4; tel. (12) 93-29-77; fax (12) 93-76-47; e-mail webmaster@mednet.az; internet www.mednet.az.

Ministry of Youth and Sport: 370072 Baku, Fhataly Khan Khoyski Ave 98A; tel. (12) 90-64-42; fax (12) 90-64-38; e-mail mys@azeri.com; internet www.mys.azeri.com.

President and Legislature

PRESIDENT
Presidential Election, 11 October 1998

Candidates	Votes	% of votes
HEYDAR ALIYEV (New Azerbaijan Party)	2,556,059	77.61
ETIBAR MAMEDOV (National Independence Party)	389,662	11.83
NIZAMI SULEYMANOV (Independent Azerbaijan Party)	270,709	8.22
FIRUDIN HASANOV (Communist Party of Azerbaijan-2)	29,244	0.89
ASHRAF MEHDIYEV (Association of Victims of Illegal Political Repressions)	28,809	0.87
KHANHUSEIN KAZYMLY (Social Welfare Party)	8,254	0.25
Blank or spoiled	10,910	0.33
Total	**3,293,647**	**100.00**

MILLI MAJLIS

Milli Majlis (National Assembly): 370152 Baku, Mehti Hussein St 2; tel. (12) 92-79-45; fax (12) 98-02-42.

Chairman (Speaker): MURTUZ ALESKEROV.

First Deputy Chairman: A. RAHIMZADE.

Elections to Azerbaijan's new 125-member Milli Majlis were held on 5 November 2000. The electoral law of August 1995 provided for a mixed system of voting: 25 seats to be filled by proportional representation, according to party lists, the remaining 100 deputies to be elected in single-member constituencies. The latter included the constituencies of Armenian-held Nagornyi Karabakh and other occupied territories: refugees from those regions cast their votes in other parts of Azerbaijan (in anticipation of the eventual return of occupied areas to Azerbaijani jurisdiction). All 25 party seats were filled: New Azerbaijan Party (NAP) 17, Popular Front of Azerbaijan

(PFA) four, Civic Solidarity Party (CSP) two. Of the 88 constituency seats filled, 62 were reported to have been taken by the NAP and 26 by independent candidates. A further round of voting was held on 7 January 2000, in order to elect members for 11 vacant seats. The NAP gained five seats, and five other parties and an independent candidate each gained a seat. Thus, following all the rounds of voting, only one seat in the Majlis remained vacant (representing the Khankendi-Khojali-Khojavend constituency in Nagornyi Karabakh).

Political Organizations

Alliance for Azerbaijan Party: Baku; f. 1994; Leader ABUTALYB SAMADOV.

Azerbaijan Democratic Independence Party: Baku, Agah-Neymatulla St 14; tel. (12) 98-78-23; in 1997 merged with Vahdat Party and one-half of the People's Freedom Party; Chair. LEYLA YUNUSOVA; Leader VAGIF KERIMOV.

Azerbaijan National Democratic Party: Baku; tel. (12) 94-89-37; fmrly the Grey Wolves Party (Boz Gurd); Leader BAKHTIYAR A. AHMADOV.

Azerbaijan National Equality Party: Baku; tel. (12) 60-05-21; Leader FAHRADDIN AYDAYEV.

Azerbaijani Democratic Left Party: Baku; f. 1999; Chair. MEHMAN AMIRALIYEV.

Azerbaijani Salvation Party: Baku; f. 1999; nationalist; supports united Azerbaijan; Chair. ELDAR GARADAGLY.

Civic Solidarity Party (CSP): Baku, H. Hajiyev St 4; tel. (12) 93-56-83; f. 1992; Chair. SABIR RUSTAMKHANLY.

Civic Unity Party of Azerbaijan–CUPA: Baku; Sec.-Gen. SABIR HAJIYEV.

Communist Party of Azerbaijan (CPA): Baku; disbanded Sept. 1991, re-established Nov. 1993; Chair. RAMIZ AHMADOV.

Communist Party of Azerbaijan-2 (CPA-2): Baku; f. 1998; deprived of legal status in Aug. 2000; Chair. FIRUDIN HASANOV.

Communist Workers' Party of Azerbaijan: Baku; formerly the United Communist Party of Azerbaijan; Leader SAYYAD SAYYADOV.

Democratic Development Party: Baku; f. 1999; Leader SABUHI ABDINOV.

Democratic Party of Azerbaijan: Baku; tel. (12) 66-79-71; f. 1994; unregistered; merged with the Democratic Way Party in November 2000; Chair. RASUL KULIYEV; Gen. Sec. SARDAR JALALOGLU.

Equality: Baku; f. 1998 to represent interests of those displaced as a result of conflict in Nagornyi Karabakh; Chair. VAGIF HADZHIBAYLI.

Heyrat Party: Baku; Sec.-Gen. ASHRAF MEHDIYEV.

Independent Azerbaijan Party: Baku, Kecid 1128; tel. (12) 39-38-51; Chair. NIZAMI SULEYMANOV.

Islamic Party of Azerbaijan: Baku; tel. (12) 93-72-61; f. 1992; Leader ALI AKRAM ALIYEV (imprisoned 1997 on charges of treason, but pardoned in 1999); 50,000 mems (1997).

Labour Party of Azerbaijan: Baku; Leader SABUTAY MARNEDOV.

Liberal Democratic Party: Baku; divisions emerged in Nov. 2000; Chair. (vacant).

Liberal Party of Azerbaijan: Baku, Azerbaijan Ave; tel. (12) 98-00-95; Chair. LALA SHOVKAT HAJIYEVA.

Modern Turan party: Baku; tel. (12) 73-16-79; Chair. ARIF ISLAM TAGIEV.

Motherland Party (Ana Vatan): Baku, Mardanov Gardashlary St 14; tel. (12) 93-82-97; Leader FAZAIL AGAMALIYEV.

Muslim Democratic Party (Musavat): Baku, Azerbaijan Ave 37; tel. (12) 98-18-70; fax (12) 98-31-66; f. 1911; in exile from 1920; re-established 1992; Chair. ISA GAMBAR; Gen. Sec. VURGUN EYYUB.

National Congress Party: Baku; f. 1997 by disaffected members of Muslim Democratic Party; Chair. IHTIYAR SHIRINOV.

National Independence Party (NIP) (Istiklal): c/o Milli Majlis, 370152 Baku, Mehti Hussein St 2; tel. (12) 62-75-76; f. 1992; Chair. ETIBAR MAMEDOV.

National Statehood Party: Baku; tel. (12) 67-71-74; f. 1994; unregistered from 1997; Chair. SABIR TARIVERDIYEV.

New Azerbaijan Party (NAP) (Yeni Azerbaijan): c/o Milli Majlis, 370152 Baku, Mehti Hussein St 2; tel. (12) 98-33-98; f. 1992; Co-Chair. HEYDAR ALIYEV; Dep. Chair. ALI TEYMUR OGLU NAGIYEV (Minister of Labour and Social Protection), ILHAM ALIYEV.

Party for National Reconciliation: Baku; f. Nov. 2000 by breakaway faction of the Liberal Democratic Party; Chair. FUAD ALIYEV.

People's Freedom Party (Halg Azadlyg): Baku; Leader PANAH SHAHSEVENLI.

People's Party of Azerbaijan: Baku; f. 1998; Chair. PANAH HUSEYNOV.

Popular Front of Azerbaijan (PFA) (Azerbaijan Xalq Cabhasi): c/o Milli Majlis, 370152 Baku, Mehti Hussein St 2; tel. (12) 98-07-94; f. 1989; following the death of Abulfaz Elchibey in Aug. 2000, divided into reformist and traditionalist factions; the reformist faction was registered for the legislative election held in November, while the traditionalist faction entered into co-operation with the Muslim Democratic Party; Chair. (reformist) ALI KERIMOV; Chair. (traditionalist) MURMAHMUD FATTAYEV.

Republican Party: f. 1999.

Social Democratic Party: 370014 Baku, 28 May St 3–11; tel. (12) 93-33-78; fax (12) 98-75-55; e-mail asdp@ngonet.baku.az; f. 1989; formed a union with the Namus Party and the Unity Party in April 2000, as the Union of Azerbaijanist Forces; Chair. ARAZ ALIZADEH, ZARDUSHT ALIZADE; Dep. Chair. ARZU ABDULLAYEVA; 2,000 mems (1990).

Social Justice Party: Baku; Leader MATLAB MUTALLIMOV.

Social Welfare Party: Baku; Chair. KHANHUSEIN KAZYMLY.

Socialist Party of Azerbaijan: Baku; f. 1997; Co-Chair. SHAPUR GASIMI, MUBARIZ IBADOV; 2,000 mems.

Turkic Nationalist Party: Baku; Leader VUGAR BEYTURAN.

Umid Party (Hope Party): Baku; tel. (12) 38-57-35; f. 1993; socialist; Chair. HUSEIN ARTIKOGLU; Leader ABULFAR AHMADOV; 5,000 mems (1998).

Vahdat Party (Unity Party): Baku, Azerbaijan Ave, Dom 23, Rm 52/54; tel. (12) 98-00-44; e-mail vahdat@box.az; f. 1995; a splinter faction, the Unity Party II, emerged in April 2000 and subsequently merged with the PFA in December; Chair. TAMIR ZAHIDAGA KARIMLI; 17,500 mems (2000).

Workers' Party of Azerbaijan: Sumgait; f. 1999; socialist; Chair. AKIF HASANOGLU.

Yurdash Party (Compatriot Party): Baku, Metbuat Ave; tel. (12) 32-10-47; f. 1991; Chair. MAIS SAFARLI.

Other political groups include the Ana Toprag (Native Soil) party, the Azerbaijan Justice Party, the Azeri Party of Popular Revival, the Democratic Enlightenment Party, the Democratic Party of Azerbaijan Business People, the People's Democratic Party and the National Movement Party. The Azerbaijan Patriots' Party was founded in July 2000 and ALIM BABAIEV was elected as its Chair.

Diplomatic Representation

EMBASSIES IN AZERBAIJAN

China, People's Republic: Baku, Azadlyg Ave 1, Hotel Azerbaijan, Rm 831; tel. (12) 98-90-10; Ambassador: ZHANG QUO QIANG.

Egypt: Baku, Azadlyg Ave 1, Hotel Azerbaijan, Rms 1434, 1439 and 1441; tel. (12) 98-92-14; Ambassador: JIHAN AMIN MEHMET ALI.

France: Baku, Hotel Respublika, Rms 8 and 17; tel. (12) 92-89-77; fax (12) 98-92-53; Ambassador: JEAN-PIERRE GUINHUT.

Georgia: Baku, Azadlyg Ave 1, Hotel Azerbaijan, Rms 1322–1325; tel. (12) 98-17-79; fax (12) 98-94-40; Ambassador: GYORGI CHANTURIA.

Germany: 370000 Baku, Mamedaliyev St 15; tel. (12) 98-78-19; fax (12) 98-54-19; Ambassador: Dr CHRISTIAN SIEBECK.

Greece: Baku, Hotel Respublika, Rms 19–20; tel. (12) 92-17-56; Ambassador: MERCOURIOS CARAFOTIAS.

Iran: Baku, B. Sadarov St 4; tel. (12) 92-64-53; Ambassador: ALI-REZA BIGDELI.

Iraq: 370000 Baku, Khagani St 9; tel. (12) 93-72-07; Chargé d'affaires a.i.: FARUQ SALMAN DAVUD.

Israel: Baku, Inshaatchylar Ave 1; tel. (12) 38-52-82; fax (12) 98-92-83; Chargé d'affaires: ARKADII MIL-MAN.

Italy: 370004 Baku, Kichic Gala Kuchesi 44; tel. (12) 97-51-33; fax (12) 97-52-02; e-mail ambbaku@azeuro.net; internet www.ambitalbaku.com; Ambassador: ALESSANDRO FALLAVOLLITA.

Kazakhstan: Baku, Azadlyg Ave 1, Hotel Azerbaijan, Rms 1524 and 1529; tel. (12) 98-87-08; fax (12) 98-87-08.

Pakistan: Baku, Azadlyg Ave 1, Hotel Azerbaijan, Rms 541 and 534; tel. (12) 98-90-04; fax (12) 98-94-85; Ambassador: PERVEZ KHANZADA.

Russian Federation: 370022 Baku, Bakikhanov St 17; tel. (12) 98-60-16; fax (12) 97-36-08; e-mail embrus@azdata.net; internet intrans.baku.az/embrus; Ambassador: NIKOLAI RYABOV.

Spain: Baku; Ambassador: JESÚS ATIENZA SERNA.

Turkey: 370000 Baku, Khagani St 57; tel. (12) 98-81-33; e-mail bakube@artel.net.az; internet www.turkbe.org.az; Ambassador: KADRI ECVET TEZCAN.

United Kingdom: 370065 Baku, Izmir St 5; tel. (12) 92-48-13; fax (12) 91-65-92; e-mail office@britemb.baku.az; internet intrans.baku.az/british; Ambassador: ANDREW TUCKER.

USA: 370007 Baku, Azadlyg Ave 83; tel. (12) 98-03-36; fax (12) 98-37-55; internet www.usembassybaku.org; Ambassador: ROSS WILSON.

Judicial System

Constitutional Court: Baku; internet www.constitutional-court-az.org; comprises a Chairman and eight judges, who are nominated by the President and confirmed in office by the Milli Majlis for a term of office of 10 years. Only the President, the Milli Majlis, the Cabinet of Ministers, the Procurator-General, the Supreme Court and the legislature of the Autonomous Republic of Nakhichevan are permitted to submit cases to the Constitutional Court.
Chairman of the Constitutional Court and of the Supreme Court: KHANLAR HAJIYEV.
Prosecutor-General: ZAKIR BEKIR OGLU GARALOV.

Religion

ISLAM

The majority (some 70%) of Azerbaijanis are Shi'ite Muslims; most of the remainder are Sunni (Hanafi school). The Spiritual Board of Muslims of the Caucasus is based in Baku. It has spiritual jurisdiction over the Muslims of Armenia, Georgia and Azerbaijan. The Chairman of the Directorate is normally a Shi'ite, while the Deputy Chairman is usually a Sunni.
Spiritual Board of Muslims of the Caucasus: Baku; Chair. Sheikh ALLASHUKUR PASHEZADE.

CHRISTIANITY
The Roman Catholic Church

The Apostolic Administrator of the Caucasus is the Holy See's Apostolic Nuncio to Georgia, Armenia and Azerbaijan, who is resident in Tbilisi, Georgia.

The Press

In 1995 there were 276 newspaper titles and 49 periodicals officially registered in Azerbaijan. Owing to financial, political and technical difficulties, many publications have reportedly suffered a sharp decrease in circulation. In August 1998 President Aliyev signed a decree abolishing censorship and ordering government bodies to provide support to the independent media.

PRINCIPAL NEWSPAPERS

In Azerbaijani, except where otherwise stated.
Adabiyat: 370146 Baku, Metbuat Ave, Block 529; tel. (12) 39-50-37; organ of the Union of Writers of Azerbaijan.
Azadliq (Liberty): 370000 Baku, Khaqani St 33; tel. (12) 98-90-81; fax (12) 93-40-01; e-mail azadliq@azeri.com; f. 1989; weekly; organ of the Popular Front of Azerbaijan; in Azerbaijani and Russian; Editor-in-Chief BAHADDIN HAZIYEV; circ. 9,034.
Azerbaijan: Baku, Metbuat Ave, Block 529; f. 1991; 5 a week; publ. by the National Assembly; in Azerbaijani and Russian; Editor-in-Chief A. MUSTAFAYEV; circ. 10,242 (Azerbaijani), 3,040 (Russian).
Azerbaijan Ganjlyari (Youth of Azerbaijan): Baku; f. 1919; 3 a week; Editor YU. A. KERIMOV.
Bakinskii Rabochii (Baku Worker): 370146 Baku, Metbuat Ave, Block 529; tel. (12) 38-00-29; f. 1906; 5 a week; govt newspaper; in Russian; Editor I. VEKILOVA; circ. 4,776.
Hayat (Life): 370146 Baku, Metbuat Ave, Block 529; f. 1991; 5 a week; publ. by the National Assembly of Azerbaijan; Editor-in-Chief A. H. ASKEROV.
Intibah (Revival): Baku; independent; 3 a week; Editor-in-Chief FAKHRI UGURLU; circ. 10,000.
Istiklal (Independence): 370014 Baku, 28 May St 3–11; tel. (12) 93-33-78; fax (12) 98-75-55; e-mail istiklal@ngonet.baku.az; 4 a month; organ of the Social Democratic Party; Editor ZARDUSHT ALIZADEH; circ. 5,000.
Khalg Gazeti: Baku; f. 1919; fmrly *Kommunist*; 6 a week; Editor M. ISMAYILOGLU.
Millat: Baku.
Molodezh Azerbaijana (Youth of Azerbaijan): 370146 Baku, Metbuat Ave, Block 529, 8th Floor; tel. (12) 39-00-51; f. 1919; weekly; in Russian; Editor V. EFENDIYEV; circ. 7,000.
Panorama: 370146 Baku, Metbuat Ave, Block 529; f. 1995; 5 a week; organ of the Centre of Strategic and International Investigations; in Azerbaijani and Russian; Editor-in-Chief A. ZEYNALOV; circ. 8,000.
Respublika (Republic): 370146 Baku, Metbuat Ave, Block 529; tel. (12) 38-01-14; fax (12) 38-01-31; f. 1996; daily; govt newspaper; Editor-in-Chief T. AHMADOV; circ. 5,500.
Veten Sesi (Voice of the Motherland): 370146 Baku, Metbuat Ave, Block 529; f. 1990; weekly; publ. by the Society of Refugees of Azerbaijan; in Azerbaijani and Russian; Editor-in-Chief T. A. AHMEDOV.
Vyshka (Oil derrick): 370146 Baku, Metbuat Ave, Block 529; tel. and fax (12) 39-96-97; e-mail vyshka@azeurotel.com; f. 1928; weekly; independent social-political newspaper; in Russian; Editor M. E. GASANOVA.
Yeni Azerbaijan: Baku, Metbuat Ave, Block 529; f. 1993; weekly; organ of the New Azerbaijan Party; Editor A. HASANOGLU; circ. 2,493.
Yeni Musavat: Baku; Editor-in-Chief (vacant).
Zerkalo: Baku; daily; Editor-in-Chief ELCIN SIXLINSKI.

PRINCIPAL PERIODICALS

Azerbaijan: Baku; tel. (12) 92-59-63; f. 1923; monthly; publ. by the Union of Writers of Azerbaijan; recent works by Azerbaijani authors; Editor-in-Chief YUSIF SAMEDOGLU.
Azerbaijan Gadyny (Woman of Azerbaijan): Baku; f. 1923; monthly; illustrated; Editor H. M. HASILOVA.
Dialog (Dialogue): Baku; f. 1989; fortnightly; in Azerbaijani and Russian; Editor R. A. ALEKPEROV.
Iki Sahil: Baku, Nobel Ave 64; f. 1965; weekly; organ of the New Baku Oil-Refining Plant; Editor-in-Chief V. RAHIMZADEH; circ. 2,815.
Kend Khayaty (Country Life): Baku; f. 1952; monthly; journal of the Ministry of Agriculture and Produce; advanced methods of work in agriculture; in Azerbaijani and Russian; Editor D. A. DAMIRLI.
Kirpi (Hedgehog): Baku; f. 1952; fortnightly; satirical; Editor A. M. AIVAZOV.
Literaturnyi Azerbaijan (Literature of Azerbaijan): 370001 Baku, Khagani St 25; tel. (12) 93-51-00; e-mail sima@azeri.com; f. 1931; monthly; journal of the Union of Writers of Azerbaijan; fiction; in Russian; Editor-in-Chief M. F. VEKILOV.
Ulus: Baku; tel. (12) 92-27-43; monthly; Editor TOFIK DADASHEV.

NEWS AGENCIES

Azadinform: Baku, F. Amirov St 1; tel. (12) 98-48-59; fax (12) 98-47-60; e-mail azadinform@azerin.com; internet www.azadinform.baku.az.com; independent information agency.
AzerTAJ (Azerbaijan State News Agency): 370000 Baku, Bul-Bul Ave 18; tel. (12) 93-59-29; fax (12) 93-62-65; e-mail office@azertac.baku.az; f. 1919; Gen. Dir SHAMIL MAMMAD OGLU SHAHMAMMADOV.
Bilik Dunyasi: Baku.
Sharg News Agency: Baku; Correspondent K. MUSTAFAYEVA.
Trend News Agency: Baku; Correspondent E. HUSEYNOV.
Turan News Agency: Baku, Khagani St 33; tel. (12) 98-42-26; fax (12) 98-38-17; e-mail root@turan.azerbaijan.su; internet www.intrans.baku.az; f. 1990; independent news agency; Dir MEHMAN ALIYEV.

Publishers

Azerbaijan Ensiklopediyasy (Azerbaijan Encyclopedia): 370004 Baku, Boyuk Gala St 41; tel. (12) 92-87-11; f. 1965; Editor-in-Chief I. O. VELIYEV (acting).
Azerneshr (State Publishing House): 370005 Baku, Gusi Hajiyev St 4; tel. (12) 92-50-15; f. 1924; various; Dir A. MUSTAFAZADE; Editor-in-Chief A. KUSEINZADE.
Elm (Azerbaijani Academy of Sciences Publishing House): 370073 Baku, Narimanov Ave 37; scientific books and journals.
Gyanjlik (Youth): 370005 Baku, Gusi Hajiyev St 4; books for children and young people; Dir E. T. ALIYEV.
Ishyg (Light): 370601 Baku, Gogol St 6; posters, illustrated publs; Dir G. N. ISMAILOV.
Maarif (Education): 370122 Baku, Tagizade St 4; educational books.
Madani-maarif Ishi (Education and Culture): 370146 Baku, Metbuat Ave, Block 529; tel. (12) 32-79-17; Editor-in-Chief ALOVSAT ATAMALY OGLY BASHIROV.
Medeniyyat (Publishing House of the 'Culture' Newspaper): 370146 Baku, Metbuat Ave 146; tel. (12) 32-98-38; Dir SHAKMAR AKPER OGLU AKPERZADE.
Sada, Literaturno-Izdatelskyi Centr: 370004 Baku, Bolshaya Krepostnaya St 28; tel. (12) 92-75-64; fax (12) 92-98-43; reference.
Shur: 370001 Baku, M. Muchtarov St 6; tel. (12) 92-93-72; f. 1992; Dir GASHAM ISA OGLU ISABEYLI.
Yazychy (Writer): 370005 Baku, Natavan St 1; fiction; Dir F. M. MELIKOV.

Broadcasting and Communications

TELECOMMUNICATIONS

Azercell Telecom: 370139 Baku, Azerbaijan Ave 41; tel. (12) 98-

30-11; fax (12) 98-30-17; provides communication services with integrated voice and data transfer; joint-venture company; Dir ERDAL OTUZBIR.

AzEuroTel: 370001 Baku, B. Sardarov St 1; tel. (12) 97-07-07; fax (12) 97-01-01; e-mail aet@azeurotel.com; f. 1995; established by the Ministry of Communication and LUKoil Europe Ltd as a joint venture with the United Kingdom.

Baku Telegraph: 370000 Baku, Azerbaijan Ave 41; tel. (12) 93-61-42; fax (12) 98-55-25; operates international telegraph, fax and telex services; Dir SABIRA AGARZAEVA.

RADIO AND TELEVISION

Radio and Television Company of Azerbaijan: 370011 Baku, Mehti Hussein St 1; tel. (12) 92-72-53; fax (12) 39-54-52; state-owned; Dir NIZAMI MANAF OGLU KHUDIYEV.

Radio Baku: f. 1926; broadcasts in Azerbaijani, Arabic, English and Turkish.

Azerbaijan National Television: f. 1956; programmes in Azerbaijani and Russian (14 hours a day).

BM–TI TV: Baku; f. 1993; first privately owned TV station in Azerbaijan; broadcasts in Azerbaijani and Russian (five hours a day); Dir MAHMUD MAMMADOV.

Finance

(cap. = capital; res = reserves; dep. = deposits; m. = million; brs = branches; amounts in manats, unless otherwise stated)

BANKING

Central Bank

National Bank of Azerbaijan: 370070 Baku, R. Bebutov St 32; tel. (12) 93-11-22; fax (12) 93-55-41; f. 1992 as central bank and supervisory authority; Chair. ELMAN ROUSTAMOV.

State-owned Banks

Amanatbank: 370014 Baku, Fizuli St 71; tel. (12) 93-18-26; fax (12) 98-31-80; f. 1992 to replace br of USSR Sberbank; 361 brs.

International Bank of Azerbaijan: 370005 Baku, Nizami St 67; tel. (12) 93-03-07; fax (12) 93-40-91; e-mail ibar@ibar.az; internet www.ibar.az; f. 1992 to succeed br of USSR Vneshekonombank; 14.4% owned by employees, 13.2% owned by the Ministry of Finance; carries out all banking services; cap. 11,456m., res 28,380m., dep. 783,693m. (Dec. 1999); Chair. FUAD AKHOUNDOV; First Dep. Chair. ZAHIR ALIYEV; 26 brs.

United Joint Stock Bank: Baku; f. 2000 by merger of Agroprombank (Agricultural bank), Prominvest (Industrial Investment Bank) and the Savings Bank; commenced operations 1 April; Pres. ZAKIR ZEYNALOV.

Other Banks

In January 2000 there were 70, mainly small, registered commercial banks operating in Azerbaijan, some of the most prominent of which are listed below:

Azakbank: 370070 Baku, R. Bebutov St 8; tel. (12) 98-31-09; fax (12) 93-20-85; f. 1991; joint-stock bank with 100% private ownership; first Azerbaijani bank with foreign shareholders; deals with crediting and settlements carried out in local currency and trade and retail banking involving all major operations in foreign currencies; cap. 1,273.5m., plus US $2.6m. (Nov. 1995); Chair. FUAD S. YUSIF-ZADEH.

Azerbaijan Central Republican Bank: 370088 Baku, Fizuli St 71; tel. (12) 93-05-61; fax (12) 93-94-89; Chair. HUSSEIN SAFROV.

Azerbaijan Industrial Bank: 370010 Baku, Fizuli St 71; tel. (12) 93-17-01; fax (12) 93-12-66; f. 1992; joint-stock commercial bank; Chair. ORUJ H. HEYDAROV; 40 brs.

Azerbaijan-Turkish Commercial Bank (Azer-Turk): 370005 Baku, Islam Seferli St 5; tel. (12) 97-43-16; fax (12) 98-37-02; e-mail azerturk@artel.net.az; f. 1995; Chair. MEMET MUSAYEV KURBANOĞLU; Gen. Man. MURAT AKSOY.

Azerdemiryolbank: 370008 Baku, Garabag St 31; tel. (12) 98-22-04; fax (12) 98-09-93; e-mail sr1954@azdata.net; f. 1989; largest private commercial bank; operates mainly in transport sector; Chair. ROMAN AMIRDJANOV; 11 brs.

Azerigazbank: 370073 Baku, Inshaatchylar Ave 3; tel. (12) 97-50-17; fax (12) 39-26-03; e-mail agbbank@azeri.com; f. 1992; joint-stock investment bank; Chair. AZER MOVSUMOV.

Bakcoopbank (Baku Co-operative Bank): 370025 Baku, Barinov St 12; tel. (12) 67-45-46; Gen. Dir ALIM I. AZIMOV.

Baybank: 370000 Baku, S. Vurgun St 14; tel. (12) 93-50-07; fax (12) 98-57-76; e-mail baybank@artel.net.az; f. 1995; joint-stock bank, carries out all banking services; cap. 4,865m., res 584m., dep.

6,450m. (Dec. 1997); Pres. and CEO A. KEMAL TOSYALI; Chair. HUSEYIN BAYRAKTAR.

Günay Bank: 370095 Baku, Rasul Rza St 4/6; tel. (12) 98-04-55; e-mail gunaybank@azerin.com; internet www.gunaybank.top.az; fax (12) 98-14-39; f. 1992; first privately owned bank in Azerbaijan; cap. 11,071m., res 684m., dep. 5,988m.; Chair. ALOVSAT GODJAYEV; 2 brs.

Inpatbank Investment Commercial Bank: 370125 Baku, Istiglaliyat St 9; tel. (12) 98-48-37.

Rabitabank: 370001 Baku, B. Sardarov St 1; tel. (12) 92-61-48; fax (12) 97-11-01; e-mail rbtbank@azest.com; f. 1993; joint-stock commercial bank; operates mainly in telecommunications sector; Chair. ZAKIR NURIYEV; 3 brs.

Ruzubank: 370055 Baku, Istiglaliyat St 27; tel. (12) 92-42-58; fax (12) 92-78-12; f. 1992; joint-stock bank; cap. 216m., res 30.4m., dep. 1,834m.; Pres. S. A. ALIYEV; Chair. of Bd V. N. MUSAYEV.

Trustbank: 370143 Baku, Firuddina Agayeva 9; tel. (12) 93-14-01; fax (12) 93-12-16; e-mail root@trustbank.baku.az; f. 1994; cap. 6,165m., res 592m., dep. 3,143m. (Dec. 1998); Pres. AZER AKHMEDO-VICH ALIYEV; Chair. BAKHRAM ASLAN OGLU SULTANOV.

Universal Commercial Bank: 370002 Baku, B. Megidov St 44/46; tel. (12) 97-30-34; fax (12) 97-30-29; e-mail bank@usal.baku.az; f. 1998; cap. 6,000m., res 620m., dep. 1,404m. (Dec. 2000); Pres. HEYDAR R. IBRAHIMOV.

Vostochniy Bank: 370070 Baku, Kirova Ave 19; tel. (12) 93-22-47; fax (12) 93-11-81; Gen. Dir RAGIMOV A. ABBAL.

Yuzhniy Bank: 373230 Shemakha, Bakiyskaya St 32.

Association

Azerbaijani Association of Banks: Baku; 49 mems.

INSURANCE

In February 1999 64 insurance companies were licensed to operate in Azerbaijan.

Azergarant Joint-Stock Insurance Company: 320001 Baku, Istiglaliyat St 31; tel. (12) 97-72-49; fax (12) 92-54-71; e-mail info@azerinvest.baku.az; Pres. Dr ALEKPER MAMEDOV; Gen. Dir FAIG HUSSE-INOV.

Azersigorta: Baku.

Günay Anadolu Sigorta JV: Baku, Terlan Aliyarbekov St 3; tel. (12) 98-13-56; fax (12) 98-13-60; f. 1992; e-mail office@gunaysigorta.in-baku.com; serves major international cos operating in Azerbaijan.

Shafag: Baku; f. 1998; medical insurance.

Trade and Industry

CHAMBER OF COMMERCE

Chamber of Commerce and Industry: 370601 Baku, Istiglaliyat St 31/33; tel. (12) 92-89-12; fax (12) 98-93-24; e-mail expo@chamber.baku.az; internet www.exhibition.azeri.com; Pres. SULEYMAN BAYRAM OGLU TATLIYEV.

INDUSTRIAL AND TRADE ASSOCIATIONS

Azerbintorg: 370004 Baku, Nekrasov St 7; tel. (12) 93-71-69; fax (12) 98-32-92; imports and exports a wide range of goods (90.4% of exports in 1995); Dir E. M. HUREYNOV.

Azerkontract: 370141 Baku, A. Alekperov St 83/23; tel. (12) 39-42-96; fax (12) 39-91-76; Chair. Minister of Trade.

Azertijaret: 370004 Baku, Genjler Sq. 3; tel (12) 92-66-67; fax (12) 98-07-56; e-mail aztij@azeri.com; Dir R. SH. ALIYEV.

Improtex: 370000 Baku, Azi Aslanov St 115; tel. (12) 98-02-27; fax (12) 90-92-25; e-mail haliyev@improtex.baku.az; internet www.improtex.baku-az.com; imports and exports a wide range of goods, incl. chemical and construction products; retail trade in consumer electronics and automobile dealership; Pres. FIZULI HASAN OGLU ALEK-PEROV.

MIT International Trade Co: 370148 Baku, Mehti Hussein St, Hotel Anba; tel. (12) 98-45-20; fax (12) 98-45-19; f. 1993; food products and consumer goods; Dir TAIR RAMAZAN OGLU ASADOV.

UTILITIES

Electricity

BakGES: Baku; electricity supply co; Head of Planning TAMILLA GULIYEVA.

Gas

Azerigaz: 370025 Baku, Yusif Safarov St 23; tel. (12) 67-74-47; fax (12) 65-12-01; f. 1992; Pres. TARIEL ABULFAZ OGLU HUSSEINOV.

STATE HYDROCARBONS COMPANIES

State Oil Company of the Azerbaijan Republic (SOCAR): 370004 Baku, Neftchilar Ave 73; tel. (12) 92-07-45; fax (12) 93-64-92; f. 1992, following a merger of the two state petroleum companies, Azerineft and Azneftkhimiya; conducts production and exploration activities, oversees refining and capital construction activities; Pres. NATIK ALIYEV; Vice-Pres. ILHAM ALIYEV; Exec. Dir. SAMIR RAUF OGLU SHARIFOV.

Azerbaijani International Operating Company (AIOC): Baku, Villa Petrolea, Neftchilar Ave 2; tel. (12) 91-21-02; f. 1994 as a consortium of: SOCAR, British Petroleum and Ramco of the United Kingdom, Amoco, Exxon and Unocal of the USA, Itocha of Japan, LUKoil of Russia, Statoil of Norway, Türkiye Petrolleri of Turkey and Delta Nimir of Saudi Arabia; exploration and development of Azerbaijani offshore petroleum reserves; Pres. DAVID WOODWARD.

TRADE UNIONS

Association of Independent Workers of Azerbaijan: Baku; Chair. NEYMAT PANAKHLI.

Confederation of Azerbaijan Trade Unions: Baku; tel. and fax (12) 92-72-68; Chair. SATTAR MEHBALIYEV.

Free Trade Union of Teachers: Baku; Chair. SEYRAN SEYRANOV.

Free Trade Unions of Oil and Gas Industry Workers: mems are employees of c. 118 enterprises in petroleum and gas sectors; Chair. JAHANGIR ALIYEV.

Trade Union of Journalists: 370105 Baku, A. Haqverdiyev St 3A/5; tel. and fax (12) 38-32-56; e-mail azeri@ajip.baku.az; f. 1998; 212 mems; Chair. AZER HASRET; not permitted to register by Govt.

Transport

RAILWAYS

In 1995 there were 2,123 km of railway track, of which 1,277 km were electrified. The overwhelming majority of total freight traffic is carried by the railways (some 78% in 1991). Railways connect Baku with Tbilisi (Georgia), Makhachkala (Dagestan, Russia) and Yerevan (Armenia). In 1997 passenger rail services between Moscow and Baku were resumed, and a service to Kiev (Ukraine) was inaugurated. The rail link with Armenia runs through the Autonomous Republic of Nakhichevan, but is currently disrupted, owing to Azerbaijan's economic blockade of Armenia. From Nakhichevan an international line links Azerbaijan with Tabriz (Iran). In 1991 plans were agreed with the Iranian Government for the construction of a rail line between Azerbaijan and Nakhichevan, which would pass through Iranian territory, thus bypassing Armenia. There is an underground railway in Baku (the Baku Metro); it comprises

two lines (total length 28 km) with 19 stations. A further 4.1 km, with three stations, is currently under construction.

Azerbaijani Railways: 370010 Baku, 1 May St 230; tel. (12) 98-44-67; fax (12) 98-85-47; f. 1992, following the dissolution of the former Soviet Railways; Pres. ZIYA MAMEDOV; First Dep. Pres. and Chief Eng. M. M. MEHTIEV.

Bakinskii Metropolitan (Baku Metro): 370602 Baku, G. Javid Ave 33A; Gen. Man. Y. I. USIFOV.

ROADS

At 31 December 1998 the total length of roads in Azerbaijan was 24,981 km (6,897 km main roads and 18,084 km secondary roads).

SHIPPING

Shipping services on the Caspian Sea link Baku with Astrakhan (Russia), Turkmenbashi (Turkmenistan) and the Iranian ports of Bandar Anzali and Bandar Nowshar. At 31 December 1998 the Azerbaijani merchant fleet comprised 287 vessels, with a combined displacement of 650,933 grt. The total included 39 petroleum tankers (176,101 grt).

Shipowning Company

Caspian Shipping Company (Caspar): 370005 Baku, Mammademin Resulzade St 5; tel. (12) 93-20-58; fax (12) 93-53-39; f. 1858; nationalized by the Azerbaijani Govt in 1991; transports crude petroleum and petroleum products; operates cargo and passenger ferries; Pres. A. A. BASHIROV.

CIVIL AVIATION

Azerbaijan Airlines (Azerbaijan Hava Yollari): 370000 Baku, Azadlyg Ave 11; tel. (12) 93-44-34; fax (12) 98-52-37; e-mail azal@azal.baku.az; internet www.azal.az; f. 1992; state airline operating scheduled and charter passenger and cargo services to the CIS, Europe and the Middle East; Gen. Dir DJAHANGIR ASGAROV.

IMAIR Airlines: 370000 Baku, Hazi Aslamov St 115; tel. (12) 93-41-71; fax (12) 93-27-77; e-mail imair@impro.baku.az; internet www.imair.com; f. 1994; independent airline operating international charter passenger and cargo services; Chair. and Pres. FIZOULI ALEKPEROV.

Tourism

Tourism is not widely developed. However, there are resorts on the Caspian Sea, including the Ganjlik international tourist centre, on the Apsheron Peninsula, near Baku, which has four hotels as well as camping facilities.

Council for Foreign Tourism: 370004 Baku, Neftchilar Ave 65; tel. (12) 92-87-13; fax (12) 98-03-68; e-mail ff-com@azdata.net; under the Cabinet of Ministers.

THE BAHAMAS

Introductory Survey

Location, Climate, Language, Religion, Flag, Capital

The Commonwealth of the Bahamas consists of about 700 islands and more than 2,000 cays and rocks, extending from east of the Florida coast of the USA to just north of Cuba and Haiti, in the West Indies. The main islands are New Providence, Grand Bahama, Andros, Eleuthera and Great Abaco. Almost 70% of the population reside on the island of New Providence. The remaining members of the group are known as the 'Family Islands'. A total of 29 of the islands are inhabited. The climate is mild and sub-tropical, with average temperatures of about 30°C (86°F) in summer and 20°C (68°F) in winter. The average annual rainfall is about 1,000 mm (39 ins). The official language is English. Most of the inhabitants profess Christianity, the largest denominations being the Anglican, Baptist, Roman Catholic and Methodist Churches. The national flag comprises three equal horizontal stripes, of blue, gold and blue, with a black triangle at the hoist, extending across one-half of the width. The capital is Nassau, on the island of New Providence.

Recent History

A former British colonial territory, the Bahamas attained internal self-government in January 1964, although the parliamentary system dates back to 1729. The first elections under universal adult suffrage were held in January 1967 for an enlarged House of Assembly. The Progressive Liberal Party (PLP), supported mainly by Bahamians of African origin and led by Lynden (later Sir Lynden) Pindling, won 18 of the 38 seats, as did the ruling United Bahamian Party (UBP), dominated by those of European origin. With the support of another member, the PLP formed a Government and Pindling became Premier (he was restyled Prime Minister in September 1968). At the next elections, in April 1968, the PLP won 29 seats and the UBP only seven.

Following a constitutional conference in September 1968, the Bahamas Government was given increased responsibility for internal security, external affairs and defence in May 1969. In the elections of September 1972, which were dominated by the issue of independence, the PLP maintained its majority. Following a constitutional conference in December 1972, the Bahamas became an independent nation, within the Commonwealth, on 10 July 1973. Pindling remained Prime Minister. The PLP increased its majority in the elections of July 1977 and was again returned to power in the June 1982 elections, with 32 of the 43 seats in the enlarged House of Assembly. The remaining 11 seats were won by the Free National Movement (FNM), which had reunited for the elections after splitting into several factions over the previous five years.

Trading in illicit drugs, mainly for the US market, has become a major problem for the country, since many of the small islands and cays are used by drugs-traffickers in their smuggling activities. According to estimates by the US Government, some 70% of cocaine and 50% of marijuana entering the USA between the early 1970s and the early 1990s passed through the Bahamas. In 1983 allegations of widespread corruption, and the abuse of Bahamian bank secrecy laws by drugs-traffickers and US tax evaders, led Pindling to appoint a Royal Commission to investigate thoroughly the drugs trade in the Bahamas. The Commission's hearings revealed the extent to which money deriving from this trade had permeated Bahamian social and economic affairs. In October 1984 two cabinet ministers, implicated by the evidence presented to the Commission, resigned, and by November 1985 a total of 51 suspects had been indicted, including the assistant police commissioner. The Commission also revealed that Pindling had received several million dollars in gifts and loans from business executives, although it found no evidence of a link to the drugs trade. After unsuccessfully demanding Pindling's resignation, the Deputy Prime Minister, Arthur Hanna, resigned, and two other ministers, Perry Christie and Hubert Ingraham, were dismissed.

Although the issue of the illegal drugs trade and of drugs-related corruption within the Government dominated the general election campaign, the PLP was returned to power for a fifth consecutive term in June 1987, winning 31 of the 49 seats in the enlarged House of Assembly. The FNM won 16 seats, while the remaining two seats were secured by Christie and Ingraham as independents.

Statistics relating to crime in 1987 indicated unprecedented levels of violent and drugs-related offences, and in February 1988 new claims of official corruption were made at the trial in Florida, USA, of a leading Colombian drugs-trafficker. Pindling and the Deputy Prime Minister were alleged to have accepted bribes, but this was vehemently denied. In March 1990 the Minister of Agriculture, Trade and Industry, Ervin Knowles, resigned, following allegations of nepotism and the misuse of public funds. He was replaced by Christie, who rejoined the PLP. The other independent member, Ingraham, subsequently joined the FNM and became its leader in May, upon the death of Sir Cecil Wallace-Whitfield.

The general election campaign in mid-1992 was disrupted by industrial unrest in the country's telephone and electricity companies, and by the continuing problems of the state airline, Bahamasair. Despite predictions of a PLP victory, the FNM won the general election on 19 August, securing 33 seats, while Pindling's party won the remaining 16. Ingraham replaced Pindling as Prime Minister, and announced a programme of measures aimed at increasing the accountability of government ministers, combating corruption and revitalizing the economy. Acknowledging responsibility for his party's defeat in the election, Pindling resigned as leader of the PLP, but, at the party's annual convention in January 1993, agreed to continue in office.

The resignation of Orville Turnquest, the Deputy Prime Minister, Minister of Foreign Affairs and Attorney-General, in January 1995, in order to assume the post of Governor-General, prompted an extensive cabinet reorganization.

In March 1995 a marked increase in violent crime in parts of New Providence led the Government to announce the creation of a special police unit to tackle the problem. Meanwhile, the trade in illegal drugs remained widespread in the country, and in late 1995 several local business leaders, as well as close relatives of a member of Parliament, were arrested in connection with a large seizure of cocaine. In October of that year the Prime Minister introduced further legislation that aimed to prevent the abuse of Bahamian banks by drugs-traffickers, and thus improve the reputation of the country's financial sector, particularly in the USA.

The decision in March 1996 to hang a man convicted of murder in early 1991 was controversial, owing to the fact that the period spent awaiting execution had exceeded five years. In recognition of a prisoner's suffering in anticipation of execution, previous cases had held five years to constitute the maximum term after which the case should be subject to review with a possible commutation to life imprisonment. However, in October 1996 the Judicial Committee of the Privy Council ruled that to await execution for more than three and a half years would amount to inhuman punishment, and that all such cases should be commuted. The ruling was believed to affect 22 of the 39 prisoners under sentence of death in the Bahamas at that time.

At a general election held on 14 March 1997, in which 91.7% of the electorate participated, the FNM won 34 of the 40 seats in a reduced House of Assembly, and the PLP six. The FNM's overwhelming victory in the election was attributed both to the Prime Minister's success in reversing the economic decline and the involvement of the PLP in various financial scandals. Most notably, Pindling was implicated in February in the findings of a public inquiry (instituted in 1993) to investigate alleged corruption and misappropriation of funds in the three principal state corporations. Following the election, Pindling, who had retained his seat in the House of Assembly, resigned as leader of the PLP and was replaced by Christie. In July Pindling announced his retirement from parliamentary politics (he died in August 2000), and his seat was won by the FNM at a by-election in September. The PLP was further damaged in January 2000 by the resignation of its deputy leader, Bernard Nottage, who subsequently formed a rival party, the Coalition for Democratic Reform.

Following its election victory in 1997, the FNM proposed establishing a commission to give detailed consideration to constitutional reforms, including a proposed limit of two terms of office for the Prime Minister. Progress was, however, slow, and although in 2000 a commission had been nominated, it had not formally been appointed.

In the late 1990s violent crime continued to be of major concern to Bahamians. In April 1998 the Government signed a convention drawn up by the Organization of American States to ban illegal guns, amid a disturbing increase in gun-related crime. The murders of several tourists in 1998 shocked the local community and provoked fears regarding the future of the tourism industry. In September the Prime Minister increased security in tourist areas, and announced plans to limit the right of appeal against death sentences (17 prisoners had had their sentences commuted in January). The hanging in October of two convicted murderers caused controversy, despite growing public demand for execution as a deterrent against crime. In carrying out the executions, the Government rejected a last-minute plea for clemency from the European Union (EU), on the grounds that both men had appeals pending at the Inter-American Commission on Human Rights (IACHR) in Washington, DC, USA. In August 1999 the Bahamian authorities were strongly criticized by human-rights groups, after they announced their intention to execute another two convicted murderers who had also submitted petitions to the IACHR. The Government justified its decision, however, by referring to a 1998 court ruling that executions could be carried out if appeals had been pending at the IACHR for more than 18 months. Despite attempts to reduce levels of crime, there were 64 murders (many of which were drugs-related) in 1999, compared with 29 during the whole of 1998. Armed robbery also rose sharply.

In mid-1999 there was vigorous public opposition in the Bahamas to the impending privatization of the state-owned telecommunications company, BaTelCo. In 2000 the Bahamas was listed by the Financial Action Task Force as a non-cooperative jurisdiction, and by the Organisation for Economic Co-operation and Development as a tax haven. The Bahamas also received the lowest grade of a bank supervision report by the Financial Stability Forum, a group of international regulators, and remained classified as a 'Country of Primary Concern' in the US International Narcotics Control Strategy Report, partly because of its banking secrecy laws and the size of its 'offshore' financial sector. In October 2000 a Financial Intelligence Unit was established to investigate suspicious financial activity.

The Bahamas suffered considerable damage in September 1999 when 'Hurricane Floyd' struck the islands; one person died and at least 2,000 were made homeless as a result of the storm. In the following month 'Hurricane Irene' caused another four deaths and inflicted further structural damage on the Bahamas.

In mid-December 1999 the Prime Minister dismissed the Minister of Consumer Welfare and Aviation, Pierre Dupuch. Later in the month the Attorney-General and Minister of Justice, Tennyson Wells, announced his resignation from both positions, in order to challenge Ingraham for the leadership of the FNM. This announcement prompted the Prime Minister, in early January 2000, to effect an extensive cabinet reorganization. In a slightly reduced Cabinet, eight ministers retained their portfolios unchanged, while the Minister of Foreign Affairs, Janet Bostwick, also assumed that of Attorney-General. Several ministries were restructured, leading to the creation of new ministries, including a Ministry of Commerce, Agriculture and Industry, aimed at the promotion of small business.

The Bahamas' traditionally close relationship with the USA has been strained by the increasingly aggressive attitude of the US Government towards the bank secrecy laws and the drugs-smuggling in the islands. Bilateral relations were damaged in August 1997, when an incendiary device exploded at a travel agency in Nassau commonly used by US tourists. Nevertheless, the USA and the Bahamas have collaborated in a series of operations to intercept drugs-traffickers, and in late 1998 the USA commended the Bahamian authorities for their efforts to curb this illegal trade.

Relations with the Bahamas' other neighbours, Haiti and Cuba, have been strained by the influx of large numbers of illegal immigrants from both countries. In 1994 the Government announced an increase its efforts to deport illegal aliens. In June 1998 the Bahamian Government agreed to inform Cuba of the arrival of illegal Cuban immigrants within 72 hours of their discovery, while Cuba agreed to their repatriation within 15 days. In mid-1998 many Cubans were deported from the Bahamas, despite an offer by Nicaragua of temporary asylum for 200 detainees. In April 2000 a boat carrying almost 300 Haitian migrants ran aground on an uninhabited cay in the southern Bahamas. By the time the migrants were discovered 14 had died of dehydration.

Government

Legislative power is vested in the bicameral Parliament. The Senate has 16 members, of whom nine are appointed by the Governor-General on the advice of the Prime Minister, four by the Leader of the Opposition and three after consultation with the Prime Minister. The House of Assembly has 40 members, elected for five years (subject to dissolution) by universal adult suffrage. Executive power is vested in the British monarch, represented by a Governor-General, who is appointed on the Prime Minister's recommendation and who acts, in almost all matters, on the advice of the Cabinet. The Governor-General appoints the Prime Minister and, on the latter's recommendation, selects the other ministers. The Cabinet is responsible to the House of Assembly.

Defence

The Royal Bahamian Defence Force, a paramilitary coastguard, is the only security force in the Bahamas, and numbered 860 (including 70 women) in August 2000. Defence expenditure in 2000 was budgeted at B $26m.

Economic Affairs

In 1995, according to estimates by the World Bank, the Bahamas' gross national product (GNP), measured at average 1993–95 prices, was US $3,297m., equivalent to US $11,940 per head (the highest level among Caribbean countries). In 1997, according to preliminary World Bank data, GNP totalled US $3,288m. (US $11,830 per head). In 1998 GNP was equivalent to US $13,990 per head on an international purchasing-power parity. During 1990–98, it was estimated, GNP per head decreased, in real terms, at an average rate of 0.8% per year. The population increased at an average annual rate of 2.0% over the same period. During 1994–98 the Bahamas' gross domestic product (GDP) increased, in real terms, at an estimated average rate of 2.7% per year. According to IMF estimates, real GDP rose by 4.2% in 1996, by 3.3% in 1997 and by 3.0% in 1998; in 1998 GDP was equivalent to US $14,450 per head.

Agriculture, hunting, forestry and fishing, which together accounted for only 3.4% of GDP in 1992 and engaged an estimated 3.8% of the employed labour force in 1997, have been developed by the Government in an attempt to reduce dependence on imports (80% of food supplies were imported in the 1980s). In 1998, however, agricultural production accounted for only 1.0% of total land area. By the late 1990s, according to official estimates, agriculture contributed less than 3% of GDP. The increase in agricultural output has resulted in the export of certain crops, particularly of cucumbers, tomatoes, pineapples, papayas, avocados, mangoes, limes and other citrus fruits. The development of commercial fishing has concentrated on conchs and crustaceans. In 1998 exports of Caribbean spiny lobster (crawfish) provided 19.1% of all export earnings, and accounted for 74.6% of the fishing total. There is also some exploitation of pine forests in the northern Bahamas.

Industry (comprising mining, manufacturing, construction and utilities) employed 14.6% of the working population in 1997 (construction accounted for 9.2%) and provided 10.9% of GDP in 1992.

Mining and manufacturing together contributed only 4.0% of GDP in 1992. Mining provided 1.4% of employment, and manufacturing 4.0%, in 1997. The islands' principal mineral resources are salt (which provided 14.5% of domestic export earnings in 1995) and aragonite.

The manufacturing sector contributed some 10% of GDP in 1982, since when it has declined, owing to the closure, in 1985, of the country's petroleum refinery. In 1992 the sector contributed 4.0% of GDP. In this year the principal branches of manufacturing, based on the value of output, were beverages (accounting for 44.7% of the total), chemicals (16.2%) and printing and publishing. Exports of rum fell from US $33.4m., or 27.5% of domestic export earnings in 1991, to only $2.9m., or 3.1% of domestic earnings in 1995, before recovering to $12.2m., or 8.8% in 1998. Petroleum transhipment on Grand Bahama remains an important activity (crude petroleum accounted for some 53% of total trade in 1990, and petroleum products for about 11% in 1988). The construction sector has, since 1986, experienced much activity, owing to hotel-building and harbour developments. In the late 1990s several major projects guaranteed strong growth in the sector.

Most of the energy requirements of the Bahamas are fulfilled by the petroleum that Venezuela and, particularly, Mexico provide under the San José Agreement (originally negotiated in 1980), which commits both the petroleum producers to selling subsidized supplies, on favourable terms, to the developing countries of the region. Excluding transhipments of petroleum, imports of mineral fuels accounted for 12.6% of total imports in 1995.

Service industries constitute the principal sectors of the economy, providing 85.7% of GDP in 1992 and 81.2% of total employment in 1997. The Bahamas established its own shipping registry in 1976, and by 1983 had one of the largest 'open-registry' fleets in the world. In 1997 an international container-transhipment was opened at Freeport, Grand Bahama. On completion of its expansion in 1999 it was capable of handling 950,000 container units per year, and was to act as an intercontinental hub port serving North America, the Caribbean and South America. At the end of 1998 a total of 1,286 vessels were registered under the Bahamian flag. With a combined displacement of 27.7m. grt, the fleet was the third largest in the world.

In 1996 the country was ranked as the 12th largest 'offshore' financial centre in the world. Banking is the second most important economic activity in the Bahamas. In May 1999 the Government introduced legislation to establish an insurance fund to protect bank depositors, following the suspension of the Gulf Union Bank's banking licence. In May 2000 a stock exchange, which planned to develop trading in global depository receipts for overseas companies, began trading the shares of nine local companies.

Despite increasing competition, the Bahamas continues to be the principal tourist destination of the Caribbean. Tourism is the predominant sector of the economy, directly accounting for 15% of GDP in 1998, and employing some 30% of the working population in 1994. In 1998 travel receipts covered 78% of the cost of goods imported. In 1997 81% of stop-over arrivals were from the USA, although attempts are being made to attract visitors from other countries and improve air access to resorts. Tourist arrivals increased steadily during the 1980s, and by 1991 amounted to some 3.7m. However, figures declined somewhat during the 1990s, as a result of recession in the important US market, an increase in the incidence of crime in the islands and competition from alternative destinations. In 1996–98 the average annual number of tourist arrivals totalled about 3.4m. However, following tourist-related investment totalling US $1,500m.–$2,000m., the sector experienced a recovery. In 1999 tourist arrivals were 3.7m., an estimated increase of 9.0%. Total arrivals were expected to increase to 4m.–5m. by 2000. Hotel-room occupancy in Nassau increased from 52% in 1992 to 77.3% in 1999. The Sun International Atlantis resort on Paradise Island completed its expansion in December 1998, providing 2,355 rooms and employment for 5,600 people—equivalent to 4% of national employment. The Bahamas received more cruise-ship arrivals than any other Caribbean destination. Receipts from tourism fell slightly in 1998, to an estimated B $1,408m., compared with B $1,416m. in 1997, but rose again in 1999 to B $1,500m. In 1997 some 81% of stop-over arrivals came from the USA. In the same year some 8% of visitors came from Europe and 6% came from Canada.

In 1999 the Bahamas recorded a visible trade deficit of US $1,428.2m., and there was a deficit of US $671.9m. on the current account of the balance of payments. The USA is the principal trading partner of the Bahamas, providing 92.8% of non-petroleum imports and taking 81.1% of total exports in 1995. Excluding the trade in petroleum and its products, the principal exports (including re-exports) in 1998 were machinery and transport equipment (26.0% of the total), food and live animals (25.1%), and chemicals (22.3%). In that year the principal imports were machinery and transport equipment (30.6% of the total), basic manufactures (19.7%), food and live animals (14.3%) and miscellaneous manufactured articles (14.2%).

In the year ending 30 June 1998 there was an estimated budgetary deficit of B $71.3m. The deficit declined to an estimated B $23.5m. in 1999. At 31 December 1998 the external debt of the central Government was B $85.0m. and in 1999 foreign-currency debt servicing cost US $69.5m., equivalent to 8.0% of the recurrent revenue of US $868.9m. The debt-service ratio, however was just 3.2% of the value of goods and services in the same year, down from 5.5% in 1997. The annual rate of inflation averaged 2.8% during 1990–98; consumer prices increased by 1.3% in 1999. The rate of unemployment declined from 13.3% of the labour force in April 1994 to 7.5% in 1999.

The Bahamas is a member of the Caribbean Community and Common Market (CARICOM, see p. 142) and the Organization of American States (OAS, see p. 261), the Association of Caribbean States (see p. 306) and is a signatory of the Lomé Convention with the EU (which expired in February 2000 and was replaced by the Cotonou Agreement—see p. 208).

Economic expansion through foreign investment continued to be restricted by fears of widespread corruption and instability, caused by the activities of illegal drugs-trafficking networks in the islands (although investor confidence was reported to be increasing by 1999). In 1995 measures were introduced in an attempt to combat corruption in the financial sector and thus improve the reputation of the country's economic institutions. In May 1999 a Securities Industry Bill was adopted. By mid-1999 all but one of the state-owned hotels had been transferred to private ownership, under a privatization programme launched in 1993, with a number of foreign companies investing in large-scale projects. The divestment of the state telecommunications and electricity companies was scheduled for 1999 and 2000 respectively. In the late 1990s the Government maintained a policy of fiscal prudence, with the aim of eliminating the recurrent budget deficit by 2001. The budget proposals for 1999/2000 included measures to raise further revenue, such as an increase in the hotel occupancy tax rate from 4% to 6%.

Social Welfare

The health service is centralized in Nassau at the government general hospital, which has 484 beds. There is also a mental hospital and rehabilitation unit (with 477 beds), a geriatric hospital (with 170 beds) and two private clinics on New Providence. There is a 92-bed hospital on Grand Bahama, and in the Family Islands several cottage hospitals and medical centres operate. A Flying Doctor Service supplies medical attention to islands that lack resident personnel. Flying Dental Services and nursing personnel from the Community Nursing Service are also provided. In 1996 there were 152 physicians and 230 nurses per 100,000 inhabitants. A National Insurance Scheme, established in 1972, provides a wide range of benefits, including sickness, maternity, retirement and widows' pensions as well as social assistance payments. The scheme is administered by the National Insurance Board (NIB), which is funded mainly by contributions and investment income. Total expenditure by the NIB in 1994 was B $74.9m., including B $56.4m. in benefit payments. An Industrial Injuries Scheme has also been established. In addition to payments by the NIB, there is some government expenditure on social welfare from the General Budget: in 1998/99 this included B $134.3m. on health (15.6% of total expenditure) and B $47.5m. on social services (5.5%).

Education

Education is compulsory between the ages of five and 16 years, and is provided free of charge in government schools. There are several private and denominational schools. Primary education begins at five years of age and lasts for six years. In 1997 enrolment at primary level was equivalent to 97% of children in the relevant age-group. Secondary education, beginning at the age of 11, also lasts for six years and is divided into two equal cycles. In 1997 enrolment at secondary level was equivalent to 85% of children in the relevant age-group. The University of the West Indies has an extra-mural department in Nassau, offering degree courses in hotel management, tourism and law. The Bahamas Law School opened, as part of the University of the West Indies, in 1998. The Bahamas Hotel Training College was established in 1992. Technical, teacher-training and professional qualifications can be obtained at the two campuses of the College of the Bahamas. In 1999 plans were under way to upgrade the college to full university status in the near future.

In 1999, according to official estimates, the average rate of adult illiteracy was 4.5% (males 5%; females 4%). This figure was estimated to have decreased to 3.9% in 2000. Government expenditure on education in 1998/99 was B $164.7m. (or 19.1% of total spending from the General Budget).

Public Holidays

2001: 1 January (New Year's Day), 13 April (Good Friday), 16 April (Easter Monday), 1 June (Labour Day), 4 June (Whit Monday), 10 July (Independence Day), 6 August (Emancipation

Day), 12 October (Discovery Day/Columbus Day), 25–26 December (Christmas).

2002: 1 January (New Year's Day), 29 March (Good Friday), 1 April (Easter Monday), 20 May (Whit Monday), 7 June (Labour Day), 10 July (Independence Day), 5 August (Emancipation

Day), 12 October (Discovery Day/Columbus Day), 25–26 December (Christmas).

Weights and Measures

The imperial system is used.

Statistical Survey

Source (unless otherwise stated): Central Bank of the Bahamas, Frederick St, POB N-4868, Nassau; tel. 322-2193; fax 322-4321.

AREA AND POPULATION

Area: 13,939 sq km (5,382 sq miles).

Population: 209,505 at census of 12 May 1980; 255,095 (males 124,992, females 130,103) at census of 2 May 1990; 298,300 (official estimate) in 1999. *By island* (1990): New Providence 172,196 (including the capital, Nassau); Grand Bahama 40,898; Andros 8,187; Eleuthera 10,586.

Density (1999): 21.4 per sq km.

Principal Town: Nassau (capital), population 172,000 (1997).

Births, Marriages and Deaths (1996): Registered live births 5,873 (birth rate 20.7 per 1,000); Registered marriages 2,628 (marriage rate 9.3 per 1,000); Registered deaths 1,537 (death rate 5.4 per 1,000). Source: UN, *Demographic Yearbook* and *Population and Vital Statistics Report*.

Expectation of Life (World Bank estimate, years at birth, 1998): 74.

Economically Active Population (sample survey, persons aged 15 years and over, excl. armed forces, April 1998): Agriculture, hunting, forestry and fishing 5,070; Mining, quarrying, electricity, gas and water 1,530; Manufacturing 5,400; Construction 15,055; Wholesale and retail trade 20,155; Hotels and restaurants 22,110; Transport, storage and communications 11,745; Finance, insurance, real estate and business services 13,960; Community, social and personal services 48,785; Activities not adequately defined 545; *Total employed* 144,355 (males 74,690, females 69,665); Unemployed 12,115 (males 4,535, females 7,580); *Total labour force* 156,470 (males, 79,225, females 77,245). Source: ILO Caribbean Office.

AGRICULTURE, ETC.

Principal Crops ('000 metric tons, 1999): Roots and tubers 1; Sugar cane 45*; Tomatoes 4; Other vegetables 18*; Lemons and limes 8*; Grapefruit and pomelos 14; Bananas 3; Other fruits 4*. *FAO estimate. Source: FAO.

Livestock ('000 head, year ending September 1999): Cattle 0.7; Pigs 5.8; Sheep 5.7; Goats 14.5; Poultry 6,000 (FAO estimate). Source: FAO.

Livestock Products ('000 metric tons, 1999): Poultry meat 9.5; Cows' milk 0.6*; Goats' milk 1.1*; Hen eggs 1.1. *FAO estimate. Source: FAO.

Forestry ('000 cu m, 1998): Roundwood removals: Sawlogs and veneer logs 17; Pulpwood 100; Total 117; Sawnwood production: Coniferous (softwood) 1. Source: FAO, *Yearbook of Forest Products*.

Fishing ('000 metric tons, live weight, 1998): Capture 10.1 (Groupers 0.7, Snappers 0.8, Caribbean spiny lobster 7.6, Stromboid conchs 0.7); Aquaculture 0 (FAO estimate); Total catch 10.1. Figures exclude marine shells (39 metric tons) and sponges (60 tons). Source: FAO, *Yearbook of Fishery Statistics*.

MINING

Production (estimates, '000 metric tons): Unrefined salt 900 in 1999; Aragonite 1,200 in 1997. Source: US Geological Survey.

INDUSTRY

Production (estimate, million kWh, 1998): Electric energy 1,227.

FINANCE

Currency and Exchange Rates: 100 cents = 1 Bahamian dollar (B $). *Sterling, US Dollar and Euro Equivalents* (29 December 2000): £1 sterling = B $1.4922; US $1 = B $1.0000; €1 = 93.05 cents; B $100 = £67.02 = US $100.00 = €107.47. *Exchange Rate:* Since February 1970 the official exchange rate, applicable to most transactions, has been US $1 = B $1, i.e., the Bahamian dollar has been at par with the US dollar. There is also an investment currency rate, applicable to certain capital transactions between residents and non-residents and to direct investments outside the Bahamas. Since 1987 this exchange rate has been fixed at US $1 = B $1.225.

General Budget (estimates, B $ million, year ending 30 June 1999): *Revenue:* Total 839.1. *Expenditure:* Education 164.7; Uniformed services 90.6; Health 134.3; Tourism 57.3; Public works 55.7; Social services 47.5; Public debt interest 106.6; Total (incl. other) 862.6 (current 767.1; capital 95.5).

1999/2000 (forecasts, B $ million): Recurrent revenue 895.6; Recurrent expenditure 838.7; Capital expenditure 95.8.

2000/01 (forecasts, B $ million): Total revenue 998; Recurrent expenditure 949; Capital expenditure 128.

International Reserves (US $ million at 31 December 1999): Reserve position in IMF 8.6; Foreign exchange 401.9; Total 410.5. Source: IMF, *International Financial Statistics*.

Money Supply (B $ million at 31 December 1999): Currency outside banks 149.1; Demand deposits at deposit money banks 587.8; Total money (incl. others) 747.7. Source: IMF, *International Financial Statistics*.

Cost of Living (consumer price index; base: 1995 = 100): 101.9 in 1997; 103.3 in 1998; 104.6 in 1999. Source: IMF, *International Financial Statistics*.

Gross Domestic Product (US $ million at current prices): 3,201 in 1995; 3,621 in 1996; 3,795 in 1997. Source: UN, *Statistical Yearbook*.

Expenditure on the Gross Domestic Product (B $ million at current prices, 1995): Government final consumption expenditure 483.9; Private final consumption expenditure 2,077.4; Increase in stocks 13.8; Gross fixed capital formation 698.5; *Total domestic expenditure* 3,273.6; Exports of goods and services 1,680.1; *Less* Imports of goods and services 1,819.6; Statistical discrepancy –64.7; *GDP in purchasers' values* 3,069.4. Source: IMF, *International Financial Statistics*.

Gross Domestic Product by Economic Activity (B $ million at current prices, 1992): Agriculture, hunting, forestry and fishing 89; Manufacturing (incl. mining and quarrying) 105; Electricity, gas and water 88; Construction 91; Trade, restaurants and hotels 705; Transport, storage and communications 227; Finance, insurance, real estate and business services 610; Government services 336; Other community, social and personal services 310; Other services 55; Statistical discrepancy 13; *Sub-total* 2,629; Import duties 268; Other indirect taxes 162; *GDP in purchasers' values* 3,059. Source: UN, *National Accounts Statistics*.

Balance of Payments* (US $ million, 1999): Exports of goods f.o.b. 379.9; Imports of goods f.o.b. –1,808.1; *Trade balance* –1,428.2; Exports of services 1,811.2; Imports of services –953.8; *Balance on goods and services* –570.8; Other income received 229.6; Other income paid –367.2; *Balance on goods, services and income* –708.4; Current transfers received 49.0; Current transfers paid –12.5; *Current balance* –671.9; Capital account (net) –14.5; Direct investment abroad –0.2; Direct investment from abroad 144.6; Other investment assets –12,487.1; Other investment liabilities 12,954.1; Net errors and omissions 140.2; *Overall balance* 65.2. Source: IMF, *International Financial Statistics*.

* The figures for merchandise imports and exports exclude petroleum and petroleum products, except imports for local consumption.

EXTERNAL TRADE*

Principal Commodities (US $ million, 1998): *Imports c.i.f.:* Food and live animals 260.1; Crude materials (inedible) except fuels 45.3; Mineral fuels, lubricants etc. 112.7; Chemicals 160.5; Basic manufactures 358.7; Machinery and transport equipment 555.8; Miscellaneous manufactured articles 257.7; Total (incl. others) 1,816.4. *Exports f.o.b.:* Food and live animals 75.3; Beverages and tobacco 12.8; Crude materials (inedible) except fuels 28.4; Chemicals 67.0; Basic manufactures 26.1; Machinery and transport equipment 78.2; Miscellaneous manufactured articles 12.4; Total (incl. others) 300.3.

1999 (US $ million): Total Imports c.i.f. 1,808; Total Exports f.o.b. 380. Source: IMF, *International Financial Statistics*.

Principal Trading Partners (US $ million, 1991): *Imports c.i.f.:* Aruba 52.2; Canada 21.2; Denmark 23.7; France 20.8; Nigeria 23.9; USA 866.0; Total (incl. others) 1,091.2. *Exports f.o.b.:* Canada 6.7; France 14.5; Germany 6.2; Mexico 4.0; United Kingdom 27.2; USA 142.5; Total (incl. others) 225.1. Source: UN, *International Trade Statistics Yearbook*.

1995 (US $ million): *Imports c.i.f.* (excl. mineral fuels): Canada 11.3; USA 1,008.7; Total (incl. others) 1,243.1. *Exports f.o.b.:* Canada 3.4; United Kingdom 4.0; USA 142.6; Total (incl. others) 175.9.

* The data exclude imports and exports of crude petroleum and residual fuel oils that are brought into the Bahamas for storage on behalf of foreign companies abroad. Also excluded is trade in certain chemical products. In 1991 total imports were valued at US $1,801.2m. and total exports at US $1,517.1m.

TRANSPORT

Road Traffic (vehicles in use, 1995): 67,100 passenger cars; 13,700 commercial vehicles. Source: UN, *Statistical Yearbook*.

Shipping: *Merchant fleet* (displacement, '000 grt at 31 December): 24,409 in 1996; 25,523 in 1997; 27,716 in 1998. (Source: Lloyd's Register of Shipping, *World Fleet Statistics*). *International sea-borne freight traffic* (estimates, '000 metric tons, 1990): Goods loaded 5,920; Goods unloaded 5,705. Source: UN, *Monthly Bulletin of Statistics*.

Civil Aviation (1997): Kilometres flown (million) 2; Passengers carried ('000) 704; Passenger-km (million) 140; Total ton-km (million) 13. Source: UN, *Statistical Yearbook*.

TOURISM

Tourist Arrivals: 3,453,769 in 1997; 3,346,329 in 1998; 3,655,839 (1,436,952 by air, 2,281,887 by sea) in 1999.

Tourism Receipts (estimates, B $ million): 1,398 in 1996; 1,416 in 1997; 1,408 in 1998.

COMMUNICATIONS MEDIA

Radio Receivers (1997): 215,000 in use.
Television Receivers (1997): 67,000 in use.
Telephones (estimate, 1997): 96,000 main lines in use.
Telefax Stations (1996): 500 in use.
Mobile Cellular Telephones (1997): 6,152 subscribers.
Daily Newspapers (1996): 3 titles (total circulation 28,000 copies).
Sources: UN, *Statistical Yearbook*; UNESCO, *Statistical Yearbook*.

EDUCATION

Pre-primary (1996/97): 20 schools; 76 teachers; 1,094 pupils.
Primary (1996/97): 113 schools; 1,540 teachers (estimate); 34,199 students.
Secondary (1996/97): 37 junior/senior high schools (1990); 1,352 teachers (public education only); 27,970 students (public education only).
Tertiary (1987): 249 teachers; 5,305 students.
In 1993 there were 3,201 students registered at the College of the Bahamas.
Source: mainly UNESCO, *Statistical Yearbook*.

Directory

The Constitution

A representative House of Assembly was first established in 1729, although universal adult suffrage was not introduced until 1962. A new Constitution for the Commonwealth of the Bahamas came into force at independence, on 10 July 1973. The main provisions of the Constitution are summarized below:

Parliament consists of a Governor-General (representing the British monarch, who is Head of State), a nominated Senate and an elected House of Assembly. The Governor-General appoints the Prime Minister and, on the latter's recommendation, the remainder of the Cabinet. Apart from the Prime Minister, the Cabinet has no fewer than eight other ministers, of whom one is the Attorney-General. The Governor-General also appoints a Leader of the Opposition.

The Senate (upper house) consists of 16 members, of whom nine are appointed by the Governor-General on the advice of the Prime Minister, four on the advice of the Leader of the Opposition and three on the Prime Minister's advice after consultation with the Leader of the Opposition. The House of Assembly (lower house) has 40 members. A Constituencies Commission reviews numbers and boundaries at intervals of not more than five years and can recommend alterations for approval of the House. The life of Parliament is limited to a maximum of five years.

The Constitution provides for a Supreme Court and a Court of Appeal.

The Government

Head of State: HM Queen ELIZABETH II (succeeded to the throne 6 February 1952).

Governor-General: Sir ORVILLE TURNQUEST (appointed 22 February 1995).

THE CABINET
(April 2001)

Prime Minister: HUBERT ALEXANDER INGRAHAM.

Deputy Prime Minister and Minister of National Security: FRANK HOWARD WATSON.

Attorney-General and Minister of Foreign Affairs: JANET G. BOSTWICK.

Minister of Tourism and Aviation: CORNELIUS ALVIN SMITH.

Minister of Finance: WILLIAM C. ALLEN.

Minister of Education and Youth: Sen. Dame IVY LEONA DUMONT.

Minister of Housing and Social Development: ALGERNON SIDNEY PATRICK BENEDICT ALLEN.

Minister of Commerce, Agriculture and Industry: THERESA MOXEY-INGRAHAM.

Minister of Public Service, Immigration and National Insurance: TOMMY TURNQUEST.

Minister of Works and Transport: JAMES F. KNOWLES.

Minister of Health: Sen. Dr RONALD KNOWLES.

Minister of Local Government, Sports and Culture: DAVID C. THOMPSON.

Minister of Labour and Maritime Affairs: DION A. FOULKES.

Minister of Economic Affairs: CARL W. BETHEL.

Minister of State for Education and Youth: ZHIVARGO LAING.

MINISTRIES

Attorney-General's Office and Ministry of Justice: East Hill, POB N-3007, Nassau; tel. 322-1141; fax 356-4179.

Office of the Prime Minister: Cecil V. Wallace-Whitfield Centre, POB CB-10980, Nassau; tel. 327-5826; fax 327-5806.

Office of the Deputy Prime Minister: Churchill Bldg, Rawson Sq., POB N-3217, Nassau; tel. 356-6792; fax 356-6087.

Ministry of Commerce, Agriculture and Industry: Levy Bldg, East Bay St, POB N-3028, Nassau; tel. 325-7502; fax 322-1767.

Ministry of Consumer Welfare and Aviation: Thompson Blvd, POB N-3002, Nassau; tel. 326-4550; fax 328-1160.

Ministry of Economic Affairs: C. A. Bain Bldg, Thompson Blvd, Nassau.

Ministry of Education and Youth: Shirley St, POB N-3913, Nassau; tel. 322-8140; fax 322-8491.

Ministry of Finance: Rawson Sq., POB N-3017, Nassau; tel. 327-1530; fax 327-1618.

Ministry of Foreign Affairs: East Hill St, POB N-3746, Nassau; tel. 322-7624; fax 328-8212.

Ministry of Health: Royal Victoria Gardens, East Hill Street, POB N-3730, Nassau; tel. 322-7425; fax 322-8389.

Ministry of Housing and Social Development: Frederick House, Frederick St, POB N 3206, Nassau; tel. 356-0765; fax 323-3883.

Ministry of Labour and Maritime Affairs: Post Office Bldg, Nassau; tel. 322-6250; fax 322-6546.

Ministry of Local Government, Sports and Culture: Pilot House, East Bay St, POB N-10114, Nassau; tel. 394-0451; fax 394-0428; e-mail minyouth.mail@batelnet.bs.

Ministry of National Security: POB N-3217, Nassau; tel. 356-6792; fax 326-7344.

Ministry of Tourism and Aviation: Bay St, POB N-3701, Nassau; tel. 322-7500; fax 328-0945; internet www.bahamas.com.

Ministry of Works and Transport: John F. Kennedy Drive, POB N-8156, Nassau; tel. 323-7240; fax 326-7344.

Legislature

PARLIAMENT

Houses of Parliament: Parliament Sq., Nassau.

Senate

President: J. HENRY BOSTWICK.
There are 16 nominated members.

House of Assembly

Speaker: ROME ITALIA JOHNSON.
The House has 40 members.

General Election, 14 March 1997

Party	Seats*
Free National Movement (FNM)	34
Progressive Liberal Party (PLP)	6
Total	40

* In a by-election in September 1997 an FNM member replaced the former PLP leader, Sir Lynden Pindling, who announced his retirement from parliamentary politics in July (he died in August 2000). Furthermore, in 2000 a PLP deputy left the party and formed the Coalition for Democratic Reform.

Political Organizations

Coalition for Democratic Reform (CDR): Nassau; f. 2000; centrist; Leader BERNARD NOTTAGE.

Free National Movement (FNM): POB N-10713, Nassau; tel. 393-7863; fax 393-7914; f. 1972; Leader HUBERT A. INGRAHAM.

Progressive Liberal Party (PLP): Nassau; tel. 325-2900; f. 1953; centrist party; Leader PERRY CHRISTIE; Chair. OBIE WILCHCOMBE.

Diplomatic Representation

EMBASSIES AND HIGH COMMISSION IN THE BAHAMAS

China, People's Republic: 17 Clipper Island, Sandyport, POB CB-13500, Nassau; tel. 327-5206; Ambassador: MA SHUXVE.

United Kingdom: Ansbacher Bldg, 3rd Floor, East St, POB N-7516, Nassau; tel. 325-7471; fax 323-3871; High Commissioner: PETER HEIGL.

USA: Mosmar Bldg, Queen St, POB N-8197, Nassau; tel. 322-1181; fax 328-7838; Ambassador: ARTHUR SCHECHTER.

Judicial System

The Judicial Committee of the Privy Council (based in the United Kingdom), the Bahamas Court of Appeal, the Supreme Court and the Magistrates' Courts are the main courts of the Bahamian judicial system.

All courts have both a criminal and civil jurisdiction. The Magistrates' Courts are presided over by professionally qualified Stipendiary and Circuit Magistrates in New Providence and Grand Bahama, and by Island Administrators sitting as Magistrates in the Family Islands.

Whereas all magistrates are empowered to try offences which may be tried summarily, a Stipendiary and Circuit Magistrate may, with the consent of the accused, also try certain less serious indictable offences. The jurisdiction of magistrates is, however, limited by law.

The Supreme Court consists of the Chief Justice, two Senior Justices and six Justices. The Supreme Court also sits in Freeport, with two Justices.

Appeals in almost all matters lie from the Supreme Court to the Court of Appeal, with further appeal in certain instances to the Judicial Committee of the Privy Council.

Supreme Court of the Bahamas: Parliament Sq., POB N-8167, Nassau; tel. 322-3315; fax 323-6895; Chief Justice JOAN SAWYER.

Court of Appeal: POB N-8167, Nassau; tel. 322-3315; fax 325-6895; Pres. JOHAQUIM C. GONZALES-SABOLA.

Magistrates' Courts: POB N-421, Nassau; tel. 325-4573; fax 323-1446; 15 magistrates and a circuit magistrate.

Registrar of the Supreme Court: ESTELLE EVANS; POB N-167, Nassau.

Attorney-General: JANET G. BOSTWICK.

Office of the Attorney-General: East Hill, POB N-3007, Nassau; tel. 322-1141; fax 322-2255; Dir of Legal Affairs RHONDA BAIN; Dir of Public Prosecutions BERNARD TURNER (acting).

Registrar-General: STERLING QUANT, POB N-532, Nassau.

Religion

Most of the population profess Christianity, but there are also small communities of Jews and Muslims.

CHRISTIANITY

According to the census of 1990, there were 79,465 Baptists (31.2% of the population), 40,894 Roman Catholics (16.0%) and 40,881 Anglicans (16.0%). Other important denominations include the Pentecostal Church (5.5%), the Church of Christ (5.0%) and the Methodists (4.8%).

Bahamas Christian Council: POB SS-4394, Nassau; tel. 393-3946; fax 394-4677; f. 1948; 27 mem. churches; Pres. Rev. SIMEON B. HALL.

The Roman Catholic Church

The Bahamas comprises the single diocese of Nassau, suffragan to the archdiocese of Kingston in Jamaica. At 31 December 1998 there were an estimated 46,922 adherents in the Bahamas. The Bishop participates in the Antilles Episcopal Conference (whose Secretariat is based in Port of Spain, Trinidad). The Turks and Caicos Islands are also under the jurisdiction of the Bishop of Nassau.

Bishop of Nassau: Rt Rev. LAWRENCE A. BURKE, The Hermitage, West St, POB N-8187, Nassau; tel. 322-8919; fax 322-2599; e-mail rcchancery@batelnet.bs.

The Anglican Communion

Anglicans in the Bahamas are adherents of the Church in the Province of the West Indies. The diocese also includes the Turks and Caicos Islands.

Archbishop of the West Indies, and Bishop of the Bahamas and the Turks and Caicos Islands: Most Rev. DREXEL GOMEZ, Bishop's Lodge, POB N-7107, Nassau; tel. 322-3015; fax 322-7943.

Other Christian Churches

Bahamas Conference of Methodist Churches: POB SS-5103, Nassau; Pres. Rev. CHARLES SWEETING.

Bahamas Conference of Seventh-day Adventists: Harrold Rd, POB N-356, Nassau; tel. 341-4021; fax 341-4088; internet www.bahamasconference.org.

Bahamas Evangelical Church Association: Carmichael Rd, POB N-1224, Nassau; tel. 362-1024.

Greek Orthodox Church: Church of the Annunciation, West St, POB N-823, Nassau; tel. 322-4382; f. 1928; part of the Archdiocese of North and South America, based in New York (USA); Priest Rev. THEOPHANIS KULYVAS.

Methodist Church Conference in the Bahamas: POB F-40021, Nassau; Superintendent Rev. RAYMOND NEILY.

Other denominations include African Methodist Episcopal, the Assemblies of Brethren, Christian Science, the Jehovah's Witnesses, the Salvation Army, Pentecostal, Presbyterian, Seventh Day Adventist, Baptist, Lutheran and Assembly of God churches.

BAHÁ'Í FAITH

Bahá'í National Spiritual Assembly: Shirley St, POB N-7105, Nassau; tel. 326-0607; e-mail nsabaha@hotmail.com.

OTHER RELIGIONS

Islam: there is a small community of Muslims in the Bahamas.

Judaism: most of the Bahamian Jewish community are based on Grand Bahama. There were 126 Jews, according to the 1990 census.

Bahamas Jewish Congregation Synagogue: POB CB-11002, Cable Beach Shopping Centre, Nassau; tel. 327-2064.

The Press

NEWSPAPERS

Bahama Journal: Media House, POB N-8610, Nassau; tel. 325-3082; fax 356-7256; internet www.love97fm.com/journal.htm; daily.

Freeport News: Cedar St, POB F-40007, Freeport; tel. 352-8321; fax 352-3449; f. 1961; daily; Gen. Man. DORLAN COLLIE; Editor ROBYN ADDERLEY; circ. 6,000.

The Nassau Guardian: 4 Carter St, Oakes Field, POB N-3011, Nassau; tel. 323-5654; fax 363-3783; internet www.thenassauguardian.com; f. 1844; daily; Gen. Man. PATRICK WALKES; Editor OSWALD BROWN; circ. 12,277.

The Punch: POB N-4081, Nassau; tel. 322-7112; fax 323-5268; twice weekly; Editor IVAN JOHNSON.

The Tribune: Shirley St, POB N-3207, Nassau; tel. 322-1986; fax 328-2398; e-mail tribune@100jamz.com; f. 1903; daily; Publr and Editor EILEEN DUPUCH CARRON; circ. 13,500.

PERIODICALS

The Bahamas Financial Digest: Miramar House, Bay and Christie Sts, POB N-4271, Nassau; tel. 356-2981; fax 356-7118; e-mail michael.symonette@batelnet.bs; f. 1973; 4 a year; business and investment; Publr and Editor MICHAEL A. SYMONETTE; circ. 15,890.

Bahamas Tourist News: Bayparl Bldg, Parliament St, POB N-4855, Nassau; tel. 322-4528; fax 322-4527; f. 1962; monthly; Editor BOBBY BOWER; circ. 360,000 (annually).

Nassau City Magazine: Miramar House, Bay and Christie Sts, POB N-4824, Nassau; tel. 356-2981; fax 326-2849.

Official Gazette: c/o Cabinet Office, POB N-7147, Nassau; tel. 322-2805; weekly; publ. by the Cabinet Office.

What's On Magazine: Woodes Rogers Wharf, POB CB-11713, Nassau; tel. 323-2323; fax 322-3428; e-mail whatson@batelnet.bs; internet www.whatsonbahamas.com; monthly; Publr NEIL ABERLE.

Publishers

Bahamas Free Press Ltd: POB CB-13309, Nassau; tel. 323-8961.

Etienne Dupuch Jr Publications Ltd: Oakes Field, POB N-7513, Nassau; tel. 323-5665; fax 323-5728; e-mail dupuch@bahamasnet.com; internet www.dupuch.com; publishes *Bahamas Handbook*, *Trailblazer* maps, *What To Do* magazines, *Welcome Bahamas*, *Tadpole* (educational colouring book) series and *Dining and Entertainment Guide*; Dirs ETIENNE DUPUCH, Jr, S. P. DUPUCH.

Media Enterprises Ltd: 31 Shirley Park Ave, POB N-9240, Nassau; tel. 325-8210; fax 325-8065; internet www.bahamasmedia.com; Publishing Dir NEIL E. SEALEY.

Printing Tours and Publishing: Miramar House, Bay and Christie Sts, POB N-4846, Nassau; tel. 356-2981; fax 356-7118.

Sacha de Frisching Publishing: POB N-7776, Nassau; tel. 362-6230; fax 362-6274; children's books.

Star Publishers Ltd: POB N-4855, Nassau; tel. 322-3724; fax 322-4537; e-mail starpub@bahamas.net.bs; internet www.supermaps.com.

Broadcasting and Communications

TELECOMMUNICATIONS

Bahamas Telecommunications Co (BaTelCo): POB N-3048, JFK Dr, Nassau; tel. 302-7000; fax 326-7474; e-mail info@batelnet.bs; internet www.batelnet.bs; state-owned; scheduled for privatization.

BROADCASTING

Radio

Broadcasting Corporation of the Bahamas: POB N-1347, Centreville, New Providence; tel. 322-4623; fax 322-3924; f. 1936; govt-owned; commercial; Chair. MICHAEL D. SMITH; Gen. Man. EDWIN LIGHTBOURNE.

Radio Bahamas: f. 1936; broadcasts 24 hours per day on four stations: the main Radio Bahamas (ZNS1), Radio New Providence (ZNS2), which are both based in Nassau, Radio Power 104.5 FM, and the Northern Service (ZNS3—Freeport; f. 1973; Station Man. ANTHONY FORSTER); Programme Man. TANYA PINDER.

Love 97 FM: East St North, POB N-3909, Nassau; tel. 356-2555.

More 95.9 FM: POB CR-54245, Nassau; tel. 361-2447; e-mail morefm94.9@batelnet.bs.

One Hundred JAMZ: Shirley and Deveaux Sts, POB N-3207, Nassau; tel. 328-4771.

Tribune Radio Ltd: Shirley and Deveaux Sts, POB N-3207, Nassau; tel. 328-4771.

Television

Broadcasting Corporation of the Bahamas: (see Radio).

Bahamas Television: f. 1977; broadcasts for Nassau, New Providence and the Central Bahamas; transmitting power of 50,000 watts; full colour; Programme Man. CARL BETHEL.

US television programmes and some satellite programmes can be received. Most islands have a cable-television service.

Finance

In recent years the Bahamas has developed into one of the world's foremost financial centres (there are no corporation, income, capital gains or withholding taxes or estate duty), and finance has become a significant feature of the economy. At June 1999 there were 416 banks and trust companies operating in the Bahamas, of which 199 had a physical presence in the islands.

BANKING

(cap. = capital; dep. = deposits; res = reserves; m. = million; brs = branches)

Central Bank

The Central Bank of the Bahamas: Frederick St, POB N-4868, Nassau; tel. 322-2193; fax 322-4321; f. 1973; bank of issue; cap. B \$3.0m., res B \$79.7m., dep. B \$146.9m. (Dec. 1998); Gov. JULIAN W. FRANCIS; Dep. Gov. WENDY CRAIG.

Development Bank

The Bahamas Development Bank: Cable Beach, West Bay St, POB N-3034, Nassau; tel. 327-5780; fax 327-5047; f. 1978 to fund approved projects and channel funds into appropriate investments; Chair. FREDERICK GOTTLIEB.

Principal Bahamian-based Banks

Bank of the Bahamas Ltd: Shirley St, POB N-7118, Nassau; tel. 326-2560; fax 325-2762; f. 1970, name changed as above in 1988, when Bank of Montreal Bahamas Ltd became jointly owned by Govt and Euro Canadian Bank; 50% owned by Govt, 50% owned by c. 4,000 Bahamian shareholders; cap. B \$10.0m., res B \$1.0m., dep. B \$172.3m. (June 1999); Chair. HUGH G. SANDS; Man. Dir P. M. ALLEN-DEAN; 8 brs.

Commonwealth Bank Ltd: 610 Bay St, POB SS-5541, Nassau; tel. 394-7373; f. 1960; Pres. WILLIAM SANDS; 8 brs.

Private Investment Bank and Trust (Bahamas) Ltd: Cumberland House, 27 Cumberland St, POB N-3918, Nassau; tel. 326-0282; fax 326-5213; f. 1984 as Bank Worms and Co International Ltd; renamed in 1990, 1996 and 1998; cap. US \$3.0m., res US \$1.8m., dep. US \$247.7m. (Dec. 1997); Chair. and Dir FRANÇOIS ROUGE.

Principal Foreign Banks

Banco Internacional de Costa Rica Ltd: Bank Lane, POB N-7768, Nassau; fax 326-5020; e-mail bicsacr@sol.racsa.co.cr; internet www.bisca.com; f. 1976; 55% owned by Banco Nacional de Costa Rica, 20% owned by Banco de Costa Rica, 10% owned by Banco Crédito de Agrícola de Cartago; Chair. ALFONSO GUARDIA M.; CEO THELMO VARGAS M.

Bank of Nova Scotia International Ltd (Canada): Scotiabank Bldg, Rawson Sq., POB N-7518, Nassau; tel. 322-1071; fax 322-7989; Vice-Pres. and Man. A. C. ALLEN; 13 brs.

Barclays Bank PLC (United Kingdom): Charlotte House, Shirley St, POB N-3221, Nassau; tel. 325-7384; fax 322-8267; internet www.bahamas.barclays.com; Dir SHARON BROWN.

BNP Paribas (Bahamas) Ltd: Beaumont House, 3rd Floor, Bay St, POB N-4883, Nassau; tel. 326-5935; fax 3265871; internet www.bnpgroup.com; Man. Dir ANDRÉ LAMOTHE.

BSI Overseas (Bahamas) Ltd (Italy): UBS House, East Bay St, POB N-7130, Nassau; tel. 394-9200; fax 394-9220; f. 1990; wholly-

owned subsid. of Banca della Svizzera Italiana; cap. US \$10.0m., res US \$44.1m., dep. US \$1,121.9m. (Dec. 1998); Chair. Dr A. GYSI; Man. IVOR J. HERRINGTON.

Canadian Imperial Bank of Commerce (CIBC) (Canada): 4th Floor, 308 East Bay St, POB N-8329, Nassau; tel. 393-4710; fax 393-4280; internet www.cibc.com; Area Man. TERRY HILTS; 9 brs.

Citibank NA (USA): Citibank Bldg, Thompson Blvd, Oakes Field, POB N-8158, Nassau; tel. 322-8510; fax 302-8555; internet www.citibank.com; Gen. Man. ALISON JOHNSTON; 2 brs.

Credit Suisse (Bahamas) Ltd (Switzerland): Bahamas Financial Centre, Shirley and Charlotte Sts, POB N-4928, Nassau; tel. 356-8100; fax 326-6589; f. 1968; subsidiary of Credit Suisse Zurich; portfolio and asset management, offshore company management, trustee services; cap. US \$12.0m., res US \$20.0m., dep. US \$500.7m. (Dec. 1997); Man. Dir GREGOR MAISSEN.

Handelsfinanz-CCF Bank International Ltd (Switzerland): Third Floor, Maritime House, Frederick St, POB N-10441, Nassau; tel. 328-8644; fax 328-8600; f. 1971; cap. US \$5.0m., res US \$11.5m., dep. US \$544.8m. (Dec. 1998); Pres. and Gen. Man. FERDINANDO M. MENCONI.

Lloyds TSB Bank International (Bahamas) Ltd (United Kingdom): Bolam House, King and George Sts, POB N-4843, Nassau; tel. 302-3000; fax 322-8719; f. 1977; cap. US \$15.0m., dep. US \$305.1 (Dec. 1998); Principal Man. and Dir DAVID G. NICOLL.

National Bank of Canada (International) Ltd: Charlotte House, Charlotte St, POB N-3015, Nassau; tel. 322-4024; fax 323-8086; e-mail nabkint@batelnet.bs; f. 1978; 100% owned by Natcan Holdings International Ltd; Gen. Man. JACQUES LATENDRESSE.

Overseas Union Bank and Trust (Bahamas) Ltd (Switzerland): 250 Bay St, POB N-8184, Nassau; tel. 322-2476; fax 323-8771; f. 1980; cap. US \$5.0m., res US \$6.2m., dep. US \$97.9m. (Dec. 1997); Chair. Dr CARLO SGANZINI; Gen. Man. URS FREI.

Pictet Bank and Trust Ltd (Switzerland): Charlotte House, Charlotte St, POB N-4837, Nassau; tel. 322-3938; fax 323-7986; e-mail pbtbah@bahamas.net.bs; internet www.pictet.com/nassau.htm; f. 1978; cap. US \$1.0m., dep. US \$10.0m., dep. US \$126.2m. (Dec. 1995); Chair. and Dir CLAUDE DEMOLE.

Royal Bank of Canada Ltd (Canada): 323 Bay St, POB N-7537, Nassau; tel. 322-8700; fax 323-6381; internet www.royalbank.com; Vice-Pres. MICHAEL F. PHELAN; 16 brs.

Royal Bank of Scotland (Nassau) Ltd (United Kingdom): 3rd Floor, Bahamas Financial Centre, Shirley and Charlotte Sts, POB N-3045, Nassau; tel. 322-4643; fax 326-7559; e-mail info@rbsint.bs; f. 1951 as E. D. Sassoon Bank and Trust Ltd, name changed 1978, 1986 and 1989; cap. US \$2.0m., res US \$7.3m., dep. US 289.5m. (Sept. 1998); Chair. JAMES D. PATON; CEO DAVID BARRON.

UBS (Bahamas) Ltd (Switzerland): Swiss Bank House, East Bay St, POB N-7757, Nassau; tel. 394-9300; fax 394-9333; f. 1968 as Swiss Bank Corpn (Overseas) Ltd, name changed as above 1998; cap. US \$4.0m., dep. US \$420.2m. (Dec. 1997); Chair. ERNST BALSIGER; Exec. Dir and Pres. PHILIP WHITE.

Principal Bahamian Trust Companies

Ansbacher (Bahamas) Ltd: Ansbacher House, Bank Lane, POB N-7768, Nassau; tel. 322-1161; fax 326-5020; e-mail ansbbah@batelnet.bs; incorporated 1957 as Bahamas International Trust Co Ltd, name changed 1994; cap. B \$1.0m., res B \$9.7m., dep. B \$190.3m. (Sept. 1998); Man. Dir DAVID L. E. FAWKES.

Bank of Nova Scotia Trust Company (Bahamas) Ltd: POB N-3016, Nassau; tel. 356-1500; fax 326-0991; e-mail scotiatr@100jamz.com; wholly owned by the Bank of Nova Scotia International Ltd.

Chase Manhattan Trust Corpn: Shirley and Charlotte Sts, POB N-3708, Nassau; tel. 356-1305; fax 325-1706; Gen. Man. KEN BROWN; 4 brs.

Leadenhall Bank and Trust Co Ltd: IBM Bldg, Bay St at Church St, POB N-1965, Nassau; tel. 325-5508; fax 328-7030; e-mail drounce@leadentrust.com; f. 1976; Man. Dir DAVID J. ROUNCE.

MeesPierson (Bahamas) Ltd: POB SS-5539, Nassau; tel. 393-8777; fax 393-0582; internet www.mpbahamas.com; f. 1987; subsidiary of MeesPierson International AG of Zug, Switzerland; Chair. IAN D. FAIR; Gen. Man. RONALD J. A. DE GRAAF.

Oceanic Bank and Trust: Euro Canadian Centre, POB N-8327, Nassau; tel. 322-7461; fax 326-6177; f. 1969.

Winterbotham Trust Co Ltd: Bolam House, King and George Sts, POB N-3026, Nassau; tel. 356-5454; fax 356-9432; e-mail nassau@winterbotham.com; internet www.winterbotham.com; cap. US \$3.8m.; CEO GEOFFREY HOOPER; 2 brs.

Bankers' Organizations

Association of International Banks and Trust Companies in the Bahamas: POB N-7880, Nassau; tel. 394-6755; Chair. BRUCE BELL.

Bahamas Institute of Bankers: Royal Palm Mall, Mackey St, POB N-3202, Nassau; tel. 393-0456; fax 394-3503; Pres. KIM BODIE.

INSURANCE

The leading British and a number of US, Canadian and Caribbean companies have agents in Nassau and Freeport. Local insurance companies include the following:

Allied Bahamas Insurance Co Ltd: 93 Collins Ave, POB N-121, Nassau; tel. 326-3537; fax 356-2192; general, aviation and marine.

Bahamas First General Insurance Co Ltd: 93 Collins Ave, POB N-1216, Nassau; tel. 326-5439; fax 326-5472.

Colina Insurance Co Ltd: 12 Village Rd, POB N-4728, Nassau; tel. 393-2224; fax 393-1710.

The Family Guardian Insurance Co Ltd: East Bay St, POB SS-6232, Nassau; tel. 393-1023; f. 1965.

Association

Bahamas General Insurance Association: POB N-860, Nassau; tel. 323-2596; fax 328-4354; Acting Co-ordinator DAVID KLEAN.

Trade and Industry

DEVELOPMENT ORGANIZATIONS

Bahamas Agricultural and Industrial Corpn (BAIC): BAIC Bldg, East Bay St, POB N-4940, Nassau; tel. 322-3740; fax 322-2123; f. 1981 as an amalgamation of Bahamas Development Corpn and Bahamas Agricultural Corpn for the promotion of greater co-operation between tourism and other sectors of the economy through the development of small- and medium-sized enterprises; Exec. Chair. ALVIN SMITH.

Bahamas Investment Authority: Cecil V. Wallace-Whitfield Centre, POB CB-10980, Nassau; tel. 327-5970; fax 327-5907; Exec. Dir BASIL H. ALBURY.

Bahamas Light Industries Development Council: POB SS-5599, Nassau; tel. 394-1907; Pres. LESLIE MILLER.

Nassau Paradise Island Promotion Board: Dean's Lane, Fort Charlotte, POB N-7799, Nassau; tel. 322-8381; fax 325-8998; f. 1970; Chair. GEORGE R. MYERS; Sec. MICHAEL C. RECKLEY; 30 mems.

CHAMBER OF COMMERCE

Bahamas Chamber of Commerce: Shirley St, POB N-665, Nassau; tel. 322-2145; fax 322-4649; f. 1935 to promote, foster and protect trade, industry and commerce; Pres. A. BISMARK COAKLEY; Exec. Dir RUBY L. SWEETING; 450 mems.

EMPLOYERS' ASSOCIATIONS

Bahamas Association of Land Surveyors: POB N-10147, Nassau; tel. 322-4569; Pres. DONALD THOMPSON; Vice-Pres. GODFREY HUMES; 30 mems.

Bahamas Boatmen's Association: POB ES-5212, Nassau; f. 1974; Pres. and Sec. FREDERICK GOMEZ.

Bahamas Contractors' Association: POB N-8049, Nassau; Pres. BRENDON C. WATSON; Sec. EMMANUEL ALEXIOU.

Bahamas Employers' Confederation: POB N-166, Nassau; tel. 393-5613; fax 322-4649; f. 1963; Pres. REGINALD LOBOSKY.

Bahamas Hotel Employers' Association: Dean's Lane, Fort Charlotte, POB N-7799, Nassau; tel. 322-2262; fax 325-8998; f. 1958; Pres. J. BARRIE FARRINGTON; Exec. Dir MICHAEL C. RECKLEY; 26 mems.

Bahamas Institute of Chartered Accountants: Star Plaza, Mackey St, POB N-7037, Nassau; tel. 394-3439; fax 394-3629; f. 1971; Pres. L. EDGAR MOXEY.

Bahamas Institute of Professional Engineers: Nassau; tel. 322-3356; fax 323-8503; Pres. ANTHONY DEAN.

Bahamas Motor Dealers' Association: POB N-3919, Nassau; tel. 328-7671; fax 328-1922; Pres. HARRY ROBERTS.

Bahamas Real Estate Association: Bahamas Chamber Bldg, POB N-8860, Nassau; tel. 325-4942; fax 322-4649; Pres. PATRICK STRACHAN.

UTILITIES

Electricity

The Bahamas Electricity Corpn (BEC): Pond and Tucker Rd, POB N-7509, Nassau; tel. 325-4101; fax 323-6852; state-owned; scheduled for privatization; provides 70% of the islands' power-generating capacity.

Freeport Power and Light Co Ltd: Mercantile Bldg, Cedar St, POB F-888, Freeport; f. 1962; tel. 352-6611; privately-owned; Pres. ALBERT J. MILLER.

Gas

Caribbean Gas Storage and Terminal Ltd: POB N-9665, Nassau; tel. 327-5587; fax 362-5006; e-mail info@caribbeangas.com; internet www.caribbeangas.com; f. 1992.

Tropigas: Nassau; tel. 322-2404.

Water

Bahamas Water and Sewerage Corpn: 87 Thompson Blvd, POB N-3905, Nassau; tel. 302-5500; fax 356-7152; e-mail wcexcoff@batelnet.bs; internet www.wsc.com.bs; Chair. MICHAEL L. BARNETT.

TRADE UNIONS

All Bahamian unions are members of one of the following:

National Congress of Trade Unions: Horseshoe Drive, POB GT-2887, Nassau; tel. 356-7457; Pres. LEROY HANNA; 20,000 mems.

Trade Union Congress: Warwick St, Nassau; tel. 394-6301; fax 394-7401; Pres. OBIE FERGUSON; 12,500 mems.

The main unions are as follows:

Bahamas Airport and Allied Workers' Union: Workers House, Harrold Rd, POB N-3364, Nassau; tel. 323-5030; f. 1958; Pres. FRANKLYN CARTER; Gen. Sec. PATRICE TYNES-RODGERS; 550 mems.

Bahamas Brewery, Distillers and Allied Workers' Union: Nassau; f. 1968; Pres. BRADICK CLEARE; Gen. Sec. DAVID KEMP; 140 mems.

Bahamas Communications and Public Officers' Union: Farrington Rd, POB N-3190, Nassau; tel. 322-1537; fax 323-8719; e-mail prebcpou@batelnet.bs; f. 1973; Pres. D. SHANE GIBSON; Sec.-Gen. ROBERT A. FARQUHARSON; 2,100 mems.

Bahamas Doctors' Union: Nassau; Pres. Dr EUGENE NEWERY; Gen. Sec. GEORGE SHERMAN.

Bahamas Electrical Workers' Union: East West Highway, POB GT-2535, Nassau; tel. 393-1431; Pres. SAMUEL MITCHELL; Gen. Sec. JONATHAN CAMBRIDGE.

Bahamas Hotel Catering and Allied Workers' Union: POB GT-2514, Nassau; tel. 323-5933; fax 325-6546; f. 1958; Pres. THOMAS BASTIAN; Gen. Sec. LEO DOUGLAS; 6,500 mems.

Bahamas Maritime Port and Allied Workers' Union: POB SS-6501, Nassau; tel. 328-7502; Pres. ANTHONY WILLIAMS; Sec.-Gen. FREDERICK N. RODGERS.

Bahamas Musicians' and Entertainers' Union: Horseshoe Drive, POB N-880, Nassau; tel. 322-3734; fax 323-3537; f. 1958; Pres. LEROY (DUKE) HANNA; Gen. Sec. PORTIA NOTTAGE; 410 mems.

Bahamas Public Services Union: Wulff Rd, POB N-4692, Nassau; tel. 325-0038; fax 323-5287; f. 1959; Pres. WILLIAM McDONALD; Sec.-Gen. SYNIDA DORSETT; 4,247 mems.

Bahamas Taxi-Cab Union: POB N-1077, Nassau; tel. 323-5952; Pres. FELIX ROLLE (acting); Gen. Sec. ROSCOE WEECH.

Bahamas Union of Teachers: 104 Bethel Ave, Stapledon Gardens, POB N-3482, Nassau; tel. 323-7085; fax 323-7086; f. 1945; Pres. KINGSLEY BLACK; Gen. Sec. HELENA CARTWRIGHT; 2,600 mems.

Eastside Stevedores' Union: POB N-1176, Nassau; f. 1972; Pres. SALATHIEL MACKEY; Gen. Sec. CURTIS TURNQUEST.

Grand Bahama Construction, Refinery and Maintenance Workers' Union: 33A Kipling Bldg, POB F-839, Freeport; tel. 352-7438; f. 1971; Pres. JAMES TAYLOR; Gen. Sec. EPHRAIM BLACK.

United Brotherhood of Longshoremen's Union: Wulff Rd, POB N-7317, Nassau; f. 1959; Pres. J. McKINNEY; Gen. Sec. W. SWANN; 157 mems.

Transport

ROADS

There are about 966 km (600 miles) of roads in New Providence and 1,368 km (850 miles) in the Family Islands, mainly on Grand Bahama, Cat Island, Eleuthera, Exuma and Long Island.

SHIPPING

The principal seaport is at Nassau (New Providence), which can accommodate the very largest cruise ships. Passenger arrivals exceed two million annually. The other main ports are at Freeport (Grand Bahama), where a container terminal opened in 1997, and Matthew Town (Inagua). There are also modern berthing facilities for cruise ships at Potters Cay (New Providence), Governor's Harbour (Eleuthera), Morgan's Bluff (North Andros) and George Town (Exuma).

The Bahamas converted to free-flag status in 1976, and by 1983 possessed the world's third-largest open-registry fleet. The fleet's displacement was 27,715,783 grt in December 1998 (the third-largest national fleet in the world).

There is a weekly cargo and passenger service to all the Family Islands.

Bahamas Maritime Authority: POB N-4679, Nassau; tel. 394-5022; fax 394-5023; f. 1995; promotes ship registration and co-ordinates maritime administration.

Freeport Harbour Co Ltd: POB F-42465, Freeport; tel. 352-9651; fax 352-6888; e-mail fhcol@batelnet.bs; Gen. Man. MICHAEL J. POWER.

Nassau Port Authority: Prince George Wharf, POB N-8175, Nassau; tel. 356-7354; fax 322-5545; regulates principal port of the Bahamas; Port Dir ANTHONY ALLENS.

Principal Shipping Companies

Cavalier Shipping: Arawak Cay, POB N-8170, New Providence; tel. 328-3035.

Dockendale Shipping Co Ltd: Dockendale House, West Bay Street, POB N-10455, Nassau; tel. 325-0448; fax 328-1542; e-mail dockship@dockendale.com; f. 1973; ship management; Man. Dir L. J. FERNANDES; Tech. Dir K. VALLURI.

Eleuthera Express Shipping Co: POB N-4201, Nassau.

Grand Master Shipping Co: POB N-4208, Nassau.

Grenville Ventures Ltd: 43 Elizabeth Ave, POB CB-13022, Nassau.

HJH Trading Co Ltd: POB N-4402, Nassau; tel. 392-3939; fax 392-1828.

Gladstone Patton: POB SS-5178, Nassau.

Pioneer Shipping Ltd: Union Wharf, POB N-3044, Nassau; tel. 325-7889; fax 325-2214.

Teekay Shipping Corporation: TK House, Bayside Executive Park, West Bay St & Blake Rd, POB AP-59213, Nassau; tel. 502-8820; fax 502-8840; internet www.teekay.com; Pres. and CEO BJORN MOLLER.

Tropical Shipping Co Ltd: POB N-8183, Nassau; tel. 322-1012; fax 323-7566.

United Shipping Co Ltd: POB F-42552, Freeport; tel. 352-9315; fax 352-4034; e-mail info@unitedship.com; internet www.unitedship.com.

CIVIL AVIATION

Nassau International Airport (15 km (9 miles) outside the capital) and Freeport International Airport (5 km (3 miles) outside the city, on Grand Bahama) are the main terminals for international and internal services. There are also important airports at West End (Grand Bahama) and Rock Sound (Eleuthera) and some 50 smaller airports and landing strips throughout the islands.

Bahamasair Holdings Ltd: Coral Harbour Rd, POB N-4881, Nassau; tel. 377-8451; fax 377-8550; e-mail astuart@bahamas air.com; internet www.bahamasair.com; f. 1973; scheduled services between Nassau, Freeport, destinations within the USA and 20 locations within the Family Islands; Chair. ANTHONY MILLER; Man. Dir PAT ROLLE (acting).

Tourism

The mild climate and beautiful beaches attract many tourists. In 1998 tourist arrivals decreased by 9.3%, compared with the previous year, to 3,655,839 (including 2,281,887 by sea) in 1999. The majority of stop-over arrivals (81% in 1997) were from the USA. Receipts from the tourist industry decreased by 0.6% in 1998, compared with the previous year, to B $1,408m. In September 1999 there were 223 hotels in the country, with a total of 14,080 rooms.

Ministry of Tourism and Aviation: Bay St, POB N-3701, Nassau; tel. 322-7500; fax 328-0945; internet www.bahamas.com; Dir-Gen. VINCENT VANDERPOOL-WALLACE.

Bahamas Hotel Association: Dean's Lane, Fort Charlotte, POB N-7799, Nassau; tel. 322-8381; fax 326-5346; e-mail bhainfo@batelnet.bs; Exec. Vice-Pres. BASIL H. SMITH.

Bahamas Tourism and Development Authority: POB SS-5256, Nassau; tel. 394-3575; Exec. Dir DIANE PHILLIPS.

Hotel Corporation of the Bahamas: West Bay St, POB N-9520, Nassau; tel. 327-8395; fax 327-6978; Chair. GEOFFREY JOHNSTONE; Chief Exec. WARREN ROLLE.

BAHRAIN

Introductory Survey

Location, Climate, Language, Religion, Flag, Capital

The State of Bahrain consists of a group of about 35 islands, situated midway along the Persian (Arabian) Gulf, approximately 24 km (15 miles) from the east coast of Saudi Arabia (to which it is linked by a causeway), and 28 km (17 miles) from the west coast of Qatar. There are six principal islands in the archipelago, the largest of these being Bahrain itself, which is about 50 km (30 miles) long, and between 13 km and 25 km (8 miles and 15 miles) wide. To the north-east of Bahrain island, and linked to it by a causeway and road, lies Muharraq island, which is approximately 6 km (4 miles) long. Another causeway links Bahrain with Sitra island. The climate is temperate from December to the end of March, with temperatures ranging from 19°C (66°F) to 25°C (77°F), but becomes very hot and humid during the summer months. In August and September temperatures can rise to 40°C (104°F). The official language is Arabic, but English is also widely spoken. Almost all Bahraini citizens are Muslims, divided into two sects: Shi'ites (almost 60%) and Sunnis (more than 40%). Non-Bahrainis comprised 39.2% of the total population at mid-1998. The national flag (proportions 5 by 3) is red, with a vertical white stripe at the hoist, the two colours being separated by a straight or (more frequently) serrated line. The capital is Manama.

Recent History

Bahrain, a traditional Arab monarchy, became a British Protected State in the 19th century. Under this arrangement, government was shared between the ruling Sheikh and his British adviser. Following a series of territorial disputes in the 19th century, Persia (now Iran) made renewed claims to Bahrain in 1928. This disagreement remained unresolved until May 1970, when Iran accepted the findings of a UN-commissioned report showing that the inhabitants of Bahrain overwhelmingly favoured complete independence, rather than union with Iran.

During the reign of Sheikh Sulman bin Hamad al-Khalifa, who became ruler of Bahrain in 1942, social services and public works were considerably expanded. Sheikh Sulman was succeeded upon his death in November 1961 by his eldest son, Sheikh Isa bin Sulman al-Khalifa. Extensive administrative and political reforms were implemented in January 1970, when a supreme executive authority, the 12-member Council of State, was established, representing the first formal derogation of the ruler's powers. Sheikh Khalifa bin Sulman al-Khalifa, the ruler's eldest brother, was appointed President of the Council.

Meanwhile, in January 1968 the United Kingdom had announced its intention to withdraw British military forces from the area by 1971. In March 1968 Bahrain joined the nearby territories of Qatar and the Trucial States (now the United Arab Emirates—UAE), which were also under British protection, in the Federation of Arab Emirates. It was intended that the Federation should become fully independent, but the interests of Bahrain and Qatar proved to be incompatible with those of the smaller sheikhdoms, and both seceded from the Federation. Bahrain thus became a separate independent state on 15 August 1971, when a new treaty of friendship was signed with the United Kingdom. Sheikh Isa took the title of Amir, while the Council of State became the Cabinet, with Sheikh Khalifa as Prime Minister. A Constituent Assembly, convened in December 1972, formulated a new Constitution providing for a National Assembly to be comprised of 14 cabinet ministers and 30 elected members. The Constitution came into force on 6 December 1973, and elections to the new Assembly were conducted the following day. In the absence of political parties, candidates sought election as independents. In August 1975 the Prime Minister submitted his resignation, complaining that the National Assembly was obstructing the Government's initiatives for new legislation, particularly regarding national security. However, Sheikh Khalifa was reappointed and, at his request, the Assembly was dissolved by Amiri decree. New elections were to be held following minor changes to the Constitution and to the electoral law, but there were few subsequent signs that the National Assembly would be reconvened.

In March 1981 Bahrain was one of the six founder members of the Co-operation Council for the Arab States of the Gulf (more generally known as the Gulf Co-operation Council—GCC, see p. 160), which was established in order to co-ordinate defence strategy and to promote freer trading and co-operative economic protection among Gulf states.

With no elected legislative body, the ruling family exercises near-absolute power. On 16 January 1993 a 30-member Consultative Council—appointed by the ruling authorities and comprising a large number of business executives and some members of the old National Assembly—held its inaugural meeting. The Council acts in a purely advisory capacity, with no legislative powers.

For many years there have been indications of tension between Shi'a Muslims, who form a slender majority in Bahrain (and many of whom are of Iranian descent), and the dominant Sunni Muslims, the sect to which the ruling family belongs. During the 1980s two plots to overthrow the Government, one of which was alleged to have Iranian support, were uncovered, as was a plan to sabotage Bahrain's petroleum installations, which was also widely reported to have received the backing of Iran. In December 1993 a prominent human rights organization, Amnesty International, published a report criticizing the Bahraini Government's treatment of Shi'ite Muslims, some of whom had been forcibly exiled. In March 1994, apparently in response to this criticism, the Amir issued a decree pardoning 64 Bahrainis who had been in exile since the 1980s and permitting them to return to Bahrain. In December 1994 Sheikh Ali Salman Ahmad Salman, a Muslim cleric, was arrested following his criticism of the Government and his public appeal for reform, particularly the restoration of the National Assembly. Widespread rioting ensued throughout Bahrain, especially in Shi'ite districts, and large-scale demonstrations were held in Manama in support of Sheikh Salman's demands and to petition for his release. Civil unrest continued despite the Amir's pledge, in mid-December, to extend the powers of the Consultative Council; 12 people died and some 2,500 demonstrators were arrested during clashes with the security forces in December and early January 1995. Sheikh Salman sought asylum in the United Kingdom, following his deportation in January. The unprecedented scale of the protests was widely attributed to a marked deterioration in socio-economic conditions in Bahrain, and in particular to a high level of unemployment.

Anti-Government demonstrations erupted in Shi'ite districts in late March 1995, and again in April, following a police search of the property of an influential Shi'ite cleric, Sheikh Abd al-Amir al-Jamri, who was subsequently placed under house arrest and later imprisoned. In mid-April, after Bahrain convened a meeting between interior ministers of GCC member states, the GCC Governments issued a statement supporting the measures adopted by Bahrain to quell civil disturbances. In May and July several people received custodial sentences, ranging from one year's detention to life imprisonment, for damaging public installations, and one Bahraini was sentenced to death for the murder of a police-officer in March. In June, in an apparent attempt to appease Shi'ite opposition leaders, the Prime Minister announced the first major cabinet reshuffle for 20 years. However, the strategic portfolios of the interior, defence, finance and national economy, and foreign affairs remained unchanged.

In August 1995 the Government initiated talks with Shi'ite opposition leaders in an effort to foster reconciliation. In the same month the Amir issued a decree pardoning 150 people detained since the unrest. However, a report issued by Amnesty International in September indicated that as many as 1,500 demonstrators remained in detention in Bahrain, and that two prisoners (including a young student) had died in police custody following torture. In mid-September talks between the Government and opposition leaders collapsed. None the less, more than 40 political prisoners were released from detention later in the month, including Sheikh al-Jamri. In late October al-Jamri and six other opposition figures began a hunger strike in protest at the Government's refusal to concede to their demands, which included the release of all political prisoners and the restoration of the National Assembly. In early November, following a large demonstration to mark the end of the hunger strike, the Government announced that it would take 'necessary action' to prevent future 'illegal' gatherings. In December the Amir declared an amnesty for nearly 150 prisoners, mostly people arrested during the disturbances earlier in the year. There were large-scale demonstrations in late December and in early January 1996, in protest at the heavy deployment of security forces in Shi'ite districts and at the closure of two mosques. Opposition activists strongly criticized the use of tear-gas and plastic bullets to disperse protesters, and also suggested that Saudi Arabian and Indian security officers had been dispatched to reinforce the Bahrain police. In mid-January eight opposition leaders, including Sheikh al-Jamri, were arrested on charges of inciting unrest. In early February Ahmad ash-Shamlan, a noted lawyer and writer, became the first prominent Sunni to be detained in connection with the disturbances, following his distribution of a statement criticizing the Government's authoritarianism. A number of bomb explosions in February and early March culminated in an arson attack on a restaurant in Sitra, in which seven Bangladeshi workers died. Also in March, jurisdiction with regard to a number of criminal offences was transferred from ordinary courts to the High Court of Appeal, acting in the capacity of State Security Court. This move effectively accelerated court proceedings, while removing the right of appeal and limiting the role of the defence. In late March Isa Ahmad Hassan Qambar was executed by firing squad, having been condemned to death for killing a policeman during clashes with security forces in March 1995 (see above). The execution, which was the first to take place in Bahrain since 1977, provoked massive popular protests, while international human rights organizations challenged the validity of Qambar's confession and trial.

Civil disturbances continued during 1996, and tensions were exacerbated by the Government's announcement, in April, of the creation of a Higher Council of Islamic Affairs (to be appointed by the Prime Minister and headed by the Minister of Justice and Islamic Affairs) to supervise all religious activity (including that of the Shi'ite community) in Bahrain. In June, however, the Amir sought to appease the demands of opposition reformers by announcing the future expansion of the Consultative Council from 30 to 40 members: a new 40-member Council was duly appointed by the Amir in late September. In July the State Security Court imposed death sentences on three of the eight Bahrainis convicted of the arson attack in Sitra, while four men were sentenced to life imprisonment. The death sentences provoked widespread domestic protests and international criticism. In response the Government agreed to allow an appeal against the ruling. In October the Court of Cassation ruled that it had no jurisdiction to overturn the verdict, and the fate of the three men seemed likely to be decided by the Amir. Towards the end of the year government plans to close a number of Shi'ite mosques resulted in further disturbances. Demonstrators gathered at the Ras Roman mosque in central Manama became involved in a violent confrontation with the security forces, during which police fired tear-gas on worshippers. The continuing unrest in December and in early 1997 prompted rumours of division within the ruling family concerning the use of force in response to the crisis. In January 1997 a National Guard was created, to provide support for the Bahraini Defence Force and the security forces of the Ministry of the Interior. The Amir's son, Hamad, was appointed to command the new force, prompting speculation that its primary duty would be to protect the ruling family. In March a week of anti-Government protests marked the first anniversary of the execution of Isa Ahmad Hassan Qambar. It was reported that since the outbreak of civil unrest at the end of 1994, some 28 people had been killed and 220 imprisoned in connection with the protests. In July and August 1997 two human rights groups produced reports criticizing the Bahrain police for allegedly making arbitrary arrests, using torture, and arresting children as young as seven years of age. The Government rejected these reports, claiming that they were based on dishonest sources. It did, however, appear to respond to the allegations when, in November, the trial *in absentia* of eight prominent exiled activists (including Sheikh Ali Salman Ahmad Salman) resulted in the imposition of prison sentences of between five and 15 years. Although the activists claimed not to have been summoned to stand trial, their sentences were considered lenient in view of the severity of the offences with which they were charged, which included attempting to overthrow the regime. In addition, during 1997 publishing restrictions were relaxed, and in December the Amir

announced plans to enlarge further the Consultative Council and to allow greater media coverage of its activities. In February 1998 opposition groups welcomed the appointment of Khalid bin Muhammad al-Khalifa as the new head of the State Security Investigation Directorate (the previous, long-serving, incumbent was not a Bahraini national) and urged the continuing 'Bahrainization' of the security apparatus as a precondition for the initiation of dialogue between the regime and the opposition.

Sheikh Isa died on 6 March 1999. He was succeeded as Amir by his son, Crown Prince Sheikh Hamad bin Isa al-Khalifa, hitherto Commander-in-Chief of the Bahrain Defence Force and National Guard; Sheikh Hamad's eldest son, Sheikh Salman bin Hamad al-Khalifa, became Crown Prince and also assumed his father's military command. Initially, opposition groups welcomed Sheikh Hamad's accession, which raised expectations of political change. In his first months in office Sheikh Hamad permitted Shi'ites to join the armed forces, allowed an investigation by Amnesty International into alleged brutality by the Sunni security forces, and released more than 300 Shi'ite prisoners being held on security-related charges. However, the opposition claimed that 1,200–1,500 political prisoners remained in detention and Sheikh Hamad failed to initiate prompt negotiations to end political unrest. At the end of May he announced a cabinet reorganization in which three new ministers were appointed, including the former Governor of the Bahrain Monetary Agency, Abdullah Hassan Saif, as Minister of Finance. Few significant changes were otherwise effected, and, despite evident tension in relations between the new Amir and the uncompromising Sheikh Khalifa, the Prime Minister retained his position. In July Sheikh al-Jamri, who was brought to trial in February, having been detained since 1996 under the terms of the State Security Act (which allows the imprisonment of suspects without trial for a period of up to three years), was sentenced to 10 years' imprisonment for spying and inciting anti-Government unrest; a substantial fine was also imposed. Following intense international pressure Sheikh Hamad granted him an official pardon the following day, although Sheikh al-Jamri was first required to read a public apology to the Amir on national television. In August 1999 Bahrain's longest-serving political prisoner, As-Sayed Jafar al-Alawi, was released from detention; he was one of 72 people convicted in 1981 for plotting against the Government, and had been sentenced to 25 years' imprisonment. The Amir ordered the release of 150 detainees in November, and of a further 195 in December. In October, meanwhile, Sheikh Hamad issued a decree ordering the Consultative Council to establish a human rights committee. None the less, Amnesty International asserted in November 2000 that while the human rights situation in Bahrain had improved since 1998 (the organization cited the release of hundreds of prisoners, the creation of the human rights body and ratification, in March 1998, of the UN Convention against Torture and Other Cruel, Inhuman or Degrading Treatment or Punishment), the mechanisms that had facilitated past human rights violations remained in place.

In December 1999 the Amir declared his intention to hold elections for municipal councils, on the basis of universal suffrage. In late May 2000 the Prime Minister stated that municipal elections would be held in early 2001 and that parliamentary elections would take place in 2004. At the end of September 2000 four women, as well as a number of non-Muslims, were, for the first time, appointed to the Consultative Council; this was interpreted by some observers as an initial step towards fuller popular representation in Bahrain. The Amir announced in November that a Supreme National Committee had been formed to prepare what was termed a Charter of National Action, which would outline the further evolution of Bahrain's political system. However, there were unconfirmed reports in early December that five political activists, most of whom were said to be Shi'ites, had withdrawn from the 46-member committee. The committee's recommendations, submitted later in the month, were that there should be a transition from an emirate to a monarchy, with a bicameral parliament; direct elections would be held to the legislative body, with women permitted both to vote and to seek election, while a consultative chamber would be appointed by the Government from all sections of society. Critics of the Bahrain regime dismissed the proposed transition to a constitutional monarchy as a pretext for the continuation of autocratic rule. The Charter was approved at a national referendum held on 14–15 February 2001. A Supreme Council for Economic Development was, meanwhile, established in April 2000, under the chairmanship of the Prime Minister.

Although relations between Bahrain and Iran were upgraded to ambassadorial level in late 1990, the situation between the two countries began to deteriorate in the mid-1990s. While there was sufficient evidence to suggest largely domestic motivation for the recent increase in popular disaffection, the Bahraini authorities continued to imply that the disturbances were fomented by Iranian-backed militant Shi'ite fundamentalists seeking to destabilize the country. These allegations were frequently dismissed by Iran. In June 1996 the Bahraini Government announced that it had uncovered details of a plot, initiated in 1993 with support from fundamentalist Shi'ite groups in Iran, to oust the Government and ruling family in Bahrain and replace them with a pro-Iran administration. It was claimed that a previously unknown Shi'ite group, Hezbollah Bahrain, had been established and financed by Iran's Revolutionary Guard. Young Bahraini Shi'ites were alleged to have received military training in Iran and at guerrilla bases in Lebanon, in preparation for a terrorist offensive in Bahrain, which had culminated in the disturbances of the previous 18 months. Within days of the Government's announcement more than 50 Bahrainis had been arrested in connection with the alleged plot. Many of the detainees, including six who made televised confessions, admitted membership of Hezbollah Bahrain. The Iranian authorities denied any involvement in the planned insurrection, but bilateral relations were severely undermined by the unprecedented directness of the Bahrain Government's accusations; the two countries' respective ambassadors were withdrawn, and diplomatic relations were downgraded. During June more than 30 Bahrainis received prison sentences of between one and 13 years—for offences connected to the disturbances—from the State Security Court (and were therefore denied the right of appeal). In March 1997 59 Bahraini Shi'ites accused of belonging to Hezbollah Bahrain were brought to trial; similar charges had been made against a further 22 Shi'ites who, according to the Bahrain Government, were to be tried *in absentia*. The State Security Court sentenced 37 of the defendants to terms of imprisonment ranging from three to 15 years, and acquitted the others. There was a period of *détente* in relations between most countries of the GCC and Iran following the election of Muhammad Khatami to the Iranian presidency in May of that year, and in December 1999 relations at ambassadorial level were formally restored between Bahrain and Iran. In late March 2000 the Ministers of Foreign Affairs of the two countries met in Manama to discuss regional security as well as political and economic co-operation; a bilateral economic commission held its first meeting in that month.

In common with other Gulf states, Bahrain consistently expressed support for Iraq at the time of the Iran–Iraq war (1980–88). However, following the Iraqi invasion of Kuwait in August 1990, Bahrain firmly supported the implementation of UN economic sanctions against Iraq and permitted the stationing of US troops and combat aircraft in Bahrain. (Military co-operation with the USA had been close for many years.) In June 1991, following the liberation of Kuwait in February, it was confirmed that Bahrain would remain a regional support base for the USA, and later in the year the two countries signed a defence co-operation agreement. In January 1994 Bahrain signed further accords of military co-operation with the USA and the United Kingdom. Relations with Iraq remained strained, and in October hopes of improved relations receded when Iraqi forces were again deployed in the Iraq–Kuwait border area. In response, Bahrain deployed combat aircraft and naval units to join GCC and US forces in the defence of Kuwait. In late 1995 Bahrain agreed to the temporary deployment on its territory of US fighter aircraft, in order to deter any possible military threat from Iraq. In February 1998 Bahrain strongly advocated a diplomatic solution to the ongoing dispute between Iraq and the UN weapons inspectors (see the chapter on Iraq) and refused to allow US military aircraft to launch attacks on Iraq from Bahraini bases. In June, as part of a wider US effort to reduce its military presence in the region, US military aircraft were withdrawn from Bahrain. In December a further US-led military campaign against Iraq was supported by the Bahraini authorities (the operation was centred in Manama, where the US Fifth Fleet is based) although Bahrain refrained from any public endorsement of the air-strikes; in August 1999 it was reported that Bahrain desired a further reduction of the US military presence in Bahrain, particularly that of the Fifth Fleet.

In April 1986 Qatari military forces raided the island of Fasht ad-Dibal, which had been artificially constructed on a coral reef (submerged at high tide), situated midway between Bahrain and Qatar; both countries claimed sovereignty over the island. Following GCC mediation, in May the two Governments agreed to destroy the island. Other areas of dispute between the two countries are Zubara (which was part of Bahraini territory until the early 20th century), in mainland Qatar, and the region of the Hawar islands, which is believed to contain potentially valuable reserves of petroleum and natural gas. In July 1991 Qatar instituted proceedings at the International Court of Justice (ICJ) in The Hague, Netherlands, regarding the issue of the Hawar islands (in 1939 a British judgment had awarded sovereignty of the islands to Bahrain), the shoals of Dibal and Qit'at Jaradah (over which the British Government had recognized Bahrain's 'sovereign rights' in 1947), together with the delimitation of the maritime border between Qatar and Bahrain. The question of sovereignty was further confused in April 1992, when the Government of Qatar issued a decree redefining its maritime borders to include territorial waters claimed by Bahrain, and tensions were exacerbated by Qatar's persistent rejection of Bahrain's insistence that the two countries should seek joint recourse to the ICJ. Moreover, it was reported that Bahrain had attempted to widen the issue to include its claim to the Zubara region. Qatar applied unilaterally to the Court, and in February 1995 the ICJ ruled that it was competent to adjudicate in the dispute. Relations between Bahrain and Qatar deteriorated in September, following the Bahrain Government's decision to construct a tourist resort on the Hawar islands, and remained tense subsequently, with the Bahrain Government advocating a regional solution to the dispute in preference to ICJ jurisdiction. In December 1996 Bahrain boycotted the GCC annual summit convened in Doha, Qatar, at which it was decided to establish a quadripartite committee (comprising those GCC members not involved in the dispute) to facilitate a solution. The committee reportedly made some progress towards resolving the territorial dispute, and following senior-level ministerial meetings between Bahrain and Qatar in London, United Kingdom, and in Manama in early 1997, it was announced that diplomatic relations at ambassadorial level were to be established between the two countries. Qatar, however, was alone in nominating its diplomatic representative shortly after. Regional efforts failed to find a solution to the territorial dispute, and the announcement of Bahraini construction plans on the Hawar islands (which, in addition to the opening of an hotel in mid-1997, included a housing complex and a causeway linking the islands to Bahrain) did little to further relations between the two countries. Bahrain emphasized that it would disregard any ruling on the issue by the ICJ, and also dismissed as a forgery a series of documents, submitted to the ICJ by the Qatar Government, supporting the Qatari claim. In September 1998 Qatar presented a report to the ICJ in support of the legitimacy of the documents, although it subsequently agreed to withdraw them from evidence. At the end of 1999 the Amir of Qatar made his first official visit to Manama, during which it was agreed that a joint committee, headed by the Crown Princes of Bahrain and Qatar, would be established to encourage bilateral co-operation. Qatar also agreed to withdraw its petition from the ICJ in the event of the joint committee's reaching a solution to the territorial disputes. Senior-level contacts were furthered in early January 2000, upon the first visit of the new Amir of Bahrain, Sheikh Hamad, to Qatar. The two countries agreed to hasten the opening of embassies in Manama and Doha, and Bahrain reportedly nominated its ambassador to Qatar. In February, following the first meeting of the Bahrain-Qatar Supreme Joint Committee, it was announced that the possibility of constructing a causeway to link the two states was to be investigated; Qatar officially named its ambassador to Bahrain on the same day. In May, however, Bahrain unilaterally suspended the Supreme Joint Committee pending the ruling of the ICJ. Hearings by the Court began later that month and were completed by the end of June; a verdict was issued in March 2001 (see the chapter on Qatar).

Government

Bahrain is ruled by an Amir through an appointed Cabinet. A Supreme National Committee was formed in late 2000 to prepare a document outlining the country's future political evolution. The committee's recommendations, published in a draft Charter of National Action in December of that year, were that there should be a transition from an emirate to a monarchy; a bicameral parliament was envisaged, comprising a directly-elected legislative body and an appointed consultative chamber. The Charter was approved by national referendum in February 2001.

Defence

Military service is voluntary. In August 2000 the active Bahraini Defence Force consisted of some 11,000 men (8,500 army, 1,000 navy, 1,500 air force). There were also paramilitary forces of an estimated 10,150 men (9,000 police, 900 national guard, 250 coastguard). The defence budget for 1999 was estimated at BD 115m.

Economic Affairs

In 1998, according to estimates by the World Bank, Bahrain's gross national product (GNP), measured at average 1996–98 prices, was US $4,909m., equivalent to $7,640 per head (or $11,556 per head on an international purchasing-power parity basis). During 1990–98, it was estimated, GNP per head increased, in real terms, at an average rate of 1.5% per year, while the population increased at an average annual rate of 3.5%. During 1993–99 the country's gross domestic product (GDP) increased, in real terms, an average rate of 3.3% per year. GDP increased by 4.8% in 1998 and, according to provisional figures, by 4.0% in 1999.

Agriculture (including hunting, forestry and fishing) engaged an estimated 1.1% of the employed labour force in 1998, and, according to provisional data, contributed 0.8% of GDP in 1999. The principal crops are dates and tomatoes. Poultry production is also important. Agricultural GDP declined by 0.7% in 1998 but, according to provisional figures, increased by 2.7% in 1999.

Industry (comprising mining, manufacturing, construction and utilities) engaged 28.2% of the employed labour force in 1991, and provided 33.2% of GDP in 1999. Industrial GDP increased by 8.4% in 1999, according to provisional data.

Mining and quarrying engaged 1.7% of the employed labour force in 1991, and, according to provisional data, contributed 16.5% of GDP in 1999. The major mining activities are the exploitation of petroleum and natural gas, which in 1999 accounted for 16.3% of GDP. At 1994 levels of production (105,000 barrels per day), Bahrain's known reserves of crude petroleum were forecast to have been exhausted by 2000. At the beginning of 1998 Bahrain's proven published reserves of petroleum were estimated to be only 200m. barrels. By the end of 1999 petroleum production had declined to 30,000 barrels per day. Bahrain's reserves of natural gas at the end of 1999 were put at 110,000m. cu m, sufficient to maintain production (at 1999 levels) for 12.9 years. The GDP of the mining sector increased by 11.3% in 1998, and by 9.2% in 1999.

In 1991 manufacturing engaged 12.6% of the employed labour force; according to provisional figures, the sector provided 11.2% of GDP in 1999. Important industries include the petroleum refinery at Sitra, aluminium (Bahrain is the region's largest producer) and aluminium-related enterprises, shipbuilding, iron and steel, and chemicals. Since the mid-1980s the Government has encouraged the development of light industry. Manufacturing GDP increased by 2.0% in 1998, and by 6.3% in 1999.

Industrial expansion has resulted in energy demand that threatens to exceed the country's 1,126-MW total installed generating capacity, particularly as not all of the installed capacity is operational, owing to the advanced age of a number of stations. (It was reported in 2000 that energy demands were increasing by more than 5% per year). A programme of refurbishment and expansion, which included private-sector funding, had begun by 1999. Despite these improvements, and an agreement with Aluminium Bahrain to provide an additional 275 MW annually until 2004, it was estimated that a further 560 MW would be required by 2006.

The services sector contributed 66.0% of GDP in 1999, according to provisional figures. The financial services industry, notably the operation of 'offshore' banking units (OBUs), is a major source of Bahrain's prosperity. However, by 2000 the number of OBUs had declined to 47, compared with 74 in 1985. A stock exchange was inaugurated in Bahrain in 1989. It is now linked to the Oman and Jordan Stock Exchanges (with each other's shares listed under reciprocal agreements), and in 1997 plans were announced to link it to the Kuwait Stock Exchange. The inauguration of the first International Islamic Financial Market, with a liquidity management centre and Islamic ratings agency based in Bahrain, is scheduled for October 2001. The GDP of the services sector increased by 1.4% in 1999.

In 1999 Bahrain recorded a visible trade surplus of US $719.1m., while there was a deficit of $420.5m. on the current account of the balance of payments. In 1998 the principal sources of non-petroleum imports were Japan (accounting for 11.5% of the total), the USA (10.4%), Australia, the United

Kingdom, Saudi Arabia, Italy and Germany. Saudi Arabia also provided most of Bahrain's petroleum imports (and accounted for 50.8% of all imports in 1990). Saudi Arabia was the principal customer for Bahrain's non-petroleum exports (18.2% of the total) in 1998; other important markets were the USA (12.6%), Japan, India and Taiwan. The principal exports are petroleum, petroleum products and aluminium. Sales of petroleum and petroleum products provided 67.2% of total export earnings in 1996. The principal import is crude petroleum (for domestic refining), accounting for 41.8% of total imports in 1996. The main category of non-petroleum imports (21.4% in 1997) is machinery and transport equipment.

In 1999 there was a budgetary deficit of BD 133.6m. (equivalent to 5.4% of GDP). The average annual rate of inflation was 1.0% in 1990–98; consumer prices increased by an annual average of 2.5% in 1997, but decreased by an annual average of 0.4% in 1998. About 63% of the labour force were expatriates in 1999. The official rate of unemployment was 2.3% in late 1999; however, unofficial sources estimated the level of unemployment to have reached 15%–30%.

Bahrain is a member of the Gulf Co-operation Council (GCC, see p. 160), which, *inter alia*, seeks to promote freer trading and co-operative economic protection among Gulf states. The country is also a member of the Organization of Arab Petroleum Exporting Countries (OAPEC, see p. 264), the Arab Monetary Fund (see p. 126) and the Islamic Development Bank (see p. 229).

In recognition of the fact that Bahrain's reserves of petroleum and natural gas are nearing exhaustion, the Government has introduced measures both to diversify the country's industrial base and to attract wider foreign investment. During the 1990s the Government continued to encourage the greater participation of the private sector in economic development and indicated that it would adopt a gradual approach to the privatization of state enterprises (excluding the petroleum sector), and would prioritize employment opportunities for Bahraini nationals. By late 2000 only 14 state enterprises had been part-privatized (one of these being a major industrial company); the World Trade Organization, of which Bahrain is a member, urged the Government to accelerate economic liberalization by increasing private investment in the petroleum and telecommunications sectors. In 1997 the Government announced a three-year development programme, which included the proposed creation of a port and free-trade zone at Hidd on Muharraq island, a new power-station and desalination plant, and the renovation of Bahrain's international airport. In 1998 plans were announced for the expansion of tourism facilities on Ad-Dar island, and for a seven-year investment programme in the power and water sector, projected to cost some BD 700m. By 1999 work had begun on the port and industrial area at Hidd as well as on the power and water complex, which was scheduled for completion by 2005. The dramatic recovery in international petroleum prices in the second half of 1999—following an agreement by both OPEC and non-OPEC producers to cut production—improved Bahrain's economic prospects markedly, with the trade surplus in 1999 reaching its highest level for a decade, strong economic growth predicted for that year, and annual GDP growth of at least 5% projected for the early years of the 21st century, combined with regular budget surpluses. As a signatory to the GCC agreement providing for the creation of a full customs union by 2005, from January 2000 the Bahrain Government abolished import duties on foodstuffs and applied a 25% reduction in tariffs on 53 essential commodities.

Social Welfare

The state-administered medical service provides comprehensive treatment for all residents, including expatriates. There are also physicians, dentists and opticians in private practice. In 1998 there were seven hospitals, 19 government health centres and five government maternity centres in Bahrain, providing a total of 1,832 hospital beds (one per 351 inhabitants). A social security law covers pensions, industrial accidents, sickness, unemployment, maternity and family allowances. In 1998 there were 709 physicians working in the country (one per 907 inhabitants). There were 289 nursing personnel per 100,000 inhabitants in the early 1990s. Of total expenditure by the central Government in 1998, BD 57.8m. (9.0%) was for health, and a further BD 27.7m. (4.3%) for social security and welfare.

Education

Education is compulsory for nine years between the ages of six and 14, and is available free of charge. Private and religious education are also available. The education system is composed of three different stages: primary and intermediate schooling, which together form 'basic education', and secondary schooling. Primary education lasts for six years from the age of six; it is divided into two cycles, each comprising three years. Intermediate education lasts for three years, between the ages of 12 and 14. Entry to secondary education, which comprises three years between the ages of 15 and 17, is conditional on obtaining the Intermediate School Certificate or its equivalent. The student chooses between five curriculums: science, literature, commerce, applied curriculums (five branches) and a technical curriculum. The University of Bahrain, established by Amiri decree in 1986, comprises five colleges: the College of Engineering, the College of Arts, the College of Science, the College of Education and the College of Business and Management. About 8,160 students were enrolled at the university in 1998. The Arabian Gulf University (AGU), funded by seven Arab governments, also provides higher education. In 1998 it comprised two colleges: the College of Medicine and Medical Sciences and the Post-Graduate College. The University campus is due to be completed at the end of 2006, and will accommodate 5,000 students. In 1998 557 students were enrolled at the AGU. The College of Health Sciences provides post-secondary education and was attended by 696 students in 1998. In 1996 enrolment at primary,

intermediate and secondary levels was 97.8% (males 97.6%; females 97.9%), 96.0% (males 96.4%; females 95.5%) and 95.0% (males 90.2%; females 99.9%), respectively, of the relevant age-groups. Expenditure on education by the central Government in 1998 was BD 85.3m. (13.2% of total expenditure). According to UNESCO estimates, the average rate of adult illiteracy in 1995 was 14.7% (males 10.8%; females 20.5%).

Public Holidays

2001: 1 January (New Year's Day), 6 March* (Id al-Adha, Feast of the Sacrifice), 26 March* (Muharram, Islamic New Year), 4 April* (Ashoura), 4 June* (Mouloud, Birth of the Prophet), 16 December (National Day), 17 December* (Id al-Fitr, end of Ramadan).

2002: 1 January (New Year's Day), 23 February* (Id al-Adha, Feast of the Sacrifice), 15 March* (Muharram, Islamic New Year), 24 March* (Ashoura), 24 May* (Mouloud, Birth of the Prophet), 6 December* (Id al-Fitr, end of Ramadan), 16 December (National Day).

* These holidays are dependent on the Islamic lunar calendar and may vary by one or two days from the dates given.

Weights and Measures

The metric system is being introduced.

Statistical Survey

Sources (unless otherwise stated): Bahrain Government; e-mail webmaster@bahrain.gov.bh; internet www.bahrain.gov.bh; Central Statistics Organization, POB 5835, Manama; tel. 725725; fax 728989; Bahrain Monetary Agency, POB 27, Manama; tel. 535535; fax 534170; e-mail bmalbr@batelco.com.bh; internet www.bma.gov.bh.

AREA AND POPULATION

Area (1999): 709.5 sq km (273.9 sq miles).

Population: 350,798 (males 204,793, females 146,005) at census of 5 April 1981; 508,037 (males 294,346, females 213,691), comprising 323,305 Bahrainis (males 163,453, females 159,852) and 184,732 non-Bahraini nationals (males 130,893, females 53,839), at census of 16 November 1991; 642,972 (males 376,210, females 266,762), comprising 391,019 Bahrainis (males 197,687, females 193,332) and 251,953 non-Bahraini nationals (males 178,523, females 73,430), at mid-1998 (official estimate).

1999 (official estimate at mid-year): 666,441.

Density (mid-1999): 939.3 per sq km.

Principal Towns (population in 1991): Manama (capital) 136,999; Muharraq Town 74,245. *Mid-1992:* Manama 140,401.

Births, Marriages and Deaths (1998): Registered live births 13,381 (birth rate 20.8 per 1,000); Registered marriages 3,677 (marriage rate 5.7 per 1,000); Registered deaths 1,997 (death rate 3.1 per 1,000).

Expectation of Life (UN estimates, years at birth, 1990–95): 71.6 (males 69.8; females 74.1). Source: UN, *World Population Prospects: The 1998 Revision.*

Economically Active Population (persons aged 15 years and over, 1991 census): Agriculture, hunting, forestry and fishing 5,108; Mining and quarrying 3,638; Manufacturing 26,618; Electricity, gas and water 2,898; Construction 26,738; Trade, restaurants and hotels 29,961; Transport, storage and communications 13,789; Financing, insurance, real estate and business services 17,256; Community, social and personal services 83,944; Activities not adequately defined 2,120; *Total employed* 212,070 (males 177,154; females 34,916); Unemployed 14,378 (males 9,703; females 4,675); *Total labour force* 226,448 (males 186,857; females 39,591), comprising 90,662 Bahrainis (males 73,118, females 17,544) and 135,786 non-Bahraini nationals (males 113,739, females 22,047). *Mid-1998* (estimates): Agriculture, etc. 3,000; Total 268,000 (Source: FAO, *Production Yearbook*).

AGRICULTURE, ETC.

Principal Crops ('000 metric tons, 1999): Tomatoes 5; Other vegetables 8; Dates 17; Other fruits 5. Source: FAO.

Livestock (FAO estimates, '000 head, year ending September 1999): Cattle 13; Camels 1; Sheep 17; Goats 16. Source: FAO.

Livestock Products ('000 metric tons, 1999): Mutton and lamb 5; Goat meat 2; Poultry meat 5; Milk 14; Poultry eggs 3. Source: FAO.

Fishing (metric tons, live weight, 1998): Total catch 9,849 (Groupers 331, Grunts and sweetlips 355, Emperors 944, Porgies and seabreams 757, Mojarras 347, Spinefeet 1,523, Carangids 359, Portunus swimcrabs 1,017, Penaeus shrimps 2,530). Source: FAO, *Yearbook of Fishery Statistics.*

MINING

Production (1999): Crude petroleum 13,472,000 barrels; Natural gas 8,789.5 million cubic metres (excluding associated gas: 2,718.4 million cubic metres).

INDUSTRY

Production ('000 barrels, unless otherwise indicated, 1998): Liquefied petroleum gas 300; Naphtha 13,087; Motor spirit (Gasoline) 6,344; Kerosene and Jet fuel 17,615; Fuel oil 19,719; Diesel oil and gas oil 31,591; Petroleum bitumen (asphalt) 1,728; Electric energy 5,773.3 million kWh; Aluminium (unwrought) 502,700 metric tons (1999).

FINANCE

Currency and Exchange Rates: 1,000 fils = 1 Bahraini dinar (BD). *Sterling, Dollar and Euro Equivalents* (29 December 2000): £1 sterling = 561.1 fils; US $1 = 376.0 fils; €1 = 349.9 fils; 100 Bahraini dinars = £178.23 = $265.96 = €285.82. *Exchange Rate:* Fixed at US $1 = 376.0 fils (BD 1 = $2.6596) since November 1980.

Budget (BD million, 1998): *Revenue:* Taxation 204.1 (Taxes on income and profits 34.4, Social security contributions 72.4, Domestic taxes on goods and services 19.3, Import duties 63.4); Entrepreneurial and property income 277.6; Other current revenue 34.8; Capital revenue 0.1; Total 516.6, excl. grants from abroad (37.6).

Expenditure: General public services 97.7; Defence 111.2; Public order and safety 94.7; Education 85.3; Health 57.8; Social security and welfare 27.7; Housing and community amenities 22.8; Recreational, cultural and religious affairs and services 11.8; Economic affairs and services 111.5 (Fuel and energy 83.6, Transport and communications 20.2); Interest payments 24.1; Total 644.6 (Current 528.0, Capital 116.6), excl. lending minus repayments (26.1). Source: IMF, *Government Finance Statistics Yearbook.*

1999 (BD million): Revenue 622.8 (excl. grants 37.6); Expenditure 723.8.

2000 (forecasts, BD million): Revenue 572; Expenditure 732.

International Reserves (US $ million at 31 December 1999): Gold (valued at $44 per troy oz) 6.6; Reserve position in IMF 85.6; Foreign exchange 1,283.4; Total 1,375.6. Source: IMF, *International Financial Statistics.*

Money Supply (BD million at 31 December 1999): Currency outside banks 113.0; Demand deposits at commercial banks 313.2; Total money 426.2. Source: IMF, *International Financial Statistics.*

Cost of Living (Consumer Price Index for Bahraini nationals; base: 1995 = 100): 99.5 in 1996; 102.0 in 1997; 101.6 in 1998. Source: IMF, *International Financial Statistics.*

Expenditure on the Gross Domestic Product (BD million, 1999): Government final consumption expenditure 518.2; Private final consumption expenditure 1,378.4; Increase in stocks 29; Gross fixed capital formation 338.4; *Total domestic expenditure* 2,264.2; Exports of goods and services 1,842.7; *Less* Imports of goods and services 1,617.7; *GDP in purchasers' values* 2,489.2. Source: IMF, *International Financial Statistics.*

Gross Domestic Product by Economic Activity (BD million at current prices, 1999, provisional): Agriculture, hunting, forestry and fishing 21.4; Mining and quarrying 453.6; Manufacturing 306.7; Electricity, gas and water 44.9; Construction 105.6; Trade, restaurants and hotels 264.3; Transport, storage and communications 196.3; Finance, insurance, real estate and business services 779.0; Government services 448.3; Other community, social and personal services 125.2; *Sub-total* 2,745.2; *Less* Imputed bank service charge 312.8; *GDP at factor cost* 2,432.3; Import duties 57.1; *GDP in purchasers' values* 2,489.4.

Balance of Payments (US $ million, 1999): Exports of goods f.o.b. 4,088.3; Imports of goods f.o.b. –3,369.1; *Trade balance* 719.1; Exports of services 763.6; Imports of services –634.6; *Balance on goods and services* 848.1; Other income received 4,988.3; Other income paid –5,437.5; *Balance on goods, services and income* 398.9; Current transfers received 36.7; Current transfers paid –856.1; *Current balance* –420.5; Capital account (net) 100.0; Direct investment abroad –163.3; Direct investment from abroad 447.6; Portfolio investment assets –2,052.7; Portfolio investment liabilities –11.7; Other investment assets 967.0; Other investment liabilities 1,012.5; Net errors and omissions 146.3; *Overall balance* 25.3. Source: IMF, *International Financial Statistics.*

EXTERNAL TRADE

Total Trade (BD million): *Imports c.i.f.:* 1,513.6 in 1997; 1,340.9 in 1998; 1,349.2 in 1999. *Exports:* 1,648.2 in 1997; 1,229.6 in 1998; 1,537.2 in 1999. Source: IMF, *International Financial Statistics.*

Principal Commodities (BD million, 1998): *Imports c.i.f.:* Live animals and animal products 46.3; Vegetable products 45.2; Prepared foodstuffs, beverages, spirits, vinegar and tobacco 64.9; Mineral products 60.9; Products of chemical or allied industries 150.6; Plastics, rubber and articles thereof 35.5; Paper-making material, paper and paperboard and articles thereof 26.4; Textiles and textile articles 71.8; Articles of stone, plaster, cement, asbestos, mica, etc., ceramic products, glass and glassware 22.3; Base metals and articles thereof 82.3; Machinery and mechanical appliances, electrical equipment, sound and television apparatus 263.9; Vehicles, aircraft, vessels and associated transport equipment 107.1; Miscellaneous manufactured articles 28.3; Total (incl. others) 1,066.9. *Exports f.o.b.:* Animal or vegetable fats and oils; prepared edible fats; animal or vegetable waxes 17.2; Mineral products 25.9; Products of chemicals and allied industries 37.6; Paper-making material, paper and paperboard, and articles thereof 12.0; Textiles and textile articles 56.1; Base metals and articles of base metal 362.6; Vehicles, aircraft, vessels and associated transport equipment 13.1; Total (incl. others) 556.9, excl. re-exports (35.7). Note: Figures exclude trade in petroleum (BD million): Imports 274.0; Exports 637.0.

1999 (BD million): Total imports c.i.f. 1,349.2 (Petroleum 469.1, Others 880.1); Total exports f.o.b. 1,537.2 (Petroleum 960.1, Others and re-exports 577.1).

Principal Trading Partners (BD million, 1998): *Imports c.i.f.:* Australia 104.0; Belgium 12.8; Brazil 22.5; China, People's Repub. 28.4; France 38.0; Germany 60.6; India 33.5; Italy 61.4; Japan 122.4; Korea Repub. 31.4; Malaysia 16.3; Netherlands 17.0; Pakistan 14.1; Saudi Arabia 76.4; Sweden 11.6; Switzerland 19.0; Taiwan 11.2; Thailand 12.2; United Arab Emirates 35.7; United Kingdom 79.3; USA 110.5; Total (incl. others) 1,066.9. *Exports f.o.b.:* India 34.7; Italy 14.9; Japan 54.2; Republic of Korea 25.9; Kuwait 20.6; Malaysia 9.0; Netherlands 18.3; Oman 6.3; Qatar 13.9; Saudi Arabia 107.6; Taiwan 32.1; Thailand 11.0; Turkey 11.1; United Arab Emirates 35.5; United Kingdom 8.0; USA 74.6; Total (incl. others) 592.6. Note: Figures exclude trade in petroleum.

TRANSPORT

Road Traffic (registered motor vehicles, 31 December 1998): Passenger cars 160,746; Buses and coaches 5,173; Lorries and vans 28,773; Motorcycles 1,894.

Shipping (international sea-borne freight traffic, '000 metric tons, 1990): *Goods loaded:* Dry cargo 1,145; Petroleum products 12,140. *Goods unloaded:* Dry cargo 3,380; Petroleum products 132. Source: UN, *Monthly Bulletin of Statistics. Merchant Fleet* (31 December 1998): Registered vessels 110; Total displacement 283,704 grt. Source: Lloyd's Register of Shipping, *World Fleet Statistics.*

Civil Aviation (1997): Kilometres flown (million) 19; Passengers carried ('000) 1,165; Passenger-km (million) 2,501; Total ton-km (million) 33.3. Figures include an apportionment (equivalent to one-quarter) of the traffic of Gulf Air, a multinational airline with its headquarters in Bahrain. Source: UN, *Statistical Yearbook.*

TOURISM

Tourist Arrivals (1998): 2,897,562*.

Tourist Receipts (1998): US $270 million.

* Figure refers to arrivals at frontiers of visitors from abroad (excluding Bahraini nationals residing abroad).

Source: World Tourism Organization, *Yearbook of Tourism Statistics.*

COMMUNICATIONS MEDIA

Radio Receivers (1997): 338,000 in use.

Television Receivers (1997): 275,000 in use.

Telephones (1998): 157,619 main lines in use.

Telefax Stations (1998): 6,687 in use.

Mobile Cellular Telephones (1998): 94,078 subscribers.

Book Production (1996, first editions only): 40 titles.

Daily Newspapers (1996): 4 (circulation 67,000 copies).

Non-daily Newspapers (1993): 5 (circulation 17,000 copies).

Other Periodicals (1993): 26 (circulation 73,000 copies).

Source: mainly UNESCO, *Statistical Yearbook.*

EDUCATION

Pre-Primary: 90 schools (1996/97); 449 teachers (1995/96); 12,308 pupils (1996/97). Source: UNESCO, *Statistical Yearbook.*

Primary (1997/98): 60,869 pupils (males 30,498; females 30,371).

Intermediate (1997/98): 27,976 pupils (males 13,647; females 14,329).

General Secondary (1997/98): 14,235 pupils (males 5,144; females 9,091).

Commercial Secondary (1997/98): 301 pupils (males 97; females 204).

Technical Secondary (1997/98): 7,561 pupils (males 5,217; females 2,344).

Directory

The Constitution

A 108-article Constitution was ratified in June 1973. It states that 'all citizens shall be equal before the law' and guarantees freedom of speech, of the press, of conscience and religious beliefs. Other provisions include the outlawing of the compulsory repatriation of political refugees. The Constitution also states that the country's financial comptroller should be responsible to the legislature and not to the Government, and allows for national trade unions 'for legally justified causes and on peaceful lines'. Compulsory free primary education and free medical care are also laid down in the Constitution. The Constitution, which came into force on 6 December 1973, also provided for a National Assembly, composed of 14 members of the Cabinet and 30 members elected by popular vote, although this was dissolved in August 1975.

A Supreme National Committee was created by amiri decree in late 2000, with the task of preparing a Charter of National Action to outline the future evolution of the Bahraini political system. In December of that year the Committee submitted its recommendations, principal among them that there should be a transition from an emirate to a monarchy, with a bicameral parliament (comprising a directly-elected legislature and an appointed consultative chamber). The proposed changes were approved in a referendum held on 14–15 February 2001.

The Government

HEAD OF STATE

Amir: Sheikh HAMAD BIN ISA AL-KHALIFA (acceded 6 March 1999).

Crown Prince and Commander-in-Chief of Bahraini Defence Force and National Guard: Sheikh SALMAN BIN HAMAD AL-KHALIFA.

CABINET
(April 2001)

Prime Minister: Sheikh KHALIFA BIN SULMAN AL-KHALIFA.

Minister of Justice and Islamic Affairs: Sheikh ABDULLAH BIN KHALIFA KHALID AL-KHALIFA.

Minister of Foreign Affairs: Sheikh MUHAMMAD BIN MUBARAK BIN HAMAD AL-KHALIFA.

Minister of the Interior: Sheikh MUHAMMAD BIN KHALIFA BIN HAMAD AL-KHALIFA.

Minister of Transport: Sheikh ALI BIN KHALIFA BIN SALMAN AL-KHALIFA.

Minister of Housing and Agriculture: Sheikh KHALID BIN ABDULLAH BIN KHALID AL-KHALIFA.

Minister of Public Works: FAHMI ALI AL-JOUDER.

Minister of Finance and National Economy: ABDULLAH HASSAN SAIF.

Minister of Defence: Maj.-Gen. Sheikh KHALIFA BIN AHMAD AL-KHALIFA.

Minister of Cabinet Affairs: MUHAMMAD IBRAHIM AL-MUTAWA.

Minister of Information: NABIL YAQUB AL-HAMER.

Minister of Oil: Sheikh ISA BIN ALI AL-KHALIFA.

Minister of Commerce and Industry: ALI SALEH ABDULLAH AS-SALEH.

Minister of Education: MUHAMMAD JASSIM AL-GHATAM.

Minister of Health: Dr FAISAL RADHI AL-MOUSAWI.

Minister of Electricity and Water: Sheikh DAIJ BIN KHALIFA BIN MUHAMMAD AL-KHALIFA.

Minister of Labour and Social Affairs: ABD AN-NABI ASH-SHULA.

Minister of Amiri Court Affairs: Sheikh ALI BIN ISA BIN SULMAN AL-KHALIFA.

Ministers of State: Brig.-Gen. ABD AL-AZIZ MUHAMMAD AL-FADHIL (Consultative Council Affairs), Dr MUHAMMAD ABD AL-GHAFFAR (Foreign Affairs), JAWAD SALIM AL-ARRAYEDH (Municipalities and Environment Affairs), MUHAMMAD HASSAN KAMALELDINE.

MINISTRIES

Amiri Court: POB 555, Riffa Palace, Manama; tel. 661252.

Office of the Prime Minister: POB 1000, Government House, Government Rd, Manama; tel. 253361; fax 533033.

Ministry of Cabinet Affairs and Information: POB 26613, Government House, Government Rd, Manama; tel. 223366; fax 225202; e-mail brtcnews@batelco.com.bh; internet www.gna.gov.bh.

Ministry of Commerce and Industry: POB 5479, Diplomatic Area, Manama; tel. 531531; fax 530455.

Ministry of Defence: POB 245, West Rifa'a; tel. 665599; fax 663923.

Ministry of Education: POB 43, Isa Town; tel. 685558; fax 680161; internet www.education.gov.bh.

Ministry of Electricity and Water: POB 2, Manama; tel. 533133; fax 533035.

Ministry of Finance and National Economy: POB 333, Diplomatic Area, Manama; tel. 530800; fax 532853; intenet www.mofne.gov.bh.

Ministry of Foreign Affairs: POB 547, Government House, Government Rd, Manama; tel. 227555; fax 212603.

Ministry of Health: POB 12, Sheikh Sulman Rd, Manama; tel. 289810; fax 289864; e-mail hid1@batelco.com.bh; internet www.batelco.com.bh/mhealth.

Ministry of Housing and Agriculture: POB 11802, Diplomatic Area, Manama; tel. 533000; fax 534115; e-mail mohvip@batelco.com.bh; internet www.mohme.gov.bh.

Ministry of the Interior: POB 13, Police Fort Compound, Manama; tel. 272111; fax 262169.

Ministry of Justice and Islamic Affairs: POB 450, Diplomatic Area, Manama; tel. 531333; fax 536343.

Ministry of Labour and Social Affairs: POB 32333, Isa Town; tel. 687800; fax 686954; e-mail jamalq@bah-molsa.com; internet www.bah-molsa.com.

Ministry of Municipalities and Environment Affairs: Manama.

Ministry of Oil: POB 1435, Manama; tel. 291511; fax 290302.

Ministry of Public Works: POB 5, Muharraq Causeway Rd, Manama; tel. 535222; fax 533095.

Ministry of Transport: POB 10325, Diplomatic Area, Manama; tel. 534534; fax 537537.

CONSULTATIVE COUNCIL

The Consultative Council is an advisory body of 40 members appointed by the ruling authorities for a four-year term, which is empowered to advise the Government but has no legislative powers. The Council held its inaugural session on 16 January 1993.

President: IBRAHIM MUHAMMAD HUMAIDAN.

Legislature

The National Assembly provided for in the 1973 Constitution was dissolved in 1975. Among the recommendations of the Supreme National Committee's draft Charter of National Action, published at the end of 2000, was that there should be a bicameral parliament, comprising a directly-elected legislature and an appointed consultative chamber. The Charter was approved in a national referendum on 14–15 February 2001.

Diplomatic Representation

EMBASSIES IN BAHRAIN

Algeria: POB 2604, Villa 579, Rd 3622, Adliya, Manama; tel. 713669; fax 713662; Ambassador: LAHSSAN BOUFARES.

Bangladesh: POB 26718, House 2280, Rd 2757, Area 327, Adliya, Manama; tel. 714717; fax 710031; e-mail bangla@batelco.com.bh; Ambassador: ANWAR UL-ALAM.

China, People's Republic: POB 3150, Bldg 158, Road 382, Juffair Ave, Block 341, Manama; tel. 723800; fax 727304; Ambassador: PAN XIANGKANG.

Egypt: POB 818, Adliya; tel. 720005; fax 721518; Ambassador: MUHAMMAD ELSAYED ABBAS.

France: POB 11134, Road 1901, Building 51, Block 319, Diplomatic Area, Manama; tel. 291734; fax 293655; Ambassador: GEORGES DUQUIN.

Germany: POB 10306, Al-Hasan Bldg, Sheikh Hamad Causeway, Manama; tel. 530210; fax 536282; Ambassador: NORBERT HEINZE.

India: POB 26106, Bldg 182, Rd 2608, Area 326, Adliya, Manama; tel. 712785; fax 715527; e-mail indemb@batelco.com.bh; internet www.indianembassy-bh.com; Ambassador: S. S. GILL.

Iran: POB 26365, Entrance 1034, Rd 3221, Area 332, Mahooz, Manama; tel. 722400; fax 722101; Ambassador: MUHAMMAD JALAL FIROUZNIA.

Iraq: POB 26477, Ar-Raqib Bldg, No 17, Rd 2001, Comp 320, King Faysal Ave, Manama; tel. 786929; fax 786220; Chargé d'affaires: AWAD FAKHRI.

Japan: POB 23720, 55 Salmaniya Ave, Manama Tower 327, Manama; tel. 716565; fax 712950; Ambassador: ONO YASUAKI.

Jordan: POB 5242, Villa 43, Rd 915, Area 309, Hoora; tel. 291109; fax 291280; Ambassador: Dr SHAKER ARABIAT.

Kuwait: POB 786, Rd 1703, Diplomatic Area, Manama; tel. 534040; fax 533579; Ambassador: ABD AL-MUHSIN SALIM AL-HARUN.

Lebanon: POB 32474, Manama; tel. 786994; fax 784998; Ambassador: ZUHAIR A. QAZAZ.

Morocco: POB 26229, Manama; tel. 740566; fax 740178; Ambassador: OMER AN-NAJEY.

Oman: POB 26414, Bldg 37, Rd 1901, Diplomatic Area, Manama; tel. 293663; fax 293540; Ambassador: SALIM ALI OMAR BAYAQOOB.

Pakistan: POB 563, Bldg 261, Rd 2807, Block 328, Segeiya, Manama; tel. 244113; fax 255960; Ambassador: Lt-Gen. (retd) MUHAMMAD SHAFIQ.

Philippines: POB 26681, Manama; tel. 710200; fax 710300; Ambassador: RODOLFO I. DUMAPIAS.

Qatar: Manama; Ambassador: ABDULLAH BIN THAMIR ATH-THANI.

Russia: POB 26612, House 877, Rd 3119, Block 331, Zinj, Manama; tel. 725222; fax 725921; Ambassador: VALERY VLASOV.

Saudi Arabia: POB 1085, Bldg 1450, Rd 4043, Area 340, Juffair, Manama; tel. 537722; fax 533261; Ambassador: ABDULLAH BIN ABD AR-RAHMAN ASH-SHEIKH.

Syria: Manama; Ambassador: MAJID ABU SALEH.

Tunisia: POB 26911, House 54, Rd 3601, Area 336, Manama; tel. 714149; fax 715702; e-mail tunisemb@batelco.com.bh; Ambassador: MUHAMMAD AOUITI.

Turkey: POB 10821, Flat 10, Bldg 81, Rd 1702, Area 317, Manama; tel. 533448; fax 536557; e-mail tcbahrbe@batelco.com.bh; Ambassador: ENGIN TÜRKER.

United Arab Emirates: POB 26505, Manama; tel. 723737; fax 727343; Ambassador: AL-ASRI SAEED AHMAD ADH-DHAHIRI.

United Kingdom: POB 114, 21 Government Ave, Area 306, Manama; tel. 534404; fax 536109; e-mail britemb@batelco.com.bh; internet www.ukembassy.gov.bh; Ambassador: PETER FORD.

USA: POB 26431, Bldg 979, Rd 3119, Block 331, Zinj, Manama; tel. 273300; fax 272594; e-mail consularmanama@state.gov.bh; internet www.usembassy.com.bh; Ambassador: JOHNNY YOUNG.

Yemen: POB 26193, House 1048, Rd 1730, Area 517, Saar; tel. 277072; fax 262358; Ambassador: NASSER M. Y. ALGAADANI.

Judicial System

Since the termination of British legal jurisdiction in 1971, intensive work has been undertaken on the legislative requirements of Bahrain. The Criminal Law is at present contained in various Codes, Ordinances and Regulations. All nationalities are subject to the jurisdiction of the Bahraini courts which guarantee equality before the law irrespective of nationality or creed.

Directorate of Courts: POB 450, Government House, Government Rd, Manama; tel. 531333.

Religion

At the November 1991 census the population was 508,037, distributed as follows: Muslims 415,427; Christians 43,237; Others 49,373.

ISLAM

Muslims are divided between the Sunni and Shi'i sects. The ruling family is Sunni, although the majority of the Muslim population (estimated at almost 60%) are Shi'ite.

CHRISTIANITY

The Anglican Communion

Within the Episcopal Church in Jerusalem and the Middle East, Bahrain forms part of the diocese of Cyprus and the Gulf. There are two Anglican churches in Bahrain: St Christopher's Cathedral in Manama and the Community Church in Awali. The congregations are entirely expatriate. The Bishop in Cyprus and the Gulf is resident in Cyprus, while the Archdeacon in the Gulf is resident in Qatar.

Provost: Very Rev. KEITH W. T. W. JOHNSON, St Christopher's Cathedral, POB 36, Al-Mutanabi Ave, Manama; tel. 253866; fax 246436; e-mail provost@batelco.com.bh; internet www.stchcathedral.org.bh.

Roman Catholic Church

A small number of adherents, mainly expatriates, form part of the Apostolic Vicariate of Arabia. The Vicar Apostolic is resident in the United Arab Emirates.

The Press

DAILIES

Akhbar al-Khaleej (Gulf News): POB 5300, Manama; tel. 620111; fax 624312; e-mail editor@akhbar-alkhaleej.com; internet www.akhbar-alkhaleej.com; f. 1976; Arabic; Chair. IBRAHIM AL-MOAYED; Man. Dir and Editor-in-Chief Dr HILAL ASH-SHAIJI; circ. 17,000.

Al-Ayam (The Days): POB 3232, Manama; tel. 727111; fax 727552; e-mail alayam@batelco.com.bh; internet www.alayam.com; f. 1989; Arabic; publ. by Al-Ayam Establishment for Press and Publications; Chair. and Editor-in-Chief NABIL YAQUB AL-HAMER; circ. 37,000.

Bahrain Tribune: POB 3232, Manama; tel. 827111; fax 827222; e-mail tribune@batelco.com.bh; internet www.bahraintribune.com; f. 1997; English; Editor-in-Chief NABIL YAQUB AL-HAMER; circ. 12,500.

Gulf Daily News: POB 5300, Manama; tel. 620222; fax 622141; e-mail gdn1@batelco.com.bh; internet www.gulf-daily-news.com; f. 1978; English; Editor-in-Chief GEORGE WILLIAMS; Deputy Editor LES HORTON; circ. 50,000.

Khaleej Times: POB 26707, City Centre Bldg, Suite 403, 4th Floor, Government Ave, Manama; tel. 213911; fax 211819; f. 1978; English; circ. 72,565.

WEEKLIES

Al-Adhwaa' (Lights): POB 250, Old Exhibition Rd, Manama; tel. 290942; fax 293166; f. 1965; Arabic; publ. by Arab Printing and Publishing House; Chair. RAID MAHMOUD AL-MARDI; Editor-in-Chief MUHAMMAD QASSIM SHIRAWI; circ. 7,000.

Akhbar BAPCO (BAPCO News): Bahrain Petroleum Co BSC, POB 25149, Awali; tel. 755055; fax 755047; e-mail khalidfm@batelco.com.bh; f. 1981; formerly known as *an-Najma al-Usbou'* (The Weekly Star); Arabic; house journal; Editor KHALID F. MEHMAS; circ. 3,000.

Al-Bahrain ath-Thaqafya: POB 26613, Manama; tel. 290210; fax 292678; internet www.al-thaqafia.com; Arabic; publ. by the Ministry of Cabinet Affairs and Information; Editor ABDULLAH YATEEM.

BAPCO Weekly News: POB 25149, Awali; tel. 755049; fax 755047; English; publ. by the Bahrain Petroleum Co BSC; Editor KATHLEEN CROES; circ. 800.

Huna al-Bahrain: POB 26005, Isa Town; tel. 731888; fax 681292; Arabic; publ. by the Ministry of Cabinet Affairs and Information; Editor HAMAD AL-MANNAI.

Al-Mawakif (Attitudes): POB 1083, Manama; tel. 231231; fax 271720; f. 1973; Arabic; general interest; Editor-in-Chief MANSOOR M. RADHI; circ. 6,000.

Oil and Gas News: POB 224, Bldg 149, Exhibition Ave, Manama; tel. 293131; fax 293400; e-mail hilalmag@batelco.com.bh; English; publ. by Al-Hilal Publishing and Marketing Co; Editor-in-Chief CLIVE JACQUES.

Sada al-Usbou' (Weekly Echo): POB 549, Manama; tel. 291234; fax 290507; f. 1969; Arabic; Owner and Editor-in-Chief ALI SAYYAR; circ. 40,000 (in various Gulf states).

OTHER PERIODICALS

Arab Agriculture: POB 10131, Manama; tel. 213900; fax 211765; e-mail fanar@batelco.com.bh; annually; English and Arabic; publ. by Fanar Publishing WLL; Editor-in-Chief ABD AL-WAHED AL-ALWANI; Gen. Man. FAYEK AL-ARRAYED.

Arab World Agribusiness: POB 10131, Manama; tel. 213900; fax 211765; e-mail fanar@batelco.com.bh; nine per year; English and Arabic; publ. by Fanar Publishing WLL; Editor-in-Chief ABD AL-WAHED AL-ALWANI; Gen. Man. FAYEK AL-ARRAYED.

Discover Bahrain: POB 10704, Manama; tel. 534587; fax 531296; f. 1988; publ. by G. and B. Media Ltd; Publr and Editor ROBERT GRAHAM.

Gulf Construction: POB 224, Exhibition Ave, Manama; tel. 293131; fax 293400; e-mail hilalmag@batelco.com.bh; monthly; English; publ. by Al-Hilal Publishing and Marketing Group; Editor BINA PRABHU GOVEAS; circ. 12,485.

Gulf Economic Monitor: POB 224, Exhibition Ave, Manama; tel. 293131; fax 293400; e-mail hilalmag@tradearabia.net; weekly; English; published by Al-Hilal Publishing and Marketing Group; Man. Dir RONNIE MIDDLETON.

Al-Hayat at-Tijariya (Commerce Review): POB 248, Manama; tel. 229555; fax 224985; e-mail bahcci@batelco.com.bh; monthly; English and Arabic; publ. by Bahrain Chamber of Commerce and Industry; Editor KHALIL YOUSUF; circ. 7,500.

Al-Hidayah (Guidance): POB 450, Manama; tel. 727100; fax 729819; f. 1978; monthly; Arabic; publ. by Ministry of Justice and Islamic Affairs; Editor-in-Chief ABD AR-RAHMAN BIN MUHAMMAD RASHID AL-KHALIFA; circ. 5,000.

Al-Mohandis (The Engineer): POB 835, Manama; e-mail mohandis @batelco.com.bh; internet www.mohandis.org; f. 1972; quarterly; Arabic and English; publ. by Bahrain Society of Engineers; Editor ISA ALI JANAHI.

Al-Musafir al-Arabi (Arab Traveller): POB 10131, Manama; tel. 213900; fax 211765; e-mail fanar@batelco.com.bh; f. 1984; six per year; Arabic; publ. by Fanar Publishing WLL; Editor-in-Chief ABD AL-WAHED AL-ALWANI; Gen. Man. FAYEK AL-ARRAYED.

Panorama: POB 3232, Manama; tel. 727111; fax 729009; monthly; Editor IBRAHIM BASHMI; circ. 15,000.

Profile: POB 10243, Manama; tel. 291110; fax 294655; f. 1992; monthly; English; publ. by Bahrain Market Promotions; Editor ISA KHALIFA AL-KHALIFA.

Al-Quwwa (The Force): POB 245, Manama; tel. 291331; fax 659596; f. 1977; monthly; Arabic; publ. by Bahrain Defence Force; Editor-in-Chief Maj. AHMAD MAHMOUD AS-SUWAIDI.

Shipping and Transport News International: POB 224, Exhibition Ave, Manama; tel. 293131; fax 293400; six per year; English; publ. by Al-Hilal Publishing and Marketing Group; Editor FREDERICK ROCQUE; circ. 5,500.

Travel and Tourism News Middle East: POB 224, Exhibition Ave, Manama; tel. 293131; fax 293400; e-mail hilalmag@ batelco.com.bh; f. 1983; monthly; English; travel trade; publ. by Al-Hilal Publishing and Marketing Group; Editorial Man. SHILPI PILLAI; circ. 6,050.

NEWS AGENCIES

Agence France-Presse (AFP): POB 5890, Kanoo Tower, Phase 3, Tijaar Ave, Manama; tel. and fax 403446; Dir JEAN-PIERRE PERRIN.

Associated Press (AP) (USA): POB 26940, Mannai Bldg, Manama; tel. 530101; fax 530249.

Gulf News Agency: POB 5421, Manama; tel. 689044; fax 683825; e-mail brtcnews@batelco.com.bh; internet www.gna.gov.bh; Chief Editor KHALID ABDULLAH AZ-ZAYANI.

Reuters (United Kingdom): POB 1030, UGB Bldg, 6th Floor, Diplomatic Area, Manama; tel. 536111; fax 536192; Bureau Man. KENNETH WEST.

PRESS ASSOCIATION

Bahrain Journalists Association: Manama; f. 2000; Chair. NABIL YAQUB AL-HAMER; 250 mems.

Publishers

Arab Communicators: POB 551, 6th Floor, Almoayyed Bldg, Government Ave, Manama; tel. 534664; fax 531837; f. 1981; publrs of annual Bahrain Business Directory; Dirs AHMAD A. FAKHRI, HAMAD A. ABUL.

Gulf Advertising: POB 5518, Manama; tel. 226262; fax 228660; e-mail gulfad@batelco.com.bh; f. 1974; advertising and marketing communications; Chair. and Man. Dir KHAMIS AL-MUQLA.

Al-Hilal Publishing and Marketing Group: POB 224, Exhibition Ave, Manama; tel. 293131; fax 293400; e-mail hilalpmg@tradearabia .net; f. 1977; specialist magazines and newspapers of commercial interest; Chair. A. M. ABD AR-RAHMAN; Man. Dir R. MIDDLETON.

Manama Publishing Co WLL: POB 1013, Manama; tel. 213223; fax 211548.

Al-Masirah Journalism, Printing and Publishing House: POB 5981, Manama; tel. 258882; fax 276178; e-mail almasera@batelco .com.bh.

Tele-Gulf Directory Publications, WLL: POB 2738, 3rd Floor, Bahrain Tower, Manama; tel. 213301; fax 210503; e-mail telegulf@ batelco.com.bh; f. 1977; publrs of annual *Gulf Directory* and *Arab Banking and Finance*.

Government Publishing House

Directorate of Publications: POB 26005, Manama; tel. 689077; Dir MUHAMMAD AL-KHOZAI.

Broadcasting and Communications

TELECOMMUNICATIONS
Regulatory Authority

Telecommunications Directorate: POB 11170, Manama; tel. 534534; fax 533544; Dir Dr RASHID JASSIM ASHOOR.

Bahrain Telecommunications Co BSC (BATELCO): POB 14, Manama; tel. 884557; fax 611898; e-mail batelco@btc.com.bh; internet www.batelco.com.bh; f. 1981; operates all telecommunications services; cap. BD 100m.; 80% owned by Government of Bahrain, financial institutions and public of Bahrain, 20% by Cable and Wireless PLC (United Kingdom); launched mobile cellular telecommunications service, Sim Sim, in 1999; Chair. Sheikh ALI BIN KHALIFA BIN SALMAN AL-KHALIFA; CEO ANDREW HEARN.

BROADCASTING
Radio

English language radio programmes, broadcast from Saudi Arabia by the US Air Force in Dhahran and by Saudi Aramco, can be received in Bahrain.

Bahrain Radio and Television Corpn: POB 702, Manama; tel. 781888; internet www.gna.gov.bh/brtc/radio.html; f. 1955; state-owned and -operated enterprise; two 10-kW transmitters; programmes are in Arabic and English, and include news, plays and discussions; Dir of Broadcasting ABD AR-RAHMAN ABDULLAH.

Radio Bahrain: POB 702, Manama; tel. 629085; fax 780911; e-mail brtcnews@batelco.com.bh; f. 1977; commercial radio station in English language; Head of Station SALAH KHALID.

Television

English language television programmes, broadcast from Saudi Arabia by Saudi Aramco, can be received in Bahrain.

Bahrain Radio and Television Corpn: POB 1075, Manama; tel. 686000; fax 681544; e-mail ceobrtc@batelco.bh; internet www.gna .gov.bh/brtc/bah-tv.html; commenced colour broadcasting in 1973; broadcasts on five channels, of which the main Arabic and the main English channel accept advertising; covers Bahrain, eastern Saudi Arabia, Qatar and the UAE; an Amiri decree in early 1993 established the independence of the Corpn, which was to be controlled by a committee; Dir H. AL-UMRAN.

Finance

(cap. = capital; res = reserves; dep. = deposits; m. = millions; brs = branches; amounts in Bahraini dinars unless otherwise stated)

BANKING
Central Bank

Bahrain Monetary Agency (BMA): POB 27, Diplomatic Area, Manama; tel. 535535; fax 534170; e-mail bmalbr@batelco.com.bh; internet www.bma.gov.bh; f. 1973, in operation from January 1975; controls issue of currency, regulates exchange control and credit policy, organization and control of banking system and bank credit; cap. and res 290.9m., dep. 136.0m. (May 2000); Governor Sheikh ABDULLAH BIN KHALIFA BIN MUHAMMAD AL-KHALIFA.

Locally-incorporated Commercial Banks

Al-Ahli Commercial Bank BSC (ACB): POB 5941, Bahrain Car Park Bldg, Government Rd, Manama; tel. 224333; fax 224322; e-mail alahli@al-ahlibank.com; internet www.al-ahlibank.com; f. 1977; full commercial bank; cap. 13.2m., res 26.2m., dep. 268.1m. (Dec. 1999); Chair. MUHAMMAD YOUSUF JALAL; CEO MICHAEL J. FULLER; 9 brs.

Bahrain Islamic Bank BSC: POB 5240, Government Rd, Manama; tel. 223402; fax 212396; e-mail bahisl@batelco.com.bh; f. 1979; cap. 11.5m., res 3.0m., dep. 137.4m. (April 1999); Chair. Sheikh ABD AR-RAHMAN AL-KHALIFA; Gen. Man. ABD AL-LATIF ABD AR-RAHIM JANAHI; 5 brs.

Bahraini Saudi Bank BSC (BSB): POB 1159, As-Saddah Bldg, Government Rd, Manama; tel. 211010; fax 210989; e-mail bsbbahr@batelco.com.bh; internet www.bahrainsaudibank.com; f. 1983; commenced operations in early 1985; licensed as a full commercial bank; cap. 20.0m., res 13.5m., dep. 121.0m. (Dec. 1999); Chair. Sheikh IBRAHIM BIN HAMAD AL-KHALIFA; Gen. Man. MANSOOR AS-SAYED; 6 brs.

Bank of Bahrain and Kuwait BSC (BBK): POB 597, 43 Government Ave, Manama; tel. 223388; fax 229822; e-mail bbk@batelco .com.bh; internet www.bbkonline.com; f. 1971; cap. 56.9m., res 49.7m., dep. 823.5m. (Mar. 2000); Chair. HASSAN KHALIFA AL-JALAHMA; Gen. Man. and CEO MURAD ALI MURAD; 22 local brs, 2 brs overseas.

Commercial Bank of Bahrain BSC (CBB): POB 793, Manama Centre, 3 Government Ave, Manama; tel. 225999; fax 224482; f. 1984; fmrly Grindlays Bahrain Bank, cap. 6.0m., res 5.0m., dep. 98.3m. (Dec. 1999); Chair. MUHAMMAD ABDULLAH AZ-ZAMIL; Gen. Man. PETER TOMKINS; 6 brs.

National Bank of Bahrain BSC (NBB): POB 106, Government Ave, Manama; tel. 228800; fax 228998; e-mail nbb@nbbonline.com; internet www.nbbonline.com; f. 1957; 49% govt-owned; cap. 40.0m., res 55.0m., dep. 858.6m. (Dec. 1999); Chair. ABDULLAH ALI KANOO; Gen. Man. ABD AR-RAZAK A. HASSAN; 25 brs.

Shamil Bank of Bahrain EC (SBB): POB 3005, Chamber of Commerce Bldg, King Faysal Rd, Manama; tel. 227040; fax 224872; e-mail general.services@shamilbank.com.bh; internet www.shamilbank.com.bh; f. 1982 as Massraf Faysal Al-Islami of Bahrain EC; renamed Faysal Islamic Bank of Bahrain in 1987 and as above in 2000; cap. US \$100.00m., res US \$18.4m., dep. US \$162.0m. (Dec. 1999); CEO Nabil A. Nassief; 2 brs.

Foreign Commercial Banks

ABN AMRO Bank NV (Netherlands): POB 350, Manama; tel. 255420; fax 262241; e-mail abnamro@batelco.com.bh; internet www.abnamro.com; Country Man. G. Loet Kniphorst; 1 br.

Arab Bank PLC (Jordan): POB 395, Government Rd, Manama; tel. 229988; fax 210443; internet www.arabbank.com; Chair. Abd al-Majeed Shoman; 4 brs.

Bank Melli Iran: POB 785, Government Rd, Manama; tel. 229910; fax 224402; e-mail bmibah@batelco.com.bh; Gen. Man. Mahdi Mahzoonieh; 2 brs.

Bank Saderat Iran: POB 825, Government Rd, Manama; tel. 210003; fax 210398; Man. Muhammad Javad Nassiri; 2 brs.

Banque du Caire, SAE (Egypt): POB 815, Manama; tel. 227454; fax 213704; Man. es-Sayed Moustafa el-Dokmawey.

Citibank NA (USA): POB 548, Government Rd, Manama; tel. 223344; fax 211323; internet www.citibank.com/bahrain; Gen. Man. Muhammad ash-Shroogi; 1 br.

Habib Bank Ltd (Pakistan): POB 566, Manama Centre, Manama; tel. 227118; fax 213421; f. 1941; Exec. Vice-Pres. and Gen. Man. Ashraf Bidiwala; 5 brs.

HSBC Bank Middle East (United Kingdom): POB 57, Al-Khalifa Rd, Manama; tel. 242555; fax 256822; e-mail bbmemnm@batelco.com.bh; internet www.britishbank.com; CEO Roger J. Jordan; 4 brs.

Rafidain Bank (Iraq): POB 607, Manama; tel. 275796; fax 255656; f. 1969; Man. Ibtisam Najem Aboud; 1 br.

Standard Chartered Bank (United Kingdom): POB 29, Government Rd, Manama; tel. 223636; fax 225001; f. in Bahrain 1920; Man. Peter Rawlings; 5 brs.

United Bank Ltd (Pakistan): POB 546, Government Rd, Manama; tel. 224030; fax 224099; e-mail ublbah@batelco.com.bh; Gen. Man. M. A. Rauf; 3 brs.

Specialized Financial Institutions

Bahrain Development Bank (BDB): POB 20501, Manama; tel. 537007; fax 534005; internet www.bd-bank.com; f. 1992; invests in manufacturing, agribusiness and services; cap. 10.0m., res 1.8m., dep. 0.1m. (Dec. 1999); Chair. Sheikh Ibrahim bin Khalifa al-Khalifa.

The Housing Bank: POB 5370, Diplomatic Area, Manama; tel. 534443; fax 533437; f. 1979; provides housing loans for Bahraini citizens and finances construction of commercial properties. Chair. Sheikh Khalid bin Abdullah bin Khalid al-Khalifa; Gen. Man. Isa Sultan adh-Dhawadi.

'Offshore' Banking Units

Bahrain has been encouraging the establishment of 'offshore' banking units (OBUs) since 1975. An OBU is not permitted to provide local banking services, but is allowed to accept deposits from governments and large financial organizations in the area and make medium-term loans for local and regional capital projects. Prior to the Iraqi invasion of Kuwait in August 1990, there were 56 OBUs in operation in Bahrain. By 2000, however, the number of OBUs had declined to 49.

Allied Banking Corporation (Philippines): POB 20493, Manama; tel. 224707; fax 210506; e-mail ally3540@batelco.com.bh; Chair. Lucio C. Tan; Gen. Man. Ramon R. Landingin.

Alubaf Arab International Bank E.C.: POB 11529, UGB Tower, Diplomatic Area, Manama; tel. 531212; fax 523100; cap. US \$50.0m., res US \$2.7m., dep. US \$178.2m. (Dec. 1998); Chair. Rashid az-Zayani.

Arab Bank plc (Jordan): POB 813, Manama; tel. 212255; fax 224475; e-mail cib@arabbank.com.bh; Senior Man. Hani Fadayel.

Arab Banking Corporation B.S.C.: POB 5698, ABC Tower, Diplomatic Area, Manama; tel. 543000; fax 533062; internet www.arabbanking.com; f. 1980; cap. US \$1,000m., res. US \$927m., dep. US \$20,210m. (March 2000); Chair. Abdulmohsen Yousef al-Hunaif; Pres. and CEO Ghazi Abd al-Jawad.

Arab Investment Co. S.A.A. (Saudi Arabia): POB 5559, Bldg 2309, Rd 2830, As-Seef District 428, Manama; tel. 588888; fax 588885; e-mail taicone@batelco.com.bh; Dir Gen. Dr Saleh al-Humaidan.

Bahrain International Bank E.C.: POB 5016, 13th Floor, As-Salam Tower, Government Ave, Manama; tel. 538777; fax 535141; f. 1982; cap. US \$182.1m., res US \$31.1m., dep. US \$467.1m. (Dec. 1999); Chair. Faisal Yousuf al-Marzouk; Vice-Chair. Sami Salman Kaiksow.

Bahrain Middle East Bank E.C.: POB 797, BMB Centre, Diplomatic Area, Manama; tel. 532345; fax 530526; e-mail corpcomm@bmb.com.bh; internet www.bmb.com.bh; cap. US \$90.8m., res US \$40.7m., dep. US \$512.8m. (Dec. 1999); Chair. Sheikh Ali Jarrah as-Sabah; CEO Albert I. Kittaneh.

Bank Kapital T.A.S. (Turkey): POB 1967, UNITAG House, Bldg 150, 8th Floor, Govt Ave, Manama; tel. 215300; fax 217900.

Bank of Tokyo-Mitsubishi, Ltd. (Japan): POB 5850, Manama; tel. 227518; fax 225013; Regional and Gen. Man. Kan Satoh.

Banque de Commerce et de Placements (Switzerland): POB 11720, Manama; tel. 530500; fax 532400; e-mail bcpsa@batelco.com.bh; Man. Waqar al-Islam.

Banque Francaise de l'Orient (France): POB 5820, Manama; tel. 229995; fax 229994; Man. Herman Dom.

BNP Paribas (France): POB 4241, Bahrain Tower, Ground Floor, Manama; tel. 225275; fax 224697; Gen. Man. Jean-Christophe Durand.

Chase Manhattan Bank N.A. (USA): POB 368, Manama; tel. 535388; fax 535135; Man. Steven J. Fullenkamp.

Credit Agricole Indosuez (France): POB 5410, Manama; tel. 531345; fax 531476; Reg. Man. Jean-Claude Kitabgi.

Demirbank T.A.S (Turkey): POB 2515, Diplomatic Area, BDB Bldg, 6th Floor, Manama; tel. 534244; fax 534245.

Gulf International Bank B.S.C. (GIB): POB 1017, Ad-Duwali, Manama; tel. 534000; fax 522633; e-mail info@gib.com.bh; internet www.gibonline.com; cap. US \$450.0m., res US \$281.0m., dep. US \$8,491m. (Dec. 1998); Chair. Ibrahim Abd al-Karim; Gen. Man. Dr Abdullah al-Kuwaiz.

Hanvit Bank (Repub. of Korea): POB 1151, Manama; tel. 223503; fax 224429; Gen. Man. Yeo Eun Youn.

Korea Exchange Bank (Repub. of Korea): POB 5767, Manama; tel. 229333; fax 225327; e-mail kebbn002@batelco.com.bh; Gen. Man. Cheon Bong Ha.

Korfezbank (Turkey): POB 1937, UNITAG House, 6th Floor, Govt Ave, Manama; tel. 216161; fax 214477.

Mashreq Bank PSC (UAE): POB 20654, Manama; tel. 210114; fax 213516; Branch Man. K. G. Datta.

Muslim Commercial Bank Ltd (Pakistan): POB 10164, Manama; tel. 533306; fax 533308; Gen. Man. Faqir Eiaz Asgher.

National Bank of Abu Dhabi (UAE): POB 5886, Manama; tel. 214450; fax 210086.

National Bank of Kuwait S.A.K. (Kuwait): POB 5290, Bahrain BMB Centre, Dipl. Area, Manama; tel. 532225; fax 530658; e-mail nbkbah@batelco.com.bh; Gen. Man. Ali Y. Fardan.

Pamukbank T.A.S. (Turkey): POB 11378, Manama; tel. 537711; fax 535463.

Saudi National Commercial Bank (Saudi Arabia): POB 10363, Manama; tel. 531182; fax 530657; Man. Saleh Hussein.

Standard Chartered Bank plc (United Kingdom): POB 29, Manama; tel. 223636; fax 225001; CEO Rupert Keeley.

State Bank of India (India): POB 5466, Manama; tel. 224956; fax 224692; CEO A. K. Sharma.

Yapi ve Kredi Bankasi A.S (Turkey): POB 1004, Manama; tel. 530313; fax 530311; Dir Sabah Tuzcu.

Investment Banks

Al-Baraka Islamic Bank BSC (EC): POB 1882, Diplomatic Area, Manama; tel. 535300; fax 533993; e-mail baraka@batelco.com.bh; internet www.barakaonline.com; f. 1984; cap. US \$50.0m., res US \$5.0m., dep. US \$33.9m. (Dec. 1998); Chair. Mahmood Jameel Hassoubah; Gen. Man. Salah Ahmad Zainalabedin; 17 brs.

ANZ Investment Bank: POB 2397, 14th Floor, Al-Jasrah Tower, Bldg no. 5, Road 1702, Manama 317, Diplomatic Area; tel. 224210; fax 224478.

INVESTCORP Bank EC: POB 5340, Investcorp House, Diplomatic Area, Manama; tel. 530000; fax 530816; internet www.investcorp.com; f. 1982 as Arabian Investment Banking Corpn (INVESTCORP) EC, current name adopted in 1990; cap. US \$100.0m., res US \$79.1m., dep. US \$762.2m. (Dec. 1999); Pres. and CEO Nemir A. Kirdar.

Nomura Investment Banking (Middle East) EC: POB 26893, 10th and 11th Floor, BMB Centre, Diplomatic Area, Manama; tel. 530531; fax 530365; f. 1982; cap. US \$25m., res US \$107.1m., dep. US \$37.1m. (Dec. 1997); Chair. Takashi Tsutsui.

TAIB Bank EC: POB 20485, Sehl Centre, Diplomatic Area, Manama; tel. 533334; fax 533174; e-mail taib@taib.com; internet www.taib.com; f. 1979 as Trans-Arabian Investment Bank EC; current name adopted in 1994; cap. US \$84.2m., res US \$17.8m., dep. US \$274.8m. (Dec. 1998); Chair. Abd ar-Rahman al-Jeraisy; Vice-Chair. and CEO Iqbal G. Mamdani.

United Gulf Bank (BSC) EC: POB 5964, UGB Tower, Diplomatic Area, Manama; tel. 533233; fax 533137; e-mail ugbbah@ batelco.com.bh; f. 1980; cap. US $171.4m., res US $15.8m., dep. US $315.9m. (Dec. 1998); Chair. FAISAL H. ALAYYAR; Gen. Man. MUHAMMAD HAROUN.

Other investment banks operating in Bahrain include the following: ABC Islamic Bank EC, Amex (Middle East) EC, Arab Financial Services Co EC, Bahrain Investment Bank BSC, Bahrain Islamic Investment Co BSC, Capital Union EC, Daiwa Middle East EC, Faysal Investment Bank of Bahrain EC, First Islamic Investment Bank EC, Man-Ahli Investment Bank EC, Merrill Lynch Int. Bank Ltd, Nikko Europe Plc, Okasan Int. (Middle East) EC, Turk-Gulf Merchant Bank EC.

STOCK EXCHANGE

Bahrain Stock Exchange: POB 3203, Manama; tel. 261260; fax 256362; e-mail bse@bahrainstock.com; internet www .bahrainstock.com; f. 1989; nine mems; linked to Muscat Securities Market (Oman) in 1995, and to Amman Financial Market (Jordan) in 1996; Dir-Gen. Sheikh AHMAD BIN MUHAMMAD AL-KHALIFA.

INSURANCE

Abdullah Yousuf Fakhro Corpn: POB 39, Government Ave, Manama; tel. 275000; fax 273947; general.

Al-Ahlia Insurance Co BSC: POB 5482, 4th Floor, Chamber of Commerce Bldg, King Faysal Rd, Manama; tel. 225860; fax 224870; e-mail marketing@alahlia.com; internet www.alahlia.com; f. 1976; Chair. ABDULLATIF MUHAMMAD SHARIF ALRAYES; Gen. Man. JAMIL M. HAJJAR.

Arab Insurance Group BSC (ARIG): POB 26992, Arig House, Diplomatic Area, Manama; tel. 544444; fax 531155; e-mail info@arig.com.bh; internet www.arig.com.bh; f. 1980; owned by Governments of Kuwait, Libya and the UAE (49.5%), and other shareholders; reinsurance and insurance; Chair. NASSER M. AN-NOWAIS; CEO UDO KRUEGER.

Arab International Insurance Co EC (AIIC): POB 10135, Manama; tel. 530087; fax 530122; f. 1981; non-life reinsurance; Chair. and Man. Dir Sheikh KHALID J. AS-SABAH.

Bahrain Kuwait Insurance Co BSC: POB 10166, Diplomatic Area, Manama; tel. 542222; fax 530799; e-mail bkicbah@ batelco.com.bh; internet www.bkic.com; f. 1975; Gen. Man. HAMEED AL-NASSER.

Bahrain National Insurance (BNI): POB 843, Manama; tel. 227800; fax 224385; e-mail bnic@batelco.com.bh; internet www.bnic.net; f. 1998 by merger of Bahrain Insurance Co and National Insurance Co; all classes including life insurance; Chair. MUHAMMAD FAKHRO; Gen. Man. PATRICK IRWIN.

Gulf Union Insurance and Reinsurance Co: POB 10949, Ground Floor, Manama Centre, Manama; tel. 215622; fax 215421; e-mail guirco@batelco.com.bh; internet www.gulfunion-bah.com; Chair. IBRAHIM BIN HAMAD AL-KHALIFA.

Trade and Industry

GOVERNMENT AGENCIES

Bahrain Promotions and Marketing Board: POB 11299, Manama; tel. 533886; fax 531117; e-mail bahrain7@batelco.com.bh; internet www.bpmb.com; f. 1993; provides national focus for Bahraini marketing initiatives; attracts inward investment; encourages development and expansion of Bahraini exports; Chair. Minister of Commerce; CEO ROBIN MARRIOT (acting).

Supreme Council for Oil: Manama; formulates Bahrain's petroleum policy; Chair. Prime Minister.

CHAMBER OF COMMERCE

Bahrain Chamber of Commerce and Industry: POB 248, New Chamber of Commerce Bldg, King Faysal Rd, Manama; tel. 229555; fax 224985; e-mail bahcci@batelco.com.bh; internet www .bahchamber.com; f. 1939; 7,300 mems (1996); Pres. ALI BIN YOUSUF FAKHROO; Sec.-Gen. JASSIM MUHAMMAD ASH-SHATTI.

STATE HYDROCARBONS COMPANIES

Bahrain National Gas Co BSC (BANAGAS): POB 29099, Rifa'a; tel. 756222; fax 756991; e-mail banagas1@batelco.com.bh; f. 1979; responsible for extraction, processing and sale of hydrocarbon liquids from associated gas derived from onshore Bahraini fields; ownership is 75% Government of Bahrain, 12.5% Caltex and 12.5% Arab Petroleum Investments Corpn (APICORP); produced 202,955 metric tons of LPG and 189,803 tons of naphtha in 1996; Chair. Sheikh HAMAD BIN IBRAHIM AL-KHALIFA; Gen. Man. Dr. Sheikh MUHAMMAD BIN KHALIFA AL-KHALIFA.

Bahrain Petroleum Co b.s.c. (BAPCO): POB 25555, Awali; tel. 704040; fax 704070; e-mail info@bapco.net; f. 2000 by merger of Bahrain National Oil Co (f. 1976) and Bahrain Petroleum Co (f. 1980); fully integrated co responsible for exploration, drilling and production of oil and gas; supply of gas to power generating plants and industries, refining crude oil, international marketing of crude oil and refined petroleum products, supply and sale of aviation fuel at Bahrain International Airport, and local distribution and marketing of petroleum products; Pres. and Man. Dir MUHAMMAD SALEH SHEIKH ALI.

Gulf Petrochemical Industries Co BSC (GPIC): POB 26730, Sitra; tel. 731777; fax 731047; f. 1979 as a joint venture between the Governments of Bahrain, Kuwait and Saudi Arabia, each with one-third equity participation; a petrochemical complex at Sitra, inaugurated in 1981; produces 1,200 tons of both methanol and ammonia per day (1990); Chair. Sheikh ISA BIN ALI AL-KHALIFA; Gen. Man. MUSTAFA AS-SAYED.

UTILITIES

Ministry of Power and Water: (see Ministries, above); provides electricity and water throughout Bahrain.

Electricity

Directorate of Electricity: POB 2, King Faysal Rd, Manama; tel. 533133; supplies domestic and industrial power and street lighting.

Water

Directorate of Water Supply: POB 326, Manama; tel. 727009; responsible for water supply to all areas except Awali.

TRADE UNIONS

There are no trade unions in Bahrain.

Transport

RAILWAYS

There are no railways in Bahrain.

ROADS

At 31 December 1998 Bahrain had 3,164 km of roads, of which 77% were hard-surfaced. Most inhabited areas of Bahrain are linked by bitumen-surfaced roads. A modern network of dual highways is being developed, and a 25-km causeway link with Saudi Arabia was opened in 1986. A three-lane dual carriageway links the causeway to Manama. Other causeways link Bahrain with Muharraq island and with Sitra island. In March 1997 the Government approved the construction of a US $80m.-causeway linking Hidd on Muharraq island with the port of Mina Salman; the new causeway was scheduled to be completed in 2001. A second 2.5-km Manama-to-Muharraq causeway was opened in early 1997.

Directorate of Roads: POB 5, Sheikh Hamad Causeway, Manama; tel. 535222; fax 532565; responsible for traffic engineering, safety, planning, road design, maintenance and construction; Dir ESSAM A. KHALAF.

SHIPPING

Numerous shipping services link Bahrain and the Gulf with Europe, the USA, Pakistan, India, the Far East and Australia.

The deep-water harbour of Mina Salman was opened in 1962; it has 13 conventional berths, two container terminals (one of which has a 400-m quay—permitting two 180-m container ships to be handled simultaneously) and a roll-on/roll-off berth. Two nearby slipways can accommodate vessels of up to 1,016 tons and 73m in length, and services are available for ship repairs afloat. During 1998 893 vessels called at Mina Salman, and in that year the port handled 1,886,151 tons of cargo.

By 1999 work had begun on the construction of a new port and industrial zone at Hidd, on Muharraq island, which had been approved by the Cabinet in March 1997. At an estimated total cost of US $330m., the port was to have an annual handling capacity of 234,000 TEUs and was to include a general cargo berth and two container berths with roll-on roll-off facilities.

Directorate of Customs and Ports: POB 15, Manama; tel. 725555; fax 725534; responsible for customs activities and acts as port authority; Pres. of Customs and Ports EID ABDULLAH YOUSUF; Dir-Gen. of Ports Capt. MAHMOOD Y. AL-MAHMOOD; Dir-Gen. of Customs JASSIM JAMSHEER.

Arab Shipbuilding and Repair Yard Co (ASRY): POB 50110, Hidd; tel. 671111; fax 670236; e-mail asry@batelco.com.bh; internet www.asry.net; f. 1974 by OAPEC members; 500,000-ton dry dock opened 1977; two floating dry docks in operation since 1992; repaired 115 ships in 1999; Chair. Sheikh DAIJ BIN KHALIFA AL-KHALIFA; CEO MUHAMMAD M. AL-KHATEEB.

Principal Shipping Agents

Dilmun Shipping Agency: POB 11664, Manama; tel. 534530; fax 531287; e-mail dilmun@batelco.com.bh; Chair. Capt. P. CARR.

The Gulf Agency Co (Bahrain) Ltd: POB 412, Manama; tel. 530022; fax 530063; Man. Dir SKJALM BANG.

Al-Jazeera Shipping Co WLL: POB 302, Manama; tel. 728837; fax 728217.

Al-Sharif Group: POB 1322, Manama; tel. 530535; fax 537637; e-mail general@bahragents.com; Dirs ALI ABDURASOOL ASH-SHARIF, KHALID ABDURASOOL ASH-SHARIF.

UCO Marine Contracting WLL: POB 1074, Manama; tel. 730816; fax 83213; e-mail ucomarin@batelco.com.bh; Man. Dirs BADER A. KAIKSOW, HASSAN AS-SABAH, ALI AL-MUSALAM.

Yusuf bin Ahmad Kanoo: POB 45, Al-Khalifa Ave, Manama; tel. 220800; fax 229122; e-mail kanoocos@batelco.com.bh; air and shipping cargo services; Chair. and CEO ABDULLAH ALI KANOO.

CIVIL AVIATION

Bahrain International Airport has a first-class runway, capable of taking the largest aircraft in use. In 1997 there were 54,314 flights to and from the airport, and in 1996 a total of 3.4m. passengers were carried. Extension work to the airport's main terminal building has been carried out during the 1990s, in order to increase the airport's cargo-handling facilities.

Department of Civil Aviation Affairs: POB 586, Bahrain International Airport, Muharraq; tel. 321095; fax 321139; e-mail bahintapt@bahrainairport.co; internet www.bahrainairport.com; Under-Sec. IBRAHIM ABDULLAH AL-HAMER.

Gulf Air Co GSC (Gulf Air): POB 138, Manama; tel. 322200; fax 338033; e-mail gfpr@batelco.com.bh; internet www.gulfairco .com.; f. 1950; jointly owned by Govts of Bahrain, Oman, Qatar and Abu Dhabi (part of the United Arab Emirates) since 1974; services to the Middle East, South-East Asia, the Far East, Australia, Africa and Europe; Chair. Sheikh ALI BIN KHALIFA AL-KHALIFA (Bahrain); Chief Exec. IBRAHIM AL-HAMR.

Tourism

There are several archaeological sites of importance in Bahrain, which is the site of the ancient trading civilization of Dilmun. There is a wide selection of hotels and restaurants, and a new national museum opened in 1989. In 1998 Bahrain received some 2.9m. visitors from abroad (excluding Bahraini nationals residing abroad). Income from tourism totalled some US $270m. in that year.

Bahrain Tourism Co (BTC): POB 5831, Manama; tel. 530530; fax 530867; e-mail bahtours@batelco.com.bh; Chair. MUHAMMAD YOUSUF JALAL.

Tourism Affairs: Ministry of Cabinet Affairs and Information, POB 26613, Manama; tel. 201203; fax 211717; e-mail btour@ bahraintourism.com; internet www.bahraintourism.com; Asst Under-Sec. for Tourism Dr KADHIM RAJAB.

BANGLADESH

Introductory Survey

Location, Climate, Language, Religion, Flag, Capital

The People's Republic of Bangladesh lies in southern Asia, surrounded by Indian territory except for a short south-eastern frontier with Myanmar (formerly Burma) and a southern coast fronting the Bay of Bengal. The country has a tropical monsoon climate and suffers from periodic cyclones. The average temperature is 19°C (67°F) from October to March, rising to 29°C (84°F) between May and September. The average annual rainfall in Dhaka is 188 cm (74 ins), of which about three-quarters occurs between June and September. About 95% of the population speak Bengali, the state language, while the remainder mostly use tribal dialects. More than 85% of the people are Muslims, Islam being the state religion, and there are small minorities of Hindus, Buddhists and Christians. The national flag (proportions 5 by 3) is dark green, with a red disc slightly off-centre towards the hoist. The capital is Dhaka (Dacca).

Recent History

Present-day Bangladesh was formerly East Pakistan, one of the five provinces into which Pakistan was divided at its initial creation, when Britain's former Indian Empire was partitioned in August 1947. East Pakistan and the four western provinces were separated by about 1,000 miles (1,600 km) of Indian territory. East Pakistan was created from the former Indian province of East Bengal and the Sylhet district of Assam. Although the East was more populous, government was based in West Pakistan. Dissatisfaction in East Pakistan at its dependence on a remote central Government flared up in 1952, when Urdu was declared Pakistan's official language. Bengali, the main language of East Pakistan, was finally admitted as the joint official language in 1954, and in 1955 Pakistan was reorganized into two wings, east and west, with equal representation in the central legislative assembly. However, discontent continued in the eastern wing, particularly as the region was under-represented in the administration and armed forces, and received a disproportionately small share of Pakistan's development expenditure. The leading political party in East Pakistan was the Awami League (AL), led by Sheikh Mujibur (Mujib) Rahman, who demanded autonomy for the East. A general election in December 1970 gave the AL an overwhelming victory in the East, and thus a majority in Pakistan's National Assembly. Sheikh Mujib should therefore have been appointed Prime Minister, but Pakistan's President, Gen. Yahya Khan, would not accept this, and negotiations on a possible constitutional compromise broke down. The convening of the new National Assembly was postponed indefinitely in March 1971, leading to violent protests in East Pakistan. The AL decided that the province should unilaterally secede from Pakistan, and on 26 March Sheikh Mujib proclaimed the independence of the People's Republic of Bangladesh ('Bengal Nation').

Civil war immediately broke out. President Yahya Khan outlawed the AL and arrested its leaders. By April 1971 the Pakistan army dominated the eastern province. In August Sheikh Mujib was secretly put on trial in West Pakistan. Resistance continued, however, from the Liberation Army of East Bengal (the Mukhti Bahini), a group of irregular fighters, who launched a major offensive in November. As a result of the conflict, an estimated 9.5m. refugees crossed into India. On 4 December India declared war on Pakistan, with Indian forces intervening in support of the Mukhti Bahini. Pakistan surrendered on 16 December, and Bangladesh became independent. Pakistan was thus confined to its former western wing. In January 1972 Sheikh Mujib was freed by Pakistan's new President, Zulfiqar Ali Bhutto, and became Prime Minister of Bangladesh. Under a provisional Constitution, Bangladesh was declared to be a secular state and a parliamentary democracy. The new nation quickly achieved international recognition, causing Pakistan to withdraw from the Commonwealth in January 1972. Bangladesh joined the Commonwealth in April. The members who had been elected from the former East Pakistan for the Pakistan National Assembly and the Provincial Assembly in December 1970 formed the Bangladesh Constituent Assembly. A new Constitution was approved by this Assembly in November 1972 and came into effect in December. A general election for the country's first Jatiya Sangsad (Parliament) was held in March 1973. The AL received 73% of the total votes and won 292 of the 300 directly-elective seats in the legislature. Bangladesh was finally recognized by Pakistan in February 1974. Internal stability, however, was threatened by opposition groups which resorted to terrorism and included extremists such as Islamic fundamentalists and Maoists. In December a state of emergency was declared and constitutional rights were suspended. In January 1975 parliamentary government was replaced by a presidential form of government. Sheikh Mujib became President, assuming absolute power, and created the Bangladesh Peasants' and Workers' Awami League. In February Bangladesh became a one-party state.

In August 1975 Sheikh Mujib and his family were assassinated in a right-wing coup, led by a group of Islamic army officers. Khandakar Mushtaq Ahmed, the former Minister of Commerce, was installed as President, declared martial law and banned political parties. A counter-coup on 3 November brought to power Brig. Khalid Musharaf, the pro-Indian commander of the Dhaka garrison, who was appointed Chief of Army Staff; on 7 November a third coup overthrew Brig. Musharaf's brief regime, and power was assumed by the three service chiefs jointly, under a non-political President, Abusadet Mohammed Sayem, the Chief Justice of the Supreme Court. A neutral non-party Government was formed, in which the reinstated Chief of Army Staff, Major-Gen. Ziaur Rahman (Gen. Zia), took precedence over his colleagues. Political parties were legalized again in July 1976.

An early return to representative government was promised, but in November 1976 elections were postponed indefinitely and, in a major shift of power, Gen. Zia took over the role of Chief Martial Law Administrator from President Sayem, assuming the presidency also in April 1977. He amended the Constitution, making Islam, instead of secularism, its first basic principle. In a national referendum in May 99% of voters affirmed their confidence in President Zia's policies, and in June 1978 the country's first direct presidential election resulted in a clear victory for Zia, who formed a Council of Ministers to replace his Council of Advisers. Parliamentary elections followed in February 1979 and, in an attempt to persuade opposition parties to participate in the elections, President Zia met some of their demands by repealing 'all undemocratic provisions' of the 1974 constitutional amendment, releasing political prisoners and withdrawing press censorship. Consequently, 29 parties contested the elections, in which President Zia's Bangladesh Nationalist Party (BNP) received 49% of the total votes and won 207 of the 300 contested seats in the Jatiya Sangsad. In April 1979 a new Prime Minister was appointed, and martial law was repealed. The state of emergency was revoked in November.

Political instability recurred, however, when Gen. Zia was assassinated on 30 May 1981 during an attempted military coup, allegedly led by Maj.-Gen. Mohammad Abdul Manzur, an army divisional commander who was himself later killed in unclear circumstances. The elderly Vice-President, Justice Abdus Sattar, assumed the role of acting President but was confronted by strikes and demonstrations in protest against the execution of several officers who had been involved in the coup, and by pressure from opposition parties to reschedule the date of the presidential election. As the only person acceptable to the different groups within the BNP, Sattar was nominated as the party's presidential candidate, gaining an overwhelming victory at the November election. President Sattar announced his intention of continuing the policies of the late Gen. Zia. He found it increasingly difficult, however, to retain civilian control over the country, and in January 1982 he formed a National Security Council, which included military personnel, led by the Chief of Army Staff, Lt-Gen. Hossain Mohammad Ershad. On 24 March Gen. Ershad seized power in a bloodless coup, claiming that political corruption and economic mismanagement had become intolerable. The country was placed under martial law, with Ershad as Chief Martial Law Administrator (in October his title was changed to Prime Minister), aided by a mainly military Council of Advisers. A retired judge, Justice Abul Chowdhury, was nominated as President by Ershad. Political activities were banned. Later in the year, several former ministers were tried and imprisoned on charges of corruption.

Although the Government's economic policies achieved some success and gained a measure of popular support for Ershad, there were increasing demands in 1983 for a return to democratic government. The two principal opposition groups that emerged were an eight-party alliance, headed by the AL under Sheikh Hasina Wajed (daughter of the late Sheikh Mujib), and a seven-party group, which was led by the BNP under the former President Sattar (who died in 1985) and Begum Khaleda Zia (widow of Gen. Zia). In September 1983 the two groups formed an alliance, the Movement for the Restoration of Democracy (MRD), and jointly issued demands for an end to martial law, for the release of political prisoners and for the holding of parliamentary elections before any other polls. In November the resumption of political activity was permitted, and it was announced that a series of local elections between December 1983 and March 1984 were to precede a presidential election and parliamentary elections later in the year. A new political party, the Jana Dal (People's Party), was formed in November 1983 to support Ershad as a presidential candidate. Following demonstrations demanding civilian government, the ban on political activity was reimposed at the beginning of December, only two weeks after it had been rescinded, and leading political figures were detained. On 11 December Ershad declared himself President.

Bangladesh remained disturbed in 1984, with frequent strikes and political demonstrations. Local elections, due to take place in March, were postponed, as the opposition objected to their holding prior to the presidential and parliamentary elections, on the grounds that Ershad was trying to strengthen his power-base. The presidential and parliamentary elections, scheduled for May, were also postponed, until December, because of persistent opposition demands for the repeal of martial law and for the formation of an interim neutral government to oversee a fair election. In October Ershad offered to repeal martial law if the opposition would participate in the elections. They responded with an appeal for a campaign of civil disobedience, which led to the elections being indefinitely postponed.

In January 1985 it was announced that parliamentary elections would be held in April, to be preceded by a partial relaxation of martial law: the Constitution was to be fully restored after the elections. The announcement was followed by the formation of a new Council of Ministers, composed entirely of military officers and excluding all members of the Jana Dal, in response to demands by the opposition parties for a neutral government during the pre-election period. Once more, the opposition threatened to boycott the elections, as President Ershad would not relinquish power to an interim government, and in March the elections were abandoned and political activity was again banned. This was immediately followed by a referendum, held in support of the presidency, in which Ershad reportedly received 94% of the total votes. Local elections were held in May, without the participation of the opposition, and Ershad claimed that 85% of the elected council chairmen were his supporters, although not necessarily of his party. In September a new five-party political alliance, the National Front (comprising the Jana Dal, the United People's Party, the Gonotantrik Party, the Bangladesh Muslim League and a breakaway section of the BNP), was established to promote government policies.

In January 1986 the 10-month ban on political activity was ended. The five components of the National Front formally became a single pro-Government entity, named the Jatiya Dal (National Party). In March President Ershad announced that parliamentary elections were to be held (under martial law) at the end of April. He relaxed martial law, however, by removing all army commanders from important civil posts and by abolishing more than 150 military courts and the martial law offices. These concessions fulfilled some of the opposition's demands and, as a result, candidates from the AL alliance (including Sheikh Hasina Wajed herself), the Jamaat-e-Islami Bangladesh and other smaller opposition parties participated in the parliamentary elections in May (postponed from April). However, the BNP alliance, led by Begum Khaleda Zia, boycotted the polls. The elections were characterized by allegations of extensive fraud, violence and intimidation. The Jatiya Dal won 153 of the 300 directly-elective seats in the Jatiya Sangsad. In addition,

the 30 seats reserved for women in the legislature were filled by nominees of the Jatiya Dal. In July a mainly civilian Council of Ministers was sworn in. Mizanur Rahman Chowdhury, former General Secretary of the Jatiya Dal, was appointed Prime Minister.

In order to be eligible to stand as a candidate in the presidential election in October 1986, Ershad retired as Chief of Army Staff in August, while remaining Chief Martial Law Administrator and Commander-in-Chief of the Armed Forces. In early September Ershad officially joined the Jatiya Dal, being elected as Chairman of the party and nominated as its presidential candidate. At the presidential election in mid-October, which was boycotted by both the BNP and the AL, Ershad won an overwhelming victory over his 11 opponents.

In November 1986 the Jatiya Sangsad approved indemnity legislation, legalizing the military regime's actions since March 1982. Ershad repealed martial law and restored the 1972 Constitution. The opposition alliances criticized the indemnity law, stating that they would continue to campaign for the dissolution of the Jatiya Sangsad and the overthrow of the Ershad Government. In December 1986, in an attempt to curb increasing dissension, President Ershad formed a new Council of Ministers, including four MPs from the AL. The Minister of Justice, Justice A. K. M. Nurul Islam, was appointed Vice-President.

In 1987 the opposition groups continued to hold anti-Government strikes and demonstrations, often with the support of the trade unions and student groups. In July the Jatiya Sangsad approved a bill enabling army representatives to participate in the district councils, along with the elected representatives. The adoption of this controversial legislation led to widespread and often violent strikes and demonstrations, organized by the opposition groups, which claimed that the bill represented an attempt by the President to secure an entrenched military involvement in the governing of the country, despite the ending of martial law in November 1986. Owing to the intensity of public opposition, President Ershad was forced to withdraw the bill in August 1987 and return it to the Jatiya Sangsad for reconsideration. Political events were overshadowed in August and September, however, when the most severe floods in the region for 40 years resulted in widespread devastation. In a renewed effort to oust President Ershad, the opposition groups combined forces and organized further protests in November. Thousands of activists were detained, but demonstrations and strikes continued, leading to numerous clashes between police units and protesters. The unrest caused considerable economic disruption. In an attempt to forestall another general strike, President Ershad declared a nation-wide state of emergency on 27 November, suspending political activity and civil rights, and banning all anti-Government protests. In spite of the imposition of curfews on the main towns, reports of disturbances continued, as the opposition maintained its campaign to force Ershad's resignation. In December, as about 6,000 activists remained in detention, opposition parties in the Jatiya Sangsad announced that their representatives intended to resign their seats. After 12 opposition members had resigned and the 73 AL members had agreed to do likewise, President Ershad dissolved the Jatiya Sangsad. In January 1988 the President announced that parliamentary elections would be held on 28 February, but leaders of the main opposition parties declared their intention to boycott the proposed poll while Ershad remained in office. Local elections, which were held throughout Bangladesh in February and which were not boycotted by the opposition, were marred by serious outbreaks of violence. The parliamentary elections (postponed until 3 March) were also characterized by widespread violence, as well as by alleged fraud and malpractice. The opposition's boycott campaign proved to be highly successful; the actual level of participation by the electorate appeared to have been considerably lower than the Government's estimate of 50%. As expected, the Jatiya Dal won a large majority of the seats.

In late March 1988 a radical reshuffle of the Council of Ministers included the appointment of a new Prime Minister, Moudud Ahmed, a long-time political ally of Ershad and hitherto the Minister of Industry and a Deputy Prime Minister, in place of Mizanur Rahman Chowdhury. Owing to an abatement in the opposition's anti-Government campaign, Ershad repealed the state of emergency in April. Despite strong condemnation by the opposition and sections of the public, legislation to amend the Constitution, establishing Islam as Bangladesh's state religion, was approved by an overall majority in the Jatiya Sangsad in June. By early September, however, political events had been completely overshadowed by new monsoon floods, which began in August and proved to be the most severe in the area's recorded history. Bangladesh suffered further flooding in December 1988 and January 1989, following a devastating cyclone in late November. At the end of 1988 the Government established a national Disaster Prevention Council.

The Government claimed that it was reinforcing constitutionality and democracy when, in July 1989, the Jatiya Sangsad approved legislation limiting the tenure of the presidency to two electoral terms of five years each and creating the post of a directly-elected Vice-President (previously appointed by the President). In August Ershad appointed Moudud Ahmed, hitherto the Prime Minister, as Vice-President, to replace Justice A.K.M. Nurul Islam, who was dismissed following charges of inefficiency. Kazi Zafar Ahmed, formerly the Minister of Information and a Deputy Prime Minister, was promoted to the post of Prime Minister. Local elections were held in March 1990; although officially boycotted by the opposition parties, many members participated on an individual basis. In April Ershad announced that he would present himself as a candidate in the presidential election, which was scheduled for mid-1991.

In late 1990 the opposition groups, with the support of thousands of students, co-operated to intensify their anti-Government campaign. In October at least eight demonstrators were shot dead by riot police, more than 500 people were arrested, and Ershad announced the closure of Dhaka University and other educational institutions. Violent incidents also occurred in Chittagong and in several other towns in southern and central Bangladesh. On 27 November President Ershad proclaimed a nation-wide state of emergency for the second time in three years, suspending civil rights, imposing strict press censorship and enforcing an indefinite curfew throughout the country. On the following day, however, army units were summoned to impose order in the capital when thousands of protesters defied the curfew and attacked police. The death toll in resultant clashes between the troops and demonstrators was estimated at between 20 and 70. Under increasing pressure from the opposition groups, President Ershad resigned on 4 December and declared that parliamentary elections would be held before the presidential election; the state of emergency was revoked, and the Jatiya Sangsad was dissolved. Following his nomination by the opposition, Justice Shahabuddin Ahmed, the Chief Justice of the Supreme Court, was appointed Vice-President. He assumed the responsibilities of acting President and was appointed to lead a neutral caretaker Government, pending fresh parliamentary elections. Shahabuddin Ahmed dismissed heads of financial institutions, purged local government and ordered a massive reshuffle in the civil service to remove Ershad's appointees from important posts. The opposition parties welcomed these developments and abandoned their protest campaigns. They also demanded that Ershad be tried for alleged corruption and abuse of power. Ershad was placed under house arrest (he was later sentenced to 20 years' imprisonment for illegal possession of firearms and other offences).

Parliamentary elections were held in February 1991. The BNP alliance won an overall majority and, following discussions with the Jamaat-e-Islami, as a result of which the BNP was ensured a small working majority in the Jatiya Sangsad, Begum Khaleda Zia assumed office as Prime Minister. In May the Government was faced with the immense problems caused by a devastating cyclone, which killed up to 250,000 people and wrought massive economic damage. In August the Jatiya Sangsad approved a constitutional amendment ending 16 years of presidential rule and restoring the Prime Minister as executive leader (under the previous system, both the Prime Minister and the Council of Ministers had been answerable to the President). The amendment, which was formally enforced when it was approved by national referendum in the following month, reduced the role of the President, who was now to be elected by the Jatiya Sangsad for a five-year term, to that of a titular Head of State. Accordingly, a new President was elected by the Jatiya Sangsad in October. The successful candidate was the BNP nominee, the erstwhile Speaker of the Jatiya Sangsad, Abdur Rahman Biswas. In September the BNP had gained an absolute majority in the Jatiya Sangsad, following the party's victory in a number of by-elections. In November, despite strong protest from the opposition parties, the Government abolished the *upazilla* (sub-district) system of rural administration, introduced by Ershad in 1982. Henceforth, all public functions at *upazilla* level were to be performed through executive orders of the central Government, pending the introduction of a new system of rural administration. To this end, the Government established a special committee to review all aspects of local government.

In early 1992 measures to transfer public-sector industries to private ownership and to curb endemic labour unrest led to strong political resistance from the opposition. In April, in an apparent attempt to destabilize the Government, accusations were made against the leader of the Jamaat-e-Islami, Golam Azam, of complicity in Pakistani war crimes in 1971 and of having remained a Pakistani citizen while participating in Bangladesh politics. The AL MPs boycotted the Jatiya Sangsad over the issue and demanded that Azam be tried immediately by a special tribunal. Under a compromise reached in June 1992, charges were to be brought against him, but only through the highly dilatory regular courts. In August the Government survived a parliamentary motion of 'no confidence', introduced by the AL, by 168 votes to 122. The opposition accused the Government of failing to curb the increasing lawlessness in the country, notably amongst university students. The anti-terrorism measures introduced in November, however, were widely criticized as being excessively harsh and undemocratic. Subsequently, the opposition parties sank their differences in pursuit of a common demand that the general election due in 1996 be held under the auspices of a neutral, caretaker government. From late 1993 and into the first half of 1994 large-scale anti-Government demonstrations were organized by the opposition, which initiated a boycott of parliamentary proceedings in February 1994. In January the AL won the mayoralties of Dhaka and Chittagong, but a by-election success in March revealed the continuing strength of the BNP elsewhere.

In 1993–94 the apparently increasing influence and popularity of Islamic fundamentalism in Bangladesh was reflected in the prominent campaign against the feminist author, Taslima Nasreen, who angered certain traditionalist sectors of the population with her allegedly anti-Islamic public stance and statements. Despite her claim that she had been misquoted in the national press, there were demands from Islamic bodies, often expressed at large demonstrations, that Nasreen should be executed. The Government issued a warrant for the author's arrest on blasphemy-related charges, although she had gone into hiding before it could be implemented. In August 1994, with the apparent complicity of government officials, Nasreen secretly fled Bangladesh and was granted refuge in Sweden.

The number of strikes and violent protests staged by the opposition increased in the latter half of 1994, and culminated in the resignation of all the opposition members from the Jatiya Sangsad *en masse* in December. In spite of the political chaos, compounded by the holding of further general strikes by the opposition, the Prime Minister, with her party's parliamentary majority, pledged to maintain constitutional government.

In June 1995 former President Ershad was acquitted of illegally possessing arms; his sentence was thus reduced to 10 years. In the following month, however, Ershad was sentenced to a further three years' imprisonment for criminal misconduct.

The opposition caused more disruption in September–October 1995 by organizing nation-wide strikes, which were, at times, marked by outbreaks of violence. In response to the intensification of the anti-Government campaign and in an attempt to break the political impasse (the opposition parties were refusing to take part in the coming by-elections), the Jatiya Sangsad was dissolved in November at the request of the Prime Minister, pending the holding of a general election in early 1996. Despite opposition demands for a neutral interim government to oversee the election, the President requested that Begum Khaleda Zia's administration continue in office in an acting capacity. Strikes and demonstrations aimed at obstructing the electoral process were organized by the opposition throughout December 1995 and into January 1996. All of the main opposition parties boycotted the general election, which was held in mid-February, and independent monitors estimated the turn-out at only about 10%–15% of the electorate. Of the 207 legislative seats declared by the end of February, the BNP had won 205 (a partial repoll had been ordered in most of the 93 remaining constituencies where violence had disrupted the electoral process). The opposition refused to recognize the legitimacy of the polls and announced the launch of a 'non-co-operation' movement against the Government. Renewed street protests rendered the country virtually ungovernable and, finally, Begum Khaleda Zia agreed to the holding of fresh elections under neutral auspices. The Prime Minister and her Government duly resigned from their posts on 30 March and the Jatiya Sangsad was dissolved. President Biswas appointed the former Chief Justice

Muhammad Habibur Rahman as acting Prime Minister and requested that a fresh general election be held, under the auspices of an interim neutral government, within three months. In the general election, which was held on 12 June, the AL won 146 of the 300 elective seats in the Jatiya Sangsad, the BNP 116, the Jatiya Dal 32 and the Jamaat-e-Islami three. An understanding was rapidly reached between the AL and the Jatiya Dal, the latter's major interest being the release of Ershad, who had gained a legislative seat from within prison. (The former President was released on bail in January 1997.) Sheikh Hasina Wajed was sworn in as the new Prime Minister on 23 June 1996. Her Council of Ministers incorporated one member from the Jatiya Dal; it also included a number of retired officials and army officers.

Meanwhile, an unsuccessful military coup attempt on 20 May 1996 indicated the continuing fragility of the country's institutions. The Chief of Army Staff, Lt-Gen. Abu Saleh Mohammed Nasim, had objected to the action of the President (who retained direct control of the armed forces during the period prior to the general election) in dismissing some senior officers for political activity, and endeavoured to seize power, but was unable to mobilize sufficient support. Lt-Gen. Nasim was immediately replaced.

On 23 July 1996 the AL's presidential nominee, retired Chief Justice and former acting President, Shahabuddin Ahmed, was elected unopposed as Bangladesh's Head of State. In early September the AL won eight of the 15 seats contested in by-elections; this result gave the AL, which was also allocated 27 of the 30 nominated women's parliamentary seats in July, an absolute majority in the Jatiya Sangsad.

On assuming power, Sheikh Hasina Wajed had vowed to bring to justice those responsible for the assassination of her father, Sheikh Mujibur Rahman, in 1975. In November 1996 the Jatiya Sangsad voted unanimously to repeal the indemnity law that had been enacted in 1975 to protect the perpetrators of the military coup in that year; the BNP and the Jamaat-e-Islami, however, boycotted the vote. The trial of 19 people accused of direct involvement in Sheikh Mujib's assassination began in March 1997, with 14 of the defendants being tried *in absentia*.

Agitation continued throughout 1997; in March the opposition launched a campaign to protest against the Government's agreement with India with regard to the sharing of the Ganga (Ganges) waters (see below), and during an anti-Government strike held at the end of the month one person was killed and many were injured. The opposition organized further general strikes in July and August in protest at the Government's imposition of higher taxes and the increase in fuel prices. Despite a subsequent government ban on street rallies and processions, a series of strikes and demonstrations, organized by the BNP in conjunction with Islamic and right-wing groups, ensued. In addition to the disruption caused by such actions (which frequently involved violent clashes between demonstrators and police), the efficacy of the Jatiya Sangsad was limited by several boycotts of parliamentary proceedings organized by BNP deputies. In mid-1998 the opposition organized public demonstrations in protest at problems of law and order and power failures. The BNP's foremost demand was for the holding of fresh elections, reiterating the AL's earlier campaign. The AL, however, strengthened its position through a series of by-election victories. The departure, therefore, of the Jatiya Dal from the coalition in March had little effect on the ruling party's hold on power. In June and August Begum Khaleda Zia was indicted on charges of corruption and abuse of power, allegedly perpetrated during her tenure of the premiership.

In August 1998 the Government appealed for international aid following devastating floods (the worst since 1988), which had caused more than 500 deaths (this figure later rose to more than 1,500) and infrastructural damage estimated at about US $220m. By late August more than 60% of the country was submerged, including large parts of the capital, and the flooding lasted an unprecedented 11 weeks.

In September 1998 the controversial author, Taslima Nasreen, was reported to have secretly returned to Bangladesh after four years in self-imposed exile. On her return, a fresh warrant for Nasreen's arrest on charges of blasphemy was issued by a Dhaka court, and the police launched a hunt for her. Islamic extremists reiterated their demand for Nasreen's immediate arrest and execution and organized street protests. In late November Nasreen voluntarily surrendered herself before the High Court in Dhaka, where she was granted bail. In

January 1999 the author left Bangladesh for Sweden, following renewed death threats from Muslim fanatics. In August her most recent book was banned.

In September 1998 three former ministers, including the former Deputy Prime Minister, Shah Moazzem Hossain, and a prominent member of the BNP, K. M. Obaidur Rahman, were arrested in connection with the murder in 1975 of four former government ministers, who were shot dead in Dhaka two months after the murder of Bangladesh's founder, Sheikh Mujib. In October 2000 they were indicted on charges of murder. In total, 22 faced trial, of whom 14 had fled the country. In November 1998 a Dhaka court sentenced to death 15 of the 19 people accused of Mujib's assassination; four of the defendants were acquitted. Only four of those convicted, however, were in custody in Bangladesh; the 11 others remained fugitives abroad. In April 2000 the Chief Justice established a two-judge bench to review the sentences. In December, after a 64-day appeal hearing and High Court review of the sentences, the two judges confirmed the death sentence against 10 of the accused, but announced a split verdict on the sentences of five defendants. The case was to be referred to a third judge.

In November 1998 the BNP organized a three-day, nation-wide general strike in protest at alleged government repression. At least two people were killed and many injured when the police clashed with protesters in Dhaka (the tension was exacerbated by the BNP's disapproval of the death sentences imposed on Mujib's assassins). The Government, in response, accused the opposition of disrupting vital post-flood rehabilitation work. In mid-December at least 100 people were injured in Dhaka in further violent clashes between police and opposition activists, following protests against alleged electoral fraud on the part of the Government during a recent by-election. Later in the month the opposition was strengthened by a decision by the BNP and the Jamaat-e-Islami to accept Ershad and the Jatiya Dal in the anti-Government movement without any condition. In March 1999 the Minister of Home Affairs was forced to resign following an escalation in violence and political instability, culminating in two bomb explosions in Jessore, as a result of which 11 people died. In July the opposition condemned the Government's proposals to spend US $115m. on eight Russian fighter aircraft as expensive and unnecessary. The announcement in the following month of government plans to permit the transhipment of Indian goods through Bangladesh to the remote states in north-eastern India provoked further protests and strikes by the opposition, which claimed that the transit proposals would pose a threat to Bangladesh's sovereignty and would allow India to transport troops across Bangladesh's borders to suppress separatists in the adjacent Indian states. In retaliation, the Government claimed that the transhipment plans could earn Bangladesh US $400m. per year and boost the importance of the port of Chittagong. The Government was also criticized in August for its plans to evict thousands of people from Dhaka's slums in response to the increasing environmental risks and rising levels of crime; a major rehabilitation programme was to be instigated for those displaced. Unrest continued throughout the latter half of 1999 and into 2000. The opposition parties boycotted parliamentary proceedings in January 2000 and persisted in their demands for the holding of early elections. The situation remained tense, despite the efforts of influential business leaders to negotiate an arrangement between the Prime Minister and the opposition parties. Street demonstrations resumed in February. The announcement in the same month of the introduction of the controversial Public Safety Act, which permitted detention without trial for up to 90 days, provoked a three-day nation-wide strike. At the end of February another opposition-led strike caused two days of serious disruption.

In June 2000 the opposition parties discontinued their boycott of the Jatiya Sangsad in order to avoid disqualification (which occurs after an absence of 90 working days from the legislature without the Speaker's approval). However, following accusations that the Government was conspiring to change the Constitution, the opposition parties promptly resumed their boycott, claiming that they were not allowed to address the legislature, an allegation denied by the Speaker. Political unrest and strikes continued; in early August an assassination attempt on the Prime Minister was foiled. In mid-August three contempt of court petitions were filed against Sheikh Hasina Wajed by members of the Supreme Court Bar Association and opposition leaders, following her criticism of the judiciary and legal profession.

At the biennial conference of the Universal Festival Celebration Committee in Dhaka in July 2000, Hindu leaders threatened to demand a separate state for the Hindu community within Bangladesh if their demands for the restoration of a secular Constitution, as originally devised immediately after Bangladesh's independence, were not met.

In late August 2000 the High Court in Dhaka reduced the sentence imposed by a lower court on Ershad to five years' imprisonment, and stipulated the payment of a fine of 54m. taka for misappropriating funds during his tenure of power between 1983 and 1990. The court also ordered the confiscation of a property, the Janata Tower. In accordance with the Constitution, Ershad lost his parliamentary seat. Following an appeal in November, and shortly after Ershad had begun his term of imprisonment, the Supreme Court reduced the sentence to three years and seven months. In early September the opposition leader, Begum Khaleda Zia, was accused by the anti-corruption unit of financial irregularities.

Bangladesh suffered from devastating floods in August–October 2000, as a result of which several hundred people died and more than 1m. were displaced.

In foreign affairs Bangladesh has traditionally maintained a policy of non-alignment. Relations with Pakistan improved in 1976: ambassadors were exchanged, and trade, postal and telecommunication links were resumed. In September 1991 Pakistan finally agreed to initiate a process of phased repatriation and rehabilitation of some 250,000 Bihari Muslims (who supported Pakistan in Bangladesh's war of liberation in 1971) still remaining in refugee camps in Bangladesh. The first group of Bihari refugees returned to Pakistan from Bangladesh in January 1993, but the implementation of the repatriation process has since been very slow. Relations with Pakistan deteriorated in September 2000 when, at the UN Millennium Summit meeting in New York, the Bangladeshi Prime Minister condemned the military leadership of Pakistan, ostensibly as part of a general request for the UN to take action against undemocratic changes of government. Pakistan's leader, Gen. Pervez Musharraf, cancelled forthcoming meetings with Bangladesh's Prime Minister. On Sheikh Hasina Wajed's return to Dhaka, she demanded that Pakistan apologize for the atrocities committed by its army during Bangladesh's war of liberation and that those involved be brought to justice. At the end of November Pakistan withdrew its Deputy High Commissioner to Bangladesh, Irfanur Rehman Raja, following his remarks that the ruling Awami League, rather than the Pakistani army, was responsible for the bloodshed. The diplomat's refusal to apologize for Pakistan's actions in 1971 led to demonstrations in Dhaka. Raja remained in the capital until the Bangladesh Government declared him *persona non grata* in mid-December and demanded his immediate departure.

Relations with India have been strained over the questions of cross-border terrorism (especially around the area of the Chittagong Hill Tracts, where Buddhist tribal rebels, the Shanti Bahini, have been waging guerrilla warfare against the Bangladeshi police and the Bengali settlers for several years) and of the Farrakka barrage, which was constructed by India on the Ganga river in 1975, so depriving Bangladesh of water for irrigation and river transport during the dry season. In December 1996, however, Indo-Bangladesh relations were given a major boost following the signing of an historic 30-year water-sharing agreement. In January 1997 the Indian Prime Minister paid an official visit to Bangladesh, the first Indian Premier to do so for 20 years. In June 1999, during a visit to Dhaka by the Indian Prime Minister, Atal Bihari Vajpayee, to celebrate the inauguration of the first direct passenger bus service between Bangladesh and India, Vajpayee promised Bangladesh greater access to Indian markets and announced that India would give its neighbour US $50m. in credits over three years to help develop its transport and industrial infrastructure. In August the Bangladesh Government was criticized by the opposition for its approval of proposals to permit the transhipment of Indian goods through Bangladesh to the north-eastern states of India by Bangladeshi transport companies. In July 2000 Bangladesh and India resumed negotiations on border-related issues.

In 1985 Bangladesh and Burma (now Myanmar) completed work on the demarcation of their common border, in accordance with a 1979 agreement. During 1991 more than 50,000 Rohingya Muslims, a Myanma ethnic minority, crossed into Bangladesh to escape political persecution in Myanmar. Despite the signing of an agreement by the Governments of Bangladesh and Myanmar in April 1992 regarding the repatriation of the Rohingyas, the influx of refugees continued unabated (by the end of June the number of Rohingya refugees in Bangladesh had increased to about 270,000). By early September 1994 about 65,000 refugees had reportedly been voluntarily repatriated. Meanwhile, in December 1993 Bangladesh and Myanmar had signed an agreement to instigate bilateral border trade. By the end of May 1995, according to government figures, more than 216,000 Rohingyas had been repatriated. In July 1999, however, about 20,000 Rohingya refugees remained in camps in Bangladesh, despite the expiry of the official deadline for their repatriation in August 1997. By March 2000 231,000 refugees had returned to Myanmar; however, owing to the high birth rate, the number of Rohingya refugees remaining in Bangladesh stood at over 21,000 in June. Tension along the border between Bangladesh and Myanmar increased in November, following reports that Myanmar was laying landmines and that Myanma troops had been deployed in the border area. The Bangladesh security forces were put on alert. In January 2001 border guards exchanged fire, amid rising tension over a controversial dam project on the River Naaf, which Bangladesh claimed would cause flooding in its territory. The shooting took place after work began in Myanmar on the construction of an embankment. The Myanma authorities agreed to suspend the project.

In 1989 the Government attempted to suppress the continuing insurgency being waged by the Shanti Bahini in the Chittagong Hill Tracts, by introducing concessions providing limited autonomy to the region in the form of three new semi-autonomous hill districts. In June voting to elect councils for the districts took place relatively peacefully, despite attempts at disruption by the Shanti Bahini, who continued to demand total autonomy for the Chakma tribals. The powers vested in the councils were designed to give the tribals sufficient authority to regulate any further influx of Bengali settlers to the districts (the chief complaint of the tribals since Bengalis were settled in the Chittagong Hill Tracts, as plantation workers and clerks, by the British administration in the 19th century). Despite these concessions, the violence continued unabated, and refugees continued to flee across the border into India (the number of refugees living in camps in Tripura reached about 56,000). In May 1992 the Governments of Bangladesh and India negotiated an agreement which was intended to facilitate the refugees' return. However, the refugees, fearing persecution by the Bangladesh security forces, proved reluctant to move. Following the conclusion of a successful round of negotiations in early 1994, the process of phased repatriation commenced in mid-February. By August, however, only about 2,000 refugees had returned. In December 1997 the Bangladesh Government signed a peace agreement with the political wing of the Shanti Bahini ending the insurgency in the Chittagong Hill Tracts. The treaty offered the rebels a general amnesty in return for the surrender of their arms and gave the tribal people greater powers of self-governance through the establishment of three new elected district councils (to control the area's land management and policing) and a regional council (the chairman of which was to enjoy the rank of a state minister). The peace agreement, which was strongly criticized by the opposition for representing a 'sell-out' of the area to India and a threat to Bangladesh's sovereignty, was expected to accelerate the process of repatriating the remaining refugees from Tripura (who totalled about 31,000 at the end of December 1997). According to official Indian sources, only about 5,500 refugees remained in Tripura by early February 1998. By the end of 2000 most of the Chakma refugees had been repatriated, the district and regional councils were in operation, and a land commission had been established. The transitional period was scheduled to end in early 2001, with the withdrawal of the army from the region and its replacement by the Bangladesh Rifles.

In June 1992 the Indian Government, under the provisions of an accord signed with Bangladesh in 1974, formally leased the Tin Bigha Corridor (a small strip of land covering an area of only 1.5 ha) to Bangladesh for 999 years. India maintained sovereignty over the corridor, but the lease gave Bangladesh access to its enclaves of Dahagram and Angarpota. In September 1997 India granted Nepal a transit route through a 60-km corridor in the Indian territory joining Nepal and Bangladesh, thus facilitating trade between the latter two countries.

In March 2000 Bill Clinton made the first ever state visit by a US President to Bangladesh, as part of a tour of South Asia. The two countries' leaders discussed development issues, as a result of which Clinton announced several aid programmes. In October Sheikh Hasina Wajed visited the USA, where the leaders focused on environmental and investment issues. In addition, Clinton gave an assurance that those indicted for murdering Sheikh Mujib and currently in hiding in the USA would be extradited.

Bangladesh is a member of the South Asian Association for Regional Co-operation (SAARC, see p. 279), formally constituted in 1985, with Bhutan, India, Maldives, Nepal, Pakistan and Sri Lanka. Included in SAARC's charter are pledges of non-interference by members in each other's internal affairs and a joint effort to avoid 'contentious' issues whenever the association meets. The SAARC Preferential Trading Arrangement (SAPTA) was signed in April 1993 and came into effect in December 1995. It was also agreed that members should work towards the objective of establishing a South Asian Free Trade Area (SAFTA) by 2005.

Government

The role of the President, who is elected by the Jatiya Sangsad (Parliament) for a five-year term, is essentially that of a titular Head of State. Executive power is held by the Prime Minister, who heads the Council of Ministers. The President appoints the Prime Minister and, on the latter's recommendation, other ministers. Three hundred of the 330-member Jatiya Sangsad are elected by universal suffrage. An additional 30 women members are appointed by the other members. The Jatiya Sangsad serves a five-year term, subject to dissolution.

For purposes of local government, the country is divided into 64 administrative districts.

Defence

Military service is voluntary. In August 2000 the armed forces numbered 137,000: an army of 120,000, a navy of 10,500 and an air force of 6,500. The paramilitary forces totalled 55,200, and included the Bangladesh Rifles (border guard) of 30,000. Budget expenditure on defence was estimated at 30,000m. taka for 1999.

Economic Affairs

In 1998, according to estimates by the World Bank, Bangladesh's gross national product (GNP), measured at average 1996–98 prices, was US $44,224m., equivalent to $350 per head (or $1,407 per head on an international purchasing-power parity basis). During 1990–98, it was estimated, GNP per head increased, in real terms, at an average annual rate of 3.2%. Over the same period, the population increased at an average annual rate of 1.9%. Bangladesh's gross domestic product (GDP) increased at an average annual rate of 4.8% in 1990–99. Compared with the previous year, GDP grew by 5.5% in 1999/2000 and was projected to increase by about 6.0% in 2000/01.

Agriculture (including hunting, forestry and fishing) contributed an estimated 21% of total GDP in 1999. About 57% of the economically active population were employed in agriculture in 1999. The principal sources of revenue in the agricultural sector are jute, tea, shrimps and fish. Raw jute and jute goods accounted for an estimated 7.0% of total export earnings in 1998/99. Output of jute, however, decreased from 1,087,000 metric tons in 1998 to 812,000 tons in 1999. World jute prices, meanwhile, continued to decline. In 1990–99, according to the World Bank, agricultural GDP rose at an average annual rate of 2.3%. Despite severe flooding, agricultural GDP rose by 4.8% in 1998/99, according to official figures. (The flood waters destroyed the summer crops, but led to bumper winter crops.) In 1999/2000 the sector continued to recover and achieved a growth rate of an estimated 6.4%. The floods in 2000, however, again hindered production. Nevertheless, domestically-produced food supplies were expected to exceed the level reached in 1999/2000.

Industry (including mining, manufacturing, power and construction) employed 9.6% of the working population in 1995/96. The industrial sector contributed an estimated 27% of total GDP in 1999. During 1990–99, according to the World Bank, industrial GDP increased at an average annual rate of 3.9%. According to official figures, the GDP of the industrial sector grew by 4.9% in 1998/99 and was estimated to have expanded by 5.6% in 1999/2000.

Bangladesh possesses small deposits of coal (estimated at more than 1,000m. metric tons) and petroleum. Production of natural gas increased from 282,007m. cu ft in 1997/98 to an estimated 307,476m. cu ft in 1998/99, most of which was consumed by the domestic market. In the late 1990s total proven reserves of natural gas amounted to around 25,000,000m. cu ft, but recent discoveries of vast gas fields indicate that actual reserves may be twice as large or more.

Manufacturing contributed an estimated 17% of total GDP in 1999. The sector employed 7.5% of the working population in 1995/96. Based on a census of establishments engaged in manufacturing (excluding hand-loom weaving), the principal branches of the sector, measured by value of output, in 1991/92 were textiles (accounting for 23.8% of the total), food products (20.4%), wearing apparel (excluding footwear) (13.6%) and chemicals (11.4%). During 1990–98 manufacturing GDP increased at an average annual rate of 7.7%. According to official figures, the GDP of the manufacturing sector grew by 3.2% in 1998/99 and by an estimated 4.3% in 1999/2000.

Energy is derived principally from natural gas and petroleum. In 1999 natural gas provided about 70% of the country's commercial energy requirement, compared with less than 40% in the early 1980s. Imports of petroleum products and crude petroleum comprised an estimated 4.8% of the cost of total imports in 1998/99.

The services sector accounted for 52% of total GDP in 1999. In 1995/96 25.0% of the employed labour force were engaged in the sector. The GDP of the services sector increased at an average annual rate of 6.3% during 1990–99, according to the World Bank. Compared with the previous year, the sector's GDP rose by 4.9% in 1998/99 and by an estimated 5.0% in 1999/2000.

In 1999, according to the IMF, Bangladesh recorded a visible trade deficit of US $1,962.1m., and there was a deficit of $291.5m. on the current account of the balance of payments. In 1997/98 the principal source of imports was India (which contributed an estimated 15% of the total), while Western Europe was the principal market for exports (accounting for an estimated 49% of the total). Other major trading partners were the USA, Japan, the People's Republic of China and Hong Kong. The principal exports in 1998/99 were ready-made garments (accounting for an estimated 56.2% of export revenue), knitwear and hosiery products, raw jute and jute goods, and frozen shrimp and fish. The principal imports were capital goods (an estimated 24.4% of the total), textiles, rice and wheat.

In 2000/01 the overall budgetary deficit was projected to amount to 64,980m. taka, equivalent to more than 6% of GDP. Bangladesh's total external debt, according to the World Bank, was US $16,376m. at the end of 1998, of which $15,804m. was long-term public debt. In that year the cost of debt-servicing was equivalent to 9.1% of the total revenue from exports of goods and services. The annual rate of inflation averaged 4.9% in 1990–99. Consumer prices increased by 6.2% in 1999. About 2.5% of the total labour force were unemployed in 1996. Remittances from Bangladeshis working abroad, which are the country's second-largest source of foreign revenue after ready-made garments, rose to an estimated $1,949m. in 1999/2000.

Bangladesh is a member of the Asian Development Bank (see p. 131) and of the South Asian Association for Regional Co-operation (SAARC, see p. 279), which seeks to improve regional co-operation, particularly in economic development. Bangladesh is also a member of the International Jute Organization, which is based in Dhaka.

The problems of developing Bangladesh include widespread poverty, malnutrition and underemployment, combined with an increasing population and a poor resource base. There are grounds, however, for cautious optimism. Despite the frequency of natural disasters, food production has improved somewhat in recent years, along with efforts to enhance storage and distribution facilities. The Ministry of Food increased its expenditure on 14 food projects by about 66.8% in 1999/2000, compared with the previous year, to 737.8m. taka. The birth rate has decreased considerably, owing to a successful nation-wide birth-control campaign. In the 1990s high rates of growth were achieved in exports of non-traditional items, particularly ready-made garments and knitwear. Nevertheless, in 2001 the increasing fiscal deficit, exacerbated by the heavy losses incurred by state-owned enterprises, continued to cause concern. Bangladesh remains heavily dependent on foreign aid. In 1999/2000 total disbursed aid amounted to $1,575m. From 1995 the social and political unrest (including frequent general strikes) had a negative impact on the level of foreign investment. The Awami League Government, which came to power in 1996, emphasized its commitment to rehabilitating the banking sector and, despite resistance from trade unionists, to accelerating the process of privatizing the country's weak state-owned enterprises. In September 1999, however, Bangladesh's international aid donors warned that funds would be reduced if the Government failed to accelerate the implementation of economic reforms.

Although the Government pledged to continue the privatization programme in 2000 and confirmed its commitment to the partial transfer to the private sector of Biman Bangladesh Airlines (40% of the carrier's assets to foreign investors and 9% to employees of the airline), little progress was actually made. In the late 1990s it was estimated that the state-owned commercial banks had outstanding bad loans of about US $3,000m. The donors also criticized the Government for increasing expenditure on defence, while the education and health sectors remained underfunded. In August 2000 the taka was devalued by around 6%, in view of the weakness of other regional currencies and in order to avoid any loss of competitiveness, particularly in the textile industry (where competition from South-East Asia had continued to increase). The recently-discovered huge reserves of natural gas appeared to offer Bangladesh the opportunity to transform itself into a middle-income country. However, international gas and oil companies that were interested in acquiring exploration licences expressed concern at the lack of transparency and accountability on the part of the Bangladesh Government. An additional problem was the Government's reluctance to commit itself to allowing gas exports to India, the most obvious large market for the product.

Social Welfare

Basic health services remain relatively undeveloped. Health programmes give particular priority to the popularization of birth control (an estimated 4.2% of public-sector development expenditure was allocated to family planning in 1997/98). In 1996 Bangladesh had 967 hospitals, with a total of 39,138 beds, equivalent to one for every 3,120 inhabitants. In 1997 there were 26,628 registered physicians (equivalent to one for every 4,671 inhabitants) and 15,408 nurses. The 2000/01 budget allocated 11,120m. taka to expenditure on health and 7,670m. taka to social security and welfare (equivalent to 5.7% and 3.9%, respectively, of total government expenditure). In late 1996 about 20m. children were inoculated against poliomyelitis as part of a mass campaign by the Bangladeshi authorities to eradicate the disease. A report published by the World Health Organization (WHO) in 2000 had found that 35m.–77m. people were exposed to naturally-occurring arsenic in water supplies. The author urged the declaration of a public health emergency, stating that the contamination, first confirmed in 1993, constituted an environmental disaster and 'the largest mass poisoning of a population in history'.

Education

The Government provides free schooling for children of both sexes for eight years. Primary education, which is compulsory, begins at six years of age and lasts for five years. Secondary education, beginning at the age of 11, lasts for up to seven years, comprising a first cycle of five years and a second cycle of two further years. In 1997 an estimated 75.1% of children (80.6% of boys; 69.6% of girls) in the relevant age-group attended primary schools, while the enrolment ratio at secondary schools was 21.6% of children (27.6% of boys; 15.6% of girls) in the relevant age-group. Secondary schools and colleges in the private sector vastly outnumber government institutions. There are seven state universities, including one for agriculture, one for Islamic studies and one for engineering. The Government launched an Open University Project in 1992 at an estimated cost of US $34.3m. In 1990 the Government initiated the Primary Education Sector Project, which aimed to help to achieve universal primary education and the eradication of illiteracy by the year 2000. In 1995, however, according to UNESCO estimates, the rate of adult illiteracy was 65.2% (males 51.1%; females 73.8%). The 2000/01 budget allocated 33,440m. taka to education (equivalent to 17.0% of total government expenditure).

Public Holidays

2001: 1 January (New Year's Day), 21 February (Shaheed Day), 6 March* (Id al-Adha, Feast of the Sacrifice), 26 March (Independence Day), 26 March* (Muharram, Islamic New Year), 13 April (Bengali New Year), May* (Buddha Purinama), 1 May (May Day), 4 June* (Birth of the Prophet), 2 July (First Monday in July), July* (Jamat Wida), 15 August (National Mourning Day), August/September (Janmashtami), September* (Shab-i-Bharat), 26 October* (Durga Puja), 7 November (National Revolution Day), 16 December (Victory Day), 17 December* (Id al-Fitr, end of Ramadan), 25 December (Christmas), 26 December (Boxing Day), 31 December (Bank Holiday).

2002: 1 January (New Year's Day), 21 February (Shaheed Day), 23 February* (Id al-Adha, Feast of the Sacrifice), 15 March* (Muharram, Islamic New Year), 26 March (Independence Day), 14 April (Bengali New Year), May* (Buddha Purinama), 1 May (May Day), 24 May* (Birth of the Prophet), 1 July (First Monday in July), July* (Jamat Wida), 15 August (National Mourning Day), August/September (Janmashtami), September* (Shab-i Bharat), September/October* (Durga Puja), 7 November (National Revolution Day), 6 December* (Id al-Fitr, end of Ramadan), 16 December (Victory Day), 25 December (Christmas), 26 December (Boxing Day), 31 December (Bank Holiday).

* Dates of certain religious holidays are subject to the sighting of the moon, and there are also optional holidays for different religious groups

Weights and Measures

The imperial system of measures is in force, pending the introduction of the metric system. The following local units of weight are also used:

1 maund = 82.28 lb (37.29 kg).
1 seer = 2.057 lb (932 grams).
1 tola = 180 grains (11.66 grams).

Statistical Survey

Source (unless otherwise stated): Bangladesh Bureau of Statistics, Statistics Division, Ministry of Planning, E- 27/A, Agargaon, Sher-e-banglanagar, Dhaka 1207; tel. (2) 9118045; fax (2) 9111064; e-mail ndbp@bangla.net; internet www.bangla.net/ndb.

Area and Population

AREA, POPULATION AND DENSITY

Area (sq km)	147,570*
Population (census results)	
6 March 1981	89,912,000†
11 March 1991‡	
Males	57,313,929
Females	54,141,256
Total	111,455,185
Population (official estimates at mid-year)	
1995	119,900,000
1996	122,100,000
1997	124,300,000
Density (per sq km) at mid-1997	842.3

* 56,977 sq miles.
† Including adjustment for net underenumeration, estimated to have been 3.2%. The enumerated total was 87,119,965.
‡ Including adjustment for net underenumeration.

ADMINISTRATIVE DIVISIONS (1991 census)*

Division	Area (sq km)	Population ('000)†	Density (per sq km)
Barisal	13,297	7,757	583.4
Chittagong	33,771	21,865	647.4
Dhaka	31,119	33,940	1,090.7
Khulna	22,274	13,243	594.5
Rajshahi	34,513	27,500	796.8
Sylhet	12,596	7,150	567.6
Total	147,570	111,455	755.3

* Data refer to the local government structure resulting from reorganizations subsequent to the census date, whereby the divisions of Barisal (formerly part of Khulna) and Sylhet (formerly part of Chittagong) were created.
† Including adjustments for net underenumeration.

PRINCIPAL TOWNS (population at 1991 census)*

Dhaka (capital) . .	3,612,850	Comilla	135,313
Chittagong . . .	1,392,860	Nawabganj . . .	130,577
Khulna	663,340	Dinajpur . . .	127,815
Rajshahi . . .	294,056	Bogra . . .	120,170
Narayanganj . . .	276,549	Sylhet	114,300
Sitakunda . . .	274,903	Brahmanbaria . .	109,032
Rangpur . . .	191,398	Tangail . . .	106,004
Mymensingh (Nasirabad)	188,713	Jamalpur . . .	103,556
Barisal (Bakerganj) .	170,232	Pabna . . .	103,277
Tongi (Tungi) . .	168,702	Naogaon . . .	101,266
Jessore	139,710	Sirajganj . . .	99,669

* Figures in each case refer to the city proper. The population of the largest urban agglomerations at the 1991 census was: Dhaka 6,487,459 (including Narayanganj and Tongi); Chittagong 2,079,968 (including Sitakunda); Khulna 921,365; Rajshahi 507,435; Mymensingh 273,350; Sylhet 225,541; Comilla 225,259; Rangpur 208,294; Barisal 202,746; Jessore 169,349; Bogra 161,155.

BIRTHS AND DEATHS*

	Registered live births Rate (per 1,000)	Registered deaths Rate (per 1,000)
1990	32.8	11.4
1991	31.6	11.2
1992	30.8	11.0
1993	28.8	10.0
1994	27.8	9.0
1995	26.5	8.4
1996	25.6	8.1

* Registration is incomplete. According to UN estimates, the average annual rates per 1,000 were: Births 38.1 in 1985–90, 27.8 in 1990–95; Deaths 13.9 in 1985–90, 10.8 in 1990–95 (Source: UN, *World Population Prospects: The 1998 Revision*).

1997 (provisional): Registered live births 3,057,000 (birth rate 24.6 per 1,000); Registered deaths 958,000 (death rate 7.7 per 1,000) (Source: UN, *Population and Vital Statistics Report*).

Expectation of life (UN estimates, years at birth, 1990–95): 55.6 (males 55.6; females 55.6). Source: UN, *World Population Prospects: The 1998 Revision*.

ECONOMICALLY ACTIVE POPULATION*
(sample survey, '000 persons aged 10 years and over, year ending June 1996)

	Males	Females	Total
Agriculture, hunting, forestry and fishing	18,382	16,148	34,530
Mining and quarrying . . .	22	1	23
Manufacturing	2,586	1,499	4,085
Electricity, gas and water. . .	90	13	103
Construction.	936	80	1,015
Trade, restaurants and hotels. .	5,573	488	6,060
Transport, storage and communications	2,263	45	2,308
Financing, insurance, real estate and business services . . .	197	16	213
Community, social and personal services	3,343	1,748	5,092
Activities not adequately defined	373	795	1,168
Total employed	33,765	20,832	54,597
Unemployed	933	484	1,417
Total labour force	34,698	21,317	56,014

* Figures exclude members of the armed forces.
Source: ILO, *Yearbook of Labour Statistics*.

Agriculture

PRINCIPAL CROPS

('000 metric tons, year ending 30 June)

	1996/97	1997/98	1998/99
Wheat	1,454	1,803	1,908
Rice (paddy)	28,152	28,293	29,857
Millet	58	57	57
Potatoes	1,508	1,553	1,702
Sweet potatoes	406	398	398*
Beans (dry)	83	85*	85*
Chick-peas	62	60	60*
Lentils	171	163	165
Other pulses	199	203	203*
Groundnuts (in shell)	40	40	40*
Rapeseed	249	254	254*
Sesame seed	49	49	49*
Linseed	50	50	50*
Seed cotton†	42	33	45
Coconuts	89	89	89*
Cabbages	107	113	113*
Lettuce	51	51	51*
Tomatoes	93	94	94*
Cauliflower	76	79	79*
Pumpkins, squash and gourds	185	187	187*
Onions (dry)	142	138	138*
Garlic	39	40	40*
Beans (green)	48	49	49*
Other vegetables	722	725	725*
Melons	97	96	96*
Sugar cane	7,521	7,379	6,951
Other sugar crops	316	323	323*
Mangoes	187	187	187*
Pineapples	148	149	149*
Bananas	628	625	625*
Papayas	39	41	41*
Other fruits and berries	399	404	404*
Tea (made)	53	51	51*
Tobacco (leaves)	38	37	37*
Pimento and allspice	53	53	53*
Ginger	39	39	39*
Other spices	47	47	47*
Jute	1,057	1,087	812

* FAO estimate.
† Unofficial figures.
Source: FAO.

LIVESTOCK ('000 head, year ending September)

	1997	1998	1999†
Cattle	23,962	23,400	23,400
Buffaloes	854*	820	820
Sheep	1,158	1,110	1,110
Goats	34,478	33,500	33,500
Chickens	152,875	138,200	138,200
Ducks	13,178	13,000†	13,000

* Unofficial figure.   † FAO estimate(s).

Source: FAO.

LIVESTOCK PRODUCTS ('000 metric tons)

	1997	1998	1999
Beef and veal	165*	161	161*
Buffalo meat*	4	4	4
Mutton and lamb*	3	3	3
Goat meat	123*	126	126*
Poultry meat*	124	110	110
Cows' milk*	780	751	751
Buffalo milk*	22	22	22
Sheeps' milk*	22	22	22
Goats' milk*	1,328	1,280	1,280
Butter and ghee*	15	15	15
Cheese*	1	1	1
Hen eggs*	136	130	130
Other poultry eggs*	26	26	26
Wool:			
greasy*	1	1	1
clean*	1	1	n.a.
Cattle and buffalo hides*	32	31	31
Goatskins*	39	38	38

* FAO estimate(s).

Source: FAO.

Forestry

ROUNDWOOD REMOVALS

('000 cubic metres, excl. bark)

	1996	1997	1998
Sawlogs, veneer logs and logs for sleepers	174	174	174
Pulpwood*	69	69	69
Other industrial wood	361	367	374
Fuel wood	31,354	31,888	32,441
Total	31,958	32,498	33,058

* Annual output assumed to be unchanged since 1986.

Source: FAO, *Yearbook of Forest Products*.

SAWNWOOD PRODUCTION ('000 cubic metres, incl. railway sleepers)

	1996	1997	1998
Total (all broadleaved)	70	70	70

Source: FAO, *Yearbook of Forest Products*.

Fishing

('000 metric tons, live weight)

	1996	1997	1998
Capture	814.8	829.4	839.1
Freshwater fishes	445.4	451.1	457.1
Hilsa shad	225.6	214.4	205.7
Marine fishes	119.5	135.9	145.3
Aquaculture	449.6	512.7	583.9
Roho labeo		82.0	95.0
Catla	340.8	66.0	77.0
Silver carp		82.0	95.0
Other freshwater fishes		157.2	181.8
Giant river prawn	59.6	48.0	48.0
Other freshwater crustaceans		21.0	21.0
Penaeus shrimps	49.3	56.5	66.1
Total catch	1,264.4	1,342.2	1,423.0

Note: The 1997 and 1998 breakdown of carp and giant river prawn is estimated on the basis of officially reported total catch for miscellaneous freshwater fishes and miscellaneous freshwater crustaceans.

Source: FAO, *Yearbook of Fishery Statistics*.

Mining

(million cubic feet, year ending 30 June)

	1996/97	1997/98	1998/99*
Natural gas	260,990	282,007	307,476

* Provisional figure.

Source: IMF, *Bangladesh: Recent Economic Developments* (March 2000).

Industry

SELECTED PRODUCTS ('000 metric tons, unless otherwise indicated; public sector only, year ending 30 June)

	1994/95	1995/96	1996/97
Jute textiles	276	275	269
Hessian	89	81	73
Sacking	145	152	157
Carpet backing . .	35	35	33
Others	7	7	6
Woven cotton fabrics (million metres) . . .	17	10	11
Pure cotton yarn . . .	49	50	50
Newsprint	43	40	28
Other paper	40	42	40
Cement	316	426	611
Steel ingots	25	21	16
Re-rolled steel products . .	10	33	27
Petroleum products . .	1,371	1,160	1,310
Urea fertilizer . . .	1,981	2,134	1,631
Ammonium sulphate . .	5	7	9
Chemicals	20	25	19
Refined sugar . . .	270	184	135
Wine and spirits ('000 litres) . .	3,650	2,196	2,747
Tea	47	51	53
Edible oil and vegetable ghee . .	30	31	26
Cigarettes ('000 million) . .	17	16	19
Electric energy (million kWh) . .	10,806	11,474	11,492

1997/98 ('000 metric tons, unless otherwise indicated): Pure cotton yarn 53.5, Woven cotton fabrics 10.7 million metres, Petroleum products 1,400, Cement 574.3, Refined sugar 195.4.

Finance

CURRENCY AND EXCHANGE RATES

Monetary Units
100 poisha = 1 taka.

Sterling, Dollar and Euro Equivalents (29 December 2000)
£1 sterling = 80.58 taka;
US $1 = 54.00 taka;
€1 = 50.25 taka;
1,000 taka = £12.41 = $18.52 = €19.90.

Average Exchange Rate (taka per US $)
1998   46.906
1999   49.085
2000   52.142

BUDGET (million taka, year ending 30 June)

Revenue	1997/98	1998/99*	1999/2000†
Taxation	147,000	158,400	185,100
Customs duties . . .	43,500	47,400	57,500
Income and profit taxes . .	20,000	23,500	27,800
Excise duties . . .	2,200	2,200	2,300
Value-added tax . .	69,800	73,200	83,700
Non-tax	38,500	39,700	56,200
Profits from non-financial enterprises . .	3,400	n.a.	n.a.
Profits from financial institutions	4,800	n.a.	n.a.
Interest receipts . . .	5,700	n.a.	n.a.
Registration fees . . .	1,800	n.a.	n.a.
Services	9,700	n.a.	n.a.
Bangladesh Telephone and Telegraph Board . .	7,700	n.a.	n.a.
Total	185,500	198,100	241,200

Expenditure	1997/98	1998/99*	1999/2000†
Goods and services . . .	78,600	83,200	88,900
Pay and allowances . .	46,500	51,000	55,800
Operations and maintenance .	6,200	8,200	8,000
Works	2,300	2,400	2,800
Interest payments . . .	23,300	29,400	28,100
Domestic	16,000	22,200	20,600
Foreign	7,300	7,200	7,500
Subsidies and current transfers	41,300	51,500	50,100
Local government transfers .	700	800	800
Grants in aid . . .	24,700	23,200	23,200
Pensions and gratuities . .	7,800	10,800	12,100
Targeted food distribution .	5,200	9,400	4,200
Other subsidies . . .	400	6,000	8,900
Operational deficits . .	1,200	1,300	1,000
Unallocated	700	3,900	10,800
Gross current expenditure .	143,900	167,800	177,900
Less Recoveries . . .	700	500	500
Net current expenditure .	143,200	167,300	177,400

* Revised figures.   †Estimates.

Source: IMF, *Bangladesh: Recent Economic Developments* (March 2000).

PUBLIC-SECTOR DEVELOPMENT EXPENDITURE
(estimates, million taka, year ending 30 June)

	1997/98	1998/99‡	1999/2000§
Agriculture	6,000	6,100	8,400
Rural development . . .	9,000	12,700	16,000
Water and flood control . .	10,400	8,800	10,200
Industry	1,200	1,000	2,000
Power, scientific research and natural resources . .	18,800	21,000	26,100
Transport*	22,600	22,500	24,700
Communications . . .	3,900	3,900	5,000
Physical planning and housing	6,000	6,700	10,200
Education	14,900	16,900	19,600
Health	5,300		
Family planning . . .	6,300	10,200	15,300
Social welfare† . . .	1,600	1,700	2,200
Other sectoral . . .	200	—	400
Total sectoral allocations .	106,400	111,400	140,100
Block allocations . . .	10,900	8,700	9,200
Food for Work . . .	5,700	5,300	2,400
Technical assistance . . .	3,000	3,200	3,200
Domestic self-financing . .	1,700	1,800	2,500
Total development expenditure	122,000	125,100	155,000

* Includes Jamuna Bridge.
† Includes employment.
‡ Revised figures.
§ Estimates.

Source: Ministry of Planning (Implementation, Monitoring and Evaluation Division).

INTERNATIONAL RESERVES (US $ million at 31 December)

	1997	1998	1999
Gold*	25.3	22.3	19.6
IMF special drawing rights .	29.2	12.9	0.9
Reserve position in IMF . .	0.1	0.2	0.3
Foreign exchange . . .	1,552.1	1,892.3	1,602.5
Total	**1,606.7**	**1,927.7**	**1,623.2**

* Valued at market-related prices.

Source: IMF, *International Financial Statistics*.

MONEY SUPPLY (million taka at 31 December)

	1997	1998	1999
Currency outside banks . . .	76,074	80,756	93,870
Demand deposits at deposit money banks*	76,559	83,214	91,055
Total money	**152,633**	**163,970**	**184,925**

* Comprises the scheduled banks plus the agricultural and industrial development banks.

Source: IMF, *International Financial Statistics*.

COST OF LIVING (Consumer Price Index for middle-class families in Dhaka, year ending 30 June; base: 1973/74 = 100)

	1994/95	1995/96	1996/97
Food	732	774	812
Fuel and lighting	1,014	1,030	1,056
Housing and household requisites	1,040	1,047	1,067
Clothing and footwear . . .	439	439	439
Miscellaneous	860	883	883
All items	**786**	**818**	**850**

All items (base: 1985/86 = 100): 195.1 in 1996/97; 208.7 in 1997/98; 227.3 in 1998/99; 236.2 in 1999/2000 (Source: Metropolitan Chamber of Commerce and Industry, Dhaka).

NATIONAL ACCOUNTS
(million taka at current prices, year ending 30 June)

Expenditure on the Gross Domestic Product

	1996/97	1997/98*	1998/99*
Government final consumption expenditure	198,225	215,110	235,540
Private final consumption expenditure	1,099,416	1,200,100	1,350,810
Gross capital formation . .	214,272	232,190	271,330
Total domestic expenditure .	**1,511,913**	**1,647,400**	**1,857,680**
Exports of goods and services . .	216,723	266,810	289,860
Less Imports of goods and services	325,591	365,880	409,930
GDP in purchasers' values . .	**1,403,045**	**1,548,330**	**1,737,620**

* Figures are rounded to the nearest 10 million taka (Source: IMF, *International Financial Statistics*).

Gross Domestic Product by Economic Activity

	1995/96	1996/97	1997/98*
Agriculture and hunting . . .	282,057	294,605	312,519
Forestry and logging . . .	43,059	45,531	50,096
Fishing	64,870	71,496	82,182
Mining and quarrying . . .	282	365	457
Manufacturing	124,411	130,496	145,115
Electricity, gas and water. . .	28,630	30,318	32,918
Construction.	76,599	82,863	91,544
Wholesale and retail trade . .	117,461	124,996	137,433
Transport, storage and communications . . .	148,238	161,161	172,946
Owner-occupied dwellings .	124,567	135,106	146,597
Finance, insurance and business services	26,373	28,512	30,285
Public administration and defence	70,742	79,950	91,577
Other services	194,311	217,646	247,254
Total	**1,301,600**	**1,403,045**	**1,540,923**

* Provisional figures.

BALANCE OF PAYMENTS (US $ million)

	1997	1998	1999
Exports of goods f.o.b. . . .	4,839.9	5,141.4	5,458.3
Imports of goods f.o.b. . . .	−6,587.6	−6,715.7	−7,420.4
Trade balance	**−1,747.7**	**−1,574.3**	**−1,962.1**
Exports of services . . .	687.3	723.9	780.2
Imports of services . . .	−1,287.9	−1,237.1	−1,431.7
Balance on goods and services.	**−2,348.3**	**−2,087.4**	**−2,613.7**
Other income received . . .	86.5	91.5	94.4
Other income paid . . .	−196.1	−206.1	−262.7
Balance on goods, services and income	**−2,457.9**	**−2,202.1**	**−2,782.0**
Current transfers received . .	2,134.9	2,172.9	2,495.8
Current transfers paid . .	−4.3	−5.9	−5.3
Current balance	**−327.3**	**−35.1**	**−291.5**
Capital account (net). . .	368.1	238.7	362.4
Direct investment abroad . .	−3.1	−3.0	n.a.
Direct investment from abroad .	141.3	190.1	178.6
Portfolio investment assets .	—	−0.3	4.4
Portfolio investment liabilities .	−14.5	−3.8	−1.0
Other investment assets . .	−674.6	−859.7	−1,146.3
Other investment liabilities .	451.1	560.7	437.4
Net errors and omissions . .	−77.3	201.0	264.2
Overall balance	**−136.3**	**288.5**	**−191.6**

Source: IMF, *International Financial Statistics*.

FOREIGN AID DISBURSEMENTS (US $ million, year ending 30 June)

	1996/97	1997/98	1998/99*
Bilateral donors	717.2	608.8	638.4
Australia	15.7	9.1	6.9
Canada	30.4	21.1	26.8
Denmark	22.7	25.0	32.6
France	27.0	20.6	10.7
Germany	33.8	40.0	36.7
Japan	368.2	301.7	235.0
Netherlands	71.9	25.0	43.1
Norway	16.7	29.3	9.5
Saudi Arabia	10.1	7.0	4.2
Sweden	22.1	23.4	22.2
United Kingdom . . .	20.6	28.0	52.1
USA	35.3	38.6	69.1
Multilateral donors . . .	764.0	809.8	834.9
Asian Development Bank .	254.9	310.0	217.5
International Development Association	313.8	327.0	477.0
European Union . . .	62.0	60.0	39.2
World Food Programme . .	18.3	43.2	82.6
UNICEF	60.2	22.0	19.2
Islamic Development Bank .	19.3	16.3	12.3
OPEC Fund	17.4	3.0	3.5
Total aid disbursements . .	**1,481.2**	**1,418.6**	**1,473.3**

* Estimates.

Source: Ministry of Finance (Economic Relations Division).

External Trade

PRINCIPAL COMMODITIES (US $ million, year ending 30 June)

Imports	1996/97	1997/98	1998/99*
Rice.	28	247	680
Wheat	156	122	351
Edible oil	216	216	287
Petroleum products . . .	341	295	270
Crude petroleum	174	140	118
Cotton	195	207	233
Yarn	395	327	283
Fertilizer	150	108	120
Cement	156	152	105
Textiles	1,098	1,264	1,109
Capital goods	1,937	2,072	1,969
Total (incl. others) . . .	**7,162**	**7,520**	**8,054**

Exports			1996/97	1997/98	1998/99*
Raw jute	.	.	116.0	107.8	71.8
Jute goods (excl. carpets)	.	.	313.3	278.6	301.9
Leather and leather products	.	.	195.0	190.3	168.2
Frozen shrimp and fish	.	.	320.0	293.8	274.3
Ready-made garments	.	.	2,238.0	2,843.3	2,984.7
Knitwear and hosiery products	.		763.3	940.3	1,035.4
Chemical fertilizers	.	.	104.1	58.7	58.7
Total (incl. others)	.	.	4,418.3	5,161.2	5,312.9

* Estimates.

Source: Bangladesh Bank.

PRINCIPAL TRADING PARTNERS (US $ million)

Imports c.i.f.			1997	1998	1999
China, People's Republic	.	.	622.1	546.5	555.7
Germany	.	.	186.1	163.5	143.6
Hong Kong	.	.	430.7	452.2	473.0
India	.	.	795.6	1,178.8	1,154.6
Japan	.	.	471.7	455.5	508.9
Korea, Republic	.	.	379.3	331.4	284.1
Saudi Arabia	.	.	117.6	71.8	55.9
Singapore	.	.	250.8	430.2	680.5
United Kingdom	.	.	207.8	313.7	245.2
USA	.	.	285.0	242.2	449.1
Total (incl. others)	.	.	6,862.5	7,369.7	8,478.9

Exports f.o.b.			1997	1998	1999
Canada	.	.	70.6	78.8	80.2
France	.	.	262.1	254.1	254.6
Germany	.	.	357.1	403.5	464.9
Hong Kong	.	.	91.3	70.1	65.0
Italy	.	.	196.8	232.2	212.3
Japan	.	.	86.9	63.7	77.4
Netherlands	.	.	177.5	189.3	182.5
United Kingdom	.	.	367.7	346.7	376.9
USA	.	.	1,289.5	1,368.2	1,465.3
Total (incl. others)	.	.	3,627.5	3,821.9	4,499.0

Source: Asian Development Bank, *Key Indicators of Developing Asian and Pacific Countries.*

Transport

RAILWAYS (traffic, year ending 30 June)

	1994/95	1995/96	1996/97
Passenger-kilometres (million) .	4,037	3,333	3,754
Freight ton-kilometres (million) .	760	689	782

Source: Bangladesh Railway.

ROAD TRAFFIC (motor vehicles in use at 31 December)

	1996	1997	1998
Passenger cars	.	.	55,034	54,784	57,068
Buses and coaches	.	.	28,347	29,310	30,361
Lorries and vans	.	.	37,322	40,084	42,425
Road tractors	.	.	2,667	2,769	2,813
Motor cycles and mopeds	.	.	140,864	145,259	145,259
Total	.	.	264,234	272,206	277,926

Source: International Road Federation, *World Road Statistics.*

SHIPPING
Merchant Fleet (registered at 31 December)

			1996	1997	1998
Number of vessels	.	.	317	314	309
Total displacement ('000 grt)	.		435.7	419.2	413.8

Source: Lloyd's Register of Shipping, *World Fleet Statistics.*

International Sea-borne Freight Traffic
('000 long tons, year ending 30 June)

	1994/95	1995/96	1996/97
Mongla			
Goods loaded .	725	396	520
Goods unloaded	2,322	2,443	2,174
Chittagong			
Goods loaded	1,417	1,451	1,435
Goods unloaded	8,638	8,738	9,063
Total goods loaded .	2,142	1,847	1,955
Total goods unloaded .	10,960	11,181	11,237

CIVIL AVIATION
(traffic on scheduled Biman Bangladesh services)

	1995	1996	1997
Kilometres flown (million) .	19.0	19	20.3
Passengers carried ('000) .	1,261	1,252	1,315
Passenger-km (million) .	3,058	2,995	3,233
Freight ton-km (million) .	n.a.	136	200.4

Source: ICAO and UN, *Statistical Yearbook for Asia and the Pacific.*

Tourism

TOURIST ARRIVALS BY COUNTRY OF NATIONALITY

			1996	1997	1998
China, People's Republic	.	.	4,016	4,869	4,379
India	.	.	53,007	61,606	57,937
Japan	.	.	5,716	6,482	7,808
Korea, Republic	.	.	6,017	6,923	6,154
Malaysia	.	.	3,927	2,680	2,857
Nepal	.	.	3,628	5,296	4,799
Netherlands	.	.	3,511	3,784	2,589
Pakistan	.	.	7,070	11,481	12,087
United Kingdom	.	.	33,463	28,115	19,605
USA	.	.	11,033	12,070	11,358
Total (incl. others)	.	.	165,887	182,420	171,961

Source: World Tourism Organization, *Yearbook of Tourism Statistics.*

Tourism receipts (US $ million): 32 in 1996; 59 in 1997.

Hotel rooms*: 4,166 in 1996; 4,249 in 1997.

Hotel beds: 8,386 in 1996; 8,552 in 1997.

* Including rooms of similar establishments.

Source: UN, *Statistical Yearbook for Asia and the Pacific.*

Communications Media

	1995	1996	1997
Radio receivers ('000 in use) . .	5,600	6,000	6,150
Television receivers ('000 in use) .	700	750	770
Telephones ('000 in use) . . .	315	388	389
Telefax stations (number in use)*†	4,000	n.a.	n.a.
Mobile cellular telephones			
(subscribers)*	2,500	4,000	26,000
Daily newspapers:			
Number of titles	51‡	37	n.a.
Average circulation ('000) . .	950‡	1,117	n.a.

* Twelve months ending 30 June of year stated.
† Provisional figures.
‡ Estimate.
Sources: mainly UNESCO, *Statistical Yearbook*; UN, *Statistical Yearbook*.

Education

(1995/96)

	Institutions	Students
Primary schools	75,595	17,580,000
Secondary schools	12,858	5,788,000
Universities (government) . . .	11	118,945

Technical colleges and institutes (government, 1990/91)*: 141 institutions, 23,722 students.

* In addition to government-owned and managed institutes, there are many privately-administered vocational training centres.

Directory

The Constitution

The members who were returned from East Pakistan (now Bangladesh) for the Pakistan National Assembly and the Provincial Assembly in the December 1970 elections formed the Bangladesh Constituent Assembly. A new Constitution for the People's Republic of Bangladesh was approved by this Assembly on 4 November 1972 and came into effect on 16 December 1972. Following the military coup of 24 March 1982, the Constitution was suspended, and the country was placed under martial law. On 10 November 1986 martial law was repealed and the suspended Constitution was revived. The main provisions of the Constitution, including amendments, are listed below.

SUMMARY

Fundamental Principles of State Policy

The Constitution was initially based on the fundamental principles of nationalism, socialism, democracy and secularism, but in 1977 an amendment replaced secularism with Islam. The amendment states that the country shall be guided by 'the principles of absolute trust and faith in the Almighty Allah, nationalism, democracy and socialism'. A further amendment in 1988 established Islam as the state religion. The Constitution aims to establish a society free from exploitation in which the rule of law, fundamental human rights and freedoms, justice and equality are to be secured for all citizens. A socialist economic system is to be established to ensure the attainment of a just and egalitarian society through state and co-operative ownership as well as private ownership within limits prescribed by law. A universal, free and compulsory system of education shall be established. In foreign policy the State shall endeavour to consolidate, preserve, and strengthen fraternal relations among Muslim countries based on Islamic solidarity.

Fundamental Rights

All citizens are equal before the law and have a right to its protection. Arbitrary arrest or detention, discrimination based on race, age, sex, birth, caste or religion, and forced labour are prohibited. Subject to law, public order and morality, every citizen has freedom of movement, of assembly and of association. Freedom of conscience, of speech, of the press and of religious worship are guaranteed.

GOVERNMENT

The President

The President is the constitutional Head of State and is elected by Parliament (Jatiya Sangsad) for a term of five years. He is eligible for re-election. The supreme control of the armed forces is vested in the President. He appoints the Prime Minister and other Ministers as well as the Chief Justice and other judges.

The Executive

Executive authority shall rest in the Prime Minister and shall be exercised by him either directly or through officers subordinate to him in accordance with the Constitution.

There shall be a Council of Ministers to aid and advise the Prime Minister.

The Legislature

Parliament (Jatiya Sangsad) is a unicameral legislature. It comprises 300 members and an additional 30 women members elected by the other members. Members of Parliament, other than the 30 women members, are directly elected on the basis of universal adult franchise from single territorial constituencies. Persons aged 18 and over are entitled to vote. The parliamentary term lasts for five years. War can be declared only with the assent of Parliament. In the case of actual or imminent invasion, the President may take whatever action he may consider appropriate.

THE JUDICIARY

The Judiciary comprises a Supreme Court with High Court and an Appellate Division. The Supreme Court consists of a Chief Justice and such other judges as may be appointed by the President. The High Court division has such original appellate and other jurisdiction and powers as are conferred on it by the Constitution and by other law. The Appellate Division has jurisdiction to determine appeals from decisions of the High Court division. Subordinate courts, in addition to the Supreme Court, have been established by law.

ELECTIONS

An Election Commission supervises elections, delimits constituencies and prepares electoral rolls. It consists of a Chief Election Commissioner and other Commissioners as may be appointed by the President. The Election Commission is independent in the exercise of its functions. Subject to the Constitution, Parliament may make provision as to elections where necessary.

The Government

HEAD OF STATE

President: Shahabuddin Ahmed (elected 23 July 1996; took office 9 October 1996).

COUNCIL OF MINISTERS

(April 2001)

Prime Minister and Minister of the Armed Forces Division, of the Cabinet Division, of Special Affairs, of Defence, of Planning, of Power, Energy and Mineral Resources, and of the Establishment: Sheikh Hasina Wajed.

Minister of Foreign Affairs: Abdus Samad Azad.

Minister of Local Government, Rural Development and Co-operatives: Mohammad Zillur Rahman.

Minister of Finance: S. A. M. S. Kibria.

Minister of Education, and of the Primary and Mass Education Division: A. S. H. K. Sadeque.

Minister of Labour and Employment: M. A. Mannan.

Minister of Science and Technology: Lt-Gen. (retd) Mohammad Nooruddin Khan.

Minister of Water Resources and Flood Control: Abdur Razzak.

Minister of Commerce: Abdul Jalil.

Minister of Industry: Tofael Ahmed.

Minister of Home Affairs and of Post and Telecommunications: Mohammad Nasim.

Minister of Agriculture: Matia Choudhury.

Minister of Food: Amir Hossain Amu.

Minister of Civil Aviation and Tourism and of Housing and Public Works: Eng. Mosharraf Hossain.

Minister of Law, Justice and Parliamentary Affairs: Abdul Matin Khasru.

Minister of Communications: Anwar Hussain.

Minister of Health and Family Welfare: Sheikh Fazlul Karim Salim.

Minister of the Environment and Forests: Syeda Sajeda Chowdhury.

Minister for Fisheries and Livestock: A. S. M. Abdur Rab.

Minister of Chittagong Hill Tracts Affairs: Kalpa Ranjan Chakma.

Ministers without Portfolio: Maj.-Gen. (retd) Rafiqul Islam Bir Uttam, Dr Salahuddin Yusuf.

Minister of State for Social Welfare: Mozammel Hossain.

Minister of State for Information: Prof. Abu Sayeed.

Minister of State for Youth and Sports and Cultural Affairs: Obaidul Kader.

Minister of State for Textiles: A. K. M. Jahangir Hossain.

Minister of State for Religious Affairs: Mohammad Nurul Islam.

Minister of State for Women's and Children's Affairs: Prof. Jinatunnessa Talukder.

Minister of State for Disaster Management and Relief: Talukder Abdul Khaleque.

Minister of State for Shipping: Mofajjal Hossain Chowdhury Maya.

Minister of State for Land: Haji Rashed Mosharraf.

Minister of State for Planning: Dr Mohiuddin Khan Alamgir.

MINISTRIES

Prime Minister's Office: Old Sangsad Bhaban, Tejgaon, Dhaka; tel. (2) 815100; fax (2) 813244; e-mail pm@pmo.bdonline.com.

Ministry of Agriculture: Bangladesh Secretariat, Bhaban 4, 2nd 9-Storey Bldg, Dhaka; tel. (2) 832137; internet www.bangladeshgov.org/moa.

Ministry of Chittagong Hill Tracts Affairs: Dhaka; internet www.bangladeshgov.org/mochta.

Ministry of Civil Aviation and Tourism: Bangladesh Secretariat, Bhaban 6, 19th Floor, Dhaka 1000; tel. (2) 866485.

Ministry of Commerce: Bangladesh Secretariat, Bhaban 3, Dhaka 1000; tel. (2) 862826; fax (2) 865741.

Ministry of Communications: Bangladesh Secretariat, Bhaban 7, 1st 9-Storey Bldg, 8th Floor, Dhaka 1000; tel. (2) 868752; fax (2) 866636.

Ministry of Cultural Affairs: Dhaka; tel. (2) 402133.

Ministry of Defence: Old High Court Bldg, Dhaka; tel. (2) 259082.

Ministry of Disaster Management and Relief: Dhaka; tel. (2) 866262.

Ministry of Education: Bangladesh Secretariat, Bhaban 7, 2nd 9-Storey Bldg, 6th Floor, Dhaka; tel. (2) 404162.

Ministry of Energy and Mineral Resources: Bangladesh Secretariat, Bhaban 6, First Floor, Dhaka 1000; tel. (2) 865918; fax (2) 861110.

Ministry of Finance: Bangladesh Secretariat, Bhaban 7, 1st 9-Storey Bldg, 3rd Floor, Dhaka 1000; tel. (2) 8690202; fax (2) 865581.

Ministry of Fisheries and Livestock: Dhaka; tel. (2) 862430.

Ministry of Food: Dhaka; internet www.bangladeshgov.org/mof.

Ministry of Foreign Affairs: Segunbagicha, Dhaka 1000; tel. (2) 9569129; fax (2) 9562163; e-mail pspmo@bangla.net; internet www.bangladeshonline.com/gob/mofa.

Ministry of Health and Family Welfare: Bangladesh Secretariat, Main Bldg, 3rd Floor, Dhaka; tel. (2) 832079.

Ministry of Home Affairs: Bangladesh Secretariat, School Bldg, 2nd and 3rd Floors, Dhaka; tel. (2) 404142.

Ministry of Housing and Public Works: Bangladesh Secretariat, Bhaban 5, Dhaka; tel. (2) 834494; fax (2) 861290.

Ministry of Industry: Shilpa Bhaban, 91 Motijheel C/A, Dhaka 1000; tel. (2) 9564250; fax (2) 860588.

Ministry of Information: Bangladesh Secretariat, 2nd 9-Storey Bldg, 8th Floor, Dhaka; tel. (2) 235111; fax (2) 834535.

Ministry of Labour and Employment: Bangladesh Secretariat, 1st 9-Storey Bldg, 4th Floor, Dhaka; tel. (2) 404106; fax (2) 813420.

Ministry of Land: Bangladesh Secretariat, Bhaban 4, 2nd 9-Storey Bldg, 3rd Floor, Dhaka.

Ministry of Local Government, Rural Development and Co-operatives: Bangladesh Secretariat, Bhaban 7, 1st 9-Storey Bldg, 6th Floor, Dhaka.

Ministry of Planning: Block No. 7, Sher-e-Bangla Nagar, Dhaka; tel. (2) 815142; fax (2) 822210.

Ministry of Post and Telecommunications: Bangladesh Secretariat, Bhaban 7, 6th Floor, Dhaka 1000; tel. (2) 864800; fax (2) 865775.

Ministry of Religious Affairs: Dhaka; tel. (2) 404346.

Ministry of Science and Technology: Dhaka; internet www.most-bd.org.

Ministry of Shipping: Bangladesh Secretariat, Bhaban 6, 8th Floor, Dhaka 1000; tel. (2) 861275.

Ministry of Social Welfare and Women's Affairs: Bangladesh Secretariat, Bhaban 6, New Bldg, Dhaka; tel. (2) 402076.

Ministry of Textiles: Bangladesh Secretariat, Bhaban 6, 11th Floor, Dhaka 1000; tel. (2) 862051; fax (2) 860600.

Ministry of Youth and Sports: Dhaka; tel. (2) 407670.

President and Legislature

PRESIDENT

On 23 July 1996 the Awami League's presidential candidate, SHAH-ABUDDIN AHMED, was elected unopposed as Bangladesh's new Head of State by the Jatiya Sangsad.

JATIYA SANGSAD
(Parliament)

Speaker: HUMAYUN RASHID CHOWDHURY.
General Election, 12 June 1996

	Seats
Awami League (AL)	146
Bangladesh Jatiyatabadi Dal (Bangladesh Nationalist Party—BNP)	116
Jatiya Dal	32
Jamaat-e-Islami Bangladesh	3
Jatiya Samajtantrik Dal (Rab)	1
Islami Oikya Jote	1
Independent	1
Total	**300**

In addition to the 300 directly-elected members, a further 30 seats are reserved for women members.

Political Organizations

Awami League (AL): 23 Bangabandhu Ave, Dhaka; f. 1949; supports parliamentary democracy; advocates socialist economy, but with a private sector, and a secular state; pro-Indian; 28-member central executive committee, 15-member central advisory committee and a 13-member presidium; Pres. Sheikh HASINA WAJED; Gen.-Sec. ZILLUR RAHMAN; c. 1,025,000 mems.

Bangladesh Jatiya League: 500A Dhanmandi R/A, Rd 7, Dhaka; f. 1970 as Pakistan National League, renamed in 1972; supports parliamentary democracy; Leader ATAUR RAHMAN KHAN; c. 50,000 mems.

Bangladesh Jatiyatabadi Dal (Bangladesh Nationalist Party—BNP): 29 Minto Rd, Dhaka; f. 1978 by merger of groups supporting Ziaur Rahman, including Jatiyatabadi Gonotantrik Dal (Jagodal—Nationalist Democratic Party); right of centre; favours multi-party democracy and parliamentary system of govt; Chair. Begum KHALEDA ZIA; Sec.-Gen. ABDUL MANNAN BHUIYAN.

Bangladesh Khelafat Andolon: 314/2 Lalbagh Kellar Morr, Dhaka 1211; tel. (2) 8612465; fax (2) 9881436; e-mail khelafat@cim-abd.com; Supreme Leader SHAH AHMADULLAH ASHRAF IBN HAFEZZEE; Sec.-Gen. Maulana MUHAMMAD ZAFRULLAH KHAN.

Bangladesh Krishak Sramik Party (Peasants' and Workers' Party): Sonargaon Bhavan, 99 South Kamalapur, Dhaka 1217; tel. (2) 834512; f. 1914, renamed 1953; supports parliamentary democracy, non-aligned foreign policy, welfare state, guarantee of fundamental rights for all religions and races, free market economy and non-proliferation of nuclear weapons; 15-mem. exec. council; Pres. A. S. M. SULAIMAN; Sec.-Gen. RASHEED KHAN MEMON; c. 125,000 mems.

Bangladesh Muslim League: Dhaka; Sec.-Gen. Alhaj MOHAMMAD ZAMIR ALI.

Bangladesh People's League: Dhaka; f. 1976; supports parliamentary democracy; Leader KHANDAKER SABBIR AHMED; c. 75,000 mems.

Communist Party of Bangladesh: 21/1 Purana Paltan, Dhaka 1000; tel. (2) 9558612; fax (2) 837464; e-mail manzur@bangla.net; f. 1948; Pres. SHAHIDULLAH CHOWDHURY; Gen. Sec. MUJAHIDUL ISLAM SELIM; c. 22,000 mems.

Democratic League: 68 Jigatola, Dhaka 9; tel. (2) 507994; f. 1976; conservative; Leader ABDUR RAZZAK.

Freedom Party: f. 1987; Islamic; Co-Chair. Lt-Col (retd) SAID FARUQ RAHMAN, Lt-Col (retd) KHANDAKAR ABDUR RASHID.

Gonoazadi League: 30 Banagran Lane, Dhaka.

Islamic Solidarity Movement: 84 East Tejturi Bazar, Tejgaon, Dhaka 1215; tel. (2) 325886; fmrly known as Islamic Democratic League; renamed as above in 1984; Chair. HAFIZ MUHAMMAD HABIBUR RAHMAN.

Jamaat-e-Islami Bangladesh: 505 Elephant Rd, Bara Maghbazar, Dhaka 1217; tel. (2) 401581; f. 1941; Islamic fundamentalist; Chair. Prof. GHULAM AZAM; Sec.-Gen. Maulana MATIUR RAHMAN NIZAMI; Asst Sec.-Gen. MUHAMMAD QUAMARUZZAMAN.

Jatiya Dal (National Party): c/o Jatiya Sangsad, Dhaka; f. 1983 as Jana Dal; reorg. 1986, when the National Front (f. 1985), a five-party alliance of the Jana Dal, the United People's Party, the Gonotantrik Dal, the Bangladesh Muslim League and a breakaway section of the Bangladesh Nationalist Party, formally converted itself into a single pro-Ershad grouping; advocates nationalism, democracy, Islamic ideals and progress; Chair. Lt-Gen. HOSSAIN MOHAMMAD ERSHAD; Sec.-Gen. NAZIUR RAHMAN MONZUR; in April 1999 a group of dissidents, led by MIZANUR RAHMAN CHOWDHURY and ANWAR HUSSAIN MANJU, formed a rival faction.

Jatiya Samajtantrik Dal (Rab): breakaway faction of JSD; Pres. A. S. M. ABDUR RAB; Gen. Sec. HASANUL HAQUE INU.

Jatiya Samajtantrik Dal (JSD—(S)) (National Socialist Party): 23 DIT Ave, Malibagh Choudhury Para, Dhaka; f. 1972; left-wing; Leader SHAJAHAN SIRAJ; c. 5,000 mems.

Jatiyo Gonotantrik Party (JAGPA): Purana Paltan, Dhaka; Jt Gen. Secs AZIZUR RAHMAN, SARDAR SHAHJAHAN.

Jatiyo Janata Party: Janata Bhaban, 47A Toyenbee Circular Rd, Dhaka 1203; tel. (2) 9567315; f. 1976; social democratic; Leader ABDULLAH NASER; Gen. Sec. MUJIBUR RAHMAN HIRO; c. 30,000 mems.

National Awami Party—Bhashani (NAP): Dhaka; f. 1957; Maoist; Leader NAZRUL ISLAM; Gen. Sec. ABDUS SUBHANI.

National Awami Party—Muzaffar (NAP—M): 21 Dhanmandi Hawkers' Market, 1st Floor, Dhaka 5; f. 1957, reorg. 1967; c. 500,000 mems; Pres. MUZAFFAR AHMED; Sec.-Gen. PANKAJ BHATTACHARYA.

Parbattya Chattagram Jana Sanghati Samity: f. 1972; political wing of the Shanti Bahini; represents interests of Buddhist tribals in Chittagong Hill Tracts; Leader JATINDRA BODDHIPRIYA ('SHANTU') LARMA.

Samyabadi Dal: Dhaka; Maoist; Leader MOHAMMAD TOAHA.

Zaker Party: f. 1989; supports sovereignty and the introduction of an Islamic state system; Leader SYED HASMATULLAH; Mem. of the Presidium MUSTAFA AMIR FAISAL.

Diplomatic Representation

EMBASSIES AND HIGH COMMISSIONS IN BANGLADESH

Afghanistan: House CWN(C)-2A Gulshan Ave, Gulshan Model Town, Dhaka 1212; tel. (2) 603232; Chargé d'affaires a.i.: ABDUL AHAD WOLASI.

Australia: 184 Gulshan Ave, Gulshan Model Town, Dhaka 1212; tel. (2) 8813105; fax (2) 8811125; e-mail julienne.iftene@dfat.gov.au; High Commissioner: ROBERT FLYNN.

Belgium: 22 Gulshan Ave, Gulshan Model Town, Dhaka 1212; tel. (2) 600138; fax (2) 883151; Ambassador: Baron OLIVIER GILLES.

Bhutan: House No. F5 (SE), Gulshan Ave, Dhaka 1212; tel. (2) 8827160; fax (2) 8823939; e-mail bhtemb@bdmail.net; Ambassador: LHATU WANGCHUK.

Canada: House 16A, Rd 48, Gulshan Model Town, POB 569, Dhaka 1212; tel. (2) 607071; fax (2) 883043; High Commissioner: JON SCOTT.

China, People's Republic: Plot NE(L)6, Rd 83, Gulshan Model Town, Dhaka 1212; tel. (2) 884862; Ambassador: HU QIANWEN.

Czech Republic: Dhaka; tel. (2) 601673.

Denmark: House NW(H)1, Rd 51, Gulshan Model Town, POB 2056, Dhaka 1212; tel. (2) 8821799; fax (2) 8823638; e-mail dandhaka@mail.citechco.net; internet www.citechco.net/dandhaka; Ambassador: FINN THILSTED.

Egypt: House NE(N)-9, Rd 90, Gulshan Model Town, Dhaka 1212; tel. (2) 882766; fax (2) 884883; Ambassador: OSSAMA MOHAMED TAWFIK.

France: POB 22, House 18, Rd 108, Gulshan Model Town, Dhaka 1212; tel. (2) 8813812; Ambassador: MICHEL LUMMAUX.

Germany: 178 Gulshan Ave, Gulshan Model Town, POB 108, Dhaka 1212; tel. (2) 8824735; fax (2) 8823141; e-mail aadhaka@citecho.net; Ambassador: UWE SCHRAMM.

Holy See: Lake Rd 2, Diplomatic Enclave, Baridhara Model Town, POB 6003, Dhaka 1212; tel. (2) 8822018; fax (2) 8823574; e-mail ve@bdonline.com; Apostolic Nuncio: Most Rev. EDWARD JOSEPH ADAMS, Titular Archbishop of Scala.

Hungary: 80 Gulshan Ave, Dhaka; tel. (2) 608101; fax (2) 883117; Chargé d'affaires a.i.: I. B. BUDAY.

India: House 120, Rd 2, Dhanmandi R/A, Dhaka 1205; tel. (2) 8615373; fax (2) 8613662; internet www.hcidhaka.org; High Commissioner: MANI LAL TRIPATHI.

Indonesia: CWS (A)-10, 75 Gulshan Ave, Gulshan Model Town, Dhaka 1212; tel. (2) 600131; fax (2) 885391; Ambassador: HADI A. WAYARABI ALHADAR.

Iran: CWN(A)-12 Kamal Ataturk Ave, Gulshan Model Town, Dhaka 1212; tel. (2) 601432; Ambassador: MOHAMMAD SADEQ FAYAZ.

Iraq: House 8, Rd 59, Gulshan 2, Dhaka 1212; tel. (2) 600298; fax (2) 8823277; Ambassador: NAHED ALI AJAJ.

Italy: Plot No. 2 & 3, Rd 74/79, POB 6062, Gulshan Model Town, Dhaka 1212; tel. (2) 882781; fax (2) 882578; e-mail ambdhaka@citechco.net; internet www.citechco.net/italydhaka; Ambassador: MARIO FILIPPO PINI.

Japan: 5 & 7, Dutabash Rd, Baridhara, Dhaka; tel. (2) 870087; fax (2) 886737; Ambassador: YOSHIKAZU KANEKO.

Korea, Democratic People's Republic: House 6, Rd 7, Baridhara Model Town, Dhaka; tel. (2) 601250; Ambassador: RI SANG IL.

Korea, Republic: 4 Madani Ave, Diplomatic Enclave, Baridhara, Dhaka; tel. (2) 872088; fax (2) 883871; e-mail rokdhaka@bangla.net; Ambassador: HAN TAE-KYU.

Kuwait: Plot 39, Rd 23, Block J, Banani, Dhaka 13; tel. (2) 600233; Ambassador: AHMAD MURSHED AL-SULIMAN.

Libya: NE(D), 3A, Gulshan Ave (N), Gulshan Model Town, Dhaka 1212; tel. (2) 600141; Secretary of People's Committee: MUSBAH ALI A. MAIMOON (acting).

Malaysia: House 4, Rd 118, Gulshan Model Town, Dhaka 1212; tel. (2) 887759; fax (2) 883115; High Commissioner: Dato' ZULKIFLY IBRAHIM BIN ABDUR RAHMAN.

Myanmar: NE(L) 3, Rd 84, Gulshan, Dhaka 1212; tel. (2) 601915; fax (2) 8823740; Ambassador: U OHN THWIN.

Nepal: United Nations Rd, Rd 2, Diplomatic Enclave, Baridhara, Dhaka; tel. (2) 601790; fax (2) 8826401; e-mail rnedhaka@bdmail.net; Ambassador: MADHU RAMAN ACHARYA.

Netherlands: House 49, Rd 90, Gulshan Model Town, POB 166, Dhaka 1212; tel. (2) 882715; fax (2) 883326; e-mail nlgovdha@bangla.net; Ambassador: D.C.B. DEN HAAS.

Pakistan: House NEC-2, Rd 71, Gulshan Model Town, Dhaka 1212; tel. (2) 885388; High Commissioner: KARAM ELAHI.

Philippines: House NE(L) 5, Rd 83, Gulshan Model Town, Dhaka 1212; tel. (2) 605945; Ambassador: CESAR C. PASTORES.

Poland: House 111, Rd 4, Banani, POB 6089, Dhaka 1213; tel. (2) 608503; fax (2) 8827568; e-mail pl_dhaka@citechco.net; Chargé d'affaires a.i.: JERZY SADOWSKI.

Qatar: House 23, Rd 108, Gulshan Model Town, Dhaka 1212; tel. (2) 604477; Chargé d'affaires a.i.: ABDULLAH AL-MUTAWA.

Romania: House 33, Rd 74, Gulshan Model Town, Dhaka 1212; tel. (2) 601467; Chargé d'affaires a.i.: ALEXANDRU VOINEA.

Russia: NE(J) 9, Rd 79, Gulshan Model Town, Dhaka 1212; tel. (2) 8828147; fax (2) 8823735; e-mail rusemb@citechco.net; Ambassador: NIKOLAI G. SHEVCHENKO.

Saudi Arabia: House 12, Rd 92, Gulshan (North), Dhaka 1212; tel. (2) 889124; fax (2) 883616; Ambassador: ABDULLAH OMAR BARRY.

Sri Lanka: House 15(NW), Rd 50, Gulshan 2, Dhaka; tel. (2) 882790; fax (2) 883971; e-mail slhc@citechco.net; High Commissioner: S. B. ATUGODA.

Sweden: House 1, Rd 51, Gulshan, Dhaka 1212; tel. (2) 884761; fax (2) 883948; Ambassador: ANDERS JOHNSON.

Thailand: House NW (D) 4, Rd 58–62, Gulshan Model Town, Dhaka 1212; tel. (2) 8812795; fax (2) 8823588; Ambassador: PITHAYA POOKAMAN.

Turkey: House 7, Rd 62, Gulshan Model Town, Dhaka 1212; tel. (2) 8823536; fax (2) 8823873; e-mail dakkabe@citechco.net; Ambassador: ERDINÇ ULUMLU.

United Arab Emirates: House CEN(H) 41, Rd 113, Gulshan Model Town, Dhaka 1212; tel. (2) 9882244; fax (2) 8823225; e-mail uaedhaka@vasdigita.com; Chargé d'affaires a.i.: ABDUL RAZAK HADI.

United Kingdom: United Nations Rd, Baridhara, POB 6079, Dhaka 1212; tel. (2) 8822705; fax (2) 8823437; e-mail press@dhaka.mail.feo.gov.uk; internet www.ukinbangladesh.org; High Commissioner: Dr DAVID CARTER.

USA: Diplomatic Enclave, Madani Ave, Baridhara, POB 323, Dhaka 1212; tel. (2) 8824700; fax (2) 8823744; e-mail dhaka@usia.gov; Ambassador: JOHN C. HOLZMAN.

Judicial System

A judiciary, comprising a Supreme Court with High Court and Appellate Divisions, is in operation (see under Constitution).

Supreme Court: Dhaka 2; tel. (2) 433585.

Chief Justice: MUSTAFA KAMAL.

Attorney-General: MAHMUDUL ISLAM.

Deputy Attorney-General: A. M. FAROOQ.

Religion

Preliminary results of the 1981 census classified 86.6% of the population as Muslims, 12.1% as caste Hindus and scheduled castes, and the remainder as Buddhists, Christians and tribals.

Freedom of religious worship is guaranteed under the Constitution but, under the 1977 amendment to the Constitution, Islam was declared to be one of the nation's guiding principles and, under the 1988 amendment, Islam was established as the state religion.

BUDDHISM

World Federation of Buddhists Regional Centre: Buddhist Monastery, Kamalapur, Dhaka 14; Leader Ven. VISUDDHANANDA MAHATHERO.

CHRISTIANITY

Jatiyo Church Parishad (National Council of Churches): 395 New Eskaton Rd, Moghbazar, Dhaka 2; tel. (2) 402869; f. 1949 as East Pakistan Christian Council; four mem. churches; Pres. Dr SAJAL DEWAN; Gen. Sec. M. R. BISWAS.

Church of Bangladesh—United Church

After Bangladesh achieved independence, the Diocese of Dacca (Dhaka) of the Church of Pakistan (f. 1970 by the union of Anglicans, Methodists, Presbyterians and Lutherans) became the autonomous Church of Bangladesh. In 1986 the Church had an estimated 12,000 members. In 1990 a second diocese, the Diocese of Kushtia, was established.

Bishop of Dhaka: Rt Rev. BARNABAS DWIJEN MONDAL, St Thomas's Church, 54 Johnson Rd, Dhaka 1100; tel. (2) 7116546; fax (2) 7118218; e-mail cbdacdio@bangla.net.

Bishop of Kushtia: Rt Rev. MICHAEL BAROI, Church of Bangladesh, 94 N.S. Rd, Thanapara, Kushtia; tel. (71) 3603.

The Roman Catholic Church

For ecclesiastical purposes, Bangladesh comprises one archdiocese and five dioceses. At 31 December 1999 there were an estimated 250,000 adherents in the country.

Catholic Bishops' Conference: Archbishop's House, 1 Kakrail Rd, Ramna, POB 3, Dhaka 1000; tel. (2) 408879; fax (2) 8314993; f. 1978; Pres. Most Rev. MICHAEL ROZARIO, Archbishop of Dhaka.

Secretariat: CBCB Centre, 24C Asad Ave, Mohammadpur, Dhaka 1207; tel. and fax (2) 9127339; e-mail cbcbsec@bdcom.com; Sec.-Gen. Rt Rev. THEOTONIUS GOMES, Titular Bishop of Zucchabar.

Archbishop of Dhaka: Most Rev. MICHAEL ROZARIO, Archbishop's House, 1 Kakrail Rd, Ramna, POB 3, Dhaka 1000; tel. (2) 408879.

Other Christian Churches

Bangladesh Baptist Sangha: 33 Senpara, Parbatta, Mirpur 10, Dhaka 1216; tel. (2) 8012967; fax (2) 9005842; e-mail bbsangha @bdmail.net; f. 1922; 31,000 mems (2000); Pres. SUSANTA ADHIKARI; Gen. Sec. (acting) Rev. ROBERT SARKAR.

In early 2000 there were about 48 denominational churches active in the country, including the Bogra Christian Church, the Evangelical Christian Church, the Garo Baptist Union, the Reformed Church of Bangladesh and the Sylhet Presbyterian Synod. The Baptist Sangha was the largest Protestant Church.

The Press

PRINCIPAL DAILIES
Bengali

Azadi: 9 C.D.A. C/A, Momin Rd, Chittagong; tel. (31) 224341; f. 1960; Editor Prof. MOHAMMAD KHALED; circ. 13,000.

Banglar Bani: 81 Motijheel C/A, Dhaka 1000; tel. (2) 237548; e-mail bani@bangla.net; f. 1972; Editor Sheikh FAZLUL KARIM SALIM; circ. 20,000.

Dainik Bangla: Dhaka; f. 1964; Editor AHMED HUMAYUN; circ. 65,000.

Dainik Bhorer Kagoj: 8 Link Rd, Banglamotor, Dhaka; tel (2) 868802; fax (2) 868801; e-mail bkagoj@bangla.net; Editor MATIUR RAHMAN; circ. 50,000.

Dainik Birol: 26 R. K. Mission Rd, Motijheel C/A, Dhaka 1203; tel. (2) 7121620; fax (2) 8013721; Chair. of Editorial Bd ABDULLAH AL-NASER.

Dainik Inquilab: 2/1 Ramkrishna Mission Rd, Dhaka 1203; tel. (2) 9563162; fax (2) 9552881; e-mail inquilab1@bangla.net; Editor A. M. M. BAHAUDDIN; circ. 180,025.

Dainik Ittefaq: 1 Ramkrishna Rd, Dhaka 1203; tel. (2) 256075; e-mail ittefaqnews@bangla.net; internet www.daily-ittefaq.com; f. 1953; Propr/Editor ANWAR HUSSAIN MANJU; circ. 200,000.

Dainik Jahan: 3/B Shehra Rd, Mymensingh; tel. (91) 5677; f. 1980; Editor MUHAMMAD HABIBUR RAHMAN SHEIKH; circ. 4,000.

Dainik Janakantha (Daily People's Voice): Dhaka; e-mail janakantha@citechco.net; internet www.daily-janakantha.com; f. 1993; Man. Editor TOAB KHAN; Exec. Editor BORHAN AHMED; circ. 100,000.

Dainik Janata: 24 Aminbagh, Shanti Nagar, Dhaka 1217; tel. (2) 400498; Editor Dr M. ASADUR RAHMAN.

Dainik Janmobhumi: 110/1 Islampur Rd, Khulna; tel. (41) 721280; fax (41) 724324; f. 1982; Editor HUMAYUN KABIR; circ. 30,000.

Dainik Karatoa: Chalkjadu Rd, Bogra; tel. (51) 3660; fax (51) 5898; f. 1976; Editor MOZAMMEL HAQUE LALU; circ. 40,000.

Dainik Khabar: 137 Shanti Nagar, Dhaka 1217; tel. (2) 406601; f. 1985; Editor MIZANUR RAHMAN MIZAN; circ. 18,000.

Dainik Millat: Dhaka; tel. (2) 242351; Editor CHOWDHURY MOHAMMAD FAROOQ.

Dainik Nava Avijan: Lalkuthi, North Brook Hall Rd, Dhaka; tel. (2) 257516; Editor A. S. M. REZAUL HAQUE; circ. 15,000.

Dainik Patrika: 85 Elephant Rd, Maghbazar, Dhaka 1217; tel. (2) 415057; fax (2) 841575; e-mail patrika@citechco.net; Publr and Chief Editor MIA MUSA HOSSAIN; Editor M. FAISAL HASSAN (acting).

Dainik Probaha: 3 KDA Ave, Khulna; tel. (41) 722552; f. 1977; Editor ASHRAF-UL-HAQUE; circ. 11,400.

Dainik Purbanchal: 38 Iqbal Nagar Mosque Lane, Khulna 9100; tel. (41) 22251; fax (41) 21432; f. 1974; Editor LIAQUAT ALI; circ. 42,000.

Dainik Rupashi Bangla: Abdur Rashid Rd, Natun Chowdhury Para, Bagicha Gaon, Comilla 3500; tel. (81) 76689; f. 1972 (a weekly until 1979); Editor Prof. ABDUL WAHAB; circ. 50,000.

Dainik Sangram: 423 Elephant Rd, Baramaghbazar, Dhaka 1217; tel. (2) 9330579; fax (2) 8315094; e-mail dsangram@bttb.net; f. 1970; Chair. ALI AHSAN MUJAHID; Editor ABUL ASAD; circ. 45,000.

Dainik Sphulinga: Amin Villa, P-5 Housing Estate, Jessore 7401; tel. (421) 6433; f. 1971; Editor Mian ABDUS SATTAR; circ. 14,000.

Dainik Uttara: Bahadur Bazar, Dinajpur Town, Dinajpur; tel. (531) 4326; f. 1974; Editor Prof. MUHAMMAD MOHSIN; circ. 8,500.

Ganakantha: Dhaka; f. 1979; morning; Editor JAHANGIR KABIR CHOWDHURY; Exec. Editor SAIYED RABIUL KARIM; circ. 15,000.

Jaijaidin Protidin: 15 New Bailey Rd, Dhaka 1000; Editor SHAFIK REHMAN.

Janabarta: 5 Babu Khan Rd, Khulna; tel. (41) 21075; f. 1974; Editor SYED SOHRAB ALI; circ. 4,000.

Jugabheri: Sylhet; tel. (821) 5461; f. 1931; Editor FAHMEEDA RASHEED CHOUDHURY; circ. 6,000.

Manav Jomeen (Human Land): Dhaka; f. 1998; tabloid.

Naya Bangla: 101 Momin Rd, Chittagong; tel. (31) 206247; f. 1978; Editor ABDULLAH AL-SAGIR; circ. 12,000.

Protidin: Ganeshtola, Dinajpur; tel. (531) 4555; f. 1980; Editor KHAIRUL ANAM; circ. 3,000.

Runner: Pyari Mohan Das Rd, Bejpara, Jessore; tel. (421) 6943; f. 1980; circ. 2,000.

Sangbad: 36 Purana Paltan, Dhaka 1000; tel. (2) 9558147; fax (2) 9562882; e-mail sangbad@bangla.net; f. 1952; Editor AHMADUL KABIR; circ. 71,050.

Swadhinata: Chittagong; tel. (31) 209644; f. 1972; Editor ABDULLAH AL-HARUN; circ. 4,000.

English

Bangladesh Observer: Observer House, 33 Toyenbee Circular Rd, Motijheel C/A, Dhaka 1000; tel. (2) 235105; e-mail bo@bangla.net; f. 1949; morning; Editor S. M. ALI; circ. 75,000.

The Bangladesh Times: Dhaka; tel. (2) 233195; f. 1975; morning; Editor MAHBUB ANAM; circ. 35,000.

Daily Evening News: 26 R. K. Mission Rd, Motijheel C/A, Dhaka 1203; tel. (2) 7121619; fax (2) 8013721; Chair. of Editorial Bd ABDULLAH AL-NASER.

Daily Star: 19 Karwan Bazar, Dhaka 1215; tel. (2) 8124944; fax (2) 8125155; e-mail dstar@bangla.net; internet www .dailystarnews.com; f. 1991; Publr and Editor MAHFUZ ANAM; circ. 30,000.

Daily Tribune: 38 Iqbal Nagar Mosque Lane, Khulna 9100; tel. (41) 21944; fax (41) 22251; f. 1978; morning; Editor FERDOUSI ALI; circ. 22,000.

Financial Express: 28/1 Toyenbee Circular Rd, 2nd Floor, POB 2526, Dhaka 1000; tel. (2) 9568154; fax (2) 9567049; e-mail tfe@bangla.net; internet www.financial-express.com; f. 1994; Editor-in-Chief REAZUDDIN AHMED.

The Independent: Beximco Media Complex, 32 Kazi Nazrul Islam Ave, Karwan Bazar, Dhaka 1215; tel. (2) 9129938; fax (2) 9127722; e-mail ind@citechco.net; internet www.independent-bangladesh.com; f. 1995; Editor MAHBUBUL ALAM.

New Nation: 1 Ramkrishna Mission Rd, Dhaka 1203; tel. (2) 256071; fax (2) 245536; e-mail newnation@nation-online.com; internet www.nation-online.com; f. 1981; Editor ALAMGIR MOHIUDDIN; circ. 15,000.

People's View: 102 Siraj-ud-Daulla Rd, Chittagong; tel. (31) 227403; f. 1969; Editor SABBIR ISLAM; circ. 3,000.

PERIODICALS
Bengali

Aachal: Dhaka; weekly; Editor FERDOUSI BEGUM.

Adhuna: 1/3 Block F, Lalmatia, Dhaka 1207; tel. (2) 812353; fax (2) 813095; e-mail adab@bdonline.com; f. 1974; quarterly; publ. by the Asscn of Devt Agencies in Bangladesh (ADAB); Exec. Editor MINAR MONSUR; circ. 10,000.

Ahmadi: 4 Bakshi Bazar Rd, Dhaka 1211; tel. (2) 9662703; fax (2) 8613414; f. 1925; fortnightly; Editor-in-Chief M. A. S. MAHMOOD; Exec. Editor MOHAMMAD M. RAHMAN.

Alokpat: 166 Arambagh, Dhaka 1000; tel. (2) 413361; fax (2) 863060; fortnightly; Editor RABBANI JABBAR.

Amod: Chowdhury Para, Comilla 3500; tel. (81) 5193; f. 1955; weekly; Editor SHAMSUN NAHAR RABBI; circ. 6,000.

Ananda Bichitra: Dhaka; tel. (2) 241639, f. 1986; fortnightly; Editor SHAHADAT CHOWDHURY; circ. 32,000.

Begum: 66 Loyal St, Dhaka 1; tel. (2) 233789; f. 1947; women's illustrated weekly; Editor NURJAHAN BEGUM; circ. 25,000.

Bichitra: Dhaka; tel. (2) 232086; e-mail bchitra@bangla.net; f. 1972; weekly; Editor SHAHADAT CHOWDHURY; circ. 42,000.

Chakra: 242A Nakhalpara, POB 2682, Dhaka 1215; tel. (2) 604568; social welfare weekly; Editor HUSNEARA AZIZ.

Chitra Desh: 24 Ramkrishna Mission Rd, Dhaka 1203; weekly; Editor HENA AKHTAR CHOWDHURY.

Chitrali: Observer House, 33 Toyenbee Circular Rd, Motijheel C/A, Dhaka 1000; tel. (2) 9550938; fax (2) 9562243; f. 1953; film weekly; Editor PRODIP KUMAR DEY; circ. 25,000.

Ekota: 15 Larmini St, Wari, Dhaka; tel. (2) 257854; f. 1970; weekly; Editor MATIUR RAHMAN; circ. 25,000.

Fashal: 28J Toyenbee Circular Rd, Motijheel C/A, Dhaka 1000; tel. (2) 233099; f. 1965; agricultural weekly; Chief Editor ERSHAD MAZUMDAR; circ. 8,000.

Ispat: Majampur, Kushtia; tel. (71) 3676; f. 1976; weekly; Editor WALIUR BARI CHOUDHURY; circ. 3,000.

Jaijaidin: 15 New Bailey Rd, Dhaka 1000; tel. (2) 8316448; fax (2) 9568598; e-mail jajadi@bangla.net; internet www.jaijaidinweekly .com; weekly; Editor SHAFIK REHMAN.

Jhorna: 4/13 Block A, Lalmatia, Dhaka; tel. (2) 415239; Editor MUHAMMAD JAMIR ALI.

Kalantar: 87 Khanjahan Ali Rd, Khulna; tel. (41) 61424; f. 1971; weekly; Editor NOOR MOHAMMAD; circ. 12,000.

Kankan: Nawab Bari Rd, Bogra; tel. (51) 6424; f. 1974; weekly; Editor Mrs SUFIA KHATUN; circ. 6,000.

Kirajagat: National Sports Control Board, 62/63 Purana Paltan, Dhaka; f. 1977; weekly; Editor ALI MUZZAMAN CHOWDHURY; circ. 7,000.

Kishore Bangla: Observer House, Motijheel C/A, Dhaka 1000; juvenile weekly; f. 1976; Editor RAFIQUL HAQUE; circ. 5,000.

Moha Nagar: 4 Dilkusha C/A, Dhaka 1000; tel. (2) 255282; Editor SYED MOTIUR RAHMAN.

Moshal: 4 Dilkusha C/A, Dhaka 1000; tel. (2) 231092; Editor MUHAMMAD ABUL HASNAT; circ. 3,000

Muktibani: Toyenbee Circular Rd, Motijheel C/A, Dhaka 1000; tel. (2) 253712; f. 1972; weekly; Editor NIZAM UDDIN AHMED; circ. 35,000.

Natun Bangla: 44/2 Free School St Bylane, Hatirpool, Dhaka 1205; tel. (2) 866121; fax (2) 863794; e-mail mujib@bangla.net; f. 1971; weekly; Editor MUJIBUR RAHMAN.

Natun Katha: 31E Topkhana Rd, Dhaka; weekly; Editor HAJERA SULTANA; circ. 4,000.

Nipun: 520 Peyarabag, Magbazar, Dhaka 11007; tel. (2) 312156; monthly; Editor SHAJAHAN CHOWDHURY.

Parikrama: 65 Shanti Nagar, Dhaka; tel. (2) 415640; Editor MOMTAZ SULTANA.

Prohar: 35 Siddeswari Rd, Dhaka 1217; tel. (2) 404206; Editor MUJIBUL HUQ.

Protirodh: Dept of Answar and V.D.P. Khilgoan, Ministry of Home Affairs, School Bldg, 2nd and 3rd Floors, Bangladesh Secretariat, Dhaka; tel. (2) 405971; f. 1977; fortnightly; Editor ZAHANGIR HABIB-ULLAH; circ. 20,000.

Purbani: 1 Ramkrishna Mission Rd, Dhaka 1203; tel. (2) 256503; f. 1951; film weekly; Editor KHONDKER SHAHADAT HOSSAIN; circ. 22,000.

Robbar: 1 Ramkrishna Mission Rd, Dhaka; tel. (2) 256071; e-mail robbar@nation-online.com; internet www.robbar.com; f. 1978; weekly; Editor ABDUL HAFIZ; circ. 20,000.

Rokshena: 13B Avoy Das Lane, Tiktuli, Dhaka; tel. (2) 255117; Editor SYEDA AFSANA.

Sachitra Bangladesh: 112 Circuit House Rd, Dhaka 1000; tel. (2) 402129; f. 1979; fortnightly; Editor A. B. M. ABDUL MATIN; circ. 8,000.

Sachitra Sandhani: 68/2 Purana Paltan, Dhaka; tel. (2) 409680; f. 1978; weekly; Editor GAZI SHAHABUDDIN MAHMUD; circ. 13,000.

Sandip: 28/A/3 Toyenbee Circular Rd, Dhaka; tel. (2) 235542; weekly; Editor MOHSEN ARA RAHMAN.

Shishu: Bangladesh Shishu Academy, Old High Court Compound, Dhaka 1000; tel. (2) 230317; f. 1977; children's monthly; Editor GOLAM KIBRIA; circ. 5,000.

Sonar Bangla: 423 Elephant Rd, Mogh Bazar, Dhaka 1217; tel. (2) 400637; f. 1961; Editor MUHAMMED QAMARUZZAMAN; circ. 25,000.

Swadesh: 19 B.B. Ave, Dhaka; tel. (2) 256946; weekly; Editor ZAKIUDDIN AHMED; circ. 8,000.

Tarokalok: Tarokalok Complex, 25/3 Green Rd, Dhaka 1205; tel. (2) 506583; fax (2) 864330; weekly; Editor AREFIN BADAL.

Tide: 56/57 Motijheel C/A, Dhaka 1000; tel. (2) 259421; Editor ENAYET KARIM.

Tilotwoma: 14 Bangla Bazar, Dhaka; Editor ABDUL MANNAN.

English

ADAB News: 1/3, Block F, Lalmatia, Dhaka 1207; tel. (2) 327424; f. 1974; 6 a year; publ. by the Asscn of Devt Agencies in Bangladesh (ADAB); Editor-in-Chief AZFAR HUSSAIN; circ. 10,000.

Bangladesh: 112 Circuit House Rd, Dhaka 1000; tel. (2) 402013; fortnightly; Editor A. B. M. ABDUL MATIN.

Bangladesh Gazette: Bangladesh Government Press, Tejgaon, Dhaka; f. 1947, name changed 1972; weekly; official notices; Editor M. HUDA.

Bangladesh Illustrated Weekly: Dhaka; tel. (2) 23358; Editor ATIQUZZAMAN KHAN; circ. 3,000.

Cinema: 81 Motijheel C/A, Dhaka 1000; Editor SHEIKH FAZLUR RAHMAN MARUF; circ. 11,000.

Detective: Polwell Bhaban, Naya Paltan, Dhaka 2; tel. (2) 402757; f. 1960; weekly; also publ. in Bengali; Editor SYED AMJAD HOSSAIN; circ. 3,000.

Dhaka Courier: Cosmos Centre, 69/1 New Circular Rd, Malibagh, Dhaka 1217; tel. (2) 408420; fax (2) 831942; e-mail cosmos@ citecho.net; internet www.dhakacourier.com; weekly; Editor ENAYET-ULLAH KHAN; circ. 18,000.

Holiday: Holiday Bldg, 30 Tejgaon Industrial Area, Dhaka 1208; tel. (2) 9122950; fax (2) 8313520; e-mail holiday@bangla.net; internet www.bangla.net/holiday; f. 1965; weekly; independent; Editor-in-Chief ENAYETULLAH KHAN; circ. 18,000.

Motherland: Khanjahan Ali Rd, Khulna; tel. (41) 61685; f. 1974; weekly; Editor M. N. KHAN.

Tide: 56/57 Motijheel C/A, Dhaka; tel. (2) 259421; Editor ENAYET KARIM.

Voice From the North: Dinajpur Town, Dinajpur; tel. (531) 3256; f. 1981; weekly; Editor Prof. MUHAMMAD MOHSIN; circ. 5,000.

NEWS AGENCIES

Bangladesh Sangbad Sangstha (BSS) (Bangladesh News Agency): 68/2 Purana Paltan, Dhaka 1000; tel. (2) 235036; Man. Dir and Chief Editor MAHBUBUL ALAM; Gen. Man. D. P. BARUA.

Eastern News Agency (ENA): Dhaka; tel. (2) 234206; f. 1970; Man. Dir and Chief Editor GOLAM RASUL MALLICK.

Islamic News Society (INS): 24 RK Mission Rd, Motijheel C/A, Dhaka 1203; tel. (2) 7121619; fax (2) 8013721; Editor ABDULLAH AL-NASER.

United News of Bangladesh: Dhaka.

Foreign Bureaux

Agence France-Presse (AFP): Shilpa Bank Bldg, 5th Floor, 8 DIT Ave, nr Dhaka Stadium, Dhaka 1000; tel. (2) 242234; Bureau Chief GOLAM TAHABOOR.

Associated Press (AP) (USA): 69/1 New Circular Rd, Dhaka 1217; tel. (2) 833717; Representative HASAN SAEED FARID HOSSAIN.

Inter Press Service (IPS) (Italy): c/o Bangladesh Sangbad Sangstha, 68/2 Purana Paltan, Dhaka 1000; tel. (2) 235036; Correspondent A. K. M. TABIBUL ISLAM.

Reuters Ltd (UK): POB 3993, Dhaka; tel. (2) 864088; fax (2) 832976; Bureau Chief ATIQUL ALAM.

South Asian News Agency (SANA): Dhaka.

United Press International (UPI) (USA): Dhaka; tel. (2) 233132.

PRESS ASSOCIATIONS

Bangladesh Council of Newspapers and News Agencies: Dhaka; tel. (2) 413256; Pres. Kazi SHAHED AHMED; Sec.-Gen. HABIBUL BASHAR.

Bangladesh Federal Union of Journalists: National Press Club Bldg, 18 Topkhana Rd, Dhaka 1000; tel. (2) 254777; f. 1973; Pres. REAZUDDIN AHMED; Sec.-Gen. SYED ZAFAR AHMED.

Bangladesh Sangbadpatra Karmachari Federation (Newspaper Employees' Fed.): Dhaka; tel. (2) 235065; f. 1972; Pres. RAFIQUL ISLAM; Sec.-Gen. MIR MOZAMMEL HOSSAIN.

Bangladesh Sangbadpatra Press Sramik Federation (Newspaper Press Workers' Federation): 1 Ramkrishna Mission Rd, Dhaka 1203; f. 1960; Pres. M. ABDUL KARIM; Sec.-Gen. BOZLUR RAHMAN MILON.

Dhaka Union of Journalists: National Press Club, Dhaka; f. 1947; Pres. ABEL KHAIR; Gen.-Sec. ABDUL KALAM AZAD.

Overseas Correspondents' Association of Bangladesh (OCAB): 18 Topkhana Rd, Dhaka 1000; e-mail naweed@ bdonline.com; f. 1979; Pres. ZAGLUL A. CHOWDHURY; Gen. Sec. NADEEM QADIR; 60 mems.

Publishers

Academic Publishers: 2/7 Nawab-Habibullah Rd, Dhaka 1000; tel. (2) 507355; fax (2) 863060; f. 1982; social sciences and sociology; Jt Man. Dir HABIBUR RAHMAN.

Agamee Prakashani: 36 Bangla Bazar, Dhaka 1100; tel. (2) 711332; fax (2) 7123945; e-mail agamee@bd.online.com; f. 1978; fiction and academic; Owner OSMAN GANI.

Ahmed Publishing House: 7 Zindabahar 1st Lane, Dhaka 1; tel. (2) 36492; f. 1942; literature, history, science, religion, children's, maps and charts; Man. Dir KAMALUDDIN AHMED; Man. MESBAHUDDIN AHMED.

Ankur Prakashani: 38/4 Bangla Bazar, Dhaka 1100; tel. (2) 9564799; e-mail ankur@bangla.net; f. 1986; academic and general.

Ashrafia Library: 4 Hakim Habibur Rahman Rd, Chawk Bazar, Dhaka 1000; Islamic religious books, texts, and reference works of Islamic institutions.

Asiatic Society of Bangladesh: 5 Old Secretariat Rd, Ramna, Dhaka; tel. (2) 9560500; f. 1952; periodicals on science, Bangla and humanities; Pres. Prof. WAKIL AHMED; Admin. Officer MD ABDUL AWAL MIAH.

Bangla Academy (National Academy of Arts and Letters): Burdwan House, 3 Kazi Nazrul Islam Ave, Dhaka 1000; tel. (2) 869577; f. 1955; higher education textbooks in Bengali, research works in language, literature and culture, language planning, popular science, drama, encyclopaedias, translations of world classics, dictionaries; Dir-Gen. Prof. MONSUR MUSA.

Bangladesh Books International Ltd: Ittefaq Bhaban, 1 Ramkrishna Mission Rd, POB 377, Dhaka 3; tel. (2) 256071; f. 1975; reference, academic, research, literary, children's in Bengali and English; Chair. MOINUL HOSSEIN; Man. Dir ABDUL HAFIZ.

Bangladesh Publishers: 45 Patuatully Rd, Dhaka 1100; tel. (2) 233135; f. 1952; textbooks for schools, colleges and universities, cultural books, journals, etc.; Dir MAYA RANI GHOSAL.

Gatidhara: 38/2-Ka Bangla Bazar, Dhaka 1100; tel. (2) 247515; fax (2) 956600; f. 1988; academic, general and fiction.

Gono Prakashani: 14/E Dhanmondhi R/A, Dhaka 1205; tel. (2) 9332245; fax (2) 863567; e-mail gk.mail@drik.bgd.toolnet.org; f. 1978; science and medicine; Man. Dir SHAFIO KHAN; Editor BAZLUR RAHIM.

International Publications: 8 Baitul Mukarram, 1st Floor, GPO Box 45, Dhaka 1000.

Muktadhara: 74 Farashganj, Dhaka 1100; tel. (2) 231374; f. 1971; educational, literary and general; Bengali and English; Dir J. L. SAHA; Man. Dir C. R. SAHA.

Mullick Brothers: 3/1 Bangla Bazar, Dhaka 1100; tel. (2) 232088; fax (2) 833983; educational.

Osmania Book Depot: 30/32 North Brook Hall Rd, Dhaka 1100.

Puthighar Ltd: 74 Farashganj, Dhaka 1100; tel. (2) 7111374; f. 1951; educational; Bengali and English; Dir J. L. SAHA; Man. Dir C. R. SAHA.

Rahman Brothers: 5/1 Gopinath Datta, Kabiraj St, Babu Bazar, Dhaka; tel. (2) 282633; educational.

Royal Library: Ispahani Bldg, 31/32 P. K. Roy Rd, Bangla Bazar, Dhaka 1; tel. (2) 250863.

Shahitya Prakash: 51 Purana Paltan, Dhaka 1000; tel. (2) 9560485; fax (2) 9565506; f. 1970; Prin. Officer MOFIDUL HOQUE.

University Press Ltd: Red Crescent Bldg, 114 Motijheel C/A, POB 2611, Dhaka 1000; tel. (2) 9565441; fax (2) 9565443; e-mail upl@bangla.net; internet www.uplbooks.com; f. 1975; educational, academic and general; Man. Dir MOHIUDDIN AHMED; Editor ABDAR RAHMAN.

Government Publishing Houses

Bangladesh Bureau of Statistics: Bldg 8, Room 14, Bangladesh Secretariat, Dhaka 1000; tel. (2) 8612833; f. 1971; statistical year book and pocket book, censuses, surveys, agricultural year book and special reports; Jt Dir S. M. TAJUL ISLAM; Sec. MAMUN-UR-RASHID.

Bangladesh Government Press: Tejgaon, Dhaka 1209; tel. (2) 606316; f. 1972.

Department of Films and Publications: 112 Circuit House Rd, Dhaka 1000; tel. (2) 402263.

Press Information Department: Bhaban 6, Bangladesh Secretariat, Dhaka 1000; tel. (2) 400958.

PUBLISHERS' ASSOCIATIONS

Bangladesh Publishers' and Booksellers' Association: 3rd Floor, 3 Liaquat Ave, Dhaka 1; f. 1972; Pres. JANAB JAHANGIR MOHAMMED ADEL; 2,500 mems.

National Book Centre of Bangladesh: 67A Purana Paltan, Dhaka 1000; f. 1963 to promote the cause of 'more, better and cheaper books'; organizes book fairs, publs a monthly journal; Dir FAZLE RABBI.

Broadcasting and Communications

TELECOMMUNICATIONS

Bangladesh Telegraph and Telephone Board: Central Office, Telejogajog Bhaban, 37/E Eskaton Garden, Dhaka 1000; tel. (2)

831500; fax (2) 832577; Chair. M.A. MANNAN CHOWDHURY; Dir (International) MD HASSANUZZAMAN.

Grameen Telecom: Dhaka; f. 1996 by Grameen Bank to expand cellular telephone service in rural areas; Head NAJMUL HUDA.

BROADCASTING

Radio

Bangladesh Betar: NBA House, 121 Kazi Nazrul Islam Ave, Shahabag, Dhaka 1000; tel. (2) 865294; fax (2) 862021; e-mail dgradio@drik.bgd.toolnet.org; f. 1971; govt-controlled; regional stations at Dhaka, Chittagong, Khulna, Rajshahi, Rangpur, Sylhet, Rangamati and Thakurgaon broadcast a total of approximately 160 hours daily; transmitting centres at Lalmai and Rangamati; external service broadcasts 8 transmissions daily in Arabic, Bengali, English, Hindi, Nepalese and Urdu; Dir-Gen. M.I. CHOWDHURY; Dep. Dir-Gen. (Programmes) ASHFAQUR RAHMAN KHAN.

Television

Bangladesh Television (BTV): Television House, Rampura, Dhaka 1219; tel. (2) 866606; fax (2) 832927; f. 1964; govt-controlled; daily broadcasts on one channel from Dhaka station for 10 hours; transmissions also from nationwide network of 14 relay stations; Dir-Gen. SAYED SALAHUDDIN ZAKI; Gen. Man. NAWAZISH ALI KHAN.

Finance

(cap. = capital; p.u. = paid up; res = reserves; dep. = deposits; m. = million; brs = branches; amounts in taka)

BANKING

Central Bank

Bangladesh Bank: Motijheel C/A, POB 325, Dhaka 1000; tel. (2) 9555000; fax (2) 9566212; e-mail banglabank@bangla.net; f. 1971; cap. 30m., res 7,757.9m., dep. 78,401.8m. (June 1998); Gov. Dr MOHAMED FARASUDDIN; 9 brs.

Nationalized Commercial Banks

Agrani Bank: Agrani Bank Bhaban, Motijheel C/A, POB 531, Dhaka 1000; tel. (2) 9566160; fax (2) 9563662; f. 1972; 100% state-owned; cap. 2,484m., res 314m., dep. 86,914m. (Dec. 1998); Chair. MD MATIUR RAHMAN; Man. Dir M. ENAMUL HAQ CHOUDHURY; 903 brs.

Janata Bank: 110 Motijheel C/A, POB 468, Dhaka 1000; tel. (2) 9565041; fax (2) 9564644; e-mail jbcomp@citecho.net; f. 1972; 100% state-owned; cap. 2,594m., res 124m., dep. 69,115m. (June 1996); Chair. MUHAMMED ALI; Man. Dir and CEO MD AMINUL ISLAM; 893 brs in Bangladesh, 4 brs in the UAE.

Rupali Bank Ltd: Rupali Bhaban, 34 Dilkusha C/A, POB 719, Dhaka 1000; tel. (2) 9551624; fax (2) 9564148; e-mail pblhocom@bdcom.com; f. 1972; 51% state-owned, 49% by public; cap. 1,250m., res 76.1m., dep. 29,585m. (June 1996); Chair. AFZALUR RAHMAN; Man. Dir MD YEASIN ALI; 516 brs in Bangladesh, 1 br. in Pakistan.

Sonali Bank: 35–44 Motijheel C/A, POB 3130, Dhaka 1000; tel. (2) 9550426; fax (2) 9561410; f. 1972; 100% state-owned; cap. 3,272.2m., res 1,938.8m., dep. 152,566.1m. (Dec. 1998); Chair. MUHAMMED ALI; Man. Dir M. ENAMUL HAQ CHOWDHURY; 1,313 brs in Bangladesh, 6 brs in United Kingdom and 1 br. in India.

Private Commercial Banks

Al-Arafah Islami Bank Ltd: Rahman Mansion, 161 Motijheel C/A, Dhaka; tel. (2) 9560198; f. 1995; 100% owned by 23 sponsors; cap. 101.2m., res 10m., dep. 534.4m. (Aug. 1996); Chair. A. Z. M. SHAMSUL ALAM; Man. Dir M. M. NURUL HAQUE.

Al-Baraka Bank Bangladesh Ltd: Kashfia Plaza, 35C Naya Paltan (VIP Rd), POB 3467, Dhaka 1000; tel. (2) 410050; fax (2) 834943; f. 1987 on Islamic banking principles; 34.68% owned by Al-Baraka Group, Saudi Arabia, 5.78% by Islamic Development Bank, Jeddah, 45.91% by local sponsors, 5.75% by Bangladesh Govt., 7.8% by general public; cap. 259.6m., res 14.9m., dep. 4,898.1m. (June 1996); Chair. Dr SALEH J. MALAIKAH; Man. Dir ANOWAR AHMED; 33 brs.

Arab Bangladesh Bank Ltd: BCIC Bhaban, 30–31 Dilkusha C/A, POB 3522, Dhaka 1000; tel. (2) 9560312; fax (2) 9564122; e-mail abbank@citecho.net; f. 1981; 95% owned by Bangladesh nationals and 5% by Bangladesh Govt; cap. 409.9m., res 315.7m., dep. 12,001.8m. (Dec. 1998); Chair. M. MORSHED KHAN; Man. Dir A. RAHIM CHOWDHURY; 58 brs, 1 br. in India..

City Bank Ltd: Jiban Bima Tower, 10 Dilkusha C/A, POB 3381, Dhaka 1000; tel. (2) 9565925; fax (2) 9562347; e-mail mail@thecity bank.com; internet www.thecitybank.com; f. 1983; 50% owned by sponsors and 50% by public; cap. p.u. 160.0m., res 263.1m., dep. 10,594.6m. (Dec. 1998); Chair. DEEN MOHAMMAD; Man. Dir MOHAMMAD FAIZ ISLAM; 76 brs.

Dhaka Bank Ltd: 1st Floor, Biman Bhaban, 100 Motijheel C/A, Dhaka 1000; tel. (2) 9556592; fax (2) 9556584; e-mail dhakabnk@bdonline.com; f. 1995; cap. 132m., res 206.3m., dep. 7,503.3m. (Dec. 1999); Chair. ABDUL HAI SARKER; Man. Dir A. I. M. IFTIKAR RAHMAN; 11 brs.

Eastern Bank Ltd: Jiban Bima Bhaban, 2nd Floor, 10 Dilkusha C/A, POB 896, Dhaka 1000; tel. (2) 9556360; fax (2) 9562364; e-mail ebank@bdcom.com; f. 1992; appropriated assets and liabilities of fmr Bank of Credit and Commerce International (Overseas) Ltd; 20% govt.-owned; cap. 600m., res 1,855.8m., dep. 12,471.0m. (Dec. 1999); Chair. NURUL HUSAIN KHAN; Man. Dir M. KHAIRUL ALAM; 21 brs.

International Finance Investment and Commerce Bank Ltd (IFICB): BSB Bldg, 17th–19th Floors, 8 Rajuk Ave, POB 2229, Dhaka 1000; tel. (2) 9563020; fax (2) 9562015; e-mail ificmd@citechco.net; f. 1983; 40% state-owned; cap. 279.4m., res 311.1m., dep. 17,229.5m. (Dec. 1998); Chair. MANZURUL ISLAM; Man. Dir ATAUL HAQ; 52 brs in Bangladesh, 2 brs in Pakistan.

Islami Bank Bangladesh Ltd (IBBL): Head Office, Islami Bank Tower, 40 Dilkusha C/A, Dhaka 1000; tel. (2) 9563046; fax (2) 9564532; e-mail ibbl@ncll.com; f. 1983 on Islamic banking principles; cap. 320.0m., res 1,115.6m., dep. 25,190.7m. (Dec. 1999); Chair. Cdre (retd) MOHAMMAD ATAUR RAHMAN; Exec. Pres. and CEO M. KAMALUDDIN CHOWDHURY; 110 brs.

National Bank Ltd: 18 Dilkusha C/A, POB 3424, Dhaka 1000; tel. (2) 9557045; fax (2) 9563953; e-mail nblho@citechco.net; f. 1983; 50% owned by sponsors, 45% by general public and 5% by Govt; cap. 430.3m., res 983.6m., dep. 20,529.4m. (Dec. 1999); Chair. A. K. M. ABU TAHER; Man. Dir RAFIQUL ISLAM KHAN; 66 brs.

National Credit and Commerce Bank Ltd: 7–8 Motijheel C/A, POB 2920, Dhaka 1000; tel. (2) 9561902; fax (2) 9566290; e-mail nccbl@bdmail.net; internet www.nccbank-bd.com; f. 1993; 50% owned by sponsors, 50% by general public; cap. 195m., res 238.1m., dep. 8,663.5m. (Dec. 1999); Chair. NURUL ISLAM; Man. Dir ANWAR AHMED; 27 brs.

Prime Bank Ltd: Adamjee Court Annex Bldg No. 2, 119–20 Motijheel C/A, Dhaka 1000; tel. (2) 9567265; fax (2) 9567230; e-mail primebnk@bangla.net; internet www.prime-bank.com; f. 1995; cap. p.u. 400m., res 268.5m., dep. 7,539.2m. (Dec. 1999); Chair. KHANDKER MOHAMMED KHALED; Man. Dir Kazi ABDUL MAZID; 20 brs.

Pubali Bank Ltd: Pubali Bank Bhaban, 26 Dilkusha C/A, POB 853, Dhaka 1000; tel. (2) 9551614; fax (2) 9564009; e-mail pubali@bdmail.net; f. 1959 as Eastern Mercantile Bank Ltd; name changed to Pubali Bank in 1972; 95% privately-owned, 5% state-owned; cap. p.u. 160m., res 442.6m., dep. 22,786.8m. (Dec. 1998); Chair. EMA-DUDDIN AHMED CHAUDHURY; Man. Dir MOHAMMAD QAMRUL HUDA; 350 brs.

Social Investment Bank: 15 Dilkusha C/A, Dhaka 1000; tel. (2) 881654; fax (2) 881654; f. 1995; cap. p.u. 118.4m., dep. 322.4m. (July 1996); Chair. Dr M. A. MANNAN; Man. Dir M. AZIZUL HUQ; 5 brs.

Southeast Bank Ltd: 1 Dilkusha C/A, Dhaka 1000; tel. (2) 9550081; fax (2) 9550093; e-mail seastbk@citechco.net; f. 1995; cap. 100m., dep. 3,341m. (Dec. 1997); Chair. M. A. KASHEM; CEO SYED ANISUL HUQ; 10 brs.

United Commercial Bank Ltd: Federation Bhaban, 60 Motijheel C/A, POB 2653, Dhaka 1000; tel. (2) 232217; fax (2) 9560587; f. 1983; 50% owned by sponsors, 45% by general public and 5% by Govt; cap. 230.2m., res 265.7m., dep. 9,451.2m. (Dec. 1997); Chair. MOHAMMAD JAHANGIR ALAM KHAN; 78 brs.

Uttara Bank Ltd: 90 Motijheel C/A, POB 818, Dhaka 1000; tel. (2) 9560820; fax (2) 8613529; e-mail ublmis@citecho.net; f. 1965 as Eastern Banking Corpn Ltd; name changed to Uttara Bank in 1972 and to Uttara Bank Ltd in 1983; 5% state-owned; cap. 99.8m., res 480.0m., dep. 20,553.6m. (Dec. 1999); Chair. A. M. ANISUZZAMAN; Man. Dir and CEO M. AMINUZAMMAN; 198 brs.

Foreign Commercial Banks

American Express Bank Ltd (USA): ALICO Bldg, 18–20 Motijheel C/A, POB 420, Dhaka 1000; tel. (2) 9561751; fax (2) 9561722; e-mail amexbd@gononet.com; res 537.5m., dep. 6,236.5m. (Dec. 1995); Chair. RICHARD HOLMES; Gen. Man. JOHN A. SMETANKA; 8 brs.

ANZ Grindlays Bank Ltd (UK): 2 Dilkusha C/A, POB 502, Dhaka 1000; tel. (2) 9550181; fax (2) 9562332; e-mail choudhun@anz.com; res 60.5m., dep. 20,060m. (1999); Gen. Man. MUHAMMAD A. ALI; 9 brs.

Citibank, NA (USA): 122–124 Motijheel C/A, POB 1000, Dhaka 1000; tel. (2) 9550060; fax (2) 642611; f. 1995; cap. p.u. 209.5m., res 5.5m., dep. 648.8m. (July 1996); Chair. JOHN S. REED; Man. Dir S. SRIDHAR; 1 br.

Crédit Agricole Indosuez (France): 47 Motijheel C/A, POB 3490, Dhaka 1000; tel. (2) 9561836; fax (2) 9565707; res 591m., dep. 5,302m. (Dec. 1997); Country Man. FRANCIS DUBUS; Chief Operating Officer S. R. VATOVEY; 2 brs.

Habib Bank Ltd (Pakistan): 53 Motijheel C/A, POB 201, Dhaka 1000; tel. (2) 9563043; fax (2) 9551674; e-mail hbldhaka@bdonline

.com; cap. 80.5m., res 14.3m., dep. 578.6m. (Dec. 1996); Man. Dir J. A. SHAHID; 2 brs.

The Hongkong and Shanghai Banking Corpn Ltd (Hong Kong): 5th Floor, Anchor Tower, 1/1B Sonargaon Rd, Dhaka, 1205; tel. (2) 9660536; fax (2) 9660554; CEO for Bangladesh DAVID HUMPHREYS.

Muslim Commercial Bank Ltd (Pakistan): 4 Dilkusha C/A, POB 7213, Dhaka 1000; tel. (2) 9568871; fax (2) 860671; cap. p.u. 100m., res 4m., dep. 650.3m. (July 1996); Man. Dir HADI ALI KHAN; 2 brs.

Standard Chartered Bank (UK): ALICO Bldg, 18–20 Motijheel C/A, POB 536, Dhaka 1000; tel. (2) 9561465; fax (2) 9561758; cap. p.u. 5,850m. (Dec. 1995); Chief Exec. (Bangladesh) GEOFF WILLIAMS; 3 brs.

State Bank of India: 24–25 Dilkusha C/A, POB 981, Dhaka 1000; tel. (2) 9559935; fax (2) 9563991; e-mail sbibd@bangla.net; cap. 190.4m., dep. 557.1m. (March 1997); CEO ASHITAVA GHOSH; 1 br.

Development Finance Organizations

Bangladesh House Building Finance Corpn (BHBFC): HBFC Bldg, 22 Purana Paltan, POB 2167, Dhaka 1000; tel. (2) 9562767; f. 1952; provides low-interest credit for residential house-building; 100% state-owned; cap. p.u. 972.9m., total investment 23,255.3m. (Dec. 1999); Chair. S. M. ATIUR RAHMAN; Man. Dir S. M. MONIAM HOSSEIN; 9 zonal offices, 13 regional offices and 6 camp offices.

Bangladesh Krishi Bank (BKB): 83–85 Motijheel C/A, POB 357, Dhaka 1000; tel. (2) 9560031; fax (2) 9561211; e-mail bkb@citechco.net; f. 1961 as the Agricultural Development Bank, name changed as above in 1973; provides credit for agricultural and rural devt; also performs all kinds of banking; 100% state-owned; cap. 1,000m., res 820.5m., dep. 31,438m. (June 2000); Chair. Dr MIRZA A. JALIL; Man. Dir MURSHID KULI KHAN; 864 brs.

Bangladesh Samabaya Bank Ltd (BSBL): 'Samabaya Sadan', 9D Motijheel C/A, POB 505, Dhaka 1000; tel. (2) 9564628; f. 1948; provides credit for agricultural co-operatives; cap. p.u. 31.6m., res 558m., dep. 22m. (June 1996); Chair. Dr ABDUL MOYEEN KHAN; Gen. Man. MD ABDUL WAHED.

Bangladesh Shilpa Bank (BSB) (Industrial Development Bank): 8 Rajuk Ave, POB 975, Dhaka; tel. (2) 9555151; fax (2) 9562061; f. 1972; fmrly Industrial Devt Bank; provides long- and short-term financing for industrial devt in the private and public sectors; also provides underwriting facilities and equity support; 51% state-owned; cap. 1,320.0m., res 643.6m., dep. 9,210.0m. (June 1999); Chair. Prof. M. SHAMSUL HAQ; 15 brs.

Bangladesh Shilpa Rin Sangstha (BSRS) (Industrial Loan Agency): BIWTA Bhaban, 5th Floor, 141-143 Motijheel C/A, POB 473, Dhaka 1000; tel. (2) 9565046; fax (2) 956705; f. 1972; 100% state-owned; cap. p.u. 700m., res 462.8m. (June 1996); Chair. Dr M. FARASHUDDIN; Man. Dir AL-AMEEN CHAUDHURY; 4 brs.

Bank of Small Industries and Commerce Bangladesh Ltd (BASIC): Suite 601/602, Sena Kalyan Bhaban, 6th Floor, 195 Motijheel C/A, Dhaka 1000; tel. (2) 956430; fax (2) 9564829; f. 1988; 100% state-owned; cap. p.u. 80m., res 106m., dep. 2,738m. (Dec. 1995); Chair. A. M. AKHTER; Man. Dir ALAUDDIN A. MAJID; 19 brs.

Grameen Bank: Head Office, Mirpur-2, POB 1216, Dhaka 1216; tel. (2) 801138; fax (2) 803559; e-mail grameen.bank@grameen.net; f. 1976; provides credit for the landless rural poor; 6.97% owned by Govt; cap. p.u. 258.1m., res 188.2m., dep. 6,063.2m. (Dec. 1998). Chair. REHMAN SOBHAN; Man. Dir Dr MUHAMMAD YUNUS; 1,140 brs.

Infrastructure Development Co Ltd (IDCOL): Dhaka; f. 1999; state-owned.

Investment Corpn of Bangladesh (ICB): BSB Bldg, 12th–14th Floor, 8 Rajuk Ave, POB 2058, Dhaka 1000; tel. (2) 9563455; fax (2) 865684; f. 1976; provides devt financing; 27% owned by Govt; cap. p.u. 200.0m., res 315.2m. (June 1996); Chair. HEDAYAT AHMED; Man. Dir KHAIRUL HUDA; 5 brs.

Rajshahi Krishi Unnayan Bank: Sadharan Bima Bhaban, Kazihata, Greater Rd, Rajshahi 6000; tel. (721) 775759; fax (721) 775947; f. 1987; 100% state-owned; cap. p.u. 980m., res 208.4m., dep. 2,622.7m. (June 1996); Chair. MD EMRAN ALI SARKAR; Man. Dir SHAH-IDUL HAQ KHAN.

STOCK EXCHANGES

Chittagong Stock Exchange: CSE Bldg, 1080 Sk Mujib Rd, Agrabad, Chittagong; tel. (31) 714100; fax (31) 714101; e-mail maroof@csebd.com; internet www.csebd.com; CEO WALI-UL-MAROOF MATIN.

Dhaka Stock Exchange Ltd: 9F Motijheel C/A, Dhaka 1000; tel. (2) 9564601; fax (2) 9564727; email dse@bol-online.com; internet www.dsebd.org; f. 1960; 196 listed cos; Chair. RAKIBUR RAHMAN.

Regulatory Authority

Bangladesh Securities and Exchange Commission: Jiban Bima Tower, 15th–16th Floor, 10 Dilkusha C/A, Dhaka 1000; tel. (2) 9568101; fax (2) 9563721; CEO M. ABU SAYEED.

INSURANCE

Bangladesh Insurance Association: Hadi Mansion, 7th Floor, 2 Dilkusha C/A, Dhaka; tel. (2) 237330; Chair. MAYEEDUL ISLAM.

Department of Insurance: 74 Motijheel C/A, Dhaka 1000; attached to Ministry of Commerce; supervises activities of domestic and foreign insurers; Controller of Insurance SHAMSUDDIN AHMAD.

In 1973 the two corporations below were formed, one for life insurance and the other for general insurance:

Jiban Bima Corpn: 24 Motijheel C/A, POB 346, Dhaka 1000; tel. (2) 256876; fax (2) 868112; state-owned; comprises 37 national life insurance cos; life insurance; Man. Dir A. K. M. MOSTAFIZUR RAHMAN.

Sadharan Bima Corpn: 33 Dilkusha C/A, POB 607, Dhaka 1000; tel. (2) 9552070; state-owned; general insurance; Man. Dir M. LUTFAR RAHMAN.

Trade and Industry

GOVERNMENT AGENCIES

Board of Investment: Jiban Bima Tower, 19th Floor, 10 Dilkusha C/A, Dhaka 1000; tel. (2) 9563570; fax (2) 9562312; e-mail ec@boi.bdmail.net; Exec. Chair. FAROOQ SOBHAN; Dep. Dir LUTFUR RAHMAN BHUIYA.

Export Promotion Bureau: 122–124 Motijheel C/A, Dhaka 1000; tel. (2) 9552245; fax (2) 9568000; e-mail epb.tic@pradeshta.net; internet www.epbbd.com; f. 1972; attached to Ministry of Commerce; regional offices in Chittagong, Khulna and Rajshahi; brs in Comilla, Sylhet, Barisal and Bogra; Dir-Gen. TAJUL ISLAM; Vice-Chair. A. B. CHOWDHURY.

Petrobangla, Bangladesh Oil, Gas and Mineral Corporation: Petrocenter Bhaban, 3 Kawran Bazar C/A, POB 849, Dhaka 1205; tel. (2) 814936; fax (2) 811613; explores and develops gas, petroleum and mineral resources, manages Bangladesh Petroleum Exploration Co Ltd and Sylhet Gas Fields Ltd; Chair S. K. MOHAMMAD ABDULLAH.

Planning Commission: Planning Commission Secretariat, G.O. Hostel, Sher-e-Bangla Nagar, Dhaka; f. 1972; govt agency responsible for all aspects of economic planning and development including the preparation of the five-year plans and annual development programmes (in conjunction with appropriate govt ministries), promotion of savings and investment, compilation of statistics and evaluation of development schemes and projects.

Privatization Board: Jiban Bima Tower, 14th Floor, 10 Dilkusha C/A, Dhaka 1000; tel. (2) 9563723; fax (2) 9563766; e-mail pb@bdonline.com; internet www.bangladeshonline.com/pb; f. 1993; Chair. KAZI ZAFRULLAH; Sec. A. M. M. NASIR UDDIN.

Trading Corpn of Bangladesh: Kawranbazar, Dhaka; tel. (2) 8111515; fax (2) 813582; e-mail tcb@bdonline.com; f. 1972; imports, exports and markets goods through appointed dealers and agents; Chair. A. M. ABDUL JABBAR; Sec. MD SHAHJAHAN MIAH.

DEVELOPMENT ORGANIZATIONS

Bangladesh Chemical Industries Corpn: BCIC Bhaban, 30–31 Dilkusha C/A, Dhaka; tel. (2) 955280; fax (2) 9564120; e-mail bciccomp@bangla.net; internet www.bangla.net/bcic; Chair. A. K. M. MOSHARRAF HOSSAIN.

Bangladesh Export Processing Zones Authority: 222 New Eskaton Rd, Dhaka 1000; tel. (2) 8312553; fax (2) 8314967; e-mail bepza@bdmail.net; internet www.bangladesh-epz.com; f. 1983 to plan, develop, operate and manage export processing zones (EPZs) in Bangladesh; in mid-2000 two state-owned EPZs (one in Chittagong and the other in Dhaka) were in operation, and another four EPZs were at the implementation stage; Exec. Chair. Brig M. A. B. SIDDIQUE TALUKDER.

Bangladesh Fisheries Development Corpn: 24–25 Dilkusha C/A, Dhaka 1000; tel. (2) 9552689; fax (2) 9563990; e-mail bfdc@citecho.net; f. 1964; under Ministry of Fisheries and Livestock; development and commercial activities; Chair. MOHAMMED MUSA; Sec. A. K. M. SHAHIDUL ISLAM.

Bangladesh Forest Industries Development Corpn: Dhaka; Chair. M. ATIKULLAH.

Bangladesh Jute Mills Corpn: Adamjee Court (Annexe), 115–120 Motijheel C/A, Dhaka 1000; tel. (2) 861980; fax (2) 863329; f. 1972; operates 35 jute mills, incl. 2 carpet mills; world's largest manufacturer and exporter of jute goods; bags, carpet backing cloth, yarn, twine, tape, felt, floor covering, etc.; Chair. MANIRUDDIN AHMAD; Man. (Marketing) MD JAHIRUL ISLAM.

Bangladesh Small and Cottage Industries Corpn (BSCIC): 137/138 Motijheel C/A, Dhaka 1000; tel. (2) 233202; f. 1957; Chair. MUHAMMAD SIRAJUDDIN.

Bangladesh Steel and Engineering Corpn (BSEC): BSEC Bhaban, 102 Kazi Nazrul Islam Ave, Dhaka 1215; tel. (2) 814616; fax (2) 812846; 16 industrial units; sales US $83m. (1994); cap.

US $52m.; Chair. A. I. M. NAZMUL ALAM; Gen. Man. (Marketing) ASHRAFUL HAQ; 8,015 employees.

Bangladesh Sugar and Food Industries Corpn: Shilpa Bhaban, Motijheel C/A, Dhaka 1000; tel. (2) 258084; f. 1972; Chair. M. NEFAUR RAHMAN.

Bangladesh Textile Mills Corpn: Dhaka; tel. (2) 252504; f. 1972; Chair. M. NURUNNABI CHOWDHURY.

CHAMBERS OF COMMERCE

Federation of Bangladesh Chambers of Commerce and Industry (FBCCI): Federation Bhaban, 60 Motijheel C/A, 4th Floor, POB 2079, Dhaka 1000; tel. (2) 9560102; fax (2) 863213; f. 1973; comprises 135 trade asscns and 58 chambers of commerce and industry; Pres. ABDUL AWAL MINTOO.

Barisal Chamber of Commerce and Industry: Asad Mansion, 1st Floor, Sadar Rd, Barisal; tel. (431) 3984; Pres. Qazi ISRAIL HOSSAIN.

Bogra Chamber of Commerce and Industry: Chamber Bhaban, 2nd Floor, Kabi Nazrul Islam Rd, Jhawtola, Bogra 5800; tel. (51) 4138; fax (51) 6257; f. 1963; Pres. AMJAD HOSSAIN TAJMA; Sr Vice-Pres. Alhaj ABUL KALAM AZAD.

Chittagong Chamber of Commerce and Industry: Chamber House, Agrabad C/A, POB 481, Chittagong; tel. (31) 713366; fax (31) 710183; f. 1959; 4,000 mems; Pres. SARWAR JAMAL NIZAM: Sec. M. H. CHOWDHURY.

Comilla Chamber of Commerce and Industry: Rammala Rd, Ranir Bazar, Comilla; tel. (81) 5444; Pres. AFZAL KHAN.

Dhaka Chamber of Commerce and Industry: Dhaka Chamber Bldg, 1st Floor, 65–66 Motijheel C/A, POB 2641, Dhaka 1000; tel. (2) 9552562; fax (2) 9560830; e-mail dcci@bangla.net; internet www.bangla1.com/dcci; f. 1958; 5,000 mems; Pres. AFTAB UL ISLAM; Sr Vice-Pres. AM MUBASH-SHAR.

Dinajpur Chamber of Commerce and Industry: Chamber Bhaban, Maldhapatty, Dinajpur 5200; tel. (531) 3189; Pres. KHAIRUL ANAM.

Faridpur Chamber of Commerce and Industry: Chamber House, Niltuly, Faridpur; tel. 3530; Pres. KHANDOKER MOHSIN ALI.

Foreign Investors' Chamber of Commerce and Industry: 'Mahbub Castle', 4th Floor, 35-1 Purana Paltan Line, Inner Circular Rd, GPO Box 4086, Dhaka 1000; tel. (2) 8319448; fax (2) 8319449; e-mail ficci@fsbd.net; f. 1963 as Agrabad Chamber of Commerce and Industry, name changed as above in 1987; Pres. WALI R. BHUIYAN; Sec. JAHANGIR BIN ALAM.

Khulna Chamber of Commerce and Industry: 6 Lower Jessore Rd, Khulna; tel. (41) 24135; f. 1934; Pres. S. K. ZAHOIUL ISLAM.

Khustia Chamber of Commerce and Industry: 15, NS Rd, Kushtia; tel. (71) 3448; Pres. DIN MOHAMMAD.

Metropolitan Chamber of Commerce and Industry: Chamber Bldg, 4th Floor, 122–124 Motijheel C/A, Dhaka 1000; tel. (2) 9565208; fax (2) 9565212; e-mail sg@citechco.net; internet www.mcci-bd.org; f. 1904; 300 mems; Sec.-Gen. C. K. HYDER.

Noakhali Chamber of Commerce and Industry: Noakhali Pourshara Bhaban, 2nd Floor, Maiydee Court, Noakhali; tel. 5229; Pres. MOHAMMAD NAZIBUR RAHMAN.

Rajshahi Chamber of Commerce and Industry: Chamber Bhaban, Station Rd, P.O. Ghoramara, Rajshahi 6100; tel. (721) 772115; fax (721) 2412; f. 1960; 800 mems; Pres. MOHAMMAD ALI SARKER.

Sylhet Chamber of Commerce and Industry: Chamber Bldg, Jail Rd, POB 97, Sylhet 3100; tel. (821) 714403; fax (821) 715210; e-mail scci@btsnet.net; Pres. MOHD SAFWAN CHOUDHURY.

INDUSTRIAL AND TRADE ASSOCIATIONS

Bangladesh Frozen Foods Exporters Association: 50/1 Inner Circular Rd, 2nd Floor, Shantinagar, Dhaka; tel. and fax (2) 837531; e-mail bffea@drik.dgd.toolnet.org.

Bangladesh Garment Manufacturers and Exporters Association: 7–9 Karwanbazar, BTMC Bhaban, Dhaka 1215; tel. (2) 815597; fax (2) 813951; e-mail bgmea@bgmea.agni.co; Pres. MOSTAFA GOLAM QUDDUS; Vice-Pres. NURUL HAQ SIKDAR.

Bangladesh Jute Association: BJA Bldg, 77 Motijheel C/A, Dhaka; tel. (2) 9552916; fax (2) 9560137; Chair. M.A. MANNAN; Sec. S. H. PRODHAN.

Bangladesh Jute Exporters Association: Nahar Mansion, 2nd Floor, 150 Motijheel C/A, Dhaka 1000; tel. (2) 9561102.

Bangladesh Jute Goods Association: 2nd Floor, Nahar Mansion, 150 Motijheel C/A, Dhaka 1000; tel. (2) 253640; f. 1979; 17 mems; Chair. M. A. KASHEM, Haji MOHAMMAD ALI.

Bangladesh Jute Mills Association: Adamjee Court, 4th Floor, 115–120 Motijheel C/A, Dhaka 1000; tel. (2) 9560071; fax (2) 9566472; Chair. A. M. ZAHIRUDDIN KHAN.

Bangladesh Jute Spinners Association: 55 Purana Paltan, 3rd Floor, Dhaka 1000; tel. (2) 9551317; fax (2) 9562772; f. 1979; 34 mems; Chair. SHABBIR YUSUF; Sec. SHAHIDUL KARIM.

Bangladesh Tea Board: 171–172 Baizid Bostami Rd, Nasirabad, Chittagong; tel. (31) 682903; fax (31) 682863; e-mail btb@spnetctg.com; f. 1951; regulates, controls and promotes the cultivation and marketing of tea, both in Bangladesh and abroad; Contact ALI OHIDUZ ZAMAN.

Bangladesh Textile Mills Association: Moon Mansion, 6th Floor, Block M, 12 Dilkusha C/A, Dhaka 1000; tel. (2) 9563790; fax 863442.

Bangladeshiyo Cha Sangsad (Tea Association of Bangladesh): 'Dar-e-Shahidi', 3rd Floor, 69 Agrabad C/A, POB 287, Chittagong 4100; tel. (31) 501009; f. 1952; Chair. QUAMRUL CHOWDHURY; Sec. G. S. DHAR.

UTILITIES
Electricity

Bangladesh Atomic Energy Commission (BAEC): 4 Kazi Nazrul Islam Ave, POB 158, Dhaka 1000; tel. (2) 502600; fax (2) 863051; f. 1964 as Atomic Energy Centre of the fmr Pakistan Atomic Energy Comm. in East Pakistan; reorg. 1973; operates an atomic energy research establishment and a 3-MW research nuclear reactor (inaugurated in January 1987) at Savar, an atomic energy centre at Dhaka, etc.; Chair. M. A. QUAIYUM; Sec. RAFIQUL ALAM.

Bangladesh Power Development Board: Dhaka; e-mail webmaster@bd-pdb.org; internet www.bd-pdb.org; f. 1972; under Ministry of Energy and Mineral Resources; installed capacity 3,603 MW (1999); Chair. QUAMRUL ISLAM SIDDIQUE.

Dhaka Electric Supply Authority: Dhaka; under Ministry of Energy and Mineral Resources.

Powergrid Company of Bangladesh: Dhaka; f. 1996; responsible for power transmission throughout Bangladesh.

Rural Electrification Board: Dhaka; under Ministry of Energy and Mineral Resources.

Water

Chittagong Water Supply and Sewerage Authority: Dampara, Chittagong; tel. (31) 621606; fax (31) 610465; f. 1963; govt corpn; Chair. SULTAN MAHMUD CHOWDHURY.

Dhaka Water Supply and Sewerage Authority: 98 Kazi Nazrul Islam Ave, Kawran Bazar, Dhaka 1215; tel. (2) 816792; fax (2) 812109; f. 1963; govt corpn; Man. Dir K. AZHARUL HAQ.

TRADE UNIONS

In 2001 only 4.3% of the non-agricultural labour force was unionized. There were about 4,200 registered unions, organized mainly on a sectoral or occupational basis. There were 23 national trade unions to represent workers at the national level.

Bangladesh Free Trade Union Congress (BFTUC): 6-A 1–19 Mirpur, Dhaka; tel. (2) 807001; fax (2) 805919; 98,000 mems.

Bangladesh Jatio Sramik League (BJSL): POB 2730, Dhaka; tel. (2) 282063; fax (2) 863470; 62,000 mems.

Transport

RAILWAYS

In late 1999 an Indian company announced plans to construct a 245-km railway line between Dhaka and Kolkata at a projected cost of US $58m. In July 2000 Bangladesh Railway and the Indian Railway Board signed an agreement to resume rail services on the Benapole–Petrapole route. The service opened fully in January 2001.

Bangladesh Railway: Rail Bhaban, Abdul Ghani Rd, Dhaka 1000; tel. (2) 9561200; fax (2) 9563413; e-mail systcan@citechco.net; f. 1862; supervised by the Railway and Road Transport Division of the Ministry of Communications; divided into East and West zones, with HQ at Chittagong (tel. (31) 711294) and Rajshahi (tel. (721) 761576; fax (721) 761982); total length of 2,734 route km (June 1999); 451 stations; Dir-Gen. M. A. RAHIM; Gen. Man. (East Zone) A. Z. M. SAZZADUR RAHMAN; Gen. Man. (West Zone) MD NURUL AMIN-KHAN.

ROADS

In 1997 the total length of roads in use was 201,182 km (19,175 km of highways, 16,772 km of secondary roads and 165,235 km of other roads), of which 9.5% were paved. In 1992 the World Bank approved Bangladesh's US $700m. Jamuna Bridge Project. The construction of the 4.8-km bridge, which was, for the first time, to link the east and the west of the country with a railway and road network, was begun in early 1994. The bridge, which was renamed the

Bangabandhu Jamuna Multipurpose Bridge, was officially opened in June 1998.

In June 1999 the first direct passenger bus service between Bangladesh (Dhaka) and India (Kolkata) was inaugurated.

Bangladesh Road Transport Corpn: Paribhaban, DIT Ave, Dhaka; f. 1961; state-owned; operates transport services, incl. truck division; transports govt foodgrain; Chair. AZMAN HOSSAIN CHOWDHURY.

INLAND WATERWAYS

In Bangladesh there are some 8,433 km of navigable waterways, which transport 70% of total domestic and foreign cargo traffic and on which are located the main river ports of Dhaka, Narayanganj, Chandpur, Barisal and Khulna. A river steamer service connects these ports several times a week. Vessels of up to 175-m overall length can be navigated on the Karnaphuli river.

Bangladesh Inland Water Transport Corpn: 5 Dilkusha C/A, Dhaka 1000; tel. (2) 257092; f. 1972; 273 vessels (1986).

SHIPPING

The chief ports are Chittagong, where the construction of a second dry-dock is planned, and Chalna. A modern seaport is being developed at Mongla.

Atlas Shipping Lines Ltd: Atlas House, 7 Sk. Mujib Rd, Agrabad C/A, Chittagong 2; tel. (31) 504287; fax (31) 225520; Man. Dir S. U. CHOWDHURY; Gen. Man. M. KAMAL HAYAT.

Bangladesh Shipping Corpn: BSC Bhaban, Saltgola Rd, POB 641, Chittagong 4100; tel. (31) 713277; fax (31) 710506; e-mail bsc–ctg@spnetctg.com; f. 1972; maritime shipping; 15 vessels, 210,672 dwt capacity (1999); Chair. MOFAZZAL HOSSAIN CHOWDHURY MAYA; Man. Dir ZULFIQAR HAIDAR CHAUDHURY.

Bengal Shipping Line Ltd: Palm View, 100A Agrabad C/A, Chittagong 4100; tel. (31) 714800; fax (31) 710362; e-mail mgt@mkrbd.com; Chair. MOHAMMED ABDUL AWWAL; Man. Dir MOHAMMED ABDUL MALEK.

Blue Ocean Lines Ltd: 1st Floor, H.B.F.C. Bldg, 1D Agrabad C/A, Agrabad, Chittagong; tel. (31) 501567; fax (31) 225415.

Broadway Shipping Line: Hafiz Estate, 65 Shiddeswari Rd, Dhaka; tel. (2) 404598; fax (2) 412254.

Chittagong Port Authority: POB 2013, Chittagong 4100; tel. (31) 505041; f. 1887; provides bunkering, ship repair, towage and lighterage facilities as well as provisions and drinking water supplies; Chair. MD SHAHADAT HUSSAIN.

Continental Liner Agencies: 3rd Floor, Facy Bldg, 87 Agrabad C/A, Chittagong; tel. (31) 721572; fax (31) 710965; Man. SAIFUL AHMED; Dir (Technical and Operations) Capt. MAHFUZUL ISLAM.

Nishan Shipping Lines Ltd: 1st Floor, Monzoor Bldg, 67 Agrabad C/A, Chittagong; tel. (31) 710855; fax (31) 710044; Dir Capt. A. K. M. ALAMGIR.

CIVIL AVIATION

There is an international airport at Dhaka (Zia International Airport) situated at Kurmitola, with the capacity to handle 5m. passengers annually. There are also airports at all major towns. In 1997 the civil aviation industry was deregulated to permit domestic competition to Biman Bangladesh Airlines. Partial privatization of the national airline was to begin at the end of 2000.

Biman Bangladesh Airlines: Head Office, Balaka, Kurmitola, Dhaka 1229; tel. (2) 8917400; fax (2) 8913005; internet www.bimanair.com/; f. 1972; 100% state-owned; domestic services to seven major towns; international services to the Middle East, the Far East, Europe, and North America; Chair. Minister of Civil Aviation and Tourism; Man. Dir Air Cmmdre M. RAFIQUL ISLAM.

GMG Airlines: ABC House, 9th Floor, 8 Kamal Ataturk Ave., Banani, Dhaka 1213; tel. (2) 8825845; fax (2) 8826115; e-mail gmgairlines@gmggroup.com; internet www.gmgairlines.com; f. 1997; private, domestic airline; Dir (Flight Operations) Capt. ISHTIAQUE AHMED; Man. Dir SHAHAB SATTAR.

Tourism

Tourist attractions include the cities of Dhaka and Chittagong, Cox's Bazar—which has the world's longest beach (120 km)—on the Bay of Bengal, and Teknaf, at the southernmost point of Bangladesh. Tourist arrivals totalled 171,961 in 1998, and earnings from tourism in 1997 reached about US $59m. The majority of visitors are from India, Pakistan, Japan, the United Kingdom and the USA.

Bangladesh Parjatan Corpn (National Tourism Organization): 233 Airport Rd, Tejgaon, Dhaka 1215; tel. (2) 8117855; fax (2) 8117235; internet www.parjatan.org; there are four tourist information centres in Dhaka, and one each in Bogra, Chittagong, Cox's Bazar, Dinajpur, Khulna, Kuakata, Rangamati, Rangpur, Rajshahi and Sylhet; Chair. MD ABU SALEH; Man. (Public Relations Division) MOHAMMAD AHSAN ULLAH.

BARBADOS

Introductory Survey

Location, Climate, Language, Religion, Flag, Capital

Barbados is the most easterly of the Caribbean islands, lying about 320 km (200 miles) north-east of Trinidad. The island has a total area of 430 sq km (166 sq miles). There is a rainy season from July to November and the climate is tropical, tempered by constant sea winds, during the rest of the year. The mean annual temperature is about 26°C (78°F). Average annual rainfall varies from 1,250 mm (49 ins) on the coast, to 1,875 mm (74 ins) in the interior. The official language is English. Almost all of the inhabitants profess Christianity, but there are small groups of Hindus, Muslims and Jews. The largest denomination is the Anglican church, but about 90 other Christian sects are represented. The national flag (proportions 3 by 2) has three equal vertical stripes, of blue, gold and blue; superimposed on the centre of the gold band is the head of a black trident. The capital is Bridgetown.

Recent History

Barbados was formerly a British colony. The Barbados Labour Party (BLP) won a general election in 1951, when universal adult suffrage was introduced, and held office until 1961. Although the parliamentary system dates from 1639, ministerial government was not established until 1954, when the BLP's leader, Sir Grantley Adams, became the island's first Premier. He was subsequently Prime Minister of the West Indies Federation from January 1958 until its dissolution in May 1962.

Barbados achieved full internal self-government in October 1961. An election in December was won by the Democratic Labour Party (DLP), formed in 1955 by dissident members of the BLP. The DLP's leader, Errol Barrow, became Premier, succeeding Dr Hugh Cummins of the BLP. When Barbados achieved independence on 30 November 1966, Barrow became the island's first Prime Minister, following another electoral victory by his party earlier in the month.

The DLP retained power in 1971, but in the general election of September 1976 the BLP, led by J. M. G. M. ('Tom') Adams (Sir Grantley's son), ended Barrow's 15-year rule. The BLP successfully campaigned against alleged government corruption, winning a large majority over the DLP. At a general election in June 1981 the BLP was returned to office with 17 of the 27 seats in the newly-enlarged House of Assembly. The DLP won the remainder of the seats. Adams died suddenly in March 1985 and was succeeded as Prime Minister by his deputy, Bernard St John, a former leader of the BLP.

At a general election in May 1986 the DLP won a decisive victory, receiving 59.4% of the total votes and winning 24 seats in the House of Assembly. Bernard St John and all except one of his cabinet ministers lost their seats, and Errol Barrow returned as Prime Minister after 10 years in opposition. In June it was announced that Barrow was to review Barbados' participation in the US-supported Regional Security System (RSS), the defence force that had been established soon after the US invasion of Grenada in October 1983. Under Adams Barbados was one of the countries whose troops had supported the invasion. In June 1987 Barrow died suddenly. He was succeeded by L. Erskine Sandiford (hitherto the Deputy Prime Minister), who pledged to continue Barrow's economic and social policies. In September 1987, however, the Minister of Finance, Dr Richard (Richie) Haynes, resigned, accusing Sandiford of failing to consult him over financial appointments. Sandiford assumed the finance portfolio, but acrimony over government policy continued to trouble the DLP. In February 1989 Haynes and three other members of Parliament resigned from the DLP and announced the formation of the National Democratic Party (NDP). Haynes was subsequently appointed as leader of the parliamentary opposition.

At a general election in January 1991 the DLP won 18 of the 28 seats in the enlarged House of Assembly, while the BLP secured the remaining 10. The creation of a Ministry of Justice and Public Safety by the new Government, and the reintroduction of flogging for convicted criminals, reflected widespread concern over increased levels of violent crime on the island. Moreover, as a result of serious economic problems, a series of austerity measures were proposed in September. However, the proposals resulted in public unrest, which continued in 1992, as large numbers of civil servants and agricultural workers were made redundant. The increasing unpopularity of Sandiford's premiership provoked continued demands for his resignation during 1993, and at the DLP's annual convention in August a leadership challenge was mounted. Sandiford, however, remained in office, and he subsequently announced a major reallocation of cabinet portfolios. Moreover, a controversial reorganization of the Barbados Tourist Authority prompted the resignation of three cabinet ministers in early 1994. Increasing dissatisfaction with the Prime Minister culminated in his narrow defeat in a parliamentary motion of confidence in June. Despite intense speculation that he would resign, Sandiford remained in office, but announced the dissolution of Parliament in preparation for a general election, which was to take place in September. At the DLP annual conference in August, David Thompson defeated Brandford Taitt in a leadership contest.

A general election took place on 6 September 1994, at which the BLP won a decisive victory, securing 19 seats in the House of Assembly, compared with the DLP's eight and the NDP's one. Owen Arthur was subsequently appointed as Prime Minister.

In May 1995 Arthur announced the formation of a 10-member commission to advise the Government on possible reforms of the country's Constitution and political institutions. In July 1996 the commission was asked to consider, in particular, the continuing role of the British monarch as Head of State in Barbados. The commission's report, which was published in December 1998, recommended, as expected, the replacement of the British monarch with a ceremonial President. It also proposed changes in the composition of the Senate and the substitution of a jointly-administered Caribbean Court for the existing highest judicial body, the Privy Council. In July 1999 Caribbean leaders agreed to establish such a court, and in August 2000 Arthur announced that there would be a referendum on the replacement of the monarchy with a republic, a move which had the clear support of all political parties.

In December 1996 the DLP retained a seat in a by-election. This development resulted in renewed pressure for the reunification of the DLP and the NDP, which together secured more votes (though fewer seats) than the BLP in the general election. In mid-1997 two prominent members of the NDP (including the influential General Secretary of the National Union of Public Workers, Joseph Goddard) rejoined the DLP. The NDP lost a further electoral candidate to the ruling BLP in November, and in September two candidates (one of whom subsequently joined the DLP) resigned from the BLP, attributing their decision to the Prime Minister's lack of control over the party. In September 1998 Hamilton Lashley, a prominent DLP member of the House of Assembly, accepted the post of consultant to the Prime Minister on matters of poverty alleviation. In October Lashley transferred political allegiance to the governing BLP.

A general election was held on 20 January 1999, even though elections were not constitutionally due until September of that year. Although the BLP was widely expected to win a second term in government, the scale of its election victory was unprecedented. The BLP received 64.8% of the total votes cast, winning 26 of the 28 seats in the House of Assembly, while the DLP received 35.1% of the votes and won only two seats (the NDP did not contest the election). The result represented an even greater defeat for the DLP than the BLP had itself experienced in the elections of 1986 (see above), and was largely attributed to the Government's recent successes in reviving the Barbadian economy, particularly in reducing unemployment. (However, although there were severe doubts over his political future, David Thompson was re-elected as the leader of the DLP in August 1999.) On 24 January the Prime Minister announced an expanded 14-member Cabinet, including the new post of Minister of Social Transformation (to which Lashley was appointed), whose major concern was to be poverty alleviation. Arthur promised to create a 'new and unprecedented prosperity' in Barbados, and declared his Government's commitment to transforming Barbados into a republic (although he simultaneously pledged to keep the country within the Commonwealth).

In April 1999 Trafalgar Square, in the centre of Bridgetown, was renamed National Heroes Square, and the decision was made to replace the statue of the British Admiral Lord Horatio Nelson which stood there, with one of Errol Barrow, the country's first Prime Minister. These developments, which reinforced existing differences between Barbados' two main ethnic communities, were seen as evidence that the country was beginning its transformation into a republic. With the aim of resolving any growing divisions, the Government organized a day of national reconciliation in July, while a 13-member Committee for National Reconciliation was also established.

In August 1999 the long-serving Minister of Health, Elizabeth Thompson, was unexpectedly dismissed by the Prime Minister. Reasons for her dismissal were unspecified, although it apparently followed derogatory remarks made by the minister about the opposition leader, David Thompson. Phillip Goddard was appointed the new Minister of Health, while the Public Works and Transport portfolio was assumed by Rommell Marshall. In November two former electoral candidates for the DLP, who had been unsuccessful in January's general election, announced their resignation from the party. Furthermore, in October 2000 five prominent opposition politicians joined the BLP at its annual conference. Three of the five, Tyrone Estwick, Kerrie Symmonds and Johnny Tudor, came from the DLP, while the other two, David Commissiong and Peter Miller, were NDP members.

In late 1997 the Government established a committee to examine alternative methods of punishing offenders, following a report which found Barbados' only prison to be grossly overcrowded. In October 1998, owing to a recent significant increase in the number of violent crimes involving firearms, the Government announced a temporary amnesty for individuals surrendering illegally-owned weapons; tougher penalties for unlawful possession were introduced as part of new firearms-control legislation enacted in November. Amid a further escalation in violent crime and fears that the country's tourism industry might be affected, it was announced in October 1999 that an anti-firearms unit was to be established in the police force. In December 2000, however, the Prime Minister was criticized for failing to meet representatives from the tourism industry to discuss the impact of crime on the sector, following an armed attack on a British couple.

Relations with Trinidad and Tobago were strained in the mid-1980s by publicly-stated differences over the 1983 intervention in Grenada (q.v.), and by Trinidad and Tobago's imposition of import restrictions (a compromise on this was reached in August 1986). In November 1990 the two Governments signed a bilateral fishing agreement; they also agreed, in late 1999, to draft a boundary delimitation treaty and to establish a negotiating mechanism to resolve trade disputes. In late 1996 Barbados signed an agreement with the USA to co-operate with a regional initiative to combat the illegal drugs trade. In mid-1998 the Government announced its intention to develop relations with countries in Asia, the Pacific region and Latin America, in order to pursue a foreign policy based on economic considerations. In March of that year Barbados began negotiations with the Organisation of Eastern Caribbean States (OECS, see p. 309) concerning the country's eventual membership in a confederation, and possible political union, of Eastern Caribbean states. Areas under discussion included health, education, diplomatic representation and the judiciary. A 14-member joint 'task force' had been appointed in February to discuss the possible incorporation of Barbados into the OECS. An inaugural meeting of the discussion group took place in April, when it was suggested that a working confederation could be instituted within 2–3 years. Although monetary union was not to be a prior condition to membership, OECS spokesmen described the adoption of a single currency as highly desirable. In June 2000 Barbados officially declared its acceptance of the compulsory jurisdiction of the Inter-American Court of Human Rights, an institution of the Organization of American States (OAS, see p. 261).

Government

Executive power is vested in the British monarch, represented by a Governor-General, who acts on the advice of the Cabinet. The Governor-General appoints the Prime Minister and, on the latter's recommendation, other members of the Cabinet. Legislative power is vested in the bicameral Parliament, comprising a Senate of 21 members, appointed by the Governor-General, and a House of Assembly with 28 members, elected by universal adult suffrage for five years (subject to dissolution) from single-member constituencies. The Cabinet is responsible to Parliament. In 1969 elected local government bodies were abolished in favour of a division into 11 parishes, all of which are administered by the central Government.

Defence

The Barbados Defence Force was established in 1978. The total strength of the Barbados armed forces in August 2000 was estimated at 610; the army consisted of 500 members and the navy (coastguard) 110. There was also a reserve force of 430. The defence budget for 2000 was estimated at Bds $26m.

Economic Affairs

In 1995, according to estimates by the World Bank, the island's gross national product (GNP), measured at average 1993–95 prices, was US $1,745m., equivalent to US $6,560 per head. Between 1990 and 1998 GNP per head increased at an average annual rate of 1.0%. In the same period the population increased at an average rate of 0.4% per year. According to preliminary estimates, GNP totalled US $2,096m. in 1998 (equivalent to US $7,890 per head, or US $12,260 on an international purchasing-power parity basis). Barbados' gross domestic product (GDP), at factor cost, increased, in real terms, at an average rate of 0.7% per year during 1990–97. Real GDP increased by 3.0% in 1997, by 4.4% in 1998 and by 2.5% in 1999. GDP totalled US $2,490.1m. (Bds $4,980.1m.) in 1999, or US $9,326 per head. In the nine months to the end of September 2000, the economy expanded by a further 2.9%, exceeding the previous official projection of 2.5%.

Agriculture (including hunting, forestry and fishing) contributed 4.0% of GDP in 1998 and engaged an estimated 4.2% of the employed labour force in 1999. Sugar remains the main commodity export, earning Bds $56.6m. in 1998; in that year, however, raw sugar production decreased by 25.7% to an estimated 48,000 metric tons. The sugar industry suffered from severe economic problems since the 1980s and was, from the late 1990s, facing increased pressure to reform, particularly as further liberalization of international trade was likely to make the island less competitive. In 1998 sugar accounted for only 1.4% of GDP, 2.3% of foreign-exchange earnings and 2.5% of total employment. Sea-island cotton, once the island's main export crop, was revived in the mid-1980s. The other principal crops, primarily for local consumption, are sweet potatoes, carrots, yams and other vegetables and fruit. Fishing was also developed in the 1980s, and in 1988 there was a fleet of about 750 fishing vessels. The GDP of the agricultural sector declined, in real terms, at an average rate of 0.5% per year during 1990–97. According to the IMF, agricultural GDP fell by 0.6% in 1997 and by 13.3% in 1998, but was estimated to have increased by 6.9% in 1999.

In 1998 industry accounted for an estimated 16.1% of GDP, and 21.5% of the working population were employed in all industrial activities (manufacturing, construction, quarrying and utilities) in 1999. In real terms, industrial GDP increased at an average rate of 0.9% annually in 1990–97. According to IMF figures, industrial GDP (including mining and quarrying) rose by 6.7% in 1997, by 10.3% in 1998 and by an estimated 2.1% in 1999.

Owing to fluctuations in international prices, the production of crude petroleum declined substantially from its peak in 1985, to 454,424 barrels in 1990, or 31% of Barbados' requirements. In late 1996 the Barbados National Oil Company signed a five-year agreement with a US company to intensify exploration activity, with the aim of increasing petroleum production from 1,000 barrels per day (b/d) to 10,000 b/d by 2001. Total annual extraction was only 328,000 barrels in 1997. As a result, however, of an onshore drilling programme begun that year production increased dramatically in 1998 and 1999, reaching 579,636 and 708,500 barrels, respectively. After a temporary suspension in drilling as a result of low international oil prices, drilling was again resumed in October 2000. Production of natural gas was 24.2m. cu m in 1998. Mining and construction contributed 6.6% of GDP and employed an estimated 11.4% of the working population in 1999.

Manufacturing contributed an estimated 9.3% of GDP and employed 8.4% of the working population in 1999. Excluding sugar factories and refineries, the principal branches of manufacturing, measured by the value of output, in 1994 were chemical, petroleum, rubber and plastic products (accounting for 27.3% of the total), food products (26.9%), and beverages and tobacco (15.0%). Manufacturing GDP increased, in real terms, at an average rate of 0.2% per year during 1990–97; it rose by 3.8% in 1997 and 3.4% in 1998, but fell by an estimated 2.4% in 1999.

Service industries are the main sector of the economy, accounting for an estimated 72.4% of GDP and 74.1% of employment in 1999. The combined GDP of the service sectors increased, in real terms, at an average rate of 0.7% per year during 1990–97. In 1998 the sector grew by 4.4% and, in 1999, by an estimated 2.3%. Business and general services contributed an estimated 16.9% of GDP in 1999. The Government has encouraged the growth of 'offshore' financial facilities, particularly through the negotiation of double taxation agreements with other countries. At the end of 1998 there were 3,073 international business companies and 2,608 foreign sales corporations operating in the country. It was estimated that the 'offshore' sector contributed almost US $150m. in foreign earnings in 1995. In the following year the Government announced a series of proposals which aimed to expand the industry. Barbados has an active anti-money-laundering regime, which was further strengthened by new legislation in 1998, although the island remained classified by the USA as a 'country of concern' with regard to money-laundering. Moreover, in May 2000 the Organisation for Economic Co-operation and Development (OECD) placed Barbados on a list of tax 'havens' which faced counter-measures from June 2001 if they failed to modify tax regimes in line with OECD requirements.

Tourism made a direct contribution of an estimated 15% to GDP in 1999 and, in 1998, employed 11.5% of the working population. Receipts from the tourist industry almost doubled between 1980 and 1988, and in 1998 totalled some Bds $1,500m. Stop-over tourist arrivals increased from 512,397 in 1998 to 517,869 in 1999, while cruise-ship passenger arrivals decreased by 12%, to 445,821. In 1999 some 39.2% of stop-over arrivals were from the United Kingdom.

In 1999 Barbados recorded an estimated visible trade deficit of US $691.7m. and there was an estimated deficit of US $125.8m. on the current account of the balance of payments. In 1999 the USA was both the principal source of imports (41.5%) and the largest single recipient of exports (17.0%). The United Kingdom accounted for 8.4% of imports and 14.4% of exports. Other major trading partners included the CARICOM countries (see below), especially Trinidad and Tobago. The principal commodity exports in 1998 were petroleum products (15.7% of total exports), chemicals (13.4%) and raw sugar (10.7%). The principal imports were machinery, transport equipment and basic manufactures.

For the financial year ending 31 March 2000 there was an estimated total budgetary deficit of Bds $65.0m.; for the year ending 31 March 2001 the deficit was projected decrease slightly, to Bds $57.2m. At December 1999 the total external debt of Barbados was US $468.8m. In 1999 the cost of foreign debt-servicing was equivalent to 7.7% of the value of exports of goods and services. The average annual rate of inflation was 3.0% in 1990–98. Average consumer prices, however, declined by 1.3% in 1998; they rose by 1.6% in 1999. By the end of September 2000 unemployment was estimated to have fallen to 9.3% of the labour force, compared with 11.1% at the beginning of 1999.

Barbados is a member of the Caribbean Community and Common Market (CARICOM, see p. 142), of the Inter-American Development Bank (IDB, see p. 212), of the Latin American Economic System (SELA, see p. 308) and of the Association of Caribbean States (see p. 306).

Political stability and consensus have contributed to the economic strengths of Barbados. Tourism dominates the economy but 'offshore' banking and sugar production are also important. The closure of major hotels for refurbishment in 1999 brought about a marginal temporary decline in tourism earnings; however, the tourism sector was expected to reach record levels in 2000. Despite the thriving tourism sector, in early 1998 the Government voiced concerns over the incidence of poverty in Barbados and established a US $5m.-Social Investment Fund and a Poverty Eradication Fund. In 1998, for the first time since 1991, a balance-of-payments deficit was recorded, owing largely to the high level of import demand in the construction sector. Moreover, the expansion of private credit, which had resulted in a significant decrease in inter-national reserves in 1998, led the Central Bank to raise the discount rate to commercial banks in May 1999, in order to curb the excess demand. The 2000/2001 budget proposals, announced in October 2000, contained plans to end the British company Cable & Wireless' monopoly of the telecommunications sector. A phased liberalization of this market was to commence at the end of 2000 and was to be completed by the end of 2002. The proposed privatization of the Barbados National Bank and the Insurance Company of Barbados were also announced (the latter was transferred to the private sector in December 2000). There were also plans to modernize the bankruptcy and insolvency laws. A Bds $5m. programme to improve export capability was also unveiled. The year 1999 was the seventh successive year of economic expansion, with real GDP growth of some 2.5%. In early 1998 negotiations were initiated regarding the proposed confederation of Barbados and the OECS (see p. 309), following the 1995 economic co-operation agreement between the two parties.

Social Welfare

A social security scheme was established in 1967, and a National Drug Plan was introduced in 1980. Old-age pensions and unemployment insurance are available. The Government has also created a building scheme of group housing for lower-income families. In 1994 Barbados had one hospital bed for every 136 citizens, and one physician for every 749 inhabitants on the island. Of total current budgetary expenditure by the central Government in the 1998/99 financial year, Bds $248.0m. (16.1%) was for health services and Bds $148.3m. (9.6%) was for social security and welfare. In addition, the national insurance scheme, funded by contributions, provides pensions and other benefits (totalling Bds $221.2m. in 1996/97). In October 2000 the Government announced that its financing of the national human immunodeficiency virus (HIV) and Acquired Immunodeficiency Syndrome (AIDS) programme was to increase to Bds $25m. The total number of AIDS cases reported between December 1984 and March 2000 was 1,199, from 2,356 HIV-infected people.

Education

Education is compulsory for 12 years, between five and 16 years of age. Primary education begins at the age of five and lasts for seven years. Secondary education, beginning at 12 years of age, lasts for six years. In 1998 enrolment of children in the primary age-group was 97% (males 99%; females 95%), while enrolment at secondary level included 69% of children in the relevant age-group (males 67%; females 71%). In that year enrolment at tertiary level was equivalent to 33.7% of the relevant age-group (males 22.2%; females 34.2%). According to UNESCO estimates, in 1996/97 3,275 students were enrolled at universities or similar institutions. Degree courses in arts, law, education, natural sciences and social sciences are offered at the Barbados branch of the University of the West Indies. The faculty of medicine administers the East Caribbean Medical Scheme, while an in-service training programme for secondary-school teachers is provided by the School of Education. The Government announced in September 2000 that it expected to realize its ambition of providing universal pre-school education by the academic year 2002. In 2000 72% of children aged three and four attended school.

In 1999, according to official estimates, adult illiteracy in Barbados was 3.0%.

Current expenditure on education by the central Government in 1998/99 was Bds $289.7m. (equivalent to 18.8% of total current spending).

Public Holidays

2001: 1 January (New Year's Day), 21 January (Errol Barrow Day), 13 April (Good Friday), 16 April (Easter Monday), 28 April (National Heroes' Day), 7 May (Labour Day), 4 June (Whit Monday), 1 August (Emancipation Day), 5 August (Kadooment Day), 30 November (Independence Day), 25–26 December (Christmas).

2002: 1 January (New Year's Day), 21 January (Errol Barrow Day), 29 March (Good Friday), 1 April (Easter Monday), 28 April (National Heroes' Day), 6 May (for Labour Day), 20 May (Whit Monday), 1 August (Emancipation Day), 4 August (Kadooment Day), 30 November (Independence Day), 25–26 December (Christmas).

Weights and Measures

The metric system is used.

Statistical Survey

Sources (unless otherwise stated): Barbados Statistical Service, National Insurance Bldg, 3rd Floor, Fairchild St, Bridgetown; tel. 427-7841; fax 435-2198; e-mail barstats@caribsurf.com; internet www.bgis.gov.bb/stats.
Central Bank of Barbados, Spry St, POB 1016, Bridgetown; tel. 436-6870; fax 427-1431; e-mail cbb.libr@caribsurf.com; internet www.centralbank.org.bb.

AREA AND POPULATION

Area: 430 sq km (166 sq miles).

Population: 252,029 (males 119,665, females 132,364) at census of 12 May 1980; 257,082 (provisional) at census of 2 May 1990; 267,900 (official estimate) at mid-1999.

Density (mid-1999): 623.0 per sq km.

Ethnic Groups (*de jure* population, excl. persons resident in institutions, 1990 census): Black 228,683; White 8,022; Mixed race 5,886; Total (incl. others) 247,288.

Principal Town: Bridgetown (capital), population 5,928 at 1990 census.

Births, Marriages and Deaths (provisional registrations, 1998): Live births 3,612 (birth rate 13.6 per 1,000); Marriages (1997) 3,377 (marriage rate 12.7 per 1,000); Deaths 2,471 (death rate 9.3 per 1,000).

Expectation of Life (UN estimates, years at birth, 1990–95): 75.3 (males 72.9; females 77.9). Source: UN, *World Population Prospects: The 1998 Revision.*

Economically Active Population (labour force sample survey, '000 persons aged 15 years and over, excl. armed forces, 1999): Agriculture, forestry and fishing 5.2; Manufacturing 10.3; Electricity, gas and water 2.0; Construction and quarrying 14.0; Wholesale and retail trade 17.2; Tourism 12.3; Transport, storage and communications 4.5; Financing, insurance, real estate and business services 7.0; Community, social and personal services 49.7; Activities not adequately defined 0.2; Total employed 122.4 (males 65.5, females 56.9); Unemployed 14.2 (males 5.5, females 8.7); Total labour force 136.6 (males 71.0, females 65.6). Source: ILO Caribbean Office.

AGRICULTURE, ETC.

Principal Crops (FAO estimates '000 metric tons, 1999): Maize 2; Sweet potatoes 5; Cassava 1; Yams 1; Pulses 1; Coconuts 2; Cabbages 1; Tomatoes 1; Pumpkins 1; Cucumbers 1; Chillies and peppers 1; String beans 1; Carrots 1; Other vegetables 5; Sugar cane 500; Bananas 1; Other fruits 2. Source: FAO.

Livestock (FAO estimates, '000 head, year ending September 1999): Horses 1; Mules 2; Asses 2; Cattle 23; Pigs 33; Sheep 41; Goats 5; Poultry 3,600. Source: FAO.

Livestock Products ('000 metric tons, 1999): Beef and veal 1*; Pig meat 4; Poultry meat 12; Cows' milk 8; Hen eggs 1*. *FAO estimate Source: FAO.

Forestry ('000 cubic metres): Roundwood removals 5 in 1996; 5 in 1997; 5 in 1998. Source: FAO, *Yearbook of Forest Products.*

Fishing (metric tons, live weight, 1998): Total catch 3,594 (Flyingfishes 2,680, Common dolphinfish 482, Yellowfin tuna 146, Marlins, sailfishes, etc. 109). Source: FAO, *Yearbook of Fishery Statistics.*

MINING

Production: Natural gas 24.2 million cu m in 1998; Crude petroleum 708,500 barrels in 1999.

INDUSTRY

Selected Products (official estimates, 1998): Raw sugar (1999) 53,196 metric tons; Rum 8,830,000 litres; Beer (1995) 7,429,000 litres; Cigarettes (1995) 65 metric tons; Batteries 17,165; Electric energy 715m. kWh.

FINANCE

Currency and Exchange Rates: 100 cents = 1 Barbados dollar (Bds $). *Sterling, US Dollar and Euro Equivalents* (29 December 2000): £1 sterling = Bds $2.984; US $1 = Bds $2.000; €1 = Bds $1.861; Bds $100 = £33.51 = US $50.00 = €53.73. *Exchange Rate:* Fixed at US $1 = Bds $2.000 since 1986.

Budget (estimates, Bds $ million, year ending 31 March 2000): *Revenue:* Tax revenue 1,562.0 (Taxes on income and profits 512.9, Levies 75.2, Taxes on property 98.2, Domestic taxes on goods and services 727.8, Taxes on international trade 134.6); Other current revenue 49.6; Total 1,611.6. *Expenditure:* Current 1,409.9 (Wages and salaries 565.2, Other goods and services 163.4, Interest payments 230.7, Transfers and subsidies 413.4); Capital (incl. net lending 4.5) 266.7; Total 1,676.6.

2000/01 (projections, Bds $ million): Total revenue and grants 1,724.7; Total expenditure 1,781.9 (Capital expenditure and net lending 291.9).

Note: Budgetary data refer to current and capital budgets only and exclude operations of the National Insurance Fund and other central government units with their own budgets.

International Reserves (US $ million at 31 December 1999): IMF special drawing rights 0.01; Reserve position in IMF 6.42; Foreign exchange 295.52; Total 301.94. Source: IMF, *International Financial Statistics.*

Money Supply (Bds $ million at 31 December 1999): Currency outside banks 302.7; Demand deposits at commercial banks 615.6; Total money (incl. others) 924.4. Source: IMF, *International Financial Statistics.*

Cost of Living (Index of Retail Prices; base: 1995 = 100): 110.3 in 1997; 108.9 in 1998; 110.6 in 1999. Source: IMF, *International Financial Statistics.*

Expenditure on the Gross Domestic Product (provisional, Bds $ million at current prices, 1999): Government final consumption expenditure 1,128.3; Private final consumption expenditure 3,134.1; Increase in stocks 10.5; Gross fixed capital formation 957.8; *Total domestic expenditure* 5,230.7; Exports of goods and services 2,509.2; *Less* Imports of goods and services 2,759.8; *GDP in purchasers' values* 4,980.1. Source: IMF, *Barbados: Statistical Appendix* (December 2000).

Gross Domestic Product by Economic Activity (Bds $ million at current prices, 1998): Agriculture, hunting, forestry and fishing 158.1; Mining and quarrying 20.1; Manufacturing 243.5; Electricity, gas and water 126.4; Construction 240.6; Wholesale and retail trade 702.2; Tourism 482.2; Transport, storage and communications 381.7; Finance, insurance, real estate and business services 715.7; Government services 674.5; Other community, social and personal services 179.8; *GDP at factor cost* 3,924.8; Indirect taxes, *less* subsidies 852.1; *GDP in purchasers' values* 4,776.9.

Balance of Payments (US $ million, 1999): Exports of goods f.o.b. 262.0; Imports of goods f.o.b. –953.7; *Trade balance* –691.7; Exports of services 1,025.4; Imports of services –454.2; *Balance on goods and services* –120.6; Other income received 66.7; Other income paid –138.1; *Balance on goods, services and income* –192.0; Current transfers received 94.0; Current transfers paid –27.7; *Current balance* –125.8; Capital account (net) 3.8; Direct investment abroad –1.3; Direct investment from abroad 17.4; Portfolio investment assets –18.6; Portfolio investment liabilities –44.9; Other investment assets –93.1; Other investment liabilities 170.2; Net errors and omissions –38.9; *Overall balance* –36.3. Source: IMF, *International Financial Statistics.*

EXTERNAL TRADE

Principal Commodities (US $ million, 1998): *Imports c.i.f.:* Food and live animals 137.3 (Cereals and cereal preparations 29.8, Vegetables and fruit 27.8); Beverages and tobacco 21.8; Crude materials (inedible) except fuels 38.3 (Cork and wood 24.2); Mineral fuels, lubricants, etc. 81.7 (Refined petroleum products 76.4); Chemicals and related products 104.5 (Medicinal and pharmaceutical products 29.8); Basic manufactures 171.8 (Paper, paperboard and manufactures 29.8, Textile yarn, fabrics, etc. 22.7, Non-metallic mineral manufactures 25.7, Iron and steel 22.3); Machinery and transport equipment 305.5 (Machinery specialized for particular industries 26.7, General industrial machinery and equipment 44.4, Office machines and automatic data-processing equipment 33.2, Telecommunications and sound equipment 31.4, Other electrical machinery, apparatus, etc. 54.8, Road vehicles and parts 101.5); Miscellaneous manufactured articles 152.6; Total (incl. others) 1,022.1. *Exports f.o.b.:* Food and live animals 61.2 (Cereals and cereal preparations 8.8, Raw sugar 27.6, Margarine and shortening 5.4); Beverages and tobacco 17.3 (Alcoholic beverages 15.2); Mineral fuels, lubricants, etc. 40.5 (Petroleum, petroleum products, etc. 40.5); Chemicals and related products 34.9 (Medicinal and pharmaceutical products 11.0, Essential oils, perfume materials and cleansing preparations 7.1, Disinfectants, insecticides, fungicides, etc. 10.4); Basic manufactures 40.1 (Paper, paperboards and manufactures 11.9, Non-metallic mineral manufactures 10.2, Metal containers for storage and transport 5.2); Machinery and transport equipment 34.0 (Electrical machinery, apparatus, etc. 24.5); Miscellaneous manufactured articles 27.9 (Unused stamps, banknotes, share certificates, etc. 6.7); Total (incl. others) 258.7. Source: UN, *International Trade Statistics Yearbook*.

Principal Trading Partners (US $ million, preliminary, 1999): *Imports:* Canada 46.2; Jamaica 11.4; Trinidad and Tobago 123.9; United Kingdom 89.3; USA 442.6; Total (incl. others) 1,067.9. *Exports:* Antigua and Barbuda 6.2; Canada 6.8; Dominica 4.6; Grenada 5.9; Guyana 5.9; Jamaica 16.8; Saint Lucia 11.0; Saint Vincent and the Grenadines 7.8; Trinidad and Tobago 27.7; United Kingdom 36.0; USA 42.5; Total (incl. others) 250.4. Source: IMF, *Barbados: Statistical Appendix* (December 2000).

TRANSPORT

Road Traffic (motor vehicles in use, 1995): Private cars 43,711; Taxis 1,405; Buses and minibuses 390; Lorries 2,215; Vans and pick-ups 3,967; Total 55,665.

Shipping (estimated freight traffic, '000 metric tons, 1990): Goods loaded 206; Goods unloaded 538. Source: UN, *Monthly Bulletin of Statistics. Total goods handled* ('000 metric tons, 1997): 1,095. Source: Barbados Port Authority. *Merchant Fleet* (vessels registered at 31 December 1998): Number of vessels 69; Total displacement 687,586 grt. Source: Lloyd's Register of Shipping, *World Fleet Statistics*.

Civil Aviation (1994): Aircraft movements 36,100; Freight loaded 5,052.3 metric tons; Freight unloaded 8,548.3 metric tons.

TOURISM

Tourist Arrivals: *Stop-overs:* 472,290 in 1997; 512,397 in 1998; 517,869 in 1999. *Cruise-ship passengers:* 517,888 in 1997; 506,610 in 1998; 445,821 in 1999.

Tourist arrivals by country ('000 persons, 1998): Canada 60.0; Germany 12.1; Trinidad and Tobago 19.3; United Kingdom 186.7; USA 106.3; Total (incl. others) 512.4. Source: Ministry of Labour, Sports and Public Sector Reform.

Tourism Receipts (US $ million): 663.4 in 1997; 711.9 in 1998; 681.1 (provisional) in 1999. Source: IMF, *Barbados: Statistical Appendix* (December 2000).

COMMUNICATIONS MEDIA

Radio Receivers (1997): 237,000 in use.

Television Receivers (1997): 76,000 in use.

Telephones (year ending 31 March 1997): 108,000 in use.

Telefax Stations (year ending 31 March 1997): 1,800 in use.

Mobile Cellular Telephones (year ending 31 March 1997): 8,013 subscribers.

Book Production (1983): 87 titles (18 books, 69 pamphlets).

Newspapers: *Daily* (1996): 2 (circulation 53,000). *Non-daily* (1990): 4 (estimated circulation 95,000).

Sources: partly UNESCO, *Statistical Yearbook*, and UN, *Statistical Yearbook*.

EDUCATION

Pre-primary (1995/96): 84 schools; 529 teachers; 4,689 pupils.

Primary (1995/96): 79 schools; 944 teachers; 18,513 pupils.

Secondary (1995/96): 21 schools; 1,263 teachers; 21,455 pupils.

Tertiary (1995/96): 4 schools; 544 teachers (1984); 6,622 students.

Directory

The Constitution

The parliamentary system has been established since the 17th century, when the first Assembly sat, in 1639, and the Charter of Barbados was granted, in 1652. A new Constitution came into force on 30 November 1966, when Barbados became independent. Under its terms, protection is afforded to individuals from slavery and forced labour, from inhuman treatment, deprivation of property, arbitrary search and entry, and racial discrimination; freedom of conscience, of expression, assembly, and movement are guaranteed.

Executive power is nominally vested in the British monarch, as Head of State, represented in Barbados by a Governor-General, who appoints the Prime Minister and, on the advice of the Prime Minister, appoints other ministers and some senators.

The Cabinet consists of the Prime Minister, appointed by the Governor-General as being the person best able to command a majority in the House of Assembly, and not fewer than five other ministers. Provision is also made for a Privy Council, presided over by the Governor-General.

Parliament consists of the Governor-General and a bicameral legislature, comprising the Senate and the House of Assembly. The Senate has 21 members: 12 appointed by the Governor-General on the advice of the Prime Minister, two on the advice of the Leader of the Opposition and seven as representatives of such interests as the Governor-General considers appropriate. The House of Assembly has (since January 1991) 28 members, elected by universal adult suffrage for a term of five years (subject to dissolution). The minimum voting age is 18 years.

The Constitution also provides for the establishment of Service Commissions for the Judicial and Legal Service, the Public Service, the Police Service and the Statutory Boards Service. These Commissions are exempt from legal investigation; they have executive powers relating to appointments, dismissals and disciplinary control of the services for which they are responsible.

The Government

Head of State: HM Queen ELIZABETH II (succeeded to the throne 6 February 1952).

Governor-General: Sir CLIFFORD HUSBANDS (appointed 1 June 1996).

THE CABINET
(April 2001)

Prime Minister and Minister of Finance and Economic Affairs, of Defence and Security and for the Civil Service: OWEN S. ARTHUR.

Deputy Prime Minister and Minister of Foreign Affairs and Foreign Trade: BILLIE A. MILLER.

Attorney-General and Minister of Home Affairs: DAVID A. C. SIMMONS.

Minister of Education, Youth Affairs and Culture: MIA A. MOTTLEY.

Minister of Health: Sen. PHILLIP GODDARD.

Minister of the Environment, Energy and Natural Resources: RAWLE C. EASTMOND.

Minister of Agriculture and Rural Development: ANTHONY P. WOOD.

Minister of Social Transformation: HAMILTON F. LASHLEY.

Minister of Tourism and of International Transport: NOEL A. LYNCH.

Minister of Housing and Lands: GLINE A. CLARKE.

Minister of Commerce, Consumer Affairs and Business Development: RONALD TOPPIN.

Minister of Industry and International Business: REGINALD R. FARLEY.

Minister of Labour, Sports and Public-Sector Reform: RUDOLPH N. GREENIDGE.

Minister of Public Works and Transport: ROMMEL MARSHALL.

Minister of State in the Office of the Prime Minister and the Ministry for the Civil Service (with responsibility for Information): GLYNE S. H. MURRAY.

MINISTRIES

Office of the Prime Minister: Government Headquarters, Bay St, St Michael; tel. 436-6435; fax 436-9280; e-mail info@primeminister .gov.bb; internet www.primeminister.gov.bb.

Ministry of Agriculture and Rural Development: Graeme Hall, POB 505, Christ Church; tel. 428-4150; fax 420-8444; internet www.barbados.gov.bb/minagri.

Ministry for the Civil Service: Roebuck Plaza, 20–23 Roebuck St, Bridgetown; tel. 426-2390; fax 228-0093.

Ministry of Commerce, Consumer Affairs and Business Development: Government Headquarters, Bay St, St Michael; tel. 427-5270.

Ministry of Defence and Security: Government Headquarters, Bay St, St Michael; tel. 436-1970.

Ministry of Education, Youth Affairs and Culture: Elsie Payne Complex, Constitution Rd, Bridgetown; tel. 430-2700; fax 436-2411.

Minister of the Environment, Energy and Natural Resources: Frank Walcott Bldg, Culloden Rd, St Michael; tel. 431-7692.

Ministry of Finance and Economic Affairs: Government Headquarters, Bay St, St Michael; tel. 436-6435; fax 429-4032.

Ministry of Foreign Affairs and Foreign Trade: 1 Culloden Rd, St Michael; tel. 436-2990; fax 429-6652; e-mail barbados@ foreign.gov.bb; internet www.foreign.barbadosgov.org.

Ministry of Health: Jemmott's Lane, St Michael; tel. 426-5080; fax 426-5570.

Ministry of Home Affairs: General Post Office Bldg, Level 5, Cheapside, Bridgetown; tel. 228-8961; fax 437-3794; e-mail mha@ caribsurf.com.

Ministry of Housing and Lands: Culloden Rd, St Michael; tel. 431-7600; fax 435-0174; e-mail psmhl@caribsurf.com.

Ministry of Industry and International Business: The Business Centre, Upton, St Michael; tel. 430-2200; fax 429-6849; e-mail mtbbar@caribsurf.com.

Ministry of International Transport: Port Authority Bldg, University Row, Bridgetown; tel. 426-9144; fax 429-3809.

Ministry of Labour, Sports and Public-Sector Reform: National Insurance Bldg, 5th Floor, Fairchild St, Bridgetown; tel. 436-6320; fax 426-8959; internet www.labour.gov.bb.

Ministry of Public Works and Transport: The Pine, St Michael; tel. 429-2191; fax 437-8133; internet www.publicworks.gov.bb.

Ministry of Social Transformation: Nicholas House, Broad St, Bridgetown; tel. 228-5878.

Ministry of Tourism: Sherbourne Conference Centre, Two Mile Hill, St Michael; tel. 430-7500; fax 436-4828.

Office of the Attorney-General: Sir Frank Walcott Bldg, Culloden Rd, St Michael; tel. 431-7707; fax 435-9533; e-mail attygen@ caribsurf.com.bb.

Legislature

PARLIAMENT
Senate

President: FRED GOLLOP.

There are 21 members.

House of Assembly

Speaker: ISHMAEL ROETT.

Clerk of Parliament: GEORGE BRANCKER.

General Election, 20 January 1999

Party	Votes	%	Seats
Barbados Labour Party (BLP) . .	83,085	64.85	26
Democratic Labour Party (DLP) .	44,974	35.10	2
Others	64	0.05	—
Total	**128,123**	**100.00**	**28**

Political Organizations

Barbados Labour Party: Grantley Adams House, 111 Roebuck St, Bridgetown; tel. 429-1990; e-mail hq@blp.org.bb; internet www.blp.org.bb; f. 1938; moderate social democrat; Leader OWEN ARTHUR; Chair. REGINALD FARLEY; Gen. Sec. MIA A. MOTTLEY.

Democratic Labour Party: George St, Belleville, St Michael; tel. 429-3104; fax 429-3007; e-mail dlp@dlpbarbados.bb; internet www.dlpbarbados.org; f. 1955; Leader DAVID THOMPSON.

National Democratic Party: 'Sueños', 3 Sixth Ave, Belleville; tel. 429-6882; f. 1989 by split from Democratic Labour Party; Leader Dr RICHARD (RICHIE) HAYNES.

Diplomatic Representation

EMBASSIES AND HIGH COMMISSIONS IN BARBADOS

Australia: Bishops Court Hill, Pine Rd, St Michael; tel. 435-2834; High Commissioner: P. M. SMITH.

Brazil: Sunjet House, 3rd Floor, Fairchild St, Bridgetown; tel. 427-1735; fax 427-1744; Ambassador: CARLOS ALFREDO PINTO DA SILVA.

Canada: Bishops Court Hill, Pine Rd, POB 404, St Michael; tel. 429-3550; fax 429-3780; High Commissioner: DUANE VAN BESELAERE.

China, People's Republic: 17 Golf View Terrace, Rockley, Christ Church; tel. 435-6890; fax 435-8300; Ambassador: ZHAN DAODE.

Colombia: 'Rosemary', Dayrells Rd, Rockley, POB 37W, Christ Church; tel. 429-6821; fax 429-6830; e-mail colombiaembassy@ sunbeach.net; Ambassador: JOSÉ JOAQUÍN GORI.

Costa Rica: Trident House, 2nd Floor, Broad St, Bridgetown; tel. 431-0250; fax 431-0261; e-mail embcr@sunbeach.net; Ambassador: SOL VILLAMICHEL MORALES.

Cuba: Cuba Erin Court, Collymore Rock, St Michael; tel. 435-2769; Ambassador: JOSÉ DE J. CONEJO.

Guatemala: Bridgetown; tel. 435-3542; fax 435-2638; Ambassador: JULIO ROBERTO PALOMO.

United Kingdom: Lower Collymore Rock, POB 676, St Michael; tel. 430-7800; fax 430-7826; e-mail britishhc@sunbeach.net; internet www.britishhc.org; High Commissioner: GORDON M. BAKER.

USA: Canadian Imperial Bank of Commerce Bldg, Broad St, POB 302, Bridgetown; tel. 436-4950; fax 429-5246; Ambassador: JAMES A. DALEY.

Venezuela: Hastings, Main Rd, Christ Church; tel. 435-7619; fax 435-7830; e-mail embaven@sunbeach.net; Ambassador: ANGEL BRITO VILLARROEL.

Judicial System

Justice is administered by the Supreme Court of Judicature, which consists of a High Court and a Court of Appeal. Final appeal lies with the Judicial Committee of the Privy Council, in the United Kingdom. There are Magistrates' Courts for lesser offences, with appeal to the Court of Appeal.

Supreme Court: Judiciary Office, Coleridge St, Bridgetown; tel. 426-3461; fax 246-2405.

Chief Justice: Sir DENYS WILLIAMS.

Justices of Appeal: G. C. R. MOE, ERROL DA COSTA CHASE, COLIN A. WILLIAMS.

Judges of the High Court: FREDERICK A. WATERMAN, MARIE A. MACCORMACK, E. GARVEY HUSBANDS, CARLISLE PAYNE, SHERMAN MOORE, LIONEL DACOSTA GREENIDGE.

Registrar of the Supreme Court: SANDRA MASON.

Office of the Attorney-General: Sir Frank Walcott Bldg, Culloden Rd, St Michael; tel. 431-7707; fax 435-9533; e-mail attygen@ caribsurf.com.bb; Dir of Public Prosecutions CHARLES LEACOCK; e-mail cbleacock@inaccs.com.bb.

Religion

More than 100 religious denominations and sects are represented in Barbados, but the vast majority of the population profess Christianity. According to the 1980 census, there were 96,894 Anglicans (or some 40% of the total population), while the Pentecostal (8%) and Methodist (7%) churches were next in importance. The regional Caribbean Conference of Churches is based in Barbados. There are also small groups of Hindus, Muslims and Jews.

Caribbean Conference of Churches: POB 616, Bridgetown; tel. 427-2681; fax 429-2075; e-mail cccbdos@cariaccess.com; internet www.cariblife.com/pub/ccc.

CHRISTIANITY

The Anglican Communion

Anglicans in Barbados are adherents of the Church in the Province of the West Indies, comprising eight dioceses. The Archbishop of the Province is the Bishop of the Bahamas and the Turks and Caicos Islands, resident in Nassau, the Bahamas. In Barbados there is a Provincial Office (St George's Church, St George) and an Anglican Theological College (Codrington College, St John).

Bishop of Barbados: Rt Rev. Dr JOHN DUNLOP HOLDER, Diocesan Office, Mandeville House, Bridgetown; tel. 426-2761; fax 427-5867.

Barbados Christian Council: Caribbean Conference of Churches Bldg, George St and Collymore Rock, St Michael; tel. 426-6014.

The Roman Catholic Church

Barbados comprises a single diocese (formed in January 1990, when the diocese of Bridgetown-Kingstown was divided), which is suffragan to the archdiocese of Port of Spain (Trinidad and Tobago). At 31 December 1998 there were an estimated 10,000 adherents in the diocese. The Bishop participates in the Antilles Episcopal Conference (currently based in Port of Spain, Trinidad and Tobago).

Bishop of Bridgetown: Rt Rev. MALCOLM GALT, St Patrick's Presbytery, Jemmott's Lane, POB 1223, Bridgetown; tel. 426-3510; fax 429-6198.

Protestant Churches

Baptist Churches of Barbados: National Baptist Convention, President Kennedy Dr., Bridgetown; tel. 429-2697.

Church of God (Caribbean Atlantic Assembly): St Michael's Plaza, St Michael's Row, POB 1, Bridgetown; tel. 427-5770; Pres. Rev. VICTOR BABB.

Church of Jesus Christ of Latter-day Saints (Mormons)—West Indies Mission: Bridgetown; tel. 435-8595; fax 435-8278.

Church of the Nazarene: District Office, Eagle Hall, Bridgetown; tel. 425-1067.

Methodist Church: Bethel Church Office, Bay St, Bridgetown; tel. 426-2223.

Moravian Church: Roebuck St, Bridgetown; tel. 426-2337; Superintendent Rev. ERROL CONNOR.

Seventh-day Adventists (East Caribbean Conference): Brydens Ave, Brittons Hill, POB 223, St Michael; tel. 429-7234; fax 429-8055.

Wesleyan Holiness Church: General Headquarters, Bank Hall; tel. 429-4864.

Other denominations include the Abundant Life Assembly, the African Orthodox Church, the Apostolic Church, the Assemblies of Brethren, the Berean Bible Brethren, the Bethel Evangelical Church, Christ is the Answer Family Church, the Church of God the Prophecy, the Ethiopian Orthodox Church, the Full Gospel Assembly, Love Gospel Assembly, the New Testament Church of God, the Pentecostal Assemblies of the West Indies, the People's Cathedral, the Salvation Army, Presbyterian congregations, the African Methodist Episcopal Church, the Mt Olive United Holy Church of America and Jehovah's Witnesses.

ISLAM

In 1996 there were an estimated 2,000 Muslims in Barbados.

Islamic Teaching Centre: Harts Gap, Hastings; tel. 427-0120.

JUDAISM

Jewish Community: Nidhe Israel and Shaara Tzedek Synagogue, Rockley New Rd, POB 651, Bridgetown; tel. 437-1290; fax 437-1303; there were 60 Jews in Barbados in 1997; Pres. RACHELLE ALTMAN; Sec. SHARON ORAN.

Caribbean Jewish Congress: POB 1331, Bridgetown; tel. 436-8163; fax 437-4992; e-mail waw@sunbeach.net; f. 1994; aims to foster closer relations between Jewish communities in the region and to promote greater understanding of the Jewish faith; Dir-Gen. W. A. WINSTON BEN ZEBEDEE.

HINDUISM

Hindu Community: Hindu Temple, Roberts Complex. Government Hill, St Michael; tel. 434-4638; there were 411 Hindus at the census of 1980.

The Press

Barbados Advocate: POB 230, St Michael; tel. 434-2000; fax 434-2020; e-mail advocate@sunbeach.net; f. 1895; daily; Pres. and CEO HUMPHREY METZGEN; Editor REUDON EVERSLEY; circ. 11,413.

The Beacon: 111 Roebuck St, Bridgetown; organ of the Barbados Labour Party; weekly; circ. 15,000.

The Broad Street Journal: Letchworth Complex, Garrison, St Michael; tel. 437-8770; fax 437-8772; e-mail bsj@sunbeach.net; internet www.broadstreetjournal.com; f. 1993; weekly; business; Editor PATRICK HOYOS.

Caribbean Week: Lefferts Place, River Rd, St Michael; tel. 436-1906; fax 436-1904; e-mail cweek@sunbeach.net; internet www.cweek.com; f. 1989; fortnightly; Editor-in-Chief JOHN E. LOVELL; Publr TIMOTHY C. FORSYTH; circ. 56,200.

The Nation: Nation House, Fontabelle, St Michael; tel. 430-5400; fax 427-6968; e-mail nationnews@sunbeach.net; internet www .nationnews.com; f. 1973; daily; Pres. and Editor-in-Chief HAROLD HOYTE; circ. 23,144 (weekday), 33,084 (weekend).

Official Gazette: Government Printing Office, Bay St, St Michael; tel. 436-6776; Mon. and Thur.

Sunday Advocate: POB 230, St Michael; tel. 434-2000; fax 434-2020; e-mail advocate@sunbeach.net; f. 1895; CEO HUMPHREY METZGEN; Editor REUDON EVERSLEY; circ. 17,490.

The Sunday Sun: Fontabelle, St Michael; tel. 436-6240; fax 427-6968; e-mail subs@sunbeach.net; f. 1977; Dir HAROLD HOYTE; circ. 42,286.

Weekend Investigator: POB 230, St Michael; tel. 434-2000; circ. 14,305.

NEWS AGENCIES

Caribbean News Agency (CANA): Culloden View, Beckles Rd, St Michael; tel. 429-2903; fax 429-4355; f. 1976; internet www .cananews.com; public and private shareholders from English-speaking Caribbean; Chair. COLIN D. MURRAY; Gen. Man. TREVOR SIMPSON.

Foreign Bureaux

Inter Press Service (IPS) (Italy): POB 697, Bridgetown; tel. 426-4474; Correspondent MARVA COSSY.

United Press International (UPI) (USA): Bridgetown; tel. 436-0465; internet www.upi.com; Correspondent RICKEY SINGH.

Xinhua (New China) News Agency (People's Republic of China): Christ Church; Chief Correspondent DING BAOZHONG.

Agence France-Presse (AFP) is also represented.

Publishers

The Advocate Publishing Co Ltd: POB 230, St Michael; tel. 434-2000; fax 434-2020.

Business Tutors: POB 800E St Michael; tel. 428-5664; fax 429-4854; e-mail pchad@caribsurf.com; business, management, computers.

Carib Research and Publications Inc: POB 556, Bridgetown; tel. 438-0580; f. 1986; regional interests; CEO Dr FARLEY BRAITHWAITE.

Nation Publishing Co Ltd: Nation House, Fontabelle, St Michael; tel. 436-6240; fax 427-6968.

Broadcasting and Communications

TELECOMMUNICATIONS

Cable & Wireless BET Ltd: POB 32, Wildey, St Michael; tel. 292-6000; fax 427-5808; e-mail bdsinfo@caribsurf.com; internet www.candwbet.com.bb; fmrly Barbados External Telecommunications Ltd; provides international telecommunications services; owned by Cable & Wireless PLC (United Kingdom).

Barbados Telephone Co Ltd (Bartel): The Windsor Lodge, Government Hill, St Michael; tel. 429-5050; fax 436-5036; provides domestic telecommunications services; subsidiary of Cable & Wireless BET Ltd, reported to have merged with parent co in March 2001.

BROADCASTING
Regulatory Authority

Caribbean Broadcasting Corporation (CBC): The Pine, POB 900, Bridgetown; tel. 429-2041; fax 429-4795; f. 1963; Chair. F. BREWSTER.

Radio

Barbados Broadcasting Service Ltd: Astoria St George, Bridgetown; tel. 437-9550; fax 437-9554; f. 1981; FM station.
Faith 102 FM; religious broadcasting.

Barbados Rediffusion Service Ltd: River Rd, Bridgetown; tel. 430-7300; fax 429-8093; f. 1935; public company; Gen. Man. VIC FERNANDES.
HOTT FM, at River Rd, Bridgetown (f. 1998), is a commercial station.
Voice of Barbados, at River Rd, Bridgetown (f. 1981), is a commercial station covering Barbados and the eastern Caribbean.
YESS Ten-Four FM, at River Rd, Bridgetown (f. 1988), is a commercial station.

CBC Radio: POB 900, Bridgetown; tel. 429-2041; fax 429-4795; e-mail CBC.@.CaribNet.Net; f. 1963; commercial; Programme Man. W. CALLENDER.
CBC Radio 900, f. 1963, broadcasts 21 hours daily.
Radio Liberty FM, f. 1984, broadcasts 24 hours daily.

Television

CBC TV: POB 900, Bridgetown; tel. 429-2041; fax 429-4795; f. 1964; Channel Eight is the main national service, broadcasting 24 hours daily; a maximum of 30 subscription channels are available through Multi Choice; Gen. Man. MELBA SMITH; Programme Man. HILDA COX.

Finance

In December 1999 there were 3,399 international business companies, 2,867 foreign sales corporations, 47 offshore banks licensees and 401 captive insurance and insurance-management companies registered in Barbados.

BANKING
(cap. = capital; auth. = authorized; dep. = deposits;
res = reserves; brs = branches; m. = million;
amounts in Barbados dollars)

Central Bank

Central Bank of Barbados: Tom Adams Financial Centre, POB 1016, Spry St, Bridgetown; tel. 436-6870; fax 427-9559; e-mail cbb.libr@caribsurf.com; internet www.centralbank.org.bb; f. 1972; bank of issue; cap. 2.0m., res 10.0m., dep. 250.9m. (Dec. 1998); Gov. MARION WILLIAMS; Deputy Gov. DARCY BOYCE.

Commercial Banks

Caribbean Commercial Bank Ltd: Lower Broad St, POB 1007C, Bridgetown; tel. 431-2500; fax 431-2530; f. 1984; cap. 25.0m., res 3.8m., dep. 146.9m. (Dec. 1998); Pres. and CEO MARIANO R. BROWNE; 4 brs.

CIBC West Indies Holdings: CIBC Centre, POB 405, Warren, St Michael; tel. 367-2500; fax 424-8923; internet www.westindies .cibc.com; operates banking network throughout Caribbean; parent co of CIBC Caribbean Ltd; Chair. JOHN HUNKIN; 9 brs.

Mutual Bank of the Caribbean Inc.: Trident House, Lower Broad St C, Bridgetown; tel. 436-8335; fax 429-5734; 4 brs.

Regional Development Bank

Caribbean Development Bank: Wildey, POB 408, St Michael; tel. 431-1600; fax 426-7269; e-mail info@caribank.org; internet www.caribank.org; f. 1970; cap. 152.1m., res 6.3m. (Dec. 1999); Pres. Sir NEVILLE V. NICHOLLS.

National Bank

Barbados National Bank (BNB): 2 Broad St, POB 1002, Bridgetown; tel. 431-5739; fax 426-5037; f. 1978 by merger; cap 47.5m., res 26.0m., dep. 595.4m., total assets 747.2m. (Dec. 1998); scheduled for privatization in 2001; Chair. GRENVILLE PHILLIPS; CEO and Man. Dir LOUIS GREENIDGE; 6 brs.

Foreign Banks

Bank of Nova Scotia (Canada): Broad St, POB 202, Bridgetown; tel. 431-3000; fax 228-8574; Man. PETER F. VAN SCHIE; 6 brs.

Barclays Bank PLC (United Kingdom): Broad Street, POB 301, Bridgetown; tel. 431-5262; fax 429-4785; f. 1837; 4 brs.

Royal Bank of Canada: Trident House, Broad St, POB 68, Bridgetown; tel. 431-6700; fax 431-4271; e-mail roycorp@caribsurf.com; f. 1911; 1 br.

Trust Companies

Bank of Nova Scotia Trust Co (Caribbean) Ltd: Bank of Nova Scotia Bldg, Broad St, POB 1003B, Bridgetown; tel. 431-3120; fax 426-0969.

Barbados International Bank and Trust Co: The Financial Services Centre, Bishop's Court Hill, POB 111, St Michael; tel. 436-7000; fax 436-7057.

Barclays Bank PLC Trustee Branch: Broad St, Bridgetown; tel. 431-5296.

CIBC Trust and Merchant Bank (Barbados) Ltd: CIBC Centre, POB 405, Warren, St Michael; tel. 367-2324; fax 421-7178.

Clico Mortgage & Finance Corporation: C L Duprey Financial Centre, Walrond St, Bridgetown; tel. 431-4719; fax 426-6168; e-mail cmfc@sunbeach.net.

Ernst & Young Trust Corporation: Bush Hill, Garrison, St Michael; tel. 430-3900.

Royal Bank of Canada Financial Corporation: Bldg 2, Chelston Park, Collymore Rock, St Michael; tel. 431-6580; fax 429-3800; e-mail roycorp@caribsurf.com; Man. N. L. SMITH.

St Michael Trust: The Financial Services Centre, Bishop's Court Hill, St Michael; tel. 436-7000; fax 436-7057; e-mail bb@ fiscglobal.com; internet www.fiscglobal.com; f. 1987.

STOCK EXCHANGE

Securities Exchange of Barbados (SEB): Tom Adams Financial Centre, 5th Floor, Church Village, Bridgetown; tel. 436-9871; fax 429-8942; e-mail sebd@caribsurf.com; f. 1987; in 1989 the Govts of Barbados, Trinidad and Tobago and Jamaica agreed to link exchanges; cross-trading began in April 1991; Chair. NEVILLE LEROY SMITH; Gen. Man. VIRGINIA MAPP.

INSURANCE

The leading British and a number of US and Canadian companies have agents in Barbados. At the end of 1995 230 captive insurance companies were registered in the country. Local insurance companies include the following:

Barbados Fire & Commercial Insurance Co: Beckwith Place, Broad St, POB 150, Bridgetown; tel. 431-2800; fax 426-0752; e-mail bf&c@caribsurf.com; f. 1996, following merger of Barbados Commercial Insurance Co. Ltd and Barbados Fire and General Insurance Co (f. 1880).

Barbados Mutual Life Assurance Society: Collymore Rock, St Michael; tel. 431-7000; fax 436-8829; f. 1840; Chair. COLIN G. GODDARD; Pres. J. ARTHUR L. BETHELL.

Insurance Corporation of Barbados: Roebuck St, Bridgetown; tel. 427-5590; fax 426-3393; f. 1978; cap. Bds $3m.; Man. Dir WISMAR GREAVES; Gen. Man. MONICA SKINNER.

Life of Barbados Ltd: Wildey, POB 69, St Michael; tel. 426-1060; fax 436-8835; f. 1971; Pres. and CEO STEPHEN ALLEYNE.

United Insurance Co Ltd: United Insurance Centre, Lower Broad St, POB 1215, Bridgetown; tel. 430-1900; fax 436-7573; e-mail united@caribsurf.com; f. 1976; Man. Dir DAVE A. BLACKMAN.

Insurance Association

Insurance Association of the Caribbean: IAC Bldg, St Michael; Collymore Rock, St Michael; tel. 427-5608; fax 427-7277; regional asscn.

Trade and Industry

GOVERNMENT AGENCY

Barbados Agricultural Management Co Ltd: Warrens, POB 719c, St Michael; tel. 425-0010; fax 425-0007; e-mail bamc@cariaccess.com; Chair. R. CARL SYLVESTER; Gen. Man. E. LEROY ROACH.

DEVELOPMENT ORGANIZATIONS

Barbados Agriculture Development and Marketing Corpn: Fairy Valley, Christ Church; tel. 428-0250; fax 428-0152; f. 1993 by merger; programme of diversification and land reforms; Chair. TYRONE POWER; CEO E. LEROY ROACH.

Barbados Investment and Development Corpn: Pelican House, Princess Alice Highway, Bridgetown; tel. 427-5350; fax 426-7802; e-mail bidc@bidc.org; internet www.bidc.com; f. 1992 by merger; facilitates the devt of the industrial sector, especially in the areas of manufacturing, information technology and financial services; offers free consultancy to investors; provides factory space for lease or rent; administers the Fiscal Incentives Legislation; Chair. TREVOR CLARKE; CEO ERROL HUMPHREY.

Department for International Development in the Caribbean: Collymore Rock, POB 167, St Michael; tel. 436-9873; fax 426-2194; Head BRIAN THOMSON.

CHAMBER OF COMMERCE

Barbados Chamber of Commerce and Industry: Nemwil House, 1st Floor, Lower Collymore Rock, POB 189, St Michael; tel. 426-2056; fax 429-2907; e-mail bdscham@caribsurf.com; internet www.bdscham.com; f. 1825; 176 mem. firms, 276 reps; Pres. HALLAM EDWARDS; Exec. Dir ROLPH JORDAN.

INDUSTRIAL AND TRADE ASSOCIATIONS

Barbados Agricultural Society: The Grotto, Beckles Rd, St Michael; tel. 436-6683; fax 435-0651; e-mail heshimu@sunbeach.net; Pres. TYRONE POWER.

Barbados Association of Medical Practitioners: BAMP Complex, Spring Garden, St Michael; tel. 429-7569; fax 435-2328; e-mail bamp@infinetworx.com; Pres. JEROME WALCOTT.

Barbados Association of Professional Engineers: POB 666, Bridgetown; tel. 425-6105; fax 425-6673; f. 1964; Pres. GLYNE BARKER; Sec. PATRICK CLARKE.

Barbados Hotel and Tourism Association: Fourth Ave, Belleville, St Michael; tel. 426-5041; fax 429-2845; e-mail bhta@maccs.com.bb; internet www.funbarbados.com/bhta; Pres. ALAN BANFIELD; Exec. Vice-Pres. SUSAN SPRINGER.

Barbados Manufacturers' Association: Bldg 1, Pelican Industrial Park, St Michael; tel. 426-4474; fax 436-5182; e-mail bmex-products@sunbeach.net; internet www.bma.org.bb; f. 1964; Pres. DERECK FOSTER; Exec. Dir CLIFTON E. MAYNARD; 100 mem. firms.

West Indian Sea Island Cotton Association (Inc): c/o Barbados Agricultural Development and Marketing Corpn, Fairy Valley, Christ Church; tel. 428-0250; Pres. E. LEROY ROACH; Sec. MICHAEL I. EDGHILL; 11 mem. asscns.

EMPLOYERS' ORGANIZATION

Barbados Employers' Confederation: Nemwil House, 1st Floor, Collymore Rock, St Michael; tel. 426-1574; fax 429-2907; e-mail bcon@sunbeach.net; internet www.barbadosemployers.com; f. 1956; Pres. HARCOURT SANDIFORD; 235 mems (incl. associate mems).

UTILITIES
Electricity

Barbados Light and Power Co (BL & P): POB 142, Garrison Hill, St Michael; tel. 436-1800; fax 436-9933; electricity generator and distributor; operates two stations with a combined capacity of 152,500 kW.

Public Utilities Board: cnr Pine Plantation Rd, Collymore Rock, St Michael; tel. 427-5693; fax 437-3542; e-mail ftchq@caribsurf.com; f. 1955; utility regulator.

Gas

Barbados National Oil Co Ltd (BNOCL): POB 175, Woodbourne, St Philip; tel. 423-0918; fax 423-0166; internet www.bnocl.com; f. 1979; extraction of petroleum and natural gas; state-owned, scheduled for privatization; Chair. HARCOURT LEWIS; 166 employees.

National Petroleum Corporation: Wildey; tel. 430-4000; gas production and distribution.

Water

Barbados Water Authority: The Pine, St Michael; tel. 427-3990.

TRADE UNIONS

Principal unions include:

Barbados Secondary Teachers' Union: Ryeburn, Eighth Ave, Belleville, St Michael; tel. 429-7676; e-mail bstumail@caribsurf.com; f. 1949; Pres. PHIL PERRY; Gen. Sec. PATRICK FROST; 382 mems.

Barbados Union of Teachers: Welches, POB 58, St Michael; tel. 436-6139; f. 1974; Pres. RONALD DA C. JONES; Gen. Sec. HARRY HUSBANDS; 2,000 mems.

Barbados Workers' Union: Solidarity House, Harmony Hall, POB 172, St Michael; tel. 426-3492; fax 436-6496; internet www.bwu-bb.org; f. 1941; operates a Labour College; Sec.-Gen. LEROY TROTMAN; 20,000 mems.

Caribbean Association of Media Workers (Camwork): Bridgetown; f. 1986; regional; Pres. RICKEY SINGH.

National Union of Public Workers: Dalkeith Rd, POB 174, Bridgetown; tel. 426-1764; fax 436-1795; e-mail nupwbarbados@sunbeach.net; f. 1944; Pres. MILLICENT M. B. SMALL; Gen. Sec. JOSEPH E. GODDARD; 6,000 mems.

Transport

ROADS

Ministry of Public Works and Transport: The Pine, St Michael; tel. 429-2191; fax 437-8133; internet www.publicworks.gov.bb; maintains a network of 1,573 km (977 miles) of roads, of which 1,496 km (930 miles) are paved; Chief Tech. Officer C. H. ARCHER.

SHIPPING

Bridgetown harbour has berths for eight ships and simultaneous bunkering facilities for five. A four-year project to extend the harbour, providing increased capacity for cruise ships, was due to begin in 1997 at a cost of Bds $120m.

Barbados Port Authority: University Row, Bridgetown Harbour; tel. 430-4700; fax 429-5348; internet www.barbadosport.com; Gen. Man. EVERTON WALTERS; Port Dir Capt. H. L. VAN SLUYTMAN.

Shipping Association of Barbados: Trident House, 2nd Floor, Broad St, Bridgetown; tel. 427-9860; fax 426-8392; e-mail shasba@caribsurf.com.

Principal Shipping Companies

Barbados Shipping and Trading Co Ltd: Musson Bldg, Hincks St, POB 1227c, Bridgetown; tel. 426-3844; fax 427-4719; e-mail richard-marshall@bsandtco.com; f. 1920; Chair. C. D. BYNOE; Man. Dir A. C. FIELDS.

Bernuth Agencies: White Park Rd, Bridgetown; tel. 431-3343.

Carlisle Shipping Ltd: Carlisle House, Bridgetown; tel. 430-4803.

DaCosta Ltd: Carlisle House, Hincks St, POB 103, Bridgetown; tel. 431-8700; fax 431-0051; shipping company; Man. Dir JOHN WILKINSON.

T. Geddes Grant Bros: White Park Rd, Bridgetown; tel. 431-3300.

Hassell, Eric and Son Ltd: Carlisle House, Hincks St, Bridgetown; tel. 436-6102; fax 429-3416; e-mail info@erichassell.com; internet www.erichassell.com; shipping agent, stevedoring contractor and cargo fowarder.

Maersk: James Fort Bldg, Hincks St, Bridgetown; tel. 430-4816.

Tec Marine: Carlisle House, Hincks St, Bridgetown; tel. 430-4816.

Tropical Shipping Kensington: Fontabelle Rd, St Michael; tel. 426-9990; fax 426-7750; internet www.tropical.com.

Windward Lines Ltd: Brighton Warehouse Complex, Black Rock, St Michael; tel. 425-7402.

CIVIL AVIATION

The principal airport is Grantley Adams International Airport, at Seawell, 18 km (11 miles) from Bridgetown.

Tourism

The natural attractions of the island consist chiefly of the warm climate and varied scenery. In addition, there are many facilities for outdoor sports of all kinds. Revenue from tourism increased from Bds $13m. in 1960 to some Bds $1,500m. in 1998. The number of stop-over tourist arrivals was 517,869 in 1999, while the number of visiting cruise-ship passengers was 445,821. There were some 6,000 hotel rooms on the island in 1999.

Barbados Tourism Authority: Harbour Rd, POB 242, Bridgetown; tel. 427-2623; fax 426-4080; e-mail btainfo@barbados.org; internet www.barbados.org; f. 1993 to replace Barbados Board of Tourism; offices in London, New York, Los Angeles, Miami, Toronto, Frankfurt, Milan, The Hague, Paris and Stockholm; Chair. HUDSON HUSBANDS; Pres. and CEO OLIVER JORDAN.

BELARUS

Introductory Survey

Location, Climate, Language, Religion, Flag, Capital

The Republic of Belarus is a land-locked state in north-eastern Europe. It is bounded by Lithuania and Latvia to the north-west, by Ukraine to the south, by the Russian Federation to the east, and by Poland to the west. The climate is of a continental type, with an average January temperature, in Minsk, of –5°C (23°F) and an average for July of 19°C (67°F). Average annual precipitation is between 560 mm and 660 mm. The official languages of the republic are Belarusian and Russian. The major religion is Christianity—the Roman Catholic Church and the Eastern Orthodox Church being the largest denominations. There are also small Muslim and Jewish communities. The national flag (proportions 2 by 1) consists of two unequal horizontal stripes, of red over light green, with a red-outlined white vertical stripe at the hoist, bearing in red a traditional embroidery pattern. The capital is Minsk (Miensk).

Recent History

Following periods of Lithuanian and Polish rule, Belarus became a part of the Russian Empire in the late 18th century. During the 19th century there was a growth of national consciousness in Belarus and, as a result of industrialization, significant migration of people from rural to urban areas. After the February Revolution of 1917 in Russia, Belarusian nationalists and socialists formed a rada (council), which sought a degree of autonomy from the Provisional Government in Petrograd (St Petersburg). In November, after the Bolsheviks had seized power in Petrograd, Red Army troops were dispatched to Minsk, and the rada was dissolved. However, the Bolsheviks were forced to withdraw by the invasion of the German army. The Treaty of Brest-Litovsk, signed in March 1918, assigned most of Belarus to Germany. On 25 March Belarusian nationalists convened to proclaim a Belarusian National Republic, but it achieved only limited autonomy. After the Germans had withdrawn, the Bolsheviks easily reoccupied Minsk, and the Belarusian Soviet Socialist Republic (BSSR) was declared on 1 January 1919.

In February 1919 the BSSR was merged with neighbouring Lithuania in a Lithuanian-Belarusian Soviet Republic (known as 'Litbel'). In April, however, Polish armed forces entered Lithuania and Belarus, and both were declared part of Poland. In July 1920 the Bolsheviks recaptured Minsk, and in August the BSSR was re-established; Lithuania became an independent state. However, the BSSR comprised only the eastern half of the lands populated by Belarusians. Western Belarus was granted to Poland by the Treaty of Rīga, signed on 18 March 1921. The Treaty also assigned Belarus's easternmost regions to the Russian Federation, but they were returned to the BSSR in 1924 and 1926. Meanwhile, the BSSR, with Ukraine and Transcaucasia, had joined with the Russian Federation to establish the Union of Soviet Socialist Republics (USSR), in December 1922.

The Soviet leadership's New Economic Policy of 1921–28, which permitted some liberalization of the economy, brought a measure of prosperity, and there was significant cultural and linguistic development, with the use of the Belarusian language officially encouraged. This period ended in 1929 with the emergence of Stalin (Iosif V. Dzhugashvili) as the dominant figure in the USSR. In that year Stalin began a campaign to collectivize agriculture, which was strongly resisted by the peasantry. In Belarus, as in other parts of the USSR, there were riots and rebellions in rural areas, and many peasants were deported or imprisoned. The purges of the early 1930s were initially targeted against Belarusian nationalists and intellectuals, but by 1936–38 they had widened to include all sectors of the population.

After the invasion of Poland by German and Soviet forces in September 1939, the BSSR was enlarged by the inclusion of the lands that it had lost to Poland and Lithuania in 1921. Between 1941 and 1944 the BSSR was occupied by Nazi German forces; an estimated 2.2m. people died, including most of the republic's large Jewish population. At the Yalta conference, in February 1945, the Allies agreed to recognize the 'Curzon line' as the

western border of the BSSR, thus endorsing the unification of western and eastern Belarus. As a result of the Soviet demand for more voting strength in the UN, the Western powers permitted the BSSR to become a member of the UN in its own right.

The immediate post-war period was dominated by the need to rehabilitate the republic's infrastructure. The reconstruction programme's requirements and the local labour shortage led to an increase in Russian immigration into the republic, thus discouraging use of the Belarusian language. During the 1960s and 1970s the process of 'russification' continued; there was a decline in the use of Belarusian in schools, and in the media. The republic was, however, one of the most prosperous in the USSR, with a wider variety of consumer goods available than in other republics.

This relative prosperity was one reason why the ruling Communist Party of Belarus (CPB) was initially able to resist implementing the economic and political reforms that were proposed by the Soviet leader, Mikhail Gorbachev, from 1985. By 1987, however, the press had become critical of the CPB's stance on cultural and ecological issues. Intellectuals and writers campaigned for the greater use of Belarusian in education. Campaigners also demanded more information about the consequences of the explosion of April 1986 at the Chornobyl (Chernobyl) nuclear power station in Ukraine, which had affected large areas of southern Belarus. Not surprisingly, the two most important unofficial groups that emerged in the late 1980s were the Belarusian Language Association and the Belarusian Ecological Union.

There was, however, little opportunity for overt political opposition. A Belarusian Popular Front (BPF) was established in October 1988, but the CPB severely restricted its activities and banned republican media reports about the new group. At the end of the month riot police were used to disperse a pro-BPF demonstration in Minsk. The BPF did have some success in the elections to the all-Union Congress of People's Deputies, which took place in March 1989, persuading voters to reject several leading officials of the CPB. However, the inaugural congress of the BPF took place in Vilnius (Lithuania) in June, the Front having been refused permission to meet in Minsk.

In early 1990, in anticipation of the elections to the republican Supreme Soviet, or Supreme Council (legislature), the CPB adopted some of the BPF's policies regarding the Belarusian language. In January the authorities approved a law declaring Belarusian to be the state language, effective from 1 September. (However, Russian was reinstated as a second state language, following the adoption of a new Constitution in November 1996.) The BPF was not officially permitted to participate in the elections to the Belarusian Supreme Council, which took place in March 1990. Instead, its members joined other pro-reform groups in a coalition known as the Belarusian Democratic Bloc (BDB). The BDB secured about one-quarter of the 310 seats that were decided by popular election; most of the remainder were won by CPB members loyal to the republican leadership. The opposition won most seats in the large cities, notably Gomel (Homiel) and Minsk, where Zyanon Paznyak, the leader of the BPF, was elected. When the new Supreme Council first convened in May the BDB deputies immediately demanded the adoption of a declaration of sovereignty. The CPB initially opposed such a move, but on 27 July, apparently after consultations with the leadership of the Communist Party of the Soviet Union in Moscow, a Declaration of State Sovereignty of the BSSR was adopted unanimously by the Supreme Council. The declaration asserted the republic's right to maintain armed forces, to establish a national currency and to exercise full control over its domestic and foreign policies. On the insistence of the opposition, the declaration included a clause stating the republic's right to compensation for the damage caused by the nuclear accident at Chornobyl, and the issue united both Communist and opposition deputies. The Belarusian Government appealed to the all-Union Government for a minimum of 17,000m. roubles to address the consequences of the disaster, but was offered only 3,000m. roubles in compensation.

The Belarusian Government took part in the negotiation of a new Treaty of Union and signed the protocol to the draft treaty on 3 March 1991. The all-Union referendum on the preservation of the USSR took place in the BSSR on 17 March; of the 83% of the electorate who participated, 83% voted in favour of Gorbachev's proposals for a 'renewed federation of equal sovereign republics'. Members of the BPF conducted a campaign advocating rejection of Gorbachev's proposals, but complained that they were denied the opportunity to present their views to the public.

In April 1991 a series of strikes threatened the continued power of the CPB. On 10 April a general strike took place, and an estimated 100,000 people attended a demonstration in Minsk. The Government finally agreed to certain economic concessions, including high wage increases, but the strikers' political demands, including the resignation of the Belarusian Government and the depoliticization of republican institutions, were rejected. Some 200,000 workers were estimated to have taken part in a second general strike on 23 April, in protest at the legislature's refusal to reconvene. The Supreme Council, which was still dominated by members of the CPB, was eventually convened in May. The authority of the conservative CPB, however, was threatened by increased internal dissent. In June 33 deputies joined the opposition as a 'Communists for Democracy' faction, led by Alyaksandr Lukashenka.

The Belarusian leadership did not strongly oppose the attempted *coup d'état* in Moscow in August 1991. The Presidium of the Supreme Council released a neutral statement on the last day of the coup, but the Central Committee of the CPB declared its unequivocal support. Following the failure of the coup attempt, an extraordinary session of the Supreme Council was convened; Mikalay Dzemyantsei, the Chairman of the Supreme Council (republican head of state), was forced to resign. He was replaced by Stanislau Shushkevich, a respected centrist politician, pending an election to the office. In addition, the Supreme Council agreed to nationalize all CPB property, to prohibit the party's activities in law-enforcement agencies, and to suspend the CPB, pending an investigation into its role in the coup. (In February 1993, however, the suspension was lifted and the CPB was permitted to re-establish itself.) On 25 August 1991 the legislature voted to grant constitutional status to the July 1990 Declaration of State Sovereignty, and declared the political and economic independence of Belarus.

On 19 September 1991 the Supreme Council voted to rename the BSSR the Republic of Belarus. The Council also elected Shushkevich as its Chairman. Shushkevich demonstrated his strong support for the continuation of some form of union by signing, in October, a treaty to establish an economic community and by agreeing, in November, to the first draft of the Treaty on the Union of Sovereign States. On 8 December Shushkevich, with the Russian and Ukrainian Presidents, signed the Minsk Agreement, establishing a new Commonwealth of Independent States (CIS—see p. 157). On 21 December the leaders of 11 former Soviet republics confirmed this decision by the Almaty (Alma-Ata) Declaration. The proposal that the headquarters of the CIS be located in Minsk was widely welcomed in Belarus as a means of attracting foreign political and economic interest.

By comparison with other former Soviet republics, Belarus experienced relative domestic stability in 1992, attributed to the country's more favourable social and economic policies, and to the comparatively homogenous nature of the population. The BPF campaigned insistently for a referendum to be held to assess the electorate's confidence in the Supreme Council and the Government. In June 1992, having collected the required number of signatures, the BPF accused the Supreme Council of seeking to obstruct such a referendum. In October the Council voted against the holding of a referendum, owing to alleged irregularities in the collection of signatures.

In March 1993 the CPB, the popularity of which had increased substantially, formed, with 17 other parties and groups opposed to Belarusian independence, an informal coalition, the Popular Movement of Belarus. Divisions between the various branches of government became more pronounced during that year. A major source of controversy was the drafting of Belarus's new Constitution, three separate versions of which were submitted to the Supreme Council in 1991–93. Shushkevich and the BPF strongly opposed the establishment of Belarus as a presidential republic; nevertheless, the new Constitution, which provided for a presidential system, was adopted in March 1994. A further point of dispute was the question of whether Belarus should adopt closer economic, military and other relations with the Russian Federation and the CIS (as advocated by the Supreme Council). Shushkevich and the BPF were opposed to Belarus's signing the Treaty on Collective Security (which had been concluded by six other CIS states in May 1992), on the grounds that this would contravene the Declaration of State Sovereignty, which defined Belarus as a neutral state, and would also lead to renewed Russian domination. None the less, in April the Supreme Council voted to sign the Treaty. Three months later the legislature passed a vote of 'no confidence' in Shushkevich, in response to his continued opposition to the Treaty; he remained in office, however, as the Council had been inquorate at the time of the vote. A second vote of confidence in Shushkevich was held in January 1994; this time the Council voted overwhelmingly to dismiss him, on charges of corruption. He was replaced by Mechislau Gryb, formerly a senior police official.

Further allegations of corruption, against the premier, Vyacheslau Kebich, and leading members of the Cabinet of Ministers, coupled with the worsening economic situation, culminated in a BPF-led general strike in Minsk in February 1994. Protesters returned to work only when Gryb announced that the presidential election would be brought forward to mid-1994. Six candidates stood for election, including Kebich, Shushkevich, Paznyak and Lukashenka, who, as head of the Supreme Council's anti-corruption committee, had been responsible for bringing the corruption charges against Shushkevich. In the first ballot, held in late June, no candidate gained an overall majority, although Lukashenka, with 47% of the valid votes, led by a considerable margin. In the second ballot, contested by Lukashenka and Kebich and held in early July, Lukashenka received 85% of the votes cast, and he was inaugurated as the first President of Belarus on 20 July. Mikhail Chigir, an economic reformist, replaced Kebich as Chairman of a new Cabinet of Ministers.

In early 1995 there were repeated confrontations between President Lukashenka and the Supreme Council over constitutional issues. In late January the Council voted for a second time to adopt legislation whereby the President could be removed by a two-thirds vote of the Council. In March Lukashenka announced that, simultaneously with the legislative election scheduled to take place in May, a referendum would be held on four policy questions. In early April, following the Council's rejection of all but one of the proposed questions (on closer integration with Russia), Lukashenka threatened to dissolve the legislature. A number of opposition deputies (including Paznyak) were forcibly evicted from the Supreme Council building, where they had declared a hunger strike in protest at the referendum. Shortly after this action, deputies voted in favour of the inclusion in the referendum of the remaining three questions: to give the Russian language equal status with Belarusian as an official language; to abandon the state insignia and flag of independent Belarus in favour of a modified version of those used in the republic during the Soviet era; and to amend the Constitution in order to empower the President to suspend the Supreme Council in the event of unconstitutional acts. Some 65% of the electorate participated in the referendum, which was held, as scheduled, on 14 May. All four questions received overwhelming popular support.

On the same occasion as the referendum, Belarus's first post-Soviet legislative election was held. However, owing to stringent electoral regulations, only 18 of the 260 seats in the Supreme Council were filled. At 'run-off' elections, held on 28 May 1995, a further 101 deputies were elected, but the two rounds of voting failed to produce the necessary two-thirds quorum, and a further round was scheduled for November. In the meantime, the confrontation between Lukashenka and the incumbent Supreme Council intensified. The Constitutional Court examined the legality of a number of decrees issued by Lukashenka, and found five to be unconstitutional. A quorum was finally achieved in the Supreme Council after two further rounds of voting, held on 29 November and 10 December; 79 new deputies were elected, bringing the total to 198. The CPB emerged with the largest number of seats in the new legislature (42), followed by the Agrarian Party (AP—33), the United Civic Party of Belarus and the Party of People's Accord. Independent candidates accounted for 95 seats. The BPF failed to win representation in the Council, as the 62 seats remaining vacant, largely owing to low electoral participation, were mostly in areas where the BPF commanded its strongest support. The Supreme Council held its inaugural session in early January 1996. Syamyon Sharetski, the leader of the AP, was appointed Chairman of the Council, replacing Mechislau Gryb.

Relations between the Constitutional Court and President Lukashenka deteriorated in early 1996, and the Court declared the observance of constitutional law in 1995 to have been unsatisfactory. Lukashenka extended his authority over the security services and the state-owned media, giving control of editorial appointments to the Cabinet of Ministers. Despite strong opposition and protests against government proposals to sign a new union treaty with Russia, President Lukashenka and the President of the Russian Federation, Boris Yeltsin, signed the Treaty on the Formation of a Community of Sovereign Republics in Moscow on 2 April 1996. Although it did not establish a single state, the treaty included extensive provisions covering military, economic and political co-operation between the two component parts of the new Community of Sovereign Republics (CSR). Following the treaty's endorsement, confrontation between Lukashenka and the opposition parties increased. A warrant was issued in April for the arrest of Paznyak, who was accused of organizing the anti-union treaty demonstrations. The offices of the BPF were searched, but Paznyak fled the country and later applied for political asylum in the USA. Several activists were arrested, and riot police clashed with demonstrators demanding their release. (They were later released on health grounds after staging a hunger strike.) Unauthorized rallies, organized by the opposition movement, were held in Minsk at the end of the month to commemorate the 10th anniversary of the disaster at the Chornobyl nuclear power station. The demonstrators used the opportunity to express publicly their dissatisfaction with the Government and, in particular, with the formation of the CSR. The rallies were reported to have been brutally dispersed by the police, and numerous arrests were made.

In early August 1996 Lukashenka, seeking to enhance his powers further, scheduled another national referendum, for early November, which was to contain, amongst other questions, proposed amendments to the 1994 Constitution; subsequently, demands for the impeachment of the President intensified. Despite disagreement between Lukashenka and the Supreme Council over the date of the referendum, it was eventually scheduled for 24 November (with polling stations to be open from 9 November for those unable to vote on the later date). Elections for the remaining vacant seats in the Supreme Council were also due to be held on 24 November. Relations between Lukashenka and the Constitutional Court deteriorated in November, following a ruling by the Court that the results of the questions concerning amendments to the Constitution could be used only for consultative purposes and would not be legally binding. Lukashenka's revocation of this decision by presidential decree provoked fierce criticism.

The referendum ballot papers contained seven questions, four of which were proposed by Lukashenka: that amendments be made to the 1994 Constitution to extend the President's term of office from 1999 to 2001, to enable the President to issue decrees that would carry legal force, and to grant him extensive powers of appointment both to the judiciary and to the envisaged bicameral National Assembly, which would replace the Supreme Council; that Belarusian Independence Day be moved from 27 July (the anniversary of the Declaration of State Sovereignty) to 3 July (the anniversary of the liberation from the Nazis); that there be an unrestricted right to purchase and sell land; and that the death penalty be abolished. The remaining three questions were submitted by the Supreme Council in an attempt to curtail the President's powers, and proposed that there be a significant reduction in the powers of the President (in effect, virtually abolishing the presidency); that the Supreme Council be allowed to elect heads of local administration (hitherto appointed by the President); and that state institutions be funded from the budget, instead of from a non-budgetary fund controlled by the President.

Despite the inclusion of questions concerning proposed constitutional changes, copies of the draft Constitution were not available to the public by the time that voting began. The Chairman of the Central Electoral Commission, Viktar Ganchar, stated that he would not approve the results of the voting, owing to this and other electoral violations; he was shortly afterwards dismissed by President Lukashenka. The crisis worsened in mid-November, when the Chairman of the Cabinet of Ministers, Mikhail Chigir, resigned, urging that the referendum be cancelled; he was replaced, in an acting capacity, by Syargey Ling, who was confirmed in the appointment in February 1997. Some 10,000 people attended an anti-Government rally in Minsk, protesting at the restrictions on their freedom of expres-

sion. Independent radio stations were closed, and as many as 200,000 issues of *Nasha Niva*, an independent newspaper containing criticisms of Lukashenka, were confiscated at the Lithuanian border. Widespread violations of the law were reported by parliamentary electoral observers—in particular, no record was kept of those who had voted early. The Organization for Security and Co-operation in Europe (OSCE, see p. 252) refused to send observers to monitor the referendum, and the Council of Europe declared that the presidential draft of the amended Constitution did not comply with European standards. Meanwhile, 75 deputies in the Supreme Council submitted a motion to the Constitutional Court to begin impeachment proceedings against the President; the Court had already found 17 decrees issued by Lukashenka to be unconstitutional.

The outcome of the voting revealed considerable support for the President, although the accuracy of this result was disputed by opposition movements and electoral observers. According to official figures, some 84% of the electorate took part, 70.5% of whom voted for the President's constitutional amendments; only 7.9% voted for those of the Supreme Council. Over 88% of participants voted to transfer Belarusian Independence Day to 3 July, while the remaining motions were rejected. The Constitutional Court was forced to abandon the impeachment proceedings, as deputies withdrew their signatures from the motion. The amended Constitution was published on 27 November 1996 and came into immediate effect.

Following the referendum, the Supreme Council divided into two factions. More than 100 deputies declared their support for Lukashenka, and adopted legislation abolishing the Supreme Council and establishing a 110-member House of Representatives, the lower chamber of the new National Assembly. Some 50 other deputies denounced the referendum as invalid and declared themselves to be the legitimate legislature. The House of Representatives convened shortly afterwards and elected Anatol Malafeyeu as its Chairman. Deputies were granted a four-year mandate, while the term of office of those opposed to the new legislature was curtailed to two months. Deputies elected in the by-elections held simultaneously with the referendum were denied registration. Legislation governing the formation of the upper house of the National Assembly, the 64-member Council of the Republic, was approved by Lukashenka in early December 1996: eight members were appointed by the President and the remaining 56 were elected by regional councils. In the event, no deputies from the former Supreme Council participated in the Council of the Republic, which convened for the first time in mid-January 1997, and elected Pavel Shypuk as its Chairman. Meanwhile, in protest at the constitutional amendments introduced by the referendum, the Chairman of the Constitutional Court, Valery Tsikhinya, and several other judges announced their resignations.

Continued opposition to the provisions of the referendum from deputies of the former legislature resulted in the formation in early January 1997 of the Public Coalition Government–National Economic Council, a form of 'shadow' cabinet, chaired by Genadz Karpenka. Structural changes to the Belarusian Government were implemented by Lukashenka, with the Chairmen of State Committees henceforth to be included in the Cabinet of Ministers. Doubts about the legitimacy of the referendum were expressed by international organizations, including the Council of Europe, which suspended Belarus's 'guest status', citing the lack of democracy in the new political structures, and the Permanent Council of the Parliamentary Assembly of the OSCE, which recognized the right of a delegation from the former Supreme Council, rather than members of the new House of Representatives, officially to represent Belarus at that organization.

Repression against opponents of the new Constitution was maintained throughout early 1997, despite the conclusion by international observers from the OSCE and the Council of Europe that the referendum and subsequent legislative elections could not be deemed legal, and that the provisions of the 1994 Constitution should be restored. Several opposition members were brought to trial for organizing unauthorized rallies and in early March 1997 a presidential decree restricted further the right to demonstrate. Moves towards greater integration with Russia (see below) continued to provoke protests from opposition parties, led, in particular, by the BPF, and in late March an anti-Lukashenka demonstration, which attracted some 10,000 participants, was violently dispersed by security forces.

The signing with Russia of the Treaty of Union, and initialling of the Charter of the Union, on 2 April 1997, by Presidents

Lukashenka and Yeltsin (see below) prompted a further anti-Union demonstration in Minsk, which was forcibly suppressed by the police, and which resulted in many arrests. Charges of violating the presidential decree on demonstrations were subsequently brought against opposition members, including Mikalay Statkevich, leader of the Belarusian Social Democratic Party. Nevertheless, support for the union treaty appeared widespread, with some 15,000 people participating in a pro-Union rally in Minsk in mid-May. The Charter of the Union was signed in Moscow on 23 May. The Treaty and Charter were ratified shortly afterwards by the respective legislatures, and came into effect in mid-June.

Negotiations mediated by the Council of Europe and the European Union (EU, see p. 181) to end the confrontation between the former Supreme Council and the new legislature were held in June 1997. A second round of talks collapsed in July, following disagreement over which constitution was to form the basis of the discussions. Despite a statement by the EU that it was willing to assist Belarus in redrafting the new Constitution, while still recognizing the 1994 version as legitimate, negotiations between the deputies of the former and current legislatures, scheduled to recommence in September, were postponed indefinitely following a severe breakdown in relations between the EU and the Belarusian authorities.

Harassment and suppression of the independent media became more persistent in mid-1997. International concern at Belarus's failure to observe human rights was expressed in August by Human Rights Watch, which declared that Lukashenka had reversed most of the progress achieved during the *perestroika* (restructuring) period. In November the UN Commission on Human Rights echoed this concern. Opposition to the Belarusian authorities descended into violence in September, when responsibility for an explosion at the Minsk District Court was claimed by the Belarusian Liberation Army, which subsequently issued a statement demanding the restoration of the 1994 Constitution and the cessation of harassment of the opposition. In October 1997 Lukashenka issued a presidential decree providing for more severe measures to combat terrorism and violent crime, following the death in a bomb attack of a senior law-enforcement official in the Mogilev region. In November, amid allegations of a connection with this murder, the Minister of Agriculture and Food was arrested on charges of embezzlement. (He was sentenced to four-and-a-half years' imprisonment in January 2000.)

In November 1997 pro-Lukashenka rallies were held to commemorate the first anniversary of the referendum that dissolved the legislature. In the same month the opposition launched a petition movement called Charter-97 (Khartyya-97–a title reminiscent of the Czechoslovak Charter-77 pro-democracy movement), which called for greater democracy in Belarus and for presidential elections to be held in 1999 as required by the 1994 Constitution. However, later that month *Svaboda*, the largest independent newspaper, was closed, following its publication of an article advocating Lukashenka's resignation. Repression of opposition figures continued unabated in 1998. A number of senior BPF members were among 40 protesters arrested in April during an unauthorized rally to protest against the Treaty of Union between Russia and Belarus, which was held on the anniversary of the signature of the Treaty. A further 30 demonstrators were arrested later in the month at a rally led by former members of the disbanded Supreme Council, urging Lukashenka's resignation for mismanaging the economy and destroying national culture; Lukashenka's campaign to institutionalize the use of the Russian language had successfully marginalized Belarusian, which had become widely associated with the opposition.

Throughout 1998 the opposition remained without access to the media or representation in public institutions. In May instructions were issued banning government agencies from making official documents available to the independent media and forbidding government officials to comment for them. Moreover, in June legislation was approved that rendered defamation of the President an offence punishable by up to five years' imprisonment.

The formation of a special committee to address the country's economic problems was decreed by Lukashenka in November 1998, relegating the Cabinet of Ministers to a subordinate role in economic policy; the new body was to be known as the National Headquarters. In the following month the Ministry of Foreign Affairs was expanded to incorporate the Ministers for CIS Affairs and for Foreign Economic Relations. In September 1998 about 30 left-wing and centrist parties, including the CPB and the Liberal Democratic Party of Belarus, formed a new alliance to promote further integration with Russia and to support Lukashenka's candidacy in the presidential election scheduled for 2001. The alliance, styled the Belarusian People's Patriotic Union, elected the CPB leader, Viktar Chykin, as its Executive Secretary and declared its intention to contest future legislative elections as a single bloc. A new law on local elections was approved by the House of Representatives in December 1998, effectively banning candidates with a police record or fine from standing in the local elections that were to be held in April 1999. Numerous opposition candidates who had incurred fines for participating in anti-Lukashenka demonstrations were, thus, excluded from the polls. In the event, the majority of the seats in the elections were each contested by a single candidate, since the opposition organized an electoral boycott, owing to the non-compliance of the polls with international standards. International observers noted irregularities in the voting procedure, in particular with regard to the participation rate, which was believed to be much lower than the officially reported 66.9% of the electorate.

Meanwhile, in January 1999 the Central Electoral Commission of the former Supreme Council called a presidential election, in accordance with the 1994 Constitution, to be held on 16 May. Throughout March the Government harassed members of the Commission and its Chairman, Viktar Ganchar, was arrested. He was charged with the offence of 'appointing oneself as an official', but was released on health grounds after a 10-day hunger strike. Nevertheless, during March the Commission registered two presidential candidates, the exiled Paznyak and the former Chairman of the Cabinet of Ministers, Mikhail Chigir. The latter was arrested in April and charged with large-scale embezzlement and abuse of office (the embezzlement charges were later dropped). Speculation naturally arose that Chigir had been arrested in order to prevent his participation in the election. Following the death of Genadz Karpenka in April, Mechislau Gryb was elected Chairman of the Public Coalition Government–National Economic Council in November. In May the Central Electoral Commission of the Supreme Council was unable to organize fixed polling stations for the presidential election, which was not recognized by Lukashenka's Government or by the international community; activists with ballot boxes therefore visited voters in their homes during 6–16 May. Paznyak withdrew his candidacy in mid-May, stating that the voting procedure had violated the law. The election results were declared invalid later in the month, owing to alleged irregularities in the polling, despite a reported participation rate of 53%. The Commission announced that the election was to be repeated within three months. In July the Chairman of the Supreme Council, Syamyon Sharetski, fled to Lithuania amid rumours of a warrant for his arrest in Belarus, following his appointment by the Supreme Council as acting President of Belarus (according to the 1994 Constitution Lukashenka's legitimate term of office expired in mid-July 1999).

The opposition was weakened by internal divisions in 1999. Following an inconclusive leadership vote in July, called by members disaffected with Paznyak, in late September Paznyak's supporters formed a breakaway faction, known as the Conservative Christian Party of the BPF, with Paznyak as Chairman. At the end of October Vintsuk Vyachorka was elected Chairman of the 'rump' BPF (he had previously held the deputy chairmanship). The opposition also suffered increased repression during 1999 and 2000. In January 1999 Lukashenka decreed that political parties, trade unions and other organizations were required to re-register by 1 July; those failing to do so were to be disbanded. Stringent minimum levels of membership penalized several political parties, and by September only 17 of the 28 existing official parties had been re-registered. In December the rump BPF changed its name to BPF–'Adradzhennye' (BPF–'Revival'), in order to comply with legislation banning the use of certain words in the names of non-governmental organizations. In early September OSCE-mediated negotiations commenced between the Government and the opposition, concerning the legislative elections to be held in 2000, reputedly prompting an increased determination on Lukashenka's part to restrict opposition activity. Further rounds of talks were subject to Government-proposed postponements, and opposition frustration was such that when talks resumed in March 2000 its participation was much reduced. Stricter security measures were implemented following a stampede in a Minsk metro station in May 1999, which resulted in 52 deaths (caused, according to Lukashenka, by 'an excess of democracy'), and following a series of bombing incidents in Russia in September. The independent press sector also came under greater scrutiny and a number of publications were closed down or had their registration revoked. Amid this atmosphere of increased control, the Government unexpectedly made a statement in August, committing itself to a number of measures to defend and improve human rights in Belarus. (In April 2000 a grouping was established to draft a national action programme for the protection of human rights, in the context of building a civil society.) Meanwhile, a number of outspoken critics of the President disappeared, in unexplained circumstances. In May 1999 a former Minister of the Interior and campaigner for Chigir, Yuriy Zakharenka, went missing. His disappearance was followed in the next months by those of Tamara Vinnikava, a former head of the central bank, who had been under house arrest since January 1997, an independent publisher and Viktar Ganchar; it was officially claimed that the four had voluntarily gone into hiding to attract attention to their political cause. In December 1999 Vinnikava was reported to be resident in the United Kingdom, prompting Belarusian protests that the host country had known of her presence, and had acted in an 'unfriendly' manner. In September 2000 Belarus requested Vinnikava's extradition.

In October 1999 15,000 people were estimated to have taken part in an anti-Government 'Freedom March' in Minsk (this constituted the largest opposition demonstration to have taken place in Belarus since April 1996). One of the protesters' demands was the release of political prisoners. Chigir, who had been held in detention for more than six months, was released in late November pending trial, which began in January 2000; the protracted trial concluded in May. Chigir received a three-year suspended sentence and a substantial fine, prompting criticism of the verdict by the EU. He was also banned from holding public office for five years; none the less, Chigir stood as a candidate in the first round of voting in the legislative elections held in October (see below), but withdrew from the second round, fearing that his notoriety would provoke electoral fraud. In December his sentence was overturned by the Supreme Court and a re-investigation of the evidence was ordered, owing to legal irregularities. Meanwhile, in April two opposition activists, Mikalai Statkevich (the leader of the Belarusian Social Democratic Party) and Valery Shchukin, were put on trial, charged with organizing the demonstration of October 1999. They were sentenced, in June 2000, to suspended sentences of two years and one year, respectively. In August, however, their convictions were overturned and a retrial was ordered to take place. Statkevich subsequently decided to maintain his candidacy in the forthcoming elections to the National Assembly. In March Andrey Klimaw, a prominent opponent of Lukashenka, was sentenced to six years' imprisonment for fraud. The charges were widely interpreted to have been politically motivated and Klimaw's violent treatment by the police attracted condemnation from Amnesty International.

In February 2000 the Consultative Council of Opposition Parties and Movements agreed not to participate in the parliamentary elections due to take place in October, in protest at not having been consulted about the preparation of a new draft electoral code. This decision appeared to prompt increased repression of both the unofficial media and opposition political parties, particularly in the wake of increased public support for the latter's cause, following the peaceful staging, in mid-March, of a second Freedom March in Minsk, which resulted in the prohibition of demonstrations in the centre of the capital. A further demonstration, to commemorate the creation of the Belarusian National Republic in 1918, which took place later that month, in contravention of the ban, was brutally suppressed by the security forces and resulted in 272 arrests. Many of those detained were journalists and international observers, and Lukashenka subsequently apologized. In the following month the Minister of Internal Affairs, Yuriy Sivakow, resigned, ostensibly for health reasons. There were suggestions, however, that he had been dismissed because of his ministry's handling of the demonstration. In mid-September the offices of *Rabochy*, an opposition publication, were raided by the authorities, following the appearance of an edition dedicated to the opposition's non-participation in the elections; the editor was detained and later fined for producing 'election boycott propaganda'. Anti-election leaflets, numbering some 115,000, were subsequently confiscated in Minsk. Later that month the headquarters of the Belarusian Social Democratic Party were broken into by masked gunmen, who removed documents and electronic data, in what was suspected to have been a politically motivated attack. Five days prior to the legislative elections, opposition politicians established a 'Choice-2001' committee to promote the interests of democratic politicians considered capable of defeating Lukashenka in the presidential election scheduled to be held in 2001.

Despite a large-scale anti-election rally by opposition activists, elections to the National Assembly took place on 15 October 2000. Out of a total of 110 constituencies, voting was declared invalid in 13, necessitating a further round of voting on 29 October. The OSCE denounced the elections as neither free, fair nor open. The official rate of participation was 60.6%, but this figure was widely believed to have been exaggerated. Numerous irregularities and violations were noted by observers in both rounds of the elections (reportedly, there were more than 5,000 in the second round alone), and the international community refused to recognize the elections as valid. In November an independent monitoring group appealed to the Supreme Court to annul the election results. In early December the Central Election Commission announced that repeat elections, to fill the 56 seats that had remained vacant in the invalid constituencies after the first round of voting, were to take place on 18 March 2001.

In February 2000 Syargey Ling resigned as Chairman of the Cabinet of Ministers, owing to his failure to resolve Belarus's economic problems. He was replaced by Uladzimir Yermoshin, hitherto the Governor of Minsk City. In late November Lukashenka made a number of changes to government and security-service personnel. Notably, Prof. Ural Latypaw, hitherto Deputy Prime Minister and Minister of Foreign Affairs, was appointed State Secretary of the Security Council; he was replaced by Mikhail Khvastow. Leanid Yeryn was appointed Chairman of the State Security Committee, replacing Uladzimir Matskevich, and the Procurator General, Alec Bazhelka, was dismissed, and later replaced by Viktar Sheyman, hitherto State Secretary of the Security Council. The changes were alleged to have resulted from Lukashenka's dissatisfaction with the progress of investigations into the disappearances of public figures, particularly that of a cameraman for Russian television, who had last been seen in Minsk in July. The opposition suspected the disappearances to be the result of criminal action on the part of the Belarusian authorities (which vigorously denied all allegations). It was also suggested that the new appointments, which resulted in a transfer of power from ethnic Belarusians to ethnic Russians, had been effected, in part, to please Russia.

Following the dissolution of the USSR in 1991, Belarus's closest relations continued to be with member states of the CIS, in particular the neighbouring Russian Federation. In April 1993 Belarus signed the CIS Treaty on Collective Security (see above), and accords on closer economic co-operation with CIS states followed. In April 1994 Belarus and Russia concluded an agreement on eventual monetary union. In March 1996 Belarus, Kazakhstan, Kyrgyzstan and Russia signed the Quadripartite Treaty, which envisaged a common market and a customs union between the four countries, as well as joint transport, energy and communications systems. (Tajikistan signed the Treaty in 1998.)

In April 1996 Belarus and Russia concluded the far-reaching and controversial Treaty on the Formation of a Community of Sovereign Republics, providing for closer economic, political and military integration. On 2 April 1997 a further Treaty of Union was signed by Yeltsin and Lukashenka in Moscow, and a Charter of the Union, detailing the process of integration, was also initialled. The stated aim of the Union was the 'voluntary unification of the member states', including the development of a common infrastructure, a single currency and a joint defence policy. The Union's ruling body was to be a Supreme Council, chaired alternately by the President of each country, and comprising the Heads of State and Government, the leaders of the legislatures and the Chairman of the Executive Committee. The Executive Committee was to be appointed by the Supreme Council. The Parliamentary Assembly (provision for which had been made in the 1996 Treaty and which had convened in March) comprised 36 members from the legislature of each country. The Charter was submitted for nation-wide discussion in both countries, before being signed in Moscow on 23 May. Ratification of the documents by the respective legislatures took place in June, and the first official session of the Parliamentary Assembly followed shortly afterwards, with the Assembly adopting the anthem of the former USSR.

Progress towards further integration appeared threatened by the deterioration in relations caused by the arrest of two Russian television crews in Belarus in mid-1997. The incidents led to strong exchanges of opinion between the two Presidents, and the cancellation of two visits by Lukashenka to Russia. Relations subsequently improved, although Lukashenka was dissatisfied with the progress of unification. In November 1998 the Parliamentary Assembly of the Russia-Belarus Union voted for the creation of a unified parliament, to consist of two chambers. The upper chamber was to include deputies delegated by the legislatures of the two countries, and the lower chamber, comprising 25 Belarusian and 75 Russian deputies, was to be elected by direct universal suffrage. The first elections to the union Parliament were expected to coincide with elections to the Russian and Belarusian legislatures. On 25 December, at a meeting in Moscow, Presidents Lukashenka and Yeltsin signed a document providing for equal rights for their citizens in Russia and Belarus and the creation of a union state within one year. A treaty on unification was to be drafted and submitted for national discussion by mid-1999. Provisions were to include the formation of the necessary governing bodies and a mechanism for pursuing a common policy in international affairs and defence and security matters, as well as further moves towards economic integration. The opposition in Belarus criticized the agreement as representing a loss of sovereignty. Agreements on enhanced military co-operation between Belarus and Russia were signed in April 1999. Lukashenka's hopes for the formation of a single state, which were much contested by the Belarusian opposition, were also not shared by Russia, and the draft treaty on unification, which was submitted for public inspection in October, did not fully satisfy the wishes of the Belarusian President. In addition, the then Russian Prime Minister, Vladimir Putin, warned that implementation might take several years. The signature of the treaty took place in Moscow on 8 December, having been postponed from November. The treaty was ratified by the two countries' respective legislatures and by Lukashenka later in December and by Putin, who had replaced Yeltsin as the President of Russia, on 3 January 2000. The treaty came into force on 26 January, when Lukashenka was appointed Chairman of the High State Council of the Union. In April Gennadii Seleznev was elected Chairman of the Parliamentary Assembly of the Union of Russia and Belarus. A union budget was passed at a session of the Parliamentary Assembly in May. Although progress towards a full union appeared to be advancing steadily, Putin remained more pragmatic than did Lukashenka, in particular in his attitude towards the formation of joint armed forces, a measure that the Belarusian President strongly favoured. On 30 November, during a CIS summit meeting in Minsk, an agreement on the introduction of a single currency was signed. Both Heads of State declared that a single currency would compel Russia and Belarus to share sovereignty, but Putin remained anxious not to rush the process of full integration. Also in November it was announced that elections to the unified parliament would take place early in 2002.

Relations with Poland deteriorated sharply in February 1998, when Poland introduced visas for travellers from Belarus, Russia and Ukraine in preparation for EU membership and the standardization of controls. The introduction of a new visa system in Latvia with regard to seven CIS states, including Belarus, in April 1999, caused tension between Belarus and Latvia, as the former was not informed of the changes prior to their implementation. The possibility of accession to the EU caused several countries to reconsider their entry requirements. Romania annulled its visa-free travel agreement with Belarus on 1 July 2000, and in November Slovakia and Hungary announced plans to implement similar measures from January and May 2001, respectively. For its part, from 1 May 2000 Belarus introduced regulations requiring foreign travellers with visas for CIS states to obtain a transit visa in order to pass through its territory. In November the Prime Ministers of Belarus, Kazakhstan, Kyrgyzstan, Tajikistan and Russia signed an agreement granting citizens from those countries the right to visa-free travel.

In June 1998 a diplomatic scandal resulted from the enforced eviction, for 'essential repairs', of 22 diplomatic families from their residences outside Minsk. This violation of the Vienna Convention, guaranteeing the inviolability of diplomatic residences, led to the recall from Belarus of the ambassadors of EU countries, a number of other European states and the USA and Japan. In a retaliatory act, Belarusian envoys were expelled from the EU in June, and in the following month Belarusian

officials (including the President) were barred from entering its member states. The ban was subsequently adopted by several other European countries and the USA. In December, however, Belarus undertook compensation procedures for those families that had been forced to relocate and Lukashenka gave assurances that, henceforth, he would comply with international agreements. All heads of diplomatic missions accredited to Belarus, with the exception of the US ambassador, returned to Minsk in January 1999. The EU ban on Belarusian officials entering its territory was repealed in February, and the US ambassador returned to Minsk in September.

In late 2000 international organizations, including the OSCE, continued to recognize the former Supreme Council as the legitimate legislature of Belarus. The OSCE, however, opened a bureau in Minsk in February 1998, the mission of which was to encourage democratization, to promote a dialogue between the Government and the opposition and to monitor human rights. In September Belarus became a permanent member of the Non-aligned Movement (see p. 318).

With the dissolution of the USSR in December 1991, Belarus effectively became a nuclear power, with approximately 80 SS-25 intercontinental ballistic missiles stationed on its territory. However, the Government consistently stressed Belarus to be, under the Declaration of State Sovereignty of July 1990, a neutral and non-nuclear state. Accordingly, in May 1992 Belarus signed the Lisbon Protocol to the Treaty on the Non-Proliferation of Nuclear Weapons (see the International Atomic Energy Agency, see p. 76), under which it pledged to transfer all nuclear missiles to the Russian Federation by 1999. In February 1993 the Supreme Council ratified the first Strategic Arms' Reduction Treaty (START 1—for further details, see chapter on the USA). Substantial amounts of financial and technical aid were pledged by the USA to help Belarus dismantle its nuclear arsenal. The last remaining nuclear warhead was transported to Russia in late November 1996. In 1998 Belarus signed the International Convention on Nuclear Safety, adopted in June 1994 in Vienna, Austria.

Government

Under the Constitution of March 1994, which was amended in November 1996, legislative power is vested in the bicameral National Assembly. The lower chamber, the 110-member House of Representatives, is elected by universal adult suffrage for a term of four years. The upper chamber, the Council of the Republic, comprises 64 members: 56 members elected by organs of local administration, and eight members appointed by the President. The President is the Head of State, and is elected by popular vote for five years. Executive authority is exercised by the Cabinet of Ministers, which is led by the Chairman (Prime Minister) and is responsible to the National Assembly. For administrative purposes, Belarus is divided into six regions (*oblasts*) and the capital city of Minsk; the regions are divided into districts (*rayons*).

Defence

In August 2000 the total strength of Belarus's armed forces was 83,100, comprising an army of 43,500, an air force of 22,500 (including air defence of 10,200), as well as 17,100 in centrally controlled units and Ministry of Defence staff. There is also a border guard numbering 12,000, which is controlled by the Ministry of Internal Affairs. Military service is compulsory and lasts for 18 months. In May 1996 it was reported that the term of military service would be reduced to 12 months from 2000. In October 1994 it was announced that two Russian non-nuclear military installations were to remain in Belarus. The defence budget for 2000 was projected at 74,000,000m. new roubles. In January 1995 Belarus joined NATO's 'Partnership for Peace' programme of military co-operation (see p. 243).

Economic Affairs

In 1998, according to estimates by the World Bank, Belarus's gross national product (GNP), measured at average 1996–98 prices, was US $22,332m., equivalent to $2,180 per head. In terms of purchasing power parity, GNP in that year was equivalent to $6,314 per head. During 1990–98, it was estimated, GNP per head declined at an average annual rate of 3.7%. Over the same period, the population increased at an average annual rate of less than 0.05%. In 1999 total GNP was estimated at $26,800m., equivalent to $2,630 per head. During 1990–98 Belarus's gross domestic product (GDP) declined, in real terms, by an average of 4.3% annually. However, GDP increased by 11.5% in 1997, by 8.4% in 1998 and by 3.0% in 1999.

Agriculture and forestry contributed an estimated 12.4% of GDP in 1998, and 16.4% of the employed labour force were engaged in the sector in that year. The principal crops are potatoes, grain and sugar beet. The livestock sector accounted for some 37% of agricultural output in 1995. Large areas of arable land (some 1.6m. ha) are still unused after being contaminated in 1986, following the accident at the Chornobyl nuclear power station in Ukraine. The Belarusian authorities have largely opposed private farming, and in 1999 collective and state farms still accounted for some 83% of agricultural land. However, in that year private farms produced the majority of Belarus's potatoes, fruit and vegetables, as well as a significant proportion of total livestock-product output. In 1998, according to the IMF, 49.8% of total crop output was produced by the private sector. During 1990–98, according to the World Bank, agricultural GDP decreased at an average annual rate of 5.4%; agricultural output declined by 0.2% in 1997. In 1999 the grain harvest totalled 3.6m. metric tons, a decline of 24% compared with 1998.

Industry (comprising mining, manufacturing, construction and power) provided an estimated 42.7% of GDP in 1998, and engaged 35.1% of the employed labour force in that year. According to the World Bank, industrial GDP decreased at an average annual rate of 5.6% during 1990–98. However, it was estimated that industrial output increased by 17.6% in 1997 and by 10% in 1998.

According to the World Bank, the manufacturing sector contributed an estimated 21.1% of GDP in 1995, and employed 26.5% of the labour force in 1994. Machine-building, power generation and chemicals are the principal branches of the sector. During 1990–98 manufacturing GDP decreased at an average annual rate of 4.4%. After several years of decline, production increased in 1996. The greatest advance was recorded in the iron and steel industry, where output rose by 23.4% in that year. The sector suffered a reverse in May 2000, when Ford, the US motor company, announced that it was to cease production at its unprofitable joint-venture truck manufacturing plant in Belarus; two months later the company sold its stake in the concern.

Belarus has relatively few mineral resources, although there are small deposits of petroleum and natural gas, and important peat reserves. Peat extraction, however, was severely affected by the disaster at Chornobyl, since contaminated peat could not be burned. Belarus produced 50% of the former USSR's output of potash. However, production of potash declined in the 1990s. In 1994 only 0.6% of the labour force were engaged in mining and quarrying.

In 1996 Belarus's supply of energy was provided by petroleum and petroleum products (58%), natural gas (34%) and electricity (8%). In 1999 the country imported 86% of its crude-oil consumption, 98% of its natural-gas consumption and 30% of its electricity consumption. In the latter half of the 1990s Belarus's principal gas supplier, the Russian company, Gazprom, threatened to reduce supplies to Belarus, owing to continuing substantial arrears in the payment of a debt estimated at US $250m. Having failed to comply with previous settlements, Belarus agreed in December 1998 to supply Russia with foodstuffs to repay the remainder of the debt. In January 1999, however, Gazprom reduced its gas supplies to Belarus by 12%. In 1999 Belarus also owed a substantial amount to Lithuania for electricity, but in early 2000 it was announced that 50% of these arrears had been repaid through the exchange of goods. Belarus's debt to Gazprom continued to increase in 2000, despite the fact that the Russian company had reduced the price of gas, a concession viewed to result from the signature of the Russia-Belarus Union Treaty. In early 2000 Gazprom announced that it was to construct two new gas pipelines across Belarus, in order to halt the alleged illicit siphoning of supplies from existing pipelines in Ukraine. Imports of energy products comprised 40.2% of the total value of imports in 1995. There are two large petroleum refineries, at Novopolotsk and Mozyr.

Services accounted for 48.5% of total employment in 1998, and provided an estimated 44.9% of GDP. The services sector is led by transport and communications and trade and catering, which accounted for 11.5% and 10.0% of GDP, respectively, in 1998. Trade and catering GDP increased by 23.0% in 1996, compared with a decline of 24.0% in 1995. During 1990–98 the GDP of the services sector declined at an average annual rate of 2.4%.

In 1999 Belarus recorded a visible trade deficit of US $598.5m., and there was a deficit of $256.7m. on the current account of the balance of payments. After the dissolution of the USSR in December 1991, Belarus endeavoured to promote economic links with non-traditional trading partners. According to the IMF, in 1999 these partners accounted for an estimated 35.7% of Belarus's imports and 38.7% of its exports, remaining trade being conducted with former Soviet republics. In 1999 Belarus's principal trading partners among countries constituting the former USSR were Russia (which accounted for 56.4% of total imports and 54.5% of exports) and Ukraine; outside the former USSR its most important trading partners were Germany and Poland. In 1999 the principal exports were machinery and metalworking, chemical and petroleum products, and light manufactures. The principal imports were chemical and petroleum products, machinery and metalworking, and metallurgy.

The 1999 state budget registered a deficit of 52,897m. readjusted new roubles. Belarus's total external debt was US $1,120m. at the end of 1998, of which $766m. was long-term public debt. In that year the cost of debt-servicing was equivalent to 2.0% of the value of exports of goods and services. During 1990–98 consumer prices increased at an average rate of 365% per year. The average annual rate of inflation was 63.8% in 1997, but it increased to 73.0% in 1998 and to 293.7% in 1999. In December 1999 the unemployment rate was 2.1% of the labour force. At the end of 1999 95,400 people were officially registered as unemployed. However, the true rate of unemployment was believed to be far higher, as many people were unwilling to register, owing to the low level of official benefits.

Belarus joined the IMF and the World Bank in 1992. It also became a member of the European Bank for Reconstruction and Development (EBRD, see p. 176).

Prior to 1991, Belarus was widely considered to have the most stable republican economy of the USSR, supported largely by a comparatively advanced engineering sector. Following the dissolution of the USSR, however, Belarus experienced serious economic problems comparable to those prevalent in other former Soviet republics, and suffered a severe contraction in output in all sectors. The introduction of market economic principles was effectively halted in 1995, causing the IMF to suspend credit to Belarus. Belarus's economic policy was influenced by its aim of integration with Russia, as envisaged in a number of treaties and agreements signed from the mid-1990s. A common currency accord was drafted in May 2000, and signed in late November; the Russian rouble was to be adopted as the Belarusian currency in 2005, and a new, single currency was to be introduced in 2008. In December 2000 the Government of Belarus and the National Bank agreed to fix a reference rate for the Belarusian currency in relation to the Russian rouble from 1 January 2001, with an established fluctuation margin of 3%, which was later to decline to 2.5%. At the end of 1999 it was announced that the Belarusian rouble was to be redenominated over a three-year period. One redenominated rouble was to be equivalent to 1,000 new roubles. In September 2000 a single rouble exchange rate was introduced, replacing the existing multiple exchange-rate system. It was hoped that these measures would help to stabilize the currency, which had depreciated considerably against the US dollar in 1998 and 1999, contributing to the high level of inflation recorded in 1999. As consumer prices increased, the standard of living declined, and in July 2000 wage arrears reached their highest level for three years. A poor grain harvest in 1999 exacerbated food shortages, which were compounded in October 2000 by difficulties in gathering the potato crop, owing to a lack of fuel supplies. In that month the IMF declined to resume lending to Belarus, owing to the absence of significant structural reform. However, in November the Fund sent a mission to Belarus, to discuss the establishment of a monitoring programme, despite a previous decision no longer to do so. Although positive growth in GDP and an increase in foreign-exchange reserves were recorded in late 1999 and early 2000, the accompanying high rate of inflation suggested that the recovery was not sustainable. Prospects for the Belarusian economy in 2000 were unfavourable, as the political situation became increasingly unstable, particularly following legislative elections in October (see Recent History), which were not recognized by the international community.

Social Welfare

From 1993 the social security system was financed by two principal funds: the Social Protection Fund (covering family allowances, pensions and sickness and disability benefits), and the Employment Fund (directing employment schemes, retraining projects and unemployment benefits). More than 2.5m. people were receiving pensions in 1998. A variety of benefits, financed through the Chornobyl tax, are paid to victims of the accident at the Chornobyl nuclear power station in April 1986. In 1996 government expenditure on social protection was 22,954,000m. new roubles (12.8% of GDP), and expenditure on health from the state budget was 9,402,000m. new roubles (5.2% of GDP). In 1998 there were 44.3 physicians, and in 1995 there were 117.1 hospital beds, per 10,000 inhabitants.

Education

Education is officially compulsory for nine years. Generally, education lasts for 11 years from six to 17 years of age. In 1999 the total enrolment at pre-primary level was equivalent to 71% of children in the relevant age group (males 72.7%; females 62.7%). Primary education generally begins at six years of age and lasts for four years (Grades 1–4). In 1999 the total enrolment at primary level was equivalent to 99.3% of the school-age population (males 99.9%; females 98.8%). Secondary education, beginning at the age of 10, lasts for a further seven years (Grades 5–11), comprising a first cycle of five years and a second of two years. In 1999 enrolment at secondary level was equivalent to 99.9% of those in the relevant age group (males 99.7%; females 99.9%). In 1998 a transition towards compulsory education for 10 years and general education lasting 12 years began. In the early 1990s, in response to public demand, the Government began to introduce greater provision for education in the Belarusian language and more emphasis on Belarusian, rather than Soviet or Russian, history and literature. In 1998/99 30.5% of all pupils were taught in Belarusian, and 69.4% were taught in Russian. Higher education institutions include seven general and 12 specialized universities, as well as nine academies. In 1999 262,000 students were enrolled in higher education. In 1996 enrolment at tertiary level was equivalent to 44.0% of people in the relevant age group (males 38.8%; females 49.3%). Research is co-ordinated by the Belarusian Academy of Sciences. Budgetary expenditure on education by all levels of government was 185,708m. readjusted new roubles (13.4% of total expenditure) in 1999. In 1989, according to census results, the average rate of adult illiteracy was 2.1% (males 0.6%; females 3.4%). According to preliminary census results, by February 1999 the rate of illiteracy had decreased to 0.4%.

Public Holidays

2001: 1 January (New Year's Day), 7 January (Orthodox Christmas), 8 March (International Women's Day), 15 March (Constitution Day), 16 April (Catholic and Orthodox Easter), 28 April (Memorial Day), 1 May (Labour Day), 9 May (Victory Day), 3 July (Anniversary of Liberation from the Nazis), 2 November (Day of Commemoration), 7 November (October Revolution Day), 25 December (Catholic Christmas).

2002: 1 January (New Year's Day), 7 January (Orthodox Christmas), 8 March (International Women's Day), 15 March (Constitution Day), 1 April (Catholic Easter), 28 April (Memorial Day), 1 May (Labour Day), 6 May (Orthodox Easter), 9 May (Victory Day), 3 July (Anniversary of Liberation from the Nazis), 2 November (Day of Commemoration), 7 November (October Revolution Day), 25 December (Catholic Christmas).

Weights and Measures

The metric system is in force.

Statistical Survey

Source: mainly Ministry of Statistics and Analysis, 220070 Minsk, pr. Partizanski 12; tel. (17) 249-52-00; fax (17) 249-22-04; e-mail minstat@mail.belpak.by; internet www.president.gov.by/Minstat/en/main.html.

Area and Population

AREA, POPULATION AND DENSITY

Area (sq km) .	207,595*
Population (census results)†	
12 January 1989	10,151,806
16 February 1999	
Males	4,717,621
Females	5,327,616
Total	10,045,237
Population (official estimates at 1 January)	
1998	10,203,837
1999‡	10,045,237
2000	10,019,000
Density (per sq km) at 1 January 2000 .	48.3

* 80,153 sq miles.
† Figures refer to the *de jure* population. The *de facto* total was 10,199,709 in 1989.
‡ Referring to the February 1999 census.

POPULATION BY NATIONALITY (1999 census)

	%
Belarusian	81
Russian	11
Polish	4
Ukrainian	2
Others	2
Total	100

PRINCIPAL TOWNS* (estimated population at 1 January 1999)

Minsk			Baranovichi	
(Miensk, capital) .	1,725,100		(Baranavichy) .	173,800
Gomel (Homiel) .	503,700		Borisov (Barysau) .	153,500
Mogilev (Mahilou) .	371,300		Pinsk .	133,500
Vitebsk (Viciebsk) .	358,700		Orsha (Vorsha) .	124,300
Grodno (Horadnia) .	308,900		Mozyr (Mazyr) .	110,000
Brest (Bierascie)† .	300,400		Soligorsk .	101,700
Bobruysk (Babrujsk) .	228,000		Lida .	99,600

* The Belarusian names of towns, in Latin transliteration, are given in parentheses after the more widely used Russian names.
† Formerly Brest-Litovsk.

1999 census (provisional): Minsk 1,680,000.

BIRTHS, MARRIAGES AND DEATHS

	Registered live births		Registered marriages		Registered deaths	
	Number	Rate (per 1,000)	Number	Rate (per 1,000)	Number	Rate (per 1,000)
1992 .	127,971	12.4	79,813	7.7	116,674	11.3
1993 .	117,384	11.3	82,326	7.9	128,544	12.4
1994 .	110,599	10.7	75,540	7.3	130,003	12.6
1995 .	101,144	9.8	77,027	7.5	133,775	13.0
1996 .	95,798	9.3	63,677	6.2	133,422	13.0
1997 .	89,586	8.8	69,735	6.8	136,653	13.4
1998 .	92,645	9.1	71,354	7.0	137,296	13.5
1999 .	93,102	9.2	n.a.	7.2	141,805	14.0

Expectation of life (official estimates, years at birth, 1999): 68.5 (males 62.7, females 74.3).

EMPLOYMENT (annual averages, '000 persons)

	1996	1997	1998
Agriculture .	760.4	735.1	695.3
Forestry .	26.4	27.4	28.7
Industry*	1,202.0	1,204.3	1,221.0
Construction .	314.1	311.8	329.5
Trade and communications .	311.2	309.1	321.4
Trade and public catering† .	460.1	461.6	483.2
Housing, public utilities and personal services .	195.5	197.6	193.4
Health care .	253.8	259.9	262.0
Physical culture and social security	45.8	48.0	51.6
Education .	433.0	441.1	454.5
Culture and arts .	69.8	71.1	73.9
Science .	47.8	44.6	43.7
Credit and insurance .	50.4	50.7	53.2
Other activities .	194.5	207.6	205.2
Total .	4,364.8	4,369.9	4,416.6
Males .	2,128.0	2,128.6	2,146.5
Females .	2,236.8	2,241.3	2,270.1

* Comprising manufacturing (except printing and publishing), mining and quarrying, electricity, gas, logging and fishing.
† Including material and technical supply and procurement.

Unemployment ('000 persons registered at December): 182.5 (males 66.1, females 116.4) in 1996; 126.2 (males 42.1, females 84.1) in 1997; 105.9 (males 35.3, females 70.6) in 1998.

1999 ('000 persons): Total employed (annual average) 4,442.0 (males 2,127.8, females 2,314.2); Unemployed (at December) 95.4 (males 34.1, females 61.3) (Source: ILO, *Yearbook of Labour Statistics*).

Agriculture

PRINCIPAL CROPS ('000 metric tons)

	1997	1998	1999
Wheat .	744	787	711
Barley .	2,359	1,623	1,181
Maize* .	5	4	3
Rye .	1,788	1,384	929
Oats .	822	501	369
Other cereals .	201	193	101
Potatoes. .	6,942	7,574	7,491
Dry beans* .	205	144	100
Dry peas* .	287	190	153
Rapeseed .	21	52	60†
Linseed† .	18	19	20
Cabbages .	490*	525*	500†
Tomatoes .	114*	126*	122†
Cucumbers and gherkins .	135*	120*	125†
Onions (dry). .	55*	45*	50†
Carrots .	54*	60*	65†
Other vegetables. .	328*	325*	330†
Sugar beet .	1,262	1,428	1,186
Apples .	243*	133*	200†
Pears .	16*	9*	13†
Plums .	49*	30*	40†
Other fruits and berries .	55*	30*	44†
Walnuts† .	10	12	12
Tobacco (leaves)†. .	2	2	2
Flax fibre .	26	36	21

* Unofficial figure(s). † FAO estimate(s).

Source: FAO.

LIVESTOCK ('000 head at 1 January)

	1997	1998	1999
Horses	232	233	229
Cattle	4,855	4,802	4,686
Pigs	3,715	3,686	3,698
Sheep	155	127	106
Goats	59	59	56
Poultry	31,540	29,871	30,425

LIVESTOCK PRODUCTS ('000 metric tons)

	1997	1998	1999
Beef and veal	256	271	261*
Mutton and lamb	3*	3	3*
Pig meat	298	320	245*
Poultry meat	70	74	72*
Cows' milk	5,133	5,232	4,762
Cheese	51	57	59†
Butter	72	74	61
Hen eggs*	194	195	190
Honey	4	3	3†
Cattle hides	28	30	29

* Unofficial figure(s).   † FAO estimate.

Source: FAO.

Forestry

ROUNDWOOD REMOVALS ('000 cubic metres, excl. bark)

	1996	1997	1998
Sawlogs, veneer logs and logs for sleepers	9,142	11,020	11,020
Other industrial wood	5,286	5,286	5,286
Fuel wood	809	809	809
Total	15,707	17,585	17,745

Source: FAO, *Yearbook of Forest Products*.

SAWNWOOD PRODUCTION ('000 cubic metres, incl. railway sleepers)

	1996	1997	1998
Coniferous (softwood)*	938	938	938
Broadleaved (hardwood)*	607	607	607
Total	1,545	1,545	1,545

* FAO estimates.

Source: FAO, *Yearbook of Forest Products*.

Fishing

(metric tons, live weight)

	1996	1997	1998
Capture	821	499	457
Freshwater bream	240	182	130
Aquaculture	6,038	4,322	4,727
Common carp	3,805	2,873	3,254
Crucian carp	396	286	410
Northern pike	1,829	1,157	1,062
Total catch	6,859	4,821	5,184

Source: FAO, *Yearbook of Fishery Statistics*.

Mining

('000 metric tons, unless otherwise indicated)

	1996	1997	1998
Crude petroleum	1,860	1,822	1,830
Natural gas (million cu metres)	249	246	252
Chalk	64	75	79
Gypsum (crude)	21	23	17
Peat: for fuel	2,847	2,768	2,035
for agriculture	533	253	99

1999: Crude petroleum ('000 metric tons) 1,840; Natural gas (million cu metres) 256.

Industry

SELECTED PRODUCTS ('000 metric tons, unless otherwise indicated)

	1996	1997	1998
Refined sugar	226	352	476
Margarine	25.3	22.7	15.0
Wheat flour	1,397	1,274	1,159
Ethyl alcohol ('000 hectolitres)	1,025	1,312	1,051
Wine ('000 hectolitres)	868.7	1,256.5	1,733.4
Beer ('000 hectolitres)	2,012.5	2,412.6	2,603.7
Mineral water ('000 hectolitres)	295.8	548.3	886.4
Soft drinks ('000 hectolitres)	1,627.0	2,031.1	1,942.0
Cigarettes (million)	6,267	6,787	7,296
Cotton yarn (pure and mixed)	11.4	10.2	18.6
Flax yarn	16.1	16.8	17.4
Wool yarn (pure and mixed)	12.8	15.5	16.3
Woven cotton fabrics (million sq metres)	42.8	47.4	66.9
Woven woollen fabrics (million sq metres)	7.0	8.9	9.5
Linen fabrics (million sq metres)	43.0	45.1	50.1
Woven fabrics of cellulosic fibres (million sq metres)	39.5	66.7	77.2
Carpets ('000 sq metres)	5,612	6,861	8,145
Footwear (excluding rubber, '000 pairs)	11,381	15,587	16,159
Plywood ('000 cu metres)	103	121	139
Paper	30	36	45
Paperboard	112	135	150
Benzene (Benzol)	34.7	35.9	16.7
Ethylene (Ethene)	78.9	104.0	108.1
Propylene (Propene)	55.1	69.8	70.5
Xylenes (Xylol)	7.6	9.3	—
Sulphuric acid (100%)	549	698	640
Nitrogenous fertilizers (a)[1]	565	490	559
Phosphate fertilizers (b)[1]	100	136	130
Potash fertilizers (c)[1]	2,716	3,247	3,451
Non-cellulosic continuous fibres	46.6	64.2	66.2
Cellulosic continuous filaments	10.7	13.2	14.3
Soap	29.7	33.7	26.1
Rubber tyres ('000)[2]	1,916	2,355	2,324
Rubber footwear ('000 pairs)	3,054	4,376	5,036
Quicklime	450	551	684
Cement	1,467	1,876	2,035
Concrete blocks ('000 cu metres)	1,370	1,996	2,134
Crude steel	886	1,220	1,412
Tractors ('000)	26.8	27.4	26.9
Refrigerators ('000)	754	795	802
Domestic washing machines ('000)	60.5	88.2	90.8
Television receivers ('000)	314	454	468
Radio receivers ('000)	138	170	114
Lorries (number)	10,671	13,002	12,792
Motor cycles ('000)	30.1	22.6	20.4
Bicycles ('000)	280	317	452
Cameras ('000)	35	15	5
Watches ('000)	4,809	4,956	4,847
Electric energy (million kWh)	23,728	26,057	23,492

[1] Production in terms of (a) nitrogen; (b) phosphoric acid; or (c) potassium oxide.

[2] For lorries and farm vehicles.

Finance

CURRENCY AND EXCHANGE RATES

Monetary Units:

100 kopeks = 1 readjusted Belarusian rouble (rubel).

Sterling, Dollar and Euro Equivalents (29 December 2000)

£1 sterling = 1,760.8 readjusted roubles;
US $1 = 1,180.0 readjusted roubles;
€1 = 1,098.0 readjusted roubles;
10,000 readjusted Belarusian roubles = £5.679 = $8.475 = €9.108.

Average Exchange Rate (readjusted Belarusian roubles per US $)
2000   876.75

Note: The Belarusian rouble was introduced in May 1992, initially as a coupon currency, to circulate alongside (and at par with) the Russian (formerly Soviet) rouble. Following the dissolution of the USSR in December 1991, Russia and several other former Soviet republics retained the rouble as their monetary unit. The parity between Belarusian and Russian currencies was subsequently ended, and the Belarusian rouble was devalued. At 30 September 1993 the exchange rate was 1 Russian rouble = 2 Belarusian roubles. The rate per Russian rouble was adjusted to 3 Belarusian roubles in October 1993, and to 4 Belarusian roubles in November. In April 1994 Belarus and Russia signed a treaty providing for the eventual union of their monetary systems. However, it was subsequently recognized that, under the prevailing economic conditions, such a union was not practicable. In August a new Belarusian rouble, equivalent to 10 old roubles, was introduced. On 1 January 1995 the Belarusian rouble became the sole national currency, while the circulation of Russian roubles ceased. On 1 January 2000 a readjusted Belarusian rouble, equivalent to 1,000 of the former units, was introduced. Some of the figures in this survey are still in terms of new roubles prior to redenomination.

STATE BUDGET (million roubles)*

Revenue	1997	1998	1999
Tax revenue	150,038	280,691	1,231,549
Taxes on income, profits and			
capital gains . . .	28,195	55,595	235,750
Social security contributions	31,639	61,480	262,858
Payroll taxes	7,794	10,803	47,232
Taxes on property . . .	4,935	9,029	18,051
Domestic taxes on goods and			
services	66,153	123,664	587,652
Taxes on international trade and			
transactions	8,964	15,269	58,011
Other current revenue . .	8,325	20,454	91,009
Capital revenue	1,533	3,019	9,546
Total	159,896	304,164	1,332,105

Expenditure	1997	1998	1999
General public services . .	8,727	15,266	59,800
Defence	6,080	9,837	38,741
Public order . . .	4,985	8,501	41,795
Education	26,283	47,610	185,708
Health	19,913	32,218	142,702
Social security and welfare . .	36,592	70,973	286,161
Housing and communal amenities	10,563	17,163	81,388
Recreation and culture . .	4,292	7,719	28,581
Industry, construction and energy	1,078	2,904	17,076
Agriculture, forestry, fishing and			
hunting	12,314	23,322	124,882
Transport and communications	11,663	22,237	103,210
Total (incl. others) . . .	164,312	307,632	1,385,001
Current expenditure . . .	130,214	248,253	1,059,185
Capital expenditure . . .	32,318	59,555	323,072
Net lending	1,780	−176	2,744

* Figures are in terms of the readjusted rouble, introduced on 1 January 2000 and equivalent to 1,000 of the former units. The data represent a consolidation of the operations of all central and local government bodies.

Source: IMF, *Republic of Belarus: Recent Economic Developments and Selected Issues* (November 2000).

INTERNATIONAL RESERVES (US $ million at 31 December)

	1997	1998	1999
IMF special drawing rights . .	—	0.42	0.42
Reserve position in IMF . .	0.03	0.03	0.03
Foreign exchange . . .	393.67	338.39	293.82
Total	393.70	338.83	294.27

Source: IMF, *International Financial Statistics*.

MONEY SUPPLY (million new roubles at 31 December)

	1997	1998	1999
Currency outside banks . .	12,300,000	27,074,000	86,852,000
Demand deposits at deposit money			
banks	21,052,000	52,487,000	140,714,000
Total money (incl. others) .	33,852,000	80,932,000	233,415,000

Source: IMF, *International Financial Statistics*.

COST OF LIVING (Consumer price index; base: 1992 = 100)

	1997	1998	1999*
Food (incl. beverages) . .	725,423	1,275,657	5,264,100
Fuel and light	1,883,617	2,675,490	4,297,400
Clothing (incl. footwear) . .	275,293	442,424	1,508,600
Rent	5,415,815	7,002,649	10,789,000
All items (incl. others) . .	606,280	1,049,047	4,130,500

* Figures are rounded to the nearest 100 (Source: ILO, *Yearbook of Labour Statistics*).

NATIONAL ACCOUNTS ('000 million new roubles at current prices)

Expenditure on the Gross Domestic Product

	1997	1998	1999
Government final consumption			
expenditure . . .	72,441	139,142	581,868
Private final consumption			
expenditure	202,875	399,844	1,685,796
Increase in stocks . . .	5,891	5,458	−47,667
Gross fixed capital formation .	92,555	182,103	740,550
Total domestic expenditure .	373,762	726,547	2,960,547
Exports of goods and services .	217,574	415,224	1,786,834
Less Imports of goods and services	239,975	449,248	1,869,663
Statistical discrepancy . .	4,718	−17,365	16,604
GDP in purchasers' values . .	356,080	675,159	2,890,320

Source: IMF, *International Financial Statistics*.

Gross Domestic Product by Economic Activity

	1996	1997	1998*
Agriculture	24,769.9	43,134.6	67,336.1
Forestry	1,303.6	2,401.9	4,252.8
Industry†	56,518.8	110,727.0	205,735.6
Construction	8,943.0	20,274.7	39,848.4
Transport	17,382.6	31,741.0	55,272.8
Communications	3,663.6	5,804.5	10,761.3
Trade and catering	14,335.8	26,401.3	57,497.0
Material supply	2,274.4	4,518.9	8,430.9
Procurement	491.9	903.5	1,417.4
Housing	4,077.8	7,608.9	12,654.5
Public utilities	3,130.4	6,114.2	11,554.1
Health care	5,694.7	11,523.3	19,203.2
Education	7,630.8	15,454.4	27,588.2
Culture and science	2,278.4	3,385.4	5,726.7
Banks and insurance	4,354.2	7,208.8	16,306.3
Public administration and defence	6,959.0	11,620.2	20,231.6
Other services	2,598.2	5,692.8	11,769.8
Sub-total	166,406.9	314,515.4	575,586.7
Less Imputed bank service charge	3,056.4	5,190.0	11,205.4
GDP at factor cost	163,350.5	309,325.4	564,381.3
Indirect taxes, *less* subsidies	20,823.4	46,753.9	97,988.6
GDP in purchasers' values	184,173.9	356,079.3	662,369.9

* Figures are preliminary.

† Principally mining, manufacturing, electricity, gas and water.

BALANCE OF PAYMENTS (US $ million)

	1997	1998	1999
Exports of goods f.o.b.	7,382.6	7,138.1	5,949.3
Imports of goods f.o.b.	−8,718.0	−8,488.2	−6,547.8
Trade balance	−1,335.4	−1,350.1	−598.5
Exports of services	918.8	925.1	733.8
Imports of services	−364.8	−443.2	−435.8
Balance on goods and services	−781.4	−868.2	−300.5
Other income received	31.2	26.8	29.0
Other income paid	−115.8	−119.7	−93.6
Balance on goods, services and income	−866.0	−961.1	−365.1
Current transfers received	106.1	120.9	136.2
Current transfers paid	−27.7	−25.3	−27.8
Current balance	−787.6	−865.5	−256.7
Capital account (net)	133.2	170.1	60.4
Direct investment abroad	−2.1	−2.3	−0.8
Direct investment from abroad	200.0	149.2	225.0
Portfolio investment assets	−61.6	28.0	−13.9
Portfolio investment liabilities	41.8	−13.4	−18.3
Other investment assets	49.8	199.4	−33.0
Other investment liabilities	358.5	−60.1	90.3
Net errors and omissions	133.1	75.3	34.3
Overall balance	65.1	−319.3	87.3

Source: IMF, *International Financial Statistics*.

External Trade

PRINCIPAL COMMODITIES ('000 million new roubles at domestic prices)*

Imports	1997	1998	1999
Industrial products	221,827	410,697	1,680,321
Electric energy	4,515	11,365	35,970
Petroleum and gas	55,299	85,872	32,660
Metallurgy	27,792	55,796	218,961
Chemical and petroleum products	38,802	70,955	606,205
Machinery and metalworking	49,934	107,686	413,427
Wood and paper products	6,436	13,323	54,232
Light industry	10,584	18,477	96,391
Food and beverages	22,093	33,717	175,541
Agricultural products (unprocessed)	8,465	12,299	73,371
Total (incl. others)	230,294	428,703	1,776,653
USSR (former)†	153,830	274,422	1,144,481
Other countries	76,463	154,281	632,172

Exports	1997	1998	1999
Industrial products	189,810	356,406	1,535,208
Petroleum and gas	15,813	18,231	132,129
Metallurgy	15,475	31,449	106,017
Chemical and petroleum products	40,440	79,765	353,885
Machinery and metalworking	64,957	112,490	534,713
Wood and paper products	13,732	25,711	103,565
Construction materials	4,809	7,837	40,800
Light industry	18,289	35,042	147,838
Food and beverages	14,599	31,672	110,214
Total (incl. others)	193,084	364,260	1,574,700
USSR (former)†	142,583	255,664	968,077
Other countries	50,501	108,596	606,623

* Figures relating to trade with Russia are compiled from enterprise surveys, while data on trade with other countries are calculated on the basis of customs declarations.

† Excluding trade with Estonia, Latvia and Lithuania.

Source: IMF, *Republic of Belarus: Recent Economic Developments and Selected Issues* (November 2000).

PRINCIPAL TRADING PARTNERS

Trade with the former USSR (excluding trade with Estonia, Latvia and Lithuania; million roubles at domestic prices)*

Imports c.i.f.	1996	1997	1998
Kazakhstan	762,711	1,525,869	1,513,100
Moldova	649,962	1,581,235	2,479,400
Russia	47,142,914	124,082,200	233,201,000
Ukraine	12,174,038	25,113,457	37,154,500
Uzbekistan	493,672	841,644	1,961,400
Total (incl. others)	61,430,171	153,830,400	277,517,600

Exports f.o.b.	1996	1997	1998
Kazakhstan	1,103,172	1,416,576	2,705,600
Moldova	920,260	1,646,513	3,185,400
Russia	39,953,600	126,763,100	229,083,200
Ukraine	6,378,435	11,181,745	21,082,400
Uzbekistan	1,020,625	796,466	995,000
Total (incl. others)	49,774,300	142,583,100	259,282,200

* Figures relating to trade with Russia are compiled from enterprise surveys, while data on trade with other countries are calculated on the basis of customs declarations.

Trade with Other Countries (US $ million)*

Imports	1996	1997	1998
Europe	1,947	2,266	2,423
Austria	54	63	61
Germany	601	691	758
Poland	195	250	283
Switzerland . . .	38	42	49
USA	152	138	125
Total (incl. others) . . .	2,369	2,872	2,995

Exports	1996	1997	1998
Europe	1,316	1,176	1,238
Austria	15	16	20
Germany	198	217	200
Italy	57	64	73
Poland	338	246	185
Switzerland . . .	20	21	8
Turkey	30	33	27
USA	84	93	103
Total (incl. others) . . .	1,889	1,922	1,910

* Figures are calculated on the basis of customs declarations.

1999 (US $ million): *Imports c.i.f.:* Germany 693; Poland 213; Russia 3,767; Ukraine 416; Total (incl. others) 6,674. *Exports f.o.b.:* Germany 215; Poland 208; Russia 3,222; Ukraine 281; Total (incl. others) 5,909. Source: IMF, *Republic of Belarus: Recent Economic Developments and Selected Issues* (November 2000).

Transport

RAILWAYS (traffic)

	1996	1997	1998
Passenger-km (million) . .	11,657	12,909	13,268
Freight ton-km (million) . .	26,018	30,636	30,370

ROAD TRAFFIC (motor vehicles in use at 31 December)

	1996	1997	1998
Passenger cars	1,035,750	1,132,843	1,279,208
Buses and coaches . . .	8,922	8,867	8,768

CIVIL AVIATION (traffic on scheduled services)

	1996	1997	1998
Passengers carried ('000) . .	362	327	274
Passenger-km (million) . .	1,085	910	729
Total ton-km (million) . .	123	84	12

Tourism

ARRIVALS BY NATIONALITY

	1996	1997	1998
Germany	12,740	12,155	15,822
Italy	5,004	4,916	7,030
Latvia	4,078	3,969	4,610
Lithuania	6,747	5,870	8,652
Moldova	2,359	1,866	4,308
Poland	30,216	9,802	12,955
Russia	112,678	145,018	211,171
Ukraine	15,115	15,183	29,129
United Kingdom . . .	9,024	10,095	11,182
USA	6,870	8,218	8,358
Total (incl. others) . . .	234,226	254,023	355,342

Tourism receipts (US $ million): 55 in 1996; 25 in 1997.

Source: World Tourism Organization, *Yearbook of Tourism Statistics.*

Communications Media

	1996	1997	1998
Telephones ('000 main lines in use)	2,128	2,313	2,490
Telefax stations (number in use) .	12,259	15,610	19,466
Book production*:			
titles	3,809	5,331	6,073
copies ('000) . . .	59,073	67,632	60,022
Daily newspapers:			
number	12	19	20
average circulation ('000) . .	1,261	1,437	1,559
Non-daily newspapers:			
number	500	539	560
average circulation ('000) . .	7,825	7,824	8,973
Other periodicals:			
number	269	302	318
average circulation ('000) . .	1,424	1,647	1,687

* Including pamphlets (1,015 titles and 16,789,000 copies in 1996).

Mobile cellular telephones (subscribers): 5,897 in 1995; 6,548 in 1996; 8,167 in 1997 (Source: UN, *Statistical Yearbook*).

Radio receivers ('000 in use): 3,031 in 1995; 3,021 in 1996; 3,020 in 1997.

Television receivers ('000 in use): 3,139 in 1995; 3,040 in 1996; 2,520 in 1997 (Source: partly UNESCO, *Statistical Yearbook*).

Education

(1998/99)

	Institutions	Teachers	Students
Pre-primary	4,483	53,700	416,700
Primary (Grades 1–4) . . }	4,796	149,600	1,601,600
Secondary (Grades 5–11) . . }			
Vocational and technical . .	249	14,000	130,700
Specialized secondary . .	157	12,400	138,400
Higher	58	18,500	244,000
Institutions offering post-graduate studies . . .	103	2,600	4,400

Directory

The Constitution

A new Constitution came into effect on 30 March 1994. An amended version of the 1994 Constitution became effective on 27 November 1996, following a referendum held on 24 November. The following is a summary of its main provisions:

PRINCIPLES OF THE CONSTITUTIONAL SYSTEM

The Republic of Belarus is a unitary, democratic, social state based on the rule of law. The people are the sole source of state power and the repository of sovereignty in the Republic of Belarus. The people shall exercise their power directly through representative and other bodies in the forms and within the bounds specified by the Constitution. Democracy in the Republic of Belarus is exercised on the basis of diversity of political institutions, ideologies and opinions. State power in the Republic of Belarus is exercised on the principle of division of powers between the legislature, executive and judiciary, which are independent of one another. The Republic of Belarus is bound by the principle of supremacy of law; it recognizes the supremacy of the universally acknowledged principles of international law and ensures that its laws comply with such principles. Property may be the ownership of the State or private. The mineral wealth, waters and forests are the sole and exclusive property of the State. Land for agricultural use is the property of the State. All religions and creeds are equal before the law. The official languages of the Republic of Belarus are Belarusian and Russian. The Republic of Belarus aims to make its territory a neutral, nuclear-free state. The capital is Minsk.

THE INDIVIDUAL, SOCIETY AND THE STATE

All persons are equal before the law and entitled without discrimination to equal protection of their rights and legitimate interests. Every person has the right to life. Until its abolition, the death penalty may be applied in accordance with the verdict of a court of law as an exceptional penalty for especially grave crimes. The State ensures the freedom, inviolability and dignity of the individual. No person may be subjected to torture or cruel, inhuman or humiliating treatment or punishment. Freedom of movement is guaranteed. Every person is guaranteed freedom of opinion and beliefs and their free expression. The right to assemble publicly is guaranteed, as is the right to form public associations, including trade unions. Citizens of the Republic of Belarus have the right to participate in the solution of state matters, both directly and through freely elected representatives; the right to vote freely and to be elected to state bodies on the basis of universal, equal, direct or indirect suffrage by secret ballot. The State shall create the conditions necessary for full employment. The right to health care is guaranteed, as is the right to social security in old age, in the event of illness, disability and in other instances. Each person has the right to housing and to education. Everyone has the right to preserve his or her ethnic affiliation, to use his or her native language and to choose the language of communication. Payment of statutory taxes and other levies is obligatory. Every person is guaranteed the protection of his or her rights and freedom by a competent, independent and impartial court of law, and every person has the right to legal assistance.

THE ELECTORAL SYSTEM AND REFERENDUMS

Elections and referendums are conducted by means of universal, free, equal and secret ballot. Citizens of the Republic of Belarus who have reached the age of 18 years are eligible to vote. Deputies are elected by direct ballot. Referendums may be held to resolve the most important issues of the State and society. National referendums may be called by the President of the Republic of Belarus, by the National Assembly or by no fewer than 450,000 citizens eligible to vote. Local referendums may be called by local representative bodies or on the recommendation of no less than 10% of the citizens who are eligible to vote and resident in the area concerned. Decisions adopted by referendum may be reversed or amended only by means of another referendum.

THE PRESIDENT

The President of the Republic of Belarus is Head of State, the guarantor of the Constitution of the Republic of Belarus, and of the rights and freedoms of its citizens. The President is elected for a term of five years by universal, free, equal, direct and secret ballot for no more than two terms.

The President calls national referendums; calls elections to the National Assembly and local representative bodies; dissolves the chambers of the National Assembly, as determined by the Constitution; appoints six members to the Central Electoral Commission; forms, dissolves and reorganizes the Administration of the President, as well as other bodies of state administration; appoints the Chairman of the Cabinet of Ministers (Prime Minister) of the Republic of Belarus with the consent of the House of Representatives; determines the structure of the Government, appoints and dismisses Ministers and other members of the Government, and considers the resignation of the Government; appoints, with the consent of the Council of the Republic, the Chairman of the Constitutional, Supreme and Economic Courts, the judges of the Supreme and Economic Courts, the Chairman of the Central Electoral Commission, the Procurator General, the Chairman and members of the board of the National Bank, and dismisses the aforementioned, having notified the Council of the Republic; appoints six members of the Constitutional Court, and other judges of the Republic of Belarus; appoints and dismisses the Chairman of the State Supervisory Committee; reports to the people of the Republic of Belarus on the state of the nation and on domestic and foreign policy; may chair meetings of the Government of the Republic of Belarus; conducts negotiations and signs international treaties, appoints and recalls diplomatic representatives of the Republic of Belarus; in the event of a natural disaster, a catastrophe or unrest involving violence or the threat of violence that may endanger people's lives or jeopardize the territorial integrity of the State, declares a state of emergency; has the right to abolish acts of the Government and to suspend decisions of local councils of deputies; forms and heads the Security Council of the Republic of Belarus, and appoints and dismisses the Supreme State Secretary of the Security Council; is the Commander-in-Chief of the Armed Forces and appoints and dismisses the Supreme Command of the Armed Forces; imposes, in the event of military threat or attack, martial law in the Republic of Belarus; issues decrees and orders which are mandatory in the Republic of Belarus. In instances determined by the Constitution, the President may issue decrees which have the force of law. The President may be removed from office for acts of state treason and other grave crimes, by a decision of the National Assembly.

THE NATIONAL ASSEMBLY

The National Assembly is a representative and legislative body of the Republic of Belarus, consisting of two chambers: the House of Representatives and the Council of the Republic. The term of the National Assembly is four years. The House of Representatives comprises 110 deputies. Deputies are elected by universal, equal, free, direct suffrage and by secret ballot. The Council of the Republic is a chamber of territorial representation with 64 members, consisting of eight deputies from every region and from Minsk, elected by deputies of local councils. Eight members of the Council of the Republic are appointed by the President. Any citizen who has reached the age of 21 years may become a deputy of the House of Representatives. Any citizen who has reached the age of 30 years, and who has been resident in the corresponding region for no less than five years, may become a member of the Council of the Republic. The chambers of the National Assembly elect their Chairmen.

The House of Representatives considers draft laws concerning amendments and alterations to the Constitution; domestic and foreign policy; the military doctrine; ratification and denunciation of international treaties; the approval of the republican budget; the introduction of national taxes and levies; local self-government; the administration of justice; the declaration of war and the conclusion of peace; martial law and a state of emergency; and the interpretation of laws. The House of Representatives calls elections for the presidency; grants consent to the President concerning the appointment of the Chairman of the Cabinet of Ministers; accepts the resignation of the President; together with the Council of the Republic, takes the decision to remove the President from office.

The Council of the Republic approves or rejects draft laws adopted by the House of Representatives; consents to appointments made by the President; elects six judges of the Constitutional Court and six members of the Central Electoral Commission; considers charges of treason against the President; takes the decision to remove the President from office; considers presidential decrees on the introduction of a state of emergency, martial law, and general or partial mobilization.

Any proposed legislation is considered initially in the House of Representatives and then in the Council of the Republic. On the proposal of the President, the House of Representatives and the Council of the Republic may adopt a law, delegating to him legislative powers to issue decrees which have the power of a law. However, he may not issue decrees making alterations or addenda to the Constitution or to policy laws.

THE GOVERNMENT

Executive power in the Republic of Belarus is exercised by the Cabinet of Ministers. The Government is accountable to the President and responsible to the National Assembly. The Chairman of the Cabinet of Ministers is appointed by the President with the consent of the House of Representatives. The Government of the Republic of Belarus formulates and implements domestic and foreign policy; submits the draft national budget to the President; and issues acts that have binding force.

THE JUDICIARY

Judicial authority in the Republic of Belarus is exercised by the courts. Justice is administered on the basis of adversarial proceedings and equality of the parties involved in the trial. Supervision of the constitutionality of enforceable enactments of the State is exercised by the Constitutional Court, which comprises 12 judges (six of whom are appointed by the President and six are elected by the Council of the Republic).

LOCAL GOVERNMENT AND SELF-GOVERNMENT

Citizens exercise local and self-government through local councils of deputies, executive and administrative bodies and other forms of direct participation in state and public affairs. Local councils of deputies are elected by citizens for a four-year term, and the heads of local executive and administrative bodies are appointed and dismissed by the President of the Republic of Belarus.

THE PROCURATOR'S OFFICE AND THE STATE SUPERVISORY COMMITTEE

The Procurator's office exercises supervision over the implementation of the law. The Procurator General is appointed by the President with the consent of the Council of the Republic, and is accountable to the President. The Supervisory Authority monitors the implementation of the national budget and the use of public property. The State Supervisory Committee is formed by the President, who appoints the Chairman.

APPLICATION OF THE CONSTITUTION AND THE PROCEDURE FOR AMENDING THE CONSTITUTION

The Constitution has supreme legal force. Amendments and supplements to the Constitution are considered by the chambers of the National Assembly on the initiative of the President, or of no fewer than 150,000 citizens of the Republic of Belarus who are eligible to vote. The Constitution may be amended or supplemented via a referendum.

The Government

HEAD OF STATE

President: ALYAKSANDR R. LUKASHENKA (took office 20 October 1994).

CABINET OF MINISTERS
(May 2001)

Chairman: ULADZIMIR YERMOSHIN.

First Deputy Chairman: ANDREY KABYAKOW.

Deputy Chairmen: ULADZIMIR ZAMYATALIN, VALERY KOKARAU, LEANID KOZIK, ALYAKSANDR PAPKOW, MIKHAIL DZYMCHUK, GENNADZ NOVITSKI.

Deputy Chairman and Minister of Foreign Affairs: MIKHAIL KHVASTOW.

Minister of Agriculture and Food: MIKHAIL I. RUSY.

Minister of Architecture and Construction: GENADZ F. KURACHKIN.

Minister of Culture: LEANID HULYAKA.

Minister of Defence: Lt-Gen. LEANID MALTSAW.

Minister of the Economy: ULADZIMIR SHYMAU.

Minister of Education: Prof. VASIL I. STRAZHAU.

Minister for Emergency Situations: VALERY P. ASTAPOU.

Minister of Entrepreneurship and Investments: ALYAKSANDR YU. SASONAU.

Minister of Finance: NIKOLAY P. KORBUT.

Minister of Forestry: VALYANTSIN P. ZORYN.

Minister of Fuel and Energy: VALYANTSIN V. GERASIMAU.

Minister of Health Care: IGAR ZELYANKEVICH.

Minister of Housing and Municipal Services: ALYAKSANDR MILKOTA.

Minister of Industry: ANATOL KHARLAP.

Minister of Internal Affairs: ULADZIMIR NAVUMAU.

Minister of Justice: GENADZ VARANTSOU.

Minister of Labour: IVAN LYAKH.

Minister for Natural Resources and Environmental Protection: LYAVONTSY KHAROUZYK.

Minister of Telecommunications and Information Technology: ULADZIMIR I. GANCHARENKA.

Minister for Social Protection: OLGA B. DARGEL.

Minister of Sports and Tourism: YAUGEN N. VORSIN.

Minister of State Property Management and Privatization: VASIL A. NOVAK.

Minister of Statistics and Analysis: VLADIMIR I. ZINOVSKY.

Minister of Trade: PYOTR A. KAZLOU.

Minister of Transport and Communications: ALYAKSANDR LUKASHOU.

Presidential Administrator of Affairs: HALINA ZHURAWKOVA.

Chairmen of State Committees

Chairman of the State Security Committee: LEANID YERYN.

Chairman of the State Committee for the Press: ZINOVI PRYGODZICH (acting).

Chairman of the State Committee for Aviation: RYGOR FYODARAW.

Chairman of the State Committee for Youth Affairs: ALYAKSANDR PAZNYAK.

Chairman of the State Customs Committee: VIKENTSI MAKAREVICH (acting).

Chairman of the State Taxation Committee: MIKALAY DZYAMCHUK.

Chairman of the State Committee for Border Troops: ALYAKSANDR PAWLOUWKI.

Chairman of the State Committee for Land Resources, Geodesy and Cartography: GEORGIY KUZNYATSOW.

Chairman of the State Committee for Energy and Energy Supervision: LEW DUBOVIK.

Chairman of the State Committee for Archives and Records: ALYAKSANDR MIKHALCHANKA.

Chairman of the State Patents Committee: VALERY KUDASHOW.

Chairman of the State Committee for Standardization, Metrology and Certification: VALERY KARASHKOW.

Chairman of the State Committee for Hydrometeorology: YURY PAKUMEYKA.

Chairman of the State Higher Appraisal Committee: ANATOL DASTANKA.

Chairman of the State Committee for Science and Technology: VIKTAR GAYSYONAK.

Chairman of the State Committee for Religious and Ethnic Affairs: ALYAKSANDR BELYK.

Chairman of the State Control Committee: ANATOL TOZIK.

Chairman of the State Committee for Material Resources: ULADZIMIR I. YARMOLIK.

MINISTRIES AND STATE COMMITTEES
Ministries

Office of the President: 220016 Minsk, vul. K. Marksa 38, Dom Urada; tel. (17) 229-33-13.

Cabinet of Ministers of the Republic of Belarus: 220010 Minsk, pl. Nezalezhnasti, Dom Urada; tel. (17) 222-69-05; fax (17) 222-66-65; e-mail contact@udsm.belpak.minsk.by; internet www .president.gov.by.

Ministry of Agriculture and Food: 220050 Minsk, vul. Kirava 15; tel. (17) 227-81-04; fax (17) 227-42-96; internet mshp.minsk.by.

Ministry of Architecture and Construction: 220048 Minsk, vul. Myasnikova 39; tel. (17) 227-26-42; fax (17) 220-74-24.

Ministry of Culture: 220600 Minsk, pr. Masherava 11; tel. (17) 223-75-74; fax (17) 223-85-15.

Ministry of Defence: 220003 Minsk, vul. Kamunistychnaya 1; tel. (17) 239-23-79; fax (17) 227-35-64.

Ministry of the Economy: 220050 Minsk, vul. Stankevicha 14; tel. (17) 222-60-48; fax (17) 222-63-35.

Ministry of Education: 220010 Minsk, vul. Savetskaya 9; tel. (17) 227-47-36; fax (17) 227-17-36; e-mail root@minedu.unibel.by; internet www.minedu.unibel.by.

Ministry for Emergency Situations: 220050 Minsk, vul. Revolutsionnaya 5; tel. (17) 206-51-70; fax (17) 223-77-81; e-mail mcs@ infonet.by.

Ministry of Entrepreneurship and Investments: 220050 Minsk, vul. Myasnikova 39; tel. (17) 220-16-23; fax (17) 227-22-40.

Ministry of Finance: 220010 Minsk, vul. Savetskaya 7; tel. (17) 222-61-37; fax (17) 220-21-72; e-mail mofb@office.un.minsk .by; internet www.ncpi.gov.by/minfin.

Ministry of Foreign Affairs: 220030 Minsk, vul. Lenina 19; tel. (17) 227-29-22; fax (17) 227-45-21; internet www.mfa.gov.by.

Ministry of Forestry: 220039 Minsk, vul. Chkalova 6; tel. (17) 224-47-05; fax (17) 224-41-83.

Ministry of Fuel and Energy: 220050 Minsk, vul. K. Marksa 14; tel. (17) 229-83-59; fax (17) 229-84-68.

Ministry of Health Care: 220010 Minsk, vul. Myasnikova 39; tel. (17) 222-60-95; fax (17) 222-62-97.

Ministry of Housing and Municipal Services: 220640 Minsk, vul. Bersana 16; tel. (17) 220-15-45; fax (17) 220-38-94.

Ministry of Industry: 220033 Minsk, pr. Partizanski 2-4; tel. (17) 224-95-95; fax (17) 224-87-84; e-mail minproml@ntc.niievm .minsk.by; internet www.niievm.minsk.by/minprom/minprom.htm.

Ministry of Internal Affairs: 220615 Minsk, Gorodskoy Val 4; tel. (17) 229-78-08; fax (17) 223-99-18.

Ministry of Justice: 220048 Minsk, vul. Kalektarnaya 10; tel. and fax (17) 220-97-55; internet ncpi.gov.by/minjust.

Ministry of Labour: 220004 Minsk, pr. Masherava 23/2; tel. (17) 206-37-97; fax (17) 206-38-84; internet www.president.gov.by/min trud.

Ministry for Natural Resources and Environmental Protection: 220048 Minsk, vul. Kalektarnaya 10; tel. (17) 220-66-91; fax (17) 220-55-83; e-mail minproos@mail.belpak.minsk.by; internet www.president.gov.by/minpriroda/english.

Ministry for Social Protection: 220010 Minsk, vul. Savetskaya 9; tel. (17) 222-69-90; fax (17) 222-62-55.

Ministry of Sports and Tourism: 220600 Minsk, vul. Kirava 8-2; tel. (17) 227-72-37; fax (17) 227-76-22.

Ministry of State Property Management and Privatization: 220050 Minsk, vul. Myasnikova 39; tel. (17) 289-11-78; fax (17) 220-65-47; internet www.president.gov.by/rus/gosim/index.htm.

Ministry of Statistics and Analysis: 220070 Minsk, pr. Partizanski 12; tel. (17) 249-52-00; fax (17) 249-22-04; e-mail minstat@ mail.belpak.by; internet www.president.gov.by/rus/minstat/en/ main.html.

Ministry of Telecommunications and Information Technology: 220050 Minsk, pr. F. Skaryny 10; tel. (17) 227-38-61; fax (17) 226-08-48; e-mail mpt@belpak.by.

Ministry of Trade: 220050 Minsk, vul. Kirava 8, kor. 1; tel. (17) 227-08-97; fax (17) 227-24-80.

Ministry of Transport and Communications: 220029 Minsk, vul. Chicherina 21; tel. (17) 239-43-00; fax (17) 232-83-91; internet www.president.gov.by/mintorg/Mintorg_site/index.htm.

State Committees

All State Committees are in Minsk.

State Committee for Archives and Record Management: 220048 Minsk, vul. Kalektarnaya 10; tel. (17) 220-51-20; fax (17) 220-57-20; e-mail nosev@minsk.sovam.com; internet www.president .gov.by/gosarchives/earh/ekomitet.htm.

State Customs Committee: 220029 Minsk, vul. Kamunistychnaya 11; tel. (17) 233-23-16; fax (17) 234-68-93.

State Security Committee: 220050 Minsk, pr. F. Skaryny 17; tel. (17) 229-94-01; fax (17) 226-00-38.

State Committee for Religious and Ethnic Affairs: 220029 Minsk, vul. Kamunistychnaya 11A; tel. (17) 284-89-65; fax (17) 284-63-44; internet www.lingoo.minsk.by/kamitet.

President and Legislature

PRESIDENT

Presidential Election, First Ballot, 23 June 1994

Candidates							Votes	%
ALYAKSANDR LUKASHENKA							2,646,140	47.10
VYACHESLAU KEBICH	.	.	.	.	.		1,023,174	18.21
ZYANON PAZNYAK			.	.	.		757,195	13.48
STANISLAU SHUSHKEVICH		.	.	.	.		585,143	10.42
ALYAKSANDR DUBKO		.	.	.	.		353,119	6.29
VASIL NOVIKAU	.	.	.	.	.		253,009	4.50
Total	.	.	.	.	.	.	**5,617,780**	**100.00**

Second Ballot, 10 July 1994 (preliminary result)

Candidates							Votes	%
ALYAKSANDR LUKASHENKA		.	.	.	.		4,219,991	84.95
VYACHESLAU KEBICH	.	.	.	.	.		747,793	15.05
Total	.	.	.	.	.	.	**4,967,784**	**100.00**

NATIONAL ASSEMBLY*

Council of the Republic

Chairman: PAVEL SHYPUK.

Deputy Chairman: (vacant).

The Council of the Republic is the upper chamber of the legislature and comprises 64 deputies. Of the total, 56 deputies are elected by regional councils and eight deputies are appointed by the President.

House of Representatives

Chairman: ANATOL MALAFEYEU.

Deputy Chairman: ULADZIMIR KANAPLYOW.

The House of Representatives is the lower chamber of the legislature and comprises 110 deputies elected by universal, equal, free, direct electoral suffrage and by secret ballot. In the first round of voting in the legislative election of 15 October 2000, 41 seats were filled and 13 constituencies were declared invalid. A second round of voting for the remaining 56 seats took place on 29 October. Owing to the high incidence of electoral violations, however, repeat elections in the invalid constituencies took place on 18 March 2001.

* The National Assembly was formed following a referendum held on 24 November 1996. Deputies who had been elected to the Supreme Council at the general election held in late 1995 were invited to participate in the new legislative body. However, many deputies regarded the new National Assembly as unconstitutional and declared themselves to be the legitimate legislature. A form of 'shadow' cabinet, the Public Coalition Government—National Economic Council, chaired by Genadz Karpenka, was established in January 1997 by opposition deputies. Following Karpenka's death in April 1999, the chairmanship of the Council was assumed, in an acting capacity, by Mechislau Gryb (he was officially elected to the post in November). International organizations continued to urge President Lukashenka to recognize the legitimacy of the Supreme Council.

Political Organizations

Following the Government's imposition of stringent measures for re-registration in January 1999, in September of that year there were only 17 political parties officially registered with the Ministry of Justice (28 had previously been registered).

Agrarian Party (AP) (Agrarnaya Partya): 220050 Minsk, vul. Kazintsa 86-2; tel. (17) 220-38-29; fax (17) 249-50-18; f. 1992; Leader SYAMYON SHARETSKI.

Belarusian Christian-Democratic Party (Belaruskaya Khrystsiyanska-Demakratychnaya Partya): Minsk, vul. Bagdanovicha 7A; f. 1994; Leader MIKALAI KRUKOUSKI.

Belarusian Christian-Democratic Union (Belaruskaya Khrystsiyanska-Demakratychnaya Zluchnasts): 220065 Minsk, vul. Avakyana 38-59; tel. and fax (17) 229-67-56; f. 1991; nationalist, reformist; Leader PETR SILKO.

Belarusian Ecological Green Party: Minsk; f. 1998 by the merger of the Belarusian Ecological Party and the Green Party of Belarus.

Belarusian Greenpeace Party (Belaruskaya Partya Zyaleny Mir): 246023 Gomel, vul. Brestskaya 6; tel. (23) 247-08-08; fax (23) 247-96-96; f. 1994; Leaders OLEG GROMYKA, NICK LEKUNOVICH.

Belarusian National Party (Belaruskaya Natsiyanalnaya Partya): 220094 Minsk, vul. Plekhanava 32-198; tel. (17) 227-43-76; f. 1994; Leader ANATOL ASTAPENKA.

Belarusian Party of Labour (Belaruskaya Partya Pratsy): Minsk, vul. Kazintsa 21-3; tel. (17) 223-82-04; fax (17) 223-97-92; e-mail acmbel@glas.apc.org; f. 1993; Leader ALYAKSANDR BUKHVOSTAU.

Belarusian Party of Women 'Hope' (Belaruskaya Partya Zhanchyn 'Nadzeya'): 220126 Minsk, pr. Masherov 21; f. 1994; tel. (17) 223-89-57; fax (17) 223-90-40; e-mail zmn@sfpb.belpak.minsk.by; internet www.nadzeya.org; Pres. VALENTINA POLEVIKOVA.

Belarusian Patriotic Party (Belaruskaya Patryatychnaya Partya): Minsk; tel. (17) 220-27-57; f. 1994; Leader ANATOL BARANKEVICH.

Belarusian Peasant Party (Belaruskaya Syalyanskaya Partya): 220068 Minsk, vul. Gaya 38-1; tel. (17) 277-19-05; fax (17) 277-96-51; f. 1991; advocates agricultural reforms; 7,000 mems; Leader YAUGEN M. LUGIN.

Belarusian People's Patriotic Union: Minsk; f. 1998; a pro-Lukashenka alliance supportive of further integration with Russia, comprising 30 left-wing and centrist organizations, incl. the CPB, the Belarusian Patriotic Party, the Liberal Democratic Party of Belarus, the White Rus Slavonic Council and the Union of Reserve Officers; Exec. Sec. VIKTAR CHYKIN.

Belarusian Popular Party (Belaruskaya Narodnaya Partya): 220050 Minsk, vul. K. Marksa 18; tel. (17) 227-89-52; fax (17) 227-13-30; e-mail imi@imibel.belpak.minsk.by; f. 1994; Leader VIKTAR TERESCHENKO.

Belarusian Republican Party (Belaruskaya Respublikanskaya Partya): 220100 Minsk, vul. Kulman 13-71; tel. (17) 234-07-49; f. 1994; Leaders VALERY ARTYSHEUSKI, ULADZIMIR RAMANAU.

Belarusian Social Democratic Assembly (Belaruskaya Satsyal-demakratychnaya Hramada): 220035 Minsk, vul. Drozda 8-52; tel. and fax (17) 226-74-37; e-mail bsdg_minsk_region@hotmail.com; f. 1998; Leader STANISLAU SHUSHKEVICH.

Belarusian Social Democratic Party (National Assembly) (Belaruskaya Satsyal-demakratychnaya Partya—Narodnaya Hramada): 220114 Minsk, pr. F. Skaryny 153-2-107; tel. and fax (17) 263-37-48; e-mail bsdp@infonet.by; f. 1903, re-established 1991; merged with Party of People's Accord (f. 1992) in 1996; centrist; Leader MIKALAI STATKEVICH; c. 2,500 mems.

Belarusian Socialist Party (Belaruskaya Satsyalistychnaya Partya): Minsk; tel. (17) 229-37-38; f. 1994; aims for a civilized society, where rights and freedoms are guaranteed for all; Leader MICHAIL PADGAINY.

Belarusian Social-Sports Party (Belaruskaya Satsyalna-Spartyunaya Partya): 220000 Minsk, pr. Partizanski 89A; tel. (17) 226-93-15; f. 1994; Leader ULADZIMIR ALYAKSANDROVICH.

BPF—'Revival' (BPF—'Adradzhennye'): 220005 Minsk, vul. Varvasheni 8; tel. (17) 231-48-93; fax (17) 233-50-12; e-mail bpf@bpf.minsk.by; internet pages.prodigy.net/dr_fission/bpf/bpfhead.htm; fmrly the Belarusian Popular Front, name changed as above Dec. 1999; f. 1988; anti-communist movement campaigning for democracy, genuine independence for Belarus and national and cultural revival; Chair. VINTSUK VYACHORKA; Exec. Sec. ANATOL KRYVAROT.

>   **Conservative Christian Party of the BPF:** Minsk; f. 1999 as a breakaway faction of the BPF; Chair. ZYANON PAZNYAK; Dep. Chair. MIKALAI ANTSIPOVICH, YURIY BELENKI, SYARGEY PAPKOW, ULADZIMIR STARCHANKA.

Christian-Democratic Choice (Khrystsiyanska-Demakratychny Vybar): 220050 Minsk, vul. Leningradskaya 3-1; tel. (17) 237-28-86; f. 1995; Leader VALERY SAROKA.

Communist Party of Belarus (CPB) (Kamunistychnaya Partya Belarusi): 220007 Minsk, vul. Varanyanskaga 52; tel. (17) 226-64-22; fax (17) 232-31-23; Leader VIKTAR CHYKIN.

Liberal Democratic Party of Belarus (Liberalna-Demakratychnaya Partya Belarusi): 220056 Minsk, vul. Platonava 22, 12th Floor; tel. and fax (17) 231-63-31; e-mail ldpb@infonet.by; f. 1994; advocates continued independence of Belarus, increased co-operation with other European countries and expansion of the private sector; Leader SYARGEY GAYDUKEVICH; 30,986 mems (2000).

National Democratic Party of Belarus (Natsyanalna-Demakratychnaya Partya Belarusi): Minsk, vul. Labanka 97-140; tel. (17) 271-95-16; fax (17) 236-99-72; f. 1990; Leader VIKTAR NAVUMENKA.

Party of Common Sense (Partya Zdarovaga Sensu): 220094 Minsk, pr. Rakasouskaga 37-40; tel. (17) 247-08-68; f. 1994; Leader IVAN KARAVAYCHYK.

Party of Communists of Belarus (Partya Kamunistau Belaruskaya): 220013 Minsk, vul. Y. Kolas 10-8; tel. (17) 232-25-73; fax (17) 231-80-36; f. 1991; Leader SERGEY KALYAKIN.

Republican Party (Respublikanskaya Partya): 220000 Minsk, vul. Pershamayskaya 18; tel. (17) 236-50-71; fax (17) 236-32-14; f. 1994; aims to build a neutral, independent Belarus; Leader ULADZIMIR BELAZOR.

Republican Party of Labour and Justice (Respublikanskaya Partya Pratsy i Spravyadlivasti): 220004 Minsk, vul. Amuratarskaya 7; tel. (17) 223-93-21; fax (17) 223-86-41; f. 1993; Leader ANATOL NYATYLKIN.

Social-Democratic Party of Popular Accord (Satsiyal-Demakratychnaya Partya Narodnay Zgody): 220050 Minsk, vul. K. Marksa 10; tel. (17) 248-02-21; f. 1997; Leader LEANID SECHKA.

United Civic Party of Belarus (UCP) (Abyadnanaya Hramadzyanskaya Partya Belarusi): 220033 Minsk, vul. Sudmalisa 10-4; tel. (17) 229-08-34; fax (17) 227-29-12; e-mail ucp@ucp.minsk.by; f. 1990; liberal-conservative; Chair. STANISLAU A. BAHDANKEVICH; Dep. Chair. ALYAKSANDR A. DABRAVOLSKI, VASILY SHLYNDZIKAV, ANATOL U. LIABEDZKA.

White Rus Slavonic Council (Slavyanski Sabor 'Belaya Rus'): 220088 Minsk, vul. Pershamayskaya 24-1-80; tel. (17) 239-52-32; fax (17) 270-09-28; f. 1992; Leader MIKALAY SYARGEEU.

Diplomatic Representation

EMBASSIES IN BELARUS

Armenia: 220050 Minsk, vul. Kirava 17; tel. and fax (17) 227-51-53; Ambassador: SUREN HAROUTUNIAN.

Bulgaria: 220034 Minsk, Branyavy per. 5; tel. (17) 227-55-02; fax (17) 236-56-61; Chargé d'affaires a.i.: VASIL PETKOV.

China, People's Republic: 220071 Minsk, vul. Berestyanskaya 22; tel. (17) 285-36-82; fax (17) 285-36-81; e-mail zbesg@belsonet.net; Ambassador: WU XIAOQUI.

Cuba: 220050 Minsk, pr. Skaryny 11, Hotel Minsk, Room 389; tel. (17) 220-03-83; fax (17) 220-23-45; Chargé d'affaires a.i.: JOSÉ FERNÁNDEZ.

Czech Republic: 220034 Minsk, Branyavy per. 5A; tel. (17) 226-52-43; fax (17) 211-01-37; Chargé d'affaires a.i.: ALES FOJTIK.

France: 220030 Minsk, pl. Svabody 11; tel. (17) 210-28-68; fax (17) 210-25-48; Ambassador: BERNARD FASSIER.

Germany: 220034 Minsk, vul. Zakharava 26B; tel. (17) 213-37-52; fax (17) 236-85-52; Ambassador: HORST WINKELMANN.

Greece: 220030 Minsk, vul. Engelsa 13, Hotel Oktyabrskaya, Room 515; tel. (17) 227-27-60; fax (17) 226-08-05; Ambassador: PANAYOTIS GOUMAS.

Holy See: Minsk, vul. Volodarsky 6, 3rd Floor; tel. (17) 289-15-84; fax (17) 289-15-17; Apostolic Nuncio: Most Rev. DOMINIK HRUŠOVSKÝ, Titular Archbishop of Tubia.

India: 220090 Minsk, vul. Kaltsova 4, kor. 5; tel. (17) 262-93-99; fax (17) 262-97-99; e-mail ambsdr@indemb.minsk.by; Ambassador: MADHU BHADURI.

Israel: 220033 Minsk, pr. Partizanski 6A; tel. (17) 230-44-44; fax (17) 210-52-70; Ambassador: MARTIN PELED-FLAX.

Italy: 220030 Minsk, vul. K. Marksa 37, Hotel Belarus; tel. (17) 229-29-69; fax (17) 234-30-46; e-mail ambitminsk@belsonet.net; Ambassador: GIOVANNI CERUTI.

Japan: 220030 Minsk, vul. Engelsa 13, Hotel Oktyabrskaya, Room 303; tel. (17) 223-60-37; fax (17) 210-41-80; Chargé d'affaires a.i.: NAOTAKE YAMASHITA.

Kazakhstan: 220029 Minsk, vul. Kuibysheva 12; tel. (17) 234-99-37; fax (17) 234-96-50; e-mail tem@kazemb.belpak.minsk.by; Ambassador: VLADIMIR ALESIN.

Kyrgyzstan: 220002 Minsk, vul. Staravilenskaya 57; tel. (17) 234-91-17; fax (17) 234-16-02; e-mail manas@nsys.minsk.by; Chargé d'affaires a.i.: BUBUIRA ABDYJAPAROVA.

Latvia: 220013 Minsk, vul. Doroshevicha 6A; tel. (17) 284-93-93; fax (17) 284-73-34; e-mail daile@belsonet.net; Ambassador: EGONS NEIMANIS.

Lithuania: 220088 Minsk, vul. Zakharova 68; tel. (17) 285-24-48; fax (17) 285-33-37; e-mail lt.embassy@belsonet.net; Ambassador: JONAS PASLAUSKAS.

Moldova: 220030 Minsk, vul. Belaruskaya 2; tel. (17) 289-14-41; fax (17) 289-11-47; Ambassador: NIKOLAE DUDAU.

Peru: 220082 Minsk, vul. Pritytskogo 34; tel.(17) 216-91-14; fax (17) 283-28-62.

Poland: 220034 Minsk, vul. Rumyantsava 6; tel. (17) 213-43-13; fax (17) 236-49-92; Ambassador: MARIUSZ MASZKIEWICZ.

Romania: 220035 Minsk, per. Moskvina 4; tel. (17) 223-77-26; fax (17) 210-40-85; Chargé d'affaires a.i.: LEONTIN PASTOR.

Russian Federation: 220002 Minsk, vul. Staravilenskaya 48; tel. (17) 234-54-97; fax (17) 250-36-64; e-mail karp@rusamb.belpak.minsk.by; Ambassador: VYACHESLAV DOLGOV.

Tajikistan: 220050 Minsk, vul. Kirava 17; tel. (17) 222-37-98; fax (17) 227-76-13; Chargé d'affaires: OLIM RAKHIMOV.

Turkey: 220050 Minsk, vul. Volodarsky 6, 4th Floor; tel. (17) 227-13-83; fax (17) 227-27-46; e-mail dtmin@comco.belpak.minsk.by; Ambassador: SULE SOYSAL.

Turkmenistan: 220050 Minsk, vul. Kirava 17; tel. (17) 222-34-27; fax (17) 222-33-67; Ambassador: ILYA VELDJANOV.

Ukraine: 220050 Minsk, vul. Kirava 17; tel. (17) 227-23-54; fax (17) 227-28-61; e-mail postmaster@am.minsk.mfa.ua; Ambassador: ANATOLII DRON.

United Kingdom: 220030 Minsk, vul. K. Marksa 37; tel. (17) 210-59-20; fax (17) 229-23-06; e-mail pia@bepost.belpak.minsk.by; Ambassador: IAIN KELLY.

USA: 220002 Minsk, vul. Staravilenskaya 46; tel. (17) 210-12-83; fax (17) 234-78-53; e-mail webmaster@usembassy.minsk.by; internet www.usis.minsk.by; Ambassador: MICHAEL KOZAK.

Yugoslavia: 220012 Minsk, vul. Surganova 28A; tel. (17) 239-90-90; fax (17) 232-51-54; e-mail embassies@smip.sv.gov.yu; Ambassador: NIKOLA PEJAKOVICH.

Judicial System

In May 1999 there were 154 courts in Belarus, employing some 200 judges.

Supreme Court: 220030 Minsk, vul. Lenina 28; tel. (17) 226-12-06; fax (17) 227-12-25; Chair. VALENTIN SUKALO; Dep. Chair. VALERII VYSHKEVICH.

Supreme Economic Court: 220050 Minsk, vul. Valadarskaga 8; tel. and fax (17) 227-16-41; Chair ULADZIMIR BOYKA.

Procuracy: 220050 Minsk, vul. Internatsionalnaya 22; tel. (17) 226-41-66; Procurator General VIKTAR SHEYMAN.

Constitutional Court: Minsk, vul. K. Marksa 32; tel. and fax (17) 227-80-12; e-mail ksrb@user.unibel.by; 12 mem. judges; Chair. RYHOR VASILEVICH; Dep. Chair. ALYAKSANDR MARYSKIN.

Religion

State Committee for Religious and Ethnic Affairs: see section on The Government.

CHRISTIANITY

The major denomination is the Eastern Orthodox Church, but there are also an estimated 1.1m. adherents of the Roman Catholic Church. Of these, some 25% are ethnic Poles and there is a significant number of Uniates or 'Greek Catholics'. There is also a growing number of Baptist churches.

The Eastern Orthodox Church

In 1990 Belarus was designated an exarchate of the Russian Orthodox Church, thus creating the Belarusian Orthodox Church.

Belarusian Orthodox Church: 220004 Minsk, vul. Osvobozhdeniya 10; tel. (17) 223-44-95; Patriarch and Exarch of All Belarus FILARET.

The Roman Catholic Church

Although five Roman Catholic dioceses, embracing 455 parishes, had officially existed since the Second World War, none of them had a bishop. In 1989 a major reorganization of the structure of the Roman Catholic Church in Belarus took place. The dioceses of Minsk and Mogilev (Mahilou) were merged, to create an archdiocese, and two new dioceses were formed, in Grodno (Horadnia) and Pinsk. The Eastern-rite, or Uniate, Church was abolished in Belarus in 1839, but was re-established in the early 1990s. At 31 December 1998 the Roman Catholic Church had an estimated 1.1m. adherents in Belarus.

Latin Rite

Archdiocese of Minsk and Mogilev: 220030 Minsk, pl. Svabody 9; tel. (17) 226-61-27; fax (17) 226-90-92; Archbishop Cardinal KAZIMIERZ SWIATEK.

Byzantine Rite

Belarusian Greek Catholic (Uniate) Church: 224014 Brest, vul. Dvornikova 63; tel. and fax (16) 224-74-82; e-mail bgkc_carkva@mail.ru; Dean Protopresbyter VIKTAR DANILAU.

Protestant Churches

Union of Evangelical Christian Baptists of Belarus: 220093 Minsk, POB 108; tel. (17) 253-92-67; fax (17) 253-82-49; e-mail beluecb@belsonet.net.

ISLAM

There are small communities of Azeris and Tatars, who are adherents of Islam. In 1994 the supreme administration of Muslims in Belarus, which had been abolished in 1939, was reconstituted. In mid-1998 there were some 4,000 Muslims and four mosques.

Muslim Society: 220004 Minsk, vul. Zaslavskaya 11, kor. 1, kv. 113; tel. (17) 226-86-43; f. 1991; Chair. ALI HALEMBEK.

JUDAISM

Before Belarus was occupied by Nazi German forces, in 1941–44, there was a large Jewish community, notably in Minsk. There were some 142,000 Jews at the census of 1989, but many have since emigrated.

Jewish Religious Society: 220030 Minsk, pr. F. Skaryny 44A.

The Press

In October 1998 there were a total of 1,001 registered periodicals in Belarus, of which 116 were in Belarusian and 295 in Russian, and 447 were in both Belarusian and Russian. Most daily newspapers are government-owned.

PRINCIPAL DAILIES

In Russian, except where otherwise stated.

Belorusskaya Niva (Belarusian Cornfield): 220013 Minsk, vul. B. Hmyalnitskaga 10A; tel. (17) 268-26-20; fax (17) 268-26-43; e-mail belniva@yandex.ru; internet belniva.chat.ru/; f. 1921; 5 a week; organ of the Council of Ministers; in Belarusian and Russian; Editor E. SEMASHKO; circ. 65,000 (2000).

Narodnaya Hazeta (The People's Newspaper): 220013 Minsk, vul. B. Hmyalnitskaga 10A; tel. (17) 268-28-70; fax (17) 268-25-29; e-mail info@ng.press.net.by; f. 1990; 5–6 a week; in Belarusian and Russian; Editor-in-Chief M. SHIMANSKIY; circ. 90,000 (2000).

Respublika (Republic): 220013 Minsk, vul. B. Hmyalnitskaga 10A; tel. (17) 268-26-12; fax (17) 268-26-15; e-mail info@republ .press.net.by; internet www.republ.press.net.by; 5 a week; in Belarusian and Russian; Editor SERGEY DUBOVIK; circ. 116,000 (2000).

Sovetskaya Belorussiya (Soviet Belorussia): 220013 Minsk, vul. B. Hmyalnitskaga 10A; tel. and fax (17) 232-14-32; e-mail admin@sb.press.net.by; internet sb.press.net.by; 5 a week; Editor-in-Chief PAVEL YAKUBOVICH; circ. 435,000 (2000).

Vechernii Minsk (Evening Minsk): 220805 Minsk, pr. F. Skaryny 44; tel. (17) 213-30-54; fax (17) 213-48-35; e-mail omp@nsys .minsk.by; internet www.belarus.net/minsk-evl; Editor S. SVERKUNOU; circ. 93,000 (2000).

Znamya Yunosti (Banner of Youth): 220013 Minsk, vul. B. Hmyalnitskaga 10A; tel. and fax (17) 268-26-84; f. 1938; 5 a week; organ of the Cabinet of Ministers; Editor-in-Chief ELENA PHILIPTCHIK; circ. 9,000 (2000).

Zvyazda (Star): 220013 Minsk, vul. B. Hmyalnitskaga 10A; tel. (17) 268-29-19; fax (17) 268-27-79; f. 1917 as *Zvezda*; 5 a week; organ of the Cabinet of Ministers; in Belarusian; Editor ULADZIMIR B. NARKEVICH; circ. 90,000 (1998).

PRINCIPAL PERIODICALS

In Belarusian, except where otherwise stated.

Advertisements Weekly: 220805 Minsk, pr. F. Skaryny 44; tel. and fax (17) 213-45-25; e-mail omp@bm.belpak.minsk.by; Editor T. ANANENKO; circ. 21,500 (1997).

Alesya: 220013 Minsk, pr. F. Skaryny 77; tel. and fax (17) 232-20-51; f. 1924; monthly; Editor MARYA KARPENKA; circ. 17,000 (1998).

Belarus: 220005 Minsk, vul. Zakharava 19, tel. (17) 284-80-01; f. 1930; monthly; publ. by the State Publishing House; journal of the Union of Writers of Belarus and the Belarusian Society of Friendship and Cultural Links with Foreign Countries; fiction and political essays; in Belarusian, English and Russian; Editor-in-Chief A. A. SHABALIN.

Belaruskaya Krinitsa: 220065 Minsk, vul. Avakyana 38-59; tel. and fax (17) 229-67-56; f. 1991; monthly; journal of the Belarusian Institute of Social Development and Co-operation; Editor-in-Chief MIKHAIL MALKO; circ. 5,000.

Byarozka (Birch Tree): 220013 Minsk, pr. F. Skaryny 77; tel. (17) 232-94-66; f. 1924; monthly; fiction; illustrated; for 10–15-year-olds; Editor-in-Chief VL. I. JAGOVDZIK.

Chyrvonaya Zmena (Red Rising Generation): 220013 Minsk, vul. B. Hmyalnitskaga 10A; tel. and fax (17) 232-21-03; e-mail czm@mail.ru; internet czm.press.net.by; f. 1921; weekly; Editor A. KARLUKIEVICH; circ. 5,000 (2000).

Gramadzyanin: Minsk; tel. (17) 229-08-34; fax (17) 272-95-05; publ. by the United Civic Party of Belarus.

Holas Radzimy (Voice of the Motherland): 220005 Minsk, pr. F. Skaryny 44; tel. (17) 213-37-82; f. 1955; weekly; articles of interest to Belarusians in other countries; Editor-in-Chief NATALIA SALUK.

Krynitsa (Spring): 220807 Minsk, vul. Kiseleva 11; tel. (17) 236-60-71; fax (17) 236-61-42; e-mail www.krynitsa@open.by; f. 1988; monthly; literary and cultural; in Belarusian; Editor ALA KANAPELKA.

Litaratura i Mastatstva (Literature and Art): 220005 Minsk, vul. Zakharava 19; tel. (17) 284-84-61; f. 1932; weekly; publ. by the Ministry of Culture and the Union of Writers of Belarus; Editor ALYAKSANDR PISMENKOV; circ. 5,000 (1998).

Maladosts (Youth): 220013 Minsk, vul. B. Hmyalnitskaga 10A; tel. (17) 268-27-54; f. 1953; monthly; journal of the Union of Writers of Belarus; novels, short stories, essays, translations, etc., for young people; Editor-in-Chief G. DALIDOVICH.

Mastatstva (Art): 220029 Minsk, vul. Chicherina 1; tel. (17) 276-94-67; fax (17) 276-94-67; e-mail masta@ibamedia.com; monthly; illustrated; Editor-in-Chief ALYAKSEY DUDARAU.

Narodnaya Asveta (People's Education): 220023 Minsk, vul. Makaenka 12; tel. (17) 264-62-68; f. 1924; publ. by the Ministry of Education; Editor-in-Chief N. I. KALESNIK.

Neman (The River Nieman): 220005 Minsk, pr. F. Skaryny 39; tel. (17) 213-40-72; fax (17) 213-44-61; f. 1945; monthly; publ. by the

Polymya (Flame) Publishing House; journal of the Union of Writers of Belarus; fiction; in Russian; Editor-in-Chief A. ZHOUK.

Polymya (Flame): 220005 Minsk, vul. Zakharava 19; tel. (17) 284-80-12; f. 1922; monthly; publ. by the Polymya (Flame) Publishing House; journal of the Union of Writers of Belarus; fiction; Editor-in-Chief S. I. ZAKONNIKOU.

Vozhyk (Hedgehog): 220013 Minsk, pr. F. Skaryny 77; tel. and fax (17) 232-12-40; f. 1941; fortnightly; satirical; Editor-in-Chief MIKHAIL POZDNYAKOV; circ. 12,000 (1998).

Vyaselka (Rainbow): 220617 Minsk, vul. Kalektarnaya 10; tel. (17) 220-92-61; fax (17) 236-62-67; f. 1957; monthly; popular; for 5–10-year-olds; Editor-in-Chief V. S. LIPSKI; circ. 30,000 (1999).

PRESS ASSOCIATIONS

Belarusian Association of Journalists: Minsk; tel. (17) 227-05-58; internet www.baj.unibel.by; f. 1995; Pres. ZHANNA LITVINA.

Belarusian Union of Journalists: 220005 Minsk, vul. Rumyantsava 3; tel. and fax (17) 236-51-95; 3,000 mems; Pres. L. EKEL.

NEWS AGENCY

BelTa (Belarusian News Agency): 220600 Minsk, vul. Kirava 26; tel. (17) 222-30-40; fax (17) 227-13-46; Dir YAKAU ALAKSEYCHYK.

Publishers

In 1998 there were 6,073 titles (books and pamphlets) published in Belarus (60m. copies).

Belarus: 220600 Minsk, pr. F. Skaryny 79; tel. (17) 223-87-42; fax (17) 223-87-31; f. 1921; social, political, technical, medical and musical literature, fiction, children's, reference books, art reproductions, etc.; Dir MIKALAY KAVALEVSKI; Editor-in-Chief ELENA ZAKONNIKOVA.

Belaruskaya Entsiklopediya (Belarusian Encyclopaedia): 220072 Minsk, vul. Akademicheskaya 15A; tel. (17) 284-17-67; fax (17) 284-09-83; f. 1967; encyclopaedias, dictionaries, directories and scientific books; Editor-in-Chief G. P. PASHKOV.

Belaruskaya Navuka (Science and Technology Publishing House): 220067 Minsk, vul. Zhodinskaya 18; tel. (17) 263-76-18; f. 1924; scientific, technical, reference books, educational literature and fiction in Belarusian and Russian; Dir LUDMILA PIETROVA.

Belaruski Dom Druku (Belarusian House of Printing): 220013 Minsk, pr. F. Skaryny 79; tel. (17) 268-27-03; fax (17) 231-67-74; f. 1917; social, political, children's and fiction in Belarusian, Russian and other European languages; Dir BARYS KUTAVY.

Belblankavyd: 220035 Minsk, vul. Timirazeva 2; tel. (17) 226-71-22; reference books in Belarusian and Russian; Dir VALENTINA MILOVANOVA.

Mastatskaya Litaratura (Art Publishing House): 220600 Minsk, pr. Masherava 11; tel. (17) 223-48-09; f. 1972; fiction in Belarusian and Russian; Dir GEORGE MARCHUK.

Narodnaya Asveta (People's Education Publishing House): 220600 Minsk, pr. Masherava 11; tel. and fax (17) 223-61-84; e-mail igpna@asveta.belpak.minsk.by; f. 1951; scientific, educational, reference literature and fiction in Belarusian, Russian and other European languages; Dir IGAR N. LAPTSYONAK.

Polymya (Flame Publishing House): 220600 Minsk, pr. Masherava 11; tel. and fax (17) 223-52-85; f. 1950; social, political, scientific, technical, religious, children's and fiction; Dir MIKHAIL A. IVANOVICH.

Universitetskae (University Publishing House): 220048 Minsk, pr. Masherava 11; tel. (17) 223-58-51; fax (17) 223-90-92; e-mail belabb@infonet.by; f. 1967; scientific, educational, art and reference; Dir ALYAKSANDR NECHAY.

Uradzhay (Harvest Publishing House): 220048 Minsk, pr. Masherava 11; tel. (17) 223-64-94; fax (17) 223-80-23; f. 1961; scientific, technical, educational, books and booklets on agriculture; in Belarusian and Russian; Dir YAUGEN MALASHEVICH.

Vysheyshaya Shkola (Higher School Publishing House): 220048 Minsk, pr. Masherava 11; tel. and fax (17) 223-54-15; f. 1954; textbooks and science books for higher educational institutions; in Belarusian, Russian and other European languages; Dir ANATOL A. ZHADAN; Editor-in-Chief T. K. MAIBORODA.

Yunatstva (Youth Publishing House): 220600 Minsk, pr. Masherava 11; tel. (17) 223-24-30; fax (17) 223-31-16; f. 1981; fiction and children's books; Dir ALYAKSANDR KOMAROVSKY; Vice Dir MIKHAIL POZDNIAKOV.

Broadcasting and Communications

TELECOMMUNICATIONS

Belcel: 22005 Minsk, vul. Zolotaya Gorka 5; tel. (17) 276-01-00; fax (17) 276-03-33; e-mail belcel@cpen.minsk.by; internet www.cplc

.com/business/euremaf/eastern/units; 50% owned by Cable and Wireless (United Kingdom); mobile telecommunications services; Gen. Man ULADZIMIR GETMANOV.

Beltelecom: 220030 Minsk, vul. Engelsa 6; tel. (17) 226-05-81; fax (17) 227-44-22; e-mail vtv@inmac.belpak.minsk.by; internet 194.226.125.34/beltelecom/beltelecom.eng/index.html; f. 1995; national telecommunications operator; Dir-Gen. VASILY T. VOLOSHCHUK.

BROADCASTING

National State Television and Radio Company of Belarus: 220807 Minsk, vul. A. Makayenka 9; tel. (17) 264-75-05; fax (17) 264-81-82; internet www.tvr.by; Chair. RYGOR KISEL.

Belarusian Television: 220807 Minsk, vul. A. Makayenka 9; tel. (17) 233-45-01; fax (17) 264-81-82; f. 1956; Pres. A. R. SITYLAROU.

Belarusian Radio: 220807 Minsk, vul. Chyrvonaya 4; tel. (17) 233-39-22; fax (17) 236-66-43; Gen. Dir A. S. ULASENKA.

Television

Television Broadcasting Network (TBN): 220072 Minsk, pr. F. Skaryny 15A; tel. and fax (17) 239-41-71; e-mail mmc@glas.apc.org; comprises 12 private television cos in Belarus's largest cities.

Minsk Television Company: Minsk; private; broadcasts to the CIS, Western Europe and North America.

A second national television channel, BT-2, was to be established in 1997. It was to use networks used by Public Russian Television (Obshchestvennoye Rossiiskoye Televideniye—ORT) and was expected to commence broadcasting by 2000.

Finance

(cap. = capital; dep. = deposits; res = reserves; m. = million; brs = branches; amounts in new Belarusian roubles, unless otherwise indicated)

BANKING

After Belarus gained its independence, the Soviet-style banking system was restructured and a two-tier system was introduced. In mid-2000 there were 28 universal commercial banks operating in Belarus.

Central Bank

National Bank of Belarus: 220008 Minsk, pr. F. Skaryny 20; tel. (17) 227-64-31; fax (17) 227-48-79; e-mail nbrb@nbrb.belpak .minsk.by; f. 1990; cap. 41,673.9m. readjusted roubles (Dec. 2000), res 5,517,686m., dep. 18,185,469m. (Dec. 1997); Chair. PYOTR PRAKAPOVICH; 6 brs.

Commercial Banks

Absolutbank: 220023 Minsk, pr. F. Skaryny 115; tel. (17) 264-24-43; fax (17) 264-60-43; f. 1993; cap. 39,234m. (Dec. 1997); Chair. DANIIL P. SVIRID; 1 br.

Bank for Foreign Economic Affairs (Belvneshekonombank—BVEB): 220050 Minsk, vul. Myasnikova 32; tel. (17) 238-11-10; fax (17) 226-48-09; e-mail chernik@bveb.belpak.minsk.by; f. 1991; cap. 401,600m., res 6,699,515m., dep. 60,320,764m. (Dec. 1999); Chair. GEORGIY YEGOROV; 23 brs.

Bank Poisk: 220009 Minsk, vul. Gamarnik 9/4; tel. (17) 228-32-49; fax (17) 228-32-48; f. 1974 (as a regional branch of Gosbank of the USSR); renamed Housing and Communal Bank (Zhilsotsbank) in 1989; present name adopted in 1992; cap. 171,820m., res 323,590m., dep. 3,896,172m. (Dec. 1998); Chair. ALGERDAS N. TABATADZE; 17 brs.

Belarusbank: 220050 Minsk, vul. Myasnikova 32; tel. (17) 220-91-16; fax (17) 226-47-50; e-mail info@belarusbank.minsk.by; internet www.belarusbank.minsk.by; f. 1995 following merger with Sberbank (Savings Bank; f. 1926); cap. 786,018m., res 1,299,329m., dep. 105,195,823m. (Dec. 1998); Chair. NADEZHDA A. YERMAKOVA; 173 brs.

Belaruski Bank Razvitiya: 220004 Minsk, vul. Melnikaite 2; tel. and fax (17) 223-93-96; e-mail bbr@belinv.minsk.by; f. 1993; cap. 1,071,334m., dep. US $2.3m. (Jan. 1999); Chair. ALYAKSANDR Y. RUTKOVSKY; 7 brs.

Belaruski Birzhevoy Bank: 220013 Minsk, vul. Surganova 48A; tel. (17) 232-47-86; fax (17) 232-67-00; e-mail kuzar@exchbank.org.by; f. 1992; cap. 50,568m. (Dec. 1997); Chair. ANDREY L. MARKOVSKY; 7 brs.

Belaruski Narodnyi Bank: 220004 Minsk, vul. Tankovaya 1; tel. and fax (17) 223-84-57; f. 1992; cap. 69,937m. (Dec. 1997); Chair. ANDREY S. TARATUKHIN; 1 br.

Belbaltia: 220050 Minsk, Privokzalnaya pl., Express Hotel, 8th Floor; tel. (17) 226-09-55; fax (17) 226-49-18; f. 1994; cap. 32,821.2m. (Dec. 1997); Chair. VASIL B. BARSEGYAN; 1 br.

Belbusinessbank: 220002 Minsk, vul. Varvasheni 81; tel. (17) 289-35-42; fax (17) 289-35-46; e-mail root@bbb.belpak.minsk.by; f. 1992 as Joint-Stock Commercial Bank for Reconstruction and Development; name changed as above Dec. 1999; cap. 745,279m., res 2,701,902m., dep. 37,428,112m. (Dec. 1999); Chair. KAZIMIR V. TURUTO; 45 brs.

Belcombank: 220007 Minsk, vul. Mogilevskaya 43; tel. (17) 229-25-28; fax (17) 229-21-94; e-mail bkb780@iname.com; f. 1991; cap. 78,265.5m. (Dec. 1997); Chair. VASIL A. DADALKO; 12 brs.

Belgazprombank: 220121 Minsk, vul. Pritytskiy 60/2; tel. (17) 259-40-24; fax (17) 259-45-25; e-mail root@bgpb.minsk.by; f. 1990; cap. 1,832.2m. readjusted roubles, res 475.2m. readjusted roubles, dep. 6,032.7m. readjusted roubles (Dec. 2000); Chair. VIKTOR D. BABARIKO; 6 brs.

Belkoopbank: 220121 Minsk, pr. Masherava 17; tel. (17) 226-96-96; fax (17) 226-97-93; f. 1992; cap. 50,741.8m. (Dec. 1997); Chair. LIDIYA A. NIKITENKO; 9 brs.

Djembank: 220012 Minsk, vul. Surganava 28; tel. (17) 268-81-04; fax (17) 268-81-90; e-mail main@djem.com.by; internet www.djem.com.by; f. 1991; cap. 132,723m., res. 3,448m., dep. 909,680m. (Dec. 1998); Pres. ALYAKSANDR V. TATARINTSEV.

Infobank: 220035 Minsk, vul. Ignatenka 11; tel. and fax (17) 253-43-88; e-mail root@infobk.belpak.minsk.by; f. 1994; cap. 110,825m., res 195,627m., dep. 1,735,511m. (Dec. 1998); Chair. ALYAKSANDR D. OSMOLOVSKIY; 4 brs.

Joint-Stock Commercial Agricultural and Industrial Bank (Belagroprombank): 220073 Minsk, vul. Olshevskaga 24; tel. (17) 228-50-01; fax (17) 228-53-19; e-mail frk@agrbank2.belpak.minsk.by; f. 1991; cap. 42,306,100m., res 15,085,300m., dep. 18,280,400m. (Dec. 1999); Chair. ALYAKSANDR GAVRUSHEV; 133 brs.

Joint-Stock Commercial Bank for Industry and Construction (Belpromstroibank): 220678 Minsk, pr. Lunacharskaga 6; tel. (17) 213-39-93; fax (17) 231-44-76; e-mail teletype@belpsb.minsk.by; internet www.belpsb.minsk.by; f. 1991; provides credit to enterprises undergoing privatization and conversion to civil production; cap. 169,800m., res 2,085,261m., dep. 41,170,766m. (Dec. 1998); Chair. GALINA P. KUKHARENKO; 58 brs.

MinskComplexbank (Joint Belarussian-Russian Bank): 220050 Minsk, vul. Myasnikova 40; tel. (17) 228-20-50; fax (17) 228-20-60; e-mail administrator@complex.nsys.minsk.by; f. 1992; cap. 153,000m. (Dec. 1997); Chair. YEVGENII I. KRAVTSOV.

Minski Tranzitnyi Bank: 220033 Minsk, pr. Partizanski 6A; tel. (17) 213-29-00; fax (17) 213-29-09; e-mail cor@mtb.minsk.by; f. 1994; cap. 36,001.9m. (Dec. 1997), res 6,570.2m., dep. 656,300m. (Dec. 1997); Chair. ANNA G. GRINKEVICH; 5 brs.

Priorbank: 220002 Minsk, vul. V. Khoruzhey 31A; tel. (17) 234-01-35; fax (17) 234-15-54; e-mail root@prior.minsk.by; internet www.prior.minsk.by; f. 1989, present name since 1992; cap. 242,000m., res 8,208,500m., dep. 48,579,300m. (Dec. 1999); Pres. MIKHAIL F. LAVRINOVICH; Chair. SYARGEY A. KOSTYUCHENKA; 30 brs.

Profbank: 220126 Minsk, vul. Melnikaite 8; tel. (17) 223-95-78; fax (17) 222-26-15; f. 1991; cap. 42,336.4m. (Dec. 1997); Chair. MIKHAIL P. SLESAREV; 5 brs.

RRB-Bank: 220037 Minsk, pr. Masherava 23; tel. (17) 226-57-27; fax (17) 226-63-93; f. 1994; cap. 51,003.3m. (Dec. 1997); Chair. IRINA A. VERETELNIKOVA.

Slavneftebank: 220815 Minsk, vul. Fabritsius 8; tel. (17) 222-07-09; fax (17) 222-07-52; e-mail snb@snbank.belpak.minsk.by; f. 1996; total assets 6,033,143.6m., cap. 82,200m. (Dec. 1998); Chair. VLADIMIR V. IVANOV; 2 brs.

Technobank: 220002 Minsk, vul. Krapotkina 44; tel. (17) 283-27-27; fax (17) 283-15-10; e-mail info@technobank.com.by; internet www.technobank.com.by; f. 1994; Chair. ZOYA I. LISHAY; 4 brs.

Trade and Industrial Bank SA: 220141 Minsk, vul. Russiyanov 8; tel. and fax (17) 268-03-45; e-mail tib_sa@anitex.by; f. 1994 as Novokom; cap. 1,141,435m. (Nov. 1999); Chair. FELIKS I. CHERNYAVSKY.

Zolotoy Taler: 220035 Minsk, vul. Tatarskaya 3; tel. (17) 226-62-98; fax (17) 223-06-40; e-mail gt_bank2@gtp.by; f. 1994; cap. and res 1,222.2m. readjusted roubles, dep. 3,270.5m. readjusted roubles (Dec. 2000); Chair. ALYAKSANDR A. ZHILINSKIY.

BANKING ASSOCIATION

Association of Belarusian Banks: 220071 Minsk, vul. Smolyachkova 9; tel. (17) 227-78-90; fax (17) 227-58-41; e-mail root@abbank.minsk.by; Chair. NIKOLAY POZNIAK.

COMMODITY AND STOCK EXCHANGES

Belagroprambirzha (Belarusian Agro-Industrial Trade and Stock Exchange): 220108 Minsk, vul. Kazintsa 86, kor. 2; tel. (17) 277-07-26; fax (17) 277-01-37; f. 1991; trade in agricultural products,

industrial goods, shares; 900 mems; Pres. ANATOL TIBOGANOU; Chair. of Bd ALYAKSANDR P. DECHTYAR.

Belarusian Currency and Stock Exchange: 220004 Minsk, vul. Melnikaite 2; tel. (17) 276-91-21; fax (17) 229-25-66; f. 1991; Gen. Dir VYACHESLAV A. KASAK.

Belarusian Universal Exchange (BUE): 220099 Minsk, vul. Kazintsa 4; tel. (17) 278-11-21; fax (17) 278-85-16; f. 1991; Pres. ULADZIMIR SHEPEL.

Gomel Regional Commodity and Raw Materials Exchange (GCME): 246000 Gomel, vul. Savetskaya 16; tel. (232) 55-73-28; fax (232) 55-70-07; f. 1991; Gen. Man. ANATOL KUZILEVICH.

INSURANCE

Belarusian Insurance Co: 220141 Minsk, vul. Zhodinskaya 1-4; tel. (17) 263-38-57; fax (17) 268-80-17; e-mail reklama@belinscosc.belpak.minsk.by; f. 1992; Dir-Gen. LEONID M. STATKEVICH.

Belgosstrakh (State Insurance Co): 220036 Minsk, vul. K. Libknekht 70; tel. (17) 259-10-21; fax (17) 286-08-05; e-mail bgs@belsonet.net; Dir-Gen. VICTOR I. SHOUST.

Belingosstrakh: 220078 Minsk, pr. Masherava 19; tel. and fax (17) 226-98-04; f. 1977; non-life, property, vehicle and cargo insurance; Dir-Gen. YURI A. GAVRILOV.

GARIS: 220600 Minsk, vul. Myasnikova 32; tel. (17) 220-37-01.

Polis: 220087 Minsk, pr. Partizansky 81; tel. (17) 245-02-91; Dir DANUTA I. VORONOVICH.

SNAMI: 220040 Minsk, vul. Nekrasova 40A; tel. and fax (17) 231-63-86; f. 1991; Dir S. N. SHABALA.

Trade and Industry

CHAMBERS OF COMMERCE

Belarusian Chamber of Commerce and Industry: 220035 Minsk, pr. Masherava 14; tel. (17) 226-91-27; fax (17) 226-98-60; e-mail gpp@cci.belpak.minsk.by; internet www.cci.by; f. 1953; brs in Brest, Gomel, Grodno, Mogilev and Vitebsk; Pres. ULADZIMIR K. LESUN.

Minsk Branch: 220113 Minsk, vul. Kolasa 65; tel. (17) 266-04-73; fax (17) 266-26-04; Man. Dir P. A. YUSHKEVICH.

EMPLOYERS' ORGANIZATION

Confederation of Industrialists and Entrepreneurs: 220004 Minsk, vul. Kalvaryskaya 1-410; tel. (17) 222-47-91; fax (17) 222-47-94; e-mail buel@user.unibel.by; f. 1990; Pres. TATYANA BYKOVA.

UTILITIES

Electricity

In November 1999 an agreement was signed on the unification of Russia's and Belarus' energy systems (including a power-grid merger).

Institute of Nuclear Energy: 223061 Minsk, Sosny Settlement; tel. (17) 246-77-12.

Gas

Belnaftagaz: Minsk; tel. (17) 233-06-75.

Beltopgaz: distributes natural gas to end-users.

Beltransgaz: imports natural gas; acts as holding co for regional transmission and storage enterprises.

TRADE UNIONS

Belarusian Congress of Democratic Trade Unions: 220005 Minsk, vul. Zaharova 24; tel. (17) 233-31-82; fax (17) 210-15-00; f. 1993; Chair. ALYAKSANDR LYSENKA; 18,000 mems.

Free Trade Union of Belarus: 220005 Minsk, vul. Zakharova 24; tel. (17) 284-31-82; fax (17) 284-59-94; e-mail spb@user.unibel.by; internet praca.promedia.minsk.by; f. 1992; Chair. GENADZ BYKOU; Vice-Chair. NIKOLAY KANAH; 6,000 mems.

Independent Trade Union of Belarus: 223710 Soligorsk, vul. Lenina 42; tel. and fax (17) 102-00-59; e-mail sol_sn@inbox.ru; f. 1991; Chair. VIKTAR BABAYED; Sec. NIKOLAY ZIMIN; 10,000 mems.

Belarusian Organization of Working Women: 220030 Minsk, pl. Svabody 23; (17) 227-57-78; fax (17) 227-13-16; f. 1992; 7,000 mems.

Belarusian Peasants' Union (Syalanski Sayuz): 220199 Minsk, vul. Brestskaya 64-327; tel. (17) 277-99-93; Chair. KASTUS YARMOLENKA.

Federation of Trade Unions of Belarus: Minsk; Chair. ULADZIMIR GANCHARYK.

Independent Association of Industrial Trade Unions of Belarus: 220013 Minsk, vul. Kulman 4; tel. (17) 223-80-74; fax (17)

223-82-04; f. 1992; Chair. ALYAKSANDR I. BUKHVOSTOU, G. F. FEDYNICH; 380,000 mems; derecognized by Govt in 1999.

Union of Electronic Industry Workers: Minsk; Leader G. F. FEDYNICH.

Union of Motor Car and Agricultural Machinery Construction Workers: Minsk; largest industrial trade union in Belarus; Leader ALYAKSANDR I. BUKHVOSTOU; 200,000 mems.

Union of Small Ventures: 220010 Minsk, vul. Sukhaya 7; tel. (17) 220-23-41; fax (17) 220-93-41; f. 1990; legal, business; Gen. Dir VIKTAR F. DROZD.

Transport

RAILWAYS

In 1995 the total length of railway lines in use was 5,543 km. Minsk is a major railway junction, situated on the east-west line between Moscow and Warsaw, and north-south lines linking the Baltic countries and Ukraine. There is an underground railway in Minsk, the Minsk Metro, which has two lines (total length 20 km), with 18 stations.

Belarusian State Railways: 220745 Minsk, vul. Lenina 17; tel. (17) 296-44-00; fax (17) 227-56-48; f. 1992, following the dissolution of the former Soviet Railways; Pres. E. I. VOLODKO; First Vice-Pres. V. BORISUK.

ROADS

At 31 December 1998 the total length of roads in Belarus was 63,355 km (including 15,462 km main roads and 47,893 km secondary roads). Some 95.6% of the total network was hard-surfaced. In September 1999 it was estimated that more than 28,000 km of Belarus' road network was in need of repair.

CIVIL AVIATION

Minsk has two airports, one largely for international flights and one for domestic connections.

Belair Belarussian Airlines: Minsk; tel. (17) 222-57-02; fax (17) 222-75-09; f. 1991; operates regional and domestic charter services.

Belavia: 220004 Minsk, vul. Nemiga 14; tel. (17) 229-24-24; fax (17) 229-23-83; e-mail belaviamarket@infonet.by; internet www.belavia.infonet.by; f. 1993 from former Aeroflot division of the USSR; became state national carrier in 1996; operates services in Europe and selected destinations in Asia; Gen. Dir ANATOLY GUSAROV.

Gomel Air Detachment: 246011 Gomel, Gomel Airport; tel. (23) 251-14-07; fax (23) 253-14-15; f. 1944; Chief Exec. VALERY N. KULAKOUSKI.

Tourism

Belintourist: 220078 Minsk, pr. Masherava 19; tel. (17) 226-98-40; fax (17) 223-11-43; e-mail belintrst@nttcmk.belpak.minsk.by; f. 1992; leading tourist org. in Belarus; Dir-Gen. VYACHESLAV V. IVANOV.

BELGIUM

Introductory Survey

Location, Climate, Language, Religion, Flag, Capital

The Kingdom of Belgium lies in north-western Europe, bounded to the north by the Netherlands, to the east by Luxembourg and Germany, to the south by France, and to the west by the North Sea. The climate is temperate. Temperatures in the capital, Brussels, are generally between 0°C (32°F) and 23°C (73°F). Flemish (closely related to Dutch), spoken in the north (Flanders), and French, spoken in the south (Wallonia), are the two main official languages. Brussels (which is situated in Flanders) has bilingual status. Nearly 60% of the population are Flemish-speaking, about 40% are French-speaking and less than 1% have German as their mother tongue. The majority of the inhabitants profess Christianity, and about four-fifths are Roman Catholics. The national flag (proportions 15 by 13) consists of three equal vertical stripes, of black, yellow and red.

Recent History

Since the Second World War, Belgium has promoted international co-operation in Europe. It is a founder member of many important international organizations, including the North Atlantic Treaty Organization (NATO, see p. 241), the Council of Europe (see p. 165), the European Union (EU, see p. 181) and the Benelux Economic Union (see p. 307).

In the latter half of the 20th century linguistic divisions were exacerbated by the political and economic polarization of Flemish-speaking Flanders in the north and francophone Wallonia in the south. The faster-growing and relatively prosperous population of Flanders has traditionally supported the conservative Flemish Christelijke Volkspartij (CVP—Christian People's Party) and the nationalist Volksunie—Vlaamse Vrije Democraten (VU—People's Union—Flemish Free Democrats), while Wallonia has traditionally been a stronghold of socialist political sympathies. Most major parties have both French and Flemish sections, as a result of a trend away from centralized administration towards greater regional control. Moderate constitutional reforms, introduced in 1971, were the first steps towards regional autonomy; in the following year further concessions were made, with the German-speaking community being represented in the Cabinet for the first time, and in 1973 linguistic parity was assured in central government. Provisional legislation, adopted in 1974, established separate Regional Councils and Ministerial Committees. The administrative status of Brussels remained contentious: the majority of the city's inhabitants are francophone, but the Flemish parties were, until the late 1980s, unwilling to grant the capital equal status with the other two regional bodies (see below).

In June 1977 the Prime Minister, Leo Tindemans, formed a coalition composed of the CVP and the francophone Parti Social Chrétien (PSC—Christian Social Party), which were collectively known as the Christian Democrats, the Socialists, the Front Démocratique des Francophones (FDF—French-speaking Democratic Front) and the VU. The Cabinet, in what became known as the Egmont Pact, proposed the abolition of the virtually defunct nine-province administration, and devolution of power from the central Government to create a federal Belgium, comprising three political and economic regions (Flanders, Wallonia and Brussels), and two linguistic communities. However, these proposals were not implemented. Tindemans resigned in October 1978 and the Minister of Defence, Paul Vanden Boeynants, was appointed Prime Minister in a transitional Government. Legislative elections in December caused little change to the distribution of seats in the Chamber of Representatives. Four successive Prime Ministers-designate failed to form a new government, the main obstacle being the future status of Brussels. The six-month crisis was finally resolved when a new coalition Government was formed in April 1979 under Dr Wilfried Martens, the President of the CVP.

During 1980 the linguistic conflict worsened, sometimes involving violent incidents. Legislation was formulated, under the terms of which Flanders and Wallonia were to be administered by regional assemblies, with control of cultural matters, public health, roads, urban projects and 10% of the national budget, while Brussels was to retain its three-member executive.

Belgium suffered severe economic difficulties during the late 1970s and early 1980s, and internal disagreement over Martens' proposals for their resolution resulted in the formation of four successive coalition Governments between April 1979 and October 1980. Proposed austerity measures, including a 'freeze' on wages and reductions in public expenditure at a time of high unemployment, provoked demonstrations and lost Martens the support of the Socialist parties. Martens also encountered widespread criticism over plans to install NATO nuclear missiles in Belgium. In April 1981 a new Government was formed, comprising a coalition of the Christian Democrats and the Socialist parties and led by Mark Eyskens (of the CVP), hitherto Minister of Finance. However, lack of parliamentary support for his policies led to Eyskens' resignation in September. In December Martens formed a new centre-right Government, comprising the Christian Democrats and the two Liberal parties. In 1982 Parliament granted special powers for the implementation of economic austerity measures; these were effective until 1984, and similar powers were approved in March 1986. Opposition to reductions in public spending was vigorous, with public-sector unions undertaking damaging strike action throughout the 1980s.

In November 1983 the Chamber of Representatives debated the controversial proposed installation of 48 US 'cruise' nuclear missiles on Belgian territory, deferring a final decision on the issue until 1985. A series of bombings, directed against NATO-connected targets, occurred during 1984. Responsibility for the attacks was claimed by an extreme left-wing organization. In March 1985 the Chamber finally adopted a majority vote in favour of the cruise sitings, and 16 missiles were installed at Florennes. Further terrorist attacks against NATO targets were perpetrated in 1985, before a number of arrests were made. The missiles were removed in December 1988, under the terms of the Intermediate-range Nuclear Forces treaty concluded by the USA and the USSR in December 1987.

In May 1985 a riot at a football match between English and Italian clubs at the Heysel Stadium in Brussels, which resulted in 39 deaths, precipitated demands for the resignation of the Minister of the Interior, Charles-Ferdinand Nothomb, over accusations of inefficient policing. In July the resignation, in connection with the issue, of six Liberal cabinet members (including the Deputy Prime Minister, Jean Gol) led to the collapse of the coalition. Martens offered the resignation of his Government, but this was 'suspended' by King Baudouin pending a general election, which was called for October. Meanwhile, however, controversy regarding educational reform provoked a dispute between the two main linguistic groups and caused the final dissolution of Parliament in September. The general election returned the Christian Democrats-Liberal alliance to power, and in November Martens formed his sixth Cabinet.

The Government collapsed in October 1987, as a result of continuing division between the French- and Flemish-speaking parties of the coalition. At the ensuing general election in December, the CVP sustained significant losses in Flanders, while the French-speaking Parti Socialiste (PS—Socialist Party) gained seats in Wallonia, and the Socialists became the largest overall grouping in the Chamber of Representatives. No party, however, had a clear mandate for power, and negotiations for a new coalition lasted 146 days. During this time, Martens assumed a caretaker role, while a series of mediators, appointed by the King, attempted to reach a compromise. In May 1988 Martens was sworn in at the head of his eighth administration, after agreement was finally reached by the French- and Flemish-speaking wings of both the Christian Democrats and Socialist parties and by the VU.

The five-party coalition agreement committed the new Government to a programme of further austerity measures, together with tax reforms and increased federalization. In August 1988 Parliament approved the first phase of the federalization plan, intended ultimately to lead to a constitutional amendment, whereby increased autonomy would be granted to the country's Communities and Regions in several areas of jurisdiction, including education and socio-economic policy. It was also agreed that Brussels would have its own Regional Council, with an executive responsible to it, giving the city equal status with Flanders and Wallonia. In January 1989 Parliament approved the second phase of the federalization programme, allocating the public funds necessary to give effect to the regional autonomy that had been approved in principle in August 1988. The federal Constitution formally came into effect in July 1989.

A brief constitutional crisis in 1990 provoked widespread demands for a review of the powers of the Monarch, as defined by the Constitution. In March proposals for the legalization of abortion (in strictly-controlled circumstances) completed their passage through Parliament. However, King Baudouin had previously stated that his religious convictions would render him unable to give royal assent to any such legislation. A compromise solution was reached in early April, whereby Article 82 of the Constitution, which makes provision for the Monarch's 'incapacity to rule', was invoked. Baudouin thus abdicated for 36 hours, during which time the new legislation was promulgated. A joint session of Parliament was then convened to declare the resumption of Baudouin's reign. However, the incident prompted considerable alarm within Belgium: it was widely perceived as setting a dangerous precedent for the reinterpretation of the Constitution.

The Government was weakened by the resignation of both VU ministers in September 1991 and by the resultant loss of its two-thirds parliamentary majority, necessary for the implementation of the third stage of the federalization programme. Further linguistic conflict between the remaining coalition partners led to Martens' resignation as Prime Minister in October and the subsequent collapse of the Government. However, King Baudouin rejected the resignations of Martens and the Cabinet. The Government remained in office until the next general election, which took place in November. The results of the election reflected a significant decline in popular support for all five parties represented in the outgoing Government. The Socialist parties remained the largest overall grouping in the Chamber of Representatives, although they sustained the highest combined loss of seats (nine). Following the election, the political parties conducted protracted negotiations, during which Martens' interim Cabinet continued in office. In early March 1992 four of the five parties that had composed the previous Government, the CVP, the PSC, the Socialistische Partij (SP) and the PS (which together controlled 120 seats in the 212-member Chamber of Representatives), agreed to form a new administration; a leading member of the CVP, Jean-Luc Dehaene, was appointed Prime Minister. The new Government committed itself to the completion of the constitutional reforms that had been initiated under Martens' premiership. For several months, however, the coalition partners repeatedly failed to reach agreement, both on proposals for the implementation of the third stage of the federalization programme and on amendments to the 1993 budget. A compromise on both issues was eventually reached at the end of September 1992.

In July 1992 the Chamber of Representatives voted, by 146 to 33, in favour of ratifying the Treaty on European Union, agreed by the heads of government of member states of the European Community (now EU) at Maastricht, in the Netherlands, in December 1991. The Senate approved ratification in November 1992.

In February 1993 (in accordance with the constitutional reforms agreed in September 1992) Parliament voted to amend the Constitution to create a federal state of Belgium, comprising the largely autonomous regions of Flanders, Wallonia and (bilingual) Brussels. The three regions, and the country's three linguistic groups, were to be represented by the following directly-elected administrations: a combined administration for Flanders and the Flemish-speaking community, regional administrations for Wallonia and Brussels, and separate administrations for French- and German-speakers. The regional administrations were to assume sole responsibility for the environment, housing, transport and public works, while the language community administrations were to supervise education policy and culture. Legislation to implement the reforms was enacted in July 1993.

In July 1993 King Baudouin died; Baudouin was succeeded by his brother, hitherto Prince Albert of Liège, in August.

In January 1994 three government ministers who were members of the PS (including a Deputy Prime Minister, Guy Coëme) resigned from their posts, following allegations that they had been involved in a bribery scandal concerning the apparently illegal receipt by the SP (the Flemish section of the party) of a substantial sum of money in connection with the award, in 1988, of a defence contract to an Italian helicopter company. The PS (the Walloon section of the party) was subsequently implicated in a similar scandal involving a French aviation company. In April 1996 Coëme and seven others were found guilty of fraud and abuse of public office; Coëme, who received a two-year suspended prison sentence, subsequently resigned from the Chamber of Representatives. The scandal also led to the suicide in March 1995 of a retired Chief of Staff of the Air Force, the resignation in the same month of Frank Vandenbroucke, a Deputy Prime Minister and the Minister of Foreign Affairs, (who claimed that he had participated unwittingly in the affair) and the resignation of Willy Claes, a prominent SP official and former Deputy Prime Minister and Minister of Foreign Affairs, as Secretary-General of NATO, and his eventual conviction in February 1999 on charges of corruption, fraud and forgery; he received a three-year suspended prison sentence.

At elections to the European Parliament in June 1994 all four parties of the governing coalition registered a decline in support, while the Liberal parties increased their number of seats. Extreme right-wing parties also performed well: the Vlaams Blok (Flemish Bloc—which had secured 12 seats in the general election of November 1991) and the Wallonia-based Front National (FN—National Front) together gained more than 10% of the total votes.

At a general election held in May 1995 the ruling centre-left coalition retained significant support, securing a total of 82 seats in the Chamber of Representatives (membership of which had been reduced from 208 to 150), despite the ongoing investigation into allegedly illegal activities by officials of the two Socialist parties. The performance of the extreme right-wing Vlaams Blok was not as strong as had been anticipated: although the party won nearly 28% of the votes cast in Antwerp, Belgium's second largest city, it received only 12% of the votes overall in Flanders. Elections to the regional assemblies took place concurrently with the national legislative elections. Following an unusually short period of negotiations the CVP-PSC-PS-SP coalition was reformed and in mid-June a new Cabinet was appointed, with Dehaene remaining as Prime Minister. The Government, which continued to be strongly committed to meeting the economic targets for future European economic and monetary union, introduced several strict economic austerity measures in late 1995; public-sector unions responded by organizing protest strike action. In April 1996 the Government, employers and trade unions agreed measures that aimed to reduce the high level of unemployment. The agreement was, however, short-lived, owing to the subsequent withdrawal of one of the main trade unions, on the grounds that the proposals for job creation were not sufficiently detailed. In the following month Parliament granted the Dehaene administration special emergency powers to implement economic austerity measures by decree.

The latter half of 1996 was dominated by extreme public concern over allegations of endemic official corruption, following the discovery, in August, of an international paedophile network based in Belgium, and subsequent widespread speculation (fuelled by the arrests in early September of several police officers) that this had received protection from the police force and from senior figures in the judicial and political establishment, who were allegedly implicated in the activities of organized crime syndicates. During September King Albert promised a thorough investigation of the network and, in an unprecedented gesture, demanded a review of the judicial system. In October, however, allegations of a judicial and political conspiracy to impede the progress of the investigation were prompted by the removal from the case of Jean-Marc Connerotte, a widely-respected senior investigating judge. The prevailing mood of national crisis was heightened by the arrests, during September, of Alain van der Biest of the PS (a former federal Minister of Pensions) and four others, on charges connected with the assassination in 1991 of a former Deputy Prime Minister, André Cools. It was alleged that Cools' murder had been ordered by PS colleagues, in order to prevent him from disclosing corruption within the party. In June 1998 a Tunisian court found two Tunisian citizens guilty of the murder; however, the background to the assassination remained unclear.

Meanwhile, in March 1997 Guy Spitaels (a former Deputy Prime Minister and an erstwhile President of the PS), having resigned in the previous month as President of the Walloon regional assembly, was indicted on bribery charges relating to the political scandals of 1994–95 (see above). In April 1997 a parliamentary committee, which had been established in October 1996 to investigate allegations of official corruption and mismanagement, issued a report that claimed that rivalry between the country's various police and judicial divisions often prevented their effective co-operation; it recommended the establishment of a single integrated national police force. However, the committee found little evidence that paedophile networks had received official protection. In February 1998 the Government announced that, in place of the recommended integrated national police force, efforts would be made to facilitate 'voluntary co-operation contracts' between the various law enforcement services.

In April 1998 Marc Dutroux, a convicted paedophile whose arrest in August 1996 on charges of child kidnapping and murder had prompted the ongoing scrutiny of Belgium's national institutions, briefly escaped from police custody. (In June 2000 Dutroux was sentenced to five years' imprisonment for his escape, but had not yet been tried for his role in the murder of at least two children. This trial was not expected to start until the third quarter of 2002.) The incident incited renewed public anger and precipitated the resignations of several high-ranking figures, including the commander of the national gendarmerie and the Ministers of the Interior and of Justice. A proposed vote of 'no confidence' in the Dehaene Government, also ensuing from Dutroux's escape, was defeated in the Chamber of Representatives. Dehaene immediately reaffirmed his commitment to restructuring the police and judiciary.

In mid-June 1998 a reorganization of the Cabinet included the appointment of a new (socialist) Minister of Finance. In late September Louis Tobback, who had been appointed Deputy Prime Minister and Minister of the Interior in April, resigned, following protests at the death of a Nigerian woman during an attempt forcibly to deport her from Belgium. Two police officers were subsequently charged with involuntary manslaughter, and the Government suspended the forced repatriation of asylum-seekers, pending further investigations.

Preparations for the general election scheduled to be held in mid-June 1999 were overshadowed by the public announcement in late May that animal feed contaminated with industrial oil containing dioxin (a carcinogenic chemical) had been supplied to farms throughout Belgium from a factory near Ghent. Following the announcement, many Belgian food products, particularly poultry and egg-based products, were withdrawn from sale in Belgium and elsewhere in Europe, while production was suspended at farms across Belgium. There was widespread public anger that, although veterinary inspectors had identified a problem as early as mid-March, it was not until May that the Ministry of Agriculture had suspended sales from the affected animal-feed suppliers, and had informed government officials in neighbouring countries. On 1 June Karel Pinxten, the Minister of Agriculture and Small and Medium-sized Enterprises, and Marcel Colla, the Minister of Consumer Affairs, Public Health and the Environment, who had been jointly blamed for the delay in informing the public of the contamination, resigned from their posts. In early June the EU announced that it was to demand the removal from sale, and subsequent destruction, of poultry, pork and cattle products from farms whose feed had been contaminated with dioxin. The Belgian Government subsequently introduced a total ban on the slaughter and transportation of all poultry, cattle and pigs until it could confirm which farms had received the affected feed. On 7 June Dehaene took the unprecedented step of halting his electoral campaign, and announced an official parliamentary enquiry into the contamination. On 10 June, in an apparent attempt to assuage farmers who were losing large amounts of income on a daily basis and demanding compensation, the Government announced that slaughtering and exports could resume at farms that had not received the contaminated feed, despite the lack of a definitive list of dioxin-free farms. This relaxation of the temporary ban on production contravened the advice of the European Commission, which had recommended that the ban should remain in place while there continued to be uncertainty about which farms had received the contaminated feed. It was alleged that the Government had believed that, for political reasons, it could not wait for the convening of the Commission's scientific and veterinary committee, whose meeting was scheduled to take place after the Belgian general election. Confusion, however, remained within Belgium as to the identification of the affected farms, and Belgian farmers blocked the roads into the country from France and the Netherlands, in an attempt to prevent agricultural imports. The Commission later announced that it

was to initiate legal proceedings against the Belgian Government over its handling of the crisis, which had led to imports of European food products being banned by many non-European countries (including the USA).

At the general election, which was held on 13 June 1999, the Christian Democrats suffered heavy losses, mainly at the hands of the Liberals and the ecologist parties. The Vlaams Blok also showed significant gains, winning more than 10% of the vote in many areas. The Vlaamse Liberalen en Demokraten—Partij van de Burger (VLD—Flemish Liberals and Democrats—Citizens' Party) emerged as the largest single party, with 23 seats in the 150-member Chamber of Representatives (having received 14.3% of the total votes cast), while the ecologist parties, Anders Gaan Leven (Agalev) and the Ecologistes Confédérés pour l'Organisation des Luttes Originales (Ecolo), almost doubled their representation, to 20 seats (with 14.4%), and the Vlaams Blok became the fifth largest party in the lower house, with 15 seats (9.9%). The CVP secured 22 seats (14.1% of the total votes) and the PSC won 10 seats (5.9%), while the Socialist parties obtained a combined total of 33 seats (19.8%). The VLD also performed well in the elections to the Senate, which (together with elections to the assemblies for the regions and linguistic communities) were held on the same day as the elections to the Chamber of Representatives; the VLD won the largest number of votes in the polling for the 40 directly-elective seats in the upper house (with 15.4% of the total votes). The defeat of the outgoing coalition in the general election was largely attributed to public anger at the authorities' perceived incompetence in their response to the dioxin scandal (which compounded general disquiet over the earlier corruption and paedophile scandals). Dehaene, who had held the premiership for eight years, tendered his resignation on 14 June and announced that he was considering leaving national politics. On 23 June the King asked the President of the VLD, Guy Verhofstadt, to form a new government. Following intensive negotiations, a new six-party coalition Government, comprising the VLD, the francophone Parti Réformateur Libéral (PRL), the two Socialist parties and the two ecologist parties, was sworn in on 12 July. The new administration was of historic note in that it was the first Belgian Government in 40 years not to include the Christian Democrats, the first to include the ecologist parties, and the first to be headed by a Liberal Prime Minister since 1884. Reflecting the right-wing programme of the Liberal parties, the new Government promised to reduce the social charges payable by employers and to reduce levels of public debt through the privatization of state assets. It also committed itself to the gradual abandonment of nuclear power (prompted by the greatly strengthened ecologist lobby), the further liberalization of the electricity sector and greater investment in the railway network. In response to the scandals that beset the previous Government, the new administration also planned to restructure Belgium's inefficient bureaucracy, making it more accountable to the public (and ending the practice of political appointments), to reform the police service and ease the tension between the Flemish and Walloon regions by granting them greater fiscal autonomy, with limited discretion to raise or lower local taxes.

Despite demonstrations staged by farmers (many of whom were reportedly on the brink of bankruptcy) in late June and in early July 1999, in protest at the authorities' handling of the dioxin crisis, the new Government announced that it was to add a further 400 farms to the list of 800 already forbidden to sell their produce. The Government also announced that it was to buy back and destroy some 80,000 metric tons of pork. In early August, in response to recommendations made by scientific advisers from the European Commission, the Belgian Government agreed to add beef to the list of livestock exports that were banned until definitively cleared of contamination. A few days later the Government promulgated a decree banning the export of food products containing more than 2% animal fat (except dairy products) that did not have a certificate guaranteeing their safety. Although the Minister of Consumer Affairs, Public Health and the Environment described the decree as unnecessarily harsh, representatives of the agricultural industry subsequently persuaded her that stringent procedures were required in order to regain consumer confidence and to avoid the imposition of a total ban on all Belgian agricultural exports by the EU. The Government, none the less, announced that, while it would comply with EU directives, it would mount a legal challenge in the hope of reducing their severity.

In late September 1999 the Belgian Government announced that some 500 Slovak Romanies who had applied for political asylum were to be repatriated. In the following month the Minister of the Interior ordered an official investigation into criticisms made by human rights groups regarding the tactics used by the authorities in Ghent to assemble the Romanies prior to deportation. In mid-October the Government announced that legislation was to be introduced, aimed at reforming the procedure of applying for asylum. The new procedure was to take no longer than one month, including the appeals process, and those applicants not granted asylum were to be repatriated without delay. The Government also announced that all outstanding asylum applications would be processed within one year. In a temporary amnesty in January 2000 asylum-seekers resident in Belgium for five years and illegal immigrants resident in Belgium for six years were granted legal status. In November, in an attempt to address the growing number of asylum-seekers (which had increased from 35,778 in 1999 to more than 40,000 in 2000, many of whom were from Eastern Europe), the Government proposed the introduction of border controls to slow the number of immigrants and an accelerated procedure for deporting those whose claims were without foundation.

In September 2000 fuel protests by road hauliers over the high price of motor spirit (petrol) brought much of Belgium to a standstill as truck drivers blockaded border crossings with France, Germany, Luxembourg and the Netherlands and prevented access to oil depots. Union leaders, however, accepted a government offer of fiscal and social measures to help ease the pressure of high fuel prices, although the agreement did not include the reductions of taxes on fuel sought by the protesters.

The general popularity of the new Government was slightly undermined by the results of the local elections, which took place on 8 October 2000. Although the government parties performed well, their achievements were overshadowed by the success of the Vlaams Blok, which had campaigned against immigration and in favour of independence for Flanders. The Vlaams Blok made significant advances in Flanders, particularly in Antwerp where it won 33% of the votes cast, securing 20 of the 55 seats on Antwerp's municipal council. It also performed well in Ghent and Mechelen, and most surprisingly in Brussels, where its share of the vote doubled to about 9% in several districts, compared with the previous election. The Vlaams Blok remained unrepresented in any municipal government owing to the refusal of any democratic party to co-operate with the party but there were fears that its extremist positions were altering political debate in Belgium.

From late 1988 Belgium's hitherto cordial relations with its former colonies underwent considerable strain. Proposals that Prime Minister Martens made in, November 1988 regarding the relief of public and commercial debts owed to Belgium by Zaire (formerly the Belgian Congo) were opposed by the Socialist parties and provoked allegations in the Belgian press of corruption within the Zairean Government and of the misappropriation of development aid. President Mobutu Sese Seko of Zaire responded by ordering the withdrawal of all Zairean state-owned businesses from Belgium and by demanding that all Zairean nationals resident in Belgium remove their assets from, and leave, their host country. In July 1989 the situation was apparently resolved following meetings between Martens and Mobutu, at which a new debt-servicing agreement was signed. However, relations again deteriorated when, in May 1990, the Mobutu regime refused to accede to demands for an international inquiry into the alleged massacre of as many as 150 students by the Zairean security forces. Mobutu accused Belgium of interfering in his country's internal affairs, and ordered the expulsion from Zaire of some 700 Belgian technical workers, together with the closure of three of Belgium's four consular offices. Following the collapse of public order in Zaire in September 1991, the Belgian Government dispatched 1,000 troops to Zaire for the protection of the estimated 11,000 Belgian nationals resident there. By the end of 1991 all the troops had been withdrawn and about 8,000 Belgian nationals had been evacuated. Prospects for the normalization of relations improved following the establishment of a transitional Government in Zaire in July 1992 and the removal of Zairean sanctions against Belgium. Relations deteriorated again, however, in January 1993, when, in response to rioting by troops loyal to President Mobutu, Belgium dispatched 520 troops to evacuate the remaining 3,000 Belgian nationals in Zaire. In October 1994 the Belgian Government pledged to resume humanitarian aid to Zaire. In August 1997, following the deposition of Mobutu's regime in May by the forces of Laurent-Désiré Kabila, it was announced that normal

relations between Belgium and the Democratic Republic of the Congo (DRC—as Zaire was now renamed) would be gradually restored. In October 1999 a high-level Belgian delegation visited the capital of the DRC, Kinshasa, to express the willingness of the Belgian Government to mediate in the ongoing crisis in the troubled African state.

In October 1990 the Martens Government dispatched 600 troops to protect some 1,600 Belgian nationals resident in Rwanda (part of the former Belgian territory of Ruanda-Urundi), when that country was invaded by exiled opponents of the incumbent regime. The Belgian Government insisted that the deployment was a purely humanitarian action, and stated that it would not agree to a request from the Rwandan Government for military assistance, citing unacceptable violations of human rights by the authorities. In late October a cease-fire agreement came into effect, and in early November Belgian forces were withdrawn from Rwanda. Nevertheless, the conflict in Rwanda continued during 1991–94. Following the signing of a peace accord in August 1993, some 420 Belgian troops were redeployed as part of a UN peace-keeping force; this was, however, unable to prevent an outbreak of extreme violence, beginning in April 1994, which resulted in the deaths of many hundreds of thousands of people. Following the execution of 10 Belgian troops in April, the Belgian Government withdrew its peace-keeping contingent. It also dispatched some 800 paratroopers to Rwanda to co-ordinate the evacuation of the estimated 1,500 Belgian expatriates remaining in the country, as well as other foreign nationals. In October 1998 three Belgian army officers were demoted, having been found negligent in not preventing the 10 troop fatalities in April 1994.

The election of a new Government in Belgium in June 1999 led to an improvement in relations between Belgium and the DRC. The new Belgian Minister of Foreign Affairs, Louis Michel, was determined to develop a new strategy towards the central African countries with which Belgium has historical ties. Following the assassination of the DRC's President Kabila in January 2001, the Belgian Government intensified its attempts to relaunch the peace initiative in the region. During a visit to Belgium by the new DRC President, Kabila's son, Joseph, as part of a tour to meet those instrumental in the DRC peace efforts, the Belgian Prime Minister urged Kabila to commit to peace negotiations under the auspices of the UN. Michel also aimed to add an 'ethical' dimension to Belgian foreign policy. Initiatives that reflected this new approach included Belgium's leading role, along with France, in calling for the EU to suspend bilateral ties with Austria following its inclusion of the far-right Freiheitliche Partei Österreichs (Freedom Party) in the government coalition; efforts to have the former Chilean dictator, Gen. Augusto Pinochet, extradited from the United Kingdom to stand trial for human rights abuses; and an apology for Belgium's role in the Rwandan genocide and the provision of funding in Rwanda for an AIDS control programme. In October 2000 the Belgian Government announced that it was to investigate the role it may have played in the murder of the Congo's first Prime Minister, Patrice Lumumba, in 1961.

In 2000 Belgium was criticized in a UN report on sanctions against diamonds used to fund anti-Government rebels in Angola for 'extremely lax controls and regulations governing the Antwerp market'. The new Government protested, however, that it had already agreed a certification scheme with Angola to ensure that it did not sell diamonds from rebel-held areas.

Government

Belgium is a constitutional and hereditary monarchy, consisting of a federation of the largely autonomous regions of Brussels, Flanders and Wallonia and of the Flemish-, French- and German-speaking language communities. The central legislature consists of a bicameral Parliament (the Chamber of Representatives and the Senate). The Chamber has 150 members, all directly elected for a term of four years by universal adult suffrage, on the basis of proportional representation. The Senate has 71 normal members, of whom 40 are directly elected at intervals of four years, also by universal suffrage on the basis of proportional representation, 21 are appointed by the legislative bodies of the three language communities (see below), and 10 are co-opted by the elected members. In addition, children of the King are entitled to honorary membership of the Senate from 18 years of age and acquire voting rights at the age of 21. Members of both Houses serve for up to four years. Executive power, nominally vested in the King, is exercised by the Cabinet. The King appoints the Prime Minister and, on the latter's advice, other Ministers. The Cabinet is responsible to the Chamber of

Representatives. The three regions and three linguistic communities are represented by the following directly-elected legislative administrations: a combined administration for Flanders and the Flemish-speaking community, regional administrations for Wallonia and Brussels, and separate administrations for French- and German-speakers. The regional administrations have sole responsibility for the environment, housing, transport and public works, while the language community administrations supervise education policy and culture.

Defence

Belgium is a member of NATO. In August 2000 the total strength of the armed forces was 39,250, including an army of 26,800, a navy of 2,600 and an air force of 8,600. The defence budget for 2000 was estimated at BF 102,300m. Compulsory military service was abolished in 1995. In 1996 the Belgian and Netherlands navies came under a joint operational command, based at Den Helder, the Netherlands. In November 2000 Belgium committed 1,000 troops to a proposed joint EU rapid reaction force, which was to be ready and able to be deployed by 2003.

Economic Affairs

In 1998, according to estimates by the World Bank, Belgium's gross national product (GNP), measured at average 1996–98 prices, was US $258,986m., equivalent to $25,380 per head (or $ 23,622 per head on an international purchasing-power parity basis). During 1990–98, it was estimated, GNP per head increased at an average rate of 1.6% per year, in real terms. Over the same period, the population increased at an average rate of 0.3% per year. The country's gross domestic product (GDP) increased, in real terms, at an average annual rate of 2.2% in 1995–99; GDP rose by 2.4% in both 1998 and 1999.

Agriculture (including forestry and fishing) contributed 1.4% of GDP and engaged 2.1% of the employed labour force in 1999. The principal agricultural products are sugar beet, cereals and potatoes. Pig meat, beef and dairy products are also important. Exports of live animals and animal and vegetable products accounted for 5.7% of Belgium's total export revenue in 1998, and for 5.2% in 1999, despite the adverse effects of the dioxin contamination scandal (see Recent History). Agricultural GDP increased, in real terms, at an average annual rate of 4.8% in 1995–99; it increased by 5.7% in 1998 and by 11.3% in 1999.

Industry (including mining and quarrying, manufacturing, power and construction) contributed 26.5% of GDP and engaged 23.7% of the employed labour force in 1999. Industrial GDP increased at an average rate of 2.9% per year in 1995–99; it rose by 2.7% in 1998 and by 2.2% in 1999.

Belgium has few mineral resources, and the country's last coal mine closed in 1992. In 1999 extractive activities accounted for only 0.2% of GDP and engaged only 0.1% of the employed labour force. Belgium is, however, an important producer of copper, zinc and aluminium, smelted from imported ores. The sector's GDP declined at an average rate of 2.5% per year during 1995–99. It declined by 3.1% in 1998 but increased by 0.7% in 1999.

Manufacturing contributed 18.7% of GDP and engaged 16.9% of the employed labour force in 1999. In 1996 the main branches of manufacturing, in terms of value added, were fabricated metal products, machinery and equipment (accounting for 29.7% of the total), food products (16.7%) and chemical products (15.4%). During 1995–99 manufacturing GDP increased at an average annual rate of 3.1%; it rose by 1.4% in 1998 and by 1.2% in 1999.

Belgium's seven nuclear reactors accounted for 60% of total electricity generation in 1997 (one of the highest levels in the world). The country's dependence on imported petroleum and natural gas has, however, increased, following the announcement by the Government in 1988 of the indefinite suspension of its nuclear programme and of the construction of a gas-powered generator. In 1999 the Government announced that it would phase out nuclear power from 2015. Imports of mineral fuels comprised 6.7% of the value of Belgium's total imports in 1999.

The services sector contributed 72.1% of GDP in 1999, and engaged 74.2% of the employed labour force in that year. The presence in Belgium of the offices of many international organizations and businesses is a significant source of revenue. In September 2000 Euronext was formed from the merger of the stock exchanges of Brussels (Brussels Exchanges), Amsterdam (Amsterdam Exchanges) and Paris (Paris Bourse). The GDP of the services sector increased at an annual average rate of 1.8% in 1995–99; it increased by 3.1% in 1998 and by 2.2% in 1999.

In 1998 the Belgo-Luxembourg Economic Union (BLEU) recorded a visible trade surplus of US $7,255m., while there was a surplus of US $11,685m. on the current account of the balance of payments. In 1999 Belgium's principal source of imports (17.5%) was Germany; other major suppliers were the Netherlands (16.7%), France (13.7%), the United Kingdom (8.6%) and the USA (7.5%). The principal market for exports (17.9%) in that year was France; other major purchasers were Germany (17.7%), the Netherlands (12.8%), the United Kingdom (10.1%), Italy (5.6%) and the USA (5.2%). The principal exports in 1999 were basic manufactures (including gem diamonds and iron and steel), machinery and transport equipment, chemicals and related products, food and live animals and miscellaneous manufactured articles. The principal imports in that year were machinery and transport equipment, basic manufactures, chemicals and related products, miscellaneous manufactured articles and food and live animals.

In 1995 there was a budget deficit of BF 259,100m., equivalent to 3.2% of GDP. By means of strict austerity measures, however, the budget deficit had decreased to 0.9% of GDP by 1999. The country's total external debt was BF 11,295,700m. in 1999, equivalent to 116.1% of GDP. The annual rate of inflation averaged 2.0% in 1990–99. Consumer prices increased by an annual average of 1.0% in 1998 and by 1.1% in 1999. At November 2000 8.6% of the labour force were unemployed; there was, however, a discrepancy between the more affluent Flanders, where, according to national statistics, unemployment stood at 6.5% in March 2000, and Wallonia, where unemployment was 16.1%.

Belgium is a member of the European Union (EU—see p. 181), including the European Monetary System (EMS, see p. 198), and of the Benelux Economic Union (see p. 307). Belgium is also a member of the European System of Central Banks (ESCB), which was inaugurated in 1998 (see European Central Bank, p. 187).

Belgium's economic priorities were dominated in the mid-1990s by the need to reduce the large budget deficit and chronic public-sector debt in order to qualify for the final stage of economic and monetary union (EMU) within the EU. The reduction of the budget deficit to the equivalent of 1.3% of GDP and the level of public debt to 116.5% of GDP by 1998 (from 7% and 135% respectively in 1993) enabled Belgium to participate in the introduction of the European single currency, the euro, which came into effect on 1 January 1999 (in 11 participating countries). Despite the damage to the economy caused by the food contamination scandal in mid-1999, greater fiscal consolidation, allied to a general economic recovery in Europe, permitted the new Government, which acceded to power in June, to reduce the social charges payable by employers (the highest in Europe) and to inaugurate a youth employment programme. The percentage of the population in work improved from 57% in 1998 to 60% in 2000; further progress was considered essential for the long-term prospects of the economy, as social security and pension payments remained a serious burden on public finances. The privatization programme, which had partly financed Belgium's progress towards EMU membership, was to be accelerated under the new Government. The new administration, which presided over strong growth in the economy, continued to reduce the budget deficit and public indebtedness: a budget deficit of only 0.1% was expected in 2000 and the first budget surplus for 50 years was projected for 2001; while public debt was expected to fall to below 100% of GDP by the end of 2002. The government surplus was to be used to finance tax reductions (the total burden of taxation and other social contributions was 46% of GDP in 1998, one of the highest in the EU), which were announced in a Fiscal Reform Plan in October 2000. The reforms (costing an estimated BF 134,500m. between 2001 and 2006), which were to contribute to a 15% reduction in income tax over the next five years, included the removal of the two highest bands of taxation and plans to phase out the 3% 'crisis surcharge' that had been introduced to ensure Belgium met the criteria for monetary union. The Government also attempted to address the imbalances in the performances of the regional economies, granting greater fiscal control to the regions (long a demand of the more affluent Flanders), with the discretion to raise or lower local taxes.

Social Welfare

Belgium maintains a very comprehensive system of social welfare, which is administered mainly by the National Office for

Social Security. Contributions are paid by employers and employees towards family allowances, health insurance, unemployment benefit and pensions. Self-employed people's contributions cover only family allowances, pensions and a more limited level of health insurance. Most allowances and pensions are periodically adjusted in accordance with changes to the consumer price index. Workers and employees are entitled to four weeks' holiday for every 12-month period of work. They are insured against accidents occurring on the work premises or on the way to and from work. Unemployment benefit is paid by trade unions to their affiliates on behalf of the National Employment Office; unemployed people without trade union affiliation are paid from a public fund. A higher rate of medical reimbursement applies to widows, pensioners, orphans and the disabled, if they fall within a designated income bracket. Ordinary and supplementary family allowances are the entitlement of all families. Social welfare is also administered at a local level by Public Assistance Commissions, which have been established in every municipality. In 1982 Belgium had 531 hospital establishments, with a total of 92,686 beds (one for every 106 inhabitants), and in 1998 there were 364 physicians and 70 dentists per 100,000 inhabitants. Current legislation restricts the number of hospital beds and establishments to the 1982 level. Government expenditure on social security, health benefits, family allowances and pensions was curtailed during the 1990s. In 1996 total expenditure by the central Government on health was equivalent to some 11.1% of total expenditure, or 6.6% of GDP.

Education

Legislation granting responsibility for the formulation of education policy to the administrations of the Flemish-, French- and German-speaking communities came into effect in 1993. Education may be provided by the Communities, by public authorities or by private interests. All educational establishments, whether official or 'free' (privately-organized), receive most of their funding from the Communities. Roman Catholic schools constitute the greatest number of 'free' establishments.

Full-time education in Belgium is compulsory between the ages of six and 16 years. Thereafter, pupils must remain in part-time education for a further two-year period. About 90% of infants attend state-financed nursery schools. Elementary education begins at six years of age and consists of three courses of two years each. Secondary education, beginning at the age of 12, lasts for six years and is divided into three two-year cycles or, in a few cases, two three-year cycles. Enrolment at elementary schools in 1995 included 98% of children in the relevant age-group (males 99%; females 98%), while the comparable ratio at secondary schools was 88% (males 89%; females 87%).

The requirement for university entrance is a pass in the 'examination of maturity', taken after the completion of secondary studies. Courses are divided into 2–3 years of general preparation followed by 2–3 years of specialization. The French Community controls four universities, while the Flemish Community controls three such institutions; in addition, there are 11 university centres or faculties (six French, five Flemish). In 1999/2000 an estimated total of 128,000 students were enrolled in university-level establishments. Non-university institutions of higher education provide arts education, technical training and teacher training; in 1999/2000 an estimated 170,000 students were enrolled in such institutions. In 1995 enrolment at tertiary level was equivalent to 56% of those in the relevant age-group (males 55%; females 57%). A national study fund provides grants where necessary and almost 20% of students receive scholarships.

Expenditure on education by all levels of government was BF 439,608m. in 1994 (equivalent to 10.2% of total government spending).

Public Holidays

2001: 1 January (New Year's Day), 16 April (Easter Monday), 1 May (Labour Day), 24 May (Ascension Day), 4 June (Whit Monday), 11 July (Flemish-speaking Community), 21 July (Independence Day), 15 August (Assumption), 27 September (French-speaking Community), 1 November (All Saints' Day), 11 November (Armistice Day), 15 November (German-speaking Community), 25 December (Christmas Day).

2002: 1 January (New Year's Day), 1 April (Easter Monday), 1 May (Labour Day), 9 May (Ascension Day), 20 May (Whit Monday), 11 July (Flemish-speaking Community), 21 July (Independence Day), 15 August (Assumption), 27 September (French-speaking Community), 1 November (All Saints' Day), 11 November (Armistice Day), 15 November (German-speaking Community), 25 December (Christmas Day).

Weights and Measures

The metric system is in force.

Statistical Survey

Source: mainly Institut National de Statistique, 44 rue de Louvain, 1000 Brussels; tel. (2) 548-62-11; fax (2) 548-63-67; e-mail info@statbel.mineco.fgov.be; internet statbel.fgov.be.

Area and Population

AREA, POPULATION AND DENSITY

Area (sq km)	30,528*
Population (census results)†	
1 March 1981	9,848,647
1 March 1991	
Males	4,875,982
Females	5,102,699
Total	9,978,681
Population (official estimates at 31 December)†	
1997	10,192,264
1998	10,213,752
1999	10,239,085
Density (per sq km) at 31 December 1999	335.4

* 11,787 sq miles.   † Population is *de jure*.

PROVINCES (31 December 1999)

	Area (sq km)	Population	Density (per sq km)	Capital (with population)
Flemish region	13,521	5,940,251	439.3	
Antwerp	2,867	1,643,972	573.4	Antwerp (446,525*)
Brabant (Flemish)	2,106	1,014,704	481.8	Leuven (88,014)
Flanders (East)	2,982	1,361,623	456.6	Ghent (224,180)
Flanders (West)	3,144	1,128,774	359.0	Brugge (116,246)
Limburg	2,422	791,178	326.7	Hasselt (68,058)
Walloon region	16,845	3,339,516	198.2	
Brabant (Walloon)	1,091	349,884	320.7	Wavre (31,033)
Hainaut	3,786	1,279,467	337.9	Mons (90,935)
Liège	3,862	1,019,442	264.0	Liège (185,639)
Luxembourg	4,440	246,820	55.6	Arlon (24,791)
Namur	3,666	443,903	121.1	Namur (105,692)
Brussels (capital)	162	959,318	5,921.7	
Total	30,528	10,239,085	335.4	

* Including suburbs.

PRINCIPAL TOWNS (population at 31 December 1999)

Bruxelles (Brussel, Brussels)	959,318*
Antwerpen (Anvers, Antwerp)	446,525†
Gent (Gand, Ghent)	224,180
Charleroi	200,827
Liège (Luik)	185,639
Brugge (Bruges)	116,246
Namur (Namen)	105,419
Mons (Bergen)	90,935
Leuven (Louvain)	88,014
Aalst (Alost)	76,313
Mechelen (Malines)	75,438
Kortrijk (Courtrai)	74,790
Sint-Niklaas (Saint-Nicolas)	68,290
Hasselt	68,058
Tournai (Doornik)	67,379
Oostende (Ostende, Ostend)	67,279

* Including Schaerbeek, Anderlecht and other suburbs.
† Including Deurne and other suburbs.

BIRTHS, MARRIAGES AND DEATHS

	Registered live births		Registered marriages*		Registered deaths†	
	Number	Rate (per 1,000)	Number	Rate (per 1,000)	Number	Rate (per 1,000)
1992	124,774	12.4	58,156	5.8	104,200	10.4
1993	120,848	12.0	54,112	5.4	106,834	10.6
1994	116,449	11.5	51,962	5.1	104,894	10.4
1995	115,638	11.4	51,402	5.1	105,933	10.5
1996	116,208	11.4	50,552	5.0	105,322	10.4
1997	116,244	11.4	47,759	4.7	104,190	10.2
1998	114,276	11.2	44,460	4.4	104,583	10.3
1999	113,469	11.1	44,171	4.3	104,904	10.2

* Including marriages among Belgian armed forces stationed outside the country and alien armed forces in Belgium, unless performed by local foreign authority.
† Including Belgian armed forces stationed outside the country but excluding alien armed forces stationed in Belgium.

Expectation of life (official estimates, years at birth, 1996–98): Males 74.81; Females 81.08.

EMPLOYMENT
(estimates, '000 persons aged 15 and over, at 30 June each year)

	1997	1998	1999
Agriculture, hunting and forestry	78.4	78.4	78.8
Fishing	2.0	2.1	2.1
Mining and quarrying	4.2	4.3	4.4
Manufacturing	654.9	657.6	651.0
Electricity, gas and water supply	27.6	28.1	28.2
Construction	221.9	222.0	229.8
Wholesale and retail trade; repair of motor vehicles, motorcycles and personal and household goods	501.7	500.1	509.5
Hotels and restaurants	105.1	104.9	104.2
Transport, storage and communications	258.5	261.5	265.5
Financial intermediation	130.3	130.4	130.0
Real estate, renting and business activities	426.8	442.4	451.2
Public administration and defence; compulsory social security	402.3	407.2	415.4
Education	305.6	305.7	306.8
Health and social work	391.6	405.4	415.3
Other community, social and personal service activities	145.9	146.3	149.5
Private households with employed persons	99.8	106.1	108.9
Total in home employment	3,756.5	3,802.3	3,850.6
Persons working abroad (net)	52.4	54.1	54.9
Total employed	3,809.0	3,856.3	3,905.5

Unemployment (ILO definition, '000 persons aged 15 years and over, at April): 375.1 in 1997; 383.7 in 1998; 375.0 in 1999.

Source: Service Statistiques financières et économiques, Banque Nationale de Belgique.

Agriculture

(Figures include totals for Luxembourg)

PRINCIPAL CROPS ('000 metric tons)

	1997	1998	1999
Wheat and spelt	1,717	1,803	1,575
Barley	441	411	388
Maize	66	251	405
Oats	57	45	43
Other cereals	112	116	82
Potatoes	2,899	2,438	3,007
Rapeseed	24	25†	29†
Cabbages	85	73	80*
Tomatoes	303	316	300*
Cauliflowers	90	96	90*
Cucumbers and gherkins	30	27	25*
Beans (green)	72	70	60*
Peas (green)	166	170*	165*
Carrots	136	131	135*
Other vegetables	797	798	788*
Sugar beet	6,545	5,366	7,112
Apples	373	421	562
Pears	131	153*	163*
Strawberries	36	48	48*
Other fruits and berries	18	30	33†

* FAO estimate.   † Unofficial figure.

Source: FAO.

LIVESTOCK ('000 head, year ending September)

	1997	1998	1999
Horses	67	67*	67*
Cattle	3,280	3,184	3,185
Pigs	7,194	7,436	7,632
Sheep	162	155†	155*
Goats	12	12	12*
Chickens	48,000	53,300	38,000*
Ducks	36	29	30*
Geese	10	9	10*
Turkeys	297	339	340*

* FAO estimate.   † Unofficial figure.

LIVESTOCK PRODUCTS ('000 metric tons)

	1997	1998	1999
Beef and veal	340	303	281
Mutton and lamb	4	4	2
Pig meat	1,033	1,085	977
Horse meat	5	5	5*
Poultry meat	337	375	371
Other meat	25	28	27
Cows' milk	3,477	3,682	3,294†
Butter	107	112	103†
Cheese	78†	75†	76*
Hen eggs	228	238	235
Cattle hides*	31	28	29

* FAO estimate(s).   † Unofficial figure.

Source: FAO.

Forestry

(Figures include totals for Luxembourg)

ROUNDWOOD REMOVALS
('000 cubic metres, excluding bark)

	1996	1997	1998
Sawlogs, veneer logs and logs for sleepers	2,470	2,400	2,480
Pulpwood	875	875	1,175
Other industrial wood	110	210	110
Fuel wood	550	500	550
Total	4,005	3,985	4,315

Source: FAO, *Yearbook of Forest Products*.

SAWNWOOD PRODUCTION
('000 cubic metres, including railway sleepers)

	1996	1997	1998
Coniferous (softwood)	880	830	880
Broadleaved (hardwood)	270	270	270
Total	1,150	1,100	1,150

Source: FAO, *Yearbook of Forest Products*.

Fishing

('000 metric tons, live weight)

	1996	1997	1998
Capture	30.8	30.5	30.8
European plaice	7.7	7.5	7.4
Common dab	0.7	0.8	1.0
Lemon sole	1.1	1.0	1.3
Common sole	5.2	4.5	4.1
Atlantic cod	4.5	5.7	6.9
Haddock	0.4	0.7	1.0
Whiting	1.3	1.0	0.9
Angler (Monk)	1.4	1.1	1.0
Rays	1.4	1.3	1.2
Aquaculture	0.9	0.8	0.8
Total catch	31.8	31.3	31.7

Source: FAO, *Yearbook of Fishery Statistics*.

Mining

('000 metric tons, unless otherwise indicated)

	1995	1996	1997
Lignite	637	560	427
Uranium (metric tons)	25	28	28
Kaolin*	300	300	300
Chalk	2,186	2,139	2,071

* Estimates.

1998: ('000 metric tons): Kaolin 300 (estimate); Chalk 2,099.

Source: partly US Geological Survey and UN, *Industrial Commodity Statistics Yearbook*.

Industry

SELECTED PRODUCTS
('000 metric tons, unless otherwise indicated)

	1996	1997	1998
Wheat flour[1]	1,319	1,343	1,332
Raw sugar	979	1,034	995
Margarine	351.5	341.5	304.3
Beer ('000 hectolitres)	n.a.	14,758.3	14,815.7
Cigarettes (million)	17,471	18,061	17,500
Cotton yarn—pure and mixed (metric tons)	20,208	22,206	20,371
Woven cotton fabrics—pure and mixed (metric tons)[2]	37,126	37,590	39,281
Flax yarn (metric tons)[3]	2,453	2,920	3,027
Wool yarn—pure and mixed (metric tons)	12,587	13,146	14,868
Woven woollen fabrics—pure and mixed (metric tons)[2]	2,106	2,632	2,971
Woven rayon and acetate fabrics—pure and mixed (metric tons)[4]	68,189	70,757	73,440
Mechanical wood pulp[5]	173	173	173
Chemical and semi-chemical wood pulp[5]	209	209	209
Newsprint[5]	104	104	104
Other paper and paperboard	1,455.6	1,621.3	1,742.3
Ethyl alcohol—Ethanol ('000 hectolitres)	150.1	64.1	102.4
Sulphuric acid (100%)	677.7	648.8	587.4
Nitric acid (100%)	48.0	50.4	55.7
Liquefied petroleum gas	605	578	598
Naphtha	1,148	1,407	1,524
Motor spirit (petrol)	5,947	6,103	6,431
Kerosene	100	113	128
White spirit	112	164	157
Jet fuel	1,739	1,644	2,067
Distillate fuel oils	12,619	12,520	12,447
Residual fuel oil	6,949.8	7,694.3	8,349.2
Petroleum bitumen (asphalt)	771.8	951.5	956.8
Coke-oven coke	3,551	3,402	300.3
Cement	9,822	9,926	9,875
Pig-iron	8,626.7	8,076.5	8,618.1
Crude steel	10,751.7	10,717.6	11,403.8
Refined copper—unwrought (metric tons)[6]	593,070	619,187	637,992
Refined lead—unwrought (metric tons)[7]	142,178	142,901	111,858
Tin: secondary (metric tons)[8]	3,000	3,000	2,500
Passenger motor cars ('000)[9]	1,153.4	1,020.4	974.9
Commercial motor vehicles ('000)[9]	78.0	81.7	n.a.
Electric energy (million kWh)	76,147.4	78,891.7	79,492.4
Manufactured gas (million cu metres)	1,510	1,366	1,334

1999: Beer ('000 hectolitres) 15,165; Cigarettes (million) 14,700; Tin (metric tons)[8] 8,000; Passenger motor cars ('000)[9] 900.

[1] Industrial production only.
[2] Including blankets and carpets.
[3] Including yarn made from tow.
[4] Including fabrics of natural silk and blankets and carpets of cellulosic fibres.
[5] Including production in Luxembourg. Source: FAO, *Yearbook of Forest Products*.
[6] Including alloys and the processing of refined copper imported from the Democratic Republic of the Congo.
[7] Primary and secondary production, including alloys and remelted lead.
[8] Estimated production. Source: US Geological Survey.
[9] Assembled wholly or mainly from imported parts.

Finance

CURRENCY AND EXCHANGE RATES

Monetary Units
100 centimes (centiemen) = 1 franc belge (frank) or Belgian franc (BF).

Sterling, Dollar and Euro Equivalents (29 December 2000)
£1 sterling = 64.691 francs;
US $1 = 43.353 francs;
€1 = 40.340 francs;
1,000 Belgian francs = £15.46 = $23.07 = €24.79.

Average Exchange Rate (francs per US $)
1998   36.299
1999   37.864
2000   43.785

Note: Since the introduction of the euro, with Belgian participation, on 1 January 1999, a fixed exchange rate of €1 = 40.3399 Belgian francs has been in operation.

BUDGET ('000 million Belgian francs)*

Revenue†	1995	1996	1997
Tax revenue	3,462.5	3,571.2	3,758.5
Taxes on income, profits and capital gains	1,262.0	1,293.0	1,382.1
Social security contributions	1,221.1	1,229.1	1,274.4
Taxes on property	89.0	102.0	115.6
Domestic taxes on goods and services	890.4	950.8	991.0
General sales, turnover or value-added taxes	553.9	581.7	605.9
Excises	193.2	202.6	210.4
Other current revenue	86.1	95.0	60.1
Entrepreneurial and property income	53.4	52.4	30.8
Capital revenue	18.9	19.0	3.9
Total	**3,567.5**	**3,685.2**	**3,822.5**

Expenditure‡	1995	1996	1997
Current expenditure	3,694.0	3,731.7	3,855.8
Expenditure on goods and services	714.3	739.0	768.4
Wages and salaries	577.0	527.7	549.3
Interest payments	695.8	682.7	668.7
Subsidies and other current transfers	2,283.9	2,310.0	2,418.7
Subsidies	149.4	157.7	135.2
Transfers to other levels of national government	228.4	240.3	241.4
Transfers to non-profit institutions and households	1,871.9	1,859.7	1,981.7
Capital expenditure	191.6	177.8	189.7
Capital transfers	118.7	117.2	123.5
Total	**3,885.6**	**3,909.5**	**4,045.6**

* Figures refer to the consolidated transactions of the central Government. In addition to the general budget, the data include the operations of social security funds, government agencies and other extrabudgetary funds.
† Excluding grants received ('000 million Belgian francs): 11.1 in 1995; 5.0 in 1996; 20.3 in 1997.
‡ Excluding lending minus repayments ('000 million Belgian francs): –47.9 in 1995; –9.1 in 1996; –26.8 in 1997.

Source: IMF, *Government Finance Statistics Yearbook*.

INTERNATIONAL RESERVES (US $ million at 31 December)*

	1998	1999	2000
Gold†‡	2,565	2,413	2,277
IMF special drawing rights . .	610	271	307
Reserve position in IMF . . .	1,899	2,290	1,699
Foreign exchange‡	15,763	8,377	7,988
Total	20,837	13,350	12,271

* From January 1999 figures were adjusted to accord with the Eurosystem's definition of reserves.
† Valued at market-related prices.
‡ Figures for gold and foreign exchange refer to the monetary association between Belgium and Luxembourg and exclude deposits made with the European Monetary Institute (now the European Central Bank).

Source: IMF, *International Financial Statistics.*

MONEY SUPPLY ('000 million Belgian francs at 31 December)

	1996	1997	1998
Notes and coins in circulation. .	435.8	440.6	438.8
Demand deposits at banking institutions	1,172.3	1,245.5	1,405.6
Total money	1,608.1	1,686.1	1,844.5

Source: Banque Nationale de Belgique.

COST OF LIVING (Consumer Price Index; base: 1990 = 100)

	1996	1997	1998
Food	104.8	107.1	109.0
Fuel and light	107.0	109.5	105.5
Clothing.	113.4	114.1	115.6
Rent	126.5	128.7	130.2
All items (incl. others) . .	115.2	117.1	118.2

1999: Food 109.3; All items 119.5.
Source: mainly ILO, *Yearbook of Labour Statistics.*

NATIONAL ACCOUNTS
(million Belgian francs at current prices)

National Income and Product

	1997	1998	1999
Compensation of employees . .	4,486,504	4,655,487	4,842,489
Operating surplus . . .	1,928,137	2,005,239	2,030,219
Domestic factor incomes .	6,414,641	6,660,726	6,872,708
Consumption of fixed capital . .	1,252,651	1,320,326	1,383,000
Gross domestic product (GDP) at factor cost.	7,667,292	7,981,052	8,255,708
Indirect taxes	1,215,333	1,262,562	1,342,191
Less Subsidies	155,614	162,069	174,619
GDP in purchasers' values. .	8,727,011	9,081,545	9,423,280
Factor income received from abroad	1,204,560	1,278,601	1,460,019
Less Factor income paid abroad	1,079,139	1,152,032	1,334,085
Subsidies received from abroad	33,334	30,017	34,690
Less Indirect taxes paid abroad	89,131	90,564	87,993
Gross national product (GNP) .	8,796,635	9,147,567	9,495,911
Less Consumption of fixed capital .	1,252,651	1,320,326	1,383,000
National income in market prices	7,543,984	7,827,241	8,112,911
Other current transfers from abroad	104,519	105,107	81,591
Less Other current transfers paid abroad	174,271	188,657	193,515
National disposable income	7,474,232	7,743,691	8,000,987

Source: Service Statistiques financières et économiques, Banque Nationale de Belgique.

Expenditure on the Gross Domestic Product

	1997	1998	1999
Government final consumption expenditure	1,857,166	1,923,916	2,016,483
Private final consumption expenditure	4,694,689	4,899,913	5,054,333
Increase in stocks . . .	−20,041	−1,146	−14,032
Gross fixed capital formation . .	1,801,597	1,895,562	2,009,000
Total domestic expenditure .	8,333,441	8,718,245	9,065,784
Exports of goods and services . .	6,608,300	6,879,100	7,213,322
Less Imports of goods and services	6,214,700	6,515,800	6,855,826
GDP in purchasers' values. .	8,727,011	9,081,545	9,423,280
GDP at constant 1995 prices .	8,510,850	8,717,501	8,955,887

Source: Service Statistiques financières et économiques, Banque Nationale de Belgique.

Gross Domestic Product by Economic Activity

	1997	1998	1999
Agriculture, hunting and forestry	132,480	128,394	122,261
Fishing	2,184	2,348	1,867
Mining and quarrying . . .	13,888	13,506	14,080
Manufacturing	1,616,434	1,650,822	1,644,106
Electricity, gas and water supply	246,914	243,107	233,994
Construction.	396,943	402,908	435,122
Wholesale and retail trade; repair of motor vehicles, motorcycles and personal and household goods	956,506	985,429	1,036,222
Hotels and restaurants . .	126,186	135,001	144,343
Transport, storage and communications . . .	559,401	584,021	596,727
Financial intermediation . .	536,522	587,058	639,335
Real estate, renting and business activities*.	1,627,187	1,754,021	1,834,103
Public administration and defence; compulsory social security	652,149	669,637	698,631
Education	536,016	551,570	562,911
Health and social work . .	499,937	516,438	535,562
Other community, social and personal service activities .	196,144	213,432	226,734
Private households with employed persons	43,951	45,808	47,378
Sub-total	8,142,842	8,483,500	8,773,376
Less Financial intermediation services indirectly measured	349,550	374,473	388,525
GDP at basic prices . . .	7,793,292	8,109,027	8,384,851
Taxes on products	1,036,204	1,076,768	1,149,287
Less Subsidies on products . .	102,485	104,250	110,858
GDP in purchasers' values. .	8,727,011	9,081,545	9,423,280

* Including imputed rents of owner-occupied dwellings.

Source: Service Statistiques financières et économiques, Banque Nationale de Belgique.

BALANCE OF PAYMENTS (US $ million)*

	1997	1998	1999
Exports of goods f.o.b.	149,497	153,558	154,069
Imports of goods f.o.b.	−141,794	−146,577	−146,814
Trade balance	7,703	6,981	7,255
Exports of services	35,503	38,081	40,144
Imports of services	−31,644	−34,411	−36,641
Balance on goods and services	11,542	10,651	10,758
Other income received	58,237	65,251	66,725
Other income paid	−51,882	−59,315	−61,238
Balance on goods, services and income	17,896	16,588	16,244
Current transfers received	7,142	7,006	6,703
Current transfers paid	−11,124	−11,426	−11,263
Current balance	13,914	12,168	11,685
Capital account (net)	403	−113	7
Direct investment abroad	−7,252	−28,845	−33,864
Direct investment from abroad	11,998	22,690	38,391
Portfolio investment assets	62,657	100,234	166,967
Portfolio investment liabilities	54,047	59,253	146,655
Financial derivatives assets	−330	489	918
Financial derivatives liabilities	444	302	1,141
Other investment assets	−48,692	7,467	−70,765
Other investment liabilities	40,352	22,836	71,199
Net errors and omissions	−1,171	1,893	−268
Overall balance	1,056	−2,095	−1,867

* Data refer to the Belgium-Luxembourg Economic Union and exclude transactions between the two countries.

Source: IMF, *International Financial Statistics*.

External Trade

PRINCIPAL COMMODITIES

(distribution by SITC, million Belgian francs)

Imports c.i.f.	1997	1998	1999
Food and live animals	487,182	505,356	486,337
Vegetables and fruit	125,063	135,033	135,678
Crude materials (inedible) except fuels	258,417	246,243	237,080
Mineral fuels, lubricants, etc.	387,638	301,215	357,025
Petroleum, petroleum products, etc.	281,591	202,852	266,133
Chemicals and related products	865,360	1,006,320	1,022,387
Organic chemicals	268,041	322,364	309,185
Medicinal and pharmaceutical products	130,863	168,750	190,325
Plastics in primary forms	160,627	172,917	168,407
Basic manufactures	1,221,227	1,267,757	1,299,643
Paper, paperboard and manufactures	121,273	135,917	135,409
Textile yarn, fabrics, etc.	151,180	157,307	142,984
Non-metallic mineral manufactures	456,370	422,554	497,812
Iron and steel	158,812	194,133	164,277
Non-ferrous metals	112,782	111,339	104,151
Other metal manufactures	133,548	149,836	153,549
Machinery and transport equipment	1,668,075	1,850,705	1,992,475
Power-generating machinery and equipment	136,297	157,570	159,363
Machinery specialized for particular industries	103,172	119,823	130,277
General industrial machinery, equipment and parts	205,439	226,369	233,989
Office machines and automatic data-processing machines	143,162	162,666	188,097

Imports c.i.f. — *continued*	1997	1998	1999
Telecommunications and sound equipment	112,690	134,770	157,965
Other electrical machinery, apparatus, etc.	243,781	251,562	274,294
Road vehicles (incl. air-cushion vehicles) and parts*	645,773	721,615	772,163
Miscellaneous manufactured articles	626,017	677,475	726,739
Clothing and accessories (excl. footwear)	170,813	183,696	189,891
Total (incl. others)	5,619,164	5,967,940	6,237,963

Exports f.o.b.	1997	1998	1999
Food and live animals	588,873	610,849	587,646
Vegetables and fruit	139,840	161,510	167,845
Crude materials (inedible) except fuels	164,493	154,986	162,440
Mineral fuels, lubricants, etc.	199,996	169,225	196,849
Petroleum, petroleum products, etc.	171,639	143,162	167,475
Chemicals and related products	1,195,734	1,282,159	1,378,609
Organic chemicals	222,063	269,799	300,928
Medicinal and pharmaceutical products	179,176	201,696	243,898
Plastics in primary forms	281,034	279,351	296,476
Basic manufactures	1,518,966	1,567,905	1,616,267
Textile yarn, fabrics, etc.	256,153	266,557	253,585
Non-metallic mineral manufactures	509,065	482,445	568,376
Iron and steel	275,273	318,028	274,402
Non-ferrous metals	128,616	125,263	122,890
Other metal manufactures	163,720	170,568	178,527
Machinery and transport equipment	1,800,266	1,954,975	2,039,660
Machinery specialized for particular industries	128,010	148,584	146,878
General industrial machinery, equipment and parts	166,974	196,137	216,762
Telecommunications and sound equipment	128,975	158,495	155,282
Other electrical machinery, apparatus, etc.	214,242	216,346	234,977
Road vehicles (incl. air-cushion vehicles) and parts*	885,648	942,360	957,895
Miscellaneous manufactured articles	572,398	642,864	684,421
Clothing and accessories (excl. footwear)	126,297	152,314	156,371
Total (incl. others)	6,142,848	6,491,340	6,780,785

* Data on parts exclude tyres, engines and electrical parts.

PRINCIPAL TRADING PARTNERS (million Belgian francs)*

Imports f.o.b.	1997	1998	1999
China, People's Repub.	91,189	93,949	119,095
France	779,104	827,380†	857,432†
Germany	971,232	1,068,867	1,089,447
Ireland	96,113	152,735	136,122
Israel	54,483	53,897	64,551
Italy	216,477	236,377	241,751
Japan	137,237	153,190	193,075
Netherlands	1,011,743	994,422	1,042,788
Spain	98,525‡	111,147	126,249
Sweden	143,094	159,007	156,926
Switzerland	60,976	59,158	56,931
United Kingdom	510,786	506,827	534,199
USA	431,081	469,433	469,559
Total (incl. others)	5,619,164	5,967,940	6,237,963

Exports f.o.b.	1997	1998	1999
Austria	65,067	72,484	76,490
France	1,063,458	1,159,937†	1,211,543†
Germany	1,146,700	1,221,486	1,201,942
India	102,533	96,814	123,945
Israel	113,858	95,717	121,843
Italy	329,870	367,751	377,823
Japan	72,383	61,462	80,296
Luxembourg	117,981	122,864	137,636
Netherlands	789,268	827,577	865,412
Spain	189,634‡	228,403	268,099
Sweden	87,955	100,501	106,349
Switzerland	101,199	102,657	98,265
United Kingdom . . .	607,314	645,195	682,344
USA	299,549	329,847	353,052
Total (incl. others) . .	6,142,848	6,491,340	6,780,785

* Imports by country of production; exports by country of last consignment.
† Including trade with Overseas Departments (French Guiana, Guadeloupe, Martinique and Réunion).
‡ Excluding trade with the Canary Islands.

Transport

RAILWAYS (traffic)

	1997	1998	1999
Passenger journeys ('000) . .	143,566	145,856	147,291
Passenger-km (million) . .	6,981	7,097	7,354
Freight carried ('000 metric tons)	58,849	60,696	59,149
Freight ton-km (million) . .	7,465	7,600	7,392

ROAD TRAFFIC (motor vehicles in use at 1 August)

	1996	1997	1998
Private cars	4,339,231	4,415,343	4,491,734
Buses and coaches . . .	14,660	14,667	14,566
Goods vehicles	416,716	435,237	453,122
Tractors (non-agricultural) . .	40,449	41,346	42,342
Motorcycles and mopeds . .	209,015	221,623	238,053

Private cars: 4,584,000 in 1999; 4,678,000 in 2000. Motorcycles and mopeds: 261,000 in 1999; 278,000 in 2000.

Sources: mainly Ministère des Communications et de l'Infrastructure.

SHIPPING

Fleet (at 30 June)

	1997	1998	1999
Merchant shipping:			
Steamships:			
number	1	1	1
displacement*	81.8	81.8	81.8
Motor vessels:			
number	27	24	14
displacement*	524	344	259
Inland waterways:			
Powered craft:			
number	1,264	n.a.	n.a.
displacement*	1,041	n.a.	n.a.
Non-powered craft:			
number	157	n.a.	n.a.
displacement*	384	n.a.	n.a.

* '000 gross registered tons.
Source: Ministère des Communications et de l'Infrastructure.

Freight Traffic ('000 metric tons)

	1997	1998	1999
Sea-borne shipping:			
Goods loaded	61,856	60,430	63,393
Goods unloaded	100,208	111,129	102,647
Inland waterways:			
Goods loaded	54,418	n.a.	n.a.
Goods unloaded	68,418	n.a.	n.a.

Source: partly Ministère des Communications et de l'Infrastructure.

CIVIL AVIATION (traffic)

	1996	1997	1998
Kilometres flown ('000) . .	118,218	121,556	167,464
Passenger-km ('000) . . .	9,099,901	11,273,577	16,971,798
Ton-km ('000)	818,990	1,014,622	1,527,490
Mail ton-km ('000) . . .	16,231	13,090	n.a.

Figures refer to SABENA Belgian Airlines.
Source: Ministère des Communications et de l'Infrastructure.

Tourism

NUMBER OF TOURIST NIGHTS BY COUNTRY OF ORIGIN*

	1996†	1998	1999
France	1,450,277	1,604,108	1,644,239
Germany	2,737,254	2,523,475	2,620,577
Italy	419,325	412,927	437,803
Japan	273,413	274,197	290,193
Netherlands	4,610,188	4,502,548	4,718,436
Spain	305,120	314,311	316,474
United Kingdom . . .	1,640,723	2,126,911	2,308,311
USA	638,099	704,789	720,474
Total (incl. others) . . .	14,440,943	14,838,367	15,365,791

* Nights spent by foreign visitors in hotels and similar establishments.
† 1997 figures not available.

Total number of tourist arrivals: 5,829,257 in 1996; 6,037,031 in 1997; 6,179,254 in 1998; 6,369,030 in 1999.

Sources: World Tourism Organization, *Yearbook of Tourism Statistics*; Office de Promotion du Tourisme Wallonie-Bruxelles.

Communications Media

	1995	1996	1997
Telephones ('000 main lines in use)	4,632	4,818	4,939
Telefax stations ('000 in use) . .	180	190	n.a.
Mobile cellular telephones ('000 subscribers)	235.3	478.1	974.5
Radio receivers ('000 in use) . .	8,000	8,050	8,075
Television receivers ('000 in use) .	4,600	4,700	4,720
Daily newspapers:			
Titles	31	30	n.a.
Average circulation ('000 copies)	1,628	1,625	n.a.

Mobile cellular telephones ('000 subscribers): 1,756.3 in 1998; 3,186.6 in 1999.

Sources: mainly UN, *Statistical Yearbook*; UNESCO, *Statistical Yearbook*.

Education

(1996/97)

	Institutions		Students	
	French*	Flemish	French*	Flemish
Pre-primary . . .	1,932	2,175	171,478	253,043
Primary	2,023	2,378	320,454	417,369
Secondary . . .	648	1,079	349,170	447,775
Non-university higher education .	105	29	73,359	94,140
University level . .	9	8	62,300	n.a.

* Figures for 1995/96.

1999/2000 (estimates): Total students: Pre-primary 399,000; Primary 778,000; Secondary 779,000; Non-university higher education 170,000; University level 128,000.

Teachers: French (1995/96): Pre-primary and primary 38,150; Secondary 57,555; Higher education 20,927. Flemish (1996/97): Pre-primary and primary 44,018; Secondary 57,707; Higher education 17,087.

Directory

The Constitution

The Belgian Constitution has been considerably modified by amendments since its creation in 1831. Belgium is a constitutional monarchy. The central legislature consists of a bicameral Parliament (the Chamber of Representatives and Senate). In July 1993 the Constitution was amended to provide for a federation of the largely autonomous regions of Brussels, Flanders and Wallonia and of the Flemish-, French- and German-speaking language communities. Article 1 of the Constitution states 'Belgium is a federal state which consists of communities and regions'. The three regions and three linguistic groups are represented by the following directly-elected legislative assemblies: a combined assembly for Flanders and the Flemish-speaking community, regional assemblies for Wallonia and Brussels, and separate assemblies for French- and German-speakers. Each assembly is elected for a term of four years. The regional administrations have sole responsibility for the local economy, the environment, housing, transport and public works, while the language community administrations supervise education policy and culture.

ELECTORAL SYSTEM

Members of Parliament must be 25 years of age, and they are elected by secret ballot according to a system of proportional representation. Suffrage is universal for citizens of 18 years or over, and voting is compulsory.

The Chamber of Representatives consists of 150 members, who are elected for four years unless the Chamber is dissolved before that time has elapsed. The Senate comprises 71 normal members, of whom 40 are directly elected, usually at intervals of four years, 21 are appointed by the legislative assemblies of the three language communities (10 each from the Flemish- and French-speaking communities and one from the German-speaking community), and 10 are co-opted by the elected members. Children of the King are entitled to honorary membership of the Senate from 18 years of age and acquire voting rights at the age of 21.

THE CROWN

The King has the right to veto legislation, but, in practice, he does not exercise it. The King is nominally the supreme head of the executive, but, in fact, he exercises his control through the Cabinet, which is responsible for all acts of government to the Chamber of Representatives. According to the Constitution, the King appoints his own ministers, but in practice, since they are responsible to the Chamber of Representatives and need its confidence, they are generally the choice of the Representatives. Similarly, the royal initiative is in the control of the ministry.

LEGISLATION

Legislation is introduced either by the federal Government or the members in the two Houses, and as the party complexion of both Houses is generally almost the same, measures passed by the Chamber of Representatives are usually passed by the Senate. Each House elects its own President at the beginning of the session, who acts as an impartial Speaker, although he is a party nominee. The Houses elect their own committees, through which all legislation passes. They are so well organized that through them the Legislature has considerable power of control over the Cabinet. Nevertheless, according to the Constitution (Article 68), certain treaties must be communicated to the Chamber only as soon as the 'interest and safety of the State permit'. Further, the Government possesses an important power of dissolution which it uses; a most unusual feature is that it may be applied to either House separately or to both together (Article 71).

Revision of the Constitution is to be first settled by an ordinary majority vote of both Houses, specifying the article to be amended. The Houses are then automatically dissolved. The new Chambers thereupon determine the amendments to be made, with the provision that in each House the presence of two-thirds of the members is necessary for a quorum, and a two-thirds majority of those voting is required.

The Government

HEAD OF STATE

King of the Belgians: HM King ALBERT II (took the oath 9 August 1993).

THE CABINET
(April 2001)

A coalition of Vlaamse Liberalen en Demokraten—Partij van de Burger (VLD), the Parti Réformateur Libéral (PRL), the Parti Social-

iste (PS), the Socialistische Partij (SP), Anders Gaan Leven (Agalev) and the Ecologistes Confédérés pour l'Organisation des Luttes Originales (Ecolo).

Prime Minister: GUY VERHOFSTADT (VLD).

Deputy Prime Minister and Minister for Employment: LAURETTE ONKELINX (PS).

Deputy Prime Minister and Minister for Foreign Affairs: LOUIS MICHEL (PRL).

Deputy Prime Minister and Minister for the Budget, Social Integration and Social Economy: JOHAN VANDE LANOTTE (SP).

Deputy Prime Minister and Minister for Mobility and Transport: ISABELLE DURANT (Ecolo).

Minister for Consumer Interests, Health and Environment: MAGDA AELVOET (Agalev).

Minister for the Interior: ANTOINE DUQUESNE (PRL).

Minister for Social Affairs and Pensions: FRANK VANDENBROUCKE (SP).

Minister for Civil Service and Modernization of Public Administration: LUC VAN DEN BOSSCHE (SP).

Minister for Defence: ANDRÉ FLAHAUT (PS).

Minister of Agriculture and the Self-employed: JAAK GABRIELS (VLD).

Minister of Justice: MARK VERWILGHEN (VLD).

Minister of Finance: DIDIER REYNDERS (PRL).

Minister for Telecommunications, Public Enterprises and Participation: RIK DAEMS (CVD).

Minister for Economic Affairs and Scientific Research, charged with Metropolitan Policy: CHARLES PICQUE (PS).

State Secretary, attached to the Minister for Foreign Affairs: ANNEMARIE NEYTS (VLD).

State Secretary for Development Co-operation, attached to the Minister for Foreign Affairs: EDDY BOUTMANS (Agalev).

State Secretary for Energy and Sustainable Development, attached to the Minister for Mobility and Transport: OLIVIER DELEUZE (Agalev).

MINISTRIES

Office of the Prime Minister: 16 rue de la Loi, 1000 Brussels; tel. (2) 501-02-11; fax (2) 512-69-53; internet www.premier.fgov.be.

Department of Development Co-operation: 45–46 blvd du Régent, 1000 Brussels; tel. (2) 549-09-20; fax (2) 512-21-23; e-mail cabos@badc.fgov.be; internet diplobel.fgov.be.

Department of Energy and Sustainable Development: 56 rue des Colonies, 1000 Brussels; tel. (2) 227-07-00; fax (2) 219-79-30.

Ministry of Agriculture and the Self-employed: 1 rue Marie-Thérèse, 1000 Brussels; tel. (2) 211-06-11; fax (2) 219-61-30; internet www.cmlag.fgov.be.

Ministry of the Budget, Social Integration and Social Economy: 180 rue Royale, 1000 Brussels; tel. (2) 210-19-11; fax (2) 217-33-28.

Ministry of Civil Service and Modernization of Public Administration: Résidence Palais, 9th floor, 155 rue de la Loi, 1040 Brussels; tel. (2) 233-05-11; fax (2) 233-05-90; internet www.mazfp.fgov.be.

Ministry of Consumer Interests, Health and Environment: 7 ave des Arts, 1210 Brussels; tel. (2) 220-20-11; fax (2) 220-20-67; e-mail marjan.leichen@minsoc.fed.be.

Ministry of Defence: 8 rue Lambermont, 1000 Brussels; tel. (2) 550-28-11; fax (2) 550-29-19; internet mcd.fgov.be.

Ministry of Economic Affairs and Scientific Research: 23 square de Meeûs, 1000 Brussels; tel. (2) 506-51-11; fax (2) 511-46-83.

Ministry of Employment: 78–80 rue du Commerce, 1040 Brussels; tel. (2) 233-51-11; fax (2) 230-10-67; e-mail info@meta.fgov.be.

Ministry of Finance: 12 rue de la Loi, 1000 Brussels; tel. (2) 233-81-11; fax (2) 233-80-03; e-mail contact@ckfin.minfin.be.

Ministry of Foreign Affairs: 15 rue des Petits Carmes, 1000 Brussels; tel. (2) 501-82-11; fax (2) 511-63-85; e-mail cab.ae@diplobel.org; internet diplobel.fgov.be.

Ministry of the Interior: 60–62 rue Royale, 1000 Brussels; tel. (2) 504-85-11; fax (2) 504-85-00; e-mail cab.affint@mibz.fgov.be; internet mibz.fgov.be.

Ministry of Justice: 115 blvd de Waterloo, 1000 Brussels; tel. (2) 542-79-11; fax (2) 538-07-67; internet www.just.fgov.be.

Ministry of Mobility and Transport: 63–65 rue de la Loi, 1040 Brussels; tel. (2) 237-67-11; fax (2) 231-18-24; internet www.vici .fgov.be.

Ministry of Social Affairs and Pensions: 62 rue de la Loi, 1040 Brussels; tel. (2) 238-28-11; fax (2) 230-38-95; e-mail cabinetas@ minsoc.fed.be; internet www.vandenbroucke.fgov.be.

Ministry of Telecommunications, Public Enterprises and Participation: 7 place Quetelet, 1210 Brussels; tel. (2) 250-03-03; fax (2) 219-09-14; internet telcobel.fgov.be.

Legislature

CHAMBRE DES REPRÉSENTANTS/KAMER VAN VOLKSVERTEGENWOORDIGERS
(Chamber of Representatives)

General Election, 13 June 1999

	% of votes	Seats
VLD	14.3	23
CVP	14.1	22
PS	10.2	19
PRL-FDF	10.1	18
Vlaams Blok	9.9	15
SP	9.6	14
Ecolo	7.4	11
PSC	5.9	10
Agalev	7.0	9
VU-ID21	5.6	8
FN	1.5	1
Total (incl. others)	100.0	150

SÉNAT/SENAAT

General Election, 13 June 1999

	% of votes	Seats
VLD	15.4	6
CVP	14.7	6
PRL-FDF	10.6	5
PS	9.7	4
Vlaams Blok	9.4	4
SP	8.9	4
Ecolo	7.4	3
Agalev	7.1	3
PSC	6.0	3
VU-ID21	5.1	2
Total (incl. others)	100.0	40

In addition, the Senate has 21 members appointed by the legislative assemblies of the three language communities and 10 members co-opted by the elected members. Children of the King are entitled to honorary membership of the Senate from 18 years of age and acquire voting rights at the age of 21.

Advisory Councils

Conseil Central de l'Economie/Centrale Raad voor het Bedrijfsleven: 17–21 ave de la Joyeuse entrée, 1040 Brussels; tel. (2) 233-88-11; fax (2) 233-89-12; e-mail mail@ccecrb.fgov.be; internet www.ccecrb.fgov.be; f. 1948; representative and consultative body; advises the authorities on economic issues; 50 mems; Pres. Baron ROBERT TOLLET.

Conseil d'Etat/Raad van Staat: 33 rue de la Science, 1040 Brussels; tel. (2) 234-96-11; e-mail webmaster@raadvst-consetat.be; internet www.raadvst.consetat.be; f. 1946; advisory body on legislative and regulatory matters; supreme administrative court; hears complaints against the actions of the legislature; 38 mems; Pres. JEAN-JACQUES STRYCKMANS.

Regional and Community Administrations

Belgium is a federal state, and considerable power has been devolved to the regional administrations of Brussels, Wallonia and Flanders, and to the French-, German- and Flemish-speaking communities. The regional authorities have sole responsibility for the environment, housing, transport and public works, and for certain aspects of social welfare, while the community administrations are primarily responsible for cultural affairs and for education. The administra-

tions of Flanders and of the Flemish-speaking community are, however, homologous.

REGION OF FLANDERS AND THE FLEMISH-SPEAKING COMMUNITY

Minister-President: PATRICK DEWAEL (VLD).

Vlaams Parlement (Flemish Parliament): 27 Leuvensweg, 1011 Brussels; tel. (2) 552-11-11; fax (2) 513-11-22; internet www .vlaamsparlement.be; f. 1980; 124 mems.

Vlaamse Overheid (Flemish Authority): 19 Martelaarsplein, 1000 Brussels; tel. (2) 553-29-11; fax (2) 553-29-05; e-mail kabinet .dewael@vlaanderen.be; internet www.vlaanderen.be.

REGION OF WALLONIA

Minister-President: JEAN-CLAUDE VAN CAUWENBERGHE (PS).

Le Parlement Wallon (Walloon Parliament): 24 rue Saint-Nicolas, 5000 Namur; tel. (81) 23-10-36; fax (2) 23-12-20; internet parlement.wallonie.be; elects Government of Wallonia; 75 mems.

Gouvernement Wallon (Walloon Government): internet www .wallonie.org; 9 mems.

REGION OF BRUSSELS-CAPITAL

Minister-President: FRANÇOIS-XAVIER DE DONNEA (PRL).

Conseil de la Région de Bruxelles-Capitale/Brussels Hoofdstedelijke Raad (Council of the Region of Brussels-Capital): 1005 Brussels; tel. (2) 549-62-11; fax (2) 549-62-12; e-mail Parlement@parlbru.irisnet.be; internet www.parlbru.irisnet.be.

Gouvernement de la Région de Bruxelles-Capitale/Brusselse Hoofdstedelijke Regering (Government of Brussels-Capital): 7–9 rue Ducale, 1000 Brussels; tel. (2) 506-32-11; fax (2) 514-40-22; internet www.bruxelles.irisnet.be.

FRENCH-SPEAKING COMMUNITY

Minister-President: HERVÉ HASQUIN (PRL).

Parlement de la Communauté française de Belgique (Parliament of the French-speaking Community): 6 rue de la Loi, 1000 Brussels; tel. (2) 506-38-11; fax (2) 506-39-78; internet www.pcf.be; comprises mems of the Walloon Parliament and the 19 francophone mems of the Council of the Region of Brussels-Capital; 94 mems.

Gouvernement de la Communauté française de Belgique (Government of the French-speaking Community): 15–17 place Surlet de Chokier, 1040 Brussels; tel. (2) 227-32-11; fax (2) 227-33-53; internet www.cfwb.be.

GERMAN-SPEAKING COMMUNITY

Minister-President: KARL-HEINZ LAMBERTZ (PS).

Rat der Deutschsprachigen Gemeinschaft Belgiens (Council of the German-speaking Community): 8 Kaperberg, 4700 Eupen; tel. and fax (87) 55-59-70; e-mail rdg@euregio.net; internet www .euregio.net/rdg.

Regierung der Deutschsprachigen Gemeinschaft Belgiens (Government of the German-speaking Community): 32 Klötzerbahn, 4700 Eupen; tel. (87) 59-64-00; fax (87) 74-02-58; e-mail juergen .heck@grenzecho.be; internet www.dglive.be.

Political Organizations

Anders Gaan Leven (Agalev) (Ecologist Party—Flemish-speaking): 23 Brialmontstraat, 1210 Brussels; tel. (2) 219-19-19; fax (2) 223-10-90; e-mail agalev@agalev.be; internet www.agalev.be; f. 1982; Gen. Sec. LUC LEMIENGRE.

Christelijke Volkspartij (CVP)/Parti Social Chrétien (PSC) (Christian Democrats): 89 Wetstraat, 1040 Brussels; tel. (2) 238-38-14; fax (2) 230-43-60 (CVP); 41 rue des Deux-Eglises, 1000 Brussels; tel. (2) 238-01-11; fax (2) 238-01-29 (PSC); e-mail inform@cvp.be; internet www.cvp.be (CVP); e-mail info@psc.be; internet www.psc.be (PSC); f. 1945; Pres. (CVP) STEFAAN DE CLERCK; Pres. (PSC) JOËLLE MILQUET; 186,000 mems.

Ecologistes Confédérés pour l'Organisation des Luttes Originales (Ecolo) (Ecologist Party—French-speaking): 12 rue Charles VI, 1210 Brussels; tel. (2) 218-30-35; fax (2) 217-52-90; e-mail service.presse@ecolo.be; internet www.ecolo.be; Fed. Secs JACQUES BAUDUIN, PHILIPPE DEFEYT, BRIGITTE ERNST.

Front Démocratique des Francophones (FDF) (French-speaking Democratic Front): 127 chaussée de Charleroi, 1060 Brussels; tel. (2) 538-83-20; fax (2) 539-36-50; e-mail fdf@fdf.be; internet www.fdf.be; f. 1964; aims to preserve the French character of Brussels; has co-operation agreement with the PRL; Pres. OLIVIER MAINGAIN; Sec.-Gen. CAROLINE PERSOONS.

Front National (FN): Clos du Parnasse 12, 1050 Brussels; tel. (2) 511-75-77; e-mail daniel.feret@frontnational.be; internet www

.frontnational.be; f. 1985; extreme right-wing nationalist party; Pres. DANIEL FERET.

ID21: 80 Noordstraat, 1000 Brussels; tel. (2) 223-39-33; fax (2) 223-39-34; e-mail info@id21.be; internet www.id21.be.

Partei der Deutschsprachigen Belgier (PDB) (German-speaking Party): 6 Kaperberg, 4700 Eupen; tel. (87) 55-59-87; fax (87) 55-59-84; internet users.skynet.be/pdb; f. 1971; promotes equality for the German-speaking minority; Pres. GUIDO BREUER.

Parti Communiste (PC) (Communist Party): 4 rue Rouppe, 1000 Brussels; tel. (2) 548-02-90; fax (2) 548-02-95; f. 1921 as Parti Communiste de Belgique–Kommunistische Partij van België, name changed 1990; Pres. PIERRE BEAUVOIS; 5,000 mems.

Parti de la Liberté du Citoyen/Parti Libéral Chretien/Partij der Liberale Christenen (PLC): 46 ave de Scheut, 1070 Brussels; tel. (2) 524-39-66; fax (2) 521-60-71; Pres. LUC EYKERMAN, PAUL MOORS.

Parti Féministe Humaniste: 35 ave des Phalènes, bte 14, 1050 Brussels; tel. (2) 648-87-38; fax (2) 376-88-63; f. 1972 as Parti Féministe Unifié, name changed 1990; aims to create a humanistic and egalitarian republic where the fundamental rights of the individual and of society are respected.

Parti Humaniste de Belgique: 131 rue du Noyer, 1000 Brussels; tel. (2) 734-37-84; fax (2) 426-03-78; e-mail parti.humaniste@euronet.be; internet www.multimania.com/phum; f. 1994; promotes social equality and human rights.

Parti Réformateur Libéral (PRL) (Liberal Party—French-speaking wing): 41 rue de Naples, 1050 Brussels; tel. (2) 500-35-11; fax (2) 500-35-09; e-mail prl@prl.be; internet www.prl.be; f. 1846 as Parti Libéral; has co-operation agreement with the FDF; Pres. DANIEL DUCARNE; 50,000 mems.

Parti Socialiste (PS) (Socialist Party—French-speaking wing): Maison du PS, 13 blvd de l'Empereur, 1000 Brussels; tel. (2) 548-32-11; fax (2) 548-33-80; e-mail secretariat@ps.be; internet www.ps.be; f. 1885 as the Parti Ouvrier Belge; split from the Flemish wing 1979; Pres. ELIO DI RUPO; Sec. JEAN-POL BARAS.

Parti Wallon (PW) (Walloon Party): 14 rue du Faubourg, 1430 Quenast; tel. (6) 767-00-19; f. 1985 by amalgamation of the Rassemblement Wallon (f. 1968), the Rassemblement Populaire Wallon and the Front Indépendantiste Wallon; left-wing socialist party advocating an independent Walloon state; Pres. JEAN-CLAUDE PICCIN.

Partij van de Arbeid van België (PvdA)/Parti du Travail de Belgique (PTB) (Belgian Labour Party): blvd M. Lemonnier 171, 1000 Brussels; tel. (2) 504-01-10; fax (2) 513-98-31; e-mail wpb@wpb.be; internet www.wpb.be; f. 1979; Marxist-Leninist; Gen. Sec. NADINE ROSA-ROSSO.

Socialistische Partij (SP) (Socialist Party—Flemish wing): 13 blvd de l'Empereur, 1000 Brussels; tel. (2) 548-32-11; fax (2) 548-35-90; e-mail info@sp.be; internet www.sp.be; f. 1885; Chair. PATRICK JANSSENS; Sec. ALAIN ANDRÉ.

Vlaams Blok (Flemish Bloc): 8 Madouplein, bus 9, 1210 Brussels; tel. (2) 219-60-09; fax (2) 219-50-47; e-mail vlblok@vlaams-blok.be; internet www.vlaams-blok.be; f. 1979 as a breakaway party from the Volksunie; advocates Flemish separatism and is anti-immigration; Chair. FRANK VANHECKE; Chief Officer ROELAND RAES.

Vlaamse Liberalen en Demokraten—Partij van de Burger (VLD) (Flemish Liberals and Democrats—Citizens' Party: Liberal Party—Flemish-speaking wing): 34 Melsensstraat, 1000 Brussels; tel. (2) 549-00-20; fax (2) 512-60-25; f. 1961 as Partij voor Vrijheid en Vooruitgang; name changed 1992; Pres. KAREL DE GENDT; 80,000 mems.

Volksunie—Vlaamse Vrije Democraten (VU) (People's Union—Flemish Free Democrats): 12 Barrikadenplein, 1000 Brussels; tel. (2) 219-49-30; fax (2) 217-35-10; e-mail secretariaat@vu.be; internet www.volksunie.be; f. 1954; Flemish nationalist party supporting national and European federalism; Acting Pres. FONS BORGINON; Sec. LAURENS APPELTANS; 16,000 mems.

Diplomatic Representation

EMBASSIES IN BELGIUM

Albania: 42 rue Alphonse Hottat, 1050 Brussels; tel. (2) 640-14-22; fax (2) 640-28-58; e-mail amba.brux@skynet.be; Ambassador: IPRIZ BASHA.

Algeria: 209 ave Molière, 1060 Brussels; tel. (2) 343-50-78; fax (2) 343-51-68; Ambassador: MISSOUM SBIH.

Andorra: 10 rue de la Montagne, 1000 Brussels; tel. (2) 513-28-06; fax (2) 513-07-41; e-mail meritxell.mateu@andorra.be; Ambassador: MERITXELL MATEU.

Angola: 182 rue Franz Merjay, 1050 Brussels; tel. (2) 346-18-72; fax (2) 344-08-94; e-mail angola.embassy.brussels@skynet.be; Ambassador: JOSÉ GUERREIRO ALVES PRIMO.

Argentina: 225 ave Louise, bte 3, 1050 Brussels; tel. (2) 647-78-12; fax (2) 647-93-19; e-mail febelg@mrecic.gov.ar; Ambassador: EDUARDO M. DE L. AIRALDI.

Armenia: 157 rue Franz Merjay, 1050 Brussels; tel. and fax (2) 346-56-67; Ambassador: V. TCHITETCHIAN.

Australia: 6–8 rue Guimard, 1040 Brussels; tel. (2) 286-05-00; fax (2) 230-68-02; e-mail austemb.brussels@dfat.gov.au; Ambassador: JOANNA HEWITT.

Austria: 5 place du Champs de Mars, 1050 Brussels; tel. (2) 289-07-10; fax (2) 513-66-41; e-mail austroamb.brussel@pophost.eunet.be; Ambassador: THOMAS MAYR-HARTING.

Azerbaijan: 464 ave Molière, 1050 Brussels; tel. (2) 345-26-60; fax (2) 345-91-58; Ambassador: MIR-HAMZA EFENDIEV.

Bangladesh: 29–31 rue Jacques Jordaens, 1000 Brussels; tel. (2) 640-55-00; fax (2) 646-59-98; Ambassador: A. S. M. KHAIRHUL ANAM.

Barbados: 78 ave Général Lartigue, 1200 Brussels; tel. (2) 732-17-37; fax (2) 732-32-66; e-mail embar@pophost.eunet.be; internet www.foreign.barbadosgov.org; Ambassador: MICHAEL IAN KING.

Belarus: 192 ave Molière, 1050 Brussels; tel. (2) 340-02-70; fax (2) 340-02-87; e-mail embbel@skynet.be; Ambassador: ULADZIMIR A. LABUNOU.

Belize: Brand Witlocklaan 136, 1200 Brussels; tel. (2) 732-62-04; fax (2) 732-62-46; e-mail embel.bru@pophost.eunet.be.

Benin: 5 ave de l'Observatoire, 1180 Brussels; tel. (2) 374-91-92; fax (2) 375-83-26; e-mail ambassade.du.benin@skynet.be; Ambassador: SALIOU ABOUDOU.

Bolivia: 176 ave Louise, bte 6, 1050 Brussels; tel. (2) 627-00-10; fax (2) 647-47-82; e-mail embolbrus@arcadis.be; Chargé d'affaires a.i.: ARTURO LIEBERS BALDIVIESO.

Bosnia and Herzegovina: 9 rue Paul Lauters, 1000 Brussels; tel. (2) 644-20-08; fax (2) 644-16-98; Ambassador: MILES V. RAGUZ.

Botswana: 169 ave de Tervueren, 1150 Brussels; tel. (2) 735-20-70; fax (2) 735-63-18; Ambassador: SASARA CHASALA GEORGE.

Brazil: 350 ave Louise, bte 5, 1050 Brussels; tel. (2) 640-20-15; fax (2) 640-81-34; e-mail brasbruxelas@beon.be; Ambassador: MARCIO DE OLIVEIRA DIAS.

Brunei: 238 ave F. D. Roosevelt, 1050 Brussels; tel. (2) 675-08-78; fax (2) 672-93-58; e-mail kedutaan-brunei.brussels@skynet.be; Ambassador: Dato KASSIM DAUD.

Bulgaria: 58 ave Hamoir, 1180 Brussels; tel. (2) 374-59-63; fax (2) 374-84-94; e-mail embassy@bulgaria.be; Ambassador: BOYKO NOEV.

Burkina Faso: 16 place Guy d'Arezzo, 1180 Brussels; tel. (2) 345-99-12; fax (2) 345-06-12; e-mail ambassade.burkina@skynet.be; Ambassador: DIEUDONNÉ KERE.

Burundi: 46 square Marie-Louise, 1000 Brussels; tel. (2) 230-45-35; fax (2) 230-78-83; Ambassador: JONATHAN NIYUNGEKO.

Cameroon: 131–133 ave Brugmann, 1190 Brussels; tel. (2) 345-18-70; fax (2) 344-57-35; Ambassador: ISABELLE BASSONG.

Canada: 2 ave de Tervueren, 1040 Brussels; tel. (2) 741-06-11; fax (2) 741-06-43; internet www.dfait-maeci.gc.ca/brussels; Ambassador: CLAUDE LAVERDURE.

Cape Verde: 29 ave Jeanne, 1050 Brussels; tel. (2) 643-62-70; fax (2) 646-33-85; e-mail emb.caboverde@skynet.be; Ambassador: FERNANDO WAHNON.

Central African Republic: 416 blvd Lambermont, 1030 Brussels; tel. (2) 242-28-80; fax (2) 215-13-11; e-mail ambassade.centrafrique@skynet.be; Chargé d'affaires a.i.: JEAN-PIERRE MBAZOA.

Chad: 52 blvd Lambermont, 1030 Brussels; tel. (2) 215-19-75; fax (2) 216-35-26; Chargé d'affaires: IDRISS ADJIDEYE.

Chile: 40 rue Montoyer, 1000 Brussels; tel. (2) 280-16-20; fax (2) 280-14-81; e-mail embachili.belgica@skynet.be; Ambassador: HUGO CUBILLOS BRAVO.

China, People's Republic: 443–445 ave de Tervueren, 1150 Brussels; tel. (2) 771-33-09; fax (2) 772-37-45; Ambassador: DING YUAN-HONG.

Colombia: 96A ave F. D. Roosevelt, 1050 Brussels; tel. (2) 649-56-79; fax (2) 646-54-91; e-mail colombia@emcolbru.org; Ambassador: ROBERTO ARENAS BONILLA.

Congo, Democratic Republic: 30 rue Marie de Bourgogne, 1000 Brussels; tel. (2) 513-66-10; fax (2) 514-04-03; Ambassador: RACHEL ALBERT KISONGA MAZAKAZA.

Congo, Republic: 16–18 ave F. D. Roosevelt, 1050 Brussels; tel. (2) 648-38-56; fax (2) 648-42-13; e-mail ambassade.congobrazza@skynet.be; Ambassador: JACQUES OBIA.

Costa Rica: 489 ave Louise, bte 13, 1050 Brussels; tel. (2) 640-55-41; fax (2) 648-31-92; e-mail embcrbel@infonie.be; Ambassador: MARIO FERNÁNDEZ SILVA.

Côte d'Ivoire: 234 ave F. D. Roosevelt, 1050 Brussels; tel. (2) 672-23-57; fax (2) 672-04-91; Ambassador: ANET N'ZI NANAN KOLIABO.

Croatia: 50 ave des Arts, 1050 Brussels; tel. (2) 500-09-20; fax (2) 512-03-38; Ambassador: Žjko Matié.

Cuba: 77 rue Roberts-Jones, 1180 Brussels; tel. (2) 343-00-20; fax (2) 344-96-91; e-mail mision@embacuba.be; Ambassador: René Juan Mujica Cantelar.

Cyprus: 2 square Ambiorix, 1000 Brussels; tel. (2) 735-35-10; fax (2) 735-45-52; e-mail chypre.pio.bxl@skynet.be; Ambassador: Nicos Agathocleous.

Czech Republic: 555 rue Engeland, 1180 Brussels; tel. (2) 373-99-69; fax (2) 375-92-72; Ambassador: Katerina Lukešová.

Denmark: 73 rue d'Arlon, 1040 Brussels; tel. (2) 233-09-00; fax (2) 233-09-30; e-mail bruamb@brubee.um.dk; Ambassador: Alf Jönsson.

Djibouti: Brugmannlaan 410, 1180 Brussels; tel. (2) 347-69-67; fax (2) 347-69-63.

Dominica: rue de Livourne 42, 1050 Brussels; tel. (2) 354-26-11; fax (2) 539-40-09; e-mail ecs.embassies@skynet.be.

Dominican Republic: 12 ave Bel Air, 1180 Brussels; tel. (2) 346-49-35; fax (2) 346-51-52; e-mail embajadombelgica@euronet.be; Ambassador: Clara Joselyn Quiñones de Longo.

Ecuador: 363 ave Louise, 1050 Brussels; tel. (2) 644-30-50; fax (2) 644-28-13; e-mail ecuador@skypro.be; Ambassador: Alfredo Pinoargote Cevallos.

Egypt: 19 ave de l'Uruguay, 1000 Brussels; tel. (2) 663-58-00; fax (2) 675-58-88; e-mail embassy.egypt@skynet.be; Ambassador: Raouf Saad.

El Salvador: 171 ave de Tervueren, 1050 Brussels; tel. (2) 733-04-85; fax (2) 735-02-11; Ambassador: Joaquín Rodezno Munguia.

Equatorial Guinea: Jupiterlaan 17, 1190 Brussels; tel. (2) 346-25-09; fax (2) 346-33-09; Ambassador: Aurelio Mba Olo.

Eritrea: Wolvendaellaan 15–17, 1180 Brussels; tel. (2) 374-44-34; fax (2) 372-07-30; Ambassador: Hanna Simon Ghebremedhin.

Estonia: 1 ave Isidore Gérard, 1160 Brussels; tel. (2) 779-07-55; fax 779-28-17; e-mail sulev.kannike@estemb.be; Ambassador: Sulev Kannike.

Ethiopia: 231 ave de Tervueren, 1150 Brussels; tel. (2) 771-32-94; fax (2) 771-49-14; Ambassador: Dr Peter Gabriel Robleh.

Fiji: 66 ave de Cortenberg, 1000 Brussels; tel. (2) 736-90-50; fax (2) 736-14-58; e-mail fijimission.brussels@skynet.be; Ambassador: Isikeli U. Mataitoga.

Finland: 58 ave des Arts, 1000 Brussels; tel. (2) 287-12-12; fax (2) 287-12-00; e-mail bry@formin.fi; Ambassador: Leif Blomqvist.

France: 65 rue Ducale, 1000 Brussels; tel. (2) 548-87-11; fax (2) 548-87-32; internet www.ambafrance.be; Ambassador: Jacques Runnelhardt.

Gabon: 112 ave Winston Churchill, 1180 Brussels; tel. (2) 340-62-10; fax (2) 346-46-69; Ambassador: René Makongo.

Gambia: 126 ave F. D. Roosevelt, 1050 Brussels; tel. (2) 640-10-49; fax (2) 646-32-77; e-mail bs175335@skynet.be; Ambassador: A. M. Ngum.

Georgia: 58 ave Orban, 1150 Brussels; tel. (2) 761-11-91; fax (2) 761-11-99; e-mail mdgade@skynet.be; Ambassador: K. Zaldastanishvili.

Germany: 190 ave de Tervueren, 1150 Brussels; tel. (2) 774-19-11; fax (2) 772-36-92; e-mail germanembassy@skynet.be; Ambassador: Peter von Butler.

Ghana: blvd Général Wahis, 1030 Brussels; tel. (2) 705-82-20; fax (2) 705-66-53; e-mail head@ghembassy.arc.be; Ambassador: Alex Ntim Abankwa.

Greece: 2 ave F. D. Roosevelt, 1050 Brussels; tel. (2) 648-17-30; fax (2) 647-45-25; e-mail ambagre@skynet.be; Ambassador: John Cambolis.

Grenada: 123 Laekenstraat, 1000 Brussels; tel. (2) 223-73-03; fax (2) 223-73-07; Chargé d'affaires a.i.: Joan-Marie Coutain.

Guatemala: 185 ave Winston Churchill, 1180 Brussels; tel. (2) 345-07-87; fax (2) 344-64-99; e-mail obguab@euronet.be; Ambassador: Claudio Riedel Telge.

Guinea: 75 ave Roger Vandendriessche, 1150 Brussels; tel. (2) 771-01-26; fax (2) 762-60-36; Ambassador: Naby Moussa Soumah.

Guinea-Bissau: 70 ave F. D. Roosevelt, 1050 Brussels; tel. (2) 647-13-51; fax (2) 640-43-12; Chargé d'affaires: José Fonseca.

Guyana: 12 ave du Brésil, 1050 Brussels; tel. (2) 675-62-16; fax (2) 675-55-98; e-mail embassy.guyana@skynet.be; Ambassador: Havelock Brewster.

Haiti: 160A ave Louise, bte 25, 1050 Brussels; tel. (2) 649-73-81; fax (2) 640-60-80; Ambassador: Yolette Azor-Charles.

Holy See: 9 ave des Franciscains, 1150 Brussels (Apostolic Nunciature); tel. (2) 762-20-05; fax (2) 762-20-32; e-mail nonciature.apostolique@euronet.be; Apostolic Nuncio: Most Rev. Pier Luigi Celata, Titular Archbishop of Doclea.

Honduras: 3 ave des Gaulois (5e étage), 1040 Brussels; tel. (2) 734-00-00; fax (2) 735-26-26; Ambassador: Ivan Romero Martínez.

Hungary: 41 rue Edmond Picard, 1050 Brussels; tel. (2) 343-67-90; fax (2) 347-60-28; e-mail huembbxl@huembbxl.be; Ambassador: László Trócsányi.

Iceland: 74 rue de Trèves, 1040 Brussels; tel. (2) 286-17-00; fax (2) 286-17-70; e-mail icemb.brussel@utn.stjr.is; internet www.islande.be; Ambassador: Gunnar Snorri Gunnarsson.

India: 217 chaussée de Vleurgat, 1050 Brussels; tel. (2) 640-91-40; fax (2) 648-96-38; e-mail eoibru@mail.interpac.be; Ambassador: P. K. Singh.

Indonesia: 294 ave de Tervueren, 1150 Brussels; tel. (2) 771-20-14; fax (2) 771-22-91; Ambassador: H. Sabana Kartasasmita.

Iran: 415 ave de Tervueren, 1150 Brussels; tel. (2) 762-37-45; fax (2) 762-39-15; e-mail eiri.bxl@skynet.be; Ambassador: Hamid Aboutalébi.

Iraq: 23 ave des Aubépines, 1180 Brussels; tel. (2) 374-59-92; fax (2) 374-76-15; Chargé d'affaires a.i.: Dr Mahdi S. Hamoudi.

Ireland: 89 rue Froissard, 1040 Brussels; tel. (2) 230-53-37; fax (2) 230-53-12; Ambassador: Padraic Cradock.

Israel: 40 ave de l'Observatoire, 1180 Brussels; tel. (2) 373-55-00; fax (2) 373-56-17; Ambassador: Senny Omer.

Italy: 28 rue Emile Claus, 1050 Brussels; tel. (2) 643-38-50; fax (2) 648-54-85; e-mail ambit.bxl.politico@ibm.net; internet www.pi.cnr.it/ambitbe; Ambassador: Francesco Corrias.

Jamaica: 2 ave Palmerston, 1000 Brussels; tel. (2) 230-11-70; fax (2) 230-37-09; e-mail emb.jam.brussels@skynet.be; Ambassador: Douglas Saunders.

Japan: 58 ave des Arts, bte 17/18, 1000 Brussels; tel. (2) 513-23-40; fax (2) 513-15-56; Ambassador: Junichi Nakamura.

Jordan: 104 ave F. D. Roosevelt, 1050 Brussels; tel. (2) 640-77-55; fax (2) 640-27-96; Ambassador: Dr Umayya Toukan.

Kazakhstan: 30 ave Van Bever, 1180 Brussels; tel. (2) 374-95-62; fax (2) 374-50-91; Ambassador: Akhmetzhan S. Yesimov.

Kenya: 208 ave Winston Churchill, 1180 Brussels; tel. (2) 340-10-40; fax (2) 340-10-50; e-mail kenbrussels@hotmail.com; Ambassador: Peter O. Nguraiyia.

Korea, Republic: 173–5 Chaussée de la Hulpe, 1170 Brussels; tel. (2) 662-23-03; fax (2) 675-52-21; Ambassador: Lee Jai Chun.

Kuwait: 43 ave F. D. Roosevelt, 1050 Brussels; tel. (2) 647-79-50; fax (2) 646-12-98; e-mail embassy.kwt@euronet.be; Ambassador: Abdulazeez al-Sharikh.

Kyrgyzstan: 47 Abdijstraat, 1050 Brussels; tel. (2) 640-18-68; fax (2) 640-01-31; Ambassador: Chingiz Torekulovitch Aitmatov.

Laos: 19–21 ave de la Brabançonne, 1000 Brussels; tel. (2) 734-16-66; fax (2) 734-16-66.

Latvia: 158 ave Molière, 1050 Brussels; tel. (2) 344-16-82; fax (2) 344-74-78; e-mail lvembassybenelux@arcadis.be; Ambassador: Aivars Groza.

Lebanon: 2 rue Guillaume Stocq, 1050 Brussels; tel. (2) 649-94-60; fax (2) 649-90-02; Ambassador: Jihad Mortada.

Lesotho: 45 blvd Général Wahis, 1030 Brussels; tel. (2) 705-39-76; fax (2) 705-67-79; e-mail boqosa@lesotho.be; Ambassador: R. V. Lechesa.

Liberia: 50 ave du Château, 1080 Brussels; tel. (2) 411-09-12; fax (2) 411-09-12; Ambassador: Dr Cecil T. O. Brandy, Sr.

Libya: 28 ave Victoria, 1050 Brussels; tel. (2) 647-37-37; fax (2) 640-90-76; Sec. of People's Bureau: Hamed Ahmed Elhouderi.

Liechtenstein: 1 place du Congrès, 1000 Brussels; tel. (2) 229-39-00; fax (2) 219-35-45; e-mail ambassade.liechtenstein@bbru.llv.li; Ambassador: Prince Nikolaus von Liechtenstein.

Lithuania: 48 rue Maurice Liétart, 1150 Brussels; tel. (2) 772-27-50; fax (2) 772-17-01; Chargé d'affaires: Arvydas Daunoravičius.

Luxembourg: 75 ave de Cortenbergh, 1000 Brussels; tel. (2) 737-57-00; fax (2) 737-57-10; Ambassador: Jean-Jacques Kasel.

Macedonia, former Yugoslav republic: 128 ave de Tervueren, 1150 Brussels; tel. (2) 732-91-08; fax (2) 732-91-11; Ambassador: Jovan Tegovski.

Madagascar: 276 ave de Tervueren, 1150 Brussels; tel. (2) 770-17-26; fax (2) 772-37-31; e-mail beriziky.jean.omer@ambassademadagascar.be; Ambassador: Jean Omer Beriziky.

Malawi: 15 rue de la Loi, 1040 Brussels; tel. (2) 231-09-80; fax (2) 231-10-66; e-mail embassy.malawi@pi.de; Ambassador: Julie Nanyoni Mphande.

Malaysia: 414A ave de Tervueren, 1150 Brussels; tel. (2) 776-03-40; e-mail mwbrusel@euronet.be; fax (2) 762-50-49; Ambassador: Dato Deva M. Ridzam.

Mali: 487 ave Molière, 1050 Brussels; tel. (2) 345-74-32; fax (2) 344-57-00; e-mail ambassade.mali@skynet.be; Ambassador: Ahmed Mohamed ag Hamani.

Malta: 65 rue Belliard, 1040 Brussels; tel. (2) 343-01-95; fax (2) 343-01-06; e-mail victor.camilleri@magnet.mt; Ambassador: VICTOR CAMILLERI.

Mauritania: 6 ave de la Colombie, 1000 Brussels; tel. (2) 672-47-47; fax (2) 672-20-51; e-mail amb.bxl.mauritanie@skynet.be; Ambassador: MOHAMED SALEM OULD LEKHAL.

Mauritius: 68 rue des Bollandistes, 1040 Brussels; tel. (2) 733-99-88; fax (2) 734-40-21; e-mail ambmaur@skynet.be; Ambassador: T. W. WAN CHAT KWONG.

Mexico: 94 ave F. D. Roosevelt, 1050 Brussels; tel. (2) 629-07-77; fax (2) 646-87-68; e-mail embamexbel@pophost.eunet.be; Ambassador: MANUEL RODRÍGUEZ ARRIAGA.

Moldova: 175 ave Emile Max, 1030 Brussels; tel. (2) 732-96-59; fax (2) 732-96-60; e-mail molda@skynet.be; Ambassador: ION CAPATINA.

Monaco: 17 place Guy d'Arezzo, bte 7, 1180 Brussels; tel. (2) 347-49-87; fax (2) 343-49-20; e-mail ambassade.monaco@skynet.be; Ambassador: JEAN ANDRÉ GRÉTHER.

Mongolia: 18 ave Besme, 1190 Brussels; tel. (2) 344-69-74; fax (2) 344-32-15; e-mail embassy.mongolia@skynet.be; Ambassador: JAGVARALYN HANIBAL.

Morocco: 29 blvd St-Michel, 1040 Brussels; tel. (2) 736-11-00; fax (2) 734-64-68; e-mail sifamabruxe@euronet.be; Ambassador: RACHAD BOUHLAL.

Mozambique: 97 blvd St-Michel, 1040 Brussels; tel. (2) 736-25-64; fax (2) 735-62-07; Ambassador: ALVARO O. DA SILVA.

Namibia: 454 ave de Tervueren, 1150 Brussels; tel. (2) 771-14-10; fax (2) 771-96-89; e-mail nam.emb@brutele.be; Ambassador: Dr ZEDEKIA J. NGAVIRUE.

Nepal: 58 ave Winston Churchill, 1180 Brussels; tel. (2) 346-26-58; fax (2) 344-13-61; e-mail rne.bru@skynet.be; Ambassador: KEDAR BHAKTA SHRESTHA.

Netherlands: 48 ave Hermann Debroux, 1160 Brussels; tel. (2) 679-17-11; fax (2) 679-17-75; Ambassador: E. RÖELL.

New Zealand: 1 Meeussquare, 1000 Brussels; tel. (2) 512-10-40; fax (2) 513-48-56; e-mail nzembbru@compuserve.com; Ambassador: DELL HIGGE.

Nicaragua: 55 ave de Wolvendael, 1180 Brussels; tel. (2) 375-65-00; fax (2) 375-71-88; e-mail sky77706@skynet.be; Ambassador: MARIO BLANDÓN LANZAS.

Niger: 78 ave F. D. Roosevelt, 1050 Brussels; tel. (2) 648-61-40; fax (2) 648-27-84; Ambassador: HOUSSEINI ABDOU-SALEYE.

Nigeria: 288 ave de Tervueren, 1150 Brussels; tel. (2) 762-52-00; fax (2) 762-37-63; Ambassador: Prof. ALABA OGUNSANWO.

Norway: 130A ave Louise (6e étage), 1050 Brussels; tel. (2) 646-07-80; fax (2) 646-28-82; e-mail ambassade-brussel@ud.dep.telemax.no; Ambassador: TOR B. NAESS.

Pakistan: 57 ave Delleur, 1170 Brussels; tel. (2) 673-80-07; fax (2) 675-83-94; Ambassador: SAIDULLA KHAN DEHLAVI.

Panama: 390–392 ave Louise, 1050 Brussels; tel. (2) 647-07-29; fax (2) 648-92-16; e-mail embajada_panama@skynet.be; Ambassador: ROLANDO A. GUEVARA ALVARADO.

Papua New Guinea: 430 ave de Tervueren, 1150 Brussels; tel. (2) 779-08-26; fax (2) 772-70-88; Ambassador: GABRIEL KOIBA PEPSON.

Paraguay: 475 ave Louise, 1050 Brussels; tel. (2) 649-90-55; fax (2) 647-42-48; e-mail embapar.belgica@skynet.be; Ambassador: MANUEL M. CÁCERES.

Peru: 179 ave de Tervueren, 1150 Brussels; tel. (2) 733-33-19; fax (2) 733-48-19; e-mail embassy.of.peru@unicall.be; Ambassador: JOSÉ URRUTIA.

Philippines: 297 ave Molière, 1050 Brussels; tel. (2) 340-33-77; fax (2) 345-64-25; e-mail bleu.pe@skynet.be; Ambassador: CLEMENCIO F. MONTESA.

Poland: 29 ave des Gaulois, 1040 Brussels; tel. (2) 735-72-12; fax (2) 736-18-81; e-mail polambbxl@free-way.net; Ambassador: JAN W. PIEKARSKI.

Portugal: 55 ave de la Toison d'Or, 1060 Brussels; tel. (2) 533-07-00; fax (2) 539-07-73; Ambassador: FRANCISCO PESSANHA DE QUEVEDO CRESPO.

Qatar: 71 ave F. D. Roosevelt, 1050 Brussels; tel. (2) 640-29-00; fax (2) 648-40-78; e-mail qatar.amb.bru@skynet.be; Chargé d'affaires: MOHAMED AL-HAIYKI.

Romania: 105 rue Gabrielle, 1180 Brussels; tel. (2) 345-26-80; fax (2) 346-23-45; e-mail amrobxl@skynet.be; Ambassador: VIRGIL N. CONSTANTINESCU.

Russia: 66 ave de Fré, 1180 Brussels; tel. (2) 374-34-00; fax (2) 374-26-13; Ambassador: SERGEI KISLYAK.

Rwanda: 1 ave des Fleurs, 1150 Brussels; tel. (2) 763-07-05; fax (2) 763-07-53; Ambassador: Dr JACQUES BIHOZAGARA.

Saint Christopher and Nevis: rue de Livourne 42, 1050 Brussels; tel. (2) 543-26-11; fax (2) 539-40-09.

Saint Lucia: 42 rue de Livourne, 1050 Brussels; tel. (2) 534-26-11; fax (2) 539-40-09; e-mail ecs.embassies@skynet.be; Ambassador: EDWIN PONTIEN JOSEPH LAURENT.

Saint Vincent and the Grenadines: 42 rue de Livourne, 1000 Brussels; tel. (2) 534-26-11; fax (2) 539-40-09; e-mail ecs.embassies@skynet.be; Ambassador: EDWIN PONTIEN JOSEPH LAURENT.

Samoa: 123 ave F. D. Roosevelt, bte 14, 1050 Brussels; tel. (2) 660-84-54; fax (2) 675-03-36; e-mail samoa.emb.bxl@skynet.be; Ambassador: TAU'ILI'ILI UILI MEREDITH.

San Marino: 62 ave F. D. Roosevelt, 1050 Brussels; tel. (2) 644-22-24; fax (2) 644-20-57; e-mail amb.rsm.bxl@skynet.be; Ambassador: SAVINA ZAFFERANI.

São Tomé and Príncipe: 175 ave de Tervueren, 1150 Brussels; tel. (2) 734-89-66; fax (2) 734-88-15; e-mail ambassade.sao.tome@skynet.be; Chargé d'affaires a.i.: ANTÓNIO DE LIMA VIEGAS.

Saudi Arabia: 45 ave F. D. Roosevelt, 1050 Brussels; tel. (2) 649-20-44; fax (2) 647-24-92; Ambassador: NASSER ASSAF HUSSEIN AL-ASSAF.

Senegal: 196 ave F. D. Roosevelt, 1050 Brussels; tel. (2) 673-00-97; fax (2) 675-04-60; Ambassador: SALOUM KANDE.

Sierra Leone: 410 ave de Tervueren, 1150 Brussels; tel. (2) 762-62-19; fax (2) 771-11-80; Chargé d'affaires a.i.: JAMES GOODWILL.

Singapore: 198 ave F. D. Roosevelt, 1050 Brussels; tel. (2) 660-29-79; fax (2) 660-86-85; e-mail amb.eu@singembbru.be; Ambassador: PANG ENG FONG.

Slovakia: 195 ave Molière, 1050 Brussels; tel. (2) 346-40-45; fax (2) 346-63-85; e-mail ambassade.slovaque@euronet.be; Ambassador: FRANTIŠEK LIPKA.

Slovenia: 179 ave Louise, 1050 Brussels; tel. (2) 646-90-99; fax (2) 646-36-67; e-mail vbr@mzz-dkp.sigov.si; Ambassador: MARIJA ADANJA.

Solomon Islands: ave de l'Yser, 13, bte 3, 1040 Brussels; tel. (2) 732-70-85; fax (2) 732-68-85; Ambassador: ROBERT SISILO.

South Africa: 26 rue de la Loi, bus 7–8, 1040 Brussels; tel. (2) 285-44-00; fax (2) 285-44-02; e-mail embassy.southafrica@online.be; Ambassador: Dr ELIAS LINKS.

Spain: 19 rue de la Science, 1040 Brussels; tel. (2) 230-03-40; fax (2) 230-93-80; e-mail ambespbe@mail.mae.es; Ambassador: FRANCISCO FERNÁNDEZ FÁBREGAS.

Sri Lanka: 27 rue Jules Lejeune, 1050 Brussels; tel. (2) 344-53-94; fax (2) 344-67-37; e-mail sri.lanka@euronet.be; Ambassador: (vacant).

Sudan: 124 ave F. D. Roosevelt, 1050 Brussels; tel. (2) 647-94-94; fax (2) 648-34-99; Ambassador: ABDELRAHIM AHMED KHALIL.

Suriname: 379 ave Louise, 1050 Brussels; tel. (2) 640-11-72; fax (2) 646-39-62; e-mail sur.amb.bru@online.be; Chargé d'affaires a.i.: JANE R. NANHU.

Swaziland: 188 ave Winston Churchill, 1180 Brussels; tel. (2) 347-47-71; fax (2) 347-46-23; Ambassador: Dr THEMBAYENA ANNASTASIA DLAMINI.

Sweden: 3 rue de Luxembourg, 1000 Brussels; tel. (2) 289-57-60; fax (2) 289-57-90; e-mail ambassaden.bryssel@foreign.ministry.se; Ambassador: ANDERS OLJELUND.

Switzerland: 26 rue de la Loi, bte 9, 1040 Brussels; tel. (2) 285-43-50; fax (2) 230-37-81; e-mail vertretung@bru.rep.admin.ch; Ambassador: ANTON THALMANN.

Syria: 3 ave F. D. Roosevelt, 1050 Brussels; tel. (2) 648-01-35; fax (2) 646-40-18; Chargé d'affaires a.i.: SAMI SALAMEH.

Tanzania: 363 ave Louise (7e étage), 1050 Brussels; tel. (2) 640-65-00; fax (2) 640-80-26; e-mail tanzania@skynet.be; Ambassador: ALI ABEID KARUME.

Thailand: 2 square du Val de la Cambre, 1050 Brussels; tel. (2) 640-68-10; fax (2) 648-30-66; e-mail thaibxl@pophost.eunet.be; internet www.waw.be/rte-be; Ambassador: SURAPONG POSAYANOND.

Togo: 264 ave de Tervueren, 1150 Brussels; tel. (2) 770-55-63; fax (2) 771-50-75; Ambassador: FOLLY-GLIDJITO AKAKPO.

Trinidad and Tobago: 14 ave de la Faisanderie, 1150 Brussels; tel. (2) 762-94-00; fax (2) 772-27-83; Ambassador: LINGSTON LLOYD CUMBERBATCH.

Tunisia: 278 ave de Tervueren, 1150 Brussels; tel. (2) 771-73-95; fax (2) 771-94-33; e-mail amb.detunisie@brutele.be; Ambassador: SLAHEDDINE BEN M'BAREK.

Turkey: 4 rue Montoyer, 1000 Brussels; tel. (2) 513-40-95; fax (2) 514-07-48; e-mail tcbrukselbe@yucom.be; Ambassador: TEMEL ISKIT.

Turkmenistan: 106 ave F. D. Roosevelt, 1050 Brussels; tel. (2) 648-18-74; fax (2) 648-19-74; e-mail turkmenistan@skynet.be.

Uganda: 317 ave de Tervueren, 1150 Brussels; tel. (2) 762-58-25; fax (2) 763-04-38; Ambassador: LEWIS BALINDA.

Ukraine: 30–32 ave Lancaster, 1180 Uccle; tel. (2) 379-21-01; fax (2) 379-21-97; e-mail embukr@planetintemet.be; Ambassador: KOSTYANTYN GRYSHCHENKO.

United Arab Emirates: 73 ave F. D. Roosevelt, 1050 Brussels; tel. (2) 640-60-00; fax (2) 646-24-73; e-mail emirates.bxl@infonie.be; Ambassador: ABDULHADI AL-KHAJAH.

United Kingdom: 85 rue d'Arlon, 1040 Brussels; tel. (2) 287-62-11; fax (2) 287-63-55; e-mail phoebe.beattie@brussels.mail.fco.gov.uk; internet www.british.embassy.be; Ambassador: DAVID HUGH COLVIN.

USA: 27 blvd du Régent, 1000 Brussels; tel. (2) 508-21-11; fax (2) 511-27-25; e-mail SniderPW@state.gov; internet www.usinfo.be; Ambassador: PAUL L. CEJAS.

Uruguay: 22 ave F. D. Roosevelt, 1050 Brussels; tel. (2) 640-11-69; fax (2) 648-29-09; e-mail uruemb@euronet.be; Ambassador: GUILLERMO E. VALLES GALMES.

Uzbekistan: 99 ave F. D. Roosevelt, 1050 Brussels; tel. (2) 672-88-44; fax (2) 672-39-46; Ambassador: SHAVKAT KHAMRAKULOV.

Venezuela: 10 ave F. D. Roosevelt, 1050 Brussels; tel. (2) 639-03-40; fax (2) 647-88-20; e-mail 100775.1735@compuserve.com; Ambassador: LUIS XAVIER GRISANTI.

Viet Nam: 130 ave de la Floride, 1080 Brussels; tel. (2) 374-91-33; fax (2) 374-93-76; Ambassador: HUYNH ANH DZUNG.

Yemen: 114 ave F. D. Roosevelt, 1050 Brussels; tel. (2) 646-52-90; fax (2) 646-29-11; Ambassador: A. K. AL-AGHBARI.

Yugoslavia: 11 ave Emile de Mot, 1000 Brussels; tel. (2) 647-57-81; fax (2) 647-29-41; e-mail rf.yougoslavie@pophost.eunet.be; Chargé d'affaires a.i.: NIKOLA CICANOVIĆ.

Zambia: 469 ave Molière, 1050 Brussels; tel. (2) 343-56-49; fax (2) 347-43-33; Ambassador: ISAIAH ZIMBA CHABALA.

Zimbabwe: 11 square Joséphine Charlotte, 1200 Brussels; tel. (2) 762-58-08; fax (2) 762-96-05; Ambassador: SIMBARASHE S. MUMBENG-EGWI.

Judicial System

The independence of the judiciary is based on the constitutional division of power between the legislative, executive and judicial bodies, each of which acts independently. Judges are appointed by the crown for life, and cannot be removed except by judicial sentence. The judiciary is organized on four levels, from the judicial canton to the district, regional and national courts. The lowest courts are those of the Justices of the Peace and the Police Tribunals. Each district has one of each type of district court, including the Tribunals of the First Instance, Tribunals of Commerce, and Labour Tribunals, and there is a Court of Assizes in each province. There are Courts of Appeal and Labour Courts in each region. The highest courts are the national civil and criminal Courts of Appeal, Labour Courts and the Supreme Court of Justice. The Military Court of Appeal is in Brussels.

COUR DE CASSATION/HOF VAN CASSATIE (SUPREME COURT OF JUSTICE)

First President: PIERRE MARCHAL.

President: I. VEROUGSTRAETE.

Counsellors: T. VERHEYDEN, R. BOES, C. PARMENTIER, P. ECHEMENT, CHR. STORCK, P. MATHIEU, METRAY, VELU, E. WAUTERS, G. SUETENS-BOURGEOIS, G. LONDERS, E. DIRIX, STASSIJNS, FETTWEIS, G. DHAEYER, E. GOETHALS, P. MAFFEI, D. DEBRUYNE, J. DE CODT, F. CLOSE, PLAS.

Attorney-General: J. DU JARDIN.

First Advocate-General: J.-F. LECLERQ.

Advocates-General: X. DE RIEMAECKER, J. SPREUTELS, A. HENKES, R. LOOP, P. GOEMINNE, M. DE SWAEFF, G. BRESSELEERS, A. DE RAEVE, G. DUBRULLE, P. DUINSLAEGER.

COURS D'APPEL/HOVEN VAN BEROEP (CIVIL AND CRIMINAL HIGH COURTS)

Antwerp: First Pres. LUCIEN JANSSENS; Attorney-Gen. CHRISTINE DEKKERS.

Brussels: First Pres. JACQUELINE COPPIN; Attorney-Gen. ANDRÉ VAN OUDENHOVE.

Ghent: First Pres. JACQUES DEGRAEVE; Attorney-Gen. FRANK SCHINS.

Liège: First Pres. ANNE MOUREAU; Attorney-Gen. ANDRÉ THILY.

Mons: First Pres. CHRISTIAN JASSOGNE; Attorney-Gen. GASTON LADRIERE.

COURS DU TRAVAIL/ARBEIDSHOVEN (LABOUR COURTS)

Antwerp: First Pres. JULES BEULS.

Brussels: First Pres. PIETER TAELMAN.

Ghent: First Pres. WALTER DECRAEYE.

Liège: First Pres. JOEL HUBIN.

Mons: First Pres. JOSEPH GILLAIN.

Religion

CHRISTIANITY
The Roman Catholic Church

Belgium comprises one archdiocese and seven dioceses. At 31 December 1998 there were an estimated 8,011,160 adherents (about four-fifths of the total population).

Bishops' Conference: Bisschoppenconferentie van België/Conférence Episcopale de Belgique, 1 rue Guimard, 1040 Brussels; tel. (2) 509-96-94; fax (2) 509-96-95; e-mail ce.belgica@catho.kerknet.be; internet www.kerknet.be; f. 1981; Pres. Cardinal GODFRIED DANNEELS, Archbishop of Mechelen-Brussels.

Archbishop of Mechelen-Brussels: Cardinal GODFRIED DANNEELS, Aartsbisdom, 15 Wollemarkt, 2800 Mechelen; tel. (15) 21-65-01; fax (15) 20-94-85; e-mail aartsbisdom@kerknet.be.

Protestant Churches

Belgian Evangelical Lutheran Church: Brussels; tel. (2) 511-92-47; f. 1950; 425 mems; Pres C. J. HOBUS.

Church of England: Holy Trinity Pro-Cathedral, 29 rue Capitaine Crespel, 1050 Brussels; tel. (2) 511-71-83; fax (2) 511-10-28; e-mail holy.trinity@arcadis.be; internet www.holytrinitybrussels.com; Rev. Canon NIGEL WALKER, Chaplain and Chancellor of the Pro-Cathedral of the Holy Trinity, Brussels.

Eglise Protestante Unie de Belgique: 5 rue du Champ de Mars, 1050 Brussels; tel. (2) 510-61-66; fax (2) 510-61-64; e-mail belpro.epub@skynet.be; internet www.protestanet.be; Pres. Rev. DANIEL VANESCOTE; Sec. Mrs B. SMETRYNS-BAETENS; 35,000 mems.

Mission Evangélique Belge: 158 blvd Lambermont, 1030 Brussels; tel. (2) 241-30-15; fax (2) 245-79-65; e-mail information@b-e-m.org; internet www.b-e-m.org; f. 1919; Pres. JOHANN LUKASSE; about 12,000 mems.

Union of Baptists in Belgium (UBB): 85 A. Liebaertstraat, 8400 Ostend; tel. (59) 32-46-10; fax (59) 32-46-10; e-mail 106466.3510@compuserve.com; f. 1922 as Union of Protestant Baptists in Belgium; Pres. SAMUEL VERHAEGHE; Sec. PATRICK DENEUT.

ISLAM

There are some 350,000 Muslims in Belgium. In December 1998 the Belgian Islamic community elected an Islamic representative body.

Leader of the Islamic Community: Imam Prof. SALMAN AL-RAHDI.

JUDAISM

There are about 35,000 Jews in Belgium.

Consistoire Central Israélite de Belgique (Central Council of the Jewish Communities of Belgium): 2 rue Joseph Dupont, 1000 Brussels; tel. (2) 512-21-90; fax (2) 512-35-78; e-mail consis@online.be; internet www.jewishcom.be; f. 1808; Chair. Prof. JULIEN KLENER; Sec. MICHEL LAUB.

The Press

Article 25 of the Belgian Constitution states: 'The Press is free; no form of censorship may ever be instituted; no cautionary deposit may be demanded from writers, publishers or printers. When the author is known and is resident in Belgium, the publisher, printer or distributor may not be prosecuted.'

There were an estimated 30 general information dailies in 1996, with an estimated combined circulation of 1,625,000 copies per issue.

There is a trend towards concentration. The Rossel ('Le Soir') group and the Médiabel group control the majority of francophone newspapers, while the principal publisher of Flemish newspapers is the VUM ('De Standaard') group. The Roularta media group is an important publisher of regional newspapers and periodicals, and the Mediaxis group is an important magazine publisher.

The most widely-circulating dailies in French in 1995 were: *Le Soir* (182,520), *L'Avenir de Luxembourg/Vers l'Avenir* (139,960) and *La Lanterne, La Meuse, La Wallonie* (129,840). (*La Wallonie* was subsequently superseded by *Le Matin*.) The corresponding figures for Flemish-language dailies were: *De Standaard/Nieuwsblad/De Gentenaar* (372,410) and, *Het Laatste Nieuws/De Nieuwe Gazet* (306,240), The major weeklies include *De Bond, Flair, Humo* and *Télémoustique*. Some periodicals are printed in both French and Flemish.

PRINCIPAL DAILIES
Antwerp

De Financieel Economische Tijd: Franklin Bldg, 3 Posthoflei, 2600 Berchem; tel. (3) 286-02-11; fax (3) 286-02-10; e-mail tijd@tijd.be; internet www.tijd.be; f. 1968; economic and financial; Gen. Man. HANS MAERTENS; circ. 51,700.

Gazet van Antwerpen: 2 Katwilgweg, 2050 Antwerp; tel. (3) 210-02-10; fax (3) 219-40-41; e-mail webmaster@gva.be; internet www.gva.be; f. 1891; Christian Democrat; Gen. Man. P. Baert; Editor Luc van Loon; circ. 123,000.

De Lloyd/Le Lloyd: 18 Vleminckstraat, 2000 Antwerp; tel. (3) 234-05-50; fax (3) 234-25-93; internet www.anlloyd.be; f. 1858; Flemish and French edns, with supplements in English; shipping, commerce, industry, finance; Dir Guy Dubois; Editor Bernard van den Bossche; circ. 10,600.

De Nieuwe Gazet: 5 Posthhoflei, 2600 Berchem; tel. (3) 286-89-30; fax (3) 286-89-40; e-mail peterverbruggen@persgroep.be; f. 1897; liberal; Chief Editor Peter Verbruggen.

Arlon

L'Avenir du Luxembourg: 38 rue des Déportés, 6700 Arlon; tel. (63) 23-10-20; fax (63) 23-42-89; e-mail info@belmail.com; f. 1897; Catholic; Chief Editor Jean-Luc Henquinet; circ. 139,960 (with *Vers l'Avenir*).

Brussels

La Dernière Heure/Les Sports: 127 blvd Emile Jacqmain, 1000 Brussels; tel. (2) 211-28-88; fax (2) 211-28-70; e-mail dhredaction@pophost.eunet.be; f. 1906; independent Liberal; Dir François le Hodey; Chief Editor Daniel van Wylick; circ. 73,130.

L'Echo: 131 rue de Birmingham, 1070 Brussels; tel. (2) 526-55-11; fax (2) 526-55-26; e-mail redaction@echonet.be; f. 1881; economic and financial; Dir R. Watson; Editor F. Melaet; circ. 22,230.

Het Laatste Nieuws: 347 Brusselsesteenweg, 1730 Asse-Kobbegem; tel. (2) 454-22-11; fax (2) 454-28-22; e-mail redactie.hln@persgroep.be; f. 1888; Flemish; independent; Dir-Gen. R. Bertels; Editors Jaak Smeets, Paul Daenen; circ. 306,279.

La Lanterne: 120 rue Royale, 1000 Brussels; tel. (2) 225-56-00; fax (2) 225-59-13; f. 1944; independent; Dir-Gen. M. Fromont; Chief Editor Guy Debisschop.

La Libre Belgique: 127 blvd Emile Jacqmain, 1000 Brussels; tel. (2) 211-27-77; fax (2) 211-28-32; e-mail lalibrebelgique@pophost.eunet.be; internet www.lalibrebelgique.com; f. 1884; European; independent; Chief Editor Jean-Paul Duchateau; circ. 80,000 (with *La Libre Belgique—Gazette de Liège*).

De Morgen: 54 Brogniezstraat, 1070 Brussels; tel. (2) 556-68-11; fax (2) 520-35-15; e-mail info@demorgen.be; Dir-Gen. Koen Clement; Editor Yves Desmet; circ. 35,000.

Het Nieuwsblad: 30 Gossetlaan, 1702 Groot Bijgaarden; tel. (2) 467-22-11; fax (2) 466-30-93; e-mail nieuwsblad@vum.be; internet www.vum.be; f. 1923; Dir-Gen. Guido Verdeyen; Chief Editor Pol van den Driessche; circ. 372,410 (with *De Standaard* and *De Gentenaar*).

Le Soir: 120 rue Royale, 1000 Brussels; tel. (2) 225-54-32; fax (2) 225-59-10; e-mail journal@lesoir.be; internet www.lesoir.com; f. 1887; independent; Chief Editor Guy Duplat; circ. 178,569.

De Standaard: 28 Gossetlaan, 1702 Groot Bijgaarden; tel. (2) 467-22-11; fax (2) 466-30-93; e-mail standaard@vum.be; internet www.standaard.be; f. 1914; Dir-Gen. Guido Verdeyen; Publisher Dirk Achten; Chief Editor Pieter Vandermeersch; circ. 77,000.

Charleroi

La Nouvelle Gazette (Charleroi, La Louvière, Philippeville, Namur, Nivelles); La Province (Mons): 2 quai de Flandre, 6000 Charleroi; tel. (71) 27-64-11; fax (71) 27-65-67; e-mail gazette@charline.be; internet www.nouvellegazette.be; f. 1878; Man. Dir Patrick Hurbain; Editor M. Frohont.

Le Rappel: 16 rue Charles Dupret, 6000 Charleroi; tel. (71) 20-00-60; fax (71) 31-43-61; f. 1900; Dir-Gen. Jacques de Thysebaert; Chief Editor Bruno Malter.

Eupen

Grenz-Echo: 8 Marktplatz, 4700 Eupen; tel. (87) 59-13-00; fax (87) 74-38-20; e-mail info@grenzecho.be; internet www.grenzecho.be; f. 1927; German; independent Catholic; Dir A. Küchenberg; Chief Editor Heinz Warny; circ. 12,040.

Ghent

De Gentenaar: 102 Lousbergskaai, 9000 Ghent; tel. (9) 265-68-51; fax (9) 265-68-50; e-mail gentenaar@vum.be; internet www.vum.be; f. 1879; Catholic; Dir-Gen. Guido Verdeyen; Chief Editor Rik Vanwalleghem; circ. 366,665 (with *Het Nieuwsblad* and *De Standaard*).

Het Volk: 22 Forelstraat, 9000 Ghent; tel. (9) 265-61-11; fax (9) 225-35-27; e-mail redactie.gent@hetvolk.be; internet www.hetvolk.be; f. 1891; Catholic; Dir-Gen. Guido Verdeyen; Chief Editor Jaki Louage; circ. 114,473.

Hasselt

Het Belang van Limburg: 10 Herckenrodesingel, 3500 Hasselt; tel. (11) 87-81-11; fax (11) 87-82-04; e-mail hbvlredactie@rug.be; internet www.hbvl.be; f. 1879; Dir Marc Vangeel; Editors Luc van Loon, Ivo Vandekerckhove, Richard Swartenbroekx; circ. 100,980.

Liège

La Libre Belgique—Gazette de Liège: 26 blvd d'Avroy, 4000 Liège; tel. (4) 223-19-33; fax (4) 222-41-26; e-mail lalibrebelgique@pophost.eunet.be; internet www.lalibrebelgique.com; f. 1840; Dir-Gen. F. le Hodey; Editor Louis Maraite; circ. 80,000 (with *La Libre Belgique*—Brussels).

Le Matin: 55 rue de la Régence, 4000 Liège; tel. (4) 230-56-56; fax (4) 223-31-17; e-mail redaction@lematin.be; f. 1998; progressive; Dir José Verdin; Editor Fabrice Jacquemart; circ. 8,000.

La Meuse: 8–12 blvd de la Sauvenière, 4000 Liège; tel. (4) 220-08-11; fax (4) 220-08-40; e-mail lameuse@mail.interpac.be; f. 1855; independent; Editor-in-Chief Marc Durand; circ. 129,840 (with *La Lanterne*).

Mons

La Province: 29 rue des Capucins, 7000 Mons; tel. (65) 31-71-51; fax (65) 33-84-77; internet www.nouvellegazette.be; Dir Philippe Dautez; Chief Editor Jean Godin.

Namur

Vers l'Avenir: 12 blvd Ernest Mélot, 5000 Namur; tel. (81) 24-88-11; fax (81) 22-60-24; f. 1918; Editor Jo Mottet; circ. 139,960 (with *L'Avenir du Luxembourg*).

Tournai

Le Courrier de l'Escaut: 24 rue du Curé Notre-Dame, 7500 Tournai; tel. (69) 88-96-20; fax (69) 88-96-61; e-mail courrier.escaut@skynet.be; f. 1829; Chief Editor Willy Thomas.

Verviers

Le Jour/Le Courrier: 14 rue du Brou, 4800 Verviers; tel. (87) 32-20-70; fax (87) 31-67-40; f. 1894; independent; Dir Jacques de Thysebaert; Chief Editor Thierry Degives.

WEEKLIES

Atlas Weekblad: Condédreef 89, 8500 Kortrijk; tel. (56) 26-10-10; fax (56) 21-35-93; e-mail atlas@atlasweekblad.be; internet www.atlasweekblad.be; classified advertising, regional news and sports.

Boer en Tuinder: 8 Minderbroedersstraat, 3000 Leuven; tel. (16) 24-21-60; fax (16) 24-21-68; internet www.boerenbond.be; f. 1891; agriculture and horticulture; circ. 38,000.

De Bond: 170 Langestraat, 1150 Brussels; tel. (2) 779-00-00; fax (2) 779-16-16; e-mail com@publicants.be; f. 1921; general interest; circ. 318,537.

Brugsch Handelsblad: 20 Sint-Jorisstraat, 8000 Brugge; tel. (50) 44-21-55; fax (50) 44-21-66; e-mail redactie.bhblad@roularta.be; f. 1906; local news; includes the Krant van West-Vlaanderen as a supplement; Dir Eddy Brouckaert; Editor-in-Chief Hedwig Dacquin; circ. 40,000.

Ciné Télé Revue: 101 ave Reine Marie-Henriette, 1190 Brussels; tel. (2) 345-99-68; fax (2) 343-12-72; e-mail redaction@cinetelerevue.be; internet www.cinetelerevue.be; f. 1944 as Theatra Ciné Revue, current name adopted 1984; TV listings, celebrity news, family issues; circ. 2,000,000.

La Cité: 26 rue St Laurent, 1000 Brussels; tel. (2) 217-23-90; fax (2) 217-69-95; f. 1950 as daily, weekly 1988; Christian Democrat; Editor Jos Schoonbroodt; circ. 20,000.

European Voice: 17–19 rue Montoyer, 1000 Brussels; tel. (2) 540-90-90; fax (2) 540-90-71; e-mail europeanvoice@compuserve.com; internet www.european-voice.com; f. 1995; EU news; Editor Jacki Davis; circ 18,000.

Femmes d'Aujourd'hui: 109 rue Neewald, 1200 Brussels; tel. (2) 776-28-53; fax (2) 776-23-99; e-mail femmesdaujourdhui@mediaxis.be; f. 1933; women's magazine; Chief Editor Robert Malies; circ. 160,000.

Flair: 82 Uitbreidingsstraat, 2600 Berchem; tel.(3) 290-13-92; fax (3) 290-13-94; e-mail flairsec@mediaxis.be; Flemish and French; women's magazine; Chief Editor A. Brouckmans; circ. 239,858.

Foot/Voetbal Magazine: 50 Raketstraat, 1130 Brussels; tel. (2) 702-45-71; fax (2) 702-45-72; e-mail voetbal@roularta.be; Flemish and French; football magazine; Chief Editors J. Sys, J. Baete.

Humo: 109 Neerveldstraat, 1200 Brussels; tel. (2) 776-24-20; fax (2) 776-23-24; e-mail humo@mediaxis.be; internet www.humo.be; general weekly and TV and radio guide in Flemish; Chief Editor Guy Mortier; circ. 278,350.

Joepie TV Plus: 2 Brandeksweg, 2627 Schelle; tel. (3) 880-84-65; fax (3) 844-61-52; f. 1973; teenagers' interest; Chief Editor Guido van Liefferinge; circ. 144,841.

Kerk en Leven: 92 Halewijnlaan, 2050 Antwerp; tel. (3) 210-08-40; fax (3) 210-08-36; e-mail redaktie.kerklev@kerknet.be; internet www.kerknet.be; f. 1942; Catholic; five regional edns; circ. 620,000.

Knack: 50–52 Raketstraat, 1130 Brussels; tel. (2) 702-46-51; fax (2) 702-46-52; e-mail knack@knack.be; internet www.knack.be; f. 1971; news magazine; Dir HUBERT VAN HUMBEECK; Chief Editors RIK VAN CAUWELAERT, FRANK DE MOOR; circ. 145,000.

Kontakt Lier: 14 Centrale Weg, 2560 Nijlen; tel. (3) 481-89-58; fax (3) 481-71-22; f. 1967; Antwerp local news.

De Kortrijks Handelsblad: 83B Doorniksewijk, 8500 Kortrijk; tel. (56) 27-00-30; fax (56) 27-00-39; e-mail khblad@roularta.be; regional news; owned by Roularta media group; includes De Krant van West-Vlaanderen as a supplement; Chief Editor LUC DEMIDDELE.

De Krant van West-Vlaanderen: 33 Meiboomlaan, 8800 Roeselares; tel. (51) 26-61-11; fax (51) 26-65-87; e-mail kvwvl@roularta.be; internet www.krantvanwestvlaanderen.be; national news and sport; owned by Roularta media group; included as a supplement with regional newspapers; Dir EDDY BROUCKAERT; circ. 331,600.

Kwik: Brusselsesteenweg 347, 1730 Kobbegem; tel. (2) 454-25-01; fax (2) 454-28-28; f. 1962; men's interest; Dir CHRISTIAN VAN THILLO; Editor FRANK SCHRAETS; circ. 55,000.

Landbouwleven/Le Sillon Belge: 92 ave Léon Grosjean, 1140 Brussels; tel. (2) 730-33-00; fax (2) 726-91-34; e-mail erulu@euronet.be; f. 1952; agriculture; Gen. Dir P. CALLEBAUT; Editorial Man. ANDRÉ DE MOL; circ. 37,300.

Libelle (Het Rijk der Vrouw): 82 Uitbreidingsstraat, 2600 Berchem; tel. (3) 290-14-42; fax (3) 290-14-44; e-mail libelle@mediaxis.be; f. 1945; Flemish; women's interest; Dir JAN VANDENWYNGAERDEN; Chief Editor KARIN BODEGOM; circ. 250,668.

Le Soir Illustré: 21 place de Louvain, 1000 Brussels; tel. (2) 225-55-55; fax (2) 225-59-11; f. 1928; independent illustrated; Chief Editor STEVE POLUS; circ. 87,000.

Spirou/Robbedoes: rue Jules Deserée 52, 6001 Marcinelle; tel. (71) 60-05-00; children's interest; circ. 80,000.

Story: 82 Uitbreidingsstraat, 2600 Berchem; tel. (3) 290-15-13; fax (3) 290-15-14; e-mail story@mediaxis.be; f. 1975; Flemish; women's interest; Dir J. VANDENWYNGAERDEN; Chief Editor L. VAN RAAK; circ. 175,111.

TeVe-Blad: 82 Uitbreidingsstraat, 2600 Berchem; tel. (3) 290-14-81; fax 290-14-82; e-mail teveblad@mediaxis.be; f. 1981; TV listings; illustrated; Chief Editor ROB JANS.

Télémoustique: Brussels; tel. (2) 537-08-00; fax (2) 537-45-63; f. 1924; radio and TV; Dir LOUIS CROONEN; Editor ALAIN DE KUYSSCHE; circ. 120,000.

Télépro/Telepro: 31 rue Saint Remacle, 4800 Verviers; tel. (87) 30-70-24; fax (87) 31-35-37; f. 1954; TV listings; owned by Roularta media group; Chief Editor GUY DARRENOUGUÉ; circ. 185,000.

Trends: 50 Raketstraat, bus 4, 1130 Brussels; tel. (2) 702-48-01; fax (2) 702-48-02; e-mail trends@trends.be; internet www.trends.be; economic analysis and business news; owned by Roularta media group; Dir FRANS CROLS; Chief Editor PIET DEPUYDT; circ. 43,514.

TV Ekspres: 82 Uitbreidingsstraat, 2600 Berchem; tel. (3) 290-14-81; fax (3) 290-14-82; e-mail tvexpres@mediaxis.be; Chief Editor ROB JANS; circ. 95,000.

Le Vif/L'Express: 33 place de Jamblinne de Meux, 1030 Brussels; tel. (2) 739-65-11; fax (2) 734-30-40; f. 1971; current affairs; owned by Roularta media group; Dir Gen. PATRICK DE BORCHGRAVE; Chief Editors JACQUES GEVERS, STÉPHANE RENARD; circ. 83,816.

De Weekbode: 33 Meiboomlaan, 8800 Roeselare; tel. (51) 26-61-11; fax (51) 26-65-87; regional news; owned by Roularta media group; includes De Krant van West-Vlaanderen as a supplement; Chief Editor NOËL MAES.

De Weekkrant: 10 Herckenrodesingel, 3500 Hasselt; tel. (11) 87-83-70; fax (11) 87-85-09; e-mail weekkrant@rug.be; f. 1949; Brabant and Limburg local news; circ. 370,000.

Het Wekelijks Nieuws: 5 Nijverheidslaan, 8970 Poperinge; tel. (57) 33-67-21; fax (57) 33-40-18; Christian news magazine; Dir WIM WAUTERS; Editor HERMAN SANSEN; circ. 56,000.

Het Wekelijks Nieuws Kust: 52–54 Torhoutsesteenweg, 8400 Ostend; tel. (59) 56-02-21; fax (59) 56-02-22; e-mail iballiu@roularta.be; Furnes, Dixmude and Belgian West coast local news; owned by Roularta media group, includes De Krant van West-Vlaanderen as a supplement.

De Zeewacht: 52–54 Torhoutsesteenweg, 8400 Ostend; tel. (59) 56-02-21; fax (59) 56-02-22; e-mail theddebauw@roularta.be; Ostend local news; owned by Roularta media group; includes *De Krant van West-Vlaanderen* as a supplement.

ZIE-Magazine: Antwerp; tel. (3) 231-47-90; fax (3) 234-34-66; f. 1930; illustrated; Dir JAN MERCKX; Chief Editor ROB JANS.

Zondag Nieuws: 2 Brandekensweg, 2627 Schelle; tel. (2) 220-22-11; fax (2) 217-98-46; f. 1958; general interest; Dir RIK DUYCK; Chief Editor LUC VANDRIESSCHE; circ. 113,567.

Zondagsblad: 22 Forelstraat, 9000 Ghent; tel. (9) 265-68-02; fax (9) 223-16-77; f. 1949; Gen. Man. WIM SCHAAP; Editor JEF NIJS; circ. 75,000.

SELECTED OTHER PERIODICALS

Alternative Libertaire: BP 103, 1050 Ixelles 1; internet www.users.skynet.be/AL; 11 a year; radical social criticism and debate.

Axelle: 170 Langestraat, 1150 Brussels; tel. (2) 799-00-00; fax (2) 799-16-16; e-mail com@publicants.be; f. 1917; monthly; women's interest; circ. 54,876.

Le Cri du Citoyen: BP 1607, 1000 Brussels 1; tel. and fax (2) 217-48-31; e-mail redaction@lecriducitoyen.com; internet www.chez.com/lecriducitoyen; social comment; 10 a year; Editor FRANCESCO PAOLO CATANIA.

Eigen Aard: 170 Langestraat, 1150 Brussels; tel. (2) 799-00-00; fax (2) 799-16-16; e-mail com@publicants.be; f. 1911; monthly; women's interest; circ. 141,414.

International Engineering News: 216 rue Verte, 1030 Brussels; tel. (2) 240-26-11; fax (2) 242-71-11; e-mail pepco@pepco.be; internet www.ien-online.com; f. 1975; 9 a year; Man. Dir A. ROZENBROEK; circ. 53,000.

Jet Limburg: 10 Herckenrodesingel, 3500 Hasselt; tel. (11) 87-84-85; fax (11) 87-84-84; fortnightly; general interest; circ. 292,000.

Marie Claire: Brussels; tel. (2) 776-25-91; monthly; women's interest; circ. 80,000.

Le Moniteur Belge/Belgisch Staatsblad: 40–42 rue de Louvain, 1000 Brussels; tel. (2) 552-24-59; fax (2) 511-01-84; internet moniteur.be; legislation and official documents; up to 5 a week.

Le Moniteur de l'Automobile: Brussels; tel. (2) 660-19-20; fortnightly; motoring; Editor ÉTIENNE VISART; circ. 85,000.

Notre Temps/Onze Tijd: 33 rue de la Concorde, 1050 Brussels; tel. (2) 514-24-24; fax (2) 514-22-44; e-mail Redaction.NT@bayard-presse.be; senior citizen's interests; monthly; circ. 96,672.

Passie/Passion: T & M, place du Congrès, 4020 Luik; tel. (4) 343-50-50; fax (4) 342-70-00; 6 a year; luxury goods; owned by Roularta media group; Dir and Chief Editor JEAN PERINI; circ. 20,000.

PC World Belgium: 70 rue Rederbachstraat, 1190 Brussels; tel. (2) 346-48-50; fax (2) 346-43-65; internet www.best.be; f. 1998; monthly; Pres. JEAN DE GHELDERE; circ. 35,000.

Santé: Drogenbos; tel. (2) 331-06-13; fax (2) 331-23-33; monthly; popular health, diet, fitness; circ. 200,000.

Sélection du Reader's Digest: 20 blvd Paepsem, 1070 Brussels; tel. (2) 526-81-85; fax (2) 526-81-89; f. 1947; monthly; general; Man. Dir CAREL ROG; circ. 80,000.

Vrouw & Wereld: 170 Langestraat, 1150 Brussels; tel. (2) 799-00-00; fax (2) 799-16-16; e-mail com@publicants.be; f. 1920; monthly; women's interest; circ. 197,794.

NEWS AGENCIES

Agence Belga (Agence Télégraphique Belge de Presse SA)—Agentschap Belga (Belgisch Pers-telegraafagentschap NV): 8B rue F. Pelletier, 1030 Brussels; tel. (2) 743-13-11; fax (2) 735-18-74; internet www.belganews.be; f. 1920; largely owned by daily newspapers; Chair. L. NEELS; Gen. Man. E. HANS.

Agence Europe SA: 36 rue de la Gare, 1040 Brussels; tel. (2) 737-94-94; fax (2) 736-37-00; internet www.agenceurope.com; f. 1952; daily bulletin on EU activities.

Centre d'Information de Presse (CIP): 199 blvd du Souverain, 1160 Brussels; tel. (2) 675-25-79; f. 1946; Dir T. SCHOLTES.

Foreign Bureaux

Agence France-Presse (AFP): Europe Center, 17/3 rue Archimède, 1000 Brussels; tel. (2) 230-83-94; fax (2) 230-23-04; e-mail afp.bru@euronet.be; internet www.afp.com; Dir PHILIPPE VALAT.

Agencia EFE (Spain): 1 blvd Charlemagne, bte 20, 1041 Brussels; tel. (2) 285-48-30; internet www.efe.com; Dir JOSÉ MANUEL SANZ MINGOTE.

Agenzia Nazionale Stampa Associata (ANSA) (Italy): 1 blvd Charlemagne, bte 7, 1040 Brussels; tel. (2) 230-81-92; fax (2) 230-60-82; internet www.ansa.it; Dir LUIGI MAYER.

Algemeen Nederlands Persbureau (ANP) (Netherlands): 1 blvd Charlemagne, bte 6, 1041 Brussels; tel. (2) 230-11-88; fax (2) 231-18-04; internet www.anp.nl; Correspondents TON VAN LIEROP, KEES PIJNAPPELS, WILMA VAN MELEREN.

Allgemeiner Deutscher Nachrichtendienst (ADN) (Germany): Brussels; tel. (2) 734-59-57; fax (2) 736-27-11; Correspondents BARBARA SCHUR, ULLRICH SCHUR.

Associated Press (AP) (USA): 1 blvd Charlemagne, bte 49, 1041 Brussels; tel. (2) 230-52-49; internet www.ap.org; Dir ROBERT WIELAARD.

Česká tisková kancelář (ČTK) (Czech Republic): 2 rue des Egyptiens, bte 6, 1050 Brussels; tel. (2) 648-01-33; fax (2) 640-31-91; internet www.ctk.cz; Correspondent M. BARTAK.

Deutsche Presse-Agentur (dpa) (Germany): 1 blvd Charlemagne, bte 17, 1041 Brussels; tel. (2) 230-36-91; fax (2) 230-98-96; e-mail dpa@dpa.be; internet www.dpa.de; Dir THOMAS SPIEKER.

Informatsionnoye Telegrafnoye Agentstvo Rossii-Telegrafnoye Agentstvo Suverennykh Stran (ITAR-TASS) (Russia): 103 rue Général Lotz, bte 10, 1180 Brussels; tel. (2) 343-86-70; fax (2) 344-83-76; e-mail mineev@arcadis.be; internet www.itar-tass.com; Correspondent ALEKSANDR I. MINEYEV.

Inter Press Service-Vlaanderen (IPS) (Italy): 21 Inquisitiestraat, 1000 Brussels; tel. (2) 732-69-16; fax (2) 735-20-89; e-mail ips@ngonet.be; internet www.ips.ngonet.be; Dirs PETER DHONDT, MAARTEN MESSIAEN.

Jiji Tsushin (Japan): 1 blvd Charlemagne, bte 26, 1041 Brussels; tel. (2) 285-09-48; fax (02) 230-14-50; Dir HIROSHI MASUDA.

Kyodo News Service (Japan): 1 blvd Charlemagne, bte 37, 1041 Brussels; tel. (2) 285-09-10; fax (02) 230-53-34; internet www.kyodo.co.jp; Dir MASARU IWATA.

Magyar Távirati Iroda (MTI) (Hungary): 41 rue Jean Chapelie, 1050 Brussels; tel. and fax (2) 343-75-35; internet www.mti.hu; Correspondents BÉLA VERES, BALÁZS LÁSZLÓ.

Reuters (United Kingdom): 61 rue de Trèves, 1040 Brussels; tel. (2) 287-66-11; fax (2) 230-55-40; internet www.reuters.com; Man. Dir PETER KAYER.

Rossiyskoye Informatsionnoye Agentstvo—Novosti (RIA—Novosti) (Russia): 74 rue du Merlo, 1180 Brussels; tel. (2) 332-24-35; fax 332-17-29; e-mail novosti@skynet.be; internet www.rian.ru; Dir VIKTOR ONOUTCHKO.

Xinhua (New China) News Agency (People's Republic of China): 32 square Ambiorix, Résidence le Pavois, bte 4, 1040 Brussels; tel. (2) 230-32-54; internet www.xinhua.org; Chief Correspondent LE ZUDE.

PRESS ASSOCIATIONS

Association belge des Editeurs de Journaux/Belgische Vereniging van de Dagbladuitgevers: 22 blvd Paepsem, bte 7, 1070 Brussels; tel. (2) 558-97-60; fax (2) 558-97-68; e-mail abej.bvdu@pressorg.be; f. 1964; 17 mems; Pres R. WATSON; Gen. Secs ALEX FORDYN (Flemish), MARGARET BORIBON (French).

Association générale des Journalistes professionnels de Belgique/Algemene Vereniging van de Beroepsjournalisten in België: 9B Quai à la Houille, 1000 Brussels; tel. (2) 229-14-60; fax (2) 223-02-72; f. 1978 by merger; 4,000 mems; affiliated to IFJ (International Federation of Journalists); Pres. PHILIPPE LERUTH; Vice-Pres. GERRIT LUTS.

Fédération Belge des Magazines/Federatie van de Belgische Magazines: 22/8 blvd Paepsemlaan, 1070 Brussels; tel. (2) 522-57-91; fax (2) 522-85-27; e-mail magazines@febelma.be; internet www.febelmn.be; Pres. PATRICK DE BORCHGRAVE; Sec. Gen. ALAIN LAMBRECHTS.

Fédération de la Presse Périodique de Belgique/Federatie van de periodieke pers van België (FPPB): 54 rue Charles Martel, 1000 Brussels; tel. (2) 230-09-99; fax (2) 231-14-59; f. 1891; Pres. P. VAN SINT JAN; Sec.-Gen. JOHAN VAN CLEEMPUT.

Principal Publishers

Acco CV: 134–136 Tiensestraat, 3000 Louvain; tel. (16) 29-11-00; fax (16) 20-73-89; e-mail rob.berrevoets@acco.be; f. 1960; general reference, scientific books, periodicals; Dir ROB BERREVOETS.

Uitgeverij Altiora Averbode NV (Publishing Dept): 1 Abdijstraat, bte 54, 3271 Averbode; tel. (13) 78-01-02; fax (13) 78-01-79; e-mail averbode.publ@verbode.be; internet www.averbode-online.be; f. 1993; children's fiction and non-fiction, religious; Man. P. HERMANS.

De Boeck & Larcier SA: 39 rue des Minimes, 1000 Brussels; tel. (10) 48-25-11; fax (10) 48-26-50; f. 1795; school, technical and university textbooks, youth, nature, legal publs and documentaries; Dirs CHR. DE BOECK, G. HOYOS.

Brepols NV: 68 Steenweg op Tielen, 2300 Turnhout; tel. (14) 40-25-00; fax (14) 42-20-22; e-mail postmaster@brepols.com; internet www.brepols.com; f. 1796; humanities, diaries; Dir PAUL VANGERVEN.

Casterman SA: 132 rue Royale, bte 2, 1000 Brussels; tel. (2) 209-83-00; fax (2) 209-83-01; f. 1780; fiction, encyclopaedias, education, history, comic books and children's books; Man. Dir J. SIMON.

D2H Didier Hatier Hachette Education SA: 412c Chaussée de Waterloo, 1050 Brussels; tel. (2) 539-26-79; fax (2) 539-26-79; e-mail d2h@infoboard.be; internet www.d2h.be; f. 1979; school books, general literature; Dir B. DELGORD.

Davidsfonds vzw: 79–81 Blijde Inkomststraat, 3000 Leuven; tel. (16) 31-06-00; fax (16) 31-06-08; e-mail informatie@davidsfonds.be; internet www.davidsfonds.be; f. 1875; general, reference, textbooks; Dir J. RENS.

Editions Dupuis SA: 52 rue Jules Destrée, 6001 Marcinelle; tel. (71) 60-50-00; fax (71) 60-05-99; internet www.editions-dupuis.com; f. 1898; children's fiction, periodicals and comic books for children and adults, multimedia and audiovisual; Dir PHILIPPE BUCK.

Etablissements Emile Bruylant: 67 rue de la Régence, 1000 Brussels; tel. (2) 512-98-45; fax (2) 511-72-02; e-mail bruylant@pophost.eunet.be; internet www.bruylant.be; f. 1838; law; Chief Man. Dir J. VANDEVELD.

Halewijn NV: 92 Halewijnlaan, 2050 Antwerp; tel. (3) 210-08-11; fax (3) 210-08-36; e-mail Jo.Cornille@kerknet.be; f. 1953; general, periodicals; Dir-Gen. J. CORNILLE.

Editions Hemma SA: 106 rue de Chevron, 4987 Chevron; tel. (86) 43-01-01; fax (86) 43-36-40; f. 1956; juveniles, educational books and materials; Dir A. HEMMERLIN.

Houtekiet NV: 33 Vrijheidstraat, 2000 Antwerp; tel. (3) 238-12-96; fax (3) 238-80-41; e-mail info@houtekiet.com; f. 1983; Dir L. DE HAES.

Die Keure NV: 108 Oude Gentweg, 8000 Brugge; tel. (50) 33-12-35; fax (50) 34-37-68; e-mail die.keure@pophost.eunet.be; f. 1948; textbooks, law, political and social sciences; Dirs J. P. STEEVENS (textbooks), R. CARTON (law, political and social sciences).

Uitgeverij De Klaproos: 4 Hostenstraat, 8670 Koksijde; tel. (58) 51-85-30; fax (58) 51-29-42; internet www.klaproos.be; f. 1992; historical works.

Kritak NV: 249 Diestsestraat, 3000 Louvain; tel. (16) 23-12-64; fax (16) 22-33-10; f. 1976; art, law, social sciences, education, humanities, literature, periodicals; Dir ANDRÉ VAN HALEWIJCK.

Editions Labor: 156–158 chaussée de Haecht, 1030 Brussels; tel. (2) 240-05-70; fax (2) 216-34-47; f. 1925; general; *L'Ecole 2000* (periodical); Gen. Man. MARIE-PAULE ESKÉNAZI.

Lannoo Uitgeverij NV: 97 Kasteelstraat, 8700 Tielt; tel. (51) 42-42-11; fax (51) 40-11-52; e-mail lannoo@lannoo.be; internet www.lannoo.be; f. 1909; general, reference.

Editions du Lombard SA: 1–11 ave Paul-Henri Spaak, 1070 Brussels; tel. (2) 526-68-11; f. 1946; juveniles, games, education, geography, history, religion; Man. Dir ROB HARREU.

Imprimerie Robert Louis Editions: 35–43 rue Borrens, 1050 Brussels; tel. (2) 640-10-40; fax (2) 640-07-39; f. 1952; science and technical; Man. PIERRE LOUIS.

Manteau NV: 147A Belgiëlei, 2018 Antwerp; tel. (3) 285-72-26; fax (3) 285-72-99; e-mail algem@standaard.com; internet www.standaard.com; f. 1932; literature, periodicals; Dir R. VANSCHOONBEEK.

Mercatorfonds: 85 Meir, 2000 Antwerp; tel. (3) 202-72-60; fax (3) 231-13-19; f. 1965; art, ethnography, literature, music, geography and history; Dir JAN MARTENS.

Nouvelles Editions Marabout SA: 30 ave de l'Energie, 4432 Alleur; tel. (41) 246-38-63; fax (41) 263-88-63; f. 1977; paperbacks; Man. Dir J. FIRMIN; Dir JEAN ARCACHE.

Peeters pvba: 153 Bondgenotenlaan, 3000 Louvain; tel. (16) 23-51-70; fax (16) 22-85-00; f. 1970; general, reference; Dir M. PEETERS-LISMOND.

Uitgeverij Pelckmans NV: 222 Kapelsestraat, 2950 Kapellen; tel. (3) 664-53-20; fax (3) 655-02-63; f. 1893 as De Nederlandsche Boekhandel, name changed 1988; school books, scientific, general; Dirs J. and R. PELCKMANS.

Roularta Books: 33 Meiboomlaan, 8800 Roeselare; tel. (51) 26-63-32; fax (51) 26-64-87; e-mail roulartabooks@roularta.be; f. 1988; owned by Roularta media group; Publr JAN INGELBEEN.

De Sikkel: 8 Nijverheidsstraat, 2390 Malle; tel. (3) 309-13-30; fax (3) 311-77-39; e-mail info@desikkel.be; internet www.desikkel.be; f. 1919; educational books and magazines; Dir K. DE BOCK.

Snoeck-Ducaju en Zoon NV: 464 Begijnhoflaan, 9000 Ghent; tel. (9) 23-48-97; fax (9) 23-68-30; f. 1948; art books, travel guides; Pres. SERGE SNOECK.

Société Belgo-Française de Presse et de Promotion (SBPP) SA: Brussels; tel. (2) 349-00-90; fax (2) 344-28-27; periodicals; Dir CLAUDE CUVELIER.

Standaard Uitgeverij NV: 147A Belgiëlei, 2018 Antwerp; tel. (3) 285-72-00; fax (3) 285-72-99; e-mail info@standaard.com; internet www.standaard.com; f. 1924; general, fiction, non-fiction, comics, dictionaries, educational, general and professional; Dirs ERIC WILLEMS, JOHAN DE KONING, DIANE DEVRIENDT, NICOLE SWYNGEDOUW.

Vlaamse Uitgeversmaatschappij (VUM): 30 Gosselaan, 1702 Groot-Bijgaarden; tel. (2) 467-22-11; internet www.vum.be; f. 1976; newspaper and magazine publishing group; Man.-Dir JO VAN CROONENBORCH.

Wolters Kluwer Belgie NV: Kovterveldstraat 14, 1831 Diegem; tel. (2) 723-11-11; fax (2) 725-13-06; e-mail ben.houdmont@wkb.be; internet www.wkb.be; law, business, school books, scientific; Dir B. HAUDMONT.

Wolters Plantyn: 21–25 Santvoortbeeklaan, 2100 Deurne; tel. (3) 360-03-37; fax (3) 360-03-30; e-mail wolters.plantyn@wpeu.wkb.be; internet www.woltersplantyn.be; f. 1959; education; Dir JACQUES GERMONPREZ.

Zuidnederlandse Uitgeverij NV: 7 Vluchtenburgstraat, 2630 Aartselaar; tel. (3) 887-14-64; fax (3) 877-21-15; f. 1956; general fiction and non-fiction, children's books; Dir J. VANDE VELDEN.

PUBLISHERS' ASSOCIATIONS

Association des Editeurs Belges (ADEB): 140 blvd Lambermont, 1030 Brussels; tel. (2) 241-65-80; fax (2) 216-71-31; f. 1922; asscn of French-language book publrs; Dir BERNARD GÉRARD.

Cercle Belge de la Librairie: 35 rue de la Chasse Royale, 1160 Brussels; tel. (2) 640-52-41; f. 1883; asscn of Belgian booksellers and publrs; 205 mems; Pres. M. DESTREBECQ.

Vlaamse Uitgevers Vereniging: Antwerp; tel. (3) 230-89-23; fax (3) 281-22-40; asscn of Flemish-language book publrs; Sec. WIM DE MONT.

Broadcasting and Communications

TELECOMMUNICATIONS

In January 1998 the Belgian telecommunications sector was fully opened to private-sector competition. More than 300 private companies have subsequently registered as service providers.

Regulatory Authority

Institut Belge des Services Postaux et de Télécommunications (IBPT)/Belgisch Instituut voor Postdiensten en Telecommunicatie (BIPT): 14 ave de l'Astronomie, 1210 Brussels; tel. (2) 226-88-88; fax (2) 223-24-77; e-mail eric.van.heesvelde@bipt.be; internet www.bipt.be; Administrator-Gen. ERIC VAN HEESVELDE.

Major Service Providers

Belgacom: 177 blvd Emile Jacqmain, 1030 Brussels; tel. (2) 202-41-11; fax (2) 203-54-93; e-mail contact@is.belgacom.be; internet www.belgacom.be; 50.1% state owned; total service operator; Chair. MICHEL DUSSENNE; Pres. and CEO JOHN J. GOOSSENS.

Belgacom Mobile SA: 177 blvd Emile Jacqmain, 1130 Brussels; tel. (2) 205-40-00; fax (2) 205-40-40; 75% owned by Belgacom, 25% by AirTouch; mobile cellular telephone operator.

BT (Worldwide) Ltd: 48–50 Excelsiorlaan, 1930 Zaventem; tel. (2) 718-22-11; e-mail olivier.servais@bt.be; internet www.bt.be.

Cable & Wireless Belgium SA: Blue Tower, 326 ave Louise, BP 17, 1050 Brussels; tel. (2) 629-03-11; fax (2) 646-82-24; internet www.cweurope.com.

Esprit Telecom Belgium BV: Bâtiment Radius, 44–46 Excelsiorlaan, 1930 Zaventem; tel. (2) 720-35-45; fax (2) 720-01-02; e-mail belgiuminfo@esprittele.com; internet www.esprittele.com; f. 1995.

KPN-Orange Belgium: 115 rue Colonel Bourg, 1140 Brussels; tel. (2) 702-42-00; fax (2) 702-42-01; mobile cellular telephone operator.

Mobistar: 149 rue Colonel Bourg, 1140 Brussels; tel. (2) 745-71-11; fax (2) 745-70-00; f. 1995; 51% owned by FTMI group; mobile cellular telephone and fixed-line operator; Pres. J. CORDIER; Dir-Gen. B. GHILLEBAERT.

Telenet Operaties NV: 4 Liersesteenweg, 2800 Mechelen; tel. (1) 533-30-00; e-mail communicatie@telenet.be; internet www.telenet.be; f. 1996; telecommunications and cable service provider; CEO PAUL VAN DER SPIEGEL.

Unisource Belgium NV: 50 Medialaan, 1800 Vilvoorde; tel. (2) 275-33-11; fax (2) 275-33-33; internet www.unisource.be; subsidiary of KPN Belgium; Man. Dir PIERRE VERBRUGEN.

VersaTel Telecom Belgium NV: 166 Koningin Astridlaan, 1780 Wemmel; internet www.versatel.be; f. 1995.

WorldCom NV: 37 Wetenschapstraat, 1040 Brussels; tel. (2) 400-83-00; e-mail worldcom.info@wcom.be; internet www.worldcom.be; subsidiary of WorldCom.Inc.

STATE BROADCASTING ORGANIZATIONS

Flemish

Vlaamse Radio- en Televisieomroep NV (VRT): 52 Auguste Reyerslaan, 1043 Brussels; tel. (2) 741-31-11; fax (2) 734-93-51; e-mail info@vrt.be; internet www.vrt.be; f. 1998; shares held by Flemish Community; operates five radio stations and three television stations; Pres. of Board of Dirs GUY PEETERS; Man. Dir BERT DE GRAEVE; Dir of Radio Programmes FRANS IEVEN; Dir of Television Programmes CHRISTINA VON WACKERBARTH.

French

Radio-Télévision Belge de la Communauté Française (RTBF): 52 blvd Auguste Reyers, 1044 Brussels; tel. (2) 737-21-11;

fax (2) 737-43-57; internet www.rtbf.be; operates five radio stations and two television stations; Chair. EDOUARD DESCAMPE; Admin-Gen. CHRISTIAN DRUITTE; Dir of Radio Programmes CLAUDE DELACROIX; Dir of Television Programmes GERRARD LOVERIOUS.

German

Belgisches Rundfunk- und Fernsehzentrum der Deutschsprachigen Gemeinschaft (BRF): 11 Kehrweg, 4700 Eupen; tel. (87) 59-11-11; fax (87) 59-11-09; e-mail info@brf.be; internet www.brf.be; Dir H. ENGELS.

COMMERCIAL, CABLE AND PRIVATE BROADCASTING

Canal Plus Belgique: 656 chaussée de Louvain, 1030 Brussels; tel. (2) 730-02-11; fax (2) 730-03-79; internet www.canalplus.be; f. 1989; 42% owned by Canal Plus Europe; broadcasts to Brussels region and Wallonia.

Regionale TV Media: Brussels; tel. (2) 467-58-77; fax (2) 467-56-54; e-mail contact@rtvm.be; internet www.rtvm.be; group of 11 regional news broadcasters within Flanders; commercial.

Télévision Indépendante (TVI): 1 ave Ariane, 1201 Brussels; tel. (2) 778-68-11; fax (2) 778-68-12; commercial station; broadcasts in French.

Vlaamse Media Maatschappij: 1 Medialaan, 1800 Vilvoorde; tel. (2) 255-32-11; fax (2) 252-37-87; f. 1987; commercial; broadcasts in Flemish; Gen. Man. ERIC CLAEYS.

Finance

(cap. = capital; m. = million; res = reserves;
dep. = deposits; brs = branches; amounts in euros, unless otherwise indicated)

BANKING

Commission bancaire et financière/Commissie voor het Bank- en Financiewezen: 99 ave Louise, 1050 Brussels; tel. (2) 535-22-11; fax (2) 535-23-23; internet www.cbf.be; f. 1935 to supervise the application of legislation relating to the legal status of credit institutions and to the public issue of securities; Acting Chair. F. T'KINT; CEOs M. CARDON, R. BONTE, G. CARTON DE TOURNAI, A. NIESTEN.

Central Bank

Banque Nationale de Belgique: 14 blvd de Berlaimont, 1000 Brussels; tel. (2) 221-21-11; fax (2) 221-31-01; e-mail secretariat@nbb.be; internet www.bnb.be; f. 1850; bank of issue; cap. BF 400m., res BF 53,184m., total assets BF 1,006,809m. (Dec. 1998); Gov. GUY QUADEN; Vice-Gov. MARCIA DE WACHTER; Exec. Dirs J.-P. PAUWELS, JAN SMETS, JEAN HILGERS, FRANÇOISE MASAL, PETER PRAET; 2 brs.

Development Bank

Investeringsmaatschappij voor Vlaanderen (GIMV): 37 Karel Oomsstraat, 2018 Antwerp; tel. (3) 290-21-00; fax (3) 290-21-05; e-mail gimv@gimv.be; internet www.gimv.com; f. 1980; promotes creation, restructuring and expansion of private cos; cap. BF 8,800,000m. (1999); Chair. HERMAN DAEMS; Dir-Gen. GERARD VAN ACKER.

Major Commercial Banks

ABN AMRO Bank NV: 53 Regentlaan, 1000 Brussels; tel. (2) 546-04-60; fax (2) 546-04-23; internet www.abnamro.be; cap. BF 1,050m., res BF 1,887m., dep. BF 106,649m. (Dec. 1996); Chair. J. KOOPMAN; Dir J. J. W. ZWEEGERS; 7 brs.

Antwerpse Diamantbank NV/Banque Diamantaire Anversoise SA: 54 Pelikaanstraat, 2018 Antwerp; tel. (3) 204-72-04; fax (3) 233-90-95; e-mail info@adia.be; f. 1934; cap. 34.4m., res 68.6m., dep. 199.8m. (Dec. 1999); Chair. JAN VANHEVEL; Man. Dir and Chair. of Exec. Cttee PAUL C. GORIS.

Artesia Banking Corporation (Artesia Bank): W.T.C. Tower 1, 30 B2 Koning Albert II-laan, 1000 Brussels; tel. (2) 204-41-11; fax (2) 203-20-14; e-mail info@artesiabc.be; internet www.artesiabc.be; f. 1999; owns Artesia Bank, BACOB Bank and DVV/AP insurance co; cap. 857.3m., res 739.7m., dep. 75,431.4m. (Dec. 1999); Chair. of Bd of Dirs PHILIPPE ROMAGNOLI.

BACOB Bank SC: 25 Trierstraat, 1040 Brussels; tel. (2) 285-20-20; fax (2) 230-71-78; e-mail bacob@bacob.be; internet www.bacob.be; f. 1924 as BACOB Savings Bank SC; Chair. DIRK BRUNEEL; 559 brs.

AXA Bank Belgium NV: 214 Grotesteenweg, 2600 Antwerp; tel. (3) 286-22-11; fax (3) 286-24-07; e-mail contact@axa-bank.be; internet www.axa.be; f. 1881, as ANHYP Bank NV, present name adopted 2000; cap. 24.8m., res 383.2m., dep 7,779.3m. (Dec. 1999); Chair. of Bd of Dirs ALFRED BOUCKAERT; Chair. of Exec. Cttee CARL HOLSTERS.

Banca Monte Paschi Belgio SA/NV: 24 rue Joseph II, 1000 Brussels; tel. (2) 220-72-11; fax (2) 218-83-91; f. 1947 as Banco di

Roma (Belgique), name changed 1992; cap. 26.0m., res 33.0m., dep. 2,061.1m. (Dec. 1999); Pres. of Exec. Cttee and Man. Dir MARIO GAETANO MAZZARINO; 6 brs.

Bank J. van Breda & Co GCV: 295 Plantin en Moretuslei, 2140 Borgerhout; tel. (3) 217-51-11; fax (3) 235-37-84; e-mail mail@bank .vanbreda.be; internet www.bank.vanbreda.be; f. 1930; cap. 16.1m., res 79.4m., dep. 1,586.1m. (Dec. 1999); Gen. Man. CARLO HENRIKSEN; 32 brs.

Bank Brussels Lambert: 24 ave Marnix, 1000 Brussels; tel. (2) 547-21-11; fax (2) 547-38-44; e-mail info@bbl.be; internet www .bbl.be; f. 1975; taken over by ING Bank NV (the Netherlands) Jan. 1998; cap. BF 34,074m., res BF 91,774m., dep. BF 3,865,595m. (Dec. 1999); Chair. of Bd JACQUES MOULAERT; Pres. and CEO MICHEL TILMANT; 953 brs.

Bank Degroof SA/Banque Degroof SCS: 44 rue de l'Industrie, 1040 Brussels; tel. (2) 287-91-11; fax (2) 230-67-00; e-mail info@ degroof.be; internet www.degroof.be; f. 1871, present name adopted 1998; cap. 31.0m., res 50.8m., dep. 1,202.4m. (Sept. 1999); Man. Dir ALAIN PHILIPPSON.

Bankunie NV: 46 Parklaan, 2300 Turnhout; tel. (14) 44-32-00; fax (14) 42-78-51; internet www.bankunie.be; f. 1966; cap. 22.8m., res 10.9m., dep. 762.5m. (Dec. 1999); Chair. LEENDERT KEEMINK; CEO PIET VERBRUGGE.

Banque Belgolaise SA: 1 Cantersteen, bte 807, 1000 Brussels; tel. (2) 551-72-11; fax (2) 551-75-15; e-mail belgolaise.brussels@ belgolaise.com; internet www.belgolaise.com; f. 1960 as Banque Belgo-Congolaise SA, present name adopted 1991; cap. BF 1,000m., res BF 2,370m., dep. BF 77,213m. (Dec. 1999); Chair. MARC YVES BLANPAIN; Vice-Chair. FILIP DIERCKX; 1 br.

Banque Européenne pour l'Amérique Latine (BEAL) SA: 166 chaussée de la Hulpe, 1170 Brussels; tel. (2) 663-69-00; fax (2) 663-69-59; internet www.westlb.com/beal; f. 1974; cap. 80.0m., res 40.6m., dep. 4,288.6m. (Dec. 1999); Chair. HANS-JÜRGEN SENGERA; Man. Dirs PHILIP WYKES, HORST R. MAGIERA.

Banque Nagelmackers 1747 SA: 23 ave de l'Astronomie, 1210 Brussels; tel. (2) 229-76-00; fax (2) 229-76-99; e-mail hilde .vernaillen@nagelmackers.be; internet www.nagelmackers.be; f. 1747; cap. 46.0m., res 52.6m., dep. 1,946.8m. (Dec. 1999); Pres. Exec. Cttee JEAN-LOUIS LUYCKX; 67 brs.

BCH Benelux SA/NV: 227 rue de la Loi, 1040 Brussels; tel. (2) 286-54-11; fax (2) 230-09-40; f. 1914, present name adopted 1998; cap. 39.6m., res 0.3m., dep. 1,962.4m. (Dec. 1999); Pres. LEOPOLDO CALVO SOTELO Y BUSTELO; Man. Dir MIGUEL SÁNCHEZ TÓVAR.

CBC Banque SA: 5 Grand-Place, 1000 Brussels; tel. (2) 547-12-15; fax (2) 547-13-12; e-mail info@cbc.be; internet www.cbc.be; f. 1958, name changed as above 1998; cap. 89.6m., res 173.0m., dep. 7,721.7m. (Dec. 1999); Chair. BAROU HUYGHEBAERT; 71 brs.

Citibank Belgium NV/SA: 263 blvd Général Jacques, 1050 Brussels; tel. (2) 626-51-11; fax (2) 626-55-84; internet www.citibank.be; f. 1919, present name adopted 1992; Gen. Man. JACK WRIGHT.

Crédit à l'Industrie/Krediet aan de Nijverheid: 14 ave de l'Astronomie, 1210 Brussels; tel. (2) 214-12-11; fax (2) 218-04-78; f. 1919; owned by Fortis Bank; cap. BF 4,500m., res BF 7,554m., dep. BF 511,133m. (Dec. 1995); Chair. FRED RAMPEN; 4 brs.

Crédit Professionnel SA/Beroepskrediet NV: 16 blvd de Waterloo, 1000 Brussels; tel. (2) 289-89-89; fax (2) 289-89-90; e-mail info@bkcp.be; internet www.bkcp.be; f. 1946 as Caisse Nationale de Crédit Professionel SA; name changed as above 1997; cap. 60.6m., res 1.3m., dep. 2,650.3m. (Dec. 1999); Chair. of Supervisory Bd GUIDO VERHAEGEN; Chair. of Exec. Cttee THIERRY FAUT.

Deutsche Bank SA/NV: 9 Lange Gasthuisstraat, 2000 Antwerp 1; tel. (2) 551-65-11; fax (2) 551-66-66; f. 1893 as Banque de Commerce SA (Handelsbank NV), renamed Crédit Lyonnais Belgium 1989, bought by Deutsche Bank 1999; cap. BF 6,587m., res BF 3,847m., dep. BF 406,231m. (Dec. 1997); Chair. CARL L. VON BOEHM-BEZING; Chief Exec. YVES DELACOLLETTE; 40 brs.

Dexia Bank SA: 44 Pachécolaan, 1000 Brussels; tel. (2) 222-11-11; fax (2) 222-31-23; internet www.dexia.be; f. 1860 as Crédit Communal de Belgique SA, present name adopted 2000; cap. 1,604m., res 410.3m., dep. 81,192.4m. (Dec. 1999); Chair. L. ONCLIN.

Europabank NV: 170 Burgstraat, 9000 Ghent; tel. (9) 224-73-11; fax (9) 223-34-72; e-mail europabank@village.uunet.be; f. 1964; owned by Staal Bank NV, The Hague; cap. 64m. Belgian francs, res. 1,384m. Belgian francs, total assets 18,156m. Belgian francs (Dec. 1999); Chair. of Supervisory Board ALBERT VAN HOUTTE; 26 brs.

Fortis Bank NV/Fortis Banque SA: 3 Montagne du Parc, 1000 Brussels; tel. (2) 565-11-11; fax (2) 565-42-22; e-mail info@ fortisbank.com; internet www.fortisbank.com; f. 1999 by merger of Generale Bank/Générale de Banque and ASLK-CGER Bank/Banque with the Fortis Group; banking, insurance and investments; cap. 2,925.4m., res 5,842.8m., dep. 292,320.2m. (Dec. 1999); Chair. of Bd of Dirs ANTON VAN ROSSUM; Chair. of Exec. Cttee HERMAN VERWILST; 3,000 brs.

ING Bank (Belgium) SA/NV: 1 rue de Ligne, 1000 Brussels; tel. (2) 229-87-11; fax (2) 229-88-10; f. 1934, present name adopted 1995; wholly-owned subsidiary of Bank Brussels Lambert; cap. BF 540m., res BF 1,560m., dep. BF 50,914m. (Dec. 1997); Chair. E. DRALANS; Man. Dirs G. COLONNA, J. DE VAUCLEROY; 1 br.

KBC Bank NV: 2 Havenlaan, 1080 Brussels 8; tel. (2) 429-11-11; fax (2) 429-81-31; e-mail kbc.telecenter@kbc.be; internet www.kbc.be; f. 1935 as Kredietbank NV; merged with Bank von Roeselare NV and CERA Investment Bank NV in 1998; cap. and res 6,042.4m., dep. 121,990.7m. (Dec. 1999); Pres. REMI VERMEIREN.

Parfibank SA: 40 blvd du Régent, 1000 Brussels; tel. (2) 513-90-20; fax (2) 512-73-20; e-mail rudi.sneyers@artesia.be; f. 1976 as Nippon European Bank SA, present name adopted 1996; cap. 75.0m., res 18.4m., dep. 879.9m. (Dec. 1999); Chair. RENAUD GREINDL; Man. Dir RUDI SNEYERS.

Banking Association

Association Belge des Banques/Belgische Vereniging van Banken (ABB): 36 rue Ravenstein, 1000 Brussels; tel. (2) 507-68-11; fax (2) 512-58-61; e-mail abb-bvb@abb-bvb.be; f. 1936; 137 mems; affiliated to Fédération des Entreprises de Belgique and Fédération Bancaire de l'UE; Pres. KAREL DE BOECK; Dir-Gen. GUIDO RAVOET.

STOCK EXCHANGE

In September 2000 Euronext was formed from the merger of the stock exchanges of Brussels (Brussels Exchanges), Amsterdam (Amsterdam Exchanges) and Paris (Paris Bourse).

Euronext Brussels: Palais de la Bourse, 1000 Brussels; tel. (2) 509-12-11; fax (2) 509-12-12; e-mail info@euronext.com; internet www.euronext.com; Sec. Gen O. LEFEBVRE.

HOLDING COMPANY

Société Générale de Belgique: 30 rue Royale, 1000 Brussels; tel. (2) 507-02-11; fax 512-18-95; f. 1822; investment and holding co with substantial interests in banking and finance, industry, mining and energy; CEO PHILIPPE LIOTIER.

INSURANCE

In 1998 there were 234 registered insurance companies active in Belgium, of which 150 were Belgian-owned.

Regulatory Authority

Office de Contrôle des Assurances/Controledienst voor de Verzekeringen: 61 ave de Cortenbergh, 1000 Brussels; tel. (2) 737-07-11; fax (2) 736-88-17; internet www.cdv-oca.be; f. 1975; supervises insurance funds and mortgage and pension cos; Chair. WILLY P. LENAERTS; Dir-Gen. GUIDO VERNAILLEN.

Principal Insurance Companies

Assurances Groupe Josi SA: 135 rue Colonel Bourg, 1140 Brussels; tel. (2) 730-12-11; fax (2) 730-16-00; f. 1955; accident, fire, marine, general, life; Pres. and Dir-Gen. J. P. LAURENT JOSI.

Aviabel, Compagnie Belge d'Assurances Aviation, SA: 10 ave Brugmann, 1060 Brussels; tel. (2) 349-12-11; fax (2) 349-12-99; e-mail insurance@aviabel.be; internet www.aviabel.be; f. 1935; aviation, insurance, reinsurance; Chair. P. GERVY; Gen. Man. J. VERWILGHEN.

AXA Royale Belge: 25 blvd du Souverain, 1170 Brussels; tel. (2) 678-61-11; fax (2) 678-93-40; e-mail webmaster@axa-royalebelge.be; internet www.axa-royalebelge.be; f. 1853; member of the AXA group; all branches; Pres. Comte JEAN-PIERRE DE LAUNOIT; Man. Dir ALFRED BOUCKAERT.

Belgamar, Compagnie Belge d'Assurances Maritimes SA: 66 Mechelsesteenweg, 2018 Antwerp; tel. (3) 247-36-11; fax (3) 247-35-90; f. 1945; marine insurance; Chair. P. H. SAVERYS; Man. Dir A. THIÉRY.

Compagnie d'Assurance de l'Escaut: 10 rue de la Bourse, Antwerp; f. 1821; fire, accident, life, burglary, reinsurance; Man E. DIERCXSENS.

Compagnie de Bruxelles 1821 SA d'Assurances: Brussels; tel. (2) 237-12-11; fax (2) 237-12-16; f. 1821; fire, life, general; Pres. C. BASECQ.

DVV Verzekeringen NV/Les AP Assurances SA: 6 ave Livingston, 1000 Brussels; tel. (2) 286-61-11; fax (2) 286-15-15; internet www.dvv.be; f. 1929; all branches; 82% owned by Artesia Banking Corporation.

EULER-COBAC Belgium NV/SA: 15 rue Montoyer, 1000 Brussels; tel. (2) 289-31-11; fax (2) 289-32-99; internet www.cobacbe .eulergroup.com; f. 1929 as Compagnie Belge d'Assurance-Crédit; name changed 1998; Chair. and Man. Dir PHILIPPE MUÛLS.

Fortis AG: 53 blvd Emile Jacqmain, 1000 Brussels; tel. (2) 220-81-11; fax (2) 220-81-50; e-mail info@fortis.com; internet www .fortisag.be; f. 1990; owned by the Fortis Group; CEO JOZEF DE MEY.

Generali Belgium SA: 149 ave Louise, 1050 Brussels; tel. (2) 533-81-11; fax (2) 533-88-99; fire, accident, marine, life, reinsurance; Pres. G. BECKERS; Dir-Gen. R. GRANDI.

KBC SA/NV: Havenlaan 2, 1080 Brussels; tel. (2) 429-71-11; fax (2) 429-81-31; e-mail kbc.telecenter@kbc.be; internet www.kbc.be; f. 1998.

Mercator & Noordstar NV: 302 Kortrijksesteenweg, 900 Ghent; tel. (9) 242-37-11; fax (9) 242-36-36; internet www.mercator.be; all branches.

Société Mutuelle des Administrations Publiques (SMAP): 24 rue des Croisiers, 4000 Liège; tel. (41) 220-31-11; internet www.smap.be; institutions, civil service employees, public administration and enterprises.

Victoire, Société Anonyme Belge d'Assurances: Brussels; tel. (2) 286-24-11; fax (2) 230-94-73; life and non-life; Chair. M. P. DE COURCEL; Gen. Man. G. DUPIN.

Insurance Associations

Fédération des Producteurs d'Assurances de Belgique (FEP-RABEL): 40 ave Albert-Elisabeth, 1200 Brussels; tel (2) 743-25-60; fax (2) 735-44-58; e-mail info@feprabel.be; internet www.feprabel.be; f. 1934; Pres. RÉGINALD VAN INGELGEM; 500 mems.

Union Professionnelle des Entreprises d'Assurances Belges et Etrangères Opérant en Belgique/Beroepsvereniging der Belgische en in België werkzame Buitenlandse Verzekeringsondernemingen: 29 square de Meeûs, 1040 Brussels; tel. (2) 547-56-11; fax (2) 547-56-01; f. 1921; affiliated to Fédération des Entreprises de Belgique; Pres. JEAN-PIERRE GÉRARD; Man. Dir MICHEL BAECKER; 137 mems.

Trade and Industry

GOVERNMENT AGENCIES

Investeren in Vlaanderen–Flanders Foreign Investment Office: 4 Leuvenseplein, 1000 Brussels; tel. (2) 227-53-11; fax (2) 227-53-10; e-mail flanders@ffio.be; internet www.ffio.com; f. 1988; promotes investment in Flanders; Man. Dir JEAN-PIERRE VANDELOO.

Société Développement Régionale de Bruxelles (SDRB): 6 rue Gabrielle Petit, 1080 Brussels; tel. (2) 422-51-11; fax (2) 422-51-12; e-mail info.sdrb@sdrb.irisnet.be; internet www.brda.irisnet.be; f. 1974; promotes economic development in the capital; Chair. P. MOUREAUX.

Société Régionale d'Investissement de Wallonie: 13 ave Destenay, 4000 Liège; tel. (4) 221-98-11; fax (4) 221-99-99; e-mail cdelevoy@sriw.be; internet www.sriw.be; f. 1979; promotes private enterprise in Wallonia; Pres. JEAN-CLAUDE DEHOVRE.

PRINCIPAL CHAMBERS OF COMMERCE

There are chambers of commerce and industry in all major towns and industrial areas.

Kamer van Koophandel en Nijverheid van Antwerpen: 12 Markgravestraat, 2000 Antwerp; tel. (3) 232-22-19; fax (3) 233-64-42; f. 1969; Pres. LUC MEURRENS; Gen. Man. L. LUWEL.

Chambre de Commerce et d'Industrie de Bruxelles: 500 ave Louise, 1050 Brussels; tel. (2) 648-50-02; fax (2) 640-93-28; f. 1875; Pres. JACQUES-ISAAC CASTIAU.

Chambre de Commerce et d'Industrie de Liège: Palais de Congrès, 2 Esplanade de l'Europe, 4020 Liège; tel. (43) 43-92-92; fax (43) 43-92-67; e-mail info@ccilg.be; internet www.ccilg.be; f. 1866; Pres. JACQUES ARNOLIS.

INDUSTRIAL AND TRADE ASSOCIATIONS

Fédération des Entreprises de Belgique (Federation of Belgian Companies): 4 rue Ravenstein, 1000 Brussels; tel. (2) 515-08-11; fax (2) 515-09-99; e-mail red@vbo-feb.be; internet www.vbo-feb.be; f. 1895; federates all the main industrial and non-industrial asscns; Pres. KAREL BOONE; CEO TONY VANDEPUTTE; 35 full mems.

Association Belge des Banques/Belgische Vereniging van Banken (ABB): (see Finance above).

Association des Exploitants de Carrières de Porphyre (Porphyry): 64 rue de Belle-Vue, 1000 Brussels; tel. (2) 648-68-60; f. 1967; Pres. GEORGES HANSEN.

Association des Fabricants de Pâtes, Papiers et Cartons de Belgique (COBELPA) (Paper): 306 Louizalaan, bus 11, 1050 Brussels; tel. (2) 646-64-50; fax (2) 646-82-97; e-mail cobelpa@unicall.be; f. 1940; Pres. FRANS WALTERS.

Confédération des Brasseries de Belgique (CBB) (Breweries): Maison des Brasseurs, 10 Grand' Place, 1000 Brussels; tel. (2) 511-49-87; fax (2) 511-32-59; e-mail cbb@beerparadise.be; internet www.beerparadise.be; f. 1971; Pres. YANNICK BOES.

Confédération Nationale de la Construction (CNC) (Civil Engineering, Road and Building Contractors and Auxiliary Trades): 34–42 rue du Lombard, 1000 Brussels; tel. (2) 545-56-00; fax (2) 545-59-00; e-mail info@confederatiebouw.be; internet www.cnc.be; f. 1946; Pres. ROB LENAERS.

Confédération Professionnelle du Sucre et de ses Dérivés (Sugar): 182 ave de Tervueren, 1150 Brussels; tel. (2) 775-80-69; fax (2) 775-80-75; e-mail info@subel.be; f. 1938; mems 10 groups, 66 firms; Pres. E. KESSELS; Dir-Gen. M. ROSIERS.

Fédération Belge de la Brique (Bricks): 13 rue des Poissonniers, bte 22, 1000 Brussels; tel. (2) 511-25-81; fax (2) 513-26-40; e-mail info@brique.be; internet www.brique.be; f. 1947; Pres. GILBERT DE BAERE.

Fédération Belge des Dragueurs de Gravier et de Sable (BELBAG-DRAGBEL) (Quarries): Hasselt; tel. (89) 56-73-45; fax (89) 56-45-42; f. 1967; Pres. CHARLES LECLUYSE.

Fédération Belge des Entreprises de la Transformation du Bois (FEBELBOIS) (Wood): 5 Hof-ter-Vleest, bte 1, 1070 Brussels; tel. (2) 556-25-55; fax (2) 556-25-70; Pres. GUSTAAF NEYT.

Fédération Belge des Industries Graphiques (FEBELGRA) (Graphic Industries): 20 rue Belliard, bte 16, 1040 Brussels; tel. (2) 512-36-38; fax (2) 513-56-76; e-mail info@febelgra.be; internet www.febelgra.be; f. 1978; Pres. ALAIN CHAUVEHEID.

Fédération Belge des Industries de l'Habillement (Clothing): 24 rue Montoyer, 1040 Brussels; tel. (2) 238-10-11; fax (2) 230-10-10; e-mail roggeman@belgianfashion.be; internet www.belgianfashion.be; f. 1946; Pres. ALAIN CHAUVEHEID.

Fédération Belgo-Luxembourgeoise de l'Industrie du Tabac (FEDETAB) (Tobacco): 7 ave Lloyd George, 1050 Brussels; tel. (2) 646-04-20; fax (2) 646-22-13; e-mail tobacco@fedetab.be; f. 1947; Pres. G. VANDERMARLIÈRE.

Fédération Charbonnière de Belgique (Coal): Brussels; tel. (2) 230-37-40; fax (2) 230-88-50; f. 1909; Pres. YVES SLEUWAEGEN; Dir JOS VAN DEN BROECK.

Fédération des Carrières de Petit Granit (Limestone): 245 rue de Cognebeau, 7060 Soignies; tel. (67) 34-78-00; fax (67) 33-00-59; f. 1948; Pres. J.-F. ABRAHAM.

Fédération d'Employeurs pour le Commerce International, le Transport et les Branches d'Activité Connexes (Employers' Federation of International Trade, Transport and Related Activities): 33 Brouwersvliet, bus 7, 2000 Antwerp; tel. (3) 221-99-90; fax (3) 226-83-71; e-mail cepa@cepa.be; f. 1937; Pres. FRANÇOIS VAN GEEL; Dir FRANS GIELEN.

Fédération des Entreprises de l'Industrie des Fabrications Métalliques, Mécaniques, Electriques, Electroniques et de la Transformation des Matières Plastiques (FABRIMETAL) (Metalwork, Engineering, Electrics, Electronics and Plastic Processing): 80 boulevard Auguste Reyers, 1030 Brussels; tel. (2) 706-78-00; fax (2) 706-78-01; e-mail info@fabrimetal.be; internet www.fabrimetal.be; f. 1946; Pres. JULIEN DE WILDE.

Fédération de l'Industrie Alimentaire/Federatie Voedingsindustrie (FEVIA) (Food and Agriculture): 172 Kortenberglaan, bte 7, 1040 Brussels; tel. (2) 743-08-00; fax (2) 733-94-26; e-mail info@fevia.be; internet www.fevia.be; f. 1937; Pres. ERIC SWENDEN; Dir-Gen. CHRIS MORIS.

Fédération de l'Industrie du Béton (FEBE) (Precast Concrete): 207–209 blvd August Reyers, 1030 Brussels; tel. (2) 735-80-15; fax (2) 734-77-95; e-mail mail@febe.be; internet www.febe.be; f. 1936; Pres. P. DECLERCK; Dir EDDY DANO.

Fédération des Industries Chimiques de Belgique (FEDICHEM) (Chemical Industries): 49 square Marie-Louise, 1000 Brussels; tel. (2) 238-97-11; fax (2) 231-13-01; e-mail postmaster@fedichem.be; internet www.fedichem.be; f. 1919; Pres. JACQUES VAN BOST; Man. Dir JEAN-MARIE BIOT.

Fédération de l'Industrie Cimentière Belge (FEBELCEM) (Cement): 8 rue Volta, 1050 Brussels; tel. (2) 645-52-11; fax (2) 640-06-70; e-mail febelcem@febelcem.be; internet www.febelcem.be; f. 1949; Pres. MARKUS OBERLE; Dir-Gen. JEAN-PIERRE JACOBS.

Fédération des Industries Extractives et Transformatrices de Roches non Combustibles (FEDIEX) (Extraction and processing of non-fuel rocks): 61 rue du Trône, 1050 Brussels; tel. (2) 511-61-73; fax (2) 511-12-84; f. 1942 as Union des Producteurs Belges de Chaux, Calcaires, Dolomies et Produits Connexes, name changed 1990; co-operative society; Pres. GILLES PLAQUET.

Fédération de l'Industrie du Gaz (FIGAZ) (Gas): 4 ave Palmerston, 1000 Brussels; tel. (2) 237-11-11; fax (2) 230-44-80; e-mail figas@figas.be; f. 1946; Pres. JEAN-PIERRE DEPAEMELAERE.

Fédération de l'Industrie Textile Belge (FEBELTEX) (Textiles): 24 rue Montoyer, 1000 Brussels; tel. (2) 287-08-11; fax (2) 230-65-85; e-mail info@febeltex.be; internet www.febeltex.be; f. 1945; Pres. FILIEP LIBEERT; Dir-Gen. JEAN-FRANÇOIS QUIX; 500 mems.

Fédération des Industries Transformatrices de Papier et Carton (FETRA) (Paper and Cardboard): 715 chaussée de Waterloo, BP 25, 1180 Brussels; tel. (2) 344-19-62; fax (2) 344-86-61; f. 1976; Pres. PAUL PISSENS.

Fédération de l'Industrie du Verre (Glass): 89 ave Louise, 1050 Brussels; tel. (2) 542-61-20; fax (2) 542-61-21; e-mail info@vgi-fiv.be; internet www.vgi-fiv.be; f. 1947; Pres. R. BUEKENHOUT; Man. Dir ROLAND DERIDDER.

Fédération Patronale des Ports Belges (Port Employers): 33 Brouwersvliet, bus 7, 2000 Antwerp; tel. (3) 221-99-85; fax (3) 226-83-71; e-mail cepa@cepa.be; f. 1937; Pres. FRANÇOIS VAN GEEL; Secs FRANS GIELEN, GUY VANKRUNKELSVEN.

Fédération Pétrolière Belge (Petroleum): 39 ave des Arts, bt 2, 1040 Brussels; tel. (2) 512-30-03; fax (2) 511-05-91; e-mail fpb-bpf@petrolfed.be; internet www.petrolfed.be; f. 1926; Pres. E. DE MENTEN DE HORNE; Sec.-Gen. G. VAN DE WERVE.

Groupement des Sablières (Sand and Gravel): 49 Quellinstraat, 2018 Antwerp; tel. (3) 223-66-83; fax (3) 223-66-47; e-mail pdn@sibelco.be; f. 1937; Pres. A. SPECKAERT; Sec. PAUL DE NIE.

Groupement de la Sidérurgie (Iron and Steel): 47 rue Montoyer, 1000 Brussels; tel. (2) 509-14-11; fax (2) 509-14-00; e-mail gsv@pophost.eunet.be; f. 1953; Pres. PAUL MATTHYS.

Union des Armateurs Belges (Shipowners): 9 Lijnwaadmarkt, 2000 Antwerp; tel. (3) 232-72-31; fax (3) 225-28-36; e-mail bru@afsnet.be; Chair. NICOLAS SAVERYS; Man. C. BETRAINS.

Union des Carrières et Scieries de Marbres de Belgique (UCSMB) (Marble): 8 Heideveld, 1654 Huizingen; tel. (2) 361-36-81; fax (2) 361-31-55; Pres. P. STONE.

Union des Exploitations Electriques et Gazières en Belgique (UEGB) (Electricity and Gas): 8 blvd du Régent, 1000 Brussels; tel. (2) 518-61-11; fax (2) 518-64-58; f. 1911; Pres. ANTOINE DECLOEDT.

Industrie des Huiles Minérales de Belgique (IHMB – IMOB) (Mineral Oils): 49 square Marie-Louise, 1000 Brussels; tel. (2) 238-97-11; fax (2) 230-03-89; f. 1921; Pres. J. VERCHEVAL; Sec. D. DE HEMPTINNE; 65 mems.

Union Professionnelle des Producteurs de Fibres-Ciment (Fibre-Cement): 114 Aerschotstraat, 9100 Sint-Niklaas; tel. (3) 760-49-00; fax (3) 777-47-84; f. 1941; Pres. MARC VANDEN BOSCH; Sec. GEORGES SANDERS.

Union de la Tannerie et de la Mégisserie Belges (UNITAN) (Tanning and Tawing): c/o 140 rue des Tanneurs, 7730 Estaimbourg; tel. (69) 36-23-23; fax (69) 36-23-10; f. 1962; Pres. BRUNO COLLE; Sec. ANNE VANDEPUTTE; 4 mems.

UTILITIES

Electricity

Electrabel: 8 Regentlaan, 1000 Brussels; tel. (2) 518-61-11; fax (2) 518-64-00; internet www.electrabel.com; f. 1905; 40% owned by Tractebel; Gen.-Dir WILLY BOSMANS.

Gas

Distrigas: 31 Kunstlaan, 1040 Brussels; tel. (2) 282-78-33; fax (2) 282-71-50; e-mail info@distri.be; internet www.distrigas.be.

Water

Société Wallonne des Distributions d'Eau: 41 rue de la Concorde, 4800 Verviers; tel. (87) 34-28-11; fax (87) 34-28-00; f. 1986; Dir-Gen. MARC DECONINCK.

Vlaamse Maatschappij voor Watervoorziening: 73 Belliardstraat, 1040 Brussels; tel. (2) 238-94-11; fax (2) 230-97-98; e-mail info@vmw.be; internet www.vmw.be.

TRADE UNIONS

Fédération Générale du Travail de Belgique (FGTB)/Algemeen Belgisch Vakverbond (ABVV): 42 rue Haute, 1000 Brussels; tel. (2) 506-82-11; fax (2) 513-47-21; internet www.abvv.be; f. 1899; affiliated to ICFTU; Pres. MICHEL NOLLET; Gen. Sec. MIA DE VITS; is an association of seven branch unions, three inter-regional organizations and 21 regional organizations with an estimated total membership of 1,200,000 (2000).
Affiliated unions:

Belgische Transportarbeidersbond/Union Belge des Ouvriers du Transport (Belgian Transport Workers' Union): 66 Paardenmarkt, 2000 Antwerp: tel. (3) 224-34-11; fax (3) 234-01-49; f. 1913; Pres. ALFONS GEERAERTS; 24,000 mems (1990).

La Centrale Générale/De Algemene Centrale (Central Union, building, timber, glass, paper, chemicals and petroleum industries): 26–28 rue Haute, 1000 Brussels; tel. (2) 549-05-49; fax (2) 514-16-91; e-mail info@accg.be; internet www.accg.be; Pres. MAURICE CORBISIER; Sec. Gen. DAN PLAUM; Fed. Secs HANS RAES,

PAUL LOOTENS, FERDY DE WOLF, JACQUES MICHIELS, RENÉ GEYBELS, JEAN CLAUDE HUMBERT; 300,000 mems (1998).

Centrale Générale des Services Publics/Algemene Centrale der Openbare Diensten (Public Service Workers): Maison des Huit Heures, 9–11 place Fontainas, 1000 Brussels; tel. (2) 508-58-11; fax (2) 508-59-02; e-mail algemeen@acod.be; internet www .acod.be; f. 1945; Pres. HENRI DUJARDIN; Vice-Pres. F. FERMON; Gen. Secs J. DUCHESNE, A. MORDANT, K. STESSENS, T. BERGS.

Centrale de l'Industrie du Métal de Belgique/Centrale der Metaalindustrie van België (Metal Workers): 17 rue Jacques Jordaens, 1000 Brussels; tel. (2) 627-74-11; fax (2) 627-74-90; f. 1887; Pres. HERWIG JORISSEN; 185,570 mems (1993).

Centrale Voeding-Horeca-Diensten (Catering and Hotel Workers): 18 rue des Alexiens, 1000 Brussels; tel. (2) 512-97-00; fax (2) 512-53-68; e-mail jean.paschenkol@horval.be; internet users.skynet.be/sky90351/horval/; f. 1912; Pres. F. DE MEY; Nat. Sec. J. PASCHENKO.

FGTB—Textile, Vêtement, et Diamant/ABVV—Textiel, Kleding – Diamant (Textile, Clothing and Diamond Workers): 143 Opvoedingstraat, 9000 Ghent; tel. (9) 242-86-86; fax (9) 242-86-96; e-mail abvvtkd.fgtbtvd@glo.be; f. 1994; Pres. DONALD WITTEVRONGEL; 60,000 mems (1999).

Syndicat des Employés, Techniciens et Cadres de Belgique/Bond der Bedienden, Technici en Kaders van België (Employees, Technicians, Administrative Workers, Graphical and Paper Workers): 42 rue Haute, 1000 Brussels; tel. (2) 512-52-50; fax (2) 511-05-08; e-mail nationaal@setca-fgtb.be; internet www .bbtk.org; f. 1891; Pres. CHRISTIAN ROLAND; Gen. Sec. ROBERT WITTEBROUCK.

Les Cadets, an organization for students and school pupils, is also affiliated to the FGTB/ABVV.

Confédération des Syndicats Chrétiens (ACV-CSC): 579 Haachtsesteenweg, POB 10, 1031 Brussels; tel. (2) 246-36-00; fax (2) 246-30-10; e-mail international@acv-csc.be; internet www.acv-csc .be; Pres. LUC CORTEBEECK; has 17 affiliated unions with an estimated total membership of 1,546,360 (1993). Affiliated unions:

CSC Bâtiment et Industrie (Building and Industrial Workers): 31 rue de Trèves, 1040 Brussels; tel. (2) 285-02-11; fax (2) 230-74-43; e-mail cchb@acv-csc.be; Pres. J. JACKERS; Sec.-Gen. JEAN-PAUL GHEYSEN; 225,000 mems (1999).

Centrale Chrétienne de l'Alimentation et des Services (Food and Service Industries): 70 Kartuizersstraat, 1000 Brussels; tel. (2) 500-28-11; fax (2) 500-28-99; e-mail ccvd-ccas@acv-csc.be; f. 1919; Pres. W. VIJVERMAN; Sec.-Gen. F. BOCKLANDT.

Centrale Chrétienne des Métallurgistes de Belgique (Metal Workers): 127 rue de Heembeek, 1120 Brussels; tel. (2) 244-99-11; fax (2) 244-99-90; e-mail ccmb@acv-csc.be; Pres. T. JANSSEN.

Centrale Chrétienne des Mines, de l'Energie, de la Chimie et du Cuir (CCMECC) (Mines, Power, Chemical and Leather Workers): 26 ave d'Auderghem, 1040 Brussels; tel. (2) 238-73-32; f. 1912; Pres. A. VAN GENECHTEN; Gen. Sec. M. ANDRÉ; Nat. Sec. A. CUYVERS; 63,155 mems (1993).

Centrale Chrétienne des Ouvriers du Textile et du Vêtement de Belgique (Textile and Clothing Workers): 27 Koning Albertlaan, 9000 Ghent; tel. (91) 22-57-01; fax (91) 20-45-59; e-mail acvtextiel@acv-csc.be; f. 1886; Pres. A. DUQUET; Gen. Sec. L. MEULEMAN.

Centrale Chrétienne des Ouvriers du Transport et des Ouvriers du Diamant (Transport and Diamond Workers): 12 Entrepotplaats, 2000 Antwerp; tel. (3) 206-95-00; fax (3) 206-95-50; e-mail cvd@acv-csc.be; Pres. JOHN JANSSENS.

Centrale Chrétienne des Professeurs de l'Enseignement Moyen et Normal Libre (Lay Teachers in Secondary and Teacher-Training Institutions): 16 rue de la Victoire, 1060 Brussels; tel. (2) 238-73-23; fax (2) 238-72-33; e-mail cemnl@acv-csc.be; Pres. WILLEM MILLER.

Centrale Chrétienne du Personnel de l'Enseignement Technique (Teachers in Technical Education): 16 rue de la Victoire, 1060 Brussels; tel. (2) 542-09-00; fax (2) 542-09-08; e-mail ccpet-uceo@acv-csc.be; Sec.-Gen. PROSPER BOULANGE; 8,500 mems (2001).

Centrale Chrétienne des Services Publics—Christelijke Centrale van de Openbare Diensten (Public Service Workers): 26-32 ave d'Auderghem, 1040 Brussels; tel. (2) 231-00-90; fax (2) 230-45-62; e-mail ccod@acv-csc.be; f. 1921; Pres. FILIP WIEERS; Sec.-Gen. GUY RASNEUR.

Centrale Nationale des Employés (CNE) (Private Sector Workers): 46 rue Pépin, 5000 Namur; tel. (81) 22-02-22; fax (81) 22-50-47; Sec.-Gen. PIERRA PRAVATA; 120,000 mems (2000).

Christelijke Centrale van Diverse Industrieen (Miscellaneous): 26–32 Oudergemselaan, 1040 Brussels; tel. (2) 238-72-11; fax (2) 238-73-12; Pres. LEO DUSOLEIL; Nat. Secs FRANÇOIS LICATA, LEON VAN HAUDT.

Christelijke Onderwijs Centrale (COC) (Teachers): 26 Oudergemselaan, 1040 Brussels; tel. (2) 238-72-68; fax (2) 230-28-83; e-mail coc.brussel@pophost.eunet.be; internet www.coc.be; f. 1993 as a result of a merger of the Flemish wings of three teachers' unions; Chair HUBERT BUYS; Gen.-Sec. GUST VAN DONGEN.

Christelijk Onderwijzersverbond van België (School teachers): 203 Koningsstraat, 1210 Brussels; tel. (2) 227-41-11; fax (2) 219-47-61; e-mail cov@acv-csc.be; internet www.cov.be; f. 1893; Pres. G. BOURDEAUD'HUI; Sec.-Gen. R. MAES; 41,000 mems (1999).

Fédération des Instituteurs Chrétiens (School teachers): 16 rue de la Victoire, 1060 Brussels; tel. (2) 539-00-01; fax (2) 534-13-36; internet www.fic.be; f. 1893; publishes twice monthly periodical 'L'éducateur'; Sec.-Gen. R. DOHOGNE; 16,000 mems (2000).

Sporta-vsb (Sport): 579 Haachtsesteenweg, 1031 Brussels; tel. (2) 246-35-41; fax (2) 246-35-42; e-mail sporta@acv-csc.be; Nat. Sec. MARCEL VAN MOL.

Syndicat Chrétien des Communications et de la Culture (Christian Trade Unions of Railway, Post and Telecommunications, Shipping, Civil Aviation, Radio, TV and Cultural Workers): Galerie Agora, 105 rue du Marché aux Herbes, bte 40, 1000 Brussels; tel. (2) 549-07-60; fax (2) 549-08-00; e-mail cvcc@acv-csc.be; f. 1919; Pres. M. BOVY; Vice-Pres. P. BERTIN.

Union Chrétienne des Membres du Personnel de l'Enseignement Officiel: 16 rue de la Victoire, 1060 Brussels; tel. (2) 542-09-00; fax (2) 542-09-08; e-mail ccpet-uceo@acv-csc.be; Sec. Gen. P. BOULANGE.

Centrale Générale des Syndicats Libéraux de Belgique (CGSLB) (General Federation of Liberal Trade Unions of Belgium): 95 Koning Albertlaan, 9000 Ghent; tel. (9) 222-57-51; fax (9) 221-04-74; e-mail cgslb@cgslb.be; internet www.cgslb.be; f. 1891; Nat. Pres. GUY HAAZE; 220,000 mems.

Fédération Nationale des Unions Professionnelles Agricoles de Belgique: 47 chaussée de Namur, 5030 Gembloux; tel. (81) 60-00-60; e-mail upa@euronet.be; Pres. L. FRANC; Sec.-Gen. J. P. CHAMPAGNE.

Landelijke Bediendencentrale-Nationaal Verbond voor Kaderpersoneel (LBC-NVK) (Employees): 5 Sudermanstraat, 2000 Antwerp; tel. (3) 220-87-11; fax (2) 231-66-64; e-mail vakbond@lbc-nvk.be; internet www.lbc-nvk.be; f. 1912; Sec-Gen. M. MAMPUYS; 270,000 mems (1998).

Nationale Unie der Openbare Diensten (NUOD)/Union Nationale des Services Publics (UNSP): 25 rue de la Sablonnière, 1000 Brussels; tel. (2) 219-88-02; fax (2) 223-38-36; f. 1983; Pres. GÉRALD VAN ACKER; Sec.-Gen. FRANCIS SACRE.

Transport

RAILWAYS

The Belgian railway network is one of the densest in the world. The main lines are operated by the Société Nationale des Chemins de Fer Belges (SNCB) under lease from the State Transport Administration. Construction of the Belgian section of a high-speed railway network for northern Europe, which will eventually link Belgium, France, Germany, the Netherlands and the United Kingdom, is expected to be completed by 2005. A high-speed link between Brussels and Paris was completed in 1997.

Société Nationale des Chemins de Fer Belges (SNCB)/ Nationale Maatschappij der Belgische Spoorwegen (NMBS): 85 rue de France, 1060 Brussels; tel. (2) 525-21-11; fax (2) 525-40-45; internet www.sncb.be; f. 1926; 147.3m. passengers were carried in 1999; 3,472 km of lines, of which 2,701 km are electrified; Chair. MICHEL DAMAR; Man. Dir ETIENNE SCHOUPPE.

ROADS

At 1 January 1998 there were 1,682 km of motorways and some 12,542 km of other main or national roads. There were also 1,326 km of secondary or regional roads and an additional 130,300 km of minor roads.

Société Régionale Wallonne du Transport: 96 ave Gouverneur Bovesse, 5100 Namur; tel. (81) 32-27-11; fax (81) 32-27-10; f. 1991; operates light railways, buses and trams; Dir-Gen. JEAN-CLAUDE PHLYPO.

Société des Transports Intercommunaux de Bruxelles: 15 ave de la Toison d'or, 1050 Brussels; tel. (2) 515-20-00; fax (2) 515-32-85; internet www.stib.be; operates a metro service, buses and trams; Dir-Gen. A. FLAUSCH.

VVM-De Lijn: 1 Hendrik Consciencestraat, 2800 Mechelen; tel. (15) 44-07-11; fax (15) 44-07-09; internet www.delijn.be; f. 1991; public transport; Dir-Gen. HUGO VAN WESEMAEL.

INLAND WATERWAYS

There are over 1,520 km of inland waterways in Belgium, of which 660 km are navigable rivers and 860 km are canals.

In 1989 waterways administration was divided between the Flemish region (1,055 km), the Walloon region (450 km) and the Brussels region (15 km):

Flemish region:
Departement Leefmilieu en Infrastructuur Administratie Waterwegen en Zeewezen: Graaf de Ferraris-Gebouw, 20 Koning Albert II-laan,, bte 5, 1000 Brussels; tel. (2) 553-77-11; fax (2) 553-77-05; e-mail awz@lin.vlaanderen.be; internet www.lin.vlaanderen.be; Dir-Gen. JAN STRUBBE.

Walloon region:
Direction Générale des Voies Hydrauliques: Centre administratif du MET, 8 blvd du Nord, 5000 Namur; tel. (81) 77-28-97; fax (81) 77-37-60; Dir-Gen. B. FAES.

Brussels region:
Haven van Brussel: 6 place des Armateurs, 1000 Brussels; tel. (2) 420-67-00; fax (2) 420-69-74; e-mail havenvanbrussel@haven.irisnet.be; internet www.havenvanbrussel.irisnet,be; f. 1993; Gen. Man. STEVEN VANACKERE; Dep. Man. Dir CHARLES HUYGENS.

SHIPPING

The modernized port of Antwerp is the second biggest in Europe and handles about 80% of Belgian foreign trade by sea and inland waterways. It is also the largest railway port and has one of the largest petroleum refining complexes in Europe. Antwerp has 98 km of quayside and 17 dry docks. A new dock for four new container terminals, with a total quay length of 6km, was under construction in 2001 and a US $580m second rail link to the port was also being built. Other ports include Zeebrugge, Ostend, Ghent, Liège and Brussels.

Ahlers Shipping NV: 139 Noorderlaan, 2030 Antwerp; tel. (3) 543-72-11; fax (3) 542-00-23; e-mail info@ahlers.com; internet www.ahlers.com; services to Finland, Poland, Latvia, Morocco; Chair. ALBERT WEYNEN; Man. Dirs LUC NATON, YVES VAN BAVEL.

ESSO Belgium: POB 100, 2060 Antwerp; tel. (3) 543-31-11; fax (3) 543-34-95; refining and marketing of petroleum products; Pres. K. O. GILJE.

De Keyser Thornton: 38 Huidevettersstraat, 2000 Antwerp; tel. (3) 205-31-00; fax (3) 234-27-86; e-mail info@multimodal.be; internet www.multimodul.be; f. 1853; shipping agency, forwarding and warehousing services; Chair. and CEO M. P. INGHAM.

Northern Shipping Service NV: 54 St Katelijnevest, 2000 Antwerp; tel. (3) 204-78-78; fax (3) 231-30-51; e-mail sales@northern-shipping.be; internet www.northern-shipping.be; forwarding, customs clearance, liner and tramp agencies, chartering, Rhine and inland barging, multi-purpose bulk/bags fertilizer, minerals and agri-bulk terminal; Pres. and Man. Dir BERNARD MONTALDIER.

P&O North Sea Ferries Ltd: Leopold II Dam, 13, 8380 Zeebrugge; tel. (50) 54-34-11; fax (50) 54-68-35; roll-on/roll-off ferry services between Zeebrugge, Felixstowe, Hull and Middlesbrough; Dirs P. V. D. BROMDHOF, R. B. LOUGH.

TotalFina SA: 52 rue de l'Industrie, 1040 Brussels; tel. (2) 288-94-49; fax (2) 288-34-45; integrated petroleum co active in exploration and production, transportation and petroleum refining, petrochemicals, etc., marketing of petroleum products and research; Vice-Chair. and Man. Dir FRANÇOIS CORNELIS.

CIVIL AVIATION

The main international airport is at Brussels, with a direct train service from the air terminal. A major programme of expansion, more than doubling the airport's passenger-handling capacity, was completed in 1994. Further expansion work was to include the construction of a new concourse by 2002. There are also international airports at Antwerp, Liège, Charleroi and Ostend.

SABENA Belgian Airlines (Société anonyme belge d'exploitation de la navigation aérienne): 2 ave E. Mounierlaan, 1200 Brussels; tel. (2) 723-31-11; fax (2) 723-80-99; internet www.sabena.com; f. 1923; 49.5% owned by Swissair; services to most parts of the world; Chair. and CEO PAUL REUTLINGER.

Delta Air Transport (DAT) NV: Airport Bldg 117, 1820 Melsbroek; tel. (2) 754-19-00; fax (2) 754-19-99; f. 1966; 100% owned by SABENA; scheduled and charter services from Brussels to many European destinations; Gen. Dir WILLY BUYSSE.

Sobelair (Société Belge de Transports par Air) NV: Bldg 45, Brussels National Airport, 1930 Zaventem; tel. (2) 754-12-11; fax (2) 754-12-88; f. 1946; 72.5% owned by SABENA; operates charter flights; Pres. and CEO SYLVIANE LUST.

Virgin Express: Airport Bldg 116, 1820 Melsbroek; tel. (2) 752-05-11; fax (2) 752-05-06; f. 1991 as EuroBelgium Airlines, name changed as above 1996; 51% owned by Virgin Group (UK), scheduled and charter services to European destinations; CEO JIM SWIGART; Man. Dir JONATHAN ORNSTEIN.

Tourism

Belgium has several towns of rich historic and cultural interest, such as Antwerp, Bruges, Brussels, Durbuy, Ghent, Liège, Namur and Tournai. The country's seaside towns attract many visitors. The forest-covered Ardennes region is renowned for hill-walking

and gastronomy. In 1999 tourist arrivals totalled an estimated 6,369,030.

Office de Promotion du Tourisme Wallonie–Bruxelles: 61 rue Marché-aux-Herbes, 1000 Brussels; tel. (2) 504-03-90; fax (2) 513-69-50; internet www.opt.net; f. 1981; promotion of tourism in French-speaking Belgium; Dir-Gen. VIVIANE JACOBS.

Tourist Information Office for Brussels (TIB): Hôtel de Ville, Grand-Place, 1000 Brussels; tel. (2) 548-04-62; fax (2) 514-11-24; Dir G. RENDERS.

Tourist Office for Flanders: 61 Grasmarkt, 1000 Brussels; tel. (2) 504-03-00; fax (2) 504-03-77; internet www.visitflanders.com; f. 1985; official promotion and policy body for tourism in Flemish region of Belgium; Gen. Commissioner URBAIN CLAEYS.

BELIZE

Introductory Survey

Location, Climate, Language, Religion, Flag, Capital

Belize lies on the Caribbean coast of Central America, with Mexico to the north-west and Guatemala to the south-west. The climate is sub-tropical, tempered by trade winds. The temperature averages 24°C (75°F) from November to January, and 27°C (81°F) from May to September. Annual rainfall ranges from 1,290 mm (51 ins) in the north to 4,450 mm (175 ins) in the south. The average annual rainfall in Belize City is 1,650 mm (65 ins). Belize is ethnically diverse, the population (according to the 1991 census) consisting of 44% Mestizos (Maya-Spanish), 30% Creoles (those of predominantly African descent), 11% Amerindian (mainly Maya), 7% Garifuna ('Black Caribs', descendants of those deported from the island of Saint Vincent in 1797) and communities of Asians, Portuguese, German Mennonites and others of European descent. English is the official language and an English Creole is widely understood. Spanish is the mother-tongue of some 15% of the population but is spoken by many others. There are also speakers of Garifuna (Carib), Maya and Ketchi, while the Mennonites speak a German dialect. Most of the population profess Christianity, with about 58% being Roman Catholics in 1997. The national flag (proportions usually 5 by 3) is dark blue, with narrow horizontal red stripes at the upper and lower edges; at the centre is a white disc containing the state coat of arms, bordered by an olive wreath. The capital is Belmopan.

Recent History

Belize, known as British Honduras until June 1973, was first colonized by British settlers (the 'Baymen') in the 17th century, but was not recognized as a British colony until 1862. In 1954 a new Constitution granted universal adult suffrage and provided for the creation of a legislative assembly. The territory's first general election, in April 1954, was won by the only party then organized, the People's United Party (PUP), led by George Price. The PUP won all subsequent elections until 1984. In 1961 Price was appointed First Minister under a new ministerial system of government. The colony was granted internal self-government in 1964, with the United Kingdom retaining responsibility for defence, external affairs and internal security. Following an election in 1965, Price became Premier and a bicameral legislature was introduced. In 1970 the capital of the territory was moved from Belize City to the newly-built town of Belmopan.

Much of the recent history of Belize has been dominated by the territorial dispute with Guatemala, particularly in the years prior to Belize's independence (see below). This was achieved on 21 September 1981, within the Commonwealth, and with Price becoming Prime Minister. However, the failure of the 1981 draft treaty with Guatemala, and the clash of opposing wings within the ruling party, undermined the dominance of the PUP. Internal disputes within the PUP intensified during 1983, although Price succeeded in keeping the factions together. However, at the general election held in December 1984 the PUP's 30 years of rule ended when the United Democratic Party (UDP) received 53% of the total votes and won 21 of the 28 seats in the enlarged House of Representatives. The remaining seven seats were won by the PUP, with 44% of the votes, but Price and several of his ministers lost their seats. The UDP's leader, Manuel Esquivel, was appointed Prime Minister. The new Government pledged itself to reviving Belize's economy through increased foreign investment.

A general election was held in September 1989. The UDP underwent a damaging selection process for candidates to contest the election, and encountered criticism that its economic successes had benefited only foreign investors and a limited number of Belizeans. The PUP campaigned for a more liberal broadcasting policy, including the establishment of a broadcasting corporation independent of direct government control, and against the sale of citizenship, of which many Hong Kong Chinese had taken advantage. At the election the PUP obtained almost 51% of the total valid votes cast, and won 15 seats in the 28-member House of Representatives. The UDP received 49% of the votes and retained 13 seats, although one of their

members subsequently joined the PUP. Price was again appointed Prime Minister, and his new Government immediately began moves to end the issue of citizenship bonds.

A general election was held in June 1993. The UDP formed an alliance with the National Alliance for Belizean Rights (NABR) to contest the election, and their campaign concentrated on concern about the security situation in the light of the imminent withdrawal of British troops and the prevailing political crisis in neighbouring Guatemala (see below). The PUP had called the election 15 months before it was constitutionally due, following recent successes at local and by-elections. However, at the election the PUP secured only 13 seats in the House of Representatives, despite obtaining more than 51% of the votes. The UDP/NABR alliance received 48.7% of the votes but secured 16 seats (the total number of seats having been increased from 28 to 29). Esquivel was sworn in as Prime Minister on 2 July. In November, at Esquivel's request, Dame Minita Gordon, who had been the Governor-General since independence, resigned from her position. She was replaced by Dr (later Sir) Colville Young, formerly President of the University College of Belize. In the same month the leader of the PUP and former Minister of Foreign Affairs, Said Musa, was among five members of the PUP who were arrested for allegedly attempting to bribe two government ministers to transfer parliamentary allegiance to the PUP. Musa was acquitted in July 1994.

In June 1994 the sale of citizenship was officially ended, following criticism that the system was open to corruption. However, a revised economic citizenship programme, including mechanisms to prevent corruption, received government approval in early 1995. In January of that year Esquivel conducted a redistribution of cabinet portfolios and in June the Minister of Human Resources, Community and Youth Development, Culture and Women's Affairs, Phillip S. W. Goldson, was relieved of responsibility for immigration and nationality affairs, following allegations implicating him in the sale of false residence and visitor permits to nationals of the People's Republic of China and the Republic of China (Taiwan). Reportedly some 5,000 such permits had been issued over the previous 12-month period, and the recipients then smuggled into the USA. In August the Judicial Committee of the Privy Council in the United Kingdom (the final court of appeal for Belize) issued stays of execution for two convicted murderers. The ruling, which came amid growing concern at rising crime in Belize, prompted widespread criticism of the British court, which was considered to be undermining the authority of the Belizean judiciary, and demands for a revision of the appeals system.

Popular discontent at economic austerity measures implemented by the Government was reflected at local elections conducted in March 1997, when the opposition PUP recorded a resounding victory over the ruling alliance. In April Esquivel conducted a reorganization of the Cabinet and created a new ministry, of National Co-ordination and Mobilisation.

In November 1997 the PUP presented proposals for the reform of the political system, including the establishment of a republican form of government, with the Governor-General to be replaced by a president elected by the National Assembly. The proposals were rejected by the Government. However, the leader of the PUP, Said Musa, pledged that, if his party should gain power at the forthcoming general election (due to be held in August 1998), preliminary proposals for political reform would be introduced within 100 days of taking office.

At the general election of August 1998 the PUP won an overwhelming victory, securing 26 of the 29 seats in the House of Representatives. The UDP obtained the remaining three seats. The result reflected popular discontent with the outgoing Government's structural-adjustment policies, including the introduction of value-added tax (VAT), which the PUP had pledged to repeal. The PUP had also promised to create 15,000 new jobs, to build 10,000 new houses and to reduce public utility tariffs. Following the defeat of his party, Esquivel, who had lost his seat in the House of Representatives, resigned as leader of the UDP. He was succeeded by Dean Barrow. On 1 September

Said Musa was sworn in as Prime Minister, and the new Cabinet was inaugurated.

In January 1999 a 14-member Political Reform Commission was established in order to review the system of governance in Belize. In March 2000 this Commission, which included representatives of the two principal political parties and of non-governmental organizations, suggested that the policy of 'economic citizenship' be abolished. In July 1999 Musa issued a statement rejecting allegations published in the British press that Michael Ashcroft, who had extensive business and banking interests in Belize and was its ambassador to the UN, as well as being treasurer of the British Conservative Party, had used improper influence in Belizean affairs and that he might have been involved in money 'laundering'. In March 2000 Ashcroft resigned his post as ambassador to the UN after receiving a life peerage in the British House of Lords.

In local elections in March 2000 the PUP reaffirmed its popular support, winning 51 seats to the UDP's five, and retaining control of six of the seven municipalities. On 5 April Belize became the eighth country to ratify the Rome Statute of the International Criminal Court, which was to be established following its ratification by 60 states.

The frontier with Guatemala was agreed by a convention in 1859 but this was declared invalid by Guatemala in 1940. Guatemalan claims to sovereignty of Belize date back to the middle of the 19th century and were written into Guatemala's Constitution in 1945. In November 1975 and July 1977 British troops and aircraft were sent to protect Belize from the threat of Guatemalan invasion, and a battalion of troops and a detachment of fighter aircraft remained in the territory. Negotiations between the United Kingdom and Guatemala began in 1977. In 1980 the United Kingdom warned that it might unilaterally grant independence to Belize if no settlement with Guatemala were forthcoming, and later that year the British Government finally excluded the possibility of any cession of land to Guatemala, although offering economic and financial concessions. In November the UN General Assembly overwhelmingly approved a resolution urging that Belize be granted independence (similar resolutions having been adopted in 1978 and 1979), and the United Kingdom decided to proceed with a schedule for independence. A tripartite conference in March 1981 appeared to produce a sound basis for a final settlement, with Guatemala accepting Belizean independence in exchange for access to the Caribbean Sea through Belize and the use of certain offshore cayes and their surrounding waters. A constitutional conference began in April. Further tripartite talks in May and July collapsed, however, as a result of renewed claims by Guatemala to Belizean land. With Belizean independence imminent, Guatemala made an unsuccessful appeal to the UN Security Council to intervene, severing diplomatic relations with the United Kingdom and sealing its border with Belize on 7 September. However, on 21 September, as scheduled, Belize achieved independence. Guatemala alone refused to recognize Belize's new status, and during 1982 requested the reopening of negotiations with the United Kingdom, alleging that Belize was not legally independent. Tripartite talks in January 1983 collapsed when Belize rejected Guatemala's proposal that Belize should cede the southern part of the country. This claim was subsequently suspended. Belize is a member of the Caribbean Community and Common Market (CARICOM—see p. 142), whose summit conferences have consistently expressed support for Belize's territorial integrity against claims by Guatemala.

At independence the United Kingdom had agreed to leave troops as protection and for training of the Belize Defence Force 'for an appropriate time'. In 1984 Prime Minister Esquivel was given renewed assurances from the British Government as regards its commitment to keep British troops in Belize until the resolution of the territorial dispute with Guatemala. Discussions with Guatemala resumed in February 1985, with greater optimism shown by all three parties. In July the new draft Guatemalan Constitution omitted the previous unconditional claim to Belize, while Esquivel had previously acknowledged Guatemala's right of access to the Caribbean Sea, but no settlement was forthcoming. In January 1986 Dr Marco Vinicio Cerezo was inaugurated as the elected President of Guatemala, representing a change from military to civilian government. In August the United Kingdom and Guatemala renewed diplomatic relations at consular level, and in December the restoration of full diplomatic relations was announced. In March 1987 the first Guatemalan trade delegation since independence visited Belize, and in April renewed discussions were held between Guatemala,

the United Kingdom and Belize (although Belize was still regarded by Guatemala as being only an observer at the meetings). Tripartite negotiations continued, and in May 1988 the formation of a permanent joint commission (which, in effect, entailed a recognition of the Belizean state by Guatemala) was announced.

In the latter half of 1991 relations between Belize and Guatemala showed considerable signs of improvement, and in September the two countries signed an accord under the terms of which Belize pledged to legislate to reduce its maritime boundaries and to allow Guatemala access to the Caribbean Sea and use of its port facilities. In return, President Jorge Serrano Elías of Guatemala officially announced his country's recognition of Belize as an independent state and established diplomatic relations. The Maritime Areas Bill was approved in January 1992 by 16 votes to 12 in the Belizean House of Representatives. The legislation, however, had caused serious divisions within the UDP, leading to the formation, in December 1991, of the Patriotic Alliance for Territorial Integrity (PATI) by certain members of the party to co-ordinate opposition to the bill. Further disagreement between PATI activists and the leaders of the UDP resulted in the expulsion or resignation of five UDP members (including two members of Parliament) in January 1992. In February these members formed a new organization, the NABR (see above), led by the former UDP Deputy Leader and Minister of Transport, Derek Aikman. In November 1992 the Guatemalan legislature voted to ratify Serrano's decision to recognize Belize. Serrano, however, indicated that the accord was not definitive and that Guatemala maintained its territorial claim over Belize.

In April 1993 Belize and Guatemala signed a non-aggression pact, affirming their intent to refrain from the threat or use of force against each other, and preventing either country from being used as a base for aggression against the other. Relations between the two countries were jeopardized when, in June, President Serrano was ousted following an attempt to suspend certain articles of the Constitution and dissolve Congress. However, in late June the new Guatemalan President, Ramiro de León Carpio, announced that Guatemala would continue to respect Belize's independence. In July the Belizean Prime Minister, Manuel Esquivel, reportedly suspended the September 1991 accord, which had been signed by the previous administration and had still not been formally ratified, stating that it involved too many concessions on the part of Belize and that the issue should be put to a referendum.

On 1 January 1994 responsibility for the defence of Belize was transferred to the Belize Defence Force, and all of the British troops were withdrawn by October, with the exception of some 180 troops, who remained to organize training for jungle warfare.

In March 1994, in a letter to the UN Secretary-General, Guatemala formally reaffirmed its territorial claim to Belize, prompting the Belizean Minister of Foreign Affairs to seek talks with the British Government regarding assistance with national defence. Concern was also expressed by the Standing Committee of CARICOM Ministers of Foreign Affairs, which reaffirmed its support for Belizean sovereignty. In mid-1994 Esquivel accused Guatemala of employing destabilizing tactics against Belize by encouraging Guatemalans to occupy and settle in areas of Belizean forest. In September 1996 the Ministers of Foreign Affairs of Belize and Guatemala conducted preliminary talks in New York, USA, concerning a resumption of negotiations on the territorial dispute. Further such discussions, involving representatives of the Governments and armed forces of both countries, were conducted in Miami, USA, in February 1997. In November 1998, at a meeting of ambassadors and officials of both countries, conducted in Miami, agreement was reached on the establishment of a joint commission to deal with immigration, cross-border traffic and respect for the rights of both countries' citizens.

In January 2000, claiming self defence, Belizean security guards shot and killed a Guatemalan civilian. In February there was an attempt to bomb the Guatemalan embassy in Belize. In the same month Guatemalan forces captured three members of the Belizean border patrol, who later escaped; the men were assisted in their escape by the Belizean ambassador, who was expelled from Guatemala as a result. Bilateral talks resumed in May and in August a panel of negotiators was installed at the headquarters of the Organization of American States. In November the two countries signed an agreement to initiate joint patrols of the unofficial common border and to hold quarterly meetings between operational commanders.

Government

Belize is a constitutional monarchy, with the British sovereign as Head of State. Executive authority is vested in the sovereign and is exercised by the Governor-General, who is appointed on the advice of the Prime Minister, must be of Belizean nationality, and acts, in almost all matters, on the advice of the Cabinet. The Governor-General is also advised by an appointed Belize Advisory Council. Legislative power is vested in the bicameral National Assembly, comprising a Senate (eight members appointed by the Governor-General) and a House of Representatives (29 members elected by universal adult suffrage for five years, subject to dissolution). The Governor-General appoints the Prime Minister and, on the latter's recommendation, other ministers. The Cabinet is responsible to the House of Representatives.

Defence

The Belize Defence Force was formed in 1978 and was based on a combination of the existing Police Special Force and the Belize Volunteer Guard. Military service is voluntary. Provision has been made for the establishment of National Service if necessary to supplement normal recruitment. In August 2000 the regular armed forces totalled 1,050, with some 700 militia reserves. In 1994 all British forces were withdrawn from Belize and in 2000 some 180 troops remained to organize training for jungle warfare. The defence budget for 2001 was an estimated BZ \$15m. In early 2000 a 'New Horizon' joint Belizean–US military exercise was held, involving some 3,500 US troops working on social infrastructure projects.

Economic Affairs

In 1998, according to estimates by the World Bank, the country's gross national product (GNP), measured at average 1996–98 prices, was US \$635m., equivalent to US \$2,660 per head (or \$4,367 per head on an international purchasing-power parity basis). During 1990–98, it was estimated, GNP per head increased, in real terms, at an annual average rate of 0.5%. Over this period, Belize's population grew at an average rate of 3.3% per year. Belize's gross domestic product (GDP) increased, in real terms, at an average rate of 4.1% per year in 1989–99, by 4.5% in 1998 and by 4.5% in 1999.

Although 38% of the country is considered suitable for agriculture, only an estimated 3.9% of total land area was used for agricultural purposes in 1997. Nevertheless, agriculture, forestry and fishing employed 31.1% of the working population in 1998, and contributed an estimated 22.1% of GDP, measured at constant 1984 prices, in 1999. The principal cash crops are sugar cane (sugar and molasses accounted for an estimated 24.8% of total domestic exports in 1999), citrus fruits (citrus concentrates accounted for an estimated 16.5%) and bananas (an estimated 16.4%). Maize, red kidney beans and rice are the principal domestic food crops, and the development of other crops, such as cocoa, coconuts and soybeans (soya beans), is being encouraged. The country is largely self-sufficient in fresh meat and eggs. Belize has considerable timber reserves, particularly of tropical hardwoods, and the forestry sector is being developed. In 1999 fishing provided export earnings of an estimated US \$27.8m. (16.7% of total domestic export revenue). According to the World Bank, the real GDP of the agricultural sector increased at an average rate of 6.4% per year during 1989–99. In 1998 real agricultural GDP decreased by 1.5%; however, it increased by 11.7% in 1999.

Industry (including mining, manufacturing, construction, water and electricity) employed 18.2% of the working population in 1997 and contributed an estimated 23.7% of GDP at constant prices in 1999. Manufacturing alone, particularly of clothing, accounted for an estimated 15.3% of GDP in 1999 and employed 11.3% of the working population in 1997. The processing of agricultural products is important, particularly sugar cane (for sugar and rum). According to the World Bank, industrial GDP increased at an average annual rate of 3.1% during 1989–99 and by an estimated 4.6% in 1999. Manufacturing GDP increased at an average rate of 3.5% per year during 1989–99, and by an estimated 4.8% in 1999. Mining accounted for an estimated 0.7% of GDP in 1999 and only 0.1% of employment in 1997.

Belize has no indigenous energy resources other than wood. Exploration for petroleum in the interior of Belize continued in the 1990s, despite increasing concern for the impact of such activity on the environment. Imports of mineral fuels and lubricants accounted for 15.3% of the total cost of retained imports in 1999. Hydroelectric power was developed in the 1990s; in 1993 construction of the Mollejón hydroelectric station, on the Macal River, began. Financed by the International Finance Corporation and the Caribbean Development Bank, the project attracted criticism over its cost and efficiency. Nevertheless, the plant opened in the late 1990s, operated by Belize Electricity Ltd.

The services sector employed 51.8% of the working population in 1997 and contributed 54.1% of GDP at constant prices in 1999. Tourist development is concentrated on promoting 'eco-tourism', based on the attraction of Belize's natural environment, particularly its rain forests and the barrier reef, the second largest in the world. In 1995 Belize had the world's largest proportion of territory dedicated to national parks. Tourist arrivals totalled an estimated 172,292 in 1999, which represented an increase of 3.3% compared with the previous year. According to the World Bank the GDP of the services sector increased, in real terms, at an average rate of 2.8% per year during 1989–99 and by an estimated 4.7% in 1999. Belize's 'offshore' financial centre opened in 1996 and by 1998 there were some 6,700 registered 'offshore' companies.

In 1999 Belize recorded a trade deficit of US \$128.8m., and a deficit of US \$77.4m. on the current account of the balance of payments. According to preliminary figures, in 1999 the principal source of imports was the USA (accounting for 52.7% of the total), while the principal markets for exports were the USA (37.7%) and the United Kingdom (28.5%). Other important trading partners are Mexico and Canada. The principal exports in 1999 were food products (86.3%). The principal imports in that year were machinery and transport equipment, basic manufactures, food and live animals and miscellaneous manufactured articles.

For the financial year ending 31 March 1998 there was a projected budgetary deficit of BZ \$32.6m. Budget proposals for the financial year ending 31 March 2000 envisaged an operating surplus of BZ \$11.8m., with the overall deficit expected to be equivalent to less than 4.0% of GDP. Belize's total external debt was US \$273.0m. at the end of 1999, according to preliminary figures, equivalent to 37.4% of GDP. The annual rate of inflation averaged 2.3% in 1990–98. Consumer prices declined by an average of 0.8% in 1998 and a further 1.2% in 1999. In mid-1998 an estimated 12.7% of the economically active population were unemployed. Many Belizeans, however, work abroad, and remittances to the country from such workers are an important source of income. Emigration, mainly to the USA, is offset by the number of immigrants and refugees from other Central American countries, particularly El Salvador.

Belize is a member of the Caribbean Community and Common Market (CARICOM, see p. 142), and in 1991 acceded to the Organization of American States (OAS, see p. 261). In September 1992 Belize was granted membership of the Inter-American Development Bank (IDB, see p. 212).

Agriculture is the dominant sector of the Belizean economy. As a member of the Commonwealth, Belize enjoys low tariffs on its exports to the European Union (EU) under the Lomé Convention (which expired in February 2000 and was replaced by the Cotonou Agreement in June—see p. 208), and tariff-free access to the USA under the Caribbean Basin Initiative. The development of tourism and the availability of foreign investment have been hindered by the uncertainties arising from the territorial dispute with Guatemala. In an effort to develop service industries, an international shipping register was established in 1989 and legislation on 'offshore' financial services was introduced in 1990. The withdrawal of British troops from Belize in 1994 had serious economic repercussions, with the loss of an estimated BZ \$60m. annually to the economy. In June 2000 Belize appealed to the United Kingdom for additional military aid. In late 1995 some 870 civil service employees (equivalent to 9% of the total central government work-force) were made redundant as the initial phase of a structural adjustment programme, introduced to address the country's serious budget deficit. As part of a reform of the tax system, value-added tax (VAT), at a basic rate of 15%, was introduced with effect from April 1996. High interest rates and low commodity prices were reflected in the lack of real GDP growth in 1998/99. However, according to the Caribbean Development Bank, the economy grew by an estimated 6.4% in 1999, the highest of the decade. On taking office in September 1998 the Musa administration inherited an extremely weak fiscal position, including a public-sector deficit of some BZ \$51m. (equivalent to 4.0% of GDP). Despite this the new Government proceeded to implement its manifesto pledges, including a restructuring of the tax system: in April 1999 VAT was replaced with a broad-based 8% sales tax. Plans for a large-scale public investment programme were also initiated. By mid-1999 prospects for economic growth had improved, based on the moderation of interest rates, expanded market opportunities for bananas (despite the phasing out of the EU preferential market for Caribbean bananas, by 2002) and increased investment in the tourism sector. The budget deficit in 1999/2000 was expected to decrease to BZ $14.8m., following the privatization of the state electricity utility and the sale of mortgages on the secondary market. However, the country was adversely affected by 'Hurricane Keith', which struck in October 2000, causing an estimated BZ $523m.-worth of damage.

Social Welfare

There were six district hospitals, a referral hospital in Belize City, and more than 30 urban and rural health centres in Belize in 1999; pre-natal and child welfare clinics are sponsored by the Ministry of Health and Public Services. In 1996 there were 554 hospital beds and 142 registered physicians. The infant mortality rate declined from 56 per 1,000 live births in 1970 to 35 per 1,000 in 1998. Of total projected budgetary expenditure by the central Government for the financial year 1997/98, BZ $29.6m. (8.2%) was for health and a further BZ $21.4m. (5.9%) for social security and welfare. The Social Security Board, established in 1981, is funded by contributions from employers and employees, as well as investment income, and provides maternity, invalidity and retirement benefits. In 2000 a US $18.1m. programme to expand and improve the health service, including the establishment of a National Health Insurance Fund, was announced. Financing was to be provided jointly by the IDB, the Caribbean Development Bank and the European Union, as well as local funds.

Education

Education is compulsory for all children for a period of 10 years between the ages of five and 14 years. Primary education, beginning at five years of age and lasting for eight years, is provided free of charge, principally through subsidized denominational schools under government control. There were 53,110 pupils enrolled at 280 primary schools in 1996/97. Secondary education, beginning at the age of 13, lasts for four years. There were 10,912 students enrolled in 30 general secondary schools in 1996/97. In 1997 primary enrolment included an estimated 99.9% of children in the relevant age-group (males 99.9%; females 99.9%), while secondary enrolment in that year was equivalent to 63.6% (males 64.6%; females 62.6%).

In 1996/97 there were 2,500 students enrolled in 11 other educational institutions, which included technical, vocational and teacher-training colleges. The University College of Belize was established in 1986 and there is also an extra-mural branch of the University of the West Indies in Belize. In early 2000 it was announced that a new University of Belize was to be formed through the amalgamation of five higher education institutions, including the University College of Belize and Belize Technical College. Budgetary expenditure on education in the financial year 1997/98 was projected at BZ $74.2m., representing 20.5% of total spending by the central Government. In 1998 the average rate of adult illiteracy was 7.3% (males 7.1%; females 7.5%).

Public Holidays

2001: 1 January (New Year's Day), 9 March (Baron Bliss Day), 13–16 April (Easter), 1 May (Labour Day), 24 May (Commonwealth Day), 10 September (St George's Caye Day), 21 September (Independence Day), 12 October (Columbus Day, anniversary of the discovery of America), 19 November (Garifuna Settlement Day), 25–26 December (Christmas).

2002: 1 January (New Year's Day), 11 March (for Baron Bliss Day), 29 March–1 April (Easter), 1 May (Labour Day), 24 May (Commonwealth Day), 10 September (St George's Caye Day), 23 September (for Independence Day), 14 October (for Columbus Day, anniversary of the discovery of America), 19 November (Garifuna Settlement Day), 25–26 December (Christmas).

Weights and Measures

Imperial weights and measures are used, but petrol and paraffin are measured in terms of the US gallon (3.785 litres).

Statistical Survey

Source (unless otherwise stated): Central Statistical Office, Ministry of Finance, Belmopan; tel. (8) 22207; fax (8) 23206; e-mail csogob@blt.net.

AREA AND POPULATION

Area: 22,965 sq km (8,867 sq miles).

Population: 144,857 at census of 12 May 1980; 189,774 (males 96,289, females 93,485) at census of 12 May 1991; 240,204 at census of 12 May 2000.

Density (May 2000): 10.5 per sq km.

Principal Towns (estimated population, April 1997): Belmopan (capital) 6,785; Belize City (former capital) 53,915; Orange Walk 15,035; San Ignacio/Santa Elena 11,375; Corozal 7,715; Dangriga (formerly Stann Creek) 7,110; Benque Viejo 5,995; Punta Gorda 4,770.

Births, Marriages and Deaths (1996, provisional figures): Registered live births 5,163 (birth rate 23.3 per 1,000); Registered marriages (1995) 1,347 (marriage rate 6.2 per 1,000); Registered deaths 964 (death rate 4.3 per 1,000). Source: partly UN, *Population and Vital Statistics Report.*

Expectation of Life (years at birth, 1998): Males 73.5; Females 76.3. Source: UNDP, *Human Development Report.*

Economically Active Population (sample survey, April 1997): Agriculture, hunting, forestry and fishing 21,140; Mining and quarrying 95; Manufacturing 7,980; Electricity, gas and water 985; Construction 3,835; Trade, restaurants and hotels 15,155; Transport, storage and communications 3,655; Financing, insurance, real estate and business services 2,360; Community, social and personal services 12,225; Private households 2,915; Other 335; Total employed 70,680.

AGRICULTURE, ETC.

Principal Crops ('000 metric tons unless otherwise stated, 1999): Sugar cane 1,181; Maize 38*; Rice (paddy) 7*; Roots and tubers 4*; Pulses (dry beans) 5*; Coconuts 3*; Other vegetables 5*; Oranges 190 (unofficial figure); Grapefruit and Pomelos 41*; Bananas 75; Other fruit 3*. *FAO estimate. Source: FAO.

Livestock (FAO estimates, '000 head, 1999): Horses 5; Mules 4; Cattle 58; Pigs 23; Sheep 3; Goats 1; Chickens 1,400. Source: FAO.

Livestock Products (FAO estimates, '000 metric tons, 1999): Meat 10; Cows' milk 7; Hen eggs 2. Source: FAO.

Forestry ('000 cu m): *Roundwood removals* (1998): Industrial wood (Sawlogs) 62, Fuel wood 126, Total 188. *Sawnwood* (1998): 20. Source: FAO, *Yearbook of Forest Products.*

Fishing (metric tons, live weight, 1998): Capture 2,206 (Porgies, seabreams 183, European pilchard 126, Other marine fishes 485, Caribbean spiny lobster 502, Penaeus shrimps 40, Stromboid conchs 252, Cuttlefish, bobtail squids 406, Octopuses, etc. 185); Aquaculture 1,809* (Tilapias 136*, Whiteleg shrimp 1,642); Total catch 4,015. *FAO estimate. Source: FAO, *Yearbook of Fishery Statistics.*

INDUSTRY

Production (preliminary figures, 1999): Raw sugar 115,205 long tons; Molasses 40,285 long tons; Cigarettes 92 million; Beer 1,455,000 gallons; Batteries 7,440; Flour 17,780,000 lb; Fertilizers 22,894 metric tons; Garments 2,134,000 items; Citrus concentrate 3,719,000 gallons; Soft drinks 1,728,000 cases. Source: IMF, *Belize: Statistical Appendix* (June 2000).

FINANCE

Currency and Exchange Rates: 100 cents = 1 Belizean dollar (BZ $). *Sterling, US Dollar and Euro Equivalents* (29 December 2000): £1 sterling = BZ $2.984; US $1 = BZ $2.000; €1 = BZ $1.861; BZ $100 = £33.51 = US $50.00 = €53.73. *Exchange rate:* Fixed at US $1 = BZ $2.000 since May 1976.

Budget (BZ $ million, year ending 31 March): *1997/98* (projections): *Revenue:* Taxation 251.3 (Taxes on income, profits, etc. 52.3, Domestic taxes on goods and services 101.3, Import duties 83.6); Other current revenue 29.8 (Entrepreneurial and property income 10.2, Administrative fees, etc. 14.9); Capital revenue 2.2; Total 283.4, excl. grants (41.2). *Expenditure:* General public services 41.3; Defence 19.7; Public order and safety 25.7; Education 74.2; Health 29.6; Social security and welfare 21.4; Housing and community amenities 9.3; Recreational, cultural and religious affairs 4.8; Econ-

omic services 101.9 (Agriculture, forestry, fishing and hunting 22.5, Transport and communications 60.8); Other purposes 34.3 (Interest payments 29.0); Total 362.3 (Current 244.8, Capital 117.4), excl. lending minus repayments (–5.1). Source: IMF, *Government Finance Statistics Yearbook.*

International Reserves (US $ million at 31 December 1999): IMF special drawing rights 1.39; Reserve position in the IMF 5.82; Foreign exchange 64.10; Total 71.31. Source: IMF, *International Financial Statistics.*

Money Supply (BZ $ million at 31 December 1999): Currency outside banks 84.15; Demand deposits at commercial banks 141.86; Total money (incl. others) 248.24. Source: IMF, *International Financial Statistics.*

Cost of Living (Consumer Price Index; base: 1995 = 100): 107.5 in 1997; 106.6 in 1998; 105.3 in 1999. Source: IMF, *International Financial Statistics.*

Expenditure on the Gross Domestic Product (BZ $ million at current prices, 1999): Government final consumption expenditure 235.2; Private final consumption expenditure 896.4; Increase in stocks 42.2; Gross fixed capital formation 408.4; *Total domestic expenditure* 1,582.2; Exports of goods and service 707.2; *Less* Imports of goods and services 870.7; *GDP in purchasers' values* 1,376.6. Source: IMF, *International Financial Statistics.*

Gross Domestic Product by Economic Activity (BZ $ million at constant 1984 prices, 1999, preliminary figures): Agriculture 122.1; Forestry and logging 14.1; Fishing 47.3; Mining 5.4; Manufacturing 127.1; Electricity and water 14.0; Construction 50.3; Trade, restaurants and hotels 140.4; Transport and communications 118.2; Finance, insurance, real estate and business services 78.9; Public administration 56.8; Other services 54.2; *Sub-total* 828.8; *Less* Imputed bank service charges 24.5; *GDP at factor cost* 804.3; Net indirect taxes 157.7; *GDP at constant market prices* 962.0. Source: IMF, *Belize: Statistical Appendix* (June 2000).

Balance of Payments (US $ million, 1999): Exports of goods f.o.b. 201.5; Imports of goods c.i.f. –330.3; *Trade balance* –128.8; Exports of services 154.1; Imports of services –105.1; *Balance on goods and services* –79.8; Other income received 7.3; Other income paid –41.5; *Balance on goods, services and income* –114.0; Current transfers received 40.0; Current transfers paid –3.5; *Current balance* –77.4; Capital account (net) –2.0; Direct investment abroad 48.9; Direct investment from abroad 3.5; Portfolio investment assets –0.7; Portfolio investment liabilities 33.6; Other investment assets –8.9; Other investment liabilities –9.5; Net errors and omissions 4.3; *Overall balance* –8.3. Source: IMF, *International Financial Statistics.*

EXTERNAL TRADE

Principal Commodities (preliminary figures, US $ million, 1999): *Imports c.i.f.:* Food and live animals 45.2; Beverages and tobacco 4.6; Mineral fuels, lubricants, etc. 47.2; Chemicals 30.9; Basic manufactures 47.7; Machinery and transport equipment 84.6; Miscellaneous manufactured articles 36.5; Total (incl. others) 309.2. *Exports f.o.b.:* Food and live animals 143.3 (Sugar 41.0, Seafood products 27.8, Bananas 27.3, Citrus concentrates 27.4, Single strength juices 9.5); Miscellaneous manufactured articles 19.6 (Garments 19.6); Total (incl. others) 166.1. Note: Figures refer to retained imports and domestic exports. The data exclude re-exports. Source: IMF, *Belize: Statistical Appendix* (June 2000).

Principal Trading Partners (preliminary figures, US $ million, 1999): *Imports c.i.f.:* Mexico 45.8; United Kingdom 17.6; USA 192.9; Total (incl. others) 366.3. *Exports f.o.b.* (excl. re-exports): United Kingdom 47.4; USA 62.7; Total (incl. others) 166.1. Source: IMF, *Belize: Statistical Appendix* (June 2000).

TRANSPORT

Road Traffic (motor vehicles licensed, 1998): 21,684. Source: IRF, *World Road Statistics.*

Shipping (sea-borne freight traffic, '000 metric tons, 1996): Goods loaded 255.4; Goods unloaded 277.1. *Merchant Fleet* (vessels registered at 31 December 1998): Number of vessels 1,308; Total displacement 2,382,478 grt. Source: Lloyd's Register of Shipping, *World Fleet Statistics.*

Civil Aviation (preliminary, 1997): Passenger arrivals 95,337.

TOURISM

Tourist Arrivals: 134,289 in 1997; 166,743 in 1998; 172,292 in 1999.

Tourist Receipts (US $ million): 75 in 1996; 88 in 1997; 99 in 1998.

Hotels: 383 in 1997; 408 in 1998; 390 in 1999.

Source: Belize Tourist Board.

COMMUNICATIONS MEDIA

Radio Receivers (1997): 133,000 in use*.

Television Receivers (1997): 41,000 in use*.

Telephones (1997): 31,000 main lines in use†.

Telefax Stations (1996): 500 in use†.

Mobile Cellular Telephones (1997): 3,023 subscribers†.

Book Production (1996): 107 titles*.

Newspapers: *Non-daily* (1996): 6 (circulation 80,000)*.

* Source: UNESCO, *Statistical Yearbook*.

† Source: UN, *Statistical Yearbook*.

EDUCATION

Pre-primary* (1994/95): 90 schools, 190 teachers, 3,311 students.

Primary (1996/97): 280 schools, 1,966 teachers (1995/96) 53,110 students.

Secondary (1996/97): 30 schools, 697 teachers (1995/96), 10,912 students.

Higher (1996/97): 11 institutions, 254 teachers (1995/96), 2,500 students.

* Source: UNESCO, *Statistical Yearbook*.

Directory

Directory

The Constitution

The Constitution came into effect at the independence of Belize on 21 September 1981. Its main provisions are summarized below:

FUNDAMENTAL RIGHTS AND FREEDOMS

Regardless of race, place of origin, political opinions, colour, creed or sex, but subject to respect for the rights and freedoms of others and for the public interest, every person in Belize is entitled to the rights of life, liberty, security of the person, and the protection of the law. Freedom of movement, of conscience, of expression, of assembly and association and the right to work are guaranteed and the inviolability of family life, personal privacy, home and other property and of human dignity is upheld. Protection is afforded from discrimination on the grounds of race, sex, etc., and from slavery, forced labour and inhuman treatment.

CITIZENSHIP

All persons born in Belize before independence who, immediately prior to independence, were citizens of the United Kingdom and Colonies automatically become citizens of Belize. All persons born outside the country having a husband, parent or grandparent in possession of Belizean citizenship automatically acquire citizenship, as do those born in the country after independence. Provision is made which permits persons who do not automatically become citizens of Belize to be registered as such. (Belizean citizenship was also offered, under the Belize Loans Act 1986, in exchange for interest-free loans of US $25,000 with a 10-year maturity. The scheme was officially ended in June 1994, following sustained criticism of alleged corruption on the part of officials. However, a revised economic citizenship programme, offering citizenship in return for a minimum investment of US $75,000, received government approval in early 1995.)

THE GOVERNOR-GENERAL

The British monarch, as Head of State, is represented in Belize by a Governor-General, a Belizean national.

Belize Advisory Council

The Council consists of not less than six people 'of integrity and high national standing', appointed by the Governor-General for up to 10 years upon the advice of the Prime Minister. The Leader of the Opposition must concur with the appointment of two members and be consulted about the remainder. The Council exists to advise the Governor-General, particularly in the exercise of the prerogative of mercy, and to convene as a tribunal to consider the removal from office of certain senior public servants and judges.

THE EXECUTIVE

Executive authority is vested in the British monarch and exercised by the Governor-General. The Governor-General appoints as Prime Minister that member of the House of Representatives who, in the Governor-General's view, is best able to command the support of the majority of the members of the House, and appoints a Deputy Prime Minister and other Ministers on the advice of the Prime Minister. The Governor-General may remove the Prime Minister from office if a resolution of 'no confidence' is passed by the House and the Prime Minister does not, within seven days, either resign or advise the Governor-General to dissolve the National Assembly. The Cabinet consists of the Prime Minister and other Ministers.

The Leader of the Opposition is appointed by the Governor-General as that member of the House who, in the Governor-General's view, is best able to command the support of a majority of the members of the House who do not support the Government.

THE LEGISLATURE

The Legislature consists of a National Assembly comprising two chambers: the Senate, with eight nominated members; and the House of Representatives, with 29 elected members. The Assembly's normal term is five years. Senators are appointed by the Governor-General: five on the advice of the Prime Minister; two on the advice of the Leader of the Opposition or on the advice of persons selected by the Governor-General; and one after consultation with the Belize Advisory Council. If any person who is not a Senator is elected to be President of the Senate, he or she shall be an ex-officio Senator in addition to the eight nominees.

Each constituency returns one Representative to the House, who is directly elected in accordance with the Constitution.

If a person who is not a member of the House is elected to be Speaker of the House, he or she shall be an ex-officio member in addition to the 29 members directly elected. Every citizen older than 18 years is eligible to vote. The National Assembly may alter any of the provisions of the Constitution.

The Government

Head of State: HM Queen ELIZABETH II (succeeded to the throne 6 February 1952).

Governor-General: Sir COLVILLE YOUNG (appointed 17 November 1993).

THE CABINET
(April 2001)

Prime Minister and Minister of Finance and of Foreign and Latin American Affairs: SAID MUSA.

Deputy Prime Minister and Minister of Natural Resources and the Environment and of Industry: JOHN BRICEÑO.

Senior Minister: GEORGE CADLE PRICE.

Minister of National Security and of Economic Development: JORGE ESPAT.

Minister of Public Utilities, Energy, Communications and Immigration: MAXWELL SAMUELS.

Minister of Budget Planning, Investment and Trade and Head of the Central Bank: RALPH FONSECA.

Minister of Health and Public Services: JOSE COYE.

Minister of the Sugar Industry, Labour and Local Government: VALDEMAR CASTILLO.

Minister of Human Development, Civil Society and Women: DOLORES BALDERAMOS GARCIA.

Minister of Agriculture, Fisheries and Co-operatives: DANIEL SILVA, Jr.

Minister of Public Works, Transport and Citrus and Banana Industries: HENRY CANTON.

Minister of Education and Sports: CORDEL HYDE.

Minister of Youth and Tourism: MARK ESPAT.

Minister of Rural Development and Culture: MARCIAL MES.

Minister of Housing, Urban Renewal and Home Affairs: RICHARD BRADLEY.

Attorney-General and Minister of Information and Broadcasting: GODFREY SMITH.

MINISTRIES

Office of the Prime Minister: New Administrative Bldg, Belmopan; tel. (8) 22346; fax (8) 20071; e-mail prime-minister@belize.gov.bz.

Ministry of Agriculture, Fisheries and Co-operatives: 2nd Floor, West Block Bldg, Belmopan; tel. (8) 22241; fax (8) 22409; e-mail mafpaeu@btl.net.

Ministry of the Attorney-General: Belmopan; tel. (8) 22504; fax (8) 23390; e-mail atgenmin@btl.net.

Ministry of Budget Planning, Investment and Trade: New Administration Bldg, Belmopan; tel. (8) 22345; fax (8) 22195.

Ministry of Economic Development: New Administration Bldg, Belmopan; tel. (8) 22526.

Ministry of Education and Sports: West Block Bldg, Belmopan; tel. (8) 23380; fax (8) 23389; e-mail educate@btl.net.

Ministry of Finance: New Administration Bldg, Belmopan; tel. (8) 22169; fax (8) 23317; e-mail finsecmof@btl.net.

Ministry of Foreign and Latin American Affairs: POB 174, New Administration Bldg, Belmopan; tel. (8) 22167; fax (8) 22854; e-mail belizemfa@btl.net.

Ministry of Health and Public Services: New Administration Bldg, Belmopan; tel. (8) 22325; fax (8) 22942.

Ministry of Housing, Urban Renewal and Home Affairs: East Block Bldg, Belmopan; tel. (1) 22016; fax (8) 23337.

Ministry of Human Development, Civil Society and Women: West Block, Independence Hill, Belmopan; tel. (8) 22161; fax (8) 23175.

Ministry of Industry: East Block Bldg, Belmopan; tel. (8) 22153.

Ministry of Information and Broadcasting: East Block Bldg, Belmopan; tel. (8) 20094.

Ministry of National Security: Curl Osmond Thompson Bldg, Belmopan; tel. (8) 22225; fax (8) 22615; e-mail mnsi@btl.net.

Ministry of Natural Resources and the Environment: Market Sq., Belmopan; tel. (8) 22249; fax (8) 22333; e-mail lincenbze@btl.net.

Ministry of Public Utilities, Energy, Communications and Immigration: Power Lane, Belmopan; tel. (8) 22817; fax (8) 23317.

Ministry of Public Works, Transport and Citrus and Banana Industries: Power Lane, Belmopan; tel. (8) 22136; fax (8) 23282; e-mail peumow@btl.net.

Ministry of Rural Development and Culture: East Block, Belmopan; tel. (8) 22444; fax (8) 20317; e-mail ruraldev@btl.net.

Ministry of the Sugar Industry, Labour and Local Government: 3rd Floor, Diamond Bldg, Constitution Drive, Belmopan; tel. (8) 23990; fax (8) 23365; e-mail msillg@belize.gov.bz.

Ministry of Youth and Tourism: Constitution Drive, Belmopan; tel. (8) 23393; fax (8) 23815; e-mail tourismmdpt@btl.net.

Legislature

NATIONAL ASSEMBLY
The Senate

President: ELIZABETH ZABANEH.

There are eight nominated members.

House of Representatives

Speaker: SYLVIA FLORES.

Clerk: JESUS KEN.

General Election, 27 August 1998

	Votes cast	% of total	Seats
People's United Party (PUP) .	50,330	59.30	26
United Democratic Party (UDP)	33,237	39.16	3
Others	1,309	1.54	—
Total	**84,876**	**100.00**	**29**

Political Organizations

National Alliance for Belizean Rights (NABR): Belize City; f. 1992 by UDP members opposed to compromise over territorial dispute with Guatemala; Chair. (vacant); Co-ordinator PHILIP S. W. GOLDSON.

People's United Party (PUP): Belize City; tel. (2) 45886; fax (2) 31940; f. 1950; based on organized labour; merged with Christian Democratic Party in 1988; Leader SAID MUSA; Chair. JORGE ESPAT; Deputy Leaders MAX SAMUELS, JOHN BRICEÑO.

United Democratic Party (UDP): South End Bel-China Bridge, POB 1898, Belize City; tel. (2) 76441; fax (2) 31004; e-mail info@udp.org.bz; internet www.udp.org.bz; f. 1974 by merger of People's Development Movement, Liberal Party and National Independence Party; conservative; Leader DEAN BARROW; Chair. ELODIO ARAGON.

Diplomatic Representation

EMBASSIES AND HIGH COMMISSION IN BELIZE

Belgium: 126 Freetown Rd, Belize City; tel. (2) 30748; fax (2) 30750; Ambassador: WILLY VERRIEST.

China (Taiwan): 3rd Floor, Blake's Bldg, cnr Hutson and Eyre Sts, POB 1020, Belize City; tel. (2) 31862; fax (2) 33082; e-mail embroc@btl.net; Ambassador: KUO-HSIUNG SHEN.

Colombia: 12 St Mathew St, POB 1805, Belize City; tel. (2) 35623; fax (2) 31972; e-mail colombia@btl.net; Chargé d'affaires: PABLO ANTONIO REBOLLEDO.

Costa Rica: 38 Princess Margaret Drive, POB 2235, Belize City; tel. (2) 32878; fax (2) 32818; e-mail cremb@btl.net; Ambassador: MARCO VINICIO VARGAS P.

Cuba: 6048 Manatee Drive, Buttonwood Bay, POB 1775, Belize City; tel. (2) 35345.

El Salvador: 49 Nanche St, POB 215, Belmopan; tel. (8) 23404; fax (8) 23569; Ambassador: MANUEL ANTONIO VÁSQUEZ MENA.

Germany: 57 South Foreshore, POB 1021, Belize City; tel. (2) 77282; fax (2) 24375; Ambassador: Dr NILS GRÜBER.

Guatemala: 8 'A' St, POB 1771, Belize City; tel. (2) 33314; fax (2) 35140; e-mail guatemb.bz@btl.net; Ambassador: JORGE SKINNER-KLEE.

Honduras: 22 Gabourel Lane, POB 285, Belize City; tel. (2) 45889; fax (2) 30562; Chargé d'affaires: CARLOS AUGUSTO MATUTÉ RIVERA.

Korea, Democratic People's Republic: Ambassador: CHOE CHUN YONG.

Mexico: 20 North Park St, POB 754, Belize City; tel. (2) 30193; fax (2) 78742; Ambassador: FEDERICO URUCHUA.

Panama: 79 Unity Blvd, POB 1692, Belize City; tel. (2) 44991; fax (2) 30654; Chargé d'affaires: JOSÉ DE LA CRUZ PAREDES.

United Kingdom: Embassy Sq., POB 91, Belmopan; tel. (8) 22146; fax (8) 22761; e-mail brithicom@btl.net; High Commissioner: TIMOTHY J. DAVID.

USA: 29 Gabourel Lane, POB 286, Belize City; tel. (2) 77161; fax (2) 30802; e-mail brithicom@btl.net; internet www.usemb-belize.gov; Ambassador: CAROLYN CURIEL.

Venezuela: 18–20 Unity Blvd, POB 49, Belmopan; tel. (8) 22384; fax (8) 22022; e-mail embaven@btl.net; Ambassador: CHRISTIAAN VAN DER REE.

Judicial System

Summary Jurisdiction Courts (criminal jurisdiction) and District Courts (civil jurisdiction), presided over by magistrates, are established in each of the six judicial districts. Summary Jurisdiction Courts have a wide jurisdiction in summary offences and a limited jurisdiction in indictable matters. Appeals lie to the Supreme Court, which has jurisdiction corresponding to the English High Court of Justice and where a jury system is in operation. From the Supreme Court further appeals lie to a Court of Appeal, established in 1967, which holds an average of four sessions per year. Final appeals are made to the Judicial Committee of the Privy Council in the United Kingdom.

Court of Appeal: KENNETH GEORGE, Dr NICHOLAS LIVERPOOL, MANUEL SOSA.

Chief Justice: ABDULAI OSMAR CONTEH (acting).

Supreme Court: Supreme Court Bldg, Belize City; tel. (2) 77256; fax (2) 70181; internet www.supremecourt.com; Registrar RAYMOND A. USHER.

Chief Magistrate: HERBERT LORD, Paslow Bldg, Belize City; tel. (2) 77164.

Religion

CHRISTIANITY

Most of the population are Christian, the largest denomination being the Roman Catholic Church (62% of the population, according to the census of 1980). The other main groups were the Anglican (12% in 1980), Methodist (6%), Mennonite (4%), Seventh-day Adventist (3%) and Pentecostal (2%) churches.

Belize Council of Churches: 149 Allenby St, POB 508, Belize City; tel. (2) 77077; f. 1957 as Church World Service Committee, present name adopted 1984; eight mem. Churches, four assoc. bodies; Pres. Maj. ERROL ROBATEAU (Salvation Army); Gen. Sec. SADIE VERNON.

The Roman Catholic Church

Belize comprises the single diocese of Belize City-Belmopan, suffragan to the archdiocese of Kingston in Jamaica. In December 1998 it was estimated that there were 132,940 adherents in the diocese. The Bishop participates in the Antilles Episcopal Conference (whose secretariat is based in Port of Spain, Trinidad and Tobago).

Bishop of Belize City-Belmopan: OSMOND PETER MARTIN, Bishop's House, 144 North Front St, POB 616, Belize City; tel. (2) 72122; fax (2) 31922.

The Anglican Communion

Anglicans in Belize belong to the Church in the Province of the West Indies, comprising eight dioceses. The Archbishop of the Province is the Bishop of North Eastern Caribbean and Aruba, resident in St John's, Antigua.

Bishop of Belize: Rt Rev. SYLVESTRE DONATO ROMERO-PALMA, Bishopthorpe, 25 Southern Foreshore, POB 535, Belize City; tel. (2) 73029; fax (2) 76898; e-mail bzediocese@btl.net.

Protestant Churches

Methodist Church (Belize/Honduras District Conference): 88 Regent St, POB 212, Belize City; tel. (2) 77173; fax (2) 75870; f. 1824; c. 2,620 mems; District Pres. Rev. Dr LESLEY G. ANDERSON.

Mennonite Congregations in Belize: POB 427, Belize City; tel. (8) 30137; fax (8) 30101; f. 1958; four main Mennonite settlements: at Spanish Lookout, Shipyard, Little Belize and Blue Creek; Bishops J. B. Loewen, J. K. Barkman, P. Thiessen, H. R. Penner, Cornelius Enns.

Other denominations active in the country include the Seventh-day Adventists, Pentecostals, Presbyterians, Baptists, Moravians, Jehovah's Witnesses, the Church of God, the Assemblies of Brethren and the Salvation Army.

OTHER RELIGIONS

There are also small communities of Hindus (106, according to the census of 1980), Muslims (110 in 1980), Jews (92 in 1980) and Bahá'ís.

The Press

Amandala: Amandala Press, 3304 Partridge St, POB 15, Belize City; tel. (2) 24476; fax (2) 24702; internet www.belizemall.com/amandala/; f. 1969; weekly; independent; Editor Evan X. Hyde; circ. 45,000.

The Belize Observer: e-mail belizeobserver@excite.com; internet www.belizeobserver.com.

The Belize Times: 3 Queen St, POB 506, Belize City; tel. (2) 45757; fax (2) 31940; e-mail editor@belizetimes.com; internet www.belize times.com; f. 1956; weekly; party political paper of PUP; Editor Andrew Steinhauer; circ. 6,000.

Belize Today: Belize Information Service, East Block, POB 60, Belmopan; tel. (8) 22159; fax (8) 23242; monthly; official; Editor Miguel H. Hernández Jr; circ. 17,000.

Government Gazette: Government Printery, 1 Power Lane, Belmopan; tel. (8) 22127; fax (8) 23367; e-mail info@gazette.gov.bz; internet www.gazette.gov.br; official; weekly; Editor L. J. Nicholas.

The Reporter: 147 cnr Allenby and West Sts, POB 707, Belize City; tel. (2) 72503; f. 1968; weekly; Editor Harry Lawrence; circ. 6,500.

The San Pedro Sun: POB 35, San Pedro Town, Ambergris Caye; fax (26) 2905; e-mail sanpedrosun@btl.net; internet www.amber griscaye.com; weekly; Editors Dan Jamison, Eileen Jamison.

NEWS AGENCY

Agencia EFE (Spain): c/o POB 506, Belize City; tel. (2) 45757; Correspondent Amalia Mai.

Publisher

Government Printery: 1 Power Lane, Belmopan; tel. (8) 22293; f. 1871; responsible for printing, binding and engraving requirements of all govt depts and ministries; publications include annual govt estimates, govt magazines and the official *Government Gazette.*

Broadcasting and Communications

TELECOMMUNICATIONS

Belize Telecommunications Ltd: Esquivel Telecom Centre, St Thomas St, POB 603, Belize City; tel. (2) 32868; fax (2) 31800; e-mail educ@btl.net; internet www.btl.net; f. 1987; Chair. Lord Ashcroft; CEO Edberto Tesecum.

Office of Telecommunications: Administration Complex, Mahogany St Extension, Belize City; tel. (2) 24938; fax (2) 24939; Dir Clifford Slusher.

RADIO

Broadcasting Corporation of Belize (BCB): Albert Cattouse Bldg, Regent St, POB 89, Belize City; tel. (2) 72468; fax (2) 75040; e-mail rbgold@btl.net; f. 1937; privatized in 1998; broadcasts in English (75%) and Spanish; also transmits programmes in Garifuna and Maya; Gen. Man. Ruth Staine-Dawson.

Love FM: Belize City; e-mail lovefm@btl.net; internet www.love fm.com; f. 1992; purchased Friends FM in 1998; Man. Dir Rene Villanueva.

Radio Krem Ltd: 3304 Partridge St, POB 15, Belize City; tel. (2) 75929; fax (2) 74079; commercial; purchased Radio Belize in 1998; Man. Eva S. Hyde.

There are a further three private radio stations broadcasting in Belize.

TELEVISION

In August 1986 the Belize Broadcasting Authority issued licences to eight television operators for 14 channels, which mainly retransmit US satellite programmes, thus placing television in Belize on a fully legal basis for the first time.

Baymen Broadcasting Network (Channel 9): 27 Baymen Ave, Belize City; tel. (2) 44400; fax (2) 31242; commercial; Man. Marie Hoare.

BCB Teleproductions: POB 89, Belize City; govt-owned; video production unit; local programmes for broadcasting.

Channel 5: POB 679, Belize City; tel. (2) 73146; fax (2) 74936; e-mail gbtv@btl.com; internet www.channel5belize.com; f. 1991.

Tropical Vision (Channels 7 and 11): 73 Albert St, Belize City; tel. (2) 77246; fax (2) 75040; commercial; Man. Nestor Vasquez.

Finance

(cap. = capital; res = reserves; dep. = deposits; brs = branches)

BANKING
Central Bank

Central Bank of Belize: Gabourel Lane, POB 852, Belize City; tel. (2) 36194; fax (2) 36226; e-mail governor@cenbank.gov.bz; f. 1982; cap. BZ $10m., res 10.8m., dep. 82.2m. (1997); Head Ralph Fonseca; Gov. Keith Arnold.

Development Bank

Development Finance Corporation: Bliss Parade, Belmopan; tel. (8) 22350; fax (8) 23096; e-mail dfc@bfl.net; internet www .dfcbelize.org; f. 1972; issued cap. BZ $10m.; Chair. Glenn Godfrey; Gen. Man. Roberto Bautista; 5 brs.

Other Banks

Atlantic Bank Ltd: POB 481, Cor Freetown Rd and Cleghorn St, Belize City; tel. (2) 34123; fax (2) 33907; e-mail atlantic@btl.net; internet www.atlabank.com; Chair. Dr Guillermo Bueso.

Barclays Bank PLC (United Kingdom): 21 Albert St, POB 363, Belize City; tel. (2) 77211; fax (2) 78572; Man. Tilvan King; 3 brs.

Belize Bank Ltd: 60 Market Sq., POB 364, Belize City; tel. (2) 77132; fax (2) 72712; e-mail bblintl@btl.net; cap. BZ $4.3m., res BZ $4.3m., dep. BZ $280.1m. (April 1997); Chair. Sir Edney Cain; Senior Vice-Pres. and Gen. Man. Louis Anthony Swasey; 10 brs.

Provident Bank and Trust of Belize: 35 Barrack Rd and Craig St, Belize City; tel. (2) 35698; fax (2) 30368; e-mail provident@btl.net; internet www.providentbelize.com.

Scotiabank (Canada): Albert St, POB 708, Belize City; tel. (2) 77027; fax 77416; e-mail cmobel@btl.net; Gen. Man. C. E. Marcel; 6 brs.

There is also a government savings bank.

INSURANCE

General insurance is provided by local companies, and British, US and Jamaican companies are also represented.

Trade and Industry

STATUTORY BODIES

Banana Control Board: c/o Dept of Agriculture, West Block, Belmopan; management of banana industry; in 1989 it was decided to make it responsible to growers, not an independent executive; Head Lalo Garcia.

Belize Beef Corporation: c/o Dept of Agriculture, West Block, Belmopan; f. 1978; semi-governmental organization to aid development of cattle-rearing industry; Dir Deedie Runkel.

Belize Marketing Board: 117 North Front St, POB 633, Belize City; tel. (2) 77402; fax (2) 77656; f. 1948 to encourage the growing of staple food crops; purchases crops at guaranteed prices, supervises processing, storing and marketing intelligence; Chair. Silas C. Caye-tano.

Belize Sugar Board: 7, 2nd St South, Corozal Town; tel. (4) 22005; fax (4) 22672; f. 1960 to control the sugar industry and cane production; includes representatives of the Government, sugar manufacturers, cane farmers and the public sector; Chair. Orlando Puga; Exec. Sec. Maria Puerto.

Citrus Control Board: c/o Dept of Agriculture, West Block, Belmopan; tel. (8) 22199; f. 1966; determines basic quota for each producer, fixes annual price of citrus; Chair. C. Sosa.

DEVELOPMENT ORGANIZATIONS

Belize Reconstruction and Development Corporation: 36 Trinity Blvd, POB 1, Belmopan; tel. (8) 22271; fax (8) 23992; e-mail recondev@btl.net; Gen. Man. Aloysius Palacio.

Belize Trade and Investment Development Service: 14 Orchid Garden St, Belmopan; tel. (8) 23737; fax (8) 20595; e-mail beltraide@belize.gov.bz; internet www.belizeinvest.org.bz; f. 1986 as a joint government and private-sector institution to encourage export and investment; Gen. Man. PETER USHER.

Department of Economic Development: Ministry of Budget Planning, Economic Development, Investment and Trade, New Administrative Bldg, Belmopan; tel. (8) 22526; fax (8) 23111; administration of public and private-sector investment and planning; statistics agency; Head HUMBERTO PAREDES.

CHAMBER OF COMMERCE

Belize Chamber of Commerce and Industry: 63 Regent St, POB 291, Belize City; tel. (2) 73148; fax (2) 74984; e-mail bcci@btl.net; internet www.belize.org/html/cont.html; f. 1920; Pres. Dr. GILBERT CANTON; Gen. Man. KEVIN HERRERA; 300 mems.

EMPLOYERS' ASSOCIATIONS

Banana Growers' Association: Big Creek, Independence Village, Stann Creek District; tel. (6) 22001; fax (6) 22112; e-mail banana@btl.net.

Belize Cane Farmers' Association: 34 San Antonio Rd, Orange Walk; tel. (3) 22005; fax (3) 23171; f. 1959 to assist cane farmers and negotiate with the Sugar Board and manufacturers on their behalf; Chair. PABLO TUN; 16 district brs.

Belize Livestock Producers' Association: 47.5 miles Western Highway, POB 183, Belmopan; tel. (8) 23202; fax (8) 23886; e-mail blpa@btl.net; Chair. PETE LIZARRAGA.

Citrus Growers' Association: 9 miles Stann Creek Valley Rd, POB 7, Stann Creek District; tel. (5) 23585; fax (5) 22686; e-mail cga@btl.net; f. 1966; CEO BRIDGET COLLERTON.

UTILITIES
Electricity

Office of Electricity Supply: Mahogany St, POB 1846, Belize City; tel. (2) 24995; fax (2) 24994; f. 1992; Dir-Gen. HERMAN CHARLESWORTH.

Belize Electricity Co Ltd (BECOL): 115 Barrack Rd, POB 327, Belize City; tel. (2) 70954; fax (2) 30891; e-mail bel@btl.net; 95% owned by Fortis Inc. (Canada); Chair. NESTOR VASQUEZ; CEO LUIS LUE.

Water

Water and Sewer Authority (WASA): 44 Regent St, Belize City; tel. (2) 77097; fax (2) 77092; f. 1971; scheduled for privatization in 2001; Man. WINSTON W. MICHAEL.

TRADE UNIONS

National Trades Union Congress of Belize (NTUCB): POB 2359, Belize City; tel. (2) 71596; fax (2) 72864; Pres. RAY DAVIS; Gen. Sec. DORENE QUIROS.

Principal Unions

United General Workers' Union: 1259 Lakeland City, Dangriga; tel. (5) 22105; f. 1979 by amalgamation of the Belize General Development Workers' Union and the Southern Christian Union; three branch unions affiliated to the central body; affiliated to ICFTU; Pres. FRANCIS SABAL; Gen. Sec. CONRAD SAMBULA.

Belize National Teachers' Union: POB 382, Belize City; tel. (2) 72857; Pres. HELEN STUART; Sec. MIGUEL WONG; 1,000 mems.

Christian Workers' Union: 107B Cemetery Rd, Belize City; tel. (2) 72150; f. 1962; general; Pres. JAMES McFOY; Gen. Sec. ANTONIO GONZÁLEZ; 1,000 mems.

Democratic Independent Union: Belize City; Pres. CYRIL DAVIS; 1,250 mems.

Public Service Union of Belize: Hilltop, POB 458, Belmopan; tel. (8) 23885; fax (8) 20283; e-mail belizepsu@btl.net; f. 1922; public workers; Pres. MARGARET VENTURA; Sec.-Gen. HUBERT ENRIQUEZ; 1,582 mems.

United Banners Banana Workers' Union: Dangriga; f. 1995; Pres. MARCIANA FUNEZ.

Transport

Department of Transport: Forest Drive, Belmopan; tel. (8) 22417; fax (8) 23379; Commissioner PHILLIP BRACKETT.

RAILWAYS

There are no railways in Belize.

ROADS

There are 1,419 km (882 miles) of all-weather main and feeder roads and 651 km (405 miles) of cart roads and bush trails. About 805 km (500 miles) of logging and forest tracks are usable by heavy-duty vehicles in the dry season. In 2000 the International Bank for Reconstruction and Development (IBRD—World Bank) approved a loan of US $13m. for road construction.

SHIPPING

There is a deep-water port at Belize City and a second port at Commerce Bight, near Dangriga (formerly Stann Creek), to the south of Belize City. There is a port for the export of bananas at Big Creek. Nine major shipping lines operate vessels calling at Belize City, including the Carol Line (consisting of Harrison, Hapag-Lloyd, Nedlloyd and CGM).

Belize Port Authority: Caesar Ridge Rd, POB 633, Belize City; tel. (2) 72439; fax (2) 73571; e-mail portbz@btl.net; f. 1980; Chair. KAY MENZIES; Ports Commr ALFRED B. COYE.

Belize Lines Ltd: 37 Regent St, Belize City.

CIVIL AVIATION

Phillip S. W. Goldson International Airport, 14 km (9 miles) from Belize City, can accommodate medium-sized jet-engined aircraft. A new terminal was completed in 1990. There are airstrips for light aircraft on internal flights near the major towns and offshore islands. The runway was extended in 2000.

Department of Civil Aviation: POB 367, Belize City; e-mail aviation@btl.net; Dir EFRAIN GOMEZ.

Maya Island Air: Municipal Airport, POB 458, Belize City; tel. (2) 35795; fax (2) 30585; e-mail mayair@btl.net; internet www.ambergriscaye.com/islandair; f. 1997 as merger between Maya Airways Ltd and Island Air; operated by Belize Air Group; internal services, centred on Belize City, and charter flights to neighbouring countries; Exec. Dir TREVOR ROE; Gen. Man. PABLO ESPAT.

Tropical Air Services (Tropic Air): San Pedro, POB 20, Ambergris Caye; tel. (2) 62012; fax (2) 62338; e-mail djonsson@btl.net; f. 1979; operates internal services and services to Mexico and Guatemala; Chair. CELI McCORKLE; Man. Dir JOHN GREIF.

Tourism

The main tourist attractions are the beaches and the barrier reef, diving, fishing and the Mayan archaeological sites. There are nine major wildlife reserves (including the world's only reserves for the jaguar and for the red-footed booby), and government policy is to develop 'eco-tourism', based on the attractions of an unspoilt environment and Belize's natural history. The country's wildlife also includes howler monkeys and 500 species of birds, and its barrier reef is the second largest in the world. However, in May 2000 scientists reported that the high sea temperatures recorded in 1998, caused by the El Niño phenomenon and global warming, had resulted in extensive damage to the coral population. There were some 390 hotels in Belize in 1999. In the same year there were an estimated 172,292 tourist arrivals and tourist receipts totalled an estimated US $99m. in 1998. In February 1996 the Mundo Maya Agreement was ratified, according to which Belize, El Salvador, Guatemala, Honduras and Mexico would co-operate in the management of Mayan archaeological remains. In February 2000 the Belize Tourist Board announced that all tour operators and guides needed to obtain a licence. In June the Inter-American Development Bank approved a loan of US $11m. towards the Government's tourism development plan. A hotel development in Belize City was to open in 2001.

Belize Tourist Board: Level 2, Central Bank Bldg, POB 325, Gabourel Lane, Belize City; tel. (2) 31913; fax (2) 31943; e-mail info@travelbelize.org; internet www.travelbelize.org; f. 1964; fmrly Belize Tourist Bureau; eight mems; Chair. PATTY ARCEO; Dir TRACY TAEGAR.

Belize Tourism Industry Association (BTIA): 10 North Park St, POB 62, Belize City; tel. (2) 75717; fax (2) 78710; e-mail btia@btl.net; internet www.btia.org; Pres. WADE BEVIER (acting).

BENIN

Introductory Survey

Location, Climate, Language, Religion, Flag, Capital

The Republic of Benin is a narrow stretch of territory in West Africa. The country has an Atlantic coastline of about 100 km (60 miles), flanked by Nigeria to the east and Togo to the west; its northern borders are with Burkina Faso and Niger. Benin's climate is tropical, and is divided into three zones: the north has a rainy season between July and September, with a hot, dry season in October–April; the central region has periods of abundant rain in May–June and in October, while there is year-round precipitation in the south, the heaviest rains being in May–October. Average annual rainfall in Cotonou is 1,300 mm. French is the official language, but each of the indigenous ethnic groups has its own language. Bariba and Fulani are the major languages in the north, while Fon and Yoruba are widely spoken in the south. It is estimated that 35% of the people follow traditional beliefs and customs; about 35% are Christians, mainly Roman Catholics, and the majority of the remainder are Muslims. The national flag (proportions 3 by 2) has a vertical green stripe at the hoist, with equal horizontal stripes of yellow over red in the fly. The administrative capital is Porto-Novo, but most government offices and other state bodies are presently in the economic capital, Cotonou.

Recent History

Benin, called Dahomey until 1975, was formerly part of French West Africa. It became a self-governing republic within the French Community in December 1958, and an independent state on 1 August 1960. The early years of independence were characterized by chronic political instability and by periodic regional unrest, fuelled by long-standing rivalries between north and south.

Elections in December 1960 were won by the Parti dahoméen de l'unité, whose leader, Hubert Maga (a northerner), became the country's first President. In October 1963, following riots by workers and students, Maga was deposed in a coup led by Col (later Gen.) Christophe Soglo, Chief of Staff of the Army. Soglo served as interim Head of State until January 1964, when Sourou-Migan Apithy, a southerner who had been Vice-President under Maga, was elected President. Another southerner, Justin Ahomadegbé, became Prime Minister. In November 1965, following a series of political crises, Gen. Soglo forced Apithy and Ahomadegbé to resign. A provisional Government was formed, but the army intervened again in December, and Soglo assumed power at the head of a military regime. In December 1967 industrial unrest, following a ban on trade union activity, precipitated another coup, led by Maj. (later Lt-Col) Maurice Kouandété. Lt-Col Alphonse Alley, hitherto Chief of Staff, became interim Head of State, and Kouandété Prime Minister.

A return to civilian rule was attempted in 1968. A referendum in March approved a new Constitution, and a presidential election followed in May. All former Heads of State and other leading politicians, banned from contesting the presidency, urged their supporters to boycott the election. Only about 26% of the electorate voted, with the abstention rate reaching 99% in the north. The election was declared void, and in June the military regime nominated Dr Emile-Derlin Zinsou, a former Minister of Foreign Affairs, as President; he was confirmed in office by referendum in the following month. In December 1969 Zinsou was deposed by Lt-Col Kouandété, then Commander-in-Chief of the Army, and a three-member military Directoire assumed power.

In March 1970 a presidential election was held amid violent incidents and widespread claims of irregularities. The poll was abandoned when counting revealed roughly equal support for the three main candidates—Ahomadegbé, Apithy and Maga—to whom the Directoire ceded power in May: it was intended that each member of this Presidential Council would act as Head of State, in rotation, for a two-year period. Maga was the first to hold this office (a concession to the north) and was succeeded in May 1972 by Ahomadegbé. In October, however, the civilian leadership was deposed by Maj. (later Brig.-Gen.) Mathieu Kérékou, Deputy Chief of Staff of the armed forces. Kérékou, a northerner, asserted that his military regime would

be based on equal representation between northern, central and southern regions. In September 1973 a Conseil national révolutionnaire (CNR), comprising representatives from each of these regions, was established.

Kérékou pursued a Marxist-based policy of 'scientific socialism'. Strategic sectors and financial institutions were acquired by the State. Between 1974 and 1978 a decentralized local administration was established, the education system was placed under government control, and the legal system was revised. A restructuring of the armed forces followed an unsuccessful coup attempt in January 1975. A further plot to depose Kérékou, allegedly initiated by the exiled Zinsou, was disclosed in October. In late 1975 the Parti de la révolution populaire du Bénin (PRPB) was established as the sole party, and Dahomey was renamed the People's Republic of Benin.

In January 1977 an airborne attack on Cotonou, led by a French mercenary, Col Robert Denard, was repelled by the armed forces. In August the CNR adopted a *Loi fondamentale* decreeing new structures in government. Elections to a new 'supreme authority', the Assemblée nationale révolutionnaire (ANR), took place in November 1979, when a single list of 336 'People's Commissioners' was approved by 97.5% of voters. At the same time a Comité exécutif national (CEN) was established to replace the CNR. The PRPB designated Kérékou as the sole candidate for President of the Republic, and in February 1980 he was unanimously elected to this office by the ANR. In April 1981 it was announced that Ahomadegbé, Apithy and Maga, imprisoned following the coup of 1972, had been released from house arrest. A gradual moderation in Benin's domestic policies followed, and subsequent ministerial changes reflected a government campaign against corruption and inefficiency. Members of the extreme left lost influence, as did the army, whose officers were by now outnumbered by civilians in the Government.

In February 1984 the ANR amended the *Loi fondamentale*, increasing the mandates of People's Commissioners and of the President from three years to five, while reducing the number of Commissioners to 196. At legislative elections in June 98% of voters approved the single list of People's Commissioners, and in July the ANR re-elected Kérékou, again the sole candidate, as President. Kérékou subsequently consolidated his position, reducing the membership of the CEN and effectively depriving southern communities of influence in government.

In January 1987 Kérékou resigned from the army to become a civilian Head of State. Concern among army officers at perceived corruption within Kérékou's civilian Government, together with opposition to the proposed establishment of a Court of State Security, were the apparent catalysts for a coup attempt in March 1988: almost 150 officers, including members of the Presidential Guard, were reportedly arrested.

Chronic economic difficulties caused Benin to seek stronger ties with the West in the second half of the 1980s. In early 1989 delays in the payment of salaries and of education grants provoked strike action by public-sector employees and students. In June economic adjustment measures were agreed with the IMF and the World Bank, prompting fears of further austerity measures. At elections to the ANR in that month a relative decline in support for the single list of PRBP-approved candidates (which was endorsed by 89.6% of voters) was attributed to dissatisfaction with the economic situation, and labour and academic unrest continued.

In August 1989 the ANR re-elected Kérékou (the sole candidate) as President. A reorganization of the CEN included the appointment of several known proponents of reform. The Government's continued failure to meet its salary commitments to public-sector workers resulted in further disruption in December. Kérékou then yielded to domestic pressure and to demands made by France and other external creditors, instituting radical political changes and abandoning Marxism-Leninism as the official ideology of the State.

A national conference of the 'active forces of the nation' was convened in Cotonou in February 1990. Delegates voted to abolish the *Loi fondamentale* and its institutions: all resolutions adopted by the conference were incorporated in a 'national charter' that was to form the basis of a new constitution. An Haut conseil de la République (HCR) was appointed to assume the functions of the ANR pending the appointment of a new legislature. Among the members of the HCR were former Presidents Ahomadegbé, Maga and Zinsou, all of whom had returned to Benin to lead opposition parties. Presidential and legislative elections, to be held on the basis of universal suffrage, in the context of a multi-party political system, were scheduled for early 1991. A former official of the World Bank (who had briefly been Minister of Finance and Economic Affairs in the mid-1960s), Nicéphore Soglo, was designated interim Prime Minister, and Kérékou subsequently relinquished the defence portfolio to Soglo. The conference also voted to change the country's name to the Republic of Benin.

In March 1990 an amnesty was announced for all political dissidents. The HCR was inaugurated, and Soglo appointed a transitional, civilian Government. Of the previous administration, only Kérékou remained in office. In May civilian administrators replaced the provincial military prefects, prior to an extensive restructuring of the armed forces. Legislation permitting the registration of political parties was promulgated in August. (The PRPB had itself been succeeded by a new party, the Union des forces du progrès, in May.)

After considerable delay, a national referendum on the draft Constitution was conducted on 2 December 1990. Voters were asked to choose between two proposed documents, one of which incorporated a clause stipulating upper and lower age-limits for presidential candidates, and would therefore prevent the candidatures of Ahomadegbé, Maga and Zinsou. It was reported that 95.8% of those who voted approved one or other of the versions, with 79.7% of voters favouring the age-restriction clause.

Some 24 political parties (many of which had formed electoral alliances) contested the legislative election on 17 February 1991. The largest grouping in the new 64-member Assemblée nationale was an alliance of three pro-Soglo parties, which secured 12 seats.

Kérékou and Soglo were among 13 candidates at the first round of the presidential election on 10 March 1991. Soglo, who took 36.2% of the total votes cast, received his greatest support in the south of the country, while Kérékou, who received 27.3% of the overall vote, was reported to have secured the support of more than 80% of voters in the north. Soglo and Kérékou proceeded to a second round of voting, which was conducted two weeks later amid violence and allegations of electoral malpractice. Soglo was elected President, obtaining 67.7% of the total votes cast. In late March, prior to its own dissolution, the HCR granted Kérékou immunity from any legal proceedings connected with actions committed since the *coup d'état* of October 1972.

Soglo was inaugurated as President on 4 April 1991. Shortly afterwards he relinquished the defence portfolio to Désiré Vieyra (his brother-in-law), who was designated Minister of State. In July the defence portfolio was transferred to Florentin Feliho, while Vieyra took the post of Senior Minister, Secretary-General at the Office of the President of the Republic.

As President, Soglo furthered attempts to address Benin's economic problems and to recover state funds allegedly embezzled by former members of the Kérékou regime. None the less, the new administration's inability to pay public-sector salary arrears provoked intermittent labour unrest. There was, moreover, considerable opposition in the Assemblée nationale to elements of the Government's programme of economic reform, notably the sale of former state-owned enterprises to foreign interests. Tensions between the executive and legislature eased somewhat following the formation, in June, of a 34-member pro-Soglo grouping, styled Le Renouveau, in the Assemblée nationale, although Soglo's economic policies continued to be a source of domestic disquiet.

In May 1992, meanwhile, several army officers were arrested following an incident outside the presidential palace in Cotonou. In August it was reported that some of the detainees, including their leader, Capt. Pascal Tawes (formerly deputy commander of the now-disbanded Presidential Guard), had escaped from custody and that Tawes was leading a mutiny at an army camp in the north. The rebellion was quickly suppressed, but Tawes was among those who evaded arrest. (In September 1994 Tawes and 15 others were sentenced *in absentia* to life imprisonment with hard labour, having been convicted of plotting to overthrow the Government.) In March 1993 more than 100 prisoners, including several soldiers who were implicated in the previous

year's disturbances, escaped from detention in Ouidah, in the south-west. The dismissal, shortly afterwards, of the armed forces Chief of Staff and of other senior members of the security forces prompted Feliho to resign the defence portfolio, protesting that Soglo had acted unconstitutionally by unilaterally making new military appointments. Following a reorganization of the Council of Ministers in September, Vieyra, now Minister of State in charge of National Defence, remained the most senior member of the Government. In the following month 15 assembly members withdrew from Le Renouveau, alleging that Soglo was consistently excluding the legislature from the decision-making process. In July Soglo, who had previously asserted his political neutrality, had made public his membership of the (Parti de la) Renaissance du Bénin (RB), formed by his wife, Rosine, in 1992. President Soglo was appointed leader of the RB in July 1994.

Social tensions re-emerged following the 50% devaluation of the CFA franc in January 1994. Following a period of severe labour unrest, in May the Government announced salary increases of 10% for all state employees, as well as the reintroduction of housing allowances (abolished in 1986) and an end to the eight-year freeze on promotions within the civil service. In July, however, the Assemblée nationale approved increases in salaries and student grants that exceeded those envisaged in the Government's draft budget. Soglo announced his intention to impose the draft budget by decree, on the grounds that the imbalanced budget arising from the legislature's amendments was unconstitutional, and would, moreover, result in the loss of funding and debt relief already agreed with external creditors. The Assemblée nationale referred the matter to the Constitutional Court, which effectively ruled that presidential recourse to the relevant article of the Constitution could not be subject to legal control. The payment of salary arrears from 1983–91 began in November 1994.

In November 1994 the Assemblée nationale voted to establish an independent electoral supervisory body, the Commission électorale nationale autonome (CENA), despite opposition from Soglo, who also opposed a planned increase in the number of deputies from 64 to 83. Some 31 political organizations participated in the legislative elections, which took place on 28 March 1995. Provisional results indicated that the RB had won the largest number of seats in the Assemblée nationale, but that opposition parties were likely, in alliance, to outnumber the President's supporters. The final composition of the new parliament remained uncertain, as the results of voting for 13 seats were annulled by the Constitutional Court on the grounds of irregularities. Voting for three seats was repeated in May, although one of the newly elected deputies (a member of the RB) was immediately disqualified by the Constitutional Court as ineligible.

The RB thus held 20 seats in the Assemblée nationale, and other supporters of Soglo held 13. Opposition parties held 49 seats, the most prominent being the Parti du renouveau démocratique (PRD), with 19 seats, and the Front d'action pour le renouveau et le développement—Alafia (FARD—Alafia), which had attracted considerable support from Kérékou supporters in the north (although the former President had not actively campaigned in the election), with 10. In June 1995 Bruno Amoussou, the leader of the opposition Parti social-démocrate, was elected President of the Assemblée nationale. A new Government was formed later in June by the RB.

In late 1995 rumours circulated of a coup plot and of attempts to sabotage a conference of Heads of State and Government of the Conseil permanent de la francophonie, which was due to take place in Cotonou in December. Tensions escalated following a rocket attack in November on the newly-built conference centre at which the summit was to take place. Although the authorities dismissed the attack as a minor act of sabotage, it was subsequently announced that one person had been killed and several arrested, and that munitions stolen during a raid on the Ouidah barracks in early 1994 had been recovered. Among those detained was Soulé Dankoro, a former minister under Kérékou. Although Dankoro and six others were released on bail in April 1996, in September of that year three defendants were sentenced to five years' enforced labour, and one to a year's imprisonment, while a fifth defendant was sentenced *in absentia* to 15 years' imprisonment.

The success of supporters of Kérékou at the 1995 parliamentary elections prompted speculation that Kérékou might again contest the presidency in 1996, and in January 1996 he announced his candidature. While Soglo's economic policies had earned his regime the respect of the international financial community, there was disquiet within Benin that growth had been achieved at the expense of social concerns and that the regime had become increasingly authoritarian. Soglo, meanwhile, asserted that the economic successes now attained would henceforth permit his administration to address unemployment and other social problems exacerbated by the adjustment policies of the first half of the decade.

In December 1995 the Assemblée nationale voted to delay ratification of the third phase of Benin's structural adjustment programme, the most contentious element of which was the planned restructuring of the state company responsible for the distribution of petroleum products, the Société nationale de commercialisation des produits pétroliers (SONACOP). Deputies rejected ratification of a modified programme twice during January 1996, and also rejected the Government's draft budget for that year, prompting Soglo to implement the budget and adjustment programme by decree.

The first round of the presidential election, on 3 March 1996, was contested by seven candidates. As had been expected, Soglo and Kérékou emerged as the leading candidates, although Soglo's supporters alleged widespread vote-rigging. Some 22.8% of the votes cast were subsequently invalidated by the Constitutional Court prior to the announcement of the official results, whereby Soglo secured 35.7% of the valid votes and Kérékou 33.9%, followed by the leader of the PRD, Adrien Houngbédji (19.7%), and Amoussou (7.8%). The rate of participation by voters was high, at 86.9%. Most of the defeated candidates quickly expressed their support for Kérékou, among them Houngbédji, who had in 1975 been sentenced *in absentia* to death for his part in a plot to overthrow Kérékou's military regime.

Indications of a clear victory for Kérékou at the second round of voting, which took place on 18 March 1996, were denounced as fraudulent by Soglo's supporters, and Soglo himself spoke of an international plot to end democracy in Benin, although international monitors declared that the overall result of the election remained credible. On 24 March the Constitutional Court issued the official results, announcing Kérékou's election, with 52.5% of the valid votes. Some 78.1% of those eligible had voted, and less than 3% of the votes had been disallowed. Kérékou won the support of a majority of voters in four of the country's six provinces, and secured more than 90% of the votes in his home province of Atakora; Soglo won some 80% of the votes in his native Zou province, in central Benin, and also performed strongly in Cotonou. On 1 April the Court stated that it had rejected all appeals against the outcome of the election, and accordingly endorsed Kérékou's victory. Soglo conceded defeat the following day.

Having sought authorization by the Constitutional Court for the appointment of a Prime Minister (provision for such a post is not stipulated in the Constitution), in April 1996 Kérékou named Houngbédji as premier in a Government mostly composed of representatives of those parties that had supported his presidential campaign. Kérékou assumed personal responsibility for defence. The Government's stated priorities were to strengthen the rule of law, and to promote economic revival and social development. Addressing a national economic conference in December, Kérékou recognized the need further to develop the private sector, and pledged measures to combat corruption in all areas of public life.

In September 1997 the Assemblée nationale approved an amnesty for electoral and media crimes and all acts seeking to undermine state security committed between January 1990 and June 1996. The amnesty, which most notably benefited members of the military as well as civilians implicated in the events of late 1995, provoked protests by the RB, which warned that the measure would exacerbate ethnic and regional divisions, as well as tensions and indiscipline within the army. The law was promulgated by Kérékou shortly afterwards, but in October 1997 the Constitutional Court invalidated the amnesty legislation, on the grounds that the failure of the Government to consult the Supreme Court rendered such legislation unconstitutional.

In late 1997 the Government was obliged to revise its budgetary provisions for 1998, after the legislature rejected proposals to end automatic promotions within the civil service. The proposed emphasis on promotions according to merit, in accordance with IMF recommendations, had prompted strike action by state employees. In March 1998, following several weeks of disruption by some 37,000 civil servants, agreement was reached on the payment of salary arrears that had accumulated since 1992, valued by the Government at 5,000m. francs CFA,

as well as on efforts to preserve jobs in recently privatized enterprises. In May, however, civil servants announced their intention to resume strike action, in protest at the State's failure to honour its commitment to pay arrears. Kérékou met with trade union leaders, undertaking personally to address the issue of salary arrears, and, moreover, invited the unions to nominate a new minister with responsibility for the civil service. A general strike none the less proceeded in mid-May. Meanwhile, Houngbédji, who was apparently dissatisfied at his exclusion from the drafting of the 1998 budget, and who was reportedly concerned that an impending government reshuffle would result in a loss of influence for himself and the PRD, resigned the premiership. Kérékou named a new Government in which there was no Prime Minister, the most senior minister being Pierre Osho (hitherto Minister of Foreign Affairs and Co-operation) as Minister-delegate to the Presidency, in charge of Defence and Relations with the Institutions.

In early March 1999 six people were sentenced to prison terms of between two and 12 years, having been convicted on charges involving forgery and fraudulent distribution of voting cards and falsification of voters' lists, in advance of legislative elections scheduled for later in the month; charges in connection with similar offences remained against about 40 defendants. A three-day strike by workers at the state radio and television broadcasting company caused some disruption to campaigning immediately prior to the elections. Polling proceeded on 30 March, with more than 2,900 candidates, representing 35 parties and alliances, contesting the 83 seats in the Assemblée nationale. International monitors reported that the elections had been conducted peacefully and democratically. Official results, issued by the CENA on 3 April and confirmed by the Constitutional Council one week later, indicated that the combined opposition parties had won a slender majority in the legislature, with 42 seats. Voting was generally divided along regional lines. The largest number of seats was won by the RB, principally in the south and centre (including eight of Cotonou's nine seats); Rosine Soglo was expected to remain as the party's parliamentary leader. FARD—Alafia (10 seats), the PSD (nine seats) and other parties loyal to the President performed strongly in the north and west. The PRD, which won 11 seats, was, however, strongly challenged in the east, particularly by the pro-Kérékou Mouvement africain pour la démocratie et le progrès, which won six seats overall. The rate of participation by voters was in excess of 70%. Both the presidential group and the new parliamentary majority expressed optimism regarding the forthcoming period of institutional 'cohabitation'. In April Houngbédji was elected Speaker of the new assembly, defeating Amoussou.

In June 1999 Kérékou effected a government reshuffle, increasing the number of parties represented in the Council of Ministers from seven to 10, in an apparent effort to consolidate his support in the Assemblée nationale. Five new ministers were appointed, most notably Bruno Amoussou, who became Minister of State, in charge of Co-ordinating Government Action, Planning, Development and Promotion of Employment; Pierre Osho remained as Minister-delegate at the Presidency, in charge of National Defence, while Abdoulaye Bio Tchané retained the finance and economy portfolio.

The findings of a commission of inquiry into official corruption in Benin, established by Kérékou following his election in 1996, were published in July 1999. The commission, which had identified 167 suspected cases of financial misappropriation, revealed that public funds valued at more than 70,000m. francs CFA had been embezzled in the three years to April 1999. At the end of July the Government instituted a code of ethics that excluded those convicted of corruption from public office and obliged the disclosure of all payments made during tendering for state projects. Kérékou announced that legal action was to be taken against those implicated in financial misappropriation, but no cases identified by the commission were taken to court within one year of the report's publication.

In October 1999 an estimated 32,000 civil servants undertook a three-day general strike after public-sector unions and the Government failed to reach agreement on the payment of salary arrears (valued by the unions at some 18,000m. francs CFA) and the abolition of the new meritocratic system of promotions. The Government, while deploring the strike action, expressed willingness to pursue negotiations with workers' representatives. In November, however, some unions began further industrial action, claiming that offers made by the Government were not satisfactory. Agreement was subsequently reached on the creation of a bipartite commission to investigate a new system of remuneration and promotion for the civil service, and on the payment of salary arrears. None the less, one trade union federation, the Centrale des organisations syndicales indépendantes, resumed strike action the following week, demanding the immediate implementation of the provisions of the agreement.

In January 2000 the President imposed the budget for 2000 by decree, after the opposition in the Assemblée nationale had rejected its provisions, claiming to have noted procedural irregularities in its preparation. In the same month members of the armed forces demonstrated in Cotonou in order to complain that they had not received the bonus payments due to them for their service in West African peace-keeping missions; the Government later admitted that sums of money due to the troops had been misappropriated by senior military figures. Kérékou subsequently announced that he suspected the armed forces and certain opposition parties of preparing a *coup d'état*. The opposition challenged the President to produce evidence of his claims, and, in its turn, accused the Government of conspiring to assassinate ex-President Soglo prior to the presidential elections due to take place in March 2001. In early 2000 Soglo and Houngbédji formed a new alliance of 10 opposition parties. The alliance condemned the perceived corruption of the Kérékou administration, particularly in relation to the privatization of SONACOP and the Government's reputed manipulation of the media.

In June 2000 one of Benin's principal trade union federations, the Centrale syndicale autonome du Bénin, undertook a 48-hour strike in order to protest at the rapid escalation of the cost of petroleum (rises of up to 77% had been announced earlier in the month), and to demand improvements in salaries and social welfare. Popular discontent at the rises continued to escalate, and in July an estimated 10,000 people attended a public demonstration in Cotonou, organized by Benin's six trade union federations. The Government later announced that funds would be made available for social measures to compensate those affected by the price rise. The trade union federations, however, rejected the Government's proposals as inadequate, and called for further demonstrations. In January 2001 a demonstration of students protesting in favour of increased scholarships led to clashes with the security forces. Civil servants also staged a 72-hour strike to protest against the non-payment of salary arrears.

In the period preceding the presidential election Soglo was widely regarded as the sole credible challenger to Kérékou, who confirmed his candidacy in early February 2001. In January a dispute had broken out between the Constitutional Court and the Assemblée nationale regarding the latter's nomination of 19 commissioners to serve on the 25-member CENA; supporters of Kérékou twice referred the matter to the court after opponents of Kérékou, who held a slender parliamentary majority, selected a majority of candidates from the opposition. In both cases the court rejected the proposed list of appointees as unrepresentative of the political composition of the assembly; a third, more balanced list was accepted in late January.

During the two weeks preceding the first round of the presidential election, which was held on 4 March 2001, corruption emerged as a leading issue, as allegations emerged of fraudulent behaviour by both Kérékou and Soglo with regard to large public-sector companies. The election was contested by 17 candidates. Early results issued by the CENA indicated that Kérékou had gained a larger share of the vote than any other candidate, with Soglo in second place; however, as no candidate had secured an absolute majority, a second round was scheduled for 18 March.

As campaigning by supporters of Soglo and Kérékou proceeded, the Constitutional Court conducted a review of the election results declared by the CENA, following the discovery of anomalies and irregularities. Revised provisional results, issued on 13 March, gave Kérékou 45.4% of the votes cast (compared with 47.1% initially announced), Soglo 27.1% (compared with 28.9%), Adrien Houngbédji 12.6% (previously 13.5%) and Bruno Amoussou (who had originally been placed fifth, with only 4.0%) 8.6%. The revised results also indicated an increase in the electoral roll by some 300,000 and a participation rate of around 80%. Following the declaration of these results, Houngbédji endorsed the candidature of Soglo, while Amoussou encouraged his supporters to vote for Kérékou, who stated that he would form a broad-based government of national unity, if re-elected.

Meanwhile, there were calls for a boycott of the second round of elections, owing to alleged irregularities in the conduct of the first round, which reputedly included incidences of vote-buying

and the use of state facilities by political parties. Soglo appealed to the Constitutional Court to annul the disputed results, and to re-run the election, either in those constituencies, or on a nation-wide basis. On 16 March, two days before the poll, Soglo, having had his appeal rejected, withdrew from the second round of the election. The Government postponed the second round of the election, which was to be contested by Kérékou and Houngbédji, firstly until 19 March and subsequently until 22 March. However, on 19 March Houngbédji also declared his dissatisfaction with the conduct of the election and withdrew from the second round. Consequently, Amoussou, who had previously declared his support for Kérékou, was now to challenge him for the presidency. Nine opposition members of the CENA resigned in protest at the organization of the election and alleged that a small group close to both Kérékou and Amoussou had effectively manipulated the commission to their own ends.

The second round duly took place on 22 March in largely peaceful conditions, although violence was reported in Zangnanado, a stronghold of support for Soglo. Voter participation, at about 55%, was, however, significantly lower than in the first round. On 24 March, the CENA announced that Kérékou had received 84.06% of valid votes cast, with Amoussou receiving 15.94%. Kérékou was thus declared President for a further term, although supporters of Soglo announced that they would appeal to the Constitutional Court to annul the result, on the grounds that the depleted CENA was not qualified to organize the elections. A government reshuffle was effected in May.

Under the Soglo administration extensive efforts were made to foster harmonious trading and diplomatic relations with external creditors. Relations with France (Benin's principal trading partner and supplier of aid, and a prominent advocate of Benin's transition to multi-party democracy) were generally cordial, as were links with the USA and other creditors. Following Kérékou's election to the presidency in March 1996, there was some initial uncertainty regarding his Government's likely conduct of external political and economic relations, particularly with the IMF (which stipulated continued spending restraint as a precondition for assistance). However, Kérékou swiftly demonstrated a pragmatic approach to international economic relations, making an official visit to France in October, during which he requested French assistance in transferring the economic capital from Cotonou to the administrative capital, Porto-Novo.

Benin has in recent years played an active role in efforts to co-ordinate regional peace-keeping and humanitarian assistance operations. In late 1998 Benin contributed some 140 troops to the peace-keeping operations in Guinea-Bissau undertaken by the ECOWAS Cease-Fire Monitoring Group (ECOMOG, see p. 172), although the force was withdrawn in mid-1999 following the *coup d'état* in Guinea-Bissau. Benin maintains generally good relations with neighbouring countries, although in mid-2000 a long-term dispute between Benin and Niger over the ownership of various small islands in the Niger river, erupted once more after Nigerien soldiers reportedly sabotaged the construction of a Beninois administrative building on the island of Lété. A meeting between representatives of the two Governments failed to resolve the dispute, which was subsequently referred to the Organization of African Unity for arbitration.

Government

The Constitution of the Republic of Benin, which was approved in a national referendum on 2 December 1990, provides for a civilian, multi-party political system. Executive power is vested in the President of the Republic, who is elected by direct universal adult suffrage with a five-year mandate, renewable only once. The legislature is the 83-member Assemblée nationale, which is similarly elected, for a period of four years, by universal suffrage. The President of the Republic appoints the Council of Ministers, subject to formal parliamentary approval.

For the purposes of local administration, Benin is divided into 12 departments, each administered by a civilian prefect.

Defence

In August 2000 the Beninois Armed Forces numbered an estimated 4,750 in active service (land army 4,500, navy about 100, air force 150). Paramilitary forces comprised a 2,500-strong gendarmerie. Military service is by selective conscription, and lasts for 18 months. The estimated defence budget for 2000 was 26,000m. francs CFA.

Economic Affairs

In 1998, according to estimates by the World Bank, Benin's gross national product (GNP), measured at average 1996–98 prices, was US $2,252m., equivalent to $380 per head (or $857 on an international purchasing-power parity basis). During 1990–98, it was estimated, GNP per head increased at an average annual rate of 1.8% in real terms. Over the same period the population was estimated to have increased at an average rate of 3.3% per year. GNP in 1999 was estimated at $2,300m., equivalent to $380 per head. Benin's gross domestic product (GDP) increased, in real terms, by an average of 4.7% per year in 1990–99. Real GDP increased by 4.5% in 1998 and by an estimated 5.0% in 1999.

Agriculture (including forestry and fishing) contributed 40.8% of GDP in 1999. In that year an estimated 55.0% of the labour force were employed in the sector. The principal cash crops are cotton (exports of which accounted for an estimated 83.9% of domestic exports and 51.6% of total exports in 1997) and oil palm. Benin is normally self-sufficient in basic foods; the main subsistence crops are yams, cassava and maize. The World Bank estimated that agricultural GDP increased at an average annual rate of 5.3% in 1990–99; growth of 4.7% was estimated in 1999.

Industry (including mining, manufacturing, construction and power) contributed 14.7% of GDP in 1999, and engaged 10.4% of the employed labour force at the time of the 1992 census. According to the World Bank, industrial GDP increased at an average annual rate of 3.8% in 1990–99; growth of 3.4% was estimated in 1999.

Mining contributed only 0.2% of GDP in 1999, and engaged less than 0.1% of the employed labour force in 1992. Petroleum extraction at Sémé was terminated on the grounds of unprofitability in 1998, although a contract signed between Benin and the multinational Zetah Oil Company in October 1999 envisaged the exploitation of Sémé's remaining petroleum reserves, estimated at some 22m. barrels. Marble and limestone are also exploited commercially. There are also deposits of gold, phosphates, natural gas, iron ore, silica sand, peat and chromium. The GDP of the mining sector was estimated to have declined by an average of 8.8% per year in 1990–97.

The manufacturing sector, which contributed 8.9% of GDP in 1999, engaged 7.8% of the employed labour force in 1992. The sector is based largely on the processing of primary products (principally cotton-ginning and oil-palm processing). Construction materials and some simple consumer goods are also produced for the domestic market. According to the World Bank, manufacturing GDP increased at an average annual rate of 5.6% in 1990–98; growth of 6.5% was estimated in 1999.

Benin is at present highly dependent on imports of electricity from Ghana (which supplied some 85% of total available production in 1996). It is envisaged that a hydroelectric installation on the Mono river, constructed and operated jointly with Togo, will reduce Benin's dependence on imported electricity, and a second such installation is under construction downstream. In 2000 the construction of a further electricity line, to run from Lagos, Nigeria, to Togo, through Benin, was proposed by the Governments of the three countries. It is also planned to construct a pipeline to supply natural gas from Nigeria to Benin, Togo and Ghana. Imports of petroleum products accounted for some 9.5% of the value of domestic imports in 1997.

The services sector contributed 44.5% of GDP in 1999, and engaged 31.8% of the employed labour force in 1992. The port of Cotonou is of considerable importance as an entrepôt for regional trade: re-exports comprised an estimated 38.5% of the value of total exports in 1997. According to the World Bank, the GDP of the services sector increased by an average of 4.4% per year in 1990–99; growth of 5.7% was estimated in 1999.

In 1999, according to provisional figures, Benin recorded a visible trade deficit of 109,200m. francs CFA, while there was a deficit of 71,000m. francs CFA on the current account of the balance of payments. In 1995 the principal source of imports (34.8%) was France; other major sources were Thailand, the USA and the Netherlands. The principal market for exports in that year was Brazil (20.0%); other important purchasers were Portugal, Morocco, India and Thailand. The principal exports in 1997 were ginned cotton (providing an estimated 79.3% of total domestic exports) and cottonseed. The main imports in 1990 were miscellaneous manufactured articles (most notably cotton yarn and fabrics), foodstuffs (particularly cereals), fuels, machinery and transport equipment, chemical products and beverages and tobacco.

In 1999 Benin recorded an overall budget surplus of an estimated 15,500m. francs CFA (equivalent to 1.1% of GDP). The country's total external debt at the end of 1998 was US $1,647m., of which $1,469m. was long-term public debt. In that year the cost of debt-servicing was equivalent to 10.6% of the value of exports of goods and services. The annual rate of inflation, which had been negligible prior to the 50% devaluation of the CFA franc in January 1994, increased to 38.5% in 1994, but slowed to an average of 3.6% per year in 1995–99; average inflation was 5.7% in 1998 and 0.3% in 1999. About one-quarter of the urban labour force was estimated to be unemployed in 1997.

Benin is a member of the Economic Community of West African States (ECOWAS, see p. 170), of the West African organs of the Franc Zone (see p. 210), of the African Petroleum Producers' Association (APPA, see p. 303), of the Conseil de l'Entente (see p. 307) and of the Niger Basin Authority (see p. 309).

Benin has experienced considerable economic growth since the beginning of the 1990s, with significant success achieved in strengthening public finances, improving the external balance-of-payments position and in reforming the financial sector. A new three-year Enhanced Structural Adjustment Facility was agreed with the IMF in August 1996, envisaging average annual growth of almost 6%. The renewal of co-operation with the IMF ensured debt relief measures, notably along concessionary terms by the 'Paris Club' of official creditors. The Government's slow progress in the privatization of a number of major state enterprises and in the reform of the civil service led the IMF to suspend disbursements during 1998. The facility was, however, resumed in January 1999, after the Government agreed to implement the agreed structural reforms. Severe electricity shortages in mid-1998, caused by generating difficulties in Ghana, slowed GDP growth in that year to 4.5%, but estimated increases of 5.0% in 1999 and 5.3% in 2000 were largely attributed to a recovery in cotton output and in manufacturing production. Allegations of corruption and malpractice in the privatization of the state enterprise responsible for the distribution of petroleum products, the Société nationale de commercialisation des produits pétroliers, heightened public concerns regarding the restructuring of the economy in 2000, although the Government remained committed to extending its privatization programme and agreed to improve divestiture procedures. In July 2000, as part of the Heavily Indebted Poor Countries (HIPC) initiative, the IMF and the World Bank cancelled some US $460m. of Benin's debt, and announced a further three-year enhanced HIPC programme for 2000–2003. Also in that month the IMF approved funding of some $35.7m., under its Poverty Reduction and Growth Facility, in support of the Government's economic programme for 2000–03. Structural reforms envisaged in the programme included the liberalization of the cotton sector, increased private-sector involvement in the management of public utilities and the reform of the civil service.

Social Welfare

In 1995 Benin had one doctor per 20,000 people and one midwife per 12,000 people. In that year only 42% of the population had access to health care. In mid-1995 the International Development Association approved funding of US $27.8m., in support of a health and population project (costing $33.4m.) a principal aim of which was to be the establishment of a nation-wide family planning programme. Moreover, a particular emphasis of economic policy for the second half of the 1990s was to be the improvement of health care and social services provisions for the poorest sectors of the population. There is a minimum wage for workers (which stood at 21,924 francs CFA per month in 1997). In 1996 the Social Security Fund's total expenditure was 5,382m. francs CFA. Spending on health in 1997 amounted to 15,100m. francs CFA.

Education

The Constitution of Benin obliges the state to make a quality compulsory primary education available to all children. All public primary and secondary schools in Benin finance themselves through school fees. Primary education begins at six years of age and lasts for six years. Secondary education, beginning at 12 years of age, lasts for up to seven years, comprising a first cycle of four years and a second of three years. Primary enrolment in 1996 included 63% of children in the appropriate age-group (males 80%; females 47%). Enrolment at secondary schools in that year was equivalent to only 17% (males 24%; females 10%). In the 1990s the Government sought to extend the provision of education. In 1993 girls in rural areas were exempted from school fees, and in 1999 the Government created a 500m. francs CFA fund to increase female enrolment. The University of Benin, at Cotonou, was founded in 1970 and had a student population of approximately 9,000 in 1999/2000. In 1996 14,055 students were enrolled at tertiary institutions. Adult illiteracy at the time of the 1992 census was 72.7% (males 60.0%; females 83.3%). In 1995, according to UNESCO estimates, the average rate of adult illiteracy was 68.4% (males 55.1%; females 80.9%). In 1995 the Government spent 31,074m. francs CFA on education (equivalent to 15.2% of total expenditure by the central Government).

Public Holidays

2001: 1 January (New Year's Day), 10 January (*Vodoun* national holiday), 16 January (Martyrs' Day, anniversary of mercenary attack on Cotonou), 6 March* (Id al-Adha, Feast of the Sacrifice), 1 April (Youth Day), 13 April (Good Friday), 16 April (Easter Monday), 1 May (Workers' Day), 24 May (Ascension Day), 4 June (Whit Monday), 1 August (Independence Day), 15 August (Assumption), 26 October (Armed Forces Day), 1 November (All Saints' Day), 30 November (National Day), 17 December* (Id al-Fitr, end of Ramadan), 25 December (Christmas Day), 31 December (Harvest Day).

2002: 1 January (New Year's Day), 10 January (*Vodoun* national holiday), 16 January (Martyrs' Day, anniversary of mercenary attack on Cotonou), 23 February* (Id al-Adha, Feast of the Sacrifice), 29 March (Good Friday), 1 April (Youth Day and Easter Monday), 1 May (Workers' Day), 9 May (Ascension Day), 20 May (Whit Monday), 1 August (Independence Day), 15 August (Assumption), 26 October (Armed Forces Day), 1 November (All Saints' Day), 30 November (National Day), 6 December* (Id al-Fitr, end of Ramadan), 25 December (Christmas Day), 31 December (Harvest Day).

* These holidays are dependent on the Islamic lunar calendar and may vary by one or two days from the dates given.

Weights and Measures

The metric system is in force.

Statistical Survey

Source (unless otherwise stated): Institut National de la Statistique et de l'Analyse Economique, Ministère du Plan, de la Restructuration Economique et de la Promotion de l'Emploi, BP 342, Cotonou; tel. 31-05-41; fax 30-16-60; e-mail insae_cici@planben.intnet.bj; internet planben.intnet.bj.

Area and Population

AREA, POPULATION AND DENSITY

Area (sq km) .	112,622*
Population (census results)	
20–30 March 1979	
Total	3,331,210
15–29 February 1992	
Males	2,390,336
Females .	2,525,219
Total	4,915,555
Population (official estimates at mid-year)	
1996	5,594,499
1997	5,828,000
1998	6,044,000
Density (per sq km) at mid-1998	53.7

* 43,484 sq miles.

ETHNIC GROUPS

1992 census (percentages): Fon 42.2; Adja 15.6; Yoruba 12.1; Bariba 8.6; Otamari 6.1; Peulh 6.1; Yoa-Lokpa 3.8; Dendi 2.8; Others 2.7.

POPULATION BY PROVINCE (1992 census)

Atakora .	649,308
Atlantique	1,066,373
Borgou	827,925
Mono .	676,377
Ouémé .	876,574
Zou .	818,998
Total	4,915,555

Note: Legislation was approved in August 1997 whereby Benin was reorganized into 12 administrative departments: Alibori, Atacora, Atlantique, Borgou, Colline, Donga, Couffo, Littoral, Mono, Ouémé, Plateau, Zou.

PRINCIPAL TOWNS (official estimates, 1994)

Cotonou	750,000	Djougou	132,000
Porto-Novo (capital)	200,000	Parakou	120,000

Source: La Zone Franc, *Rapport Annuel 1997*.

BIRTHS AND DEATHS (UN estimates, annual averages)

	1980–85	1985–90	1990–95
Birth rate (per 1,000)	51.4	49.0	44.2
Death rate (per 1,000)	17.7	16.2	14.4

Expectation of life (UN estimates, years at birth, 1990–95): 52.5 (males 50.7; females 54.5).
Source: UN, *World Population Prospects: The 1998 Revision*.
1998 (official estimates at mid-year): Birth rate (per 1,000) 45.82; Death rate (per 1,000) 12.77; Expectation of life (years at birth) 53.61.

ECONOMICALLY ACTIVE POPULATION
(persons aged 10 years and over, 1992 census)

	Males	Females	Total
Agriculture, hunting, forestry and fishing	780,469	367,277	1,147,746
Mining and quarrying	609	52	661
Manufacturing	93,157	67,249	160,406
Electricity, gas and water	1,152	24	1,176
Construction .	50,959	696	51,655
Trade, restaurants and hotels	36,672	395,829	432,501
Transport, storage and communications	52,228	609	52,837
Finance, insurance, real estate and business services	2,705	401	3,106
Community, social and personal services	126,122	38,422	164,544
Activities not adequately defined	25,579	12,917	38,496
Total employed	1,169,652	883,476	2,053,128
Unemployed .	26,475	5,843	32,318
Total labour force	1,196,127	889,319	2,085,446

Source: ILO, *Yearbook of Labour Statistics*.

Mid-1999 (estimates in '000): Agriculture, etc. 1,488; Total 2,706 (Source: FAO).

Agriculture

PRINCIPAL CROPS ('000 metric tons)

	1997	1998	1999
Rice (paddy) .	29	36	37
Maize	728	662	679
Millet .	27	29	30
Sorghum	120	138	142
Sweet potatoes	60	41	40
Cassava (Manioc)	1,926	1,989	2,063
Yams .	1,514	1,584	1,628
Taro (Coco yam) .	4	4	4
Dry beans	77	75	77
Groundnuts (in shell) .	107	99	101
Coconuts*	20	20	20
Palm kernels*	14	14	14
Tomatoes	127	106	108
Chillies and peppers (green) .	24	20	20*
Other vegetables .	158	159	173
Oranges*	12	12	12
Mangoes*	12	12	12
Bananas*	13	13	13
Pineapples*	59	45	78
Other fruit* .	108	108	108
Cotton (lint) .	155	150	150

* FAO estimate(s).
Source: FAO.

LIVESTOCK ('000 head, year ending September)

	1997	1998	1999
Horses*	6	6	6
Asses*	1	1	1
Cattle	1,399	1,345	1,438
Pigs	580*	470	470*
Sheep	668*	634	645
Goats	1,020*	1,087	1,183
Poultry* .	27,000	29,000	29,000

* FAO estimate(s).
Source: FAO.

LIVESTOCK PRODUCTS ('000 metric tons)

	1997	1998	1999
Beef and veal	20	20	23
Mutton and lamb	3	3	2
Goat meat	4	4	4
Pig meat	8	6	6
Poultry meat	30	33	22
Other meat	6	6	6
Cows' milk	20	19	19*
Goats' milk	5	6	6
Poultry eggs	19	19	19
Cattle hides	3	3	3
Goatskins	1	1	1

* FAO estimate.

Source: FAO.

Forestry

ROUNDWOOD REMOVALS
('000 cubic metres, excl. bark)

	1996	1997	1998
Sawlogs, veneer logs and logs for sleepers	50	50	50
Other industrial wood	274	282	289
Fuel wood	5,361	5,506	5,655
Total	5,685	5,838	5,994

Source: FAO, *Yearbook of Forest Products*.

SAWNWOOD PRODUCTION
('000 cubic metres, incl. railway sleepers)

	1996	1997	1998
Total (all broadleaved)	24	24	24

Source: FAO, *Yearbook of Forest Products*.

Fishing

('000 metric tons, live weight)

	1996	1997	1998
Tilapias*	10.7	10.3	10.2
Torpedo-shaped catfishes*	2.1	2.0	2.0
Groupers and seabasses*	1.6	2.2	2.1
Threadfins and tasselfishes*	1.1	1.5	1.4
Madeiran sardinella*	1.5	2.1	2.0
Bonga shad*	1.8	1.7	1.7
Freshwater crustaceans*	4.3	4.1	4.1
Penaeus shrimps	2.9	2.8*	2.8*
Total catch (incl. others)	42.2	43.8	43.2

* FAO estimate(s).

Note: Figures exclude catches by Beninois canoes operating from outside the country.

Source: FAO, *Yearbook of Fishery Statistics*.

Mining

('000 barrels)

	1996	1997	1998
Crude petroleum	552.1	455.1	355.9

Source: Banque centrale des états de l'Afrique de l'ouest.

Industry

SELECTED PRODUCTS ('000 metric tons, unless otherwise indicated)

	1993	1994	1995
Salted, dried or smoked fish*	2.0	2.0	2.0
Cement†	380	380	380
Electric energy (million kWh)‡	5	6	6

1996: Electric energy (million kWh): 6‡.

* Data from FAO.
† Data from the US Bureau of Mines.
‡ Provisional or estimated figure(s).

Source: UN, *Industrial Commodity Statistics Yearbook*.

Cement (estimates, '000 metric tons): 360 in 1996; 450 in 1997; 520 in 1998; 520 in 1999 (Source: US Geological Survey).
Palm oil and palm kernel oil ('000 metric tons): 10.8 in 1993; 10.3 in 1994; 5.4 in 1995; 7.4 in 1996; 6.6 in 1997 (Source: IMF, *Benin: Selected Issues and Statistical Appendix*, September 1998).

Finance

CURRENCY AND EXCHANGE RATES

Monetary Units
100 centimes = 1 franc de la Communauté financière africaine (CFA).

Sterling, Dollar and Euro Equivalents (29 December 2000)
£1 sterling = 1,051.93 francs CFA;
US $1 = 704.95 francs CFA;
€1 = 655.96 francs CFA;
10,000 francs CFA = £9.506 = $14.185 = €15.245.

Average Exchange Rate (francs CFA per US $)
1998   589.95
1999   615.70
2000   711.98

Note: An exchange rate of 1 French franc = 50 francs CFA, established in 1948, remained in force until January 1994, when the CFA franc was devalued by 50%, with the exchange rate adjusted to 1 French franc = 100 francs CFA. This relationship to French currency remained in effect with the introduction of the euro on 1 January 1999. From that date, accordingly, a fixed exchange rate of €1 = 655.957 francs CFA has been in operation.

BUDGET ('000 million francs CFA)

Revenue	1997	1998	1999
Tax revenue	158.9	182.6	200.8
Direct taxation	44.5	49.7	n.a.
Indirect taxation	114.4	132.9	n.a.
Taxes on goods and services	81.2	83.9	n.a.
Taxes on international transactions	22.9	37.9	n.a.
Non-tax revenue	23.1	28.7	34.1
Total	182.0	211.3	234.9

Expenditure*	1997	1998	1999
Current expenditure	151.4	144.7	159.5
Salaries	62.0	64.6	66.3
Interest due	21.1	13.6	13.8
Domestic debt	2.7	2.6	2.4
External debt	18.4	11.0	11.4
Capital expenditure	83.7	77.5	87.6
Internal financing	11.9	15.0	22.8
External financing	71.8	62.5	64.8
Total	235.1	222.1	247.1

* Excluding net lending ('000 million francs CFA): –0.7 in 1997; 1.9 in 1998; 4.5 in 1999.

Source: Banque centrale des états de l'Afrique de l'ouest.

2000 (draft budget, '000 million francs CFA): Revenue 251.3; Expenditure 375.8.

INTERNATIONAL RESERVES (US $ million at 31 December)

	1997	1998	1999
Gold*	3.4	3.3	3.3
IMF special drawing rights . .	0.1	0.1	0.2
Reserve position in IMF . .	2.9	3.1	3.0
Foreign exchange . . .	250.1	258.4	396.8
Total	256.5	264.9	403.3

* Valued at market-related prices.

Source: IMF, *International Financial Statistics*.

MONEY SUPPLY ('000 million francs CFA at 31 December)

	1997	1998	1999
Currency outside banks . .	80.8	70.4	160.3
Demand deposit at deposit money banks	107.5	108.4	104.2
Checking deposits at post office .	4.4	4.7	5.1
Total money (incl. others) . .	193.4	184.2	270.6

Source: IMF, *International Financial Statistics*.

COST OF LIVING
(Consumer price index; base: 1992 = 100)

	1997	1998	1999
Food (incl. beverages) . . .	189.2	203.0	202.4
All items	172.6	182.6	183.1

Source: UN, *Monthly Bulletin of Statistics*.

NATIONAL ACCOUNTS
('000 million francs CFA at current prices)

Expenditure on the Gross Domestic Product

	1998	1999	2000
Government final consumption expenditure . . .	119.6	125.6	132.0
Private final consumption expenditure . . .	1,099.4	1,155.2	1,237.2
Increase in stocks . . .	6.8	7.2	7.9
Gross fixed capital formation . .	242.0	271.5	311.1
Total domestic expenditure .	1,467.8	1,559.5	1,688.2
Exports of goods and services .	367.8	398.3	439.3
Less Imports of goods and services	474.8	504.7	546.5
GDP in purchasers' values .	1,360.6	1,453.2	1,581.0

Source: IMF, *International Financial Statistics*.

Gross Domestic Product by Economic Activity

	1997	1998	1999
Agriculture, livestock, forestry, hunting and fishing . .	479.8	524.8	553.5
Mining	4.6	4.4	3.3
Manufacturing and handicrafts .	104.9	111.9	120.4
Water, gas and electricity . .	10.1	9.6	10.9
Construction and public works .	54.6	58.5	64.4
Trade and hotels . . .	222.5	245.4	267.2
Transport and communications .	87.8	97.1	101.2
Financial services . . .	115.7	129.4	139.1
Other services . . .	86.5	90.9	95.5
GDP at factor cost . . .	1,166.5	1,271.9	1,355.5
Indirect taxes, *less* subsidies .	83.3	88.7	97.7
GDP in purchasers' values	1,249.8	1,360.6	1,453.2

Source: Banque centrale des états de l'Afrique de l'ouest.

BALANCE OF PAYMENTS ('000 million francs CFA)

	1997	1998	1999*
Exports of goods f.o.b. . .	247.5	244.4	237.2
Imports of goods f.o.b. . .	−336.7	−337.8	−346.4
Trade balance	−89.2	−93.4	−109.2
Services and other income (net)	−44.6	−36.8	−42.3
Balance on goods, services and income	−133.8	−130.2	−151.5
Private unrequited transfers (net)	35.6	42.2	59.4
Public unrequited transfers (net) .	8.3	9.9	21.1
Current balance . . .	−89.8	−78.1	−71.0
Capital account . . .	49.3	39.3	27.5
Direct investments . . .	8.0	19.3	14.4
Portfolio investments . . .	−5.4	15.6	101.4
Other investments . . .	79.5	−17.6	22.5
Net errors and omissions . .	3.9	4.2	—
Overall balance . . .	45.6	−17.3	94.8

* Provisional figures.

Source: Banque centrale des états de l'Afrique de l'ouest.

External Trade

PRINCIPAL COMMODITIES (million francs CFA)

Imports c.i.f.*	1988	1989	1990
Food products	25,743	12,814	17,863
Food products of animal origin . .	2,856	2,040	1,300
Food products of plant origin . .	19,655	8,579	15,020
Rice	13,523	4,753	9,110
Wheat	2,170	1,769	3,562
Processed foodstuffs . . .	3,222	2,195	1,543
Beverages and tobacco . . .	4,643	4,688	5,268
Alcoholic beverages . . .	1,863	1,199	2,241
Manufactured tobacco products .	2,760	3,482	2,983
Energy products	13,343	10,113	10,393
Refined petroleum products . .	9,355	5,795	6,158
Other raw materials (inedible) .	4,500	2,449	2,410
Machinery and transport equipment	13,302	9,593	7,860
Non-electrical machinery . . .	5,478	3,486	n.a.
Electrical machinery . . .	4,239	2,251	n.a.
Road transport equipment . .	3,454	3,812	n.a.
Other industrial products . .	34,774	25,036	28,026
Chemical products . . .	7,726	4,710	7,235
Fertilizers	866	3	1,533
Miscellaneous manufactured articles	27,048	20,326	20,791
Cotton yarn and fabrics . .	14,988	11,160	7,715
Total (incl. others) . . .	97,257	66,132	72,192

* Excluding imports for re-export.

Source: Banque centrale des états de l'Afrique de l'ouest.

Exports f.o.b.*†	1995	1996	1997‡
Crude petroleum	4,700	5,200	5,000
Cottonseed	8,500	4,800	6,500
Cotton (ginned)	86,400	107,600	112,700
Palm and palm-kernel oil . .	3,200	900	1,200
Total (incl. others) . . .	117,300	134,300	142,100

* Excluding re-exports (million francs CFA†): 85,000 in 1995; 81,700 in 1996; 89,000‡ in 1997.

† Figures rounded to the nearest 100 million francs CFA.

‡ Estimate(s).

Source: IMF, *Benin: Selected Issues and Statistical Appendix* (September 1998).

PRINCIPAL TRADING PARTNERS (US $ '000)

Imports c.i.f.	1993	1994	1995
China, People's Repub. . . .	33,151	17,730	20,420
Côte d'Ivoire. . . .	10,138	12,506	23,353
France (incl. Monaco) . . .	148,499	111,522	225,347
Germany	16,798	21,588	22,758
Japan	33,844	24,772	28,637
Netherlands	52,046	22,749	31,125
Senegal	8,988	5,675	21,596
Thailand	99,249	69,562	64,459
United Kingdom	15,502	14,265	21,833
USA	24,175	18,519	31,755
Total (incl. others) . . .	571,719	431,558	647,065

Exports f.o.b.	1993	1994	1995
Brazil	10,662	31,162	32,914
China, People's Repub. . . .	13,298	966	4,147
France (incl. Monaco) . . .	5,953	11,586	4,578
India	7,199	3,635	10,597
Indonesia	2,579	7,138	7,258
Italy	13,476	7,141	7,064
Morocco	63,923	15,091	16,801
Nigeria	5,873	11,654	4,336
Portugal	9,230	17,868	24,242
Southern African Customs Union* .	5,199	2,500	4,291
Thailand	3,390	4,806	8,419
Total (incl. others) . . .	181,589	163,260	164,955

* Comprising Botswana, Lesotho, Namibia, South Africa and Swaziland.

Source: UN, *International Trade Statistics Yearbook.*

Transport

RAILWAYS (traffic)

	1995	1996	1997
Passenger-km (million) . . .	116.0	117.0	121.8
Freight ton-km (million) . . .	388.4	269.7	311.4

Source: IMF, *Benin: Selected Issues and Statistical Appendix* (September 1998).

ROAD TRAFFIC (motor vehicles in use)

	1994	1995	1996
Passenger cars	26,507	30,346	37,772
Buses and coaches . . .	353	405	504
Lorries and vans . . .	5,301	6,069	7,554
Road tractors	2,192	2,404	2,620
Motor cycles and mopeds . . .	220,800	235,400	250,000

Source: IRF, *World Road Statistics.*

SHIPPING
Merchant Fleet (registered at 31 December)

	1996	1997	1998
Number of vessels . . .	7	8	6
Total displacement ('000 grt) . .	1.0	1.2	0.9

Source: Lloyd's Register of Shipping, *World Fleet Statistics.*

International Sea-borne Freight Traffic
(at Cotonou, including goods in transit, '000 metric tons)

	1996	1997	1998
Goods loaded	423.9	370.3	379.0
Goods unloaded	1,795.8	1,877.9	2,004.6

Source: Banque centrale des états de l'Afrique de l'ouest.

CIVIL AVIATION (traffic on scheduled services)*

	1995	1996	1997
Kilometres flown (million) . .	3	3	3
Passengers carried ('000) . .	74	75	86
Passenger-km (million) . .	223	225	242
Total ton-km (million) . .	36	37	38

* Including an apportionment of the traffic of Air Afrique.

Source: UN, *Statistical Yearbook.*

Tourism

	1995	1996	1997
Tourist arrivals ('000) . . .	138	143	148
Tourism receipts (US $ million) .	27	29	31

Source: World Tourism Organization, *Yearbook of Tourism Statistics.*

Communications Media

	1994	1995	1996
Radio receivers ('000 in use) . .	480	500	600
Television receivers ('000 in use) .	30	32	50
Telephones ('000 main lines in use)	24	28	33
Telefax stations (number in use) .	600	800	1,064
Mobile cellular telephones (subscribers) . . .	n.a.	1,050	2,587
Daily newspapers			
Number	1	1	1
Average circulation ('000 copies)	1	3	12
Non-daily newspapers			
Number	n.a.	10	4
Average circulation ('000 copies)	n.a.	51	66
Book production*			
Titles	84	n.a.	n.a.
Copies ('000)	42	n.a.	n.a.

* First editions.

1997: Radio receivers ('000 in use) 620; Television receivers ('000 in use) 60; Telephones ('000 main lines in use) 36; Mobile cellular telephones (subscribers) 4,295.

Sources: UNESCO, *Statistical Yearbook*; UN, *Statistical Yearbook.*

Education

(1996/97)

	Institutions	Teachers	Students Males	Students Females	Students Total
Pre-primary . .	283*	622	9,106	8,335	17,441
Primary . .	3,088*	13,957	492,826	286,503	779,329
Secondary					
General . .	145§	5,352	102,011	44,124	146,135
Vocational§ . .	14	283	3,553	1,320	4,873
Higher . .	9	962‡	11,398†	2,657†	14,055†

*1995/96.　†1996.　‡1995.　§1993/94.

Source: mainly UNESCO, *Statistical Yearbook.*

Directory

The Constitution

A new Constitution was approved in a national referendum on 2 December 1990.

The Constitution of the Republic of Benin guarantees the basic rights and freedoms of citizens. The functions of the principal organs of state are delineated therein.

The President of the Republic, who is Head of State and Head of Government, is directly elected, by universal adult suffrage, for a period of five years, renewable only once. The President appoints government members, who are responsible to the Head of State. The legislature is the 83-member Assemblée nationale, which is elected, also by direct universal suffrage, for a period of four years.

The Constitution upholds the principle of an independent judiciary. The Constitutional Court, the Economic and Social Council and Higher Audiovisual and Communications Authority are intended to counterbalance executive authority.

The Government

HEAD OF STATE

President: Gen. (retd) MATHIEU KÉRÉKOU (took office 4 April 1996; re-elected 22 March 2001).

COUNCIL OF MINISTERS
(May 2001)

President: Gen. (retd) MATHIEU KÉRÉKOU.

Minister of State in charge of Co-ordinating Government Action, Future Planning and Development: BRUNO AMOUSSOU.

Minister of State of Defence: PIERRE OSHO.

Minister of Justice, Legislation and Human Rights: JOSEPH GNONLONFOUN.

Minister of the Interior, Public Security and Local Government: DANIEL TAWÉMA.

Minister of Foreign Affairs and African Integration: ANTOINE KOLAWOLÉ IDJI.

Minister of Finance and the Economy: ABDOULAYE BIO TCHANÉ.

Minister in charge of Relations with the Institutions, Civil Society and Benin Nationals Abroad: SYLVAIN ADÉKPÉDJOU AKINDÈS.

Minister of Agriculture, Stockbreeding and Fishing: THÉOPHILE NATA.

Minister of the Family, Social Protection and Solidarity: CLAIRE AYÉMONA HOUGAN.

Minister of Mining, Energy and Water Resources: FASSASSI KAMAROU.

Minister of Public Works and Transport: JOSEPH SOUROU ATTIN.

Minister of the Environment, Housing and Urban Development: LUC-MARIE CONSTANT GNACADJA.

Minister of the Civil Service, Labour and Administrative Reform: OUSMANE BATOKO.

Minister of Higher Education and Scientific Research: DOROTHÉE SOSSA.

Minister of Communication and the Promotion of Information Technology: GASTON ZOSSOU.

Minister of Public Health: CÉLINE KANDISSOUNON.

Minister of Culture, Handicrafts and Tourism: AMOS ELEGBE.

Minister of Trade, Industry, Community Development and the Promotion of Employment: LAZARE SEHOUETO.

Minister of Primary and Secondary Education: JEAN BIO TCHABI OROU.

Minister of Technical and Professional Education: DOMINIQUE C. SOHOUNHLOUE.

Minister of Youth, Leisure and Sport: VALENTIN ADITI HOUDE.

MINISTRIES

Office of the President: BP 1288, Cotonou; tel. 30-02-28; fax 30-06-36.

Ministry of Agriculture, Stockbreeding and Fishing: 03 BP 2900, Cotonou; tel. 30-19-55; fax 30-03-26.

Ministry of the Civil Service, Labour and Administrative Reform: BP 907, Cotonou; tel. 31-26-18.

Ministry of Communication and the Promotion of Information Technology: Cotonou.

Ministry for the Co-ordination of Government Action, Future Planning and Development: BP 342, Cotonou; tel. 30-15-53; fax 30-16-60; e-mail meccagpdpe@planben.internet.bj.

Ministry of Culture, Handicrafts and Tourism: BP 120, Cotonou; fax 31-59-31.

Ministry of Defence: BP 2493, Cotonou; tel. 30-08-90.

Ministry of the Environment, Housing and Urban Development: 01 BP 308, Cotonou; tel. 33-05-85; fax 33-14-27.

Ministry of the Family, Social Protection and Solidarity: Cotonou.

Ministry of Finance and the Economy: BP 302, Cotonou; tel. 30-10-20; fax 31-58-98.

Ministry of Foreign Affairs and African Integration: BP 319, Cotonou; tel. 30-04-00.

Ministry of Higher Education and Scientific Research: BP 348, Cotonou; tel. 30-06-81; fax 30-18-48.

Ministry of the Interior, Public Security and Local Government: BP 925, Cotonou; tel. 30-10-06.

Ministry of Justice, Legislation and Human Rights: BP 967, Cotonou; tel. 31-31-46; fax 31-34-48.

Ministry of Mining, Energy and Water Resources: 03 BP 2184, Cotonou; tel. 30-40-18.

Ministry of Primary and Secondary Education: Cotonou.

Ministry of Public Health: BP 882, Cotonou; tel. 33-08-70.

Ministry of Public Works and Transport: BP 351, Cotonou; tel. 31-56-96.

Ministry of Technical and Professional Education: Cotonou.

Ministry of Trade, Industry, Community Development and the Promotion of Employment: BP 2493, Cotonou; tel. 30-05-02.

Ministry of Youth, Leisure and Sport: 03 BP 2103, Cotonou; tel. 31-46-00.

President and Legislature

PRESIDENT

Presidential Election, First Ballot, 4 March 2001*

Candidate	Votes	% of votes
MATHIEU KÉRÉKOU	1,127,200	45.42
NICÉPHORE SOGLO (RB)	672,927	27.12
ADRIEN HOUNGBÉDJI (PRD)	313,186	12.62
BRUNO AMOUSSOU (PSD)	213,136	8.59
Others	155,080	6.25
Total	**2,481,529**	**100.00**

* Revised provisional results.

Second Ballot, 22 March 2001*

Candidate	Votes	% of votes
MATHIEU KÉRÉKOU	1,286,465	84.06
BRUNO AMOUSSOU	244,032	15.94
Total	**1,530,497**	**100.00**

* Following the withdrawals of Nicéphore Soglo and Adrien Houngbédji, the second-round ballot took place, in accordance with the Constitution, between Bruno Amoussou and Mathieu Kérékou.

ASSEMBLÉE NATIONALE

President: ADRIEN HOUNGBÉDJI (PRD).

Elections, 30 March 1999

Party	Seats
RB.	27
PRD	11
FARD—Alafia	10
PSD	9
MADEP	6
Alliance Etoile	4
Alliance IPD	4
CAR—DUNYA	3
MERCI	2
Alliance RPR—UNSD	1
Alliance SURU	1
PDB	1
PN Ensemble	1
PS	1
RDP	1
RUND	1
Total	**83**

Advisory Councils

Cour Constitutionnelle: (see Judicial System, below).

Conseil Economique et Social (ECOSOC): Cotonou; f. 1994; 30 mems, representing the executive, legislature and 'all sections of the nation'; reviews all legislation relating to economic and social affairs; competent to advise on proposed economic and social legislation, as well as to recommend economic and social reforms; Pres. RAFIOU TOUKOUROU.

Political Organizations

The registration of political parties commenced in August 1990. In late 1999 there were 116 registered parties. The following 35 parties and coalitions contested the March 1999 legislative election:

The **Alliance étoile**; the **Alliance fraternité**; the **Alliance pour la démocratie et le progrès (ADP)**: Leader SYLVAIN ADÉKPÉDJOU AKINDÈS; the **Alliance des patriotes**; the **Alliance impulsion pour le progrès et la démocratie (Alliance IPD)**; the **Alliance pour le progrès (Alliance APP)**: eight mem. parties; Leader EMILE DERLIN ZINSOU; the **Alliance rassemblement pour la république—Union nationale pour la solidarité et le développement (Alliance RPR—UNSD)**; the **Alliance républicaine**; the **Alliance SURU**: four mem. parties; Leader GADO GUIRIGISSIOU; the **Alliance union pour le développement économique et social (Alliance UDES)**; the **Congrès africain pour le renouveau—DUNYA (CAR—DUNYA)**; the **Congrès du peuple pour le progrès (CPP)**; the **Front d'action pour le renouveau, la démocratie et le développement—Alafia (FARD—Alafia)**: Leader SAKA KINA; the **Front pour la république (FPR)**; the **Mouvement africain pour la démocratie et le progrès (MADEP)**: Leader SEFOU FAGBOHOUN; the **Mouvement africain pour le progrès (MAP)**; the **Mouvement pour l'engagement et le réveil des citoyens (MERCI)**: five mem. parties; Leader SEVERIN ADJOVI; **Notre cause commune (NCC)**: Leader FRANÇOIS ODJO TANKPINON; the **Parti africain pour la rédemption et l'indépendance (PARI)**; the **Parti communiste du Bénin (PCB)**: Leader PASCAL FANTONDJI; the **Parti démocratique du Bénin (PDB)**; the **Parti national campagne pour la moralité et la démocratie (PN CMD)**; the **Parti national 'ensemble' (PN Ensemble)**; the **Parti du renouveau démocratique (PRD)**: Leader ADRIEN HOUNGBÉDJI; the **Parti du salut (PS)**; the **Parti social démocrate (PSD)**: Leader BRUNO AMOUSSOU; the **Parti social démocrate—Bélier (PSD—Bélier)**; the **Parti socialiste du Bénin (PSB)**; the **Rassemblement pour la démocratie et le panafricanisme (RDP)**: Leader DOMINIQUE HOYMINOU; the **Rassemblement pour l'unité nationale et la démocratie (RUND)**; the **Rassemblement national pour la démocratie (RND)**; the **Renaissance du Bénin (RB)**: Leader NICÉPHORE SOGLO; the **Union pour la patrie et le travail (UPT)**; the **Union républicaine du peuple (URP)**; the **Union pour le triomphe de la république (UTR)**.

The **Coalition des forces démocratiques** (Pres. GATIEN HOUNG-BÉDJI) is an alliance of parties and organizations supporting President Kérékou.

Diplomatic Representation

EMBASSIES IN BENIN

China, People's Republic: 2 blvd de France, 01 BP 196, Cotonou; tel. 30-12-92; fax 30-08-41; Ambassador: CHUNLAI DUAN.

Congo, Democratic Republic: Carré 221, Ayélawadjè, Derrière la maison du Peuple d'Akpakpa à côté de l'école Ronsard, Cotonou; tel. 30-00-01; Chargé d'affaires: NDOMPETELO DEKA.

Cuba: ave de la Marina, face Hôtel du Port, 01 BP 948, Cotonou; tel. and fax 31-52-97; Ambassador: FERNANDO PRATS MARI.

Denmark: Lot P7, Les Cocotiers, 04 BP 1223, Cotonou; tel. 30-38-62; fax 30-38-60; e-mail ambdan@bow.intnet.bj; Chargé d'affaires: JOHNNY FLENTØ.

Egypt: route de l'Aéroport, Lot G26, BP 1215, Cotonou; tel. 30-08-42; fax 30-14-25; Ambassador: MOHAMED MAHMOUD NAGUIB.

France: ave Jean-Paul II, BP 966, Cotonou; tel. 30-02-25; fax 30-15-47; e-mail ambafrance@serv.eit.bj; internet www.eit.bj/ambafrance-benin; Ambassador: FRANÇOIS MIMIN.

Germany: 7 ave Jean-Paul II, 01 BP 504, Recette Principale, Cotonou; tel. 31-29-68; fax 31-29-62; Ambassador: VOLKER SEITZ.

Ghana: route de l'Aéroport, Lot F, Les Cocotiers, BP 488, Cotonou; tel. 30-07-46; fax 30-03-45; Ambassador: AGYOGBE ACHAAB.

Korea, Democratic People's Republic: Cotonou; Ambassador: RI IN SOK.

Libya: Les Cocotiers, BP 405, Cotonou; tel. 30-04-52; Ambassador: TOUFIK ASHOUR ADAM.

Netherlands: ave Jean-Paul II, 08 BP 0783, Cotonou; tel. 30-41-52; fax 30-41-50; e-mail nlgovcot@intnet.bj; Chargé d'affaires: SASKIA N. BAKKER.

Niger: derrière l'Hôtel de la Plage, BP 352, Cotonou; tel. 31-56-65; Ambassador: MAHAMAN BACHIR ZADAA.

Nigeria: blvd de France—Marina, BP 2019, Cotonou; tel. 30-11-42; Chargé d'affaires a.i.: M. S. ADOLI.

Russia: BP 2013, Cotonou; tel. 31-28-34; fax 31-28-35; Ambassador: YURII TCHEPIK.

USA: rue Caporal Anani Bernard, BP 2012, Cotonou; tel. 30-06-50; fax 30-19-74; e-mail amemb.coo@intnet.bj; Ambassador: PAMELA E. BRIDGEWATER.

Judicial System

The Constitution of December 1990 establishes the judiciary as an organ of state whose authority acts as a counterbalance to that of the executive and of the legislature.

Cour Constitutionnelle: BP 2050, Cotonou; tel. 31-16-10; fax 31-37-12; f. 1990, inaug. 1993; seven mems (four appointed by the Assemblée nationale, three by the President of the Republic); exercises highest jurisdiction in constitutional affairs; determines the constitutionality of legislation, oversees and proclaims results of national elections and referendums, responsible for protection of individual and public rights and obligations, charged with regulating functions of organs of state and authorities; Pres. CONCEPTIA L.-D. OUINSOU; Sec.-Gen. JEAN-BAPTISTE MONSI.

Haute Cour de Justice: comprises the members of the Cour constitutionnelle (other than its President), six deputies of the Assemblée nationale and the President of the Cour suprême; competent to try the President of the Republic and members of the Government in cases of high treason, crimes committed in, or at the time of, the exercise of their functions, and of plotting against state security.

Cour Suprême: highest juridical authority in administrative and judicial affairs and in matters of public accounts; competent in disputes relating to local elections; advises the executive on jurisdiction and administrative affairs; comprises a President (appointed by the President of the Republic, after consultation with the President of the Assemblée nationale, senior magistrates and jurists), presidents of the component chambers and counsellors.

Religion

At the time of the 1992 census it was estimated that some 35% of the population held animist beliefs; another 35% were Christians (mainly Roman Catholics) and the remainder were mostly Muslims. Religious and spiritual cults, which were discouraged under Kérékou's military regime, re-emerged as a prominent force in Beninois society during the early 1990s.

CHRISTIANITY

The Roman Catholic Church

Benin comprises two archdioceses and eight dioceses. At 31 December 1998 there were an estimated 1.3m. Roman Catholics (about 21.4% of the population), mainly in the south of the country.

Bishops' Conference: Conférence Episcopale du Bénin, Archevêché, BP 491, Cotonou; tel. 31-31-45; fax 30-07-07; Pres. Rt Rev. LUCIEN MONSI-AGBOKA, Bishop of Abomey.

Archbishop of Cotonou: Most Rev. NESTOR ASSOGBA, Archevêché, 01 BP 491, Cotonou; tel. 30-01-45; fax 30-07-07; e-mail cotonou@cef.fr; internet evry.cefm.net/evry/cotonou/index.html.

Archbishop of Parakou: Most Rev. FIDÈLE AGBATCHI, Archevêché, BP 75, Parakou; tel. 61-02-54; fax 61-01-99.

Protestant Church

There are an estimated 257 Protestant mission centres in Benin.

Eglise protestante méthodiste en République du Bénin: 54 ave Mgr Steinmetz, BP 34, Cotonou; tel. 31-11-42; fax 31-25-20; f. 1843; Pres. Rev. Dr MOÏSE SAGBOHAN; Sec. Rev. MATHIEU D. OLODO; 95,827 mems (1996).

VODOUN

The origins of the traditional *vodoun* religion can be traced to the 14th century. Its influence is particularly strong in Latin America and the Caribbean, owing to the shipment of slaves from the West African region to the Americas in the 18th and 19th centuries.

Communauté nationale du culte vodoun (CNCV): Ouidah; Pres. ADAN YOSSI GUÉDÉHOUNGUÉ.

The Press

In early 2001 there were 18 daily newspapers and 37 periodicals published in Benin.

DAILIES

L'Aurore: Face Clinique Boni, Akpakpa, 05 BP 464, Cotonou; tel. 33-70-43; Dir PATRICK ADJAMONSI; circ. 1,500.

Bénin-Presse Info: 01 BP 72, Cotonou; tel. 31-26-55; bulletin of Agence Bénin-Presse; Dir YAOVI HOUNKPONOU; Chief Editor EMMANUEL AGBOKOU.

La Cloche: Carré 2248, Zogbo, 07 BP 65, Cotonou; tel. 30-56-04; e-mail lacloche@h2com.com; Dir VINCENT METONNOU; Chief Editor JOS-PERZO ANAGO.

La Dépêche du Soir: Carré 555, Jericho, 03 BP 1100, Cotonou; tel. 33-51-53; Dir EUSÈBE SOTON.

Les Echos du Jour: Akpakpa, 08 BP 718, Cotonou; tel. 33-18-33; fax 33-71-27; e-mail echos@netcourrier.com; independent; Dir MAURICE CHABI; Editor-in-Chief MICHEL TCHANOU; circ. 3,000.

Le Journal: Sikècodji, 01 BP 2141, Cotonou; f. 1999; independent; Dir MAXIMIN TCHIBOZO; Chief Editor ANIQUE DJIMADJA.

Liberté: Carré 478, Bar Tito, 03 BP 3555; tel. 32-55-19; e-mail liberte@avu.org; Dir SYLVESTRE FOHOUNGO.

Le Matin: Carré 54, Tokpa Hoho; tel. 31-10-80; fax 33-42-62; f. 1994; independent; Dir MOÏSE DATO; Editor-in-Chief PIERRE MATCHOUDO.

Le Matinal: 06 BP 1989, Cotonou; tel. 31-49-20; fax 31-49-19; e-mail lematinal@h2com.com; internet www.h2com.com/lematinal; Dir CHARLES TOKO; Editor-in-Chief ASPAVITA R. NOUNAGNON.

La Nation: Cadjèhoun, 01 BP 1210, Cotonou; tel. 30-02-99; fax 30-34-63; e-mail lanation@elodia.intnet.bj; internet elodia.intnet.bj/nation.htm; f. 1990; official newspaper; Dir INNOCENT M. ADJAHO; Editor-in-Chief ALFRED AHOUNOU; circ. 4,000.

L'Oeil du Peuple: Carré 743, Gbégamey, rue PTT, 01 BP 5538; tel. 30-22-07; Dir CELESTIN ABISSI; Editor-in-Chief PAUL AGBOYIDOU.

Le Point au Quotidien: 322 rue du Renouveau, 05 BP 934, Cotonou; tel. and fax 32-50-55; e-mail lepointq@leland.bj; internet www.lepointauquotidien.com; independent; Dir VINCENT FOLY; Editor-in-Chief CÉLESTIN AKPOVO; circ. 2,000.

Le Progrès: Sikècodji, 05 BP 708, Cotonou; tel. and fax 32-52-73; e-mail journaleprogres@hotmail.com; Dir EDOUARD LOKO; Chief Editor SEPTIME TOLLI.

La Pyramide: Carré 1145, Ste Rita, 07 BP 828, Cotonou; tel. 32-28-89; Dir CHRISTOPHE HODONOU; Editor-in-Chief RENÉ ADENIYI.

Le Soleil: Carré 850, Sikècodji, 02 BP 8187, Cotonou; tel. 32-69-96; Dir MAURILLE GNANSOUNOU; Editor-in-Chief MATINI MARCOS.

PERIODICALS

Africa Visages: BP 2297, Porto-Novo; tel. 22-40-25; fax 21-25-25; fortnightly; Dir ERICK HOUNTONDJI; Editor-in-chief PHILIPPE D'ALMEIDA.

L'Avenir: 02 BP 8143, Cotonou; tel. 30-29-70; fortnightly; Dir FIRMIN GANGBE.

Bénin Info: 06 BP 590, Cotonou; tel. 32-52-64; fortnightly; Dir ROMAIN TOI.

Bénin Santé: 06 BP 1905, Cotonou; tel. 33-26-38; fax 33-18-23; bi-monthly.

Le Canard du Golfe: 06 BP 59, Cotonou; tel. 32-72-33; satirical; 2 a month; Dir. F. L. TINGBO; Editor-in-Chief CHARLES MIGAN.

Le Continental: BP 4419, Cotonou; Dir ARNAULD HOUNDETE.

La Croix du Bénin: 01 BP 105, Cotonou; tel. and fax 32-11-19; e-mail lacroixbenin@excite.fr; f. 1946; fortnightly; Roman Catholic; Dir BARTHÉLÉMY ASSOGBA CAKPO.

La Dernière Barque—Creuset de la Jeunesse Chrétienne: 06 BP 446, Cotonou; tel. 30-32-82; fax 33-42-14.

Emotion: 06 BP 1404, Cotonou; tel. and fax 32-25-34; e-mail houannou.sessinou@carammail.com; monthly; women's interest; Dir ERIC SESSINOU HOUANNOU; Editor-in-Chief FLORENT EUSTACHE HESSOU; circ. 1,500.

L'Enjeu: 04 BP 0454, Cotonou; tel. 30-47-18; Dir MATHURIN ASSOGBA.

La Flamme: 01 BP 2582, Cotonou; Dir PHILIPPE NOUDJENOUME.

Flash Info: Carré 55, Akpakpa derrière Stade Pleven, Cotonou; tel. 31-51-53; 2 a month; Dir-Gen. SOTON E. MOULÉRO.

La Gazette du Golfe: Immeuble La Gazette du Golfe, Carré 902 E Sikècodji, 03 BP 1624, Cotonou; tel. 32-42-08; fax 32-52-26; e-mail gazettedugolfe@serv.eit.bj; internet www.eit.bj/gazettedugolfe.htm; f. 1987; weekly; Dir ISMAËL Y. SOUMANOU; Editor MARCUS BONI TEIGA; circ. 18,000 (nat. edn), 5,000 (international edn).

Le Gongonneur: 04 BP 1432, Cotonou; tel. 35-04-91; e-mail dahoun@yahoo.com; Dir MATHIAS C. SOSSOU; Editor-in-Chief ASSANE M. YOUSSOUF.

Le Heraut: 03 BP 3417, Cotonou; tel. 36-00-64; Dir HYACINTHE OUINGNON; Editor-in-Chief ADAM OBATOKI.

Journal Officiel de la République du Bénin: BP 59, Porto-Novo; tel. 21-39-77; f. 1890; official govt bulletin; fortnightly; Dir AFIZE D. ADAMON.

Labari: BP 816, Parakou; tel. and fax 61-09-10; f. 1997; weekly; Dir DRAMANE AMITOURE; circ. 3,000.

Le Label: 03 BP 3190, Cotonou; tel. 30-04-72; weekly; Dir GASPARD KODJO; Chief Editor YVES AGONDANOU.

La Lumière de l'Islam: Carré 163, 01 BP 4022, Cotonou; tel. and fax 31-34-59; monthly; Dir MOHAMED BACHIROU SOUMANOU.

Madame Afrique: 08 BP 274, Cotonou; tel. 32-21-22; fax 32-21-23; Dir BERNARD ZANCLAN.

MC (Cinq Millions de Consommateurs): 04 BP 142, Cotonou; tel. 33-58-53; Dir BERNARD DOUSSOU DOSSA.

Nouvel Essor: Carré 497, Jéricho, 06 BP 1182, Cotonou; tel. 32-43-13; monthly; Dir JEAN-BAPTISTE HOUNKONNOU.

Nouvelle Vision: BP 73, Abomey-Calavi; Dir CLÉMENT AHOSSI.

Opérateur Économique: ave du Général de Gaulle, 01 BP 31, Cotonou; tel. 31-20-81; fax 31-22-99; monthly; published by Chambre de Commerce et d'Industrie du Bénin; Dir WASSI MOUFTAOU.

Le Pélican: 03 BP 0432, Cotonou; tel. 30-33-97; monthly; Dir OSCAR S. GBAGUIDI.

Le Perroquet: Carré 478, 03 BP 0880, Cotonou; tel. 32-18-54; e-mail perro@intnet.bj; f. 1996; 2 a month; independent; news and analysis; Dir DAMIEN P. HOUESSOU; Chief Editor ADRIEN HOUNKOUÉ; circ. 2,500.

Le Point de la Semaine: 01 BP 2288, Houinmè; tel. 22-50-39; weekly; Dir JEAN-CHRISTOPHE HOUNGBO.

Le Radical: 03 BP 0408, Cotonou; Dir ALASSANE BAWA.

Le Recadaire: 02 BP 308, Cotonou; tel. 22-60-11; e-mail lerecadaire@yahoo.com; Dir GUTEMBERT HOUNKANRIN.

La Réplique: BP 1087, Porto-Novo; tel. and fax 21-45-77; Dir EMILE ADECHINA; Editor-in-Chief JERÔME AKLAMAVO.

La République: 02 BP 508, Cotonou; Dir PARFAIT AGBALE; Editor-in-Chief JACQUES GBEKA.

La Sirène: Carré 357, Sènadé, 01 BP 122, Cotonou; tel. 33-40-17; Dir ETIENNE HOUSSOU.

Le Télégramme: 06 BP 1519, Cotonou; tel. 33-04-18; fortnightly; Dir ETIENNE SAGBE AHO; Chief Editor RAYMOND MONOKE.

Le Temps: 04 BP 43, Cotonou; tel. 30-55-06; Dir YAYA YOLOU.

Vérité Hebdo: 03 BP 432, Cotonou; tel. 32-70-50; fax 32-70-51; e-mail veritehebdo@h2com.com; internet www.h2com.com/veritehebdo; weekly; Dir CHRISTOPHE DAVÁKAN; Editor-in-Chief ANGELO AHOUANMAGNA.

Press Association

Union des Journalistes de la Presse Privée du Bénin (UJPB): Blvd de la République près Cadmes Plus, 03 BP 383, Cotonou; tel. 32-52-73; e-mail ujpb@h2com.com; internet www.h2com.com/ujpb; association of independent journalists; Pres AGAPIT N. MAFORIKAN.

NEWS AGENCIES

Agence Bénin-Presse (ABP): BP 72, Cotonou; tel. and fax 31-26-55; e-mail abpben@intnet.bj; f. 1961; national news agency; section of the Ministry of Culture and Communication; Dir YAOVI R. HOUNKPONOU.

Foreign Bureaux

Agence France-Presse (AFP): 06 BP 1382, Cotonou; tel. 33-51-32; fax 33-39-23; Correspondent VIRGILE C. AHISSOU.

Associated Press (USA) and Reuters (UK) are also represented in Benin.

Publishers

Les Editions de l'ACACIA: 06 BP 1978, Cotonou; tel. and fax 31-49-40; f. 1997; fmrly Les Editions du Flamboyant; Man. OSCAR DE SOUZA.

Graphitec: 04 BP 825, Cotonou; tel. and fax 30-46-04; e-mail padonou@bow.intnet.bj.

Government Publishing House

Office National de Presse et d'Imprimerie (ONPI): BP 1210, Cotonou; tel. 30-02-99; fax 30-11-52; f. 1975; Dir-Gen. INNOCENT ADJAHO.

Broadcasting and Communications

TELECOMMUNICATIONS

Office des Postes et des Télécommunications (OPT): Cotonou; tel. 31-20-45; fax 31-38-43; internet www.opt.bj; f. 1890; state-owned; Dir-Gen. BARTHÉLEMY AGNAN.

Libercom: Villa Fadoul 4, Cotonou; tel. 30-54-84; fax 30-54-85; f. 2000; mobile cellular telephone operator initially operating solely in Cotonou; jt venture between the OPT and Titan Africa; 3,300 subscribers.

Three mobile cellular telephone operators (Belgolaise, Spacetel-Bénin and Télécel Bénin) were awaiting interconnection with the OPT network in mid-2000. In July 2000 proposals to divide OPT into separate postal and telecommunications companies were announced; the privatization of the latter, to be known as Bénin Telecom, was also foreseen.

BROADCASTING

Regulatory Authority

Since 1997 the HAAC has issued licences to private radio and television stations.

Haute Autorité de l'Audiovisuel et de la Communication (HAAC): 01 BP 3567, Cotonou; tel. 31-52-12; fax 31-17-42; e-mail haac@planben.intnet.bj; f. in accordance with the 1990 Constitution to act as the highest authority for the media; Pres. TIMOTHÉE ADANLIN.

Radio

Office de Radiodiffusion et de Télévision du Bénin (ORTB): 01 BP 366, Cotonou; tel. 30-10-96; fax 30-04-48; state-owned; radio programmes broadcast from Cotonou and Parakou in French, English and 18 local languages; Dir-Gen. JEAN N'TCHA; Dir of Radio PELU C. DIOGO.

Atlantic FM: 01 BP 366, Cotonou; tel. 30-30-41; Dir JOSEPH OGOUNCHI.

Radio Cotonou: 01 BP 306, Cotonou; tel. 30-04-81; Dir PELU CHRISTOPHE DIOGO.

Radio Régionale de Parakou: BP 128, Parakou; tel. 61-07-73; Dir DIEUDONNÉ METOZOUNVÉ.

Radio Adja Ouèrè FM Ouémé: 01 BP 1509, Cotonou; tel. 25-02-88; Dir FAÏZOU FAGBOHOUN.

Radio Afrique Espoir: C123, Porto-Novo; tel. 21-34-55; Dir ROUMANOU KOUFERIDJI.

Ahémé FM: Centre Africa OBOTA, Possotomè; Promoter RUFIN GODJO.

CAPP FM: 06 BP 2076, Cotonou; tel. 31-08-10; Promoter JERÔME CARLOS.

Radio Carrefour: 03 BP 432, Cotonou; tel. 32-53-10; Dir CHRISTOPHE DAVAKAN.

Gerddes FM: 01 BP 1258, Cotonou; tel. 33-43-33; Man. ALEXANDRE DURAND.

Golfe FM-Magic Radio: 03 BP 1624, Cotonou; tel. 32-42-08; fax 32-52-26; e-mail golfefm@serv.eit.bj; internet www.eit.bj/golfefm.htm; Dir ISMAËL SOUMANOU.

Radio Iléma: 01 BP 3609, Cotonou; tel. 32-46-67; fax 53-01-37; Promoter FRANÇOIS SOUROU OKIOH.

Radio Immaculée Conception: BP 49, Cotonou; tel. 37-10-23; operated by the Roman Catholic Church of Benin; Promoter Mgr ISADORE DE SOUZA.

Radio Maranatha: 03 BP 4113, Cotonou; tel. 32-53-23; fax 31-06-91; e-mail phouessou@firstnet.bj; operated by the Conseil des Eglises Protestantes évangéliques du Bénin; Dir Rev. ROMAIN ZANNOU.

Noon-Sina FM: BP 04, Bembèrèkè; Man. ALI ZATO.

Radio Planète: 06 BP 537, Cotonou; tel. 30-30-30; Dir JANVIER YAHOUEDEHOU.

Radio Solidarité FM: BP 135, Djougou; tel. 80-01-95; fax 80-15-63; Promoter DAOUDA TAKPARA.

Radio Star: 04 BP 0553, Cotonou; tel. 32-53-22; Dir MARCELLIN Y. ATINDEGLA.

Radio Tokpa: Carré 233, 01 BP 2445, Cotonou; tel. 31-45-32; Man. GUY KPAKPO.

La Voix de la Lama: BP 21, Porto-Novo; tel. 31-11-61; Promoter SÉRAPHINE DADY.

La Voix de l'Islam: 08 BP 134, Cotonou; tel. 31-11-34; operated by the Communauté musulmane de Zongo; Man. El Hadj MAMAN YARO.

Radio Wêkê: 03 BP 2753, Cotonou; tel. 33-13-82; Promoter SOULÉ ISSA BADAROU.

Benin also receives broadcasts from Africa No. 1, BBC World Service and Radio France International.

Television

ORTB: (see radio); Dir of Television MAMA SOUMAÏLA.

ATVS: BP 7101, Cotonou; tel. 31-43-19; owned by African Television System-Sobiex; Promoter JACOB AKINOCHO.

La Cellule 2 (LC2): 05 BP 427, Cotonou; tel. 33-47-49; fax 33-46-75; e-mail lc2@intnet.bj; internet www.vn.refer.org/benin_ct/med/lc2/lc2.htm; commenced broadcasts 1997; Promoter CHRISTIAN LAGNIDÉ.

Telco: 01 BP 1241, Cotonou; tel. 31-37-72; e-mail telco@serv.eit.bj; internet www.eit.bj/telco.htm; relays five international channels; Promoter JOSEPH JÉBARA.

TV+ International: 01 BP 2376, Cotonou; tel. 31-53-54; Promoter CLAUDE KARAM.

Finance

(cap. = capital; res = reserves; m. = million; br. = branch; amounts in francs CFA)

BANKING

Central Bank

Banque Centrale des Etats de l'Afrique de l'Ouest (BCEAO): ave Jean-Paul II, BP 325, Cotonou; tel. 31-24-66; fax 31-24-67; e-mail akangni@bceao.int; internet www.bceao.int; HQ in Dakar, Senegal; f. 1962; bank of issue for the mem. states of the Union économique et monétaire ouest-africaine (UEMOA, comprising Benin, Burkina Faso, Côte d'Ivoire, Guinea-Bissau, Mali, Niger, Senegal and Togo); cap. and res 806,918m., total assets 4,084,464m. (Dec. 1998); Gov. CHARLES KONAN BANNY; Dir in Benin IDRISS LYASSOU DAOUDA; br. at Parakou.

Commercial Banks

Bank of Africa—Bénin: ave Jean-Paul II, 08 BP 0879, Cotonou; tel. 31-32-28; fax 31-31-17; e-mail boa.benin@firstnet.bj; f. 1990; 28% owned by African Financial Holding; cap. and res 11,047m., total assets 129,335m. (Dec. 1998); Pres. FRANÇOIS TANKPINOU; Man. Dir RENÉ FORMEY DE SAINT-LOUVENT; 4 brs.

Banque Internationale du Bénin (BIBE): carrefour des Trois Banques, ave Giran, 03 BP 2098, Jéricho, Cotonou; tel. 31-55-49; fax 31-23-65; e-mail bibe@intnet.bj; f. 1989; owned by Nigerian commercial interests; cap. 3,000m., total assets 46,222m. (Dec. 1998); Pres. Chief ARTHUR C. I. MBANEFO; Man. Dir OLADÉLÉ R. ADEBOLU; 4 brs.

Continental Bank—Bénin: ave Jean-Paul II, carrefour des Trois Banques, 01 BP 2020, Cotonou; tel. 31-24-24; fax 31-51-77; e-mail contbk@intnet.bj; internet www.ad-net.fr/cbb; f. 1995 to assume activities of Crédit Lyonnais Bénin; 25% state-owned; cap. and res 4,647m., total assets 38,421m. (Dec. 1998); Pres. WASSI MOUFTAOU; Man. Dir MICHEL SABATH D'ALMEIDA; 1 br.

Ecobank—Bénin SA: rue Gouverneur Bayol, 01 BP 1280, Cotonou; tel. 31-40-23; fax 31-33-85; e-mail ecobank@ecobank.bj; internet www.ecobank.com; f. 1989; 84% owned by Ecobank Transnational Inc (operating under the auspices of the Economic Community of West African States); cap. and res 3,452m., total assets 83,960m. (Dec. 1998); Pres. GILBERT MEDJE; Gen. Man. M. F. SOSSAH; 3 brs.

Financial Bank Bénin (FBB): Immeuble Adjibi, rue du Commandant Decoeur, 01 BP 2700, Cotonou; tel. 31-31-00; fax 31-31-02; e-mail financial@ment.fr; f. 1988; 85% owned by Financial BC (Switzerland); cap. and res 2,392m., total assets 45,002m. (Dec. 1998); Pres. and Man. Dir RÉMY BAYSSET; 8 brs.

Savings Bank

Caisse Nationale d'Epargne: Cadjèhoun, route Inter-Etat Cotonou-Lomé, Cotonou; tel. 30-18-35; fax 31-38-43; state-owned; cap. and res 736m., total assets 15,738m. (Dec. 1997); Pres. MARCELLIN DOSSOU KPANOU; Dir ANDRÉ H. AFFEDJOU.

Credit Institutions

Crédit du Bénin: 08 BP 0936, Cotonou; tel. 31-30-02; fax 31-37-01; Man. Dir GILBERT HOUNKPAIN.

Crédit Promotion Bénin: 03 BP 1672, Cotonou; tel. 31-31-44; fax 31-31-66; wholly owned by private investors; cap. 150m., total assets 409m. (Dec. 1998); Pres. BERNARD ADIKPETO; Man. Dir DÉNIS OBA CHABI.

Equipbail Bénin: blvd Jean-Paul II, 08 BP 0690, Cotonou; tel. 31-11-45; fax 31-31-17; 49% owned by Bank of Africa—Bénin; cap. and res 486m., total assets 3,041m. (Dec. 1998); Pres. PAUL DERREUMAUX; Man. Dir CLAUDE D'ALMEIDA.

Financial Institution

Caisse Autonome d'Amortissement du Bénin: BP 59, Cotonou; tel. 31-47-81; fax 31-53-56; manages state funds; Man. Dir IBRAHIM PEDRO-BONI.

STOCK EXCHANGE

Bourse Régionale des Valeurs Mobilières (BRVM): Immeuble Chambre de Commerce et d'Industrie du Bénin, ave Charles de Gaulle, 01 BP 2985, Cotonou; tel. 31-21-26; fax 31-20-77; f. 1998; national branch of BRVM (regional stock exchange based in Abidjan, Côte d'Ivoire, serving the member states of UEMOA); Man. in Benin YVETTE GNIGLA.

INSURANCE

A&C Benin SA: Cotonou; internet elodia.intnet.bj/acb/index .htm; all branches; Dir Gen. JUSTIN HERBERT AGBOTON.

Gras Savoye Benin: Immeuble Goussanou, rue du Rev. Père Colineau, BP 294, Cotonou; tel. 31-24-34; fax 31-25-32; Man. YVES MEHOU-LOKO.

Société Nationale d'Assurances et de Réassurances (SONAR): BP 2030, Cotonou; tel. 30-16-49; fax 30-09-84; parastatal co; Pres. S. ATTOLOU.

Union Béninoise d'Assurance-Vie: Cotonou; f. 1994; cap. 400m.; 51% owned by Union Africaine Vie (Côte d'Ivoire).

Trade and Industry

GOVERNMENT AGENCIES

Centre Béninois de la Recherche Scientifique et Technique (CBRST): 03 BP 1665, Cotonou; tel. 32-12-63; fax 30-14-66; internet www.refer.org/benin_ct/rec/cbrst/cbrst.htm; f. 1986 to promote scientific and technical research.

Centre Béninois du Commerce Extérieur: Place du Souvenir, BP 1254, Cotonou; tel. 30-13-20; fax 30-04-36; f. 1988; provides information to export cos.

Centre de Promotion pour l'Emploi, la Petite et Moyenne Entreprise (CEPEPE): Face à la Mairie de Xlacondji, BP 2093, Cotonou; tel. 31-44-47; fax 31-59-50; promotes business and employment.

Commission Technique de Dénationalisation: 02 BP 8140, Cotonou; tel. 31-59-18; fax 31-23-15; Co-ordinator VICTORIN DOSSOU-SOGNON.

Institut National de Recherches Agricoles du Bénin (INRAB): Cotonou; fax 30-37-70; internet www.refer.org/benin_ct/rec/inrab/inrab.htm; f. 1992; undertakes research into agricultural improvements; publicizes advances in agriculture.

Office Béninois de Recherches Géologiques et Minières (OBRGM): Ministère des mines, de l'energie et de l'hydraulique, 01 BP 249, Cotonou; tel. 31-03-09; fax 31-41-20; e-mail obrgm@ planben.intnet.bj; f. 1996 as govt agency responsible for mining policy, exploitation and research; Dir-Gen. ALIOU MORIBA DJIBRIL.

Office National d'Appui à la Sécurité Alimentaire (ONASA): 06 BP 2544, Cotonou; tel. 33-15-02; fax 33-02-93; f. 1992; distribution of cereals; state-owned; Pres. IMAROU SALÉ; Dir-Gen. MOUSSA ASSOUMA.

Office National du Bois (ONAB): BP 1238, Recette Principale, Cotonou; tel. 33-16-32; fax 33-19-56; f. 1983; forest development and management, manufacture and marketing of wood products; transfer of industrial activities to private ownership pending; Man. Dir PASCAL PATINVOH.

DEVELOPMENT ORGANIZATIONS

Agence Française de Développement (AFD): blvd Jean-Paul II, BP 38, Cotonou; tel. 31-35-80; fax 31-20-18; fmrly Caisse Française de Développement; Dir HENRI PHILIPPE DE CLERCQ.

Mission de Coopération et d'Action Culturelle (Mission Française d'Aide et de Coopération): BP 476, Cotonou; tel. 30-08-24; administers bilateral aid from France according to the co-operation agreement of 1975; Dir BERNARD HADJADJ.

CHAMBER OF COMMERCE

Chambre de Commerce et d'Industrie du Bénin (CCIB): ave du Général de Gaulle, 01 BP 31, Cotonou; tel. 31-20-81; fax 31-32-99; e-mail albert.tevoedjre@planben.intnet.bj; internet planben .intnet.bj/pne/ccib.htm; Pres. WASSI MOUFTAOU; Sec.-Gen. N. A. VIADENOU; brs at Parakou, Abomey and Porto-Novo.

EMPLOYERS' ORGANIZATIONS

Association des Syndicats du Bénin (ASYNBA): Cotonou; Pres. PIERRE FOURN.

Fondation de l'Entrepreneurship du Bénin (FEB): Place du Québec, 08 BP 1155, Cotonou; tel. 31-35-37; fax 31-37-26; e-mail fonda@intnet.bj; internet elodia.intnet.bj/feb.htm; non profit-making org.; encourages the devt of the private sector and of small and medium-sized businesses.

Groupement Interprofessionnel des Entreprises du Bénin (GIBA): BP 6, Cotonou; Pres. A. JEUKENS.

Organisation Nationale des Employeurs du Bénin (ONEB): BP 41, Cotonou; tel. 33-13-00; fax 31-39-50.

Syndicat des Commerçants Importateurs et Exportateurs du Bénin: BP 6, Cotonou; Pres. M. BENCHIMOL.

Syndicat Interprofessionnel des Entreprises Industrielles du Bénin: Cotonou; Pres. M. DOUCET.

Syndicat National des Commerçants et Industriels Africains du Bénin (SYNACIB): BP 367, Cotonou; Pres. URBAIN DA SILVA.

UTILITIES
Electricity and Water

Communauté Electrique du Bénin (CEB): BP 385, Cotonou; f. 1968 as a jt venture between Benin and Togo to exploit energy resources in the two countries.

Société Béninoise d'Electricité et d'Eau (SBEE): BP 123, Cotonou; tel. 31-21-45; fax 31-50-28; f. 1973; state-owned; privatization scheduled for 2001; production and distribution of electricity and water; Man. Dir GODEFROY CHEKETE.

TRADE UNIONS

In early 2001 there were six trade union federations active in Benin:

Centrale des Organisations Syndicales Indépendantes (COSI): Cotonou; principally active in the health and education sectors; Sec.-Gen. JOSÉ DE SOUZA.

Centrale Syndicale Autonome du Bénin (CSA—Bénin): Cotonou; principally active in private-sector enterprises; Sec.-Gen. GUILLAUME ATTIGBÉ.

Centrale Syndicale des Travailleurs du Bénin (CSTB): Cotonou; actively opposes privatization and the influence of the international financial community; linked to the Parti Communiste du Bénin; Sec.-Gen. GASTON AZOUA.

Centrale Syndicale Unie des Travailleurs du Bénin (CSUB): Cotonou; f. 1999.

Confédération Générale des Travailleurs du Bénin (CGTB): Cotonou; principally active in public administration; Sec.-Gen. PASCAL TODJINOU.

Union Nationale des Syndicats de Travailleurs du Bénin (UNSTB): 1 blvd Saint-Michel, BP 69, Cotonou; tel. and fax 30-36-13; principally active in public administration; sole officially-recognized trade union 1974–90; Sec.-Gen. LAWANI AMINOU.

Transport

In 1996 the World Bank approved a credit of US $40m., to be issued through the International Development Association, in support of a major programme of investment in Benin's transport network. The integrated programme aimed to enhance Benin's status as an entrepôt for regional trade, and also to boost domestic employment and, by improving the infrastructure and reducing transport costs, agricultural and manufacturing output.

RAILWAYS

In 1997 the network handled 311,400 metric tons of goods. Plans for a 650-km extension, linking Parakou to Niamey (Niger), via Gaya, were postponed in the late 1980s, owing to lack of finance. In January 1999 the line between Cotonou and Porto-Novo was re-opened after nine years of closure.

Organisation Commune Bénin-Niger des Chemins de Fer et des Transports (OCBN): BP 16, Cotonou; tel. 31-33-80; fax 31-41-50; f. 1959; 50% owned by Govt of Benin, 50% by Govt of Niger; total of 579 track-km; main line runs for 438 km from Cotonou to Parakou in the interior; br. line runs westward via Ouidah to

Segboroué (34 km); also line of 107 km from Cotonou via Porto-Novo to Pobé (near the Nigerian border); Man. Dir ISAAC ENIDÉ KILANYOSSI.

ROADS

In 1996 there were 6,787 km of roads, including 10 km of motorway, 3,425 km of main roads and 3,352 km of secondary roads. About one-fifth of the network was paved.

AGETRAC: BP 1933, Cotonou; tel. 31-32-22; e-mail agetrac@leland.bj; f. 1967; goods transportation and warehousing.

Compagnie de Transit et de Consignation du Bénin (CTCB Express): route de l'Aéroport, BP 7079, Cotonou; f. 1986; Pres. SOULÉMAN KOURA ZOUMAROU.

SHIPPING

The main port is at Cotonou. In 1998 the port handled some 2,383,600 metric tons of goods.

Port Autonome de Cotonou (PAC): BP 927, Cotonou; tel. 31-28-90; fax 31-28-91; e-mail pac@leland.bj; f. 1965; state-owned port authority; private-sector involvement planned in late 2000; Dir-Gen. FERDINAND ASSOGBA-DOGNON.

> **Association pour la Défense des Intérêts du Port de Cotonou (AIPC) (Communauté Portuaire du Bénin):** Port Autonome de Cotonou; tel. 31-17-26; fax 31-28-91; f. 1993; promotes, develops and co-ordinates port activities at Cotonou; Pres. ISSA BADAROU-SOULÉ; Sec.-Gen. CAMILLE MÉDÉGAN.

Compagnie Béninoise de Navigation Maritime (COBENAM): Place Ganhi, 01 BP 2032, Cotonou; tel. 31-32-87; fax 31-09-78; f. 1974; 51% state-owned, 49% by Govt of Algeria; Pres. ABDEL KADER ALLAL; Man. Dir COCOU THÉOPHILE HOUNKPONOU.

Maersk Line: BP 2826, Cotonou; tel. 31-43-30; Danish co.

SDV Bénin: route du Collège de l'Union, Akpakpa, Cotonou; tel. 33-11-78; fax 33-06-11; e-mail sdvbenin@bow.intnet.bj; f. 1986; Pres. J. F. MIGNONNEAU; Dir-Gen. R. PH. RANJARD.

Société Béninoise d'Entreprises Maritimes: blvd de France, Zone Portuaire, BP 1733, Cotonou; tel. 31-21-19; fax 31-59-26; warehousing, storage and transportation.

Société Béninoise des Manutentions Portuaires (SOBEMAP): place des Martyrs, BP 35, Cotonou; tel. 31-39-83; state-owned; Pres. GEORGES SEKLOKA; Man. Dir THÉODORE AHOUMÉNOU AHOUASSOU.

Société Béninoise Maritime (SOBEMAR): Carré 8, Cruintomé, 08 BP 0956, Cotonou; tel. 31-50-26; fax 31-52-51; e-mail sobemarn@intnet.bj.

CIVIL AVIATION

The international airport at Cotonou (Cotonou-Cadjehoun) has a 2.4-km runway, and there are secondary airports at Parakou, Natitingou, Kandi and Abomey.

Air Afrique: ave du Gouverneur Ballot, BP 200, Cotonou; tel. 31-21-07; fax 31-53-41; see the chapter on Côte d'Ivoire; Dir in Benin JOSEPH KANZA.

Bénin Inter-Régional: Cotonou; f. 1991 as a jt venture by private Beninois interests and Aeroflot (then the state airline of the USSR); operates domestic and regional flights.

Tourism

Benin's rich cultural diversity and its national parks and game reserves are the principal tourist attractions. About 148,000 tourists visited Benin in 1997, when receipts from tourism were estimated at US $31m.

Conseil National du Tourisme: Cotonou; f. 1993.

BHUTAN

Introductory Survey

Location, Climate, Language, Religion, Flag, Capital

The Kingdom of Bhutan lies in the Himalaya range of mountains, with Tibet (the Xizang Autonomous Region), part of China, to the north and India to the south. Average monthly temperature ranges from 4.4°C (40°F) in January to 17°C (62°F) in July. Rainfall is heavy, ranging from 150 cm (60 ins) to 300 cm (120 ins) per year. The official language is Dzongkha, spoken mainly in western Bhutan. Written Dzongkha is based on the Tibetan script. The state religion is Mahayana Buddhism, primarily the Drukpa school of the Kagyupa sect, although Nepalese settlers, who comprise about one-quarter of the country's total population, practise Hinduism. The Nepali-speaking Hindus dominate southern Bhutan and are referred to as southern Bhutanese. The national flag (proportions 3 by 2) is divided diagonally from the lower hoist to the upper fly, so forming two triangles, one orange and the other maroon, with a white dragon superimposed in the centre. The capital is Thimphu.

Recent History

The first hereditary King of Bhutan was installed in December 1907. An Anglo-Bhutanese Treaty, signed in 1910, placed Bhutan's foreign relations under the supervision of the Government of British India. After India became independent, that treaty was replaced in August 1949 by the Indo-Bhutan Treaty of Friendship, whereby Bhutan agrees to seek the advice of the Government of India with regard to its foreign relations, but remains free to decide whether or not to accept such advice. King Jigme Dorji Wangchuk, installed in 1952, established the National Assembly (Tshogdu Chenmo) in 1953 and a Royal Advisory Council (Lodoi Tsokde) in 1965. He formed the country's first Council of Ministers (Lhengye Zhungtshog) in 1968. He died in 1972 and was succeeded by the Western-educated 16-year-old Crown Prince, Jigme Singye Wangchuk. The new King stated his wish to preserve the Indo-Bhutan Treaty and further to strengthen friendship with India. In 1979, however, during the Non-Aligned Conference and later at the UN General Assembly, Bhutan voted in opposition to India, in favour of Chinese policy. In 1983 India and Bhutan signed a new trade agreement concerning overland trade with Bangladesh and Nepal. India raised no objection to Bhutan's decision to negotiate directly with the People's Republic of China over the Bhutan–China border, and discussions between Bhutan and China were begun in 1984 (see below).

When Chinese authority was established in Tibet (Xizang) in 1959, Bhutan granted asylum to more than 6,000 Tibetan refugees. As a result of the discovery that many refugees were allegedly engaged in spying and subversive activities, the Bhutanese Government decided in 1976 to disperse them in small groups, introducing a number of Bhutanese families into each settlement. In June 1979 the National Assembly approved a directive establishing the end of the year as a time-limit for the refugees to decide whether to acquire Bhutanese citizenship or accept repatriation to Tibet. By September 1985 most of the Tibetans had chosen Bhutanese citizenship, and the remainder were to be accepted by India. A revised Citizenship Act, adopted by the National Assembly in 1985, confirmed residence in Bhutan in 1958 as a fundamental basis for automatic citizenship (as provided for by the 1958 Nationality Act), but this was to be flexibly interpreted. Provision was also made for citizenship by registration for Nepalese immigrants who had resided in the country for at least 20 years (15 years if employed by the Government) and who could meet linguistic and other tests of commitment to the Bhutanese community.

The violent ethnic Nepalese agitation in India for a 'Gurkha homeland' in the Darjeeling-Kalimpong region during the late 1980s and the populist movement in Nepal in 1988–90 (see chapters on India and Nepal respectively) spread into Bhutan in 1990. Ethnic unrest became apparent in that year when a campaign of intimidation and violence, directed by militant Nepalese against the authority of the Government in Thimphu, was initiated. In September thousands of southern Bhutanese villagers, and Nepalese who entered Bhutan from across the Indian border, organized demonstrations in border towns in southern Bhutan to protest against domination by the indigenous Buddhist Drukpa. The 'anti-nationals' ('ngolops'), as they were called by the Bhutanese authorities, demanded a greater role in the country's political and economic life and were bitterly opposed to official attempts to strengthen the Bhutanese sense of national identity through an increased emphasis on Tibetan-derived, rather than Nepalese, culture and religion (including a formal dress code, Dzongkha as the sole official language, etc.). Bhutanese officials, on the other hand, viewed the southerners as recent arrivals who abused the hospitality of their hosts through acts of violence and the destruction of development infrastructure.

Most southern villagers are relatively recent arrivals from Nepal and many of them have made substantial contributions to the development of the southern hills. The provision of free education and health care by the Bhutanese Government for many years attracted Nepalese who had been struggling to survive in their own country and who came to settle illegally in Bhutan. This population movement was largely ignored by local administrative officials, many of whom accepted incentives to disregard the illegal nature of the influx. The Government's policy of encouraging a sense of national identity, together with rigorous new procedures (introduced in 1988) to check citizenship registration, revealed the presence of thousands of illegal residents in southern Bhutan, many of whom had lived there for a decade or more, married local inhabitants and raised families. During the ethnic unrest in September 1990, the majority of southern villagers were coerced into participating in the demonstrations by groups of armed and uniformed young men (including many of Nepalese origin who were born in Bhutan). Many of these dissidents, including a large number of students and former members of the Royal Bhutan Army and of the police force, had fled Bhutan in 1989 and early 1990. In 1988–90 a large number of the dissidents resided in the tea gardens and villages adjoining southern Bhutan. Following the demonstrations that took place in Bhutan in September–October 1990, other ethnic Nepalese left Bhutan. In January 1991 some 234 persons, who claimed to be Bhutanese refugees, reportedly arrived in the Jhapa district of eastern Nepal. In September, at the request of the Nepalese Government, the United Nations High Commissioner for Refugees (UNHCR) inaugurated a relief programme providing food and shelter for more than 300 people in the *ad hoc* camps. By December the number of people staying in the camps had risen to about 6,000. This number was substantially augmented by landless and unemployed Nepalese, who had been expelled from Assam and other eastern states of India. The small and faction-ridden ethnic Nepalese Bhutan People's Party (BPP), which was founded in Kathmandu in 1990 (as a successor to the People's Forum on Democratic Rights, an organization established in 1989), purported to lead the agitation for 'democracy', but presented no clear set of objectives and attracted little support from within Bhutan itself. Schools and bridges became principal targets for arson and looting during 1990–92. Most of the schools in southern Bhutan were closed indefinitely from the end of September 1990, in response to threats to the lives of teachers and students' families, but the majority of pupils affected by these closures were provided with temporary places in schools in northern Bhutan. By mid-1995, despite the continuing security problems, some 74 schools and 89 health facilities had been reopened in the five southern districts.

Between 1988 and the end of 1999 King Jigme personally authorized the release of more than 1,700 militants captured by the authorities. The King asserted that, while he had an open mind regarding the question of the pace and extent of political reform (including a willingness to hold discussions with any discontented minority group), his Government could not tolerate pressures for change if based on intimidation and violence. Although several important leaders of the dissident movement remained in custody, the King stated that they would be released upon a return to normal conditions of law and order. Some leaders of the BPP declared that they had no differences with the King, but with 'corrupt officials'; on the other hand, certain militants strongly condemned the King as their 'main enemy'.

A number of southern Bhutanese officials (including the Director-General of Power, Bhim Subba, and the Managing Director of the State Trading Corporation, R. B. Basnet) absconded in June 1991 (on the eve of the publication of departmental audits) and went directly to Nepal, where they reportedly sought political asylum on the grounds of repression and atrocities against southern Bhutanese. These accusations were refuted by the Government in Thimphu. The former Secretary-General of the BPP, D. K. Rai, was tried by the High Court in Thimphu in May 1992 and was sentenced to life imprisonment for terrorist acts; a further 35 defendants received lesser sentences. Teknath Rizal, who was alleged to be responsible for the ethnic unrest and who had been held in prison since November 1989, came to trial, and was sentenced to life imprisonment in November 1993, having been found guilty of offences against the Tsawa Sum ('the country, the King, and the people'). (Rizal, together with 40 other 'political prisoners', was pardoned by the King and released from prison in December 1999; he decided to remain in Thimphu.)

Violence continued in the disturbed areas of Samtse, Chhukha, Tsirang, Sarpang and Gelephu throughout the early 1990s, and companies of trained militia volunteers were posted to these areas to relieve the forces of the regular army. The state government of West Bengal in India, whose territory abuts much of southern Bhutan, reaffirmed in 1991 and 1992 that its land would not be used as a base for any agitation against Bhutan.

In late 1991 and throughout 1992 several thousand legally-settled villagers left southern Bhutan for the newly-established refugee camps in eastern Nepal. The Bhutanese Government alleged that the villagers were being enticed or threatened to leave their homes by militants based outside Bhutan, in order to augment the population of the camps and gain international attention; the dissidents, on the other hand, claimed that the Bhutanese Government was forcing the villagers to leave. The formation of the Bhutan National Democratic Party (BNDP), including members drawn from supporters of the BPP and with the leading dissident R. B. Basnet as its President, was announced in Kathmandu in February 1992. Incidents of ethnic violence, almost all of which involved infiltration from across the border by ethnic Nepalese who had been trained and dispatched from the camps in Nepal, reportedly diminished substantially in the first half of 1993, as talks continued between Bhutanese and Nepalese government officials regarding proposals to resolve the issues at stake. The Nepalese Government steadfastly refused to consider any solution that did not include the resettlement in Bhutan of all ethnic Nepalese 'refugees' living in the camps (by November 1993 the number of alleged ethnic Nepalese refugees from Bhutan totalled about 85,000). This proposal was rejected by the Bhutanese Government, which maintained that the majority of the camp population merely claimed to be from Bhutan, had absconded from Bhutan (and thus forfeited their citizenship, according to Bhutan's citizenship laws), or had voluntarily departed after selling their properties and surrendering their citizenship papers and rights. The apparent deadlock was broken, however, when a joint statement was signed by the Ministers of Home Affairs of Bhutan and Nepal in July, which committed each side to establishing a 'high-level committee' to work towards a settlement and, in particular, to fulfilling the following mandate prior to undertaking any other related activity: to determine the different categories of people claiming to have come from Bhutan in the refugee camps in eastern Nepal (which now numbered eight); and to specify the positions of the two Governments on each of these categories, which would provide the basis for the resolution of the problem. The two countries held their first ministerial-level meeting regarding the issue in Kathmandu in October, at which it was agreed that four categories would be established among the people in the refugee camps: '(i) bona fide Bhutanese who have been evicted forcefully; (ii) Bhutanese who emigrated; (iii) non-Bhutanese; and (iv) Bhutanese who have committed criminal acts' henceforth referred to as Category I, II, III and IV). Further meetings were held in 1994. Following the election of a new Government in Nepal in November of that year, however, little progress was made at joint ministerial meetings held in the first half of 1995. Nepal's communist Government demanded that all persons in the camps be accepted by Bhutan; the Bhutanese authorities, on the other hand, were prepared to accept only the unconditional return of any bona fide Bhutanese citizens who had left the country involuntarily. Nevertheless, diplomatic exchanges continued in the latter half of the year, despite serious political instability in Nepal.

In January 1996 the new Nepalese Prime Minister, Sher Bahadur Deuba, proposed a resumption of intergovernmental talks, this time at foreign minister level. King Jigme welcomed the proposal, but the seventh round of talks, which was held in April, resulted in demands by Nepal that went beyond the mandate drawn up by the joint ministerial committee in mid-1993. It was widely understood that the Nepalese Government had again reverted to a requisition that all persons in the camps be accepted by Bhutan, regardless of status. This demand remained unacceptable to the Bhutanese Government, which stated that the problem of the people in the camps would not have arisen in the first place, if conditions (such as prospects of free food, shelter, health and education, and 'moral support' by the Nepalese authorities for all persons claiming to be Bhutanese refugees) had not been created when there were reportedly only 234 persons in Jhapa making such claims. In addition, the Bhutanese Government stated that even with such conditions attracting people to the refugee camps, a well-organized screening process would have prevented the sheer scale of ethnic Nepalese claiming to be Bhutanese refugees. (Until June 1993 no screening of claimants to refugee status had been enforced on the Indo-Nepalese border.) In August 1996 a UNHCR delegation visited Bhutan at the invitation of the authorities and received detailed information from the Bhutan Government regarding the issue of the camps. Talks at ministerial level were held in 1997, without any public communiqué. Following informal discussions during the summit meeting of the South Asian Association for Regional Co-operation (SAARC) in Colombo in July 1998, the new Chairman of the Council of Ministers and Head of Government in Bhutan, Lyonpo Jigmi Y. Thinley, held talks with the Nepalese Prime Minister, G. P. Koirala; both leaders stated that their meeting had been 'very positive.' Thinley and Koirala agreed that bilateral negotiations would continue through their respective Foreign Ministers on the issue of persons claiming refugee status in Nepal (who now numbered about 100,000). The 77th National Assembly session, which took place in June–August 1999, unanimously reiterated that the Bhutanese Government accepted full responsibility for any Bhutanese found to have been forcefully evicted (Category I—see above): such persons would be recognized and accepted as genuine refugees, while those responsible for their eviction would be punished. Category II people who had voluntarily emigrated from the country would be dealt with according to the respective immigration and citizenship laws of Bhutan and Nepal; Category III people 'must return to their own country'; and the repatriation of those in Category IV was to be conducted in accordance with the laws of the two countries. At the eighth round of joint ministerial negotiations between Bhutan and Nepal, which was held in Kathmandu in September, the Bhutanese Minister of Foreign Affairs agreed that some of those previously classified as voluntary emigrants (under Category II) might be reclassified as belonging to Category I (according to the Bhutanese Government, the number of people in this category totalled only about 3,000, while the Nepalese Government claimed that all of the camp dwellers had been compelled to leave Bhutan). In 1999 the Bhutanese Government was reported to have resettled people from the central and eastern hill regions of Bhutan in the southern areas of the country. No real progress was reported to have been made with regard to the refugee crisis at the ninth round of joint ministerial talks held in Thimphu in March 2000. European donor states strongly urged the two countries to resolve the refugee issue. This encouragement was repeated in early December during the visit of a delegation of senior US officials. At the 10th round of joint ministerial negotiations, held in late December, the Bhutanese and Nepalese Ministers of Foreign Affairs agreed that nationality would be verified on the basis of the head of the refugee family. Joint verification teams were formed to conduct the process. This important advance in bilateral negotiations signified a major concession by Bhutan, which had hitherto insisted that verification be conducted on an individual basis.

From December 1995 terrorist incidents in Bhutan were fewer, coinciding with the adoption of the 'peace march' tactic by persons claiming to be Bhutanese and seeking to travel from Nepal into Bhutan. These marches continued throughout 1996; a small group of marchers actually reached Phuentsholing in mid-August and again in December before being forced to return to India (which maintained a neutral stance with regard to the refugee issue). The Bhutanese Minister of Home Affairs asserted that those participating in the marches were not Bhutanese, but were non-nationals and emigrants who were attempting to enter the country illegally. A number of isolated bombing incidents occurred in Bhutan during 1998–99, most notably in Thimphu's main stadium in November 1998; the Government claimed that Nepalese militants were responsible for the attacks. In June 1999 it was reported that the Bhutanese police had arrested 80 alleged Bhutanese refugees who were conducting a peaceful demonstration (organized by the Bhutan Gurkha National Liberation Front) in Phuentsholing; the demonstrators claimed to be genuine Bhutanese citizens who were seeking to travel from the camps in Nepal back into Bhutan.

In 1991 'Rongthong' Kinley Dorji (also styled Kuenley or Kunley), a former Bhutanese businessman accused of unpaid loans and of acts against the State, had absconded to Nepal and joined the anti-Government movement. In 1992 he established and became President of the Druk National Congress, claiming human-rights violations in Bhutan. The Bhutan Government's 74th Assembly held in July 1996 discussed Kinley Dorji's case at length, and unanimously demanded his extradition from Nepal in conjunction with the Bhutan-Nepal talks. Following the signing of an extradition treaty between India and Bhutan in December, Kinley was arrested by the Indian authorities during a visit to Delhi in April 1997, and remained in detention until June 1998, when he was released on bail while his case was being examined by the Indian courts. Meanwhile, the extradition treaty was read to the 75th Assembly in July 1997, when Kinley Dorji's case was again discussed at length and demands for his return to Bhutan for trial were unanimously supported (as they were also at the 76th Assembly in mid-1998 and the 77th Assembly in mid-1999). At the same time the Assembly resolved that all relatives of alleged 'anti-national militants' in government service should be compulsorily retired as soon as possible. The 75th Assembly also discussed the intrusions into Bhutan's south-eastern border forests by Bodo and Maoist extremists from the neighbouring Indian state of Assam. In September a group of Bodo militants attacked a Bhutanese police station in the south-eastern district of Sam-drup Jongkhar, killing four policemen and looting large quantities of arms and ammunition.

During 1997 anti-Government activities (culminating in rallies in south-eastern Bhutan in October) were alleged to have been organized by several lay-preacher (Gomchen) students of Lam Dodrup in Sikkim, India; a number of arrests were subsequently made. Part of the famous historic retreat of Taktsang Monastery was badly damaged by fire under suspicious circumstances in April 1998. Despite the instability of the cliff face on which the monastery is positioned, reconstruction work commenced in mid-2000.

Important institutional changes were introduced in mid-1998, whereby King Jigme relinquished his role as Head of Government (while remaining Head of State) in favour of a smaller elected Council of Ministers, which was to enjoy full executive power under the leadership of a Chairman (elected by ministers, on a rotational basis, for a one-year term in office) who would be Head of Government. On 16 June the King informed the members of the existing Council of Ministers that it was to be dissolved on 26 June, and stated that he had issued a royal decree to the Speaker of the National Assembly, which was to be discussed at the pending 76th session. In the decree the King stressed the necessity to promote greater popular participation in the decision-making process, to strengthen the Government's mandate, and to enhance the administration's transparency and efficiency with integral checks and balances. He said that the Council of Ministers should now be restructured as an elected body 'vested with full executive powers', and he presented three key points—(i) All government ministers should henceforth be elected by the National Assembly, with the first election to take place during the 76th session; (ii) a decision should be taken on the exact role and responsibilities of the Council of Ministers; and (iii) the National Assembly should have a mechanism to move a vote of confidence in the King. In elaboration, King Jigme advised that the Council of Ministers should henceforth consist of six elected ministers and all nine members of the Royal Advisory Council, ministers should be elected by secret ballot, candidates should be selected from those who had held senior government posts at the rank of Secretary or above, and

a candidate must secure a majority of the votes cast to be considered elected. The portfolios for the elected ministers were to be awarded by the King. A minister's term in office was to be five years, after which he would undergo a vote of confidence in the National Assembly (previously there was no time limit on the tenure of ministerial posts). All decisions adopted by the Council of Ministers were to be based on consensus, and, while the Council was to govern Bhutan with full executive powers, it was also to be obliged to keep the King fully informed on all matters concerning the security and sovereignty of the country. The procedures of the Council of Ministers were to be supervised by a Cabinet Secretary appointed by the Council. The 76th session of the National Assembly voted by secret ballot on six new ministerial nominees; all were successful, but all received some negative votes.

An act to regulate the Council of Ministers, which was framed by a committee comprising members of the Government, clergy and people's representatives of the 20 districts, was presented to the 77th session of the National Assembly in mid-1999 and was subjected to extensive discussion and amendment. The rules as finally endorsed explicitly specified that the King had full power to dissolve the Council of Ministers. Procedures for a confidence vote (with regard to the King) were also drafted by the aforementioned committee and presented to the 77th session of the National Assembly, where members unanimously expressed regret over (and opposition to) the draft and repeatedly requested that King Jigme withdraw the proposal. Following a further earnest plea by the King, however, a key draft provision that a confidence vote regarding the monarch should only be placed on the agenda of an assembly session if a minimum of 50% of the districts requested it, was amended to allow the initiative if supported by at least one-third of the assembly members. The 77th session also agreed that ministers should serve a maximum of two consecutive five-year terms.

King Jigme told the Council of Ministers at a special sitting in mid-August 1999 (held for the formal change of Chairman) that it should streamline the Government and create mobility in the higher levels of the civil service when staffing ministries and other organizations, and that it must be responsive to the needs of the people. He also stressed that while governance was the responsibility of the Council of Ministers, the Royal Advisory Council was empowered to ensure that all the policies, laws and resolutions passed by the National Assembly were implemented by the Government. The outgoing Chairman of the Council, Lyonpo Jigmi Yozer Thinley, stated that all the elements were now in place for a democratic system of decision-making, while government was being institutionalized and made more accountable and transparent.

The activities of the militant 'anti-nationals' were unanimously condemned at the 76th session of the National Assembly in mid-1998, but the most pressing security issue was judged to be the perceived threat from the presence of Assamese tribal (Bodo) and Maoist (United Liberation Front of Assam—ULFA) militants, who had established military training bases in the jungle border regions of south-eastern Bhutan. Particular concern was expressed regarding the Indian military incursions into Bhutanese territory in an attempt to expel the militants. A serious incident, which took place in May in Sarpang and was reported to have involved 165 armed Indian soldiers, was discussed during the session, and was to be investigated by the Bhutanese and Indian authorities. In late November Bhutan and India launched an unprecedented joint military offensive against tribal insurgents, following an attack on a Bhutanese army convoy in Assam by members of the National Democratic Front of Bodoland (NDFB), which left four soldiers dead. In mid-1999 the Minister of Home Affairs reported that talks with ULFA leaders (in November 1998 and May 1999) had elicited the response that members of the ULFA had been forced to enter Bhutanese territory in 1992, but that they were not ready to leave Bhutanese territory for at least another 18 months. They asserted that they were determined to fight until independence for Assam was achieved, but offered to reduce their military presence in Bhutan. The Government of Bhutan reiterated to the ULFA leaders that its concern was at the very presence of any number of armed militants on Bhutanese soil. After detailed discussion, assembly members decided that all supplies of food and other essentials to the ULFA and Bodo militants must be stopped, that any Bhutanese who assisted the militants should be punished according to the National Security Act, and that discussions should continue with the ULFA to seek a peaceful withdrawal of these foreign forces from Bhutan. At the 78th session of the National Assembly in July 2000, members passed a resolution stating that the problem should be solved through peaceful means, but that if negotiations failed, military force should be used to evict the insurgents from Bhutanese territory. This decision placed pressure on militant groups to close their camps. Supplies of rations had already been halted, and the police had taken action against Bhutanese citizens found to be helping the militants. Some groups of militants began to return to India. However, most ULFA and Bodo militants, who had hitherto refrained from carrying out violent activities in Bhutan, were angered by the decision. Bhutan's security forces were put on maximum alert in September, amid fears that the King of Bhutan might be a target of the insurgents. In late December members of the Bodo Liberation Tigers (BLT) attacked a convoy of Bhutanese vehicles on the Bhutan–India border. Some 13 people were killed. The act was perceived as a warning to the Bhutanese Government not to shelter ULFA and NDFB militants. The Indian Government agreed to escort Bhutanese vehicles travelling to Assam.

Reflecting the increasing complexities of contemporary administration, the 77th Assembly also passed an unprecedented number of acts in mid-1999 to enhance the prevailing legal framework relating to telecommunications (providing for the creation of a state-owned public corporation, Bhutan Telecom, from the existing Telecommunications Division), the postal sector (enabling Bhutan Post to become an autonomous public-sector corporation), bankruptcy (giving a contemporary context for the rights and duties of borrowers and lenders), property (setting a legal framework for the management of loans, mortgages and related securities and financial services), legal deposit, municipalities (establishing legal authority for municipalities to enforce rules relating to urban development), and road safety. Further indications of the modernization of Bhutan were the inauguration of (limited) television and internet services in mid-1999, and the election of nine women to attend the 1999 session of the National Assembly. At the end of 1999 a government-endorsed report proposed the rationalization of government under 10 ministries; the proposals were to be fully implemented by 2002. In addition, in late 1999 two new government agencies—the Office of Legal Affairs and the National Employment Board—were established, and a new Department of Aid and Debt Management was created. The 78th session of the National Assembly in mid-2000 approved new legislation regarding the environment.

Bhutan suffered from devastating floods in August 2000. Landslides destroyed at least seven villages in southern Bhutan and killed more than 200 people.

Following the relaxation of many policies in the People's Republic of China from 1978, and anticipating improved relations between India and China, Bhutan moved cautiously to assert positions on regional and world affairs that took into account the views of India but were not necessarily identical to them. Discussions with China regarding the formal delineation and demarcation of Bhutan's northern border were begun in 1984, and substantive negotiations commenced in 1986. At the 12th round of talks, held in Beijing in December 1998, the Ministers of Foreign Affairs of Bhutan and China signed an official interim agreement (the first agreement ever to be signed between the two countries) to maintain peace and tranquillity in the Bhutan–China border area and to observe the status quo of the border as it was prior to May 1959, pending a formal agreement on the border alignment. The disputed area, which was 1,128 sq km during the early rounds of bilateral talks, was subsequently reduced to 269 sq km in three areas in the northwest of Bhutan. Meanwhile, demarcation of Bhutan's southern border was agreed with India, except for small sectors in the middle zone (between Sarpang and Gelephu) and in the eastern zone of Arunachal Pradesh and the *de facto* Sino-Indian border. Further sessions of bilateral discussions took place in Thimphu in September 1999. The Chinese ambassador to India paid a goodwill visit to Bhutan in October 2000, and in November the 14th round of 'satisfactory' border discussions was held in Beijing.

Bhutan has asserted itself as a fully sovereign, independent state, becoming a member of the UN in 1971 and of the Non-aligned Movement in 1973. By 1993 Bhutan had established diplomatic relations with 17 countries and with the European Union, and maintained diplomatic missions at the UN in New York and Geneva, in New Delhi, Dhaka and Kuwait; it is also represented by several honorary consulates.

In 1983 Bhutan was an enthusiastic founder-member of the South Asian Regional Co-operation (SARC) organization, with Bangladesh, India, Maldives, Nepal, Pakistan and Sri Lanka. In 1985 Bhutan was host to the first meeting of ministers of foreign affairs from SARC member countries, which agreed to give their grouping the formal title of South Asian Association for Regional Co-operation (SAARC, see p. 279).

Government

Bhutan's state system is a modified form of constitutional monarchy, without a formal, written constitution. The system of government is unusual in that power is shared by the monarchy (assisted by the Royal Advisory Council—Lodoi Tsokde), the Council of Ministers (Lhengye Zhungtshog), the National Assembly (Tshogdu Chenmo) and the Head Abbot (Je Khempo) of Bhutan's 3,000–4,000 Buddhist monks.

Important institutional changes were introduced at the 76th session of the National Assembly in July 1998. In accordance with a royal decree, King Jigme relinquished his role as Head of Government (while remaining Head of State) in favour of an elected Council of Ministers, which was to enjoy full executive powers (although the King was to retain authority with regard to strategic security issues) and was to be headed by a Chairman (elected by ministers, on a rotational basis, for a one-year period), who would be Head of Government. The new Council of Ministers was subsequently elected by the National Assembly by secret ballot and the portfolios of the elected ministers were awarded by the King. The term in office of a minister was to be five years, after which he would be obliged to undergo a vote of confidence in the National Assembly. In 1999 the National Assembly agreed that ministers should serve a maximum of two consecutive five-year terms.

The National Assembly, which serves a three-year term, has 150 members, including 105 directly elected by adult suffrage. Ten seats in the Assembly are reserved for religious bodies, while the remainder are occupied by officials, ministers and members of the Royal Advisory Council.

There are 20 local districts (dzonkhags), each headed by a Dzongda (district officer, in charge of administration and law and order) and a Thrimpon (magistrate, in charge of judicial matters). Dzongdas are appointed by the Royal Civil Service Commission and are responsible to the commission and the Ministry of Home Affairs. Thrimpons are responsible to the High Court. The principal officers under the Dzongda are the Dzongda Wongma and the Dzongrab, responsible for locally administered development projects and fiscal matters respectively. Seven of the districts are further sub-divided into sub-districts (dungkhags), and the lowest administrative unit in all districts is the block (geog) of several villages. There are Geog Yargye Tshogchungs (GYT—Geog Development Committees) in each of the geogs (of which there were 202 in July 1998). Committee members (geog yargye tshogpas) number between five and 13, depending on the size of the block, and are directly elected, on the basis of merit, by the villagers. Each GYT also elects a representative to the Dzongkhag Yargye Tshogchungs (DYTs—District Development Committees). Public meetings (zomdue) are held periodically, at the village level, to discuss local issues.

Defence

The strength of the Royal Bhutanese Army, which is under the direct command of the King, is officially said to number just over 6,000, and is based on voluntary recruitment augmented by a form of conscription. Army training facilities are provided by an Indian military training team. Although India is not directly responsible for the country's defence, the Indian Government has indicated that any act of aggression against Bhutan would be regarded as an act of aggression against India. Militia courses, lasting up to two years, have been provided since 1990 with the aim of establishing a 'home guard' corps to protect public and government installations and facilities.

Economic Affairs

In 1998, according to estimates by the World Bank, Bhutan's gross national product (GNP), measured at average 1996–98 prices, was US $354m., equivalent to $470 per head (or $1,438 per head on an international purchasing-power parity basis). In 1990–98 GNP per head increased, in real terms, at an average annual rate of 2.1%. During the same period the population increased by an average rate of 3.4% per year. In 1999 GNP totalled an estimated $399m., equivalent to $510 per head. Bhutan's gross domestic product (GDP) increased, in real terms, at an average annual rate of an estimated 5.8% in 1990–99. Real GDP growth was estimated at 5.3% in 1999 and was projected to remain at a similar level in 2000.

Agriculture (including livestock and forestry) contributed an estimated 34.8% of GDP in 1999. About 94% of the economically active population were employed in agriculture in that year. The principal sources of revenue in the agricultural sector are apples, oranges and cardamom. Timber production is also important; about 60% of the total land area is covered by forest. According to the Asian Development Bank (ADB), agricultural GDP increased at an average annual rate of an estimated 3.0% in 1990–99.

Industry (including mining, manufacturing, utilities and construction) employed only about 1% of the labour force in 1981/82, but contributed an estimated 34.7% of GDP in 1999. The production of low-cost electricity by the Chhukha hydroelectric project (see below) helped to stimulate growth in the industrial sector in the 1990s. Industrial GDP increased at an average annual rate of an estimated 9.0% in 1990–99.

Mining and quarrying contributed an estimated 1.4% of GDP in 1999. Calcium carbide remained the major mineral export in 1999 (contributing 13.1% of total export revenue in 1998). Gypsum, coal, limestone, slate and dolomite are also mined. Mining GDP increased by an average rate of an estimated 9.9% per year in 1990–99.

Manufacturing contributed an estimated 9.5% of GDP in 1999. The most important sector is cement production. Commercial production began at a calcium carbide plant and a ferro-alloy plant at Pasakha, near Phuentsholing, in 1988 and 1995, respectively. Bhutan also has some small-scale manufacturers, producing, for example, textiles, soap, matches, candles and carpets. Manufacturing GDP increased at an average annual rate of an estimated 9.9% in 1990–99.

The services sector, which employed only about 3.4% of the labour force in 1981/82, contributed an estimated 30.6% of GDP in 1999. The GDP of the services sector increased at an average annual rate of an estimated 7.0% in 1990–99.

Energy is derived principally from hydroelectric power. The Chhukha hydroelectric project, with a generating capacity of about 338 MW, began production in 1986 and was formally inaugurated in 1988. The project provides about 40% of Bhutan's national revenue. The Indian-financed Tala hydroelectric project, when completed in 2004 at an estimated cost of Nu 20,000m., was to have an installed capacity of 1,020 MW. Damage to the project, caused by the floods in 2000, incurred further costs of Nu 450m.; however, the development was still expected to be completed by the end of 2004. The Kurichhu power project was scheduled for completion in April 2001. In 1997 the cost of imports of diesel oil and petroleum totalled Nu 236.2m. (equivalent to 4.7% of total import costs).

In the financial year ending 30 June 1999, according to the ADB, Bhutan recorded a visible trade deficit of US $59.4m., and there was a deficit of $102.2m. on the current account of the balance of payments. In 1997/98 the principal source of imports (70.5%) was India, which was also the principal market for exports (94.5%). The principal exports in 1999 were electricity, calcium carbide, cement and particle board. Exports of electric energy to India commenced in 1988, with the inauguration of the Chhukha hydroelectric project. The principal imports in 1997 were telecommunications equipment, rice and diesel oil.

The 2000/01 budget envisaged a deficit of Nu 981.6m. (revenue Nu 8,342.1m., expenditure Nu 9,323.7m.). Grants from the Government of India provided 23.8% of Bhutan's total budgetary revenue in that year, while other grants accounted for 14.4% of the total. Bhutan's total external debt amounted to US $119.6m. at the end of 1998, all of which was long-term public debt. In that year the cost of debt-servicing was equivalent to 6.3% of the value of exports of goods and services. The average annual rate of inflation was 9.8% in 1990–99. Consumer prices rose by an estimated 6.8% in 1999. Inflation remained below 10% in 2000. By 2000 the rising level of unemployment was beginning to cause concern; an estimated 50,000 school-leavers were expected to join the labour force over the next five years.

Bhutan is a member of the Asian Development Bank (ADB, see p. 131) and of the South Asian Association for Regional Co-operation (SAARC, see p. 279), which seeks to improve regional co-operation, particularly in economic development.

The Seventh Plan (1992–97) asserted seven main objectives: self-reliance, with emphasis on internal resource mobilization; sustainability, with emphasis on environmental protection; private-sector development; decentralization and popular participation; human resources' development; balanced development in all districts; and national security. The Eighth Plan (1997–2002) further refined the seven objectives of the Seventh Plan and explicitly added another: 'the preservation and promotion of cultural and traditional values'. During these five years, GDP was expected to grow at an average annual rate of 6.7%, while the population growth rate was projected to decline to 2.56%. Revenue, which was forecast to reach Nu 15,912m. during the plan, was to cover 53% of the total plan outlay of Nu 30,000m. The agricultural sector was projected to expand by 2.5% per year over the plan period through productivity gains and horticultural development. Exports to India and third countries were expected to increase by 15% and 10%, respectively, by 2002. The guiding goal was declared as the establishment of sustainability in development, while balancing achievements with the popular sense of contentment. Core areas were to be the further development of hydro-power (long-term potential was assessed at 20,000 MW) and further industrialization. The Plan also provided for further development of the infrastructure (18.6% of outlay) and social services (22.0%), human resource development (10.7%), and renewable natural resources. Development partners meeting in Geneva, Switzerland, in January 1997 pledged US $450m. (about 50% of the projected plan outlay). The mid-term review of the Eighth Plan, which was carried out in February 2000, indicated that the Government had made satisfactory progress in reaching its targets. Fund utilization had reached around 40% of the original outlay of Nu 30,000m.; total outlay was expected to increase by 10%, while domestic revenue was projected to increase to Nu 18,673m., largely owing to the power tariff increase. This review was to serve as the basis for the Ninth Plan (2002–07), which was expected to give greater autonomy to local bodies with regard to project development.

Multilateral investment in Bhutan's financial sector was agreed by the Government for the first time in September 1998, when the ADB and Citibank purchased shares in the Bhutan National Bank. Two important measures were implemented in 1999: a proper personal income tax (to be levied only on wealthier Bhutanese) was introduced, and the country was opened up to foreign investment (foreign investors were to be permitted up to 51% ownership in a joint venture). The stock exchange remained closed to external investors. In September 2000 Bhutan and Bangladesh renewed their trade agreement for a further three years and pledged to increase the volume of bilateral trade. Bangladesh exporters were granted duty-free access to the Bhutanese market. Representatives of the two countries agreed to establish a Trade Promotional Council to deal with trade issues, infrastructure development and promote co-operation.

Social Welfare

In 1998 there were 28 hospitals (including one indigenous and five leprosy hospitals, providing general health services also), with a total of 1,001 beds (one for every 599 inhabitants), and there were 98 doctors (one for every 6,510 inhabitants). Nurses totalled 386. In December 1997 there were 1,093 village health workers in the country. Because of a shortage of medical personnel and a lack of funds, local dispensaries are being converted into basic health units (of which there were 145 by the end of 1997), providing basic medical services. In 1990 the World Health Organization declared that universal child immunization had been achieved in Bhutan. Malaria and tuberculosis are, however, still widespread. In December 2000 Bhutan was awarded a grant from the Global Fund for Children's Vaccines in order to improve basic immunization services and systems. The budget for the financial year 1998/99 allocated an estimated Nu 883m. (12.5% of total projected expenditure) to health. A total of Nu 2,410m. (25.9% of budgetary expenditure) was allocated to health and education in 2000/01. A national pension plan was due to be implemented in 2000.

Education

Education is not compulsory. Pre-primary education usually lasts for one year. Primary education begins at six years of age and lasts for seven years. Secondary education, beginning at the age of 13, lasts for a further four years, comprising two cycles of two years each. Virtually free education is available (nominal fees are demanded), but there are insufficient facilities to accommodate all school-age children. In order to accommodate additional children, community schools (established in 1989 as 'extended classrooms'—ECRs, but renamed, as above, in 1991) were set up as essentially one-teacher schools for basic primary classes, whence children were to be 'streamed' to other schools. In 1988 the total enrolment at primary schools was equivalent to an estimated 26% of children in the relevant age-group (31% of boys; 20% of girls), while the comparable ratio for secondary schools was only 5% (boys 7%; girls 2%). All schools are co-educational. English is the language of instruction and Dzongkha is a compulsory subject. Bhutan has no mission schools. Since 1988 seven privately-operated schools have been established (the majority in Thimphu); these schools are under the supervision of the Department of Education. Owing to a shortage of qualified staff (despite the existence of two teacher-training institutes with a combined enrolment of 660 students in 1999), many Indian teachers are employed. In July 2000 the total number of enrolled pupils was 112,320, and the total number of teachers was 3,025. In 1999 there were more than 320 educational institutions under the supervision of the Department of Education, including 254 community and pri-

mary schools, 51 junior high schools, 21 high schools, one degree college and nine other post-secondary institutions. Some Bhutanese students were receiving higher education abroad. The 1998/99 budget allocated an estimated Nu 912m. (12.9% of total projected expenditure) to education. In 1995, according to UNESCO estimates, the rate of adult illiteracy in Bhutan averaged 57.8% (males 43.7%; females 71.8%).

Public Holidays

2001 and 2002: The usual Buddhist holidays are observed, as well as Paru Tsechu, which falls on the 10th to the 15th day of the second lunar month, Independence Day (8 August), the Birthday of HM Jigme Singye Wangchuck (11 November), the movable Hindu feast of Dussehra and the National Day of Bhutan (17 December).

Weights and Measures

The metric system is in operation.

Statistical Survey

Source (unless otherwise stated): Royal Government of Bhutan, Thimphu.

Area and Population

AREA, POPULATION AND DENSITY

Area (sq km)	46,500*
Population (official estimates)†	
1999	657,594
2000	677,979
2001	698,996
Density (per sq km) in 2001	15.0

* 17,954 sq miles.

† These figures (which are based on the 1995 estimate of 582,000 and assume an annual population growth rate of 3.1%) are much lower than former estimates. It was previously reported that a census in 1969 enumerated a population of 931,514, and a 1980 census recorded a total of 1,165,000. On the basis of the latter figure, a mid-1988 population of 1,375,400 was projected. Other figures in this Survey are derived from the earlier, higher estimates of Bhutan's population.

Capital: Thimphu (estimated population 27,000 at 1 July 1990).

POPULATION OF DISTRICTS*
(mid-1985 estimates, based on 1980 census)

Bumthang	23,842
Dagana	28,352
Gasa†	16,907
Gelephu	111,283
Ha	16,715
Lhuentse	39,635
Mongar	73,239
Paro	46,615
Pemagatshel	37,141
Punakha†	16,700
Samdrup Jongkhar	73,044
Samtse	172,109
Zhemgang	44,516
Thimphu	58,660
Trashigang	177,718
Trongsa	26,017
Tsirang	108,807
Wangdue Phodrang	47,152
Total rural population	**1,119,452**
Total urban population	**167,823**
Total	**1,286,275**

* The above figures are approximate, and predate the creation of a new district, Chhukha, in 1987. Chhukha has an estimated total population of about 13,372 (based on the figure of 3,343 households, with an estimated average of four persons per household), who were formerly included in Samtse, Paro or Thimphu districts. The above figures also predate the creation of a further two new districts, Gasa (previously within Punakha) and Trashi Yangtse (previously within Trashigang), in 1992.

† Gasa and Punakha were merged into a single district, which was to be known as Punakha, in 1987.

BIRTHS AND DEATHS (UN estimates, annual averages)

	1980–85	1985–90	1990–95
Birth rate (per 1,000) . . .	41.5	40.9	39.8
Death rate (per 1,000) . . .	17.6	14.4	11.5

Expectation of life (UN estimates, years at birth, 1990–95): 57.6 (males 56.5; females 59.0).

Source: UN, *World Population Prospects: The 1998 Revision*.

ECONOMICALLY ACTIVE POPULATION
(estimates, '000 persons, 1981/82)

Agriculture, etc.	613
Industry	6
Trade	9
Public services	22
Total	**650**

1984 (estimates, '000 persons): Agriculture, hunting, forestry and fishing 629; Total 721 (Source: UN, *Statistical Yearbook for Asia and the Pacific*).

Agriculture

PRINCIPAL CROPS (FAO estimates, '000 metric tons)

	1997	1998	1999
Rice (paddy)	50	50	50
Wheat	20*	20*	20*
Barley	5*	5*	5*
Maize	85*	85*	70*
Millet	7	7	7
Other cereals	7	7	7
Potatoes	34	34	34
Other roots and tubers . .	22	22	22
Pulses	2	2	2
Vegetables and melons . .	10	10	10
Oranges	58	58	58
Other fruits (excl. melons) . .	6	6	6

* Unofficial figure.

Source: FAO.

LIVESTOCK (FAO estimates, '000 head, year ending September)

	1997	1998	1999
Horses	30	30	30
Mules	10	10	10
Asses	18	18	18
Cattle	435	435	435
Buffaloes	4	4	4
Pigs	75	75	75
Sheep	59	59	59
Goats	42	42	42
Poultry	310	310	310

Source: FAO.

Yaks ('000 head): 35 in 1993; 39* in 1994; 40† in 1995.

* Provisional.   † Estimate.

Source: IMF, *Bhutan—Selected Issues* (February 1997).

LIVESTOCK PRODUCTS ('000 metric tons)

	1997	1998	1999
Beef and veal	5.8	5.8	5.8
Buffalo meat	0.1	0.1	0.1
Mutton and lamb . . .	0.2	0.2	0.2
Goat meat	0.2	0.2	0.2
Pig meat	1.2	1.2	1.2
Poultry meat	0.3	0.3	0.3
Cows' milk	29.0	29.0	29.0
Buffaloes' milk . . .	2.7	2.7	2.7
Goats' milk	0.2	0.2	0.2
Hen eggs	0.4	0.4	0.4
Cattle hides (fresh) . . .	1.2	1.2	1.2
Sheepskins (fresh) . . .	0.1	0.1	0.1

Source: FAO.

Forestry

ROUNDWOOD REMOVALS ('000 cubic metres, excl. bark)

	1996	1997	1998
Sawlogs, veneer logs and logs for sleepers	18	18	18
Other industrial wood	27	27	27
Fuel wood	1,565	1,608	1,657
Total	1,610	1,653	1,702

Sawnwood production ('000 cubic metres, incl. railway sleepers): 18 in 1996; 18 in 1997; 18 in 1998.

Source: FAO, *Yearbook of Forest Products*.

Fishing

(FAO estimates, metric tons, live weight)

	1996	1997	1998
Capture			
Freshwater fishes	300	300	300
Aquaculture			
Freshwater fishes	30	30	30
Total catch	330	330	330

Source: FAO, *Yearbook of Fishery Statistics*.

Mining

(metric tons, unless otherwise indicated, year ending 30 June)

	1995/96	1996/97	1997/98
Dolomite	249,253	276,700	240,300
Limestone	266,591	297,900	376,700
Gypsum	52,102	66,600	62,300
Coal	67,994	63,900	53,200
Marble chips (sq ft)	12,841	35,400	n.a.
Slate (sq ft)	92,148	44,100	48,400
Quartzite	50,226	98,100	39,500
Talc	9,158	9,200	11,400
Iron ore	5,516	4,000	5,000
Pink shale/quartzite	5,112	1,400	2,700

Source: Geology and Mines Division, Ministry of Trade and Industry, Royal Government of Bhutan.

Industry

GROSS SALES AND OUTPUT OF SELECTED INDUSTRIES (million ngultrum)

	1997	1998	1999
Penden Cement Authority	265.5	564.7	433.7
Bhutan Ferro Alloys	522.9	488.4	534.7
Bhutan Fruit Products	107.2	112.3	124.9
Army Welfare Project*	232.0	237.9	234.9
Bhutan Carbide and Chemicals	560.3	583.6	569.3
Bhutan Board Products	428.7	383.8	257.8

* Manufacturer of alcoholic beverages.

Source: Royal Monetary Authority.

Electric energy (million kWh, year ending 30 June): 1,972.2 in 1995/96; 1,838.4 in 1996/97; 1,800.0 in 1997/98.

Revenue from the Chhukha Hydroelectric Project (million ngultrum): 1,404.8 (Internal consumption 116.7, Exports 1,288.1) in 1997; 1,489.6 (Internal consumption 150.8, Exports 1,338.8) in 1998; 2,141.7 (Internal consumption 122.5, Exports 2,019.1) in 1999.

Source: Department of Power, Royal Government of Bhutan.

Finance

CURRENCY AND EXCHANGE RATES

Monetary Units
100 chetrum (Ch) = 1 ngultrum (Nu).

Sterling, Dollar and Euro Equivalents (29 December 2000)
£1 sterling = 69.76 ngultrum;
US $1 = 46.75 ngultrum;
€1 = 43.50 ngultrum;
1,000 ngultrum = £14.33 = $21.39 = €22.99.

Average Exchange Rate (ngultrum per US $)
1998   41.259
1999   43.055
2000   44.942

Note: The ngultrum is at par with the Indian rupee, which also circulates freely within Bhutan. The foregoing figures relate to the official rate of exchange, which is applicable to government-related transactions alone. Since April 1992 there has also been a market rate of exchange, which values foreign currencies approximately 20% higher than the official rate of exchange.

BUDGET (estimates, million ngultrum, year ending 30 June)

Revenue	1996/97	1997/98*	1998/99†
Domestic revenue	2,425	3,079	3,094
Tax	869	1,246	1,285
Non-tax	1,556	1,832	1,809
Grants from Government of India	948	1,335	2,271
Grants from UN and other international agencies	1,284	820	1,479
Total	4,657	5,234	6,844

Expenditure	1996/97	1997/98*	1998/99†
General public services	1,427	1,562	1,985
Economic services	2,205	1,834	3,187
Agriculture and irrigation	430	199	320
Animal husbandry	135	78	149
Forestry	122	132	190
Industries, mining, trade and commerce	36	34	74
Public works, roads and housing	668	502	626
Transport and communication	252	250	161
Power	562	639	1,667
Social services	999	1,119	1,827
Education	517	543	912
Health	469	558	883
Urban development and municipal corporations	13	17	32
Net lending	327	231	45
Total expenditure and net lending	4,958	4,745	7,044

* Provisional figures.   † Projected figures.

Source: IMF, *Bhutan – Statistical Annex* (July 1999).

1999/2000 (million ngultrum, revised figures): *Revenue:* Domestic revenue 3,866.0; Other receipts 273.0; Grants 3,616.3; Total 7,755.3. *Expenditure:* Current expenditure 3,743.7; Capital expenditure 4,514.6; Net lending 54.2; Repayment 209.3; Total 8,521.8.

2000/01 (million ngultrum, provisional figures): *Revenue:* Domestic revenue 4,210.6; Other receipts 566.4; Grants 3,565.2; Total 8,342.1. *Expenditure:* Current expenditure 4,158.6; Capital expenditure 4,922.6; Net lending 27.1; Repayment 215.4; Total 9,323.7.

Source: Royal Government of Bhutan.

FOREIGN EXCHANGE RESERVES (at 30 June)

	1998	1999†	2000
Indian rupee reserves (million Indian rupees). . . .	1,629.1	2,725.4	3,356.9
Royal Monetary Authority .	152.8	278.4	293.9
Bank of Bhutan . . .	1,404.4	1,863.7	1,819.5
Bhutan National Bank . .	72.0	583.3	1,191.9
Royal Insurance Corporation of Bhutan	—	—	51.5
Convertible currency reserves (US $ million)	177.2	195.6	217.5
Royal Monetary Authority* . .	171.0	189.0	193.4
Bank of Bhutan . . .	4.0	3.0	11.4
Bhutan National Bank . .	2.2	3.6	12.6
Royal Insurance Corporation of Bhutan	—	0.1	—

* Includes tranche position in the International Monetary Fund.

† Revised figures.

Source: Royal Monetary Authority of Bhutan.

MONEY SUPPLY (million ngultrum at 31 December)

	1998	1999	2000*
Currency outside banks† . . .	768.8	969.2	1,119.4
Demand deposits at the Bank of Bhutan	1,860.4	2,754.9	2,474.8
Total money‡	2,792.0	12,665.8	14,000.4

* Figures at 30 June.

† Including an estimate for Indian rupees.

‡ Including non-monetary deposits with the Royal Monetary Authority by financial institutions.

Source: Royal Monetary Authority of Bhutan.

COST OF LIVING
(Consumer Price Index at 31 December; base: 1979 = 100)

	1997	1998	1999
All items (excl. rent). . . .	501.2	561.7	587.0*

* Revised figure.

Source: Central Statistical Office of the Planning Commission, Royal Government of Bhutan.

NATIONAL ACCOUNTS (million ngultrum at current prices)
Expenditure on the Gross Domestic Product

	1994	1995	1996
Government final consumption expenditure	2,106.0	2,727.0	3,445.0
Private final consumption expenditure	3,136.0	3,147.0	4,224.0
Increase in stocks . . .	229.3	155.7	157.3
Gross fixed capital formation .	3,871.1	4,416.5	5,046.4
Total domestic expenditure	9,342.4	10,446.2	12,872.7
Exports of goods and services .	2,508.0	3,712.0	3,973.0
Less Imports of goods and services	3,349.0	4,190.0	5,133.0
GDP in purchasers' values . .	8,501.4	9,968.2	11,712.7
GDP at constant 1990 prices .	5,917.8	6,362.3	6,767.6

GDP in purchasers' values (million ngultrum): 14,477 in 1997; 16,420 in 1998.

Source: IMF, *International Financial Statistics*.

Gross Domestic Product by Economic Activity

	1997	1998*	1999†
Agriculture, forestry and livestock	5,276.0	6,023.6	6,896.1
Mining and quarrying . . .	308.7	262.3	272.0
Manufacturing	1,588.5	1,778.2	1,889.0
Electricity	1,729.5	1,937.1	2,333.6
Construction.	1,466.4	1,756.4	2,380.1
Trade, restaurants and hotels. .	1,014.4	1,159.7	1,278.9
Transport, storage and communications	1,022.6	1,336.1	1,752.3
Finance, insurance and real estate	729.2	1,004.0	1,157.4
Community, social and personal services	1,362.7	1,436.9	1,873.1
Sub-total	14,498.0	16,694.3	19,832.5
Less Imputed bank service charges	526.9	458.3	559.0
GDP at factor cost	13,971.1	16,236.0	19,273.5
GDP at constant 1980 factor cost	3,320.1	3,490.2	3,700.4

* Revised figures.

† Projected figures.

Source: Royal Monetary Authority of Bhutan.

BALANCE OF PAYMENTS (US $ million, year ending 30 June)

	1996/97	1997/98*	1998/99†
Merchandise exports f.o.b.‡ . .	99.3	111.3	108.8
Merchandise imports c.i.f.‡ . .	−131.2	−136.1	−165.2
Trade balance	−31.9	−24.8	−56.4
Services and transfers:			
Receipts.	27.8	45.2	47.7
Payments	−52.2	−66.9	−78.2
Current balance	−56.4	−46.5	−86.9
Grants	74.4	85.4	124.8
Loans (net)	5.4	4.4	2.3
Foreign direct investment . .	—	—	1.1
Net errors and omissions . . .	−1.2	2.1	—
Total (net monetary movements) .	22.2	45.4	41.4

* Provisional figures.

† Projected figures.

‡ On a calendar year basis.

Source: IMF, *Bhutan — Statistical Annex* (July 1999).

OFFICIAL DEVELOPMENT ASSISTANCE (US $ million)

	1995	1996	1997
Bilateral donors	55.3	42.1	44.5
Multilateral donors . . .	18.5	20.3	25.5
Total	73.8	62.4	70.0
Grants	68.5	58.5	59.9
Loans	5.3	3.9	10.1
Per caput assistance (US $) . .	45.1	34.4	37.6

Source: UN, *Statistical Yearbook for Asia and the Pacific*.

SELECTED COMMODITIES (million ngultrum, provisional)

Imports c.i.f.	1995	1996	1997
Wood charcoal	n.a.	122.3	139.6
Telecommunications equipment .	n.a.	302.0	491.0
Beer	n.a.	66.0	86.3
Coal	n.a.	44.6	103.3
Diesel oil	136.1	138.8	163.2
Petroleum	64.0	67.4	73.0
Rice.	217.3	209.1	215.3
Wheat	39.3	89.0	100.0
Vegetable fats and oils . .	134.7	134.4	121.1
Cotton fabric	41.9	38.2	n.a.
Industrial machinery. . .	142.0	77.5	54.3
Tyres for buses and trucks .	37.5	34.5	n.a.
Iron and steel	115.4	109.6	117.0
Electricity	10.7	7.6	n.a.
Total (incl. others) . . .	3,802.3	4,250.0	4,980.0

Exports f.o.b.	1995	1996	1997
Electricity	721.9	747.6	1,290.0
Calcium carbide	497.9	533.0	546.3
Cement	278.4	253.0	371.4
Particle board	329.1	286.0	329.0
Non-coniferous plywood	32.8	2.2	n.a.
Sawn logs (hard)	71.8	79.1	78.1
Sawn timber (soft)	60.7	27.1	76.5
Cardamom	73.8	68.2	36.9
Wheat and flour	23.8	58.0	n.a.
Mixed fruit/vegetable juice	119.5	86.7	7.8
Coal (bituminous)	n.a.	19.9	25.6
Rum	n.a.	65.0	58.8
Total (incl. others)	3,349.1	3,553.8	4,270.0

1998 (million ngultrum): Electricity 1,338.7; Calcium carbide 583.6; Cement 547.3; Particle board 285.8.

1999 (million ngultrum): Electricity 2,019.1; Calcium carbide 546.8; Cement 433.7; Particle board 247.6. Source: Asian Development Bank, *Key Indicators of Developing Asian and Pacific Countries.*

PRINCIPAL TRADING PARTNERS
(estimates, US $ million, year ending 30 June)

Imports c.i.f.	1995/96	1996/97	1997/98
India	81.4	85.8	96.0
Other countries	29.5	45.5	40.1
Total	110.9	131.3	136.1

Exports f.o.b.	1995/96	1996/97	1997/98
India	89.8	90.2	105.3
Other countries	7.9	9.1	6.1
Total	97.7	99.4	111.4

Source: Royal Monetary Authority of Bhutan.

Transport

ROAD TRAFFIC
In 1997 there were 2,559 registered, roadworthy vehicles—764 light four-wheeled vehicles, 1,170 two-wheeled vehicles (motor cycles and scooters), 442 heavy vehicles (trucks, buses, bulldozers, etc.) and 183 taxis. Source: Central Statistical Office, Ministry of Planning.

CIVIL AVIATION (traffic, year ending 30 June)

	1985	1986	1987
Kilometres flown ('000)	152	201	n.a.
Passengers	5,928	7,776	8,700
Passenger-km ('000)	3,349	4,381	n.a.

Paying passengers: 19,608 in 1993, 21,115 in 1994, 22,286 in 1995.
Revenue (million ngultrum, year ending 30 June): 241.5 in 1992/93, 188.3 in 1993/94, 210.0 in 1994/95.
Source: Central Statistical Office, Ministry of Planning, Royal Government of Bhutan.

Tourism

FOREIGN VISITORS BY COUNTRY OF ORIGIN*

	1997	1998	1999
Australia	121	64	131
Austria	156	270	197
France	229	366	236
Germany	533	520	574
Italy	186	218	276
Japan	1,173	1,032	1,102
Netherlands	234	370	362
Spain	9	109	n.a.
Switzerland	186	170	296
Taiwan	83	135	n.a.
Thailand	140	19	71
United Kingdom	642	686	646
USA	910	1,471	2,122
Total (incl. others)	5,362	6,203	7,158

* Figures relate to tourists paying in convertible currency.

Receipts (US $ million): 6.55 in 1997; 7.84 in 1998; 8.65 in 1999.

Sources: Tourism Authority of Bhutan; World Tourism Organization, *Yearbook of Tourism Statistics.*

Government hotel rooms: 560 in 1996; 560 in 1997; 560 (provisional) in 1998 (Source: IMF, *Bhutan—Statistical Annex* (July 1999)).

Communications Media

In 1996 there were 6,000 telephone lines and 1,000 telefax stations in use. There were 37,000 radio receivers and 11,000 television receivers in 1997.

Education

	Institutions at 1 April 1999	Students at 15 July 2000		
		Males	Females	Total
Community schools	254 {	9,607	7,723	17,330
Primary schools		17,956	14,788	32,744
Junior high schools	51	21,368	19,140	40,508
High schools	21	9,829	7,652	17,481
Degree college*	1	433	147	580
Other post-secondary institutions (incl. Sanskrit Pathsalas)	9	n.a.	n.a.	n.a.
Private schools	7	1,300	1,149	2,449
Non-formal education (NFE) centres	81	n.a.	n.a.	n.a.

* Affiliated with University of Delhi.

15 July 2000: Total teachers 3,025 (of whom 2,867 at schools, 158 at higher institutes). Total students at higher institutes 1,808.

Source: Ministry of Health and Education, Thimphu.

Directory

The Constitution

The Kingdom of Bhutan has no formal constitution. However, the state system is a modified form of constitutional monarchy. Written rules, which are changed periodically, govern procedures for the election of members of the Council of Ministers, the Royal Advisory Council and the Legislature, and define the duties and powers of those bodies.

The Government

Head of State: HM Druk Gyalpo ('Dragon King') JIGME SINGYE WANGCHUK (succeeded to the throne in July 1972).

LODOI TSOKDE
(Royal Advisory Council)
(March 2001)

The Royal Advisory Council (Lodoi Tsokde), established in 1965, comprises nine members: two monks representing the Central and District Monastic Bodies (Rabdeys), six people's representatives and a Chairman (Kalyon), nominated by the King. Each geog (group of villages, known also as a block) within a dzongkhag (district) selects one representative, from whom the respective Dzongkhag Yargye Tshogchungs (DYTs—District Development Committees) each agree on one nomination to be forwarded to the National Assembly (Tshogdu Chenmo). From these 20 nominees, the National Assembly, in turn, elects six persons to serve on the Royal Advisory Council as people's representatives for the whole country. The Council's principal task is to advise the Chairman of the Council of Ministers (Lhengye Zhungtshog), as head of government, and to supervise all aspects of administration. The Council is in permanent session, virtually as a government department, and acts, on a daily basis, as the *de facto* Standing Committee of the National Assembly. Representatives of the monastic bodies serve for one year, representatives of the people for three years, and the duration of the Chairman's term of office is at the discretion of the King. Representatives may be re-elected, but not for consecutive terms; they are all full members of the Council of Ministers.

Chairman: Dasho RINZIN GYELTSHEN.

Councillors*: Dasho PHANCHUNG, Dasho TASHI DORJI, Dasho JAMBAY NGEDUB, Dasho PENPA, Dasho NOB TSHERING, Dasho UGYEN DORJI.

* From November 1998 to November 2001.

LHENGYE ZHUNGTSHOG
(Council of Ministers)
(March 2001)

Chairman (August 2000–July 2001) **and Minister of Finance:** Lyonpo YESHEY ZIMBA.

Minister of Foreign Affairs: Lyonpo JIGMI YOZER THINLEY.

Minister of Health and Education: Lyonpo SANGYE NGEDUP DORJI.

Minister of Agriculture: Lyonpo KUNZANG DORJI.

Minister of Trade and Industry: Lyonpo KHANDU WANGCHUK.

Minister of Home Affairs: Lyonpo THINLEY GYAMTSHO.

Cabinet Secretary: Aum NETEN ZANGMO.

All members of the Royal Advisory Council are also members of the Council of Ministers.

MINISTRIES AND OTHER MAJOR GOVERNMENT BODIES

Ministry of Agriculture: POB 252, Thimphu; tel. 322129; fax 323153; internet www.moa.gov.bt.

Ministry of Communications: Tashichhodzong, POB 278, Thimphu; tel. 322218; fax 322184; internet www.dit.gov.bt.

Ministry of Finance: Tashichhodzong, POB 117, Thimphu; tel. 322223; fax 323154.

Ministry of Foreign Affairs: Convention Centre, POB 103, Thimphu; tel. 324119; fax 323240.

Ministry of Health and Education: Tashichhodzong, POB 726, Thimphu; tel. 322351; fax 324649 (Health Services division); tel. 325146; fax 324823; internet www.rim.edu.bt (Education Division).

Ministry of Home Affairs: Tashichhodzong, POB 133, Thimphu; tel. 322301; fax 322214.

Ministry of Trade and Industry: Tashichhodzong, POB 141, Thimphu; tel. 322211; fax 323617; internet www.cdb.gov.bt.

National Commission for Cultural Affairs: Thimphu; tel. 322001; fax 323040; fmrly Special Commission for Cultural Affairs; Chair. Lyonpo THINLEY GYAMTSHO; Sec. Dasho SANGAY WANGCHUCK.

National Environment Commission: Thimphu; tel. 323384; fax 323385; Hon. Dep. Minister Dasho NADO RINCHEN.

Office of the Royal Advisory Council: Tashichhodzong, POB 200, Thimphu; tel. 312339; fax 325343.

Legislature
TSHOGDU CHENMO

A National Assembly (Tshogdu Chenmo) was established in 1953. The Assembly has a three-year term and meets (in recent years) at least once a year (usually in June–July). The size of the membership is based, in part, on the population of the districts; although the size is, in principle, subject to periodic revision, in practice the popular representation has remained unchanged since 1953. In 2000 the Assembly had 152 members, including the Speaker and Deputy Speaker. Of this number, 99 were elected by direct popular consensus in the districts (formal voting is used, however, in the event of a deadlock). Six were members of the Royal Advisory Council (RAC), elected by secret ballot; the Chairman (Kalyon) of the RAC also sits in the Assembly. Ten seats were reserved for representatives of the Central and District Monk Bodies (of whom two sit as members of the RAC), one was reserved for a representative of industry (elected by the Bhutan Chamber of Commerce and Industry), and the remainder (35) were occupied by officials (including the 20 Dzongdas) selected by the King in conjunction with the National Assembly Secretariat. Not all of the public members (chimis) are elected simultaneously; there are, therefore, overlaps in tenure. The Assembly elects its own Speaker from among its members, for a three-year (renewable) term. It enacts laws, advises on constitutional and political matters and debates all important issues. There is provision for a secret ballot on controversial issues, but, in practice, decisions are reached by consensus. Ministers and the six public members of the RAC are chosen by the entire Assembly in a secret ballot. Both the RAC and the Council of Ministers are responsible to the Assembly.

Speaker: Dasho UGYEN DORJI.

Political Organizations

Political parties are banned in Bhutan, in accordance with long-standing legislation. There are, however, a small number of anti-Government organizations, composed principally of Nepali-speaking former residents of Bhutan, which are based in Kathmandu, Nepal.

Bhutan Gurkha National Liberation Front (BGNLF): Nepal; f. 1994; Sec.-Gen. R. P. SUBBA.

Bhutan National Democratic Party (BNDP): POB 3334, Kathmandu, Nepal; tel. 525682; f. 1992; also has offices in Delhi and Varanasi, India, and in Thapa, Nepal; Pres. R. B. BASNET; Gen. Secs HARI P. ADHIKARI (Organization), Dr D. N. S. DHAKAL (Planning and External Affairs).

Bhutan People's Party (BPP): f. 1990 as a successor to the People's Forum on Democratic Rights (f. 1989); advocates unconditional release of all political prisoners, judicial reform, freedom of religious practices, linguistic freedom, freedom of press, speech and expression, and equal rights for all ethnic groups; Pres. R. K. BUDATHOKI; Gen. Sec. R. K. CHETTRI.

Druk National Congress (DNC): Maharagunj, Chakrapath, Kathmandu, Nepal; f. 1992; claims to represent 'all the oppressed people of Bhutan'; Pres. 'RONGTHONG' KINLEY DORJI.

Human Rights Organization of Bhutan (HUROB): POB 172, Patan Dhoka, Lalitpur, Kathmandu, Nepal; tel. 525046; fax 526038; f. 1991; documents alleged human rights violations in Bhutan and co-ordinates welfare activities in eight refugee camps in Nepal for ethnic Nepalese claiming to be from Bhutan; Chair. S. B. SUBBA; Gen. Sec. OM DHUNGEL.

United Liberation People's Front: f. 1990; Leader BALARAM POUDYAL.

Diplomatic Representation
EMBASSIES IN BHUTAN

Bangladesh: POB 178, Upper Choubachu, Thimphu; tel. 322362; fax 322629; e-mail bdoot@druknet.net.bt; Ambassador: SARADINDU SEKHAR CHAKMA.

India: India House, Lungtenzampa, Thimphu; tel. 322100; fax 323195; Ambassador: KANWAR SINGH JASROTIA.

Judicial System

Bhutan has Civil and Criminal Codes, which are based on those laid down by the Shabdrung Ngawang Namgyal in the 17th century. An independent judicial authority was established in 1961, but law was mostly administered at the district level until 1968, when the High Court was set up. Existing laws were consolidated in 1982, although annual or biennial conferences of Thrimpons are held to keep abreast of changing circumstances and to recommend (in the first instance, to the King) amendments to existing laws. Most legislation is sent by the Council of Ministers to the National Assembly for approval and enactment. During 1995–99 substantial revisions to the civil and criminal codes were being drafted.

Appeal Court: The Supreme Court of Appeal is the King.

High Court (Thrimkhang Gongma): Thimphu; tel. 322344; fax 322921; established 1968 to review appeals from Lower Courts, although some cases are heard at the first instance. The Full Bench is presided over by the Chief Justice. There are normally seven other judges, who are appointed by the King on the recommendation of the Chief Justice and who serve until their superannuation. Three judges form a quorum. The judges are assisted by senior rabjams/ramjans (judges in training). Assistance to defendants is available through jabmis (certificated pleaders). The operation of the legal system and proposed amendments are considered by regular meetings of all the judges and Thrimpons (usually annually, or at least once every two years). Under the mid-1998 grant of governance to an elected Council of Ministers and pending the adoption of detailed regulations, proposed amendments are expected to be submitted to the Council of Ministers for consideration.

Chief Justice: Lyonpo SONAM TOBGYE.

Judges of the High Court: Dasho THINLEY YOEZER, Dasho PASANG TOBGYE, Dasho KARMA D. SHERPA, Dasho D. N. KATWAL*, Dasho K. B. GHALEY*, Dasho GAGEY LHAM, Dasho DORJI WANGDI.

* Originally nominated as public representative.

Magistrates' Courts (Dzongkhag Thrimkhang): Each district has a court, headed by the thrimpon (magistrate) and aided by a junior rabjam/ramjam, which tries most cases. Appeals are made to the High Court, and less serious civil disputes may be settled by a gup or mandal (village headman) through written undertakings by the parties concerned.

All citizens have the right to make informal appeal for redress of grievances directly to the King, through the office of the gyalpoi zimpon (court chamberlain).

Department of Legal Affairs: f. 2000; to consist of a prosecution division, with civil and criminal sections, to indict offenders on behalf of the Government; and a legal services division, to assist in the drafting of laws and acts, advance Bhutan's interest internationally in accordance with public international laws, develop the legal profession, and create public awareness of laws and acts; Dir-Gen. Dasho TASHI PHUNTSOG.

Religion

The state religion is Mahayana Buddhism, but the southern Bhutanese are predominantly followers of Hinduism. Buddhism was introduced into Bhutan in the eighth century AD by the Indian saint Padmasambhava, known in Bhutan as Guru Rimpoche. In the 13th century Phajo Drugom Shigpo made the Drukpa school of Kagyupa Buddhism pre-eminent in Bhutan, and this sect is still supported by the dominant ethnic group, the Drukpas. The main monastic group, the Central Monastic Body (comprising 1,160 monks), is led by an elected Head Abbot (Je Khenpo), is directly supported by the State and spends six months of the year at Tashichhodzong and at Punakha respectively. A further 2,120 monks, who are members of the District Monastic Bodies, are sustained by the lay population. The Council for Ecclesiastical Affairs oversees all religious bodies. Monasteries (Gompas) and shrines (Lhakhangs) are numerous. Religious proselytizing, in any form, is illegal.

Council for Ecclesiastical Affairs (Dratshang Lhentshog): POB 254, Thimphu; tel. 322754; fax 323867; f. 1984, replacing the Central Board for Monastic Studies, to oversee all Buddhist meditational centres and schools of Buddhist studies, as well as the Central and District Monastic Bodies; daily affairs of the Council are run by the Central Monastic Secretariat; Chair. His Holiness the Je Khenpo JIGME CHOEDRA; Sec. SANGAY WANGCHUK; Dep. Sec. SANGAY TENZIN.

The Press

The Bhutan Review: POB 172, Patan Dhoka, Lalitpur, Kathmandu, Nepal; tel. 525046; fax 523819; f. 1993; monthly organ of the Human Rights Organization of Bhutan (HUROB); opposed to existing government policies.

Kuensel: POB 204, Thimphu; tel. 322483; fax 322975; internet www.kuensel.com.bt; f. 1965 as a weekly govt bulletin; reorg. as a national weekly newspaper in 1986; became autonomous corporation in 1992 (previously under Dept of Information), incorporating former Royal Government Press; in English, Dzongkha and Nepali; Editor-in-Chief KINLEY DORJI; Editors R. N. MISHRA (Nepali), TENZIN RIGDEN (English), MINDU DORJI (Dzongkha); circ. 280 (Nepali), 12,875 (English), 4,280 (Dzongkha).

Broadcasting and Communications

TELECOMMUNICATIONS

Bhutan Telecom Corporation: POB 134, Thimphu; tel. 322678; fax 323041; e-mail info@telecom.net.bt; internet www.telecom.net.bt; f. 2000; state-owned public corpn; regulation authority; Dir SANGEY TENZING.

DrukNet: Bhutan Telecom, Thimphu; tel. 326999; fax 322098; e-mail info@druknet.net.bt; internet www.druknet.net.bt; f. 1999; internet service provider; Head GANGA SHARMA.

BROADCASTING

Radio

In 1994 there were 52 radio stations for administrative communications. Of these, 34 were for internal communications (to which the public had access), and three were external stations serving Bhutan House at Kalimpong and the Bhutanese diplomatic missions in India and Bangladesh.

BBS Corporation (Bhutan Broadcasting Service): POB 101, Thimphu; tel. 323071; fax 323073; f. 1973 as Radio National Youth Association of Bhutan (NYAB); became autonomous corporation in 1992 (previously under Dept of Information); short-wave radio station broadcasting daily in Dzongkha, Sharchopkha, Nepali (Lhotsamkha) and English; a daily FM programme (for Thimphu only) began in 1987; Chair. Lyonpo YESHEY ZIMBA; Exec. Dir KUENGA SINGYE.

Television

In June 1999 the BBS Corporation started operating a television service (in Dzongkha and English) in Thimphu; the service was gradually to be expanded throughout the country. Broadcasts were to be limited to a few hours a day and were to consist entirely of national news and documentaries about the Bhutanese. By March 2000, according to the Ministry of Communications, each of the two cable television operators was providing 25 channels.

Finance

(cap. = capital; auth. = authorized; p.u. = paid up;
res = reserves; dep. = deposits; m. = million; brs = branches;
amounts in ngultrum)

BANKING

Central Bank

Royal Monetary Authority (RMA): POB 154, Thimphu; tel. 322540; fax 322847; f. 1982; bank of issue; frames and implements official monetary policy, co-ordinates the activities of financial institutions and holds foreign-exchange deposits on behalf of the Govt; cap. 1.5m.; Chair. Lyonpo YESHEY ZIMBA; Man. Dir SONAM WANGCHUK.

Commercial Banks

Bank of Bhutan: POB 75, Phuentsholing; tel. 252225; fax 252641; f. 1968; 20%-owned by the State Bank of India and 80% by the Govt of Bhutan; wholly managed by Govt of Bhutan from 1997; auth. cap. 100m., cap. p.u. 50m., res 361.7m., dep. 4,921.5m. (Dec. 1998); Dirs nominated by the Bhutan Govt: Chair. Lyonpo YESHEY ZIMBA; Dirs KINLEY D. DORJI, SONAM WANGCHUK, Dasho UGYEN DORJI; Dirs nominated by the State Bank of India: D. K. JAIN, V. RAMAMOORTY; Man. Dir TSHERING DORJI; 25 brs and 3 extension counters.

Bhutan National Bank (BNB): POB 439, Thimphu; tel. 322767; fax 323601; e-mail mdbnb@druknet.net.bt; Bhutan's second commercial bank, in 1996; partially privatized in 1998; 27% owned by Govt, 20.1% by Asian Development Bank and 19.9% by Citibank; auth. cap. 200m., cap. p.u. 59.5m. (1999); Chair. Lyonpo YESHEY ZIMBA; Man. Dir KIPCHU TSHERING; 4 brs.

Development Bank

Bhutan Development Finance Corporation (BDFC): POB 256, Thimphu; tel. 322579; fax 323428; e-mail krangdol@druknet.net.bt; f. 1988; provides industrial loans and short- and medium-term agricultural loans; cap. p.u. 100m., loans 422m. (1998); Chair. Lyonpo YESHEY ZIMBA; Man. Dir KARMA RANGDOL.

STOCK EXCHANGE

Royal Securities Exchange of Bhutan Ltd (RSEB): POB 742, Thimphu; tel. 323995; fax 323849; e-mail rseb@druknet.net.bt; f. 1993; supervised by the Royal Monetary Authority; open to Bhutanese nationals only; 13 listed cos (1998); Chair. SONAM WANGCHUK; CEO TASHI YEZER.

INSURANCE

Royal Insurance Corporation of Bhutan: POB 77, Phuentsholing; tel. 252869; fax 252640; e-mail ricbho@druknet.net.bt; f. 1975; Chair. Lyonpo YESHEY ZIMBA; Man. Dir LAMKEY TSHERING; 10 brs and development centres.

Trade and Industry

GOVERNMENT AGENCIES

Food Corporation of Bhutan (FCB): POB 80, Phuentsholing; tel. 322877; fax 323957; f. 1974; activities include procurement and distribution of food grains and other essential commodities through appointed Fair Price Shop Agents; marketing of surplus agricultural and horticultural produce through FCB-regulated market outlets; logistics concerning World Food Programme food aid; accumulation of buffer stocks to offset any emergency food shortages; maintenance of SAARC Food Security Reserve Stock; Man. Dir TSHERING WANGDI; Man. ZEKO DORJI.

Forestry Development Corporation: Man. Dir NAMGAY WANGCHUK.

Planning Commission: Convention Centre, POB 127, Thimphu; tel. 323176; fax 322928; e-mail plansect@druknet.net.bt; headed by the King until 1991, formally reconstituted 1999; consists of 21 officials; proposes socio-economic policy guidelines, issues directives for the formulation of development plans, ensures efficient and judicious allocation of resources, directs socio-economic research, studies and surveys, and appraises the Government on the progress of development plans and programmes; Chair. Lyonpo SANGAY NGEDUP; Sec. DAW TENZIN.

State Trading Corpn of Bhutan Ltd (STCB): POB 76, Phuentsholing; tel. 252286; fax 252619; e-mail stcbl@druknet.net.bt; manages imports and exports on behalf of the Govt; Man. Dir Dasho DORJI NAMGAY; Jt Man. Dir (Automobile Div.) SONAM GYAMTSHO; brs in Thimphu (POB 272; tel. 322953; fax 323781; e-mail stcbthim@druknet.net.bt) and Calcutta, India.

CHAMBER OF COMMERCE

Bhutan Chamber of Commerce and Industry (BCCI): POB 147, Thimphu; tel. 322742; fax 323936; e-mail bcci@druknet.net.bt; f. 1980; reorg. 1988; promotion of trade and industry, information dissemination, private-sector human resource development; 434 registered mems; 12-mem. technical advisory committee; 25-mem. executive committee; 20 liaison offices; Pres. Dasho UGYEN DORJI; Sec.-Gen. Dasho TSHERING DORJI.

UTILITIES

Electricity

Department of Power: c/o Ministry of Trade and Industry, Tashichhodzong, POB 141, Thimpu; tel. 22159; fax 223507.

Chhukha Hydropower Corporation: Phuentsholing; tel. 252575; fax 252582; f. 1991; state-owned; Chair. Lyonpo YESHEY ZIMBA; Man. Dir YESHEY WANGDI.

Kurichhu Project Authority: Mongar; tel. 744113; fax 744130; e-mail chhewang@druknet.net.bt; co-ordinates construction of hydroelectric power-generating facilities at Gyelpozhing; Man. Dir. CHHEWANG RINZIN.

Tala Hydroelectric Project: Tala; tel. 325498; fax 325499; co-ordinates construction of dam and hydroelectric power-generating facilities; Gen. Man. R. N. KHAZANCHI.

Water

Thimphu City Corporation (Water Supply Unit): POB 215, Thimphu; tel. 22265; fax 24315; f. 1982; responsible for water supply of Thimphu municipality (population 32,000); Head BHIMLAL DHUNGEL.

TRADE UNIONS

Under long-standing legislation, trade union activity is illegal in Bhutan.

Transport

ROADS AND TRACKS

In December 1997 there were 3,375 km of roads in Bhutan, of which 65.9% were paved. Surfaced roads link the important border towns of Phuentsholing, Gelephu, Sarpang and Samdrup Jongkhar in southern Bhutan to towns in West Bengal and Assam in India. There is a shortage of road transport. Yaks, ponies and mules are still the chief means of transport on the rough mountain tracks. By 1990 most of the previously government-operated transport facilities (mainly buses and minibuses) on major and subsidiary routes had been transferred to private operators on the basis of seven-year contracts.

Road Safety and Transport Authority: Thimphu; tel. 321282; fax 322538; under Ministry of Communications; regulates condition of goods and passenger transport services; Dir YESHI TSHERING.

Transport Corpn of Bhutan: Phuentsholing; tel. 252476; f. 1982; subsidiary of Royal Insurance Corpn of Bhutan; operates direct coach service between Phuentsholing and Kolkata (Calcutta) via Siliguri.

Other operators are Barma Travels (f. 1990), Dawa Transport (Propr SHERUB WANGCHUCK), Dhendup Travel Service (Phuentsholing; tel. 252437), Gyamtsho Transport, Gurung Transport Service, Namgay Transport, Nima Travels (Phuentsholing; tel. 252384), and Rimpung Travels (Phuentsholing; tel. 252354).

Lorries for transporting goods are operated by the private sector.

CIVIL AVIATION

There is an international airport at Paro. There are also numerous helicopter landing pads, which are used, by arrangement with the Indian military and aviation authorities, solely by government officials.

Department of Civil Aviation: c/o Ministry of Communications, Tashichhodzong, POB 278, Thimphu; tel. 22499; fax 22987; Dir RIN GYELTSHEN.

Druk-Air Corpn Ltd (Royal Bhutan Airlines): POB 209, Old Bhutan Hotel, Thimphu; tel. 322825; fax 322775; internet www.drukair.com; national airline; f. 1981; became fully operational in 1983; services from Paro to Bangladesh, India, Nepal and Thailand; charter services also undertaken; Chair. Dasho LEKI DORJI; Man. Dir (vacant).

Tourism

Bhutan was opened to tourism in 1975. In 1999 the total number of foreign visitors was 7,158. Receipts from tourism in 1999 totalled US $8.65m. Tourists travel in organized 'package' or trekking tours, or individually, accompanied by government-appointed guides. Hotels have been constructed at Phuentsholing, Paro, Bumthang and Thimphu, with lodges at Trongsa, Trashigang and Mongar. In addition, there are many small privately-operated hotels and guesthouses. The Government exercises close control over the development of tourism. In 1987 the National Assembly resolved that all monasteries, mountains and other holy places should be inaccessible to tourists from 1988 (this resolution is flexibly interpreted, however—e.g. Japanese Buddhist tour groups are permitted to visit 'closed' monasteries). In 1991 the Government began transferring the tourism industry to the private sector and licences were issued to new private tourism operators. New rules were introduced in 1995, asserting more stringent controls over private operators, through the Tourism Authority of Bhutan.

Tourism Authority of Bhutan: POB 126, Thimphu; tel. 323252; fax 323695; e-mail tab@druknet.net.bt; f. 1991; under regulatory authority of Ministry of Trade and Industry; exercises overall authority over tourism policy, pricing, hotel, restaurant and travel agency licensing, visa approvals, etc.; Man. Dir TSHERING YONTEN; Dep. Man. Dir THUJI D. NADIK.

Bhutan Tourism Corporation Ltd: POB 159, Thimphu; tel. 322854; fax 323392; e-mail btcl@druknet.net.bt; internet www.kingdomofbhutan.com.

BOLIVIA

Introductory Survey

Location, Climate, Language, Religion, Flag, Capital

The Republic of Bolivia is a land-locked state in South America, bordered by Chile and Peru to the west, by Brazil to the north and east, and by Paraguay and Argentina to the south. The climate varies, according to altitude, from humid tropical conditions in the northern and eastern lowlands, which are less than 500 m (1,640 ft) above sea-level, to the cool and cold zones at altitudes of more than 3,500 m (about 11,500 ft) in the Andes mountains. The official languages are Spanish, Quechua and Aymará. Almost all of the inhabitants profess Christianity, and the great majority are adherents of the Roman Catholic Church. The national civil flag (proportions 3 by 2) has three equal horizontal stripes, of red, yellow and green. The state flag has, in addition, the national coat of arms in the centre of the yellow stripe. The legal capital is Sucre. The administrative capital and seat of government is La Paz.

Recent History

The Incas of Bolivia were conquered by Spain in 1538 and, although there were many revolts against Spanish rule, independence was not achieved until 1825. Bolivian history has been characterized by recurrent internal strife, resulting in a lengthy succession of presidents, and frequent territorial disputes with its neighbours, including the 1879–83 War of the Pacific between Bolivia, Peru and Chile, and the Chaco Wars of 1928–30 and 1932–35 against Paraguay.

At a presidential election in May 1951 the largest share of the vote was won by Dr Víctor Paz Estenssoro, the candidate of the Movimiento Nacionalista Revolucionario (MNR), who had been living in Argentina since 1946. He was denied permission to return to Bolivia and contested the election in absentia. However, he failed to gain an absolute majority, and the incumbent President transferred power to a junta of army officers. This regime was itself overthrown in April 1952, when a popular uprising, supported by the MNR and a section of the armed forces, enabled Dr Paz Estenssoro to return from exile and assume the presidency. His Government, a coalition of the MNR and the Labour Party, committed itself to profound social revolution. The coalition nationalized the tin mines and introduced universal suffrage (the franchise had previously been limited to literate adults) and land reform. Dr Hernán Siles Zuazo, a leading figure in the 1952 revolution, was elected President for the 1956–60 term, and Dr Paz Estenssoro was again elected President in 1960. However, the powerful trade unions came into conflict with the Government, and in November 1964, following widespread strikes and disorder, President Paz Estenssoro was overthrown by the Vice-President, Gen. René Barrientos Ortuño, who was supported by the army. After serving with Gen. Alfredo Ovando Candía as Co-President under a military junta, Gen. Barrientos resigned in January 1966 to campaign for the presidency; he was elected in July 1966.

President Barrientos encountered strong opposition from left-wing groups, including mineworkers' unions. There was also a guerrilla uprising in south-eastern Bolivia, led by Dr Ernesto ('Che') Guevara, the Argentine-born revolutionary who had played a leading role in the Castro regime in Cuba. However, the insurgency was suppressed by government troops, with the help of US advisers, and guerrilla warfare ended in October 1967, when Guevara was captured and killed. In April 1969 President Barrientos was killed in an air crash and Dr Luis Adolfo Siles Salinas, the Vice-President, succeeded to the presidency. In September, however, President Siles Salinas was deposed by the armed forces, who reinstated Gen. Ovando. He was forced to resign in October 1970, when, after a power struggle between right-wing and left-wing army officers, Gen. Juan José Torres González, who had support from leftists, emerged as President, pledging support for agrarian reform and worker participation in management. A 'People's Assembly', formed by Marxist politicians, radical students and leaders of trade unions, was allowed to meet and demanded the introduction of extreme socialist measures, causing disquiet in right-wing circles. President Torres was deposed in August 1971 by Col (later Gen.) Hugo Bánzer Suárez, who drew support from

the right-wing Falange Socialista Boliviana and a section of the MNR, as well as from the army. In June 1973 President Bánzer announced an imminent return to constitutional government, but elections were later postponed to June 1974. The MNR withdrew its support and entered into active opposition.

Following an attempted military coup in June 1974, all portfolios within the Cabinet were assigned to military personnel. After another failed coup attempt in November, President Bánzer declared that elections had been postponed indefinitely and that his military regime would retain power until at least 1980. All political and union activity was banned. Political and industrial unrest in 1976, however, led President Bánzer to announce that elections would be held in July 1978. Allegations of fraud rendered the elections void, but Gen. Juan Pereda Asbún, the armed forces candidate in the elections, staged a successful military coup. In November 1978 his right-wing Government was overthrown in another coup, led by Gen. David Padilla Aranciba, Commander-in-Chief of the Army, with the support of national left-wing elements.

Presidential and congressional elections were held in July 1979. The presidential poll resulted in almost equal support for two ex-Presidents, Dr Siles Zuazo (with 36.0% of the vote) and Dr Paz Estenssoro (with 35.9%), who were now leading rival factions of the MNR. Congress, which was convened in August to resolve the issue, failed to award a majority to either candidate. An interim Government was formed under Walter Guevara Arce, President of the Senate (the upper house of Congress), but this administration was overthrown on 1 November by a right-wing army officer, Col Alberto Natusch Busch. He withdrew 15 days later after failing to gain the support of Congress, which elected Dra Lidia Gueiler Tejada, President of the Chamber of Deputies (the lower house of Congress), as interim Head of State pending presidential and congressional elections scheduled for June 1980.

The result of the 1980 presidential election was inconclusive, and in July, before Congress could meet to decide between the two main contenders (again Siles Zuazo and Paz Estenssoro), a military junta led by an army commander, Gen. Luis García Meza, staged a coup—the 189th in Bolivia's 154 years of independence. In August 1981 a military uprising forced Gen. García to resign. In September the junta transferred power to another army commander, Gen. Celso Torrelio Villa, who declared his intention to fight official corruption and to return the country to democracy within three years. Labour unrest, provoked by Bolivia's severe economic crisis, was appeased by restitution of trade union and political rights, and a mainly civilian Cabinet was appointed in April 1982. Elections were scheduled for April 1983. The political liberalization disturbed the armed forces, who attempted to create a climate of violence, and President Torrelio resigned in July 1982, amid rumours of an impending coup. The junta installed the less moderate Gen. Guido Vildoso Calderón, the Army Chief of Staff, as President. Unable to resolve the worsening economic crisis or to control a general strike, in September the military regime announced that power would be handed over in October to the Congress that had originally been elected in 1980. Dr Siles Zuazo, who had obtained most votes in both 1979 and 1980, was duly elected President by Congress, and was sworn in for a four-year term in October 1982.

President Siles Zuazo appointed a coalition Cabinet consisting of members of his own party, the Movimiento Nacionalista Revolucionario de Izquierda (MNRI), the Movimiento de la Izquierda Revolucionaria (MIR) and the Partido Comunista de Bolivia (PCB). Economic aid from the USA and Europe was resumed, but the Government found itself unable to fulfil the expectations that had been created by the return to democratic rule. The entire Cabinet resigned in August 1983, and the President appointed a Cabinet in which the number of portfolios that were held by the right-wing of the MNRI, the Partido Demócrata Cristiano (PDC) and independents was increased. The MIR joined forces with the MNR and with business interests in rejecting the Government's policy of complying with IMF conditions for assistance, which involved harsh economic measures. The Government lost its majority in Congress and was confronted by strikes and mass labour demonstrations. In November the opposition-dominated Senate approved an increase of 100% in the minimum wage, in defiance of the Government's austerity measures. Following a 48-hour general strike, the whole Cabinet resigned once again in December, in anticipation of an opposition motion of censure; the ministers accused the Senate of planning a 'constitutional coup' and urged the formation of a government of 'national unity'. In January 1984 President Siles Zuazo appointed a new coalition Cabinet, including 13 members of the previous Government.

The new Cabinet's main priority was to reverse Bolivia's grave economic decline. However, constant industrial agitation by the trade union confederation, the Central Obrera Boliviana (COB), coupled with rumours of an imminent coup, seriously undermined public confidence in the President. In June 1984 the country was again thrown into turmoil by the temporary abduction of President Siles Zuazo. Two former cabinet ministers and some 100 right-wing army officers were arrested in connection with the kidnapping, which was believed to have been supported by leading figures in the illicit drugs trade.

In September 1984 another crisis beset the Government following the discovery of a plot by extreme right-wing groups to overthrow the President. The disclosure that Congress had ordered an inquiry into suspected links between the Government and cocaine dealers prompted President Siles Zuazo to undertake a five-day hunger strike in a bid to secure national unity and stability. In January 1985 a new Cabinet was formed, comprising only members of the MNRI and independents. In the same month it was announced that an attempted coup by former military officers had been thwarted.

At elections in July 1985, amid reports of electoral malpractice and poor organization, the right-wing Acción Democrática Nacionalista (ADN), whose presidential candidate was Gen. Hugo Bánzer Suárez (the former dictator), received 28.6% of the votes cast, and the MNR obtained 26.4%, while the MIR was the leading left-wing party. At a further round of voting in Congress in August, an alliance between the MNR and the leading left-wing groups, including the MIR, enabled Dr Víctor Paz Estenssoro of the MNR to secure the presidency (which he had previously held in 1952–56 and 1960–64). The armed forces pledged their support for the new Government.

On taking office in August 1985, the new Government immediately introduced a very strict economic programme, designed to reduce inflation, which was estimated to have reached 14,173% in the year to August. The COB rejected the programme and called an indefinite general strike in September. The Government responded by declaring the strike illegal and by ordering a 90-day state of siege throughout Bolivia. Leading trade unionists were detained or banished, and thousands of strikers were arrested. The strike was called off in October, when union leaders agreed to hold talks with the Government. The conclusion of the strike was regarded as a considerable success for the new administration which, in spite of having achieved office with the assistance of left-wing parties, had subsequently found a greater ally in the right-wing ADN.

In July 1986 the Government was strongly criticized by opposition groups and trade unions when 160 US soldiers arrived in Bolivia to participate in a joint campaign with the Bolivian armed forces to eradicate illegal coca plantations. The Government was accused of having contravened the Constitution and of compromising national sovereignty. The allocation of US aid, however, was to be conditional upon the elimination of Bolivia's illegal cocaine trade. In October the US administration agreed to provide more than US $100m. in aid to continue the coca-eradication campaign, and US troops were withdrawn, so that the Bolivian authorities could assume responsibility for the campaign. However, within a few months of the troops' withdrawal, cocaine production was once again flourishing.

Throughout 1986 demonstrations and strikes were held by the COB in protest at the Government's austerity measures. Following a general strike in August, the Government imposed another 90-day state of siege. Social discontent persisted in 1987 and extensive unrest continued in 1988 (following a further increase in the price of petrol in February of that year), which culminated in April with a national hunger strike, called by the COB, to protest against the continuing austerity measures. These problems led to the resignation of the Cabinet in August, although all except four ministers were reappointed.

Presidential and congressional elections took place in May 1989. Of the votes cast in the presidential election, Gonzalo Sánchez de Lozada of the MNR obtained 23.1%, Gen. Hugo

Bánzer Suárez of the ADN 22.7%, and Jaime Paz Zamora of the MIR 19.6%. As no candidate had gained the requisite absolute majority, responsibility for the choice of President passed to the newly-elected Congress, which was to convene in August. Shortly before the second stage of the election, Bánzer withdrew his candidacy in order to support his former adversary, Paz Zamora. The 46 ADN and 41 MIR seats in Congress were sufficient to assure a majority vote for Paz Zamora, who assumed the presidency. A coalition Government of 'national unity', the Acuerdo Patriótico, was then formed. At the same time, a joint political council (with undefined powers), headed by Bánzer, was established. In his inaugural speech, President Paz Zamora gave assurances that fiscal discipline would be maintained, and a state of siege, banning strikes, was imposed in November.

Meanwhile, further measures to reduce the production of coca were taken during 1988. An anti-narcotics department was established in April. The drugs-control troops, Unidad Móvil de Patrullaje Rural (UMOPAR), were provided with greater resources and were further supported by a coca limitation law, restricting the area of land allowed for coca production (the leaves to be used for 'traditional' purposes only). In the same month, Roberto Suárez, Bolivia's leading cocaine-trafficker, was arrested and imprisoned for trading in illicit drugs. Suárez's arrest led to the exposure of drugs-trading involving leading members of the ADN, and was linked to a bomb attack on US Secretary of State George Shultz's motorcade in La Paz in August, during a visit undertaken to demonstrate support for the campaign against coca production.

By mid-1989, however, the Government had failed to attain the targets of its coca-eradication programme, having encountered staunch opposition from the powerful coca-growers' organizations. Clashes between UMOPAR and drugs-traffickers had become increasingly violent, especially in the coca-processing region of northern Beni. Paz Zamora was critical of the militaristic approach of the USA to coca eradication and emphasized the need for economic and social support. In May 1990, however, he accepted US $35m. in military aid from the USA. In late 1990 reaction to US involvement in Bolivia became increasingly violent. The left-wing Nestor Paz Zamora guerrilla group claimed responsibility for several bomb attacks, declaring that its actions were in response to the violation of Bolivia's political and territorial sovereignty by the USA.

In December 1989 a serious institutional conflict arose when the Government allowed a former Minister of the Interior, Migration and Justice, Col Luis Arce Gómez, to be taken to Miami, Florida (USA), to be tried on drugs-trafficking charges, despite the absence of a formal extradition treaty between Bolivia and the USA. Arce Gómez had been on trial in Bolivia since 1986, accused of violating human rights. His extradition, therefore, constituted a contravention of Bolivian law, which states that a Bolivian cannot be extradited while undergoing trial in Bolivia. Following an acrimonious conflict between the Government and the judiciary, Congress temporarily suspended eight of the 12 supreme court judges in late 1990. In retaliation, the court threatened to annul the 1989 elections. The conflict was resolved in early 1991 with the signing by the country's five main political parties of a pact affirming the independence of the Supreme Court. In January 1991 a federal jury in Miami found Arce Gómez guilty on two charges of drugs-trafficking, and in March he was sentenced to 30 years' imprisonment.

In March 1991 the reputation of the Government was seriously undermined when three of its senior officials were forced to resign amid allegations of corruption. Moreover, the appointment in February of Col. Faustino Rico Toro as the new head of Bolivia's Special Force for the Fight Against Drugs-Trafficking (FELCN) had provoked widespread outrage. In addition to his alleged connections with illegal drugs-traffickers, Rico was accused of having committed human-rights abuses during his tenure as chief of army intelligence under the regime of Gen. Luis García Meza (1980–81). On 4 March, after considerable pressure from the USA (including the suspension of all military and economic aid), Rico resigned from his new position. On 13 March, following accusations by the USA linking them with illegal drugs-traffickers, the Minister of the Interior, Migration and Justice and the Chief of Police resigned from their posts, although both maintained their innocence. In July the Government announced a decree granting a period of amnesty, lasting 120 days, for drugs-traffickers to surrender voluntarily. A condition of the amnesty was that those giving themselves up confess their crimes and contribute effectively to the apprehension of other such criminals. In return, they were offered minimum prison sentences and the guarantee that they would not risk extradition to the USA. In the months that followed, as many as seven of the country's most powerful drugs-traffickers were reported to have taken advantage of the amnesty.

Government plans to privatize state-owned enterprises, including the state mining corporation, COMIBOL, resulted in a series of strikes, organized by the COB, in late 1991 and early 1992. In July the COB called a further general strike, and in October, in what was regarded as a major reversal for the Government and a considerable victory for the mining union, Federación Sindical de Trabajadores Mineros de Bolivia (FSTMB), the Government suspended its programme of joint ventures between COMIBOL and private companies. Continued social unrest led to violent confrontation between protesters and troops throughout the country in early 1993, and the military occupation of La Paz in March of that year.

In April 1993 the Supreme Court found the former military dictator Gen. Luis García Meza guilty on 49 charges of murder, human-rights abuses, corruption and fraud, and sentenced him, *in absentia*, to 30 years' imprisonment. Similar sentences were imposed on 14 of his collaborators. García Meza was arrested in Brazil in March 1994 and, following his extradition to Bolivia in October of that year, began his prison sentence in March 1995.

Presidential and congressional elections were held in June 1993. Sánchez de Lozada was the MNR's presidential candidate, while Bánzer Suárez was supported by both the ADN and the MIR, as Paz Zamora was ineligible for re-election. Of the votes cast in the presidential election, Sánchez received 33.8%, Bánzer secured 20.0% and Carlos Palenque Aviles, a popular television presenter and leader of Conciencia de Patria (Condepa), received 13.6%. Since no candidate had secured the requisite absolute majority, a congressional vote was scheduled to take place in August to decide between the two main contenders. However, Bánzer withdrew from the contest, thereby leaving Sánchez de Lozada's candidacy unopposed. At legislative elections, conducted simultaneously, the MNR secured 69 of the 157 seats in the bicameral Congress, while the ruling Acuerdo Patriótico coalition won only 43. The MNR subsequently concluded a pact with the Unión Cívica Solidaridad (UCS) and the Movimiento Bolivia Libre, thus securing a congressional majority. Sánchez de Lozada was sworn in as President on 6 August.

In March 1994 the leader of the opposition MIR, former President Jaime Paz Zamora, announced his retirement from political life. His statement followed the presentation of a report by the FELCN to Congress alleging his co-operation with drugs-traffickers. The report, which also implicated several of Paz Zamora's political allies and family members, was largely based on information provided by one of the country's most notorious drugs-traffickers, Carmelo 'Meco' Domínguez, and his former associate, Isaac 'Oso' Chavarría, who had been a paramilitary leader during Gen. García Meza's military regime in 1980–81 and was arrested in January 1994. Despite his earlier statement, Paz Zamora announced his return to political life in January 1995, while denying the allegations against him in the FELCN report.

Despite the new Government's stated intention to combat corruption in Bolivia's political and public life, evidence of fraudulent practice continued to feature widely in the country's affairs. In June 1994 the President of the Supreme Court and its third judge were found guilty of bribery by the Senate and were dismissed and banned from holding public office for 10 years. In the same month it was revealed that a large proportion of the US $20m. seized from drugs-traffickers between 1988 and 1993 had disappeared. Members of the FELCN, trustees from the Attorney-General's office and local government officials were implicated in the affair.

Meanwhile, the US-funded coca-eradication programme (see above) continued to cause serious unrest during 1994, particularly in the Chapare valley of Cochabamba, where UMOPAR forces were occupying the area. Large-scale demonstrations throughout the year culminated in August and September in protests across the country by teachers, students and COB members, as well as coca-producers. The unrest subsided in late September, when the Government pledged to cease forcible eradication of coca and to withdraw its forces gradually from Chapare.

In early 1995 some 80,000 teachers across the country undertook a campaign of industrial action in opposition to a proposed programme of education reforms, which advocated the privatization of much of the education system and the restriction of teachers' rights to union membership. In March the COB called

an indefinite strike. In response, and in an attempt to quell several weeks of civil unrest, the Government declared a state of siege for 90 days. Military units were deployed throughout the country, and 370 union leaders (including the Secretary-General of the COB, Oscar Salas) were arrested and banished to remote areas. However, protests continued nation-wide, and some 70,000 teachers remained on strike. In April COB leaders agreed to sign a memorandum of understanding with the Government to end the strike in return for the release of trade-union officials and the initiation of negotiations. The state of siege, however, was extended by a further 90 days in July, owing to continued civil unrest, which had become particularly intense in the Chapare valley, where, despite of the introduction of a voluntary coca-eradication programme, UMOPAR forces had begun to occupy villages and to destroy coca plantations. Violent clashes between peasant farmers and UMOPAR personnel between July and September resulted in the arrest of almost 1,000 coca-growers. Human rights organizations expressed alarm at the force with which UMOPAR was conducting its operations and at the number of peasants killed and injured in the campaign. In October the state of siege was revoked, and negotiations between the Government and the coca-growers were undertaken, although the talks soon broke down, and further violent clashes were reported. Despite sustained resistance by coca-growers throughout 1995, a total of 5,520 ha of the crop were destroyed during the year (some 120 ha more than the target set by the US Government in its eradication programme).

Meanwhile, allegations implicating senior public officials in the illegal drugs trade continued to emerge in 1995. Four members of the FELCN, including the organization's second-in-command, Col Fernando Tarifa, were dismissed in September, following an investigation into their links with drugs-traffickers. A further 100 FELCN members were detained in November on drugs-related charges. Also in September, 13 police officers and 10 civilians were arrested in connection with a large haul of cocaine seized from a Bolivian aircraft in Peru. Moreover, a serious political scandal erupted in October, following allegations that Guillermo Bedregal, the President of the Senate and a deputy leader of the MNR, had co-operated with leading drugs-traffickers. The MNR suffered serious losses in municipal elections held in December, winning control in only one of the 10 principal cities.

In December 1995 a team of experts from Argentina began a search for the body of the guerrilla leader and revolutionary, Ernesto ('Che') Guevara, at the request of Sánchez de Lozada, following revelations by a retired general concerning the whereabouts of his remains. The Government of Cuba had long sought to recover Guevara's remains. In July 1997 Guevara's remains, together with those of three of his comrades, were finally located and returned to Cuba.

The issue of fraudulent practice in political and public life re-emerged in early 1996, when allegations concerning the abuse of the personal expenses system resulted in the resignation of 10 MNR members of Congress and the suspension of 12 others on criminal charges. Moreover, a supreme court judge who had presided over numerous cases involving drugs-related offences was arrested by the FELCN in March after having been filmed accepting money from a defendant's relative.

Continued opposition to the Government's capitalization programme led to further industrial unrest and a general strike in early 1996. In April more than 100,000 transport workers undertook a series of strikes and demonstrations in protest at the sale of the Eastern Railway to a Chilean company. Riots in La Paz resulted in damage to Chilean-owned railway property, which prompted threats from the Chilean Government to withdraw its investment from Bolivia. During violent clashes with the police several protesters were injured and one was killed. The dispute ended later in the month, when the COB signed an agreement with the Government which provided for modest public-sector wage increases, but did not include concessions in the Government's plans to continue implementation of its capitalization policies.

The proposed introduction of an agrarian reform law proved highly controversial and led to a series of protests in September and October 1996 by indigenous and peasant groups who feared that their land rights would be undermined by measures contained in the proposed legislation. In early October the leaders of several peasant farmers' groups began a hunger strike, while the COB called an indefinite general strike. Shortly afterwards Sánchez de Lozada agreed to hold discussions with representatives of some of the indigenous and peasant groups (although not with the COB) and subsequently secured their support for the law by making a number of significant concessions. The most important of these was the modification of the proposed role of the Agrarian Superintendency, such that it would not be authorized to rule on issues of land ownership. The law was approved by Congress later that month.

Dissatisfaction with the continued privatization of major industrial companies in Bolivia, particularly in the mining sector, resulted in further unrest in late 1996. In mid-December a group of miners occupied a pit at Amayapampa in northern Potosí to protest at the actions of the mine's Canadian operators, who, they alleged, had failed to pay local taxes and had caused damage to the environment. When troops arrived at the site to remove the miners 10 protesters were killed and 50 others injured in ensuing violent clashes. The incident provoked outrage throughout the country and was the subject of an investigation by the Organization of American States' Inter-American Human Rights Commission in early 1997. A similar occupation by miners opposed to private development of the Cerro Rico site in Potosí took place in January 1997.

Ten presidential candidates announced their intention to contest the elections scheduled for 1 June 1997. The MNR confirmed Juan Carlos Durán as its candidate (owing to the fact that Sánchez de Lozada was ineligible for re-election), the MIR presented Paz Zamora, while Bánzer Suárez was to make a fourth attempt to gain the presidency by democratic means, on behalf of the ADN. An often acrimonious election campaign was characterized by expressions of increasing discontent with the Government's radical economic reform programme and repeated criticism of Bánzer, who was held responsible for numerous human rights abuses during his dictatorship in the 1970s. In the event, Bánzer secured 22.3% of the total votes, Durán won 17.7% and Paz Zamora received 16.7%. At legislative elections held concurrently the ADN won a total of 46 congressional seats, the MIR won 31, the MNR secured 29 and the UCS and Condepa secured 23 and 20 seats, respectively. The ADN subsequently concluded a pact with the MIR, the UCS and Condepa to form a congressional majority. The inclusion of the MIR in the coalition prompted concern among some observers, as it was feared that previous allegations of corruption and of involvement in the illegal drugs trade against the party and, in particular, against Paz Zamora (see above) would jeopardize the country's ability to attract international aid and investment. However, the grouping remained, and on 5 August Bánzer was elected President for a newly-extended term of five years with 118 congressional votes. The new administration pledged to consolidate the free-market reforms introduced by the previous Government and sought to assure the USA that the alliance with the MIR would not compromise its commitment to combating the illegal drugs trade.

In late August 1997 the newly-elected Government signed a financial co-operation agreement with the USA for continued action to combat the illegal drugs trade. The agreement, which provided finance for the implementation of eradication programmes, was criticized for its emphasis on the suppression of coca cultivation rather than on the development of alternative crops. The previous Government's commitment to destroy 7,000 ha of coca plantations during 1997 in order to keep Bolivia's 'certification' status led to concern that violence might erupt if the new Government felt under pressure to implement an aggressive eradication programme in order to meet this target. Moreover, many observers believed the policy to be ineffective, as, despite the provision of US finance worth US \$500m. since 1990 to eradicate the crop, there had been no real reduction in coca production in Bolivia. There was also evidence that compensation payments given to coca growers for the destruction of their crops had been used to replant coca in more remote areas. Meanwhile, discontent with some of the new Government's economic policies, particularly an increase in petrol prices and taxes announced in November, prompted several COB-organized strikes in late 1997 and early 1998.

In February 1998 coca-producers in the Cochabamba region announced their rejection of the Government's new anti-coca policy (the so-called 'Dignity Plan', which aimed to eradicate all illegal coca plantations by 2002), claiming that an agreement, signed in October 1997, to provide alternative development programmes had not been honoured. Coca-growers also stated that groups of peasant farmers, styled 'self-defence committees', created to defend the coca crop but disbanded in mid-1997, would be reactivated. Violent clashes ensued, in which some 13 peasant farmers were killed and many more injured, when army and police personnel converged on the region in April to implement the eradication programme. In the following month the Government agreed temporarily to suspend the measures. Further clashes, however, were reported in May.

In late May 1998 central Bolivia was struck by a series of earthquakes which left more than 120 people dead and some 15,000 homeless.

In July 1998 Freddy Conde, the Minister of Agriculture, resigned his post after publicly criticizing the leaders of his party, Condepa. Internal divisions within Condepa subsequently led Bánzer to announce the removal of the party from the governing coalition, and to make several new appointments to the Cabinet.

More than 1,000 coca-growers undertook a 800-km march of protest from Chapare to La Paz in August 1998. The protesters demanded that the Government review its coca-eradication programme and denounced new measures including the confiscation of land used for coca cultivation, the incarceration of new coca-growers and the reduction, by more than 50%, of compensation rates paid to farmers who voluntarily ceased to grow coca. The Government rejected the demands of the coca-producers, reiterating its intention to eradicate more than 9,000 ha of the crop by the end of the year. Demonstrations and roadblocks by protesters in La Paz and Cochabamba during September were disrupted by security forces, leading to violent confrontation in many cases. The announcement in late 1998 that the headquarters of the armed forces were to be moved from La Paz to Cochabamba during 1999 was interpreted by some observers as a further measure to suppress the activities of the coca-growing community. The Government, however, denied that a process of militarization of the Cochabamba region was being implemented. In late 1998 it was announced that the 'Dignity Plan' was progressing successfully, with more than 11,500 ha of coca having been destroyed during that year. The Bolivian Government stated that funding for the programme had been received from the USA and the European Union (EU), but that a further US \$300m. was required to develop alternative resources to replace revenue lost from the illegal sale of coca. In 1999 the amount of eradicated coca crops increased to 14,000 ha.

During the first half of 1999 there were a number of high-profile resignations: in March the Minister of Labour, Leopoldo López, resigned following revelations, in a report published by the Ministry of Finance, that he had been involved in smuggling activities; in the subsequent month the commander of the national police force, Ivar Narváez, was forced to stand down from his post as a result of accusations of corruption and misuse of funds; and in June the resignation of the Minister of the Interior, Guido Nayor, prompted a major cabinet reorganization, including the appointment of eight new ministers. In mid-1999 a number of reforms of the judicial system were announced, including the appointment of a people's ombudsman, a constitutional tribunal and an independent judicial council. It was hoped that these measures would help to reduce levels of corruption, particularly with regard to the accountability of the police force. The new system was not expected to be fully implemented, however, until 2001. Bolivia's new penal code, which came into effect at the end of May 1999, was groundbreaking in that it formally incorporated into the country's legal system the customary law of indigenous Indian peoples.

In December 1999 a sharp increase in water charges in Cochabamba prompted violent demonstrations, which spread to other areas. Further violent protests in April 2000 led to the imposition of a state of emergency by the Government. In the same month a brief strike by the police, coinciding with a general strike in protest at the water charges, forced the Government to withdraw the measure, which had been intended to help the newly privatized water authority fund improvements in supply. The reverse in policy precipitated a cabinet reshuffle, which increased the representation of the ADN by one post at the expense of the MIR, while the UCS retained its two ministerial posts. The Government was put under further pressure in September when striking teachers demanding higher salaries were joined by peasants protesting against the Government's plan to tax water used for crop irrigation. As coca-growers were already protesting against the Government's plans to restrict the cultivation of the coca leaf, the combination of roadblocks and demonstrations brought the country to a standstill. Violence ensued between the protesters and riot police, resulting in at least 10 fatalities. A settlement was achieved in October, whereby the teachers received bonus payments and the Government signed a 50-point agreement with the peasant farmers' union, which included a pledge to draft new agrarian reform legislation and to review the controversial water privatization law. Later in the month the Government acceded to coca-growers' demands for a halt to the construction of new military bases in the Chapare region; however, the process of coca eradication intensified. In response to the unrest in the country a further government reshuffle was implemented in late October. In December President Bánzer announced that most of the coca leaf in the Chapare region had been eradicated, with only 1,500 acres remaining. He pledged to destroy the remaining 5,000 acres of coca leaf in the rest of the country by August 2002.

In September 1990, following the completion of a 650-km march of protest by 700 indigenous Indians from the town of Trinidad, in Beni, to the capital, La Paz, the Government issued four decrees in an unprecedented act of recognition of Indian land rights. Besides acknowledging as Indian territory more than 1.6m. ha of tropical rainforest in northern Bolivia, a multi-party commission was to be established in order to draft a new Law for Indigenous Indians of the East and Amazonia. In October 2000 a new Ministry for Peasants', Indigenous Peoples' and Ethnic Affairs was created, headed by Wigberto Rivero.

Bolivia's relations with Peru and Chile have been dominated by the long-standing issue of possible Bolivian access to the Pacific Ocean. An agreement with Peru, completed in 1993, granted Bolivia free access from the border town of Desaguadero, Bolivia, to the Pacific port of Ilo, Peru, until 2091. Bolivia's desire to regain sovereign access to the sea, however, continued to impair relations with Chile in 1997, when the Bolivian Government repeatedly requested that discussions on the subject take place and sought Peru's assistance as a mediator in the dispute. In February Bolivia's Minister of Foreign Affairs directly accused Gen. Augusto Pinochet Ugarte, the Commander-in-Chief of the Chilean Army, of being the main obstacle in Bolivia's quest for access to the sea. Moreover, talks which aimed to improve trade arrangements between the two countries were suspended in March and again in May following failure to reach agreement. Relations deteriorated further in late 1997 when the Bolivian Government filed an official protest note to Chile regarding its failure to remove land-mines along the common border (planted during the 1970s). However, following a meeting between government representatives in August 1998 Bolivia announced that it was to abandon its policy of actively pursuing access to the sea in Chile and, after discussions with the Chilean Minister of Foreign Affairs in June 1999, President Bánzer announced that Bolivia was considering the resumption of diplomatic relations with Chile. However, subsequent talks between representatives of the two countries appeared to collapse later in the year, when the Chilean Government indicated that it would not be willing to resume negotiations over Bolivia's access to the Chilean coastline.

In 1992 Bolivia signed an agreement with Brazil for the construction of a 3,150-km pipeline to carry natural gas from Bolivia to southern Brazil. The outlines of the project, which was expected to cost US $1,800m. and was the largest of its kind in South America, were finalized, following considerable delay, in mid-1996. The pipeline (the first 1,970 km of which were completed in early 1999) was expected to transport an initial 3.7m. cu m of natural gas per day to Brazil, increasing to 9.1m. cu m by 2000, when the pipeline was due to be fully operational. Concern was expressed by numerous environmental groups throughout the world that the project would threaten the tropical Chiquitano forest, through which the pipeline was to pass. Protests groups claimed that the scheme was in breach of a US law prohibiting support for projects harmful to the environment. However, these claims were rejected by the US Overseas Private Investment Corporation, which was expected to approve a US $200m.-loan for the construction of the pipeline.

In November 1994 an agreement to provide a waterway linking Bolivia with the Atlantic coast in Uruguay was concluded. However, by 2001 the controversial project, which involved dredging a deep-water channel in the Paraguay and Paraná Rivers, still had not begun, owing to Brazilian fears that the scheme would devastate a large, undeveloped area of ecological importance in south-western Brazil, known as the Pantanal.

Government

Legislative power is held by the bicameral Congress, comprising a Senate (27 members) and a Chamber of Deputies (130 members). Both houses are elected for a four-year term by universal adult suffrage. Executive power is vested in the President and the Cabinet, which is appointed by the President. The President is directly elected for five years (extended from four years in 1997). If no candidate gains an absolute majority of votes, the President is chosen by Congress. The country is divided, for administrative purposes, into nine departments, each of which is governed by a prefect, appointed by the President.

Defence

Military service, for one year, is selective. In August 2000 the armed forces numbered 32,500 men (there were plans to increase this to 35,000), of whom the army had 25,000 (including 18,000 conscripts), the air force 3,000, and the navy 4,500. Expenditure on defence by the central Government in 1999 was 864m. bolivianos.

Economic Affairs

In 1998, according to World Bank estimates, Bolivia's gross national product (GNP), measured at average 1996–98 prices, totalled US $8,013m., equivalent to about $1,010 per head (or $2,205 per head on an international purchasing-power parity basis). In the period 1990–98 real GNP per head grew by an average of 2.0% per year. During the same period the population increased at an annual rate of 2.7%. Bolivia's gross domestic product (GDP) increased, in real terms, at an average annual rate of 4.2% in 1990–99; GDP increased by some 2.0% in 1999.

Agriculture (including forestry and fishing) contributed an estimated 16% of GDP in 1999. In 1998 an estimated 44.7% of the economically active population were employed in agriculture. Wood accounted for 5.1% of export earnings in 1998. The principal cash crops are soybeans (which, together with soybean oil, accounted for 17.5% of export earnings in 1998), sugar, chestnuts and coffee. Beef and hides are also important exports. In the period 1990–96 agricultural GDP increased at an average annual rate of 3.7%; it rose by 4.1% in 1997, but declined by 3.5% in 1998.

Industry (including mining, manufacturing, construction and power) provided some 31% of GDP in 1999. In 1997 18.4% of the working population were employed in industry. During the period 1990–97 industrial GDP increased at an average annual rate of 4.3%; it rose by 2.6% in 1997 and by 3.9% in 1998.

Mining (including petroleum exploration) contributed an estimated 9.9% of GDP (at constant 1990 prices) in 1997 and employed about 1% of the working population in that year. Investment in mineral exploitation increased 10-fold between 1991 and 1996. Funding for gold-exploration projects, however, decreased from US $45m. in 1996 to $20m. in 1997, while investment in polymetallic projects increased from $8m. in 1996 to $15m. in the following year. Investment in petroleum exploration totalled US $129m. in 1997. Zinc, tin, silver, gold, lead and antimony are the major mineral exports. Tungsten and copper continue to be mined. Exports of zinc and tin earned $158.2m. and $66.1m., respectively, in 1998. In 1990–97 the GDP of the mining sector increased at an average annual rate of 2.7%; mining GDP decreased by 1.0% in 1996 and by 0.3% in 1997.

In 1999 manufacturing accounted for some 17% of GDP, and in 1997 some 11.0% of the working population were employed in manufacturing. The GDP of this sector increased during 1990–97 at an average annual rate of 4.2%; it rose by 3.9% in 1996 and by 4.2% in 1997. Measured by the value of output, the principal branches of manufacturing in 1995 were food products (30.9%—including meat preparations 10.5% and beverages 9.1%), petroleum refineries (20.7%), jewellery and related articles (5.7%) and cement (3.8%).

Energy is derived principally from petroleum and natural gas, although hydroelectricity is also important. In 1998 production of crude petroleum increased by an estimated 15.1% to 12.6m. barrels. In 1998 imports of fuels comprised an estimated 4.0% of total merchandise imports, compared with 7.1% in the previous year. Earnings from exports of petroleum and petroleum products accounted for 3.0% of the total in 1998. Exports of natural gas accounted for 26.1% of total export earnings in 1991, but only 4.2% in 1998. Reserves of natural gas were estimated at 4,600,000m. cu ft at the end of 1997. During the late 1990s several major new natural gas deposits were discovered, which significantly increased the country's total known reserves.

The services sector accounted for some 54% of GDP in 1999 and engaged 38.5% of the employed population in 1997. During the period 1990–97 the GDP of this sector increased at an average annual rate of 4.4%; services GDP increased by 4.9% in 1996 and by 5.1% in 1997.

In 1999 Bolivia recorded a visible trade deficit of US $488.0m., and there was a deficit of $556.0m. on the current account of the balance of payments. In 1998 the main sources of imports were the USA (23.4%), Japan (19.7%), Brazil (10.9%) and Argentina (9.9%). The USA, the United Kingdom, Argentina and Peru were the major recipients of Bolivian exports in 1998 (22.9%, 15.0%, 10.7% and 10.6%, respectively). The principal imports in that year included industrial materials and machinery, transport equipment and consumer goods. The principal legal exports were metallic minerals, natural gas, soybeans and wood. In 1997 the United Nations claimed that more than 50% of Bolivia's export earnings came from the illegal trade in coca and its derivatives (mainly cocaine).

In 1998 Bolivia's overall budget deficit (including regional and local governments) amounted to 1,275m. bolivianos (equivalent to 2.7% of GDP). Bolivia's total external debt at the end of 1998 was US $6,078m., of which $4,307m. was long-term public debt. The cost of debt-servicing in that year was equivalent to 30.2% of the total value of exports of goods and services. In 1990–98 the average annual rate of inflation was 8.0%. Consumer prices increased by an average of 4.7% in 1997, 7.7% in 1998 and 2.2% in 1999. In 1996 an estimated 4.2% of the labour force were unemployed.

In May 1991 Bolivia was one of five Andean Pact countries to sign the Caracas Declaration providing the foundation for a common market. In October 1992 Bolivia officially joined the Andean free-trade area, removing tariff barriers to imports from Colombia, Ecuador and Venezuela. Bolivia also agreed to sign a free-trade accord with Mexico in September 1994. In late 1996 Bolivia concluded a free-trade agreement with Mercosur (see p. 284), equivalent to associate membership of the organization, with effect from January 1997. In mid-1999 an agreement on the rationalization of their respective customs systems (thus moving closer to the formation of a regional free-trade area) was reached between Mercosur and the Andean Community (see p. 122); the two-year accord came into effect in August. Bolivia is a member of the Andean Community, and in 1989 the Andean Social Development Fund was established. The country is also a member of the Organization of American States (OAS, see p. 261), and of the Latin American Integration Association (ALADI, see p. 230). Bolivia became the 97th contracting party to GATT (which was superseded by the World Trade Organization, WTO, in 1995—see p. 292) in 1989.

A public-sector capitalization programme, which aimed to attract more private-sector involvement in Bolivia's principal industries by selling a 50% controlling share in several state-owned companies to private investors, began in early 1995; the process was expected to be completed by the end of 2002.

The continued success of exploratory missions in locating new sources of petroleum and natural gas, in particular, resulted in a series of projects in the late 1990s, which aimed to develop Bolivia's potential as one of the region's most important energy-producing countries. A major new gas deposit near Santa Cruz, with total reserves estimated at 1,700,000m. cu ft, was discovered in 1998. Official development assistance was equivalent to some 10% of GNP annually in the mid-1990s. The country's severe debt burden is widely acknowledged to be a major factor in inhibiting economic growth, and in recognition of this the World Bank and the IMF approved a debt-relief package worth US $760m. (under its Heavily Indebted Poor Countries' Initiative), which was released in October 1998. Also in late 1998 a three-year loan worth US $138m. was secured from the IMF. In early 1999 the Government announced that, despite severe drought conditions, the economy had again shown strong growth in 1998 and that the rate of inflation had fallen to its lowest

level for nine years. It also confirmed that the programme for the transfer of state-owned companies to private ownership (launched in 1990) was expected to be finally completed by mid-2000, and that the process would provide an estimated US $150m. in revenue. However, on the negative side, the trade deficit in 1998 rose to its highest level for several years, partly owing to a 10.5% decrease in export revenue (one of the reasons for which was the effects of the Asian financial crisis). Economic growth, which was forecast at 4% for 2000 and subsequently reduced to 2.5%, was adversely affected by social unrest which paralysed the country in April and September 2000. Despite demands for increased public spending to alleviate social ills, the Government committed itself to the maintenance of strict fiscal economic policies.

Social Welfare

There are benefits for unemployment, accident, sickness, old age and death. In 1993 there were 51 physicians and 25 nurses for every 100,000 inhabitants. A privately-managed national pension scheme was established in 1995, as a result of the Government's capitalization programme, in which a 50% share in several state-owned industries was sold to private-sector investors while the remaining 50% was invested in a pension fund for all Bolivian citizens. In May 1997 some 300,000 Bolivians over the age of 65 years began to receive a bonus payment (*bono solidaridad*) of US $248 from the pension fund. Of total expenditure by the central Government in 1998, 352.0m. bolivianos (3.4%) was for health, and a further 2,682.3m. bolivianos (25.9%) for social security and welfare.

Education

Primary education, beginning at six years of age and lasting for eight years, is officially compulsory and is available free of charge. Secondary education, which is not compulsory, begins at 14 years of age and lasts for up to four years. In 1990 the total enrolment at primary and secondary schools was equivalent to 77% of the school-age population (81% of boys; 73% of girls). In that year enrolment at primary schools included an estimated 91% of children in the relevant age-group (95% of boys; 87% of girls), while the comparable ratio for secondary enrolment was only 29% (32% of boys; 27% of girls). There are eight state universities and two private universities. In 1995, according to UNESCO estimates, the average rate of adult illiteracy was 16.9% (males 9.5%; females 24.0%). Expenditure on education by the Central Government in 1998 was 2,023.4m. bolivianos, representing 19.6% of total spending.

Public Holidays

2001: 1 January (New Year), 4–7 February (Carnival), 22 February (Oruro only), 13 April (Good Friday), 15 April (Tarija only), 1 May (Labour Day), 25 May (Sucre only), 14 June (Corpus Christi), 16 July (La Paz only), 6 August (Independence), 14 September (Cochabamba only), 24 September (Santa Cruz and Pando only), 1–2 November (All Saints' Day), 10 November (Potosí only), 18 November (Beni only), 25 December (Christmas).

2002: 1 January (New Year), 4–7 February (Carnival), 22 February (Oruro only), 29 March (Good Friday), 15 April (Tarija only), 1 May (Labour Day), 25 May (Sucre only), 30 May (Corpus Christi), 16 July (La Paz only), 6 August (Independence), 14 September (Cochabamba only), 24 September (Santa Cruz and Pando only), 1–2 November (All Saints' Day), 10 November (Potosí only), 18 November (Beni only), 25 December (Christmas).

Weights and Measures

The metric system is officially in force, but various old Spanish measures are also used.

Statistical Survey

Sources (unless otherwise indicated): Instituto Nacional de Estadística, Plaza Mario Guzmán Aspiazu No. 1, Casilla 6129, La Paz; tel. (2) 36-7443; internet www.ine.gov.bo; Banco Central de Bolivia, Ayacucho esq. Mercado, Casilla 3118, La Paz; tel. (2) 37-4151; fax (2) 39-2398; internet www.bcb.gov.bo.

Area and Population

AREA, POPULATION AND DENSITY

Area (sq km)	
Land	1,084,391
Inland water	14,190
Total	1,098,581*
Population (census results)†	
29 September 1976	4,613,486
3 June 1992	
Males	3,171,265
Females	3,249,527
Total	6,420,792
Population (official estimates at mid-year)	
1998	7,949,933
1999	8,137,113
2000	8,328,700
Density (per sq km) at mid-2000	7.6

* 424,164 sq miles.

† Figures exclude adjustment for underenumeration. This was estimated at 6.99% in 1976 and at 6.92% in 1992.

DEPARTMENTS (official estimates at mid-2000)

	Area (sq km)	Population	Density (per sq km)	Capital
Beni	213,564	366,047	1.7	Trinidad
Chuquisaca	51,524	589,948	11.4	Sucre
Cochabamba	55,631	1,524,724	27.4	Cochabamba
La Paz	133,985	2,406,377	18.0	La Paz
Oruro	53,588	393,991	7.4	Oruro
Pando	63,827	57,316	0.8	Cobija
Potosí	118,218	774,696	6.6	Potosí
Santa Cruz	370,621	1,812,522	4.9	Santa Cruz de la Sierra
Tarija	37,623	403,079	10.7	Tarija
Total	**1,098,581**	**8,328,700**	**7.6**	

PRINCIPAL TOWNS (estimated population at mid-2000)

Santa Cruz de la Sierra	1,034,070	Sucre (legal capital)	223,436
La Paz (administrative capital)	1,004,440	Tarija	162,973
		Potosí	162,212
Cochabamba	616,022	Sacaba	108,377
El Alto	568,919	Quillacollo	102,138
Oruro	248,273		

BIRTHS AND DEATHS (UN estimates, annual averages)

	1980–85	1985–90	1990–95
Birth rate (per 1,000)	38.2	36.6	35.7
Death rate (per 1,000)	13.5	11.5	10.2

Expectation of life (UN estimates, years at birth, 1990–95): 59.3 (males 57.7, females 61.0).

Source: UN, *World Population Prospects: The 1998 Revision.*

ECONOMICALLY ACTIVE POPULATION

(labour force surveys, '000 persons aged 10 years and over, at November)

	1996	1997
Agriculture	1,620.7	1,518.7
Forestry and fishing	14.6	23.1
Mining and quarrying	53.7	63.9
Manufacturing	403.6	393.5
Electricity, gas and water supply	9.9	11.0
Construction	172.4	187.0
Wholesale and retail trade; repair of motor vehicles, motorcycles and personal and household goods	562.3	505.9
Hotels and restaurants	135.2	126.5
Transport, storage and communications	147.6	170.5
Financial intermediation	18.1	20.1
Real estate, renting and business activities	51.9	58.8
Public administration and defence; compulsory social security	91.8	78.8
Education	137.9	158.8
Health and social work	59.9	62.9
Other community, social and personal service activities	67.5	70.4
Private households with employed persons	127.0	117.8
Extra-territorial organizations and bodies	1.6	2.1
Total employed	**3,675.7**	**3,569.7**
Unemployed	65.0	75.4
Total labour force	**3,740.7**	**3,645.2**
Males	2,008.7	2,048.8
Females	1,731.9	1,596.4

Agriculture

PRINCIPAL CROPS ('000 metric tons)

	1997	1998	1999
Wheat	143	164	141
Rice (paddy)	253	301	189
Barley	69	41	50
Maize	678	424	613
Sorghum	76	121	148
Potatoes	843	495	783
Cassava (Manioc)	348	357	400
Other roots and tubers*	95	95	95
Pulses	32	26	28
Soya beans	1,038	1,071	762
Groundnuts (in shell)	13	12	13
Sunflower seeds	81	115	95
Tomatoes	80	80	84
Pumpkins, squash and gourds	105	104	107
Onions (dry)	49	48	49
Peas (green)	25	20	26
Carrots	34	33	36
Other vegetables	189	177	192
Watermelons	21	21	21
Sugar cane	4,126	4,241	4,160
Oranges	100	101	106
Tangerines, mandarins, clementines and satsumas	53	55	60
Lemons and limes	62	62	63
Grapefruit and pomelos	29	29	29
Pineapples	45	46	53
Papayas	22	22	23
Peaches and nectarines	36	36	36*
Grapes	23	23	24
Bananas*	396	403	419
Plantains*	170	173	180
Other fruits and berries*	46	46	49
Chestnuts	40	32	34
Coffee (green)	23	24	23
Cotton (lint)	22	19	19†
Natural rubber†	11	11	11

* Unofficial figure(s).   † FAO estimate(s).

Source: FAO.

LIVESTOCK ('000 head, year ending September)

	1997	1998	1999
Horses*	322	322	322
Mules*	81	81	81
Asses*	631	631	631
Cattle	6,238	6,387	6,556
Pigs	2,569	2,637	2,715
Sheep	8,232	8,409	8,575
Goats	1,496	1,496	1,500*
Chickens	66,686	77,717	85,000
Ducks*	270	270	280
Turkeys*	150	150	150

* FAO estimate(s).

Source: FAO.

LIVESTOCK PRODUCTS ('000 metric tons)

	1997	1998	1999
Beef and veal	147	151	155
Mutton and lamb	15	15	15
Goat meat	6	6	6
Pig meat	69	72	74
Poultry meat	117	136	145
Cows' milk	202	193	202
Sheep's milk	29	29	29*
Goats' milk	11	11	11
Cheese	7	7	7
Hen eggs*	68	68	68
Wool: greasy*	8	8	9
Cattle hides (fresh)	17	18	18
Sheepskins (fresh)	5	5	5

* FAO estimates.

Source: FAO.

Forestry

ROUNDWOOD REMOVALS ('000 cubic metres, excl. bark)

	1996	1997	1998
Sawlogs, veneer logs and logs for sleepers	491	489	233
Pulpwood	383	383	383
Other industrial wood	18	18	18
Fuel wood	1,293	1,323	1,355
Total	2,185	2,213	1,989

Source: FAO, *Yearbook of Forest Products*.

SAWNWOOD PRODUCTION ('000 cubic metres, incl. railway sleepers)

	1996	1997	1998
Coniferous (softwood)*	15	15	15
Broadleaved (hardwood)	166	165	203
Total	181	180	218

* FAO estimates.

Source: FAO, *Yearbook of Forest Products*.

Fishing

(metric tons, live weight)

	1996	1997	1998
Capture	5,988	6,038	6,055
Freshwater fishes	4,800	4,850	4,865
Rainbow trout	338	338	340
Silversides (sand smelts)	850	850	850
Aquaculture	380	387	385
Rainbow trout	300	312	320
Total catch	6,368	6,425	6,440

Note: Figures exclude crocodiles and alligators, recorded by number rather than by weight. The number of spectacled caimans caught was: 15,961 in 1997; 1,757 in 1998.

Source: FAO, *Yearbook of Fishery Statistics*.

Mining*

(metric tons, unless otherwise indicated)

	1997	1998	1999
Crude petroleum ('000 barrels)	10,971	12,628	n.a.
Natural gas (million cu feet)	106,285	109,673	n.a.
Copper	190	48	n.a.
Tin	12,898	11,308	12,417
Lead	18,608	13,848	10,153
Zinc	154,491	152,110	146,144
Tungsten (Wolfram)	647	627	421
Antimony	5,999	4,735	2,790
Silver	387	404	423
Gold (kg)	13,292	14,445	11,782

* Figures for metallic minerals refer to the metal content of ores.
† Provisional figures.

Source: partly IMF, *Bolivia: Statistical Annex* (March 2000).

Industry

SELECTED PRODUCTS ('000 metric tons, unless otherwise indicated)

	1997	1998	1999*
Flour	465	549	576
Cement	970	1,095	1,163
Refined sugar	332	285	294
Carbonated drinks ('000 hectolitres)	1,867	2,368	2,281
Beer ('000 hectolitres)	1,702	1,922	1,840
Cigarettes (packets)	73,166	69,949	67,332
Alcohol ('000 litres)	27,678	31,154	26,412
Diesel oil ('000 barrels)	2,866	3,034	3,063
Motor spirit (petrol) ('000 barrels)	3,941	4,003	4,176
Electric energy (million kWh)	3,528	n.a.	n.a.

* Provisional figures.

Tin (primary metal, metric tons): 16,853 in 1997; 11,102 in 1998; 11,000 (estimate) in 1999 (Source: US Geological Survey).

Finance

CURRENCY AND EXCHANGE RATES

Monetary Units

100 centavos = 1 boliviano (B).

Sterling, Dollar and Euro Equivalents (29 December 2000)

£1 sterling = 9.535 bolivianos;
US $1 = 6.390 bolivianos;
€1 = 5.946 bolivianos;
1,000 bolivianos = £104.88 = $156.49 = €168.18.

Average Exchange Rate (bolivianos per US $)

1998	5.5101
1999	5.8124
2000	6.1835

BUDGET (million bolivianos)*

Revenue†	1996	1997	1998
Taxation	5,483.9	6,266.3	7,111.3
Taxes on income, profits and capital gains	416.6	524.2	617.8
Social security contributions	869.2	1,010.7	768.5
Taxes on property	604.6	562.5	666.8
Sales taxes	2,553.6	2,880.4	3,279.8
Excises	618.9	787.6	798.4
Import duties	377.9	472.0	556.7
Entrepreneurial and property income	575.3	181.0	182.1
Administrative fees, charges, etc.	243.8	342.7	735.0
Other current revenue	141.2	280.0	200.0
Capital revenue	120.5	22.3	72.4
Total	**6,564.7**	**7,092.3**	**8,300.8**

Expenditure‡	1996	1997	1998
General public services	1,037.1	1,219.9	1,211.2
Defence	630.2	783.7	992.7
Public order and safety	650.8	782.9	746.4
Education	1,511.9	1,830.3	2,023.4
Health	347.0	314.9	352.0
Social security and welfare	1,580.4	2,543.7	2,682.3
Housing and community amenities	35.0	74.7	106.6
Recreational, cultural and religious affairs and services	27.5	35.3	54.2
Economic services	1,827.6	851.0	1,341.4
Fuel and energy	25.2	13.8	40.6
Agriculture, forestry and fishing	69.6	90.3	207.9
Mining and mineral resources, manufacturing and construction	68.4	47.2	42.7
Transport and communications	1,028.1	473.1	771.7
Other purposes	979.8	757.3	829.6
Total	**8,627.4**	**9,193.7**	**10,339.8**
Current§	6,749.2	7,712.7	8,723.1
Capital	1,878.2	1,481.0	1,616.7

* Figures refer to the transactions of central government units covered by the General Budget, plus the operations of other units (government agencies and social security institutions) with their own budgets.
† Excluding grants received (million bolivianos): 1,093.0 in 1996; 816.7 in 1997; 701.3 in 1998.
‡ Excluding lending minus repayments (million bolivianos): −63.7 in 1996; −320.0 in 1997; −260.5 in 1998.
§ Including interest payments (million bolivianos): 749.5 in 1996; 709.2 in 1997; 775.7 in 1998.

Source: IMF, *Government Finance Statistics Yearbook*.

INTERNATIONAL RESERVES (US $ million at 31 December)

	1998	1999	2000
Gold*	234.9	235.7	234.7
IMF special drawing rights	37.7	37.4	35.6
Reserve position in IMF	12.5	12.2	11.6
Foreign exchange	834.4	866.9	777.1
Total	**1,119.5**	**1,152.2**	**1,058.9**

* National valuation (US $ 250 per troy oz each year).

Source: IMF, *International Financial Statistics*.

MONEY SUPPLY (million bolivianos at 31 December)

	1997	1998	1999
Currency outside banks	2,061	2,193	2,173
Demand deposits at commercial banks	1,036	1,124	1,031
Total money	**3,636**	**3,895**	**3,670**

Source: IMF, *International Financial Statistics*.

COST OF LIVING

(Consumer Price Index for urban areas; base: 1991 = 100)

	1998	1999	2000
Food and beverages	185.94	183.89	186.89
Fuel and light	192.12	210.02	238.90
Clothing and footwear	161.76	168.44	177.45
Rent	130.52	138.09	145.32
All items (incl. others)	**184.71**	**188.70**	**197.39**

NATIONAL ACCOUNTS

Expenditure on the Gross Domestic Product
(million bolivianos at current prices)

	1997	1998*	1999*
Government final consumption expenditure	5,790	6,624	7,088
Private final consumption expenditure	30,113	35,312	37,050
Increase in stocks	276	143	−278
Gross fixed capital formation	7,899	10,721	9,451
Total domestic expenditure	44,078	52,800	53,311
Exports of goods and services	8,791	9,417	8,446
Less Imports of goods and services	12,226	15,217	13,153
GDP in purchasers' values	41,644	47,001	48,605
GDP at constant 1990 prices	20,677	21,817	21,949

* Provisional.

Source: IMF, *International Financial Statistics*.

Gross Domestic Product by Economic Activity
(million bolivianos at constant 1990 prices)

	1995	1996	1997
Agriculture, hunting, forestry and fishing	2,810	2,999	3,135
Mining and quarrying	1,925	1,887	2,002
Manufacturing	3,220	3,376	3,445
Electricity, gas and water	389	402	421
Construction	634	691	725
Trade	1,622	1,710	1,794
Restaurants and hotels	609	635	647
Transport, storage and communications	1,880	2,009	2,194
Finance, insurance, real estate and business services	2,029	2,202	2,480
Government services	1,766	1,793	1,879
Other community, social and personal services	718	754	796
Other producers	104	106	109
Sub-total	17,706	18,564	19,626
Import duties	1,625	1,681	1,778
Less Imputed bank service charge	454	544	727
Total	18,877	19,701	20,677

BALANCE OF PAYMENTS (US $ million)

	1997	1998	1999
Exports of goods f.o.b.	1,166.5	1,104.0	1,051.1
Imports of goods f.o.b.	−1,643.6	−1,759.4	−1,539.1
Trade balance	−477.1	−655.4	−488.0
Exports of services	247.2	253.5	259.3
Imports of services	−418.7	−441.1	−449.5
Balance on goods and services	−648.5	−843.1	−678.3
Other income received	98.2	127.4	157.1
Other income paid	−294.7	−289.4	−358.5
Balance on goods, services and income	−845.0	−1,005.1	−879.6
Current transfers received	300.3	341.6	352.2
Current transfers paid	−8.8	−11.7	−28.6
Current balance	−553.5	−675.2	−556.0
Capital account (net)	25.3	9.9	—
Direct investment abroad	−2.5	−2.6	−2.5
Direct investment from abroad	730.7	872.4	953.5
Portfolio investment assets	−53.2	−74.5	−44.4
Portfolio investment liabilities	—	—	−16.9
Other investment assets	−19.9	−106.2	125.1
Other investment liabilities	234.8	309.9	−32.4
Net errors and omissions	−260.6	−232.1	−218.0
Overall balance	101.0	101.7	−41.8

Source: IMF, *International Financial Statistics*.

External Trade

PRINCIPAL COMMODITIES (distribution by SITC, US $ million)

Imports c.i.f.	1996	1997	1998
Food and live animals	156.6	142.2	162.2
Cereals and cereal preparations	86.3	65.9	72.5
Wheat (including spelt) and meslin, unmilled	60.2	38.4	32.2
Crude materials (inedible) except fuels	52.0	52.4	38.1
Mineral fuels, lubricants, etc.	48.0	144.2	110.9
Petroleum, petroleum products, etc.	47.9	144.2	110.8
Refined petroleum products	39.8	136.5	104.1
Gas oils (distillate fuels)	30.9	109.4	78.8
Chemicals and related products	202.7	232.2	253.3
Essential oils, perfume materials and cleansing preparations	31.3	35.9	36.1
Artificial resins, plastic materials, etc.	42.6	48.3	46.1
Products of polymerization, etc.	34.2	39.6	36.3
Basic manufactures	230.0	251.0	421.7
Paper, paperboard and manufactures	35.8	45.2	45.7
Iron and steel	68.9	78.8	225.3
Tubes, pipes and fittings	18.3	26.7	163.5
'Seamless' tubes and pipes	8.4	16.7	149.6
Machinery and transport equipment	788.8	931.0	1,170.4
Power-generating machinery and equipment	47.2	22.6	32.7
Machinery specialized for particular industries	101.4	122.4	187.7
Civil engineering and contractors' plant and equipment	35.2	56.1	111.6
Construction and mining machinery	24.4	30.0	49.1
General industrial machinery, equipment and parts	67.9	92.5	122.9
Telecommunications and sound equipment	117.2	180.9	117.4
Electrical line telephonic and telegraphic apparatus	49.6	86.5	55.4
Other electrical machinery, apparatus, etc.	49.7	66.5	63.9
Road vehicles and parts*	233.3	352.4	524.9
Passenger motor cars (excl. buses)	107.3	148.7	238.8
Motor vehicles for the transport of goods, etc.	75.7	126.9	189.2
Goods vehicles	69.6	118.9	177.8
Other road motor vehicles	32.1	56.2	73.7
Public-service vehicles (e.g. buses)	27.6	47.7	52.0
Other transport equipment and parts*	150.4	61.7	91.6
Aircraft, associated equipment and parts*	150.0	60.0	86.6
Miscellaneous manufactured articles	113.1	103.8	147.0
Non-monetary gold (excl. ores and concentrates	42.0	43.7	36.5
Total (incl. others)	1,643.1	1,909.2	2,350.2

* Excluding tyres, engines and electrical parts.

Exports f.o.b.	1996	1997	1998
Food and live animals . . .	179.1	230.7	216.8
Vegetables and fruit	42.3	53.0	48.9
Fresh or dried fruit and nuts			
(excl. oil nuts)	29.3	31.5	31.4
Edible nuts	28.4	31.1	30.9
Brazil nuts	27.6	30.8	28.3
Sugar, sugar preparations and			
honey.	28.1	22.3	23.8
Sugar and honey . . .	27.9	22.1	23.6
Coffee, tea, cocoa and spices .	17.1	27.0	15.9
Feeding-stuff for animals (excl.			
unmilled cereals) . . .	81.7	117.7	106.0
Oil-cake and other residues from			
the extraction of vegetable oils	81.1	117.7	105.9
Oil-cake and residues from			
soya beans	78.2	112.2	100.8
Crude materials (inedible)			
except fuels . . .	428.7	468.5	379.1
Oil seeds and oleaginous fruit. .	84.6	75.8	64.6
Soya beans	64.8	61.6	47.3
Cork and wood	68.9	67.2	50.5
Simply worked wood and railway			
sleepers	68.9	67.1	50.4
Sawn non-coniferous wood .	64.6	61.8	45.1
Textile fibres (excl. wool tops) and			
waste	32.4	40.5	16.5
Cotton	31.3	39.3	15.5
Raw cotton (excl. linters) .	31.3	39.3	15.5
Metalliferous ores and metal			
scrap	235.0	275.3	238.1
Base metal ores and concentrates	182.5	226.8	178.7
Zinc ores and concentrates .	151.7	200.1	157.8
Precious metal ores and			
concentrates	52.2	48.0	58.8
Mineral fuels, lubricants etc. .	142.1	107.1	96.4
Petroleum, petroleum products, etc.	47.4	37.0	40.1
Crude petroleum oils, etc. .	38.5	28.2	30.3
Gas (natural and manufactured) .	94.5	70.1	56.3
Petroleum gases and other			
gaseous hydrocarbons .	94.5	69.9	55.5
Animal and vegetable oils, fats			
and waxes	40.5	59.3	72.6
Fixed vegetable oils and fats . .	40.5	59.3	72.5
Soya bean oil	39.5	55.1	68.7
Basic manufactures . . .	146.0	142.9	115.5
Non-ferrous metals . . .	113.9	102.1	74.1
Tin and tin alloys . . .	101.2	90.4	58.3
Unwrought tin and alloys. .	100.2	90.0	57.8
Machinery and transport			
equipment	76.7	14.8	189.0
Transport equipment and parts*	62.2	5.6	156.1
Aircraft, associated equipment			
and parts*	59.4	4.0	148.7
Miscellaneous manufactured			
articles	49.6	115.1	115.6
Clothing and accessories (excl.			
footwear)	28.5	26.6	27.2
Jewellery, goldsmiths' and			
silversmiths' wares, etc. .	11.4	74.6	61.6
Non-monetary gold (excl. ores			
and concentrates) . .	n.a.	110.6	112.7
Total (incl. others) . . .	1,087.0	1,272.1	1,323.3

* Excluding tyres, engines and electrical parts.

Source: UN, *International Trade Statistics Yearbook*.

PRINCIPAL TRADING PARTNERS (US $ million)*

Imports c.i.f.	1996	1997	1998
Argentina	136.6	259.4	232.4
Brazil	181.6	227.6	256.8
Canada	42.7	36.1	27.7
Chile	110.6	122.5	141.9
Colombia	33.8	40.0	46.2
Denmark	4.4	3.2	25.7
Germany	60.9	58.7	57.9
Italy	55.6	43.2	37.8
Japan	199.1	236.2	463.0
Korea, Republic . . .	20.4	20.4	29.0
Mexico	25.5	37.2	38.8
Peru	89.1	97.5	94.9
Spain	35.0	25.2	36.9
Sweden	48.2	89.4	108.0
United Kingdom . . .	12.4	23.3	18.0
USA	455.7	443.5	550.7
Venezuela	13.2	23.2	23.5
Total (incl. others) . . .	1,643.1	1,909.2	2,350.2

Exports f.o.b.	1996	1997	1998
Argentina	143.4	183.0	141.3
Belgium-Luxembourg . .	49.4	70.4	64.0
Brazil	36.3	37.4	30.1
Chile	43.5	59.3	34.2
Colombia	116.0	87.6	86.5
Ecuador	7.8	3.7	80.2
Germany	24.4	56.9	21.4
Mexico	11.9	11.2	6.6
Peru	138.8	158.5	140.5
Switzerland-Liechtenstein .	52.0	115.5	83.8
United Kingdom . . .	155.6	154.7	198.9
USA	237.4	264.1	303.2
Uruguay	8.5	2.8	50.1
Total (incl. others) . . .	1,087.0	1,272.1	1,323.3

* Imports by country of provenance; exports by country of last consignment.

Source: UN, *International Trade Statistics Yearbook*.

Transport

RAILWAYS (traffic)

	1996	1997	1998
Passenger-kilometres (million) .	197	225	270
Freight ton-kilometres (million) .	780	839	908

Source: UN, *Statistical Yearbook*.

ROAD TRAFFIC (motor vehicles in use at 31 December)

	1994	1995	1996
Passenger cars	198,734	213,666	223,829
Buses	18,884	19,627	20,322
Lorries and vans	108,214	114,357	118,214
Tractors	9	9	10
Motorcycles	62,725	64,936	66,113

Source: IRF, *World Road Statistics*.

1997: Passenger cars ('000 in use) 234.1; Commercial vehicles ('000 in use) 124.8.
1998: Passenger cars ('000 in use) 235.7; Commercial vehicles ('000 in use) 122.2. (Source: UN, *Statistical Yearbook*).

CIVIL AVIATION (traffic on scheduled services)

				1995	1996	1997
Kilometres flown (million)	.		.	16	24	28
Passengers carried ('000)	.		.	1,224	1,783	2,251
Passenger-km (million)	.		.	1,234	1,634	2,143
Freight ton-km (million)	.		.	187	223	274

Source: UN, *Statistical Yearbook*.

Tourism

ARRIVALS AT HOTELS (regional capitals only, '000)

Country of origin					1996	1997	1998
Argentina	.	.	.	.	41.0	51.0	53.7
Brazil	.	.	.	.	34.8	36.8	36.1
Chile	.	.	.	.	23.4	28.6	28.9
France	.	.	.	.	20.2	19.6	21.9
Germany	.	.	.	.	23.8	22.8	22.9
Israel	.	.	.	.	12.7	9.6	10.6
Italy	.	.	.	.	8.4	7.8	8.4
Japan	.	.	.	.	7.7	6.8	6.3
Netherlands	.	.	.	.	10.9	10.8	11.5
Peru	.	.	.	.	56.2	62.5	66.2
Spain	.	.	.	.	11.4	10.2	11.2
Switzerland	.	.	.	.	10.8	9.7	9.3
United Kingdom	.	.	.	.	12.2	12.0	13.2
USA	.	.	.	.	39.6	40.4	45.0
Total (incl. others)		.	.	.	376.9	397.5	420.5

Total tourism receipts (US $ million): 159 in 1996; 170 in 1997.

Source: World Tourism Organization, *Yearbook of Tourism Statistics*.

Communications Media

		1995	1996	1997
Radio receivers ('000 in use)	.	4,980	5,100	5,250
Television receivers ('000 in use)	.	850	875	900
Telephones ('000 main lines in use)		295*	425	535
Mobile cellular telephones				
(subscribers)	. . .	10,000	20,300	116,000
Daily newspapers:				
Number	. . . .	17	18	n.a.
Average circulation ('000 copies)		410	420	n.a.

* Installed lines.

Sources: UNESCO, *Statistical Yearbook*; UN, *Statistical Yearbook*.

Education

(1998)

				Institutions	Teachers	Students
Pre-primary	.	.	.	2,294*	4,168	188,145
Primary	.	.	.	12,639†	63,056	1,547,203
Secondary	.	.	.	n.a.	15,132	320,736
Higher	.	.	.			
Universities and equivalent				n.a.	4,261‡	184,169§
Other	.	.	.	n.a.	1,302‖	34,889‖

* 1988.   † 1987.   ‡ 1991.   § 1997.   ‖ 1989.

Source: partly UNESCO, *Statistical Yearbook*.

Directory

The Constitution

Bolivia became an independent republic in 1825 and received its first Constitution in November 1826. Since that date a number of new Constitutions have been promulgated. Following the *coup d'état* of November 1964, the Constitution of 1947 was revived. Under its provisions, executive power is vested in the President, who chairs the Cabinet. According to the revised Constitution, the President is elected by direct suffrage for a five-year term (extended from four years in 1997) and is not eligible for immediate re-election. In the event of the President's death or failure to assume office, the Vice-President or, failing the Vice-President, the President of the Senate becomes interim Head of State.

The President has power to appoint members of the Cabinet and diplomatic representatives from a panel proposed by the Senate. The President is responsible for the conduct of foreign affairs and is also empowered to issue decrees, and initiate legislation by special messages to Congress.

Congress consists of a Senate (27 members) and a Chamber of Deputies (130 members). Congress meets annually and its ordinary sessions last only 90 working days, which may be extended to 120. Each of the nine departments (La Paz, Chuquisaca, Oruro, Beni, Santa Cruz, Potosí, Tarija, Cochabamba and Pando), into which the country is divided for administrative purposes, elects three senators. Members of both houses are elected for five years.

The supreme administrative, political and military authority in each department is vested in a prefect appointed by the President. The sub-divisions of each department, known as provinces, are administered by sub-prefects. The provinces are further divided into cantons. There are 94 provinces and some 1,000 cantons. The capital of each department has its autonomous municipal council and controls its own revenue and expenditure.

Public order, education and roads are under national control.

A decree issued in July 1952 conferred the franchise on all persons who had reached the age of 21 years, whether literate or illiterate. Previously the franchise had been restricted to literate persons. (The voting age for married persons was lowered to 18 years at the 1989 elections.)

The Government

HEAD OF STATE

President: HUGO BÁNZER SUÁREZ (ADN) (took office 6 August 1997).
Vice-President: JORGE FERNANDO QUIROGA RAMÍREZ (ADN).

THE CABINET
(April 2001)

A coalition comprising members of the Acción Democrática Nacionalista (ADN), the Movimiento de la Izquierda Revolucionaria (MIR) and the Unión Cívica Solidaridad (UCS).

Minister of Foreign Affairs and Worship: JAVIER MURILLO DE LA ROCHA (ADN).
Minister of the Interior: GUILLERMO FORTÚN (ADN).
Minister of National Defence: OSCAR VARGAS LORENZETTI (ADN).
Minister of the Presidency: MARCELO PÉREZ MONASTERIOS (ADN).
Minister of Sustainable Development and Planning: RONALD MACLEAN ABAROA (ADN).
Minister of Justice and Human Rights: LUIS VÁSQUEZ VILLAMOR (MIR).
Minister of Finance: JOSÉ LUIS LUPO FLORES (ADN).
Minister of Health and Social Welfare: GUILLERMO CUENTAS YAÑEZ (MIR).
Minister of Labour and Small Enterprises: JORGE PACHECO FRANCO.
Minister of Education, Culture and Sport: TITO HOZ DE VILA QUIROGA (ADN).
Minister of Agriculture, Livestock and Rural Development: HUGO CARVAJAL.
Minister of Foreign Trade and Investment: CLAUDIO MANSILLA.
Minister for Economic Development: CARLOS ARMANDO SAAVEDRA BRUNO (MIR).
Minister of Housing and Basic Services: RUBÉN POMA ROJAS (UCS).
Minister of Peasants', Indigenous Peoples' and Ethnic Affairs: WIGBERTO RIVERO (ADN).

Minister for Government Information: MANFREDO KEMPFF SUÁREZ (ADN).

MINISTRIES

Ministry of Agriculture, Livestock and Rural Development: Avda Camacho 1471, La Paz.

Ministry of Economic Development: Edif. Palacio de Comunicaciones, Avda Mariscal Santa Cruz, La Paz; tel. (2) 37-7234; fax (2) 35-9955; e-mail contactos@desarrollo.gov.bo; internet www.desarrollo.gov.bo.

Ministry of Education, Culture and Sport: Casilla 6500, La Paz.

Ministry of Finance: Edif. Palacio de Comunicaciones, Avda Mariscal Santa Cruz, La Paz; tel. (2) 37-7234; fax (2) 35-9955.

Ministry of Foreign Affairs and Worship: Calle Ingavi, esq. Junin, La Paz; tel. (2) 37-1150; fax (2) 37-1155; e-mail mreuno@rree.gov.bo; internet www.rree.gov.bo.

Ministry of Foreign Trade and Investment: Edif. Palacio de las Comunicaciones, Avda Mariscal Santa Cruz, La Paz; tel. (2) 37-7222; fax (2) 37-7451; e-mail despacho@mcei-bolivia.com; internet www.mcei-bolivia.com.

Ministry of Government Information: Edif. La Urbana, 5°, Avda Camacho 1485, La Paz; tel. (2) 33-9027; fax (2) 39-1607; internet www.comunica.gov.bo.

Ministry of Health and Social Welfare: Plaza del Estudiante, La Paz; tel. (2) 37-1373; fax (2) 39-1590; e-mail minsalud@ceibo.entelnet.bo; internet www.sns.gov.bo.

Ministry of Housing and Basic Services: Avda Edif. Ex-Conavi, 20 de Octubre 2230, La Paz; tel. (2) 36-0469; fax (2) 37-1335; e-mail minviv@ceibo.entelnet.bo.

Ministry of the Interior: Avda Arce 2409, esq. Belisario Salinas, La Paz; tel. (2) 37-0460; fax (2) 37-1334.

Ministry of Justice and Human Rights: Casilla 6966, La Paz; tel. (2) 36-1083; fax (2) 36-530; e-mail minjust@caoba.entelnet.bo.

Ministry of Labour and Small Enterprises: Calle Yanacocha, esq. Mercado, La Paz; tel. (2) 36-4164; fax (2) 37-1387; e-mail mintrabajo@unete.com.

Ministry of National Defence: Plaza Avaroa, esq. 20 de Octubre, La Paz; tel. (2) 37-7130; fax (2) 35-3156; e-mail mindef2@ceibo entelnet.bo.

Ministry of Peasants', Indigenous Peoples' and Ethnic Affairs: La Paz.

Ministry of the Presidency: Palacio de Gobierno, Plaza Murillo, La Paz; tel. (2) 37-1082; fax (2) 37-1388.

Ministry of Sustainable Development and Planning: Avda Mariscal Santa Cruz, Edif. De la Ex-Comibol, 8°, Casilla 12814, La Paz; tel. and fax (2) 31-0860; e-mail sdnp@coord.rds.org.bo; internet www.rds.org.bo.

President and Legislature

PRESIDENT

At the presidential election that took place on 1 June 1997 the majority of votes were spread between five of the 10 candidates. Gen. (retd) Hugo Bánzer Suárez of the Acción Democrática Nacionalista (ADN) obtained 22.3% of the votes cast, Juan Carlos Durán of the Movimiento Nacionalista Revolucionario (MNR) won 17.7%, Jaime Paz Zamora of the Movimiento de la Izquierda Revolucionaria (MIR) won 16.7%, Ivo Kuljis of the Unión Cívica Solidaridad (UCS) secured 15.9% and Remedios Loza of Conciencia de Patria (Condepa) won 15.8%. As no candidate obtained the requisite absolute majority, responsibility for the selection of the President passed to the new National Congress. As a result of the formation of a coalition between the ADN, the MIR, the UCS, the NFR, Condepa and an Independent, Bánzer was elected President with 118 votes on 5 August and took office the following day. Condepa was removed from the governing coalition in mid-1998.

CONGRESO NACIONAL

President of the Senate: LEOPOLDO FERNÁNDEZ.
President of the Chamber of Deputies: JALIL MELGAR.

General Election, 1 June 1997

	Seats	
Party	Chamber of Deputies	Senate
Acción Democrática Nacionalista (ADN)	33	13
Movimiento Nacionalista Revolucionario (Histórico) (MNR) .	26	3
Movimiento de la Izquierda Revolucionaria (MIR)	25	6
Unión Cívica Solidaridad (UCS) . .	21	2
Conciencia de Patria (Condepa) . .	17	3
Movimiento Bolivia Libre (MBL) . .	4	—
Izquierda Unida	4	—
Total	130	27

Political Organizations

Acción Democrática Nacionalista (ADN): La Paz; internet www.bolivian.com/adn; f. 1979; right-wing; Leader HUGO BÁNZER SUÁREZ; Nat. Exec. Sec. JORGE LANDÍVAR.

Alianza de Renovación Boliviana (ARBOL): La Paz; f.1993; conservative; Leader CASIANO ACALLE CHOQUE.

Bolivia Insurgente: La Paz; f. 1996; populist party; Leader MÓNICA MEDINA.

Conciencia de Patria (Condepa): La Paz; f. 1988; populist party; Leader REMEDIOS LOZA.

Frente Revolucionario de Izquierda (FRI): La Paz; left-wing; Leader OSCAR ZAMORA.

Movimiento Bolivariano: La Paz; f. 1999; Leader CRISTINA CORRALES.

Movimiento Bolivia Libre (MBL): Edif. Camiri, Of. 601, Calle Comercio 972 esq. Yanacocha, Casilla 10382, La Paz; tel. (2) 34-0257; fax (2) 39-2242; f. 1985; left-wing; breakaway faction of MIR; Pres. MIGUEL URIOSTE.

Movimiento Hacia el Socialismo (MAS): La Paz; left-wing.

Movimiento de la Izquierda Revolucionaria (MIR): Avda América 119, 2°, La Paz; e-mail mir@ceibo.entelnet.bo; internet www.cibergallo.com; f. 1971; split into several factions in 1985; left-wing; Leader JAIME PAZ ZAMORA; Sec.-Gen. OSCAR EID FRANCO.

Movimiento sin Miedo: La Paz; f. 1999; left-wing; Leader JUAN DEL GRANADO.

Movimiento Nacionalista Revolucionario (Histórico)—MNR: Calle Nicolás Acosta 574, tel. (2) 49-0748; fax (2) 49-0009; e-mail mnr2002@ceibo.entelnet.bo; La Paz; formerly part of the Movimiento Nacionalista Revolucionario (MNR, f. 1942); centre-right; Leader GONZALO SÁNCHEZ DE LOZADA; Sec.-Gen. CARLOS SÁNCHEZ BERZAIN; 360,000 mems.

Movimiento Revolucionario Túpac Katarí de Liberación (MRTKL): Avda Baptista 939, Casilla 9133, La Paz; tel. 35-4784; f. 1978; peasant party; Leader VÍCTOR HUGO CÁRDENAS CONDE; Sec.-Gen. NORBERTO PÉREZ HIDALGO; 80,000 mems.

Nueva Fuerza Republicana (NFR): Cochabamba; Leader MANFRED REYES VILLA.

Partido Comunista de Bolivia (PCB): La Paz; f. 1950; Leader MARCOS DOMIC; First Sec. SIMÓN REYES RIVERA.

Partido Demócrata Cristiano (PDC): Casilla 4345, La Paz; f. 1954; Pres. BENJAMÍN MIGUEL HARB; Sec. ANTONIO CANELAS-GALATOIRE; 50,000 mems.

Partido Obrero Revolucionario (POR): Correo Central, La Paz; f. 1935; Trotskyist; Leader GUILLERMO LORA.

Partido Revolucionario de la Izquierda Nacionalista (PRIN): Calle Colón 693, La Paz; f. 1964; left-wing; Leader JUAN LECHIN OQUENDO.

Partido Socialista-Uno (PS-1): La Paz; Leader JERJES JUSTINIANO.

Partido de Vanguardia Obrera: Plaza Venezuela 1452, La Paz; Leader FILEMÓN ESCOBAR.

Unión Cívica Solidaridad (UCS): Calle Mercado 1064, 6°, La Paz; tel. (2) 36-0297; fax (2) 37-2200; f. 1989; populist; Leader JOHNNY FERNÁNDEZ.

Vanguardia Revolucionaria 9 de Abril: Avda 6 de Agosto 2170, Casilla 5810, La Paz; tel. (2) 32-0311; fax 39-1439; Leader Dr CARLOS SERRATE REICH.

Other parties include the Alianza de Renovación Boliviana, the Alianza Democrática Socialista and the Eje Patriótica.

Diplomatic Representation

EMBASSIES IN BOLIVIA

Argentina: Calle Aspiazu 497, La Paz; tel. (2) 35-3233; fax (2) 39-1083; Ambassador: ARTURO E. OSSORIO ARANA.

Belgium: Avda Hernando Siles 5290, Casilla 2433, La Paz; tel. (2) 78-4925; fax (2) 78-6764; e-mail amblapaz@entelnet.bo; Ambassador: ALAIN KUNDYCKI.

Brazil: Edif. Metrobol, Calle Capitán Ravelo 2334, Casilla 429, La Paz; tel. (2) 44-0202; fax (2) 44-0043; internet www.embajadabrasil.org.bo; Ambassador: STELIO MARCOS AMARANTE.

China, People's Republic: Los Pinos 8532, Casilla 10005, La Paz; tel. (2) 79-3851; fax (2) 79-7121; e-mail emb-china@kolla.net; Ambassador: WONG YONGZHAN.

Colombia: Calle 20 de Octubre 2427, Casilla 1418, La Paz; tel. (2) 78-4491; fax 78-6510; e-mail emcol@caoba.entelnet.bo; Ambassador: LAURA OCHOA DE ARDILA.

Costa Rica: Avda 14 de Septiembre 4850, Casilla 2780, La Paz; tel. and fax (2) 79-3201; Ambassador: ISABEL CARAZO SABORÍA DE SAENZ.

Cuba: Avda Arequipa 8037, Calacoto, La Paz; tel. (2) 72-1157; fax (2) 72-3419; e-mail embacuba@ceibo.entelnet.bo; Ambassador: RAÚL BARZAGA NAVAS.

Denmark: Edif. Fortaleza, Avda Arce 2799 esq. Cordero, 9°, Casilla 9860, La Paz; tel. (2) 43-2070; fax (2) 43-3150; e-mail ambdklp@ceibo.entelnet.bo; Chargé d'affaires: MICHAEL HJORTS.

Ecuador: Edif. Herrman, 14°, Plaza Venezuela, Casilla 406, La Paz; tel. (2) 33-1588; fax (2) 39-1932; e-mail mecuabol@caoba.entelnet.bo; Ambassador: LUIS MORENO GUERRA.

Egypt: Avda Ballivián 599, Casilla 2956, La Paz; tel. (2) 78-6511; fax (2) 78-4325; Ambassador: Dr MAHMOUD AMIN HASSANEIN.

France: Avda Hernando Silés 5390, esq. Calle 8, Obrajes, Casilla 717, La Paz; tel. (2) 78-6114; fax (2) 78-6746; e-mail amfrabo@ceibo.entelnet.bo; internet www.ambafrance-bo.org.bo; Ambassador: GÉRARD DUMONT.

Germany: Avda Arce 2395, Casilla 5265, La Paz; tel. (2) 44-0066; fax (2) 44-1441, e-mail germany@ceibo.entelnet.bo; Ambassador: JOACHIM KAUSCH.

Holy See: Avda Arce 2990, Casilla 136, La Paz; tel. (2) 43-1007; fax (2) 43-2120; e-mail nunzibol@caoba.entelnet.bo; Apostolic Nuncio: Most Rev. JÓZEF WESOŁOWSKI, Titular Archbishop of Slebte (Slebty).

Israel: Edif. Esperanza, 10°, Avda Mariscal Santa Cruz, Casilla 1309, La Paz; tel. (2) 39-1126; fax 39-1712; email emisrabo@ceibo.entelnet.bo; Ambassador: ISAAC LAVIE BACHMAN.

Italy: Avda 6 de Agosto 2575, Casilla 626, La Paz; tel. (2) 43-4929; fax 43-4975; e-mail ambitlap@ceibo.entelnet.bo; Ambassador: Dr EUGENIO CAMPO.

Japan: Calle Rosendo Gutiérrez 497, Casilla 2725, La Paz; tel. (2) 37-3151; fax (2) 39-1052; Ambassador: HIROYUKI KIMOTO.

Korea, Democratic People's Republic: La Paz; Ambassador: KIM CHAN SIK.

Mexico: Sánchez Bustamente 509, Casilla 430, La Paz; tel. (2) 77-2212; fax (2) 77-1855; e-mail embamex@kolla.net; internet www.embamex-bolivia.org; Ambassador: Lic. MARGARITA DIEGUEZ ARMA.

Panama: Avda Ballivián 1110, Casilla 678, La Paz; tel. (2) 79-2036; fax (2) 79-7290; e-mail empanbol@ceibo.entelnet.bo; Ambassador: CARMEN G. MENÉNDEZ.

Paraguay: Edif. Illimani II, Avda 6 de Agosto y Pedro Salazar, Casilla 882, La Paz; tel. (2) 43-3176; fax (2) 43-2201; e-mail emparabo@ceibo.entelnet.bo; Ambassador: EMILIO LORENZO G. FRANCO.

Peru: Calle F. Guachalla 300, Casilla 668, La Paz; tel. (2) 44-1250; fax (2) 44-1240; e-mail embbol@caoba.entelnet.bo; Ambassador: Dr HARRY BELEVAN-MCBRIDE.

Russia: Avda Walter Guevara Arce 8129, Casilla 5494, La Paz; tel. (2) 78-6419; fax (2) 78-6531; e-mail embrusia@ceibo.entelnet.bo; Ambassador: GUENNADI VASILIEVICH SIZOV.

Spain: Avda 6 de Agosto 2860, Casilla 282, La Paz; tel. (2) 43-3518; fax (2) 43-2752; e-mail riolui@ceibo.entelnet.bo; Ambassador: MANUEL VITURRO DE LA TORRE.

Switzerland: Edif. Petrolero, Avda 16 de Julio 1616, Casilla 657, La Paz; tel. (2) 31-5471; fax (2) 39-1462; e-mail swiembol@ceibo.entelnet.bo; Ambassador ERIC MARTIN.

United Kingdom: Avda Arce 2732–2754, Casilla 694, La Paz; tel. (2) 43-3424; fax (2) 43-1073; e-mail ppa@mail.rds.org.bo; Ambassador: GRAHAM MINTER.

USA: Avda Arce 2780, Casilla 425, La Paz; tel. (2) 43-0251; fax (2) 43-3900; internet www.megalink.com/usemblapaz; Ambassador: MANUEL ROCHA.

Uruguay: Avda 6 de Agosto 2577, Casilla 441, La Paz; tel. (2) 43-0080; fax 43-0087; e-mail urulivia@datacom-bo.net; Ambassador: JUAN A. PACHECO RAMÍREZ.

Venezuela: Edif. Illimani, 4°, Avda Arce esq. Campos, Casilla 960, La Paz; tel. (2) 43-1365; fax (2) 43-2348; e-mail hecmaldo@ceibo .entelnet.bo; Ambassador: OTTO R. VEITIA MATOS.

Judicial System

SUPREME COURT

Corte Suprema: Calle Pilinco 352, Sucre; tel. (64) 21883; fax (64) 32696.

Judicial power is vested in the Supreme Court. There are 12 members, appointed by Congress for a term of 10 years. The court is divided into four chambers of three justices each. Two chambers deal with civil cases, the third deals with criminal cases and the fourth deals with administrative, social and mining cases. The President of the Supreme Court presides over joint sessions of the courts and attends the joint sessions for cassation cases.

President of the Supreme Court: Dr GUILLERMO ARANCIBIA.

DISTRICT COURTS

There is a District Court sitting in each Department, and additional provincial and local courts to try minor cases.

ATTORNEY-GENERAL

In addition to the Attorney-General at Sucre (appointed by the President on the proposal of the Senate), there is a District Attorney in each Department as well as circuit judges.

Attorney-General: OSCAR CRESPO.

Religion

The majority of the population are Roman Catholics; there were an estimated 6.9m. adherents at 31 December 1998, equivalent to 89.5% of the population. Religious freedom is guaranteed. There is a small Jewish community, as well as various Protestant denominations, in Bolivia.

CHRISTIANITY

The Roman Catholic Church

Bolivia comprises four archdioceses, six dioceses, two Territorial Prelatures and five Apostolic Vicariates.

Bishops' Conference: Conferencia Episcopal Boliviana, Calle Potosí 814, Casilla 2309, La Paz; tel. (2) 40-6855; fax (2) 40-6798; e-mail comceb@ceibo.entelnet.bo; f. 1972; Pres. Cardinal JULIO TERRAZAS SANDOVAL, Archbishop of Santa Cruz de la Sierra.

Archbishop of Cochabamba: Most Rev. RENÉ FERNÁNDEZ APAZA, Avda Heroínas esq. Zenteno Anaya, Casilla 129, Cochabamba; tel. (42) 56562; fax (42) 50522.

Archbishop of La Paz: Most Rev. EDMUNDO LUIS FLAVIO ABASTOFLOR MONTERO, Calle Ballivián 1277, Casilla 259, La Paz; tel. (2) 34-1920; fax (2) 39-1244.

Archbishop of Santa Cruz de la Sierra: Cardinal JULIO TERRAZAS SANDOVAL, Calle Ingavi 49, Casilla 25, Santa Cruz; tel. (3) 32-4286; fax (3) 33-0181; e-mail asc@scbbs-bo.com.

Archbishop of Sucre: Most Rev. JESÚS GERVASIO PÉREZ RODRÍGUEZ, Calle Bolívar 702, Casilla 205, Sucre; tel. (64) 51587; fax (64) 60336.

The Anglican Communion

Within the Iglesia Anglicana del Cono Sur de América (Anglican Church of the Southern Cone of America), Bolivia forms part of the diocese of Peru. The Bishop is resident in Lima, Peru.

Protestant Churches

Baptist Union of Bolivia: Casilla 2199; tel. (2) 22-9538, La Paz; Pres. Rev. AUGUSTO CHUIJO.

Convención Bautista Boliviana (Baptist Convention of Bolivia): Casilla 3147, Santa Cruz; tel. (3) 340717; fax (3) 340717; f. 1947; Pres. EIRA SORUCO DE FLORES.

Iglesia Evangélica Metodista en Bolivia (Evangelical Methodist Church in Bolivia): Casillas 356 y 8347, La Paz; tel. (2) 34-2702; fax (2) 35-7046; autonomous since 1969; 10,000 mems; Bishop Rev. EFRAÍN YANAPA.

BAHÁ'Í FAITH

National Spiritual Assembly of the Bahá'ís of Bolivia: Casilla 1613, La Paz; tel. (2) 78-5058; fax (2) 78-2387; e-mail aebahais@ caoba.entelnet.bo; mems resident in 6,229 localities.

The Press

DAILY NEWSPAPERS

Cochabamba

Opinión: General Acha 0252, Casilla 287, Cochabamba; tel. (42) 54402; fax (42) 15121; f. 1985; Dir EDWIN TAPIA FRONTANILLA; Man. Editor JAIME BUITRAGO.

Los Tiempos: Plaza Quintanilla-Norte, Casilla 525, Cochabamba; tel. (42) 54561; fax (42) 54577; e-mail lostiempos@lostiempos.bo.net; internet www.lostiempos.com; f. 1943; morning; independent; Dir FERNANDO CANELAS; Man. Editor MIGUEL LORA; circ. 19,000.

La Paz

El Diario: Calle Loayza 118, Casilla 5, La Paz; tel. (2) 39-0900; fax (2) 36-3846; e-mail contacto@eldiario.net; internet www.eldiario.net; f. 1904; morning; conservative; Dir JORGE CARRASCO JAHNSEN; Man. Editor MAURICIO CARRASCO; circ. 55,000.

Hoy: Pasaje Carrasco 1718, Casilla 477, La Paz; tel. (2) 24-4154; fax (2) 24-4147; e-mail hoy@wara.bolnet.bo; f. 1968; morning and midday editions; independent; Pres. SAMUEL DORIA MEDINA; Dir HERNÁN PAREDES MUÑOZ; circ. 12,000.

Jornada: Edif. Almirante Grau 672, Casilla 1628, La Paz; tel. (2) 35-3844; fax (2) 35-6213; e-mail jornada@ceibo.entelnet.bo; f. 1964; evening; independent; Dir JAIME RÍOS CHACÓN; circ. 11,500.

Presencia: Avda Mariscal Santa Cruz 2150, Casilla 3276, La Paz; tel. (2) 37-2340; fax (2) 39-1040; e-mail prsencia@caoba.entelnet.bo; f. 1952; morning and evening; Catholic; Pres. JESÚS LÓPEZ DE LAMA; Dir Lic. JUAN CRISTÓBAL SORUCO; Man. Lic. MARÍA LUISA URDAY; circ. 20,000.

La Razón: Jorge Sáenz 1330, Casilla 13100, La Paz; tel. (2) 22-2727; fax (2) 22-2049; internet www.la-razon.com; f. 1990; Pres. RAÚL GARAFULIC GUTIÉRREZ; Dir JORGE CANELAS SÁENZ; circ. 27,000.

Ultima Hora: Avda Camacho 1372, Casilla 5920, La Paz; tel. (2) 39-2115; fax (2) 39-2139; e-mail uhora@wara.bolnet.bo; f. 1939; evening; independent; Propr LUIS MERCADO ROCABADO; Pres. MAURO BERTERO; Dir MARIANO BAPTISTA GUMUCIO; circ. 15,000.

Oruro

El Expreso: Potosí 4921 esq. Villarroel, Oruro; f. 1973; morning; independent; right-wing; Dir ALBERTO FRONTANILLA MORALES; circ. 1,000.

La Patria: Avda Camacho 1892, Casilla 48, Oruro; tel. (52) 50761; fax (52) 50781; f. 1919; morning; independent; Pres. MARCELO MIRRALLES BOVÁ; Dir ENRIQUE MIRALLES BONNECARRERE; circ. 6,000.

Potosí

El Siglo: Calle Linares 99, Casilla 389, Potosí; f. 1975; morning; Dir WILSON MENDIETA PACHECO; circ. 1,500.

Santa Cruz

El Deber: Avda El Trompillo 1144, Casilla 2144, Santa Cruz; tel. (3) 53-8000; fax (3) 53-9053; e-mail info.eldeber@eldeber.com; internet www.eldeber.com; f. 1955; morning; independent; Dir PEDRO RIVERO MERCADO; Man. Editor GUILLERMO RIVERO JORDÁN; circ. 35,000.

La Estrella del Oriente: Calle Sucre 558, Casilla 736, Santa Cruz; tel. (3) 37-0707; fax (3) 37-0557; e-mail estrella@mitai.nrs.bolnet.bo; internet www.laestrella.com; f. 1864; Pres. JORGE LANDÍVAR ROCA; Man. Editor TUFFI ARÉ.

El Mundo: Parque Industrial PI-7, Casilla 1984, Santa Cruz; tel. (3) 46-4646; fax (3) 46-5057; e-mail elmundo@mitai.nrs.bolnet.bo; f. 1979; morning; owned by Santa Cruz Industrialists' Association; Pres. WALTER PAREJAS MORENO; Dir JUAN JAVIER ZEBALLOS GUTIÉRREZ; circ. 15,000.

El Nuevo Día: Calle Independencia 470, Casilla 5344, Santa Cruz; tel. (3) 33-7474; fax (3) 36-0303; f. 1987; Dir NANCY EKLUND VDA DE GUTIÉRREZ; Man. Editor JORGE ORÍAS HERRERA.

Trinidad

La Razón: Avda Bolívar 295, Casilla 166, Trinidad; tel. (46) 21377; f. 1972; Dir CARLOS VÉLEZ.

PERIODICALS

Actualidad Boliviana Confidencial (ABC): Fernando Guachalla 969, Casilla 648, La Paz; f. 1966; weekly; Dir HUGO GONZÁLEZ RIOJA; circ. 6,000.

Aquí: Casilla 10937, La Paz; tel. (2) 34-3524; fax (2) 35-2455; f. 1979; weekly; circ. 10,000.

Bolivia Libre: Edif. Esperanza, 5°, Avda Mariscal Santa Cruz 2150, Casilla 6500, La Paz; fortnightly; govt organ.

Carta Cruceña de Integración: Casilla 3531, Santa Cruz de la Sierra; weekly; Dirs HERNÁN LLANOVARCED A., JOHNNY LAZARTE J.

Comentarios Económicos de Actualidad (CEA): Casilla 312097, La Paz; tel. (2) 43-0122; fax (2) 43-2554; e-mail veceba@caoba .entelnet.bo; f. 1983; fortnightly; articles and economic analyses; Editor GUIDO CESPEDES.

Información Política y Económica (IPE): Calle Comercio, Casilla 2484, La Paz; weekly; Dir GONZALO LÓPEZ MUÑOZ.

Informe R: La Paz; weekly; Editor SARA MONROY.

Notas: Casilla 5782, La Paz; tel. (2) 37-3773; fax (2) 36-5153; weekly; political and economic analysis; Editor JOSÉ GRAMUNT DE MORAGAS.

El Noticiero: Sucre; weekly; Dir DAVID CABEZAS; circ. 1,500.

Prensa Libre: Sucre; tel. (64) 41293; fax (64) 32768; f. 1989; weekly; Dir JORGE ENCERAS DIAZ.

Servicio de Información Confidencial (SIC): Elías Sagárnaga 274, Casilla 5035, La Paz; weekly; publ. by Asociación Nacional de Prensa; Dir JOSÉ CARRANZA.

Siglo XXI: La Paz; weekly.

Unión: Sucre; weekly; Dir JAIME MERILES.

Visión Boliviana: Calle Loayza 420, Casilla 2870, La Paz; 6 a year.

PRESS ASSOCIATIONS

Asociación Nacional de la Prensa: Avda 6 de Agosto 2170, Casilla 477, La Paz; tel. (2) 36-9916; Pres. Dr CARLOS SERRATE REICH.

Asociación de Periodistas de La Paz: Avda 6 de Agosto 2170, Casilla 477, La Paz; tel. (2) 36-9916; fax (2) 32-3701; f. 1929; Pres. MARIO MALDONADO VISCARRA; Vice-Pres. MARÍA EUGENIA VERASTEGUI A.

NEWS AGENCIES

Agencia de Noticias Fides (ANF): Edif. Mariscal de Ayacucho, 5°, Of. 501, Calle Loayza, Casilla 5782, La Paz; tel. (2) 36-5152; fax (2) 36-5153; owned by Roman Catholic Church; Dir JOSÉ GRAMUNT DE MORAGAS.

Foreign Bureaux

Agencia EFE (Spain): Edif. Esperanza, Avda Mariscal Santa Cruz 2150, Casilla 7403, La Paz; tel. (2) 36-7205; fax (2) 39-1441; e-mail fvv@caoba.entelnet.bo; Bureau Chief FERNANDO DE VALENZUELA.

Agenzia Nazionale Stampa Associata (ANSA) (Italy): La Paz; tel. (2) 35-5521; fax (2) 36-8221; Correspondent RAÚL PENARANDA UNDURRAGA.

Associated Press (AP) (USA): Edif. Mariscal de Ayacucho, Of. 1209, Calle Loayza, Casilla 9569, La Paz; tel. (2) 37-0128; Correspondent PETER J. MCFARREN.

Deutsche Presse-Agentur (dpa) (Germany): Edif. Esperanza, 9°, Of. 3, Av. Mariscal Santa Cruz 2150, Casilla 13885, La Paz; tel. (2) 35-2684; fax (2) 39-2488; Correspondent ROBERT BROCKMANN.

Informatsionnoye Telegrafnoye Agentstvo Rossii-Telegrafnoye Agentstvo Suverennykh Stran (ITARTASS) (Russia): Casilla 6839, San Miguel, Bloque 0–33, Casa 958, La Paz; tel. (2) 79-2108; Correspondent ELDAR ABDULLAEV.

Inter Press Service (IPS) (Italy): Edif. Esperanza, 6°, Of. 6, Casilla 4313, La Paz; tel. (2) 36-1227; Correspondent RONALD GREBE LÓPEZ.

Prensa Latina (Cuba): La Paz; tel. (2) 32-3479; Correspondent MANUEL ROBLES SOSA.

Reuters (United Kingdom): Edif. Loayza, 3°, Of. 301, Calle Loayza 349, Casilla 4057, La Paz; tel. (2) 35-1106; fax (2) 39-1366; Correspondent RENÉ VILLEGAS MONJE.

Rossiyskoye Informatsionnoye Agentstvo—Novosti (RIA—Novosti) (Russia): La Paz; tel. (2) 37-3857; Correspondent VLADIMIR RAMÍREZ.

United Press International (UPI) (USA): Plaza Venezuela 1479, 7°, Of. 702, Casilla 1219, La Paz; tel. (2) 78-4172; fax (2) 78-4066; Correspondent ALBERTO ZUAZO NATHES.

Agence France-Presse and Telam (Argentina) are also represented.

Publishers

Editora Khana Cruz SRL: Avda Camacho 1372, Casilla 5920, La Paz; tel. (2) 37-0263; Dir GLADIS ANDRADE.

Editora Lux: Edif. Esperanza, Avda Mariscal Santa Cruz, Casilla 1566, La Paz; tel. (2) 32-9102; fax (2) 34-3968; f. 1952; Dir FELICISIMO TARILONTE PÉREZ.

Editorial los Amigos del Libro: Avda Heroínas E-0311, Casilla 450, Cochabamba; tel. (42) 51140; fax (41) 15128; e-mail amigol@ amigol.bo.net; f. 1945; general; Man. Dir WERNER GUTTENTAG.

Editorial Bruño: Loayza 167, Casilla 4809, La Paz; tel. (2) 33-1254; fax (2) 33-5043; f. 1964; Dir IGNACIO LOMAS.

Editorial Don Bosco: Calle Tiahuanacu 116, Casilla 4458, La Paz; tel. (2) 37-1757; fax (2) 36-2822; f. 1896; social sciences and literature; Dir GIAMPAOLO MARIO MAZZON.

Editorial Icthus: La Paz; tel. (2) 35-4007; f. 1967; general and textbooks; Man. Dir DANIEL AQUIZE.

Editorial Popular: Plaza Pérez Velasco 787, Casilla 4171, La Paz; tel. (2) 35-0701; f. 1935; textbooks, postcards, tourist guides, etc; Man. Dir GERMÁN VILLAMOR.

Editorial Puerta del Sol: Edif. Litoral Sub Suelo, Avda Mariscal Santa Cruz, La Paz; tel. (2) 36-0746; f. 1965; Man. Dir OSCAR CRESPO.

Empresa Editora Proinsa: Avda Saavedra 2055, Casilla 7181, La Paz; tel. (2) 22-7781; fax (2) 22-6671; f. 1974; school books; Dirs FLOREN SANABRIA G., CARLOS SANABRIA C.

Gisbert y Cía, SA: Calle Comercio 1270, Casilla 195, La Paz; tel. (2) 20-2626; fax (2) 20-2911; e-mail libgis@ceibo.entelnet.bo; f. 1907; textbooks, history, law and general; Pres. JAVIER GISBERT; Dirs MARÍA DEL CARMEN SCHULCZEWSKI, ANTONIO SCHULCZEWSKI.

Ivar American: Calle Potosí 1375, Casilla 6016, La Paz; tel. (2) 36-1519; Man. Dir HÉCTOR IBÁÑEZ.

Librería Editorial Juventud: Plaza Murillo 519, Casilla 1489, La Paz; tel. (2) 40-6248; fax (2) 40-7033; f. 1946; textbooks and general; Dir GUSTAVO URQUIZO MENDOZA.

Librería El Ateneo SRL: Calle Ballivián 1275, Casilla 7917, La Paz; tel. (2) 36-9925; fax (2) 39-1513; Dirs JUAN CHIRVECHES D., MIRIAN C. DE CHIRVECHES.

Librería Dismo Ltda: Calle Comercio 806, Casilla 988, La Paz; tel. (2) 35-3119; fax (2) 31-6545; Dir TERESA GONZÁLEZ DE ALVAREZ.

Librería La Paz: Calle Campos y Villegas, Edif. Artemis, Casilla 539, La Paz; tel. (2) 43-4927; fax (2) 43-5004; e-mail liblapaz@ ceibo.entelnet.bo; f. 1900; Dirs EDUARDO BURGOS R., CARLOS BURGOS M.

Librería La Universal SRL: Calle Genaro Sanjines 538, Casilla 2888, La Paz; tel. (2) 34-2961; f. 1958; Man. Dir ROLANDO CONDORI.

Librería San Pablo: Calle Colón 627, Casilla 3152, La Paz; tel. (2) 32-6084; f. 1967; Man. Dir MARÍA DE JESÚS VALERIANO.

PUBLISHERS' ASSOCIATION

Cámara Boliviana del Libro: Calle Capitán Ravelo 2116, Casilla 682, La Paz; tel. (2) 44-4239; fax (2) 44-1523; e-mail cabolib@ceibo .entelnet.bo; f. 1947; Pres. CARMEN TEJERINA DE TERRAZAS; Gen. Man. VERONICA FLORES BEDREGAL.

Broadcasting and Communications

TELECOMMUNICATIONS

Cámara Nacional de Medios de Comunicación: Casilla 2431, La Paz.

Empresa Nacional de Telecomunicaciones (ENTEL): Edif. Palacio de Comunicaciones, Federico Zuazo 1771, Casilla 4450, La Paz; tel. (2) 31-3030; fax (2) 39-1789; internet www.entelnet.bo; f. 1965; privatized under the Govt's capitalization programme in 1995; Exec. Pres. FRANCO BERTONI; Gen. Man. MICHAEL ANGELO ORDÓÑEZ.

Superintendencia de Telecomunicaciones: Edif. M. Cristina, Plaza España, Casilla 6692, La Paz; tel. (2) 41-6641; fax (2) 41-8183; e-mail supertel@ceibo.entelnet.bo; f. 1995; govt-controlled broadcasting authority; Superintendent Ing. GUIDO LOAYZA.

BROADCASTING
Radio

There were 145 radio stations in 1990, the majority of which were commercial. Broadcasts are in Spanish, Aymará and Quechua.

Asociación Boliviana de Radiodifusoras (ASBORA): Edif. Jazmin, 10°, Avda 20 de Octubre 2019, Casilla 5324, La Paz; tel. (2) 36-5154; fax (2) 36-3069; broadcasting authority; Pres. TERESA SANJINÉS L.; Vice-Pres. LUIS ANTONIO SERRANO.

Educación Radiofónica de Bolivia (ERBOL): Calle Ballivian 1323, 4°, Casilla 5946, La Paz; tel. (2) 35-4142; fax (2) 39-1985; asscn of 28 educational radio stations in Bolivia; Gen. Sec. RONALD GREBE LÓPEZ.

Television

Corporación Boliviana de Televisión Canal 30: Calle Obispo Cárdenas 1475, Casilla 8980, La Paz; tel. (2) 31-5031; fax (2) 31-9563; f. 1996; Pres. RICARDO CLAURE; Dir ALEX MEJÍA.

Empresa Nacional de Televisión Boliviana Canal 7: Edif. La Urbana, 6° y 7°, Avda Camacho 1486, Casilla 900, La Paz; tel. (2) 37-6356; fax (2) 35-9753; f. 1969; govt network operating stations in La Paz, Oruro, Cochabamba, Potosí, Chuquisaca, Pando, Beni, Tarija and Santa Cruz; Gen. Man. MIGUEL M. MONTERO VACA.

Televisión Boliviano Canal 2: Casilla 4837, La Paz.

Televisión Universitaria Canal 13: Edif. 'Hoy', 12°–13°, Avda 6 de Agosto 2170, Casilla 13383, La Paz; tel. (2) 35-9297; fax (2) 35-9298; f. 1980; educational programmes; stations in Oruro, Cochabamba, Potosí, Sucre, Tarija, Beni and Santa Cruz; Dir Lic. ROBERTO CUEVAS RAMÍREZ.

Finance

(cap. = capital; p.u. = paid up; res = reserves;
dep. = deposits; m. = million; brs = branches; amounts are in
bolivianos unless otherwise stated)

BANKING

Supervisory Authority

Superintendencia de Bancos y Entidades Financieras: Plaza Isabel la Católica 2507, Casilla 447, La Paz; tel. (2) 43-1919; fax (2) 43-0028; e-mail supban@lp.superbancos.gov.bo; internet www .superbancos.gov.bo; f. 1928; Supt Lic. JACQUES TRIGO LOUBIÈRE.

State Banks

Banco Central de Bolivia: Avda Ayacucho esq. Mercado, Casilla 3118, La Paz; tel. (2) 37-4151; fax (2) 39-2398; e-mail vmarquez@ mail.bcb.gov.bo; internet www.bcb.gov.bo; f. 1911 as Banco de la Nación Boliviana, name changed as above 1928; bank of issue; cap. 96.6m., res 215.6m. (Dec. 1996); Pres. Dr JUAN ANTONIO MORALES ANAYA; Gen. Man. Lic. JAIME VALENCIA VALENCIA.

Banco del Estado: Calle Colón esq. Mercado, Casilla 1401, La Paz; tel. (2) 35-2868; fax (2) 39-1682; f. 1970; state bank incorporating banking department of Banco Central de Bolivia; cap. and res 51.1m., dep. 92.5m. (June 1990); Pres. Lic. RAMÓN RADA VELASCO; Gen. Man. JUAN LUIS PACHECO RAMÍREZ; 55 brs.

Banco Agrícola de Bolivia: Avda Mariscal Santa Cruz esq. Almirante Grau, Casilla 1179, La Paz; tel. (2) 36-5876; fax (2) 35-5940; f. 1942; cap. and res 100.4m. (June 1990); Pres. Lic. WALTER NÚÑEZ R.; Gen. Man. Lic. JUAN CARLOS PEREDO P.

Banco Minero de Bolivia: Calle Comercio 1290, Casilla 1410, La Paz; tel. (2) 35-2168; fax (2) 36-8870; f. 1936; finances private mining industry; cap. and res 44.6m. (June 1990); Pres. Ing. JAIME ASCARRUNZ E.; Gen. Man. Ing. RENÉ SANZ M.

Banco de la Vivienda: La Paz; tel. (2) 34-3510. 1964; to encourage and finance housing developments; 51% state participation; initial cap. 100m. Bolivian pesos; Pres. (vacant); Gen. Man. Lic. JOSÉ RAMÍREZ MONTALVA.

Commercial Banks

Banco Bisa SA: Avda 16 de Julio 1628, Casilla 1290, La Paz; tel. (2) 35-9471; fax (2) 39-1735; e-mail mcastellanos@grupobisa.com; internet www.grupobisa.com; f. 1963; cap. 285m., res 34m., dep. 2,800m. (Dec. 1998); Pres. Ing. JULIÓ LEÓN PRADO; Gen. Man. JOSÉ LUIS ARANGUREN AGUIRRE.

Banco Boliviano Americano: Avda Camacho esq. Loayza, Casilla 478, La Paz; tel. (2) 35-0886; fax (2) 39-1056; e-mail nuevobba@wara .bolnet.bo; f. 1957; cap. and res US $13.4m., dep. US $186m. (June 1997); Pres. DAVID BLANCO; Gen. Man. ELIZABETH DE BADINI; 5 brs.

Banco de Cochabamba, SA: Warnes 40, Casilla 4107, Santa Cruz; tel. (3) 351036; fax (3) 340871; f. 1962; cap. 7.8m., dep. 112.0m. (July 1994); Exec. Pres. GUILLERMO GUTIÉRREZ SOSA; Gen. Man. MARÍA ELENA BLANCO DE ESTENSSORO; 5 brs.

Banco de Crédito de Bolivia, SA: Calle Colón esq. Mercado 1308, Casilla 907, La Paz; tel. (2) 36-0025; fax (2) 39-1044; f. 1993 as Banco Popular, SA, name changed as above 1994; 61% owned by Banco de Crédito del Perú; cap. US $26.1m., res US $1.9m., dep. US $511.3m. (Dec. 1998); Chair. DIONISIO ROMERO SEMINARIO; Gen. Man. RUBÉN LOAIZA NEGREIROS; 6 brs.

Banco Económico SA-SCZ: Calle Ayacucho 166, Santa Cruz; tel. (3) 36-1177; fax (3) 36-1184; e-mail bcneco@roble.scz.entelnet.bo; f. 1990; dep. US $290.4m., total assets US $328.1m. (Dec. 1998); Pres. ALEX JOSÉ CUÉLLAR CHÁVEZ; Gen. Man. Ing. JUSTO YEPEZ KAKUDA; 14 brs.

Banco de Financiamiento Industrial, SA: Plaza 10 de Febrero acera Adolfo Mier esq. La Plata, Casilla 51, Oruro; tel. (52) 53759; f. 1974 to encourage and finance industrial development; cap. p.u. 2.6m. Bolivian pesos, dep. 1.1m. Bolivian pesos; Pres. Lic. HUGO CAMPOS; Man. FRANCISCO BERMÚDEZ.

Banco Ganadero SA-Santa Cruz: Calle Bolivar 99, Casilla 4492, Santa Cruz; tel. (3) 36-1616; fax (3) 34-0825; e-mail hkrutzfeldt@ bancoganadero.co.bo; internet www.bancoganedero.com; f. 1994; cap. and res 108.1m.; dep. 1,078.1m. (Dec. 2000); Pres. FERNANDO MONASTERIO NIEME; Gen. Man. HERMANN KRUTZFELDT.

Banco Industrial, SA: Avda 16 de Julio 1628, 12°, Casilla 1290, La Paz; tel. (2) 35-9471; fax (2) 31-6597; e-mail bancbisa@caoba .entelnet.bo; f. 1963; industrial credit bank; cap. 153.2m., res 16.7m., dep. 2,194.2m. (Dec. 1996); Pres. JULIO LEÓN PRADO; CEO JUAN OTERO; 18 brs.

Banco Industrial y Ganadero del Beni, SA: Edif. Bigbeni, Avda 6 de Agosto, Casilla 54, Trinidad; tel. (46) 21476; cap. and res 22.4m., dep. 121.8m. (June 1990); Pres. Dr ISAAC SHIRIQUI V.; 11 brs.

Banco Internacional de Desarrollo, SA: Calle Nuflo de Chávez 150, Santa Cruz; tel. (3) 361555; fax (3) 338485; f. 1991; cap. 13.5m., res 11.8m., dep. 545.2m. (Dec. 1993); Pres. CARLOS LANDIVAR GIL; Gen. Man. Lic. ROBERTO LANDIVAR ROCA; 2 brs.

Banco de Inversión Boliviano, SA: Avda 16 de Julio 1571, Casilla 8639, La Paz; tel. (2) 35-4233; fax (2) 32-6536; f. 1977; cap. and res 11.2m., dep. 126.8m. (June 1991); Pres. JAIME GUTIÉRREZ MOSCOSO; Exec. Vice-Pres. MAURICIO URQUIDI URQUIDI.

Banco de La Paz, SA: Avda 16 de Julio 1473, Casilla 6826, La Paz; tel. (2) 39-0991; fax (2) 32-6536; f. 1975; cap. 53.1m., res 8.4m., dep. 767.5m. (Dec. 1995); Pres. LUIS VISCARRA; Gen. Man. GLENN KLEIN; 14 brs.

Banco Mercantil, SA: Calle Ayacucho esq. Mercado 295, Casilla 423, La Paz; tel. (2) 31-5131; fax (2) 37-4483; e-mail bercant@caoba .entelnet.bo; internet www.mercantil.com.bo; f. 1905; cap. and res 38.5m., dep. 379m. (Sept. 1997); Pres. EDUARDO QUINTANILLA; Gen. Man. MARCELO DÍEZ DE MEDINA; 39 brs.

Banco Nacional de Bolivia: Avda Camacho esq. Colón, Casilla 360, La Paz; tel. (2) 35-4616; fax (2) 37-1279; e-mail info@bnb.com.bo; internet www.bnb.bolivia.com; f. 1871; cap. 189.3m., res 46.1m., dep. 3,108.9m. (Dec. 1998); Pres. FERNANDO BEDOYA B.; Gen. Man. EDUARDO ALVAREZ LEMAITRE; 10 brs.

Banco Santa Cruz, SA: Calle Junín 154, Casilla 865, Santa Cruz; tel. (3) 36-9911; fax (3) 35-0114; e-mail bancruz@mailbsc.com.bo; internet www.bsc.com.bo; f. 1965; 90% owned by Banco Central Hispanoamericano (Spain); cap. and res 44.2m., dep. 315.4m. (June 1990); Pres. LYDERS PAREJA EGÜEZ; Gen. Man. ALFONSO ALVAREZ NÚÑEZ; 44 brs.

Banco Solidario, SA: Calle Nicolás Acosta esq. Cañada Strongest 289, Casilla 13176, La Paz; tel. (2) 48-4242; fax (2) 48-6468; e-mail info@bancosol.com.bo; f. 1992; Pres. ROBERTO CAPRILES; 43 brs.

Banco Unión, SA: Calle Libertad 165, Casilla 4057, Santa Cruz; tel. (3) 36-6869; fax (3) 34-0684; e-mail info@bancounion.com.bo; f. 1982; cap. 48.8m., res 7.6m., dep. 1,056.5m. (Dec. 1994); Pres. Ing. ANDRÉS PETRICEVIC; Gen. Man. Ing. LUIS SAAVEDRA BRUNO; 31 brs.

Caja Central de Ahorros y Préstamos para la Vivienda: Avda Mariscal Santa Cruz 1364, 20°, Casilla 4808, La Paz; tel. (2) 37-1280; fax (2) 36-1346; f. 1967; assets US $51m. (1993); Gen. Man. EDUARDO FRIAS T.

Foreign Banks

Banco ABN AMRO Real, SA (USA): Avda 16 de Julio 1642, Casilla 10008, La Paz; tel. (2) 33-4477; fax (2) 33-5588; e-mail real@caoba.entelnet.bo; f. 1978 as Banco Real, name changed as above 2000; dep. US $8.3m.; total assets US $17.5m. (Dec. 1997); Operations Man. BRIGITTE LAURA SCHIMUNEK GUEVERA.

Banco do Brasil, SA: Avda Camacho 1468, Planta Baja, Casilla 1650, La Paz; tel. (2) 37-7272; fax (2) 39-1036; e-mail bblapaz@caoba .entelnet.bo; f. 1961; Gen. Man. LEO SCHNEIDERS; 1 br.

Banco de la Nación Argentina: Avda 16 de Julio 1486, Casilla 2745-4312, La Paz; tel. (2) 35-9218; fax (2) 39-1392; e-mail bancnalp @caoba.entelnet.bo; internet www.bna.com.ar; f. 1891; Man. EDUARDO CASADO; 2 brs.

Citibank NA (USA): Edif. Multicentro Torre B, Calle Rosendo Gutiérrez esq. Arce 146, La Paz; tel. (2) 43-0099; fax (2) 44-0433; e-mail juan.leyes@citicorp.com; f. 1966; Vice-Pres MARIO BEDOYA GARLAND, MARCELO CELERINO; 2 brs.

Dresdner Bank Lateinamerika AG: Calle Rosendo Gutiérrez esq. Arce 136, Edif. Multicentro Torre B, La Paz; tel. (2) 43-4114; fax (2) 43-4115; fmrly Deutsch-Südamerikanische Bank AG and Dresdner Bank AG; Gen. Man. NILS HUPKA.

Banking Association

Asociación de Bancos Privados de Bolivia (ASOBAN): Edif. Cámara Nacional de Comercio, 15°, Avda Mariscal Santa Cruz esq. Colombia 1392, Casilla 5822, La Paz; tel. (2) 36-1308; fax (2) 39-1093; e-mail asoban@wara.bdnet.bo; f. 1957; Pres. JAVIER ZUAZO CH.; Exec. Sec. CARLOS ITURRALDE B.; 18 mems.

STOCK EXCHANGE

Supervisory Authority

Superintendencia de Pensiones, Valores y Seguros: Calle Reyes Ortiz esq. Federico Zuazo, Torres Gundlach, 3°, Casilla 6118, La Paz; tel. (2) 33-1212; fax (2) 33-0001; e-mail spvs@caoba .entelnet.bo; Superintendent Dr PABLO GOTTRET VALDÉS; Intendent FRANCISCO GÓMEZ.

Bolsa Boliviana de Valores SA: Edif. Zambrana P.B., Calle Montevideo 142, Casilla 12521, La Paz; tel (2) 39-2911; fax (2) 35-2308; e-mail info@bolsa-valores-bolivia.com; internet www.bolsa-valores

-bolivia.com; f. 1989; Pres. Lic. Luis Felipe Rivero Mendoza; Gen. Man. Lic. Armando Alvarez Arnal.

INSURANCE

Supervisory Authority

Superintendencia de Pensiones, Valores y Seguros: (see above).

National Companies

Adriatica Seguros y Reaseguros, SA: Avda Cristóbal de Mendoza 250, Santa Cruz; tel. (3) 36-6667; fax (3) 36-0600; e-mail adriatica@cotas.com.bo; Pres. Antonio Olea Baudoin; Gen. Man. Eduardo Landívar Roca.

Alianza, Cía de Seguros y Reaseguros, SA: Avda 20 de Octubre 2680, esq. Campos Zona San Jorge, Casilla 11873, La Paz; tel. (2) 43-2121; fax (2) 43-2511; e-mail alianza@ceibo.entelnet.bo; Pres. Juan Manuel Peña Roca; Gen. Man. César Eyzaguirre Angeles.

Alianza Vida Seguros y Reaseguros, SA: Avda Viedma 19, Casilla 1043, Santa Cruz; tel. (3) 37-5656; fax (3) 37-5666; e-mail alejandro@sc.alianzaseguros.com; Pres. Raúl Adler K.; Gen. Man. Alejandro Ybarra C.

Aseguranza Internacional, SA: Avda San Martín 1000-B esq. Calle Pablo Sanz, Casilla 1188, Santa Cruz; tel. (3) 43-7443; fax (3) 43-7439; Pres. Davida Gutiérrez.

Bisa Seguros y Reaseguros, SA: Edif. San Pablo, 13°, Avda 16 de Julio 1479, Casilla 3669, La Paz; tel. (2) 35-2123; fax (2) 39-2500; e-mail bisaseguros@grupobisa.com; Pres. Julio León Prado; Exec. Vice-Pres. Alejandro Maclean C.

Bolívar de Seguros, SA: Edif. Bolívar, Avda Mariscal Santa Cruz 1287, Casilla 1459, La Paz; tel. (2) 36-3688; fax (2) 32-2158; Pres. Freddy Oporto Méndez.

La Boliviana Ciacruz de Seguros y Reaseguros, SA: Calle Colón, esq. Mercado 288, Casilla 5959, La Paz; tel. (2) 20-3131; fax (2) 20-4087; e-mail bolseg@caoba.entelnet.bo; f. 1946; all classes; Pres. Gonzalo Bedoya Herrera.

Compañía de Seguros y Reaseguros Cruceño, SA: Calle René Moreno esq. Lemoyne 607, Santa Cruz; tel. (3) 33-8985; fax (3) 33-8984; e-mail seg.crycena@mail.cotas.com.bo; Pres. Lic. Guido Hinojosa; Gen. Man. Nelson Hinojosa.

Credinform International SA de Seguros: Edif. Credinform, Calle Potosí esq. Ayacucho 1220, Casilla 1724, La Paz; tel. (2) 31-5566; fax (2) 39-1225; e-mail credinfo@caoba.entelnet.bo; f. 1954; all classes; Pres. Dr Robín Barragán Peláez; Gen. Man. Miguel Angel Barragán Ibarguen.

Delta Insurance Co, SA: Calle España, Casilla 920, Cochabamba; tel. (42) 25-7765; fax (42) 22-0451; f. 1965; all classes except life; Pres. Carlos Christie Justiniano.

La Fenix Boliviana, SA de Seguros y Reaseguros: Calle Potosí, Edif. Naira Mezzanine Of 5, Casilla 4409, La Paz; tel. (2) 35-3708; fax (2) 37-0187; Pres. Orlando Nogales.

Nacional de Seguros y Reaseguros, SA: Calle Libertad esq. Cañoto 879, Casilla 6794, Santa Cruz; tel. (3) 34-6969; fax (3) 34-2415; e-mail nalseg@bibosi.scz.entelnet.bo; f. 1977; fmrly known as Condor, SA de Seguros y Reaseguros; Pres. Tonchi Eterovic Niegovic; Gen. Man. Luis Alberto Flor Cortez.

Seguros Illimani, SA: Edif. Mariscal de Ayacucho, 10°, Calle Loayza, Casilla 133, La Paz; tel. (2) 20-3040; fax (2) 39-1149; e-mail sisalp@ceibo.entelnet.bo; f. 1979; all classes; Pres. Fernando Arce Grandchant; Gen. Man. Luis Arce Ostria.

Unicruz Cía de Seguros de Vida, SA: Zona El Trompillo 76 Perimetral y Río Grande, Santa Cruz; tel. (3) 54-0707; fax (3) 53-9549; e-mail unicruz@bibosi.scz.entelnet.bo; Pres. Francisco Nalda Mujica.

Unión de Seguros, SA: Edif. El Cóndor, 16°, Calle Batallón Colorados, Casilla 2922, La Paz; tel. (2) 35-8155; fax (2) 39-2049; all classes; Pres. Dr Jorge Rengel Sillerico; Man. Víctor Rosas.

La Vitalicia Seguros y Reaseguros de Vida, SA: Avda 6 de Agosto 2170, Edif. Hoy Mezzanine, La Paz; tel. (2) 33-4303; fax (2) 33-3792; e-mail vitalseg@ceibo.entelnet.bo; Pres. Julio César L. Prado.

There are also four foreign-owned insurance companies operating in Bolivia: American Life Insurance Co, American Home Assurance Co, United States Fire Insurance Co and International Health Insurance Danmarck.

Insurance Association

Asociación Boliviana de Aseguradores: Edif. Castilla, 5°, Of. 506, Calle Loayza esq. Mercado 250, Casilla 4804, La Paz; tel. (2) 31-0056; fax (2) 20-1088; e-mail abasegu@ceibo.entelnet.bo; f. 1962; Pres. Alfonso Ibáñez; Gen. Man. Carlos Baudoin D.

Trade and Industry

GOVERNMENT AGENCIES

Cámara Nacional de Exportadores (CAMEX): Avda Arce 2017, esq. Goitia, Casilla 12145, La Paz; tel. (2) 34-1220; fax (2) 36-1491; e-mail camex@caoba.entelnet.bo; internet www.camex-lpb.com; f. 1970; Pres. Luis Nemtala Yamin; Gen. Man. Jorge Adriazola Reimers.

Centro de Promoción Bolivia (CEPROBOL): Calle Mercado 1328, 18°, Casilla 10871, La Paz; tel. (2) 33-6886; fax (2) 33-6996; e-mail ceprobol@ceprobol.gov.bo; internet www.ceprobol.gov.bo; f. 1998 as a successor to the Instituto Nacional de Promoción de Exportaciones (INPEX).

Instituto Nacional de Inversiones (INI): Edif. Cristal, 10°, Calle Yanacocha, Casilla 4393, La Paz; tel. (2) 37-5730; fax (2) 36-7297; e-mail abeseg@kolla.net.bo; f. 1971; state institution for the promotion of new investments and the application of the Investment Law; Exec. Dir Ing. José Mario Fernández Irahola.

Sistema de Regulación Sectorial (SIRESE): Edif. Capitán Ravelo, 8°, Casilla 9647, La Paz; tel. (2) 44-4545; fax (2) 44-4017; e-mail sg@sirese.gov.bo; internet www.sirese.gov.bo; f. 1994; regulatory body for the formerly state-owned companies and utilities; oversees the general co-ordination and growth of the regulatory system and the work of its Superintendencies of Electricity, Hydrocarbons, Telecommunications, Transport and Water; Superintendent Gen. Claude Besse Arze.

DEVELOPMENT ORGANIZATIONS

Consejo Nacional de Acreditación y Medición de la Calidad Educativa (CONAMED): La Paz; f. 1994; education quality board.

Consejo Nacional de Planificación (CONEPLAN): Edif. Banco Central de Bolivia, 26°, Calle Mercado esq. Ayacucho, Casilla 3118, La Paz; tel. (2) 37-4151; fax (2) 35-3840; e-mail claves@mail.bcb.gov.bo; internet www.bcb.gov.bo; f. 1985.

Corporación de las Fuerzas Armadas para el Desarrollo Nacional (COFADENA): Avda 6 de Agosto 2649, Casilla 1015, La Paz; tel. (2) 37-7305; fax (2) 36-0900; f. 1972; industrial, agricultural and mining holding company and development organization owned by the Bolivian armed forces; Gen. Man. Col Juan Manuel Rosales.

Corporación Regional de Desarrollo de La Paz (CORDEPAZ): Avda Arce 2529, Edif. Santa Isabel, Casilla 6102, La Paz; tel. (2) 43-0313; fax (2) 43-2152; f. 1972; decentralized government institution to foster the development of the La Paz area; Pres. Lic. Ricardo Paz Ballivián; Gen. Man. Ing. Juan G. Carrasco R.

Instituto para el Desarrollo de la Pequeña Unidad Productiva: La Paz.

CHAMBERS OF COMMERCE

Cámara Nacional de Comercio: Edif. Cámara Nacional de Comercio, Avda Mariscal Santa Cruz 1392, 1°, Casilla 7, La Paz; tel. (2) 35-0042; fax (2) 39-1004; e-mail cnc@boliviacomercio.org.bo; internet www.boliviacomercio.org.bo; f. 1890; 30 brs and special brs; Pres. Alejandro Yaffar de la Barra; Gen. Man. José Kuhn Poppe.

Cámara de Comercio de Oruro: Pasaje Guachalla s/n, Casilla 148, Oruro; tel. and fax (52) 50606; f. 1895; e-mail camacor@coteor.net.bo; Pres. Alvaro Cornejo Gazcón; Gen. Man. Luis Camacho Vargas.

Cámara Departamental de Industria y Comercio de Santa Cruz: Calle Suárez de Figueroa 127, 3°, Casilla 180, Santa Cruz; tel. (3) 33-4555; fax (3) 34-2353; e-mail cainco@cainco.org.bo; internet www.cainco.org.bo; f. 1915; Pres. Zvonko Matkovic Fleig; Gen. Man. Lic. Oscar Ortiz Antelo.

Cámara Departamental de Comercio de Cochabamba: Calle Sucre E-0336, Casilla 493, Cochabamba; tel. (42) 57715; fax (42) 57717; e-mail camcom@pino.cbb.entelnet.bo; internet www.camind.com/cadeco; f. 1922; Pres. Ing. Carlos Olmedo Z.; Gen. Man. Lic. Juan Carlos Avila S.

Cámara Departamental de Comercio e Industria de Potosí: Calle Matos 12, Casilla 149, Potosí; tel. (62) 22641; fax (62) 22641; Pres. Javier Flores Castro; Gen. Man. Walter Zabala Ayllon.

Cámara Departamental de Industria y Comercio de Chuquisaca: Calle España 64, Casilla 33, Sucre; tel. (64) 51194; fax (64) 51850; e-mail cicch@camara.scr.entelnet.bo; f. 1923; Pres. Marco Mihaic; Gen. Man. Lic. Alfredo Yáñez Mercado.

Cámara Departamental de Comercio e Industria de Cobija—Pando: Plaza Germán Busch, Casilla 110, Cobija; tel. (842) 3139; fax (842) 2291; Pres. Nemesio Ramírez.

Cámara Departamental de Industria y Comercio de Tarija: Avda Bolívar 0413, 1°, Casilla 74, Tarija; tel. (66) 22737; fax (66) 24053; e-mail metfess@olivo.tja.entelnet.bo; Pres. Rene Silbermann U.; Gen. Man. Víctor Aramayo.

Cámara Departamental de Comercio de Trinidad—Beni: Casilla 96, Trinidad; tel. (46) 22365; fax (46) 21400; Pres. EDUARDO AVILA ALVERDI.

INDUSTRIAL AND TRADE ASSOCIATIONS

Cámara Agropecuaria del Oriente: 3 anillo interno zona Oeste, Casilla 116, Santa Cruz; tel. (3) 52-2200; fax (3) 52-2621; e-mail caosrz@bibosi.scz.entelnet.bo; f. 1964; agriculture and livestock association for eastern Bolivia; Pres. RICARDO FRERKING ORTIZ; Gen. Man. WALTER NÚÑEZ RODRÍGUEZ.

Cámara Agropecuaria de La Paz: Avda 16 de Julio 1525, Casilla 12521, La Paz; tel. (2) 39-2911; fax (2) 35-2308; Pres. ALBERTO DE OLIVA MAYA; Gen. Man. JUAN CARLOS ZAMORANO.

Cámara Forestal de Bolivia: Prolongación Manuel Ignacio Salvatierra 1055, Casilla 346, Santa Cruz; tel. (3) 33-2699; fax (3) 33-1456; e-mail foresbol@cotas.com.bo; internet www.cadex.org/camaraforestal; f. 1969; represents the interests of the Bolivian timber industry; Pres. MARIO BARBERY SCIARONI; Gen. Man. Lic. ARTURO BOWLES OLHAGARAY.

Cámara Nacional de Industrias: Edif. Cámara Nacional de Comercio, 14°, Avda Mariscal Santa Cruz 1392, Casilla 611, La Paz; tel. (2) 37-4476; fax (2) 36-2766; e-mail cni@mail.megalink.com; internet www.bolivia-industry.com; f. 1931; Pres. ROBERTO MUSTAFÁ; Man. GERARDO VELASCO T.

Cámara Nacional de Minería: Pasaje Bernardo Trigo 429, Casilla 2022, La Paz; tel. (2) 35-0623; f. 1953; mining institute; Pres. Ing. LUIS PRADO BARRIENTOS; Sec.-Gen. GERMÁN GORDILLO S.

Comité Boliviano de Productores de Antimonio: Pasajes Bernardo Trigo 429, Casilla 14451, La Paz; tel. (2) 44-2140; fax (2) 44-1653; f. 1978; controls the marketing, pricing and promotion policies of the antimony industry; Pres. ALBERTO BARRIOS MORALES; Sec.-Gen. Dr ALCIDES RODRÍGUEZ J.

Comité Boliviano del Café (COBOLCA): Calle Nicaragua 1638, Casilla 9770, La Paz; tel. (2) 22-3883; fax (2) 24-4591; e-mail cobolca@ceibo.entelnet.bo; controls the export, quality, marketing and growing policies of the coffee industry; Gen. Man. MAURICIO VILLARROEL.

EMPLOYERS' ASSOCIATIONS

Asociación Nacional de Mineros Medianos: Calle Pedro Salazar 600 esq. Presbítero Medina, Casilla 6190, La Paz; tel. (2) 41-7522; fax (2) 41-4123; e-mail anmm@caoba.entelnet.bo; f. 1939; association of the 14 private medium-sized mining companies; Pres. RAÚL ESPAÑA-SMITH; Sec.-Gen. ROLANDO JORDÁN.

Confederación de Empresarios Privados de Bolivia (CEPB): Edif. Cámara Nacional de Comercio, 7°, Avda Mariscal Santa Cruz 1392, Casilla 20439, La Paz; tel. (2) 35-6831; e-mail cepbol@ceibo.entelnet.bo; internet www.cepb.org; largest national employers' organization; Pres. Lic. CARLOS CALVO GALINDO; Exec. Sec. Lic. JOHNNY NOGALES VIRUEZ.

There are also employers' federations in Santa Cruz, Cochabamba, Oruro, Potosí, Beni and Tarija.

UTILITIES

Electricity

Superintendencia de Electricidad: Avda 16 de Julio 1571, La Paz; tel. (2) 31-2401; fax (2) 31-2393; e-mail superele@superele.gov.bo; internet www.superele.gov.bo; f. 1996; regulates the electricity sector; Superintendent ALEJANDRO NOWOTNY VERA; Gen. Sec. ROLANDO LÓPEZ.

Compañía Boliviana de Energía Eléctrica, SA (COBEE): Avda Hernando Siles 5635, Casilla 353, La Paz; tel. (2) 78-2474; fax (2) 78-5920; e-mail cobee@cobee.com; f. 1925; second largest private producer and distributor of electricity serving the areas of La Paz and Oruro; in 1998 the company generated 25.9% of all electricity produced in Bolivia; Chair. D. H. BUSWELL.

Electropaz: Avda Illimani 1987, La Paz; tel. (2) 22-2200; fax (2) 22-3756; Gen. Man. Ing. ANGEL GÓMEZ.

Empresa Nacional de Electricidad, SA (ENDE): Colombia 655, esq. Falsuri, Casilla 565, Cochabamba; tel. (4) 25-9500; fax (4) 25-9509; f. 1962; former state electricity company; privatized under the Govt's capitalization programme in 1995 and divided into three arms concerned with generation, transmission and distribution, respectively; Pres. Ing. Dr ENRIQUE GÓMEZ DE ANGELO; Gen. Man. Ing. JORGE DE LA VEGA BARNECHEA.

Gas

Numerous distributors of natural gas exist throughout the country, many of which are owned by the petroleum distributor, Yacimientos Petrolíferos Fiscales Bolivianos (YPFB).

CO-OPERATIVES

Instituto Nacional de Co-operativas (INALCO): Edif. Lotería Nacional, 4°, Avda Mariscal Santa Cruz y Cochabamba, La Paz; tel. (2) 37-4366; fax (2) 37-2104; e-mail inalcolp@ceibo.entelnet.bo; f. 1974; Pres. DAVID AYAVIRI.

TRADE UNIONS

Central Obrera Boliviana (COB): Edif. COB, Calle Pisagua 618, Casilla 6552, La Paz; tel. (2) 28-3220; fax (2) 28-0420; f. 1952; main union confederation; 800,000 mems; Exec. Sec. ALBERTO CAMACHO PARDO; Sec.-Gen. OSCAR SALAS MOYA.

Affiliated unions:

Central Obrera Departamental de La Paz: Estación Central 284, La Paz; tel. (2) 35-2898; Exec. Sec. GENARO TORRICO.

Confederación Sindical Unica de los Trabajadores Campesinos de Bolivia (CSUTCB): Calle Sucre, esq. Yanacocha, La Paz; tel. (2) 36-9433; f. 1979; peasant farmers' union; Exec. Sec. JUAN DE LA CRUZ VILLCA.

Federación de Empleados de Industria Fabril: Edif. Fabril, 5°, Plaza de San Francisco, La Paz; tel. (2) 40-6799; fax (2) 40-7044; Exec. Sec. ALEX GÁLVEZ.

Federación Sindical de Trabajadores Mineros de Bolivia (FSTMB): Plaza Venezuela 1470, Casilla 14565, La Paz; tel. (2) 35-9656; fax (2) 48-4948; f. 1944; mineworkers' union; Exec. Sec. MILTON GONZÁLEZ; Gen. Sec. EDGAR RAMÍREZ SANTIESTÉBAN; 27,000 mems.

Federación Sindical de Trabajadores Petroleros de Bolivia: Calle México 1504, La Paz; tel. (2) 35-1748; Exec. Sec. NEFTALY-MENDOZA DURÁN.

Confederación General de Trabajadores Fabriles de Bolivia (CGTFB): Avda Armentia 452, Casilla 21590, La Paz; tel. (2) 37-1603; fax (2) 32-4302; e-mail dirabc@bo.net; f. 1951; manufacturing workers' union; Exec. Sec. ANGEL ASTURIZAGA; Gen. Sec. ROBERTO ENCINAS.

Transport

RAILWAYS

Empresa Nacional de Ferrocarriles (ENFE): Estación Central de Ferrocarriles, Plaza Zalles, Casilla 428, La Paz; tel. (2) 35-9935; fax (2) 39-2106; f. 1964; administers most of the railways in Bolivia; privatized under the Government's capitalization programme in 1995. Total networks: 3,698 km (1995); Andina network: 2,274 km; Eastern network: 1,424 km; Gen. Man. RAFAEL ECHAZU BROWN.

A former private railway, Machacamarca–Uncia, owned by Corporación Minera de Bolivia (105 km), merged with the Andina network of ENFE in 1987. There are plans to construct a railway line with Brazilian assistance, to link Cochabamba and Santa Cruz. There were also plans for the construction of a rail link between Santa Cruz and Mutún on the border with Brazil.

ROADS

In 1996 Bolivia had some 49,400 km of roads, of which an estimated 2,500 km were paved. Almost the entire road network is concentrated in the altiplano region and the Andes valleys. A 560-km highway runs from Santa Cruz to Cochabamba, serving a colonization scheme on virgin lands around Santa Cruz. The Pan-American Highway, linking Argentina and Peru, crosses Bolivia from south to north-west. In late 1997 the Government announced the construction of 1,844 km of new roads in the hope of improving Bolivia's connections with neighbouring countries.

INLAND WATERWAYS

By agreement with Paraguay in 1938 (confirmed in 1939), Bolivia has an outlet on the River Paraguay. This arrangement, together with navigation rights on the Paraná, gives Bolivia access to the River Plate and the sea. The River Paraguay is navigable for vessels of 12-ft draught for 288 km beyond Asunción, in Paraguay, and for smaller boats another 960 km to Corumbá in Brazil. In late 1994 plans were finalized to widen and deepen the River Paraguay, providing a waterway from Bolivia to the Atlantic coast in Uruguay. However, in 2000 work on the project had still not begun, owing largely to environmental concerns.

In 1974 Bolivia was granted free duty access to the Brazilian coastal ports of Belém and Santos and the inland ports of Corumbá and Port Velho. In 1976 Argentina granted Bolivia free port facilities at Rosario on the River Paraná. In 1992 an agreement was signed with Peru, granting Bolivia access to (and the use, without customs formalities, of) the Pacific port of Ilo. Most of Bolivia's foreign trade is handled through the ports of Matarani (Peru), Antofagasta and

Arica (Chile), Rosario and Buenos Aires (Argentina) and Santos (Brazil). An agreement between Bolivia and Chile to reform Bolivia's access arrangements to the port of Arica came into effect in January 1996.

Bolivia has over 14,000 km of navigable rivers, which connect most of Bolivia with the Amazon basin.

Bolivian River Navigation Company: f. 1958; services from Puerto Suárez to Buenos Aires (Argentina).

OCEAN SHIPPING

Líneas Navieras Bolivianas (LINABOL): Edif. Hansa, 16°, Avda Mariscal Santa Cruz, Apdo 11160, La Paz; tel. (2) 37-9459; fax (2) 39-1079; Pres. Vice-Adm. LUIS AZURDUY ZAMBRANA; Vice-Pres. WOLFGANG APT.

CIVIL AVIATION

Bolivia has 30 airports including the two international airports at La Paz (El Alto) and Santa Cruz (Viru-Viru).

Dirección General de Aeronaútica Civil: Avda Mariscal Santa Cruz 1278, Casilla 9360; La Paz; tel. (2) 37-4142; e-mail dgacbol@ceibo-entelnet.bo; internet www.dgac.gov.bo; f. 1947; Dir-Gen. ORLANDO MONTOYA KOËSTER.

AeroSur: Calle Colón y Avda Irala, Casilla 3104, Santa Cruz; tel. (3) 36-4446; fax (3) 33-0666; e-mail javiedr.gonzalez@aerosur.com; f. 1992 by the merger of existing charter cos following deregulation; privately-owned; Pres. OSCAR ALCOCER; Gen. Man. FERNANDO PRUDENCIO.

Lloyd Aéreo Boliviano, SAM (LAB): Casilla 132, Aeropuerto 'Jorge Wilstermann', Cochabamba; tel. (4) 25-1270; fax (4) 25-0766; e-mail lider@labairlines.bo.net; internet www.labairlines.bo.net; f. 1925; privatized under the Government's capitalization programme in 1995; owned by Bolivian Govt (48.3%), VASP-Brazil (49%), private interests (2.7%); operates a network of scheduled services to 12 cities within Bolivia and to 21 international destinations in South America, Central America and the USA; Pres. ULISSES CANHEDO AZEVEDO; Gen. Man. ANTONIO SANCHES.

Transportes Aéreos Bolivianos (TAB): Casilla 12237, La Paz; tel. (42) 37-8325; fax (42) 35-9660; f. 1977; regional scheduled and charter cargo services; Gen. Man. LUIS GUERECA PADILLA; Chair. CARLO APARICIO.

Transportes Aéreos Militares: Avda Montes 738, La Paz; tel. (2) 37-9286; internal passenger and cargo services; Dir-Gen. REMBERTO DURÁN.

Tourism

Bolivia's tourist attractions include Lake Titicaca, at 3,810 m (12,500 ft) above sea-level, pre-Incan ruins at Tiwanaku, Chacaltaya in the Andes mountains, which has the highest ski-run in the world, and the UNESCO World Cultural Heritage Sites of Potosí and Sucre. In 1998 420,491 foreign visitors arrived at hotels in Bolivian regional capitals. In 1996 receipts from tourism totalled US \$161m. Tourists come mainly from South American countries, the USA and Europe.

Asociación Boliviana de Agencias de Viajes y Turismo: Edif. Litoral, Avda Mariscal Santa Cruz 1351, Casilla 3967, La Paz; f. 1984; Pres. EUGENIO MONROY VÉLEZ.

Viceministerio de Turismo: Avda Mariscal Santa Cruz, 16°, Casilla 1868, La Paz; tel. (2) 35-8312; fax (2) 37-4630; e-mail etorres@mcei-gov.bo; internet www.bolivia-travel.gov.bo; Vice-Minister of Tourism EDGAR TORRES SARAVIA.

BOSNIA AND HERZEGOVINA

Introductory Survey

Location, Climate, Language, Religion, Flag, Capital

Bosnia and Herzegovina is situated in south-eastern Europe. It is bounded by Croatia to the north and west, by Serbia to the east and by Montenegro to the south-east, and has a short (20 km—12 miles) western coastline on the Adriatic Sea. It is a largely mountainous territory with a continental climate and steady rainfall throughout the year; in areas nearer the coast, however, the climate is more Mediterranean. The principal language is Serbo-Croat. Although it is a single spoken language, Serbo-Croat has two written forms: the Muslims (Bosniaks) and Croats use the Roman alphabet, while the Serbs use Cyrillic script. The Muslims (the majority of whom belong to the Sunni sect) are the largest religious grouping in Bosnia and Herzegovina, comprising 43.7% of the population in 1991. Religious affiliation is roughly equated with ethnicity, the Serbs (31.4% of the population) belonging to the Serbian Orthodox Church and the Croats (17.3%) being members of the Roman Catholic Church. The national flag (proportions 2 by 1) consists of two unequal vertical sections of blue, separated by a yellow triangle, which is bordered on the left by a diagonal line of nine white five-pointed stars. The capital is Sarajevo.

Recent History

The provinces of Bosnia and Herzegovina formed part of the Turkish (Ottoman) Empire for almost 400 years before annexation to the Austro-Hungarian Empire in 1878. The population of the provinces was composed of an ethnic mixture of Orthodox Serbs, Roman Catholic Croats and Muslims (mainly Bosnian Slavs who had converted to Islam). Serbian expansionist aims troubled the area from the beginning of the 20th century, and in 1914 Austria-Hungary attempted to end the perceived Serbian threat by declaring war on Serbia; this conflict was to escalate into the First World War. On 4 December 1918 the Kingdom of Serbs, Croats and Slovenes was proclaimed when the Serbs and Croats agreed with other ethnic groups to establish a common state under the Serbian monarchy. The provinces of Bosnia and Herzegovina formed part of the new kingdom. Bitter disputes ensued between Serbs and Croats, however, and in January 1929 King Alexander imposed a dictatorship, changing the name of the country to Yugoslavia later that year.

Although officially banned in 1921, the Communist Party of Yugoslavia (CPY) operated clandestinely, and in 1937 Josip Broz (alias Tito) became its General Secretary. During the Second World War (1939–45) Tito's communist-led Partisan movement, comprising members from a variety of ethnic groups, dominated most of Bosnia and Herzegovina. Following Tito's victory in 1945, Bosnia and Herzegovina became one of the six constituent republics of the Yugoslav federation (despite Serbian pressure to limit the region to provincial status, as with Kosovo and the Vojvodina). In the 1960s Tito established Muslim power in Bosnia and Herzegovina in an effort to counter the growing ethnic tension between the Serbs and Croats of the republic. Slav Muslims were granted a distinct ethnic status, as a nation of Yugoslavia, for the 1971 census, and a collective state presidency was established in that year, with a regular rotation of posts.

Increasing ethnic tension in Bosnia and Herzegovina became evident in September 1990. Followers of the Party of Democratic Action (PDA), the principal Muslim party of the republic, demonstrated in the neighbouring Sandjak area of Serbia in support of Muslim rights in the Novi Pazar district, clashing with Serb nationalists. Ethnic affiliation proved to be a decisive factor in the republican elections in November and December. The ruling League of Communists of Bosnia and Herzegovina was ousted, and three main nationalist parties subsequently emerged: the Muslim (Bosniak) PDA, with 86 seats; the Serbian Democratic Party (SDP), with 72 seats; and the Croatian Democratic Union of Bosnia and Herzegovina (CDU—BH), an affiliate of the ruling CDU party of Croatia, with 44 seats. The three nationalist parties also took all seven seats on the directly-elected collective Presidency and formed a coalition administration for the republic. On 20 December they announced that Dr Alija Izetbegović of the PDA was to be President of the Presidency, Jure

Pelivan of the CDU—BH was to be President of the Executive Council (Prime Minister) and Momčilo Krajišnik of the SDP was to be President of the Assembly.

In 1991 the politics of Bosnia and Herzegovina were increasingly dominated by the Serb–Croat conflict. Following the declarations of independence by Slovenia and Croatia in June, Serb-dominated territories in Bosnia and Herzegovina declared their intent to remain within the Yugoslav federation (or in a 'Greater Serbia'). On 27 June the self-proclaimed Serb 'Municipal Community of Bosanska Krajina' in Bosnia announced its unification with the 'Serbian Autonomous Region (SAR) of Krajina' in Croatia. An SAR of Bosanska Krajina was proclaimed on 16 September. The republican Government rejected these moves and declared the inviolability of the internal boundaries of Yugoslavia. Armed incidents contributed to the rising tension throughout mid-1991 and many Serb areas announced the formation of further 'Autonomous Regions'. Other ethnic groups accused the Serbs of planning a 'Greater Serbia', with the support of the Jugoslavenska Narodna Armija (JNA—Yugoslav People's Army). In October the JNA assumed effective control of Mostar, to the north-west of the Serb 'Old' Herzegovina, and began a siege of the Croatian city of Dubrovnik.

In October 1991 both the republican Presidency (with the dissenting votes of the Serb members) and the PDA proposed to the Assembly that the republic declare its independence (Macedonia had done so in September). During a debate in the Assembly later that month the Serbs (mainly the SDP) rejected any such declaration as a move towards secession, claiming that all Serbs should live in one state. No compromise was reached, and the Serb representatives subsequently withdrew from the chamber. However, the other deputies, dominated by the members of the PDA and the CDU—BH, continued the session; on 15 October the remaining members of the Assembly approved a resolution declaring that the Republic of Bosnia and Herzegovina was a sovereign state within its existing borders.

The 'Autonomous Regions' of the Serbs rejected the republican Assembly's resolution and declared that only the federal laws and Constitution would apply on their territory. On 24 October 1991 the Serb deputies of the Bosnia and Herzegovina Assembly constituted an 'Assembly of the Serb Nation' (Serb Assembly). In early November another SAR was proclaimed, comprising the Serbs of Northern Bosnia, with an Assembly based in Doboj (an area without a Serb majority). On 9–10 November a referendum, organized by the Serb Assembly, indicated overwhelming support for remaining in a common Serb State. However, in another referendum on 29 February and 1 March 1992, which was boycotted by the Serbs, 99.4% of the 63% of the electorate who participated were in favour of full independence. President Izetbegović immediately declared the republic's independence and omitted the word 'socialist' from the new state's official title.

Following the declaration of independence, there was renewed Serb–Muslim tension, leading to clashes in Sarajevo, the republican capital, and elsewhere. On 18 March 1992, following mediation by the European Community (EC, now European Union—EU—see p. 181), the leaders of the Serb, Croat and Muslim communities of Bosnia and Herzegovina signed an agreement providing for the division of the republic into three autonomous units. The EC and the USA recognized Bosnia and Herzegovina's independence on 7 April. On 27 March the Serbs announced the formation of a 'Serbian Republic of Bosnia and Herzegovina', which comprised Serbian-held areas of the republic (about 65% of the total area), including the SARs, and which was to be headed by Dr Radovan Karadžić. The Bosnian Government immediately declared this secessionist republic, the headquarters of which were based in Banja Luka, to be illegal. In April fighting between the Serbian-dominated JNA in Bosnia and Herzegovina and Muslim and Croatian forces intensified; several cities, including Sarajevo, were besieged by Serbian troops. In early May, however, the newly-established Federal Republic of Yugoslavia (FRY—comprising solely the republics of Serbia and Montenegro), in an apparent attempt to disclaim any responsibility for Bosnia and Herzegovina's internal strife, ordered all of its citizens in the JNA to withdraw from the republic within 15 days. Early EC and UN efforts at mediation proved unsuccessful, and their respective peace monitors were withdrawn from Sarajevo in mid-May after a state of emergency had been declared and successive cease-fires had failed to take effect. Izetbegović requested foreign military intervention, but the UN, while deploying 14,000 troops (the United Nations Protection Force—UNPROFOR, see p. 62) in Croatia and demanding a halt to the fighting and the withdrawal of Yugoslav and Croat troops from Bosnia and Herzegovina, decided against the deployment of a peace-keeping force in the republic under prevailing conditions. On 20 May the Government of Bosnia and Herzegovina declared the JNA to be an 'occupying force' and announced the formation of a republican army. Two days later Bosnia and Herzegovina was accepted as a member of the UN. On 30 May the UN imposed economic sanctions against the FRY for its continuing involvement in the Bosnian conflict. In early June, in an apparent effort to placate the UN, Serb leaders in Belgrade (the FRY capital) ordered the Bosnian Serbs to end the siege of Sarajevo and to surrender Sarajevo airport to UN control. In the same month the UN Security Council decided to redeploy 1,000 of the UNPROFOR troops in Croatia to protect Sarajevo airport. An additional 500 troops were dispatched to Sarajevo in mid-July.

On 7 July 1992 there was a major development in the Bosnian conflict, when a breakaway Croat state, 'The Croatian Union of Herzeg-Bosna', was declared. The new state covered about 30% of the territory of Bosnia and Herzegovina and was headed by Mate Boban. Izetbegović's Government promptly declared it illegal, and Karadžić proposed that Serbs and Croats partition Bosnia and Herzegovina among themselves. Despite their political differences, Izetbegović and President Franjo Tudjman of Croatia (who supported the establishment of 'The Croatian Union of Herzeg-Bosna') signed a co-operation agreement in late July.

Revelations concerning the predominantly Serb policy of 'ethnic cleansing' (involving the expulsion by one ethnic group of other ethnic groups in an attempt to create a homogenous population) and the discovery of a number of detention camps in Bosnia and Herzegovina led to the unanimous adoption by the UN Security Council, in early August 1992, of a resolution condemning the camps and those responsible for abuses of human rights.

In an annex to the agreement signed in July 1992, the Governments of Bosnia and Herzegovina and of Croatia formed a Joint Defence Committee in late September, and repeated demands that the UN remove its arms embargo on Bosnia and Herzegovina and Croatia (the embargo was imposed on the whole of the former Yugoslavia in September 1991). Within Bosnia and Herzegovina, however, hostilities erupted between Bosnian Croats and Muslims in mid-October, and the towns of Mostar, Novi Travnik and Vitez were captured by the Croats. Mostar was subsequently proclaimed the capital of 'The Croatian Union of Herzeg-Bosna'. In early November the Croat Jure Pelivan resigned as Prime Minister of Bosnia and Herzegovina, and was replaced by Mile Akmadžić. In mid-November the Croatian Government admitted for the first time that Croatian regular army units had been deployed in Bosnia and Herzegovina, and agreed to withdraw them. In accordance with this official admission, Croatia became a signatory to the latest cease-fire agreement in Bosnia and Herzegovina. In early December the UN Human Rights Commission declared that the Serbs were largely responsible for violations of human rights in Bosnia and Herzegovina. Following allegations of the organized rape of more than 20,000 Muslim women by Serb forces, the UN Security Council unanimously adopted, in mid-December, a resolution condemning the atrocities and demanding access to all Serb detention camps.

Meanwhile, in mid-December 1992 the Serbian enclave in Bosnia and Herzegovina, the self-proclaimed 'Serbian Republic', unilaterally declared that the conflict was at an end and that the Serbs had won their own 'independent and sovereign state'. However, by late December Muslim forces appeared to be regaining territory. In early January 1993 the co-Chairmen of the Geneva Peace Conference (a permanent forum for talks on the conflict, established in 1992), Lord (David) Owen (a former British Secretary of State for Foreign and Commonwealth Affairs) and Cyrus Vance (the UN mediator and a former US Secretary of State), visited Belgrade for talks with the newly re-elected President of Serbia, Slobodan Milošević. Their aim was to persuade him to convince the Bosnian Serbs to agree to

a division of Bosnia and Herzegovina into 10 provinces (with three provinces allocated to each faction and Sarajevo as a province with special status). The peace plan was approved by the leader of the Bosnian Croats, Mate Boban, and, in part, by Izetbegović, but was rejected by the Bosnian Serb leader, Karadžić, who insisted on the establishment of an autonomous Serbian state within the territory of Bosnia and Herzegovina.

In mid-January 1993 Milošević attended the peace talks in Geneva, Switzerland, for the first time. Karadžić, under pressure from Milošević and President Dobrica Cosić of the FRY, agreed to the constitutional proposals included in the plan and, subsequently, to the military arrangements. On 19–20 January the Bosnian Serb Assembly voted to accept the general principles of the Vance-Owen plan. Hostilities between Croats and Muslims intensified, however, in central Bosnia.

In February 1993 the UN Security Council adopted a resolution providing for the establishment of an international court to try alleged war criminals for acts committed since 1991 in the former Yugoslav republics. In the following month the UN Security Council adopted a resolution to allow NATO aircraft to fire on any aircraft violating the 'no-fly zone' imposed on Bosnian airspace in October 1992.

During March 1993, at further peace talks, Izetbegović agreed to both the military arrangements and the proposed territorial divisions included in the Vance-Owen plan, leaving the Bosnian Serbs as the only party not to have signed the section on the division of Bosnia and Herzegovina. In April the Bosnian Serb Assembly rejected the territorial arrangements, incurring international disapproval (including that of Serbia, which had endorsed the plan under pressure from UN and EC sanctions). In early May Karadžić signed the Vance-Owen plan in Geneva, but two days later it was decisively rejected by the Serb Assembly at Pale, since under the terms of the plan the Bosnian Serbs would be forced to surrender some territory that they had seized during the fighting. In late May the USA, France, Russia, Spain and the United Kingdom signed a communiqué declaring that the arms embargo on the former Yugoslavia would continue and that international armed forces would not intervene in the conflict on behalf of the Muslims; they proposed instead the creation of six UN 'safe areas' (Sarajevo, Bihać, Tuzla, Goražde, Srebreniča and Zepa) to protect the Muslim population from Serb attack, to take effect from 22 July. Cease-fires negotiated by the UN collapsed in May, as both the Bosnian Serbs and Croats initiated offensives to expand and consolidate their territorial holdings. In mid-June new peace proposals were announced in Geneva by Lord Owen and Thorvald Stoltenberg (formerly Norwegian Minister of Foreign Affairs, who had replaced Vance as the UN mediator in May), under which Bosnia and Herzegovina would become a confederation of three states divided on ethnic grounds. Izetbegović refused to discuss the tripartite division of Bosnia and boycotted the remainder of the Geneva talks, although other members of the Presidency continued discussions.

In early June 1993 the UN adopted a resolution to allow UNPROFOR to use force, including air power, in response to attacks against 'safe areas', but later that month failed to approve a resolution, supported by the USA, on the exemption of the Bosnian Muslims from the UN arms embargo. In late June a joint Serb-Croat offensive began against the northern Muslim town of Maglaj, and in the following month Muslims and Croats commenced hostilities for control of the city of Mostar. On 30 July the three warring factions reached a constitutional agreement in Geneva on the reconstruction of Bosnia and Herzegovina into a confederation of three ethnically-based states, styled the 'Union of Republics of Bosnia and Herzegovina', under a central government with powers limited to foreign policy and foreign trade. Under this agreement, Sarajevo, except for the municipality of Pale, would be placed under UN administration during a two-year transitional period. Despite this agreement and numerous negotiated cease-fires, fighting continued, and in early August the three Croat members of the Bosnian State Presidency (including Mile Akmadžić, the Prime Minister of Bosnia and Herzegovina) left the Bosnian Geneva delegation, in protest at Muslim attacks on Croat populations, and joined the Croatian negotiating team. On 27 August Akmadžić was dismissed from the premiership. On the following day the 'Croatian Republic of Herzeg-Bosna' was proclaimed by a Croat 'House of Representatives of the Assembly of the Croatian Republic of Herzeg-Bosna' (Croat Assembly) in Grude, which proceeded to accept the Owen-Stoltenberg plan on condition that the Serbs and Muslims also accepted it. On the same day the Serb Assembly in Pale also voted in favour of the plan. On 31 August, however, a session of the Assembly of Bosnia and Herzegovina rejected the Geneva plan in its existing form, while agreeing to use it as a basis for further peace negotiations.

On 10 September 1993 Fikret Abdić, a Muslim member of the Bosnian State Presidency and a rival of President Izetbegović, announced the creation of an 'Autonomous Province of Western Bosnia' in the Muslim region around Bihać, which was to form part of the 'Union of Republics of Bosnia and Herzegovina'. On 27 September, in Velika Kladusa, the Province was declared to have been established and Abdić was elected President by a 'Constituent Assembly'. Abdić was subsequently dismissed from the Bosnian State Presidency, Izetbegović imposed martial law on the area and fighting erupted between Abdić's followers and government forces. The Muslim Democratic Party was founded in Bihać, with Abdić as Chairman.

In late September 1993 the Croat and Serb Assemblies announced their intention to withdraw concessions offered during negotiations earlier that month: the Croats had allowed Bosnian access to the sea; the Serbs had agreed to accept a territorial division awarding them 52% of Bosnia's territory (rather than the existing 70%). During September Izetbegović had agreed, in a significant concession, that after two years the Serb and Croat republics in a future confederation would be permitted to hold a referendum on whether to remain in the 'Union' or to join Serbia and Croatia, respectively.

On 23 October 1993 Abdić and the Bosnian Croat leader, Mate Boban, officially declared their intent to establish peace in Western Bosnia; Abdić and Karadžić subsequently announced their commitment to peace between their two 'republics'. Later in the month two Croats and one Muslim were elected to the three vacant positions in the Bosnian State Presidency, while Dr Haris Silajdžić, formerly the Minister of Foreign Affairs, was appointed Prime Minister of the Bosnian Government, replacing Akmadžić. Silajdžić's Government took office on 30 October.

At further talks in late December 1993 the Bosnian Serbs refused to accept the establishment of a UN administration in Sarajevo and the reopening of Tuzla airport (which was surrounded by Serb positions) to accelerate the passage of aid. The Bosnians demanded access through Croatian territory to the Adriatic (thus interrupting continuous Croatian control of the coast) and, although they accepted the proposed division of the country, they remained opposed to the specific areas allocated to Bosnian Muslims.

The massacre, in early February 1994, of 68 civilians in Sarajevo prompted the EU and the USA to draft a joint French-US proposal that NATO set a deadline for Serb forces to cease their bombardment or risk being subjected to air attacks. Following a Russian initiative, the Bosnian Serbs withdrew most of their heavy weaponry, and Russian peace-keeping troops were deployed in the 'exclusion zone' around Sarajevo. However, the city remained effectively blockaded. In late February NATO aircraft shot down four Serb light attack aircraft near Banja Luka, which had violated the UN 'no-fly zone' over Bosnia and Herzegovina. The incident represented the first aggressive military action taken by NATO since its establishment. There was continuous Serb shelling of the Maglaj area in northern Bosnia throughout March, while other UN-designated 'safe areas' were also shelled. In the same month UNHCR officials accused the Serbs of the 'ethnic cleansing' of Banja Luka's Muslim population.

Following a cease-fire, which was agreed by the Bosnian Government and the Bosnian Croats in late February 1994, Silajdžić and Kresimir Zubak (who had replaced Mate Boban as the leader of the Bosnian Croats) signed an agreement on 18 March, in Washington, DC, the USA, providing for the creation of a Federation of Bosnia and Herzegovina, with power shared equally between Muslims and Croats. Under the federal Constitution (finalized earlier in the month), a federal government was to be responsible for defence, foreign affairs and the economy. Greater executive power was to be vested in the prime ministerial post than in the presidency; the offices were to rotate annually between the two ethnic groups. Until the full implementation of the Federation and the holding of elections, Izetbegović was to remain President of the collective Presidency of Bosnia and Herzegovina; the emerging federal institutions were to operate in parallel during the interim period. At the same ceremony a second 'preliminary' agreement was signed by Presidents Izetbegović and Tudjman, which provided for the eventual creation of a loose confederation of the Federation and Croatia. As well as the establishment of a 'Confederative Council', closer

economic ties between the two states were to be introduced, with the eventual aim of establishing a common market and monetary union. In late March the accords were approved by the Bosnian Croat Assembly, while the new Constitution was ratified by the Bosnian Assembly. However, the Bosnian Serb Assembly in Pale vetoed Serb participation in the agreements.

In April 1994, in response to the continued shelling of the 'safe area' of Goražde by Bosnian Serb forces, UN-sanctioned air strikes were launched by NATO aircraft on Serb ground positions. However, Serb forces captured Goražde later that month, prompting strong criticism from the Russian Government, which hitherto had been perceived as sympathetic towards the Serbs, but which had now indicated that it would not oppose the use of force against them. Bosnian Serb forces withdrew from Goražde in late April. On 26 April a new negotiating forum was established in London, United Kingdom; the 'Contact Group' comprised representatives from Russia, the USA, France, Germany and the United Kingdom.

In late May 1994 the Constituent Assembly of the Federation of Bosnia and Herzegovina held its inaugural meeting, at which it elected Kresimir Zubak to the largely ceremonial post of President of the Federation. Ejup Ganić, a Muslim, was elected Vice-President of the Federation (he was concurrently Vice-President of the collective Presidency of Bosnia and Herzegovina) and Silajdžić was appointed Prime Minister of the Federation. A joint Government of the Republic of Bosnia and Herzegovina and the Federation, led by Silajdžić, was appointed in late June. Earlier in the month it was announced that the existing Bosnian Assembly would act, additionally, as the interim legislature of the Federation.

Following peace negotiations in Geneva in early June 1994, a one-month cease-fire was declared throughout Bosnia and Herzegovina. Repeated violations were reported by the end of the month, however, by which time Bosnian government forces had captured Serb-held areas of central Bosnia in an attempt to link the region with the Adriatic coast. Fighting also escalated in the Bihać enclave between the Bosnian army and rebel forces led by Abdić.

The Contact Group presented new peace proposals in early July 1994, after its members had reached agreement on a territorial division of Bosnia and Herzegovina in late June. According to the new plan, the Federation of Bosnia and Herzegovina would be granted 51% of the territory of Bosnia and Herzegovina, while the Bosnian Serbs would yield approximately one-third of the territory they controlled. Key sensitive areas, including Sarajevo, Srebrenica, Goražde and Brčko, would be placed under UN and EU administration. In an indication of the international community's increasing impatience with the warring factions, the Contact Group warned of various measures that would be taken in the event of the parties' refusal of the plan. These included the relaxation of economic sanctions against Serbia and Montenegro if the Bosnian Government rejected the proposal, and the lifting of the arms embargo against Bosnia and Herzegovina in the event of Bosnian Serb refusal.

On 17 July 1994 Izetbegović and Tudjman endorsed the Contact Group plan, which was also approved by the Bosnian Assembly. However, the proposed territorial division was rejected by the Bosnian Serb Assembly at Pale. The Serbs' refusal to accept the plan centred on the question of Serb access to the Adriatic Sea, the status of Sarajevo and the right of the Bosnian Serbs to enter a confederation with the FRY. President Milošević of Serbia subsequently criticized the Bosnian Serbs for rejecting the plan, and in early August the FRY announced the closure of its border with Serb-occupied Bosnia and Herzegovina. On 5 August NATO air strikes (the first since April) were launched against Bosnian Serb targets, following Serb attacks against UN forces and the renewed shelling of Sarajevo. In late August the Bosnian Serbs held a referendum in which 96% of participants voted to reject the Contact Group plan; the result was unanimously approved by the Bosnian Serb Assembly on 1 September. Meanwhile, on 21 August the Bihać enclave, held by Abdić's forces, was captured by the Bosnian government army.

In early October 1994 Bosnian government troops infiltrated the demilitarized zone of Mount Igman, near Sarajevo, and attacked Serb forces there, to be repelled shortly afterwards by UNPROFOR troops. Later in the month government forces took control of tracts of Serb-held land around the Bihać enclave. In early November government forces, supported by Bosnian Croat troops, launched offensives on three fronts: in central Bosnia, in the Bihać area and around Sarajevo. The fall of the strategic

Serb-held town of Kupres on 3 November represented the first significant military gain for the Muslim-Croat alliance. By late November, however, the Serbs had regained most of the Bihać territory. Meanwhile, in early November the USA announced that its warships in the Adriatic Sea would no longer enforce the international arms embargo.

On 30 November 1994 an attempt by the UN Secretary-General, Dr Boutros Boutros-Ghali, to protect the Bihać 'safe area' from further Bosnian Serb attack and to salvage the UN peace-keeping operation in Bosnia and Herzegovina met with failure when Karadžić refused to meet him at Sarajevo airport and boycotted the proposed discussions, owing to the UN's refusal to recognize the 'Serbian Republic'. In early December the Contact Group issued a text based on the July peace plan (dividing Bosnia between the Federation and the Bosnian Serbs), which indicated the possibility of confederal links between the Bosnian Serbs and the FRY. President Milošević supported the proposals. In mid-December the former US President, Jimmy Carter (acting in a non-official capacity), visited Bosnia and Herzegovina with the aim of persuading the Bosnian Serb leadership to accept the Contact Group plan. The Bosnian Serbs and the Bosnian Government subsequently agreed to a four-month cease-fire, to take effect from 1 January 1995. Both sides expressed their readiness to resume peace negotiations based on the revised Contact Group plan; there were also agreements on the exchange of prisoners. The cease-fire agreement was formally signed by both parties on 31 December.

The cease-fire was generally observed throughout Bosnia and Herzegovina during January 1995. However, intense fighting continued in the Bihać enclave between government forces and troops loyal to Abdić, supported by troops from the self-proclaimed 'Republic of Serbian Krajina' (RSK) in Croatia (adjoining the Bihać enclave). There were renewed disagreements between Muslims and Croats over the implementation of the new Federation, the most controversial issues being the co-ordination of a joint military command, the division of power and territorial reorganization. In early February, however, Zubak and Silajdžić were signatories to an accord allowing grievances concerning the implementation of the Federation of Bosnia and Herzegovina to be submitted to some form of (as yet unspecified) international arbitration. In the same month the USA refused to continue negotiations with Karadžić until the Bosnian Serbs accepted the Contact Group plan.

In early 1995 hostilities continued in the Bihać enclave, where Bosnian Serb and Bosnian government troops had resumed fighting around Bosanska Krupa, with the 'safe area' of Bihać town being directly targeted by the Serbs. In mid-February the UN announced that Serb and rebel Muslim attacks on humanitarian aid convoys into the Bihać enclave were resulting in the starvation of Muslim civilians within the 'safe area'. On 20 February representatives of the Bosnian Serbs and the Croatian Serbs signed a military pact, guaranteeing mutual assistance in the event of attack and providing for the establishment of a joint Supreme Defence Council, which was to be led by Karadžić and the Croatian Serb leader, Milan Martić. In late February the Bosnian Government introduced new restrictions on the movements of peace-keepers within its borders, preventing UN observers from monitoring front lines. In early March, following talks in Zagreb, Croatia, a formal military alliance was announced between the armies of Croatia, the Bosnian Croats and the Bosnian Government.

In late March 1995 the UN threatened to order further NATO air strikes against Serb targets unless the Bosnian Serbs halted their shelling of the UN 'safe areas' of Sarajevo, Tuzla, Bihać and Goražde. The Contact Group appealed to the warring factions to respect and work towards the extension of the four-month cease-fire, while Russia presented a fresh peace plan to the US Secretary of State, Warren Christopher, in Geneva. The plan, involving Serbian recognition of Bosnia and Herzegovina in exchange for the simultaneous lifting of UN sanctions against the FRY, had reportedly been drafted by President Milošević and the Russian Minister of Foreign Affairs, Andrei Kozyrev.

On 8 April 1995 an agreement was signed between President Zubak of the Federation and Ejup Ganić, the Vice-President of both the Federation and of Bosnia and Herzegovina, aimed at accelerating the establishment of federal institutions. The inaugural session of the Federation's Constituent Assembly duly took place in Novi Travnik on 4 May, during which the Bonn Agreement on the implementation of federal principles was unanimously adopted. In mid-May heavy fighting was reported around the Serb-held corridor near Brčko and hostilities intensified around Sarajevo, with Bosnian government forces regaining territory to the south-east of the capital. Reflecting increasing UN impatience, on 24 May Lt-Gen. Smith issued a formal ultimatum to both the Bosnian Serbs and the Bosnian Government, which threatened NATO air strikes unless all heavy weapons were removed from the 20-km 'exclusion zone' around Sarajevo (or surrendered to peace-keepers) by midday on 26 May. On 25 May, however, NATO aircraft carried out strikes on Serb ammunition depots near Pale, a move that was openly criticized by Russia. Within hours of the NATO air strikes, Serb forces responded by shelling five of the six UN 'safe areas' and, following further NATO air strikes against Serb positions on 26 May, retaliated with a massive bombardment of Tuzla, which resulted in at least 70 deaths. Over the next few days Serb troops disarmed and took hostage 222 UNPROFOR personnel in the Goražde 'safe area', thereby preventing the UN and NATO from taking retaliatory action against fighting in the region. However, the UN rejected the Serbs' offer of conditional negotiations on the release of the hostages. In early June defence ministers from NATO and other European states agreed on the creation of a 10,000-strong 'rapid reaction force', which was to operate in Bosnia and Herzegovina under UN command from mid-July and the mandate of which was to provide 'enhanced protection' to UNPROFOR. The ongoing hostage crisis, led, however, to a withdrawal of UNPROFOR troops from Bosnian Serb territory around Sarajevo in mid-June and the consequent collapse of the 20-km 'exclusion zone'. Although the UN denied that any deal had been struck with the Bosnian Serbs, the release of the remaining hostages roughly coincided with the withdrawal of UNPROFOR from around the capital.

On 11 July 1995 the 'safe area' of Srebreniča in south-eastern Bosnia was captured by the Bosnian Serbs after Dutch peace-keeping troops based in the town were taken hostage, prompting NATO air strikes on Serb tanks approaching the town. The fall of Srebreniča was followed by the capture of the nearby 'safe area' of Zepa on 25 July. Bihać was attacked on 20 July; the assault involved a concerted effort by Bosnian Serbs, Croatian Serbs and rebel Bosnian Muslims led by Abdić. The situation in Bihać prompted the signature of a military co-operation agreement between Izetbegović and Tudjman in Split, Croatia, on 22 July. Croatian and Bosnian Croat troops subsequently launched attacks on Serb positions around Bihać, as a result of which Serb supply routes into the Krajina enclave were blocked.

Croatian government forces invaded Serb-held Krajina on 4 August 1995; by 9 August the whole of the enclave had been recaptured by Croatia, resulting in a massive exodus of Serb civilians from the region into Serb-held areas of Bosnia and Herzegovina and into Serbia itself. On 6–7 August the siege of Bihać was effectively broken by Bosnian government and Croatian troops. On 9 August a fresh peace initiative (devised by Richard Holbrooke, the then US Assistant Secretary of State for European and Canadian Affairs) was announced by the US Government; the proposals, which were based on the Contact Group plan of 1994, allowed the Bosnian Serbs to retain control of Srebreniča and Zepa.

On 28 August 1995 a suspected Serb mortar attack near a market place in central Sarajevo resulted in 37 deaths, prompting Silajdžić to demand a clarification of the UN peace-keeping role in the 'safe area' of Sarajevo. NATO responded to the mortar attack by launching a series of air strikes (codenamed 'Operation Deliberate Force') on Serb positions across Bosnia and Herzegovina on 30 August and 5 September.

On 8 September 1995 major progress in the peace process was achieved when, at a meeting in Geneva, chaired by the Contact Group, the Ministers of Foreign Affairs of Bosnia and Herzegovina, Croatia and the FRY (the latter acting on behalf of the Bosnian Serbs), signed an agreement determining basic principles for a peace accord. These principles incorporated the territorial division of Bosnia and Herzegovina as earlier proposed by the Contact Group, with 51% apportioned to the Federation and 49% to the Bosnian Serbs. They also included the continuing existence of Bosnia and Herzegovina within its present borders, but the country was to comprise two entities, namely the Federation of Bosnia and Herzegovina (as stated in the Washington Agreements of 1994) and a Serb Republic, with each entity retaining its existing Constitution. In mid-September 'Operation Deliberate Force' was suspended, following the withdrawal of Bosnian Serb weaponry from the 'exclusion zone' around Sarajevo. Agreement on further basic principles for a peace accord was reached by the foreign ministers of Bosnia and Herzegovina, Croatia and the FRY, meeting in New York, the USA, on 26 September. These included a one-third share in the republican parliamentary seats for the Serb Republic, while the Federation was to control two-thirds of the seats (legislative decisions were only to be implemented, however, with the approval of at least one-third of the deputies of each entity). A collective presidency was also to be organized according to the one-third Serb to two-thirds Muslim-Croat proportional division, with all decisions to be taken by majority vote. It was decided, furthermore, that free elections, under international auspices, would be held in Bosnia and Herzegovina at the earliest opportunity. A 60-day cease-fire came into effect on 12 October; the UN simultaneously announced its intention to reduce the number of peace-keeping troops in the area. In late October, at a summit meeting between President Bill Clinton of the USA and his Russian counterpart, Boris Yeltsin, it was agreed that Russian peace-implementation troops would co-operate with, but work independently of, the NATO Peace Implementation Force, which was to be deployed in the country following the signature of a formal peace accord.

On 1 November 1995 peace negotiations between the three warring parties in the Bosnian conflict began in Dayton, Ohio, the USA, attended by Presidents Izetbegović, Tudjman and Milošević (the latter representing both the FRY and the Bosnian Serbs), and representatives of the Contact Group and the EU. On 10 November Izetbegović and Tudjman signed an accord aimed at reinforcing the 1994 federation agreement, which included a provision for the unification of the divided city of Mostar as the federal capital and seat of the federal presidency. The Croatian Government and the Croatian Serbs of Eastern Slavonia subsequently concluded an accord providing for the eventual reintegration of Serb-held Eastern Slavonia into Croatia. The most comprehensive peace agreement was achieved on 21 November, when Izetbegović, Tudjman and Milošević initialled a definitive accord, dividing Bosnia and Herzegovina between the Federation, with 51% of the territory, and the Serb Republic (Republika Srpska), which would control 49% of the area; it was stressed, however, that relations with neighbouring countries should honour the sovereignty and territorial integrity of Bosnia and Herzegovina. The Dayton agreement, which was based on the agreements that had been signed in Geneva and New York in September, included provisions for a central government with a democratically-elected collective presidency and a parliament, based in Sarajevo, and provisions for a single monetary system, central bank and other institutions for the economic reconstruction of Bosnia and Herzegovina. It also stipulated the right of all refugees and displaced persons to return to their homes and either to have seized property returned to them or to receive fair compensation. Sarajevo was granted special status as a united city within the Federation and it was also envisaged that each of the warring factions would relinquish some of the territory under its control at the time of the October cease-fire. Serb-held suburbs of Sarajevo were to be transferred to the administration of the Federation, while Bosnian Serbs were to retain control of Srebreniča and Zepa; Goražde was to remain under the control of the Federation and was to be linked to Sarajevo via a Federation-administered land corridor. No agreement was reached, however, regarding the width of the strategically vital Posavina corridor, connecting the northern sector of the Serb Republic with the southern sector, and control of the town of Brčko, located at this point; the three sides agreed to place the issue under international arbitration. Under the Dayton agreement, UNPROFOR troops were to be replaced by an international, NATO-commanded, 60,000-strong 'Implementation Force' (IFOR, see p. 244). The agreement provided IFOR with a mandate to oversee the withdrawal of the warring parties from zones of separation and to monitor the agreed exchanges of territory.

Following the initialling of the Dayton peace agreement, the UN voted to suspend the remaining economic sanctions against the FRY and to phase out gradually the arms embargo imposed on all of the former Yugoslav republics in September 1991. At the end of November 1995 the UN Security Council established the deadline of 31 January 1996 for the withdrawal of UNPROFOR troops from Bosnia and Herzegovina. At a conference on the implementation of the Dayton peace agreement, which took place in London in early December 1995, it was agreed that an Organization for Security and Co-operation in Europe (OSCE, see p. 252) mission would organize and oversee parliamentary elections in Bosnia and Herzegovina and that the Contact Group would be replaced by a Peace Implementation

Council based in Brussels, Belgium. The former Swedish Prime Minister and EU envoy to the Bosnian peace talks, Carl Bildt, was appointed High Representative of the International Community in Bosnia and Herzegovina, with responsibility for the implementation of the civilian aspects of the Dayton agreement. On 14 December the Dayton peace agreement was formally signed by Izetbegović, Tudjman and Milošević and by President Clinton and a number of European political leaders in Paris, France. The formal transfer of power from UNPROFOR to IFOR took place on 20 December.

In mid-December 1995 the People's Assembly of the Serb Republic elected a new Government, headed by Rajko Kasagić. On 30 January 1996 Hasan Muratović was elected by the republican Assembly as Prime Minister of the Republic of Bosnia and Herzegovina, following the resignation from the premiership of Silajdžić, apparently in protest at the increasing Bosniak nationalism of the ruling PDA; a new central Government was appointed on the same day. On 31 January the Constituent Assembly of the Federation appointed a new federal government, with Izudin Kapetanović as Prime Minister. In mid-February, in response to unrest in the city of Mostar and isolated attacks elsewhere, an emergency summit meeting took place in Rome, Italy, during which Izetbegović, Tudjman and Milošević reaffirmed their adherence to the Dayton agreement. A joint Croat-Muslim police patrol, accompanied by officers from the UN International Police Task Force (IPTF) and Western European Union (WEU) subsequently began operating in Mostar.

By the end of April 1996 substantial progress had been made in the implementation of the military aspects of the Dayton agreement. The former warring parties completed staged withdrawals from the IFOR-controlled zone of separation; agreement was reached, under the auspices of the OSCE in Vienna, Austria, on the exchange of information on weaponry and the submission of arsenals to OSCE inspection; and the majority of prisoners of war were released, albeit with some delays. However, the exchange of territory between the two Bosnian 'entities' did not proceed as envisaged in the peace agreement. From mid-January there was a mass exodus from the Serb-held suburbs of Sarajevo that were passing to the control of the Bosnian Federation. The Serb authorities in Pale were criticized for using intimidation to coerce the Serb inhabitants of these districts into leaving and to resettle in towns in the Serb Republic from which Muslims had been driven during the war. By late March only about 10% of the previous Serb population in the Sarajevo area remained.

In early April 1996 Muslim and Croat leaders agreed on a customs union linking the two parts of the Bosnian Federation. They also agreed on a single state budget and a unitary banking system. In mid-May further agreement was reached between the two sides, meeting in Washington, on the merger of their armed forces and the return of refugees. The agreement on a unified federation army was the principal precondition for the implementation of the controversial US programme to train and equip the Federation's army in order to place it on an equal military footing with that of the Serb Republic. Also in mid-May Karadžić dismissed Kasagić as Serb Prime Minister and appointed Gojko Klicković, a former Serb Minister for Health, in his place; Klicković's appointment was endorsed by the Bosnian Serb People's Assembly. Kasagić, who was considered a moderate among Serbs, had been co-operating to a large extent with the international community and high-level diplomatic efforts were undertaken both to effect Kasagić's reinstatement and to oust Karadžić from the presidency. Karadžić had been indicted by the International Criminal Tribunal for the former Yugoslavia (ICTY, see p. 15), based in The Hague, the Netherlands, for his part in the siege of Sarajevo and the alleged massacre at Srebreniča in July 1995. His continued position as President—as well as that of Gen. Ratko Mladić, also indicted for war crimes, as head of the armed forces—was in breach of the Dayton agreement, which prohibited indicted war criminals from holding public office. In response to international pressure, Karadžić announced the delegation of some of his powers to his deputy, Dr Biljana Plavšić. In early June 1996 the USA threatened Milošević with renewed sanctions against the FRY unless he effected the removal from office of Karadžić and Mladić and their extradition to the Netherlands to stand trial. At the Peace Implementation Conference on Bosnia and Herzegovina held in Florence, Italy, in mid-June, the holding of all-Bosnia elections in September was approved. Later in the same month the Chairman-in-Office of the OSCE, which was given responsibility under the Dayton accord for the organization and supervision of the Bosnian elections, formally announced that these would proceed on 14 September.

In mid-June 1996 Bosnian Croats in Mostar announced a new government of Herzeg-Bosna, in defiance of agreements that the separate Croat state would be dissolved; Pero Marković was named as Prime Minister of the new Government. Municipal elections in Mostar were held on 30 June: the PDA-dominated List for a United Mostar gained 21 of the council seats, while the CDU−BH secured 16 seats. At a summit meeting of the Presidents of Bosnia and Herzegovina, Croatia and Serbia, which was convened by the USA in Geneva in mid-August, Tudjman and Izetbegović agreed on the full establishment of the Bosnian Federation by the end of the month. Tudjman vouched for the dismantling of Herzeg-Bosna, while Izetbegović agreed that the functions of the current Bosnian Government that would not pass to the tripartite Presidency would revert to the Federation. The three Presidents signed a fresh declaration committing themselves to the Dayton agreement.

In late June 1996 western European countries issued an ultimatum to Karadžić to resign, on penalty of the reimposition of sanctions against the Serb Republic (suspended in April, following the Serb withdrawal behind IFOR's line of separation). In defiance of this, the SDP re-elected Karadžić as their party leader. At the end of June Karadžić sent a letter to Bildt announcing his temporary resignation and the appointment of Plavšić as the acting Serb President. It was then confirmed that Karadžić would not stand in the election to the Serb presidency in September, and Plavšić was nominated as the SDP candidate. None the less, it was deemed unacceptable that Karadžić should retain the powerful position of party leader, and the OSCE Bosnian mission declared that the SDP would be excluded from the elections if Karadžić retained any office in the party. In mid-July the ICTY issued arrest warrants for Karadžić and Mladić; however, IFOR's mandate was not changed, and NATO remained cautious regarding pursuit of the indicted men. A few days later the USA dispatched Holbrooke to the former Yugoslavia in an attempt to bring about Karadžić's removal. Following intensive negotiations with Milošević and Bosnian Serb leaders, Holbrooke secured Karadžić's resignation on 19 July both from the presidency and as head of the SDP. Plavšić remained acting President, while Aleksa Buha succeeded Karadžić as leader of the SDP.

During the electoral campaign there were increasing reports of harassment and violence perpetrated by the PDA and its supporters against members of the opposition. Opposition candidates in the Serb Republic were also subjected to intimidation, and many international observers, as well as opposition activists, protested that the conditions would prevent free and fair elections from being conducted. In late August 1996 the OSCE announced that the Bosnian municipal elections, which were to have been held concurrently with the other elections, were to be postponed, in response to evidence that the Serb authorities were forcibly registering displaced Serbs in formerly Muslim-dominated localities. This arose from the provision included in the Dayton agreement permitting refugees and displaced persons to vote either in their former homes or in the place where they chose to settle. National elections were held on 14 September for the republican Presidency and legislature, the presidency and legislature of the Serb Republic, and the legislature and cantonal authorities of the Bosnian Federation. The elections were monitored by about 1,200 OSCE observers, while IFOR and the IPTF forces maintained security.

At the elections for the republican Presidency, Izetbegović won 80% of the Bosniak votes cast; Kresimir Zubak (CDU−BH) 88% of the Croat votes; and Momčilo Krajišnik (SDP), the former Speaker of the Serb Assembly, 67% of the Serb votes. Having received the largest number of votes of the three winning presidential candidates, Izetbegović became Chairman of the Presidency. The Federation section of the republican House of Representatives and the Federation's own House of Representatives were dominated by the PDA and the CDU−BH. None the less, the Joint List of Bosnia and Herzegovina, comprising an alliance of social-democrat Bosniak and Croat parties, and the Party for Bosnia and Herzegovina (established earlier that year by the former Prime Minister, Haris Silajdžić) won a significant number of votes in the elections to both the republican and federation Houses. Although the SDP secured a majority of votes in both the Serb section of the House of Representatives and in the Serb National Assembly, the PDA polled about one-sixth of the votes cast on the territory of the Serb Republic. The People's Alliance for Peace and Progress also gained a significant share of the Serb votes cast in the elections to the House of Representatives and the Serb National Assembly. Plavšić was elected President of the Serb Republic and Dragolub Mirjanić the Vice-President, securing some 59% of the votes. The validity of the election results was questioned by the International Crisis Group, comprising senior western European politicians, who claimed that a large number of voting papers had been fraudulently added to the ballot boxes. The OSCE subsequently revised its estimate of the Bosnian electorate upwards and refused to order a recount of the ballot papers. Following the OSCE's endorsement of the election results, the UN Security Council decided on 1 October 1996 to remove the sanctions imposed against the FRY and the Serb Republic. A few days later Izetbegović and Milošević, meeting in Paris, agreed to establish full diplomatic relations; Milošević pledged to respect the territorial integrity of Bosnia and Herzegovina, while Izetbegović consented to recognize the FRY as the successor state to Yugoslavia. The inaugural session of the Presidency was held on 5 October; however, Krajišnik failed to attend, claiming that his personal safety might be threatened in Sarajevo (where the ceremony was held). The inaugural session of the republican Assembly was to have been held on the same day, but was boycotted by the Serb deputies. The new National Assembly of the Serb Republic held its inaugural session on 19 October; the inaugural session of the federation House of Representatives took place on 6 November.

In mid-October 1996 the OSCE changed the regulations regarding voting in the delayed municipal elections, ruling that people could only vote in their places of residence prior to 1992. The municipal elections, which were due to have taken place in November 1996, were rescheduled for early 1997 (when, however, they were again postponed). In early November 1996 Plavšić announced that she had dismissed Gen. Mladić as commander of the Serb armed forces, replacing him with a little-known officer, Maj.-Gen. Pero Colić. A large number of the members of Mladić's general staff were also replaced, but Mladić and the other officers refused to accept their dismissal. After a power struggle, during which the Minister of Defence of the Serb Republic was taken captive for a short time by Mladić's supporters, Mladić agreed to surrender his position at the end of November.

In mid-November 1996 clashes were reported between Muslims and Serbs along the inter-entity boundary near the Serb-held village of Gajevi, to which the Muslims were attempting to return. There were repeated incidents in which Muslims attempting to return home on Serb-held territory were forcibly repulsed. In many parts of the country hostility between the ethnic groups continued, with minority elements being intimidated and often driven out from their homes. At a conference on Bosnia and Herzegovina, hosted by the French Government in mid-November, it was agreed that the post of High Representative of the International Community would be maintained for a further two years, and that Bildt's powers would be increased to make him the final arbiter in the interpretation of the civilian provisions of the Dayton agreement. A Bosnian Peace Implementation Conference was held in London in early December; the NATO Secretary-General announced the establishment of a successor contingent to IFOR, to be known as the Stabilization Force (SFOR), which was to have a mandate of 18 months, with six-monthly reviews. SFOR officially replaced IFOR on 20 December. In mid-December, after some delay, the Presidency appointed the two Co-Prime Ministers of the republican Council of Ministers: Haris Silajdžić of the Party for Bosnia and Herzegovina and Boro Bosić of the SDP. One week later the federal House of Representatives elected Edhem Bičakčić as the federal Prime Minister, replacing Izudin Kapetanović. (On the previous day the Bosnian Croats had announced that 'Herzeg-Bosna' had ceased to exist.) The republican Council of Ministers was appointed by the Co-Prime Ministers and approved by the inaugural session of the Bosnian Assembly, which was finally held on 3 January 1997. The Council of Ministers comprised Ministers for Foreign Affairs, for Foreign Trade and Economic Relations, and for Communications and Civilian Affairs. Each post had two Deputy Ministers, with each of the Bosnian ethnic groups holding an equal number of offices. In February a ruling on the future status of the disputed town of Brčko was postponed until March 1998 by an international arbitration commission; however, in March 1998 the commission announced a further deferral of judgment. In March 1997 Robert Farrand, a US diplomat, was appointed to act as supervisor of the town in the interim period. In the same month Vladimir

Soljić was elected to replace Kresimir Zubak as President of the Federation. (Soljić, in turn, was succeeded by the Vice-President, Dr Ejup Ganić, in December.)

On 28 February 1997 Krajišnik signed, on behalf of the Serb Republic, an agreement with the FRY to foster mutual economic co-operation and to collaborate on regional security. The accord was ratified by the National Assembly of the Serb Republic in March, despite opposition voiced by Plavšić and by a number of Bosnian Muslim and Bosnian Croat leaders. In July Plavšić announced the dissolution of the National Assembly and scheduled parliamentary elections for the beginning of September. Although this action was supported by both the UN and the OSCE, it was sharply criticized by Gojko Klicković, the Prime Minister of the Serb Republic, and a number of resolutions designed to undermine Plavšić were approved by the National Assembly. In mid-August the Constitutional Court ruled that Plavšić's decision to dissolve the legislature had been illegal: the Assembly proceeded to vote to disregard future decrees by Plavšić. (It subsequently emerged that one of the Constitutional Court judges had been subject to physical intimidation, allegedly by supporters of Karadžić, prior to the judgment.) Plavšić's position was strengthened in August, following a decision by the Serb Republic's Vice-President, Dragolub Mirjanić, to abandon the Assembly in Pale and join the presidential team in Banja Luka. In late September a constitutional crisis was averted, following a meeting in Belgrade hosted by President Milošević and attended by Plavšić and Krajišnik. A joint statement was issued detailing an agreement, whereby elections to the National Assembly would be held in November under the aegis of the OSCE, and presidential elections for both the Serb Republic and the Bosnian collective Presidency would be held on 7 December. In October Carlos Westendorp, who had replaced Bildt as High Representative in June, announced his intention to reorganize the Bosnian Serb television service and to demand the resignation of the management board, including Krajišnik.

At a further Bosnian Peace Implementation Conference, held in Sintra, Portugal, in May 1997, NATO stipulated deadlines for the approval by the entities of a number of laws on property, passports and citizenship. In addition a new list of ambassadors was demanded better to reflect the ethnic diversity of the country. Following the expiry on 1 August of the deadline for the submission of the new diplomatic list, the USA and the EU suspended recognition of Bosnia and Herzegovina's ambassadors. In July, at a conference of international donors, the Serb Republic was warned that the supply of economic aid might be disrupted if suspected war criminals were not extradited to the ICTY. Earlier in the month the EU had announced the suspension of aid to the Republic for its failure to comply with this requirement. In late November the collective Presidency accepted a Croatian proposal for the creation of a joint committee to improve co-operation between the two countries. On 17 December the Bosnian Assembly approved the law on passports within the deadline established by the international community, but failed to ratify the law on citizenship; the following day Westendorp announced that the citizenship law would be imposed on Bosnian territory from 1 January 1998. (An agreement had been signed earlier in the month by Krajišnik and the FRY Government, which accorded Bosnian Serbs citizenship of both Bosnia and Herzegovina and the FRY.) In late December 1997 it was announced that NATO had agreed to extend indefinitely the mandate of the peace-keeping forces; in November Westendorp had warned that renewed hostilities might ensue, following the scheduled withdrawal of SFOR troops at the expiry of their mandate in June 1998. In February 1998 NATO formally approved the establishment of a new peace-keeping force for Bosnia and Herzegovina, which was to be deployed in the country following the expiry of SFOR's mandate; the force was to comprise 33,000 troops, but was to be reduced after presidential and legislative elections in September of that year.

Municipal elections for both entities finally took place in September 1997 under the aegis of the OSCE. Although some 91 parties contested the elections (in which voter participation was estimated at about 60%) the three main nationalist parties, the PDA, the CDU—BH and the SDP, received the vast majority of the votes cast. Parliamentary elections to the National Assembly of the Serb Republic were held during 22–23 November, under the supervision of the OSCE. Participating parties included the Serb National Alliance (SNA), which had been established by Plavšić in September, following her expulsion from the SDP in July. In the elections the SDP secured 24 seats (compared with 45 in 1996), but still remained the largest party

in the Assembly. A newly-formed electoral alliance, the Coalition for a Single and Democratic Bosnia and Herzegovina, which included the PDA and the Party for Bosnia and Herzegovina, secured 16 seats, while the SNA and the Serb Radical Party (SRP) each achieved 15 seats. At the inaugural session of the new Assembly on 27 December, Plavšić nominated as prime minister-designate Mladen Ivanić, an economist with no political affiliation. The nomination was immediately challenged by the leadership of the SDP, which considered that as the largest party in the new Assembly it should have the first opportunity to propose a new prime minister and government; accordingly, the SDP proposed Klicković, the outgoing Prime Minister, and Aleksa Buha, the acting Chairman of the party. Ivanić declared, however, that he would continue negotiating with all the parties represented in the new Assembly to try to form an interim government of 'national unity'. On 18 January 1998, however, following the failure of Ivanić's inter-party talks, Milorad Dodik, who was considered to be a proponent of moderate rather than extremist policies, secured sufficient parliamentary support to form a new government. Following the announcement of the new administration, which contained a large number of Bosnian Muslims, Dodik assured the international community of his determination to govern according to the terms of the Dayton peace agreement. His appointment was condemned, however, by Krajišnik, who warned that it would lead to the destabilization of the Serb Republic. At the end of January Dodik announced that government bodies were to be transferred from Pale to Banja Luka.

A number of accused war criminals were put on trial in The Hague in 1997. In May Dušan Tadić, who had been indicted in 1996 for organizing 'ethnic cleansing' in Omarska concentration camp (see above), was convicted of torturing Bosnian Muslims and sentenced to 20 years' imprisonment. In July 1997 an indicted Serbian war criminal, Simo Drljaca, was killed following an exchange of fire with SFOR members, who had sought to arrest him. For many observers the operation demonstrated an increased determination on the part of the international community, and in particular Westendorp, to enforce indictments issued by the ICTY; to this end it had been decided not to publish the identity of accused war criminals (the policy was entitled 'sealed indictments') to facilitate their apprehension. The shooting of Drljaca was condemned as murder, however, by President Plavšić and other Bosnian Serb leaders, and the actions of SFOR were strongly criticized by Russia, which claimed that SFOR had exceeded its mandate. In February 1998 the arrest by SFOR troops of two Bosnian Serb suspected war criminals at the boundary between the Serb and Muslim regions of Sarajevo prompted protests from Bosnian Serbs in the town. In the same month three Bosnian Serbs who had been indicted for war crimes were the first to surrender to SFOR troops for trial at the ICTY.

In early April 1998 the OSCE dissolved the Serb-dominated municipal assembly of Srebrenica, owing to its failure to assist in the resettlement of displaced Muslims in the town; a provisional executive council, headed by a senior OSCE official, was established to replace the assembly. In May the Government issued a warrant for the arrest of Gojko Klicković (who had served as Prime Minister of the Serb Republic in 1996–97) on charges of embezzlement and abuse of office. In mid-June the UN Security Council officially voted in favour of extending the mandate of SFOR to remain in the country indefinitely, with six-monthly reviews.

In June 1998 Krajišnik criticized a motion by the National Assembly of the Serb Republic expressing 'no confidence' in its Speaker, Dragan Kalinić, and Deputy Speaker, Buha subsequently resigned from the chairmanship of the SDP, citing what he claimed to be interference in his leadership by Krajišnik; Kalinić was elected as the new Chairman of the SDP. In early September, following lengthy negotiations, the Governments of Bosnia and Croatia signed an agreement (subject to approval by the legislatures of both countries), which would allow Bosnia and Herzegovina to use the Croatian port of Ploce, while permitting Croatia transit through the village of Neum (Bosnia's only access to the Adriatic Sea).

In September 1998 elections took place, as scheduled, for a new Bosnian collective Presidency and national legislature, for the presidency and National Assembly of the Serb Republic, and for the Federation House of Representatives. Izetbegović was re-elected as the Bosniak member of the collective Presidency, while the Chairman of the Socialist Party of the Bosnian Serb Republic (Socijalistička partija za Republiku Srpsku—

SPRS), which was a member of the SNA-led Accord Coalition, Zivko Radišić, replaced Krajišnik, and the Chairman of the CDU—BH, Ante Jelavić, was elected as the Croat member of the Presidency. In the election to the Serb presidency the Chairman of the SRP, Dr Nikola Poplasen (who represented a coalition of the SRP and the SDP), defeated Plavšić. The SDP retained 19 of the 83 seats in the National Assembly of the Serb Republic, while the Coalition for a Single and Democratic Bosnia and Herzegovina won 15 seats; the latter also secured 14 of the 42 seats in the Bosnian House of Representatives and 68 of the 140 seats in the Federation House of Representatives.

On 13 October 1998 the newly-elected Presidency of Bosnia and Herzegovina was inaugurated. Radišić became the first Serb to chair the Presidency (replacing Izetbegović) for an eight-month term, in accordance with the rotational schedule. At the end of October Dodik replaced the Serbian Minister of the Interior and Minister of Justice. Poplasen was inaugurated as President of the Serb Republic; he pledged to maintain good relations with western Governments and to comply with the Dayton agreement. The major parties represented in the Serb National Assembly subsequently conducted negotiations regarding the appointment of a new Council of Ministers in the Serb Republic. The Accord Coalition, which held 32 seats in the National Assembly, rejected Poplasen's nomination of Kalinić as Prime Minister, while supporting the reappointment of Dodik to the post.

In December 1998 the Federation Parliament re-elected Ganić as President, while Ivo Andrić-Luzanski (a member of the CDU—BH) became Federation Vice-President; a new Federation Council of Ministers, nominated by Bičakčić, was established. Following the continued failure of the National Assembly of the Serb Republic to agree on a new government, in early January 1999 Poplasen nominated Brane Miljus, a member of the Party of Independent Social Democrats (Stranko Nezavisnih Socijaldemokrata—SNSD) as Prime Minister-Designate. The Accord Coalition objected to Miljus' candidacy, and Dodik (the leader of the SNSD) announced his expulsion from the party. (Miljus subsequently formed a breakaway organization, which was entitled the Party of Independent Social Democrats of the Serb Republic.) Later in January the National Assembly rejected Miljus' nomination to the office of Prime Minister (while continuing to support Dodik). Also in January SFOR troops killed a Bosnian Serb suspected of war crimes, after he resisted arrest near the town of Foca, in the east of the country; Bosnian Serbs subsequently staged violent protests at UN headquarters in Foca.

In February 1999 the Council of Ministers of the Presidency was reorganized. Later that month Westendorp declared that supreme command of the armed forces of the Federation and the Serb Republic was to be transferred to the members of the collective Presidency. However, the Government of the Serb Republic contested the decision, and announced that Poplasen would remain Commander of the Serb armed forces, pending a ruling by the Constitutional Court of Bosnia and Herzegovina. In early March Poplasen proposed a motion in the Serb Republic National Assembly in an attempt to instigate Dodik's dismissal. Westendorp announced Poplasen's removal from office, on the grounds that he had exceeded his authority. In the same month international arbitrators, who had met in Vienna in February, ruled that Serb control of Brčko would end, and that the town would henceforth be governed jointly by the Serb Republic and the Federation, under international supervision. Dodik tendered his resignation (which he later withdrew) in protest at the announcement, and the National Assembly rejected both the ruling on Brčko and Westendorp's decision to remove Poplasen from office. (The National Assembly subsequently withdrew its opposition to Poplasen's dismissal, and Mirko Sarović, the incumbent Vice-President, provisionally assumed the presidential office.) In mid-April a new municipal government, comprising Serbs, Muslims and Croats, was elected in Brčko, with an SPRS candidate as mayor.

In May 1999 the ICTY sentenced a former Bosnian Croat detention camp commander to 30 months' imprisonment for war crimes, but acquitted him of charges brought under the 1949 Geneva Convention governing international warfare, on the grounds that the Muslim–Croat conflict had been internal. In June, in accordance with the Constitution, Jelavić became Chairman of the Bosnia and Herzegovina Presidency, replacing Radišić. In the same month the UN Security Council voted to extend the mandate of SFOR and the principally civilian security force, the UN Mission in Bosnia and Herzegovina

(UNMIBH), for a further year; NATO announced that the strength of the SFOR contingent was to be reduced to about 16,500. In July SFOR members arrested Radislav Brdjanin, a former Bosnian Serb official (who had served as Deputy Prime Minister under Karadžić), following his indictment by the ICTY in connection with massacres of Muslims and Croats near Banja Luka by Serb forces in 1992. In August 1999 a prominent Bosnian Serb army commander, Col-Gen. Momir Talić, was arrested in Vienna (where he was attending a military conference), prompting protests from the Serb Republic Government; Talić had been secretly indicted by the ICTY for war crimes committed against Muslims and Croats during the Bosnian conflict.

In August 1999 Wolfgang Petritsch, hitherto the Austrian ambassador to the FRY, succeeded Westendorp as High Representative in Bosnia (following Westendorp's appointment to the European Parliament). In September Plavšić was re-elected leader of the SNA at a party congress. In October Petritsch prohibited Poplasen and a further two SRP officials from contesting forthcoming local elections, on the grounds that they had obstructed the implementation of the Dayton peace agreement. In December Andrić Luzanski assumed the Federation presidency, in accordance with the one-year rotational mandate stipulated in the Constitution. In February 2000 Izetbegović replaced Jelavić as Chairman of the collective Presidency. In the same month legislation allowing for a reconstituted state Presidency, comprising a Chairman (with a rotational mandate) and two other members, was agreed. Later in February the SPRS withdrew from the governing Accord Coalition of the Serb Republic, in protest at the dismissal in January of the SPRS Deputy Prime Minister, Tihomir Gligorić, by Dodik, who had accused him of provoking dissension within the Government. In March a senior Bosnian Croat commander, Gen. Tihomir Blaskić, was sentenced by the ICTY to 45 years' imprisonment (the most severe sentence issued by the Tribunal) for war crimes perpetrated against Muslims in 1992–93. In early April Krajišnik was arrested in Pale by SFOR troops and extradited to the ICTY.

At local government elections, which took place on 8 April 2000, the SDP won control of 49 of the country's 145 municipal councils (mainly in the Serb Republic), while the CDU—BH secured 25 and the PDA 23; the multi-ethnic Social Democratic Party of Bosnia and Herzegovina (Socijaldemokratska Partija BiH—SDP BiH) made significant electoral gains in the Federation. In the same month the national House of Representatives adopted legislation providing for the restructuring of the Bosnian Council of Ministers, which would henceforth comprise a Chairman (appointed by the collective Presidency for an eight-month term) and five ministers. In late May a motion, proposed by the SDP, expressing 'no confidence' in the Federation Government was defeated in the entity's House of Representatives. The Federation Vice-President, Ejup Ganić, was expelled from the PDA, after failing to comply with the Party's decision that he resign from his government office. In early June a new Bosnian Council of Ministers was appointed, after the national House of Representatives confirmed the nomination of Spasoje Tusevljak (a non-party candidate) to the office of prime minister. In July Dodik announced his candidacy in the election to the Serb Republic presidency, which was scheduled for 11 November; elections to the national House of Representatives and to the legislatures of both entities were to take place concurrently.

In July 2000 the Minister of Information of the Serb Republic resigned, after the international community criticized his alleged interference in the appointment of television officials. Later that month Petritsch replaced the Federation Minister of Agriculture, Water Management and Forestry, owing to his opposition to proposed economic reforms. In early August the Minister of Refugees and Displaced Persons of the Serb Republic resigned, after international representatives expressed dissatisfaction concerning the Republic's implementation of the Dayton peace accord. In early September the National Assembly of the Serb Republic adopted a motion, proposed by the SDP, expressing 'no confidence' in Dodik's administration. However, the Government submitted a legal challenge to the entity's Constitutional Court and announced that it would remain in office pending the forthcoming legislative election. In October Izetbegović retired from the collective Presidency on grounds of age; Halid Genjac, a senior official of the PDA, replaced him as the Bosniak member of the Presidency, while the Serb representative, Zirko Radišić, became Chairman. A member of the CDU—BH, Martin Raguz, subsequently replaced Tusevljak as

Introductory Survey

Prime Minister, owing to a constitutional stipulation that the Chairman of the collective Presidency and that of the Council of Ministers should not belong to the same ethnic group.

In October 2000 a Bosnian war crimes suspect, who had been indicted by the ICTY for involvement in atrocities against Muslim women in 1992–93, killed himself and injured four members of SFOR, after peace-keeping troops attempted to arrest him. Also in October violent clashes between Muslims and Serbs were reported in Brčko, after Serb students protested against sharing educational facilities with Muslims.

On 11 November 2000 simultaneous elections to the national House of Representatives, the legislatures of both entities and the presidency of the Serb Republic took place. At the national legislative election the SDP BiH secured nine seats, the PDA eight seats, the SDP six seats and the CDU−BH five seats in the 42-member House of Representatives. At the federal election the PDA won 38 seats, the SDP BiH 37 seats, the CDU−BH 25 seats and the Party for Bosnia and Herzegovina 21 seats in the 140-member legislature. The SDP secured 31 of the 83 seats in the republican National Assembly, while the SPRS and the Party of Democratic Progress of the Serb Republic (PDP) each received 11 seats. Mirko Sarović, the SDP candidate who had reportedly been selected by Karadžić, was elected, with some 49.8% of votes cast, to the presidency of the Serb Republic, defeating Dodik. The SDP subsequently announced that it was to establish a parliamentary coalition with the PDP, the SPRS and the PDA, thereby securing a majority in the National Assembly.

In December 2000 Sarović designated Mladen Ivanić, a member of the PDP, as Prime Minister of the Serb Republic. In mid-January 2001 Ivanić formed the Republic's first multi-ethnic Council of Ministers. However, the inclusion in the Council of Ministers of several SDP representatives proved controversial, following warnings by the USA that it might suspend financial aid to the Serb Republic if the SDP entered the Government. Ivanić subsequently requested that government members suspend party activities, and replaced the newly-appointed Minister of Trade and Tourism (a prominent SDP member), in an attempt to address international concerns over SDP representation. In the same month Raguz was redesignated as national Prime Minister; he was expected to form a new Council of Ministers. Meanwhile, the SDP BiH had established a parliamentary coalition with a further nine non-nationalist parties (known as the Alliance for Change), which held 17 seats in the national House of Representatives and 69 seats in the federal legislature. The CDU−BH and six other allied Croat parties subsequently threatened to withdraw from Federation government institutions, after members of the Alliance for Change were elected Speaker and Deputy Speaker of the federal House of Representatives.

In January 2001 Plavšić surrendered to the ICTY, following her indictment in April 2000, but subsequently denied charges that she, together with other Serb officials, had planned a campaign of genocide and deportation against the Muslim and Croat inhabitants of Bosnia and Herzegovina from July 1991 to December 1992. By the beginning of 2001 the ICTY had convicted 14 Bosnian Serbs, Croats and Muslims for war crimes. On 22 February the national House of Representatives approved a new Bosnian Council of Ministers, which had been nominated by the elected Chairman, Bozidar Matić (a member of the SDP BiH).

Government

In accordance with the General Framework Agreement for Peace in Bosnia and Herzegovina, signed in December 1995, Bosnia and Herzegovina is a single state, which consists of two independent political entities: the Federation of Bosnia and Herzegovina, comprising the Bosniak (Muslim)- and Croat-majority areas, and the Serb Republic (Republika Srpska), comprising the Serb-majority area. The central Government of Bosnia and Herzegovina has a three-member collective presidency of one Bosniak, one Croat and one Serb. Members of the Presidency are directly elected for a term of four years, and are eligible to serve for only two consecutive terms. Chairmanship of the Presidency is rotated between the members every eight months. The bicameral Parliamentary Assembly of Bosnia and Herzegovina comprises the House of Peoples and the House of Representatives. The House of Representatives has 42 deputies, of whom 28 are directly elected from the Federation and 14 directly elected from the Serb Republic for a two-year term. The House of Peoples has 15 deputies, of whom 10 are selected by the Federation legislature and five by the Serb Republic

legislature for a two-year term. The Presidency appoints a Prime Minister (subject to the approval of the House of Representatives), who subsequently appoints the national Council of Ministers.

The Federation of Bosnia and Herzegovina and the Serb Republic each retain an executive presidency, government and legislature. The bicameral parliament of the Federation comprises a 140-member House of Representatives, which is elected for a two-year term by proportional representation, and a 74-member House of Peoples, which has one-half Bosniak and one-half Croat representation. The unicameral legislature of the Serb Republic, known as the National Assembly, has 83 deputies, who are elected for a two-year term by proportional representation. The Federation is divided into 10 cantons, each headed by a zupan or governor.

Defence

In October 2000 it was estimated that government forces in Bosnia and Herzegovina numbered about 30,000 (with some 150,000 reserves). In addition, the Serb Republic had an army of about 30,000 and the Federation an army (comprising the former Croatian Defence Council−HVO−and Bosniak forces) of more than 10,000. The armies of the Serb Republic and the Federation were to be reduced in size by a further 15% in early 2001.

On 20 December 1995 power was formally transferred to an international NATO-commanded 60,000-strong 'Implementation Force' (IFOR), which was granted authority to oversee the implementation of the peace accord. In December 1996 IFOR was superseded by a Stabilization Force (SFOR), which initially comprised about 32,000 troops. In early 1998 NATO agreed to extend SFOR's mandate to remain in the region indefinitely, with six-monthly reviews. About 2,300 members of the International Police Task Force were deployed in Bosnia and Herzegovina in 1998. At May 2000, following restructuring, SFOR numbered about 20,000 troops. At 1 December the UN Mission in Bosnia and Herzegovina (UNMIBH) comprised 1,769 civilian police officers and four army personnel; the contingent had a total authorized strength of 2,057 civilian police and five military personnel. Government expenditure on defence was estimated at 371m. konvertibilna marka (convertible marka) in 1998.

Economic Affairs

In 1998, according to official estimates, Bosnia and Herzegovina's gross national product (GNP) was US $3,789m., equivalent to $1,024 per head. According to the World Bank, the population of Bosnia and Herzegovina declined at an average annual rate of 2.4% in 1990–98. According to official estimates, real GDP growth in Bosnia and Herzegovina was 18.6% in 1998; growth in the Bosnian Federation in that year was estimated at 12.4%, while growth in the Serb Republic was estimated at 39.3%.

Agriculture (including forestry and fishing) contributed an estimated 16.0% of GDP in Bosnia and Herzegovina in 1998 (accounting for 12.1% of GDP in the Bosnian Federation and 26.6% of GDP in the Serb Republic in that year). In 1998 about 6.1% of the labour force were employed in the agricultural sector in Bosnia and Herzegovina. The major agricultural products were tobacco and fruit, while the livestock sector was also significant. Imports of foodstuffs comprised 4.1% of total imports in 1997. According to official estimates, agricultural GDP in Bosnia and Herzegovina declined by 9.7% in 1995, but increased by 28.4% in 1996, by 22.8% in 1997 and by 8.6% in 1998. It was estimated that agricultural GDP in the Bosnian Federation increased by 40.9% in 1995, with growth slowing to 12.6% in 1996, to 18.6% in 1997 and to 4.9% in 1998; agricultural GDP in the Serb Republic declined by 48.1% in 1995, but increased by 61.0% in 1996, by 28.8% in 1997 and by 13.6% in 1998.

Industry (mining and manufacturing) contributed an estimated 22.4% of GDP in Bosnia and Herzegovina in 1998 (with equivalent levels in the Bosnian Federation and in the Serb Republic). According to official estimates, industrial GDP in Bosnia and Herzegovina increased by 33.0% in 1995, by 38.1% in 1996 and by 51.4% in 1997, with growth slowing to 18.5% in 1998. It was estimated that industrial GDP in the Federation increased by 127.2% in 1995, by 43.3% in 1996, by 73.2% in 1997 and by only 12.0% in 1998; industrial GDP in the Serb Republic declined by 24.8% in 1995, but increased by 28.4% in 1996, by 6.4% in 1997 and by 40.1% in 1998.

The mining and manufacturing sectors accounted for an estimated 70.7% of total exports in 1997. Bosnia and Herzegovina possesses extensive mineral resources, including iron ore, lignite, copper, lead, zinc and gold. The manufacturing sector is based largely on the processing of iron ore, non-ferrous metals, coal, and wood and paper products.

The civil conflict in 1992–95 resulted in the destruction of much of the electric power system in Bosnia and Herzegovina. Prior to the conflict, the system comprised 13 hydroelectric installations and 12 coal- and lignite-fuelled thermal power installations. Imports of electric power accounted for 3.2% of total imports in 1997.

The services sector contributed an estimated 55.8% of GDP in Bosnia and Herzegovina in 1998 (accounting for 59.0% of GDP in the Bosnian Federation and 47.1% of GDP in the Serb Republic). In that year entrepôt trade accounted for an estimated 14.8% of GDP in Bosnia and Herzegovina (17.1% of GDP in the Bosnian Federation and 8.7% of GDP in the Serb Republic). According to official estimates, the GDP of the services sector in Bosnia and Herzegovina increased by 68.3% in 1995, by 71.3% in 1996, by 46.5% in 1997 and by 20.8% in 1998. It was estimated that the GDP of the services sector increased by 118.6% in the Federation in 1995, with growth slowing to 76.1% in 1996, to 48.0% in 1997 and to 12.4% in 1998; the GDP of the sector in the Serb Republic declined by 14.7% in 1995, but increased by 52.3% in 1996, by 39.5% in 1997 and by 62.0% in 1998.

In 1999 Bosnia and Herzegovina recorded a visible trade deficit of US $1,414.7m., while there was a deficit of $767.0m. on the current account of the balance of payments. The principal exports in 1997 were wood and paper products, iron and steel, electric power and fabricated metal products. The main imports in that year were foodstuffs and electric power.

Bosnia and Herzegovina's overall budget deficit for 1999 was estimated at 466m. konvertibilna marka (convertible marka). The country's total external debt was estimated at US $2,981.4m. at the end of 1998 (equivalent to some 73.7% of annual GDP). According to official estimates, the cost of debt-servicing was equivalent to about 16.6% of the value of exports of goods and services. Consumer prices in the Federation of Bosnia and Herzegovina declined by 4.4% in 1995 and by 24.5% in 1996, but increased by an estimated 14.3% in 1997. The annual rate of inflation in the Serb Republic averaged 117.6% in 1995, but fell to 65.9% in 1996 and to an estimated 2.7% in 1997. In the year to September 2000 consumer prices increased by an estimated 3.5% in the Federation and by an estimated 16.9% in the Serb Republic. The rate of unemployment in Bosnia and Herzegovina was estimated at 40% in late 1999.

Bosnia and Herzegovina became a member of the IMF in December 1995 and was admitted to the International Bank for Reconstruction and Development (the World Bank) in April 1996. In July 1999 the first summit meeting of the Stability Pact for South-Eastern Europe (see p. 255) took place in Bosnia and Herzegovina, with the aim of adopting a common strategy for regional stability.

The civil conflict in 1992–95 resulted in extensive damage to the economy of Bosnia and Herzegovina. Following the signing of the Dayton peace agreement in December 1995, the official reconstruction of the economy commenced; Bosnia and Herzegovina was subsequently admitted to the IMF. An early priority of the reconstruction programme was the resolution of the considerable foreign debt that Bosnia and Herzegovina had inherited from the former Yugoslavia. In May 1998 the IMF approved a stand-by credit to support the Bosnian Government's economic programme. The World Bank subsequently granted further assistance in economic reconstruction and development.

The new national currency, fixed at par with the German Deutsche Mark, was officially introduced in June 1998. In October agreement was reached with the so-called Paris Club of creditor governments on the reduction of external debt. By the end of 2000, following large inflows of foreign assistance, the country had made some recovery from the civil war, and from the subsequent adverse affects of the conflict in Kosovo and Metohija in March–June 1999 (see chapter on Yugoslavia), which had a particularly severe impact on the trade of the Serb Republic. Real GDP was estimated to have increased by 9% in 1999, and was projected to grow by a further 10% in 2000. Nevertheless, with production in most traditional industries remaining at less than one-half of its pre-war level, unemployment remained high. While progress in some areas of reform, particularly that of the financial sector, was achieved, the implementation of privatization measures was slow (owing, in part, to obstruction from local politicians). The Government's principal objectives remained the attainment of greater fiscal sustainability through tax and expenditure reform and the encouragement of market development. However, the unfavourable business environment continued to deter significant private investment, which was essential for a reduction in the rate of unemployment and complete recovery from post-war poverty. In addition, the international community criticized persistent administrative corruption and announced a reduction in assistance to the country.

Social Welfare

Bosnia and Herzegovina has a state-administered health service, which is open to all. The health service was greatly disrupted by the war. Following the end of hostilities in December 1995, budgetary funds allocated to the health service were used principally for emergency relief and humanitarian aid. In 1998 there were 143 physicians, 452 nurses, 19 dentists and 11 pharmacists per 100,000 people working in the country. At mid-2000 some 809,000 internally-displaced persons and 39,500 Croatian Serb refugees remained in Bosnia and Herzegovina; economic and social reconstruction continued to be supported by international aid.

Education

Elementary education is free and compulsory for all children between the ages of seven and 15 years, when children attend the 'eight-year school'. Various types of secondary education are available to all who qualify, but the vocational and technical schools are the most popular. Alternatively, children may attend a general secondary school (gymnasium), where they follow a four-year course to prepare them for university entrance. At the secondary level there are also a number of art schools, apprentice schools and teacher-training schools. There are four universities, situated in Sarajevo, Banja Luka, Mostar and Tuzla.

Public Holidays

2001: 1–2 January (New Year), 1 March (Independence Day), 1 May (Labour Day), 9 May (V. E. Day), 21 November (National Statehood Day).

2002: 1–2 January (New Year), 1 March (Independence Day), 1 May (Labour Day), 9 May (V. E. Day), 21 November (National Statehood Day).

Weights and Measures

The metric system is in force.

Statistical Survey

Source (unless otherwise stated): *Yugoslav Survey*, Belgrade, POB 677, Moše Pijade 8/I; tel. (11) 333610; fax (11) 332295.

Area and Population

AREA, POPULATION AND DENSITY

Area (sq km)	51,129*
Population (census results)	
31 March 1981	4,124,008
31 March 1991	
Males	2,183,795
Females	2,193,238
Total	4,377,033
Population (official estimates at mid-year)†	
1997	4,204,000
1998	4,211,000
Density (per sq km) at mid-1998	82.4

* 19,741 sq miles.

† Figures include refugees outside the country. The number of people living in the country was estimated to be 3,750,000 at 31 December 1999.

Source: mainly UN, *Demographic Yearbook* and *Population and Vital Statistics Report*.

PRINCIPAL ETHNIC GROUPS (1991 census, provisional)

	Number	% of total population
Muslims	1,905,829	43.7
Serbs	1,369,258	31.4
Croats	755,892	17.3
'Yugoslavs'	239,845	5.5
Total (incl. others) . . .	4,364,574	100.0

PRINCIPAL TOWNS (population at 1991 census): Sarajevo (capital) 415,631; Banja Luka 142,644 (Source: *Statistički godišnjak Jugoslavije—Statistical Yearbook of Yugoslavia*).

1991 (estimates): Doboj 102,624; Mostar 127,034; Prijedor 112,635 (Source: UN, *Demographic Yearbook*).

Sarajevo (estimated population in 1993): 383,000.

BIRTHS, MARRIAGES AND DEATHS

1989: Registered live births 66,809 (birth rate 14.9 per 1,000); Registered deaths 30,383 (death rate 6.8 per 1,000).

1990: Registered live births 66,952; Registered marriages 29,990; Registered deaths 29,093.

1991: Registered live births 64,769; Registered deaths 31,411 (Source: UN, *Population and Vital Statistics Report*).

1995: Registered deaths 114,670 (death rate 13.6 per 1,000) (Source: UN, *Demographic Yearbook*).

1990–95 (UN estimates, annual averages): Birth rate 12.6 per 1,000; Death rate 7.1 per 1,000 (Source: UN, *World Population Prospects: The 1998 Revision*).

Expectation of life (UN estimates, years at birth, 1990–95): 72.2 (males 69.5; females 75.1) (Source: UN, *World Population Prospects: The 1998 Revision*).

EMPLOYMENT (Federation of Bosnia and Herzegovina, average for December)

	1997	1998	1999*
Activities of the material sphere . .	173,857	204,117	217,000
Non-material services	113,723	131,945	127,345
Total	287,580	336,062	344,345

Source: IMF, *Bosnia and Herzegovina: Selected Issues and Statistical Appendix* (June 2000).

Agriculture

PRINCIPAL CROPS (metric tons)

	1997	1998	1999
Wheat	287,372	340,931	257,764
Barley	58,032	63,402	56,295
Maize	830,445	846,638	888,845
Rye	7,384	9,389	9,031
Oats	58,826	66,275	61,650
Potatoes	390,000*	380,000*	380,000†
Dry beans†	12,000	14,000	14,000
Soybeans (Soya beans)	7,369	8,117	8,701
Cabbages†	85,000	80,000	80,000
Tomatoes†	35,000	40,000	40,000
Onions (dry)† . . .	32,000	35,000	35,000
Garlic†	8,000	8,000	8,000
Carrots†	10,000	11,200	11,200
Watermelons† . . .	3,000	3,000	3,000
Grapes†	15,000	17,000	17,000
Apples†	16,000	18,000	18,000
Pears†	5,500	6,400	6,400
Plums	23,300	25,000†	25,000†
Strawberries† . . .	4,800	4,800	4,800
Tobacco (leaves)† . .	4,000	4,300	4,300

* Unofficial figure. † FAO estimate(s).

Source: FAO.

LIVESTOCK
(FAO estimates, '000 head, year ending September)

	1997	1998	1999
Horses	50	50	50
Cattle	380	350	350
Pigs	70	80	80
Sheep	276	285	285
Chickens	3,870	3,870	3,870
Ducks	120	120	120
Geese	150	150	150
Turkeys	120	120	120

Source: FAO.

LIVESTOCK PRODUCTS (metric tons)

	1997	1998	1999
Beef and veal	12,701	8,800*	8,800†
Mutton and lamb† . . .	2,700	2,700	2,700
Pig meat	4,900	4,500†	4,500†
Poultry meat	8,200	8,200†	8,200†
Cows' milk	202,000	210,000†	210,000†
Sheep's milk†	3,250	3,500	3,500
Cheese†	14,000	14,000	14,000
Eggs†	7,100	8,000	8,000
Cattle and buffalo hides . .	2,432	1,664	1,664

* Unofficial figure. † FAO estimate(s).

Source: FAO.

Forestry

ROUNDWOOD REMOVALS ('000 cubic metres, excluding bark)

	1996	1997	1998
Total (all sawlogs, veneer logs and logs for sleepers)	40	40	40

Source: FAO, *Yearbook of Forest Products*.

SAWNWOOD PRODUCTION
('000 cubic metres, including railway sleepers)

	1996	1997	1998
Total (all broadleaved) . . .	20	20	20

Source: FAO, *Yearbook of Forest Products.*

Fishing

(FAO estimates, metric tons, live weight)

	1996	1997	1998
Total catch (capture, freshwater fish)	2,600	2,550	2,500

Source: FAO, *Yearbook of Fishery Statistics.*

Mining

('000 metric tons)

	1992	1993	1994
Lignite	2,000*	1,500*	1,400
Barite (Barytes)	10	n.a.	n.a.
Gypsum (crude)	150	n.a.	n.a.

* Estimated production.

Lignite ('000 metric tons): 1,640 in 1995; 1,640 in 1996.

Source: UN, *Industrial Commodity Statistics Yearbook.*

Industry

SELECTED PRODUCTS ('000 metric tons, unless otherwise indicated)

	1990
Electric energy (million kWh)	14,632
Crude steel	1,421
Aluminium	89
Machines	16
Tractors (number)	34,000
Lorries (number)	16,000
Motor cars (number)	38,000
Cement	797
Paper and paperboard	281
Television receivers (number)	21,000

Electric energy (million kWh): 1,921 in 1994; 2,203 in 1995; 2,203 in 1996 (Source: UN, *Industrial Commodity Statistics Yearbook*).

Finance

CURRENCY AND EXCHANGE RATES

Monetary Units
100 pfeninga = 1 konvertibilna marka (KM or convertible marka).

Sterling, Dollar and Euro Equivalents (29 December 2000)
£1 sterling = KM 3.1365;
US $1 = KM 2.1019;
€1 = KM 1.9558;
KM 100 = £31.88 = $47.58 = €51.13.

Average Exchange Rate (KM per US $)
1998   1.7597
1999   1.8358
2000   2.1229

Note: The new Bosnia and Herzegovina dinar (BHD) was introduced in August 1994, with an official value fixed at 100 BHD = 1 Deutsche Mark (DM). The DM, the Croatian kuna and the Yugoslav dinar also circulated within Bosnia and Herzegovina. On 22 June 1998 the BHD was replaced by the KM, equivalent to 100 of the former units. The KM was thus at par with the DM. Since the introduction of the euro, on 1 January 1999, the German currency has had a fixed exchange rate of €1 = DM 1.95583.

BUDGET (KM million)*

Revenue	1996	1997	1998
Tax revenue	1,381	1,615	2,035
Taxes on goods and services .	767	976	1,190
Trade taxes	296	349	407
Taxes on income . . .	296	284	377
Other taxes	22	7	60
Other revenue (incl. grants) . .	609	789	1,113
Total	1,992	2,398	3,148

Expenditure	1996	1997	1998
Wages and contributions . . .	235	293	462
Goods and services . . .	92	73	133
Military	188	348	371
Debt service	27	75	87
Reconstruction expenditure . .	24	109	149
Subsidies	46	8	20
Other transfers to households . .	402	745	373
Transfers to war invalids . .	198	271	347
Transfers to cantons or municipalities	1	9	—
Social fund expenditure . . .	—	—	912
Other expenditure (incl. unallocated)†	1,158	770	830
Total	2,173	2,429	3,657

* Figures represent a consolidation of the budgetary accounts of the central Government and the authorities in the Federation of Bosnia and Herzegovina and (except for local and district administration) the Serb Republic.
† Including district, canton and municipal expenditure.

1999 (KM million): Total revenue 3,628; Total expenditure 4,094.

Source: IMF, *Bosnia and Herzegovina: Selected Issues and Statistical Appendix* (June 2000).

MONEY SUPPLY (KM million at 31 December)

	1997	1998	1999
Currency outside banks	113	162	515
Demand deposits at banks	139	148	585
Total money	252	310	1,100

Source: Central Bank of Bosnia and Herzegovina.

COST OF LIVING (Retail Price Index, Federation of Bosnia and Herzegovina; base: December 1995 = 100)

	1997	1998	1999
All items	114.5	120.3	119.9

Source: IMF, *Bosnia and Herzegovina: Selected Issues and Statistical Appendix* (June 2000).

NATIONAL ACCOUNTS

Expenditure on the Gross Domestic Product (US $ million at current prices)

	1996	1997	1998
Government final consumption expenditure			
Private final consumption expenditure	3,237	3,589	3,914
Increase in stocks			
Gross fixed capital formation	1,124	1,438	1,481
Total domestic expenditure	4,361	5,027	5,396
Exports of goods and services	658	1,002	1,367
Less Imports of goods and services	−2,278	−2,606	−2,864
GDP in purchasers' values	2,741	3,423	3,899

1999 (US $ million): GDP 4,418.

Source: IMF, *Bosnia and Herzegovina: Selected Issues and Statistical Appendix* (June 2000).

BALANCE OF PAYMENTS (estimates, US $ million).

	1997	1998	1999
Exports of goods f.o.b.	575.0	816.8	972.8
Imports of goods f.o.b.	−2,333.2	−2,573.2	−2,387.5
Trade balance	−1,758.2	−1,756.4	−1,414.7
Exports of services	427.0	549.8	590.5
Imports of services	−273.0	−291.3	−260.7
Balance on goods and services	−1,604.2	−1,497.9	−1,084.9
Other income (net)	−228.0	−110.6	−79.4
Balance on goods, services and income	−1,832.2	−1,608.5	−1,164.3
Unrequited transfers received	852.0	550.0	397.3
Unrequited transfers paid	−80.0	−40.0	−
Current balance	−1,060.2	−1,098.4	−767.0
Capital account (net)	593.0	933.1	1,203.9
Net errors and omissions	252.1	−91.1	94.4
Overall balance	−215.1	−256.5	531.2

Source: IMF, *Bosnia and Herzegovina: Selected Issues and Statistical Appendix* (June 2000).

External Trade

SELECTED COMMODITIES (US $ million)*

Imports	1996	1997
Electric power	19.7	39.6
Fabricated metal products	33.9	22.9
Electrical machinery and equipment	5.1	28.7
Wood and paper products	11.5	29.9
Foodstuffs	39.9	50.2
Total (inc. others)	1,172.6	1,225.0

Exports	1996	1997
Electric power	0.3	5.7
Iron and steel	7.0	12.4
Non-metallic minerals	1.3	0.9
Fabricated metal products	4.5	5.3
Transport equipment	6.5	3.4
Electrical machinery and equipment	0.3	4.6
Chemical products	1.4	1.6
Wood and paper products	18.2	18.1
Textile products	2.1	0.8
Footwear and fancy goods	1.6	2.2
Total (incl. others)	57.8	87.3

* Figures are provisional and refer only to the Federation of Bosnia and Herzegovina (the Bosniak- and Croat-majority areas, excluding the Serb Republic).

1999 (Federation and Serb Republic, KM million): Total imports 6,047; Total exports 1,375 (Source: Office of the High Representative).

Transport

RAILWAYS (traffic)

	1996	1997	1998
Passenger-km ('000)			
Federation	30,150	5,869	5,118
Republika Srpska	31,000	33,331	50,059
Freight ton-km ('000)			
Federation	18,677	46,339	72,589
Republika Srpska	7,000	2,963	12,292

Source: IMF, *Bosnia and Herzegovina: Selected Issues and Statistical Appendix* (June 2000).

Communications Media

	1994	1995	1996
Telephones ('000 main lines in use)	250	238	272
Radio receivers ('000 in use)	800	840	900
Daily newspapers*:			
Number	n.a.	2	3
Average circulation ('000 copies)	n.a.	520	n.a.
Mobile cellular telephones (subscribers)	n.a.	n.a.	1,500

* Figures refer to government-controlled areas only.

Non-daily newspapers (1992): 22 (average circulation 2,508,000 copies).

1997: Radio receivers ('000 in use) 940; Telephones ('000 main lines in use) 303; Mobile cellular telephones (subscribers) 9,000.

Sources: UN, *Statistical Yearbook*; UNESCO, *Statistical Yearbook*.

Directory

The Constitution

The Constitution of Bosnia and Herzegovina was Annexe 4 to the General Framework Agreement for Peace in Bosnia and Herzegovina, signed in Paris (France) on 14 December 1995. These peace accords were negotiated at Dayton, Ohio (USA), in November and became the Elysées or Paris Treaty in December. Annexe 4 took effect as a constitutional act upon signature, superseding and amending the Constitution of the Republic of Bosnia and Herzegovina.

The previous organic law, an amended version of the 1974 Constitution of the then Socialist Republic of Bosnia and Herzegovina (part of the Socialist Federal Republic of Yugoslavia—the name was changed to the Republic of Bosnia and Herzegovina upon the declaration of independence following a referendum on 29 February–1 March 1992), provided for a collective State Presidency, a Government headed by a Prime Minister and a bicameral Assembly.

The institutions of the Republic continued to function until the firm establishment of the bodies provided for by the Federation of Bosnia and Herzegovina, which was formed on 31 March 1994. This was an association of the Muslim- or Bosniak-led Republic and the Croat Republic of Herzeg-Bosna. The federal Constitution provided for a balance of powers between Bosniak and Croat elements in a Federation divided into cantons. The federal Government was to be responsible for defence, foreign and economic affairs, and its head, the Prime Minister, was to have a greater executive role than the President. These two posts were to rotate between the two ethnic groups.

According to the General Framework Agreement, the Federation was one of the two constituent 'entities' of the new union of Bosnia and Herzegovina, together with the Serb Republic (Republika Srpska) of Bosnia and Herzegovina. The Serb Republic was proclaimed by the Serb deputies of the old Bosnian Assembly on 27 March 1992. Its Constitution provided for an executive President (with two Vice-Presidents), a Government headed by a Prime Minister and a unicameral National Assembly. Under the terms of the General Framework Agreement, known as the Dayton accords (after Dayton, Ohio, the US town where the treaty was negotiated in November 1995), the two Entities were to exist under their current Constitutions, which were to be amended to conform with the peace agreement.

The Dayton accords included 12 annexes on: the military aspects of the peace settlement (including the establishment of an international Implementation Force—IFOR, superseded by a Stabilization Force—SFOR in 1996); regional stabilization; inter-entity boundaries; elections; arbitration; human rights; refugees and displaced persons; a Commission to Preserve National Monuments; Bosnia and Herzegovina public corporations (specifically a Transportation Corporation); civilian implementation (including the office of a High Representative of the International Community); and an international police task force. One of the annexes was the Constitution of Bosnia and Herzegovina, summarized below, and it was signed by representatives of the Republic, the Federation and the Serb Republic.

CONSTITUTION OF BOSNIA AND HERZEGOVINA

The Preamble declares the basic, democratic principles of the country and its conformity with the principles of international law. The Bosniaks, Croats and Serbs are declared to be the constituent peoples (along with Others) of Bosnia and Herzegovina.

Article I affirms the continuation of Bosnia and Herzegovina with the Republic of Bosnia and Herzegovina, within its existing international boundaries, but with its internal structure modified. Bosnia and Herzegovina is a democratic state, consisting of two Entities, the Federation of Bosnia and Herzegovina and the Serb Republic. The capital of the country is Sarajevo and the symbols are to be determined by the legislature. Citizenship is to exist both for Bosnia and Herzegovina and for the Entities.

Article II guarantees human rights and fundamental freedoms, and makes specific mention of the Human Rights Commission to be established under Annexe 6 of the General Framework Agreement. The provisions of a number of international agreements are assured and co-operation and access for the international war-crimes tribunal specified. The provisions of this Article, according to Article X, are incapable of diminution or elimination by any amendment to the Constitution.

The responsibilities of and relations between the Entities and the institutions of Bosnia and Herzegovina are dealt with in Article III. The institutions of Bosnia and Herzegovina are responsible for foreign policy (including trade and customs), overall financial policy, immigration and refugee issues, international and inter-entity law enforcement, common and international communications facilities, inter-entity transportation and air-traffic control. Any governmental functions or powers not reserved to the institutions of Bosnia and Herzegovina by this Constitution are reserved to the Entities, unless additional responsibilities are agreed between the Entities or as provided for in the General Framework Agreement (Annexes 5–8). The Entities may establish special, parallel relations with neighbouring states, provided this is consistent with the sovereignty and territorial integrity of Bosnia and Herzegovina. The Constitution of Bosnia and Herzegovina has primacy over any inconsistent constitutional or legal provisions of the Entities.

The Parliamentary Assembly

Bosnia and Herzegovina has a bicameral legislature, known as the Parliamentary Assembly. It consists of a House of Peoples and a House of Representatives. The House of Peoples comprises 15 members, five each from the Bosniaks, the Croats and the Serbs. The Bosniak and Croat Delegates are selected by, respectively, the Bosniak and Croat Delegates to the House of Representatives of the Federation, and the Serb Delegates by the National Assembly of the Serb Republic. The first House of the Peoples selected under the Constitution is protected from an early dissolution.

The House of Representatives consists of 42 Members, two-thirds to be directly elected from the territory of the Federation and one-third from the territory of the Serb Republic. The first general election was conducted in September 1998 in accordance with Annexe 3 of the General Framework Agreement, which provided for a Permanent Election Commission then to be appointed.

The Parliamentary Assembly convenes in Sarajevo and each chamber rotates its chair between three members, one from each of the constituent peoples. The Parliamentary Assembly is responsible for: necessary legislation under the Constitution or to implement Presidency decisions; determining a budget for the institutions of Bosnia and Herzegovina; and deciding whether to ratify treaties.

The Presidency

Article V concerns the state Presidency of Bosnia and Herzegovina. The head of state consists of three Members: one Bosniak and one Croat, each directly elected from the Federation; and one Serb, directly elected from the Serb Republic. Elections will be in accordance with legislation of the Parliamentary Assembly, but the first elections, in September 1998, were held as agreed in Annexe 3 of the General Framework Agreement. The first elected Members will have a term of two years, but, thereafter, a Member's term shall be for four years. The Chair for the first term of the Presidency will be the Member to receive the largest number of votes, thereafter the method of selection must be determined by parliamentary legislation. A Presidency decision, if declared to be destructive of a vital interest of an Entity, can be vetoed by a two-thirds majority in the relevant body: the National Assembly of the Serb Republic if the declaration was made by the Serb Member; or by the Bosniak or Croat Delegates in the Federation House of Peoples if the declaration was made by, respectively, the Bosniak or Croat Members of the Presidency. The Presidency is responsible for the foreign policy and international relations of Bosnia and Herzegovina. It is required to execute the decisions of the Parliamentary Assembly and to propose an annual central budget to that body, upon the recommendation of the Council of Ministers.

The Chair of the Council of Ministers is nominated by the Presidency and confirmed in office by the House of Representatives. The post of Chair rotates between Bosniak, Croat and Serb representatives every eight months. Each appointed Chair of the Council of Ministers is to be from a different constituent people to the Chair of the Presidency. In addition, the Chair holds one of the six ministerial posts in the Council of Ministers. Other Ministers and Deputy Ministers are nominated by the Chair of the Council of Ministers, and also approved by the House of Representatives. The Council of Ministers is responsible for carrying out the policies and decisions of Bosnia and Herzegovina and reporting to the Parliamentary Assembly. There are also guarantees that no more than two-thirds of Ministers be from the territory of the Federation, and Deputy Ministers are to be from a different constituent people to their Minister.

Each Member of the Presidency has, *ex officio*, civilian command authority over armed forces. Each Member is a member of a Standing Committee on Military Matters, appointed by the Presidency and responsible for co-ordinating the activities of armed forces in the country. The inviolability of each Entity to any armed force of the other is assured.

Other Institutions and Provisions

Article VI is on the Constitutional Court, which is to have nine members, four selected by the House of Representatives of the Federation and two by the National Assembly of the Serb Republic. The three remaining judges, at least initially, are to be selected by the President of the European Court of Human Rights. The first judges will have a term of office of five years; thereafter judges will usually serve until they are 70 years of age (unless they retire or are removed by the consensus of the other judges). The Constitutional Court of Bosnia and Herzegovina is to uphold the Constitution, to resolve the jurisdictions of the institutions of Bosnia and Herzegovina and the Entities, to ensure consistency with the Constitution and to guarantee the legal sovereignty and territorial integrity of the country. Its decisions are final and binding.

The Central Bank of Bosnia and Herzegovina is the sole authority for issuing currency and for monetary policy in Bosnia and Herzegovina. For the first six years of the Constitution, however, it is not authorized to extend credit by creating money; moreover, during this period the first Governing Body will consist of a Governor, appointed by the International Monetary Fund, and three members appointed by the Presidency (a Bosniak and a Croat, sharing one vote, from the Federation, and one from the Serb Republic). The Governor, who may not be a citizen of Bosnia and Herzegovina or any neighbouring state, will have a deciding vote. Thereafter, the Governing Body shall consist of five members, appointed by the Presidency for a term of six years, with a Governor selected by them from among their number.

Article VIII concerns the finances of Bosnia and Herzegovina and its institutions. Article IX concerns general provisions, notably forbidding anyone convicted or indicted by the International Tribunal on war crimes in the former Yugoslavia from standing for or holding public office in Bosnia and Herzegovina. These provisions also guarantee the need for all public appointments to be generally representative of the peoples of Bosnia and Herzegovina. Amendments to the Constitution need a two-thirds majority of those present and voting in the House of Representatives.

The penultimate Article XI is on transitional arrangements provided for in an annexe to the Constitution. This is mainly concerned to legitimize the parallel competence of existing authorities and legislation until such time as the institutions of Bosnia and Herzegovina are properly established. A Joint Interim Commission is to co-ordinate the implementation of the Constitution of Bosnia and Herzegovina and of the General Framework Agreement and its Annexes. It is to be composed of four members from the Federation, three from the Serb Republic and one representative of Bosnia and Herzegovina. Meetings of the Commission are to be chaired by the High Representative of the International Community.

The Government

(May 2001)

HIGH REPRESENTATIVE OF THE INTERNATIONAL COMMUNITY IN BOSNIA AND HERZEGOVINA

Under the terms of the treaty and annexes of the General Framework Agreement for Peace in Bosnia and Herzegovina, signed in December 1995, the international community, as authorized by the UN Security Council, was to designate a civilian representative to oversee the implementation of the peace accords and the establishment of the institutions of the new order in Bosnia and Herzegovina.

High Representative: WOLFGANG PETRITSCH; 71000 Sarajevo, Emerika Bluma 1; tel. (33) 283500; fax (33) 283501; internet www.ohr.int.

BOSNIA AND HERZEGOVINA
Presidency

The Dayton accords, which were signed into treaty in December 1995, provide for a three-member Presidency for the state, comprising one Bosniak (Muslim), one Croat and one Serb. The Presidency has responsibility for governing Bosnia and Herzegovina at the state level. The Presidency was subsequently reconstituted to comprise a Chairman and a further two members, with the post of Chairman rotating every eight months between Bosniak, Croat and Serb representatives. The Presidency nominates a Prime Minister (subject to the approval of the legislature), who appoints a Council of Ministers.

Chairman of the Presidency: ZIVKO RADIŠIĆ (SPRS).

Member of the Presidency: BERIZ BELKIĆ (Party for Bosnia and Herzegovina).

Member of the Presidency: JOZO KRIŽANOVIĆ (SDP BiH).

Council of Ministers
(May 2001)

Prime Minister and Minister of the Treasury of the Institutions of Bosnia and Herzegovina: BOZIDAR MATIĆ.

Minister of Civil Affairs and Communications: SVETOZAR MIHAJLOVIĆ.

Minister of European Integration: DRAGAN MIKEREVIĆ.

Minister of Foreign Affairs: ZLATKO LAGUMDZIJA.

Minister of Foreign Trade and Economic Relations: AZRA HADZIAHMETOVIĆ.

Minister of Human Rights and Refugees: KRESIMIR ZUBAK.

There are, in addition, 12 Deputy Ministers.

Ministries

Office of the Presidency: 71000 Sarajevo, Musala 5; tel. (33) 664941; fax (33) 472491.

Office of the Prime Minister: 71000 Sarajevo, Vojvode Putnika 3; tel. (33) 664941; fax (33) 443446.

Ministry of Civil Affairs and Communications: 71000 Sarajevo, Vojvode Putnika 3; tel. (33) 786822; fax (33) 786944.

Ministry of European Integration: 71000 Sarajevo.

Ministry of Foreign Affairs: 71000 Sarajevo, Musala 2; tel. (33) 663813; fax (33) 472188; e-mail info@mvp.gov.ba; internet www.mvp.gov.ba.

Ministry of Foreign Trade and Economic Relations: 71000 Sarajevo, trg Oktobra bb; tel. (33) 445750; fax (33) 655060.

Ministry of the Treasury of the Institutions of Bosnia and Herzegovina: 71000 Sarajevo.

THE FEDERATION OF BOSNIA AND HERZEGOVINA

Following an agreement reached in Washington, DC (USA), by representatives of the Republic of Bosnia and Herzegovina and the 'Croat Republic of Herzeg-Bosna' (declared on 28 August 1993), the Federation of Bosnia and Herzegovina was formed on 31 March 1994. The President and Vice-President of the Federation were elected in May 1994. The Federation was reorganized as one of the two constituent entities of Bosnia and Herzegovina in the peace agreements of 1995.

President: KARLO FILIPOVIĆ (SDP BiH).

Vice-President: SAFET HALILOVIĆ (Party for Bosnia and Herzegovina).

Government
(May 2001)

Prime Minister: Dr ALIJA BEHMEN.

Deputy Prime Minister and Minister of Finance: Dr NIKOLA GRABOVAC.

Minister of Defence: MIJO ANIĆ.

Minister of Internal Affairs: MUHAMED BEŠIĆ.

Minister of Justice: ZVONKO MIJAN.

Minister of Energy, Mining and Industry: HASAN BECIROVIĆ.

Minister of Transport and Communications: BESIM MEHMEDIĆ.

Minister of Social Welfare, Displaced Persons and Refugees: SEFER HALILOVIĆ.

Minister of Health: ŽELJKO MIŠANOVIĆ.

Minister of Education, Science, Culture and Sport: Dr MUJO DEMIROVIĆ.

Minister of Trade: ANDRIJA JURKOVIĆ.

Minister of Physical Planning and the Environment: RAMIZ MEHMEDAGIĆ.

Minister of Issues of Veterans and Disabled: SUADA HADŽOVIĆ.

Minister of Agriculture, Water Management and Forestry: BEHIJA HADŽIHAJDAREVIĆ.

Ministers without Portfolio: MLADEN IVANKOVIĆ, GAVRILO GRAHOVAC.

Ministries

Office of the President: 71000 Sarajevo; tel. and fax (33) 472618.

Office of the Prime Minister: 71000 Sarajevo, Alipašina 41; tel. (33) 663649; fax (33) 444718; e-mail ebicakcic@fbihvlada.gov.ba.

Ministry of Agriculture, Water Management and Forestry: 71000 Sarajevo, Hamdije Kresevljakovica 3/III; tel. (33) 443338; fax (33) 663659; e-mail fmpvs@bih.net.ba.

Ministry of Defence: 71000 Sarajevo, Hamdije Kresevljakovica 98; tel. (33) 664926; fax (33) 663785; e-mail cabmod@bih.net.ba.

Ministry of Education, Science, Culture and Sport: 71000 Sarajevo, Obala Maka Dizdara 2; tel. (33) 663691; fax (33) 664381; e-mail fmonks@bih.net.ba.

Ministry of Energy, Mining and Industry: 71000 Sarajevo, Alipašina 41; tel. (33) 663779; fax (33) 642064; e-mail fmeri-mo@bih.net.ba.

Ministry of Finance: 71000 Sarajevo, Mehmeda Spahe 5; tel. (33) 2034117; fax (33) 203152; e-mail dcovic@fbihvlada.gov.ba.

Ministry of Health: 71000 Sarajevo, Titova 9; tel. and fax (33) 664245; e-mail moh@bih.net.ba.

Ministry of Internal Affairs: 71000 Sarajevo, Mehmeda Spahe 7; tel. (33) 667246; fax (33) 472976.

Ministry of Issues of Veterans and Disabled: 71000 Sarajevo, Alipašina 41; tel. (33) 212932; fax (33) 209333; e-mail fpurisevic@fbihvlada.gov.ba.

Ministry of Justice: 71000 Sarajevo, Valtera Perica 15; tel. and fax (33) 213151; e-mail zeljas@pris.gov.ba.

Ministry of Physical Planning and the Environment: 71000 Sarajevo, Marsala Tita 9A; tel. and fax (33) 473124.

Ministry of Social Welfare, Displaced Persons and Refugees: 71000 Sarajevo, Alipašina 41/II; tel. (33) 663977; e-mail povratak@bih.net.ba.

Ministry of Trade: Mostar, Kneza Domagoja 12; tel. (36) 310148; fax (36) 318684.

Ministry of Transport and Communications: 71000 Sarajevo, Alipašina 41; tel. (33) 668907; fax (33) 667866; internet www.fmpik.gov.ba.

SERB REPUBLIC (REPUBLIKA SRPSKA) OF BOSNIA AND HERZEGOVINA

On 27 March 1992 a 'Serb Republic of Bosnia and Herzegovina' was proclaimed. It was immediately declared illegal by the President of the State Presidency. The Republic comprised Serb-held areas of Bosnia and Herzegovina, including the 'Serb Autonomous Regions' of Eastern and Old Herzegovina, Bosanska Krajina, Romanija and Northern Bosnia. According to the peace treaty of December 1995, the Serb Republic constituted one of the two territorial entities comprising Bosnia and Herzegovina, with 49% of the country's area. It retained its own executive presidency, government and parliament (henceforth known as the National Assembly—see below).

President: MIRKO SAROVIĆ.

Vice President: DRAGAN CAVIĆ.

Government
(May 2001)

Prime Minister: MLADEN IVANIĆ.

Deputy Prime Minister: PETAR KUNIĆ.

Minister of Justice: BILJANA MARIĆ.

Minister of the Police: PERICA BUNDALO.

Minister of Education: GOJKO SAVANOVIĆ.

Minister of Finance: MILENKO VRACAR.

Minister of Defence: SLOBODAN BILIĆ.

Minister of Administration and Local Government: PETAR KUNIĆ.

Minister of Industry and Technology: PERO BUKEJLOVIĆ.

Minister of Health and Social Welfare: MILORAD BALABAN.

Minister of Energy and Mining: BOSKO LEMES.

Minister of Agriculture, Water Resources and Forestry: RAJKO LATINOVIĆ.

Minister of Transport and Communications: BRANKO DOKIĆ.

Minister of Science and Culture: MITAR NOVAKOVIĆ.

Minister of Trade and Tourism: ZELJKO TADIĆ.

Minister of Urban Planning, Utilities and the Environment: NEDJO DJURIĆ.

Minister of War Veterans and Casualties, and Labour Affairs: DRAGAN SOLAJA.

Minister of Foreign Economic Relations: FUAD TURALIĆ.

Minister of Refugees and Displaced Persons: MICO MICIĆ.

Minister of Religion: DUSAN ANTELJ.

Minister of Sports and Youth: ZORAN TESANOVIĆ.

Ministries

Office of the Prime Minister: 78000 Banja Luka; tel. (51) 46474; fax (51) 30103.

Ministry of Administration and Local Government: 78000 Banja Luka; tel. (51) 218641; fax (51) 218674.

Ministry of Agriculture, Water Resources and Forestry: 76000 Bijelina; tel. (51) 471412; fax (51) 472353.

Ministry of Defence: 78000 Banja Luka; tel. and fax (51) 12025.

Ministry of Education: 78000 Banja Luka, Vuka Karadžica 1; tel. and fax (51) 218287.

Ministry of Energy and Mining: 78000 Banja Luka, trg Srpskih Junaka 4/3; tel. (51) 15118; fax (51) 218657.

Ministry of Finance: 78000 Banja Luka, Vuka Karadžica 4; tel. (51) 17626; fax (51) 218634.

Ministry of Foreign Economic Relations: 78000 Banja Luka, Vuka Karadžica 4; tel. (51) 215651; fax (51) 217115; e-mail boda@blic.net.

Ministry of Health and Social Welfare: 78000 Banja Luka, Zdravke Korde 8; tel. (51) 36740; fax (51) 36472.

Ministry of Industry and Technology: 78000 Banja Luka; tel. (51) 218649; fax (51) 218657.

Ministry of Information: 78000 Banja Luka, Vuka Karadžica 4; tel. (51) 218816; fax (51) 218831.

Ministry of the Interior: Neznanih junaka, 76000 Bijeljina; tel. (65) 471633; fax (65) 472685.

Ministry of Justice: 78000 Banja Luka; tel. (51) 218835; fax (51) 218847.

Ministry of Refugees and Displaced Persons: 78000 Banja Luka, Kralja Petra I; tel. (51) 43224; fax (51) 17924.

Ministry of Religion: 78000 Banja Luka; tel. and fax (51) 17262.

Ministry of Science and Culture: 78000 Banja Luka; tel. (51) 17071; fax (51) 17003.

Ministry of Sports and Youth: 78000 Banja Luka; tel. (51) 18689; fax (51) 30103.

Ministry of Trade and Tourism: 78000 Banja Luka; tel. and fax (51) 12720.

Ministry of Transport and Communications: 78000 Banja Luka; tel. and fax (51) 18912.

Ministry of Urban Planning, Utilities and the Environment: 78000 Banja Luka; tel. (51) 39287; fax (51) 47218.

Ministry of War Veterans and Casualties, and Labour Affairs: 78000 Banja Luka; tel. (51) 17074; fax (51) 17003.

Presidency and Legislature

PRESIDENCY OF BOSNIA AND HERZEGOVINA

Election, 12–13 September 1998

	Votes
Bosniak Candidates	
Dr ALIJA IZETBEGOVIĆ (Party of Democratic Action)	511,309
FIKRET ABDIĆ (Democratic People's Union) . . .	36,446
SEFER HALILOVIĆ	33,680
HARIJA HALILOVIĆ	7,690
Croat Candidates	
ANTE JELAVIĆ (Croatian Democratic Union of Bosnia and Herzegovina)	189,408
GRADIMIR GOJER	n.a.
KRESIMIR ZUBAK (New Croatian Initiative) . . .	40,811
Serb Candidates	
ZIVKO RADIŠIĆ (Socialist Party of the Serb Republic)	360,286
MOMČILO KRAJIŠNIK (Serbian Democratic Party) . .	315,480
ZORAN TADIĆ	27,427

PARLIAMENTARY ASSEMBLY

The General Framework Agreement, signed in December 1995, provided for a Parliamentary Assembly of Bosnia and Herzegovina, comprising two chambers, the House of Peoples and the House of Representatives. In both houses two-thirds of the deputies were to be drawn from the territory of the Federation of Bosnia and Herzegovina, while one-third were to come from the Serb Republic.

Dom Naroda
(House of Peoples)

There are 15 deputies in the House of Peoples, of whom 10 are elected by the Federation legislature and five by the Serb Republic legislature.

Speaker: MOMIR TOSIĆ.

Zastupnièki dom
(House of Representatives)

Speaker: Dr SEAD AVDIĆ.

General Election, 11 November 2000

Party	Votes	% of votes	Seats
Social Democratic Party of Bosnia and Herzegovina	268,270	18.0	9
Party of Democratic Action	279,548	18.8	8
Serbian Democratic Party of Bosnia and Herzegovina	248,579	16.7	6
Croatian Democratic Union of Bosnia and Herzegoniva	169,821	11.4	5
Party for Bosnia and Herzegovina	168,995	11.3	5
Party of Democratic Progress of the Serb Republic	n.a.	6.4	2
Party of Independent Social Democrats	n.a.	5.1	1
Democratic Socialist Party			
Socialist Party of the Serb Republic	n.a.	2.6	1
Serbian People's Party of the Serb Republic	n.a.	1.9	1
New Croatian Initiative	n.a.	1.6	1
Democratic People's Union	n.a.	1.4	1
Patriotic Party of Bosnia and Herzegovina	n.a.	1.2	1
Democratic Party of Pensioners of Bosnia and Herzegovina	n.a.	1.1	1
Total*	1,491,101	100.0	42

* Including other parties.

ZASTUPNIÈKI DOM FEDERACIJE
(House of Representatives of the Federation)

Speaker: ENVER KRESO.

General Election, 11 November 2000

	Votes	% of votes	Seats
Party of Democratic Action	232,674	26.8	38
Social Democratic Party of Bosnia and Herzegovina	226,440	26.1	37
Croatian Democratic Union of Bosnia and Herzegovina	151,812	17.5	25
Party for Bosnia and Herzegovina	128,883	14.9	21
Democratic People's Union	17,999	2.1	3
Patriotic Party of Bosnia and Herzegovina	14,681	1.7	2
New Croatian Initiative	14,014	1.6	2
Pensioners' Party of the Bosnia and Herzegovina Federation	11,213	1.3	2
Bosnian Party	9,439	1.1	2
Croatian Rights Party	9,026	1.0	1
Democratic Party of Pensioners of Bosnia and Herzegovina	7,774	0.9	1
Liberal Democratic Party	7,441	0.9	1
Republican Party	5,301	0.6	1
Croatian Peasants' Party	3,948	0.5	1
Croatian Christian Democratic Union—Bosnia and Herzegovina	3,559	0.4	1
Civic Democratic Party	3,684	0.4	1
Party of Independent Social Democrats	n.a.	n.a.	1
Total*	867,712	100.0	140

* Including other parties.

PRESIDENCY OF THE SERB REPUBLIC (REPUBLIKA SRPSKA)

Election, 11 November 2000

Candidate	Votes	% of votes
MIRKO SAROVIĆ (Serbian Democratic Party of Bosnia and Herzegovina)	313,572	49.8
MILORAD DODIK (Party of Independent Social Democrats)	161,942	25.7
MOMČILO TEPIĆ (Party of Democratic Progress of the Serb Republic)	54,392	8.6
ZIJAD MUJKIĆ (Civic Democratic Party)	48,992	7.8
SLOBODAN POPOVIĆ (Social Democratic Party of Bosnia and Herzegovina)	37,614	6.0
ALJO DUGONJIĆ (Bosnian Party)	12,851	2.0
Total	629,363	100.0

NARODNA SKUPŠTINA REPUBLIKA SRPSKA
(National Assembly of the Serb Republic)

Speaker: DRAGAN KALINIĆ.

Election, 11 November 2000

Party	Votes	% of votes	Seats
Serbian Democratic Party of Bosnia and Herzegovina	224,562	36.0	31
Party of Independent Social Democrats	81,089	13.0	11
Party of Democratic Progress of the Serb Republic	76,147	12.2	11
Party of Democratic Action	47,254	7.6	6
Party for Bosnia and Herzegovina	32,305	5.2	4
Social Democratic Party of Bosnia and Herzegovina	31,774	5.1	4
Socialist Party of the Serb Republic	30,361	4.9	4
Democratic Socialist Party	25,899	4.2	4
Democratic People's League	22,012	3.5	3
Serbian People's Party of the Serb Republic	14,052	2.3	2
Pensioners' Party of the Serb Republic	8,315	1.3	1
New Croatian Initiative	4,533	0.7	1
Democratic Party of the Serb Republic	3,830	0.6	1
Total*	623,711	100.0	83

* Including other parties.

Political Organizations

Association of the Democratic Initiative of Sarajevo Serbs (Udruženje demokratske inicijative Srba iz Sarajeva): Sarajevo; f. 1996 to affirm and protect the rights of Serbs in Muslim-held Sarajevo; Chair. MAKSIM STANISIĆ.

Bosnia and Herzegovina Democratic Alternative: Sarajevo; f. 1990; Chair. MUHAMED CENGIĆ.

Bosnian Party (Bosanska Stranka): Tuzla, Stari Grad 9; tel. and fax (35) 251035; e-mail boss.bh@delta.com.ba; Chair. MIRNES AJANOVIĆ.

Bosnian Rights Party of Bosnia and Herzegovina (Bosanska Stranka Prava Bosne i Hercegovine—BSP BiH): Sarajevo.

Civic Democratic Party (Gradjanska Demokratska Stranka): Sarajevo, Maršala Tita 9A; tel. (33) 666621; fax (33) 213435; Chair. IBRAHIM SPAHIĆ.

Croatian Christian Democratic Union—Bosnia and Herzegovina (Hrvatska Kršćanska Demokratska Unija—Bosne i Hercegovine): 80240 Tomislavgrad; tel. and fax (80) 52051; e-mail bihdem@posluh.hr; internet www.posluh.hr; Pres. ANTE PASALIĆ.

Croatian Democratic Union of Bosnia and Herzegovina (CDU—BH) (Hrvatska Demokratska Zajednica Bosne i Hercegovine—HDZ BiH): 71000 Sarajevo, Titova 16; tel. (33) 471213; internet www.hdzbih.org; f. 1990; affiliate of the CDU in Croatia; adopted new party statute July 2000; Croat nationalist party; Chair. ANTE JELAVIĆ; Gen.-Sec. MARKO TOKIĆ.

Croatian Peasants' Party (Hrvatska Seljacka Stranka): Sarajevo, Radićeva 4; tel. and fax (33) 441987; affiliated to Croatian Peasants' Party in Croatia; Chair. ILIJA SIMIĆ.

Croatian Rights Party (Hrvatska Stranka Prava): Ljubuški, Fra Petra Bakule 2; tel. and fax (36) 834917; contested 1996 elections; nationalist; Pres. ZDRAVKO HRSTIĆ.

Democratic National Alliance: Banja Luka; f. 2000, by fmr mems of the Serb National Alliance (q.v.); Chair. DRAGAN KOSTIĆ.

Democratic Party for Banja Luka and Krajina: Banja Luka; f. 1997, by fmr mems of Serb Radical Party of the Serb Republic (q.v.); Chair. NIKOLA SPIRIĆ.

Democratic Party of Pensioners of Bosnia and Herzegovina (Demokratska Stranka Penzionera BiH): Tuzla, 6 Basanske 51; tel. (66) 151390; e-mail dsp.bih@bih.net.ba; Pres. ALOJZ KNEZOVIĆ.

Democratic Party of the Serb Republic (Demokratska Stranka Republike Srpske): Banja Luka.

Democratic Patriotic Bloc of the Serb Republic (Demokratski Patriotski Blok Republike Srpske): contested 1996 elections; Chair. PREDRAG RADIĆ.

Democratic People's League (Demokratski Narodni Savez).

Democratic People's Union (Narodna Demokratska Zajednica— NDZ): Velika Kladuša, D. Pucara Starog 23; tel. and fax (77) 770407; e-mail dnzbih@bih.net.ba; f. 1996; Chair. FIKRET ABDIĆ.

Democratic Socialist Party: Bijeljina; f. 2000, by fmr mems of Socialist Party of the Bosnian Serb Republic (q.v.); member of the Accord Coalition; Pres. NEBOJSA RADMANOVIĆ.

Eastern Bosnian Muslim Party (Istočnobosanska Muslimanska Stranka): Sarajevo; f. 1997; Chair. IBRAN MUSTAFIĆ.

Homeland Party: Banja Luka; f. 1996 by fmr members of Serb Democratic Union—Homeland Front; nationalist; Chair. PREDRAG RASIĆ.

Liberal Democratic Party (LDP) (Liberalna Demokratska Stranka): Sarajevo, Maršala Tita 9A; tel. (33) 664540; e-mail liberali @bih.net.ba; f. 2000 by merger of Liberal Party of Bosnia and Herzegovina and the Liberal Bosniak Organization; Chair. RASIM KADIĆ.

Liberal Social Party of Bosnia and Herzegovina (Liberalna Socijalna Partija—LSP): Sarajevo; f. 1998; centre party; Chair. HIDAJET REPOVAĆ; Deputy Chairs JADRANKA MIKIĆ, NAMIK TERZIMEHEC, VINKO CURO.

Muslim Democratic Alliance (Muslimanski Demokratski Savez— MDS): Bihać; f. 1994; seeks to promote equality between the ethnic groups of Bosnia and Herzegovina.

New Croatian Initiative (Nova Hrvatska Inicijativa): Sarajevo, Sime Milutinovića 2/II; tel. (33) 214602; fax (33) 214603; e-mail nhi@nhi.ba; f. 1998 by fmr mems of the Croatian Democratic Union of Bosnia and Herzegovina (q.v.); Chair. KREŠIMIR ZUBAK.

New Radical Party: member of the People's Alliance for Peace and Progress electoral coalition; Chair. GORAN ZMIJANAĆ.

Party for Bosnia and Herzegovina: Sarajevo, Maršala Tita 7A; tel. and fax (33) 214417; f. 1996; integrationist; member of the Coalition for a Single and Democratic Bosnia electoral alliance; Pres. Dr HARIS SILAJDŽIĆ; Sec. SAFET REDZEPAGIC.

Party of Democratic Action (PDA) (Stranka Demokratske Akcije—SDA): 71000 Sarajevo, Mehmeda Spahe 14; tel. (33) 667274; fax (33) 650429; e-mail sda@bih.net.ba; internet www.sda.ba; f. 1990; leading Muslim nationalist party; has brs in Yugoslavia; member of the Coalition for a Unified and Democratic Bosnia electoral alliance; Chair. Dr ALIJA IZETBEGOVIĆ; Deputy Chair. EDHEM BIĆAKĆIĆ, SULEJMAN TIHIC; Sec.-Gen. MIRSAD CEMAN.

Party of Democratic Progress of the Serb Republic (PDP): Banja Luka; Chair. MLADEN IVANIĆ.

Party of Economic Prosperity (Stranka Privednog Prosperita— SPP): Zenica; f. 1996; Chair. PANE SKRBIĆ; Sec.-Gen. SAFET REDZEPAGIC.

Party of Independent Social Democrats (Stranka Nezavisnih Socijaldemokrata—SNSD): Banja Luka; e-mail snsd@inecco.net; internet www.snsd.tripod.com; member of the Accord Coalition; Chair. MILORAD DODIK; Deputy Chair. DOBROSLAV CUK; Sec.-Gen. SLAVKO MITROVIĆ.

Party of Independent Social Democrats of the Serb Republic: f. 1999; breakaway faction of the Party of Independent Social Democrats; Leader BRANE MILJUS.

Party of Serb Unity (Stranka Srpskog Jedinstva): Bijeljina; extreme nationalist; Chair. (vacant).

Patriotic Party of Bosnia and Herzegovina (Patriotska Stranka BiH): Sarajevo, Hakije Kulenovića 9; tel. and fax (33) 216881; Pres. SEFER HALILOVIĆ.

Pensioners' Party of the Bosnia and Herzegovina Federation (Stranka Penzionera Federacije BiH).

Pensioners' Party of the Serb Republic (Penzionerska Stranka Republike Srpske).

People's Party of the Serb Republic (Narodna Stranka Republicka Srpska): Leader MILAN TRBOJEVIĆ.

Radical Party of the Serb Republic (Radikalna Stranka Republika Srpska).

Republican Party (Republikanska Stranka BiH): Sarajevo, Antuna Hangija 35, tel. and fax (33) 834917; e-mail republ94@bih .net.ba; integrationist; Chair. STJEPAN KLJUIĆ.

Serbian Civic Council: Sarajevo; anti-nationalist; org. of Serbs in the Federation of Bosnia and Herzegovina; Chair. Dr MIRKO PEJANOVIĆ.

Serbian Democratic Party of Bosnia and Herzegovina (SDP) (Srpska Demokratska Stranka Bosne i Hercegovine—SDS BiH): c/o Pale, National Assembly of the Serb Republic; f. 1990; allied to SDP of Croatia; Serb nationalist party; member of the Serb Coalition of the Serb Republic electoral alliance; Chair. ALEXANDER BUHA (acting); Deputy Chair. DRAGAN CAVIĆ.

Serb Democratic Union—Homeland Front: nationalist; Pres. BOŽIDAR BOJANIĆ.

Serb National Alliance (SNA) (Srpski Narodni Savez—SNS): Banja Luka; f. 1997; member of the Accord Coalition; Chair. Dr BILJANA PLAVŠIĆ.

Serb Patriotic Party (Srpska Patriotska Stranka): contested 1996 elections; Chair. STOJAN ZUPLJANIN; Vice-Chair. PETAR DJAKOVIĆ.

Serb Party of Krajina (Srpska Stranka Krajina—SSK): Banja Luka; f. 1996; regional party in favour of the creation of clear borders between nations; Pres. PREDRAG LAZAREVIĆ; Chair. of Exec. Cttee DJORDJE UMICEVIĆ.

Serbian People's Party of the Serb Republic (Srpski Narodni Savez): moderate; Pres. BILJANA PLAVŠIĆ.

Serb Radical Party of the Serb Republic (Srpska Radikalna Stranka Srpske Republike—SRS SR): internet www.srpskastrars .org; br. of SRS in Serbia; member of the Serb Coalition of the Serb Republic; Chair. MIRKO BLAGOJEVIĆ (acting); Vice-Chair. PANTELIJA DAMJANOVIĆ; Gen. Sec. OGNJEN TADIĆ.

Social Alliance: c/o 71000 Sarajevo, trg Dure Pucara bb; fmr communist mass organization; allies of Social Democratic Party; left-wing.

Social Democratic Party of Bosnia and Herzegovina (Socijaldemokratska Partija BiH—SDP BiH): 71000 Sarajevo, Branislava Durdeva 8; tel. (33) 203667; fax (33) 210942; e-mail sdp@ sdpbih-centar.com; internet www.sdpbih-centar.com; f. 1908; merged with Social Democrats of Bosnia and Herzegovina; Chair. Dr ZLATKO LAGUMDŽIJA; Sec.-Gen. KARLO FILIPOVIĆ.

Social Liberal Party: Banja Luka; reintegrationist; member of the People's Alliance for Peace and Progress electoral coalition; merged with the Party of Independent Social Democrats in Dec. 1999; Chair. MIODRAG ŽIVANOVIĆ; Gen. Sec. MILAN TUKIĆ.

Socialist Party of the Serb Republic (Socijalistička partija za Republiku Srpsku—SPRS): Kralja Petra 1 Karadorćevića 103/1; tel. and fax (51) 231643; e-mail sprs@inecco.net; f. 1993; br. of the Socialist Party of Serbia; member of the Accord Coalition until Feb. 2000; Chair. ŽIVKO RADIŠIĆ; Sec.-Gen. ŽELJKO MIRJANIĆ; 40,000 mems.

Yugoslav Left of the Serb Republic: Bijeljina; f. 1996; branch of pro-Communist party based in Belgrade (Yugoslavia); Pres. MILORAD IVOSEVIĆ.

Diplomatic Representation

EMBASSIES IN BOSNIA AND HERZEGOVINA

Austria: 71000 Sarajevo, Džidžikovac 7; tel. (33) 668337; fax (33) 668339; Ambassador: Dr VALENTIN INZKO.

Belgium: Sarajevo, Abdesthana 4; tel. (33) 532190; fax (33) 532125.

Bulgaria: Sarajevo, Trampina 14/11; tel. (33) 668191; fax (33) 668182; Ambassador: MARKO MARKOV.

Canada: Sarajevo, Logavina 7; tel. (33) 447900; fax (33) 447901; Ambassador: SERGE MARCOUX.

China, People's Republic: Sarajevo, Braće Begića 17; tel. (33) 215102; fax (33) 215108; Ambassador: WEN XIGUI.

Croatia: 71000 Sarajevo, Mehmeda Spahe 20; tel. (33) 444330; fax (33) 472434; Ambassador: DAMIR ZORIĆ.

Czech Republic: 71000 Sarajevo, Potoklinica 6; tel. (33) 447525; fax (33) 447526; Ambassador: JIŘÍ KUDĚLA.

Denmark: 71000 Sarajevo, Skenderija 4; tel. (33) 665901; fax (33) 665902; e-mail danamb@bih.net.ba; Ambassador: HENRIK WØHLK.

Egypt: Sarajevo, Nurudina Gackića 58; tel. (33) 666498; fax (33) 666499; Ambassador: HEDR SALAH ELASHRVI.

France: 71000 Sarajevo, Kapetanović Ljubušaka 18; tel. (33) 668149; fax (33) 668103; e-mail france-1@bih.net.ba; internet www.ambafrance.com.ba; Ambassador: BERNARD BAJOLET.

Germany: 71000 Sarajevo, Ulica Buka 11-13; tel. (33) 666584; fax (33) 652978; e-mail debosara@bih.net.ba; Ambassador: HANS JOCHIN PETERS.

Greece: Sarajevo, Obala Maka Dizdara I; tel. (33) 203516; fax (33) 203512; e-mail greekemb@bih.net.ba; Ambassador: PROCOPIOS MANTZOURANIS.

Holy See: Pehlivanuša 9, 71000 Sarajevo, Nadbiskupa Josipa Stadlera 5; tel. (33) 207867; fax (33) 207863; e-mail apnunbh@utic.net.ba; Apostolic Nuncio: Mgr GIUSEPPE LEANZA.

Hungary: 71000 Sarajevo, Hasana Bibera 53; tel. (33) 205302; fax (33) 205303; e-mail hung.emb@bih.net.ba; Ambassador: KÁLMÁN KOCSIS.

Iran: 71000 Sarajevo, Obala Maka Dizdara 6; tel. (33) 650210; fax (33) 663910; e-mail iries1@bih.net.ba; Ambassador: SEYED HOMAYOUN AMIRKHALILI.

Italy: 71000 Sarajevo, Čekaluša 39; tel. (33) 218021; fax (33) 659368; e-mail ambsara@bih.net.ba; Ambassador: ENRICO PIETROMARCHI.

Japan: Sarajevo, Mula Mustafe Bašeskije 2; tel. (33) 209580; fax (33) 209583; Ambassador: TAKASHIMA YUSHU.

Libya: 71000 Sarajevo, Tahtali sokak 17; tel. (33) 657534; fax (33) 663620; Head of People's Bureau: IBRAHIM ALI TAGIURI.

Macedonia, former Yugoslav republic: Sarajevo, Splitska 6; tel. (33) 206004; Chargé d'affaires a.i.: STOJAN RUMENOVSKI.

Malaysia: Sarajevo, UNIS Business Centre, Fra Andela Zvizdovića 1; tel. (33) 667712; fax (33) 667713; e-mail malsrjevo@bih.net.ba; Ambassador: ZAKARIA BIN SULONG.

Malta: 71000 Sarajevo, Mula Mustafe Baseskije 12; tel. and fax (33) 668632; e-mail lor.tac@tiscalinet.it; Ambassador: Dr LORENZO TACCHELLA.

Netherlands: Sarajevo, Obala Kulina Bana 4/2; tel. (33) 668422; fax (33) 668423; Ambassador: VALERIE STEFANIE MARIE SLUITER.

Norway: 71000 Sarajevo, Ferhadija 20; tel. (33) 666373; fax (33) 666505; Ambassador: KNUT MØRKVED.

Pakistan: 71000 Sarajevo, Emerika Bluma 17; tel. (33) 211836; fax (33) 211837; e-mail parep@bih.net.ba; Ambassador: Maj.-Gen. (retd) SYED ZAFAR MEHDI.

Romania: Sarajevo, Isaka Samokovlije 89; tel. and fax (33) 679344; Chargé d'affaires a.i.: Dr VASILE LECA.

Russia: Sarajevo, Kemal Begova 4; tel. (33) 668147; fax (33) 668148; Ambassador: FILIP FILIPOVICH SIDORSKII.

Saudi Arabia: Sarajevo, Koševo 44; tel. (33) 211861; fax (33) 211744; Chargé d'affaires a.i.: HAZEM KARAKOTLY.

Slovenia: 71000 Sarajevo, Bentbaša 7; tel. (33) 271260; fax (33) 271270; Ambassador: DRAGO MIROŠIĆ.

Spain: Sarajevo, Čekaluša 16; tel. (33) 278560; fax (33) 208758; Ambassador: JOSÉ ANGEL LÓPEZ JORRÍN.

Sweden: 71000 Sarajevo, Ferhadija 20; tel. (33) 276030; fax (33) 276060; e-mail ambassaden.sarajevo@foreign.ministry.se; Ambassador: HANS JORG KRETSCHMER.

Switzerland: 71000 Sarajevo, Josipa Štadlera 15; tel. (33) 665250; fax (33) 665246; Ambassador: WILHELM SCHMID.

Turkey: 71000 Sarajevo, Hamdije Kreševljakovića 5; tel. (33) 445260; fax (33) 472437; e-mail turksa@bih.net.ba; Ambassador: AHMET EROZAN.

United Kingdom: 71000 Sarajevo, Tina Vjevica 8; tel. (33) 444429; fax (33) 666131; e-mail fco.gov.uk; Ambassador: GRAHAM HAND.

USA: 71000 Sarajevo, Alipašina 43; tel. (33) 659969; fax (33) 659722; Ambassador: THOMAS MILLER.

Yugoslavia: Sarajevo; Chargé d'affaires a.i.: RADOSLAV JANKOVIĆ.

Judicial System

The judicial system in Bosnia and Herzegovina comprises a State Court and a Constitutional Court, which has three international judges (selected by the President of the European Court of Human Rights) and three national judges. The Constitutional Court has competence regarding constitutional matters in both entities, but there are separate judicial systems in the Bosnian Federation and the Serb Republic. In April 2000 the National Assembly of the Serb Republic passed legislation on the development of an independent judicial system.

Constitutional Court of the Republic of Bosnia and Herzegovina: 71000 Sarajevo, Save Kovačevića 6; tel. (33) 214555; nine mems; mems elected for five-year term; Pres. Dr KASIM TRNKA: Vice-Pres. (vacant).

Constitutional Court of the Serb Republic: Banja Luka; eight mems; Pres. RAJKO KUZMANOVIĆ; Sec. MIODRAG SIMOVIĆ.

Supreme Court of the Federation of Bosnia and Herzegovina: 71000 Sarajevo, Valtera Perića 15; tel. (33) 664754; Pres. VENCESLAV ILIĆ.

Supreme Court of the Serb Republic: Banja Luka; Pres. JOVO ROSIĆ.

Office of the Federal Prosecutor: 71000 Sarajevo, Valtera Perića 11; tel. (33) 214990; Federal Prosecutor SULJO BABIĆ.

Religion

Bosnia and Herzegovina has a diversity of religious allegiances. Just over one-half of the inhabitants are nominally Christian, but these are divided between the Serbian Orthodox Church and the Roman Catholic Church. The dominant single religion is Islam. The Reis-ul-ulema, the head of the Muslims in the territory comprising the former Yugoslavia, is resident in Sarajevo. Most of the Muslims are ethnic Muslims or Bosniaks (Slavs who converted to Islam under the Ottomans). There are, however, some ethnic Albanian and Turkish Muslims. Virtually all are adherents of the Sunni persuasion. There is a small Jewish community; since 1966, however, there has been no rabbi in the community. In June 1997 an agreement to establish an interreligious council was signed by the leaders of the Roman Catholic, Serbian Orthodox, Jewish and Islamic communities.

ISLAM

Islamic Community of the Sarajevo Region: 71000 Sarajevo, Save Kovačevića 2; Pres. of Massahat SALIH EFENDIJA COLAKOVIĆ; Mufti of Bosnia and Herzegovina Hadži MUSTAFA TIRIĆ; Reis-ul-ulema MUSTAFA EFENDI CERIĆ.

CHRISTIANITY

The Serbian Orthodox Church

Metropolitan of Dabrobosna: NICOLAJ; (c/o Serbian Patriarchate, 11001 Belgrade, Kralja Petra 5, POB 182, Yugoslavia).

The Roman Catholic Church

For ecclesiastical purposes, Bosnia and Herzegovina comprises one archdiocese and three dioceses. At 31 December 1998 adherents of the Roman Catholic Church represented about 16.2% of the total population.

Bishops' Conference (Biskupska Konferencija Bosne i Hercegovine): Nadbiskupski Ordinarijat, 71000 Sarajevo, Kaptol 7; tel. and fax (33) 472178; f. 1995; Pres. Cardinal VINKO PULJIĆ, Archbishop of Vrhbosna-Sarajevo; Vice-Pres. Rt Rev. FRANJO KOMARICA, Bishop of Banja Luka.

Archbishop of Vrhbosna-Sarajevo: Cardinal VINKO PULJIĆ, Nadbiskupski Ordinarijat Vrhbosanski, 71000 Sarajevo, Kaptol 7; tel. (33) 664784; fax (33) 472178.

JUDAISM

Jewish Community of the Sarajevo Region: 71000 Sarajevo, Hamdije Kreševljekoviće 59; tel. (33) 663472; fax (33) 663473; e-mail la-bene@open.net.ba; internet www.soros.org.ba; Pres. JAKOB FINCI.

The Press

In early 1997 145 publications, 92 radio stations, 29 television stations and six news agencies were in existence in Bosnia and Herzegovina.

PRINCIPAL DAILIES

Dnevni Avaz: 71000 Sarajevo.

Glas Srpski: Banja Luka; Serb Republic government newspaper; Editor-in-Chief TOMO MARIĆ; Deputy Editor-in-Chief NIKOLA GUZIJAN.

Horizont: Mostar; f. 1996; Croat independent.

Oslobodjenje (Liberation): 71000 Sarajevo, Džemala Bijedića 185; tel. (33) 454144; fax (33) 460982; e-mail info@obodjenje .net; f. 1943; morning; Editor MEHMED HALILOVIĆ; circ. 56,000.

Slobodna Dalmacija BH: 71000 Sarajevo; f. 1998; aimed at Croat population in Bosnia and Herzegovina; Exec. Editor ANTE SULJAK; Deputy Editor JOSKO DADIĆ.

Večernje novine: 71000 Sarajevo, Pruščakova St 13; tel. (71) 664874; fax (71) 664875; f. 1964; special edition published daily in Serb Republic; privatized in May 2000; Editor-in-Chief AHMED BOSNIĆ; Dir IRFAN LJEVAKOVIĆ; circ. 15,000.

WEEKLY NEWSPAPERS

Hratska Rijec: 71000 Sarajevo; Croat weekly.

Ljiljan: 71000 Sarajevo; official newspaper of the PDA; Chair. MENSUR BRDAR; Editor-in-Chief DŽEMALUDIN LATIĆ.

Nezavisne novine (The Independent): Banja Luka; f. 1995; Editor-in-Chief ŽELJKO KOPANJA.

Reporter: Banja Luka; independent; Editor PERICA VUCINIĆ.

Slobodna Bosna: 71000 Sarajevo, Muhameda Kantardžića 3; tel. (33) 444041; fax (33) 444895; e-mail slobo-bosna@zamir-sa.ztn.atc .org; Editor SENAD AVDIĆ.

PERIODICALS

Alternativa: Doboj; f. 1996; fortnightly; Editor-in-Chief PAVLE STANISIĆ; Deputy Editor-in-Chief ZIVKO SAVKOVIĆ; Dir SLOBODAN BABIĆ; circ. 5,000.

Dani: 71000 Sarajevo; e-mail bhdani@bih.net.ba; independent; political and cultural; 4 a week; Editor-in-Chief SENAD PECANIN.

Front Slobode: Tuzla; formerly Communist; became independent in 1993; 2 a week.

Novi prelom: Banja Luka; monthly.

Svijet: Sarajevo; illustrated; weekly; Editor-in-Chief JELA JEVREMOVIĆ; circ. 115,000.

Tuzla List: Tuzla; f. 1993; independent; regional political information.

Zadrugar: Sarajevo, Omladinska 1; f. 1945; weekly; journal for farmers; Editor-in-Chief FADIL ADEMOVIĆ; circ. 34,000.

NEWS AGENCIES

Alternativna Informativna Mreza (AIM—Alternative Information Network): Sarajevo; exchange of information between independent media in the former Yugoslavia; non-commercial and dependent on financial support from abroad.

BH Press: Sarajevo; state news agency.

HABENA: 88000 Mostar, Kralja Tvrtka 9; tel. (36) 319222; fax (36) 319422; e-mail habena@habena.ba; f. 1993; Bosnian Croat news agency; Man. MARKO DRAGIĆ; Editor-in-Chief ZDRAVKO NIKIĆ.

Novinska Agencija Bosne i Hercegovine: 71000 Sarajevo, Branilaca grada 21; tel. (33) 445336; fax (33) 445312; e-mail bhpres@bih.net.ba; internet www.bihpress.ba.

ONASA (Oslobodjenje News Agency): Sarajevo, Hasana Kikića 3; tel. (33) 276580; fax (33) 276590; e-mail onasa@onasa.com.ba; internet www.onasa.com.ba; f. 1994; Gen. Man. MEHMED HUSIĆ.

SNRA: Banja Luka; Bosnian Serb news agency; Man. Dir DRAGAN DAVIDOVIĆ.

Publishers

Novi Glas: 78000 Banja Luka, Borisa Kidriča 1; tel. (51) 12766; fax (51) 12758; general literature; Dir MIODRAG ŽIVANOVIĆ.

Public Company for Newspaper Publication Organization, Official Gazette of Bosnia and Herzegovina: Sarajevo, Magribija 3; tel. (33) 663470; e-mail slist@bih.net.ba; publishes legislation for official newspapers, and books and other material from the field of newspaper-publication activities.

Student's Printing House of the University of Sarajevo: Sarajevo, Obala Kulina Bana 7; tel. and fax (33) 526138; university textbooks; Dir EMIR KADRIĆ; Chief Editor DRAGAN S. MARKOVIĆ.

Svjetlost: 71000 Sarajevo, Petra Preradovića 3; tel. (33) 212144; fax (33) 272352; f. 1945; textbooks and literature; Dir SAVO ZIROJEVIĆ.

Veselin Masleša (Sarajevo Publishing): 71000 Sarajevo, Obala Kulina Bana 4; tel. (33) 521476; fax (33) 272369; f. 1950; school and university textbooks, general literature; Dir RADOSLAV MIJATOVIĆ.

PUBLISHERS' ASSOCIATION

Association of Publishers and Booksellers of Bosnia and Herzegovina: 71000 Sarajevo, M. Tita brigade 9A; tel. and fax (33) 207945; Pres. IBRAHIM SPAHIĆ; Gen. Sec. DRAGAN S. MARKOVIĆ.

Broadcasting and Communications

TELECOMMUNICATIONS

Director of Telecommunications: 71000 Sarajevo, Musala 2; tel. (33) 472657; fax (33) 441248; Dir EMIN SKOPLJAK.

Telekom Srpske: Banja Luka; Bosnian Serb telecommunications company; Deputy Dir-Gen. MILE BAJALICA.

BROADCASTING

In the late 1990s broadcasting in Bosnia and Herzegovina was largely controlled by the three nationalist parties: the Party of Democratic Action (PDA); the Croatian Democratic Union of Bosnia and Herzegovina (CDU—BH); and the Serbian Democratic Party (SDP). There were, however, a number of locally based independent radio and television stations. In May 1996 two such organizations, NTV Zetel and ITV Hayat (both television companies), had created, with the Mostar and Tuzla branches of Radio-Televizija Bosne i Hercegovine, the TVIN-TV International Network. This was to be open to media and correspondents from the Bosniak–Croat Federation and the Serb Republic, in accordance with the aims of the Dayton accords.

Regulatory Authority

Open Media Commission: Sarajevo; Dir-Gen. KRISTER THELIN.

Radio

Croat Radio Herzeg-Bosna: Mostar; Dir TOMISLAV MAZALO; Editor-in-Chief IVAN KRISTIĆ.

Open Serb Network (OSM): Pale; Editor-in-Chief MIRKO DESPIĆ.

Radio Kameleon: 75000 Tuzla, Milana Jovanovića 6; tel. and fax (35) 250055; e-mail kameleon@kameleon.ba; internet www.kameleon.ba; f. 1992; independent radio station; Gen. Dir ZLATKO BERBIĆ.

Radio-Televizija (RTV) Bosne i Hercegovine: 71000 Sarajevo, Bulevar Meše Selimovića 12; tel. (33) 455124; fax (33) 455104; f. 1945; 4 radio programmes; broadcasts in Serbo-Croat; Dir-Gen. JOHN SHEARER; Dir of Radio NADJA PAŠIĆ; Editor-in-Chief ESAD CEROVIĆ.

Radio-Televizija Republika Srpska (RTRS): Banja Luka; Editor-in-Chief DRAGOLJUB MILANOVIĆ.

Radio ZID: Sarajevo; f. Dec. 1992; commenced broadcasts March 1993; independent radio station; cultural and educative programmes; Chair. ZDRAVKO GREBO; Editor-in-Chief VLADO AZINOVIĆ.

Serb Radio Banja Luka: Banja Luka; f. 1997 as independent radio station following breakaway from Serb Radio and Television (q.v.); eight-mem. editorial council; Chair. RADOMIR NESKOVIĆ.

Studio 99: Sarajevo; f. 1991; independent radio station; broadcast political information during the civil conflict; Editor-in-Chief ADIL KULENOVIĆ; Editor of Programmes ZORAN ILIĆ.

Television

Independent TV Tuzla: Tuzla; f. 1991 by a group of journalists; promotes the values of democratic society.

ITV Hayat: Sarajevo; e-mail itvhayat@bih.net.ba; internet www.ntvhayat.com; Muslim influences; broadcasts 18 hours daily; Dir and Editor-in-Chief ELVIR SVRAKIĆ.

Konjic Radio-TV: Konjic; fmrly a public-service station, sold in April 2000; Owners ERMIN MUSTAFIC, ENES RATKUSIĆ.

NTV Zetel: Zenica; f. 1991; cultural, political, educative and sports programmes.

Radio-Televizija (RTV) Bosne i Hercegovine: 71000 Sarajevo, Bulevar Meše Selimovića 12; tel. (33) 652333; fax (33) 461569; e-mail radio@rtvbih.ba; internet www.rtvbih.ba; f. 1969; 2 TV programmes; Dir-Gen. JOHN SHEARER; Dir of TV AMILA OMERSOFTIĆ; Editor-in-Chief ESAD CEROVIĆ.

Radio-Televizija Republika Srpska (RTRS): Banja Luka; Editor-in-Chief DRAGOLJUB MILANOVIĆ.

Serb Radio and Television (SRT): Pale; Dir-Gen. SLAVIŠA SABLJIĆ; Editor-in-Chief DUSKO OLJACA.

Finance

(d.d. = dioničko društvo (joint-stock company); cap. = capital; res = reserves; dep. = deposits; m. = million; amounts in Yugoslav dinars unless otherwise stated; brs = branches)

BANKING

In 1999 there were 70 banks operating in Bosnia and Herzegovina, of which 55 were in the Federation and 15 in the Serb Republic. In the Federation 13 majority-owned banks controlled nearly 77% of total banking assets, while in the Serb Republic the four largest of the 11 majority-owned public banks controlled nearly two-thirds of all assets.

Central Bank

Central Bank of Bosnia and Herzegovina: 71000 Sarajevo, 25 Maršala Tita; tel. (33) 278100; fax (33) 201517; e-mail contact@cbbh.gov.ba; internet www.cbbh.gov.ba; replaced the National Bank of the Federation of Bosnia and Herzegovina, and the National Bank of the Republika Srpska, which ceased monetary operations in August 1997; Gov. PETER NICHOLL.

Selected Banks

Central Profit Banka d.d. Sarajevo: Sarajeva, Zelenih Beretki 24; tel. (33) 533688; fax (33) 663855; internet www.centralprofitbanka.com; cap. 17.7m. konvertibilna marka (1999); Gen. Man. FEHIM F. KAPIDŽIĆ.

Export Banka a.d., Bijeljina: Bijeljina, ul. Svetog Save br. 46; tel. (65) 401409; fax (65) 401410; f. 1992; Pres. JOVO STANKIĆ; Chair. SLAVKO ROGULJIĆ; Man. Dir MILADIN VIDIĆ.

Federation Investment Bank: 71000 Sarajevo, Igmanska 1; tel. (33) 277900; fax (33) 668952; e-mail info@ibf-bih.com; internet www.ibf-bih.com; Gen. Man. ASIM OMANIĆ.

Glumina Banka d.d. Mostar: Ljubuški, a Šimića b.b.; tel. (36) 835451; fax (36) 835450; e-mail glumba-ljubuski@int.tel.hr; f. 1996; cap. 41.0m., res 0.9m., dep. 305.8m. (Dec. 1997); Pres. ANTE ZDILAR; Gen. Man. LEON BEGIĆ.

Hrvatska Banka d.d. Mostar: 88000 Mostar, Kardinala Štepinca b.b.; tel.(36) 312121; fax (36) 312123; cap. 86.9m., res 0.1m., dep. 571.6m. (Dec. 1998); Pres. DRAGAN COVIĆ; Gen. Man. BERISLAV KUTLE.

Investiciono-Komercijalna Banka d.d., Zenica: 72000 Zenica, POB 62, trg Samoupravljača 1; tel. (32) 21804; fax (32) 417022; f. 1990; cap. 10.7m., res 24.4m., dep. 131.2m. (Dec. 1998); Gen. Man. UZEIR FETIĆ.

Privredna Banka Brčko d.d.: Brčko, Kralja Petra I Oslobodioca broj 1; tel. (49) 204222; fax (49) 204055; f. 1993; Pres. JOVICA SOPIĆ; Chair. MILAN KARANOVIĆ; Gen. Man. STOJAN MAJSTOROVIĆ.

Privredna Banka Gradiška d.d.: Gradiška, Vidovdanska bb; tel. (51) 813333; fax (51) 813205; e-mail pbgrad@inecco.net; f. 1953, registered as independent bank since 1992; privatization commenced in early 2001; cap. 5.9m., res 3.0m., dep. 53.2m. (Dec. 1998); Pres. STOJAN TODOROVIĆ.

Privredna Banka Sarajevo a.d.: ul. Srpskih Ratnika br. 14, Pale; tel. (33) 664852; fax (33) 663807; f. 1970 by merger of five banks; Man. Dir MOMČILO MANDIĆ.

Privredna Banka Sarajevo d.d., Sarajevo: 71000 Sarajevo, Alipašina 6; tel. (33) 209804; fax (33) 218511; f. 1971; cap. 3,713.1m., res 1,131.1m., dep. 35,471.6m. (Dec. 1990); Pres. and Gen. Man. MEVSUDIN DREKOVIĆ; 14 brs.

Razvojna Banka a.d.: 78000 Banja Luka, Bana Milosavljevica 4; tel. (51) 12012; fax (51) 17575; e-mail sdb@inecco.net; f. 1996; cap. 18m., res 4.6m., dep. 3.9m.; Gen. Dir RANKO TRAVAR; 12 brs.

Semberska Banka d.d., Bijeljina: Bijeljina, Karadjordjeva 3; tel. (65) 471588; fax (65) 472247; Pres. MILAN MIHAJLOVIĆ; Chair. ARSEN TEŠIĆ; Man. Dir CVIJETIN NIKIĆ.

Turkish Ziraat Bank Bosnia d.d.: 71000 Sarajevo, Strossmayerova 10; tel. (33) 230619; fax (33) 441902; e-mail ziraat@bin.net.ba; f. 1996; cap. 10.3m., dep. 11.3m. (Dec. 1998); Pres. METIN ERTÜRK.

Banking Agencies

Agency for Banking of the Federation of Bosnia and Herzegovina (Agencija za Bankarstvo Federacije Bosne i Hercegovine): 71000 Sarajevo, Ćemaluša 6/2; f. 1996; Dir ZLATKO BARŠ.

Banking Agency of Republika Srpska: Banja Luka, Marije Bursac 4; tel. (58) 218111; fax (58) 216675.

Trade and Industry

GOVERNMENT AGENCIES

Foreign Investment Promotion Agency: 71000 Sarajevo, Strossmayerova 3; tel. (33) 278000; fax (33) 278081; e-mail fipa@fipa.gov.ba; internet www.fipa.gov.ba; f. July 1999; provides services to foreign investors.

Privatization Agency of the Federation of Bosnia and Herzegovina: Sarajevo, Alipašina 41; tel. (33) 212884; fax (33) 212883; e-mail apfbih@bih.net.ba; internet www.apf.com.ba; Dir ADNAD MUJAGIĆ.

Republika Srpska Directorate for Privatization: 51000 Banja Luka, Mladena Stoganovića 4; tel. (51) 308311; fax (51) 311245; e-mail dip@inecco.net; internet www.rsprivatizacija.com; Dir BORISLAV OBRADOVIĆ.

Securities Commission of the Federation of Bosnia and Herzegovina: 71000 Sarajevo, Ćemaluša 9; tel. (33) 665897; fax (33) 211655; e-mail komvp@bih.net.ba; internet www.komvp.gov.ba; f. 1999; Pres. EDIB BASIĆ.

DEVELOPMENT ORGANIZATION

Federation Development Planning Institute: Sarajevo, Alipašina 41; tel. (33) 212884; fax (33) 212883; e-mail fzzprfbh@bih.net.ba.

CHAMBERS OF COMMERCE

Chamber of Economy of Bosnia and Herzegovina: 71000 Sarajevo, Branislava Durdeva 10; tel. (33) 663370; fax (33) 663635; e-mail cis@komorabih.com; internet www.komorabih.com; Pres. MENSUR SMAJLOVIĆ.

Chamber of Economy of Sarajevo Canton: 71000 Sarajevo, Hamdije Kreševljakovića 3; tel. and fax (33) 664597; e-mail webmaster@pksa.com.ba; internet www.pksa.com.ba; Pres. KEMAL GREBO.

UTILITIES
Electricity

Elektroprivreda of Bosnia and Herzegovina Ltd: 71000 Sarajevo, Vilsonovo šetalište 15; tel. (33) 472481; fax (33) 654266; e-mail b.edhem@ep.org.ba; internet www.eletroprivreda.ba; generation, transmission and distribution of electric energy; Dir-Gen. MEHO OBRADOVIĆ.

Gas

Bosnia and Herzegovina Gas (BH—Gas): Sarajevo, Hamdije Cemerlića 2; tel. (33) 279011; fax (33) 231621; e-mail bhgassa@bih.net.ba; internet www.bh-gas.ba; Dir MIRSAD HANOVIĆ.

TRADE UNIONS

Independent Union of Professional Journalists: Sarajevo; f. Dec. 1994; Chair. MEHMED HALILOVIĆ; Vice-Pres. BORO KONTIĆ.

Trade Unions of Bosnia and Herzegovina: Sarajevo, Obala Kulina Bana 1; tel. (33) 664872.

Trade Unions of Republika Srpska: Banja Luka, Srpska 32; tel. (58) 40711; fax (58) 34241.

Transport
RAILWAYS

At the beginning of the 1990s the railway system consisted of some 1,030 km of track, of which 75% was electrified. Much of the system was damaged or destroyed during the civil war, but in July 1996 the Sarajevo–Mostar service was restored and in 1997 the Tuzla–Doboj and Tuzla–Brčko services were reopened. Following the outbreak of hostilities, the state railway company was divided into three regional state-owned companies: the **Bosnia and Herzegovina Railway Company (ZBH)**, based in Sarajevo; the **Herzeg-Bosnia Railway Company (ZHB)**, based in the Croat-majority part of the Federation; and the **Serb Republic Railway and Transport Company (ZTP)**, based in Banja Luka. In March 2000 the presidents of Bosnia and Herzegovina and Croatia signed an agreement to recommence railway traffic between the two countries. By the end of that year post-war reconstruction assistance had resulted in the restoration of about 85% of track; however, regular train services between the Federation and the Serb Republic remained suspended.

ROADS

The transport infrastructure in Bosnia and Herzegovina was badly damaged during the civil war of 1992–95. Some 35% of the country's roads and 40% of its bridges were affected by the conflict. A new Transportation Corporation was established (with its headquarters in Sarajevo), under the terms of the Dayton accords, in order to organize and operate roads, ports and railways on the territory of the two entities. The agreement also provided for the construction of a new road linking the Goražde enclave, in the east of Bosnia and Herzegovina, with the rest of the Federation. There were 21,846 km of roads in Bosnia and Herzegovina in 1996, of which 3,722 km were principal roads and 4,104 km were secondary roads; 52.3% of the network was paved. In 1997 an internationally-funded project to rehabilitate and rebuild the road network in the Serb Republic commenced. In June 2000 the Governments of Bosnia and Herzegovina and Croatia signed an accord on the construction of the Ploče–Budapest corridor, linking the Croatian seaport with the Hungarian capital through Bosnian territory.

Transportation Corporation: Sarajevo; public corporation.

CIVIL AVIATION

The country has an international airport at Sarajevo, and three smaller civil airports, at Tuzla, Banja Luka and Mostar. Civil aviation was severely disrupted by the 1992–95 civil war. Commercial flights resumed to Sarajevo in August 1996, to Banja Luka in November 1997 and to Mostar in July 1998. In June 1997 it was announced that a new airport at Dubrave, near Tuzla, was to be built.

Department of Civil Aviation of Bosnia and Herzegovina: 33000 Sarajevo, Envera Sehovića 2; tel. (71) 653016; fax (71) 653008; e-mail bhdca@bhdca.gov.ba; internet www.bhdca.gov.ba.

Air Bosna: 71000 Sarajevo, 6 Cemalasa; tel. (33) 650794; fax (33) 667953; e-mail marketing@airbosna.ba; internet www.airbosna.ba; regular services to Croatia, Germany, Slovenia, Sweden, Turkey and the Federal Republic of Yugoslavia; Man. Dir OMER KULIĆ.

Air Srpska: 78000 Banja Luka; f. 1999; flights from Banja Luka airport to Yugoslavia.

Mast Air: 78000 Banja Luka; tel. (51) 304551; flights from Tuzla airport to Hungary, Italy, Slovenia and Turkey.

RS Airlines: Pale; f. 1997; flights from Banja Luka airport to Yugoslavia, Greece, Hungary, Romania, Bulgaria and Russia; Dir JOVAN TINTOR.

BOTSWANA

Introductory Survey

Location, Climate, Language, Religion, Flag, Capital

The Republic of Botswana is a land-locked country in southern Africa, with South Africa to the south and east, Zimbabwe to the north-east and Namibia to the west and north. A short section of the northern frontier adjoins Zambia. The climate is generally sub-tropical, with hot summers. Annual rainfall averages about 457 mm (18 ins), varying from 635 mm (25 ins) in the north to 228 mm (9 ins) or less in the western Kalahari desert. The country is largely near-desert, and most of its inhabitants live along the eastern border, close to the main railway line. English is the official language, and Setswana the national language. Most of the population follow traditional animist beliefs, but several Christian churches are also represented. The national flag (proportions 3 by 2) consists of a central horizontal stripe of black, edged with white, between two blue stripes. The capital is Gaborone.

Recent History

Botswana was formerly Bechuanaland, which became a British protectorate, at the request of the local rulers, in 1885. It was administered as one of the High Commission Territories in southern Africa, the others being the colony of Basutoland (now Lesotho) and the protectorate of Swaziland. The British Act of Parliament that established the Union of South Africa in 1910 also allowed for the inclusion in South Africa of the three High Commission Territories, on condition that the local inhabitants were consulted. Until 1960 successive South African Governments asked for the transfer of the three territories, but the native chiefs always objected to such a scheme.

Within Bechuanaland, gradual progress was made towards self-government, mainly through nominated advisory bodies. A new Constitution was introduced in December 1960, and a Legislative Council (partly elected, partly appointed) first met in June 1961. Bechuanaland was made independent of High Commission rule in September 1963, and the office of High Commissioner was abolished in August 1964. The seat of government was transferred from Mafeking (now Mafikeng), in South Africa, to Gaberones (now Gaborone) in February 1965. On 1 March 1965 internal self-government was achieved, and the territory's first direct election, for a Legislative Assembly, was held on the basis of universal adult suffrage. Of the Assembly's 31 seats, 28 were won by the Bechuanaland Democratic Party (BDP or Domkrag), founded in 1962. The leader of the BDP, Seretse Khama, was sworn in as the territory's first Prime Minister. Bechuanaland became the independent Republic of Botswana, within the Commonwealth, on 30 September 1966, with Sir Seretse Khama (as he had become) taking office as the country's first President, while the Legislative Assembly was renamed the National Assembly. The BDP, restyled the Botswana Democratic Party at independence, won elections to the National Assembly, with little opposition, in 1969, 1974 and 1979.

Khama died in July 1980, and was succeeded as President by Dr Quett Masire (later Sir Ketumile Masire), hitherto Vice-President and Minister of Finance. Following elections to the National Assembly in September 1984, at which the BDP again achieved a decisive victory, Masire was re-elected President by the legislature. However, the BDP fared badly in local government elections, which were held simultaneously with the parliamentary elections, apparently reflecting discontent at the country's high level of unemployment. An unprecedented outbreak of rioting, in March 1987, was similarly attributed by observers to popular dissatisfaction with the Government as a result of increasing unemployment; the Government accused the principal opposition party, the Botswana National Front (BNF), of fomenting the unrest. At a referendum in September a large majority endorsed amendments to the electoral system, as defined by the Constitution, although the BNF boycotted the vote.

Despite widespread labour unrest during 1989, in October the BDP received 65% of the votes cast at a general election to the National Assembly, winning 27 of the 30 elective seats (the remaining three seats were won by the BNF), and the new

legislature re-elected Masire for a third term as President. In November 1991 the Government dismissed some 12,000 members of public-service trade unions who had been campaigning for wage increases.

In March 1992 the Vice-President and Chairman of the BDP, Peter Mmusi, resigned as Vice-President and Minister of Local Government and Lands, while the party's Secretary-General, Daniel Kwelagobe, resigned as Minister of Agriculture, having been accused of corruption involving the illegal transfer of land. Festus Mogae, the Minister of Finance and Development Planning, was appointed as the new Vice-President. In June Mmusi and Kwelagobe were suspended from the Central Committee of the BDP; both were, however, re-elected to their former positions within the party at the BDP congress in July 1993. In 1993 it was revealed that seven government ministers were among the debtors of the National Development Bank, which was reported to be in financial difficulties. (In July 1995 the Minister of Presidential Affairs and Public Administration, Ponatshego Kedikilwe, was elected Chairman of the BDP—a post which had remained vacant since the death of Mmusi in October 1994.)

For the general election of 15 October 1994 the number of directly-elective seats in the National Assembly was increased to 40. The BDP, which received 53.1% of the votes cast, won 26 seats (three government ministers failed to secure re-election, and several members were returned with considerably reduced majorities), while the BNF, which obtained 37.7% of the votes, increased its representation to 13 seats. More than 70% of registered voters participated in the election. In general, the BDP retained its dominance in rural areas, while the BNF received strong support in urban constituencies. The National Assembly re-elected Masire to the presidency on 17 October. One week later the Assembly elected four additional parliamentary members. The new Cabinet, the composition of which was announced on the same day, included two of these, as well as Kwelagobe, who had been acquitted by the High Court in connection with the 1992 allegations.

Rioting, which had begun in January 1995 in Mochudi (to the north of Gaborone) following the release without charge of three people who had been detained on suspicion of involvement in a ritual murder, spread to the capital in February. One person was killed during three days of violent confrontations; shops were looted and government vehicles damaged. The BNF denied government assertions that it had incited the unrest, countering that the demonstrations reflected frustrations at the high level of unemployment and other social problems.

A number of constitutional amendments, which had been proposed during 1995–96, were adopted in August and September 1997. In August the National Assembly formally approved revisions restricting the presidential mandate to two terms of office and providing for the automatic succession to the presidency of the Vice-President, in the event of the death or resignation of the President. Further amendments approved by the National Assembly, reforming aspects of the electoral system, were endorsed in a national referendum in September. The reforms reduced the age of eligibility to vote from 21 to 18 years and provided for the introduction of votes for Batswana resident abroad, and for the establishment of an independent electoral commission; opposition parties had hitherto been critical of the prevailing system, whereby the election supervisor was an appointee of the President's office.

In November 1997 Masire announced his intention to retire from politics in March 1998; in accordance with the constitutional amendment adopted three months earlier, Vice-President Mogae was temporarily to assume the presidency pending the holding of elections in 1999. Mogae was inaugurated as President on 1 April 1998 and subsequently appointed a new Cabinet, in which the only new minister was Lt-Gen. Seretse Ian Khama, son of Botswana's first President (the late Sir Seretse Khama) and hitherto Commander of the Botswana Defence Force (BDF). Khama received the portfolio of presidential affairs and public administration, and was later designated as Mogae's Vice-President, subject to his election to the National Assembly. Kedikilwe, who had been favoured for the vice-presidency by certain prominent members of the BDP leadership, was appointed Minister of Finance and Development Planning. Khama was elected to the National Assembly in July, and was sworn in as Vice-President in the same month.

Meanwhile, hostility between Kenneth Koma, the leader of the BNF, and his deputy, Michael Dingake, had led to a split in the party. At the BNF's annual congress in April 1998 relations deteriorated over the issue of dissident members who had been expelled from the party. Koma, supported by the dissidents, ordered the expulsion from the party of central committee members. His actions were upheld by the party's constitution, and ultimately on appeal by the High Court. In June members of the dissolved central committee formed the Botswana Congress Party (BCP), under the leadership of Dingake. The BCP was declared the official opposition in mid-July, after 11 of the BNF's 13 deputies joined the new party.

In August 1999 President Mogae dissolved the National Assembly in preparation for the holding of a general election in mid-October. In early September, to the surprise and consternation of the opposition parties, Mogae declared a state of emergency, the purpose of which was to reconvene the legislature in order to amend the Electoral Act, thus permitting the Independent Electoral Commission (IEC) to complete its work and prevent the disenfranchisement of around 60,000 Batswana. The general election was held, as scheduled, on 16 October, despite opposition demands that it be postponed owing to the Government's apparent disregard for correct electoral procedure. The BDP, which received 57.2% of the votes, increased its representation in the National Assembly from 26 to 33 seats, while the number of seats held by the BNF (with 26.0% of the votes) fell significantly to only six seats, and the BCP (having received 11.9%) obtained just one seat. The IEC declared that the election had been conducted in a free and fair manner and recorded that 77.3% of the electorate had participated in the polls. Mogae was re-elected to the presidency by the new National Assembly on 20 October and announced the formation of a new Cabinet the following day.

In December 1999 Mogae provoked outrage among the opposition parties, and tension within the ruling party, when he granted Vice-President Khama an unprecedented one-year sabbatical leave, effective from 1 January 2000. In July Kedikilwe resigned as Minister of Education, a position he had held since October 1999. Khama resumed his duties as Vice-President in September 2000, and a minor cabinet reshuffle was effected.

The Government's attempts to relocate Bushmen from their homeland within the Central Kalahari Game Reserve to a new settlement outside the reserve provoked international concern in 1996–2000; it was claimed that officials had forced many Bushmen to move by disconnecting water supplies and threatening military intervention.

Although, as one of the 'front-line' states, Botswana did not have diplomatic links with the apartheid regime in South Africa, it was (and remains) heavily dependent on its neighbour for trade and communications. Botswana is a member of the Southern African Development Community (SADC—see p. 280), which superseded the Southern African Development Co-ordination Conference (SADCC), in 1992. The SADC, of which South Africa became a member in 1994, has its headquarters in Gaborone.

From independence, it was the Botswana Government's stated policy not to permit any guerrilla groups to operate from its territory. Relations with South Africa deteriorated in May 1984, when Masire accused the South African Government of exerting pressure on Botswana to sign a non-aggression pact, aimed at preventing the alleged use of Botswana's territory by guerrilla forces of the (then outlawed) African National Congress of South Africa (ANC). In the second half of the 1980s South African forces launched a number of raids on alleged ANC bases in Botswana, causing several deaths. Owing to Botswana's vulnerable position, however, the Government did not commit itself to the imposition of economic sanctions against South Africa when this was recommended by the SADCC in August 1986. In 1988–89 Botswana took action against the extension onto its territory of hostilities between South African government and anti-apartheid forces. Two South African commandos, who had allegedly opened fire on Botswana security forces, while engaged in a raid, were sentenced to 10 years' imprisonment; nine South Africans were expelled for 'security reasons', and five ANC members were convicted on firearms charges. It was reported in August 1989 that the South African army had erected an electrified fence along a 24-km section of the South Africa–Botswana border, in order to halt the reputed threat of guerrilla infiltration into South Africa via Botswana.

With the dismantling of apartheid in the first half of the 1990s, Botswana's relations with South Africa improved markedly and full diplomatic relations were established in June 1994. President Nelson Mandela of South Africa visited Botswana in September 1995; the need for the two countries to co-operate in combating crime was identified as a priority during discussions on issues of mutual concern. Meanwhile, in August 1994 it was announced that the 'front-line' states were to form a political and security wing within the SADC. In April 1999 Botswana and South Africa signed a bilateral agreement on the administrative merger of their adjacent national parks. The Kgalagadi Transfrontier Park was formally opened in May 2000 by President Mogae and President Thabo Mbeki of South Africa. In November 2000 the inaugural meeting of the Botswana-South Africa joint permanent commission on defence and security was held in Gaborone.

In August 1998 Botswana participated in attempts made by the SADC to resolve a political crisis in Lesotho, where opposition parties were demanding the annulment of elections held in May of that year. Following an increase in civil and military unrest and reports of an imminent coup attempt, on 22 September 200–300 members of the BDF and 600 South African troops entered Lesotho, in response to requests from the Prime Minister, Pakalitha Mosisili. The SADC-sponsored military intervention encountered strong resistance from dissident members of the Lesotho armed forces and civilians, who resented what was perceived as an unwarranted foreign invasion. After three days of heavy fighting and looting, in which more than 70 people died, relative calm was restored to the devastated capital, Maseru. In early 1999 the role of the BDF troops in Lesotho was the subject of debate in Botswana itself, and in May all the remaining SADC forces were withdrawn. A group of instructors from Botswana and South Africa remained in Lesotho, in an advisory and training capacity, until May 2000.

In 1983, following allegations that armed dissidents from Zimbabwe were being harboured among Zimbabwean refugees encamped in Botswana, the Botswana Government agreed to impose stricter restrictions on the refugees. In May Botswana and Zimbabwe established full diplomatic relations. The first meeting of the Botswana-Zimbabwe joint commission for co-operation was held in October 1984. A new influx of refugees, following the Zimbabwe general election in July 1985, threatened to strain relations between the two countries. In May 1988, however, Masire expressed confidence that the Zimbabwean refugees would return to their country as a result of an apparent improvement in the political climate in Zimbabwe. Nevertheless, in April 1989 about 600 Zimbabwean refugees remained in Botswana; at the end of that month the Botswana Government announced that refugee status for Zimbabwean nationals was to be revoked; by September almost all former Zimbabwean refugees had reportedly left Botswana. In the mid-1990s, however, the Government expressed concern at the growing number of illegal immigrants in the country, the majority of whom were from Zimbabwe; of more than 40,000 illegal immigrants repatriated during 1995, more than 14,000 were Zimbabwean. Relations between the two countries were again strained in 2000, when Zimbabwe's construction of a railway line from Bulawayo (its second largest city) to Beitbridge (on the border with South Africa) severely reduced transit freight traffic on Botswana Railways.

Following Namibian independence, in July 1990 it was announced that a commission for bilateral co-operation was to be established by Botswana and Namibia. In 1992, however, a border dispute developed between the two countries regarding their rival territorial claims over a small island (Sedudu-Kasikili) in the Chobe river. In early 1995 the two states agreed to present the issue of the demarcation of their joint border for arbitration at the International Court of Justice (ICJ, in The Hague, Netherlands), and in February 1996 the two countries signed an agreement committing themselves in advance to the Court's eventual judgment. Meanwhile, Namibia appealed to Botswana to remove its troops—stated by the Botswana authorities to be anti-poaching patrols—and national flag from the island. In the following month the two countries agreed joint measures aimed at deterring smuggling and illegal border crossings. None the less, what were perceived as attempts by Botswana to extend the role and capabilities of its armed forces remained a source of friction between the two countries, although Botswana emphasized that a principal aim of such expansion was to enable its military to fulfil a wider regional and international peace-keeping role. Namibia's decision to construct a pipeline to take water from the Okavango river caused some concern in Botswana in 1996–97. (The river feeds the Okavango delta, which is an important habitat for Botswana's varied wildlife, and therefore of great importance to the tourist industry.) In early 1997 it was reported that Namibia had been angered by Botswana's erection of a fence along Namibia's Caprivi Strip, which separates the two countries to the north; Botswana insisted, however, that the fence was simply a measure to control the spread of livestock diseases. In January 1998 an emergency meeting of the Botswana-Namibia joint commission on defence and security was held to discuss ownership of another island (Situngu) in the Chobe river, following allegations by Namibia that the BDF had occupied the island and was stealing crops planted by Namibian farmers resident there. In December 1999 the ICJ granted Botswana control over Sedudu-Kasikili. A joint technical commission was subsequently established to consider other demarcation disputes between Botswana and Namibia.

In late 1998 relations between the two countries were further strained by the arrival of refugees (a number of whom were reportedly leading political dissidents) in Botswana from the Caprivi Strip in Namibia. President Mogae rejected Namibian demands for the extradition of the refugees, whose number had increased to more than 2,000 by early 1999. In May, however, a formal agreement was signed by the two Governments under which prominent dissidents among the refugees would be allowed to leave Botswana for another country and an amnesty extended to other refugees returning to Namibia. In December 2000 a court hearing was scheduled to take place in Gaborone to consider a request from the Namibian Government for the extradition of a group of suspected Caprivi separatists who were wanted to stand trial for alleged high treason.

Government

Legislative power is vested in Parliament, consisting of the President and the National Assembly. The National Assembly is elected for a term of five years and comprises 40 members directly elected by universal adult suffrage, together with four members who are elected by the National Assembly from a list of candidates submitted by the President; the President and the Attorney-General are also *ex-officio* members of the Assembly. Executive power is vested in the President, elected by the Assembly for its duration. The President is restricted to two terms of office. He appoints and leads a Cabinet, which is responsible to the Assembly. The President has powers to delay implementation of legislation for six months, and certain matters also have to be referred to the 15-member House of Chiefs for approval, although this advisory body has no power of veto. Local government is effected through nine district councils and four town councils.

Defence

Military service is voluntary. In August 2000 the total strength of the Botswana Defence Force was some 9,000, comprising an army of 8,500 and an air force of 500. In addition, there was a paramilitary police force of 1,000. There are plans to enlarge the strength of the army to 10,000 men. Projected budgetary expenditure on defence for 2000 was P1,243m.

Economic Affairs

In 1998, according to estimates by the World Bank, Botswana's gross national product (GNP), measured at average 1996–98 prices, was US $4,795m., equivalent to $3,070 per head (or $5,796 on an international purchasing-power parity basis). During 1990–98, it was estimated, GNP per head increased, in real terms, at an average annual rate of 0.9%. Over the same period the population increased by an average of 2.9% per year. In 1999 GNP was estimated at $5,100m. ($3,240 per head). Botswana's gross domestic product (GDP) increased, in real terms, at an average annual rate of 10.3% during 1980–90 (one of the highest growth rates in the world), and by an average of 4.3% yearly in 1990–99. Real GDP growth in 1998/99 was 4.2%.

Agriculture (including hunting, forestry and fishing) contributed 2.9% of GDP in 1998/99, according to provisional figures, and engaged 15.6% of the employed labour force in 1996. The principal agricultural activity is cattle-raising (principally beef production), which supports about one-half of the population and contributes more than 80% of agricultural GDP. The main subsistence crops are vegetables, pulses and roots and tubers.

Botswana, which is not self-sufficient in basic foods, imported some 133,000 metric tons of cereals in 1993. According to the World Bank, agricultural GDP rose at an average annual rate of 0.3% in 1990–99. The GDP of the sector decreased by 3.0% in 1998/99, according to provisional figures.

Industry (including mining, manufacturing, construction and power) engaged 25.6% of the employed labour force in 1996 and, according to provisional figures, provided 49.2% of GDP in 1998/99. According to the World Bank, industrial GDP increased at an average annual rate of 2.8% in 1990–99. Industrial GDP declined by 0.8% in 1998/99, according to provisional figures.

Mining contributed 36.3% of GDP in 1998/99, according to provisional figures, although the sector engaged only 4.3% of the employed labour force in 1996. In terms of value, Botswana is the world's largest producer of diamonds (which accounted for 79.4% of export earnings in 1999, according to provisional figures); copper-nickel matte and soda ash are also exported. In addition, coal, gold, cobalt and salt are mined, and there are known reserves of plutonium, asbestos, chromite, fluorspar, iron, manganese, potash, silver, talc and uranium. In 1998 a new minerals code included measures to encourage non-diamond mining projects. According to provisional figures, the GDP of the mining sector increased, in real terms, at an average rate of 2.3% per year in 1990/91–1998/99. The GDP of the sector increased by 9.5% in 1997/98, but declined by 4.4% in 1998/99.

Manufacturing engaged 8.5% of the employed labour force in 1996 and provided 4.9% of GDP in 1998/99, according to provisional figures. Based on the gross value of output, the principal branches of manufacturing in the year to June 1994 were food products (accounting for 36.4% of the total), beverages (15.3%) and metal products, machinery and transport equipment (13.4%). The GDP of the manufacturing sector increased at an average rate of 3.5% per year in 1990–98; growth of 5.4% was recorded in 1998/99, according to provisional figures.

The services sector contributed 47.9% of GDP in 1998/99, according to provisional figures, and engaged 58.7% of the employed labour force in 1996. Within the sector, tourism is of considerable importance, and the tourist industry is the third largest source of total foreign exchange. According to the World Bank, the GDP of the services sector increased at an average annual rate of 6.3% in 1990–99. Growth was 8.8% in 1998/99, according to provisional figures.

Energy is derived principally from fuel wood and coal; the use of solar power is currently being promoted as an alternative source of energy. According to provisional figures, imports of fuels accounted for 4.9% of the value of total imports in 1999.

In 1998 Botswana recorded a visible trade surplus of US $77.5m., and there was a surplus of $170.1m. on the current account of the balance of payments. In 1999, according to provisional figures, countries of the Southern African Customs Union (SACU—see below) provided 76.6% of imports. European countries took 84.7% of exports in 1999; other important purchasers were the countries of SACU. The principal exports in that year were diamonds, vehicles and copper-nickel matte. The principal imports were machinery and electrical equipment, food, beverages and tobacco, vehicles and transport equipment, chemicals and rubber products, metals and metal products, wood and paper products, and textiles and footwear.

In the financial year to 31 March 2000, according to provisional figures, the central Government recorded a budgetary surplus of P1,611.4m. Botswana's external debt totalled US $548.2m. at the end of 1998, of which $508.2m. was long-term public debt. In 1998 the cost of debt-servicing was equivalent to 2.7% of the value of exports of goods and services. The average annual rate of inflation was 10.6% in 1990–99; consumer prices increased by an annual average of 7.2% in 1999. Some 19.6% of the labour force were unemployed in 1998.

Botswana is a member of the Southern African Development Community (SADC, see p. 280) and (with Lesotho, Namibia, South Africa and Swaziland) of SACU. In September 2000 the SADC implemented a free-trade agreement, whereby all trade tariffs between member countries were to be eliminated gradually over a 12-year period.

Botswana's high rate of growth during the 1980s was based predominantly on the successful exploitation of diamonds and other minerals. However, domestic factors, such as a vulnerability to drought, in conjunction with the world-wide economic recession of the early 1990s, depressed Botswana's economy and exemplified the need to reduce dependence on diamond-mining, to diversify agricultural production and to broaden the manufacturing base. By the mid-1990s, a return to growth had enabled the resumption of both public and private construction projects, which were expected to generate much-needed employment opportunities. The encouragement of private-sector growth, particularly in the manufacturing sector, was a key element of Botswana's eighth National Development Plan (1997/98–2002/03), which was presented in 1997 with the theme 'sustainable economic diversification'. Diamond exports declined in 1998, as a result of reduced demand from major Asian markets (most significantly Japan), which were experiencing an economic crisis, but recovered in 1999. The expansion of the Orapa diamond mine, which was completed in early 2000, was expected to double its annual output. However, Botswana's persistent dependence on the diamond sector has remained a source of potential weakness. In 2000, in an attempt to diversify the economic base and create sustainable employment, the Government introduced measures aimed at establishing the country as an international financial services centre for southern Africa; Botswana's proximity to South Africa, substantial tax incentives, and the stability of a well-established democratic system of government were all expected to aid the realization of this plan.

Social Welfare

Compared with those of many other countries of the region, Botswana's health services are well-developed. In 1997 there were 14 primary hospitals, six district hospitals, three mission hospitals, three mine hospitals, two national referral hospitals, one private hospital and one mental hospital. In addition, there were 209 clinics, 314 health posts and 687 mobile health stops. In that year 94 registered medical specialists, 292 medical officers, 34 dentists and 3,866 nurses were working in the country. Medical treatment for children under 12 years of age is provided free of charge. Old-age pensions for all persons over 65 years of age were introduced in 1996. Acquired Immunodeficiency Syndrome (AIDS) had reached epidemic proportions in Botswana by the mid-1990s and, according to UN estimates released in 1998, was projected to reduce life expectancy from 61 years in 1990–95 to some 41 years by 2000–05. The UN estimated that 35.8% of Botswana's adult population (aged between 15 and 49 years) was infected with Human Immunodeficiency Virus (HIV) at the end of 1999. Expenditure on health by the central Government in 1999/2000 was estimated at P576.0m. (equivalent to 5.0% of total government spending).

Education

Although education is not compulsory in Botswana, enrolment ratios are high. Primary education, which is provided free of charge, begins at seven years of age and lasts for up to seven years. Secondary education, beginning at the age of 13, lasts for a further five years, comprising a first cycle of three years and a second of two years. As a proportion of the school-age population, the total enrolment at primary and secondary schools increased from 52% in 1975 to the equivalent of 91% (boys 90%; girls 93%) in 1996. Enrolment at primary schools in 1997 included 96.7% of children in the relevant age-group (boys 95.7%; girls 97.7%), while the comparable ratio for secondary enrolment was 53.3% (boys 51.0%; girls 55.5%). By the late 1990s the Government provided universal access to 10 years of basic education. Botswana has the highest teacher-pupil ratio in Africa, but continues to rely heavily on expatriate secondary school teachers. In 1999 tertiary education was provided by 30 technical and vocational training centres, including health institutes, four teacher-training colleges, two further education colleges and a university (which was attended by 8,598 students in 1998).

According to estimates by UNESCO, the average rate of adult illiteracy in 1995 was 27.3% (males 30.0%; females 24.9%). Expenditure on education by the central Government in 1999/2000 was estimated at P2,580.3m. (representing 22.6% of total government spending).

Public Holidays

2001: 1–2 January (New Year), 13–16 April (Easter), 1 May (Labour Day), 24 May (Ascension Day), 1 July (Sir Seretse Khama Day), 15–16 July (for President's Day), 30 September (Botswana Day), 25–26 December (Christmas).

2002: 1–2 January (New Year), 29 March–1 April (Easter), 1 May (Labour Day), 9 May (Ascension Day), 1 July (Sir Seretse Khama Day), 15–16 July (for President's Day), 30 September (Botswana Day), 25–26 December (Christmas).

Weights and Measures

The metric system is in use.

Statistical Survey

Source (unless otherwise stated): Central Statistics Office, Private Bag 0024, Gaborone; tel. 352200; fax 352201; e-mail csobots@gov.bw; internet www.cso.gov.bw/cso.

Area and Population

AREA, POPULATION AND DENSITY

Area (sq km)	581,730*
Population (census results)	
16 August 1981	941,027†
21 August 1991	
Males	634,400
Females	692,396
Total	1,326,796
Population (official estimates at 19 August)	
1997	1,533,393
1998	1,571,728
1999	1,611,021
Density (per sq km) at August 1999	2.8

* 224,607 sq miles.
† Excluding 42,069 citizens absent from the country during enumeration.

POPULATION BY ADMINISTRATIVE DISTRICT
(August 1997 estimates)

Barolong . . .	19,837	Lobatse . . .	29,872
Central . . .	457,349	Ngamiland . .	62,403
Chobe . . .	16,845	Ngwaketse . .	143,370
Francistown . .	88,195	North-East . .	47,312
Gaborone . .	183,487	Okavango . .	41,687
Ghanzi . . .	27,099	Orapa . . .	10,244
Jwaneng . . .	14,866	Selebi-Phikwe .	45,651
Kgalagadi . .	34,537	South-East . .	54,091
Kgatleng . .	63,712	Sowa . . .	3,154
Kweneng . .	189,672		

PRINCIPAL TOWNS (estimated population, August 1999)

Gaborone (capital) .	202,680	Serowe . . .	32,940
Francistown . .	97,050	Mahalapye . .	31,865
Selebi-Phikwe . .	47,868	Lobatse . . .	31,323
Molepolole . .	45,811	Maun . . .	31,104
Kanye . . .	36,189	Mochudi . .	30,040

BIRTHS AND DEATHS (UN estimates, annual averages)

	1980–85	1985–90	1990–95
Birth rate (per 1,000) . . .	44.1	40.2	36.8
Death rate (per 1,000) . . .	9.5	7.7	8.0

Expectation of life (UN estimates, years at birth, 1990–95): 61.2 (males 59.5; females 62.9).

Source: UN, *World Population Prospects: The 1998 Revision*.

1999 (projected rates per 1,000): Birth 32.1; Death 10.6.

ECONOMICALLY ACTIVE POPULATION*
(sample survey, persons aged 12 years and over, year ending August 1996)

	Males	Females	Total
Agriculture, hunting, forestry and fishing	37,050	16,729	53,779
Mining and quarrying . . .	12,754	2,379	15,133
Manufacturing	14,157	15,373	29,530
Electricity, gas and water supply .	2,633	172	2,805
Construction	28,096	12,929	41,025
Wholesale and retail trade; repair of motor vehicles, motorcycles and personal and household goods	19,526	24,615	44,141
Hotels and restaurants . .	2,524	7,491	10,015
Transport, storage and communications	5,778	1,937	7,715
Financial intermediation . . .	1,781	2,315	4,096
Real estate, renting and business services	5,766	1,875	7,641
Public administration and defence; compulsory social security	37,928	22,029	59,957
Education	12,377	20,854	33,231
Health and social work . . .	2,096	7,280	9,376
Other community, social and personal service activities . .	4,330	2,977	7,307
Private households with employed persons	1,957	16,997	18,954
Extra-territorial organizations and bodies	197	27	224
Activities not adequately defined .	351	125	476
Total employed	189,301	156,104	345,405
Unemployed	45,461	49,067	94,528
Total labour force . . .	234,762	205,171	439,933

* Excluding members of the armed forces and those not actively seeking work.

Source: Labour Statistics Unit, Central Statistics Office.

Mid-1999 (estimates, '000 persons): Agriculture, etc. 314; Total labour force 703. (Source: FAO).

Agriculture

PRINCIPAL CROPS ('000 metric tons)

	1997	1998	1999
Wheat*	1	1	1
Maize	12	1	5†
Millet	2*	1	1†
Sorghum	17	9	13†
Roots and tubers* . . .	10	11	12
Pulses*	15	15	16
Cottonseed*	3	2	2
Cotton (lint)*	1	1	1
Vegetables*	16	15	16
Fruit*	11	8	10

* FAO estimate(s).   † Unofficial figure.

Source: FAO.

LIVESTOCK (FAO estimates, '000 head, year ending September)

	1997	1998	1999
Cattle	2,420	2,370	2,380
Horses	33	32	33
Asses	233	234	235
Sheep	250	240	250
Goats	1,870	1,820	1,835
Pigs	5	6	7

Poultry (FAO estimates, million): 3 in 1997; 3 in 1998; 4 in 1999.

Source: FAO.

LIVESTOCK PRODUCTS (FAO estimates, '000 metric tons)

	1997	1998	1999
Beef and veal	39	40	41
Goat meat	5	5	5
Poultry meat	9	10	10
Other meat	12	13	13
Cows' milk	102	100	102
Goats' milk	3	3	3
Cheese	3	3	3
Butter and ghee	1	1	1
Hen eggs	2	3	3
Cattle hides	5	5	5

Source: FAO.

Forestry

ROUNDWOOD REMOVALS ('000 cubic metres, excl. bark)

	1996	1997	1998
Industrial wood	99	102	103
Fuel wood	1,509	1,541	1,570
Total	1,608	1,643	1,673

Source: FAO, *Yearbook of Forest Products*.

Fishing

(FAO estimates, metric tons, live weight)

	1996	1997	1998
Tilapias	1,050	1,000	1,000
Other freshwater fishes	1,050	1,000	1,000
Total catch	2,100	2,000	2,000

Source: FAO, *Yearbook of Fishery Statistics*.

Mining

(metric tons, unless otherwise indicated)

	1996	1997	1998
Diamonds ('000 carats)	17,707	20,121	19,733
Copper*	20,979	18,350	19,432
Nickel*	17,461	14,996	15,593
Cobalt*	405	348	352
Soda ash	119,137	199,990	195,500
Salt	93,886	184,533	214,700
Coal	763,000	776,917	928,100
Clay (cu metres)	81,900	73,700	82,500
Crushed stone (cu metres)	845,526	1,091,877	997,244

1999 (metric tons, unless otherwise indicated): Diamonds ('000 carats) 21,348; Copper* 18,239; Nickel* 15,820; Cobalt* 329.

* Figures refer to the metal content of ores.

Source: The Mining Journal Ltd, *Mining Annual Review 2000*.

Industry

SELECTED PRODUCTS

	1995	1996	1997
Beer ('000 hectolitres)	1,366	1,351	1,005
Soft drinks ('000 hectolitres)	293	308	348
Electric energy (million kWh)	1,114*	807	925

* Provisional or estimated figure.

Source: UN, *Industrial Commodity Statistics Yearbook*.

Electric energy (million kWh): 1,608 in 1998; 1,817 in 1999.

Finance

CURRENCY AND EXCHANGE RATES

Monetary Units
100 thebe = 1 pula (P).

Sterling, Dollar and Euro Equivalents (29 December 2000)
£1 sterling = 7.997 pula;
US $1 = 5.359 pula;
€1 = 4.987 pula;
100 pula = £12.51 = $18.66 = €20.05.

Average Exchange Rate (pula per US $)
1997   3.6508
1998   4.2259
1999   4.6244

BUDGET (million pula, year ending 31 March)

Revenue*	1997/98	1998/99	1999/2000†
Taxation	6,766.1	5,636.5	10,467.7
Mineral revenues	4,681.1	3,186.6	6,699.9
Customs pool revenues	1,186.1	1,261.3	1,931.2
Non-mineral income tax	537.4	739.3	767.6
General sales tax	327.9	400.5	485.0
Other current revenue	1,401.8	1,900.3	1,909.5
Interest	257.1	208.6	207.3
Other property income	984.5	1,252.9	1,231.7
Fees, charges, etc.	133.5	378.0	417.7
Sales of fixed assets and land	32.5	60.8	52.8
Total	8,167.9	7,536.8	12,377.2

* Excluding grants received (million pula): 112.1 in 1997/98; 137.7 in 1998/99; 118.8 in 1999/2000.
† Provisional figures.

Expenditure*	1997/98	1998/99	1999/2000
General services (incl. defence)	2,027.9	2,485.5	3,164.4
Education	1,786.2	2,275.7	2,580.3
Health	411.2	468.4	576.0
Housing, urban and regional development	554.9	669.7	992.4
Food and social welfare programme	160.2	320.9	201.2
Other community and social services	131.4	270.4	424.8
Economic services	1,796.8	1,800.2	2,335.4
Agriculture, forestry and fishing	379.2	440.0	496.0
Mining	58.5	201.2	161.9
Electricity and water supply	704.4	451.1	654.0
Roads	321.8	390.9	590.1
Interest on public debt	86.2	94.6	100.6
Deficit grants to local authorities	567.5	706.5	872.4
Other grants	102.0	108.0	168.0
Total	7,624.3	9,199.3	11,409.9

* Figures refer to recurrent and development expenditure, excluding net lending (million pula): −218.1 in 1997/98; −134.3 in 1998/99; −46.7 in 1999/2000.

Source: Bank of Botswana, Gaborone.

INTERNATIONAL RESERVES (US $ million at 31 December)

	1997	1998	1999
IMF special drawing rights . .	40.96	45.63	38.50
Reserve position in IMF . . .	24.46	38.87	31.00
Foreign exchange . . .	5,675.00	5,940.67	6,229.21
Total	**5,740.42**	**6,025.17**	**6,298.72**

Source: IMF, *International Financial Statistics*.

MONEY SUPPLY (million pula at 31 December)

	1997	1998	1999
Currency outside banks . .	276	353	404
Demand deposits at commercial banks	762	1,160	1,371
Total money	**1,038**	**1,513**	**1,775**

Source: IMF, *International Financial Statistics*.

COST OF LIVING (Consumer Price Index; base: 1990 = 100)

	1996	1997	1998
Food (incl. beverages) . .	207.0	228.3	242.4
Clothing (incl. footwear) . .	219.1	239.9	254.4
All items (incl. others) . .	**199.8**	**217.2**	**231.4**

Source: ILO, *Yearbook of Labour Statistics*.

1999: Food 259.0; All items 248.0 (Source: UN, *Monthly Bulletin of Statistics*).

NATIONAL ACCOUNTS
(million pula at current prices, year ending 30 June)
National Income and Product (provisional)

	1995/96	1996/97	1997/98
Compensation of employees . .	3,990.7	4,486.3	5,337.8
Operating surplus . . .	7,221.4	9,560.0	11,141.6
Domestic factor incomes .	**11,212.1**	**14,046.3**	**16,479.4**
Consumption of fixed capital . .	1,972.3	2,268.5	2,479.8
Gross domestic product (GDP) at factor cost . . .	**13,184.4**	**16,314.7**	**18,959.2**
Indirect taxes	1,096.6	1,266.2	1,578.4
Less Subsidies	79.2	78.0	109.3
GDP in purchasers' values .	**14,201.8**	**17,502.9**	**20,428.3**
Factor income received from abroad . . . . . *Less* Factor income paid abroad .	−465.7	−685.1	−427.7
Gross national product . .	**13,736.2**	**16,817.9**	**20,000.6**
Less Consumption of fixed capital .	1,972.3	2,268.5	2,479.8
National income in market prices	**11,763.9**	**14,549.4**	**17,520.8**
Other current transfers from abroad . . . . *Less* Other current transfers paid abroad	−293.8	−61.1	−80.1
National disposable income .	**11,470.1**	**14,488.3**	**17,440.7**

Expenditure on the Gross Domestic Product (provisional figures)

	1996/97	1997/98	1998/99
Government final consumption expenditure	4,908.1	5,812.2	6,705.7
Private final consumption expenditure	5,410.5	6,587.8	8,673.2
Increase in stocks . . .	−162.5	699.5	1,730.8
Gross fixed capital formation .	4,176.5	5,047.1	6,433.8
Total domestic expenditure .	**14,332.6**	**18,146.6**	**23,543.4**
Exports of goods and services . .	9,988.0	11,359.7	9,863.9
Less Imports of goods and services	6,834.9	9,143.2	10,148.5
GDP in purchasers' values .	**17,485.7**	**20,363.1**	**23,258.9**
GDP at constant 1993/94 prices	**12,838.4**	**13,868.6**	**14,451.0**

Source: Bank of Botswana, Gaborone.

Gross Domestic Product by Economic Activity (provisional figures)

	1996/97	1997/98	1998/99
Agriculture, hunting, forestry and fishing	602.7	635.3	644.2
Mining and quarrying . . .	6,469.1	7,682.2	8,148.8
Manufacturing	866.1	988.2	1,093.6
Water and electricity . . .	316.0	366.3	440.8
Construction	1,016.5	1,152.7	1,382.3
Trade, restaurants and hotels .	2,046.1	2,313.4	2,750.6
Transport	686.5	791.5	946.6
Finance, insurance and business services	1,816.1	2,068.6	2,438.9
Government services . . .	2,473.1	2,908.9	3,722.1
Social and personal services . .	682.0	785.7	911.3
Sub-total	**16,974.2**	**19,692.8**	**22,479.2**
Customs duties	973.5	1,209.7	1,419.2
Less Imputed bank service charge .	462.1	539.3	639.6
GDP in purchasers' values . .	**17,485.7**	**20,363.1**	**23,258.8**

Source: Bank of Botswana, Gaborone.

BALANCE OF PAYMENTS (US $ million)

	1996	1997	1998
Exports of goods f.o.b. . . .	2,217.5	2,819.8	2,060.6
Imports of goods f.o.b. . . .	−1,467.7	−1,924.4	−1,983.1
Trade balance	**749.8**	**895.4**	**77.5**
Exports of services . . .	163.0	210.2	255.3
Imports of services . . .	−343.6	−440.7	−522.4
Balance on goods and services	**569.2**	**664.9**	**−189.6**
Other income received . . .	501.7	622.1	622.7
Other income paid . . .	−754.8	−766.9	−503.1
Balance on goods, services and income	**316.1**	**520.1**	**−70.0**
Current transfers received . .	355.4	456.8	460.9
Current transfers paid . . .	−176.6	−255.5	−220.8
Current balance . . .	**495.0**	**721.5**	**170.1**
Capital account (net) . . .	6.2	16.9	31.8
Direct investment abroad . .	1.1	−4.1	−3.5
Direct investment from abroad .	71.2	100.1	95.3
Portfolio investment assets . .	−35.5	−28.5	−42.8
Portfolio investment liabilities .	28.9	10.8	−14.1
Financial derivatives assets . .	n.a.	−15.4	5.2
Financial derivatives liabilities .	2.1	n.a.	n.a.
Other investment liabilities . .	70.3	109.3	68.2
Net errors and omissions . . .	−32.9	−108.9	63.0
Overall balance . . .	**510.7**	**635.1**	**62.6**

Source: IMF, *International Financial Statistics*.

External Trade

PRINCIPAL COMMODITIES (million pula)

Imports c.i.f.	1997	1998	1999*
Food, beverages and tobacco . .	1,083.0	1,247.4	1,411.6
Fuels	464.8	433.3	494.9
Chemicals and rubber products .	749.4	843.0	940.6
Wood and paper products . .	511.8	653.2	819.4
Textiles and footwear . . .	533.3	570.2	596.2
Metals and metal products . .	880.7	957.8	877.1
Machinery and electrical			
equipment	1,453.2	2,018.5	2,142.0
Vehicles and transport equipment	1,648.5	1,546.2	1,373.7
Total (incl. others) . . .	8,255.8	9,513.1	10,163.9

Exports f.o.b.	1997	1998	1999*
Meat and meat products . . .	231.4	298.5	223.4
Diamonds	7,670.0	6,040.5	9,706.4
Copper-nickel matte . . .	480.6	435.9	557.6
Textiles	248.4	302.6	248.5
Vehicles and parts . . .	1,182.7	965.7	666.8
Total (incl. others) . . .	10,390.7	8,696.9	12,227.5

* Provisional figures.

PRINCIPAL TRADING PARTNERS (million pula)

Imports c.i.f.	1997	1998	1999*
SACU†	5,981.6	7,111.4	7,783.1
Zimbabwe	368.1	374.6	396.6
United Kingdom . . .	162.6	350.5	272.5
Other Europe	580.0	643.7	664.3
Korea, Repub.	785.4	456.4	264.0
USA	89.1	134.5	188.0
Total (incl. others) . . .	8,256.0	9,513.1	10,163.9

Exports f.o.b.	1997	1998	1999*
SACU†	1,485.3	1,494.6	1,270.9
Zimbabwe	382.5	249.9	291.0
Other Africa	113.6	110.5	137.2
United Kingdom . . .	5,839.9	4,830.0	8,130.1
Other Europe	2,444.2	1,873.5	2,220.6
USA	101.8	90.0	86.5
Total (incl. others) . . .	10,390.7	8,696.9	12,227.5

* Provisional figures.
† Southern African Customs Union, of which Botswana is a member; also including Lesotho, Namibia, South Africa and Swaziland.

Transport

RAILWAYS (traffic)

	1996/97	1997/98	1998/99
Number of passengers ('000) . .	574	494	360
Passenger-km (million) . .	96	94	89
Freight ('000 metric tons) . .	1,967	2,568	2,812
Freight net ton-km (million) . .	795	1,111	1,282

Source: Botswana Railways.

ROAD TRAFFIC (registered vehicles)

	1996	1997	1998
Passenger cars	27,328	28,843	37,622
Lorries and vans	51,031	54,680	59,530
Buses	3,026	3,667	4,189
Tractors	3,455	3,669	3,357
Others	8,996	8,302	9,317
Total	93,836	99,161	114,015

CIVIL AVIATION (traffic on scheduled services)

	1995	1996	1997
Kilometres flown (million) . . .	2	2	2
Passengers carried ('000) . .	100	104	116
Passenger-km (million). . .	53	51	55
Total ton-km (million) . . .	5	5	5

Source: UN, *Statistical Yearbook.*

Tourism

FOREIGN TOURIST ARRIVALS

Country of origin	1996	1997	1998
South Africa	402,147	429,020	637,120
Zimbabwe	243,256	291,745	311,702
Total (incl. others) . . .	1,071,121	1,162,774	1,351,798

Receipts from tourism (US $ million): 162 in 1995; 181 in 1996; 184 in 1997 (Source: World Tourism Organization, *Yearbook of Tourism Statistics*).

Communications Media

	1994	1995	1996
Radio receivers ('000 in use) . .	180	190	230
Television receivers ('000 in use) .	24	27	29
Daily newspapers:			
Number	1	1	1
Average circulation ('000 copies)	35	45	40
Non-daily newspapers:			
Number	n.a.	5	3
Average circulation ('000 copies)	n.a.	79	51

Book production (first editions only, 1991): 158 titles, including 61 pamphlets.

Other periodicals (1992): 14 titles (average circulation 177,000 copies).

1997: Radio receivers ('000 in use) 237; Television receivers ('000 in use) 31.

Source: UNESCO, *Statistical Yearbook.*

Telephones ('000 main lines in use, year ending 31 March): 60 in 1995/96; 72 in 1996/97; 86 in 1997/98 (Source: UN, *Statistical Yearbook*).

Telefax stations (estimated number in use, year ending 31 March): 3,149 in 1995/96; 3,413 in 1996/97; 3,529 in 1997/98 (Source: UN, *Statistical Yearbook*).

Education

(1998)

	Institutions	Teachers	Students
Primary	721	11,617	323,348
Secondary	272	7,977	143,503
Brigades*	31	492	4,022
Teacher training	4	207	1,056
Technical education . . .	15	524	5,917
Colleges of education . . .	2	170	1,257
Agricultural college . . .	1	87†	392†
University	1	507‡	8,598

* Semi-autonomous units providing craft and practical training.
† 1997 figure.
‡ 1994 figure.

Source: Ministry of Education, Gaborone.

1999: *Primary:* 738 institutions; 11,864 teachers. *Secondary:* 270 institutions; 8,298 teachers.

Directory

The Constitution

The Constitution of the Republic of Botswana took effect at independence on 30 September 1966; it was amended in August and September 1997.

EXECUTIVE

President

Executive power lies with the President of Botswana, who is also Commander-in-Chief of the armed forces. Election for the office of President is linked with the election of members of the National Assembly. The President is restricted to two terms of office. Presidential candidates must be over 30 years of age and receive at least 1,000 nominations. If there is more than one candidate for the Presidency, each candidate for office in the Assembly must declare support for a presidential candidate. The candidate for President who commands the votes of more than one-half of the elected members of the Assembly will be declared President. In the event of the death or resignation of the President, the Vice-President will automatically assume the Presidency. The President, who is an *ex-officio* member of the National Assembly, holds office for the duration of Parliament. The President chooses four members of the National Assembly.

Cabinet

There is also a Vice-President, whose office is ministerial. The Vice-President is appointed by the President and deputizes in the absence of the President. The Cabinet consists of the President, the Vice-President and other Ministers, including Assistant Ministers, appointed by the President. The Cabinet is responsible to the National Assembly.

LEGISLATURE

Legislative power is vested in Parliament, consisting of the President and the National Assembly, acting after consultation in certain cases with the House of Chiefs. The President may withhold assent to a Bill passed by the National Assembly. If the same Bill is again presented after six months, the President is required to assent to it or to dissolve Parliament within 21 days.

House of Chiefs

The House of Chiefs comprises the Chiefs of the eight principal tribes of Botswana as *ex-officio* members, four members elected by sub-chiefs from their own number, and three members elected by the other 12 members of the House. Bills and motions relating to chieftaincy matters and alterations of the Constitution must be referred to the House, which may also deliberate and make representations on any matter.

National Assembly

The National Assembly consists of 40 members directly elected by universal adult suffrage, together with four members who are elected by the National Assembly from a list of candidates submitted by the President; the President and the Attorney-General are also *ex-officio* members of the Assembly. The life of the Assembly is five years.

The Constitution contains a code of human rights, enforceable by the High Court.

The Government

HEAD OF STATE

President: FESTUS G. MOGAE (took office 1 April 1998; sworn in 20 October 1999).
Vice-President: Lt.-Gen. SERETSE IAN KHAMA (sworn in 13 July 1998).

CABINET
(April 2001)

President: FESTUS G. MOGAE.
Vice-President: Lt.-Gen. SERETSE IAN KHAMA.
Minister of Presidential Affairs and Public Administration: THEBE MOGAMI.
Minister of Health: JOY PHUMAPHI.
Minister of Agriculture: JOHNNIE SWARTZ.
Minister of Foreign Affairs: Lt.-Gen. MOMPATI MERAFHE.
Minister of Minerals, Energy and Water Affairs: BOOMETSWE MOKGOTHU.

Minister of Commerce and Industry: TEBELELO SERETSE.
Minister of Local Government: MARGARET NASHA.
Minister of Works, Transport and Communications: DAVID MAGANG.
Minister of Finance and Development Planning: BALEDZI GAOLATHE.
Minister of Education: GEORGE KGOROBA.
Minister of Labour and Home Affairs: DANIEL KWELAGOBE.
Minister of Lands and Housing: JACOB NKATE.
In addition, there are four Assistant Ministers.

MINISTRIES

Office of the President: Private Bag 001, Gaborone; tel. 350800; fax 312525.
Ministry of Agriculture: Private Bag 003, Gaborone; tel. 350603; fax 356027.
Ministry of Commerce and Industry: Private Bag 004, Gaborone; tel. 3601200; fax 371538.
Ministry of Education: Private Bag 005, Gaborone; tel. 3655400; fax 3655458.
Ministry of Finance and Development Planning: Private Bag 008, Gaborone; tel. 350100; fax 356086; e-mail kbaleseng@gov.bw.
Ministry of Foreign Affairs: Private Bag 00368, Gaborone; tel. 3600700; fax 313366.
Ministry of Health: Private Bag 0038, Gaborone; tel. 352000; fax 353100; e-mail lmanthe@gov.bw.
Ministry of Labour and Home Affairs: Private Bag 002, Gaborone; tel. 611100; fax 313584.
Ministry of Lands and Housing: Private Bag 006, Gaborone; tel. 354100; fax 352382.
Ministry of Local Government: Private Bag 006, Gaborone; tel. 354100; fax 352091.
Ministry of Minerals, Energy and Water Affairs: Khama Crescent, Private Bag 0018, Gaborone; tel. 3656600; fax 372738.
Ministry of Presidential Affairs and Public Administration: Private Bag 001, Gaborone; tel. 350800.
Ministry of Works, Transport and Communications: Private Bag 007, Gaborone; tel. 358500; and fax 313303.

Legislature

HOUSE OF CHIEFS

The House has a total of 15 members.
Chairman: Chief TAWANA II.

NATIONAL ASSEMBLY

Speaker: RAY MATLAPENG MOLOMO.

General Election, 16 October 1999

Party	Votes	%	Seats
Botswana Democratic Party	192,598	57.2	33
Botswana National Front	87,457	26.0	6
Botswana Congress Party	40,096	11.9	1
Botswana Alliance Movement	15,805	4.7	—
Others	1,026	0.3	—
Total	336,982	100.0	40*

* The President and the Attorney-General are also *ex-officio* members of the National Assembly.

Political Organizations

Botswana Alliance Movement (BAM): Private Bag BO 210, Gaborone; tel. 313476; fax 314634; f. 1998 as an alliance of three opposition parties to contest the 1999 general election; Botswana People's Party withdrew in July 2000; Leader LEPETU SETSHWAELO.

Independence Freedom Party (IFP): POB 3, Maun; f. by merger of Botswana Freedom Party and Botswana Independence Party; Pres. MOTSAMAI K. MPHO.

United Action Party (UAP): Private Bag BO 210, Gaborone; f. 1998; Leader LEPETU SETSHWAELO.

Botswana Congress Party (BCP): POB 2918, Gaborone; tel. and fax 581805; f. 1998, following a split in the Botswana National Front; Leader MICHAEL DINGAKE.

Botswana Democratic Party (BDP): POB 28, Tsholetsa House, Gaborone; tel. 352564; fax 313911; e-mail domkrag@info.bw; f. 1962; Pres. FESTUS G. MOGAE; Chair. PONATSHEGO KEDIKILWE; Sec.-Gen. DANIEL K. KWELAGOBE.

Botswana Labour Party: POB 140, Mahalapye; f. 1989; Pres. LENYELETSE KOMA.

Botswana National Front (BNF): POB 1720, Gaborone; tel. 351789; fax 584970; f. 1966; Pres. Dr KENNETH KOMA; Sec.-Gen. Dr BADZIYILI NFILA.

Botswana People's Party (BPP): POB 484, Francistown; f. 1960; Pres. MOTLATSI MOLAPISI; Chair. JOSEPH MOGOTLE; Sec.-Gen. KOPANO CHINGAPANE.

Botswana Progressive Union (BPU): POB 328, Nkange; f. 1982; Leader G. KAELO.

Botswana Workers' Front (BWF): POB 597, Jwaneng; tel. 380420; f. 1993; Leader M. M. AKANYANG.

MELS Movement of Botswana: POB 501818, Gaborone; tel. and fax 306005; f. 1993; Leader T. JOINA.

Social Democratic Party (SDP): POB 201818, Gaborone; tel. 356516; f. 1994; Leader Ms O. MARUMO.

United Socialist Party (USP): POB 233, Lobatse; f. 1994; Leader N. MODUBULE.

Diplomatic Representation

EMBASSIES AND HIGH COMMISSIONS IN BOTSWANA

Angola: 5131 Kopanyo House, Nelson Mandela Dr., Private Bag BR 111, Gaborone; tel. 300204; fax 375089; Ambassador: EVARISTO DOMINGOS KIMBA.

China, People's Republic: 3096 North Ring Rd, POB 1031, Gaborone; tel. 352209; fax 300156; e-mail chnemb@info.bw; Ambassador: BAO SHUSHENG.

Cuba: Plot 5158, Gaborone; tel. 351750; fax 311485; Ambassador: ANA VILMA VALLEJERA.

Germany: Professional House, Broadhurst, Segodithsane Way, POB 315, Gaborone; tel. 353143; fax 353038; Ambassador: Dr IRENE HINRICHSEN.

India: 5375 President's Dr., Private Bag 249, Gaborone; tel. 372676; fax 374636; e-mail hicomind@global.bw; High Commissioner: RAJEET MITTER.

Kenya: Plot 5373, President's Dr., Private Bag 0297, Gaborone; tel. 351408; fax 351409; e-mail kenya@info.bw; High Commissioner: RICHARD OKWARO.

Libya: POB 180, Plot 8851 (Government Enclave), Gaborone; tel. 352481; Ambassador: JUMA MOHAMED JUBAIL.

Namibia: POB 987, Plot 186, Morara Close, Gaborone; tel. 302181; fax 302248; e-mail nhc.gabs@info.bw; High Commissioner: JOSUA HOEBEB.

Nigeria: POB 274, The Mall, Gaborone; tel. 313561; fax 313738; High Commissioner: Ms HARRISON-OBAFEMI.

Russia: Plot 4711, Tawana Close, POB 81, Gaborone; tel. 353389; fax 352930; e-mail embarus@info.bw; Ambassador: VALERII A. KALUGIN.

South Africa: Private Bag 00402, Kopanyo House, Plot 5131, Nelson Mandela Dr., Gaborone; tel. 304800; fax 305501; High Commissioner: (vacant).

Sweden: Development House, Private Bag 0017, Gaborone; tel. 353912; fax 353942; e-mail ambassaden.gaborone@foreign.ministry.se Ambassador: CHRISTINA REHLEN.

United Kingdom: Private Bag 0023, Gaborone; tel. 352841; fax 356105; e-mail british@bc.bw; internet www.british.global.bw; High Commissioner: JOHN WILDE.

USA: POB 90, Gaborone; tel. 353982; fax 356947; Ambassador: Dr JOHN E. LANGE.

Zambia: POB 362, Gaborone; tel. 351951; fax 353952; High Commissioner: J. PHIRI.

Zimbabwe: Plot 8850, POB 1232, Gaborone; tel. 314495; fax 305863; High Commissioner: Z. W. NSIMBI.

Judicial System

There is a High Court at Lobatse and a branch at Francistown, and Magistrates' Courts in each district. Appeals lie to the Court of Appeal of Botswana. The Chief Justice and the President of the Court of Appeal are appointed by the President.

High Court: Private Bag 1, Lobatse; tel. 330396; fax 332317.
Chief Justice: JULIAN NGANUNU.
President of the Court of Appeal: A. N. E. AMISSAH.
Justices of Appeal: T. A. AGUDA, W. H. R. SCHREINER, J. STEYN, P. H. TEBBUTT, W. COWIE, G. G. HOEXTER, W. ALLANBRIDGE.
Puisne Judges: I. R. ABOAGYE, J. B. GITTINGS, M. DIBOTELO, M. GAEFELE, J. Z. MASOJANE, I. K. B. LESETEDI (acting).
Registrar and Master: W. G. GRANTE.
Office of the Attorney-General: Private Bag 009, Gaborone; tel. 354700; fax 357089.
Attorney-General: PHANDU SKELEMANI.

Religion

The majority of the population hold animist beliefs; an estimated 30% are thought to be Christians. There are Islamic mosques in Gaborone and Lobatse. The Bahá'í Faith is also represented.

CHRISTIANITY

Lekgotla la Sekeresete la Botswana (Botswana Christian Council): POB 355, Gaborone; tel. 351981; f. 1966; comprises 34 churches and organizations; Pres. Rev. K. F. MOKOBIJ; Gen. Sec. DAVID J. MODIEGA.

The Anglican Communion

Anglicans are adherents of the Church of the Province of Central Africa, comprising 12 dioceses and covering Botswana, Malawi, Zambia and Zimbabwe. The Province was established in 1955, and the diocese of Botswana was formed in 1972.

Archbishop of the Province of Central Africa and Bishop of Botswana: Most Rev. WALTER PAUL KHOTSO MAKHULU, POB 769, Gaborone; fax 313015; e-mail acenter@info.bw.

Protestant Churches

African Methodist Episcopal Church: POB 141, Lobatse; Rev. L. M. MBULAWA.

Evangelical Lutheran Church in Botswana: POB 1976, Gaborone; tel. 352227; fax 313966; Bishop Rev. PHILIP ROBINSON; 16,305 mems.

Evangelical Lutheran Church in Southern Africa (Botswana Diocese): POB 400, Gaborone; tel. 353976; Bishop Rev. M. NTUPING.

Methodist Church in Botswana: POB 260, Gaborone; Dist. Supt Rev. Z. S. M. MOSAI.

United Congregational Church of Southern Africa (Synod of Botswana): POB 1263, Gaborone; tel. 352491; Synod status since 1980; Chair. Rev. D. T. MAPITSE; Sec. Rev. M. P. P. DIBEELA; 24,000 mems.

Other denominations active in Botswana include the Church of God in Christ, the Dutch Reformed Church, the United Methodist Church and the Seventh-day Adventists.

The Roman Catholic Church

Botswana comprises one diocese and an apostolic vicariate. The metropolitan see is Bloemfontein, South Africa. The church was established in Botswana in 1928, and had an estimated 76,587 adherents (some 5.5% of the total population) in the country at 31 December 1998. The Bishop participates in the Southern African Catholic Bishops' Conference, currently based in Pretoria, South Africa.

Bishop of Gaborone: Rt Rev. BONIFACE TSHOSA SETLALEKGOSI, POB 218, Bishop's House, Gaborone; tel. 312958; fax 356970.

Vicar Apostolic of Francistown: Rt Rev. FRANKLYN NUBUASAH.

The Press

DAILY NEWSPAPER

Dikgang tsa Gompieno (Daily News): Private Bag 0060, Gaborone; tel. 352541; f. 1964; publ. by Dept of Information and Broadcasting; Setswana and English; Mon.–Fri.; Editor LAMONG LESHAGA; circ. 40,000.

PERIODICALS

Agrinews: Private Bag 003, Gaborone; f. 1971; monthly; agriculture and rural development; circ. 6,000.

Botswana Advertiser: POB 130, 5647 Nakedi Rd, Broadhurst, Gaborone; tel. 312844; weekly.

Botswana Business Month Magazine: POB 1605, Gaborone; fax 312774; bimonthly; Editor CLARA OLSEN; circ. 500.

Botswana Business News: Private Bag 00367, Gaborone; fax 305375; monthly; publ. by Ministry of Commerce and Industry; Editors MUKRAM SHEIKH, MONTY LETSHWITI; circ. 3,000.

The Botswana Gazette: Private Bag 0081, Gaborone; tel. 312833; fax 312774; weekly; Editor ALFRED P. MULENGA; circ. 14,000.

Botswana Guardian: POB 1641, Gaborone; tel. 308408; fax 308457; e-mail guardsun@info.bw; f. 1982; weekly; Editor OUTSA MOKONE; circ. 20,792.

Business and Financial Times: POB 402396, Gaborone; tel. 586397; fax 561700; e-mail bftimes@info.bw.

Government Gazette: Private Bag 0081, Gaborone; tel. 314441; fax 312001; weekly.

Kutlwano: Private Bag 0060, Gaborone; tel. 352541; fax 352971; monthly; Setswana and English; publ. by Dept of Information and Broadcasting; Editor RUSS MOLOSIWA; circ. 24,000.

The Midweek Sun: POB 1641, Gaborone; tel. 308408; fax 308457; e-mail guardsun@info.bw; f. 1989; weekly; Editor MIKE MOTHIBI; circ. 18,108.

Mmegi/The Reporter: Private Bag BR50, Gaborone; tel. 374784; fax 305508; e-mail mmegi@info.bw; internet www.mmegi.bw; f. 1984; weekly; Setswana and English; publ. by Dikgang Publishing Co; Man. Editor TITUS MBUYA; circ. 20,000.

Motswana Woman: 686 Botswana Rd, Gaborone; tel. 375362; fax 375378; monthly; women's interests; circ. 4,000.

Northern Advertiser: POB 402, Francistown; tel. 212265; fax 213769; e-mail rsfish@global.bw; f. 1985; weekly; advertisements, local interest, sport; Editor GRACE FISH; circ. 6,000.

The Zebra's Voice: Private Bag 00114, National Museum, 331 Independence Ave, Gaborone; tel. 374616; fax 302797; f. 1982; quarterly; cultural affairs; Editor RUDOLPH MOJALEMOTHO; circ. 5,000.

NEWS AGENCIES

Botswana Press Agency (BOPA): Private Bag 0060, Gaborone; tel. 313601; f. 1981.

Foreign Bureaux

Deutsche Presse-Agentur (Germany) and **Reuters** (UK) are represented in Botswana.

Publishers

A. C. Braby (Botswana) (Pty) Ltd: POB 1549, Gaborone; tel. 371444; fax 373462; telephone directories.

The Botswana Society: POB 71, Gaborone; tel. 351500; fax 359321; f. 1968; archaeology, arts, history, law, sciences.

Department of Information and Broadcasting: Private Bag 0060, Gaborone; tel. 352541; fax 357138.

Heinemann Educational Botswana (Pty) Ltd: POB 10103, Gaborone; tel. 372305; fax 371832; Man. Dir LESEDI SEITEI.

Longman Botswana (Pty) Ltd: POB 1083, Lobatse Rd, Gaborone; tel. 313969; fax 322682; e-mail joe@info.bw; f. 1981; educational; Man. Dir J. K. CHALASHIKA.

Macmillan Botswana Publishing Co (Pty) Ltd: POB 1155, Gaborone; tel. 314379; fax 374326; Gen. Man. W. UITERWIJK.

Magnum Press (Pty) Ltd: Gaborone; tel. 372852; fax 374558.

Morula Press: Business School of Botswana, POB 402492, Gaborone; tel. 353499; fax 304809; f. 1994; business, law.

Printing and Publishing Co (Botswana) (Pty) Ltd: POB 130, 5647 Nakedi Rd, Broadhurst, Gaborone; tel. 312844.

Sygma Publishing: POB 753, Gaborone; tel. 372532; fax 372531; e-mail sygma@info.bw.

Government Publishing House

Department of Government Printing and Publishing Services: Private Bag 0081, Gaborone; tel. 314441; fax 312001.

Broadcasting and Communications

TELECOMMUNICATIONS

In early 1998 two companies were granted licences to operate mobile cellular telephone networks.

Botswana Telecommunications Authority (BTA): Private Bag 00495, Gaborone; tel. 357755; fax 357976; e-mail bta@info.bw; f. 1996; Chair. C. M. LEKAUKAU.

Botswana Telecommunications Corporation: POB 700, Gaborone; tel. 358411; fax 352777; e-mail jramutsh@btc.bw; internet www.btc.bw; f. 1980; state-owned; Chair. A. V. LIONJANGA; CEO M. T. CURRY.

BROADCASTING

Department of Information and Broadcasting: Private Bag 0060, Gaborone; Dir ANDREW SESINYI.

Radio

Radio Botswana: Private Bag 0060, Gaborone; tel. 352541; fax 357138; e-mail rbeng@info.bw; broadcasts in Setswana and English; govt-owned; f. 1965; Dir ANDREW SESINYI; Chief Eng. HABUJI SOSOME.

Radio Botswana II: Private Bag 0060, Gaborone; tel. 352541; fax 371588; f. 1992; commercial service.

Yarona FM: Gaborone; f. 1999; independent; Gen. Man. MORAKI MOKGASANA.

Television

Botswana Television: Department of Information & Broadcasting, Private Bag 0060, Gaborone; tel. 300050; fax 300051; e-mail simon .higman@btv.bw; govt-funded national TV service; broadcasts commenced in July 2000; Gen. Man. SIMON HIGMAN.

TV Association of Botswana: Gaborone; relays SABC-TV and BOP-TV programmes from South Africa.

Finance

(cap. = capital; res = reserves; dep. = deposits;
m. = million; brs = branches; amounts in pula)

BANKING

Central Bank

Bank of Botswana: POB 712, Private Bag 154, Plot 1863, Khama Crescent, Gaborone; tel. 360600; fax 301100; e-mail rakhudme@ bob.bw; internet www.bankofbotswana.bw; f. 1975; bank of issue; cap. 25m., res 3,362.3m., dep. 24,502.5m. (Dec. 1999); Gov. LINAH MOHOHLO.

Commercial Banks

Barclays Bank of Botswana Ltd: POB 478, Barclays House, 6th Floor, Plot 8842, Khama Crescent, Gaborone; tel. 352041; fax 353699; f. 1975; 74.9% owned by Barclays Bank PLC (UK); cap. 8.5m., res 174.3m., dep. 2,019.4m. (Dec. 1998); Chair. C. TIBONE; Man. Dir C. LOWE; 48 brs, etc.

First National Bank of Botswana Ltd: POB 1552, Finance House, 5th Floor, Plot 8843, Khama Crescent, Gaborone; tel. 311669; fax 306130; e-mail jchibuye@fnb.co.za; f. 1991; 70% owned by First National Bank Holdings Botswana Ltd; cap. and res 172.7m., dep. 1,487.5m. (June 1999); Chair. P. C. H. THOMPSON; Man. Dir J. K. MACASKILL; 11 brs.

Stanbic Bank Botswana Ltd: Private Bag 00168, Travaglini House, Plot 1271, Old Lobatse Rd, Gaborone; tel. 301600; fax 300171; f. 1992 by merger; subsidiary of Standard Bank Investment Corpn Africa Holdings Ltd; cap. 23.1m., res 2.3m., dep 553.2m. (Dec. 1999); Chair. J. N. LEGGETT; Man. Dir W. L. V. PRICE; 4 brs.

Standard Chartered Bank Botswana Ltd: POB 496, Standard House, 5th Floor, Plots 1124–1127, The Mall, Gaborone; tel. 353111; fax 372933; internet www.standardcharteredbank.com; f. 1975; 75% owned by Standard Chartered Holdings (Africa) BV, Amsterdam; cap. and res 109.9m. (Dec. 1997), dep. 881.7m. (Dec. 1995); Chair. P. L. STEENKAMP; CEO D. N. T. KUWANA; 15 brs.

Other Banks

Botswana Savings Bank: POB 1150, Gaborone; tel. 312555; fax 352608; e-mail bsb@info.bw; cap. and res 48.4m., dep. 101.5m. (March 2000); Chair. F. MODISE; Man. Dir E. B. MATHE.

Investec Bank: Gaborone; f. 1998; merchant bank; Man. Dir KUMBULANI MUNAMTI.

National Development Bank: POB 225, Development House, Queens Rd, Gaborone; tel. 352801; fax 374446; f. 1964; cap. 77.7m., res 17.2m., total assets 247.6m. (March 1999); priority given to agricultural credit for Botswana farmers, and co-operative credit and loans for local business ventures; Chair. F. MODISE; Gen. Man. T. JOHNSON; 5 brs.

STOCK EXCHANGE

Botswana Stock Exchange: Private Bag 00417, 4th Floor, Finance House, Khama Crescent, Gaborone; tel. 374078; fax 374079; e-mail stockex@ncs.com.gh; f. 1989; commenced formal functions of a stock exchange in 1995; Chair. LOUIS NCHINDO; CEO R. MCCAMMON.

INSURANCE

Botswana Co-operative Insurance Co Ltd: POB 199, Gaborone; tel. and fax 313654; Man. Dir PHILIP MAKGALEMELE.

Botswana Eagle Insurance Co Ltd: POB 1221, 501 Botsalano House, Gaborone; tel. 319910; fax 319911; Gen. Man. JOHN MAIN.

Botswana Insurance Holdings: POB 336, Gaborone; tel. 351791; fax 306386; Chair. W. A. JACK; Man. Dir J. A. BURDIDGE.

Botswana Life: Private Bag 00296, Gaborone; tel. 351791; fax 305884; e-mail blil@lifeinsurance.bw.

Mutual and Federal Insurance Co of Botswana Ltd: Private Bag 00347, Gaborone; tel. 303333; fax 303400; Gen. Man. JEAN WALKIN.

Sedgwick James Insurance Brokers (Pty) Ltd: POB 103, Plot 730, The Mall, Botswana Rd, Gaborone; tel. 314241; fax 373120.

Tshireletso Insurance Brokers: POB 1967, Gaborone; tel. 357064; fax 371558.

Trade and Industry

GOVERNMENT AGENCIES

Botswana Housing Corporation: POB 412, Gaborone; tel. 3605102; fax 314101; f. 1971; e-mail bhc@info.bw; provides housing for central govt and local authority needs and assists with private-sector housing schemes; Gen. Man. E. M. MAPHANYANE; 950 employees.

Department of Food Resources: POB 96, Gaborone; tel. 354124. 1982; procurement, storage and distribution of food commodities under the Drought Relief Programme; Admin. Officer M. S. SEHLULANE.

Department of Town and Regional Planning: Private Bag 0042, Gaborone; tel. 351935; e-mail infoterra@info.bw; f. 1972; responsible for physical planning matters throughout the country, including formulation of national physical planning policy; prepares devt plans for settlements and regions and provides physical planning advice to govt and local authorities as well as private bodies.

DEVELOPMENT ORGANIZATIONS

Botswana Development Corporation Ltd: Private Bag 160, Moedi, Plot 50380, Gaborone International Showgrounds, off Machel Drive, Gaborone; tel. 351811; fax 303105; e-mail bdc@bdc.bw; f. 1970; Chair. O. K. MATAMBO; Man. Dir. M. O. MOLEFANE.

Botswana Enterprise Development Unit (BEDU): Plot No. 1269, Lobatse Rd, POB 0014, Gaborone; f. 1974; promotes industrialization and rural devt; Dir J. LINDFORS.

Botswana Export Development and Investment Authority (BEDIA): BIC House, 4th Floor, The Main Mall, POB 3122, Gaborone; tel. 581931; fax 581941; f. 1998; promotes and facilitates local and foreign investment.

Department of Trade and Investment Promotion (TIPA), Ministry of Commerce and Industry: Private Bag 00367, Gaborone; tel. 351790; fax 305375; e-mail tipa@info.bw; internet www.tipa.bw; promotes industrial and commercial investment, diversification and expansion; offers consultancy, liaison and information services; participates in overseas trade fairs and trade and investment missions; Dir D. TSHEKO.

Financial Services Co of Botswana (Pty) Ltd: POB 1129, Finance House, Khama Crescent, Gaborone; tel. 351363; fax 357815; f. 1974; hire purchase, mortgages, industrial leasing and debt factoring; Chair. M. E. HOPKINS; Man. Dir R. A. PAWSON.

Integrated Field Services: Private Bag 004, Ministry of Commerce and Industry, Gaborone; tel. 353024; fax 371539; promotes industrialization and rural development; Dir B. T. TIBONE.

CHAMBER OF COMMERCE

Botswana National Chamber of Commerce and Industry: POB 20344, Gaborone; tel. 52677.

INDUSTRIAL AND TRADE ASSOCIATIONS

Botswana Agricultural Marketing Board (BAMB): Private Bag 0053, 1227 Haile Selassie Rd, Gaborone; tel. 351341; fax 352926; Chair. the Perm. Sec., Ministry of Agriculture; Gen. Man. S. B. TAUKOBONG.

Botswana Meat Commission (BMC): Private Bag 4, Lobatse; tel. 330321; fax 330504; e-mail bmc_gm_finance@info.bw; f. 1966; slaughter of livestock, export of hides and skins, carcasses, frozen and chilled boneless beef; operates tannery and beef products cannery; Chair. Dr MARTIN M. MANNATHOKO; CEO O. K. NIELSEN.

EMPLOYERS' ORGANIZATION

Botswana Confederation of Commerce, Industry and Manpower (BOCCIM): POB 432, BOCCIM House, Gaborone; f. 1971; Chair. D. N. MOROKA; Dir MODIRI J. MBAAKANYI; 1,478 affiliated mems.

UTILITIES

Electricity

Botswana Power Corporation: POB 48, Motlakase House, Macheng Way, Gaborone; tel. 3603203; fax 373563; f. 1971; operates power stations at Selebi-Phikwe (capacity 65 MW) and Moropule (132 MW); Chair. the Dep. Perm. Sec., Ministry of Minerals, Energy and Water Affairs; CEO KETANE SITHOLE.

Water

Department of Water Affairs: Gaborone; provides public water supplies for rural areas.

Water Utilities Corporation: Private Bag 00276, Gaborone; tel. 3604400; fax 373852; e-mail metsi@wuc.bw; f. 1970; 100% state-owned; supplies water to main urban centres; Chair. the Perm. Sec., Ministry of Minerals, Energy and Water Affairs; Chief Exec. B. MPHO.

CO-OPERATIVES

Department of Co-operative Development: POB 86, Gaborone; f. 1964; promotes marketing and supply, consumer, dairy, horticultural and fisheries co-operatives, thrift and loan societies, credit societies, a co-operative union and a co-operative bank.

Botswana Co-operative Union: Gaborone; f. 1970; Dir AARON RAMOSAKO.

TRADE UNIONS

Botswana Federation of Trade Unions: POB 440, Gaborone; tel. and fax 352534; f. 1977; Gen. Sec. MARANYANE KEBITSANG.

Affiliated Unions

Air Botswana Employees' Union: POB 92, Gaborone; Gen. Sec. DANIEL MOTSUMI.

Barclays Management Staff Union: POB 478, Gaborone; Gen. Sec. TEFO LIONJANGA.

BCL Senior Staff Union: POB 383, Selebi-Phikwe; Gen. Sec. KABELO MATTHEWS.

Botswana Agricultural Marketing Board Workers' Union: Private Bag 0053, Gaborone; Gen. Sec. M. E. SEMATHANE.

Botswana Bank Employees' Union: POB 111, Gaborone; Gen. Sec. KEOLOPILE GABORONE.

Botswana Beverages and Allied Workers' Union: POB 41358, Gaborone; Gen. Sec. S. SENWELO.

Botswana Brigade Teachers' Union: Private Bag 007, Molepolole; Gen. Sec. SADIKE KGOKONG.

Botswana Commercial and General Workers' Union: Gaborone; Gen. Sec. KEDIRETSE MPETANG.

Botswana Construction Workers' Union: POB 1508, Gaborone; Gen. Sec. JOSHUA KESIILWE.

Botswana Diamond Sorters-Valuators' Union: POB 1186, Gaborone; Gen. Sec. FELIX T. LESETEDI.

Botswana Housing Corporation Staff Union: POB 412, Gaborone; Gen. Sec. GORATA DINGALO.

Botswana Meat Industry Workers' Union: POB 181, Lobatse; Gen. Sec. JOHNSON BOJOSI.

Botswana Mining Workers' Union: Gaborone; Gen. Sec. BALEKA-MANG S. GANASIANE.

Botswana Postal Services Workers' Union: POB 87, Gaborone; Gen. Sec. AARON MOSWEU.

Botswana Power Corporation Workers' Union: Private Bag 0053, Gaborone; Gen. Sec. MOLEFE MODISE.

Botswana Railways and Artisan Employees' Union: POB 1486, Gaborone; Gen. Sec. PATRICK MAGOWE.

Botswana Railways Senior Staff Union: Mahalapye; Gen. Sec. LENTSWE LETSWELETSE.

Botswana Railways Workers' Union: POB 181, Gaborone; Gen. Sec. ERNEST T. G. MOHUTSIWA.

Botswana Telecommunications Employees' Union: Gaborone; Gen. Sec. SEDIBANA ROBERT.

Botswana Vaccine Institute Staff Union: Private Bag 0031, Gaborone; Gen. Sec. ELLIOT MODISE.

Central Bank Union: POB 712, Gaborone; Gen. Sec. GODFREY NGIDI.

National Amalgamated Local and Central Government, Parastatal, Statutory Body and Manual Workers' Union: POB 374, Gaborone; Gen. Sec. DICKSON KELATLHEGETSWE.

National Development Bank Employees' Union: POB 225, Gaborone; Sec.-Gen. MATSHEDISO FOLOGANG.

Non-Academic Staff Union: Private Bag 0022, Gaborone; Gen. Sec. ISAAC THOTHE.

Transport

RAILWAYS

The 960-km railway line from Mafikeng, South Africa, to Bulawayo, Zimbabwe, passes through Botswana and has been operated by

Botswana Railways (BR) since 1987. In 1997 there were 888 km of 1,067-mm-gauge track within Botswana, including three branches serving the Selebi-Phikwe mining complex (56 km), the Morupule colliery (16 km) and the Sua Pan soda-ash deposits (175 km). BR derives 85%–90% of its earnings from freight traffic, although passenger services do operate between Gaborone and Francistown, and Lobatse and Bulawayo. Through its links with Spoornet, which operates the South African railways system and the National Railways of Zimbabwe, BR provides connections with Namibia and Swaziland to the south, and an unbroken rail link to Zambia, the Democratic Republic of the Congo, Angola, Mozambique, Tanzania and Malawi to the north. Freight traffic on BR has been severely reduced, however, since Zimbabwe's construction in 1999 of a rail link from Bulawayo to Beitbridge, on its border with South Africa.

Botswana Railways (BR): Private Bag 52, Mahalapye; tel. 411375; fax 411385; e-mail botrail@info.bw; f. 1987; Gen. Man. C. B. BOTANA.

ROADS

In 1996 there were 18,482 km of roads, including 4,350 km of main roads, and 4,566 km of secondary roads; some 23.5% of the road network was bituminized (including a main road from Gaborone, via Francistown, to Kazungula, where the borders of Botswana, Namibia, Zambia and Zimbabwe meet). The construction of a 340-km road between Nata and Maun is currently under way. Construction of the 600-km Trans-Kalahari Highway, from Jwaneng to the port of Walvis Bay on the Namibian coast, commenced in 1990 and was completed in 1998. A car-ferry service operates from Kazungula across the Zambezi river into Zambia.

Department of Road Transport and Safety: Private Bag 0026, Gaborone; tel. 55515; responsible for national road network; responsible to the Ministry of Works, Transport and Communications.

CIVIL AVIATION

The main international airport is at Gaborone. Four other major airports are located at Kasane, Maun, Francistown and Ghanzi. In 2000 there were also 108 airfields throughout the country. Scheduled services of Air Botswana are supplemented by an active charter and business sector.

Air Botswana: POB 92, Sir Seretse Khama Airport, Gaborone; tel. 352812; fax 375408; f. 1972; govt-owned; transfer to private sector to be completed by mid-2001; domestic services and regional services to countries in eastern and southern Africa, Dir-Gen. CORNWELL MULEYA.

Tourism

There are five game reserves and three national parks, including Chobe, near Victoria Falls, on the Zambia–Zimbabwe border. Efforts to expand the tourism industry include plans for the construction of new hotels and the rehabilitation of existing hotel facilities. In 1998 foreign tourist arrivals totalled 1,351,798; receipts from tourism amounted to US $184m. in 1997.

Department of Tourism: Ministry of Commerce and Industry, Private Bag 0047, Standard House, 2nd Floor, Main Mall, Gaborone; tel. 353024; fax 308675; e-mail botswanatourism@gov.bw; internet www.botswana-tourism.gov.bw; f. 1994; Dir GAYLARD KOMBANI.

Department of Wildlife and National Parks: POB 131, Gaborone; tel. 371405; fax 312354; e-mail dwnp@gov.bw; Dir. J. MATLHARE.

Hotel and Tourism Association of Botswana: Gaborone; Dir MODISA MOTHOAGAE.

BRAZIL

Introductory Survey

Location, Climate, Language, Religion, Flag, Capital

The Federative Republic of Brazil, the fifth largest country in the world, lies in central and north-eastern South America. To the north are Venezuela, Colombia, Guyana, Suriname and French Guiana, to the west Peru and Bolivia, and to the south Paraguay, Argentina and Uruguay. Brazil has a very long coastline on the Atlantic Ocean. Climatic conditions vary from hot and wet in the tropical rain forest of the Amazon basin to temperate in the savannah grasslands of the central and southern uplands, which have warm summers and mild winters. In Rio de Janeiro temperatures are generally between 17°C (63°F) and 29°C (85°F). The official language is Portuguese. Almost all of the inhabitants profess Christianity, and about 90% are adherents of the Roman Catholic Church. The national flag (proportions 10 by 7) is green, bearing, at the centre, a yellow diamond containing a blue celestial globe with 26 white five-pointed stars (one for each of Brazil's states), arranged in the pattern of the southern firmament, below an equatorial scroll with the motto 'Ordem e Progresso' ('Order and Progress'), and a single star above the scroll. The capital is Brasília.

Recent History

Formerly a Portuguese possession, Brazil became an independent monarchy in 1822, and a republic in 1889. A federal constitution for the United States of Brazil was adopted in 1891. Following social unrest in the 1920s, the economic crisis of 1930 resulted in a major revolt, led by Dr Getúlio Vargas, who was installed as President. He governed the country as a benevolent dictator until forced to resign by the armed forces in December 1945. During Vargas's populist rule, Brazil enjoyed internal stability and steady economic progress. He established a strongly authoritarian corporate state, similar to fascist regimes in Europe, but in 1942 Brazil entered the Second World War on the side of the Allies.

A succession of ineffectual presidential terms (including another by Vargas, who was re-elected in 1950) failed to establish stable government in the late 1940s and early 1950s. President Jânio Quadros, elected in 1960, resigned after only seven months in office, and in September 1961 the Vice-President, João Goulart, was sworn in as President. Military leaders suspected Goulart, the leader of the Partido Trabalhista Brasileiro (PTB), of communist sympathies, and they were reluctant to let him succeed to the presidency. As a compromise, the Constitution was amended to restrict the powers of the President and to provide for a Prime Minister. However, following the appointment of three successive premiers during a 16-month period of mounting political crisis, the system was rejected when a referendum, conducted in January 1963, approved a return to the presidential system of government, whereupon President Goulart formed his own Cabinet.

Following a period of economic crisis, exacerbated by allegations of official corruption, the left-wing regime of President Goulart was overthrown in April 1964 by a bloodless right-wing military coup led by Gen. (later Marshal) Humberto Castelo Branco, the Army Chief of Staff, who was promptly elected President by the National Congress. In October 1965 President Castelo Branco assumed dictatorial powers, and all 13 existing political parties were banned. In December, however, two artificially-created parties, the pro-Government Aliança Renovadora Nacional (ARENA) and the opposition Movimento Democrático Brasileiro (MDB), were granted official recognition. President Castelo Branco nominated as his successor the Minister of War, Marshal Artur da Costa e Silva, who was elected in October 1966 and took office in March 1967 as President of the redesignated Federative Republic of Brazil (a new Constitution was introduced simultaneously). The ailing President da Costa e Silva was forced to resign in September 1969 and was replaced by a triumvirate of military leaders.

The military regime granted the President wide-ranging powers to rule by decree. In October 1969 the ruling junta introduced a revised Constitution, vesting executive authority in an indirectly-elected President. The Congress, suspended since December 1968, was recalled and elected Gen. Emílio Garrastazú Médici as President. Médici was succeeded as President by Gen. Ernesto Geisel and Gen. João Baptista de Figueiredo, respectively. Despite the attempts of both Presidents to pursue a policy of *abertura*, or opening to democratization (legislation to end the controlled two-party system was approved in 1979), opposition to military rule intensified throughout the 1970s and early 1980s. In November 1982 the government-sponsored Partido Democrático Social (PDS) suffered significant losses at elections to the Chamber of Deputies, state governorships and municipal councils. However, the PDS secured a majority of seats in the Federal Senate and, owing to pre-election legislation, seemed likely to enjoy a guaranteed majority in the electoral college, scheduled to choose a successor to Gen. Figueiredo in 1985.

However, in July 1984 Vice-President Chaves de Mendonça and the influential Marco de Oliveira Maciel, a former Governor of Pernambuco State, announced the formation of an alliance of liberal PDS members with members of the Partido do Movimento Democrático Brasileiro (PMDB). This offered the opposition a genuine opportunity to defeat the PDS in the electoral college. In August Senator Tancredo Neves, the Governor of Minas Gerais State (who had been Prime Minister in 1961–62), was named presidential candidate for the liberal alliance, while the former President of the PDS, José Sarney, was declared vice-presidential candidate. In December the liberal alliance formed an official political party, the Partido Frente Liberal (PFL). At the presidential election, conducted in January 1985, Neves was elected as Brazil's first civilian President for 21 years, winning 480 of the 686 votes in the electoral college. Prior to the inauguration ceremony in March 1985, however, Neves was taken ill, and in April, following a series of operations, he died. José Sarney, who had assumed the role of Acting President in Neves' absence, took office as President in April. President Sarney made no alterations to the Cabinet selected by Neves, and he affirmed his commitment to fulfilling the objectives of the late President-designate. In May the Congress approved a constitutional amendment restoring direct elections by universal suffrage. The right to vote was also extended to illiterate adults. The first direct elections, to municipal councils in 31 cities, took place in November.

The introduction in February 1986 of an anti-inflation programme, the Cruzado Plan, proved, initially, to be successful and boosted the popularity of President Sarney. Support for the Government was further demonstrated in November 1986 at elections to the Congress, which was to operate as a Constitutional Assembly. The Constitutional Assembly was installed in February 1987, and the constitutional debate was dominated by the issue of the length of the presidential mandate. In June 1988 the Constitutional Assembly finally approved a presidential mandate of five years. The first round of voting for the presidential election was provisionally set for 15 November 1989, thereby enabling Sarney to remain in office until March 1990. This *de facto* victory for the President precipitated a series of resignations from the PMDB by some of its leading members, who subsequently formed a new centre-left party, the Partido da Social Democracia Brasileira (PSDB). The Constitution was approved by the Congress on 22 September 1988, and was promulgated on 5 October. Among its 245 articles were provisions transferring many hitherto presidential powers to the legislature. In addition, censorship was abolished; the National Security Law, whereby many political dissidents had been detained, was abolished; the minimum voting age was lowered to 16 years; and the principle of habeas corpus was recognized. However, the Constitution offered no guarantees of land reform, and was thought by many to be nationalistic and protectionist.

In April 1988 the Government revealed its commitment to drastic reductions in planned public-sector expenditure, primarily based on a 'freeze' on salary increases for state employees. The combination of industrial unrest and social tension which resulted was thought to have been a decisive factor in the PMDB's poor results at municipal elections held on 15 November, when the centre-left Partido Democrático

Trabalhista (PDT) and the left-wing Partido dos Trabalhadores (PT) made important gains at the expense of the ruling party.

Brazil's first presidential election by direct voting since 1960 took place on 15 November 1989. The main contenders were the conservative, Fernando Collor de Mello of the newly-formed Partido de Reconstrução Nacional (PRN), Luiz Inácio (Lula) da Silva of the PT and Leonel Brizola of the PDT. Since no candidate received the required overall majority, a second round of voting was held on 17 December, contested by Collor de Mello and da Silva, who were first and second, respectively, in the November poll. Collor de Mello was declared the winner, with 53% of the votes cast. Following his inauguration as President on 15 March 1990, Collor de Mello announced an ambitious programme of economic reform, entitled 'New Brazil' (or, more commonly, the 'Collor Plan'), with the principal aim of reducing inflation, which had reached a monthly rate of more than 80%. A new currency, the cruzeiro (to replace, at par, the novo cruzado) was also introduced. The results of elections to 31 senatorial seats, 503 seats in the Chamber of Deputies and 27 state governorships, conducted in October 1990, were interpreted as a rejection of extreme left- and right-wing parties in favour of familiar candidates from small, centre-right parties. Nevertheless, the President was confident of securing sufficient support to continue to pursue a programme of radical economic reform. However, the results of a second round of voting, on 25 November, to elect governors in those states where candidates had received less than the required 50% of the votes on 3 October represented a serious reversal for the Government. Few candidates associated with or supported by the Government were successful, and particularly damaging defeats were suffered by government-favoured candidates in the crucial states of São Paulo, Rio Grande do Sul, Rio de Janeiro and Espírito Santo.

The Government's dramatic loss of popularity was largely attributed to the severity and apparent failure of its economic austerity programme. A second economic plan, announced by the Minister of the Economy, Zélia Cardoso de Mello, and presented as a simple intensification of the first Collor Plan, had been implemented in February 1991. In March Collor de Mello announced a new Plan for National Reconstruction, which envisaged further deregulation and rationalization of many state-controlled areas, including the ports, and the communications and fuel sectors. By May 1991, despite a considerable decrease in the monthly rate of inflation, Cardoso de Mello's political popularity had been undermined by her confrontational style of negotiation, and she was forced to resign.

Collor de Mello's position became increasingly precarious towards the end of 1991, after allegations of mismanagement of federal funds were made against his wife and against several associates in the President's home state of Alagoas. In September 1991 the President embarked upon a series of informal multi-party negotiations in an attempt to achieve greater congressional consensus and to reinforce his own mandate. Following lengthy discussions at a specially-convened meeting of the emergency Council of the Republic in the same month, Collor de Mello presented a comprehensive series of proposals for constitutional amendment, before the Congress.

Allegations of high-level corruption persisted into 1992 and despite attempts, in January and April, to restore public confidence in the integrity of the Government with the implementation of comprehensive cabinet changes, the President failed to dispel suspicions sufficiently to attract the wider political participation in government which was considered necessary to facilitate the passage of legislation through an increasingly ineffectual Congress. In May, moreover, the President became the focus of further allegations, following a series of disclosures made by Collor de Mello's younger brother, which appeared to implicate the President in a number of corrupt practices orchestrated by Paulo César Farias, Collor de Mello's 1989 election campaign treasurer. While the President dismissed the allegations as false, in late May the Congress approved the creation of a special commission of inquiry to investigate the affair. In early September, acting upon the report of the special commission of inquiry, and bolstered by massive popular support, a 49-member congressional committee authorized the initiation of impeachment proceedings against the President, within the Chamber of Deputies. On 29 September the Chamber voted to proceed with the impeachment of the President for abuses of authority and position, prompting the immediate resignation of the Cabinet. On 2 October Collor de Mello surrendered authority to Vice-President Itamar Franco for a six-month period, pending the final pronouncement regarding his future in office, to be decided by the Senate. Following lengthy negotiations, Franco announced the composition of a new Cabinet in October, representing a broad political base. A final round of municipal elections, conducted in November, revealed a significant resurgence of support for left-wing parties.

Meanwhile, in December 1992, the Senate had voted overwhelmingly to proceed with Collor de Mello's impeachment and to indict the President for 'crimes of responsibility'. Within minutes of the opening of the impeachment trial on 29 December, however, Collor de Mello announced his resignation from the presidency. Itamar Franco was immediately sworn in as President (to serve the remainder of Collor de Mello's term). On the following day the Senate, which had agreed to continue with proceedings against Collor de Mello (despite his resignation), announced that the former President's political rights (including immunity from prosecution and the holding of public office for an eight-year period) were to be removed. In January 1993 Collor de Mello was notified by the Supreme Court that he was to stand trial, as an ordinary citizen, on charges of 'passive corruption and criminal association'. Proceedings against Collor de Mello were initiated in June, and in December the Supreme Federal Tribunal endorsed the Senate's eight-year ban on his holding public office. In December 1994, however, the Tribunal voted to acquit Collor de Mello of the charges, owing to insufficient evidence. In January 1998 the former President was cleared of charges of illegal enrichment.

At a referendum conducted in April 1993 voters overwhelmingly rejected the introduction of a parliamentary system of government or the restoration of the monarchy, opting instead to retain the presidential system.

Following several unsuccessful attempts in late 1992 and early 1993 to address the problems of burgeoning inflation and massive budget deficit, in June 1993 the new Minister of the Economy, Fernando Henrique Cardoso, announced the terms of the Government's latest economic programme, the 'plano de verdade' (real plan). A new currency, the cruzeiro real, was introduced in August. A programme for economic stability, announced in December 1993, sought to regulate the flow of federal resources to states and municipalities. Congressional approval for the establishment of a Social Emergency Fund (providing for further centralization of control over the expenditures and revenue of states and government agencies) prompted the activation of a transitional index, the Unidade Real de Valor (URV), linked to the US dollar, on 1 March 1994. On 1 July the new currency, the real, was introduced, at par with the dollar.

In April 1993 the PDT leader, Leonel Brizola, announced the party's withdrawal from the ruling coalition, following Franco's decision to proceed with the privatization of the prestigious National Steel Company (Companhia Siderúrgica Nacional—CSN). Minister of Justice and PDT member Maurício Corrêa Lima subsequently resigned from the party rather than relinquish the justice portfolio. In August the Partido Socialista Brasileiro (PSB) withdrew from the coalition, and in the following month the PMDB national council narrowly defeated a motion to end its association with the Government. The fragility of the Government was exacerbated by the emergence of a new corruption scandal in October, in which 22 deputies, four senators, two incumbent ministers, two former ministers and three governors were implicated in a fraudulent scheme in which political influence was allegedly exercised in order to secure state projects for individual construction companies, in exchange for bribes. A congressional committee of inquiry was established which, in January 1994 recommended the expulsion of 18 federal deputies, and the further investigation of 12 deputies, three governors and one senator. In mid-April the Chamber of Deputies voted to expel three of the 18 named deputies and to continue investigations into four deputies who had recently resigned, in order to prevent their participation in the October elections. In May, Ibsen Pinheiro, a former leader of the Chamber of Deputies, was similarly expelled from the Congress. In the same month Congress concluded a review of the Constitution, having adopted just six amendments, including a reduction in the length of the presidential term from five to four years.

A number of ministerial changes were made in late 1993 and early 1994, largely to enable ministers to seek election in the forthcoming polls. In March 1994 Cardoso resigned from the finance portfolio in order to meet the 2 April deadline for registration as presidential candidate of the PSDB. Lula da Silva was formally endorsed as presidential candidate of the PT-led Frente Popular (FP) on 1 May. Political events in the months preceding the election were dominated by numerous allegations of corruption and misconduct, which forced the replacement of the vice-presidential running mates of both Cardoso and da Silva, the withdrawal from the contest of the presidential candidate of the PL and the resignation of the Ministers of Finance and Mines and Energy.

Presidential, gubernatorial and legislative elections were conducted on 3 October 1994. Cardoso, whose candidacy was supported by the PFL, the PTB, the PL and the business community, won the presidential contest in the first round, with an overall majority of 54.3% of the votes, following a campaign that had focused largely on the success of his economic initiatives. The PT candidate, da Silva, with the support of the PSB, was second with 27.0% of the votes cast. The discovery of large-scale, organized electoral fraud in the State of Rio de Janeiro forced the annulment of elections for state and federal deputies there, which were reorganized to coincide with the 15 November run-off elections for governorships in states where no overall majority had been achieved in the October poll. PSDB candidates were also successful in the gubernatorial contests, securing six of the 27 state governorships, including the crucial industrial centres of São Paulo, Minas Gerais and Rio de Janeiro. While the PMDB increased its number of state governorships from seven to nine, and continued to boast the largest single-party representation in the Congress, the party's presidential candidate, Orestes Quércia, had attracted only 4.4% of the votes cast.

Cardoso was inaugurated as President on 1 January 1995 and a new Cabinet was installed on the following day. The multi-party composition of the Cabinet (with portfolios allocated not only to those parties that had supported his candidacy, but also to the PT and the PMDB) demonstrated the new President's need to maintain a broad base of congressional support in order to secure prompt endorsement for proposed constitutional reform of the taxation and social security systems. Cardoso immediately made clear his intention to continue the programme of economic reform in order to control public expenditure and reduce inflation. In February he vetoed a draft congressional proposal to increase the minimum monthly wage. In March the currency was devalued, and the privatization programme, suspended by Franco during 1994, was reactivated; interest rates and tariffs on consumer durables were raised and the increase in the minimum wage, previously vetoed by the President, was approved. However, opposition to the programme of economic stabilization and to renewed efforts by the Government to introduce constitutional amendments, including those that would end state monopolies in the telecommunications and petroleum sectors, resulted in the organization, by the Central Unica dos Trabalhadores (CUT) trade-union confederation, of a general strike in May 1995. The President's decision to order military intervention in a number of crucial petroleum refineries was widely interpreted as evidence of the Government's intent to undermine the concerted action of the political opposition and the trade unions. By early June, however, employees in the petroleum sector had begun to return to work, and on 20 June (despite vociferous congressional opposition) the Chamber of Deputies approved the proposal to open the sector to private participation. (The amendment relating to the petroleum sector was subsequently approved by the Senate in November; constitutional amendments providing for an end to state control of telecommunications, natural gas distribution and a number of shipping routes, were formally promulgated by the Congress in August.)

In September 1995 three existing right-wing parties merged to create the Partido Progressista Brasileiro (PPB), which expressed cautious support for the Government. By December, however, Cardoso's integrity had been seriously compromised by the alleged involvement of a number of his political associates in irregular financial transactions organized by the Banco Econômico in support of recent electoral campaigns, and by an influence-peddling scandal arising from the award to a US company, Raytheon, of the contract for development of an Amazon Regional Surveillance System (Sivam), which resulted in the resignation, in November, of the Minister of the Air Force. A congressional inquiry into the Sivam affair was initiated during November 1995. In February 1996 a special committee of the Senate made a recommendation, supported by Cardoso, that the Government should negotiate a substantial foreign loan to honour the Sivam contract with Raytheon, and in October 1996 the President was able to endorse the agreement.

Meanwhile, investigation of the so-called 'pink folder' of politicians, recovered from the ailing Banco Econômico, continued

during 1996, as the banking sector was plunged into further crisis. In March it was revealed that the Government had withheld details of a US $5,000m.-fraud perpetrated at the Banco Nacional a decade earlier. Moreover, it emerged that the Government had extended a recent credit facility of US $5,800m. to the bank in order to facilitate its merger with UNIBANCO in November 1995. Also in March the Government announced emergency financing for the Banco do Brasil, which, in common with many Brazilian banks, had suffered huge losses during 1995.

During 1996 renewed attempts by the Government to secure congressional approval for constitutional reforms relating to taxation, public administration and social security were repeatedly obstructed, delayed or defeated in the Congress, despite the adoption of a number of concessionary clauses and the successful negotiation of a compromise agreement on social security with trade-union organizations in January. A minor reorganization of the Cabinet was implemented in April 1996 to accommodate the introduction of the new Ministry of Political Co-ordination and there were further ministerial resignations throughout the year, including, in November, that of the Minister of Health, Abid Jatene, in protest at inadequate levels of state funding for the health sector.

The results of municipal elections conducted on 3 October 1996 revealed a reduction in support for the PSDB; José Serra was third in the contest for the São Paulo mayorship, with only 15.6% of the votes. Celso Pitta of the PPB was finally elected to the post at a second round of voting conducted on 15 November. The results of other run-off elections, conducted concurrently, also demonstrated a significant level of support for the PPB. The elections represented a disappointment for many veteran parties. The PPB, the PFL and the PSB, however, all made significant gains. None the less, Cardoso's own popularity continued to benefit from the success of the Government's attempts to control inflation. In January 1997 a legislative document, sponsored by the President, which sought to amend the Constitution in order to allow the incumbent head of state, state governors and mayors to seek re-election, received tentative endorsement from the Chamber of Deputies, despite vociferous opposition from the PMDB.

In mid-1996 the moderate Força Sindical trade union organization joined the CUT in urging workers to observe Brazil's first general strike in five years, on 21 June. Despite the Government's announcement, in April, of a job-creation programme to provide employment for 3m. Brazilians, the unions were dissatisfied with the Government's failure to halt rising levels of unemployment. However, the strike was only partially observed, and on the same day the Government announced details of the next phase of its massive divestment programme. Several companies in the power sector, 31 ports (including Santos and Rio de Janeiro) and the prestigious mining company, Companhia Vale do Rio Doce (CVRD) were among those state concerns to be offered for sale. In July the Government announced that the state telecommunications company, Telebrás, together with large sections of the rail and power networks, would be privatized by the end of 1998. Further reductions in public spending were announced in August and a new programme of economic measures designed to further reduce the fiscal deficit was introduced, by executive decree, in October. The Social Emergency Fund was again extended, to the end of 1999.

In February 1997 the Chamber of Deputies confirmed its approval of a constitutional amendment to permit the President to stand for re-election in 1998, Cardoso's position having been strengthened by the election of two of his supporters to the presidencies of both chambers of the Congress. Following the Senate vote in favour of the legislation (despite allegations of bribery relating to its passage through the lower house), the constitutional amendment received the upper house's final approval in June and was swiftly ratified by President Cardoso.

In March 1997, meanwhile, controversial legislation to end the long-standing monopoly of PETROBRAS over the petroleum industry was approved by the Chamber of Deputies, which, in the following month, voted narrowly in favour of proposals to reform the civil service. The Senate rejection of the latter item of legislation in June, however, was a major set-back to the Government's programme of economic reform and in particular to its attempts to reduce the budget deficit. Nevertheless, a series of compromises enabled the Government to renew its plans for civil-service reform, and in July an opposition amendment to the proposed legislation was narrowly defeated in the legislature. In November the lower house gave its final approval to the legislation.

As public confidence in the integrity of the country's police force continued to diminish, in mid-1997 thousands of troops were deployed in response to a strike by police officers protesting against low rates of pay. President Cardoso denounced as an 'uprising' the illegal strikes, which, in some areas, resulted in a complete breakdown of law and order.

In June 1997 the PT ordered an inquiry into allegations of corruption on the part of its presidential candidate, Lula da Silva. Although da Silva was exonerated by the investigation (thus permitting him to renew his candidacy for the 1998 election), other financial irregularities were uncovered, leading to a sharp decline in the PT's popularity. As the 1998 presidential election approached, various potential candidates announced changes in their party affiliation. In August 1997 Ciro Gomes, a former Minister of Finance, defected from the PSDB to the smaller Partido Popular Socialista (PPS), thereby exacerbating the internal crisis within the PSDB. (In the same month the Minister of Communications, Sérgio Vieira da Motta, announced his resignation from the party.) Former President Itamar Franco, meanwhile, declared his affiliation to the PMDB, and in October the incumbent President Cardoso's candidacy was endorsed by the PMDB.

In July 1997, meanwhile, an investigation by the Senate into a financial scandal arising from fraudulent bond issues concluded that 20 prominent politicians and senior officials (including three state governors, the mayor of São Paulo, Celso Pitta, and his predecessor, Paulo Maluf) had been involved in a criminal operation. A total of 161 financial institutions, including Banco Bradesco, Brazil's largest private bank, were implicated in the scandal. In January 1998 Celso Pitta was found guilty of fraud, but remained in office pending an appeal.

In March 1998 three ministers were obliged to resign in order to permit their participation in the forthcoming elections. The Minister of Planning, Budget and Co-ordination, Antônio Kandir, was replaced by Paulo Paiva of the PTB. President Cardoso announced the reallocation of several other cabinet portfolios in April. The deaths in rapid succession in April of two of the President's closest associates, however, was a major set-back to Cardoso's campaign for re-election. (The loss of Sérgio Motta, the dynamic Minister of Communications and co-founder of the PSDB, was followed by that of Luis Eduardo Magalhães, leader of government business in the Chamber of Deputies and son of Antônio Carlos Magalhães, President of the Senate.)

Despite his declared commitment to further economic austerity measures, at the presidential election held on 4 October 1998 Cardoso became the first President to be re-elected for a second consecutive term, securing almost 53.1% of the valid votes cast. Lula da Silva of the PT won 31.7% of the votes, while Ciro Gomes of the PPS received 11.0%. A high rate of abstention was recorded. At the concurrent legislative elections, the PSDB also performed well, securing 99 of the 513 seats in the lower chamber, while its electoral allies won a total of 278 seats (PFL 105, PMDB 82, PPB 60 and PTB 31), bringing the coalition's total representation to 377. Following the simultaneous first stage of the gubernatorial elections in 13 states, the second round was conducted where necessary on 25 October. Opposition candidates defeated the incumbent governors of the populous states of Rio de Janeiro, Rio do Sul and Minas Gerais, although the São Paulo governorship was retained by Mário Covas, a close ally of President Cardoso.

In November 1998 the Minister of Communications, Luís Carlos Mendonça de Barros, and three other officials resigned as a result of the exposure of a scandal involving illegal tape recordings of telephone conversations detailing their alleged attempts to influence (through their support for the establishment of consortia) the sale to the private sector of Telebrás in July 1998.

Prior to formally resuming office on 1 January 1999, President Cardoso announced the composition of his Cabinet. Although most ministers, including Pedro Malan, the Minister of Finance, retained their portfolios, changes included the creation of a new development ministry (which assumed some of the functions of the Ministry of Industry and Trade, a separate tourism portfolio being established); the new Ministry, headed by Celso Láfer, was to be responsible for the co-ordination of all government policies relating to production, its initiation being regarded as necessary to improve relations with the business community. A civilian was appointed Minister of Defence.

In January 1999 Itamar Franco, the newly-elected Governor of Minas Gerais, declared that the state was defaulting on its debt to the federal Government, indirectly precipitating the devaluation of the Brazilian currency. In the same month, however, having rejected the legislation on four occasions in the previous three years, the Chamber of Deputies finally endorsed the proposed reforms to the country's munificent pension system. The passage of the controversial legislation through the Senate in late January considerably enhanced the prospects of President Cardoso's programme of fiscal austerity.

In April 1999 Francisco Lopes, briefly President of the Central Bank until his removal in January 1999, was arrested, owing to his refusal to give evidence to a senate inquiry into corruption allegations at the bank. He was acquitted of charges of contempt, but remained under investigation over allegations that officials of the Central Bank had accepted illicit payments in exchange for the disclosure of privileged information. In a separate inquiry, a senate committee continued its investigations into allegations of corruption within the country's judiciary.

Following the withdrawal of the PTB from the ruling coalition in March 1999 as a result of the unexpected removal from his post of the Minister of the Budget and Administration, Paulo Paiva, the Government of President Cardoso came under further pressure in May when the PFL announced its intention to present its own candidate at the next presidential election, scheduled for 2002. In July, in an attempt to promote unity within the administration and to give impetus to the programme of economic reform, President Cardoso announced a reorganization of the Cabinet. A new Ministry of National Integration was established. The administration's popularity continued to decline, however, and in August anti-Government demonstrations culminated in the arrival in Brasília of as many as 100,000 marchers, comprising political opponents led by the PT, trade unionists and landless individuals, all protesting against economic and social policies. In early September, furthermore, Clovis Covilho, Minister of Development, Industry and Trade, was dismissed by the President, following a public disagreement over the policy of economic austerity. He was replaced by Alcides Tápias.

Meanwhile, in April 1999 a congressional commission had commenced investigations into allegations of organized criminal activities. In September 1999 Hildebrando Pascoal became the second deputy that year to be expelled from the lower house as a result of accusations of murder. It was alleged that Pascoal had been the leader of a cocaine-trafficking gang involved in the torture and murder of numerous victims in the remote state of Acre. Moreover, in October the congressional commission exposed a nation-wide criminal network that allegedly encompassed politicians, government officials, judges, police officers, business executives and banking officials. Embarrassed by the scale of the revelations (which even extended to reports of drugs-trafficking within the National Congress building), in November President Cardoso announced the establishment of a new anti-corruption force to combat the growing problem of organized crime. In the following month, in an effort to improve accountability and to strengthen congressional powers of investigation, the Senate approved a constitutional amendment to restrict presidential use of provisional measures, to which successive Governments had frequently resorted as a means to circumvent the cumbersome legislative process.

In January 2000 the Minister of Defence, Elcio Alvares, was dismissed by President Cardoso, allegedly as a result of cabinet disagreements; he was replaced by the former Attorney-General, Geraldo Magela da Cruz Quintão. Furthermore, in April, the Minister of Justice, José Carlos Dias, resigned following a disagreement over a joint drugs-control programme with Bolivia. He was replaced by the former National Secretary for Human Rights, José Gregori; in May the Minister of Sports and Tourism, Rafael Greca de Macedo, was dismissed and replaced by Carlos Melles, a PFL member. In mid-February the PSDB announced a new congressional alliance with the centrist PTB, thus becoming the largest legislative bloc in the Chamber of Deputies and further bolstering support for the ruling executive.

In late March 2000 the Mayor of São Paulo, Celso Pitta, was accused by his wife of bribing members of the city council to reject a move for his dismissal proposed in 1997. (Pitta had been involved in a senate investigation into alleged fraudulent bond issues; he was subsequently found guilty of fraud, but remained in office pending an appeal.). It was later alleged that Pitta had received a substantial loan from a businessman in return for favourable treatment from his administration and

Pitta was dismissed as Mayor. However, he was again permitted to remain in office, pending a further appeal and, following a ruling in mid-June by the federal court of appeal, he was reinstated. A further corruption scandal in July, which implicated President Cardoso in the funding and illegal awarding of contracts surrounding the construction of a regional labour tribunal headquarters in São Paulo, threatened to further damage the Government. Moreover, in the following month the announcement by the PTB that it was to dissolve the recently-formed alliance with the PSDB owing to the Government's increasing unpopularity, re-established the PFL as the largest party in the Chamber of Deputies. A report on organized drugs-trafficking and crime, published in November 2000, implicated a number of state deputies and mayors; legal proceedings were expected to commence against those allegedly involved.

At municipal elections held in October 2000 the PT made significant gains, obtaining 14.1% of votes cast (compared with 10.6% in 1996); the PSDB received 15.9% of votes and the PMDB 15.7%. A second round of voting was required in 16 cities, where no candidate secured more than 50% of the vote. In the same month Pedro Simon was selected as the PMDB's candidate in presidential elections scheduled to be held in October 2002. In December the Minister of Foreign Affairs, Luiz Felipe Lampréia, resigned and was replaced by the former development minister, Celso Láfer.

In February 2001 the Ministers of Social Security and Assistance, and of Mines and Energy, were dismissed following an internal disagreement. Moreover, in early May the Minister of National Integration, Fernando Bezerra, resigned following allegations of corruption. Shortly after, the Minister of Labour and Employment, Francisco Oswaldo Neves Dornelles, left the Government after a disagreement over the creation of a congressional committee to investigate public-sector corruption.

Meanwhile, in late February 1995, Cardoso launched a social improvement programme, Comunidade Solidária, with a consultative council headed by the President's wife, and with a budget of US $3,000m. In September the President announced a new programme for the defence of human rights and later in the month a government-sponsored bill was approved by the Chamber of Deputies, whereby responsibility for the deaths of more than 100 left-wing politicians and activists during the military regimes of the 1960s and 1970s was assumed by the State, which also approved financial compensation for the relatives of the victims. A National Plan for Human Rights, introduced in May 1996, contained 168 recommendations, including proposals to increase protection for the rights of children and workers. However, the absence of a financial or procedural framework for adoption of the plan prompted a cautious response to the document from human-rights organizations. During 1995 the Government suffered from repeated criticism of its failure to address burgeoning urban crime (particularly in Rio de Janeiro) and the demands of the Landless Peasant Movement, the Movimento dos Sem-Terra (MST), which organized a number of illegal occupations of disputed land during the year in support of demands for an acceleration of the Government's programme of expropriation of uncultivated land for distribution to landless rural families. Tensions arising from land ownership and reallocation disputes persisted. In January 1996 protests and land occupations were renewed following the enactment, by presidential decree, of a new law regulating the demarcation of Indian lands, which many indigenous groups interpreted as a serious erosion of the previously-existing land rights of the Indian population. Meanwhile, landless peasant groups challenged government claims that 100,000 itinerant families had been resettled during 1995 and 1996, and described the Government's reallocation programme as inadequate. (Official estimates of the number of landless families in Brazil were considerably lower than the figure of 4.8m. quoted by the MST.) Rapidly deteriorating relations between the authorities and the MST were further exacerbated in April 1996 by the violent intervention of the local military police in a demonstration, organized by the MST and supported by some 1,500 protesters at Eldorado de Carajás in the State of Pará, which resulted in the deaths of 19 demonstrators. (It was subsequently alleged that a number of those killed had been summarily executed.) Widespread public outrage prompted Cardoso to request immediate congressional priority for legislation relating to land expropriation, and to afford full cabinet status to the former agriculture ministry department responsible for executing the agrarian reform programme. Raúl Jungmann of the PPS was appointed to the new post of Minister of Agrarian Reform. José Eduardo de Andrade Vieira, who had attributed responsibility for the April massacre to the increasingly confrontational operations of the MST, was replaced as Minister of Agriculture and Supplies by Arlindo Porto of the PTB. However, Cardoso's attempts to propel land reform legislation through the Congress were promptly obstructed, and the emergence of a number of reports detailing the creation of close associations between local military police units and powerful rural landowners seemed likely to undermine efforts to bring to justice those responsible for the Eldorado de Carajás atrocity. Despite Jungmann's stated intention to facilitate dialogue amongst opposing groups in the dispute through the creation of a discussion council, by late 1996 the MST-sponsored campaign of illegal land seizures and occupations of federal and state government buildings had intensified, particularly in the States of São Paulo and Santa Catarina.

In April 1997, in response to the growing unrest and the arrival in Brasília of 1,500 MST members at the conclusion of a two-month march, the Government announced new measures to accelerate the process of land reform. At the end of April landless peasants threatened to occupy land belonging to the CVRD, in protest at the company's forthcoming transfer to the private sector. In May, however, despite various legal challenges, the sale of assets in this major producer of iron ore proceeded. In the following month José Rainha Júnior, an MST leader, was sentenced to more than 26 years' imprisonment for his involvement in the murder in 1989 of a landowner and of a police officer (he was acquitted of the charges in April 2000). In August 1997 a clash between riot police and illegal occupants of public land in Brasília resulted in 49 arrests and 20 persons injured. In the same month some 200 landless families seized two ranches in the state of São Paulo. In early 1998 the MST intensified its campaign for land reform. In March thousands of activists occupied government premises. In the same month Adelson Silva de Brito, an MST leader who had recently headed a land invasion, was shot dead in Barra Mansa. In September the head of the agrarian reform institute in São Paulo was obliged to suspend the state's land-expropriation proceedings when the organization's offices were occupied by 500 MST members.

In August 1999 the trial of 150 military policemen accused of participation in the 1996 killings in Eldorado de Carajás opened in Belém. Three commanding officers were promptly acquitted of the charges on the grounds of insufficient evidence. President Cardoso expressed regret at the ruling. The acquittal provoked outrage among the families of the victims of the massacre and led to rioting on the streets of Belém. Proceedings against the other 147 defendants were suspended.

In May 2000 in one of the largest demonstrations in history by the movement, over 30,000 members of the MST occupied a number of public buildings, including the Ministry of Finance and the Ministry of Agrarian Reform, to demand land reform. The occupations were widely condemned and prompted the Government to introduce legislation preventing further land invasions. Following inconclusive negotiations with the Government, the MST scaled down its protest and ministers agreed to resume talks with the MST leaders at the end of that month. However, following renewed occupations by the MST in September (the MST claimed that the Government had failed to honour a number of agreements reached in July), the Government suspended its negotiations on land reform. A constitutional crisis ensued, provoked by the request by the Governor of Minas Gerais, Itamar Franco, that federal troops, sent to protect the President's estate, withdraw. When his request was not met, Franco threatened to mobilize state military police to remove the troops; moreover, the Supreme Federal Tribunal ruled that the state Government had acted within the Constitution. However, it was reported later that month that, following the temporary withdrawal of MST activists, the Government had agreed to resume negotiations with the movement, and in early October the Government announced that loans of R $2,000 per family were to be made available for those already settled on their own land.

In December 1988 the murder of Francisco (Chico) Mendes, the leader of the rubber-tappers' union and a pioneering ecologist brought Brazil's environmental problems to international attention. Widespread concern was expressed that large-scale development projects, together with the 'slash-and-burn' farming techniques of cattle ranchers, peasant smallholders and loggers, and the release of large amounts of mercury into the environment by an estimated 60,000 gold prospectors (or *garimpeiros*) in the Amazon region, presented a serious threat to the survival of both the indigenous Indians and the rain forest. International criticism of the Government's poor response to the threat to the environment persisted throughout the 1990s. Of particular concern to many international observers was the plight of the Yanomami Indian tribe in Roraima. It was estimated that, since the arrival of the *garimpeiros* in the region, some 10%–15% of the Yanomami's total population had been exterminated as a result of pollution and disease, introduced to the area by the gold prospectors. The Fundação Nacional do Indio (FUNAI—National Indian Foundation) was heavily criticized for its role in the affair and was accused of failing to provide effective protection and support for Brazil's Indian population. In June 1992, however, national prestige was heightened when Brazil successfully hosted the UN Conference on Environment and Development or 'Earth Summit'. In August 1993 international attention was again focused on the region, following the slaughter of 73 members of the Yanomami tribe by *garimpeiros*, in the context of the ongoing territorial dispute prompted by the miners' attempts to exploit the rich mineral deposits of the Yanomami land. A new cabinet post of Minister with Special Responsibility for the Brazilian Amazon was subsequently created. In March 1996 a US $5,700m.-rain forest protection programme (to be funded by the Brazilian Government, the European Union and the G-7 group of industrialized countries over a five-year period) was concluded between President Cardoso and the Secretary-General of the United Nations. At a meeting in Manaus in October 1997, the G-7 group pledged an additional US $68m. In July 1997 Júlio Gaiger, the head of FUNAI, resigned, claiming that the Government had failed to honour its commitment to assist indigenous people. Legislation to provide greater protection for Brazil's natural resources, through the establishment of criminal penalties for illegal activities, was approved by the President in February 1998.

In 1990 a series of bilateral trade agreements was signed with Argentina, representing the first stage in a process leading to the eventual establishment of a Southern Cone Common Market (Mercado Comum do Sul—Mercosul), also to include Paraguay and Uruguay. In March 1991, in Paraguay, the four nations signed the Asunción treaty whereby they reaffirmed their commitment to the creation of such a market by the end of 1994. Mercosul duly came into effect on 1 January 1995, following the signing, by the Presidents of the four member nations, of the Ouro Prêto Protocol, in Brazil, in December 1994. While a complete common external tariff was not expected until 2006, customs barriers on 80%–85% of mutually exchanged goods were removed immediately. In 1999, however, Brazil's commercial relations with Argentina, in particular, were severely strained by the devaluation of the real, which prompted the latter country to impose curbs on certain Brazilian exports.

In May 1994 Brazil declared its full adherence to the 1967 Tlatelolco Treaty for the non-proliferation of nuclear weapons in Latin America and the Caribbean. The Treaty was promulgated by presidential decree in September 1994. Brazil signed the international Treaty on the Non-Proliferation of Nuclear Weapons in June 1997. The President ratified this and also the Comprehensive Test Ban Treaty (see p. 77) in July 1998.

Government

Under the 1988 Constitution, the country is a federal republic comprising 26 States and a Federal District (Brasília). Legislative power is exercised by the bicameral Congresso Nacional (National Congress), comprising the Senado Federal (Federal Senate—members elected by a system of proportional representation for four years) and the Câmara dos Deputados (Chamber of Deputies—members elected by the majority principle in rotation for eight years). The number of deputies is based on the size of the population. Election is by universal adult suffrage. Executive power is exercised by the President, elected by direct ballot for four years. The President appoints and leads the Cabinet. Each State has a directly elected Governor and an elected legislature. For the purposes of local government, the States are divided into municipalities.

Defence

Military service, lasting 12 months, is compulsory for men between 18 and 45 years of age. In August 2000 the armed forces totalled 287,600 (including 48,200 conscripts): army 189,000 (40,000 conscripts), navy 48,600 and air force 50,000. Public security forces number about 385,600. Defence expenditure for 2000 was budgeted at R $17,900m.

Economic Affairs

In 1998, according to estimates by the World Bank, Brazil's gross national product (GNP), measured at average 1996–98 prices, was US $767,568m., equivalent to US $4,630 per head. During 1990–98, it was estimated, GNP per head increased, in real terms, at an average rate of 1.7% per year. Over the same period, the population increased at an average annual rate of 1.6%. In 1999 GNP totalled about US $742,800m., equivalent to $4,420 per head (or $6,460 on an international purchasing-power parity basis). Brazil's gross domestic product (GDP) increased, in real terms, at an average annual rate of 2.9% in 1990–99. According to the IMF, GDP increased by an estimated 0.3% in 1998, and by 0.8% in 1999.

Agriculture (including hunting, forestry and fishing) engaged 24.2% of the employed labour force and contributed 7.9% of GDP in 1999. The principal cash crops are soya beans, coffee, tobacco, sugar cane and cocoa beans. Subsistence crops include wheat, maize, rice, potatoes, beans, cassava and sorghum. Beef and poultry production are also important, as is fishing (particularly tuna, crab and shrimp). During 1990–99, according to the World Bank, agricultural GDP increased at an average annual rate of 3.0%. Agricultural GDP increased by an estimated 2.7% in 1997 and by 0.2% in 1998. In late 1999 coffee production, in particular, was affected by drought.

Industry (including mining, manufacturing, construction and power) employed 19.3% of the working population and provided 33.8% of GDP in 1999. During 1990–99 industrial GDP increased at an average annual rate of 3.2%. Estimated growth of 5.5% was recorded in the sector in 1997. In 1998, however, industrial GDP declined by an estimated 0.9%.

Mining contributed 1.6% of GDP in 1999. The major mineral exports are iron ore (haematite—in terms of iron content, Brazil is the largest producer in the world), tin and aluminium (Brazil was the world's third largest producer of bauxite in 1997). Gold, phosphates, platinum, uranium, manganese, copper and coal are also mined. In 1990 deposits of niobium, thought to be the world's largest, were discovered in the state of Amazonas. Brazil's reserves of petroleum were estimated at 657m. metric tons in 1997.

Manufacturing contributed 20.5% of GDP in 1999. In the same year the sector engaged 11.5% of the total employed population. There is considerable state involvement in a broad range of manufacturing activity. While traditionally-dominant areas, including textiles and clothing, footwear and food- and beverage-processing, continue to contribute a large share to the sector, more recent developments in the sector have resulted in the emergence of machinery and transport equipment (including road vehicles and components, passenger jet aircraft and specialist machinery for the petroleum industry), construction materials (especially iron and steel), wood and sugar cane derivatives, and chemicals and petrochemicals as significant new manufacturing activities. According to the World Bank, manufacturing GDP increased at an average rate of 2.5% per year in 1990–98. The sector's production increased by 3.6% in 1997, but fell by 3.3% in 1998.

By the mid-1980s some 32% of total energy was derived from electricity (90% of which was hydroelectric), 30% from petroleum, 18% from wood and charcoal and 12% from fuel alcohol. Other energy sources, including coal and natural gas, accounted for some 8%. Attempts to exploit further the country's vast hydroelectric potential (estimated at 213,000 MW) were encouraged by the completion of ambitious dam projects at Itaipú, on the border with Paraguay (expected to produce as much as 35% of Brazil's total electricity requirements when fully operational), and at Tucuruí, on the Tocantins river. In late 2000 it was announced that plans were underway to further expand the hydroelectric power-station at Itaipú, increasing its generating capacity to 14,000 MW. By 1998 electricity production by hydroelectric sources was more than 50 times that of 1989. The construction of 49 thermal power stations was expected to be completed by 2003, and the Government was reported to be considering the development of windpower and of sugar-derived bagasse as alternative sources of energy. The Angra I nuclear power plant, inaugurated in 1985, has subsequently operated only intermittently, while financial constraints hindered the completion of the Angra II plant, which became operational in mid-2000, preventing further development of the country's nuclear programme. Imports of petroleum comprised 8.8% of the value of total merchandise imports in 1999.

The services sector contributed an estimated 58.3% of GDP and engaged 56.5% of the employed labour force in 1999.

According to the World Bank, the GDP of the services sector increased at an average rate of 2.7% per year in 1990–99. Growth in the sector's GDP was estimated at 1.7% in 1997 and 0.7% in 1998.

In 1999 Brazil recorded a visible trade deficit of US $1,207m. There was a deficit of US $25,073m. on the current account of the balance of payments. In 1999 the principal source of imports (23.5%) was the USA, which was also the principal market for exports (22.2%). Other major trading partners were Germany, Japan, Italy, the Netherlands and Argentina. The principal exports in 1999 were food and food-processing products (notably coffee), iron ore and concentrates, iron and steel products, machinery, and road vehicles and parts. The principal imports were mineral fuels, machinery and mechanical appliances, road vehicles and parts, and chemical products.

The 1999 federal budget recorded expenditure of R $163,709m. and revenue of R $158,781m. Brazil's external debt was US $232,004m. at the end of 1998, of which US $98,959m. was long-term public debt. In that year the cost of debt-servicing was equivalent to 74.1% of revenue from exports of goods and services. The annual rate of inflation averaged 289% in 1990–98. Consumer prices increased by an average of 3.2% in 1998 and by 4.9% in 1999. Official figures indicated an unemployment rate of 9.6% of the labour force in 1999. (Unemployment in São Paulo was estimated at a record 16.3% in September 1997.)

Brazil is a member of ALADI (see p. 230), Mercosul (p. 284), the Association of Tin Producing Countries (ATPC, p. 303) and the Cairns Group (p. 354). Brazil also joined the Comunidade dos Países de Língua Portuguesa (CPLP, p. 317), founded in 1996.

An economic stabilization programme, implemented during 1994 with the aim of balancing the budget and controlling inflation, was bolstered by the success of a new currency (the real), introduced on 1 July of that year, and by the reactivation of the privatization programme in early 1995. Upon his re-election to office in October 1998, President Cardoso immediately reiterated his pledge to reform the public sector and announced details of a three-year programme of fiscal adjustment, including drastic cuts in budgetary expenditure. In December of that year, in support of the Government's programme, the IMF formally approved Brazil's request for a three-year stand-by credit equivalent to US $18,100m. In January 1999, however, the unexpected resignation of the President of the Central Bank and his successor's decision to devalue the Brazilian currency (thus abandoning the exchange-rate policy agreed with the IMF) precipitated a period of renewed capital flight, seriously depleting the country's reserves and leading to turmoil on international financial markets. Brazil and the IMF subsequently reached agreement on a revised programme for 1999–2001, thus permitting lending to resume. Requirements included an increase in Brazil's budgetary surplus, which was to be raised from 2.6% of GDP to 3.1%, a reduction of the country's public debt to a level below the original specification of 46.5% of GDP, the introduction of a new monetary policy, incorporating a formal target for the restriction of inflation, and the acceleration of the Government's privatization programme. Also in March 1999 the first reduction in interest rates, which had reached 45%, was made. The economy grew by 4.0% in 2000 and was expected to expand by 4.5%–5.0% in 2001 and 2002. According to the IMF, consumer prices were projected to increase by 7.5% in 2000 and by 5.0% in 2001. Following its failure to achieve its projected US $2,800m. surplus for 2000, partly as a consequence of an increase in petroleum prices, the Government introduced a series of measures aimed at reducing the country's significant trade deficit, incorporating means for reducing export costs and developing the production of goods destined for export. The budget for 2001 projected total revenue of R $268,900m. and expenditure of R $240,800m., of which R $42,400m. was to be allocated to the social services sector (a 28% increase on the previous year), notably in the areas of education and health.

Social Welfare

The social security system, in existence since 1923, was rationalized in 1960, and the Instituto Nacional de Previdência Social (INPS) was formed in 1966. All social welfare programmes were consolidated in 1977 under the National System of Social Insurance and Assistance (SINPAS). The INPS administers benefits to urban and rural employees and their dependants. Benefits include sickness benefit, invalidity, old age, length of service and widows' pensions, maternity and family allowances and grants. There are three government agencies: the Instituto de Administração Financeira da Previdência e Assistência Social collects contributions and revenue and supplies funds, the Instituto Nacional de Assistência Médica da Previdência Social is responsible for medical care, and CEME (Central Medicines) supplies medicines at a low price. According to official sources, the state social security budget for 2000 was projected at R $3,800m. In the early 1990s privatization of pension fund management, based on the Chilean model, was implemented. By 1997 it was estimated that some US $70,000m. were being managed by pension funds in Brazil (including US $17,600m. controlled by Previ—the pension fund for the Banco do Brasil, and US $7,000m. controlled by the 260 members of the private funds association—the Associação Brasileira das Entidades Fechadas de Previdência Privada). Total assets controlled by pension funds were expected to exceed US $400,000m. by 2010.

In 1996 there were 127.2 physicians and 41.3 nurses per 100,000 people in Brazil. The private medical sector controls 90% of Brazil's hospitals. Budget forecasts for 2000 envisaged expenditure on health services of R $14,100m.

The welfare of the dwindling population of indigenous American Indians is the responsibility of the Fundação Nacional do Índio (FUNAI), which was formed to assign homelands to the Indians, most of whom are landless and threatened by the exploitation of the Amazon forest.

Education

Education is free in official pre-primary schools and is compulsory between the ages of seven and 14 years. Primary education begins at seven years of age and lasts for eight years. Secondary education, beginning at 15 years of age, lasts for three years and is also free in official schools. In 1998 95.8% of children in the relevant age-group were enrolled at primary schools, but only 30.7% of those aged 15 to 17 were enrolled at secondary schools. The Federal Government is responsible for higher education, and in 1997 there were 150 universities, of which 77 were state-administered. Numerous private institutions exist at all levels of education. Expenditure on education by the central Government was forecast at R $5,100m. for 2000.

Despite an anti-illiteracy campaign, initiated in 1971, according to official estimates in 1996 the adult illiteracy rate was 14.7%.

Public Holidays

2001: 1 January (New Year's Day—Universal Confraternization Day), 26–28 February (Carnival), 13 April (Good Friday), 21 April (Tiradentes Day—Discovery of Brazil) 1 May (Labour Day), 24 May (Ascension Day), 14 June (Corpus Christi), 7 September (Independence Day), 12 October (Our Lady Aparecida, Patron Saint of Brazil), 2 November (All Souls' Day), 15 November (Proclamation of the Republic), 25 December (Christmas Day).

2002: 1 January (New Year's Day—Universal Confraternization Day), 11–13 February (Carnival), 29 March (Good Friday), 21 April (Tiradentes Day—Discovery of Brazil), 1 May (Labour Day), 9 May (Ascension Day), 30 May (Corpus Christi), 7 September (Independence Day), 12 October (Our Lady Aparecida, Patron Saint of Brazil), 2 November (All Souls' Day), 15 November (Proclamation of the Republic), 25 December (Christmas Day).

Other local holidays include 20 January (Foundation of Rio de Janeiro) and 25 January (Foundation of São Paulo).

Weights and Measures

The metric system is in force.

Statistical Survey

Sources (unless otherwise stated): Economic Research Department, Banco Central do Brasil, SBS, Q 03, Bloco B, Brasília, DF; tel. (61) 414-1074; fax (61) 414-2036; e-mail coace.depec.@bcb.gov.br; internet www.bcb.gov.br/; Instituto Brasileiro de Geografia e Estatística (IBGE), Centro de Documentação e Disseminação de Informações (CDDI), Rua Gen. Canabarro 706, 4° andar, 20271-201 Maracanã, Rio de Janeiro, RJ; tel. (21) 569-2901; fax (21) 284-1959; internet www.ibge.gov.br.

Area and Population

AREA, POPULATION AND DENSITY

Area (sq km)	8,547,403.5*
Population (census results)†	
1 September 1991	146,825,475
1 August 1996	
Males	77,442,865
Females	79,628,298
Total	157,070,163
Population (official estimates at mid-year)†	
1997	159,636,400
1998	161,790,300
1999	163,947,600
Density (per sq km) at mid-1999	19.2

* 3,300,170.9 sq miles.

† Excluding Indian jungle population, numbering 45,429 in 1950.

ADMINISTRATIVE DIVISIONS
(population at census of 1 August 1996)

State	Population	Capital
Acre (AC)	483,593	Rio Branco
Alagoas (AL)	2,633,251	Maceió
Amapá (AP)	379,459	Macapá
Amazonas (AM) . . .	2,389,279	Manaus
Bahia (BA)	12,541,675	Salvador
Ceará (CE)	6,809,290	Fortaleza
Espírito Santo (ES) . .	2,802,707	Vitória
Goiás (GO)	4,514,967	Goiânia
Maranhão (MA) . . .	5,222,183	São Luís
Mato Grosso (MT) . .	2,235,832	Cuiabá
Mato Grosso do Sul (MS) .	1,927,834	Campo Grande
Minas Gerais (MG) . .	16,672,613	Belo Horizonte
Pará (PA)	5,510,849	Belém
Paraíba (PB) . . .	3,305,616	João Pessoa
Paraná (PR) . . .	9,003,804	Curitiba
Pernambuco (PE) . .	7,399,071	Recife
Piauí (PI)	2,673,085	Teresina
Rio de Janeiro (RJ) . .	13,406,308	Rio de Janeiro
Rio Grande do Norte (RN) .	2,558,660	Natal
Rio Grande do Sul (RS) .	9,634,688	Porto Alegre
Rondônia (RO) . . .	1,229,306	Porto Velho
Roraima (RR) . . .	247,131	Boa Vista
Santa Catarina (SC) . .	4,875,244	Florianópolis
São Paulo (SP) . . .	34,119,110	São Paulo
Sergipe (SE) . . .	1,624,020	Aracaju
Tocantins (TO) . . .	1,048,642	Palmas
Distrito Federal (DF) . .	1,821,946	Brasília
Total	**157,070,163**	—

PRINCIPAL TOWNS (population at census of 1 August 1996)*

São Paulo . . .	9,839,066	Campo Grande .	600,069
Rio de Janeiro . .	5,551,538	João Pessoa . .	549,363
Salvador . . .	2,211,539	Jaboatão . .	529,966
Belo Horizonte . .	2,091,371	Contagem . .	492,214
Fortaleza . .	1,965,513	São José dos	
Brasília (capital) .	1,821,946	Campos . .	486,167
Curitiba . .	1,476,253	Ribeirão Preto .	456,252
Recife . . .	1,346,045	Feira de Santana .	450,487
Porto Alegre .	1,288,879	Niterói . .	450,364
Manaus . .	1,157,357	São João de	
Belém . . .	1,144,312	Meriti . .	434,323
Goiânia . .	1,003,477	Cuiabá . .	433,355
Guarulhos . .	972,197	Sorocaba . .	431,561
Campinas . .	908,906	Aracaju . .	428,194
São Gonçalo .	833,379	Juíz de Fora .	424,479
Nova Iguaçu . .	826,188	Londrina . .	421,343
São Luís . .	780,833	Uberlândia . .	438,986
Maceió . .	723,142	Santos . .	412,243
Duque de Caxias .	715,089	Joinville . .	397,951
São Bernardo do		Campos dos	
Campo . .	660,396	Goytacazes . .	389,547
Natal . . .	656,037	Olinda . .	349,380
Teresina . .	655,473	Diadema . .	323,116
Santo André . .	624,820	Porto Velho .	294,227
Osasco . .	622,912	Jundiai . .	293,373

* Figures refer to *municípios,* which may contain rural districts.

BIRTHS AND DEATHS (official estimates)

	Birth rate (per 1,000)	Death rate (per 1,000)
1992	22.09	7.04
1993	21.37	6.98
1994	20.75	6.92
1995	20.14	6.87
1996	19.69	6.82
1997	19.25	6.78
1998	20.30	6.75
1999	20.10	6.72

Expectation of life (official estimates, years at birth, mid-1999): 66.97 (males 63.35; females 70.76).

ECONOMICALLY ACTIVE POPULATION (household surveys, September each year, '000 persons aged 10 years and over)*

	1997	1998	1999
Agriculture, hunting, forestry and fishing	16,770.7	16,338.1	17,372.1
Manufacturing	8,507.0	8,230.6	8,278.1
Mining and quarrying . . }	774.3	861.6	783.1
Electricity, gas and water . }			
Construction	4,583.5	4,980.0	4,743.1
Wholesale and retail trade . .	9,222.8	9,417.0	9,618.4
Transport and communications .	2,759.0	2,786.6	2,815.2
Community, social and personal services (incl. restaurants and hotels)	25,436.4	26,040.5	26,721.3
Financing, insurance, real estate and business services . . }	1,277.9	1,308.7	1,344.3
Activities not adequately defined }			
Total employed . . .	**69,331.5**	**69,963.1**	**71,676.2**
Unemployed	5,881.8	6,922.6	7,639.1
Total labour force . . .	**75,213.3**	**76,885.7**	**79,315.3**
Males	44,832.2	45,614.0	46,480.9
Females	30,381.1	31,271.7	32,834.4

* Figures exclude the rural population of the States of Rondônia, Acre, Amazonas, Roraima, Pará and Amapá.

Agriculture

PRINCIPAL CROPS ('000 metric tons)

	1997	1998	1999
Wheat	2,489	2,270	2,438
Rice (paddy)	8,352	7,716	11,783
Barley	259	300	315
Maize	32,948	29,602	32,038
Oats	229	207	288
Sorghum	543	590	574
Potatoes	2,670	2,784	2,843
Sweet potatoes	490	445	650*
Cassava (Manioc)	19,896	19,503	20,892
Yams*	225	225	225
Dry beans	2,840	2,191	2,817
Soybeans (Soya beans)	26,391	31,307	30,901
Groundnuts (in shell)	141	193	173
Castor beans	97	17	31
Cottonseed†	526	754	n.a.
Coconuts	1,451	1,505	1,723
Babassu kernels	790	752	n.a.
Tomatoes	2,718	2,784	3,251
Onions (dry)	881	838	990
Other vegetables†	2,209	2,204	2,892
Water-melons	625	770*	770*
Sugar cane	331,613	345,255	337,165
Grapes	891	774	895
Apples‡	3,968	3,957	4,724
Peaches and nectarines	128	146†	195*
Oranges‡	115,234	104,252	113,841
Tangerines, mandarins, clementines and satsumas	782	721†	760†
Lemons and limes	509	470*	470*
Avocados	84	75*	75*
Mangoes	508	600*	600*
Pineapples	1,073	1,094	1,175
Bananas§	541,236	532,220	552,778
Papayas	1,531	1,621	1,700*
Cashew nuts	125	54	131
Coffee beans (green)‖	2,457	3,379	3,268
Cocoa beans	278	281	205
Tobacco (leaves)	597	505	626
Jute and allied fibres	4	9	8
Sisal	138	116	194
Cotton (lint)†	280	380	455
Other fibre crops*	88	88	88
Natural rubber*	54	55	55

* FAO estimate(s).
† Unofficial figure(s).
‡ In '000 fruit.
§ In '000 bunches.
‖ Official figures, reported in terms of dry cherries, have been converted into green coffee beans at 50%.

Source: partly FAO.

LIVESTOCK ('000 head, year ending September)

	1997	1998	1999
Cattle	156,289	159,752	163,470
Buffaloes*	1,700	1,700	1,700
Horses*	6,400	6,400	6,400
Asses*	1,350	1,350	1,350
Mules*	2,000	2,000	2,000
Pigs	27,670	27,542	27,425
Sheep*	18,300	18,300	18,300
Goats*	12,600	12,600	12,600
Chickens*	892,000	900,000	950,000
Ducks*	8,800	8,800	8,800
Turkeys*	7,500	8,200	8,700

* FAO estimates.
Source: FAO.

LIVESTOCK PRODUCTS ('000 metric tons)

	1997	1998	1999
Beef and veal	5,922	5,794	6,182
Mutton and lamb*	88	88	88
Goat meat*	43	43	43
Pig meat	1,518	1,652	1,752
Horse meat*	14	14	14
Poultry meat	4,584	4,983	5,661
Cows' milk†	20,600	21,630	22,495
Goats' milk	141	141	141
Butter and ghee†	68	68	69
Cheese	34	39	9
Dried milk	231†	240†	247*
Hen eggs*	1,500	1,500	1,500
Other poultry eggs*	25	25	25
Honey*	18	18	18
Wool:			
greasy*	25	25	25
scoured	16	16	n.a.
Cattle hides (fresh)	515	590*	600*

* FAO estimate(s). † Unofficial figure(s).
Source: FAO.

Forestry

ROUNDWOOD REMOVALS
('000 cubic metres, excl. bark)

	1996	1997	1998
Sawlogs, veneer logs and logs for sleepers	47,779	47,779	46,779
Pulpwood	30,701	30,701	30,701
Other industrial wood	6,121	6,204	6,284
Fuel wood	114,052	114,052	114,052
Total	198,653	198,736	197,816

Source: FAO, *Yearbook of Forest Products*.

SAWNWOOD PRODUCTION
(FAO estimates, '000 cubic metres, incl. railway sleepers)

	1996	1997	1998
Coniferous (softwood)	8,591	8,591	8,591
Broadleaved (hardwood)	10,500	10,500	10,000
Total	19,091	19,091	18,591

Source: FAO, *Yearbook of Forest Products*.

Fishing

('000 metric tons, live weight)

	1996	1997	1998
Capture	715.5	744.6	760.0
Characins	84.9	68.1	68.5
Freshwater siluroids	47.3	52.6	52.9
Weakfishes	26.5	26.0	29.1
Whitemouth croaker	23.4	23.3	26.2
Brazilian sardinella	97.1	117.6	82.3
Skipjack tuna	22.5	26.6	23.8
Penaeus shrimps	23.8	25.3	28.3
Aquaculture	77.7*	87.7	95.0*
Common carp	23.9*	35.5	38.5*
Total catch	793.2*	832.3	855.0*

* FAO estimate.

Note: Figures exclude aquatic mammals, recorded by number rather than by weight. The number of baleen whales caught was: 1 in 1997; 1 in 1998. The number of toothed whales caught was: 171 in 1997; 136 in 1998. Also excluded are crocodiles. The number of spectacled caimans caught was: 659 in 1996; 7,307 in 1997; 242 in 1998.

Source: FAO, *Yearbook of Fishery Statistics*.

Mining

('000 metric tons, unless otherwise indicated)

	1997	1998	1999
Hard coal	5,632	5,571	5,720
Crude petroleum ('000 cubic metres)	50,446	58,279	65,451
Natural gas (million cubic metres)	9,865	10,833	11,855
Iron ore:			
gross weight[1]	185,128	207,017	190,345
metal content[1]	122,184	124,210	114,207
Copper concentrates (metric tons)[2]	39,952	34,446	31,371
Nickel ore (metric tons)[2]	31,936	36,764	43,784
Bauxite	11,671	11,961	12,880
Lead concentrates (metric tons)[2]	8,729	7,567	10,281
Zinc concentrates (metric tons)[2]	152,634	87,475	98,590
Tin concentrates (metric tons)[2]	18,291	14,238	13,202
Manganese ore[2]	977	988	770
Chromium ore (metric tons)[3]	112,274	160,742	190,000
Tungsten concentrates (metric tons)[2]	40	—	—
Ilmenite (metric tons)	97,174	103,000	96,000
Rutile (metric tons)	1,742	1,800	4,300
Zirconium concentrates (metric tons)[4]	19,252	20,132	29,448
Silver (kilograms)[5]	26,598	34,000	42,000
Gold (kilograms)[6]	58,488	49,567	40,943
Bentonite (beneficiated)	230.0	220.0	274.6
Kaolin (beneficiated)	1,165.0	1,373.9	1,516.7
Magnesite (beneficiated)	294.6	308.3	259.8
Phosphate rock[7]	4,275.6	4,421.4	4,300.6
Potash salts[8]	280.2	326.5	348.2
Fluorspar (Fluorite) (metric tons)[9,10]	78,032	72,082	44,926
Barite (Barytes) (beneficiated) (metric tons)	51,961	46,632	44,906
Salt (unrefined):			
marine	5,064	5,353	4,528
rock	1,452	1,484	1,430
Gypsum and anhydrite (crude)	1,507.1	1,632.0	1,456.3
Graphite (natural) (metric tons)[1,9]	40,587	61,369	n.a.
Asbestos (fibre)[1,9,11]	170	170	170
Mica (metric tons)	4,000	4,000	5,000
Talc and pyrophyllite (crude)	444.3	452.2	460.0
Diamonds ('000 carats):			
gem[1,11]	300	300	300
industrial[1,11]	600	600	600

[1] Data from the US Geological Survey.
[2] Figures refer to the metal content of ores and concentrates.
[3] Figures refer to the chromic oxide (Cr_2O_3) content.
[4] Including production of baddeleyite-caldasite.
[5] Figures refer to primary production only. The production of secondary silver (in kilograms) was: 32,000 in 1997; 40,000 in 1998; 50,000 in 1999.
[6] Including production by independent miners (garimpeiros): 17,426 kg in 1997; 11,780 kg in 1998; 2,556 kg in 1999.
[7] Figures refer to the gross weight of concentrates. The phosphoric acid (P_2O_5) content (in '000 metric tons) was: 1,510 in 1997; 1,561 in 1998; 1,528 in 1999.
[8] Figures refer to the potassium oxide (K_2O) content.
[9] Figures refer to marketable products.
[10] Acid-grade and metallurgical-grade concentrates.
[11] Estimated production.

Source (unless otherwise indicated): Departamento Nacional de Produção Mineral, Ministério de Minas e Energia.

Industry

SELECTED PRODUCTS ('000 metric tons, unless otherwise indicated)

	1997	1998	1999
Asphalt	1,572	2,060	n.a.
Electric power (million kWh)	330,358	341,880	n.a.
Pig-iron	25,013	25,111	25,549
Crude steel	26,153	25,760	24,996
Cement*	38,096	39,942	40,270
Passenger cars ('000 units)	1,678	1,254	1,102
Commercial vehicles (units)	390,800	331,614	248,367
Tractors (units)	24,494	25,167	22,157
Newsprint	265	273	n.a.

* Portland cement only.

Finance

CURRENCY AND EXCHANGE RATES

Monetary Units
100 centavos = 1 real (plural: reais).

Sterling, Dollar and Euro Equivalents (29 December 2000)
£1 sterling = 2.9167 reais;
US $1 = 1.9546 reais;
€1 = 1.8188 reais;
100 reais = £34.29 = $51.16 = €54.98.

Average Exchange Rates (reais per US $)
1998   1.161
1999   1.815
2000   1.830

Note: In March 1986 the cruzeiro (CR $) was replaced by a new currency unit, the cruzado (CZ $), equivalent to 1,000 cruzeiros. In January 1989 the cruzado was, in turn, replaced by the new cruzado (NCZ $), equivalent to CZ $1,000 and initially at par with the US dollar (US $). In March 1990 the new cruzado was replaced by the cruzeiro (CR $), at an exchange rate of one new cruzado for one cruzeiro. In August 1993 the cruzeiro was replaced by the cruzeiro real, equivalent to CR $1,000. On 1 March 1994, in preparation for the introduction of a new currency, a transitional accounting unit, the Unidade Real de Valor (at par with the US $), came into operation, alongside the cruzeiro real. On 1 July 1994 the cruzeiro real was replaced by the real (R $), also at par with the US $ and thus equivalent to 2,750 cruzeiros reais.

BUDGET (R $ million)*

Revenue	1997	1998	1999
Tax revenue	108,731	130,681	147,366
Income tax	32,244	41,675	46,471
Value-added tax on industrial products	16,551	16,092	16,084
Tax on financial operations	3,769	3,514	4,843
Import duty	5,103	6,490	7,806
Tax on financial and share transactions	6,908	8,113	7,948
Social security contributions	18,405	17,732	30,935
Tax on profits of legal entities	7,241	7,183	9,477
Contributions to Social Integration Programme and Financial Reserve Fund for Public Employees	7,228	6,783	6,776
Repayment of loans	7,200	8,278	11,386
Transfer of profits from Banco do Brasil	103	127	29
Total	**116,034**	**139,086**	**158,781**

Expenditure	1997	1998	1999
Earmarked expenditures . . .	32,193	38,468	40,062
Transfers to state and local governments†	25,042	29,166	33,432
Other expenditures . .	86,965	107,471	121,233
Wages and social contributions	42,848	47,296	50,169
Interest payments . . .	17,975	27,706	35,439
Funding and investment . .	24,252	32,469	35,625
Lending	2,522	2,394	2,414
Total	**121,680**	**148,333**	**163,709**

* Figures refer to cash operations of the National Treasury, including the collection and transfer of earmarked revenues for social expenditure purposes. The data exclude the transactions of other funds and accounts controlled by the Federal Government.
† Constitutionally mandated participation funds.

CENTRAL BANK RESERVES (US $ million at 31 December)

	1998	1999	2000
Gold*	1,358	929	523
IMF special drawing rights . .	2	10	—
Foreign exchange . . .	42,578	34,786	32,488
Total	**43,938**	**35,725**	**33,011**

* Valued at market-related prices.
Source: IMF, *International Financial Statistics*.

MONEY SUPPLY (R $ million at 31 December)

	1997	1998	1999
Currency outside banks . . .	18,141	21,185	25,978
Demand deposits at deposit money banks.	27,912	29,059	36,251
Total money (incl. others) . .	**50,999**	**54,819**	**62,287**

Source: IMF, *International Financial Statistics*.

COST OF LIVING
(Consumer Price Index at December; base: December 1992 = 100)

	1997	1998	1999
Food	32,214.0	32,842.0	35,510.4
All items (incl. others) . .	**36,967.1**	**37,579.2**	**40,938.8**

NATIONAL ACCOUNTS (R $ '000 at current prices)
Composition of the Gross National Product

	1997	1998	1999
Compensation of employees	318,785,117	328,210,516	360,096,000
Operating surplus Consumption of fixed capital }	419,503,163	445,594,317	446,596,000
Gross domestic product (GDP) at factor cost	738,288,280	773,804,833	806,692,000
Indirect taxes . . .	129,541,930	129,464,334	157,273,000
Less Subsidies . . .	3,719,184	3,455,035	3,106,000
GDP in purchasers' values	864,111,026	899,814,132	960,859,000
Factor income received from abroad	5,579,926	5,396,135	7,353,000
Less Factor income paid abroad	22,690,178	27,758,308	42,176,000
Gross national product .	**847,000,774**	**877,451,959**	**926,036,000**

Expenditure on the Gross Domestic Product

	1997	1998	1999
Government final consumption expenditure	154,238,952	159,920,518	181,160,000
Private final consumption expenditure	545,113,309	572,390,773	593,938,000
Increase in stocks . .	15,342,520	12,271,254	14,639,000
Gross fixed capital formation .	172,212,039	179,202,590	181,813,000
Total domestic expenditure .	**886,906,820**	**923,785,135**	**971,550,000**
Exports of goods and services .	65,490,952	66,862,010	101,809,000
Less Imports of goods and services	88,286,746	90,833,013	112,501,000
GDP in purchasers' values .	**864,111,026**	**899,814,132**	**960,858,000**
GDP at constant 1999 prices	**951,234,004**	**953,326,719**	**960,858,000**

Gross Domestic Product by Economic Activity (at factor cost)

	1997	1998	1999
Agriculture, hunting, forestry and fishing .	68,005,538	75,764,350	79,405,305
Mining and quarrying . .	7,776,999	5,758,810	15,950,243
Manufacturing . . .	183,882,826	182,662,269	206,238,561
Electricity, gas and water .	22,898,942	24,744,889	27,480,539
Construction	86,411,103	92,320,930	91,185,424
Trade, restaurants and hotels	66,363,727	65,236,525	73,793,894
Transport, storage and communications . .	43,724,018	50,389,591	52,366,761
Finance, insurance, real estate and business services	56,858,506	58,847,844	61,206,655
Government services . .	131,863,343	139,291,228	155,082,481
Rents	131,344,876	138,031,488	138,267,466
Other community, social and personal services . .	109,310,045	113,286,599	106,174,809
Sub-total	**908,439,922**	**946,334,523**	**1,007,075,270**
Less Imputed bank service charge	44,328,896	46,520,391	46,217,270
Total	**864,111,026**	**899,814,132**	**960,858,000**

BALANCE OF PAYMENTS (US $ million)

	1997	1998	1999
Exports of goods f.o.b. . .	53,189	51,136	48,012
Imports of goods f.o.b. . .	−59,841	−57,739	−49,219
Trade balance	**−6,652**	**−6,603**	**−1,207**
Exports of services . .	5,989	7,631	7,734
Imports of services . . .	−15,298	−16,676	−14,429
Balance on goods and services	**−15,961**	**−15,648**	**−7,902**
Other income received . .	5,344	4,914	3,929
Other income paid . . .	−21,688	−24,531	−22,788
Balance on goods, services and income	**−32,305**	**−35,265**	**−26,761**
Current transfers received . .	2,130	1,795	1,968
Current transfers paid . .	−316	−359	−280
Current balance . . .	**−30,491**	**−33,829**	**−25,073**
Capital account (net) . .	482	375	339
Direct investment abroad . .	−1,042	−2,721	−1,680
Direct investment from abroad .	19,650	31,913	32,659
Portfolio investment assets . .	−335	−594	259
Portfolio investment liabilities .	10,393	19,013	1,664
Financial derivatives assets . .	n.a.	n.a.	627
Financial derivatives liabilities .	n.a.	n.a.	−733
Other investment assets . .	2,251	−5,992	−11,155
Other investment liabilities . .	−5,999	−21,556	−14,418
Net errors and omissions . .	−3,160	−2,911	746
Overall balance . . .	**−8,251**	**−16,302**	**−16,765**

Source: IMF, *International Financial Statistics*.

External Trade

PRINCIPAL COMMODITIES

(distribution by SITC, US $ million, excl. military goods)

Imports f.o.b.	1997	1998	1999
Food and live animals . . .	4,226.2	4,626.7	3.280
Cereals and cereal preparations .	1,569.3	1,939.8	1,440
Crude materials (inedible) except fuels	2,364.8	1,925.8	1,569
Mineral fuels, lubricants, etc. .	6,783.1	5,110.0	5,433
Petroleum, petroleum products, etc.	5,549.2	3,925.0	4,336
Chemicals and related products	9,255.7	9,554.0	9,274
Organic chemicals . . .	3,289.8	3,158.5	2,942
Medicinal and pharmaceutical products	1,410.6	1,582.0	1,916
Plastics in primary forms . .	1,091.0	1,117.1	1,009
Basic manufactures . . .	6,257.8	6,171.4	4,776
Machinery and transport equipment	26,021.3	25,777.0	21,450
Power-generating machinery and equipment	1,979.8	2,331.0	2,290
Machinery specialized for particular industries . . .	3,355.9	2,976.0	2,322
General industrial machinery, equipment and parts . .	3,582.5	3,624.0	2,748
Office machines and automatic data-processing machines . .	1,718.3	1,733.0	1,541
Telecommunications and sound equipment . . .	3,277.4	2,773.0	2,575
Other electrical machinery, apparatus, etc. . . .	4,877.0	4,745.5	4,452
Road vehicles and parts* . .	5,319.7	5,607.3	3,409
Other transport equipment* . .	1,018.9	1,125.1	1,210
Miscellaneous manufactured articles	4,238.8	3,903.2	3,020
Professional, scientific and controlling instruments, etc. .	1,212.3	1,258.5	1,117
Total (incl. others) . . .	59,757.7	57,734.0	49,224

* Excluding tyres, engines and electrical parts.

Exports f.o.b.	1997	1998	1999
Food and live animals . . .	11,438.8	10,363.3	10,386.0
Meat and meat preparations . .	1,556.3	1,591.5	1,928.6
Vegetables and fruit . . .	1,428.5	1,667.6	1,691.4
Sugar, sugar preparations and honey	1,863.6	2,030.7	2,011.3
Coffee, tea, cocoa and spices . .	3,426.3	2,939.3	2,761.0
Feeding-stuff for animals (excl. unmilled cereals) . . .	2,841.9	1,800.7	1,586.9
Beverages and tobacco . .	1,755.4	1,624.6	1,017.8
Tobacco and tobacco manufactures	1,664.8	1,559.0	961.2
Crude materials (inedible) except fuels	7,700.8	7,949.0	7,163.5
Oil seeds and oleaginous fruit .	2,453.6	2,180.4	1,595.1
Pulp and waste paper . . .	1,024.2	1,049.4	1,243.6
Metalliferous ores and metal scrap	3,190.5	3,661.6	3,168.2
Chemicals and related products	3,402.7	3,195.6	3,019.8
Organic chemicals . . .	1,155.1	1,054.7	1,016.2
Basic manufactures . . .	11,223.0	10,184.4	9,776.3
Textile yarn, fabrics, etc. . .	1,021.9	891.0	819.9
Iron and steel	3,889.2	3,671.1	3,103.1
Non-ferrous metals . . .	1,668.0	1,276.0	1,499.3
Machinery and transport equipment	11,992.6	12,600.5	11,386.7
Power-generating machinery and equipment	1,488.6	1,550.2	1,384.3
Machinery specialized for particular industries . .	1,289.0	1,163.1	854.7

Exports f.o.b. — *continued*	1997	1998	1999
General industrial machinery, equipment and parts . . .	1,595.3	1,508.4	1,411.8
Electrical machinery, apparatus, etc.	1,640.5	1,534.5	1,682.1
Road vehicles and parts* . . .	4,453.3	4,827.8	3,499.6
Other transport equipment* . .	1,000.1	1,481.3	1,937.7
Miscellaneous manufactured articles	3,084.1	2,869.0	2,888.9
Footwear	1,594.5	1,387.1	1,342.3
Total (incl. others) . . .	52,994.3	51,139.9	48,011.4

* Excluding tyres, engines and electrical parts.

PRINCIPAL TRADING PARTNERS (US $ million)*

Imports f.o.b.	1997	1998	1999
Algeria	766	624	988
Argentina	7,941	8,031	5,814
Belgium-Luxembourg . . .	638	718	493
Canada	1,416	1,338	973
Chile	974	817	718
China, People's Republic . . .	1,166	1,034	865
France	1,641	1,977	1,989
Germany	4,959	5,239	4,714
Italy	3,407	3,232	2,598
Japan	3,534	3,277	2,576
Korea, Republic	1,355	988	1,019
Mexico	1,173	983	618
Netherlands	576	697	594
Nigeria	520	612	738
Paraguay	518	350	260
Saudi Arabia	1,100	727	615
Spain	1,141	1,195	1,179
Sweden	857	1,104	924
Switzerland	854	902	773
Taiwan	801	699	540
United Kingdom	1,451	1,489	1,222
USA	13,706	13,512	11,730
Uruguay	967	1,042	647
Venezuela	1,006	756	974
Total (incl. others) . . .	59,746	57,734	49,843

Exports f.o.b.	1997	1998	1999
Argentina	6,770	6,748	5,364
Belgium-Luxembourg . . .	1,483	2,195	1,817
Canada	584	544	513
Chile	1,197	1,024	896
China, People's Republic . .	1,088	905	676
France	1,113	1,231	1,200
Germany	2,608	3,006	2,544
Iran	245	493	495
Italy	1,709	1,931	1,845
Japan	3,068	2,205	2,193
Korea, Republic	737	467	628
Mexico	828	1,002	1,068
Netherlands	3,998	2,745	2,594
Paraguay	1,407	1,249	744
Russia	761	647	746
Spain	1,057	1,056	1,169
United Kingdom	1,259	1,339	1,437
USA	9,276	9,747	10,675
Uruguay	870	881	670
Venezuela	768	706	537
Total (incl. others) . . .	52,994	51,140	48,011

* Imports by country of purchase; exports by country of last consignment.

Source: Ministério do Desenvolvimento, Indústria e Comércio Exterior, Brasília, DF.

Transport

RAILWAYS*

	1997	1998	1999
Passengers (million) .	1,221	1,255	n.a.
Passenger-km (million) .	12,688	12,667	n.a.
Freight ('000 metric tons) .	267,795	271,829	271,799
Freight ton-km (million) .	138,724	142,446	140,817

* Including suburban and metro services.

Source: Empresa Brasileira de Planejamento de Transportes (GEIPOT), Brasília, DF.

ROAD TRAFFIC (motor vehicles in use at 31 December)

	1997	1998	1999
Passenger cars .	20,194,882	21,313,351	22,347,423
Buses and coaches .	348,168	430,062	400,048
Light goods vehicles .	3,158,695	3,313,774	3,193,058
Heavy goods vehicles .	1,699,338	1,755,877	1,778,084
Motorcycles and mopeds .	3,365,121	3,854,646	4,222,705

Source: Empresa Brasileira de Planejamento de Transportes (GEIPOT).

SHIPPING

Merchant Fleet (registered at 31 December)

	1996	1997	1998
Number of vessels .	539	536	504
Total displacement ('000 grt) .	4,530	4,372	4,171

Source: Lloyd's Register of Shipping, *World Fleet Statistics*.

International Sea-borne Freight Traffic ('000 metric tons)

	1997	1998	1999
Goods loaded .	259,238	269,935	269,863
Goods unloaded .	155,002	173,070	165,847

Source: Empresa Brasileira de Planejamento de Transportes (GEIPOT).

CIVIL AVIATION (embarked passengers, mail and cargo)

	1997	1998	1999
Number of passengers ('000) .	25,149	32,179	30,678
Passenger-km (million) .	44,930	49,291	44,158
Freight ton-km ('000)* .	5,657,255	6,023,161	5,380,194

* Including mail.

Source: Empresa Brasileira de Planejamento de Transportes (GEIPOT), Brasília, DF.

Tourism

FOREIGN TOURIST ARRIVALS

Country of origin	1997	1998	1999
Argentina .	938,973	1,467,922	1,548,571
Bolivia .	n.a.	150,242	145,070
Chile .	92,233	159,673	170,564
France .	84,552	121,272	131,978
Germany .	140,578	262,740	282,846
Italy .	123,114	169,566	177,589
Paraguay .	146,581	451,693	501,425
Portugal .	63,315	105,593	115,088
Spain .	63,809	91,968	99,677
United Kingdom .	62,308	117,518	125,607
USA .	402,200	524,093	559,367
Uruguay .	206,468	359,186	383,741
Total (incl. others) .	n.a.	4,818,084	5,107,169

Receipts from tourism (US $ million): 2,594.9 in 1997; 3,678 in 1998; 3,994 in 1999.

Source: Instituto Brasileiro de Turismo—EMBRATUR, Brasília, DF.

Communications Media

	1995	1996	1997
Radio receivers ('000 in use)* .	63,500	70,000	71,000
Television receivers ('000 in use)* .	35,000	36,000	36,500
Daily newspapers*			
Number .	352	380	n.a.
Average circulation ('000 copies)	6,551	6,472	n.a.
Non-daily newspapers*			
Number .	703	938	n.a.
Telephones in use ('000 main lines)†	14,875	17,729	n.a.
Telefax stations‡ .	270,000§	350,000§	500,000
Mobile cellular telephones (subscribers)‡ .	1,285,533	2,498,154	4,400,000

* Source: UNESCO, *Statistical Yearbook*.
† Source: Fundação Instituto Brasileiro de Geografia e Estatística (IBGE).
‡ Source: UN, *Statistical Yearbook*.
§ Provisional figure.

1998 ('000): Fixed telephone lines 22,599.9; Mobile cellular telephones 9,099.9 (Source: ANATEL, Ministério das Comunicações, Brasília, DF).

Education

(1998)

	Institutions	Teachers	Students
Pre-primary .	78,107	219,594	4,111,153
Literacy classes (Classe de Alfabetização) .	34,064	46,126	806,288
Primary .	187,497	1,460,469	35,845,742
Secondary .	17,602	380,222	6,968,531
Higher* .	900	173,705	1,948,200

* 1997 figures (preliminary).

Source: Ministério da Educação, Brasília, DF.

Directory

The Constitution

A new Constitution was promulgated on 5 October 1988. The following is a summary of the main provisions:

The Federative Republic of Brazil, formed by the indissoluble union of the States, the Municipalities and the Federal District, is constituted as a democratic state. All power emanates from the people. The Federative Republic of Brazil seeks the economic, political, social and cultural integration of the peoples of Latin America.

All are equal before the law. The inviolability of the right to life, freedom, equality, security and property is guaranteed. No one shall be subjected to torture. Freedom of thought, conscience, religious belief and expression are guaranteed, as is privacy. The principles of habeas corpus and 'habeas data' (the latter giving citizens access to personal information held in government data banks) are granted. There is freedom of association, and the right to strike is guaranteed.

There is universal suffrage by direct secret ballot. Voting is compulsory for literate persons between 18 and 69 years of age, and optional for those who are illiterate, those over 70 years of age and those aged 16 and 17.

Brasília is the federal capital. The Union's competence includes maintaining relations with foreign states, and taking part in international organizations; declaring war and making peace; guaranteeing national defence; decreeing a state of siege; issuing currency; supervising credits, etc.; formulating and implementing plans for economic and social development; maintaining national services, including communications, energy, the judiciary and the police; legislating on civil, commercial, penal, procedural, electoral, agrarian, maritime, aeronautical, spatial and labour law, etc. The Union, States, Federal District and Municipalities must protect the Constitution, laws and democratic institutions, and preserve national heritage.

The States are responsible for electing their Governors by universal suffrage and direct secret ballot for a four-year term. The organization of the Municipalities, the Federal District and Territories is regulated by law.

The Union may intervene in the States and in the Federal District only in certain circumstances, such as a threat to national security or public order, and then only after reference to the National Congress.

LEGISLATIVE POWER

The legislative power is exercised by the Congresso Nacional (National Congress), which is composed of the Câmara dos Deputados (Chamber of Deputies) and the Senado Federal (Federal Senate). Elections for deputies and senators take place simultaneously throughout the country; candidates for the Congresso must be Brazilian by birth and have full exercise of their political rights. They must be at least 21 years of age in the case of deputies and at least 35 years of age in the case of senators. The Congresso meets twice a year in ordinary sessions, and extraordinary sessions may be convened by the President of the Republic, the Presidents of the Câmara and the Senado, or at the request of the majority of the members of either house.

The Câmara is made up of representatives of the people, elected by a system of proportional representation in each State, Territory and the Federal District for a period of four years. The total number of deputies representing the States and the Federal District will be established in proportion to the population; each Territory will elect four deputies.

The Senado is composed of representatives of the States and the Federal District, elected according to the principle of majority. Each State and the Federal District will elect three senators with a mandate of eight years, with elections after four years for one-third of the members and after another four years for the remaining two-thirds. Each Senator is elected with two substitutes. The Senado approves, by secret ballot, the choice of Magistrates, when required by the Constitution; of the Attorney-General of the Republic, of the Ministers of the Accounts Tribunal, of the Territorial Governors, of the president and directors of the central bank and of the permanent heads of diplomatic missions.

The Congresso is responsible for deciding on all matters within the competence of the Union, especially fiscal and budgetary arrangements, national, regional and local plans and programmes, the strength of the armed forces and territorial limits. It is also responsible for making definitive resolutions on international treaties, and for authorizing the President to declare war.

The powers of the Câmara include authorizing the instigation of legal proceedings against the President and Vice-President of the Republic and Ministers of State. The Senado may indict and impose sentence on the President and Vice-President of the Republic and Ministers of State.

Constitutional amendments may be proposed by at least one-third of the members of either house, by the President or by more than one-half of the legislative assemblies of the units of the Federation. Amendments must be ratified by three-fifths of the members of each house. The Constitution may not be amended during times of national emergency, such as a state of siege.

EXECUTIVE POWER

Executive power is exercised by the President of the Republic, aided by the Ministers of State. Candidates for the Presidency and Vice-Presidency must be Brazilian-born, be in full exercise of their political rights and be over 35 years of age. The candidate who obtains an absolute majority of votes will be elected President. If no candidate attains an absolute majority, the two candidates who have received the most votes proceed to a second round of voting, at which the candidate obtaining the majority of valid votes will be elected President. The President holds office for a term of four years and (under an amendment adopted in 1997) is eligible for re-election.

The Ministers of State are chosen by the President and their duties include countersigning acts and decrees signed by the President, expediting instructions for the enactment of laws, decrees and regulations, and presentation to the President of an annual report of their activities.

The Council of the Republic is the higher consultative organ of the President of the Republic. It comprises the Vice-President of the Republic, the Presidents of the Câmara and Senado, the leaders of the majority and of the minority in each house, the Minister of Justice, two members appointed by the President of the Republic, two elected by the Senado and two elected by the Câmara, the latter six having a mandate of three years.

The National Defence Council advises the President on matters relating to national sovereignty and defence. It comprises the Vice-President of the Republic, the Presidents of the Câmara and Senado, the Minister of Justice, military Ministers and the Ministers of Foreign Affairs and of Planning.

JUDICIAL POWER

Judicial power in the Union is exercised by the Supreme Federal Tribunal; the Higher Tribunal of Justice; the Regional Federal Tribunals and federal judges; Labour Tribunals and judges; Electoral Tribunals and judges; Military Tribunals and judges; and the States' Tribunals and judges. Judges are appointed for life; they may not undertake any other employment. The Tribunals elect their own controlling organs and organize their own internal structure.

The Supreme Federal Tribunal, situated in the Union capital, has jurisdiction over the whole national territory and is composed of 11 ministers. The ministers are nominated by the President after approval by the Senado, from Brazilian-born citizens, between the ages of 35 and 65 years, of proved judicial knowledge and experience.

The Government

HEAD OF STATE

President: FERNANDO HENRIQUE CARDOSO (took office 1 January 1995, re-elected 4 October 1998).

Vice-President: MARCO ANTÔNIO DE O. MACIEL.

THE CABINET
(May 2001)

Minister of Foreign Affairs: CELSO LÁFER.

Minister of Justice: JOSÉ GREGORI.

Minister of Finance: PEDRO SAMPAIO MALAN.

Minister of Defence: GERALDO MAGELA DA CRUZ QUINTÃO.

Minister of Agriculture and Food Supply: MARCUS VINICIUS PRATINI DE MORÃES.

Minister of Agrarian Reform: RAÚL BELENS JUNGMANN PINTO.

Minister of Civilian Household: PEDRO PARENTE.

Minister of Military Household: Gen. ALBERTO CARDOSO.

Minister of Labour and Employment: PAULO JOBÍM, Filho (acting).

Minister of Transport: ELISEU LEMOS PADILHA.

Minister of Planning, Budget and Administration: MARTUS ANTÔNIO RODRIGUES TAVARES.

Minister of Mines and Energy: JOSÉ JORGE DE VASCONCELOS LIMA.

Minister of Culture: FRANCISCO CORRÊA WEFFORT.

Minister of the Environment: JOSÉ SARNEY, Filho.

Minister of Development, Industry and Trade: ALCIDES TÁPIAS.

Minister of Education: PAULO RENATO DE SOUZA.

Minister of Health: JOSÉ SERRA.

Minister of National Integration: (vacant).

Minister of Social Security and Assistance: ROBERTO LÚCIO ROCHA BRANT.

Minister of Communications: JOÃO PIMENTA DA VEIGA, Filho.

Minister of Science and Technology: RONALDO SARDENBERG.

Minister of Sport and Tourism: CARLOS MELLES.

Minister of Urban Policies: OVÍDIO ANTÓNIO DE ANGELIS.

MINISTRIES

Office of the President: Palácio do Planalto, 4° andar, 70150-900 Brasília, DF; tel. (61) 411-1573; fax (61) 323-1461; e-mail casacivil@planalto.gov.br; internet www.planalto.gov.br.

Office of the Civilian Cabinet: Palácio do Planalto, 4° andar, Praça dos Três Poderes, 70150 Brasília, DF; tel. (61) 211-1034; fax (61) 321-5804.

Ministry of Agrarian Reform: Edif. Palacio do Desenvolvimento, 70057 Brasília, DF; tel. (61) 223-8852; fax (61) 226-3855; internet www.incra.gov.br.

Ministry of Agriculture and Food Supply: Esplanada dos Ministérios, Bloco D, 8° andar, 70043 Brasília, DF; tel. (61) 226-5161; fax (61) 218-2586; internet www.agricultura.gov.br.

Ministry of Communications: Esplanada dos Ministérios, Bloco R, 8° andar, 70044 Brasília, DF; tel. (61) 311-6000; fax (61) 226-3980; internet www.mc.gov.br.

Ministry of Culture: Esplanada dos Ministérios, Bloco B, 3° andar, 70068-900 Brasília, DF; tel. (61) 316-2172; fax (61) 225-9162; internet www.minc.gov.br.

Ministry of Defence: Esplanada dos Ministérios, Bloco Q, 70049-900 Brasília, DF; tel. (61) 223-5356; fax (61) 321-2477; e-mail faleconosco@defesa.gov.br; internet www.defesa.gov.br.

Ministry of Development, Industry and Trade: Esplanada dos Ministérios, Bloco J, 7° andar, Sala 700, 70056-900 Brasília, DF; tel. (61) 325-2056; fax (61) 325-2063; internet www.mdic.gov.br.

Ministry of Education: Esplanada dos Ministérios, Bloco L, 8° andar, 70047-900 Brasília, DF; tel. (61) 225-6515; fax (61) 223-0564; e-mail acordabr@acb.mec.gov.br; internet www.mec.gov.br.

Ministry of the Environment: SAIN, Av. L4 Norte, Edif. Sede Terreo, 70800 Brasília, DF; tel. (61) 226-8221; fax (61) 322-1058; internet www.mma.gov.br.

Ministry of Finance: Esplanada dos Ministérios, Bloco P, 5° andar, 70048 Brasília, DF; tel. (61) 412-2548; fax (61) 226-9084; internet www.fazenda.gov.br.

Ministry of Foreign Affairs: Palácio do Itamaraty, Esplanada dos Ministérios, 70170 Brasília, DF; tel. (61) 224-2773; fax (61) 226-1762; internet www.mre.gov.br.

Ministry of Health: Esplanada dos Ministérios, Bloco G, 5° andar, 70058 Brasília, DF; tel. (61) 223-3169; fax (61) 224-8747; internet www.saude.gov.br.

Ministry of Justice: Esplanada dos Ministérios, Bloco T, 4° andar, 70064-900 Brasília, DF; tel. (61) 226-4404; fax (61) 322-6817; internet www.mj.gov.br.

Ministry of Labour and Employment: Esplanada dos Ministérios, Bloco F, 5° andar, 70059-900 Brasília, DF; tel. (61) 225-0041; fax (61) 226-3577; e-mail internacional@mtb.gov.br; internet www.mtb.gov.br.

Ministry of Mines and Energy: Esplanada dos Ministérios, Bloco U, 7° andar, 70000 Brasília, DF; tel. (61) 225-8106; fax (61) 225-5407; internet www.mme.gov.br.

Ministry of National Integration: Esplanada dos Ministérios, 70000 Brasília, DF; internet www.integracao.gov.br.

Ministry of Planning, Budget and Administration: Esplanada dos Ministérios, Bloco K, 70040-602 Brasília, DF; tel. (61) 215-4100; fax (61) 321-5292; internet www.planejamento.gov.br.

Ministry of Science and Technology: Esplanada dos Ministérios, Bloco E, 4° andar, 70062-900 Brasília, DF; tel. (61) 224-4364; fax (61) 225-7496; internet www.mct.gov.br.

Ministry of Social Security and Assistance: Esplanada dos Ministérios, Bloco A, 6° andar, 70054-900 Brasília, DF; tel. (61) 224-7300; fax (61) 226-3861; internet www.previdenciasocial.gov.br.

Ministry of Sport and Tourism: Esplanada dos Ministérios, Brasília, DF; internet www.met.gov.br.

Ministry of Transport: Esplanada dos Ministérios, Bloco R, 70000 Brasília, DF; tel. (61) 218-6335; fax (61) 218-6315; internet www.transportes.gov.br.

President and Legislature

PRESIDENT

Election, 4 October 1998

Candidate	Valid votes cast	% valid votes cast
FERNANDO HENRIQUE CARDOSO (PSDB)	35,936,916	53.06
LUIZ INÁCIO 'LULA' DA SILVA (PT)	21,475,348	31.71
CIRO GOMES (PPS)	7,426,235	10.97
Others	2,884,528	4.26
Total	67,723,027	100.00

CONGRESSO NACIONAL
(National Congress)

Câmara dos Deputados
(Chamber of Deputies)

President: MICHEL MIGUEL ELIAS TEMER LULIA (PMDB).

The Chamber has 513 members who hold office for a four-year term.

General Election, 4 October 1998

Party	Seats
Partido da Frente Liberal (PFL)	106
Partido da Social Democracia Brasileira (PSDB)	99
Partido do Movimento Democrático Brasileiro (PMDB)	82
Partido Progressista Brasileiro (PPB)	60
Partido dos Trabalhadores (PT)	58
Partido Trabalhista Brasileiro (PTB)	31
Partido Democrático Trabalhista (PDT)	25
Partido Socialista Brasileiro (PSB)	19
Partido Liberal (PL)	12
Partido Comunista do Brasil (PC do B)	7
Partido Popular Socialista (PPS)	3
Others	11
Total	513

Senado Federal
(Federal Senate)

President: ANTÔNIO CARLOS PEIXOTO DE MAGALHÃES (PFL).

The 81 members of the Senate are elected by the 26 States and the Federal District (three Senators for each) according to the principle of majority. The Senate's term of office is eight years, with elections after four years for one-third of the members and after another four years for the remaining two-thirds.

Following the elections of 4 October 1998, the PMDB was represented by 27 senators, the PFL by 19, the PSDB by 16, the PT by 7 and the PPB by 5. The PSB, the PDT, the PTB and the PPS were also represented.

Governors

STATES

Acre: JORGE NEY VIANA (PT).

Alagoas: RONALDO AUGUSTO LESSA (PSB).

Amapá: JOÃO ALBERTO RODRIGUES CAPIBERIBE (PSB).

Amazonas: AMAZONINO ARMANDO MENDES (PFL).

Bahia: CÉSAR AUGUSTO RABELO BORGES (PFL).

Ceará: TASSO RIBEIRO JEREISSATI (PSDB).

Espírito Santo: JOSÉ IGNÁCIO FERREIRA (PSDB).

Goiás: MARCONI FERREIRA PERILLO (PSDB).

Maranhão: ROSEANA SARNEY MURAD (PFL).

Mato Grosso: DANTE MARTINS DE OLIVEIRA (PSDB).

Mato Grosso do Sul: ANTÔNIO ZECA (PT).

Minas Gerais: ITAMAR AUGUSTO CAUTIERO FRANCO (PMDB).

Pará: ALMIR DE OLIVEIRA GABRIEL (PSDB).

Paraíba: JOSÉ TARGINO MARANHÃO (PMDB).

Paraná: JAIME LERNER (PFL).

Pernambuco: JARBAS DE ANDRADE VASCONCELOS (PMDB).

Piauí: MÃO SANTA (PMDB).

Rio de Janeiro: ANTHONY WILLIAM GAROTINHO MATHEUS DE OLIVEIRA (PDT).

Rio Grande do Norte: GARIBALDI ALVES, Filho (PMDB).

Rio Grande do Sul: OLÍVIO DUTRA (PT).

Rondônia: José de Abreu Bianco (PFL).
Roraima: Neudo Ribeiro Campos (PTB).
Santa Catarina: Esperidião Amin Helou, Filho (PPB).
São Paulo: Geraldo Alckmin.
Sergipe: Albano do Prado Pimentel Franco (PSDB).
Tocantins: José Wilson Siqueira Campos (PFL).

FEDERAL DISTRICT
Brasília: Joaquim Domingos Roriz (PMDB).

Political Organizations

In May 1985 the National Congress approved a constitutional amendment providing for the free formation of political parties.

Partido Comunista do Brasil (PC do B): Rua Major Diogo 834, Bela Vista, 01324-000 São Paulo, SP; tel. (11) 232-1622; fax (11) 3106-4104; e-mail pcdobcc@uol.com.br; internet www.pcdob.org.br; f. 1922; Leader Aldo Rebelo ; Sec.-Gen. João Amazonas; 185,000 mems.

Partido Democrático Trabalhista (PDT): Rua Marechal Câmara 160, 4°, 20050 Rio de Janeiro, RJ; fax (21) 262-8834; e-mail pdtnac@domain.com.br; internet www.pdt.org.br; f. 1980; formerly the PTB (Partido Trabalhista Brasileiro), renamed 1980 when that name was awarded to a dissident group following controversial judicial proceedings; member of Socialist International; Pres. Leonel Brizola; Gen. Sec. Manoel Dias.

Partido da Frente Liberal (PFL): Câmara dos Deputados, 70160-900 Brasília, DF; internet www.pfl.org.br; f. 1984 by moderate members of the PDS and PMDB; Pres. Jorge Bornhausen; Gen. Sec. José Carlos Aleluia.

Partido Liberal (PL): Câmara dos Deputados, 70160-900 Brasília, DF; Tel. (61) 318-5899; internet www.pl.org.br; Pres. Valdemar Costa Neto.

Partido do Movimento Democrático Brasileiro (PMDB): Câmara dos Deputados, Edif. Principal, 70160-900 Brasília, DF; tel. (61) 318-5120; e-mail pmdb@tba.com.br; internet www.pmdb.org.br; f. 1980; moderate elements of former MDB; merged with Partido Popular February 1982; Pres. Jader Barbalho; Sec.-Gen. Sarana Felipe; factions include: the **Históricos** and the **Movimento da Unidade Progressiva (MUP)**.

Partido Popular Socialista (PPS): Rua Coronel Lisboa 260, Vila Mariana, 04020-040, São Paulo, SP; tel. (11) 570-2182; fax (11) 549-9841; internet www.pps.com.br; f. 1922; Pres. Roberto Freire.

Partido Progressista Brasileiro (PPB): Senado Federal, Anexo 1, 17° andar, 70165-900 Brasília, DF; tel. (61) 311-3041; fax (61) 226-8192; internet www.ppb.org.br; f. 1995 by merger of Partido Progressista Reformador (PPR), Partido Progressista (PP) and the Partido Republicano Progressista (PRP); right-wing; Pres. Paulo Salim Maluf; Sec.-Gen. Benedito Domingos.

Partido de Reconstrução Nacional (PRN): Brasília, DF; f. 1988; right-wing; Leader Fernando Collor de Mello.

Partido da Social Democracia Brasileira (PSDB): SCN, Quadro 04, Bloco B, Torre C, Sala 303/B, Centro Empresarial Varig, 70710-500 Brasília, DF; tel. (61) 328-0045; fax (61) 328-2120; e-mail tucano@psdb.org.br; internet www.psdb.org.br; f. 1988; centre-left; formed by dissident members of the PMDB (incl. Históricos), PFL, PDS, PDT, PSB and PTB; Pres. Teotonio Vilela, Filho; Sec.-Gen. Márcio Fortes.

Partido Socialista Brasileiro (PSB): Brasília, DF; tel. (61) 318-6951; fax (61) 318-2104; internet www.psb.org.br; f. 1947; Pres. Miguel Arraes; Sec.-Gen. Renato Soares.

Partido dos Trabalhadores (PT): Congresso Nacional, 70160, Brasília, DF; tel. (61) 224-1699; internet www.pt.org.br; f. 1980; first independent labour party; associated with the *autêntico* branch of the trade union movement; 350,000 mems; Pres. José Dirceu de Oliveira e Silva; Vice-Pres. Jacó Bittar.

Partido Trabalhista Brasileiro (PTB): SCLN 303, Bloco C, Sala 105, Asa Norte, 70735-530 Brasília, DF; tel. (61) 226-0477; fax (61) 225-4757; e-mail ptb@ptb.org.br; internet www.ptb.org.br; f. 1980; Pres. José Eduardo Andrade Vieira; Sec.-Gen. Rodrigues Palma.

Other political parties represented in the Congresso Nacional include the Partido Social Cristão (PSC; internet www.psc.org.br), the Partido Social-Democrático (PSD), the Partido Verde (PV; internet www.pv.org.br) and the Partido da Mobilização Nacional (PMN; internet www.pmn.org.br).

Diplomatic Representation

EMBASSIES IN BRAZIL

Algeria: SHIS, QI 09, Conj. 13, Casa 01, Lago Sul, 70472-900 Brasília, DF; tel. (61) 248-4039; fax (61) 248-4691; Ambassador: Hocine Meghaloui.

Angola: SHIS, QI 07, Conj. 11, Casa 9, 71625-160 Brasília, DF; tel. (61) 248-4489; fax (61) 248-1567; Ambassador: Alberto Correia Neto.

Argentina: SHIS, QL 02, Conj. 1, Casa 19, Lago Sul, 70442-900 Brasília, DF; tel. (61) 356-3000; fax (61) 365-2109; Ambassador: Juan José Uranga.

Australia: SHIS, QI 09, Conj. 16, Casa 01, Lago Sul, 70469-900 Brasília, DF; tel. (61) 248-5569; fax (61) 248-1066; e-mail embaustr@nutecnet.com.br; Ambassador: Gary Alfred Conroy.

Austria: SES, Quadra 811, Av. das Nações, Lote 40, 70426-900 Brasília, DF; tel. (61) 443-3111; fax (61) 443-5233; e-mail emb .austria@zaz.com.br; Ambassador: Daniel Krumholz.

Bangladesh: SHIS, QI 07, Conj. 03, Casa 04, 71615-230 Brasília, DF; tel. (61) 248-4905; fax (61) 248-4609; e-mail bdoot.bz@nutecnet .com.br; Ambassador: Syed Noor Hossain.

Belgium: SES, Av. das Nações, Lote 32, 70422-900 Brasília, DF; tel. (61) 443-1133; fax (61) 443-1219; Ambassador: Jean-Miguel Veranneman de Watervliet.

Bolivia: SHIS, QI 19, Conj. 13, Casa 19, Lago Sul, Brasília, DF; tel. (61) 366-3432; fax (61) 366-3136; e-mail embol@vol.com.br; Ambassador: Gonzalo Montenegro Irigoyen.

Bulgaria: SEN, Av. das Nações, Lote 8, 70432-900 Brasília, DF; tel. (61) 223-6193; fax (61) 323-3285; e-mail tchavo@tba.com.br; Ambassador: Ventzislav Anguelov Ivanov.

Cameroon: SHIS, QI 11, Conj. 10, Casa 06, Lago Sul, 71600-900 Brasília, DF; tel. (61) 248-5403; fax (61) 248-0443; Ambassador: Martin Nguele Mbarga.

Canada: SES, Av. das Nações, Quadra 803, Lote 16, 70410-900 Brasília, DF; CP 00961, 70359-970 Brasília, DF; tel. (61) 321-2171; fax (61) 321-4529; e-mail brsla@dfait-maeci.gc.ca; Ambassador: Jean-Pierre Juneau.

Cape Verde: SHIS, QL 07, Conj. 01, Casa 06, 71615-210 Brasília, DF; tel. (61) 248-0543; fax (61) 248-1210; e-mail embcaboverde@rudah.com.br; Ambassador: Manuel Augusto Amante de Rosa.

Chile: SES, Av. das Nações, Quadra 803, Lote 11, 70407-900 Brasília, DF; tel. (61) 322-5151; fax (61) 322-2966; e-mail embchile@terra.com.br; Ambassador: Carlos Eduardo Mena Keymer.

China, People's Republic: SES, Av. das Nações, Lote 51, 70443-900 Brasília, DF; tel. (61) 346-4436; fax (61) 346-3299; Ambassador: Wan Yongxiang.

Colombia: SES, Av. das Nações, Quadra 803, Lote 10, 70444-900 Brasília, DF; tel. (61) 226-8997; fax (61) 224-4732; e-mail emb-col@zaz.com.br; Ambassador: Samuel Navas Pinzón.

Congo, Democratic Republic: SMPW, Quadra 11, Conj. 2, Lote 06, Lago Sul, CP 07-041, 71600 Brasília, DF; tel. (61) 338-7386; Chargé d'affaires a.i. : Lumba Mfulunkatu.

Costa Rica: SRTVN 701, Conj. C, Ala A, Salas 308/310, Edifício Centro Empresarial Norte, 70710-200, Brasília, DF; tel. (61) 328-2219; fax (61) 328-2243; e-mail embrica@solar.com.br; Ambassador: Javier Sancho Bonilla.

Côte d'Ivoire: SEN. Av. das Nações, Lote 9, 70473-900, Brasília, DF; tel. (61) 321-4656; fax (61) 321-1306; Ambassador: Djibo Felicien Abdoulaye.

Croatia: SHIS QI 9, Conj. 11, Casa 3, 71625-110 Brasília, DF; tel. (61) 248-0610; fax (61) 248-1708; Ambassador: Zelimir Urban.

Cuba: SHIS, QI 15, Conj. 18, Casa 01, Lago Sul, 70481-900 Brasília, DF; tel. (61) 248-4710; fax (61) 248-6778; Ambassador: Jorge Lezcano Pérez.

Czech Republic: Av. das Nações, Quadra 805, Lote 21, 70414-900, CP 970 Brasília, DF; tel. (61) 242-7785; fax (61) 242-7833; e-mail czech@brnet.com.br; Ambassador: Ladislav Skerik.

Denmark: SES, Av. das Nações, Lote 26, 70416-900 Brasília, DF; tel. (61) 443-8188; fax (61) 443-5232; e-mail danmark@tba.com.br; Ambassador: Anita Hugau.

Dominican Republic: SHIS, QL 8, Conj. 5, Casa 14, Lago Sul, 70460-900 Brasília, DF; tel. and fax (61) 248-1405; e-mail embajdar gan@nutcnet.com.br; Ambassador: Ciro Amaury Dargam Cruz.

Ecuador: SHIS, QI 11, Conj. 9, Casa 24, 71625-290 Brasília, DF; tel. (61) 248-5560; fax (61) 248-1290; e-mail embec@solar .com.br; Ambassador: Diego Ribadeneira Espinosa.

Egypt: SEN, Av. das Nações, Lote 12, Asa Norte, 70435-900 Brasília, DF; tel. (61) 323-8800; fax (61) 323-1039; e-mail embegypt@tba .com.br; internet www.tba.com.br/pages/embegypt; Ambassador: Hatem Aziz Seif en-Nasr.

El Salvador: SHIS, QI 07, Conj. 6, Casa 14, 71615-260 Brasília, DF; tel. (61) 364-4141; fax (61) 364-2459; e-mail embelsalvador@tba .com.br; Ambassador: Martín Alberto Rivera Gómez.

Finland: SES, Av. das Nações, Lote 27, 70417-900 Brasília, DF; tel. (61) 443-7151; fax (61) 443-3315; e-mail suomi@tba.com.br/ finlandia; Ambassador: Asko Henrik Numminen.

France: SES, Av. das Nações, Lote 4, 70404-900 Brasília, DF; tel. (61) 312-9100; fax (61) 312-9108; Ambassador: ALAIN ROUQUIÉ.

Gabon: SHIS QI 9, Conj. 11, Casa 24, 71615-300, Brasília, DF; tel. (61) 248-3536; fax (61) 248-2241; e-mail mgabao@nutecnet.com.br; Ambassador: MARCEL ODONGUI-BONNARD.

Germany: SES, Av. das Nações, Lote 25, 70415-900 Brasília, DF; tel. (61) 443-7330; fax (61) 443-7508; Ambassador: HANS-BODO BERTRAM.

Ghana: SHIS, QL 10, Conj. 8, Casa 2, CP 07-0456, 70466-900 Brasília, DF; tel. (61) 248-6047; fax (61) 248-7913; Chargé d'affaires a.i.: SAMMIE PESKY EDDICO .

Greece: SES, Av. das Nações, Quadra 805, Lote 22, 70480-900 Brasília, DF; tel. (61) 443-6573; fax (61) 443-6902; e-mail emb-grecia@zaz.com.br; internet www.emb-grecia.org; Ambassador: STRATOS DOUKAS.

Guatemala: SHIS, QI 09, Conj. 2, Casa 08, 71625-020 Brasília, DF; tel. (61) 248-3318; fax (61) 248-4383; Ambassador: HERBERT ESTUARDO MENESES CORONADO.

Guyana: SBN, Quadra 2, Bloco J, Edif. Paulo Maurício, 13° andar, salas 1310–1315, 70438-900 Brasília, DF; tel. (61) 326-9728; fax (61) 326-3022; e-mail embguyana@apis.com.br; Ambassador: MARILYN CHERYL MILES.

Haiti: SHIS, QI 17, Conj. 4, Casa 19, Lago Sul, 70465-900 Brasília, DF; tel. (61) 248-6860; fax (61) 248-7472; Chargé d'affaires: JEAN-VICTOR HARVEL JEAN-BAPTISTE.

Holy See: SES, Av. das Nações, Lote 1, CP 153, 70359-970 Brasília, DF (Apostolic Nunciature); tel. (61) 223-0794; fax (61) 224-9365; e-mail nunapost@sdar.com.br; Apostolic Nuncio: Most Rev. ALFIO RAPISARDA, Titular Archbishop of Cannae.

Honduras: SBN, Edif. Engenheiro Paulo Maurício, Salas 712–716, 70040-905 Brasília, DF; tel. (61) 248-1200; fax (61) 248-1425; Ambassador: GERARDO MARTÍNEZ BLANCO.

Hungary: SES, Av. das Nações, Quadra 805, Lote 19, 70413-900 Brasília, DF; tel. (61) 443-0836; fax (61) 443-3434; e-mail huembbrz@uninet.com.br; internet www.hungria.org.br; Ambassador: TAMÁS RÓZSA.

India: SHIS, QL 08, Conj. 8, Casa 01, 71625-285 Brasília, DF; tel. (61) 248-4006; fax (61) 248-7849; Ambassador: MUTHAL PUREDATH M. MENON.

Indonesia: SES, Av. das Nações, Quadra 805, Lote 20, 70479-900 Brasília, DF; tel. (61) 443-1788; fax (61) 443-8020; Ambassador: SUTADI DJAJAKUSUMA.

Iran: SES, Av. das Nações, Lote 31, 70421-900 Brasília, DF; tel. (61) 242-5733; fax (61) 224-9640; Ambassador: MANSOUR MOAZAMI.

Iraq: SES, Av. das Nações, Quadra 815, Lote 64, 70430-900 Brasília, DF; tel. (61) 346-2822; fax (61) 346-7034; Ambassador: AHMAD J. ABDULLA AD-DABBAGH.

Israel: SES, Av. das Nações, Lote 38, 70424-900 Brasília, DF; tel. (61) 244-7675; fax (61) 244-6129; e-mail embisrae@solar.com.br; Ambassador: DANIEL GAZIT.

Italy: SES, Av. das Nações, Lote 30, 70420 Brasília, DF; tel. (61) 443-0044; fax (61)443-1231; e-mail embitalia@zaz.com.br; internet www.embitalia.org.br; Ambassador: VINCENZO PETRONE.

Japan: SES, Av. das Nações, Lote 39, 70425-900 Brasília, DF; tel. (61) 242-6866; fax (61) 242-0738; Ambassador: KATSUNARI SUZUKI.

Jordan: SHIS, QI 9, Conj. 18, Casa 14, 70483-900 Brasília, DF; tel. (61) 248-5407; fax (61) 248-1698; Ambassador: FARIS SHAWKAT MUFTI.

Korea, Republic: SEN, Av. das Nações, Lote 14, 70436-900 Brasília, DF; tel. (61) 321-2500; fax (61) 321-2508; Ambassador: WON-YOUNG LEE.

Kuwait: SHIS, QI 05, Chácara 30, 71600-750 Brasília, DF; tel. (61) 248-2323; fax (61) 248-0969; Ambassador: NASSER SABEEH B. AS-SABEEH.

Lebanon: SES, Av. das Nações, Quadra 805, Lote 17, 70411-900 Brasília, DF; tel. (61) 443-9837; fax (61) 443-8574; e-mail emblibano @uol.com.br; Ambassador: ISHAYA EL-KHOURY.

Libya: SHIS, QI 15, Chácara 26, CP 3505, 70462-900 Brasília, DF; tel. (61) 248-6710; fax (61) 248-0598; Chargé d'affaires a.i.: ALHASSAN ALI ALBAROUNI.

Malaysia: SHIS, QI 05, Chácara 62, Lago Sul, 70477-900 Brasília, DF; tel. (61) 248-5008; fax (61) 248-6307; e-mail mwbrasilia@ persocom.com.br; Ambassador: S. THANARAJASINGAM.

Malta: Av. W3 Norte, Quadra 507, Bloco C, 70740-535 Brasília, DF; tel. (61) 272-0402; fax (61) 347-4940; Ambassador: WOLFGANG FRANZ JOSEF SAUER.

Mexico: SES, Av. das Nações, Lote 18, 70412-900 Brasília, DF; tel. (61) 244-1011; fax (61) 443-6275; e-mail embamexbra@brnet.com.br; Ambassador: JORGE EDUARDO NAVARRETE LÓPEZ.

Morocco: SEN, Av. das Nações, Lote 2, 70432-900 Brasília, DF; tel. (61) 321-4487; fax (61) 321-0745; e-mail sifamabr@tba.com.br;

internet www.mincom.gov.ma; Ambassador: ABDELMALEK CHARKAOUI GHAZOUANI.

Mozambique: SHIS, QL 12, Conj. 7, Casa 9, 71630-275 Brasília, DF; tel. (61) 248-4222; fax (61) 248-3917; Ambassador: FELIZARDA ISAURA MONTEIRO.

Myanmar: SHIS, QL 8, Conj. 4, Casa 5, 71620-245 Brasília, DF; tel. (61) 248-3747; fax (61) 248-1922; e-mail mebrsl@brnet.com.br; Ambassador: U. KYAW MIYNT.

Netherlands: SES, Av. das Nações, Quadra 801, Lote 05, 7045-900 Brasília, DF; tel. (61) 321-4769; fax (61) 321-1518; e-mail nlgovbra@ pepz.brnet.com.br; Ambassador: FRANCISCUS BENEDICTUS ANTONIUS MARIA VAN HAREN.

Nicaragua: SHIS, QI 03, Conj. 01, Casa 06, Lago Sul, 71605-210 Brasília, DF; tel. (61) 365-2555; fax (61) 365-2562; Ambassador: EDGARD SOLÍS MARTÍNEZ.

Nigeria: SEN, Av. das Nações, Lote 05, CP 03-710, 70459-900 Brasília, DF; tel. (61) 226-1717; fax (61) 224-0320; Ambassador: THADDEUS DANIEL HART.

Norway: SES, Av. das Nações, Lote 28, CP 07-0670, 70418-900 Brasília, DF; tel. (61) 443-8720; fax (61) 443-2942; e-mail embno@ tba.com.br; Ambassador: LIV AGNES KERR.

Pakistan: SHIS, QL 12, Conj. 02, Casa 19, 71615-140 Brasília, DF; tel. (61) 364-1632; fax (61) 248-0246; Ambassador: MUHAMMAD NASSER MIAN.

Panama: SHIS, QL 6, Conj. 11, Casa 18, 71625-260 Brasília, DF; tel. (61) 248-7309; fax (61) 248-2834; e-mail empanama@nettur.com.br; Ambassador: OLIMPO ANÍBAL SAEZ MARCUCCI.

Paraguay: SES, Av. das Nações, Quadra 811, Lote 42, CP 14-2314, 70427-900 Brasília, DF; tel. (61) 242-3742; fax (61) 242-4605; Ambassador: CARLOS ALBERTO GONZÁLEZ GARABELLI.

Peru: SES, Av. das Nações, Lote 43, 70428-900 Brasília, DF; tel. (61) 242-9933; fax (61) 244-9344; e-mail emb-peru@nutecnet.com.br; Ambassador: EDUARDO PONCE VIVANCO.

Philippines: SEN, Av. das Nações, Lote 1, 70431 Brasília, DF; tel. (61) 223-5143; fax (61) 226-7411; e-mail pr@pop.persocom.com.br; Ambassador: OSCAR G. VALENZUELA.

Poland: SES, Av. das Nações, Lote 33, 70423-900 Brasília, DF; tel. (61) 443-3438; fax (61) 242-8543; Ambassador: BOGUSŁAW ZAKRZEWSKI.

Portugal: SES, Av. das Nações, Lote 2, 70402-900 Brasília, DF; tel. (61) 321-3434; fax (61) 224-7347; e-mail embporbr@abordo.com.br; Ambassador: FRANCISCO KNOPFLI.

Romania: SEN, Av. das Nações, Lote 6, 70456 Brasília, DF; tel. (61) 226-0746; fax (61) 226-6629; e-mail romenia@tha.com.br; Ambassador: ION FLOROIU.

Russia: SES, Av. das Nações, Quadra 801, Lote A, 70476-900 Brasília, DF; tel. (61) 223-3094; fax (61) 223-5094; e-mail embrus@brnet.com.br; internet www.brnet.com.br/pages/embrus; Ambassador: VASSILII PETROVICH GROMOV.

Saudi Arabia: SHIS, QL 10, Conj. 9, Casa 20, 70471-900 Brasília, DF; tel. (61) 248-3523; fax (61) 284-2905; Ambassador: YAHYA AHMED AL-YAHYA.

Slovakia: Av. das Nações, Quadra 805, Lote 21, 70414-900 Brasília, DF; tel. (61) 443-1263; fax (61) 443-1267; Ambassador: JOZEF ADAMEC.

South Africa: SES, Av. das Nações, Lote 6, CP 11-1170, 70406 Brasília, DF; tel. (61) 312-9500; fax (61) 322-8491; e-mail saemb@brnet.com.br; Ambassador: MBULELO RAKWENA.

Spain: SES, Av. das Nações, Lote 44, 70429-900 Brasília, DF; tel. (61) 244-2121; fax (61) 242-1781; Ambassador: CÉSAR ALBA Y FUSTER.

Suriname: SHIS, QI 09, Conj. 8, Casa 24, 70457-900 Brasília, DF; tel. (61) 248-6706; fax (61) 248-3791; e-mail sur.emb@persocom .com.br; Chargé d'affaires a.i.: ROBBY D. RAMLAKHAN.

Sweden: SES, Av. das Nações, Lote 29, 70419-900 Brasília, DF; tel. (61) 443-1444; fax (61) 443-1187; e-mail swebra@tba.com.br; Ambassador: CHRISTER MANHUSEN.

Switzerland: SES, Av. das Nações, Lote 41, 70448-900 Brasília, DF; CP 08671, 70312-970 Brasília, DF; tel. (61) 443-5500; fax (61) 443-5711; e-mail swissembra@brasilia.com.br; Ambassador: JÜRG LEUTERT.

Syria: SEN, Av. das Nações, Lote 11, 70434-900 Brasília, DF; tel. (61) 226-0970; fax (61) 223-2595; Ambassador: MUHAMMAD TAUFIK JUHANI.

Thailand: SEN, Av. das Nações Norte, Lote 10, 70433-900 Brasília, DF; tel. (61) 224-6943; fax (61) 321-2994; Ambassador: SAMROENG LAKSANASUT.

Trinidad and Tobago: SHIS, QL 02, Conj. 02, Casa 01, 71665-028 Brasília, DF; tel. (61) 365-1132; fax (61) 365-1733; e-mail trinbago@tba.com.br; Ambassador: ROBERT M. TORRY.

Tunisia: SHIS, QI 9, Conj. 16, Casa 20, 71625-160 Brasília, DF; tel. (61) 248-3725; fax (61) 248-7355; Ambassador: HASSINE BOUZID.

Turkey: SES, Av. das Nações, Lote 23, 70452-900 Brasília, DF; tel. (61) 242-1850; fax (61) 242-1448; e-mail emb.turquia@conectanet .com.br; Ambassador: SEVINÇ DALYANOĞLU.

Ukraine: SHIS, QL 6, Conj. 2, Casa 17, 71620-025 Brasília, DF; tel. (61) 365-3889; fax (61) 365-3898; e-mail brucremb@zaz.com.br; Chargé d'Affaires: ROSTYSLAV TRONENKO.

United Arab Emirates: SHIS, QI 5, Chácara 18, 70486-901 Brasília, DF; tel. (61) 248-0717; fax (61) 248-7543; Ambassador: SAEED HAMED AL-JUNAIBI.

United Kingdom: SES, Quadra 801, Conj. K, Lote 8, CP 07-0586, 70408-900 Brasília, DF; tel. (61) 225-2710; fax (61) 225-1777; e-mail britemb@nutecnet.com.br; Ambassador: ROGER BRIDGELAND BONE.

USA: SES, Av. das Nações, Quadra 801, Lote 3, 70403-900 Brasília, DF; tel. (61) 321-7272; fax (61) 225-9136; Ambassador: ANTHONY STEPHEN HARRINGTON.

Uruguay: SES, Av. das Nações, Lote 14, 70450-900 Brasília, DF; tel. (61) 322-1200; fax (61) 322-6534; e-mail urubras@tba.com.br; Ambassador: AUGUSTIN ESPINOSA LLOVERAS.

Venezuela: SES, Av. das Nações, Quadra 803, Lote 13, 70451-900 Brasília, DF; tel. (61) 322-1011; fax (61) 226-5633; e-mail embvenbr@nutecnet.com.br; Ambassador: MILOS ALCALAY.

Viet Nam: SHIS, QI 05, Conj. 07, Casa 21, 71615-070 Brasília, DF; tel. and fax (61) 364-5587.

Yugoslavia: SES, Av. das Nações, Quadra 803, Lote 15, 70409-900 Brasília, DF; tel. (61) 223-7272; fax (61) 223-8462; e-mail embiugos@ nutecnet.com.br; Chargé d'affaires a.i.: LJUBOMIR MILIĆ.

Judicial System

The judiciary powers of the State are held by the following: the Supreme Federal Tribunal, the Higher Tribunal of Justice, the five Regional Federal Tribunals and Federal Judges, the Higher Labour Tribunal, the 24 Regional Labour Tribunals, the Conciliation and Judgment Councils and Labour Judges, the Higher Electoral Tribunal, the 27 Regional Electoral Tribunals, the Electoral Judges and Electoral Councils, the Higher Military Tribunal, the Military Tribunals and Military Judges, the Tribunals of the States and Judges of the States, the Tribunal of the Federal District and of the Territories and Judges of the Federal District and of the Territories.

The Supreme Federal Tribunal comprises 11 ministers, nominated by the President and approved by the Senate. Its most important role is to rule on the final interpretation of the Constitution. The Supreme Federal Tribunal has the power to declare an act of Congress void if it is unconstitutional. It judges offences committed by persons such as the President, the Vice-President, members of the Congresso Nacional, Ministers of State, its own members, the Attorney General, judges of other higher courts, and heads of permanent diplomatic missions. It also judges cases of litigation between the Union and the States, between the States, or between foreign nations and the Union or the States; disputes as to jurisdiction between higher Tribunals, or between the latter and any other court, in cases involving the extradition of criminals, and others related to the writs of habeas corpus and habeas data, and in other cases.

The Higher Tribunal of Justice comprises at least 33 members, appointed by the President and approved by the Senado. Its jurisdiction includes the judgment of offences committed by State Governors. The Regional Federal Tribunals comprise at least seven judges, recruited when possible in the respective region and appointed by the President of the Republic. The Higher Labour Tribunal comprises 27 members, appointed by the President and approved by the Senado. The judges of the Regional Labour Tribunals are also appointed by the President. The Higher Electoral Tribunal comprises at least seven members: three judges from among those of the Supreme Federal Tribunal, two from the Higher Tribunal of Justice (elected by secret ballot) and two lawyers appointed by the President. The Regional Electoral Tribunals are also composed of seven members. The Higher Military Tribunal comprises 15 life members, appointed by the President and approved by the Senate; three from the navy, four from the army, three from the air force and five civilian members. The States are responsible for the administration of their own justice, according to the principles established by the Constitution.

SUPREME FEDERAL TRIBUNAL

Supreme Federal Tribunal: Praça dos Três Poderes, 70175-900 Brasília, DF; tel. (61) 316-5000; fax (61) 316-5483; internet www.stf.gov.br.

President: CARLOS MÁRIO DA SILVA VELLOSO.

Vice-President: MARCO AURÉLIO MENDES DE FARIAS MELLO.

Justices: JOSÉ CARLOS MOREIRA ALVES, JOSÉ NÉRI DA SILVEIRA, SYDNEY SANCHES, LUIZ OCTAVIO PIRES E ALBUQUERQUE GALLOTTI, JOSÉ PAULO SEP-

ÚLVEDA PERTENCE, JOSÉ CELSO DE MELLO, Filho, ILMAR NASCIMENTO GALVÃO, MAURÍCIO JOSÉ CORRÊA, NELSON DE AZEVEDO JOBIM.

Attorney-General: GERALDO BRINDEIRO.

Director-General (Secretariat): JOSÉ GERALDO DE LANA TÒRRES.

Religion

CHRISTIANITY

Conselho Nacional de Igrejas Cristãs do Brasil—CONIC (National Council of Christian Churches in Brazil): SCS, Quadra 01, Bloco E, Edif. Ceará, Sala 713, 70303-900 Brasília, DF; tel. (61) 321-8341; fax (61) 321-4034; f. 1982; seven mem. churches; Pres. GLAUCO SOARES DE LIMA; Exec. Sec. P. ERVINO SCHMIDT.

The Roman Catholic Church

Brazil comprises 38 archdioceses, 204 dioceses (including one each for Catholics of the Maronite, Melkite and Ukrainian Rites), 14 territorial prelatures and two territorial abbacies. The Archbishop of São Sebastião do Rio de Janeiro is also the Ordinary for Catholics of other Oriental Rites in Brazil (estimated at 10,000 in 1994). The great majority of Brazil's population are adherents of the Roman Catholic Church (around 106m. at the time of the 1980 census), although a report published by the Brazilian weekly, *Veja*, in July 1989 concluded that since 1950 the membership of non-Catholic Christian Churches had risen from 3% to 6% of the total population, while membership of the Roman Catholic Church had fallen from 93% to 89% of Brazilians.

Bishops' Conference: Conferência Nacional dos Bispos do Brasil, SE/Sul Q 801, Conj. B, CP 02067, 70259-970 Brasília, DF; tel. (61) 313-8300; fax (61) 313-8303; e-mail cnbb@cnbb.org.br; f. 1980 (statutes approved 1986); Pres. JAYME HENRIQUE CHEMELLO, Bishop of Pelotas, RS; Sec.-Gen. RAYMUNDO DAMASCENO ASSIS.

Latin Rite

Archbishop of São Salvador da Bahia, BA: Cardinal GERALDO MAJELLA AGNELO, Primate of Brazil, Rua Martin Afonso de Souza 270, 40100-050 Salvador, BA; tel. and fax (71) 247-5987.

Archbishop of Aparecida, SP: Cardinal ALOÍSIO LORSCHEIDER.

Archbishop of Aracajú, SE: JOSÉ PALMEIRA LESSA.

Archbishop of Belém do Pará, PA: VICENTE JOAQUIM ZICO.

Archbishop of Belo Horizonte, MG: Cardinal SERAFIM FERNANDES DE ARAÚJO.

Archbishop of Botucatú, SP: ANTÔNIO MARIA MUCCIOLO.

Archbishop of Brasília, DF: Cardinal JOSÉ FREIRE FALCÃO.

Archbishop of Campinas, SP: GILBERTO PEREIRA LOPES.

Archbishop of Campo Grande, MS: VITÓRIO PAVANELLO.

Archbishop of Cascavel, PR: LÚCIO IGNÁCIO BAUMGAERTNER.

Archbishop of Cuiabá, MT: BONIFÁCIO PICCININI.

Archbishop of Curitiba, PR: PEDRO ANTÔNIO MARCHETTI FEDALTO.

Archbishop of Diamantina, MG: PAULO LOPES DE FARIA.

Archbishop of Florianópolis, SC: EUSÉBIO OSCAR SCHEID.

Archbishop of Fortaleza, CE: JOSÉ ANTÔNIO APARECIDO TOSI MARQUES.

Archbishop of Goiânia, GO: ANTÔNIO RIBEIRO DE OLIVEIRA.

Archbishop of Juiz de Fora, MG: CLÓVIS FRAINER.

Archbishop of Londrina, PR: ALBANO BORTOLETTO CAVALLIN.

Archbishop of Maceió, AL: EDVALDO GONÇALVES AMARAL.

Archbishop of Manaus, AM: LUIZ SOARES VIEIRA.

Archbishop of Mariana, MG: LUCIANO PEDRO MENDES DE ALMEIDA.

Archbishop of Maringá, PR: MURILO SEBASTIÃO RAMOS KRIEGER.

Archbishop of Natal, RN: HEITOR DE ARAÚJO SALES.

Archbishop of Niterói, RJ: CARLOS ALBERTO ETCHANDY GIMENO NAVARRO.

Archbishop of Olinda e Recife, PE: JOSÉ CARDOSO SOBRINHO.

Archbishop of Palmas, PR: ALBERTO TAVEIRA CORRÊA.

Archbishop of Paraíba, PB: MARCELO PINTO CARVALHEIRA.

Archbishop of Porto Alegre, RS: ALTAMIRO ROSSATO.

Archbishop of Porto Velho, RO: MOACYR GRECHI.

Archbishop of Pouso Alegre, MG: RICARDO PEDRO CHAVES PINTO, Filho.

Archbishop of Ribeirão Prêto, SP: ARNALDO RIBEIRO.

Archbishop of São Luís do Maranhão, MA: PAULO EDUARDO DE ANDRADE PONTE.

Archbishop of São Paulo, SP: Cardinal CLAUDIO HUMMES.

Archbishop of São Sebastião do Rio de Janeiro, RJ: Cardinal EUGÊNIO DE ARAÚJO SALES.

Archbishop of Sorocaba, SP: José Lambert.
Archbishop of Teresina, PI: Miguel Fenelon Câmara, Filho.
Archbishop of Uberaba, MG: Aloísio Roque Oppermann.
Archbishop of Vitória, ES: Silvestre Luís Scandian.

Maronite Rite
Bishop of Nossa Senhora do Líbano em São Paulo, SP: Joseph Mahfouz.

Melkite Rite
Bishop of Nossa Senhora do Paraíso em São Paulo, SP: Fares Maakaroun.

Ukrainian Rite
Bishop of São João Batista em Curitiba, PR: Efraim Basílio Krevey.

The Anglican Communion

Anglicans form the Episcopal Anglican Church of Brazil (Igreja Episcopal Anglicana do Brasil), comprising seven dioceses.
Igreja Episcopal Anglicana do Brasil: CP 11-510, 90841-970 Porto Alegre, RS; tel. and fax (51) 318-6200; f. 1890; 103,021 mems (1997); Primate Most Rev. Glauco Soares de Lima, Bishop of São Paulo-Brazil; Gen. Sec. Rev. Mauricio J. A. de Andrade; e-mail m_andrade@ieab.org.br.

Protestant Churches

Igreja Cristã Reformada do Brasil: CP 2808, 01000 São Paulo, SP; Pres. Rev. Janos Apostol.
Igreja Evangélica de Confissão Luterana no Brasil (IECLB): Rua Senhor dos Passos 202, 2° andar, CP 2876, 90020-180 Porto Alegre, RS; tel. (51) 221-3433; fax (51) 225-7244; e-mail secretariageral@ieclb.org.br; internet www.iedb.org.br; f. 1949; 714,000 mems; Pres. Pastor Huberto Kirchheim.
Igreja Evangélica Congregacional do Brasil: CP 414, 98700 Ijuí, RS; tel. (55) 332-4656; f. 1942; 41,000 mems, 310 congregations; Pres. Rev. H. Hartmut W. Hachtmann.
Igreja Evangélica Luterana do Brasil: Rua Cel. Lucas de Oliveira 894, 90440-010 Porto Alegre, RS; tel. (51) 332-2111; fax (51) 332-8145; e-mail ielb@ielb.org.br; internet www.ielb.org.br; f. 1904; 218,600 mems; Pres. Rev. Carlos Walter Winterle.
Igreja Metodista do Brasil: General Communication Secretariat, Rua Artur Azevedo 1192, Apdo 81, Pinheiros, 05404 São Paulo, SP; Exec. Sec. Dr Onésimo de Oliveira Cardoso.
Igreja Presbiteriana Unida do Brasil (IPU): CP 01-212, 29001-970 Vitória, ES; tel. (27) 222-8024; f. 1978; Sec. Paulo Rückert.

BAHÁ'Í FAITH

Bahá'í Community of Brazil: SHIS, QL 08, Conj. 2, Casa 15, 71620-285, Brasília, DF; CP 7035, 71620-225 Brasília, DF; tel. (61) 364-3594; fax (61) 364-3470; e-mail secext@bahai.org.br; f. 1921; Sec. Iradj Roberto Eghrari.

BUDDHISM

Federação das Seitas Budistas do Brasil: Av. Paulo Ferreira 1133, 02915-100, São Paulo, SP; tel. (11) 876-5771; fax (11) 877-8687.
Sociedade Budista do Brasil (Rio Buddhist Vihara): Dom Joaquim Mamede 45, Lagoinha, Santa Tereza, 20241-390 Rio de Janeiro, RJ; tel. (21) 205-4400; f. 1972; Principal Dr Puhulwelle Vipassi.

The Press

The most striking feature of the Brazilian press is the relatively small circulation of newspapers in comparison with the size of the population. The newspapers with the largest circulations are *O Día* (250,000), *O Globo* (350,000), *Fôlha de São Paulo* (560,000), and *O Estado de São Paulo* (242,000). The low circulation is mainly owing to high costs resulting from distribution difficulties. In consequence there are no national newspapers. In 1996 a total of 380 daily newspaper titles were published in Brazil.

DAILY NEWSPAPERS
Belém, PA

O Liberal: Rua Gaspar Viana 253, 66020 Belém, PA; tel. (91) 222-3000; fax (91) 224-1906; f. 1946; Pres. Lucidea Maiorana; circ. 20,000.

Belo Horizonte, MG

Diário da Tarde: Rua Goiás 36, 30190 Belo Horizonte, MG; tel. (31) 273-2322; fax (31) 273-4400; f. 1931; evening; Dir-Gen. Paulo C. de Araújo; total circ. 150,000.

Diário de Minas: Rua Francisco Salles 540, 30150-220 Belo Horizonte, MG; tel. (31) 222-5622; f. 1949; Pres. Marco Aurílio F. Carone; circ. 50,000.
Diário do Comércio: Av. Américo Vespúcio 1660, 31.230 Belo Horizonte, MG; tel. (31) 469-1011; fax (31) 469-1080; f. 1932; Pres. José Costa.
Estado de Minas: Rua Goiás 36, 30190 Belo Horizonte, MG; tel. (31) 273-2322; fax (31) 273-4400; f. 1928; morning; independent; Pres. Paulo C. de Araújo; circ. 65,000.

Blumenau, SC

Jornal de Santa Catarina: Rua São Paulo 1120, 89010-000 Blumenau, SC; tel. (2147) 340-1400; e-mail redacao@santa.com.br; f. 1971; Dir Alvaro Iahnig; circ. 25,000.

Brasília, DF

Correio Brasiliense: SIG, Q2, Lotes 300/340, 70610-901 Brasília, DF; tel. (61) 321-1314; fax (61) 321-2856; f. 1960; Dir-Gen. Paulo C. de Araújo; circ. 30,000.
Jornal de Brasília: SIG, Trecho 1, Lotes 585/645, 70610-400 Brasília, DF; tel. (61) 225-2515; f. 1972; Dir-Gen. Fernando Côma; circ. 25,000.

Campinas, SP

Correio Popular: Rua Conceição 124, 13010-902 Campinas, SP; tel. (192) 32-8588; fax (192) 31-8152; f. 1927; Pres. Sylvino de Godoy Neto; circ. 40,000.

Curitiba, PR

O Estado do Paraná: Rua João Tschannerl 800, 80820-000 Curitiba, PR; tel. (41) 335-8811; fax (41) 335-2838; f. 1951; Pres. Paulo Cruz Pimentel; circ. 15,000.
Gazeta do Povo: Praça Carlos Gomes 4, 80010 Curitiba, PR; tel. (41) 224-0522; fax (41) 225-6848; f. 1919; Pres. Francisco Cunha Pereira; circ. 40,000.
Tribuna do Paraná: Rua João Tschannerl 800, 80820-010 Curitiba PR; tel. (41) 335-8811; fax (41) 335-2838; f. 1956; Pres. Paulo Cruz Pimentel; circ. 15,000.

Florianópolis, SC

O Estado: Rodovia SC-401, Km 3, 88030 Florianópolis, SC; tel. (482) 388-8888; fax (482) 380-0711; f. 1915; Pres. José Matusalém Comelli; circ. 20,000.

Fortaleza, CE

Jornal O Povo: Av. Aguanambi 282, 60055 Fortaleza, CE; tel. (85) 211-9666; fax (85) 231-5792; f. 1928; evening; Pres. Demócrito Rocha Dummar; circ. 20,000.
Tribuna do Ceará: Av. Desemb. Moreira 2900, 60170 Fortaleza, CE; tel. (85) 247-3066; fax (85) 272-2799; f. 1957; Dir José A. Sancho; circ. 12,000.

Goiânia, GO

Diário da Manhã: Av. Anhanguera 2833, Setor Leste Universitário, 74000 Goiânia, GO; tel. (62) 261-7371; f. 1980; Pres. Julio Nasser Custódio dos Santos; circ. 16,000.
Jornal O Popular: Rua Thómas Edson Q7, Setor Serrinha, 74835-130 Goiânia, GO; tel. (62) 250-1000; fax (62) 241-1018; f. 1938; Pres. Jaime Câmara Júnior; circ. 65,000.

Londrina, PR

Fôlha de Londrina: Rua Piauí 241, 86010 Londrina, PR; tel. (432) 24-2020; fax (432) 21-1051; f. 1948; Pres. João Milanez; circ. 40,000.

Manaus, AM

A Crítica: Av. André Araújo, Km 3, 69060 Manaus; tel. (92) 642-2000; fax (92) 642-1501; f. 1949; Dir Umberto Caderaro; circ. 19,000.

Niterói, RJ

O Fluminense: Rua Visconde de Itaboraí 184, 24030 Niterói, RJ; tel. (21) 719-3311; fax (21) 719-6344; f. 1978; Dir Alberto Francisco Torres; circ. 80,000.
Jornal de Icarai: Rua Barão de Amazonas 31, 24030111 Niterói, RJ; tel. (21) 719-1886; e-mail icarai@urbi.com.br; f. 1926; daily.
A Tribuna: Rua Barão do Amazonas 31, 24030111 Niterói, RJ; tel. (21) 719-1886; e-mail icarai@urbi.com.br; f. 1926; daily; Dir-Gen. Jourdan Amóra; circ. 10,000.

Porto Alegre, RS

Zero Hora: Av. Ipiranga 1075, 90169-900 Porto Alegre, RS; tel. (51) 218-4101; fax (51) 218-4405; internet www.rbs.com.br; f. 1964; Pres. Nelson Sirotsky; circ. 165,000 (Mon.), 170,000 weekdays, 240,000 Sunday.

Recife, PE

Diário de Pernambuco: Praça da Independência 12, 2° andar, 50010-300 Recife, PE; tel. (81) 424-3666; fax (81) 424-2527; f. 1825; morning; independent; Pres. ANTÔNIO C. DA COSTA; circ. 31,000.

Ribeirão Preto, SP

Diário da Manhã: Rua Duque de Caxias 179, 14015 Ribeirão Preto, SP; tel. (16) 634-0909; f. 1898; Dir PAULO M. SANT'ANNA; circ. 17,000.

Rio de Janeiro, RJ

O Dia: Rua Riachuelo 359, 20235 Rio de Janeiro, RJ; tel. (21) 272-8000; fax (21) 507-1038; f. 1951; morning; centrist labour; Pres. ANTÔNIO ARY DE CARVALHO; circ. 250,000 weekdays, 500,000 Sundays.

O Globo: Rua Irineu Marinho 35, CP 1090, 20233-900 Rio de Janeiro, RJ; tel. (21) 534-5000; fax (21) 534-5510; f. 1925; morning; Dir FRANCISCO GRAELL; circ. 350,000 weekdays, 600,000 Sundays.

Jornal do Brasil: Av. Brasil 500, 6° andar, São Cristovão, 20949-900 Rio de Janeiro, RJ; tel. (21) 585-4422; f. 1891; morning; Catholic, liberal; Pres. M. F. DO NASCIMENTO BRITO; circ. 200,000 weekdays, 325,000 Sundays.

Jornal do Comércio: Rua do Livramento 189, 20221 Rio de Janeiro, RJ; tel. (21) 253-6675; f. 1827; morning; Pres. AUSTREGÉSILO DE ATHAYDE; circ. 31,000 weekdays.

Jornal dos Sports: Rua Tenente Possolo 15/25, 20230-160 Rio de Janeiro, RJ; tel. (21) 232-8010; e-mail esportes@vol.com.br; f. 1931; morning; sporting daily; Dir MILTON COELHO DA GRAÇA; circ. 39,000.

Ultima Hora: Rua Equador 702, 20220 Rio de Janeiro, RJ; tel. (21) 223-2444; fax (21) 223-2444; f. 1951; evening; Dir K. NUNES; circ. 56,000.

Salvador, BA

Jornal da Bahia: Rua Peruvia Carneiro 220, 41100 Salvador, BA; tel. (71) 384-2919; fax (71) 384-5726; f. 1958; Pres. MÁRIO KERTÉSZ; circ. 20,000.

Jornal Correio da Bahia: Av. Luis Viana Filho s/n, 41100 Salvador, BA; tel. (71) 371-2811; fax (71) 231-3944; f. 1979; Pres. ARMANDO GONÇALVES.

Jornal da Tarde: Av. Tancredo Neves 1092, 41820-020 Salvador, BA; tel. (71) 231-9683; fax (71) 231-1064; f. 1912; evening; Pres. REGINA SIMÕES DE MELLO LEITÃO; circ. 54,000.

Santo André, SP

Diário do Grande ABC: Rua Catequese 562, 09090-900 Santo André, SP; tel. (11) 715-8112; fax (11) 715-8257; e-mail Maury Dotto@dgabc.com.br; internet www.dgabc.com.br; f. 1958; Pres. MAURY DE CAMPOS DOTTO; circ. 78,500.

Santos, SP

A Tribuna: Rua General Câmara 90/94, 11010-903 Santos, SP; tel. (13) 211-7000; fax (13) 219-6783; f. 1984; Dir ROBERTO M. SANTINI; circ. 40,000.

São Luís, MA

O Imparcial: Rua Afonso Pena 46, 65000 São Luís, MA; tel. (98) 222-5120; fax (98) 222-5120; f. 1926; Dir-Gen. PEDRO BATISTA FREIRE.

São Paulo, SP

Diário Comércio e Indústria: Rua Alvaro de Carvalho 354, 01050-020 São Paulo, SP; tel. (11) 256-5011; fax (11) 258-1989; f. 1933; morning; Pres. HAMILTON LUCAS DE OLIVEIRA; circ. 50,000.

Diário Popular: Rua Major Quedinho 28, 1°-6° andares, 01050 São Paulo, SP; tel. (11) 258-2133; fax (11) 256-1627; f. 1884; evening; independent; Dir RICARDO GURAL DE SABEYA; circ. 90,000.

O Estado de São Paulo: Av. Eng. Caetano Álvares 55, 02550 São Paulo, SP; tel. (11) 856-2122; fax (11) 266-2206; f. 1875; morning; independent; Dir FRANCISCO MESQUITA NETO; circ. 242,000 weekdays, 460,000 Sundays.

Fôlha de São Paulo: Alameda Barão de Limeira 425, Campos Elíseos, 01202-900 São Paulo, SP; tel. (11) 224-3222; fax (11) 223-1644; f. 1921; morning; Editorial Dir OCTAVIO FRIAS, Filho; circ. 557,650 weekdays, 1,401,178 Sundays.

Gazeta Mercantil: Rua Major Quedinho 90, 5° andar, 01050 São Paulo, SP; tel. (11) 256-3133; fax (11) 258-5864; f. 1920; business paper; Pres. LUIZ FERREIRA LEVY; circ. 80,000.

Jornal da Tarde: Rua Peixoto Gomidi 671, 01409 São Paulo, SP; tel. (11) 284-1944; fax (11) 289-3548; f. 1966; evening; independent; Dir R. MESQUITA; circ. 120,000, 180,000 Mondays.

Notícias Populares: Alameda Barão de Limeira 425, 01202 São Paulo, SP; tel. (11) 874-2222; fax (11) 223-1644; f. 1963; Dir RENATO CASTANHARI; circ. 150,000.

Vitória, ES

A Gazeta: Rua Charic Murad 902, 29050 Vitória, ES; tel. (27) 222-8333; fax (27) 223-1525; f. 1928; Pres. MARIO LINDENBERG; circ. 19,000.

PERIODICALS

Rio de Janeiro, RJ

Amiga: Rua do Russel 766/804, 22214 Rio de Janeiro, RJ; tel. (21) 285-0033; fax (21) 205-9998; weekly; women's interest; Pres. ADOLPHO BLOCH; circ. 83,000.

Antenna-Eletrônica Popular: Av. Marechal Floriano 143, CP 151, 20080-005 Rio de Janeiro, RJ; tel. (21) 223-2442; fax (21) 263-8840; e-mail antenna@unisys.com.br; internet www.anep.com.br; f. 1926; monthly; telecommunications and electronics, radio, TV, hi-fi, amateur and CB radio; Dir GILBERTO AFFONSO PENNA, Filho; circ. 15,000.

Carinho: Rua do Russel 766/804, 22214 Rio de Janeiro, RJ; tel. (21) 285-0033; fax (21) 205-9998; monthly; women's interest; Pres. ADOLPHO BLOCH; circ. 65,000.

Conjuntura Econômica: Praia de Botafogo 190, Sala 923, 22253-900 Rio de Janeiro, RJ; tel. (21) 536-9267; fax (21) 551-2799; f. 1947; monthly; economics and finance; published by Fundação Getúlio Vargas; Pres. JORGE OSCAR DE MELLO FLÔRES; Editor LAURO VIEIRA DE FARIA; circ. 20,000.

Desfile: Rua do Russel 766/804, 22214 Rio de Janeiro, RJ; tel. (21) 285-0033; fax (21) 205-9998; f. 1969; monthly; women's interest; Dir ADOLPHO BLOCH; circ. 120,000.

Ele Ela: Rua do Russel 766/804, 22214 Rio de Janeiro RJ; tel. (21) 285-0033; fax (21) 205-9998; f. 1969; monthly; men's interest; Dir ADOLPHO BLOCH; circ. 150,000.

Manchete: Rua do Russel 766/804, 20214 Rio de Janeiro, RJ; tel. (21) 285-0033; fax (21) 205-9998; f. 1952; weekly; general; Dir ADOLPHO BLOCH; circ. 110,000.

São Paulo, SP

Capricho: Rua Geraldo Flausino Gomes 61, 6°, 04573-900 São Paulo, SP; tel. (11) 534-5231; monthly; youth interest; Dir ROBERTO CIVITA; circ. 250,000.

Carícia: Av. das Nações Unidas 5777, 05479-900 São Paulo, SP; tel. (11) 211-7866; fax (11) 813-9115; monthly; women's interest; Dir ANGELO ROSSI; circ. 210,000.

Casa e Jardim: B. Machado 82, 01230-010 São Paulo, SP; fax (11) 824-9079; f. 1953; monthly; homes and gardens, illustrated; Pres. LUCIANA JALONETSKY; circ. 120,000.

Claudia: Rua Geraldo Flausino Gomes 61, CP 2371, 04573-900 São Paulo, SP; tel. (11) 534-5130; fax (11) 534-5638; f. 1962; monthly; women's magazine; Dir ROBERTO CIVITA; circ. 460,000.

Criativa: Rua do Centúria 655, 05065-001, São Paulo, SP; tel. (11) 874-6003; fax (11) 864-0271; monthly; women's interest; Dir-Gen. RICARDO A. SÁNCHEZ; circ. 121,000.

Digesto Econômico: Associação Comercial de São Paulo, Rua Boa Vista 51, 01014-911 São Paulo, SP; tel. (11) 234-3322; fax (11) 239-0067; every 2 months; Pres. ELVIO ALIPRANDI; Chief Editor JOÃO DE SCANTIMBURGO.

Disney Especial: Av. das Nações Unidas 7221, 05477-000 São Paulo, SP; tel. (11) 3037-2000; fax (11) 3037-4124; every 2 months; children's magazine; Dir ROBERTO CIVITA; circ. 211,600.

Elle: Av. das Nações Unidas 7221, 05425-902 São Paulo; tel. (11) 3037-5197; fax (11) 3037-5451; f. 1988; internet www.uol.com.br/elle; monthly; women's magazine; Editor CARLOS COSTA; circ. 100,000.

Exame: Av. Octaviano Alves de Lima, 4400, 02909-900 São Paulo, SP; tel. (11) 877-1421; fax (11) 877-1437; f. 1967; e-mail publicidade .exame@email.abril.com.br; two a week; business; Dir JOSÉ ROBERTO GUZZO; circ. 168,300.

Iris, A Revista da Imagem: Rua Brito Peixoto 322, Brooklin, 04582-020 São Paulo, SP; tel. (11) 531-1299; fax (11) 531-1627; e-mail irisfoto@totalnet.com.br; internet www.totalnet.com.br /irisfoto; f. 1947; monthly; photography and general pictures; Dirs BEATRIZ AZEVEDO MARQUES, HÉLIO M. VALENTONI; circ. 50,000.

Manequim: Rua Geraldo Flausino Gomes 61, 04573-900 São Paulo, SP; tel. (11) 534-5668; fax (11) 534-5632; monthly; fashion; Dir ROBERTO CIVITA; circ. 300,000.

Máquinas e Metais: Alameda Olga 315, 01155-900, São Paulo, SP; tel. (11) 3824-5300; fax (11) 3662-0103; e-mail info@arandanet .com.br; internet www.arandanet.com.br; f. 1964; monthly; machine and metal industries; Editor JOSÉ ROBERTO GONÇALVES; circ. 15,000.

Marie Claire: Rua Dr Renato Paes Barros 613, 04530-000 São Paulo, SP; tel. (11) 866-3373; monthly; women's magazine; Publr REGINA LEMUS; circ. 273,000.

Mickey: Av. das Nações Unidas 7221, 05477-000 São Paulo, SP; tel. (11) 3037-2000; fax (11) 3037-4124; monthly; children's magazine; Dir ROBERTO CIVITA; circ. 76,000.

Micromundo-Computerworld do Brasil: Rua Caçapava 79, 01408 São Paulo, SP; tel. (11) 289-1767; monthly; computers; Gen. Dir ERIC HIPPEAU; circ. 38,000.

Nova: Rua Geraldo Flausino Gomes 61, 04573-900 São Paulo, SP; tel. (11) 534-5712; fax (11) 534-5187; f. 1973; monthly; women's interest; Dir ROBERTO CIVITA; circ. 300,000.

Pato Donald: Av. das Nações Unidas 7221, 05477-000 São Paulo, SP; tel. (11) 3037-2000; fax (11) 3037-4124; every 2 weeks; children's magazine; Dir ROBERTO CIVITA; circ. 120,000.

Placar: Av. das Nações Unidas 7221, 14° andar, 05477-000 São Paulo, SP; tel. (11) 3037-5816; fax (11) 3037-5597; e-mail placar .leitor@email.abril.com.br; f. 1970; monthly; soccer magazine; Dir MARCELO DURATE; circ. 127,000.

Quatro Rodas: Rua Geraldo Flausino Gomes 61, Brooklin, 04573-900 São Paulo, SP; tel. (11) 534-5491; fax (11) 530-8549; f. 1960; monthly; motoring; Pres. ROBERTO CIVITA; circ. 250,000.

Revista O Carreteiro: Rua Palacete das Aguias 239, 04035-021 São Paulo, SP; tel. (11) 542-9311; monthly; transport; Dirs JOÃO ALBERTO ANTUNES DE FIGUEIREDO, EDSON PEREIRA COELHO; circ. 80,000.

Saúde: Av. das Nações Unidas 5777, 05479-900 São Paulo, SP; tel. (11) 211-7675; fax (11) 813-9115; monthly; health; Dir ANGELO ROSSI; circ. 180,000.

Veja: Rua do Copturno 571, 6°, São Paulo, SP; tel. (11) 877-1322; fax (11) 877-1640; internet www.veja.com.br; f. 1968; news weekly; Dirs JOSÉ ROBERTO GUZZO, TALES ALVARENGA, MÁRIO SERGIO CONTI; circ. 800,000.

Visão: São Paulo, SP; tel. (11) 549-4344. 1952; weekly; news magazine; Editor HENRY MAKSOUD; circ. 148,822.

NEWS AGENCIES

Editora Abril, SA: Av. Otaviano Alves de Lima 4400, CP 2372, 02909-970 São Paulo, SP; tel. (11) 877-1322; fax (11) 877-1640; f. 1950; Pres. ROBERTO CIVITA.

Agência ANDA: Edif. Correio Brasiliense, Setor das Indústrias Gráficas 300/350, Brasília, DF; Dir EDILSON VARELA.

Agência o Estado de São Paulo: Av. Eng. Caetano Alvares 55, 02588-900 São Paulo, SP; tel. (11) 856-2122; Rep. SAMUEL DIRCEU F. BUENO.

Agência Fôlha de São Paulo: Alameda Barão de Limeira 425, 4° andar, 01290-900 São Paulo; tel. (11) 224-3790; fax (11) 221-0675; Dir MARION STRECKER.

Agência Globo: Rua Irineu Marinho 35, 2° andar, Centro, 20233-900 Rio de Janeiro, RJ; tel. (21) 292-2000; fax (21) 292-2000; Dir CARLOS LEMOS.

Agência Jornal do Brasil: Av. Brasil 500, 6° andar, São Cristóvão, 20949-900 Rio de Janeiro, RJ; tel. (21) 585-4453; fax (21) 580-9944; f. 1966; Exec. Dir. EDGAR LISBOA.

Foreign Bureaux

Agence France-Presse (AFP) (France): CP 2575-ZC-00, Rua México 21, 7° andar, 20031-144 Rio de Janeiro, RJ; tel. (21) 533-4555; fax (21) 262-7933; e-mail afprio@unisys.com.br; Bureau Chief (Brazil) ALAIN BOEBION.

Agencia EFE (Spain): Praia de Botafogo 228, Bloco B, Gr. 1106, 22359-900 Rio de Janeiro, RJ; tel. (21) 553-6355; fax (21) 553-8823; e-mail redario@efebrasil.com.br; Bureau Chief FRANCISCO R. FIGUÉROA.

Agenzia Nazionale Stampa Associata (ANSA) (Italy): Av. São Luís 258, 23° andar, Of. 1302, São Paulo, SP; tel. (11) 256-5835; Bureau Chief RICCARDO CARUCCI.

Associated Press (AP) (USA): Av. Brasil 500, sala 847, CP 72-ZC-00, 20001 Rio de Janeiro, RJ; tel. (21) 580-4422; Bureau Chief BRUCE HANDLER; Rua Major Quedinho Sala 707, CP 3815, 01050 São Paulo, SP; tel. (11) 256-0520; fax (11) 256-4135; Correspondent STAN LEHMAN; a/c Sucursal Fôlha de São Paulo, CLS 104 Bloco C Loja 41, CP 14-2260, 70343 Brasília, DF; tel. (61) 223-9492; Correspondent JORGE MEDEROS.

Deutsche Presse-Agentur (dpa) (Germany): Rua Abade Ramos 65, 22461-90 Rio de Janeiro, RJ; tel. (21) 266-5937; fax (21) 537-8273; Bureau Chief ESTEBAN ENGEL.

Inter Press Service (IPS) (Italy): Rua Vicente de Souza 29, 2° andar, 22251-070 Rio de Janeiro; tel. (21) 286-5605; fax (21) 286-5324; Correspondent MARIO CHIZUO OSAVA.

Jiji Tsushin-Sha (Jiji Press) (Japan): Av. Paulista 854, 13° andar, Conj. 133, Bela Vista, 01310-913 São Paulo, SP; tel. (11) 285-0025; fax (11) 285-3816; e-mail jijisp@nethall.com.br; f. 1958; Chief Correspondent MUTSUHIRO TAKABAYASHI.

Kyodo Tsushin (Japan): Praia do Flamengo 168-701, Flamengo, 22210 Rio de Janeiro, RJ; tel. (21) 285-2412; fax (21) 285-2270; Bureau Chief TAKAYOSHI MAKITA.

Prensa Latina (Cuba): Marechal Mascarenhas de Moraís 121, Apto 602, Copacabana, 22030-040 Rio de Janeiro, RJ; tel. and fax (21) 237-1766; Correspondent FRANCISCO FORTEZA.

Reuters (United Kingdom): Av. Nações Unidas 17891, 8° andar, 04795-100 São Paulo, SP; tel. (11) 232-4411; fax (11) 604-6538; Rua

Sete de Setembro 99, 4° andar, sala 401, 20050-005 Rio de Janeiro, RJ; tel. (21) 507-4151; fax (21) 507-2120; Bureau Chief (News and Television): ADRIAN DICKSON.

United Press International (UPI) (USA): Rua Uruguaina 94, 18°, Centro, 20050 Rio de Janeiro, RJ; tel. (21) 224-4194; fax (21) 232-8293; Rua Sete de Abril 230, Bloco A, 816/817, 01044 São Paulo, SP; tel. (11) 258-6869; Edif. Gilberto Salamão, Sala 805/806, 70305 Brasília, DF; tel. (61) 224-6413. Man. ANTÔNIO PRAXEDES; Chief Correspondent H. E. COYA HONORES.

Xinhua (New China) News Agency (People's Republic of China): SHIS QI 15, Conj. 16, Casa 14, CP 7089, 71.600 Brasília, DF; tel. (61) 248-5489; Chief Correspondent WANG ZHIGEN.

Central News Agency (Taiwan) and Rossiyskoye Informatsionnoye Agentstvo—Novosti (Russia) are also represented in Brazil.

PRESS ASSOCIATIONS

Associação Brasileira de Imprensa: Rua Araújo Porto Alegre 71, Castelo, 20030 Rio de Janeiro, RJ; f. 1908; 4,000 mems; Pres. (vacant); Sec. JOSUÉ ALMEIDA.

Associação Nacional de Editores de Revistas: SCS, Edif. Bandeirantes 201/204, 70300-910 Brasília, DF; tel. (61) 322-5511; fax (61) 321-8348; e-mail redshoes@embratel.net.br; Pres. JOSÉ CARLOS SALLES NETO; Exec. Dir Dr MURILLO DE ARAGÃO.

Federação Nacional dos Jornalistas—FENAJ: Higs 707, Bloco R, Casa 54, 70351-718 Brasília, DF; tel. (61) 244-0650; fax (61) 242-6616; f. 1946; represents 31 regional unions; Pres. AMÉRICO CÉSAR ANTUNES.

Publishers

Rio de Janeiro, RJ

Ao Livro Técnico Indústria e Comércio Ltda: Rua Sá Freire 36/40, São Cristóvão, 20930-430 Rio de Janeiro, RJ; tel. (21) 580-1168; fax (21) 580-9955; internet www.editoraaolivrotécnico .com.br; f. 1933; textbooks, children's and teenagers' fiction and non-fiction, art books, dictionaries; Man. Dir REYNALDO MAX PAUL BLUHM.

Bloch Editores, SA: Rua do Russell 766/804, Glória, 22214 Rio de Janeiro, RJ; tel. (21) 265-2012; fax (21) 205-9998; f. 1966; general; Pres. ADOLPHO BLOCH.

Distribuidora Record de Serviços de Imprensa, SA: Rua Argentina 171, São Cristóvão, CP 884, 20921 Rio de Janeiro, RJ; tel. (21) 585-2000; fax (21) 580-4911; e-mail sacm@record.com.br; internet www.record.com.br; f. 1941; general fiction and non-fiction, education, textbooks, fine arts; Pres. SÉRGIO MACHADO.

Ediouro Publicações, SA: Rua Nova Jerusalém 345, CP 1880, Bonsucesso, 21042-230 Rio de Janeiro, RJ; tel. (21) 260-6122; fax (21) 280-2438; e-mail editoriallivros@ediouro.com.br; internet www.ediouro.com.br; f. 1939; general; Pres. JORGE CARNEIRO.

Editora Artenova, SA: Rua Pref. Olímpio de Mello 1774, Benfica, 20000 Rio de Janeiro, RJ; tel. (21) 264-9198; f. 1971; sociology, psychology, occultism, cinema, literature, politics and history; Man. Dir ALVARO PACHECO.

Editora Brasil-América (EBAL), SA: Rua Gen. Almério de Moura 302/320, São Cristóvão, 20921-060 Rio de Janeiro, RJ; tel. (21) 580-0303; fax (21) 580-1637; f. 1945; children's books; Dir PAULO ADOLFO AIZEN.

Editora Campus: Rua Sete de Setembro 111, 16° andar, 20050-002 Rio de Janeiro; tel. (21) 509-5340; fax (21) 507-1991; e-mail c.rothmuller@campus.com.br; internet www.campus.com.br; business, computing, non-fiction; Man. Dir CLAUDIO ROTHMULLER.

Editora Delta, SA: Av. Almirante Barroso 63, 26° andar, CP 2226, 20031 Rio de Janeiro, RJ; tel. (21) 240-0072; f. 1958; reference books.

Editora Expressão e Cultura—Exped Ltda: Estrada dos Bandeirantes 1700, Bloco E, 22710-113, Rio de Janeiro, RJ; tel. (21) 444-0676; fax (21) 444-0700; e-mail exped@ggh.com.br; f. 1967; textbooks, literature, reference; Gen. Man. RICARDO AUGUSTO PAMPLONA VAZ.

Editora e Gráfica Miguel Couto, SA: Rua da Passagem 78, Loja A, Botafogo, 22290-030 Rio de Janeiro, RJ; tel. (21) 541-5145; f. 1969; engineering; Dir PAULO KOBLER PINTO LOPES SAMPAIO.

Editora Nova Fronteira, SA: Rua Bambina 25, Botafogo, 22251-050 Rio de Janeiro, RJ; tel. (21) 537-8770; fax (21) 286-6755; e-mail nova2@embratel.net.br; f. 1965; fiction, psychology, history, politics, science fiction, poetry, leisure, reference; Pres. CARLOS AUGUSTO LACERDA.

Editora Vozes, Ltda: Rua Frei Luís 100, CP 90023, 25689-900 Petrópolis, RJ; tel. (242) 43-5112; fax (242) 31-4676; e-mail editorial@ vozes.com.br; f. 1901; Catholic publishers; management, theology, anthropology, fine arts, history, linguistics, science, fiction, education, data processing, etc.; Dir STEPHEN OTTENBREIT.

Livraria Francisco Alves Editora, SA: Rua Uruguaiana 94/13°, 20050-002 Rio de Janeiro, RJ; tel. (21) 221-3198; fax (21) 242-3438; f. 1854; textbooks, fiction, non-fiction; Pres. CARLOS LEAL.

Livraria José Olympio Editora, SA: Rua da Glória 344, 4° andar, Glória, 20241-180 Rio de Janeiro, RJ; tel. (21) 221-6939; fax (21) 242-0802; f. 1931; juvenile, science, history, philosophy, psychology, sociology, fiction; Dir MANOEL ROBERTO DOMINGUES.

São Paulo, SP

Atual Editora, Ltda: Av. Gen. Valdomiro de Lima 833, Pq. Jabaquara, 04344-070 São Paulo, SP; tel. (11) 5071-2288; fax (11) 5071-3099; e-mail www.atualeditora.com.br; f. 1973; school and children's books, literature; Dirs GELSON IEZZI, OSVALDO DOLCE.

Cia Editora Nacional: Rua Joli 294, Brás, CP 5312, 03016 São Paulo, SP; tel. (11) 291-2355; fax (11) 291-8614; f. 1925; textbooks, history, science, social sciences, philosophy, fiction, juvenile; Dirs JORGE YUNES, PAULO C. MARTI.

Cia Melhoramentos de São Paulo: Rua Tito 479, 05051-000 São Paulo, SP; tel. (11) 3874-0854; fax (11) 3874-0855; f. 1890; general non-fiction; e-mail blerner@melhoramentos.com.br; internet www.melhoramentos.com.br; Dir BRENO LERNER.

Ebid-Editora Páginas Amarelas Ltda: Av. Liberdade 956, 5° andar, 01502-001 São Paulo, SP; tel. (11) 278-6622; fax (11) 279-8723; e-mail mail@guiaspaginasamarelas.com.br; f. 1947; commercial directories.

Editora Abril, SA: Av. da Nações Unidas 7221, 05425-902 São Paulo, SP; tel. (11) 3037-2000; fax (11) 3037-5638; f. 1950; Pres. ROBERTO CIVITA.

Editora Atica, SA: Rua Barão de Iguape 110, 01507-900 São Paulo, SP; tel. (11) 3346-3000; fax (11) 3277-4146; e-mail editora@atica.com.br; f. 1965; textbooks, Brazilian and African literature; Pres. VICENTE PAZ FERNANDEZ.

Editora Atlas, SA: Rua Conselheiro Nébias 1384, Campos Elíseos, 01203-904 São Paulo, SP; tel. 221-9144; fax (11) 220-7830; e-mail edatlas@editora-atlas.com.br; f. 1944; business administration, data-processing, economics, accounting, law, education, social sciences; Pres. LUIZ HERRMANN.

Editora Brasiliense, SA: Mariano de Sousa 664, 03411-090 São Paulo, SP; tel. (11) 6942-0545; fax (11) 6942-0813; e-mail brasilse@uol.com.br; f. 1943; education, racism, gender studies, human rights, ecology, history, literature, social sciences; Man. YOLANDA C. DA SILVA PRADO.

Editora do Brasil, SA: Rua Conselheiro Nébias 887, Campos Elíseos, CP 4986, 01203-001 São Paulo, SP; tel. (11) 222-0211; fax (11) 222-9655; e-mail editora@editoradobrasil.com.be; internet www.editoradobrasil.com.br; f. 1943; education; Pres. Dr CARLOS COSTA.

Editora FTD, SA: Rua Manoel Dutra 225, 01328-010 São Paulo, SP; tel. (11) 253-5011; fax (11) 288-0132; e-mail ftd@dial&ta.com.br; f. 1897; textbooks; Pres. JOÃO TISSI.

Editora Globo, SA: Av. Jaguare 1485/1487, 05346-902 São Paulo, SP; tel. (11) 874-6000; fax (11) 836-7098; e-mail dflmkt@edglobo.com.br; f. 1957; fiction, engineering, agriculture, cookery, environmental studies; Gen. Man. RICARDO A. FISCHER.

Editora Luzeiro Ltda: Rua Almirante Barroso 730, Brás, 03025-001 São Paulo, SP; tel. (11) 292-3188; f. 1973; folklore and literature.

Editora Michalany Ltda: Rua Biobedas 321, Saúde, 04302-010 São Paulo, SP; tel. (11) 585-2012; fax (11) 276-8775; e-mail editora@editoramichalany.com.br; internet www.editoramichalany.com.br; f. 1965; biographies, economics, textbooks, geography, history, religion, maps; Dir DOUGLAS MICHALANY.

Editora Moderna, Ltda: Rua Padre Adelino 758, Belenzinho, 03303-904, São Paulo, SP; tel. (11) 6090-1316; fax (11) 6090-1369; e-mail moderna@moderna.com.br; internet www.moderna.com.br; Pres. RICARDO ARISSA FELTRE.

Editora Pioneira: Praça Dirceu de Lima 313, Casa Verde, 02515-050 São Paulo, SP; tel. (11) 858-3199; fax (11) 858-0443; e-mail pioneira@virtual-net.com.br; f. 1960; architecture, computers, political and social sciences, business studies, languages, children's books; Dirs ROBERTO GUAZZELLI, LILIANA GUAZZELLI.

Editora Revista dos Tribunais Ltda: Rua Conde do Pinhal 78, CP 8153, 01501 São Paulo, SP; tel. (11) 37-8689; f. 1955; law and jurisprudence, administration, economics and social sciences; Man. Dir NELSON PALMA TRAVASSOS.

Editora Rideel Ltda: Alameda Afonso Schmidt 879, Santa Terezinha, 02450-001 São Paulo, SP; tel. (11) 6977-8344; fax (11) 6976-7415; e-mail sac@rideel.com.br; internet www.rideel.com.br; f. 1971; general; Dir ITALO AMADIO.

Editora Scipione Ltda: Praça Carlos Gomes 46, 01501-040 São Paulo, SP; tel. (11) 239-2255; fax (11) 239-1700; e-mail scipione@scipione.com.br; internet www.scipione.com.br; f. 1983; school-books, literature, reference; Dir LUIZ ESTEVES SALLUM.

Encyclopaedia Britannica do Brasil Publicações Ltda: Rua Rego Freitas 192, Vila Buarque, CP 299, 01059-970 São Paulo, SP; tel. (11) 250-1900; fax (11) 250-1960; e-mail vicepresidencia@barsa.com.br; f. 1951; reference books.

Instituto Brasileiro de Edições Pedagógicas, Ltda: Rua Joli 294, 03016-020 São Paulo, SP; tel. (11) 6099-7799; fax (11) 6694-5338; e-mail editoras@ibep-nacional.com.br; internet www.ibep-nacional.com.br; f. 1965; textbooks, foreign languages and reference books.

Lex Editora, SA: Rua Machado de Assis 47/57, Vila Mariana, 04106-900 São Paulo, SP; tel. (11) 549-0122; fax (11) 575-9138; e-mail adm@lexli.com.br; internet www.lexli.com.br; f. 1937; legislation and jurisprudence; Dir MILTON NICOLAU VITALE PATARA.

Saraiva SA Livreiros Editores: Av. Marquês de São Vicente 1697, CP 2362, 01139-904 São Paulo, SP; tel. (11) 861-3344; fax (11) 861-3308; f. 1914; education, textbooks, law, economics; Pres. JORGE EDUARDO SARAIVA.

Belo Horizonte, MG

Editora Lê, SA: Av. D. Pedro II, 4550 Jardin Montanhês, CP 2585, 30730 Belo Horizonte, MG; tel. (31) 34131720. 1967; textbooks.

Editora Lemi, SA: Av. Nossa Senhora de Fátima 1945, CP 1890, 30000 Belo Horizonte, MG; tel. (31) 201-8044; f. 1967; administration, accounting, law, ecology, economics, textbooks, children's books and reference books.

Editora Vigília, Ltda: Rua Felipe dos Santos 508, Bairro de Lourdes, CP 1068, 30180-160 Belo Horizonte, MG; e-mail lerg@planetarium.com.br; tel. (31) 337-2744; fax (31) 337-2834; f. 1960; general.

Curitiba, PR

Editora Educacional Brasileira, SA: Rua XV de Novembro 178, salas 101/04, CP 7498, 80000 Curitiba, PR; tel. (41) 223-5012; f. 1963; biology, textbooks and reference books.

PUBLISHERS' ASSOCIATIONS

Associação Brasileira do Livro: Av. 13 de Maio 23, 16°, 20031-000 Rio de Janeiro, RJ; tel. (21) 240-9115; fax (21) 532-6678; e-mail abralivro@uol.com.br; Pres. MARCOS DAVID GOMES.

Câmara Brasileira do Livro: Av. Ipiranga 1267, 10° andar, 01039-907 São Paulo, SP; tel. (11) 3315-8277; fax (11) 229-7463; e-mail cbl@cbl.org.br; internet www.cbl.org.br; f. 1946; Pres. RAUL WASSERMANN.

Sindicato Nacional dos Editores de Livros—SNEL: Av. Rio Branco 37, 1503/6 and 1510/12, 20090-003 Rio de Janeiro, RJ; tel. (21) 233-6481; fax (21) 253-8502; e-mail snel@snel.org.br; internet www.snel.org.br; 200 mems; Pres. PAULO ROBERTO ROCCO; Man. ANTÔNIO LASKOS.

There are also regional publishers' associations.

Broadcasting and Communications

TELECOMMUNICATIONS

BCP Telecomunicações: São Paulo; internet www.bcp.com.br; f. 1997; mobile services in São Paulo area; Pres. ROBERTO PEÓN.

Empresa Brasileira de Telecomunicações, SA (EMBRATEL): Av. Pres. Vargas 1012, CP 2586, 20179-900 Rio de Janeiro, RJ; tel. (21) 519-8182; e-mail cmsocial@embratel.net.br; internet www.embratel.com.br; f. 1965; operates national and international telecommunications system; controlled by MCI WorldCom of USA; Chair. DANIEL CRAWFORD.

Empresa Brasileira de Comunicação, SA (Radiobrás): CP 04-0340, 70710 Brasília, DF; tel. (61) 321-3949; fax (61) 321-7602; internet www.radiobras.gov.br; f. 1988 following merger of Empresa Brasileira de Radiodifusão and Empresa Brasileira de Notícias; Pres. MARCELO AMORIM NETTO.

Telecomunicações Brasileiras, SA (Telebrás): SAS Quadra 6, Conjunto Sede, Brasília, DF; tel. (61) 215-2120; fax (61) 322-1213; internet www.telebras.com.br; f. 1972; transferred to the private sector in July 1998; 28 divisions.

Telecomunicações de Rio de Janeiro (Telerj): Rio de Janeiro; internet www.telerj.com.br.

Telecomunicações de São Paulo, SA (Telesp): Rua Martiniano de Carvalho 851, 01321-001 São Paulo; tel. (11) 285-8011; fax (11) 253-3050; e-mail webmaster@telesp.com.br; internet www.telesp.com.br; services operated by Telefónica, SA, of Spain; Pres. FERNANDO XAVIER FERREIRA; Chief Exec. SAMPAIO DORIA.

Regulatory Authority

Agência Nacional de Telecomunicações (ANATEL): SAS Quadra 06, Bloco H, 3° andar, 70313-900, Brasília, DF; tel. (61) 312-2336; fax (61) 312-2211; e-mail biblioteca@anatel.gov.br; internet www.anatel.gov.br/default.htm; f. 1998; Pres. RENATO GUERREIRO.

RADIO

In April 1992 there were 2,917 radio stations in Brazil, including

20 in Brasília, 38 in Rio de Janeiro, 32 in São Paulo, 24 in Curitiba, 24 in Porto Alegre and 23 in Belo Horizonte.

The main broadcasting stations in Rio de Janeiro are: Rádio Nacional, Rádio Globo, Rádio Eldorado, Rádio Jornal do Brasil, Rádio Tupi and Rádio Mundial. In São Paulo the main stations are Rádio Bandeirantes, Rádio Mulher, Rádio Eldorado, Rádio Gazeta and Rádio Excelsior; and in Brasília: Rádio Nacional, Rádio Alvorada, Rádio Planalto and Rádio Capital.

Rádio Nacional do Brásil (RADIOBRÁSIL): CP 070747, 70359-970 Brasília; tel. 321-3949; fax 321-7602; e-mail maurilio@radiobras.gov.br; internet www.radiobras.gov.br; Pres. MAURÍLIO FERREIRA LIMA.

TELEVISION

In April 1992 there were 256 television stations in Brazil, of which 118 were in the state capitals and six in Brasília.

The main television networks are:

TV Bandeirantes—Canal 13: Rádio e Televisão Bandeirantes Ltda, Rua Radiantes 13, 05699 São Paulo, SP; tel. (11) 842-3011; fax (11) 842-3067; 65 TV stations and repeaters throughout Brazil; Pres. JOÃO JORGE SAAD.

RBS TV-TV Gaúcha, SA: Rua Rádio y TV Gaúcha 189, 90850-080 Porto Alegre, RS; tel. (51) 218-5002; fax (51) 218-5005; Vice-Pres WALMOR BERGESCH.

TV Globo—Canal 4: Rua Lopes Quintas 303, Jardim Botânico, 22460-010 Rio de Janeiro, RJ; tel. (21) 511-1711; fax (21) 511-4305; e-mail apm@domain.com.br; internet www.redeglobo.com.br; f. 1965; 8 stations; national network; Dir ADILSON PONTES MALTA.

TV Manchete-Canal 6: Rua do Russel 766, 20000 Rio de Janeiro, RJ; tel. (21) 265-2012; Dir-Gen. R. FURTADO.

TV Record—Rede Record de Televisão—Radio Record, SA: Rua de Várzea 240, Barra Funda, 01140-080 São Paulo, SP; tel. (11) 824-7000; Pres. JOÃO BATISTA R. SILVA; Exec. Vice-Pres. H. GONÇALVES.

TVSBT—Canal 4 de São Paulo, SA: Rua Dona Santa Veloso 535, Vila Guilherme, 02050 São Paulo, SP; tel. (11) 292-9044; fax (11) 264-6004; Vice-Pres. GUILHERME STOLIAR.

BROADCASTING ASSOCIATIONS

Associação Brasileira de Emissoras de Rádio e Televisão (ABERT): Centro Empresarial Varig, SCN Quadra 04, Bloco B, Conjunto 501, Pétala A, 70710-500 Brasília, DF; tel. (61) 327-4600; fax (61) 327-3660; e-mail abert@abert.org.br; internet www.abert.org.br; f. 1962; mems: 32 shortwave, 1,275 FM, 1,574 medium-wave and 80 tropical-wave radio stations and 258 television stations (1997); Pres. PAULO MACHADO DE CARVALHO NETO; Exec. Dir OSCAR PICONEZ.

There are regional associations for Bahia, Ceará, Goiás, Minas Gerais, Grande do Sul, Santa Catarina, São Paulo, Amazonas, Distrito Federal, Mato Grosso and Mato Grosso do Sul (combined) and Sergipe.

Finance

(cap. = capital; dep. = deposits; res = reserves; m. = million; brs = branches; amounts in reais, unless otherwise stated)

BANKING

Conselho Monetário Nacional: SBS, Q.03, Bloco B, Edif. Sede do Banco do Brasil, 21° andar, 70074-900 Brasília, DF; tel. (61) 414-1945; fax (61) 414-2528; f. 1964 to formulate monetary policy and to supervise the banking system; Pres. Minister of Finance.

Central Bank

Banco Central do Brasil: SBS, Q 03, Bloco B, CP 04-0170, 70074-900 Brasília, DF; tel. (61) 414-1000; fax (61) 223-1033; e-mail secre.surel@bcb.gov.br; internet www.bcb.gov.br; f. 1965 to execute the decisions of the Conselho Monetário Nacional; bank of issue; Pres. ARMÍNIO FRAGA NETO; 10 brs.

State Commercial Banks

Banco do Brasil, SA: Setor Bancário Sul, SBS, Quadra 4, Bloco C, Lote 32, 70089-900 Brasília, DF; tel. (61) 310-3400; fax (61) 310-2563; internet www.bancobrasil.com.br; f. 1808; cap. 6,629.9m., dep. 78,743.8m. (Dec. 1998); Pres. PAOLO CESAR XIMENES ALVES FERREIRA; 2,778 brs.

Banco do Estado do Rio Grande do Sul, SA: Rua Capitão Montanha 177, CP 505, 90010-040 Porto Alegre, RS; tel. (51) 215-2501; fax (51) 215-1715; e-mail banrisul@banrisul.com.br; internet www.banrisul.com.br; f. 1928; cap. 1,667.2m., res –1,190.3m., dep. 13,214.9 (Dec. 1998); Pres. JOÃO ALCIR VERLE; 303 brs.

Banco do Estado de Santa Catarina SA: Rua Padre Miguelinho 80, CEP 88010-550, Florianópolis, SC; tel. (48) 224-2100; fax (48) 223-4962; e-mail decam/dinte@besc.com.br; internet www.besc.com.br; f. 1962; cap. 158.1m., res 104.3m., dep. 1,329.6m. (Dec. 1997); Pres. VITOR FONTANA.

Banco do Estado de São Paulo, SA (Banespa): Praça Antônio Prado 6, 01010-010 São Paulo, SP; tel. (11) 259-7722; fax (11) 239-2409; e-mail presidencia@banespa.com; f.1926; cap. 2,409.3m., res 1,733.9m., dep. 12,650.7m. (Dec. 1998); scheduled for privatization; Chair. EDUARDO AGUSTO DE ALMEIDA GUIMARÃES; 1,404 brs.

Banco do Nordeste do Brasil, SA: Av. Paranjana 5700, Passaré, 60740-000 Fortaleza, CE; tel. (85) 299-3022; fax (85) 299-3585; e-mail info@banconordeste.gov.br; internet www.banconordeste.gov.br; f. 1954; cap. 831.0m., res 124.7m., dep. 1,474.9m. (Dec. 1999); Pres. and CEO BYRON COSTA DE QUEIROZ; 186 brs.

Private Banks

Banco ABN AMRO SA: Av. Paulista 1374, 3° andar, 01310-916 São Paulo, SP; tel. (11) 525-6000; fax (11) 525-6387.

Banco da Amazônia, SA: Av. Presidente Vargas 800, 66017-000 Belém, PA; tel. (91) 216-3000; fax (91) 223-5403; internet www.bancoamazonia.com.br; f. 1942; cap. 88,211m., res 78,957m., dep. 638,953m. (Dec. 1998); Pres. ANIVALDO JUVENIL VALE; 109 brs.

Banco América do Sul, SA: Av. Brigadeiro Luís Antônio 2020, 01318-911 São Paulo, SP; tel. (11) 3170-9899; fax (11) 3170-9564; e-mail bas@bas.com.br; internet www.bas.com.br; f. 1940; cap. 214.6m., dep. 2,832.8m. (Dec. 1997); CEO YVES L. J. LEJEUNE; 139 brs.

Banco Barclays e Galicia, SA: Av. Paulista 1842, Edif. Cetenco Plaza, Torre Norte 24°–25° andares, 01310-200 São Paulo, SP; tel. (11) 269-2700; fax (11) 283-3168; e-mail barclays@barclays.com.br; internet www.barclays.com; f. 1967 as Banco de Investimento; cap. 170.1m., res 22.9m., dep. 197.8m. (Dec. 1999); Pres. PETER ANDERSON.

Banco BBA-Creditanstalt, SA: Av. Paulista 37, 20°, 01311-902 São Paulo, SP; tel. (11) 281-8000; fax (11) 284-2158; e-mail bancobba@bba.com.br; internet www.bba.com.br; f. 1988; cap. 161.6m., res 747.7m., dep. 5,019.9m. (Dec. 1999); Pres. FERNÃO CARLOS BOTELHO BRACHER; 5 brs.

Banco BMC, SA: Av. das Nações Unidas 12.995, 24° andar, 04578-000 São Paulo, SP; tel. (11) 5503-7807; fax (11) 5503-7676; e-mail bancobmc@bmc.com.br; internet www.bmc.com.br; f.1939, adopted current name in 1990; cap. 159.8m., res 13.5m., dep. 1,134.8m. (Dec. 1999); Chair. FRANCISCO JAIME NOGUEIRA PINHEIRO; 9 brs.

Banco BMG, SA: Av. Alvares Cabral 1707, Santo Agostinho, 30170-001 Belo Horizonte, MG; tel. (31) 290-3000; fax (31) 290-3315; f. 1988; cap. 89.8m., res 50.9m., dep. 305.0m. (Dec. 1996); Pres. FLÁVIO PENTAGNA GUIMARÃES; 4 brs.

Banco Bandeirantes, SA: Rua Boa Vista 162, 01014-902 São Paulo, SP; tel. (11) 233-7155; fax (11) 233-7329; e-mail band@bandeirantes.com.br; f. 1944; cap. 546.4m., res –225.8m., dep. 3,534.7m. (Dec. 1998); acquired by Unibanco in 2000; Pres. Dr CARLOS TRAGUELHO; 167 brs.

Banco Bilbao Vizcaya Argentaria Brasil, SA: Av. Antônio Carlos Magalhães 2728, 41840-000 Salvador, BA; tel. (71) 354-7000; fax (71) 354-7106; internet www.exceleconomico.com.br; f. 1996 as a result of merger of Excel Banco and Banco Econômico; name changed in 2000; cap. 1,000.0m., res 353.6m., dep. 4,868.3m. (Dec. 1999); Pres. EZEQUIEL NASSER; 232 brs.

Banco Boavista Interatlântico, SA: Praça Pio X 118, 20091-040 Rio de Janeiro, RJ; tel. (21) 849-1661; fax (21) 253-1579; e-mail boavista@ibm.net; internet www.boavista.com.br; f. 1997; cap. 627.9m., res –111.8m., dep. 4,050.6m. (Dec. 1998); acquired by Banco Bradesco in 2000; Pres. and Gen. Man. JOSÉ LUIZ SILVEIRA MIRANDA.

Banco Bozano, Simonsen, SA: Av. Rio Branco 138-Centro, 20057-900 Rio de Janeiro, RJ; tel. (21) 508-4711; fax (21) 508-4479; e-mail info@bozano.com.br; f. 1967; cap. 248.2m., res 266.4m., dep. 5,103.1m. (Dec. 1998); Pres. PAULO VEIGA FERRAZ PEREIRA; 4 brs.

Banco Bradesco, SA: Cidade de Deus, Vila Yara, 06029-900 Osasco, SP; tel. (11) 708-14011; fax (11) 708-44630; internet www.bradesco.com.br; f. 1943; fmrly Banco Brasileiro de Descontos; cap. 3,800.0m., res 2,969.2m., dep. 49,974.3m. (Dec. 1999); Chair. LÁZARO DE MELLO BRANDÃO; VICE-CHAIR. ANTÔNIO BORNIA; 2,106 brs.

Banco CCF Brasil SA: Av. Brigadeiro Faria Lima 3064, 1°–4° andares, Itaim Bibi, 01451-000 São Paulo, SP; tel. (11) 827-5000; fax (11) 827-5299; internet www.ccfbrasil.com.br; f. 1980; cap. 409.2m., res 189.4m., dep. 537.8m. (Dec. 1999); Pres. BERNARD MENCIER.

Banco Chase Manhattan, SA: Rua Verbo Divino, 04719-002 São Paulo, SP; tel. (11) 546-4433; fax (11) 546-4624; f. 1925; fmrly Banco Lar Brasileiro, SA; Chair. PETER ANDERSON.

Banco Cidade, SA: Praça Dom José Gaspar 106, 01047-010 São Paulo, SP; tel. (11) 3150-5000; fax (11) 255-4176; e-mail cambio.comercial@bancocidade.com.br; internet www.bancocidade.com.br; f. 1965; cap. 75.0m., res 99.5m., dep. 1,278.1m. (Dec. 1998); Pres. EDMUNDO SAFDIÉ; 25 brs.

Banco Credibanco, SA: Av Paulista 1294, 21° andar, 01310-915 São Paulo, SP; tel. (11) 3150-5000; fax (11) 285-3431; e-mail crediban@credibanco.com.br; internet www.credibanco.com.br; f. 1967; cap. 120.0m., res 63.6m., dep. 458.1m. (Dec. 1998); CEO PETER ANDERSON; 2 brs.

Banco de Crédito Nacional, SA (BCN): Av. das Nações Unidas 12901, CENU-Torre Oeste, 04578-000 Vila Cordeiro, SP; tel. (11) 5509-2801; fax (11) 5509-2802; internet www.bcn.com.br; f. 1924; acquired by Banco Bradesco in 1997; cap. 580.0m., res 327.3m., dep. 7,713.5m. (Dec. 1999); Pres. JOSÉ LUIZ ACAR PEDRO; 122 brs.

Banco Dibens, SA: Alameda Santos 200, Cerqueira Cesar, 01418-000 São Paulo, SP; tel. (11) 253-2177; fax (11) 284-3132; f. 1989; cap. 81.7m., res 84.0m., dep. 760.9m. (Dec. 1996); Pres. MAURO SADDI; 23 brs.

Banco do Estado de Minas Gerais, SA: Rua Rio de Janeiro 471, Centro Belo Horizonte, 30160-910 Belo Horizonte, MG; tel. (31) 239-1211; fax (31) 239-1859; f. 1967; acquired by Banco de Crédito Nacional in 1997; cap. 240.8m., res −157.6m., dep. 2,450.3m. (Dec. 1997); Pres. JOSÉ AFONSO B. BELTRÃO DA SILVA; 755 brs.

Banco do Estado do Paraná, SA (Banestado): Rua Máximo João Kopp 274, Santa Cândida, 82630-900 Curitiba, PR; tel. (41) 351-8745; fax (41) 351-7252; e-mail helphb@email.banestado.com.br; internet www.banestado.com.br; f. 1928; cap. 3,988.9m., res −3,555.3m., dep. 4,203.5m. (Dec. 1999); acquired by Banco Itaú in 2000; Pres. REINHOLD STEPHANES; 389 brs.

Banco Fibra: Av. Brigadeiro Faria Lima 3064, 7° andar, Itaim Bibi, 01451-000, São Paulo, SP; tel. (11) 3827-6700; fax (11) 3827-6620; e-mail internacional@bancofibra.com.br; f. 1988; cap. 106.1m., res 111.4m., dep. 1,334.0m. (Dec. 1998); Pres. BENJAMIN STEINBRUCH; CEO JOÃO AYRES RABELLO, Filho.

Banco Francês e Brasileiro, SA: Av. Paulista 1294, 01310-915 São Paulo, SP; tel. (11) 238-8216; fax (11) 238-8622; e-mail bfb.international@itau.com.br; internet www.bfb.com.br; f. 1948; affiliated with Crédit Lyonnais; cap. 472.3m., res 29.5m., dep. 1,152.0m. (Dec. 1997); Pres. ROBERTO EGYDIO SETÚBAL; 32 brs.

Banco Industrial e Comercial, SA: Rua Boa Vista 192, 01014-030 São Paulo, SP; tel. (11) 237-6904; fax (11) 3107-5290; e-mail bicbanco.dinte@uol.com.br; internet www.bicbanco.com.br; f. 1938; cap. 191.7m., res 62.9m., dep. 725.6m. (June 2000); Pres. JOSÉ BEZERRA DE MENEZES; 38 brs.

Banco Itaú, SA: Rua Boa Vista 176, CP 30341, 01014-919 São Paulo, SP; tel. (11) 237-3000; fax (11) 277-1044; e-mail info@itau.com.br; internet www.itau.com.br; f. 1944; cap. 2,500.0m., res 3,406.7m., dep. 28,288.8m. (Dec. 1999); Chair. OLAVO EGYDIO SETÚBAL; Pres. and CEO ROBERTO EGYDIO SETÚBAL; 1,070 brs.

Banco Mercantil de São Paulo: CP 4077, Av. Paulista 1450, 01310-917 São Paulo; tel. (11) 252-2121; fax (11) 284-3312; e-mail finasa@finasa.com.br; internet www.finasa.com.br; f. 1938; name changed 2000; cap. 817.4m., res 189.6m., dep. 3,832.6m. (Dec. 1999); Pres. Dr GASTÃO EDUARDO DE BUENO VIDIGAL.

Banco Pactual: Av. República do Chile 230, 28° e 29° andares, 20031-170 Rio de Janeiro, RJ; tel. (21) 272-1100; fax (21) 533-1661; e-mail webmaster@pactual.com.br; internet www.pactual.com.br; f. 1983; cap. 175.9m., res 92.5m., dep. 1,767.0m. (Dec. 1998); Pres. LUÍS CEZAR FERNANDES.

Banco Safra, SA: Av. Paulista 2100, 16° andar, 01310-930 São Paulo, SP; tel. (11) 3175-7575; fax (11) 3175-8605; f. 1940; e-mail safrapact@uol.com.br; internet www.safra.com.br; cap. 314.5m., res 706.9m., dep. 10,808.4m. (Dec. 1999); Pres. CARLOS ALBERTO VIEIRA; 68 brs.

Banco Santander Brasil, SA: Rua Funchal 160, 04551-903 São Paulo, SP; tel. (11) 828-7322; fax (11) 828-7208; f. 1942; fmrly Banco Geral do Comercio; Pres. LUIZ ROBERTO ORTIZ NASCIMENTO; 41 brs.

Banco Santander Meridional, SA: Rua General Câmara 156, Centro, 90010-230 Porto Alegre, RS; tel. (51) 287-5700; fax (51) 508-5769; internet www.meridional.com.br; f. 1985, formerly Banco Sulbrasileiro, SA; taken over by the Government in Aug. 1985; acquired by Banco Bozano, Simonsen in 1997; name changed 2000; cap. 1,200.5m., res −121.1m., dep. 5,782.5m. (Dec. 1998); Pres. PAULO VEIGA FERRAZ PEREIRA; 227 brs.

Banco Sogeral, SA: Rua Verbo Divino 1207, 3° e 4° andares, CP 8785, 04719-002 São Paulo, SP; tel. (11) 5180-5052; fax (11) 5180-5258; f. 1981; internet www.sogeral.com.br; cap. 83.0m., res 18.7m., dep. 457.2m. (Dec. 1998); Pres. ERIC DHOSTE; 1 br.

Banco Sudameris Brasil, SA: Av. Paulista 1000, 2°, 10°–16° andares, 01310-100 São Paulo, SP; tel. (11) 3170-9899; fax (11) 289-1239; internet www.sudameris.com.br; f. 1910; cap. 742.6m., res 93.6m., dep. 4,803.3m. (Dec. 1998); Exec. Dirs YVES L. J. LEJEUNE, SEBASTIÃO G. T. CUNHA; 153 brs.

BankBoston SA: Rua Líbero Badaró 487-3°, 01009-000 São Paulo, SP; tel. (11) 3118-5622; fax (11) 3118-4438; internet www.bankboston.com.br; Pres. GERALDO JOSÉ CARBONE; 31 brs.

HSBC Bank Brasil, SA, Banco Multiplo: Travessa Oliveira Belo 34, Centro, 80020-030 Curitiba, PR; tel. (41) 321-6161; fax (41) 321-6081; internet www.hsbc.com.br; f. 1997; cap. 874.5m., res 106.6m., dep. 7,633.8m. (Dec. 1998); Pres. M. F. GEOGHEGAN; 1,214 brs.

UNIBANCO—União de Bancos Brasileiros, SA: Av. Eusébio Matoso 891, 22° andar, CP 8185, 05423-901 São Paulo, SP; tel. (11) 867-4461; fax (11) 814-0528; e-mail investor.relations@unibanco.com.br; internet www.unibanco.com.br; f. 1924; cap.2,324.1m., res 1,677.6m., dep. 13,476.2m. (Dec. 1999); Chair. PEDRO MOREIRA SALLES; 639 brs.

Development Banks

Banco de Desenvolvimento de Minas Gerais, SA—BDMG: Rua da Bahia 1600, CP 1026, 30160-011 Belo Horizonte, MG; tel. (31) 226-3292; fax (31) 273-5084; f. 1962; long-term credit operations; cap. 250.5m., res −124.6m., dep. 3.3m. (Dec. 1997); Pres. MARCOS RAYMUNDO PESSÔA DUARTE.

Banco de Desenvolvimento do Espírito Santo, SA: Av. Princesa Isabel 54, Edif. Caparão, 12° andar, CP 1168, 29010-906 Vitória, ES; tel. (27) 223-8333; fax (27) 223-6307; total assets US $12.5m. (Dec. 1993); Pres. SÉRGIO MANOEL NADER BORGES.

Banco Nacional de Crédito Cooperativo, SA: Brasília, DF; tel. (61) 224-5575; established in association with the Ministry of Agriculture and guaranteed by the Federal Government to provide co-operative credit; cap. 4.7m. (cruzeiros, July 1990); Pres. ESUPÉRIO S. DE CAMPOS AGUILAR (acting); 41 brs.

Banco Nacional do Desenvolvimento Econômico e Social (BNDES): Av. República do Chile 100, 20139-900 Rio de Janeiro, RJ; tel. (21) 277-7447; fax (21) 533-1665; internet www.bndes.gov.br; f. 1952 to act as main instrument for financing of development schemes sponsored by the Government and to support programmes for the development of the national economy; charged with supervision of privatization programme of the 1990s; Pres. FRANCISCO GROS; 2 brs.

Banco Regional de Desenvolvimento do Extremo Sul (BRDE): Rua Uruguai 155, 3°–4° andares, CP 139, 90010-140 Porto Alegre, RS; tel. (51) 121-9200. 1961; cap. 15m. (Dec. 1993); development bank for the states of Paraná, Rio Grande do Sul and Santa Catarina; finances small- and medium-sized enterprises; Dir-Pres. NELSON WEDEKIN; 3 brs.

Investment Bank

Banco de Investimentos CSFB Garantia, SA: Av. Brigadeiro Faria Lima 3064, 13° andar, Itaim Bibi, 01451-020 São Paulo, SP; tel. (11) 821-6000; fax (11) 821-6900; f. 1971; fmrly Banco de Investimentos Gerais; cap. 956.6m., res 107.2m., dep. 1,794.7m. (Dec. 1996); Dir LUIS ALBERTO MENDES RODRIGUES; 1 br.

State-owned Savings Bank

Caixa Econômica Federal: SBS, Q 04, Lote 3/4, Edif. Sede de Caixa Econômica, 70070-000 Brasília, DF; tel. (61) 321-9209; fax (61) 225-0215; f. 1860; cap. 60,247,000m. (cruzeiros, May 1993); dep. 796,113,000m. (April 1993); Pres. EMÍLIO CARRAZAI; 1,752 brs.

Foreign Banks

Banco de la Nación Argentina: Av. Paulista 2319, Sobreloja, 01310 São Paulo, SP; tel. (11) 883-1555; fax (11) 881-4630; e-mail bnaspbb@dialdata.com.br; f. 1891; Dir-Gen. GERARDO LUIS PONCE; 2 brs.

Banco Unión (Venezuela): Av. Paulista 1708, 01310 São Paulo, SP; tel. (11) 283-3722; fax (11) 283-2434; f.1892; Dir-Gen. DONALDISON MARQUES DA SILVA.

The Chase Manhattan Bank (USA): Rua Verbo Divino 1400, São Paulo, SP; tel. (11) 546-4433; fax (11) 546-44624.

Dresdner Bank Lateinamerika AG (Germany): Rua Verbo Divino 1488, Centro Empresarial Transatlântico, CP 3641, 01064-970 São Paulo, SP; e-mail brazil.rep-office@dresdner-bank.com; fmrly Deutsch-Sudamerikanische Bank; tel. (11) 5188-6700; fax (11) 5188-6900; f. 1969; Chair. WALTER U. HAAGEN; 3 brs.

Lloyds TSB Bank PLC (United Kingdom): Av. Brig. Faria Lima 2020, 01452 São Paulo, SP; tel. (11) 818-8311; fax (11) 818-8403; e-mail lloyds.dmkt@lloyds.com.br; Gen. Man. DAVID V. THOMAS; 11 brs.

Banking Associations

Federação Brasileira das Associações de Bancos: Rua Líbero Badaró 425, 17° andar, 01069-900 São Paulo, SP; tel. (11) 239-3000; fax (11) 607-8486; f. 1966; Pres. MAURÍCIO SCHULMAN; Vice-Pres ROBERTO EGYDIO SETÚBAL, JOSÉ AFONSO SANCHO.

Sindicato dos Bancos dos Estados do Rio de Janeiro e Espírito Santo: Av. Rio Branco 81, 19° andar, Rio de Janeiro, RJ; Pres. THEÓPHILO DE AZEREDO SANTOS; Vice-Pres. Dr NELSON MUFARREJ.

Sindicato dos Bancos dos Estados de São Paulo, Paraná, Mato Grosso e Mato Grosso do Sul: Rua Líbero Badaró 293, 13° andar, 01905 São Paulo, SP; f. 1924; Pres. PAULO DE QUEIROZ.

There are other banking associations in Maceió, Salvador, Fortaleza, Belo Horizonte, João Pessoa, Recife and Porto Alegre.

STOCK EXCHANGES

Comissão de Valores Mobiliários CVM: Rua Sete de Setembro 111, 32° andar, 20159-900 Rio de Janeiro, RJ; tel. (21) 212-0200; fax (21) 212-0524; e-mail pte@cvm.gov.br; f. 1977 to supervise the operations of the stock exchanges and develop the Brazilian securities market; Chair. José Luiz Osorio de Almeida, Filho.

Bolsa de Valores do Rio de Janeiro: Praça XV de Novembro 20, 20010-010 Rio de Janeiro, RJ; tel. (21) 514-1010; fax (21) 242-8066; e-mail info@bvrj.com.br; internet www.bvrj.com.br; f. 1845; focuses on the trading of fixed income government bonds and foreign exchange; Chair. Sergio Luiz Berardi.

Bolsa de Valores de São Paulo (BOVESPA): Rua XV de Novembro 275, 01013-001 São Paulo, SP; tel. (11) 233-2000; fax (11) 233-2099; e-mail bovespa@bovespa.com.br; internet www.bovespa.com.br; f. 1890; 550 companies listed in 1997; CEO Gilberto Mifano.

There are commodity exchanges at Porto Alegre, Vitória, Recife, Santos and São Paulo.

INSURANCE

Supervisory Authorities

Superintendência de Seguros Privados (SUSEP): Rua Buenos Aires 256, 4° andar, 20061-000 Rio de Janeiro, RJ; tel. (21) 297-4415; fax (21) 221-6664; f. 1966; within Ministry of Finance; Superintendent Helio Portocarrero.

Conselho Nacional de Seguros Privados (CNSP): Rua Buenos Aires 256, 20061-000 Rio de Janeiro, RJ; tel. (21) 297-4415; fax (21) 221-6664; f. 1966; Sec. Theresa Christina Cunha Martins.

Federação Nacional dos Corretores de Seguros e de Capitalização (FENACOR): Av. Rio Branco 147, 6° andar, 20040-006 Rio de Janeiro, RJ; tel. (21) 507-0033; fax (21) 507-0041; e-mail leoncio@fenacor.com.br; Pres. Leôncio de Arruda.

Federação Nacional das Empresas de Seguros Privados e de Capitalização (FENASEG): Rua Senador Dantas 74, 20031-200 Rio de Janeiro, RJ; tel. (21) 524-1204; fax (21) 220-0046; e-mail fenaseg@fenaseg.org.br; Pres. João Elisio Ferraz de Campos.

IRBBrasil Resseguros: Av. Marechal Câmara 171, 20023-900 Rio de Janeiro, RJ; tel. (21) 272-0200; fax (21) 240-6261; e-mail info@irb brasilre.com.br; f. 1939; fmrly Instituto de Resseguros do Brasil; reinsurance; Pres. Demósthenes Madureira de Pinho, Filho.

Principal Companies

The following is a list of the principal national insurance companies, selected on the basis of assets.

AGF Brasil Seguros, SA: Rua Luís Coelho 26, 01309-000 São Paulo; tel. (11) 281-5572; fax (11) 283-1401; internet www.agf.com.br; Dir Eugênio de Oliveira Mello.

Cia de Seguros Aliança da Bahia: Rua Pinto Martins 11, 2° andar, 40015-020 Salvador, BA; tel. (71) 242-1055; fax (71) 242-8998; f. 1870; general; Pres. Paulo Sérgio Freire de Carvalho Gonçalves Tourinho.

Cia de Seguros Aliança do Brasil: Rua Senador Dantas 105, 32° andar, 20031-201 Rio de Janeiro; tel. (21) 533-1080; fax (21) 220-2105; Pres. Khalid Mohammed Raouf.

Allianz-Bradesco Seguros, SA: Rua Barão de Itapagipe 225, 20269-900 Rio de Janeiro; tel. (21) 563-1101; fax (21) 293-9489.

BCN Seguradora, SA: Alameda Santos 1940, 9° andar, 01418-100 São Paulo; tel. (11) 283-2244; fax (11) 284-3415; internet www.bcn.com.br/seguro.htm; f. 1946; Pres. Antônio Grisi, Filho.

Bradesco Previdência e Seguros, SA: Av. Deputado Emílio Carlos 970, 06028-000 São Paulo; tel. (11) 704-4466; fax (11) 703-3063; internet www.bradesco.com.br/prodserv/bradprev.html; f. 1989; Pres. Antônio Lopes Cristóvão.

Bradesco Seguros, SA: Rua Barão de Itapagipe 225, 20269-900 Rio de Janeiro, RJ; tel. (21) 563-1199; fax (21) 503-1466; internet www.bradesco.com.br/prodserv/bradseg.html; f. 1935; general; Pres. Eduardo Vianna.

CGU Cia de Seguros: Av. Almirante Barroso 52, 23° e 24° andares, 20031-000 Rio de Janeiro; tel. (21) 292-1125; fax (21) 262-0291; internet www.york.com.br/york0700.html; Pres. Robert Charles Wheeler.

Finasa Seguradora, SA: Alameda Santos 1827, 6° andar, CJS 61, 01419-002 São Paulo; tel. (11) 253-8181; fax (11) 285-1994; internet www.finasa.com.br/ficoli02.html; f. 1939; Pres. Marcello de Camargo Vidigal.

Golden Cross Seguradora, SA: Rua Maestro Cardim 1164, 013200-301 Rio de Janeiro, RJ; tel. (21) 283-4922; fax (21) 289-4624; e-mail comunica@goldencross.com.br; internet www.golden.com.br; f. 1971; Pres. Albert Bullus.

HSBC Seguros (Brasil), SA: Travessa Oliveira Belo 11-B, 2° andar, 80020-030 Curitiba, PR; tel. (41) 321-6162; fax (41) 321-8800; f. 1938; all classes; Pres. Simon Lloyd Brett.

Itaú Seguros, SA: Praça Alfredo Egydio de Souza Aranha 100, Bloco A, 04344-920 São Paulo, SP; tel. (11) 5582-3322; fax (11) 5582-3514; e-mail itauseguros@itauseguros.com.br; internet www .itauseguros.com.br; f. 1921; all classes; Pres. Luiz de Campos Salles.

Cia de Seguros Minas-Brasil: Rua dos Caetés 745, 5° andar, 30120-080 Belo Horizonte, MG; tel. (31) 219-3882; fax (31) 219-3820; f. 1938; life and risk; Pres. José Carneiro de Araújo.

Cia Paulista de Seguros: Rua Dr Geraldo Campos Moreira 110, 04571-020 São Paulo, SP; tel. (11) 5505-2010; fax (11) 5505-2122; internet www.pauliseg.com.br; f. 1906; general; Pres. Phillip Norton Moore.

Porto Seguro Cia de Seguros Gerais: Rua Guaianazes 1238, 01204-001 São Paulo, SP; tel. (11) 224-6129; fax (11) 222-6213; internet www.porto-seguro.com.br; f. 1945; life and risk; Pres. Rosa Garfinkel.

Sasse, Cia Nacional de Seguros Gerais: SCN Qd. 01, Bl. A, 15°–17° andares, 70710-500 Brasília, DF; tel. (61) 329-2400; fax (61) 321-0600; internet www.sasse.com.br; f. 1967; general; Pres. Pedro Pereira de Freitas.

Sul América Aetna Seguros e Previdência, SA: Rua Anchieta 35, 9° andar, 01016-030 São Paulo; tel. (11) 232-6131; fax (11) 606-8141; internet www.sulaamerica.com.br; f. 1996; Pres. Rony Castro de Oliveira Lyrio.

Sul América, Cia Nacional de Seguros: Rua da Quitanda 86, 20091-000 Rio de Janeiro, RJ; tel. (21) 276-8585; fax (21) 276-8317; f. 1895; life and risk; Pres. Rony Castro de Oliveira Lyrio.

Sul América Santa Cruz Seguros, SA: Tv. Franc. Leonardo Truda 98, 6° andar, 90010-050 Porto Alegre; tel. (51) 211-5455; fax (51) 225-5894; f. 1943; Pres. Rony Castro de Oliveira Lyrio.

Unibanco Seguros, SA: Av. Eusébio Matoso 1375, 13° andar, 05423-180 São Paulo, SP; tel. (11) 819-8000; fax (11) 3039-4005; internet www.unibancoseguros.com.br; f. 1946; life and risk; Pres. José Castro Araújo Rudge.

Vera Cruz Seguradora, SA: Av. Maria Coelho Aguiar 215, Bloco D, 3° andar, 05804-906 São Paulo, SP; tel. (11) 3741-3815; fax (11) 3741-3827; internet www.veracruz.com.br; f. 1955; general; Pres. Alfredo Fernandez de L. Ortiz de Zarate.

Trade and Industry

GOVERNMENT AGENCIES

Agência Nacional de Petróleo (ANP): Brasília, DF; internet www.anp.gov.br; f. 1998; regulatory body of the petroleum industry; Chair. David Zylberstajn.

Comissão de Fusão e Incorporação de Empresa (COFIE): Ministério da Fazenda, Edif. Sede, Ala B, 1° andar, Esplanada dos Ministérios, Brasília, DF; tel. (61) 225-3405; mergers commission; Pres. Sebastião Marcos Vital; Exec. Sec. Edgar Bezerra Leite, Filho.

Conselho de Desenvolvimento Comercial (CDC): Bloco R, Esplanada dos Ministérios, 70044 Brasília, DF; tel. (61) 223-0308; commercial development council; Exec. Sec. Dr Ruy Coutinho do Nascimento.

Conselho de Desenvolvimento Econômico (CDE): Bloco K, 7° andar, Esplanada dos Ministérios, 70063 Brasília, DF; tel. (61) 215-4100; f. 1974; economic development council; Gen. Sec. João Batista de Abreu.

Conselho de Desenvolvimento Social (CDS): Bloco K, 3° andar, 382, Esplanada dos Ministérios, 70063 Brasília, DF; tel. (61) 215-4477; social development council; Exec. Sec. João A. Teles.

Conselho Nacional do Comércio Exterior (CONCEX): Fazenda, 5° andar, Gabinete do Ministro, Bloco 6, Esplanada dos Ministérios, 70048 Brasília, DF; tel. (61) 223-4856; f. 1966; responsible for foreign exchange and trade policies and for the control of export activities; Exec. Sec. Namir Salek.

Conselho Nacional de Desenvolvimento Científico e Tecnológico (CNPq): Brasília, DF; tel. (61) 348-9401; fax (61) 273-2955; f. 1951; scientific and technological development council; Pres. José Galizia Tundisi.

Conselho Nacional de Desenvolvimento Pecuário (CONDEPE): to promote livestock development.

Conselho de Não-Ferrosos e de Siderurgia (CONSIDER): Ministério da Indústria e Comércio, Esplanada dos Ministérios, Bloco 7, 7° andar, 70056-900 Brasília, DF; tel. (61) 224-6039; f. 1973; exercises a supervisory role over development policy in the non-ferrous and iron and steel industries; Exec. Sec. William Rocha Cantal.

Fundação Instituto Brasileiro de Geografia e Estatística (IBGE): Centro de Documentação e Disseminação de Informações

(CDDI), Rua Gen. Canabarro 706, 2° andar, Maracanã, 20271-201 Rio de Janeiro, RJ; tel. (21) 569-5997; fax (21) 569-1103; e-mail webmaster@ibge.gov.br; internet www.ibge.gov.br; f. 1936; produces and analyses statistical, geographical, cartographic, geodetic, demographic and socio-economic information; Pres. (IBGE) Sérgio Besserman Vianna; Superintendent (CDDI) David Wu Tai.

Instituto Nacional de Metrologia, Normalização e Qualidade Industrial (INMETRO): Rua Santa Alexandrina 416, Rio Comprido, 20261-232 Rio de Janeiro, RJ; tel. (21) 273-9002; fax (21) 293-0954; e-mail pusi@inmetro.gov.br; in 1981 INMETRO absorbed the Instituto Nacional de Pesos e Medidas (INPM), the weights and measures institute; Pres. Dr Júlio Cesar Carmo Bueno.

Instituto de Planejamento Econômico e Social (IPEA): SBS, Edif. BNDE, 6° andar, 70076 Brasília, DF; tel. (61) 225-4350; planning institute; Pres. Ricardo Santiago.

Secretaria Especial de Desenvolvimento Industrial: Brasília, DF; tel. (61) 225-7556; fax (61) 224-5629; f. 1969; industrial development council; offers fiscal incentives for selected industries and for producers of manufactured goods under the Special Export Programme; Exec. Sec. Dr Ernesto Carrara.

REGIONAL DEVELOPMENT ORGANIZATIONS

Companhia de Desenvolvimento dos Vales do São Francisco e do Parnaíba (CODEVASF): SGAN, Q 601, Lote 1, Edif. Manoel Novaes, 70830-901 Brasília, DF; tel. (61) 312-4758; fax (61) 226-8819; e-mail divulgacao@codevasf.gov.br; internet www.codevasf.gov.br/indice.html; f. 1974; promotes integrated development of resources of São Francisco and Parnaíba Valley.

Superintendência do Desenvolvimento da Amazônia (SUDAM): Av. Almirante Barroso 426, Bairro do Marco, 66000 Belém, PA; tel. (91) 226-0044; f. 1966 to develop the Amazon regions of Brazil; supervises industrial, cattle breeding and basic services projects; Superintendent Eng. Henry Checralla Kayath.

Superintendência do Desenvolvimento do Nordeste (SUDENE): Edif. SUDENE s/n, Praça Ministro João Gonçalves de Souza, Cidade Universitária, 50670-900 Recife, PE; tel. (81) 416-2880; fax (81) 453-1277; f. 1959; attached to the Ministry of Planning, Budget and Co-ordination; assists development of north-east Brazil; Superintendent Nilton Moreira Rodrigues.

Superintendência do Desenvolvimento da Região Centro Oeste (SUDECO): SAS, Quadra 1, Bloco A, Lotes 9/10, 70070 Brasília, DF; tel. (61) 225-6111; f. 1967 to co-ordinate development projects in the states of Goiás, Mato Grosso, Mato Grosso do Sul, Rondônia and Distrito Federal; Superintendent Ramez Tebet.

Superintendência da Zona Franca de Manaus (SUFRAMA): Rua Ministro João Gonçalves de Souza s/n, Distrito Industrial, 69075-770 Manaus, AM; tel. (92) 237-1691; fax (92) 237-6549; e-mail 15dinf@internet.com.br; to assist in the development of the Manaus Free Zone; Superintendent Mauro Ricardo Machado Costa.

AGRICULTURAL, INDUSTRIAL AND TRADE ORGANIZATIONS

ABRASSUCOS: São Paulo, SP; association of orange juice industry; Pres. Mário Branco Peres.

Associação do Comércio Exterior do Brasil (AEB): Av. General Justo 335, 4° andar, Rio de Janeiro, RJ; tel. (21) 240-5048; fax (21) 240-5463; e-mail aebbras@embratel.net.br; internet www.probrazil.com/aeb.html; exporters' association.

Companhia de Pesquisa de Recursos Minerais (CPRM): Esplanada dos Ministérios, Bloco U, 7° andar, 70055-900 Brasília, DF; mining research, attached to the Ministry of Mining and Energy; Pres. Carlos Berbert.

Confederação das Associações Comerciais do Brasil: Brasília, DF; confederation of chambers of commerce in each state; Pres. Amaury Temporal.

Confederação Nacional da Agricultura (CNA): Brasília, DF; tel. (61) 225-3150; national agricultural confederation; Pres. Alysson Paulinelli.

Confederação Nacional do Comércio (CNC): SCS, Edif. Presidente Dutra, 4° andar, Quadra 11, 70327 Brasília, DF; tel. (61) 223-0578; national confederation comprising 35 affiliated federations of commerce; Pres. Antônio José Domingues de Oliveira Santos.

Confederação Nacional da Indústria (CNI): Av. Nilo Peçanha 50, 34° andar, 20044 Rio de Janeiro, RJ; tel. (21) 292-7766; fax (21) 262-1495; f. 1938; national confederation of industry comprising 26 state industrial federations; Pres. Dr Albano do Prado Franco; Vice-Pres. Mário Amato.

Conselho dos Exportadores de Café Verde do Brasil (CECAFE): internet www.coffee.com.br/cecafe/; in process of formation in 1999/2000 through merger of Federação Brasileira dos Exportadores de Café and Associação Brasileira dos Exportadores de Café; council of green coffee exporters.

Departamento Nacional da Produção Mineral (DNPM): SAN, Quadra 1, Bloco B, 3° andar, 70040-200 Brasília, DF; tel. (61) 224-7097; fax (61) 225-8274; e-mail webmaster@dnpm.gov.br; internet www.dnpm.gov.br; f. 1934; responsible for geological studies and control of exploration of mineral resources; Dir-Gen. João R. Pimentel.

Empresa Brasileira de Pesquisa Agropecuária (EMBRAPA): SAIN, Parque Rural, W/3 Norte, CP 040315, 70770-901 Brasília, DF; tel. (61) 348-4433; fax (61) 347-1041; f. 1973; attached to the Ministry of Agriculture; agricultural research; Pres. Alberto Duque Portugal.

Federação das Indústrias do Estado de São Paulo (FIESP): Av. Paulista 1313, 01311-923 São Paulo, SP; tel. (11) 252-4200; fax (11) 284-3611; regional manufacturers' association; Pres. Carlos Eduardo Moreira Ferreira.

Instituto Brasileiro do Meio Ambiente e Recursos Naturais Renováveis (IBAMA): Ed. Sede IBAMA, Av. SAIN, L4 Norte, Bloco C, Subsolo, 70800-200 Brasília, DF; tel. (61) 316-1205; fax (61) 226-5094; e-mail cnia@sede.ibama.gov.br; internet www.ibama.gov.br; f. 1967; responsible for the annual formulation of national environmental plans; merged with SEMA (National Environmental Agency) in 1988 and replaced the IBDF in 1989; Pres. Eduardo Mallius.

Instituto Brasileiro do Mineração (IBRAM): Brasília, DF; Pres. João Sérgio Marinho Nunes.

Instituto Nacional da Propriedade Industrial (INPI): Praça Mauá 7, 18° andar, 20081-240 Rio de Janeiro, RJ; tel. (21) 223-4182; fax (21) 263-2539; e-mail inpipres@inpi.gov.br; internet www.inpi.gov.br; f. 1970; intellectual property, etc.; Pres. Jorge Machado.

Instituto Nacional de Tecnologia (INT): Av. Venezuela 82, 8° andar, 20081-310 Rio de Janeiro, RJ; tel. (21) 206-1100; fax (21) 263-6552; e-mail int@ riosoft.softex.br; internet www.int.gov.br; f. 1921; co-operates in national industrial development; Dir João Luiz Hanriot Selasco.

UTILITIES

Electricity

Centrais Elétricas Brasileiras, SA (ELETROBRÁS): Edif. Petrobrás, Rua Dois, Setor de Autarquias Norte, 70040-903 Brasília, DF; tel. (61) 223-5050; fax (61) 225-5502; e-mail maryann@eletrobras.gov.br; internet www.eletrobras.gov.br; f. 1962; government holding company responsible for planning, financing and managing Brazil's electrical energy programme; scheduled for division into eight generating cos and privatization; Pres. Firmino Ferreira Sampaio Neto.

Centrais Elétricas do Norte do Brasil, SA (ELETRONORTE): SCN, Quadra 6, Conj. A, Blocos B /C, sala 602, Super Center Venâncio 3000, 70718-500 Brasília, DF; tel. (61) 429-5151; fax (61) 328-1566; e-mail elnweb@eln.gov.br; internet www.eln.gov.br; f. 1973; Pres. Benedito Aparecido Carraro.

Centrais Elétricas do Sul do Brasil, SA (ELETROSUL): Rua Deputado Antônio Edu Vieira 999, Pantanal, 88040-901 Florianópolis, SC; tel. (48) 231-7000; fax (48) 234-3434; Gerasul responsible for generating capacity; f. 1968; Pres. Firmino Ferreira Sampaio Neto.

Companhia Hidro Elétrica do São Francisco (CHESF): 333 Edif. André Falcão, Bloco A, sala 313 Bongi, Rua Delmiro Golveia, 50761-901 Recife, PE; tel. (81) 228-3160; fax (81) 227-4970; e-mail chesf@cr.pe.rnp.br; f. 1945; Pres. Júlio Sérgio de Maya Pedrosa Moreira.

Furnas Centrais Elétricas, SA: Rua Real Grandeza 219, Bloco A, 16° andar, Botafogo, 22281-031 Rio de Janeiro, RJ; tel. (21) 528-3112; fax (21) 528-3438; internet www.furnas.com.br; f. 1957; Pres. Luiz Laércio Simões Machado .

Associated companies include:

Espírito Santo Centrais Elétricas, SA (ESCELSA): Rua Sete de Setembro 362, Centro, CP 01-0452, 29015-000 Vitória, ES; tel. (27) 321-9000; fax (27) 322-0378; internet www.escelsa.com.br; f. 1968; Pres. José Gustavo de Souza.

Nuclebrás Engenharia, SA (NUCLEN): Rua Visconde de Ouro Preto 5, 12° andar, Botafogo, 22250-180 Rio de Janeiro, RJ; tel. (21) 552-2345; fax (21) 552-1745; f. 1975; nuclear-power generation/distribution; Pres. Evaldo Césari de Oliveira.

Centrais Elétricas de Santa Catarina, SA (CELESC): Rodovia SC 404, Km 3, Itacorubi, 88034-900 Florianópolis, SC; tel. (48) 231-5000; fax (48) 231-6530; e-mail celesc@celesc.com.br; internet www.celesc.com.br; production and distribution of electricity throughout state of Santa Catarina; Chair. Oscar Falk.

Comissão Nacional de Energia Nuclear (CNEN): Rua General Severiano 90, Botafogo, 22294-900 Rio de Janeiro, RJ; tel. (21) 295-2232; fax (21) 546-2442; e-mail corin@cnen.gov.br; internet www.cnen.gov.br; f. 1956; state organization responsible for management of nuclear power programme; Pres. MARCIO COSTA.

Companhia de Eletricidade do Estado da Bahia (COELBA): Av. Edgard Santos 300, Cabula IV, 41186-900 Salvador, BA; tel. (71) 370-5130; fax (71) 370-5132; CEO ERALDO TINOCO MELO.

Companhia de Eletricidade do Estado do Rio de Janeiro (CERJ): Rua Visconde do Rio Branco 429, Centro, 24020-003 Niterói, RJ; tel. (21) 613-7120; fax (21) 613-7196; internet www.cerj.com.br; f. 1907; Man. JULIO CESAR DE SOUZA FONSECA.

Companhia Energética Ceará (COELCE): Av. Barão de Studart 2917, 60120-002 Fortaleza, CE; tel. (85) 247-1444; fax (85) 272-4711; internet www.coelce.com.br; f. 1971; Pres. CARLOS EDUARDO CARVALHO ALVES.

Companhia Energética de Minas Gerais (CEMIG): Av. Barbacena 1200, 30123-970 Belo Horizonte; tel. (31) 349-2111; fax (31) 299-3700; e-mail mail@cemig.com.br; internet www.cemig.com.br; fmrly state-owned, sold to a Brazilian-US consortium in May 1997; Pres. JOSÉ DA COSTA CARVALGO NETO.

Companhia Energética de Pernambuco (CELPE): Av. João de Barros 111, Sala 301, 50050-902 Recife, PE; tel. (81) 231-0221; fax (81) 231-1253; internet www.celpe.com.br; state distributor of electricity; CEO J. BOSCO DE ALMEIDA.

Companhia Energética de São Paulo (CESP): Al. Ministro Rocha Azevedo 25, 01410-900 São Paulo, SP; tel. (11) 252-3560; fax (11) 287-0871; e-mail presiden@cesp.com.br; internet www.cesp.com.br; f. 1966; Pres. GUILHERME AUGUSTO CIRNE DE TOLEDO.

Companhia Força Luz Cataguases Leopoldina: Praça Rui Barbosa 80, 36770-000 Cataguases, MG; tel. (32) 429-6000; fax (32) 421-4240; internet www.cataguazes.com.br; f. 1905; Pres. MANOEL OTONI NEIVA.

Companhia Paranaense de Energia (COPEL): Rua Coronel Dulcídio 800, 80420-170 Curitiba, PR; tel. (41) 322-3535; fax (41) 331-4145; f. 1954; state distributor of electricity and gas; Pres. NEY AMINTHAS DE BARROS BRAGA.

Companhia Paulista de Força e Luz: Rodovia Campinas Mogi-Mirim Km 2.5, Campinas, SP; tel. (192) 253-8704; fax (192) 252-7644; provides electricity through govt concessions.

Eletricidade de São Paulo (ELETROPAULO): Av. Alfredo Egidio de Souza Aranha 100, 04791-900 São Paulo, SP; tel. (11) 546-1467; fax (11) 239-1387; e-mail administracao@eletropaulo.com.br; internet www.eletropaulo.com.br; f. 1899; state-owned, but partially privatized in 1998; Pres. MARC ANDRÉ PERREIRA.

Itaipú Binacional: Av. Tancredo Neves 6731, 85856-970 Foz de Iguaçu, PR; tel. (45) 520-5252; e-mail itaipu@itaipu.gov.br; internet www.itaipu.gov.br; f. 1974; 1,490 employees (Itaipú Brasil–1998); Dir-Gen. (Brazil) EUCLIDES SCALCO.

LIGHT—Serviços de Eletricidade, SA: Av. Marechal Floriano 168, CP 0571, 20080-002 Rio de Janeiro, RJ; tel. (21) 211-7171; fax (21) 233-1249; e-mail light@lightrio.com.br; internet www.lightrio.com.br; f. 1905; electricity generation and distribution in Rio de Janeiro; formerly state-owned, sold to a Brazilian-French-US consortium in 1996; Pres. LUIZ DAVID TRAVESSO.

Regulatory Agency

Agência Nacional de Energia Elétrica (ANEEL): SGAN 603, Módulo J, 70830-030 Brasília, DF; e-mail aneel@aneel.gov.br; internet www.aneel.gov.br; Dir JOSÉ MARIA ABDO.

Gas

Companhia Estadual de Gás do Rio de Janeiro (CEG): Av. Pres. Vargas 2610, 20210 Rio de Janeiro, RJ; tel. (21) 284-5622; fax (21) 284-5742; f. 1969; gas distribution in the Rio de Janeiro region; privatized in July 1997.

Companhia de Gás de São Paulo (COMGÁS): Rua Augusta 1600, 01304-901 São Paulo, SP; tel. (11) 289-0344; fax (11) 288-1862; internet www.comgas.com.br; f. 1978 distribution in São Paulo of gas; sold in April 1999 to consortium including British Gas PLC and Royal Dutch/Shell Group; Pres. JULIO CESAR LAMOUNIER NAPA.

Water

The first transfers to private ownership of state-owned water and sewerage companies were scheduled to commence in 2000.

Agua e Esgostos do Piauí (AGESPISA): Av. Mal Castelo Branco 101, Cabral, 64000 Teresina, PI; tel. (862) 239-300; f. 1962; state-owned; water and waste management; Pres. OLIVÃO GOMES DA SOUSA.

Companhia de Agua e Esgosto de Ceará (CAGECE): Rua Lauro Vieira Chaves 1030, Fortaleza; tel. (85) 247-2422; internet www.cagece.com.br; state-owned; water and sewerage services; Gen. Man. JOSÉ DE RIBAMAR DA SILVA.

Companhia Algoas Industrial (CINAL): Rodovia Divaldo Suruagy, Km 12, 57160-000 Marechal Deodoro, AL; tel. (82) 269-1100; fax (82) 269-1199; f. 1982; management of steam and treated water; Dir PAULO ALBERQUERQUE MARANHÃO.

Companhia Espírito Santense de Saneamento (CESAN): Av. Governador Bley, Edif. BEMGE, 29010-150 Vitória ES; tel. (27) 322-8399; internet www. cesan.com.br; f. 1968; state-owned; construction, maintenance and operation of water supply and sewerage systems; Pres. CLÁUDIO DE MORAES MACHADO.

Companhia Estadual de Aguas e Esgostos (CEDAE): Rua Sacadura Cabral 103, 9° andar, 20081-260 Rio de Janeiro, RJ; tel. (21) 296-0025; fax (21) 296-0416; state-owned; water supply and sewerage treatment; Pres. RAYMUNDO THEODORO OLIVEIRA.

Companhia Pernambucana Saneamento (COMPESA): Av. Cruz Cabugá 1387, 50040-905 Recife, PE; tel. (81) 421-1711; fax (81) 421-2712; state-owned; management and operation of regional water supply in the state of Pernambuco; Pres. JOÃO CORREA VILAR.

Companhia Riograndense de Saneamento (CORSAN): Rua Caldas Júnior 120, 18° andar, 90010-260 Porto Alegre, RS; tel. (51) 228-5622; fax (51) 228-7870; internet www.corsan.com.br; f. 1965; state-owned; management and operation of regional water supply and sanitation programmes.

Companhia de Saneamento Básico do Estado de São Paulo (SABESP): Rua Costa Carvalho 300, 05429-000 São Paulo, SP; tel. (11) 3030-4000; internet www.sabesp.com.br; f. 1973; state-owned; supplies basic sanitation services for the state of São Paulo, including water treatment and supply; Pres. ARIOVALDO CARMIGNANI.

TRADE UNIONS

Central Unica dos Trabalhadores (CUT): Rua São Bento 405, Edif. Martinelli, 7° andar, 01011 São Paulo, SP; tel. (11) 255-7500; fax (11) 37-5626; f. 1983; central union confederation; left-wing; Pres. VINCENTE PAULO DA SILVA; Gen. Sec. GILMAR CARNEIRO.

Confederação General dos Trabalhadores (CGT): São Paulo, SP; f. 1986; fmrly Coordenação Nacional das Classes Trabalhadoras; represents 1,258 labour organizations linked to PMDB; Pres. LUÍS ANTÔNIO MEDEIROS.

Confederação Nacional dos Metalúrgicos (Metal Workers): f. 1985; Pres. JOAQUIM DOS SANTOS ANDRADE.

Confederação Nacional das Profissões Liberais (CNPL) (Liberal Professions): SAU/SUL, Edif. Belvedere Gr. 202, 70070-000 Brasília, DF; tel. (61) 223-1683; fax (61) 223-1944; e-mail cnpliber@nutecnet.com.br; internet www.bsb.nutecut.com.br/web/cnpl; f. 1953; confederation of liberal professions; Pres. LUÍS EDUARDO GAUTÉRIO GALLO; Exec. Sec. JOSÉ ANTÔNIO BRITO ANDRADE.

Confederação Nacional dos Trabalhadores na Indústria (CNTI) (Industrial Workers): Av. W/3 Norte, Quadra 505, Lote 01, 70730-517 Brasília, DF; tel. (61) 274-4150; fax (61) 274-7001; f. 1946; Pres. JOSÉ CALIXTO RAMOS.

Confederação Nacional dos Trabalhadores no Comércio (CNTC) (Commercial Workers): Av. W/5 Sul, Quadra 902, Bloco C, 70390 Brasília, DF; tel. (61) 224-3511; f. 1946; Pres. ANTÔNIO DE OLIVEIRA SANTOS.

Confederação Nacional dos Trabalhadores em Transportes Marítimos, Fluviais e Aéreos (CONTTMAF) (Maritime, River and Air Transport Workers): Av. Pres. Vargas 446, gr. 2205, 20071 Rio de Janeiro, RJ; tel. (21) 233-8329; f. 1957; Pres. MAURÍCIO MONTEIRO SANT'ANNA.

Confederação Nacional dos Trabalhadores em Comunicações e Publicidade (CONTCOP) (Communications and Advertising Workers): SCS, Edif. Serra Dourada, 7° andar, gr. 705/709, Q 11, 70315 Brasília, DF; tel. (61) 224-7926; fax (61) 224-5686; f. 1964; 350,000 mems; Pres. ANTÔNIO MARIA THAUMATURGO CORTIZO.

Confederação Nacional dos Trabalhadores nas Empresas de Crédito (CONTEC) (Workers in Credit Institutions): SEP-SUL, Av. W4, EQ 707/907 Lote E, 70351 Brasília, DF; tel. (61) 244-5833; f. 1958; 814,532 mems (1988); Pres. LOURENÇO FERREIRA DO PRADO.

Confederação Nacional dos Trabalhadores em Estabelecimentos de Educação e Cultura (CNTEEC) (Workers in Education and Culture): SAS, Quadra 4, Bloco B, 70302 Brasília, DF; tel. (61) 226-2988; f. 1967; Pres. MIGUEL ABRAHÃO.

Confederação Nacional dos Trabalhadores na Agricultura (CONTAG) (Agricultural Workers): SDS, Ed Venâncio VI, 1° andar, 70393-900 Brasília, DF; tel. (61) 321-2288; fax (61) 321-3229; f. 1964; Pres. FRANCISCO URBANO ARAÚJO, Filho.

Força Sindical (FS): São Paulo, SP; f. 1991; 6m. mems (1991); Pres. LUÍS ANTÔNIO MEDEIROS.

Transport

Ministério dos Transportes (MT): see section on the Government (Ministries).

Empresa Brasileira de Planejamento de Transportes (GEIPOT): SAN, Quadra 3, Blocos N/O, Edif. Núcleo dos Transportes, 70040-902 Brasília, DF; tel. (61) 315-4890; fax (61) 315-4895; e-mail deind@geipot.gov.br; internet www.geipot.gov.br; f. 1973;

agency for the promotion of an integrated modern transport system; advises the Minister of Transport on transport policy; Pres. CARLOS ALBERTO WANDERLEY NÓBREGA.

RAILWAYS

Rede Ferroviária Federal, SA (RFFSA) (Federal Railway Corporation): Praça Procópio Ferreira 86, 20221-030 Rio de Janeiro, RJ; tel. (21) 516-1890; fax (21) 516-1390; internet www.rffsa.gov.br; f.1957; holding company for 18 railways grouped into regional networks, with total track length of 20,500 km in 1998; privatization of federal railways was completed in 1997; freight services; Pres. ISAAC POPOUTCHI.

Companhia Brasileira de Trens Urbanos (CBTU): Estrada Velha da Tijuca 77, Usina, 20531-080 Rio de Janeiro, RJ; tel. (21) 575-3399; fax (21) 571-6149; fmrly responsible for surburban networks and metro systems throughout Brazil; 252 km in 1998; the transfer of each city network to its respective local government is currently under way; Pres. LUIZ OTAVIO MOTA VALADARES.

> **Belo Horizonte Metro (CBTU/STU/BH-Demetrô):** Av. Afonso Pena 1500, 11° andar, 30130-921 Belo Horizonte, MG; tel. (31) 250-4002; fax (31) 250-4004; e-mail metrobh@gold.horizontes.com.br; f. 1986; 21.2 km open in 1997; Gen. Man. M. L. L. SIQUEIRA.

> **Trem Metropolitano de Recife:** Rua José Natário 478, Areias, 50900-000 Recife, PE; tel. (81) 455-4655; fax (81) 455-4422; f.1985; 53 km open in 1997; Supt FERNANDO ANTÔNIO C. DUEIRE.

There are also railways owned by state governments and several privately-owned railways:

Companhia Fluminense de Trens Urbanos (Flumitrens): Praça Cristiano Otoni, sala 445, 20221 Rio de Janeiro, RJ; tel. (21) 233-8594; fax (21) 253-3089; f. 1975 as operating division of RFFSA, current name adopted following takeover by state government in 1994; suburban services in Rio de Janeiro and its environs; 293 km open in 1998; Supt MURILO JUNQUEIRA.

Companhia do Metropolitano do Rio de Janeiro: Av. Nossa Senhora de Copacabana 493, 22021-031 Rio de Janeiro, RJ; tel. (21) 235-4041; fax (21) 235-4546; 2-line metro system, 42 km open in 1997; Pres. ALVARO J. M. SANTOS.

Companhia do Metropolitano de São Paulo: Rua Augusta 1626, 03310-200 São Paulo, SP; tel. (11) 283-7411; fax (11) 283-5228; f. 1974; 3-line metro system, 56 km open in 1998; Pres. PAULO CLARINDO GOLDSCHMIDT.

Companhia Paulista de Trens Metropolitanos (CPTM): Av. Paulista 402, 5° andar, 01310-903 São Paulo, SP; tel. (11) 281-6101; fax (11) 288-2224; f. 1993 to incorporate suburban lines fmrly operated by the CBTU and FEPASA; 286 km; Pres. Eng. OLIVER HOSSEPIAN SALLES DE LIMA.

Departamento Metropolitano de Transportes Urbanos: SES, Quadra 4, Lote 6, Brasília, DF; tel. (61) 317-4090; fax (61) 226-9546; the first section of the Brasília metro, linking the capital with the western suburb of Samambaia, was inaugurated in 1994; 38.5 km open in 1997; Dir LEONARDO DE FARIA E SILVA.

Empresa de Trens Urbanos de Porto Alegre, SA: Av. Ernesto Neugebauer 1985, 90250-140 Porto Alegre, RS; tel. (51) 371-5000; fax (51) 371-1219; e-mail secos@trensurb.com.br; internet www .trensurb.com.br; f. 1985; 31 km open in 1998; Pres. PEDRO BISCH NETO.

Estrada de Ferro do Amapá: Praia de Botafogo 300, 11° andar, ala A, 22250-050 Rio de Janeiro, RJ; tel. (21) 552-4422; f. 1957; operated by Indústria e Comércio de Minérios, SA; 194 km open in 1998; Pres. OSVALDO LUIZ SENRA PESSOA.

Estrada de Ferro Campos do Jordão: Rua Martin Cabral 87, CP 11, 12400-000 Pindamonhangaba, SP; tel. (22) 242-4233; fax (22) 242-2499; operated by the Tourism Secretariat of the State of São Paulo; 47 km open in 1998; Dir ARTHUR FERREIRA DOS SANTOS.

Estrada de Ferro Carajás: Av. dos Portugueses s/n, 65085-580 São Luís, MA; tel. (98) 218-4000; fax (98) 218-4530; f. 1985 for movement of minerals from the Serra do Carajás to the new port at Ponta da Madeira; operated by the Companhia Vale do Rio Doce; 955 km open in 1998; Supt JUARES SALIBRA.

Estrada de Ferro do Jari: Monte Dourado, 68230-000 Pará, PA; tel. (91) 735-1155; fax (91) 735-1475; transportation of timber and bauxite; 68 km open; Dir ARMINDO LUIZ BARETTA.

Estrada de Ferro Mineração Rio do Norte, SA: Praia do Flamengo 200, 5° e 6° andares, 22210-030 Rio de Janeiro, RJ; tel. (21) 205-9112; fax (21) 545-5717; 35 km open in 1998; Pres. ANTÔNIO JOÃO TORRES.

Estrada de Ferro Paraná-Oeste, SA (Ferroeste): Av. Iguaçu 420-7°, 80230-902 Curitiba, PR; tel. (41) 322-1811; fax (41) 233-2147; f. 1988 to serve the grain-producing regions in Paraná and Mato Grosso do Sul; 248 km inaugurated in 1995; privatized in late 1996, Brazilian company, Ferropar, appointed as administrator; Pres. JOSÉ HERALDO CARNEIRO LOBO.

Estrada de Ferro Vitória-Minas: Av. Dante Michelini 5.500, 29090-900 Vitória, ES; tel. (27) 335-3666; fax (27) 226-0093; f. 1942; operated by Companhia Vale de Rio Doce; transport of iron ore, general cargo and passengers; 898 km open in 1998; Dir THIER BARSOTTI MANZANO.

Ferrovia Bandeirante, SA (Ferroban): Rua Mauá 51, 01018-900 São Paulo, SP; tel. (11) 222-3392; fax (11) 220-8852; f. 1971 by merger of five railways operated by São Paulo State; transferred to private ownership, Nov. 1998; fmrly Ferrovia Paulista; 4,235 km open in 1998.

ROADS

In 1998 there were an estimated 1,659,000 km of roads in Brazil, of which 3,630 km were main roads. Brasília has been a focal point for inter-regional development, and paved roads link the capital with every region of Brazil. The building of completely new roads has taken place predominantly in the north. Roads are the principal mode of transport, accounting for 63% of freight and 96% of passenger traffic, including long-distance bus services, in 1998. Major projects include the 5,000-km Trans-Amazonian Highway, running from Recife and Cabedelo to the Peruvian border, the 4,138-km Cuibá–Santarém highway, which will run in a north–south direction, and the 3,555-km Trans-Brasiliana project, which will link Marabá, on the Trans-Amazonian highway, with Aceguá, on the Uruguayan frontier. A 20-year plan to construct a highway linking São Paulo with the Argentine and Chilean capitals was endorsed in 1992 within the context of the development of the Southern Cone Common Market (Mercosul).

Departamento Nacional de Estradas de Rodagem (DNER) (National Roads Development): SAN, Quadra 3, Blocos N/O, 4° andar, Edif. Núcleo dos Transportes, 70040-902 Brasília, DF; tel. (61) 315-4100; fax (61) 315-4050; f. 1945 to plan and execute federal road policy and to supervise state and municipal roads with the aim of integrating them into the national network; Dir GENÉSIO B. SOUZA.

INLAND WATERWAYS

River transport plays only a minor part in the movement of goods. There are three major river systems, the Amazon, Paraná and the São Francisco. The Amazon is navigable for 3,680 km, as far as Iquitos in Peru, and ocean-going ships can reach Manaus, 1,600 km upstream. Plans have been drawn up to improve the inland waterway system and one plan is to link the Amazon and Upper Paraná to provide a navigable waterway across the centre of the country. In October 1993 the member governments of Mercosul, together with Bolivia, reaffirmed their commitment to a 10-year development programme (initiated in 1992) for the extension of the Tietê Paraná river network along the Paraguay and Paraná Rivers as far as Buenos Aires, improving access to Atlantic ports and creating a 3,442 km waterway system, navigable throughout the year.

Secretaria de Transportes Aquaviários: Ministério dos Transportes, SAN, Quadra 3, Blocos N/O, 70040-902 Brasília, DF; tel. (61) 315-8102; Sec. WILDJAN DA FONSECA MAGNO.

Administração da Hidrovia do Paraguai (AHIPAR): Rua Treze de Junho 960, Corumbá, MS; tel. (67) 231-2841; fax (67) 231-2661; Supt. PAULO CÉSAR C. GOMES DA SILVA.

Administração da Hidrovia do Paraná (AHRANA): Rua Vinte e Quatro de Maio 55, 9° andar, Conj. B, 01041-001 São Paulo, SP; tel. (11) 221-3230; fax (11) 220-8689; Supt LUIZ EDUARDO GARCIA.

Administração da Hidrovia do São Francisco (AHSFRA): Praça do Porto 70, Distrito Industrial, 39270-000 Pirapora, MG; tel. (38) 741-2555; fax (38) 741-2510; Supt JOSÉ H. BORATO JABUR JÚNIOR.

Administração das Hidrovias do Sul (AHSUL): Praça Oswaldo Cruz 15, 3° andar, 90030-160 Porto Alegre, RS; tel. (51) 228-3677; fax (51) 226-9068; Supt JOSÉ LUIZ F. DE AZAMBUJA.

Empresa de Navegação da Amazônia, SA (ENASA): Av. Pres. Vargas 41, 66000-000 Belém, PA; tel. (91) 223-3878; fax (91) 224-0528; f. 1967; cargo and passenger services on the Amazon river and its principal tributaries, connecting the port of Belém with all major river ports; Pres. ANTÔNIO DE SOUZA MENDONÇA; 48 vessels.

SHIPPING

There are more than 40 deep-water ports in Brazil, all but two of which (Luis Correia and Imbituba) are directly or indirectly administered by the Government. The majority of ports are operated by eight state-owned concerns (Cia Docas do Pará, Maranhão, Ceará, Rio Grande do Norte, Bahia, Espírito Santo, Rio de Janeiro and Estado de São Paulo), while a smaller number (including Suape, Cabedelo, Barra dos Coqueiros, São Sebastião, Paranaguá, Antonina, São Francisco do Sul, Porto Alegre, Pelotas and Rio Grande) are administered by state governments. In late 1996 the Government announced plans to privatize 31 ports (including Santos and Rio de Janeiro).

The ports of Santos, Rio de Janeiro and Rio Grande have specialized container terminals handling more than 1,200,000 TEUs (20-ft equivalent units of containerized cargo) per year. Santos is the major container port in Brazil, accounting for 800,000 TEUs annually. The ports of Paranaguá, Itajaí, São Francisco do Sul, Salvador, Vitória and Imbituba cater for containerized cargo to a lesser extent.

Total cargo handled by Brazilian ports in 1998 amounted to 443m. tons, of which 250m. was bulk cargo, 148m. was liquid cargo and 45m. was general cargo. Some 43,000 vessels used Brazil's ports in 1998.

Brazil's merchant fleet comprised 504 vessels totalling 4,170,577 grt in December 1998.

Departamento de Marinha Mercante: Coordenação Geral de Transporte Maritimo, Av. Rio Branco 103, 6° e 8° andar, 20040-004 Rio de Janeiro, RJ; tel. (21) 221-4014; fax (21) 221-5929; Dir PAULO OCTÁVIO DE PAIVA ALMEIDA.

Port Authorities

Departamento de Portos: SAN, Quadra 3, Blocos N/O, CEP 70040-902, Brasília, DF; Dir PAULO ROBERTO K. TANNFNBAUM.

Paranaguá: Administração dos Portos de Paranaguá e Antonina (APPA), BR-277, km 0, 83206-380 Paranaguá, PR; tel. (41) 420-1102; fax (41) 423-4252; Port Admin. Eng. OSIRIS STENGHEL GUIMARÃES.

Recife: Administração do Porto do Recife, Praça Artur Oscar, 50030-370 Recife, PE; tel. (81) 424-4044; fax (81) 224-2848; Port Dir CARLOS DO REGO VILAR.

Rio de Janeiro: Companhia Docas do Rio de Janeiro (CDRJ), Rua do Acre 21, 20081-000 Rio de Janeiro, RJ; tel. (21) 296-5151; fax (21) 253-0528; CDRJ also administers the ports of Forno, Niterói, Sepetiba and Angra dos Reis; Pres. MAURO OROFINO CAMPOS.

Rio Grande: Administração do Porto de Rio Grande, Av. Honório Bicalho, CP 198, 96201-020 Rio Grande do Sul, RS; tel. (532) 31-1996; fax (532) 31-1857; Port Dir LUIZ FRANCISCO SPOTORNO.

Santos: Companhia Docas do Estado de São Paulo (CODESP), Av. Conselheiro Rodrigues Alves s/n, 11015-900 Santos, SP; tel. (13) 222-5485; fax (13) 222-3068; e-mail codesp@carrier.com.br; internet www.portodesantos.com; CODESP also administers the ports of Charqueadas, Estrela, Cáceres, Corumbá/Ladário, and the waterways of Paraná (AHRANA), Paraguai (AHIPAR) and the South (AHSUL); Pres. WAGNER GONÇALVES ROSSI.

São Francisco do Sul: Administração do Porto de São Francisco do Sul, Av. Eng. Leite Ribeiro 782, CP 71, 89240-000 São Francisco do Sul, SC; tel. (474) 44-0200; fax (474) 44-0115; Dir-Gen. ARNALDO S. THIAGO.

Tubarão: Companhia Vale do Rio Doce, Porto de Tubarão, Vitória, ES; tel. (27) 335-5727; fax (27) 228-0612; Port Dir CANDIDO COTTA PACHECO.

Vitória: Companhia Docas do Espírito Santo (CODESA), Av. Getúlio Vargas 556, Centro, 29020-030 Vitória, ES; tel. (27) 321-1311; fax (27) 222-7360; e-mail assecs@codesa.com.br; internet www.codesa.com.br; f. 1983; Pres. FÁBIO NUNES FALCE.

Other ports are served by the following state-owned companies:

Companhia Docas do Estado de Bahia: Av. da França 1551, 40010-000 Salvador, BA; tel. (71) 243-5066; fax (71) 241-6712; administers the ports of Aracaju, Salvador, Aratu, Ilhéus and Pirapora, and the São Francisco waterway (AHSFRA); Pres. JORGE FRANCISCO MEDAUAR.

Companhia Docas do Estado de Ceará (CDC): Praça Amigos da Marinha s/n, 60182-640 Fortaleza, CE; tel. (85) 263-1551; fax (85) 263-2433; administers the port of Fortaleza; Dir MARCELO MOTA TEIXEIRA.

Companhia Docas de Maranhão (CODOMAR): Porto do Itaquí, Rua de Paz 561, 65085-370 São Luís, MA; tel. (98) 222-2412; fax (98) 221-1394; administers ports of Itaquí and Manaus, and waterways of the Western Amazon (AHIMOC) and the North-East (AHINOR); Dir WASHINGTON DE OLIVEIRA VIEGAS.

Companhia Docas do Pará (CDP): Av. Pres. Vargas 41, 2° andar, 66010-000 Belém, PA; tel. (91) 216-2011; fax (91) 241-1741; f. 1967; administers the ports of Belém, Macapá, Porto Velho, Santarém and Vila do Conde, and the waterways of the Eastern Amazon (AHIMOR) and Tocantins and Araguaia (AHITAR); Dir-Pres. CARLOS ACATAUSSÚ NUNES.

Companhia Docas do Estado do Rio Grande do Norte (CODERN): Av. Hildebrando de Góis 2220, Ribeira, 59010-700 Natal, RN; tel. (84) 211-5311; fax (84) 221-6072; administers the ports of Areia Branca, Natal, Recife and Maceió; Dir EMILSON MEDEIROS DOS SANTOS.

Other State-owned Companies

Companhia de Navegação do Estado de Rio de Janeiro: Praça 15 de Novembro 21, 20010-010 Rio de Janeiro, RJ; tel (21) 533-6661; fax (21) 252-0524; Pres. MARCOS TEIXEIRA.

Frota Nacional de Petroleiros—Fronape: Rua Carlos Seidl 188, CP 51015, 20931, Rio de Janeiro, RJ; tel. (21) 585-3355; f. 1953; fleet of tankers operated by the state petroleum company, PETROBRÁS, and the Ministry of Transport; Chair. ALBANO DE SOUZA GONÇALVES.

Private Companies

Companhia Docas de Imbituba (CDI): Porto de Imbituba, Av. Presidente Vargas s/n, 88780-000 Imbituba, SC; tel. (482) 55-0080; fax (482) 55-0701; administers the port of Imbituba; Exec. Dir. MANUEL ALVES DO VALE.

Companhia de Navegação do Norte (CONAN): Av. Rio Branco 23, 25° andar, 20090-003 Rio de Janeiro, RJ; tel. (21) 223-4155; fax (21) 253-7128; f. 1965; services to Brazil, Argentina, Uruguay and inland waterways; Chair. J. R. RIBEIRO SALOMÃO.

Empresa de Navegação Aliança, SA: Av. Pasteur 110, Botafogo, 22290-240 Rio de Janeiro, RJ; tel. (21) 546-1112; fax (21) 546-1161; f. 1950; cargo services to Argentina, Uruguay, Europe, Baltic, Atlantic and North Sea ports; Pres. CARLOS G. E. FISCHER.

Companhia de Navegação do São Francisco: Av. São Francisco 1517, 39270-000 Pirapora, MG; tel. (38) 741-1444; fax (38) 741-1164; Pres. JOSÉ HUMBERTO BARATA JABUR.

Frota Oceânica Brasileira, SA: Av. Venezuela 110, CP 21-020, 20081-310 Rio de Janeiro, RJ; tel. (21) 291-5153; fax (21) 263-1439; f. 1947; Pres. JOSÉ CARLOS FRAGOSO PIRES; Vice-Pres. LUIZ J. C. ALHANATI.

Serviço de Navegação Bacia Prata: Av. 14 de Março 1700, 79370-000 Ladário, MS; tel. (67) 231-4354; Dir LUIZ CARLOS DA SILVA ALEXANDRE.

Vale do Rio Doce Navegação, SA (DOCENAVE): Rua Voluntários da Pátria 143, Botafogo, 22279-900 Rio de Janeiro, RJ; tel. (21) 536-8002; fax (21) 536-8276; bulk carrier to Japan, Arabian Gulf, Europe, North America and Argentina; Pres. AKIRA KATSUGARI.

CIVIL AVIATION

There are about 1,500 airports and airstrips. Of the 67 principal airports 22 are international, although most international traffic is handled by the two airports at Rio de Janeiro and two at São Paulo.

Empresa Brasileira de Infra-Estrutura Aeroportuária (INFRAERO): SCS, Q 04, NR 58, Edif. Infraero, 6° andar, 70304-902 Brasília, DF; tel. (61) 312-3170; fax (61) 312-3105; e-mail fernandalima@infraero.gov.br; internet www.infraero.gov.br; Pres. EDUARDO BOGALHO PETTENGILL.

Principal Airlines

Lider Taxi Aéreo, SA: Av. Santa Rosa 123, 31270-750 Belo Horizonte, MG; tel. (31) 490-4500; fax (31) 490-4600; internet www.lidertaxiaereo.com.br; f. 1958; Pres. JOSÉ AFONSO ASSUMPÇÃO.

Nordeste Linhas Aéreas Regionais: Av. Tancredo Neves 1672, Edif. Catabas Empresarial, 1° andar, Pituba, 41820-020 Salvador, BA; tel. (71) 341-7533; fax (71) 341-0393; e-mail nordeste@provider.com.br; internet www.nordeste.com.br; f. 1976; services to 26 destinations in north-east Brazil; Pres. PERCY LOURENÇO RODRIGUES.

Pantanal Linhas Aéreas Sul-Matogrossenses, SA: Av. das Nações Unidas 10989, 8° andar, São Paulo, SP; tel. (11) 3040-3900; fax (11) 866-3424; e-mail pantanal@uninet.com.br; internet www.pantanal-airlines.com.br; f. 1993; regional services; Pres. MARCOS FERREIRA SAMPAIO.

Rio-Sul Serviços Aéreos Regionais, SA: Av. Rio Branco 85, 11° andar, 20040-004 Rio de Janeiro, RJ; tel. (21) 263-4282; fax (21) 253-2044; internet www.rio-sul.com; f. 1976; subsidiary of VARIG; domestic passenger services to cities in southern Brazil; Pres. PAULO ENRIQUE MORÃES COCO.

TAM—Transportes Aéreos Regionais (TAM): Av. Pedro Bueno 1400, 04342-001 São Paulo, SP; tel. (11) 5582-8811; fax (11) 578-5946; e-mail tamimprensa@tam.com.br; internet www.tam-airlines.com.br; f. 1976; scheduled passenger and cargo services from São Paulo to destinations throughout Brazil; Pres. DANIEL MANDELLI MARTIN.

Transbrasil SA Linhas Aéreas: Zona C 01, Lotes 8/9, Aeroporto Internacional, 71608 Brasília, DF; tel. (61) 248-0900; fax (61) 242-5893; internet www.transbrasil.com.br; f. 1955 as Sadia, renamed 1972; scheduled passenger and cargo services to major Brazilian cities and Orlando; cargo charter flights to the USA; Pres. OMAR FONTANA.

Transportes Aéreos Regionais da Bacia Amazônica (TABA): Av. Governador José Malcher 883, 66055-260 Belém, PA; tel. (91) 223-6300; fax (91) 223-0471; f. 1976; domestic passenger services throughout north-west Brazil; Chair. MARCÍLIO JACQUES GIBSON.

VARIG, SA (Viação Aérea Rio Grandense): Rua 18 de Novembro 120, 90240-040 Porto Alegre, RS; tel. (51) 358-4233; fax (51) 358-7001; internet www.varig.com.br; f. 1927; international services throughout North, Central and South America, Africa, Western

Europe and Japan; domestic services to major Brazilian cities; cargo services; Chair. and Pres. FERNANDO PINTO.

VASP, SA (Viação Aérea São Paulo): Praça Comte-Lineu Gomes s/n, Aeroporto Congonhas, 04626-910 São Paulo, SP; tel. (11) 532-3000; fax (11) 542-0880; internet www.vasp.com.br; f. 1933; privatized in Sept. 1990; domestic services throughout Brazil; international services to Argentina, Belgium, the Caribbean, South Korea and the USA; Pres. WAGNER CANHEDO.

Tourism

In 1999 some 5.1m. tourists visited Brazil. Receipts from tourism totalled US $3,678m. in 1998. Rio de Janeiro, with its famous beaches, is the centre of the tourist trade. Like Salvador, Recife and other towns, it has excellent examples of Portuguese colonial and modern architecture. The modern capital, Brasília, incorporates a new concept of city planning and is the nation's show-piece. Other attractions are the Iguaçu Falls, the seventh largest (by volume) in the world, the tropical forests of the Amazon basin and the wildlife of the Pantanal.

Instituto Brasileiro de Turismo—EMBRATUR: SCN, Q 02, Bloco G, 3° andar, 70710-500 Brasília, DF; tel. (61) 224-9100; fax (61) 223-9889; internet www.embratur.gov.br; f. 1966; Pres. CAIO LUIZ DE CARVALHO.

Seção de Feiras e Turismo/Departamento de Promoção Comercial: Ministério das Relações Exteriores, Esplanada dos Ministérios, 5° andar, Sala 523, 70170-900 Brasília, DF; tel. (61) 411-6394; fax (61) 322-0833; e-mail docstt@mre.gov.br; internet www.braziltradenet.gov.br; f. 1977; organizes Brazil's participation in trade fairs and commercial exhibitions abroad; Principal Officer ANTÔNIO J. M. DE SOUZA E SILVA.

BRUNEI

Introductory Survey

Location, Climate, Language, Religion, Flag, Capital

The Sultanate of Brunei (Negara Brunei Darussalam) lies in South-East Asia, on the north-west coast of the island of Borneo (most of which is comprised of the Indonesian territory of Kalimantan). It is surrounded and bisected on the landward side by Sarawak, one of the two eastern states of Malaysia. The country has a tropical climate, characterized by consistent temperature and humidity. Annual rainfall averages about 2,540 mm (100 ins) in coastal areas and about 3,300 mm (130 ins) in the interior. Temperatures are high, with average daily temperatures ranging from 24°C (75°F) to 32°C (90°F). The principal language is Malay, although Chinese is also spoken and English is widely used. The Malay population (an estimated 67.6% of the total in 1999) are mainly Sunni Muslims. Most of the Chinese in Brunei (14.9% of the population) are Buddhists, and some are adherents of Confucianism and Daoism. Europeans and Eurasians are predominantly Christians, and the majority of indigenous tribespeople (Iban, Dayak and Kelabit—5.9% of the population) adhere to various animist beliefs. The flag (proportions 2 by 1) is yellow, with two diagonal stripes, of white and black, running from the upper hoist to the lower fly; superimposed in the centre is the state emblem (in red, with yellow Arabic inscriptions). The capital is Bandar Seri Begawan (formerly called Brunei Town).

Recent History

Brunei, a traditional Islamic monarchy, formerly included most of the coastal regions of North Borneo (now Sabah) and Sarawak, which later became states of Malaysia. During the 19th century the rulers of Brunei ceded large parts of their territory to the United Kingdom, reducing the sultanate to its present size. In 1888, when North Borneo became a British Protectorate, Brunei became a British Protected State. In accordance with an agreement made in 1906, a British Resident was appointed to the court of the ruling Sultan as an adviser on administration. Under this arrangement, a form of government that included an advisory body, the State Council, emerged.

Brunei was invaded by Japanese forces in December 1941, but reverted to its former status in 1945, when the Second World War ended. The British-appointed Governor of Sarawak was High Commissioner for Brunei from 1948 until the territory's first written Constitution was promulgated in September 1959, when a further agreement was made between the Sultan and the British Government. The United Kingdom continued to be responsible for Brunei's defence and external affairs until the Sultanate's declaration of independence in 1984.

In December 1962 a large-scale revolt broke out in Brunei and in parts of Sarawak and North Borneo. The rebellion was undertaken by the 'North Borneo Liberation Army', an organization linked with the Parti Rakyat Brunei (PRB—Brunei People's Party), led by Sheikh Ahmad Azahari, which was strongly opposed to the planned entry of Brunei into the Federation of Malaysia. The rebels proclaimed the 'revolutionary State of North Kalimantan', but the revolt was suppressed, after 10 days' fighting, with the aid of British forces from Singapore. A state of emergency was declared, the PRB was banned, and Azahari was given asylum in Malaya. In the event, the Sultan of Brunei, Sir Omar Ali Saifuddin III, decided in 1963 against joining the Federation. From 1962 he ruled by decree, and the state of emergency remained in force. In October 1967 Saifuddin, who had been Sultan since 1950, abdicated in favour of his son, Hassanal Bolkiah, who was then 21 years of age. Under an agreement signed in November 1971, Brunei was granted full internal self-government.

In December 1975 the UN General Assembly adopted a resolution advocating British withdrawal from Brunei, the return of political exiles and the holding of a general election. Negotiations in 1978, following assurances by Malaysia and Indonesia that they would respect Brunei's sovereignty, resulted in an agreement (signed in January 1979) that Brunei would become fully independent within five years. Independence was duly proclaimed on 1 January 1984, and the Sultan took office as Prime Minister and Minister of Finance and of Home Affairs,

presiding over a Cabinet of six other ministers (including two of the Sultan's brothers and his father, the former Sultan).

The future of the Chinese population, which controlled much of Brunei's private commercial sector but had become stateless since independence, appeared threatened in 1985, when the Sultan indicated that Brunei would become an Islamic state in which the indigenous, mainly Malay, inhabitants, known as *bumiputras* ('sons of the soil'), would receive preferential treatment. Several Hong Kong and Taiwan Chinese, who were not permanent Brunei residents, were repatriated.

In May 1985 a new political party, the Parti Kebangsaan Demokratik Brunei (PKDB—Brunei National Democratic Party), was formed. The new party, which comprised business executives loyal to the Sultan, based its policies on Islam and a form of liberal nationalism. However, the Sultan forbade employees of the Government (about 40% of the country's working population) to join the party. Persons belonging to the Chinese community were also excluded from membership. Divisions within the new party led to the formation of a second group, the Parti Perpaduan Kebangsaan Brunei (PPKB—Brunei National Solidarity Party), in February 1986. This party, which also received the Sultan's official approval, placed greater emphasis on co-operation with the Government, and was open to both Muslim and non-Muslim ethnic groups.

Although the Sultan was not expected to allow any relaxation of restrictions on radical political activities, it became clear during 1985 and 1986 that a more progressive style of government was being adopted. The death of Sir Omar Ali Saifuddin, the Sultan's father, in September 1986 was expected to accelerate modernization. In October the Cabinet was enlarged to 11 members, and commoners and aristocrats were assigned portfolios that had previously been given to members of the royal family. In February 1988, however, the PKDB was dissolved by the authorities after it had demanded the resignation of the Sultan as Head of Government (although not as Head of State), an end to the 26-year state of emergency and the holding of democratic elections. The official reason for the dissolution of the party was its connections with a foreign organization, the Pacific Democratic Union. The leaders of the PKDB, Abdul Latif Hamid and Abdul Latif Chuchu, were arrested, under the provisions of the Internal Security Act, and detained until March 1990. Abdul Latif Hamid died in May of that year. In January 1990 the Government ordered the release of six political prisoners, who had been detained soon after the revolt in 1962.

In 1990 the Government encouraged the population to embrace *Melayu Islam Beraja* (Malay Islamic Monarchy) as the state ideology. This affirmation of traditional Bruneian values for Malay Muslims was widely believed to be a response to an increase in social problems, including the abuse of alcohol and mild narcotics. Muslims were encouraged to adhere more closely to the tenets of Islam, greater emphasis was laid on Islamic holiday celebrations, and the distribution of alcohol was discouraged.

Extremely moderate progress towards reform was apparent in subsequent years. In 1994 a constitutional committee, appointed by the Government and chaired by the Minister of Foreign Affairs, Prince Mohamad Bolkiah, submitted a recommendation that the Constitution be amended to provide for an elected legislature. In February 1995 the PPKB was given permission to convene a general assembly, at which Abdul Latif Chuchu, the former Secretary-General of the PKDB, was elected President. Latif Chuchu was, however, compelled to resign shortly afterwards, owing to a condition of his release from detention in 1990. In May 1998 the PKDB was permitted to hold a further annual general meeting, at which Hatta Zainal Abidin, the son of a former opposition leader, was elected party President.

In February 1997 the Sultan replaced his brother, Prince Jefri Bolkiah, as Minister of Finance. It was rumoured that the Sultan's assumption of the finance portfolio was due to alleged financial disagreements rather than Prince Jefri's frequently criticized extravagant lifestyle. In March the Sultan and Prince Jefri denied accusations of misconduct made by a former winner of a US beauty contest, Shannon Marketic. A US court granted the Sultan immunity from legal action in August, owing to his status as a foreign head of state; this immunity was extended to Prince Jefri in March 1998. Similar allegations against Prince Jefri, submitted to a court in Hawaii, resulted in an undisclosed financial settlement, following the judge's rejection of Prince Jefri's claims to immunity. Marketic subsequently appealed against the granting of exemption from prosecution in her case. Further allegations concerning the extravagant lifestyle of Prince Jefri emerged in a court case in the United Kingdom in February, in which Jefri was being sued for £80m. by two former business associates, Watche (Bob) and Rafi Manoukian. The Manoukian brothers claimed that Prince Jefri had reneged on two property agreements; Prince Jefri was counter-suing them for £100m., alleging that they had exploited their relationship with him to amass considerable wealth. The case, which was unreported in Brunei, was also settled out of court for an undisclosed sum.

Following the dismissal in March 1998, after 14 years in office, of Dato' Dr Haji Johar bin Dato' Haji Noordin, reportedly owing to the inadequacy of his response to the haze over Brunei caused by forest fires in Indonesia and Malaysia, Abdul Aziz assumed responsibility for the health portfolio. The resignations of the Attorney-General, Pengiran Haji Bahrin bin Pengiran Haji Abbas (who was granted leave from his position as Minister of Law), and of the Solicitor-General were accepted by the Sultan in June. An acting Attorney-General and Solicitor-General were appointed, while the Sultan assumed temporary responsibility for the law portfolio. On 10 August the Sultan's son, Prince Al-Muhtadee Billah Bolkiah, was installed as the heir to the throne.

Prince Jefri, who had left Brunei in April 1998, was removed as Chairman of the Brunei Investment Agency (BIA), which controls the country's overseas investments, at the end of July, following the collapse earlier in the month of his business conglomerate, the Amedeo Development Corporation. (The Amedeo Development Corporation was formally liquidated by the High Court of Brunei in July 1999, with reported debts of at least US $3,500m.) Prince Jefri was also removed from the boards of seven communications companies. He claimed that he was the victim of a conspiracy of conservative Islamists, led by his estranged brother, Prince Mohamad Bolkiah (the Minister of Foreign Affairs), and the Minister of Education, Pehin Dato' Haji Abdul Aziz bin Pehin Haji Umar. Prince Jefri's removal from positions of authority took place amid a more rigorous enforcement of the ban on alcohol and the confiscation from retailers of non-Islamic religious artefacts. Abdul Aziz, who replaced Prince Jefri as Chairman of the BIA, also headed an investigation (which was initiated in June) into the finances of the BIA. In September Abdul Aziz announced that large amounts of government funds had been misappropriated during Prince Jefri's tenure as Chairman. In January 2000, following a long period during which the Government made no significant comment about the misappropriation of BIA funds or about the role of the Sultan's younger brother in the affair, Prince Jefri returned to Brunei after many months of self-imposed exile. Private negotiations ensued between Prince Jefri and the parties involved in the investigation. These negotiations failed, however, and in February the Government and the BIA began civil proceedings against Prince Jefri, alleging his improper withdrawal and use of substantial BIA funds during the period in which he had served as Minister of Finance and Chairman of the BIA; 71 other people were named in the action, including Prince Jefri's eldest son, Prince Muda Abdul Hakeem, and his private secretary. It was subsequently announced by the Government that Prince Jefri's assets had been 'frozen' worldwide, and in April a Brunei court dismissed an appeal lodged by the Prince against the disclosure of his assets. In May, however, an out-of-court settlement was reached between Prince Jefri and the prosecuting parties, in accordance with which all of Prince Jefri's assets, both in Brunei and overseas, that had been acquired with funds derived from the BIA were to be returned to the State; observers speculated that this would only partially recoup the funds squandered by Prince Jefri.

In February 2000 the Brunei Darussalam Economic Council (BDEC), which had been established in September 1998 to explore ways of improving the Sultanate's economy, released a report in which it warned that Brunei's economy was becoming increasingly unsustainable. The report was approved by the Sultan, who appointed Prince Mohamad to oversee the implementation of the economic recovery plan recommended by the BDEC. In his address to mark Brunei's 16th National Day, also

in February, the Sultan focused on the issue of the economy and the importance of the development of alternative sources of revenue, in an unprecedented acknowledgement of the country's fundamental economic problems.

Relations with the United Kingdom, meanwhile, had become strained during 1983, following the Brunei Government's decision, in August, to transfer the management of its investment portfolio from the British Crown Agents to the newly-created BIA. However, normal relations were restored in September, when the British Government agreed that a battalion of Gurkha troops, stationed in Brunei since 1971, should remain in Brunei after independence, at the Sultanate's expense, specifically to guard the oil and gas fields.

Brunei has developed close relations with the members of the Association of South East Asian Nations (ASEAN—see p. 134), in particular Singapore, and became a full member of the organization immediately after independence. Brunei also joined the UN, the Commonwealth (see p. 150) and the Organization of the Islamic Conference (see p. 266) in 1984. In September 1992 Brunei was formally admitted to the Non-aligned Movement (see p. 318). In late 1991 Brunei established diplomatic relations with the People's Republic of China at ambassadorial level. As a member of ASEAN, Brunei's relations with Viet Nam improved during 1991 (following Viet Nam's withdrawal from Cambodia in September 1989). In February 1992 diplomatic relations were formally established with Viet Nam during a visit to Brunei of the Vietnamese Prime Minister. In October 1993 the Brunei Government announced the establishment of diplomatic relations at ambassadorial level with Myanmar.

In July 1990, in response to the uncertainty over the future of US bases in the Philippines (see chapter on the Philippines, Vol. II), Brunei joined Singapore in offering the USA the option of operating its forces from Brunei. A bilateral memorandum of understanding was subsequently signed, providing for up to three visits a year to Brunei by US warships. Under the memorandum, Brunei forces were to train with US personnel.

Conflicting claims (from Brunei, Viet Nam, the People's Republic of China, the Philippines, Malaysia and Taiwan) to all, or some, of the uninhabited Spratly Islands, situated in the South China Sea, remained a source of tension in the region. Brunei is the only claimant not to have stationed troops on the islands, which are both strategically important and possess potentially large reserves of petroleum. During the 1990s attempts to resolve the dispute through a negotiated settlement resulted in little progress, and military activity in the area increased.

In February 2000 Brunei hosted its first Asia-Pacific Economic Co-operation (APEC—see p. 128) Senior Officials' Meeting, attended by 3,000 delegates from 21 countries. In April an ASEAN Regional Forum meeting to discuss security issues was held in Brunei. In November Brunei hosted the annual summit meeting of APEC leaders.

Government

The 1959 Constitution confers supreme executive authority on the Sultan. He is assisted and advised by four Constitutional Councils: the Religious Council, the Privy Council, the Council of Cabinet Ministers and the Council of Succession. Since the rebellion of 1962, certain provisions of the Constitution (including those pertaining to elections and to a fifth Council, the Legislative Council) have been suspended, and the Sultan has ruled by decree.

Defence

At 1 August 2000 the Royal Brunei Malay Regiment numbered 5,000 (including 600 women): army 3,900; navy 700; air force 400. Military service is voluntary, but only Malays are eligible for service. Paramilitary forces comprised 1,750 Royal Brunei Police. Defence expenditure in 2000 was budgeted at an estimated B $484m. One Gurkha battalion of the British army, comprising about 1,050 men, has been stationed in Brunei since 1971. There are also about 500 troops from Singapore, operating a training school in Brunei.

Economic Affairs

In 1994, according to estimates by the World Bank, Brunei's gross national product (GNP), measured at average 1992–94 prices, was US $3,975m., equivalent to US $14,240 per head. During 1985–94, it was estimated, GNP per head declined, in real terms, at an average rate of 1.5% per year. In 1990–98 the population increased by an average of 2.7% annually. According to preliminary World Bank data, GNP in 1997 was US $7,151m.

Brunei's gross domestic product (GDP) increased at an estimated average annual rate of 2.3% during 1990–97. Real GDP growth in 1998 was estimated at 1.0%.

Agriculture (including forestry and fishing) employed an estimated 0.9% of the working population in 1998 and provided an estimated 2.8% of GDP in that year. In 1998 an estimated 1.2% of the total land area was cultivated; the principal crops include rice, cassava, bananas and pineapples. In the 1990s Brunei imported about 80% of its total food requirements. Owing to the increasing emphasis on Islamic values in Brunei, a severe shortage of meat was caused in 1999 following a decision to ensure that all food was *halal* (slaughtered in accordance with Islamic traditions) by either imposing supervisors in foreign abattoirs or by slaughtering imported livestock in Brunei. During 1990–97 agricultural GDP increased, in real terms, at an average annual rate of 2.7%. Agricultural GDP increased by an estimated 2.9% in 1998.

Industry (comprising mining, manufacturing, construction and utilities) employed 24.1% of the working population in 1991 and contributed an estimated 39.1% of GDP in 1998. Total industrial GDP declined at an average annual rate of 1.6% in 1985–95. Industrial GDP, including oil and gas services, increased by an average of 6.6% per year in 1993–97. Industrial GDP growth was estimated at 4.1% in 1998.

Brunei's economy depends almost entirely on its petroleum and natural gas resources. Mining and quarrying employed only 5.0% of the working population in 1991, but the petroleum sector provided an estimated 36% of GDP in 1996. Production of crude petroleum from the eight offshore and two onshore fields averaged 157,000 barrels per day in 1998. In that year output of natural gas totalled 10,751m. cu m. In the 1990s there were significant further discoveries of both petroleum and natural gas reserves. Crude petroleum, natural gas and petroleum products together accounted for an estimated 88.6% of total export earnings in 1998. Reserves of petroleum and natural gas were sufficient to enable production to be maintained at current levels until 2018 and 2033 respectively. The GDP of the mining sector declined at an average rate of 5.3% per year in 1985–89, but rose by 1.4% in 1990 and by 10.0% in 1991. The GDP of the petroleum and gas sector declined by an annual average of 0.3% in 1990–97 and by an estimated 1.6% in 1998.

Manufacturing is dominated by petroleum refining. The sector employed 3.8% of the working population in 1991 (increasing to 5.4% in 1995) and contributed an estimated 8.1% of GDP in 1991. Since the mid-1980s Brunei has attempted to expand its manufacturing base. In the mid-1990s the textile industry provided the largest non-oil and -gas revenue; other industries included cement, mineral water, canned food, dairy products, silica sands products, footwear and leather products, the design and manufacture of printed circuits, publishing and printing. Manufacturing GDP increased at an average annual rate of 4.8% in 1985–89 and by 5.3% in 1990, but fell by 22.6% in 1991.

Services employed 73.7% of the working population in 1991 and provided an estimated 58.1% of GDP in 1998. In 1998 the sector comprising wholesale and retail trade, restaurants and hotels contributed 12.6% of GDP, and the finance sector 8.3%. Plans are under way to develop Brunei as a regional centre for finance and banking. The GDP of the banking and finance sector increased by an annual average of 7.7% in 1993–97 and by an estimated 3.8% in 1998. The tourism sector is also being actively promoted as an important part of Brunei's policy of diversification away from its reliance on petroleum and natural gas; 2001 was designated 'Visit Brunei Year'. During 1985–96 the combined GDP of the service sectors increased, in real terms, at an average rate of 5.5% per year.

In 1998 Brunei recorded a visible trade surplus of US $175m., while, as a result of high investment income from abroad, there was a surplus of US $2,085m. on the current account of the balance of payments. In 1998 the principal source of imports (25.2%) was Malaysia; other major suppliers were Singapore (which accounted for 20.4%), the USA (13.5%), the United Kingdom and Japan. The principal market for exports in that year was Japan, which accounted for 53.1% of total exports (mainly natural gas on a long-term contract); other significant purchasers were the Republic of Korea (also a purchaser of natural gas), the USA, Singapore and Thailand. Principal imports comprised machinery and transport equipment, basic manufactures, food and live animals and miscellaneous manufactured articles; principal exports were crude petroleum and natural gas.

In 1997 there was a budgetary deficit of B $27m. (equivalent to 0.3% of GDP). Brunei has no external public debt. International reserves were unofficially estimated at US $38,000m. in 1997 but were estimated to have declined to US $20,000m. in late 1998. Consumer prices increased at an average rate of 2.7% per year in 1990–97, but declined by 0.4% in 1998. Foreign workers, principally from Malaysia and the Philippines, have helped to ease the labour shortage resulting from the small size of the population, and comprised about 30% of the labour force in 1998, compared with 41% in 1995 (owing to an exodus of foreign workers in 1998). However, the rate of unemployment was estimated at 5.1% in 1998, reflecting a shortage of non-manual jobs for the well-educated Bruneians.

Brunei is a member of the Association of South East Asian Nations (ASEAN—see p. 134). In October 1991 the member states formally announced the establishment of the ASEAN Free Trade Area, which was to be implemented over 15 years (later reduced to 10), and, as a member of ASEAN, Brunei endorsed Malaysia's plan for an East Asia Economic Caucus. Brunei was a founder member of the Asia-Pacific Economic Co-operation forum (APEC—see p. 128), initiated in November 1989, and is also a member of the UN Economic and Social Commission for Asia and the Pacific (see p. 28), which aims to accelerate economic progress in the region. In 1994 the East ASEAN Growth Area (EAGA) was established, encompassing Mindanao, in the Philippines, Sarawak and Sabah, in Malaysia, Kalimantan and Sulawesi, in Indonesia, and Brunei. The EAGA was modelled on the Singapore-Johore-Riau 'growth triangle'. In October 1995 Brunei joined the International Monetary Fund (IMF—see p. 92) and the World Bank.

The seventh (1996–2000) National Development Plan continued the emphasis of the fifth (1986–1990) and sixth (1991–95) Plans on diversification of the economy to reduce the country's dependence on income from petroleum and natural gas. In 1996 the Government announced proposals to develop Brunei as a 'Service Hub for Trade and Tourism' by the year 2003, following earlier plans for the development of the private sector and the conversion of Brunei into a regional centre for banking and finance. Various measures were taken to accelerate the broadening of Brunei's economic base, which had been extremely slow, owing to the constraints of high labour costs, the small domestic market and a lack of entrepreneurial skills and motivation in the indigenous population. However, the regional financial crisis, which began in 1997, resulted in the depreciation of the Brunei dollar, a decrease in income from the stock market and a sharp reduction in tourist arrivals, owing to the recession in other Asian countries. The situation was compounded by a significant decline in the price of petroleum from mid-1997 and by the huge financial losses caused by alleged mismanagement of the Brunei Investment Agency (BIA) by the Sultan's brother, Prince Jefri Bolkiah. Another factor was the collapse of Prince Jefri's Amedeo Development Corporation, which was responsible for many building projects in Brunei. In an attempt to address the economic situation, budgetary allocations were drastically reduced, halting much government investment (although complaints from the business community caused the Government to reverse some decisions). Service industries were then also adversely affected by the exodus of thousands of unemployed foreign workers. Amedeo's liquidation in July 1999, without compensating its 25 creditors (mostly foreign construction companies), was expected to have an adverse effect on investor confidence in Brunei. A recovery in petroleum prices in 1999 offered the prospect of an economic revival. However, concerns over the future of the Sultanate's economy increased in 1999 and 2000. A report released by the Brunei Darussalam Economic Council (BDEC) in February 2000 warned of the unsustainable nature of the economy. The Sultan, who had personally approved the BDEC's report, further underlined these concerns when he emphasized the importance of the development of sources of revenue other than petroleum and natural gas in an address delivered to the nation during the same month.

Social Welfare

Free medical services are provided by the Government. In 1997 there were 318 physicians working in the country and 874 hospital beds. In the same year there were 49 dentists, 23 pharmacists and 1,276 nurses. The main central referral hospital is in Bandar Seri Begawan, but there are three other hospitals (in Kuala Belait, Tutong and Temburong), as well as private facilities provided by Brunei Shell in Seria. For medical care not available in Brunei, citizens are sent abroad at the

Government's expense. There is a 'flying doctor' service, as well as various clinics, travelling dispensaries and dental clinics. A non-contributory state pensions scheme for elderly and disabled persons came into operation in 1955. The State also provides financial assistance to the poor, the destitute and widows. Of total ordinary expenditure by the Government in 1997, B $178m. (6.9%) was for the Ministry of Health.

Education

Education is free and is compulsory for 12 years from the age of five years. Islamic studies form an integral part of the school curriculum. Pupils who are Brunei citizens and reside more than 8 km (5 miles) from their schools are entitled to free accommodation in hostels, free transport or a subsistence allowance. Schools are classified according to the language of instruction, i.e. Malay, English or Chinese (Mandarin). In 1996 enrolment at pre-primary level was equivalent to 53% of children in the relevant age-group (males 53%; females 53%). Primary education lasts for six years from the age of six years. Secondary education, usually beginning at 12 years of age, lasts for seven years, comprising a first cycle of three years (lower secondary), a second of two years (upper secondary) and a third of two years (pre-tertiary). In 1996 enrolment at primary level was equivalent to 106% of children in the relevant age-group (males 109%; females 104%), while the comparable enrolment ratio at secondary level was 77% (males 72%; females 82%). In 1998 there were eight vocational colleges, one teacher-training college, three institutes of higher education and one university. The University of Brunei Darussalam was formally established in 1985, but many students continue to attend universities abroad, at government expense. In 1994 enrolment at tertiary level was equivalent to 6.6% of the relevant age-group (males 5.3%; females 8.0%). In 1995, according to UNESCO estimates, the adult illiteracy rate averaged 10.9% (males 6.8%; females

15.4%). Of total ordinary expenditure by the Government in 1997, B $347m. (13.5%) was for the Ministry of Education.

Public Holidays

2001: 1 January (New Year's Day), 25 January* (Chinese New Year), 23 February (National Day), 6 March† (Hari Raya Aidiladha, Feast of the Sacrifice), 26 March† (Hijrah, Islamic New Year), 31 May (Royal Brunei Armed Forces Day), 4 June† (Hari Mouloud, Birth of the Prophet), 15 July (Sultan's Birthday), 15 October† (Israk Mikraj, Ascension of the Prophet Muhammad), 17 November† (Beginning of Ramadan), 3 December† (Memperingati Nuzul Al-Quran, Anniversary of the Revelation of the Koran), 17 December† (Hari Raya Aidilfitri, end of Ramadan), 25 December (Christmas).

2002: 1 January (New Year's Day), 13 February* (Chinese New Year), 23 February (National Day), 23 February† (Hari Raya Aidiladha, Feast of the Sacrifice), 15 March† (Hijrah, Islamic New Year), 24 May (Hari Mouloud, Birth of the Prophet), 31 May (Royal Brunei Armed Forces Day), 15 July (Sultan's Birthday), 4 October† (Israk Mikraj, Ascension of the Prophet Muhammad), 6 November† (Beginning of Ramadan), 22 November† (Memperingati Nuzul Al-Quran, Anniversary of the Revelation of the Koran), 6 December† (Hari Raya Aidilfitri, end of Ramadan), 25 December (Christmas).

* The first day of the first moon of the lunar calendar.

† These holidays are dependent on the Islamic lunar calendar and may vary by one or two days from the dates given.

Weights and Measures

The imperial system is in operation but local measures of weight and capacity are used. These include the gantang (1 gallon), the tahil (1⅓ oz) and the kati (1⅓ lb).

Statistical Survey

Source (unless otherwise stated): Department of Economic Planning and Development, Ministry of Finance, Bandar Seri Begawan 2012; tel. (2) 241991; fax (2) 226132.

AREA AND POPULATION

Area: 5,765 sq km (2,226 sq miles); *by district:* Brunei/Muara 570 sq km (220 sq miles), Seria/Belait 2,725 sq km (1,052 sq miles), Tutong 1,165 sq km (450 sq miles), Temburong 1,305 sq km (504 sq miles).

Population (excluding transients afloat): 192,832 (males 102,942, females 89,890) at census of 25 August 1981; 260,482 (males 137,616, females 122,866) at census of 7 August 1991; 330,700 (males 175,200, females 155,000) at mid-1999 (official estimates). *By district* (mid-1999): Brunei/Muara 218,800; Seria/Belait 66,800; Tutong 35,700; Temburong 9,400; Total 330,700.

Density (mid-1999): 57.3 per sq km.

Ethnic Groups (1991 census): Malay 174,319, Chinese 40,621, Other indigenous 15,665, Others 29,877, Total 260,482; (official estimates at mid-1999): Malay 223,500, Chinese 49,300, Other indigenous 19,600, Others 38,300, Total 330,700.

Principal Town: Bandar Seri Begawan (capital), population 45,867 at 1991 census, 50,000 in 1995 (estimate).

Births, Marriages and Deaths (registrations, 1998): Live births 7,411 (birth rate 22.9 per 1,000), Deaths 928 (death rate 2.9 per 1,000); (1995): Marriages 1,793 (marriage rate 6.1 per 1,000).

Expectation of Life (years at birth, 1998): Males 72.1; Females 76.5.

Economically Active Population (persons aged 15 years and over, 1991 census): Agriculture, hunting, forestry and fishing 2,162; Mining and quarrying 5,327; Manufacturing 4,070; Electricity, gas and water 2,223; Construction 14,145; Trade, restaurants and hotels 15,404; Transport, storage and communications 5,392; Financing, insurance, real estate and business services 5,807; Community, social and personal services 52,121; Activities not adequately defined 95; *Total employed* 106,746 (males 72,338; females 34,408); Unemployed 5,209 (males 2,745; females 2,464); *Total labour force* 111,955 (males 75,083; females 36,872).

1998 (estimate): Total labour force 132,390.

AGRICULTURE, ETC.

Principal Crops (FAO estimates, '000 metric tons, 1999): Rice (paddy) 0.4, Cassava (Manioc) 1.6, Vegetables (incl. melons) 9.0, Fruit 5.4.

Livestock (FAO estimates, '000 head, 1999): Cattle 2.1, Buffaloes 5.9, Goats 3.5, Poultry 5,500.

Livestock Products (metric tons, 1999): Poultry meat 6,156; Hen eggs 3,800 (FAO estimate).

Forestry ('000 cu m, 1998): *Roundwood removals:* Sawlogs, veneer logs and logs for sleepers 108.0; Other industrial wood 131.6; Fuel wood 66.2; Total 305.8.

Sawnwood production: Total (incl. railway sleepers) 90 in 1998 (Source: FAO, *Yearbook of Forest Products*).

Fishing (metric tons, live weight, 1998): Inland waters 21.1 (Giant river prawn 21.1); Pacific Ocean 1,925.2 (Marine fishes 1,473.2, Shrimps 367.7, Other crustaceans and molluscs 84.3); Total catch 1,946.3.

MINING

Production (1998): Crude petroleum ('000 cu m) 8,329; Natural gas (million cu m) 10,751.

INDUSTRY

Production ('000 metric tons, unless otherwise indicated, 1998): Motor spirit (petrol) 187.6; Distillate fuel oils 147.8; Kerosene 76.5; Electric energy (million kWh) 1,528.5.

FINANCE

Currency and Exchange Rates: 100 sen (cents) = 1 Brunei dollar (B $). *Sterling, US Dollar and Euro Equivalents* (29 December 2000): £1 sterling = B $2.5837; US $1 = B $1.7315; €1 = B $1.6112; B $100 = £38.70 = US $57.75 = €62.07. *Average Exchange Rate* (Brunei dollars per US $): 1.6736 in 1998; 1.6950 in 1999; 1.7240 in 2000. Note: The Brunei dollar is at par with the Singapore dollar.

Budget (B $ million, 1997): *Revenue:* Tax revenue 1,561 (Import duty 224, Corporate income tax 1,333); Non-tax revenue 1,282 (Commercial receipts 303, Property income 957); Transfers from

Brunei Investment Agency 1,146; Total 3,989. *Expenditure:* Ordinary expenditure 2,564 (Prime Minister's Office 183, Defence 548, Foreign Affairs 116, Finance 502, Home Affairs 94, Education 347, Industry and Primary Resources 43, Religious Affairs 113, Development 286, Health 178); Other current expenditure 36; Capital expenditure 1,350; Investment in public enterprises by Brunei Investment Agency 67; Total 4,016.

(B $ million, 1998, estimates): *Revenue:* 2,775 (excl. transfers from Brunei Investment Agency); *Expenditure:* 4,295 (excl. investment by Brunei Investment Agency).

Source: IMF, *Brunei Darussalam: Recent Economic Developments* (April 1999).

Money Supply (B $ million, 1998): Currency in circulation 627.2; Demand deposits of private sector 1,637.6; Total money 2,264.8.

Cost of Living (Consumer Price Index; base: 1990 = 100): All items 120.8 in 1997; 120.3 in 1998 (Food 118.0; Clothing and footwear 127.2; Rent, fuel and power 110.4); 119.8 in 1999 (Food 117.3). Source: partly UN, *Monthly Bulletin of Statistics*.

Gross Domestic Product by Economic Activity (B $ million in current prices, 1998, provisional): Agriculture, hunting, forestry and fishing 231.9; Mining, quarrying and manufacturing 2,633.6; Electricity, gas and water 87.5; Construction 539.2; Trade, restaurants and hotels 1,049.0; Transport, storage and communications 422.4; Finance, insurance, real estate and business services 693.9; Community, social and personal services 2,673.1; *Sub-total* 8,330.7; *Less* Imputed bank service charge 219.7; *GDP in purchasers' values* 8,111.0.

Balance of Payments (US $ million, 1998, estimates): Exports of goods 1,894; Imports of goods –1,718; *Trade balance* 175; Exports of services 486; Imports of services –774; *Balance on goods and services* –112; Other income received 2,439; Other income paid –58; *Balance on goods, services and income* 2,269; Current transfers received 8; Current transfers paid –192; *Current balance* 2,085; Foreign investment (net) 151; Long-term capital (net) –2,610; Short-term capital (net) 376; *Overall balance* 3. Source: IMF, *Brunei Darussalam: Recent Economic Developments* (April 1999).

EXTERNAL TRADE

Principal Commodities: *Imports* (B $ million, 1997, estimates): Food and live animals 352; Beverages and tobacco 62; Crude materials (inedible) except fuels 108; Chemicals 201; Basic manufactures 804; Machinery and transport equipment 1,229; Miscellaneous manufactured articles 364; Total (incl. others) 3,154. *Exports* (US $ million, 1998): Mineral fuels and lubricants 2,043.3; Machinery and transport equipment 111.9; Miscellaneous manufactured articles 107.3; Total (incl. others) 2,306.9.

Principal Trading Partners (US $ million, 1998): *Imports:* Australia 58.2; People's Republic of China 23.0; France 18.9; Germany 49.6; Hong Kong 67.8; Indonesia 52.6; Italy 28.5; Japan 100.5; Republic of Korea 22.0; Malaysia 439.5; Netherlands 17.8; Singapore 355.4; United Kingdom 103.5; USA 235.2; Total (incl. others) 1,740.7. *Exports:* Japan 1,225.4; Republic of Korea 414.0; Malaysia 19.2; Singapore 180.0; Thailand 140.8; USA 210.4; Total (incl. others) 2,306.8.

Source: mainly UN, *International Trade Statistics Yearbook*.

TRANSPORT

Road Traffic (registered vehicles, 1998): Private cars 170,247, Goods vehicles 17,091, Motorcycles and scooters 6,386, Buses and taxis 2,016, Others 4,432.

Merchant Fleet (displacement, '000 grt at 31 December): 368.9 in 1996; 368.6 in 1997; 361.9 in 1998. Source: Lloyd's Register of Shipping, *World Fleet Statistics*.

International Sea-borne Shipping (freight traffic, '000 metric tons, 1998): Goods loaded (excl. petroleum and gas) 25.9; Goods unloaded 1,195.2; Registered boats 249.

Civil Aviation (1998): Passenger arrivals 490,700, passenger departures 489,900; freight loaded 1,494.4 metric tons, freight unloaded 5,749.5 metric tons; mail loaded 24.6 metric tons, mail unloaded 175.2 metric tons.

TOURISM

Visitor Arrivals by Nationality (1998): Australia 10,464; Cambodia 30,062; Japan 6,639; Malaysia 789,093; Nepal 5,939; Philippines 30,751; Singapore 23,718; Thailand 8,751; United Kingdom 31,500; USA 5,806; Total (incl. others) 964,080 (Source: Ministry of Industry and Primary Resources, Bandar Seri Begawan).

Tourist Receipts (US $ million): 37 in 1995; 38 in 1996; 39 in 1997 (Source: World Tourism Organization, *Yearbook of Tourism Statistics*).

COMMUNICATIONS MEDIA

Radio Receivers (1998, estimate): 329,000 in use.

Television Receivers (1998, estimate): 201,900 in use.

Telephones (1998): 79,800 direct exchange lines in use.

Telefax Stations (1996, estimate): 2,000 in use (Source: UN, *Statistical Yearbook*).

Mobile Cellular Telephones (1996): 43,524 subscribers (Source: UN, *Statistical Yearbook*).

Book Production (1992): 45 titles. (1990): 25 titles; 56,000 copies (Source: UNESCO, *Statistical Yearbook*).

Daily Newspaper (1998): 1 (estimated circulation 12,000 copies per issue).

Non-daily Newspapers (1998): 3 (estimated combined circulation 63,000 copies per issue).

Other Periodicals (1998): 15 (estimated combined circulation 132,000 copies per issue).

EDUCATION
(1998)

Pre-primary and Primary: 184 schools; 3,858 teachers; 58,548 pupils.

General Secondary: 38 schools; 2,636 teachers; 30,956 pupils.

Teacher Training: 1 college; 46 teachers; 568 pupils.

Vocational: 8 colleges; 470 teachers; 1,985 pupils.

Higher Education: 4 institutes (incl. 1 university); 370 teachers; 2,080 students.

Directory

The Constitution

Note: Certain sections of the Constitution relating to elections and the Legislative Council have been in abeyance since 1962.

A new Constitution was promulgated on 29 September 1959 (and amended significantly in 1971 and 1984). Under its provisions, sovereign authority is vested in the Sultan and Yang Di-Pertuan, who is assisted and advised by five Councils: the Religious Council, the Privy Council, the Council of Cabinet Ministers, the (inactive) Legislative Council and the Council of Succession. Power of appointment to the Councils is exercised by the Sultan.

The 1959 Constitution established the Chief Minister as the most senior official, with the British High Commissioner as adviser to the Government on all matters except those relating to Muslim and Malay customs.

In 1971 amendments were introduced reducing the power of the British Government, which retained responsibility for foreign affairs, while defence became the joint responsibility of both countries.

In 1984 further amendments were adopted as Brunei acceded to full independence and assumed responsibility for defence and foreign affairs.

THE RELIGIOUS COUNCIL

In his capacity as head of the Islamic faith in Brunei, the Sultan and Yang Di-Pertuan is advised on all Islamic matters by the Religious Council, whose members are appointed by the Sultan and Yang Di-Pertuan.

THE PRIVY COUNCIL

This Council, presided over by the Sultan and Yang Di-Pertuan, is to advise the Sultan on matters concerning the Royal prerogative of mercy, the amendment of the Constitution and the conferment of ranks, titles and honours.

THE COUNCIL OF MINISTERS

Presided over by the Sultan and Yang Di-Pertuan, the Council of Cabinet Ministers considers all executive matters.

THE LEGISLATIVE COUNCIL

The role of the Legislative Council is to scrutinize legislation. However, following political unrest in 1962, provisions of the Constitution relating, *inter alia*, to the Legislative Council were amended, and the Legislative Council has not met since 1984. In the absence of the Legislative Council, legislation is enacted by royal proclamation.

THE COUNCIL OF SUCCESSION

Subject to the Constitution, this Council is to determine the succession to the throne, should the need arise.

The State is divided into four administrative districts, in each of which is a District Officer responsible to the Prime Minister and Minister of Home Affairs.

The Government

HEAD OF STATE

Sultan and Yang Di-Pertuan: HM Sultan Haji HASSANAL BOLKIAH (succeeded 4 October 1967; crowned 1 August 1968).

COUNCIL OF CABINET MINISTERS
(April 2001)

Prime Minister, Minister of Defence and of Finance: HM Sultan Haji HASSANAL BOLKIAH.

Minister of Foreign Affairs: HRH Prince MOHAMED BOLKIAH.

Minister of Home Affairs and Special Adviser to the Prime Minister: Pehin Dato' Haji ISA BIN Pehin Haji IBRAHIM.

Minister of Education and Acting Minister of Health: Pehin Dato' Haji ABDUL AZIZ BIN Pehin Haji UMAR.

Minister of Industry and Primary Resources: Dato' Haji ABDUL RAHMAN TAIB.

Minister of Religious Affairs: Pehin Dato' Dr Haji MOHAMAD ZAIN BIN Haji SERUDIN.

Minister of Development: Pengiran Dato' Dr Haji ISMAIL BIN Haji DAMIT.

Minister of Culture, Youth and Sports: Pehin Dato' Haji HUSSEIN BIN Pehin Haji MOHAMAD YOSOF.

Minister of Communications: Pehin Dato' Haji ZAKARIA BIN Haji SULEIMAN.

There are, in addition, eight deputy ministers.

MINISTRIES

Office of the Prime Minister (Jabatan Perdana Menteri): Istana Nurul Iman, Bandar Seri Begawan BA 1000; tel. (2) 229988; fax (2) 241717; e-mail info@jpm.gov.bn; internet www.pmo.gov.bn.

Ministry of Communications (Kementerian Perhubungan): Jalan Menteri Besar, Bandar Seri Begawan BB 3910; tel. (2) 383838; fax (2) 380127; e-mail info@mincom.gov.bn; internet www .mincom.gov.bn.

Ministry of Culture, Youth and Sports (Kementerian Kebudayaan, Belia dan Sukan): Simpang 336, Jalan Kebangsaan, Bandar Seri Begawan BC 4415; tel. (2) 380911; fax (2) 380653; e-mail info@kkbs.gov.bn.

Ministry of Defence (Kementerian Pertahanan): Bolkiah Garrison, Bandar Seri Begawan BB 3510; tel. (2) 386000; fax (2) 382110; e-mail info@mindef.gov.bn.

Ministry of Development (Kementerian Pembangunan): Old Airport Rd, Jalan Berakas, Bandar Seri Begawan 1190; tel. (2) 241911; e-mail info@mod.gov.bn.

Ministry of Education (Kementerian Pendidikan): Old Airport, Jalan Berakas, Bandar Seri Begawan BB 3510; tel. (2) 382233; fax (2) 380050; e-mail info@moe.gov.bn.

Ministry of Finance (Kementerian Kewangan): Bandar Seri Begawan 1130; tel. (2) 241991; fax (2) 226132; e-mail info@finance .gov.bn.

Ministry of Foreign Affairs (Kementerian Hal Ehwal Luar Negeri): Jalan Subok, Bandar Seri Begawan BD 2710; tel. (2) 261177; fax (2) 262904; e-mail info@mfa.gov.bn.

Ministry of Health (Kementerian Kesihatan): Jalan Menteri Besar, Bandar Seri Begawan BB 3910; tel. (2) 226640; fax (2) 240980; e-mail moh2@brunet.bn.

Ministry of Home Affairs (Kementerian Hal Ehwal Dalam Negeri): Bandar Seri Begawan 1140; tel. (2) 223225; e-mail info@home-affairs.gov.bn.

Ministry of Industry and Primary Resources (Kementerian Perindustrian dan Sumber-sumber Utama): Jalan Menteri Besar, Bandar Seri Begawan BB 3910; tel. (2) 382822; fax (2) 244811; e-mail MIPRS2@brunet.bn.

Ministry of Religious Affairs (Kementerian Hal Ehwal Ugama): Jalan Menteri Besar, Jalan Berakas, Bandar Seri Begawan BB 3910; tel. (2) 382525; fax (2) 382330; e-mail info@religious-affairs.gov.bn.

Political Organizations

Parti Perpaduan Kebangsaan Brunei—PPKB (Brunei National Solidarity Party—BNSP): Bandar Seri Begawan; f. 1986, after split in PKDB (see below); ceased political activity in 1988, but re-emerged in 1995; Pres. HATTA ZAINAL ABIDIN.

Former political organizations included: **Parti Rakyat Brunei—PRB** (Brunei People's Party), banned in 1962, leaders are all in exile; **Barisan Kemerdeka'an Rakyat—BAKER** (People's Independence Front), f. 1966 but no longer active; **Parti Perpaduan Kebangsaan Rakyat Brunei—PERKARA** (Brunei People's National United Party), f. 1968 but no longer active, and **Parti Kebangsaan Demokratik Brunei—PKDB** (Brunei National Democratic Party—BNDP), f. 1985 and dissolved by government order in 1988.

Diplomatic Representation

EMBASSIES AND HIGH COMMISSIONS IN BRUNEI

Australia: Teck Guan Plaza, 4th Floor, Jalan Sultan, Bandar Seri Begawan BS 8811; tel. (2) 229435; fax (2) 221652; High Commissioner: DOUG CHESTER.

Bangladesh: AAR Villa, 5 Simpang 308, Kampong Lambak Kanan, Jalan Berakas, Bandar Seri Begawan BB 1714; tel. (2) 394716; fax (2) 394715; High Commissioner: MUHAMMAD MUMDAZ HUSSAIN.

Canada: 5th Floor, Jalan McArthur Bldg, 1 Jalan McArthur, Bandar Seri Begawan BS 8711; tel. (2) 220043; fax (2) 220040; e-mail hicomcda@brunet.bn; High Commissioner: NEIL REEDER.

China, People's Republic: 1, 3 & 5, Simpang 462, Kampong Sungai Hanching, Jalan Muara, Bandar Seri Begawan BC 2115; tel. (2) 334163; e-mail embproc@brunet.bn; Ambassador: WANG JIANLI.

France: Kompleks Jalan Sultan, Units 308–310, 3rd Floor, 51–55 Jalan Sultan, Bandar Seri Begawan BS 8811; tel. (2) 220960; fax (2) 243373; e-mail france@brunet.bn; Ambassador: JEAN-PIERRE LAFOSSE.

Germany: Bangunan Yayasan Sultan Haji Hassanal Bolkiah, 2nd Floor, Jalan Pretty, Bandar Seri Begawan BS 8711; POB 3050, Bandar Seri Begawan BS 8711; tel. (2) 225547; fax (2) 225583; e-mail prgerman@brunet.bn; Ambassador: KLAUS PETER BRANDES.

India: Baitussyifaa, Simpang 40–42, Jalan Sungai Akar, Bandar Seri Begawan BC 3915; tel. (2) 339947; fax (2) 339783; e-mail hicomind@brunet.bn; High Commissioner: DINESH K. JAIN.

Indonesia: Simpang 528, Lot 4498 Jalan Sungai Hanching Baru, off Jalan Muara, Bandar Seri Begawan BC 3031; tel. (2) 330180; fax (2) 330646; Ambassador: KOESNADI POEDJIWINARTO.

Iran: 19 Simpang 477, Kampong Sungai Hanching, Jalan Muara, BC 2115 Bandar Seri Begawan; tel. (2) 330021; fax (2) 331744; Ambassador: JAVAD ANSARI.

Japan: 33 Lot 37355, Simpang 122, Kampong Kiulap, Bandar Seri Begawan; tel. (2) 229265; fax (2) 229481; Ambassador: SHIGENOBI YOSHIDA.

Korea, Republic: No. 9, Lot 21652, Simpang 623; Kampong Beribi, Jalan Gadong, Bandar Seri Begawan BE 1118; POB 2169, Bandar Seri Begawan 1921; tel. (2) 650471; fax (2) 650299; Ambassador: SA BOO-SUNG.

Laos: Lot 19824, 11 Simpang 480, Jalan Kebangsaan Lama, off Jalan Muara, Bandar Seri Begawan BC 4115; tel. (2) 345666; fax (2) 345888; Ambassador: Dr AMMONE SINGHAVONG.

Malaysia: 27–29 Simpang 396–39, Lot 9075, Kampong Sungai Akar, Mukim Berakas B, Jalan Kebangsaan, POB 2826, Bandar Seri Begawan BC 4115; tel. (2) 345652; fax (2) 345654; High Commissioner: WAN YUSOF EMBONG.

Myanmar: 14 Lot 2185/46292, Simpang 212, Jalan Kampong Rimba, Gadong, Bandar Seri Begawan BE 3119; tel. (2) 450506; fax (2) 451008; Ambassador: U THAN TUN.

Oman: 35, Simpang 100, Kampong Pengkalan, Jalan Tungku Link, Gadong, Bandar Seri Begawan BE 3719; tel. (2) 446953; fax (2) 449646; e-mail omnembsb@brunet.bn; Ambassador: AHMAD BIN MOHAMMED AL-RIYAMI.

Pakistan: No. 6, Simpang 23, Kampong Serusop, Muara Berakas, POB 3026, Bandar Seri Begawan BB 2313; tel. (2) 339797; fax (2) 334990; e-mail lateef@brunet.com; High Commissioner: ABDUL LATEEF (acting).

Philippines: Room 1, 4th & 6th Floors, Badiah Bldg, Mile 1, Jalan Tutong, Bandar Seri Begawan BNA 2111; tel. (2) 241465; fax (2) 237707; e-mail bruneipe@brunet.bn; Ambassador: ENRIQUE A. ZALDIVAR.

Saudi Arabia: 1, Simpang 570, Kampong Salar, Muara, Bandar Seri Begawan BT 2528; tel. (2) 792821; fax (2) 792826; Ambassador: (vacant).

Singapore: RBA Plaza, 5th Floor, Jalan Sultan, Bandar Seri Begawan BS 8811; tel. (2) 227583; fax (2) 220957; High Commissioner: ANTHONY CH'NG CHYE TONG.

Thailand: No. 2, Simpang 682, Jalan Tutong, Kampong Bunut, Bandar Seri Begawan BF 1320; tel. (2) 653108; fax (2) 653032; Ambassador: MAITRI CHULADUL.

United Kingdom: Unit 2.01, Block D, Bangunan Yayasan Sultan Haji Hassanal Bolkiah, 2nd Floor, Jalan Pretty, Bandar Seri Begawan BS 8711; POB 2197, Bandar Seri Begawan BS 8674; tel. (2) 222231; fax (2) 226002; e-mail brithc@brunet.bn; internet www.britain-brunei.org.bn; High Commissioner: STUART LAING.

USA: Teck Guan Plaza, 3rd Floor, Jalan Sultan, Bandar Seri Begawan BS 8811; tel. (2) 229670; fax (2) 225293; Ambassador: GLEN ROBERT RASE.

Viet Nam: No. 10, Simpang 485, Kampong Sungai Hanching, Jalan Muara, Bandar Seri Begawan BC 2115; tel. (2) 343167; fax (2) 343169; Ambassador: NGUYEN NGOC DIEN.

Judicial System

SUPREME COURT

The Supreme Court consists of the Court of Appeal and the High Court. Syariah (Shari'a) courts coexist with the Supreme Court and deal with Islamic laws.

Supreme Court: Km 1½, Jalan Tutong, Bandar Seri Begawan BA 2056; tel. (2) 225853; fax (2) 241984; e-mail supcourt@brunet.bn.

Chief Registrar: Datin Paduka HAYATI SALLEH.

The Court of Appeal: composed of the President and two Commissioners appointed by the Sultan. The Court of Appeal considers criminal and civil appeals against the decisions of the High Court and the Intermediate Court. The Court of Appeal is the highest appellate court for criminal cases. In civil cases an appeal may be referred to the Judicial Committee of Her Majesty's Privy Council in London if all parties agree to do so before the hearing of the appeal in the Brunei Court of Appeal.

President: Dato' Seri Paduka KUTLU TEKIN FUAD.

The High Court: composed of the Chief Justice and judges sworn in by the Sultan as Commissioners of the Supreme Court. In its appellate jurisdiction, the High Court considers appeals in criminal and civil matters against the decisions of the Subordinate Courts. The High Court has unlimited original jurisdiction in criminal and civil matters.

Chief Justice: Dato' Seri Paduka Sir DENYS TUDOR EMIL ROBERTS.

OTHER COURTS

Intermediate Courts: have jurisdiction to try all offences other than those punishable by the death sentence and civil jurisdiction to try all actions and suits of a civil nature where the amount in dispute or value of the subject/matter does not exceed B $100,000.

The Subordinate Courts: presided over by the Chief Magistrate and magistrates, with limited original jurisdiction in civil and criminal matters and civil jurisdiction to try all actions and suits of a civil nature where the amount in dispute does not exceed B $50,000 (for Chief Magistrate) and B $30,000 (for magistrates).

Chief Magistrate: HAIROLARNI Haji ABDUL MAJID.

The Courts of Kathis: deal solely with questions concerning Islamic religion, marriage and divorce. Appeals lie from these courts to the Sultan in the Religious Council.

Chief Kathi: Dato' Seri Setia Haji SALIM BIN Haji BESAR.

Attorney-General: KIFRAWI BIN Dato' Paduka Haji KIFLI; Attorney-General's Chambers, Office of the Prime Minister, Bandar Seri Begawan 1160; tel. (2) 244872; fax (2) 241428.

Solicitor-General: MAGDELENE CHONG.

Religion

The official religion of Brunei is Islam, and the Sultan is head of the Islamic community. The majority of the Malay population are Muslims of the Shafi'is school of the Sunni sect; at the 1991 census Muslims accounted for 67.2% of the total population. The Chinese population is either Buddhist (accounting for 12.8% of the total population at the 1991 census), Confucianist, Daoist or Christian. Large numbers of the indigenous ethnic groups practise traditional animist forms of religion. The remainder of the population are mostly Christians, generally Roman Catholics, Anglicans or members of the American Methodist Church of Southern Asia. At the 1991 census Christians accounted for 10.0% of the total population.

ISLAM

Supreme Head of Islam: Sultan and Yang Di-Pertuan.

CHRISTIANITY

The Anglican Communion

Within the Church of the Province of South East Asia, Brunei forms part of the diocese of Kuching (Malaysia).

The Roman Catholic Church

Brunei became an apostolic prefecture on 21 November 1997; at December 1998 an estimated 6.7% of the population were adherents.

Prefect Apostolic: Rev. CORNELIUS SIM, St John's Church, POB 53, Kuala Belait KA 1131; tel. (3) 334207; fax (3) 342817; e-mail frcsim@brunet.bn.

The Press

NEWSPAPERS

Borneo Bulletin: Locked Bag No. 2, MPC (Old Airport Rd, Berakas), Bandar Seri Begawan 3799; tel. (2) 451468; fax (2) 451461; f. 1953; daily; English; independent; owned by QAF Group; Editor CHARLES REX DE SILVA; circ. 25,000.

Brunei Darussalam Newsletter: Dept of Information, Prime Minister's Office, Istana Nurul Iman, Bandar Seri Begawan BA 1000; tel. (2) 229988; fortnightly; English; govt newspaper; distributed free; circ. 14,000.

Daily News Digest: Dept of Information, Prime Minister's Office, Istana Nurul Iman, Bandar Seri Begawan BA 1000; English; govt newspaper.

News Express: Bandar Seri Begawan; f. 1999; daily; English; Propr PETER WONG; Eidtor-in-Chief R. NADESWARAN.

Pelita Brunei: Dept of Information, Prime Minister's Office, Istana Nurul Iman, Bandar Seri Begawan BA 1000; tel. (2) 229988; fax (2) 225942; f. 1956; weekly (Wed.); Malay; govt newspaper; distributed free; Editor TIMBANG BIN BAKAR; circ. 45,000.

Salam: c/o Brunei Shell Petroleum Co Sdn Bhd, Seria 7082; tel. (3) 4184; fax (3) 4189; f. 1953; monthly; Malay and English; distributed free to employees of the Brunei Shell Petroleum Co Sdn Bhd; circ. 46,000.

Publishers

Borneo Printers & Trading Sdn Bhd: POB 2211, Bandar Seri Begawan BS 8674; tel. (2) 651387; fax (2) 654342; e-mail bptl@ brunet.bn.

Brunei Press Sdn Bhd: Lots 8 and 11, Perindustrian Beribi II, Jalan Gadong, Bandar Seri Begawan BE 1118; tel. (2) 451468; fax (2) 451460; e-mail brupress@jtb.brunet.bn; internet web3.asia1.com .sg/borneo; f. 1953; Gen. Man. REGGIE SEE.

Capital Trading & Printing Pte Ltd: POB 1089, Bandar Seri Begawan; tel. (2) 244541.

Leong Bros: 52 Jalan Bunga Kuning, POB 164, Seria; tel. (3) 22381.

Offset Printing House: POB 1111, Bandar Seri Begawan; tel. (2) 224477.

The Star Press: Bandar Seri Begawan; f. 1963; Man. F. W. ZIMMERMAN.

Government Publishing House

Government Printer: Government Printing Department, Office of the Prime Minister, Bandar Seri Begawan BB 3510; tel. (2) 382541; fax (2) 381141; e-mail info@printing.gov.bn; Dir WAHID Haji SALLEH.

Broadcasting and Communications

TELECOMMUNICATIONS

DST Communications Sdn Bhd: Block D, Yayasan Sultan Haji Hassanal Bolkiah Kompleks, Bandar Seri Begawan; tel. (2) 232323; mobile service provider.

Jabatan Telecom Brunei (Department of Telecommunications of Brunei): Ministry of Communications, Jalan Berakas, Bandar Seri Begawan BB 3510; tel. (2) 382382; fax (2) 382445; Dir of Telecommunications BUNTAR BIN OSMAN.

BROADCASTING

Radio

Radio Televisyen Brunei (RTB): Prime Minister's Office, Jalan Elizabeth II, Bandar Seri Begawan BS 8610; tel. (2) 243111; fax (2) 241882; e-mail rtbdir@brunet.bn; internet www.rtb.gov.bn; f. 1957; five radio networks: four broadcasting in Malay, the other in English, Chinese (Mandarin) and Gurkhali; Dir Pengiran Dato' Paduka Haji ISMAIL BIN Pengiran Haji MOHAMED.

The British Forces Broadcasting Service (Military) broadcasts a 24-hour radio service to a limited area.

Television

Radio Televisyen Brunei (RTB): Prime Minister's Office, Jalan Elizabeth II, Bandar Seri Begawan BS 8610; tel. (2) 243111; fax (2) 227204; f. 1957; programmes in Malay and English; a satellite service relays RTB television programmes to the South-East Asian region for nine hours per day; Dir Pengiran Dato' Paduka Haji ISMAIL BIN Pengiran Haji MOHAMED.

Finance

BANKING

The Department of Financial Services (Treasury), the Brunei Currency Board and the Brunei Investment Agency (see Government Agencies, below), under the Ministry of Finance, perform most of the functions of a central bank.

Commercial Banks

Baiduri Bank Bhd: 145 Jalan Pemancha, POB 2220, Bandar Seri Begawan BS 8674; tel (2) 233233; fax (2) 237575; e-mail baiduri@brunet.bn; internet www.baiduri.com; Gen. Man. LUC ROUSSELET; 6 brs.

Islamic Bank of Brunei Bhd: Lot 159, Bangunan IBB, Jalan Pemancha, POB 2725, Bandar Seri Begawan BS 8711; tel. (2) 235686; fax (2) 235722; e-mail ibb@brunet.bn; f. 1981 as Island Development Bank; name changed from International Bank of Brunei Bhd to present name in January 1993; practises Islamic banking principles; Chair. Haji ABDUL RAHMAN BIN Haji ABDUL KARIM; Man. Dir Haji ZAINASALLEHEN BIN Haji MOHAMED TAHIR; 10 brs.

Islamic Development Bank of Brunei Bhd: Ground–4th Floor, Kompleks Setia Kenangan, Kampong Kiulap, Jalan Gadong, Bandar Seri Begawan BE 1518; tel. (2) 233430; fax (2) 233429; e-mail dbb@brunet.bn; f. 1995 as Development Bank of Brunei Bhd; name changed to present in July 2000; practises Islamic banking principles; Man. Dir Dayangku Hajah URAI Pengiran ALI; 1 br.

Foreign Banks

Citibank NA (USA): Darussalam Complex 12–15, Jalan Sultan, Bandar Seri Begawan BS 8811; tel. (2) 243983; fax (2) 237344; e-mail glen.rase@citicorp.com; Vice-Pres. and Country Head PAGE STOCKWELL; 1 br.

The Hongkong and Shanghai Banking Corpn Ltd (Hong Kong): Jalan Sultan, cnr Jalan Pemancha, Bandar Seri Begawan BS 8811; POB 59, Bandar Seri Begawan BS 8670; tel. (2) 242305; fax (2) 241316; e-mail hsbc@brunet.bn; internet www.hsbc.com; f. 1947; acquired assets of National Bank of Brunei in 1986; CEO WARNER G. N. MANNING; 10 brs.

Malayan Banking Bhd (Malaysia): 148 Jalan Pemancha, Bandar Seri Begawan BS 8811; tel. (2) 242494; fax (2) 226101; f. 1960; Branch Man. BURHAN BIN LASA; 2 brs.

Overseas Union Bank Ltd (Singapore): Unit G5, RBA Plaza, Jalan Sultan, Bandar Seri Begawan BS 8811; POB 2218, Bandar Seri Begawan BS 8674; tel. (2) 225477; fax (2) 240792; f. 1973; Vice-Pres. and Man. SAW BENG; 1 br.

RHB Bank Bhd (Malaysia): Unit G02, Block D, Bangunan Yayasan Sultan Haji Hassanal Bolkiah, Ground Floor, Jalan Pretty, Bandar Seri Begawan BS 8711; tel. (2) 222515; fax (2) 237487; fmrly Sime Bank Bhd; Branch Man. SHAFIK YUSSOF; 1 br.

Standard Chartered Bank (United Kingdom): 51–55 Jalan Sultan, Bandar Seri Begawan BS 8811; POB 186, Bandar Seri Begawan BS 8670; tel. (2) 242386; fax (2) 242390; f. 1958; CEO DAVID KNIGHT; 10 brs.

INSURANCE

In 1998 there were 18 general, three life and two composite (takaful) insurance companies operating in Brunei, including:

General Companies

AGF Insurance (S) Pte Ltd: c/o A&S Associates Sdn Bhd, Bangunan Gadong Properties, 03-01, Jalan Gadong, Bandar Seri Begawan BE 4119; tel. (2) 420766; fax (2) 440279; Man. SEBASTIAN TAN.

The Asia Insurance Co Ltd: Unit A1 & A2, 1st Floor, Block A, Bangunan Hau Man Yong Complex, Simpang 88, Kg. Kiulap BE 1518, POB 2226, Bandar Seri Begawan BS 8674; tel. (2) 236108; fax (2) 236102; Man. DAVID WONG KOK MIN.

BALGI Insurance (B) Sdn Bhd: Unit 13, Kompleks Haji Tahir II, 1st Floor, Jalan Gadong, Bandar Seri Begawan BE 4119; tel. (2) 422736; fax (2) 445204; Man. Dir PATRICK SIM SONG JUAY.

Borneo Insurance Sdn Bhd: Unit 103, Bangunan Kambang Pasang, Km 2, Jalan Gadong, Bandar Seri Begawan BE 4119; tel. (2) 420550; fax (2) 428550; Man. LIM TECK LEE.

CGU Insurance Berhad: Unit 311, 3rd Floor, Kompleks Mohamad Yussof, Km 4, Jalan Tutong, Bandar Seri Begawan BA 1712; tel. (2) 223632; fax (2) 220965; e-mail cgu@brunet.bn; Man. PETER SHAK.

Citystate Insurance Pte Ltd: c/o Dominic Choong & Sons, Bangunan Guru-Guru Melayu Brunei, 3rd Floor, Jalan Kianggeh, Bandar Seri Begawan BS 8711; tel. (2) 242361; fax (2) 226203; Man. BETTY CHOONG.

Commercial Union Assurance (M) Sdn Bhd: c/o Jasra Harrisons Sdn Bhd, Jalan McArthur, cnr Jalan Kianggeh, Bandar Seri Begawan BS 8711; tel. (2) 242361; fax (2) 226203; Man. WHITTY LIM.

Cosmic Insurance Corpn Sdn Bhd: Block J, Unit 11, Abdul Razak Complex, 1st Floor, Jalan Gadong, Bandar Seri Begawan BE 3919; tel. (2) 427112; fax (2) 427114; Man. RONNIE WONG.

GRE Insurance (B) Sdn Bhd: Unit 608, 6th Floor, Jalan Sultan Complex, 51-55 Jalan Sultan, Bandar Seri Begawan BS 8811; tel. (2) 226138; fax (2) 243474; Man. MOK HAI TONG.

ING General Insurance International NV: Shop Lot 86, 2nd Floor, Jalan Bunga Raya, Kuala Belait 6082; tel. (3) 335338; fax (3) 335338; Man. SHERRY SOON PECK ENG.

Malaysia National Insurance Bhd: No 9, Bangunan Haji Mohd Salleh Simpang 103, 1st Floor, Jalan Gadong, Bandar Seri Begawan BE 4119; tel. (2) 443393; fax (2) 427451; Man. ROBERT LAI CHIN YIN.

MBA Insurance Co Sdn Bhd: 7 Bangunan Hasbullah I, 1st Floor, Km 4, Jalan Gadong, Bandar Seri Begawan BE 3519; tel. (2) 441535; fax (2) 441534; e-mail cheahmbabrunei@brunet.bn; Man. CHEAH LYE CHONG.

Motor and General Insurance Sdn Bhd: 6 Bangunan Hasbullah II, Km 4, Jalan Gadong, Bandar Seri Begawan BE 3919; tel. (2) 440797; fax (2) 420336; Man. Dir Haji ABDUL AZIZ BIN ABDUL LATIF.

National Insurance Co Bhd: 6th Floor, Wisma Raya, Jalan Sultan, Bandar Seri Begawan BS 8811; tel. (2) 226555; fax (2) 227496; e-mail national@brunet.bn; Dep. Man. TIMOTHY ONG.

The Royal Insurance (Global) Ltd: c/o H C Lau & Sons, Khoon Foh Bldg, Bangunan Maju, Jalan Bunga Raya, Kuala Belait KA 1131; tel. (3) 334599; fax (3) 334671; Gen. Man. TOMMY LEONG TONG KAW.

South East Asia Insurance (B) Sdn Bhd: Unit 2, Block A, Abdul Razak Complex, 1st Floor, Jalan Gadong, Bandar Seri Begawan BE 3919; tel. (2) 443842; fax (2) 420860; Man. BILLINGS TEO.

Standard Insurance (B) Sdn Bhd: 11 Bangunan Hasbullah II, Ground Floor, Bandar Seri Begawan BE 3919; tel. and fax (2) 445348; Man. PAUL KONG.

Winterthur Insurance (Far East) Pte Ltd: c/o Borneo Co (B) Sdn Bhd, Lot 9771, Km 3½, Jalan Gadong, Bandar Seri Begawan BE 4119; tel. (2) 422561; fax (2) 424352; Man. HII CHANG WOO.

Life Companies

American International Assurance Co Ltd: Unit 509A, Wisma Jaya Building, 5th Floor, No 85/94, Jalan Pemancha, Bandar Seri Begawan BS 8511; tel. (2) 239112; fax (2) 221667; Man. PHILIP TAN.

The Asia Life Assurance Society Ltd: Unit 2, Block D, Abdul Razak Complex, Gadong, Bandar Seri Begawan BE 4119; tel. (2) 423755; fax (2) 423754; e-mail brunei@asialife.com.sg; Exec. Officer PATRICIA CHIN YUNG YIN.

The Great Eastern Life Assurance Co Ltd: Suite 1, Badi'ah Complex, 2nd Floor, Jalan Tutong, Bandar Seri Begawan BA 2111; tel. (2) 243792; fax (2) 225754; Man. HELEN YEO.

Takaful (Composite Insurance) Companies

Syarikat Insurans Islam TAIB Sdn Bhd: Bangunan Pusat Komersil dan Perdagangan Bumiputera, Ground Floor, Jalan Cator, Bandar Seri Begawan BS 8811; tel. (2) 237724; fax (2) 237729; Man. Dir Haji MOHAMED ROSELAN BIN Haji MOHAMED DAUD.

Takaful IBB Bhd: Unit 5, Block A, Kiarong Complex, Lebuhraya Sultan Hassanal Bolkiah, Bandar Seri Begawan BE 1318; tel. (2) 451804; fax (2) 451808; e-mail takaful@brunet.bn; f. 1993; Man. Dir Haji MUSIB Haji MOHD YUSOF.

Trade and Industry

GOVERNMENT AGENCIES

Brunei Currency Board: c/o Ministry of Finance, Secretariat Bldg, POB 660, Bandar Seri Begawan BS 8670; tel. (2) 222095; fax (2) 241559; e-mail bcb@brunet.bn; f. 1967; maintains control of currency circulation; Dir Dato' YAAKUB BIN ABU BAKAR.

Brunei Darussalam Economic Council (BDEC): Bandar Seri Begawan; internet www.brudirect.com/BruneiInfo/info/BD_EconomicCouncil.htm; f. 1998; convened to examine the economic situation in Brunei and to recommend short- and long-term measures designed to revitalize the economy; Chair. HRH Prince MOHAMED BOLKIAH.

Brunei Investment Agency: Ministry of Finance, Bandar Seri Begawan 1130; f. 1973; Chair. YAHYA BAKAR.

Brunei Oil and Gas Authority: Bandar Seri Begawan; f. 1993 to oversee the hydrocarbons sector; Chair. Minister of Finance.

DEVELOPMENT ORGANIZATIONS

Brunei Industrial Development Authority (BINA): Ministry of Industry and Primary Resources, Jalan Gadong, BE 1118 Bandar Seri Begawan; tel. (2) 444100; fax (2) 423300; e-mail binal1@brunet.bn; f. 1996: Dir Haji RAZALI MOHD YUSSOF.

Brunei Islamic Trust Fund (Tabung Amanah Islam Brunei): Bandar Seri Begawan; f. 1991; promotes trade and industry.

Industrial and Trade Development Council: Bandar Seri Begawan; facilitates the industrialization of Brunei; Chair. Minister of Industry and Primary Resources.

Semaun Holdings Sdn Bhd: Unit 2.02, Block D, 2nd Floor, Yayasan Sultan Haji Hassanal Bolkiah Complex, Jalan Pretty, Bandar Seri Begawan BS 8711; tel. (2) 232950; e-mail semaun@brunet.bn; internet www.semaun.gov.bn; promotes industrial and commercial development through direct investment in key industrial sectors; 100% govt-owned; the board of directors is composed of ministers and senior govt officials; Chair. Minister of Industry and Primary Resources; Man. Dir Haji KAMIS Haji TAMIN (acting).

CHAMBERS OF COMMERCE

Brunei Darussalam International Chamber of Commerce and Industry: POB 2246, Bandar Seri Begawan 8674; tel. (2) 236601;

fax (2) 228382; Chair. SULAIMAN Haji AHAI; Sec. Haji SHAZALI BIN Dato' Haji SULAIMAN; 108 mems.

Brunei Malay Chamber of Commerce and Industry: Unit 15, First Floor, Bangunan Halimadul Saadiah, Jalan Gadong, Bandar Seri Begawan BE 3519; POB 1099, Bandar Seri Begawan BS 8672; tel. (2) 422752; fax (2) 422753; f. 1964; Pres. Dato' A. A. HAPIDZ; 160 mems.

Chinese Chamber of Commerce: Chinese Chamber of Commerce Bldg, 72 Jalan Roberts, Bandar Seri Begawan; POB 281, Bandar Seri Begawan BS 8670; tel. (2) 235494; fax (2) 235492; Chair. LIM ENG MING.

National Chamber of Commerce and Industry of Brunei Darussalam: Unit 10–14, 1st Floor, Bangunan Halimadul Saadiah, Jalan Gadong, Bandar Seri Begawan 2086; POB 1099, Bandar Seri Begawan BE 3519; POB 1099, Bandar Seri Begawan BS 8672; tel. (2) 440898; fax (2) 422998.

HYDROCARBON COMPANIES

Brunei LNG Sdn Bhd: Lumut KC 2935, Seria; tel. (3) 378125; fax (3) 236919; e-mail hamdillah.b.wahab@shell.com.bn; f. 1969; natural gas liquefaction; owned jointly by the Brunei Govt, Shell and Mitsubishi Corpn; operates LNG plant at Lumut, which has a capacity of 7.2m. tons per year; merged with Brunei Coldgas Sdn Bhd in 1995; Exec. Dir H. A. W. HAMDILLAH.

Brunei Shell Marketing Co Bhd: Maya Puri Bldg, 36/37 Jalan Sultan, POB 385, Bandar Seri Begawan; tel. (2) 25739; fax (2) 240470; f. 1978 (from the Shell Marketing Co of Brunei Ltd), when the Govt became equal partner with Shell; markets petroleum and chemical products throughout Brunei; Marketing Man. HAMIDON Haji ABD LATIF.

Brunei Shell Petroleum Co Sdn Bhd: Seria 7082; tel. (3) 73999; fax (3) 72883; f. 1957; the largest industrial concern in the country; 50% state holding; petroleum output 150,000 barrels per day (1989); Man. Dir GEORGE INNES.

Jasra International Petroleum Sdn Bhd: RBA Plaza, 2nd floor, Jalan Sultan, Bandar Seri Begawan; tel. (2) 228968; fax (2) 228929; petroleum exploration and production; Man. Dir ROBERT A. HARRISON.

TRADE UNIONS

Brunei Government Junior Officers' Union: Bandar Seri Begawan; tel. (2) 241911; Pres. Haji ALI BIN Haji NASAR; Gen. Sec. Haji OMARALI BIN Haji MOHIDDIN.

Brunei Government Medical and Health Workers' Union: Bandar Seri Begawan; Pres. Pengiran Haji MOHIDDIN BIN Pengiran TAJUDDIN; Gen. Sec. HANAFI BIN ANAI.

Brunei Oilfield Workers' Union: XDR/11, BSP Co Sdn Bhd, Seria KB 3534; f. 1964; 470 mems; Pres. SUHAINI Haji OTHMAN; Sec.-Gen. ABU TALIB BIN Haji MOHAMAD.

Royal Brunei Custom Department Staff Union: Badan Sukan dan Kebajikan Kastam, Royal Brunei Customs and Excise, Kuala Belait KA 1131; tel. (3) 334248; fax (3) 334626; Chair. Haji MOHD DELI BAKAR; Sec. HAMZAH Haji ABD. HAMID.

Transport

RAILWAYS

There are no public railways in Brunei. The Brunei Shell Petroleum Co Sdn Bhd maintains a 19.3-km section of light railway between Seria and Badas.

ROADS

In 1997 there were 2,693 km of roads in Brunei, comprising 1,945 km with a bituminous or concrete surface, 588 km surfaced with gravel and 160 km passable only in dry conditions. The main highway connects Bandar Seri Begawan, Tutong and Kuala Belait. A 59-km coastal road links Muara and Tutong.

Land Transport Department: 451979 Km 6, Jalan Gadong, Beribi, Bandar Seri Begawan BE 1110; tel. (2) 451979; fax (2) 424775; e-mail latis@brunet.bn; Dir Haji HAMIDON BIN Haji MOHD TAHIR.

SHIPPING

Most sea traffic is handled by a deep-water port at Muara, 28 km from the capital, which has a 611-m wharf and a draught of 8 m. The port has a container terminal, warehousing, freezer facilities and cement silos. In October 2000 a plan to deepen the port to enable its accommodation of larger vessels was announced. The original, smaller port at Bandar Seri Begawan itself is mainly used for local river-going vessels, for vessels to Malaysian ports in Sabah and Sarawak and for vessels under 30 m in length. There is a port at Kuala Belait, which takes shallow-draught vessels and serves mainly the Shell petroleum field and Seria. Owing to the shallow waters at Seria, tankers are unable to come up to the shore to load, and crude petroleum from the oil terminal is pumped through an underwater loading line to a single buoy mooring, to which the tankers are moored. At Lumut there is a 4.5-km jetty for liquefied natural gas (LNG) carriers.

Four main rivers, with numerous tributaries, are an important means of communication in the interior, and boats or water taxis the main form of transport for most residents of the water villages. Larger water taxis operate daily to the Temburong district.

Bee Seng Shipping Co: 7, Block D, Sufri Complex, Km 2, Jalan Tutong, POB 92, Bandar Seri Begawan; tel. (2) 220033; fax (2) 224495.

Belait Shipping Co (B) Sdn Bhd: B1, 2nd Floor, 94 Jalan McKerron, Kuala Belait 6081; POB 632, Kuala Belait; tel. (3) 335418; fax (3) 330239; f. 1977; Man. Dir Haji FATIMAH BINTE Haji ABDUL AZIZ.

Brunei Shell Tankers Sdn Bhd: Seria KB 3534; tel. (3) 373999; f. 1986; vessels operated by Shell International Trading and Shipping Co Ltd; Man. Dir CHRIS FINLAYSON.

Harper Wira Sdn Bhd: B2 Bangunan Haji Mohd Yussof, Jalan Gadong, Bandar Seri Begawan 3188; tel. (2) 448529; fax (2) 448529.

Inchcape Borneo: Bangunan Inchcape Borneo, Km 4, Jalan Gadong, Bandar Seri Begawan; tel. (2) 422561; fax (2) 424352; f. 1856; Dir LO FAN KEE.

New Island Shipping: Unit 5, 1st Floor, Block C, Kiarong Complex, Jalan Kiarong, Bandar Seri Begawan 3186; POB 850, Bandar Seri Begawan 1908; tel. (2) 451800; fax (2) 451480; f. 1975; Chair. TAN KOK VOON; Man. JIMMY VOON.

Pansar Co Sdn Bhd: Muara Port; tel. (2) 445246; fax (2) 445247.

Seatrade Shipping Co: Muara Port; tel. (2) 421457; fax (2) 421453.

Silver Line (B) Sdn Bhd: Muara Port; tel. (2) 445069; fax (2) 430276.

Wei Tat Shipping and Trading Co: Mile 4½, Jalan Tutong, POB 103, Bandar Seri Begawan; tel. 65215.

CIVIL AVIATION

There is an international airport near Bandar Seri Begawan, which can handle up to 1.5m. passengers and 50,000 metric tons of cargo a year. The Brunei Shell Petroleum Co Sdn Bhd operates a private airfield at Anduki for helicopter services.

Department of Civil Aviation: Brunei International Airport, Bandar Seri Begawan BB 2513; tel. (2) 330142; fax (2) 331706; Dir Haji KASIM BIN Haji LATIP.

Royal Brunei Airlines Ltd: RBA Plaza, POB 737, Bandar Seri Begawan 1907; tel. (2) 240500; fax (2) 244737; internet www .bruneiair.com; f. 1974; operates services within the Far East and to the Middle East, Australia and Europe; Chair. Dato' Paduka Awang Haji ALIMIN WAHAB; Exec. Dir Pengiran ALI Pengiran Haji AHMAD.

Tourism

Tourist attractions in Brunei include the flora and fauna of the rainforest and the national parks, as well as mosques and water villages. There were 964,080 foreign visitor arrivals (including same-day visitors) in 1998. In 1997 international tourist receipts totalled US $39m. The year 2001 was designated 'Visit Brunei Year'.

Brunei Tourism: c/o Ministry of Industry and Primary Resources, Jalan Menteri Besar, Bandar Seri Begawan BB 3910; tel. (2) 382822; fax (2) 383811; internet www.visitbrunei.com; Dir-Gen. Sheikh JAMALUDDIN BIN Sheikh MOHAMED.

BULGARIA

Introductory Survey

Location, Climate, Language, Religion, Flag, Capital

The Republic of Bulgaria lies in the eastern Balkans, in south-eastern Europe. It is bounded by Romania to the north, by Turkey and Greece to the south, by Yugoslavia (Serbia) to the west and by the former Yugoslav republic of Macedonia to the south-west. The country has an eastern coastline on the Black Sea. The climate is one of fairly sharp contrasts between winter and summer. Temperatures in Sofia are generally between–5°C (23°F) and 28°C (82°F). The official language is Bulgarian, a member of the Slavonic group, written in the Cyrillic alphabet. Minority languages include Turkish and Macedonian. The majority of the population are Christian, most of whom adhere to the Bulgarian Orthodox Church, although there is a substantial minority of Muslims. The national flag (proportions 3 by 2) has three equal horizontal stripes, of white, green and red. The capital is Sofia.

Recent History

After almost 500 years of Ottoman rule, Bulgaria declared itself an independent kingdom in 1908. In both the First and Second World Wars Bulgaria allied itself with Germany, and in 1941 joined in the occupation of Yugoslavia. Soviet troops occupied Bulgaria in 1944. In September of that year the Fatherland Front, a left-wing alliance formed in 1942, seized power, with help from the USSR, and installed a Government, led by Kimon Georgiev. In September 1946 the monarchy was abolished, following a popular referendum, and a republic was proclaimed. The first post-war election was held in October, when the Fatherland Front received 70.8% of the votes cast and won 364 seats, of which 277 were held by the Bulgarian Communist Party (BCP), in the 465-member National Assembly. In November Georgi Dimitrov, the First Secretary of the BCP and a veteran international revolutionary, became Chairman of the Council of Ministers (Prime Minister) in a Government that comprised members of the Fatherland Front. All opposition parties were abolished and a new Constitution, based on the Soviet model, was adopted in December 1947, when Bulgaria was designated a People's Republic. Dimitrov was replaced as Prime Minister by Vasil Kolarov in March 1949, but remained leader of the BCP until his death in July. His successor as Party leader, Vulko Chervenkov, became Prime Minister in February 1950.

Todor Zhivkov succeeded Chervenkov as leader of the BCP in March 1954, although the latter remained Prime Minister until April 1956, when he was replaced by Anton Yugov. Following an ideological struggle within the BCP, Zhivkov became Prime Minister in November 1962. In May 1971 a new Constitution was adopted, and in July Zhivkov relinquished his position as Prime Minister to become the first President of the newly formed State Council. He was re-elected in 1976, 1981 and 1986. At the 12th BCP Congress, held in March and April 1981, the Party's leader was restyled General Secretary. In June, following elections to the National Assembly, a new Government was formed; Grisha Filipov, a member of the BCP's Political Bureau, succeeded Stanko Todorov, who had been Prime Minister since 1971. In March 1986 Filipov was replaced in this post by Georgi Atanasov, a former Vice-President of the State Council.

In local elections in March 1988, the nomination of candidates other than those endorsed by the BCP was permitted for the first time. Candidates presented by independent public organizations and workers' collectives obtained about one-quarter of the total votes cast. At a plenum of the BCP, held in July, several prominent proponents of the Soviet-style programme of reform were dismissed from office.

On 10 November 1989 Zhivkov was unexpectedly removed from his post of General Secretary of the BCP and from the Political Bureau. He was replaced as General Secretary by Petur Mladenov, hitherto the Minister of Foreign Affairs (since 1971), and a member of the BCP's Political Bureau since 1977. Mladenov also replaced Zhivkov as President of the State Council. In mid-November 1989 the National Assembly voted to abolish part of the penal code prohibiting 'anti-State propaganda' and to grant an amnesty to persons who had been convicted under the code's provisions. Zhivkov was subsequently denounced by the BCP and divested of his party membership, and an investigation into corruption during his tenure of power was initiated. In 1990 Zhivkov was arrested on charges of embezzlement of state funds.

In early December 1989 Angel Dimitrov became leader of the Bulgarian Agrarian People's Union (BAPU, the sole legal political party apart from the BCP, with which it was originally allied); the BAPU was subsequently reconstituted as an independent opposition party. In mid-December the BCP proposed amendments to the Constitution and the adoption of a new electoral law to permit free and democratic elections to be held in the second quarter of 1990. In January 1990 the National Assembly voted overwhelmingly to remove from the Constitution the article guaranteeing the BCP's dominant role in society. It also approved legislation permitting citizens to form independent groups and to stage demonstrations.

Discussions regarding political and economic reforms commenced in early January 1990 between the BCP, the BAPU and the Union of Democratic Forces (UDF), a co-ordinating organization (established in December 1989), which comprised several dissident and independent groups, including Ecoglasnost and the Podkrepa (Support) Trade Union Confederation. In early February the BCP adopted a new manifesto, pledging the Party's commitment to extensive political and economic reforms, the separation of party and state, and the introduction of a multi-party system. It was stressed, however, that the BCP would retain its Marxist orientation. The Party's Central Committee was replaced by a Supreme Council, chaired by Aleksandur Lilov, who was formerly head of the BCP's ideology department and who had been expelled from the Party in 1983 for criticism of Zhivkov. The Political Bureau and Secretariat of the Central Committee were replaced by the Presidium of the Supreme Council, also with Lilov as Chairman. The President of the State Council, Mladenov, proposed the formation of an interim coalition government, pending elections to the National Assembly (which were subsequently scheduled for June 1990). The UDF and the BAPU, however, rejected Mladenov's invitation to participate in such a coalition. Accordingly, the new Council of Ministers, appointed on 8 February 1990, was composed solely of BCP members, chaired by Andrei Lukanov, the former Minister of Foreign Economic Relations, who was regarded as an advocate of reform.

There was unrest in mid-February 1990, when an estimated 200,000 supporters of the UDF gathered in Sofia to demand the end of BCP rule. Following discussions on reform in late March, with the participation of the BAPU and other political and public organizations, it was finally agreed that Mladenov was to be re-elected as President, pending elections to the National Assembly in June and the subsequent approval of a new constitution. The participants in the talks also decided to dissolve the State Council. In early April the National Assembly adopted an electoral law, together with legislation that provided for political pluralism and guaranteed the right to form political parties. Also in early April the BCP voted overwhelmingly to rename itself the Bulgarian Socialist Party (BSP).

Following an electoral campaign, which was marred by acts of intimidation and violence, elections to the 400-member Grand National Assembly were held in two rounds, on 10 and 17 June 1990. The BSP won 211 seats, but failed to gain the two-thirds majority of seats in the legislature necessary to secure support for the approval of constitutional and economic reforms. The UDF, which won the majority of votes in urban areas, obtained 144 seats in the Assembly. The Movement for Rights and Freedoms (MRF), which had been established earlier in 1990 to represent the country's Muslim minority, won a large percentage of the votes in areas populated by ethnic Turks, and secured 23 seats. The BAPU won 16 seats in the legislature, considerably fewer than had been expected. The UDF, after initial protests against alleged electoral fraud, accepted the validity of the result, although it again rejected the BSP's invitation to join a coalition government.

In July 1990 Mladenov announced his resignation as President, following a campaign of protests and strikes, led by students. Zhelyu Zhelev, the Chairman of the UDF, was elected to replace him in early August. Zhelev was succeeded as Chairman of the UDF first by Petur Beron, hitherto the party's Secretary, and, from December, by Filip Dimitrov, a lawyer and the Vice-President of the Green Party.

In 1990 the severe deterioration in the economy resulted in widespread shortages of food and fuel. In October Lukanov proposed that the Grand National Assembly approve a programme of extensive economic reforms. The UDF (which held more than one-third of the seats in the legislature) refused to support the reforms, and proceeded to organize rallies in many parts of Bulgaria to demand the resignation of Lukanov's Government.

In mid-November 1990 the Grand National Assembly voted to rename the country the Republic of Bulgaria, and voted to remove from the national flag the state emblem, which included Communist symbols.

Increasing division between conservative and reformist elements within the BSP became manifest in early November 1990, when 16 BSP delegates to the Grand National Assembly announced their decision to form a separate parliamentary group, as a result of which the Party no longer held an absolute majority in the legislature. A motion expressing 'no confidence' in the Government, proposed by the UDF in late November, was defeated by 201 votes to 159. However, following a four-day general strike organized by Podkrepa, Lukanov and his Government resigned at the end of the month. Subsequent discussions between representatives of all the political forces in the Grand National Assembly resulted in the formation of a new 'government of national consensus' in mid-December, comprising members of the BSP, the UDF, the BAPU and four independents. Dimitur Popov, a lawyer with no party affiliation, had been elected in early December to chair the new Council of Ministers.

The Grand National Assembly adopted a new Constitution in mid-July 1991; it subsequently voted to dissolve itself, although it continued sessions in an interim capacity, pending a legislative election. The Constitution stipulated, *inter alia*, a five-year residency qualification for presidential candidates, effectively disqualifying the candidacy of Simeon II, the pretender to the Bulgarian throne, who had lived in exile since 1946. In the months preceding the parliamentary election, internal divisions arose in many of the major parties, including the UDF. Nevertheless, at the election to the new, 240-seat National Assembly, held on 13 October, the majority UDF obtained the largest share of the votes cast (34.4%), defeating the BSP (which contested the election in alliance with a number of smaller parties) by a narrow margin of just over 1%. The UDF won a total of 110 seats in the legislature, while the BSP obtained 106 seats. The ethnic Turkish MRF became the third-strongest political force, securing a total of 24 seats. The new Council of Ministers, composed of UDF members and six independents, was announced in early November. Filip Dimitrov, the leader of the UDF, was elected Chairman of the new Government. A direct presidential election was held in January 1992. Following an inconclusive first round, a second ballot, involving the two leading candidates (the incumbent President, Zhelev, and Velko Valkanov, an independent supported by the BSP), took place. Zhelev was re-elected for a five-year term, receiving 53% of the votes cast.

In March 1992 attempts by the Government to introduce legislation that would further reduce the power of former Communists was opposed by the BSP, with the support of President Zhelev, who maintained that the apparent restriction of political freedom could undermine Bulgaria's application for membership of the Council of Europe (see p. 165). In the same month a compromise solution was agreed by the Minister of Foreign Affairs, Stoyan Ganev, and President Zhelev, whereby the National Intelligence Service was eventually to be placed under the jurisdiction of the Government, rather than the Office of the Presidency. In early April, despite BSP opposition, the Government adopted legislation restoring ownership of land and property that had been transferred to the state sector during 1947–62; this was followed by legislation approving the privatization of state-owned companies. In the same month a government programme of price liberalization, which had been adopted in early 1991 in fulfilment of IMF conditions, caused further trade-union disaffection, and the main trade-union federations, the Confederation of Independent Trade Unions in

Bulgaria (CITUB) and Podkrepa, abandoned talks with the Government.

In May 1992 Dimitrov threatened to resign as Prime Minister, unless the Minister of Defence, Dimitur Ludzhev, relinquished his post. This was widely believed to be indicative of a broader struggle for control of the increasingly factional UDF. Ludzhev resigned later that month, and Dimitrov implemented an extensive reorganization of the Council of Ministers. In July the former BCP Prime Minister, Lukanov (now a BSP deputy of the National Assembly), was arrested, prompting the BSP deputies to withdraw from a meeting of the National Assembly in protest. Legal proceedings were initiated against Lukanov and a further 60 senior officials (including two other former Prime Ministers, Grisha Filipov and Georgi Atanasov) on charges of misappropriating state funds. (Atanasov was officially pardoned by President Zhelev in August 1994 on the grounds of ill health.)

In mid-July 1992 there were further strikes, supported by Podkrepa, and miners were joined by other public-sector employees. In early August the Chairman of Podkrepa, Konstantin Trenchev, was arrested with 37 others, and charged with incitement to destroy public property in 1990. Meanwhile, relations between President Zhelev and the UDF became increasingly strained. In late August 1992 Zhelev publicly criticized Dimitrov's Government and received support for his position from both the MRF and the CITUB. In September the UDF convened a national conference and agreed to initiate discussions with the President and the MRF, but reaffirmed its support for Dimitrov. In late September the MRF declared a lack of confidence in Dimitrov's leadership. At the end of October MRF and BSP deputies in the National Assembly defeated the Government by 121 votes to 111 in a motion of confidence, proposed by Dimitrov; the Government subsequently resigned.

In November 1992 President Zhelev invited Dimitrov (as the nominee of the party with the largest representation in the National Assembly) to form a new government. The MRF, however, declined to form a coalition with the UDF, and Dimitrov's nomination was thus defeated in the National Assembly. The BSP was then assigned a mandate to nominate a candidate for the premiership. President Zhelev, however, rejected the candidacy of the BSP nominee, Petur Boyadzhiev, on the grounds that he held dual nationality (Bulgarian and French), in contravention of the terms of the Constitution. Following the failure of the UDF and the MRF to reach agreement for a coalition under the MRF mandate, in December the MRF nominated an academic, Prof. Lyuben Berov, hitherto an economic adviser to President Zhelev, to the office of Prime Minister. The UDF accused Berov of collaborating with the former communist regime and organized a large rally to protest against his candidacy, while threatening to expel members who voted in his favour in the National Assembly. In the event, the majority of UDF deputies abstained, but Berov was approved as Prime Minister on 30 December by 124 votes to 25, in a secret ballot. Berov's proposed Council of Ministers, principally composed of 'experts' without party political allegiances, was also accepted by the National Assembly. On the same day, the BSP and the MRF voted in the National Assembly to discharge Lukanov from custody. It was widely speculated that BSP support for Berov's Government had been, in part, conditional on Lukanov's release.

In March 1993 internal divisions within the UDF became more apparent when a breakaway faction of the party formed a new, pro-Berov organization, known as the New Union for Democracy (NUD); in response, the UDF intensified its campaign of opposition, claiming, in particular, that the Government was planning to reintroduce socialism. In May the former Speaker of the National Assembly, Stefan Savov, was injured by a policeman during a demonstration, organized by the UDF, outside the parliamentary building in Sofia; the UDF claimed that he had been attacked on government orders. In early June a UDF deputy, Edvin Sugarev, began a hunger strike to demand President Zhelev's resignation. In the same month large demonstrations were staged by the UDF in Sofia and several other cities to denounce Zhelev for allegedly attempting the restoration of Communism and to demand immediate elections. The situation improved slightly later that month, when Sugarev ended his hunger strike. On 29 June, however, the Vice-President, Blaga Dimitrova, resigned, claiming that she had been insufficiently consulted while in office. The crisis finally subsided when two votes expressing 'no confidence' in Berov's Government, which were proposed by the UDF in the National Assembly, proved unsuccessful. Political unrest continued, however, and in November the Berov administration survived another motion of 'no confidence', proposed by the UDF. In the same month Berov's National Security Adviser was dismissed from his post, and in December further allegations of government corruption were presented to the Chief Prosecutor.

In January 1994 Zhivkov was sentenced to seven years in prison for embezzlement of government funds. (In February 1996, however, the Supreme Court upheld his appeal against the sentence.) In February 1994 the Berov Government survived a fifth motion of 'no confidence', proposed by the UDF in protest against the Government's apparent inability to control the dramatic increase in the crime rate. In early April Zhelev announced that he could no longer give his political support to Berov's administration, citing its failure to implement objectives such as an accelerated privatization programme. Following the controversial introduction of value-added tax (VAT), unpopular increases in fuel prices and the dramatic fall of the national currency, the lev, thousands of demonstrators protested in Sofia against government policies. In mid-May a proposal by Berov for the appointment of a new Council of Ministers was rejected by the National Assembly; it was claimed by certain political groups that Berov wished to install a BSP-dominated administration. Later that month Berov's Government survived a further vote of 'no confidence', again proposed by the UDF. In late May the Government narrowly won a vote of confidence presented in the National Assembly. The UDF deputies subsequently boycotted National Assembly sessions throughout June.

In late June 1994 the Government finally launched the delayed May privatization programme, whereby each Bulgarian citizen was offered a 500-leva voucher, which could be invested either directly into state enterprises or into private investment funds. In early September, however, Berov's Government submitted its resignation, following increasing criticism of the poor organization of the privatization programme. Both the BSP and the UDF refused presidential mandates to form a new Government. In October President Zhelev dissolved the National Assembly and announced that a general election would take place on 18 December. Later in October Zhelev appointed an interim neutral Government, headed by Reneta Indzhova.

At the general election, which was held as scheduled on 18 December 1994, the BSP (in alliance, as the Democratic Left, with two small parties, the Aleksandur Stamboliyski Bulgarian Agrarian People's Union and the Ecoglasnost Political Club—the political wing of the Ecoglasnost National Movement) obtained an outright majority in the National Assembly, with 125 seats (43.5% of the total votes cast); the UDF won 69 seats (24.2%). Other groups that gained more than the 4% of votes required for representation in the legislature were: the People's Union (an alliance of the BAPU and the Democratic Party), the MRF and the Bulgarian Business Bloc (BBB). A new Government, headed by the Chairman of the BSP, Zhan Videnov, was appointed at the end of January 1995; the majority of the ministers were members of the BSP.

In February 1995 the National Assembly passed a bill that amended the 1992 property restitution law (see above), extending for a further three years the deadline by which certain properties had to be restored to their rightful owners. In March the National Assembly abolished a law, adopted by the UDF Government in 1992, prohibiting former Communists from senior academic positions. In the same month the Government drafted a programme for mass privatization in 1995, which envisaged payment through a combination of cash, debt bonds and investment vouchers (the vouchers were made available from early January 1996). Mass demonstrations took place throughout March 1995, however, reflecting widespread dissatisfaction with government amendments to the Agricultural Land Tenure Act, on the grounds that they would restrict landowners' rights to dispose of their property and would encourage the restoration of Communist-style collective farms. In late April President Zhelev exercised his right of veto against the highly unpopular amendments, which had been adopted by the National Assembly in mid-April; the President claimed that the amendments contravened the constitutional right of Bulgarian citizens to own private property. The case was subsequently examined by the Constitutional Court, which in June rejected the amendments as unconstitutional.

In late June 1995 the Government removed the heads of the state television and radio services and the Director-General of the national news agency; the opposition alleged that the dismissals represented an attempt by the BSP to control the state media. In late September the Government survived a

motion of 'no confidence' (by 130 votes to 102), which was introduced by the opposition in the National Assembly, in protest at the continued failure of Videnov's administration to control the rapid increase in levels of crime.

At municipal elections in late October and early November 1995, the ruling coalition won 195 of a total of 255 mayoralties, although the UDF secured the mayoralties in the country's three main cities. In mid-November President Zhelev announced that he would seek re-election in 1997.

On 10 January 1996 a further motion of 'no confidence' in the Videnov administration was proposed by the opposition, in protest at a severe shortage of grain, which had resulted from the Government's repeal of a ban on grain exports in July 1995. The motion was defeated, but the situation prompted the resignation of the Deputy Prime Minister and a further two ministers. In February 1996 the MRF staged a demonstration in Sofia in protest at the annulment, owing to alleged irregularities, of the result of the municipal elections in the south-eastern town of Kurdzhali (where the MRF had narrowly secured a victory). In April, however, the Supreme Court upheld the election result. In May the Minister of the Interior resigned, following an incident in which three members of the security forces were killed by criminals. Meanwhile, a sharp devaluation of the lev resulted in further economic hardship. In June the UDF proposed a motion expressing 'no confidence' in the Government's management of the economy, which was, however, defeated by a large majority in the National Assembly.

In primary elections for a UDF presidential candidate, which were conducted in early June 1996, Petar Stoyanov, a lawyer and senior member of the opposition alliance, secured 66% of the votes cast, defeating Zhelev. Zhelev subsequently announced that he would support Stoyanov's candidature for the presidency. In July the National Assembly scheduled the presidential election for 27 October. In the same month the Constitutional Court ruled that Georgi Pirinski, nominated in June to contest the election on behalf of the BSP, was ineligible, on the grounds that he was not a Bulgarian citizen by birth, as stipulated in the Constitution. Pirinski (who had been considered to be the most popular nominee) declared that political bias had influenced the decision. In September, following a ruling by the Supreme Court that confirmed the invalidity of Pirinski's candidature, the BSP selected the Minister of Culture, Ivan Marazov, as its presidential candidate; Marazov was to represent a newly-formed electoral alliance, known as Together for Bulgaria, which comprised the parties in the Democratic Left parliamentary coalition (the BSP, Aleksandur Stamboliyski and the Ecoglasnost Political Club).

In early October 1996 the former Prime Minister, Andrei Lukanov (who had remained an influential member of the BSP), was assassinated. Ensuing speculation regarding the motive for the killing focused, in particular, on Lukanov's critical stance towards the Videnov administration's slow implementation of economic reforms. Later that month the CITUB and Podkrepa organized a demonstration in Sofia to demand the resignation of the Government. In the first round of the presidential election, which was contested by 14 political groups on 27 October (as scheduled), Stoyanov secured 44.1% of the votes cast; Marazov received only 27.0% of the votes, while the candidate of the BBB, Georgi Ganchev, won 21.9%. Only 61% of the electorate voted in the second round, which took place on 3 November, reflecting increasing public disaffection with the Government's management of the critical economic situation. Stoyanov was elected to the presidency, with 59.7% of the votes cast. Stoyanov (who was believed to favour Bulgaria's entry into NATO) subsequently announced that he was to establish a Council of National Salvation, which would devise measures to improve financial stability.

Following the election of Stoyanov, the political council of the UDF agreed to initiate a campaign to demand that a parliamentary election be conducted later that year (earlier than scheduled). The electoral defeat of the BSP in the presidential election aggravated existing divisions within the organization; in early November 1996 several senior members of the BSP accused Videnov of causing the Party's unpopularity and demanded the resignation of the Government. However, a joint convention of the BSP and its allied parties subsequently rejected a motion of 'no confidence' in the Government. Later in November Pirinski, who was a leading opponent of Videnov within the BSP, submitted his resignation from the post of Minister of Foreign Affairs, on the grounds that the Government no longer commanded public support and that the party vote had failed to indicate sufficient confidence in Videnov.

In December 1996 the UDF staged a series of demonstrations to demand an early legislative election and the resignation of the Government. On 21 December, at an extraordinary congress of the BSP, Videnov unexpectedly tendered his resignation from the office of Prime Minister and the post of party leader. (The incumbent Council of Ministers was to remain in office, pending the formation of a new administration.) Georgi Purvanov, who was a supporter of Videnov, subsequently replaced him as Chairman of the BSP. At the end of December the National Assembly voted by a large majority to accept the resignation of Videnov's Government. In January 1997 the BSP designated the Minister of the Interior, Nikolai Dobrev, to replace Videnov as Prime Minister. The UDF, however, intensified its campaign of demonstrations; in early January an attempt by protesters to seize the parliamentary building was suppressed by security forces. Zhelev subsequently announced that he would not invite Dobrev to form a new government as expected. Later that month the UDF, with the support of Podkrepa, organized a series of one-hour strikes to demand an early parliamentary election. On 19 January Stoyanov was inaugurated as President. At the end of January the BSP accepted a proposal by Stoyanov that the Party form a new government, pending a legislative election, which was expected to take place in the second half of 1997. In early February the BSP announced the appointment of a new Council of Ministers; following continued protests and strikes by supporters of the UDF, however, Dobrev agreed to relinquish the Party's mandate to form a new government (owing to increasing concern that the disorder might escalate into civil conflict). The Consultative National Security Council adopted recommendations (which were approved by the National Assembly) that, in the absence of agreement between the political parties represented in the legislature on the formation of a government, the President should appoint an interim council of ministers, dissolve the incumbent National Assembly and schedule a legislative election. Stoyanov subsequently nominated the mayor of Sofia, Stefan Sofianski, to the office of Prime Minister, and formed an interim Council of Ministers, pending the election, which was scheduled to be held on 19 April; the National Assembly was dissolved on 19 February. Following the resumption of negotiations between the new Government and the IMF, agreement was reached in March regarding the establishment of a currency control board, as a prerequisite to economic and financial stability. Later in March the interim Government announced that Videnov was to be charged with criminal negligence as a result of government policies that had caused the severe shortage of grain in 1995–96; the Minister of Agriculture in the Videnov administration and three of his deputies were also prosecuted.

At the election to the National Assembly, which took place as scheduled on 19 April 1997, the UDF secured 137 seats, while the BSP (which again contested the elections in the Democratic Left alliance) obtained only 58 seats; the Alliance for National Salvation (a coalition comprising the MRF and other monarchist and centrist groups) won 19 seats, a newly-established left-wing organization, known as Euro-Left, gained 14 seats and the BBB 12 seats. Later in April the UDF formally nominated the party Chairman, Ivan Kostov, to the office of Prime Minister (subject to the approval of the National Assembly). At the first session of the new National Assembly, which was convened in early May, deputies adopted, despite some opposition, a seven-point declaration of national consensus, which had been proposed by the UDF; the stated policies included the implementation of economic reforms that had been agreed with the IMF, the acceleration of measures to restore agricultural land to rightful ownership and support for Bulgaria's accession to the European Union (EU, see p. 181) and NATO (see p. 241). Later in May the National Assembly elected Kostov to the office of Prime Minister; only deputies belonging to the Democratic Left alliance opposed his nomination. The new Council of Ministers, which had been formed by Kostov, included five members of the outgoing interim administration.

Following its installation, the new Government replaced the President of the State Savings Bank. In June 1997 the National Assembly adopted legislation providing for the establishment of the currency control board, which was installed at the beginning of July. In a further effort to impose fiscal discipline, the Government replaced the senior officials of the Bulgarian National Bank; Svetoslav Gavriyski, who had served as Minister of Finance in the interim Council of Ministers, was appointed

Governor. At the end of July the National Assembly voted in favour of declassifying security files on politicians and public officials, and adopted legislation to expedite the restoration of land to rightful ownership. In early September two parliamentary representatives of the BBB were expelled from the party after criticizing the leadership of Ganchev, who, they claimed, intended to establish links with the BSP; another deputy resigned in protest at their removal. The BBB was consequently obliged to dissolve its parliamentary group, which had been reduced to below the required minimum of 10 representatives. In October a government commission announced that 23 prominent public officials, including 14 members of the National Assembly, had been members of the security services of former Communist governments. In early November, following protests from deputies belonging to the Democratic Left, the Constitutional Court ruled that the appointment of directors of the national radio and television stations by the National Assembly (rather than by an independent media council) was in contravention of the Constitution. In January 1998 the National Assembly rejected a motion expressing 'no confidence' in the Government, which had been proposed by Democratic Left deputies in protest at the Council of Ministers' policy on health care. In March Stoyanov replaced a senior army official, who (apparently with the support of many other army officers) had publicly opposed plans by the Government to reduce the size of the armed forces under structural reforms. The senior commanders of the armed forces were reorganized in May. At an annual congress of the BSP in the same month Purvanov was re-elected as Chairman of the Party, obtaining 58% of the votes cast. In late September a Security Council, chaired by the Prime Minister, was established to advise on state security activities.

In April 1999 the Government, accused of nepotism and corruption, survived a second vote of 'no confidence' in the National Assembly, by 139 votes to 87. Local government elections took place on 16 and 23 October: the UDF narrowly won, with 31.3% of the votes cast; the BSP secured 29.4%. In December Stoyanov accepted a reorganization of the Council of Ministers by Kostov, including a reduction in the number of deputy premiers, from three to one, and the appointment as defence minister of Boiko Noev, who replaced Georgi Ananiev. In May 2000 Kostov's administration survived a third vote of 'no confidence', and in February 2001 the National Assembly rejected, by 135 votes to 74, a further confidence motion, proposed by the opposition in response to the worsening crime situation. Meanwhile, in advance of presidential and legislative elections, due to be held later in 2001, in January the BSP attempted to consolidate support by forming an alliance, known as Coalition for Bulgaria, with 14 other, smaller leftist and nationalist groups.

Bulgaria maintained close links with other Eastern European countries through its membership of the Warsaw Pact and of the Council for Mutual Economic Assistance (CMEA). Following the political upheavals that took place in Eastern Europe in 1989 and 1990, both the Warsaw Pact and the CMEA were dissolved in mid-1991. Diplomatic relations with several Western nations were re-established in 1990 and 1991, and in mid-1992 Bulgaria became a member of the Council of Europe (see p. 165). In May 1994 Bulgaria was granted associate partnership status by the Western European Union (WEU—see p. 286). In June 1992 Bulgaria, together with 10 other countries (including six of the former Soviet republics), signed a pact to establish the Organization of the Black Sea Economic Co-operation (see p. 265), which envisaged the creation of a Black Sea economic zone that would complement the European Community (now EU). In 1996 Bulgaria submitted an official application for membership of the EU. In October of that year Bulgaria joined the World Trade Organization (see p. 292). Negotiations on Bulgaria's accession to the EU, which were conditional on the Government's fulfilment of certain criteria (see Economic Affairs), began in March 2000.

Bulgaria's establishment of formal relations with the former Yugoslav republic of Macedonia (FYRM) in January 1992 prompted harsh criticism from the Greek Government. Relations with Greece appeared to improve, however, after the visit of the Bulgarian Minister of Foreign Affairs to Athens in May. In November 1993 the FYRM expressed its desire to establish full diplomatic relations with Bulgaria. In the following month Bulgaria announced that it was to open an embassy in the FYRM and relax border procedures between the two states. In February 1999 Kostov and the Prime Minister of the FYRM, Ljubčo Georgievski, signed a declaration pledging that neither country had a territorial claim on the other. In March the Ministers of Defence of Bulgaria and the FYRM signed a joint declaration providing for increased military co-operation, including joint exercises and the supply of military equipment to the FYRM, in connection with the aim of both countries to join NATO. Public opposition in Bulgaria to the NATO air bombardment of Yugoslavia that commenced in late March 1999 (see chapter on Yugoslavia), increased, after a misdirected NATO missile damaged a private residence in the outskirts of Sofia in April. Nevertheless, the Bulgarian National Assembly approved a decision made by the Council of Ministers to allow NATO use of the country's airspace (despite opposition from the BSP). It was reported that public support for Bulgaria's proposed membership of NATO had declined in response to the bombardment.

In June 2000, after eight years of discussions, relations with Romania were significantly improved by the signature of an agreement on the construction of a second bridge over the River Danube, from Vidin to Calafat, in Romania; the link was to improve road connections between the Balkans and western Europe.

Relations between Bulgaria and Russia improved in 1992, following the signature of co-operation agreements, and the visit of the Russian President, Boris Yeltsin, to Sofia in August. Reciprocal visits by the premiers of Bulgaria and Russia in 1995 further improved relations between the two countries. In late 1996 a Russian parliamentary delegation visited Sofia to meet Bulgarian deputies; it was agreed that joint Bulgarian-Russian debates would be conducted on significant issues of mutual concern. In April 1998 the Bulgarian Government signed a significant agreement with the Russian national gas company, Gazprom, providing for the supply and transit of Russian gas (see Economic Affairs). In December 2000 Russia expressed its disappointment at Bulgaria's decision to terminate, in accordance with conditions for accession to the EU, a 1978 bilateral agreement on visa-free travel, with effect from June 2001.

Relations with neighbouring Turkey have been intermittently strained since the mid-1980s, when the Zhivkov regime began a campaign of forced assimilation of Bulgaria's ethnic Turkish minority (which constitutes an estimated 10% of the total population). The ethnic Turks were forced to adopt Slavic names prior to the December 1985 census, and were banned from practising Islamic religious rites. In February 1988, on the eve of a conference of Ministers of Foreign Affairs of the six Balkan nations, Bulgaria and Turkey signed a protocol to further bilateral economic and social relations. However, the situation deteriorated in May 1989, when Bulgarian militia units violently suppressed demonstrations by an estimated 30,000 ethnic Turks in eastern Bulgaria against the assimilation campaign. In June more than 80,000 ethnic Turks were expelled from Bulgaria, although the Bulgarian authorities claimed that the Turks had chosen to settle in Turkey, following a relaxation in passport regulations to ease foreign travel. In response, the Turkish Government opened the border and declared its commitment to accepting all the ethnic Turks as refugees from Bulgaria. By mid-August an estimated 310,000 Bulgarian Turks had crossed into Turkey. In late August the Turkish Government, alarmed by the continued influx of refugees, closed the border. In the following month a substantial number of the Bulgarian Turks, disillusioned with conditions in Turkey, began to return to Bulgaria.

The Turkish Government repeatedly proposed that discussions with the Bulgarian Government be held, under the auspices of the UN High Commissioner for Refugees, to establish the rights of the Bulgarian Turks and to formulate a clear immigration policy. Finally, Bulgaria agreed to negotiations and friendly relations between Bulgaria and Turkey had apparently been restored by late 1991. In March 1992 a bilateral defence agreement was signed. In May Prime Minister Dimitrov visited Turkey, and the two countries signed a treaty of friendship and co-operation.

Meanwhile, in December 1989, some 6,000 Pomaks (ethnic Bulgarian Muslims who form a community of about 300,000 people) held demonstrations to demand religious and cultural freedoms, as well as an official inquiry into alleged atrocities against Pomaks during Zhivkov's tenure of office. In January 1990 anti-Turkish demonstrations were held in the Kurdzhali district of southern Bulgaria, in protest at the Government's declared intention to restore civil and religious rights to the ethnic Turkish minority. Despite continuing demonstrations by Bulgarian nationalist protesters, in March the National

Assembly approved legislation that permitted ethnic Turks and Pomaks to use their original Islamic names. This development was welcomed by the Turkish Government. Nevertheless, inter-ethnic disturbances continued, particularly in the Kurdzhali region, during 1990. Proposals in early 1991 to introduce the teaching of Turkish in schools in predominantly Turkish regions led to renewed inter-ethnic conflict. In November of that year the Government finally decreed that Turkish be taught as an optional subject four times weekly in the regions concerned, following which the MRF ended a boycott on school attendance, which it had imposed in mid-1991. By 1993 ethnic tensions had generally been contained in Bulgaria, although there were reports of some disturbances between ethnic Turks and ethnic Bulgarian Muslims in the south of the country in September. In July 1995 a visit by President Demirel of Turkey to Bulgaria, during which regional security and economic relations between the two countries were discussed, indicated a significant improvement in Bulgarian-Turkish relations. Following a visit to Bulgaria by the Turkish Minister of Foreign Affairs in May 1998, it was announced that a number of co-operation agreements had been signed. In June the National Assembly ratified an agreement demarcating the border between Bulgaria and Turkey (which had been signed during an official visit to Sofia by the Turkish Prime Minister, Mesut Yılmaz, in December 1997).

Government

Legislative power is held by the unicameral National Assembly, comprising 240 members, who are elected for four years by universal adult suffrage. The President of the Republic (Head of State) is elected directly by the voters for a period of five years, and is also Supreme Commander-in-Chief of the Armed Forces. The Council of Ministers, the highest organ of state administration, is elected by the National Assembly. For local administration, Bulgaria comprises 29 regions (divided into a total of 259 municipalities).

Defence

Military service is compulsory and lasts for 18 months. The total strength of the armed forces in August 2000 was 79,760 (including an estimated 49,000 conscripts), comprising an army of 42,400, an air force of 18,300, a navy of an estimated 5,260, 12,500 centrally-controlled staff and 1,300 Ministry of Defence staff. Paramilitary forces include an estimated 12,000 border guards, 18,000 railway and construction troops and 4,000 security police. The state budget proposals for 2001 allocated 802m. new leva to defence. Bulgaria joined NATO's 'Partnership for Peace' programme of military co-operation (see p. 243) in 1994. In late 1999 the Government announced plans to reduce the armed forces to number 45,000 by 2004.

Economic Affairs

In 1998, according to estimates by the World Bank, Bulgaria's gross national product (GNP), measured at average 1996–98 prices, was US $10,085m., equivalent to $1,220 per head (or $4,683 per head on an international purchasing-power parity basis). During 1990–98, it was estimated, GNP per head decreased, in real terms, at an average annual rate of 1.8%. Over the same period the population decreased at an average rate of 0.4% per year. According to the World Bank, Bulgaria's gross domestic product (GDP) declined, in real terms, by an average of 3.1% annually during 1990–98. However, according to official figures, GDP decreased by 6.9% in 1997, but increased by 26.5% in 1998 and by 5.6% in 1999.

Agriculture (including forestry and fishing) contributed 17.3% of GDP in 1999. In that year the sector engaged 26.6% of the employed labour force. In 1990 private farming was legalized, and farmland was restituted, in its former physical boundaries, to former owners and their heirs; by the end of 1999 96% of land restitution had been completed. In 1996 privately owned farms supplied 75.4% of total agricultural production. The principal crops are wheat, maize, barley, sunflower seeds, potatoes, tomatoes and melons. Bulgaria is a major exporter of wine, although grape production declined in the late 1990s. There is a large exportable surplus of processed agricultural products. During 1990–98, according to the World Bank, the real GDP of the agricultural sector declined at an average annual rate of 0.7%. According to official estimates, however, agricultural GDP rose by 32.9% in 1997, by 1.4% in 1998 and by 0.6% in 1999.

Industry (including mining, manufacturing, construction and utilities) provided 26.8% of GDP and engaged 29.1% of the employed labour force in 1999. According to the World Bank, industrial GDP declined, in real terms, at an average annual rate of 4.9% in 1990–98. Industrial GDP declined, according to official estimates, by 11.3% in 1997, but increased by 4.3% in 1998, before declining again, by 4.4%, in 1999.

In 1999 mining and quarrying engaged 1.6% of the employed labour force. Coal, iron ore, copper, manganese, lead and zinc are mined, while petroleum is extracted on the Black Sea coast. Bulgaria's annual output of coal (including brown coal—lignite) decreased from 31.3m. metric tons in 1996 to 29.7m. tons in 1997 and 29.9m. tons in 1998. In 1986 the construction of a gas pipeline, linking Bulgaria to the USSR, was completed. In April 1998 Bulgaria and Russia signed an agreement providing for Russia's delivery of natural gas to Bulgaria until 2010; the volume of gas transported across Bulgaria to neighbouring countries was to be increased, and the existing pipeline network upgraded.

The manufacturing sector engaged 21.6% of the employed labour force in 1999. Based on the value of output, the main branches of manufacturing in 1998 were food products, beverages and tobacco products, refined petroleum products, basic metals, and chemicals and chemical products. The GDP of the manufacturing sector declined by 14.9% in 1997, but increased by 6.5% in 1998, before declining once more, by 5.9%, in 1999.

Bulgaria's production of primary energy in 1998 was equivalent to 51.3% of gross consumption. Coal and nuclear power are the main domestic sources of energy. The country's sole nuclear power station, at Kozloduy, provided some 40% of electric energy in 1990. Imports of mineral fuels and lubricants comprised 30.5% of the value of the merchandise imports in 1997.

The services sector contributed an estimated 55.9% of GDP and engaged 44.3% of the employed labour force in 1999. Trade represented an estimated 7.5% of GDP in that year. According to the World Bank, the real GDP of the services sector declined at an average rate of 2.0% per year in 1990–98. The sector's GDP declined, according to official estimates, by 19.3% in 1997, but increased by 0.5% in 1998 and by 5.8% in 1999.

In 1999 Bulgaria recorded a visible trade deficit of US $1,081m., and there was a deficit of $685m. on the current account of the balance of payments. In that year the principal source of imports was Russia, which provided 20.1% of the total; Germany and Italy were also major suppliers. The main market for exports was Italy (taking 13.9% of the total) in 1999; Germany, Greece and Turkey were also significant purchasers. The principal exports in 1997 were basic manufactures, chemicals and related products, and miscellaneous manufactured articles. The principal imports in that year were mineral fuels and lubricants (particularly petroleum and petroleum products), basic manufactures and machinery and transport equipment.

Bulgaria's overall budget surplus for 1999 was 348.7m. leva (equivalent to 1.5% of GDP). Bulgaria's total external debt at the end of 1998 was US $9,907m., of which $7,781m. was long-term public debt. In that year the cost of debt-servicing was equivalent to 22.1% of revenue from exports of goods and services. The annual rate of inflation averaged 149% in 1990–98. Consumer prices increased by 1,061.6% in 1997, but by only 22.3% in 1998 and 1.8% in 1999, before increasing by 10.4% in 2000. Some 16.6% of the labour force were registered unemployed at the end of 1999.

Bulgaria is a member of the International Bank for Economic Co-operation (see p. 308), the UN Economic Commission for Europe (see p. 27) and the Organization of the Black Sea Economic Co-operation (see p. 265). In 1990 Bulgaria became a member of the IMF and the World Bank. Bulgaria made a formal application for membership of the European Union (EU, see p. 181) in 1996, and in 1999 was admitted to the Central European Free Trade Association (CEFTA, see p. 307). Bulgaria is a founding member of the European Bank for Reconstruction and Development (EBRD, established in 1990, see p. 176).

In the late 1980s the Bulgarian economy entered a severe decline. The economy was further affected, in the early 1990s, by UN sanctions against Iraq, Libya and Yugoslavia. In an effort to prevent total economic collapse, the Government introduced an extensive programme of privatization and restructuring of the banking system, to effect the transition to a market economy, and in 1991 adopted austerity measures in fulfilment of conditions stipulated by the IMF. In May 1996 there was a collapse in the value of the lev; in September the IMF suspended the disbursement of funds, pending progress in the implementation of reforms. Following the resumption of negotiations between a new interim administration (see Recent History) and the IMF, agreement was reached in March 1997 regarding the adoption of structural reforms, which included the acceleration of the privatization programme, the liberalization of trade and price controls and the rationalization of state-sector employees, to reduce government expenditure on loss-making companies. In an effort to impose fiscal discipline, the Government established a currency control board in July, which fixed the exchange rate of the lev to that of the Deutsche Mark. In May 1998 legislation ending state subsidies to the agricultural sector was approved. In September the IMF approved a further three-year credit to finance debt-servicing repayments and to support additional reforms. Following its accession to the CEFTA in January 1999, Bulgaria was to remove gradually tariffs on industrial products traded with other CEFTA countries. Negotiations on Bulgaria's accession to the EU were conditional on the achievement of growth of 3.4%, greater progress in economic reform and agreement on closure dates for four of the six reactors of the Kozloduy nuclear power installation (on the grounds that they were unsafe). Bulgaria pledged that the first two reactors would be closed by 2003, and the other two by 2010; the country was to be granted financial assistance from the EU for restructuring the energy sector and upgrading the remaining two nuclear reactors. Bulgaria began accession talks with the EU in March 2000 and by the end of 2000 it was the first candidate country to meet conditions for participation in the Special Accession Programme for Agriculture and Rural Development (SAPARD); Bulgaria was to receive €52.1m. each year until 2006, in addition to €17.6m. annually from the state budget. In 2000 the balance of trade recorded a positive result for the first time in 10 years. Despite the Government's continued success in curbing the rate of inflation, however, lack of private investment (and, consequently, growth) remained major impediments to progress; critics blamed this on the inefficient privatization programme and a lack of transparency. Although considerable progress in privatization was achieved in 1999, the planned privatization of energy companies lost momentum in 2000. Rising energy costs in conjunction with a relatively high rate of unemployment eroded living standards. However, the relaxation of rigorous budget controls in 2000 provided some relief; in June of that year the IMF agreed to the 'freezing' of electricity prices for one year and to public-sector wage increases of up to 10% in the following year. A new financing arrangement was to be negotiated with the IMF in mid-2001, following the disbursement of the final tranche of the previous loan agreement; principal objectives until that time constituted the completion of a unified revenue agency, the ongoing reform of pensions and health care, and the establishment of a fully-functioning treasury. The Government also aimed to decrease unemployment. The budget for 2001 envisaged GDP growth of some 5% and a reduction in average consumer-price inflation to around 6%.

Social Welfare

The Bulgarian health service is administered by the Ministry of Health, with the assistance of local government and the Bulgarian Red Cross; medical care is provided free of charge. The development of the private health sector is also encouraged (private medical and dentistry practices were banned between 1972 and November 1989). A health insurance system for primary care commenced operations in July 2000, and more than 16,000 medical specialists were transferred from the state-financed to the commercial sector. All primary-care facilities and hospitals were transformed into commercial partnerships, as a precursor to privatization. A restructuring of the emergency care system was also completed in this year. In 1999 there were 27,940 doctors and 4,684 dentists working in the country. In the same year there were 276 hospital establishments, with 62,404 beds, and 3,890 sanatoriums and other institutions, with 38,712 beds. State provision is made for social benefits, including sickness and unemployment allowances, maternity leave payments and pensions. The retirement age is 60 years for men and 55 years for women; many employees are entitled to early retirement.

State social insurance is directed by the Department of Public Insurance and the Directorate of Pensions. In 1997 there were 196 social welfare institutions. Of total government expenditure in 1998, 341.7m. leva (4.7%) was for health, and a further 2,343.7m. leva (32.4%) for social security and welfare. Pension Fund expenditure for 2001 was projected at 2,600m. leva. According to government estimates there were 2,370,938 pensioners at the beginning of 2001. Pension reform was undertaken from 1999.

Education

Education is free and compulsory between the ages of seven and 16 years. Children between the ages of three and six years may attend kindergartens (in 1995 62% of pre-school age children attended). Primary education, beginning at seven years of age, lasts for four years. Secondary education, from 11 years of age, lasts for up to eight years, comprising two cycles of four years each. Secondary education is undertaken at general schools, which provide a general academic course, or vocational and technical schools, and art schools, which offer specialized training. In 1997 primary enrolment included 97.9% of children in the relevant age-group, while enrolment at secondary schools included 77.6% of those in the relevant age-group. In 1999/2000 there were a total of 41 higher educational institutions, with a total enrolment of 242,860 students, and an additional 47 colleges.

In 1997 enrolment in higher education courses was equivalent to 41.2% of those in the relevant age-group. The 1999 state budget allocated 319.1m. leva to education (representing 4.4% of total expenditure by the central Government). In 1998, according to UNDP estimates, 1.8% of the adult population were illiterate (males 1.1%; females 2.4%).

Public Holidays

2001: 1 January (New Year), 3 March (National Day), 16 April (Easter Monday), 1 May (Labour Day), 6 May (St George's Day), 24 May (Education Day), 6 September (Union of Eastern Rumelia and the Bulgarian Principality), 22 September (Independence Day), 1 November (Commemoration of the Leaders of the Bulgarian National Revival), 24–25 December (Christmas).

2002: 1 January (New Year), 3 March (National Day), 1 April (Easter Monday), 1 May (Labour Day), 6 May (St George's Day), 24 May (Education Day), 6 September (Union of Eastern Rumelia and the Bulgarian Principality), 22 September (Independence Day), 1 November (Commemoration of the Leaders of the Bulgarian National Revival), 24–25 December (Christmas).

Weights and Measures

The metric system is in force.

Statistical Survey

Source (unless otherwise stated): National Statistical Institute, 1000 Sofia, Shesti Septemvri St 10; tel. (2) 98-57-27-27; fax (2) 98-57-20-02; e-mail iilarionov@nsi.bg; internet www.nsi.bg.

Area and Population

AREA, POPULATION AND DENSITY

Area (sq km)*	110,994†
Population (census results)	
4 December 1985	8,948,649
4 December 1992	
Males	4,170,622
Females	4,316,695
Total	8,487,317
Population (official estimates at 31 December)	
1997	8,283,200
1998	8,230,371
1999	8,190,876
Density (per sq km) at 31 December 1999	73.8

* Including territorial waters of frontier rivers (261.4 sq km).
† 42,855 sq miles.

ETHNIC GROUPS (1992 census)

	Number	%
Bulgarian	7,271,185	85.67
Turkish	800,052	9.43
Gypsy	313,396	3.69
Armenian	13,677	0.16
Others	80,526	0.95
Unknown	8,481	0.10
Total	**8,487,317**	**100.00**

ADMINISTRATIVE REGIONS (31 December 1997)

	Area (sq km)	Estimated population	Density (per sq km)
Sofia (town)*	1,310.8	1,190,547	908.3
Burgas	14,724.3	834,367	56.7
Khaskovo	13,824.1	889,849	64.4
Lovech	15,150.0	971,938	64.2
Montana†	10,606.8	603,024	56.9
Plovdiv	13,585.4	1,199,423	88.3
Ruse	10,842.5	748,840	69.1
Sofia (region)*	19,021.1	953,335	50.1
Varna	11,928.6	891,877	74.8
Total	**110,993.6**	**8,283,200**	**74.6**

* The city of Sofia, the national capital, has separate regional status. The area and population of the capital region are not included in the neighbouring Sofia region.
† Formerly Mikhailovgrad.

PRINCIPAL TOWNS
(estimated population at 31 December 1997)

Sofia (capital) .	1,114,168	Pleven . . .	122,625
Plovdiv . .	339,744	Sliven . . .	105,793
Varna . . .	298,571	Dobrich* . .	100,902
Burgas (Bourgas) .	194,301	Shumen . . .	94,537
Ruse (Roussé) . .	166,416	Yambol . . .	88,835
Stara Zagora . .	148,103	Pernik	87,172

* Dobrich was renamed Tolbukhin in 1949, but its former name was restored in 1990.

BIRTHS, MARRIAGES AND DEATHS

	Registered live births		Registered marriages		Registered deaths	
	Number	Rate (per 1,000)	Number	Rate (per 1,000)	Number	Rate (per 1,000)
1992 . .	89,134	10.4	44,806*	5.2	107,998	12.6
1993 . .	84,987	10.0	40,022*	4.7	109,540	12.9
1994 . .	79,934	9.4	37,910*	4.5	111,787	13.2
1995 . .	72,428	8.6	36,795*	4.4	114,670	13.6
1996 . .	72,743	8.6	n.a.	4.3	117,056	14.0
1997 . .	64,609	7.7	n.a.	4.2	121,861	14.7
1998 . .	65,360	7.9	n.a.	4.3	118,193	14.3
1999 . .	68,989	8.4	35,540	4.3	107,865	13.1

* Including marriages of Bulgarian nationals outside the country but excluding those of aliens in Bulgaria.

Source: partly UN, *Population and Vital Statistics Report* and *Monthly Bulletin of Statistics*.

Expectation of life (years at birth, 1998): Males 67; Females 75 (Source: World Bank, *World Development Indicators*).

EMPLOYMENT
(annual averages, excluding armed forces)

	1997	1998	1999
Agriculture, hunting, forestry and fishing . .	776,822	825,185	818,195
Mining and quarrying . .	60,463	55,453	47,941
Manufacturing	755,647	723,184	662,963
Electricity, gas and water supply	57,906	57,802	57,860
Construction	157,291	129,088	123,736
Wholesale and retail trade; repair of motor vehicles, motorcycles and personal and household goods . .	319,435	337,243	337,696
Hotels and restaurants . .	76,255	70,545	68,200
Transport and communications .	245,972	236,681	232,857
Financial intermediation . .	40,055	37,613	35,799
Real estate, renting and business activities . .	96,086	102,912	95,188
Public administration; compulsory social security . .	77,139	80,723	91,744
Education	247,551	233,045	231,977
Health and social work . .	183,787	167,138	165,096
Other community, social and personal service activities .	103,725	95,942	102,661
Total employees . . .	**3,198,134**	**3,152,554**	**3,071,913**

Unemployment (persons registered at 31 December): 523,507 in 1997; 465,202 in 1998; 610,551 in 1999.

Agriculture

PRINCIPAL CROPS ('000 metric tons)

	1997	1998	1999
Wheat	3,575	5,345	5,132
Rice (paddy)	11	10	7
Barley	810	717	652
Maize	1,659	1,303	1,719
Rye	27	27	30*
Oats	54	64	52*
Potatoes	463	478	566
Dry beans	25	23	24
Dry peas	8	8	10*
Soybeans	6	6	5*
Sunflower seed	438	524	610
Seed cotton	9	7	9
Cabbages	122	143	143†
Tomatoes	242	490	446†
Pumpkins, squash and gourds	60†	47	52†
Cucumbers and gherkins	134	193	170
Green peppers	180	242	207
Dry onions	70	107	104
Green beans	20	17	20†
Green peas	4†	6	7†
Melons and watermelons	246	288	384
Grapes	636	396	371
Apples	161	129	92
Pears	23	20	18†
Plums	113	62	66
Peaches and nectarines	50	42	38
Apricots	12	9	10†
Strawberries	5	8	10
Sugar beets	80	62	53
Tobacco (leaves)	61*	39	34*

* Unofficial figure. † FAO estimate.

Source: FAO.

LIVESTOCK ('000 head at 1 January each year)

	1997	1998	1999
Horses	170	126	126*
Asses	287	225	225*
Cattle	582	612	671
Pigs	1,500	1,480	1,721
Sheep	3,020	2,848	2,744
Goats	849	966	1,048
Buffaloes	11	11	10
Chickens†	15,127	13,766	14,626
Ducks†	350	320	340
Geese†	250	230	240
Turkeys†	500	450	480

* FAO estimate. † Unofficial figures.

Source: FAO.

LIVESTOCK PRODUCTS ('000 metric tons)

	1997	1998	1999
Beef and veal	56*	55*	64†
Buffalo meat†	2	1	1
Mutton and lamb	44	46*	46†
Goat meat†	6	7	7
Pig meat	227	247*	258*
Poultry meat	101	107	100*
Cows' milk	1,197	1,327	1,389
Buffaloes' milk	11†	11	11
Sheeps' milk	110	109	106
Goats' milk	162	191	200
Butter	2	2	1
Cheese	66	72	58
Hen eggs	87	93*	90*
Other poultry eggs	2	2†	2†
Honey	5	5†	6
Wool: greasy	7	8	8
Cattle and buffalo hides†	9	9	10

* Unofficial figure. † FAO estimate(s).

Source: FAO.

Forestry

ROUNDWOOD REMOVALS ('000 cubic metres, excl. bark)

	1996	1997	1998
Sawlogs, veneer logs and logs for sleepers	869	810	810
Pulpwood	1,001	927	927
Other industrial wood	150	125	125
Fuel wood	1,185	1,179	1,179
Total	3,205	3,041	3,041

Source: FAO, *Yearbook of Forest Products.*

SAWNWOOD PRODUCTION ('000 cubic metres, incl. sleepers)

	1996	1997	1998
Coniferous (softwood)*	186	186	186
Broadleaved (hardwood)*	67	67	67
Total	253	253	253

* FAO estimates.

Source: FAO, *Yearbook of Forest Products.*

Fishing

('000 metric tons, live weight)

	1996	1997	1998
Capture	8.9	11.2	10.8
Silver carp	0.5	0.5	0.6
Other cyprinids	0.2	1.0	1.3
Gobies	0.5	0.4	0.4
European sprat	3.5	3.6	3.3
Sea snails	3.3	4.9	4.3
Aquaculture	4.7*	5.4	4.3
Common carp	3.5*	3.7	1.5
Other cyprinids	0.6*	0.9	1.7
Rainbow trout	0.6	0.7	0.6
Total catch	13.6	16.6	15.0

* FAO estimate.

Source: FAO, *Yearbook of Fishery Statistics.*

Mining

('000 metric tons, unless otherwise indicated)

	1995	1996	1997
Anthracite	24	19	14
Other hard coal	170	119	88
Lignite	27,449	28,104	26,929
Other brown coal	3,187	3,060	2,677
Iron ore*	270	282	264
Copper ore*†	75.5	84.8	84.8
Lead ore*†	32.5	28.5	28.8
Zinc ore*†	30.0	28.0	28.0
Manganese ore*	5.6	13.1	14.2
Crude petroleum	43	32	28
Natural gas (million cu metres)	22.5	18.8	12.9

* Figures relate to the metal content of ores. Data for copper, lead and zinc are from *World Metal Statistics* (London).
† Source: UN, *Industrial Commodity Statistics Yearbook.*

1998 ('000 metric tons): Anthracite and other hard coal 88; Lignite 27,117; Other brown coal 2,666.

Industry

SELECTED PRODUCTS
('000 metric tons, unless otherwise indicated)

	1996	1997	1998
Flour	875	757	681
Refined sugar	292	114	130
Wine ('000 hectolitres)	2,264	1,943	2,333
Beer ('000 hectolitres)	4,402	3,031	3,796
Cigarettes and cigars (metric tons)	57,300	43,300	33,200
Cotton yarn (metric tons)[1]	26,000	28,200	21,700
Woven cotton fabrics ('000 metres)[2]	68,800	75,700	80,100
Flax and hemp yarn (metric tons)	800	500	400
Wool yarn (metric tons)[1]	12,900	11,600	8,600
Woven woollen fabrics ('000 metres)[2]	12,100	11,200	6,100
Woven fabrics of man-made fibres ('000 metres)[3]	19,300	16,500	16,400
Leather footwear ('000 pairs)	8,200	8,200	7,400
Rubber footwear ('000 pairs)	1,000	500	n.a.
Chemical wood pulp	84.7	92.4	88.7
Paper and paperboard	202.3	178.4	114.7
Rubber tyres ('000)[4]	532	391	314
Sulphuric acid (100%)	524.7	556.2	498.9
Soda ash (98%)	866.1	n.a.	n.a.
Nitrogenous fertilizers[5]	468.2	375.6	262.8
Phosphate fertilizers[5]	90.4	110.2	91.4
Coke (gas and coke-oven)	1,157	1,239	n.a.
Unworked glass—rectangles ('000 sq metres)	12,300	10,500	9,500
Clay building bricks (million)	622	412	361
Cement	2,137	1,654	1,742
Pig-iron and ferro-alloys	1,513	1,654	n.a.
Crude steel	2,457	2,628	n.a.
Refined copper—unwrought (metric tons)	22,300	34,500	32,100
Refined lead—unwrought (metric tons)	74,700	72,600	79,900
Zinc—unwrought (metric tons)	68,000	70,400	72,700
Metal-working lathes (number)	2,513	2,315	1,761
Fork-lift trucks (number)[6]	3,900	3,100	2,400
Refrigerators—household (number)	36,400	21,100	55,100
Washing machines—household (number)	23,700	4,900	n.a.
Radio receivers (number)	300	30	n.a.
Television receivers (number)	10,600	5,900	2,800
Construction: dwellings completed (number)[7]	8,099	7,452	4,942
Electric energy (million kWh)	42,716	42,803	41,712

[1] Pure and mixed yarn. Figures for wool include yarn of man-made staple.
[2] Pure and mixed fabrics, after undergoing finishing processes.
[3] Finished fabrics, including fabrics of natural silk.
[4] Tyres for road motor vehicles (passenger cars and commercial vehicles).
[5] Figures for nitrogenous fertilizers are in terms of nitrogen, and for phosphate fertilizers in terms of phosphoric acid. Data for nitrogenous fertilizers include urea.
[6] Including hoisting gears.
[7] Including restorations and conversions.

Finance

CURRENCY AND EXCHANGE RATES

Monetary Units
100 stotinki (singular: stotinka) = 1 new lev (plural: leva).

Sterling, Dollar and Euro Equivalents (29 December 2000)
£1 sterling = 3.1365 new leva;
US $1 = 2.1019 new leva;
€1 = 1.9558 new leva;
100 new leva = £31.88 = $47.58 = €51.13.

Average Exchange Rate (new leva per US$)
1998	1.7604
1999	1.8364
2000	2.1233

Note: On 5 July 1999 a new lev, equivalent to 1,000 old leva, was introduced. In January 1999 the value of the old lev had been linked to the German currency, the Deutsche Mark (DM), when an official exchange rate of DM1 = 1,000 old leva was established. The new lev was thus at par with the DM. Since the establishment of the euro, on 1 January 1999, the German currency has had a fixed exchange rate of €1 = 1.95583. Most of the figures in this Survey are still in terms of old leva.

STATE BUDGET ('000 million old leva)*

Revenue[†]	1996	1997	1998
Taxation	424.4	4,303.4	5,827.6
Taxes on income, profits, etc.	107.7	1,222.0	1,104.6
Social security contributions	118.2	1,171.4	1,663.1
From employers	109.0	1,146.8	1,531.7
Taxes on payroll or work-force	12.4	116.7	—
Domestic taxes on goods and services	146.9	1,424.3	2,526.1
Sales, turnover or value-added taxes	118.8	1,050.0	1,836.0
Excises	28.0	374.3	674.1
Taxes on international trade and transactions	38.2	363.6	443.0
Import duties	29.1	351.4	440.5
Other current revenue	143.8	1,169.8	1,491.1
Entrepreneurial and property income	71.2	614.6	260.2
Administrative fees and charges, non-industrial and incidental sales	50.3	276.5	758.6
Fines and forfeits	9.5	104.0	188.6
Contributions to government employee pension and welfare funds	—	—	193.3
Capital revenue	1.2	84.9	61.7
Total revenue	569.4	5,558.0	7,380.4

Expenditure[‡]	1996	1997	1998
General public services	19.7	327.6	518.9
Defence	41.4	460.3	580.4
Public order and safety	24.2	279.5	452.9
Education	28.6	323.9	319.1
Health	23.1	326.7	341.7
Social security and welfare	157.1	1,552.3	2,343.7
Housing and community amenities	4.3	24.5	116.1
Recreational, cultural and religious affairs and services	6.1	62.4	104.0
Economic affairs and services	127.4	934.6	860.3
Fuel and energy	6.1	184.1	170.6
Agriculture, forestry, fishing and hunting	10.7	146.2	145.6
Transport and communications	13.4	167.1	329.5
Other purposes	408.8	1,441.5	1,590.5
Total expenditure	840.6	5,733.2	7,227.6
Current[§]	818.3	5,284.0	6,580.3
Capital	22.3	449.2	647.3

* Figures refer to the consolidated accounts of the central Government (including social security funds and other extrabudgetary units).
[†] Excluding grants received ('000 million old leva): 4.1 in 1996; 104.1 in 1997; 150.3 in 1998.
[‡] Excluding lending minus repayments ('000 million old leva): 2.6 in 1996; −424.4 in 1997; −296.2 in 1998.
[§] Including interest payments ('000 million old leva): 353.3 in 1996; 1,439.3 in 1997; 952.0 in 1998.

Source: IMF, *Government Finance Statistics Yearbook*.

INTERNATIONAL RESERVES (US $ million at 31 December)

	1998	1999	2000
Gold*	296	265	245
IMF special drawing rights	30	82	85
Reserve position in IMF	46	45	43
Foreign exchange	2,755	2,957	3,215
Total	3,127	3,348	3,587

* Valued at market-related prices.

Source: IMF, *International Financial Statistics*.

MONEY SUPPLY (million new leva at 31 December)

	1998	1999	2000
Currency outside banks	1,742.0	1,957.4	2,373.6
Demand deposits at deposit money banks	1,013.6	1,039.3	1,258.6
Total money	2,755.6	2,996.6	3,632.2

Source: Bulgarian National Bank.

COST OF LIVING
(Consumer Price Index; base: 1990=100)

	1997	1998	1999
Food	106,100	128,552	118,044
Fuel and light	145,080	175,382	208,619
Clothing	71,375	84,109	81,286
Rent	69,484	128,903	164,591
All items (incl. others)	98,132	120,008	122,155

Source: ILO, *Yearbook of Labour Statistics*.

NATIONAL ACCOUNTS (million old leva at current prices)
Expenditure on the Gross Domestic Product

	1997	1998	1999†
Government final consumption expenditure	2,188,117	3,255,264	3,612
Private final consumption expenditure	11,981,707	15,733,740	17,037
Increase in stocks	100,768	785,633	707
Gross fixed capital formation	1,840,974	2,850,802	3,632
Adjustment*	0	−418,052	−447
Total domestic expenditure	16,111,566	22,207,387	24,541
Exports of goods and services	10,555,860	10,360,948	10,054
Less Imports of goods and services	9,612,221	10,991,315	11,819
GDP in purchasers' values	17,055,205	21,577,020	22,776

* Referring to consumption by Bulgarian residents abroad, less consumption by non-residents in Bulgaria.

† In million new leva.

Gross Domestic Product by Economic Activity

	1997	1998	1999*
Agriculture	4,008,331	3,980,383	3,363
Forestry	54,367	64,992	77
Mining	344,731	294,011	336
Manufacturing	2,857,613	3,664,261	3,303
Electricity, gas and water	689,325	832,850	950
Construction	424,637	717,629	737
Trade	1,304,910	1,470,290	1,486
Transport	814,387	1,025,663	959
Communications	340,634	551,610	778
Financial services	398,232	407,244	585
Other services	4,057,315	6,194,271	7,317
Sub-total	15,294,482	19,203,204	19,891
Excises and value-added tax	1,754,786	2,351,362	2,896
Import duties	368,131	389,903	299
Less Imputed bank service charge	362,194	367,449	310
GDP in purchasers' values	17,055,205	21,577,020	22,776

* In million new leva.

BALANCE OF PAYMENTS (US $ million)

	1997	1998	1999
Exports of goods f.o.b.	4,940	4,194	4,006
Imports of goods f.o.b.	−4,559	−4,574	−5,087
Trade balance	380	−381	−1,081
Exports of services	1,337	1,788	1,786
Imports of services	−1,171	−1,415	−1,471
Balance on goods and services	547	−8	−767
Other income received	211	307	266
Other income paid	−567	−590	−484
Balances on goods, services and income	190	−292	−985
Current transfers received	276	261	329
Current transfers paid	−39	−32	−29
Current balance	427	−62	−685
Capital account (net)	—	—	−2
Direct investment abroad	2	—	−17
Direct investment from abroad	505	537	806
Portfolio investment assets	−14	−130	−208
Portfolio investment liabilities	147	−112	8
Other investment assets	−54	222	17
Other investment liabilities	−123	−251	171
Net errors and omissions	256	−299	6
Overall balance	1,145	−94	96

Source: IMF, *International Financial Statistics*.

External Trade

PRINCIPAL COMMODITIES (US $ million)

Imports c.i.f.	1995	1996	1997
Food and live animals	357.4	312.9	362.8
Sugar, sugar preparations and honey	140.3	100.0	107.7
Sugar and honey	n.a.	98.5	106.2
Crude materials (inedible) except fuels	379.0	283.6	347.5
Textile fibres and waste	164.4	79.1	92.5
Cotton	114.5	32.7	48.7
Metalliferous ores and metal scrap	124.6	120.0	170.9
Mineral fuels, lubricants, etc.	1,525.4	1,716.1	1,503.7
Coal, coke and briquettes	n.a.	201.2	188.4
Coal, lignite and peat	n.a.	181.4	170.0
Petroleum, petroleum products, etc.	n.a.	969.2	832.2
Crude petroleum oils, etc.	n.a.	917.7	771.2
Gas (natural and manufactured)	n.a.	545.8	483.1
Petroleum gases, etc. (liquefied)	n.a.	545.8	483.1
Chemicals and related products	729.1	547.4	509.8
Organic chemicals	139.4	97.6	94.2
Inorganic chemicals	143.1	80.1	89.4
Artificial resins, plastic materials, etc.	142.6	86.3	73.8
Basic manufactures	1,010.2	883.5	958.5
Leather, leather manufactures and dressed furskins	50.5	92.9	99.3
Paper, paperboard, etc.	179.6	119.7	99.3
Textile yarn, fabrics, etc.	250.7	292.2	352.4
Woven synthetic fabrics	n.a.	82.8	105.2
Iron and steel	141.1	124.7	142.7
Non-ferrous metals	185.3	71.4	81.0
Machinery and transport equipment	1,067.9	808.2	800.5
Machinery specialized for particular industries	n.a.	117.7	172.5

Imports c.i.f. — *continued*	1995	1996	1997
General industrial machinery, equipment and parts .	n.a.	160.7	151.2
Electrical machinery, apparatus, etc. (excl. telecommunications and sound equipment) .	n.a.	147.1	128.2
Road vehicles and parts (excl. tyres, engines and electrical parts)	250.1	155.3	115.9
Miscellaneous manufactured articles . . .	308.3	261.8	280.3
Total (incl. others) . . .	5,469.5	5,074.0	4,932.0

Exports f.o.b.	1995	1996	1997
Food and live animals . .	561.7	413.9	327.7
Cereals and cereal preparations .	161.5	17.2	27.0
Vegetables and fruit . .	75.7	133.3	111.0
Beverages and tobacco. .	500.9	431.4	306.5
Beverages . . .	195.0	175.3	141.7
Alcoholic beverages . .	n.a.	170.3	136.9
Wine of fresh grapes . .	n.a.	137.3	121.3
Tobacco and tobacco manufactures	306.0	256.2	164.9
Manufactured tobacco . .	n.a.	195.1	128.1
Cigarettes . . .	n.a.	191.5	124.8
Crude materials (inedible) except fuels . . .	336.5	239.5	260.5
Mineral fuels, lubricants, etc.	325.0	318.3	375.3
Petroleum, petroleum products, etc.	n.a.	309.8	372.6
Refined petroleum products. .	n.a.	308.3	371.1
Chemicals and related products	921.4	893.6	837.2
Organic chemicals . . .	185.4	141.2	175.4
Inorganic chemicals . .	121.5	128.9	117.7
Medicinal and pharmaceutical products . . .	n.a.	112.7	137.2
Medicaments (incl. veterinary)	n.a.	93.2	113.3
Essential oils, perfume materials and cleansing preparations. .	88.1	106.4	100.1
Manufactured fertilizers . .	243.9	271.8	172.5
Nitrogenous mineral or chemical fertilizers . . .	n.a.	242.6	142.2
Ammonium nitrate . .	n.a.	99.3	51.5
Urea . . .	n.a.	130.7	81.5
Artificial resins, plastic materials, etc. . . .	151.2	101.5	100.8
Basic manufactures . .	1,476.2	1,339.6	1,518.4
Textile yarn, fabrics, etc. .	148.9	180.1	178.5
Non-metallic mineral manufactures . . .	108.9	125.4	135.3
Iron and steel . . .	552.2	399.9	521.1
Ingots and other primary forms	n.a.	158.9	239.0
Coils for re-rolling . .	n.a.	112.4	186.7
Universals, plates and sheets	n.a.	147.4	208.5
Non-ferrous metals . . .	409.8	395.4	446.7
Copper and copper alloys .	280.4	257.5	280.9
Unwrought copper and alloys	n.a.	223.3	250.9
Unrefined copper (excl. cement copper) .	n.a.	169.2	173.7
Machinery and transport equipment . .	614.1	608.4	548.4
General industrial machinery, equipment and parts . .	n.a.	154.5	138.4
Electrical machinery, apparatus, etc. (excl. telecommunications and sound equipment) . .	n.a.	139.5	136.2
Miscellaneous manufactured articles . .	435.9	499.3	569.2
Clothing and accessories (excl. footwear) . .	239.8	281.4	354.2
Women's, girls' and infants' outer garments of non-knitted textile fabrics . .	n.a.	82.3	104.5
Total (incl. others) . .	5,220.5	4,890.3	4,939.7

Source: UN, *International Trade Statistics Yearbook*.

PRINCIPAL TRADING PARTNERS (US $ million)*

Imports c.i.f.	1997	1998	1999
Austria	119.8	140.8	164.3
Belgium	64.2†	89.6†	91.5
Brazil	69.3	54.9	n.a.
Czech Republic . .	63.5	96.5	99.6
France	158.2	227.1	287.7
Germany	580.0	686.1	821.2
Greece	207.7	295.1	311.7
Iran	52.8	13.1	n.a.
Iraq	43.9	58.5	n.a.
Italy	354.1	385.2	463.4
Japan	37.2	41.9	65.5
Netherlands . . .	91.7	102.3	110.8
Poland	57.4	43.0	75.7
Romania	48.8	58.2	74.4
Russia	1,382.2	1,003.2	1,109.7
Spain	25.8	50.1	n.a.
Sweden	41.0	45.7	74.1
Switzerland . . .	79.7	72.9	74.4
Turkey	102.5	131.2	167.0
Ukraine	182.0	193.6	144.3
United Kingdom . . .	128.8	120.7	132.5
USA	185.0	197.9	193.8
Total (incl. others) . .	4,932.0	4,995.0	5,515.1

Exports f.o.b.	1997	1998	1999
Austria	54.2	71.0	68.3
Belgium	78.2†	154.2†	176.8
Egypt	43.3	54.4	n.a.
France	134.8	147.1	181.2
Georgia	123.0	67.6	41.1
Germany	469.0	448.7	395.1
Greece	407.1	377.1	346.0
Italy	577.9	544.5	558.2
Macedonia, former Yugoslav republic . .	98.1	98.0	105.4
Malta	18.0	43.0	n.a.
Moldova. . . .	100.0	46.1	n.a.
Netherlands . . .	75.7	79.2	83.3
Poland	29.7	55.3	29.5
Romania	66.0	52.8	55.8
Russia	392.6	234.1	189.6
Slovenia. . . .	14.0	28.7	44.6
Spain	129.2	121.0	108.2
Switzerland . . .	33.5	28.1	48.8
Turkey	445.2	341.3	293.2
Ukraine	147.0	113.6	67.4
United Kingdom . . .	131.0	108.1	100.3
USA	129.4	111.3	146.6
Yugoslavia, Federal Republic .	124.8	95.6	164.0
Total (incl. others) . .	4,939.7	4,293.0	4,006.4

* Imports by country of purchase; exports by country of sale.
† Including trade with Luxembourg.

Source: partly UN, *International Trade Statistics Yearbook*.

Transport

RAILWAYS (traffic)

	1997	1998	1999
Passengers carried ('000) . .	82,656	64,260	53.112
Passenger-kilometres (million) .	5,886	4,740	3,819
Freight carried ('000 metric tons) .	29,220	24,461	21,090
Freight net ton-kilometres (million)	7,444	6,152	5,297

ROAD TRAFFIC (motor vehicles in use at 31 December)

	1996	1997	1998
Passenger cars . . .	1,707,023	1,730,506	1,809,350
Buses and coaches . .	40,835	40,422	41,487
Lorries and vans. . .	207,258	210,960	220,948
Motorcycles and mopeds . .	521,710	524,950	515,701

Source: International Road Federation, *World Road Statistics*.

INLAND WATERWAYS (traffic)

	1997	1998	1999
Passengers carried ('000) . . .	10	10	10
Passenger-kilometres (million) .	11	13	12
Freight carried ('000 metric tons) .	919	836	439
Freight ton-kilometres (million) .	677	711	274

SHIPPING

Merchant Fleet (registered at 31 December)

	1996	1997	1998
Number of vessels	192	187	181
Total displacement ('000 grt) . .	1,149.7	1,128.2	1,091.2

Source: Lloyd's Register of Shipping, *World Fleet Statistics*.

Sea-borne Traffic (international and coastal)

	1997	1998	1999
Passengers carried ('000) . .	21	7	n.a.
Freight ('000 metric tons). .	19,623	16,446	16,822

CIVIL AVIATION (traffic)

	1997	1998	1999*
Passengers carried ('000) . . .	1,209	1,269	1,354
Passenger-kilometres (million) .	2,711	2,868	2,680
Freight carried ('000 metric tons) .	13	14	30
Freight ton-kilometres (million) .	41	39	63

* Including the private sector.

Tourism

ARRIVALS OF FOREIGN VISITORS

Country of origin	1997	1998	1999
Czech Republic	61,345	58,144	63,299
Germany	228,662	212,919	239,173
Greece	210,963	389,759	407,269
Macedonia, former Yugoslav			
republic	487,641	714,195	976,734
Poland*	70,511	101,863	93,754
Romania*	1,202,325	1,225,776	1,238,708
Russia	548,572	212,576	102,188
Slovakia*	57,312	89,189	69,141
Turkey*	2,587,223	784,465	514,137
Ukraine*	846,005	243,840	170,501
United Kingdom	79,206	80,974	65,032
Yugoslavia, Federal Republic . .	601,134	393,710	415,308
Total (incl. others)	7,543,185	5,239,691	5,056,250

* Mainly visitors in transit, totalling 4,562,948 in 1997 and 2,565,535 in 1999.

Receipts from tourism (US $ million): 388 in 1996; 369 in 1997; 437 in 1998 (Source: mainly World Tourism Organization, *Yearbook of Tourism Statistics*).

Communications Media

	1997	1998	1999
Telephone subscribers . . .	3,118,800	3,186,500	3,254,700
Book production:*			
Titles	3,773	4,863	4,850
Copies ('000)	10,400	11,900	10,800
Newspapers:			
Titles	673	644	622
Total circulation ('000 copies)	383,800	428,400	411,500
Magazines:†			
Titles	611	639	631
Total circulation ('000 copies)	9,600	14,100	13,500

* Including pamphlets.
† Including bulletins.

Telefax stations (number in use): 15,000 in 1995 (provisional data).
Mobile cellular telephones (subscribers): 20,920 in 1995; 26,588 in 1996; 70,000 in 1997.
Radio licences (at 31 December): 1,448,000 in 1995; 1,390,700 in 1996; 1,329,900 in 1997.
Television licences (at 31 December): 1,479,100 in 1995; 1,470,700 in 1996; 1,462,500 in 1997.

Sources: partly UNESCO, *Statistical Yearbook*, and UN, *Statistical Yearbook*.

Education

(1999/2000)

	Institutions	Teachers	Students
Kindergartens	3,434	20,022	212,000
General schools. . . .	3,011	65,885	887,213
Special.	146	2,597	15,984
Vocational technical. . .	2	26	2,376
Secondary vocational . .	150	3,206	50,727
Technical colleges and			
schools of arts . .	369	14,264	132,240
Semi-higher institutes* . .	47	2,367	18,461
Higher educational . . .	41	24,368	242,860†

* Including technical, teacher-training, communications and librarians' institutes.
† Including post-graduate students.

Directory

The Constitution

The Constitution of the Republic of Bulgaria, summarized below, took effect upon its promulgation, on 13 July 1991, following its enactment on the previous day.

FUNDAMENTAL PRINCIPLES

Chapter One declares that the Republic of Bulgaria is to have a parliamentary form of government, with all state power derived from the people. The rule of law and the life, dignity and freedom of the individual are guaranteed. The Constitution is the supreme law; the power of the State is shared between the legislature, the executive and the judiciary. The Constitution upholds principles such as political and religious freedom (although no party may be formed on separatist, ethnic or religious lines), free economic initiative and respect for international law.

FUNDAMENTAL RIGHTS AND OBLIGATIONS OF CITIZENS

Chapter Two establishes the basic provisions for Bulgarian citizenship and fundamental human rights, such as the rights of privacy and movement, the freedoms of expression, assembly and association, and the enfranchisement of Bulgarian citizens aged over 18 years. The Constitution commits the State to the provision of basic social welfare and education and to the encouragement of culture, science and the health of the population. The study and use of the Bulgarian language is required. Other obligations of the citizenry include military service and the payment of taxes.

THE NATIONAL ASSEMBLY

The National Assembly is the legislature of Bulgaria and exercises parliamentary control over the country. It consists of 240 members, elected for a four-year term. Only Bulgarian citizens aged over 21 years (who do not hold a state post or another citizenship and are not under judicial interdiction or in prison) are eligible for election to parliament. A member of the National Assembly ceases to serve as a deputy while holding ministerial office. The National Assembly is a permanently-acting body, which is free to determine its own recesses and elects its own Chairman and Deputy Chairmen. The Chairman represents and convenes the National Assembly, organizes its proceedings, attests its enactments and promulgates its resolutions.

The National Assembly may function when more than one-half of its members are present, and may pass legislation and other acts by a majority of more than one-half of the members present, except where a qualified majority is required by the Constitution. Ministers are free to, and can be obliged to, attend parliamentary sessions. The most important functions of the legislature are: the enactment of laws; the approval of the state budget; the scheduling of presidential elections; the election and dismissal of the Chairman of the Council of Ministers (Prime Minister) and of other members of the Council of Ministers; the declaration of war or conclusion of peace; the foreign deployment of troops; and the ratification of any fundamental international instruments to which the Republic of Bulgaria has agreed. The laws and resolutions of the National Assembly are binding on all state bodies and citizens. All enactments must be promulgated in the official gazette, *Durzhaven Vestnik*, within 15 days of their passage through the legislature.

THE PRESIDENT OF THE REPUBLIC

Chapter Four concerns the Head of State, the President of the Republic of Bulgaria, who is assisted by a Vice-President. The President and Vice-President are elected jointly, directly by the voters, for a period of five years. A candidate must be eligible for election to the National Assembly, but also aged over 40 years and a resident of the country for the five years previous to the election. To be elected, a candidate must receive more than one-half of the valid votes cast, in an election in which more than one-half of the eligible electorate participate. If necessary, a second ballot must then be conducted, contested by the two candidates who received the most votes. The one who receives more votes becomes President. The President and Vice-President may hold the same office for only two terms and, during this time, may not engage in any unsuitable or potentially compromising activities. If the President resigns, is incapacitated, impeached or dies, the Vice-President carries out the presidential duties. If neither official can perform their duties, the Chairman of the National Assembly assumes the prerogatives of the Presidency, until new elections take place.

The President's main responsibilities include the scheduling of elections and referendums, the conclusion of international treaties and the promulgation of laws. The President is responsible for appointing a Prime Minister-designate (priority must be given to the leaders of the two largest parties represented in the National Assembly), who must then attempt to form a government.

The President is Supreme Commander-in-Chief of the Armed Forces of the Republic of Bulgaria and presides over the Consultative National Security Council. The President has certain emergency powers, usually subject to the later approval of the National Assembly. Many of the President's actions must be approved by the Chairman of the Council of Ministers. The President may return legislation to the National Assembly for further consideration, but can be overruled.

THE COUNCIL OF MINISTERS

The principal organ of executive government is the Council of Ministers, which supervises the implementation of state policy and the state budget, the administration of the country and the Armed Forces, and the maintenance of law and order. The Council of Ministers is headed and co-ordinated by the Chairman (Prime Minister), who is responsible for the overall policy of government. The Council of Ministers, which also includes Deputy Chairmen and Ministers, must resign upon the death of the Chairman or if the National Assembly votes in favour of a motion of no confidence in the Council or in the Chairman.

JUDICIAL POWER

The judicial branch of government is independent. All judicial power is exercised in the name of the people. Individuals and legal entities are guaranteed basic rights, such as the right to contest administrative acts and the right to legal counsel. One of the principal organs is the Supreme Court of Cassation, which exercises supreme judicial responsibility for the precise and equal application of the law by all courts. The Supreme Administrative Court rules on all challenges to the legality of acts of any organ of government. The Chief Prosecutor supervises all other prosecutors and ensures that the law is observed, by initiating court actions and ensuring the enforcement of penalties, etc.

The Supreme Judicial Council is responsible for appointments within the ranks of the justices, prosecutors and investigating magistrates, and recommends to the President of the Republic the appointment or dismissal of the Chairmen of the two Supreme Courts and of the Chief Prosecutor (they are each appointed for a single, seven-year term). These last three officials are, *ex officio*, members of the Supreme Judicial Council, together with 22 others, who must be practising lawyers of high integrity and at least 15 years of professional experience. These members are elected for a term of five years, 11 of them by the National Assembly and 11 by bodies of the judiciary. The Supreme Judicial Council is chaired by the Minister of Justice, who is not entitled to vote.

LOCAL SELF-GOVERNMENT AND LOCAL ADMINISTRATION

Chapter Seven provides for the division of Bulgaria into regions and municipalities. Municipalities are the basic administrative territorial unit at which local self-government is practised; their principal organ is the municipal council, which is elected directly by the population for a term of four years. The council elects the mayor, who is the principal organ of executive power. Bulgaria is also divided into regions. Regional government, which is entrusted to regional governors (appointed by the Council of Ministers) and administrations, is responsible for regional policy, the implementation of state policy at a local level and the harmonization of local and national interests.

THE CONSTITUTIONAL COURT

The Constitutional Court consists of 12 justices, four of whom are elected by the National Assembly, four appointed by the President of the Republic and four elected by the justices of the two Supreme Courts. Candidates must have the same eligibility as for membership of the Supreme Judicial Council. They serve a single term of nine years, but a part of the membership changes every three years. A chairman is elected by a secret ballot of the members.

The Constitutional Court provides binding interpretations of the Constitution. It rules on the constitutionality of: laws and decrees; competence suits between organs of government; international agreements; national and presidential elections; and impeachments. A ruling of the Court requires a majority of more than one-half of the votes of all the justices.

CONSTITUTIONAL AMENDMENTS AND THE ADOPTION OF A NEW CONSTITUTION

Chapter Nine provides for constitutional changes. Except for those provisions reserved to the competence of a Grand National Assembly (see below), the National Assembly is empowered to amend the Constitution with a majority of three-quarters of all its Members, in three ballots on three different days. Amendments must be proposed by one-quarter of the parliamentary membership or by the President. In some cases, a majority of two-thirds of all the Members of the National Assembly will suffice.

Grand National Assembly

A Grand National Assembly consists of 400 members, elected by the generally-established procedure. It alone is empowered to adopt a new constitution, to sanction territorial changes to the Republic of Bulgaria, to resolve on any changes in the form of state structure or form of government, and to enact amendments to certain parts of the existing Constitution (concerning the direct application of the Constitution, the domestic application of international agreements, the irrevocable nature of fundamental civil rights and of certain basic individual rights even in times of emergency or war, and amendments to Chapter Nine itself).

Any bill requiring the convening of a Grand National Assembly must be introduced by the President of the Republic or by one-third of the members of the National Assembly. A decision to hold elections for a Grand National Assembly must be supported by two-thirds of the members of the National Assembly. Enactments of the Grand National Assembly require a majority of two-thirds of the votes of all the members, in three ballots on three different days. A Grand National Assembly may resolve only on the proposals for which it was elected, whereupon its prerogatives normally expire.

The Government

HEAD OF STATE

President: PETAR STOYANOV (elected 3 November 1996; took office 19 January 1997).

COUNCIL OF MINISTERS

(March 2001)

Prime Minister and Minister of State Administration: IVAN KOSTOV.

Deputy Prime Minister and Minister of Economy: PETUR ZHOTEV.

Minister without Portfolio: ALEKSANDUR PRAMATARSKI.

Minister of Transport and Communications: ANTONI SLAVINSKI.

Minister of Defence: BOIKO NOEV.

Minister of Education and Science: Prof. DIMITER DIMITROV.

Minister of the Interior: EMANUIL YORDANOV.

Minister of Culture: EMMA MOSKOVA.

Minister of the Environment and Water: EVDOKIA MANEVA.

Minister of Regional and Urban Development: EVGENI CHACHEV.

Minister of Health: ILKO SEMERDJIEV.

Minister of Labour and Social Policy: IVAN NEIKOV.

Minister of Finance: MOURAVEI RADEV.

Minister of Foreign Affairs: NADEZHDA MIHAILOVA.

Minister of Justice: TEODOSSIY SIMEONOV.

Minister of Agriculture and Forestry: VENTSISLAV VURBANOV.

MINISTRIES

Council of Ministers: 1000 Sofia, Blvd Dondukov 1; tel. (2) 940-27-70; fax (2) 980-20-56; e-mail iprd@government.bg; internet www.government.bg.

Ministry of Agriculture and Forestry: 1040 Sofia, Blvd Botev 55; tel. (2) 980-99-27; fax (2) 980-62-56; internet www.mzgar .government.bg.

Ministry of Culture: 1040 Sofia, Blvd A. Stamboliiski 17; tel. (2) 980-53-84; fax (2) 981-81-45; e-mail press.culture@bta.bg.

Ministry of Defence: 1000 Sofia, Aksakov St 1; tel. (2) 987-95-62; fax (2) 87-32-28; internet www.md.government.bg.

Ministry of the Economy: 1000 Sofia, Slavyanska St 8; tel. (2) 988-55-32; fax (2) 980-26-90; e-mail s.bozukova@mi.government.bg; internet www.mi.government.bg.

Ministry of Education and Science: 1540 Sofia, A. Stamboliiski 18; tel. (2) 84-87-44; fax (2) 988-26-93; internet www.minedu .government.bg.

Ministry of the Environment and Water: 1000 Sofia, William Gladstone St 67; tel. (2) 940-62-31; fax (2) 988-59-13; internet www.moew.govrn.bg.

Ministry of Finance: 1000 Sofia, Rakovski St 102; tel. (2) 985-920-20; fax (2) 87-05-81; internet www.minfin.government.bg.

Ministry of Foreign Affairs: 1113 Sofia, Al. Zhendov St 2; tel. (2) 73-79-97; fax (2) 70-30-41; internet www.mfa.government.bg.

Ministry of Health: 1000 Sofia, Sveta Nedelya Sq. 5; tel. (2) 930-01-107; fax (2) 981-26-39; e-mail press@mh.government.bg; internet www.mh.government.bg.

Ministry of the Interior: 1000 Sofia, Shesti Septemvri St 29; tel. (2) 982-20-14; fax (2) 982-20-47; e-mail spvo@mvr.bg; internet www.mvr.bg.

Ministry of Justice: 1040 Sofia, Slavyanska St 1; tel. (2) 988-48-23; fax (2) 981-91-57; e-mail pr@mjeli.government.bg; internet www.mjeli.government.bg.

Ministry of Labour and Social Policy: 1000 Sofia, Triaditza St 2; tel. (2) 87-33-94; fax (2) 986-13-18; e-mail inter.coop@mlsp .government.bg.

Ministry of Regional and Urban Development: Sofia, Kirili Metodi 17–19; tel. (2) 988-29-54; fax (2) 987-58-56.

Ministry of Transport and Communications: 1000 Sofia, Levski St 9; tel. and fax (2) 988-53-29; e-mail vluleva@mtc.government.bg; internet www.mt.government.bg.

President and Legislature

PRESIDENT

Presidential Election, First Ballot, 27 October 1996

Candidates	% of votes
PETAR STOYANOV (Union of Democratic Forces) . . .	44.07
IVAN MARAZOV (Together for Bulgaria)* . . .	27.01
GEORGI GANCHEV (Bulgaria Business Bloc) . . .	21.87
Others.	7.05
Total	**100.00**

Second Ballot, 3 November 1996

Candidates	% of votes
PETAR STOYANOV	59.73
IVAN MARAZOV	40.27
Total	**100.00**

* An electoral alliance, comprising the Bulgarian Socialist Party, the Aleksandur Stamboliyski Bulgarian Agrarian People's Union and the Ecoglasnost Political Club.

NARODNO SOBRANIYE
(National Assembly)

National Assembly: 1000 Sofia, Narodno Sobraniye Sq. 3; tel. (2) 980-85-01; fax (2) 981-01-81; e-mail infocenter@nt52.parliament.bg; internet www.parliament.bg.

Chairman: YORDAN SOKOLOV.

General Election, 19 April 1997

Parties	% of votes	Seats
Union of Democratic Forces . . .	52.57	137
Bulgarian Socialist Party* . .	22.08	58
Alliance for National Salvation† . .	7.60	19
Euro-Left	5.50	14
Bulgarian Business Bloc . .	4.93	12
Others	7.32	—
Total	**100.00**	**240**

* The BSP contested the election in alliance (as the Democratic Left) with the Aleksandur Stamboliyski Bulgarian Agrarian People's Union and the Ecoglasnost Political Club.
† An alliance comprising the Movement for Rights and Freedoms and other groups.

Political Organizations

There are over 80 registered political parties in Bulgaria, many of them incorporated into electoral alliances. The most significant political forces are listed below:

Aleksandur Stamboliyski Bulgarian Agrarian People's Union (Bulgarski Zemedelski Naroden Sayuz 'Aleksandur Stamboliyski'): c/o National Assembly, 1000 Sofia, Narodno Sobraniye Sq. 3; contested 1994 general election and 1996 presidential election in alliance with the Bulgarian Socialist Party and the Ecoglasnost Political Club.

Alliance for National Salvation (ONS): c/o National Assembly, 1000 Sofia, Narodno Sobraniye Sq. 3; f. 1997; electoral coalition of Movement for Rights and Freedoms and other monarchist and centrist groups; Leader AHMED DOGAN.

Bulgarian Communist Party (Bulgarska Komunisticheska Partiya): 1404 Sofia, Blvd P. J. Todorov; tel. and fax (2) 59-16-73; e-mail spasov@internet-bg.net; f. 1990 by conservative mems of the former, ruling Bulgarian Communist Party (now the Bulgarian Socialist Party); First Sec. of the Central Cttee VLADIMIR SPASSOV.

Bulgarian Socialist Party—BSP (Bulgarska Sotsialisticheska Partiya): Sofia, Positano St 20; POB 382; tel. (2) 980-12-91; fax (2) 980-52-91; e-mail BSP@mail.bol.bg; internet www.bsp.bg; f. 1891 as the Bulgarian Social Democratic Party (BSDP); renamed the Bulgarian Communist Party (BCP) in 1919; renamed as above in 1990; 320,000 mems (Jan. 1996); Chair. GEORGI PURVANOV.

Christian Republican Party: Sofia; f. 1989; Chair. KONSTANTIN ADZHAROV.

Civic Party: Sofia; f. 2000; centre-right; Chair. BOGOMIL BONEV.

Confederation—Kingdom Bulgaria (Tsarstvo Bulgaria): 7000 Ruse, Vassil Kolarov 45; tel. (82) 299-64; f. 1990; advocates the restoration of the former King, Simeon II; Chair. GEORGI BAKARDZHIEV.

Democratic Alternative for the Republic—DAR: c/o National Assembly, 1000 Sofia, Narodno Sobraniye Sq. 3; left-of-centre coalition.

Democratic Party of Justice: Sofia; f. 1994; ethnic Turkish group; frmly part of the Movement for Rights and Freedoms; Chair. NEDIM GENDZHEV.

Ecoglasnost National Movement: 1000 Sofia, Blvd Kniaz Dondukov 9, 4th Floor, Rm 45; tel. (2) 986-22-21; fax (2) 88-15-30; e-mail ekogl@bulnet.bg; f. 1989; contested 1994 general election and 1996 presidential election in alliance with the BSP and Aleksandur Stamboliyski (BAPU); represented in more than 140 clubs and organizations in Bulgaria; Chair. IVAN SUNGARSKY; Sec. LUCHEZAR TOSHEV.

Euro-Left: c/o National Assembly, 1000 Sofia, Narodno Sobraniye Sq. 3; internet www.euroleft.bg.org; f. 1997 by the Civic Union of the Republic, the Movement for Social Humanism, and former mems of the Bulgarian Socialist Party; Leader ALEKSANDUR TOMOV.

Fatherland Party of Labour: 1000 Sofia, Slavyanska St 3, Hotel Slavyanska Beseda; tel. (2) 65-83-10; nationalist; Chair. RUMEN POPOV.

Fatherland Union: Sofia, Blvd Vitosha 18; tel. (2) 88-12-21; f. 1942 as the Fatherland Front (a mass organization unifying the BAPU, the BCP—now the BSP—and social organizations); named as above when restructured in 1990; a socio-political organization of independents and individuals belonging to different political parties; Chair. GINYO GANEV.

Georgi Ganchev Bloc: 1000 Sofia, Shipka 13; tel. (2) 44-61-28; f. 2000 as a successor to the Bulgarian Business Bloc; Leader GEORGI GANCHEV; Chair. DOBRI DOBREV.

Inner Macedonian Revolutionary Organization (IMRO): 1301 Sofia, Pirotska St 5; tel. (2) 980-25-82; fax (2) 980-25-83; e-mail vmro@vmro.org; internet www.vmro.org; f. 1893; Chair. KRASSIMIR KARAKACHANOV.

Liberal Congress Party: Sofia; f. 1989 as the Bulgarian Socialist Party, renamed Bulgarian Social Democratic Party (non-Marxist) in 1990 and as above in 1991; membership of the Union of Democratic Forces suspended 1993; c. 20,000 mems; Chair. YANKO N. YANKOV.

Liberal Democratic Union: 1408 Sofia, Petko Karavelov St 1A; tel. (2) 66-05-35; fax (2) 66-04-03; e-mail zhelev@bgnet.bg; f. 1998; electoral alliance; Pres. ZHELYU ZHELEV.

> **Free Radical Democratic Party:** Sofia.
>
> **Liberal Democratic Alternative:** 1000 Sofia, Triaditsa St 4; tel. (2) 986-37; e-mail lda@bulgarianspace.com; internet www .bulgarianspace.com/lda/; f. 1997; Leader ZHELYU ZHELEV.

Movement for Rights and Freedoms—MRF (Dvizhenie za Prava i Svobodi—DPS): 1408 Sofia, Ivan Vazov, Tzarigradsko St 47/1; tel. (2) 88-18-23; f. 1990; represents the Muslim minority in Bulgaria; 95,000 mems (1991); Pres. AHMED DOGAN.

> **New Choice Liberal Alliance:** f. 1994 by a former faction of the Union of Democratic Forces; Co-Chair. DIMITUR LUDZHEV, IVAN PUSHKAROV.

National Movement for Rights and Freedoms: f. 1999; breakaway faction of the MRF; Leader GYUNER TAHIR.

New Union for Democracy—NUD: Sofia; f. 1993; fmrly section of the Union of Democratic Forces.

Party of Free Democrats (Centre): 6000 Stara Zagora; tel. (42) 2-70-42; f. 1989; Chair. Asst Prof. KHRISTO SANTULOV.

Union of Democratic Forces—UDF (Sayuz na Demokratichni Sili—SDS): 1000 Sofia, Blvd Rakovski 134; tel. (2) 88-25-01; fax (2) 981-05-22; e-mail fortuna@infotel.bg; internet www.sds.bg; f. 1989; Chair. IVAN KOSTOV; alliance of the following parties, organizations and movements:

> **Bulgarian Agrarian People's Union—'Nikola Petkov'** (Bulgarski Zemedelski Naroden Sayuz—'Nikola Petkov'): 1000 Sofia, Vrabtcha St 1; tel. (2) 87-80-81; fax (2) 981-09-49; f. 1899; in govt coalition from April 1997; Leader GEORGI PINCHEV.
>
> **Bulgarian Democratic Forum:** 1505 Sofia; tel. (2) 890-22-85; Chair. VASSIL ZLATAREV.
>
> **Bulgarian Social Democratic Party (United—BSDP):** 1504 Sofia, Ekzarkh Yosif St 37; tel. (2) 80-15-84; fax (2) 39-00-86; e-mail biltd@vt.bia-bg.com; internet www.bsdp.dir.bg; f. 1891; re-established 1989; Chair. PETUR DERTLIEV.
>
> **Christian Democratic Union:** Sofia; Chair. JULIUS PAVLOV.
>
> **Christian 'Salvation' Union:** Sofia; Chair. Bishop KHRISTOFOR SAHEV.
>
> **Citizens' Initiative Movement:** Sofia; tel. (2) 39-01-93; Chair. TODOR GAGALOV.
>
> **Conservative Ecological Party:** Sofia; Chair. KHRISTO BISSEROV.
>
> **Democratic Party 1896:** f. 1994 by a former faction of the Democratic Party; Chair. STEFAN RAYCHEVSKI.
>
> **Federation of Democracy Clubs:** Sofia; f. 1988 as Club for the Support of Glasnost and Perestroika; merged with other groups, as above in 1990; Chair. YORDAN VASSILEV.
>
> **Federation of Independent Student Committees:** Sofia; Leader ANDREI NENOV.
>
> **New Social Democratic Party:** 1504 Sofia, POB 14; tel. (2) 44-99-47; f. 1990; membership of UDF suspended 1991, resumed 1993; Chair. Dr VASSIL MIKHAILOV.
>
> **New United Labour Bloc:** f. 1997; Chair. KRUSTYU PETKOV.
>
> **People's Union:** c/o National Assembly, 1000 Sofia, Narodno Sobraniye Sq. 3; tel. (2) 987-90-32; fax (2) 981-09-49; f. 1994 as an electoral alliance between the following:
>
>> **Bulgarian Agrarian People's Union (BAPU)** (Bulgarski Zemedelski Naroden Sayuz—BZNS): 1000 Sofia, Yanko Zabunov St 1; tel. (2) 88-19-51; fax (2) 80-09-91; f. 1899; in ruling coalition 1946–89; Leader ANASTASIA MOSER.
>>
>> **Democratic Party:** 1000 Sofia, Blvd Kniaz Dondukov 34; tel. (2) 80-01-87; re-formed 1990; Chair. (vacant).
>
> **Radical Democratic Party:** 1000 Sofia, Blvd Kniaz Dondukov 8, 3rd Floor, Rms 6–8; tel. (2) 980-54-91; fax (2) 980-34-85; Chair. Dr KYRIL BOYADZHIEV.
>
> **Real Reform Movement (DESIR):** f. 1997; Leader RENATA INDZHOVA.
>
> **Republican Party:** Sofia; Chair. LENKO RUSSANOV.
>
> **United Christian Democratic Centre:** 1000 Sofia, Blvd Kniaz Dondukov 34; tel. (2) 80-04-09; Chair. STEFAN SOFIANSKI.

The Independent Association for Human Rights in Bulgaria (Leader STEFAN VALKOV), the Union of Victims of Repression (Leader IVAN NEVROKOPSKY) and the Union of Non-Party Members (Leader BOYAN VELKOV) all enjoy observer status in the UDF.

Diplomatic Representation

EMBASSIES IN BULGARIA

Afghanistan: 1618 Sofia, Boryana St 61, Bl. 216A; tel. (2) 55-61-96; fax (2) 955-99-76; Chargé d'affaires: FAZEL SAIFI.

Albania: Sofia, Dimitur Polyanov St 10; tel. (2) 44-33-81; Ambassador: KOCO KOTE.

Algeria: Sofia, Slavyanska St 16; tel. (2) 87-56-83; Ambassador: ZINE EL-ABIDINE HACHICHI.

Argentina: Sofia, Dragan Tsankov 36, 2nd Floor; POB 635; tel. (2) 971-25-39; fax (2) 71-61-30-28; Ambassador: ARTURO HOTTON RISLER.

Austria: 1000 Sofia, Shipka St 4; tel. (2) 80-35-72; fax (2) 87-22-60; Ambassador: Dr ERICH KRISTEN.

Belarus: 1421 Sofia, Kokitche St 20; tel. (2) 65-28-43; fax (2) 963-40-23; Ambassador: ALYAKSANDR GERASIMENKA.

Belgium: 1126 Sofia, Velchova Zavera St 1; tel. (2) 963-36-22; fax (2) 963-36-38; e-mail ambabel@einet.bg; Ambassador: EDMOND DE WILDE.

Brazil: 1113 Sofia, Frédéric Joliot Curie St 19, Bl. 156/1; tel. (2) 72-35-27; fax (2) 971-28-18; e-mail sofbrem@main.infotel.bg; Ambassador: CARLOS ALBERTO PESSÔA PARDELLAS.

Cambodia: Sofia, Mladost 1, Blvd S. Allende, Res. 2; tel. (2) 75-71-35; fax (2) 75-40-09 Ambassador: BO RASSI.

China, People's Republic: Sofia, Blvd Ruski 18; tel. (2) 87-87-24; Ambassador: TAO MIAOFA.

Colombia: 1113 Sofia, Aleksandur Zhendov St 1; POB 562; tel. (2) 971-31-03; fax (2) 72-76-60; e-mail emcolsof@mbox.digsys.bg; Ambassador: (vacant).

Cuba: 1113 Sofia, Mladezhka St 1; tel. (2) 72-09-96; fax (2) 72-07-94; Ambassador: LUIS FELIPE VÁZQUEZ.

Cyprus: Sofia, G. Gagarin St, Bl. 154A, Flat 2; tel. (2) 70-10-77; fax (2) 73-99-95; e-mail cyembsof@fintech.bg; Chargé d'affaires: PHILIPPOS KRITIOTIS.

Czech Republic: 1000 Sofia, Yanko Sakazov St 9; tel. (2) 946-11-10; fax (2) 946-18-00; e-mail sofia@embassy.mzv.cz; Ambassador: DANIEL ZÁMASKÝ.

Denmark: 1000 Sofia, Blvd Dondukov 54, POB 1393; tel. (2) 980-08-30; fax (2) 980-08-31; e-mail dkemb_sofia@attglobal.net; Ambassador: CHRISTIAN FABER-ROD.

Egypt: 1000 Sofia, Shesti Septemvri St 5; tel. (2) 87-02-15; fax (2) 980-12-63; Ambassador: MAY ABOUL-DAHAB.

Finland: 1126 Sofia, Simeonovsko St 57, Res. 3; tel. (2) 962-58-70; fax (2) 962-51-70; Ambassador: TAPIO SAARELA.

France: 1054 Sofia, Oborishte St 27–29; tel. (2) 946-15-41; fax: (2) 946-15-58; internet www.ambafranc.bg; Ambassador: DOMINIQUE CHASSARD.

Germany: 1113 Sofia, Frédéric Joliot Curie St 25, POB 869; tel. (2) 91-83-80; fax (2) 963-16-58; e-mail gemb@vilmat.com; internet www.german-embassy.bg; Ambassador: URSULA SEILER-ALBRING.

Ghana: Sofia; tel. (2) 70-65-09; Chargé d'affaires a.i.: HENRY ANDREW ANUM AMAH.

Greece: Sofia, Blvd Klement Gottwald 68; tel. (2) 44-37-70; Ambassador: ANASTASIOS SIDHERIS.

Holy See: 1000 Sofia, 11 August 6, POB 9; tel. (2) 981-17-43; fax (2) 981-61-95; e-mail segretario@mbox.digsys.bg; Apostolic Nuncio: Most Rev. ANTONIO MENNINI, Titular Archbishop of Ferento.

Hungary: Sofia, Shesti Septemvri St 57; tel. (2) 963-04-60; fax (2) 963-21-10; Ambassador: BELA KOLOZSI.

India: Sofia, Blvd Patriiarkh Evtimii 31; tel. (2) 981-17-02; fax (2) 981-41-24; e-mail india@inet.bg; Ambassador: NIRUPAM SEN.

Indonesia: 1126 Sofia, Simeonovsko St 53; tel. (2) 962-52-40; fax (2) 962-58-42; Ambassador: R. SUHARJONO.

Iran: Sofia, Blvd Vassil Levski 77; tel. (2) 44-10-13; Ambassador: MOHAMMAD ALI KORMI-NOURI.

Iraq: 1113 Sofia, Anton Chekhov St 21; tel. (2) 973-33-48; fax (2) 971-11-91; e-mail iraqiyah@asico.net; internet www.bgnet.bg/-iraqiyah; Ambassador: HASSAN MAJID AS-SAFFAR.

Italy: Sofia, Shipka St 2; tel. (2) 980-45-07; fax (2) 980-37-17; e-mail italdiplsofia@online.bg; Ambassador: ALESSANDRO GRAFFINI.

Japan: Sofia, Lyulyakova Gradina St 14; tel. (2) 72-39-84; fax (2) 49-210-95; Ambassador: YOSHIHIRO JIBIKI.

Korea, Democratic People's Republic: Sofia, Mladost 1, Blvd S. Allende, Res. 4; tel. (2) 77-53-48; Ambassador: KIM MAN-IK.

Korea, Republic: 1414 Sofia, Bulgaria Sq. 1, National Palace of Culture; tel. (2) 650-162; Ambassador: PILL-JOO SUNG.

Kuwait: Sofia, Blvd Klement Gottwald 47; tel. (2) 44-19-92; Ambassador: TALIB JALAL AD-DIN AN-NAQIB.

Laos: Sofia, Ovcha Kupel, Buket St 80; tel. (2) 56-55-08; Ambassador: SOMSAVAT LENGSAVAD.

Lebanon: 1113 Sofia, Frédéric Joliot Curie St 19; tel. (2) 971-31-69; fax (2) 973-32-56; e-mail amliban@bgnet.bg; Ambassador: HUSSEIN MOUSSAWI.

Libya: 1784 Sofia, Blvd Andrei Sakharov 1; tel. (2) 974-35-56; fax (2) 974-32-73; Secretary of People's Bureau: FARAG GIBRIL.

Macedonia, former Yugoslav republic: 1113 Sofia, Frédéric Joliot Curie St 17, Block 2, Floor 1, Suite 1; Ambassador: LJUBISA GEORGIEVSKI.

Moldova: Sofia; Ambassador: MIHAI COSCODAN.

Morocco: Sofia, Blvd Evlogui Gueorguiev 129; tel. (2) 44-27-94; fax (2) 946-10-43; e-mail sifmasof@bulnet.bg; Ambassador: ABDESSELAM ALEM.

Mozambique: Sofia; Ambassador: GONÇALVES RAFAEL SENGO.

Netherlands: 1126 Sofia, Galichitsa St 38; tel. (2) 962-57-90; fax (2) 962-59-88; e-mail nlgovsof@mbox.digsys.bg; Ambassador: W. SIX.

Nicaragua: Sofia, Mladost 1, Blvd Allende, Res. 1; tel. (2) 75-41-57; Ambassador: UMBERTO CARIÓN.

Peru: Sofia, Volokolamsko Shose 11; tel. (2) 68-32-43; Chargé d'affaires: JULIO VEGA ERAUSQUÍN.

Poland: Sofia, Khan Krum St 46; tel. (2) 987-26-10; fax (2) 987-29-39; e-mail polamba@internet-bg.net; Ambassador: JAROSLAW LINDENBERG.

Portugal: 1124 Sofia, Ivatz Voivoda St 6; tel. (2) 943-36-67; fax (2) 943-30-89; Ambassador: ANTÓNIO CARVALHO DE FARIA.

Romania: Sofia, Minai Eminescu St 4; tel. (2) 971-28-58; e-mail ambsofro@exco.net; Ambassador: CONSTANTIN GRIGORIE.

Russian Federation: Sofia, Blvd Dragan Tsankov 28; tel. (2) 963-44-58; fax (2) 963-41-03; Ambassador: VLADIMIR TITOV.

Slovakia: Sofia, Blvd Janko Sakazov 9; tel. (2) 943-32-81; fax (2) 943-38-37; e-mail svkemba@mbox.ttm.bg; Ambassador: JÁN KOVÁČ.

Spain: Sofia, Sheinovo 27; tel. (2) 943-30-32; fax (2) 946-12-01; Ambassador: JOSÉ CORDERCH.

Sweden: Sofia, Alfred Nobel St 4; tel. (2) 971-24-31; fax (2) 973-37-95; Ambassador: STEN ASK.

Switzerland: 1504 Sofia, Shipka St 33; tel. (2) 946-01-97; fax (2) 946-11-86; Ambassador: GAUDENZ RUF.

Syria: Sofia, Khristo Georgiev 10; tel. (2) 44-15-85; fax (2) 946-14-31; Chargé d'affaires: SADDIK SADDIKNI.

Turkey: 1000 Sofia, Blvd Vassil Levski 80; tel. (2) 987-14-64; fax (2) 981-93-58; e-mail turkel@techno-link.com; Ambassador: MEHMET ALI IRTEMCELIK.

Ukraine: 1618 Sofia, Ovcha Kupel, Boriana 29; tel. (2) 95-55-247; e-mail emailIN@ukr.cit.bg; Ambassador: OLEKSANDR VOROBYOV.

United Kingdom: 1000 Sofia, Blvd Vassil Levski 38; tel. (2) 980-12-20; fax (2) 980-12-29; e-mail britembsof@mbox.cit.bg; internet www.british-embassy.bg; Ambassador: RICHARD STAGG.

USA: Sofia, Suborna St 1; tel. (2) 980-52-41; fax (2) 981-89-77; Ambassador: AVIS T. BOHLEN.

Uruguay: Sofia, Tsar Ivan Asen II St 91; POB 213; tel. (2) 943-45-45; fax (2) 943-40-40; e-mail urubulg@mbox.digsys.bg; Ambassador: OLGA BARBAROV.

Venezuela: 1504 Sofia, Tulovo St 1, Flat 2; tel. (2) 943-30-61; fax (2) 943-30-10; e-mail embavenez@mbox.digsys.bg; internet www.embavenez-sofia.bgi; Ambassador: GERARDO E. WILLS.

Viet Nam: Sofia, Ilya Petrov St 1; tel. (2) 65-83-34; Ambassador: NGUYEN TIEN THONG.

Yemen: Sofia, Blvd S. Allende, Res. 3; tel. (2) 75-61-63; Ambassador: ALI MUNASSAR MUHAMMAD.

Yugoslavia: Sofia, Veliko Turnovo St 3; tel. (2) 44-32-37; Ambassador: CEDOMIR RADOJKOVIĆ.

Judicial System

The 1991 Constitution provided for justice to be administered by the Supreme Court of Cassation, the Supreme Administrative Court, courts of appeal, courts of assizes, military courts and district courts. The main legal officials are the justices, or judges, of the higher courts, the prosecutors and investigating magistrates. The judicial system is independent, most appointments being made or recommended by the Supreme Judicial Council. The Ministry of Justice coordinates the administration of the judicial system and the prisons. There is also the Constitutional Court, which is the final arbiter of constitutional issues. Under transitional arrangements attached to the 1991 Constitution, the existing Supreme Court of Bulgaria was to exercise the prerogatives of the two new Supreme Courts until the new judicial system was enacted and established.

Supreme Court of Cassation: 1000 Sofia, Blvd Vitosha 2, Sudebna Palata; tel. (2) 987-76-98; fax (2) 88-39-85; Pres. IVAN GRIGOROV.

Supreme Administrative Court: Sofia, Blvd A. Stamboliyski 18; tel. (2) 981-30-42; fax (2) 981-87-51; Pres. VLADISLAV SLAVOV.

Constitutional Court: 1194 Sofia, Blvd Dondukov 1; tel. (2) 88-47-66; fax (2) 87-19-86; Pres. ZHIVKO STALEV; Sec.-Gen. KIRIL A. MANOV.

Supreme Judicial Council: Sofia; Head TEODOSSIY SIMEONOV, Minister of Justice; tel. (2) 981-79-74.

Ministry of Justice: see The Government (Ministries).

Office of the Prosecutor-General: 1040 Sofia, Blvd Vitocha 2; tel. and fax (2) 988-52-13; Prosecutor-General NIKOLA FILTCHEV; Deputy Prosecutor-General CHRISTO MANCHEV.

Religion

Most of the population profess Christianity, the main denomination being the Bulgarian Orthodox Church, with a membership of more than 80% of the population. The 1991 Constitution guarantees freedom of religion, although Eastern Orthodox Christianity is declared to be the 'traditional religion in Bulgaria'. In accordance with the 1949 Bulgarian Law on Religious Faith, all new religious denominations must be registered by a governmental board before being allowed to operate freely. There is a significant Muslim minority (some 9% of the population), most of whom are ethnic Turks, although there are some ethnic Bulgarian Muslims, known as Pomaks. There is a small Jewish community.

Directorate of Religious Affairs: 1000 Sofia, Blvd Dondukov 1; tel. and fax (2) 88-04-88; a dept of the Council of Ministers; conducts relations between govt and religious organizations; Chair. Dr KHRISTO MATANOV.

CHRISTIANITY

In 1992 a schism occurred in the Bulgarian Orthodox Church, although this was resolved in October 1998.

Bulgarian Orthodox Church: 1090 Sofia, Oborishte St 4, Synod Palace; tel. (2) 87-56-11; fax (2) 89-76-00; f. 865; autocephalous Exarchate 1870 (recognized 1945); administered by the Bulgarian Patriarchy; 11 dioceses in Bulgaria and two dioceses abroad (Diocese of North and South America and Australia, and Diocese of West Europe), each under a Metropolitan; Chair. of the Bulgarian Patriarchy His Holiness Patriarch MAKSIM.

Armenian Apostolic Orthodox Church: Sofia 1080, Nishka St 31; tel. (2) 88-02-08; 20,000 adherents (1996); administered by Bishop DIRAYR MARDIKIYAN (resident in Bucharest, Romania); Chair. of the Diocesan Council in Bulgaria OWANES KIRAZIAN.

The Roman Catholic Church

Bulgarian Catholics may be adherents of either the Latin (Western) Rite, which is organized in two dioceses, or the Byzantine-Slav (Eastern) Rite (one diocese). All three dioceses are directly responsible to the Holy See.

Bishops' Conference (Mejduritualna Episcopska Konferenzia vâv Bâlgaria): 1606 Sofia, Liulin Planina 5; tel. (2) 953-04-06; fax (2) 952-61-86; Pres. CHRISTO PROYKOV (Titular Bishop of Briula).

Western Rite

Bishop of Nicopolis: PETKO CHRISTOV; 7000 Ruse, Ivan Vazov St 26A; tel. (82) 22-52-45; fax (82) 82-28-81; e-mail dio_nicop@elits.rousse.bg; 30,000 adherents (1998).

Diocese of Sofia and Plovdiv: GEORGI IVANOV YOVCHEV (Apostolic Administrator); 4000 Plovdiv, Nezavisimost St 3; tel. and fax (32) 62-20-42; 35,000 adherents (1996).

Eastern Rite

Apostolic Exarch of Sofia: CHRISTO NIKOLOV PROYKOV (Titular Bishop of Briula), 1606 Sofia, Liulin Planina 5; tel. (2) 953-04-06; fax (2) 952-61-86; e-mail cproikov@techno-link-com; 10,000 adherents (1998).

The Protestant Churches

Bulgarian Church of God: Sofia 1408, Petko Karavelov St 1; tel. (2) 65-75-52; fax (2) 51-91-31; 30,000 adherents (1992); Head Pastor PAVEL IGNATOV.

Bulgarian Evangelical Church of God: Plovdiv, Velbudge St 71; tel. (32) 43-72-92; 300 adherents (1992); Head Pastor BLAGOI ISEV.

Bulgarian Evangelical Methodist Episcopal Church: 1000 Sofia, Rakovski St 86; tel. (2) 981-37-83; fax (2) 980-94-83; e-mail umc-supint@mbox.digsys.bg; 2,000 adherents (2000); Gen. Superintendent Rev. BEDROS G. ALTUNIAN.

Church of Jesus Christ of Latter-day Saints in Bulgaria: Sofia, Drugba estate, Bl. 82/B/6, Flat 54; tel. (2) 74-08-06; f. 1991; 64 adherents (1992); Pres. VENTSESLAV LAZAROV.

Open Biblical Confraternity: 9300 Dobrich, General Kolev St 8; f. 1991; Head Pastor ANTONIA POPOVA.

Union of the Churches of the Seventh-day Adventists: Sofia, Solunska St 10; tel. (2) 88-12-18; fax (2) 980-17-09; e-mail sda.bg@sbline.net; 6,700 adherents (1997); Head Pastor AGOP TACHMISSJAN.

Union of Evangelical Baptist Churches: 1303 Sofia, Ossogovo St 63; tel. and fax (2) 931-06-82; 4,000 adherents (1999); Pres. Dr THEODOR ANGELOV.

Union of Evangelical Congregational Churches: Sofia, Solunska St 49; tel. (2) 980-56-85; fax (2) 980-69-02; e-mail sesc@yahoo.com; f. 1888; 4,000 adherents (1998); Head Pastor Rev. Dr HRISTO KULICHEV.

Union of Evangelical Pentecostal Churches: 1557 Sofia, Bacho Kiro St 21; tel. (2) 83-51-69; f. 1928; 30,000 adherents (1991); Head Pastor VIKTOR VIRCHEV.

Universal White Fraternity: 1612 Sofia, Balshik St 8B, Flat 27; tel. (2) 54-69-43; f. 1900; unifies the principles of Christianity with the arts and sciences; more than 6,000 adherents (1994); Chair. Dr ILIYAN STRATEV.

ISLAM

Supreme Muslim Theological Council: Sofia, Bratya Miladinovi St 27; tel. (2) 87-73-20; fax (2) 39-00-23; adherents estimated at 9% of the actively religious population, with an estimated 708 acting regional imams; Chair. Hadzhi NEDIM GENDZHEV; Chief Mufti of the Muslims in Bulgaria HADZHIBASRI HADZHISHARIF.

JUDAISM

Central Jewish Theological Council: 1000 Sofia, Ekzarkh Yosif St 16; tel. (2) 83-12-73; fax (2) 83-50-85; 5,000 adherents (1992); Head YOSSIF LEVI.

The Press

PRINCIPAL DAILIES

24 Chasa (24 Hours): 1504 Sofia, Tzarigradsko St 47; tel. (2) 44-19-45; fax (2) 433-93-39; f. 1991; privately-owned; Editor-in-Chief VALERI NAIDENOV; circ. 330,000.

Bulgarska Armiya (Bulgarian Army): 1080 Sofia, Ivan Vasov St 12, POB 629; tel. (2) 87-47-93; fax (2) 987-91-26; f. 1944 as Narodna Armiya, name changed 1991; organ of the Ministry of Defence; Editor-in-Chief Col VLADI VLADKOV; circ. 30,000.

Chernomorsky Far (Black Sea Lighthouse): 8000 Burgas, Milin Kamak St 9; tel. and fax (56) 423-96; f. 1950; independent regional from 1988; Editor-in-Chief GALENTIN VLAHOV; circ. 37,000.

Demokratsiya (Democracy): 1000 Sofia, Rakovski St 134; tel. (2) 981-29-79; fax (2) 980-73-42; e-mail demnews@sficit.bg; f. 1990; newspaper of the Union of Democratic Forces; Editor-in-Chief NEVEN KOPANDANOVA; circ. 45,000.

Duma (Word): 1000 Sofia, Tzarigradsko St 47; tel. (2) 43-431; fax (2) 87-50-73; f. 1927; fmrly *Rabotnichesko Delo*; organ of the Bulgarian Socialist Party; Editor-in-Chief STEFAN PRODEV; circ. 130,000.

Kontinent: 1000 Sofia, Tzarigradsko St 47A; tel. (2) 943-44-46; fax (2) 44-19-04; e-mail kont@bgnet.bg; internet www.tetracom.com/kontinent; f. 1992; independent; Editor-in-Chief BOIKO PANGELOV; circ. 12,000.

Maritza: 4000 Plovdiv, Blvd Khristo Botev 27A; tel. (32) 60-34-50; fax (32) 60-34-22; e-mail maritsa@plovdiv.techno-link.com; f. 1991; Editor-in-Chief ANTON BAYEV; circ. 30,000.

Narodno Delo (People's Cause): 9000 Varna, Blvd Khristo Botev 3; tel. (52) 23-10-71; fax (52) 23-90-67; f. 1944; 6 a week; regional independent; business, politics and sport; Editor-in-Chief DIMITUR KRASIMIROV; circ. 56,000.

Noshten Trud (Night Labour): 1000 Sofia, Blvd Kniyas Dondukov 52; tel. and fax (2) 87-70-63; f. 1992; 5 a week; Editor-in-Chief PLAMEN KAMENOV; circ. 332,000.

Nov Glas (New Voice): 5500 Lovech, G. Dimitrov St 24, 3rd Floor; tel. (68) 2-22-42; f. 1988; regional independent; Editor-in-Chief VENETSII GEORGIEV; circ. 50,000.

Otechestven Vestnik (Fatherland Newspaper): 1504 Sofia, Tzarigradsko St 47; tel. (2) 43-431; fax (2) 46-31-08; f. 1942 as *Otechestven Front*; published by the journalists' co-operative 'Okchestvo'; Editor-in-Chief KONSTANCE ANSCHVA; total circ. 16,000.

Pari (Money): 1504 Sofia, Tzarigradsko St 47A; POB 46; tel. (2) 943-31-47; fax (2) 943-31-88; e-mail office@pari.bg; internet www.pari.bg; f. 1991; daily; financial and economic news online; Editor-in-Chief EVGENII PETROV; circ. 13,500.

Podkrepa (Support): 1000 Sofia, Ekzarkh Yosif St 37; tel. (2) 83-12-27; fax (2) 46-73-74; f. 1991; organ of the Podkrepa (Support) Trade Union Confederation; Editor-in-Chief (vacant); circ. 18,000.

Shipka: 6300 Khaskovo, Georgi Dimitrov St 14; tel. (38) 12-52-52; fax (38) 3-76-28; f. 1988; independent regional newspaper; Editor-in-Chief DIMITUR DOBREV; circ. 25,000.

Sport: 1000 Sofia, National Stadium 'Vassil Levski', Sektor V; POB 88; tel. (2) 88-03-43; fax (2) 81-49-70; f. 1927; Editor-in-Chief IVAN NANKOV; circ. 80,000.

Standart News Daily: 1303 Sofia, Tzarigradsko St 113A; tel. (2) 975-36-88; fax (2) 76-28-77; e-mail root@standart.news.com; internet www.standartnews.com; f. 1992; Editor-in-Chief YULY MOSKOV; circ. 110,000.

Telegraf: 1113 Sofia, Tzarigradsko St 72; POB 135; tel. (2) 75-11-22; fax (2) 77-04-11; f. 1990; privately-owned independent newspaper; Editor-in-Chief PLAMEN DIMITROV; circ. 30,000.

Trud (Labour): 1000 Sofia, Blvd Dondukov 52; tel. (2) 987-98-05; fax (2) 80-11-40; f. 1923; organ of the Confederation of Independent Trade Unions in Bulgaria; Editor-in-Chief TOSHO TOSHEV; circ. 200,000.

Vecherni Novini (Evening News): Sofia; f. 1951; independent newspaper; centre-left; publ. by the Vest Publishing House; Dir GEORGI GANCHEV; Editor-in-Chief LYUBOMIR KOLAROV; circ. 35,000.

Vselena (Universe): 34000 Montana, Geravitza Sq.; tel. (96) 2-25-06; fmrly *Delo*; Editor-in-Chief BOYAN MLADENOV.

Zemedelsko Zname (Agrarian Banner): Sofia, Yanko Zabunov St 23; tel. (2) 87-38-51; fax (2) 87-45-35; f. 1902; organ of the Bulgarian Agrarian People's Union; circ. 178,000.

Zemya (Earth): Sofia, 11 August St 18; tel. (2) 88-50-33; fax (2) 83-52-27; f. 1951 as *Kooperativno Selo*; renamed 1990; fmrly an organ of the Ministry of Agriculture, BSP daily; Editor-in-Chief KOSTA ANDREEV; circ. 53,000.

PRINCIPAL PERIODICALS

168 Chasa (168 Hours): 1504 Sofia, Tzarigradsko St 47; tel. (2) 43-39-288; fax (2) 43-39-315; f. 1990; weekly; business, politics, entertainment; Editor-in-Chief VASELKA VALILEVA; circ. 93,000.

166 Politzeiski Vesti (166 Police News): 1680 Sofia, J. K. Belite Brezi, Solun St, Bl. 25 and 26, Ground Floor; tel. (2) 82-30-30; fax 82-30-28; f. 1945; fmrly *Naroden Strazh*; weekly; criminology and public security; Editor-in-Chief PETUR VITANOV; circ. 22,000.

Anti: 1000 Sofia, Blvd Dondukov 9; tel. and fax (2) 80-43-03; f. 1991; weekly; Editor-in-Chief VASIL STANILOV; circ. 7,000.

Avto-moto Svyat (Automobile World): 1000 Sofia, Sveta Sofia St 6, POB 1348; tel. and fax (2) 88-08-08; f. 1957; monthly; illustrated publication on cars and motor sports; Editor-in-Chief ILJA SELIKTAR; circ. 33,600.

Az Buki (Alphabet): 1113 Sofia, Tzarigradsko St 125; tel. (2) 71-65-73; f. 1991; weekly; education and culture; for schools; sponsored by the Ministry of Education and Science; Editor-in-Chief MILENA STRAKOVA; circ. 11,800.

Bulgarski Biznes (Bulgarian Business): 1505 Sofia, Oborishte St 44, POB 15; tel. (2) 46-70-23; fax (2) 44-63-61; weekly; organ of National Union of Employers; Editor-in-Chief DETELIN SERTOV; circ. 10,000–15,000.

Bulgarski Fermer (Bulgarian Farmer): 1797 Sofia, Blvd Dr G. M. Dimitrov 89; tel. (2) 71-04-48; fax (2) 73-10-08; f. 1990; weekly; Editor-in-Chief VASSIL ASPARUHOV; circ. 20,000.

Computer: 1504 Sofia, Panayot Volov St 11; tel. and fax (2) 943-41-28; e-mail office@newteck.bg; internet www.newteck.bg; f. 1991; monthly; information technology; Editor-in-Chief PETAR PETROV; circ. 7,000.

Computer World: 1421 Sofia, Blvd Hr. Smirnenski 1, Bl. B, Flat 1111; tel. (2) 81-42-70; fax (2) 80-26-52; internet www.eunet.bg/idg/; f. 1990; weekly; US-Bulgarian joint venture; information technology; Editor-in-Chief TATIANA HINOVA; circ. 7,000.

Domashen Maistor (Household Manager): 1000 Sofia, Blvd Tolbu-khin 51A; tel. (2) 87-09-14; f. 1991; monthly; magazine for household repairs; Editor-in-Chief GEORGI BALANSKI; circ. 12,000.

Durzhaven Vestnik (State Gazette): 1169 Sofia; tel. (2) 80-01-27; 2 a week; official organ of the National Assembly; 2 bulletins of parliamentary proceedings and the publication in which all legislation is promulgated; Editor-in-Chief PLAMEN MLADENOV; circ. 73,000.

Edinstvo (Unity): 1000 Sofia, Blvd Khristo Botev 48; tel. (2) 84-101 Ext. 218; f. 1991; weekly; Editor-in-Chief GENCHO BUCHVAROV.

Ekho (Echo): 1000 Sofia, 'Vassil Levski' St 75; tel. (2) 87-54-41; f. 1957; weekly; organ of the Bulgarian Tourist Union; tourism publication; Editor-in-Chief LUBOMIR GLIGOROV; circ. 7,000.

Emigrant: Sofia; tel. (2) 87-23-08; fax (2) 87-46-17; f. 1991 (to replace *Kontakti*); weekly; magazine for Bulgarians living abroad; Editor-in-Chief MANOL MANOV; circ. 20,000.

Futbol (Football): 1000 Sofia, Blvd Bulgaria 1, Vassil Levski Stadium; tel. (2) 87-19-51; fax (2) 65-72-57; f. 1988; weekly; independent soccer publication; Editor-in-Chief IVAN CHOMAKOV; circ. 132,500.

Ikonomicheski Zhivot (Economic Life): 1000 Sofia, Alabin St 33; tel. (2) 87-95-06; fax (2) 87-65-60; f. 1970; weekly; independent; marketing and advertising; Editor-in-Chief VASIL ALEKSIEV; circ. 21,000.

Kompyutar (Computer): 1142 Sofia, Blvd Vlevski 54; tel. (2) 87-50-45; e-mail newteck@ttm.bg; internet www.newteck.bg; f. 1985; monthly; hardware and software; Editor-in-Chief GEORGI BALANSKI; circ. 9,000.

Komunistichesko Delo (Communist Cause): 1000 Sofia, Central Post Office; POB 183; tel. (2) 59-16-73; organ of the Bulgarian Communist Party; Editor-in-Chief VLADIMIR SPASSOV; circ. 15,000–20,000.

Krile (Wings): 1184 Sofia, Tzarigradsko St 111; tel. (2) 70-45-73; f. 1911; fmrly *Kam Nebeto*, renamed 1991; monthly; official organ; civil and military aviation; Editor-in-Chief TODOR ANDREEV; circ. 20,000.

Kultura (Culture): 1040 Sofia, Blvd Aleksandur Battenberg 4; tel. (2) 83-33-22; fax (2) 87-40-27; e-mail kultura@online.bg; internet www.online.bg.com/kultura/; f. 1957; weekly; issue of the Ministry of Culture; arts, publicity and cultural affairs; Editor-in-Chief KOPRINKA CHERVENKOVA; circ. 10,000.

Kurier 5 (Courier 5): 1000 Sofia, Tzarigradsko St 47; tel. (2) 46-30-26; f. 1991; weekdays; advertising newspaper; Editor-in-Chief STEPAN ERAMIAN; circ. 30,000.

Liberalen Kongres (Liberal Congress): Sofia; tel. (2) 39-00-18; fax (2) 68-77-14; f. 1990; weekly; organ of the Liberal Congress Party; Editor-in-Chief ROSSEN ELEZOV; circ. 12,000.

LIK: Sofia, Tzarigradsko St 49; weekly; publication of the Bulgarian Telegraph Agency; literature, art and culture; Editor-in-Chief SIRMA VELEVA; circ. 19,000.

Literaturen Forum (Literary Forum): 1000 Sofia, Blvd Aleksandur Battenberg 4; tel. (2) 88-10-69; fax (2) 88-10-69; f. 1990; weekly; independent; Editor-in-Chief ATANAS SVILENOV; circ. 5,300.

Makedonia (Macedonia): 1301 Sofia, Pirotska St 5; tel. (2) 80-05-32; fax 87-46-64; e-mail mpress@virbus.bg; f. 1990; weekly; organ of the Inner Macedonian Revolutionary Organization (IMRO)—Union of Macedonian Societies; Editor-in-Chief DINKO DRAGANOV; circ. 22,000.

Missul (Thought): 1000 Sofia, Pozitano St 20, POB 382; tel. (2) 85-141; f. 1990; weekly; organ of the Marxist Alternative Movement; politics, culture; Editor-in-Chief GEORGI SVEZHIN; circ. 15,000.

Napravi Sam (Do It Yourself): 1504 Sofia, Panayot Volov St 11; tel. and fax (2) 943-41-28; e-mail newteck@einet.bg; internet www.newteck.bg; f. 1981; monthly; Editor-in-Chief GEORGI BALANSKI; circ. 8,000.

Nie Zhenite (We the Women): 1000 Sofia, Blvd Patriarch Evtimii 84; tel. (2) 52-31-98; f. 1990; weekly; organ of the Democratic Union of Women; Editor-in-Chief EVGINIA KIRANOVA; circ. 176,600.

Nov Den (New Day): 1000 Sofia, Lege St 5; tel. (2) 77-39-82; e-mail ivan_kalchev@yahoo.com; f. 1991; weekly; organ of the Union of Free Democrats; Editor-in-Chief IVAN KALCHEV; circ. 25,000.

Paraleli: Sofia, Tzarigradsko St 49; tel. (2) 87-40-35; f. 1964; weekly; illustrated publication of the Bulgarian Telegraph Agency; Editor-in-Chief KRASSIMIR DRUMEV; circ. 50,000.

Pardon: 1000 Sofia, Tzarigradsko St 47; tel. (2) 43-431; f. 1991; weekly; satirical publication; Editor-in-Chief CHAVDAR SHINOV; circ. 8,560.

Pogled (Review): 1090 Sofia, Slaveikov Sq. 11; tel. (2) 87-70-97; fax (2) 65-80-23; f. 1930; weekly; organ of the Union of Bulgarian Journalists; Editor-in-Chief EVGENII STANCHEV; circ. 47,300.

Prava i Svobodi (Rights and Freedoms): 1408 Sofia, Ivan Vazov, Tzarigradsko St 47/1; tel. (2) 46-72-12; fax (2) 46-73-35; f. 1990; weekly; organ of the Movement for Rights and Freedoms; politics, culture; Editor-in-Chief (vacant); circ. 7,500.

Progres (Progress): 1000 Sofia, Gurko St 16; tel. (2) 89-06-24; fax (2) 89-59-98; f. 1894; fmrly *Tekhnichesko Delo*; weekly; organ of the Federation of Scientific and Technical Societies in Bulgaria; Editor-in-Chief PETKO TOMOV; circ. 35,000.

Start: 1000 Sofia, Vassil Levski Stadium, POB 797; tel. (2) 980-25-17; fax (2) 981-29-42; f. 1971; weekly; sports, illustrated; Editor-in-Chief NIKOLAY RANGELOV; circ. 21,300.

Sturshel (Hornet): 1504 Sofia, Tzarigradsko St 47; tel. (2) 44-35-50; fax (2) 443-550; f. 1946; weekly; humour and satire; Editor-in-Chief YORDAN POPOV; circ. 45,200.

Svoboden Narod (Free People): 1000 Sofia, Ekzarkh Yosif St 37, 8th Floor; f. 1990; weekly; organ of the Bulgarian Social Democratic Party; Editor-in-Chief TEODOR DETCHEV; circ. 10,000.

Televiziya i Radio (Television and Radio): 1504 Sofia, Bulgarska Natsionalna Televiziya, San Stefano St 29; tel. (2) 44-32-94; fax (2) 946-12-10; f. 1964; weekly; broadcast listings; Editor-in-Chief LUBOMIR YANKOV; circ. 70,300.

Tsarkoven Vestnik (Church Newspaper): 1000 Sofia, Oborishte St 4; tel. (2) 87-56-11; f. 1900; weekly; organ of the Bulgarian Orthodox Church; Editor-in-Chief DIMITUR KIROV; circ. 4,000.

Uchitelsko Delo (Teachers' Cause): 1113 Sofia, Tzarigradsko St 125, Studentski Obshtezhitiya, Bl. 5; tel. (2) 70-00-12; f. 1905; weekly; organ of the Union of Bulgarian Teachers; Editor-in-Chief MARGARITA CHOLAKOVA; circ. 12,700.

Vek 21 (21st Century): 1000 Sofia, Kaloyan St 10; tel. (2) 46-54-23; fax (2) 46-61-23; f. 1990; weekly; organ of the Radical Democratic Party; liberal politics and culture; Editor-in-Chief ALEKSANDUR YORDANOV; circ. 5,900.

Zdrave (Health): 1421 Sofia, Blvd Chr Smirnenski 44; tel. (2) 44-30-26; fax (2) 65-68-35; f. 1955; monthly; published by Bulgarian Red Cross; Editor-in-Chief YAKOV YANAKIEV; circ. 55,000.

Zhenata Dnes (Women Today): 1000 Sofia, Narodno Sobraniye Sq. 12; tel. (2) 89-16-00; f. 1946; monthly; organ of Zhenata Dnes Ltd; Editor-in-Chief BOTIO ANGELOV; circ. 50,000.

Zname (Banner): 1184 Sofia, Blvd Kniyas Korsakov 34; tel. (2) 80-01-83; f. 1894, publ. until 1934 and 1945–49, resumed publishing 1990; weekly; Editor-in-Chief BOGDAN MORFOV; circ. 20,000.

NEWS AGENCIES

Bulgarska Telegrafna Agentsia—BTA (Bulgarian Telegraph Agency): 1024 Sofia, Tzarigradsko St 49; tel. (2) 87-73-63; fax (2)

80-24-88; f. 1898; official news agency; publishes weekly surveys of science and technology, international affairs, literature and art; Gen. Dir MILEN VULKOV.

Bulnet: 1000 Sofia, Rakovski St 127; tel. (2) 987-11-22; fax (2) 980-30-71; e-mail support@bulnet.bg; f. 1994; provides on-line access, internet services, communications software, hardware and consultancy; photo service; Exec. Dir INA STOIANOVA.

LEFF Information Service: 1000 Sofia, Rakovski St 127; tel. (2) 87-11-22; fax (2) 81-34-42; e-mail leffnews@bulnet.bg; private and independent news agency via internet; publishes daily economic and current affairs newsletters; Pres. BORIS BASMADJIYEV.

Sofia-Press Agency: 1040 Sofia, Slavyanska St 29; tel. (2) 88-58-31; fax (2) 88-34-55; internet sun.iecs.bas.bg/press; f. 1967 by the Union of Bulgarian Writers, the Union of Bulgarian Journalists, the Union of Bulgarian Artists and the Union of Bulgarian Composers; publishes socio-political and scientific literature, fiction, children's and tourist literature, publications on the arts, a newspaper, magazines and bulletins in foreign languages; also operates **Sofia-Press Info** (tel. (2) 87-66-80; Pres. ALEKSANDUR NIKOLOV), which provides up-to-date information on Bulgaria, in print and for broadcast; Dir-Gen. KOLIO GEORGIEV.

Foreign Bureaux

Agence France-Presse (AFP): 1000 Sofia, Blvd Tolbukhin 16; tel. (2) 71-91-71; Correspondent VESSELA SERGEVA-PETROVA.

Agencia EFE (Spain): Sofia; tel. (2) 87-29-63; Correspondent SAMUEL FRANCÉS.

Allgemeiner Deutscher Nachrichtendienst (ADN) (Germany): Sofia; tel. (2) 87-82-73; fax 87-53-16; Correspondent HANS-PETKO TEUCHERT.

Česká tisková kancelář (ČTK) (Czech Republic): Sofia; tel. (2) 70-91-36; Correspondent VĚRA IVANOVIČOVÁ.

Deutsche Presse Agentur (dpa) (Germany): Sofia; tel. (2) 72-02-02; Correspondent ELENA LALOVA.

Informatsionnoye Telegrafnoye Agentstvo Rossii—Telegrafnoye Agentstvo Suverennykh Stran (ITAR—TASS) (Russia): 1000 Sofia, A. Gendov St 1, Flat 29; tel. (2) 87-38-03; Correspondent ALEKSANDR STEPANENKO.

Magyar Távirati Iroda (MTI) (Hungary): Sofia, Frédéric Joliot Curie St 15, Bl. 156/3, Flat 28; tel. (2) 70-18-12; Correspondent TIVADAR KELLER.

Novinska Agencija Tanjug (Yugoslavia): 1000 Sofia, L. Koshut St 33; tel. (2) 71-90-57; Correspondent PERO RAKOSEVIĆ.

Polska Agencja Prasowa (PAP) (Poland): Sofia; tel. (2) 44-14-39; Correspondent BOGDAN KORNEJUCK.

Prensa Latina (Cuba): Sofia; tel. (2) 71-91-90; Correspondent SUSANA UGARTE SOLER.

Reuters (United Kingdom): 1000 Sofia, Ivan Vazov 16; tel. (2) 911-88; fax (2) 980-91-31; e-mail sofia.newsroom@reuters.com; Correspondent THALIA GRIFFITHS.

Rossiyskoye Informatsionnoye Agentstvo—Novosti (RIA—Novosti) (Russia): Sofia; Bureau Man. YEVGENII VOROBYOV.

United Press International (UPI) (USA): Sofia; tel. (2) 62-24-65; Correspondent GUILLERMO ANGELOV.

Xinhua (New China) News Agency (People's Republic of China): Sofia; tel. (2) 88-49-41; Correspondent U. SIZIUN.

The following agencies are also represented: SANA (Syria) and Associated Press (USA).

PRESS ASSOCIATIONS

Union of Bulgarian Journalists: 1000 Sofia, Graf Ignatiev St 4; tel. (2) 87-27-73; fax (2) 88-30-47; f. 1955; Pres. ALEKSANDUR ANGELOV; 5,600 mems.

Union of Journalists in Bulgaria: 1000 Sofia, Ekzarkh Yosif St 37; tel. and fax (2) 83-19-95; Chair. CHAVDAR TONCHEV.

Publishers

Darzhavno Izdatelstvo 'Khristo G. Danov' ('Khristo G. Danov' State Publishing House): 4005 Plovdiv, Stoyan Chalakov St 1; tel. (32) 23-12-01; fax (32) 26-05-60; f. 1855; fiction, poetry, literary criticism; Dir NACHO HRISTOSKOV.

Darzhavno Izdatelstvo 'Meditsina i Fizkultura': 1080 Sofia, Slaveikov Sq. 11; tel. (2) 87-13-08; fax (2) 987-99-75; f. 1948; medicine, physical culture and tourism; Dir PETKO PETKOV.

Darzhavno Izdatelstvo 'Prosveta': 1184 Sofia, Tzarigradsko St 117; tel. (2) 76-11-82; fax (2) 76-44-51; e-mail prosveta@tradel.net; f. 1945; educational publishing house; Man. Dir JOANA TOMOVA.

Darzhavno Izdatelstvo 'Tekhnika': 1000 Sofia, Slaveikov Sq. 1; tel. (2) 87-12-83; fax (2) 87-49-06; f. 1958; textbooks for technical and higher education and technical literature; Dir NINA DENEVA.

Darzhavno Izdatelstvo 'Zemizdat': 1504 Sofia, Tzarigradsko St 47; tel. (2) 44-18-29; f. 1949; specializes in works on agriculture, shooting, fishing, forestry, livestock-breeding, environmental studies and popular scientific literature and textbooks; Dir PETUR ANGELOV.

Galaktika: 9000 Varna, Nezavissimost Sq. 6; tel. (52) 24-11-56; fax (52) 23-47-50; f. 1960; science fiction, economics, Bulgarian and foreign literature; Dir ASSYA KADREVA.

Izdatelstvo na Bulgarskata Akademiya na Naukite 'Marin Drinov': 1113 Sofia, Acad. Georgi Bonchev St, Bl. 6; tel. (2) 72-09-22; fax (2) 70-40-54; f. 1869; scientific works and periodicals of the Bulgarian Academy of Sciences; Dir TODOR RANGELOV.

Izdatelstvo 'Bulgarski Houdozhnik': 1504 Sofia, Shipka St 6; tel. (2) 46-72-85; fax (2) 946-02-12; e-mail filchev@bulnet.bg; f. 1952; art books, children's books; Dir BOUYAN FILCHEV.

Izdatelstvo 'Bulgarsky Pisatel': Sofia, Shesti Septemvri St 35; tel. (2) 87-58-73; fax (2) 87-24-95; publishing house of the Union of Bulgarian Writers; Bulgarian fiction and poetry, criticism; Dir GERTCHO ATANASOV.

Izdatelstvo 'Khristo Botev': 1504 Sofia, Tzarigradsko St 47; tel. (2) 44-14-08; f. 1944; fmrly the Publishing House of the Bulgarian Communist Party, renamed as above 1990; Dir IVAN DINKOV.

Izdatelstvo na Ministerstvo na Otbrana (Ministry of Defence Publishing House): 1000 Sofia, Ivan Vazov St 12; tel. (2) 88-44-31; fax (2) 88-15-68; Head Maj. BOYAN SULTANOV.

Izdatelstvo Mladezh, (Youth Publishing House): Sofia; tel. (2) 88-21-37; fax (2) 87-61-35; f. 1945; art, history, original and translated fiction, political science and sociology; Gen. Dir STANIMIR ILCHEV.

Izdatelstvo 'Profizdat' (Publishing House of the Central Council of Bulgarian Trade Unions): Sofia; specialized literature and fiction; Dir STOYAN POPOV.

'Narodna Kultura' Publishers: 1000 Sofia, Angel Kanchev St 1; POB 421; tel. (2) 987-80-63; e-mail nauk-izk@sigma-bg.com; f. 1944; general; Dir PETAR MANOLOV.

Nauka i Izkustvo: 1000 Sofia, Slaveikov Sq. 11; tel. and fax (2) 87-24-96; f. 1948; general publishers; Man. LORETA PUCHKAROVA.

Reporter Ltd Publishing Co: 1184 Sofia, Tzarigradsko St; tel. (2) 76-90-28; fax (2) 71-83-77; e-mail reporter@techno-link.com; private publishers of fiction and documentary literature.

Sinodalno Izdatelstvo: Sofia, Oboriste St 4; tel. (2) 87-56-11; religious publishing house; Dir ANGEL VELITEHKOV.

STATE ORGANIZATION

Jusautor: Sofia; tel. (2) 87-28-71; fax (2) 87-37-40; state organization of the Council of Ministers; Bulgarian copyright agency; represents Bulgarian authors of literary, scientific, dramatic and musical works, and deals with the grant of options, authorization for translations, and drawing up of contracts for the use of works by foreign publishers and producers; Dir-Gen. YANA MARKOVA.

PUBLISHERS' ASSOCIATION

Bulgarian Book Publishers' Association: 1000 Sofia, Slaveikov Sq. 11; POB 1046; tel. and fax (2) 986-79-93; e-mail bba@otel.net; internet bba.hit.bg; f. 1994; Exec. Dir MADLENA ROMANOVA; Chair. RAYMOND WAGENSTEIN.

WRITERS' UNION

Union of Bulgarian Writers: Sofia, Slaveikov Sq. 2; tel. (2) 88-06-85; fax (2) 87-47-57; f. 1913; Chair. NIKOLAI HAITOV; 501 mems.

Broadcasting and Communications

TELECOMMUNICATIONS

In October 1997 there were 32 telephone lines for every 100 residents. Approximately 5% of the telephone network was digitized; there were 17 digital exchanges, with a total capacity of 107,000 subscribers.

Committee of Posts and Telecommunications: 1000 Sofia, Gourko St 6; POB 1352; tel. (2) 981-29-49; fax (2) 980-61-05; internet www.cpt.bg; supervises and regulates the post and telecommunications systems; Pres. ANTONI SLAVINSKI.

Bulgarian Telecommunications Company (BTC): 1606 Sofia, Blvd Totleben 8; tel. (2) 88-94-38; fax (2) 87-58-85; e-mail central.office.@btc.bg; internet www.btc.bg; scheduled for privatization in 2000; provides telecommunications and information services; Pres. MARIAN DRAGOSTINOV; 23,000 employees.

BROADCASTING

National Radio and Television Council: 1504 Sofia, San Stefano St 29, tel. (2) 46-81; internet www.bild.net/nsrt; Dir IVAN BORISLAVOV.

Radio

An estimated nine private local radio stations were broadcasting in 1995.

Bulgarsko Nationalno Radio: 1040 Sofia, Blvd Dragan Tzankov 4; tel. (2) 985-24; fax (2) 65-72-98; e-mail bgintrel@nationalradio.bg; internet www.nationalradio.bg; f. 1929; two Home Service programmes; local stations at Blagoevgrad, Plovdiv, Shumen, Stara Zagora and Varna. The Foreign Service broadcasts in Bulgarian, Turkish, Greek, Serbo-Croat, French, Italian, German, English, Portuguese, Spanish, Albanian and Arabic; Dir-Gen. ALEKSANDUR VELEV.

Radio Alma Mater: 1000 Sofia, Moskovska St 49; tel. (2) 986-16-07; fax (2) 930-84-80; f. 1993; cable radio service introduced by Sofia Univ.; from July 1998 24-hour broadcasting at 87.7 MHz in Sofia; culture and science programmes; Editor-in-Chief DILIANA KIRKOVSKA.

Television

Balkan News Corporation: Sofia; daily news transmission of commercial news, family entertainment and locally-produced programmes, on bTV channel; Chief Exec. MARTY POMPADUR.

Bulgarska Natsionalna Televiziya: 1504 Sofia, San Stefano St 29; tel. (2) 44-63-29; fax (2) 946-12-10; internet www.bnt.bg; f. 1959; daily transmission of programmes on Channel 1 and Efir 2 and on the satellite channel—TV Bulgaria; Dir-Gen. LILYANA POPOVA; 3,000 employees.

Nova Televiziya: 1000 Sofia, Sveta Nedela Sq. 16; tel. (2) 80-50-25; fax (2) 87-02-98; f. 1994; first private television channel in Bulgaria; commercial news and entertainment.

Finance

(cap. = capital; dep. = deposits; res = reserves;
m. = million; amounts in old leva, unless otherwise indicated)

BANKING

The Bulgarian banking system was restructured during the 1990s as part of a comprehensive reform of the entire economic system, in order to establish a market economy. By late 1991 the transition to a two-tier banking sector had been achieved. In September 1992 almost 80 commercial banks were organized as self-managing joint-stock companies. However, only 16 of these were licensed for cross-border foreign-exchange operations, with most of the remainder less important in terms of size and activities. In late 1992 21 commercial banks merged to form the United Bulgarian Bank, which opened in 1993. In early 1993 two new banks emerged, Commercial Bank Expressbank (formed from the merger of 12 banks) and Hebrosbank (a merger of eight banks). In 1996 14 banks, including five state-owned banks, collapsed. In May 1996 the total number of banks was 47, and in October 1997 state-owned banks accounted for 73% of the total. A currency board was established in July 1997.

Currency Board

Currency Board of the Republic of Bulgaria: Sofia; f. 1997; monetary supervision; Head MARTIN ZAIMOV.

Central Bank

Bulgarian National Bank (Bulgarska Narodna Banka): 1000 Sofia, Aleksandur Battenberg Sq. 1; tel. (2) 914-51-203; fax (2) 980-24-25; e-mail press_office@bnbank.org; internet www.bnb.bg; f. 1879; bank of issue; cap. 20,000m., res 865,538m., dep. 2,082,918m. (Dec. 1999); Gov. SVETOSLAV GAVRIYSKI; 6 brs; 1,200 employees.

State Savings Bank

DSK Bank plc: 1000 Sofia, Moskovska St 19; tel. (2) 985-57-220; fax (2) 980-64-77; e-mail office@dskbank.bg; f. 1951 as State Savings Bank; name changed as above in 1998; provides general retail banking services throughout the country; scheduled for privatization; cap. 329.1m., res 93,552.7m., dep. 834,312.5m. (Dec. 1998); Pres. SPAS DIMITROV; 126 brs.

Commercial Banks Licensed for Cross-border Foreign-Exchange Operations

BNP-Ak-Dresdner Bank: 1000 Sofia, Narodno Sobraniye Sq. 1; POB 11; tel. (2) 980-12-37; fax (2) 981-69-91; e-mail pobox@bnpdreba.ddm.bg; f. 1994; cap. 16,000m., dep. 258,867.9m., res 9,087.7m. (Dec. 1999); Gen. Man. ULLRICH GUENTER SCHUBERT.

BRIBANK AD: 1000 Sofia, Saborna St 11A; tel. (2) 98-50-02-40; fax (2) 981-25-26; e-mail nkratchounova@hq.bribank.bg; f. 1994; formerly Bulgarian Russian Investment Bank; cap. 13,386m., res 3,887m., dep. 100,198m. (Dec. 1999); Chair. ROSSITZA LISSITCHKOVA; 10 brs.

Bulbank (Bulgarian Foreign Trade Bank): 1000 Sofia, Sveta Nedelya Sq. 7; tel. (2) 98-41-11-11; fax (2) 988-46-36; e-mail info@sof.bulbank.bg; internet www.bulbank.bg; f. 1964; privatized in 2000; cap. 166,370m., res 276,341m., dep. 1,582,777m. (Dec. 1999); Chair. and Chief Exec. CHAVDAR KANTCHEV; 104 brs.

Bulgarian Investment Bank plc: 1606 Sofia, Laoish Koshut St 4; tel. (2) 917-17-17; fax (2) 917-11-56; e-mail icb@internet-bg.net; f. 1994; assets 28.5m. (1998); Chief Exec. STEPHEN B. STRAUSS.

Bulgarian Post Bank: 1414 Sofia, Bulgaria Sq. 1; tel. (2) 963-20-96; fax (2) 963-04-82; e-mail intldiv@postbank.bg; f. 1991; privatized in 1999; cap. 89,316m., dep. 366,824m. (Dec. 1999); Chair. VLADIMIR VLADIMIROV.

CB Unionbank Ltd: 1606 Sofia, Damyan Gruev St 10–12; tel. (2) 980-20-05; fax (2) 980-20-04; e-mail mainmail@unionbank.bg; internet www.unionbank.bg; f. 1992; cap. 10,000m., res 14,146m., dep. 39,865m. (Dec. 1999); Chair. and Exec. Dir IVAN TOTEV RADEV; 4 brs.

Central Co-operative Bank Ltd: 1000 Sofia, G. S. Rakovski St 103; tel. (2) 926-62-37; fax (2) 987-19-48; e-mail centralccb@ccb.bg; internet www.ccbank.bg; f. 1991; cap. 15,000m., res 7,399.4m., dep. 198,733.2m. (Dec. 1998); Chief Exec. TENCHO TENEV.

Commercial Bank Biochim: 1026 Sofia, Ivan Vazov St 1; tel. (2) 926-92-10; fax (2) 926-94-40; e-mail info@biochim.com; internet www.biochim.com; f. 1987; scheduled for privatization; cap. 28,757.2m., dep. 371,552m. (1999); Exec. Dirs VENTZISLAV LYUBOMIROV, PLAMEN DOBREV, TSVETAN TSEKOV; 40 brs.

Commercial Bank Bulgaria Invest Ltd: 1202 Sofia, Blvd Maria Louiza 65; tel. (2) 988-54-88; fax (2) 981-93-07; e-mail bginvid@mail.erix.net; f. 1989 as Yambol Commercial Bank; cap. 12,000m., res 16,000m., dep. 66,000m. (Dec. 1999); Chair. DIMITAR ZHELEV.

Corporate Commercial Bank: 1000 Sofia, Ekzarkh Yosif St 65; POB 632; tel. (2) 980-93-62; fax (2) 980-89-48; f. 1989 as BSFK Bulgarsovinvest; cap. 10,000m., res 1,315.3m., dep. 2,282.6m. (Dec. 1998); Chair. VENTZISLAV ANTONOV.

Demirbank (Bulgaria) AD: 1000 Sofia, Blvd Tsar Osvoboditel 8; tel. (2) 989-44-44; fax (2) 989-48-48; e-mail info@demirbank.bg; internet www.demirbank.bg; f. 1999; cap. 15,000m., dep. 48,501m.; Pres. SELAMATTIN SERBEST; Gen. Man. ÇANER ÇELIK.

ELITBANK: 1000 Sofia, Hristo Belchev St 7; tel. (2) 845-41-31; fax (2) 81-01-13; f. 1994; cap. 1,000m., res 346.5m., dep. 9,002.2m. (Dec. 1995); Chair. and Exec. Pres. IVO GEORGIEV.

Eurobank plc: 1407 Sofia, Blvd Cherni Vrach 43; tel. (2) 62-33-66; fax (2) 68-10-86; e-mail eurobank@nat.bg; internet www.eurobank.bg; f. 1993 as Commercial Bank Mollov Ltd; cap. 36,597m., dep. 38,144m. (1998); Chief Exec. JAN TUŠIM.

First East International Bank: 1504 Sofia, Blvd Vassil Levski 103; tel. (2) 946-16-82; fax (2) 946-16-83; e-mail feib@asico.net; f. 1991 as Trade Bank Kremikovzi; cap. 12,098.1m., res 294.4m., dep. 53,432.2m. (1998); Pres. ANNA SABEVA; 27 brs; 800 employees.

First Investment Bank Ltd: 1000 Sofia, St Karadja St 10; tel. (2) 910-01-00; fax (2) 980-50-33; e-mail fib@fibank.bg; internet www.fibank.bg; f. 1993; cap. 48.5m., dep. 130.7m. (Dec. 2000); Exec. Dirs MAJA GEORGIEVA, MATTHEW MATTEEV; Chair. GEORGI DIMITROV MUTAFCHIEV.

Hebrosbank: 4018 Plovdiv, Blvd Tsar Boris III Obedinitel 37; tel. (32) 56-26-68; fax (32) 62-39-64; e-mail hebros@hebros.bg; internet www.hebros.bg; f. 1993 following merger of eight banks; cap. and res 58,939m. (Dec. 1999); Chair. and Exec. Dir JAMIE GIBSON; 1,784 employees.

International Bank for Trade and Development: 1000 Sofia, Ivan Vazov St 2; tel. (2) 987-15-16; fax (2) 87-30-41; e-mail biededp@bsbg.net; cap. 13,000m. (1998); Chief Exec. PLAMEN BONEV; 8 brs.

Municipal Bank plc: 1000 Sofia, 6 Vrabcha St; tel. (2) 930-01-85; fax (2) 981-51-47; f. 1986 as Sofia Municipal Bank Plc; name changed Jan. 1998; cap. 20,767.2m., res 5,354.4m., dep. 140,280.0m. (Dec. 1998); Exec. Dir VANYA GEORGIEVA VASSILEVA.

Neftinvestbank plc: 1000 Sofia, 155 Rakovski St; POB 1138; tel. (2) 981-69-38; fax (2) 980-77-22; e-mail neftinvestbank@sps-elsys.com; internet www.nib.bg; f. 1994 as International Orthodox Bank 'St Nikola'; cap. 68,996.8m., dep. 21,136.2m. (Dec. 1998); Chair. PETIA IVANOVA BARAKOVA-SLAVOVA; 9 brs.

Raiffeisenbank (Bulgaria): 1504 Sofia, Gogol St 18–20; tel. (2) 919-85-101; fax (2) 943-45-28; e-mail ibgakgi@rbb-sofia.raiffeisen.at; internet www.raiffeisen.bg; f. 1994; cap. 50,373m., dep. 160,914m. (Dec. 1999); Pres. JOHN HARRIS.

Rosexim Bank plc: 1000 Sofia, Blvd Dondukov 4–6; tel. (2) 930-71-36; fax (2) 980-26-23; e-mail info@roseximbank.bg; internet www.roseximbank.bg; f. 1994; cap. 33,618.3m., res 18,100.4m., dep. 78,265.2m. (Dec. 1998); Chair. DIANA MLADENOVA; Exec. Dirs MINCHO MIMOV, IVAN ISKROV.

SG Expressbank AD: 9000 Varna, Blvd Vl. Varnenchik 92; tel. (52) 66-04-80; fax (52) 60-13-24; e-mail eurobank@nat.bg; internet www.expressbank.bg; f. 1987 as Transport Bank, name changed following merger of 12 banks in 1993; privatized in 1999; cap. 14,264.8m., res 56,345.0m., dep. 275,846.6m. (Dec. 1998); Chair. and Exec. Dir IVAN KONSTANTINOV; 70 brs; 1,350 employees.

Teximbank: 1202 Sofia, Blvd Maria Louiza 107, Sredetz Municipality; tel. (2) 31-40-38; fax (2) 931-12-07; e-mail texim@omega.bg; f. 1992; private entrepreneurial bank; cap. 10,000m., res 982,500m., dep. 2,869.1m. (Dec. 1998); Pres. MARIA VIDOLOVA.

United Bulgarian Bank AD: 1000 Sofia, Sveta Sofia St 5; tel. (2) 98-54-00; fax (2) 988-08-22; e-mail info@sof.ubb.bg; internet www.ubb.bg; f. 1993 following a merger of 22 commercial banks; universal commercial bank; privatized in 1999; cap. 75,964.0m., res 33,935.0m., dep. 628,977.0m. (Dec. 1998); Chief Exec. STILIAN VATEV; 53 brs; 2,250 employees.

STOCK EXCHANGE

Bulgarian Stock Exchange: 1040 Sofia, Makedonia Sq. 1; tel. (2) 986-59-15; fax (2) 986-58-63; e-mail bsemail@online; internet www.online.bg/bs; Chair. GEORGE PROHASKI; Chief Exec. APOSTOL APOSTOLOV.

INSURANCE

In 1947 all insurance firms were nationalized, and reorganized into a single state insurance company (see below). In 1989 private insurance companies began to reappear.

State Insurance Institute (DZI): 1000 Sofia, Blvd Tzar Osvoboditel 6; tel. (2) 981-57-99; fax (2) 987-45-33; e-mail general.ins@dzi.bg; internet www.dzi.bg; f. 1946; all areas of insurance; Chair. BOGISLAV MIKHAILOV; 101 brs.

Bulstrad Insurance and Reinsurance: 1000 Sofia, Pozitano Sq. 5, POB 627; tel. (2) 985-66-100; fax (2) 985-66-103; f. 1961; all classes of insurance and reinsurance; Chief Exec. RUMEN YANCHEV.

Trade and Industry

GOVERNMENT AGENCIES

Privatization Agency: 1000 Sofia, Aksakov St 29; tel. (2) 897-75-79; fax (2) 981-62-01; e-mail bgpriv@mbox.digsys.bg; internet www.privatization.bg; f. 1992; organizes the privatization of state-owned enterprises whose assets exceed 70m. leva; Exec. Dir LEVON HAMPARTSUMIAN.

INTERNATIONAL FREE-TRADE ZONES

Burgas Free-Trade Zone: 8000 Burgas, Trapezitza St 5, POB 154; tel. (56) 84-20-47; fax (56) 84-15-62; e-mail freezone@bse.bg; internet www.freetradezone-bourgas.com; f. 1989; Exec. Dirs AN-GELIN POPOV, KRASIMIR GRUDOV.

Dobrotitza Free-Trade Zone: 4649 Kranevo, Dobrich District.

Dragoman Free-Trade Zone: 2210 Dragoman; tel. (9971) 72-20-14.

Plovdiv Free-Trade Zone: 4003 Plovdiv, Vassil Levski St 242A; POB 75; tel. (32) 90-62-33; fax (32) 65-08-33; e-mail frzone@plovdiv.techno-link.com; internet www.freezone-plovdiv.com; f. 1990; Chief Exec. ALEKSANDUR NIKOLOV.

Rousse International Free-Trade Zone: 7000 Rousse, Knyazheska St 5; POB 107; tel. (82) 27-22-47; fax (82) 27-00-84; e-mail freezone@elits.rousse.bg; internet www.freezone.rousse.bg; f. 1988; Gen. Man. NIKOLAY KORFONOZOV.

Svilengrad Free-Trade Zone: 6500 Svilengrad; tel. (359) 379-74-45; fax (359) 379-75-41; e-mail sbz@svilengrad.com; internet www.svilengrad.com/sbz; f. 1990; Exec. Dir DIMO HARAKCHIEV.

Vidin Free-Trade Zone: 3700 Vidin; tel. (94) 228-37; fax (94) 309-47; f. 1988; Gen. Man. K. MARINOV.

CHAMBER OF COMMERCE

Bulgarian Chamber of Commerce and Industry: 1000 Sofia, Parchevich St 42; tel. (2) 987-26-31; fax (2) 987-32-09; e-mail bcci@bcci.org; internet www.bcci.bg; f. 1895; promotes economic relations and business contacts between Bulgarian and foreign cos and orgs; organizes participation in international fairs and exhibitions; publishes economic publs in Bulgarian and foreign languages; organizes foreign trade advertising and publicity; provides legal and economic consultations, etc.; registers all Bulgarian cos trading internationally (more than 40,000 at the end of 2000); Pres. BOJIDAR BOJINOV; 27 regional chambers.

EMPLOYERS' ASSOCIATIONS

Bulgarian Industrial Association (BISA): 1000 Sofia, Alabin St 16–20; tel. (2) 980-99-14; fax (2) 87-26-04; e-mail office@bia.bol.bg; internet www.bia-bg.com; f. 1980; assists Bulgarian economic enterprises with promotion and foreign contacts; analyses economic situation; formulates policies for legislative and commercial projects; assists development of small and medium-sized firms; organizes

privatization and investment operations; Chair. and Pres. BOJIDAR DANEV.

National Union of Employers: 1505 Sofia, Oborishte St 44, POB 15; f. 1989; federation of businessmen in Bulgaria.

Union of Private Owners in Bulgaria: Sofia; f. 1990; Chair. DIMITUR TODOROV.

Vuzrazhdane Union of Bulgarian Private Manufacturers: 1618 Sofia, Blvd Todor Kableshkov 2; tel. (2) 55-00-16; Chair. DRAGOMIR GUSHTEROV.

UTILITIES

Electricity

Central Laboratory of Solar Energy and New Energy Sources: 1784 Sofia, Tzarigradsko St 72; tel. and fax (2) 75-40-16; e-mail solar@phys.bas.bg; research into alternative energy production; Dir Assoc. Prof. PETKO VITANOV.

Committee on Energy: 1000 Sofia, Blvd Kniyas Dondukov 1; Chair. KONSTANTIN ROSINOV.

Committee on the Use of Atomic Energy for Peaceful Purposes: 1574 Sofia, Blvd Shipchenski Prokhod 69; tel. (2) 72-02-17; fax (2) 70-21-43; f. 1957; Chair. LUCHEZAR KOSTOV.

National Electricity Company (Natsionalna Elektricheska Kompania): 1040 Sofia, Vestlets St 5; tel. (2) 549-09; fax (2) 980-12-43; e-mail nek@nek.bg; internet www.nek.bg; f. 1991; scheduled for privatization, companies were to demerge by mid-2000; responsible for all thermal, nuclear and hydroelectric electricity production; Chair. M. GOLEMEKOV; Exec. Dir D.TAFROV.

Gas

Bulgargaz: Sofia; tel. (2) 25-90-74; Chair. KRASIMIR NIKOLOV; Dir KIRIL GEGOV.

Topenergy Joint-Stock Co: Sofia; f. 1995; owned by Gazprom of Russia; responsible for supply of Russian natural gas to Bulgaria; Chair. BOGDAN BUDZULIAK; Dir SERGEI PASHIN.

CO-OPERATIVE

Central Union of Workers' Productive Co-operatives: 1000 Sofia, Blvd Dondukov 11; POB 55; tel. (2) 80-39-38; fax (2) 87-03-20; f. 1988; umbrella organization of 164 workers' productive co-operatives; Pres. STILIAN BALASSOPOULOV; 60,000 mems.

TRADE UNIONS

Confederation of Independent Trade Unions in Bulgaria (CITUB): Sofia, D. Blagoev Sq. 1; tel. (2) 86-61; fax (2) 87-17-87; f. 1904; name changed from Bulgarian Professional Union and independence declared from all parties and state structures in 1990; in 1998 remained the main trade-union organization; approx. 75 mem. federations and four associate mems (principal mems listed below); Chair. Prof. Dr KRUSTYU PETKOV; Sec. MILADIN STOYNOV; some 3m. mems.

Edinstvo (Unity) People's Trade Union: 1000 Sofia, Moskovska St 5; tel. (2) 87-96-40; f. 1990; co-operative federation of Clubs, based on professional interests, grouped into 84 asscns, 2 prof. asscns and 14 regional groups; Chair. OGNYAN BONEV; 384,000 mems.

Podkrepa (Support) Trade Union Confederation: 1000 Sofia, Angel Kanchev St 2; tel. (2) 988-78-39; fax (2) 988-87-38; e-mail fciw@mail.techno-link.com; f. 1990 as an opposition trade union (affiliated to the Union of Democratic Forces); organized into territorial (31 regions) and professional asscns (33 syndicates); Pres. Dr KONSTANTIN TRENCHEV; Gen. Sec. PETUR GANCHEV; 15,000 mems (1997).

Principal CITUB Trade Unions

Federation of Independent Agricultural Trade Unions: 1606 Sofia, Dimo Hadzhidimov St 29; tel. (2) 52-15-40; Pres. LYUBEN KHARALAMPIEV; 44,600 mems (mid-1994).

Federation of Independent Trade Unions of Construction Workers: Sofia; tel. (2) 80-16-003; Chair. NIKOLAI RASHKOV; 220,000 mems.

Federation of the Independent Trade Unions of Employees of the State and Social Organizations: 1000 Sofia, Alabin Sq. 52; tel. (2) 87-98-52; Chair. PETUR SUCHKOV; 144,900 mems.

Federation of Independent Mining Trade Unions: 1233 Sofia, 32 Veania St; tel. (2) 931-07-00; fax (2) 931-00-50; f. 1992; Pres. PENCHO TOKMAKCHIEV; 20,000 mems.

Federation of Light Industry Trade Unions: 1040 Sofia, Makedonia Sq. 1; tel. (2) 88-15-70; fax (2) 88-15-20; Chair. IORDAN VASSILEV IVANOV; 64,320 mems (1997).

Federation of Metallurgical Trade Unions: Sofia; tel. (2) 88-48-21; fax (2) 88-27-10; f. 1992; Pres. VASSIL YANACHKOV; 20,000 mems.

Federation of Trade Unions in the Chemical Industry: 1040 Sofia, Makedonia Sq. 1; tel. (2) 87-39-07; Pres. LYUBEN MAKOV; 60,000 mems (mid-1993).

Federation of Trade Union Organizations in the Forestry and Woodworking Industries: 1606 Sofia, Vladayska St 29; tel. (2) 52-31-21; fax (2) 51-73-97; Pres. PETER IVANOV ABRACHEV; 16,570 mems (mid-1999).

Federation of Trade Unions of Health Services: 1202 Sofia, Blvd Maria Louiza 45; tel. (2) 988-20-97; fax (2) 83-18-14; e-mail fsz-citub@mail.orbitel.bg; f. 1990; Pres. Dr IVAN KOKALOV; 24,065 mems (2000).

Independent Trade Union Federation of the Co-operatives: 1000 Sofia, Rakovski St 99; tel. (2) 87-36-74; Chair. NIKOLAI NIKOLOV; 96,000 mems.

Independent Trade Union Federation for Trade, Co-operatives, Services and Tourism: 1000 Sofia, 6 September St 4; tel. (2) 88-02-51; Chair. PETUR TSEKOV; 212,221 mems.

Independent Trade Union of Food Industry Workers: 1606 Sofia, Dimo Hadzhidimov St 29; tel. (2) 52-30-72; fax (2) 52-16-70; Pres. SLAVCHO PETROV; 53,000 mems (mid-1994).

National Federation of Energy Workers: 1040 Sofia, Makedonia Sq. 1; tel. (2) 88-48-22; f. 1927; Pres. BOJIL PETROV; 15,000 mems.

National Trade Union Federation 'Metal-elektro': 1040 Sofia, Makedonia Sq. 1; POB 543; tel. (2) 987-48-06; fax (2) 987-75-38; e-mail nsf-me@netbg.com; Pres. ASSEN ASSENOV; 40,000 mems (1999).

Union of Bulgarian Teachers: 1000 Sofia; tel. (2) 87-78-18; f. 1905; Chair. IVAN YORDANOV; 186,153 mems.

Union of Transport Workers: 1233 Sofia, Blvd Maria Louiza 106; tel. (2) 31-51-24; fax (2) 31-71-24; f. 1911; Pres. IOROLANKA MILANOVA RADEVA; 70,000 mems (mid-1991).

Other Principal Trade Unions

Bulgarian Military Legion 'G. S. Rakovski': 1000 Sofia, Blvd Ruski 9; tel. (2) 87-72-96; Chair. DOICHIN BOYADZHIEV.

Construction, Industry and Water Supply Federation 'Podkrepa': 1000 Sofia, Uzundjovska St 12; tel. (2) 987-96-70; fax (2) 98-87-38; e-mail fciw@mail.techno-link.com; Pres. IOANIS PARTENIOTIS; 15,000 mems (2000).

Podkrepa National Union of Petrochemical Workers: 8000 Bourgas, Neftohim EAD; tel. (56) 80-09-01; fax (56) 80-12-89.

Podkrepa Professional Trade Union for Chemistry, Geology and Metallurgy Workers: 1000 Sofia, Angel Kanchev St 2; Chair. LACHEZAR MINKOV (acting); 15,000 mems.

Podkrepa Professional Trade Union for Doctors and Medical Personnel: 1000 Sofia, Angel Kanchev St 2; Chair. Dr K. KRASTEV; 20,000 mems.

Podkrepa Union of Journalists: 1000 Sofia, Angel Kanchev St 2; tel. (2) 87-21-98.

Union of Architects in Bulgaria: 1504 Sofia, Krakra St 11; tel. (2) 46-31-09; fax (2) 946-08-00; e-mail sab@bguet.bg; internet www.bulgarianarchitects.org; f. 1893; Chair. TANKO SERAFIMOV.

Union of Bulgarian Lawyers: 1000 Sofia, Treti April St 7; tel. (2) 87-58-59; Chair. PETUR KORNAZHEV.

Transport

Ministry of Transport and Communications: 1000 Sofia, Levski St 9; tel. and fax (2) 988-53-29; directs the state rail, road, water and air transport organizations.

Despred International Freight Forwarders Ltd: 1080 Sofia, Slavyanska St 2; tel. (2) 87-60-16; fax (2) 981-33-40; e-mail despcu@mail.techno-link.com; internet www.despted.com; Exec. Dir DIMITAR NESTOROV.

RAILWAYS

In 1996 there were 4,293 km of track in Bulgaria, of which 2,708 km were electrified. The international and domestic rail networks are centred on Sofia. In 1995 a US $45m.-loan from the European Bank for Reconstruction and Development was granted to Bulgarian State Railways. Construction of a 52-km underground railway system for Sofia commenced in 1979; the first section, comprising 6.1 km, was opened in January 1998.

Bulgarian State Railways (BDZ): 1080 Sofia, Ivan Vazov St 3; tel. (2) 87-30-45; fax (2) 87-71-51; e-mail bdzboev@bg400.bg; f. 1988; owns and controls all railway transport; manufacture of railway coaches and equipment; Pres. VASKO RAICHEV; Gen. Dir VLADIMIR DUNCHEV; 57,850 employees.

ROADS

There were 36,759 km of roads in Bulgaria in 1998, of which 3,080 km were principal roads and 10,060 km were secondary roads;

92% of the network was paved. Two important international motorways traverse the country and a major motorway runs from Sofia to the coast.

General Road Administration: 1606 Sofia, Blvd Makedonia 3; tel. (2) 52-17-68; fax (2) 951-54-22; e-mail ktaushanov@gra.bg; f. 1952; develops, manages and maintains the national road network; provides conditions for the realization of state road policy; Gen. Dir KOSTADIN TAUSHANOV.

SHIPPING AND INLAND WATERWAYS

The Danube (Dunav) River is the main waterway, with Ruse and Lom the two main ports. There are external services from Black Sea ports (the largest being Varna and Burgas) to the former USSR, the Mediterranean and Western Europe. The port of Tsarevo was opened to international shipping in 1995. In September 1998 it was announced that the port of Burgas was to be modernized, with financial assistance from the Japanese Government.

Bulgarian River Shipping Company: 7000 Ruse, Otets Paisi Sq. 2; tel. (82) 220-81; fax (82) 22-26-08; f. 1935; shipment of cargo and passengers on the Danube; storage, handling and forwarding of cargo; Chair. STEFAN ZAGOROV; Gen. Dir VRANGEL NIKIFOROV; 1,260 employees.

Bulgarski Morski Flot Co.: 9000 Varna, Panaguirishte St 17; tel. (52) 22-63-16; fax (52) 22-53-94; organization of sea and river transport; carriage of goods and passengers on waterways; controls all aspects of shipping and shipbuilding; research, design and personnel training; Dir-Gen. ATANAS YONKOV.

Burgas Port Authority: Burgas; Chief Exec. GEORGE DERELIEV.

Navigation Maritime Bulgare Ltd: 9000 Varna, Blvd Primorski 1; tel. (52) 22-24-74; fax (52) 22-24-91; e-mail office@navbul.com; internet www.navbul.com; f. 1892; major enterprise in Bulgaria employed in sea transport; owns 103 tankers, bulk carriers and container, ferry, cargo and passenger vessels with a capacity of 1,817,169 dwt (1995); Dir-Gen. Capt. IVAN BORISSOV; 7,100 employees.

CIVIL AVIATION

There are three international airports in Bulgaria; at Sofia, Varna and Burgas, and seven other airports for domestic services. In mid-1995 construction work began on the modernization of Sofia Airport.

Air Via Bulgarian Airways (Via): Sofia, Blvd Dimitros 54; tel. (2) 72-25-87; fax (2) 72-05-84; f. 1990, began services in 1997; first private charter airline, internal charter services to Burgas, Plovdiv and Varna.

Balkan Bulgarian Airlines: 1540 Sofia, Sofia Airport; tel. (2) 98-44-89; fax (2) 79-12-06; e-mail balkan@balkanairlines.bg; internet www.balkan.com; f. 1947; restructured and split in 1991; privatized in 1999; designated national carrier; passenger and cargo services; services to 52 international destinations; also operates domestic routes; Exec. Dir TSVI FRANK; Chair. YOSIF NOVAK; 3,700 employees.

Heli Air Services: 1540 Sofia, Sofia Airport North; tel. (2) 79-50-36; fax (2) 71-75-26; e-mail heliair@intech.bg; f. 1991; Exec. Dir GEORGI SPASSOV.

Hemus Airlines: 1540 Sofia, Sofia Airport; tel. (2) 70-20-76; fax (2) 79-63-80; f. 1991; Dir-Gen. ZDRAVKO VELICHKOV.

Jes Air: 1540 Sofia, Sofia Airport; f. 1991; Exec. Dir TATIANA STOICHKOVA.

Tourism

Bulgaria's tourist attractions include the resorts on the Black Sea coast, mountain scenery and historic centres. Under the Communist regime most visitors to Bulgaria were from former Eastern bloc countries, or in transit to or from Turkey. Following the end of Communist rule, fewer Eastern Europeans holidayed within Eastern Europe, and there was, overall, a severe reduction in the numbers of tourists staying at Black Sea resorts. The EC granted aid for developing tourism in 1993–95. In 1999 there were 5,056,250 foreign visitor arrivals (including 2,565,535 visitors in transit). Tourism receipts totalled US $369m. in 1997. In that year the tourism authorities promoted the creation of a national system of tourist offices, to be managed by local governments.

Bulgarian Tourist Chamber: 1000 Sofia, Sveta Sofia St 8; tel. (2) 87-40-59; fax (2) 986-51-33; some 800 firms are mems, incl. state enterprises, which are in the process of privatization; Chair. TSVETAN TONCHEV.

Balkantourist: 1040 Sofia, Blvd Vitosha 1; tel. (2) 4-33-31; fax (2) 981-01-14; f. 1948; Bulgaria's first privatized travel company; leading tour operator and travel agent; Chair. and Man. Dir VLADIMIR ANGELOU.

BURKINA FASO

Introductory Survey

Location, Climate, Language, Religion, Flag, Capital

Burkina Faso (formerly the Republic of Upper Volta) is a land-locked state in West Africa, bordered by Mali to the west and north, by Niger to the east, and by Benin, Togo, Ghana and Côte d'Ivoire to the south. The climate is hot and mainly dry, with an average temperature of 27°C (81°F) in the dry season (December–May). A rainy season occurs between June and October. Levels of rainfall are generally higher in the south than in the north; average annual rainfall in Ouagadougou is 894 mm (35 ins). The official language is French, and there are numerous indigenous languages (principally Mossi), with many dialects. The majority of the population follow animist beliefs; about 30% are Muslims and some 10% Christians, mainly Roman Catholics. The national flag (proportions 3 by 2) has two equal horizontal stripes, of red and green, with a five-pointed gold star in the centre. The capital is Ouagadougou.

Recent History

Burkina Faso (Upper Volta until August 1984) was formerly a province of French West Africa. It became a self-governing republic within the French Community in December 1958 and achieved full independence on 5 August 1960, with Maurice Yaméogo as President. In January 1966 Yaméogo was deposed in a military coup, led by Lt-Col (later Gen.) Sangoulé Lamizana, the Chief of Staff of the army, who took office as President and Prime Minister. The new regime dissolved the legislature, suspended the Constitution and established a Conseil suprême des forces armées. Political activities were suspended between September 1966 and November 1969. A new Constitution, approved by referendum in June 1970, provided for a return to civilian rule after a four-year transitional period. Elections for an Assemblée nationale took place in December, at which the Union démocratique voltaïque (UDV) won 37 of the 57 seats. In early 1971 Lamizana appointed the UDV leader, Gérard Ouédraogo, as Prime Minister at the head of a mixed civilian and military Council of Ministers.

A series of conflicts between the Government and the legislature prompted Lamizana, in February 1974, to announce that the army had again assumed power. Ouédraogo was dismissed, the legislature was dissolved, and the Constitution and all political activity were suspended. The Assemblée was replaced in July by a Conseil national consultatif pour le renouveau, with 65 members nominated by the President. Political parties were allowed to resume their activities from October 1977. A referendum in November of that year approved a draft Constitution providing for a return to civilian rule. Seven parties contested elections for a new Assemblée nationale in April 1978. The UDV won 28 of the 57 seats, while the Union nationale pour la défense de la démocratie (UNDD), led by Hermann Yaméogo, the son of the former President, secured 13 seats. In accordance with the Constitution, the seven parties grouped themselves into three alliances in the legislature, with the main opposition front being formed by the UNDD and the Union progressiste voltaïque. In May Lamizana was elected President, and in July the Assemblée elected the President's nominee, Dr Joseph Conombo, as Prime Minister.

In November 1980, following protracted industrial unrest, Lamizana was overthrown in a bloodless coup, led by Col Saye Zerbo, who had been Minister of Foreign Affairs during the previous period of military rule. A 31-member Comité militaire de redressement pour le progrès national (CMRPN) was established, and the regime formed a new Government comprising both army officers and civilians. The Constitution was suspended, the legislature was dissolved, and political parties were banned. Opposition to the Zerbo regime, most notably to its attempts to suppress trade union activity, soon emerged, and in November 1982 Zerbo was deposed by a group of non-commissioned army officers. Maj. Jean-Baptiste Ouédraogo, President of the Conseil de salut du peuple (CSP), emerged as leader of the new regime. The CMRPN was dissolved, and a predominantly civilian Government was formed. A power struggle within the CSP became apparent with the arrest, in May 1983, of radical left-wing elements within the Government, including the recently-appointed Prime Minister, Capt. Thomas Sankara. Ouédraogo announced the withdrawal of the armed forces from political life, and disbanded the CSP. Sankara and his supporters were released following a rebellion by pro-Sankara commandos at Pô, near the border with Ghana, under the leadership of Capt. Blaise Compaoré.

In August 1983 Sankara seized power in a violent coup. A Conseil national révolutionnaire (CNR) was established, and Jean-Baptiste Ouédraogo and other perceived opponents of the new administration were placed under house arrest. Compaoré, as Minister of State at the Presidency, became the regime's second-in-command. In September ex-President Zerbo was arrested after his supporters attempted to overthrow the new Government. Administrative, judicial and military reforms were announced, and Tribunaux populaires révolutionnaires (TPRs) were inaugurated to consider cases of alleged corruption. Several former politicians, including Zerbo, appeared before these tribunals and were subsequently imprisoned. Meanwhile, citizens were urged to join Comités pour la défense de la révolution (CDRs), which, by imposing government policies and organizing local affairs, played an important role in consolidating Sankara's position.

In June 1984 seven army officers were executed, convicted of plotting to overthrow the Government. Sankara accused an outlawed left-wing political group, the Front progressiste voltaïque, of complicity in the plot, alleging that it had been supported by France and other foreign powers: the French Government vigorously denied any involvement, and relations between the two countries underwent some strain. In August the country was renamed Burkina Faso ('Land of the Incorruptible Men'). In response to growing factionalism within the CNR, Sankara made efforts to reduce the influence of Marxist elements that had begun to oppose his populist rhetoric.

In December 1985 a long-standing border dispute with Mali erupted into a six-day war which left some 50 people dead. The conflict centred on a reputedly mineral-rich area known as the Agacher strip. Following a cease-fire, arranged by the regional defence grouping, Accord de non-agression et d'assistance en matière de défense, and as a result of an interim decision on the dispute delivered by the International Court of Justice (ICJ) in January 1986, troops were withdrawn from the Agacher area. Ambassadors were exchanged in June, and both countries accepted the ICJ's ruling, made in December, that the territory be divided equally between the two.

Amnesty measures for Sankara's political opponents were gradually effected. However, tensions between the Government and trade unions were exacerbated by policies aimed at developing the rural economy and by the introduction, from 1985, of austerity measures. In May 1987 several prominent trade unionists were detained on charges of 'counter-revolutionary' activities, and at the same time a major tax-recovery operation reportedly led to the closure of many small businesses. There was, moreover, evidence of growing disharmony within the CNR (in part engendered by Sankara's suppression of the trade unions), and in August two members of a leading communist faction were dismissed from the Government. On 15 October a self-styled Front populaire (FP), led by Compaoré, overthrew the CNR in a violent coup, in which Sankara and 13 of his entourage were killed. The new regime pledged to continue the revolutionary process, but emphasized the need for 'rectification', principally in the area of economic policy. A predominantly civilian Council of Ministers included seven members of the previous administration. Compaoré became Head of State, with the title of Chairman of the FP. Many of Sankara's close associates were arrested and detained without trial in the months following the coup, although most had been released by mid-1988.

Among institutional reforms instigated in the aftermath of the coup, the CDRs were disarmed and replaced by Comités révolutionnaires (which had only limited success in recruiting members), and the powers of the TPRs were curtailed. Civilian government members, meanwhile, had considerable influence in the implementation of the FP's economic programme. In

April 1989 a new political grouping, the Organisation pour la démocratie populaire/Mouvement du travail (ODP/MT), was established, under the leadership of Clément Oumarou Ouédraogo. The swift dismissal of government members who had declined to join the new party was an apparent indication that the ODP/MT was intended to assume a prominent role in Compaoré's regime.

In August 1989 an amnesty was proclaimed for all political prisoners. In the following month it was announced that the Commander-in-Chief of the Armed Forces and Minister of Popular Defence and Security, Maj. Jean-Baptiste Boukary Lingani, and the Minister of Economic Promotion, Capt. Henri Zongo (both of whom had been prominent at the time of the 1983 and 1987 coups), had been executed, together with two others, following the discovery of a plot to overthrow Compaoré. It was widely believed that Boukary Lingani and Zongo had been opposed to aspects of the 'rectification' process, notably the promotion of private enterprise and the principle of co-operation with the IMF and the World Bank (funding negotiations with which had begun in 1988). Compaoré subsequently assumed personal responsibility for defence. In December 1989 it was announced that a further attempt to overthrow the Government had been thwarted; in November 1990 19 people (including a former Minister of Justice under Sankara) were officially said to be awaiting trial in connection with the alleged plot.

The first congress of the FP, in March 1990, was attended by delegates from seven political tendencies. The congress sanctioned the establishment of a commission to draft a new constitution that would define a process of 'democratization'. Hermann Yaméogo, widely regarded as a political moderate, was appointed to the Executive Committee of the FP. (Three months later, however, Yaméogo and his supporters were expelled from the organization.) In April Clément Oumarou Ouédraogo was dismissed from prominent posts within the FP, the ODP/MT and the Council of Ministers. He was replaced as Secretary for Political Affairs of the FP and as Secretary-General of the ODP/MT by Roch Marc-Christian Kaboré, hitherto Minister of Transport and Communications and, unlike Ouédraogo, a known supporter of Compaoré's ideals. In September Kaboré was appointed Minister of State within the Government.

The final draft of the Constitution, which was completed in late 1990, delineated the division of power between the executive, legislature and judiciary, in a 'revolutionary, democratic, unitary and secular state'. Multi-party elections, by universal suffrage, would take place for a President and legislative Assemblée des députés du peuple (ADP), while provision was made for the establishment of a second, consultative chamber of the legislature, to be composed of the 'active forces of the nation'.

In March 1991 the first congress of the ODP/MT adopted Compaoré as the party's presidential candidate. The party also renounced its Marxist-Leninist ideology, embracing instead policies of free enterprise. In the following month an amnesty was proclaimed for the alleged perpetrators of the coup attempt of late 1989. In May 1991 a congress was convened to restructure the FP and to provide for the separation, upon the adoption of the new Constitution, of the functions of the FP and the organs of state. Compaoré, redesignated Secretary-General of the FP, was confirmed in office as Head of State pending the presidential election. Delegates also approved the rehabilitation of Maurice Yaméogo, and an appeal was made to all political exiles to return to Burkina. In June plans were announced for the construction of a memorial honouring Sankara.

About 49% of the registered electorate voted in the constitutional referendum, which took place on 2 June 1991: of these, 93% were reported to have endorsed the Constitution of what was to be designated the Fourth Republic. The new document took effect on 11 June, whereupon the Council of Ministers was dissolved. A transitional Government was subsequently appointed, its most senior member being Kaboré (as Minister of State, with responsibility for the Co-ordination of Government Action). The dominant role of the ODP/MT was widely criticized, and several nominated government members declined their posts. In July Hermann Yaméogo, now leader of the Alliance pour la démocratie et la fédération (ADF), and several other representatives of parties outside the FP were appointed to the Government. In August, however, Yaméogo (who had announced his intention to contest the presidency) was one of three government members who resigned in protest against proposed electoral procedures. Seven further opposition members resigned from the transitional administration in September, when Compaoré failed to accede to demands for a national conference.

Grouped in a Coordination des forces démocratiques (CFD), the opposition organized rallies and demonstrations in support of the campaign for a national conference. Attempts to achieve a compromise failed, and in October five CFD candidates withdrew from the presidential contest.

The presidential election proceeded on 1 December 1991, whereupon Compaoré (who had resigned from the army to contest the presidency as a civilian) was elected, unopposed, with the support of 90.4% of those who voted. The CFD claimed that an abstention rate of 74.7% reflected the success of its appeal for a boycott of the poll. Compaoré emphasized the need for national reconciliation, but shortly after the election Clément Oumarou Ouédraogo was assassinated while leaving a CFD meeting; attacks on other opposition members were also reported. Although the Government condemned the violence, the CFD denounced Compaoré as personally responsible for the incidents, and further disturbances followed Ouédraogo's funeral. Apparently in response, the Government announced the indefinite postponement of the legislative elections, which had been scheduled for January 1992: the CFD had been advocating a boycott of the elections, and few political parties had registered their intention to contest the poll.

Compaoré was inaugurated as President of the Fourth Republic on 24 December 1991, and in the following month it was announced that some 4,000 people who had been convicted in connection with political or trade union activities since the time of Sankara's accession to power were to be rehabilitated. By contrast, Compaoré imposed restrictions on the remit of a 'national reconciliation forum', which convened in February 1992 but was suspended by the Government within two weeks, following disagreements regarding the broadcasting of debates by the state-owned media. None the less, four opposition members were appointed to the Government later in the month, including Hermann Yaméogo as Minister of State.

The legislative election finally took place on 24 May 1992, contested by 27 political parties. According to official results, the ODP/MT won 78 of the ADP's 107 seats. Nine other parties secured representation: of these, the most successful was Pierre Tapsoba's Convention nationale des patriotes progressistes— Parti social-démocrate (CNPP–PSD), which took 12 seats, while the ADF won four seats. The rate of participation by voters was reported to have been little more than 35%. In June Compaoré appointed Youssouf Ouédraogo, hitherto President of the country's Economic and Social Council, as Prime Minister. His Council of Ministers included representatives of seven political parties, although the ODP/MT was allocated most strategic posts—among them the finance and planning portfolio, which was assigned to Kaboré. In September 1993 Kaboré was redesignated Minister of State, with responsibility for Relations with the Organs of State.

Following the 50% devaluation of the CFA franc, in January 1994, trade unions denounced the Government's emergency measures as inadequate compensation, and began a campaign for salary increases of 40%–50%. Negotiations between the Government and workers' representatives failed to reach a compromise, and in March Ouédraogo resigned. He was replaced as Prime Minister by Kaboré.

Municipal elections took place in February 1995, at which the ODP/MT won control of 24 of the country's 33 major towns. However, fewer than 10% of those eligible were reported to have registered to vote. Several opposition parties had refused to present candidates, in protest at what they claimed were inadequate preparations for the elections.

In February 1996 Kadré Désiré Ouédraogo, hitherto Deputy Governor of the regional Banque centrale des états de l'Afrique de l'ouest, replaced Kaboré as Prime Minister. Kaboré was named Special Adviser to the Presidency, and also First Vice-President of a new, pro-Compaoré political party, the Congrès pour la démocratie et le progrès (CDP). The CDP, termed a social-democratic party, grouped the ODP/MT and some 10 other parties (including the CNPP–PSD). Named as its President was a long-time ally of Compaoré, Arsène Bognessan Yè, the President of the legislature and the former head of the ODP/MT. Most of the members of the outgoing administration were reappointed to Ouédraogo's first Council of Ministers. The new premier (who at the time claimed to have no party political affiliation, but later joined the CDP) stated that his Government's priority would be to strengthen and revitalize economic development. Ouédraogo assumed personal responsibility for the economy and finance in a government reshuffle in September 1996.

Constitutional amendments and a new electoral code were approved by the ADP in January 1997. Restrictions were removed on the renewal of the Head of State's mandate (hitherto renewable only once); with effect from the forthcoming elections, the number of parliamentary seats was to be increased to 111, while the ADP was renamed the Assemblée nationale. In addition, the number of provinces was increased from 30 to 45.

Legislative elections took place on 11 May 1997, at which some 569 candidates from 13 parties contested seats in the Assemblée nationale. As expected, the CDP won a resounding victory, with 101 seats in the enlarged assembly. The results of voting for four seats, all of which had been won by the CDP, were annulled by the Supreme Court, but these were regained by the party at re-run elections in June. The Parti pour la démocratie et le progrès (PDP), led by veteran politician Joseph Ki-Zerbo, secured six seats, and the ADF and Gérard Kango Ouédraogo's Rassemblement démocratique africain (RDA) each won two. Mélégué Maurice Traoré was elected President of the incoming legislature in June, and a new Government, under Kadré Désiré Ouédraogo, was appointed. Hermann Yaméogo left the Council of Ministers, while Arsène Bognessan Yè was named Minister of State at the Presidency of the Republic.

New legislation regarding rights of assembly and public procession, adopted by the Assemblée nationale in October 1997, was denounced by opposition parties and trade unions. Further controversy was provoked by the announcement that, from the end of the year, private radio stations would no longer be authorized to relay broadcasts from abroad. In December there was a strike by civil servants, in protest at the likely effects on jobs of the Government's privatization programme and at new regulations favouring contract employment.

In April 1998, following consultations with pro-Government and opposition parties, the Council of Ministers adopted legislation providing for the establishment of an independent electoral commission: the 26-member Commission électorale nationale indépendante (CENI) was to be composed of six representatives of the political majority and an equal number of opposition delegates, together with civic representatives. However, when the CENI was inaugurated in July, several opposition parties, among them the PDP, refused to take up their seats, and indicated their intention to boycott the forthcoming presidential election. The Groupe du 14 février (G-14f) opposition coalition protested about a lack of transparency in the electoral process, alleging corruption and unfair provisions for campaign funding, and disputing the impartiality of the CENI, the judiciary and the media regulatory authority, the Conseil supérieur de l'information. The national human rights movement, the Mouvement burkinabè des droits de l'homme et des peuples (MBDHP), also declined representation on the electoral commission.

Several key opposition figures, among them Hermann Yaméogo, whose party had absorbed a faction of the RDA to form the Alliance pour la démocratie et la fédération—Rassemblement démocratique africain (ADF—RDA), and Joseph Ki-Zerbo, refused to participate in the approaching presidential election. Compaoré was challenged by Ram Ouédraogo, leader of the ecologist Union des verts pour le développement du Burkina (UVDB), and Frédéric Guirma, a retired ambassador representing the faction of the RDA that remained outside Yaméogo's party. Despite demands by the G-14f that the election be postponed, voting proceeded, as scheduled, on 15 November 1998. The opposition denounced the election as fraudulent, but international monitors and national observers pronounced themselves satisfied with the conduct of the campaign and voting (although the latter expressed some concerns, mainly regarding the compilation of voters' lists and the distribution of ballot cards). The provisional results, issued by the CENI on 18 November 1998, confirmed a decisive victory for Compaoré, with 87.53% of the valid votes cast; Ram Ouédraogo took 6.61%, and Guirma 5.86%. Despite the appeal by the G-14f for a boycott, the rate of voter participation, at 56.08%, was considerably higher than in 1991. A new Government, again headed by Kadré Désiré Ouédraogo, was appointed in January 1999.

The political climate deteriorated rapidly after Norbert Zongo, the managing editor of the weekly *l'Indépendant* newspaper, was found dead, together with three colleagues, in December 1998. Zongo, a frequent critic of the Compaoré regime, had been investigating the death of David Ouédraogo, a driver employed by François Compaoré, younger brother and special adviser of the President; Ouédraogo had allegedly been tortured to death by members of the presidential guard for having stolen money from his employer. Opposition parties and human rights organi-

zations, grouped in a Collectif d'organisations démocratiques de masse et de partis politiques, demanded a full investigation of the case. The deaths provoked violent demonstrations, and a curfew was imposed in Koudougou (Zongo's birthplace) after several CDP properties were set on fire. It was subsequently reported that Hermann Yaméogo had been detained, accused of fomenting the Koudougou unrest. Students and school pupils boycotted classes in Ouagadougou, as part of the protest movement. Meanwhile, opposition groups refused to participate in an independent commission of inquiry into Zongo's apparent murder, established by presidential decree in January 1999, stating that a similar commission had failed to bring to justice those responsible for the assassination of Clément Oumarou Ouédraogo in 1991. Furthermore, the MBDHP suspended participation in the commission, on the grounds that its preconditions for membership, including an end to legal proceedings against activists involved in recent protests, had not been met. Shortly afterwards a three-day general strike, organized by the opposition collective, was widely observed in the capital.

In its final report, submitted in May 1999, the commission of inquiry stated that it had been unable to prove the identity of the culprits, but indicated the likelihood that the members of the presidential guard implicated in the death of François Compaoré's driver were also responsible for the murders of the journalists. Shortly afterwards the only foreign member of the commission of inquiry, Robert Ménard, the head of an international press freedom group, Reporters sans frontières, was placed under house arrest and deported. The announcement of the commission's findings provoked renewed unrest. In mid-May three prominent members of the opposition, including Halidou Ouédraogo, the Chairman of the Collectif, and Hermann Yaméogo, were arrested by the security forces, accused of having repeated Ménard's denunciation of the presidential guard and of having plotted a *coup d'état*. Two were released after a brief detention, but Yaméogo remained in custody for three days. Shortly afterwards Compaoré stated that the examining magistrate responsible for the Zongo case would be given his full support. He further announced a reorganization of the presidential guard, an amnesty for all those arrested in the recent protests, the reopening of the educational establishments closed during the unrest, and compensation for the relatives of victims of the murders that had provoked the political crisis. The Collectif welcomed these measures, but criticized what they perceived as official pressure on the judiciary.

Public discontent intensified in mid-1999. In June state electricity workers observed a 24-hour strike in protest at the alleged murder of one of their colleagues by the security forces, and in July the entrances to the Ministry of Defence and the headquarters of the armed forces were blocked for a short time by unarmed soldiers and junior officers, who were demanding the payment of outstanding allowances. Meanwhile, two-day general strikes were organized by trade unions in late June and mid-August to protest against low wages, labour reforms and the privatization of parastatal enterprises, as well as alleged human rights abuses by the state.

In June 1999 Compaoré established a Collège des sages, composed of 16 Burkinabè state elders, together with religious and ethnic leaders. The Collège was to promote national reconciliation, and, most notably, to investigate unpunished political crimes since independence. In mid-June the Collège ordered the arrest of the three members of the presidential guard accused of the murder of David Ouédraogo. The Collège published its report in August. Its main recommendations were that a government of national unity should be formed, as well as a 'commission of truth and justice' to oversee the transition to a truly plural political system and to investigate unresolved political murders, including that of Sankara. The Collège also suggested that an amnesty should be granted to those implicated during the investigations of the commission, and that compensation should be paid to the families of victims. The Collège further recommended the creation of a commission to examine certain clauses of the Constitution and to formulate rules governing political parties; also that Compaoré should not seek re-election, and that fresh elections should be held for the Assemblée nationale. Compaoré praised the work of the Collège, describing it as having acted with 'a sense of fairness, honour and dignity'. However, opposition organizations rejected the proposed amnesty and criticized the need for Compaoré's assent to any of the proposed reforms. Meanwhile, on the eve of the publication of the elders' report, Roch Marc-Christian Kaboré was appointed to the new post of Executive Secretary of the CDP, replacing both the former President, Arsène Bognessan Yè, and Secretary-General, Simon Compaoré.

In September 1999 the Prime Minister, Kadré Désiré Ouédraogo, began consultations with the leaders of the major political parties in order to identify the key objectives of any government of national unity. Most opposition parties stipulated that participation in such a government would be conditional upon the expedition of legal action in the cases of David Ouédraogo and Norbert Zongo. Thus, the reshuffled Council of Ministers, announced in October, included just two opposition leaders: Ram Ouédraogo of the moderate UVDB and Noyabtigungu Congo Kaboré of the Mouvement pour la tolérance et le progrès (MTP). Ouédraogo, who had retained his post as Prime Minister, subsequently reiterated the Government's willingness to maintain a dialogue with the G-14f.

In late 1999 students demonstrated in Ouagadougou to demand the reinstatement of pupils who had been expelled from secondary schools in Sabou and Koudougou for participating in protests against the assassination of Zongo. Meanwhile, workers in the health care sector undertook strike action to demand improved allowances and higher salaries for the emergency services. There was also much criticism of the Government's handling of the enforced repatriation of Burkinabè citizens from Côte d'Ivoire (see below).

In November 1999, in accordance with the recommendations of the Collège des sages, two advisory commissions were inaugurated: one to examine certain clauses of the Constitution and to formulate rules governing political parties, and another to promote national reconciliation. Despite official assurances that the commissions' findings would be binding, the G-14f refused to participate, claiming that debate would be restricted and that their conclusions would carry little weight. Shortly afterwards the Collectif organized a series of mass demonstrations intended to commemorate the first anniversary of the murder of Zongo. In December it was reported that several important figures in the Collectif had been detained by the police and accused of 'inciting revolt and sedition in the army' by publishing a letter in *Le Pays* urging the security forces to guarantee the security of protesters and to reject the 'terrorist tactics' of the authorities. A court subsequently dismissed the case against the men.

In January 2000 Compaoré offered to bring forward the legislative elections scheduled for 2002, in the hope of resolving the political crisis. Many opposition leaders, however, rejected this proposal, suggesting that the establishment of a political solution and the prosecution of suspects in the Ouédraogo and Zongo cases should precede the elections. In late January the ruling CDP organized a public demonstration in favour of the proposals of the advisory commission on political reform, which had recommended the modification of the electoral code and the reform of the judiciary and the Constitution. Most notably, the commission proposed the restriction of the presidential mandate to no more than two successive terms. The Assemblée nationale subsequently voted to revise the electoral code, to accord greater powers to the CENI, and to postpone the municipal elections scheduled for February in order to allow the implementation of the revisions. The opposition, however, criticized what they perceived to be the limited nature of the reforms, and expressed their continued determination to boycott any elections until the Ouédraogo and Zongo cases had been fully resolved.

In February 2000 the advisory commission on national reconciliation published its report, which urged the prosecution of those suspected of involvement in the embezzlement of public funds and in so-called political killings. The report also recommended that victims of political violence or their relations receive an official apology, compensation and a guarantee regarding their future security. The commission also called for greater freedom of speech and of assembly, the resolution of legal proceedings in the Ouédraogo and Zongo cases, the strengthening of press freedom, the introduction of an amnesty law, and the construction of a monument to former President Sankara. The commission's final proposal was that a further commission be established to monitor the implementation of its recommendations.

In April 2000 a demonstration in Ouagadougou, held in support of demands for the resolution of the Zongo case, resulted in violent clashes between student demonstrators and the security forces. The opposition subsequently called for a three-day general strike and a series of protests against the intervention of the security forces. Halidou Ouédraogo, the Chairman of the Collectif, and 38 other activists were briefly detained on charges

of endangering public order, and the Government announced the temporary closure of all schools and universities in Ouagadougou and Bobo-Dioulasso. Later that month the Government sought to defuse the tension with the announcement that it was to encourage the return to Burkina Faso of political exiles, and that a mausoleum for former President Sankara was to be constructed.

The Assemblée nationale approved revisions to the electoral code in April 2000; under the new regulations, which introduced a system of proportional representation, 91 deputies would be elected from regional lists, while 21 would be elected from a national list. The new legislation also reduced the presidential mandate from seven to five years, renewable only once. However, the opposition, while broadly welcoming the reforms, noted that, as the new limits were not to be introduced until the next election, it would be possible for Compaoré to stand again in 2005 and 2010. A new law regulating opposition parties was also introduced, which defined their responsibilities and rights, in particular regarding public funding. In the same month Hermann Yaméogo was expelled from the G-14f for having criticized the group's policy of not co-operating with the Government on reform until the Ouédraogo and Zongo cases had been resolved.

In early May 2000 the Government announced that the postponed municipal elections would be held on 30 July. Several opposition parties criticized the date as unfeasible in view of the political climate and reiterated their demand for the Ouédraogo and Zongo cases to be resolved prior to the elections. In late May Compaoré held a meeting with Halidou Ouédraogo and other members of the Collectif in order to discuss the process of reform. However, the death of a police officer who had been implicated in attempts to conceal the murder of David Ouédraogo was widely viewed as suspicious by the opposition, and in June the Collectif refused to meet Ram Ouédraogo, the Chairman of the commission for national reconciliation, whom they accused of having reneged on agreements reached at their previous meeting. The opposition continued to reject the proposed date for the municipal elections, and in mid-July the Chairman of the CENI also urged the postponement of the elections by at least one month in order to allow the commission time to resolve difficulties in the compilation of electoral registers and the distribution of ballot cards. The elections were postponed, initially until 24 August, and subsequently until 24 September, although the Collectif and the G-14f continued to call for a further delay. However, by mid-August, dissent within the radical opposition regarding the policy of boycotting elections had prompted several constituent parties of the Collectif and the G-14f to nominate candidates. As a result, the ADF—RDA, the Union des démocrates et patriotes indépendants and the Convention panafricaine sankariste were expelled from the Collectif and the G-14f. The increasingly fragmented nature of the opposition was also evident in the formation of several breakaway groups by former ADF—RDA members.

Meanwhile, the trial of the soldiers accused of murdering David Ouédraogo began in mid-August 2000. Two of the defendants were acquitted by the military tribunal, but two members of Compaoré's presidential guard, including Marcel Kafando, head of the guard at the time of Ouédraogo's death, were sentenced to 20 years' imprisonment, with a third member sentenced to 10 years'. Reporters sans frontières welcomed the sentences, but condemned as inadmissible the failure to implicate President Compaoré's brother in the trial. The G-14f expressed dissatisfaction at the resolution of the case, and at what it termed 'ongoing economic crimes'.

The CDP won a clear victory in the municipal elections on 24 September 2000, securing 802 of the 1,100 available seats, and retaining outright control of 40 of the 49 municipalities. Twenty-five parties contested the elections, although the G-14f and the PDP boycotted the poll. The ADF—RDA gained 133 seats, while two breakaway factions from the party, the pro-Compaoré Union des libéraux pour la démocratie (ULD) and the opposition Union pour la démocratie et la fédération, won 49 and 22 seats respectively. A total of 14 parties gained representation as a result of the elections, in which the rate of voter participation was reported to be 68.4%.

In October 2000, following five months of strikes by students, who were protesting in support of demands for improved facilities and living conditions, the Government closed the University of Ouagadougou and declared the 1999/2000 academic year invalid. At the same time government proposals for educational reform, which envisaged a greater emphasis on selection by merit, were denounced by trade-union leaders and students. Following the appointment of a new university Chancellor, Alfred Traoré, in late October, the opposition Collectif organized a campaign of protests to demand the reopening of the university.

In early November 2000, amid ongoing social unrest, Kadré Désiré Ouédraogo resigned as Prime Minister and was replaced by Paramanga Ernest Yonli, hitherto the Minister of the Civil Service and Institutional Development. President Compaoré subsequently announced the formation of a 36-member Council of Ministers, one-third of which was composed of members of the opposition. The new appointments resulted from an agreement reached by Yonli and representatives from seven political parties, including the ruling CDP, the ADF—RDA and the ULD, but not the principal opposition party, the PDP, which refused to participate. The agreement specified the parties' conditions for joining the Government, notably the prompt and thorough completion of pending legal cases and the reopening of the University of Ouagadougou. It was stated that the new administration was to serve as a focus of national unity and to govern by consensus. The leaders of the participating parties were to meet with the Prime Minister every three months to evaluate the implementation of the accord.

Meanwhile, the protests continued, and in late November 2000 three days of demonstrations erupted into riots between secondary-school pupils and the police. In early December the Government issued a decree prohibiting all demonstrations, except those of a religious nature, in public places across Burkina Faso. It was suggested that this decree was in part a response to the death of a school pupil who had been shot during violent clashes between demonstrators and the security forces in Boussé, some 50 km north-west of Ouagadougou. Nevertheless, demonstrations to commemorate the second anniversary of Norbert Zongo's murder were held, as planned, later that month, leading to clashes with the security forces. The University of Ouagadougou was reopened in mid-December, after a postponement of more than two weeks prompted by the November riots. In early February 2001 the inquiry into the death of Norbert Zongo charged Marcel Kafando with his murder.

Compaoré has, in recent years, gained wide recognition for his efforts as a regional mediator and as a proponent of inter-African conflict-resolution initiatives. In the early 1990s, however, relations with some members of the Economic Community of West African States (ECOWAS, see p. 170) suffered a reverse, owing to the Compaoré Government's support for Charles Taylor's rebel National Patriotic Front of Liberia (NPFL) and Burkina's refusal to participate in the military intervention by the ECOWAS cease-fire monitoring group (ECOMOG, see p. 172) in Liberia. In September 1991 Compaoré admitted that Burkinabè troops had been dispatched to Liberia to assist the NPFL in the overthrow of Samuel Doe's regime in mid-1990. However, his assertion that the country's involvement in Liberia had ended contrasted with reports that Burkina was continuing to assist the NPFL with arms and training facilities. In November 1992 the US Government recalled its ambassador to Burkina, and announced that the recently-appointed Burkinabè ambassador to the USA would not be welcome in Washington, DC, owing to Burkina's alleged role in transporting arms from Libya to the NPFL. Allegations of Burkinabè support for the NPFL persisted, but in September 1995 the Compaoré administration, stating that it regarded the peace agreement that had been signed in Abuja, Nigeria, in the previous month as more 'credible' than earlier peace settlements for Liberia, announced that Burkina would contribute peace-keeping troops to ECOMOG. In early February 1997 the Burkinabè legislature approved legislation authorizing the participation of Burkinabè military personnel in the cease-fire monitoring group, in preparation for the forthcoming elections in Liberia. Members of the Burkinabè military subsequently remained in Liberia to assist in the training of new armed forces. In May 1998 the Government of Burkina vehemently denied allegations (made by Sierra Leonean refugees entering Guinea) that Burkinabè forces were assisting anti-government fighters in Sierra Leone. In early 1999 accusations were made by President Kabbah of Sierra Leone, by the Nigerian Government and by the international press that Burkina and Liberia were co-operating to provide support to the rebels in Sierra Leone and to supply them with arms. The Burkinabè Government continued to deny its involvement. In early 2000 a report to the United Nations (UN) Security Council accused Burkina Faso of having supplied weapons to the rebels in Sierra Leone in exchange for diamonds

on several occasions. It was also alleged that Burkina Faso had supplied weapons to Liberia and to Angolan rebel groups, despite international embargoes on the supply of weapons to those countries. The report, which further accused Compaoré of having conducted personal negotiations with the Angolan rebel leader Jonas Savimbi, was strenuously denied by the Burkinabè Government, which stated that the external policy of Burkina Faso was entirely motivated by a desire to establish peace in the region. Two missions from the UN Security Council visited Burkina Faso in mid-2000, at the invitation of the Burkinabè Government, to investigate the claims regarding the breaching of arms embargoes against Angola and Sierra Leone. In December it was reported that Burkina Faso was to introduce measures aimed at controlling its weapons imports in an attempt to allay international concern.

In early November 1999 a dispute over land rights between Burkinabè settlers in the south-west of Côte d'Ivoire and the indigenous minority Krou population, which caused two deaths, led to the violent and systematic expulsion from the region of several hundred Burkinabè plantation workers by militant Krou. Several deaths were reported, and it was estimated that between 9,000 and 12,000 expatriates had returned to Burkina in subsequent weeks. In late November the Burkinabè Minister of Foreign Affairs, Youssouf Ouédraogo, visited Côte d'Ivoire in order to discuss the expulsions with the Ivorian authorities. The two Governments emphasized, however, that the problem was a local one and that relations between the two countries remained cordial. Following the *coup d'état* in Côte d'Ivoire in December 1999, the military authorities assured the Government of Burkina that the expulsions would cease and that measures would be taken in order to allow workers to return.

Compaoré visited France in June 1993 (his first official visit to that country) and in April 1994, and attended the Franco-African summit meeting in Biarritz, France, in November 1994. Burkina swiftly established close relations with Jacques Chirac following his election to the French presidency in May 1995. The 1996 summit meeting of Franco-African Heads of State took place in Ouagadougou in December. Compaoré subsequently participated in a regional mediation effort, conceived at the meeting, to resolve the political crisis in the Central African Republic (CAR). The Assemblée nationale authorized the dispatch of a Burkinabè military contingent to the surveillance mission for the CAR in February 1997, and a Burkinabè force remained in the CAR as part of the UN peace-keeping operation that succeeded the regional mission in April 1998. Burkina was one of eight regional countries to participate in the Cohésion Kompienga '98 military exercises in April, in the context of efforts to establish a regional crisis-response force. The 34th Assembly of Heads of State and Government of the Organization of African Unity took place in Ouagadougou in June; Compaoré, as incoming Chairman, subsequently played an active role in mediation initiatives in the dispute between Eritrea and Ethiopia.

Links with Libya have generally been strong under the Compaoré regime; Burkina was, notably, a founder member of the Community of the Sahel-Saharan States (COMESSA, now CENSAD, see p. 307), established in Tripoli in 1997. In April 1999 Compaoré attended the first COMESSA summit held in Sirte, Libya, and in July 2000 the Libyan leader, Col Muammar al-Qaddafi, visited Burkina Faso. In August 2000 President Chen Shui-bian of the Republic of China (Taiwan) became the first Asian leader to make a state visit to Burkina Faso.

Government

Under the terms of the Constitution of June 1991, executive power is vested in the President and in the Government, and is counterbalanced by a legislative Assemblée nationale (until 1997 the Assemblée des députés du peuple), and by an independent judiciary. Presidential and legislative elections are conducted by universal adult suffrage, in the context of a multiparty political system. The President is elected for a seven-year term, and delegates to the Assemblée nationale are elected for a five-year term. In April 2000 the Assemblée nationale adopted legislation, effective from the next elections, which reduced the presidential mandate from seven to five years, renewable only once, and introduced a system of proportional representation for elections to the Assemblée nationale, according to which 91 deputies would be elected from a regional list, while 21 would be elected from a national list. The President is empowered to appoint a Prime Minister; however, the Assemblée nationale has the right to veto any such appointment. Both the Government and the Assemblée nationale are competent to initiate legislation. There is also a second, consultative chamber—the Chambre des représentants—whose 178 members are nominated from among the 'active forces of the nation' to serve a three-year term of office. These 'active forces' include regional councils, religious communities, women's associations, trade unions, presidential representatives, military and paramilitary forces, sports associations and non-governmental organizations.

Burkina is divided into 45 provinces, each of which is administered by a civilian governor.

Defence

National service is voluntary, and lasts for two years on a part-time basis. In August 2000 the active armed forces numbered 10,000 (army 5,600, air force 200, gendarmerie 4,200). Other units include a 'security company' of 250 and a part-time people's militia of 45,000. The defence budget for 2000 was estimated at 49,000m. francs CFA.

Economic Affairs

In 1998, according to estimates by the World Bank, Burkina Faso's gross national product (GNP), measured at average 1996–98 prices, was US $2,575m., equivalent to $240 per head (or $866 on an international purchasing-power parity basis). During 1990–98, it was estimated, GNP per head increased, in real terms, at an average annual rate of 1.1%. Over the same period the population increased by an average of 2.7% per year. GNP in 1999 was an estimated $2,600m. ($240 per head). During 1990–99 Burkina's gross domestic product (GDP) increased, in real terms, at an average annual rate of 3.8%. According to the IMF, real GDP increased by 6.2% in 1998, and by an estimated 5.8% in 1999.

According to IMF estimates, agriculture (including livestock-rearing, forestry and fishing) contributed 31.3% of GDP in 1999. About 92.2% of the labour force were employed in agriculture in that year. The principal cash crop is cotton (exports of which accounted for an estimated 53.4% of the value of total exports in 1999). Smaller amounts of other crops, including shea-nuts (karité nuts) and sesame seed, are also exported. The main subsistence crops are millet, sorghum, maize and rice. Burkina is almost self-sufficient in basic foodstuffs in non-drought years; however, accumulated surpluses of cereals were eliminated as a result of poor rainfall in 1997/98, when a deficit of 159,800 metric tons was recorded. Livestock-rearing is of considerable significance, contributing an estimated 9.4% of GDP and an estimated 18.7% of export revenue in 1999. During 1990–99 agricultural GDP increased at an average annual rate of 3.5%. Agricultural GDP was estimated to have declined by 1.3% in 1997, but increased by 5.5% in 1998, and by an estimated 3.1% in 1999.

Industry (including mining, manufacturing, construction and power) contributed 28.3% of GDP, according to IMF estimates, in 1999, but engaged only 1.5% of the employed labour force in 1991. During 1990–99 industrial GDP increased at an average annual rate of 3.9%. Growth in industrial GDP was estimated at 10.8% in 1999.

Although Burkina has considerable mineral resources, extractive activities accounted for 1.0% of GDP in 1997, and engaged only 0.6% of the employed labour force in 1991. However, the development of reserves of gold (exports of which contributed an estimated 5.9% of the value of total exports in 1999) has since brought about an increase in the sector's economic importance, while there is considerable potential for the exploitation of manganese, zinc and limestone. The country's other known mineral reserves include phosphates, silver, lead and nickel.

The manufacturing sector engaged only 1.1% of the employed labour force in 1991, and—together with mining—contributed an estimated 21.7% of GDP in 1999. The sector is dominated by the processing of primary products: major activities are cotton-ginning, the production of textiles, food-processing (including milling and sugar-refining), brewing and the processing of tobacco and of hides and skins. Motorcycles and bicycles are also assembled. According to IMF estimates, the combined GDP of the mining and manufacturing sectors increased at an average annual rate of 3.9% in 1990–98; growth was estimated at 12.9% in 1999.

Two hydroelectric stations supplied about one-third of Burkina's electricity output in 1998; the remainder was derived from thermal power stations (using imported fuel). The country's hydropower capacity is being expanded, and in 2000 the interconnection of the south of Burkina Faso with the electricity network of Côte d'Ivoire was finalized; a link with Ghana's electricity grid is also planned. Imports of petroleum products

comprised an estimated 16.9% of the value of merchandise imports in 1999.

The services sector contributed an estimated 40.4% of GDP in 1999, and engaged 5.4% of the employed labour force in 1991. The GDP of the services sector increased at an average annual rate of 3.5% in 1990–99, with growth of 6.7% in 1999.

In 1999 Burkina recorded an estimated visible trade deficit of 212,000m. francs CFA, while there was a deficit of 200,300m. francs CFA on the current account of the balance of payments. In 1998 the principal source of imports was France (29.9%), followed by Côte d'Ivoire and Japan. The principal markets for exports in that year were France (23.1%), Belgium-Luxembourg (10.9%) and Côte d'Ivoire (9.8%). The principal exports in 1999 were cotton, livestock and livestock products (including hides and skins) and gold. In the same year the principal imports were capital equipment, petroleum products, food products and raw materials.

In 1999 Burkina recorded an overall budget deficit of 63,800m. francs CFA, equivalent to an estimated 4.0% of GDP. Burkina's total external debt was US $1,399m. at the end of 1998, of which $1,229m. was long-term public debt. In that year the cost of debt-servicing was equivalent to 10.7% of the value of exports of goods and services. Inflation was negligible prior to the 50% devaluation of the CFA franc in January 1994 (averaging 0.4% per year in 1990–93). Consumer prices increased by an average of 25.1% in 1994, but the rate of inflation slowed to 7.4% in 1995 and averaged 3.7% annually in 1996–98. In 1999 consumer prices decreased by an average of 1.1%. Some 26,631 people were registered as unemployed in 1994.

Burkina is a member of numerous regional organizations, including the Economic Community of West African States (ECOWAS, see p. 170), the West African organs of the Franc Zone (see p. 210), the Conseil de l'Entente (see p. 307), the Liptako–Gourma Integrated Development Authority (see p. 308), and the Permanent Inter-State Committee on Drought Control in the Sahel (CILSS, see p. 309).

Burkina Faso has experienced strong growth since the devaluation of the CFA franc in 1994, as the competitiveness notably of cotton, livestock and gold have been enhanced, and from 1995 the decline in GDP per head has been reversed. An Enhanced Structural Adjustment Facility (ESAF) was agreed with the IMF in 1996, and GDP growth of 4.8% in 1997, 6.2% in 1998 and 5.8% in 1999 was achieved. In September 1999 the IMF approved funding under a further ESAF (later replaced by the Poverty Reduction and Growth Facility) in support of the Government's economic programme for 1999–2002. Policies of economic liberalization instituted at the beginning of the decade were to continue to emphasize privatization, the elimination of monopolies, particularly in the agricultural sector, and efficiency in taxation collection. A principal priority was to improve living standards for the poorest sections of the population, notably by improving infrastructure and access to basic health care and education. In July 2000 the IMF and the World Bank announced that Burkina Faso was to receive some US $400m. in debt-service relief under their original Heavily Indebted Poor Countries initiative (for which Burkina was deemed eligible in 1997) and a further $ 300m. under an enhanced framework. In 2000 lower economic growth than forecast (an estimated 4.0% rather than 5.7%) was attributed to a decrease in agricultural output, resulting from drought conditions, an increase in world petroleum prices and a decline in workers' remittances from Côte d'Ivoire. The introduction at the beginning of that year of a common external tariff within the Union économique et monétaire ouest-africaine (see p. 211) and reductions in petroleum taxation contributed to a decline in fiscal revenue in the second half of 2000, prompting the Government to introduce a number of emergency measures. For 2001 real GDP growth of 6.2% was forecast, based on an anticipated recovery in the agricultural sector, while the Government was to continue with its programme of structural reform, including the restructuring of the cotton sector, the privatization of state-owned enterprises and the promotion of the private sector.

Social Welfare

The Government provides hospitals and rural medical services. In 1990 there were 314 physicians, 325 midwives, 19 dentists and 112 pharmacists. In 1987 there were 11 hospitals and 59 health centres. Old-age and veterans' pensions are provided by the State, and workers' insurance schemes are also in operation. A minimum wage is in force. Of total planned budgetary expenditure by the central Government in 1990, 7,963m. francs CFA (7.2%) was for health, and a further 130m. francs CFA (0.1%)

was for social security and welfare. Further payments are made from social security funds. Government spending on health in 1999 was equivalent to 13.9% of total domestic expenditure, excluding foreign-financed investment and debt.

Education

Education is provided free of charge, and is officially compulsory for six years between the ages of seven and 14. Primary education begins at seven years of age and lasts for six years. Secondary education, beginning at the age of 13, lasts for a further seven years, comprising a first cycle of four years and a second of three years. Enrolment levels are among the lowest in the region. In 1995 primary enrolment included only 40% of children in the relevant age-group (males 48%; females 31%). Secondary education in 1993 included only 7% of children in the appropriate age-group (males 9%; females 5%). The Government aimed to increase the rate of primary enrolment to 48% by1999/2000. There is a university in Ouagadougou, a polytechnic university at Bobo-Dioulasso and an École Normale Supérieure at Koudougou. The number of students enrolled at tertiary-level institutions in 1996/97was 8,911, compared with 1,520 in 1980/81. In 1995, according to UNESCO estimates, adult illiteracy averaged 80.8% (males 70.5%; females 90.8%). Expenditure on education by the central Government in 1994 totalled 36,315m. francs CFA, representing 11.1% of total government spending in that year. Spending on primary education in 1999 was equiva-lent to 16.9% of total domestic expenditure, excluding foreign-financed investment and debt.

Public Holidays

2001: 1 January (New Year's Day), 6 March* (Aid el Kebir—Tabaski, Feast of the Sacrifice), 8 March (International Women's Day), 16 April (Easter Monday), 1 May (Labour Day), 24 May (Ascension Day), 4 June* (Mouloud, Birth of the Prophet), 4 August (National Day), 15 August (Assumption), 15 October (Anniversary of the 1987 *coup d'état*), 1 November (All Saints' Day), 11 December (Proclamation of the Republic), 17 December* (Aid es Segheir, end of Ramadan), 25 December (Christmas).

2002: 1 January (New Year's Day), 23 February* (Aid el Kebir—Tabaski, Feast of the Sacrifice), 8 March (International Women's Day), 1 April (Easter Monday), 1 May (Labour Day), 9 May (Ascension Day), 24 May* (Mouloud, Birth of the Prophet), 4 August (National Day), 15 August (Assumption), 15 October (Anniversary of the 1987 *coup d'état*), 1 November (All Saints' Day), 6 December* (Aid es Segheir, end of Ramadan), 11 December (Proclamation of the Republic), 25 December (Christmas)

* These holidays are dependent on the Islamic lunar calendar and may vary by one or two days from the dates given.

Weights and Measures

The metric system is in force.

Statistical Survey

Source (except where otherwise stated): Institut National de la Statistique et de la Démographie, 555 blvd de la Révolution, 01 BP 374, Ouagadougou 01; tel. 32-49-76; fax 31-07-60.

Area and Population

AREA, POPULATION AND DENSITY

Area (sq km)	274,200*
Population (census results)	
10–20 December 1985	7,964,705
10 December 1996	
Males	4,970,882
Females	5,341,727
Total	10,312,609
Population (official estimate at mid-year)	
1998	10,683,000
Density (per sq km) at mid-1998	38.9

* 105,870 sq miles.

Ethnic Groups (percentage of total, 1993): Mossi 48.6; Fulani (Peul) 7.8; Gourmantché 7; Bobo 6.8; Bisa-Samo 6.5; Gourounsi 6; Dagari-Lobo 4.3; Bwa (Bwamu) 3.0; Sénoufo-Marka-Dioula 2.2; Others 7.8.

POPULATION BY PROVINCE (estimates, 1997)

Province	Population	Capital
Balé	169,543	Boromo
Bam	212,295	Kongoussi
Banwa	214,234	Solenzo
Bazèga	214,450	Kombissiri
Bougouriba	76,444	Diébougou
Boulgou	415,414	Tenkodogo
Boulkiemdé	421,083	Koudougou
Comoé	240,942	Banfora
Ganzourgou	257,707	Zorgho
Gnagna	307,386	Bogandé
Gourma	221,956	Fada N'Gourma
Houet	674,916	Bobo-Dioulasso
Ioba	159,422	Dano
Kadiogo	976,513	Ouagadougou
Kénédougou	198,936	Orodara
Komondjari	49,389	Gayéri
Kompienga	73,949	Pama
Kossi	217,866	Nouna
Koulpélogo.	188,760	Ouargaye
Kouritenga	250,699	Koupéla
Kourwéogo.	117,370	Boussé
Léraba	93,351	Sindou
Loroum	111,707	Titao
Mouhoun	237,048	Dédougou
Nahouri	121,314	Pô
Namentenga	251,909	Boulsa
Nayala	136,273	Toma
Noumbiel	51,449	Batié
Oubritenga	198,130	Ziniaré
Oudalan	136,583	Gorom-Gorom
Passoré	271,216	Yako
Poni	196,568	Gaoua
Sanguié	249,169	Réo
Sanmatenga	460,684	Kaya
Séno	202,972	Dori
Sissili	153,560	Léo
Soum	253,867	Djibo
Sourou	189,726	Tougan
Tapoa	235,288	Diapaga
Tuy	160,249	Houndé
Yagha	116,985	Sebba
Yatenga	443,967	Ouahigouya
Ziro	117,774	Sapouy
Zondoma	127,580	Gourcy
Zoundwéogo	196,698	Manga
Total	10,373,341	

Source: Ministère des Affaires Etrangères, Ouagadougou.

PRINCIPAL TOWNS (population at 1985 census)

Ouagadougou			Ouahigouya . . .	38,902
(capital) . .	441,514	Banfora	35,319
Bobo-Dioulasso. .	228,668	Kaya	25,814
Koudougou . .	51,926		

1993 (official estimates,'000): Ouagadougou 690; Bobo-Dioulasso 300; Koudougou 105.

Source: Secrétariat du Comité Monétaire de la Zone Franc, *Rapport Annuel*.

BIRTHS AND DEATHS (UN estimates, annual averages)

	1980–85	1985–90	1990–95
Birth rate (per 1,000) . .	50.1	48.9	47.7
Death rate (per 1,000) . .	20.1	18.9	18.9

Expectation of life (UN estimates, years at birth, 1990–95): 45.0 (males 44.1; females 46.1).

Source: UN, *World Population Prospects: The 1998 Revision*.

ECONOMICALLY ACTIVE POPULATION
(sample survey, persons aged 10 years and over, 1991)

	Males	Females	Total
Agriculture, hunting, forestry and fishing	2,162,759	2,131,025	4,293,784
Mining and quarrying . .	2,286	304	2,590
Manufacturing	26,996	24,698	51,694
Electricity, gas and water . .	3,038	806	3,844
Construction	10,988	28	11,016
Trade, restaurants and hotels. .	48,117	72,197	120,314
Transport, storage and communications	14,620	421	15,041
Finance, insurance, real estate and business services . . .	1,650	425	2,075
Community, social and personal services	84,136	27,420	111,556
Activities not adequately defined .	8,355	9,105	17,460
Total employed	2,362,945	2,266,429	4,629,374
Unemployed	38,515	11,304	49,819
Total labour force	2,401,460	2,277,733	4,679,193

Source: ILO, *Yearbook of Labour Statistics*.

Mid-1999 (estimates in '000): Agriculture, etc. 5,292; Total 5,738 (Source: FAO).

Agriculture

PRINCIPAL CROPS ('000 metric tons)

	1997	1998	1999*
Maize	332	378	378
Millet	737	973	973
Sorghum	1,094	1,203	1,203
Rice (paddy)	99	89	89
Sweet potatoes	16	14	14
Yams	36	46	46
Other roots and tubers	3	4	4
Tomatoes	9	9*	9
Other vegetables	219	219*	219
Fruit*	73	73	73
Pulses*	66	66	66
Groundnuts (in shell)	152	215	215
Sesame seed	8	13	13
Sugar cane*	400	400	400
Cotton (lint)	144	136	136

* FAO estimate(s).
Source: FAO.

LIVESTOCK ('000 head, year ending September)

	1997	1998*	1999*
Cattle	4,522	4,550	4,550
Sheep	6,207	6,350	6,350
Goats	7,914	7,950	7,950
Pigs	587	590	590
Horses*	25	25	25
Asses*	475	475	475
Camels*	14	14	14
Poultry	20,517	21,000	21,000

* FAO estimates.
Source: FAO.

LIVESTOCK PRODUCTS ('000 metric tons)

	1997	1998	1999
Beef and veal	50	45	45*
Mutton and lamb	13	13	13*
Goat meat	22	22	22*
Pig meat	8	8	8*
Poultry meat	23	24	24
Other meat	8	8	8*
Cows' milk	157	160	160*
Goats' milk	52	52	52
Butter	1	1	1
Hen eggs*	17	17	17
Cattle hides	8	7	7
Sheepskins	3	3	3
Goatskins	6	6	6

* FAO estimate(s).
Source: FAO.

Forestry

ROUNDWOOD REMOVALS
('000 cubic metres, excluding bark)

	1996	1997	1998
Sawlogs, veneer logs and logs for sleepers	1	1	1
Other industrial wood	469	482	496
Fuel wood	9,750	10,020	10,297
Total	10,220	10,503	10,794

Source: FAO, *Yearbook of Forest Products*.

SAWNWOOD PRODUCTION ('000 cubic metres)

	1996	1997	1998
Total (all broadleaved)	2	2	2

Source: FAO, *Yearbook of Forest Products*.

Fishing

(metric tons, live weight)

	1996	1997	1998
Capture	8,000	8,000	8,335
Freshwater fishes	8,000	8,000	8,335
Aquaculture	30	45	60*
Total catch	8,030	8,045	8,395*

* FAO estimate.
Source: FAO, *Yearbook of Fishery Statistics*.

Mining

	1997	1998	1999
Gold (kilograms)	1,088	1,091	869

Source: IMF, *Burkina Faso: Recent Economic Developments* (August 2000).

Industry

SELECTED PRODUCTS

	1997	1998	1999
Edible oils (metric tons)	14,475	16,070	11,850
Shea (karité) butter (metric tons)	—	316	121
Flour (metric tons)	33,669	41,577	21,454
Pasta (metric tons)	870	257	496
Sugar (metric tons)	30,906	44,088	29,905
Beer ('000 hl)	460	501	387
Soft drinks ('000 hl)	168	195	155
Cigarettes (million packets)	60	74	60
Printed fabric ('000 sq metres)	4,141	3,818	1,462
Soap (metric tons)	11,580	12,349	9,910
Matches (cartons)	6,234	8,814	8,056
Bicycles (units)	36,030	35,924	24,079
Mopeds (units)	17,283	20,875	17,364
Tyres ('000)	480	314	417
Inner tubes ('000)	2,604	1,755	2,540
Electric energy ('000 kWh)	305,531	267,961	n.a.

Source: IMF, *Burkina Faso: Recent Economic Developments* (August 2000).

Finance

CURRENCY AND EXCHANGE RATES

Monetary Units

100 centimes = 1 franc de la Communauté financière africaine (CFA).

Sterling, Dollar and Euro Equivalents (29 December 2000)

£1 sterling = 1,051.93 francs CFA;
US $1 = 704.95 francs CFA;
€1 = 655.96 francs CFA;
10,000 francs CFA = £9.506 = $14.185 = €15.245.

Average Exchange Rate (francs CFA per US $)

1998	589.95
1999	615.70
2000	711.98

Note: An exchange rate of 1 French franc = 50 francs CFA, established in 1948, remained in force until January 1994, when the CFA franc was devalued by 50%, with the exchange rate adjusted to 1 French franc = 100 francs CFA. This relationship to French currency remained in effect with the introduction of the euro on 1 January 1999. From that date, accordingly, a fixed exchange rate of €1 = 655.957 francs CFA has been in operation.

BUDGET ('000 million francs CFA)

Revenue	1997	1998	1999
Current revenue .	181.3	199.2	238.0
Tax revenue .	166.4	183.5	222.2
Income and profits .	39.8	43.5	53.7
Domestic goods and services .	72.3	82.0	103.0
International trade .	50.0	52.2	60.2
Other tax revenue .	4.3	5.9	5.3
Non-tax revenue .	14.9	15.6	15.8
Capital revenue .	0.1	0.2	0.1
Total .	181.5	199.4	238.1

Expenditure and net lending	1997	1998	1999
Domestic expenditure and net lending .	177.8	205.1	246.9
Wages and salaries .	67.7	72.0	82.6
Goods and services .	28.0	34.6	37.6
Interest payments .	11.7	12.7	13.7
Current transfers .	33.1	38.7	45.4
Budgetary contribution to investment .	39.7	47.6	67.3
Net lending* .	-2.5	-0.6	0.3
Foreign-financed government investment .	135.0	140.4	185.3
Restructuring operations .	10.5	2.4	1.4
Total .	323.3	347.9	433.7

* Including proceeds from privatization, which are excluded from revenue and are treated as a deduction from expenditure.

Source: IMF, *Burkina Faso: Recent Economic Developments* (August 2000).

INTERNATIONAL RESERVES (US $ million at 31 December)

	1997	1998	1999
Gold* .	3.4	3.3	3.3
IMF special drawing rights .	2.2	0.8	0.7
Reserve position in IMF .	9.7	10.2	9.9
Foreign exchange .	332.9	362.4	284.3
Total .	348.2	376.7	298.2

* Valued at market-related prices.

Source: IMF, *International Financial Statistics*.

MONEY SUPPLY ('000 million francs CFA at 31 December)

	1997	1998	1999
Currency outside banks .	170.1	165.0	142.5
Demand deposits at deposit money banks* .	90.7	89.5	107.7
Checking deposits at post office .	2.1	2.3	2.3
Total money (incl. others) .	268.9	261.9	256.9

* Excluding the deposits of public establishments of an administrative or social nature.

Source: IMF, *International Financial Statistics*.

COST OF LIVING (Consumer Price Index for African households in Ouagadougou; base: 1996 = 100)

	1997	1998	1999
Food, beverages and stimulants .	104.6	114.4	107.3
Clothing .	101.6	104.8	107.2
Housing .	101.2	101.5	103.7
All items (incl. others) .	102.9	108.0	106.8

Source: IMF, *Burkina Faso: Recent Economic Developments* (August 2000).

NATIONAL ACCOUNTS
('000 million francs CFA at current prices)

Expenditure on the Gross Domestic Product

	1997	1998	1999*
Government final consumption expenditure .	198.0	218.4	215.7
Private final consumption expenditure .	1,041.2	1,110.7	1,218.0
Increase in stocks .	-4.7	—	—
Gross fixed capital formation .	384.8	450.4	442.4
Total domestic expenditure .	1,619.3	1,779.5	1,876.1
Exports of goods and services .	155.8	213.2	179.6
Less Imports of goods and services	385.0	470.5	467.1
GDP in purchasers' values .	1,390.1	1,522.4	1,588.6
GDP at constant 1985 prices .	951.6	1,010.2	1,068.8

* Estimates.

Source: IMF, *Burkina Faso: Recent Economic Developments* (August 2000).

Gross Domestic Product by Economic Activity

	1997	1998	1999*
Agriculture, livestock, forestry and fishing .	415.7	459.9	469.0
Mining .	} 266.2	307.7	325.4
Manufacturing .			
Electricity, gas and water .	11.5	12.8	13.8
Construction and public works .	74.0	79.3	85.2
Trade .	175.6	189.0	189.2
Transport and communications .	55.9	60.3	65.0
Non-marketable services .	138.3	146.5	153.0
Other services .	169.9	180.9	199.4
Sub-total .	1,306.8	1,436.4	1,500.0
Import taxes and duties .	83.3	86.0	88.6
GDP in purchasers' values .	1,390.1	1,522.4	1,588.6

* Estimates.

Source: IMF, *Burkina Faso: Recent Economic Developments* (August 2000).

BALANCE OF PAYMENTS ('000 million francs CFA)

	1997	1998	1999*
Exports of goods f.o.b.	133.7	190.4	156.6
Imports of goods f.o.b.	−297.7	−374.2	−368.7
Trade balance	−164.0	−183.8	−212.0
Exports of services	22.1	22.8	23.0
Imports of services	−87.3	−96.3	−98.4
Balance on goods and services	−229.1	−257.3	−287.4
Other income received	10.0	8.5	8.9
Other income paid	−17.8	−15.6	−16.7
Balance on goods, services and income	−236.9	−264.3	−295.3
Private unrequited transfers (net)	43.4	43.9	41.0
Official unrequited transfers (net)	52.2	67.6	54.0
Current balance	−141.4	−152.8	−200.3
Capital transfers (net)	91.6	89.5	122.9
Official capital (net)	21.9	46.1	56.9
Private capital (net)	6.6	−7.8	7.8
Net errors and omissions	−1.7	2.6	−0.7
Overall balance	−23.0	−22.4	−13.5

* Estimates.

Source: IMF, *Burkina Faso: Recent Economic Developments* (August 2000).

External Trade

PRINCIPAL COMMODITIES (estimates, '000 million francs CFA)

Imports f.o.b.	1997	1998	1999*
Food products	41.3	83.7	45.5
Petroleum products	40.1	42.0	62.4
Capital equipment	90.4	114.5	135.8
Raw materials	23.4	40.0	35.0
Total (incl. others)	297.7	374.2	368.7

Exports f.o.b.	1997	1998	1999*
Livestock and livestock products	27.1	27.0	29.3
Live animals	14.6	14.6	15.8
Hides and skins	11.1	10.9	11.8
Cotton	74.6	120.9	83.6
Gold	9.0	9.5	9.2
Total (incl. others)	133.7	190.4	156.6

* Estimates.

Source: IMF, *Burkina Faso: Recent Economic Developments* (August 2000).

PRINCIPAL TRADING PARTNERS ('000 million francs CFA)*

Imports c.i.f.	1996	1997	1998
Belgium-Luxembourg	9.0	7.6	8.9
China, People's Repub.	3.5	3.5	5.9
Côte d'Ivoire	51.3	58.1	67.0
France	81.9	88.5	115.2
Germany	13.3	8.4	11.1
Ghana	2.7	3.0	3.5
India	12.0	3.2	9.8
Italy	13.2	12.2	12.8
Japan	17.3	17.0	20.7
Netherlands	5.8	10.1	11.4
Nigeria	13.8	8.4	3.7
Pakistan	2.9	6.8	5.0
Senegal	2.1	4.8	4.2
Togo	3.0	4.4	5.3
United Kingdom	5.9	4.1	5.3
USA	12.6	13.4	14.1
Viet Nam	5.5	5.6	6.4
Total (incl. others)	301.8	309.3	385.9

Exports f.o.b.	1996	1997	1998
Belgium-Luxembourg	3.5	10.8	15.2
Benin	n.a.	0.4	2.6
Colombia	—	1.3	3.7
Côte d'Ivoire	11.2	11.7	13.7
France	13.5	16.7	32.3
Ghana	2.7	3.7	3.0
Indonesia	23.2	7.1	—
Italy	2.9	3.0	0.3
Japan	0.1	1.1	0.4
Mali	1.1	1.3	2.4
Niger	1.1	1.5	1.4
Singapore	0.5	5.4	7.8
Taiwan	0.8	4.1	—
Togo	3.5	3.6	2.1
United Kingdom	1.3	0.9	0.2
USA	0.3	1.8	0.2
Total (incl. others)	96.5	106.9	140.0

* Figures refer to recorded trade only.

Source: Banque centrale des états de l'Afrique de l'ouest in IMF, *Burkina Faso: Recent Economic Developments* (August 2000).

Transport

RAILWAYS (international freight traffic, '000 metric tons)

	1997	1998	1999
To Côte d'Ivoire	54.0	48.5	39.5
From Côte d'Ivoire	459.0	427.2	333.3

Source: IMF, *Burkina Faso: Recent Economic Developments* (August 2000).

Passenger-km (million, 1993): 403 (Source: UN Economic Commission for Africa, *African Statistical Yearbook*).

ROAD TRAFFIC (motor vehicles in use)

	1994	1995	1996*
Passenger cars	32,224	35,460	38,220
Buses and coaches	1,939	2,237	2,460
Lorries and vans	14,439	14,985	15,520
Road tractors	2,087	2,251	2,400
Motor cycles and mopeds	97,900	100,591	105,000

* Estimates.

Source: IRF, *World Road Statistics*.

CIVIL AVIATION (traffic on scheduled services)*

	1995	1996	1997
Kilometres flown (million)	3	4	3
Passengers carried ('000)	137	138	97
Passenger-km (million)	256	258	248
Total ton-km (million)	40	40	39

* Including an apportionment of the traffic of Air Afrique.

Source: UN, *Statistical Yearbook*.

Tourism

FOREIGN VISITORS BY COUNTRY OF ORIGIN*

	1996	1997	1998
Côte d'Ivoire	14,381	15,172	12,906
France	29,972	31,621	45,136
Germany	4,661	4,918	4,810
Mali	8,143	8,591	5,774
Niger	4,990	5,265	5,629
Senegal	5,190	5,476	4,545
Togo	4,329	4,567	4,223
USA	3,854	4,066	5,310
Total (incl. others) . . .	131,113	138,364	160,284

* Arrivals at hotels and similar establishments.

Receipts from tourism ('000 million francs CFA): 13.2 in 1996; 17.6 in 1997; 25.1 in 1998.

Source: Direction du Tourisme et de l'Hôtellerie: *Statistiques du Tourisme (Année 1994–1998)*.

Communications Media

	1994	1995	1996
Radio receivers ('000 in use) . .	280	290	350
Television receivers ('000 in use) .	57	60	90
Telephones ('000 main lines in use)	26	30	34
Mobile cellular telephones (subscribers)	n.a.	n.a.	525
Daily newspapers			
Number	4	3	4
Average circulation ('000 copies)	16	15	14
Non-daily newspapers			
Number	n.a.	9	n.a.
Average circulation ('000 copies)	n.a.	42	n.a.
Book production*			
Titles	4	17	12
Copies ('000)	n.a.	37	14

* All first editions.

1997: Radio receivers ('000 in use) 370; Television receivers ('000 in use) 100; Telephones ('000 main lines in use) 36; Mobile cellular telephones (subscribers) 1,503.

Sources: UNESCO, *Statistical Yearbook*; UN, *Statistical Yearbook*.

Education

(1995/96)

	Institu-tions	Teachers	Students		
			Males	Females	Total
Primary . . .	3,568	14,037	426,869	275,335	702,204
Secondary					
General . . .	252	4,162	89,609	47,648	137,257
Vocational* . .	41	731	4,890	4,703	9,539
Tertiary . . .	9	632†	7,245	2,286	9,531

* Including teacher training.

† Teachers at the Universities of Ouagadougou and Bobo-Dioulasso.

Pre-primary (1996/97): Institutions 141; Teachers 423; Students 17,005 (Males 8,347; Females 8,658).

Pre-primary (1997/98): Institutions 147; Teachers 441; Students 18,045 (Males 8,921; Females 9,124).

Tertiary (1996/97): Teachers 352; Students 8,911 (Males 6,889; Females 2,022).

Sources: Ministère de l'Enseignement de Base et de l'Alphabétisation, Ouagadougou; UNESCO, *Statistical Yearbook*.

Directory

The Constitution

The present Constitution was approved in a national referendum on 2 June 1991, and was formally adopted on 11 June. The following are its main provisions:

The Constitution of the 'revolutionary, democratic, unitary and secular' Fourth Republic of Burkina Faso guarantees the collective and individual political and social rights of Burkinabè citizens, and delineates the powers of the executive, legislature and judiciary.

Executive power is vested in the President, who is Head of State, and in the Government, which is appointed by the President upon the recommendation of the Prime Minister. The President is elected, by universal suffrage, for a seven-year term; as amended in January 1997, there are no restrictions on the renewal of the presidential mandate. Under proposals introduced in April 2000 the Presidential mandate was to be reduced to five years, renewable only once.

Legislative power is exercised by the multi-party Assemblée nationale (Assemblée des députés du peuple until a constitutional amendment in January 1997). Deputies are elected, by universal suffrage, for a five-year term. An increase in the number of deputies, from 107 to 111, was provided for by constitutional amendment in January 1997. Under proposals introduced in April 2000 91 members of the Assemblée nationale would be elected from regional lists, while 21 would be elected from a national list. Both elections would be conducted under the rules of proportional representation. The President is empowered to appoint a Prime Minister; however, the Assemblée nationale has the right to veto any such appointment. The second chamber of the Parlement is the consultative Chambre des représentants, comprising 178 members, nominated from among the 'active forces of the nation' for a three-year term of office.

Both the Government and the Assemblée nationale may initiate legislation.

The judiciary is independent. Judges are accountable to a Higher Council, under the chairmanship of the Head of State.

The Constitution also makes provision for a Conseil économique et sociale, for a Conseil supérieur de l'information, and for a national ombudsman.

The Constitution denies legitimacy to any regime that might take power as the result of a *coup d'état*.

The Government

HEAD OF STATE

President: BLAISE COMPAORÉ (assumed power as Chairman of the Front populaire 15 October 1987; elected President 1 December 1991; re-elected 15 November 1998).

COUNCIL OF MINISTERS
(April 2001)

President: BLAISE COMPAORÉ.

Prime Minister, Minister of the Economy and Finance: PARAMANGA ERNEST YONLI.

Minister of State, Minister of Foreign Affairs: YOUSSOUF OUÉDRAOGO.

Minister of State: RAM OUÉDRAOGO.

Minister of Agriculture: SALIF DIALLO.

Minister of Health: PIERRE JOSEPH EMMANUEL TAPSOBA.

Minister of Defence: KOUAMÉ LOUGUE.

Minister of Justice and the Promotion of Human Rights: BOUREIMA BADINI.

Minister of Security: DJIBRILL YIPENÉ BASSOLE.

Minister of Territorial Administration and Decentralization: BERNARD T. NABARE.

Minister of the Environment and Water Resources: FIDÈLE HIEN.

Minister of Trade, the Promotion of Business and Crafts: BEDOUMA ALAIN YODA.

Minister of Mines, Quarries and Energy: ABDOULAYE ABDOULKADER CISSÉ.

Minister of Secondary and Higher Education and Scientific Research: LAYA SAWADOGO.

Minister of Primary Education and Literacy: FIDÈLE KIENTGA.

Minister of Infrastructure, Housing and Town Planning: HIPPOLYTE LINGANI.

Minister of Transport and Tourism: SALVADOR YAMÉOGO.

Minister of the Civil Service and Institutional Development: JEAN EMILE SOMDA.

Minister of Employment, Labour and Social Security: ALAIN LUDOVIC TOU.

Minister of Posts and Telecommunications: JUSTIN TIÈBA THIOMBIANO.

Minister of Regional Integration: NOYABTIGUNGU CONGO KABORÉ.

Minister responsible for Relations with Parliament: SANNÉ MOHAMED TOPAN.

Minister of Arts and Culture: MAHAMOUDOU OUÉDRAOGO.

Minister of Information, Spokesperson for the Government: KILIMITÉ THÉODORE HIEN.

Minister of Youth and Sports: RENÉ EMILE KABORÉ.

Minister of Social Action and National Solidarity: GILBERT OUÉDRAOGO.

Minister of Animal Resources: ALPHONSE BONOU.

Minister for the Promotion of Women: GISÈLE GUIGMA.

There are, in addition, six Ministers-Delegate responsible for Finance and the Budget, Economic Development, Housing, Water Resources, Labour and Professional Training, and Tourism Promotion. There are also three Secretaries of State responsible for the Promotion of Human Rights, Literacy and Informal Education, and Youth.

MINISTRIES

Office of the President: 03 BP 7030, Ouagadougou 03; tel. 30-66-30; fax 31-49-26; internet www.primature.gov.bf.

Office of the Prime Minister: 03 BP 7027, Ouagadougou 03; tel. 32-48-89; fax 31-47-61; internet www.primature.gov.bf.

Ministry of Agriculture: 03 BP 7005, Ouagadougou 03; tel. 32-49-63.

Ministry of Animal Resources: 03 BP 7026, Ouagadougou 03; tel. 32-46-51; fax 31-84-75.

Ministry of Arts and Culture: 03 BP 7045, Ouagadougou 03; tel. 32-48-86; fax 31-55-99.

Ministry of the Civil Service and Institutional Development: 03 BP 7006, Ouagadougou 03; tel. 32-40-10.

Ministry of Defence: 01 BP 496, Ouagadougou 01; tel. 30-72-14; fax 31-36-10.

Ministry of the Economy and Finance: 03 BP 7012, Ouagadougou 03; tel. 30-69-98; fax 31-27-15; e-mail finances@cenatrin.bf; internet www.finances.gov.bf.

Ministry of Employment, Labour and Social Security: 03 BP 7016, Ouagadougou 03; tel. 30-09-60; fax 31-88-01; internet www.metss.gov.bf.

Ministry of the Environment and Water Resources: 565 rue Agostino Neto, Secteur 4, Koulouba, 03 BP 7044, Ouagadougou 03; tel. 32-40-74; fax 31-46-05; e-mail diallo@ouaga.orstom.bf; internet aochycos.ird.ne/htmlf/partnat/mee.

Ministry of Foreign Affairs: 03 BP 7038, Ouagadougou 03; tel. 32-47-34; fax 30-87-92; e-mail mamadou.kone@mae.gov.bf; internet www.mae.gov.bf/newdefault.htm.

Ministry of Health: 03 BP 7009, Ouagadougou 03; tel. 32-41-71.

Ministry of Information: 03 BP 7045, Ouagadougou 03; tel. 31-45-72.

Ministry of Infrastructure, Housing and Town Planning: 03 BP 7011, Ouagadougou 03; tel. 32-49-54; fax 31-84-08.

Ministry of Justice and the Promotion of Human Rights: 01 BP 526, Ouagadougou 01; tel. 32-48-33.

Ministry of Mines, Quarries and Energy: 01 BP 644, Ouagadougou 01; tel. 31-84-29; fax 31-84-30.

Ministry of Posts and Telecommunications: Ouagadougou.

Ministry of Primary Education and Literacy: 03 BP 7032, Ouagadougou 03; tel. 30-78-53; fax 30-80-86.

Ministry of the Promotion of Women: Ouagadougou.

Ministry of Regional Integration: 01 BP 06, Ouagadougou 01; tel. 32-48-33; fax 31-41-90.

Ministry responsible for Relations with Parliament: 03 BP 2079, Ouagadougou 03; tel. 32-40-70.

Ministry of Secondary and Higher Education and Scientific Research: 03 BP 7047, Ouagadougou 03; tel. 32-48-68; fax 31-41-41.

Ministry of Security: Ouagadougou.

Ministry of Social Action and National Solidarity: 01 BP 515, Ouagadougou 01; tel. 30-68-75; fax 31-67-37.

Ministry of Territorial Administration and Decentralization: 03 BP 7034, Ouagadougou 03; tel. 32-47-83; fax 30-84-17.

Ministry of Trade, the Promotion of Business and Crafts: 01 BP 514, Ouagadougou 01; tel. 32-47-86; fax 32-48-28.

Ministry of Transport and Tourism: 03 BP 7048, Ouagadougou 03; tel. 30-62-11.

Ministry of Youth and Sports: 03 BP 7035, Ouagadougou 03; tel. 32-47-86.

President and Legislature

PRESIDENT

Presidential Election, 15 November 1998

Candidate	Votes	% of votes
Blaise Compaoré	1,996,151	87.53
Ram Ouédraogo	150,793	6.61
Frédéric Guirma	133,552	5.86
Total	**2,280,496***	**100.00**

* There were, in addition, 89,458 blank votes.

PARLEMENT
Assemblée Nationale

President: Mélégué Maurice Traoré.

General Election, 11 May 1997

Party	Seats
Congrès pour la démocratie et le progrès (CDP)	101*
Parti pour la démocratie et le progrès (PDP)	6
Alliance pour la démocratie et la fédération (ADF)	2
Rassemblement démocratique africain (RDA)	2
Total	**111**

* This total includes the results of voting in four constituencies won by the CDP at a further round of voting on 18 June, after the Supreme Court annulled the previous results.

Chambre des Représentants

President: Moussa Sanogo.

The second chamber comprises 178 members, nominated from among the 'active forces of the nation' for a three-year term. The Chambre des Représentants, which has advisory functions, was inaugurated in December 1995.

Advisory Council

Conseil Economique et Social: 01 BP 6162, Ouagadougou 01; tel. 30-89-28; fax 31-06-54; f. 1985 as Conseil Révolutionnaire Economique et Social, present name adopted in 1992; 90 mems; Pres. Juliette Bonkougou-Yaméogo.

Political Organizations

There were 27 political parties officially registered in March 2000, although a number of splits and realignments subsequently occurred. The following are amongst the most important:

Alliance pour la démocratie et la fédération—Rassemblement démocratique africain (ADF–RDA): 01 BP 2061, Ouagadougou 01; tel. 31-15-15; f. 1990 as Alliance pour la démocratie et la fédération, absorbed faction of Rassemblement démocratique africain in 1998; several factions broke away in mid-2000; Pres. Me Hermann Yaméogo.

Congrès pour la démocratie et le progrès (CDP): 01 BP 1605, Ouagadougou; tel. 31-50-18; e-mail cdp@cenatrin.bf; internet www.cdp.bf; f. 1996, by merger of more than 10 parties, to succeed the Organisation pour la démocratie populaire/Mouvement du travail as the prin. political org. supporting Pres. Compaoré; social democratic; Exec. Sec. Roch Marc-Christian Kaboré.

Convention africaine pour la démocratie (CAD): Ouagadougou; Leader Lassané Ouangrawa.

Convention des démocrates et patriotes (CNDP): Ouagadougou; f. 2000.

Convention panafricaine sankariste (CPS): Ouagadougou; tel. 35-74-11; f. 1999 by merger of four parties, expanded in 2000 to include two other parties; promotes the policies of former President Sankara; Pres. Ernest Nongma Ouédraogo.

Convention pour la démocratie et la fédération (CDF): Ouagadougou; tel. 36-23-63; f. 1998; Leader Amadou Diemdioda Dicko.

Front des forces sociales (FFS): Ouagadougou; e-mail tino8@caramail.com; internet membres.tripod.fr/FFS; f. 1996; Sankarist; member of the Groupe du 14 février and opposition Collectif d'organisations démocratiques de masse et de partis politiques; boycotted 2000 municipal elections; Chair. Norbert Michel Tiendrebeogo.

Mouvement pour la tolérance et le progrès (MTP): Ouagadougou; tel. 31-85-11; f. 2000; Sankarist; Leader Noyabtigungu Congo Kaboré.

Parti africain de l'indépendance (PAI): Ouagadougou; tel. 36-10-56; f. 2000; Leader Soumane Touré.

Parti pour la démocratie et le progrès (PDP): BP 606, Ouagadougou; tel. 31-16-46; f. 1993, expanded in 1996 to include three other parties; Pres. Joseph Ki-Zerbo.

Parti pour la démocratie sociale (PDS): Ouagadougou; Sankarist; Leader Valère Somé.

Parti pour le progrès social (PPS): Ouagadougou; f. 2000.

Parti de la renaissance nationale (PAREN): Ouagadougou; tel. 30-65-87; f. 2000; Leader Laurent Bado.

Rassemblement démocratique africain (RDA): BP 345, Ouagadougou; tel.30-68-53; pre-independence party; self-styled Front de refus du Rassemblement démocratique africain represented by Frédéric Guirma at 1998 presidential election; Leader Gérard Kango Ouédraogo.

Union des libéraux pour la démocratie (ULD): supports President Compaoré; f. 2000; breakaway faction from ADF–RDA.

Union des démocrates et patriotes indépendants (UDPI): Ouagadougou; expelled from Groupe du 14 février in mid-2000.

Union des verts pour le développement du Burkina (UVDB): Ouagadougou; tel. 36-39-08; ecologist party; Leader Ram Ouédraogo.

Union pour la démocratie et la fédération (UDF): f. 2000; breakaway faction from ADF–RDA.

The **Groupe du 14 février (G-14f)**, an alliance of opposition parties including the PDP and (until mid-2000) the ADF–RDA, boycotted the 1998 presidential election and the municipal elections of Sept. 2000; several parties were expelled in mid-2000.

Diplomatic Representation

EMBASSIES IN BURKINA FASO

Algeria: 01 BP 3893, Ouagadougou 01; tel. 30-64-01; fax 30-37-46 Ambassador: Ahcene Boukhelfa.

Belgium: 01 BP 1264, Ouagadougou 01; tel. 31-21-64; fax 31-06-60; e-mail ouagadougou@diplobel.org; Ambassador: Jacques Henin.

Canada: 01 BP 548, Ouagadougou 01; tel. 31-18-94; fax 31-19-00; e-mail ouaga@dfait-maeci.gc.ca; Ambassador: Jules Savaria.

China (Taiwan): 01 BP 5563, Ouagadougou 01; tel. 31-61-95; fax 31-61-97; Ambassador: Sainting Kung.

Côte d'Ivoire: 01 BP 20, Ouagadougou 01; tel. 31-82-28; fax 31-82-30; Ambassador: Valama Georges Bakayoko.

Cuba: 01 BP 3422, Ouagadougou 06; tel. 30-64-91; Chargé d'affaires a.i.: José Luis Noriega Sánchez.

Denmark: rue Agostino Neto, 01 BP 1760, Ouagadougou 01; tel. 31-31-92; fax 31-31-89; e-mail ouaamb@ouaamb.dk; Ambasssador: Stig Barlyng.

Egypt: Zone du Conseil de L'Entente, Secteur 4, 03 BP 3893, Ouagadougou 03; tel. 30-66-37; Ambassador: Dr Mohamed Said Abdel Hamid.

France: 33 rue Yalgado Ouédraogo, 01 BP 504, Ouagadougou 01; tel. 30-67-74; fax 31-41-66; e-mail ambassade.france@cenatrin.bf; internet www.france-burkina.bf; Ambassador: Maurice Portiche.

Germany: 01 BP 600, Ouagadougou 01; tel. 30-67-31; fax 31-39-91; e-mail amb.allemagne@fasonet.bf; Ambassador: Dr Helmut Rau.

Ghana: 22 ave d'Oubritenga, 01 BP 212, Ouagadougou 01; tel. 30-76-35; Ambassador: Baffour Assasie-Gyimah.

India: 167 rue Joseph Badoua, BP 6648, Ouagadougou; tel. 31-43-67; Chargé d'affaires a.i.: Mohan Lal.

Korea, Democratic People's Republic: Ouagadougou; Ambassador: (vacant).

Libya: 01 BP 1601, Ouagadougou 01; tel. 30-67-53; fax 31-34-70.

Mali: 01 BP 1911, Ouagadougou 01; tel. 38-19-22; Chargé d'affaires a.i.: Diarra Daouda.

Netherlands: 415 ave du Dr Kwamé N'Krumah, 01 BP 1302, Ouagadougou 01; tel. 30-61-34; fax 30-76-95; Ambassador: Alphons J. M. G. Hennekens.

Nigeria: 01 BP 132, Ouagadougou 01; tel. 36-30-15; Ambassador: Alhaji BABA AHMAD JIDDA.

Senegal: Ouagadougou; tel. 31-14-18; Ambassador: CHEIKH SYLLA.

USA: 01 BP 35, Ouagadougou 01; tel. 30-67-23; fax 30-38-90; e-mail amembouaga@ouagadougb.us-state.gov; Ambassador: JIMMY J. KOLKER.

Judicial System

The Constitution provides for the independence of the judiciary. Judges are to be accountable to a Higher Council, under the chairmanship of the President of the Republic.

Supreme Court: 01 BP 5577, Ouagadougou 01; tel. 31-08-35; fax 31-08-96; Pres. SAMBO ANTOINE KOMI.

Religion

The Constitution provides for freedom of religion, and the Government respects this right in practice. The country is a secular state. Islam, Christianity, and traditional religions operate freely without government interference. More than 50% of the population follow animist beliefs.

ISLAM

An estimated 30% of the population are Muslims.

CHRISTIANITY
The Roman Catholic Church

Burkina comprises one archdiocese and ten dioceses. At 31 December 1998 Roman Catholics comprised an estimated 10.5% of the total population.

Bishops' Conference: Conférence des Evêques de Burkina Faso et du Niger, BP 1195, Ouagadougou; tel. 30-60-26; f. 1966, legally recognized 1978; Pres. Rt Rev. JEAN-BAPTISTE SOMÉ, Bishop of Diébougou.

Archbishop of Ouagadougou: Most Rev. JEAN-MARIE UNTAANI COMPAORÉ, Archevêché, 01 BP 1472, Ouagadougou 01; tel. 30-67-04; fax 30-72-75; e-mail untaani@fasonet.bf.

Protestant Churches

At 31 December 1986 there were an estimated 106,467 adherents.

The Press

Direction de la presse écrite: Ouagadougou; govt body responsible for press direction.

DAILIES

L'Express du Faso: Ouagadougou; privately-owned.

Le Journal du Soir: 02 BP 5468, Ouagadougou 02; tel. 31-59-20; fax 31-59-22; Dir ISSA TAPSOBA; Editor NOEL OUANZA LIEHOUN; circ. 3,000.

L'Observateur Paalga (New Observer): 01 BP 584, Ouagadougou 01; tel. 33-27-05; fax 31-45-79; e-mail lobs@fasonet.bf; internet www.lobservateur.bf; f. 1974; also a Sunday edn; Dir EDOUARD OUÉDRAOGO; circ. 8,000.

Le Pays: 01 BP 4577, Ouagadougou 01; tel. 31-35-46; fax 31-45-40; f. 1991; privately-owned; Dir BOUREIMA SIGUE; circ. 5,000.

Sidwaya Quotidien (Daily Truth): 5 rue du Marché, 01 BP 507, Ouagadougou 01; tel. 30-63-07; fax 31-03-62; e-mail sidwayas@mcc.gov.bf; internet www.sidwaya.bf; f. 1984; state-owned; Editor-in-Chief ISSAKA SOURWEMA; circ. 3,000.

24 Heures: Ouagadougou; privately-owned.

PERIODICALS

Bendré (Drum): 02 BP 2625, Ouagadougou; tel. 31-28-54; fax 31-28-53; weekly; Dir SY MOUMINA CHERIFF.

Le Berger: Zone commerciale, ave Binger, Bobo-Dioulasso; f. 1992; weekly; Dir KOULIGA BLAISE YAMÉOGO.

Bulletin de l'Agence d'Information du Burkina: 01 BP 2507, Ouagadougou 01; tel. 30-70-52; fax 30-70-56; 2 a week; Editor-in-Chief JAMES DABIRÉ; circ. 200.

La Clef: Ouagadougou; tel. 31-38-27; f. 1992; weekly; Dir KY SATURNIN; circ. 6,000.

Fitla: 5 rue du Marché, 01 BP 507, Ouagadougou 01; tel. 30-63-07; fax 31-03-62; f. 2000.

L'Hébdomadaire: Ouagadougou; tel. 31-47-62; e-mail hebdcom@fasonet.bf; internet www.fasonet.bf/hebdo; f. 1999; weekly on Fridays; Dir ZÉPHIRIN KPODA; Editor- in-Chief DJIBRIL TOURÉ.

L'Indépendant: 01 BP 4809, Ouagadougou 01; tel. 30-74-93; fax 31-44-58; f. 1993; weekly.

L'Intrus Toujours: 01 BP 2009, Ouagadougou 01; f. 1985; weekly; satirical; Dir JEAN HUBERT BAZIÉ; circ. 10,000.

Le Journal du Jeudi: 01 BP 3654, Ouagadougou 01; tel. 31-41-08; fax 31-38-74; e-mail jj@liptinfor.bf; internet www.journaldujeudi.com; f. 1991; weekly; Dir BOUBAKAR DIALLO; Editor-in-Chief DAMIEN GLEZ; circ. 10,000.

Le Matin: BP 339, Bobo-Dioulasso; tel. 97-16-93; f. 1992; weekly; Dir DOFINITA FLAURENT BONZI.

Nekr Wagati: Ouagadougou; six a year; Dir SIMON COMPAORÉ.

La Nouvelle Tribune: Ouagadougou; weekly; Dir KYALBABOUÉ BAYILI.

L'Opinion: 01 BP 6459, Ouagadougou 01; tel. 30-89-48; fax 30-89-47; e-mail zedcom@fasonet.bf; internet www.zedcom.bf/actualite/actualite.htm; weekly; Editor ISSAKA LINGANI.

L'Ouragan: 06 BP 9276, Ouagadougou 06; weekly; Dir LOHÉ ISSA KONATÉ; circ. 4,000.

Regard: 01 BP 4707, Ouagadougou 01; tel. 31-16-70; fax 31-57-47; weekly; Dir CHRIS VALÉA; Editor PATRICK ILBOUDO; circ. 4,000.

San Finna: Ouagadougou 01; privately-owned; weekly; Editor-in-Chief PAULIN YAMÉOGO; circ. 3,000.

Sidwaya Hebdo: 5 rue du Marché, 01 BP 507, Ouagadougou 01; tel. 30-63-07; fax 31-03-62; e-mail sidwayas@mcc-gov.bf; internet www.sidwaya.bf; f. 1997; weekly.

Sidwaya Magazine: 5 rue du Marché, 01 BP 507, Ouagadougou 01; tel. 30-63-07; fax 31-03-62; e-mail sidwayas@mcc.gov.bf; internet www.sidwaya.bf; f. 1989; state-owned; monthly; Editor-in-Chief BONIFACE COULIBALY; circ. 2,500.

Le Tam Tam: 01 BP 6660, Ouagadougou 01; tel. 30-70-01; f. 1992; weekly; Dir ZANGA OUATTARA; Editor ZONGO BOUREIMA; circ. 3,500.

Yeelen (Light): Ouagadougou; monthly; pro-Govt.

NEWS AGENCIES

Agence d'Information du Burkina (AIB): 03 BP 2507, Ouagadougou 03; tel. 32-46-39; fax 32-46-40; e-mail aib.redaction@mcc.gov.fc; internet www.aib.bf; f. 1964; fmrly Agence Voltaïque de Presse; state-controlled; Dir JAMES DABIRÉ.

Foreign Bureaux

Agence France-Presse (AFP): BP 391, Ouagadougou; tel. 33-56-56.

Reuters (UK) is also represented in Burkina Faso.

PRESS ASSOCIATIONS

Association des Journalistes du Burkina: 01 BP 507, Ouagadougou 01; tel. 31-01-14; fax 31-62-03; e-mail cnpress@fasonet.bf; also operates a Press centre; Pres. JEAN-CLAUDE MÉDA.

Centre National de Presse—Norbert Zongo (CNP—NZ): 04 BP 8524, Ouagadougou 04; tel. and fax 34-37-45; e-mail cnpress@fasonet.bf; internet www.cemu.sn/cnpnz; Man. ABDOULAYE DIALLO.

Publishers

Presses Africaines SA: BP 1471, Ouagadougou; tel. 33-43-07; general fiction, religion, primary and secondary textbooks; Man. Dir A. WININGA.

Société Nationale d'Edition et de Presse (SONEPRESS): BP 810, Ouagadougou; f. 1972; general, periodicals; Pres. MARTIAL OUÉDRAOGO.

Government Publishing House

Imprimerie Nationale du Burkina Faso (INBF): route de l'Hôpital Yalgado, BP 7040, Ouagadougou; tel. 33-52-92; f. 1963; Dir LATY SOULEYMANE TRAORÉ.

Broadcasting and Communications

TELECOMMUNICATIONS

The introduction of a regulatory framework for the telecommunications industry is ongoing and the increased liberalization of the sector is expected.

Office National des Télécommunications (ONATEL): ave Nelson Mandela, 01 BP 10000, Ouagadougou 01; tel. 33-40-01; fax 31-03-31; e-mail webmaster@onatel.bf; internet www.onatel.bf; privatization scheduled for mid-2001; Dir-Gen. JACQUES LOUARI.

Telecel-Faso: Ouagadougou; f. 2000; mobile cellular telephone operator; subsid. of Telecel International, South Africa; operates in Ouagadougou and Bobo-Dioulasso.

In mid-2000 the authorities were considering the application for a mobile cellular telephone licence of Mobile System International Cellular Investments Holding (MSI/CI).

BROADCASTING

Regulatory Authority

Conseil Supérieur de l'Information (CSI): 290 ave Ho Chi Minh, 01 BP 6618, Ouagadougou 01; tel. 30-11-24; fax 30-11-33; internet www.primature.gov.bf/republic/acc_csi.htm; f. 1995; Pres. ADAMA FOFANA.

Radio

Twelve state-owned radio stations and 30 private radio stations operated in Burkina Faso in mid-2000.

Radiodiffusion Nationale du Burkina: 03 BP 7029, Ouagadougou 03; tel. 32-40-55; fax 31-04-41; f. 1959; state radio service; operates nationally; Dir RODRIGUE BARRY.

Canal Arc-en-Ciel: Ouagadougou; tel. 32-41-41; state-owned; br. at Bobo-Dioulasso.

Horizon FM: 01 BP 2714, Ouagadougou 01; tel. 31-28-58; fax 31-39-34; private commercial station; broadcasts in French, English and eight vernacular languages; operates eight stations nationally; Dir MOUSTAPHA LAABLI THIOMBIANO.

Radio CEDICOM Fréquence Espoir: Dédougou; religious broadcaster.

Radio ABGA (Radio Energie): Ouagadougou; tel. 31-61-69; operates five stations nationally.

Radio Bobo-Dioulasso: BP 392, Bobo-Dioulasso; tel. 97-14-13; daily programmes in French and vernacular languages; regional broadcaster; Dir of Programmes SITA KAM.

Radio Evangile Développement (RED): 04 BP 8050, Ouagadougou 04; tel. 43-51-56; fax 36-43-39; e-mail apaong@centrin.bf; three stations at Ouagadougou; Bobo-Dioulasso and Ouahigouya; religious broadcaster.

Radio Gaoua: Gaoua; state-owned regional broadcaster.

Radio Maria: Ouagadougou; tel. 31-70-70; religious broadcaster; br. at Koupéla.

Radio Palabre: BP 196, Kougoudou; tel. 53-84-86; fax 53-83-65; community broadcaster.

Radio Toamba: Fada N'Gourma; tel. 77-02-33; religious broadcaster.

Radio Vive le Paysan: Saponé; tel. 40-56-21; community broadcaster.

Radio la Voix du Paysan: BP 100, Ouahigouya; tel. 55-04-11; fax 55-01-62; community broadcaster.

Television

Télévision Nationale du Burkina: 29 blvd de la Révolution, 01 BP 2530, Ouagadougou 01; tel. 31-83-53; fax 32-48-09; e-mail tnb@mcc.gov.bf; internet www.tnb.bf; f. 1963; Dir ALINE KOALA.

Télévision Canal Viim Koéga: Ouagadougou; private broadcaster.

Télévision Multi Media: Ouagadougou; commercial broadcaster.

Finance

(cap. = capital; res = reserves; m. = million; brs = branches; amounts in francs CFA)

BANKING

Central Bank

Banque Centrale des Etats de l'Afrique de l'Ouest (BCEAO): ave Gamal-Abdel-Nasser, BP 356, Ouagadougou; tel. 30-60-15; fax 31-01-22; e-mail akangni@bceao.int; internet www.bceao.int; HQ in Dakar, Senegal; f. 1962; bank of issue for the mem. states of the Union économique et monétaire ouest-africaine (UEMOA, comprising Benin, Burkina Faso, Côte d'Ivoire, Guinea-Bissau, Mali, Niger, Senegal and Togo); cap. and res 806,918m., total assets 4,084,464m. (December 1998); Gov. CHARLES KONAN BANNY; Dir in Burkina Faso CÉLESTIN KOUKA ZALLE; br. in Bobo-Dioulasso.

Other Banks

Bank of Africa—Burkina Faso (BOA—Burkina Faso): ave de la Résistance du 17 mai, 01 BP 1319, Ouagadougou 01; tel. 30-88-70; fax 30-88-74; e-mail boadg@fasonet.bf; f. 1998; cap. 1,250m., total assets 22,623m. (Dec. 2000); Pres. LASSINÉ DIAWARA; Man. Dir PHILIPPE NADAUD.

Banque Commerciale du Burkina (BCB): 800 ave de la Nation, 01 BP 1336, Ouagadougou 01; tel. 30-79-00; fax 31-06-28; e-mail bcb@fasonet.bf; f. 1988; 50% owned by Libyan Arab Foreign Bank, 25% state-owned, 25% owned by Caisse Nationale de Sécurité Sociale; cap. and res 3,841m., total assets 30,859m. (Dec. 2000); Pres. IBRAHIMA OUATTARA; Man. Dir MAHMUD HAMMUDA.

Banque Internationale du Burkina (BIB): ave Dimdolobsom, 01 BP 362, Ouagadougou 01; tel. 30-61-69; fax 31-00-94; e-mail bibouaga@fasonet.bf; f. 1974; 25% owned by Banque Belgolaise SA (Belgium), 23% state-owned; cap. and res 9,688m., total assets 112,281m. (Dec. 1998); Pres. and Man. Dir GASPARD OUÉDRAOGO; 21 brs.

Banque Internationale pour le Commerce, l'Industrie et l'Agriculture du Burkina (BICIA—B): ave Dr Kwamé N'Krumah, 01 BP 08, Ouagadougou 01; tel. 30-62-26; fax 31-19-55; e-mail biciadg@fasonet.bf; f. 1973; 25% state-owned; cap. 5,000m., res 3,374m., dep. 118,070m. (Dec. 1999); Chair. AMADOU TRAORÉ; Dir-Gen. AMADÉ OUÉDRAOGO; 11 brs.

Caisse Nationale de Crédit Agricole du Burkina (CNCA—B): 2 ave Gamal-Abdel-Nasser, 01 BP 1644, Ouagadougou 01; tel. 33-33-33; fax 31-43-52; e-mail cncabf@cenatrin.bf; f. 1979; 26% state-owned; cap. and res 9,829m., total assets 39,549m. (Dec. 1997); Pres. ANGÈLE SOUDRE; Man. Dir CÉLESTIN KOUKA ZALLE; 4 brs.

Ecobank—Burkina SA: 633 rue Maurice Bishop, 01 BP 145, Ouagadougou 01; tel. 31-89-75; fax 31-89-81; e-mail ecobank@ecobank.com; f. 1997; 48% owned by Ecobank Transnational Inc, 12% by Ecobank Benin, 12% by Ecobank Togo; cap. and res. 1,575m., total assets 22,452m. (Dec. 1998); Pres. PAUL BALKOUMA; Man. Dir OLAYEMI ALAMU AKAPO.

Société Générale de Banques au Burkina (SGBB): 4 rue du Marché, 01 BP 585, Ouagadougou 01; tel. 30-60-35; fax 31-06-28; f. 1998 by restructuring of Banque pour le Financement du Commerce et des Investissements du Burkina; cap. and res 2,100m., total assets 34,078m. (Dec. 1998); Pres. and Man. Dir EMILE PARÉ.

Credit Institutions

Burkina Bail SA: Immeuble BIB, 1340 ave Dimdolobsom, 01 BP 1913, Ouagadougou 01; tel. 30-69-87; fax 30-70-02; e-mail burkina.bail@fasonet.bf; internet www.burkinabail.com; 52% owned by BIB; cap. 500m.; Man. Dir ABDOULAYE K. SORY.

Réseau des Caisses Populaires du Burkina (RCPB): 01 BP 5282, Ouagadougou 01; tel. 30-48-41.

Société Burkinabè de Financement (SOBFI): Immeuble Nassa, 1242 ave Dr Kwamé N'Krumah, 10 BP 13876, Ouagadougou 10; tel. 31-80-04; fax 33-71-62; e-mail sobfi@fasonet.bf; cap. 300m., total assets 397m. (Dec. 1998); Pres. M. DIACK; Man. Dir M. GUILLEMOT.

Bankers' Association

Association Professionnelle des Banques et Etablissements Financiers (APBEF): Ouagadougou; Pres. HAMADÉ OUÉDRAOGO.

STOCK EXCHANGE

Bourse Régionale des Valeurs Mobilières (BRVM): s/c Chambre de Commerce, d'Industrie et d'Artisanat du Burkina, 180/220 rue 3-119, 01 BP 502, Ouagadougou 01; tel. 30-87-73; fax 30-87-19; f. 1998; national branch of BRVM (regional stock exchange based in Abidjan, Côte d'Ivoire, serving the member states of UEMOA); Man. LÉOPOLD OUÉDRAOGO.

INSURANCE

Fonci-Assurances (FONCIAS): ave Léo Frobénius, 01 BP 398, Ouagadougou 01; tel. 30-62-04; fax 31-01-53; f. 1978; 51% owned by Athena Afrique (France), 20% state-owned; cap. 140m.; Pres. El Hadj OUMAROU KANAZOE; Man. Dir GÉRARD G. MANTOUX.

Société Nationale d'Assurances et de Réassurances (SONAR): 01 BP 406, Ouagadougou 01; tel. 33-46-66; fax 30-89-75; e-mail sonar@cenatrin.bf; f. 1973; 25% state-owned; cap. 240m.; Man. Dir ANDRÉ BAYALA.

Union des Assurances du Burkina (UAB): 08 BP 11041, Ouagadougou 08; tel. 31-26-15; fax 31-26-20; f. 1991; 20% owned by l'Union Africaine—IARD (Côte d'Ivoire); cap. 270m.; Man. Dir J. V. ALFRED YARÉOGO.

Trade and Industry

GOVERNMENT AGENCIES

Bureau des Mines et de la Géologie du Burkina (BUMIGEB): 01 BP 601, Ouagadougou 01; tel. 36-48-02; fax 36-48-88; e-mail bumigeb@cenatrin.bf; f. 1978, restructured 1997; research into geological and mineral resources; Pres. S. KY; Man. Dir JEAN-LÉONARD COMPAORÉ.

Caisse de Stabilisation des Prix des Produits Agricoles du Burkina (CSPPAB): 01 BP 1453, Ouagadougou 01; tel. 30-62-17; fax 31-06-14; f. 1964; responsible for purchase and marketing of shea-nuts (karité nuts), sesame seeds, cashew nuts and groundnuts; transfer pending to private ownership; Admin. DIANGO CHARLY HEBIE (acting); br. at Bobo-Dioulasso, representation at Boromo, Fada N'Gourma and Gaoua.

Comptoir Burkinabè des Métaux Précieux (CBMP): Ouagadougou; promotes gold sector, liaises with artisanal producers.

Office National d'Aménagement des Terroirs (ONAT): 01 BP 524, Ouagadougou 01; tel. 30-61-10; fax 30-61-12; f. 1974; fmrly Autorité des Aménagements des Vallées des Voltas; integrated rural development, including economic and social planning; Man. Dir ZACHARIE OUÉDRAOGO.

Office National des Barrages et des Aménagements Hydroagricoles (ONBAH): 03 BP 7056, Ouagadougou 03; tel. 30-89-82; fax 31-04-26; e-mail onbah@cenatrin.bf; f. 1976; control and development of water for agricultural use, construction of dams, water and soil conservation; state-owned; Dir-Gen. AÏZO TINDANO.

Office National du Commerce Extérieur (ONAC): 30 ave Léo Frobénius, 01 BP 389, Ouagadougou 01; tel. 31-13-00; fax 31-14-69; e-mail sekou.ba@gov.bf; internet www.tradepoint.bf; f. 1974; promotes and supervises external trade; Man. Dir SÉRIBA OUATTARA (acting).

DEVELOPMENT ORGANIZATIONS

Agence Française de Développement (AFD): 52 ave de la Nation, 01 BP 529, Ouagadougou 01; tel. 30-60-92; fax 30-19-66; e-mail afd@cenatrin.bf; fmrly Caisse Française de Développement; Dir M. GLEIZES.

Association Française des Volontaires du Progrès (AFVP): 01 BP 947, Ouagadougou 01; tel. 30-70-43; supports unofficial small business.

Bureau d'Appui aux Micro Entreprises (BAME): BP 610, Bobo-Dioulasso; tel. 97-16-28; fax 97-21-76; supports small business.

Cellule d'Appui à la Petite et Moyenne Entreprise d'Ouagadougou (CAPEO): 01 BP 6443, Ouagadougou 01; tel. 31-37-62; supports small and medium-sized enterprises, in particular those owned by women.

Fondation pour la Promotion de l'Entreprise et de l'Emploi (FEE): 01 BP 6466, Ouagadougou 01; tel. 31-27-90; promotes private enterprise.

Promotion du Développement Industriel, Artisanal et Agricole (PRODIA): 01 BP 2344, Ouagadougou; tel. 30-26-29; fax 34-23-80; supports small business.

CHAMBER OF COMMERCE

Chambre de Commerce, d'Industrie et d'Artisanat du Burkina: 180/220 rue 3-119, 01 BP 502, Ouagadougou 01; tel. 30-61-14; fax 30-61-16; e-mail ccia-bf@cenatrin.bf; internet www.ccia.bf; f. 1948; Pres. El Hadj OUMAROU KANAZOÉ; Dir-Gen. BENOIT OUATTARA; brs in Bobo-Dioulasso, Koupéla and Ouahigouya.

EMPLOYERS' ORGANIZATIONS

Association Femmes Solidaritées (AFS): 01 BP 1749, Ouagadougou 01; tel. 30-01-50; association of female employers.

Conseil National du Patronat Burkinabè: 02 BP 660, Ouagadougou 02; tel. 31-29-24; fax 30-25-21; Pres. BRUNO ILBOUDO.

Groupement Professionnel des Industriels: BP 810, Ouagadougou; tel. 30-28-19; f. 1974; Pres. MARTIAL OUÉDRAOGO.

Syndicat des Commerçants Importateurs et Exportateurs (SCIMPEX): 01 BP 552, Ouagadougou 01; tel. 31-18-70; fax 31-30-36; e-mail scimpex@cenatrin.bf; Pres. OLE KAM.

UTILITIES
Electricity

Société Générale de Travaux et de Constructions Electriques (SOGETEL): Zone Industrielle, Quartier S.O. Gounghin, 01 BP 429, Ouagadougou 01; tel. 30-23-45; fax 34-25-70; e-mail sogetel@cenatrin.bf; internet www.cenatrin.bf/sogetel; transport and distribution of electricity; installation of electrical apparatus.

Société Nationale Burkinabè d'Electricité (SONABEL): ave Nelson Mandela, 01 BP 54, Ouagadougou 01; tel. 30-61-00; fax 31-03-40; f. 1954; state-owned; privatization scheduled for 2002; production and distribution of electricity; Dir-Gen. EUGÈNE MEDA.

Water

Office National de l'Eau et de l'Assainissement (ONEA): 01 BP 170, Ouagadougou 01; tel. 30-60-73; fax 30-33-60; f. 1977; storage, purification and distribution of water; Dir ALY CONGO.

CO-OPERATIVES

Société de Commercialisation du Burkina 'Faso Yaar': ave du Loudun, Ouagadougou; tel. 30-61-28; f. 1967; 99% state-owned; transfer pending to private ownership; import-export and domestic trade; Pres. Minister of Trade, the Promotion of Business and Crafts.

Union des Coopératives Agricoles et Maraîchères du Burkina (UCOBAM): 01 BP 277, Ouagadougou 01; tel. 30-65-27; fax 30-65-28; e-mail ucobam@cenatrin.bf; f. 1968; comprises 8 regional co-operative unions (20,000 mems); production and marketing of fruit, vegetables, jams and conserves.

TRADE UNIONS

There are more than 20 autonomous trade unions. The five trade union syndicates are:

Confédération Générale du Travail Burkinabè (CGTB): Ouagadougou; f. 1988; confed. of several autonomous trade unions; Sec.-Gen. TOLE SAGNON.

Confédération Nationale des Travailleurs Burkinabè (CNTB): BP 445, Ouagadougou; f. 1972; Leader of Governing Directorate ABDOULAYE BÂ.

Confédération Syndicale Burkinabè (CSB): Ouagadougou; f. 1974; mainly public service unions; Sec.-Gen. YACINTHE OUÉDRAOGO.

Organisation Nationale des Syndicats Libres (ONSL): BP 99, Ouagadougou; f. 1960; 6,000 mems.

Union Syndicale des Travailleurs Burkinabè (USTB): BP 381, Ouagadougou; f. 1958; Sec.-Gen. BONIFACE SOMDAH; 35,000 mems in 45 affiliated orgs.

Transport

RAILWAY

At the end of 1991 there were some 622 km of track in Burkina Faso. A 105-km extension from Donsin to Ouagadougou was inaugurated in December of that year. Plans exist for the construction of an extension to the manganese deposits at Tambao. Responsibility for operations on the railway line linking Abidjan (Côte d'Ivoire) and Kaya, via Ouagadougou, was transferred to SITARAIL (a consortium of French, Belgian, Ivorian and Burkinabè interests) in 1995.

SITARAIL—Transport Ferroviaire de Personnes et de Marchandises: 01 BP 1192, Ouagadougou 01; tel. 30-60-50; fax 30-85-21; national branch of SITARAIL (based in Abidjan, Côte d'Ivoire); Rep. in Burkina S. YAMÉOGO.

Société de Gestion du Patrimoine Ferroviaire du Burkina (SOPAFER—B): 01 BP 192, Ouagadougou 01; tel. 31-35-99; fax 31-35-94; railway network services; Dir-Gen. OUMAR ZONGO.

ROADS

In 1996 there were an estimated 12,100 km of roads, including 5,720 km of main roads and 3,030 km of secondary roads; about 16% of the road network was paved in 1995. A major aim of current road projects is to improve transport links with other countries of the region. In 1999 a US $37m. project was begun to upgrade the road linking Ouagadougou with the Ghanaian border via the more isolated southern provinces.

Burkina Transit: 01 BP 1947, Ouagadougou 01; tel. 30-79-88; fax 31-05-15; passenger transport.

Interafricaine de Transport et de Transit (IATT): 04 BP 8242, Ouagadougou 04; tel. 30-25-12; fax 30-37-04.

Régie Nationale des Transports en Commun (RNTC X9): Ouagadougou 01; tel. 30-42-96; f. 1984; urban, national and international public transport co; Dir FRANÇOIS KONSEIBO.

Société Africaine de Transit (SAT): 01 BP 4249, Ouagadougou 01; tel. 31-09-16.

Société Africaine de Transports Routiers (SATR): 01 BP 5298, Ouagadougou 01; tel. 34-08-62.

Société Nationale du Transit du Burkina (SNTB): 474 ave Bishop, 01 BP 1192, Ouagadougou 01; tel. 30-60-54; fax 30-85-21; f. 1977; privatized 1999; road haulage and warehousing; Dir-Gen. SEYDOU DIAKITÉ.

CIVIL AVIATION

There are international airports at Ouagadougou and Bobo-Dioulasso, 49 small airfields and 13 private airstrips. Ouagadougou airport handled an estimated 176,400 passengers and 7,000 metric tons of freight in 1997.

Air Afrique: BP 141, Ouagadougou; tel. 30-60-20; see under Côte d'Ivoire.

Air Burkina: ave Loudun, 01 BP 1459, Ouagadougou 01; tel. 30-76-76; fax 31-48-80; f. 1967 as Air Volta; sold, in 2000, to a strategic partner, which was expected to take over operations in early 2001; operates domestic and regional services; Man. Dir MATHIEU BOUDA.

Air Inter-Burkina: Ouagadougou; f. 1994; operates domestic passenger and postal services.

Tourism

Burkina Faso, which possesses some 2.8m. hectares of nature reserves, is considered to provide some of the best opportunities to observe wild animals in West Africa. Some big game hunting is also permitted. Several important cultural events are also held in Burkina Faso: the biennial pan-African film festival is held in Ouagadougou, as is the biennial international exhibition of handi-crafts, while Bobo-Dioulasso hosts the biennial week of national culture. In 1998 there were 160,284 foreign visitors (28.2% of whom were from France), and receipts from tourism were estimated at 25.1m. francs CFA.

Association des Hôteliers et Restaurateurs du Burkina Faso (Association of Hotel and Restaurant Owners): 02 BP 5044, Ouagadougou 02; fax 34-29-41; e-mail ahrbf@ahrbf.com; internet www.ahrbf.com; f. 1980.

Direction du Tourisme et de l'Hôtellerie: 01 BP 624, Ouagadougou 01; tel. 30-63-96; Dir JEAN-PIERRE SIMPORE.

Office National du Tourisme Burkinabè: BP 1318, Ouagadougou; tel. 31-19-59; fax 31-44-34; e-mail faroleroy@yahoo.fr; internet www.zedcom.bf/annonces/ontb/ontb.htm; Dir-Gen. ISIDORE NABALOUM.

BURUNDI

Introductory Survey

Location, Climate, Language, Religion, Flag, Capital

The Republic of Burundi is a land-locked country lying on the eastern shore of Lake Tanganyika, in central Africa, a little south of the Equator. It is bordered by Rwanda to the north, by Tanzania to the south and east, and by the Democratic Republic of the Congo (formerly Zaire) to the west. The climate is tropical (hot and humid) in the lowlands, and cool in the highlands, with an irregular rainfall. The population is composed of three ethnic groups: the Hutu (85%), the Tutsi (14%) and the Twa (1%). The official languages are French and Kirundi, while Swahili is used, in addition to French, in commercial circles. More than 65% of the inhabitants profess Christianity, with the great majority of the Christians being Roman Catholics. A large minority still adhere to traditional animist beliefs. The national flag (proportions 5 by 3) consists of a white diagonal cross on a background of red (above and below) and green (hoist and fly), with a white circle, containing three green-edged red stars, in the centre. The capital is Bujumbura.

Recent History

Burundi (formerly Urundi) became part of German East Africa in 1899. In 1916, during the First World War, the territory was occupied by Belgian forces from the Congo (now the Democratic Republic of the Congo). Subsequently, as part of Ruanda-Urundi, it was administered by Belgium under a League of Nations mandate and later as a UN Trust Territory. Elections in September 1961, conducted under UN supervision, were won by the Union pour le progrès national (UPRONA), which had been formed in 1958 by Ganwa (Prince) Louis Rwagasore, the son of the reigning Mwami (King), Mwambutsa IV. As leader of UPRONA, Prince Rwagasore became Prime Minister later in the month, but was assassinated after only two weeks in office. He was succeeded by his brother-in-law, André Muhirwa. Internal self-government was granted in January 1962 and full independence on 1 July, when the two parts of the Trust Territory became separate states, as Burundi and Rwanda. Tensions between Burundi's two main ethnic groups, the Tutsi (traditionally the dominant tribe, despite representing a minority of the overall population) and the Hutu, escalated during 1965. Following an unsuccessful attempt by the Hutu to overthrow the Tutsi-dominated Government in October, nearly all the Hutu political élite were executed, eliminating any significant participation by the Hutu in Burundi's political life until the late 1980s (see below). In July 1966 the Mwami was deposed, after a reign of more than 50 years, by his son Charles, and the Constitution was suspended. In November Charles, now Mwami Ntare V, was himself deposed by his Prime Minister, Capt. (later Lt-Gen.) Michel Micombero, who declared Burundi a republic.

Several alleged plots against the Government in 1969 and 1971 were followed, in 1972, by an abortive coup during which Ntare V was killed. Hutu activists were held responsible for the attempted coup, and this served as a pretext for the Tutsi to conduct a series of large-scale massacres of the rival tribe, in which, it was estimated, about 100,000 were killed; large numbers of the Hutu fled to neighbouring countries.

In 1972 Micombero began a prolonged restructuring of the executive, which resulted in 1973 in an appointed seven-member Presidential Bureau, with Micombero as President and Prime Minister. In July 1974 the Government introduced a new republican Constitution, which vested sovereignty in UPRONA, the sole legal political party. Micombero was elected Secretary-General of the party and re-elected for a seven-year presidential term.

On 1 November 1976 an army coup deposed Micombero, who died in exile in July 1983. The leader of the coup, Lt-Col (later Col) Jean-Baptiste Bagaza, was appointed President by the Supreme Revolutionary Council (composed of army officers), and a new Council of Ministers was formed. In October 1978 Bagaza announced a ministerial reorganization in which he abolished the post of Prime Minister. The first national congress of UPRONA was held in December 1979, and a party Central Committee, headed by Bagaza, was elected to take over the functions of the Supreme Revolutionary Council in January 1980. A new Constitution, adopted by national referendum in November 1981, provided for the establishment of a national assembly, to be elected by universal adult suffrage. The first legislative elections were held in October 1982. Having been re-elected President of UPRONA at the party's second national congress in July 1984, Bagaza, the sole candidate, was elected President of Burundi by direct suffrage in August, winning 99.63% of the votes cast.

On 3 September 1987 a military coup deposed Bagaza while he was attending a conference in Canada. The coup was led by Maj. Pierre Buyoya, who accused Bagaza of corruption and immediately formed a Military Committee for National Salvation (CMSN) to administer the country, pending the appointment of a new President. The Constitution was suspended, and the National Assembly was dissolved. On 2 October Buyoya was sworn in as President of the Third Republic. His Council of Ministers included mostly civilians, retaining no minister from the previous regime.

In August 1988 tribal tensions erupted into violence in the north of the country when groups of Hutus, claiming Tutsi provocation, slaughtered hundreds of Tutsis in the towns of Ntega and Marangara. The Tutsi-dominated army was immediately dispatched to the region to restore order, and large-scale tribal massacres occurred. In October Buyoya announced changes to the Council of Ministers, including the appointment of a Hutu, Adrien Sibomana, to the newly-restored post of Prime Minister. For the first time the Council included a majority of Hutu representatives. Buyoya subsequently established a Committee for National Unity (comprising an equal number of Tutsis and Hutus) to investigate the massacres and make recommendations for national reconciliation. Following the publication of the Committee's report, Buyoya announced plans to combat all forms of discrimination against the Hutu and to introduce new regulations to ensure equal opportunities in education, employment and in the armed forces. Notwithstanding Buyoya's efforts to achieve ethnic reconciliation, political tension remained at a high level in 1989.

In May 1990, in response to a new draft charter on national unity, Buyoya announced plans to introduce a 'democratic constitution under a one-party government' in place of military rule. A charter designed to reconcile the Tutsi and the Hutu was to be the subject of a referendum. In December, at an extraordinary national congress of UPRONA, the CMSN was abolished and its functions transferred to an 80-member Central Committee, with Buyoya as Chairman and with a Hutu, Nicolas Mayugi, as Secretary-General. At a referendum conducted in February 1991 the draft charter on national unity was overwhelmingly approved, despite vociferous criticism from opposition groups. Later in the month a ministerial reorganization, whereby Hutus were appointed to 12 of the 23 government portfolios, was viewed with scepticism by political opponents. In March a commission was established to prepare a report on the democratization of national institutions and political structures, in preparation for the drafting of a new constitution. The commission's report, presented in September, recommended the establishment of a parliamentary system to operate in conjunction with a presidential system of government, a renewable five-year presidential mandate, the introduction of proportional representation, freedom of the press, the compilation of a declaration of human rights and a system of 'controlled multipartyism' whereby political groupings seeking legal recognition would be forced to fulfil specific requirements, including subscription to the Charter of Unity (adopted in February). The proposals received the support of more than 90% of the voters in a referendum held on 9 March 1992, and the new Constitution was promulgated on 13 March.

In an extensive ministerial reshuffle in April 1992, seven ministers left the Government, Buyoya relinquished the defence portfolio, and Hutus were appointed to 15 of the 25 portfolios. In the same month Buyoya approved legislation relating to the creation of new political parties in accordance with the provisions of the new Constitution. New political parties were to be obliged to demonstrate impartiality with regard to ethnic or regional origin, gender and religion, and were to refrain from militarization. In October Buyoya announced the creation of the National Electoral Preparatory Commission (NEPC), a 33-member body comprising representatives of the eight recognized political parties, together with administrative, judicial, religious and military officials. The NEPC was convened for the first time at the end of November. By early December Buyoya had appointed a new 12-member technical commission, charged with drafting an electoral code and a communal law.

Presidential elections, which took place on 1 June 1993, were won, with 64.8% of the votes cast, by Melchior Ndadaye, the candidate of the Front pour la démocratie au Burundi (FRO-DEBU), with the support of the Rassemblement du peuple burundien (RPB), the Parti du peuple and the Parti libéral; Buyoya received 32.4% of the vote as the UPRONA candidate, with support from the Rassemblement pour la démocratie et le développement économique et social (RADDES) and the Parti social démocrate. Legislative elections for 81 seats in the National Assembly were conducted on 29 June. FRODEBU again emerged as the most successful party, with 71% of the votes and 65 of the seats in the new legislature. UPRONA, with 21.4% of the votes, secured the remaining 16 seats. None of the other four parties contesting the elections secured the minimum 5% of votes needed for representation in the legislature. Ndadaye, Burundi's first Hutu Head of State, assumed the presidency on 10 July. A new Council of Ministers was subsequently announced. The new Prime Minister, Sylvie Kinigi, was one of seven newly-appointed Tutsi ministers.

On 21 October 1993 more than 100 army paratroopers, supported by armoured vehicles, swiftly overwhelmed supporters of the Government and occupied the presidential palace and the headquarters of the national broadcasting company. Ndadaye and several other prominent Hutu politicians and officials were detained and subsequently killed by the insurgents, who later proclaimed François Ngeze, one of the few Hutu members of UPRONA and a minister in the Government of former President Buyoya, as head of a National Committee for Public Salvation (CPSN). While members of the Government sought refuge abroad and in the offices of foreign diplomatic missions in Bujumbura, the armed forces declared a state of emergency, closing national borders and the capital's airport. However, immediate and unanimous international condemnation of the coup, together with the scale and ferocity of renewed tribal violence (fuelled by reports of Tutsi-dominated army units seeking out and eliminating Hutu intellectuals), undermined support for the insurgents from within the armed forces, and precipitated the collapse of the CPSN, which was disbanded on 25 October. Kinigi announced the ending of the curfew, but remained in hiding and urged the deployment of an international force in Burundi to protect the civilian Government. Communications were restored on 27 October, and on the following day the UN confirmed that the Government had resumed control of the country. Ngeze and 10 coup leaders were arrested, while some 40 other insurgents were believed to have fled to Zaire (now the Democratic Republic of the Congo). In December a commission of judicial inquiry was created to investigate the insurgency.

Meanwhile, in early November 1993 several members of the Government, including the Prime Minister, had left the French Embassy (where they had remained throughout the uprising) with a small escort of French troops, and on 8 November Kinigi met with 15 of the 17 surviving ministers in an attempt to address the humanitarian crisis arising from the massacre and displacement of hundreds of thousands of Burundians following the failed coup. On the same day the Constitutional Court officially recognized the presidential vacancy resulting from the murder of both Ndadaye and his constitutional successor, Giles Bimazubute, the Speaker of the National Assembly, and stated that presidential power should be exercised by the Council of Ministers, acting in a collegiate capacity, pending a presidential election which was to be conducted within three months. However, the Minister of External Relations and Co-operation, Sylvestre Ntibantunganya (who succeeded Ndadaye as leader of FRODEBU), suggested that no electoral timetable should be considered before the resolution of internal security difficulties and the initiation of a comprehensive programme for the repatriation of refugees. In December Ntibantunganya was elected Speaker of the National Assembly. The foreign affairs portfolio was assumed by Jean-Marie Ngendahayo, previously Minister of Communications and Government Spokesman.

Meanwhile, in November 1993, following repeated requests by the Government for an international contribution to the protection of government ministers in Burundi, the Organization of African Unity (OAU, see p. 256) agreed to the deployment of a 200-strong protection force (MIPROBU), to comprise civilian and military personnel, for a period of six months. In December opposition parties, including UPRONA and the RADDES, organized demonstrations in protest at the arrival of the 180-strong military contingent, scheduled for January 1994, claiming that Burundi's sovereignty and territorial integrity were being infringed. As a compromise, in March the Government secured a significant reduction in the size of the force. The mandate of the mission (comprising a military contingent of 47 and 20 civilian observers) was subsequently extended at three-monthly intervals.

In early January 1994 FRODEBU deputies in the National Assembly approved a draft amendment to the Constitution, allowing a President of the Republic to be elected by the National Assembly, in the event of the Constitutional Court's recognition of a presidential vacancy. UPRONA deputies, who had boycotted the vote, challenged the constitutionality of the amendment, and expressed concern that such a procedure represented election by indirect suffrage, in direct contravention of the terms of the Constitution. The continued boycott of the National Assembly by UPRONA deputies, together with procedural impediments to the immediate ratification of the amendment, forced the postponement on 10 January of an attempt by FRODEBU deputies to elect their presidential candidate, the Minister of Agriculture and Livestock, Cyprien Ntaryamira. Three days later, none the less, following the successful negotiation of a political truce with opposition parties, Ntaryamira was elected President by the National Assembly (with 78 of the 79 votes cast). He assumed the post on 5 February; a Tutsi Prime Minister, Anatole Kanyenkiko, was appointed two days later, while the composition of a new multi-party Council of Ministers was finally agreed in mid-February. During that month ethnic tension was renewed as armed Hutu and Tutsi extremist factions attempted to establish territorial strongholds.

On 6 April 1994, returning from a regional summit meeting in Dar es Salaam, Tanzania, Ntaryamira was killed (together with the Ministers of Development, Planning and Reconstruction and of Communications) when the aircraft of Rwandan President Juvénal Habyarimana, in which he was travelling at Habyarimana's invitation, was the target of a rocket attack above Kigali airport, Rwanda, and crashed on landing. Habyarimana was also killed, and was widely acknowledged to have been the intended victim of the attack. In contrast to the violent political and tribal chaos that erupted in Rwanda (q.v.) in the aftermath of the death of Habyarimana, Burundians responded positively to appeals for calm issued by Ntibantunganya, the Speaker of the National Assembly, who, on 8 April, was confirmed (in accordance with the Constitution) as interim President for a three-month period. However, violent exchanges between Hutu extremist rebels and factions of the armed forces continued in April, claiming numerous victims. The failure of the warring militias to respond to an ultimatum, issued by the interim President, Ntibantunganya, in late April, to surrender all illegal arms by 1 May, resulted in the military bombardment of several rebel strongholds, forcing the withdrawal and surrender of a number of insurgents. Relations between the Government and the armed forces subsequently improved, and were further cemented by the Prime Minister's announcement, in early May, that the Minister of State for the Interior and Public Security, Léonard Nyangoma, had forfeited his position in the Council of Ministers, having failed to return from official business abroad; he had earlier been accused of attempting to provoke large-scale civil confrontation.

Having discounted the possibility of organizing a general election, owing to security considerations, in June 1994 all major political parties joined lengthy negotiations to establish a procedure for the restoration of the presidency. The mandate of the interim President was extended for three months by the Constitutional Court in July, and by the end of August it had been decided that a new President would be elected by a broadly representative commission, with a composition yet to be decided. A new agreement on power-sharing was announced on 10 September. This Convention of Government, which detailed the terms of government for a four-year transitional period (including the allocation of 45% of cabinet posts to opposition parties), was incorporated into the Constitution on 22 September. The Convention also provided for the creation of a

National Security Council (Conseil de sécurité nationale, CSN), which was formally inaugurated on 10 October to address the national security crisis. On 30 September the Convention elected Ntibantunganya to the presidency from a list of six candidates including Charles Mukasi, the UPRONA leader. Ntibantunganya's appointment was endorsed by the National Assembly, and he was formally inaugurated on 1 October. Anatole Kanyenkiko was reappointed as Prime Minister, and a coalition Government was announced in accordance with the terms of the Convention. In December, however, UPRONA announced its intention to withdraw from the Government and from the legislature, following the election earlier that month of Jean Minani (a prominent FRODEBU member) to the post of Speaker of the National Assembly. UPRONA members accused Minani of having incited Hutu attacks against Tutsis in the aftermath of the October 1993 attempted coup. In January 1995 the political crisis was averted by agreement on a compromise FRODEBU candidate, Léonce Ngendakumana. Minani subsequently assumed the FRODEBU party leadership. UPRONA then declared its willingness to rejoin the Government, but later in January Kanyenkiko resisted attempts by the UPRONA leadership to expel him from the party for having failed to comply with party demands for the withdrawal from the Government of all party members over the Minani affair. Two UPRONA ministers were subsequently dismissed from the Council of Ministers, in apparent retaliation, prompting Mukasi, in mid-February, to demand the resignation of the Prime Minister and to declare an indefinite general strike in support of this demand. Increased political opposition to Kanyenkiko forced the Prime Minister to acknowledge that he no longer commanded the necessary mandate to continue in office, and on 22 February Antoine Nduwayo, a UPRONA candidate selected in consultation with other opposition parties, was appointed Prime Minister by presidential decree. A new coalition Council of Ministers was announced on 1 March, but political stability was undermined immediately by the murder, in early March, of the Hutu Minister of Energy and Mines, Ernest Kabushemeye.

Ethnic tension persisted in the second half of 1994, exacerbated by the scale and proximity of the violence in Rwanda and by the presence in Burundi of an estimated 200,000 Rwandan Hutu refugees. Ethnically-motivated atrocities became a daily occurrence in parts of the country (several prominent politicians and government officials were murdered), resulting in the imposition of a partial curfew in the capital in December. Fears that the security crisis in Burundi would develop into civil war were aggravated, in late 1994, by reports that the 30,000-strong Force pour la défense de la démocratie (FDD), the armed wing of Nyangoma's extremist Conseil national pour la défense de la démocratie (CNDD), were making preparations for an armed struggle against the armed forces in Burundi. In early November the CSN had urged all political and civilian groups to dissociate themselves from Nyangoma, who was believed to be co-ordinating party activities from Zaire.

An escalation in the scale and frequency of incidents of politically- and ethnically-motivated violence during 1995 prompted renewed concern that the security crisis would precipitate a large-scale campaign of ethnic massacres similar to that in Rwanda during 1994. Government-sponsored military initiatives were concentrated in Hutu-dominated suburbs of Bujumbura and in the north-east, where an aggressive campaign was waged against the alleged insurgent activities of the Parti de libération du peuple hutu (PALIPEHUTU—a small, proscribed, Hutu opposition group based in Tanzania), resulting in the deaths of hundreds of Hutu civilians. The Government accused Hutu extremist militias of conducting an intimidating and violent programme of recruitment of Hutu males in the region. Anti-insurgency operations were intensified in June in several suburbs of the capital, where an estimated 2,000 heavily-armed troops sought to apprehend members of the FDD. It was reported that as many as 130 civilians were killed in the ensuing hostilities. Also in June a report published by the human rights organization, Amnesty International, claimed that national security forces in Burundi had collaborated with extremist Tutsi factions in the murder of thousands of Hutus since 1993. Increased security measures announced by Ntibantunganya in the same month included restrictions on a number of civil liberties and the regrouping of many communes into administrative sectors to be administered jointly by civilian and military personnel. Notwithstanding the latest security initiative, in late June the Minister of State in charge of External Relations and Co-operation, Jean-Marie Ngendahayo, announced his resignation, expressing dissatisfaction at the Government's inability to guarantee the safety and basic rights of the population. Later in the month a meeting of the OAU, convened in Addis Ababa, Ethiopia, concluded that some degree of military intervention in Burundi would be necessary should ethnic violence continue to escalate. (In April the Burundian Government had declined an OAU offer of military intervention in favour of increasing the number of MIPROBU personnel to 67.)

By early 1996 reports of atrocities perpetrated against both Hutu and Tutsi civilians by rogue elements of the Tutsi-led armed forces (including militias known as the *Sans Echecs*), and by extremist Hutu rebel groups had become almost commonplace in rural areas. It was believed that the capital had been effectively 'cleansed' of any significant Hutu presence by the end of 1995. In late December the UN Secretary-General had petitioned the Security Council to sanction some form of international military intervention in Burundi to address the crisis, and in February 1996 these efforts were renewed after the UN Special Rapporteur on Human Rights concluded that no discernible improvement had been made in the protection of human rights since mid-1995 and that a state of near civil war existed in many areas of the country. However, the Burundian Government (and the weight of political opinion in Burundi) remained vehemently opposed to a foreign military presence.

In early April 1996 representatives of the US Agency for International Development and the Humanitarian Office of the European Union (EU, see p. 181) visited Burundi. Their findings—which were severely critical of the administration's failure to reconcile the country's various ethnic and political interests within government, and expressed doubts that effective power-sharing could be achieved within the terms of the 1994 Convention of Government and under the leadership of a Tutsi premier with considerable executive power—prompted the USA and the EU to announce the immediate suspension of aid to Burundi. Despite an undertaking by Ntibantunganya in late April 1996 that a human rights commission was to be established and a comprehensive reform of the security forces and the judiciary was to be undertaken, violence continued to escalate, prompting the suspension of French military co-operation with Burundi at the end of May.

In November 1995 the Presidents of Burundi, Rwanda, Uganda and Zaire, together with a Tanzanian presidential envoy, met in Cairo, Egypt, to discuss the crises in Burundi and Rwanda. The Great Lakes' representatives announced a subregional peace initiative for Burundi, to be led by the former President of Tanzania, Julius Nyerere. A further Great Lakes summit took place in Tunisia in mid-March 1996, at which Ntibantunganya reiterated his commitment to the restoration of internal security and the organization of democratic, multiparty elections in 1998. Representatives of some 13 political parties (including FRODEBU and UPRONA) participated in inter-party discussions conducted in Mwanza, Tanzania, in April 1996. Talks resumed in Mwanza in early June; the leader of UPRONA, Charles Mukasi, with support from an informal coalition of seven smaller, predominantly Tutsi parties (the Rassemblement unitaire), accused FRODEBU deputies of seeking to abrogate the Convention of Government, a charge which was strenuously denied by FRODEBU spokesmen following the talks. At a conference of regional powers in Arusha, Tanzania, in late June, it was reported that Ntibantunganya and Nduwayo had requested foreign intervention to protect politicians, civil servants and strategic installations. By early July a regional technical commission to examine the request for 'security assistance' (comprising regional defence ministers, but not representatives of the Burundian armed forces) had convened in Arusha and had reached preliminary agreement, with the support of the UN, for an intervention force to be composed of units of the Ugandan and Tanzanian armed forces and police officers from Kenya. Meanwhile, significant differences of interpretation with regard to the purpose and mandate of such a force had emerged between Ntibantunganya and Nduwayo (who suggested that the President was attempting to neutralize the country's military capability). At a mass rally in Bujumbura of Tutsi-dominated opposition parties, the Prime Minister joined Mukasi and other anti-Government figures in rejecting foreign military intervention and condemning what they regarded as Ntibantunganya's encouragement of external interference in domestic affairs. Some days later, however, full endorsement of the Arusha proposal for intervention was recorded by member nations of the OAU at a summit meeting convened in Yaoundé, Cameroon.

Political and ethnic enmities intensified still further when reports of a massacre of more than 300 Tutsi civilians at Bugendana, allegedly committed by Hutu extremists including heavily-armed Rwandan Hutu refugees, emerged shortly after the UN accused the Burundian authorities of collaborating with the Rwandan administration in a new initiative of (largely enforced) repatriation of Rwandan refugees in Burundi. While FRODEBU members made an urgent appeal for foreign military intervention to contain the increasingly violent civil and military reaction to these events, the former President, Bagaza, urged civil resistance to foreign intervention; his appeal for a general strike in Bujumbura was partially observed. Meanwhile, students (with the support of the political opposition) began a second week of protests against regional military intervention, and demonstrated in support of demands for the removal of the country's leadership. On 23 July 1996 Ntibantunganya was forced to abandon an attempt to attend the funeral of the victims of the Bugendana massacre when mourners stoned the presidential helicopter. The following day, amid strong indications that UPRONA intended to join a number of smaller opposition parties that had already withdrawn from the Convention of Government, it was reported that Ntibantunganya had sought refuge in the US embassy building. Several government Ministers and the Speaker of the National Assembly similarly sought refuge within the German embassy compound, while the FRODEBU Chairman, Jean Minani, fled the country.

On 25 July 1996 the armed forces were extensively deployed in the capital in a military coup. A statement made by the Minister of National Defence, Lt-Col Firmin Sinzoyiheba, criticized the failure of the administration to safeguard national security, and announced the suspension of the National Assembly and all political activity, the imposition of a nation-wide curfew and the closure of national borders and the airport at Bujumbura. Former President Buyoya was declared to be interim President of a transitional republic. On the same day Buyoya stated his immediate aim to be the restoration of peace and national security, and sought to reassure former ministers and government officials that their safety would be guaranteed by the new regime. Ntibantunganya conveyed his refusal to relinquish office, but Nduwayo immediately resigned, attributing his failure to effect national reconciliation principally to Ntibantunganya's ineffective leadership. In response to widespread external condemnation of the coup, Buyoya announced that a largely civilian, broadly-based government of national unity would be promptly installed, and that future negotiations with all Hutu groups would be considered. The forced repatriation of Rwandan Hutu refugees was halted with immediate effect.

Despite the appointment at the end of July 1996 of Pascal-Firmin Ndimira, a Hutu member of UPRONA, as Prime Minister, and an urgent attempt by Buyoya to obtain regional support, the leaders of Ethiopia, Kenya, Rwanda, Tanzania, Uganda and Zaire, meeting in Arusha, under OAU auspices, declared their intention to impose stringent economic sanctions against the new regime unless constitutional government was restored immediately. In early August the composition of a new 23-member, multi-ethnic Cabinet was announced. In mid-August Buyoya announced that an expanded transitional national assembly, incorporating existing elected deputies, would be inaugurated during September for a three-year period. A consultative council of elders was also to be established to oversee a period of broad political debate, during which time formal political activity would remain proscribed. Buyoya was formally inaugurated as President on 27 September.

Despite some evidence of violations, the regional sanctions that were imposed in early August 1996 resulted in the suspension of all significant trade and in Burundi's virtual economic isolation. However, the threat of a humanitarian crisis prompted the sanctions co-ordinating committee, meeting in Arusha in September, to authorize a relaxation of the embargo to facilitate the distribution of food and medical aid. An attempt, later in the month, by Buyoya to secure the repeal of all sanctions, by announcing an end to the ban on political parties and the restoration of the National Assembly, was received with scepticism by opponents, given the continued suspension of the Constitution and Buyoya's refusal to address preconditions to the ending of sanctions that required the organization of unconditional peace negotiations. In October Buyoya agreed to enter into negotiations with the CNDD, but a subsequent meeting, in Arusha, of regional leaders decided that sanctions should be maintained until evidence emerged of constructive progress in the negotiations. This prompted the Burundian Government to denounce the actions and motives of the group, and to withdraw the offer of unconditional dialogue with the CNDD as long as sanctions remained in place. Meanwhile, in early October some 37 deputies had attended the formal reopening of the National Assembly, which was boycotted by the majority of FRODEBU deputies. (It was reported that 22 of the Assembly's original 81 deputies had been murdered during the recent hostilities, while a large number remained in exile or in hiding.)

Reports emerged that the armed forces were targeting Hutus (thousands were estimated to have been killed since the coup), in an attempt to safeguard rural and border regions for Tutsi communities, to which the CNDD and other Hutu militia retaliated with attacks against military installations near Bujumbura as well as against Tutsi civilians. A UN report on the causes of the 1993 coup, published in August, implicated two of Buyoya's military leaders, who were subsequently dismissed. By late 1996 the military action in eastern Zaire had led to the repatriation of 30,000 Burundians and had severely weakened FDD fighting capacity, although some activists continued the fight from Tanzania. A report issued by the office of the UN High Commissioner for Refugees (UNHCR) in December estimated that more than 1,100 individuals (predominantly Hutu refugees) had been killed by the armed forces during October and November alone. Also in December Amnesty International denounced what it termed a 'policy of systematic extermination of a section of population' on the part of the armed forces, alleging that the army had massacred as many as 500 Hutu civilians in Butaganza, in the north-west, earlier in the month. Such reports were denied by the Burundian Government. In January 1997 UNHCR reported that the army had massed more than 100,000 (mainly Hutu) civilians in camps, as part of a 'regroupment' scheme stated by the authorities to protect villagers in areas of rebel activity. Although the authorities asserted that the 'regroupment' programme was voluntary, and that members of all ethnic groups were seeking the protection of the camps, it was widely believed that Hutu civilians were being coerced into 'regroupment' centres by the armed forces, under threat that they would be treated as guerrillas should they fail to comply. Furthermore, the policy was frequently interpreted as a means of isolating rebel militia from their support base within the civilian population. By mid-1997, according to government figures, some 200,000 civilians had been 'regrouped' in about 50 camps, while non-governmental organizations variously estimated the number of civilians affected at 350,000–500,000.

The security situation was, meanwhile, further troubled by the return of CNDD fighters among large numbers of Hutu refugees effectively expelled by the Tutsi-led rebellion in eastern Zaire, as well as by the enforced repatriation of refugees from Tanzania. In January 1997 Buyoya condemned the killing of some 120 Hutu refugees who had apparently been expelled from Tanzania, accused of fomenting unrest in camps there. In late May UNHCR appealed to bordering countries to cease repatriating Burundian refugees, owing to renewed massacres notably in the 'regroupment' centres. (Confrontations between the army and Hutu fighters had intensified in recent weeks, and there were frequent reports of massacres of civilians as fighting neared the capital.)

The trial began in mid-May 1997 of some 79 military officers accused of involvement in the October 1993 coup attempt. (Of those charged, 22 were reportedly at large, while four of the accused had died.) In May 1999 five of those accused were sentenced to death and a number of others received prison terms; however, all of the senior officers, including Bikomagu, were acquitted. Meanwhile, at the end of July 1997 it was reported that six people convicted of involvement in acts of genocide perpetrated in 1993 had been executed. In all during July–August 1997, the Burundian courts issued 30 death sentences in relation to such crimes; 10 defendants were sentenced to life imprisonment, and 19 to 20 years' custody.

Six ministers were replaced in a reorganization of Ndimira's Government in early May 1997, and in August Ambroise Niyonsaba was allocated the new post of Minister of the Peace Process. Meanwhile, the introduction of a new law regulating the press was denounced by opposition groups, human rights activists and journalists' representatives as seeking to curb the freedom of the media.

Civil unrest continued in late 1997, and on 1 January 1998 an attack on Bujumbura airport by more than 1,000 Hutu rebels resulted in at least 250 deaths. Similar attacks, although on a smaller scale, continued during early 1998. On 18 February the second stage of the inter-Burundian peace talks was held. The talks, which had been delayed following the death of the Minister of Defence in a helicopter crash, were attended by representatives of the Government, the political parties and the National Assembly, and prominent civilians. The CNDD, however, suspended its participation in protest at the human rights' violations on the part of the Government. Following the announcement in late February that a regional summit, held in Kampala, had voted to maintain the sanctions on Burundi, President Buyoya announced the impending repeal of travel restrictions which had been applied to former Presidents Bagaza and Ntibantunganya, and to the Speaker of the National Assembly, Ngendakumana. In mid-March the courts dismissed a case against Ngendakumana, on charges of genocide.

Following negotiations between the Government and the National Assembly concerning the expiry of FRODEBU's electoral mandate in June 1998, Buyoya and Ngendakumana publicly signed a political accord, and a new Transitional Constitution was promulgated on 6 June, replacing the law (enabling him to rule by decree) enacted by Buyoya after he took power in July 1996. The new charter provided for institutional reforms, including the creation of two vice-presidencies to replace the office of Prime Minister, the enlargement of the National Assembly from 81 to 121 seats, and the creation of a seven-member Constitutional Court, which was sworn in on 24 June 1998. In accordance with the Transitional Constitution, Buyoya was inaugurated as President on 11 June. On the following day the two Vice-Presidents were appointed: Frédérique Bavuginyumvira, a senior member of FRODEBU, who was allocated responsibility for political and administrative affairs, and Mathias Sinamenye (a Tutsi and hitherto the Governor of the Central Bank), with responsibility for economic and social issues. A new 22-member Council of Ministers, sworn in on 13 June, included 13 Hutus and eight Tutsis. The newly-enlarged National Assembly was inaugurated on 18 July, incorporating nine representatives from smaller political parties (with four further seats remaining vacant, owing to internal party disputes or the lack of a candidate) as well as 27 civilian representatives and 21 new representatives of FRODEBU to replace those who had been killed or gone into exile. On 22 July the inter-Burundian peace talks were adjourned at the request of the Government, as the parties were unable to reach agreement on the structure of the negotiations.

Meanwhile, little substantive progress was made in regional efforts to bring about direct peace talks between the Buyoya Government and its opponents. Consultations in Arusha in December 1996 were attended by representatives of the Buyoya administration, FRODEBU, the CNDD, PALIPEHUTU and other organizations. However, the Government's stipulation that fighting must be brought to a formal halt prior to any negotiations effectively precluded direct contacts. The first of a series of national discussions on the peace process began in January 1997, attended by academics, religious leaders, politicians and representatives of civil society. However, prominent political organizations, notably FRODEBU, refused to attend the talks, and the credibility of the discussions was undermined when the UN Development Programme, which had initially agreed to finance the negotiations, withdrew its support, on the grounds that all parties were not represented. Buyoya attended the fourth Arusha summit meeting on the Burundi conflict, in April, in his capacity as Head of State. The leaders of the Great Lakes countries agreed to an easing of the economic sanctions in the interests of alleviating conditions for the civilian population. The summit made the full revocation of sanctions dependent on the opening of direct, unconditional peace talks between the Burundian Government and opposition, and, in its final communiqué, urged the Government to dismantle the 'regroupment' camps.

Initial optimism that planned inter-party talks, scheduled to take place in Arusha in August 1997, would achieve progress in ending the political crisis diminished as the Buyoya Government became increasingly hostile to the mediation of Nyerere, claiming him to be biased in favour of the opposition. After it became clear that the sanctions would not be revoked immediately upon the opening of negotiations (a decision for which the Burundian authorities appeared to blame Nyerere), the Buyoya Government announced that it would not be attending the Arusha talks, stating that it required more time to prepare. The session was effectively abandoned after the Burundian authorities refused to allow an aircraft that had been sent to carry other delegates from Burundi to the meeting to land at Bujumbura. Nyerere openly condemned the stance of the Buyoya regime, announcing that the peace process had reached a stalemate and appealing for wider international assistance in resolving the crisis. A meeting of regional leaders, convened (in Buyoya's absence) in the Tanzanian capital in early September, reaffirmed its support for Nyerere's mediation, criticized the Burundian Government for its intransigence, and resolved to maintain all existing sanctions. The Government was represented at informal discussions between parties involved in the Burundian conflict, organized under UNESCO auspices in Paris, France, in late September.

In May 1998 Nyerere conducted discussions with Burundian political leaders, in preparation for the peace negotiations, which commenced in mid-June in Arusha. At the Arusha talks, which were attended by 17 groupings involved in the conflict, it was agreed that the next round of discussions would take place on 20 July, and that all factions would suspend hostilities on that date. The Government, however, expressed reservations concerning the cease-fire, citing the need to maintain state security. The FDD, which had rejected the political leadership of the CNDD and subsequently became a separate rebel movement, also refused to accept the cease-fire. It was agreed that the negotiations were to continue for three months, and that commissions would be established to negotiate each of the main issues of contention. At the July discussions, however, little progress was made. Prior to the third round of negotiations, a split emerged in UPRONA between those who supported Mukasi's opposition to the Arusha talks and those who were prepared to negotiate with the Hutu opposition. In October some moderate members of the UPRONA central committee elected a rival Chairman, Dr Luc Rukingama, the Minister of Information and a supporter of Buyoya. Mukasi was arrested in August, following outspoken criticism of the Government. At the third round of talks, which took place in October, three of the envisaged commissions were established. A fourth round of discussions took place in January 1999; a further commission was constituted, but no substantive progress was achieved.

At a regional summit meeting, which took place in Arusha in January 1999, following an appeal from the UN Security Council earlier in the month, regional Heads of State voted to suspend the economic sanctions, in recognition of the progress made in the peace negotiations, although they emphasized that the eventual lifting of the sanctions would be dependent on the progress made at the peace talks. In May Buyoya announced his proposals for reconciliation; these included a 10-year transitional period during which he would occupy the presidency for the first five years and a Hutu representative would assume the post for the second five years. The plan also envisaged the extension of the National Assembly to include Hutu rebel factions, the creation of a senate, the establishment of communal police forces, to resolve the issue of Tutsi-dominated defence and security forces, and the establishment of a national truth commission. Buyoya's opponents dismissed the proposals, citing his failure to honour his commitment to return the country swiftly to civilian rule in 1996 and the absence of any reference to elections in his plan. A round of discussions took place in Arusha in July; Nyerere criticized the lack of progress achieved at the negotiations, and the failure of the commissions to reach agreement. The absence from the negotiations of the two most significant rebel movements, the FDD and an armed wing of PALIPEHUTU, known as Forces nationales de libération (FNL), was also viewed as a major impediment to agreement on a peace plan. (The CNDD had rejoined the discussions.) Further talks at Arusha in September were impeded by the escalation of violence throughout the country, particularly around Bujumbura. Subsequent discussions were postponed owing to the death of Nyerere in mid-October. All the participating parties expressed their commitment to the process and nine organizations, including FRODEBU and UPRONA, created a movement for peace and solidarity, the Convergence nationale pour la paix et réconciliation (CNPR), which proposed that negotiations continue on neutral territory, owing to the alleged role of Tanzania in sheltering Hutu rebels. In December regional Heads of State, meeting in Arusha, nominated the former President of South Africa, Nelson Mandela, as the new mediator of the peace negotiations.

In June 1999 a new penal code was adopted by the National Assembly; the code, which was to enter into effect on 1 January 2000, protected civil rights and liberties, and introduced controls to prohibit torture and reduce the length of detention. In August 169 suspects, who had been detained for two years, were released pending their court appearance, under the terms of the new code.

Unrest continued throughout 1999 and increased in the second half of the year. In August rebel militia attacked Kanyosha, near Bujumbura; hundreds of civilians were killed in a counter-insurgency operation by the armed forces, according to human rights groups. The escalation of Hutu-led attacks around the capital led to the alleged rearming of Tutsi militias by the Tutsi-dominated security forces. A further response to increased Hutu rebel activity was the enforced relocation of more than 320,000 Hutus into 'regroupment' camps. The Government claimed that the camps provided protection for the civilian population and would prevent members from seeking shelter in the community. However, the UN, the USA and the EU all expressed their concern at the Government's enforced 'regroupment' of Hutu civilians in these camps, which lacked basic supplies and medical assistance. In mid-October, following an ambush in which two UN aid workers were killed attempting to inspect a 'regroupment' camp, the UN announced that it was to restrict its operations and confine its staff to Bujumbura. Insecurity continued during October and November, with further clashes between government and rebel forces. A UN human rights' report, issued in October, criticized Burundi for its 'regroupment' policy and for the continuing massacres. At this time it was estimated that more than 200,000 people, mainly civilians, had been killed since the outbreak of hostilities in 1993 and a further 1.1m. displaced. In November the aid agency, Médecins sans Frontières, announced the suspension of its programme in the camps, and Amnesty International issued a warning that conditions in Burundi resembled those that had preceded the genocide in Rwanda in 1994.

In January 2000 a major cabinet reorganization was effected. Peace negotiations (the first to be attended by Mandela) resumed in Arusha in late February. Mandela criticized Tutsi domination of public office and urged equal representation of Hutu and Tutsi in the armed forces, while also denouncing Hutu rebel attacks on civilians. At a further round of discussions, which commenced in Arusha in late March, agreement was reached on draft proposals for a new ethnically-balanced armed force. (Nevertheless, government forces continued attacks against Hutu rebel positions, prompting fierce fighting south of Bujumbura.) In April Mandela visited Burundi for the first time, meeting government and militia leaders. Following a further meeting with Buyoya in Johannesburg in June, Mandela announced that the Burundian President had agreed to ensure equal representation of Hutu and Tutsi in the armed forces, and the closure of 'regroupment' camps by the end of July.

In July 2000 the leader of the FDD, Jean-Bosco Ndayikengurukiye, for the first time accepted an invitation by Mandela to participate in the peace negotiations. In the same month the drafting of a peace accord was finalized; the agreement stipulated the terms for the establishment of a transitional government for a period of three years, the integration of former Hutu rebels into the armed forces, and the creation of an electoral system that would ensure power-sharing between the Tutsi and the Hutu. Mandela announced that, since a number of points of disagreement remained, the peace plan would be signed on 28 August (rather than later in July, as originally scheduled) to allow time for its consideration. At a summit meeting, which was attended by several regional Heads of State in Arusha, negotiating groups were presented with the draft peace agreement, which included compromise proposals on unresolved issues. However, the FDD demanded the release by the authorities of political prisoners, the fulfilment of the pledge to dismantle the 'regroupment' camps, and bilateral negotiations with the armed forces, as a precondition to the cessation of hostilities. (The FNL had again failed to attend the discussions.) On 28 August the peace agreement was formally endorsed by representatives of the Government, the National Assembly, seven Hutu political associations and seven Tutsi parties. The remaining three Tutsi groups that had attended the previous negotiations subsequently signed the accord at cease-fire discussions, which took place in Nairobi, Kenya, in late September, following assurances by Mandela that measures would be taken to ensure that the Hutu rebels cease hostilities. At the same time an Implementation and Monitoring Committee, comprising representatives of the negotiating parties, and international and civil society representatives, was established. Following the conclusion of these discussions, a statement was issued demanding that the FDD and FNL suspend rebel activity and sign the peace agreement.

In December 2000 continuing Hutu rebel attacks included the killing of a British aid worker, together with a number of other civilians, on a principal road near Bujumbura. Meanwhile, negotiations on the establishment of power-sharing structures continued. In late January 2001 14 of the 19 signatories of the peace accord agreed on the composition of a new National Assembly, which would allocate Hutu parties 60% and Tutsi 40% representation in the legislature. Six candidates for the transitional presidency had emerged; however, the negotiating groups had failed to agree to return Buyoya to the office. In early February a meeting of the Implementation and Monitoring Committee ended without achieving significant progress in reaching agreement on transitional institutions. A further regional summit meeting was scheduled to commence in Arusha later that month.

The cross-border movement of vast numbers of refugees, provoked by regional ethnic and political violence, has dominated recent relations with Rwanda, Tanzania and the Democratic Republic of the Congo (DRC, formerly Zaire), and has long been a matter of considerable concern to the international aid community. In October and November 1993, following the abortive coup by factions of the Tutsi-dominated armed forces (see above), ethnic violence erupted on a massive scale throughout the country, claiming an estimated 150,000 lives and displacing an estimated 800,000 civilians, including 500,000 who fled into Tanzania, Rwanda and Zaire. Limited relief resources were overburdened in April 1994 by the exodus into Burundi of thousands of Rwandans, and by the repatriation of vast numbers of Burundians from refugee camps in Rwanda, as a result of the political violence and accompanying massacres following the death of President Habyarimana. In July 1995 UNHCR estimated that some 50,000 Rwandan refugees had been repatriated since the beginning of the year. By 31 December 1996, following a programme of forced repatriation in July of that year, the refugee population in Burundi had declined to less than 1,000 (although this estimate excluded Zairean refugees, the number of whom was unknown to UNHCR). At that time some 882,900 internally displaced Burundians and 71,031 returnees from Tanzania were of concern to UNHCR. In early 1999 UNHCR estimated that there was a total of 299,400 Burundian refugees, although this figure excluded some 200,000 long-term Burundian residents in Tanzania, who were increasingly vulnerable to expulsion. According to UNHCR, some 5,000 refugees were repatriated to Burundi between January and April 1999. Following the killing of two UN personnel in October 1999, however, the repatriation programme to Burundi from neighbouring countries was suspended.

The uprising by Laurent-Désiré Kabila's Alliance des forces démocratiques pour la libération du Congo-Zaïre (AFDL) in eastern Zaire resulted in the return of large numbers of refugees: an estimated 300,000 returned to Burundi from late 1996, severely undermining the operations from Zaire of large numbers of FDD fighters who were believed to have been massed in refugee camps there. Moreover, the seizure of power by the AFDL in May 1997 was welcomed by the Buyoya regime, which moved to forge close relations with Kabila's DRC. In April 1998 Burundi, the DRC and Uganda agreed to establish a combined police force to provide security along their common borders. Burundi initially denied any involvement in the civil war, which commenced in the DRC in August, but by May 1999 some 3,000 Burundian troops were believed to be stationed there with the aim of destroying FDD camps in the eastern DRC. The FDD has supported the DRC Government in the civil war and has used the conflict as an opportunity to regroup and rearm. In June the DRC instituted proceedings against Burundi, together with Rwanda and Uganda, at the ICJ, accusing them of acts of armed aggression in contravention of the terms of both the UN Charter and the Charter of the OAU. In early February 2001, however, the DRC abandoned proceedings against Burundi and Rwanda.

Meanwhile, the continued presence of large numbers of Burundian refugees in Tanzania, and increasingly strong accusations on the part of the Buyoya Government that Tanzania was supporting the Hutu rebellion, prompted tension between the two countries in mid-1997. These allegations were strenuously denied by the Tanzanian Government, which stated that it would never allow the use of refugee camps on its territory for military training. Mutual suspicion was exacerbated by Tanzania's refusal to allow a representative of the Buyoya regime to take the position of Chargé d'affaires at the Burundian embassy in Dar es Salaam. In late August Tanzania announced that it had placed its armed forces on alert, stating that Burundian forces were mobilizing near the border in preparation for an invasion of the refugee camps. Meanwhile, the Buyoya Government's assertions that Nyerere was unduly biased in his role as mediator in the Burundian conflict further strained bilateral ties. In late 1997 Burundian allegations that the Tanzanian Government was involved in cross-border raids by Hutu militias, based in Tanzania, adversely affected relations, and in November there were reports of clashes between troops on the Tanzanian-Burundian border. In the same month Burundi's ambassador-designate to Tanzania, Clavera Mayegara, was sent to assume control of the Burundian embassy in Dar es Salaam, which was occupied by members of the CNDD and FRODEBU. She was, however, arrested by the Tanzanian authorities and subsequently expelled. In 1998 bilateral relations improved slightly, and in July Tanzania agreed to the reopening of the Burundian embassy. Relations appeared to improve further in early 1999 and, following a meeting of the Burundian and Tanzanian ministers of foreign affairs, it was announced that a tripartite commission was to be established (with representatives from Burundi, Tanzania and UNHCR) to investigate allegations that armed militia groups had used Tanzania as a base from which to launch attacks on Burundi. Exchanges of fire between members of the Tanzanian armed forces and Burundian rebels on the border between the two countries were reported in September 2000.

Government

Under the Constitution of March 1992, executive power is vested in the President, who is elected directly, by universal adult suffrage, for a five-year term, renewable only once. Statutory power is shared with the Prime Minister, who appoints a Council of Ministers. Legislative power is exercised by the National Assembly, whose members are elected directly, by universal adult suffrage, for a five-year renewable mandate. Following the coup of 25 July 1996, the Constitution was suspended. On 6 June 1998 a Transitional Constitution was promulgated. The membership of the National Assembly was increased from 81 to 121, and two vice-presidencies were created to replace the post of Prime Minister. A peace agreement, which was signed by representatives of the incumbent Government, the National Assembly and 17 political groupings on 28 August 2000, provided for the installation of a transitional administration, in which power-sharing between the Hutu and Tutsi ethnic groups would be guaranteed (see Recent History).

For the purposes of local government, Burundi comprises 15 provinces (administered by civilian governors), each of which is divided into districts and further subdivided into communes.

Defence

The total strength of the armed forces in August 2000 was 45,500, comprising an army of an estimated 40,000 (including an air wing of 200), and a paramilitary force of an estimated 5,500 gendarmes (including a 50-strong marine police force). Defence expenditure for 1999 was budgeted at 24,564m. Burundian francs (equivalent to 23.4% of total expenditure).

Economic Affairs

In 1998, according to estimates by the World Bank, Burundi's gross national product (GNP), measured at average 1996–98 prices, was US $911m., equivalent to $140 per head (or $561 per head on an international purchasing-power parity basis). During 1990–98, it was estimated, GNP per head decreased, in real terms, at an average rate of 5.5% per year. Over the same period the population increased by an average of 2.6% annually. GNP totalled an estimated $800m. in 1999, equivalent to $120 per head. Burundi's gross domestic product (GDP) declined, in real terms, at an average annual rate of 1.5% in 1990–99, according to IMF estimates; GDP registered growth of 4.8% in 1998, but declined by 1.0% in 1999.

Agriculture (including forestry and fishing) contributed an estimated 52.2% of GDP in 1999. An estimated 90.4% of the labour force were employed in the sector at mid-1999. The principal cash crops are coffee (which accounted for 76.3% of export earnings in 1999) and tea. Hides and skins are also exported. The main subsistence crops are cassava and sweet potatoes. Although Burundi is traditionally self-sufficient in food crops, population displacement as a result of the political crisis has resulted in considerable disruption in the sector, while the economic sanctions imposed following the 1996 coup further affected production. The livestock-rearing sector was also severely affected by the civil war. During 1990–99, according to

IMF estimates, agricultural GDP decreased at an average annual rate of 1.2%; growth of 5.3% was recorded in 1998, but a decline of 3.0% was registered in 1999.

Industry (comprising mining, manufacturing, construction and utilities) engaged only 2.1% of the employed labour force in 1990, but contributed an estimated 16.2% of GDP in 1999. Industrial GDP decreased at an average annual rate of 3.7% in 1990–99, according to IMF estimates, although growth of 6.9% was recorded in 1999.

Mining and power engaged 0.1% of the employed labour force in 1990 and contributed an estimated 0.8% of GDP in 1999. Gold (alluvial), tin, tungsten and columbo-tantalite are mined in small quantities, although much activity has hitherto been outside the formal sector. Burundi has important deposits of nickel (estimated at 5% of world reserves), vanadium and uranium. In addition, petroleum deposits have been discovered. The GDP of the mining sector increased by an average annual rate of 8.4% in 1990–99, according to IMF estimates, but remained at a constant level in 1998 and 1999.

Manufacturing engaged 1.2% of the employed labour force in 1990 and contributed an estimated 10.1% of GDP in 1999. The sector consists largely of the processing of agricultural products (coffee, cotton, tea and the extraction of vegetable oils). A number of small enterprises also produce beer, flour, cement, footwear and textiles. According to IMF estimates, manufacturing GDP decreased at an average annual rate of 17.4% in 1990–99, although growth of 5.6% was registered in 1999.

Energy is derived principally from hydroelectric power (an estimated 39.1% of electricity consumed in 1999 was imported). Peat is also exploited as an additional source of energy. Imports of petroleum products comprised 17.3% of the value of imports in 1999.

The services sector contributed an estimated 31.7% of GDP in 1999, but engaged just 4.4% of the employed labour force in 1990. According to IMF estimates, the GDP of the services sector decreased at an average annual rate of 1.3% in 1990–99; growth of 3.0% was estimated in 1999.

In 1999 Burundi recorded a visible trade deficit of US $42.3m., and there was a deficit of $27.0m. on the current account of the balance of payments. In 1999 the principal source of imports (16.9%) was Belgium; other important suppliers in that year were Zambia, Kenya, France and Germany. The principal market for exports in 1999 (33.2%) was the United Kingdom; other important markets were Germany and Belgium. The main imports in 1993 were machinery and transport equipment, basic manufactures, chemicals, mineral fuels and food. The principal exports in 1999 were coffee, tea, cocoa and spices, and hides and skins.

In 1999 the budget deficit, after adjustment, was 12,244.6m. Burundian francs, equivalent to 2.7% of GDP. Burundi's external debt at the end of 1998 was US $1,119m., of which $1,079m. was long-term public debt. In that year the cost of debt-servicing was equivalent to 10.0% of revenue from the export of goods and services. External debt at the end of 1999 was estimated at $1,207m. (including $84m. of arrears). The annual rate of inflation averaged 13.8% in 1990–99. Consumer prices increased by an average of 3.4% in 1999.

Burundi, with its neighbours Rwanda and the Democratic Republic of the Congo, is a member of the Economic Community of the Great Lakes Countries (CEPGL, see p. 307). Burundi is also a member of the Common Market for Eastern and Southern Africa (COMESA, see p. 148), and of the International Coffee Organization (see p. 304).

Burundi's acute economic decline after 1993, owing to the severe political upheaval and accompanying population displacement, was further exacerbated by the regional economic sanctions imposed following the coup of July 1996. By early 1999, when the sanctions were revoked, a sustained decline in government revenue had resulted in the depletion of official reserves; capital expenditure was minimal, and the Government was borrowing heavily in order to meet its financing requirements. As a result, domestic and foreign debts had accumulated at an unsustainable level, and Burundi was defaulting on its debt-servicing obligations. Meanwhile, smuggling and tax evasion were largely unchecked, and a 'black market' for both goods and currency was flourishing. The ending of the regional blockade had little positive impact during 1999, as aid inflows and international co-operation, on which the economy depended, remained at a very low level compared with that of the early 1990s. The recovery especially of agricultural activity was, furthermore, effectively prevented by the worsening security situation and consequent increase in population displacement. Despite the reopening of regional trading links, Burundi's principal export commodity, coffee, remained uncompetitive at a time of low international prices, although a 15% devaluation of the Burundian franc in August 1999 was intended partially to offset this impediment to trade. Meanwhile, the revival of plans to exploit important nickel reserves at Musongati, in the south of the country, was accompanied by prospects for much-needed investment and infrastructural development. In May 2000 the IMF and World Bank announced the resumption of international credit to Burundi. In September, following further dramatic increases in external debt, the UN initiated an appeal for emergency humanitarian funds to finance a plan for economic recovery. In December an international donor conference pledged considerable support to enable the country to commence economic reconstruction. Long-term assistance towards the servicing of the country's external debt was envisaged. However, the normalization of economic activity, and thus the eventual return of sustained growth, continued to depend on the realization of a peace agreement acceptable to all factions involved in the conflict (see Recent History).

Social Welfare

Medical facilities in Burundi are limited. In the mid-1990s there were 34 hospitals, with one bed for every 1,526 inhabitants. Some 329 physicians were working in hospitals (one per 17,210 inhabitants), and there was one nurse for every 4,800 inhabitants. Of total expenditure by the central Government in 1999, 2,271m. Burundian francs (2.2%) was allocated to health, and a further 2,401m. Burundian francs (2.3%) to social security and welfare. In 2000 it was reported that the health situation in the country had worsened dramatically, while the resources allocated in the state budget to health had declined by some 70% since the beginning of the civil conflict in October 1993.

Education

Education is provided free of charge. Kirundi is the language of instruction in primary schools, while French is used in secondary schools. Primary education, which is officially compulsory, begins at seven years of age and lasts for six years. Secondary education begins at the age of 13 and lasts for up to seven years, comprising a first cycle of four years and a second of three years. In 1995 the total enrolment at primary schools included 51% of children in the relevant age-group (males 55%; females 46%). Enrolment at secondary schools included only 7% of the population in the appropriate age-group (males 9%; females 5%). There is one university, in Bujumbura; in 1996 4,379 students were enrolled in higher education. According to UNESCO estimates, the average rate of illiteracy among the population aged 15 years and over was 57.7% (males 47.8%; females 66.8%) in 1995. Expenditure on education by the central Government in 1999 was 15,990m. Burundian francs (15.2% of total government expenditure).

Public Holidays

2001: 1 January (New Year's Day), 5 February (Unity Day), 16 April (Easter Monday), 1 May (Labour Day), 24 May (Ascension Day), 1 July (Independence Day), 15 August (Assumption), 18 September (Victory of UPRONA Party), 13 October (Rwagasore Day), 21 October (Ndadaye Day), 1 November (All Saints' Day), 25 December (Christmas).

2002: 1 January (New Year's Day), 5 February (Unity Day), 1 April (Easter Monday), 1 May (Labour Day), 9 May (Ascension Day), 1 July (Independence Day), 15 August (Assumption), 18 September (Victory of UPRONA Party), 13 October (Rwagasore Day), 21 October (Ndadaye Day), 1 November (All Saints' Day), 25 December (Christmas).

Weights and Measures

The metric system is in force.

Statistical Survey

Area and Population

AREA, POPULATION AND DENSITY

Area (sq km)	27,834*
Population (census results)†	
15–16 August 1979	4,028,420
16–30 August 1990	
Males	2,473,599
Females	2,665,474
Total	5,139,073
Population (official estimates at mid-year)	
1997	6,194,000
1998	6,300,000
1999	6,483,000
Density (per sq km) at mid-1999	232.9

* 10,747 sq miles.
† Excluding adjustment for underenumeration.

PRINCIPAL TOWNS

Bujumbura (capital), population 235,440 (census result, August 1990); Gitega 15,943 (1978).

Source: Banque de la République du Burundi.

BIRTHS AND DEATHS (UN estimates, annual averages)

	1980–85	1985–90	1990–95
Birth rate (per 1,000) . . .	46.2	46.7	46.2
Death rate (per 1,000) . . .	17.9	18.1	21.5

Expectation of life (UN estimates, years at birth, 1990–95): 41.6 (males 40.1; females 43.0).

Source: UN, *World Population Prospects: The 1998 Revision.*

ECONOMICALLY ACTIVE POPULATION*
(persons aged 10 years and over, 1990 census)

	Males	Females	Total
Agriculture, hunting, forestry and			
fishing	1,153,890	1,420,553	2,574,443
Mining and quarrying . . .	1,146	39	1,185
Manufacturing	24,120	9,747	33,867
Electricity, gas and water. .	1,847	74	1,921
Construction.	19,447	290	19,737
Trade, restaurants and hotels. .	19,667	6,155	25,822
Transport, storage and			
communications . . .	8,193	311	8,504
Financing, insurance, real estate			
and business services . .	1,387	618	2,005
Community, social and personal			
services	68,905	16,286	85,191
Activities not adequately defined .	8,653	4,617	13,270
Total labour force . . .	1,307,255	1,458,690	2,765,945

* Figures exclude persons seeking work for the first time, totalling 13,832 (males 9,608; females 4,224).

Source: UN, *Demographic Yearbook.*

Mid-1999 (estimates in '000): Agriculture, etc. 3,178; Total 3,514 (Source: FAO).

Agriculture

PRINCIPAL CROPS ('000 metric tons)

	1997	1998	1999
Wheat	10*	10	7
Rice (paddy)	65*	41	59
Maize	145*	132	129
Millet	17*	11	10
Sorghum	68*	67	60
Potatoes	49*	23	24
Sweet potatoes . . .	681*	590	734
Cassava (Manioc) . .	603*	622	617
Yams	11*	11	13
Taro (Coco yam) . .	105*	76	90
Dry beans	271*	275	227
Dry peas	37*	36	32
Groundnuts (in shell) .	11†	9*	10
Vegetables and melons† . .	220	215	210
Sugar cane	175	190	175
Bananas and plantains . .	1,543*	1,399	1,511
Other fruits (excl. melons) .	86*	85	84
Coffee (green) . . .	18*	17	30
Tea (made)	4	7	7
Cotton (lint) . . .	1*	1*	1

* Unofficial figure.   † FAO estimate(s).

Source: FAO.

LIVESTOCK ('000 head, year ending September)

	1997	1998	1999
Cattle	311*	346	329
Pigs.	70†	73	61
Sheep	200†	163	165†
Goats	650†	659	594
Poultry	4,400†	4,600	4,400†

* Unofficial figure.   † FAO estimate.

Source: FAO.

LIVESTOCK PRODUCTS (FAO estimates, '000 metric tons)

	1997	1998	1999
Beef and veal . . .	10	11	9
Mutton and lamb . . .	1	1	1
Goat meat	3	3	3
Pig meat	4	4	4
Poultry meat	6	6	6
Cows' milk	24	27	23
Sheep's milk	1	1	1
Goats' milk	8	8	8
Poultry eggs	3	3	3
Cattle hides	2	2	2
Goatskins	1	1	1

Source: FAO.

Forestry

ROUNDWOOD REMOVALS ('000 cubic metres, excl. bark)

	1996	1997	1998
Sawlogs, veneer logs and logs for			
sleepers	47	80	222
Other industrial wood . .	65	65	67
Fuel wood	1,465	1,487	1,510
Total	1,577	1,632	1,799

Source: FAO, *Yearbook of Forest Products.*

SAWNWOOD PRODUCTION ('000 cubic metres, incl. railway sleepers)

	1996	1997	1998
Coniferous (softwood).	7	7	7
Broadleaved (hardwood)	26	26	26
Total	33	33	33

* FAO estimate.

Source: FAO, *Yearbook of Forest Products*.

Fishing

(metric tons, live weight)

	1996	1997	1998
Capture.	3,041	20,296	32,039
Freshwater perches	1,205	2,378	2,845
Dagaas	1,508	17,868	28,853
Aquaculture*	10	10	10
Total catch (incl. others)	3,051	20,306	32,049

* FAO estimates.

Source: FAO, *Yearbook of Fishery Statistics*.

Mining

	1995	1996	1997
Gold (kilograms)*	2,000	2,200	1,500†
Tin ore (metric tons)*	15	25	—
Kaolin ('000 metric tons)*.	1†	1†	1
Peat ('000 metric tons)*	10	10	5

* Data from the US Bureau of Mines. Figures for gold and tin refer to the metal content of ores.
† Estimates.

Source: UN, *Industrial Commodity Statistics Yearbook*.

Industry

SELECTED PRODUCTS ('000 metric tons, unless otherwise indicated)

	1996	1997	1998*
Beer ('000 hectolitres)	1,227.9	1,161.2	1,036.3
Soft drinks ('000 hectolitres)	179.1	146.6	62.6
Cottonseed oil ('000 hectolitres)	234.6	199.7	133.6
Sugar	17.8	19.6	21.7
Paint	0.4	0.4	0.5
Insecticides	2.4	2.4	1.8
Soap	3.4	2.8	3.7
Bottles	2.5	1.8	3.3
Blankets ('000)	116.2	217.3	174.4
Fibro-cement products	0.2	0.5	1.6
Batteries ('000 cartons)†	14.5	2.2	5.6
Electric energy (million kWh)	103.1	85.8	107.1

* Estimates.
† Cartons of 240 batteries.

1999: Electric energy 99.1 million kWh (estimate).

Source: IMF, *Burundi: Statistical Annex* (April 2000).

Finance

CURRENCY AND EXCHANGE RATES

Monetary Units
100 centimes = 1 Burundian franc.

Sterling, Dollar and Euro Equivalents (29 December 2000)
£1 sterling = 1,161.2 francs;
US $1 = 778.2 francs;
€1 = 724.1 francs;
10,000 Burundian francs = £8.612 = $12.850 = €13.810.

Average Exchange Rate (Burundian francs per US dollar)
1998   447.77
1999   563.56
2000   720.67

BUDGET (million Burundian francs)*

Revenue†	1997	1998	1999
Tax revenue.	42,880	61,554	66,627
Taxes on income and profits	10,322	13,139	15,122
Social security contributions	3,731	4,281	5,357
Domestic taxes on goods and services	20,744	25,305	31,640
Transaction tax	7,281	11,435	12,643
Excise tax	13,155	13,870	18,997
Taxes on international trade	7,229	18,829	14,508
Import duties	6,527	10,726	11,022
Export tax	702	4,562	28
Entrepreneurial and property income	1,920	3,106	3,071
Other current revenue	1,345	1,610	2,238
Capital revenue	108	64	111
Total	46,253	66,334	72,047

Expenditure‡	1997	1998	1999
General public services	18,154	20,513	25,122
Defence.	21,100	23,325	24,564
Public order and safety	1,344	2,153	2,502
Education	11,204	14,080	15,990
Health	2,085	2,421	2,271
Social security and welfare	4,718	6,510	2,401
Recreational, cultural and religious affairs and services	334	286	345
Economic affairs and services.	n.a.	3,062	3,721
Fuel and energy	n.a.	232	543
Agriculture, forestry, fishing and hunting.	n.a.	1,499	1,941
Mining, manufacturing and construction	n.a.	995	1,068
Transport and communications	n.a.	336	169
Other purposes	n.a.	25,711	28,265
Interest payments	6,071	6,844	9,507
Total	80,800	98,061	105,181
Current	58,207	74,082	80,966
Capital	12,322	23,979	24,215
Adjustment to total expenditure	10,271	—	—

* Figures refer to the consolidated operations of the central Government, comprising the general budget, social security funds and extrabudgetary accounts (covering transactions undertaken through foreign borrowing arrangements and grants not recorded in treasury accounts). The data exclude the operations of other central government units with individual budgets.
† Excluding grants received.
‡ Excluding lending minus repayments.

CENTRAL BANK RESERVES (US $ million at 31 December)

	1997	1998	1999
Gold*	4.99	4.95	5.00
IMF special drawing rights	0.06	0.09	0.10
Reserve position in IMF	7.91	8.25	8.04
Foreign exchange	105.07	57.18	39.84
Total	118.03	70.47	52.98

* Valued at market-related prices.

Source: IMF, *International Financial Statistics*.

MONEY SUPPLY (million Burundian francs at 31 December)

	1997	1998	1999
Currency outside banks . .	23,693	24,180	32,087
Deposits at central bank . .	749	860	710
Demand deposits at commercial banks	22,235	22,180	34,296
Demand deposits at other monetary institutions	1,527	1,595	2,200
Total money	**48,203**	**48,816**	**69,293**

Source: IMF, *International Financial Statistics*.

COST OF LIVING
(Consumer Price Index for Bujumbura; base: January 1991 = 100)

	1996	1997	1998
Food	199.0	268.7	302.3
Clothing	199.3	308.7	342.2
Housing, heating and light . .	192.1	235.4	276.0
Transport	176.4	229.1	217.1
All items (incl. others) . .	**193.4**	**253.6**	**285.3**

Source: IMF, *Burundi: Statistical Annex* (April 2000).

All items (base: 1995 = 100): 186.5 in 1998; 192.8 in 1999 (Source: IMF, *International Financial Statistics*).

NATIONAL ACCOUNTS

Composition of the Gross National Product (million Burundian francs at current prices)

	1997	1998	1999
GDP in purchasers' values .	337,333	396,366	451,549
Net factor income from abroad .	-4,416	-3,699	-5,315
Gross national product .	**332,917**	**392,667**	**446,234**

Source: IMF, *International Financial Statistics*.

Expenditure on the Gross Domestic Product (million Burundian francs at current prices)

	1997	1998	1999
Government final consumption expenditure	51,300	59,900	74,638
Private final consumption expenditure	274,507	351,810	378,377
Increase in stocks . . .	2,739	3,211	2,443
Gross fixed capital formation . .	24,500	26,620	34,314
Total domestic expenditure .	**353,046**	**441,541**	**489,772**
Exports of goods and services .	33,760	32,018	34,506
Less Imports of goods and services	49,473	77,193	72,729
GDP in purchasers' values .	**337,333**	**396,366**	**451,549**
GDP at constant 1980 prices	105,512	110,249	n.a.

Source: IMF, *International Financial Statistics*.

Gross Domestic Product by Economic Activity ('000 million Burundian francs at current prices, estimates)

	1997	1998	1999
Agriculture, hunting, forestry and fishing	163.4	191.1	183.0
Mining and quarrying . .⎫ Electricity, gas and water . .⎭	2.4	2.8	2.9
Manufacturing*	29.6	37.5	35.4
Construction	19.2	17.5	18.4
Trade, restaurants and hotels .	13.2	15.0	14.8
Transport, storage and communications . . .	13.6	14.5	14.2
Government services . . .	57.8	65.1	72.5
Other services . . .	7.3	9.4	9.6
GDP at factor cost . .	**306.4**	**352.8**	**350.8**
Indirect taxes, *less* subsidies . .	30.9	43.5	44.1
GDP in purchasers' values .	**337.3**	**396.4**	**394.9**

* Including handicrafts ('000 million francs): 9.3 in 1997; 9.0 in 1998; 9.0 in 1999.

Source: IMF, *Burundi: Statistical Annex* (April 2000).

BALANCE OF PAYMENTS (US $ million)

	1997	1998	1999
Exports of goods f.o.b. . . .	87.5	64.0	55.0
Imports of goods f.o.b. . . .	-96.1	-123.5	-97.3
Trade balance	**-8.6**	**-59.5**	**-42.3**
Exports of services . . .	8.7	7.6	6.3
Imports of services . . .	-45.4	-49.5	-32.6
Balance on goods and services	**-45.3**	**-101.3**	**-68.7**
Other income received . .	4.3	3.6	1.9
Other income paid . . .	-16.8	-11.9	-11.3
Balance on goods, services and income	**-57.8**	**-109.6**	**-78.1**
Current transfers received . .	61.3	59.3	52.9
Current transfers paid . .	-4.5	-3.3	-1.8
Current balance . . .	**-1.0**	**-53.6**	**-27.0**
Capital account (net)	-0.1	—	—
Direct investment from abroad .	—	—	0.2
Other investment assets . .	15.3	45.8	35.4
Other investment liabilities . .	-1.6	18.1	3.1
Net errors and omissions . .	-2.4	-29.7	-13.0
Overall balance . . .	**10.2**	**-19.5**	**-1.2**

Source: IMF, *International Financial Statistics*.

External Trade

PRINCIPAL COMMODITIES (distribution by SITC, US $ '000)

Imports c.i.f.	1991	1992	1993
Food and live animals . .	22,675	19,706	20,312
Cereals and cereal preparations .	14,424	12,520	13,341
Wheat meal and flour of wheat and meslin	6,453	3,904	3,859
Flour of wheat or meslin .	6,445	3,835	3,859
Cereal preparations, etc. . .	6,447	7,116	7,480
Malt (incl. malt flour) . .	6,290	6,962	7,365
Crude materials (inedible) except fuels	8,081	4,915	5,478
Mineral fuels, lubricants, etc. . .	31,183	27,992	25,387
Petroleum, petroleum products, etc.	31,044	27,888	25,346
Refined petroleum products .	29,603	27,248	24,538
Motor spirit (gasoline) and other light oils .	12,511	10,570	8,630
Gas oils	9,893	8,966	7,993

Imports c.i.f. — *continued*	1991	1992	1993
Chemicals and related products	33,890	32,475	28,807
Medicinal and pharmaceutical products	10,289	11,554	8,523
Manufactured fertilizers . . .	3,228	4,865	4,562
Artificial resins, plastic materials, etc.	4,774	4,721	5,401
Disinfectants, insecticides, fungicides, weed-killers, etc., for retail sale	5,809	3,581	2,785
Insecticides	5,713	3,451	2,635
Basic manufactures . .	52,433	48,948	42,868
Rubber manufactures . .	6,641	5,383	7,077
Rubber tyres, tubes, etc. .	5,334	4,059	5,215
Paper, paperboard and manufactures . . .	6,062	5,777	5,556
Non-metallic mineral manufactures	13,512	12,898	9,445
Lime, cement, etc. . .	11,093	10,896	7,145
Cement	10,481	10,226	6,820
Machinery and transport equipment . . .	70,144	63,206	43,603
General industrial machinery, equipment and parts . .	29,926	23,147	20,484
Electrical machinery, apparatus and appliances . . .	12,351	14,437	3,894
Road vehicles and parts (excl. tyres, engines and electrical parts)	26,388	23,999	18,265
Passenger motor cars (excl. buses)	9,687	8,202	5,350
Motor vehicles for the transport of goods or materials . .	9,557	7,530	5,984
Parts and accessories for cars, buses, lorries, etc. . .	4,326	5,543	4,194
Miscellaneous manufactured articles . . .	12,105	16,798	8,188
Photographic apparatus, optical goods, watches and clocks . .	6,725	10,154	4,182
Special transactions and commodities not classified according to kind . .	14,291	13,406	19,877
Total (incl. others) . . .	247,087	229,508	204,525

Source: UN, *International Trade Statistics Yearbook.*

1994 (US $ million): *Imports c.i.f.*: Capital goods 53.3; Intermediate goods 82.9 (Petroleum products 27.6); Consumption goods 87.3 (Food 30.0); Total 223.5.
1995 (US $ million): *Imports c.i.f.*: Capital goods 62.8; Intermediate goods 87.2 (Petroleum products 24.8); Consumption goods 82.9 (Food 28.8); Total 232.9.
1996 (US $ million): *Imports c.i.f.*: Capital goods 31.2; Intermediate goods 55.3 (Petroleum products 17.3); Consumption goods 36.8 (Food 10.9); Total 123.3.
1997 (US $ million): *Imports c.i.f.*: Capital goods 31.7; Intermediate goods 46.9 (Petroleum products 13.6); Consumption goods 44.0 (Food 11.2); Total 122.6.
1998 (US $ million): *Imports c.i.f.*: Capital goods 46.2; Intermediate goods 60.5 (Petroleum products 18.5); Consumption goods 50.2 (Food 14.4); Total 156.9.
1999 (estimates, US $ million): *Imports c.i.f.*: Capital goods 30.0; Intermediate goods 50.2 (Petroleum products 20.3); Consumption goods 37.4 (Food 10.0); Total 117.6.
Source: IMF, *Burundi: Statistical Annex* (April 2000).

Exports f.o.b.	1997	1998	1999
Food and live animals . .	86,094	62,933	53,761
Coffee, tea, cocoa and spices . .	85,583	62,015	52,836
Coffee (incl. husks and skins)	76,567	51,048	41,953
Tea	9,015	10,967	10,883
Total (incl. others) . . .	87,320	63,950	54,956

Source: Banque de la République du Burundi.

PRINCIPAL TRADING PARTNERS

Imports c.i.f. (US $ '000)	1997	1998	1999
Belgium	22,358	30,254	19,851
China, People's Repub. . .	2,812	6,403	3,961
France	11,645	14,217	5,980
Germany	8,042	9,585	5,901
Italy	4,220	4,811	3,423
Japan	7,567	5,989	3,677
Kenya	5,305	8,784	6,199
Netherlands	5,234	4,656	2,246
Tanzania	3,057	3,113	5,118
United Arab Emirates . .	5,445	5,224	3,909
United Kingdom	2,041	2,314	2,511
USA	2,281	2,339	2,557
Zambia	6,761	12,530	6,734
Zimbabwe	2,806	1,562	2,208
Total (incl. others) . . .	122,745	156,944	117,658

Exports (million Burundian Francs)	1997	1998	1999
Belgium-Luxembourg . . .	4,929.3	2,624.8	995.5
France	37.3	17.8	358.1
Germany	6,579.5	2,968.8	1,520.9
United Kingdom	8,305.7	8,125.9	10,278.9
Total (incl. others) . . .	30,767.2	28,634.8	30,970.8

Source: Banque de la République du Burundi.

Transport

ROAD TRAFFIC (estimates, '000 motor vehicles in use)

	1992	1993	1994
Passenger cars	17.5	18.5	17.5
Commercial vehicles . . .	11.8	12.3	10.2

Source: UN, *Statistical Yearbook.*

LAKE TRAFFIC (Bujumbura—'000 metric tons)

	1997	1998	1999
Goods:			
Arrivals	70.9	123.1	142.5
Departures	28.1	28.1	28.2

Source: Banque de la République du Burundi.

CIVIL AVIATION (traffic on scheduled services)

	1995	1996	1997
Passengers carried ('000) . . .	9	9	12
Passenger-km (million) . . .	2	2	8

Source: UN, *Statistical Yearbook.*

Tourism

TOURIST ARRIVALS BY REGION*

	1996	1997	1998
Africa	13,004	5,011	7,394
Americas	1,660	639	1,092
Asia	2,213	852	1,218
Europe	10,514	4,051	5,700
Total	27,391	10,553	15,404

* Including Burundian nationals residing abroad.

Tourism receipts (US $ million): 1 in 1995; 1 in 1996; 1 in 1997.

Source: World Tourism Organization, *Yearbook of Tourism Statistics.*

Communications Media

	1995	1996	1997
Radio receivers ('000 in use) . .	410	425	440
Television receivers ('000 in use) .	12	20	25
Telephones ('000 main lines in use)	17	15	16
Telefax stations (number in use) .	3,000	4,000	n.a.
Mobile cellular telephones (subscribers)	564	561	619
Daily newspapers:			
Number	1	1	n.a.
Circulation ('000 copies) . .	20	20	n.a.

Sources: UNESCO, *Statistical Yearbook,* and UN, *Statistical Yearbook.*

Education

(1992/93, unless otherwise indicated)

	Teachers	Students		
		Males	Females	Total
Pre-primary*	49	1,220	1,161	2,381
Primary	10,400	358,180	292,906	651,086
Secondary:				
General . . . . }	2,060 {	28,706	17,675	46,381
Teacher-training . . . }		1,237	1,233	2,470
Vocational . . .	502	4,170	2,692	6,862
Higher	556	3,129	1,127	4,256

* Figures refer to 1988/89.

Primary (1995/96): Institutions 1,501; Teachers 10,316; Students 518,144 (males 283,516; females 234,628).

Source: UNESCO, *Statistical Yearbook.*

1996 (students): *Primary* 453,746; *Secondary (General)* 56,887; *Secondary (Teacher-training and Vocational)* 5,712; *Higher* 4,379 (Source: IMF, *Burundi: Statistical Annex* (February 1999)).

Directory

The Constitution

The Constitution was promulgated on 13 March 1992 and provided for the establishment of a plural political system. The Constitution seeks to guarantee human rights and basic freedoms for all citizens, together with the freedom of the press. Executive powers are vested in the President, who (under normal circumstances—see below) is elected directly, by universal adult suffrage, for a five-year term, renewable only once. Statutory power is shared with the Prime Minister, who appoints a Council of Ministers. Legislative power is exercised by a National Assembly, whose members are elected directly, by universal adult suffrage, for a five-year renewable mandate. In September 1994 a Convention of Government was agreed among the country's major political parties. The Convention, which defines the terms of government for a four-year transitional period, provides for the establishment of a National Security Council whose members include the President, the Prime Minister and the Ministers of State with responsibility for External Affairs, Interior and Public Security, and National Defence. The Convention was incorporated into the Constitution on 22 September 1994. However, the Convention disintegrated in July 1996, prompting the military coup which returned Maj. Pierre Buyoya to power.

On 6 June 1998 a Transitional Constitution was promulgated. It combined elements of the 1992 Constitution and the terms of office introduced by Buyoya in 1996, and provided for the enlargement of the National Assembly from 81 to 121 seats and the creation of two vice-presidencies to replace the post of Prime Minister.

The Government

HEAD OF STATE

President: Maj. PIERRE BUYOYA (assumed power 25 July 1996).

COUNCIL OF MINISTERS
(April 2001)

Vice-President responsible for Political and Administrative Affairs: FRÉDÉRIQUE BAVUGINYUMVIRA.

Vice-President responsible for Economic and Social Affairs: MATHIAS SINAMENYE.

Minister of External Relations and Co-operation: SÉVÉRIN NTAHOMVUKIYE.

Minister of the Interior and Public Security: Col ASCENSION TWAGIRAMUNGU.

Minister of Justice: TÉRENCE SINUNGURUZA.

Minister of National Defence: Col CYRILLE NDAYIRUKIYE.

Minister of Development, Planning and Reconstruction: LÉON NIMBONA.

Minister of Communal Development and Handicrafts: DENIS NSHIMIRIMANA.

Minister of Relocation and Resettlement of Displaced and Repatriated Persons: PASCAL NKURUNZIZA.

Minister of the Peace Process: AMBROISE NIYONSABA.

Minister of Territorial Development and the Environment: JEAN-PACIFIQUE NSENGIYUMVA.

Minister of Agriculture and Livestock: SALVATOR NTIHABOSE.

Minister of Labour, the Public Service and Professional Training: EMMANUEL TUNGAMWESE.

Minister of Finance: CHARLES NIHANGAZA.

Minister of Commerce, Industry and Tourism: JOSEPH NTANYOTORA.

Minister of Education: PROSPER MPAWENAYO.

Minister of Social Action and Women's Affairs: ROMAINE NDORIMANA.

Minister of Culture, Youth and Sport: GÉRARD NYAMWIZA.

Minister of Public Health: Dr STANISLAS NTAHOBARI.

Minister of Information and Government Spokesman: Dr LUC RUKINGAMA.

Minister of Public Works and Housing: GASPARD NTIRAMPEBA.

Minister of Transport, Posts and Telecommunications: CYPRIEN MBONIGABA.

Minister of Energy and Mines: BERNARD BARANDEREKA.

Minister of Human Rights, Institutional Reforms and Relations with the National Assembly: EUGÈNE NINDORERA.

There are also two Secretaries of State.

MINISTRIES

Office of the President: Bujumbura; tel. 226063.

Ministry of Agriculture and Livestock: Bujumbura; tel. 222087.

Ministry of Commerce, Industry and Tourism: BP 492, Bujumbura; tel. 225330; fax 225595.

Ministry of Communal Development: Bujumbura.

Ministry of Culture, Youth and Sport: Bujumbura; tel. 226822.

Ministry of Development, Planning and Reconstruction: BP 1830, Bujumbura; tel. 223988.

Ministry of Education: Bujumbura.

Ministry of Energy and Mines: BP 745, Bujumbura; tel. 225909; fax 223337.

Ministry of External Relations and Co-operation: Bujumbura; tel. 222150.

Ministry of Finance: BP 1830, Bujumbura; tel. 225142; fax 223128.

Ministry of Human Rights, Institutional Reforms and Relations with the National Assembly: Bujumbura.

Ministry of Information: BP 2870, Bujumbura.

Ministry of the Interior and Public Security: Bujumbura.

Ministry of Justice: Bujumbura; tel. 222148.

Ministry of Labour, the Public Service and Professional Training: BP 1480, Bujumbura; tel. 225645; fax 228715; e-mail mtpe@cbinf.com; internet www.burundi.gov.bi/appofre.htm.

Ministry of National Defence: Bujumbura.

Ministry of the Peace Process: Bujumbura.

Ministry of Public Health: Bujumbura.

Ministry of Public Works and Housing: BP 1860, Bujumbura; tel. 225645; fax 226840; e-mail mtpe@cbinf.com; internet www.burundi.gov.bi/appoffre.htm.

Ministry of Relocation and Resettlement of Displaced and Repatriated Persons: Bujumbura.

Ministry of Social Action and Women's Affairs: Bujumbura; tel. 225039.

Ministry of Territorial Development and the Environment: Bujumbura.

Ministry of Transport, Posts and Telecommunications: BP 2000, Bujumbura; tel. 222923; fax 226900.

President and Legislature

PRESIDENT

On 13 January 1994 Cyprien Ntaryamira, a member of FRODEBU, was elected President by 78 of the 79 votes cast by the National Assembly. Following Ntaryamira's death in April 1994, the Speaker of the National Assembly, Sylvestre Ntibantunganya, assumed the presidency for an interim, three-month period (subsequently extended for a further three months), in accordance with the Constitution. Ntibantunganya was subsequently appointed to the presidency for a four-year transitional term, by broad consensus in accordance with the Convention of Government adopted in September 1994. In July 1996 Ntibantunganya was deposed by a military coup and replaced by Maj. Pierre Buyoya.

NATIONAL ASSEMBLY*

Speaker: Léonce Ngendakumana (FRODEBU).

Legislative Elections, 29 June 1993

Party	Votes cast	% of votes cast	Seats
FRODEBU	1,532,107	71.04	65
UPRONA	462,324	21.44	16
RPB	35,932	1.67	—
PRP	29,966	1.39	—
RADDES	26,631	1.23	—
PP	24,372	1.13	—
Independents	853	0.04	—
Invalid votes	44,474	2.06	—
Total	2,156,659	100.00	81

* The National Assembly was suspended following the July 1996 coup, but was reconvened in October. Under the Transitional Constitution promulgated in June 1998, the membership of the National Assembly was enlarged from 81 to 121 members in order to incorporate representatives of smaller parties and the civilian population. The composition of the new National Assembly, which was inaugurated on 18 July, was as follows: FRODEBU controlled 65 seats, UPRONA 16, other political parties 13 seats (although four remained vacant, owing to internal party problems) and civilians 27 seats.

Political Organizations

Political parties are required to demonstrate firm commitment to national unity, and impartiality with regard to ethnic or regional origin, gender and religion, in order to receive legal recognition. The principal political associations participating in the peace negotiations (see Recent History) comprised a grouping of 10 Tutsi parties (G10) and seven Hutu organizations (G7).

Alliance burundaise-africaine pour le salut (ABASA): Bujumbura; f. 1993; Tutsi; Leader Serge Mukamarakiza.

Alliance nationale pour les droits et le développement economique (ANADDE): Bujumbura; f. 1992; Tutsi; Leader Patrice Nsababaganwa.

AV–Intware (Alliance of the Brave): Bujumbura: f. 1993; Tutsi; Leader André Nkundikije.

Convergence nationale pour la paix et la réconciliation (CNPR): Bujumbura; f. Oct. 1999; alliance comprising Union pour le progrès national, a faction of Front pour la démocratie au Burundi and several Tutsi parties; Pres. Augustin Nzojibwami.

Forum démocratique (FODE): Bujumbura; f. Nov. 1999; Leader Deogratias Baburifato.

Front pour la démocratie au Burundi (FRODEBU): Bujumbura; f. 1992; split in June 1999; Hutu; Chair. Jean Minani; Sec.-Gen. Domitien Ndayizeye.

Inkinzo y'Ijambo Ry'abarundi (Inkinzo) (Guarantor of Freedom of Speech in Burundi): Bujumbura; f. 1993; Tutsi; Pres. Dr Alphonse Rugambarara.

Parti indépendant des travailleurs (PIT): Bujumbura; f. 1993; Tutsi; Leader Etienne Nyahoza.

Parti libéral (PL): Bujumbura; f. 1992; Hutu; Leader Gaetan Nikombaye.

Parti du peuple (PP): Bujumbura; f. 1992; Hutu; Leader Shadraik Niyonkuru.

Parti pour la réconciliation du peuple (PRP): Bujumbura; f. 1992; Tutsi; Leader Mathias Hitimana.

Parti pour le redressement national (PARENA): Bujumbura; f. 1994; Leader Jean-Baptiste Bagaza; Sec.-Gen. Rémy Nkengurutse.

Parti social démocrate (PSD): Bujumbura; f. 1993; Tutsi; Leader Godefroid Hakizimana.

Rassemblement pour la démocratie et le développement économique et social (RADDES): Bujumbura; f. 1992; Tutsi; Chair. Joseph Nzeyzimana.

Rassemblement pour le peuple du Burundi (RPB): Bujumbura; f. 1992; Hutu; Leader Balthazar Bigirimana.

Solidarité pour la defénce des minorités (SOJEDEM): Bujumbura.

Union pour le progrès national (UPRONA): BP 1810, Bujumbura; tel. 225028; f. 1958; following the 1961 elections, the numerous small parties which had been defeated merged with UPRONA, which became the sole legal political party in 1966; party activities were suspended following the coup of Sept. 1987, but resumed in 1989; Chair. Charles Mukasi; in Oct. 1999 moderate mems of the cen. cttee who opposed Mukasi's rejection of the Arusha talks elected Dr Luc Rukingama as a rival Chair.

The exclusion of political organizations advocating 'tribalism, divisionalism or violence' and the requirement that party leaderships be equally representative of Hutu and Tutsi ethnic groups have been opposed by some externally-based opposition parties. These include the **Parti de libération du peuple hutu (PALIPEHUTU,** f. 1980 and based in Tanzania), which seeks to advance the interests of the Hutu ethnic group. An armed dissident wing of PALIPE-HUTU, known as the **Forces nationales de libération (FNL),** led by Kabora Khossan, is based in southern Rwanda. Another grouping representing the interests of Hutu extremists, the **Conseil national pour la défense de la démocratie (CNDD)** is led by Léonard Nyangoma (e-mail cndd_bur@usa.net). The 30,000-strong armed wing of the CNDD, the **Force pour la défence de la démocratie (FDD),** rebelled against the political leadership of the CNDD in 1998 and was led by its Commander-in-Chief, Jean-Bosco Ndayikengurukiye.

Diplomatic Representation

EMBASSIES IN BURUNDI

Belgium: 10 blvd de la Liberté, BP 1920, Bujumbura; tel. 223676; fax 223171; e-mail bujumbura@diplobel.org; Ambassador: Jan Mouton.

China, People's Republic: 675 sur la Parcelle, BP 2550, Bujumbura; tel. 224307; fax 213735; Ambassador: Shi Tongning.

Egypt: 31 ave de la Liberté, BP 1520, Bujumbura; tel. 223161; Ambassador: Muhammad Mousa.

France: 60 ave de l'Uprona, BP 1740, Bujumbura; tel. 226767; fax 221793; Ambassador: Christian Daziano.

Germany: 22 rue 18 septembre, BP 480, Bujumbura; tel. 226412; Ambassador: Dr Bernd Morast.

Holy See: 46 chaussée Prince Louis-Rwagasore, BP 1068, Bujumbura (Apostolic Nunciature); tel. 222326; fax 223176; Apostolic Nuncio: Most Rev. Emil Paul Tscherrig, Titular Archbishop of Voli.

Korea, Democratic People's Republic: BP 1620, Bujumbura; tel. 222881; Ambassador: Pae Sok Jun.

Russia: 78 blvd de l'UPRONA, BP 1034, Bujumbura; tel. 226098; fax 222984; Ambassador: Igor S. Liakin-Frolov.

Rwanda: 24 ave du Zaïre, BP 400, Bujumbura; tel. 223140; Ambassador: Sylvestre Uwibajije.

Tanzania: BP 1653, Bujumbura; Ambassador: Anthony Nyakyi.

USA: ave des Etats-Unis, BP 1720, Bujumbura; tel. 223454; fax 222926; Ambassador: Mary Carlin Yates.

Judicial System

Constitutional Court: Bujumbura.

Supreme Court: BP 1460, Bujumbura; tel. 222571; fax 222148. Court of final instance; four divisions: ordinary, cassation, constitutional and administrative.

Courts of Appeal: Bujumbura, Gitega and Ngozi.

Tribunals of First Instance: There are 17 provincial tribunals and 123 smaller resident tribunals in other areas.

Tribunal of Trade: Bujumbura.

Tribunals of Labour: Bujumbura and Gitega.

Administrative Courts: Bujumbura and Gitega.

Religion

More than 65% of the population are Christians, the majority of whom (an estimated 61%) are Roman Catholics. Anglicans number about 60,000. There are about 200,000 other Protestant adherents, of whom about 160,000 are Pentecostalists. Fewer than 40% of the population adhere to traditional beliefs, which include the worship of the God 'Imana'. About 1% of the population are Muslims. The Bahá'í Faith is also active in Burundi.

CHRISTIANITY

Conseil National des Eglises protestantes du Burundi (CNEB): BP 17, Bujumbura; tel. 224216; fax 227941; f. 1970; five mem. churches; Pres. Rt. Rev. Jean Nduwayo (Anglican Bishop of Gitega); Gen. Sec. Rev. Osias Habingabwa.

The Anglican Communion

The Church of the Province of Burundi, established in 1992, comprises five dioceses.

Archbishop of Burundi and Bishop of Buye: Most Rev. SAMUEL NDAYISENGA, BP 94, Ngozi; fax 302317.

Provincial Secretary: Rev. PASCAL BIGIRIMANA, BP 2098, Bujumbura; tel. 224389; fax 229129; e-mail eebprov@cbinf.com.

The Roman Catholic Church

Burundi comprises one archdiocese and six dioceses. At 31 December 1998 there were an estimated 3,763,923 adherents, equivalent to 62.6% of the total population.

Bishops' Conference: Conférence des Evêques Catholiques du Burundi, 5 blvd de l'UPRONA, BP 1390, Bujumbura; tel. 223263; fax 223270; e-mail cecab@cbinf.com; f. 1980; Pres. Most Rev. SIMON NTAMWANA, Archbishop of Gitega.

Archbishop of Gitega: Most Rev. SIMON NTAMWANA, Archevêché, BP 118, Gitega; tel. 402160; fax 402620.

Other Christian Churches

Union of Baptist Churches of Burundi: Rubura, DS 117, Bujumbura 1; Pres. PAUL BARUHENAMWO.

Other denominations active in the country include the Evangelical Christian Brotherhood of Burundi, the Free Methodist Church of Burundi and the United Methodist Church of Burundi.

BAHÁ'Í FAITH

National Spiritual Assembly: BP 1578, Bujumbura.

The Press

NEWSPAPERS

Burundi chrétien: BP 232, Bujumbura; Roman Catholic weekly; French.

Le Renouveau du Burundi: Ministry of Information, BP 2870, Bujumbura; f. 1978; publ. by UPRONA; daily; French; circ. 20,000; Dir JEAN NZEYIMANA.

Ubumwe: BP 1400, Bujumbura; tel. 223929; f. 1971; weekly; Kirundi; circ. 20,000.

PERIODICALS

Au Coeur de l'Afrique: Association des conférences des ordinaires du Rwanda et Burundi, BP 1390, Bujumbura; fax 223027; e-mail cnid@cbinf.com; bimonthly; education; circ. 1,000.

Bulletin économique et financier: BP 482, Bujumbura; bi-monthly.

Bulletin mensuel: Banque de la République du Burundi, Service des études, BP 705, Bujumbura; tel. 225142; monthly.

Bulletin officiel du Burundi: Bujumbura; monthly.

Le Burundi en Images: BP 1400, Bujumbura; f. 1979; monthly.

Culture et Sociétés: BP 1400, Bujumbura; f. 1978; quarterly.

Ndongozi Y'uburundi: Catholic Mission, BP 690, Bujumbura; tel. 222762; fax 228907; fortnightly; Kirundi.

Revue administration et juridique: Association d'études administratives et juridiques du Burundi, BP 1613, Bujumbura; quarterly; French.

PRESS ASSOCIATION

Burundian Association of Journalists (BAJ): Bujumbura; Pres. FRANÇOIS SENDAZIRASA.

NEWS AGENCY

Agence burundaise de Presse (ABP): ave Nicolas Mayugi, BP 2870, Bujumbura; tel. 213083; fax (2) 22282; e-mail abp@cbinf.com; internet cni.cbinf.com/abp.htm; f. 1975; publ. daily bulletin.

Publishers

BURSTA: BP 1908, Bujumbura; tel. 231796; fax 232842; f. 1986; Dir RICHARD KASHIRAHAMWE.

Editions Intore: 14 ave Patrice Emery Lumumba, BP 2524, Bujumbura; tel. 223499; f. 1992; philosophy, history, journalism, literature, social sciences; Dir Dr ANDRÉ BIRABUZA.

GRAVIMPORT: BP 156, Bujumbura; tel. 222285; fax 226953.

IMPARUDI: ave du 18 septembre 3, BP 3010, Bujumbura; tel. 223125; fax 222572; f. 1982; Dir THÉONESTE MUTAMBUKA.

Imprimerie la Licorne: 29 ave de la Mission, BP 2942, Bujumbura; tel. 223503; fax 227225; f. 1991.

Imprimerie MAHI: BP 673, Bujumbura.

MICROBU: BP 645, Bujumbura.

Imprimerie Moderne: BP 2555, Bujumbura.

Imprimerie du Parti: BP 1810, Bujumbura.

Les Presses Lavigerie: 5 ave de l'UPRONA, BP 1640, Bujumbura; tel. 222368; fax 220318.

Régie de Productions Pédagogiques: BP 3118, Bujumbura II; tel. 226111; fax 222631; f. 1984; school textbooks; Dir LÉONARD BIZONGWAKO.

SASCO: BP 204, Bujumbura.

Government Publishing House

Imprimerie nationale du Burundi (INABU): BP 991, Bujumbura; tel. 224046; fax 225399; f. 1978; Dir NICOLAS NIJIMBERE.

Broadcasting and Communications

TELECOMMUNICATIONS

Direction générale des transports, postes et télécommunications: BP 2390, Bujumbura; tel. 225422; fax 226900; govt telecommunications authority; Dir-Gen. APOLLINAIRE NDAYIZEYE.

Office nationale des télécommunications (ONATEL): BP 60, Bujumbura; tel. 223196; fax 226917; service provider; privatization pending; Dir-Gen. Lt-Col NESTOR MISIGARO.

Téléphonie Cellulaire du Burundi (TELECEL): Bujumbura; 40% govt-owned; mobile telephone service provider.

BROADCASTING

Radio

Radio Umwizero/Radio Hope: BP 5314, Bujumbura; tel. 217068; e-mail umwizero@cbinf.com; f. 1996; EU-funded, private station promoting national reconciliation, peace and development projects; broadcasts nine hours daily in Kirundi, Swahili and French; Dir. HUBERT VIEILLE.

Voix de la Révolution/La Radiodiffusion et Télévision Nationale du Burundi (RTNB): BP 1900, Bujumbura; tel. 223742; fax 226547; e-mail rtnb@cbinf.com; f. 1960; govt-controlled; daily radio broadcasts in Kirundi, Swahili, French and English; Dir-Gen. INNOCENT MUHOZI; Dir (Radio) EMMANUEL NZEYIMANA; Dir (Television) DAVID HICUBURUMAI.

Television

Voix de la Révolution/La Radiodiffusion et Télévision Nationale du Burundi (RTNB): BP 1900, Bujumbura; tel. 223742; fax 226547; f. 1960; govt-controlled; television service in Kirundi, Swahili, French and English; Dir (Television) CLÉMENT KIRAHAGAZWI.

Finance

(cap. = capital; res = reserves; dep. = deposits; m. = million; brs = branches; amounts in Burundian francs)

BANKING

Central Bank

Banque de la République du Burundi (BRB): BP 705, Bujumbura; tel. 225142; fax 223128; e-mail brb@cbinf.com; f. 1964 as Banque du Royaume du Burundi; state-owned; bank of issue; cap. and res 12,164.8m., dep. 13,032.5m. (Dec. 1998); Gov. GRÉGOIRE BANYIYEZAKO; Vice-Gov. CYPRIEN SINZOBAHAMVYA; 2 brs.

Commercial Banks

Banque Burundaise pour le Commerce et l'Investissement SARL (BBCI): blvd du Peuple Murundi, BP 2320, Bujumbura; tel. 223328; fax 223339; f. 1988; cap. and res 507.4m., total assets 3,451.0m. (Dec. 1998); Pres. ZACHARIE GASABANYA; Vice-Pres. CLÔTILDE NIZIGAMA.

Banque Commerciale du Burundi SARL (BANCOBU): 84 chaussée Prince Louis-Rwagasore, BP 990, Bujumbura; tel. 222317; fax 221018; e-mail bancobu@cbinf.com; f. 1988 by merger; cap. and res 2,914.6m., total assets 27,155.4m. (Sept. 1999); Pres. N. BARUTWANAYO; Dir-Gen. LIBÈRE NDABAKWAJE; 6 brs.

Banque de Commerce et de Développement (BCD): ave de Grèce, BP 2020, Bujumbura;; tel. 210950; fax 210952; e-mail bcd@cbinf.com; f. 1999; cap. and res 1,016.0m., total assets 5,024.7m. (June 1999); Pres. FRANÇOIS BUTOKE; Man. Dir ANTOINE NDUWAYO.

Banque de Crédit de Bujumbura SMei: ave Patrice Emery Lumumba, BP 300, Bujumbura; tel. 222091; fax 223007; f. 1964; cap. and res 3,282.4m., total assets 22,546.8m. (Dec. 1998); Pres. CHARLES NIHANGAZA; Man. ATHANASE GAHUNGU; 6 brs.

Banque de Gestion et de Financement: 1 blvd de la Liberté, BP 1035, Bujumbura; tel. 221352; fax 221351; e-mail bgf@cbinf.com; f. 1992; cap. and res 760.1m., total assets 3,847.8m. (Dec. 1998); Pres. DIDACE NZOHABONAYO; Dir-Gen. MATHIAS NDIKUMANA.

Banque Populaire du Burundi (BPB): 10 ave du 18 Septembre, BP 1780, Bujumbura; tel. 221257; fax 221256; e-mail bpb@cbinf.com; internet www.cbinf.com; f. 1992; cap. and res 834.0m., dep. 5,546.6m. (Dec. 1999); Pres. THÉODORE KAMWENUBUSA; Dir-Gen. D. BUKOBERO.

Interbank Burundi SARL: 15 ave de l'Industrie, BP 2970, Bujumbura; tel. 220629; fax 220461; e-mail interb@cbinf.com; cap. and res 1,623.6m., total assets 14,545.7m. (Dec. 1997); Pres. GEORGES COUCOULIS.

Development Bank

Banque Nationale pour le Développement Economique SARL (BNDE): 3 ave du Marché, BP 1620, Bujumbura; tel. 222888; fax 223775; e-mail bnde@cbinf.com; f. 1966; cap. and res 2,112m., total assets 12,533m. (Dec. 1998); Pres. and Dir-Gen. GASPARD SINDIYIGAYA; Gen. Sec. FRANÇOIS BARWENDERE.

Co-operative Bank

Banque Coopérative d'Epargne et de Crédit Mutuel (BCM): BP 1340, Bujumbura; operating licence granted in April 1995; Vice-Pres. JULIEN MUSARAGANY.

INSURANCE

Burundi Insurance Corporation (BICOR): BP 2377, Bujumbura.

Société d'Assurances du Burundi (SOCABU): 14–18 rue de l'Amitié, BP 2440, Bujumbura; tel. 226520; fax 226803; e-mail socabu@cbinf.com; f. 1977; partly state-owned; cap. 180m.; Dir-Gen. (Admin.) SÉRAPHINE RUVAHAFI.

Société Générale d'Assurances et de Réassurance (SOGEAR): BP 2432, Bujumbura; tel. 222345; fax 229338; f. 1991; Pres. BENOIT NDORIMANA; Dir-Gen. L. SAUSSEZ.

Union Commerciale d'Assurances et de Réassurance (UCAR): BP 3012, Bujumbura; tel. 223638; fax 223695; f. 1986; cap. 150m.; Chair. Lt-Col EDOUARD NZAMBIMANA; Man. Dir HENRY TARMO.

Trade and Industry

GOVERNMENT AGENCIES

Agences de Promotion des Echanges Extérieurs (APEE): Bujumbura; promotes and supervises foreign exchanges.

Office des Cultures Industrielles du Burundi (Office du Café du Burundi) (OCIBU): BP 450, Bujumbura; tel. 224017; fax 225532; e-mail ocibu3@cbinf.com; f. 1964; supervises coffee plantations and coffee exports; Dir-Gen. BARTHÉLÉMY NIYIKIZA.

Office du Thé du Burundi (OTB): 52 blvd de l'UPRONA, Bujumbura; tel. 224228; fax 224657; f. 1979 supervises production and marketing of tea; Man. Dir SALVATORE NIMUBONA.

Office National du Commerce (ONC): Bujumbura; f. 1973; supervises international commercial operations between the Govt of Burundi and other states or private orgs; also organizes the import of essential materials; subsidiary offices in each province.

Office National du Logement (ONL): BP 2480, Bujumbura; tel. 226074; f. 1974 to supervise housing construction.

DEVELOPMENT ORGANIZATIONS

Compagnie de Gérance du Coton (COGERCO): BP 2571, Bujumbura; tel. 222208; fax 224370; e-mail cogerco@cbinf.com; f. 1947; promotion and development of cotton industry; Pres. SÉBASTIEN NDAVIZEYE; Dir FRANÇOIS KABURA.

Fonds de Développement Communal (FDC): Bujumbura; funds local development.

Institut des Sciences Agronomiques du Burundi (ISABU): BP 795, Bujumbura; tel. 223390; fax 225798; e-mail isabu@cni.cbinf.com.; f. 1962 for the scientific development of agriculture and livestock.

Office National de la Tourbe (ONATOUR): BP 2360, Bujumbura; tel. 226480; fax 226709; f. 1977 to promote the exploitation of peat deposits.

Société d'Exploitation du Quinquina du Burundi (SOKINABU): 16 blvd Mwezi Gisabo, BP 1783, Bujumbura; tel. 223469; f. 1975 to develop and exploit cinchona trees, the source of quinine; Dir RAPHAËL REMEZO.

Société de Financement et Développement de l'Habitat Urbain (SOFIDHAR): Bujumbura; urban development.

Société Régionale de Développement de l'IMBO (SRDI): Bujumbura; promotes development of IMBO region.

Société Régionale de Développement de Kayanza (SRD KAYANZA): Kayanza; promotes development of Kayanza region.

Société Régionale de Développement de Kirimiro (SRD KIRIMIRO): Bujumbura; promotes development of Kirimiro region.

Société Régionale de Développement de Kirundo (SRD KIRUNDO): Bujumbura; promotes development of Kirundo region.

Société Régionale de Développement de Mumirwa (SRD MUMIRWA): Bujumbura; promotes development of Mumirwa region.

Société Régionale de Développement de Rumonge (SRD RUMONGE): Bujumbura; promotes development of Rumonge region.

Société Sucrière du Mosso (SOSUMO): BP 835, Bujumbura; tel. 275002; fax 275004; e-mail sosumo@cbinf.com; f. 1982 to develop and manage sugar cane plantations; Pres. BONAVENTURE KIDWINGIRA; Dir-Gen. (Admin.) NUMÉRIEN BARUTWANAYO.

CHAMBER OF COMMERCE

Chambre de Commerce, d'Industrie, d'Agriculture et d'Artisanat du Burundi: BP 313, Bujumbura; tel. 222280; fax 227895; f. 1923; Pres. DIDACE NZOHABONAYO; Sec.-Gen. CYRILLE SINGEJEJE; 130 mems.

UTILITIES

Régie de Distribution d'Eau et d'Electricité (REGIDESCO): Bujumbura; state-owned distributor of water and electricity services.

MAJOR COMPANY

Complexe Textile de Bujumbura (COTEBU): BP 2899, Bujumbura; tel. 231900; fax 231750; textile mfrs; Dirs JEAN KABURA, DÉO NDABANEZE, ANICET NDAYISABA.

TRADE UNIONS

Confédération des Syndicats du Burundi (COSIBU): Bujumbura; Chair. Dr PIERRE-CLAVIER HAJAYANDI.

Union des Travailleurs du Burundi (UTB): BP 1340, Bujumbura; tel. 223884; f. 1967 by merger of all existing unions; closely allied with UPRONA; sole authorized trade union prior to 1994, with 18 affiliated nat. professional feds; Sec.-Gen. MARIUS RURAHENYE.

Transport

RAILWAYS

There are no railways in Burundi. Plans have been under consideration since 1987 for the construction of a line passing through Uganda, Rwanda and Burundi, to connect with the Kigoma–Dar es Salaam line in Tanzania. This rail link would relieve Burundi's isolated trade position.

ROADS

In 1996 Burundi had a total of 14,480 km of roads, of which 1,950 km were national highways and 2,530 km secondary roads. A new crossing of the Ruzizi River, the Bridge of Concord (Burundi's longest bridge), was opened in early 1992.

Office des Transports en Commun (OTRACO): Bujumbura; 100% govt-owned; operates public transport.

INLAND WATERWAYS

Bujumbura is the principal port for both passenger and freight traffic on Lake Tanganyika, and the greater part of Burundi's external trade is dependent on the shipping services between Bujumbura and lake ports in Tanzania, Zambia and the Democratic Republic of the Congo.

Exploitation du Port de Bujumbura (EPB): Bujumbura; 43% state-owned; controls Bujumbura port.

CIVIL AVIATION

The international airport at Bujumbura is equipped to take large jet-engined aircraft.

Air Burundi: 40 ave du Commerce, BP 2460, Bujumbura; tel. 224609; fax 223452; e-mail airbdi@cbinf.com; f. 1971 as Société de Transports Aériens du Burundi; state-owned; operates charter and scheduled passenger services to destinations throughout central Africa; CEO Col ANTOINE GATOTO; Dir C. KAGARI.

Tourism

Tourism is relatively undeveloped. The annual total of tourist arrivals declined from 125,000 in 1991 (with receipts amounting to US \$4m.) to only 10,553 in 1997 (receipts \$1m.); total arrivals recovered somewhat, to reach 15,404 in 1998. However, the worsening security situation in 1999 proved a continuing impediment to tourism.

CAMBODIA

Introductory Survey

Location, Climate, Language, Religion, Flag, Capital

The Kingdom of Cambodia occupies part of the Indo-Chinese peninsula in South-East Asia. It is bordered by Thailand and Laos to the north, by Viet Nam to the east and by the Gulf of Thailand to the south. The climate is tropical and humid. There is a rainy season from June to November, with the heaviest rainfall in September. The temperature is generally between 20°C and 36°C (68°F to 97°F), with March and April generally the hottest months; and the annual average temperature in Phnom-Penh is 27°C (81°F). The official language is Khmer, which is spoken by everybody except the Vietnamese and Chinese minorities. The state religion is Theravada Buddhism. The national flag (proportions 3 by 2) consists of three horizontal stripes, of dark blue, red (half the depth) and dark blue, with a stylized representation (in white) of the temple of Angkor Wat, with three towers, in the centre. The capital is Phnom-Penh.

Recent History

The Kingdom of Cambodia became a French protectorate in the 19th century and was incorporated into French Indo-China. In April 1941 Norodom Sihanouk, then aged 18, succeeded his grandfather as King. In May 1947 he promulgated a Constitution which provided for a bicameral Parliament, including an elected National Assembly. Cambodia became an Associate State of the French Union in November 1949 and attained independence on 9 November 1953. In order to become a political leader, King Sihanouk abdicated in March 1955 in favour of his father, Norodom Suramarit, and became known as Prince Sihanouk. He founded a mass movement, the Sangkum Reastr Niyum (Popular Socialist Community), which won all the seats in elections to the National Assembly in 1955, 1958, 1962 and 1966. King Suramarit died in April 1960, and in June Parliament elected Prince Sihanouk as Head of State. Prince Sihanouk's Government developed good relations with the People's Republic of China and with North Viet Nam, but it was highly critical of the USA's role in Asia. From 1964, however, the Government was confronted by an underground Marxist insurgency movement, the Khmers Rouges, while it also became increasingly difficult to isolate Cambodia from the war in Viet Nam.

In March 1970 Prince Sihanouk was deposed by a right-wing coup, led by the Prime Minister, Lt-Gen. (later Marshal) Lon Nol. The new Government pledged itself to the removal of foreign communist forces and appealed to the USA for military aid. Sihanouk went into exile and formed the Royal Government of National Union of Cambodia (GRUNC), supported by the Khmers Rouges. Sihanoukists and the Khmers Rouges formed the National United Front of Cambodia (FUNC). Their combined forces, aided by South Viet Nam's National Liberation Front and North Vietnamese troops, posed a serious threat to the new regime, but in October 1970 Marshal Lon Nol proclaimed the Khmer Republic. In June 1972 he was elected the first President. During 1973 several foreign states recognized GRUNC as the rightful government of Cambodia. In 1974 the republican regime's control was limited to a few urban enclaves, besieged by GRUNC forces, mainly Khmers Rouges, who gained control of Phnom-Penh on 17 April 1975. Prince Sihanouk became Head of State again but did not return from exile until September. The country was subjected to a pre-arranged programme of radical social deconstruction immediately after the Khmers Rouges' assumption of power; towns were largely evacuated, and their inhabitants forced to work in rural areas. During the following three years an estimated 1.7m. people died as a result of ill-treatment, hunger, disease and executions.

A new Constitution, promulgated in January 1976, renamed the country Democratic Kampuchea, and established a republican form of government; elections for a 250-member People's Representative Assembly were held in March 1976. In April Prince Sihanouk resigned as Head of State, and GRUNC was dissolved. The Assembly elected Khieu Samphan, formerly Deputy Prime Minister, to be President of the State Presidium (Head of State). The little-known Pol Pot (formerly Saloth Sar) became Prime Minister. In September 1977 it was officially disclosed that the ruling organization was the Communist Party of Kampuchea (CPK), with Pol Pot as the Secretary of its Central Committee.

After 1975 close links with the People's Republic of China developed, while relations with Viet Nam deteriorated. In 1978, following a two-year campaign of raids across the Vietnamese border by the Khmers Rouges, the Vietnamese army launched a series of offensives into Kampuchean territory. In December the establishment of the Kampuchean National United Front for National Salvation (KNUFNS, renamed Kampuchean United Front for National Construction and Defence—KUFNCD—in December 1981, and United Front for the Construction and Defence of the Kampuchean Fatherland—UFCDKF—in 1989), a communist-led movement opposed to Pol Pot and supported by Viet Nam, was announced. Later in the month, Viet Nam invaded Kampuchea, supported by the KNUFNS.

On 7 January 1979 Phnom-Penh was captured by Vietnamese forces, and three days later the People's Republic of Kampuchea was proclaimed. A People's Revolutionary Council was established, with Heng Samrin, leader of the KNUFNS, as President. It pledged to restore freedom of movement, freedom of association and of religion, and to restore the family unit. The CPK was replaced as the governing party by the Kampuchean People's Revolutionary Party (KPRP). The Khmer Rouge forces, however, remained active in the western provinces, near the border with Thailand, and conducted sporadic guerrilla activities elsewhere in the country. Several groups opposing both the Khmers Rouges and the Heng Samrin regime were established, including the Khmer People's National Liberation Front (KPNLF), headed by a former Prime Minister, Son Sann. In July, claiming that Pol Pot's regime had been responsible for 3m. deaths, the KPRP administration sentenced Pol Pot and his former Minister of Foreign Affairs, Ieng Sary, to death *in absentia*. In January 1980 Khieu Samphan assumed the premiership of the deposed Khmer Rouge regime, while Pol Pot became Commander-in-Chief of the armed forces. In 1981 the CPK was reportedly dissolved and was replaced by the Party of Democratic Kampuchea (PDK).

During the first few years of the KPRP regime Viet Nam launched regular offensives on the Thai-Kampuchean border against the united armed forces of Democratic Kampuchea, the coalition Government-in-exile of anti-Vietnamese resistance groups formed in June 1982. As a result of the fighting, and the prevalence of starvation and disease, thousands of Kampuchean refugees crossed the border into Thailand; in turn, a large number of Vietnamese citizens subsequently settled on Kampuchean territory. The coalition Government-in-exile, of which Prince Sihanouk became President, Khieu Samphan (PDK) Vice-President and Son Sann (KPLNF) Prime Minister, received the support of the People's Republic of China and of member states of the Association of South East Asian Nations (ASEAN—see p. 134), whilst retaining the Kampuchean seat in the UN General Assembly.

In the mid-1980s an increasingly conciliatory attitude between the USSR and the People's Republic of China led to a number of diplomatic exchanges, aimed at reconciling the coalition Government-in-exile with the Government in Phnom-Penh, led by the General Secretary of the KPRP, Heng Samrin. Largely, however, because of mistrust of the PDK (due to Pol Pot's continuing influence), the Heng Samrin Government rejected peace proposals from ASEAN and the coalition Government-in-exile in 1985 and 1986. In September 1987 the Government of the People's Republic of China stated that it would accept a Kampuchean 'government of national reconciliation' under Prince Sihanouk, but that the presence of Vietnamese troops in Kampuchea remained a major obstacle. In the same month the USSR also declared that it was 'prepared to facilitate a political settlement' in Kampuchea. In October, after having announced its readiness to conduct negotiations with some PDK leaders (but not Pol Pot), the Heng Samrin Government offered Prince Sihanouk a government post and issued a set of peace proposals which included the complete withdrawal of Vietnamese troops, internationally-observed elections and the formation of a coalition government. In December 1987 Prince Sihanouk and Hun Sen, the Chairman of the Council of Ministers in the Heng Samrin Government, met in France for private discussions for the first time since the invasion by Viet Nam. The meeting ended in a joint communiqué, stating that the conflict was to be settled politically by negotiations among all the Kampuchean parties, and that any resulting agreement should be guaranteed by an international conference.

Under increasing pressure from the USSR and the People's Republic of China, the four Kampuchean factions participated in a series of 'informal meetings', held in Indonesia, which were also attended by representatives of Viet Nam, Laos and the six ASEAN members. At the first of these meetings, in July 1988, Viet Nam, under pressure from the USSR, advanced its deadline for a complete withdrawal of its troops from Kampuchea to late 1989. In April 1989 the National Assembly in Phnom-Penh ratified several constitutional amendments, whereby the name of the country was changed to the State of Cambodia, a new national flag, emblem and anthem were introduced, Buddhism was reinstated as the state religion, and the death penalty was abolished. In July 1989 the Paris International Conference on Cambodia (PICC) met for the first time. The PICC agreed to send a UN reconnaissance party to Cambodia to study the prospects for a cease-fire and the installation of a peace-keeping force.

The withdrawal of Vietnamese forces, completed on schedule in September 1989, was followed by renewed offensives into Cambodia by the resistance forces, particularly the PDK. In November, following substantial military gains by the PDK, the UN General Assembly adopted a resolution supporting the formation of an interim government in Cambodia which would include members of the PDK, but which retained a clause, introduced in 1988, relating to past atrocities committed by the organization. The resolution also cast doubt on the Vietnamese withdrawal (since it had not been monitored by the UN) and, in reference to the alleged presence of 1m. Vietnamese settlers in Cambodia, condemned 'demographic changes' imposed in the country. An Australian peace initiative was unanimously approved by the five permanent members of the UN Security Council in January 1990. In February Prince Sihanouk declared that the coalition Government-in-exile would henceforth be known as the National Government of Cambodia.

In July 1990 the USA withdrew its support for the National Government of Cambodia's occupation of Cambodia's seat at the UN. In August the UN Security Council endorsed the framework for a comprehensive settlement in Cambodia. The agreement provided for UN supervision of an interim government, military arrangements for the transitional period, free elections and guarantees for the future neutrality of Cambodia. A special representative of the Secretary-General of the UN was to control the proposed United Nations Transitional Authority in Cambodia (UNTAC). The UN would also assume control of the Ministries of Foreign Affairs, National Defence, Finance, the Interior and Information, Press and Culture. China and the USSR pledged to cease supplies of military equipment to their respective allies, the PDK and the Phnom-Penh Government.

At a fourth 'informal meeting' in Jakarta in September 1990 the four Cambodian factions accepted the UN proposals. They also agreed to the formation of the Supreme National Council (SNC), with six representatives from the Phnom-Penh Government and six from the National Government of Cambodia. SNC decisions were to be taken by consensus, effectively allowing each faction the power of veto, and the SNC was to occupy the Cambodian seat at the UN General Assembly. Prince Sihanouk was subsequently elected to the chairmanship of the SNC (a position in which he would have final arbitration if a consensus could not be reached), and resigned as leader of the resistance coalition and as President of the National Government of Cambodia (positions to which Son Sann was appointed). Agreement was also reached on the four factions reducing their armed forces by 70% and the remaining 30% being placed in cantonments under UN supervision; the introduction of a system of multi-party democracy; the Phnom-Penh Government abandoning its demand for references to genocide to be included in a draft plan; and the holding of elections to a constituent assembly which would subsequently become a legislative assembly comprising 120 seats.

Following the release of political prisoners by the Phnom-Penh Government in October 1991, including former 'reformist' associates of Hun Sen (who had been arrested in 1990 and replaced by supporters of the more conservative chairman of

the National Assembly, Chea Sim), a congress of the KPRP was convened at which the party changed its name to the Cambodian People's Party (CPP). The communist insignia was removed from its emblem, Heng Samrin was replaced as Chairman of the Central Committee (formerly the Politburo) by Chea Sim and Hun Sen was elected as Vice-Chairman.

On 23 October 1991 the four factions signed the UN peace accord in Paris, under the auspices of the PICC. UNTAC was expected to be in place by August 1992. As an interim measure, the mainly military UN Advance Mission in Cambodia (UNAMIC), comprising 300 men, was in place by the end of 1991. The peace-keeping operation was expected to be completed in 1993. The agreement also provided for the repatriation, under the supervision of the UN High Commissioner for Refugees, of the estimated 340,000 Cambodian refugees living in camps in Thailand. There were continuing fears that the PDK would, in an attempt to ensure electoral support, endeavour forcibly to repatriate refugees to areas of western Cambodia under their control.

In November 1991 Prince Sihanouk returned to Phnom-Penh, accompanied by Hun Sen. The CPP and the United National Front for an Independent, Neutral, Peaceful and Co-operative Cambodia (FUNCINPEC), led by Prince Sihanouk, subsequently formed an alliance and announced their intention to establish a coalition government. (The alliance was abandoned in December, in response to objections from the KPNLF and the PDK.) On 23 November the four factions endorsed the reinstatement of Prince Sihanouk as the Head of State of Cambodia, pending a presidential election in 1993. Political protest increased towards the end of 1991. An attack by demonstrators on Khieu Samphan on his return to Phnom-Penh in late November led senior PDK officials to flee to Bangkok where the SNC met and agreed that, henceforth, officials of the party would occupy the SNC headquarters in Phnom-Penh with members of UNAMIC. Further demonstrations took place in December and in January 1992 in protest against corruption and in support of human rights, during which the security forces killed several protesters. The authorities closed all schools and colleges in the capital, imposed a curfew and prohibited any unauthorized demonstrations. Later in January, the assassination of an official critical of the CPP and the attempted assassination of a prominent dissident, Oung Phan, further served to intimidate government critics. However, following an agreement with representatives of the UN Security Council, the Phnom-Penh Government released all remaining political prisoners between January and March 1992.

In early January 1992 the Japanese UN Under-Secretary-General for Disarmament Affairs, Yasushi Akashi, was appointed the UN Special Representative to Cambodia in charge of UNTAC. The UN Security Council expanded UNAMIC's mandate to include mine-clearing operations, and in late February authorized the dispatch of a 22,000-member peace-keeping force to Cambodia to establish UNTAC, at an estimated cost of nearly US $2,000m. In mid-March UNAMIC, whose efforts had been impeded by a lack of funds and personnel and the refusal of the PDK to allow free access to the zones it controlled, transferred responsibility for the implementation of the peace agreement to UNTAC.

The refugee repatriation programme which began in March 1992 was threatened by continued cease-fire violations. The fighting, concentrated in the central province of Kompong Thom, was widely believed to be an attempt by the PDK to delay implementation of the peace plan in order to make territorial gains and thereby increase its representation in the proposed National Assembly. In June the continued obduracy of the PDK disrupted the implementation of the second phase of the peace-keeping operation, which comprised the cantonment and disarmament of the four factions' forces. Although by mid-July about 12,000 troops from three of the factions had reported to the designated areas, the PDK intensified its violations of the cease-fire agreement, continued to deny the UN access to its zones, and failed to attend meetings on the implementation of the peace agreement. At the Ministerial Conference on the Rehabilitation and Reconstruction of Cambodia, which was convened in Tokyo in late June, the application of economic sanctions against the PDK was considered. Despite criticism from the People's Republic of China, the PDK reiterated demands that power be transferred from the Phnom-Penh Government to the SNC and that both the SNC and UNTAC should co-operate in ensuring that all Vietnamese forces had withdrawn from Cambodia. During August Akashi affirmed that the elections would proceed without the participation of the PDK if it continued to refuse to co-operate. The UN set a deadline for compliance of 15 November. By the end of November, however, no consensus had been reached, and the Security Council adopted a resolution condemning PDK obduracy. The Security Council approved an embargo on the supplies of petroleum products to the PDK and endorsed a ban on the export of timber (a principal source of income for the party) from 31 December. On the day the sanctions were adopted, however, the PDK announced the formation of a subsidiary party to contest the forthcoming elections, the Cambodian National Unity Party, led by Khieu Samphan and Son Sen.

In December 1992 the seizure of six members of the UN peace-keeping forces in PDK-controlled areas reflected a growing distrust of UNTAC by the PDK, which had previously alleged UN bias in favour of the Phnom-Penh Government. The slow progress of the peace initiative, coupled with the poor conduct of UN troops, resulted in widespread disaffection with UNTAC, and in the latter part of 1992 resentment towards ethnic Vietnamese intensified, largely as a result of PDK and, subsequently, KPLNF propaganda.

In January 1993 Prince Sihanouk announced that he would no longer co-operate with UNTAC, owing to the increasing level of violence against FUNCINPEC personnel; these attacks were widely attributed to the Phnom-Penh Government. Prince Sihanouk subsequently resumed co-operation after Akashi signed a directive establishing procedures for indicting and prosecuting alleged violators of human rights independently of the Phnom-Penh Government. The PDK continued to violate the terms of the cease-fire (and abducted further groups of UN troops seeking access to areas under its control), claiming that 2m. Vietnamese remained in Cambodia and that the SNC had not been empowered to administer the country prior to the elections.

By the final deadline at the end of January 1993 20 parties, excluding the PDK, had registered to contest the elections. The Phnom-Penh Government subsequently launched an offensive against the PDK in northern and western Cambodia, recovering much of the territory gained by the PDK since the signing of the peace agreement in October 1991. In early February 1993 Prince Sihanouk returned to Phnom-Penh from Beijing amidst intensifying politically-motivated violence. There were also continuing attacks by the PDK on ethnic Vietnamese, and, following several rural massacres, thousands of Vietnamese took refuge in Viet Nam. Despite the violence, UNTAC's voter registration campaign, which ended in February, had been extremely successful; 4.7m. Cambodians were registered, constituting about 97% of the estimated eligible electorate. The repatriation programme for refugees on the Thai border was also successfully concluded; 360,000 refugees had been returned to Cambodia on schedule by the end of April.

On 23–28 May 1993 about 90% of the electorate participated in the elections to the Constituent Assembly. The PDK offered support to the FUNCINPEC Party, in the hope of securing a role in government following the elections but, owing to the massive voter participation in the election, Prince Sihanouk abandoned his proposals for the inclusion of the PDK in a future Government. Early results from the election, indicating a FUNCINPEC victory, prompted CPP allegations of electoral irregularities. UNTAC, however, rejected CPP requests for fresh elections in at least four provinces. In early June, without prior consultation with the UN and disregarding the incomplete election results, Prince Sihanouk announced the formation of a new Government, with himself as Prime Minister and Prince Ranariddh and Hun Sen as joint Deputy Prime Ministers. The coalition was created and renounced within hours, owing to objections from Prince Ranariddh, who had not been consulted, and to suggestions by UN officials that it was tantamount to a coup. Two days later the official results of the election were released: the FUNCINPEC Party secured 58 seats with 46% of the votes, the CPP 51 seats with 38% of the votes, the Buddhist Liberal Democratic Party (BLDP, founded by the KPNLF) 10 seats (3%) and a breakaway faction from the FUNCINPEC Party, MOLINAKA (National Liberation Movement of Cambodia), one seat. Despite the UN's endorsement of the election as fair, the CPP refused to dissolve the State of Cambodia Government in Phnom-Penh and announced that certain eastern provinces were threatening to secede unless demands for an independent examination of the results were met. Prince Norodom Chakkrapong (a son of Prince Sihanouk who had been appointed to the Council of Ministers of the Phnom-Penh Government in December 1991) subsequently led a secessionist

movement in seven provinces in the east and north-east of the country, which was reportedly sanctioned by the CPP leadership in an attempt to secure a power-sharing agreement with the FUNCINPEC Party.

On 14 June 1993, at the inaugural session of the Constituent Assembly, Prince Sihanouk was proclaimed Head of State, and 'full and special' powers were conferred on him. The Assembly adopted a resolution declaring null and void the overthrow of Prince Sihanouk 23 years previously and recognizing him retroactively as Head of State of Cambodia during that period. The secessionist movement in the eastern provinces collapsed, and on the following day an agreement was reached on the formation of an interim government, with Hun Sen and Prince Ranariddh as Co-Chairmen of the Provisional National Government of Cambodia, pending the drawing up of a new constitution. Prince Chakkrapong returned to Phnom-Penh, where he was reconciled with Prince Sihanouk. A few days later the CPP officially recognized the results of the election.

The PDK had immediately accepted the results of the election and supported the formation of a coalition government, but continued to engage in military action to support its demands for inclusion in a future government. In July 1993 the PDK offered to incorporate its forces into the newly-formed Cambodian National Armed Forces (later restyled the Royal Cambodian Armed Forces), which had been created through the merger of the forces of the other three factions in June. PDK offensives escalated, however, after the party was denied a role in government, largely owing to US threats to withhold economic aid from Cambodia if the PDK were included prior to a renunciation of violence. In late August Cambodia's united armed forces initiated a successful offensive against PDK positions in north-western Cambodia. The Government rejected an appeal for urgent discussions by the PDK after government forces had captured PDK bases, insisting that the party surrender unconditionally the estimated 20% of Cambodian territory under its control. The PDK suffered from defections as disillusioned troops were offered the same rank in the Cambodian National Armed Forces under a government amnesty, which ended in January 1995.

On 21 September 1993 the Constituent Assembly adopted a new Constitution, which provided for an hereditary monarchy. On 24 September Prince Sihanouk promulgated the Constitution, thus terminating the mandate of UNTAC (whose personnel left the country by mid-November). The Constituent Assembly became the National Assembly, and Prince Sihanouk acceded to the throne of the new Kingdom of Cambodia. Chea Sim was re-elected Chairman of the National Assembly. Government ministers were to be chosen from parties represented in the National Assembly, thus precluding the involvement of the PDK. In October talks scheduled between the Cambodian Government and the PDK were postponed indefinitely, owing to the ill health of King Sihanouk, who was undergoing medical treatment in Beijing (Chea Sim assumed the position of acting Head of State while the King was out of the country). At the end of October the National Assembly approved the new Royal Government of Cambodia (previously endorsed by King Sihanouk), in which Prince Ranariddh was named First Prime Minister and Hun Sen Second Prime Minister. Between November 1993 and January 1994 initiatives to incorporate the PDK into the new Government failed, owing to objections from various parties. In May 1994 King Sihanouk threatened to stop negotiating with the PDK and the Government to end the fighting in the north-west of the country, which had reached a severity not witnessed since 1989, and forced the postponement of proposed peace talks in Pyongyang, the Democratic People's Republic of Korea. Following the failure of peace talks held in May and June 1994, the Government ordered the PDK to leave Phnom-Penh and closed the party's mission in the capital.

In July 1994 the Government claimed to have suppressed a coup attempt led by Prince Chakkrapong and Gen. Sin Song, a former Minister of National Security under the State of Cambodia. Following a personal appeal from King Sihanouk, Prince Chakkrapong, who protested his innocence, was exiled from Cambodia, while Gen. Sin Song was placed under arrest. (Gen. Sin Song escaped from prison in September and was captured by Thai authorities in November.) Hun Sen also suspected his rival, Sar Kheng, a Deputy Prime Minister and Minister of the Interior, of involvement in the alleged revolt. Sar Kheng was, however, protected by his powerful brother-in-law, Chea Sim. The coup attempt was also used by the increasingly divided Government as a pretext to suppress criticism of the regime.

Newspapers were closed, editors fined and imprisoned and in September an editor renowned as an outspoken critic of the Government was killed by unidentified assailants. Hun Sen continued to fear a possible coup attempt from rival CPP members, and in August the armed forces mistakenly opened fire on four tourists at a road block.

Despite King Sihanouk's continued advocacy of national reconciliation, in July 1994 legislation providing for the outlawing of the PDK was adopted by the National Assembly (whilst allowing for an immediate six-month amnesty for the lower ranks of the party). The proposed legislation was initially opposed by a group led by the Minister of Finance, Sam Rainsy and the Minister of Foreign Affairs, Prince Norodom Sirivudh but, following the inclusion of guarantees safeguarding civil liberties, the bill was approved. In response, the PDK announced the formation of a Provisional Government of National Unity and National Salvation of Cambodia (PGNUNSC), under the premiership of Khieu Samphan, which was to co-ordinate opposition to the Government in Phnom-Penh from its headquarters in Preah Vihear in the north of the country. In October Sam Rainsy, who was highly regarded by independent foreign observers, was dismissed as Minister of Finance, apparently owing to his efforts to combat high-level corruption. Prince Sirivudh subsequently resigned as Minister of Foreign Affairs in protest at Rainsy's removal, which also demonstrated the decline in King Sihanouk's political influence—Prince Ranariddh and Hun Sen had jointly proposed Rainsy's dismissal in March, but King Sihanouk had withheld his consent. Prince Sirivudh also criticized the FUNCINPEC Party, of which he was Secretary-General, for submitting too readily to CPP demands, as it became increasingly apparent that real power lay with the former communists.

In May 1995 Rainsy was expelled from the FUNCINPEC Party, following his continued criticism of corruption in the Government; and in April he was expelled from the National Assembly. This caused international disquiet and provoked criticism from human rights groups since there was no provision in the Constitution for such an expulsion. Rainsy, who refused to accept the decision, formed a new party, the Khmer Nation Party (KNP), which was officially launched in November. The Government declared the KNP illegal but refrained from action to disband it. Rainsy's expulsion from the National Assembly coincided with the adoption of the revised draft of a draconian press law, which imposed substantial fines and prison sentences for reporting issues affecting 'national security' or 'political stability'. Since these terms remained undefined, it was widely believed that the law would be used to stifle criticism of the Government. Chea Sim signed the bill into law in August, during King Sihanouk's absence from the country.

Politically-motivated violence, organized crime and drugs-trafficking all developed as serious problems in Cambodia. The situation was exacerbated by the inadequacies of law enforcement, the lack of any specific legislation to deter 'money-laundering' and endemic corruption among senior government officials and the armed forces. The security forces were increasingly accused both of criminal activity and of perpetrating violence against opponents of the Government. The restructuring of the ranks of the national police and the armed forces, which were completed in October and December 1995 respectively, had little impact on the situation. In October Prince Sirivudh was expelled from the National Assembly (and thus deprived of diplomatic immunity) and charged with conspiring to assassinate Hun Sen. Human rights groups declared that Prince Sirivudh, who protested his innocence, was a political prisoner. Under an agreement reached with King Sihanouk's intervention, Prince Sirivudh was allowed to go into exile in France in December on condition that he refrain from political activity. In January 1996 Prince Sirivudh was convicted and sentenced to 10 years' imprisonment *in absentia* on charges of criminal conspiracy and possession of unlicensed firearms.

In January 1996 the Government began to adopt repressive measures against the KNP, raiding the organization's headquarters and detaining some 150 supporters. In March Rainsy nominally merged the KNP with a defunct but still legally-registered party, in an attempt to gain legal status. However, in April the Government ordered all parties without parliamentary representation to close their offices (in an effort to prevent Rainsy from legalizing the KNP); in June KNP requests for permission to open a radio station were refused. Several KNP officials were assassinated in 1996, including, in May, the editor of a

newspaper that supported the KNP and had frequently criticized the two Prime Ministers.

In August 1996 the prominent PDK leader, Ieng Sary, together with two military divisions that controlled the significant PDK strongholds of Pailin and Malai, defected from the movement and negotiated a peace agreement with the Government. Ieng Sary subsequently denied responsibility for the atrocities committed during Pol Pot's regime, and was granted a royal amnesty in September, at the request of both Hun Sen and Prince Ranariddh. Following his defection, Ieng Sary formed a new political organization, the Democratic National United Movement (DNUM), while his supporters retained control of Pailin and Malai, despite efforts by troops loyal to the PDK leadership to recapture the region (where lucrative mineral and timber resources were situated). Former PDK troops (numbering about 4,000) were integrated into the national army in November. Ieng Sary's departure from the PDK precipitated further major defections, with an estimated 2,500 PDK troops transferring allegiance to the Government in October.

Throughout 1996 political instability increased, mainly as a result of the CPP's failure to fulfil power-sharing agreements at district level. In September the partial dissolution of the PDK increased tensions within the ruling coalition, as both the CPP and the FUNCINPEC Party attempted to attract former PDK troops. However, as the FUNCINPEC Party appeared more successful than the CPP at recruiting former PDK commanders and cadres, Hun Sen became concerned that the alliance between the royalists and the PDK as former resistance forces would be re-established. In February 1997 Prince Ranariddh sent a helicopter to Anlong Veng to negotiate with the central PDK faction. However, PDK members opposed to peace talks ambushed the helicopter, killing the majority of the Prince's emissaries. Meanwhile, the two Prime Ministers were stockpiling weapons, violations of human and civil rights were becoming increasingly prevalent, corruption was rampant, and labour unrest was widespread, as strikes were organized in both the public sector and the garment industry. King Sihanouk announced his concern for the welfare of the country and raised the possibility of his abdication. The potential involvement of the popular monarch in the forthcoming polls provoked a threat from Hun Sen to cancel both the local and national elections and to amend the Constitution to prohibit all members of the royal family from participating in politics, to guarantee the neutrality of the constitutional monarchy. In March 1997 Rainsy, who had increased his attacks against Hun Sen and the CPP-controlled judicial system and police force, led a demonstration outside the National Assembly. The meeting was attacked by assailants who threw four grenades, killing 19 and injuring more than 100 protesters in a presumed attempt to assassinate Rainsy. Rainsy accused Hun Sen of orchestrating the attack and expressed no confidence in the commission established to investigate the incident.

In April 1997 Ung Phan, a former CPP member who had joined the FUNCINPEC Party in the early 1990s, led a rebellion against the party leadership of Prince Ranariddh, with the support of Hun Sen. The National Assembly, which was due to adopt legislation pertaining to local and national elections scheduled for 1998, was unable to convene, as the FUNCINPEC Party refused to attend until its dissident members were expelled from the Assembly, whereas the CPP insisted on their retention. In June the dissident FUNCINPEC members organized a party congress and formed a rival FUNCINPEC Party, with Toan Chhay, the Governor of Siem Reap, as its chairman. Also in June Prince Sirivudh was prevented from returning to Cambodia, as he was refused permission to board flights to Cambodia in Hong Kong, owing to threats by Hun Sen, who had earlier refused to support a royal pardon for the Prince.

In May 1997, following negotiations with representatives of Prince Ranariddh, Khieu Samphan announced the creation of a new political party, the National Solidarity Party, which would support the National United Front (an alliance founded in February by Prince Ranariddh) at the next election. Prince Ranariddh declared that, if the notorious former leadership of the PDK were excluded, he would welcome such an alliance. Hun Sen, however, deemed the potential alliance to be a threat to the CPP and, following the seizure of a seven-ton shipment of weapons destined for Prince Ranariddh, accused the Prince of illegally importing weapons to arm PDK soldiers to create unrest. The PDK was divided over the issue of peace negotiations, with certain factions sympathetic to reconciliation with the FUNCINPEC Party, while others, notably that of Pol Pot, were opposed. Pol Pot therefore began a violent purge, ordering the death of Son Sen and also that of Ta Mok. Following the execution of Son Sen and his family, many PDK commanders rallied behind Ta Mok, and fighting erupted between the two factions. Pol Pot and his supporters fled into the jungle, with Khieu Samphan as a hostage, but were captured by Ta Mok's forces and returned to the PDK base at Anlong Veng, near the Thai border. In late July a US journalist, Nate Thayer, was invited by the PDK to Anlong Veng to witness the trial of Pol Pot. He was condemned by a 'people's court' for 'destroying national unity' and for the killing of Son Sen and his family. In October Thayer, who was the first journalist to see Pol Pot for 18 years, was permitted to interview the former leader, who denied that atrocities had occurred under his regime.

In June 1997 Prince Ranariddh announced in Phnom-Penh that Pol Pot was under arrest and that Khieu Samphan would surrender, but the statement was received with widespread scepticism, while Hun Sen condemned Ranariddh for his relations with the PDK. Hun Sen had demanded that Ranariddh choose between himself and Khieu as a partner in government. Tensions between Prince Ranariddh and Hun Sen increased, as FUNCINPEC military forces were strengthened. Hun Sen continued to warn that PDK defectors were massing in Phnom-Penh and there was crossfire between CPP and FUNCINPEC security units close to Ranariddh's residence. On 3 July, following several attempts by CPP troops to detect the presence of PDK soldiers in FUNCINPEC units, CPP forces disarmed a unit of Prince Ranariddh's bodyguards, on the grounds that they were allegedly PDK troops. On the following day Prince Ranariddh left the country. On 5 July (on which day Hun Sen returned from a holiday in Viet Nam) serious fighting erupted in Phnom-Penh, and on 6 July, the day on which Khieu Samphan had been scheduled to broadcast the PDK's agreement with the FUNCINPEC Party to end its resistance and rejoin the political system, Hun Sen appeared on television to demand Prince Ranariddh's arrest (on charges of negotiating with the PDK, introducing proscribed PDK troops into Phnom-Penh and secretly importing weapons to arm those forces) and to urge FUNCINPEC officials to select another leader. More than 24 hours of pillage then ensued, in which the airport and many shops and factories were raided and looted. The UN subsequently claimed that it had documentary evidence showing that at least 43 people, principally from the royalist army structure, had been murdered by forces loyal to Hun Sen after the events of 5–6 July. Many more FUNCINPEC and KNP officials, as well as many FUNCINPEC members of the legislature, fled the country. Despite assurances by Hun Sen of a full investigation, no one was arrested or charged for the killings.

King Sihanouk's appeals for both sides to travel to the People's Republic of China to negotiate a settlement were rejected by Hun Sen. Prince Ranariddh announced from Paris that a resistance movement was being organized in western Cambodia. Meanwhile, Hun Sen began negotiations with certain prominent members of the FUNCINPEC Party who remained in Phnom-Penh (the General Secretary, Loy Simchheang, the Co-Minister of the Interior, You Hockry, and the Minister of Defence, Tie Chamrat) in an effort to attain the two-thirds' majority of the National Assembly necessary for the investiture of a new government. By the end of July 1997 the National Assembly had reconvened, with 98 of the 120 deputies present, including 40 of the 58 FUNCINPEC deputies. Hun Sen protested to the international community that his actions did not constitute a *coup d'état*, as he had not abolished the Constitution or the monarchy and had not dissolved the Government or the National Assembly. He also declared that he was in favour of free elections in 1998. Despite these assurances, aid was temporarily suspended by the USA, Japan, Germany and later Australia. However, the UN refused to condemn Hun Sen by name, although it expressed a 'grave preoccupation' with the situation in Cambodia. King Sihanouk, who had been in the People's Republic of China since February, also insisted on remaining neutral and accepted that Chea Sim should continue to sign royal decrees in his absence. In August the National Assembly voted to remove Ranariddh's legal immunity (a warrant subsequently being issued for his arrest) and elected Ung Huot, the FUNCINPEC Minister of Foreign Affairs, to the post of First Prime Minister. The USA opposed his election as undemocratic, but Japan resumed its aid programme, and China also accepted Prince Ranariddh's replacement.

In July 1997 troops loyal to Prince Ranariddh, led by Gen. Nhiek Bunchhay (the former military Deputy Chief of Staff and a principal negotiator with the PDK), were swiftly forced into the north-west of the country by CPP troops. They regrouped near the Thai border in an effective alliance with PDK troops under Ta Mok. Prolonged fighting took place for control of the town of O'Smach, about 70 km west of Anlong Veng, which was the last base for the resistance coalition led by Prince Ranariddh, the Union of Cambodian Democrats. At the end of August the King arrived in Siem Reap on a mission of peace and was welcomed at the airport by Chea Sim, Hun Sen and Ung Huot. Hun Sen rejected another proposal from the King to act as a mediator in peace talks, insisting that Ranariddh had to be tried for his alleged crimes. At the end of October the King left the country but returned in early December.

In September 1997 Hun Sen announced a cabinet reorganization that effectively removed remaining supporters of Prince Ranariddh from the Government. However, in a secret ballot the National Assembly failed by 13 votes to approve the changes by the required two-thirds' majority. Hun Sen continued his efforts to encourage the return of all opposition representatives who had fled the country in July, except Ranariddh and Gen. Nhiek Bunchhay. In November Rainsy returned to Cambodia, whereupon he organized a peace march through Phnom-Penh, which was attended by several thousand supporters. In a conciliatory gesture in December, Hun Sen and Rainsy held a cordial meeting, at which they agreed to co-operate in the national interest.

In mid-December 1997 the National Assembly voted, for technical reasons, to postpone local and legislative elections from May until July 1998 and to increase the number of seats from 120 to 122, owing to Ieng Sary's decision in October 1997 to transfer nominal control of Pailin and Malai to the Government. At the beginning of February 1998 Rainsy withdrew the KNP from the electoral process in protest at the unlawful methods allegedly employed by Hun Sen, including the registration of a breakaway faction of the KNP bearing an identical title and logo and the fatal shooting in January of a KNP official and his daughter. Rainsy subsequently restyled the KNP the Sam Rainsy Party.

Hun Sen and Ranariddh agreed to the terms of a Japanese peace proposal in February 1998, which provided for the severance of Ranariddh's links with the PDK, the implementation of a ceasefire in the north-west (which came into effect on 27 February), a royal pardon for Ranariddh if he were convicted *in absentia* of the charges against him and his guaranteed safe return to participate in the general election. Ranariddh was convicted in March of illegally importing weapons and of conspiring with the proscribed PDK, and sentenced to 30 years' imprisonment and a fine of US $54m. for damage caused on 5–6 July. At the formal request of Hun Sen, Sihanouk granted Ranariddh a royal pardon, but no amnesty was accorded to Nhiek Bunchhay or Serei Kosal, the commanders of Ranariddh's troops in the north-west, who were found guilty on the same day. Ranariddh returned to Phnom-Penh at the end of March 1998, but the FUNCINPEC Party had been severely weakened by the killing of many of its senior personnel, the closure of its offices across the country and the defection of some principal officials, including Loy Simchheang and You Hockry.

In March 1998 two divisions of PDK troops mutinied against their leader, Ta Mok; further divisions rebelled in the following week, surrendering control of the PDK headquarters, Anlong Veng, to government troops. During the ensuing clashes thousands of civilians were evacuated to Thailand. Pol Pot died on 15 April, shortly after his comrades had offered to surrender him for trial by an international tribunal. It was later reported that he had committed suicide. Ta Mok announced that he was prepared to reach agreement with the Government but demanded autonomy for Anlong Veng. Sporadic clashes between the remnants of the PDK and government forces continued in late 1998. The grouping was practically defunct, however, by the end of the year, following further significant defections in October and December. In late December Nuon Chea (Pol Pot's former deputy) and Khieu Samphan defected to the Government, seeking sanctuary in Pailin, an area effectively controlled by Ieng Sary. In February 1999 a final 4,332 PDK troops surrendered to the Co-Ministers of National Defence in Anlong Veng. Ta Mok, however, remained in the border area.

The election campaign period was characterized by escalating political intimidation and violence. All demonstrations were banned, as was the dissemination of political information by private news media. Ranariddh and, more particularly, Rainsy (who did finally contest the election) sought to exploit traditional

Cambodian hatred of the Vietnamese. Hun Sen refused to campaign, but the ruling CPP dominated the National Election Committee, the Constitutional Council, the armed forces and the judiciary, as well as central and local government. However, the general election, which took place on 26 July 1998, was characterized by the UN-co-ordinated Joint International Observer Group as free and fair. Voting took place relatively peacefully, except for an attack on a polling station by PDK remnants, in which 10 people were killed. Ninety per cent of the 5,395,024 registered voters (representing 98% of the population of voting age) participated in the election, which was contested by 39 parties. Under a newly-introduced modified system of proportional representation that favoured larger parties, the CPP secured 64 seats (with 41.4% of the popular vote), the FUNCINPEC Party 43 seats (31.7%) and the Sam Rainsy Party 15 seats (14.3%). At an audience with the King at the end of July Hun Sen proposed a three-party coalition, but this was rejected by Ranariddh and Rainsy, who demanded a national recount, on the grounds of electoral fraud, and threatened to boycott the new National Assembly.

In August 1998 Rainsy was detained for questioning, following a grenade explosion at the Ministry of the Interior. Several thousand Cambodians took part in a demonstration in Phnom-Penh, organized by Sam Rainsy, to denounce electoral fraud and to demand the removal of Hun Sen. Despite a ruling by the Constitutional Court upholding the National Election Committee's decision to reject allegations of electoral fraud, the peaceful demonstration outside the National Assembly lasted for more than two weeks. Talks between the three principal parties failed to produce a resolution. On 8 September, however, following a grenade attack on a disused residence of Hun Sen, the protesters were violently dispersed by security forces, and Hun Sen ordered the arrest of Rainsy on charges of murder. The opposition accused Hun Sen of staging the incident in order to justify his suppression of the peaceful protest. Rainsy took refuge under the protection of the UN, and both Rainsy and Ranariddh abandoned claims for a recount. Sporadic violence continued, and Hun Sen announced that the FUNCINPEC Party and the Sam Rainsy Party would be expelled from the National Assembly if they failed to attend its inauguration on 24 September. Prior to the inauguration Hun Sen, Rainsy and Ranariddh met, under the chairmanship of Sihanouk, in Siem Reap Province, but failed to resolve the crisis. Tension was further heightened by a rocket-propelled grenade attack on a convoy of vehicles en route to the convening ceremony of the National Assembly. Hun Sen, who claimed to be the intended victim of the attack, issued retaliatory threats prompting Ranariddh and Rainsy to flee to Thailand. Following the failure of further negotiations in early October, a declaration was issued, stating that the present Government, which was due to leave office, would continue to administer the country until a new government was formed. The situation continued to deteriorate in October 1998 with the arrest, torture and execution of many opposition supporters. Human rights' groups estimated that more than 200 people had disappeared during September. Skirmishes took place on the Thai border between government forces and those loyal to Ranariddh in October, and sporadic clashes continued in early November.

Ranariddh agreed to return to Cambodia to attend a meeting with Hun Sen, under the auspices of King Sihanouk, from which Rainsy was excluded. On 13 November 1998 agreement was reached on the formation of a coalition Government, which would be supported by 107 of the 122 deputies, with Hun Sen as Prime Minister and Ranariddh as the Chairman of the National Assembly. The accord also provided for the creation of a Senate (to be presided over by Chea Sim), the reintegration of resistance soldiers into the armed forces, royal pardons for Gen. Nhiek Bunchhay and Serei Kosal, as well as Prince Sirivudh and Prince Chakkrapong, and restitution for property damaged during fighting in July 1997. On Rainsy's return to Phnom-Penh in November 1998, a large crowd of his supporters was violently dispersed by security forces. On 25 November the National Assembly convened, and Ranariddh was duly elected Chairman of the Assembly, with two CPP deputies. The new Royal Government was approved on 30 November and included Co-Ministers for the influential Ministries of Defence and of the Interior, while the CPP controlled the foreign affairs and finance portfolios, and the FUNCINPEC Party assumed responsibility for information and health. Rainsy became the official leader of the opposition. The Senate, which was empowered to scrutinize and amend bills passed by the National Assembly, held its inaugural session on 25 March 1999. Representation in the 61-member upper chamber was proportionate to elected strength in the National Assembly; the CPP was allocated 31 seats, the FUNCINPEC Party 21 and the Sam Rainsy Party seven, whilst a further two members were appointed by the King. Chea Sim was duly elected as Chairman, and Nhiek Bunchhay became one of the three Deputy Chairmen.

Reform of the Royal Cambodian Armed Forces began in January 1999 with Hun Sen's resignation as Commander-in-Chief, to demonstrate the neutrality of the armed forces. He was replaced by the former Chief of the General Staff, Gen. Ke Kimyan. By the end of September 15,551 'ghost' troops (soldiers who had been killed or had deserted, but whose pay continued to be collected by senior officers) had been removed from the army payroll. Plans announced in November 1999 provided for the demobilization of 11,500 troops in 2000, followed by a further 10,000 in both 2001 and 2002. The coalition Government also expressed its commitment to administrative and environmental reforms.

In March 1999 Ta Mok was captured near the Thai border and placed in detention. In April Kang Kek Ieu, known as Duch, the director of the Tuol Sleng detention centre where 16,000 detainees had been tortured and executed during the Democratic Kampuchean regime, was located by a journalist; he was arrested in May and charged with belonging to a proscribed organization. These detentions intensified domestic and international pressure for the establishment of a tribunal to try former Khmer Rouge leaders for atrocities committed during 1975–79. Three jurists, commissioned by the UN to assess the evidence against the leaders of the PDK, recommended that 20–30 Khmer Rouge leaders be brought to trial and reparations be made to their victims. The Cambodian Government, however, in the interests of national reconciliation, was reluctant to indict former Khmer Rouge leaders who had surrendered to the Government, for fear that former PDK members might revert to armed insurrection. The Cambodian Government and the UN also differed as to the composition and structure of a tribunal. The UN doubted Cambodia's ability to conduct a trial in accordance with international standards and thus favoured an international tribunal, whereas Hun Sen claimed that this would constitute an infringement of Cambodian sovereignty and insisted that any trials take place within the existing Cambodian court structure. In April, however, Hun Sen conceded that UN-appointed foreign judges could take part in a trial in Cambodia, although he still favoured the nomination of a Cambodian prosecutor. Cambodia submitted draft legislation recommending a majority of Cambodian judges to the UN for approval in December. Hun Sen announced in January 2000 that the trials would begin on 17 April, the 25th anniversary of Pol Pot seizing control of Phnom-Penh, with or without UN support. The Government approved draft legislation establishing a court in January, but the UN finally issued its rejection of the draft in February, stating that the legislation did not conform to international standards. In December 1999 the office of the UN Secretary-General's special envoy to Cambodia was closed at the request of the Cambodian Government, despite UN pleas that it remain open for a further year. The Cambodian Government had, however, agreed in August to extend the mandate of the representative of the UN High Commissioner for Human Rights based in Cambodia, Thomas Hammarberg. Following the delays in establishing a tribunal, in August 1999 the National Assembly approved legislation extending pre-trial detention for those accused of genocide and crimes against humanity from six months to three years, effectively postponing the trials of Ta Mok and Duch. In September both Ta Mok and Duch were formally charged with genocide under a 1979 decree of the People's Republic of Kampuchea; the pair remained in government custody, awaiting trial, in early 2001. In June 1999, following pressure from Australia and the United Kingdom, Gen. Nuon Paet, a senior Khmer Rouge commander, was convicted in connection with the abduction and murder of three foreign tourists (Australian, British and French nationals) in July 1994 and sentenced to life imprisonment. Gen. Nuon Paet's sentence was upheld by the appeals court in September 2000. In July Col Chhouk Rin, one of a number of other Khmer Rouge leaders charged in connection with the murder of the three tourists, was freed after it was announced that he was covered by the amnesty granted to Khmer Rouge cadres who surrendered to the Cambodian Government. However, following formal protests from the Australian, British and French Governments, the

Cambodian Government announced that it was to appeal against the court's decision.

In April 2000 US Senator John Kerry announced that, following extensive negotiations between the Cambodian Government and the UN, an agreement had been reached on a formula for the establishment of a tribunal to try former Khmer Rouge leaders for atrocities committed under the regime. The details of a draft accord on the establishment of the tribunal were finalized in July, whereupon the requisite legislation was to be submitted to the Cambodian National Assembly. In early August the Sam Rainsy Party presented a petition containing the signatures of all the party's 15 deputies in the lower chamber and of its seven senators, expressing unreserved support for the Government's agreement with the UN. Despite the opposition's support for the legislation, however, significant delays ensued, and in September the UN Secretary-General, Kofi Annan, expressed impatience at the slow pace of progress. The National Assembly finally approved the legislation on 2 January 2001. However, the Assembly specified that only those individuals deemed 'most responsible' for the atrocities would face the tribunal, thereby implicitly exempting significant numbers of middle- and lower-ranking former Khmer Rouge officials from prosecution. The legislation was approved by the Cambodian Senate later the same month. Before the tribunal could be established, it remained for the legislation to be passed by the Constitutional Council and signed by King Sihanouk (although it was not anticipated that the legislation would be rejected at either of these stages). Moreover, it was speculated that the preparation of prosecutions could take up to a further two years. On 7 January a number of people were injured in clashes in Phnom-Penh between thousands of demonstrators marking the 22nd anniversary of the overthrow of the Khmer Rouge regime and a group protesting at the subsequent Vietnamese occupation of Cambodia and alleged Vietnamese influence on the Cambodian Government.

In late November 2000 dozens of armed men launched an attack on official buildings in Phnom-Penh. At least seven of the gunmen were killed and a number of others injured in the raid, which government officials initially attributed to unspecified 'terrorists'; however, some of those involved alleged that they had been brought to Phnom-Penh under false pretences and forced to carry weapons. Two days after the violence, the leader of the Cambodian Freedom Fighters, US citizen Chhun Yasith, issued a statement in Bangkok claiming responsibility for the attack on behalf of his organization and alleging that the principal intention of the Cambodian Freedom Fighters had been to disrupt the forthcoming visit to Cambodia of the President of Viet Nam, Tran Duc Luong (which had originally been scheduled for late November, but which was then postponed indefinitely). Forty-seven people, including two members of the Sam Rainsy Party, were subsequently reported to have been charged with terrorism in connection with the attack. The arrest of two of its members provoked an angry response from the opposition party, and some observers expressed concerns that the Government was attempting to discredit the political opposition by connecting it with the violence.

International relations were severely affected by the events of 5–6 July 1997. The USA, Germany and Japan suspended all but humanitarian assistance, and in October 1998 the US House of Representatives adopted a resolution accusing Hun Sen of genocide. One of the most serious international consequences of the events of 5–6 July 1997 was the decision by ASEAN to postpone indefinitely Cambodia's admission to the grouping. Cambodia had attended an ASEAN meeting in July 1995 with official observer status, had its application for membership accepted in July 1996 and had been due to join in late July 1997. Hun Sen was angered by ASEAN's decision and initially rejected the grouping's attempts to negotiate a diplomatic solution to the Cambodian crisis. However, at the end of July Hun Sen invited ASEAN to mediate in the dispute and held talks with the grouping in early August. At the end of August the Prime Minister of Singapore announced that Cambodia would not be considered for admission to ASEAN until after elections had been held. Prior to the ASEAN summit meeting in Hanoi in December 1998, despite the formation of a Cambodian coalition Government in November, Singapore, Thailand and the Philippines remained opposed to Cambodia's immediate accession to the organization. However, in the event, the host country, Viet Nam, announced that Cambodia had been accepted as the 10th member of ASEAN, although the formal admission was to take place at a later unspecified date. Cambodia duly acceded to

ASEAN on 30 April 1999. A further significant consequence of the events of 5–6 July 1997 was the decision of the UN Accreditation Committee to leave Cambodia's seat at the UN vacant. However, following the formation of a coalition Government in November 1998, Cambodia regained its seat at the UN in December.

Relations between Cambodia and the People's Republic of China (which had formerly supported the PDK) had already improved during the mid-1990s. However, following the events of 5–6 July 1997, Hun Sen deliberately aligned himself with China, possibly as a reaction to the disapproval of ASEAN, which considered itself to be a counterbalance to the influence of China in the region. China continued to provide political and limited financial support, and in November 2000 President Jiang Zemin paid a two-day official visit to Cambodia, the first by a Chinese Head of State in more than 35 years. On the first day of Jiang's visit, China defended its support of the Khmers Rouges during the 1970s, claiming that its limited assistance had been intended to help maintain Cambodia's independence from foreign powers.

In January 1994 Chuan Leekpai undertook the first-ever official visit to Cambodia by a Thai Prime Minister. Relations between Cambodia and Thailand had been strained by the Thai armed forces' unauthorized links with the PDK (which controlled illicit trade in gems and timber along the Thai border) and by Cambodian allegations of Thai involvement in the July 1994 coup attempt, but improved in September 1995 when the two countries signed an agreement to establish a joint border commission. Thailand remained neutral following the events of 5–6 July 1997, but extended humanitarian assistance to the estimated 35,000 refugees who crossed into Thailand to avoid the fighting in the north-west of Cambodia. The Thai Deputy Minister of Foreign Affairs, Sukhumbhand Paribatra, was instrumental in securing the coalition agreement between the CPP and the FUNCINPEC Party in November 1998.

In August 1994 the National Assembly adopted an immigration bill which prompted concern that it might be used to enforce the mass expulsion of ethnic Vietnamese from Cambodia, given that the legislation had no provision for the definition of Cambodian citizenship. In January 1995 Prince Ranariddh held talks in Viet Nam on improving bilateral relations, following an increase in tension over the issue of ethnic Vietnamese in Cambodia. The Vietnamese President made an official state visit to Cambodia in August. In early 1996 Cambodia accused Viet Nam of encroaching on disputed border territory, but in April discussions in Phnom-Penh resulted in an agreement providing for the settlement of all border issues through further negotiations.

In April 1995 Cambodia, Thailand, Viet Nam and Laos signed an agreement providing for the establishment of the Mekong River Commission (see p. 309), which was to co-ordinate the sustainable development of the resources of the Lower Mekong River Basin. In October 1999 the leaders of Cambodia, Laos and Viet Nam convened in the Laotian capital for their first 'unofficial' Indo-Chinese summit meeting.

Government

The Kingdom of Cambodia is a constitutional monarchy. The monarch is the Head of State and is selected by the Throne Council from among descendants of three royal lines. Legislative power is vested in the 122-member National Assembly, the lower chamber, which is elected for a term of five years by universal adult suffrage, and the 61-member Senate, the upper chamber, whose members are appointed by political parties in proportion to their representation in the National Assembly. Executive power is held by the Cabinet (the Royal Government of Cambodia), headed by the Prime Minister, who is appointed by the King at the recommendation of the Chairman of the National Assembly from among the representatives of the winning party.

For local administration the Kingdom of Cambodia is divided into provinces, municipalities, districts, khan, khum and sangkat.

Defence

In August 2000 the total strength of the Royal Cambodian Armed Forces was estimated to be 140,000, comprising an army of 90,000, a navy of 3,000, an air force of 2,000 and provincial forces of about 45,000. A system of conscription was in force, for those aged between 18 and 35, for five years. However, conscription has not been implemented since 1993. In 2000 government expenditure on defence was budgeted at an estimated 460,000m. riels.

Economic Affairs

In 1998, according to the World Bank, Cambodia's gross national product (GNP), measured at average 1996–98 prices, was US $2,945m., equivalent to $260 per head (or $1,246 per head on an international purchasing-power parity basis). During 1990–98, it was estimated, GNP per head increased, in real terms, at an average annual rate of 2.0%. Over the same period, the population increased at an average rate of 3.3% per year. In 1999 GNP was estimated at $3,000m., equivalent to $260 per head. Cambodia's gross domestic product (GDP) increased, in real terms, at an average annual rate of 4.8% during 1990–99; GDP increased by 7.0% in 1996 but by only 2.0% in 1997 and 1998. In 1999, according to the IMF, GDP increased by 4.5%.

Agriculture (including forestry and fishing) contributed 34.4% of GDP in 1999. In 1998 the sector engaged 76.8% of the economically active population, but remained extremely vulnerable to adverse weather conditions, this problem being compounded by inadequate rural infrastructure and a lack of farm inputs such as fertilizers. However, production of the staple crop, rice, rose in 1999, partly because of an increase in the total cultivated area, owing to the reclamation of previously land-mined fields. In October 1999 Cambodia announced its intention to export rice for the first time since 1970, owing to an estimated rice surplus of 140,000 metric tons. Other principal crops include cassava, maize, sugar cane and bananas. Timber and rubber are the two principal export commodities. The forestry sector accounted for only an estimated 2.7% of GDP in 1998, as reserves continued to be depleted and reafforestation remained inadequate. The sector lacked a coherent policy, with poorly-observed periodic logging and export bans subject to ad hoc exemptions. However, from 1999 it was hoped that following agreements with the IMF and multilateral donors for conditional loans, Cambodia would take measures to enforce bans and forestry regulations imposed in conjunction with the aid donors. In February 2000 it was reported that 20 government officials had been suspended from office for involvement in illegal logging. The fishing sector was also adversely affected by deforestation, which caused reductions in freshwater fishing catches, owing to the silting up of lakes and rivers. According to estimates published by the IMF, the GDP of the fishing sector declined at an average annual rate of 4.1% in 1990–98 and contributed only an estimated 2.5% of GDP in 1998. According to the IMF, agricultural GDP increased, in real terms, at an average annual rate of 2.2% during 1990–98. Compared with the previous year, growth in agricultural GDP was estimated by the Asian Development Bank (ADB) to be 2.4% in 1999.

Industry (including mining, manufacturing, construction and power) contributed 21.9% of GDP in 1999, and employed 3.4% of the labour force in 1998. According to estimates published by the IMF, in real terms, industrial GDP increased at an average annual rate of 8.7% during 1990–98. According to the ADB, growth in industrial GDP was an estimated 12.9% in 1999.

In 1999 mining and quarrying contributed only 0.3% of GDP. Cambodia has limited mineral resources, including phosphates, gem stones, iron ore, bauxite, silicon and manganese ore, of which only phosphates and gem stones are, at present, being exploited. In the 1990s several agreements on petroleum exploration were signed with foreign enterprises. Cambodia's resources of natural gas were unofficially estimated to be 1,500,000m.–3,500,000m. cu m in 1992, and petroleum reserves were estimated to be between 50m. and 100m. barrels. According to estimates published by the IMF, the GDP of the mining sector increased, in real terms, at an average annual rate of 6.1% during 1990–98; growth in mining GDP was an estimated 0.5% in 1998.

The manufacturing sector contributed 14.0% of GDP in 1999. The sector is dominated by rice milling and the production of ready-made garments, household goods, textiles, tyres and pharmaceutical products. The manufacture of garments, mostly for export, grew rapidly during the 1990s; employment in the sector increased from 2,270 workers in 1994 to 36,717 in 1997. Exports of clothing rose in value by more than 50% in 1999, compared with the previous year, to reach US $598m. The Government was also attempting to promote the establishment of agro-industrial enterprises (sugar and vegetable oil refineries and factories producing paper pulp) and to encourage the production of fertilizers, petroleum and heavy construction and mechanical equipment. According to estimates published by the IMF, the GDP of the manufacturing sector increased, in real

terms, at an average annual rate of 7.8% during 1990–98. Growth in manufacturing GDP was an estimated 6.0% in 1998.

Energy is derived principally from timber. All commercial energy used in Cambodia is imported. In the late 1990s the country had an installed capacity of 28.7 MW, of which 15 MW was accounted for by an oil-fired thermal power plant and the rest by diesel generating units. Owing to a lack of spare parts and a shortage of fuel, only a small percentage of the generating capacity can be utilized. Cambodia has considerable hydropower potential, and two hydropower plants were under construction in the late 1990s.

The services sector contributed 42.9% of GDP in 1999 and engaged 19.8% of the economically active population in 1998. The tourism sector has become increasingly significant. In 2000 greater political stability led to an increase in tourist arrivals to an estimated 440,000. Receipts from tourism in that year were estimated at almost US $200m. In real terms, according to estimates published by the IMF, the GDP of the services sector increased at an average annual rate of 6.3% during 1990–98. Growth in the sector rose by an estimated 2.6% in 1999, according to the ADB.

In 1999 Cambodia recorded a visible trade deficit of US $209.5m., while there was a deficit of $66.0m. on the current account of the balance of payments. In 1999 the principal sources of imports were Thailand (15.9%) and Hong Kong (15.1%); other major sources were Singapore, Viet Nam, and Japan. In the same year, the principal market for exports was Singapore (17.7%); other important purchasers were Hong Kong, Thailand and Viet Nam. The principal exports in 1999 were garments (accounting for 58.3% of the total), sawn timber, logs and rubber. The principal imports were petroleum products (accounting for 12.3% of the total), cigarettes and motorcycles. Re-exports (which were a result of the differences in tariffs on goods imported by Cambodia and its neighbours) remained important, although they declined from 53% of total exports in 1993 to an estimated 39.6% in 1998.

Cambodia's overall budget deficit in 1999 was 508,000m. riels, equivalent to 4.3% of GDP. Cambodia's external debt at the end of 1998 totalled US $2,210m., of which $2,102m. was long-term public debt. In that year the cost of debt-servicing was equivalent to 1.5% of revenue from exports of goods and services. The annual rate of inflation averaged 6.5% during 1994–99; declining to 4.0% in 1999.

Cambodia is a member of the Asian Development Bank (see p. 131). Cambodia was formally admitted to the Association of South East Asian Nations (ASEAN, see p. 134) in April 1999.

Prospects for economic development in Cambodia were greatly enhanced by the formation of the coalition Government in November 1998, owing both to the resumption of lending by foreign donors (who had suspended aid in mid-1997) and to the possibility of the sustained implementation of reformist policies. In 1999 economic growth exceeded expectations, the rate of inflation decreased sharply and export growth was maintained. Despite these positive developments, however, Cambodia conceded that it could be many years before its economy reached the level of those of its regional neighbours. In February 2000 the Government announced a three-year US $1,400m. economic development programme intended to promote growth and to reduce poverty. At the annual meeting of bilateral and multilateral donors in Paris in May, US $548m. of fresh aid was pledged to Cambodia in response to the Government's appeals. (This aid, however, was partly dependent upon the fulfilment of government pledges to reduce military spending, to address the problem of illegal logging and to decrease expenditure on the civil service payroll.) During 2000 the currency remained stable, and revenue from the services sector (and, in particular, from tourism) continued to rise. Severe flooding in September, however, damaged unharvested rice crops; it was anticipated, therefore, that GDP growth for 2000 would be somewhat lower than the Government's stated target of 5.5%. Moreover, it was widely recognized that the Government needed to make further positive efforts to accelerate the reform of key areas, including forestry management, public finance, trade, banking and public administration.

Social Welfare

In 1988 there were 188 hospitals in the country, containing 12,953 beds (equivalent to 1 bed per 612 inhabitants). In the same year there were 425 physicians, 7,271 nurses and 2,332 midwives. Under the 1993 Constitution, a social security system was envisaged for workers and employees. In 1999 government expenditure on health was 125,600m. riels (6.8% of total expenditure); in the same year the Ministry of Social Affairs, Labour, Professional Training and Youth Rehabilitation was allocated 18,900m. riels (1.0% of total expenditure).

Education

Education is compulsory for six years between the ages of six and 12. Primary education begins at six and lasts for six years. In 1997 enrolment at primary level was equivalent to 113% of children in the relevant age-group (males 123%; females 104%). Secondary education comprises two cycles, each lasting three years. In 1997 enrolment at secondary level was equivalent to 24% of the relevant age-group (males 31%; females 17%). In the same year enrolment at tertiary level was equivalent to 1.0% of the relevant age-group (males 2.0%; females 0.5%). In 1993, according to a sample survey, the average rate of adult illiteracy was 34.7% (males 20.3%; females 46.6%). In 1999 the Ministry

of Education, Youth and Sport was allocated 155,700m. riels (8.5% of total expenditure).

Public Holidays

2001: 1 January (International New Year's Day), 7 January (Remembrance Day), April (Cambodian New Year), 1 May (Labour Day), 20 May (Day of Remembrance), 24 September (Constitution Day), 23 October (Anniversary of Paris Peace Agreement on Cambodia), 9 November (Independence Day).

2002: 1 January (International New Year's Day), 7 January (Remembrance Day), April (Cambodian New Year), 1 May (Labour Day), 20 May (Day of Remembrance), 24 September (Constitution Day), 23 October (Anniversary of Paris Peace Agreement on Cambodia), 9 November (Independence Day).

Weights and Measures

The metric system is in force.

Statistical Survey

Note: Some of the statistics below represent only sectors of the economy controlled by the Government of the former Khmer Republic. During the years 1970–75 no figures were available for areas controlled by the Khmers Rouges.

Area and Population

AREA, POPULATION AND DENSITY

Area (sq km)	181,035*
Population (census results)	
17 April 1962	5,728,771
Prior to elections of 1 May 1981	6,682,000
3 March 1998	
Males	5,511,408
Females	5,926,248
Total	11,437,656
Density (per sq km) at census of 3 March 1998 . . .	63.2

* 69,898 sq miles.

Principal Towns: Phnom-Penh (capital), population 900,000 in 1991 (estimate); Sihanoukville (Kompong-Som), population 75,000 in 1990 (estimate).

BIRTHS AND DEATHS (annual averages)

	1980–85	1985–90	1990–95
Birth rate (per 1,000) . . .	45.9	44.2	38.2
Death rate (per 1,000) . . .	17.9	16.5	14.1

Source: Ministry of Economy and Finance, Phnom-Penh.

Expectation of life (UN estimates, years at birth, 1997): Males 51.8; Females 59.7 (Source: UN, *Statistical Yearbook for Asia and the Pacific*).

ECONOMICALLY ACTIVE POPULATION
('000 persons, 1998 census)

	Males	Females	Total
Agriculture, etc.	1,694.5	2,076.5	3,771.0
Industry.	82.1	86.4	168.5
Services	612.2	357.4	969.6
Total	2,388.7	2,520.4	4,909.1

Source: Ministry of Economy and Finance, Phnom-Penh.

Agriculture

PRINCIPAL CROPS ('000 metric tons)

	1997	1998	1999
Rice (paddy)	3,414.9	3,509.9	3,800.0
Maize	42.4	48.5	50.0
Sweet potatoes	28.9	25.5	25.0*
Cassava (Manioc) . . .	69.4	66.5	67.5
Other roots and tubers . .	18.0	18.5	18.5*
Dry beans	15.3	9.2	10.5
Soybeans (Soya beans) . .	56.3	27.7	35.1†
Groundnuts (in shell) . .	7.0	6.6	6.9
Sesame seed	3.1	5.1	5.1
Coconuts*	58.0	56.0	56.0
Sugar cane	187.5	133.1	138.0
Tobacco (leaves) . . .	10.5	10.1	10.0
Jute	2.3	2.5*	2.5*
Natural rubber . . .	37.8	40.8	42.0*
Vegetables*	460.0	465.0	470.0
Oranges*	62.0	63.0	63.0
Mangoes*	33.0	34.0	35.0
Pineapples*	15.5	16.0	16.0
Bananas*	145.0	146.0	147.0
Other fruits and berries* . .	56.7	58.0	59.2

* FAO estimate(s).
† Unofficial figure.

Source: FAO.

LIVESTOCK ('000 head, year ending September)

	1997	1998*	1999*
Horses	22*	23	25
Cattle	2,821	2,860	2,860
Buffaloes	694	695	695
Pigs	2,438	2,500	2,550
Chickens	12,098	12,500	12,500
Ducks	4,400*	4,500	4,600

* FAO estimate(s).
Source: FAO.

LIVESTOCK PRODUCTS ('000 metric tons)

	1997	1998	1999
Beef and veal	41.0	41.8	42.1
Buffalo meat	12.6	13.1	13.1
Pig meat	97.0	100.0	102.5
Poultry meat	23.3	24.1	25.0
Cows' milk	19.6	20.1	20.4
Hen eggs*	11.0	11.5	11.7
Other poultry eggs . . .	3.1	3.2	3.3
Cattle hides (fresh) . . .	10.3	10.4	10.5
Buffalo hides (fresh) . . .	2.6	2.7	2.7

* FAO estimates.
Source: FAO.

Forestry

ROUNDWOOD REMOVALS ('000 cu m, excl. bark)

	1996	1997	1998
Sawlogs, veneer logs and logs for sleepers	410	410	410
Other industrial wood . .	630	630	630
Fuel wood	6,655	6,813	6,968
Total	**7,695**	**7,853**	**8,008**

Source: FAO, *Yearbook of Forest Products.*

SAWNWOOD PRODUCTION
('000 cu m, incl. railway sleepers)

	1996	1997	1998
Total (all broadleaved) . . .	100	71	40

Source: FAO, *Yearbook of Forest Products.*

Fishing

('000 metric tons, live weight)

	1997	1998	1999
Capture	102.8	107.9	109.0
Freshwater fishes . . .	73.0	75.7	71.0
Marine fishes . . .	29.8	32.2	38.0
Aquaculture	11.5	14.1	15.0
Total catch	**114.3**	**122.0**	**124.0**

Source: Ministry of Economy and Finance, Phnom-Penh.

Note: Figures exclude crocodiles, recorded by number rather than by weight. The total of estuarine crocodiles caught was: 17,000 in 1997; 40,700 in 1998 (Source: FAO, *Yearbook of Fishery Statistics*).

Mining

('000 metric tons)

	1995*	1996*	1997
Salt (unrefined)†	40	40	40

* Estimates.
† Data supplied by US Bureau of Mines.
Source: UN, *Industrial Commodity Statistics Yearbook.*

Industry

SELECTED PRODUCTS ('000 metric tons, unless otherwise indicated)

	1971	1972	1973
Distilled alcoholic beverages ('000 hectolitres)	45	55	36
Beer ('000 hectolitres) . . .	26	23	18
Soft drinks ('000 hectolitres) . .	25	25*	25*
Cigarettes (million) . . .	3,413	2,510	2,622
Cotton yarn—pure and mixed (metric tons)	1,068	1,094	415
Bicycle tyres and tubes ('000) . .	208	200*	200*
Rubber footwear ('000 pairs) . .	1,292	1,000*	1,000*
Soap (metric tons) . . .	469	400*	400*
Motor spirit (petrol) . . .	2	—	—
Distillate fuel oils . . .	11	—	—
Residual fuel oils . . .	14	—	—
Cement	44	53	78
Electric energy (million kWh)† .	148	166	150

Cigarettes (million): 4,175 in 1987; 4,200 annually in 1988–92 (estimates by US Department of Agriculture).
Cement ('000 metric tons): 200 in 1996; 200 in 1997; 300 in 1998 (estimates by the US Geological Survey).
Electric energy (million kWh): 187 in 1994*; 194 in 1995*; 201 in 1996.
Plywood ('000 cu m): 29 in 1995; 29 in 1996; 29 in 1997.
* Estimate.   † Production by public utilities only.
(Source: partly UN, *Industrial Commodity Statistics Yearbook*.)

Finance

CURRENCY AND EXCHANGE RATES
Monetary Units
  100 sen = 1 riel.

Sterling, Dollar and Euro Equivalents (29 December 2000)
  £1 sterling = 5,827.0 riels;
  US $1 = 3,905.0 riels;
  €1 = 3,633.6 riels;
  10,000 riels = £1.716 = $2.561 = €2.752.

Average Exchange Rate (riels per US $)
  1998   3,744.4
  1999   3,807.8
  2000   3,840.8

BUDGET ('000 million riels)

Revenue	1997	1998	1999
Tax revenue	597.4	679.4	961.4
Direct taxes	43.6	54.6	82.7
Profit tax	35.0	42.1	61.2
Indirect taxes	206.5	248.5	445.3
Turnover tax . . .	46.6	65.9	21.8
Value-added tax . . .	75.2	90.1	328.6
Excise duties . . .	74.1	76.0	91.8
Taxes on international trade .	347.3	376.3	433.4
Import duties . . .	337.5	373.6	415.3
Other current revenue . . .	236.8	225.9	354.8
Forestry	37.4	22.8	36.3
Royalties	33.6	3.5	1.8
Posts and telecommunications	83.0	87.2	108.9
Capital revenue	12.3	33.2	13.7
Total	**846.5**	**938.5**	**1,330.0**

Expenditure	1997	1998	1999
Council of Ministers . . .	46.1	57.4	53.8
Ministry of Defence . . .	304.7	312.2	335.7
Ministry of the Interior . . .	141.2	169.0	146.6
Ministry of Economy and Finance	334.3	114.4	144.6
Ministry of Public Works and Transport . . .	19.8	13.1	23.7
Ministry of Agriculture, Forestry, Hunting and Fisheries . . .	23.8	18.4	21.5
Ministry of Education, Youth and Sport . . .	155.5	102.4	155.7
Ministry of Industry, Mines and Energy . . .	3.7	3.0	4.1
Ministry of Health . . .	94.2	44.3	125.6
Ministry of Posts and Telecommunications . . .	52.9	53.6	113.8
Ministry of Social Affairs, Labour, Professional Training and Youth Rehabilitation . . .	50.6	47.6	18.9
Total (incl. others) . . .	1,260.0	1,569.0	1,838.0
Current expenditure . . .	808.0	940.0	1,110.0
Capital expenditure . . .	452.0	629.0	728.0

Source: Ministry of Economy and Finance, Phnom-Penh.

INTERNATIONAL RESERVES (US $ million at 31 December)

	1998	1999	2000
IMF special drawing rights . .	9.78	5.19	0.18
Foreign exchange . . .	314.50	388.00	501.50
Total . . .	324.28	393.19	501.68

Source: IMF, *International Financial Statistics*.

MONEY SUPPLY (million riels at 31 December)

	1998	1999	2000*
Currency outside banks . . .	509,057	489,862	494,600
Demand deposits at deposit money banks	34,215	42,092	45,040
Total money . . .	543,272	531,954	539,640

* Figures are rounded to the nearest 10 million riels.

Sources: Ministry of Economy and Finance, Phnom-Penh, and IMF, *International Financial Statistics*.

COST OF LIVING
(Consumer Price Index; base: 1994 = 100)

	1997	1998	1999
All items	124.8	143.1	148.8

Source: Ministry of Economy and Finance, Phnom-Penh.

2000 (base: 1999 = 100): All items 99.2 (Source: IMF, *International Financial Statistics*).

NATIONAL ACCOUNTS (US $ million at current prices)
Expenditure on the Gross Domestic Product

	1997	1998	1999
Government final consumption expenditure	269	245	291
Private final consumption expenditure . . .	2,454	2,333	2,483
Gross capital formation . .	624	613	680
Total domestic expenditure	3,347	3,191	3,454
Exports of goods and services . .	865	847	1,118
Less Imports of goods and services	1,179	1,169	1,483
GDP in purchasers' values .	3,033	2,868	3,089
GDP at constant 1993 prices .	2,365	2,389	2,498

Source: Ministry of Economy and Finance, Phnom-Penh.

Gross Domestic Product by Economic Activity

	1997	1998	1999
Agriculture, hunting, forestry and fishing . . .	1,247	1,137	1,064
Mining and quarrying . . .	8	7	8
Manufacturing . . .	325	346	432
Electricity, gas and water . .	26	27	31
Construction . . .	180	170	205
Trade, restaurants and hotels .	516	484	590
Transport, storage and communications . . .	198	190	206
Owner-occupied dwellings . .	145	138	146
Government services . . .	129	118	139
Other services . . .	239	229	244
GDP in purchasers' values .	3,033	2,868	3,089

Source: Ministry of Economy and Finance, Phnom-Penh.

BALANCE OF PAYMENTS (US $ million)

	1997	1998	1999
Exports of goods f.o.b. . .	736.0	705.4	1,002.1
Imports of goods f.o.b. . .	−1,064.0	−1,096.8	−1,211.6
Trade balance . . .	−328.0	−391.4	−209.5
Exports of services . . .	160.4	109.8	128.9
Imports of services . . .	−188.0	−189.4	−195.0
Balance on goods and services	−355.6	−471.0	−275.6
Other income received . . .	16.0	17.9	20.5
Other income paid . . .	−58.5	−68.2	−45.4
Balance on goods, services and income . . .	−398.1	−521.3	−300.5
Current transfers received . .	188.5	298.0	235.9
Current transfers paid . . .	−0.3	−0.6	−1.4
Current balance . . .	−209.9	−223.9	−66.0
Capital account (net) . . .	65.2	61.6	44.0
Direct investment from abroad .	203.7	120.7	125.5
Other investment assets . .	−23.6	−41.6	−61.1
Other investment liabilities . .	39.7	43.7	39.6
Net errors and omissions . .	−41.2	−55.3	−32.8
Overall balance . . .	33.9	15.8	49.2

Source: IMF, *International Financial Statistics*.

External Trade

PRINCIPAL COMMODITIES (US $ million)

Imports c.i.f.	1997	1998	1999
Cigarettes	188	142	119
Petroleum products . . .	136	140	151
Motorcycles	17	44	36
Vehicles	26	15	27
Gold	136	3	28
Total (incl. others) . . .	1,224	1,127	1,227

Exports f.o.b.	1997	1998*	1999
Crude rubber†	23	25	24
Logs and sawn timber† . .	224	178	33
Clothing	279	390	598
Total (incl. others)‡ . .	874	999	1,026

* Estimates.

† Including estimates for illegal exports.

‡ Including re-exports (US $ million): 338 in 1997; 396 (estimate) in 1998.

Sources: IMF, *Cambodia: Statistical Annex* (April 1999); Ministry of Economy and Finance, Phnom-Penh.

PRINCIPAL TRADING PARTNERS (US $ million)

Imports c.i.f.	1997	1998	1999
Australia	11.0	10.5	6.6
France	40.7	39.9	41.8
Hong Kong	65.8	127.9	185.1
Indonesia	14.5	27.6	50.7
Japan	82.2	70.1	73.7
Singapore	112.8	94.4	98.8
Thailand	194.6	166.0	194.7
Viet Nam	105.9	89.4	85.4
Total (incl. others)	1,041.6	1,127.0	1,227.0

Exports f.o.b.	1997	1998	1999
Hong Kong	12.5	26.4	38.1
Malaysia	10.7	6.1	6.6
Singapore	72.6	131.0	181.1
Taiwan	18.8	20.5	9.4
Thailand	129.2	75.8	18.5
Viet Nam	34.5	41.3	12.8
Total (incl. others)	874.0	999.0	1,026.0

Source: Ministry of Economy and Finance, Phnom-Penh.

Transport

RAILWAYS (traffic)

	1997	1998	1999
Freight carried ('000 metric tons)	16	294	259
Freight ton-km ('000)	36,514	75,721	76,171
Passengers ('000)	553	438	431
Passenger-km ('000)	50,992	43,847	49,894

Source: Ministry of Economy and Finance, Phnom-Penh.

ROAD TRAFFIC (motor vehicles in use at 31 December)

	1995	1996	1997
Passenger cars	42,210	46,800	52,919
Buses and coaches	720	790	868
Lorries and vans	8,712	11,000	12,706
Road tractors	390	463	513
Motorcycles and mopeds	378,783	397,300	456,800

Source: International Road Federation, *World Road Statistics*.

SHIPPING
Merchant Fleet (registered at 31 December)

	1996	1997	1998
Number of vessels	43	125	195
Displacement ('000 grt)	206.2	438.7	616.4

Source: Lloyd's Register of Shipping, *World Fleet Statistics*.

International Sea-borne Freight Traffic (estimates, '000 metric tons)

	1988	1989	1990
Goods loaded	10	10	11
Goods unloaded	100	100	95

Source: UN, *Monthly Bulletin of Statistics*.

CIVIL AVIATION (traffic on scheduled services)

	1975	1976	1977
Passenger-kilometres (million)	42	42	42
Freight ton-kilometres ('000)	400	400	400

Source: Statistisches Bundesamt, Wiesbaden, Germany.

Tourism

ARRIVALS BY NATIONALITY

Country	1997	1998	1999
Australia	7,434	6,690	9,443
Canada	3,781	3,298	5,415
China, People's Repub.	17,738	18,035	26,788
France	17,967	18,613	23,754
Germany	4,572	4,096	6,431
Japan	25,447	13,422	17,885
Korea, Repub.	8,805	4,467	6,377
Malaysia	18,682	11,016	12,541
Singapore	13,931	9,123	10,634
Taiwan	28,627	18,232	20,607
Thailand	15,433	10,859	15,283
United Kingdom	9,385	11,164	13,847
USA	18,173	17,595	30,375
Total (incl. others)	255,124	212,935	271,100

Source: Ministry of Economy and Finance, Phnom-Penh.

Tourism receipts (US $ million): 100 in 1995; 118 in 1996; 143 in 1997.
Source: World Tourism Organization, *Yearbook of Tourism Statistics*.

Communications Media

	1995	1996	1997
Radio receivers ('000 in use)	1,120	1,300	1,340
Television receivers ('000 in use)	85	90	94
Telephones ('000 main lines in use)	5	8	19
Telefax stations (number in use)	884	1,470	2,995
Mobile cellular telephones (subscribers)	15,000	23,000	33,550

Sources: UNESCO, *Statistical Yearbook*, and UN, *Statistical Yearbook*.

Education

(1998/99)

	Insti-tutions	Teachers	Pupils/Students Males	Females	Total
Pre-primary	806	1,793	22,878	22,186	45,064
Primary	5,156	43,530	1,137,916	956,084	2,094,000
Secondary	487	17,324	202,999	105,168	308,167
Vocational	26	n.a.	n.a.	n.a.	5,187
Higher education	9	n.a.	n.a.	n.a.	7,333

Source: Ministry of Economy and Finance, Phnom-Penh.

Directory

The Constitution

The Constitution was promulgated on 21 September 1993; a number of amendments were passed on 4 March 1999. The main provisions are summarized below:

GENERAL PROVISIONS

The Kingdom of Cambodia is a unitary state in which the King abides by the Constitution and multi-party liberal democracy. Cambodian citizens have full right of freedom of belief; Buddhism is the state religion. The Kingdom of Cambodia has a market economy system.

THE KING

The King is Head of State and the Supreme Commander of the Khmer Royal Armed Forces. The monarchist regime is based on a system of selection: within seven days of the King's death the Royal Council of the Throne (comprising the Chairman of the Senate, the Chairman of the National Assembly, the Prime Minister, the Supreme Patriarchs of the Mohanikay and Thoammayutikanikay sects, the First and Second Vice-Chairmen of the Senate and the First and Second Vice-Chairmen of the National Assembly) must select a King. The King must be at least 30 years of age and be a descendant of King Ang Duong, King Norodom or King Sisowath. The King appoints the Prime Minister and the Cabinet. In the absence of the King, the Chairman of the Senate assumes the duty of acting Head of State.

THE LEGISLATURE

Legislative power is vested in the National Assembly (the lower chamber) and the Senate (the upper chamber). The National Assembly has 122 members who are elected by universal adult suffrage. A member of the National Assembly must be a Cambodian citizen by birth over the age of 25 years and has a term of office of five years, the term of the National Assembly. The National Assembly may not be dissolved except in the case where the Royal Government (Cabinet) has been dismissed twice in 12 months. The National Assembly may dismiss cabinet members or remove the Royal Government from office by passing a censure motion through a two-thirds majority vote of all the representatives in the National Assembly. The Senate comprises nominated members, the number of which does not exceed one-half of all of the members of the National Assembly; two are nominated by the King, two are elected by the National Assembly and the remainder are elected by universal adult suffrage. A member of the Senate has a term of office of six years. The Senate reviews legislation passed by the National Assembly and acts as a co-ordinator between the National Assembly and the Royal Government. In special cases, the National Assembly and the Senate can assemble as the Congress to resolve issues of national importance.

CABINET

The Cabinet is the Royal Government of the Kingdom of Cambodia, which is led by a Prime Minister, assisted by Deputy Prime Ministers, with state ministers, ministers and state secretaries as members. The Prime Minister is designated by the King at the recommendation of the Chairman of the National Assembly from among the representatives of the winning party. The Prime Minister appoints the members of the Cabinet, who must be representatives in the National Assembly or members of parties represented in the National Assembly.

THE CONSTITUTIONAL COUNCIL

The Constitutional Council's competence is to interpret the Constitution and laws passed by the National Assembly and reviewed completely by the Senate. It has the right to examine and settle disputes relating to the election of members of the National Assembly and the Senate. The Constitutional Council consists of nine members with a nine-year mandate. One-third of the members are replaced every three years. Three members are appointed by the King, three elected by the National Assembly and three appointed by the Supreme Council of the Magistracy.

The Government

HEAD OF STATE

HM King Norodom Sihanouk; acceded to the throne on 24 September 1993.

ROYAL GOVERNMENT OF CAMBODIA
(April 2001)

A coalition of the Cambodian People's Party (CPP) and the FUNCINPEC Party.

Prime Minister: Hun Sen (CPP).

Deputy Prime Minister and Co-Minister of the Interior: Sar Kheng (CPP).

Deputy Prime Minister and Minister of Education, Youth and Sport: Tol Lah (FUNCINPEC).

Senior Ministers:

Tea Banh (CPP)   Lu Lay Sreng (FUNCINPEC)
Keat Chhon (CPP)   Chhim Seak Leng (FUNCINPEC)
Sok An (CPP)   Hong Sun Huot (FUNCINPEC)
Hor Nam Hong (CPP)   You Hockry (FUNCINPEC)

Minister in charge of the Council of Ministers: Sok An (CPP).

Co-Ministers of Defence: Tea Banh (CPP), Prince Sisowath Sireirath (FUNCINPEC).

Co-Minister of the Interior: You Hockry (FUNCINPEC).

Minister of Relations with the National Assembly and Inspection: Khun Haing (FUNCINPEC).

Minister of Foreign Affairs and International Co-operation: Hor Nam Hong (CPP).

Minister of Economy and Finance: Keat Chhon (CPP).

Minister of Information: Lu Lay Sreng (FUNCINPEC).

Minister of Health: Hong Sun Huot (FUNCINPEC).

Minister of Industry, Mines and Energy: Suy Sem (CPP).

Minister of Planning: Chhay Than (CPP).

Minister of Commerce: Cham Prasidh (CPP).

Minister of Agriculture, Forestry, Hunting and Fisheries: (vacant).

Minister of Culture and Fine Arts: Princess Norodom Bopha Devi (FUNCINPEC).

Minister of Environment: Dr Mok Mareth (CPP).

Minister of Rural Development: Chhim Seak Leng (FUNCINPEC).

Minister of Social Affairs, Labour, Professional Training and Youth Rehabilitation: Ith Sam Heng (CPP).

Minister of Posts and Telecommunications: So Khun (CPP).

Minister of Cult and Religious Affairs: Chea Savoeurn (FUNCINPEC).

Minister of Women's Affairs and Veterans: Mou Sok Huor (FUNCINPEC).

Minister of Public Works and Transport: Khy Taing Lim (FUNCINPEC).

Minister of Justice: Uk Vithun (FUNCINPEC).

Minister of Tourism: Veng Sereivuth (FUNCINPEC).

Minister of Territorial Organization and Urbanization: Im Chhun Lim (CPP).

Minister of Water Resources and Meteorology: Lim Kean Hor (CPP).

Secretary of State for Public Civil Servants: Pich Bun Thin (CPP).

Secretary of State for Civil Aviation: Pok Sam El (FUNCINPEC).

There are also 52 further Secretaries of State.

MINISTRIES

Ministry of Agriculture, Forestry, Hunting and Fisheries: 200 blvd Norodom, Phnom-Penh; tel. and fax (23) 427320.

Ministry of Commerce: 20 blvd Norodom, Phnom-Penh; tel. (23) 723775; fax (23) 426396; internet www.moc.gov.kh.

Ministry of Cult and Religious Affairs: blvd Sisowath, rue 240, Phnom-Penh; tel. (23) 725699.

Ministry of Culture and Fine Arts: 274 blvd Monivong, cnr rue Red Cross, Phnom-Penh; tel. (23) 362647.

Ministry of Defence: blvd Pochentong, Phnom-Penh; tel. (23) 366170; fax (23) 366169.

Ministry of Economy and Finance: 60 rue 92, Phnom-Penh; tel. (23) 722863; fax (23) 427798.

Ministry of Education, Youth and Sport: 80 blvd Norodom, Phnom-Penh; tel. (23) 360233; fax (23) 426791.

Ministry of Environment: 48 blvd Sihanouk; tel. (23) 426814; fax (23) 427844; e-mail minenvlb@forum.org.kh.

Ministry of Foreign Affairs and International Co-operation: 161 Preah Sisowath Quay, Phnom-Penh; tel. (23) 426122; fax (23) 426144; e-mail mfaicasean@bigpond.com.kh.

Ministry of Health: 128 blvd Kampuchea Krom, Phnom-Penh; tel. (23) 366553; fax (23) 426841.

Ministry of Industry, Mines and Energy: 45 blvd Norodom, Phnom-Penh; tel. and fax (23) 428263.

Ministry of Information: 62 blvd Monivong, Phnom-Penh; tel. (23) 427475; fax (23) 426059.

Ministry of the Interior: 275 blvd Norodom, Phnom-Penh; tel. (23) 363653; fax (23) 212708.

Ministry of Justice: blvd Sothearos, cnr rue 240, Phnom-Penh; tel. (23) 360320; fax (23) 360327.

Ministry of Planning: 386 blvd Monivong, Phnom-Penh; tel. (23) 362307.

Ministry of Posts and Telecommunications: cnr rue Preah Ang Eng and rue Ang Non, Phnom-Penh; tel. (23) 426510; fax (23) 426011; e-mail koyks@camnet.com.kh; internet www.mptc.gov.kh.

Ministry of Public Works and Transport: blvd Khsattreiani Kossomak, Phnom-Penh; tel. (23) 420813; fax (23) 427862.

Ministry of Rural Development: blvd Czechoslovakia/blvd Pochentong, Phnom-Penh; tel. (23) 722425; fax (23) 722425.

Ministry of Social Affairs, Labour, Professional Training and Youth Rehabilitation: 68 blvd Norodom, Phnom-Penh; tel. (23) 725191; fax (23) 427322.

Ministry of Tourism: 3 blvd Monivong, Phnom-Penh; tel. (23) 215292; fax (23) 214483; e-mail tourism@camnet.com.kh; internet www.cambodia-web.net/camtourist.

Ministry of Water Resources and Meteorology: Phnom-Penh.

Ministry of Women's Affairs and Veterans: Phnom-Penh; tel. (23) 366412.

Legislature

NATIONAL ASSEMBLY

National Assembly, blvd Samdech Sothearos, cnr rue 240, Phnom-Penh; tel. (23) 214136; fax (23) 217769; e-mail kolpheng@camnet.com.kh.

Chairman: Prince NORODOM RANARIDDH (FUNCINPEC).

Election, 26 July 1998

	% of Votes	Seats
Cambodian People's Party	41.4	64
FUNCINPEC Party	31.7	43
Sam Rainsy Party	14.3	15
Others	12.6	—
Total	100.0	122

SENATE

Senate, Chamcarmon Palace, blvd Norodom, Phnom-Penh; e-mail cheasim@khmersenate.org.

Chairman: CHEA SIM (CPP).

First Vice-Chairman: CHIVAN MONIRAK (FUNCINPEC).

Second Vice-Chairman: NHEK BUN CHHAY (FUNCINPEC).

25 March 1999

	Seats
Cambodian People's Party	31
FUNCINPEC Party	21
Sam Rainsy Party	7
King's appointees	2
Total	61

Political Organizations

Buddhist Liberal Party (Kanakpak Serei Niyum Preah Put Sasna): Phnom-Penh; internet www.blp.org; f. 1998; Chair. IENG MULI; Gen. Sec. SIENG LAPRESSE.

Cambodian Freedom Fighters: f. 1998 in opposition to Hun Sen's leadership; Leader CHHUN YASITH; Sec.-Gen. RICHARD KIRI KIM.

Cambodian People's Party (CPP) (Kanakpak Pracheachon Kampuchea): Chamcarmon, blvd Norodom, Phnom-Penh; tel. (23) 725403; fax (23) 722906; internet www.cambodianpeopleparty.org;

(known as the Kampuchean People's Revolutionary Party 1979–91); 20-mem. Standing Cttee of the Cen. Cttee; Cen. Cttee of 153 full mems; Hon. Chair. of Cen. Cttee HENG SAMRIN; Chair. of Cen. Cttee CHEA SIM; Vice-Chair. HUN SEN.

Democratic National United Movement (DNUM): Pailin; f. 1996 by IENG SARY, following his defection from the PDK; not a national political party, did not contest 1998 election; DNUM members are also free to join other political parties.

FUNCINPEC Party (United National Front for an Independent, Neutral, Peaceful and Co-operative Cambodia Party): 11 blvd Monivong (93), Sangkat Sras Chak, Khan Daun Penh, Phnom Penh; tel. (23) 426053; internet www.funcinpec.org; FUNCINPEC altered its title to the FUNCINPEC Party when it adopted political status in 1992; the party's military wing was the National Army of Independent Cambodia (fmrly the Armée Nationale Sihanoukiste—ANS); merged with the Son Sann Party in Jan. 1999; Pres. Prince NORODOM RANARIDDH; Gen. Sec. TOL LAH.

Khmer Citizens' Party (Kanakpak Pulroat Khmer): Phnom-Penh; f. 1996; breakaway faction of Khmer Nation Party (now Sam Rainsy Party); Chair. NGUON SOEUR; Sec.-Gen. IEM RA.

Khmer Democracy Party (Kanakpak Pracheathippatei Khmer): Phnom-Penh; Pres. UK PHURI.

Khmer Neutral Party (Kanakpak Kampuchea Appyeakroet): 14A rue Keo Chea, Phnom-Penh; tel. (23) 62365; fax (23) 27340; e-mail smasavan@pratique.fr; internet pages.pratique.fr/~smasavan/; Pres. BUO HEL.

Khmer Republican Democratic Party (KRDP): Phnom-Penh; f. 1997; supports CPP; Chair. NHUNG SEAP.

Liberal Democratic Party: Phnom-Penh; f. 1993; receives support from members of the armed forces; pro-Government; Chair. Gen. CHHIM OM YON.

MOLINAKA (National Liberation Movement of Cambodia): c/o National Assembly, blvd Sothearos, cnr rue 240, Phnom-Penh; a breakaway faction of FUNCINPEC; Pres. PRUM NEAKAREACH.

National Union Party (Kanakpak Ruop Ruom Cheat): Phnom-Penh; established by rebel mems of FUNCINPEC Party; Chair. TOAN CHHAY; Sec.-Gen. UNG PHAN.

New Society Party: see Sangkum Thmei Party.

Reastr Niyum (Nationalist Party): blvd Norodom, Phnom-Penh; tel. (23) 215659; fax (23) 215279; f. 1998; breakaway faction of the FUNCINPEC Party; Pres. UNG HUOT; Sec.-Gen. PU SOTHIRAK.

Sangkum Thmei Party (New Society Party): 4 rue 310, Phnom-Penh; f. 1997 by Loy Simchheang, formerly the Gen. Sec. of FUNCINPEC.

Sam Rainsy Party (SRP): 71 blvd Sothearos, Phnom-Penh; tel. and fax (23) 217452; e-mail samrainsy@bigpond.com.kh; internet www.samrainsyparty.org; f. 1995 as the Khmer Nation Party; name changed as above in 1998; 427,524 mems (Jan. 2001); Pres. SAM RAINSY; Gen. Sec. ENG CHHAY EANG.

United Front for the Construction and Defence of the Kampuchean Fatherland (UFCDKF): Phnom-Penh; f. 1978 as the Kampuchean National United Front for National Salvation (KNUFNS), renamed Kampuchean United Front for National Construction and Defence (KUFNCD) in 1981, present name adopted in 1989; mass organization supporting policies of the CPP; an 89-mem. Nat. Council and a seven-mem. hon. Presidium; Chair. of Nat. Council CHEA SIM; Sec.-Gen. ROS CHHUN.

Uphold the Cambodian Nation Party: Phnom-Penh; f. 1997 by Pen Sovan, fmr Sec.-Gen. of the Cen. Cttee of the CPP, to contest the 1998 legislative elections; Chair. PEN SOVAN.

Diplomatic Representation

EMBASSIES IN CAMBODIA

Australia: Villa 11 R. V., Senei Vinnavaut Oum (rue 254), Chartaumuk, Khan Daun Penh, Phnom-Penh; tel. (23) 213470; fax (23) 213413; Ambassador: LOUISE HAND.

Brunei: Office 5, Hotel Sofitel Cambodiana, Ground Floor, 313 quai Sisowath, Phnom-Penh; tel. (23) 363331; fax (23) 363332; Ambassador: Pengiran Haji SALLEHUDDIN.

Bulgaria: 177/227 blvd Norodom, Phnom-Penh; tel. (23) 723181; fax (23) 426491; Chargé d'affaires a.i.: STOYAN DAVIDOV.

Canada: Villa 9, R.V. Senei Vinnavaut Oum, Sangkat Chartaumuk, Khan Daun Penh, Phnom-Penh; tel. (23) 213470 (ext. 426); fax (23) 211389; e-mail cdnemb@bigpond.com.kh; Ambassador: NORMAND MAILHOT.

China, People's Republic: 256 blvd Mao Tse Toung, Phnom-Penh; tel. (15) 911062; fax (23) 426271; Ambassador: YAN TINGAI.

Cuba: 98 route 214, Phnom-Penh; tel. (23) 724181; fax (23) 427428; Ambassador: RUBÉN PÉREZ VALDÉS.

France: 1 blvd Monivong, Phnom-Penh; tel. (23) 430020; fax (23) 430037; Ambassador: ANDRÉ-JEAN LIBOUREL.

Germany: rue Yougoslavie 76–78 (Street 214), BP 60, Phnom-Penh; tel. (23) 216381; fax (23) 427746; e-mail germ.emb.phnomph@bigpond.com.kh; Ambassador: Dr HARALD LOESCHNER.

Hungary: 463 blvd Monivong, Phnom-Penh; tel. (23) 722781; fax (23) 426216; Ambassador: ERNŐ BOHÁR.

India: Villa 777, blvd Monivong, Phnom-Penh; tel. (23) 210912; fax (23) 364489; Ambassador: JASJIT SINGH RANDHAWA.

Indonesia: 90 blvd Norodom, Phnom-Penh; tel. (23) 216148; fax (23) 217566; Ambassador: HAMID ALHADAD.

Japan: 75 blvd Norodom, Phnom-Penh; tel. (23) 217161; fax (23) 216162; e-mail eojc@bigpond.com.kh; Ambassador: MASAKI SAITO.

Korea, Democratic People's Republic: 39 rue 268, Phnom-Penh; tel. (15) 912567; fax (23) 426230; Ambassador: KIM YOUNG SOP.

Korea, Republic: 64 rue 214, Sangkar Beung Rain, Khan Daun Penh, Phnom-Penh; tel. (23) 211901; fax (23) 211903; Ambassador: LEE WUN-HYUNG.

Laos: 15–17 blvd Mao Tse Toung, POB 19, Phnom-Penh; tel. (23) 982632; fax (23) 720907; Ambassador: LY SOUTHAVILAY.

Malaysia: Villa 161, rue 51, Khan Daun Penh, Phnom-Penh; tel. (23) 216176; fax (23) 216004; Ambassador: MOHD KAMAL ISMAUN.

Myanmar: 181 blvd Norodom, Phnom-Penh; tel. (23) 213664; fax (23) 213665; Ambassador: U TINT LWIN.

Philippines: 33 rue 294, Khan Chamcarmon, Sangkat Tonle Bassac, Phnom-Penh; tel. (23) 215145; fax (23) 215143; e-mail phnompenhpe@bigpond.com.kh; Ambassador: FRANCISCO E. ATAYDE.

Poland: 767 blvd Monivong, Phnom-Penh; tel. (23) 217782; fax (23) 217781; e-mail emb.pol.pp@bigpond.com.kh; Chargé d'affaires a.i.: KAZIMIERZ A. DUCHOWSKI.

Russia: 213 blvd Sotheáros, Phnom-Penh; tel. (23) 210931; fax (23) 216776; e-mail russemba@forum.org.kh; Ambassador: VICTOR V. SAMOILENKO.

Singapore: 92 blvd Norodom, Phnom-Penh; tel. (23) 360855; fax (23) 360850; e-mail singemb@bigpond.com.kh; Ambassador: VERGHESE MATHEWS.

Thailand: 196 blvd Norodom, Sangkat Tonle Bassac, Khan Chamkarmon, Phnom-Penh; tel. (23) 363869; fax (18) 810860; e-mail thaipnp@mfa.go.th; Ambassador: ASIPHOL CHABCHITRCHAIDOL.

United Kingdom: 27–29 rue 75, Sras Chak, Dom Penh, Phnom-Penh; tel. (23) 427124; fax (23) 427125; e-mail BRITEMB@bigpond.com.kh; Ambassador: STEPHEN BRIDGES.

USA: 27 rue 240—Box P, Phnom-Penh; tel. (23) 216436; fax (23) 216811; Ambassador: KENT WIEDEMANN.

Viet Nam: 436 blvd Monivong, Phnom-Penh; tel. (23) 725481; fax (23) 427385; Ambassador: NGUYEN DU HONG.

Judicial System

An independent judiciary was established under the 1993 Constitution.

Supreme Court: rue 134, cnr rue 63, Phnom-Penh; tel. 17816663; Chair. DID MONTY.

Religion

BUDDHISM

The principal religion of Cambodia is Theravada Buddhism (Buddhism of the 'Tradition of the Elders'), the sacred language of which is Pali. A ban was imposed on all religious activity in 1975. By a constitutional amendment, which was adopted in April 1989, Buddhism was reinstated as the national religion and was retained as such under the 1993 Constitution. By 1992 2,800 monasteries (of a total of 3,369) had been restored and there were 21,800 Buddhist monks. In 1992 about 90% of the population were Buddhists.

Supreme Patriarchs: Ven. Patriarch TEP VONG, Ven. Patriarch BOU KRI.

Patriotic Kampuchean Buddhists' Association: Phnom-Penh; mem. of UFCDKF; Pres. LONG SIM.

CHRISTIANITY

The Roman Catholic Church

Cambodia comprises the Apostolic Vicariate of Phnom-Penh and the Apostolic Prefectures of Battambang and Kompong-Cham. At 31 December 1998 there were an estimated 18,900 adherents in the country, equivalent to about 0.2% of the population. An Episcopal Conference of Laos and Kampuchea was established in 1971. In 1975 the Government of Democratic Kampuchea banned all religious

practice in Cambodia, and the right of Christians to meet to worship was not restored until 1990.

Vicar Apostolic of Phnom-Penh: Rt Rev. YVES-GEORGES-RENÉ RAMOUSSE (Titular Bishop of Pisita), 787 blvd Monivong (rue 93), BP 123, Phnom-Penh; tel. (23) 368367; fax (23) 427986.

ISLAM

Islam is practised by a minority in Cambodia. Islamic worship was also banned in 1975, but it was legalized in 1979, following the defeat of the Democratic Kampuchean regime.

The Press

NEWSPAPERS

Newspapers are not widely available outside Phnom-Penh.

Areyathor (Civilization): Phnom-Penh; tel. (23) 913662; Editor CHIN CHAN MONTY.

Bayon Pearnik: POB 2279, Phnom-Penh); tel. (23) 219189; fax (23) 213401; English; monthly; Editor CRAIG MAPLESTON.

Cambodia Daily: 50B, rue 240, Phnom-Penh; tel. (23) 426602; fax (23) 426573; e-mail aafc@forum.org.kh; internet www.cambodiadaily.com; f. 1993; in English and Khmer; Mon.–Sat.; Editor-in-Chief BRIAN MOCKENHAUPT; Publr BERNARD KRISHER.

Cambodia Times: Phnom-Penh; tel. (23) 723405; fax (23) 426647; f. 1992 (in Kuala Lumpur, Malaysia); English-language weekly.

Chakraval: Phnom-Penh; tel. (23) 720410; fax (23) 720141; Editor SO SOVAN RITH.

Commercial News: 75 rue 134, Phnom-Penh; tel. (23) 725506; fax (23) 725135; f. 1993; Chinese; Chief Editor EANG SOVAN; circ. 3,000.

Construction (Kasang): Phnom-Penh; tel. 18818292; Khmer; Editor CHHEA VARY.

Equality Voice: Phnom-Penh; tel. 12842471; Khmer; Publr HUON MARA.

Intervention: Phnom-Penh; tel. 12843285; Khmer; Editor NGUON THAI DAY.

Kampuchea: 158 blvd Norodom, Phnom-Penh; tel. (23) 725559; f. 1979; weekly; Chief Editor KEO PRASAT; circ. 55,000.

Khmer Wisdom: Phnom-Penh; tel. 12850690; Khmer; CHUM SOPHAL.

Khmer Youth Voice: Phnom-Penh; tel. 15917153; Khmer; Editor KEO SOKHA.

Koh Santepheap (Island of Peace): Phnom-Penh; tel. (23) 801149; fax (23) 364515; Khmer.

Moneaksekar Khmer: Phnom-Penh; tel. (23) 16880389; Editor DAM SITHIK.

Neak Chea: 1 rue 158, Daun Penh, Phnom-Penh; tel. (23) 428653; fax (23) 427229; e-mail adhoc@forum.org.kh.

Phnom Penh: Phnom-Penh; tel. 15917682; Khmer; Editor VA DANE.

Phnom Penh Post: 10A rue 264, Phnom-Penh; tel. (23) 210309; fax (23) 426568; e-mail michael.pppost@bigpond.com.kh; internet www.phnompenhpost.com; f. 1992; English; fortnightly; Editor-in-Chief MICHAEL HAYES; Publrs MICHAEL HAYES, KATHLEEN HAYES.

Pracheachon (The People): 101 blvd Norodom, Phnom-Penh; f. 1985; 2 a week; organ of the CPP; Editor-in-Chief SOM KIMSUOR; circ. 50,000.

Reaksmei Kampuchea: 476 blvd Monivong, Phnom-Penh; tel. (23) 362881; fax (23) 362472; daily; local newspaper in northern Cambodia; Editor PEN PHENG.

Samleng Thmei (New Voice): Phnom-Penh; tel. 15920589; Khmer; Editor KHUN NGOR.

NEWS AGENCIES

Agence Kampuchia de Presse (AKP): 62 blvd Monivong, Phnom-Penh; tel. and fax (23) 427945; e-mail akp@camnet.com.kh; internet www.camnet.com.kh/akp; f. 1978; Dir-Gen. KIT-KIM HUON.

Foreign Bureaux

Agence France-Presse (AFP) (France): 18 rue 214, Phnom-Penh; tel. (23) 426227; fax (23) 426226; Correspondent STEFAN SMITH.

Associated Press (AP) (USA): 18C rue 19, BP 870, Phnom-Penh; tel. (23) 426607; e-mail ap@bigpond.com.kh; Correspondent CHRIS FONTAINE.

Deutsche Presse-Agentur (dpa): 5E rue 178, Phnom-Penh; tel. (23) 427846; fax (23) 427846; Correspondent JOE COCHRANE.

Reuters (UK): 15 rue 246, Phnom-Penh; tel. (23) 427854; fax (23) 723405; Bureau Chief ROBERT BIRSEL.

Xinhua (New China) News Agency (People's Republic of China): 19 rue 294, Phnom-Penh; tel. (23) 211608; fax (23) 426613; Correspondent LEI BOSONG.

ASSOCIATIONS

Khmer Journalists' Association: 101 blvd Preah Norodom, Phnom-Penh; tel. (23) 725459; f. 1979; mem. of UFCDKF; Pres. PIN SAMKHON.

League of Cambodian Journalists (LCJ): Phnom-Penh; tel. 15917682; fax (23) 360612; Pres. CHUM KANAL.

Broadcasting and Communications

TELECOMMUNICATIONS

Cambodian Samart Communication: 33 blvd Samdech Sothearos, Phnom-Penh; tel. (15) 910022; fax (15) 911703; operates a national mobile telephone network.

Camintel: 1 quai Sisowath, Phnom-Penh; tel. (23) 981234; fax (23) 981277; a jt venture between the Ministry of Posts and Telecommunications and the Indonesian co, Indosat; operates domestic telephone network; Chair. STEVE YANUAN.

Camshin Corporation: 26 rue Preah Monivong, Phnom-Penh; tel. (23) 60001; fax (23) 61234; a jt venture between the Ministry of Posts and Telecommunications and the Thai co, Shinawatra International Co Ltd; telephone communications co.

Telstra Corpn: 58 blvd Norodom, Phnom-Penh; tel. (23) 426022; fax (23) 426023; e-mail Paul.Blanche-Horgan@team.telstra.com; Australian corpn contracted to manage the international calls system until Oct. 2001; Man. PAUL BLANCHE-HORGAN.

BROADCASTING

Radio

Apsara: 69 rue 360, Phnom-Penh; tel. (23) 361197; fax (23) 721888; Head of Admin. KEO SOPHEAP; News Editor SIN SO CHEAT.

Bayon: c/o Bayon Media Group, 954 rue 2, Takhmau, Kandal Province; tel. (23) 983435; fax (23) 363895; Dir-Gen. KEM KUNNAVATH.

Bee Hive Radio: 41 rue 214, Phnom-Penh; tel. (23) 720401; Dir-Gen. MAM SONANDO.

FM 90 MHZ: 65 rue 178, Phnom-Penh; tel. (23) 363699; fax (23) 368623; Dir-Gen. NHIM BUN THON; Dep. Dir-Gen. TUM VANN DET.

FM 99 MHZ: 41 rue 360, Phnom-Penh; tel. (23) 426794; Gen. Man. SOM CHHAYA.

FM 107 MHZ: 81 rue 562, Phnom-Penh; tel. (23) 428047; fax (23) 368212; Dir-Gen. KHUN HANG.

Phnom-Penh Municipality Radio: 131–132 blvd Pochentong, Phnom-Penh; tel. (23) 725205; fax (23) 360800; Gen. Man. KHAMPUN KEOMONY.

RCAF Radio: c/o Borei Keila, rue 169, Phnom-Penh; tel. (23) 366061; fax (23) 366063; f. 1994; Royal Cambodian Armed Forces radio station; Dir THA TANA; News Editor SENG KATEKA.

Vithyu Cheat Kampuchea (National Radio of Cambodia): rue Preah Kossamak, Phnom-Penh; tel. (23) 368140; fax (23) 427319; f. 1978; fmrly Vithyu Samleng Pracheachon Kampuchea (Voice of the Cambodian People); controlled by the Ministry of Information and the Press; home service in Khmer; daily external services in English, French, Lao, Vietnamese and Thai; Dir-Gen. VANN SENG LY; Dep. Dir Gen. TAN YAN.

There are also eight private local radio stations based in Phnom-Penh, Battambang Province, Sihanoukville, and Stung Treng Province.

Television

Apsara Television (TV11): 69 rue 360, Phnom-Penh; tel. (23) 724402; fax (23) 724302; Dir-Gen. TEN SIMAN.

Bayon Television (TV27): 954 rue 2, Takhmau, Kandal Province; tel. (23) 983435; fax (23) 982232; Dir-Gen. KEM KUNNAVATH.

National Television of Cambodia (Channel 7): 19 rue 242, Phnom-Penh; tel. (23) 722983; fax (23) 426407; opened 1983; broadcasts for 10 hours per day in Khmer; Dir-Gen. (Head of Television) MAO AYUTH.

Phnom-Penh Television (TV3): 131–132 blvd Pochentong, Phnom-Penh; tel. (23) 725205; fax (23) 360800; Dir-Gen. KHAMPHUN KEOMONY.

RCAF Television (TV5): 165 rue 169, Phnom-Penh; tel. (23) 366061; fax (23) 366063; Editor-in-Chief PRUM KIM.

TV Khmer (TV9): 81 rue 562, Phnom-Penh; tel. (23) 428047; fax (23) 368212; Dir-Gen. KHUN HANG; News Editor PHAN TITH.

Finance

BANKING

The National Bank of Cambodia, which was established as the sole authorized bank in 1980 (following the abolition of the monetary system by the Government of Democratic Kampuchea in 1975), is the central bank, and assumed its present name in February 1992. The adoption of a market economy led to the licensing of privately-owned and joint-venture banks from July 1991. At June 1999 there were a further 32 banks operating in Cambodia, including two state-owned banks, 22 locally-incorporated private banks and eight branches of foreign banks. Rural financing was often provided by a decentralized system of non-governmental organizations. Plans were confirmed in early 1998 to establish a Rural Development Bank. These institutions are under the supervision of the National Bank of Cambodia.

Central Bank

National Bank of Cambodia: 22–24 blvd Norodom, BP 25, Phnom-Penh; tel. (23) 722563; fax (23) 426117; e-mail nbc2@bigpond.com.kh; f. 1980; cap. 1,550m. riels; Gov. CHEA CHANTO; Dep. Gov. ENG THAYSAN.

State Banks

Foreign Trade Bank: 24–26 blvd Norodom, Phnom-Penh; tel. (23) 525866; scheduled for privatization; Man. TIM BO PHOL.

Rural Development Bank: 5 rue Preah Ang Eng St & rue Preah Ang No, Sangkat Watt Phnom Khan Daun Penh, Phnom-Penh; tel. (23) 982434.

Private Banks

Advanced Bank of Asia Ltd: 97–99 blvd Norodom, Khan Daun Penh, Phnom-Penh; tel. (23) 720434; fax (23) 720435; Dir CHAE WAN CHO.

Agriculture and Commercial Bank of Cambodia (ACBC) Ltd: 49 rue 214, Samdach Pann, Phnom-Penh; tel. (23) 722272; fax (23) 426683; e-mail 012812428@mobitel.com.kh; Man. THAI SOVANA.

Cambodia Agriculture, Industrial and Merchant Bank: 87 blvd Norodom, Phnom-Penh; tel. 366856; Man. CHHOR SANG.

Cambodia Asia Bank Ltd: 252 blvd Monivong, Phnom-Penh; tel. (23) 722105; fax (23) 426647; Man. WONG TOW FOCK.

Cambodia Farmers Bank: 45 rue Kampuchea Viet Nam, Phnom-Penh; tel. (23) 426183; fax (23) 426801; f. 1992; joint venture by Thai business executives and the National Bank of Cambodia; Man. PHOT PUNYARATABANDHU; Dep. Man. NORODOM ARUNRASMY; 2 brs.

Cambodia International Bank Ltd: 21 rue 128, 107 S. Monorom, Khan 7 Makara, Phnom-Penh; tel. (23) 725920; Man. CHIEE YOON CHENG.

Cambodia Mekong Bank: 1 rue Kramuon Sar, Khan Daun Penh, Phnom-Penh; tel. (23) 217112; fax (23) 217122; e-mail ho.mailbox@mekongbank.com; Man. KHOV BOUN CHHAY.

Cambodian Commercial Bank Ltd: 26 blvd Monivong, Phnom-Penh; tel. (23) 25644; fax (23) 426116; f. 1991; Man. BHENGBHASANG KRISHMMSA; 4 brs.

Cambodian Public Bank (Campu Bank): Villa 23, rue 114, BP 899, Phnom-Penh; tel. (23) 426067; fax (23) 426068; e-mail campu@bigpond.com.kh; Man. CHAN KOK CHOY.

Canadia Bank Ltd: 265–269 rue Ang Duong, Sangkat Wat Phnom, Khan Daun Penh, Phnom-Penh; tel. (23) 215286; fax (23) 427064; e-mail canadia@camnet.com.kh; internet www.canadiabank.com; Man. PUNG KHEAV SE; 8 brs.

Chansavangwong Bank: 145A–145B rue 154–51, Khan Daun Penh, Phnom-Penh; tel. (23) 427464; fax (23) 427461; Man. TAING LI PHENG.

Emperor International Bank Ltd: 230–232 blvd Monivong, Phnom-Penh; tel. (23) 426254; fax (23) 426417; e-mail eib@bigpond.com.kh; Man. VAN SOU IENG.

First Overseas Bank Ltd: 20 rue 114, Phnom-Penh; tel. (23) 213023; fax (23) 427439; e-mail firstoverseas@worldmail.com.kh; Man. CHOY SOOK KUEN; 3 brs.

Global Commercial Bank Ltd: 337 blvd Monivong, Sangkat Orassey 4, Khan 7 Makara, Phnom-Penh; tel. (23) 364258; fax (23) 426612; e-mail gcb@camnet.com.kh; Man. WELLSON HSIEH.

Great International Bank Ltd: 320A–320B blvd Monivong, Khan Daun Penh, Phnom-Penh; tel. (23) 427282; Man. LY TAK BOUALAY.

Khmer Bank (Thaneakar Khmer): 116 rue Sihanouk, Phnom-Penh; tel. (23) 724853; Man. HENG KIM Y.

Pacific Commercial Bank Ltd: 350 rue 217, Sangkat Orassey 2, Khan 7 Makara, Phnom-Penh; tel. (23) 426896; Man. TENG DANNY.

Phnom-Penh City Bank Ltd: 101 blvd Norodom, rue 214, Phnom-Penh; tel. (23) 427354; fax (23) 427353; Man. THEERAYUT SEANG AROON.

Rich Nation Bank Ltd: 272–278 Charles de Gaulle, Sangkat Orassey 2, Khan 7 Makara, Phnom-Penh; tel. (23) 720100; fax (23) 720118; e-mail richbank@bigpond.com.kh; Man. HENRY SHI CALLE; Dep. Man. DANIEL CHAN.

Singapore Banking Corporation Ltd: 68 rue 214, Sangkat Boeung Reang, Khan Daun Penh, Phnom-Penh; tel. (23) 723366; fax (23) 427277; f. 1993; Exec. Dir ANDY KUN.

Singapore Commercial Bank Ltd: 316 blvd Preah Monivong, Khan Daun Penh, BP 1199, Phnom-Penh; tel. and fax (23) 427471; cap. US $5m.; Pres. Kong Look Sen; Gen. Man. Teoh Sam Ming; 1 br.

Union Commercial Bank Ltd: UCB Building, 61 rue 130, Psa Chas Quarter, Khan Daun Penh, Phnom-Penh; tel. (23) 427995; fax (23) 427997; e-mail ucb@bigpond.com.kh; internet www.cambodia-web.net/banking/ucb; f. 1994; cap. US $10m., res US $2m., dep. US $13m. (1999); CEO Yum Sui Sang; 2 brs.

Foreign Banks

Bangkok Bank Ltd (Thailand): 26 M.V. Preah Norodom, P.O.B. 106, Phnom-Penh; tel. (23) 723598; fax (23) 426593; Man. Thewakun Chanakun.

Crédit Agricole Indosuez (France): 70 blvd Norodom, POB 923, Phnom-Penh; tel. (23) 427233; fax (23) 214481; Man. Bernard Pardigon.

Krung Thai Bank PLC (Thailand): 149 rue 215 Jawaharlal Nehru, Depot Market 1, Tuolkok Division, Phnom-Penh; tel. (23) 366005; fax (23) 428737; e-mail ktbpmp@camnet.com.kh; Man. Nakxob U-Setthasakdi.

Lippo Bank (Indonesia): 273 Preah Andoung, S.K. Wat Phnom, Khan Daun Penh, Phnom-Penh; Man. Markus Parmadi.

Maybank Bhd (Malaysia): 2 blvd Norodom, Phnom-Penh; tel. (23) 217590; fax (23) 217594; Man. Abdul Malek Mohd Khair.

Standard Chartered Bank (UK): 89 blvd Norodom, POB 46, Phnom-Penh; tel. (23) 216685; fax (23) 216687; CEO Ong Teng Hoon; 1 br.

Thai Farmers Bank Ltd (Thailand): 335 Blvd Preah Monivong, Sangkat Orussey 4, Khan 7, Makara, Phnom-Penh; tel. (23) 426536; fax (23) 426548; Man. Perawap Sing Tong.

INSURANCE

Commercial Union: 28 rue 47, Phnom-Penh; tel. (23) 426694; fax (23) 427171; general insurance; Gen. Man. Paul Cable.

Indochine Insurance Ltd: 55 rue 178, BP 808, Phnom-Penh; tel. (23) 210701; fax (23) 210501; e-mail insurance@indochine.com.kh; internet www.indochine.net; Dir Philippe Lenain.

Trade and Industry
DEVELOPMENT ORGANIZATIONS

Cambodian Development Council (CDC): Government Palace, quai Sisowath, Wat Phnom, Phnom-Penh; tel. (23) 981156; fax (23) 361516; f. 1993; sole body responsible for approving foreign investment in Cambodia, also grants exemptions from customs duties and other taxes, and provides other facilities for investors; Chair. Hun Sen; Sec.-Gen. Sok Chenda.

Cambodian Investment Board: Phnom-Penh; Sec.-Gen. Ith Vichit.

CHAMBER OF COMMERCE

Phnom-Penh Chamber of Commerce: 22 rue Kramuon Sar, Psar Thmei 2, Phnom-Penh; tel. (23) 722744; fax (23) 427207; Pres. Sok Kong.

INDUSTRIAL AND TRADE ASSOCIATIONS

Cambodian Garment Factory Association (CGFA): Phnom-Penh; tel. 12888222; fax (23) 427983; Pres. Van Sou Ieng; Sec. Roger Tan.

Export Promotion Department: Ministry of Commerce, 20A blvd Norodom, Phnom-Penh; tel. (23) 210365; fax (23) 217353; e-mail ogawa@bigpond.com.kh; internet www.moc.gov.kh/depts/epd.htm; f. 1997; Dir Prak Nork.

UTILITIES
Electricity

Electricité du Cambodge: rue 19, Wat Phnom, Phnom-Penh; tel. (23) 811327; fax (23) 426018; Dir-Gen. Tan Kim Vin.

Water

Phnom-Penh Water Supply Authority: nr Railway Station, Phnom-Penh; tel. (23) 427657; fax (23) 428969; e-mail ppwsa@

bigpond.com.kh; f. 1996 as an autonomous public enterprise; Dir-Gen. Ek Sonn Chan.

TRADE UNIONS

Cambodian Federation of Independent Trade Unions (CFITU): Phnom-Penh; e-mail CFITU@bigpond.com.kh; f. 1979 as Cambodian Federation of Trade Unions; changed name as above in 1999; Chair. Ros Sok; Vice-Chair. Tep Kim Vannary, Kieng Thisotha.

Cambodian Union Federation: f. 1997 with the support of the CPP in response to the formation of the FTUWKC.

Free Trade Union of Workers of the Kingdom of Cambodia (FTUWKC): f. 1997 with the assistance of Sam Rainsy; Leader Chea Vichea.

Transport
RAILWAYS

Royal Railway of Cambodia: Moha Vithei Pracheathippatay, Phnom-Penh; tel. (23) 725156; comprises two 1,000 mm-gauge single track main lines with a total length of 649 km: the 385-km Phnom-Penh to Poipet line, the 264-km Phnom-Penh to Sihanoukville line and branch lines and special purpose sidings; the condition of the lines is very poor, with many temporary repairs, owing to mine damage, and the service also suffers from other operational difficulties, such as a shortage of rolling stock; there are 14 'Gares' (main stations), 19 stations and 38 halts; Dir Sokhom Pheakavanmony.

ROADS

In 1997 the total road network was 35,769 km in length, of which 4,165 km were highways and 3,604 km were secondary roads; about 7.5% of the road network was paved.

INLAND WATERWAYS

The major routes are along the Mekong river, and up the Tonlé Sap river into the Tonlé Sap (Great Lake), covering, in all, about 2,400 km. The inland ports of Neak Luong, Kompong Cham and Prek Kdam have been supplied with motor ferries, and the ferry crossings have been improved.

SHIPPING

The main port is Sihanoukville, on the Gulf of Thailand, which has 11 berths and can accommodate vessels of 10,000–15,000 tons. Phnom-Penh port lies some distance inland. Steamers of up to 4,000 tons can be accommodated.

CIVIL AVIATION

There is an international airport at Pochentong, near Phnom-Penh. In August 1997 the Government announced the formation of a second state-owned airline, Kampuchea Airlines. Prince Norodom Chakkrapong established a new airline named Phnom-Penh Airline in 1999.

State Secretariat of Civil Aviation (SSCA): 62 blvd Norodom, Phnom-Penh; tel. (23) 724167; fax (23) 426169; Gen. Dir Keo Saphal.

Royal Air Cambodge (RAC): 24 ave Kramuonsar, blvd Monivong, Phnom-Penh; tel. (23) 428831; fax (17) 428895; internet www.royalaircambodge.com; re-established 1994; national airline; joint venture between the Govt (60%) and Malaysian Helicopter Services (now known as Naluri Bhd, 40%); operates flights to six domestic destinations and routes to Malaysia, Singapore, Thailand, Viet Nam, Hong Kong and the People's Republic of China; Chair. and CEO (vacant).

Tourism

Tourism continued to be adversely affected by civil unrest in 1998, with arrivals declining to 212,935. However, arrivals increased to 271,100 in 1999, owing to the improvement in the security situation, and to an estimated 440,000 in 2000, in which year tourist receipts reached almost US $200m.

General Directorate for Tourism: 3 blvd Monivong, Phnom-Penh; tel. (23) 427130; fax (23) 426107; e-mail tourism@camnet.com.kh; f. 1988; Dir So Mara.

CAMEROON
Introductory Survey

Location, Climate, Language, Religion, Flag, Capital

The Republic of Cameroon lies on the west coast of Africa, with Nigeria to the west, Chad and the Central African Republic to the east, and the Republic of the Congo, Equatorial Guinea and Gabon to the south. The climate is hot and humid in the south and west, with average temperatures of 26°C (80°F). Annual rainfall in Yaoundé averages 4,030 mm (159 ins). The north is drier, with more extreme temperatures. The official languages are French and English; many local languages are also spoken, including Fang, Bamileke and Duala. Approximately 53% of Cameroonians profess Christianity, 25% adhere to traditional religious beliefs, and about 22%, mostly in the north, are Muslims. The national flag (proportions 3 by 2) has three equal vertical stripes, of green, red and yellow, with a five-pointed gold star in the centre of the red stripe. The capital is Yaoundé.

Recent History

In 1884 a German protectorate was established in Cameroon (Kamerun). In 1916, during the First World War, the German administration was overthrown by invading British and French forces. Under an agreement reached between the occupying powers in 1919, Cameroon was divided into two zones: a French-ruled area in the east and south, and a smaller British-administered area in the west. In 1922 both zones became subject to mandates of the League of Nations, with France and the United Kingdom as the administering powers. In 1946 the zones were transformed into UN Trust Territories, with British and French rule continuing in their respective areas.

French Cameroons became an autonomous state within the French Community in 1957. Under the leadership of Ahmadou Ahidjo, a northerner who became Prime Minister in 1958, the territory became independent, as the Republic of Cameroon, on 1 January 1960. The first election for the country's National Assembly, held in April 1960, was won by Ahidjo's party, the Union camerounaise. In May the new National Assembly elected Ahidjo to be the country's first President.

British Cameroons, comprising a northern and a southern region, was attached to neighbouring Nigeria, for administrative purposes, prior to Nigeria's independence in October 1960. Plebiscites were held, under UN auspices, in the two regions of British Cameroons in February 1961. The northern area voted to merge with Nigeria (becoming the province of Sardauna), while the south voted for union with the Republic of Cameroon, which took place on 1 October 1961.

The enlarged country was named the Federal Republic of Cameroon, with French and English as joint official languages. It comprised two states: the former French zone became East Cameroon, while the former British portion became West Cameroon. John Ngu Foncha, the Prime Minister of West Cameroon and leader of the Kamerun National Democratic Party, became Vice-President of the Federal Republic. Under the continuing leadership of Ahidjo, who (as the sole candidate) was re-elected President in May 1965, the two states became increasingly integrated. In September 1966 the two governing parties and several opposition groups combined to form a single party, the Union nationale camerounaise (UNC). The only significant opposition party, the extreme left-wing Union des populations camerounaises (UPC), was suppressed in 1971 (although it was allowed to operate again when multi-party politics was reintroduced in the early 1990s). Meanwhile, Ahidjo was re-elected as President in March 1970, and Solomon Muna (who had replaced Foncha as Prime Minister of West Cameroon in 1968) became Vice-President.

In June 1972, following the approval by referendum of a new Constitution, the federal system was ended and the country was officially renamed the United Republic of Cameroon. The office of Vice-President was abolished. A centralized political and administrative system was rapidly introduced, and in May 1973 a new National Assembly was elected for a five-year term. After the re-election of Ahidjo as President in April 1975, the Constitution was revised, and a Prime Minister, Paul Biya (a bilingual Christian southerner), was appointed in June. In April 1980 Ahidjo was unanimously re-elected to the presidency for a fifth five-year term of office.

Ahidjo announced his resignation as President in November 1982, and nominated Biya as his successor. In subsequent cabinet reorganizations Biya removed a number of supporters of the former President. In August 1983 Biya announced the discovery of a conspiracy to overthrow his Government, and simultaneously dismissed the Prime Minister and the Minister of the Armed Forces, both northern Muslims. Later in August Ahidjo resigned as President of the UNC and strongly criticized Biya's regime. In September Biya was elected President of the ruling party, and in January 1984 he was re-elected as President of the Republic, reportedly obtaining 99.98% of the votes cast. In a subsequent reorganization of the Cabinet the post of Prime Minister was abolished, and it was announced that the country's name was to revert from the United Republic of Cameroon to the Republic of Cameroon.

In February 1984 Ahidjo and two of his close military advisers were tried (Ahidjo *in absentia*) for their alleged complicity in the coup plot of August 1983, and received death sentences, which were, however, commuted to life imprisonment. On 6 April 1984 rebel elements in the presidential guard, led by Col Saleh Ibrahim (a northerner), attempted to overthrow the Biya Government. After three days of intense fighting, in which hundreds of people were reported to have been killed, the rebellion was suppressed by forces loyal to the President; a total of 51 defendants received death sentences at trials held in May and November. Following extensive changes within the military hierarchy, the UNC Central Committee and the leadership of state-controlled companies, Biya reorganized his Government in July and introduced more stringent press censorship.

In March 1985 the UNC was renamed the Rassemblement démocratique du peuple camerounais (RDPC). In January 1986 members of the exiled UPC movement claimed that 200–300 opponents of the Biya Government (most of whom were anglophones or members of clandestine opposition movements) had been arrested in the preceding months, and that some of those in detention were being subjected to torture. A number of detainees were subsequently released. In July 1987 the National Assembly approved a new electoral code providing for multiple candidacy in public elections, and in October voters had a choice of RDPC-approved candidates in local government elections.

Ostensibly for reasons of economy, the presidential election, originally scheduled for January 1989, was brought forward to coincide with elections to the National Assembly in April 1988. Biya was re-elected unopposed to the presidency, securing 98.75% of the votes cast. In the legislative elections voters were presented with a choice of RDPC-approved candidates; 153 of those elected were new members. (In accordance with constitutional amendments agreed in March 1988, the number of members in the National Assembly was increased from 150 to 180.)

In February 1990 11 people, including the former President of the Cameroonian Bar Association, Yondo Black, were arrested in connection with their alleged involvement in an unofficial opposition organization, the Social Democratic Front (SDF). In April Black was sentenced to three years' imprisonment on charges of 'subversion'. Later that month Biya announced that all the prisoners who had been detained in connection with the 1984 coup attempt were to be released. In May 1990 a demonstration organized by the SDF was violently suppressed by security forces, and six deaths were subsequently reported. Furthermore the Government suspended the publication of an independent newspaper that had implied support for the SDF. In June the Vice-President of the RDPC, John Ngu Foncha, resigned, alleging corruption and human rights violations on the part of the Government, while the Congress of the RDPC re-elected Biya as President of the party. In response to continued civil unrest, Biya stated that he envisaged the future adoption of a multi-party system and announced a series of reforms, including the abolition of laws governing subversion, the revision of the law on political associations, and the reinforcement of press freedom. In the same month a committee

908

was established to revise legislation on human rights. In August several political prisoners, including Black, were released.

In September 1990 Biya announced an extensive cabinet reshuffle, in which a new ministry to implement the Government's economic stabilization programme was created. In December the National Assembly adopted legislation whereby Cameroon officially became a multi-party state. Under the new legislation, the Government was required to provide an official response within three months to any political organization seeking legal recognition. However, the recruitment of party activists on an ethnic or regional basis and the financing of political parties from external sources remained illegal. Legislative elections, which were due in April 1993, were rescheduled to take place by the end of 1991 (but were later postponed).

In January 1991 anti-Government demonstrators protested at Biya's failure (despite previous undertakings) to grant an amnesty to prisoners implicated in the 1984 coup attempt. In the same month the trial of two journalists, who had criticized Biya in an independent publication, *Le Messager*, provoked violent rioting. Meanwhile, opposition leaders reiterated demands for Biya's resignation and the convening of a national conference to formulate a timetable for multi-party elections. Biya's continued opposition to the holding of a conference provoked a series of demonstrations, which were violently suppressed by the security forces. In April the principal anti-Government groups created an informal alliance, the National Co-ordination Committee of Opposition Parties (NCCOP), which organized a widely-observed general strike. Later in April, in response to increasing pressure for political reform, the National Assembly approved legislation granting a general amnesty for political prisoners and reintroducing the post of Prime Minister. Biya subsequently appointed Sadou Hayatou, hitherto Secretary-General at the Presidency, to the position. Hayatou named a 32-member transitional Government, principally composed of members of the former Cabinet. The Government's refusal to comply with the NCCOP's demands for an unconditional amnesty for all political prisoners (the existing provisions for an amnesty excluded an estimated 400 political prisoners jailed for allegedly non-political crimes) and for the convening of a national conference prompted the alliance to organize a campaign of civil disobedience, culminating in a general strike in June, which halted commercial activity in most towns. The Government placed seven of Cameroon's 10 provinces under military rule, prohibited opposition gatherings, and later in June, following continued civil disturbances, banned the NCCOP and several opposition parties, alleging that the opposition alliance was responsible for terrorist activities. Although opposition leaders announced that the campaign of civil disobedience would continue, the effect of the general strike declined in subsequent months. In September several opposition leaders were temporarily detained, following violent demonstrations in Douala.

In October 1991 Biya announced that legislative elections were to be held in February 1992, and that a Prime Minister would be appointed from the party that secured a majority in the National Assembly. Tripartite negotiations between the Government, opposition parties and independent officials commenced at the end of October 1991. In mid-November the Government and about 40 of the 47 registered opposition parties (including some parties belonging to the NCCOP) signed an agreement providing for the establishment of a committee to draft constitutional reforms. The opposition undertook to suspend the campaign of civil disobedience, while the Government agreed to end the ban on opposition meetings and to release all prisoners who had been arrested during anti-Government demonstrations. However, several principal opposition parties belonging to the NCCOP, including the SDF, subsequently declared the agreement to be invalid, and stated that the campaign of civil disobedience would continue. The Government revoked the ban on opposition gatherings later in November, and in December ended the military rule that had been imposed in seven provinces.

In January 1992 the Government postponed the legislative elections until March (opposition leaders had demanded that the elections take place in May), in order to allow parties sufficient time for preparation. However, several opposition movements, including two of the principal parties, the SDF and the Union démocratique du Cameroun (UDC), refused to contest the elections, on the grounds that the scheduled date was too early and therefore benefited the RDPC. In February more than 100 people were killed in the northern town of Kousseri,

following violent clashes between the Kokoto and Arab Choa ethnic groups during the registration of voters. In the same month those opposition parties that had not accepted the tripartite agreement in November 1991 formed the Alliance pour le redressement du Cameroun (ARC), and announced that they were to boycott the elections.

The legislative elections, which took place on 1 March 1992, were contested by 32 political parties; the RDPC won 88 of the National Assembly's 180 seats, while the Union nationale pour la démocratie et le progrès (UNDP) obtained 68, the UPC 18 and the Mouvement pour la défense de la République (MDR) six seats. The RDPC subsequently formed an alliance with the MDR, thereby securing an absolute majority in the National Assembly. In April Biya formed a 25-member Cabinet, principally comprising members of the previous Government; Simon Achidi Achu, an anglophone member of the RDPC who had served in the Ahidjo administration, was appointed Prime Minister. Five members of the MDR, including the party leader, Dakolle Daissala, also received ministerial portfolios.

In August 1992 Biya announced that the forthcoming presidential election, scheduled for May 1993, was to be brought forward to 11 October 1992. In September Biya promulgated legislation regulating the election of the President that prohibited the formation of electoral alliances. Shortly before the election two of the seven opposition candidates withdrew in favour of the Chairman of the SDF, John Fru Ndi, who received the support of the ARC alliance. The presidential election, which took place as scheduled, immediately provoked opposition allegations of malpractice on the part of the Government. In mid-October Fru Ndi proclaimed himself President, following unconfirmed reports that he had won the election. Later that month, however, the Government announced that Biya had been re-elected by 39.9% of the votes cast, while Fru Ndi had secured 35.9%, prompting violent demonstrations by opposition supporters in many areas, particularly in the north-west and in Douala. The Supreme Court rejected a subsequent appeal by Fru Ndi that the results of the election be declared invalid. At the end of October, in response to the continued unrest, the Government placed Fru Ndi and several of his supporters under house arrest, and imposed a three-month state of emergency in North-West Province. Biya was inaugurated as President on 3 November and pledged to implement further constitutional reforms. Later that month international condemnation of the Government increased, following the death by torture of a detained opposition member; the USA and Germany suspended economic aid to Cameroon in protest at the continued enforcement of the state of emergency. At the end of November Biya appointed a new 30-member Cabinet, which, in addition to three members of the MDR, included representatives of the UPC, the UNDP and the Parti national du progrès. In late December the state of emergency was revoked in North-West Province. In January 1993 the Government granted an amnesty to a number of political prisoners who had been arrested in October 1992.

In March 1993 an informal alliance of opposition parties (led by the SDF), the Union pour le changement, organized a series of demonstrations and a boycott of French consumer goods (in protest at the French Government's involvement with Biya) in support of demands for a new presidential election. The Government accused the alliance of incitement to civil disorder and continued efforts to suppress opposition activity. Later in March three people were killed in clashes between members of the armed forces and opposition supporters in Bamenda, in North-West Province, while a number of members of a prominent opposition movement, the Union des forces démocratiques du Cameroun, were arrested shortly before a demonstration was due to take place. In response to international pressure, however, the Government announced its intention to conduct a national debate on constitutional reform. In April a gathering organized by the Cameroon Anglophone Movement (CAM) in Buéa, in South-West Province, demanded the restoration of a federal system of government, in response to the traditional dominance of the French-speaking section of the population. In the following month the Government promulgated draft constitutional amendments which provided for the installation of a democratic political system, with the establishment of new organs of government, including an upper legislative chamber, to be known as the Senate, and restricted the power vested in the President (who was to serve a maximum of two five-year terms of office). The draft legislation retained a unitary state, but, in recognition of demands by supporters of federalism, envisaged a more decentralized system of local government.

During the second half of 1993 the opposition organized a series of anti-Government strikes and demonstrations, which led to the detention of many activists. In December public-sector workers initiated a general strike, with the support of the opposition, after the Government announced substantial reductions in state-sector salaries. In early 1994, however, strike action in protest at the devaluation of the CFA franc subsided, following the imposition of sanctions against striking civil servants. Meanwhile, in September 1993 a peace agreement was signed between the Kokoto and Arab Choa ethnic groups in Kousseri, although further clashes were reported later in the year. In February 1994 security forces killed some 50 members of the Arab Choa ethnic group at the village of Karena in northern Cameroon, apparently in retaliation for acts of armed banditry in the region, which were, however, widely attributed to former Chadian rebels. In March some 1,200 citizens took refuge in Chad, in response to continuing clashes between security forces and bandits in northern Cameroon.

In July 1994, in accordance with the Government's aim of promoting economic recovery, a new ministerial department with responsibility for the economy and finance was created as part of an extensive cabinet reorganization. In September an informal alliance of 16 opposition movements, the Front des alliés pour le changement (FAC), was established, effectively replacing the Union pour le changement; the FAC denounced alleged human rights violations on the part of the authorities, together with the indefinite postponement of municipal elections and the transfer of state-owned enterprises to the private sector. The UNDP and the UDC refused to join the alliance, however, on the grounds that it was dominated by the SDF. (In February 1995 the leader of the Mouvement pour la démocratie et le progrès (MDP), Samuel Eboua, was elected President of the FAC, replacing Fru Ndi of the SDF.) In November 1994 Biya announced that discussions on the revision of the Constitution were to resume, following the establishment of a Consultative Constitutional Review Committee, and that municipal elections were to take place in 1995. Constitutional discussions commenced in December 1994, but were boycotted by the opposition, which cited limitations in the agenda of the debate. In early 1995, however, the Consultative Constitutional Review Committee submitted revised constitutional amendments to Biya for consideration.

In July 1995 members of a new anglophone organization, the Southern Cameroons National Council (SCNC, which demanded that the former portion of the British Cameroons that had amalgamated with the Republic of Cameroon in 1961 be granted autonomy), staged a demonstration in Bamenda, at which they clashed with security forces. In the same month a number of independently-owned newspapers temporarily suspended publication in protest at alleged increasing press censorship and intimidation of journalists. In August representatives of anglophone movements, including the SCNC and the CAM, officially presented their demands for the establishment of an independent, English-speaking republic of Southern Cameroons at the UN, and urged the international community to assist in resolving the issue in order to avert civil conflict in Cameroon; the organizations claimed that the plebiscite of 1961, whereby the former southern portion of British Cameroons had voted to merge with the Republic of Cameroon on terms of equal status, had been rendered invalid by subsequent francophone domination.

In October 1995 a special congress of the RDPC re-elected Biya as leader of the party for a further term of five years. Meanwhile, Cameroon's pending application for membership of the Commonwealth (which had been accepted, in principle, in 1993, subject to the Government's fulfilment of certain democratic conditions) prompted further controversy; opposition movements urged the Commonwealth to refuse admission to Cameroon on the grounds that no progress had been achieved with regard to human rights and the democratic process, while the SCNC submitted a rival application for membership on behalf of the proposed independent republic of Southern Cameroons. In November, however, Cameroon was formally admitted to the Commonwealth. In the same month Biya announced that the long-awaited municipal elections were to take place in January 1996 (although both opposition movements and parties belonging to the government coalition had demanded that the elections be preceded by constitutional reform and the establishment of an independent electoral commission). In December 1995 the National Assembly adopted the revised constitutional amendments, submitted by Biya earlier

that month, which increased the presidential mandate from five to seven years (while restricting the maximum tenure of office to two terms) and provided for the establishment of a Senate. Municipal elections, in which some 38 political parties participated, duly took place in January 1996; the RDPC won the majority of seats in 56% of local councils, and the SDF in 27%, while the UNDP received popular support in the north of the country. (The two main opposition parties performed well in the elections, despite having both suffered internal division during 1994–95.) In March 1996 the SDF and the UNDP urged a campaign of civil disobedience in protest at the Government's appointment by decree of representatives to replace the elected mayors in principal towns (following the municipal elections, the opposition had gained control of 13 towns). At the beginning of that month at least two people were killed in a demonstration, which had been organized by the SDF in the south-western town of Limbe. In April the Government imposed a total ban on all media reports of the SDF/UNDP campaign of civil disobedience. In May–June the two parties organized general strikes, which were principally observed in western and northern regions. In September Simon Achidi Achu was replaced as Prime Minister by Peter Mafany Musonge, the General Manager of the Cameroon Development Corporation, and a new Cabinet was appointed.

In January 1997 the Government postponed the legislative elections (which had been scheduled to take place in March) owing to organizational difficulties, following opposition complaints that its supporters had been allowed insufficient time for registration; Biya's subsequent failure to extend the mandate of the incumbent National Assembly (which expired in March) prompted criticism from a number of opposition deputies. At the end of March some 10 people were killed when unidentified armed groups staged attacks against government and security buildings in Bamenda and other towns in North-West Province; the violence was generally attributed to members of the SCNC. In April the Government announced that the elections were to take place on 17 May. Pre-election violence, in which some five people were killed, prompted the imposition of increased security measures, including the closure of the country's borders. The elections, which were contested by 46 political parties, were monitored by a Commonwealth observer mission. The announcement of provisional results (which attributed a large majority of seats to the RDPC) prompted claims from the opposition parties of widespread electoral malpractice; the observer group also expressed general dissatisfaction with the election process. The Supreme Court, however, rejected opposition appeals against RDPC victories. Three people were killed in clashes between RDPC and SDF members in South-West Province, where the election result was disputed by the two parties. In early June the Supreme Court announced the official election results: the RDPC had secured 109 of the 180 seats in the legislature, while the SDF had obtained 43, the UNDP 13 and the UDC five seats; the Mouvement pour la jeunesse du Cameroun (MLJC), the UPC and the MDR obtained one seat each. The Cabinet remained virtually unchanged from the previous administration and Musonge was retained as Prime Minister. In August further polls were conducted in seven constituencies where the results had been annulled, owing to alleged irregularities; the RDPC won all of the seats, thus increasing its representation in the National Assembly to 116 seats.

In July 1997 it was reported that the former Minister of Public Health, Titus Edzoa, who in April had resigned from the Cabinet in order to contest the forthcoming presidential election, had been arrested and charged with embezzlement; his supporters claimed, however, that Edzoa (a leading figure in the RDPC) was being held as a political prisoner at a 'torture centre'. It was announced in September that the election would be held on 12 October. Shortly afterwards the three major opposition parties, the SDF, UNDP and UDC, declared a boycott of all elections, including the imminent presidential election, in protest at the absence of an independent electoral commission; a fourth opposition party, the Union du peuple africain, later joined the boycott. In mid-September Biya was officially elected as the RDPC presidential candidate. At the election, which was contested by seven candidates, Biya was re-elected, winning 92.6% of the votes cast. The level of voter participation in the election was much disputed, with official sources asserting that a record 81.4% of the electorate took part, while opposition leaders claimed that the abstention rate was higher than 80%, and dismissed the poll as an 'electoral masquerade'. Biya was formally inaugurated on 3 November, beginning, in accordance with the revised Constitution, a seven-year term in presidential office. Following talks with various opposition groups, the RDPC reached an agreement with the UNDP on the creation of a coalition government; the SDF, however, refused to co-operate with the ruling party. In December, having reappointed Musonge as Prime Minister, Biya effected a major cabinet reshuffle. The new Government included representatives from four of the country's many political groups, although the RDPC retained 45 of the 50 ministerial posts.

At the end of December 1997 the editor of *Le Messager*, Pius Njawe, was arrested, following the publication of an article in which he alleged that President Biya had suffered a heart attack. In January 1998 Njawe was fined and sentenced to two years' imprisonment; this was widely condemned, as were the convictions of three other journalists for similar offences. In April, as a result of an appeal, Njawe's prison sentence was reduced to one year, and, following reports that the editor had been denied medical attention, he was granted presidential clemency and released in October.

In March 1998 renewed communal clashes were reported in Bamenda. In July 10 of the 43 SDF parliamentary deputies resigned from the party, in protest at the perceived tribalism and authoritarianism of its leadership. In October the SDF expelled its First National Vice-President, Soulaimane Mahamad, following the latter's criticism of Fru Ndi as authoritarian. In January 1999 Fru Ndi announced that he was prepared to initiate direct dialogue with President Biya. It was, however, alleged that the leader of the SDF had announced this radical change of policy in the hope of securing a favourable verdict in his imminent court appearance on charges of defamation. In April Fru Ndi was, none the less, found guilty and was fined and given a three-year suspended sentence. At the SDF party conference in the same month Fru Ndi was re-elected Chairman of the party by an overwhelming majority of delegates, despite accusations made by opponents that he had presided over the disintegration of the SDF as a political force. The conference also voted not to enter into dialogue with the Government until an independent electoral commission had been established, and to improve internal party discipline.

Meanwhile, in September 1998 it was reported that some 60 English-speaking Cameroonians, who were alleged to be secessionists campaigning for the independence of Southern Cameroons, were being detained and tortured in Yaoundé, following attacks on police premises. There were counter-accusations made by the opposition, however, that the raids had been staged by government agents as a pretext for further suppression of demands for increased decentralization. In January 1999 the opposition condemned the Government for the alleged marginalization of the anglophone minority in Cameroon, noting that only three of the 2,000 soldiers recently recruited by the armed forces were English-speaking. In June the trial of the alleged anglophone secessionists (the majority of whom had been arrested in 1997) began in Yaoundé. The trial was notable for frequent adjournments and complaints by defence lawyers relating to the competence of the military tribunal to hear the case. In July several of the defendants claimed that confessions that they were members of the separatist SCNC had been extracted under torture and threats of summary execution. The human rights organization Amnesty International later claimed that, prior to the start of the trial, several of the detainees had died in prison either from torture or from lack of medical care. In August the accused formally denied all charges against them, although several individuals admitted to being members of a cultural association linked to the SCNC. In October three of the defendants were sentenced to life imprisonment, others received lengthy prison sentences, while 29 were acquitted. Amnesty International criticized the verdicts, alluding to the alleged bias of the military court and the reported torture of detainees, and in November the UN Human Rights Committee criticized Cameroon for its alleged failure to protect and to respect fundamental human rights.

In September 1999 Mounchipou Seydou was dismissed from his post as Minister of Posts and Telecommunications and was subsequently arrested on charges of embezzlement of public funds. In October a report by a German non-governmental organization, Transparency International (see p. 319), rated Cameroon as the most corrupt country in the world. The Government strenuously denied the allegations of Transparency International; none the less, a meeting was held in November of the National Commission on Corruption, which had met

infrequently since its creation in 1997, at which senior government officials outlined strategies to curb corruption in their areas of responsibility.

There was a cabinet reshuffle in March 2000, which was widely interpreted as a response to an escalation in urban crime (several foreign diplomats, including the ambassadors of the USA and the Netherlands, had been attacked). All ministers linked to security matters were involved in the reshuffle, most notably the Minister of Territorial Administration, Samson Ename, who was replaced by Ferdinand Kougou Edima, a former Governor of Littoral Province. Furthermore, some 70% of senior police officers were reportedly replaced. In November deputies staged a sit-in outside the National Assembly after the security forces prevented a protest march, from the legislative building to the presidential palace, from proceeding. The march had been organized by the SDF in support of demands for the creation of an independent electoral commission. In the following month the National Assembly adopted legislation on the establishment of a national elections observatory and on the regulation of state funding for political parties and electoral campaigns. However, five opposition parties boycotted the vote on the elections observatory, claiming that it would be unconstitutional, as it would perform the same functions as the Constitutional Council, and criticizing the President's role in appointing its 11 members. President Biya subsequently postponed municipal elections, due on 21 January 2001, until January 2002, ostensibly on the grounds that the new electoral legislation had yet to become fully operational, and that the 21st Franco-African summit was to convene in Yaoundé a few days prior to the original date. In April 2001 another cabinet reshuffle was implemented, following accusations of corruption against several ministers.

Relations with Nigeria, which had become strained as a result of a series of border disputes, showed signs of improvement following a state visit by the Nigerian President in late 1987, when it was announced that joint border controls were to be established. In 1991, however, the Nigerian Government claimed that Cameroon had annexed nine Nigerian fishing settlements, following a long-standing border dispute, based on a 1913 agreement between Germany and the United Kingdom that ceded the Bakassi peninsula in the Gulf of Guinea to Cameroon. Subsequent attempts by the Governments of Nigeria and Cameroon to resolve the dispute achieved little progress. In December 1993 some 500 Nigerian troops were dispatched to the region, in response to a number of incidents in which Nigerian nationals had been killed by Cameroonian security forces. Later that month the two nations agreed to establish a joint patrol in the disputed area, and to investigate the incidents. In February 1994, however, Cameroon announced that it was to submit the dispute for adjudication by the UN, the Organization of African Unity (OAU—see p. 256) and the International Court of Justice (ICJ), and requested military assistance from France. Subsequent reports of clashes between Cameroonian and Nigerian forces in the region prompted fears of a full-scale conflict between the two nations. In March Cameroon agreed to enter into negotiations with Nigeria (without the involvement of international mediators) to resolve the issue. In the same month the OAU issued a resolution urging the withdrawal of troops from the disputed region. In May negotiations between the two nations, with mediation by the Togolese Government, resumed in Yaoundé. In September the Cameroonian Government submitted additional claims to territory in north-eastern Nigeria to the ICJ.

In February 1996 renewed hostilities between Nigerian and Cameroonian forces in the Bakassi region resulted in several casualties. Later that month, however, Cameroon and Nigeria agreed to refrain from further military action, and delegations from the two countries resumed discussions, with Togolese mediation, in an attempt to resolve the dispute. In March the ICJ ruled that Cameroon had failed to provide sufficient evidence to substantiate its contention that Nigeria had instigated the border dispute, and ordered both nations to cease military operations in the region, to withdraw troops to former positions, and to co-operate with a UN investigative mission, which was to be dispatched to the area. In April, however, clashes continued, with each Government accusing the other of initiating the attacks. Claims by Nigeria that the Cameroonian forces were supported by troops from France were denied by the French Government. Diplomatic efforts to avoid further conflict increased. Nevertheless, both nations continued to reinforce their contingents in the region (where some 5,000 Cameroonian and 3,000 Nigerian troops were deployed at the end of May). Further tension arose in July, when Nigeria accused Cameroon of substantially increasing troops and artillery on the Bakassi peninsula. In September both countries assured the UN investigative mission of their commitment to a peaceful settlement of the dispute. In December and again in May 1997, however, the Nigerian authorities claimed that Cameroonian troops had resumed attacks in the region. In May 1997 the UN requested that the Togolese Government continue efforts to mediate in the dispute. Further clashes were reported in late 1997 and early 1998.

In March 1998, at the preliminary ICJ hearing on the dispute, Nigeria argued that the ICJ did not have jurisdiction in the matter since the two countries had agreed to settle the dispute through bilateral discussion. In June, however, the ICJ declared itself competent to examine the case. In May, and again in September, Cameroon denied reports that it was massing troops on the peninsula. In October further contention arose when Nigeria alleged that Cameroon had awarded a Canadian company a concession to prospect for petroleum in the disputed area. Cameroon insisted that no such concession had been granted.

From late 1998 relations between Cameroon and Nigeria began to improve, and in November the International Committee of the Red Cross organized an exchange of prisoners between the two sides. In April 1999 the President-elect of Nigeria, Gen. Olusegun Obasanjo, visited Cameroon, the first such visit since the beginning of the border conflict in 1994, and in May 1999 the outgoing Nigerian Head of State, Gen. Abdulsalami Abubakar, held further talks with President Biya in Yaoundé. The two countries reportedly agreed to resolve the dispute 'in a fraternal way'. It was, however, announced that ICJ proceedings would be continued, and in late May Nigeria filed its defence. In July the ICJ ruled that it would allow counter-claims from Nigeria relating to the apportioning of responsibility for border incidents; the counter-claims were to be examined alongside Cameroonian complaints. However, relations between the two countries deteriorated in October 2000 following allegations of an armed attack by Cameroonian security forces on Nigerian citizens resident on the peninsula.

Government

Under the amended 1972 Constitution, the Republic of Cameroon is a multi-party state. Executive power is vested in the President, as Head of State, who is elected by universal adult suffrage for a term of seven years, and may serve a maximum of two terms. Legislative power is held by the National Assembly, which comprises 180 members and is elected for a term of five years. In December 1995 constitutional amendments provided for the establishment of an upper legislative chamber (to be known as the Senate). The Cabinet is appointed by the President. Local administration is based on 10 provinces, each with a governor who is appointed by the President.

Defence

In August 2000 Cameroon's armed forces were estimated to total 22,100 men, including 9,000 in paramilitary forces. The army numbered 11,500, the navy about 1,300 and the air force 300. Cameroon has a bilateral defence agreement with France. The defence budget for 2000 was estimated at US $155m.

Economic Affairs

In 1998, according to estimates by the World Bank, Cameroon's gross national product (GNP), measured at average 1996–98 prices, was US $8,736m., equivalent to $610 per head (or $1,395 per head on an international purchasing-power parity basis). During 1990–98, it was estimated, GNP per head declined, in real terms, at an average annual rate of 2.3%. Over the same period the population increased at an average annual rate of 3.2%. In 1999 estimated GNP totalled $8,500m. (equivalent to $580 per head). Cameroon's gross domestic product (GDP) increased, in real terms, at an average annual rate of 1.3% in 1990–99. Real GDP rose by 5.0% in 1997/98 and by an estimated 4.4% in 1998/99.

Agriculture (including hunting, forestry and fishing) contributed an estimated 43.5% of GDP in 1998/99. An estimated 60.6% of the labour force were employed in agriculture in 1999. The principal cash crops are cocoa beans (which accounted for 8.6% of export earnings in 1998/99), coffee and cotton. The principal subsistence crops are roots and tubers (mainly cassava), maize and sorghum; Cameroon is not, however, self-sufficient in cereals. In 1995 an estimated 42% of the country's land area was covered by forest, but an inadequate transport

infrastructure has impeded the development of the forestry sector. Livestock-rearing makes a significant contribution to the food supply. During 1990–99, according to the World Bank, the real GDP of the agricultural sector increased at an average annual rate of 5.3%. Agricultural GDP rose by 6.8% in 1997/98 and again by an estimated 6.8% in 1998/99.

Industry (including mining, manufacturing, construction and power) employed 6.7% of the working population in 1985, and contributed an estimated 20.2% of GDP in 1998/99. During 1990–99, according to the World Bank, industrial GDP declined at an average annual rate of 2.0%. Industrial GDP rose by 7.7% in 1997/98 and by an estimated 6.3% in 1998/99.

Mining contributed an estimated 4.0% of GDP in 1998/99, but employed only 0.05% of Cameroon's working population in 1985. Receipts from the exploitation of the country's petroleum reserves constitute a principal source of government revenue. Deposits of limestone are also quarried. Significant reserves of natural gas, bauxite, iron ore, uranium and tin remain largely undeveloped. According to the IMF, the GDP of the mining sector increased by 7.3% in 1997/98 and by an estimated 3.7% in 1998/99.

Manufacturing contributed an estimated 10.9% of GDP in 1998/99, and employed an estimated 7% of the working population in 1995. The sector is based on the processing of both indigenous primary products (petroleum-refining, agro-industrial activities) and of imported raw materials (an aluminium-smelter uses alumina imported from Guinea). In the financial year ending June 1996, according to a survey of industrial enterprises in the modern sector, the main branches of manufacturing, based on the value of output, were food products (accounting for 16.2% of the total), beverages (13.1%), petroleum and coal products (13.0%) and wood products (12.6%). Manufacturing GDP declined by an average of 1.0% per year in 1990–98, according to the World Bank. However, the GDP of the sector increased by 7.9% in 1997/98 and by an estimated 6.7% in 1998/99.

In the early 1990s about 95% of Cameroon's energy was derived from hydroelectric power installations. Imports of fuel products accounted for only an estimated 0.6% of the value of total imports in 1995.

Services contributed an estimated 36.2% of GDP in 1998/99. During 1990–99, according to the World Bank, the GDP of the services sector increased at an average annual rate of 0.1%. It rose by 9.1% in 1997/98 and by an estimated 1.8% in 1998/99.

In 1998/99 Cameroon recorded a visible trade surplus of an estimated 112,400m. francs CFA, but there was a deficit of 231,300m. francs CFA on the current account of the balance of payments. In 1998/99 the principal source of imports (27.7%) was France; other major suppliers were Nigeria, Germany and the USA. The principal market for exports in that year (24.0%) was Italy; other significant purchasers were France, Spain and the Netherlands. The principal exports in 1998/99 were petroleum and petroleum products (accounting for 36.3% of the total), timber and timber products, cocoa beans and coffee. The principal imports in that year were enterprise consumption goods (accounting for 17.7% of the total), semi-finished goods, industrial equipment, food, beverages and tobacco, and mineral and other raw materials.

In the financial year ending June 1999 there was a budget deficit of 221,000m. francs CFA (equivalent to an estimated 4.1% of GDP). Cameroon's total external debt at the end of 1998 was US $9,829m., of which $8,096m. was long-term public debt. In that year the cost of debt-servicing was equivalent to 22.3% of revenue from exports of goods and services. The annual rate of inflation averaged 5.8% in 1990–99; consumer prices increased by an average of 0.1% in 1998 and by an average of 5.3% in 1999. An estimated 5.8% of the labour force were unemployed in mid-1985.

Cameroon is a member of the Central African organs of the Franc Zone (see p. 210), of the International Cocoa Organization (see p. 304) and of the International Coffee Organization (see p. 304).

The devaluation of the CFA franc in January 1994 (by 50% in relation to the French franc) resulted in an immediate increase in economic hardship, but also in an increase in real growth. Increases in international prices for Cameroon's major export commodities contributed to an improvement in economic conditions in 1995–96, while a number of structural reforms were implemented in compliance with IMF requirements. In 1997 the IMF approved a three-year loan for Cameroon, equivalent to about US $221m., under the Enhanced Structural Adjustment Facility. The 1997/98 and 1998/99 programmes supported a series of macroeconomic reforms, which contributed to increased economic activity and reduced inflation rates. The 1999/2000 programme sought to continue the process of reform, to limit the annual rate of inflation to 2% and to contain the external current-account deficit to 3.5% of GDP. In October 2000 the IMF and the World Bank's International Development Association agreed to support a debt-reduction package for Cameroon, worth an estimated $2000m., under the enhanced Heavily Indebted Poor Countries initiative, thus substantially reducing Cameroon's debt-service obligations and allowing increased expenditure on social and welfare services. In December the IMF approved another three-year loan, equivalent to about $144m., under the Poverty Reduction and Growth Facility, in support of efforts to improve social services, reduce poverty and maintain a stable macroeconomic environment. Real GDP growth was estimated at 4.2% for 1999/2000. None the less, fraud and corruption remained a hindrance to the economic development of Cameroon, as did the country's poor physical infrastructure.

Social Welfare

The Government and Christian missions maintain hospitals and medical centres. In the early 1990s there were three central hospitals in Cameroon, 73 general hospitals, 46 private hospitals and 792 health centres (112 of which were privately owned). There were also 49 maternal and child health centres, and 11 centres for the treatment of leprosy. At that time Cameroon had 28,000 hospital beds, 618 physicians and 135 pharmacists. A long-term national health development plan was inaugurated in April 1999 for the period 1999–2008. The main aims of the plan were to rehabilitate Cameroon's 135 health districts and to secure their financing, and to curb the infection rate of the human immunodeficiency virus (HIV). Expenditure on health by the central Government in 1998/99 was an estimated 31,000m. francs CFA (3.0% of total spending).

Education

Since independence, Cameroon has achieved one of the highest rates of school attendance in Africa, but provision of educational facilities varies according to region. Education, which is bilingual, is provided by the Government, missionary societies and private concerns. Education in state schools is available free of charge, and the Government provides financial assistance for other schools. Primary education begins at six years of age. It lasts for six years in Eastern Cameroon (where it is officially compulsory), and for seven years in Western Cameroon. Secondary education, beginning at the age of 12 or 13, lasts for a further seven years, comprising two cycles of four years and three years in Eastern Cameroon and five years and two years in Western Cameroon. In 1994 primary enrolment was equivalent to 88% of children in the appropriate age-group (males 93%; females 84%), while enrolment at secondary schools was equivalent to only 27% (males 32%; females 22%). In 1995, according to estimates by UNESCO, the average rate of adult illiteracy was 30.7% (males 22.8%; females 38.4%). Expenditure on education by the central Government in 1998/99 was an estimated 102,000m. francs CFA (10.0% of total spending).

Public Holidays

2001: 1 January (New Year), 11 February (Youth Day), 6 March* (Festival of Sheep), 13 April (Good Friday), 16 April (Easter Monday), 1 May (Labour Day), 20 May (National Day), 24 May (Ascension Day), 15 August (Assumption), 17 December* (Djoulde Soumae, end of Ramadan), 25 December (Christmas).

2002: 1 January (New Year), 11 February (Youth Day), 23 February* (Festival of Sheep), 29 March (Good Friday), 1 April (Easter Monday), 1 May (Labour Day), 9 May (Ascension Day), 20 May (National Day), 15 August (Assumption), 6 December* (Djoulde Soumae, end of Ramadan), 25 December (Christmas).

* These holidays are dependent on the Islamic lunar calendar and may vary by one or two days from the dates given.

Weights and Measures

The metric system is in force.

Statistical Survey

Source (unless otherwise stated): Direction de la Prévision, Ministère de l'Economie et des Finances, BP 18, Yaoundé; tel. 23-40-40; fax 23-21-50.

Area and Population

AREA, POPULATION AND DENSITY

Area (sq km)	475,442*
Population (census results)	
9 April 1976†	7,663,246
9 April 1987	
Males	5,162,878
Females	5,330,777
Total	10,493,655
Population (official estimates at mid-year)	
1997	14,044,000
1998	14,439,000
1999	14,859,000
Density (per sq km) at mid-1999	31.3

* 183,569 sq miles.
† Including an adjustment for underenumeration, estimated at 7.4%. The enumerated total was 7,090,115.

PROVINCES (population at 1987 census)

	Urban	Rural	Total
Centre	877,481	774,119	1,651,600
Littoral	1,093,323	259,510	1,352,833
West	431,337	908,454	1,339,791
South-West	258,940	579,102	838,042
North-West	271,114	966,234	1,237,348
North	234,572	597,593	832,165
East	152,787	364,411	517,198
South	104,023	269,775	373,798
Adamaoua	178,644	316,541	495,185
Far North	366,698	1,488,997	1,855,695
Total	3,968,919	6,524,736	10,493,655

PRINCIPAL TOWNS (population at 1987 census)

Douala . . .	810,000	Bamenda . . .	110,000
Yaoundé (capital) .	649,000	Nkongsamba . .	85,420
Garoua . . .	142,000	Kumba . . .	70,112
Maroua . . .	123,000	Limbé . . .	44,561
Bafoussam . . .	113,000		

1999 (estimated population, '000): Douala 1,448.3; Yaoundé 1,372.8 (Source: Ministry of Public Investments and Regional Planning, *Indicateurs démographiques sur le Cameroun*).

BIRTHS AND DEATHS (official estimates, annual averages)

	1987–92	1993–97	1998–2000
Birth rate (per 1,000). . . .	41.7	39.7	38.2
Death rate (per 1,000) . . .	12.8	11.4	10.1

Expectation of life (official estimates, years at birth, 1998–2000): 59.0 (males 56.7; females 61.3).

Source: Ministry of Public Investments and Regional Planning, *Indicateurs démographiques sur le Cameroun*.

ECONOMICALLY ACTIVE POPULATION
(official estimates, persons aged six years and over, mid-1985)

	Males	Females	Total
Agriculture, hunting, forestry and fishing	1,574,946	1,325,925	2,900,871
Mining and quarrying . . .	1,693	100	1,793
Manufacturing	137,671	36,827	174,498
Electricity, gas and water . .	3,373	149	3,522
Construction	65,666	1,018	66,684
Trade, restaurants and hotels .	115,269	38,745	154,014
Transport, storage and communications . . .	50,664	1,024	51,688
Financing, insurance, real estate and business services .	7,447	562	8,009
Community, social and personal services . . .	255,076	37,846	292,922
Activities not adequately defined .	18,515	17,444	35,959
Total in employment . . .	2,230,320	1,459,640	3,689,960
Unemployed	180,016	47,659	227,675
Total labour force . . .	2,410,336	1,507,299	3,917,635

Source: ILO, *Yearbook of Labour Statistics*.

Mid-1999 (estimates in '000): Agriculture, etc. 3,621; Total labour force 5,980 (Source: FAO).

Agriculture

PRINCIPAL CROPS ('000 metric tons)

	1997	1998	1999
Rice (paddy)	65*	73	65*
Maize	760*	855	650*
Millet	71†	71†	71†
Sorghum	400*	500*	500*
Potatoes†	38	42	49
Sweet potatoes†	150†	148	150†
Cassava (Manioc)*	1,848	1,918	1,991
Yams†	150	180	200
Other roots and tubers . .	600†	541†	550†
Dry beans†	90	95	98
Groundnuts (in shell)* . . .	90	90	95
Sesame seed†	16	16	17
Palm kernels*	58	60	60
Tomatoes	65†	69	70†
Onions (dry)	40†	41	42†
Other vegetables	442†	455	466†
Sugar cane†	1,350	1,350	1,350
Avocados†	47	48	49
Pineapples	50†	52*	48†
Bananas	800†	730	800†
Plantains†	1,290*	1,332	1,364*
Other fruit†	108	108	110
Coffee (green)	55	113	78*
Cocoa beans	127	125	150*
Tea (made)	4	4	4†
Tobacco (leaves)	3†	4†	5*
Cotton lint	75*	75*	79*
Natural rubber	58	53	61*

* Unofficial figure(s).   † FAO estimate(s).

Source: FAO.

LIVESTOCK ('000 head, year ending September)

	1997	1998	1999
Horses*	16	16	17
Asses*	37	37	37
Cattle*	5,700	5,900	5,900
Pigs*	1,420	1,425	1,430
Sheep*	3,840	3,860	3,880
Goats*	3,830	3,840	3,850
Poultry†.	25,000	28,000	31,000

* FAO estimates. † Unofficial figures.

Source: FAO.

LIVESTOCK PRODUCTS ('000 metric tons)

	1997	1998	1999
Beef and veal* . . .	88	90	90
Mutton and lamb . . .	17	17	17
Goat meat	14	14	15
Pig meat	18	18	18
Poultry meat* . . .	22	23	24
Other meat	46	46	46
Cows' milk	125	125	125
Sheep's milk. . . .	17	17	17
Goats' milk	42	42	42
Poultry eggs . . .	13	14	14
Honey*	3	3	3
Cattle hides	13	13	13
Sheepskins	3	3	3
Goatskins	1	1	1

* FAO estimates.

Source: FAO.

Forestry

ROUNDWOOD REMOVALS ('000 cubic metres, excl. bark)

	1996	1997	1998
Sawlogs, veneer logs and logs for sleepers	2,820	2,317	2,016
Other industrial wood . .	913	938	964
Fuel wood	11,547	11,867	12,192
Total	15,280	15,122	15,172

Source: FAO, *Yearbook of Forest Products*.

SAWNWOOD PRODUCTION
(FAO estimates, '000 cubic metres, incl. railway sleepers)

	1996	1997	1998
Total (all broadleaved) . .	685	560	588

Source: FAO, *Yearbook of Forest Products*.

Fishing

('000 metric tons, live weight)

	1996	1997*	1998*
Capture	92.5*	94.0	97.0
Freshwater fishes . .	28.5*	30.0	32.0
Bobo croaker . . .	4.4	4.4	4.4
Other croakers and drums . .	6.1	6.1	6.2
Sardinellas . . .	24.0	24.0	24.4
Bonga shad . . .	24.0	24.0	24.4
Aquaculture	0.1*	0.1	0.1
Total catch	92.5*	94.1	97.1

* FAO estimate(s).

Source: FAO, *Yearbook of Fishery Statistics*.

Mining

	1995	1996	1997
Crude petroleum ('000 metric tons)	5,380*	5,835	5,890
Tin ore (metric tons)† . . .	2	1	1
Gold (kilograms)†	1,000	1,000	1,000

* Estimate.
† Estimates of metal content (data from the US Bureau of Mines).

Source: UN, *Industrial Commodity Statistics Yearbook*.

Crude petroleum (estimate, million barrels): 43.8 in 1998/99 (Source: Société Nationale des Hydrocarbures. Yaoundé).

Industry

SELECTED PRODUCTS ('000 metric tons, unless otherwise indicated)

	1994	1995	1996
Palm oil*	125	125	161
Raw sugar*	60	53	44
Veneer sheets ('000 cu metres)	31	31	31
Plywood ('000 cu metres) . .	43	43	43
Paper and paperboard . .	5	5	5
Aviation gasoline . . .	14†	15†	17
Jet fuels	9	10†	10
Motor spirit (petrol) . . .	296	298†	301
Kerosene	245	243†	245
Gas-diesel (distillate fuel) oil .	287	288†	290
Residual fuel oils† . . .	135	153	155
Lubricating oils† . . .	28	38	40
Petroleum bitumen (asphalt) .	10	10†	10
Liquefied petroleum gas . .	20†	21†	22
Cement	620‡	522	n.a.
Aluminium (unwrought) . .	81.1§	71.4	82.3§
Electric energy (million kWh) .	2,740†	2,746†	2,753

1997 ('000 metric tons, unless otherwise indicated): Palm oil* 135 (unofficial estimate); Raw sugar* 46 (unofficial figure); Veneer sheets ('000 cu metres) 31; Plywood ('000 cu metres) 43; Aviation gasoline 17; Jet fuels 10; Lubricating oils† 42; Petroleum bitumen (asphalt) 12; Aluminium (unwrought) 91.0§.
1998 ('000 metric tons, unofficial figures): Palm oil* 136; Raw sugar* 52.
1999 ('000 metric tons, unofficial figures): Palm oil* 140; Raw sugar* 54.

* Data from the FAO.
† Provisional or estimated figure(s).
‡ Data from the US Bureau of Mines.
§ Data from *World Metal Statistics* (London).

Sources: UN, *Industrial Commodity Statistics Yearbook*; FAO, *Production Yearbook*.

Finance

CURRENCY AND EXCHANGE RATES

Monetary Units
100 centimes = 1 franc de la Coopération financière en Afrique central (CFA).

Sterling, Dollar and Euro Equivalents (29 December 2000)
£1 sterling = 1,051.93 francs CFA;
US $1 = 704.95 francs CFA;
€1 = 655.96 francs CFA;
10,000 francs CFA = £9.506 = $14.185 = €15.245.

Average Exchange Rate (francs CFA per US $)
1998   589.95
1999   615.70
2000   711.98

Note: An exchange rate of 1 French franc = 50 francs CFA, established in 1948, remained in force until January 1994, when the CFA franc was devalued by 50%, with the exchange rate adjusted to 1 French franc = 100 francs CFA. This relationship to French currency remained in effect with the introduction of the euro on 1 January 1999. From that date, accordingly, a fixed exchange rate of €1 = 655.957 francs CFA has been in operation.

BUDGET ('000 million francs CFA, year ending 30 June)

Revenue	1996/97	1997/98	1998/99
Oil revenue	204	204	133
National oil company's contributions . . .	187	166	113
Profit taxes . . .	17	39	21
Non-oil revenue . . .	563	644	716
Tax revenue	486	578	652
Taxes on income and profits .	101	130	174
Individual income taxes .	35	44	52
Wages and salaries .	18	23	28
Progressive surcharge .	17	22	25
Profit taxes . . .	35	45	63
Taxes on goods and services .	258	304	340
Domestic taxes . .	125	142	169
Turnover taxes . .	84	97	128
Excise taxes . . .	17	22	23
Taxes collected by customs .	75	104	99
Turnover taxes . .	73	103	97
Excise taxes . . .	1	1	2
Excise tax on petroleum products . . .	58	58	65
Taxes on international trade .	127	143	138
Import duties . . .	75	94	101
Export duties . . .	48	43	26
Non-tax revenue . . .	77	67	64
Privatization proceeds . .	22	1	11
Total	**767**	**849**	**849**

Expenditure*	1996/97	1997/98	1998/99
General government services . .	60	58	65
Defence	57	73	83
Public order and justice . .	47	47	55
Education	94	85	102
Health	30	25	31
Social security	4	3	4
Housing and community affairs .	11	7	9
Recreational and cultural affairs .	7	7	8
Economic affairs and services . .	483	634	666
Energy and mining . .	3	1	1
Agriculture, forestry and fishing	41	22	25
Public works, transport and communications . .	49	29	37
Other economic services . .	390	582	603
Interest on public debt . .	299	299	282
Total	**793**	**937**	**1,023**
Current	719	784	828
Capital	74	153	194

* Excluding adjustment for changes in payments arrears.

Source: IMF, *Cameroon: Statistical Appendix* (July 2000).

INTERNATIONAL RESERVES

(US $ million, excluding gold, at 31 December)

	1996	1997	1998
Gold*	11.04	8.72	8.61
IMF special drawing rights . .	0.16	—	0.02
Reserve position in IMF . .	0.53	0.55	0.63
Foreign exchange . . .	2.08	0.31	0.64
Total	**13.81**	**9.58**	**9.90**

* Valued at market-related prices.

Source: IMF, *International Financial Statistics*.

MONEY SUPPLY ('000 million francs CFA at 31 December)

	1997	1998	1999
Currency outside banks . .	180.28	205.76	237.40
Demand deposits at deposit money banks . . .	237.72	271.06	294.49
Total money (incl. others) .	**423.90**	**485.29**	**537.73**

Source: IMF, *International Financial Statistics*.

COST OF LIVING

(Consumer Price Index for Africans in Yaoundé; base: 1995 = 100)

	1997	1998	1999
All items	105.8	105.9	111.5

Source: IMF, *International Financial Statistics*.

NATIONAL ACCOUNTS

('000 million francs CFA at current prices, year ending 30 June)

National Income and Product

	1986/87	1987/88	1988/89
Compensation of employees . .	1,142.4	1,091.2	1,055.1
Operating surplus . . .	2,197.7	2,003.0	1,934.5
Domestic factor incomes . .	**3,340.1**	**3,094.3**	**2,989.7**
Consumption of fixed capital . .	190.8	232.6	230.4
Gross domestic product (GDP) at factor cost	**3,530.9**	**3,326.9**	**3,220.1**
Indirect taxes	430.2	337.9	299.3
Less Subsidies	39.2	20.2	6.3
GDP in purchasers' values .	**3,921.9**	**3,644.5**	**3,513.0**
Factor income received from abroad	5.3	3.4	−121.0
Less Factor income paid abroad .	88.1	103.5	
Gross national product . .	**3,839.1**	**3,544.5**	**3,392.0**
Less Consumption of fixed capital .	190.8	232.6	230.4
National income in market prices	**3,648.4**	**3,311.9**	**3,161.6**
Other current transfers received from abroad . . .	13.1	8.9	−60.0
Less Other current transfers paid abroad	57.0	82.8	
National disposable income .	**3,604.5**	**3,238.0**	**3,101.6**

Source: UN, *National Accounts Statistics*.

Expenditure on the Gross Domestic Product

	1996/97	1997/98	1998/99*
Government final consumption expenditure	406	480	542
Private final consumption expenditure	3,585	3,718	3,871
Gross capital formation . . .	798	964	1,017
Total domestic expenditure .	**4,789**	**5,162**	**5,430**
Exports of goods and services . .	1,248	1,388	1,323
Less Imports of goods and services	1,104	1,310	1,347
GDP in purchasers' values . .	**4,932**	**5,240**	**5,406**
GDP at constant 1989/90 prices	**3,367**	**3,537**	**3,693**

* Estimates.

Source: IMF, *Cameroon: Statistical Appendix* (July 2000).

Gross Domestic Product by Economic Activity

	1996/97	1997/98	1998/99*
Agriculture, hunting, forestry and fishing	2,018	2,159	2,288
Mining and quarrying . . .	315	288	211
Manufacturing	506	545	572
Electricity, gas and water . .	75	78	81
Construction	163	189	200
Services	1,716	1,829	1,903
GDP at factor cost . . .	**4,793**	**5,088**	**5,255**
Indirect taxes, *less* subsidies . .	138	152	152
GDP in purchasers' values . .	**4,932**	**5,240**	**5,406**

* Estimates.

Source: IMF, *Cameroon: Statistical Appendix* (July 2000).

BALANCE OF PAYMENTS (million francs CFA, year ending 30 June)

	1996/97	1997/98	1998/99
Exports of goods f.o.b.	982,900	1,083,900	993,900
Imports of goods f.o.b.	−729,000	−874,500	−881,500
Trade balance	253,900	209,400	112,400
Services and other income (net)	−440,100	−413,800	−412,600
Balance on goods, services and income	−186,200	−204,400	−300,200
Transfers (net)	46,800	63,200	68,900
Current balance	−139,300	−141,300	−231,300
Long-term capital (net)	−191,300	−28,300	−87,400
Short-term capital (net)	−2,300	−33,700	4,200
Net errors and omissions	78,800	—	—
Overall balance	−254,000	−203,000	−314,500

Source: IMF, *Cameroon: Statistical Appendix* (July 2000).

External Trade

PRINCIPAL COMMODITIES
(million francs CFA, year ending 30 June)

Imports c.i.f.	1996/97	1997/98	1998/99
Food, beverages and tobacco	64,200	94,300	99,500
Animal and vegetable raw materials	23,900	35,400	40,600
Mineral and other raw materials	111,000	108,200	93,500
Semi-finished goods	117,900	143,500	140,300
Transportation equipment	77,300	115,800	90,600
Industrial equipment	91,800	123,500	117,200
Household consumption	74,400	87,700	91,000
Enterprise consumption	132,600	152,400	146,700
Total (incl. others)	708,300	873,400	827,700

Exports f.o.b.	1996/97	1997/98	1998/99
Petroleum and petroleum products	401,900	356,300	314,300
Cocoa beans	63,200	89,800	74,000
Cocoa products	16,900	22,200	18,200
Coffee (robusta)	47,900	58,200	50,800
Coffee (arabica)	20,500	8,500	5,500
Raw cotton	65,400	59,000	47,100
Sawlogs, veneer logs, etc.	102,900	158,900	119,900
Aluminium	50,900	52,500	49,600
Total (incl. others)	955,700	979,800	864,800

Source: IMF, *Cameroon: Statistical Appendix* (July 2000).

PRINCIPAL TRADING PARTNERS
(estimates, '000 million francs CFA)

Imports c.i.f.	1996/97	1997/98	1998/99
Brazil	7	5	6
Belgium-Luxembourg	34	39	42
Canada	4	9	15
China, People's Repub.	10	16	18
Côte d'Ivoire	21	19	14
Equatorial Guinea	26	18	2
France	177	226	226
Germany	47	58	57
Guinea	20	26	19
India	6	5	9
Italy	27	34	38
Japan	34	50	44
Netherlands	20	23	23
Nigeria	60	68	65
Pakistan	5	9	8
Senegal	8	10	12
South Africa	7	10	9
Spain	13	16	14
Turkey	2	9	11
United Kingdom	21	24	23
USA	60	79	50
Total (incl. others)	704	875	816

Exports f.o.b.	1996/97	1997/98	1998/99
Belgium-Luxembourg	21	25	18
Central African Republic	9	12	9
Chad	3	12	21
China, People's Repub.	27	30	20
Congo, Repub.	10	10	10
Equatorial Guinea	14	14	13
France	158	173	168
Gabon	16	31	18
Germany	21	20	19
Hong Kong	5	6	11
Ireland	2	3	11
Italy	250	269	223
Korea, Repub.	21	7	13
Netherlands	70	100	93
Philippines	12	9	1
Portugal	13	33	33
Spain	201	166	125
Taiwan	11	33	10
Thailand	12	8	5
United Kingdom	15	24	21
USA	22	10	12
Total (incl. others)	979	1,084	929

Source: IMF, *Cameroon: Statistical Appendix* (July 2000).

Transport

RAILWAYS (traffic, year ending 30 June)

	1990/91	1991/92	1992/93
Freight ton-km (million)	679	613	653
Passenger-km (million)	530	445	352

Source: UN, *Statistical Yearbook*.

ROAD TRAFFIC (estimates, motor vehicles in use at 31 December)

	1994	1995	1996
Passenger cars	89,000	93,000	98,000
Goods vehicles	57,000	60,000	64,350

Source: International Road Federation, *World Road Statistics*.

SHIPPING

Merchant Fleet (registered at 31 December)

	1996	1997	1998
Number of vessels	50	48	58
Total displacement ('000 grt)	36.7	11.4	12.9

Source: Lloyd's Register of Shipping.

International Sea-borne Freight Traffic
(freight traffic at Douala, '000 metric tons)

	1995	1996	1997
Goods loaded	1,841	1,967	2,385
Goods unloaded	2,317	2,211	2,497

Source: Banque des états de l'Afrique centrale, *Etudes et Statistiques*.

CIVIL AVIATION (traffic on scheduled services)

	1995	1996	1997
Kilometres flown (million)	7	7	6
Passengers carried ('000)	345	362	279
Passenger-km (million)	615	649	547
Total ton-km (million)	94	100	84

Source: UN, *Statistical Yearbook*.

Tourism

FOREIGN VISITORS BY COUNTRY OF ORIGIN*

	1995	1996	1997
Belgium	2,562	2,597	3,696
Canada	2,650	2,687	2,763
France	35,612	36,096	35,626
Germany	6,211	6,296	6,659
Italy	4,237	4,295	3,083
Switzerland	2,516	2,550	5,443
United Kingdom . . .	3,798	3,849	4,106
USA	4,974	5,041	11,317
Total (incl. others) . . .	99,749	101,106	132,839

* Arrivals at hotels and similar establishments.

Receipts from tourism (US $ million): 36 in 1995; 38 in 1996; 39 in 1997.

Source: World Tourism Organization, *Yearbook of Tourism Statistics*.

Communications Media

	1995	1996	1997
Radio receivers ('000 in use) . .	2,000	2,200	2,270
Television receivers ('000 in use) .	320	400	450
Telephones ('000 main lines in use)	66	71	75
Mobile cellular telephones:			
(subscribers)	2,800	3,500	4,200
Daily newspapers:			
Number	2	2	n.a.
Average circulation ('000) .	85	91	n.a.
Non-daily newspapers:			
Number	n.a.	7	n.a.
Average circulation ('000) .	n.a.	152	n.a.

Mobile cellular telephones (subscribers, July 1999): 4,800.

Sources: mainly UNESCO, *Statistical Yearbook*; UN, *Statistical Yearbook*.

Education

(1996/97, unless otherwise indicated)

	Institutions	Teachers	Students
Pre-primary	1,109	4,545	87,318
Primary	8,514	39,384	1,921,186
Secondary			
General*	700	19,148	484,461
Vocational*	324	7,245	108,519
Universities	6	761†	42,199

* 1995/96 figures.

† 1990/91 figure.

Sources: UNESCO, *Statistical Yearbook*; *Annuaire statistique du Cameroun*.

Directory

The Constitution*

The Republic of Cameroon is a multi-party state. The main provisions of the 1972 Constitution, as amended, are summarized below:

The Constitution declares that the human being, without distinction as to race, religion, sex or belief, possesses inalienable and sacred rights. It affirms its attachment to the fundamental freedoms embodied in the Universal Declaration of Human Rights and the UN Charter. The State guarantees to all citizens of either sex the rights and freedoms set out in the preamble of the Constitution.

SOVEREIGNTY

1. The Republic of Cameroon shall be one and indivisible, democratic, secular and dedicated to social service. It shall ensure the equality before the law of all its citizens. Provisions that the official languages be French and English, for the motto, flag, national anthem and seal, that the capital be Yaoundé.

2–3. Sovereignty shall be vested in the people who shall exercise it either through the President of the Republic and the members returned by it to the National Assembly or by means of referendum. Elections are by universal suffrage, direct or indirect, by every citizen aged 21 or over in a secret ballot. Political parties or groups may take part in elections subject to the law and the principles of democracy and of national sovereignty and unity.

4. State authority shall be exercised by the President of the Republic and the National Assembly.

THE PRESIDENT OF THE REPUBLIC

5. The President of the Republic, as Head of State and Head of the Government, shall be responsible for the conduct of the affairs of the Republic. He shall define national policy and may charge the members of the Government with the implementation of this policy in certain spheres.

6–7. Candidates for the office of President must hold civic and political rights, be at least 35 years old and have resided in Cameroon for a minimum of 12 consecutive months, and may not hold any other elective office or professional activity. The President is elected for seven years, by a majority of votes cast by the people, and may serve a maximum of two terms. Provisions are made for the continuity of office in the case of the President's resignation.

8–9. The Ministers and Vice-Ministers are appointed by the President to whom they are responsible, and they may hold no other appointment. The President is also head of the armed forces, he negotiates and ratifies treaties, may exercise clemency after consultation with the Higher Judicial Council, promulgates and is responsible for the enforcement of laws, is responsible for internal and external security, makes civil and military appointments, provides for necessary administrative services.

10. The President, by reference to the Supreme Court, ensures that all laws passed are constitutional.

11. Provisions whereby the President may declare a state of emergency or state of siege.

THE NATIONAL ASSEMBLY

12. The National Assembly shall be renewed every five years, though it may at the instance of the President of the Republic legislate to extend or shorten its term of office. It shall be composed of 180 members elected by universal suffrage.

13–14. Laws shall normally be passed by a simple majority of those present, but if a bill is read a second time at the request of the President of the Republic a majority of the National Assembly as a whole is required.

15–16. The National Assembly shall meet twice a year, each session to last not more than 30 days; in one session it shall approve the budget. It may be recalled to an extraordinary session of not more than 15 days.

17–18. Elections and suitability of candidates and sitting members shall be governed by law.

RELATIONS BETWEEN THE EXECUTIVE AND THE LEGISLATURE

19. Bills may be introduced either by the President of the Republic or by any member of the National Assembly.

20. Reserved to the legislature are: the fundamental rights and duties of the citizen; the law of persons and property; the political, administrative and judicial system in respect of elections to the National Assembly, general regulation of national defence,

authorization of penalties and criminal and civil procedure etc., and the organization of the local authorities; currency, the budget, dues and taxes, legislation on public property; economic and social policy; the education system.

21. The National Assembly may empower the President of the Republic to legislate by way of ordinance for a limited period and for given purposes.

22–26. Other matters of procedure, including the right of the President of the Republic to address the Assembly and of the Ministers and Vice-Ministers to take part in debates.

27–29. The composition and conduct of the Assembly's programme of business. Provisions whereby the Assembly may inquire into governmental activity. The obligation of the President of the Republic to promulgate laws, which shall be published in both languages of the Republic.

30. Provisions whereby the President of the Republic, after consultation with the National Assembly, may submit to referendum certain reform bills liable to have profound repercussions on the future of the nation and national institutions.

THE JUDICIARY

31. Justice is administered in the name of the people. The President of the Republic shall ensure the independence of the judiciary and shall make appointments with the assistance of the Higher Judicial Council.

THE SUPREME COURT

32–33. The Supreme Court has powers to uphold the Constitution in such cases as the death or incapacity of the President and the admissibility of laws, to give final judgments on appeals on the Judgment of the Court of Appeal and to decide complaints against administrative acts. It may be assisted by experts appointed by the President of the Republic.

IMPEACHMENT

34. There shall be a Court of Impeachment with jurisdiction to try the President of the Republic for high treason and the Ministers and Vice-Ministers for conspiracy against the security of the State.

THE ECONOMIC AND SOCIAL COUNCIL

35. There shall be an Economic and Social Council, regulated by the law.

AMENDMENT OF THE CONSTITUTION

36–37. Bills to amend the Constitution may be introduced either by the President of the Republic or the National Assembly. The President may decide to submit any amendment to the people by way of a referendum. No procedure to amend the Constitution may be accepted if it tends to impair the republican character, unity or territorial integrity of the State, or the democratic principles by which the Republic is governed.

* In December 1995 the National Assembly formally adopted constitutional amendments that provided for a democratic system of government, with the establishment of an upper legislative chamber (to be known as the Senate), a Council of Supreme Judiciary Affairs, a Council of State, and a Civil Service High Authority, and restricted the power vested in the President, who was to serve a maximum of two seven-year terms. The restoration of decentralized local government areas was also envisaged.

The Government

HEAD OF STATE

President: PAUL BIYA (took office 6 November 1982; elected 14 January 1984; re-elected 24 April 1988, 11 October 1992 and 12 October 1997).

CABINET
(April 2001)

A coalition of the Rassemblement démocratique du peuple camerounais (RDPC), the Union nationale pour la démocratie et le progrès (UNDP) and the Union des populations camerounaises (UPC). With the exception of those specified, all cabinet members belong to the RDPC.

Prime Minister: PETER MAFANY MUSONGE.

Ministers of State

Minister of State, Delegate at the Presidency in charge of Defence: LAURENT ESSO.

Minister of State in charge of Justice: AMADOU ALI.

Minister of State in charge of External Relations: FRANÇOIS XAVIER GOUBEYOU.

Minister of State in charge of Culture: FERDINAND LÉOPOLD OYONO.

Minister of State in charge of Industrial and Commercial Development: BELLO BOUBA MAÏGARI (UNDP).

Minister of State in charge of Economy and Finance: MICHEL MEVA'A.

Ministers

Minister of National Education: JOSEPH OWONA.

Minister of Territorial Administration: FERDINAND KOUNGOU EDIMA.

Minister of Scientific and Technical Research: HENRI HOGBE NLEND (UPC).

Minister of Youth and Sports: BIDOUNG MKPATT.

Minister of Public Health: URBAIN OLANGUENA AWONO.

Minister of Agriculture: TEREVET ZACHARIE.

Minister of the Environment and Forests: SYLVESTER NAAH ONDOA.

Minister of Town Planning and Housing: BOUBARY YÉRIMA HALILOU.

Minister of Urban Affairs: CLAUDE JOSEPH MBAFOU.

Minister of Higher Education: JEAN-MARIE ATANGANA MEBARA.

Minister of Tourism: PIERRE HELLE (UNDP).

Minister of Public Service and Administrative Reform: RENÉ ZE NGUELE.

Minister of Communication: JACQUES FAME NDONGO.

Minister of Social Affairs: MARIE MADELEINE FOUDA.

Minister of Women's Affairs: CATHERINE BAKANG.

Minister of Public Investments and Regional Planning: MARTIN OKOUDA.

Minister of Public Works: JÉRÔME ETAH.

Minister of Transport: CHRISTOPHER NSALAI.

Minister of Employment, Labour and Social Welfare: PIUS ONDOUA.

Minister of Mines, Water Resources and Energy: Dr YVES MBELLE.

Minister of Livestock, Fisheries and Animal Industries: Dr HAMAJOUDA HAJOUDJI.

Minister of Posts and Telecommunications: KOUÉ KONGO.

Ministers responsible for Special Duties at the Presidency: PETER ABETY, JUSTIN NDIORO, RAFAËL ONAMBÉLÉ, BABA HAMADOU, ELVIS NGOLE NGOLE.

Ministers-delegate

Minister-delegate at the Presidency in charge of Relations with the Assemblies and with the Economic and Social Council: GRÉGOIRE OWONA.

Minister-delegate at the Presidency in charge of the Supreme State Audit: NJIEMOUM MAMA.

Minister-delegate at the Ministry of External Relations in charge of Relations with the Commonwealth: JOSEPH NDION NGUTE.

Minister-delegate at the Ministry of External Relations in charge of Relations with the Islamic World: ADOUM GARGOUM.

Minister-delegate at the Ministry of Economy and Finance in charge of the Budget: ROGER MELINGUI.

Minister-delegate at the Ministry of Economy and Finance in charge of the Stabilization Plan: JEAN-MARIE GANKOU.

Secretaries of State

Secretary of State for Territorial Administration in charge of Prisons Administration: ADAMA MODI BAKARI.

Secretary of State for Agriculture: ABOUBAKARY ABDOULAYE.

Secretary of State for Defence in charge of Gendarmerie: RÉMY ZE MÉKA.

Secretary of State for Industrial and Commercial Development: EDMOND MOUAMPÉA MBIO.

First Secretary of State for National Education: JOSEPH YUNGA TEGHEN.

Second Secretary of State for National Education: HAMAN ADAMA.

Secretary of State for Public Investments and Regional Development: SHEY JOHN YEMBE.

Secretary of State for Posts and Telecommunications: DENIS OUMAROU.

Secretary of State for Public Health: ALIM HAYATOU.

Secretary of State for Transport: Dr NANA ABOUBAKAR DJALLOH (UNDP).

Secretary of State for Public Works: EMMANUEL BONDE.

Secretary of State for Town Planning and Housing in charge of Lands: TSALA MESSI.

Other officials with the rank of Minister

Secretary-General of the Presidency: YAYA MARAFA HAMIDOU.

Assistant Secretary-General of the Presidency: EPHRAIM INONI.

Assistant Secretary-General of the Presidency: RENÉ OWONA.

Director of the Cabinet of the President of the Republic: NGO'O MEBE.

MINISTRIES

Correspondence to ministries not holding post boxes should generally be addressed c/o the Central Post Office, Yaoundé.

Office of the President: Palais de l'Unité, Yaoundé; tel. 23-40-25; internet www.camnet.cm/celcom/homepr.htm.

Office of the Prime Minister: Yaoundé; tel. 23-80-05; fax 23-57-35; e-mail spm@spm.gov.cm; internet www.spm.gov.cm.

Ministry of Agriculture: Yaoundé; tel. 22-05-53.

Ministry of City Affairs: Yaoundé; tel. 20-15.58.

Ministry of Communication: BP 1588, Yaoundé; tel. 23-34-67.

Ministry of Culture: Yaoundé; tel. 22-65-79; fax 23-30-22.

Ministry of Defence: Yaoundé; tel. 23-40-55.

Ministry of Economy and Finance: BP 18, Yaoundé; tel. and fax 23-20-99; internet www.camnet.cm/investir/minfi/.

Ministry of Education: Yaoundé; tel. 23-40-50.

Ministry of Employment, Labour and Social Welfare: Yaoundé; tel. 22-01-86; fax 23-18-20.

Ministry of the Environment and Forests: Yaoundé; BP 1341, tel. 20-42-58; fax 21-53-50; e-mail onadef@camnet.cm; internet www.camnet.cm/investir/envforet/index.htm.

Ministry of External Relations: Yaoundé; tel. 20-38-50; fax 20-79-18.

Ministry of Higher Education: 2 ave du 20 Mai, BP 1457, Yaoundé; tel. 22-17-70; fax 22-97-24; e-mail aowono@uycdc.uninet.cm; internet www.uninet.cm.

Ministry of Industrial and Commercial Development: Yaoundé; tel. 23-23-88; fax 22-27-04; e-mail mindic@camnet.cm; internet www.camnet.cm/investir/mindic.

Ministry of Justice: Yaoundé; tel. 22-01-89; fax 23-59-61.

Ministry of Livestock, Fisheries and Animal Industries: Yaoundé; tel. 22-33-11.

Ministry of Mines, Water Resources and Energy: Yaoundé; tel. 23-34-04; fax 22-34-00; e-mail minmee@camnet.cm; internet www.camnet.cm/investir/minmee.

Ministry of Posts and Telecommunications: Yaoundé; tel. 23-06-15; fax 23-31-59; internet www.camnet.cm/investir/minposte/minpost.htm.

Ministry of Public Health: Yaoundé; tel. 22-29-01; internet www.camnet.cm/investir/hgy/index.htm.

Ministry of Public Investments and Regional Planning: Yaoundé; tel. 23-36-37; fax 22-15-01.

Ministry of the Public Service and Administrative Reform: Yaoundé; tel. 22-03-56; fax 23-08-00.

Ministry of Public Works: Yaoundé; tel. 22-19-16; fax 22-01-56.

Ministry of Scientific and Technical Research: Yaoundé; tel. 22-13-31; fax 22-13-36.

Ministry of Social Affairs and of Women's Affairs: Yaoundé; tel. 22-58-67; fax 22-58-69.

Ministry of Territorial Administration: Yaoundé; tel. 23-40-90.

Ministry of Tourism: BP 266, Yaoundé; tel. 22-44-11; fax 22-12-95; e-mail mintour@camnet.cm; internet www.camnet.cm/mintour/tourisme.

Ministry of Town Planning and Housing: Yaoundé; tel. 23-22-82.

Ministry of Transport: Yaoundé; tel. 22-87-09; fax 23-45-20; e-mail mintrans@camnet.cm; internet www.camnet.cm/investir/transport.

Ministry of Youth and Sports: Yaoundé; tel. 23-32-57; internet www.camnet.cm/minjes3/accueil.htm.

President and Legislature

PRESIDENT

Election, 12 October 1997

Candidate	Votes	% of votes
Paul Biya (RDPC)	3,167,820	92.57
Henri Hogbe Nlend (UPC)	85,693	2.50
Samuel Eboua (MDP)	83,506	2.44
Albert Dzongang (PPD)	40,814	1.19
Joachim Tabi Owono (AMEC)	15,817	0.46
Antoine Demannu (RDPF)	15,490	0.45
Gustave Essaka (DIC)	12,915	0.38
Total*	**3,422,055**	**100.00**

* Excluding invalid votes.

NATIONAL ASSEMBLY

President: Djibril Cavayé Yeguie.

General Election, 17 May 1997

Party	Seats
Rassemblement démocratique du peuple camerounais	109
Social Democratic Front	43
Union nationale pour la démocratie et le progrès	13
Union démocratique du Cameroun	5
Mouvement pour la défense de la République	1
Mouvement pour la jeunesse du Cameroun	1
Union des populations camerounaises (K)	1
Total*	**180**

* On 3 August 1997 further elections took place in seven constituencies, where the results had been annulled; all the seats were won by the RDPC.

Political Organizations

In early 2001 there were 169 active political parties, of which the most important are listed below:

Action for Meritocracy and Equal Opportunity Party (AMEC): Leader Joachim Tabi Owono.

Alliance pour la démocratie et le développement (ADD): Sec.-Gen. Garga Haman Adji.

Alliance démocratique pour le progrès du Cameroun (ADPC): Garoua; f. 1991.

Alliance pour le progrès et l'émancipation des dépossédés (APED): Yaoundé; f. 1991; Leader Bohin Bohin.

Alliance pour le redressement du Cameroun (ARC): f. 1992 by a number of opposition movements.

Association social-démocrate du Cameroun (ASDC): Maroua; f. 1991.

Cameroon Anglophone Movement (CAM): advocates a federal system of govt.

Congrès panafricain du Cameroun (CPC): Douala; f. 1991.

Convention libérale (CL): f. 1991; Leader Pierre-Flambeau Ngayap.

Démocratie intégrale au Cameroun (DIC): Douala; f. 1991; Leader Gustave Essaka.

Front des alliés pour le changement (FAC): Douala; f. 1994; alliance of 16 opposition movements; Leader Samuel Eboua.

Front démocratique et patriotique (FDP): f. 1994; alliance of six opposition parties.

Liberal Democratic Alliance (LDA): Buéa; Pres. Henri Fossung.

Mouvement pour la défense de la République (MDR): f. 1991; Leader Dakole Daissala.

Mouvement pour la démocratie et le progrès (MDP): f. 1992; Leader Samuel Eboua.

Mouvement pour la jeunesse du Cameroun (MLJC): Leader Dieudonné Tina.

Mouvement pour la libération et le développement du Cameroun (MLDC): f. by a breakaway faction of the MLJC; Leader Marcel Yondo.

Mouvement social pour la nouvelle démocratie (MSND): Leader Yondo Black.

Nouvelle convention (NC): Yaoundé.

Parti des démocrates camerounais (PDC): Yaoundé; f. 1991; Leader Louis-Tobie Mbida.

Parti libéral-democrate (PLD): f. 1991; Leader Njoh Litumbe.

Parti populaire pour le développement (PPD): f. 1997.

Parti républicain du peuple camerounais (PRPC): Bertoua; f. 1991; Leader Ateba Ngoua.

Parti socialiste camerounais (PSC): Leader Jean-Pierre Dembele.

Parti socialiste démocratique (PSD): Douala; f. 1991; Leader Ernest Koum Bin Biltik.

Parti socialiste démocratique du Cameroun (PSDC): Leader Jean Michel Tekam.

Rassemblement démocratique du peuple camerounais (RDPC): BP 867, Yaoundé; tel. 23-27-40. 1966 as Union nationale camerounaise by merger of the Union camerounaise, the Kamerun National Democratic Party and four opposition parties; adopted present name in 1985; sole legal party 1972–90; Pres. Paul Biya; Sec.-Gen. Joseph-Charles Doumba.

Rassemblement démocratique du peuple sans frontières (RDPF): f. 1997.

Social Democratic Front (SDF): Bamenda; f. 1990; e-mail webmaster@sdfparty.org; internet www.sdfparty.org; Chair. John Fru Ndi; Sec.-Gen. Prof. Tazoacha Asonganyi.

Social Democratic Movement (SDM): f. 1995; breakaway faction of the Social Democratic Front; Leader Siga Asanga.

Southern Cameroons National Council (SCNC): f. 1995; supports the establishment of an independent republic in anglophone Cameroon; Chair. Sam Ekontang Elad.

Union démocratique du Cameroun (UDC): f. 1991; Leader Adamou Ndam Njoya.

Union des forces démocratiques du Cameroun (UFDC): Yaoundé; f. 1991; Leader Victorin Hameni Bieleu.

Union nationale pour la démocratie et le progrès (UNDP): f. 1991; split in 1995; Chair. Bello Bouba Maigari.

Union des populations camerounaises (UPC): Douala; f. 1948; split into two main factions in 1996: UPC (N), led by Ndeh Ntumazah, and UPC (K), led by Augustin Frédéric Kodock.

Diplomatic Representation

EMBASSIES AND HIGH COMMISSIONS IN CAMEROON

Algeria: BP 1619, Yaoundé; tel. 21-53-51; fax 21-53-54; Ambassador: Mohamed Achache.

Belgium: BP 816, Yaoundé; tel. 20-67-47; fax 20-05-21; Ambassador: Baudouin Vanderhulst.

Brazil: BP 348, Yaoundé; tel. 21-45-67; fax 21-19-57; Chargé d'affaires a.i.: Sergio Couri Elias.

Canada: Immeuble Stamatiades, BP 572, Yaoundé; tel. 23-02-03; fax 22-10-90; e-mail Honore.Mondomobe@dfait-maeci.gc.ca; internet www.infoexport.gc.ca/cm; High Commissioner: Michel Perrault.

Central African Republic: BP 396, Yaoundé; tel. and fax 20-51-55; Ambassador: Jean Poloko.

Chad: BP 506, Yaoundé; tel. and fax 21-06-24; Ambassador: Homsala Ouangmotching.

China, People's Republic: BP 1307, Yaoundé; tel. 21-00-83; fax 21-43-95; e-mail ambchine@camnet.cm; Ambassador: Xu Mengshui.

Congo, Democratic Republic: BP 632, Yaoundé; tel. 22-51-03; Ambassador: (vacant).

Congo, Republic: BP 1422, Yaoundé; tel. 21-24-58; Ambassador: Marcel Makome.

Egypt: BP 809, Yaoundé; tel. 20-39-22; fax 20-26-47; Ambassador: Nofal Ibrahim el-Sayed.

Equatorial Guinea: BP 277, Yaoundé; tel. and fax 21-14-04; Ambassador: Angue Ondo Purificación.

France: Plateau Atémengué, BP 1631, Yaoundé; tel. 23-40-13; fax 23-50-43; e-mail ambafrancecam@camnet.cm; internet www.france-cam.cm; Ambassador: Jean-Paul Véziant.

Gabon: BP 4130, Yaoundé; tel. 20-29-66; fax 21-02-24; Ambassador: Ferdinand Massala Malonga.

Germany: rue Charles de Gaulle, BP 1160, Yaoundé; tel. 20-05-66; fax 20-73-13; Ambassador: Jürgen Dröge.

Greece: BP 82, Yaoundé; tel. and fax 20-39-36; Ambassador: Ionnis Georgiadis.

Holy See: rue du Vatican, BP 210, Yaoundé (Apostolic Nunciature); tel. 20-04-75; fax 20-75-13; Apostolic Pro-Nuncio: Most Rev. Félix del Blanco Prieto, Titular Archbishop of Vannida.

Israel: BP 5934, Yaoundé; tel. 20-16-44; fax 21-08-23; Ambassador: Yoram Elron.

Italy: Quartier Bastos, BP 827, Yaoundé; tel. 20-33-76; fax 21-52-50; e-mail ambyaounde@gcnet.com; Ambassador: FRANCESCO LANATA.

Japan: Bastos-Ekoudou, Yaoundé; tel. 20-62-02; fax 20-62-03; Ambassador: TAKERU SASAGUCHI.

Korea, Republic: BP 301, Yaoundé; tel. 21-32-23; fax 20-17-25; Ambassador: DAE-TAEK LIM.

Liberia: Ekoudou, Quartier Bastos, BP 1185, Yaoundé; tel. 21-12-96; fax 20-97-81; Ambassador: CARLTON ALEXWYN KARPEH.

Libya: Quartier Bastos, BP 1980, Yaoundé; tel. 22-41-38.

Morocco: BP 1629, Yaoundé; tel. 20-50-92; fax 20-37-93; Ambassador: OMAR EL-NASRI.

Nigeria: BP 448, Yaoundé; tel. 22-34-55; High Commissioner: EMMANUEL CHAME QUILTON TOMI NJWAH.

Romania: rue de Joseph Mballa Elounden, BP 6212, Yaoundé; tel. and fax 21-39-86; Chargé d'affaires a.i.: ION MOGOS.

Russia: BP 488, Yaoundé; tel. 20-17-14; fax 20-78-91; e-mail conrusse@camnet.cm; Ambassador: POULATE ABDOULAYEV.

Saudi Arabia: BP 1602, Yaoundé; tel. 21-26-75; fax 20-66-89; Ambassador: ABDULAZIZ FAHD AR-REBDI.

Spain: BP 877, Yaoundé; tel. 20-35-43; fax 20-64-91; Ambassador: JOSÉ LUIS SOLANO.

Tunisia: rue de Rotary, BP 6074, Yaoundé; tel. 20-33-68; fax 21-05-07; Chargé d'affaires a.i.: MOHAMED AMIRI.

United Kingdom: ave Winston Churchill, BP 547, Yaoundé; tel. 22-05-45; fax 22-01-48; e-mail BHC@yaounde.mail.fco.gov.uk; High Commissioner: PETER BOON.

USA: rue Nachtigal, BP 817, Yaoundé; tel. 23-40-14; fax 23-07-53; internet www.usembassy.state.gov/yaounde/wwwhmain.html; Ambassador: JOHN M. YATES.

Judicial System

Supreme Court: Yaoundé; tel. 22-01-64; fax 22-05-76; consists of a president, nine titular and substitute judges, a procureur général, an avocat général, deputies to the procureur général, a registrar and clerks.

President: ALEXANDRE DIPANDA MOUELLE.

High Court of Justice: Yaoundé; consists of 9 titular judges and 6 substitute judges, all elected by the National Assembly.

Attorney-General: RISSOUCK A. MOULLONG.

Religion

It is estimated that 53% of the population are Christians (mainly Roman Catholics), 25% adhere to traditional religious beliefs and 22% are Muslims.

CHRISTIANITY
Protestant Churches

There are about 1m. Protestants in Cameroon, with about 3,000 church and mission workers, and four theological schools.

Fédération des Eglises et missions évangéliques du Cameroun (FEMEC): BP 491, Yaoundé; tel. 22-30-78; f. 1968; 10 mem. churches; Pres. Rev. Dr JEAN KOTTO (Evangelical Church of Cameroon); Admin. Sec. Rev. Dr GRÉGOIRE AMBADIANG DE MENDENG (Presbyterian Church of Cameroon).

Eglise évangélique du Cameroun (Evangelical Church of Cameroon): BP 89, Douala; tel. 42-36-11; fax 42-40-11; f. 1957; 500,000 mems (1992); Pres. Rev. CHARLES E. NJIKE; Sec. Rev. HANS EDJENGUELE.

Eglise presbytérienne camerounaise (Presbyterian Church of Cameroon): BP 519, Yaoundé; tel. 32-42-36; independent since 1957; comprises four synods and 16 presbyteries; 200,000 mems (1985); Gen. Sec. Rev. GRÉGOIRE AMBADIANG DE MENDENG.

Eglise protestante africaine (African Protestant Church): BP 26, Lolodorf; f. 1934; 8,400 mems (1985); Dir-Gen. Rev. MARNIA WOUNGLY-MASSAGA.

Presbyterian Church in Cameroon: BP 19, Buéa; tel. 32-23-36; 300,000 mems (1996); 302 ministers; Moderator Rev. NYANSAKO-NI-NKU.

Union des Eglises baptistes au Cameroun (Union of Baptist Churches of Cameroon): BP 6007, New Bell, Douala; tel. 42-41-06; autonomous since 1957; 37,000 mems (1985); Gen. Sec. Rev. EMMANUEL MBENDA.

Other Protestant churches active in Cameroon include the Cameroon Baptist Church, the Cameroon Baptist Convention, the Church of the Lutheran Brethren of Cameroon, the Evangelical Lutheran Church of Cameroon, the Presbyterian Church in West Cameroon and the Union of Evangelical Churches of North Cameroon.

The Roman Catholic Church

Cameroon comprises five archdioceses and 18 dioceses. At 31 December 1998 adherents represented some 23.6% of the total population. There are several active missionary orders, and four major seminaries for African priests.

Bishops' Conference: Conférence Episcopale Nationale du Cameroun, BP 1963, Yaoundé; tel. 31-15-92; fax 31-29-77; e-mail basc@rctmail.net; f. 1989; Pres. Rt Rev. ANDRÉ WOUKING, Bishop of Bafoussam; Sec.-Gen. Fr PATRICK LAFON.

Archbishop of Bamenda: Most Rev. PAUL VERDZEKOV, Archbishop's House, BP 82, Bamenda; tel. 36-12-41; fax 36-34-87; e-mail abpbda@compuserve.com.

Archbishop of Bertoua: Most Rev. LAMBERTUS JOHANNES VAN HEYGEN, Archevêché, BP 40, Bertoua; tel. 24-17-48; fax 24-25-85.

Archbishop of Douala: Cardinal CHRISTIAN WIYGHAN TUMI, Archevêché, BP 179, Douala; tel. 42-37-14; fax 42-18-37.

Archbishop of Garoua: Most Rev. ANTOINE NTALOU, Archevêché, BP 272, Garoua; tel. 27-13-53; fax 27-29-42.

Archbishop of Yaoundé: Most Rev. ANDRÉ WOUKING, Archevêché, BP 185, Yaoundé; tel. 22-24-89; fax 23-50-58; e-mail procure.yde@rctmail.net.

BAHÁ'Í FAITH

National Spiritual Assembly: BP 145, Limbe; tel. 33-21-46; mems in 1,744 localities.

The Press

Restrictions on the press have operated since 1966.

DAILIES

Cameroon Tribune: BP 1218, Yaoundé; tel. 30-36-89; fax 30-43-62; e-mail camtrib@gcnet.cm; internet www.cameroon-tribune.cm/accueil.asp; f. 1974; govt-controlled; French and English; Dir JÉRÔME MVONDO; Editor-in-Chief DAVID WAFFO MONGO; circ. 20,000.

Politiks Matinal: Yaoundé; f. 1999; independent; French; circ. 10,000.

Le Quotidien: BP 13088, Douala; tel. 39-11-89; fax 39-18-19; French.

PERIODICALS

Affaires Légales: BP 3681, Douala; tel. 42-58-38; fax 43-22-59; monthly; legal periodical.

Afrique en Dossiers: BP 1715; Yaoundé; f. 1970; French and English; Dir EBONGUE SOELLE.

Cameroon Outlook: BP 124, Limbe; f. 1969; 3 a week; independent; English; Editor JEROME F. GWELLEM; circ. 20,000.

Cameroon Panorama: BP 46, Buéa; tel. 32-22-40; f. 1962; monthly; English; Roman Catholic; Editor Sister MERCY HORGAN; circ. 1,500.

Cameroon Post: Yaoundé; weekly; independent; English; Publr PADDY MBAWA; Editor JULIUS WAMEY; circ. 50,000.

Cameroon Review: BP 408, Limbe; monthly; Editor-in-Chief JEROME F. GWELLEM; circ. 70,000.

Cameroon Times: BP 408, Limbe; f. 1960; weekly; English; Editor-in-Chief JEROME F. GWELLEM; circ. 12,000.

Challenge Hebdo: BP 1388, Douala; weekly; Editor BENJAMIN ZEBAZE.

Le Combattant: Yaoundé; weekly; independent; Editor BENYIMBE JOSEPH; circ. 21,000.

Courrier Sportif du Bénin: BP 17, Douala; weekly; Dir HENRI JONG.

Dikalo: BP 4320, Douala; tel. 37-00-32; fax 37-19-06; independent; 2 a week; French; Dir EMMANUEL NOUBISSIE NGANKAM.

L'Effort Camerounais: BP 15231, Douala; tel. 43-27-26; fax 43-18-37; weekly; Catholic.

L'Expression: BP 15333, Douala; tel. 43-22-27; fax 43-26-69; e-mail expression@cybernum.com; 3 times a week.

La Gazette: BP 5485, Douala; 2 a week; Editor ABODEL KARIMOU; circ. 35,000.

The Herald: BP 3659, Yaoundé; tel. 31-55-22; fax 31-81-61; 3 a week; English; Dir Dr BONIFACE FORBIN; circ. 8,000.

Al Houda: BP 1638, Yaoundé; quarterly; Islamic cultural review.

L'Indépendant Hebdo: Yaoundé; Chief Editor EVARISTE MENONGA.

Le Jeune Observateur: Yaoundé; f. 1991; Editor JULES KOUM.

Journal Officiel de la République du Cameroun: BP 1603, Yaoundé; tel. 23-12-77; fortnightly; official govt notices; circ. 4,000.

Le Messager: 266 blvd de la Liberté, BP 5925, Douala; tel. 42-04-39; fax 42-02-14; e-mail lemessager@camnet.cm; internet wagne.net/messager; f. 1979; 3 a week; independent; Man. Editor PIUS N. NJAWE; circ. 39,000.

Le Messager Popoli: 266 blvd de la Liberté, BP 5925, Douala; tel. 42-04-39; fax 42-02-14; f. 1993; 2 a week; independent; Man. Editor PIUS N. NJAWE; circ. 24,000.

The Messenger: BP 15043, Douala; English edn of *Le Messager*; Editor HILARY FOKUM.

Mutations: BP 12348, Yaoundé; tel. 22-51-04; fax 22-51-04; e-mail mutations@cybernum.com; 2 a week; French.

Nleb Ensemble: Imprimerie Saint-Paul, BP 763, Yaoundé; tel. 23-97-73; fax 23-50-58; f. 1935; fortnightly; Ewondo; Dir Most Rev. JEAN ZOA; Editor JOSEPH BEFE ATEBA; circ. 6,000.

La Nouvelle Expression: BP 15333, Douala; independent; 3 a week; French; Man. Editor SÉVERIN TCHOUNKOU.

Presbyterian Newsletter: BP 19, Buéa; quarterly.

Que Savoir: BP 1986, Douala; monthly; industry, commerce and tourism.

Recherches et Études Camerounaises: BP 193, Yaoundé; monthly; publ. by Office National de Recherches Scientifiques du Cameroun.

La Révélation: Yaoundé; Dir BOSCO TCHOUBET.

Le Serment: Yaoundé; newspaper; Editor-in-Chief ANSELME MBALLA.

Le Serviteur: BP 1405, Yaoundé; monthly; Protestant; Dir Pastor DANIEL AKO'O; circ. 3,000.

Le Travailleur/The Worker: BP 1610, Yaoundé; tel. 22-33-15; f. 1972; monthly; French and English; journal of Organisation Syndicale des Travailleurs du Cameroun/Cameroon Trade Union Congress; Sec.-Gen. LOUIS SOMBES; circ. 10,000.

L'Unité: BP 867, Yaoundé; weekly; French and English.

Weekly Post: Obili, Yaoundé; Publr Chief BISONG ETAHOBEN.

NEWS AGENCIES

CamNews: c/o SOPECAM, BP 1218, Yaoundé; tel. 30-38-30; fax 30-43-62; Dir JEAN NGANDJEU.

Foreign Bureaux

Xinhua (New China) News Agency (People's Republic of China): ave Joseph Omgba, BP 1583, Yaoundé; tel. 20-25-72; Chief Correspondent SUN XINGWEN.

Agence France-Presse (France), Reuters (UK) and ITAR—TASS (Russia) are also represented.

Publishers

Editions Buma Kor: BP 727, Yaoundé; tel. 22-48-99; fax 23-29-03; f. 1977; general, children's, educational and Christian; English and French; Man. Dir B. D. BUMA KOR.

Editions Clé: BP 1501, Yaoundé; tel. 22-35-54; fax 23-27-09; e-mail cle@a–vip.com; f. 1963; African and Christian literature and studies; school textbooks; medicine and science; general non-fiction; Gen. Man. COMLAN PROSPER DEH.

Editions Le Flambeau: BP 113, Yaoundé; tel. 22-36-72; f. 1977; general; Man. Dir JOSEPH NDZIE.

Editions Semences Africaines: BP 5329, Yaoundé-Nlongkak; tel. 22-40-58; f. 1974; fiction, history, religion, textbooks; Man. Dir PHILIPPE-LOUIS OMBEDE.

New Times Publishing House: Presbook Compound, BP 408, Limbe; tel. 33-32-17; f. 1983; publishing and book trade reference; Dir and Editor-in-Chief J. F. GWELLEM.

Presses Universitaires d'Afrique: BP 7136, Yaoundé; tel. 22-00-30; fax 22-23-25; f. 1986; literature, social sciences and law.

Government Publishing Houses

Centre d'Edition et de Production pour l'Enseignement et la Recherche (CEPER): BP 808, Yaoundé; tel. 22-13-23; f. 1967; transfer pending to private ownership; general non-fiction, science and technology, tertiary, secondary and primary textbooks; Man. Dir JEAN CLAUDE FOUTH.

Imprimerie Nationale: BP 1603, Yaoundé; tel. 23-12-77; scheduled for transfer to private ownership; Dir AMADOU VAMOULKE.

Société de Presse et d'Editions du Cameroun (SOPECAM): BP 1218, Yaoundé; tel. 30-40-12; fax 30-43-62; f. 1977; under the supervision of the Ministry of Communication; Dir-Gen. PAUL CÉLESTIN NDEMBIYEMBE; Man. Editor PIERRE ESSAMA ESSOMBA.

Broadcasting and Communications

TELECOMMUNICATIONS

A Telecommunications Regulation Agency was established in early 1999.

Cameroon Telecommunications (CAMTEL): BP 1571, Yaoundé; tel. 23-40-65; fax 23-03-03; e-mail camtel@camnet.cm; internet www.camnet.cm; f. 1999 by merger of INTELCAM and the Dept of Telecommunications; 51% privatization pending; Pres. NFON VICTOR MUKETE; Dir-Gen. EMMANUEL NGUIAMBA NLOUTSIRI.

Mobile Telephone Networks Cameroon (MTNC): Douala; f. 1999 as CAMTEL Mobile; mobile cellular telephone operator; 70% owned by MTN South Africa.

Société Camerounaise de Mobiles: Yaoundé; internet www.fcr.fr/fr/identite/pays/cameroun.htm; f. 1999; mobile cellular telephone operator; operates in Yaoundé, Douala and Bafoussam; 100% owned by France Câbles et Radio; Dir-Gen. JEAN-PAUL GANDET.

BROADCASTING

Radio

Office de Radiodiffusion-Télévision Camerounaise (CRTV): BP 1634, Yaoundé; tel. 21-40-88; fax 20-43-40; internet www.ditof.cm/crtv; f. 1987 by merger; broadcasts in French and English; satellite broadcasts commenced in Jan. 2001, reaching some 80% of the national territory; Pres. HENRI BANDOLO; Dir-Gen. Prof. GERVAIS MENDOZE.

Radio Bertoua: BP 260, Bertoua; tel. 24-14-45.

Radio Buéa: POB 86, Buéa; tel. 32-26-15; programmes in English, French and 15 vernacular languages; Man. PETERSON CHIA YUH; Head of Station GIDEON MULU TAKA.

Radio Douala: BP 986, Douala; tel. 42-60-60; programmes in French, English, Douala, Bassa, Ewondo, Bakoko and Bamiléké; Dir BRUNO DJEM; Head of Station LINUS ONANA MVONDO.

Radio Garoua: BP 103, Garoua; tel. 27-11-67; programmes in French, Hausa, English, Foulfoudé, Arabic and Choa; Dir BELLO MALGANA; Head of Station MOUSSA EPOPA.

Radio Ngaoundéré: BP 135, Ngaoundéré; tel. 25-21-48.

Radio Yaoundé: BP 1634, Yaoundé; tel. 20-25-02.

There are also provincial radio stations at Abong Mbang, Bafoussam, Bamenda, Ebolowa and Maroua.

Television

Television programmes from France were broadcast by the Office de Radiodiffusion-Télévision Camerounaise from early 1990.

Office de Radiodiffusion-Télévision Camerounaise (CRTV): see Radio.

Finance

(cap. = capital; res = reserves; dep. = deposits; m. = million; brs = branches; amounts in francs CFA)

BANKING

Central Bank

Banque des Etats de l'Afrique Centrale (BEAC): rue du Dr Jamot, BP 1917, Yaoundé; tel. 23-40-30; fax 23-33-29; f. 1973; bank of issue for mem. states of the Communauté économique et monétaire de l'Afrique centrale (CEMAC, fmrly Union douanière et économique de l'Afrique centrale) Cameroon, the Central African Repub., Chad, the Repub. of the Congo, Equatorial Guinea and Gabon; cap. 45,000m., res 172,198m., total assets 1,407,908m. (Dec. 1999); Gov. JEAN-FÉLIX MAMALEPOT; Dir in Cameroon SADOU HAYATOU; 5 brs in Cameroon.

Commercial Banks

Amity Bank Cameroon SA: Commercial Ave, BP 2171, Bamenda; tel. 36-36-51; fax 36-36-59; e-mail amibac@camnet.cm; internet www.afrika.com/amity-bank; f. 1990; cap. and res 1,106m., total assets 19,071m. (June 1999); Pres. LAWRENCE LOWEH TASHA, Vice-Pres. Prof. VICTOR ANOMAH NGU; 4 brs.

Banque Internationale pour le Commerce et l'Industrie du Cameroun SA: ave du Général de Gaulle, BP 4070, Douala; tel. 23-40-07; fax 42-41-16; f. 1962; 51% owned by Banque Populaire de France; cap. 3,000m. (March 1997); Pres. RAYMOND MALOUMA; Dir-Gen. SADOU HAYATOU; 34 brs.

Citibank N.A. Cameroon: 96 rue Flatters, Bonanjo, BP 4571, Douala; tel. 42-42-72; fax 42-40-74; f. 1997; Dir-Gen. LOUIS ADANDE; Asst Dir-Gen. OSMAN EL TOUM.

Commercial Bank of Cameroon: BP 4004, Douala; tel. 42-02-02; fax 43-38-00; e-mail cbcbank@camnet.cm; f. 1997; cap. and res

1,450.1m., total assets 41,602.1m. (March 1999); Pres. VICTOR FOTSO; Dir-Gen. JEAN LOUIS CHAPUIS.

Highland Corporation Bank SA: Immeuble Hotel Hilton, blvd du 20 mai, BP 10039, Yaoundé; tel. 23-92-87; fax 23-92-91; e-mail hicobk@camnet.cm; f. 1995; 100% privately owned; cap. 600m. (Dec. 1996); Exec. Pres. PAUL ATANGA NJI; Asst Dir-Gen. JOHANES MBATI.

Société Commerciale de Banque—Crédit Lyonnais Cameroun (SCB–CLC): 220 ave Monseigneur Vogt, BP 700, Yaoundé; tel. 23-40-05; fax 22-41-32; e-mail andré .roggemans@camnet.cm; f. 1989; 35% state-owned; cap. and res 12,817.5m., total assets 185,237.7m. (June 1998); Pres. MARTIN OKOUDA; Dir-Gen. BERNARD FOURNIER; 18 brs.

Société Générale de Banques au Cameroun (SGBC): 78 rue Joss, BP 4042, Douala; tel. 42-70-10; fax 43-03-53; e-mail sgbcdla@ camnet.cm; f. 1963; 25.6% state-owned; cap. 6,250.0m., res 3,300.2m., dep. 195,225.8m. (June 1999); Pres. AHMADOU NJIFENDJOU MOULIOM; Dir-Gen. MICHEL SAUVAGNAC; 15 brs.

Standard Chartered Bank Cameroon SA: blvd de la Liberté, BP 1784, Douala; tel. 43-52-00; fax 42-27-89; internet www .standardchartered.com/cm/index.html; f. 1980 as Boston Bank Cameroon; 100% owned by Standard Chartered Bank (United Kingdom); cap. 3,500m., total assets 116,873m. (June 2000); Pres. EPHRAIM INONI; Man. Dir GREG FLETCHER; 3 brs.

Development Banks

Banque de Développement des États de l'Afrique Centrale: (see Franc Zone, p. 211).

Crédit Foncier du Cameroun (CFC): 484 blvd du 20 mai 1972, BP 1531, Yaoundé; tel. 23-52-15; fax 23-52-21; f. 1977; 70% owned by Banque des Etats de l'Afrique Centrale; cap. and res 7,913.1m., total assets 77,963.7m. (June 1997); provides assistance for low-cost housing; Pres. GEORGES NGANGO; Dir-Gen. SYLVESTRE NAAH ONDOA.

Société Nationale d'Investissement du Cameroun (SNI): place de la Poste, BP 423, Yaoundé; tel. 22-44-22; fax 23-13-32; f. 1964; state-owned investment and credit agency; cap. and res 12,510.2m., total assets 37,392.9m. (June 1995); Pres. VICTOR AYISSI MVODO; Dir-Gen. ESTHER BELIBI DANG.

Financial Institutions

Caisse Autonome d'Amortissement du Cameroun: BP 7167, Yaoundé; tel. 22-22-26; fax 22-01-29; f. 1985; e-mail camtis@ camnet.cm; cap. 5,000m. (1998); Dir-Gen. DANIEL LAMERE NJANKOUO.

Caisse Commune d'Epargne et d'Investissement (CCEI): place de l'Indépendance, BP 11834, Yaoundé; tel. 23-30-68; fax 22-17-85; cap. and res 7,400m., total assets 76,700m. (June 1998); Pres. Dr PAUL KANMOGNE FOKAM; Dir-Gen. BONIFACE KACYEM.

Fonds d'Aide et de Garantie des Crédits aux Petites et Moyennes Entreprises (FOGAPE): BP 1591, Yaoundé; tel. 23-38-59; fax 22-32-74; f. 1984; cap. 1,000m. (Oct. 1997); Pres. JOSEPH HENGA; Vice-Pres. ARMAND FIRMIN MVONDO.

Société Camerounaise de Crédit Automobile (SOCCA): rue du Roi Albert, BP 554, Douala; tel. 42-74-78; fax 42-12-19; cap. and res 2,059.6m., total assets 15,239.6m. (June 1998); Pres. VALENTIN MOUYOMBON; Dir-Gen. PHILIPPE DE LAPLAGNOLLE.

Société Camerounaise de Crédit-Bail (SOCABAIL): rue du Roi Albert, BP 554, Douala; tel. 42-74-78; fax 42-12-19; cap. and res 1,347.8m., total assets 5,059.6m. (June 1998); Pres. ALAIN GUYON.

INSURANCE

Activa Assurances: Douala; f. 1999; all branches except life insurance; cap. 400m.; 66% owned by Cameroonian investors, 33% by Ivorian investors; Chair. JEAN DIAGOU; Gen. Man. RICHARD LOWE.

Assurances Mutuelles Agricoles du Cameroun (AMACAM): BP 962, Yaoundé; tel. 22-49-66; f. 1965; cap. 100m.; state-owned; privatization pending; Pres. SAMUEL NGBWA NGUELE; Dir-Gen. LUC CLAUDE NANFA.

Caisse Nationale de Réassurances (CNR): ave Foch, BP 4180, Yaoundé; tel. 22-37-99; fax 23-36-80; f. 1965; all classes of reinsurance; cap. 1,000m.; state-owned; scheduled for transfer to private ownership by 2000; Pres. JEAN KEUTCHA; Man. Dir ANTOINE NTSIMI.

Compagnie Camerounaise d'Assurances et de Réassurances (CCAR): 11 rue Franqueville, BP 4068, Douala; tel. 42-31-59; fax 42-64-53; f. 1974; cap. 499.5m.; Pres. YVETTE CHASSAGNE; Dir Gen. CHRISTIAN LE GOFF.

Compagnie Nationale d'Assurances (CNA): BP 12125, Douala; tel. 42-44-46; fax 42-47-27; f. 1986; all classes of insurance; cap. 600m.; Chair. THÉODORE EBOBO; Man. Dir. PROTAIS AYANGMA AMANG.

General and Equitable Assurance Cameroon Ltd (GEACAM): 56 blvd de la Liberté, BP 426, Douala; tel. 42-59-85; fax 42-71-03; cap. 300m.; Pres. V. A. NGU; Man. Dir J. CHEBAUT.

Société Camerounaise d'Assurances et de Réassurances (SOCAR): 1450 blvd de la Liberté, BP 280, Douala; tel. 42-55-84; fax 42-13-35; f. 1973; cap. 800m.; state-owned; scheduled for transfer to private ownership by 2000; Chair. J. YONTA; Man. Dir R. BIOUELE.

Société Nouvelle d'Assurances du Cameroun (SNAC): rue Manga Bell, BP 105, Douala; tel. 42-92-03; fax 43-03-24; 1974; all classes of insurance; cap. 700m.; Dir-Gen. JEAN CHEBAUT.

Trade and Industry

GOVERNMENT AGENCY

Economic and Social Council: BP 1058, Yaoundé; tel. 23-24-74; advises the Govt on economic and social problems; comprises 150 mems and a perm. secr.; mems serve a five-year term; Pres. LUC AYANG; Sec.-Gen. FRANÇOIS EYOK.

DEVELOPMENT ORGANIZATIONS

Agence Française de Développement (AFD): BP 46, Yaoundé; tel. 22-23-24; fax 23-57-07; fmrly Caisse Française de Développement; Dir DOMINIQUE DORDAIN.

Cameroon Development Corporation (CAMDEV): Bota, Limbe; tel. 33-22-51; fax 43-17-40; f. 1947, reorg. 1982; cap. 15,626m. francs CFA; state-owned; statutory corpn established to acquire and develop plantations of tropical crops for local and export markets; operates two oil mills, seven banana-packing stations, three tea and seven rubber factories; owned by Del Monte, USA; Chair. NERIUS NAMASO MBILE; Gen. Man. NJALLU QUAN.

Direction Générale des Grands Travaux du Cameroun (DGTC): BP 6604, Yaoundé; tel. 22-18-03; fax 22-13-00; f. 1988; commissioning, implementation and supervision of public works contracts; Chair. JEAN FOUMAN AKAME; Man. Dir MICHEL KOWALZICK.

Hévéa-Cameroun (HEVECAM): BP 1298, Douala and BP 174, Kribi; tel. 42-75-64. 1975; cap. 16,518m. francs CFA; state-owned; development of 15,000 ha rubber plantation; 4,500 employees; transferred to private ownership in 1997; Pres. NYOKWEDI MALONGA; Man. Dir PAUL DE KIPPELEYR.

Mission d'Aménagement et d'Equipement des Terrains Urbains et Ruraux (MAETUR): BP 1248, Yaoundé; tel. 22-31-13. 1977; Pres. LÉOPOLD FERDINAND OYONO; Dir-Gen. ANDRÉ MAMA FOUDA.

Mission de Développement de la Province du Nord-Ouest (MIDENO): BP 442, Bamenda; Dir ANDREW WAINDIM NDONYI.

Mission Française de Coopération et d'Action Culturelle: BP 1616, Yaoundé; tel. 23-04-12; fax 22-50-65; e-mail mission.coop@ camnet.cm; administers bilateral aid from France; Dir LUC HALLADE.

Office Céréalier dans la Province du Nord: BP 298, Garoua; tel. 27-14-38. 1975 to combat effects of drought in northern Cameroon and stabilize cereal prices; Pres. Alhadji MAHAMAT; Dir-Gen. GILBERT GOURLEMOND.

Société de Développement du Cacao (SODECAO): BP 1651, Yaoundé; tel. 30-45-44; fax 30-33-95; f. 1974, reorg. 1980; cap. 425m. francs CFA; development of cocoa, coffee and food crop production in the Littoral, Centre, East and South provinces; Pres. JOSEPH-CHARLES DOUMBA; Dir-Gen. JOSEPH INGWAT II.

Société de Développement de l'Elevage (SODEVA): BP 50, Kousseri; cap. 50m. francs CFA; Dir Alhadji OUMAROU BAKARY.

Société de Développement et d'Exploitation des Productions Animales (SODEPA): BP 1410, Yaoundé; tel. 22-24-28; f. 1974; cap. 375m. francs CFA; development of livestock and livestock products; Man. Dir ETIENNE ENGUELEGUELE.

Société de Développement de la Haute-Vallée du Noun (UNVDA): BP 25, N'Dop, North-West Province; f. 1970; cap. 1,380m. francs CFA; rice, maize and soya bean cultivation; Dir-Gen. SAMUEL BAWE CHI WANKI.

Société d'Expansion et de Modernisation de la Riziculture de Yagoua (SEMRY): BP 46, Yagoua; tel. 29-62-13; f. 1971; cap. 4,580m. francs CFA; commercialization of rice products and expansion of rice-growing in areas where irrigation is possible; Pres. ALBERT EKONO; Dir-Gen. LIMANGANA TORI.

Société Immobilière du Cameroun (SIC): BP 387, Yaoundé; tel. 23-34-11; fax 22-51-19; f. 1952; cap. 1,000m. francs CFA; housing construction and development; Pres. ENOCH KWAYEB; Dir-Gen. GILLES-ROGER BELINGA.

CHAMBERS OF COMMERCE

Chambre d'Agriculture, d'Elevage et des Forêts du Cameroun: Parc Repiquet, BP 287, Yaoundé; tel. 23-14-96; f. 1955; 120 mems; Pres. PHILÉMON ADJIBOLO; Sec.-Gen. SOLOMON NFOR GWEI; other chambers at Yaoundé, Ebolowa, Bertoua, Douala, Ngaoundéré, Garoua, Maroua, Buéa, Bumenda and Bafoussam.

Chambre de Commerce, d'Industrie et des Mines du Cameroun (CCIM): rue de Chambre de Commerce, BP 4011, Douala; tel. 42-68-55; fax 42-55-96; internet www.g77tin.org/ccimhp.html; f. 1921; also at BP 36, Yaoundé; BP 211, Limbe; BP 59, Garoua; BP 944, Bafoussam; BP 551, Bamenda; 138 mems; Pres. PIERRE TCHANQUE; Sec.-Gen. SAÏDOU ABDOULAYE BOBBOY.

EMPLOYERS' ORGANIZATIONS

Association Professionnelle des Établissements Financiers (APECAM): Yaoundé; tel. 23-54-01; fax 23-54-02.

Groupement des Femmes d'Affaires du Cameroun (GFAC): BP 1940, Douala; tel. 42-4-64; Pres. FRANÇOISE FONING.

Groupement Interpatronal du Cameroun (GICAM): ave Konrad Adenauer, BP 1134, Yaoundé; tel. 20-27-22; fax 20-96-94; e-mail gicam-yde@camnet.cm; also at BP 829, Douala; tel. and fax 42-31-41; f. 1957; Pres. ANDRÉ SIAKA; Sec.-Gen. FRANCIS SANZOUANGO.

Syndicat des Commerçants Importateurs-Exportateurs du Cameroun (SCIEC): 16 rue Quillien, BP 562, Douala; tel. 42-03-04; Sec.-Gen. G. TOSCANO.

Syndicat des Industriels du Cameroun (SYNDUSTRICAM): 17 blvd de Liberté, BP 673, Douala; tel. 42-30-58; fax 42-56-16; f. 1953; Pres. SAMUEL KONDO EBELLÉ.

Syndicat des Producteurs et Exportateurs de Bois du Cameroun: BP 570, Yaoundé; tel. 20-27-22; fax 20-96-94; Pres. CARLO ORIANI.

Syndicat Professionnel des Entreprises du Bâtiment, des Travaux Publics et des Activités Annexes: BP 1134, Yaoundé; also at BP 660, Douala; tel. and fax 20-27-22; Pres. (vacant).

Syndicats Professionnels Forestiers et Activités connexes du Cameroun: BP 100, Douala.

Union des Syndicats Professionnels du Cameroun (USPC): BP 829, Douala; Pres. MOUKOKO KINGUE.

West Cameroon Employers' Association (WCEA): BP 97, Tiko.

UTILITIES

Electricity

Société Nationale d'Electricité du Cameroun (SONEL): BP 4077, 63 ave de Gaulle, Douala; tel. 42-54-44; fax 42-22-09; e-mail sonel@camnet.cm; internet www.camnet.cm/investir/minmee/sonelind.htm; f. 1974; 93.1% state owned; scheduled for transfer to the private sector in 2001; CEO JEAN FOUMAN AKAME; Dir-Gen. MARCEL NIAT NJI FENJI.

Water

Société Nationale des Eaux du Cameroun (SNEC): BP 157, Douala; tel. 42-87-11; fax 42-29-45; e-mail snec@camnet.cm; internet www.camnet.cm/investir/minmee/snec.htm; f. 1967; 73% state owned; scheduled for transfer to the private sector by 2000; Pres. AMADOU ALI; Dir-Gen. CLÉMENT OBOUH FEGUE.

PRINCIPAL CO-OPERATIVE ORGANIZATIONS

Centre National de Développement des Entreprises Coopératives (CENADEC): Yaoundé; f. 1970; promotes and organizes the co-operative movement; bureaux at BP 43, Kumba and BP 26, Bamenda; Dir JACQUES SANGUE.

Union Centrale des Coopératives Agricoles de l'Ouest (UCCAO): ave Samuel Wonko, BP 1002, Bafoussam; tel. 44-14-39; fax 44-11-01; f. 1957; marketing of cocoa and coffee; 110,000 mems; Pres. VICTOR GNIMPIEBA; Dir-Gen. PIERRE NZEFA TSACHOUA.

West Cameroon Co-operative Association Ltd: BP 135, Kumba; founded as cen. financing body of the co-operative movement; provides short-term credits and agricultural services to mem. socs; policy-making body for the co-operative movement in West Cameroon; 142 mem. unions and socs representing c. 45,000 mems; Pres. Chief T. E. NJEA.

TRADE UNION FEDERATION

Confederation of Cameroon Trade Unions (CCTU): BP 1610, Yaoundé; tel. 22-33-15; f. 1985; fmrly the Union National des Travailleurs du Cameroun (UNTC); Pres. EMMANUEL BAKOD; Sec.-Gen. LOUIS SOMBES.

Transport

RAILWAYS

There are some 1,104 km of track—the West Line running from Douala to Nkongsamba (166 km) with a branch line leading south-west from Mbanga to Kumba (29 km), and the Transcameroon railway which runs from Douala to Ngaoundéré (885 km), with a branch line from Ngoumou to Mbalmayo (30 km).

Cameroon Railways (CAMRAIL): Gare Centrale de Bessengue, blvd de la Réunification, BP 766, Douala; tel. 40-60-45; fax 40-82-52; e-mail camrail@camnet.cm; internet www.camnet.cm/investir/transport/regie/regie.htm; f. 1999; Pres. ETIENNE GIROS; Dir-Gen. PATRICK CLAES.

Office du Chemin de Fer Transcamerounais: BP 625, Yaoundé; tel. 22-44-33; supervises the laying of new railway lines and improvements to existing lines, and undertakes relevant research; Dir-Gen. LUC TOWA FOTSO.

ROADS

In 1999 there were an estimated 49,300 km of roads, of which about 4,100 km were paved.

SHIPPING

There are seaports at Kribi and Limbé-Tiko, a river port at Garoua, and an estuary port at Douala-Bonabéri, the principal port and main outlet, which has 2,510 m of quays and a minimum depth of 5.8 m in the channels and 8.5 m at the quays. In 1997 the port handled 4,882,000 metric tons of cargo. Total handling capacity is 7m. metric tons annually. Plans are under way to increase the annual capacity of the container terminal. There are also plans to modernize Limbé–Tiko and to promote it internationally.

Office National des Ports/National Ports Authority: Centre des Affaires Maritimes, 18 rue Joffre, BP 4002, Douala; tel. 42-01-33; fax 42-67-97; e-mail onpc@camnet.cm; internet www.camnet.cm/investir/transport/onpc; f. 1971; Chair. JOSEPH TSANGA ABANDA (Minister of Transport); Dir Gen. ALPHONSE SIYAM SIEW.

Cameroon Shipping Lines SA (CAMSHIP): Centre des Affaires Maritimes, BP 4054, Douala; tel. 42-00-38; fax 42-01-14; f. 1975; scheduled for transfer to private-sector ownership by 2000; 6 vessels trading with western Europe, USA, Far East and Africa; Chair. FRANÇOIS SENGAT KUO; Man. Dir RENÉ MBAYEN.

Camafrica Liner Ltd: Centre des Affaires Maritimes, BP 4054, Douala; non-vessel owner container carrier co. trading between West Africa and Europe.

Compagnie Maritime Camerounaise SA (CMC): BP 3235, Douala; tel. 42-85-40; fax 42-58-42.

Conseil National des Chargeurs du Cameroun (CNCC): BP 1588, Douala; tel. 42-32-06; fax 42-89-01; f. 1986; promotion of the maritime sector; Gen. Man. EMMANUEL EDOU.

Delmas Cameroun: rue Kitchener, BP 263, Douala; tel. 42-47-50; fax 42-88-51; f. 1977; Pres. JEAN-GUY LE FLOCH; Dir-Gen. DANY CHUTAUX.

Société Africaine de Transit et d'Affrètement (SATA): Douala; tel. 42-82-09; f. 1950; Man. Dir RAYMOND PARIZOT.

Société Agence Maritime de l'Ouest Africain Cameroun (SAMOA): 5 blvd de la Liberté, BP 1127, Douala; tel. 42-16-80; f. 1953; shipping agents; Dir JEAN PERRIER.

Société Camerounaise de Manutention et d'Acconage (SOCAMAC): BP 284, Douala; tel. 42-40-51; f. 1976; freight handling; Pres. MOHAMADOU TALBA; Dir-Gen. HARRY J. GHOOS.

Société Camerounaise de Transport et d'Affrètement (SCTA): BP 974, Douala; tel. 42-17-24; f. 1951; Pres. JACQUES VIAULT; Dir-Gen. GONTRAN FRAUCIEL.

Société Ouest-Africaine d'Entreprises Maritimes—Cameroun (SOAEM—Cameroun): 5 blvd de la Liberté, BP 4057, Douala; tel. 42-52-69; fax 42-05-18; f. 1959; Pres. JACQUES COLOMBANI; Man. Dir JEAN-LOUIS GRECIET.

Société de Transports Urbains du Cameroun (SOTUC): BP 1697, Yaoundé; tel. 21-38-07; fax 20-77-84; f. 1973; 58% owned by Société Nationale d'Investissement du Cameroun; operates urban transport services in Yaoundé and Douala; Dir-Gen. MARCEL YONDO; Mans JEAN-VICTOR OUM (Yaoundé), GABRIEL VASSEUR (Douala).

SOCOPAO (Cameroun): BP 215, Douala; tel. 42-64-64; f. 1951; shipping agents; Pres. VINCENT BOLLORE; Man. Dir E. DUPUY.

Transcap Cameroun: BP 4059, Douala; tel. 42-72-14; f. 1960; Pres. RENÉ DUPRAZ; Man. Dir MICHEL BARDOU.

CIVIL AVIATION

There are international airports at Douala, Garoua and Yaoundé; there are, in addition, 11 domestic airports, as well as a number of secondary airfields.

Aéroports du Cameroun (ADC): Aéroport de Douala; tel. 42-35-26; fax 42-37-58; f. 1999; manages major airports; 35% owned by Aéroports de Paris, 29% state-owned.

Air Affaires Afrique: BP 1225, Douala; tel. 42-29-77; fax 42-99-03; f. 1978; regional and domestic charter passenger services; CEO BYRON BYRON-EXARCOS.

Cameroon Airlines (CAMAIR): 151 rue de l'Hôtel de Ville, BP 4092, Douala; tel. 42-25-25; fax 42-34-59; e-mail camair@camnet.cm; internet www.camnet.cm/investir/transpor/camair/index.htm; f. 1971; domestic flights and services to Africa and Europe; privatization pending; Chair. JÉRÔME EMILIEN ABONDO; CEO CYRILLE ETOUNDI ATANGANA.

Tourism

Tourists are attracted by Cameroon's cultural diversity and by its national parks, game reserves and sandy beaches. In 1997 an estimated 132,839 tourists visited Cameroon. In that year receipts from tourism totalled some US $39m.

Ministère du Tourisme: BP 266, Yaoundé; tel. 22-44-11; fax 22-12-95; e-mail mintour@camnet.cm; internet www.camnet.cm/mintour/tourisme.

CANADA

Introductory Survey

Location, Climate, Language, Religion, Flag, Capital

Canada occupies the northern part of North America (excluding Alaska and Greenland) and is the second largest country in the world, after Russia. It extends from the Atlantic Ocean to the Pacific. Except for the boundary with Alaska in the north-west, Canada's frontier with the USA follows the upper St Lawrence Seaway and the Great Lakes, continuing west along latitude 49°N. The climate is an extreme one, particularly inland. Winter temperatures drop well below freezing but summers are generally hot. Rainfall varies from moderate to light and there are heavy falls of snow. The two official languages are English and French, the mother tongues of 59.3% and 23.2%, respectively, at the general census in 1996. Immigration during the 1990s has made a profound impact on languages spoken in Canadian homes; at the 1996 census Chinese was the language most commonly spoken at home, after English and French. About 45% of the population are Roman Catholics. The main Protestant churches are the United Church of Canada and the Anglican Church of Canada. Numerous other religious denominations are represented. The national flag (proportions 2 by 1) consists of a red maple leaf on a white field, flanked by red panels. The capital is Ottawa.

Recent History

The Liberals, led by Pierre Trudeau, were returned to office at general elections in 1968, 1972, 1974, and again in 1980 after a short-lived minority Progressive Conservative Party (PCP) administration. Popular support for the Liberals, however, was undermined by an economic recession, and the PCP, led by Brian Mulroney, obtained a substantial legislative majority at general elections held in September 1984.

During 1986 the persistence of high rates of unemployment, together with the resignations in discordant circumstances of five cabinet ministers, led to a fall in the PCP Government's popularity. Popular support for the Government further declined, in response to criticism by the Liberals and the New Democratic Party (NDP) of the Government's negotiation of a new US–Canadian trade treaty, which the Liberals and the NDP viewed as overly advantageous to US business interests and potentially damaging to Canada's national identity, and which was approved by the House of Commons in August 1988. Nevertheless, in general elections in November the PCP was re-elected, although with a reduced majority, and full legislative ratification of the trade agreement followed in December. In February 1990 the federal Government opened negotiations with Mexico, to achieve a lowering of trade barriers. These discussions were joined by the US Government, and in December 1992, Canada, the USA and Mexico finalized terms for a tripartite North American Free Trade Agreement (NAFTA, see p. 240), with the aim of creating a free trade zone encompassing the whole of North America.

In the province of Québec, where four-fifths of the population speak French as a first language and which maintains its own cultural identity, the question of political self-determination has long been a sensitive issue. At provincial elections in 1976 the separatist Parti Québécois (PQ) came to power, and in 1977 made French the official language of education, business and government in Québec. In December 1985 the PQ was replaced by the Liberals as the province's governing party. The Liberals retained power at the next provincial elections, held in September 1989. However, political support for separatist aspirations was extended to the federal Parliament in May 1990, when seven PCP members representing Québec constituencies, led by Lucien Bouchard (a former member of Mulroney's Cabinet), formed an independent Bloc Québécois (BQ) with the object of acting in the interests of a 'sovereign Québec'. The BQ later expanded, with disaffected Liberal support, to nine members.

In 1982 the British Parliament transferred to Canada authority over all matters contained in British statutes relating to Canada, opening the way for institutional reform and the redistribution of legislative powers between Parliament and the provincial legislatures. All the provinces except Québec eventually accepted constitutional provisions that included a charter of rights and a formula for constitutional amendments, whereby such amendments would require the support of at least seven provinces representing more than 50% of the population. Québec, however, maintained that its legislature could exercise the right to veto constitutional provisions.

Following the return to office in 1985 of the Liberals in Québec, the federal Government adopted new initiatives to include Québec in the constitutional arrangements. In April 1987 Mulroney and the provincial premiers met at Meech Lake, Québec, to negotiate a constitutional accommodation for Québec. The resultant agreement, the Meech Lake Accord, recognized Québec as a 'distinct society' within the Canadian federation, and granted each of the provinces substantial new powers in the areas of federal parliamentary reform, judicial appointments and the creation of new provinces. The Accord was subject to ratification, not later than June 1990, by the federal Parliament and all provincial legislatures. By early 1990 the federal Parliament and each of the 10 provincial legislatures, except for New Brunswick and Manitoba, had approved the Accord.

Opposition to the Meech Lake arrangements, on the grounds that they afforded too much influence to Québec and failed to provide Inuit and Indian minorities with the same measure of protection as francophone groups, began to emerge in March 1990, when the Newfoundland legislature rescinded its earlier endorsement of the Accord. Following a meeting in June between Mulroney and the provincial premiers (at which a number of compromise amendments were adopted), the New Brunswick legislature agreed to accept the Accord, but the provinces of Manitoba and Newfoundland upheld their opposition. The Meech Lake Accord duly lapsed in late June, and the Québec Government, which had opposed any changes to the earlier terms of the Accord, responded by refusing to participate in future provincial conferences, and by appointing a commission to examine the province's political choices. In October Mulroney appointed a consultative panel to ascertain public opinion both on constitutional reform and on the wider issue of Canada's national future.

In September 1991 the federal Government announced a new series of constitutional reform proposals, which, unlike the Meech Lake Accord, would require the assent of only seven provinces representing 50% of the total population. Under the new plan, Québec was to be recognized as a distinct society in terms of its language, culture and legal system, while each province would have full control of its cultural affairs. Native peoples were to receive full self-government within 10 years, inter-provincial trade barriers were to be abolished, and the federal Senate was to become an elected body with limited powers of legislative veto, except in matters involving natural resources, in which it would have full powers of veto. The reform proposals also included the creation of a Council of Federation to resolve disputes between the provinces and federal Government. A National Unity Committee, comprising an inter-party group of 30 federal legislators, was formed to ascertain public reaction to the plan, about which the Québec provincial government expressed initial reservations on economic grounds.

In March 1992 an all-party committee of the federal Parliament recommended new constitutional proposals providing for a system of 'co-operative federalism', which would grant Québec powers of veto over future constitutional changes, together with exclusive jurisdiction over the main areas of its provincial affairs. This plan was rejected by the Québec Government.

Further, inconclusive, discussions among the provincial premiers (in which Québec refused to participate) took place in mid-1992. Mulroney proposal to revive the Meech Lake proposals was opposed by the western provinces, which sought increased representation in a reformed Senate and were unwilling to concede a constitutional veto to Québec until after these changes were carried out. In late August 1992, following resumed consultations between Mulroney and the provincial premiers, a new programme of constitutional reforms, known as the Charlottetown Agreement, was finalized for submission to a national referendum. The proposals, which were endorsed by all of the provincial premiers as well as the leaders of the three main political parties, provided for an equal and elected Senate, a guarantee in perpetuity to Québec of one-quarter of the seats in the federal House of Commons (regardless of future movements in population), as well as three of the nine seats on the Supreme Court of Canada. There was also to be recognition of provincial jurisdiction in cultural affairs, and increased provincial powers over certain economic affairs and immigration. The inherent right to self-government of the Indian and Inuit population was also to be recognized.

Despite the apparent political consensus, considerable opposition to the Charlottetown Agreement became evident during the national debate that preceded the referendum, which took place in October 1992. Disagreements emerged on a regional basis, as well as among NDP and Liberal supporters (among whom Pierre Trudeau denounced the Agreement). Aspects of the proposed constitution were opposed by the PQ and the BQ, and by the Reform Party (RP), a conservative-populist movement which led opposition in the western provinces. Nationally, the proposals were defeated by a margin of 54.4% to 44.6%; only four of the provinces (Ontario, New Brunswick, Newfoundland and Prince Edward Island) and the Northwest Territories (NWT) endorsed the Agreement.

The defeat of the Charlottetown Agreement, together with the persistence of adverse economic conditions, led to a rapid erosion in the prestige of the Government, and in Mulroney's personal popularity. A reorganization of Cabinet posts in January 1993 failed to restore public confidence, and in the following month Mulroney announced that he was to relinquish office in June. He was succeeded by the former Minister of Defence and Veterans' Affairs, Kim Campbell, who became Canada's first woman Prime Minister.

The Campbell Government proved unable to restore the PCP's political standing, and, faced with the expiry in November 1993 of its five-year parliamentary mandate, general elections were scheduled for October. The outcome of the elections, which were contested primarily on domestic economic issues, resulted in a decisive victory for the Liberals, led by Jean Chrétien. A significant realignment of political forces was reflected in the new Parliament, in which PCP representation was reduced to only two seats. The RP, which attracted support from disaffected PCP voters, emerged with 52 seats, while the BQ, with 54 seats, became the official opposition party. The BQ, which had diverted support from the PCP in Québec, declared that it would pursue the achievement of full sovereignty for Québec. Kim Campbell, who lost her seat in the federal Parliament, resigned as PCP leader and was succeeded by Jean Charest.

The new Liberal Government set out to implement an economic recovery programme. Substantial reductions in defence expenditure were announced, as well as a C $6,000m. job-creation scheme, and in December 1993, following the renegotiation of certain treaty protocols with the US Government, NAFTA, which had received Canadian legislative ratification in June, was formally promulgated, to take effect from January 1994. The Liberals were re-elected at general elections held in June 1997, although with a reduced majority in the House of Commons. The RP replaced the BQ as the main opposition party.

The issue of separatism in Québec was reopened by provincial elections held in September 1994, in which the PQ, led by Jacques Parizeau, defeated the incumbent Liberal administration by a margin of 44.7% to 44.3%. Parizeau, whose campaign had included an undertaking that a new referendum on independence would be held during 1995, was supported at federal level by the BQ, although the federal Government asserted that considerable uncertainty was felt within Québec over the possible economic consequences of secession. In June 1995 the PQ and the BQ, together with a smaller provincial nationalist group, the Action Démocratique du Québec, agreed a framework for the province's proposed independence and in mid-September the referendum received provincial legislative approval.

During the six-week referendum campaign, indications of growing support within Québec for secession led to considerable anxiety nationally about the political and economic implications of the independence plan. On the eve of the referendum, held on 30 October 1995, Chrétien issued an appeal for national unity, and undertook to reinstate negotiations for a new constitutional accord. The sovereignty proposals were defeated by a margin of only 50,000 votes; in a turnout of 93% of eligible voters, 49.4% were in favour of the sovereignty plan, and 50.6% opposed. Parizeau, who blamed the defeat on economic special interest groups and the non-francophone 'ethnic' vote,

announced on the following day that he was to relinquish the provincial premiership. In January 1996 Chrétien carried out an extensive reshuffle of his Cabinet and reaffirmed the federal Government's commitment to the maintenance of Canadian federation and national unity. In the following month Lucien Bouchard, having resigned from the federal House of Commons and relinquished the leadership of the BQ, succeeded Parizeau as Premier of Québec and leader of the PQ. Bouchard indicated that his administration viewed the sovereignty issue as less urgent than the resolution of Québec's immediate economic problems. In September 1997 Bouchard refused to attend a conference of provincial premiers and territorial commissioners, at which a seven-point framework on Canadian unity was agreed. The conference, held in Calgary, recognized the 'unique character' of Québec, but asserted that any future change in the constitutional powers of one province should be applicable to all provinces. By June 1998 the resultant 'Calgary Declaration' had been endorsed by the legislatures of all provinces except Québec.

The Supreme Court, which had been requested in February 1998 to rule on the legality of a unilateral secession by Québec, declared in August that no province had the right, in constitutional or international law, to leave the federation without prior negotiations with the federal and provincial governments, and that secession would require the approval of the federal legislature, together with that of seven of the 10 provinces. It was further stated that an obligation would exist for negotiation with Québec if a clear majority of its voters expressed a wish to leave the federation.

In March 1998 Jean Charest resigned as leader of the PCP, to accept the leadership of the Liberal Party of Québec, which had been perceived as losing popular support for its anti-separatist policy. The PQ Government, which was further encouraged by its success in addressing the province's economic problems, called a provincial legislative election in November, with the implication that a substantial victory for the PQ would open the way to a further referendum on independence. At the election, however, an unexpected rise in support for the Liberals awarded them 43.7% of the popular vote, against 42.7% for the PQ, which, none the less, obtained 76 seats in the 125-seat legislature, compared with 48 seats for the Liberals. Following the election, Bouchard conceded that the PQ had failed to attract sufficient support to merit an early referendum.

In November 1999 Chrétien proposed the introduction of legislation requiring the agreement of 60% of Québec voters in any future provincial referendum on independence as a precondition to federal–provincial negotiations of terms of separation. This plan, however, was postponed following objections from members of the Cabinet and from Liberal MPs representing Québec constituencies in the Federal House of Commons.

In March 2000 members of the RP voted to join the Canadian Alliance (CA), an organization based on a convention held in September 1998 with the aim of uniting the major right-wing parties. The PCP declined to join the CA, although a number of that party's prominent members chose to do so. Deborah Grey, formerly of the RP, became the temporary Leader of the Opposition, pending a formal contest for the leadership of the CA. In July Stockwell Day, a former PCP member, was elected leader of the CA, defeating Preston Manning, the last leader of the RP. Day was elected to the House of Commons at a by-election in September.

In October 2000 Chrétien undertook a reorganization of the Government; Lloyd Axworthy, the Minister of Foreign Affairs, was replaced by John Manley, hitherto Minister of Industry. The industry portfolio was awarded to Brian Tobin, the former Premier of Newfoundland and Labrador. The Ministers of Veterans' Affairs and of State for the Atlantic Canada Opportunities Agency were also replaced. Chrétien subsequently announced that a general election would be held on 27 November, despite his Government's mandate being valid until June 2002.

At the general election of 27 November 2000 Chrétien's Liberals received 40.8% of the votes cast and won 172 of the 301 seats in the House of Commons. The CA secured 25.5% of the votes cast and 66 parliamentary seats, compared with the 58 seats won by the RP at the election of June 1997. The BQ obtained 38 seats, compared with 44 at the previous election, the NDP 13 seats and the PCP 12. Observers noted an increasing political polarization between the country's east and centre and its west—the CA won 50 of the 60 seats available in the two westernmost provinces, British Columbia and Alberta, but only two in Ontario (the Liberals being elected in 100 of the 103 constituencies in that province).

In January 2001 Bouchard announced his resignation as Premier of Québec, once a successor had been elected. He also resigned as a member of the provincial legislature and as leader of the PQ, stating that he had failed in his intention to achieve independence for the province and that he lacked both popular and party support. The BQ had lost several seats in Québec to the Liberals at the November 2000 federal general election and opinion polls continued to show a decline in support for the PQ's policy on independence.

The question of land treaty claims by Canada's indigenous peoples came to prominence during the early 1990s, when disputes over land rights arose in Ontario, Manitoba and, most notably, Québec, where armed confrontations took place in 1990 between the civil authorities and militant indigenous groups. During the 1980s debate began to intensify in the formulation of a new constitutional status for the NWT, in which a population of only 58,000 (of which Inuit and other indigenous peoples comprised about one-half) occupied an area comprising one-third of Canada's land mass. In November 1982 the Federal Government agreed in principle to implement the decision of a territorial referendum held in April, in which 56% of the voters approved a division of the NWT. Proposals to replace the NWT with two self-governing units: Nunavut (to the east of a proposed boundary running northwards from the Saskatchewan–Manitoba border), and a second newly-constituted territory to the west, were approved by the NWT legislature in January 1987 and were endorsed in May 1992 by a plebiscite among NWT residents. In December 1991 specific terms for the creation of a semi-autonomous Nunavut Territory, covering an area of 2.2m. sq km, were agreed by Inuit representatives and the Federal Government. In September 1988, following 13 years of negotiations, the Federal Government formally transferred to indigenous ownership an area covering 673,000 sq km in the NWT. In the Yukon Territory, an area of 41,000 sq km (representing 8.6% of the Territory's land) was transferred to indigenous control.

In April 1991 the Federal Government undertook that all outstanding land treaty claims would be resolved by 2000. A formal agreement to this effect was finalized in May 1993, providing for Nunavut and a second territory, as yet unnamed, to come into official existence on 1 April 1999. In October 1997 the NWT Government recommended that the Federal Government approve the establishment of a 17-seat Legislature for Nunavut, to be located at Iqaluit. Elections to the new Legislature were held in February 1999, and the new Territorial Government took office in April. In November 1996 an official inquiry into the social and economic condition of Canada's indigenous peoples recommended the creation of a new chamber of the Federal Parliament to function as a permanent commission to review issues affecting the indigenous groups, and that these communities receive increased powers of self-government. In December 1997 the Supreme Court awarded legal title to 57,000 sq km of ancestral land to two native groups in British Columbia, and in the following month the Federal Government offered a formal apology to all native groups for past mistreatment and injustices. The principle of 'aboriginal title', established by the Supreme Court ruling, was again exercised in April 1999 with the transfer, together with substantial powers of self-government, of a further 2,000 sq km of land to native ownership in British Columbia.

During his period in office, Mulroney sought to re-establish Canada's traditional 'special relationship' with the USA, which had operated until the Trudeau period. Subsequent administrations sought to emphasize Canada's independence from the USA in matters of foreign policy, while continuing the increased co-operation in areas such as trade and environmental protection. There was considerable support in Canada for efforts by successive Governments to secure effective control of the emission of gases from industrial plants, both domestically and in the USA (the gases move northwards into Canada to produce environmentally destructive 'acid rain'). In the 1980s and 1990s a number of bilateral environmental agreements were signed, including accords on gaseous emissions and the elimination of industrial pollution from the Great Lakes, in conjunction with the implementation of a number of domestic environmental-improvement programmes. In 1991 Canada, with the USA and 23 European countries, signed an international treaty on cross-border pollution control, under which the signatories undertook to prevent, reduce and control environmental degradation caused by industrial activity. A further agreement with the USA on the reduction of industrial pollution was signed in April 1997. In December of that year, at the third Conference of the Parties to the Framework Convention on Climate Change (see UN Environment Programme, p. 48), held in Kyoto, Japan, Canada undertook to implement reductions of its emissions of 'greenhouse gases' to 6% below 1990 levels by the year 2012. Canada assumed a leading role in the establishment, with seven other circumpolar countries, of the Arctic Council (see p. 306), which commenced operation in September 1996. The aims of the Council include the protection of the environment of the polar region, the formation of co-ordinated policies governing its future, and the safeguarding of the interests of its indigenous population groups.

Relations between the USA and Canada came under strain in August and September 1985, when a US coastguard ice-breaker traversed the Northwest Passage without seeking prior permission from Canada, in assertion of long-standing US claims that the channels within this 1.6m. sq km tract of ice-bound islands are international waters. The Canadian Government declared sovereignty of this area as from 1 January 1986, and in January 1988 the USA recognized Canadian jurisdiction over the Arctic islands (but not over their waters) and undertook to notify the Canadian Government in advance of all Arctic passages by US surface vessels. There have also been recurrent disagreements between Canada and France concerning the boundary of disputed waters near the French-controlled islands of St Pierre and Miquelon, off the southern coast of Newfoundland. In June 1992 an international arbitration tribunal presented its report, generally regarded as favourable to Canada, on this dispute. It was reported in December 1994 that the two countries had agreed a 10-year accord on the allocation of fishing rights around the islands.

In December 1992 Canada and the EC (European Community, now European Union—EU) announced the resolution of a seven-year disagreement over the allocation of fishing rights to European commercial fleets in the north-west Atlantic Ocean. In 1994, however, the EU unilaterally awarded itself almost 70% of the internationally agreed quota of Greenland halibut (also sometimes known as turbot) caught in the north-west Atlantic fishing grounds. This action was not recognized by other members of the Northwest Atlantic Fishing Organization (NAFO), and was vigorously contested by the Canadian Government, which declared that it would act to prevent EU fishing trawlers (principally from Spain and Portugal) from overfishing the already seriously depleted stocks of Greenland halibut. It was also announced that Canada was extending its maritime jurisdiction beyond its Exclusive Economic Zone (EEZ), already extending 200 nautical miles (370 km) from the coastline. This action was rejected by the EU as contrary to international law.

In February 1995 the Canadian Government formally notified the EU that its fishing fleets would not be permitted to increase their Greenland halibut catches in the Grand Banks, off the eastern coast of Canada, and warned that force would be used if necessary to ensure that total catches by EU vessels did not exceed 3,400 tons of the NAFO-agreed world Greenland halibut quota of 27,000 tons. On 6 March the Canadian Government declared a 60-day moratorium on all trawling for this fish in the north-west Atlantic, and three days later its enforcement vessels fired on and impounded a Spanish trawler fishing in international waters. The EU responded by suspending all official political contacts with Canada, pending the release of the trawler, and the Spanish Government responded by instituting proceedings against Canada in the International Court of Justice (ICJ). The impasse was eased by the release of the trawler on 15 March, when it was agreed to initiate quota allocation negotiations. In late March, however, a further three Spanish vessels were prevented by the Canadian coast guard from fishing in international waters. Divisions began to emerge within the EU when the British Government refused to endorse an EU protest against these interceptions, and declared its support of Canada's desire to conserve north-west Atlantic fishing stocks. A resolution was eventually reached in mid-April, under which Canada and EU countries each agreed to accept 41% of the 1996 Greenland halibut quota. It was agreed that independent observers would monitor the activities of trawlers in the north-west Atlantic fishing zone. However, during the negotiation of an accord in June 1996 governing bilateral relations between Canada and the EU, the Canadian Government rejected a Spanish request that it suspend the enforcement of its fishing regulations outside Canadian territorial waters. In December

1998 the ICJ accepted the contention by Canada that it had no jurisdiction to deal with the complaint by Spain over the trawler incident in 1995.

Canada, which maintains significant economic and commercial links with Cuba and operates a policy of 'constructive engagement' in its relations with that country, adopted a prominent role in international opposition to efforts, initiated by the US Government in March 1996, to penalize investors whose business in any way involves property in Cuba that was confiscated from US citizens following the 1959 revolution. The imposition of these measures, known as the Helms-Burton Act, led in July 1996 to the exclusion from the USA of nine Canadian businessmen involved in nickel-mining operations in Cuba. The Canadian Government responded by introducing legislation prohibiting Canadian companies from compliance with the Helms-Burton Act, and refused to recognize foreign court rulings arising from the Act, or to assist in the enforcement of judgments obtained against Canadian businesses under the Act. With Mexico, which also conducts significant trade with Cuba, Canada co-ordinated a joint challenge to the US Government through NAFTA dispute procedures. In November 1996 Canada actively promoted a resolution by the UN General Assembly condemning the US trade sanctions against Cuba, and in the same month joined the EU in a complaint against the embargo to the World Trade Organization (WTO, see p. 292). In late 1997 the Canadian Government protested to the USA over its penalization of a Canadian petroleum company with business interests in Iran. In April 1998, following an official visit to Cuba by Chrétien, the Canadian Government signed a series of co-operation agreements with Cuba. However, relations between the two countries subsequently experienced a sharp decline, owing to increasing official and public concern in Canada at the Cuban Government's human-rights record, particularly in relation to the treatment of political prisoners. In July 1999 the Canadian Government stated that it would implement no further assistance programmes to Cuba that did not clearly further the protection of human rights, and it was indicated that Canada would not support, or encourage other countries to support, the admission of Cuba to the Organization of American States (see p. 261).

Relations with the USA improved in June 1999 following the resolution of a long-standing disagreement over the demarcation of salmon-fishing rights off the Pacific coast. However, in October the US Government criticized a Canadian petroleum company, Talisman Energy, Inc., for its presence in Sudan. The USA, which maintained sanctions against Sudan, claimed that Talisman's activities contributed to the continued conflict in that country. It also criticized the Canadian Government for allowing Talisman to operate there. The Canadian Government rejected such criticism and, in July 2000, re-established full diplomatic relations with Sudan. In September a dispute arose over export restrictions imposed by the USA on Canadian timber and termed as subsidies. Canada requested a WTO investigation into US anti-subsidy policies, which would allow the USA to impose duties on imports from Canada in response.

Relations with Brazil were strained in 2000 when Canada requested, and was granted, permission from the WTO to impose sanctions in response to subsidies given by the Brazilian Government to the country's aircraft industry. Bilateral negotiations aimed at avoiding the imposition of sanctions failed, and in December Canada received final permission to impose tariffs to the value of C $344.2m. on goods imported from Brazil, the largest such award made by the WTO.

In the mid-1990s Canada actively sought to obtain an international ban on the manufacture and use of land-mines. At a conference held in Ottawa in December 1997, Canada became the first signatory of a treaty, agreed by 121 countries, undertaking to discontinue the use of these armaments and providing for the destruction of existing stockpiles. However, by early 2001 the USA, the Russian Federation and the People's Republic of China had not become parties to the agreement. Humanitarian concerns remained at the forefront of Canadian foreign policy: during 1999 and 2000 the Government contributed forces to humanitarian and peace-keeping operations in Kosovo, East Timor and Sierra Leone and in October 1999 the Canadian Minister of Foreign Affairs led a Commonwealth delegation to Pakistan to seek the restoration of democratic government following a military coup. In September 2000 the Canadian Government strongly urged governments of creditor nations to accelerate programmes of debt relief for Heavily Indebted Poor Countries—in December the Government announced a morato-

rium on debt repayments due from 11 such countries, with effect from January 2001.

Government

Canada is a federal parliamentary state. Under the Constitution Act 1982, executive power is vested in the British monarch, as Head of State, and exercisable by her representative, the Governor-General, whom she appoints on the advice of the Canadian Prime Minister. The Federal Parliament comprises the Head of State, a nominated Senate (a maximum of 112 members, appointed on a regional basis) and a House of Commons (301 members, elected by universal adult suffrage for single-member constituencies). A Parliament may last no longer than five years. The Governor-General appoints the Prime Minister and, on the latter's recommendation, other ministers to form the Cabinet. The Prime Minister should have the confidence of the House of Commons, to which the Cabinet is responsible. Canada comprises 10 provinces (each with a Lieutenant-Governor and a legislature, which may last no longer than five years, from which a Premier is chosen), and three territories constituted by Act of Parliament.

Defence

Canada co-operates with the USA in the defence of North America and is a member of NATO. Military service is voluntary. In August 2000 the armed forces numbered 59,100: army 20,900, navy 9,000, air force 13,500, and 15,700 not identified by service. There were 43,300 reserve troops. The Federal Government's defence budget for 2000 was C $11,200m.

Economic Affairs

In 1998, according to estimates by the World Bank, Canada's gross national product (GNP), measured at average 1996–98 prices, was US $580,872m., equivalent to US $19,170 per head. Between 1990 and 1998, it was estimated, GNP per head increased, in real terms, at an average rate of 1.1% per year. The country's population increased at an average annual rate of 1.2% in 1990–99. According to preliminary estimates, GNP in 1999 was about US $591,400m. (equivalent to US $19,320 per head). Canada's gross domestic product (GDP) increased, in real terms, at an average rate of 2.3% per year in 1990–99; GDP increased by 3.1% in 1998 and by 4.3% in 1999.

Agriculture (including forestry and fishing) contributed 2.5% of GDP (in constant 1992 prices), and engaged 3.6% of the labour force, in 1999. The principal crops are wheat, barley and other cereals, which, together with livestock production (chiefly cattle and pigs) and timber, provide an important source of export earnings. Canada is a leading world exporter of forest products and of fish and seafood. The production of furs is also important. In real terms, the GDP of the agricultural sector increased at an average annual rate of 2.4% in 1995–99. Agricultural GDP increased by 3.2% in 1998 and by 8.0% in 1999.

Industry (including mining, manufacturing, construction and power) provided 30.2% of GDP (in constant 1992 prices), and employed 22.3% of the labour force, in 1999. Industrial GDP increased, in real terms, at an average annual rate of 3.2% in 1995–99. Industrial GDP increased by 1.9% in 1998 and by 4.4% in 1999.

Mining provided 3.4% of GDP (in constant 1992 prices), but employed only 1.3% of the labour force, in 1999. Canada is a major world producer of zinc, asbestos, nickel, potash and uranium. Gold, silver, iron, copper, cobalt and lead are also exploited. There are considerable reserves of petroleum and natural gas in Alberta, off the Atlantic coast and in the Canadian Arctic islands. The GDP of the mining sector increased, in real terms, at an average rate of 1.3% per year during 1980–90, and by 3.8% per year in 1990–94. However, it declined at an average annual rate of 0.2% in 1995–99. Mining GDP declined by 1.6% in 1998 and by 3.3% in 1999.

Manufacturing contributed 18.0% of GDP (in constant 1992 prices), and employed 14.9% of the labour force, in 1999. The principal branches of manufacturing in 1995, measured by the value of output, were transport equipment (accounting for 22.9% of the total), food products (11.6%), paper and allied products (7.0%), chemical products (7.0%), electrical and electronic products (6.8%) and primary metal industries (6.5%). The GDP of the sector increased, in real terms, at an average rate of 4.3% per year in 1995–99. Manufacturing GDP increased by 4.1% in 1998 and by 6.3% in 1999.

Energy is derived principally from hydroelectric power (which provided 67% of the electricity supply in 1985) and from coal-fired and nuclear power-stations. Canada is an important source of US energy supplies, accounting in 1989 for 7.0% of the USA's requirements of natural gas and for 5.0% of its petroleum imports. In 1999 energy products accounted for 8.2% of Canada's exports and 3.3% of imports.

Services engaged 71.6% of the labour force, and provided 67.3% of GDP (in constant 1992 prices), in 1999. The combined GDP of the service sectors increased, in real terms, at an average rate of 3.3% per year in 1995–99. Services GDP increased by 3.7% in 1998 and by 4.2% in 1999.

In 1999 Canada recorded a visible trade surplus of US $22,756m., but there was a deficit of US $2,273m. on the current account of the balance of payments. In 1999 the USA accounted for 86.8% of Canada's total exports and 67.2% of total imports; the European Union (EU, see p. 181) and Japan were also important trading partners. The principal exports in that year were motor vehicles and parts, machinery and equipment and industrial goods. The principal imports were machinery and equipment, motor vehicles and parts and industrial goods. In January 1989 a free-trade agreement with the USA entered into force, whereby virtually all remaining trade tariffs imposed between the two countries were to be eliminated over a 10-year period. Negotiations with the USA and Mexico, aimed at the eventual creation of a full North American free-trade area, began in 1991 and concluded in December 1992 with the signing of an agreement. Following its formal ratification in December 1993, the North American Free Trade Agreement (NAFTA, see p. 240) entered into operation on 1 January 1994. Since the implementation of NAFTA, however, disagreements have persisted between Canada and the USA over alleged violations of the Agreement by the US Government in relation to bilateral trade in softwood lumber, wheat and other commodities. Since the mid-1990s the Canadian Government has implemented measures aimed at expanding trade in the Far East, notably with the People's Republic of China, the Republic of Korea, Indonesia and Viet Nam. In November 1996 Canada finalized a trade agreement with Chile, which will, with effect from June 1997, phase out most customs duties by 2002. In October 1998 negotiations began with the members of the European Free Trade Association (EFTA, see p. 178) for the creation of a free-trade area, while Canada has also pursued efforts to develop similar arrangements with the EU.

In the financial year ending 31 March 1999 there was a federal budget surplus of C $2,566m. The annual rate of inflation averaged 1.9% in 1990–98. Consumer prices increased by an average of 1.6% in 1997, by 1.0% in 1998 and by 1.7% in 1999. The rate of unemployment, which exceeded 10% of the labour force in 1991–94, declined to 9.5% in 1995 before rising to 9.7% in 1996. It averaged 9.1% in 1997, 8.3% in 1998 and 7.6% in 1999. The rate of unemployment stood at 6.3% in December 2000.

Many sectors of Canadian industry rely heavily on foreign investment. Following the international recession of the mid-1970s, Canada's average annual rate of inflation remained above 4% throughout the 1980s. A series of budgetary deficits were attributable largely to high interest rates, which continued into the early 1990s, to the detriment of a sustained economic recovery. The persistence of substantial budgetary deficits both at federal and provincial level, together with political uncertainties surrounding the future of Québec, necessitated further rises in interest levels during 1994, despite the achievement at mid-year of a negative rate of inflation. Government spending and foreign borrowing were reduced in the mid-1990s, as part of a series of deflationary measures. This emphasis on fiscal stringency led, in part, in August 1996, to the country's first current-account surplus in the balance of payments since 1984. The recovery was further aided by low rates of domestic inflation and by the beneficial effects of NAFTA on Canadian export sales to the USA and continued strongly throughout the late 1990s and early 2000s. Proposals for the 1999/2000 budget included provisions for increased expenditure on health care and for reductions in personal rates of taxation, while achieving a budgetary surplus for the second successive year. The Government indicated that it intended to retain a target annual inflation rate of 1%–3%, announced in February 1998, to December 2001. Further reductions in personal taxation were announced in the budget for 2000/01 and the Government projected a combined budgetary surplus of C $95,000m. for the period 2000–05. Eight of the 10 provinces projected a budgetary surplus in 2000/01. An additional series of budget proposals, again including reductions in personal taxation, were announced in October 2000. The predominance of trade with the USA (in which Canada, assisted by currency fluctuations favourable to its exports, maintained a substantial surplus in the late 1990s and early 2000s) compensated for deficits with other major trading partners, including the EU and Japan, and allowed Canada to record substantial trade surpluses in the early 2000s. However, in spite of its strong recovery, the Canadian economy remains vulnerable to adverse movements in world prices for its major exports of raw materials.

Social Welfare

The Federal Government administers family allowances, unemployment insurance and pensions. Other services are provided by the provinces. A federal medical care insurance programme covers all Canadians against medical expenses, and a federal-provincial hospital insurance programme covers over 99% of the insurable population. In 1994/95 there were 978 hospitals, with a total of 156,547 beds. In 1997 there were 187 active physicians per 100,000 population. Of total budgetary expenditure by the Federal Government in the financial year 1999/2000, C $1,710m. (1.0%) was for health, and a further C $50,252m. (29.6%) for social services. In addition, substantial welfare payments are made by social security funds under federal government control. Expenditure by the governments of the provinces and territories in 1999/2000 included C $55,920m. (29.4% of the total) for health services and C $32,141m. (16.9%) for social services.

Education

Education policy is a provincial responsibility, and the period of compulsory school attendance varies. French-speaking students are entitled by law, in some provinces, to instruction in French. Primary education is from the age of five or six years to 13–14, followed by three to five years at secondary or high school. In 1995 an estimated 95% of children aged six to 11 years (males 96%; females 94%) attended primary schools, while 91% of those aged 12 to 17 (males 92%; females 90%) were enrolled at secondary schools. In 1997/98 there were 75 universities and 270 other institutions of post-secondary education. Federal government budgetary expenditure on education totalled C $4,434m. (2.6% of total spending) in 1999/2000, compared with C $4,126m. (2.5%) in 1998/99. Expenditure on education by provincial and territorial governments was C $37,955m. (19.9% of total spending) in 1999/2000.

Public Holidays*

2001: 1 January (New Year's Day), 13 April (Good Friday), 16 April (Easter Monday), 21 May (Victoria Day), 1 July (Canada Day), 3 September (Labour Day), 8 October (Thanksgiving Day), 11 November (Remembrance Day), 25 December (Christmas Day), 26 December (Boxing Day).

2002: 1 January (New Year's Day), 29 March (Good Friday), 1 April (Easter Monday), 20 May (Victoria Day), 1 July (Canada Day), 2 September (Labour Day), 14 October (Thanksgiving Day), 11 November (Remembrance Day), 25 December (Christmas Day), 26 December (Boxing Day).

*Standard public holidays comprise the listed days, together with any other day so proclaimed by individual provinces.

Weights and Measures

The metric system is in force.

Statistical Survey

Source (unless otherwise stated): Statistics Canada, Ottawa, ON K1A 0T6; tel. (613) 951-8116; fax (613) 951-0581; internet www.statcan.ca.

Area and Population

AREA, POPULATION AND DENSITY

Area (sq km)
Land	9,203,210
Inland water	755,109
Total	9,958,319*

Population (census results)†
4 June 1991	27,296,860
14 May 1996	
Males	14,170,030
Females	14,676,735
Total	28,846,761

Population (official estimates at 1 July)
1997	29,987,214
1998	30,247,949
1999	30,493,433

Density (per sq km) at 1 July 1999 . . . 3.1

* 3,844,928 sq miles.
† Excluding census data for one or more incompletely enumerated Indian reserves or Indian settlements. The overall extent of underenumeration at the 1991 census was estimated to be 2.8%.

PROVINCES AND TERRITORIES (census results, 14 May 1996)

	Land area (sq km)	Population*	Capital
Provinces:			
Alberta	638,233	2,696,826	Edmonton
British Columbia	892,677	3,724,500	Victoria
Manitoba	547,704	1,113,898	Winnipeg
New Brunswick	71,569	738,133	Fredericton
Newfoundland	371,635	551,792	St John's
Nova Scotia	52,841	909,282	Halifax
Ontario	916,734	10,753,573	Toronto
Prince Edward Island	5,660	134,557	Charlottetown
Québec	1,357,812	7,138,795	Québec
Saskatchewan	570,113	990,237	Regina
Territories:			
Northwest Territories	1,004,471	39,672	Yellowknife
Nunavut Territory†	2,241,919	24,730	Iqaluit
Yukon Territory	531,844	30,766	Whitehorse
Total	9,203,210	28,846,761	—

* Excluding census data for one or more incompletely enumerated Indian reserves or Indian settlements.
† Formerly part of Northwest Territories. Constituted as a separate Territory with effect from 1 April 1999.

PRINCIPAL METROPOLITAN AREAS (census results, 14 May 1996)

Toronto	4,263,757		London	398,616
Montréal*	3,326,510		Kitchener	382,940
Vancouver	1,831,665		St Catharines-	
Ottawa (capital)	1,010,498†		Niagara	372,406
Edmonton*	862,597		Halifax	332,518
Calgary*	821,628		Victoria*	304,287
Québec	671,889		Windsor	278,685
Winnipeg	667,209		Oshawa	268,773
Hamilton	624,360		Saskatoon	219,056

* Excluding census data for one or more incompletely enumerated Indian reserves or Indian settlements.
† Including Hull.

BIRTHS, MARRIAGES AND DEATHS

	Registered live births*		Registered marriages		Registered deaths*	
	Number	Rate (per 1,000)	Number	Rate (per 1,000)	Number	Rate (per 1,000)
1991	402,258	14.4	172,251	6.1	195,568	7.0
1992	398,642	14.0	164,573	5.8	196,535	6.9
1993	388,394	13.5	159,316	5.6	204,912	7.1
1994	385,112	13.3	159,959	5.5	207,077	7.1
1995	378,011	12.9	160,251	5.5	210,733	7.2
1996	366,200	12.3	156,692	5.3	212,859	7.2
1997	348,598	11.6	153,306	5.1	215,669	7.2
1998	343,371	11.4	153,190	5.0	219,834	7.3

* Including Canadian residents temporarily in the USA but excluding US residents temporarily in Canada.

Expectation of life (years at birth, 1992): Males 74.6; Females 80.9 (Source: UN, *Demographic Yearbook*).

IMMIGRATION

Country of Origin	1997	1998	1999
United Kingdom	4,846	4,036	4,626
USA	5,036	4,755	5,522
Other	206,163	164,380	179,817
Total	216,045	173,191	189,965

ECONOMICALLY ACTIVE POPULATION*
(annual averages, '000 persons aged 15 years and over)

	1997	1998	1999
Agriculture, hunting, forestry and fishing	582.8	594.1	567.9
Mining and quarrying	194.7	194.7	169.7
Manufacturing	2,143.6	2,248.0	2,344.8
Utilities	120.1	119.3	118.3
Construction	834.6	836.5	866.1
Trade, restaurants and hotels	3,210.4	3,273.0	3,363.7
Transport and storage	737.0	750.5	777.7
Financing, insurance, real estate and business services	2,205.1	2,288.2	2,380.4
Community, social and personal services	4,596.0	4,657.0	4,730.8
Unclassified†	528.9	456.7	401.9
Total labour force	15,153.0	15,417.7	15,721.2
Males	8,277.5	8,380.2	8,534.0
Females	6,875.5	7,037.5	7,187.2

* Figures exclude military personnel, inmates of institutions, residents of the Yukon and Northwest Territories, and Indian reserves. The data include unemployed persons, totalling (in '000): 1,378.6 in 1997; 1,277.3 in 1998; 1,190.1 in 1999.
† Referring to unemployed persons without previous work experience or those whose last activity was not adequately defined.

Agriculture

PRINCIPAL CROPS ('000 metric tons)

	1997	1998	1999
Wheat	24,280.3	24,076.3	26,850.2
Barley	13,527.3	12,708.7	13,196.0
Maize (Corn)*	7,179.8	8,952.4	9,096.3
Rye	320.0	398.1	386.6
Oats	3,484.7	3,957.5	3,641.3
Buckwheat	16.5	14.8	12.5
Mixed grain	602.8	548.0	446.8
Potatoes	4,171.0	4,329.1	4,253.0
Beans (dry)	82.6	73.9	149.1
Peas (dry)	1,762.3	2,336.8	2,251.9
Soybeans	2,737.7	2,736.6	2,765.9
Sunflower seed	65.1	111.8	121.9
Rapeseed (Canola)	6,393.1	7,643.3	8,798.3
Linseed	895.4	1,080.9	1,049.1
Mustard seed	243.4	238.6	306.4
Sugar beets	635.0	880.0	743.9
Tame hay	20,865.3	21,436.8	26,739.2

* Maize for grain only, excluding fodder maize.

LIVESTOCK ('000 head at 1 July)

	1997	1998	1999
Milch cows	1,206.3	1,174.0	1,157.6
Beef cattle	4,679.4	4,593.1	4,541.4
Sheep	821.5	829.8	880.2
Pigs	11,668.0	12,353.0	12,392.0

LIVESTOCK PRODUCTS

	1997	1998	1999
Beef and veal (metric tons)	1,076,374	1,148,123	1,238,192
Mutton and lamb (metric tons)	10,183	9,885	10,816
Pig meat (metric tons)	1,256,696	1,389,741	1,562,109
Poultry meat (metric tons)	917,063	962,658	1,012,431
Milk (kilolitres)*	7,421,376	7,456,000	7,501,093
Creamery butter (metric tons)	89,537	85,935	88,824
Cheddar cheese (metric tons)	129,220	127,466	128,245
Ice-cream mix (kilolitres)†	154,974	154,802	151,947
Eggs ('000 dozen)	494,269	498,847	512,596

* Farm sales of milk and cream.

† Excluding Newfoundland.

Forestry

ROUNDWOOD REMOVALS (1997, '000 cubic metres)*

	Softwoods	Hard-woods	Total
Alberta	14,482	7,745	22,227
British Columbia	66,904	2,393	69,298
Manitoba	1,583	599	2,183
New Brunswick	7,668	3,585	11,253
Newfoundland	2,409	150	2,558
Nova Scotia	6,190	799	6,989
Ontario	19,609	6,986	26,595
Québec	32,653	9,794	42,447
Saskatchewan	2,718	1,486	4,205
Total	154,216	33,537	187,754

* Figures exclude Prince Edward Island: 1995 ('000 cubic metres): Softwoods 490; Hardwoods 148.

SAWNWOOD PRODUCTION
('000 cubic metres, incl. railway sleepers)

	1997	1998	1999
Coniferous (softwood)	65,014.7	65,142.7	68,379.3
Broadleaved (hardwood)	1,061.7	1,110.7	1,131.6
Total	66,076.3	66,253.5	69,510.9

Fur Industry

NUMBER OF PELTS PRODUCED

	1996	1997	1998
Newfoundland	27,043	n.a.	n.a.
Prince Edward Island	34,033	36,350	41,429
Nova Scotia	358,129	366,856	383,107
New Brunswick	72,809	n.a.	n.a.
Québec	309,665	342,242	294,193
Ontario	724,021	695,895	599,020
Manitoba	238,427	250,786	138,940
Saskatchewan	204,123	189,594	82,887
Alberta	218,522	n.a.	n.a.
British Columbia	188,122	228,451	231,332
Northwest Territories	46,801	55,429	22,392
Yukon	12,217	9,179	7,195
Total	2,433,912	2,581,938	2,061,848

Fishing

('000 metric tons, live weight)

	1996	1997	1998
Capture	910.7	963.5	995.0
Atlantic cod	15.5	30.0	36.8
Capelin	32.6	22.0	40.8
Atlantic herring	188.8	186.6	187.7
Pacific herring	22.2	31.5	23.3
Queen crab	65.8	71.4	72.2
American lobster	39.4	39.3	40.1
Northern prawn	31.3	48.3	78.9
Other Pandalus shrimps	24.1	28.3	36.8
American sea scallop	47.6	53.9	55.5
Clams	33.5	35.3	31.7
Aquaculture	71.1	82.5	90.6
Atlantic salmon	36.4	51.0	49.5
Total catch	981.8	1,046.0	1,085.6

Note: Figures exclude aquatic plants ('000 metric tons, capture only): 24.3 in 1996; 34.7 in 1997; 12.5 in 1998. Also excluded are aquatic mammals, recorded by number rather than weight. The number of whales caught was: 11 in 1996; 15 in 1997; 1 in 1998. The number of seals caught was: 269,376, in 1996; 273,100 in 1997; 261,368 in 1998.

Source: FAO, *Yearbook of Fishery Statistics*.

Mining

('000 metric tons, unless otherwise indicated)

	1997	1998	1999*
Metallic			
Bismuth (metric tons)	196	186	264
Cadmium (metric tons)	1,272	1,179	1,212
Cobalt (metric tons)	2,168	2,262	2,015
Copper (metric tons)	647,779	690,762	580,036
Gold (kilograms)	171,479	164,773	157,790
Iron ore	38,928	36,586	33,004
Lead (metric tons)	170,847	150,019	156,102
Molybdenum (metric tons)	7,794	8,099	6,293
Nickel (metric tons)	180,624	197,947	177,229
Platinum group (kilograms)	11,836	15,588	14,012
Selenium (metric tons)	592	398	438
Silver (metric tons)	1,194	1,140	1,173
Uranium (metric tons)	11,127	9,992	9,892
Zinc (metric tons)	1,026,864	991,584	960,099
Non-metallic			
Asbestos	420	321	345
Gypsum	8,628	8,307	8,935
Nepheline syenite	648	636	693
Potash (K_2O)	9,235	8,884	8,345
Salt	13,497	13,034	12,643
Sulphur, in smelter gas	800	836	846
Sulphur, elemental	8,272	8,404	8,792
Fuels			
Coal	78,670	75,360	72,310
Natural gas (million cubic metres)†	156,171	160,515	163,384
Natural gas by-products ('000 cubic metres)†‡	26,427	26,666	26,075
Petroleum, crude ('000 cubic metres)†	123,827	128,401	122,448
Structural materials			
Cement	11,736	12,124	12,604
Sand and gravel§	225,495	225,338	218,458
Stone	99,265	108,924	104,026

* Preliminary.
† Marketable production.
‡ Excludes sulphur.
§ Includes quartz.

Industry

VALUE OF SHIPMENTS (preliminary figures, C $ million)

	1997	1998	1999*
Food industries	50,469.3	51,828.1	52,352.8
Beverage industries	7,183.3	7,504.5	8,042.4
Tobacco products industries	2,810.1	2,933.3	3,034.9
Rubber products industries	4,406.6	4,698.6	5,019.4
Plastic products industries	9,819.9	10,370.7	11,864.0
Leather and allied products industries	951.0	872.7	849.4
Primary textile industries	3,752.1	3,690.2	3,510.5
Textiles products industries	3,440.0	3,453.4	3,683.3
Clothing industries	6,905.5	6,997.6	6,996.3
Wood industries	26,810.4	26,335.7	30,600.6
Furniture and fixture industries	6,464.6	7,727.4	8,506.4
Paper and allied products industries	30,405.4	31,486.5	33,150.3
Printing, publishing and allied industries	15,759.1	16,389.6	16,526.3
Primary metal industries	27,919.1	27,424.4	27,528.0
Fabricated metal products industries	23,791.2	25,656.2	26,883.9
Machinery industries (excl. electrical machinery)	17,930.1	18,041.7	16,890.5
Transportation equipment industries	97,007.3	104.551.9	125,034.3
Electrical and electronic products industries	30,007.1	32,978.9	36,760.6
Non-metallic mineral products industries	8,389.2	8,920.1	9,719.8

— continued	1997	1998	1999*
Refined petroleum and coal products industries	21,037.4	16,745.5	21,237.5
Chemical and chemical products industries	31,005.6	31,089.2	32,351.3
Other manufacturing industries	8,766.7	9,057.2	9,800.6
Total	435,030.8	448,753.1	490,343.2

Electric Energy (net production, million kWh): 575,150 in 1997; 543,100 in 1998; 541,900 in 1999.

Finance

CURRENCY AND EXCHANGE RATES

Monetary Units
100 cents = 1 Canadian dollar (C $).

Sterling, US Dollar and Euro Equivalents (29 December 2000)
£1 sterling = C $2.2386;
US $1 = C $1.5002;
€1 = C $1.3959;
C $100 = £44.67 = US $66.66 = €71.64.

Average Exchange Rate (C $ per US $)
1998   1.4835
1999   1.4857
2000   1.4851

FEDERAL BUDGET (C $ million, year ending 31 March)

Revenue	1997/98	1998/99	1999/2000
Taxes on income and profits	101,265	102,614	108,301
Personal income tax	76,139	78,203	82,501
Corporation income tax	22,152	21,509	22,500
Taxes on payments to non-residents	2,974	2,901	3,300
Taxes on goods and services	33,807	34,342	34,940
General sales taxes	22,324	23,468	24,868
Gasoline and motive fuel tax	4,626	4,742	4,539
Alcoholic beverages and tobacco taxes	3,119	3,309	3,152
Custom duties	2,766	2,359	2,200
Contributions to social security plans	18,831	19,390	18,685
Sales of goods and services	3,696	4,077	3,730
Investment income	4,519	5,316	4,674
Total (incl. others)	164,398	168,167	172,532

Expenditure	1997/98	1998/99	1999/2000
General services	5,648	6,173	6,047
Protection of persons and property	15,612	16,509	18,405
Transport and communications	3,141	1,911	1,530
Health	1,328	1,667	1,710
Hospital care	26	50	17
Social services	47,818	48,711	50,252
Social assistance	45,377	46,401	47,007
Education	3,416	4,126	4,434
Resource conservation and industrial development	6,124	5,524	6,236
Foreign affairs and international assistance	3,690	4,046	4,623
General purpose transfers to other levels of government	20,204	22,749	24,260
Debt charges	43,443	43,898	41,565
Total (incl. others)	159,891	165,576	169,966

INTERNATIONAL RESERVES (US $ million at 31 December)

	1998	1999	2000
Gold*	122	524	323
IMF special drawing rights	1,098	527	574
Reserve position in IMF	2,299	3,168	2,509
Foreign exchange	19,911	24,432	28,841
Total	23,430	28,650	32,247

* National valuation.
Source: IMF, *International Financial Statistics*.

MONEY SUPPLY (C $ '000 million at 31 December)

	1997	1998	1999
Currency outside banks	30.15	32.32	38.72
Demand deposits at deposit money banks	139.61	147.08	160.95
Total money (incl. others)	169.92	179.62	199.95

Source: IMF, *International Financial Statistics*.

COST OF LIVING (Consumer Price Index; base: 1992 = 100)

	1997	1998	1999
Food	107.6	109.3	110.7
Housing	103.3	103.7	105.1
Household expenses and furnishings	106.6	108.2	109.0
Clothing	102.7	103.9	105.3
Transport	121.5	120.5	124.5
Health and personal care	105.9	108.1	110.2
Recreation, education and reading	114.9	117.5	119.6
Tobacco and alcohol	89.3	92.6	94.5
All items	107.6	108.6	110.5

NATIONAL ACCOUNTS

National Income and Product (C $ million at current prices)

	1997	1998	1999
Compensation of employees	453,103	474,571	498,836
Operating surplus	197,992	193,240	216,013
Domestic factor incomes	651,095	667,811	714,849
Consumption of fixed capital	111,005	115,545	120,098
Gross domestic product at factor cost	762,100	783,356	834,947
Indirect taxes, *less* subsidies	116,069	118,818	123,522
Statistical discrepancy	−248	−369	−558
GDP at market prices	877,921	901,805	957,911
Factor income from abroad *Less* Factor income paid abroad	−28,300*	−29,550*	−29,620*
Gross national product	849,621	872,255	928,291
Less Consumption of fixed capital	111,005	115,545	120,098
Statistical discrepancy	248	369	558
National income at market prices	738,864	757,079	808,751
Other current transfers from abroad‡	5,056	4,953	5,435
Less Other current transfers paid abroad‡	4,289	4,185	4,433
National disposable income	739,631	757,847	809,753

* Figure is rounded to the nearest 10 million Canadian dollars.
Source: IMF, *International Financial Statistics*.

Expenditure on the Gross Domestic Product
(C $ million at current prices)

	1997	1998	1999
Government final consumption expenditure	171,744	175,864	179,999
Private final consumption expenditure	512,454	532,926	558,567
Increase in stocks	10,595	5,740	3,884
Gross fixed capital formation	167,876	174,082	186,554
Total domestic expenditure	862,669	888,612	929,004
Exports of goods and services	346,513	373,184	414,291
Less Imports of goods and services	331,509	360,359	385,941
Statistical discrepancy	248	368	557
GDP at market prices	877,921	901,805	957,911
GDP at constant 1992 prices	815,013	842,002	880,254

Gross Domestic Product by Economic Activity
(C $ million at constant 1992 prices)

	1997	1998	1999
Agriculture, hunting, forestry and fishing	16,801	17,344	18,732
Mining and quarrying	27,062	26,590	25,700
Manufacturing	122,320	127,335	135,419
Electricity, gas and water	24,876	24,499	25,250
Construction	39,398	39,336	40,974
Trade, restaurants and hotels	101,906	108,378	116,163
Transport, storage and communications	54,677	57,368	62,046
Finance, insurance, real estate and business services*	153,693	160,114	166,505
Other services	159,306	160,915	162,258
GDP at factor cost	700,039	721,879	753,047

* Including imputed rents of owner-occupied dwellings.

BALANCE OF PAYMENTS (US $ million)

	1997	1998	1999
Exports of goods f.o.b.	217,739	217,406	242,820
Imports of goods f.o.b.	−200,516	−204,631	−220,064
Trade balance	17,223	12,775	22,756
Exports of services	31,407	32,907	34,854
Imports of services	−38,182	−37,660	−38,921
Balance on goods and services	10,448	8,022	18,690
Other income received	22,501	20,772	21,283
Other income paid	−43,564	−40,435	−42,923
Balance on goods, services and income	−10,615	−11,641	−2,950
Current transfers received	3,653	3,342	3,654
Current transfers paid	−3,104	−2,834	−2,978
Current balance	−10,065	−11,133	−2,273
Capital account (net)	5,429	3,335	3,428
Direct investment abroad	−22,521	−31,041	−17,842
Direct investment from abroad	11,758	21,677	25,129
Portfolio investment assets	−8,568	−15,106	−15,443
Portfolio investment liabilities	11,487	16,973	3,686
Other investment assets	−16,282	10,253	8,396
Other investment liabilities	27,962	6,641	−5,796
Net errors and omissions	−1,592	3,397	6,647
Overall balance	−2,393	4,996	5,933

Source: IMF, *International Financial Statistics*.

External Trade

PRINCIPAL COMMODITIES (C $ million)

Imports f.o.b.	1997	1998	1999
Agricultural and fishing products	15,655.3	17,264.5	17,643.4
Energy products	10,627.6	8,624.2	10,708.7
Crude petroleum	7,189.4	5,217.6	7,160.3
Forestry products	2,386.1	2,500.8	2,740.8
Industrial goods and materials	54,560.3	60,292.1	62,130.9
Metals and metal ores	14,393.9	15,328.3	14,086.7
Chemicals and plastics	19,610.1	21,521.1	22,675.8
Machinery and equipment (excl. automotive products)	91,346.8	101,126.1	108,168.2
Industrial and agricultural machinery	25,625.5	28,234.4	27,768.2
Aircraft and other transportation equipment	10,988.1	12,488.3	13,226.0
Office machines and equipment	14,881.0	15,741.7	16,908.1
Automotive products	60,825.7	66,785.9	75,916.1
Passenger automobiles and chassis	17,688.8	17,630.0	19,587.3
Trucks and other motor vehicles	8,598.5	9,652.6	10,644.6
Motor vehicle parts	34,538.4	39,503.3	45,684.2
Other consumer goods	29,733.3	34,578.6	36,954.2
Apparel and footwear	5,818.3	6,618.8	6,844.7
Special transactions trade	6,954.4	6,326.1	6,325.3
Unallocated adjustments	5,661.6	5,922.4	6,233.4
Total	277,751.1	303,420.4	326,820.9

Exports f.o.b.	1997	1998	1999
Agricultural and fishing products	24,963.0	25,202.3	25,567.7
Energy products	27,125.7	23,765.7	29,722.4
Crude petroleum	10,371.2	7,834.1	11,015.4
Natural gas	8,625.6	8,967.1	10,951.4
Forestry products	34,847.8	35,173.2	39,116.5
Lumber and sawmill products	16,803.8	16,563.1	19,659.5
Wood pulp and other wood products	6,505.1	6,226.0	6,961.9
Newsprint and other paper and paperboard products	11,538.9	12,384.1	12,495.1
Industrial goods and materials	56,067.1	57,580.1	57,429.3
Metals and metal ores	5,960.5	5,420.5	5,081.7
Chemicals, plastics and fertilizers	17,096.6	17,529.0	18,518.1
Metals and alloys	20,048.5	19,752.9	18,292.6
Machinery and equipment (excl. automotive products)	68,265.4	78,947.1	85,985.3
Industrial and agricultural machinery	14,811.2	16,597.0	16,591.0
Aircraft and other transportation equipment	12,961.1	16,381.5	17,852.9
Automotive products	69,095.2	77,381.1	95,493.8
Passenger automobiles and chassis	35,685.2	41,840.2	51,054.6
Trucks and other motor vehicles	14,422.2	13,988.7	19,375.7
Motor vehicle parts	18,987.8	21,552.2	25,063.5
Other consumer goods	10,667.4	12,400.8	13,470.7
Special transactions trade	4,074.5	5,563.4	7,348.4
Unallocated adjustments	6,438.1	6,503.4	6,474.8
Total	301,544.3	322,517.0	360,608.8

PRINCIPAL TRADING PARTNERS (C $ million)

Imports f.o.b.	1997	1998	1999
China, People's Repub.	6,342	7,655	8,915
France	5,137	4,875	5,311
Germany	5,410	6,120	7,006
Italy	3,069	3,437	3,645
Japan	12,555	13,999	15,031
Korea, Repub.	2,838	3,314	3,574
Mexico	7,019	7,681	9,521
Norway	3,317	2,528	2,548
Taiwan	3,475	4,030	4,583
United Kingdom	6,502	6,314	8,151
USA	184,344	203,548	215,111
Total (incl. others)	272,856	298,382	319,910

Exports f.o.b.	1997	1998	1999
Japan	11,043	8,551	8,251
Korea, Repub.	2,986	1,794	1,934
United Kingdom	3,641	4,158	4,412
USA	229,279	251,094	286,761
Total (incl. others)	281,226	297,451	330,410

Transport

RAILWAYS (revenue traffic)*

	1996	1997	1998
Passenger-km (million)	1,513	1,515	1,458
Freight ton-km (million)	282,482	306,943	299,508

* Seven major rail carriers only.

ROAD TRAFFIC ('000 vehicles registered at 31 December)

	1996	1997	1998
Passenger cars (incl. taxis and for car hire)	13,251	13,487	13,887
Trucks and truck tractors (commercial and non-commercial)	3,476	3,527	3,626
Buses (school and other)	65	64	68
Motorcycles	291	299	314
Other (ambulances, fire trucks, etc.)	79	80	73

INLAND WATER TRAFFIC (St Lawrence Seaway, '000 metric tons)

	1998	1999	2000
Montréal—Lake Ontario	39,246	36,400	35,398
Welland Canal	40,657	37,422	36,577

Source: St Lawrence Seaway Management Corporation.

SHIPPING
Merchant Fleet (registered at 31 December)

	1996	1997	1998
Number of vessels	872	852	835
Total displacement ('000 grt)	2,406.2	2,526.6	2,501.3

Source: Lloyd's Register of Shipping, *World Fleet Statistics*.

International Sea-borne Freight Traffic

	1997	1998	1999
Goods ('000 metric tons)			
Loaded	187,945	179,107	178,872
Unloaded .	94,704	100,377	101,555
Vessels (number)			
Arrived	27,614	27,856	26,097
Departed .	27,549	27,959	25,889

CIVIL AVIATION (Canadian carriers—revenue traffic, '000)*

	1997	1998	1999
Passengers	24,363	24,571	24,047
Passenger-km	62,479,410	64,426,065	65,700,046
Goods ton-km	2,058,953	2,340,594	2,016,503

* Figures refer to the operations of 'Level I' air carriers.

Tourism

	1997	1998	1999
Travellers from the USA:			
Number ('000) .	13,401	14,893	15,180
Expenditure (C $ million) .	5,355	6,703	7,149
Travellers from other countries:			
Number ('000) .	4,234	3,935	4,187
Expenditure (C $ million) .	4,516	4,462	4,892

Communications Media

('000)

	1996	1997	1998
Total households	11,412	11,473	11,690
Homes with radio	11,268	n.a.	n.a.
Homes with television	11,258	11,314	11,545
Homes with telephone	11,305	11,282	11,481

Daily newspapers in French and English 105 (1996); total circulation 5,200,000.

Telefax stations ('000 in use): 700 in 1995; 800 in 1996; 1,000 in 1997 (Source: UN, *Statistical Yearbook*).

Mobile cellular telephones (subscribers): 2,589,780 in 1995; 3,420,318 in 1996; 4,207,000 in 1997 (Source: UN, *Statistical Yearbook*).

Book production (titles): 17,931 in 1995; 19,900 in 1996 (Source: UNESCO, *Statistical Yearbook*).

Non-daily newspapers (1996, provisional): 1,071; average circulation 21,235,000 copies (Source: UNESCO, *Statistical Yearbook*).

Education

(1997/98)

	Institutions	Teachers*	Pupils*
Primary and secondary .	15,566	296,901	5,386,302
Post-secondary colleges .	270	65,429	971,742
Universities	75	33,702	573,099

* Full-time only.

Directory

The Constitution

Under the Constitution Act 1982, which entered into force on 17 April 1982, executive authority is vested in the Sovereign, and exercised in her name by a Governor-General and Privy Council. Legislative power is exercised by a Parliament of two Houses, the Senate and the House of Commons. The Constitution includes a Charter of Rights and Freedoms, and provisions which recognize the nation's multicultural heritage, affirm the existing rights of native peoples, confirm the principle of equalization of benefits among the provinces and strengthen provincial ownership of natural resources.

THE GOVERNMENT

The national government operates through three main agencies: Parliament (consisting of the Sovereign as represented by the Governor-General, the Senate and the House of Commons), which makes the laws; the Executive (the Cabinet or Ministry), which applies the laws; and the Judiciary, which interprets the laws.

The Prime Minister is appointed by the Governor-General and is habitually the leader of the political party commanding the confidence of the House of Commons. He chooses the members of his Cabinet from members of his party in Parliament, principally from those in the House of Commons. Each Minister or member of the Cabinet is usually responsible for the administration of a department, although there may be Ministers without portfolio whose experience and counsel are drawn upon to strengthen the Cabinet, but who are not at the head of departments. Each Minister of a department is responsible to Parliament for that department, and the Cabinet is collectively responsible before Parliament for government policy and administration generally.

Meetings of the Cabinet are presided over by the Prime Minister. From the Cabinet signed orders and recommendations go to the Governor-General for his or her approval, and the Crown acts only on the advice of its responsible Ministers. The Cabinet takes the responsibility for its advice being in accordance with the support of Parliament and is held strictly accountable.

THE FEDERAL PARLIAMENT

Parliament must meet at least once a year, so that 12 months do not elapse between the last meeting in one session and the first meeting in the next. The duration of Parliament may not be longer than five years from the date of election of a House of Commons. Senators (normally a maximum of 104 in number) are appointed until age 75 by the Governor-General in Council. They must be at least 30 years of age, residents of the province they represent and in possession of C $4,000 of real property over and above their liabilities. Members of the House of Commons are elected by universal adult suffrage for the duration of a Parliament.

Under the Constitution, the Federal Parliament has exclusive legislative authority in all matters relating to public debt and property; regulation of trade and commerce; raising of money by any mode of taxation; borrowing of money on the public credit; postal service, census and statistics; militia, military and naval service and defence; fixing and providing for salaries and allowances of the officers of the Government; beacons, buoys and lighthouses; navigation and shipping; quarantine and the establishment and maintenance of marine hospitals; sea-coast and inland fisheries; ferries on an international or interprovincial frontier; currency and coinage; banking, incorporation of banks, and issue of paper money; savings banks; weights and measures; bills of exchange and promissory notes; interest; legal tender; bankruptcy and insolvency; patents of invention and discovery; copyrights; Indians and lands reserved for Indians; naturalization and aliens; marriage and divorce; the criminal law, except the constitution of courts of criminal jurisdiction but including the procedure in criminal matters; the establishment, maintenance and management of penitentiaries; such classes of subjects as are expressly excepted in the enumeration of the classes of subjects exclusively assigned to the Legislatures of the provinces by the Act. Judicial interpretation and later amendment have, in certain cases, modified or clearly defined the respective powers of the Federal Government and provincial governments.

Both the Parliament of Canada and the legislatures of the provinces may legislate with respect to agriculture and immigration, but provincial legislation shall have effect in and for the provinces as long and as far only as it is not repugnant to any Act of Parliament. Both Parliament and the provincial legislatures may legislate with respect to old age pensions and supplementary benefits, but no federal law shall affect the operation of any present or future law of a province in relation to these matters.

PROVINCIAL AND MUNICIPAL GOVERNMENT

In each of the 10 provinces the Sovereign is represented by a Lieutenant-Governor, appointed by the Governor-General in Council, and acting on the advice of the Ministry or Executive Council, which is responsible to the Legislature and resigns office when it ceases to enjoy the confidence of that body. The Legislatures are unicameral, consisting of an elected Legislative Assembly and the Lieutenant-Governor. The duration of a Legislature may not exceed five years from the date of the election of its members.

The Legislature in each province may exclusively make laws in relation to: amendment of the constitution of the province, except as regards the Lieutenant-Governor; direct taxation within the province; borrowing of money on the credit of the province; establishment and tenure of provincial offices and appointment and payment of provincial officers; the management and sale of public lands belonging to the province and of the timber and wood thereon; the establishment, maintenance and management of public and reformatory prisons in and for the province; the establishment, maintenance and management of hospitals, asylums, charities and charitable institutions in and for the province other than marine hospitals; municipal institutions in the province; shop, saloon, tavern, auctioneer and other licences issued for the raising of provincial or municipal revenue; local works and undertakings other than interprovincial or international lines of ships, railways, canals, telegraphs, etc., or works which, though wholly situtated within the province are declared by the Federal Parliament to be for the general advantage either of Canada or two or more provinces; the incorporation of companies with provincial objects; the solemnization of marriage in the province; property and civil rights in the province; the administration of justice in the province, including the constitution, maintenance and organization of provincial courts both in civil and criminal jurisdiction, and including procedure in civil matters in these courts; the imposition of punishment by fine, penalty or imprisonment for enforcing any law of the province relating to any of the aforesaid subjects; generally all matters of a merely local or private nature in the province. Further, provincial Legislatures may exclusively make laws in relation to education, subject to the protection of religious minorities; and to non-renewable natural resources, forestry resources and electrical energy, including their export from one province to another, and to the right to impose any mode or system of taxation thereon, subject in both cases to such laws not being discriminatory.

Under the Constitution Act, the municipalities are the creations of the provincial governments. Their bases of organization and the extent of their authority vary in different provinces, but almost everywhere they have very considerable powers of local self-government.

The Government

Head of State: HM Queen Elizabeth II (succeeded to the throne 6 February 1952).

Governor-General: Adrienne Clarkson (took office 7 October 1999).

FEDERAL MINISTRY
(April 2001)

Prime Minister: Jean Chrétien.

Deputy Prime Minister: Herbert Gray.

Minister of Transport: David Collenette.

Minister of the Environment: David Anderson.

Minister of Natural Resources and Minister responsible for the Canadian Wheat Board: Ralph Goodale.

Minister of Industry: Brian Tobin.

Minister of Canadian Heritage: Sheila Copps.

Minister of Foreign Affairs: John Manley.

Minister of Finance: Paul Martin.

Minister of National Defence: Arthur Eggleton.

Minister of Justice and Attorney-General: Anne McLellan.

Minister of Health: Allan Rock.

Solicitor-General: Lawrence MacAulay.

Minister of Public Works and Government Services: Alfonso Gagliano.

President of the Treasury Board and Minister responsible for Infrastructure: Lucienne Robillard.

Minister of National Revenue and Secretary of State (Economic Development Agency of Canada for the Regions of Québec): Martin Cauchon.

Minister of Human Resources Development: JANE STEWART.

President of the Queen's Privy Council for Canada and Minister of Intergovernmental Affairs: STÉPHANE DION.

Minister for International Trade: PIERRE PETTIGREW.

Leader of the Government in the House of Commons: DON BOUDRIA.

Minister of Agriculture and Agri-Food: LYLE VANCLIEF.

Minister of Fisheries and Oceans: HERB DHALIWAL.

Minister of Veterans' Affairs and Secretary of State (Western Economic Diversification and Francophonie): RONALD DUHAMEL.

Minister of Labour: CLAUDETTE BRADSHAW.

Minister of Indian Affairs and Northern Development: ROBERT NAULT.

Minister for International Co-operation: MARIA MINNA.

Minister of Citizenship and Immigration: ELINOR CAPLAN.

Leader of the Government in the Senate: SHARON CARSTAIRS.

Minister of State (Atlantic Canada Opportunities Agency): ROBERT THIBAULT.

Secretary of State (Children and Youth): ETHEL BLONDIN-ANDREW.

Secretary of State (Multiculturalism and Status of Women): HEDY FRY.

Secretary of State (Latin America and Africa): DAVID KILGOUR.

Secretary of State (International Financial Institutions): JAMES PETERSON.

Secretary of State (Rural Development and Federal Economic Development Initiative for Northern Ontario): ANDREW MITCHELL.

Secretary of State (Science, Research and Development): GILBERT NORMAND.

Secretary of State (Amateur Sport): DENIS CODERRE.

Secretary of State (Asia–Pacific): REY PAGTAKHAN.

MINISTRIES

Office of the Prime Minister: Langevin Block, 80 Wellington St, Ottawa, ON K1A 0A3; tel. (613) 992-4211; fax (613) 941-6900; e-mail pm@pm.gc.ca; internet www.pm.gc.ca.

Agriculture and Agri-Food Canada: Sir John Carling Bldg, 930 Carling Ave, Ottawa, ON K1A 0C5; tel. (613) 759-1000; fax (613) 759-6726; e-mail PIRS@em.agr.ca; internet www.agr.ca.

Canadian Heritage: Immeuble Jules Léger, 25 rue Eddy, Hull, QC K1A 0M5; tel. (819) 997-0055; fax (819) 953-5382; internet www.pch.gc.ca.

Citizenship and Immigration Canada: Jean Edmonds Towers, 365 ave Laurier ouest, Hull, QC K1A 1L1; tel. (613) 954-9019; fax (613) 954-2221; internet www.cicnet.ingenia.com/english/index.html.

Department of Justice Canada: East Memorial Bldg, 284 Wellington St, Ottawa, ON K1A 0H8; tel. (613) 957-4222; fax (613) 954-0811; internet www.canada.justice.gc.ca.

Environment Canada: Ottawa, ON K1A 0H3; tel. (819) 997-2800; fax (819) 953-2225; e-mail enviroinfo@ec.gc.ca; internet www.ec.gc.ca.

Finance Canada: L'Esplanade Laurier, 140 O'Connor St, Ottawa, ON K1A 0G5; tel. (613) 992-1573; fax (613) 996-8404; internet www.fin.gc.ca.

Fisheries and Oceans Canada: 200 Kent St, Ottawa, ON K1A 0E6; tel. (613) 993-0999; fax (613) 990-1866; e-mail info@www.ncr.dfo.ca; internet www.dfo-mpo.gc.ca.

Foreign Affairs and International Trade Canada: Lester B. Pearson Bldg, 125 Sussex Drive, Ottawa, ON K1A 0G2; tel. (613) 996-9134; fax (613) 952-3904; e-mail infotech@dfait-maeci.gc.ca; internet www.dfait-maeci.gc.ca.

Health Canada: Brooke Claxton Bldg, Tunney's Pasture, Ottawa, ON K1A 0K9; tel. (613) 957-2991; fax (613) 941-5366; internet www.hwc.ca/links/english/html.

Human Resources Development Canada: 140 promenade du Portage, Hull, QC K1A 0J9; tel. (819) 994-6013; fax (819) 953-3981; internet www.hrdc-drhc.gc.ca.

Indian and Northern Affairs Canada: Les Terrasses de la Chaudière, Bureau 1400, 10 rue Wellington, Hull, QC K1A 0H4; tel. (819) 997-0811; fax (819) 953-5491; e-mail reference@inac.gc.ca; internet www.inac.gc.ca.

Industry Canada: C. D. Howe Bldg, 235 Queen St, Ottawa, ON K1A 0H5; tel. (613) 954-2788; fax (613) 954-2303; internet www.info.ic.gc.ca.

National Defence (Canada): Maj.-Gen. George R. Pearkes Bldg, 101 Colonel By Drive, Ottawa, ON K1A 0K2; tel. (613) 992-4581; fax (613) 992-4241; internet www.dnd.ca.

Natural Resources Canada: 580 Booth St, Ottawa, ON K1A 0E4; tel. (613) 995-0947; fax (613) 996-9094; internet www.NRCan.gc.ca/.

Public Works and Government Services Canada: place du Portage, rue Laurier, Hull, QC K1A 0S5; tel. (819) 956-3115; internet www.pwgsc.gc.ca.

Revenue Canada: 871 Heron Rd, Ottawa, ON K1A 0L8; tel. (613) 952-0384; internet www.rc.gc.ca.

Solicitor-General Canada: Sir Wilfrid Laurier Bldg, 340 Laurier Ave West, Ottawa, ON K1A 0P8; tel. (613) 991-3283; fax (613) 993-7062; internet www.sgc.gc.ca.

Transport Canada: Transport Canada Bldg, 330 Sparks St, Ottawa, ON K1A 0N5; tel. (613) 990-2309; fax (613) 954-4731; e-mail mintc@tc.gc.ca; internet www.tc.gc.ca.

Treasury Board: East Tower, L'Esplanade Laurier, 140 O'Connor St, Ottawa, ON K1A 0R5; tel. (613) 957-2400; fax (613) 952-3658; internet www.tbs-sct.gc.ca.

Veterans Affairs Canada: 161 Grafton St, POB 7700, Charlottetown, PE C1A 8M9; tel. (902) 566-8888; fax (902) 566-8508; internet www.vac-acc.gc.ca.

Western Economic Diversification Canada: Canada Place, 9700 Jasper Ave, Suite 1500, Edmonton, AB T5J 4H7; tel. (780) 495-4164; fax (403) 495-6876; internet www.wd.gc.ca.

Federal Legislature

THE SENATE

Speaker: DANIEL HAYS.

Seats at January 2001

Liberal	54
Progressive Conservative	35
Independent	5
Canadian Alliance	1
Vacant	10
Total	**105**

HOUSE OF COMMONS

Speaker: PETER MILLIKEN.

General Election, 27 November 2000

	% of votes at election	Seats at election
Liberal	40.8	172
Canadian Alliance	25.5	66
Bloc Québécois	10.7	38
New Democratic Party	8.5	13
Progressive Conservative	12.2	12
Others	2.3	—
Total	**100.0**	**301**

Provincial Legislatures

ALBERTA

Lieutenant-Governor: LOIS HOLE.

Premier: RALPH KLEIN.

Election, March 2001

	Seats at election
Progressive Conservative	74
Liberal	7
New Democratic Party	2
Total	**83**

BRITISH COLUMBIA

Lieutenant-Governor: GARDE B. GARDOM.

Premier-designate: GORDON CAMPBELL.

Election, May 2000

	Seats at election
Liberal	76
New Democratic Party	3
Total	79

MANITOBA

Lieutenant-Governor: PETER LIBA.

Premier: GARY DOER.

Election, September 1999

	Seats at election	Seats at May 2001
New Democratic Party	31	32
Progressive Conservative	25	24
Liberal	1	1
Total	57	57

NEW BRUNSWICK

Lieutenant-Governor: MARILYN TRENHOLME COUNSELL.

Premier: BERNARD LORD.

Election, June 1999

	Seats at election	Seats at May 2001
Progressive Conservative	44	47
Liberal	10	7
New Democratic Party	1	1
Total	55	55

NEWFOUNDLAND AND LABRADOR

Lieutenant-Governor: Dr A. M. (MAX) HOUSE.

Premier: BEATON TULK.

Election, February 1999

	Seats at election	Seats at May 2001
Liberal	32	29
Progressive Conservative	14	16
New Democratic Party	2	2
Vacant	—	1
Total	48	48

NOVA SCOTIA

Lieutenant-Governor: MYRA A. FREEMAN.

Premier: JOHN F. HAMM.

Election, July 1999

	Seats at election	Seats at May 2001
Progressive Conservative	30	31
New Democratic Party	11	11
Liberal	11	10
Total	52	52

ONTARIO

Lieutenant-Governor: HILARY WESTON.

Premier: MICHAEL D. HARRIS.

Election, June 1999

	Seats at election	Seats at May 2001
Progressive Conservative	59	57
Liberal	35	35
New Democratic Party	9	9
Independent	—	1
Vacant	—	1
Total	103	103

PRINCE EDWARD ISLAND

Lieutenant-Governor: GILBERT R. CLEMENTS.

Premier: PAT BINNS.

Election, April 2000

	Seats at election	Seats at May 2001
Progressive Conservative	26	26
Liberal	1	1
Total	27	27

QUÉBEC

Lieutenant-Governor: LISE THIBAULT.

Premier: BERNARD LANDRY.

Election, November 1998

	Seats at election	Seats at April 2001
Parti Québécois	76	72
Liberal	48	49
Action Démocratique du Québec	1	1
Vacant	—	3
Total	125	125

SASKATCHEWAN

Lieutenant-Governor: LYNDA HAVERSTOCK.

Premier: LORNE CALVERT.

Election, September 1999

	Seats at election	Seats at May 2001
New Democratic Party	29	29
Saskatchewan Party	26	26
Liberal	3	2
Independent	—	1
Total	58	58

Territorial Legislatures

NORTHWEST TERRITORIES

Commissioner: GLENNA HANSEN.

Premier and Minister of the Executive Department: STEPHEN KAKFWI.

The Legislative Assembly, elected in December 1999, consists of 19 independent members without formal party affiliation.

NUNAVUT TERRITORY

Commissioner: HELEN MAGSAGAK.

Premier: PAUL OKALIK.

The Legislative Assembly, elected in February 1999, consists of 19 independent members without formal party affiliation.

YUKON TERRITORY

Commissioner: JACK CABLE.

Government Leader and Minister of the Executive Council Office: PAT DUNCAN.

Election, April 2000

	Seats at election	Seats at May 2001
Liberal	10	11
New Democratic Party	6	5
Yukon Party	1	1
Total	17	17

Political Organizations

Action Démocratique du Québec: 1050 rue de la Montagne, 3e étage, Montréal, QC H3G 1Y7; tel. (514) 932-5505; e-mail adq@dq.qc.ca; internet www.adq.qc.ca; f. 1994; provincial nationalist; Leader MARIO DUMONT; Pres. ISABELLE MARQUIS.

Bloc Québécois: 1200 ave Papineau, Montréal, QC H2K 4R5; tel. (514) 526-3000; fax (514) 526-2868; e-mail infobloc@bloc.org; internet www.blocquebecois.org; f. 1990 by group of seven Progressive Conservative MPs representing Québec constituencies in fed. parl.; subsequently attracted Liberal support; main opposition party in Federal House of Commons during 1993–97; seeks negotiated sovereignty for Québec; Leader GILLES DUCEPPE; Dir-Gen. YVES DUFOUR.

Canadian Action Party: 99 Atlantic Ave, Suite 302, Toronto ON M6K 3J8; tel. (416) 535-4144; fax (416) 535-6325; e-mail cap-pac@istar.ca; internet www.canadianactionparty.ca; Leader PAUL HELLYER.

Canadian Alliance: 833 4th ave SW, Suit 600, Calgary, AB T2P 3T5; tel. (403) 269-1990; fax (403) 269-4077; internet www.canadian-alliance.ca; f. 2000; incorporates the Reform Party; supports decentralization of fed. govt, with provincial jurisdiction over language and culture; advocates fiscal reform; main opposition party in Federal House of Commons since March 2000; Leader STOCKWELL DAY; Co-Chairs KEN KALOPSIS, CLAYTON MANNESS.

Christian Heritage Party of Canada: 155 Queen St, Suite 200, Ottawa, ON K1P 6L1; tel. (613) 788-3716; fax (613) 457-9242; internet www.chp.ca; f. 1986; Pres. THOMAS KROESBERGEN; Leader RONALD O. GRAY.

Communist Party of Canada (Marxist-Leninist): 396 Cooper St, Suite 405, Ottawa, ON K2P 2H7; tel. (613) 565-6446; fax (613) 565-8787; e-mail office@cpcml.ca; internet www.cpcml.ca; f. 1970; Nat. Leader SANDRA SMITH.

Confederation of Regions Party: 6155 99th St, Edmonton, AB T6E 3P1; tel. (780) 435-4185; fax (780) 437-2297; Nat. Leader ELMER S. KNUTSON.

COR (Confederation of Regions) Party of New Brunswick: POB 3322,Station B, Fredericton, NB E3A 5H1; tel. (506) 444-4040; fax (506) 444-4053; e-mail cor@nbnet.nb.ca; f. 1989 to promote populist democratic principles; opposes legislation and govt subsidies relating to linguistic and cultural matters; Leader JAMES A. WEBB (acting); Pres. DOLORES COOK.

Equality Party: Box 21, Station NDG, Montréal, QC H4A 3P4; tel. (514) 488-7586; fax (514) 488-7306; e-mail canadian@equality.qc.ca; internet www.equality.qc.ca; f. 1989; represents interests of federalists in Québec; Leader KEITH HENDERSON.

Green Party of Canada: 244 Gerrard St E, Toronto, ON M5A 2G2; tel. (416) 929-2397; fax (416) 929-7709; internet www.green.ca; f. 1983; environmentalist; Leader JOAN RUSSOW.

Liberal Party of Canada: 81 Metcalfe St, Suite 400, Ottawa, ON K1P 6M8; tel. (613) 237-0740; fax (613) 235-7208; e-mail info@liberal.ca; internet www.liberal.ca; supports comprehensive social security, economic growth and a balanced economy; Leader JEAN CHRÉTIEN; Pres. STEPHEN LEDREW; Nat. Dir GEORGE YOUNG.

New Democratic Party of Canada: 85 Albert St, Suite 802, Ottawa, ON K1P 6A4; tel. (613) 236-3613; fax (613) 230-9950; e-mail ndpadmin@fed.ndp.ca; internet www.ndp.ca; f. 1961; social democratic; Leader ALEXA MCDONOUGH; Pres. DAVE MACKINNON; Sec. JILL MARZETTI; 100,000 mems. (1996).

Parti Québécois: 1200 ave Papineau, Bureau 150, Montréal, QC H2K 4R5; tel. (514) 526-0200; fax (514) 526-0272; e-mail info@pq.org; internet www.pq.org; f. 1968; social democratic; seeks political sovereignty for Québec; governing party of Québec in 1976–85 and since Sept. 1994; Pres. BERNARD LANDRY; 200,000 mems (2001).

Progressive Conservative Party of Canada: 275 Slater St, Suite 501, Ottawa, ON K1P 5H9; tel. (613) 238-6111; fax (613) 238-7429; e-mail pcinfo@pcparty.ca; internet www.pcparty.ca; f. 1854; advocates individualism and free enterprise; Leader C. JOSEPH CLARK; Pres. JACQUES LÉGER; Nat. Dir SUSAN ELLIOTT.

Saskatchewan Party: POB 546, Regina, SK S4P 3A2; tel. (306) 359-1638; fax (306) 359-9832; e-mail skparty@sk.sympatico.ca; internet www.skparty.ca; Leader ELWIN HERMANSON.

Socialist Party of Canada: POB 4280, Victoria, BC V8X 3X8; tel. (250) 595-2144; fax (250) 676-7417; e-mail spc@iname.com; internet www.worldsocialism.org/canada/; f. 1931; Gen. Sec. DON POIRIER.

Yukon Party: POB 31113, Whitehorse, YT Y1A 5P7; tel. (867) 668-6505; fax (867) 667-7660; e-mail yukonparty@mailcity.com; internet www.angelfire.com/yt2/yukonparty/home.html; Leader JOHN OSTASHEK.

Diplomatic Representation

EMBASSIES AND HIGH COMMISSIONS IN CANADA

Algeria: 435 Daly Ave, Ottawa, ON K1N 6H3; tel. (613) 789-8505; fax (613) 789-1406; e-mail ambalgott@sympatico.ca; internet www.ambalgott.com; Ambassador: ABDESSELAIM BEDRANE.

Angola: 75 Albert St, Suite 900, Ottawa, ON K1P 5E7; tel. (613) 234-1152; fax (613) 234-1179; Chargé d'affaires a.i.: ANDRÉ PANZO.

Antigua and Barbuda, Dominica, Grenada, Montserrat, Saint Christopher and Nevis, Saint Lucia and Saint Vincent and the Grenadines: 130 Albert St, Suite 700, Ottawa, ON K1P 5G4; tel. (613) 236-8952; fax (613) 236-3042; e-mail echcc@travel-net.com; High Commissioner: GEORGE R. E. BULLEN.

Argentina: Royal Bank Centre, 90 Sparks St, Suite 910, Ottawa, ON K1P 5B4; tel. (613) 236-2351; fax (613) 235-2659; Ambassador: CÉSAR F. MAYORAL.

Armenia: 7 Delaware Ave, Ottawa, ON K2P 0Z2; tel. (613) 234-3710; fax (613) 234-3444; Ambassador: LEVON BARKHUDARYAN.

Australia: 50 O'Connor St, Suite 710, Ottawa, ON K1P 6L2; tel. (613) 236-0841; fax (613) 236-4376; internet www.ahc-ottawa.org; High Commissioner: GREGORY S. R. WOOD.

Austria: 445 Wilbrod St, Ottawa, ON K1N 6M7; tel. (613) 789-1444; fax (613) 789-3431; e-mail embassy@austro.org; internet www.austro.org; Ambassador: Dr WENDELIN ETTMAYER.

Bahamas: 50 O'Connor St, Suite 1313, Ottawa, ON K1P 6L2; tel. (613) 232-1724; fax (613) 232-0097; e-mail ottawa-mission@bahighco.com; Chargé d'affaires a.i.: JULIE ANN CAMPBELL.

Bangladesh: 275 Bank St, Suite 302, Ottawa, ON K2P 2L6; tel. (613) 236-0138; fax (613) 567-3213; e-mail bdootcanda@iosphere.net; internet www.iosphere.net/~bhc/; High Commissioner: M. AMINUL ISLAM.

Barbados: 130 Albert St, Suite 302, Ottawa, ON K1P 5G4; tel. (613) 236-9517; fax (613) 230-4362; e-mail barhcott@travel-net.com; High Commissioner: VICTOR LEROY JOHNSON.

Belgium: 80 Elgin St, 4th Floor, Ottawa, ON K1P 1B7; tel. (613) 236-7267; fax (613) 236-7882; internet www.diplobel.org/canada/; Ambassador: LUC CARBONEZ.

Benin: 58 Glebe Ave, Ottawa, ON K1S 2C3; tel. (613) 233-4429; fax (613) 233-8952; Ambassador: LÉOPOLD DAVID-GNAHOUI.

Bolivia: 130 Albert St, Suite 416, Ottawa, ON K1P 5G4; tel. (613) 236-5730; fax (613) 236-8237; e-mail bolcan@iosphere.net; internet www.iosphere.net/~bolcan/; Ambassador: RENÉ A. SORIA GALVARRO HAENSEL.

Bosnia and Herzegovina: 130 Albert St, Suite 805, Ottawa, ON K1P 5G4; tel. (613) 236-0028; fax (613) 236-1139; e-mail embassyofbih@magma.ca; Ambassador: KRUNOSLAV VASILJ.

Brazil: 450 Wilbrod St, Ottawa, ON K1N 6M8; tel. (613) 237-1090; fax (613) 237-6144; e-mail brasemb@ottawa.net; Ambassador: HENRIQUE RODRIGUES VALLE JÚNIOR.

Brunei: Hongkong Bank Bldg, 395 Laurier Ave East, Suite 400, Ottawa, ON K1N 6R4; tel. (603) 234-5656; fax (603) 234-4397; High Commissioner: Dato' JOCKLIN KONG PAW.

Bulgaria: 325 Stewart St, Ottawa, ON K1N 6K5; tel. (613) 789-3215; fax (613) 789-3524; Ambassador: SLAV DANEV.

Burkina Faso: 48 Range Rd, Ottawa, ON K1N 8J4; tel. (613) 238-4796; fax (613) 238-3812; e-mail burkina.faso@sympatico.ca; internet www.amba.burkina-canada.org; Ambassador: MOUHOUSSINE NACRO.

Burundi: Ottawa; Ambassador: EDONIAS NIYONGABO.

Cameroon: 170 Clemow Ave, Ottawa, ON K1S 2B4; tel. (613) 236-1522; fax (613) 238-3885; High Commissioner: PHILÉMON YUNJI YANG.

Chile: 50 O'Connor St, Suite 1413, Ottawa, ON K1N 6L2; tel. (613) 235-4402; fax (613) 235-1176; e-mail echileca@chile.ca; internet www.embachile-canada.com; Ambassador: JOSÉ TOMÁS LETELIER.

China, People's Republic: 515 St Patrick St, Ottawa, ON K1N 5H3; tel. (613) 789-3434; fax (613) 789-1911; Ambassador: PING MEI.

Colombia: 360 Albert St, Suite 1002, Ottawa, ON K1R 7X7; tel. (613) 230-3760; fax (613) 230-4416; e-mail embcolot@travel-net.com; internet www.travel-net.com/~embcolot; Ambassador: FANNY KERTZMANN.

Congo, Democratic Republic: 18 Range Rd, Ottawa, ON K1N 8J3; tel. (613) 236-7103; fax (613) 567-1404; Chargé d'affaires a.i.: LEYAN' SIMBI M'FUMU KANUNU.

Costa Rica: 135 York St, Suite 208, Ottawa, ON K1N 5T4; tel. (613) 562-2855; fax (613) 562-2582; e-mail embcrica@travel-net.com; Ambassador: CARLOS MIRANDA.

Côte d'Ivoire: 9 Marlborough Ave, Ottawa, ON K1N 8E6; tel. (613) 236-9919; fax (613) 563-8287; e-mail ambaci@ican.net; Ambassador: JEAN OBÉO-COULIBALY.

Croatia: 229 Chapel St, Ottawa, ON K1N 7Y6; tel. (613) 562-7820; fax (613) 562-7821; e-mail info@croatiaemb.net; internet www.croatiaemb.net; Ambassador: ANDRIJA JAKOČEVIĆ.

Cuba: 388 Main St, Ottawa, ON K1S 1E3; tel. (613) 563-0141; fax (613) 563-0068; e-mail cuba@embacuba.ca; internet www.embacuba.ca; Ambassador: CARLOS FERNÁNDEZ DE COSSIO DOMÍNGUEZ.

Czech Republic: 251 Cooper St, Ottawa, ON K2P 0G2; tel. (613) 562-3875; fax (613) 562-3878; e-mail ottawa@embassy.mzv.cz; Ambassador: VLADIMÍR KOTZY.

Denmark: 47 Clarence St, Suite 450, Ottawa, ON K1N 9K1; tel. (613) 562-1811; fax (613) 562-1812; e-mail danemb@cyberus.ca; internet www.danish-embassy-canada.com; Ambassador: SVEND ROED NIELSEN.

Dominican Republic: 130 Albert St, Suite 418, Ottawa, ON K1P 5G4; tel. (613) 569-9893; fax (613) 569-8673; e-mail info@drembassy.org; internet www.drembassy.org; Ambassador: JULIO ORTEGA TOUS.

Ecuador: 50 O'Connor St, Suite 316, Ottawa, ON K1P 6L2; tel. (613) 563-8206; fax (613) 235-5776; e-mail mecucan@inasec.ca; internet www.ncf.carleton.ca/ecuador; Ambassador: MANUEL A. PESANTES.

Egypt: 454 Laurier Ave East, Ottawa, ON K1N 6R3; tel. (613) 234-4931; fax (613) 234-9347; Ambassador: HAMDY NADA.

El Salvador: 209 Kent St, Suite 504, Ottawa, ON K2P 1Z8; tel. (613) 238-2939; fax (613) 238-6940; e-mail 103234.607@compuserve.com; Ambassador: Dr MAURICIO ROSALES RIVERA.

Ethiopia: 151 Slater St, Suite 210, Ottawa, ON K1P 5H3; tel. (613) 235-6637; fax (613) 235-4638; e-mail infoethi@magi.com; internet www.ethiopia.ottawa.on.ca; Ambassador: Dr FECADU GADAMU.

Finland: 55 Metcalfe St, Suite 850, Ottawa, ON K1P 6L5; tel. (613) 236-2389; fax (613) 238-1474; e-mail finembott@synapse.net; internet www.finemb.com; Ambassador: ILKKA K. RISTIMÄKI.

France: 42 Sussex Drive, Ottawa, ON K1M 2C9; tel. (613) 789-1795; fax (613) 562-3735; internet www.ambafrance-ca.org; Ambassador: DENIS BAUCHARD.

Gabon: 4 Range Rd, Ottawa, ON K1N 8J5; tel. (613) 232-5301; fax (613) 232-6916; Ambassador: ALPHONSE OYABI-GNALA.

Germany: 1 Waverley St, Ottawa, ON K2P 0T8; tel. (613) 232-1101; fax (613) 594-9330; e-mail 100566.2620@compuserve.com; internet www.germanembassyottawa.org; Ambassador: Dr ERNST JÜRGEN PÖHLMANN.

Ghana: 1 Clemow Ave, Ottawa, ON K1S 2A9; tel. (613) 236-0871; fax (613) 236-0874; High Commissioner: OLIVER K. K. LAWLUVI.

Greece: 76–80 MacLaren St, Ottawa, ON K2P 0K6; tel. (613) 238-6271; fax (613) 238-5676; e-mail greekembott@travel-net.com; Ambassador: LEONIDAS CHRYSANTHOPOULOS.

Guatemala: 130 Albert St, Suite 1010, Ottawa, ON K1P 5G4; tel. (613) 233-7237; fax (613) 233-0135; e-mail embguate@webruler.com; Ambassador: CARLOS JIMÉNEZ LICONA.

Guinea: 483 Wilbrod St, Ottawa, ON K1N 6N1; tel. (613) 789-8444; fax (613) 789-7560; e-mail ambguineaott@sympatico.ca; Ambassador: AMARA DJABAR SOUMAH.

Guyana: Burnside Bldg, 151 Slater St, Suite 309, Ottawa, ON K1P 5H3; tel. (613) 235-7249; fax (613) 235-1447; High Commissioner: RAJNARINE SINGH.

Haiti: Place de Ville, Tower B, 112 Kent St, Suite 205, Ottawa, ON K1P 5P2; tel. (613) 238-1628; fax (613) 238-2986; e-mail bohio@sympatico.ca; Chargé d'affaires a.i.: LHANDE HENRIQUEZ.

Holy See: Apostolic Nunciature, 724 Manor Ave, Rockcliffe Park, Ottawa, ON K1M 0E3; tel. (613) 746-4914; fax (613) 746-4786; e-mail nuncioap@istar.ca; Nuncio: Most Rev. PAOLO ROMEO, Titular Archbishop of Vulturia.

Honduras: 151 Slater St, Suite 805, Ottawa, ON K1P 5H3; tel. (613) 233-8900; fax (613) 232-0193; e-mail embhonca@magma.ca; Chargé d'affaires a.i.: BERTHA MARÍA REINA GARCÍA.

Hungary: 299 Waverley St, Ottawa, ON K2P 0V9; tel. (613) 230-2717; fax (613) 230-7560; e-mail h2embott@docuweb.ca; internet www.docuweb.ca/hungary/; Ambassador: SÁNDOR PAPP.

India: 10 Springfield Rd, Ottawa, ON K1M 1C9; tel. (613) 744-3751; fax (613) 744-0913; e-mail hicomind@ottawa.net; internet www.docuweb.ca/India; High Commissioner: RAJANIKANTA VERMA.

Indonesia: 55 Parkdale Ave, Ottawa, ON K1Y 1E5; tel. (613) 724-1100; fax (613) 724-1105; e-mail kbri@indonesia-ottawa.org; internet www.indonesia-ottawa.org; Chargé d'affaires a.i.: ARTAULI TOBING.

Iran: 245 Metcalfe St, Ottawa, ON K2P 2K2; tel. (613) 235-4726; fax (613) 232-5712; e-mail iranemb@salamiran.org; internet www.salamiran.org; Ambassador: MOHAMMAD ALI MOUSSAVI.

Iraq: 215 McLeod St, Ottawa, ON K2P 0Z8; tel. (613) 236-9177; fax (613) 567-1101; Chargé d'affaires a.i.: MOHAMMAD H. RADHI AL-SAFAR.

Ireland: 130 Albert St, Suite 1105, Ottawa, ON K1P 5G4; tel. (613) 233-6281; fax (613) 233-5835; e-mail emb.ireland@sympatico.ca; Ambassador: PAUL DEMPSEY.

Israel: 50 O'Connor St, Suite 1005, Ottawa, ON K1P 6L2; tel. (613) 567-6450; fax (613) 237-8865; e-mail embisrott@cyberus.ca; internet www.israelca.org; Ambassador: DAVID SULTAN.

Italy: 275 Slater St, 21st Floor, Ottawa, ON K1P 5H9; tel. (613) 232-2401; fax (613) 233-1484; e-mail ambital@italyincanada.com; internet www.italyincanada.com; Ambassador: ROBERTO NIGIDO.

Jamaica: 275 Slater St, Suite 800, Ottawa, ON K1P 5H9; tel. (613) 233-9311; fax (613) 233-0611; High Commissioner: RAYMOND WOLFE.

Japan: 255 Sussex Drive, Ottawa, ON K1N 9E6; tel. (613) 241-8541; fax (613) 241-7415; e-mail infocul@embassyjapancanada.org; internet www.embassyjapancanada.org; Ambassador: KATSUHISA UCHIDA.

Jordan: 100 Bronson Ave, Suite 701, Ottawa, ON K1R 6G8; tel. (613) 238-8090; fax (613) 232-3341; Ambassador: SAMIR M. KHALIFEH.

Kenya: 415 Laurier Ave East, Ottawa, ON K1N 6R4; tel. (613) 563-1773; fax (613) 233-6599; e-mail kenrep@on.aibn.com; Chargé d'affaires a.i.: JOSEPH O. O. KISEREMA.

Korea, Republic: 150 Boteler St, Ottawa, ON K1N 5A6; tel. (613) 244-5010; fax (613) 244-5043; internet www.emb-korea.ottawa.on.ca; Ambassador: SAM HOON KIM.

Kuwait: 80 Elgin St, Ottawa, ON K1P 1C6; tel. (613) 780-9999; fax (613) 780-9905; e-mail info@embassyofkuwait.com; internet www.embassyofkuwait.com; Ambassador: MAJDI AHMAD E. AL-DAFIRI.

Latvia: 280 Albert Street, Suit 300, Ottawa, ON K1P 5G8; tel. (613) 238-6014 fax (613) 238-7044; e-mail latvia-embassy@magmacom.com; internet www.magma.ca/-latemb/; Ambassador: JĀNIS LŪSIS.

Lebanon: 640 Lyon St, Ottawa, ON K1S 3Z5; tel. (613) 236-5825; fax (613) 232-1609; e-mail emblebanon@synapse.net; internet www.synapse.net/~emblebanon/; Ambassador: RAYMOND BAAKLINI.

Lithuania: 130 Albert St, Suite 204, Ottawa, ON K1P 5G4; tel. (613) 567-5458; fax (613) 567-5315; Ambassador: Dr ALFONSAS EIDINTAS.

Macedonia, former Yugoslav republic: 130 Albert St, Suite 1006, Ottawa, ON K1P 5G4; tel. (613) 234-3882; fax (613) 233-1852; Ambassador: JORDAN VESELINOV.

Madagascar: 649 Blair Rd, Gloucester, ON K1J 7M4; tel. (613) 744-7995; fax (613) 744-2530; e-mail ambamadott@on.aibn.com; Ambassador: ROLLAND BESOA RAZAFIMAHARO.

Malawi: 7 Clemow Ave, Ottawa, ON K1S 2A9; tel. (613) 236-8931; fax (613) 236-1054; e-mail malawihighcommission@sympatico.ca; High Commissioner: HENRY R. CHIRWA.

Malaysia: 60 Boteler St, Ottawa, ON K1N 8Y7; tel. (613) 241-5182; fax (613) 241-5214; e-mail mwottawa@istar.ca; internet home .istar.ca/~mwottawa; High Commissioner: Datuk A. W. OMARDIN.

Mali: 50 Goulburn Ave, Ottawa, ON K1N 8C8; tel. (613) 232-1501; fax (613) 232-7429; Ambassador: MANASSA DANIOKO DIAKITÉ.

Mauritania: 121 Sherwood Dr., Ottawa, ON K1Y 3V1; tel. (613) 237-3283; fax (613) 237-3287; e-mail info@ambarimca.org; internet www.ambarimca.org; Ambassador: ABDERRAHIM OULD HADRAMI.

Mexico: 45 O'Connor St, Suite 1500, Ottawa, ON K1P 1A4; tel. (613) 233-8988; fax (613) 235-9123; e-mail info@embamexcan.com; internet www.embamexcan.com; Ambassador: EZEQUIEL PADILLA.

Morocco: 38 Range Rd, Ottawa, ON K1N 8J4; tel. (613) 236-7391; fax (613) 236-6164; e-mail info@ambassade-maroc.ottawa.on.ca; internet www.ambassade-maroc.ottawa.on.ca; Ambassador: ABDEL-KADER LECHEHEB.

Myanmar: 85 Range Rd, Ottawa, ON K1N 8J6; tel. (613) 232-6434; fax (613) 232-6435; Chargé d'affaires a.i.: Mme YIN YIN OO.

Netherlands: 350 Albert St, Suite 2020, Ottawa, ON K1R 1A4; tel. (613) 237-5030; fax (613) 237-6471; e-mail nlgovott@netcom.ca; internet www.netherlandsembassy.ottawa.org; Ambassador: D. J. VAN HOUTEN.

New Zealand: Metlife Centre, 99 Bank St, Suite 727, Ottawa, ON K1P 6G3; tel. (613) 238-5991; fax (613) 238-5707; e-mail nzhcott@istar.ca; internet www.nzhcottawa.org; High Commissioner: WADE ARMSTRONG.

Niger: 38 Blackburn Ave, Ottawa, ON K1N 8A3; tel. (613) 232-4291; fax (613) 230-9808; Ambassador: RAKIATOU MAYAKI.

Nigeria: 295 Metcalfe St, Ottawa, ON K2P 1R9; tel. (613) 236-0522; fax (613) 236-0529; High Commissioner: ABDUL-AZIZ GARUBA.

Norway: 90 Sparks St, Suite 532, Ottawa, ON K1P 5B4; tel. (613) 238-6571; fax (613) 238-2765; e-mail emb.ottawa@mfa.no; internet www.emb-norway.ca; Ambassador: INGVARD HAVNEN.

Pakistan: Burnside Bldg, 151 Slater St, Suite 608, Ottawa, ON K1P 5H3; tel. (613) 238-7881; fax (613) 238-7296; e-mail hcpak@sprint.com; High Commissioner: RAFAT MAHDI.

Panama: 130 Albert St, Suite 300, Ottawa, ON K1P 5G4; tel. (613) 236-7177; fax (613) 236-5775; e-mail pancanem@travel-net.com; Ambassador: MARIANELA DÍAZ.

Papua New Guinea: 130 Albert St, Suite 300, Ottawa, ON K1A 5G4; fax (613) 236-5775; High Commissioner: NAGORA Y. BOGAN.

Paraguay: 151 Slater St, Suite 501, Ottawa, ON K1P 5H3; tel. (613) 567-1283; fax (613) 567-1679; e-mail embapar@magmacom .com; internet www.magma.ca/~embapar; Chargé d'affaires a.i.: VICTOR HUGO AQUINO FORNERA.

Peru: 130 Albert St, Suite 1901, Ottawa, ON K1P 5G4; tel. (613) 238-1777; fax (613) 232-3062; e-mail emperuca@sprint.ca; Ambassador: JOSÉ E. ROMERO.

Philippines: 130 Albert St, Suite 606, Ottawa, ON K1P 5G4; tel. (613) 233-1121; fax (613) 233-4165; e-mail ottawape@istar.ca; internet www.philembassyca.org; Ambassador: FRANCISCO L. BENEDICTO.

Poland: 443 Daly Ave, Ottawa, ON K1N 6H3; tel. (613) 789-0468; fax (613) 789-1218; e-mail polamb@alphainter.net; internet www.polonianet.com/pol/ambasada/; Ambassador: BOGDAN GRZELONSKI.

Portugal: 645 Island Park Drive, Ottawa, ON K1Y 0B8; tel. (613) 729-0883; fax (613) 729-4236; Ambassador: JOSÉ PACHECO LUÍZ GOMES.

Romania: 655 Rideau St, Ottawa, ON K1N 6A3; tel. (613) 789-3709; fax (613) 789-4365; e-mail romania@cyberus.ca; internet www.cyberus.ca/~romania; Ambassador: GABRIEL GAFIŢA.

Russia: 285 Charlotte St, Ottawa, ON K1N 8L5; tel. (613) 235-4341; fax (613) 236-6342; e-mail rusemb@magma.ca; internet www.magma.ca/~rusemb; Ambassador: VITALY CHURKIN.

Rwanda: Ambassador: LAURENT NKONGOLI.

Saudi Arabia: 99 Bank St, Suite 901, Ottawa, ON K1P 6B9; tel. (613) 237-4100; fax (613) 237-0567; Ambassador: Dr MOHAMMED R. AL-HUSANI AL-SHARIF.

Senegal: 57 Marlborough Ave, Ottawa, ON K1N 8E8; tel. (613) 238-6392; fax (613) 238-2695; Ambassador: PIERRE DIOUF.

Slovakia: 50 Rideau Terrace, Ottawa, ON K1M 2A1; tel. (613) 749-4442; fax (613) 749-4989; e-mail slovakemb@sprint.ca; internet www.slovakembassy.com; Ambassador: Dr MIROSLAV MIKOLÁŠIK.

Slovenia: 150 Metcalfe St, Suite 2101, Ottawa, ON K2P 1P1; tel. (613) 565-5781; fax (613) 565-5783; Ambassador: Dr BOŽO CERAR.

South Africa: 15 Sussex Drive, Ottawa, ON K1M 1M8; tel. (613) 744-0330; fax (613) 741-1639; e-mail rsafrica@sympatico.ca; internet www.docuweb.ca/SouthAfrica; High Commissioner: ANDRÉ JAQUET.

Spain: 74 Stanley Ave, Ottawa, ON K1M 1P4; tel. (613) 747-2252; fax (613) 744-1224; e-mail spain@docuweb.ca; internet www .docuweb.ca/SpainInCanada/; Ambassador: JOSÉ CUENCA ANAYA.

Sri Lanka: 333 Laurier Ave West, Suite 1204, Ottawa, ON K1P 1C1; tel. (613) 233-8449; fax (613) 238-8448; e-mail lankacom@ magi.com; internet infoweb.magi.com/~lankacom; High Commissioner: A. C. GOONASEKERA.

Sudan: 85 Range Rd, Suite 507, Ottawa, ON K1N 8J6; tel. (613) 235-4000; fax (613) 235-6880; Chargé d'affaires a.i.: ABD EL-HANI E. AWAD EL-KARIM.

Swaziland: 130 Albert St, Suite 1204, Ottawa, ON K1P 5G4; tel. (613) 567-1480; fax (613) 567-1058; High Commissioner: BREMER M. NXUMALO.

Sweden: Mercury Court, 377 Dalhousie St, Ottawa, ON K1N 9N8; tel. (613) 241-8553; fax (613) 241-2277; e-mail info@sweden-suede -can.org; internet www.sweden-suede-can.org; Ambassador: LENNART ALVIN.

Switzerland: 5 Marlborough Ave, Ottawa, ON K1N 8E6; tel. (613) 235-1837; fax (613) 563-1394; e-mail vertretung@ott.rep.admin.ch; Ambassador: URS ZISWILER.

Syria: 151 Slater St, Suite 1000, Ottawa, ON K1P 5H3; tel. (613) 569-5556; fax (613) 569-3800; Chargé d'affaires a.i.: AHMAD FAROUK ARNOUS.

Tanzania: 50 Range Rd, Ottawa, ON K1N 8J4; tel. (613) 232-1500; fax (613) 232-5184; High Commissioner: FADHIL D. MBAGA.

Thailand: 180 Island Park Drive, Ottawa, ON K1Y 0A2; tel. (613) 722-4444; fax (613) 722-6624; e-mail thaiott@magma.ca; internet www.magma.ca/~thaiott/mainpage.htm; Ambassador: SUNAI BUNYASIRIPHANT.

Togo: 12 Range Rd, Ottawa, ON K1N 8J3; tel. (613) 238-5916; fax (613) 235-6425; Ambassador: (vacant).

Trinidad and Tobago: 200 First Ave, Ottawa, ON K1S 2G6; tel. (613) 232-2418; fax (613) 232-4349; e-mail ottawa@ttmissions .com; internet www.ttmissions.com; High Commissioner: ROBERT M. SABGA.

Tunisia: 515 O'Connor St, Ottawa, ON K1S 3P8; tel. (613) 237-0330; fax (613) 237-7939; Ambassador: HABIB LAZREG.

Turkey: 197 Wurtemburg St, Ottawa, ON K1N 8L9; tel. (613) 789-4044; fax (613) 789-3442; Ambassador: ERHAN ÖGÜT.

Ukraine: 310 Somerset St West, Ottawa, ON K2P 0J9; tel. (613) 230-2961; fax (613) 230-2400; e-mail ukremb@cyberus.ca; internet 209.82.14.226/ukremb; Ambassador: YURIY SCHERRAK.

United Arab Emirates: World Exchange Plaza, 45 O'Connor St, Suite 1800, Ottawa, ON K1P 1A4; tel. (613) 565-7272; fax (613) 565-8007; e-mail safara@uae-embassy.com; internet www.uae-embassy .com; Ambassador: HASSAN M. O. AL-SUWAIDI.

United Kingdom: 80 Elgin St, Ottawa, ON K1P 5K7; tel. (613) 237-1530; fax (613) 237-7980; e-mail generalenquiries@britain-in -canada.org; internet www.britain-in-canada.org; High Commissioner: Sir ANDREW BURNS.

USA: 490 Sussex Drive, POB 866, Station B, Ottawa, ON K1N 1G8; tel. (613) 238-5335; internet www.usembassycanada.gov; Ambassador: GORDON D. GIFFIN.

Uruguay: 130 Albert St, Suite 1905, Ottawa, ON K1P 5G4; tel. (613) 234-2727; fax (613) 233-4670; e-mail urott@iosphere.net; internet www.iosphere.net/~uruott/; Ambassador: GASTON LASARTE.

Venezuela: 32 Range Rd, Ottawa, ON K1N 8J4; tel. (613) 235-5151; fax (613) 235-3205; e-mail embavene@travel-net.com; internet www.travel-net.com/~embavene/; Ambassador: JORGE OSORIO.

Viet Nam: 470 Wilbrod St, Ottawa, ON K1M 6M8; tel. (613) 236-0772; fax (613) 236-2704; Ambassador: THANH QUANG TRINH.

Yemen: 788 Island Park Drive, Ottawa, ON K1Y 0C2; tel. (613) 729-6627; fax (613) 729-8915; Chargé d'affaires a.i.: ABDULMALEK ABDULGHANI SALEH.

Yugoslavia: 17 Blackburn Ave, Ottawa, ON K1N 8A2; tel. (613) 233-6289; fax (613) 233-7850; e-mail embotava@capitalnet.com; Ambassador: Dr PAVLE TODOROVIĆ.

Zimbabwe: 332 Somerset St West, Ottawa, ON K2P 0J9; tel. (613) 237-4388; fax (613) 563-8269; e-mail zim.highcomm@sympatico.ca; internet www.docuweb.ca/zimbabwe; High Commissioner: LILLIE CHITAURO.

Judicial System

FEDERAL COURTS

The Supreme Court of Canada: Supreme Court Bldg, 301 Wellington St, Ottawa, ON K1A 0J1; tel. (613) 995-4330; fax (613) 996-3063; e-mail reception@scc-csc.gc.ca; internet www.scc-csc.gc.ca; ultimate court of appeal in both civil and criminal cases throughout Canada. The Supreme Court is also required to advise on questions referred to it by the Governor-General in Council. Important questions concerning the interpretation of the Constitution Act, the constitutionality or interpretation of any federal or provincial law, the powers of Parliament or of the provincial legislatures, among other matters, may be referred by the Government to the Supreme Court for consideration.

In most cases, appeals are heard by the Court only if leave to appeal is given from any final judgement of the highest court of last resort in a province or territory, or of the Federal Court of Appeal. Such leave, or permission, will be given by the Court when a case involves a question of public importance. There are cases, however, where leave is not required. In criminal cases, there is an automatic right of appeal where an acquittal has been set aside in the provincial court of appeal or where one judge in the provincial court of appeal dissents on a question of law.

Chief Justice of Canada: BEVERLEY MCLACHLIN.

Puisne Judges: CLAIRE L'HEUREUX-DUBÉ, CHARLES DOHERTY GONTHIER, FRANK IACOBUCCI, JOHN C. MAJOR, MICHEL BASTARACHE, W. IAN BINNIE, LOUISE ARBOUR, LOUIS LEBEL.

The Federal Court of Canada: Supreme Court Bldg, Wellington St, Ottawa, ON K1A 0H9; tel. (613) 992-4238; has jurisdiction in claims against the Crown, claims by the Crown, miscellaneous cases involving the Crown, claims against or concerning crown officers and servants, relief against Federal Boards, Commissions, and other tribunals, interprovincial and federal-provincial disputes, industrial or industrial property matters, admiralty, income tax and estate tax appeals, citizenship appeals, aeronautics, interprovincial works and undertakings, residuary jurisdiction for relief if there is no other Canadian court that has such jurisdiction, jurisdiction in specific matters conferred by federal statutes.

The Federal Court of Appeal: Supreme Court Bldg, Wellington St, Ottawa, ON K1A 0H9; tel. (613) 996-6795; has jurisdiction on appeals from the Trial Division, appeals from Federal Tribunals, review of decisions of Federal Boards and Commissions, appeals from Tribunals and Reviews under Section 28 of the Federal Court Act, and references by Federal Boards and Commissions. The Court has one central registry and consists of the principal office in Ottawa and local offices in major centres throughout Canada.

Chief Justice: JOHN D. RICHARD.

Associate Chief Justice: ALLAN LUTFY.

Court of Appeal Judges: ARTHUR STONE, BARRY STRAYER, ALICE DESJARDINS, ROBERT DÉCARY, ALLEN LINDEN, GILLES LÉTOURNEAU, MARC NOËL, F. JOSEPH MCDONALD, J. EDGAR SEXTON, JOHN EVANS, KAREN SHARLOW, J. BRIAN MALONE.

Trial Division Judges: PAUL ROULEAU, FRANCIS MULDOON, PIERRE DENAULT, YVON PINARD, MAX TEITELBAUM, WILLIAM MACKAY, DONNA MCGILLIS, WILLIAM MCKEOWN, FREDERICK GIBSON, SANDRA SIMPSON, MARC NADON, DANIÈLE TREMBLAY-LAMER, DOUGLAS CAMPBELL, PIERRE BLAIS, FRANÇOIS LEMIEUX, J. D. DENIS PELLETIER, JOHN O'KEEFE, ELIZABETH HENEGHAN, DOLORES HANSEN, ELEANOR DAWSON, EDMOND BLANCHARD.

PROVINCIAL COURTS
Alberta
Court of Appeal

Chief Justice of Alberta: CATHERINE A. FRASER.

Court of Queen's Bench

Chief Justice: WILLIAM K. MOORE.
Associate Chief Justice: ALLAN H. J. WACHOWICH.

British Columbia
Court of Appeal

Chief Justice of British Columbia: ALLAN MCEACHERN.

Supreme Court

Chief Justice: D. I. BRENNER.
Associate Chief Justice: P. D. DOHM.

Manitoba
Court of Appeal

Chief Justice of Manitoba: R. J. SCOTT.

Court of Queen's Bench

Chief Justice: B. HEWAK.
Associate Chief Justice: J. J. OLIPHANT.
Associate Chief Justice (Family Division): G. W. MERCIER.

New Brunswick
Court of Appeal

Chief Justice of New Brunswick: JOSEPH Z. DAIGLE.

Court of Queen's Bench

Chief Justice: D. D. SMITH.

Newfoundland
Supreme Court—Court of Appeal

Chief Justice: CLYDE K. WELLS.

Trial Division

Chief Justice: J. D. GREEN.

Nova Scotia
Court of Appeal

Chief Justice of Nova Scotia: CONSTANCE R. GLUBE.

Supreme Court

Chief Justice: J. P. KENNEDY.
Associate Chief Justice: J. M. MACDONALD.

Supreme Court (Family Division)

Associate Chief Justice: R. F. FERGUSON.

Ontario
Court of Appeal

Chief Justice of Ontario: ROY R. MCMURTRY.
Associate Chief Justice of Ontario: COULTER A. OSBORNE.

Court of Justice

Chief Justice: P. J. LESAGE.
Associate Chief Justice: Madam H. J. SMITH.

Prince Edward Island
Supreme Court—Appeal Division

Chief Justice: G. E. MITCHELL.

Supreme Court—Trial Division

Chief Justice: KENNETH R. MACDONALD.

Québec
Court of Appeal

Chief Justice of Québec: PIERRE A. MICHAUD.

Superior Court

Chief Justice: LYSE LEMIEUX.
Senior Associate Chief Justice: RENÉ W. DIONNE.
Associate Chief Justice: ANDRÉ DESLONGCHAMPS.

Saskatchewan
Court of Appeal

Chief Justice of Saskatchewan: E. D. BAYDA.

Court of Queen's Bench

Chief Justice: W. F. GEREIN.

Northwest Territories
Court of Appeal

Chief Justice: CATHERINE A. FRASER (Alberta).

Supreme Court

Judges of the Supreme Court: J. E. RICHARD, J. Z. VERTES.

Nunavut Territory
Court of Appeal

Chief Justice: CATHERINE A. FRASER (Alberta).

Court of Justice

Judges of the Court of Justice: B. A. BROWNE, R. G. KILPATRICK.

Yukon Territory
Court of Appeal

Chief Justice: ALLAN MCEACHERN (British Columbia).

Supreme Court

Judges of the Supreme Court: RALPH E. HUDSON.

Religion
CHRISTIANITY

About 75% of the population belong to the three main Christian churches: Roman Catholic, United and Anglican. Numerous other religious denominations are active in Canada.

Canadian Council of Churches/Conseil canadien des Eglises: 3250 Bloor St West, 2nd Floor, Etobicoke, ON M8X 2Y4; tel. (416) 232-6070; fax (416) 236-4532; e-mail cccadmin@web.net; internet www.web.net/~ccchurch; f. 1944; 18 mem. churches, one assoc. mem; Pres. Most Rev. ANDRÉ VALLÉE (Roman Catholic Bishop of Hearst); Gen. Sec. JANET SOMERVILLE.

The Anglican Communion

The Anglican Church of Canada (L'Eglise anglicane du Canada) comprises 30 dioceses in four ecclesiastical provinces (each with a Metropolitan archbishop). The Church had 780,897 members in 1,740 parishes in 1997.

General Synod of the Anglican Church of Canada: Church House, 600 Jarvis St, Toronto, ON M4Y 2J6; tel. (416) 924-9192; fax (416) 968-7983; e-mail info@national.anglican.ca; internet www.anglican.ca; Gen. Sec. Archdeacon JAMES BOYLES.

Primate of the Anglican Church of Canada: Most Rev. MICHAEL G. PEERS.

Province of British Columbia and Yukon: Metropolitan Most Rev. DAVID P. CRAWLEY, Archbishop of Kootenay.

Province of Canada: Metropolitan Most Rev. ARTHUR PETERS, Archbishop of Nova Scotia.

Province of Ontario: Metropolitan Most Rev. PERCY R. O'DRISCOLL, Archbishop of Huron.

Province of Rupert's Land: Acting Metropolitan Rt Rev. THOMAS O. MORGAN, Bishop of Saskatoon.

The Orthodox Churches

Greek Orthodox Metropolis of Toronto (Canada): 1 Patriarch Bartholomew Way, Toronto, ON M4H 1C6; tel. (416) 429-5757; fax (416) 429-4588; e-mail gocanada@total.net; internet www.gocanada.org; 350,000 mems (1997); Metropolitan Archbishop SOTIRIOS ATHANASSOULAS.

Ukrainian Orthodox Church of Canada: 9 St John's Ave, Winnipeg, MB R2W 1G8; tel. (204) 586-3093; fax (204) 582-5241; e-mail consistory@uocc.ca; internet www.uocc.ca; f. 1918; 281 parishes, 120,000 mems (1998); Metropolitan of Winnipeg and of all Canada His Beatitude WASYLY (FEDAK); Chancellor Rt Rev WILLIAM MAKARENKO.

The Romanian, Serbian, Coptic, Antiochian and Armenian Churches are also represented in Canada.

The Roman Catholic Church

For Catholics of the Latin rite, Canada comprises 18 archdioceses (including one directly responsible to the Holy See), 46 dioceses and one territorial abbacy. There are also one archdiocese and four dioceses of the Ukrainian rite. In addition, the Maronite, Melkite and Slovak rites are each represented by one diocese (all directly responsible to the Holy See). In December 1998 the Roman Catholic Church had about 11.5m. adherents in Canada.

Canadian Conference of Catholic Bishops/Conférence des évêques catholiques du Canada: 90 Parent Ave, Ottawa, ON K1N 7B1; tel. (613) 241-9461; fax (613) 241-8117; e-mail cecc@cccb.ca; internet www.cccb.ca; Pres. Most Rev. GERALD WIESNER, Bishop of Prince George; Vice-Pres. Most Rev. JACQUES BERTHELET, Bishop of St-Jean-Longueuil.

Latin Rite

Archbishop of Edmonton: Most Rev. THOMAS COLLINS.

Archbishop of Gatineau-Hull: Most Rev. ROGER ÉBACHER.

Archbishop of Grouard-McLennan: Most Rev. ARTHÉ GUIMOND.

Archbishop of Halifax: Most Rev. TERRENCE PRENDERGAST.

Archbishop of Keewatin-Le Pas: Most Rev. PETER ALFRED SUTTON.

Archbishop of Kingston: Most Rev. FRANCIS J. SPENCE.

Archbishop of Moncton: Most Rev. ERNEST LÉGER.

Archbishop of Montréal: Most Rev. Cardinal JEAN-CLAUDE TURCOTTE.

Archbishop of Ottawa: Most Rev. MARCEL A. GERVAIS.

Archbishop of Québec: Most Rev. MAURICE COUTURE.

Archbishop of Regina: Most Rev. PETER J. MALLON.

Archbishop of Rimouski: Most Rev. BERTRAND BLANCHET.

Archbishop of St Boniface: (vacant).

Archbishop of St John's, Nfld: Most Rev. BRENDAN O'BRIEN.

Archbishop of Sherbrooke: Most Rev. ANDRÉ GAUMOND.

Archbishop of Toronto: Cardinal ALOYSIUS M. AMBROZIC.

Archbishop of Vancouver: Most Rev. ADAM J. EXNER.

Archbishop of Winnipeg: Most Rev. JAMES V. WEISGERBER.

Ukrainian Rite

Ukrainian Catholic Church in Canada: 233 Scotia St, Winnipeg, MB R2V 1V7; tel. (204) 338-7801; fax (204) 339-4006; 133,490 mems (1991 census); Archeparch-Metropolitan of Winnipeg Most Rev. MICHAEL BZDEL.

The United Church of Canada

The United Church of Canada (L'Eglise unie du Canada) was founded in 1925 with the union of Methodist, Congregational and Presbyterian churches in Canada. The Evangelical United Brethren of Canada joined in 1968. In 1999 there were 3,764 congregations and 1,748,875 mems.

Moderator: MARION PARDY.

General Secretary: K. VIRGINIA COLEMAN, 3250 Bloor St West, Suite 300, Toronto, ON M8X 2Y4; tel. (416) 231-5931; fax (416) 231-3103; e-mail info@uccan.org; internet www.uccan.org.

Other Christian Churches

Canadian Baptist Ministries: 7185 Millcreek Drive, Mississauga, ON L5N 5R4; tel. (905) 821-3533; fax (905) 826-3441; e-mail dphillips@cbmin.org; internet www.cbmin.org; 1,133 churches; 129,000 mems (1996); Pres. Dr BRUCE MILNE; Gen. Sec. Rev. DAVID PHILLIPS.

Christian Reformed Church in North America (Canadian Council): 3475 Mainway, POB 5070, Burlington, ON L7R 3Y8; tel. (905) 336-2920; fax (905) 336-8344; internet www.crcna.org; f. 1857; 237 congregations; 82,000 mems (2000); Dir in Canada Rev. WILLIAM VEENSTRA.

Church of Jesus Christ of Latter-day Saints (Mormon): 1185 Eglinton Ave East, POB 116, Toronto, ON M3C 3C6; tel. (416) 424-2485; fax (416) 424-3326; 391 congregations; 130,000 mems in Canada (1996).

Evangelical Lutheran Church in Canada: 393 Portage Ave, Suite 302, Winnipeg, MB R3B 3H6; tel. (204) 984-9150; fax (204) 984-9185; e-mail sartison@elcic.ca; internet www.elcic.ca/; f. 1967; 640 congregations, 193,915 mems (1998); Bishop Rev. TELMOR G. SARTISON.

Lutheran Church–Canada: 3074 Portage Ave, Winnipeg, MB R3K 0Y2; tel. (204) 895-3433; fax (204) 897-4319; e-mail lcc@mts.net; internet www.lutheranchurch-canada.ca; f. 1988; 325 congregations; 80,000 mems (1997); Pres. Rev. RALPH MAYAN.

Mennonite Central Committee–Canada: 134 Plaza Drive, Winnipeg, MB R3T 5K9; tel. (204) 261-6381; fax (204) 269-9875; e-mail mcc@mennonitecc.ca; f. 1963; 120,000 mems in 600 congregations; Exec. Dir MARVIN FREY.

Pentecostal Assemblies of Canada: 2450 Milltower Ct, Mississauga, ON L5N 5Z6; tel. (905) 542-7400; fax (905) 542-7313; e-mail info@paoc.org; internet www.paoc.org; 1,938 congregations, 237,000 mems (1998); Gen. Supt Dr WILLIAM D. MORROW.

Presbyterian Church in Canada: 50 Wynford Drive, Toronto, ON M3C 1J7; tel. (416) 441-1111; fax (416) 441-2825; e-mail pccadmin@presbycan.ca; internet www.presbyterian.ca; f. 1875; 1,000 congregations; 134,683 mems (1999); Moderator Rev. GLEN DAVIS; Prin. Clerk Rev. STEPHEN KENDALL.

Religious Society of Friends: 91A Fourth Ave, Ottawa, ON K1S 2L1; tel. (613) 235-8553; fax (613) 235-1753; e-mail cym-office@quaker.ca; internet www.quaker.ca; Clerk of Canadian Yearly Meeting GORDON McCLURE.

Seventh-day Adventists: 1148 King St East, Oshawa, ON L1H 1H8; tel. (905) 433-0011; fax (905) 433-0982; internet www.sdacc.org; 325 congregations; 48,000 mems (1998); Pres. ORVILLE PARCHMENT; Sec. NILTON AMORIM.

BAHÁ'Í FAITH

Bahá'í Community of Canada: 7200 Leslie St, Thornhill, ON L3T 6L8; tel. (905) 889-8168; fax (905) 889-8184; e-mail secretariat@cdnbnc.org; internet www.ca.bahai.org; f. 1902; 29,000 mems (1998); Sec. JUDY FILSON.

BUDDHISM

Buddhist Churches of Canada: 11786 Fentiman Place, Richmond, BC V7E 6M6; tel. (604) 272-3330; fax (604) 272-6865; internet www.bcc.ca; Jodo Shinshu Hongwanji-ha of Mahayana Buddhism; Bishop KYOJO IKUTA.

ISLAM

There are an estimated 260,000 Muslims in Canada.

Ahmadiyya Movement in Islam (Canada): 10610 Jane St, Maple, ON L6A 1S1; tel. (416) 832-2669; fax (416) 832-3220; e-mail info@islam.ahmadiyya.org; Pres. and Missionary-in-Charge NASEEM MAHDI.

Canadian Islamic Organization Inc: 2069 Kempton Park Drive, Mississauga, ON L5M 2Z4; tel. (905) 820-4655; fax (905) 820-0832; Gen. Sec. FAREED AHMAD KHAN.

Council of Muslim Communities of Canada: 1250 Ramsey View Court, Suite 504, Sudbury, ON P3E 2E7; co-ordinating agency; Dir MIR IQBAL ALI.

Federation of Islamic Associations: 73 Patricia Ave, North York, ON M2M 1J1; tel. (416) 222-2794; fax (416) 674-8168; Pres. AYUBE ALLY.

Organization of North American Shi'a Itha-Asheri Muslim Communities (NASIMCO): 300 John St, POB 87629, Thornhill, ON L3T 5W0; tel. (905) 763-7512; fax (905) 763-7509; e-mail nasimco@idirect.com; f. 1980; Pres. GHULAM ABBAS SAJAN.

JUDAISM

The Jews of Canada are estimated to number 320,000.

Canadian Council for Conservative Judaism: 1250 Steeles Ave, Suite 112, Concord, ON L4K 3B9; tel. (905) 738-1717; fax (905) 738-1331; e-mail 71263.302@compuserve.com; Pres. DAVID GREENBERG; Exec. Sec. RHONDA SCHILD.

Canadian Council for Reform Judaism: 36 Atkinson Ave, Thornhill, ON L4J 8C9; tel. (905) 709-2275; fax (905) 709-1895; Pres. CHARLES ROTHSCHILD.

Canadian Jewish Congress: 100 Sparks St, Suite 650, Ottawa, ON K1P 5B7; tel. (613) 233-8703; fax (613) 233-8748; e-mail canadianjewishcongress@cjc.ca; f. 1919; 10 regional offices; Exec. Vice-Pres. JACK SILVERSTONE.

SIKHISM

There are an estimated 250,000 Sikhs in Canada.

Federation of Sikh Societies of Canada: POB 91, Station B, Ottawa, ON K1P 6C3; tel. (613) 737-7296; fax (613) 739-7153; f. 1981; Pres. MOHINDER SINGH GOSAL.

The Press

The daily press in Canada is essentially local and regional in coverage, influence and distribution. Chain ownership has traditionally been predominant: at the beginning of 2000 63.4% of daily newspaper circulation was represented by two major groups: Hollinger Inc (42.0% of daily newspaper circulation) and Quebecor Inc (21.4%). However, in 2000 both Hollinger and the Thomson Corpn (10.5%) divested themselves of significant proportions of their newspaper interests—Thomson retaining only the Toronto *Globe and Mail,* control of which was subsequently transferred to Bell Globemedia, Inc, a joint venture between companies including Thomson and the telecommunications operator, BCE, Inc. In November 2000 CanWest Global Communications Corpn acquired 14 daily metropolitan newspapers, a number of community newspapers and a 50% interest in the National Post (Canada's first national daily newspaper, launched by Hollinger's Southam Inc division in October 1998). Torstar (which owns the *Toronto Star*) accounted for 13.8% of total circulation in 2000.

In 2000 there were 101 daily newspapers with a combined circulation exceeding 5m., and about 1,100 weekly and twice-weekly community newspapers serving mainly the more remote areas of the country. A significant feature of the Canadian press is the number of newspapers catering for immigrant groups: there are over 80 of these daily and weekly publications appearing in over 20 languages.

There are numerous periodicals for business, trade, professional, recreational and special interest readership, although periodical publishing, particularly, encounters substantial competition from publications originating in the USA.

The following are among the principal newspaper publishing groups:

Quebecor Inc: 612 rue St-Jacques, Montréal, QC H3C 1C8; tel. (514) 877-9777; fax (514) 877-9790; internet www.quebecor.com; f. 1965; Pres. and CEO PIERRE PELADIEU.

Southam Inc: 1450 Don Mills Rd, Don Mills, ON M3B 2X7; tel. (416) 445-6641; fax (416) 442-2077; internet www.southam.com; Pres. and CEO DON BABICK.

Thomson Corporation: POB 24, Toronto-Dominion Centre/Bank Tower, Toronto, ON M5K 1A1; tel. (416) 360-8700; fax (416) 360-8812; Chair. K. R. THOMSON; Pres. and CEO RICHARD HARRINGTON.

PRINCIPAL DAILY NEWSPAPERS

(D = all day; E = evening; M = morning; S = Sunday)

Alberta

Calgary Herald: 215 16th St, SE, POB 2400, Station M, Calgary, AB T2P 0W8; tel. (403) 235-7100; internet www.calgaryherald.com; f. 1883; Publr DAN GAYNOR; Editor-in-Chief PETER MENZIES; circ. 122,000 (M); 116,000 (S).

Calgary Sun: 2615 12th St, NE, Calgary, AB T2E 7W9; tel. (403) 250-4200; fax (403) 250-4180; e-mail calpromo@sunpub.com; internet www.canoe.ca; f. 1980; Publr GUY HUNTINGFORD; Editor-in-Chief CHRIS NELSON; circ. 70,000 (M), 101,000 (S).

Daily Herald–Tribune: 10604 100th St, Postal Bag 3000, Grande Prairie, AB T8V 6V4; tel. (403) 532-1110; fax (403) 532-2120; e-mail bowes@telusplanet.net; internet www.bowesnet.com/dht; f. 1913; Publr PETER J. WOOLSEY; Man. Editor FRED RINNE; circ. 9,000 (E).

Edmonton Journal: POB 2421, Edmonton, AB T5J 2S6; tel. (780) 429-5100; fax (780) 429-5536; e-mail bcox@the-journal.southam.ca; internet www.edmontonjournal.com; f. 1903; Publr LINDA HUGHES; Editor-in-Chief MURDOCH DAVIS; circ. 141,000 (M); 134,000 (S).

Edmonton Sun: 4990 92nd Ave, Suite 250, Edmonton, AB T6B 3A1; tel. (780) 468-0100; fax (780) 468-0128; e-mail edmonton .sun@ccinet.ab.ca; internet www.canoe.ca; f. 1978; Publr CRAIG MARTIN; Editor PAUL STANWAY; circ. 73,000 (M), 110,000 (S).

Fort McMurray Today: 8550 Franklin Ave, Fort McMurray, AB T9H 3G1; tel. (403) 743-8186; fax (403) 790-1006; e-mail today@ ccinet.ab.ca; Publr TIM O'ROURKE; Editor DARRELL SKIDNUK; circ. 5,000 (E).

Lethbridge Herald: 504 Seventh St South, POB 670, Lethbridge, AB T1J 3Z7; tel. (403) 328-4411; fax (403) 328-4536; internet www .lethbridgeherald.com; f. 1907; Publr PETER SCOTT; Man. Editor MICHAEL J. HERTZ; circ. 22,000 (E), 19,000 (S).

Medicine Hat News: 3257 Dunmore Rd, SE, POB 10, Medicine Hat, AB T1A 7E6; tel. (403) 527-1101; fax (403) 527-6029; internet www.medicinehatnews.com; f. 1887; Publr MICHAEL J. HERTZ; Man. Editor GORDON WRIGHT; circ. 14,000 (E).

Red Deer Advocate: 2950 Bremner Ave, Bag 5200, Red Deer, AB T4N 5G3; tel. (403) 343-2400; fax (403) 341-4772; e-mail editorial@ advocate.red-deer.ab.ca; Editor JOE MCLAUGHLIN; circ. 19,000 (M).

British Columbia

Alaska Highway News: 9916 89th St, Fort St John, BC V1J 3T8; tel. (250) 785-5631; fax (250) 785-3522; Publr BRUCE LANTZ; Editor JOE PAVLIN; circ. 4,000 (E).

Alberini Valley Times: 4918 Napier St, POB 400, Port Alberini, BC V9Y 7N1; tel. (250) 723-8171; fax (250) 723-0586; e-mail avtimes @arrowsmith.net; internet www.arrowsmith.net/~avtimes; Publr NIGEL E. HANNAFORD; circ. 7,000 (M).

Daily Bulletin: 335 Spokane St, Kimberley, BC V1A 1Y9; tel. (250) 427-5333; fax (250) 427-5336; e-mail bulletin@cyberlink.bc.ca; f. 1932; Publr STEEN JORGENSEN; Editor CHRIS DOUAN; circ. 2,000 (E).

Daily Courier: 550 Doyle Ave, Kelowna, BC V1Y 7V1; tel. (250) 762-4445; fax (250) 763-0194; e-mail alison.yesilcimen@ok.bc.ca;

internet www.ok.bc.ca; f. 1904; Publr ALISON YESILCIMEN; Exec Editor ROSS FREAKE; circ. 18,000 (E); 16,000 (S).

Daily News: 2575 McCullough Rd, Nanaimo, BC V9S 5W5; tel. (250) 758-4917; fax (250) 758-4513; f. 1874; Publr NIGEL LARK; Man. Editor DOYLE MACKINNON; circ. 9,000 (E).

Daily Townsman: 822 Cranbrook St North, Cranbrook, BC V1C 3R9; tel. (250) 426-5201; fax (250) 426-5003; e-mail townsman@ cyberlink.bc.ca; Publr STEEN JORGENSEN; Editor DAVID SANDS; circ. 4,000 (E).

Kamloops Daily News: 393 Seymour St, Kamloops, BC V2C 6P6; tel. (250) 372-2331; fax (250) 374-3884; e-mail kamnews@ wkpowerlink.com; internet www.southam.com/kamloopsdailynews/; f. 1930; Publr DALE BRIN; Editor MEL ROTHENBURGER; circ. 14,000 (E).

Nelson Daily News: 266 Baker St, Nelson, BC V1L 4H3; tel. (250) 352-3552; fax (250) 352-2418; e-mail adnews@netidea.com; internet www.nelsondailynews.com; f. 1902; Publr JOHN A. SMITH; Editor DREW EDWARDS; circ. 4,000 (E).

Peace River Block News: 901 100th Ave, Dawson Creek, BC V1G 1W2; tel. (250) 782-4888; fax (250) 782-6770; e-mail prbnews@ pris.bc.ca; f. 1930; Publr MARGARET FORBES; Editor JEREMY HAINS-WORTH; circ. 3,000 (E), 11,000 (S).

Penticton Herald: 186 Nanaimo Ave West, Suite 101, Penticton, BC V2A 1N4; tel. (250) 492-4002; fax (250) 492-2403; e-mail jhcoady@ok.bc.ca; internet www.ok.bc.ca/ph; Publr ALISON YESIL-CIMEN; Man. Editor DAVID MARSDEN; circ. 9,000 (E).

Prince George Citizen: 150 Brunswick St, POB 5700, Prince George, BC V2L 5K9; tel. (250) 562-2441; fax (250) 562-7453; e-mail pgcnews@prg.southam.ca; internet www.princegeorgecitizen.com; f. 1957; Publr DEL LAVERDURE; Man. Editor JOHN HARDING; circ. 18,000 (E).

The Province: 200 Granville St, Suite 1, Vancouver, BC V6C 3N3; tel. (604) 605-2222; fax (604) 605-2720; internet www .vancouverprovince.com; f. 1898; Publr DENNIS SKULSKY; Editor-in-Chief VIVIENNE SOSNOWSKI; circ. 160,000 (M), 196,000 (S).

Sing Tao Daily News: 8874 Hudson St, Vancouver, BC V6A 2V1; tel. (604) 261-5066; fax (604) 261-7093; Chinese; Editor PAUL TSANG; circ. 15,000 (M).

Times Colonist: 2621 Douglas St, POB 300, Victoria, BC V8T 4M2; tel. (250) 380-5211; fax (250) 380-5353; e-mail timesc@ interlink.bc.ca; f. 1858; Publr PETER BAILLIE; Editor-in-Chief BOB POOLE; circ. 76,000 (M), 76,000 (S).

Trail Daily Times: 1163 Cedar Ave, Trail, BC V1R 4B8; tel. (250) 368-8551; fax (250) 368-8550; e-mail konschuk@wkpowerlink.com; Publr JON JARRETT; Editor TRACY KONSCHUK; circ. 7,000 (E).

The Vancouver Sun: 200 Granville St, Suite 1, Vancouver, BC V6C 3N3; tel. (604) 732-2111; fax (604) 732-2323; internet www .vancouversun.com; f. 1886; Editor-in-Chief NEIL REYNOLDS; circ. 190,000 (M), 247,000 (Sat.).

World Journal (Vancouver): 2288 Clark Drive, Vancouver, BC V5N 3G8; tel. (604) 876-1338; fax (604) 876-9191; Chinese; Publr WILSON CHIEN; circ. 10,000 (M).

Manitoba

Brandon Sun: 501 Rosser Ave, Brandon, MB R7A 0K4; tel. (204) 727-2451; fax (204) 727-0385; e-mail bmarshall@brandonsun.com; internet www.brandonsun.com; f. 1882; Publr RUDY REDEKOP; Man. Editor BRIAN D. MARSHALL; circ. 18,000 (E), 24,000 (S).

Daily Graphic: 1941 Saskatchewan Ave West, POB 130, Portage La Prairie, MB R1N 3B4; tel. (204) 857-3427; fax (204) 239-1270; e-mail plpnews@mb.sympatico.ca; Publr W. J. HAMILTON; Editor IAN R. WHITE; circ. 4,000 (E).

Flin Flon Reminder: 10 North Ave, Flin Flon, MB R8A 0T2; tel. (204) 687-3454; fax (204) 687-4473; e-mail reminder@mb .sympatico.ca; f. 1946; Publr RANDY DANELIUK; Editor RICH BILLY; circ. 4,000 (E).

Winnipeg Free Press: 1355 Mountain Ave, Winnipeg, MB R2X 3B6; tel. (204) 697-7000; fax (204) 697-7375; internet www .winnipegfreepress.com; f. 1874; Publr H. R. REDEKOP; Editor NICH-OLAS HIRST; circ. 131,000 (E), 187,000 (Sat.), 144,000 (S).

Winnipeg Sun: 1700 Church Ave, Winnipeg, MB R2X 3A2; tel. (204) 694-2022; fax (204) 632-8709; e-mail editor@wpgsun.com; internet www.canoe.ca/winnipegsun/home.html; f. 1980; Publr GORDAN NORRIE; Man. Editor BILL DAVIDSON; circ. 45,000 (M), 58,000 (S).

New Brunswick

L'Acadie Nouvelle: 476 blvd St-Pierre ouest, CP 5536, Caraquet, NB E1W 1B7; tel. (506) 727-4444; fax (506) 727-7620; e-mail infos@acadienouvelle.com; internet www.capacadie.com/ acadienouvelle/index.cfm; f. 1984; Publr GILLES GAGNÉ; Editor LORIO ROY; circ. 17,000 (M).

Daily Gleaner: POB 3370, Fredericton, NB E3B 5A2; tel. (506) 452-6671; fax (506) 452-7405; e-mail dgnews@nbnet.nb.ca; internet www.nbnews.com/dailygleaner; f. 1880; Publr BRIAN BUTTERS; Editor-in-Chief HAL WOOD; circ. 30,000 (E).

Telegraph–Journal (M), **St John Times–Globe** (E): 210 Crown St, POB 2350, Saint John, NB E2L 3V8; tel. (506) 632-8888; fax (506) 648-2654; e-mail tjetg@nbnet.nb.ca; internet www.nbnews .com; Publr JONATHAN FRANKIN (Telegraph–Journal), VICTOR MLODECKI (Times–Globe); circ. 21,000 (M), 23,000 (E).

Times–Transcript: 939 Main St, POB 1001, Moncton, NB E1C 8P3; tel. (506) 859-4900; fax (506) 859-4899; e-mail news@ timestranscript.com; internet www.nbnews.com/timestranscript; f. 1983; Publr JONATHAN FRANKLIN; Man. Editor MIKE BEMBRIDGE; circ. 39,000 (E), 46,000 (Sat.).

Newfoundland

Telegram: Columbus Drive, POB 5970, St John's, NF A1C 5X7; tel. (709) 364-6300; fax (709) 364-9333; e-mail telegram@ thetelegram.com; internet www.thetelegram.com; f. 1879; Publr MILLER H. AYRE; Man. Editor BRETTON LONEY; circ. 33,000 (E), 57,000 (Sat.).

Western Star: 106 West St, POB 460, Corner Brook, NF A2H 6E7; tel. (709) 634-4348; fax (709) 634-9824; e-mail star@thezone.net; f. 1900; Publr IAN BAIRD; Editor RICHARD WILLIAMS; circ. 9,000 (M).

Nova Scotia

Amherst Daily News: POB 280, Amherst, NS B4H 3Z2; tel. (902) 667-5102; fax (902) 667-0419; e-mail cumbpub@istar.ca; f. 1893; Publr EARL J. GOUCHIE; Editor JOHN CONRAD; circ. 5,000 (M).

Cape Breton Post: 255 George St, POB 1500, Sydney, NS B1P 6K6; tel. (902) 564-5451; fax (902) 562-7077; e-mail maned@cbpost.com; internet www.capebretonpost.com; f. 1900; Publr MILTON ELLIS; Man. Editor FRED JACKSON; circ. 28,000 (M).

Chronicle–Herald (M), **Mail–Star** (E): 1650 Argyle St, POB 610, Halifax, NS B3J 2T2; tel. (902) 426-2811; fax (902) 426-3014; e-mail ombud@herald.ns.ca; internet www.herald.ns.ca; Publr GRAHAM W. DENNIS; Man. Editor TERRY O'NEIL; circ. 90,000 (M), 54,000 (Sat.), 21,000 (E).

Daily News: POB 8330, Station A, Halifax, NS B3K 5M1; tel. (902) 468-1222; fax (902) 468-3609; e-mail citydesk@hfxnews.southam.ca; internet www.hfxnews.southam.ca/; f. 1974; Publr. MARK RICH-ARDSON; Editor-in-Chief BILL TURPIN; circ. 24,000 (M), 33,000 (S).

Evening News: 352 East River Rd, POB 159, New Glasgow, NS B2H 5E2; tel. (902) 752-3000; fax (902) 752-1945; f. 1910; Publr RICHARD RUSSELL; Man. Editor DOUG MACNEIL; circ. 8,000 (E).

Truro Daily News: 6 Louise St, POB 220, Truro, NS B2N 5C3; tel. (902) 893-9405; fax (902) 893-0518; e-mail editor.news@north .nsis.com; internet www.truro.canada.com; f. 1891; Publr LEITH ORR; Man. Editor BILL MCGUIRE; circ. 8,000 (E).

Ontario

Barrie Examiner: 16 Bayfield St, Barrie, ON L4M 4T6; tel. (705) 726-6537; fax (705) 726-7706; e-mail examiner@sympatico.ca; f. 1864; Publr RON LAURIN; Man. Editor JOANNE KUSHNIER; circ. 9,000 (M).

Beacon–Herald: 108 Ontario St, POB 430, Stratford, ON N5A 6T6; tel. (519) 271-2220; fax (519) 271-1026; e-mail beacan@cyg.net; f. 1854; Publr CHARLES W. DINGMAN; Man. Editor JOHN KASTNER; circ. 12,000 (E).

Brockville Recorder and Times: 23 King St West, POB 10, Brockville, ON K6V 5T8; tel. (613) 342-4441; fax (613) 342-4456; e-mail editor@recorder.ca; internet www.recorder.ca; f. 1821; Publr BOB DOORNEBAL; Editor BARRY RAISON; circ. 13,000 (E).

Cambridge Reporter: 26 Ainslie St South, POB 1510, Cambridge, ON N1R 5T2; tel. (519) 621-3810; fax (519) 621-8239; e-mail news@ cambridge-reporter.com; internet www.cambridge-reporter.com; f. 1846; Publr L. R. (VERNE) SHAULL; Editor CLYDE WARRINGTON; circ. 7,000 (E).

Chatham Daily News: 45 Fourth St, POB 2007, Chatham, ON N7M 5M6; tel. (519) 354-2000; fax (519) 436-0949; e-mail chathamnews@cha.southam.ca; f. 1862; Publr JOHN CHEEK; Man. Editor JIM BLAKE; circ. 14,000 (E).

Chronicle–Journal: 75 Cumberland St South, Thunder Bay, ON P7B 1A3; tel. (807) 343-6200; fax (807) 345-5991; e-mail cj-editorial@ cwconnect.ca; Publr COLIN BRUCE; Man. Editor PETER HAGGERT; circ. 32,000 (M), 38,000 (S).

Cobourg Daily Star: 415 King St West, POB 400, Cobourg, ON K9A 4L1; tel. (905) 372-0131; fax (905) 372-4966; e-mail starletters @eagle.ca; internet www.eagle.ca/cobourgstar; Publr MIKE WALSH; Editorial Dir JIM GROSSMITH; circ. 6,000 (E).

Daily Observer: 186 Alexander St, Pembroke, ON K8A 4L9; tel. (613) 732-3691; fax (613) 732-2645; e-mail observer@webhart.net; f. 1855; Publr STEVE GLOSTER; Man. Editor PETER LAPINSKIE; circ. 6,000 (E).

Daily Press: 187 Cedar St South, POB 560, Timmins, ON P4N 2G9; tel. (705) 268-5050; fax (705) 268-7373; e-mail tdp@nt.net;

internet www.timminspress.com; f. 1933; Publr SYL BÉLISLE; Man. Editor DAVE MCGEE; circ. 10,000 (M).

Le Droit: 47 rue Clarence, Pièce 222, CP 8860, succursale Terminus, Ottawa, ON K1G 3J9; tel. (613) 562-0111; fax (613) 562-6280; e-mail publicite@ledroit.com; internet www.ledroit.com; f. 1913; Publr PIERRE BERGERON; Man. Editor FRANÇOIS ROY; circ. 35,000 (M), 42,000 (Sat.).

The Expositor: 53 Dalhousie St, POB 965, Brantford, ON N3T 5S8; tel. (519) 756-2020; fax (519) 756-4911; e-mail expnews@ brtsoutham.ca; internet www.southam.com/brantfordexpositor/; f. 1852; Publr MICHAEL PEARCE; Editor DAVID SCHULTZ; circ. 23,000 (E).

Financial Post: 333 King St East, Toronto, ON M5A 4N2; tel. (416) 350-6300; fax (416) 350-6301; e-mail letters@ finpost.com; f. 1907; Publr and CEO WILLIAM NEILL; Editor ARTHUR JOHNSON; circ. 91,000 (M).

The Globe and Mail: 444 Front St West, Toronto, ON M5V 2S9; tel. (416) 585-5000; fax (416) 585-5085; e-mail newsroom@ globeandmail.ca; internet www.globeandmail.com; f. 1844; Publr PHILIP CRAWLEY; Editor RICHARD ADDIS; circ. 321,000 (M), 395,000 (Sat.).

Guelph Mercury: 14 Macdonnell St, POB 3604, Guelph, ON N1H 6P7; tel. (519) 822-4310; fax (519) 767-1681; e-mail mercury@ in.on.ca; f. 1854; Publr STEPHEN RHODES; Editor ED CASSAVOY; circ. 13,000 (E).

Hamilton Spectator: 44 Frid St, POB 300, Hamilton, ON L8N 3G3; tel. (905) 526-3333; fax (905) 526-1139; internet www .hamiltonspectator.com; f. 1846; Publr PATRICK J. COLLINS; Editor-in-Chief DANA ROBBINS; circ. 111,000 (M).

Intelligencer: 45 Bridge St East, POB 5600, Belleville, ON K8N 5C7; tel. (613) 962-9171; fax (613) 962-9652; e-mail intel@intranet .on.ca; f. 1870; Publr MICHAEL A. POWER; Man. Editor NICK PALMER; circ. 17,000 (M).

Kingston Whig–Standard: 6 Cataraqui St, POB 2300, Kingston, ON K7L 1Z7; tel. (613) 544-5000; fax (613) 530-4119; e-mail kinwhig@ thewhig.com; internet www.kingstonwhigstandard.com; f. 1834; Publr FRED LAFLAMME; Man. Editor STEVE LUKITS; circ. 28,000 (D).

Lindsay Daily Post: 15 William St North, Lindsay, ON K9V 3Z8; tel. (705) 324-2114; fax (705) 324-0174; e-mail lindsaypost@ .sympatico.ca; Publr MIKE WALKER; Editor TED MCFADDEN; circ. 9,000 (E).

London Free Press: 369 York St, POB 2280, London, ON N6A 4G1; tel. (519) 679-1111; fax (519) 667-5520; e-mail letters@lfpress.com; internet www.lfpress.com; f. 1849; Publr LES PYETTE; Editor ROB PAYNTER; circ. 99,000 (M), 125,000 (Sat.).

Ming Pao Daily News: 1355 Huntingwood Drive, Scarborough, ON M1S 3J1; tel. (416) 321-0093; fax (416) 321-3499; Chinese; Editor-in-Chief K. M. LUI; circ. 33,000 (M), 51,000 (S).

National Post: 1450 Don Mills Rd, Suite 300, Don Mills, ON M3B 2X7; tel. (416) 510-6748; fax (416) 510-6743; f. 1998; internet www.nationalpost.com; Publr DON BABICK; Editor-in-Chief KEN WHYTE; national newspaper with printing centres in nine cities; circ. 285,000 (M), 336,000 (Sat.).

Niagara Falls Review: 4801 Valley Way, POB 270, Niagara Falls, ON L2E 6T6; tel. (905) 358-5711; fax (905) 356-0785; e-mail review@nfreview.com; internet www.nfreview.com; f. 1879; Publr DAVID A. BEATTIE; Man. Editor MICHAEL BROWN; circ. 18,000 (E).

North Bay Nugget: 259 Worthington St, POB 570, North Bay, ON P1B 8J6; tel. (705) 472-3200; fax (705) 472-5128; e-mail nugnews@ onlink.net; f. 1909; Publr ROBERT HULL; Man. Editor BRUCE COWAN; circ. 18,000 (E).

Northern Daily News: 8 Duncan Ave, POB 1030, Kirkland Lake, ON P2N 3L4; tel. (705) 567-5321; fax (705) 567-6162; f. 1922; Publr SYL BELISLE; Editor TOM PERRY; circ. 6,000 (E).

Ottawa Citizen: 1101 Baxter Rd, POB 5020, Ottawa, ON K2C 3M4; tel. (613) 829-9100; fax (613) 596-3755; internet www .ottawacitizen.com; f. 1845; Publr RUSSELL A. MILLS; Editor SCOTT ANDERSON; circ. 141,000 (M), 185,000 (Sat.).

Ottawa Sun: 380 Hunt Club Rd, POB 9729, Station T, Ottawa, ON K1G 5H7; tel. (613) 739-7000; fax (613) 739-9383; internet www.canoe.ca/OttawaSun/home.html; Publr JUDY BULLIS; Editor-in-Chief MICHAEL THERIEN; circ. 50,000 (M), 56,000 (S).

The Packet and Times: 31 Colborne St East, Orillia, ON L3V 1T4; tel. (705) 325-1355; fax (705) 325-7691; e-mail packet@barint.on.ca; f. 1953; Publr KEN KOYAMA; Man. Editor MARK BISSET; circ. 8,000 (E).

Peterborough Examiner: 730 Kingsway, Peterborough, ON K9J 8L4; tel. (705) 745-4641; fax (705) 743-4581; e-mail news1@ ptbo.igs.net; f. 1884; Publr JIM AMBROSE; Man. Editor ED ARNOLD; circ. 22,000 (E).

The Record: 225 Fairway Rd, Kitchener, ON N2G 4E5; tel. (519) 894-2231; fax (519) 894-3912; internet www.therecord.com; f. 1878; Publr WAYNE MACDONALD; Editor LYNN HADDRALL; circ. 71,000 (E).

St Catharines Standard: 17 Queen St, St Catharines, ON L2R 5G5; tel. (905) 684-7251; fax (905) 684-6670; e-mail akrulik@scs .southam.ca; internet www.scstandard.com; f. 1891; Publr DAN GAYNOR; Man. Editor DOUG FIRBY; circ. 34,000 (E).

St Thomas Times–Journal: 16 Hincks St, St Thomas, ON N5R 5Z2; tel. (519) 631-2790; fax (519) 631-5653; internet www .bowesnet.com/timesjournal; f. 1882; Publr BRENT SPILAK; Man. Editor ROSS PORTER; circ. 9,000 (E).

Sarnia Observer: 140 Front St South, POB 3009, Sarnia, ON N7T 7M8; tel. (519) 344-3641; fax (519) 332-2951; e-mail observer@ xcelco.on.ca; f. 1917; Publr DARYL C. SMITH; Man. Editor TERRY SHAW; circ. 22,000 (E).

Sault Star: 145 Old Garden River Rd, POB 460, Sault Ste Marie, ON P6A 5M5; tel. (705) 759-3035; fax (705) 759-0102; ssmstar@ ssmsoutham.ca; internet www.saultstar.comssm; f. 1912; Publr ROBERT W. RICHARDSON; Man. Editor JOHN HALUCHA; circ. 22,000 (E).

Sentinel–Review: 18 Brock St, POB 1000, Woodstock, ON N4S 8A5; tel. (519) 537-2341; fax (519) 537-3049; e-mail sentinel@ annexweb.com; internet www.annexweb.com/sentinel; f. 1886; Publr PAT LOGAN; Man. Editor ALISON DOWNIE; circ. 9,000 (E).

Simcoe Reformer: 105 Donly Drive South, POB 370, Simcoe, ON N3Y 4L2; tel. (519) 426-5710; fax (519) 426-9255; e-mail refedit@ annexweb.com; internet www.annexweb.com/reformernet; f. 1858; Publr MICHAEL FREDERICKS; Man. Editor KIM NOVAK; circ. 9,000 (E).

Sing Tao Daily News: 417 Dundas St West, Toronto, ON M5T 1G6; tel. (416) 596-8168; fax (416) 861-8169; Chinese; Editor-in-Chief TONY KU; circ. 38,000 (M).

Standard–Freeholder: 44 Pitt St, Cornwall, ON K6J 3P3; tel. (613) 933-3160; fax (613) 933-7168; e-mail publisher@standard-freeholder .southam.ca; Publr MILTON S. ELLIS; Editor ALF LAFAVE; circ. 15,000 (M).

Sudbury Star: 33 MacKenzie St, Sudbury, ON P3C 4Y1; tel. (705) 674-5271; fax (705) 674-0624; e-mail editorial@sightseer.ca; f. 1909; Publr KEN D. SEGUIN; Man. Editor ROGER CAZABON; circ. 22,000 (E).

Sun Times: 290 9th St East, POB 200, Owen Sound, ON N4K 5P2; tel. (519) 376-2250; fax (519) 376-7190; e-mail owtimes@southam.ca; internet www.southam.com/owensoundsuntimes; f. 1853; Publr CLYDE T. WICKS; Editor JIM MERRIAM; circ. 19,000 (E).

Toronto Star: One Yonge St, Toronto, ON M5E 1E6; tel. (416) 367-2000; fax (416) 869-4328; e-mail newsroom@webramp.net; internet www.thestar.com; f. 1892; Publr JOHN A. HONDERICH; Man. Editor MARY DEANNE SHEARS; circ. 453,000 (M), 702,000 (Sat.), 501,000 (S).

Toronto Sun: 333 King St East, Toronto, ON M5A 3X5; tel. (416) 947-2221; fax (416) 361-1205; internet www.canoe.ca; f. 1971; Publr and CEO MARK STEVENS; Editor-in-Chief MIKE STROBEL; circ. 231,000 (M), 400,000 (S).

Welland-Port Colborne Tribune: 228 East Main St, POB 278, Welland, ON L3B 5P5; tel. (905) 732-2411; fax (905) 732-4883; e-mail tribune@iaw.on.ca; f. 1863; Publr L. R. (VERNE) SHAULL; Editor GARY MANNING; circ. 15,000 (M).

Windsor Star: 167 Ferry St, Windsor, ON N9A 4M5; tel. (519) 256-5533; fax (519) 255-5515; e-mail letters@win.southam.ca; internet www.southam.com/windsorstar; f. 1918; Publr JIM MCCORMACK; Editor WAYNE MORIARTY; circ. 77,000 (M).

World Journal (Toronto): 415 Eastern Ave, Toronto, ON M4M 1B7; tel. (416) 778-0889; fax (416) 778-4889; Chinese; Editor-in-Chief LOUIS CHU; circ. 38,000 (M).

Prince Edward Island

Guardian: 165 Prince St, POB 760, Charlottetown, PE C1A 4R7; tel. (902) 629-6000; fax (902) 566-3808; f. 1887; Publr DON BRANDER; Editor G. MACDOUGALL; circ. 22,000 (M).

Journal–Pioneer: 4 Queen St, POB 2480, Summerside, PE C1N 4K5; tel. (902) 436-2121; fax (902) 436-0784; e-mail dshea@itas.net; f. 1865; Publr SANDY RUNDLE; Editor DARLENE SHEA; circ. 11,000 (E).

Québec

Le Devoir: 2050 rue de Bleury, 9e étage, Montréal, QC H3A 3M9; tel. (514) 985-3333; fax (514) 985-3360; e-mail redaction@ledevoir .com; internet www.ledevoir.com; Publr BERNARD DESCÔTEAUX; Editor-in-Chief JEAN ROBERT SANSFAÇON; circ. 27,000 (M), 34,000 (Sat.).

The Gazette: 250 rue St-Antoine ouest, Montréal, QC H2Y 3R7; tel. (514) 987-2222; fax (514) 987-2270; internet www .montrealgazette.com; f. 1778; Publr MICHAEL GOLDBLOOM; Editor-in-Chief ALAN ALLNUTT; circ. 140,000 (M), 188,000 (Sat.), 133,000 (S).

Le Journal de Montréal: 4545 rue Frontenac, Montréal, QC H2H 2R7; tel. (514) 521-4545; fax (514) 525-542; f. 1964; Publr and Editor PIERRE FRANCOEUR; circ. 267,000 (M), 334,000 (Sat.).

Le Journal de Québec: 450 ave Béchard, Vanier, QC G1M 2E9; tel. (418) 683-1573; fax (418) 683-1027; f. 1967; Publr JEAN-CLAUDE L'ABBÉE; Chief Editor SERGE CÔTÉ; circ. 98,000 (M), 126,000 (Sat.), 101,000 (S).

Le Nouvelliste: 1920 rue Bellefeuille, CP 668, Trois Rivières, QC G9A 5J6; tel. (819) 376-2501; fax (819) 376-0946; e-mail information@lenouvelliste.qc.ca; internet www.lenouvelliste.qc.ca; f. 1920; Pres. and Publr JEAN SISTO; Editor-in-Chief ANDRÉ POITRAS; circ. 43,000 (M).

La Presse: 7 rue St-Jacques, Montréal, QC H2Y 1K9; tel. (514) 285-7272; fax (514) 285-6808; f. 1884; Pres. and Editor ROGER D. LANDRY; circ. 187,000 (M), 286,000 (Sat.), 196,000 (S).

Le Quotidien du Saguenay-Lac-St-Jean: 1051 blvd Talbot, Chicoutimi, QC G7H 5C1; tel. (418) 545-4474; fax (418) 690-8824; internet www.lequotidien.com; f. 1973; Pres. and Editor CLAUDE GAGNON; circ. 29,000 (M).

The Record: CP 1200, Sherbrooke, QC J1H 5L6; tel. (819) 569-9525; fax (819) 569-3945; internet www.sherbrookerecord.com; f. 1837; Publr RANDY KINNEAR; Editor SHARON MCCULLY; circ. 6,000 (M).

Le Soleil: 925 chemin St-Louis, CP 1547, succursale Terminus, Québec, QC G1K 7J6; tel. (418) 686-3394; fax (418) 686-3374; internet www.lesoleil.com; f. 1896; Pres. and Editor CLAUDE THIBODEAU; circ. 80,000 (M), 126,000 (Sat.), 89,000 (S).

La Tribune: 1950 rue Roy, Sherbrooke, QC J1K 2X8; tel. (819) 564-5454; fax (819) 564-8098; e-mail redaction@latribune.qc.ca; internet www.latribune.qc.ca; f. 1910; Pres. and Publr RAYMOND TARDIF; Editor-in-Chief MAURICE CLOUTIER; circ. 31,000 (M), 39,000 (Sat.).

La Voix de L'Est: 76 rue Dufferin, Granby, QC J2G 9L4; tel. (450) 375-4555; fax (450) 777-4865; e-mail redaction@lavoixdelest.qc.ca; internet www.lavoixdelest.qc.ca; f. 1945; Pres. and Publr JACQUES PRONOVOST; circ. 16,000 (M).

Saskatchewan

Daily Herald: 30 10th St East, POB 550, Prince Albert, SK S6V 5R9; tel. (306) 764-4276; fax (306) 763-3331; e-mail pa@dailyherald @sk.sympatico.ca; internet www.paherald.sk.ca; f. 1894; Publr CURT DUDDY; Man. Editor BARB GUSTAFSON; circ. 10,000 (M).

Leader–Post: 1964 Park St, POB 2020, Regina, SK S4P 3G4; tel. (306) 565-8211; fax (306) 565-2588; internet www.leaderpost.com; f. 1883; Publr GREG MCLEAN; Editor BOB HUGHES; circ. 58,000 (M).

StarPhoenix: 204 5th Ave North, Saskatoon, SK S7K 2P1; tel. (306) 652-9200; fax (306) 664-0433; e-mail spnews@thesp.com; internet www.thestarphoenix.com; f. 1902; Publr LYLE SINKEWICZ; Editor STEVE GIBB; circ. 62,000 (M).

Times–Herald: 44 Fairford St West, POB 3000, Moose Jaw, SK S6H 6E4; tel. (306) 692-6441; fax (306) 692-2101; e-mail editorial@mjtimes.sk.ca; internet www.mjtimes.sk.ca; f. 1889; Publr AB CALVERT; Editor LESLEY SHEPPARD; circ. 9,000 (E).

Yukon Territory

Whitehorse Star: 2149 2nd Ave, Whitehorse, Yukon, YT Y1A 1C5; tel. (867) 667-4481; fax (867) 668-7130; e-mail star@hypertech.yk.ca; internet www.whitehorsestar.com; f. 1985; Publr ROBERT ERLAM; Editor JIM BUTLER; circ. 3,000 (E).

SELECTED PERIODICALS

(W = weekly; F = fortnightly; M = monthly; Q = quarterly)

Alberta

Alberta FarmLIFE: 250 Shawville Blvd, SE, Calgary, AB T2Y 2Z7; tel. (403) 274-4002; fax (403) 274-4116; e-mail farmlife@ cadvision.com; Man. BRUCE TUNNICLIFFE; circ. 65,000; 24 a year.

Ukrainski Visti (Ukrainian News): 12227 107th Ave, Suite 1, Edmonton, AB T5M 1Y9; tel. (780) 488-3693; fax (780) 488-3859; e-mail ukrnews@compusmart.ab.ca; f. 1929; Ukrainian and English; Editor MARCO LEVYTSKY; circ. 4,000 (F).

British Columbia

BC Outdoors: 780 Beatty St, Suite 300, Vancouver, BC V6B 2M1; tel. (604) 687-1581; fax (604) 687-1925; e-mail oppubl@istar.ca; internet www.oppublishing.com; f. 1945; Editor GEORGE GRUENEFELD; circ. 37,000; 8 a year.

Pacific Yachting: 780 Beatty St, Suite 300, Vancouver, BC V6B 2M1; tel. (604) 606-4644; fax (604) 687-1925; e-mail oppubl@istar.ca; internet www.oppublishing.com; f. 1968; Editor DUART SNOW; circ. 15,000 (M).

Vancouver Magazine: 555 West 12th Ave, SE Tower, Suite 300, Vancouver, BC V5Z 4L4; tel. (604) 877-7732; fax (604) 877-4823; e-mail vanmag@vanmag.com; internet www.vanmag.com; f. 1957; Editor NICK ROCKEL; circ. 60,000; 9 a year.

Western Living: 555 West 12th Ave, SE Tower, Suite 300, Vancouver, BC V5Z 4L4; tel. (604) 877-7732; fax (604) 877-4849; e-mail westernliving@ican.net; f. 1971; Editor CAROLANN RULE; circ. 253,000 (M).

WestWorld BC: 4180 Lougheed Hwy, 4th Floor, Burnaby, BC V5C 6A7; tel. (604) 299-7311; fax (604) 299-9188; f. 1974; Editor PAT PRICE; circ. 495,000 (Q).

Manitoba

The Beaver: Exploring Canada's History: 167 Lombard Ave, Suite 478, Winnipeg, MB R3B 0T6; tel. (204) 988-9300; fax (204) 988-9309; e-mail beaver@cyberspc.mb.ca; f. 1920; Canadian social history; Editor ANNALEE GREENBERG; circ. 40,000; 6 a year.

Cattlemen: 201 Portage Ave, Suite 2500, Winnipeg, MB R3C 3A7; tel. (204) 944-5750; fax (204) 942-8463; e-mail gwinslow@fbc .unitedgrain.ca; internet www.agcanada.com; f. 1938; animal husbandry; Editor GREN WINSLOW; circ. 27,000 (M).

Country Guide: 201 Portage Ave, Suite 2500, Winnipeg, MB R3C 3A7; tel. (204) 944-5750; fax (204) 942-8463; internet www.agcanada .com; f. 1882; agriculture; Editor DAVID WREFORD; circ. 61,000; 11 a year.

Grainews: 201 Portage Ave, Suite 2500, POB 6600, Winnipeg, MB R3C 3A7; tel. (204) 944-5587; fax (204) 944-5416; e-mail dbedard@ fbc.unitedgrain.ca; internet www.agcanada.com; f. 1975; grain and cattle farming; Editor ANDY SIRSKI; circ. 47,000; 17 a year.

Kanada Kurier: 955 Alexander Ave, POB 1054, Winnipeg, MB R3C 2X8; tel. (204) 774-1883; fax (204) 783-5740; f. 1889; German; Editor RENATE ACHENBACH; circ. 25,000 (W).

The Manitoba Co-operator: 220 Portage Ave, POB 9800, Main Station, Winnipeg, MB R3C 3K7; tel. (204) 954-1400; fax (204) 954-1422; e-mail news@co-operator.mb.ca; f. 1925; farming; Editor JOHN W. MORRISS; circ. 17,000 (W).

Northwest Territories

L'Aquilon: POB 1325, Yellowknife, NT X1A 2N9; tel. (403) 873-6603; fax (403) 873-2158; e-mail aquilon@internorth.com; f. 1985; Editor ALAIN BESSETTE; circ. 1,000 (W).

The Hub: 3 Capital Drive, Suite 105, MacKenzie Hwy, Hay River, NT X0E 1Q2; tel. (867) 874-8577; fax (867) 874-2679; e-mail hub@ cancom.net; f. 1973; Editor CHRIS BRODEUR; circ. 3,000 (W).

News/North: 5108 50th St, Yellowknife, NT X1A 2R1; tel. (403) 873-4031; fax (403) 873-8507; e-mail newsnorth@nnsl.yk.ca; f. 1945; Editor JACK SIGVALDASON; circ. 11,000 (W).

Slave River Journal: 207 McDougal Rd, POB 990, Fort Smith, NT X0E 0P0; tel. (867) 872-2784; fax (867) 872-2754; e-mail srj@ aurora.net.nt.ca; Publr DON JAQUE; Editor BRENT KERRIGAN; circ. 2,000 (W).

Yellowknifer: 5108 50th St, Yellowknife, NT X1A 2R1; tel. (403) 873-4031; fax (403) 873-8507; e-mail yellowknifer@nnsl.yk.com; Editor BRUCE VALPY; circ. 5,000 (W).

Nova Scotia

Atlantic Progress Magazine: 1660 Hollis St, Suite 603, Halifax, NS B3J 1V7; tel. (902) 494-0999; fax (902) 494-0997; f. 1993; regional business; Editor DAVID HOLT; circ. 22,000; 8 a year.

Canadian Forum: 5502 Atlantic St, Halifax, NS B3H 1G4; tel. (902) 421-7022; fax (902) 425-0166; f. 1920; political, literary and economic; Editor ROBERT CLUDOS; circ. 9,000; 10 a year.

Nunavut

Nunatsiaq News: POB 8, Iqaluit, NT X0A 0H0; tel. (867) 979-5357; fax (867) 979-4763; e-mail nunat@nunanet.com; internet www.nunatsiaq.com; f. 1972; English and Inuktitut; Publr STEVEN ROBERTS; Editor JIM BELL; circ. 9,000 (W).

Ontario

Anglican Journal: 600 Jarvis St, Toronto, ON M4Y 2J6; tel. (416) 924-9199; fax (416) 921-4452; e-mail editor@national.anglican.ca; internet www.anglicanjournal.com; f. 1871; official publ. of the Anglican Church of Canada; Editor Rev. VIANNEY CARRIERE; circ. 250,000; 10 a year.

Books in Canada: 50 St Clair Ave East, 4th Floor, Toronto, ON M4T 1M9; tel. (416) 925-1543; fax (416) 925-7682; e-mail binc@ istar.ca; f. 1971; Editor DIANA KUPREL; circ. 8,000; 9 a year.

CA magazine: The Canadian Institute of Chartered Accountants, 277 Wellington St West, Toronto, ON M5V 3H2; tel. (416) 977-3222; fax (416) 204-3409; e-mail christian.bellavance@cica.ca; internet www.camagazine.com; f. 1911; Editor-in-Chief CHRISTIAN BELLAVANCE; circ. 69,000 (M).

Campus Canada: 287 MacPherson Ave, Toronto, ON M4V 1A4; tel. (416) 928-2909; fax (416) 966-1181; f. 1983; 30 campus edns; Man. Editor SARAH MOORE; circ. 125,000 (Q).

Canada Gazette: Canada Gazette Division, Public Works and Government Services, 350 Albert St, Ottawa, ON K1A 0S5; tel. (613) 991-1347; fax (613) 991-3540; f. 1867; official bulletin of the Govt of Canada; (W).

Canadian Architect: 1450 Don Mills Rd, Don Mills, ON M3B 2X7; tel. (416) 442-3390; fax (416) 442-2213; e-mail cdnarchitect@ southam.ca; internet www.cdnarchitect.com; f. 1955; Editor MARCO POLO; circ. 11,000 (M).

Canadian Art: 56 The Esplanade, Suite 310, Toronto, ON M5E 1R2; tel. (416) 368-8854; fax (416) 368-6135; e-mail rhodes@ canadianart.ca; internet www.canadianart.ca; Editor RICHARD RHODES; circ. 24,000 (Q).

Canadian Aviation & Aircraft for Sale: POB 47555, Hamilton, ON L8H 7S7; tel. (909) 544-0560; fax (909) 544-8121; e-mail jhminc@cml.com; f. 1928; Editor GARTH WALLACE; circ. 10,000; 6 a year.

Canadian Bar Review: Canadian Bar Asscn, 50 O'Connor St, Suite 902, Ottawa, ON K1P 6L2; tel. (613) 237-2925; fax (613) 237-0185; e-mail CBA:info@cba.org; internet www.cba.org; f. 1923; Editor Prof. EDWARD VEITCH; circ. 36,000 (Q).

Canadian Business: 777 Bay St, 5th Floor, Toronto, ON M5W 1A7; tel. (416) 596-5100; fax (416) 596-5152; internet www.canbus.com; f. 1927; Editor JOE CHIDLEY; circ. 81,000; 21 a year.

Canadian Chemical News: 130 Slater St, Suite 550, Ottawa, ON K1P 6E2; tel. (613) 232-6252; fax (613) 232-5862; e-mail info@cheminst.ca; internet www.accn.ca; f. 1949; Editor DINAH LAPRARIE; circ. 5,000; 10 a year.

Canadian Defence Quarterly: 310 Dupont St, Toronto, ON M5R 1V9; tel. (416) 968-7252; fax (416) 968-2377; e-mail cdq@baxter.net; Editor MARTIN SHADWICK; circ. 6,000.

Canadian Dental Association Journal: 1815 Alta Vista Drive, Ottawa, ON K1G 3Y6; tel. (613) 523-1770; fax (613) 523-7736; e-mail reception@cda-adc.ca; internet www.cda-adc.ca; f. 1935; Editor Dr JOHN O'KEEFE; (M).

Canadian Electronics: 135 Spy Court, Markham, ON L3R 5H6; tel. (905) 447-3222; fax (905) 477-4320; e-mail ce@actioncom .com; f. 1986; Editor TIM GOULDSON; circ. 22,000; 6 a year.

Canadian Geographic: 39 McArthur Ave, Ottawa, ON K1L 8L7; tel. (613) 745-4629; fax (613) 744-0947; e-mail editorial@cangeo.ca; internet www.canadiangeographic.ca; f. 1930; publ. of the Royal Canadian Geographical Soc.; Editor RICK BOYCHUK; circ. 227,000; 7 a year.

Canadian Home Workshop: 340 Ferrier St, Suite 210, Markham, ON L3R 2Z5; tel. (905) 475-8440; fax (905) 475-9246; e-mail letters@canadianworkshop.ca; f. 1977; do-it-yourself; Editorial Dir TOM HOPKINS; circ. 104,000 (M).

Canadian House & Home: 511 King St West, Suite 120, Toronto, ON M5V 2Z4; tel. (416) 593-0204; fax (416) 591-1630; e-mail exec@ canhomepub.com; internet www.canadianhouseandhome.com; f. 1982; Editor COBI LADNER; circ. 142,000; 9 a year.

Canadian Jewish News: 1500 Don Mills Rd, Suite 205, North York, ON M3B 3KY; tel. (416) 391-1836; fax (416) 391-0829; e-mail torcjn1@aol.com; Editor MORDECHAI BEN-DAT; circ. 44,000; 50 a year.

Canadian Medical Association Journal: 1867 Alta Vista Drive, Ottawa, ON K1G 3Y6; tel. (613) 731-8610; fax (613) 565-5471; e-mail pubs@cma.ca; internet www.cma.ca; f. 1911; Editor Dr JOHN HOEY; circ. 59,000; 24 a year.

Canadian Musician: 23 Hannover Drive, Suite 7, St Catharines, ON L2W 1A3; tel. (905) 641-1512; fax (905) 641-1648; e-mail info@nor.com; internet www.canadianmusician.com; f. 1979; Man. Editor JIM NORRIS; circ. 30,000; 6 a year.

Canadian Nurse/L'infirmière canadienne: 50 Driveway, Ottawa, ON K2P 1E2; tel. (613) 237-2133; fax (613) 237-3520; e-mail cnj@cna-nurses.ca; f. 1905; journal of the Canadian Nurses' Asscn; Editor-in-Chief JUDITH HAINES; circ. 111,000; 10 a year.

Canadian Pharmaceutical Journal: c/o C. K. Goodman, Inc, 1382 Hurontario St, Mississauga, ON L5G 3H4; tel. (905) 278-6700; fax (905) 278-4850; f. 1868; Editor ANDREW REINBOLDT; circ. 13,000; 10 a year.

Canadian Public Policy/Analyse de Politiques: School of Policy Studies, Rm 409, Queen's University, Kingston, ON K7L 3N6; tel. (613) 533-6644; fax (613) 533-6960; e-mail cpp@qsilver .queensu.ca; internet www.qsilver.queensu.ca/~cpp/; Editor CHARLES M. BEACH; circ. 1,000 (Q).

Canadian Travel Press Weekly: 310 Dupont St, Toronto, ON M5R 1V9; tel. (416) 968-7252; fax (416) 968-2377; e-mail ctp@baxter.net; Editor-in-Chief EDITH BAXTER; circ. 13,000; 46 a year.

Chatelaine: 777 Bay St, Suite 405, Toronto, ON M5W 1A7; tel. (416) 596-5891; fax (416) 596-5158; e-mail chatcour@maclean .hunter-quebec.qc.ca; internet www.chatelaine.com; f. 1928; women's journal; Editor RONA MAYNARD; circ. 803,000 (M).

ComputerWorld Canada: 55 Town Centre Court, Scarborough, ON M1P 4X4; tel. (416) 290-0240; fax (416) 290-0238; internet www.lti.on.ca; f. 1984; Editor-in-Chief NORMAN TOLLINSKY; circ. 47,000; 25 a year.

Elm Street: 665 Bay St, Suite 1100, Toronto, ON M5G 2K4; tel. (416) 595-9944; fax (416) 595-7217; e-mail elmstreet@m-v-p.com; f. 1996; women's interest; Editor-in-Chief GWEN SMITH; circ. 600,000; 8 a year.

Farm & Country: One Yonge St, Suite 1504, Toronto, ON M5E 1E5; tel. (416) 364-5324; fax (416) 364-5857; e-mail agpub@inforamp.net; f. 1936; Editor RICHARD CHARTERIS; circ. 43,000; 23 a year.

Flare: 777 Bay St, Suite 405, Toronto, ON M5W 1A7; tel. (416) 596-5891; fax (416) 596-5158; e-mail editors@flare.com; internet www.flare.com; f. 1964; women's interest; Editor-in-Chief SUZANNE BOYD; cir. 174,000 (M).

Hockey News: 777 Bay St, Suite 2700, Toronto, ON M5G 2N1; tel. (416) 340-8000; fax (416) 340-2786; internet www.thn.com; f. 1947; Editor-in-Chief STEVE DRYDEN; circ. 205,000; 42 a year.

Holstein Journal: 9120 Leslie St, Unit 105, Richmond Hill, ON L4B 3J9; tel. (905) 886-4222; fax (905) 886-0037; e-mail subs@holsteinjournal.com; internet www.holsteinjournal.com; f. 1938; Editor BONNIE COOPER; circ. 5,000 (M).

Kanadai Magyarsag (Canadian Hungarians): 74 Advance Rd, Etobicoke, ON M8Z 2T7; tel. (416) 233-3131; fax (416) 233-5984; e-mail csabogal@dhost.com; circ. 10,000 (W).

Legion Magazine: 359 Kent St, Suite 407, Ottawa, ON K2P 0R6; tel. (613) 235-8741; fax (613) 233-7159; e-mail magazine@legion.ca; f. 1926; internet www.legionmagazine.com; Editor MAC JOHNSTON; circ. 383,000; 5 a year.

Maclean's Canada's Weekly Newsmazagine: 777 Bay St, Suite 405, Toronto, ON M5W 1A7; tel. (416) 596-5891; fax (416) 596-5158; e-mail letters@macleans.ca; internet www.macleans.co; f. 1905; Editor-in-Chief ROBERT LEWIS; circ. 500,000.

Northern Miner: 1450 Don Mills Rd, Don Mills, ON M3B 2X7; tel. (416) 510-6744; fax (416) 442-2181; e-mail tnm@southam.ca; internet www.northernminer.com; f. 1915; Editor VIVIAN DANIELSON; circ. 23,000 (W).

Ontario Medical Review: 525 University Ave, Suite 300, Toronto, ON M5G 2K7; tel. (416) 599-2580; fax (416) 340-2232; e-mail jeff_henry@oma.org; internet www.oma.org; f. 1922; Editor JEFF HENRY; circ. 24,000 (M).

Oral Health: 1450 Don Mills Rd, Don Mills, ON M3B 2X7; tel. (416) 442-2193; fax (416) 442-2214; e-mail cwilson@corporate.southam.ca; f. 1911; dentistry; Man. Editor CATHERINE WILSON; circ. 17,000 (M).

Photo Life: 1 Dundas St West, Suite 2500, POB 84, Toronto, ON M5G 1G3; tel. (800) 905-7468; fax (800) 664-2739; e-mail write@photolife.com; internet www.photolife.com; f. 1976; Editor-in-Chief SUZY KETENE; circ. 74,000; 6 a year.

Quill & Quire: 70 The Esplanade, Suite 210, Toronto, ON M5E 1R2; tel. (416) 360-0044; fax (416) 955-0794; e-mail quill@idirect.com; f. 1935; book-publishing industry; Editor SCOTT ANDERSON; circ. 7,000 (M).

Style: 1448 Lawrence Ave East, Suite 302, Toronto, ON M4A 2V6; tel. (416) 755-5199; fax (416) 755-9123; e-mail style@style.ca; internet www.style.ca; f. 1888; Editor DORIS MONTANERA; circ. 12,000 (M).

Style at Home: 25 Sheppard Ave West, Suite 100, Toronto, ON M2N 6S7; tel. (416) 733-7600; fax (416) 218-3632; f. 1997; e-mail letters@styleathome.com; Editor GAIL JOHNSTON HABS; circ. 204,000; 8 a year.

Sympatico Netlife: 25 Sheppard Ave West, Suite 100, North York, ON M2N 6S7; tel. (416) 733-7600; fax (416) 733-8272; e-mail giffen@sympatico.ca; internet www.sympatico.ca/netlife; computer technology; Editor PETER GIFFEN; circ. 450,000; 6 a year.

Toronto Life Magazine: 59 Front St East, 3rd Floor, Toronto, ON M5E 1B3; tel. (416) 364-3333; fax (416) 861-1169; internet www.torontolife.com; f. 1966; Editor JOHN MACFARLANE; circ. 97,000 (M).

Tribute Magazine: 71 Barber Greene Rd, Don Mills, ON M3C 2A2; tel. (416) 445-0544; fax (416) 445-2894; internet www.tribute.ca; f. 1984; entertainment; Publr and Editor SANDRA STEWART; circ. 500,000; 9 a year.

TV Guide: 25 Sheppard Ave West, Suite 100, North York, ON M2N 6S7; tel. (416) 733-7600; fax (416) 733-3632; e-mail tvguide@telemedia.org; internet www.tvguide.ca; f. 1976; Editor CHRISTOPHER LOUDON; circ. 838,000 (W).

TV Times: 1450 Don Mills Rd, Don Mills, ON M3B 2X7; tel. (416) 442-3444; fax (416) 442-2088; f. 1969; 14 regional edns; circ. 1,941,000 (W).

Québec

L'Actualité: 1001 blvd de Maisonneuve ouest, Montréal, QC H3A 3E1; tel. (514) 845-2543; fax (514) 845-7503; e-mail ucteour@maclean-hunter-quebec.qc.ca; f. 1976; current affairs; Editor DAVID A. LADKIN; circ. 191,000 (M).

Affaires Plus: 1100 blvd René-Lévesque ouest, 24e étage, Montréal, QC H3B 4X9; tel. (514) 392-9000; fax (514) 392-4726; e-mail aplus@transcontinental.ca; internet www.transcontinental-gtc.com; f. 1978; Editor-in-Chief MARIE-AGNÈS THELLIER; circ. 96,000 (M).

Le Bulletin des Agriculteurs: 1001 blvd de Maisonneuve ouest, Montréal, QC H3A 3E1; tel. (514) 845-5141; fax (514) 845-6261; e-mail info@lebulletin.com; internet www.lebulletin.com; f. 1918; Editor SIMON M. GUERTIN; circ. 24,000 (M).

Canadian Forest Industries: 1 rue Pacifique, Ste-Anne-de-Bellevue, QC H9X 1C5; tel. (514) 457-2211; fax (514) 457-2558; e-mail jcft@aei.ca; f. 1880; Editor SCOTT JAMIESON; circ. 13,000; 8 a year.

Châtelaine: 1001 blvd de Maisonneuve ouest, 11e étage, Montréal, QC H3A 3E1; tel. (514) 843-2504; fax (514) 845-4302; e-mail lettres@chatelaine-quebec.com; internet www.chatelaine-quebec.com; f. 1960; Editor CATHERINE ELIE; circ. 207,000 (M).

CIM Bulletin: 3400 blvd de Maisonneuve ouest, Bureau 1210, Montréal, QC H3Z 3B8; tel. (514) 939-2710; fax (514) 939-2714; internet www.cim.org; publ. by the Canadian Inst. of Mining, Metallurgy and Petroleum; Editor PERLA GANTZ; circ. 10,000 (M).

Il Cittadino Canadese: 5960 Jean-Talon est, Bureau 209, Montréal, QC H1S 1M2; tel. (514) 253-2332; fax (514) 253-6574; f. 1941; Italian; Editor BASILIO GIORDANO; circ. 46,000 (W).

Equinox: 11450 blvd Albert-Hudon, Montréal-Nord, QC H1G 3J9; tel. (514) 327-4464; fax (514) 327-7592; e-mail eqxmag@globetrotter.net; internet www.equinox.ca; f. 1982; Editor ALAN MORANTZ; circ. 130,000; 6 a year.

Harrowsmith Country Life: 11450 blvd Albert-Hudon, Montréal-Nord, QC H1G 3J9; tel. (514) 327-4464; fax (514) 327-0514; e-mail hclmag@globetrotter.net; f. 1986; Editor TOM CRUICKSHANK; circ. 190,000; 6 a year.

Le Lundi: 7 chemin Bates, Outremont, QC H2V 1A6; tel. (514) 270-1100; fax (514) 270-4810; f. 1976; Editor MICHAEL CHOINIÈRE; circ. 62,000 (W).

Le Producteur de Lait Québécois: 555 blvd Roland-Thérrien, Longueuil, QC J4H 3Y9; tel. (514) 679-0530; fax (514) 670-4788; e-mail rioiseau@tcn.upa.qc.ca; f. 1980; dairy farming; Editor-in-Chief JEAN VIGNEAULT; circ. 12,000 (M).

Progrès-Dimanche: 1051 blvd Talbot, Chicoutimi, QC G7H 5C1; tel. (418) 545-4474; fax (418) 690-8805; internet www.lequotidien.com; f. 1964; Pres. and Editor CLAUDE GAGNON; circ. 45,000 (W).

Québec Science: 3430 rue St-Denis, Bureau 300, Montréal, QC H2X 3L3; tel. (514) 843-6888; fax (514) 843-4897; e-mail courrier@QuebecScience.qc.ca; internet www.cybersciences.com; f. 1969; Editor-in-Chief RAYMOND LEMIEUX; circ. 32,000; 10 a year.

Rénovation Bricolage: 7 chemin Bates, Outremont, QC H2V 1A6; tel. (514) 270-1100; fax (514) 270-9618; e-mail renobrico@publicor.ca; f. 1976; Editor NICOLE LABBÉ; circ. 35,000; 10 a year.

Revue Commerce: 1100 blvd René-Lévesque ouest, 24e étage, Montréal, QC H3B 4X9; tel. (514) 392-9000; fax (514) 392-4726; e-mail commerce@transcontinental.ca; internet www.transcontinental-gtc.com; f. 1898; Editor-in-Chief PIERRE DUHAMEL; circ. 44,000 (M).

Sélection du Reader's Digest: 1100 blvd Réne-Lévesque ouest, Montréal, QC H3B 5H5; tel. (514) 940-7328; fax (514) 940-7340; e-mail manon.sylvain@readersdigest.com; internet www.readersdigest.ca; f. 1947; Editor-in-Chief LISE VERSCHELDEN; circ. 321,000 (M).

La Terre de Chez Nous: 555 blvd Roland-Thérrien, Longueuil, QC J4H 3Y9; tel. (514) 679-0530; fax (514) 679-5436; e-mail rioiseau@tcn.upa.qc.ca; f. 1929; agriculture and forestry; Editor REJEAN POULIOT; circ. 40,000 (W).

TV Hebdo: 2020 rue Université, 20e étage, Montréal, QC H3A 2A5; tel. (514) 848-7000; fax (514) 848-7070; e-mail tv@trustar.com; f. 1960; Editor-in-Chief JEAN-LOUIS PODLESAK; circ. 223,000 (W).

Saskatchewan

Farm Light & Power: 2352 Smith St, Regina, SK S4P 2P6; tel. (306) 525-3305; fax (306) 757-1810; f. 1959; Editor TOM BRADLEY; circ. 71,000 (M).

Western Producer: 2310 Millar Ave, POB 2500, Saskatoon, SK S7K 2C4; tel. (306) 665-3500; fax (306) 934-2401; internet www.producer.com; f. 1923; agriculture; Editor BARB GLEN; circ. 96,000 (W).

Yukon Territory

Yukon News: 211 Wood St, Whitehorse, YT Y1A 2E4; tel. (867) 667-6285; fax (867) 668-3755; e-mail plesniak@yukon-news.com; internet www.yukon-news.com; f. 1960; Editor PETER LESNIAK; circ. 8,000; 3 a week.

NEWS AGENCIES

The Canadian Press: 36 King St East, Toronto, ON M5C 2L9; tel. (416) 364-0321; fax (416) 364-0207; internet www.cp.org; f. 1917; national news co-operative; 102 newspaper mems; Chair. MICHAEL G. SIFTON; Pres. ERIC MORRISON.

Foreign Bureaux

Agence France-Presse (AFP): 231 rue St-Jacques, Bureau 1201, Montréal, QC H2Y 1M6; tel. (514) 288-2777; fax (514) 288-3506; e-mail afpcanada@afp.com; internet www.afp.com; Bureau Chief CHRISTINE COURCOL; also office in Toronto.

Agenzia Nazionale Stampa Associata (ANSA) (Italy): 150 Wellington St, Press Gallery, Rm 703, Ottawa, ON K1P 5A4; tel. (613) 235-4248; fax (613) 235-4248; Rep. ELIO COPPOLA.

Associated Press (USA): 36 King St East, Toronto, ON M5C 2L9; tel. (416) 368-1388.

Deutsche Presse-Agentur (dpa) (Germany): 702 National Press Bldg, 150 Wellington St, Ottawa, ON K1P 5A4; tel. (613) 234-6024; Correspondent BARBARA HALSIG.

Informatsionnoye Telegrafnoye Agentstvo Rossii—Telegrafnoye Agentstvo Suverennykh Stran (ITAR—TASS) (Russia): 200 Rideau Terrace, Suite 1305, Ottawa, ON K1M OZ3; tel. (613) 745-4310; fax (613) 745-5581; Correspondent NIKOLAI SETOUNSKI.

Inter-Press Service (IPS) (Italy): 1262 Kingston Ave, Ottawa, ON K1Z 8K6; tel. (613) 992-4517; also office in Montréal.

Reuters (United Kingdom): 2020 rue Université, Bureau 1020, Montréal, QC H3A 2A5; tel. (514) 282-0744; fax (514) 844-2327; also office in Vancouver.

Agencia EFE (Spain), Jiji Tsushin (Japan), Prensa Latina (Cuba), United Press International (USA) and Xinhua (New China) News Agency (People's Republic of China) are also represented.

PRESS ASSOCIATIONS

Canadian Business Press: 40 Shields Court, Suite 201, Markham, ON L3R 0M5; tel. (905) 946-8889; fax (905) 479-1711; e-mail JJCBP@passport.ca; Chair. TERRY MALDEN; Pres. JUDY JOHNSON; 125 mems.

Canadian Community Newspapers Association: 90 Eglinton Ave East, Suite 206, Toronto, ON M4P 2Y3; tel. (416) 482-1090; fax (416) 482-1908; e-mail info@ccna.ca; internet www.ccna.ca; f. 1919; Exec. Dir SERGE LAVOIE; 692 mems.

Canadian Newspaper Association: 890 Yonge St, Suite 200, Toronto, ON M4W 3P4; tel. (416) 923-3567; fax (416) 923-7206; e-mail bcantley@cna-acj.ca; internet www.cna-acj.ca/; f. 1996; Chair. RUSS MILLS; 102 mems.

Canadian Magazine Publishers Association: 130 Spadina Ave, Suite 202, Toronto, ON M5V 2L4; tel. (416) 504-0274; fax (416) 504-0437; e-mail cminfo@cmpa.ca; internet www.cmpa.ca/; f. 1973; Chair. MICHAEL REA.

Magazines Canada (The Magazine Asscn of Canada): 777 Bay St, 4th Floor, Toronto, ON M5W 1A7; tel. (416) 596-5382; fax (416) 596-6043; e-mail info@magazinescanada.com; internet www.magazinescanada.com; Chair. LARRY THOMAS.

Publishers

Annick Press Ltd: 15 Patricia Ave, Willowdale, ON M2M 1H9; tel. (416) 221-4802; fax (416) 221-8400; e-mail annick@annickpress.com; internet www.annickpress.com; f. 1976; children's; Dir RICK WILKS.

Arsenal Pulp Press Book Publishers Ltd: 1014 Homer St, Suite 103, Vancouver, BC V6B 2W9; tel. (604) 687-4233; fax (604) 669-8250; e-mail contact@arsenalpulp.com; internet www.arsenalpulp.com; f. 1982; literary, native, cultural studies; Publr BRIAN LAM.

Black Rose Books: CP 1258, succursale place du Parc, Montréal, QC H2W 1Y5; tel. (514) 844-4076; fax (514) 849-1956; e-mail blackrose@web.net; internet www.web.net/blackrosebooks; f. 1969; social studies, humanities; Pres. JACQUES ROUX.

Blizzard Publishing: 73 Furby St, Winnipeg, MB R3C 2A2; tel. (204) 775-2923; fax (204) 775-2947; e-mail info@blizzard.mb.ca; internet www.blizzard.mb.ca/catalog; drama and criticism; Man. Editor PETER ATWOOD.

Borealis Press Ltd/The Tecumseh Press Ltd: 8 Mohawk Cres., Nepean, ON K2H 7G6; tel. (613) 829-0150; fax (613) 829-7783; e-mail borealis@istar.ca; internet www.borealispress.com; f. 1972; Canadian fiction and non-fiction, drama, juveniles, poetry; Pres. FRANK TIERNEY.

Breakwater Books/Softwares Ltd: 100 Water St, POB 2188, St John's, NF A1C 6E6; tel. (709) 722-6680; fax (709) 753-0708; e-mail info@breakwater.nf.net; internet www.breakwater.nf.net; f. 1973; fiction, non-fiction, children's, educational, folklore; Pres. CLYDE ROSE.

Canada Law Book Inc: 240 Edward St, Aurora, ON L4G 3S9; tel. (905) 841-6472; fax (905) 841-5085; internet www.canadalawbook.ca; f. 1855; law reports, law journals, legal textbooks, etc.; Pres. S. G. CORBETT.

Carswell-Thomson Professional Publishing Canada: 2075 Kennedy Rd, Scarborough, ON M1T 3V4; tel. (416) 609-8000; fax (416) 298-5094; internet www.carswell.com/carswell.home; f. 1864; Pres. and CEO DON VAN MEER.

CDG Books Canada, Inc: 99 Yorkville Ave, Suite 400, Toronto, ON M5R 3K5; tel. (416) 963-8830; fax (416) 923-4821; e-mail info@cdgbooks.com; internet www.cdgbooks.com; f. 1998; trade, reference, publishing; Pres. TOM BEST.

Chenelière/McGraw-Hill: 7001 blvd St-Laurent, Montréal, QC H2S 3E3; tel. (514) 273-1066; fax (514) 276-0324; e-mail chene@dlcmcgrawhill.ca; textbooks; Pres. MICHEL DE CHENELIÈRE.

Coach House Books: 401 Huron St, Toronto, ON M5S 2G5; tel. (416) 979-2217; fax (416) 977-1158; internet www.chbooks.com; f. 1965; fiction, poetry, drama; Publr STAN BEVINGTON.

Crabtree Publishing Co Ltd: 612 Welland Ave, St Catharines, ON L2M 5V6; tel. (905) 682-5221; fax (905) 682-7166; e-mail letters@crabtreebooks.com; internet www.crabtreebooks.com; f. 1978; children's; Pres. PETER A. CRABTREE.

Doubleday Canada Ltd: 105 Bond St, Toronto, ON M5B 1Y3; tel. (416) 340-0777; fax (416) 977-8488; internet www.randomhouse.ca; f. 1944; general, trade, textbooks, mass market; Pres. JOHN NEALE.

Douglas & McIntyre Ltd: 2323 Québec St, Suite 201, Vancouver, BC V5T 4S7; tel. (604) 254-7191; fax (604) 254-9099; e-mail dm@douglasmcintyre.com; f. 1964; fiction, general non-fiction, juvenile; Pres. SCOTT MCINTYRE.

The Dundurn Group: 8 Market St, Suite 200, Toronto, ON M5E 1M6; tel. (416) 214-5544; fax (416) 214-5556; e-mail info@dundurn.com; internet www.dundurn.com; f. 1972; drama and performing arts, history, reference, fiction and non-fiction; Pres. KIRK HOWARD.

Editions d'Acadie: 236 rue St-Georges, Moncton, NB E1C 8N8; tel. (506) 857-8490; fax (506) 855-3130; e-mail edacadie@nbnet.nb.ca; f. 1972; Gen. Dir MARCEL OUELLETTE.

Editions Bellarmin: 165 rue Deslauriers, Ville St-Laurent, QC H4N 2S4; tel. (514) 745-4290; fax (514) 745-4299; e-mail editions@fides.qc.ca; internet www.fides.qc.ca; f. 1891; religious, educational, politics, sociology, ethnography, history, sport, leisure; Dir-Gen. ANTOINE DEL BUSSO.

Les Editions CEC Inc: 8101 blvd Métropolitain est, Anjou, Montréal, QC H1J 1J9; tel. (514) 351-6010; fax (514) 351-3534; f. 1956; textbooks; Pres. and Dir-Gen. JACQUES ROCHEFORT.

Editions Fides: 165 rue Deslauriers, Ville St-Laurent, PQ H4N 2S4; tel. (514) 745-4290; fax (514) 745-4299; e-mail editions@fides.qc.ca; internet www.fides.qc.ca; f. 1937; juvenile, history, theology, textbooks and literature; Dir-Gen. ANTOINE DEL BUSSO.

Editions de l'Hexagone: 1010 rue de la Gauchetière est, Montréal, QC H2L 2N5; tel (514) 523-1182; fax (514) 282-7530; internet www.edhexagone.com; f. 1953; literature; Pres. PIERRE LESPÉRANCE.

Editions du Noroît Ltée: 6694 ave Papineau, Montréal, QC H2G 2X2; tel. (514) 727-0005; fax (514) 72-6660; e-mail lenoroit@ca.inter.net; f. 1971; poetry; Admin. Dir ANDRÉ PAUL.

Editions du Renouveau Pédagogique Inc: 5757 rue Cyphiot, St-Laurent, QC H4S 1R3; tel. (514) 334-2690; fax (514) 334-4720; e-mail info@erpi.com; internet www.erpi.com; f. 1965; textbooks; Pres. NORMAND CLÉROUX.

Editions du Septentrion: 1300 ave Maguire, Sillery, QC G1T 1Z3; tel. (418) 688-3556; fax (418) 527-4978; internet www.septentrion.qc.ca; f. 1988; history, essays, general; Man. DENIS VAUGEOIS.

Fenn Publishing Co Ltd: 34 Nixon Rd, Bolton, ON L7E 1W2; internet www.hbfenn.com; fiction and non-fiction; Publr C. JORDAN FENN.

Fifth House Publishers Ltd: 6125 11th St, SE, No. 9, Calgary, AB T2H 2L6; tel. (403) 571-5230; fax (403) 571-5235; f. 1982; native, literary and non-fiction; Publr FRASER SEELY.

Fitzhenry & Whiteside Ltd: 195 Allstate Pkwy, Markham, ON L3R 4T8; tel. (416) 477-9700; fax (416) 477-9179; e-mail godwit@fitzhenry.ca; internet www.fitzhenry.ca; f. 1966; textbooks, trade, educational; Pres. SHARON FITZHENRY.

Gage Educational Publishing Co: 164 Commander Blvd, Agincourt, ON M1S 3C7; tel. (416) 293-8141; fax (416) 293-9009; e-mail info@gage.canpub.ca; internet www.cornerstones.gagepub.ca; f. 1844; Pres. CHRIS R. BESSE.

General Publishing Co Ltd: 895 Don Mills Rd, Toronto, ON M3C 1W3; tel. (416) 445-3333; fax (416) 445-5991; e-mail sleeshew@genpub.com; internet www.genpub.com; fiction and non-fiction; Pres. NELSON DOUCET.

Grolier Ltd: 12 Banigan Drive, Toronto, ON M4H 1A6; tel. (416) 425-1924; fax (416) 425-4015; f. 1912; reference, children's; Gen. Man. ROB FURLONGER.

Harcourt Brace & Co Canada: 55 Horner Ave, Toronto, ON M8Z 4X6; tel. (416) 255-4491; fax (416) 255-4046; internet www.harcourtcanada.com; f. 1922; medical, educational, scholarly; Pres. JEAN-GUY BLANCHETTE.

Harlequin Books: 225 Duncan Mill Rd, Don Mills, ON M3B 3K9; tel. (416) 445-5860; fax (416) 445-8655; internet eharlequin.com; f. 1949; fiction, paperbacks; Chair. and CEO BRIAN HICKEY.

HarperCollins Canada Ltd: Hazleton Lanes, 55 Avenue Rd, Suite 2900, Toronto, ON M5R 3L2; tel. (416) 975-9334; fax (416) 975-9884; e-mail hccanada@harpercollins.com; internet www .harpercanada.com; f. 1932; trade, bibles, dictionaries, juvenile, paperbacks; Pres. CLAUDE PRIMEAU.

Hyperion Press Ltd: 300 Wales Ave, Winnipeg, MB R2M 2S9; tel. (204) 256-9204; fax (204) 255-7845; e-mail tamos@escape.ca; internet www.escape.ca/~tamos; children's illustrated; Pres. MARVIS TUTIAH.

Institut de Recherches psychologiques, inc/Institute of Psychological Research, Inc: 34 rue Fleury ouest, Montréal, QC H3L 1S9; tel. (514) 382-3000; fax (514) 382-3007; f. 1964; educational and psychological tests; Gen. Dir MARIE-PAULE CHEVRIER.

Irwin Publishing Ltd: 325 Humber College Blvd, Toronto, ON M9W 7C3; tel. (416) 798-0424; fax (416) 798-1384; e-mail irwin@irwin-pub.com; internet www.irwin-pub.com; f. 1945; educational; Pres. BRIAN O'DONNELL.

Jesperson Publishing: 39 James Lane, St John's, NF A1E 3H3; tel. (709) 753-0633; fax (709) 753-5507; f. 1974; educational and trade; Pres. and Publr JOHN SYMONDS.

Key Porter Books: 70 The Esplanade, 3rd Floor, Toronto, ON M5E 1R2; tel. (416) 862-7777; fax (416) 862-2304; e-mail srenouf@ keyporter.com; internet www.keyporter.com; f. 1980; general trade; Pres. SUSAN RENOUF.

Lancelot Press Ltd: POB 425, Hantsport, NS B0P 1P0; tel. (902) 684-9129; fax (902) 684-3685; e-mail lancelot@atcon.com; internet www.atcon.com/lancelot; f. 1966; non-fiction, regional; Pres. WILLIAM POPE.

Leméac Editeur: 1124 Marie-Anne est, Montréal, QC H2J 2B7; tel. (514) 524-5558; fax (514) 524-3145; e-mail lemeac@lemeac.qc.ca; f. 1957; literary, academic, general; Pres. JULES BRILLANT.

Lidec Inc: 4350 ave de l'Hôtel-de-Ville, Montréal, QC H2W 2H5; tel. (514) 843-5991; fax (514) 843-5252; e-mail lidec@lidec.qc.ca; internet www.lidec.qc.ca; f. 1965; educational, textbooks; Pres. MARC-AIME GUÉRIN.

James Lorimer & Co Ltd: 35 Britain St, Toronto, ON M5A 1R7; tel. (416) 362-4762; fax (416) 362-3939; e-mail jlc@sympatico.ca; f. 1971; urban and labour studies, children's, general non-fiction; Pres. JAMES LORIMER.

McClelland and Stewart Ltd: 481 University Ave, Suite 900, Toronto, ON M5G 2E9; tel. (416) 598-1114; fax (416) 598-7764; internet www.mcclelland.com; f. 1906; trade, illustrated and educational; Pres. and Publr DOUGLAS M. GIBSON.

McGill-Queen's University Press: 3430 rue McTavish, Montréal, QC H3A 1X9; tel. (514) 398-3750; fax (514) 398-4333; e-mail mqup@ mqup.mcgill.ca; internet www.mcgill.ca/mqup; f. 1960; scholarly and general interest; Exec. Dir PHILLIP J. CERCONE.

McGraw-Hill Ryerson Ltd: 300 Water St, Whitby, ON L1N 9B6; tel. (416) 430-5000; fax (416) 430-5020; e-mail johnd@mcgrawhill.ca; internet www.mcgrawhill.ca; f. 1944; educational and general; Pres. and CEO JOHN DILL.

Nelson–A Division of Thomson Learning: 1120 Birchmount Rd, Scarborough, ON M1K 5G4; tel. (416) 752-9100; fax (416) 752-9646; internet www.nelson.com; f. 1914; retailing, consumer affairs, textbooks; Pres. GEORGE W. BERGQUIST.

Oberon Press: 350 Sparks St, Suite 400, Ottawa, ON K1R 7S8; tel. and fax (613) 238-3275; f. 1966; poetry, children's, fiction and general non-fiction; Pres. MICHAEL MACKLEM.

Oxford University Press Canada: 70 Wynford Drive, Don Mills, ON M3C 1J9; tel. (416) 441-2941; fax (416) 444-0427; e-mail custserv@oupcan.com; internet www.oupcan.com; f. 1904; general, education, scholarly, Canadiana; Pres. JOANNA GERTLER.

Pearson Education Canada Inc: 26 Prince Andrew Pl, Toronto, ON M3C 2T8; tel. (416) 447-5101; fax (416) 443-0948; internet www.pearsoned.ca; educational; Pres. and CEO TONY VANDER WOUDE.

Penguin Books Canada Ltd: 10 Alcorn Ave, Suite 300, Toronto, ON M4V 3B2; tel. (416) 925-2249; fax (416) 925-0068; e-mail oper@ penguin.ca; internet www.penguin.ca; f. 1974; Pres. STEVEN PARR.

Pippin Publishing Corpn: 85 Ellesmere Rd, Suite 232, Toronto, ON M1R 4B9; tel. (416) 510-2918; fax (416) 510-3359; e-mail jld@ pippinpub.com; internet www.pippinpub.com; f. 1995; educational; Pres. JONATHAN LOVAT DICKSON.

Pontifical Institute of Mediaeval Studies: 59 Queen's Park Crescent East, Toronto, ON M5S 2C4; tel. (416) 926-7144; fax (416) 926-7258; e-mail pontifex@chass.utoronto.ca; f. 1939; scholarly publs concerning the Middle Ages; Dir of Publs RON B. THOMSON.

Prentice Hall Canada Inc: 1870 Birchmount Rd, Scarborough, ON M1P 2J7; tel. (416) 293-3621; fax (416) 299-2529; e-mail pub_canada@prenhall; internet www.prenhall.com/; f. 1960; trade, textbooks; Pres. BRIAN HEER.

Les Presses de l'Université Laval: Cité Universitaire, Ste-Foy, QC G1K 7P4; tel. (418) 656-2803; fax (418) 656-3305; f. 1950; scholarly; Publr BENOIT BERNIER.

Les Presses de l'Université de Montréal: CP 6128, succursale Centre-Ville, Montréal, QC H3C 3J7; tel. (514) 343-6933; fax (514) 343-2232; e-mail pum@umontreal.ca; internet www.pum .umontreal.ca; f. 1962; scholarly and general; Gen. Man. ANTOINE DEL BUSSO.

Les Presses de l'Université du Québec: 2875 blvd Laurier, Suite 450, Ste-Foy, QC G1V 2M2; tel. (418) 657-4399; fax (418) 657-2096; e-mail admin@puq.uquebec.ca; internet www.puq.uquebec.ca; f. 1969; scholarly and general; Dir-Gen. ANGÈLE TREMBLAY.

Random House of Canada Ltd: 1265 Aerowood Drive, Mississauga, ON L4W 1B9; tel. (905) 624-0672; fax (905) 624-6217; internet www.randomhouse.ca; f. 1944; Pres. DAVID KENT.

Scholastic Canada Ltd: 175 Hillmount Rd, Markham, ON L6C 1Z7; tel. (905) 887-7323; fax (905) 887-1131; internet www.scholastic .ca; Pres. F. C. L. MULLER.

Sélection du Reader's Digest (Canada) Ltée/The Reader's Digest Association (Canada) Ltd: 1100 blvd René-Lévesque ouest, Montréal, QC H3B 5H5; tel. (514) 940-0751; fax (514) 940-3637; internet www.readersdigest.ca; Pres. and CEO PIERRE DION.

Sogides Ltée: 955 rue Amherst, Montréal, QC H2L 3K4; tel. (514) 523-1182; fax (514) 597-0370; e-mail franvin@sogides.com; internet www.sogides.com; f. 1958; general interest, fiction, psychology, biography; Pres. PIERRE LESPÉRANCE.

Stoddart Publishing Co Ltd: 895 Don Mills Rd, Suite 400, Toronto ON M3C 1W3; tel. (416) 445-3333; fax (416) 445-5967; e-mail bhowson@stoddartpub.com; internet www.stoddartpub.com; internet www.genpub.com; f. 1984; general fiction and non-fiction, textbooks, children's; Pres. JACK STODDART.

Thistledown Press Ltd: 633 Main St, Saskatoon, SK S7H 0J8; tel. (306) 244-1722; fax (306) 244-1762; e-mail thistle@sk.sympatico.ca; internet www.thistledown.sk.ca; f. 1975; Canadian fiction, non-fiction and poetry; Pres. GLEN SORESTAD.

Thompson Educational Publishing Inc: 6 Ripley Ave, Suite 200, Toronto, ON M6S 3N9; tel. (416) 766-2763; fax (416) 766-0398; e-mail publisher@thompsonbooks.com; internet www .thompsonbooks.com; f. 1989; textbooks; Pres. KEITH THOMPSON.

University of Alberta Press: Ring House 2, Edmonton, AB T6G 2E1; tel. (780) 492-3662; fax (780) 492-0719; e-mail uap@ualberta.ca; internet www.ualberta.ca/~uap; f. 1969; scholarly, general non-fiction; Dir JANINE ANDREWS (acting).

University of British Columbia Press: 6344 Memorial Rd, Vancouver, BC V6T 1Z2; tel. (604) 822-3259; fax (604) 822-6083; e-mail info@ubcpress.ubc.ca; internet www.ubcpress.ubc.ca; f. 1971; humanities, forestry, social science; Dir PETER MILROY.

University of Manitoba Press: 423 University Crescent, Winnipeg, MB R3T 2N2; tel. (204) 474-9495; fax (204) 474-7566; internet www.umanitoba.ca/uofmpress; f. 1967; regional history, Native, Icelandic and women's studies; Dir DAVID CARR.

University of Ottawa Press/Presses de l'Université d'Ottawa: 542 ave King Edward, Ottawa, ON K1N 6N5; tel. (613) 562-5246; fax (613) 562-5247; e-mail press@uottawa.ca; internet www .uopress.uottawa.ca; f. 1936; university texts, scholarly works in English and French; general; Editor-in-Chief VICKI BENNETT.

University of Toronto Press Inc: 100 Queen's Park, Toronto, ON M5S 2C6; tel. (416) 586-5581; fax (416) 586-5827; internet www.utpress.utoronto.ca; f. 1901; scholarly books and journals; Pres. and Publr GEORGE MEADOWS.

Weigl Educational Publishers: 1902 11th St, SE, Calgary, AB T2G 3G2; tel. (403) 233-7747; fax (403) 33-7769; e-mail calgary@ weigl.com; internet www.weigl.com; f. 1979; textbooks; Publr LINDA WEIGL.

John Wiley and Sons Canada Ltd: 22 Worcester Rd, Etobicoke, ON M9W 1L1; tel. (416) 236-4433; fax (416) 236-8743; e-mail canada@wiley.com; internet www.wiley.com; f. 1968; Pres. DIANE WOOD.

Government Publishing House

Canada Communications Group Publishing: 45 blvd Sacre-Coeur, D2200, Hull, QC K1A 0S9; tel. (819) 956-4800; fax (819) 994-1498; e-mail publishing@ccg.gcc.ca; internet www.ccg.gcc.ca; f. 1876; books and periodicals on numerous subjects, incl. agriculture, economics, environment, geology, history and sociology; Dir LESLIE-ANN SCOTT.

ORGANIZATIONS AND ASSOCIATIONS

Association of Canadian Publishers: 110 Eglinton Ave West, Suite 401, Toronto, ON M4R 1A3; tel. (416) 487-6116; fax (416) 487-8815; internet www.publishers.ca; f. 1976; trade asscn of Canadian-owned English-language book publrs; represents Canadian publishing internationally; 145 mems; Exec. Dir MONIQUE SMITH.

Association of Canadian University Presses: c/o University of Toronto Press, 10 Saint Mary St, Suite 700, Toronto, ON M4Y 2W8; tel. (416) 978-2239; Exec. Dir BILL HARNUM.

Canadian Copyright Institute: 192 Spadina Ave, Suite 107, Toronto, ON M5T 2C2; tel. (416) 975-1756; fax (416) 975-1839; e-mail bkper@interlog.com; 83 mems; Chair. RON B. THOMSON.

Canadian Publishers' Council: 250 Merton St, Suite 203, Toronto, ON M4S 1B1; tel. (416) 322-7011; fax (416) 322-6999; e-mail pubadmin@pubcouncil.ca; internet www.pubcouncil.ca; f. 1910; trade asscn of Canadian-owned publrs and Canadian-incorp. subsidiaries of UK and USA publrs; 24 mems; Pres. GEORGE BERQUIST.

Broadcasting and Communications

The 1968 Broadcasting Act established the Canadian Broadcasting Corporation (CBC) as the national, publicly-owned, broadcasting service and created the Canadian Radio-Television and Telecommunications Commission (CRTC) as the agency regulating radio, television and cable television. The CRTC's telecommunications authority is currently derived from the 1985 Canadian Radio-Television and Telecommunications Act. Subsequent Broadcasting Acts, introduced in 1991 and 1993, reconfirmed the CRTC's regulatory powers.

Many privately-owned television and radio stations have affiliation agreements with the CBC and help to distribute the national services. A number of the major private television networks (see below) also have affiliates.

Canadian Broadcasting Corporation/Société Radio Canada (CBC/SRC): 250 Lanark Ave, POB 3220, Station C, Ottawa, ON K1Y 1E4; tel. (613) 724-1200; internet www.cbc.radio-canada.ca; f. 1936; financed mainly by public funds, with supplementary revenue from commercial advertising on CBC television; services in French, English, Dene and Inuktitut languages; Pres. and CEO ROBERT RABINOVITCH.

Canadian Radio-Television and Telecommunications Commission (CRTC): Ottawa, ON K1A 0N2; tel. (819) 997-0313 (Information); fax (819) 994-0218; e-mail info@crtc.gc.ca; internet www.crtc.gc.ca; f. 1968; offices in Halifax, Winnipeg and Vancouver; Chair. FRANÇOISE BERTRAND; Vice-Chair. DAVID COLVILLE (Telecommunications), A. P. WYLIE (Broadcasting); Sec.-Gen. URSULA MENKE.

TELECOMMUNICATIONS

Principal Telecommunications Networks

Aliant Inc: POB 880, Halifax, NS B3J 2W3; tel. (877) 225-4268; fax (877) 429-8755; internet www.aliant.ca; f. 1999 by merger of telecommunications providers in New Brunswick, Nova Scotia, Prince Edward Is. and Nfld; 39.2% owned by Bell Canada, 14.0% owned by BCE Inc; Pres. and CEO STEPHEN WETMORE.

BCE Inc: 1000 rue de la Gauchetière ouest, Montréal, QC, H3B 4Y7; tel. (514) 397-7056; fax (514) 397-7157; internet www.bce.ca; holding company with numerous telecommunications and media interests; Pres. and CEO JEAN C. MONTY.

> **Teleglobe Inc:** 1000 rue de la Gauchetière ouest, Montréal, QC H3B 4X5; tel. (514) 868-7272; fax (514) 868-7234; internet www.teleglobe.ca; operates international telecommunications network; CEO TERENCE J. JARMAN.

BCT.Telus Inc (Telus): 3777 Kingsway, Burnaby, BC V5H 3Z7; tel (604) 432-2413; fax (604) 432-2949; internet www.telus.com; f. 1999 by merger of BC Telecom Inc and Telus Corporation; supplies services to residents of Alberta and British Columbia; Chair. BRIAN CANFIELD; Pres. and CEO GEORGE PETTY.

Bell Canada: 1800 ave Collège McGill, Montréal, QC H3B 4Y7; tel. (514) 870-6434; fax (514) 870-2630; internet www.bell.ca; Canada's largest regional telephone operating co; holds a monopoly in most of Québec and Ontario; also supplies services to the Northwest Territories and Nunavut; 80% owned by BCE Inc; Chair. and CEO JEAN C. MONTY.

Manitoba Telecom Services Inc (MTS): 333 Main St, POB 6666, Winnipeg, MB R3C 3V6; internet www.mts.mb.ca; formerly Manitoba Telephone System; supplies services to residents of Manitoba; 21.7% owned by BCE Inc; Pres. and CEO CEO W. C. FRASER.

Nortel Networks Corpn: 8200 Dixie Rd, Suite 1000, Brompton, ON L6T 5P6; tel. (905) 863-0000; fax (905) 863-8505; internet www.nortelnetworks.com; formerly Northern Telecom Ltd; operates international telecommunications network; Pres. and CEO JOHN ROTH.

Saskatchewan Telecommunications (SaskTel): 2121 Saskatchewan Drive, Regina, SK S4P 3Y2; tel. (306) 777-2201; fax (306) 777-1812; internet www.sasktel.com; supplies services to residents of Saskatchewan; Pres. and CEO DONALD R. CHING.

RADIO

The CBC operates two AM and two FM networks, one each in English and French. The CBC's Northern Service provides both national network programming in English and French, and special local and short-wave programmes, some of which are broadcast in the eight principal languages of the Indian and Inuit peoples. In March 1996 there were 576 outlets for AM radio and 1,229 outlets for FM radio (including private affiliates and rebroadcasters). The CBC radio service, which is virtually free of commercial advertising, is within reach of 99.5% of the population. Radio Canada International, the CBC's overseas short-wave service, broadcasts daily in 11 languages and distributes recorded programmes for use worldwide.

TELEVISION

The CBC operates two television networks, one in English and one in French. CBC's Northern Service provides both radio and television service to 98% of the 90,000 inhabitants of northern Québec, the Northwest Territories, Nunavut and the Yukon. Almost 41% of these inhabitants are native Canadians, and programming is provided in Dene and Inuktitut languages as well as English and French. As of March 1996, CBC television was carried on 881 outlets (22 CBC-owned stations, 613 CBC-owned rebroadcasters, 160 community-owned rebroadcasters, 25 private affiliates and 61 private affiliated rebroadcasters). CBC television is available to approximately 99% of the English- and French-speaking population.

Canadian Satellite Communication Inc (Cancom) of Toronto has been licensed since 1981 by the CRTC to conduct a multi-channel television and radio broadcasting operation via satellite for the distribution of CTV programme output, Réseau de Télévision (TVA) and independent television and radio programmes to remote and under-served communities. Cancom also distributes by satellite the programme output of five US television networks. A second satellite broadcaster, Star Choice, was licensed by the CRTC in June 1998.

In March 1999 there were 2,091 licensed cable operators. There are five educational services: TV-Ontario in Ontario and Radio-Québec in Québec operate their own television stations and networks; the Learning and Skills Television of Alberta provides educational programming in that province; the Saskatchewan Communications Network Corporation distributes educational programming in Saskatchewan; and the Open Learning Agency (OLA) provides child and adult education by television in British Columbia. Programmes obtainable by pay television services have been in operation since 1983.

Canadian Satellite Communications Inc (Cancom): 50 Burnhamthorpe Rd West, Suite 1000, Mississauga, ON L5B 3C2; tel. (905) 272-4960; fax (905) 272-3399; e-mail pdumas@cancom.ca; internet www.cancom.ca; a division of Shaw Communications Inc; Chair. HAROLD ROOZEN; Pres. and CEO PETER CLASSON.

CTV Television Network: 9 Channel Nine Court, POB 9, Station O, Toronto, ON M4A 2M9; tel. (416) 299-2000; fax (416) 299-2643; internet www.ctv.ca; 25 privately-owned affiliated stations from coast to coast, with 247 rebroadcasters; covers 99% of Canadian TV households; Pres. and CEO JOHN CASSADAY.

Global Television Network: 81 Barber Greene Rd, Don Mills, ON M3C 2A2; tel. (416) 446-5311; fax (416) 446-5447; internet www.globaltv.com; 11 stations in eight provinces; a subsidiary of CanWest Global Communications Corpn; Pres. KEVIN SHEA.

Réseau de Télévision (TVA): 1600 blvd de Maisonneuve est, CP 368, succursale C, Montréal, QC H2L 4P2; tel. (514) 526-0476; fax (514) 526-4285; f. 1971; French-language network, with 10 stations in Québec and 19 rebroadcasters serving 98% of the province, together with francophone communities in Ontario and New Brunswick; Pres. and CEO JEAN GOUEPY.

Réseau TQS Inc: 612 rue St-Jacques, Bureau 100, Montréal, QC H3C 5R1; tel. (514) 390-6035; fax (514) 390-6067; e-mail tvpublic@tqs.qc.ca; internet www.tqs.qc.ca; f. 1986; French-language; 2 stations, 6 rebroadcasters and 2 retransmitters serving 95% of the province of Québec; Pres. RENÉ GUIMOND.

Telesat Canada: 1601 Telesat Court, Gloucester, ON K1B 5P4; tel. (613) 748-0123; fax (613) 748-8712; e-mail info@telesat.ca; internet www.telesat.ca; a subsidiary of BCE Inc; f. 1969; Chair. J. MONTY; Pres. L. J. BOISVERT.

ASSOCIATIONS

Canadian Association of Broadcasters: 350 Sparks St, Suite 306, Ottawa, ON K1R 7S2; tel. (613) 233-4035; fax (613) 233-6961; e-mail cab@cab-acr.ca; internet www.cab-acr.ca; f. 1926; Pres. and CEO MICHAEL McCABE; 500 mem. broadcasting stations.

Canadian Cable Television Association: 360 Albert St, Suite 1010, Ottawa, ON K1R 7X7; tel. (613) 232-2631; fax (613) 232-2137; e-mail ccta@ccta.com; internet www.ccta.ca; Pres. JANET YALE; 846 mems.

Television Bureau of Canada, Inc: 160 Bloor St E, Suite 1005, Toronto, ON M4W 1B9; tel. (416) 923-8813; fax (416) 923-8739; e-mail tvb@tvb.ca; internet www.tvb.ca; f. 1962; Pres. JIM PATTERSON; 101 mems.

Finance

(cap. = capital; auth. = authorized; res = reserves;
dep. = deposits; m. = million; brs = branches; amounts in
Canadian dollars)

BANKING

Since Confederation in 1867, the Federal Government has exercised jurisdiction over banking operations throughout Canada. The Bank Act of 1980 created two categories of banking institution: Schedule 'I' banks, and in which no one interest is allowed to own more than 10% of the shares; and Schedule 'II' banks, which are either subsidiaries of foreign financial institutions, or are banks controlled by Canadian non-bank financial institutions. In June 1999 there were eight Schedule 'I' banks and 46 Schedule 'II' banks. At the end of June 1999 there were 8,247 bank branches in Canada.

Major revisions to the Bank Act, the federal Trust and Loans Companies Act, the federal Insurance Companies Act and the Co-operative Credit Associations Act came into force in June 1992. This legislation permits federal financial institutions, with some restrictions, to diversify into each other's markets through subsidiaries. By 1 January 1995, following ratification of the North American Free Trade Agreement (NAFTA) and the enactment of the World Trade Organization Implementation Act, the domestic asset limitations on foreign-owned Schedule 'II' banks in the Canadian market were removed.

In the past, the Bank Act was generally reviewed once every 10 years. As a result of extensive revisions to the federal financial institutions legislation in 1992, a further review of the Bank Act was carried out in 1997. In addition, a Task Force on the Future of the Canadian Financial Services Sector was appointed by the Federal Government in 1996 to review the legislative framework of the financial services sector. The report of the Task Force, published in September 1998, recommended the abolition of existing barriers preventing financial institutions from providing unified services in banking, insurance and motor vehicle leasing. It was also proposed that commercial banks and trust companies (see below) be permitted to market all classes of insurance through their branch networks by 2002. The Task Force expressed support for the entry of foreign banks into the commercial loans market, and for the adoption of new regulations for consumer protection. No recommendations, however, were made concerning the proposed mergers between the Royal Bank of Canada and the Bank of Montréal (announced in January 1998) and between the Canadian Imperial Bank of Commerce and the Toronto-Dominion Bank (announced in April). The merger plans were subsequently considered by a committee of the Federal House of Commons, which in December recommended that they be allowed to proceed. In the following week, however, the Minister of Finance announced that the Government had rejected the merger plans on the grounds that they would create an unacceptably high concentration of economic power and market dominance by the merged groups. It was stated that the Government was to initiate a further review of the financial services industry, during which time no new bank merger proposals would be considered. The Government was also to introduce legislation to stimulate competition within the banking sector, and to ease the existing restraints on the operation of foreign banks in Canada.

Trust and loan companies, which were originally formed to provide mortgage finance and private customer loans, now occupy an important place in the financial system, offering current account facilities and providing access to money transfer services.

Central Bank

Bank of Canada: 234 Wellington St, Ottawa, ON K1A 0G9; tel. (613) 782-8111; fax (613) 782-8655; e-mail paffairs@bank-banque-canada.ca; internet www.bank-banque-canada.ca; f. 1934; bank of issue; cap. and res 30m., dep. 2,387.6m. (Dec. 1999); Gov. DAVID DODGE.

Commercial Banks
Schedule 'I' Banks

Bank of Montréal: 129 rue St-Jacques ouest, Montréal, QC H2Y 1L6; tel. (514) 877-1285; fax (514) 877-6922; e-mail info@bmo.com; internet www.bmo.com; f. 1817; cap. and res 10,981m., dep. 156,874m. (Oct. 1999); Chair. and CEO ANTHONY F. COMPER; 1,163 brs.

Bank of Nova Scotia (Scotiabank): Scotia Plaza, 44 King St West, Toronto, ON M5H 1H1; tel. (416) 866-6161; fax (416) 866-3750; e-mail email@scotiabank.ca; internet www.scotiabank.ca; f. 1832; cap. and res 11,406m., dep. 156,618m. (Oct. 1999); Chair. and CEO PETER C. GODSOE; Pres. BRUCE R. BIRMINGHAM; 1,272 brs.

Canadian Imperial Bank of Commerce: Commerce Court, Toronto, ON M5L 1A2; tel. (416) 980-2211; internet www.cibc.com; f. 1867; cap. and res 11,058m. (Oct. 1999); Chair. and CEO JOHN S. HUNKIN; 1,453 brs.

Canadian Western Bank: 10303 Jasper Ave, Suite 2300, Edmonton, AB T5J 3X6; tel. (780) 423-8888; fax (780) 423-8897; e-mail comments@cwb.com; internet www.cwbank.com; f. 1988; cap. and res 159.6m., dep. 2,371.1m. (Oct. 1999); Chair. JACK C. DONALD; Pres. and CEO LARRY M. POLLOCK; 24 brs.

Laurentian Bank of Canada: 1981 ave Collège McGill, Montréal, QC H3A 3K3; tel. (514) 284-5996; fax (514) 284-3396; e-mail laurentianbank@com; internet www.laurentianbank.com; f. 1846; cap. and res 613.4m., dep. 10,469.5m. (Oct. 1999); Chair. JEANNINE G. WOOD; Pres. and CEO HENRI-PAUL ROUSSEAU; 204 br.

National Bank of Canada: 600 rue de la Gauchetière ouest, Montréal, QC H3B 4L2; tel. (514) 394-5000; fax (514) 394-8434; internet www.nbc.ca; f. 1979; cap. and res 3,301m., dep. 49,984m. (Oct. 1999); Chair. and CEO ANDRÉ BÉRARD; Pres. LÉON COURVILLE; 637 brs.

Royal Bank of Canada: 1 place Ville Marie, CP 6001, Montréal, QC H3C 3A9; tel. (514) 874-2110; internet www.royalbank.com; f. 1869; cap. and res 12,615m., dep. 187,897m. (Oct. 1999); Chair. and CEO JOHN E. CLEGHORN; 1,400 brs.

Toronto-Dominion Bank: Toronto-Dominion Centre, POB 1, Toronto, ON M5K 1A2; tel. (416) 982-8222; fax (416) 982-5671; internet www.tdbank.ca; f. 1855; cap. and res 11,533m., dep. 140,386m. (Oct. 1999); Chair., Pres. and CEO A. CHARLES BAILLIE; 907 brs.

Principal Schedule 'II' Banks

ABN Amro Bank Canada: TD Centre, Aetna Tower, 15th Floor, Toronto-Dominion Centre, POB 114, Toronto, ON M5K 1G8; tel. (416) 367-0850; fax (416) 363-1312; internet www.abnamro.com; f. 1981; subsidiary of ABN AMRO Bank NV (The Netherlands); total assets 5,262.2m. (April 1998); Pres. and CEO TH. BARK; 5 brs.

Bank of America Canada: 130 Adelaide St West, Suite 1800, Toronto, ON M5H 3P5; tel. (416) 366-8101; internet www.bankamerica.com; f. 1981; subsidiary of Bank of America NT & SA (USA); total assets 4,476.2m. (April 1998); Pres. and CEO J. C. MASTERS; 4 brs.

Bank of Tokyo-Mitsubishi (Canada): Royal Bank Plaza, South Tower, Suite 2100, POB 42, Toronto, ON M5J 2J1; tel. (416) 865-0220; fax (416) 865-9511; internet www.btm.co.jp; f. 1981; subsidiary of Bank of Tokyo-Mitsubishi (Japan); total assets 2,565.9m. (October 1999); Chair., Pres. and CEO YOSHIO SAIHARA; 3 brs.

Citibank Canada: Citibank Place, 123 Front St West, Suite 1900, Toronto, ON M5J 2M3; tel. (416) 947-5500; fax (416) 947-5813; internet www.citibank.com/canada; f. 1981; subsidiary of Citibank NA (USA); total assets 9,148.1m. (April 1998); Chair. and CEO P. LABBÉ; 17 brs.

Deutsche Bank Canada: 222 Bay St, Suite 1200, POB 196, Toronto, ON M5K 1E7; tel. (416) 682-8400; fax (416) 682-8484; internet www.db-dmg.com; f. 1981; subsidiary of Deutsche Bank AG (Germany); incorporated BT Bank of Canada 1999; total assets 7,945.7m. (April 1998); Pres. and CEO N. ZELENCZUK.

HSBC Bank Canada: 885 West Georgia St, Vancouver, BC V6C 3E9; tel. (604) 685-1000; fax (604) 641-1849; e-mail info@hsbc.ca; internet www.hsbc.ca; f. 1981; subsidiary of HSBC Holdings plc (United Kingdom); total assets 29,400m. (Dec. 2000); Pres. and CEO MARTIN GLYNN; 120 brs.

Société Générale (Canada): 1501 ave Collège McGill, Bureau 1800, Montréal, QC H3A 3M8; tel. (514) 841-6000; fax (514) 841-6250; internet www.socgen.com; f. 1981; subsidiary of Société Générale SA (France); total assets 3,778.3m. (October 1999); Pres. and CEO A. JOYET; 3 brs.

Development Bank

Business Development Bank of Canada: 5 place Ville Marie, Plaza Level, Bureau 12525, Montréal, PQ H3B 2G2; tel. (514) 496-7966; fax (514) 496-7974; internet www.bdc.ca; f. 1975; fed. govt corpn; auth. cap. 1,500m. (1995); Pres. and CEO MICHEL VENNAT; 80 brs.

Principal Trust and Loan Companies

Canada Trustco Mortgage Co: Canada Trust Tower, 275 Dundas St, London, ON N6A 4S4; tel. (519) 663-1500; fax (519) 663-5114; f. 1855; total assets 46,000m. (1997); Pres. and CEO W. EDMUND CLARK; 421 brs.

Montréal Trustco Inc: Scotia Plaza, 44 King St West, Toronto, ON M5H 1H1; tel. (416) 866-3675; fax (416) 866-5090; f. 1889; subsidiary of Scotiabank; total assets 18,044.3m. (1994); Chair. and CEO ROBERT W. CHISHOLM.

National Trust Co Ltd: 1 Adelaide St East, Toronto, ON M5C 2W8; tel. (416) 361-3611; fax (416) 361-4037; f. 1898; subsidiary of Scotiabank; cap. and res 253.7m., dep. 13,849.1m. (Oct. 1996); Chair. and CEO ROBERT W. CHISHOLM.

Royal Trust Corporation of Canada: Royal Trust Tower, POB 7500, Station A, Toronto, ON M5W 1P9; tel. (416) 974-1400; fax

(416) 861-9658; f. 1899; total assets 11,500m. (July 1997); Pres. ANTHONY A. WEBB.

Trust Général du Canada Inc: 1100 rue Université, 12e étage, Montréal, QC H3B 2G7; tel. (514) 871-7200; fax (514) 871-8525; f. 1928; Pres. and CEO MICHEL W. PETIT.

Savings Institutions with Provincial Charters

Alberta Treasury Branches: 9888 Jasper Ave, Edmonton, AB T5J 1P1; tel. (780) 493-7309; fax (780) 422-4178; internet www.atb.com; f. 1938; assets 11,464m. (Dec. 2000); Pres. and CEO PAUL G. HAGGIS; 144 brs.

Province of Ontario Savings Office: 33 King St West, 6th Floor, Oshawa, ON L1H 8H5; tel. (905) 433-5788; fax (905) 433-6519; e-mail poso@ofina.ca; internet www.ofina.on.ca/poso; f. 1921; assets 2,600m. (March 1996); Chair. Dr BRIAN B. PURCHASE; 23 brs.

Bankers' Organization

Canadian Bankers Association: Commerce Court West, Box 348, Suite 3000, Toronto, ON M5L 1G2; tel. (416) 362-6092; fax (416) 362-7705; e-mail inform@cba.ca; internet www.cba.ca; f. 1891; Pres. RAYMOND PROTTI; 5 regional brs, 48 mems.

STOCK EXCHANGES

Bourse de Montréal/Montreal Exchange: Tour de la Bourse, CP 61, 800 square Victoria, Montréal, QC H4Z 1A9; tel. (514) 871-2424; fax (514) 871-3553; e-mail info@me.org; internet www.me.org; f. 1874; 75 mems; Pres. and CEO LUC BERTRAND.

Canadian Venture Exchange (CDNX): 609 Granville Street, POB 10333, Vancouver, BC V7Y 1H1; tel. (604) 689-3334; fax (604) 688-6051; e-mail information@cdnx.ca; internet www.cdnx.ca; f. 1999 by merger of Alberta and Vancouver Stock Exchanges, incorporated Winnipeg Stock Exchange 2000; 66 mems; Chair. G. SCOTT PATERSON; Pres. and CEO WILLIAM L. HESS.

Toronto Stock Exchange: The Exchange Tower, 130 King St West, Toronto, ON M5X 1J2; tel. (416) 947-4700; fax (416) 947-4662; e-mail info@tse.com; internet www.tse.com; f. 1852; 101 mems; Pres. and CEO BARBARA STYMIEST.

INSURANCE
Principal Companies

Aetna Life Insurance Co of Canada: TD Centre, 79 Wellington St West, POB 120, Toronto, ON M5K 1N9; tel. (416) 864-6000; fax (416) 864-8189; internet www.aetna.ca; Pres. and CEO NICK VILLANI.

Allianz Canada: 10 York Mills Rd, Suite 700, Toronto, ON M2P 2G5; tel. (416) 227-7800; fax (416) 227-9837; e-mail info@allianz.ca; internet www.allianz.ca; f. 1928; Pres. CHRISTIAN CASSEBAUM.

Assurance vie Desjardins–Laurentienne: 200 ave des Commandeurs, Lévis, QC G6V 6R2; tel. (418) 838-7701; fax (418) 835-9171; f. 1994; Pres. FRANÇOIS JOLY.

Blue Cross Life Insurance Co of Canada: POB 220, Moncton, NB E1C 8L3; tel. (506) 853-1811; fax (506) 853-4651; internet www.bluecross.ca; Pres. and CEO LEON R. FURLONG.

Canada Life Assurance Co: 330 University Ave, Toronto, ON M5G 1R8; tel. (416) 597-1456; fax (416) 597-1940; e-mail info@canadalife.com; internet www.canadalife.com; f. 1847; Pres. DAVID NIELD.

Canadian General Insurance Co: 2206 Eglinton Ave East, Suite 500, Scarborough, ON M1L 4S8; tel. (416) 288-1800; fax (416) 288-9756; f. 1907; Pres. and CEO R. LEWIS DUNN.

Clarica: 227 King St South, Waterloo, ON N2J 4C5; tel. (519) 888-2290; fax (519) 888-2990; e-mail service@clarica.com; internet www.clarica.com; f. 1999 following demutualization of The Mutual Group (f. 1870); Pres. and CEO ROBERT ASTLEY.

Crown Life Insurance Co: 1901 Scarth St, POB 827, Regina, SK S4P 3B1; tel. (306) 751-6000; fax (306) 751-6150; internet www.crownlife.ca; f. 1900; Pres. and CEO R. F. RICHARDSON.

Dominion of Canada General Insurance Co: 165 University Ave, Toronto, ON M5H 3B9; tel. (416) 362-7231; fax (416) 362-9918; f. 1887; Pres. and CEO GEORGE L. COOKE.

Federation Insurance Co of Canada: 1000 rue de la Gauchetière ouest, Bureau 500, Montréal, QC H3B 4W5; tel. (514) 875-5790; fax (514) 875-9769; f. 1947; Pres. WILLIAM GREEN.

General Accident Group of Canada: 2206 Eglinton Ave East, Toronto, ON M1L 4S8; tel. (416) 288-1800; fax (416) 288-9756; internet www.genacc.ca; f. 1906; Pres. R. LEWIS DUNN.

Gerling Canada Insurance Co: 480 University Ave, Suite 1600, Toronto, ON M5G 1V6; tel. (416) 598-4651; fax (416) 598-5478; f. 1955; Pres. A. H. HENKE.

Gore Mutual Insurance Co: 262 Dundas St, Cambridge, ON N1R 5T3; tel. (519) 623-1910; fax (519) 623-8348; e-mail vision@

goremutual.ca; internet www.goremutual.ca; f. 1839; Pres. and CEO KEVIN W. MCNEIL.

Guardian Insurance Co of Canada: 181 University Ave, Toronto, ON M5W 3M7; tel. (416) 941-5050; fax (416) 941-9791; f. 1911; Pres. and CEO HENRY J. CURTIS.

Halifax Insurance Co: 75 Eglinton Ave East, Toronto, ON M4P 3A4; tel. (416) 440-1000; fax (416) 440-0799; internet www.halifaxinsurance.com; f. 1809; Pres. and CEO DONALD K. LOUGH.

Imperial Life Assurance Co of Canada: 95 St Clair Ave West, Toronto, ON M4V 1N7; tel. (416) 926-2600; fax (416) 923-1599; f. 1896; Pres. and CEO MARCEL PEPIN.

Industrial Alliance Pacific Life Insurance Co: 2165 Broadway West, POB 5900, Vancouver, BC V6B 5H6; tel. (604) 734-1667; fax (604) 734-8221; e-mail intouch@iapacificlife.com; internet www.iapacificlife.com; f. 2000 by merger; Pres. and CEO ROBERT SMITH.

ING Canada: 2450 rue Girouard ouest, St-Hyacinthe, QC J2S 3B3; tel. (514) 773-9701; fax (514) 773-3515; Pres. and CEO YVES BROUILLETTE.

Kings Mutual Insurance Co: POB 10, Berwick, NS B0P 1E0; tel. (902) 538-3187; fax (902) 538-7271; e-mail kings.mutual@ns.sympatico.com; f. 1904; Pres. J. J. UEFFING.

Manufacturers Life Insurance Co (Manulife Financial): 200 Bloor St East, Toronto, ON M4W 1E5; tel. (416) 926-0100; fax (416) 926-5454; e-mail webmaster@manulife.com; internet www.manulife.com; f. 1887; Pres. and CEO DOMINIC D'ALESSANDRO.

Metropolitan Life Insurance Co of Canada: 99 Bank St, Ottawa, ON K1P 5A3; tel. (613) 560-7446; fax (613) 560-7668; Pres. and CEO WILLIAM R. PRUETER.

The National Life Assurance Co of Canada: 522 University Ave, Toronto, ON M5G 1Y7; tel. (416) 598-2122; fax (416) 598-4948; internet www.nationallife.ca; f. 1897; Pres. VINCENT TONNA.

Portage La Prairie Mutual Insurance Co: 749 Saskatchewan Ave East, Portage La Prairie, MB R1N 3B8; tel. (204) 857-3415; fax (204) 239-6655; f. 1884; Pres. T. W. MCCARTNEY.

Royal and Sun Alliance Co of Canada: 10 Wellington St East, Toronto, ON M5E 1L5; tel. (416) 366-7511; fax (416) 367-9869; f. 1851; Pres. and CEO ROBERT J. GUNN.

Société Nationale d'Assurance Inc: 425 blvd de Maisonneuve ouest, Bureau 1500, Montréal, QC H3A 3G5; tel. (514) 288-8711; fax (514) 288-8269; f. 1940; Pres. ANDRÉ NADON.

Sun Life Assurance Co of Canada: POB 4150, Station A, Toronto, ON M5W 2C9; tel. (416) 979-9966; fax (416) 585-9546; internet www.sunlife.ca; f. 1871; Chair. and CEO DONALD A. STEWART.

Toronto Mutual Life Insurance Co: 112 St Clair Ave West, Toronto, ON M4V 2Y3; tel. (416) 960-3463; fax (416) 960-0531; Pres. and CEO VAN M. CAMPBELL.

Wawanesa Mutual Insurance Co: 191 Broadway, Winnipeg, MB R3C 3P1; tel. (204) 985-3923; fax (204) 972-7724; internet www.wawanesa.com; f. 1896; Pres. and CEO G. J. HANSON.

Western Assurance Co: 10 Wellington St East, Toronto, ON M5E 1L5; tel. (416) 366-7511; fax (416) 367-9869; f. 1851; Pres. and CEO ROBERT J. GUNN.

Zurich Life of Canada: 2225 Sheppard Ave East, Willowdale, ON M2J 5C4; tel. (416) 502-3600; fax (416) 502-3488; Pres. and CEO MICHAEL P. STRAMAGLIA.

Insurance Organizations

Canadian Association of Mutual Insurance Companies: 325 Dalhousie St, Suite 907, Box 117, Station B, Ottawa, ON K1P 6C3; tel. (613) 789-6851; fax (613) 789-6854; e-mail nflafreniere@camic.ca; internet www.camic.ca; Pres. NORMAN LAFRENIÈRE; 103 mems.

Canadian Life and Health Insurance Association: 1 Queen St East, Suite 1700, Toronto, ON M5C 2X9; tel. (416) 777-2221; fax (416) 777-1895; internet www.clhia.ca; f. 1894; Pres. MARK DANIELS.

Insurance Brokers Association of Canada: 181 University Ave, Suite 1902, Toronto, ON M5H 3M7; tel. (416) 367-1831; fax (416) 367-3681; e-mail info@ibac.ca; internet www.ibac.ca; f. 1921; Exec. Dir BRENDAN WYCKS; 11 mem. asscns.

Insurance Bureau of Canada: 151 Yonge St, Suite 1800, Toronto, ON M5C 2W7; tel. (416) 362-2031; fax (416) 361-5952; internet www.ibc.ca; f. 1964; Pres. and CEO GEORGE ANDERSON; 110 corporate mems.

Insurance Institute of Canada: 18 King St East, 6th Floor, Toronto, ON M5C 1C4; tel. (416) 362-8586; fax (416) 362-4239; e-mail iican@ibm.net; internet www.iic-iac.org; f. 1952; Pres. J. CHRIS RHIND; 31,000 mems.

Life Insurance Institute of Canada: 1 Queen St East, Suite 1600, Toronto, ON M5C 2X9; tel. (416) 359-2020; fax (416) 359-9173; e-mail dcgauer@liic.ca; internet www.liic.ca; f. 1935; Exec. Dir DEBBIE COLE-GAUER; 57 mem. asscns.

Life Underwriters' Association of Canada: 41 Lesmill Rd, North York, ON M3B 2T3; tel. (416) 444-5251; fax (416) 444-8031; f. 1906; Chair. and CEO JOHN DEAN; 18,000 mems.

Trade and Industry

CHAMBER OF COMMERCE

The Canadian Chamber of Commerce: 350 Sparks St, Suite 501, Ottawa, ON K1R 7S8; tel. (613) 238-4000; fax (613) 238-7643; e-mail info@chamber.ca; internet www.chamber.ca; f. 1925; mems: 500 community chambers of commerce and boards of trade, 80 nat. trade asscns and 2,500 business corpns; Nat. Pres. NANCY HUGHES ANTHONY.

INDUSTRIAL AND TRADE ASSOCIATIONS

Alliance of Manufacturers and Exporters Canada: 75 International Blvd, 4th Floor, Toronto, ON M9W 6L9; tel. (416) 798-8000; fax (416) 798-8050; e-mail national@the-alliance.com; internet www.palantir.ca/the-alliance/; f. 1871; the nat. org. of mfrs and exporters of Canada; Pres. STEPHEN VAN HOUTEN; 3,500 mems.

Agriculture and Horticulture

Canada Grains Council: 330–360 Main St, Winnipeg, MB R3C 3Z3; tel. (204) 942-2254; fax (204) 947-0992; e-mail office@canadagrainscouncil.ca; internet www.canadagrainscouncil.ca; f. 1969; Chair. JIM WILSON; 27 mems.

Canadian Federation of Agriculture: 75 Albert St, Suite 1101, Ottawa, ON K1P 5E7; tel. (613) 236-3633; fax (613) 236-5749; e-mail cfafca@fox.nstn.ca; internet www.cfa-fca.ca; f. 1935; Exec. Dir (vacant); 20 mems.

Canadian Horticultural Council: 1101 Prince of Wales Drive, Suite 310, Ottawa, ON K2C 3W7; tel. (613) 226-4187; fax (613) 226-2984; f. 1922; Exec. Vice-Pres. DAN DEMPSTER.

Canadian Nursery Landscape Association: 7856 Fifth Lane South, RR 4, Stn Main, Milton, ON L9T 2X8; tel. (905) 875-1399; fax (905) 875-1840; e-mail cnla@canadanursery.com; internet www.canadanursery.com; Exec. Dir CHRIS D. ANDREWS; 1,500 mems.

Canadian Seed Growers' Association: POB 8455, Ottawa, ON K1G 3T1; tel. (613) 236-0497; fax (613) 563-7855; e-mail seeds@seedgrowers.ca; internet www.seedgrowers.ca; f. 1904; Exec. Dir W. K. ROBERTSON; 4,300 mems.

National Dairy Council of Canada: 221 Laurier Ave East, Ottawa, ON K1N 6P1; tel. (613) 238-4116; fax (613) 238-6247; e-mail info@ndcc.ca; internet www.ndcc.ca; f. 1918; Pres. KEMPTON MATTE; 69 mem asscns, 250 individual mems.

National Farmers Union (NFU): 2717 Wentz Ave, Saskatoon, SK S7K 4B6; tel. (306) 652-9465; fax (306) 664-6226; e-mail nfu@sk.sympatico.ca; internet www.nfu.ca; f. 1969; Pres. CORY OLLIKKA; 10,000 mems.

L'Union des producteurs agricoles: 555 blvd Roland-Therrien, Longueuil, QC J4H 3Y9; tel. (514) 679-0530; fax (514) 679-4943; e-mail upa@upa.qc.ca; internet www.upa.qc.ca; f. 1924; Dir-Gen. JEAN LAROSE; 37 institutional mems, 45,000 individual mems.

Building and Construction

Canadian Construction Association: 75 Albert St, Suite 400, Ottawa, ON K1P 5E7; tel. (613) 236-9455; fax (613) 236-9526; e-mail cca@cca-acc.com; internet www.cca-acc.com; f. 1918; Pres. MICHAEL ATKINSON; over 20,000 mems.

Canadian Institute of Steel Construction: 201 Consumers Rd, Suite 300, Willowdale, ON M2J 4G8; tel. (416) 491-4552; fax (416) 491-6461; e-mail info@compuserve.com; internet www.cisc-icca.ca; f. 1930; Pres. TED TEMPLE; 245 mems.

Canadian Paint and Coatings Association: 9900 blvd Cavendish, Bureau 103, St-Laurent, QC H4M 2V2; tel. (514) 745-2611; fax (514) 745-2031; e-mail cpca@cdnpaint.org; internet www.cdnpaint.org; f. 1913; Pres. RICHARD MURRY; 132 mems.

Canadian Precast/Prestressed Concrete Institute: 196 Bronson Ave, Suite 100, Ottawa, ON K1R 6H4; tel. (613) 232-2619; fax (613) 232-5139; e-mail info@cpci.ca; internet www.cpci.ca; Pres. JOHN R. FOWLER; 300 mems.

Ontario Painting Contractors Association: 211 Consumers Rd, Suite 305, Willowdale, ON M2J 4G8; tel. (416) 498-1897; fax (416) 498-6757; e-mail mmarquardt@attglobal.net; internet www.ontpca.org; f. 1967; Exec. Dir MAUREEN MARQUARDT; 100 mems.

Clothing and Textiles

Canadian Apparel Federation: 130 Slater St, Suite 1050, Ottawa, ON K1P 6E2; tel. (613) 231-3220; fax (613) 231-2305; e-mail info@apparel.ca; internet www.apparel.ca; f. 1977.

Canadian Carpet Institute: 130 Slater St, Suite 1050, Ottawa, ON K1P 6E2; tel. (613) 232-7183; fax (613) 232-3072; e-mail carpet@magi.com; f. 1961; Exec. Dir JEAN-CLAUDE CARISSE; 7 mems.

Canadian Textiles Institute: 66 Slater St, Suite 1720, Ottawa, ON K1P 5H1; tel. (613) 232-7195; fax (613) 232-8722; e-mail cti@textiles.ca; f. 1935; Pres. ELIZABETH SIWICKI; 60 mems.

Men's Clothing Manufacturers Association: 555 rue Chabanel ouest, Bureau 801, Montréal, QC H3N 2H8; tel. (514) 382-3846; fax (514) 382-3846; e-mail mcma@macten.net; f. 1961; Exec. Dir DAVID BALINSKY; 67 mems.

Textile Federation of Canada: c/o CTT, 3000 rue Boullé, St-Hyacinthe, QC J2S 1H9; tel. (450) 778-1870; fax (450) 778-3901; e-mail rleclerc@ctt.ca; Exec. Sec. ROGER LECLERC; 1,950 mems.

Electrical and Electronics

Canadian Electrical Contractors Assocation: 23 Lesmill Rd, Suite 207, North York, ON M3B 3P6; tel. (416) 391-3226; fax (416) 391-3926; Exec. Sec. ERYL M. ROBERTS.

Canadian Electricity Association: see Utilities—Electricity.

Electrical and Electronic Manufacturers Association of Canada: 10 Carlson Court, Suite 500, Rexdale, ON M9W 6L2; tel. (905) 674-7410; fax (905) 674-7412; f. 1976; Pres. NORMAN ASPIN; 175 mems.

Fisheries

Canadian Association of Fish Exporters: 1770 Woodward Drive, Suite 212, Ottawa, ON K2C 0P8; tel. (613) 228-9220; fax (613) 228-9223; e-mail jbarnett@seafood.ca; internet www.seafood.ca/index.htm; f. 1978; Pres. Dr JANE BARNETT.

Fisheries Council of Canada: 38 Antares Drive, Suite 110, Nepean, ON K2E 7V2; tel. (613) 727-7450; fax (613) 727-7453; e-mail ronbulmer@fisheriescouncil.org; f. 1945; Pres. R. W. BULMER; 200 mems.

Food and Beverages

Baking Association of Canada: 7895 Tranmere Drive, Mississauga, ON L5S 1V9; tel. (905) 405-0288; fax (905) 405-0993; e-mail info@baking.ca; internet www.baking.ca; f. 1947; Pres. and CEO PAUL HETHERINGTON; 1,400 institutional mems, 200 assoc. mems.

Brewers Association of Canada: 155 Queen St, Suite 1200, Ottawa, ON K1P 6L1; tel. (613) 232-9601; fax (613) 232-2283; e-mail office@brewers.ca; internet www.brewers.ca; f. 1943; Pres. and CEO R. A. MORRISON; 29 mems.

Canadian Council of Grocery Distributors: CP 1082, succursale place-du-Parc, Montréal, QC H2W 2P4; tel. (514) 982-0267; fax (514) 849-3021; f. 1919; Pres. and CEO JOHN F. GECI; 69 institutional mems, 115 assoc. mems.

Canadian Food Brokers Association: 58 Meadowbrook Ave, Suite 100, Unionville, ON L3R 2N9; tel. (905) 477-4644; fax (905) 477-9580; e-mail kbray@idirect.com; f. 1942; Pres. KEITH BRAY; 70 mems, 60 assoc mems.

Canadian Meat Council: 875 Carling Ave, Suite 410, Ottawa, ON K1S 5P1; tel. (613) 729-3911; fax (613) 729-4997; internet www.cmc-cvc.com; f. 1919; Gen. Man. ROBERT WEAVER; 65 mems.

Canadian National Millers' Association: 90 Sparks St, Suite 1127, Ottawa, ON K1P 5B4; tel. (613) 238-2293; fax (613) 235-5866; f. 1920; Pres. GORDON HARRISON; 17 mems.

Canadian Pork Council: 75 Albert St, Suite 1101, Ottawa, ON K1P 5E7; tel. (613) 236-9239; fax (613) 236-6658; e-mail cpc@fox.nstn.ca; Exec. Dir. MARTIN RICE; 8 mems.

Confectionery Manufacturers Association of Canada: 885 Don Mills Rd, Suite 301, Don Mills, ON M3C 1V9; tel. (416) 510-8034; fax (416) 510-8044; e-mail carolh@fcpmc.com; f. 1919; Pres. CAROL L. HOCHU; 81 corporate mems.

Food and Consumer Products Manufacturers of Canada: 885 Don Mills Rd, Suite 301, Don Mills, ON M3C 1V9; tel. (416) 510-8024; fax (416) 510-8043; e-mail info@cpmc.com; internet www.fcpmc.com; Pres. GEORGE FLEISCHMANN; 180 corporate mems.

Food Institute of Canada: 1600 Scott St, Suite 415, Ottawa, ON K1Y 4N7; tel. (613) 722-1000; fax (613) 722-1404; e-mail fic@foodnet.fic.ca; internet www.fic.ca; f. 1989; Pres. JEAN GATTUSO; 200 mems.

Forestry, Lumber and Allied Industries

Canadian Lumbermen's Association: 27 Goulburn Ave, Ottawa, ON K1N 8C7; tel. (613) 233-6205; fax (613) 233-1929; e-mail info@cla-ca.ca; internet www.cla-ca.ca; f. 1907; Pres. and Exec. Dir ROBERT RIVARD; 200 mems.

Canadian Pulp and Paper Association: Immeuble Sun Life, 1155 rue Metcalfe, 19e étage, Montréal, QC H3B 4T6; tel. (514) 866-6621; fax (514) 866-3035; e-mail cppacda@ibm.net; internet www.open.doors.cppa.ca/; f. 1913; Pres. LISE LACHAPELLE; 60 mems.

Canadian Wood Council: 1400 Blair Pl, Suite 210, Ottawa, ON K1J 9B8; tel. (613) 247-7077; fax (613) 247-7856; internet www.cwc.ca; f. 1959; Pres. CATHERINE LALONDE.

Council of Forest Industries: 1200-555 Burrard St, POB 276, Vancouver, BC V7X 1S7; tel. (604) 684-0211; fax (604) 687-4930; e-mail info@cofi.org; internet www.cofi.org; f. 1960; CEO RON MCDONALD.

Ontario Forest Industries Association: 130 Adelaide St West, Suite 1700, Toronto, ON M5H 3P5; tel. (416) 368-6188; fax (416) 368-5445; e-mail info@ofia.com; internet www.ofia.com; f. 1943; Pres. R. MARIE RAUTER; 20 corporate mems.

Hotels and Catering

Canadian Restaurant and Foodservices Association: 316 Bloor St West, Toronto, ON M5S 1W5; tel. (416) 923-8416; fax (416) 923-1450; e-mail info@crfa.ca; internet www.crfa.ca; f. 1944; Pres. DOUGLAS NEEDHAM; 14,000 mems.

Hotel Association of Canada Inc: 130 Albert St, Suite 1016, Ottawa, ON K1P 5G4; tel. (613) 237-7149; fax (613) 237-8928; e-mail hac@hotels.ca; internet www.hotels.ca; f. 1929; Pres. ANTHONY POLLARD.

Mining

Canadian Association of Petroleum Producers: 350 7th Ave, SW, Suite 2100, Calgary, AB T2P 3N9; tel. (403) 267-1100; fax (403) 261-4622; e-mail communication@capp.ca; internet www.capp.ca; f. 1952; Pres. PIERRE ALVAREZ; 200 institutional mems, 120 assoc. mems.

Canadian Gas Association: See Utilities—Gas.

Canadian Mining Contractors Association: 1088 Staghorn Court, Mississauga, ON L5C 3R2; tel. (905) 279-0104; fax (905) 279-1646; e-mail bcampbell@istar.ca; Pres. BRUCE CAMPBELL.

Mining Association of Canada: 350 Sparks St, Suite 1105, Ottawa, ON K1R 7S8; tel. (613) 233-9391; fax (613) 233-8897; e-mail gpeeling@mining.ca; internet www.mining.ca; f. 1935; Chair. GUY DUFRESNE; 75 mems.

Northwest Territories Chamber of Mines: POB 2818, Yellowknife, NT X1A 2R1; tel. (403) 873-5281; fax (403) 920-2145; e-mail nwtmines@ssimicro.com; f. 1967; Gen. Man. MIKE VAYDIK; 380 mems.

Ontario Mining Association: 110 Yonge St, 15th Floor, Toronto, ON M5C 1T4; tel. (416) 364-9301; fax (416) 364-5986; f. 1920; Pres. PATRICK REID; 47 mems.

Petroleum Services Association of Canada: 800 6th Ave SW, Suite 1150, Calgary, AB T2P 3G3; tel. (403) 264-4195; fax (403) 263-7174; e-mail infor@psac.ca; internet www.psac.ca; Pres. ROGER SOUCY.

Yukon Chamber of Mines: 3151B 3rd Ave, Whitehorse, YT Y1A 1G1; tel. (867) 667-2090; fax (867) 668-7127; e-mail ycmines@yukon.net; internet www.yukon.net/ycmines; f. 1956; Man. Dir DAVE AUSTIN; 350 mems.

Pharmaceutical

Canada's Research-Based Pharmaceuticals (Rx & D): 1111 Prince of Wales Drive, Suite 302, Ottawa, ON K2C 3T2; tel. (613) 727-1380; fax (613) 727-1407; e-mail info@canadapharma.org; internet www.canadapharma.org; f. 1914 as Pharmaceutical Mfrs Asscn of Canada; Pres. MURRAY J. ELSTON; 65 mems.

Canadian Drug Manufacturers Association: 4120 Yonge St, Suite 409, Toronto, ON M2P 2B8; tel. (416) 223-2333; fax (416) 223-2425; e-mail info@cdma-acfpp.org; internet www.cdma-acfpp.org; Pres. JIM KEON; 18 mems.

Retailing

Retail Council of Canada: 121 Bloor St, Suite 1210, Toronto, ON M4W 3M5; tel. (416) 922-6678; fax (416) 922-8011; internet www.retailcouncil.org; f. 1963; Pres. and CEO DIANE J. BRISEBOIS; 8,500 mems.

Retail Merchants' Association of Canada Inc: 1780 Birchmount Rd, Scarborough, ON M1P 2H8; tel. (416) 291-7903; fax (416) 291-5635; f. 1896; Pres. SEAN MCMAHON; 3,000 mems.

Transport

Air Transport Association of Canada: see Transport—Civil Aviation.

Canadian Institute of Traffic and Transportation: 10 King St East, 4th Floor, Toronto, ON M5C 1C3; tel. (416) 363-5696; fax (416) 363-5698; e-mail citt@citt.ca; internet www.citt.ca; f. 1958; Chair. SUSAN COLLINS; 2,000 mems.

Canadian Shippers' Council: see Transport—Shipping.

Canadian Trucking Alliance: National Bldg, 130 Slater St, Suite 1025, Ottawa, ON K1P 6E2; tel. (613) 236-9426; fax (613) 563-2701; e-mail dugas@cantruck.com; internet www.cantruck.com; f. 1937; CEO DAVID BRADLEY.

Canadian Vehicle Manufacturers' Association: 25 Adelaide St East, Suite 1602, Toronto, ON M5C 3A1; tel. (416) 364-9333; fax

(416) 367-3221; e-mail info@cvma.ca; internet www.cvma.ca; f. 1926; Pres. MARK A. NANTAIS; 5 mems.

Railway Association of Canada: see Transport—Railways.

Shipping Federation of Canada: see Transport—Shipping.

Miscellaneous

Canadian Association of Importers and Exporters, Inc: 438 University Ave, Suite 1618, Box 60, Toronto, ON M5G 2K8; tel. (416) 595-5333; fax (416) 595-8226; internet www.importers.ca; f. 1932; Pres. BOB ARMSTRONG; 550 mems.

Canadian Printing Industries Association: 75 Albert St, Suite 906, Ottawa, ON K1P 5E7; tel. (613) 236-7208; fax (613) 236-8169; Pres. PIERRE BOUCHER; 650 mems.

Canadian Tobacco Manufacturers' Council: 99 Bank St, Suite 701, Ottawa, ON K1P 6B9; tel. (613) 238-2799; fax (613) 238-4463; f. 1963; Pres. ROBERT PARKER.

Shipbuilding Association of Canada: 222 Queen St, Suite 1502, Ottawa, ON K1P 5V9; tel. (613) 232-7127; fax (613) 238-5519; internet www.shipbuilding.ca; f. 1995; Pres. PETER CAIRNS; 20 mems.

UTILITIES

Regulatory Authorities

Alberta Energy and Utilities Board: 640 Fifth Ave, SW, Calgary, AB T2P 3G4; tel. (403) 297-8311; fax (403) 297-8398; Chair. CÉLINE BELANGER.

British Columbia Utilities Commission: 900 Howe St, 6th Floor, Box 250, Vancouver, BC V6Z 2N3; tel. (604) 660-4700; fax (604) 660-1102; e-mail commission.secretary@bcuc.com; internet www.bcuc.com; Chair. PETER OSTERGAARD.

Manitoba Public Utilities Board: 280 Smith St, 2nd Floor, Winnipeg, MB R3C 1K2; tel. (204) 945-2638; fax (204) 945-2643; Exec. Dir G. O. BARRON.

National Energy Board: 444 Seventh Ave, SW, Calgary, AB T2P 0X8; tel. (403) 292-4800; fax (403) 292-5503; internet www.neb.gc.ca; fed. regulatory agency; Chair. KENNETH W. VOLLMAN.

New Brunswick Board of Commissioners of Public Utilities: 110 Charlotte St, POB 5001, Saint John, NB E2L 4Y9; tel. (506) 658-2504; fax (506) 633-0163; e-mail dnichols@nbnet.nb.ca; Chair. DAVID C. NICHOLSON.

Newfoundland and Labrador Board of Commissioners of Public Utilities: POB 21040, St John's, NF A1A 5B2; tel. (709) 726-8600; fax (709) 726-9604; e-mail cheryl@pub.nf.ca; Dir and Board Sec. G. CHERYL BLUNDON.

Nova Scotia Utility and Review Board: POB 1692, Postal Unit M, Halifax, NS B3J 3S3; tel. (902) 424-4448; fax (902) 424-3919; e-mail uarb@board.gov.ns.ca; Chair. J. A. MORASH.

Ontario Energy Board: 2300 Yonge St, 26th Floor, Box 2319, Toronto, ON M4P 1E4; tel. (416) 481-1967; fax (416) 440-7656; Chair. MARIE C. ROUNDING.

Prince Edward Island Regulatory and Appeals Commission: 134 Kent St, Suite 501, POB 577, Charlottetown PE C1A 7L1; tel. (902) 892-3501; fax (902) 566-4076; e-mail irac@irac.pe.ca; internet www.irac.pe.ca; Chair. WAYNE D. CHEVERIE.

Québec Electricity and Gas Board: 800 place Victoria, CP 001, succursale de la Bourse, Montréal, QC H4Z 1A2; tel. (514) 873-2070.

Saskatchewan Municipal Board: 2151 Scarth St, 4th Floor, Regina, SK S4P 3V7; Chair. B. G. MCNAMEE.

Electricity

ATCO Electric: 10035 105th St, POB 2426, Edmonton, AB T5J 2V6; internet www.atcoelectric.com; formerly Alberta Power Ltd; generates and distributes electricity in Alberta.

BC Hydro: 6911 Southpoint Drive, Burnaby, BC V3N 4X8; tel. (604) 528-1600; fax (604) 623-3901; e-mail info.serv@bchydro.bc.ca; internet www.bchydro.bc.ca; generation, transmission and distribution of energy in British Columbia; Chair. BRIAN R. D. SMITH; Pres. and CEO MICHAEL COSTELLO.

Canadian Electricity Association: 1155 rue Metcalfe, Bureau 1120, Montréal, QC H3Z 2P9; tel. (514) 866-6121; fax (514) 866-1880; e-mail info@canelect.ca; internet www.intertower.com/cea.html; mems include 36 corporate utility enterprises accounting for c. 95% of Canada's installed generating capacity; Pres. and CEO HANS R. KONOW.

Hydro-Québec: 75 blvd René-Lévesque ouest, Montréal, QC H2Z 1A4; tel. (514) 289-2211; fax (514) 843-3163; Pres. ANDRÉ CAILLÉ.

Manitoba Hydro: 820 Taylor Ave, POB 815, Winnipeg, MB R3C 2P4; tel. (204) 474-3311; fax (204) 475-9044; e-mail publicaffairs@hydro.mb.ca; internet www.hydro.mb.ca; Pres. and CEO ROBERT B. BRENNAN.

Newfoundland and Labrador Hydro: POB 12400, St John's NF A1B 4K7; tel. (709) 737-1400; fax (709) 737-1231; internet www.nlh.nf.ca; Pres. and CEO WILLIAM E. WELLS.

Northwest Territories Power Corporation: 4 Capital Drive, Hay River, NT X0E 1G2; tel. (867) 874-5200; fax (867) 874-5251; e-mail info@ntpc.com; internet www.ntpc.com; f. 1988; Chair. GORDON STEWART; Pres. and CEO LEON COURNEYA.

Nova Scotia Power Inc: POB 910, Halifax, NS B3J 2W5; tel. (902) 428-6230; fax (902) 428-6110.

Ontario Power Generation: 700 University Ave, Toronto, ON M5G 1X6; tel. (416) 592-5111; fax (416) 971-3691; internet www .ontariopowergeneration.com; Canada's largest public utility corpn; also the prin. producer of nuclear power; Chair. WILLIAM FARLINGER; Pres. and CEO RONALD OSBORNE.

Prince Edward Island Energy Corporation: Shaw Bldg, 105 Rochford St, 5th Floor, POB 2000, Charlottetown, PE C1A 7N8; tel. (902) 894-0288; fax (902) 368-4242; e-mail dwmacquarrie@gov.pe.ca; internet www.gov.pe.ca; CEO WAYNE MACQUARRIE.

SaskPower: 2025 Victoria Ave, Regina, SK S4P 0S1; tel. (306) 566-2121; fax (306) 566-2330; f. 1930; Pres. and CEO JOHN R. MESSER.

Gas

Canadian Gas Association: 20 Eglinton Ave West, Suite 1305, POB 1305, Toronto, ON M4R 1K8; tel. (416) 481-1828; fax (416) 481-2625; e-mail info@cga.ca; internet www.cga.ca; f. 1907; Pres. and CEO MARIE C. ROUNDING; 220 corporate mems.

Ontario Natural Gas Association: 77 Bloor St, Suite 1104, Toronto, ON M5S 1M2; tel. (416) 961-2339; fax (416) 961-1173; e-mail onga@sympatico.ca; Chair. J. W. WELLARD.

TransCanada Pipelines Ltd: 111 Fifth Ave, SW, POB 1000, Station M, Calgary, AB T2P 4K5; tel. (403) 267-6100; fax (403) 267-6444; internet www.transcanada.com; production, storage, transmission and sale of natural gas through six subsidiary cos; Pres. and CEO DOUGLAS D. BALDWIN.

Westcoast Energy Inc: 666 Burrard St, Suite 3400, Park Place, Vancouver, BC V6C 3M8; tel. (604) 488-8000; fax (604) 488-8500; internet www.westcoastenergy.com; production, storage, transmission and sale of natural gas through four operating cos in British Columbia, Alberta and Manitoba; Chair. and CEO MICHAEL E. J. PHELPS.

Water

Northwest Territories Water Board: POB 1500, Yellowknife, NT X1A 2R3; tel. (867) 669-2772; fax (867) 669-2719.

Nunavut Water Board: Gjoa Haven, NT X0E 1J0.

Resource Management and Environmental Protection Branch, Nova Scotia Department of Environment and Labour: 5151 Terminal Rd, 5th Floor, POB 2107, Halifax, NS B3J 3B7; tel. (902) 424-2554; fax (902) 424-0503; internet www.gov.ns.ca/enla.

SaskWater: Victoria Place, 111 Fairford St East, Moose Jaw, SK 6SH 7X9; tel. (306) 694-3900; fax (306) 694-3944; e-mail saskwater .cd@sasknet.sk.ca; Pres. BRIAN KAUKINEN.

Water Management Branch, British Columbia Ministry of Environment, Lands and Parks: 2975 Jutland Rd, POB 9340, Victoria, BC V8W 9M1; tel. (250) 952-6806; internet www.elp.-gov.bc.ca/wat/; Dir JAMES S. MATTISON.

Water Resources Branch, Manitoba Natural Resources: 200 Saulteaux Crescent, POB 80, Winnipeg, MB R3J 3W3; tel. (204) 945-7488; fax (204) 945-7419; Dir STEVEN TOPPING.

Water Resources Branch, Ontario, Ministry of Environment and Energy: 135 St Clair Ave West, 2nd Floor, Toronto, ON M4V 1P5; tel. (416) 323-4917; fax (416) 965-9807; Dir JIM ASHMAN.

Water Resources Division, Newfoundland Department of Environment and Labour: Confederation Bldg, POB 8700, St John's NF A1B 4J6; tel. (709) 729-2563; fax (709) 729-0320; internet www.gov.nf.ca/env/env/water_resources.asp; Dir MARTIN GOEBEL.

Water Resources Division, Prince Edward Island Department of the Environment: Jones Bldg, 11 Kent St, POB 2000, Charlottetown, PE C1A 7N8; tel. (902) 368-5028; fax (902) 368-5982; e-mail cemurphy@gov.pe.ca; Dir CLAIR MURPHY.

Water Resources Planning Branch, New Brunswick Department of the Environment: 364 Argyle St, POB 6000, Fredericton, NB E3B 5H1; tel. (506) 457-4846; fax (506) 453-2390; Man. WILLIAM C. AYER.

TRADE UNIONS

At the beginning of 2000 there were 4,057,000 union members in Canada, representing 25.8% of the civilian labour force. Of these, 29.5% belonged to unions with headquarters in the USA.

In 2000 unions affiliated to the Canadian Labour Congress represented 69.4% of total union membership.

Canadian Labour Congress: 2841 Riverside Drive, Ottawa, ON K1V 8X7; tel. (613) 521-3400; fax (613) 521-4655; internet www .clc-ctc.ca; f. 1956; Pres. KEN GEORGETTI; Sec.-Treas. NANCY RICHE; 2,300,000 mems (2000).

Affiliated unions with more than 15,000 members:

Amalgamated Transit Union: 1450 Meyerside Drive, Suite 701, Mississauga, ON L5T 2N5; tel. (905) 670-4710; fax (905) 670-3659; e-mail kfoster@netcom.ca; internet www.cdn-council-atu .org; Canadian Dir KEN FOSTER; 24,000 mems (2000).

American Federation of Musicians of the United States and Canada: 75 The Donway West, Suite 1010, Don Mills, ON M3C 2E9; tel. (416) 391-5161; fax (416) 391-5165; Vice-Pres. in Canada DAVID J. JANDRISCH; 18,000 mems (2000).

British Columbia Nurses' Union: 4060 Regent St, Burnaby, BC V5C 6P5; tel. (604) 433-2268; fax (604) 433-7945; Pres. CATHY FERGUSON; 25,000 mems (2000).

Canadian Union of Postal Workers: 337 Bank St, Ottawa, ON K2P 1Y3; tel. (613) 236-7238; fax (613) 563-7861; f. 1965; Nat. Pres. DALE CLARK; 54,000 mems (2000).

Canadian Union of Public Employees: 21 Florence St, Ottawa, ON K2P 0W6; tel. (613) 237-1590; fax (613) 237-5508; internet www.cupe.ca; Nat. Pres. JUDY DARCY; 485,000 mems (2000).

Communications, Energy and Paperworkers Union of Canada: 350 Albert St, 19th Floor, Ottawa, ON K1R 1A4; tel. (613) 230-5200; fax (613) 230-5801; internet www.cep.ca; Pres. BRIAN PAYNE; 144,000 mems (2000).

Hotel Employees and Restaurant Employees International Union: 1140 blvd de Maisonneuve ouest, Bureau 1150, Montréal, QC H3A 1M8; tel. (514) 844-4167; fax (514) 844-1536; e-mail jamesstamos@herecanadianoffice.com; Canadian Dir JAMES STAMOS; 34,000 mems (2000).

International Association of Fire Fighters: 350 Sparks St, Suite 403, Ottawa, ON K1R 7S8; tel. (613) 567-8988; fax (613) 567-8986; Canadian Dir SEAN MCMANUS; 17,000 mems (2000).

International Association of Machinists and Aerospace Workers: 100 Metcalfe St, Suite 300, Ottawa, ON K1P 5M1; tel. (613) 236-9761; fax (613) 563-7830; Gen. Vice-Pres. in Canada DAVE L. RITCHIE; 45,000 mems (2000).

International Brotherhood of Electrical Workers: 1450 Meyerside Dr., Suite 300, Mississauga, ON L5T 2N5; tel. (905) 564-5441; fax (905) 564-8114; e-mail ivpd_oi@ibew.org; Int.Vice-Pres. DON E. LOUNDS; 59,000 mems (1999).

International Union of Operating Engineers: 28 Aberdeen St, Kentville, NS B4N 3X9; tel. (902) 678-9950; fax (902) 678-1838; e-mail iuoe@glinx.com; Canadian Dir EDGAR DOULL; 40,000 mems (2000).

IWA Canada (Industrial Wood and Allied Workers of Canada): 1285 Pender St, Suite 500, Vancouver, BC V6E 4B2; tel. (604) 683-1117; fax (604) 688-6416; internet www.iwa.ca; f. 1937; Pres. D. C. HAGGARD; 40,000 mems (2000).

Labourers' International Union of North America: 44 Hughson St South, Hamilton, ON L8N 2A7; tel. (905) 522-7177; fax (905) 522-9310; Canadian Dir and Vice-Pres. ENRICO H. MANCINELLI; 60,000 mems (2000).

National Automobile, Aerospace Transportation and General Workers Union of Canada (CAW–Canada): 205 Placer Court, North York, Willowdale, ON M2H 3H9; tel. (416) 497-4110; fax (416) 495-6552; e-mail caw@caw.ca; internet www.caw.ca; f. 1985; Nat. Pres. BASIL HARGROVE; 220,000 mems (2000).

National Union of Public and General Employees: 15 Auriga Drive, Nepean, ON K2E 1B7; tel. (613) 228-9800; fax (613) 228-9801; e-mail national@nupge.ca; internet www.nupge.ca; Nat. Pres. JAMES CLANCY; 325,000 mems (2000).

Office and Professional Employees' International Union: 1200 ave Papineau, Bureau 250, Montréal, QC H2K 4S6; tel. (514) 522-6511; fax (514) 522-9000; Canadian Dir MICHEL LAJEUNESSE; 33,000 mems (2000).

Ontario English Catholic Teachers' Association: 65 St Clair Ave East, Suite 400, Toronto, ON M4T 2Y8; tel. (416) 925-2493; fax (416) 925-7764; internet www.oecta.on.ca; Pres. JIM SMITH; 30,000 mems (2000).

Ontario Secondary School Teachers' Federation: 60 Mobile Drive, Toronto, ON M4A 2P3; tel. (416) 751-8300; fax (416) 751-3394; Pres. EARL MANNERS; 51,000 mems (2000).

Public Service Alliance of Canada: 233 Gilmour St, Ottawa, ON K2P 0P1; tel. (613) 560-4200; fax (613) 567-0385; internet www.psac-afpc.com; f. 1966; Nat. Pres. NYCOLE TURMEL; 150,000 mems (2000).

Service Employees International Union: 75 The Donway West, Suite 810, North York, ON M3C 2E9; tel. (416) 447-2311; fax

(416) 447-2428; e-mail brownk@seiu.ca; internet www.seiu.org; Vice-Pres. in Canada SHARLEEN STEWART; 90,000 mems (2000).

Teamsters Canada: 2540 Daniel-Johnson, Bureau 804, Laval, QC H7T 2S3; tel. (514) 682-5521; fax (514) 681-2244; internet www.teamsters-canada.org; Canadian Pres. LOUIS LACROIX; 95,000 mems (2000).

Union of Needletrades, Industrial and Textile Employees–Canada: 15 Gervais Drive, Suite 700, Toronto, ON M3C 1Y8; tel. (416) 441-1806; fax (416) 441-9680; internet www.unite-svti.org; Canadian Dir JOHN ALLERUZZO; 25,000 mems (2000).

United Association of Journeymen and Apprentices of the Plumbing and Pipe Fitting Industry of the United States and Canada: 1959 152nd St, Suite 316, Surrey, BC V4A 9E3; tel. (604) 531-0516; fax (604) 531-0547; e-mail uacanada@direct.ca; internet www.ua.org; Vice-Pres. and Canadian Dir GEORGE MESERVIER; 37,000 mems (2000).

United Brotherhood of Carpenters and Joiners of America: 5799 Young St, Suite 807, Willowdale, ON M2M 3V3; tel. (416) 225-8885; fax (416) 225-5390; Gen. Exec. Bd Mem. JAMES E. SMITH; 56,000 mems (2000).

United Food and Commercial Workers Canada: 61 International Blvd, Suite 300, Rexdale, ON M9W 6K4; tel. (416) 675-1104; fax (416) 675-6919; e-mail ufcw@.ufcw.ca; internet www.ufcw.ca; f. 1979; Canadian Dir MICHAEL J. FRASER; 220,000 mems (2000).

United Steelworkers of America: 234 Eglinton Ave East, 7th Floor, Toronto, ON M4P 1K7; tel. (416) 487-1571; fax (416) 482-5548; internet www.uswa.org; Nat. Dir in Canada LAWRENCE MCBREARTY; 190,000 mems (2000).

Other Central Congresses

Centrale des syndicats du Québec: 9405 rue Sherbrooke est, Montréal, QC H1L 6P3; tel. (514) 356-8888; fax (514) 356-9999; internet www.csq.qc.net; f. 1974, name changed as above 2000; Pres. MONIQUE RICHARD; 17 affiliated unions:

Affiliated union with over 15,000 members:

Fédération des syndicats de l'enseignment: 320 rue St-Joseph est, Bureau 100, Québec, QC G1K 9E7; tel. (418) 649-8888; fax (418) 649-1914; Pres. JOHANNE FORTIER; 80,000 mems (2000).

Centrale des syndicats démocratiques: 801 rue Québec, 4e étage, Québec, QC G1J 2T7; tel. (418) 529-2956; fax (418) 529-6323; f. 1972; Pres. FRANÇOIS VAUDREUIL; 2 federated and 382 affiliated unions (2000).

Confederation of Canadian Unions: 155 Skinner St, Suite 206, Nanaimo, BC V9R 5E8; tel. (250) 753-1060; fax (250) 753-1062; e-mail ccu@island.net; f. 1969; Pres. JOE ELWORTHY; 9 affiliated unions (1999).

Confédération des syndicats nationaux: 1601 ave de Lorimier, Montréal, QC H2K 4M5; tel. (514) 598-2121; fax (514) 598-2052; e-mail intcsn@total.net; internet www.csn.qc.ca; f. 1921; Pres. MARC LAVIOLETTE; 9 federated unions.

Federated unions with over 15,000 members:

Fédération des employées et employés de services publics inc: 1601 ave de Lorimier, Montréal, QC H2K 4M5; tel. (514) 598-2231; fax (514) 598-2398; Pres. GINETTE GUÉRIN; 36,000 mems (2000).

Fédération du commerce inc: 1601 ave de Lorimier, Montréal, QC H2K 4M5; tel. (514) 598-2181; fax (514) 598-2304; Pres. JEAN LORTIE; 34,000 mems (2000).

Fédération de la métallurgie: 2100 blvd de Maisonneuve est, Bureau 204, Montréal, QC H2K 4S1; tel. (514) 529-4937; fax (514) 529-4935; Pres. ALAIN LAMPRON; 20,000 mems (1998).

Fédération de la santé et des services sociaux: 1601 ave de Lorimier, Montréal, QC H2K 4M5; tel. (514) 598-2210; fax (514) 598-2223; Pres. LOUIS ROY; 97,000 mems (2000).

Fédération nationale des enseignantes et des enseignants du Québec (FNEEQ): 1601 ave de Lorimier, Montréal, QC H2K 4M5; tel. (514) 598-2241; fax (514) 598-2190; e-mail fneeq@videotron.net; internet www.fneeq.qc.ca; f. 1969; Pres. PIERRE PATRY; 20,000 mems (2000).

The American Federation of Labor and Congress of Industrial Organizations (AFL–CIO), with headquarters in Washington, DC, USA, represented 0.4% of the total union membership in Canada, at the beginning of 1997.

Affiliated union with over 15,000 members:

International Association of Bridge, Structural and Ornamental Iron Workers: 1350 L'Heritage Drive, Sarnia, ON N7S 6H8; tel. (519) 542-1413; fax (519) 542-3790; Gen. Vice-Pres. JAMES PHAIR; 15,000 mems (2000).

Principal Unaffiliated Unions

Alberta Teachers' Association: 11010 142nd St, Edmonton, AB T5N 2R1; tel. (780) 447-9400; fax (780) 455-6481; e-mail postmaster@teachers.ab.ca; internet www.teachers.ab.ca; Pres. LARRY BOOI; 30,000 mems (2000).

British Columbia Teachers' Federation: 550 West 6th Ave, Suite 100, Vancouver, BC V5Z 4P2; tel. (604) 871-2283; fax (604) 871-2294; internet www.bctf.bc.ca; Pres. DAVID CHUDNOVSKY; 44,000 mems (2000).

Canadian Telephone Employees' Association: place du Canada, Bureau 360; Montréal, QC H3B 2N2; tel. (514) 861-9963; Pres. JUDITH KING; 16,000 mems (2000).

Christian Labour Association of Canada: 5920 Atlantic Drive, Mississauga, ON L4W 1N6; tel. (905) 670-7383; fax (905) 670-8416; e-mail headoffice@clac.ca; internet www.clac.ca; Pres. STAN BAKER; 22,000 mems (2000).

Elementary Teachers' Federation of Ontario: POB 1100, Station F, Toronto, ON M4Y 2T7; tel. (416) 962-3836; fax (416) 964-0512; f. 1998; Pres. PHYLLIS BENEDICT; 52,000 mems (2000).

Fédération des infirmières et d'infirmiers du Québec: 2050 rue de Bleury, 4e étage, Montréal, QC H3A 2J5; tel. (514) 987-1141; fax (514) 987-7273; Pres. JENNIE SKENE; 48,000 mems (1998).

Ontario Nurses' Association: 85 Grenville St, Suite 400, Toronto, ON M5S 3A2; tel. (416) 964-8833; fax (416) 964-8864; e-mail onamail@mail.ona.on; internet www.ona.org; Pres. BARB WAHL; 45,000 mems (2000).

Professional Institute of the Public Service of Canada: 53 Auriga Drive, Nepean, ON K2E 8C3; tel. (613) 228-6310; fax (613) 228-9048; internet www.pipsc.ca; Pres. STEVE HINDLE; 35,000 mems (1999).

Syndicat de la fonction publique Québec: 5100 blvd des Gradins, Québec, QC G2J 1N4; tel. (418) 623-2424; fax (418) 623-6109; Gen. Pres. SERGE ROY; 39,000 mems (2000).

United Nurses of Alberta: Park Plaza, 9th Floor, 10611 98th Ave, Edmonton, AB T5K 2P7; tel. (403) 425-1025; fax (403) 426-2093; Pres. HEATHER SMITH; 17,000 mems (2000).

Transport

Owing to the size of the country, Canada's economy is particularly dependent upon its transport infrastructure. The St Lawrence Seaway allows ocean-going ships to reach the Great Lakes. In addition to an extensive railway network, the country's transport facilities are being increasingly augmented by new roads, air services and petroleum pipelines. The Trans-Canada Highway forms a main feature of a network of more than 900,000 km of roads and highways.

Canadian Transportation Agency (CTA): 15 rue Eddy, Hull, QC K1A 0N9; tel. (819) 997-0344; fax (819) 953-8353; internet www.cta-otc.gc.ca; f. 1996 to oversee the economic regulation of transport; Chair. MARIAN L. ROBSON.

RAILWAYS

BC Rail: POB 8770, Vancouver, BC V6B 4X6; tel. (604) 986-2012; fax (604) 984-5004; internet www.bcrail.com; f. 1912; publicly-owned; 2,314 km of track; Chair. J. GOLDSMITH; Pres. and CEO (vacant).

CN Rail: 935 rue de la Gauchetière ouest, CP 8100, succursale A, Montréal, QC H3C 3N4; tel. (514) 399-4937; fax (514) 399-6910; internet www.cn.ca; f. 1919; investor-owned; 32,500 km of track; Chair. DAVID G. A. MCLEAN; Pres. and CEO PAUL TELLIER.

CP Rail System (Canadian Pacific Railway): 401 Ninth Av, SW, Calgary, AB T2P 4Z4; tel. (403) 319-7000; internet www.cpr.ca; f. 1881; 24,000 km of track; Pres. ROBERT RITCHIE.

Ontario Northland Transportation Commission: 555 Oak St East, North Bay, ON P1B 8L3; tel. (705) 472-4500; fax (705) 476-5598; internet www.ontc.on.ca; an agency of the Govt of Ontario; operates rail services over 1,211 km of track; Chair. ROYAL POULIN; Pres. and CEO K. J. WALLACE.

VIA Rail Canada Inc: 2 place Ville-Marie, CP 8116, succursale A, Montréal, QC H3C 3N3; tel. (514) 871-6000; fax (514) 871-6463; internet www.viarail.ca; f. 1977; fed. govt corpn; proposed transfer to private sector pending in 2000; operates passenger services over rail routes covering 13,822 km of track throughout Canada; Chair. MARC LEFRANÇOIS; Pres. and CEO (vacant).

Association

Railway Association of Canada: 99 Bank St, Suite 1401, Ottawa ON K1P 6B9; tel. (613) 567-8591; fax (613) 567-6726; e-mail rac@railcan.ca; internet www.railcan.ca; f. 1917; Pres. WILLIAM ROWAT; 54 mems.

ROADS

Provincial governments are responsible for roads within their boundaries. The Federal Government is responsible for major roads in the

Yukon, the Northwest Territories and Nunavut and in National Parks. In 1995 there were an estimated 912,200 km of roads (including 15,000 km of federal roads and highways). The Trans-Canada Highway extends from St John's, NF, to Victoria, BC.

INLAND WATERWAYS

The St Lawrence River and the Great Lakes provide Canada and the USA with a system of inland waterways extending from the Atlantic Ocean to the western end of Lake Superior, a distance of 3,769 km (2,342 miles). There is a 10.7-m (35-foot) navigation channel from Montréal to the sea and an 8.25-m (27-foot) channel from Montréal to Lake Erie. The St Lawrence Seaway (see below), which was opened in 1959, was initiated partly to provide a deep waterway and partly to satisfy the increasing demand for electric power. Power development has been undertaken by the provinces of Québec and Ontario, and by New York State. In 1998 cargo traffic through the Seaway exceeded 50m. metric tons. The navigation facilities and conditions are within the jurisdiction of the federal governments of the USA and Canada.

St Lawrence River and Great Lakes Shipping

St Lawrence Seaway Management Corporation: 202 Pitt St, Cornwall, ON K6J 3P7; tel. (613) 932-5170; fax (613) 932-7286; e-mail marketing@seaways.ca; internet www.seaway.ca; f. 1998; responsible for supervision of marine traffic through Canadian section of St Lawrence Seaway, which is operated jtly with the USA; Chair. ROBERT J. SWENOR; Pres. and CEO GUY VÉRONNEAU.

Algoma Central Corpn: 289 Bay St, POB 7000, Sault Ste Marie, ON P6A 5P6; tel. (705) 964-7200; fax (705) 946-7302; f. 1899; Pres. and CEO P. R. CRESSWELL; 24 bulk cargo vessels.

Canada Steamship Lines Inc (CSL Group): 759 square Victoria, CP 100, Montréal, QC H2Y 2K3; tel. (514) 982-3800; fax (514) 982-3802; e-mail ships@csltml.com; internet www.csl.ca; f. 1913; Pres. and CEO RAYMOND JOHNSTON; 19 vessels.

Paterson, N. M., and Sons Ltd: POB 664, Station F, Thunder Bay, ON P7C 4W6; tel. (807) 577-8421; fax (807) 475-3493; f. 1908; bulk carriers; Pres. and CEO R. J. PATERSON; 7 vessels; 95,536 grt.

SHIPPING

At 31 December 1998 the Canadian merchant fleet comprised 835 vessels, with a total displacement of 2,501,274 grt.

British Columbia Ferry Corporation: 1112 Fort St, Victoria, BC V8V 4V2; tel. (250) 386-3431; fax (250) 381-5452; internet www.bcferries.bc.ca; passenger and vehicle ferries; Pres. and CEO BOB LINGWOOD; 40 vessels.

Fednav Ltd: 1000 rue de la Gauchetière ouest, Bureau 3500, Montréal, QC H3B 4W5; tel. (514) 878-6500; fax (514) 878-6642; e-mail info@fednav.com; internet www.fednav.com; f. 1944; ship-owners, operators, contractors, terminal operators; Pres. L. G. PATHY; owned and chartered fleet of 60 vessels.

Groupe Desagnés Inc: 21 rue du Marché-Champlain, Bureau 100, Québec, QC G1K 8Z8; tel. (418) 692-1000; fax (418) 692-6044; Chair. and CEO LOUIS-MARIE BEAULIEU; 10 vessels.

Marine Atlantic Inc: 355 Purves St, North Sydney, NS B2A 3V2; tel. (800) 341-7891; fax (902) 564-7480; internet www.marine-atlantic.ca; Chair. SID HYNES; vehicle and passenger ferries connecting Nova Scotia with Nfld and Labrador.

Associations

Canadian Shipowners Association: 350 Sparks St, Suite 705, Ottawa, ON K1R 7S8; tel. (613) 232-3539; fax (613) 232-6211; e-mail csa@shipowners.ca; internet www.shipowners.ca; f. 1953; Pres. DONALD N. MORRISON; 9 mems.

Canadian Shippers' Council: 48 Balsam Drive, Baie d'Urfé, QC H9X 3K5; tel. (514) 457-7268; fax (514) 457-7269; Sec. WALTER MUELLER; 12 institutional mems, 2 assoc. mems.

Shipping Federation of Canada: 300 rue St-Sacrement, Bureau 326, Montréal, QC H2Y 1X4; tel. (514) 849-2325; fax (514) 849-6992; f. 1903; Pres. Capt. FRANCIS C. NICOL; 75 mems.

CIVIL AVIATION

Principal Company

Air Canada: CP 14000, succursale St-Laurent, Montréal, QC H4Y 1H4; tel. (514) 422-5000; fax (514) 422-5909; internet www.aircanada.ca; f. 1937; investor-owned; acquired Canadian Airlines International in Jan. 2000; Pres. and CEO ROBERT MILTON; operates scheduled and charter services throughout Canada and to the USA; also serves Europe, the Middle East and the Caribbean.

Association

Air Transport Association of Canada: 255 Albert St, Suite 1100, Ottawa, ON K1P 6A9; tel. (613) 233-7727; fax (613) 230-8648; e-mail atac@atac.ca; internet www.atac.ca; f. 1934; Pres. J. CLIFFORD MACKAY; 300 mems.

Tourism

Most tourist visitors (15.2m. of a total 19.4m. in 1999) are from the USA. Expenditure by tourists in 1998 amounted to C $13,300m.

Canadian Tourism Commission: 235 Queen St, 8th Floor West, Ottawa, ON K1A 0H6; tel. (613) 946-1000; fax (613) 954-3964; internet www.canadatourism.com; fed. govt org.; Chair. J. BUDD BUCHANAN; Pres. and CEO JIM WATSON.

Tourism Industry Association of Canada: 130 Albert St, Suite 1608, Ottawa, ON K1P 5G4; tel. (613) 238-3883; fax (613) 238-3878; e-mail info@tiac-aitc.ca; internet www.tiac-aitc.ca; f. 1931; private-sector asscn; encourages travel to and within Canada; promotes devt of travel facilities and services; Pres. ADAM BELYEA.

CAPE VERDE

Introductory Survey

Location, Climate, Language, Religion, Flag, Capital

The Republic of Cape Verde is an archipelago of 10 islands and five islets in the North Atlantic Ocean, about 500 km (300 miles) west of Dakar, Senegal. The country lies in a semi-arid belt, with little rain and an average annual temperature of 24°C (76°F). The official language is Portuguese, of which the locally spoken form is Creole (Crioulo). Virtually all of the inhabitants profess Christianity, and more than 95% are Roman Catholics. The national flag, adopted in 1992 (proportions 5 by 3), comprises five horizontal stripes: blue (half the depth) at the top, white, red, white (each one-twelfth) and blue. Superimposed, to the left of centre, is a circle of 10 five-pointed gold stars (four on the white stripes and three each on the blue stripes above and below). The capital is Cidade de Praia.

Recent History

The Cape Verde Islands were colonized by the Portuguese in the 15th century. From the 1950s liberation movements in Portugal's African colonies were campaigning for independence, and, in this context, the archipelago was linked with the mainland territory of Portuguese Guinea (now Guinea-Bissau) under one nationalist movement, the Partido Africano da Independência do Guiné e Cabo Verde (PAIGC). The independence of Guinea-Bissau was recognized by Portugal in September 1974, but the PAIGC leadership in the Cape Verde Islands decided to pursue its independence claims separately, rather than enter into an immediate federation with Guinea-Bissau. In December 1974 a transitional Government, comprising representatives of the Portuguese Government and the PAIGC, was formed; members of other political parties were excluded. On 30 June 1975 elections for a legislative body, the Assembléia Nacional Popular (ANP—National People's Assembly) were held, in which only PAIGC candidates were allowed to participate. Independence was granted to the Republic of Cape Verde on 5 July 1975, with Aristides Pereira, Secretary-General of the PAIGC, becoming the country's first President. Cape Verde's first Constitution was approved in September 1980.

Although Cape Verde and Guinea-Bissau remained constitutionally separate, the PAIGC supervised the activities of both states. Progress towards the ultimate goal of unification was halted by the November 1980 coup in Guinea-Bissau (during which the President, Luiz Cabral, himself a Cape Verdean, was placed under house arrest). The Cape Verde Government condemned the coup, and in January 1981 the Cape Verde wing of the PAIGC was renamed the Partido Africano da Independência de Cabo Verde (PAICV). In February Pereira was re-elected as President by the ANP, and all articles concerning an eventual union with Guinea-Bissau were removed from the Constitution. Discussions concerning reconciliation were held in June 1982, however, after the release of Cabral, and diplomatic relations between the two countries were subsequently normalized. Cape Verde's relations with Guinea-Bissau improved further in 1988, when an agreement on bilateral co-operation was signed.

Meanwhile, elections to the ANP took place in December 1985. The 83 candidates on the PAICV-approved list, not all of whom were members of the PAICV, obtained 94.5% of the votes cast. In January 1986 Pereira was re-elected for a further five-year term as President by the ANP. At the PAICV Congress in November 1988, Pereira and the Prime Minister, Gen. Pedro Verona Rodrigues Pires, were re-elected Secretary-General and Deputy Secretary-General, respectively, of the party. In 1989 two political commissions were established, to regulate legislative elections and to consider proposals for constitutional changes, and it was subsequently announced that, although elections to the ANP were to be held (as scheduled) in 1990, local elections were to be deferred until 1991. The postponement was criticized by the opposition Catholic newspaper, *Terra Nova*, which accused the Government of perpetuating its monopoly of power. In February 1990, in an apparent response to increasing pressure from church and academic circles, the PAICV announced the convening of an emergency congress to discuss the possible abolition of Article 4 of the Constitution, which guaranteed the supremacy of the PAICV. In April a newly-formed political organization, the Movimento para a Democracia (MPD), issued a manifesto in Paris, France, which advocated the immediate introduction of a multi-party system. Pereira subsequently announced that the next presidential election, which was planned for December 1990, would be held, for the first time, on the basis of universal suffrage.

In July 1990 Pires implemented an extensive ministerial reshuffle, in which seven new state secretariats were created. In the same month a special congress of the PAICV reviewed proposals for new party statutes and the abolition of Article 4 of the Constitution. Pereira also announced his resignation as Secretary-General of the PAICV, and was later replaced by Pires. In September the ANP approved a constitutional amendment abolishing the PAICV's monopoly of power and permitting a multi-party system. The legislative elections were rescheduled for January 1991. The MPD subsequently received official recognition as a political party. In November 1990 the MPD announced its support for an independent candidate, António Mascarenhas Monteiro (a former judge), in the presidential election, which had been postponed until February 1991. On 13 January 1991 the legislative elections, the first multi-party elections to take place in lusophone Africa, resulted in a decisive victory for the MPD, which secured 56 of the 79 seats in the ANP. In late January Dr Carlos Alberto Wahnon de Carvalho Veiga, the leader of the MPD, was sworn in as Prime Minister at the head of an interim Government, mostly comprising members of the MPD, pending the result of the presidential election. This was duly held in mid-February, and resulted in victory for Mascarenhas, who secured 73.5% of the votes cast. The new President was sworn in on 22 March, and the Government was officially inaugurated in April. The first multi-party local elections, held in December, resulted in another decisive victory for the MPD, which secured control of 10 of the 14 local councils. In January 1992 Veiga reorganized the Council of Ministers and created four new ministries.

On 25 September 1992 a new Constitution came into force, enshrining the principles of multi-party democracy. Under the new Constitution of the Republic of Cape Verde (also referred to as the 'Second Republic'), a new national flag and emblem were adopted, and the ANP became the Assembléia Nacional (AN). In August 1993 the opposition PAICV elected Aristides Lima to the post of Secretary-General of the party, replacing Pires, who was appointed party Chairman. In December the Minister of Justice and Labour, Dr Eurico Correia Monteiro, was dismissed, following his announcement that he would be contesting the leadership of the MPD at an extraordinary national convention of the party, called by Veiga to take place in February 1994. At the convention Carlos Veiga was re-elected Chairman of the MPD. However, increasing conflict within the party resulted in some 30 party delegates, led by Monteiro and former Minister of Foreign Affairs, Jorge Carlos Almeida Fonseca, boycotting the convention and holding a convention of their own. That month Monteiro announced the establishment of a new political party, the Partido da Convergência Democrática (PCD). In May 1994, in view of the split within the ruling MPD, a motion of confidence in the Government was debated by the legislature. The motion was carried in the Government's favour by a narrow margin.

At legislative elections conducted in December 1995 the MPD secured an outright majority, taking 50 of the 72 seats in the AN (reduced from 79 seats under electoral legislation approved in 1994). The PAICV won 21 seats, while the remaining seat was obtained by the PCD. At a presidential election conducted in February 1996 António Mascarenhas Monteiro, the sole candidate and incumbent President, was re-elected. However, despite appeals for the electorate to demonstrate its support for Mascarenhas' second term of office, the turn-out was low, at only 45%. Veiga, meanwhile, expressed his intention to continue the policies of liberal economic and social reform that had been pursued in his previous term in office.

In May 1998, as part of a reorganization of the Council of Ministers, Veiga created several new ministries and appointed the Minister of Economic Co-ordination, António Gualberto do Rosário, to the newly-created post of Deputy Prime Minister. In March 1999 Veiga confirmed speculation that he would not seek re-election as the Chairman of the MPD at the next party convention. Do Rosário and the Mayor of Praia, Jacinto Santos, subsequently announced their candidacies for the chairmanship of the MPD, and thus the premiership. However, in November 1999 Veiga dismissed the Minister of Education, Science, Youth and Sports, José Luis Livramento, the Minister of Justice, Simão Gomes Monteiro, as well as the Secretary of State for Decentralization, César Barbosa de Almeida, who were considered to be close associates of Santos. Nevertheless, the MPD sustained substantial losses in municipal elections held in February 2000. The MPD retained eight of a possible 17 local councils, but lost the capital, Praia, to the PAICV, which re-emerged as a credible political force. Following the resignation of Pedro Pires, who announced his candidacy for the presidential election, the PAICV elected José Maria Neves as its new President in June. In the following month do Rosário was elected Chairman of the MPD, and Santos subsequently formed a new political party, the Partido da Renovação Democratica.

In late July 2000 Veiga announced his resignation as Prime Minister and confirmed his candidacy for the presidential election scheduled to take place in early 2001; he was replaced by do Rosário. Veiga's decision to stand down was criticized by both President Monteiro and Neves, who argued that the unelected do Rosário had no mandate, and that his appointment was therefore unconstitutional. In August the Minister of Education, Youth and Sports and of Infrastructure and Housing, António Joaquim Fernandes, resigned, following protests by students. In October 2000 it was announced that the PCD, the União Caboverdiana Independente e Democrática and the Partido de Trabalho e Solidariedade were to form a coalition (the Aliança Democrática para a Mudança—ADM) to participate in the forthcoming legislative elections.

At the legislative elections, held on 14 January 2001, the opposition PAICV obtained 49.5% of the votes and 40 seats in the AN, compared with 40.5% (30 seats) for the MPD and 6.1% (two seats) for the ADM. A new Government, headed by Prime Minister José Maria Neves, was announced at the end of January, with a number of portfolios either abolished or merged. At the presidential elections, held on 11 February, no candidate received an overall majority, necessitating a second round, held on 25 February, at which Pedro Pires narrowly defeated the former Prime Minister, Carlos Veiga, receiving 50.05% of votes cast (compared with 49.95% for Veiga).

Cape Verde has traditionally professed a non-aligned stance in foreign affairs and maintains relations with virtually all the power blocs. On taking office in 1991, the MPD Government successfully sought to extend Cape Verde's range of international contacts, with special emphasis on potential new sources of development aid: substantial assistance has been received from both Israel and the Gulf states. The MPD Government enlarged the scope of Cape Verde's diplomatic contacts, establishing embassies in South Africa and Sweden, as well as diplomatic presences in Hong Kong, Macau, Singapore, Spain, the United Kingdom and the USA. The country has continued to maintain particularly close relations with Portugal and Brazil, and with other lusophone African former colonies—Angola, Guinea-Bissau, Mozambique and São Tomé and Príncipe, known collectively, with Cape Verde, as the Países Africanos da Língua Oficial Portuguesa (PALOP). Cape Verde is regularly represented at meetings of PALOP, whose principal aid donors include the EU, the IMF, the World Bank and the African Development Bank. In July 1996 a 'lusophone commonwealth', known as the Comunidade dos Países de Língua Portuguesa (CPLP), comprising the five PALOP countries together with Portugal and Brazil, was formed with the intention of benefiting each member state through joint co-operation on technical, cultural and social matters. In December 1996 Cape Verde became a full member of the Sommet francophone, a commonwealth comprising all the French-speaking nations of the world, and benefits in turn from membership of this body's Agence de coopération culturelle et technique, an agency which promotes cultural and technical co-operation among francophone countries. Although a lusophone nation, Cape Verde had been an observer at annual meetings of the Sommet francophone since 1977.

Government

Under the 1992 Constitution, Cape Verde is a multi-party state, although the formation of parties on a religious or geographical basis is prohibited. Legislative power is vested in the Assembléia Nacional (AN—National Assembly), which comprises 72 deputies, elected by universal adult suffrage for a five-year term. The Head of State is the President of the Republic, who is elected by universal suffrage for a five-year term. Executive power is vested in the Prime Minister, who is nominated by the deputies of the AN, appointed by the President and governs with the assistance of a Council of Ministers.

Defence

The armed forces, initially formed from ex-combatants in the liberation wars, totalled about 1,150 (army 1,000, air force less than 100, coastguard 50) in August 2000. There is also a police force, the Police for Public Order, which is organized by the local municipal councils. National service is by selective conscription. Government defence expenditure in 2000 was budgeted at an estimated 925m. escudos (US $8m.).

Economic Affairs

In 1998, according to estimates from the World Bank, Cape Verde's gross national product (GNP), measured at average 1996–98 prices, was US $499m., equivalent to $1,200 per head (or $3,192 per head on international purchasing-power parity basis). During 1990–98, it was estimated, GNP per head increased, in real terms, by an average of 2.5% per year. Over the same period, the population increased at an average annual rate of 2.8%. Estimated GNP in 1999 was $569m. ($1,330 per head). During 1991–98, according to IMF estimates, Cape Verde's gross domestic product (GDP) increased, in real terms, at an average rate of 5.5% per year. Real GDP growth was estimated at 8.0% in both 1998 and 1999.

Agriculture (including forestry and fishing) contributed 12.2% of GDP in 1998, and employed an estimated 23.8% of the economically active population in 1999. The staple crops are maize and beans; potatoes, sweet potatoes, cassava, coconuts, dates, sugar cane, mangoes and bananas are also cultivated. Fish, crustaceans and molluscs provided almost one-half of total export earnings in 1994, although their contribution declined to 17.7% in 1998. Lobster and tuna are among the most important exports. Moreover, the total catch declined from 14,730 metric tons in 1981 to 6,573 tons in 1992. In 1994 a five-year project was announced for the redevelopment of the fishing industry, with investment of US $28m., largely funded by international development agencies. By 1998 the annual catch had recovered somewhat to 9,999 tons. During 1991–95 the GDP of the agricultural sector increased, in real terms, at an average rate of 0.7% per year; an increase of 6.6% was recorded in 1995.

Industry (including mining, manufacturing, construction, power and 'new industries') contributed some 19.1% of GDP in 1998. Industry employed 24.5% of the labour force in 1990. During 1991–95 industrial GDP increased, in real terms, at an average rate of 2.7% per year; an increase of 8.3% was recorded in 1995.

Mining employed 0.3% of the labour force in 1990 and contributed an estimated 0.3% of GDP in 1993. Salt and pozzolana, a volcanic ash used in cement manufacture, are the main nonfuel minerals produced.

Manufacturing contributed some 7% of GDP in 1997 and employed about 6% of the labour force in 1995. The most important branches, other than fish-processing, are clothing, footwear, rum distilling and bottling. Legislation enacted in 1999 provided for the transformation of industrial parks at Mindelo and Praia into free-trade zones, and for the establishment of a further free-trade zone on Sal island. During 1985–93 the GDP of the manufacturing sector increased, in real terms, at an average rate of 5.9% per year.

Energy is derived principally from hydroelectric power and gas. Imports of mineral fuels comprised 2.2% of the value of total imports in 1998.

Services accounted for 68.7% of GDP in 1998. Tourism has been identified as the area with the most potential for economic development. Legislation introduced since 1991 has aimed to provide increased incentives and guarantees to investors. The construction of a new international airport at Praia, due for completion in 2001, was expected to give considerable impetus to the development of the tourism sector. The airport on São Vicente island was upgraded to international capacity in 2000. Plans were also being prepared for the construction of an international airport on Boa Vista island. During 1991–95 the combined GDP of the service sectors increased, in real terms, at an average rate of 8.1% per year; an increase of 7.4% was recorded in 1995.

In 1998 Cape Verde recorded a trade deficit of US $185.6m., and there was a deficit of $58.0m. on the current account of the balance of payments. In 1999 the principal source of imports was Portugal (52.7%); other major suppliers were the Netherlands (17.8%) and the USA (3.4%). Portugal was also the principal market for exports (89.7%) in that year. The principal exports in 1998 were footwear (59.5%) and clothing (18.8%). Large-scale exports of bananas were interrupted during 1994–98, owing to quality restrictions imposed by the EU. The major imports in 1998 were machinery and electrical equipment (17.4%), food and beverage products (14.4%) and vegetable products (11.0%).

In 1999 there was an estimated budgetary deficit of 4,503m. escudos (equivalent to 7.6% of GDP). Cape Verde's total external debt at the end of 1998 was US $243.7m., of which $237.3m. was long-term public debt. In that year the cost of debt-servicing was equivalent to 9.9% of the value of exports of goods and services. The annual rate of inflation averaged 5.8% in 1990–99. Consumer prices increased by an average of 8.7% in 1997, 4.2% in 1998 and 4.3% in 1999. In 1995 unemployment was estimated to affect about 25% of the labour force, with a further 26% underemployed.

Cape Verde is a member of the Economic Community of West African States (ECOWAS—see p. 170), which promotes trade and co-operation in West Africa, and is a signatory to the Lomé Convention and subsequent Cotonou Agreement (see p. 208).

Cape Verde's agricultural economy is highly vulnerable to severe periodic drought, making self-sufficiency in food production impossible; approximately 85% of the country's total food requirements are imported. The country benefits from considerable external assistance (which totalled US $109.6m. in 1997) and substantial remittances from emigrants. There are about 700,000 Cape Verdeans living outside the country, principally in the USA, the Netherlands, Portugal, Italy and Angola. In 1995 private remittances from emigrants provided an estimated 7,369m. escudos; annual remittances averaged some 20% of GDP during 1992–95. The Government has attempted to attract emigrants' capital into the light-industry and fishing sectors in Cape Verde by offering favourable tax conditions to investors. A national development plan was adopted in 1997, the key aim of which was to alleviate poverty, which was estimated to affect some 45% of the population. The plan aimed to create jobs and wealth by developing the private sector, in particular the light-manufacturing and service-sector industries. In March 1998 Cape Verde and Portugal signed an agreement providing for their respective currencies to become linked through a fixed exchange rate, thus transforming the Cape Verde escudo into a convertible currency, which would, in turn, encourage foreign investment and trade. GDP was projected to grow by 8% in 2000, supported by private and public investment, and by the expansion of manufactures destined for export. Domestic revenue was budgeted at 14,300m. escudos for 2000 (equivalent to 21.7% of GDP), and this was expected to be supplemented by a further increase in external grants. Government expenditure was to focus primarily on health, security and education (notably, the number of teachers was to be increased by 7%). The Government's privatization programme, scheduled for conclu-sion by early 2001, was expected to provide some US $80m. in extra funds. However, Cape Verde would still remain highly dependent on external grants and aid for the foreseeable future.

Social Welfare

Medical facilities are limited and there is a severe shortage of staff and buildings, although plans for a national health service are being implemented. In 1980 Cape Verde had 21 hospital establishments, with a total of 632 beds, and in 1996, according to estimates by the World Health Organization, there were 17.1 physicians and 55.6 nurses per 100,000 population working in the country. Development plans include the construction of more than 300 small local health units. In 1997 the Ministry of Health received 8.4% of the central Government's total current expenditure and 2.9% of capital expenditure. Social security is available through the Instituto Nacional de Previdência Social (INPS), established in 1991. The INPS provides a range of benefits, including retirement and disability pensions. In 1995 the scheme covered about 23,000 workers, who contributed 23% of their earnings.

Education

Primary education, beginning at seven years of age and lasting for six years, comprises a first cycle of four years, which is compulsory, and a second cycle of two years. Secondary education, beginning at 13 years of age, is also divided into two cycles, the first comprising a three-year general course, the second a three-year pre-university course. There are three teacher-training units and two industrial and commercial schools of further education. In 1997 the total enrolment at primary and secondary schools was equivalent to 103% of all school-age children (males 104%; females 103%). In 1997/98 91,777 pupils attended primary schools, and 31,602 attended secondary schools. Primary enrolment in 1997 was equivalent to 148% of children in the relevant age-group (males 150%; females 147%). In that year secondary enrolment included 48% of children in the relevant age-group (males 47%; females 48%). In 1996/97 there were 1,660 Cape Verdean students studying at overseas universities. In 1995, according to estimates by UNESCO, the average rate of illiteracy among the population aged 15 years and over was 30.6% (males 19.3%; females 39.3%). In 1997 the Ministry of Education received 19.7% of the central Government's total current expenditure and 17.8% of capital expenditure.

Public Holidays

2001: 1 January (New Year), 20 January (National Heroes' Day), 1 May (Labour Day), 5 July (Independence Day), 15 August (Assumption), 1 November (All Saints' Day), 25 December (Christmas Day).

2002: 1 January (New Year), 20 January (National Heroes' Day), 1 May (Labour Day), 5 July (Independence Day), 15 August (Assumption), 1 November (All Saints' Day), 25 December (Christmas Day).

Weights and Measures

The metric system is in force.

Statistical Survey

Sources (unless otherwise stated): Instituto Nacional de Estatística, CP 116, Praia, Santiago; tel. 61-38-27; e-mail inecv@mail.cvtelecom.cv; internet www.ine.cv; Statistical Service, Banco de Cabo Verde, 117 Avda Amílcar Cabral, CP 101, Praia, Santiago; tel. 60-70-00; fax 61-19-14; internet www.bcv.cv.

AREA AND POPULATION

Area: 4,033 sq km (1,557 sq miles).

Population: 341,491 (males 161,494; females 179,997) at census of 23 June 1990; 434,812 (males 210,569; females 224,243) at census of 16 June 2000. *By island* (2000 census): Boa Vista 4,193; Brava 6,820; Fogo 37,409; Maio 6,742; Sal 14,792; Santo Antão 47,124; São Nicolau 13,536; Santiago 236,352; São Vicente 67,844.

Density (2000 census): 107.8 per sq. km.

Principal Towns: (population at 2000 census): Praia (capital) 94,757; Mindelo 62,970.

Births, Marriages and Deaths (1998, provisional): Registered live births 15,460 (birth rate 37.1 per 1,000); Registered marriages (1994) 1,200 (marriage rate 3.2 per 1,000); Registered deaths 2,811 (death rate 6.7 per 1,000). Source: partly UN, *Demographic Yearbook* and *Population and Vital Statistics Report*.

Expectation of Life (years at birth, 1990): Males 63.53; Females 71.33. Source: UN, *Demographic Yearbook*.

Economically Active Population (persons aged 10 years and over, 1990 census): Agriculture, hunting, forestry and fishing 29,876; Mining and quarrying 410; Manufacturing 5,520; Electricity, gas and water 883; Construction 22,722; Trade, restaurants and hotels 12,747; Transport, storage and communications 6,138; Financing, insurance, real estate and business services 821; Community, social and personal services 17,358; Activities not adequately defined 24,090; Total labour force 120,565 (males 75,786; females 44,779), including 31,049 unemployed persons (males 19,712; females 11,337). Source: International Labour Office, *Yearbook of Labour Statistics*.

AGRICULTURE, ETC.

Principal Crops (FAO estimates, '000 metric tons, 1999): Maize 10; Potatoes 2; Sweet potatoes 4; Cassava 3; Pulses 2; Coconuts 5; Cabbages 6; Tomatoes 4; Onions (dry) 1; Green beans 2; Other vegetables 3; Sugar cane 13; Mangoes 5; Bananas 6; Other fruits 5. Source: FAO.

Livestock ('000 head, year ending September 1999): Cattle 22; Pigs 636*; Sheep 9; Goats 112; Asses 14*.
* FAO estimate.
Source: FAO.

Livestock Products ('000 metric tons, 1999): Pig meat 8*; Other meat 1; Cows' milk 6; Goats' milk 5.
* FAO estimate.
Source: FAO.

Fishing (metric tons, live weight, 1998): Total catch 9,999 (Wahoo 429, Skipjack tuna 682, Yellowfin tuna 1,417). Source: FAO, *Yearbook of Fishery Statistics*.

MINING

Production (estimates, '000 metric tons, 1999): Salt (unrefined) 7; Pozzolana 1. Source: US Geological Survey.

INDUSTRY

Production (metric tons, unless otherwise indicated, 1998): Biscuits 348 (1990 figure); Bread 5,628 (1995 figure); Canned fish 250 (1997 figure); Frozen fish 932 (1997 figure); Flour 65,916; Beer 4,234,560 litres; Soft drinks 922,714 litres (1996 figure); Cigarettes and tobacco 43 kg (1996 figure); Paint 628,243 kg (1996 figure); Footwear 670,676 pairs (1996 figure); Soap 1,722,114 kg (1996 figure); Electric energy 41m. kWh (1996 figure). Sources: mainly UN, *Industrial Commodity Statistics Yearbook*, and IMF, *Cape Verde: Recent Economic Developments* (July 1999).

FINANCE

Currency and Exchange Rates: 100 centavos = 1 Cape Verde escudo; 1,000 escudos are known as a conto. *Sterling, Dollar and Euro Equivalents* (29 December 2000): £1 sterling = 177.21 escudos; US $1 = 118.76 escudos; €1 = 110.51 escudos; 1,000 Cape Verde escudos = £5.643 = $8.420 = €9.049. *Average Exchange Rate* (escudos per US dollar): 98.158 in 1998; 102.700 in 1999; 115.877 in 2000.

Budget (preliminary, million escudos, 1999): *Revenue:* Taxation 10,318 (Taxes on income and profits 3,924, Taxes on international trade 5,818, Stamp and liquor tax 576); Other revenue 3,415 (Licences and miscellaneous fees 449, Property income 959,

Transfers 687, Reimbursement of debt principal by public enterprises 519, Sales of fixed assets and services 146, Autonomous revenue 300); Total 13,733, excl. external grants (4,416) and receipts from privatization (3,708). *Expenditure:* Recurrent 12,097 (Wages and salaries 6,372, Goods and services 590, Interest on public debt 944, Subsidies and transfers 2,673, Other current 613, Autonomous 905); Capital 8,561; Emergency social expenditure 1,994; Total 22,652. Source: Ministério da Finanças.

International Reserves (US $ million at 31 December 1999): IMF special drawing rights 0.02; Foreign exchange 60.37; Total 60.39. Source: IMF, *International Financial Statistics*.

Money Supply (million escudos at 31 December 1999): Currency outside banks 6,026.1; Demand deposits at commercial banks 12,216.4; Total money (incl. others) 18,332.6. Source: IMF, *International Financial Statistics*.

Cost of Living (Consumer Price Index; base: 1990 = 100): 153.0 in 1997; 159.5 in 1998; 166.4 in 1999. Source: International Labour Office, *Yearbook of Labour Statistics*.

Expenditure on the Gross Domestic Product (estimates, million escudos at current prices, 1998): Government final consumption expenditure 11,317; Private final consumption expenditure 33,327; Gross capital formation 19,580; *Total domestic expenditure* 64,224; *Exports of goods and services* 12,139; *Less* Imports of goods and services 27,696; *GDP in purchasers' values* 48,667. Source: IMF, *Cape Verde: Recent Economic Developments* (July 1999).

Gross Domestic Product by Economic Activity (estimates, million escudos at current prices, 1998): Agriculture, forestry and livestock 5,212; Fishing 740; Industry and energy 4,711; Construction 4,304; Commerce 7,571; Hotels 1,669; Transport and communications 8,575; Banks and insurance 2,605; Housing 3,099; Public service 6,577; Other services 3,315; New industries 289; *GDP at market prices* 48,667. Source: IMF, *Cape Verde: Recent Economic Developments* (July 1999).

Balance of Payments (US $ million, 1998): Exports of goods f.o.b. 32.69; Imports of goods f.o.b. –218.33; *Trade balance* –185.64; Exports of services 86.45; Imports of services –90.57; *Balance on goods and services* –189.76; Other income received 2.51; Other income paid –8.07; *Balance on goods, services and income* –195.32; Current transfers received 142.46; Current transfers paid –5.15; *Current balance* –58.00; Capital account (net) 19.01; Direct investment from abroad 9.04; Other investment assets –22.44; Other investment liabilities 50.39; Net errors and omissions 12.77; *Overall balance* 10.76. Source: IMF, *International Financial Statistics*.

EXTERNAL TRADE

Total Trade (million escudos): *Imports c.i.f.:* 21,936 in 1997; 22,395 in 1998; 25,484 in 1999. *Exports f.o.b.*: 1,309 in 1997; 1,024 in 1998; 1,185 in 1999.

* Figures exclude stores and bunkers for ships (million escudos): 2,449 in 1997; 1,678 in 1998.

Source: partly IMF, *Cape Verde: Recent Economic Developments* (July 1999).

Principal Commodities (million escudos, 1998): *Imports c.i.f.:* Live animals and animal products 1,025 (Milk 616); Vegetable products 2,472 (Maize 599, Rice 625); Animal or vegetable fats and oils; prepared edible fats; animal or vegetable waxes 1,079; Prepared foodstuffs; beverages, spirits and vinegar; tobacco and manufactured substitutes 3,222 (Sugar 665); Mineral products 1,949 (Cement 815, Diesel oil 483); Products of chemical or allied industries 1,375; Plastics, rubber and articles thereof 798; Wood, cork and articles thereof; wood charcoal; manufactures of straw, esparto, etc. 518; Paper-making material; paper and paperboard and articles thereof 558; Textiles and textile articles 560; Articles of stone, plaster, cement, asbestos, mica, etc.; ceramic products; glass and glassware 721; Base metals and articles thereof 1,632; Machinery and mechanical appliances; electrical equipment; sound and television apparatus 3,887; Vehicles, aircraft, vessels and associated transport equipment 1,510; Total (incl. others) 22,395. *Exports f.o.b.*: Fish 105; Crustaceans 76; Footwear (incl. parts) 609; Clothing 193; Total (incl. others)* 1,024. * Excluding stores and bunkers for ships (million escudos): 1,678. Source: IMF, *Cape Verde: Recent Economic Developments* (July 1999).

Principal Trading Partners (million escudos, 1999): *Imports c.i.f.:* France 612.5; Germany 498.2; Netherlands 4,531.0; Portugal 13,436.7; Spain 618.5; United Kingdom 726.6; USA 865.8; Total (incl. others) 25,483.9. *Exports f.o.b.*: Guinea-Bissau 24.9; Portugal 1,062.8; Spain 34.2; Total (incl. others) 1,184.9.

TRANSPORT

Road Traffic (motor vehicles in use, 31 December 1999): Passenger cars 13,473; Commercial vehicles 3,085; Motorcycles 1,296.

Shipping: Merchant fleet (registered at 31 December 1998): Number of vessels 37, total displacement ('000 grt) 19.9 (Source: Lloyd's Register of Shipping, *World Fleet Statistics*); International freight traffic (estimates, '000 metric tons, 1993): Goods loaded 144, goods unloaded 299 (Source: UN Economic Commission for Africa, *African Statistical Yearbook*).

Civil Aviation (traffic on scheduled services, 1997): Kilometres flown 5,000,000; passengers carried 237,000; passenger-km 268,000,000; total ton-km 25,000,000. Source: UN, *Statistical Yearbook*.

TOURISM

Tourist Arrivals (estimates): 52,000 in 1998; 67,000 in 1999; 100,000 in 2000. Source: Centro de Promoção Turística, do Investimento Externo e das Exportações (PROMEX).

Tourist Arrivals by Country of Residence (1997): France 4,762, Germany 5,560, Italy 13,750, Portugal 13,762; Total (incl. others) 45,000. Source: World Tourism Organization, *Yearbook of Tourism Statistics*.

Tourism Receipts (US $ million): 10 in 1995; 11 in 1996; 15 in 1997. Source: World Tourism Organization, *Yearbook of Tourism Statistics*.

COMMUNICATIONS MEDIA

Radio Receivers* (1997): 73,000 in use.

Television Receivers* (1997): 2,000 in use.

Telephones† (1997): 33,000 main lines in use.

Mobile Cellular Telephones† (1997): 20 subscribers.

Telefax Stations† (1996): 1,000 in use.

Non-daily Newspapers* (1996): 4 titles (average circulation 20,000 copies).

Book Production* (1989): 10 titles.

* Source: UNESCO, *Statistical Yearbook*.

† Source: UN, *Statistical Yearbook*.

EDUCATION

Pre-primary (1986/87): 58 schools; 136 teachers; 4,523 pupils.

Primary (1997/98): 370 schools (1990/91); 3,219 teachers; 91,777 pupils.

Total Secondary (1997/98): 1,372 teachers; 31,602 pupils.

   General Secondary (1993/94): 438 teachers; 11,808 pupils.

   Teacher Training: 25 teachers (1987/88); 889 pupils (1993/94).

   Vocational Schools (1993/94): 94 teachers; 1,400 pupils.

Source: UNESCO, *Statistical Yearbook*.

Directory

The Constitution

A new constitution of the Republic of Cape Verde ('the Second Republic') came into force on 25 September 1992. The constitution defines Cape Verde as a sovereign, unitary and democratic republic, guaranteeing respect for human dignity and recognizing the inviolable and inalienable rights of man as a fundament of humanity, peace and justice. It recognizes the equality of all citizens before the law, without distinction of social origin, social condition, economic status, race, sex, religion, political convictions or ideologies and promises transparency for all citizens in the practising of fundamental liberties. The constitution gives assent to popular will, and has a fundamental objective in the realization of economic, political, social and cultural democracy and the construction of a society which is free, just and in solidarity.

The head of state is the president of the republic, who is elected by universal adult suffrage and must obtain two-thirds of the votes cast to win in the first round of the election. If no candidate secures the requisite majority, a new election is held within 21 days and contested by the two candidates who received the highest number of votes in the first round. Voting is conducted by secret ballot. Legislative power is vested in the national assembly, which is also elected by universal adult suffrage. The Prime Minister is nominated by the national assembly, to which he is responsible. On the recommendation of the prime minister, the president appoints the council of ministers, whose members must be elected deputies of the national assembly. There are 17 local government councils, elected by universal suffrage for a period of five years.

A constitutional revision, adopted in July 1999, gave the president the right to dissolve the national assembly, established a constitutional court (tribunal de constitução), created a new advisory chamber (conselho económico e social), and adopted *Crioulo* as the country's second official language.

The Government

HEAD OF STATE

President: PEDRO PIRES (elected 25 February 2001).

COUNCIL OF MINISTERS
(April 2001)

Prime Minister and Minister of Defence: JOSÉ MARIA PEREIRA NEVES.

Minister of Foreign Affairs, Co-operation and Communities: MANUEL INOCÊNCIO SOUSA.

Minister of Finance and Planning: CARLOS AUGUSTO DUARTE BURGO.

Minister of Justice and Internal Administration: CRISTINA FONTES.

Minister of Agriculture and Fisheries: MÁRIO ANSELMO COUTO DE MATOS.

Minister of Education, Culture and Sports: VÍCTOR MANUEL BARBOSA BORGES.

Minister of Health, Employment and Solidarity: DARIO LAVAL RESENDE DANTAS DOS REIS.

Minister of Infrastructure and Transport: JORGE LIMA DELGADO LOPES.

Minister of Tourism, Industry and Commerce: JOSÉ ARMANDO FILOMENO FERREIRA DUARTE.

Secretary of State for Foreign Affairs: FÁTIMA LIMA VEIGA.

Secretary of State for Parliamentary Affairs and National Defence: ARMINDO CIPRIANO MAURÍCIO.

Secretary of State in Assistance to the Prime Minister: JORGE HOMERO TOLENTINO ARAÚJO.

Secretary of State for State Reform, Public Administration and Local Government: EDELTRUDES RODRIGUES PIRES NEVES.

Secretary of State for Youth: MARIA DE JESUS VEIGA MIRANDA MASCARENHAS.

MINISTRIES

Office of the President: Presidência da República, Plateau, Praia, Santiago; tel. 61-65-66.

Office of the Prime Minister: Palácio do Governo, Várzea, CP 16, Praia, Santiago; tel. 61-05-13; fax 61-30-99.

Ministry of Agriculture and Fisheries: Ponta Belém, Praia, Santiago; tel. 61-57-13; fax 61-40-54.

Ministry of Education, Culture and Sports: Palácio do Governo, Várzea, CP 111, Praia, Santiago; tel. 61-02-11; fax 61-56-75; internet www.gov.cv/contacto.

Ministry of Finance and Planning: 107 Avda Amílcar Cabral, CP 30, Praia, Santiago; tel. 61-43-50.

Ministry of Foreign Affairs, Co-operation and Communities: Praça Dr Lorena, Praia, Santiago; tel. 61-57-27; fax 61-39-52.

Ministry of Health, Employment and Solidarity: Palácio do Governo, Várzea, Praia, Santiago; tel. 61-05-01.

Ministry of Infrastructure and Transport: Ponta Belém, Praia, Santiago; tel. 61-56-99; fax 61-56-99.

Ministry of Justice and Internal Administration: Rua Serpa Pinto, Praia, Santiago; tel. 62-32-62; fax 61-56-78.

Ministry of National Defence: Palácio do Governo, Várzea, Praia, Santiago; tel. 61-03-44; fax 61-05-15.

Ministry of Tourism, Industry and Commerce: Palácio do Governo, Várzea, Praia, Santiago; tel. 61-17-70; fax 61-17-70.

President and Legislature

PRESIDENT

Presidential Election, First Ballot, 11 February 2001

Candidate	Votes	% of votes
PEDRO VERONA RODRIGUES PIRES (PAICV) .	61,389	46.51
CARLOS ALBERTO DE CARVALHO VEIGA (MPD) .	60,472	45.82
JORGE CARLOS DE ALMEIDA FONSECA (PCD) .	5,182	3.93
DAVID HOPFFER DE CORDEIRO ALMADA (Ind)	4,936	3.74
Total	**131,979**	**100.00**

Second Ballot, 25 February 2001

Candidate	Votes	% of votes
PEDRO VERONA RODRIGUES PIRES (PAICV) .	75,900	50.05
CARLOS ALBERTO DE CARVALHO VEIGA (MPD) .	75,736	49.95
Total	**151,636**	**100.00**

ASSEMBLÉIA NACIONAL

Speaker: ARISTIDES RAIMUNDO LIMA.

Legislative Election, 14 January 2001

Party	Votes	% of votes	Seats
Partido Africano da Independência de Cabo Verde (PAICV)	67,862	49.5	40
Movimento para a Democracia (MPD)	55,581	40.5	30
Aliança Democrática para a Mudança (ADM) . . .	8,382	6.1	2
Partido da Renovação Democrática (PRD) . . .	4,644	3.4	—
Partido Socialista Democrático (PSD)	622	0.5	—
Total	**137,091**	**100.0**	**72**

Political Organizations

Aliança Democrática para a Mudança (ADM): Praia, Santiago; f. 2000; coalition of the PCD, the UCID and the PTS; Leader Dr EURICO CORREIA MONTEIRO.

Partido da Convergência Democrática (PCD): Praia, Santiago; f. 1994 by fmr mems of the MPD; Pres. Dr EURICO CORREIA MONTEIRO.

Partido de Trabalho e Solidariedade (PTS): Praia, Santiago; f. 1998; Leader ONESIMO SILVEIRA.

União Caboverdiana Independente e Democrática (UCID): Praia, Santiago; f. 1974 by emigrants opposed to the PAICV; obtained legal recognition in 1991; Pres. CELSO CELESTINO.

Movimento para a Democracia (MPD): Achada Santo António, CP 90A, Praia, Santiago; tel. 61-40-82; fax 61-41-22; f. 1990; advocates administrative decentralization; governing party since Jan. 1991; Chair. ANTÓNIO GUALBERTO DO ROSÁRIO.

Partido Africano da Independência de Cabo Verde (PAICV): Avda Amílcar Cabral, CP 22, Praia, Santiago; tel. 61-27-20; fax 61-14-10; internet www.paicv.org; f. 1956 as the Partido Africano da Independência do Guiné e Cabo Verde (PAIGC); name changed in 1981, following the 1980 coup in Guinea-Bissau; sole authorized political party 1975–90; Pres. JOSÉ MARIA NEVES; Sec.-Gen. ARISTIDES LIMA.

Partido da Renovação Democrática (PRD): Praia, Santiago; f. 2000 by fmr mems of the MPD; Pres. JACINTO SANTOS.

Partido Socialista Democrático (PSD): Praia, Santiago; f. 1992; Sec.-Gen. JOÃO ALÉM.

Diplomatic Representation
EMBASSIES IN CAPE VERDE

Angola: Praia, Santiago; Ambassador: CÉSAR A. KILUANGE.

Brazil: Chã de Areia, CP 93, Praia, Santiago; tel. 61-56-07; fax 61-56-09; Ambassador: ROMEO ZERO.

China, People's Republic: Achada de Santo António, Praia, Santiago; tel. 61-55-86; Ambassador: LIAO QIPING.

Cuba: Prainha, Praia, Santiago; tel. 61-55-97; fax 61-55-90; Ambassador: PABLO REIS DOMINGUES.

France: CP 192, Praia, Santiago; tel. 61-55-89; fax 61-55-90; Ambassador: ANDRÉ BARBE.

Korea, Democratic People's Republic: Praia, Santiago; Ambassador: RI IN SOK.

Portugal: Achada de Santo António, CP 160, Praia, Santiago; tel. 61-56-02; fax 61-40-58; Ambassador: RUI QUARTIN SANTOS.

Russia: Achada de Santo António, CP 31, Praia, Santiago; tel. 62-27-39; fax 62-27-38; Ambassador: VLADIMIR E. PETUKHOV.

Senegal: Prainha, Praia, Santiago; tel. 61-56-21; e-mail silcarneyni@homeviewsenegal.com; Ambassador: SILCARNEYNI GUEYE.

USA: Rua Hoji Ya Yenna 81, CP 201, Praia, Santiago; tel. 61-56-16; fax 61-13-55; Ambassador: MICHAEL METELITS.

Judicial System

Tribunal de Constitução: f. 1999; the supreme court.

Supremo Tribunal de Justiça: Rua Cesário de Lacerda, CP 117, Praia, Santiago; tel. 61-58-10; fax 61-17-51; established 1975; the highest court.

President: Dr OSCAR GOMES.

Attorney-General: Dr HENRIQUE MONTEIRO.

Religion
CHRISTIANITY

At 31 December 1998 there were an estimated 432,424 adherents of the Roman Catholic Church, representing 95.7% of the total population. Protestant churches, among which the Church of the Nazarene is prominent, represent about 1% of the population.

The Roman Catholic Church

Cape Verde comprises the single diocese of Santiago de Cabo Verde, directly responsible to the Holy See. The Bishop participates in the Episcopal Conference of Senegal, Mauritania, Cape Verde and Guinea-Bissau, currently based in Senegal.

Bishop of Santiago de Cabo Verde: Rt Rev. PAULINO DO LIVRAMENTO ÉVORA, Avda Amílcar Cabral, Largo 5 de Outubro, CP 46, Praia, Santiago; tel. 61-11-19; fax 61-45-99.

The Anglican Communion

Cape Verde forms part of the diocese of The Gambia, within the Church of the Province of West Africa. The Bishop is resident in Banjul, The Gambia.

The Press

Agaviva: Mindelo, São Vicente; tel. 31-21-21; f. 1991; monthly; Editor GERMANO ALMEIDA; circ. 4,000.

Boletim Informativo: CP 126, Praia, Santiago; f. 1976; weekly; publ. by the Ministry of Foreign Affairs; circ. 1,500.

Boletim Oficial da República de Cabo Verde: Imprensa Nacional, CP 113, Praia, Santiago; tel. 61-41-50; weekly; official announcements.

O Cidadão: Praça Dr António Aurélio Gonçalves 2, CP 669, Mindelo, São Vicente; tel. 32-50-24; fax 32-50-22; e-mail ocidadao@mail.cvtelecom.cv; Editor JOSÉ MÁRIO CORREIA.

Contacto: CP 89C, Praia, Santiago; tel. 61-57-52; fax 61-14-42; f. 1993; quarterly; economic bulletin publ. by Centro de Promoção Turística, do Investimento Externo e das Exportações (PROMEX); Dir of Investment and Exports: Dr JOÃO SANTOS; circ. 1,500.

Horizonte: Achada de Santo António, CP 40, Praia, Santiago; tel. 62-24-47; fax 62-33-30; e-mail infopress@cvtelecom.cv; f. 1999; weekly; pro-government; Editor FERNANDO MONTEIRO; circ. 5,000.

Perspectiva: Achada de Santo António, CP 89C, Praia, Santiago; tel. 62-27-41; fax 62-27-37; f. 1995; annual; economic bulletin publ. by Centro de Promoção Turística, do Investimento Externo e das Exportações (PROMEX); Dir of Marketing and Promotion: Dr SILVINO CASTRO, Jr; circ. 5,000.

Raízes: CP 98, Praia, Santiago; tel. 319; f. 1977; quarterly; cultural review; Editor ARNALDO FRANÇA; circ. 1,500.

A Semana: CP 36C, Avda Cidade de Lisboa, Praia, Santiago; tel. 61-39-50; fax 61-52-91; e-mail asemana@mail.cvtelecom.cv; weekly; independent; Editor FILOMENA SILVA; circ. 5,000.

Terra Nova: CP 166, São Vicente; tel. 32-24-42; fax 32-14-75; e-mail terranova@cabonet.cv; f. 1975; monthly; Roman Catholic; Editor P. ANTÓNIO FIDALGO BARROS; circ. 3,000.

NEWS AGENCIES

Cabopress: Achada de Santo António, CP 40/A, Praia, Santiago; tel. 62-30-21; fax 62-30-23; f. 1988.

Foreign Bureaux

Agence France-Presse (AFP): CP 26/118 Praia, Santiago; tel. 61-38-89; Rep. FÁTIMA AZEVEDO.

Agência Portuguesa de Notícias (LUSA): Prainha, Praia, Santiago; tel. 61-35-19.

Inter Press Service (IPS) (Italy): CP 14, Mindelo, São Vicente; tel. 31-45-50; Rep. JUAN A. COLOMA.

Publisher
Government Publishing House

Imprensa Nacional: CP 113, Praia, Santiago; tel. 61-42-09; Admin. JOÃO DE PINA.

Broadcasting and Communications
TELECOMMUNICATIONS

Cabo Verde Telecom: CP 220, Varzea, Praia, Santiago; tel. 61-55-79; e-mail cvtelecom@mail.cvtelecom.cv; internet www.cvtelecom.cv; f. 1995; Chief Exec. ANTÓNIO PIRES CORREIA.

BROADCASTING

Rádio Televisão de Cabo Verde (RTC): Praça Albuquerque, CP 26, Praia, Santiago; tel. 61-57-55; fax 61-57-54; govt-controlled; five radio transmitters and five solar relay radio transmitters; FM transmission only; radio broadcasts in Portuguese and Creole for 18 hours daily; one television transmitter and seven relay television transmitters; television broadcasts in Portuguese and Creole for eight hours daily with co-operation of RTPI (Portugal); Chair. ROMEU MODESTO.

Praia FM: Rua Justino Lopes 1, CP 276-C, Praia, Santiago; tel. 61-63-56; fax 61-63-57; e-mail gccomunicacoes@mail.cvtelecom.cv; Dir GIORDANO CUSTÓDIO.

Rádio Comercial: Achada Santo António, Prédio Gomes Irmãos 3c, Santiago; tel. 62-31-56; fax 62-24-13; e-mail multimedia.rc@cvtelecom.cv; Dir CARLOS FILIPE GONÇALVES.

Rádio Educativa de Cabo Verde: Achada de Santo António, Praia, Santiago; tel. 61-11-61.

Rádio Nova—Emissora Cristã/Cabo Verde: CP 426, Mindelo, São Vicente; tel. 32-20-83; fax 32-14-75; Dir ANTONIO FIDALGO BARROS.

Voz de São Vicente: CP 29, Mindelo, São Vicente; fax 31-10-06; f. 1974; govt-controlled; Dir JOSÉ FONSECA SOARES.

Finance

(cap. = capital; res = reserves; dep. = deposits; m. = million; †brs = branches; amounts in Cape Verde escudos)

BANKING
Central Bank

Banco de Cabo Verde (BCV): 117 Avda Amílcar Cabral, CP 101, Praia, Santiago; tel. 60-70-00; fax 61-19-14; e-mail bcv@mail.cvtelecom.cv; internet www.bcv.cv; f. 1976; bank of issue; cap. and res 3,169m., dep. 5,143m. (Dec. 1998); Gov. OLAVO CORREIA.

Other Banks

Banco Comercial do Atlântico (BCA): Avda Amílcar Cabral, CP 214, Praia, Santiago; tel. 61-30-93; fax 61-31-00; f. 1993; privatized in 2000; main commercial bank; cap. 1,000m., res 275.5m., dep. 22,499m. (1998); Chair. ADALBERTO HIGINO TAVARES SILVA; 22 brs.

Banco Interatlântico (Caixa Geral de Depósitos) (Portugal): Avda Cidade de Lisboa, CP 131A, Varzea, Praia, Santiago; tel. 61-38-29; fax 61-47-52; e-mail cgdcv@mail.cvtelecom.cv; f. 1999; Pres. Dr ANTÓNIO MIGUEL ORNELAS AFONSO.

Banco Mello (Portugal): Avda Amílcar Cabral 84, CP 33, Plateau, Praia, Santiago; tel. 61-72-50; fax 61-72-51.

Banco Nacional Ultramarino: Edifício Socotril, Avda Cidade de Lisboa, Varzea, Praia, Santiago; tel. 61-42-32; fax 61-42-53.

Banco Totta e Açores (BTA) (Portugal): Rua Roberto Silva, CP 593, Praia, Santiago; tel. 61-16-62; fax 61-40-06; e-mail bta@cvtelecom.cv; f. 1996; cap. 300m. (Dec. 1998); Gen. Man. RODRIGO NASCIMENTO; 3 br.

Caixa Económica de Cabo Verde (CECV): Avda Cidade de Lisboa, CP 193, Praia, Santiago; tel. 61-55-61; fax 61-55-60; e-mail cecv@mail.cvtelecom.cv; f. 1928; privatized in 1999; commercial bank; cap. 348m., res 494m., dep. 6,538.6m. (Dec. 1999); Pres. ADALGIOSA BARBOSA VAZ.

The **Fundo de Solidariedade Nacional** is the main savings institution; the **Fundo de Desenvolvimento Nacional** channels public investment resources; and the **Instituto Caboverdiano** administers international aid.

STOCK EXCHANGE

Bolsa de Valores de Cabo Verde: Achada de Santo António, CP 115-A, Praia, Santiago; tel. 60-30-30; fax 60-30-35; e-mail bcv@mail.cvtelecom.cv; f. 1998.

INSURANCE

Companhia Caboverdiana de Seguros (IMPAR): Praça Amílcar Cabral, CP 344, Mindelo, São Vicente; tel. 31-20-27; fax 31-19-36; f. 1992; Pres. Dr CORSINO FORTES.

Garantia Companhia de Seguros: Rua Guerra Mendes, CP 138, Praia, Santiago; tel. 61-56-61; fax 61-25-55; f. 1991; privatized in 2000.

Trade and Industry

GOVERNMENT AGENCIES

Centro de Promoção Turística, do Investimento Externo e das Exportações (PROMEX): CP 89C, Achada de Santo António, Praia, Santiago; tel. 62-27-41; fax 62-27-37; e-mail promex@mail.cvtelecom.cv; internet www.promex.cv; f. 1990; promotes tourism, foreign investment and exports; Pres. Dr PEDRO BARROS.

Gabinete de Apoio à Reestruturação do Sector Empresarial do Estado (GARSEE; Cabo Verde Privatization): Praia, Santiago; tel. 61-47-48; fax 61-23-34; e-mail cvprivatization@mail.cvtelecom.cv; internet http://cvprivatization.org; bureau in charge of planning and supervising restructuring and divestment of public enterprises; Project Dir Dr SÉRGIO CENTEIO.

DEVELOPMENT ORGANIZATION

Instituto Nacional de Investigação e Desenvolvimento Agrário: CP 84, Praia, Santiago; tel. 71-11-47; fax 71-11-33; e-mail inida@mail.cvtelecom.cv; f. 1979; under the supervision of the Ministry of Agriculture and Fisheries; research and training on agricultural issues.

CHAMBERS OF COMMERCE

Associação Comercial Industrial e Agrícola de Barlavento (ACIAB): CP 62, Mindelo, São Vicente; tel. 31-32-81; fax 32-36-58; f. 1918.

Associação Comercial de Sotavento (ACAS): Rua Serpa Pinto 23, 1°, CP 78, Praia, Santiago; tel. 61-29-91; fax 61-29-64; e-mail acs@milton.cvtelecom.cv.

STATE INDUSTRIAL ENTERPRISES

Correios de Cabo Verde, SARL: CP 92, Praia, Santiago; tel. 61-10-49; fax 61-34-78.

Empresa de Comercialização de Produtos do Mar-INTERBASE, EP: CP 59, Mindelo, São Vicente; tel. 32-66-89; fax 32-66-91; e-mail interbase-sv@mail.cvtelecom.sv; supervises marketing of seafood; shipping agency and ship chandler; Man. Dir CARLOS ALBERTO RAMOS FARIA.

Empresa Nacional de Conservação e Reparação de Equipamentos (SONACOR): Praia, Santiago; tel. 61-25-57.

Empresa Nacional de Produtos Farmacêuticos (EMPROFAC): CP 59, Praia, Santiago; tel. 62-78-95; fax 62-78-99; f. 1979; state monopoly of pharmaceuticals and medical imports.

UTILITIES

Electricity

Empresa Pública de Electricidade e Agua (ELECTRA): 10 Avda Unidade Africana, CP 137, Mindelo, São Vicente; tel. 32-44-48; fax 32-44-46; e-mail electra@milton.cvtelecom.cv; f. 1982; privatized in 1999; Chair. MARTINHO CRISTOGOMO RAMOS.

CO-OPERATIVES

Instituto Nacional das Cooperativas: Fazenda, CP 218, Praia, Santiago; tel. 61-41-12; fax 61-39-59; central co-operative organization.

TRADE UNIONS

Confederação Cabo-Verdiana dos Sindicatos Livres (CCSL): Rua Dr Júlio Abreu, Praia, Santiago; tel. 61-63-19; Sec.-Gen. JOSÉ MANUEL VAZ.

Sindicato da Indústria, Agricultura e Pesca (SIAP): Plateau, Praia, Santiago; tel. 61-63-19.

Sindicato dos Transportes, Comunicações e Turismo (STCT): Praia, Santiago; tel. 61-63-38.

União Nacional dos Trabalhadores de Cabo Verde—Central Sindical (UNTC—CS): Estrada do Aeroporto, Praia, Santiago; tel. 61-43-05; fax 61-36-29; f. 1978; Chair. JÚLIO ASCENSÃO SILVA.

Transport

ROADS

In 1996 there were an estimated 1,100 km of roads, of which 858 km were paved.

SHIPPING

Cargo-passenger ships call regularly at Porto Grande, Mindelo, on São Vicente, and Praia, on Santiago. In 1993 plans were announced for the upgrading of Porto Grande, and for the re-establishment of the port of Vale dos Cavaleiros, on Fogo island. There are small ports on the other inhabited islands.

Comissão de Gestão dos Transportes Marítimos de Cabo Verde: CP 153, São Vicente; tel. 31-49-79; fax 31-20-55.

Empresa Nacional de Administração dos Portos, EP (ENAPOR): Avda Marginal, CP 82, Mindelo, São Vicente; tel. 31-44-14; fax 31-46-61; f. 1982; Chair. and Man. Dir MANUEL VICENTE A. SILVA; 499 employees.

Companhia Cabo-Verdiana de Transportes Marítimos: CP 150, Praia, Santiago; tel. 61-22-84; fax 61-60-95.

Companhia Nacional de Navegação Arca Verde: Rua 5 de Julho, CP 41, Praia, Santiago; tel. 61-10-60; fax 61-54-96; f. 1975.

Companhia de Navegação Estrela Negra: Avda 5 de Julho 17, CP 91, São Vicente; tel. 31-54-23; fax 31-53-82.

Companhia Portuguesa de Transportes Marítimos: Agent in Santiago: João Benoliel de Carvalho, Lda, CP 56, Praia, Santiago.

CS Line: Praia, Santiago.

Linhas Marítimas Caboverdianas (LINMAC): Dr João Battista Ferreira Medina, CP 357, Praia, Santiago; tel. 61-43-52; fax 61-37-15; Man. ESTHER SPENCER.

Mare Verde: Mindelo, São Vicente.

Seage Agência de Navegação de Cabo Verde: Avda Cidade de Lisboa, CP 232, Praia, Santiago; tel. 61-57-58; fax 61-25-24; Chair. CÉSAR MANUEL SEMEDO LOPES.

CIVIL AVIATION

The Amílcar Cabral international airport, at Espargos, on Sal island, can accommodate aircraft of up to 50 tons and 1m. passengers per year. The airport's facilities were expanded during the 1990s. A second international airport, under construction on Santiago, capable of accommodating long-range aircraft, was due for completion in 2001. There is also a small airport on each of the other inhabited islands. The airport on São Vicente was upgraded to international capacity in 2000. Plans were also under way for the construction of an international airport on Boa Vista.

Empresa Nacional de Aeroportos e Segurança Aérea, EP (ASA): Aeroporto Amílcar Cabral, CP 58, Ilha do Sal; tel. 41-13-94; fax 41-15-70; e-mail asacv@mail.cvtelecom.cv; airports and aircraft security; Pres. VALDEMAR CORREIA; 344 employees.

CABOVIMO: 32 Avda Unidade Guiné-Cabo Verde, Praia, Santiago; tel. 61-33-14; fax 61-55-59; f. 1992; internal flights; Gen. Man. JORGE DANIEL SPENCER LIMA.

Transportes Aéreos de Cabo Verde (TACV): Avda Amílcar Cabral, CP 1, Praia, Santiago; tel. 61-58-13; fax 61-35-85; e-mail cv.airline@milton.cvtelecom.cv; internet www.tacv.com; f. 1958; internal services connecting the nine inhabited islands; also operates regional services to Senegal, Guinea, the Gambia and Guinea-

Bissau, and long-distance services to Europe and the USA; Dir ALFREDO CARVALHO.

Tourism

The islands of Santiago, Santo Antão, Fogo and Brava offer attractive mountain scenery. There are extensive beaches on the islands of Santiago, Sal, Boa Vista and Maio. There are nine hotels on Sal, three on Boa Vista, three on São Vicente, and nine on Santiago. In 1999 there were some 1,825 hotel rooms in Cape Verde, with 3,165 beds. Some 52,000 tourists visited Cape Verde during 1998, mainly

from Italy, Portugal, Germany, Austria, France, the Netherlands, Belgium and Spain. In 2000 an estimated 100,000 tourists visited Cape Verde. In 1997 tourism receipts totalled US $15m. The sector is undergoing rapid expansion, with tourist arrivals projected to increase to about 400,000 annually by 2008.

Centro de Promocão Turística, do Investimento Externo e das Exportações (PROMEX): CP 89c, Achada de Santo António, Praia, Santiago; tel. 62-27-36; fax 62-27-37; e-mail promex@ mail.cvtelecom.cv; internet www.promex.cv; f. 1990; promotes tourism, foreign investment and exports; Dir of Tourism AIDA DUARTE SILVA.

THE CENTRAL AFRICAN REPUBLIC

Introductory Survey

Location, Climate, Language, Religion, Flag, Capital

The Central African Republic is a land-locked country in the heart of equatorial Africa. It is bordered by Chad to the north, by Sudan to the east, by the Democratic Republic of the Congo (formerly Zaire) and the Republic of the Congo to the south and by Cameroon to the west. The climate is tropical, with an average annual temperature of 26°C (79°F) and heavy rainfall in the south-western forest areas. The national language is Sango, but French is the official language and another 68 languages and dialects have been identified. It is estimated that about one-half of the population are Christian; another 15% are Muslims, while animist beliefs are held by an estimated 24%. The national flag (proportions 5 by 3) has four equal horizontal stripes, of blue, white, green and yellow, divided vertically by a central red stripe, with a five-pointed yellow star in the hoist corner of the blue stripe. The capital is Bangui.

Recent History

The former territory of Ubangi-Shari (Oubangui-Chari), within French Equatorial Africa, became the Central African Republic (CAR) on achieving self-government in December 1958. Barthélemy Boganda, the first Prime Minister, died in March 1959. He was succeeded by his nephew, David Dacko, who led the country to full independence, and became the first President, on 13 August 1960. In 1962 a one-party state was established, with the ruling Mouvement d'évolution sociale de l'Afrique noire (MESAN) as the sole authorized party. President Dacko was overthrown on 31 December 1965 by a military coup which brought to power his cousin, Col (later Marshal) Jean-Bédel Bokassa, Commander-in-Chief of the armed forces.

In January 1966 Bokassa formed a new Government, rescinded the Constitution and dissolved the National Assembly. Bokassa, who became Life President in March 1972 and Marshal of the Republic in May 1974, forestalled several alleged coup attempts and employed increasingly repressive measures against dissidents. From January 1975 to April 1976 Elisabeth Domitien, the Vice-President of MESAN, was Prime Minister; she was the first woman to hold this position in any African country.

In September 1976 the Council of Ministers was replaced by the Council for the Central African Revolution, and the former President, Dacko, was appointed personal adviser to the President. In December the Republic was renamed the Central African Empire (CAE), and a new Constitution was instituted. Bokassa was proclaimed the first Emperor, and Dacko became his Personal Counsellor. The Imperial Constitution provided for the establishment of a national assembly, but no elections were held. The elaborate preparations for Bokassa's coronation in December 1977 were estimated to have consumed about one-quarter of the country's income. In May 1978 Bokassa reorganized the army leadership and strengthened its powers. In July he appointed a new Council of Ministers, headed by a former Deputy Prime Minister, Henri Maidou. In January 1979 violent protests, led by students, were suppressed, reportedly with the help of Zairean troops. Following a protest by schoolchildren against compulsory school uniforms (made by a company owned by the Bokassa family), many children were arrested in April. About 100 were killed in prison, and Bokassa himself allegedly participated in the massacre. On 20 September, while Bokassa was in Libya, Dacko deposed him in a bloodless coup, which received considerable support from France. The country was again designated a republic, with Dacko as its President and Maidou as Vice-President.

President Dacko's principal concern was to establish order and economic stability, but his Government encountered opposition, particularly from students who objected to the continuation in office of CAE ministers. In August 1980 Dacko accepted demands for the dismissal of both Maidou and the Prime Minister, Bernard Christian Ayandho. Bokassa, at that time in exile in Côte d'Ivoire (and subsequently in Paris), was sentenced to death *in absentia* in December. In February 1981 a new Constitution, providing for a multi-party system, was approved by referendum and promulgated by President Dacko. He won a presidential election in March, amid allegations of electoral malpractice, and was sworn in for a six-year term in April. Political tension intensified in subsequent months, and on 1 September the Chief of Staff of the Armed Forces, Gen. André Kolingba, deposed Dacko in a bloodless coup. Kolingba was declared President, and a ruling Comité militaire pour le redressement national (CMRN) and an all-military Government were formed. All political activity was suspended.

In March 1982 the exiled leader of the banned Mouvement pour la libération du peuple centrafricain (MLPC), Ange-Félix Patassé, returned to Bangui and was implicated in an unsuccessful coup attempt. Patassé, who had been the Prime Minister under Bokassa in 1976–78 and who had contested the 1981 presidential election, sought asylum in the French embassy in Bangui, from where he was transported to exile in Togo. A visit by President Mitterrand of France to the CAR in October 1982 normalized bilateral relations, which had been strained by French support for Patassé. Domestic opposition to Kolingba's regime continued, and in August 1983 elements of the three main opposition parties formed a united front. In September 1984 Kolingba announced an amnesty for the leaders of banned political parties, who had been under house arrest since January.

In September 1985 the CMRN was dissolved and, for the first time since Kolingba's assumption of power, civilians were appointed to the Council of Ministers. In early 1986 a specially-convened commission drafted a new Constitution, which provided for the creation of a sole legal political party, the Rassemblement démocratique centrafricain (RDC), and conferred extensive executive powers on the President, while defining a predominantly advisory role for the legislature. At a referendum in November some 91.17% of voters approved the draft Constitution and granted Kolingba a mandate to serve a further six-year term as President. The Council of Ministers was reorganized in December to include a majority of civilians. The RDC was officially established in February 1987, with Kolingba as founding President, and elections to the new Assemblée nationale took place in July, at which 142 candidates, all nominated by the RDC, contested the 52 seats.

In October 1986 Bokassa returned unexpectedly to the CAR and was immediately arrested. His new trial opened in November and continued until June 1987, when the former Emperor was sentenced to death, having been convicted on charges of murder, conspiracy to murder, the illegal detention of prisoners and embezzlement. In February 1988 Kolingba commuted the sentence to one of life imprisonment with hard labour.

The appointment during 1988 of former associates of Bokassa, Dacko and Patassé to prominent public offices appeared to represent an attempt by Kolingba to consolidate national unity. In August 1989, however, 12 opponents of his regime, including members of the Front patriotique oubanguien-Parti du travail and the leader of the Rassemblement populaire pour la reconstruction de la Centrafrique, Brig.-Gen. (later Gen.) François Bozize, were arrested in Benin, where they had been living in exile, and extradited to the CAR. Bozize was subsequently found guilty of complicity in the 1982 coup attempt.

During 1990 demands for higher salaries, improved working conditions and the payment of salary arrears owed to public-sector workers created unrest, which escalated into a general strike in November. In the same year opposition movements exerted pressure on the Government to introduce a plural political system, and in October violent anti-Government demonstrations were suppressed by the security forces. In December the Executive Council of the RDC recommended a review of the Constitution and the re-establishment of the premiership. Accordingly, in March 1991 Edouard Franck, a former Minister of State at the Presidency, was appointed Prime Minister, and in July the Assemblée nationale approved a constitutional amendment providing for the establishment of a multi-party political system. Kolingba resigned from the presidency of the RDC in the following month, in order to remain 'above parties'. In October the Kolingba administration agreed to convene a national debate on the country's political future, with representatives of opposition movements invited to attend. In December Kolingba pardoned Brig.-Gen. Bozize.

The Grand National Debate took place in August 1992, but was boycotted by the influential Concertation des forces démocratiques (CFD), an alliance of opposition groupings, which announced that it would only participate in a multi-party national conference with sovereign powers. At the end of August the Assemblée nationale approved legislation in accordance with decisions taken by the Grand National Debate: constitutional amendments provided for the strict separation of executive, legislative and judicial powers and Kolingba was granted temporary powers to rule by decree until the election of a new multi-party legislature. Concurrent legislative and presidential elections commenced in October, but were suspended by presidential decree and subsequently annulled by the Supreme Court, owing to alleged sabotage of the electoral process. In December Franck resigned as Prime Minister and was replaced by Gen. Timothée Malendoma, the leader of the Forum civique.

In February 1993 Malendoma, who had accused Kolingba of curtailing his powers, was dismissed from the premiership and replaced by Enoch Derant Lakoué, the leader of the Parti social-démocrate. In June, in response to mounting pressure from both the opposition and the French Government, Kolingba announced that elections would commence in August. Accordingly, two rounds of concurrent legislative and presidential elections were held in late August and mid-September. At the legislative elections the MLPC won 34 of the 85 seats in the Assemblée nationale while the RDC, in second place, secured 13 seats. Patassé, the MLPC leader and former Prime Minister, was elected President, winning 52.47% of the votes cast at a second round of elections. The seven other presidential candidates included Kolingba, Prof. Abel Goumba (the leader of the CFD) and former President Dacko. In late August Kolingba, who had been defeated at the first round of presidential elections, attempted to delay the publication of the election results by issuing two decrees which modified the electoral code and altered the composition of the Supreme Court; however, the decrees were revoked, after the French Government threatened to suspend all co-operation with the CAR in protest.

In September 1993 Bokassa was released from prison under a general amnesty for convicts; however, the former Emperor was banned for life from participating in elections and demoted from the military rank of marshal. He died in November 1996.

In October 1993 Patassé was inaugurated as President. Soon afterwards he appointed Jean-Luc Mandaba, Vice-President of the MLPC, as Prime Minister; Mandaba formed a coalition Government, which had a working majority of 53 seats in the Assemblée nationale. In December the Government announced the establishment of a commission of inquiry into the conduct of Kolingba during his 12-year presidency, which was to include an audit of government finances. In March 1994, following the arrest of two senior members of the RDC on charges of provoking popular discontent, Kolingba was stripped of his army rank.

In December 1994 a draft Constitution was approved by 82% of voters in a national referendum. The new Constitution, which was adopted in January 1995, included provisions empowering the President to nominate senior military, civil service and judicial officials, and requiring the Prime Minister to implement policies decided by the President. In addition, provision was made for the creation of directly-elected regional assemblies and for the establishment of an advisory State Council, which was to deliberate on administrative issues. Several groups in the governing coalition (notably the Mouvement pour la démocratie et le développement—MDD, led by Dacko) expressed concern at the powers afforded to the President.

In April 1995 Mandaba resigned as Prime Minister, pre-empting a threatened vote of 'no confidence' in his administration (initiated by his own party), following accusations of corruption and incompetence. Patassé appointed Gabriel Koyambounou, formerly a civil servant, as the new Prime Minister. Koyambounou subsequently nominated a new Council of Ministers, with an enlarged membership. In August supporters of the RDC staged a peaceful demonstration in protest at perceived abuses of power by the Government, such as the imposition of a two-year term of imprisonment on the editor of the RDC newspaper, who had been found guilty of treason following the publication of an article critical of Patassé. In December several opposition movements (including the MDD, but not the RDC) united to form the Conseil démocratique des partis politiques de l'opposition (CODEPO), which aimed to campaign against alleged corruption and mismanagement by the Patassé regime.

In the mid-1990s the Government repeatedly failed to pay the salaries of public-sector employees and members of the security forces, prompting frequent strikes and mounting political unrest. In mid-April 1996 CODEPO staged an anti-Government rally in Bangui. Shortly afterwards part of the national army mutinied in the capital and demanded the immediate settlement of all salary arrears. Patassé promised that part of the overdue salaries would be paid and that the mutineers would not be subject to prosecution. The presence of French troops (the Elements français d'assistance opérationelle—EFAO) in Bangui, with a mandate to secure the safety of foreign nationals and (in accordance with a bilateral military accord) to protect the presidential palace and other key installations, contributed to the swift collapse of the rebellion. About nine people, including civilians, were reported to have died in the uprising. In late April Patassé appointed a new Chief of Staff of the Armed Forces, Col Maurice Regonessa, and banned all public demonstrations. In mid-May, however, discontent again resurfaced and CODEPO organized another rally in Bangui, at which it demanded the resignation of the Government. Soon afterwards, in an attempt to tighten his hold on power, the President ordered that control of the national armoury should be transferred from the regular army to the presidential guard. However, adverse reaction to this move within the ranks of the armed forces rapidly escalated into a second, more determined insurrection. Once again EFAO troops were deployed to protect the Patassé administration; some 500 reinforcements were brought in from Chad and Gabon to consolidate the resident French military presence (numbering 1,400). Five hostages were taken by the mutineers, including Col Regonessa, a government minister and the President of the Assemblée nationale. After five days of fierce fighting between dissident and loyalist troops, the French forces intervened to suppress the rebellion. France's military action (which allegedly resulted in civilian deaths) prompted intense scrutiny of the role of the former colonial power, and precipitated large pro- and anti-French demonstrations in Bangui. In total, 11 soldiers and 32 civilians were reported to have been killed in the second army mutiny. Following extended negotiations between the mutineers and government representatives, the two sides eventually signed an accord, providing for an amnesty for the rebels (who were to return to barracks under EFAO guard), the immediate release of hostages, and the installation of a new government of national unity. The political opposition rejected the proposed government of national unity, however, demanding instead a transitional government leading to fresh legislative and presidential elections. The opposition also requested a revision of the Constitution to remove some executive powers from the President and enhance the role of the Prime Minister.

In June 1996 the Government and the opposition signed a protocol providing for the establishment of a government of national unity led by a civilian Prime Minister with no official party ties. Although the Constitution was not to be amended to alter the balance of power between the President and the Prime Minister, Patassé agreed to permit 'some room for manoeuvre'. Meanwhile, France agreed to assist the CAR authorities with the payment of salary arrears. Following the publication of the protocol, Koyambounou's Government resigned. Jean-Paul Ngoupandé, hitherto Ambassador to France and with no official political affiliation (although he had been Secretary-General of the RDC in the late 1980s), was appointed as the new Prime Minister. Ngoupandé immediately nominated a new Council of Ministers. National co-operation, however, remained elusive, as CODEPO, dissatisfied with the level of its ministerial representation, immediately withdrew from the Government of National Unity. Moreover, a growing animosity was reported between Patassé and Ngoupandé, with the former refusing to transfer any effective power to the latter.

At a conference on national defence held in August/September 1996, several resolutions were adopted regarding restructuring and improving conditions within the army. In October, however, it was reported that troops who had been involved in the insurrections of April and May were refusing to be transferred from their barracks in the capital to a more remote location; Patassé insisted that their departure would take place none the less. However, in mid-November a further mutiny erupted among these troops. A substantial part of Bangui was occupied by the rebels, and a number of hostages were taken. The latest uprising appeared to have a strong tribal and political motivation: the mutineers, who demanded the resignation of Patassé, belonged to the Yakoma ethnic group of Kolingba. EFAO troops were deployed once again, ostensibly to maintain order and protect foreign residents; however, by guarding key installations and government buildings, they also effectively prevented the overthrow of the Patassé administration. More than 100 people were killed in the unrest during late November and early December.

In December 1996 the Presidents of Burkina Faso, Chad, Gabon and Mali negotiated a 15-day truce, which was supervised by the former transitional President of Mali, Brig.-Gen. Amadou Toumani Touré; a one-month extension to the cease-fire was subsequently agreed. In January 1997, following the killing of two French soldiers in Bangui (reportedly by mutineers), EFAO troops retaliated by killing at least 10 members of the rebel forces; French military involvement in the CAR was condemned by the opposition, which also sought (without success) to initiate impeachment proceedings against Patassé. Subsequent to the renewal of violence, Touré again came to Bangui as mediator and helped to create a cross-party Committee of Consultation and Dialogue. The 'Bangui Accords', drawn up by this committee, were signed towards the end of January; these, as well as offering an amnesty to the mutineers, agreed upon the formation of a new government of national unity and on the replacement of the EFAO troops by peace-keeping forces from African nations. The opposition at first threatened to boycott the new Government, largely owing to the appointment of Michel Gbezera-Bria (a close associate of Patassé and hitherto the Minister of Foreign Affairs) as Prime Minister. However, with the creation of new ministerial posts for opposition politicians, a 'Government of Action' (which did not include Ngoupandé) was formed on 18 February; soon afterwards Gen. Bozize replaced Gen. Regonessa as Chief of Staff of the Armed Forces.

In February 1997 responsibility for peace-keeping operations was transferred from the EFAO to forces of the newly-formed Mission interafricaine de surveillance des accords de Bangui (MISAB), comprising some 700 soldiers from Burkina Faso, Chad, Gabon, Mali, Senegal and Togo (with logistical support from 50 French military personnel). MISAB soldiers were also to assist in disarming the former mutineers; however, when in late March they attempted to do so, fighting broke out in which some 20 MISAB soldiers were killed. A spokesman for the rebels, Capt. Anicet Saulet, claimed that the lack of representation of the former mutineers in the new Government constituted a breach of the Bangui Accords. Following a meeting between Saulet and Patassé in early April, the Council of Ministers was expanded to include two military officers as representatives of the rebels. Later that month several hundred former mutineers attended a ceremony marking their reintegration into the regular armed forces.

In mid-April 1997 a curfew was imposed on Bangui, owing to a serious escalation in violent crime, much of which was allegedly perpetrated by groups of former mutineers. In May, following the deaths in police custody of three former rebels suspected of criminal activities, nine ministers representing the G11 (a grouping of 11 opposition parties, including the MDD—which had left CODEPO in November 1996—and the RDC), as well as the two representatives of the former mutineers, suspended participation in the Government. In June violent clashes erupted once again between MISAB forces and former mutineers. In response to several attacks on the French embassy by the rebels, several hundred EFAO troops were redeployed on the streets of Bangui, and MISAB forces launched a major offensive in the capital, capturing most of the rebel-controlled districts. This assault led to the arrest of more than 80 former mutineers, but also to some 100 deaths, both of soldiers and of civilians, while numerous homes and business premises were destroyed. Soon afterwards some 500 demonstrators gathered outside the French embassy to protest against alleged abuses of human rights by MISAB troops; MISAB officials claimed that criminals were impersonating their soldiers in order to perpetrate atrocities. On the same day Touré returned to Bangui in his capacity as Chairman of MISAB, and negotiated a four-day truce, which took effect at the end of June, followed by a 10-day cease-fire agreement, signed at the beginning of July; all of the former mutineers were to be reintegrated into the regular armed forces, and their safety and that of the people living in the districts under their control was guaranteed; the rebels, for their part, were to relinquish their weaponry. Towards the end of July many of the people who had been held in custody in relation to the previous month's violence were

released by the authorities, and the curfew in Bangui was eased, while it was reported that almost all of the former mutineers had rejoined the regular armed forces. In September the nine representatives of opposition parties in the Council of Ministers resumed their vacant posts.

In July 1997, in accordance with a foreign policy decision to disengage forces from its former African colonies, France announced its intention to withdraw its troops from the CAR by April 1998; the first troops left the country in October 1997. France campaigned vigorously for the formation of a UN force, but encountered initial resistance from the USA. A National Reconciliation Conference, held in Bangui, in February 1998 led to the signing on 5 March of a National Reconciliation Pact by President Patassé and 40 representatives of all the country's political and social groups. The accord was countersigned by Brig.-Gen. Touré and witnessed by many other African Heads of State. The Pact restated the main provisions of the Bangui Accords and of the political protocol of June 1996. It provided for military and political restructuring, to be implemented by a civilian Prime Minister, supported by all of the country's social and political groups. The powers and position of the President were, however, guaranteed, and a presidential election was scheduled for late 1999.

The signature of the Pact facilitated the authorization later in March 1998 by the UN Security Council of the establishment of a peace-keeping mission, the UN Mission in the Central African Republic (MINURCA), to replace MISAB. MINURCA comprised 1,345 troops from Benin, Burkina Faso, Canada, Chad, Côte d'Ivoire, Egypt, France, Gabon, Mali, Portugal, Senegal and Togo, and was granted a mandate to remain in the country for an initial period of three months. MINURCA's initial mandate was to maintain security and stability around Bangui, to supervise the final disposition of weapons retrieved under the disarmament programme, to assist in efforts to train a national police force, and to provide advice and technical assistance for the legislative elections. The mission was subsequently extended until the end of February 1999 in order to support and verify the legislative elections.

There was substantial support for the new political solution and, significantly, when in April 1998 the principal trade union, the Union Syndicale des Travailleurs de la Centrafrique, called for a 48-hour general strike to protest against outstanding pay arrears, their action received little support. However, preparations for the legislative elections were marked by disagreement between the Government and the G11 group of opposition parties over electoral procedure. When the authorities announced in August that the elections were to be postponed, owing to the difficulties of registering rural voters, the opposition claimed that there was little political will for the elections in government circles. Demonstrations took place outside the Assemblée nationale in September to protest against the indefinite postponement of the legislative elections and the subsequent extension of the term of office of deputies.

Elections to the newly-reorganized Assemblée nationale finally took place on 22 November and 13 December 1998. A reportedly large number of the electorate participated in the polls, which were contested by 29 parties. The MPLC won 47 of the 109 seats in the legislature, but secured the co-operation of seven independent members. The opposition won 55 seats; however, the defection, amid allegations of bribery, of a newly-elected deputy belonging to the Parti social-démocrate (PSD) gave the ruling MPLC a majority in the Assemblée. The opposition called for the defector to give up his seat, and the opening of the Assemblée nationale was delayed. Most of the opposition representatives boycotted the opening of the legislature, which was eventually held on 4 January 1999, and MINURCA troops were deployed to protect deputies from anti-Government protesters gathered outside. Patassé's decision to call on a close associate, the nominally independent erstwhile Minister of Finance, Anicet Georges Dologuélé, to form a new Government provoked public demonstrations, and caused the opposition formally to withdraw from the legislature (the boycott lasted until March). Dologuélé announced the composition of a new coalition Council of Ministers in early January, but 10 opposition ministers immediately resigned in protest at the MPLC's alleged disregard for the results of the election. In mid-January Dologuélé announced the formation of another Council of Ministers, which included four members of the MDD, despite an earlier agreement made by the opposition not to accept posts in the new Government. The MDD leadership subsequently ordered its members to resign from their government positions; three of the four ministers did so, but Armand Sama, the nominated Minister of Town Planning, Housing and Public Buildings, defied his party's directives and retained his portfolio. In March two PSD deputies resigned from the party, announcing their intention to retain their seats in the Assemblée nationale as independents.

In February 1999 the UN Security Council extended MINURCA's mandate until mid-November in order that it might assist in the preparations and conduct of the presidential election, which was scheduled to be held on 29 August. It was simultaneously agreed, however, that the force would gradually be reduced after the successful conclusion of the election with the aim of withdrawing all troops prior to the end of MINURCA's mandate. France was reported to have opposed an extension of the mandate, and in February the French contingent withdrew from MINURCA (as did the troops from Côte d'Ivoire in April). The UN Secretary-General, Kofi Annan, called on all factions in the CAR to co-operate in preparations for the presidential election. In particular, Annan criticized delays in the appointment of the independent electoral commission, the Commission électorale mixte indépendante (CEMI), the 27 members of which were finally approved in May. In July the Constitutional Court authorized 10 candidates to stand in the presidential election. President Patassé was to seek re-election, while other candidates included two former Presidents, Gen. André Kolingba and David Dacko, two former Prime Ministers, Jean-Paul Ngoupandé and Enoch Derant Lakoué, as well as Prof. Abel Goumba, the opposition candidate in the 1993 presidential election. In the same month MINURCA supervised the destruction in Bangui of hundreds of weapons collected under the disarmament programme. In August a 45-member body was established, at the request of bilateral creditors and the UN, in order to supervise the activities of the CEMI, which comprised members of both opposition and pro-Patassé parties, and was intended to ensure transparency in the conduct of the election. In mid-August the opposition grouping, the Union des forces acquises à la paix (UFAP), requested that voting be postponed until late September because of the delay in the appointment of the CEMI. Patassé later postponed the election until 12 September. In the event, the election was not held until 19 September, owing to organizational problems. The voting procedure was conducted in a peaceful manner and international observers reported that, despite some attempts at fraud by a number of individuals, no widespread irregularities had been discovered. On 2 October the Constitutional Court announced that Patassé had won 517,993 votes, equivalent to 51.6% of the total votes cast, and had, therefore, by attaining more than 50% of the vote, been re-elected President without the need for a second round of voting. Patassé's nearest rivals were Kolingba, who won 194,486 votes (19.4%), Dacko, who received 111,886 votes (11.2%), and Goumba, who obtained 60,778 votes (6.1%). The nine defeated candidates subsequently demanded the annulment of the election results, which they claimed had been manipulated; however, they asked their supporters to remain calm, and on 22 October Patassé was sworn in as President for a further six-year term. In early November the recently-reappointed Prime Minister Dologuélé announced the formation of a new Council of Ministers, which included members of parties loyal to Patassé as well as independents, three opposition representatives and two members of the armed forces. The Government stated that its main priorities were to improve human development in the CAR and to combat poverty; particular emphasis was also laid on the restructuring of the public sector and of the armed forces.

In October 1999 Kofi Annan requested that the UN Security Council authorize the gradual withdrawal of MINURCA from the CAR over a three-month period following the end of its mandate on 15 November. Annan highlighted the important role of MINURCA in guaranteeing stability in the post-electoral period, while he also noted that a delayed withdrawal would enable MINURCA units to complete a training course for local police recruits. In December the UN announced proposals to establish a Bureau de soutien à la consolidation de la paix en Centrafrique (BONUCA), in Bangui, the role of which would be to monitor developments in the CAR in the areas of politics, socio-economics, human rights and security issues, as well as to facilitate dialogue between political figures. BONUCA began its operation on the same day as the final withdrawal of MINURCA, 15 February 2000, with a mandate for a one-year period.

In April 2000 there was a ministerial reshuffle, which included the appointment of Antoine Grothe as the new Minister of Justice to replace Denis Wangao Kizmalé, who was transferred to the Ministry of the Civil Service and Employment. In the same month the Dologuélé Government survived a vote of 'no confidence', which was proposed by the opposition, in the Assemblée nationale: 40 deputies voted in favour of the motion, 58 against and four abstained. The Government was subject to further pressure in November when thousands of civil servants staged a strike in support of their demands for the payment of at least 12 of the 30 months' salary arrears owed to them. The paralysis of public services exacerbated social tensions and youths joined the protest movement, erecting barricades. Later that month 15 opposition parties united to demand the resignation of President Patassé and to announce, in December, the formation of a co-ordination committee with the aim of organizing a peaceful transfer of power. In mid-December the security forces dispersed a mass demonstration, organized by trade unions and opposition political parties, arresting some 65 people, including four deputies of the Assemblée nationale. A subsequent sit-in planned by striking civil servants to protest against the arrests was banned by the Government. In April 2001 Patassé dismissed the Dologuélé administration. Martin Ziguélé was appointed as Prime Minister, and a new Government was formed.

In May 1997 the CAR recognized the administration of President Laurent Kabila in the Democratic Republic of the Congo (DRC, formerly Zaire). In the same month the CAR and the DRC signed a mutual assistance pact, which provided for permanent consultation on internal security and defence. The pact also sought to guarantee border security; however, during mid-1997 armed soldiers of what had been the Zairean army were reported to be fleeing troops loyal to Kabila and crossing the Oubangui river into the CAR. In 1998 the CAR authorities blamed the country's rapidly escalating AIDS problem on the continuing influx of refugees from the DRC, the Republic of the Congo, Rwanda, Chad and Sudan, and in January 1999 there was a further influx of DRC civilians to the CAR. The refugees crossed the Oubangui river to escape the fighting between government and rebel soldiers, who were occupying the northern part of the DRC. DRC troops also entered the CAR, with the agreement of the CAR authorities, to try to halt the rebel advance in the northern part of the DRC. By early August, following significant rebel advances, it was reckoned that as many as 20,000 DRC refugees had entered the CAR, including around 6,000 members of the DRC armed forces, prompting fears of a humanitarian disaster. In mid-August the regional office of the UN High Commissioner for Refugees estimated that the CAR was sheltering about 54,000 refugees from the DRC, Chad and Sudan.

In late 1994 the CAR and Chad agreed to establish a bilateral security structure to ensure mutual border security. In 1994 the CAR also became the fifth member of the Lake Chad Basin Commission (see p. 308). Attacks on Chadian nationals resident in Bangui and on the Chadian contingent of the MISAB forces in late 1996 and early 1997 led the Chadian Government to issue a communiqué in March 1997 warning that further incidences of such aggression would not be tolerated. In June 1999 President Patassé issued an official apology to Chad following a disturbance at a market in Bangui in which five Chadian nationals were killed by members of the CAR security forces. In August the CAR Government agreed to pay compensation to the families of the victims. None the less, in December it was reported that some 1,500 Chadian refugees were preparing to leave the CAR, allegedly owing to fears for their security following the scheduled departure of MINURCA forces.

The CAR maintains amicable relations with Nigeria, and in June 1999 the two countries signed a bilateral trade agreement. The CAR is also a close ally of Libya, and in April 1999 joined the Libyan-sponsored Community of Sahel–Saharan States (see p. 307).

Government

Executive power is vested in the President of the Republic, and legislative power in the Congress. The Congress consists of a 109-seat Assemblée nationale, sessions of which are held at the summons of the President, an advisory Economic and Regional Council, one-half of the members of which are elected by the Assembly and one-half appointed by the President, and an advisory State Council, which deliberates on matters that are referred to it by the President of the Assemblée nationale. Both the President and the Assemblée nationale are elected by direct universal suffrage, the former for a six-year term and the latter for a five-year term. The Prime Minister, who presides over a Council of Ministers, is appointed by the President.

For administrative purposes, the country is divided into 14 prefectures, two economic prefectures (Gribingui and Sangha), and one commune (Bangui). It is further divided into 67 sub-prefectures and two postes de contrôle administratif. At community level there are 65 communes urbaines, 102 communes rurales and seven communes d'élevage. The 1995 Constitution provided for the election of new regional assemblies by universal suffrage.

Defence

In August 2000 the armed forces numbered about 3,150 men (army 3,000; air force 150), with a further 1,000 men in paramilitary forces. There are plans to enlarge the strength of the army to some 4,200 men, as part of a general restructuring of the armed forces. Military service is selective and lasts for two years. The full withdrawal of the 1,345 troops of the United Nations Mission in the Central African Republic (MINURCA) was completed in mid-February 2000. Government expenditure on defence in 2000 was estimated at 31,000m. francs CFA.

Economic Affairs

In 1998, according to estimates by the World Bank, the CAR's gross national product (GNP), measured at average 1996–98 prices, was US $1,053m., equivalent to $300 per head (or $1,098 per head on an international purchasing-power parity basis). During 1990–98, it was estimated, GNP per head declined, in real terms, at an average rate of 0.7% per year. Over the same period, the population increased at an average annual rate of 2.4%. GNP in 1999 was estimated at $1,000m., equivalent to $290 per head. The country's gross domestic product (GDP) increased, in real terms, at an average annual rate of 1.8% in 1990–99. The IMF estimated real GDP growth at 4.8% in 1998 and at 3.4% in 1999.

Agriculture (including hunting, forestry and fishing) contributed 53.4% of GDP in 1999. About 73.5% of the economically active population were employed in the sector in that year. The principal cash crops are coffee (which accounted for an estimated 10.2% of export earnings in 1999) and cotton (an estimated 10.4% of total exports in 1999). Livestock and tobacco are also exported. The major subsistence crops are cassava (manioc) and yams. The Government is encouraging the cultivation of horticultural produce for export. The exploitation of the country's large forest resources represents a significant source of export revenue (exports of wood accounted for an estimated 18.2% of the total in 1999); however, the full potential of this sector has yet to be realized, owing to the inadequacy of the transport infrastructure. Rare butterflies are also exported. Agricultural GDP increased at an average annual rate of 3.7% during 1990–99, and by an estimated 4.0% in 1999.

Industry (including mining, manufacturing, construction and power) engaged 3.3% of the employed labour force in 1988 and provided 18.8% of GDP in 1999. Industrial GDP increased at an average annual rate of 0.4% in 1990–99, but declined by an estimated 2.0% in 1997. It increased, however, by 1.7% in 1998 and by 4.3% in 1999, according to IMF estimates.

Mining and quarrying engaged a labour force estimated at between 40,000 and 80,000 in the late 1990s, and contributed 4.3% of GDP in 1999. The principal activity is the extraction of predominantly gem diamonds (exports of diamonds provided an estimated 45.9% of total export revenue in 1999). The introduction of gem-cutting facilities and the eradication of widespread 'black market' smuggling operations would substantially increase revenue from diamond mining. The reopening in 1997 of the Bangui diamond bourse, which had been established in 1996, was intended to increase revenue by levying a 10% sales tax on transactions. Deposits of gold are also exploited. The development of uranium resources may proceed. Reserves of iron ore, copper, tin and zinc have also been located. According to IMF estimates, the GDP of the mining sector increased at an average rate of 7.0% per year during 1992–94, but declined by an average of 4.6% per year in 1994–97, before increasing by 0.8% in 1998 and by 3.5% in 1999.

The manufacturing sector engaged 1.6% of the employed labour force in 1988. Manufacturing, which contributed 8.9% of GDP in 1999, is based upon the processing of primary products. In 1997 the major activities were the processing of foods, beverages and tobacco, furniture, fixtures and paper and textiles. According to IMF estimates, in real terms, the GDP of the manufacturing sector increased at an average annual rate of 7.9% in 1992–95, but declined by an average of 8.5% per year in 1995–97, before recording an increase of 2.0% in 1998 and 3.5% in 1999.

In 1999, according to preliminary figures, 97.7% of electrical energy generated within the CAR was derived from the country's two hydroelectric power installations. Imports of petroleum products comprised an estimated 10.6% of the cost of merchandise imports in 1999.

Services engaged 15.5% of the employed labour force in 1988 and provided 27.8% of GDP in 1999. In real terms, the GDP of the services sector decreased at an average rate of 0.7% per year during 1990–99. It increased, however, by an estimated 3.7% in 1999.

In 1998 the CAR recorded a visible trade deficit of an estimated 13,700m. francs CFA and a deficit of an estimated 4,000m. francs CFA on the current account of the balance of payments. In 1996 the principal source of imports was France (providing 39.5% of the total), while the principal markets for exports were the Belgo-Luxembourg Economic Union (accounting for 60.1% of the total) and France (30.9%). Other major trading partners in that year were Cameroon, Japan and the United Kingdom. The principal exports in 1999 were diamonds, wood products, cotton and coffee. The principal imports in 1996 were road vehicles, machinery, basic manufactures, cotton, mineral fuels and lubricants, chemical products and food.

In 1997 there was an estimated budget deficit of 58,900m. francs CFA (equivalent to 9.0% of GDP). At the end of 1998 the CAR's external debt was US $921.3m., of which $829.8m. was long-term public debt. In that year the cost of debt-servicing was equivalent to 20.9% of revenue from exports of goods and services. Consumer prices rose by 24.5% in 1994, following the devaluation of the currency, and by 19.2% in 1995. In 1996 and 1997 the annual rate of inflation averaged 3.7% and 0.9% respectively, but consumer prices decreased by an average of 1.2% in 1998 and 1.4% in 1999. At the December 1988 census 7.5% of the labour force were unemployed.

The CAR is a member of the Central African organs of the Franc Zone (see p. 210) and of the Communauté economique des états de l'Afrique centrale (CEEAC, see p. 307).

The CAR's land-locked position, the inadequacy of the transport infrastructure and the country's vulnerability to adverse climatic conditions and to fluctuations in international prices for its main agricultural exports have impeded sustained economic growth. The January 1994 devaluation of the CFA franc had a profound effect on the economy, increasing export competitiveness, but also increasing consumer prices. Economic growth recovered in 1994–95, partly reflecting an improvement in prices for the CAR's agricultural exports. By late 1995, however, the Government was unable to control its mounting budgetary deficit and failed to pay the salaries of public-sector employees and the armed forces, thereby precipitating serious political instability during 1996–97, which, in turn, badly disrupted economic activity, destroying much of Bangui's industry. In mid-1998, following the signing of the National Reconciliation Pact and the appointment of an economist, Anicet Georges Dologuélé, as Prime Minister, the IMF approved a three-year Enhanced Structural Adjustment Facility (ESAF), valued at US $66m., to support the CAR's economic programme for 1998–2000. In order to normalize relations with external creditors, the CAR undertook to eliminate arrears on external payments in 1998 and to make regular payments on all external obligations. In September 1998 the 'Paris Club' of creditor nations expressed its approval of these plans by rescheduling and reducing the CAR's external debt. In July 1999 the IMF noted that, while progress had been less than envisaged under the terms of the ongoing economic programme, the CAR had succeeded in significantly improving budgetary receipts, from 6.1% of GDP in 1996 to an estimated 9.0% of GDP in mid-1999; the IMF subsequently agreed to the early release of the second tranche of ESAF funding. However, economic growth in 2000 was lower than projected, partly owing to higher international petroleum prices and a doubling in petroleum transportation costs following a suspension of imports from the Democratic Republic of the Congo. The accumulation of external and domestic payments arrears aggravated social tensions and led to mass protests by public-sector workers in late 2000 and early 2001. In January 2001 the IMF approved an increase in the second annual allocation of funds to the CAR, thus allowing the Government to draw some $10m. to cover the shortfalls in state revenue.

Social Welfare

The Government's commitments to the social welfare and health sectors were neglected during the 1990s, owing to a severe lack of funds. The provision of health-care facilities in rural areas is minimal. In 1991 there were three hospitals in Bangui, four regional hospitals and 11 prefectoral hospitals, of which four were privately operated. In addition, there were 413 other health centres and five leper hospitals. An estimated 4,030 beds were available in that year, equivalent to a ratio of 718 inhabitants per bed. In the early 1990s there were only 6 physicians and 45 nurses per 100,000 population working in the country. Government expenditure on health was estimated at an average annual rate of 1.9% of GDP in 1990–95.

Education

Education is officially compulsory for eight years between six and 14 years of age. Primary education begins at the age of six and lasts for six years. Secondary education begins at the age of 12 and lasts for up to seven years, comprising a first cycle of four years and a second of three years. In 1991 an estimated 58% of children in the relevant age-group (71% of boys; 46% of girls) attended primary schools, while secondary enrolment was equivalent to only 10% (boys 15%; girls 6%). According to estimates by the World Bank, the adult illiteracy rate in 1997 averaged 44% among males and 70% among females. Current expenditure by the Ministry of Education in 1995 totalled 8,820m. francs CFA, equivalent to 1.6% of GNP. The provision of state-funded education was severely disrupted during the 1990s, owing to the inadequacy of the Government's resources.

Public Holidays

2001: 1 January (New Year), 29 March (Anniversary of death of Barthélemy Boganda), 16 April (Easter Monday), 1 May (May Day), 24 May (Ascension Day), 4 June (Whit Monday), 30 June (National Day of Prayer), 13 August (Independence Day), 15 August (Assumption), 1 November (All Saints' Day), 1 December (National Day), 25 December (Christmas).

2002: 1 January (New Year), 29 March (Anniversary of death of Barthélemy Boganda), 1 April (Easter Monday), 1 May (May Day), 9 May (Ascension Day), 20 May (Whit Monday), 30 June (National Day of Prayer), 13 August (Independence Day), 15 August (Assumption), 1 November (All Saints' Day), 1 December (National Day), 25 December (Christmas).

Weights and Measures

The metric system is officially in force.

Statistical Survey

Source (unless otherwise stated): Division des Statistiques et des Etudes Economiques, Ministère de l'Economie, du Plan et de la Coopération Internationale, Bangui.

Area and Population

AREA, POPULATION AND DENSITY

Area (sq km)	622,984*
Population (census results)	
8 December 1975	2,054,610
8 December 1988	
Males	1,210,734
Females	1,252,882
Total	2,463,616
Population (UN estimates at mid-year)†	
1997	3,420,000
1998	3,485,000
1999	3,550,000
Density (per sq km) at mid-1999	5.7

* 240,535 sq miles.
† Source: UN, *World Population Prospects: The 1998 Revision.* The official estimate of the mid-1997 population is 3,245,000.

PRINCIPAL TOWNS (estimated population at mid-1994)

Bangui (capital). .	524,000	Carnot . . .		41,000
Berbérati . . .	47,000	Bambari . . .		41,000
Bouar	43,000	Bossangoa . . .		33,000

BIRTHS AND DEATHS (UN estimates, annual averages)

	1980–85	1985–90	1990–95
Birth rate (per 1,000). . .	42.4	42.1	39.6
Death rate (per 1,000) . .	18.5	17.9	17.4

Source: UN, *World Population Prospects: The 1998 Revision.*

1994: Registered live births 124,707 (birth rate 41.6 per 1,000); Registered deaths 50,063 (death rate 16.7 per 1,000) (Source: UN, *Population and Vital Statistics Report*).

Expectation of life (UN estimates, years at birth, 1990–95): 47.5 (males 45.9; females 49.3) (Source: UN, *World Population Prospects: The 1998 Revision*).

ECONOMICALLY ACTIVE POPULATION
(persons aged 6 years and over, 1988 census)

	Males	Females	Total
Agriculture, hunting, forestry and fishing	417,630	463,007	880,637
Mining and quarrying . . .	11,823	586	12,409
Manufacturing	16,096	1,250	17,346
Electricity, gas and water . .	751	58	809
Construction	5,583	49	5,632
Trade, restaurants and hotels .	37,435	54,563	91,998
Transport, storage and communications	6,601	150	6,751
Financing, insurance, real estate and business services . .	505	147	652
Community, social and personal services	61,764	8,537	70,301
Activities not adequately defined .	7,042	4,627	11,669
Total employed	565,230	532,974	1,098,204
Unemployed.	66,624	22,144	88,768
Total labour force . . .	631,854	555,118	1,186,972

Source: International Labour Office, *Yearbook of Labour Statistics.*

Mid-1999 (estimates in '000): Agriculture, etc. 1,244; Total labour force 1,692 (Source: FAO).

Agriculture

PRINCIPAL CROPS ('000 metric tons)

	1997	1998	1999
Rice (paddy)	17	19	21
Maize	82	88	95
Millet	11*	12*	12†
Sorghum	28*	29*	45
Cassava (Manioc) . . .	579	608	552
Yams†	340	360	360
Taro (Coco yam)† . . .	90	100	100
Pulses†	28	29	29
Groundnuts (in shell) . .	97	102	110
Sesame seed	32	33	36
Palm kernels	5†	5†	3
Pumpkins, squash and gourds	18	19	23*
Other vegetables (incl. melons) .	57	57	57
Sugar cane	79	91*	91
Oranges†	22	22	22
Mangoes†	9	9	9
Pineapples†	13	14	14
Bananas†	110	115	115
Plantains†	80	82	82
Other fruits (excl. melons)† . .	11	10	10
Coffee (green)	15	13*	13*
Cotton (lint)	22	17*	7†

* Unofficial figure.   † FAO estimate(s).

Source: FAO.

LIVESTOCK ('000 head, year ending September)

	1997	1998	1999
Cattle	2,926	2,992*	2,951
Goats	2,213	2,339*	2,473*
Sheep	191	201*	211*
Pigs.	596	622*	649*
Chickens	3,718*	3,875	4,040*

* Unofficial figure.

Source: FAO.

LIVESTOCK PRODUCTS ('000 metric tons)

	1997	1998	1999
Beef and veal	50*	51*	51†
Mutton and lamb . . .	1	1	1
Goat meat	8	8†	8†
Pig meat	12	12†	12†
Poultry meat	3	3*	3
Other meat*	7	7	7
Cows' milk	60†	60†	60†
Cattle hides (fresh)* . . .	7	8	8
Goatskins (fresh)* . . .	1	1	1
Hen eggs	1	1	1
Honey†	11	11	11

* Unofficial figure(s).   † FAO estimate(s).

Source: FAO.

Forestry

ROUNDWOOD REMOVALS ('000 cubic metres, excluding bark)

	1996	1997	1998
Sawlogs, veneer logs and logs for sleepers	305	461	529
Other industrial wood . . .	291	297	302
Fuel wood	2,606	2,687	2,687
Total	3,202	3,445	3,518

Source: FAO, *Yearbook of Forest Products*.

SAWNWOOD PRODUCTION
('000 cubic metres, including railway sleepers)

	1996	1997	1998
Total (all broadleaved) . . .	61	72	91

Source: FAO, *Yearbook of Forest Products*.

Fishing

('000 metric tons, live weight)

	1996*	1997	1998
Capture	12.7	12.5*	13.0*
Aquaculture.	0.2	0.1	0.1
Total catch (freshwater fishes) . .	12.8	12.6	13.1

* FAO estimate(s).

Source: FAO, *Yearbook of Fishery Statistics*.

Mining

	1997	1998	1999
Gold (kg, metal content of ore) . .	35.1	23.8	38.7
Diamonds ('000 carats) . . .	486.8	420.0	431.1

Source: Banque des Etats de l'Afrique Centrale, *Etudes et Statistiques*.

Industry

SELECTED PRODUCTS

	1996	1997	1998
Beer ('000 hectolitres) . . .	156.4	208.6	218.8
Soft drinks and syrups ('000 hectolitres)	60.6	93.2	46.8
Cigarettes (million packets) . .	7.8	—	—
Palm oil ('000 metric tons) . .	n.a.	2.6	3.3
Groundnut oil ('000 metric tons) .	n.a.	2.3	2.7
Plywood ('000 cubic metres) . .	1.5	1.4	1.0
Electric energy (million kWh) .	98.7	100.7	114.7

Source: IMF, *Central African Republic: Statistical Annex* (August 2000).

Raw sugar (FAO estimates, '000 metric tons): 9 in 1997; 10 in 1998; 10 in 1999 (Source: FAO).

Finance

CURRENCY AND EXCHANGE RATES

Monetary Units
100 centimes = 1 franc de la Coopération financière en Afrique centrale (CFA).

Sterling, Dollar and Euro Equivalents (29 December 2000)
£1 sterling = 1,051.93 francs CFA;
US $1 = 704.95 francs CFA;
€1 = 655.96 francs CFA;
10,000 francs CFA = £9.506 = $14.185 = €15.245.

Average Exchange Rate (francs CFA per US $)
1998   589.95
1999   615.70
2000   711.98

Note: The exchange rate of 1 French franc = 50 francs CFA, established in 1948, remained in force until January 1994, when the CFA franc was devalued by 50%, with the exchange rate adjusted to 1 French franc = 100 francs CFA. This relationship to French currency remained in effect with the introduction of the euro on 1 January 1999. From that date, accordingly, a fixed exchange rate of €1 = 655.957 francs CFA has been in operation.

BUDGET (million francs CFA)

Revenue	1997*	1998*	1999*
Tax revenue	42,400	50,300	52,500
Taxes on income and profits .	8,700	7,900	11,900
Domestic taxes on goods and services . . .	16,500	17,200	18,000
Taxes on international trade	17,100	25,200	22,700
Import duties and taxes . .	15,400	18,000	15,400
Other receipts	2,600	6,100	7,200
Total	45,000	56,300	59,700

Expenditure	1997	1998	1999*
Current expenditure . . .	51,200	50,200	56,900
Wages and salaries. . .	26,600	26,500	27,000
Other goods and services .	12,900	11,300	13,200
Transfers and subsidies . .	3,800	4,100	7,600
Interest payments . . .	7,800	8,300	9,100
Capital expenditure . . .	30,700	59,300	59,100
Sub-total	81,900	109,500	116,100
Adjustment for payments arrears†	−21,100	69,800	2,600
Total	60,800	179,300	118,700

* Estimates.
† Minus sign indicates an increase in arrears.

Source: IMF, *Central African Republic: Statistical Annex* (August 2000).

INTERNATIONAL RESERVES (US $ million at 31 December)

	1996	1997	1998
Gold*	4.10	3.24	3.20
IMF special drawing rights . .	0.01	—	0.01
Reserve position in IMF . .	0.14	0.13	0.13
Foreign exchange	232.09	178.43	145.56
Total	236.34	181.80	148.90

* National valuation.

Source: IMF, *International Financial Statistics*.

MONEY SUPPLY (million francs CFA at 31 December)

	1997	1998	1999
Currency outside banks . . .	92,963	75,247	81,115
Demand deposits at commercial and development banks . .	14,223	12,332	17,529
Total money	107,186	87,579	98,644

Source: Banque des Etats de l'Afrique Centrale, *Etudes et Statistiques*.

COST OF LIVING
(Consumer Price Index for Bangui; base: 1981 = 100)

	1997	1998	1999
Food	190.6	186.6	180.7
Fuel and light . . .	161.2	173.6	171.8
Clothing.	226.4	228.4	241.2
All items (incl. others)* . .	196.2	193.8	191.0

* Excluding rent.

Source: IMF, *Central African Republic: Statistical Annex* (August 2000).

NATIONAL ACCOUNTS
(IMF estimates, million francs CFA at current prices)

Expenditure on the Gross Domestic Product*

	1997	1998	1999
Government final consumption expenditure . .	63,800	72,200	74,800
Private final consumption expenditure . . .	494,800	521,600	529,800
Increase in stocks . . }	57,300	84,300	94,000
Gross fixed capital formation . . }			
Total domestic expenditure .	615,900	678,100	698,600
Exports of goods and services .	114,000	100,400	109,500
Less Imports of goods and services	145,700	156,000	155,500
GDP in purchasers' values .	584,300	622,600	652,500
GDP at constant 1985 prices .	411,600	430,700	445,300

* Figures are rounded to the nearest 100 million francs CFA.

Source: IMF, *Central African Republic: Statistical Annex* (August 2000).

Gross Domestic Product by Economic Activity*

	1997	1998	1999
Agriculture, hunting, forestry and fishing	283,200	306,900	326,800
Mining and quarrying . .	33,300	23,500	26,200
Manufacturing . . .	51,600	52,600	54,500
Electricity, gas and water . .	4,100	4,500	4,600
Construction . . .	26,700	28,000	29,500
Trade, restaurants and hotels .	75,500	75,600	78,800
Transport, storage and communications . . .	14,800	14,800	15,400
Other private services . .	28,100	28,200	28,300
Government services . .	43,200	46,000	46,800
GDP at factor cost . .	550,600	580,200	611,900
Indirect taxes . . .	33,600	42,400	40,700
GDP in purchasers' values . .	584,300	622,600	652,500

* Figures are rounded to the nearest 100 million francs CFA.

Source: IMF, *Central African Republic: Statistical Annex* (August 2000).

BALANCE OF PAYMENTS ('000 million francs CFA)

	1996	1997	1998*
Exports of goods	73.5	89.7	80.2
Imports of goods	−64.2	−84.4	−93.9
Trade balance . . .	9.3	5.2	−13.7
Services and other income (net)	−39.5	−46.0	−66.2
Balance on goods, services and income	−30.2	−40.8	−79.9
Private unrequited transfers (net)	−4.1	−4.4	−5.2
Public unrequited transfers (net)	25.2	29.4	81.1
Current balance . . .	−9.1	−15.8	−4.0
Long-term capital (net) . .	−5.4	−8.1	−5.2
Short-term capital (net) . .	7.8	−5.7	−2.0
Net errors and omissions . .	−1.8	3.3	−22.0
Overall balance . . .	−8.6	−26.3	−33.2

* Estimates.

Source: La Zone Franc, *Rapport Annuel 1998*.

External Trade

PRINCIPAL COMMODITIES (distribution by SITC, US $'000)

Imports c.i.f.	1994	1995	1996
Food and live animals . . .	24,635	27,587	12,585
Cereals and cereal preparations	17,183	15,010	5,915
Flour of wheat or meslin . .	13,990	7,999	3,442
Beverages and tobacco. . .	14,238	12,128	8,977
Tobacco and tobacco manufactures	12,216	9,244	6,709
Unmanufactured tobacco and tobacco refuse . .	4,417	8,510	3,632
Cigarettes	7,799	734	3,077
Crude materials (inedible) except fuels	10,353	27,184	25,177
Cork and wood	97	2,466	4,365
Coniferous sawlogs and veneer logs. . . .	90	1,921	3,901
Textile fibres (excl. wool tops) and waste	9,361	22,443	19,132
Cotton	7,951	20,547	17,501
Mineral fuels, lubricants, etc.	11,606	23,063	14,594
Petroleum, petroleum products, etc.	11,374	22,755	14,550
Refined petroleum products. .	11,223	22,715	14,447
Motor spirit (gasoline) and other light oils. .	3,223	8,364	4,756
Kerosene and other medium oils	3,948	4,239	2,973
Gas oils (distillate fuels) . .	2,242	7,651	4,809
Chemicals and related products	25,037	20,721	14,056
Medicinal and pharmaceutical products	16,759	9,522	6,416
Medicaments . . .	15,912	8,300	5,960
Disinfectants, insecticides, fungicides, etc. . . .	2,824	3,760	4,039
Basic manufactures . . .	21,404	29,201	19,118
Paper, paperboard and manufactures . . .	3,483	4,169	3,970
Non-ferrous metals . . .	4,685	3,548	1,812
Aluminium and aluminium alloys	4,393	3,204	1,210
Plates, sheets and strip . .	3,985	2,575	1,066
Machinery and transport equipment	36,668	112,122	67,289
Power-generating machinery and equipment	1,424	3,897	3,704
Machinery specialized for particular industries . .	2,809	26,240	7,912
Civil engineering and contractors' plant and equipment	876	23,753	4,939
Construction and mining machinery . . .	460	20,437	3,685
Self-propelled bulldozers, angledozers and levellers .	366	14,872	472
General industrial machinery, equipment and parts . .	5,969	9,441	5,042
Telecommunications and sound equipment . . .	3,131	12,119	4,777
Television and radio transmitters, etc. . .	983	6,170	2,496
Other electrical machinery, apparatus, etc. . .	4,120	5,494	4,180
Road vehicles and parts* . .	16,456	49,770	33,043
Passenger motor cars (excl. buses) . . .	2,948	8,935	5,473
Motor vehicles for goods transport and special purposes	4,847	17,160	13,314
Goods vehicles (lorries and trucks)	4,500	11,006	11,387
Special-purpose motor lorries and vans . .	347	6,154	1,927
Public-service passenger motor vehicles (buses, etc.) . .	1,071	5,987	2,815
Parts and accessories for cars, buses, lorries, etc.*	4,204	9,836	7,056
Other transport equipment* . .	557	1,963	5,771
Aircraft, associated equipment and parts*	548	1,791	5,771

Imports c.i.f. — *continued*	1994	1995	1996
Miscellaneous manufactured articles	7,040	12,019	10,386
Printed matter	1,544	2,582	3,890
Armoured fighting vehicles, arms of war and ammunition	17	6	7,152
Tanks and other armoured fighting vehicles, motorized, and parts	—	—	6,830
Total (incl. others)	154,162	265,499	179,942

* Excluding tyres, engines and electrical parts.

Exports f.o.b.	1994	1995	1996
Food and live animals	2,605	4,142	1,295
Coffee, tea, cocoa and spices	2,054	3,109	872
Coffee and coffee substitutes	2,049	3,103	872
Unroasted coffee, husks and skins	2,049	3,103	872
Crude materials (inedible) except fuels	42,858	59,829	57,334
Cork and wood	1,299	2,790	4,756
Coniferous sawlogs and veneer logs	142	1,736	3,883
Textile fibres (excl. wool tops) and waste	7,531	20,351	22,379
Cotton	7,528	20,309	22,379
Crude fertilizers and crude minerals (excl. coal, petroleum and precious stones)	33,545	35,998	29,437
Industrial diamonds (sorted)	33,545	35,998	29,435
Basic manufactures	31,114	41,776	40,107
Non-metallic mineral manufactures	30,839	39,887	39,725
Diamonds (excl. sorted industrial diamonds), unmounted	30,836	39,880	39,715
Sorted non-industrial diamonds, rough or simply worked	29,877	39,812	39,663
Machinery and transport equipment	2,239	10,543	8,663
Road vehicles and parts*	2,008	9,259	7,119
Public-service passenger motor vehicles (buses, etc.)	74	3,277	823
Parts and accessories for cars, buses, lorries, etc.*	1,237	3,351	4,141
Armoured fighting vehicles, arms of war and ammunition	692	—	6,992
Tanks and other armoured fighting vehicles, motorized, and parts	—	—	6,829
Total (incl. others)	81,451	119,522	115,128

* Excluding tyres, engines and electrical parts.

Source: UN, *International Trade Statistics Yearbook*.

PRINCIPAL TRADING PARTNERS (US $'000)*

Imports c.i.f.	1994	1995	1996
Belgium-Luxembourg	2,675	6,589	2,805
Cameroon	8,448	12,880	7,103
Congo, Dem. Repub.	1,386	1,841	1,938
Congo, Repub.	18,047	4,738	3,371
France (incl. Monaco)	59,149	90,739	71,137
Germany	3,213	7,626	2,792
Italy	1,332	2,921	1,674
Japan	8,586	52,303	15,676
Netherlands	1,685	2,815	1,845
United Kingdom	1,437	1,563	3,148
USA	2,447	4,871	2,971
Total (incl. others)	154,162	265,499	179,942

Exports f.o.b.	1994	1995	1996
Belgium-Luxembourg	64,906	75,487	69,192
Cameroon	226	1,825	1,184
Congo, Dem. Repub.	437	1,917	1,904
Congo, Repub.	1,012	1,374	850
France (incl. Monaco)	9,862	30,207	35,556
Spain	1,154	4	—
United Kingdom	270	2,069	3,996
Total (incl. others)	81,451	119,522	115,128

* Imports by country of production; exports by country of consumption.

Source: UN, *International Trade Statistics Yearbook*.

Transport

ROAD TRAFFIC (motor vehicles in use)

	1993	1994	1995
Passenger cars	10,400	11,900	8,900
Commercial vehicles	2,400	2,800	3,500

Source: UN, *Statistical Yearbook*.

INLAND WATERWAYS TRAFFIC—INTERNATIONAL SHIPPING (metric tons)

	1996	1997	1998
Freight unloaded at Bangui	60,311	56,206	57,513
Freight loaded at Bangui	5,348	5,907	12,524
Total	63,659	62,113	70,037

Source: Banque des Etats de l'Afrique Centrale, *Etudes et Statistiques*.

CIVIL AVIATION (traffic on scheduled services)*

	1995	1996	1997
Kilometres flown (million)	3	3	3
Passengers carried ('000)	74	75	86
Passenger-km (million)	223	225	242
Total ton-km (million)	36	37	38

* Including an apportionment of the traffic of Air Afrique.

Source: UN, *Statistical Yearbook*.

Tourism

	1995	1996	1997
Tourist arrivals ('000)	26	21	17
Tourism receipts (US $ million)	5	5	5

Source: World Tourism Organization, *Yearbook of Tourism Statistics*.

Communications Media

	1995	1996	1997
Radio receivers ('000 in use) . .	245	270	283
Television receivers ('000 in use) .	16	17	18
Telephones ('000 main lines in use)	8	10	10
Telefax stations (number in use) .	136	222	281
Mobile cellular telephones (subscribers)	44	471	570
Daily newspapers			
Number	1	3	n.a.
Average circulation ('000 copies)	2	6	n.a.

Non-daily newspapers (1995): 1 (estimated circulation 2,000 copies).

Sources: UNESCO, *Statistical Yearbook;* UN, *Statistical Yearbook.*

Education

(1990/91, unless otherwise indicated)

	Schools	Teachers	Pupils
Pre-primary	162	572*	15,734
Primary	930	4,004	308,409
Secondary			
General	46† }	1,005 {	46,989
Vocational	n.a.		1,862
Higher	n.a.	136	2,823

* 1987/88 figure.

† State-funded general secondary schools.

1991/92: Primary pupils 277,961; General secondary pupils 42,263; Vocational secondary pupils 1,477; University teachers 139; University students 2,923.

Source: UNESCO, *Statistical Yearbook.*

Directory

The Constitution

A new Constitution was adopted on 7 January 1995, following approval by a national referendum held on 28 December 1994. It replaced the 1986 Constitution and all subsequent amendments. The new Constitution provided for decentralization, through the election of regional assemblies by direct universal adult suffrage, and the establishment of a Constitutional Court (whose officials were to be appointed by the President), and it redefined the separation of sovereign and executive powers between the President and the Prime Minister.

THE PRESIDENCY

The President of the Republic is Head of State and Commander-in-Chief of the national armed forces. The President is elected for a six-year term by direct universal suffrage and may serve for a maximum of two consecutive terms*. Election of the President is determined by an absolute majority of votes cast. If such is not obtained at the first ballot, a second ballot is to take place, contested by the two candidates gaining the largest number of votes in the first ballot. The election of the new President is to take place not less than 20 days and not more than 40 days before the expiration of the mandate of the President in office. However, the President may choose to hold a referendum to determine whether or not his mandate is to be renewed. Should the electorate reject the proposal, the President is to resign and a new presidential election is to be held two weeks after the publication of the results of the referendum. The Presidency is to become vacant only in the event of the President's death, resignation, condemnation by the High Court of Justice or permanent physical incapacitation, as certified by a Special Committee comprising the presidents of the Assemblée nationale, the Economic and Regional Council and the Supreme Court (see below). The election of a new President must take place not less than 20 days and not more than 40 days following the occurrence of a vacancy, during which time the president of the Assemblée nationale is to act as interim President, with limited powers.

The President appoints the Prime Minister, who presides over the Council of Ministers. The President promulgates laws adopted by the Assemblée nationale or by the Congress and has the power to dissolve the Assemblée nationale, in which event legislative elections must take place not less than 20 and not more than 40 days following its dissolution.

PARLIAMENT

This is composed of the Assemblée nationale, the Economic and Regional Council and the State Council, which, when sitting together, are to be known as the Congress. The primary function of the Congress is to pass organic laws in implementation of the Constitution, whenever these are not submitted to a referendum.

Assemblée nationale

The Assemblée nationale is composed of 109 deputies elected by direct universal suffrage for a five-year term. Its president is designated by, and from within, its bureau. Legislation may be introduced either by the President of the Republic or by a consensus of one-third of the members of the Assemblée. Provisions are made for the rendering inadmissible of any law providing for the execution of projects carrying a financial cost to the State which exceeds their potential value. The Assemblée nationale holds two ordinary sessions per year of 60 days each, at the summons of the President of the Republic, who may also summon it to hold extraordinary sessions with a pre-determined agenda. Sessions of the Assemblée nationale are opened and closed by presidential decree.

The Economic and Regional Council

The Economic and Regional Council is composed of representatives from the principal sectors of economic and social activity. One-half of its members are appointed by the President, and the remaining half are elected by the Assemblée nationale on the nomination of that body's president. It acts as an advisory body in all legislative proposals of an economic and social nature.

The State Council

The State Council is an advisory body which deliberates on administrative matters that are referred to it by the president of the Assemblée nationale.

The Congress

The Congress has the same president and bureau as the Assemblée nationale. An absolute majority of its members is needed to pass organic laws, as well as laws pertaining to the amendment of the Constitution which have not been submitted to a referendum. It defines development priorities and may meet, at the summons of the President, to ratify treaties or to declare a state of war.

* A special clause was incorporated in the 1995 Constitution, whereby the incumbent President, Ange-Félix Patassé, was to be permitted to remain in office, if re-elected, for three consecutive terms.

The Government

HEAD OF STATE

President: ANGE-FÉLIX PATASSÉ (elected 19 September 1993; re-elected 19 September 1999).

COUNCIL OF MINISTERS
(April 2001)

A coalition comprising members of the Mouvement pour la libération du peuple centrafricain (MLPC), the Parti libéral-démocrate (PLD), the Parti africain de développement (PAD), the Convention nationale (CN), the Union démocratique pour le renouveau—Fini Kodro (UDR—FK) and an independent (Ind.).

Prime Minister: MARTIN ZIGUÉLÉ (MLPC).

Minister of State in charge of Communication, Posts and Telecommunications, New Technologies and Francophone Affairs: GABRIEL JEAN-EDOUARD KOYANBOUNOU (MLPC).

Minister of State in charge of Finance and the Budget: ERIC SORONGOPÉ (MLPC).

Minister of the Environment, Water Resources, Forestry, Hunting and Fisheries: CONSTANCE NATHALIE GOUNÉBANA (PLD).

Minister for the Promotion of Rural Life: SALOMON NAMKO-SERENA (MLPC).

Minister of the Interior and Public Security: THÉODORE BIKO (PLD).

Minister of Social Affairs and the Promotion of Women: FRANÇOISE IBRAHIM (CN).

Minister in charge of Relations with Parliament: MICHEL DOKO (PLD).

Minister of Equipment, Transport, Urban Planning and Housing: DÉSIRÉ PÉNDÉMOU (MLPC).

Minister of Foreign Affairs: OTIPKO MEZODE (Ind.).

Minister of National Defence: JEAN-JACQUES DÉMAFOUTH (MLPC).

Minister of Justice: MARCEL MÉTÉFARA (MLPC).

Minister of the Civil Service and Employment: LAURENT NGON BABA (PAD).

Minister of Energy and Hydraulics: ANDRÉ NALKÉ DOROGO (MLPC).

Minister of Education: TIMOLÉON M'BAIKOUA (MLPC).

Minister of Youth and Sports: JEAN DOMINIQUE N'DARATA (UDR—FK).

Minister of Public Health and Population: JOSEPH KALITÉ (MLPC).

Minister of Trade, Industry and the Promotion of the Private Sector: JACOB M'BAITADJM (MLPC).

Minister of Planning and International Co-operation: ALEXIS N'GOMBA (PLD).

Minister-delegate for Public Security: ROBERT ZANA (MLPC).

Minister-delegate of Finance responsible for the Budget: LAZARA DOKOULA (MLPC).

Minister-delegate of Planning and International Co-operation: CLÉMENT ÉREGANI (MLPC).

Minister-delegate of Foreign Affairs: VICTOR BOUCHER (MLPC).

Minister-delegate of Disarmament: MICHEL DOYÉNÉ (MLPC).

MINISTRIES

Office of the President: Palais de la Renaissance, Bangui; tel. 61-46-63; internet www.socatel.cf/patasse.htm.

Ministry of the Civil Service and Employment: Bangui; tel. 61-01-44.

Ministry of Communication, Posts and Telecommunications, New Technologies and Francophone Affairs: BP 940, Bangui; tel. 61-27-66; fax 61-59-85.

Ministry of Education: BP 791, Bangui.

Ministry of Energy and Hydraulics: Bangui; tel. 61-20-54; fax 61-60-76.

Ministry of the Environment, Water Resources, Forestry, Hunting and Fisheries: Bangui.

Ministry of Equipment, Transport, Urban Planning and Housing: BP 941, Bangui.

Ministry of Finance and the Budget: BP 912, Bangui; tel. 61-70-55; fax 61-63-98.

Ministry of Foreign Affairs: Bangui; tel. 61-35-55; fax 61-20-76.

Ministry of the Interior and Public Security: Bangui.

Ministry of Justice: Bangui; tel. 61-16-44.

Ministry of National Defence: Bangui; tel. 61-46-11.

Ministry for Planning and International Co-operation: Bangui.

Ministry for the Promotion of Rural Life: Bangui; tel. 61-28-00.

Ministry of Public Health and Population: Bangui; tel. 61-29-01.

Ministry for Relations with Parliament: Bangui.

Ministry of Social Affairs and the Promotion of Women: Bangui.

Ministry of Trade, Industry and the Promotion of the Private Sector: Bangui.

Ministry of Youth and Sports: Bangui.

President and Legislature

PRESIDENT

Presidential Election, 19 September 1999

Candidate	% of votes
ANGE-FÉLIX PATASSÉ (MLPC)	51.6
Gen. ANDRÉ KOLINGBA (RDC)	19.4
DAVID DACKO (MDD)	11.2
ABEL GOUMBA (FPP)	6.1
HENRI POUZÈRE (Independent)	4.1
JEAN-PAUL NGOUPANDÉ (PUN)	3.1
ENOCH DERANT LAKOUÉ (PSD)	1.3
CHARLES MASSI (Independent)	1.3
FIDÈLE NGOUANDJIKA (Independent)	0.9
JOSEPH ABOSSOLO (Independent)	0.8
Total	**100.00**

ASSEMBLÉE NATIONALE

President: LUC-APOLLINAIRE DONDON-KONAMABAYÉ.

General Election, 22 November and 13 December 1998

	Seats
MLPC	47
RDC	20
MDD	8
FPP	7
PSD	6*
ADP	5
PUN	3
PLD	2
FODEM	2
FC	1
UPR	1
Independents	7
Total	**109**

* In December 1998 one member of the PSD left the party, declaring his intention to support the parties loyal to the President. In March 1999 two further PSD representatives left the parliamentary party to vote as independents.

Political Organizations

Alliance pour la démocratie et le progrès (ADP): Bangui; f. 1991; progressive; Leader FRANÇOIS PEHOUA; Nat. Sec. TCHAPKA BRÉDÉ.

Conseil démocratique des partis politiques de l'opposition (CODEPO): Bangui; f. 1995; political alliance led by AUGUSTE BOUKANGA; comprises the following parties:

Mouvement démocratique pour la renaissance et l'évolution de la République Centrafricaine (MDRERC): Bangui; Chair. JOSEPH BENDOUNGA; Sec.-Gen. LÉON SEBOU;

Parti républicain centrafricain (PRC): Bangui.

Convention nationale (CN): Bangui; f. 1991; Leader DAVID GALIAMBO.

Forum civique (FC): Bangui; Leader Gen. TIMOTHÉE MALENDOMA.

Forum démocratique pour la modernité (FODEM): Bangui; f. 1998; Pres. CHARLES MASSI.

Front patriotique pour le progrès (FPP): BP 259, Bangui; tel. 61-52-23; fax 61-10-93; f. 1972; aims to promote political education and debate; Leader Prof. ABEL GOUMBA.

G11: Bangui; f. 1997; alliance of 11 opposition parties led by Prof. ABEL GOUMBA; prin. mems: ADP, FPP, MDD and RDC.

Mouvement d'évolution sociale de l'Afrique noire (MESAN): Bangui; f. 1949; comprises two factions, led respectively by PROSPER LAVODRAMA and JOSEPH NGBANGADIBO.

Mouvement pour la démocratie et le développement (MDD): Bangui; f. 1993; aims to safeguard national unity and the equitable distribution of national wealth; Leader DAVID DACKO.

Mouvement pour la démocratie, l'indépendance et le progrès social (MDI–PS): BP 1404, Bangui; tel. 61-18-21; e-mail mdicentrafrique@chez.com; internet www.chez.com/mdicentrafrique; Sec. Gen. DANIEL NDITIFEI BOYSEMBE.

Mouvement pour la libération du peuple centrafricain (MLPC): Bangui; f. 1979; leading party in govt since Oct. 1993; Pres. ANGE-FÉLIX PATASSÉ.

Parti africain de développement (PAD): Bangui.

Parti libéral-démocrate (PLD): Bangui; Leader NESTOR KOMBO-NAGUEMON.

Parti social-démocrate (PSD): BP 543, Bangui; tel. 61-59-02; fax 61-58-44; Leader ENOCH DERANT LAKOUÉ.

Parti pour l'union nationale (PUN): Bangui; Leader JEAN-PAUL NGOUPANDÉ.

Rassemblement démocratique centrafricain (RDC): BP 503, Bangui; tel. 61-53-75; f. 1987; sole legal political party 1987–91; Leader Gen. ANDRÉ KOLINGBA.

Rassemblement populaire pour la reconstruction de la Centrafrique (RPRC): Bangui; Leader Gen. FRANÇOIS BOZIZE.

Union démocratique pour le renouveau—Fini Kodro (UDR—FK): Bangui.

Union des forces acquises à la paix (UFAP): Bangui; f. 1998; opposition alliance, including political parties, trade unions and human rights orgs; weakened by withdrawals in Nov. 1999; Pres. PAUL BELLÉT.

Union nationale démocratique du peuple centrafricain (UNDPC): Bangui; f. 1998; Islamic fundamentalist; based in southeast CAR; Leader MAHAMAT SALEH.

Union pour la république (UPR): Bangui.

Diplomatic Representation

EMBASSIES IN THE CENTRAL AFRICAN REPUBLIC

Cameroon: rue du Languedoc, BP 935, Bangui; tel. 61-18-57; fax 61-16-87; Chargé d'affaires a.i.: GILBERT NOULA.

Chad: ave Valérie Giscard d'Estaing, BP 461, Bangui; tel. 61-46-77; Ambassador: HASSAN-MICHEL DJANGDEÏ (recalled June 2000).

China, People's Republic: Bangui; tel. 61-36-28; fax 61-37-41; Chargé d'affaires: CUI YONGQUIAN.

Congo, Democratic Republic: BP 989, Bangui; tel. 61-33-44; Ambassador: EMBE ISEA MBAMBE.

Congo, Republic: BP 1414, Bangui; tel. 61-18-77; fax 61-03-09; Chargé d'affaires a.i.: ANTOINE DELICA.

Egypt: BP 1422, Bangui; tel. 61-46-88; fax 61-35-45; Ambassador: SAMEH SAMY DARWICHE.

France: blvd du Général de Gaulle, BP 884, Bangui; tel. 61-30-00; fax 61-74-04; Ambassador: GILDAS LE LIDEC.

Gabon: BP 1570, Bangui; tel. 61-29-97; Ambassador: FRANÇOIS DE PAULE MOULENGUI.

Germany: ave G. A. Nasser, BP 901, Bangui; tel. 61-07-46; fax 61-19-89; Ambassador: REINHARD BUCHHOLZ.

Holy See: ave Boganda, BP 1447, Bangui; tel. 61-26-54; fax 61-03-71; e-mail nonrca@intnet.cf; Apostolic Nuncio: Most Rev. DIEGO CAUSERO, Titular Archbishop of Meta.

Japan: ave Barthélemy Boganda, BP 1367, Bangui; tel. 61-16-10; fax 61-06-68; e-mail japonamb@intnet.cf; Ambassador: YOICHI HAYASHI.

Libya: Bangui; tel. 61-46-62; fax 61-12-79; Head of Mission: (vacant).

Nigeria: ave des Martyrs, BP 1010, Bangui; tel. 61-40-97; fax 61-12-79; Chargé d'affaires a.i.: AYODELE J. BAKARE.

Russia: rue Fourreau-lamy, BP1405, Bangui; tel. 61-03-11; Ambassador: BORIS KRASNIKOV.

Sudan: ave de l'Indépendance, BP 1351, Bangui; tel. 61-38-21; Ambassador: TIJANI SALIH FADAYL.

USA: ave David Dacko, BP 924, Bangui; tel. 61-02-00; fax 61-44-94; Ambassador: ROBERT C. PERRY.

Judicial System

Supreme Court: BP 926, Bangui; tel. 61-41-33; highest judicial organ; acts as a Court of Cassation in civil and penal cases and as Court of Appeal in administrative cases; comprises four chambers: constitutional, judicial, administrative and financial; Pres. EDOUARD FRANCK.

There is also a Court of Appeal, a Criminal Court, 16 tribunaux de grande instance, 37 tribunaux d'instance, six labour tribunals and a permanent military tribunal. A High Court of Justice was established under the 1986 Constitution, with jurisdiction in all cases of crimes against state security, including high treason by the President of the Republic.

In August 1992 constitutional amendments were introduced which provided for the strict separation of executive, legislative and judicial powers.

The 1995 Constitution established a Constitutional Court, the judges of which are appointed by the President.

Religion

It is estimated that 24% of the population hold animist beliefs, 50% are Christians (25% Roman Catholic, 25% Protestant) and 15% are Muslims. There is no official state religion.

CHRISTIANITY
The Roman Catholic Church

The Central African Republic comprises one archdiocese and seven dioceses. There were an estimated 708,808 adherents at 31 December 1998.

Bishops' Conference: Conférence Episcopale Centrafricaine, BP 1518, Bangui; tel. 50-24-84; f. 1982; Pres. Rt Rev. PAULIN POMODIMO, Bishop of Bossangoa.

Archbishop of Bangui: Most Rev. JOACHIM N'DAYEN, Archevêché, BP 1518, Bangui; tel. 61-31-48; fax 61-46-92; e-mail cent_afr@intnet.cf.

Protestant Church
Eglise Protestante de Bangui: Bangui.

The Press

The independent press is higly regulated. Independent publications must hold a trading licence and prove their status as a commercial enterprise. They must also have proof that they fulfil taxation requirements. There is little press activity outside Bangui.

DAILIES

E le Songo: Bangui; f. 1986.

Le Citoyen: BP 974, Bangui; tel. 61-89-16; independent; Publr MAKA GBOSSOKOTTO; circ. 3,000.

Le Novateur: BP 913, Bangui; tel. 61-48-84; fax 61-87-03; e-mail ccea-ln@intnet.cf; independent; Publr MARCEL MOKWAPI; circ. 750.

PERIODICALS

Bangui Match: Bangui; monthly.

Le Courrier Rural: BP 850, Bangui; publ. by Chambre d'Agriculture.

Le Delit d'Opinion: Bangui; independent.

Demain le Monde: BP 650, Bangui; tel. 61-23-15; f. 1985; fortnightly; independent; Editor-in-Chief NGANAM NÖEL.

Journal Officiel de la République Centrafricaine: BP 739, Bangui; f. 1974; fortnightly; economic data; Dir-Gen. GABRIEL AGBA.

Nations Nouvelles: BP 965, Bangui; publ. by Organisation Commune Africaine et Mauricienne; politics and current affairs.

Le Peuple: BP 569, Bangui; tel. 61-76-34; f. 1995; weekly; Editor-in-Chief VERMOND TCHENDO.

Le Progrès: BP 154, Bangui; tel. 61-70-26; f. 1991; monthly; Editor-in-Chief BELIBANGA CLÉMENT; circ. 2,000.

Le Rassemblement: Bangui; organ of the RDC; Editor-in-Chief MATHIAS GONEVO REAPOGO.

La Tortue Déchainée: Bangui; independent; satirical; Publr MAKA GBOSSOKOTTO.

PRESS ASSOCIATION
Groupement des Editeurs de la Presse privée indépendante de Centrafrique (GEPAIC): Bangui; Pres. MAKA GBOSSOKOTO.

NEWS AGENCIES
Agence Centrafricaine de Presse (ACAP): BP 40, Bangui; tel. 61-10-88; f. 1974; Gen. Man. VICTOR DETO TETEYA.

Informatsionnoye Telegrafnoye Agentstvo Rossii—Telegrafnoye Agentstvo Suverennykh Stran (ITAR—TASS) (Russia) and Agence France-Presse are represented in the CAR.

Publisher

Government Publishing House
Imprimerie Centrafricaine: BP 329, Bangui; tel. 61-00-33; f. 1974; Dir-Gen. PIERRE SALAMATE-KOILET.

Broadcasting and Communications

TELECOMMUNICATIONS
Société Centrafricaine de Télécommunications (SOCATEL): BP 939, Bangui; tel. 61-74-69; fax 61-44-49; e-mail postmaster@intnet.cf; internet www.socatel.intnet.cf; f. 1990; 60% state-owned; 40% owned by France Cables et Radio.

CARATEL Entreprises: BP 2439, Bangui; tel. 61-44-10; fax 61-44-49; e-mail telecomp@intnet.cf; internet www.socatel.intnet.cf/carat.html; mobile cellular telephone operator.

BROADCASTING
Radiodiffusion-Télévision Centrafricaine: BP 940, Bangui; tel. 61-25-88; f. 1958 as Radiodiffusion Nationale Centrafricaine; govt-controlled; broadcasts in French and Sango; Man. Dir PAUL SERVICE.

Radio Rurale: community stations operating in Bouar, Nola, Berbérati and Bambari.

Finance

(cap. = capital; res = reserves; dep. = deposits; m. = million; amounts in francs CFA)

BANKING
Central Bank
Banque des Etats de l'Afrique Centrale (BEAC): BP 851, Bangui; tel. 61-24-00; fax 61-19-95; HQ in Yaoundé, Cameroon; f. 1973; bank of issue for mem. states of the Communauté économique et monétaire de l'Afrique centrale (CEMAC, fmrly Union douanière et économique de l'Afrique centrale), comprising Cameroon, the Central African Repub., Chad, the Repub. of the Congo, Equatorial Guinea and Gabon; cap. 45,000m., res 172,198m., total assets 1,407,908m. (Dec. 1999); Gov. JEAN-FÉLIX MAMALEPOT; Dir in CAR JONAS YOLOGAZA.

Commercial Banks
Banque Internationale pour le Centrafrique (BICA): place de la République, BP 910, Bangui; tel. 61-00-42; fax 61-61-36; e-mail bica@intnet.cf; internet www.socatel.intnet.cf/bica.html; f. 1946; present name adopted 1996; 35% owned by Banque Belgolaise SA, Brussels, 15% by group of African investors (COFIPA), 40.4% by private citizens, 9.6% by Govt; cap. and res 497.1m., dep. 17,352.6m. (Dec. 1998); Pres. MARTIN BABA; Dir-Gen. JEAN-PAUL LE CALM; 1 br.

Banque Populaire Maroco-Centrafricaine (BPMC): rue Guerillot, BP 844, Bangui; tel. 61-12-90; fax 61-62-30; f. 1991; 50% owned by Banque Centrale Populaire (Morocco), 12.5% owned by Banque Marocaine du Commerce Extérieur, 50% owned by Banque Centrale Populaire du Maroc and 37.5% state-owned; cap. and res 5,622.2m., total assets 6,353.7m. (Dec. 1998); Chair. MARTIN BABA; Dir-Gen. MOHAMED BENZIANI.

Union Bancaire en Afrique Centrale SA (UBAC): rue de Brazza, BP 59, Bangui; tel. 61-29-90; fax 61-34-54; e-mail rcubac@intnet.cf; internet www.socatel.intnet.cf/ubac.html; f. 1962; state-owned; 49% privatization pending; cap. 1,000.0m., res –615.3m., dep. 15,289.3m. (Dec. 1998); Pres. JEAN-SERGE WAFIO; Gen. Man. ETIENNE DJIMARIM; 1 br.

Development Bank

Banque de Developpement des Etats de l'Afrique Centrale: (see Franc Zone, p. 211).

Investment Bank

Banque Centrafricaine d'Investissement (BCI): Bangui; tel. 61-00-64; f. 1976; 34.8% state-owned; cap. 1,000m.; Pres. ALPHONSE KONGOLO; Man. Dir GÉRARD SAMBO.

Financial Institutions

Caisse Autonome d'Amortissement de la République Centrafricaine: Bangui; fax 61-21-82; management of state funds; Dir-Gen. JOSEPH PINGAMA.

Caisse Nationale d'Epargne (CNE): Office national des postes et de l'épargne, Bangui; tel. 61-22-96; fax 61-78-80; Pres. JUSTIN SALAMATE; Dir-Gen. AMBROISE DAOUDA; Man. RAPHAÏL OLONGA.

Bankers' Association

Association Professionnelle des Banques: Bangui.

Development Agencies

Agence Française de Développement: rue de la Moyenne corniche, BP 817, Bangui; tel. 61-03-06; fax 61-22-40; e-mail afd@intnet.cf; administers economic aid and finances specific development projects; Man. JEAN-FRANÇOIS VAVASSEUR.

Mission Française de Coopération et d'Action Culturelle: BP 934, Bangui; tel. 61-63-34; fax 61-28-24; administers bilateral aid from France; Dir HERVÉ CRONEL.

INSURANCE

Agence Centrafricaine d'Assurances (ACA): BP 512, Bangui; tel. 61-06-23; f. 1956; Dir Mme R. CERBELLAUD.

Assureurs Conseils Centrafricains Faugère et Jutheau: rue de la Kouanga, BP 743, Bangui; tel. 61-19-33; fax 61-44-70; f. 1968; Dir JEAN CLAUDE ROY.

Entreprise d'Etat d'Assurances et de Réassurances (SIRIRI): Bangui; tel. 61-36-55; f. 1972; Pres. EMMANUEL DOKOUNA; Dir-Gen. JEAN-MARIE YOLLOT.

Legendre, A. & Cie: rue de la Victoire, BP 896, Bangui; Pres. and Dir-Gen. ANDRÉ LEGENDRE.

Union Centrafricaine d'Assurances et de Réassurances: BP 343, Bangui; tel. 61-36-66; fax 61-33-40.

Trade and Industry

DEVELOPMENT ORGANIZATION

Société Centrafricaine de Développement Agricole (SOCADA): ave David Dacko, BP 997, Bangui; tel. 61-30-33; f. 1964; reorg. 1980; 75% state-owned, 25% Cie Française pour le Développement des Fibres Textiles (France); purchasing, transport and marketing of cotton, cotton-ginning, production of cottonseed oil and groundnut oil; Pres. MAURICE METHOT.

INDUSTRIAL AND TRADE ASSOCIATIONS

Agence de Développement de la Zone Caféière (ADECAF): BP 1935, Bangui; tel. 61-47-30; coffee producers' asscn; assists coffee marketing co-operatives; Dir-Gen. J. J. NIMIZIAMBI.

Agence Nationale pour le Développement de l'Élevage (ANDE): BP 1509, Bangui; tel. 61-69-60; fax 61-50-83; assists with development of livestock.

Caisse de Stabilisation et de Péréquation des Produits Agricoles (CAISTAB): BP 76, Bangui; tel. 61-08-00; supervises marketing and pricing of agricultural produce; Dir-Gen. M. BOUNANDELE-KOUMBA.

Fédération Nationale des Éleveurs Centrafricains (FNEC): ave des Martyrs, BP 588, Bangui; tel. 61-23-97; fax 61-47-24.

Office National des Forêts (ONF): BP 915, Bangui; tel. 61-38-27; f. 1969; reafforestation, development of forest resources; Dir-Gen. C. D. SONGUET.

CHAMBERS OF COMMERCE

Chambre d'Agriculture, d'Elevage, des Eaux, Forêts, Chasses, Pêches et Tourisme: BP 850, Bangui; tel. 61-09-33; f. 1964; Pres. FRANÇOIS T. BEYÉLÉ; Sec.-Gen. MOÏSE DENISSIO.

Chambre de Commerce, d'Industrie, des Mines et de l'Artisanat (CCIMA): BP 813, Bangui; tel. 61-16-68; fax 61-35-70; Pres. RIGOBERT YOMBO; Sec. GERTRUDE ZOUTA-YAMANDJA.

EMPLOYERS' ORGANIZATION

Union Nationale du Patronat Centrafricain (UNPC): Bangui; Pres. RIGOBERT YOMBO.

UTILITIES

Electricity

Société Energie de Centrafrique (ENERCA): ave de l'Indépendance, BP 880, Bangui; tel. 61-20-22; f. 1967; state-owned; privatization pending; production and distribution of electric energy.

Water

Société Nationale des Eaux (SNE): BP 1838, Bangui; tel. 61-20-28; f. 1975; state-owned co responsible for supply, treatment and distribution of water; Dir-Gen. FRANÇOIS FARRA-FROND.

TRADE UNIONS

There are five officially recognized trade union federations, including:

Organization of Free Public-Sector Unions: Bangui.

Union Syndicale des Travailleurs de la Centrafrique (USTC): Bangui; affiliated with the International Confed. of Free Trade Unions; Sec.-Gen. THÉOPHILE SONNY KOLLE.

Transport

RAILWAYS

There are no railways at present. There are long-term plans to connect Bangui to the Transcameroon railway. A line linking Sudan's Darfur region with the CAR's Vakaga province has also been proposed.

ROADS

In 1998 there were an estimated 24,307 km of roads, including 5,398 km of main roads and 3,909 km of secondary roads. Only about 2.7% of the total network is paved. Eight main routes serve Bangui, and those that are surfaced are toll roads. Both the total road length and the condition of the roads are inadequate for current requirements. In 1997 the European Union provided 32,500m. francs CFA to improve infrastructure in the CAR. In September a vast road improvement scheme was launched, concentrating initially on roads to the south and north-west of Bangui. The CAR is linked with Cameroon by the Transafrican Lagos–Mombasa highway. Roads are frequently impassable in the rainy season (May to October).

Bureau d'Affrètement Routier Centrafricain (BARC): BP 523, Bangui; tel. 61-20-55; fax 61-37-44; Dir-Gen. J. M. LAGUEREMA-YADINGUIN.

Compagnie Nationale des Transports Routiers (CNTR): Bangui; tel. 61-46-44; state-owned; Dir-Gen. GEORGES YABADA.

INLAND WATERWAYS

There are some 2,800 km of navigable waterways along two main water courses. The first, formed by the Congo river and its tributary the Oubangui, can accommodate convoys of barges (of up to 800 metric tons load) between Bangui and Brazzaville and Pointe-Noire in the Republic of the Congo, except during the dry season, when the route is impassable. The second is the river Sangha, also a tributary of the Congo, on which traffic is again seasonal. There are two ports, at Bangui and Salo, on the rivers Oubangui and Sangha respectively. Bangui port has a handling capacity of 350,000 tons, with 350 m of wharfs and 24,000 sq m of warehousing. Efforts are being made to develop the Sangha upstream from Salo to increase the transportation of timber from this area, and to develop Nola as a timber port.

Agence Centrafricaine des Communications Fluviales (ACCF): BP 822, Bangui; tel. 61-31-10; f. 1969; state-owned; supervises development of inland waterways transport system; Man. Dir JUSTIN NDJAPOU.

Société Centrafricaine de Transports Fluviaux (SOCATRAF): BP 1445, Bangui; tel. and fax 61-43-15; f. 1980; 51%-owned by ACCF; Man. Dir FRANÇOIS TOUSSAINT.

CIVIL AVIATION

The international airport is at Bangui-M'Poko. There are also 37 small airports for internal services.

Agence pour la sécurité de la navigation aérienne en Afrique et Madagascar (ASECNA): BP 828, Bangui; tel. 61-33-80; fax 61-49-18.

Air Afrique: BP 875, Bangui; tel. 60-47-00; fax 61-44-29; see under Côte d'Ivoire; Dir in Bangui ALBERT BAGNERES.

Centrafrican Airlines (CAL): Aéroport Bangui-M'Poko; f. 1999; privately-owned; internal flights.

Mondial Air Fret (MAF): BP 1883, Bangui; tel. 61-14-58; fax 61-62-62; f. 1998; Dir THÉOPHILE SONNY COLE.

Tourism

Although tourism remains relatively undeveloped, the Central African Republic possesses considerable scenic attractions in its waterfalls, forests and wildlife. Tourist arrivals were estimated at 17,000 in 1997, compared with only 1,599 in 1990. In 1997 receipts from tourism were estimated at US $5m.

Office National Centrafricain du Tourisme (OCATOUR): BP 655, Bangui; tel. 61-45-66.

CHAD

Introductory Survey

Location, Climate, Language, Religion, Flag, Capital

The Republic of Chad is a land-locked country in north central Africa, bordered to the north by Libya, to the south by the Central African Republic, to the west by Niger, Nigeria and Cameroon, and to the east by Sudan. The climate is hot and arid in the northern desert regions of the Sahara but very wet, with annual rainfall of 5,000 mm (197 ins) in the south. The official languages are French and Arabic, and various African languages are also widely spoken. Almost one-half of the population are Muslims, living in the north. About 30% of the population are Christians. Most of the remainder follow animist beliefs. The national flag (proportions 3 by 2) has three equal vertical stripes, of dark blue, yellow and red. The capital is N'Djamena.

Recent History

Formerly a province of French Equatorial Africa, Chad became an autonomous state within the French Community in November 1958, and achieved full independence on 11 August 1960. Its first President was François (later Ngarta) Tombalbaye, a southerner and leader of the Parti progressiste tchadien (PPT). In 1962 the PPT was declared the sole political party. In 1965 a full-scale insurgency began, concentrated mainly in the north. The Muslims of northern Chad have traditionally been in conflict with their black southern compatriots, who are mainly Christians or animists. The banned Front de libération nationale du Tchad (FROLINAT, founded in Sudan in 1966) assumed leadership of the revolt. The rebellion was partially quelled in 1968, following French military intervention.

In 1973 several prominent figures in the regime, including Gen. Félix Malloum, the Army Chief of Staff, were imprisoned on charges of conspiracy. In August of the same year the PPT was reconstituted as the Mouvement national pour la révolution culturelle et sociale (MNRCS). Also in 1973 Libyan troops occupied the so-called 'Aozou strip', an apparently mineral-rich region of some 114,000 sq km (44,000 sq miles) in northern Chad. Libya's claim to sovereignty over the region was based on an unratified treaty signed by France and Italy in 1935.

In April 1975 Tombalbaye was killed in a military coup. Malloum was released and appointed President, at the head of a Conseil militaire suprême, and the MNRCS was dissolved. FROLINAT remained in opposition, receiving clandestine military assistance from Libya. In early 1978 FROLINAT seized control of a large area of the north before its advance was halted by French military intervention. In August, after negotiations with President Malloum, Hissène Habré, a former leader of FROLINAT, was appointed Prime Minister. However, disagreements developed between Habré (a Muslim from the north) and Malloum over the status of Muslims in Chad.

In February 1979 armed conflict broke out between Habré's Forces armées du nord (FAN) and the government armed forces, the Forces armées tchadiennes (FAT). The FAN gained control of the capital, N'Djamena, and in March Malloum resigned and fled the country. In April a provisional Government was formed, comprising representatives of several groups, including FROLINAT, the FAN and the FAT, but sporadic fighting continued between rival political factions and between Muslims and non-Muslims. In August 11 factions formed a Gouvernement d'union nationale de transition (GUNT), with Goukouni Oueddei, the leader of FROLINAT, as President, and Lt-Col (later Gen.) Wadal Abdelkader Kamougué as Vice-President.

Goukouni's authority was undermined by continual disagreements with Habré, and in March 1980 fighting resumed. In October, after numerous attempts at reconciliation had failed, Libyan forces intervened directly in the hostilities, in support of Goukouni. By December Habré had been defeated, and a Libyan force of some 15,000 men was established in the country. In November 1981 Libyan troops were withdrawn, and a peace-keeping force was installed under the auspices of the Organization of African Unity (OAU—see p. 256). The conflict intensified, however, and in June 1982 Habré's forces captured N'Djamena. Habré was formally inaugurated as President in October, and in the same month Goukouni formed a rival government in Bardai.

In January 1983 some members of the FAT joined the ranks of Habré's FAN to form the Forces armées nationales tchadiennes (FANT). In August, after protracted fighting, Goukouni's rebel forces, with Libyan support, captured the northern administrative centre of Faya-Largeau. France dispatched a further 3,000 troops to Chad, and an 'interdiction line' was imposed by the French to separate the warring factions. In mid-September it was announced that fighting had ceased.

In June 1984, in an attempt to consolidate his political support in the south of the country, Habré dissolved the FROLINAT-FAN movement and replaced it with a new organization, the Union nationale pour l'indépendance et la révolution (UNIR). In July a more broadly-based Government was formed, with greater participation by politicians from the south. The opposition, meanwhile, was becoming increasingly fragmented, following the defection of several groups from Goukouni's GUNT. In August, however, the southern-based *commandos rouges* (or *codos*) resumed guerrilla activities, which were harshly repressed by the government forces. In September Libya and France agreed to a simultaneous withdrawal of their troops from Chad. By mid-November all French troops had left the country; however, it was reported that some 3,000 Libyan troops remained in Chad.

By the end of 1985 the *codos* rebellion had collapsed and hostilities in southern Chad had ceased. In February 1986, however, GUNT forces, with support from Libya, attacked government positions south of the 'interdiction line'. Habré appealed for French military assistance, and France agreed to establish a defensive air-strike force (designated Opération Epervier) in N'Djamena. The USA also provided additional military aid. Hostilities ceased temporarily in the following month, following the capture by government forces of a rebel base at Chicha.

During 1985–86 Habré continued to consolidate his regime by securing support from former opponents, including erstwhile *codos* rebels, and in March 1986 several former opponents of the regime were given government posts. The GUNT, meanwhile, began to disintegrate. Kamougué resigned as Goukouni's Vice-President in June, and in February 1987 declared his support for Habré. In August 1986, meanwhile, Acheikh Ibn Oumar's Conseil démocratique révolutionnaire (CDR) also withdrew support from Goukouni, leaving him politically isolated. In October, following armed clashes between the Libyan-supported CDR and his own Forces armées populaires (FAP), Goukouni declared himself willing to seek a reconciliation with Habré.

In December 1986 clashes began in the Tibesti region between Libyan forces and the (now pro-Habré) FAP. Habré's FANT troops moved into northern Chad, and, with increased logistical support from France and the USA, forced Libya to withdraw from Faya-Largeau. In May 1987 Libyan troops retreated to the disputed 'Aozou strip'. In August FANT troops attacked and occupied Aozou, the administrative centre of the area, but Libyan forces recaptured the town three weeks later. This was followed, in September, by an incursion into southern Libya by the FANT. An OAU-brokered cease-fire took effect, but sporadic fighting continued, and the Chadian Government claimed that Libyan aircraft were repeatedly violating Chadian airspace.

In May 1988 Col Muammar al-Qaddafi, the Libyan leader, failed to attend a scheduled meeting with Habré to discuss the dispute between the two countries. However, he subsequently declared his willingness to recognize the Habré regime, and invited Habré and Goukouni to hold reconciliation talks in Libya. Following negotiations between the Ministers of Foreign Affairs of the two countries, held in Gabon in July, agreement was reached, in principle, to restore diplomatic relations. However, the issues of the sovereignty of the Aozou region, the fate of Libyan prisoners of war in Chad, and the security of common borders remained unresolved. In October 1988 diplomatic relations were resumed and the September 1987 cease-fire agreement was reaffirmed, although Chad continued to accuse Libya of violating the conditions of the agreement.

The cohesion of the GUNT was undermined in 1988 by a dispute between Goukouni and Acheikh Ibn Oumar regarding its leadership. Several former opposition groups transferred their support to Habré, and in November, following negotiations with UNIR, Acheikh Ibn Oumar and his supporters returned to Chad. He was appointed Minister of Foreign Affairs in March 1989. In April Mahamat Itno, the Minister of the Interior and Territorial Administration, was arrested following the discovery of an alleged plot to overthrow Habré. Idriss Deby, a former Commander-in-Chief of the Armed Forces, who was also implicated in the attempted coup, fled to Sudan, where he established a new opposition group.

In June 1989 the Government accused Libya of planning a military offensive against Chad, with the complicity of Sudan. In July Qaddafi and Habré met for the first time, in Mali, but their negotiations were inconclusive. On 31 August, however, Acheikh Ibn Oumar met his Libyan counterpart in Algiers, where they signed an outline peace accord. Under its terms, if a negotiated settlement to the dispute over sovereignty of the 'Aozou strip' was not achieved within one year, the issue was to be submitted to the International Court of Justice (ICJ) for adjudication. Provision was made for the withdrawal of all armed forces from the Aozou region and the release of all prisoners of war. The accord also reaffirmed the principles of the September 1987 cease-fire agreement. Military engagements between FANT troops and pro-Libyan forces were none the less reported in late 1989, and attempts to resolve the dispute were undermined by mutual recriminations regarding each side's commitment to the negotiation process. No agreement was reached at discussions between Habré and Qaddafi in Morocco in August 1990, and the territorial dispute was referred for adjudication by the ICJ.

In December 1989 a new Constitution, which granted greater powers to the President, was approved by a reported 99.94% of voters in a national referendum. In endorsing the document, the electorate also approved Habré in the office of President for a further seven-year term. The new Constitution confirmed UNIR as the sole legal party, and provided for the establishment of an elected legislature. Elections to this 123-seat Assemblée nationale followed in July 1990.

In March 1990 Idriss Deby and his supporters, the Forces patriotiques du salut (subsequently styled the Mouvement patriotique du salut—MPS), invaded Chad from Sudan and occupied or destroyed many villages in the east of the country. Although this attack was successfully countered by government forces, the MPS launched a second invasion in November, during which a number of FANT troops transferred allegiance to Deby. France reiterated its policy of non-interference in Chad's internal affairs. The MPS subsequently advanced rapidly towards N'Djamena, and on 30 November Habré and his associates fled the country. Deby arrived in N'Djamena two days later. The Assemblée nationale was dissolved, and the Constitution suspended: Deby declared his intention to introduce a multi-party political system, stating that new legislative and presidential elections were to be held at a future date. A provisional Conseil d'Etat was installed, with Deby as interim Head of State. Several members of the former Habré regime, including Acheikh Ibn Oumar, were included in the new Government.

Following Deby's accession to power, many political organizations that had opposed Habré announced their support for the MPS. Goukouni indicated his willingness to negotiate with Deby, and denied persistent reports that he was massing forces in northern Chad. Deby announced that the FANT was to be restructured to form a smaller national army, designated the Armée nationale tchadienne (ANT). The French Government responded favourably to the new administration, and the Libyan and Sudanese Governments declared their support for the MPS, undertaking not to allow forces hostile to Deby to operate on their territory. Deby, however, reiterated Chad's claim to the sovereignty of the Aozou region, which remained under consideration by the ICJ.

In March 1991 the Government promulgated a National Charter to operate for a 30-month transitional period, at the end of which a constitutional referendum was to take place. The National Charter confirmed Deby's appointment as President, Head of State and Chairman of the MPS, and replaced the provisional Conseil d'Etat by a Council of Ministers (with Jean Bawoyeu Alingué as Prime Minister) and a 31-member legislative Conseil de la République. In May Deby announced that a national conference would be convened in May 1992 to prepare a new Constitution. Interim arrangements permitting the registration of political parties would enter into force in January 1992. Requirements for such registration, including the prohibi-

tion of parties formed on an ethnic or regional basis, were announced in October 1991.

In September 1991 forces loyal to Habré apparently entered Chad from Niger and attacked military garrisons in northern Chad. In December some 3,000 pro-Habré rebels attacked towns in the Lake Chad region. These operations were ascribed to the Mouvement pour la démocratie et le développement (MDD), an opposition group based in Libya, led by Goukouni Guët. In early 1992 the Chadian Government reported that the rebels had been defeated. Several prominent members of opposition groups were subsequently arrested on suspicion of complicity in the rebellion, and a number of these were reported to have been summarily executed. France (which had dispatched reinforcements for the Epervier contingent) condemned such violations of human rights and indicated that its continued support for Deby was dependent on the implementation of political reforms. The Deby regime responded by reiterating its commitment to the democratic process and declaring a general amnesty for political prisoners.

Meanwhile, in October 1991 disaffected troops attacked an arsenal at N'Djamena airport in an attempt to seize power; some 40 people were killed in the ensuing fighting. Several officials, including the Minister of the Interior, Maldoum Bada Abbas, were arrested on charges connected with the incident. Although the Government asserted that Abbas had been motivated by personal ambition, there was speculation that the coup attempt had been provoked by discontent within his ethnic group, the Hadjerai, who considered themselves under-represented in Government. France reaffirmed its support for the MPS, and announced that the 'Opération Epervier' contingent would be reinforced by an additional 300 troops. Following the coup attempt, Chad abrogated a recent co-operation agreement with Libya, on the grounds that the sovereignty of the Aozou region remained in dispute. In February 1992 a further *coup d'état* was attempted by members of the armed forces who attacked a police station in N'Djamena. In April, following the expulsion from Chad of four French citizens suspected of involvement in this coup attempt, the French Government announced that it was to reduce its military support, although some 750 troops were to remain in the country to assist in the planned restructuring of the Chadian armed forces.

In May 1992 the Government announced that the national conference was to be postponed until September, stating that the work of the preparatory commission had not been completed. Also in May a number of amendments to the National Charter were adopted, and Joseph Yodoyman, a member of an opposition movement, the Alliance nationale pour la démocratie et le développement (ANDD), was appointed Prime Minister. A new Council of Ministers included, for the first time, members of several opposition parties and human rights organizations.

In April 1992 the MDD claimed that more than 40 of its activists, including Goukouni Guët, had been arrested in Nigeria, extradited to Chad, and subsequently imprisoned or executed. In May MDD rebels, reportedly led by a former minister in the GUNT, Moussa Medella Mahamat, launched a new offensive in the region of Lake Chad. In June an agreement between the Government and the Comité de sursaut national pour la paix et la démocratie (CSNPD), the dissident faction of the armed forces responsible for the abortive coup attempt in February, provided for the release of detained members of the CSNPD and their reintegration into the ANT. Later that month the Government announced that it had forestalled a coup attempt by insurgents of the Conseil national de redressement du Tchad (CNRT). In June an agreement was signed in Libreville, Gabon, providing for a cessation of hostilities between government forces and the MDD.

In July 1992 Yodoyman was expelled from the ANDD for allegedly failing to support the democratic process. Another member of the ANDD subsequently left the Government. A reorganization of the Council of Ministers took place in August, after three representatives of human rights organizations in the Government, including a member of the Ligue tchadienne des droits de l'homme (LTDH), resigned in protest at the continued violence perpetrated against civilians. In the same month clashes between members of the CSNPD and government forces were reported in Doba, in the south. In September an agreement was reached by the Government and an opposition group based in Sudan, the Front national du Tchad (FNT), which granted the FNT the status of a political party. Later that month the Government signed further peace agreements with the MDD, which had resumed activities in the Lake Chad region, and with the CSNPD. In October, however, the MDD was reported to have begun a renewed offensive against government forces at Bagassola, near Lake Chad; at the end of that month the MDD officially declared the peace agreement to be invalid, alleging that the Government had received armaments from Libya and was preparing to resume hostilities. In December further clashes between government forces and members of the MDD were reported in the Lake Chad region.

In October 1992 public-sector workers of the Union des syndicats du Tchad (UST) organized a one-month general strike in support of demands for higher salaries and the convening of the national conference on the country's political future. Two representatives of former opposition parties resigned their ministerial portfolios in protest at the Government's subsequent suspension of the activities of the UST. Despite an announcement by the Government that the conference would take place in January 1993, the UST extended the general strike for a further month. The Government subsequently revoked the ban on the UST and the strike ended in January 1993.

The national conference (comprising representatives of the organs of state, political parties, trade unions and professional organizations) was finally convened in January 1993 to prepare for the establishment of a democratic system of government. In April the conference, which had been accorded sovereign status, adopted a Transitional Charter, elected Dr Fidèle Moungar, hitherto Minister of National and Higher Education, as Prime Minister, and established a 57-member interim legislature, the Conseil supérieur de la transition (CST). The leader of the Rassemblement pour la démocratie et le progrès (RDP), Lol Mahamat Choua (who had briefly been President in 1979), was elected Chairman of the CST. Under the terms of the Transitional Charter, Deby was to remain in office as Head of State and Commander-in-Chief of the Armed Forces for a period of one year (with provision for one extension), while a Transitional Government, under the supervision of the CST, was to implement economic, political and social programmes as drafted by the Conference. The Transitional Government included representatives of a number of opposition parties. In June 1993 the CST refused to ratify a co-operation agreement that had been signed with Libya in November 1992, in view of the unresolved issue of the sovereignty of the Aozou region.

In January 1993 troops loyal to Habré attempted a coup; several of the rebels were subsequently arrested. In February government troops, who were engaged in conflict with the MDD in the region of Lake Chad, clashed with members of the Nigerien armed forces, after attacking rebel bases in Niger. In the same month, following renewed military engagements between ANT and CSNPD forces in southern Chad, opposition groups claimed that the Republican Guard (a special unit of the ANT, under the direct supervision of Deby) had massacred civilians in the region of Goré, in retaliation for local support for the CSNPD; by March some 15,000 people had fled to the Central African Republic (CAR). In May, in response to the findings of a commission of inquiry, the Government confirmed that its forces had carried out massacres of civilians in southern Chad earlier that year. Moungar announced that members of the armed forces who were implicated in the violence had been arrested, that military units in the region were to be replaced, and that a judicial investigation was to be instituted. Meanwhile, the CSNPD refuted claims by the Government that it had launched further attacks against the ANT in the Goré region.

In mid-1993 the Government announced that the ANT and other security forces were to be reorganized, in response to widespread public concern at the increasing incidence of violence involving the armed and security forces. In August, however, armed men killed some 82 civilians in the region of Chokoyam, in the southern prefecture of Ouaddaï. Shortly afterwards it was reported that some 41 people had been killed when a demonstration by residents of N'Djamena originating from Ouaddaï, in protest at the massacre, was violently suppressed by the Republican Guard. The CST subsequently accused the Government of exceeding its powers by deploying the Republican Guard to disperse the demonstration and by imposing a nation-wide curfew in response to the unrest. Also in August the leader of the CNRT, Abbas Koti, returned to Chad, following an agreement with Deby mediated by the Governments of Sudan and Libya. In October Koti agreed to the integration of CNRT forces into the ANT. Shortly afterwards, however, he was killed by security forces while allegedly resisting arrest on charges of implication in a conspiracy to overthrow the Government.

In October 1993 a motion expressing 'no confidence' in the Moungar administration, apparently initiated by supporters of Deby, was approved by the CST. Moungar subsequently resigned, and in November the CST elected Kassire Delwa Koumakoye, hitherto Minister of Justice and Keeper of the Seals, as Prime Minister. In January 1994 the Government threatened to implement sanctions against teachers and other government employees who had begun strike action in the previous month, in protest at the Government's failure to pay salary arrears. The 50% devaluation of the CFA franc, shortly afterwards, precipitated further unrest.

Meanwhile, rebel activities by the so-called 'politico-military' movements continued. In January 1994 members of the FNT (who were to have been integrated into the ANT following the peace agreement with the Government) attacked a military garrison at Abéché, in the north-east. In February negotiations between the Chadian authorities and the CSNPD, with mediation by the CAR, failed to secure a lasting peace, and there were further clashes between government and CSNPD forces in southern Chad at the end of March.

In February 1994 the ICJ ruled in favour of Chad in the issue of the sovereignty of the Aozou region, upholding a treaty concluded in 1955 by France and Libya. In April 1994 Libya agreed to commence the withdrawal of troops from the region, and at the end of May the Governments of Chad and Libya issued a joint statement confirming that the withdrawal had been completed as scheduled. In June a co-operation agreement consolidated relations between the two nations. France stated that its military support force (which then numbered some 800 troops) was to remain in Chad, despite demands from the Libyan Government for its withdrawal.

In March 1994 an Institutional Committee submitted constitutional recommendations, which included provisions for the election of a President for a term of five years, the installation of a bicameral legislature and a Constitutional Court, and the establishment of a decentralized administrative structure. In April the CST extended the transitional period for one year, on the grounds that the Government had achieved little progress in preparing for democratic elections. A new electoral timetable was adopted, whereby the Government was obliged to provide funds for the organization of the elections, to reach an agreement with the UST in order to end industrial unrest, and to implement further preparatory measures by June, including the adoption of an electoral code, the establishment of a national reconciliation council (to negotiate a peace settlement with the rebel movements), and the appointment of electoral and human rights commissions. It was expected that the constitutional recommendations would be submitted for approval at a national referendum in December, and that democratic elections would take place in early 1995.

Government efforts to negotiate a settlement with the UST were impeded by further strike action, initiated by public-sector workers at the end of April 1994, in support of salary demands to compensate for the devaluation of the CFA franc. A presidential decree declared the strike illegal, but industrial action continued until July, when agreement was reached on limited salary increases and the payment of arrears. A 12-member Conseil de la réconciliation nationale (CRN), which was to initiate negotiations with insurgent opposition groups, was established in May. In the same month Deby effected a comprehensive reorganization of the Government.

In August 1994 the Chadian authorities and the CSNPD signed a cease-fire agreement, providing for the recognition of the CSNPD as a legal political organization and the integration of its forces into the ANT. Later that month, however, it was reported that government troops had killed some 26 civilians in southern Chad, in reprisal for attacks by members of another rebel faction, the Forces armées pour la République fédérale (FARF). In October the Government and the FNT negotiated a peace agreement, which was, however, subsequently repudiated by the leader of the FNT. In November a number of former members of the CSNPD were integrated into the ANT in accordance with the August peace agreement.

In September 1994 it was reported that the Minister of Mines and Energy, Lt-Col Mahamat Garfa (who had apparently resented his dismissal from the post of Chief of Army Staff), had fled N'Djamena with substantial government funds, and, together with some 600 members of the ANT, had joined CNRT forces in eastern Chad. In October Choua was replaced as Chairman of the CST by a member of the MPS, Mahamat Bachar Ghadaia. Choua subsequently accused the Government of human rights violations, including the assassination of two prominent members of the RDP.

Deby officially announced in November 1994 that the process of democratic transition would conclude on 9 April 1995, following presidential and legislative elections. In December 1994 Deby declared a general amnesty for political prisoners and opposition members in exile, notably excluding Habré; a number of political detainees were subsequently released. Nevertheless, the LTDH continued to allege violations of human rights by the ANT in its suppression of rebel activity. In the same month an independent national electoral commission was established. In January 1995 the CST adopted a new electoral code and subsequently approved the draft Constitution, which had been amended in accordance with recommendations made by a national conference in August 1994.

In February 1995 a population census was conducted, in preparation for the compilation of a new electoral register. There were reports of widespread irregularities, and opposition parties accused the MPS of attempted electoral malpractice, demanding a new census. At the end of March the CST extended the transitional period for a further year, and amended the National Charter to debar the incumbent Prime Minister from contesting the forthcoming presidential election or from belonging to a political party. In April the CST, which had criticized the Government's lack of progress in organizing democratic elections, voted to remove Koumakoye from the office of Prime Minister. The CST subsequently elected Djimasta Koibla, a prominent member of the Union pour la démocratie et la République, as Prime Minister. In the same month the results of the population census were annulled by the Court of Appeal, on the grounds of procedural irregularities.

In May 1995 a prominent human rights organization, Amnesty International, and the LTDH claimed that members of the ANT had perpetrated violations of human rights against civilians in retaliation for rebel attacks. In June security forces raided the premises of an independent newspaper, *N'Djamena-Hebdo*, which had published an article criticizing the activities of the ANT. Later that month the authorities prohibited a planned demonstration by opposition groups to protest at the Government's continued failure to improve democratic conditions. In July a unilateral government declaration of a national cease-fire was received with caution by the rebel movements.

In July 1995 Koumakoye announced that he was to contest the forthcoming presidential election. In August the Chairman and other members of the Executive Bureau of the CST resigned, following accusations of the misappropriation of funds. At the end of that month security forces raided the home of Saleh Kebzabo, the leader of the opposition Union nationale pour le développement et le renouveau (UNDR). In protest, the Concertation des partis politiques, an informal alliance of opposition parties to which the UNDR belonged, announced that it was to suspend participation in the CST and the CRN, and demanded the resignation of the head of the security forces. In September Kebzabo was arrested and charged with endangering state security by associating with rebel groups; he was released on bail later that month.

In November 1995 Deby announced that Gabon was to act as a mediator in forthcoming reconciliation talks between the Government and political organizations and armed opposition groups. In the same month the Government and the MDD agreed to a cease-fire, an exchange of prisoners and the integration of a number of MDD troops into the ANT. The reconciliation discussions between the Government and its opponents were convened in Franceville, Gabon, in January 1996. In March the Government and 13 opposition parties signed an agreement providing for a cease-fire and the establishment of a special security force to maintain order during the electoral period. Although it appeared that the majority of the armed movements had rejected the agreement, the conclusion of the Franceville accord allowed the electoral programme to proceed. A number of opposition parties, particularly the southern-based organizations that favoured the adoption of a federal system of government, urged their supporters to reject the draft Constitution (which enshrined a unitary state). However, the new Constitution was endorsed by 63.5% of votes cast at a national referendum on 31 March 1996.

Deby was among the 15 candidates authorized to contest the presidential election: five contenders (among them former Prime Minister Moungar) had been rejected on the grounds that they failed to meet residency criteria. Deby secured 43.9% of the votes cast in the first round of voting, which took place on 2 June, followed by Kamougué, who had contested the election on behalf of the Union pour le renouveau et la démocratie (URD), with 12.4%, and Kebzabo (8.5%). Deby and Kamougué proceeded to a second round of voting on 3 July. Most of the unsuccessful first-round candidates urged a boycott of the vote. However, Kebzabo announced his support for Deby, and the incumbent won a decisive victory, with, according to the official results, 69.1% of votes cast. The rate of participation by voters exceeded 75% of the registered electorate. Deby was inaugurated as President on 8 August, and subsequently reappointed Koibla as Prime Minister. Koibla named an interim Council of Ministers, which included several former opposition members, notably Kebzabo as Minister of Foreign Affairs. Kamougué, however, refused to join the Government until the legislative elections had taken place.

In August 1996 the CNRT merged with another 'politico-military' group, the Front d'action pour l'installation de la démocratie au Tchad, to form the Congrès pour le renouveau et la démocratie. Later that month the Government and elements of the FARF signed a peace agreement, providing for a cease-fire and an amnesty for members of the faction, which was to be reconstituted as a legal political organization, the Front patriotique pour la démocratie. In September a further armed movement, the Front national du Tchad renové (FNTR), threatened to abandon plans for peace negotiations with the Chadian authorities, after claiming that government forces had launched attacks against FNTR positions in eastern Chad. The Government and the MDD signed a peace agreement in Niger in the same month, and in October Deby announced that he had dispatched an adviser to meet representatives of other dissident factions, in an attempt to initiate peace negotiations.

The French Government denied allegations, made in an Amnesty International report issued in October 1996, of complicity in violations of human rights in Chad. In January 1997 the International Federation of Human Rights Leagues expressed its concern at a recent increase in summary executions by the Chadian security forces. In March, following the adoption by the European Parliament of a resolution condemning Chad for serious violations of human rights, the Government announced an end to the executions.

Legislative elections, which had been postponed in October and again in November 1996, eventually took place in two rounds on 5 January and 23 February 1997, contested by some 30 political organizations. Preliminary results were announced in early March, but were challenged by both the MPS and opposition parties (who claimed that there had been serious irregularities in the second round of voting). Later that month the Court of Appeal announced the final election results, in which a further eight seats were allocated to the MPS. The MPS thus secured an absolute majority in the 125-member Assemblée nationale, with a final total of 65 seats, while the URD won 29 seats and the UNDR 15. The new Assemblée nationale was inaugurated on 4 April, and in May Kamougué was elected as its President, with the support of deputies of Deby's MPS and Kebzabo's UNDR, as well as those of his own URD. Koibla's Transitional Government resigned in the same month. Nassour Guelengdouksia Ouaidou, hitherto Secretary-General at the Presidency, was named as the new Prime Minister. His Government retained Kebzabo, as Minister of State for Public Works, Transport, Housing and Town Planning, although most strategic portfolios remained under the control of the MPS.

In April 1997 the Government and the FARF signed a peace agreement, providing for the cessation of all hostilities between the ANT and the FARF, a general amnesty for FARF members, the integration of its civilian and armed members into the state apparatus, and the legalization of the movement as a political party. In August the Government was reported to have negotiated a peace agreement with the Forces armées populaires, the military wing of Goukouni's FROLINAT. A new 'politico-military' group, the Résistance armée contre les forces antidémocratiques (RAFAD), was formed in Nigeria in the same month, with the stated aim of deposing the Deby regime by force. Reconciliation talks took place in N'Djamena in October between representatives of the Government, the FNT, the FNTR and the Mouvement pour la justice sociale et la démocratie. Agreement was reached on a general amnesty for the three groups, which received similar concessions to those previously granted to the FARF. However, the reconciliation between the Government and the FARF appeared to be in jeopardy at the end of the month, when fighting erupted between government forces and members of the FARF in the Logone Occidental prefecture of southern Chad; according to official figures, 42 FARF rebels, 52 civilians and four members of the ANT were killed. The FARF accused the Government of reneging on commitments made under the terms of the April peace agreement, notably concerning the integration of fighters into the regular armed forces. In December Deby expressed his willingness for reconciliation with the FARF, but emphasized that he could not agree to 'peace gained by blackmail'.

The restoration of peace, particularly in the south, was regarded as imperative as efforts continued to secure funding for the development of petroleum resources. However, insecurity persisted in 1998. Responsibility for the kidnap, in February, of four French nationals in Moyen Chari prefecture was claimed by the Union des forces démocratiques (UFD). It was subsequently reported that 11 rebels had been killed, and 19 arrested, in an operation to liberate the hostages. French Epervier forces were mobilized in support of the Chadian security forces, although the military attaché at the French embassy in N'Djamena, said to be an associate of the UFD leader, Dr Mahamout Nahour, was declared *persona non grata* by the Chadian authorities after Nahour demanded only to negotiate with him.

In March 1998 it was revealed that discreet talks had been taking place since January between Kamougué and the FARF leader, Laokein Barde; the petroleum-rich Logone region, a centre for FARF activities, was a stronghold of Kamougué's URD. In the same month, however, Amnesty International claimed that at least 100 civilians had been killed in what the organization termed 'extrajudicial executions' by security forces in the south. The Government, acknowledging an increase in violence in the south, stated that it had assumed its responsibilities in dispatching forces to restore peace. The FNTR, demanding the withdrawal from Chadian territory of French troops and petroleum companies, claimed responsibility for the kidnapping of eight Europeans in late March. (All had been released by the end of the month.)

Despite the renewed violence by the 'politico-military' groups, and the issuing, in March 1998, of a warrant for the arrest of Laokein Barde, negotiations between the President of the Assemblée nationale and the FARF continued. In May a presidential envoy and the FARF chief of general staff signed an agreement envisaging an immediate end to rebel activity; the Government undertook to withdraw élite elements of the nomadic and national security guards from the south and there was to be a general amnesty for FARF militants. The terms of the April 1997 peace accord, whereby the FARF was to be legalized as a political party, were also to be renewed. (Reports later in the year stated that Barde had been presumed dead since April.)

In an extensive government reshuffle announced in January 1998 Kebzabo was redesignated Minister of State, Minister of Mines, Energy and Petroleum (a new post, apparently emphasizing the importance attached by the Deby regime to the development of the petroleum and industrial mining sectors). In May, however, Kebzabo was removed from the Government, as were two UNDR secretaries of state.

In February 1998 Dieudonné Djonabaye, the editor-in-chief of *N'Djamena Hebdo*, received a two-year suspended prison sentence, having been found guilty of libel against the Head of State: this was the first conviction for libel imposed on the media since the installation of the new organs of state. In the following month Djonabaye was reportedly detained and severely beaten by security forces while attempting, in his capacity as correspondent for Radio France Internationale, to visit the headquarters of the Epervier force. In July Ngarledjy Yorongar, the sole parliamentary representative of the Front d'action pour le renouveau, was sentenced to three years' imprisonment (although Deby announced his release in January 1999, reportedly following a meeting with political representatives from Yorongar's native Logone Orientale region). Yorongar, who had been an outspoken critic of provisions for the exploitation of petroleum in southern Chad, had claimed that Kamougué had received 1,500m. francs CFA from a French petroleum company, and had also alleged that Deby and his family were mismanaging the country's petroleum resources.

In September 1998 a faction of the MDD issued a communiqué asserting that it had ousted Moussa Medella Mahamat as its leader, with the aim of engaging in peace talks with the Government. Medella denounced this rallying to the Government, and further condemned a joint offensive against MDD fighters by the security forces of Chad, Niger and Nigeria. In November Goukouni Oueddei appealed from Algiers for a general mobiliza-

tion against the Deby regime. In the same month, however, the FARF, now apparently led by Dienambaye Barde, the brother of the former leader, rallied to the MPS.

Reports emerged from late 1998 of a rebellion in the Tibesti region of northern Chad by the Mouvement pour la démocratie et la justice au Tchad (MDJT), led by Youssouf Togoimi—a former government member who had been dismissed as Minister of Defence in June 1997. Despite MDJT claims of significant military and territorial successes, the Government did not acknowledge the existence of any rebellion in Tibesti until March 1999; even then, the authorities asserted that Togoimi was leading a group of only some 30 Toubou rebels. It was confirmed that military reinforcements, including a 3,000-strong élite force, had been deployed to prevent infiltration by Toubou sympathizers from neighbouring countries, and the authorities admitted that the ANT had suffered some losses in operations against the MDJT. However, claims by Togoimi that his movement was in control of much of the north of the country were categorically denied. In June 1999 FROLINAT announced that it was giving political and logistical support to the Tibesti rebellion.

In July 1999 Medella returned to N'Djamena, following the signing in Khartoum, Sudan, of a reconciliation accord with the Deby regime. MDD dissidents, however, denounced Medella, and the leadership of the movement was assumed by Issa Faki Mahamat and Gaileth Gatoul Bourkoumandah. At the end of September the MDD alleged that joint forces from Chad, Niger and Nigeria were waging a 'campaign of terror' in the region of Lake Chad against suspected opposition sympathizers. Meanwhile, Deby dispatched a group of negotiators to the north, in an effort to establish contacts with the rebels. In October Togoimi expressed his willingness to meet with the presidential envoys, although no such meeting occurred until September 2000 (see below). In November 1999 the MDJT, the MDD and the CDR alleged that the Chadian Government had acquired what were termed 'dirty weapons', such as chemicals to poison wells, from countries of the former communist bloc, in order to 'decimate' the population of Tibesti. In a communiqué issued later in November, furthermore, the MDJT claimed to have defeated ANT forces in Aozou, killing 80 and capturing 47 (a further 42 ANT troops were said to have defected to the rebellion). The MDJT asserted that its victory followed heavy fighting precipitated by an ambush by ANT forces who had allegedly used the cover of civilian negotiators in order to access MDJT positions.

Ouaidou resigned as Prime Minister in December 1999. He was replaced by Nagoum Yamassoum, whose new Government included five UNDR members, among them Saleh Kebzabo as Minister of State and Minister of Agriculture. A minor government reshuffle was effected in March 2000.

In the first half of 2000 claims made by the MDJT of further military successes around the strongholds of Yebibon, Guizinti and Bardai were dismissed or diminished by the Government. In February the Government admitted that its mediation mission to the north, led by the former Prime Minister Djimasta Koibla, had proved fruitless. In the same month it was reported that the former armed wing of the MDD had renamed itself the Mouvement pour l'unité et la République, under the leadership of Bourkoumandah, and had allied itself with the MDJT and the CDR. Meanwhile, in December 1999 it was announced that 13 'politico-military groups', including FROLINAT and the FNTR, had formed a new alliance in opposition to the Deby regime, the Coordination des mouvements armés et partis politiques de l'opposition, led by Antoine Bangui. No significant progress was achieved at talks held in Libya in April 2000 between Deby and Goukouni Oueddei, the leader of FROLINAT.

In June 2000 the Chadian Government signed a peace accord with the RAFAD in Cotonou, Benin, in which it was agreed that RAFAD members would be incorporated into the state military and civil services. In July the MDJT attacked a garrison in Bardai and proclaimed their control of four towns in Tibesti. Official military sources stated that 57 rebels and 13 government troops were killed during the fighting. The Prime Minister visited the region and invited MDJT negotiators to take part in peace discussions. In September it was reported that Moïse Ketté Nodji, the leader of the CSNPD, had been killed during clashes with ANT forces in Logone Orientale. It was further reported that the group had attacked a vehicle near Goré in July, indicating the end of its cease-fire, but this was denied by government sources. In September Youssouf Togoimi met with Deby for the first time, in Sirte, Libya. Togoimi's proposal for multilateral peace discussions, incorporating all opposition groups and Deby's administration, was followed later that month by a conference at which Deby met with representatives of some 30 opposition organizations, which were reportedly united in their disapproval of the new electoral code (see below). However, renewed fighting broke out in October between members of the MDJT and government forces in the far north of Chad and intensified in December. In November it was reported that more than 50 people had been killed during fighting between rival cattle-herding groups in the central province of Batha.

Meanwhile, in July 2000 the Assemblée nationale approved proposals for the creation of an independent electoral body, the Commission électorale nationale indépendant (CENI), which was to plan a reorganization of constituencies in advance of presidential and legislative elections due to be held in 2001. The Government was to appoint 16 of the 31 CENI members, with a further 12 to be nominated by parties represented in the legislature, and the remaining three by non-parliamentary parties. Several opposition parties were concerned by their apparent exclusion from the CENI and threatened to boycott the forthcoming elections in protest against the new arrangements, while fears were expressed that certain northern regions would be over-represented in comparison with those in the south. An extensive reshuffle of the Government at the end of August 2000 followed the dismissal of ministers belonging to the URD, owing to their party's rejection of the new electoral code. Furthermore, a number of members of the MPS resigned from the ruling party, reportedly in protest against violent acts committed by government forces. Government reshuffles were effected in February and April 2001; in the latter Deby removed all UNDR ministers from office, reportedly in response to Kebzabo's announcement that he was to contest the forthcoming presidential election. Deby was re-elected to the presidency on 20 May, winning 67.35% of votes cast, according to provisional figures, although opposition candidates alleged fraud. Of the remaining six candidates, the most successful were Yorongar, with 13.94%, and Kebzabo, with 6.53%.

In early 1998 it was reported that Chad was to seek the extradition from Senegal of former President Habré, with a view to his prosecution in relation to human rights abuses and in connection with the embezzlement of state funds. A committee of inquiry, established by the Deby regime, had held Habré's 'political police' responsible for the deaths of some 40,000 people and the torture of 200,000 others; the deposed President was also alleged to have taken some 7,000m. francs CFA in state funds when he fled the country in 1990. In February 2000, following a ruling by a Senegalese court that he could be tried in that country for alleged crimes committed in Chad under his leadership, Habré was charged with complicity in acts of torture and barbarity, and placed under house arrest. The charges were dismissed in July, however, on the grounds that Senegal lacked the appropriate penal procedure to process such an international case. The rejection of the charges followed the removal of the judge presiding over the case by a panel headed by the Senegalese President, Abdoulaye Wade. Allegations of political interference in the case ensued, and an appeal was made to Senegal's highest court, the Cour de cassation. In addition, in October and November more than 50 lawsuits were reportedly filed in N'Djamena accusing members of Habré's Government and 'political police' of involvement in reputed cases of torture, murder and disappearance. Despite allegations that members of his administration were implicated in a number of these cases, Deby attended his first meeting with an association for the victims of torture, the Association des victimes des crimes et de la répression politique au Tchad, in September.

Relations with France appeared uneasy in the first half of 1998, particularly following the expulsion of a French military attaché, accused of maintaining dangerous contacts with the opposition (see above). In May Deby denounced what he termed the 'neo-imperialism' of the international media and human rights groups, accusing the West of imposing multi-party politics on Africa. In June 30 agents of the French Direction générale de la sécurité extérieure, who had apparently been operating as Deby's protection agents, were dismissed. Deby none the less met with President Jacques Chirac during a visit to France in July, and in September the French army Chief of Staff visited Chad in an effort to ease tensions. It was generally believed that France regarded the maintenance of its military presence in Chad as a priority, given the country's proximity to potential conflict zones in central Africa, and also, notably, to Libya. However, in March 2000 the Chadian Government demanded the recall of the French ambassador in N'Djamena, Alain du Boispéan, reputedly because of his personality and working methods, although it was subsequently alleged that France's refusal to provide military support to government forces in Tibesti was a factor in the dispute.

During the late 1990s, meanwhile, Chad developed closer relations with its neighbours, particularly Libya. Chad was a founder member of the Community of the Sahel-Saharan States (CEN-SAD, formerly COMESSA, see p. 307), established in Tripoli in 1997, and Deby and members of his administration made several visits to Libya during 1997–2000, including some by air prior to the ending of the UN embargo on air links with Libya in April 1999. In May 1998, meanwhile, Qaddafi made what was reported as his first visit to Chad since 1981. However, tension in Libya between Libyan nationals and migrant workers from west and central Africa in September–October 2000 led to at least 12 Chadians being killed in clashes, with another 80 declared missing, according to the Chadian Government, which subsequently undertook to repatriate some 8,000 of the 500,000 Chadians resident in Libya. The Government rejected allegations, made by the FNTR, of involvement in the execution of Chadian opposition members, as they fled the attacks in Libya.

Chad dispatched troops to the CAR in early 1997, as part of a regional surveillance mission (q.v.), and Chadian forces remained in the CAR as part of the UN peace-keeping mission that began operations in April 1998. In September 1998 the Chadian authorities confirmed that troops had been deployed in the Democratic Republic of the Congo (DRC, q.v.), in support of President Laurent-Désiré Kabila. The Chadian Government asserted that the military had intervened to assist in the restoration of peace and recovery of territorial integrity in the DRC. It was denied, furthermore, that Libya was lending logistical support for the Chadian intervention. However, there was considerable domestic opposition to Chad's involvement in the DRC. Following discussion of the DRC conflict at a summit meeting held under the auspices of COMESSA in Sirte, Libya, in April 1999, Chad announced the withdrawal of its troops from the DRC, with effect from late May. The Chadian Ministry of Defence specified in June that 2,227 troops had been deployed in the DRC; the number of deaths within the Chadian contingent was confirmed as 105. The Government denied that its decision to withdraw from the Congolese conflict reflected concern at the security situation in Tibesti (see above).

Government

A new Constitution was adopted by national referendum on 31 March 1996. Under the terms of the Constitution, the Republic of Chad is a unitary state with a multi-party political system. Executive power is vested in the President, who is the Head of State and Commander-in-Chief of the Armed Forces. The President is elected by direct universal suffrage for a maximum of two five-year terms of office. The President appoints the Prime Minister, who nominates the Council of Ministers. Legislative power is vested in a bicameral legislature, comprising the 125-member Assemblée nationale, which is elected by direct universal suffrage for a four-year term, and a Sénat, which has a six-year mandate (with one-third of the membership renewable every two years). By early 2001 the Sénat had not yet been established.

Chad is divided into 28 administrative departments.

Defence

In August 2000 the Armée nationale tchadienne (ANT) was estimated to number 30,350 (army approximately 25,000, air force 350, Republican Guard 5,000). In addition, there was a 4,500-strong gendarmerie. The army has been undergoing restructuring since 1996. Military service is by conscription. Under defence agreements with France, the army receives technical and other aid: in August 2000 the number of troops deployed in Chad by France numbered 990. Direct aid from France to the Chadian army in 1999 was an estimated 6,160m. francs CFA. Defence expenditure for 2000 was budgeted at an estimated 34,000m. francs CFA.

Economic Affairs

In 1998, according to estimates by the World Bank, Chad's gross national product (GNP), measured at average 1996–98 prices, was US $1,658m., equivalent to $230 per head (or $843 on an international purchasing-power parity basis). During 1990–98, it was estimated, GNP per head declined, in real terms, at an average annual rate of 1.1%. Over the same period the population increased by an annual average of 3.4%. GNP in 1999 was estimated at \$1,600m., equivalent to \$200 per head. Chad's gross domestic product (GDP) increased, in real terms, by an average of 2.3% annually in 1990–99. Real GDP increased by 6.7% in 1998, but, according to preliminary estimates by the World Bank, declined by 0.7% in 1999.

Agriculture contributed 36.0% of GDP in 1999, according to preliminary estimates; some 76.1% of the labour force were employed in the sector in that year. The principal cash crop is cotton (exports of which contributed 59.3% of total export revenue in 1997). The principal subsistence crops are sorghum, millet and groundnuts. In response to low rainfall, which was expected to lead to food shortages in many regions of Chad, the Government appealed for international food aid in November 2000. Livestock-rearing, which contributed 12.0% of GDP in 1998, makes an important contribution both to the domestic food supply and to export earnings, although illicit trade accounts for a significant proportion of the output. During 1990–99 agricultural GDP increased by an annual average of 4.9%; agricultural GDP increased by 11.1% in 1998, but declined by an estimated 6.5% in 1999.

Industry contributed an estimated 14.7% of GDP in 1999. About 4.6% of the population were employed in the sector in 1980. During 1990–99 industrial GDP increased by an average of 2.2%; the sector's GDP expanded by 9.0% in 1998, but declined by an estimated 4.1% in 1999.

The mining sector (including fishing) contributed 3.0% of GDP in 1998. For many years the only minerals exploited were natron, salt, alluvial gold and materials for the construction industry. However, long-delayed plans to develop sizeable petroleum reserves in the Doba Basin and at Sedigi, in the south of the country, were being pursued in 2000 (see below). There is believed to be considerable potential for the further exploitation of gold, bauxite and uranium.

The manufacturing sector, which contributed an estimated 11.8% of GDP in 1999, operates mainly in the south of the country, and is dominated by agro-industrial activities, notably the processing of the cotton crop by the state-controlled Société Cotonnière du Tchad (COTONTCHAD). Work commenced in mid-2000 on the construction of a pipeline from petroleum reserves at Sedigi to supply a new refinery in N'Djamena. During 1994–98 manufacturing GDP increased by an annual average of 12.4%. The GDP of the sector increased by 9.9% in 1998, but declined by an estimated 7.0% in 1999.

Chad is heavily dependent on imports of mineral fuels (principally from Cameroon and Nigeria) for the generation of electricity. Imports of mineral fuels comprised an estimated 17.9% of the total value of imports in 1995. The use of wood-based fuel products by most households has contributed to the severe depletion of Chad's forest resources. In November 2000 the Cameroonian Prime Minister announced the creation of a technical committee to instigate the export of electricity to Chad.

Services contributed an estimated 49.3% of GDP in 1999. The GDP of the sector increased by an average of 0.8% per year in 1990–99; the sector's GDP increased by 2.8% in 1998 and by an estimated 5.1% in 1999.

In 1998 Chad recorded a visible trade deficit of 29,700m. francs CFA, and there was a deficit of 121,600m. francs CFA on the current account of the balance of payments. In 1995 Chad's principal source of imports (41.3%) was France; other major suppliers were Cameroon, Nigeria and the USA. The principal markets for exports include Cameroon and France. The principal exports are cotton and livestock. The principal imports in 1995 were petroleum products, road vehicles and parts, sugar and cereals.

In 1998 Chad recorded an overall budgetary deficit of 65,161m. francs CFA (equivalent to 6.6% of GDP). Chad's external debt at the end of 1998 totalled US \$1,091m., of which \$1,005m. was long-term public debt. In that year the cost of debt-servicing was equivalent to 10.6% of earnings from exports of goods and services. Consumer prices declined by an annual average of 2.1% in 1990–93. There was a sharp increase in the rate of inflation in 1994, to an average of 40.4%, following the 50% devaluation of the currency. Thereafter, the rate of inflation slowed to an average of 8.1% in 1995–98, consumer prices increased by an average of 6.5% in 1998, before decreasing by an average of 6.8% in 1999.

Chad is a member of the Central African organs of the Franc Zone (see p. 210) and of the Communauté économique des états de l'Afrique centrale (CEEAC, see p. 307); the Lake Chad Basin Commission (see p. 308) is based in N'Djamena.

Economic growth in Chad has been inhibited by a number of factors: conflict has deterred investment that could allow the development of considerable mineral wealth and other resources, leaving the economy over-dependent on the cotton sector, while the country's land-locked position has been compounded by infrastructural deficiencies. Chad thus remains among the world's least developed countries, with severely inadequate levels of education and health care. However, the 50% devaluation of the CFA franc in 1994 was of considerable benefit to the cotton and livestock sectors, and GDP increased by 10.2% in that year. Growth was at a slower rate in 1995–97, but was accompanied by some success in reducing inflation and in containing the fiscal and current-account deficits. Good rains and a consequent increase in food output contributed to strong growth in 1998. The IMF, which in 1995 granted support under its Enhanced Structural Adjustment Facility, has sought efforts to enhance government revenue and improve the efficiency of the agricultural sector, as well as banking reforms and measures to foster private investment. Notable privatizations have included the state abattoir and the sugar company, although there has been considerable domestic opposition to the dismantling of the COTONTCHAD monopoly. In January 2000 the IMF approved further funding under its Poverty Reduction and Growth Facility in support of the Government's economic programme for 1999–2002. It has been hoped that the abatement of civil conflict and the installation of elected organs of government in the second half of the 1990s would facilitate the exploitation of mineral reserves. A consortium led by the US Exxon Corporation and supported, from April 2000, by the US Chevron Corporation and Petronas of Malaysia has begun work to develop the substantial petroleum resources in the Doba Basin in southern Chad, with peak output of 225,000 barrels per day anticipated. The construction of a 1,070-km pipeline to transport petroleum to the port of Kribi in Cameroon began in October. However, while the project was expected to generate considerable revenue, controversy has surrounded not only the potentially adverse environmental and social consequences of the scheme, but also the ethics of partial World Bank funding for a commercial project. The Assemblée nationale has adopted legislation whereby 70% of Chad's earnings from petroleum would be dedicated to the development of health, education, agriculture and infrastructure, with a further 10% saved for future generations. However, in late 2000 the Government was criticized for reportedly spending some US \$3m of a bonus paid by the petroleum companies on armaments. In February 2001 the World Bank appointed an international advisory group to monitor the implementation of the project. The successful pursuit of this and other efforts to develop the Chadian economy will largely depend on the Government's ability to maintain domestic peace and, increasingly, to satisfy the international community of its commitment to transparent governance and respect for human rights.

Social Welfare

An Employment Code guarantees a minimum wage and other rights for employees. There are four hospitals, 28 medical centres and several hundred dispensaries. In 1978 there were 3,373 beds in government-administered hospital establishments (one per 1,278 inhabitants), while only 90 physicians were employed in official medical services. In 1994 the International Development Association approved loans of US \$18.5m. to finance improvements to Chad's health system. A comprehensive reform of Chad's social security system is planned.

Education

Education is officially compulsory for six years between six and 12 years of age. Primary education begins at the age of six and lasts for six years. Secondary education, from the age of 12, lasts for seven years, comprising a first cycle of four years and a second of three years. In 1996 the total enrolment at primary and secondary schools was equivalent to 35% of the school-age population (males 47%; females 23%). In 1996 primary enrolment included 46% of children in the relevant age-group (males 59%; females 33%), while secondary enrolment was equivalent to only 9% of children in the appropriate age-group (males 15%; females 4%). The Université du Tchad was opened at N'Djamena in 1971. In addition, there are several technical colleges. Some 3,274 students were enrolled at higher education institutions in 1995/96. Total expenditure on education by the central Government (including foreign-financed investment) in 1996 was 32,196m. francs CFA (21.2% of total government expenditure). At the 1993 census the average rate of adult illiteracy was 86.5%.

Public Holidays

2001: 1 January (New Year), 6 March* (Id al-Adha, Feast of the Sacrifice), 16 April (Easter Monday), 1 May (Labour Day), 25 May ('Liberation of Africa', anniversary of the OAU's foundation), 4 June (Whit Monday and Maloud, Birth of the Prophet*), 11 August (Independence Day), 15 August (Assumption), 1 November (All Saints' Day), 28 November (Proclamation of the Republic), 1 December (Liberation and Democracy Day, anniversary of the 1990 *coup d'état*), 17 December* (Id al-Fitr, end of Ramadan), 25 December (Christmas).

2002: 1 January (New Year), 23 February* (Id al-Adha, Feast of the Sacrifice), 1 April (Easter Monday), 1 May (Labour Day), 20 May (Whit Monday), 24 May* (Maloud, Birth of the Prophet), 25 May ('Liberation of Africa', anniversary of the OAU's foundation), 11 August (Independence Day), 15 August (Assumption), 1 November (All Saints' Day), 28 November (Proclamation of the Republic), 1 December (Liberation and Democracy Day, anniversary of the 1990 *coup d'état*), 6 December* (Id al-Fitr, end of Ramadan), 25 December (Christmas).

* These holidays are dependent on the Islamic lunar calendar and may vary by one or two days from the dates given.

Weights and Measures

The metric system is officially in force.

Statistical Survey

Source (unless otherwise stated): Direction de la Statistique, des Etudes Economiques et Démographiques, BP 453, N'Djamena.

Area and Population

AREA, POPULATION AND DENSITY

Area (sq km)	
Land	1,259,200
Inland waters	24,800
Total	1,284,000*
Population (sample survey)	
December 1963–August 1964	3,254,000†
Population (census result)	
8 April 1993‡	
Males	2,950,415
Females	3,208,577
Total	6,158,992
Population (official estimate at mid-year)	
1999	7,557,000
Density (per sq km) at mid-1999	5.9

* 495,800 sq miles.

† Including areas not covered by the survey.

‡ Figures are provisional. The revised total, including an adjustment for underenumeration (estimated at 1.4%), is 6,279,931.

PREFECTURES (1993 census)

	Area (sq km)	Population*	Density (per sq km)
Batha	88,800	288,458	3.2
Biltine	46,850	184,807	3.9
Borkou-Ennedi-Tibesti (BET) . .	600,350	73,185	0.1
Chari-Baguirmi†	82,910	1,251,906	15.1
Guera	58,950	306,253	5.2
Kanem	114,520	279,927	2.4
Lac	22,320	252,932	11.3
Logone Occidental . . .	8,695	455,489	52.4
Logone Oriental	28,035	441,064	15.7
Mayo-Kebbi	30,105	825,158	27.4
Moyen Chari	45,180	738,595	16.3
Ouaddaï	76,240	543,900	7.1
Salamat	63,000	184,403	2.9
Tandjilé	18,045	453,854	25.2
Total	1,284,000	6,279,931	4.9

* Including adjustment for underenumeration.

† Including the capital district, N'Djamena (population 530,965).

Note: As a result of administrative reform, Chad's former prefectures have been replaced by the following departments: Assongha (capital Adre), Bahr el Gazal (Moussoro), Bahr Koh (Sarh), Baguirmi (Massenya), Batha Est (Oum-Hadjer), Batha Ouest (Ati), Biltine (Biltine), Bourkou (Faya), Dababa (Bokoro), Ennedi (Fada), Guéra (Mongo), Hadjer Lamis (Massaguet), Kabia (Gonou Gaya), Kanem (Mao), Lac (Bol), Lac Iro (Kyabe), Logone Occidental (Moundou), Logone Oriental (Doba), Mandoul (Koumra), Mayo-Dala (Pala), Mayo Boneye (Bongor), Monts de Lam (Mbaibokoum), Ouaddaï (Abéché), Salamat (Am-Timan), Sila (Goz-Beida), Tandjilé Est (Lai), Tandjilé Ouest (Kélo), Tibesti (Bardai).

PRINCIPAL LOCALITIES (population at 1993 census)

N'Djamena (capital)	. 530,965	Koumra	. . .	26,702
Moundou	. . 99,530	Pala	. . .	26,115
Sarh	. . . 75,496	Am Timan	. .	21,269
Abéché	. . 54,628	Bongor	. . .	20,448
Kelo	. . . 31,319	Mongo	. . .	20,443

BIRTHS AND DEATHS (UN estimates, annual averages)

	1980–85	1985–90	1990–95
Birth rate (per 1,000) . . .	49.1	47.7	46.7
Death rate (per 1,000) . . .	22.4	20.5	19.3

Expectation of life (UN estimates, years at birth, 1990–95): 45.9 (males 44.4; females 47.5).

Source: UN, *World Population Prospects: The 1998 Revision.*

ECONOMICALLY ACTIVE POPULATION
(ILO estimates, '000 persons at mid-1980)

	Males	Females	Total
Agriculture, etc.	1,043	318	1,361
Industry	72	4	76
Services	154	44	197
Total labour force . . .	1,269	366	1,635

Source: ILO, *Economically Active Population Estimates and Projections, 1950–2025.*

1993 census (persons aged six years and over): Total labour force 2,719,443 (males 1,416,449; females 1,302,994) (Source: ILO, *Yearbook of Labour Statistics*).

Mid-1999 (estimates in '000): Agriculture, etc. 2,639; Total 3,467 (Source: FAO).

Agriculture

PRINCIPAL CROPS ('000 metric tons)

	1997	1998	1999
Wheat	4	5	5
Rice (paddy)	112	121	131
Maize	99	180	97
Millet	248	357	347
Sorghum	521	555	436
Other cereals	95	135	138
Potatoes*	8	8	8
Sweet potatoes* . . .	60	65	65
Cassava (Manioc) . . .	279†	275	275*
Yams*	240	240	240
Taro (Coco yam)* . . .	38	38	38
Dry beans	24	53	53*
Other pulses	20	21	21*
Groundnuts (in shell) . .	352	471	471*
Sesame seed	26	15	15*
Dry onions*	14	14	14
Other vegetables* . . .	87	87	87
Dates*	18	18	18
Mangoes*	32	32	32
Other fruit*	65	65	65
Sugar cane*	330	280	280
Cotton (lint)	86	103	103*

* FAO estimate(s).   † Unofficial figure.

Source: FAO.

LIVESTOCK ('000 head, year ending September)

	1997	1998	1999*
Cattle	5,451	5,582	5,582
Goats	4,824	4,968	4,968
Sheep	2,361	2,432	2,432
Pigs	19†	23*	23
Horses	228†	230*	230
Asses	280†	285*	285
Camels	677†	700*	700
Poultry*	4,700	4,800	4,800

* FAO estimate(s).   † Unofficial figure.

Source: FAO.

LIVESTOCK PRODUCTS (FAO estimates, '000 metric tons)

	1997	1998	1999
Beef and veal	39	40	40*
Mutton and lamb	11	12	12*
Goat meat	13	14	14*
Poultry meat	4	5	5
Other meat	5	5	5
Cows' milk	123	123	123
Sheep's milk	9	9	9
Goats' milk	29	30	30
Poultry eggs	4	4	4
Cattle hides	6	6	6
Sheepskins	2	2	2
Goatskins	2	3	3

* FAO estimate.

Source: FAO.

Forestry

ROUNDWOOD REMOVALS ('000 cubic metres, excl. bark)

	1996	1997	1998
Sawlogs, veneer logs and logs for sleepers	14	14	14
Other industrial wood	691	710	728
Fuel wood	1,117	1,147	1,177
Total	1,822	1,871	1,919

Source: FAO, *Yearbook of Forest Products*.

SAWNWOOD PRODUCTION ('000 cubic metres, incl. railway sleepers)

	1996	1997	1998
Total (all broadleaved)	2	2	2

Source: FAO, *Yearbook of Forest Products*.

Fishing

('000 metric tons, live weight)

	1996	1997	1998
Total catch (freshwater fishes)	100.0	85.0	84.0

Source: FAO, *Yearbook of Fishery Statistics*.

Industry

SELECTED PRODUCTS

	1996	1997	1998
Edible oil ('000 hectolitres)	114.1	156.1	160.0
Sugar ('000 metric tons)	35.0	33.0	29.0
Beer ('000 hectolitres)	118.2	123.0	135.0
Cigarettes (million)	700	780	860
Woven cotton fabrics (million metres)	0.8	1.0	1.1
Electric energy (million kWh)	92.1	81.2	74.9

Source: IMF, *Chad: Recent Economic Developments* (May 1999).

Finance

CURRENCY AND EXCHANGE RATES

Monetary Units
100 centimes = 1 franc de la Coopération financière en Afrique centrale (CFA).

Sterling, Dollar and Euro Equivalents (29 December 2000)
£1 sterling = 1,051.93 francs CFA;
US $1 = 704.95 francs CFA;
€1 = 655.96 francs CFA;
10,000 francs CFA = £9.506 = $14.185 = €15.245.

Average Exchange Rate (francs CFA per US $)
1998   589.95
1999   615.70
2000   711.98

Note: An exchange rate of 1 French franc = 50 francs CFA, established in 1948, remained in force until January 1994, when the CFA franc was devalued by 50%, with the exchange rate adjusted to 1 French franc = 100 francs CFA. This relationship to French currency remained in effect with the introduction of the euro on 1 January 1999. From that date, accordingly, a fixed exchange rate of €1 = 655.957 francs CFA has been in operation.

BUDGET ('000 million francs CFA)

Revenue*	1996	1997	1998†
Tax revenue	53.0	61.3	69.8
Taxes on income and profits	21.5	21.6	22.6
Companies	11.9	9.7	10.7
Individuals	8.5	10.8	10.6
Employers' payroll tax	1.1	1.0	1.4
Taxes on goods and services	11.1	17.0	14.4
Turnover tax	6.5	10.8	8.5
Tax on petroleum products	2.9	3.4	3.5
Taxes on international trade	18.6	20.7	27.4
Import taxes	17.0	18.7	25.7
Export taxes	0.9	1.4	1.3
Other tax revenues	1.9	2.1	5.4
Other revenue	6.5	7.1	6.5
Property income	0.4	1.3	1.3
Total	59.6	68.4	76.2

Expenditure‡	1996	1997	1998†
Current expenditure . . .	77.2	73.5	75.4
Primary current expenditure .	64.4	61.3	65.7
Wages and salaries . .	30.8	30.8	31.5
Materials and supplies . .	17.1	14.6	16.1
Transfers	3.9	6.1	8.6
Defence	12.7	9.7	9.5
Salaries	10.7	8.4	8.3
Elections	3.8	0.3	0.0
Interest	8.4	8.5	8.9
External	7.1	7.0	7.5
Investment expenditure . . .	74.6	85.4	78.4
Foreign-financed . . .	74.0	81.4	73.3
Total	151.8	158.9	153.8

* Excluding grants received ('000 million francs CFA): 50.6 in 1996; 56.4 in 1997; 50.9 (provisional) in 1998.
† Preliminary figures.
‡ Excluding adjustment for payments arrears.

Source: IMF, *Chad: Recent Economic Developments* (May 1999).

INTERNATIONAL RESERVES (US $ million at 31 December)

	1998	1999	2000
Gold*	3.20	n.a.	n.a.
IMF special drawing rights . .	0.01	0.03	—
Reserve position in IMF . . .	0.40	0.39	0.37
Foreign exchange . . .	119.68	94.60	177.50
Total	123.29	n.a.	n.a.

* Valued at market-related prices.

Source: IMF, *International Financial Statistics*.

MONEY SUPPLY ('000 million francs CFA at 31 December)

	1997	1998	1999
Currency outside banks . .	78.81	73.62	68.25
Demand deposits at commercial and development banks .	27.11	25.38	27.80
Total money (incl. others) . .	108.47	99.75	96.67

Source: IMF, *International Financial Statistics*.

COST OF LIVING (Consumer Price Index for African households in N'Djamena; base: 1995 = 100)

	1998	1999	2000
All items	133.1	124.1	128.8

Source: IMF, *International Financial Statistics*.

NATIONAL ACCOUNTS
('000 million francs CFA at current prices)
Expenditure on the Gross Domestic Product

	1996	1997	1998
Government final consumption expenditure	100.4	97.0	94.1
Private final consumption expenditure	752.9	803.9	887.8
Increase in stocks . . .	13.0	16.8	5.0
Gross fixed capital formation . .	98.8	128.0	144.6
Total domestic expenditure .	965.2	1,045.7	1,131.5
Exports of goods and services .	144.7	155.7	180.5
Less Imports of goods and services .	279.2	313.5	327.8
GDP in purchasers' values . .	830.7	887.9	984.2

Gross Domestic Product by Economic Activity

	1996	1997	1998
Agriculture*	285.0	306.1	348.6
Mining and quarrying† . . .	23.5	25.8	28.1
Electricity, gas and water. . .	5.4	5.5	5.4
Manufacturing	92.5	110.6	117.8
Construction	13.8	14.4	15.4
Wholesale and retail trade, restaurants and hotels . .	204.2	214.2	239.9
Transport and communications			
Public administration . . .	98.6	95.0	104.7
Other services	85.2	91.0	92.1
GDP at factor cost	808.2	862.6	951.9
Indirect taxes, *less* subsidies . .	22.5	25.3	32.3
GDP in purchasers' values . .	830.7	887.9	984.2

* Excluding fishing.   † Including fishing.

Source: IMF, *Chad: Recent Economic Developments* (May 1999).

BALANCE OF PAYMENTS ('000 million francs CFA)

	1996	1997	1998
Exports of goods f.o.b. . . .	113.1	123.2	145.3
Imports of goods f.o.b. . . .	−148.0	−165.5	−175.0
Trade balance	−34.9	−42.3	−29.7
Exports of services . . .	31.6	32.5	35.2
Imports of services . . .	−131.2	−148.0	−152.8
Balance on goods and services	−134.4	−157.8	−147.2
Other income (net) . . .	−16.6	−17.0	−17.9
Balance on goods, services and income	−151.0	−174.8	−165.1
Current transfers (net) . . .	50.0	41.6	43.5
Current balance	−101.0	−133.2	−121.6
Capital account	36.4	36.1	28.4
Direct investment (net) . . .	7.6	9.2	15.8
Other investment (net) . . .	64.1	75.4	81.9
Net errors and omissions . . .	13.7	6.3	−9.6
Overall balance	20.7	−6.2	−5.1

Source: IMF, *Chad: Recent Economic Developments* (May 1999).

External Trade

PRINCIPAL COMMODITIES

Imports c.i.f. (US $'000)	1995
Food and live animals	41,182
Cereals and cereal preparations	16,028
Rice (semi- or wholly-milled)	4,589
Wheat and meslin (unmilled)	8,945
Sugar, sugar preparations and honey . . .	17,078
Sugar and honey	16,970
Refined sugars, etc..	16,825
Beverages and tobacco	7,175
Beverages	4,526
Mineral fuels, lubricants, etc.	38,592
Petroleum, petroleum products, etc..	38,574
Refined petroleum products	38,551
Motor spirit (gasoline) and other light oils . .	6,490
Kerosene and other medium oils . . .	8,456
Gas oils	23,318
Chemicals and related products	15,507
Medicinal and pharmaceutical products . . .	7,789
Medicaments (incl. veterinary medicaments) . .	6,351
Basic manufactures	26,190
Non-metallic mineral manufactures	7,654
Lime, cement and fabricated construction materials .	6,394
Cement	6,247
Metal manufactures	8,804

Imports c.i.f. (US $'000) — *continued*	1995
Machinery and transport equipment . . .	51,246
General industrial machinery, equipment and parts . .	8,175
Telecommunications and sound recording and reproducing	
equipment and parts	4,572
Telecommunications equipment and parts . .	4,375
Road vehicles (incl. air-cushion vehicles) and parts* . .	17,873
Motor vehicles for the transport of goods or materials,	
etc.	4,444
Lorries and trucks	4,338
Parts and accessories for cars, lorries, buses, etc.* .	8,253
Miscellaneous manufactured articles . . .	27,335
Professional, scientific and controlling instruments and	
apparatus	5,073
Printed matter	13,565
Postage stamps, banknotes, etc.	11,622
Total (incl. others)	215,171

* Excluding tyres, engines and electrical parts.

Source: UN, *International Trade Statistics Yearbook.*

Exports (million francs CFA)	1983
Live cattle	49.5
Meat	23.5
Fish	2.0
Oil-cake	8.1
Natron	8.1
Gums and resins	0.4
Hides and skins	16.6
Raw cotton	3,753.7
Total (incl. others)	4,120.0

Total exports (million francs CFA): 27,781 in 1985; 34,145 in 1986; 32,892 in 1987; 42,900 in 1988; 49,570 in 1989; 51,202 in 1990; 54,600 in 1991; 48,250 in 1992; 37,330 in 1993; 82,160 in 1994; 125,600 in 1995; 117,230 in 1996; 138,100 in 1997; 154,250 in 1998 (Source: Banque des Etats de l'Afrique Centrale).

Cotton exports ('000 million francs CFA): 26.8 in 1991; 25.3 in 1992.

PRINCIPAL TRADING PARTNERS

Imports c.i.f. (US $'000)	1995
Belgium-Luxembourg	4,771
Cameroon	33,911
Central African Repub.	3,010
China, People's Repub.	6,251
France	88,887
Germany	2,988
Italy	6,452
Japan	5,121
Malaysia	2,234
Netherlands	2,843
Nigeria	25,269
Spain	3,402
USA	13,966
Total (incl. others)	215,171

Source: UN, *International Trade Statistics Yearbook.*

Exports (million francs CFA)	1984	1985	1986
Cameroon	929	1,711	2,661
Central African Repub. . .	64	1,219	321
Congo, Democratic Repub. . .	125	5	n.a.
France	6,950	1,432	1,774
Nigeria	113	1,981	425
Sudan	8	47	101
Total (incl. others) . . .	8,231	6,446	5,374

Transport

ROAD TRAFFIC (motor vehicles in use at 31 December)

	1994	1995*	1996*
Passenger cars	8,720	9,700	10,560
Buses and coaches . . .	708	760	820
Lorries and vans	12,650	13,720	14,550
Tractors	1,413	1,500	1,580
Motorcycles and mopeds . .	1,855	2,730	3,640

* Estimates.

Source: International Road Federation, *World Road Statistics.*

CIVIL AVIATION (traffic on scheduled services*)

	1995	1996	1997
Kilometres flown (million) . .	3	3	3
Passengers carried ('000) . .	92	93	93
Passengers-km (million) . .	231	233	247
Total ton-km (million) . . .	37	37	39

* Including an apportionment of the traffic of Air Afrique.

Source: UN, *Statistical Yearbook.*

Tourism

	1996	1997	1998
Tourist arrivals ('000) . . .	8	9	11
Tourism receipts (US $ million) .	10	9	n.a.

Source: World Tourism Organization, *Yearbook of Tourism Statistics.*

Communications Media

	1995	1996	1997
Radio receivers ('000 in use) . .	1,570	1,620	1,670
Television receivers ('000 in use) .	9	9	10
Telephones ('000 main lines in use)	5	6	7
Telefax stations (number in use) .	174	175	185
Daily newspapers:			
Number	1	1	n.a.
Average circulation ('000 copies)	2	2	n.a.
Non-daily newspapers:			
Number	2	n.a.	n.a.
Average circulation ('000 copies)	10	n.a.	n.a.

Sources: UNESCO, *Statistical Yearbook*; UN *Statistical Yearbook.*

Education

(1996/97, unless otherwise indicated)

	Insti-tutions	Teachers	Students Males	Females	Total
Pre-primary* . .	24	67	938	735	1,673
Primary . . .	2,660†	10,151	447,685	233,224	680,909
Secondary:					
General . .	153†	2,598	77,622	19,389	97,011
Teacher training . .	6†	46	360	265	625
Vocational . .	12†	148	1,506	647	2,153
University-level† . .	n.a.	288	2,868‡	406‡	3,274‡

* 1994/95 figures; public education only.

† 1995/96 figures.

‡ Provisional figure.

Source: mainly UNESCO, *Statistical Yearbook.*

Directory

The Constitution

The Constitution of the Republic of Chad, which was adopted by national referendum on 31 March 1996, enshrines a unitary state. The President is elected for a term of five years by direct universal adult suffrage, and is restricted to a maximum of two terms in office. The Prime Minister, who is appointed by the President, nominates the Council of Ministers. The bicameral legislature includes a 125-member Assemblée nationale, which is elected by direct universal adult suffrage for a term of four years. Provision is also made for an upper legislative chamber, the Sénat, with one-third of members renewed every two years. The Constitution provides for an independent judicial system, with a High Court of Justice, and the establishment of a Constitutional Court and a High Council for Communication.

The Government

HEAD OF STATE

President and Commander-in-Chief of the Armed Forces: IDRISS DEBY (assumed office 4 December 1990; elected President 3 July 1996; re-elected 20 May 2001).

COUNCIL OF MINISTERS
(April 2001)

Prime Minister: NAGOUM YAMASSOUM.

Minister of Agriculture: MOCTAR MOUSSA MAHAMAT.

Minister of Economic Promotion and Development: MAHAMAT ALI HASSAN.

Minister of Foreign Affairs: MAHAMAT SALEH ANNADIF.

Minister of Mines, Energy and Petroleum: ALBERT PAHIM.

Minister of Finance: MAHAMAT LOUANI.

Minister of National Defence and Reintegration: MAHAMAT NOURI.

Minister of the Interior and Security: ABDERAMANE MOUSSA.

Minister of Justice, Keeper of the Seals: MAHAMAT AHMAT ALHABO.

Minister of Livestock: WEIDING ASSI ASSOUÉ.

Minister of Public Health: FATIME KIMTO.

Minister of Higher Education: RAMAT ISSAKA.

Minister of National Education: ABDERAHIM BIREME HAMID.

Minister of Trade, Industry and Crafts: KALZEUBE PAHIMI.

Minister of Communications, Spokesperson for the Government: NADJO ABDELKARIM.

Minister of Social Welfare and the Family: MARIAM ATAHIR.

Minister of the Environment and Water Resources: OUMAR BOUKAR KADJALAMI.

Minister of Tourism Development: MAHAMAT AHMAT CHOUCOU.

Minister of the Civil Service, Labour, Employment Promotion and Modernization: ROUTOUANG YOMA GOLOM.

Minister of Public Works, Transport, Housing and Town Planning: MOUSSA MUSTAPHA TERAP.

Minister of Posts and Telecommunications: SALIBOU GARBA.

Minister of Culture, Youth and Sports: MOUSSA WAYOR.

Minister, Secretary-General of the Government, in charge of Relations with Parliament: DAVID HOUDEINGAR.

Minister-delegate to the Prime Minister, in charge of Decentralization: DJIMTIBAYE LAPIA.

In addition, there are six Secretaries of State.

MINISTRIES

Office of the President: BP 74, N'Djamena; tel. 51-44-37; fax 51-45-01.

Ministry of Agriculture: BP 441, N'Djamena; tel. 52-24-48; fax 52-51-19.

Ministry of the Civil Service, Labour, Employment Promotion and Modernization: BP 437, N'Djamena; tel. and fax 52-21-98.

Ministry of Communications: BP 154, N'Djamena; tel. 51-41-64; fax 51-60-94.

Ministry of Culture, Youth and Sports: N'Djamena.

Ministry of Economic Promotion and Development: N'Djamena.

Ministry of the Environment and Water Resources: N'Djamena.

Ministry of Finance: BP 144, N'Djamena; tel. 52-21-61; fax 52-49-08.

Ministry of Foreign Affairs: N'Djamena; tel. 51-50-82.

Ministry of Higher Education: N'Djamena

Ministry of the Interior and Security: N'Djamena.

Ministry of Justice: BP 426, N'Djamena; tel. 52-21-72; fax 52-21-39; e-mail justice@intnet.td.

Ministry of Livestock: N'Djamena; tel. 51-59-07.

Ministry of Mines, Energy and Petroleum: BP 94, N'Djamena; tel. 52-38-50; fax 52-25-65.

Ministry of National Defence and Reintegration: N'Djamena; tel. 51-58-89.

Ministry of National Education: N'Djamena.

Ministry of Posts and Telecommunications: BP 154, N'Djamena; tel. 52-41-64; fax 52-15-34; e-mail dabye@intnet.td.

Ministry of Public Health: N'Djamena; tel. 51-39-60.

Ministry of Public Works, Transport, Housing and Town Planning: BP 984, N'Djamena; tel. 52-37-67.

Ministry of Social Welfare and the Family: N'Djamena.

Ministry of Tourism Development: N'Djamena.

Ministry of Trade, Industry and Crafts: BP 458, N'Djamena; tel. 52-30-49; fax 52-27-33.

President and Legislature

PRESIDENT

Election, 20 May 2001*

Candidate	% of vote
IDRISS DEBY (MPS†)	67.35
NGARLEDJY YORONGAR (FAR)	13.94
SALEH KEBZABO (UNDR)	6.53
Gen. WADAL ABDELKADER KAMOUGUÉ (URD)	5.13
IBN OUMAR MAHAMAT SALEH (PLD)	2.79
KASSIRE DELWA KOUMAKOYE (RNDP)	2.22
Dr JEAN BAWOYEU ALINGUÉ (UDR)	2.05
Total	100.00

* Provisional results.
† In coalition with 27 other parties.

ASSEMBLÉE NATIONALE

President: Gen. WADAL ABDELKADER KAMOUGUÉ.

General Election, 5 January and 23 February 1997

Party	Seats
Mouvement patriotique du salut	65
Union pour le renouveau et la démocratie	29
Union nationale pour le développement et le renouveau	15
Union pour la démocratie et la République	4
Parti pour la liberté et le développement	3
Rassemblement pour la démocratie et le progrès	3
Other opposition parties	6
Total	125

Note: The Constitution also makes provision for an upper house of the legislature, the Sénat.

Political Organizations

Legislation permitting the operation of political associations, subject to official registration, took effect in October 1991. In late 2000 there were about 60 active political organizations, of which the most important are listed below.

Action tchadienne pour l'unité et le socialisme (ACTUS): N'Djamena; f. 1992; Leader Dr FIDÈLE MOUNGAR.

Alliance nationale pour la démocratie et le développement (ANDD): BP 4066, N'Djamena; tel. 51-46-72; f. 1992; Leader SALIBOU GARBA.

Comité de sursaut national pour la paix et la démocratie (CSNPD): fmr dissident faction; obtained legal recognition in Sept. 1994; Leader (vacant).

Concertation nationale pour la démocratie sociale (CNDS): N'Djamena; Leader ADOUM MOUSSA SEIF.

Front d'action pour le renouveau (FAR): Leader NGARLEDJY YORONGAR.

Mouvement patriotique du salut (MPS): N'Djamena; f. 1990 as a coalition of several opposition movements; other opposition groups joined during the Nov. 1990 offensive against the regime of Hissène Habré, and following the movement's accession to power in Dec. 1990; Chair. MALDOM BADA ABBAS; Sec.-Gen. MAHAMAT SALEH AHMAT.

Mouvement pour la démocratie et le socialisme du Tchad (MDST): N'Djamena; Leader Dr SALOMON NGARBAYE TOMBALBAYE.

Parti pour la liberté et le développement (PLD): N'Djamena; f. 1993; Leader IBN OUMAR MAHAMAT SALEH.

Rassemblement pour la démocratie et le progrès (RDP): N'Djamena; f. 1992; Leader LOL MAHAMAT CHOUA.

Rassemblement pour le développement et le progrès: f. 1992; Leader MAMADOU BISSO.

Rassemblement national pour la démocratie et le progrès (RNDP): N'Djamena; f. 1992; Pres. KASSIRE DELWA KOUMAKOYE.

Union pour la démocratie et la République (UDR): N'Djamena; f. 1992; Leader Dr JEAN BAWOYEU ALINGUÉ.

Union nationale pour le développement et le renouveau (UNDR): Leader SALEH KEBZABO.

Union pour le renouveau et la démocratie (URD): BP 92, N'Djamena; tel. 51-44-23; fax 51-41-87; f. 1992; Leader Gen. WADAL ABDELKADER KAMOUGUÉ.

A number of unregistered dissident groups (some based abroad) are also active. These 'politico-military' organizations include the **Conseil démocratique révolutionnaire (CDR)**, led by ACHEIKH IBN OUMAR; the **Front de libération nationale du Tchad (FROL-INAT)**, based in Algeria and led by GOUKOUNI OUEDDEI; the **Front national du Tchad (FNT)**, based in Sudan and led by Dr FARIS BACHAR; the **Front national du Tchad renové (FNTR)**, led by AHMAT YACOUB (internet www.maxpages.com/tchad); the **Mouvement pour la démocratie et le développement (MDD)**, led by ISSA FAKI MAHAMAT; the **Mouvement pour la démocratie et la justice au Tchad (MDJT)**, led by YOUSSOUF TOGOIMI; the **Mouvement pour l'unité et la République (MUR**; f. 2000 as a break-away faction of the MDD), led by GAILETH GATOUL BOURKOUMANDAH; and the **Union des forces démocratiques (UFD)**, led by Dr MAHAMAT NAHOUR. In December 1999 13 'politico-military' organizations formed the **coordination des movements armés et partis politiques de l'opposition (CMAP)**, led by ANTOINE BANGUI.

Under the terms of a peace agreement signed by the Chadian Government and the **Forces armées pour la République fédérale (FARF)** in April 1997 (the terms of which were renewed in May 1998), the FARF was to cease armed activities and was to be legalized as a political organization. The FARF, reportedly under the leadership of DIENAMBAYE BARDE, rallied to the MPS in November 1998. The former MDD leader, MOUSSA MEDELLA MAHAMAT, signed a reconciliation document, on behalf of the movement, with the Government in July 1999, but the accord was denounced by the present MDD leadership. In June 2000 the Government signed a peace agreement with the **Résistance armée contre les forces antidémocratiques (RAFAD)**, led by ADOUM MOUSSA SEIF.

Diplomatic Representation

EMBASSIES IN CHAD

Algeria: N'Djamena; tel. 52-38-15; Ambassador: BOUBAKEUR OGAB.

Central African Republic: BP 115, N'Djamena; tel. 51-32-06; Ambassador: DAVID NGUINDO.

China (Taiwan): BP 1150, N'Djamena; tel. 52-44-05; fax 52-44-02; Ambassador: CHIU JONG-JEN.

Congo, Democratic Republic: ave du 20 août, BP 910, N'Djamena; tel. 51-59-35; Ambassador: (vacant).

Egypt: BP 1094, N'Djamena; tel. 51-36-60; Ambassador: AZIZ M. NOUR EL-DIN.

France: BP 431, N'Djamena; tel. 51-25-75; fax 52-28-55; e-mail amba-france@intnet.td; Ambassador: JACQUES COURBIN.

Germany: ave Félix Eboué, BP 893, N'Djamena; tel. 51-62-02; fax 51-48-00; Chargé d'affaires a.i.: DIETER FREUND.

Holy See: BP 490, N'Djamena; tel. 52-31-15; fax 52-38-27; Apostolic Nuncio: Most Rev. JOSEPH CHENNOTH, Titular Archbishop of Milevi.

Korea, Democratic People's Republic: N'Djamena; Ambassador: RI YONG HAK.

Libya: N'Djamena; Sec. of People's Bureau: GHAYTH SALIM.

Nigeria: 35 ave Charles de Gaulle, BP 752, N'Djamena; tel. 51-24-98; Chargé d'affaires a.i.: A. M. ALIYU BIU.

Sudan: BP 45, N'Djamena; tel. 51-34-97; Ambassador: TAHA MAK-KAWI.

USA: ave Félix Eboué, BP 413, N'Djamena; tel. 51-70-09; fax 51-56-54; e-mail paschallrc@ndjamenab.us-state.gov; internet usembassy.state.gov/posts/cd1/wwwhindex.html: CHRISTOPHER E. GOLDTHWAITE.

Judicial System

The highest judicial authority is the Supreme Court. There is also a Constitutional Council, with final jurisdiction in matters of state. The legal structure also comprises the Court of Appeal, and Magistrate and Criminal Courts. Under the terms of the Constitution adopted in 1996, a High Court of Justice was to be established.

President of the Supreme Court: AHMAT BATCHIRET.

President of the Constitutional Council: NAGOUM YAMASSOUM.

Religion

It is estimated that some 50% of the population are Muslims and about 30% Christians. Most of the remainder follow animist beliefs.

ISLAM

Conseil Suprème des Affaires Islamiques: POB 1101, N'Djamena; tel. 51-81-80; fax 52-58-84.

Head of the Islamic Community: Imam MOUSSA IBRAHIM.

CHRISTIANITY
The Roman Catholic Church

Chad comprises one archdiocese and six dioceses. At 31 December 1998 Roman Catholics numbered an estimated 463,103 (about 6.8% of the total population).

Bishops' Conference: Conférence Episcopale du Tchad, BP 456, N'Djamena; tel. 51-44-43; fax 51-28-60; f. 1991; Pres. Most Rev. CHARLES VANDAME, Archbishop of N'Djamena.

Archbishop of N'Djamena: Most Rev. CHARLES VANDAME, Archevêché, BP 456, N'Djamena; tel. 51-74-44; fax 52-50-51; e-mail diocndja@intnet.td.

Protestant Churches

Entente des Eglises et Missions Evangéliques au Tchad: BP 2006, N'Djamena; tel. and fax 51-53-93; an asscn of churches and missions working in Chad; includes Assemblées Chrétiennes au Tchad (ACT), Eglise Evangélique des Frères au Tchad (EEFT), Eglise Evangélique au Tchad (EET), Eglise Fraternelle Luthérienne au Tchad (EFLT); also five assoc. mems.

BAHÁ'Í FAITH

National Spiritual Assembly: BP 181, N'Djamena; tel. 51-47-05; mems in 1,125 localities.

The Press

Al-Watan: BP 407, N'Djamena; tel. 51-57-96; weekly; Editor-in-Chief MOUSSA NDORKOÏ.

Bulletin Mensuel de Statistiques du Tchad: BP 453, N'Djamena; monthly.

Comnat: BP 731, N'Djamena; tel. 51-46-75; fax 51-46-71; quarterly; publ. by Commission Nationale Tchadienne for UNESCO.

Contact: N'Djamena; f. 1989; current affairs; Dir KOULAMALO SOU-RADJ.

Info-Tchad: BP 670, N'Djamena; tel. 51-58-67; news bulletin issued by Agence Tchadienne de Presse; daily; French.

Informations Economiques: BP 458, N'Djamena; publ. by the Chambre de Commerce, d'Agriculture et d'Industrie; weekly.

N'Djamena Hebdo: BP 760, N'Djamena; tel. 51-53-14; fax 52-14-98; internet www.chez.com/ndjamenahebdo; weekly; Arabic and French; f. 1989; Dir YALDET BÉGOTO OULATAR; Editor-in-Chief DIEU-DONNÉ DJONABAYE.

L'Observateur: BP 2031, N'Djamena; tel. and fax 51-80-05; fortnightly; Editor-in-Chief SINGA GALI KOUMBA.

Le Progrès: BP 3055, N'Djamena; tel. 51-55-86; fax 51-02-56; f. 1993; daily.

NEWS AGENCIES

Agence Tchadienne de Presse (ATP): BP 670, N'Djamena; tel. 52-37-74; f. 1966.

Agence France-Presse (AFP): N'Djamena; tel. 51-54-71; Correspondent ALDOM NADJI TITO.

Publisher

Government Publishing House: BP 453, N'Djamena.

Broadcasting and Communications

TELECOMMUNICATIONS

Office Nationale des Postes et des Télécommunications (ONPT): BP 1132, N'Djamena; tel. 52-10-13; fax 52-10-12; state-owned; Dir-Gen. ALHOKI BLAMKAKOU.

The ONPT was to be reorganized into two structures, the **Société des Télécommunications du Tchad (SOTE—TCHAD)** and the **Société Tchadienne des Postes et de l'Epargne (STPE)**, prior to the privatization of the telecommunications sector. A tender was issued in late 1998 for a licence to operate the country's first cellular telephone network.

Société des Télécommunications Internationales du Tchad (TIT): BP 1132, N'Djamena; tel. 52-14-41; fax 52-14-05; internet www.tit.td; f. 1976; 52% state-owned, 43% owned by France Câbles et Radio; privatization pending; Man. Dir MAHAMAT S. ANNADIF.

BROADCASTING

Radio

Radiodiffusion Nationale Tchadienne (RNT): BP 892, N'Djamena; tel. 51-53-53; f. 1957; state-controlled; programmes in French, Arabic and eight vernacular languages; there are four transmitters; Dir KHAMIS TOGOÏ.

Radio Abéché: BP 36, Abéché; tel. 69-81-49; Dir DIMANANGAR DJAINTA.

Radio Moundou: BP 122, Moundou; tel. 69-13-22; daily programmes in French, Sara and Arabic; Dir DIMANANGAR DJAÏNTA.

Radio Sarh: BP 270, Sarh; tel. 68-13-61; daily programmes in French, Sara and Arabic; Dir BIANA FOUDA NACTOUANDI.

Television

Télé-Chad: Commission for Information and Culture, BP 748, N'Djamena; tel. 52-29-23; fax 52-51-63; state-controlled; broadcasts c. 12 hours per week in French and Arabic; Dir HOURMADJI HOUSSA DOUMGOR.

Finance

(cap. = capital; res = reserves; m. = million; br. = branch; amounts in francs CFA)

BANKING

Central Bank

Banque des Etats de l'Afrique Centrale (BEAC): BP 50, N'Djamena; tel. 52-41-76; fax 51-44-87; HQ in Yaoundé, Cameroon; f. 1973; bank of issue for mem. states of the Communauté économique et monétaire de l'Afrique centrale (CEMAC, fmrly Union douanière et économique de l'Afrique centrale), comprising Cameroon, the Central African Repub., Chad, the Repub. of the Congo, Equatorial Guinea and Gabon); cap. 45,000m., res 172,198m., total assets 1,407,908m. (Dec. 1999); Gov. JEAN-FÉLIX MAMALEPOT; Dir in Chad MAHAMAD AMINE BEN BARKA; 2 brs.

Other Banks

Banque de Développement du Tchad (BDT): rue Capitaine Ohrel, BP 19, N'Djamena; tel. 52-28-29; fax 52-33-18; e-mail exp .bdt@intnet.td; f. 1962; 25.9% state-owned; transfer to private ownership pending; cap. and res 3,386m., total assets 13,536m. (Dec. 1998); Pres. MAHAMAT AHMAT SALEH; Dir-Gen. ABDESSIT MAHAMAT.

Banque Internationale pour l'Afrique au Tchad (BIAT): ave Charles de Gaulle, BP 87, N'Djamena; tel. 51-43-14; fax 51-23-45; e-mail biat@intnet.td; f. 1980; fmrly Banque Meridien BIAO Tchad; Dir-Gen. GILLES D'HALLUIN.

Financial Bank Tchad: ave Charles de Gaulle, BP 804, N'Djamena; tel. 52-33-89; fax 52-29-05; e-mail fbt@intnet.td; f. 1992; 97.9% owned by Financial BC SA (Switzerland); cap. and res 1,000m., total assets 9,675m. (Dec. 1998); Pres. RÉMY BAYSSET; Dir-Gen. PIERRE LECLAIRE.

Société Générale Tchadienne de Banque (SGTB): 2–6 rue Robert Lévy, BP 461, N'Djamena; tel. 52-28-76; fax 52-37-13; internet www.socgen.com; f. 1963; fmrly Banque Tchadienne de Crédit et de Dépôts; 30% owned by Société Générale, SA (France),

20% state-owned, cap. and res 2,189m., total assets 33,233m. (Dec. 1998); Pres. and Dir-Gen. CHEMI KOGRIMI; br. at Moundou.

Bankers' Organizations

Association Professionnelle des Banques au Tchad: 2–6 rue Robert Lévy, BP 461, N'Djamena; tel. 52-41-90; fax 52-17-13; Pres. CHEMI KOGRIMI.

Conseil National de Crédit: N'Djamena; f. 1965 to formulate a national credit policy and to organize the banking profession.

INSURANCE

Assureurs Conseils Tchadiens Cécar & Jutheau: BP 139, N'Djamena; tel. 52-21-15; fax 52-35-39; e-mail biliou.alikeke@intnet.td; Dir BILIOU ALI-KEKE.

Société Mutuelle d'Assurances des Cadres des Professions Libérales et des Indépandants (SMAC): N'Djamena; tel. 51-70-19; fax 51-70-61.

Société de Représentation d'Assurances et de Réassurances Africaines (SORARAF): N'Djamena; Dir Mme FOURNIER.

Société Tchadienne d'Assurances et de Réassurances (STAR): BP 914, N'Djamena; tel. 51-56-77; Dir PHILIPPE SABIT.

Trade and Industry

DEVELOPMENT ORGANIZATIONS

Agence Française de Développement: BP 478, N'Djamena; tel. 51-40-71; fax 51-28-31; fmrly Caisse Française de Développement; Dir JACBIE BATHANY.

Association Tchadienne pour le Développement: BP 470, Quartier Sabangali, N'Djamena; tel. 51-43-69; fax 51-89-23.

Mission Française de Coopération et d'Action Culturelle: BP 898, N'Djamena; tel. 52-42-87; fax 52-44-38; administers bilateral aid from France; Dir EDOUARD LAPORTE.

Office National de Développement Rural (ONDR): BP 896, N'Djamena; tel. 51-48-64; f. 1968; Dir MICKAEL DJIBRAEL.

Société pour le Développement de la Région du Lac (SOD-ELAC): BP 782, N'Djamena; tel. 51-35-03; f. 1967; cap. 180m. francs CFA; Pres. CHERIF ABDELWAHAB; Dir-Gen. MAHAMAT MOCTAR ALI.

CHAMBER OF COMMERCE

Chambre de Commerce, d'Industrie, d'Agriculture, des Mines et d'Artisanat: BP 458, N'Djamena; tel. 52-52-64; fax 52-14-98; f. 1935; fmrly Chambre Consulaire; Dir. YOUSSOUF ABASSALLAH; brs at Sarh, Moundou, Bol and Abéché.

TRADE ASSOCIATIONS

Office National des Céréales (ONC): BP 21, N'Djamena; tel. 51-37-31; f. 1978; production and marketing of cereals; Dir YBRAHIM MAHAMAT TIDEI; 11 regional offices.

Société Nationale de Commercialisation du Tchad (SON-ACOT): N'Djamena; f. 1965; cap. 150m. francs CFA; 76% state-owned; nat. marketing, distribution and import-export co; Man. Dir MARBROUCK NATROUD.

UTILITIES

Electricity and Water

Société Tchadienne d'Eau et d'Electricité (STEE): 11 rue du Colonel Largeau, BP 44, N'Djamena; tel. 51-28-81; fax 51-21-34; f. 1968; state-owned; transfer to private ownership pending; production and distribution of electricity and water; Pres. GOMON MAWATA WAKAG; Dir-Gen. ISMAEL MAHAMAT ADOUM.

TRADE UNIONS

Union des Syndicats du Tchad (UST): BP 1143, N'Djamena; tel. 51-76-72; f. 1988 by merger; Pres. DOMBAL DJIMBAGUE; Sec.-Gen. DJIBRINE ASSALI HAMDALLAH.

Groupement Professionnel de Transport Routier Tchadien: BP 326, N'Djamena; tel. 51-43-55.

Union des Transportateurs Tchadiens: BP 529, N'Djamena; tel. 51-45-27.

Transport

RAILWAYS

There are no railways in Chad. In 1962 the Governments of Chad and Cameroon signed an agreement to extend the Transcameroon railway from Ngaoundéré to Sarh, a distance of 500 km. Although the Transcameroon reached Ngaoundéré in 1974, its proposed extension into Chad remains indefinitely postponed.

ROADS

The total length of the road network in 1996 was an estimated 33,400 km, of which 7,880 km were principal roads and 5,380 km were secondary roads. There are also some 20,000 km of tracks suitable for motor traffic during the October–July dry season. The European Union is contributing to the construction of a highway connecting N'Djamena with Sarh and Léré, on the Cameroon border, and of a 400-km highway linking Moundou and Ngaoundéré.

Coopérative des Transportateurs Tchadiens (CTT): BP 336, N'Djamena; tel. 51-43-55; road haulage; Pres. SALEH KHALIFA; brs at Sarh, Moundou, Bangui (CAR), Douala and Ngaoundéré (Cameroon).

Société Générale d'Entreprise Routière (SGER): BP 175, N'Djamena; tel. and fax 51-55-12; devt and maintenance of roads; transfer to private ownership pending in 2000.

INLAND WATERWAYS

The Chari and Logone rivers, which converge to the south of N'Djamena, are navigable. These waterways connect Sarh with N'Djamena on the Chari and Bongor and Moundou with N'Djamena on the Logone.

CIVIL AVIATION

The international airport is at N'Djamena. There are also more than 40 smaller airfields.

Air Afrique: BP 466, N'Djamena; tel. 51-40-20; fax 51-38-59; see under Côte d'Ivoire.

Air Tchad: 27 ave du Président Tombalbaye, BP 168, N'Djamena; tel. 51-50-90; f. 1966; 98% govt-owned; liquidation pending; international charters and domestic passenger, freight and charter services; Chair. DJIBANGAR MADJIREBAYE; Man. Dir MAHAMAT NOURI.

Tourism

Chad's potential attractions for tourists include a variety of scenery from the dense forests of the south to the deserts of the north. Receipts from tourism in 1997 totalled an estimated US $9m. A total of 11,249 tourists visited Chad in 1998, compared with about 9,000 in 1997.

Direction du Tourisme: BP 86, N'Djamena; tel. 52-23-03; fax 52-22-61.

CHILE

Introductory Survey

Location, Climate, Language, Religion, Flag, Capital

The Republic of Chile is a long, narrow country lying along the Pacific coast of South America, extending from Peru and Bolivia in the north to Cape Horn in the far south. Isla de Pascua (Rapa Nui or Easter Island), about 3,780 km (2,350 miles) off shore, and several other small islands form part of Chile. To the east, Chile is separated from Argentina by the high Andes mountains. Both the mountains and the cold Humboldt Current influence the climate; between Arica in the north and Punta Arenas in the extreme south, a distance of about 4,000 km (2,500 miles), the average maximum temperature varies by no more than 13°C. Rainfall varies widely between the arid desert in the north and the rainy south. The language is Spanish. There is no state religion but the great majority of the inhabitants profess Christianity, and some 79% are adherents of the Roman Catholic Church. The national flag (proportions 3 by 2) is divided horizontally: the lower half is red, while the upper half has a five-pointed white star on a blue square, at the hoist, with the remainder white. The capital is Santiago.

Recent History

Chile was ruled by Spain from the 16th century until its independence in 1818. For most of the 19th century it was governed by a small oligarchy of landowners. Chile won the War of the Pacific (1879–83) against Peru and Bolivia. The greater part of the 20th century was characterized by the struggle for power between right- and left-wing forces.

In September 1970 Dr Salvador Allende Gossens, the Marxist candidate of Unidad Popular (a coalition of five left-wing parties, including the Partido Comunista de Chile), was elected to succeed Eduardo Frei Montalva, a Christian Democrat who was President between 1964 and 1970. Allende promised to transform Chilean society by constitutional means, and imposed an extensive programme of nationalization. The Government failed to obtain a congressional majority in the elections of March 1973 and encountered a deteriorating economic situation as well as an intensification of violent opposition to its policies. Accelerated inflation led to food shortages and there were repeated clashes between pro- and anti-Government activists. The armed forces finally intervened in September 1973. President Allende died during the coup. The Congreso (Congress) was subsequently dissolved, all political activity banned and strict censorship introduced. The military Junta dedicated itself to the eradication of Marxism and the reconstruction of Chile, and its leader, Gen. Augusto Pinochet Ugarte, became Supreme Chief of State in June 1974 and President in December. The Junta was widely criticized abroad for its repressive policies and violations of human rights. Critics of the regime were tortured and imprisoned, and several thousand were abducted or 'disappeared'. Some of those who had been imprisoned were released, as a result of international pressure, and sent into exile.

In September 1976 three constitutional acts were promulgated with the aim of creating an 'authoritarian democracy'. All political parties were banned in March 1977, when the state of siege was extended. Following a UN General Assembly resolution, adopted in December 1977, which condemned the Government for violating human rights, President Pinochet organized a referendum in January 1978 to seek endorsement of the regime's policies. Since more than 75% of the voters supported the President in his defence of Chile 'in the face of international aggression', the state of siege (in force since 1973) was ended and was replaced by a state of emergency.

At a plebiscite held in September 1980, 67% of voters endorsed a new Constitution, drafted by the Government, although dubious electoral practices were allegedly employed. The new Constitution was described as providing a 'transition to democracy' but, although President Pinochet ceased to be head of the armed forces, additional clauses allowed him to maintain his firm hold on power until 1989. The new Constitution became effective from March 1981. Political parties, which were still officially outlawed, began to re-emerge, and in July 1983 five moderate parties formed a coalition, the 'Alianza Democrática', which advocated a return to democratic rule within 18 months. A left-wing coalition was also created.

In February 1984 the Council of State, a government-appointed consultative body, began drafting a law to legalize political parties and to prepare for elections in 1989. Despite the Government's strenuous attempts to eradicate internal opposition through the introduction of anti-terrorist legislation and extensive security measures, a campaign of explosions and public protests continued throughout 1984 and 1985. A number of protesters were killed in violent clashes with security forces during this period, and many opposition leaders and trade unionists were detained and sent into internal exile.

Throughout 1986 President Pinochet's regime came under increasing attack from the Roman Catholic Church, guerrilla organizations (principally the Frente Patriótico Manuel Rodríguez—FPMR) and international critics, including the US administration, which had previously refrained from condemning the regime's notorious record of violations of human rights. In September the FPMR made an unsuccessful attempt to assassinate President Pinochet. The regime's immediate response was to impose a state of siege throughout Chile, under which leading members of the opposition were detained and strict censorship was introduced. One consequence of the state of siege was the reappearance of right-wing 'death squads', which were implicated in a series of murders following the assassination attempt.

By mid-1987 President Pinochet had clearly indicated his intention to remain in office beyond 1989 by securing the presidential candidacy to be rejected or approved by the same plebiscite which would decide the future electoral timetable; a cabinet reshuffle in July enabled him to appoint staunch supporters of his policies. By mid-1988 several political parties and opposition groups had established the Comando por el No to co-ordinate the campaign for the anti-Government vote at the forthcoming referendum. The hopes of the opposition were encouraged by the high level of popular registration for the plebiscite and by the Government's repeal, in August, of the states of exception, which had prohibited opposition groups from organizing public rallies. Pinochet was named by the Junta as the single candidate at the plebiscite, scheduled for 5 October. Despite reports of electoral malpractice, the plebiscite took place without major incident. The official result recorded 54.7% of the votes cast for the anti-Pinochet campaign, and 43.1% for the President. Following the plebiscite, the opposition made repeated demands for changes to the Constitution, in order to accelerate the democratic process, and sought to initiate discussions with the armed forces. However, President Pinochet rejected the opposition's proposals, and affirmed his intention to remain in office until March 1990.

In mid-1989 Patricio Aylwin Azócar, a lawyer and former senator who had been a vociferous supporter of the 'no' vote in the October 1988 plebiscite, emerged as the sole presidential candidate for the centre-left Concertación de los Partidos de la Democracia (CPD, formerly the Comando por el No), an alliance of 17 parties, including the Partido Demócrata Cristiano (PDC), of which Aylwin had hitherto been President. Throughout 1989 the election campaign was dominated by demands from both the CPD and right-wing parties for constitutional reform, and by the ensuing lengthy negotiations with Carlos Cáceres Contreras, the Minister of the Interior. A document detailing 54 amendments (including the legalization of Marxist political parties) ratified by the Junta was finally accepted by the opposition, with some reservations, and the constitutional reforms (see p. 1015) were approved by 85.7% of voters in a national referendum in July 1989.

The electoral campaign was conducted amidst intermittent outbursts of political violence and government intervention. Uncertainty regarding President Pinochet's own intentions concerning the forthcoming elections was finally dispelled in mid-1989, when he dismissed the possibility of his candidacy as unconstitutional, but reiterated his intention to continue as Commander-in-Chief of the Army for at least four years. Opposition leaders interpreted subsequent actions by the Government (including the implementation of a law providing for the autonomy of the Banco Central de Chile, the appointment of directors to state-owned companies with mandates of up to 10 years and curbs on the Government's power to remove state officials from their posts) as an attempt by the President to retain a degree of influence beyond his term of office.

The presidential and congressional elections were conducted on 14 December 1989. Patricio Aylwin Azócar of the centre-left CPD secured 55.2% of the valid votes cast in the presidential election, thus achieving a clear victory over the former Minister of Finance, Hernán Büchi Buc, who was supported by the Government and won 29.4%. The transfer of power took place on 11 March. Two members of the outgoing Junta remained as commanders of the air force and police.

Having failed to obtain the support of the two-thirds' majority in the Congreso necessary to amend the 1981 Constitution significantly, Aylwin's new CPD administration was forced to reconcile attempts to fulfil campaign promises as quickly as possible with the need to adopt a conciliatory approach towards more right-wing parties in the Congreso. Agreement was reached almost immediately on a series of modifications to the tax laws, but attempts to amend existing legislation considered repressive by the new administration (including the death penalty and provisions for the censorship of the press) were less successful.

In April 1990 the Government created the National Commission for Truth and Reconciliation (Comisión Nacional de Verdad y Reconciliación—CNVR) to document and investigate alleged violations of human rights during the previous administration. Although Pinochet, before leaving office, had provided for the impunity of the former military Junta with regard to abuses of human rights, it was suggested by human rights organizations that such safeguards might be circumvented by indicting known perpetrators of atrocities on charges of 'crimes against humanity', a provision which gained considerable public support following the discovery, during 1990, of a number of mass graves containing the remains of political opponents of the 1973–90 military regime. The army High Command openly condemned the Commission for undermining the prestige of the armed forces and attempting to contravene the terms of a comprehensive amnesty declared in 1978. Although a new accord between military leaders and the Government-Elect had been negotiated in January 1990 (whereby the role of the armed forces redefined as essentially subservient to the Ministry of Defence), relations between the new Government and the army High Command remained tense. Pinochet became the focus for widespread disaffection with the military élite, but resisted repeated demands for his resignation, reiterating his intention to continue as Commander-in-Chief of the Army until 1997.

Throughout 1990 and 1991 escalating public and political antagonism towards the former military leadership was fuelled by further revelations of abuses of human rights and financial corruption, and erupted into widespread popular outrage and renewed political violence following the publication, in March 1991, of the findings of the CNVR The report documented the deaths of 2,279 alleged political opponents of the former regime who were executed, died as a result of torture or disappeared (and were presumed to be dead) in 1973–90. In accordance with President Aylwin's recommendation that the report should foster national reconciliation and fulfil an expositionary rather than judicial function, those responsible for the deaths were identified only by the institutions to which they belonged. However, President Aylwin pledged full government co-operation for families wishing to pursue private prosecutions. The report concluded that the military Government had embarked upon a 'systematic policy of extermination' of its opponents through the illegal activities of the covert military intelligence agency, Dirección de Inteligencia Nacional (Dina), and was also highly critical of the Chilean judiciary for failing to protect the rights of individuals by refusing thousands of petitions for habeas corpus submitted by human rights lawyers. Later in the month, Pinochet publicly denounced the document and declared his opposition to government plans, to make material reparation to the families of the victims named in the report.

In November 1992, following a prolonged investigation, former Dina officials Gen. Manuel Contreras and Col. Pedro Espinoza were charged with the murder of Orlando Letelier, a former cabinet minister (and Chile's ambassador to the USA during the government of Salvador Allende in the early 1970s), who was assassinated, together with an associate, by a car bomb in Washington, DC, in 1976. (In November 1993 Contreras and Espinoza received prison sentences of seven and six years, respectively. An appeal was rejected by the Supreme Court in May 1995, although their sentences were reduced by 15 months as a result of a Supreme Court ruling on technicalities.) In October 1999 the Supreme Court granted an Italian court permission to pursue the extradition of Contreras—on completion of his sentence in Chile—on charges connected to the murders of Chilean politician Bernardo Leighton and his wife in Italy in 1975. Hopes that this development might herald an end to the apparent impunity of the former military regime were somewhat frustrated, however, following the decision of the Supreme Court, announced later in the month, to withdraw charges, recently brought against former police chief and Junta member, César Mendoza Durán, of complicity in the kidnap and murder of three members of the Partido Comunista de Chile (PCCh) in 1985. (In March 1994 15 former members of the subsequently-disbanded paramilitary police intelligence unit, Dicomcar, were sentenced to varying terms of imprisonment, having been convicted on charges connected with the murders in July 1993.) Furthermore, in December 2000 the Supreme Court rejected an Italian request for the extradition of Contreras.

Notwithstanding increasing frustration at the Government's reluctance or inability to bring to justice the perpetrators of the atrocities documented in the report, the conclusions of the CNVR were widely welcomed. However, following the publication of the report, a series of terrorist attacks by left-wing extremists against right-wing opponents threatened to undermine the process of national reconciliation. Fears of an escalation in extremist violence were partially dispelled, however, by the announcement, in late May 1991, of the FPMR's intention to renounce its armed struggle and join the political mainstream as the Movimiento Patriótico Manuel Rodríguez.

In November 1991, as part of the new Government's commitment to political decentralization, the Congreso approved constitutional amendments to local government statutes, which provided for the replacement of centrally-appointed local officials with directly-elected representatives. Elections to the 326 municipalities in June 1992 demonstrated clear public endorsement of the ruling coalition, which received some 53% of the votes, compared with 29% for the right-wing opposition. However, the considerable right-wing opposition in the Congreso continued to frustrate Aylwin's attempts to enact legislation. Proposals to accelerate the prosecution of military personnel accused of human rights abuses, while safeguarding their anonymity, put forward by the President in August 1993, were rejected by the right as ill-considered and precipitate, while left-wing groups challenged the concessionary nature of the legislation, with regard to the military. In September Aylwin was forced to withdraw the proposals from the Congreso, following a declaration of opposition to the legislation, made by two member parties of the ruling coalition, in response to the petitions of human rights organizations.

A presidential election, held on 11 December 1993, was won by the CPD candidate Eduardo Frei Ruiz-Tagle, a PDC senator, with 58% of the votes cast, ahead of Arturo Alessandri Besa, the candidate of the right-wing coalition, the Unión para el Progreso de Chile (UPC), who received 24% of the votes. However, the ruling coalition failed to make significant gains at concurrently conducted congressional elections, attributing the disappointing results to the binomial electoral system, which requires each party to secure two-thirds of the votes in each district for the successful election of its two candidates to the legislature. Frei's electoral campaign had identified the need for increased spending on health and education, the consolidation of municipalities, and greater support for small businesses. In February 1994 formal congressional endorsement was secured for constitutional reform whereby the length of the non-renewable presidential term would be henceforth fixed at six years.

On 11 March 1994 Frei assumed the presidency. Some days later he identified the immediate aims of his presidency as the alleviation of poverty, the elimination of corrupt government, and the fostering of significant economic growth. However, the President's affirmation of Pinochet's right to remain in office until 1997, appeared to compromise his pre-election demands for greater powers for the executive to nominate and remove the military High Command. In August 1994 Frei presented several constitutional reform proposals to the Congreso, including the abolition of the nine appointed senators (installed by the former military regime) and the introduction of an electoral system based on proportional representation (to replace the unrepresentative binomial system). However, Frei encountered the same level of opposition to constitutional reform (particularly from the right and from the upper house), that had undermined most attempts at constitutional amendment made by the previous administration.

In August 1995 a number of congressional bills, presented by the President as a crucial step towards national reconciliation, sought once again to remove the institutionalized influence of the military High Command (implemented by the outgoing military regime) and to accelerate the prosecution of armed forces personnel implicated in abuses of human rights by the report of the CNVR.

In November 1995 the Government secured the support of the opposition Renovación Nacional (RN) for revised proposals for new legislation relating to human rights and constitutional reform. However, the compromised nature of the agreement provoked considerable disaffection within the RN, and within the opposition UPC alliance in general, which was effectively dissolved following the departure of the Unión Demócrata Independiente (UDI) and the Unión de Centro-Centro (UCC) in protest at the actions of the RN. Concern was also expressed by members of the Partido Socialista (PS—within the ruling coalition) that the human rights legislation had been severely compromised.

During 1997 efforts by the Government to abolish the designated seats in the Senado were intensified, in response to Pinochet's stated intention to assume one of the seats assigned to former Presidents on retirement as Commander-in-Chief of the Army in March 1998, and by speculation that Pinochet would seek to exert considerable influence over future legislation by installing close military associates in other designated seats. In July 1997 the Senado rejected the Government's latest petition for reform to the system of appointments to the Senado.

In October 1997 it was announced that Maj.-Gen. Ricardo Izurieta, previously chief of defence staff, was to succeed Pinochet as Commander-in-Chief of the Army. The announcement was made amid a number of changes in the military High Command, which appeared to confirm earlier predictions that military influence was henceforth to be concentrated in the Senado, where it would bolster the political right wing.

Legislative elections to renew all 120 seats in the Cámara de Diputados and 20 of the elective seats in the Senado were conducted on 11 December 1997. The Government expressed satisfaction with the performance of parties within the governing Concertación, which secured 50.5% of the votes for deputies and retained (with 70 seats) a comfortable majority in the lower house. However, political analysts noted an erosion of support for the centre-left alliance (which had attracted 55.4% of votes for the lower house at the 1993 elections) and observed that the group's disappointing showing at elections to the Senado (where one seat was lost to the UDI) would make future attempts to effect constitutional reform as problematic as those undertaken in the past, particularly given the predominance of right-wing sympathizers among the nine designated senators (three nominated by the Supreme Court, four by the National Security Council—from a list of former chiefs of the armed forces—and two by the President), named later in December, who were scheduled to take their seats, together with the newly-elected senators, in March 1998. The elections revealed a shifting balance of power within the two major political groupings (support for the UDI, in particular, appeared to have superseded that for the RN within the Unión por Chile), and prompted renewed criticism of the country's binomial system of voting, the PCCh having failed to secure congressional representation despite attracting 8.4% and 6.9% of the votes to the upper and lower houses, respectively.

During December 1997 Pinochet reiterated his intention to assert his constitutional right, on retirement, to assume an *ex-officio* seat (for life) in the Senado (in addition to the nine designated senators). Expressing the opinion that to extend such an opportunity to Pinochet, who had headed an administration that had suspended all legislative processes for many years, would be wholly inappropriate, a number of centre-left politicians pledged to obstruct Pinochet's accession to the Senado. During January 1998 separate attempts were made by junior members of the Concertación (despite the declarations of senior members of the Government—anxious to ensure a peaceful exchange of offices in March—that such action was untimely and politically inconvenient) and by the leadership of the PCCh to begin judicial proceedings against Pinochet on charges related to gross abuses of human rights. Pinochet responded by announcing that he would not retire as Commander-in-Chief of the Army on 26 January, as previously suggested,

but would continue in office until 10 March, thereby preserving the immunity from prosecution provided by the position for as long as possible. Pinochet's announcement and a perceived entrenchment of the divergent interests of the Government and the armed forces prompted the resignation of the Minister of National Defence, Edmundo Pérez Yoma.

On 6 March 1998 the military High Command announced that Pinochet had been named an honorary commander-in-chief—a position with no historical precedent. On 11 March Pinochet assumed his seat in the Senado. A largely symbolic, and unsuccessful, attempt by 11 Concertación deputies to instigate a formal impeachment action against Pinochet was initiated in the Cámara in March. The motion's defeat prompted a crisis within the Concertación—the majority of PDC deputies having voted against it.

Preparations for the December presidential poll dominated domestic affairs during 1999. In January the RN and the UDI announced that they would present a joint presidential candidate to represent a new political alliance, the Alianza por Chile. In April Joaquín Lavín of the UDI was chosen as its candidate. In May a primary election to select the presidential candidate of the ruling Concertación was won by the former Minister of Public Works, Ricardo Lagos Escobas of the PS, with 71.3% of the estimated 1.4m. votes. The poor showing of the PDC candidate, Andrés Zaldívar, resulted in that party's adoption of a new reformist manifesto and the selection of a new national executive in July. Meanwhile, in June a minor cabinet reshuffle had been implemented, in which the recall to government of Eduardo Pérez Yoma as Minister of National Defence was widely interpreted as an attempt to foster improved relations with the armed forces.

Although it was widely expected that a clear margin favouring Lagos would emerge in the presidential poll held on 12 December 1999, he received 47.96% of the total votes cast, with Lavín obtaining 47.52%. Four minor candidates, among whom only Gladys Marín (representing the PCCh) received more than 3.0% of the poll, were eliminated. At the second round of voting, which took place on 16 January 2000, Lagos emerged victorious with 51.3% of the total votes, while Lavín received 48.7%. (Lavín was subsequently elected Mayor of Santiago in local elections held in October.) Lagos was sworn in as President on 11 March. He set out a reduction in unemployment and an increase in economic growth to be the main priorities for his new Government.

The treatment of the Mapuche indigenous peoples was another problem that faced the incoming administration. Mining, dam and forestry projects prompted violent protests by the Mapuche indigenous peoples who were campaigning for the restitution of their ancestral lands. In May 2000 a Historical Truth and New Deal Commission was created to consider the demands and needs of the Mapuche communities. However, in October the Cámara de Diputados rejected legislation, drafted over a period of nine years, that would have granted constitutional recognition to the Mapuche peoples.

As the controversy surrounding the detention of former President Pinochet in the United Kingdom continued (see below), domestic attentions were once again focused on the actions of the security forces during the post-1973 military regime. In June 1999 the arrest of five retired army officers (former commanders of a notorious élite army unit popularly referred to as the 'caravan of death') was ordered by an appeal court judge following renewed investigation into the disappearance of 72 political prisoners in the immediate aftermath of the 1973 military coup. The decision to arrest and prosecute the five men on charges of aggravated kidnapping was considered a breakthrough in Chilean judicial practice, since the absence of physical or documented evidence of the deaths of the prisoners meant that the crimes were technically in continuance, and that the accused men were not protected by the 1978 amnesty which guaranteed the impunity of military personnel for crimes committed before that year. In July 1999 the legality of the arrests was confirmed by the Supreme Court, and the indictment (and extradition from the USA) of a sixth former army officer was sought in connection with the case in August. Attempts by the Government to stem the resurgence of popular resentment of the past actions of the armed forces included, in August, the first direct discussions of the fate of the 'disappeared' between representatives of the armed forces and human rights organizations. However, tensions were exacerbated by the US National Security Council's declassification, in June, of some 5,800 CIA documents which recorded abuses of human rights during

1973–78, and appeared to support claims that the Chilean armed forces had falsified evidence purporting to demonstrate the threat posed by the Allende administration in order to justify the 1973 coup. A further 1,100 US documents were declassified in October 1999, and later in the same month a Chilean court issued an arrest warrant against Gen. (retd) Hugo Salas Wendel, a former Director of Dina, on charges of complicity in the killings in 1987 of 12 alleged members of a left-wing guerrilla group. Meanwhile, in September the Supreme Court had ruled in favour of criminal proceedings brought against two retired generals, Humberto Gordon Rubio and Roberto Schmied, earlier in the month for their alleged involvement in the murder of trade union leader Tucapel Jiménez in 1982. (Gordon Rubio, a former head of covert national intelligence operations, was the most senior military officer to date to face prosecution in Chile for crimes committed during the period of military rule.)

On 16 October 1998 former President Pinochet was arrested at a private clinic in London (United Kingdom), where he was receiving medical treatment for a back injury. The arrest was prompted by a preliminary request, made to the British authorities by Spanish magistrates, that Pinochet should be extradited to Spain to answer charges of 'genocide and terrorism' committed against some 4,000 individuals, including Spanish nationals, by his administration during 1973–90. A second Spanish request for Pinochet's extradition, received on 23 October 1998, cited his alleged involvement in institutionalized torture, conspiracy and the taking of hostages. On 28 October, however, a unanimous judgment of the British High Court rejected the Spanish petitions (presented by the British Crown Prosecution Service—CPS), largely on the ground that Pinochet enjoyed the 'sovereign immunity' of a former head of state. However, leave to appeal to the British House of Lords (the upper house of parliament and the supreme judicial authority) was granted to those wishing to pursue the extradition. In early November a formal request for extradition was made, although the Spanish Government (like the British Government) was anxious to emphasize its neutrality in what it considered to be a purely judicial affair.

In Chile the Frei Government protested that Pinochet's diplomatic immunity had been infringed by the British authorities, while the British Government denied Pinochet's status as an accredited diplomat. Meanwhile, supporters and opponents of Pinochet clashed during demonstrations in Santiago, and there were concerns that Pinochet's detention was threatening to undermine the country's delicate political and military balance.

The House of Lords' hearing of the extradition appeal concluded on 25 November 1998 with a 3–2 majority judgment by the panel of five senior law lords overturning the October ruling of the High Court on the basis that Pinochet's sovereign immunity did not extend to functions of office deemed unacceptable under international law. Despite the remonstrances of the Chilean Minister of Foreign Affairs, José Miguel Insulza, and pressure from the US Secretary of State, Madeleine Albright, to allow Pinochet to return to Chile, on 9 December the British Secretary of State for the Home Department, Jack Straw, authorized the start of formal extradition proceedings.

President Frei reacted angrily to Straw's decision, recalling the Chilean ambassador in London for consultations, and suspending travel permits to London and Madrid for Chilean nationals. Pinochet appeared in a British court in person for the first time on 11 December 1998, where initially he refused to recognize the competence of any court outside of Chile to try him with the 'lies of Spain'. Prior to the announcement of Straw's decision, meanwhile, it had emerged that Lord Hoffmann, one of the three law lords who had rejected Pinochet's immunity in the November ruling, had failed to declare potentially compromising personal links to the London-based human rights organization Amnesty International. A submission made by Pinochet's lawyers to the House of Lords, for a review of the November ruling in the light of this revelation, was accepted, and on 17 December a new panel of five senior judges unanimously suspended the November pronouncement and ordered the case to be re-submitted to a new appellate committee of seven law lords. Meanwhile, Pinochet remained under effective house arrest in the United Kingdom.

The new House of Lords' hearing began on 18 January 1999. In a change of defence strategy, the Chilean Government announced that it would be arguing that Pinochet's detention amounted to an infringement of Chilean sovereignty. The hearing ended on 4 February. The ruling of the appellate committee, announced on 24 March, supported the November 1998 pronouncement overturning Pinochet's claims to immunity, by

a majority of six to one. However, the committee also found that only charges relating to events subsequent to December 1988 (at which time the 1984 UN Convention against Torture and Other Cruel, Inhuman or Degrading Treatment or Punishment had entered into British law) should be considered relevant, thus reducing the number of draft charges brought by Spain from 33 to three. (In response, the Spanish magistrate responsible for the prosecution attempt, Baltasar Garzón, announced that additional pertinent charges, relating to crimes committed after December 1988 were being prepared.) In the light of this diminution of evidence, the committee urged Jack Straw to reconsider his decision to allow extradition proceedings to continue. Nevertheless, in April Straw confirmed his decision to allow the petition to proceed, contending that the serious nature of the three remaining charges from the original draft petition was sufficient to justify the extradition. Pinochet's legal representatives announced that they would challenge Straw's decision in the High Court, but this challenge was rejected on 27 May. Formal extradition proceedings were initiated in a London magistrates' court on 27 September. On 8 October the court found that Pinochet could be lawfully extradited to Spain to answer some 35 charges. Pinochet's lawyers made a formal appeal against the decision on 22 October.

Attempts by the Chilean Government to persuade Spain to allow international arbitration in the case against Pinochet had been dismissed by the Spanish judiciary in September, prompting the Chilean Minister of Foreign Affairs, Juan Gabriel Valdés, to announce that Chile would ask the International Court of Justice in The Hague (Netherlands) to examine Spain's claims to jurisdiction in the matter. Meanwhile, international media attention was riveted to the affair by the succession of prominent political figures (including George Bush, Margaret Thatcher and Dr Henry Kissinger) who expressed support for Pinochet's return to Chile, by the involvement of the Roman Catholic Church (in response to petitions from the Chilean Government, in November 1999 the Vatican had written to the British authorities requesting Pinochet's release in the interest of humanitarianism and of national reconciliation in Chile) and by widespread discussion of the advisability and profitability of continuing with prolonged legal proceedings, given Pinochet's advanced years and failing health. In January 2000, having considered an independent doctors' report that Pinochet was medically unfit to undergo further legal proceedings, Straw indicated that he was inclined to order Pinochet's release, although he agreed to defer his final decision pending further representations from those seeking Pinochet's extradition. Such representations swiftly followed from legal authorities in Belgium, France, Spain and Switzerland, and from six human rights organizations. However, on 2 March Straw announced that Pinochet was to be released, and on the following day the former President returned by air to Chile.

The return of Pinochet to Chile was interpreted as a triumph for the former dictator and included a public welcome by the heads of the armed forces but no representation from the civilian Government. Both the outgoing and incoming Governments were reported to be embarrassed by Pinochet's robust appearance on landing in Chile and by the jubilant welcome given to him by the armed forces. Initially, expectations that Pinochet would ever stand trial in Chile were very low; however, these were raised in June 2000 following the Santiago Appeal Court's ruling to lift the former dictator's political immunity. In August, in an historical judgement, the Supreme Court confirmed the decision, by 14 votes to six. The judgement was made possible by changes to Chile's judiciary, several members of which had retired and had been replaced by more independent-minded judges. Foremost among these was Juan Guzmán Tapia, who vigorously took up the legal case against Pinochet and others accused of human rights infringements. Over 200 lawsuits were filed against Pinochet. In Chile citizens over the age of 70 must be subject to a medical examination to determine whether they are mentally fit to stand trial. Pinochet's lawyers argued that to submit to such an examination would be too undignified for the former President. In October an Argentine judge requested the extradition of Pinochet to stand trial for the 1974 killing, in Buenos Aires, of former Chilean army chief Carlos Prats and his wife. However, in November the Supreme Court ruled that Pinochet must not leave the country and placed him under court supervision. On 1 December Judge Guzmán indicted Pinochet on charges of aggravated kidnapping and murder in the 'caravan of death' case (see above) and placed him under house arrest. While human rights activists were jubilant at the news, Pinochet's supporters denounced the indictment as a travesty of justice. Although President Lagos promised not to interfere in the due process of law, he did accede to a request by the military to convene the National Security Council in order to discuss human rights issues. Before the meeting could take place, however, the Santiago Appeal Court overturned the house arrest order on the grounds that his case had been improperly handled (he was not questioned before being charged), a decision subsequently confirmed by the Supreme Court. However, the Supreme Court also ruled that Pinochet must face interrogation by Judge Guzmán within 20 days though not before undergoing the medical tests required by law. In early January 2001, after failing to appear for previously scheduled tests, Pinochet finally consented to the medical examination and was subsequently questioned. On 30 January Judge Guzmán issued an order for the former General's arrest on charges of kidnap and murder.

Meanwhile, in June 2000 the Mesa de Diálogo, a round-table discussion between human rights lawyers and the military, agreed to guarantee the anonymity of any military person offering information on the whereabouts of any 'disappeared' person. The Relatives of the Disappeared organization condemned this agreement, as the discovery of bodies would mean that a charge of homicide, which was covered by the amnesty law, would replace the legal abduction charge. The first official report as a result of the agreement was issued by President Lagos in January 2001 and disclosed information on the fate of 200 people—151 were allegedly thrown into the sea, 20 were buried in a mass grave and 29 were scattered in graves around central Chile.

In August 1991 Argentina and Chile reached a settlement regarding disputed territory in the Antarctic region. Responsibility for the contentious Laguna del Desierto region, however, was to be decided by international arbitration. In October 1994 Argentina's claim to the territory was upheld by a five-member international arbitration panel. In July 1997 it was announced unexpectedly that the two countries were to conduct joint military exercises in 1998, and in September it was agreed to proceed with the creation of a conciliation commission, originally envisaged within the terms of a peace and friendship treaty concluded in 1984. Joint naval exercises began in August 1998. In December agreement on border demarcation of the still contentious 'continental glaciers' territory in the Antarctic region was reached by the Presidents of the two countries. In September 2000 both countries ratified the Mining and Co-operation Integration Treaty, signed in 1997, which allows joint exploitation of mineral deposits along their shared border.

Prospects for renewed diplomatic relations with Bolivia (which severed relations with Chile in 1978 over the issue of Bolivian access to the Pacific Ocean) were encouraged during 1993 by the successful conclusion of a comprehensive trade agreement and by a series of bilateral co-operation treaties. By 1997, however, relations had deteriorated again. The Bolivian Government made repeated requests during the year for the renewal of discussions on Bolivian access to the sea, and sought Peru's assistance in the dispute. Relations between the two countries deteriorated further in late 1997 when the Bolivian Government made an official protest to Chile regarding its failure to remove land-mines (planted during the 1970s) from the two countries' border. Subsequent ministerial discussions failed to produce an effective formula for the restoration of diplomatic relations. In November 1999, following an Iberio-American summit meeting in Havana, Cuba, at which Bolivia sought to initiate a regional discussion of the dispute, Chile stated that the issue was a matter for bilateral, rather than international, negotiation. In the same month it was announced that Chile was to take immediate action to remove land-mines on all its borders.

A free-trade agreement with Colombia, the Acuerdo de Complementación Económica (ACE), took effect from 1 January 1994, and was expected to have eliminated tariffs on most goods by the time of its full implementation on 1 January 1999. A free-trade agreement with Ecuador came into effect on 1 January 1995. In December 1994 the signatory nations to the North American Free Trade Agreement (NAFTA) issued a formal invitation to Chile to join the group. Formal discussions on Chile's accession to the Agreement by late 1996, began in June 1995. However, despite the removal of contentious clauses relating to labour and the environment, US President Bill Clinton failed to secure US congressional support for 'fast track' authorization for Chile's accession to the Agreement. In November 2000 President Clinton announced that the USA would negotiate a bilateral trade deal with Chile, as opposed to it formally becoming a full member of NAFTA. In the context of this delay, Chile intensified attempts to negotiate a bilateral free-trade agreement with Canada and a formal trade agreement with the Mercado Común del Sur (Mercosur—see p. 284). In November 1996 agreement was reached with Canada on the imminent removal of tariffs on three-quarters of bilateral trade, with the gradual removal of remaining duties over a five-year period. The agreement received formal congressional approval in mid-1997 and came into effect in July of that year; the terms of the agreement were modified and expanded in early 1998. Meanwhile, in June 1996, at a summit meeting of Mercosur member nations in San Luis (Argentina), Chile had secured associate membership of the group following negotiations which established the immediate reduction of tariffs on 90% of Chilean goods, and the subsequent elimination of tariffs on 'sensitive' goods including meat, sugar, edible oils and wheat, over an 18-year period. Chile's associate membership became effective from 1 October. However, Chile's decision to negotiate a bilateral free trade accord with the USA caused tension with Brazil at the Mercosur summit in Florianópolis (Brazil) in December 2000 and effectively stalled further negotiations on full membership.

In April 1998 Chile and Mexico signed a free-trade agreement, expanding the terms of an ACE in force since 1992. In June 1998 Chile signed an ACE agreement with Peru, whereby customs duties were to be abolished on 2,500 products from 1 July. The agreement also envisaged the free passage of 50% of all products by 2003 and the creation of a free-trade area within 18 years. With the exception of Bolivia, Chile has now negotiated free-trade agreements throughout the South American continent. During 1998 agreements to facilitate and increase trade between Chile and the countries of Central America were also signed. A second 'Summit of the Americas' was convened in Santiago on 18–19 April 1998, and was attended by representatives of all nations in the region (with the exception of Cuba), who reiterated commitments to establishing a 'Free-Trade Area of the Americas' by 2005.

In January 1994 Chile declared its full adherence to the 1967 Tlatelolco Treaty, which proscribes nuclear weapons in Latin America and the Caribbean. In April 1995 full diplomatic relations with Cuba, severed as a result of the 1973 military coup in Chile, were restored. From late 1998 Chile's relations with both the United Kingdom and Spain came under strain as a result of the detention of former President Pinochet (see above).

Government

Chile is a republic, divided into 12 regions and a metropolitan area. Under the terms of the Constitution, executive power is vested in the President, who is directly elected for a six-year term. The President is assisted by a Cabinet. Legislative power is vested in the bicameral Congreso Nacional (National Congress), comprising the 47-member Senado (Senate) and the 120-member Cámara de Diputados (Chamber of Deputies).

Defence

Military service is for one year (army) or 22 months (navy and air force) and is compulsory for men at 19 years of age. In August 2000 the army had a strength of 51,000, the navy 24,000 and the air force 12,000. Paramilitary security forces numbered about 29,500 carabineros. Defence expenditure for 2000 was budgeted at 1,096,000m. pesos.

Economic Affairs

In 1998, according to estimates by the World Bank, Chile's gross national product (GNP), measured at average 1996–98 prices, was US $73,935m., equivalent to $4,990 per head (or $8,507 per head on an international purchasing-power parity basis). Total GNP for 1999 was estimated at $71,000m. ($4,740 per head). During 1990–98, it was estimated, GNP per head increased, in real terms, at an average annual rate of 6.5%. Over the same period, the population increased by an average of 1.8% per year. Chile's gross domestic product (GDP) increased, in real terms, by an average of 7.2% per year in 1990–99; real GDP grew by an estimated at 3.4% in 1998, but contracted by 1.1% in 1999.

Agriculture (including forestry and fishing) contributed an estimated 8.1% of GDP in 1999. About 14.4% of the employed labour force were engaged in this sector in that year. Important subsistence crops include wheat, oats, barley, rice, beans, lentils, maize and chick-peas. Industrial crops include sugar beet, sunflower seed and rapeseed. Fruit and vegetables are also important export commodities (together contributing 9.7% of total export revenues in 1998), particularly, beans, asparagus, onions, garlic, grapes, citrus fruits, avocados, pears, peaches, plums and nuts. The production and export of wine has increased significantly in recent years. Forestry and fishing, and derivatives from both activities, also make important contributions to the sector. During 1990–99 agricultural GDP increased, in real terms, by an average of 1.3% per year. Agricultural GDP increased by 3.0% in 1998, but declined by 0.6% in 1999.

Industry (including mining, manufacturing, construction and power) contributed an estimated 35.1% of GDP in 1999 and accounted for 23.4% of the employed labour force in the same year. During 1990–99 industrial GDP increased by an annual average of 6.3% per year. GDP growth in all industrial sectors was just 0.6% in 1998 and 2.8% in 1999.

Mining contributed an estimated 11.1% of GDP in 1999 and engaged 1.4% of the employed labour force in that year. Chile, with some 28% of the world's known reserves, is the world's largest producer and exporter of copper. Copper accounted for 87.5% of Chile's total export earnings in 1970, but the proportion had decreased to around 38% by 1998. Gold, silver, iron ore, nitrates, molybdenum, manganese, lead and coal are also mined, and the whole sector contributed some 47% of total export earnings in 1998. In real terms, the sector's GDP increased by an estimated 4.1% in 1998 and by a much more significant 16.9% in 1999. Petroleum and natural gas deposits have been located in the south, and plans to exploit significant reserves of lithium are under consideration.

Manufacturing contributed an estimated 16.3% of GDP in 1999, and engaged 14.3% of the employed labour force in that year. The most important branches of manufacturing, measured by gross value of output, are food (22.3% of the total) and nonferrous metals (15.4%). Manufacturing GDP increased by an average of 6.3% per year in 1990–99. The sector's GDP declined by an estimated 1.5% in 1998 and by a further 0.7% in 1999.

Energy is derived mainly from petroleum and natural gas (some 55%), hydroelectric power (26%) and coal (18%). Chile produces some 40% of its national energy requirements. Plans are under consideration to develop Chile's vast hydroelectric potential (estimated at 18,700 MW—the largest in the world). Meanwhile, Chile imported fuel and energy products equivalent to some 9% of the value of total merchandise imports in 1998.

The services sector contributed an estimated 56.8% of GDP in 1999 and engaged some 62.1% of the employed labour force in that year. The financial sector continued to expand in the 1990s, fuelled, in part, by the success of private pension funds (AFPs—see section on Social Welfare). During 1990–99 services GDP increased by an average of 7.5% per year. The sector's GDP increased, in real terms, by an estimated 5.2% in 1998, but decreased by 0.8% in 1999.

In 1999 Chile recorded a visible trade surplus of US $1,664m., but there was a deficit of $80m. on the current account of the balance of payments. In 1998 the principal source of imports (23.3%) was the USA, which was also the principal market for exports (17.7%). Other major trading partners were Japan, Italy, Mexico, Brazil, Germany, Argentina and the United Kingdom. The principal exports in 1998 were copper and copper manufactures (37.5% of total export revenue), fish (8.4%), fruit (7.2%) and wood pulp (4.7%). The principal imports in that year were machinery and transport equipment, and chemical and mineral products.

In 1998 there was a budgetary surplus of some 131,310m. pesos (equivalent to 0.4% of GDP). Chile's external debt totalled US $36,302m. at the end of 1998, of which $4,986m. was long-term public debt. Debt-servicing costs in that year were equivalent to some 22.3% of the value of exports of goods and services. The annual rate of inflation averaged 11.0% in 1990–98, and stood at 3.3% in 1999. An average 9.8% of the labour force were unemployed in 1999.

Chile is a member of the Latin American Integration Association (ALADI—see p. 230) and was admitted to the Rio Group (see p. 318) in 1990 and to the Asia-Pacific Economic Co-operation group (APEC—see p. 128) in 1994. Chile is also among the founding members of the World Trade Organization (WTO, see p. 292).

Owing to the relaxation of import duties in the early 1980s, Chile's potential in the agricultural and manufacturing sectors was stifled by cheaper imported goods. Exports of fruit, seafoods and wines, however, have expanded considerably, yet Chile remains heavily dependent on exports of copper and on the stability of the world copper market. The 1990–94 Aylwin administration successfully maintained significant economic growth while reducing inflation from 26% in 1990 to 12.7% in 1993. In September 1997 a report published by the WTO praised the economic achievements of the previous two decades in liberalizing trade and reducing inflation, but warned that recent preoccupation with the creation of regional trade associations was leading to the perpetuation of serious imbalances in the structure of Chile's trade. As a result of the 1997–98 economic crisis in Asia (one of Chile's principal markets), economic growth was less than predicted. Chile entered a period of recession during 1999, largely as a result of depressed world prices for copper; the economy contracted by some 6% in April, and by 1.1% over the whole year. In June President Frei announced a number of new initiatives to reactivate the economy, including the immediate creation of 150,000 jobs; these measures were supported by a reduction in interest rates. In September, in an attempt to stimulate exports, the Central Bank abandoned its strict regulation of the peso, allowing the currency to float against the US dollar. Confidence returned to the economy in 2000 with GDP growth estimated at 5.6%. However, high unemployment and low investment levels continued to stifle consumer demand. In an attempt to stimulate recovery, the new Government of President Lagos initiated a public works programme, designed to increase the incomes of skilled and semi-skilled workers, and introduced tax rebates of up to $400 for about 1m. people. Other government initiatives included encouraging foreign investment in growth areas such as tourism and new technology and promoting investment in Chile's disparate regions.

Social Welfare

Employees, including agricultural workers, may receive benefits for sickness, unemployment, accidents at work, maternity and retirement, and there are dependants' allowances, including family allowances. In May 1981 the management of social security was opened to the private sector. By the mid-1990s some 90% of Chile's 5m. pensions contributors were participating in the private pension system operated by Administradoras de Fondos de Pensiones (AFPs), while responsibility for the remainder was assumed by the Instituto de Normalización Previsional, a transitional state organization. In late 1997 it was estimated that Chile's AFPs were managing more than US $30,000m. of funds. However, the Government retains ultimate control of the sector, monitoring the performance of AFP managers and regulating the proportion of assets to be invested at home and abroad. A National Health Service (Sistema Nacional de Servicios de Salud—SNSS) was established in 1952. In March 1998 President Frei announced an ambitious two-year social reform programme. There were 17,467 medical personnel in 1998; in 1997 there were 182 hospital establishments, with a total of 42,222 beds. There were an estimated 110 doctors for every 100,000 Chileans in 1994 and an estimated 47 nurses for every 100,000 Chileans in 1996. Of total expenditure by the central Government in 1998, about 917,025m. pesos (11.8%) was for health services, and a further 2,574,210m. pesos (33.1%) for social security and welfare.

Education

Pre-primary education is widely available for all children from five years of age. Primary education is officially compulsory, and is provided free of charge, for eight years, beginning at six or seven years of age. It is divided into two cycles: the first lasts for four years and provides a general education; the second cycle offers more specialized schooling. Secondary education, beginning at 13 or 14 years of age, is divided into the humanities-science programme (lasting for four years), with the emphasis on general education and possible entrance to university, and the technical-professional programme (lasting for between four and six years), designed to fulfil the requirements of specialist training. In 1996 the total enrolment at primary schools included an estimated 88% of children in the relevant age-group, while the comparable ratio for secondary enrolment was 58%. Higher education is provided by three kinds of institution: universities, professional institutes and centres of technical information. An intensive national literacy campaign, launched in 1980, reduced the rate of adult illiteracy from 11% in 1970 to an estimated 4.8% (males 4.6%; females 5.0%) in 1995. Expenditure on education by the central Government in 1998 was about 1,252,143m. pesos (16.1% of total spending).

Public Holidays

2001: 1 January (New Year's Day), 13–14 April (Good Friday and Easter Saturday), 1 May (Labour Day), 21 May (Battle of Iquique), 15 August (Assumption), 4 September (National Unity

Day), 18 September (Independence Day), 12 October (Day of the Race, anniversary of the discovery of America), 1 November (All Saints' Day), 8 December (Immaculate Conception), 25 December (Christmas).

2002: 1 January (New Year's Day), 29–30 March (Good Friday and Easter Saturday), 1 May (Labour Day), 21 May (Battle of Iquique), 15 August (Assumption), 4 September (National Unity

Day), 18 September (Independence Day), 12 October (Day of the Race, anniversary of the discovery of America), 1 November (All Saints' Day), 8 December (Immaculate Conception), 25 December (Christmas Day).

Weights and Measures

The metric system is officially in force.

Statistical Survey

Sources (unless otherwise stated): Instituto Nacional de Estadísticas, Avda Bulnes 418, Casilla 498-3, Correo 3, Santiago; tel. (2) 366-7777; fax (2) 671-2169; e-mail inesdadm@reuna.cl; internet www.ine.cl; Banco Central de Chile, Agustinas 1180, Santiago; tel. (2) 696-2281; fax (2) 698-4847; e-mail bcch@bcentral.cl; internet www.bcentral.cl.

Area and Population

AREA, POPULATION AND DENSITY*

Area (sq km)	756,096†
Population (census results)‡	
21 April 1982	11,329,736
22 April 1992	
Males	6,553,254
Females	6,795,147
Total	13,348,401
Population (official estimates at mid-year)	
1998	14,821,714
1999	15,017,760
2000	15,211,308
Density (per sq km) at mid-2000	20.1

* Excluding Chilean Antarctic Territory (approximately 1,250,000 sq km).
† 291,930 sq miles.
‡ Excluding adjustment for underenumeration.

REGIONS (30 June 2000)

		Area (sq km)	Population ('000)	Capital
I	De Tarapacá . . .	59,099.1	398.9	Iquique
II	De Antofagasta .	126,049.1	468.4	Antofagasta
III	De Atacama . .	75,176.2	273.6	Copiapó
IV	De Coquimbo . .	40,579.9	577.9	La Serena
V	De Valparaíso . .	16,396.1	1,561.4	Valparaíso
VI	Del Libertador Gen. Bernardo O'Higgins	16,387.0	788.8	Rancagua
VII	Del Maule . .	30,296.1	915.2	Talca
VIII	Del Bíobío . .	37,062.6	1,936.3	Concepción
IX	De la Araucanía .	31,842.3	874.2	Temuco
X	De Los Lagos . .	67,013.1	1,061.5	Puerto Montt
XI	Aisén del Gen. Carlos Ibáñez del Campo .	108,494.4	95.0	Coihaique
XII	De Magallanes y Antártica Chilena .	132,297.2	157.8	Punta Arenas
	Metropolitan Region (Santiago) . .	15,403.2	6,102.2	—
	Total . . .	756,096.3	15,211.3	—

PRINCIPAL TOWNS (provisional figures, population at 30 June 2000)

Gran Santiago (capital) . .	5,493,062	Arica	185,622
Puente Alto . .	425,056	Talca	182,445
Concepción . .	379,860	Chillán . . .	171,207
Viña del Mar . .	342,715	Iquique . . .	169,997
Valparaíso . .	285,262	Puerto Montt . .	138,138
Talcahuano . .	280,941	Coquimbo . . .	135,622
Temuco . .	273,223	Osorno . . .	131,666
Antofagasta . .	251,868	La Serena . . .	130,426
San Bernardo . .	246,491	Calama . . .	128,073
Rancagua . .	213,735	Valdivia . . .	125,999
		Punta Arenas . .	124,246

BIRTHS, MARRIAGES AND DEATHS

	Registered live births		Registered marriages		Registered deaths	
	Number	Rate (per 1,000)	Number	Rate (per 1,000)	Number	Rate (per 1,000)
1991 . .	299,456	22.5	91,732	6.9	74,862	5.6
1992 . .	293,787	21.7	89,370	6.6	74,090	5.5
1993 . .	290,438	21.1	92,821	6.7	76,261	5.5
1994 . .	288,175	20.6	91,555	6.5	75,445	5.4
1995 . .	279,928	19.7	87,205	6.1	78,531	5.5
1996 . .	264,793	18.4	83,547	5.8	79,123	5.5
1997 . .	259,959	17.8	78,077	5.3	78,472	5.4
1998 . .	257,105	17.3	73,456	5.0	80,257	5.4

Expectation of Life (official estimates, years at birth, 1997): Males 72.13; Females 78.10.

Source: partly UN, *Demographic Yearbook*.

ECONOMICALLY ACTIVE POPULATION*
('000 persons aged 15 years and over, October–December)

	1997	1998	1999
Agriculture, hunting, forestry and fishing	775.9	784.4	780.1
Mining and quarrying . .	87.9	81.8	73.3
Manufacturing . . .	860.8	818.6	775.5
Electricity, gas and water . .	31.1	37.6	28.5
Construction	488.8	448.5	388.6
Trade, restaurants and hotels .	975.9	1,005.5	1,027.2
Transport, storage and communications . . .	401.0	432.7	403.2
Financing, insurance, real estate and business services . . .	376.5	405.7	390.4
Community, social and personal services	1,382.4	1,417.7	1,537.7
Total employed . . .	5,380.2	5,432.3	5,404.5
Unemployed	303.6	419.2	529.1
Total labour force . . .	5,683.8	5,851.5	5,933.6
Males	3,812.5	3,895.9	3,926.5
Females	1,871.3	1,955.7	2,007.0

* Figures are based on sample surveys, covering 36,000 households, and exclude members of the armed forces. Estimates are made independently, therefore totals are not always the sum of the component parts.

Agriculture

PRINCIPAL CROPS ('000 metric tons)

	1997	1998	1999
Wheat	1,677	1,682	1,197
Rice (paddy)	88	104	61
Barley	81	115	81
Oats	347	250	281
Maize	881	943	624
Dry beans	42	55	31
Potatoes	1,114	792	995
Sugar beet	2,707	3,085	3,100
Rapeseed	30	52	72
Tomatoes*	1,121†	1,205	1,243
Pumpkins, etc.	160	111	100†
Onions (dry)	198*	219	263*
Watermelons	70*	63	63
Melons†	68	60	60
Grapes	1,669	1,642	1,575
Apples	940	1,000	1,165
Peaches and nectarines	305	269	310

* Unofficial figure.   † FAO estimate(s).

Source: FAO.

LIVESTOCK ('000 head, year ending September)

	1997	1998	1999
Horses*	590	590	590
Cattle	4,142	4,160	4,134
Pigs	1,655	1,962	2,221
Sheep	3,835	3,754	4,116
Goats	738	740*	740*

* FAO estimate(s).

Poultry (FAO estimates, million): 68 in 1997; 70 in 1998; 70 in 1999.

Source: FAO.

LIVESTOCK PRODUCTS ('000 metric tons)

	1997	1998	1999
Beef and veal	262	256	226
Mutton and lamb	10	11	12
Pig meat	209	235	244
Horse meat	12	11	11*
Poultry meat	314	339	344
Cows' milk	2,050	2,080	2,050
Goats' milk*	10	10	10
Butter	10	11	12
Cheese	50	53	53
Hen eggs*	95	95	95
Wool: greasy	16	15	17*

* FAO estimate(s).

Source: FAO.

Forestry

ROUNDWOOD REMOVALS ('000 cubic metres, excluding bark)

	1996	1997	1998
Sawlogs, veneer logs and logs for sleepers	11,024	12,132	10,313
Pulpwood	7,765	7,063	10,738
Other industrial wood	593	375	263
Fuel wood	10,449	10,407	10,356
Total	29,831	29,977	31,670

Source: FAO, *Yearbook of Forest Products*.

SAWNWOOD PRODUCTION
('000 cubic metres, including railway sleepers)

	1996	1997	1998
Coniferous (softwood)	3,744	4,274	4,222
Broadleaved (hardwood)	396	387	329
Total	4,140	4,661	4,551

Source: FAO, *Yearbook of Forest Products*.

Fishing

('000 metric tons, live weight)

	1996	1997	1998
Capture	6,691.0	5,811.6	3,265.3
Patagonian grenadier	379.0	71.5	354.2
Chilean jack mackerel	3,883.3	2,917.1	1,612.9
Araucanian herring	446.7	441.2	317.6
Anchoveta (Peruvian anchovy)	1,400.6	1,757.5	522.7
Chub mackerel	146.6	211.6	71.8
Aquaculture	217.9	272.3	293.0
Atlantic salmon	77.3	96.7	107.1
Total catch	6,908.9	6,083.9	3,558.4

Note: Figures exclude aquatic plants ('000 metric tons): 322.0 (capture 216.8, aquaculture 105.2) in 1996; 281.6 (capture 178.8, aquaculture 102.8) in 1997; 265.9 (capture 197.5, aquaculture 68.4) in 1998. Also excluded are aquatic mammals, recorded by number rather than by weight. The number of South American sea lions caught was: 96 in 1996; 16 in 1997.

Source: FAO, *Yearbook of Fishery Statistics*.

Mining

('000 metric tons, unless otherwise indicated)

	1997	1998	1999
Copper (metal content)	3,511.5	3,757.8	4,421.6
Coal	1,387.2	319.0	513.8
Iron ore*	8,738	9,112	8,345
Calcium carbonate	5,618	5,999	n.a.
Sodium sulphate (metric tons)	1,335	1,298	n.a.
Zinc—metal content (metric tons)	34,350	16,066	32,263
Molybdenum—metal content (kilograms)	21,337	25,297	27,269
Manganese (kilograms)†	62,750	48,931	40,507
Gold (kilograms)	49,486	44,990	46,668
Silver (metric tons)	1,091.5	1,340.6	1,380.4
Petroleum ('000 cubic metres)	489.0	468.7	446.0
Natural gas ('000 cubic metres)	3,211	3,218	n.a.

* Gross weight. The estimated iron content is 61%.
† Gross weight. The estimated metal content is 32%.

Source: partly Servicio Nacional de Geología y Minería.

Industry

SELECTED PRODUCTS ('000 metric tons, unless otherwise indicated)

	1997	1998	1999
Refined sugar	470	470	434
Beer (million litres)	364	367	333
Soft drinks (million litres)	1,195	1,197	1,154
Cigarettes (million)	12,522	12,904	13,174
Non-rubber footwear ('000 pairs)	7,638	6,777	5,940
Particle board ('000 cu metres)	315	242	257
Mattresses ('000)	1,131	1,100	1,082
Sulphuric acid	1,864	1,983	2,436
Motor spirit (petrol)	1,972	2,078	2,153
Kerosene and jet fuel	814	753	831
Distillate fuel oils	2,937	3,544	3,840
Residual fuel oils	1,663	n.a.	n.a.
Cement	3,191	3,280	2,508
Tyres ('000)	2,509	2,350	2,551
Glass sheets ('000 sq metres)	21,075	21,313	21,523
Blister copper	181	165	177
Refined fire copper	125	129	163
Electrolytic copper	1,261	1,437	1,463

Electric Energy: (million kWh): 32,549 in 1997; 34,886 in 1998; 38,019 in 1999.

Finance

CURRENCY AND EXCHANGE RATES

Monetary Units
100 centavos = 1 Chilean peso.

Sterling, Dollar and Euro Equivalents (29 December 2000)
£1 sterling = 854.6 pesos;
US $1 = 572.7 pesos;
€1 = 532.9 pesos;
1,000 Chilean pesos = £1.170 = $1.746 = €1.877.

Average Exchange Rate (pesos per US $)
1998   460.29
1999   508.78
2000   535.47

BUDGET (million pesos)

Revenue	1997	1998	1999
Current revenue	7,342,126	7,713,838	7,741,513
Taxation	6,122,304	6,449,178	6,332,835
Taxes on income, profits and capital gains	1,302,365	1,431,404	1,312,195
Social security contributions	449,471	496,839	527,042
Domestic taxes on goods and services	3,395,782	3,585,474	3,629,354
Sales or turnover taxes	2,726,764	2,845,357	2,811,585
Excises	669,018	740,117	817,769
Taxes on international trade and transactions	615,723	612,817	535,490
Other taxes	358,962	322,644	328,754
Administrative fees and charges, non-industrial and incidental sales	470,910	559,516	650,311
Other current revenue*	748,912	705,146	758,367
Capital revenue	24,516	19,223	7,139
Total revenue	7,366,642	7,733,061	7,748,652

Expenditure*	1997	1998	1999
General public services	269,235	309,805	340,902
Defence	564,636	633,496	679,392
Public order and safety	375,528	428,476	477,136
Education	1,069,653	1,252,143	1,384,085
Health	806,542	917,025	976,662
Social security and welfare	2,311,247	2,574,210	2,913,285
Housing	351,387	376,728	432,779
Economic services	1,020,972	1,056,790	1,099,923
Interest payments	140,777	233,225	120,712
Sub-total	6,909,976	7,781,898	8,424,877
Less Lending included in expenditure	214,631	205,590	187,890
Total expenditure	6,695,345	7,576,308	8,236,987
Current	5,575,812	6,324,627	6,882,153
Capital	1,119,533	1,251,681	1,354,833

* Excluding net lending.

INTERNATIONAL RESERVES (US $ million at 31 December)

	1997	1998	1999
Gold*	533.0	321.9	316.9
IMF special drawing rights	1.3	8.3	18.5
Reserve position in IMF	313.1	604.9	411.0
Foreign exchange	16,991.4	15,049.4	13,977.3
Total	17,838.8	15,984.5	14,723.7

* National valuation.

Source: IMF, *International Financial Statistics*.

MONEY SUPPLY ('000 million pesos at 31 December)

	1997	1998	1999
Currency outside banks	985.3	977.3	1,185.6
Demand deposits at commercial banks	2,242.6	1,821.9	2,533.0
Total money (incl. others)	2,686.7	2,799.4	3,718.9

Source: IMF, *International Financial Statistics*.

COST OF LIVING
(Consumer Price Index for Santiago; base: 1990 = 100)

	1997	1998	1999
Food (incl. beverages)	222.3	230.6	231.2
Rent, fuel and light	214.3	224.0	229.6
Clothing (incl. footwear)	136.4	130.9	126.8
All items (incl. others)	217.8	228.9	236.5

Source: ILO, *Yearbook of Labour Statistics*.

NATIONAL ACCOUNTS

Expenditure on the Gross Domestic Product
('000 million pesos at current prices)

	1997	1998	1999
Government final consumption expenditure	3,319.5	3,708.3	4,060.4
Private final consumption expenditure	20,514.8	22,382.5	22,382.5
Increase in stocks	550.5	413.1	−47.2
Gross fixed capital formation	8,044.0	8,461.0	7,302.2
Total domestic expenditure	32,428.8	34,964.9	33,697.9
Exports of goods and services	8,878.2	9,004.4	9,989.3
Less Imports of goods and services	9,739.9	10,382.9	9,360.5
GDP in purchasers' values	31,567.3	33,513.3	34,326.7
GDP at constant 1986 prices	7,845.1	8,109.4	8,020.7

Source: IMF, *International Financial Statistics*.

Gross Domestic Product by Economic Activity
('000 million pesos at constant 1986 prices)

	1997	1998*	1999*
Agriculture and forestry . . .	452.1	465.5	460.0
Fishing	120.0	123.9	126.0
Mining and quarrying . .	659.3	686.0	801.9
Manufacturing	1,203.6	1,185.5	1,177.5
Electricity, gas and water . .	177.6	186.2	189.5
Construction	416.9	415.3	374.0
Trade, restaurants and hotels .	1,356.4	1,425.9	1,375.4
Transport, storage and communications . . .	644.5	716.7	735.8
Financial services . . .	1,053.6	1,090.9	1,079.8
Real estate, renting and business activities†	253.5	261.6	269.2
Personal services. . . .	461.7	476.7	475.0
Public administration . .	167.4	169.7	172.0
Sub-total	6,966.8	7,203.9	7,236.3
Value-added tax	742.4	773.4	749.9
Import duties	647.3	658.8	551.3
Less Imputed bank service charge .	511.3	526.7	516.8
GDP in purchasers' values	7,845.1	8,109.4	8,020.7

* Figures are provisional.
† Including imputed rents of owner-occupied dwellings.

BALANCE OF PAYMENTS (US $ million)

	1997	1998	1999
Exports of goods f.o.b. . .	16,663	14,831	15,616
Imports of goods f.o.b. . .	−18,221	−17,347	−13,951
Trade balance . . .	−1,558	−2,516	1,664
Exports of services . . .	4,109	4,122	3,790
Imports of services . . .	−4,063	−4,236	−4,106
Balance on goods and services .	−1,512	−2,630	1,348
Other income received . .	1,086	1,135	1,103
Other income paid . . .	−3,823	−3,107	−2,983
Balance on goods, services and income	−4,249	−4,602	−532
Current transfers received .	877	815	793
Current transfers paid . .	−356	−352	−341
Current balance . . .	−3,728	−4,139	−80
Direct investment abroad . .	−1,865	−2,798	−4,855
Direct investment from abroad .	5,219	4,638	9,221
Portfolio investment assets .	−238	−1,420	−2,366
Portfolio investment liabilities .	2,603	591	2,496
Other investment assets . .	−843	−2,546	−6,390
Other investment liabilities .	2,479	4,716	1,065
Net errors and omissions . .	−443	−1,177	151
Overall balance . . .	3,184	−2,135	−758

Source: IMF, *International Financial Statistics*.

External Trade

PRINCIPAL COMMODITIES (distribution by SITC, US $ million)

Imports c.i.f.	1996	1997	1998
Food and live animals . .	1,026.2	1,024.1	995.9
Mineral fuels, lubricants, etc. .	1,847.5	1,818.3	1,506.3
Petroleum, petroleum products, etc.	1,536.1	1,504.5	1,140.4
Crude petroleum oils, etc. . .	1,158.8	1,131.2	845.2
Chemicals and related products	1,959.4	2,024.6	1,934.4
Artificial resins, plastic materials, etc. .	443.4	498.9	439.3
Products of polymerization, etc. .	345.0	390.5	333.6
Basic manufactures . .	2,471.9	2,740.2	2,739.8
Paper, paperboard and manufactures	337.4	387.4	381.2
Textile yarn, fabrics, etc. . .	500.2	500.8	461.0
Iron and steel	480.9	577.4	605.9
Machinery and transport equipment	7,147.5	7,875.1	7,362.5

Imports c.i.f. — *continued*	1996	1997	1998
Power-generating machinery and equipment	406.7	460.1	413.9
Machinery specialized for particular industries . . .	1,174.2	1,228.8	1,152.1
General industrial machinery, equipment and parts . .	1,236.4	1,450.1	1,297.5
Office machines and automatic data-processing equipment . .	530.0	619.2	595.5
Automatic data-processing equipment	369.3	451.3	407.9
Telecommunications and sound equipment	699.2	865.1	1,023.0
Other electrical machinery, apparatus, etc. . . .	710.4	836.7	801.8
Road vehicles and parts* . .	2,043.4	2,217.7	1,794.8
Passenger motor cars (excl. buses)	862.0	915.2	689.3
Lorries and trucks . . .	663.5	717.0	617.6
Miscellaneous manufactured articles	1,663.2	1,891.5	1,875.6
Clothing and accessories (excl. footwear)	416.4	441.8	468.8
Total (incl. others) . . .	16,810.0	18,110.9	17,082.5

* Data on parts exclude tyres, engines and electrical parts.

Exports f.o.b.	1996	1997	1998
Food and live animals . .	3,733.6	3,634.7	3,564.4
Fish, crustaceans and molluscs, and preparations thereof .	1,042.9	1,216.3	1,244.7
Fish, fresh (live or dead), chilled or frozen . . .	736.2	854.3	920.7
Fish, frozen (excl. fillets) .	333.9	397.7	397.5
Vegetables and fruit . . .	1,568.6	1,388.2	1,434.8
Fruit and nuts (excl. oil nuts), fresh or dried . .	1,083.5	1,006.5	1,066.0
Grapes, fresh or dried .	463.8	455.6	440.7
Grapes, fresh . . .	429.4	414.0	403.5
Feeding-stuff for animals (excl. unmilled cereals) . .	639.3	583.5	371.8
Flours and meals of fish, crustaceans or mulluscs, unfit for human consumption . .	612.6	555.4	348.9
Beverages and tobacco. .	319.9	452.1	567.2
Beverages	300.4	439.2	553.9
Alcoholic beverages . .	297.4	434.4	548.9
Wine of fresh grapes . .	293.8	424.0	510.5
Crude materials (inedible) except fuels . . .	3,947.5	4,150.9	3,367.8
Cork and wood . . .	619.6	700.3	525.6
Simply worked wood and railway sleepers	332.5	429.7	360.9
Coniferous wood, sawn, etc.	318.1	414.5	344.7
Pulp and waste paper . .	764.9	690.5	693.8
Chemical wood pulp, soda or sulphate	764.4	689.3	692.4
Metalliferous ores and metal scrap	2,278.2	2,473.9	1,859.4
Copper ores and concentrates (excl. matte) . . .	1,879.5	2,017.7	1,399.5
Chemicals and related products	545.2	762.2	765.1
Inorganic chemicals . . .	253.5	319.8	369.4
Basic manufactures . .	5,339.3	6,111.9	5,085.3
Non-ferrous metals . . .	4,563.2	5,277.3	4,307.1
Copper	4,401.0	5,142.5	4,162.8
Copper and copper alloys, refined or not, unwrought .	4,263.8	5,019.3	4,068.1
Unrefined copper (incl. blister copper but excl. cement copper) . .	532.8	370.7	264.7
Refined copper (incl. copper alloys other than master alloys), unwrought . .	3,731.0	4,648.5	3,803.4

Exports f.o.b. — *continued*	1996	1997	1998
Machinery and transport equipment	372.2	428.6	492.0
Miscellaneous manufactured articles	344.8	378.3	371.2
Non-monetary gold (excl. ores and concentrates) . . .	427.6	382.1	275.3
Total (incl. others) . . .	15,406.8	16,678.3	14,841.7

Source: UN, *International Trade Statistics Yearbook*.

1999 (US $ million): *Imports c.i.f.:* 15,137; *Exports f.o.b.:* 15,616. Source: IMF, *International Financial Statistics*.

PRINCIPAL TRADING PARTNERS (US $ million)*

Imports c.i.f.	1996	1997	1998
Argentina	1,634.2	1,837.2	1,900.5
Brazil	1,065.7	1,242.8	1,092.3
Canada	408.1	432.5	494.5
China, People's Republic . . .	635.8	721.3	753.1
Colombia	222.4	201.2	176.0
Ecuador	224.9	258.6	149.6
France	582.0	502.1	680.5
Germany	729.9	842.7	811.7
Italy	550.8	699.7	680.3
Japan	949.7	1,054.7	994.6
Korea, Republic . . .	556.8	558.8	545.2
Mexico	927.2	1,076.2	849.9
Spain	530.4	621.1	656.0
Sweden	271.3	352.0	246.7
Taiwan	220.9	225.1	200.2
United Kingdom	281.7	320.2	256.3
USA	4,109.5	4,332.6	4,025.8
Venezuela	313.2	273.4	236.1
Total (incl. others) . . .	16,975.0	18,330.7	17,277.5

Exports f.o.b.	1996	1997	1998
Argentina	699.9	780.9	735.1
Belgium-Luxembourg . .	247.7	272.6	345.6
Bolivia	207.8	228.5	249.6
Brazil	934.5	957.2	781.2
China, People's Republic . .	467.2	598.1	459.7
Colombia	194.1	227.9	211.2
France	392.8	458.0	443.5
Germany	742.3	747.0	538.4
Italy	475.3	499.5	668.5
Japan	2,495.7	2,675.8	1,959.3
Korea, Republic . . .	864.1	989.7	384.7
Mexico	146.2	376.3	488.5
Netherlands	393.6	423.2	432.6
Peru	321.3	347.8	352.9
Spain	281.8	345.2	275.1
Taiwan	629.1	785.6	525.0
United Kingdom	886.5	1,061.6	1,161.2
USA	2,559.1	2,710.5	2,609.7
Venezuela	141.2	158.3	176.8
Total (incl. others) . . .	15,396.2	17,024.8	14,757.1

* Imports by country of purchase; exports by country of sale.

Transport

PRINCIPAL RAILWAYS

	1997	1998	1999*
Passenger journeys ('000) .	8,271	9,659	10,008
Passenger-kilometres ('000) .	551,830	518,226	637,120
Freight ('000 metric tons) .	18,012	20,634	21,250
Freight ton-kilometres (million) .	2,330	2,650	2,896

* Figures are provisional.

ROAD TRAFFIC (motor vehicles in use)

	1997	1998	1999
Passenger cars (excl. taxis) .	1,061,122	1,121,262	1,206,986
Buses and coaches (incl. taxis) .	163,946	168,695	173,228
Lorries and vans .	585,959	619,086	652,059
Specialized vehicles (incl. tractors)	14,475	14,310	13,714
Motor cycles and mopeds . . .	34,051	30,893	31,419

SHIPPING
Merchant Fleet (registered at 31 December)

	1996	1997	1998
Number of vessels . . .	456	469	472
Total displacement ('000 grt) . .	691	722	753

Source: Lloyd's Register of Shipping, *World Fleet Statistics*.

International Sea-borne Shipping (freight traffic, '000 metric tons)

	1997	1998	1999*
Goods loaded	30,126	28,178	31,208
Goods unloaded	18,487	19,193	19,455

* Figures are provisional.

CIVIL AVIATION (traffic on scheduled services)

	1997	1998	1999
Kilometres flown (million) . .	109	139	107
Passengers ('000) . . .	4,693	5,102	5,188
Passenger-km (million) . .	8,597	9,698	10,650
Freight (million ton-km) . .	1,030	1,248	1,139

Source: Dirección de Aeronaútica Civil.

Tourism

ARRIVALS BY NATIONALITY

	1997	1998	1999
Argentina	754,001	815,601	801,660
Bolivia	127,470	150,895	118,619
Brazil	86,712	83,132	67,751
Germany	39,493	40,073	42,233
Peru	199,785	180,684	122,929
Spain	33,398	35,902	32,831
USA	108,542	127,652	124,044
Total (incl. others) . . .	1,643,640	1,759,279	1,622,252

Tourism receipts (US $ million): 1,019 in 1997; 1,062 in 1998; 894 in 1999.

Sources: World Tourism Organization, *Yearbook of Tourism Statistics*; Servicio Nacional de Turismo.

Communications Media

	1995	1996	1997
Radio receivers ('000 in use) . .	4,950	5,100	5,180
Television receivers ('000 in use) .	3,050	3,100	3,150
Telephones ('000 main lines in use)	1,885	2,248	2,630
Telefax stations (number in use) .	25,000	32,000	40,000
Mobile cellular telephones			
(subscribers)	197,314	335,430	410,000
Book production: titles . . .	2,469	n.a.	n.a.
Daily newspapers	56	52	n.a.

Source: mainly UNESCO, *Statistical Yearbook*.

Education*

(1998)

	Students		
	Males	Females	Total
Pre-primary	137,518	132,749	270,267
Primary	1,172,740	1,101,674	2,274,414
Special primary	24,616	15,888	40,504
Secondary	422,280	426,656	848,936
Higher (incl. universities) . .	217,152	185,791	402,943

* Figures are provisional.

Directory

The Constitution

The 1981 Constitution, described as a 'transition to democracy', separated the presidency from the Junta and provided for presidential elections and for the re-establishment of the bicameral legislature, consisting of an upper chamber (Senado) of both elected and appointed Senators, who are to serve an eight-year term, and a lower chamber (Cámara de Diputados) of 120 Deputies elected for a four-year term. All former Presidents are to be Senators for life. There is a National Security Council consisting of the President of the Republic, the heads of the armed forces and the police, and the Presidents of the Supreme Court and the Senado.

In July 1989 a national referendum approved 54 reforms to the Constitution, including 47 proposed by the Government and seven by the Military Junta. Among provisions made within the articles were an increase in the number of directly elected senators from 26 to 38, the abolition of the need for the approval of two successive Congresos for constitutional amendments (the support of two-thirds of the Cámara de Diputados and the Senado being sufficient), the reduction in term of office for the President to be elected in 1989 from eight to four years, with no immediate re-election possible, and the redrafting of the provision that outlawed Marxist groups so as to ensure 'true and responsible political pluralism'. The President's right to dismiss the Congreso and sentence to internal exile were eliminated.

In November 1991 the Congreso approved constitutional changes to local government. The amendments provided for the replacement of centrally appointed local officials with directly elected representatives.

In February 1994 an amendment to the Constitution was approved whereby the length of the presidential term was reduced from eight to six years.

The Government

HEAD OF STATE

President: RICARDO LAGOS ESCOBAR (took office 10 March 2000).

THE CABINET
(April 2001)

A coalition of parties represented in the Concertación de los Partidos de la Democracia (CPD), including the Partido Demócrata Cristiano (PDC), the Partido Socialista de Chile (PS), the Partido Por la Democracia (PPD) and the Partido Radical Socialdemócrata (PRSD).

Minister of the Interior: JOSÉ MIGUEL INSULZA SALINAS (PS).

Minister of Foreign Affairs: MARIA SOLEDAD ALVEAR VALENZUELA (PDC).

Minister of National Defence: MARIO FERNÁNDEZ BAEZA (PDC).

Minister of Finance: NICOLÁS EYZAGUIRRE GUZMÁN (PPD).

Minister, Secretary-General of the Presidency: ALAVARO GARCÍA HURTADO (PPD).

Minister, Secretary-General to the Government: CLAUDIO HUEPE GARCÍA (PDC).

Minister of Economy, Mining and Energy: JOSÉ DE GREGORIO REBECO (PDC).

Minister of Planning and Co-operation: ALEJANDRA KRAUSS VALLE (PDC).

Minister of Education: MARIANA AYLWIN ORYARZÚN (PDC).

Minister of Justice: JOSÉ ANTONIO GÓMEZ URRUTIA (PRSD).

Minister of Labour and Social Security: RICARDO SOLARI SAAVEDRA (PS).

Minister of Public Works, Transport and Telecommunications: CARLOS CRUZ LORENZEN.

Minister of Health: Dr MICHELLE BACHELET JERIA (PS).

Minister of Housing and Urban Planning: JAIME RAVINET DE LA FUENTE (PDC).

Minister of Agriculture: JAIME CAMPOS QUIROGA (PRSD).

Minister of the National Women's Service (Sernam): ADRIANA DELPIANO PUELMA (PS).

MINISTRIES

Ministry of Agriculture: Teatinos 40, Santiago; tel. (2) 696-5698; fax (2) 696-4496; e-mail prensa@minagri.gob.cl; internet www.minagri.gob.cl.

Ministry of Economy, Mining and Energy: Teatinos 120, 10°, Santiago; tel. (2) 672-5522; fax (2) 672-6040.

Ministry of Education: Alameda 1371, 7°, Santiago; tel. (2) 698-3351; fax (2) 688-2300.

Ministry of Finance: Teatinos 120, 12°, Santiago; tel. (2) 675-5800; fax (2) 671-6479.

Ministry of Foreign Affairs: Catedral 1158, Santiago; tel. (2) 679-4200; fax (2) 696-8796.

Ministry of Health: Enrique MacIver 541, 3°, Santiago; tel. (2) 639-4001; fax (2) 633-2405.

Ministry of Housing and Urban Development: Alameda 924, Santiago; tel. (2) 638-3366; fax (2) 633-3892.

Ministry of the Interior: Palacio de la Moneda, Santiago; tel. (2) 690-4000; fax (2) 699-2165.

Ministry of Justice: Morandé 107, Santiago; tel. (2) 674-3100; fax (2) 695-4558.

Ministry of Labour and Social Security: Huérfanos 1273, 6°, Santiago; tel. (2) 695-5133; fax (2) 698-8473; e-mail mintrab@mintrab.gob.cl; internet www.mintrab.gob.cl.

Ministry of National Defence: Villavicencio 364, 22°, Edif. Diego Portales, Santiago; tel. (2) 222-1202; fax (2) 634-5339.

Ministry of the National Women's Service (Sernam): Teatinos 950, 5°, Santiago; tel. (2) 549-6100; fax (2) 549-6248; e-mail clopez@sernam.cl; internet www.mujereschile.cl.

Ministry of Planning and Co-operation (MIDEPLAN): Ahumada 48, 7°, Santiago; tel. (2) 675-1400; fax (2) 672-1879; internet www.mideplan.cl.

Ministry of Public Works: Morandé 59, 2°, Santiago; tel. (2) 361-3000; fax (2) 672-5281.

Ministry of Transport and Telecommunications: Amunátegui 139, 3°, Santiago; tel. (2) 421-3000; fax (2) 672-2785; e-mail mtt@mtt.cl.

Office of the Minister Secretary-General of Government: Palacio de la Moneda, Santiago; tel. (2) 690-4160; fax (2) 697-1756; e-mail cmladini@segegob.cl; internet www.segegob.cl.

Office of the Minister Secretary-General of the Presidency: Palacio de la Moneda, Santiago; tel. (2) 690-4218; fax (2) 690-4329.

President and Legislature

PRESIDENT

Election, 12 December 1999 and 16 January 2000

	% of votes cast, 12 Dec. 1999	% of votes cast, 16 Jan. 2000
RICARDO LAGOS ESCOBAR (CPD)	48.0	51.3
JOAQUÍN LAVÍN INFANTE (Alianza por Chile)	47.5	48.7
GLADYS MARÍN MILLIE (PCCh)	3.2	—
TOMÁS HIRSCH GOLDSCHMIDT (PH)	0.5	—
SARA LARRAÍN RUIZ-TAGIE	0.4	—
ARTURO FREI BOLÍVAR (UCCP)	0.4	—
Total	**100.0**	**100.0**

CONGRESO NACIONAL

Senado*
(Senate)

President: ANDRÉS ZALDÍVAR LARRAÍN (PDC).

General Election, 11 December 1997*

	Valid votes	% of valid votes	Seats
Partido Demócrata Cristiano (PDC)	1,223,495	29.24	10
Unión Demócrata Independiente (UDI)	717,919	17.16	3
Renovación Nacional (RN)	620,799	14.84	2
Partido Socialista de Chile (PS)	609,725	14.57	1
Partido Comunista de Chile (PCCh)	352,327	8.42	4
Independents	293,429	7.02	—
Partido por la Democracia (PPD)	180,468	4.31	—
Partido Humanista (PH)	92,880	2.22	—
Partido Radical Socialdemócrata (PRSD)	75,680	1.81	—
Unión de Centro-Centro Progresista (UCCP)	17,725	0.42	—
Total	4,184,447	100.00	20

In addition, there were 220,945 blank and 632,538 spoiled votes.

* Results of elections to renew 20 of the 39 elective seats in the Senado. In addition, there are eight (originally nine) designated senators, and a constitutional provision for former Presidents to assume a seat for life, in an *ex-officio* capacity. In March 1998 former President Pinochet assumed a senatorial seat, bringing the total number of senators to 48.

Cámara de Diputados
(Chamber of Deputies)

President: CARLOS MONTES CISTERNA (PS).

General Election, 11 December 1997

	Valid votes	% of valid votes	Seats
Partido Demócrata Cristiano (PDC)	1,317,441	22.98	39
Renovación Nacional (RN)	962,247	16.78	23
Unión Demócrata Independiente (UDI)	827,324	14.43	17
Partido por la Democracia (PPD)	719,575	12.55	16
Partido Socialista de Chile (PS)	636,357	11.10	11
Independents	433,210	7.56	8
Partido Comunista de Chile (PCCh)	393,523	6.86	—
Partido Radical Socialdemócrata (PRSD)	179,701	3.13	4
Partido Humanista (PH)	166,569	2.91	—
Unión de Centro-Centro Progresista (UCCP)	68,185	1.19	1
Partido Democracia del Sur (PDS)	20,635	0.36	1
Nueva Alianza Popular (NAP)	8,947	0.16	—
Total	5,733,714	100.00	120

In addition, there were 295,581 blank and 943,235 spoiled votes.

Political Organizations

The most prominent political organizations are:

Partido Comunista de Chile (PCCh): San Pablo 2271, Santiago; tel. (2) 695-4791; fax (2) 695-1150; achieved legal status in October 1990; Pres. GLADYS MARÍN MILLIE.

Partido Democracia Social: San Antonio 220, Of. 604, Santiago; tel. (2) 39-4244; democratic socialist party; Pres. LUIS ANGEL SANTIBÁÑEZ; Sec.-Gen. JAIME CARMONA DONOSO.

***Partido Demócrata Cristiano (PDC):** Alameda B. O'Higgins 1460, 2°, Santiago; tel. (2) 252-7408; fax (2) 697-3465; f. 1957; member of CPD; Pres. GUTENBERG MARTÍNEZ; Vice-Pres. MARÍA ROZAS.

***Partido Democrático de Izquierda ((PDI):** Londres 37, Of. 16, Santiago; tel. and fax (2) 632-144; Pres. LUIS GODOY GÓMEZ.

Partido Humanista (PH): Alameda B. O'Higgins 129, 4°, Santiago; tel. (2) 632-6787; fax (2) 223-9016; internet www.partidohumanista .cl; Pres. CARLOS DONOSO PACHECO; Sec.-Gen. WILFREDO ALFGEN.

Partido Izquierda Cristiana (PIC): Compañia 2404, Santiago; tel. (2) 671-8410; fax (2) 671-7837; e-mail naitun@entelchile.net; Pres. CARLOS DONOSO PACHECO; Sec.-Gen. PATRICIO VÉJAR MERCADO.

***Partido Liberal:** Huelén 102, 2°, Providencia, Santiago; liberal party; tel. (2) 235-3752; fax (2) 264-0792; f. 1998 by dissident centrist politicians; Pres. ADOLFO BALLA.

***Partido Mapu Obrero Campesino:** Eleuterio Ramírez 1463, Santiago; tel. and fax (2) 696-6342; Pres. SAMUEL BELLO SEPÚLVEDA; Sec.-Gen. HUMBERTO SOLAR DÁVILA.

***Partido por la Democracia (PPD):** Erasmo Escala 2154, Santiago; tel. and fax (2) 671-2320; internet www.ppd.cl; Pres. SERGIO BITAR CHACRA; Sec.-Gen. RICARDO BRODSKY BAUDET.

***Partido Radical Socialdemócrata (PRSD):** Miraflores 495, Santiago; tel. (2) 639-4769; fax (2) 639-1053; centre-left; allied to CPD; Pres. ANSELMO SULE CANDIA; Sec.-Gen. PATRICIO MORALES AGUIRRE.

†Partido Renovación Nacional: Antonio Varas 454, Providencia, Santiago; tel. (2) 235-2436; fax (2) 244-3966; e-mail rn@carn.cl; internet www.rn.cl; f. 1987; right-wing; Pres. ALBERTO CARDEMIL HERRERA; Sec.-Gen. ALBERTO HAUDÓN DEL RÍO.

Partido Social Demócrata (PSD): París 815, Casilla 50.220, Correo Central, Santiago; tel. (2) 39-9064; f. 1973; Pres. ARTURO VENEGAS GUTIÉRREZ; Sec.-Gen. LEVIÁN MUÑOZ PELLICER.

***Partido Socialista de Chile (PS):** Concha y Toro 36, Santiago; tel. (2) 696-4106; fax (2) 699-5429; e-mail pschile@reuna.cl; f. 1933; left-wing; member of Socialist International; Pres. RICARDO NÚÑEZ MUÑOZ; Sec.-Gen. CAMILO ESCALONA MEDINA.

†Partido Unión Demócrata Independiente (UDI): Suecia 286, Santiago; tel. (2) 233-0037; fax (2) 233-6189; e-mail udi@caudi.cl; internet www.udi.cl; f. 1989; right-wing; Pres. PABLO LONGUEIRA MONTES; Sec.-Gen. JUAN ANTONIO COLOMA CORREA.

* Members of the **Concertación de Partidos por la Democracia (CPD):** Londres 57, Santiago; tel. and fax (2) 633-1691; e-mail concert@ctcreuna.cl; f. 1988 as the Comando por el No, an opposition front to campaign against the military regime in the plebiscite of 5 October 1988; name changed to above following plebiscite; Leader RICARDO LAGOS ESCOBAR.

† Members of the **Alianza por Chile:** Santiago; f. 1996 as the Unión por Chile; name changed to above in 1999; right-wing alliance; Leader JOAQUÍN LAVÍN.

Diplomatic Representation

EMBASSIES IN CHILE

Argentina: Miraflores 285, Santiago; tel. (2) 633-1076; fax (2) 639-3321; e-mail embajada.dearg001@chilnet.cl; Ambassador: JOSÉ MARÍA ALVAREZ DE TOLEDO.

Australia: Gertrudis Echeñique 420, Casilla 33, Correo 10, Las Condes, Santiago; tel. (2) 228-5065; fax (2) 208-1707; e-mail cancilau @bellsouth.cl; Ambassador: SUSAN TANNER.

Austria: Barros Errázuriz 1968, 3°, Santiago; tel. (2) 233-4281; fax (2) 204-9382; e-mail santiagodechile@bmaa.gv.at; Ambassador: PETER WILFLING.

Belgium: Providencia 2653, 11°, Of. 1104, Santiago; tel. (2) 232-1070; fax (2) 232-1073; e-mail santiago@diplobel.org; Ambassador: JOHAN BALLEGEER.

Brazil: Alonso Ovalle 1665, Santiago; tel. (2) 672-5000; fax (2) 698-1021; e-mail embrasil@brasembsantiago.cl; Ambassador: GUILHERME LEITE-RIBEIRO.

Bulgaria: Rodolfo Bentjerodt 4895, Santiago; tel. (2) 228-3110; fax (2) 208-0404; e-mail embajada.debul0001@chilnet.cl.

Canada: Nueva Tajamar 481, 12°, Santiago; tel. (2) 362-9660; fax (2) 362-9665; e-mail stago@dfait-maeci.gc.ca; internet www.dfait maeci.gc.ca/santiago; Ambassador: PAUL D. DURAND.

China, People's Republic: Pedro de Valdivia 550, Santiago; tel. (2) 233-9880; fax (2) 234-1129; e-mail em.na@ctcinternet.cl; Ambassador: ZHANG SHAYING.

Colombia: Presidente Errázuriz 3943, Santiago; tel. (2) 206-1314; fax (2) 208-0712; e-mail emcolchi@entelchile.net; Ambassador: RAFAEL PÉREZ M.

Costa Rica: Concepción 65, Of. 801, Santiago; tel. (2) 235-1869; fax (2) 235-1326; e-mail embajada.decas001@chilnet.cl; Ambassador: MARIO GARNIER BORELLA.

Croatia: Jorge VI 306, Santiago; tel. (2) 211-4518, fax (2) 212-4998; e-mail embajada@croatia.cl; Ambassador: IVE LIVLJANIĆ.

Cuba: Los Leones 1346, Providencia, Santiago; tel. (2) 274-5021; fax (2) 274-5708; Ambassador: ARAMÍS FUENTE HERNÁNDEZ.

Czech Republic: Avda El Golf 254, Santiago; tel. (2) 231-1910; fax (2) 232-0707; e-mail santiago@embassy.mzv.cz; Ambassador: JIRI JIRANEK.

Denmark: Jacques Cazotte 5531, Casilla 13430, Vitacura, Santiago; tel. (2) 218-5949; fax (2) 218-1736; e-mail santiago@danish-embassy.cl; Ambassador: BENT KIILERICH.

Dominican Republic: Augusto Leguia Norte 79, Santiago; tel. (2) 245-0667; fax (2) 245-1648; e-mail consulad.odere001@chilnet .cl; Ambassador: RAFAEL VÁLDEZ HICARIO.

Ecuador: Avda Providencia 1979, 5°, Santiago; tel. (2) 231-5073; fax (2) 232-5833; e-mail eecuador@ctc-mundo.cl; Ambassador: JAIME MARCHANT.

Egypt: Roberto del Río 1871, Providencia, Santiago; tel. (2) 274-8881; fax (2) 274-6334; e-mail embajada.deegi001@ chilnet.cl; Ambassador: TALAAT SELMY.

El Salvador: Coronel 2330, Of. 51, Santiago; tel. (2) 233-8324; fax (2) 231-0960; e-mail embajada.deels001@chilnet.cl; Ambassador: HUGO CARRILLO CORLETO.

Finland: Alcántara 200, Of. 201, Las Condes, Santiago; tel. (2) 263-4917; fax (2) 263-4701; e-mail embfin@ctc-mundo.net; Ambassador: RISTO KAUPPI.

France: Condeu 65, Providencia, Santiago; tel. (2) 225-1030; fax (2) 274-1353; e-mail ambassade@ambafrance-cl.org; internet www .france.cl; Ambassador: JEAN-MICHEL GAUSSOT.

Germany: Agustinas 785, 7° y 8°, Casilla 9949, Santiago; tel. (2) 463-2500; fax (2) 463-2525; e-mail emb.alemana.stgo@bellsouth.cl; internet www.embajadadealemania.cl; Ambassador: GEORG CLEMENS DICK.

Greece: Isidora Goyenechea 3356, Of. 21; tel. (2) 231-1244; fax (2) 231-1246; e-mail embgrel@chilesat.net; Ambassador DIMITRIOS MANOLÓPOULOS.

Guatemala: Nuncio Sótero Sonz 55, 8°, Santiago; tel. (2) 335-1565; fax (2) 335-1285; e-mail embajada.degua001@chilnet.cl; Ambassador: JOSE MAURICIO RODRÍGUEZ W.

Haiti: Zurich 255, Of. 21, Los Condes, Santiago; tel. (2) 231-8233; fax (2) 231-0967; e-mail embajada.dehai001@chilnet.cl; Ambassador: GUY PIERRE ANDRÉ.

Holy See: Calle Nuncio Sótero Sanz 200, Casilla 16.836, Correo 9, Santiago (Apostolic Nunciature); tel. (2) 231-2020; fax (2) 231-0868; e-mail nunciatu@entelchile.net; Nuncio: Most Rev. LUIGI VENTURA, Titular Archbishop of Equilio.

Honduras: Rosario Sur 269, Santiago; tel. (2) 212-3682; fax (2) 224-1291; e-mail embajada.dehon001@chilnet.cl; Ambassador: ROBERTO MARTÍNEZ ORDÓÑEZ.

Hungary: Avda los Leones 2279, Providencia, Santiago; tel (2) 204-7977; fax (2) 234-1277; e-mail huembstg@entelchile-net; internet www.chilenet.net/huembstg; Ambassador: TAMÁS TÓTH.

India: Triana 871, Casilla 10433, Santiago; tel. (2) 235-2633; fax (2) 235-9607; e-mail embindia@entelchile.net; Ambassador: K. P. ERNEST.

Indonesia: Nueva Costanera 3318, Santiago; tel. (2) 207-6266; fax (2) 207-9901; e-mail embajada.delar003@chilnet.cl; Ambassador: NOOR HANDONO.

Iran: Luis Thayer Ojeda 1955, Santiago; tel. (2) 209-5373; fax (2) 209-5236; e-mail zagro@cmet.net; Chargé d'affaires: SAYED MUHAMMAD HASHEM HASHEMI.

Israel: San Sebastián 2812, 5°, Casilla 1224, Santiago; tel. (2) 750-0500; fax (2) 750-0555; e-mail eisraelp@rdc.cl; Ambassador: ORI NOY.

Italy: Clemente Fabres 1050, Santiago; tel. (2) 225-9439; fax (2) 223-2467; e-mail italcom@entelchile.net; Ambassador: EMILIO BARBARANI.

Japan: Avda Ricardo Lyon 520, Santiago; tel. (2) 232-1807; fax (2) 232-1812; e-mail embajada.dejap001@chilnet.cl; Ambassador: SHUICHI NOMIYAMA.

Jordan: San Pascual 446, Santiago; tel. (2) 228-8989; fax (2) 228-8783; e-mail embajada.dejor001@chilnet.cl; Ambassador: ATEF HALASA.

Korea, Republic: Alcántara 74, Casilla 1301, Santiago; tel. (2) 228-4214; fax (2) 206-2355; e-mail embajada.decor001@chilnet.cl; Ambassador: CHO YOUNG-HA.

Lebanon: Alianza 1728, Santiago; tel. (2) 232-5027; fax (2) 219-3502; e-mail líbano@netline.cl; Ambassador: MASSOUD MALUF.

Malaysia: Tajamar 183, Of. 1002, Santiago; tel. (2) 233-6698; fax (2) 234-3853; e-mail embajada.demal001@chilnet.cl; Ambassador: LILY ZACHARIAH.

Mexico: Félix de Amesti 128, Santiago; tel. (2) 206-6133; fax (2) 206-6146; e-mail embamex@ia.cl; Ambassador: RAÚL VALDÉS AGUILAR.

Morocco: Los Leones 668, Providencia, Santiago; tel. (2) 366-1050; fax (2) 266-1052; e-mail ambmarch@entelchile.net; Ambassador: ABDELLATIF EL ALOUI.

Netherlands: Las Violetas 2368, Casilla 56-D, Santiago; tel. (2) 223-6825; fax (2) 225-2737; e-mail nlqoustq@holanda-paisesbajos-cl; Ambassador: JOHN C. F. VON MÜHLEN.

New Zealand: Avda Isidora Goyenechea 3516, Casilla 112, Las Condes, Santiago; tel. (2) 231-4204; fax (2) 231-9040; e-mail embajada.denue001@chilnet.cl; Ambassador: DAVID G. MCKEE.

Nicaragua: El Bosque Norte 0140, Of. 33, Santiago; tel. (2) 231-2034; e-mail embajada.denic001@chilnet.cl; Chargé d'affaires a.i.: MARÍA JOSEFINA LAGOS DE CARDENAL.

Norway: San Sebastián 2839, Of. 509, Casilla 2431, Santiago; tel. (2) 234-2888; fax (2) 234-2201; e-mail ambassade-santiago@ud.dep .telemax.no; Ambassador: MARTIN TORE BJØRNDAL.

Panama: Lota 2257, Of. 203, Santiago; tel. (2) 231-1641; fax (2) 234-4086; e-mail embajada.depan001@chilnet.cl; Ambassador: RICARDO MORENO VILLALAZ.

Paraguay: Huérfanos 886, 5°, Ofs 514-515, Santiago; tel. (2) 639-4640; fax (2) 633-4426; e-mail embajada.delpa001@chilnet.cl; Ambassador: CARLOS VILLAGRA MARSAL.

Peru: Avda Andrés Bello 1751, Providencia, Santiago 9, Casilla 16277, Santiago; tel. (2) 235-2356; fax (2) 235-8139; e-mail embajada .peru@chilnet.cl; Ambassador: JORGE COLUNGE VILLACORTA.

Philippines: Félix de Amesti 367, Santiago; tel. (2) 208-1313; fax (2) 208-1400; e-mail embajada.defil001@chilnet.cl; Ambassador: HERMENEGILDO C. CRUZ.

Poland: Mar del Plata 2055, Santiago; tel. (2) 204-1213; fax (2) 204-9332; e-mail embchile@entelchile.net; Ambassador: DANIEL PASSENT.

Portugal: Nuncio Sótero Sanz 35, 5°, Santiago; tel. (2) 232-3034; fax (2) 231-8809; e-mail embajada.depor001@chilnet.cl; Ambassador: RUI FÉLIX-ALVES.

Romania: Benjamín 2955, Santiago; tel. (2) 231-1893; fax (2) 231-2325; e-mail embajada.derum001@chilnet.cl; Ambassador: VASILE DAN.

Russia: Cristobal Colón 4152, Las Condes, Santiago; tel. (2) 208-3413; fax (2) 206-1386; e-mail embrusia@mcl.cl; internet www.rucl.virtualave.net; Ambassador: ALEXEI G. KVASVOV.

South Africa: Avda 11 de Septiembre 2353, 16°, Torre San Ramón, Santiago; tel. (2) 231-2860; fax (2) 231-3185; e-mail embajada .desud001@chilnet.cl; Ambassador: C. S. C. VENTER.

Spain: Avda Andrés Bello 1895, Casilla 16456, Providencia, Santiago; tel. (2) 235-2755; fax (2) 236-1547; e-mail embajada.deesp001@chilnet.cl; internet www.embajada-sudafrica .cl; Ambassador: JUAN MANUEL EGEA IBÁÑEZ.

Sweden: 11 de Septiembre 2353, 4°, Santiago; tel. (2) 231-2733; fax (2) 232-4188; e-mail ambassaden.santiago-de-chile@foreign .ministry.se; Ambassador: ARNE RODIN.

Switzerland: Avda Américo Vespucio Sur 100, 14°, Santiago; tel. (2) 263-4211; fax (2) 263-4094; e-mail vertretung@san.rep.admin.ch; Ambassador: HANS-PETER ERISMANN.

Syria: Carmencita 111, Casilla 12, Correo 10, Santiago; tel. (2) 232-7471; Ambassador: HISHAM HALLAJ.

Thailand: Avda Americo Vespucio 100, 15°, Las Condes, Santiago; tel. (2) 263-0710; fax (2) 263-0803; e-mail thaichil@ctcreuna.cl; internet www.rte-chile.thaiembdc.org; Ambassador: BUSBA BUNNAG.

Turkey: Calle Nuncio Sótero Sanz 136, Providencia, Santiago; tel. (2) 233-6066; fax (2) 206-6146; e-mail embajada .delar006@chilnet.cl; Ambassador: SADI CALISLAR.

Ukraine: Los Conquistadores 1700, 28°, Santiago; tel. (2) 334-5689; fax (2) 334-4556.

United Kingdom: Avda el Bosque Norte 0125, Casilla 72 D, Santiago; tel. (2) 370-4100; fax (2) 370-2140; e-mail consulate@santiago .mail.fco.gov.uk; internet www.britemb.cl; Ambassador: L. GREGORY FAULKNER.

USA: Andrés Bello 2800, Las Condes, Santiago; tel. (2) 232-2600; fax (2) 330-3710; internet www.usembassy.cl; Ambassador: JOHN O'LEARY.

Uruguay: Avda Pedro de Valdivia 711, Casilla 2636, Santiago; tel. (2) 204-7988; fax (2) 204-7772; e-mail urusgo@mailnet.rdl.cl; Ambassador: ALFREDO BIANCHI PALAZZO.

Venezuela: Bustos 2021, Santiago; tel. (2) 225-0021; fax (2) 209-9117; e-mail embajada.deven001@chilnet.cl; Ambassador: HÉCTOR VARGAS ACOSTA.

Yugoslavia: Exequías Allende 2370, Providencia, Casilla 16597, Santiago 9; tel. (2) 223-0510; fax (2) 233-9890; e-mail embajada .deyug001@chilnet.cl; Chargé d'affaires: SVETISLAV RAJEVIC.

Judicial System

The Supreme Courts consist of 21 members.

There are Courts of Appeal (in the cities or departments of Arica, Iquique, Antofagasta, Copiapó, La Serena, Valparaíso, Santiago, San Miguel, Rancagua, Talca, Chillán, Concepción, Temuco, Valdivia, Puerto Montt, Coyhaique and Punta Arenas) whose members are appointed from a list submitted to the President of the Republic by the Supreme Court. The number of members of each court varies. Judges of the lower courts are appointed in a similar manner from lists submitted by the Court of Appeal of the district in which the vacancy arises. Judges and Ministers of the Supreme Court do not continue in office beyond the age of 75 years.

In March 1998 a major reform of the judiciary was implemented, including an increase, from 17 to 21, in the number of Ministers of the Supreme Court.

Corte Suprema: Plaza Montt Varas, Santiago; tel. (2) 698-0561; fax (2) 695-2144.

President of the Supreme Court: HERNÁN ALVAREZ GARCÍA.

Ministers of the Supreme Court:
SERVANDO JORDÁN LÓPEZ
OSCAR CARRASCO ACUÑA
ENRIQUE TAPIA WITTING
ELEODORO ORTIZ SEPÚLVEDA
JORGE RODRÍGUEZ ARIZTÍA
LUIS CORREA BULO
GUILLERMO NAVAS BUSTAMANTE
ALBERTO CHAIGNEAU DEL CAMPO
ENRIQUE CURY URZÚA
JOSÉ LUIS PÉREZ ZAÑARTU
OSVALDO FAÚNDEZ VALLEJOS
HUMBERTO ESPEJO ZÚÑIGA
RICARDO GÁLVEZ BLANCO
ORLANDO ALVAREZ HERNÁNDEZ
DOMINGO YURAC SOTO
MARIO GARRIDO MONTT
MARCOS LIBEDINSKY TSCHORNE
URBANO MARÍN VALLEJO
JOSÉ BENQUIS CAMHI
JORGE MEDINA CUEVAS

Attorney-General: GUILLERMO PIEDRABUENA.

Secretary of the Court: CARLOS A. MENESES PIZARRO.

Corporación Nacional de Reparación y Reconciliación: f. 1992 in order to co-ordinate and implement the recommendations of the **Comisión Nacional de Verdad y Reconciliación,** which was established in 1990 to investigate violations of human rights committed during the military dictatorship, and which delivered its report in 1991; Pres. ALEJANDRO GONZÁLEZ POBLETE; Exec. Sec. ANDRÉS DOMÍNGUEZ VIAL.

Religion

Some 80% of the population are Roman Catholics; there were an estimated 12.0m. adherents at 31 December 1998.

CHRISTIANITY
The Roman Catholic Church

Chile comprises five archdioceses, 17 dioceses, two territorial prelatures and two apostolic vicariates.

Bishops' Conference: Conferencia Episcopal de Chile, Cienfuegos 47, Casilla 517-V, Correo 21, Santiago; tel. (2) 671-7733; fax (2) 698-1416; e-mail sge@cechnet.cl; internet www.cechnet.cl; f. 1955; Pres. Cardinal FRANCISCO JAVIER ERRÁZURIZ OSSA, Archbishop of Santiago de Chile.

Archbishop of Antofagasta: PATRICIO INFANTE ALFONSO, San Martín 2628, Casilla E, Antofagasta; tel. (55) 26-8856; fax (55) 22-3021; e-mail arzoanto@cechnet.cl.

Archbishop of Concepción: ANTONIO MORENO CASAMITJANA, Calle Barros Arana 544, Casilla 65-C, Concepción; tel. (41) 22-8173; fax (41) 25-4121; e-mail arconcep@cechnet.cl.

Archbishop of La Serena: MANUEL DONOSO DONOSO, Los Carrera 450, Casilla 613, La Serena; tel. (51) 21-2325; fax (51) 22-5886; e-mail mdonoso@cechnet.cl.

Archbishop of Puerto Montt: SAVINO M. BERNARDO CAZZARO BERTOLLO, Calle Benavente 385, Casilla 17, Puerto Montt; tel. (65) 25-2215; fax (65) 27-1861; e-mail pmontt@cechnet.cl.

Archbishop of Santiago de Chile: Cardinal FRANCISCO JAVIER ERRÁZURIZ OSSA, Erasmo Escala 1884, Casilla 30-D, Santiago; tel. (2) 696-3275; fax (2) 698-9137.

The Anglican Communion

Anglicans in Chile come within the Diocese of Chile, which forms part of the Anglican Church of the Southern Cone of America, covering Argentina, Bolivia, Chile, Paraguay, Peru and Uruguay.

Bishop of Chile: Rt Rev. H. F. ZAVALA M., Iglesia Anglicana, Casilla 50675, Santiago; tel. (2) 639-1509; fax (2) 639-4581; e-mail fzavala@evangel.cl.

Other Christian Churches

Baptist Evangelical Convention: Casilla 41-22, Santiago; tel. (2) 222-4085; fax (2) 635-4104; f. 1908; Pres. MOISÉS PINTO; Gen. Sec. VÍCTOR OLIVARES.

Evangelical Lutheran Church: Pedro de Valdivia 3420-H, Depto 33, Ñuñoa, Casilla 15167, Santiago; tel. (2) 225-0091; fax (2) 205-2193; f. 1937 as German Evangelical Church in Chile; present name adopted in 1959; Pres. MARTIN JUNGE; 2,500 mems.

Jehovah's Witnesses: Avda Concha y Toro 3456, Puente Alto; tel. (2) 288-1264; fax (2) 288-1257; Dir PEDRO J. LOVATO GROSSO.

Methodist Church: Sargento Aldea 1041, Casilla 67, Santiago; tel. (2) 556-6074; fax (2) 554-1763; autonomous since 1969; 7,317 mems; Bishop NEFTALÍ ARAVENA BRAVO.

Orthodox Chruch of the Patriarch of Antioch: Avda Perú 502, Recoleta, Santiago; tel. and fax (2) 737-4697; Archbishop Mons. SERGIO ABAD.

Pentecostal Church: Calle Pena 1103, Casilla de Correo 2, Curicó; tel. (75) 1035; f. 1945; 90,000 mems; Bishop ENRIQUE CHÁVEZ CAMPOS.

Pentecostal Church Mission: Calle Passy 032, Casilla 238, Santiago; tel. (2) 634-6785; fax (2) 634-6786; f. 1952; Sec. Rev. DANIEL GODOY FERNÁNDEZ; Pres. Rev. ERASMO FARFÁN FIGUEROA; 12,000 mems.

JUDAISM

Comité Representativo de las Entidades Judías en Chile (CREJ): Ricardo Lyon 812, Providencia, Santiago; tel. (2) 274-7101; fax (2) 269-7005; Pres. ELIMAT Y. JASON.

Comunidad Israelita Sefardi de Chile: Ricardo Lyon 812, Providencia, Santiago; tel. (2) 209-8086; fax (2) 204-7382; Pres. SALOMON CAMHI AVAYU; Rabbi IOSEF GABAY.

ISLAM

Sociedad Unión Musulmana: Mezquita As-Salam, Campoamor 2975, esq. Chile-España, Ñuñoa, Santiago; tel. (2) 343-1376; fax (2) 343-11378; Pres. OUSAMA ABUGHAZALÉ.

BAHÁ'Í FAITH

National Spiritual Assembly: Casilla 3731, Manuel de Salas 356, Ñuñoa, Santiago; tel. (2) 269-2005; fax (2) 225-8276; e-mail nsachile@chileat.net; internet www.bci.ord/nsachile; Co-ordinator ROBERTO JARA B.

The Press

Most newspapers of nationwide circulation in Chile are published in Santiago.

DAILIES

Circulation figures listed below are supplied mainly by the Asociación Nacional de la Prensa. Other sources give much lower figures.

Santiago

La Cuarta: Diagonal Vicuña Mackenna 2004, Santiago; tel. (2) 555-0034; fax (2) 556-8727; morning; Gen. Man. JUAN CARLOS LARRAÍN WORMALD.

El Diario: San Crescente 81, 3°, Las Condes, Santiago; tel. (2) 339-1000; fax (2) 231-3340; e-mail buzon@eldiario; internet www .eldiario.cl; f. 1988; morning; Gen. Man. JOSÉ MIGUEL RESPALDIZA CHICHARNO; circ. 20,000.

Diario Oficial de la República de Chile: Agustinas 1269, Santiago; tel. (2) 695-5500; fax (2) 698-2222; internet www.diarioficial .cl; f. 1877; Dir FLORENCIO CEBALLOS B.; circ. 10,000.

Estrategia: Rafael Cañas 114, Providencia, Santiago; tel. (2) 252-4000; fax (2) 236-1114; e-mail estrategia@reuna.cl; internet www.reuna.estrategia.cl; f. 1978; morning; Dir VÍCTOR MAÑUEL O. MÉNDEZ.

El Mercurio: Avda Santa María 5542, Casilla 13-D, Santiago; tel. (2) 330-1111; fax (2) 228-9042; e-mail mercurio@mercurio.cl; internet www.emol.com; f. 1827; morning; conservative; Gen. Man. FERNANDO CISTERNAS BRAVO; circ. 120,000 (weekdays), 280,000 (Sun.).

La Nación: Agustinas 1269, Casilla 81-D, Santiago; tel. (2) 787-0100; fax (2) 698-1059; f. 1917 to replace govt-subsidized *El Cronista*; morning; financial; Propr Soc. Periodística La Nación; Dir GUILLERMO HORMAZÁBAL SALGADO; circ. 45,000.

La Segunda: Avda Santa María 5542, Casilla 13-D, Santiago; tel. (2) 330-1111; fax (2) 228-9289; internet www.lasegunda.com; f. 1931; evening; Dir CRISTIÁN ZEGERS ARIZTÍA; circ. 40,000.

La Tercera: Vicuña Mackenna 1870, Santiago; tel. (2) 551-7067; fax (2) 550-7999; e-mail latercera@copesa.cl; internet www .latercera.cl; f. 1950; morning; Dir FERNANDO PAULSEN; circ. 200,000.

Las Ultimas Noticias: Bellavista 0112, Providencia, Santiago; tel. (2) 730-3000; fax (2) 730-3331; f. 1902; morning; Gen. Man. JUAN ENRIQUE CANALES BESA; owned by the Proprs of *El Mercurio*; circ. 150,000 (except Sat. and Sun.).

Antofagasta

La Estrella del Norte: Manuel Antonio Matta 2112, Antofagasta; tel. (55) 26-4835; f. 1966; evening; Dir CAUPOLICÁN MÁRQUEZ VERGARA; circ. 5,000.

El Mercurio: Manuel Antonio Matta 2112, Antofagasta; tel. (55) 26-4815; fax (55) 25-1710; f. 1906; morning; conservative independent; Proprs Soc. Chilena de Publicaciones; Dir ROBERTO RETAMAL PACHECO; circ. 9,000.

Arica

La Estrella de Arica: San Marcos 580, Arica; tel. (58) 22-5024; fax (58) 25-2890; f. 1976; Dir REINALDO NEIRA RUIZ; circ. 10,000.

Atacama

Chañarcillo: Los Carrera 801, Chañaral, Atacama; tel. (52) 21-9044; f. 1992; morning; Dir LUIS CERPA HIDALGO.

Calama

El Mercurio: Sotomayor 2025, Calama; tel. (56) 25-1090; f. 1968; Propr Soc. Chilena de Publicaciones; Dir ROBERTO RETAMAL PACHECO; circ. 4,500 (weekdays), 7,000 (Sun.).

Chillán

La Discusión de Chillán, SA: Calle 18 de Septiembre 721, Casilla 479, Chillán; tel. (42) 21-2650; fax (42) 21-3578; e-mail ladiscu@ctcreuna.cl; f. 1870; morning; independent; Dir TITO CASTILLO PERALTA; circ. 5,000.

Concepción

El Sur: Calle Freire 799, Casilla 8-C, Concepción; tel. (41) 23-5825; f. 1882; morning; independent; Dir RAFAEL MAIRA LAMAS; circ. 28,000 (weekdays), 45,000 (Sun.).

Copiapó

Atacama: Manuel Rodríguez 740, Copiapó; tel. (52) 2255; morning; independent; Dir SAMUEL SALGADO; circ. 6,500.

Coyhaique

El Diario de Aisén: 21 de Mayo 410, Coyhaique; tel. (67) 234-850; fax (67) 232-318; Dir ALDO MARCHESSE COMPODÓNICO.

Curicó

La Prensa: Merced 373, Casilla 6-D, Curicó; tel. (75) 31-0453; fax (75) 31-1924; e-mail laprensa@entelchile.net; internet diariolaprensa.cl; f. 1898; morning; right-wing; Man. Dir MANUEL MASSA MAUTINO; circ. 4,000.

Iquique

La Estrella de Iquique: Luis Uribe 452, Iquique; tel. (57) 42-2805; fax (57) 42-7975; f. 1966; evening; Dir ARCADIO CASTILLO ORTÍZ; circ. 10,000.

El Nortino: Baquedano 1470, Iquique; tel. (57) 41-6666; fax (57) 41-2997; e-mail nortino@entelchile.net; f. 1992; morning; Dir-Gen. REYNALDO BERRÍOS GONZÁLEZ.

La Serena

El Día: Brasil 431, La Serena; tel. (51) 22-2863; fax (51) 22-2844; f. 1944; morning; Dir ANTONIO PUGA RODRÍGUEZ; circ. 10,800.

Los Angeles

La Tribuna: Calle Colo Colo 464, Casilla 15-D, Los Angeles; tel. (43) 31-3315; fax (43) 31-1040; independent; Dir CIRILO GUZMÁN DE LA FUENTE; circ. 4,500.

Osorno

El Diario Austral: Avda B. O'Higgins 870, Osorno; tel. (64) 23-5191; fax (64) 23-5192; f. 1982; Dir CARLOS NOLI A.; circ. 6,500 (weekdays), 7,300 (Sun.).

Ovalle

El Ovallino: Victoria 323-B, Ovalle; tel. and fax (53) 627-557; Dir JORGE CONTADOR ARAYA.

Puerto Montt

El Llanquíhue: Antonio Varas 167, Puerto Montt; tel. (65) 25-5115; fax (65) 432-401; e-mail ellanquihue@123click.cl; f. 1885; Dir ERNESTO MONTALBA; circ. 4,800 (weekdays), 5,700 (Sun.).

Punta Arenas

La Prensa Austral: Waldo Seguel 636, Casilla 9-D, Punta Arenas; tel. (61) 24-3166; fax (61) 24-7406; e-mail prensa@webcom.com; internet www.prensaaustral.com; f. 1941; morning; independent; Dir MANUEL GONZÁLEZ ARAYA; circ. 10,000, Sunday (*El Magallanes*; f. 1894) 12,000.

Quillota

El Observador: La Concepción 277, Casilla 1-D, Quillota; tel. (33) 312-096; fax (33) 311-417; Dir ROBERTO SILVA BIJIT.

Rancagua

El Rancagüino: O'Carroll 518, Rancagua; tel. (72) 23-0345; fax (72) 22-1483; f. 1915; independent; Dirs HÉCTOR GONZÁLEZ, ALEJANDRO GONZÁLEZ; circ. 10,000.

Talca

El Centro: Tres Oriente 798, Talca; tel. (71) 22-0946; fax (71) 22-0924; f. 1989; Gen. Man. HUGO SAAVEDRA OTEIZA.

Temuco

El Diario Austral: Antonio Varas 945, Casilla 1-D, Temuco; tel. (45) 21-2575; fax (45) 23-9189; f. 1916; morning; commercial, industrial and agricultural interests; Dir MARCO ANTONIO PINTO ZEPEDA; Propr Soc. Periodística Araucanía, SA; circ. 15,100 (weekdays), 23,500 (Sun.).

Tocopilla

La Prensa de Tocopilla: Bolívar 1244, Tocopilla; tel. (83) 81-3036; f. 1924; morning; independent; Gen. Man. JORGE LEIVA CONCHA; circ. 3,000.

Valdivia

El Diario Austral: Yungay 499, Valdivia; tel. (63) 21-3353; fax (63) 21-2236; f. 1982; Dir GUSTAVO SERRANO COTAPOS; circ. 5,600.

Valparaíso

La Estrella: Esmeralda 1002, Casilla 57-V, Valparaíso; tel. (32) 26-4230; fax (32) 26-4241; e-mail estrell@entelchile.net; f. 1921; evening; independent; Dir ALFONSO CASTAGNETO; owned by the Proprs of *El Mercurio*; circ. 28,000 (weekdays), 35,000 (Sat.).

El Mercurio: Esmeralda 1002, Casilla 57-V, Valparaíso; tel. (32) 25-8011; fax (32) 21-8287; f. 1827; morning; Dir ENRIQUE SCHRÖDER VICUÑA; owned by the Proprs of *El Mercurio* in Santiago; circ. 65,000.

Viña del Mar

El Expreso: 3 Poniente 61, Casilla 617, Viñar del Mar; tel. (32) 972-020; fax (32) 972-217; e-mail editor@entelchile.net; internet www.imaginativa.cl/expreso; Man. Dir ENRIQUE ALVARADO AGUILERA.

PERIODICALS

Santiago

Apsi: Gen. Alberto Reyes 032, Providencia, Casilla 9896, Santiago; tel. (2) 77-5450; f. 1976; fortnightly; Dir MARCELO CONTRERAS NIETO; circ. 30,000.

La Bicicleta: José Fagnano 614, Santiago; tel. (2) 222-3969; satirical; Dir ANTONIO DE LA FUENTE.

CA (Ciudad/Arquitectura) Revista Oficial del Colegio de Arquitectos de Chile AG: Manuel Montt 515, Santiago; tel. (2) 235-3368; fax (2) 235-8403; f. 1964; 4 a year; architects' magazine; Editor Arq. JAIME MÁRQUEZ ROJAS; circ. 3,500.

Carola: San Francisco 116, Casilla 1858, Santiago; tel. (2) 33-6433; fortnightly; women's magazine; published by Editorial Antártica, SA; Dir ISABEL MARGARITA AGUIRRE DE MAINO.

Cauce: Huérfanos 713, Of. 604–60, Santiago; tel. (2) 38-2304; fortnightly; political, economic and cultural affairs; Dir ANGEL FLISFICH; circ. 10,000.

Chile Agrícola: Teresa Vial 1172, Casilla 2, Correo 13, Santiago; tel. and fax (2) 522-2627; e-mail chileagricola@agroneg.com; f. 1975; 6 per year; farming; Dir Ing. Agr. RAÚL GONZÁLEZ VALENZUELA; circ. 10,000.

Chile Forestal: Avda Bulnes 259, Of. 406, Santiago; tel. (2) 671-1850; fax (2) 696-6724; f. 1974; monthly; technical information and features on forestry sector; Dir MARIELA ESPEJO SUAZO; circ. 4,000.

Cosas: Almirante Pastene 329, Providencia, Santiago; tel. (2) 364-5100; fax (2) 235-8331; f. 1976; fortnightly; international affairs; Dir MÓNICA COMANDARI KAISER; circ. 40,000.

Creces: Manuel Montt 1922, Santiago; tel. (2) 223-4337; monthly; science and technology; Dir SERGIO PRENAFETA; circ. 12,000.

Deporte Total: Santiago; tel. (2) 251-6236; fax (2) 204-7420; f. 1981; weekly; sport, illustrated; Dir JUAN IGNACIO OTO LARIOS; circ. 25,000.

Economía y Sociedad: MacIver 125, 10°, Santiago; tel. (2) 33-1034; Dir JOSÉ PIÑERA; circ. 10,000.

Ercilla: Luis Thayer Ojeda 1626, Providencia, Santiago; tel. (2) 251-6236; f. 1936; weekly; general interest; Dir JOAQUÍN GONZÁLEZ; circ. 28,000.

Gestión: Luis Carrera 1289, Vitacura, Santiago; tel. (2) 655-6100; fax (2) 655-6408; internet www.estrategia.cl/gestion.htm; f. 1975; monthly; business matters; Dir VÍCTOR MANUEL OJEDA MÉNDEZ; circ. 38,000.

Hoy: María Luisa Santander 0436, Clasificador 654, Correo Central, Santiago; tel. (2) 225-6926; fax (2) 225-4669; e-mail hoy@mailnet.rdc.cl; internet www.reuna.cl/hoy; f. 1977; weekly; general interest; Dir ASCANIO CAVALLO CASTRO; circ. 30,000.

Internet: Avda Carlos Valdovinos 251; tel. (2) 552-5599; e-mail director@interra.cl; monthly; internet and new technology; Dir FLORENCIO UTERAS.

Jurídica del Trabajo: Avda Bulnes 180, Of. 80, Casilla 9447, Santiago; tel. (2) 696-7474; fax (2) 672-6320; f. 1930; 10 a year; Editor IVÁN K. HERNÁNDEZ; circ. 1,000.

Mensaje: Almirante Barroso 24, Casilla 10445, Santiago; tel. (2) 696-0653; fax (2) 698-0617; e-mail mensaje@interaccess.cl; internet www.mensaje.cl; f. 1951; monthly; national, church and international affairs; Dir ANTONIO DELFAU; circ. 7,000.

Microbyte: Avda Condell 1879, Ñuñoa, Santiago; tel. (2) 341-7507; fax (2) 341-7504; f. 1984; monthly; computer science; Dir JOSÉ KAFFMAN; circ. 6,000.

News Review: Casilla 151/9, Santiago; tel. (2) 236-9511; fax (2) 236-0887; e-mail newsrevi@netline.cl; f. 1991; weekly; English language news; Dir GRAHAM A. WIGG.

Paula: Avda Santa María 0120, Providencia,, Santiago; tel. (2) 200-0585; fax (2) 200-0490; e-mail revpaula@paula.cl; 1967; monthly; women's interest; Dir PAULA RECART; circ. 85,000.

Punto Final: San Diego 31, Of. 606, Casilla 13954, Correo 21, Santiago; tel. (2) 697-0615; e-mail punto@interaccess.cl; internet www.puntofinal.cl; f. 1965; fortnightly; politics; left-wing; Dir MANUEL CABIESES; circ. 15,000.

¿Qué Pasa?: Vicuña Mackenna 1870, Ñuñoa, Santiago; tel. (2) 551-7067; fax (2) 550-7529; f. 1971; weekly; general interest; Dir BERNADITA DEL SOLAR VERA; circ. 30,000.

El Siglo: Diagonal Paraguay 458, Casilla 13479, Santiago; tel.and fax (2) 633-0074; f. 1989; fortnightly; published by the Communist Party of Chile (PCCh); Dir CLAUDIO DENEGRI QUINTANA.

Super Rock: Luis Thayer Ojeda 1626, Casilla 3092, Providencia, Santiago; tel. (2) 74-8231. 1985; weekly; Latin and European rock music, illustrated; Dir DARÍO ROJAS MORALES; circ. 40,000.

The Clinic: Las Claras 195, Providencia, Santiago; tel. (2) 343-5850; fax (2) 343-4088; e-mail theclinic@bigfoot.com; forthnightly; political and social satire; Dir PATRICIO FERNÁNDEZ.

Vea: Luis Thayer Ojeda 1626, Casilla 3092, Providencia, Santiago; tel. (2) 74-9421. 1939; weekly; general interest, illustrated; Dir DARÍO ROJAS MORALES; circ. 150,000.

PRESS ASSOCIATION

Asociación Nacional de la Prensa: Agustinas 1357, 12°, Santiago; tel. (2) 696-6431; fax (2) 698-7699; Pres. CARLOS PAUL LAMAS; Sec. FERNANDO SILVA VARGAS.

NEWS AGENCIES

Agencia Chile Noticias (ACN): Dr Pedro Lautaro 2048, Providencia, Santiago; tel. (2) 209-2640; fax (2) 341-4336; e-mail chilenoticias@entelchile.com; internet www.chilenoticias.cl; Dir NORBERTO PARRA HIDALGO.

Chile Information Project (CHIP): Avda Santa María 227, Recoleta, Santiago; tel. (2) 777-5376; e-mail anderson@chip.mic.cl; internet www.santiagotimes.cl; English language; Dir STEPHEN J. ANDERSON..

Europa Press: Biarritz 1913, Providencia, Santiago; tel. and fax (2) 274-3552; e-mail europapress@rdc.cl; Dir JOSÉ RÍOS VIAL.

Orbe Servicios Informativos, SA: Phillips 56, 6°, Of. 66, Santiago; tel. (2) 39-4774; Dir SEBASTIANO BERTOLONE GALLETTI.

Foreign Bureaux

Agence France-Presse (France): Avda B. O'Higgins 1316, 9°, Apt. 92, Santiago; tel. (2) 696-0559; Correspondent HUMBERTO ZUMARÁN ARAYA.

Agencia EFE (Spain): Coronel Santiago Bueras 188, Santiago; tel. (2) 638-0179; fax (2) 633-6130; e-mail direccion@agenciaefe.tie.cl; internet www.efe.es; f. 1966; Bureau Chief Mn MANUEL FUENTES GARCÍA.

Agenzia Nazionale Stampa Associata (ANSA) (Italy): Moneda 1040, Of. 702, Santiago; tel. (2) 698-5811; fax (2) 698-3447; f. 1945; Bureau Chief GIORGIO BAGONI BETTOLLINI.

Associated Press (AP) (USA): Tenderini 85, 10°, Of. 100, Casilla 2653, Santiago; tel. (2) 33-5015; Bureau Chief KEVIN NOBLET.

Bloomberg News (USA): Miraflores 222, Santiago; tel. (2) 638-6820; fax (2) 698-3447; Dir MIKE SMITH.

Deutsche Presse-Agentur (dpa) (Germany): San Antonio 427, Of. 306, Santiago; tel. (2) 639-3633; Correspondent CARLOS DORAT.

Inter Press Service (IPS): Santiago; tel. (2) 39-7091; Dir and Correspondent GUSTAVO GONZÁLEZ RODRÍGUEZ.

Prensa Latina (Cuba): Bombero Ossa 1010, Of. 1104, Santiago; tel. (2) 671-8222; fax (2) 695-8605; Correspondent LIDIA SEÑARIS CEJAS.

Reuters (United Kingdom): Neuva York 33, 11°, Casilla 4248, Santiago; tel. (2) 672-8800; fax (2) 696-0161; Correspondent ROGER ATWOOD.

United Press International (UPI) (USA): Nataniel 47, 9°, Casilla 71-D, Santiago; tel. (2) 696-0162; fax (2) 698-6605; Bureau Chief FERNANDO LEPÉ.

Xinhua (New China) News Agency (People's Republic of China): Biarritz 1981, Providencia, Santiago; tel. (2) 25-5033; Correspondent SUN KUOGUOWEIN.

Association

Asociación de Corresponsales de la Prensa Extranjera en Chile: Coronel Santiago Bueras 188, Santiago; tel. (2) 632-1890; fax (2) 633-6130; Pres. OMAR RUZ.

Publishers

Distribuidora Molino, SA: Abtao 574, Santiago; tel. (2) 776-2295; fax (2) 776-6425; e-mail distribuidoramolino@chilnet.cl; internet www.chilnet.cl/distmolino; Admin. Man. JORGE VARGAS ARAYA.

Ediciones y Comunicaciones Ltda: Luis Thayer Ojeda 0115, Santiago; tel. (2) 232-1241; fax (2) 234-9467; e-mail edicom@chilnet.cl; internet www.chilnet.cl/edicom/; publs include *Anuario Farmacológico*; Gen. Man. MARIO SILVA MARTÍNEZ.

Ediciones San Pablo: Vicuña MacKenna 10777, Casilla 3746, Santiago; tel. (2) 288-2025; fax (2) 288-2026; e-mail dgraledi@cnet.net; Catholic texts; Dir-Gen. P. LUIS NEIRA RAMÍREZ.

Ediciones Técnicas Ltda: Matilde Salamanca 736, 6°, Santiago; tel. (2) 209-8100; fax (2) 209-8101; e-mail editec@editec.cl; internet www.editec.cl; Pres. RICARDO CORTES DONOSO; Gen. Man. ROLY SOLIS SEPÚLVEDA.

Ediciones Universidad Católica de Valparaíso: Universidad Católica de Valparaíso, 12 de Febrero 187, Casilla 1415, Valparaíso; tel. (32) 25-3087; fax (32) 27-3429; also Moneda 673, 8°, Santiago; tel. (2) 633-2230; f. 1970; general literature, social sciences, engineering, education, music, arts, textbooks; Gen. Man. KARLHEINZ LAAGE H.

Editora Nacional Gabriel Mistral Ltda: Santiago; tel. (2) 77-9522; literature, history, philosophy, religion, art, education; government-owned; Man. Dir JOSÉ HARRISON DE LA BARRA.

Editorial Andrés Bello/Jurídica de Chile: Avda Ricardo Lyon 946, Casilla 4256, Providencia, Santiago; tel. (2) 204-9900; fax (2) 225-3600; e-mail mmallea@entelchile.net; internet www .juridicadechile.com; f. 1947; history, arts, literature, politics, economics, textbooks, law and social science; Gen. Man. JULIO SERRANO LAMAS.

Editorial Antártica, SA: San Francisco 116, Santiago; tel. (2) 639-4650; fax (2) 633-4475; f. 1978; Gen. Man. HERNÁN AGUIRRE MACKAY.

Editorial Cuatro Vientos Ltda: Errázuriz 3293, Nuñoa, Santiago; tel. (2) 225-5343; fax (2) 341-3107; e-mail 4vientos@netline.cl; internet www.cuatrovientos.net; Man. Editor JUAN FRANCISCO HUNEEUS COX.

Editorial El Sembrador: Sargento Aldea 1041, Casilla 2037, Santiago; tel. (2) 556-9454; Dir ISAÍAS GUTIÉRREZ.

Editorial Evolución, SA: General del Canto 105, Of. 707, Santiago; tel. (2) 236-4789; fax (2) 236-4796; e-mail evoluc@entelchile.net; internet www.evolucion.cl.

Editorial Nascimento, SA: Chiloé 1433, Casilla 2298, Santiago; tel. (2) 555-0254; f. 1898; general; Man. Dir CARLOS GEORGE NASCIMENTO MÁRQUEZ.

Editorial Renacimiento: Huérfanos 623, Santiago; tel. (2) 639-6621; fax (2) 633-9374; internet www.feriachilenodellibro.cl; Gen. Man. ALBERTO ALDEA.

Editorial San Lucas Ltda: Guardia Vieja 293, Of. 201, Santiago; tel. (2) 334-1583; fax (2) 233-2457; e-mail sanlucas@chilesat.net; internet www.muyinteresante.com/; Gen. Man. CHRISTIAN MIDDLETON O.

Editorial Terra Chile: Ernesto Pinto Lagarrigue 156-H, Recoleta, Santiago; tel. (2) 737-4455; fax (2) 738-0445; Gen. Man. ORLANDO MILESI.

Editorial Texido: Manuel Antonio Tocornal 1487, Santiago; tel. (2) 555-5534; fax (2) 555-5466; Gen. Man. ELSA ZLATER.

Editorial Tiempo Presente Ltda: Almirante Pastene 329, Providencia, Santiago; tel. (2) 364-5100; fax (2) 235-8331; e-mail cosas@mailnet.rdc.cl; internet www.cosas.com; Gen. Man. JUAN LUIS SOMMERS.

Editorial Trineo, SA: Los Olmos 3685, Macul, Santiago; tel. (2) 272-5945; fax (2) 272-0212; e-mail triven@crnet.net; internet www.cmet.net/trineo/; Gen. Man. CARLOS JÉREZ HERNÁNDEZ.

Editorial Universitaria, SA: María Luisa Santander 0447, Casilla 10220, Providencia, Santiago; tel. (2) 223-4555; fax (2) 209-9455; e-mail edituniv@reuna.cl; f. 1947; general literature, social science, technical, textbooks; Man. Dir EDUARDO CASTRO.

Empresa Editora Zig-Zag SA: Los Conquistadores 1700, 17°-B, Providencia, Santiago; tel. (2) 335-7477; fax (2) 335-7445; e-mail zigzag@zigzag.cl; f. 1934; general publishers of literary works, reference books and magazines; Pres. GONZALO VIAL C.; Gen. Man. FRANCISCO PÉREZ FRUGONE.

McGraw-Hill/Interamericana de Chile Ltda: Avda Seminario 541, Santiago; tel;. (2) 222-9405; (2) 635-4467; e-mail mcgrawhill .int001@chilnet.cl; internet www.bookshop.co.uk.

Publicaciones Técnicas, SA (PUBLITECSA): Serrano 172, Santiago; tel. (2) 365-8000; fax (2) 365-8010; e-mail acliente@publitecsa .cl; internet www.publitecsa.cl/; Commercial Man. CARLOS MUNIZAGA.

Red Internacional del Libro Ltda: Avda Eliodoro Yáñez 1934, Of. 14, Santiago; tel. (2) 223-8100; fax (2) 225-4269; e-mail redil@ interactiva.cl; internet www.riledutores.cl; Commercial Man. ELEONORA FINKELSTEIN.

PUBLISHERS' ASSOCIATION

Cámara Chilena del Libro AG: Avda B. O'Higgins 1370, Of. 502, Casilla 13526, Santiago; tel. (2) 672-0348; fax (2) 687-4271; e-mail camlibro@terra.cl; internet www.camilbro.cl; Pres. EDUARDO CASTILLO GARCÍA; Exec. Sec. RAQUEL TORNERO GÓMEZ.

Broadcasting and Communications

TELECOMMUNICATIONS
Regulatory Authority

Subsecretaría de Telecomunicaciones (Department of Telecommunications, Ministry of Public Works, Transport and Telecommunications): Amunátegui 139, 5°, Casilla 120, Correo 21, Santiago; tel. (2) 672-6502; fax (2) 421-3553; e-mail subtel@ subtel.cl; Under-Sec. CHRISTIAN NICOLAI ORELLANA.

Major Operators

Alcatel de Chile: Monseñor Sótero Sanz 55, 3°, Providencia, Santiago; tel. (2) 230-3000; fax (2) 231-1862; internet www.alcatel.com; Pres. SERGE TCHURUK; Gen. Man. MARCEL MAFILLE.

AT&T Chile: Vitacura 2939, 8° y 9°, Vitacura, Santiago; tel. (2) 380-0171; fax (2) 382-5142; e-mail info@firstcom.cl; internet www.attla.cl; Pres. PATRICIO NORTHLAND; Gen. Man. CARLOS FERNÁNDEZ.

Chilesat: Rinconada El Salto 202, Huechuraba, Santiago; tel. (2) 380-0171; fax (2) 382-5142; e-mail tlchile@chilesat.net; internet www.chilesat.net; Pres. JUAN EDUARDO IBÁÑEZ; Gen. Man. RAMÓN VALDIVIESO.

CMET Compañía de Telefónos: Avda Los Leones 1412, Providencia, Santiago; tel. (2) 251-333; fax (2) 274-9573; Pres. JULIO YUBERO; Gen. Man. AGUSTIN CASTELLON.

Empresa Nacional de Telecomunicaciones, SA—ENTEL Chile, SA: Andrés Bello 2687, 14°, Casilla 4254, Santiago; tel. (2) 360-0123; fax (2) 661-7299; internet www.entel.cl; f. 1964; operates the Chilean land satellite stations of Longovilo, Punta Arenas and Coihaique, linked to INTELSAT system; 52% owned by Telecom Italia; Pres. JUAN HURTADO.

PTT Comunicaciones: Marín 0193, Providencia, Santiago; tel. (2) 665-1000; fax (2) 665-1004; e-mail pttsa@ctinternet.cl; internet wwww.pttsa.com; Gen. Man. JAVIER MOLINOS.

Telefónica Chile: Apoquindo 4499, 10°, Casilla 16-D, Santiago; tel. (2) 691-2020; fax (2) 691-2009; formerly Compañía de Telecomunicaciones de Chile, SA; Gen. Man. JACINTO DÍAZ SÁNCHEZ.

TELEX-CHILE, SA: Rinconada El Salto 202, Santiago; tel. (2) 380-0171; fax (2) 382-5142; internet www.telex.cl; Pres. JUAN EDUARDO IBÁÑEZ; Gen. Man. RAMÓN VALDIVIESO.

VTR Gobal Com: Reyes Lavalle 3340, 9°, Las Condes, Santiago; tel. (2) 310-1000; fax (2) 310-1560; internet www.aldea.com; Pres. BLAS TOMIC.

BROADCASTING
Regulatory Authority

Asociación de Radiodifusores de Chile (ARCHI): Pasaje Matte 956, Of. 801, Casilla 10476, Santiago; tel. (2) 639-8755; fax (2) 639-4205; f. 1936; 455 broadcasting stations; Pres. CÉSAR MOLFINO MENDOZA.

Radio

In 1999, according to official sources, there were 1,046 radio stations (867 FM and 179 AM) transmitting in Chile.

Agricultura (AM y FM): Avda Manuel Rodríguez 15, Santiago; tel. (2) 695-3088; fax (2) 672-2749; owned by Sociedad Nacional de Agricultura; Pres. MANUEL VALDÉS VALDÉS; Gen. Man. GUIDO ERRÁZURIZ MORENO.

Aurora FM (Iberoamerican Radio Chile): Phillips 40, 2°, Of. 26, Santiago; tel. (2) 632-4104; fax (2) 639-8868; f. 1982; Pres. ERNESTO CORONA BOZZO; Gen. Man. JUAN CARRASCO HERNÁNDEZ.

Beethoven FM: Garibaldi 1620, Ñuñoa, Santiago; tel. (2) 274-7951; fax (2) 274-3323; internet www.beethovenfm.cl; f. 1981; affiliate stations in Viña del Mar and Temuco; Dir ADOLFO FLORES SAYLER.

Belén AM: Benavente 385, 3°, Casilla 17, Puerto Montt; tel. (65) 25-8048; e-mail radiobel.en001@chilnet.cl; f. 1990; owned by Archbishopric of Puerto Montt; Dir NELSON GONZÁLEZ ANDRADE; Gen. Man. CARLOS WAGNER CATALÁN.

Bío Bío La Radio: Pedro de Valdivia 37, Santiago; tel. (2) 231-2757; fax (2) 233-7997; affiliate stations in Concepción, Los Angeles, Temuco, Ancud, Castro, Osorno, Puerto Montt and Valdivia.

Chilena Solonoticias (AM y FM): Phillips 40, 2°, Casilla 10277; tel. (2) 463-5000; fax (2) 463-5100; e-mail radio@radiochilena.cl; internet www.radiochilena.com; f. 1922; Dir DANIEL LESCOT.

Radio El Conquistador FM: El Conquistador del Monte 4644, Huechuraba, Santiago; tel. (2) 740-9090; fax (2) 740-4992; e-mail rconquis@entelchile.net; internet www.openbox.com/conquistador; f. 1962; affiliate stations in Santiago, Iquique, Antofagasta, La Serena, Viña del Mar, Rancagua, Talca, Chillán, Concepción, Talcahuano, Pucón, Temuco, Villarrica, Lago Llanquihue, Osorno, Puerto Montt, Puerto Varas, Valdivia and Punta Arenas; Gen. Man. URSULA BURKERT FALK.

Radio Cooperativa (AM y FM): Antonio Bellet 223, Casilla 16367, Correo 9, Santiago; tel. (2) 235-2695; fax (2) 235-2320; f. 1936; affiliate stations in Copiapó, Bahía Inglesa, Coquimbo, La Serena, Valparaíso, Concepción, Talcahuano, Temuco and Villarrica; Pres. LUIS AJENJO I.; Gen. Man. SERGIO PARRA G.

La Clave FM: Monjitas 454, Of. 406, Santiago; tel. (2) 633-1621; fax (2) 639-2914; f. 1980; Pres. MIGUEL NASUR ALLEL; Gen. Man. VÍCTOR IBARRA NEGRETE.

Duna FM: Dr Torres Boonen 136, Casilla 13962, Santiago; tel. (2) 225-5494; fax (2) 225-6901; e-mail dunafm@entelchile.net; affiliate stations in Viña del Mar and Concepción; Pres. FELIPE LAMARCA CLARO; Gen. Man. ANA HOLUIGUE BARROS.

Estrella del Mar AM: Ramírez 207, Ancud-Isla de Chiloé; tel. (65) 62-2095; fax (65) 62-2722; e-mail estrella@telsur.cl; f. 1982; affiliate stations in Castro and Quellón; Dir MIGUEL ANGEL MILLAR SILVA.

Festival AM: Paseo Cousiño 8, Casilla 337, Viña del Mar; tel. (32) 88-1229; fax (32) 68-0266; e-mail radiofes.tival002@chilnet.cl; f. 1976; Pres. LUIS MUÑOZ AHUMADA; Gen. Man. SANTIAGO CHIESA HOWARD.

Finísima FM: Luis Thayer Ojeda 1145, Casilla 67, Santiago; tel. (2) 233-5771; fax (2) 231-0611; affiliate stations in Santiago, Arica, Iquique, Calama, Copiapó, La Serena, Ovalle, Isla de Pascua, Quilpe, San Antonio, San Felipe, Villa Alemana, Viña del Mar, Rancagua, Talca, Chillán, Concepción, Los Angeles, Temuco, Puerto Montt, Coihayque, Puerto Aysen and Punto Arenas; Gen. Man. CRISTIÁN WAGNER MUÑOZ.

FM-Hit: Eliodoro Yáñez 1783, Providencia, Santiago; tel. (2) 274-6737; fax (2) 274-8928; internet www.concierto.cl; affiliate stations in Santiago, Iquique, Antofagasta, San Antonio, La Serena, Viña del Mar, Concepción, Temuco, Osorno and Puerto Montt; Gen. Man. JAIME VEGA DE KUYPER.

Horizonte: Avda Los Leones 1625, Providencia, Santiago; tel. (2) 274-6737; fax (2) 274-8900; internet www.concierto.cl/horizon .htm; f. 1985; affiliate stations in Iquique, La Serena, Viña del Mar, Concepción, Temuco and Osorno.

Infinita FM: Avda Los Leones 1285, Casilla Los Leones 1285, Providencia, Santiago; tel. (2) 204-2813; fax (2) 341-6737; f. 1977; affiliate stations in Santiago, Viña del Mar, Concepción and Valdivia; Gen. Man. CARLOS ALBERTO PEÑAFIEL GUARACHI.

Radio Nacional de Chile: Argomedo 369, Santiago; tel. (2) 638-1348; fax (2) 632-1065; affiliate stations in Arica and Punta Arenas; Gen. Man. SANTIAGO AGLIATI.

Para Ti FM: El Conquistador del Monte 4644, Huechuraba, Santiago; tel. (2) 740-9393; fax (2) 740-9051; internet www.openbox.com/ manquehue; affiliate stations in La Serena and Viña del Mar; Gen. Man. FELIPE MOLFINO BURKERT.

Radio Polar: Bories 871, 2°, Punta Arenas; tel. (61) 24-1417; fax (61) 22-8344; f. 1940; Pres. RENÉ VENEGAS OLMEDO.

Pudahuel FM: Eliodoro Yáñez 1783, Providencia, Santiago; tel. (2) 223-0704; fax (2) 223-7589; e-mail radio@pudahuel.cl; internet www.pudahuel.cl; f. 1966; affiliate stations in Arica, Iquique, Antofagasta, Calama, Copiapó, Coquimbo, La Serena, Ovalle, San Felipe, Valparaíso, Viña del Mar, Rancagua, Curico, Linares, Talca, Chillán, Concepción, Los Angeles, Talcahuano, Pucón, Temuco, Villarrica, Ancud-Castro, Osorno, Puerto Montt, Valdivia and Punta Arenas; Pres. SUSANA MUTINELLI ANCHUBIDART; Gen. Man. JOAQUÍN BLAYA BARRIOS.

Santa María de Guadalupe: Miguel Claro 161, Casilla 2626, Santiago; tel. (2) 235-7996; fax (2) 235-8527; affiliate stations in Arica, Iquique, Antofagasta, La Serena, Viña del Mar, Temuco, Puerto Varas, Coihayque and Punta Arenas; Dir ALFONSO CHADWICK.

Superandina FM: Santa Rosa 441, Of. 34, Casilla 401, Los Andes; tel. (34) 42-2515; fax (34) 42-4095; f. 1987; Dir JOSÉ ANDRÉS GÁLVEZ.

Universo FM: Félix de Amesti 124, 8°, Santiago; tel. (2) 206-6065; fax (2) 206-6049; affiliate stations in Iquique, Copiapó, La Serena, Ovalle, Concepción, Temuco, Puerto Montt, Coihayque and Punta Arenas; Pres. ALVARO LARRAÍN.

Television

Canal 2°Rock & Pop: Chucre Manzur 15, Providencia, Santiago; tel. (2) 73-7880; fax (2) 73-5845; Exec. Dir LUIS AJENJO ISAS.

Corporación de Televisión de la Universidad Católica de Chile—Canal 13: Inés Matte Urrejola 0848, Casilla 14600, Providencia, Santiago; tel. (2) 251-4000; fax (2) 630-2040; e-mail dasein@reuna.cl; internet www.reuna.cl/teletrece/corpora.html; f. 1959; non-commercial; Exec. Dir ELEODORO RODRÍGUEZ MATTE; Gen. Man. MANUEL VEGA RODRÍGUEZ.

La Red Televisión, S.A./TV Azteca Chile, S.A.: Manquehue Sur 1201, Las Condes, Santiago; tel. (2) 212-1111; fax (2) 246-5881; e-mail administracion@lared.cl; f. 1991; Pres. JUAN CARLOS LATORRE; Gen. Man. MARCELO PAMDOLFO.

Megavisión, S.A.—Canal 9: Avda Vicuña Mackenna 1348, Santiago; tel. (2) 555-5400; fax (2) 551-8916; e-mail mega@mcl.cl; internet www.mcl.cl./megavision; f. 1990; Pres. RICARDO CLARO VALDÉS; Gen. Man. JOSÉ DÍAZ DEL RÍO.

Red de Televisión S.A./Chilevisión—Canal 11: Inés Matte Urrejola 0825, Casilla 16547, Correo 9, Providencia, Santiago; tel. (2) 737-2227; fax (2) 737-7923; e-mail chu@cmet.net; internet www.chilevision.emet.net; News Dir FELIPE POZO.

Red de Televisión Universidad del Norte, SA: Carrera 1625, Casilla 1045, Antofagasta; tel. (83) 22-6725. 1981; operates Canal 11-Arica, Canal 12-Iquique, Canal 4-Antofagasta and Canal 5-La Serena; Dir SERGIO HERRERA.

Televisión Nacional de Chile—Canal 7: Bellavista 0990, Casilla 16104, Providencia, Santiago; tel. (2) 707-7777; fax (2) 707-7766; e-mail rrpp@tvn.cl; internet www.tvn.cl; government network of 145 stations and an international satellite signal; Chair. LUIS ORTIZ QUIROGA; Gen. Man. MARIO CONCA ROSENDE.

Corporación de Televisión de la Universidad Católica de Valparaíso: Agua Santa Alta 2455, Casilla 247; Viña del Mar; tel. (32) 616-000; fax (32) 610-505; e-mail tv@ucv.cl; f. 1957; Dir JORGE A. BORNSCHEUER.

Finance

(cap. = capital; p.u. = paid up; dep. = deposits; res = reserves; m. = million; amounts in pesos unless otherwise specified)

BANKING
Supervisory Authority

Superintendencia de Bancos e Instituciones Financieras: Moneda 1123, 6°, Casilla 15-D, Santiago; tel. (2) 442-6200; fax (2) 441-0914; e-mail superintendente@sbif.cl; internet www.sbif.cl; f. 1925; affiliated to Ministry of Finance; Superintendent ENRIQUE MARSHALL RIVERA.

Central Bank

Banco Central de Chile: Agustinas 1180, Santiago; tel. (2) 670-2000; fax (2) 698-4647; e-mail bcch@bcentral.cl; internet www.bcentral.cl; f. 1926; under Ministry of Finance until Dec. 1989, when autonomy was granted; bank of issue; cap. 717,470.3m., total assets 16,717,758.1m. (Dec. 2000); Pres. CARLOS MASSAD; Gen. Man. CAMILO CARRASCO.

State Bank

Banco del Estado de Chile: Avda B. O'Higgins 1111, Santiago; tel. (2) 670-7000; fax (2) 670-5094; e-mail mforno@bech.cl; internet www.bancoestado.cl; f. 1953; state bank; cap. 274,801.1m., res 2,086,100m., dep. 3,970,190.3m. (Dec. 1998); Pres. JAIME ESTÉVEZ; Gen. Man. JOSÉ MANUEL MENA; 214 brs.

Commercial Banks

Banco de A. Edwards: Huérfanos 740, Santiago; tel. (2) 388-3000; fax (2) 388-4428; internet www.banedwards.cl; f. 1851; cap. 73,649m., res 8,649m. (Dec. 1995); Pres. ANDRONICO LUKSIC; Gen. Man. GUSTAVO FAVRE DOMÍNGUEZ; 61 brs.

Banco BICE: Teatinos 220, Santiago; tel. (2) 692-2000; fax (2) 696-5324; e-mail webmaster@bice.cl; internet www.bice.cl; f. 1979 as Banco Industrial y de Comercio Exterior; name changed as above in 1988; cap. and res 60,065.4m., dep. 851,465.4m. (Dec. 1998); Pres. and Chair. BERNARDO MATTE; Gen. Man. CRISTIAN EYZAGUIRRE; 13 brs.

Banco de Chile: Ahumada 251, Casilla 151-D, Santiago; tel. (2) 637-1111; fax (2) 637-3434; internet www.bancochile.cl; f. 1894; 55% owned by the Luksic group; cap. and res 302,272.3m., dep.

3,917,410.2m. (Dec. 1999); Chair. SEGISMUNDO SCHULIN-ZEUTHEN SERRANO; Gen. Man. RENÉ LEHUEDÉ; 102 brs.

Banco de Crédito e Inversiones: Huérfanos 1134, Casilla 136-D, Santiago; tel. (2) 692-7000; fax (2) 695-3777; e-mail webmaster@bci.cl; internet www.bci.cl; f. 1937; cap. and res 132,329.6m., dep. 2,619,703.0m. (Dec. 1998); Pres. LUIS ENRIQUE YARUR REY; Gen. Man. HUMBERTO BÉJARES; 112 brs.

Banco del Desarrollo: Avda B. O'Higgins 949, 3°, Casilla 320-V, Correo 21, Santiago; tel. (2) 674-5000; fax (2) 671-5547; e-mail bdd@bandes.cl; internet www. bdesarrollo.cl; f. 1983; cap. US $119.7m., dep. US $2,108.4m. (Dec. 1998); Pres. VICENTE CARUZ MIDDLETON; Gen. Man. HUGO TRIVELLI; 80 brs.

Banco Internacional: Moneda 818, Casilla 135-D, Santiago; tel. (2) 369-7000; fax (2) 369-7367; e-mail infor@binter.cl; f. 1944; placed under state control Jan. 1983 but returned to the private sector in May 1986; cap. 6,845.4m., res 5,870.7m., dep. 132,219.4m. (Dec. 1998); Pres. ALEJANDRO L. FURMAN SIHMAN; Gen. Man. ALVARO ACHONDO GONZÁLEZ; 11 brs.

Banco Santander-Chile: Bandera 140, Casilla 57-D, Santiago; tel. (2) 320-2000; fax (2) 330-8877; internet www.bsantander.cl; f. 1926; cap. 56,745.0m., res 11,015.1m., dep. 900,891.9m. (Dec. 1994); subsidiary of Banco de Santander (Spain); incorporated Banco Osorno y La Unión in 1996; Pres. EMILIO BOTÍN SANZ DE SAUTUOLA Y GARCÍA DE LOS RÍOS; Gen. Man. OSCAR VON CHRISMAR; 72 brs.

Banco Santiago: Bandera 201, 3°, Casilla 14437, Santiago; tel. (2) 647-4000; fax (2) 671-7152; e-mail comelec@bancosantiago.cl; internet www.bancosantiago.cl; f. 1997 by merger of Banco O'Higgins and Banco de Santiago; cap. 373,203.3m., res 11,940.5m., dep. 4,621,991m. (Dec. 1999); Chair. CARLOS OLIVOS MARCHANT; Gen. Man. FERNANDO CAÑAS; 163 brs.

Banco Security: Agustinas 621, Santiago; tel. (2) 270-4000; fax (2) 270-4001; e-mail banco@security.cl; internet www.security.cl; f. 1981; fmrly Banco Urquijo de Chile; cap. and res 54,300.6m., dep. 661,327.2m. (Dec. 1998); Pres. FRANCISCO SILVA S.; Gen. Man. RAMÓN ELUCHANS O.; 11 brs.

Banco Sud Americano: Morandé 226, Casilla 90-D, Santiago; tel. (2) 692-6000; fax (2) 698-6008; e-mail bsa@bsa.cl; internet www.bsa.cl; f. 1944; cap. 57,300.9m., res 35,035.8m., dep. 1,090,037.7m. (Dec. 1998); Chair. RICHARD E. WAUGH; CEO LUIS FERNANDO TOBÓN; 49 brs.

BBV Banco BHIF: Huérfanos 1234, Casilla 517, Santiago; tel. (2) 679-1000; fax (2) 698-5640; internet www.bhif.cl; f. 1883; was merged with Banco Nacional in 1989; acquired Banesto Chile Bank in Feb. 1995; controlling interest acquired by Banco Bilbao Vizcaya (Spain) in Sept. 1998; name changed as above in 1999; cap. 103,849.5m., res 44,387.2m., dep. 1,178,799.1m. (Dec. 1998); Pres. JOSÉ SAID SAFFIE; CEO CARLOS SENENT-SALES; 78 brs.

Corpbanca: Huérfanos 1072, Casilla 80-D, Santiago; tel. (2) 696-2741; fax (2) 696-0271; e-mail fburgos@corpbanca.cl; internet www.corpbanca.cl; f. 1871 as Banco de Concepción, current name adopted in March 1997; cap. and res 106,951.5m., dep. 1,144,161.2m. (Dec. 1999); Chair. CARLOS ABUMOHOR; Gen. Man. JORGE SELUME; 65 brs.

Dresdner Banque Nationale de Paris: Huérfanos 1219, Casilla 10492, Santiago; tel. (2) 731-4444; fax (2) 460-8177; e-mail info@dresbnp.cl; internet www.dresbnp.cl; f. 1958 as Banco Continental; bought by Crédit Lyonnais in Sept. 1987; current name adopted in 1996; cap. and res 23,319.8m., dep. 249,655.1m. (Dec. 1999); Pres. WALTER SIEBEL; Gen. Man. EWALD DOERNER; 1 br.

ING Bank (Chile), SA: Avda Nueva Tajamar 481, 17°, Of. 1701, Casilla 500-V, Las Condes, Santiago; tel. (2) 330-0600; fax (2) 699-1113; cap. and res 10.1m. (Oct. 1995); Pres. ALBERT JACOB STAAL; Gen. Man. GERMÁN TAGLE O'RYAN; 1 br.

Foreign Banks

Foreign banks with branches in Chile include the following:

ABN AMRO Bank (Netherlands), American Express Bank Ltd (USA), Banco do Brasil, Banco do Estado de São Paulo (Brazil), Banco de la Nación Argentina, Banco Real (Brazil), Banco Sudameris (France and Italy), Bank of America NT & SA (USA), Bank of Boston (USA), Bank of Tokyo-Mitsubishi Ltd (Japan), BBVA Banco BHIF (Spain), Chase Manhattan Bank NA, Citibank NA (USA), HSBC Bank (United Kingdom), Republic National Bank of New York (USA).

Finance Corporations

Financiera Atlas, SA: Nueva de Lyon 72, 7°, Santiago; tel. (2) 233-3151; fax (2) 233-3152; Gen. Man. NEIL A. DENTON FEILMANN.

Financiera Condell, SA: Ahumada 179, 9°, Santiago; tel. (2) 672-1222; fax (2) 699-2590; Gen. Man. ANTONIO S. UNDURRAGA OLIVOS.

Financiera Conosur: Avda B. O'Higgins 1980, 7°, Santiago; tel. (2) 697-1491; fax (2) 696-3133; internet www.financieraconosur.cl; Pres. JOSÉ LUIS DEL RÍO; Gen. Man. EDMUNDO HERMOSILLA.

Banking Association

Asociación de Bancos e Instituciones Financieras de Chile AG: Ahumada 179, 12°, Santiago; tel. (2) 699-3977; fax (2) 698-8945; internet www.abif.cl; f. 1945; Pres. HERNÁN SOMERVILLE SENN; Gen. Man. ALEJANDRO ALARCÓN PÉREZ.

Other Financial Supervisory Bodies

Superintendencia de Administradoras de Fondos de Pensiones (AFPs) (Superintendency of Pensions Fund Administrators): Huérfanos 1273, 9°, Casilla 3955, Santiago; tel. (2) 753-0122; fax (2) 753-0122; e-mail info@safp.cl; internet www.safp.cl; f. 1981; CEO ALEJANDRO FERREIRO Y.

Superintendencia de Previsión Social (Superintendency of Social Security): Huérfanos 1376, 5°, Santiago; tel. (2) 696-8092; fax (2) 696-4672; CEO LUIS ORLANDINI MOLINA.

STOCK EXCHANGES

Bolsa de Comercio de Santiago: La Bolsa 64, Casilla 123-D, Santiago; tel. (2) 698-2001; fax (2) 697-2236; e-mail fledermann @comercio.bolsantiago; internet www.bolsantiago.cl; f. 1893; 44 mems; Pres. PABLO YRARRÁZAVAL VALDÉS; Gen. Man. JOSÉ ANTONIO MARTÍNEZ Z.

Bolsa de Corredores—Valores de Valparaíso: Prat 798, Casilla 218-V, Valparaíso; tel. (32) 25-0677; fax (32) 21-2764; e-mail bolsadec.orred001@chilnet.cl; f. 1905; Pres. CARLOS F. MARÍN ORREGO; Man. ARIE JOEL GELFENSTEIN FREUNDLICH.

Bolsa Electrónica de Chile: Huérfanos 770, 14°, Santiago; tel. (2) 639-4699; fax (2) 639-9015; e-mail info@bolchile.cl; internet www.bolchile.cl; Gen. Man. JUAN CARLOS SPENCER OSSA.

INSURANCE

In 1999 there were 60 general, life and reinsurance companies operating in Chile.

Supervisory Authority

Superintendencia de Valores y Seguros: Teatinos 120, 6°, Santiago; tel. (2) 549-5900; fax (2) 549-5965; e-mail svalseg@ibm.net; internet www.svs.cl; f. 1931; under Ministry of Finance; Supt ALVARO CLARK DE LA CERDA.

Principal Companies

Aetna Chile Seguros de Vida, SA: Suecia 211, 7°, Santiago; tel. (2) 364-2000; fax (2) 364-2010; e-mail jdupre@aetna.cl; internet www.aetna.cl; f. 1981; life; Pres. SERGIO BAEZA VALDÉS; Gen. Man. FERNANDO HASENBERG NATOLI.

Aseguradora Magallanes, SA: Agustinas 1022, Of. 722; tel. (2) 365-4800; fax (2) 365-4860; e-mail fvarela@magallanes.cl; internet www.magallanes.cl; f. 1957; general; Pres. SERGIO LARRAÍN; Gen. Man. FERNANDO VARELA.

Axa Seguros Generales, SA: Huérfanos 1189, 2°, 3° y 4°, Casilla 429-V, Santiago; tel. (2) 679-9200; fax (2) 679-9300; internet www.axa.cl; f. 1936; general; Gen. Man BARNARDO SERRANO LOPEZ.

Chubb de Chile, SA: Gertrudis Echeñique 30, 4°, Santiago; tel. (2) 206-2191; fax (2) 206-2735; internet www.chubb.com/chile; f. 1992; general; Gen. Man. CLAUDIO M. ROSSI.

Cía de Seguros de Crédito Continental, SA: Avda Isidora Goyenechea 3162, 6°, Edif. Parque 1 Golf, Santiago; tel. (2) 636-4000; fax (2) 636-4001; e-mail comer@continental.cl; f. 1990; general; Gen. Man. FRANCISCO ARTIGAS CELIS.

Cía de Seguros Generales Aetna Chile, SA: Suecia 211, Santiago; tel. (2) 364-2000; fax (2) 364-2060; internet www.aetna.cl; f. 1899; general; Pres. SERGIO BAEZA VALDÉS; Gen. Man. MAXIMO ERRÁZURIZ DE SOLMINIHAC.

Cía de Seguros Generales Consorcio Nacional de Seguros, SA: Apoquindo 3039, Casilla 28, Correo 10, Santiago; tel. (2) 250-2500; fax (2) 364-2525; f. 1992; general; Gen. Man. ARMANDO BRICEÑO NEFF.

Cía de Seguros Generales Cruz del Sur, SA: Paseo Puente 574, 7°, Casilla 2682, Santiago; tel. (2) 690-6000; fax (2) 698-9126; f. 1974; general; Pres. ROBERTO ANGELINI; Gen. Man. MIKEL URIARTE.

Cía de Seguros Generales Euroamérica, SA: Agustinas 1127, 2°, Casilla 180-D, Santiago; tel. (2) 672-7242; fax (2) 696-4086; internet www.euroamerica.cl; f. 1986; general; Gen. Man. JUAN ENRIQUE BUDINICH SANTANDER.

Cía de Seguros Generales La Chilena Consolidada, SA: Pedro de Valdivia 195, Casilla 16587, Correo 9, Providencia, Santiago; tel. (2) 200-7000; fax (2) 274-9933; f. 1905; general; Gen. Man. IGNACIO BARRIGA UGARTE.

Cía de Seguros de Vida Consorcio Nacional de Seguros, SA: Avda El Bosque Sur 180, 3°, Casilla 232, Correo 35, Providencia, Santiago; tel. (2) 230-4000; fax (2) 230-4050; e-mail

guillermomartinez@consorcio.cl; f. 1916; life; Pres. JUAN BILBAO HORMAECHE; Gen. Mn. MARCOS BÜCHI BUC.

Cía de Seguros de Vida La Construcción, SA: Avda Providencia 1806, 11°–18°, Providencia, Santiago; tel. (2) 340-3000; fax (2) 340-3024; e-mail seguros@laconstruccion.sa.cl; f. 1985; life; Pres. VÍCTOR MANUEL JARPA RIVEROS; Gen. Man. MANUEL ZEGERS IRARRÁZAVAL.

Cía de Seguros de Vida Cruz del Sur, SA: Paseo Puente 574, 4°, Casilla 2682, Santiago; tel. (2) 690-6000; fax (2) 698-9126; internet www.cruzdelsur.cl; f. 1992; life; Pres. ROBERTO ANGELINI; Gen. Man. MIKEL URIARTE.

Cía de Seguros de Vida Euroamérica, SA: Agustinas 1127, 3°, Casilla 21-D, Santiago; tel. (2) 782-7000; fax (2) 699-0732; e-mail deptoservicio@eurovida.cl; internet www.eurovida.cl; f. 1962; life; Pres. BENJAMIN DAVIS CLARKE; Gen. Man. PATRICIA JAIME VÉLIZ.

Cía de Seguros de Vida Santander, SA: Bandera 150, Santiago; tel. (2) 640-1177; fax (2) 640-1377; e-mail servicio@santanderseg.cl; internet www.netra.santanderseg.cl/index; f. 1989; life; Pres. FRANCISCO MARTÍN LÓPEZ-QUESADA.

ING, Seguros de Vida, SA: Nueva Tajamar 555; 18°, Casilla 70, Correo 10, Santiago; tel. (2) 252-1500; fax (2) 252-1504; internet www.INGgrupo.com; f. 1989; life; Gen. Man. ANDRÉS TAGLE DOMINGUEZ.

La Interamericana Compañía de Seguros de Vida: Agustinas 640, 9°, Casilla 163, Correo Central, Santiago; tel. (2) 630-3000; fax (2) 633-3222; internet www.intervida.cl/interamerica; f. 1980; life; Pres. RICARDO PERALTA VALENZUELA; Gen. Man. ANDRÉS SAAVEDRA ECHEVERRÍA.

Le Mans—ISE Compañia Seguros Generales, SA: Encomenderos 113, Casilla 185-D, Centro 192, Las Condes, Santiago; tel. (2) 230-9000; fax (2) 232-8209; e-mail lemans@lemans.cl; internet www.lemans.cl; f. 1888; general; Pres. IGNACIO WALKER CONCHA; Gen. Man. MARC GARÇON.

Mapfre Garanías y Crédito, SA: Teatinos 280, 5°, Santiago; tel. (2) 870-1500; fax (2) 870-1501; e-mail mapfreg@entelchile.net; f. 1991; general; Gen. Man. RODRIGO CAMPERO PETERS.

Renta Nacional Compañía de Seguros de Vida, SA: Amunátegui 178, 1° y 2°, Santiago; tel. (2) 670-0200; fax (2) 670-0399; e-mail renta@rentanac.cl; f. 1982; life; Pres. JORGE SIMS SAN ROMÁN; Gen. Man. ROBERTO MORA.

Seguros Previsión Vida, SA: Hendaya 60, 7°, Casilla 134, Correo 34, Santiago; tel. (2) 750-2400; fax (2) 750-2440; e-mail seguro@prevision.cl; internet www.prevision.cl; f. 1981; life; Pres. FRANCISCO SILVA; Gen. Man. CARLOS FERNÁNDEZ.

Reinsurance

American Re-Insurance Company (Chile), SA: Avda Nueva Tajamar 481, Torre Norte, Of. 505, Santiago; tel. (2) 339-7171; fax (2) 339-7117; f. 1981; general; Pres. MAHMOUD ABDALLAH; Gen. Man. MAURICIO RIESCO VALDÉS.

Caja Reaseguradora de Chile, SA (Generales): Apoquindo 4449, 8°, Casilla 2753, Santiago; tel. (2) 338-1200; fax (2) 206-4063; f. 1927; general; Pres. ANDRÉS JIMÉNES; Gen. Man. ANDRÉS CHAPARRO KAUFMAN.

Caja Reaseguradora de Chile, SA: Apoquindo 4449, 8°, Santiago; tel. (2) 228-6106; fax (2) 698-9730; f. 1980; life; Pres. ANDRÉS JIMÉNES.

Cía de Reaseguros de Vida Soince, SA: Bandera 150, Santiago; tel. (2) 640-1177; internet www.santanderseg.cl; f. 1990; life; Pres. FRANCISCO MARTÍN LÓPEZ-QUESADA.

Insurance Association

Asociación de Aseguradores de Chile, AG: La Concepción 322, Of. 501, Providencia, Santiago; tel. (2) 236-2596; fax (2) 235-1502; e-mail seguros@aach.cl; internet www.aach.cl; f. 1931; Pres. MARCOS BÜCHI BUC; Gen. Man. JOAQUÍN ECHENIQUE RIVERA.

Trade and Industry

GOVERNMENT AGENCIES

Corporación de Fomento de la Producción—CORFO: Moneda 921, Casilla 3886, Santiago; tel. (2) 638-0521; fax (2) 671-1058; f. 1939; holding group of principal state enterprises; grants loans and guarantees to private sector; responsible for sale of non-strategic state enterprises; Gen. Man. EDUARDO BITRÁN COLODRO.

PROCHILE (Dirección General de Relaciones Económicas Internacionales): Avda B. O'Higgins 1315, 2°, Casilla 14087, Correo 21, Santiago; tel. (2) 565-9000; fax (2) 696-0639; e-mail info@prochile.cl; internet www.uxdirecon.prochile.cl; f. 1974; bureau of international economic affairs; Dir HÉCTOR CASANUEVA OJEDA.

Servicio Nacional de Capacitación y Empleo (National Training and Employment Service): Huérfanos 1273, planta 11, Santiago; tel. (2) 696-8213; fax (2) 696-5039; internet www.sence.cl; attached to Ministry of Labour and Social Security; Dir IGNACIO LARRAECHEA LOESSER.

STATE CORPORATION

Corporación Nacional del Cobre de Chile (CODELCO—Chile): Huérfanos 1270, Casilla 150-D, Santiago; tel. (2) 690-3000; fax (2) 690-3059; internet www.codelcochile.com; f. 1976 as a state-owned enterprise with five copper-producing operational divisions at Chuquicamata, Radomiro Tomić, Salvador, Andina and El Teniente; attached to Ministry of Mines; Exec. Pres. JUAN VILLARZÚ RHODE; 17,403 employees.

DEVELOPMENT ORGANIZATIONS

Comisión Chilena de Energía Nuclear: Amunátegui 95, Casilla 188-D, Santiago; tel. (2) 699-0070; fax (2) 699-1618; e-mail gtorres@ gopher.cchen.cl; internet www.cchen.cl; f. 1965; government body to develop peaceful uses of atomic energy; concentrates, regulates and controls all matters related to nuclear energy; Exec. Dir GONZALO TORRES OVIEDO.

Corporación Nacional de Desarrollo Indígena (Conadi): Manuel Mott 1070, Temuco; tel. (45) 324-111; fax (45) 234-323; internet www.conadi.cl; promote the economic and social development of indigenous communities.

Corporación Nacional Forestal—CONAF: Avda Bulnes 285, Of. 501, Santiago; tel. (2) 672-2724; fax (2) 671-5881; f. 1970 to promote forestry activities, to enforce forestry law, to promote afforestation, to administer subsidies for afforestation projects and to increase and preserve forest resources; manages 13.97m. ha designated as National Parks, Natural Monuments and National Reserves; under Ministry of Agriculture; Exec. Dir Ing. CRISTIÁN PALMA ARANCIBIA.

Empresa Nacional de Minería—ENAMI: MacIver 459, 2°, Casilla 100-D, Santiago; tel. (2) 637-5000; fax (2) 637-5436; promotes the development of the small- and medium-sized mines; attached to Ministry of Mines; partially privatized; Exec. Vice-Pres. PATRICIO ARTIAGOITIA ALTI.

CHAMBERS OF COMMERCE

Cámara de Comercio de Santiago de Chile, AG: Santa Lucía 302, 3°, Casilla 1297, Santiago; tel. (2) 360-7000; fax (2) 633-3395; f. 1919; 1,300 mems; Pres. PETER T. HILL; Man. CLAUDIO ORTIZ T.

Cámara de la Producción y del Comercio de Concepción: Cauplicán 567, 2°, Concepción; tel. (41) 241-440; fax (41) 227-903; e-mail bseguel@cpcc.cl; internet www.cpcc.cl; Pres. HERNÁN ASCUI; Gen. Man. LEONCIO TÍO.

Cámara Nacional de Comercio, Servicios y Turismo de Chile: Merced 230, Santiago; tel. (2) 365-4000; fax (2) 365-4001; internet www.cnc.cl; f. 1858; Pres. FERNANDO LIHN CONCHA; Gen. Sec. JOSÉ MANUEL MELERO ABAROA; 120 mems.

There are chambers of commerce in all major towns.

INDUSTRIAL AND TRADE ASSOCIATIONS

Servicio Agrícola y Ganadero (SAG): Avda Bulnes 140, Santiago; tel. (2) 698-2244; fax (2) 672-1812; e-mail sag@sag.minagri.gob.cl; internet www.sag.gob.cl; under Ministry of Agriculture; responsible for the protection and development of safe practice in the sector; Exec. Dir ANTONIO YAKSIC SOULÉ.

Sociedad Agrícola y Servicios Isla de Pascua: Alfredo Lecannelier 1940, Providencia, Santiago; tel. (2) 232-7497; fax (2) 232-7497; administers agriculture and public services on Easter Island; Gen. Man. GERARDO VELASCO.

Subsecretaría de Pesca: Bellavista 168, 16-18°, Valparaíso; tel. (32) 21-2187; fax (32) 21-2790; f. 1976; controls and promotes fishing industry; Sub-Sec. PATRICIO BERNAL PONCE.

EMPLOYERS' ORGANIZATIONS

Confederación de la Producción y del Comercio: Monseñor Sótero Sanz 182, Providencia, Santiago; tel. (2) 231-9764; fax (2) 231-9808; f. 1936; Pres. WALTER RIESCO SALVO; Gen. Man. CRISTIÁN PIZARRO ALLARD.

Affiliated organizations:

Asociación de Bancos e Instituciones Financieras de Chile (q.v.).

Cámara Chilena de la Construcción: Marchant Pereira 10, 3°, Providencia, Casilla Clasificador 679, Santiago; tel. (2) 233-1131; fax (2) 232-7600; f. 1951; Pres. VÍCTOR MANUEL JARPA RIVEROS; Gen. Man. BLAS BELLOLIO RODRÍGUEZ; 3,000 mems.

Sociedad de Fomento Fabril, FG: Avda Andrés Bello 2777, 3°, Casilla 37, Correo 35, Tobalaba, Santiago; tel. (2) 203-3100; fax (2) 203-3101; f. 1883; largest employers' organization; Pres. PEDRO LIZANA GREVE; Man. FREDERICO MONTES LIRA; 2,000 mems.

Sociedad Nacional de Agricultura—Federación Gremial (SNA): Tenderini 187, 2°, Casilla 40-D, Santiago; tel. (2) 639-6710; fax (2) 633-7771; f. 1838; landowners' association; controls Radio Stations CB 57 and XQB8 (FM) in Santiago, CB-97 in

Valparaíso, CD-120 in Los Angeles, CA-144 in La Serena, CD-127 in Temuco; Pres. RICARDO ARIZTÍA DE CASTRO; Gen. Sec. LUIS QUIROZA ARRAU.

Sociedad Nacional de Minería—SONAMI: Teatinos 20, 3°, Of. 33, Casilla 1807, Santiago; tel. (2) 695-5626; fax (2) 697-1778; f. 1883; Pres. WALTER RIESCO SALVO; Man. MANUEL CERECEDA VIDAL.

Confederación de Asociaciones Gremiales y Federaciones de Agricultores de Chile: Lautaro 218, Los Angeles; registered with Ministry of Economic Affairs in 1981; Pres. DOMINGO DURÁN NEUMANN; Gen. Sec. ADOLFO LARRAÍN V.

Confederación del Comercio Detallista de Chile, AG: Merced 380, 8°, Of. 74, Santiago; tel. (2) 39-5719; fax (2) 38-0338; f. 1938; retail trade; registered with Ministry of Economic Affairs in 1980; Nat. Pres. RAFAEL CUMSILLE ZAPAPA; Sec.-Gen. JAIME PÉREZ RODRÍGUEZ.

Confederación Gremial Nacional Unida de la Mediana y Pequeña Industria, Servicios y Artesanado—CONUPIA: Santiago; registered with Ministry of Economic Affairs in 1980; small-and medium-sized industries and crafts; Pres. FÉLIX LUQUE PORTILLA.

There are many federations of private industrialists, organized by industry and region.

UTILITIES

Comisión Nacional de Energía: Teatinos 120, 7°, Santiago; tel. (2) 365-6842; fax (2) 365-6834; Pres. OSCAR LANDERRETCHE GACITÚA.

General

COLBUN: Avda 11 de Septiembre 2353, 9°, Santiago; tel. (2) 231-3414; fax (2) 231-6609; state power utility; scheduled for privatization once anti-monopoly legislation was in place.

Electricity

Arauco Generación: Vitacura 2771, 9°, Las Condes, Santiago; tel. (2) 560-6700; fax (2) 236-5090; e-mail gic@arauco.cl; Pres. ARMANDO LOLAS; Gen. Man. HERNÁN ARRIAGADA.

BMV Industrias Electricas: Avda Vicuña Mackenna 1540, Nuñoa, Santiago; tel. (2) 555-8806; fax (2) 555-8807; Gen. Man. ANGÉLICA PADOVANI.

Chilectra, SA: Santo Domingo 789, Casilla 1557, Santiago; tel. (2) 632-2000; fax (2) 639-3280; e-mail rrpp@chilectra.cl; internet www.chilectra.cl; f. 1921; transmission and distribution of electrical energy; supplies distribution companies including the Empresa Eléctrica Municipal de Lo Barnechea, Empresa Municipal de Til-Til, Empresa Eléctrica de Colina, SA and the Cía Eléctrica del Río Maipo, SA; holds overseas distribution concessions in Argentina, Peru and Brazil; Pres. JORGE ROSENBLUT; Gen. Man. JULIO VALENZUELA.

Chilquinta Energía, SA: General Cruz 222, Valparaíso; tel. (32) 502-000; fax (32) 210-723; f. 1995; Pres. HÉCTOR MADARIAGA; Gen. Man. CRISTIÁN ARNOLDS.

Compañía Eléctrica del Litoral, SA: San Sebastián 2952, Of. 202, Las Condes, Santiago; tel. (2) 362-1436; fax (2) 362-1437; e-mail litoral@litoral.cl.

Compañía General de Electricidad—CGE: Teatinos 280, Santiago; tel. (2) 680-7000; fax (2) 680-7104; e-mail cge@cge.cl; internet www.cge.cl; Pres. JOSÉ CLARO; Gen. Man. GUILLERMO MATTA FUENZALIDA.

EMELAT (Empresa Eléctrica Atacama, SA): Circunvalación Ignacio Carrera, Copiapó; tel. (52) 21-3551; fax (52) 21-3393; f. 1981; distribution company; Pres. DAURÓPEDIS GARCÍA DE LA PASTORA; Gen. Man. JUAN JAIME DÍAZ CARRASCO.

EMELSA (Empresa Eléctrica de Melpilla, Colchagua y Maule, SA): Alameda 886, 5° y 6°, Santiago; tel. (2) 633-3852; fax (2) 633-6944; Gen. Man. EDUARDO VALENZUELA.

Empresa Eléctrica de Antofagasta, SAELECDA: Orella 643, Antofagasta; tel. (55) 541-9209; Dir L. BITRAN.

Empresa Eléctrica de Arica, SA: Baquedano 731, Arica; tel. (58) 23-1880; fax (58) 23-1105; Dir DAURÓPEDIS GARCÍA DE LA PASTORA.

Empresa Eléctrica de Aysen, SA: Francisco Bilbao 412, Casilla 280, Coyhaique; tel. (67) 23-1293; fax (67) 23-1293; f. 1983; Gen. Man. JORGE BARRIENTOS TECA.

Empresa Eléctrica Emec, SA: Los Talleres 1831, Barrio Industrial, Coquimbo; tel. (51) 20-1000; fax (51) 24-0200; e-mail emecsa@ entelchile.net; f. 1980; Pres. RAMÓN ABOITIZ M.; Gen. Man. PABLO GUARDA B.

Empresa Eléctrica de Iquique, SA: Zegeres 469, Iquique; tel. (57) 42-3053; fax (57) 42-7181; CEO ALEJANDRO BLANCO SCHULER.

Empresa Eléctrica del Norte Grande (EDELNOR): Avda Grecia 750, Antofagasta; tel. (55) 24-8500; fax (55) 28-8094; f. 1981; Dir J. W. HOLDEN, III.

Empresa Eléctrica Pehuenche, SA—EEP: Moneda 1025, Santiago; fax (2) 696-5568; f. 1986; Gen. Man. ERNESTO SILVA BAFALLUY.

Empresa Eléctrica Pilmaiquen, SA: Las Bellotas 199, Of. 104, Providencia, Santiago; tel. (2) 233-4072; fax (2) 231-9780; Dir A. C. RODRÍGUEZ.

Empresa Nacional de Electricidad, SA—ENDESA: Santa Rosa 76, Casilla 1392, Santiago; tel. (2) 630-9000; fax (2) 635-3938; e-mail comunicacion@endesa.cl; internet www.emdea.cl; f. 1943; installed capacity 2,428,310 MW; ENERSIS (see below) obtained majority control of ENDESA in April 1999; Gen. Man. HECTOR LÓPEZ.

ENERSIS, SA: Santo Domingo 789, Casilla 1557, Correo Central, Santiago; tel. (2) 638-0840; fax (2) 633-4661; e-mail enersis@chil net.cl; internet www.enersis.com; f. 1981; holding company generating and distributing electricity through its subsidiaries throughout South America, including ENDESA of Chile (see above); 32% interest acquired by ENDESA of Spain in 1997, a further 31.78% acquired in 1999; Gen. Man. PABLO IHNEN DE LA FUENTE.

Gener, SA: Miraflores 222, 4°, Casilla 3514, Santiago; tel. (2) 632-3909; fax (2) 633-4499; f. 1981 as Chilectra Generación, SA following the restructuring of Compañía Chilena de Electricidad, SA; privatized in 1988 and Chilgener, SA adopted in 1989; current name adopted in 1998; owned by AES Corp. (USA); responsible for operation of power plants Renca, Ventanas, Laguna Verde, El Indio, Altalfal, Maitenes, Queltehues and Volcán; total generating capacity 1,746.2 MW (Dec. 1997); Pres. NAVEED ISMAIL; Gen. Man. ANDRÉS GLUSKI.

> **Empresa Eléctrica Guacolda, SA:** Agustinas 1022, Of. 1022, Santiago; tel. (2) 697-3212; fax (2) 671-5343; operates a thermoelectric power-station in Huasco; installed capacity of 304 MW.

> **Empresa Eléctrica Santiago:** Miraflores 222, 4°, Santiago; tel. (2) 686-8664; fax (2) 686-8447; operates the Nueva Renca thermoelectric plant in Santiago; installed capacity of 370 MW.

> **Energía Verde:** O'Higgins 940, Of. 90, Concepción; tel. (41) 25-3228; fax (41) 25-3227; operates two co-generation power stations at Constitución and Laja and a steam plant at Nacimiento; supplies the Cabrero industrial plant.

> **Norgener, SA:** Miraflores 222, 5°, Santiago; tel. (2) 632-6291; fax (2) 696-8810; northern subsidiary supplying the mining industry; operates power plants with installed capacity of 274.4 MW.

SAESA (Sociedad Austral de Electricidad, SA): Manuel Bulnes 441, Osorno; tel. (64) 23-3531; fax (64) 23-6256; CEO FELIPE LAMARCA CLARO.

Gas

Abastecedora de Combustible: Vicuña Mackenna 55, Providencia, Santiago; tel. (2) 639-9251; fax (2) 693-9249; internet www.abastible.cl; Pres. FELIPE LAMARCA; Gen. Man. JOSÉ ODONE.

AGA Chili, SA: Juan Bautista Pistene 2344, Santiago; tel. (2) 232-8711; natural-gas utility.

Compañía de Consumidores de Gas de Santiago—GASCO, SA: Rosas 1062, Casilla 8-D, Santiago; tel. (2) 698-2121; fax (2) 695-2685; e-mail gasco@chilnet.cl; internet www.gasco.cl; natural-gas utility; supplies Santiago and Punta Arenas regions; Pres. GABRIEL DEL REAL; Gen. Man. CARLOS ROCCA.

Compañía de Gas de Concepción, SA: En Continuidad De Giro, Avda Artura Prat 175, Concepción; tel. (41) 235-133; natural-gas utility.

Electrogas: Apoquindo 3076, Of. 402, Las Condes, Santiago; tel. (2) 232-1839; fax (2) 233-4931; Gen. Man. CARLOS ANDREANI.

Gas Valpo: Valparaíso; tel. (32) 27-7000; fax (32) 21-3092; e-mail info@gasvalpo.cl.

GasAndes: Santiago; distributes gas transported from the Argentine province of Mendoza via a 463-km pipeline.

Industrias Codigas: Camino a Melipilla 11000, Maipú, Santiago; tel.(2) 557-8870; fax (92) 538-6647; Pes. EDUARDO CABELLO; Gen. Man. CHRISTIAN CORNEJO.

Lipigas: Avda Libertad 51, Viña del Mar; tel. (32) 689-668; fax (32) 656-595; e-mail info@lipigas.cl; internet www.lipigas.cl; Pres. JAIME SANTA CRUZ; Gen. Man. MARIO FERNÁNDEZ.

Metrogas: El Bosque Norte 0177, 11°, Las Condes, Santiago; tel. (2) 337-8000; fax (2) 332-0348; internet www.metrogas.cl; natural-gas utility; Pres. JUAN CLARO; Gen. Man. EDUARDO MORANDÉ.

Water

Desalari Ltda: Arturo Prat 391, Of. 73, Arica; tel. (58) 25-0179; fax (58) 25-6652; e-mail desalari.ltda001@chilnet.cl.

Empresa Metropolitana de Obras Sanitarias, SA (EMOS): Avda Presidente Balmaceda 1398, Santiago; tel. (2) 688-1000; fax (2) 698-5871; e-mail info@emos.cl; internet www.emos.cl; water supply and sanitation services to Santiago and the surrounding area; sold to a French-Spanish consortium in June 1999; Gen. Man. ANGEL SIMON.

Sigsig Ltda (Tecnagent): Presidente Errázuriz 3262, Santiago; tel. (2) 335-2001; fax (2) 334-8466; e-mail tecnagent@tecnagent.cl;

internet www.tecnagent.cl; Pres. RAÚL SIGREN BINDHOFF; Gen. Man. RAÚL A. SIGREN O.

TRADE UNIONS

There are more than 50 national labour federations and unions.

Central Unions

Central Autónoma de Trabajadores (CAT): Sazié 1761, Casilla 6510480, Santiago; tel. and fax (2) 695-3388; e-mail catchile@entelchile.net; Pres. OSVALSO ERBACH ALVAREZ, Sec. Gen. PEDRO SAAVEDRA.

Central Unitaria de Trabajadores de Chile (CUT): Avda B. O'Higgins 1346, Santiago; tel. (2) 695-8053; fax (2) 695-8055; e-mail cutchile@chilesat.net; f. 1988; two associations, 27 confederations, 49 federations; 36 regional headquarters; Pres. ARTURO MARTÍNEZ MOLINA; 411,000 mems.

Movimiento Unitario Campesino y Etnias de Chile (MUCECH): Portugal 623, Of. 1-A, Santiago; tel. (2) 222-6572; fax 635-1518; e-mail mucech@ia.cl; Pres. EUGENIO LEÓN GAJARDO; Nat. Sec. RIGOBERTO TURRA PAREDES.

Union Confederations

There are 37 union confederations, of which the following are among the most important:

Agrupación Nacional de Empleados Fiscales (ANEF): Avda B. O'Higgins 1603, Santiago; tel. (2) 696-2957; fax 699-3806; affiliated to CUT; Pres. RAÚL DE LA PUENTE PEÑA; Sec.-Gen. FRESIA AROCS ALBARRACÍN.

Confederación Bancaria: Agustinas 1185, Of. 92, Santiago; tel. (2) 699-5597; affiliated to CUT; Pres. DIEGO OLIVARES ARAVENA; Sec.-Gen. RAÚL REQUENA MARTÍNEZ.

Confederación de Empleados Particulares de Chile (CEPCH): Teatinos 20, Of. 1, Casilla 1771, Santiago; tel. (2) 72-2093; trade union for workers in private sector; affiliated to CUT; Pres. ANGÉLICA CARVALLO PRENAFETA; Sec.-Gen. ANDRÉS BUSTOS GONZÁLEZ.

Confederación de Personal en Retiro y Montepío de las Fuerzas Armadas (CAPREDENA): Nataniel Cox 265, Casilla 14988, Santiago; tel. (2) 698-4657; fax (2) 671-5980; Pres. OSCAR HEILCALEO CHEUQUE; Sec. Gen. OSCAR SÁEZ TRONCOSO.

Confederación General de Trabajadores del Transporte Terrestre (CGTT): Almirante Latorre 355, 2°, Of. 3, Santiago; tel. and fax (2) 695-9551; affiliated to CUT; Pres. ULISES MARTÍNEZ SEPÚLVEDA; Sec.-Gen. RODOLFO DOSSETTO UGALDE.

Confederación National Campesina: Gorbea 1769, Santiago; tel. and fax (2) 695-2017; affiliated to CUT; Pres. EUGENIO LEÓN GAJARDO; Sec.-Gen. RENÉ ASTUDILLO R.

Confederación Nacional de Federaciones y Sindicatos de Empresas e Interempresas de Trabajadores del Transporte Terrestre y Afines (CONATRACH): Concha y Toro 2-A, 2°, Santiago; tel. (2) 698-0810; fax (2) 698-0810; Pres. PEDRO MONSALVE FUENTES; Sec. Gen. PEDRO JARA ESPINOZA.

Confederación Nacional de Federaciones y Sindicatos de Trabajadores Textiles y Ramos Similares (CONTEXTIL): Nataniel Cox 152 B, 1°, Santiago; tel. and fax (2) 696-8098; affiliated to the CUT; Pres. PATRICIA C. CARRILLO; Sec.-Gen. MARIA FELISA GARAY ASTUDILLO.

Confederación Nacional de Gente de Mar, Marítimos, Portuarios y Pesqueros (CONGEMAR): Tomás Ramos 158-172, Casilla 2210, Valparaíso; tel. (32) 255-430; fax (32) 257-580; affiliated to CUT; Pres. WALTER ASTORGA LOBOS; Sec.-Gen. JUAN GUZMÁN CARRASCO.

Confederación Nacional de Sindicatos Agrícolas—Unidad Obrero Campesina (UOC): Eleuterio Ramírez 1463, Santiago; tel. and fax (2) 696-6342; affiliated to CUT; Pres. OSCAR VALLADARES GONZÁLEZ; Sec.-Gen. DANIEL SAN MARTÍN VALLEJOS.

Confederación Nacional de Sindicatos de Trabajadores de la Construcción, Maderas, Materiales de Edificación y Actividades Conexas: Almirante Hurtado 2069, Santiago; tel. (2) 695-3908; fax (2) 696-4536; affiliated to CUT; Pres. MIGUEL ANGEL SOLÍS VIERA; Sec.-Gen. ADRIAN FUENTES HERMOSILLA.

Confederación Nacional de Sindicatos y Federaciones de Trabajadores Metalúrgicos (CONSTRAMET): Avda Francia 1317, Independencia, Santiago; tel. (2) 737-6875; fax (2) 443-0039; e-mail contrame@mailnet.rdc.cl; affiliated to CUT; Pres. MIGUEL SOTO ROA; Sec.-Gen. MIGUEL CHÁVEZ SOAZO.

Confederación Nacional de Trabajadores de la Alimentación y Afines (CONTALCH): Lizt 3082, San Joaquín, Santiago; tel. and fax (2) 553-2193; affiliated to CUT; Pres. CIJIFREDO VERA VERA.

Confederación Nacional de Trabajadores de la Industria del Pan (CONAPAN): Tucapel Jiménez 32, 2°, Santiago; tel. and fax (2) 672-1622; affiliated to CUT; Pres. LUIS ALEGRÍA ALEGRÍA; Sec. LUIS PALACIOS CAMPOS.

Confederación Nacional de Trabajadores de la Industria Textil (CONTEVECH): Agustinas 2349, Santiago; tel. (2) 699-3442, fax (2) 687-3269; affiliated to CUT; Pres. MIGUEL VEGA FUENTES; Sec.-Gen. OSCAR CÁCERES YÁÑEZ.

Confederación Nacional de Trabajadores del Comercio (CONATRADECO): Londres 73, Santiago; tel. and fax (2) 638-6718; Pres. EDMUNDO LILLO ARAVENA; Sec.-Gen. FEDERICO MUJICA CANALES.

Confederación Nacional de Trabajadores del Comercio (CONSFECOVE): Monjitas 454, Of. 606, Santiago; tel. (2) 632-2950; fax (2) 632-2884; affiliated to CUT; Pres. CLAUDIO ARAVENA ALVAREZ; Sec.-Gen. SUSANA ROSAS VALDEBENITO.

Confederación Nacional de Trabajadores del Cuero y Calzado (FONACC): Arturo Prat 1490, Santiago; tel. (2) 556-9602; affiliated to CUT; Pres. MANUEL JIMÉNEZ TORRES; Sec.-Gen. VÍCTOR LABBÉ SILVA.

Confederación Nacional de Trabajadores Electrometalúrgicos, Mineros, Automotrices (CONSFETEMA): Vicuña Mackenna 3101, Casilla 1803, Correo Central, San Joaquín, Santiago; tel. (2) 238-1732; fax 553-6494; Pres. LUIS SEPÚLVEDA DEL RÍO.

Confederación Nacional de Trabajadores Forestales (CTF): Rengo 884, Casilla 2717, Concepción; tel. and fax (41) 220-0407; Pres. JORGE GONZÁLEZ CASTILLO; Sec.-Gen. GUSTAVO CARRASO SALAZAR.

Confederación Nacional de Trabajadores Independientes Suplementeros: Roberto Pretot 18, Santiago; tel. (2) 699-4390; Pres. IVAN ENCINA CARO; Sec. RAMÓN GONZÁLEZ.

Confederación Nacional de Trabajadores Molineros: Bascuñan Guerrero 1739, Casilla 703, Correo 21, Santiago; tel. and fax (2) 683-8882; Pres. JOSÉ VÁSQUEZ ALIAGA.

Confederación Nacional Minera: Príncipe de Gales 88, Casilla 10361, Correo Central, Santiago; tel. (2) 696-6945; fax (2) 696-6945; Pres. MOISÉS LABRAÑA MENA; Sec.-Gen. JOSÉ CARRILLO BERMEDO.

Confederación Nacional Sindical Campesina y del Agro 'El Surco': Chacabuco 625, Santiago; tel. and fax (2) 681-1032; e-mail asurco@entelchile.net; affiliated to CUT; Pres. FERNANDO VALÁSQUEZ SERRANO; Sec.-Gen. SERGIO DÍAZ TAPIA.

There are also 45 union federations and over 100 individual unions.

Transport

RAILWAYS

State Railways

Empresa de los Ferrocarriles del Estado: Avda B. O'Higgins 3170, Santiago; tel. (2) 779-0707; fax (2) 689-8434; f. 1851; 3,427 km of track (1997); the State Railways are divided between the Ferrocarril Regional de Arica (formerly Ferrocarril Arica–La Paz), Ferrocarriles del Pacífico (cargo division), Metro Regional de Valparaíso (passenger service only) and Ferrovía (formerly the Ferrocarril del Sur); several lines scheduled for privatization; Pres. H. TRIVELLI; Gen. Man. DANIEL F. KOPRICH.

Parastatal Railways

Ferrocarriles del Pacífico (FEPASA): Alfredo Barros Errázuriz 1960, 6°, Providencia, Santiago; tel. (2) 330-4900; fax (2) 330-4905; e-mail fepasa@chilnet.cl; f. 1993; freight services; scheduled for privatization; Gen. Man. F. LANGER.

Metro de Santiago: Empresa de Transporte de Pasajeros Metro, SA, Avda B. O'Higgins 1414, Santiago; tel. (2) 698-8218; fax (2) 252-6364; e-mail gerencia.marketing@metro-chile.cl; internet www.metro-chile.cl; started operations 1975; 40.4 km (2000); 3 lines; Pres. FERNANDO BUSTAMENTE HUENTA; Gen. Man. R. AZÓCAR HIDALGO.

Private Railways

Antofagasta (Chile) and Bolivia Railway PLC: Bolívar 255, Casillas ST, Antofagasta; tel. (55) 20-6700; fax (55) 20-6220; e-mail webmaster@fcab.cl; internet www.fcab.com; f. 1888; British-owned; operates an internat. railway to Bolivia and Argentina; cargo forwarding services; total track length 934 km; Chair. ANDRÓNICO LUKSIC ABAROA; Gen. Man. M. V. SEPÚLVEDA.

Empresa de Transporte Ferroviario, SA (Ferronor): Avda Alessandri 042, Coquimbo; tel. (51) 31-2442; fax (51) 31-3460; 2,200 km of track (1995); established as a public/private concern, following the transfer of the Ferrocarril Regional del Norte de Chile to the Ministry of Production Development (CORFO) as a *Sociedad Anónima* in 1989; controlling interest purchased by RailAmerica of the USA in 1997; operates cargo services only; Pres. G. MARINO; Gen. Man. P. ESPY.

Ferrocarril Codelco-Chile: Barquito, Region III, Atacama; tel. (52) 48-8521; fax (52) 48-8522; Gen. Man. B. BEHN THEUNE.

Diego de Almagro a Potrerillos: transport of forest products, minerals and manufactures; 99 km.

Ferrocarril Rancagua–Teniente: transport of forest products, livestock, minerals and manufactures; 68 km.

Ferrocarril Tocopilla–Toco: Calle Arturo Prat 1060, Casilla 2098, Tocopilla; tel. (55) 81-2139; fax (55) 81-2650; owned by Sociedad Química y Minera de Chile, SA; 117 km (1995); Gen. Man. SEGISFREDO HURTADO GUERRERO.

Association

Asociación Chilena de Conservación de Patrimonio Ferroviario (Chilean Railway SocietyACCPF): Casilla 179-D, Santiago; tel. (2) 210-2280; fax (2) 280-0252; Pres. H. VENEGAS.

ROADS

The total length of roads in Chile in 1998 was an estimated 79,200 km, of which some 6,350 km were highways and some 16,700 km were secondary roads. The road system includes the completely paved Pan American Highway extending 3,455 km from north to south. Toll gates exist on major motorways. The 1,200 km-Carretera Austral (Southern Highway), linking Puerto Montt and Puerto Yungay, was completed in March 1996, at an estimated total cost of US $200m.

SHIPPING

As a consequence of Chile's difficult topography, maritime transport is of particular importance. In 1997 90% of the country's foreign trade was carried by sea (51m. metric tons). The principal ports are Valparaíso, Talcahuano, Antofagasta, San Antonio, Arica, Iquique, Coquimbo, San Vicente, Puerto Montt and Punta Arenas. Most port operations were privatized in the late 1990s.

Chile's merchant fleet amounted to 753,432 grt (comprising 472 vessels) at December 1998.

Supervisory Authorities

Asociación Nacional de Armadores: Blanco 869, 3°, Valparaíso; tel. (32) 21-2057; fax (32) 21-2017; e-mail armadore@entelchile.net; f. 1931; shipowners' association; Pres. JUAN FERNANDO WAIDELE; Gen. Man. ARTURO SIERRA MERINO.

Cámara Marítima y Portuaria de Chile, AG: Blanco 869, 3°, Valparaíso; tel. (32) 25-3443; fax (32) 25-0231; e-mail camport@entelchile.net; Pres. JAIME BARAHONA VARGAS; Vice-Pres. RODOLFO GARCÍA SÁNCHEZ.

Dirección General de Territorio Marítimo y Marina Mercante: Errázuriz 537, 4°, Valparaíso; tel. (32) 25-8061; fax (32) 25-2539; maritime admin. of the coast and national waters, control of the merchant navy; Dir Rear Adm. FERNANDO LAZCANO.

Empresa Portuaria Antofagasta: Grecia s/n, Antofagasta; tel. (55) 25-1737; fax (55) 22-3171; e-mail epa@puertoantofagasta.cl; Pres. BLAS ENRIQUE ESPINOZA SEPÚLVEDA; Dir EDUARDO SALVADOR ABEDRAPO BUSTOS.

Empresa Portuaria Arica: Máximo Lira 389, Arica; tel. (58) 25-5078; fax (58) 23-2284; e-mail puertoarica@entelchile.net; Pres. CARLOS EDUARDO MENA KEYMER; Dir RAÚL RICARDO BALBONTÍN FERNÁNDEZ.

Empresa Portuaria Austral: B. O'Higgins 1385, Punta Arenas; tel. (61) 24-1760; fax (61) 24-1822; e-mail portspug@ctc-mundo.net; Pres. LAUTARO HERNÁN POBLETE KNUDTZON-TRAMPE; Dir FERNANDO ARTURO JOFRÉ WEISS.

Empresa Portuaria Chacabuco: B. O'Higgins s/n, Puerto Chacabuco; tel. (67) 35-1198; fax (67) 35-1174; e-mail ptochb@entelchile.net; Pres. LUIS MUSALEM MUSALEM; Dir RAIMUNDO CRISTI SAAVEDRA.

Empresa Portuaria Coquimbo: Melgareja 676, Coquimbo; tel. (51) 31-3606; fax (51) 32-6146; e-mail ptoqq@entelchile.net; Pres. ARMANDO ARANCIBIA CALDERÓN; Gen. Man. MIGUEL ZUVIC MUJICA.

Empresa Portuaria Iquique: Jorge Barrera 62, Iquique; tel. (57) 40-0100; fax (57) 41-3176; e-mail epi@port-iquique.cl; internet www.port-iquique.cl; f. 1998; Pres. PATRICIO ARRAU PONS; Gen. Man. PEDRO DÁVILA PINO.

Empresa Portuaria Puerto Montt: Angelmó 1673, Puerto Montt; tel. (65) 25-2247; e-mail puertomont@telsur.cl; Pres. JOSÉ DANIEL BARRETA SÁEZ; Gen. Man. RICARDO GHIORZI CARCEY.

Empresa Portuaria San Antonio: Alan Macowan 0245, San Antonio; tel.(35) 21-2159; fax (35) 21-2114; e-mail correo@saiport.cl; internet www.saiport.cl; f. 1960; Pres. JOSÉ MANUEL MORALES TALLAR; Gen. Man. FERNANDO CRISÓSTOMO BURGOS.

Empresa Portuaria Talcahuano-San Vicente: Latorre 1590, Talcahuano; tel. (41) 54-1419; fax (41) 54-1807; e-mail eportuaria@ptotalsve.co.cl; Pres. JUAN ENRIQUE COEYMANS AVARIA; Gen. Man. PATRICIO CAMPAÑA CUELLO.

Empresa Portuaria Valparaíso: Errázuriz 25, 4°, Of. 1, Valparaíso; tel. (32) 44-8700; fax (32) 23-4427; e-mail hjaeger@portvalparaiso.cl; internet www.portvalparaiso.cl; Pres. GABRIEL ALDONEY V.; Gen. Man. HARALD JAEGER KARL.

Principal Shipping Companies
Santiago

Cía Chilena de Navegación Interoceánica, SA: Avda Andrés Bello 2687, 17°, Las Condes, Santiago; tel. (2) 339-1300; fax (2) 203-9060; e-mail info@ccni.cl; internet www.ccnl.cl; f. 1930; regular sailings to Japan, Republic of Korea, Taiwan, Hong Kong, USA, Mexico, South Pacific, South Africa and Europe; bulk and dry cargo services; Chair. BELTRAN F. URENDA; CEO ALEJANDRO PATTILLO.

Marítima Antares, SA: MacIver 225, Of. 2001, 2°, Santiago; tel. (2) 38-3036; Pres. ALFONSO GARCÍA-MIÑAUR G.; Gen. Man. LUIS BEDRIÑANA RODRÍGUEZ.

Naviera Magallanes, SA (NAVIMAG): Avda El Bosque, Norte 0440, 11°, Of. 1103/1104, Las Condes, Santiago; tel. (2) 203-5180; fax (2) 203-5191; f. 1979; Chair. PEDRO LECAROS MENÉNDEZ; Gen. Man. EDUARDO SALAZAR RETAMALES.

Nisa Navegación, SA: Avda El Bosque Norte 0440, 11°, Casilla 2829, Santiago; tel.(2) 203-5180; fax (2) 203-5190; Chair. PEDRO LECAROS MENÉNDEZ; Gen. Man. SERGIO VIAL.

Valparaíso

A. J. Broom y Cía, SAC: Blanco 951, Casilla 910, Valparaíso and MacIver 225, 10°, Casilla 448, Santiago; e-mail genmanager@ajbroom.cl; f. 1920; Pres. GASTÓN ANRÍQUEZ; Man. Dir JAMES C. WELLS M.

Agencias Universales, SA (AGUNSA): Urriola 87, 3°, Valparaíso; tel. (32) 21-7333; fax (32) 25-4261; maritime transportation and shipping, port and docking services; Dir JOSÉ URENDA; Gen. Man. FRANCO MONTALBETTI.

Cía Sud-Americana de Vapores: Plaza Sotomayor 50, Casilla 49-V, Valparaíso; tel. (32) 20-3000; fax (32) 20-3333; also Hendaya 60, 12°, Santiago; tel. (2) 330-7000; fax (2) 330-7700; f. 1872; regular service between South America and US/Canadian ports, US Gulf ports, North European, Mediterranean, Scandinavian and Far East ports; bulk carriers, tramp and reefer services; Pres. RICARDO CLARO VALDÉS; Gen. Man. FRANCISCO SILVA DONOSO.

Empresa Marítima, SA (Empremar Chile): Almirante Gómez Carreño 49, Casilla 105-V, Valparaíso; tel. (32) 25-0563; fax (32) 21-3904; f. 1953; international and coastal services; Chair. LORENZO CAGLEVIC.

Naviera Chilena del Pacífico, SA: Almirante Señoret 70, 6°, Casilla 370, Valparaíso; tel. (32) 25-0563; fax (32) 25-3869; e-mail nachipav@entelchile.net; also Serrano 14, Of. 502, Casilla 2290, Santiago; tel. (2) 633-3063; fax (2) 639-2069; e-mail nachipa@entelchile.net; cargo; Pres. ARTURO FERNÁNDEZ ZEGERS; Gen. Man. PABLO SIMIAN ZAMORANO.

Sociedad Anónima de Navegación Petrolera (SONAP): Cochrane 813, 6°, Casilla 1870, Valparaíso; tel. (32) 25-9476; fax (32) 25-1325; e-mail valsonap@sonap.cl; f. 1954; tanker services; Chair. FELIPE VIAL C.; Gen. Man. JOSÉ THOMSEN Q.

Transmares Naviera Chilena Ltda: Moneda 970, 20°, Edif. Eurocentro, Casilla 193-D, Santiago; tel. (2) 630-1000; fax (2) 698-9205; e-mail transmares@transmares.cl; also Cochrane 813, 8°, Casilla 52-V, Valparaíso; tel. (32) 20-2000; fax (32) 25-6607; f. 1969; dry cargo service Chile–Uruguay–Brazil; Chair. WOLF VON APPEN; CEO RICARDO SCHLECHTER.

Several foreign shipping companies operate services to Valparaíso.

Punta Arenas

Cía Marítima de Punta Arenas, SA: Avda Independencia 830, Casilla 337, Punta Arenas; tel. (61) 24-1702; fax (61) 24-7514; also Casilla 2829, Santiago; tel. (2) 203-5180; fax (2) 203-5191; f. 1949; shipping agents and owners operating in the Magellan Straits; Pres. PEDRO LECAROS MENÉNDEZ; Gen. Man. ARTURO STORAKER MOLINA.

Puerto Montt

Transporte Marítimo Chiloé-Aysén, SA: Angelmo 2187, Puerto Monttjel. (65) 27-0419; Deputy Man. PEDRO HERNÁNDEZ LEHMAN.

San Antonio

Naviera Aysén Ltda: San Antonio; tel. (35) 32578; also Huérfanos 1147, Of. 542, Santiago; tel. (2) 698-8680; Man. RAÚL QUINTANA A.

CIVIL AVIATION

There are 325 airfields in the country, of which eight have long runways. Arturo Merino Benítez, 20 km north-east of Santiago, and Chacalluta, 14 km north-east of Arica, are the principal international airports.

Aero Continente: Marchant Pereira 357; tel. (2) 204-2424; fax (2) 209-2358; internet www.aerocontinente.com.

Aerocardal: José Arrieta 7808, Casilla 9630, La Reina, Santiago; tel. (2) 279-3535; fax (2) 279-4272; f. 1989; charter services; Chair. ALEX CASASEMPERE.

Aerovías DAP: Casilla 633, Punta Arenas; tel. (61) 22-3340; fax (61) 22-1693; f. 1980; domestic services; CEO ALEX PISCEVIC.

Avant Airlines: e-mail reservas@avant.cl; internet www.avant.cl; Gen. Man. ROLANDO UAUY.

Lineas Aéreas Chilenas: B. O'Higgins 107, 7°, Santiago; tel. (2) 290-5140; fax (2) 290-5144; Man. RICARDO MARDONES.

Línea Aérea Nacional de Chile (LAN-Chile): Américo Vespucio 901, Renca, Santiago; tel. (2) 565-2525; fax (2) 565-1729; internet www.lanchile.com; f. 1929; operates scheduled domestic passenger and cargo services, also Santiago–Easter Island; international services to French Polynesia, Spain, and throughout North and South America; under the Govt's privatization programme, 99% of LAN-Chile shares have been sold to private interests since 1989; Pres. JORGE AWAD MEHECH; CEO ENRIQUE CUETO.

Línea Aérea del Cobre SA—LADECO: Américo Vespucio 901, Renca, Santiago; tel. (2) 565-3131; fax (2) 639-9115; internet www.ladeco.cl; f. 1945; affiliated to LAN-Chile in 1996; internal passenger and cargo services; international passenger and cargo services to the USA and throughout South America; Chair. JOSÉ LUIZ IBÁÑEZ; CEO GASTÓN CUMMINS.

Tourism

Chile has a wide variety of attractions for the tourist, including fine beaches, ski resorts in the Andes, lakes, rivers and desert scenery. There are many opportunities for hunting and fishing in the southern archipelago, where there are plans to make an integrated tourist area with Argentina, requiring investment of US $120m. Isla de Pascua (Easter Island) may also be visited by tourists. In 1998 there were an estimated 1.76m. tourist arrivals, and receipts from tourism totalled US $1,062m.

Servicio Nacional de Turismo—SERNATUR: Avda Providencia 1550, Casilla 14082, Santiago; tel. (2) 731-8300; fax (2) 251-8469; e-mail info@sernatur.cl; internet www.senatur.cl; f. 1975; Pres. MARÍA EUGENIA CASTRO; Man. ISABEL BACHLER.

Asociación Chilena de Empresas de Turismo—ACHET: Moneda 973, Of. 647, Casilla 3402, Santiago; tel. (2) 696-5677; fax (2) 699-4245; f. 1945; 240 mems; Pres. IVONNE LAHAYE DE MONTES MARDONES; Man. CARLOS MESCHI MONTALDO.

THE PEOPLE'S REPUBLIC OF CHINA

Introductory Survey

Location, Climate, Language, Religion, Flag, Capital

The People's Republic of China covers a vast area of eastern Asia, with Mongolia and Russia to the north, Tajikistan, Kyrgyzstan and Kazakhstan to the north-west, Afghanistan and Pakistan to the west, and India, Nepal, Bhutan, Myanmar (formerly Burma), Laos and Viet Nam to the south. The country borders the Democratic People's Republic of Korea in the north-east, and has a long coastline on the Pacific Ocean. The climate ranges from subtropical in the far south to an annual average temperature of below 10°C (50°F) in the north, and from the monsoon climate of eastern China to the aridity of the north-west. The principal language is Northern Chinese (Mandarin); in the south and south-east local dialects are spoken. The Xizangzu (Tibetans), Wei Wuer (Uygurs), Menggus (Mongols) and other groups have their own languages. The traditional religions and philosophies of life are Confucianism, Buddhism and Daoism. There are also Muslim and Christian minorities. The national flag (proportions 3 by 2) is plain red, with one large five-pointed gold star and four similar but smaller stars, arranged in an arc, in the upper hoist. The capital is Beijing (Peking).

Recent History

The People's Republic of China was proclaimed on 1 October 1949, following the victory of Communist forces over the Kuomintang (KMT) Government, which fled to the island province of Taiwan. The new Communist regime received widespread international recognition, but it was not until 1971 that the People's Republic was admitted to the United Nations, in place of the KMT regime, as the representative of China. Most countries now recognize the People's Republic.

With the establishment of the People's Republic, the leading political figure was Mao Zedong, who was Chairman of the Chinese Communist Party (CCP) from 1935 until his death in 1976. Chairman Mao, as he was known, also became Head of State in October 1949, but he relinquished this post in December 1958. His successor was Liu Shaoqi, First Vice-Chairman of the CCP, who was elected Head of State in April 1959. Liu was dismissed in October 1968, during the Cultural Revolution (see below), and died in prison in 1969. The post of Head of State was left vacant, and was formally abolished in January 1975, when a new Constitution was adopted. The first Premier (Head of Government) of the People's Republic was Zhou Enlai, who held this office from October 1949 until his death in 1976. Zhou was also Minister of Foreign Affairs from 1949 to 1958.

The economic progress of the early years of Communist rule enabled China to withstand the effects of the industrialization programmes of the late 1950s (called the 'Great Leap Forward'), the drought of 1960–62 and the withdrawal of Soviet aid in 1960. To prevent the establishment of a ruling class, Chairman Mao launched the Great Proletarian Cultural Revolution in 1966. The ensuing excesses of the Red Guards caused the army to intervene; Liu Shaoqi and Deng Xiaoping, General Secretary of the CCP, were disgraced. In 1971 an attempted coup by the Defence Minister, Marshal Lin Biao, was unsuccessful, and by 1973 it was apparent that Chairman Mao and Premier Zhou Enlai had retained power. In 1975 Deng Xiaoping re-emerged as first Vice-Premier and Chief of the General Staff. Zhou Enlai died in January 1976. Hua Guofeng, hitherto Minister of Public Security, was appointed Premier, and Deng was dismissed. Mao died in September 1976. His widow, Jiang Qing, tried unsuccessfully to seize power, with the help of three radical members of the CCP's Politburo. The 'gang of four' and six associates of Lin Biao were tried in November 1980. All were found guilty and were given lengthy terms of imprisonment. (Jiang Qing committed suicide in May 1991.) The 10th anniversary of Mao's death was marked in September 1986 by an official reassessment of his life; while his accomplishments were praised, it was now acknowledged that he had made mistakes, although most of the criticism was directed at the 'gang of four'.

In October 1976 Hua Guofeng succeeded Mao as Chairman of the CCP and Commander-in-Chief of the People's Liberation Army (PLA). The 11th National Congress of the CCP, held in August 1977, restored Deng Xiaoping to his former posts. In September 1980 Hua Guofeng resigned as Premier, but retained his chairmanship of the CCP. The appointment of Zhao Ziyang, a Vice-Premier since April 1980, to succeed Hua as Premier confirmed the dominance of the moderate faction of Deng Xiaoping. In June 1981 Hua Guofeng was replaced as Chairman of the CCP by Hu Yaobang, former Secretary-General of the Politburo, and as Chairman of the party's Central Military Commission by Deng Xiaoping. A sustained campaign by Deng to purge the Politburo of leftist elements led to Hua's demotion to a Vice-Chairman of the CCP and, in September 1982, to his exclusion from the Politburo.

In September 1982 the CCP was reorganized and the post of Party Chairman abolished. Hu Yaobang became, instead, General Secretary of the CCP. A year later a 'rectification' (purge) of the CCP was launched, aimed at expelling 'Maoists', who had risen to power during the Cultural Revolution, and those opposed to the pragmatic policies of Deng. China's new Constitution, adopted in December 1982, restored the office of Head of State, and in June 1983 Li Xiannian, a former Minister of Finance, became President of China. In September 1986 the sixth plenary session of the 12th CCP Central Committee adopted a detailed resolution on the 'guiding principles for building a socialist society', which redefined the general ideology of the CCP, to provide a theoretical basis for the programme of modernization and the 'open door' policy of economic reform.

In January 1986 a high-level 'anti-corruption' campaign was launched, to investigate reports that many officials had exploited the programme of economic reform for their own gain. The field of culture and the arts underwent significant liberalization in 1986, with a revival of the 'Hundred Flowers' movement of 1956–57, which had encouraged the development of intellectual debate. However, a series of student demonstrations in major cities in late 1986 was regarded by China's leaders as an indication of excessive 'bourgeois liberalization'. In January 1987 Hu Yaobang unexpectedly resigned as CCP General Secretary, being accused of 'mistakes on major issues of political principles'. Zhao Ziyang became acting General Secretary. At the 13th National Congress of the CCP, which opened in October, Deng Xiaoping retired from the Central Committee, but amendments to the Constitution of the CCP permitted him to retain the influential positions of Chairman of the State and of the CCP Central Military Commissions. A new Politburo was appointed by the Central Committee in November. The majority of its 18 members were relatively young officials, who supported Deng Xiaoping's policies. The membership of the new Politburo also indicated a decline in military influence in Chinese politics. The newly-appointed Standing Committee of the Politburo was regarded, on balance, as being 'pro-reform'. In late November Li Peng was appointed Acting Premier of the State Council, in place of Zhao Ziyang. At the first session of the Seventh National People's Congress (NPC), held in March–April 1988, Li Peng was confirmed as Premier, and Yang Shangkun (a member of the CCP Politburo) was elected President.

The death of Hu Yaobang in April 1989 led to the most serious student demonstrations ever seen in the People's Republic. The students criticized the alleged prevalence of corruption and nepotism within the Government, and sought a limited degree of Soviet-style *glasnost* in public life. When negotiations between government officials and the students' leaders had failed to satisfy the protesters' demands, workers from various professions joined the demonstrations in Tiananmen Square, Beijing, which had now become the focal point of the protests. At one stage more than 1m. people congregated in the Square, as demonstrations spread to more than 20 other Chinese cities. In mid-May some 3,000 students began a hunger strike in Tiananmen Square, while protesters demanded the resignation of both Deng Xiaoping and Li Peng, and invited President Gorbachev of the USSR, who was visiting Beijing, to address them. The students ended their hunger strike at the request of Zhao Ziyang, who was generally regarded as being sympathetic to the students' demands. On 20 May a state of martial law was declared in Beijing. Within days, some 300,000 troops had assembled. At the end of May the students erected a 30 m-high replica of the US Statue of Liberty in the Square.

On 3 June 1989 a further unsuccessful attempt was made to dislodge the demonstrators, but on the following day troops of the PLA attacked protesters on and around Tiananmen Square, killing an unspecified number of people. Television evidence and eye-witness accounts estimated the total dead at between 1,000 and 5,000. The Government immediately rejected these figures and claimed, furthermore, that the larger part of the casualties had been soldiers and that a counter-revolutionary rebellion had been taking place. Arrests and executions ensued, although some student leaders eluded capture and fled to Hong Kong. Zhao Ziyang was dismissed from all his party posts and replaced as General Secretary of the CCP by Jiang Zemin, hitherto the secretary of the Shanghai municipal party committee. Zhao was accused of participating in a conspiracy to overthrow the CCP and placed under house arrest. In November Deng resigned as Chairman of the CCP Central Military Commission, his sole remaining party position, and was succeeded by Jiang Zemin, who was hailed as the first of China's 'third generation' of communist leaders (Mao being representative of the first, and Deng of the second). In January 1990 martial law was lifted in Beijing, and it was announced that a total of 573 prisoners, detained following the pro-democracy demonstrations, had been freed. Further groups of detainees were released subsequently. In March Deng Xiaoping resigned from his last official post, that of Chairman of the State Central Military Commission, and was succeeded by Jiang Zemin. An extensive military reshuffle ensued. At the CCP's 14th National Congress, held in October 1992, a new 319-member Central Committee was elected. The Politburo was expanded and a new Secretariat was chosen by the incoming Central Committee. Many opponents of Deng Xiaoping's support for a 'socialist market economy' were replaced.

At the first session of the Eighth NPC, convened in March 1993, Jiang Zemin was elected as the country's President, remaining CCP General Secretary. Li Peng was reappointed as Premier, and an extensive reorganization of the State Council was announced. The Congress also approved amendments to the 1982 Constitution. Changes included confirmation of the State's practice of a 'socialist market economy'. During 1993, however, the Government became concerned at the growing disparity between urban and rural incomes (exacerbated by the heavy taxes imposed on farmers) and the resultant problem of rural migration, and at the decline in support for the CCP in the countryside. In June thousands of peasants took part in demonstrations in Sichuan Province to protest against excessive official levies. In response to the ensuing riots, the central Government banned the imposition of additional local taxes.

In March 1995, at the third session of the Eighth NPC, the appointment of Wu Bangguo and of Jiang Chunyun as Vice-Premiers of the State Council was approved. In an unprecedented display of opposition, however, neither nominee received the NPC's full endorsement. Nevertheless, the position of Jiang Zemin, now regarded by many as the eventual successor to the 'paramount' leadership of the ailing Deng Xiaoping, appeared to have been strengthened. Personnel changes in the military hierarchy later in the year were also viewed as favourable to Jiang Zemin.

The death of Deng Xiaoping, on 19 February 1997, precipitated a period of uncertainty regarding China's future direction. President Jiang Zemin, however, declared that the economic reforms would continue, and this was reiterated in Premier Li Peng's address to the fifth session of the Eighth NPC in March 1997, which included a commitment to restructure state-owned enterprises (SOEs). Delegates at the Congress approved legislation reinforcing the CCP's control over the PLA, and revisions to the criminal code were also promulgated, whereby statutes concerning 'counter-revolutionary' acts (under which many of the pro-democracy demonstrators had been charged in 1989) were removed from the code, but were replaced by 11 crimes of 'endangering state security'. Financial offences, such as money laundering, were also included for the first time.

At the 15th National Congress of the CCP, convened in September 1997, emphasis was placed on radical reform of the 370,000 SOEs. No substantial commitment to political reform, however, was made. Delegates approved amendments to the party Constitution, enshrining the 'Deng Xiaoping Theory' of socialism with Chinese characteristics alongside 'Mao Zedong Thought' as the guiding ideology of the CCP. The Congress

elected a new 344-member Central Committee, which re-elected Jiang Zemin as General Secretary of the CCP, and appointed a 22-member Politburo. The composition of the new Politburo appeared to confirm Jiang Zemin's enhanced authority: Qiao Shi, a reformist and Jiang's most influential rival, who was ranked third in the party hierarchy, was excluded, reportedly because of his age, as was Gen. Liu Huaqing, China's most senior military figure. Zhu Rongji, a former mayor of Shanghai, replaced Qiao Shi, and was also widely regarded as the likely successor to Li Peng, on Li's retirement as Premier of the State Council in March 1998. Gen. Liu was replaced by a civilian, Wei Jinxiang, who was responsible for combating corruption within the CCP. The absence of the military from the Politburo, and the composition of the new Central Military Commission, confirmed Jiang's increased authority over the PLA.

At the first session of the Ninth NPC, which commenced in early March 1998, the number of ministry-level bodies was reduced from 40 to 29, mainly through mergers. On 16 March Jiang Zemin was re-elected President of the State Council, and Hu Jintao was elected Vice-President. Li Peng resigned as Premier and was replaced by Zhu Rongji, who received overwhelming support from the NPC delegates. Li Peng replaced Qiao Shi as Chairman of the NPC, despite a lack of support from a number of delegates. Zhu's appointments to a new 39-member State Council included a number of associates of Jiang Zemin. Zhu also promoted a number of technocrats who were supportive of his own policies, most notably Xiang Huaicheng, hitherto a Vice-Minister of Finance, who was allocated the finance portfolio.

At the second session of the Ninth NPC, held in March 1999, a number of constitutional amendments were ratified, including the elevation in status of private-sector and other non-state enterprises to 'important components of the socialist market economy', a recommendation for adherence to the rule of law, and the incorporation of Deng Xiaoping's ideology into the Constitution alongside Marxism-Leninism and 'Mao Zedong thought'. In October Hu Jintao was appointed a Vice-Chairman of the Central Military Commission, and in December Zeng Qinghong became a full member of the Politburo, replacing Xie Fei, who had died in September.

Meanwhile, public disquiet over corruption within the CCP, the state bureaucracy and economic enterprises was acknowledged in August 1993, when the Party initiated an anti-corruption campaign. Hundreds of executions of officials were subsequently reported, and in April 1995, following allegations of corruption, Wang Baosen, a deputy mayor of Beijing, committed suicide. In the same month Chen Xitong, Secretary of the Beijing Municipality Committee, was arrested. An extensive inquiry concluded that Wang Baosen, a protégé of Chen Xitong, had been responsible for serious irregularities, including the embezzlement of the equivalent of millions of US dollars. In September, having been similarly disgraced, Chen Xitong was expelled from the Politburo and from the Central Committee of the CCP, later being expelled from the CCP itself. Owing to his implication in the scandal, the mayor of Beijing, Li Qiyan, finally resigned in October 1996. The campaign against corruption intensified in 1997 with the sentencing in August of Chen Xiaotong, son of Chen Xitong, to 12 years' imprisonment for the misappropriation of public funds. Lengthy prison terms were also conferred on two former senior officials in the Beijing administration for accepting bribes. In August 1998 Chen Xitong was sentenced to 16 years' imprisonment for corruption and dereliction of duty; a subsequent appeal was rejected by the Supreme People's Court. It was reported that between October 1992 and June 1997 121,000 people had been expelled from the CCP for corruption, while 37,500 others had faced criminal charges. In an attempt to eradicate illicit trade, in July 1998 President Jiang Zemin ordered the closure of all the business interests of the PLA, comprising some 15,000 companies across all sections of the economy. The divestment of all the PLA's enterprises to a state body, styled the Takeover Office for Military, Armed Police, Government and Judiciary Businesses, was completed by mid-December.

An extensive operation to counter the sharp increase in crimes such as drugs-trafficking, prostitution and the distribution of pornography continued, resulting in hundreds of executions. In April 1996 the Government initiated 'Strike Hard', a new campaign against crime, executing hundreds of people. In September 1998 Amnesty International, the human rights organization, released a report stating that China had executed 1,876 people in 1997, more than the rest of the world combined. This represented, however, a considerable reduction compared with the 4,367 executions documented in 1996.

China's treatment of political dissidents attracted international attention in November 1997, with the release on medical grounds into exile in the USA of Wei Jingsheng. Wei had been imprisoned in 1979, but was released on parole in September 1993. He was rearrested, however, in April 1994, and detained incommunicado until December 1995, when he was convicted of conspiring to overthrow the Government. His sentencing to 14 years' imprisonment provoked an international outcry, and he was released shortly after Jiang Zemin's visit to the USA in October 1997 (see below). Bao Ge, a prominent Shanghai dissident and campaigner for compensation for Chinese victims of Japanese war aggression, was released from three years' imprisonment without trial in June. He left for the USA in November.

In January 1991, meanwhile, the trials of many of those arrested during the pro-democracy protests of 1989 commenced. Most activists received relatively short prison sentences. In July 1992 Bao Tong, a senior aide of Zhao Ziyang, the former General Secretary of the CCP, was found guilty of involvement in the pro-democracy unrest of mid-1989. At the end of his seven-year prison sentence, Bao Tong was released in May 1996 and placed under house arrest. He was freed from house arrest in May 1997, but remained under constant police surveillance.

In February 1994 Asia Watch, an independent New York-based human rights organization, issued a highly critical report of the situation in China, which detailed the cases of more than 1,700 detainees, imprisoned for their political, ethnic or religious views. In April, shortly before the USA was due to decide upon a renewal of China's favourable trading status, Wang Juntao, imprisoned for his part in the 1989 protests, was unexpectedly released and permitted to travel to the USA for medical treatment. Other releases followed. In July, however, the trial on charges of counter-revolutionary activity of 14 members of a dissident group, in detention since 1992, commenced. In December 1994 nine of the defendants received heavy prison sentences.

In February 1993 Wang Dan and Guo Haifeng, leading student activists in the 1989 demonstrations, were freed. In late 1994, however, complaining of police harassment, Wang Dan filed a lawsuit against the authorities. He was rearrested in May 1995. The imposition of an 11-year sentence on Wang Dan at the conclusion of his cursory trial on charges of conspiracy, in October 1996, received international condemnation. Appeals for his release on medical grounds in 1997 were rejected, but in April 1998 he was released on medical parole and was sent into exile in the USA on the following day. In May 1993, having served 12 years of a 15-year sentence, Xu Wenli was released from prison. He was rearrested in April 1994, but released shortly afterwards. In August 1993 the arrest and expulsion from China of Han Dongfang, a trade union activist who had attempted to return to his homeland after a year in the USA, attracted much international attention.

In June 1995 Liu Gang, a leader of the 1989 uprising, was released from prison, and in May 1996 he was granted temporary asylum in the USA. Two further dissidents, Ren Wanding and Zhang Xianliang, were freed upon completion of their prison terms in June 1996. Having been released in the same month, Wang Xizhe escaped from Guangzhou and was permitted to enter the USA in October. His fellow activist, Liu Xiaobo, was arrested in Beijing, however, and ordered to serve three years in a labour camp. In November Chen Zeming, another alleged leader of the 1989 pro-democracy demonstrations, was released on medical parole.

In 1997 there was increasing pressure on the CCP to reconsider its assessment of the 1989 Tiananmen Square pro-democracy demonstrations as a 'counter-revolutionary rebellion'. In June 1997, in an unprecedented decision, a court in Liaoning Province overturned convictions of 'counter-revolution' against four dissidents imprisoned for their role in the 1989 pro-democracy movement. However, an appeal to the CCP National Congress by Zhao Ziyang (who remained under house arrest) to reassess the official verdict was dismissed. During President Jiang's visit to the USA, in October 1997, having first described the brutal treatment of the 1989 demonstrators as a 'necessary measure', a subsequent acknowledgement that mistakes might have been made was not, according to the Chinese authorities, to be regarded as an apology. In mid-1997 Beijing refuted Amnesty International reports that several pro-democracy activists remained among the numerous political prisoners in

China, classifying as criminals the estimated 2,000 people imprisoned on charges of 'counter-revolution'.

The UN Commissioner for Human Rights, Mary Robinson, made an unprecedented official visit to China, including Tibet, and Hong Kong in September 1998. Following the visit, in October China signed the International Covenant on Civil and Political Rights in New York, guaranteeing freedom of expression, a fair trial and protection against arbitrary arrest. Although the Government's signing of the Covenant was hailed as a great advance in its attitude towards human rights, the treaty would only come into force once ratified by the NPC. No date was set for ratification. Following a further visit by Robinson to Beijing in March 2000 (during which China refuted her right to criticize its conduct of internal affairs), in November a human rights training agreement was signed which, it was hoped, would be a precursor to ratification.

In 1998 attempts by dissidents in Beijing and the provinces to create and register an opposition party, the Chinese Democratic Party (CDP), with the principal aim of democratic elections, were suppressed by the Government. The exiled dissident, Wang Binzhang, was deported to the USA in February after entering the country to meet fellow opposition activists. In November the Government published a judicial interpretation of the crimes of political subversion (thereby expanding existing punishable offences), specifying that 'incitement to subvert state power' would result in imprisonment for between three years and life for any publisher, musician, author, artist or film-maker found guilty of the charge. In December at least 30 members of the CDP were detained, and three veteran activists, Xu Wenli, Qin Yongmin and Wang Youcai, were sentenced to 13, 12 and 11 years' imprisonment, respectively, provoking strong international condemnation. Human rights groups declared the release on medical parole and subsequent exile to the USA of the prominent dissident, Liu Nianchun, shortly before the conviction of the CDP activists, to be an attempt to deflect criticism of their trials. A speech by President Jiang Zemin in December appeared to confirm the end of a period of relative tolerance of political dissent. By November 1999 a further 18 CDP leaders had been convicted of subverting state power and sentenced to lengthy terms of imprisonment.

At the first Sino-US discussions on human rights for four years in Washington, DC, in January 1999 members of the US delegation urged their Chinese counterparts to halt the harsh treatment of dissidents. In February of that year two dissidents, Gao Yu (a journalist) and Sun Weibang, who had received substantial sentences, were released ahead of schedule, prompting speculation that Beijing was attempting to counter criticism before the imminent visit to the People's Republic by the US Secretary of State and the forthcoming meeting of the UN Commission on Human Rights in Geneva. None the less, China continued its suppression of dissent. In late April, however, a US-sponsored resolution at the aforementioned UN Commission meeting, condemning China's human rights record, was defeated. The resolution was again defeated in April 2000. A number of activists were detained in June 1999 in advance of the 10th anniversary of the killings in Tiananmen Square; despite official fears, the day passed without major incident in Beijing. (In Hong Kong, however, thousands attended a commemorative rally.) The Square had been closed for some time, ostensibly for repairs before the 50th anniversary of the founding of the People's Republic in October, and did not reopen until late June.

The CCP's desire to protect its supremacy became increasingly apparent when it banned the popular Falun Gong religious cult in July 1999, on the grounds that it constituted a threat to society. The ban was prompted by demonstrations, attended by tens of thousands of supporters in numerous towns and cities, in protest at the arrest of more than 100 adherents of the sect. The authorities embarked on a campaign of harsh persecution of those who refused to renounce their faith, and by the end of the month more than 6,000 arrests had been made. The authorities had initially been alarmed by a peaceful protest in central Beijing, attended by some 10,000 practitioners in April. Four members of the sect were imprisoned in December, with sentences ranging from seven to 18 years, for their part in organizing the demonstration. This followed the conviction and imprisonment of four of Falun Gong's provincial leaders in November. The authorities were also concerned by the high level of Falun Gong membership among CCP and PLA officials. The CCP took the opportunity to demonstrate its continuing power on 1 October 1999, with lavish but strictly-controlled, celebrations of the 50th anniversary of the foundation of the People's Republic of China. In a highly symbolic gesture, a picture of Jiang Zemin was paraded alongside portraits of Mao Zedong and Deng Xiaoping: the first time that the current President had been publicly placed on a par with his predecessors. In January 2000 five Catholic bishops were ordained in a display of strength by the state-controlled Chinese Catholic Church, impeding any improvement in relations with the Vatican, which opposed the ordination. In August 1999 Beijing had refused to grant permission for the Pope to visit Hong Kong, owing to the Vatican's links with Taiwan.

According to a US-based Catholic organization, the arrest of an archbishop belonging to the clandestine Roman Catholic Church in February 2000 was part of an attempt by China to undermine allegiance to the Vatican. During the year there was substantial evidence of the CCP's intensification of repression of all non-official religious movements, many of which were classified as 'evil cults', with widespread arrests and church closures. In October the situation was exacerbated when, on China's National Day, the Pope canonized 120 missionary and Chinese Roman Catholic martyrs. Beijing responded with allegations of serious crimes perpetrated by several of the new saints. Despite a subsequent apology by the Pope for any errors committed by missionaries in China, prospects for the establishment of relations between the two sides were severely damaged. Despite condemnation and prosecution by the full force of the law, meanwhile, Falun Gong members continued to make quiet protests on a regular basis during 2000. Many practitioners were detained, and a Hong Kong human rights group claimed in June that, thus far, 22 members of the sect had died while in custody. The CCP's fear of losing its authority in the face of this increasing religious adherence became evident in October, when Falun Gong was declared to be a political rival to the CCP and an enemy of the nation. In February, in an attempt definitively to refute the growing belief that China must eventually abandon one-party rule, Jiang Zemin had launched a new political theory entitled 'The Three Representations', which declared that the CCP would 'always represent the development needs of China's advanced social productive forces, always represent the onward direction of China's advanced culture and always represent the fundamental interests of the largest number of Chinese people'. It appeared, however, that with the advent of significant social change the CCP was finding it increasingly difficult to maintain control over its members.

Attempts were made by the Government in February and in November 2000 to regulate the publication of material on the internet, with the issuing of new rules first granting the regime the right to 'reorganize' or close down offending websites, and then requiring government approval prior to the posting of news bulletins. It was feared that the only permitted information would be that already published in the official media, particularly after the earlier fining and temporary suspension of a financial news website for publishing material that might damage the Government's image. In April it was reported that four academics had been dismissed from a Chinese Academy, accused of being 'a branch of opposition within the Party' following the publication of an essay by one of them advocating political reform. In the following months there was harsh repression of provincial labour unrest. In April 2000 it was reported that labour disputes had totalled more than 120,000 in 1999. Workers had become increasingly restless since 1998, when SOE restructuring began to result in widespread redundancies.

The firmest repressive action, however, proved to be necessary in regional and central government circles. The third session of the Ninth NPC, which convened in Beijing in March 2000, focused mainly on economic issues but also made a commitment to ending official corruption and smuggling. Earlier that month a former provincial deputy governor had been executed for bribery and possession of property acquired from unidentified sources. Corruption appeared to be rife throughout 2000 in many areas of government, including customs, finance, the military and the Three Gorges dam project. Among the most notable cases was that of former Vice-Chairman of the Standing Committee of the NPC, Cheng Kejie, who was executed in September for accepting huge bribes. Also in September, Maj.-Gen. Ji Shengde, the former head of military intelligence of the PLA, was formally charged with taking massive bribes while in office. His trial formed part of the biggest corruption and smuggling case in the history of the People's Republic, with several senior officials in various Chinese cities facing prosecution. Fourteen were executed, while other defendants received

sentences of life imprisonment. The leader of the smuggling ring, Lai Changxing, evaded capture and escaped to Canada, from where China was attempting to extradite him in late 2000. Meanwhile, at its Plenary Session in October, the CCP announced a new five-year plan, under which China was to concentrate on rural development, the creation of employment, economic modernization and combating corruption. Later that month, following a two-year investigation, government auditors reported the embezzlement or serious misuse of the equivalent of more than US \$11,000m. of public funds by government officials.

In August 2000 a group of Chinese dissidents filed a lawsuit in the USA accusing Li Peng of crimes against humanity for sanctioning the events of 4 June 1989 in Tiananmen Square. China made a request to the USA that the case be abandoned, describing it as 'political farce'.

Tibet (Xizang), a semi-independent region of western China, was occupied in October 1950 by Chinese Communist forces. In March 1959 there was an unsuccessful armed uprising by Tibetans opposed to Chinese rule. The Dalai Lama, the head of Tibet's Buddhist clergy and thus the region's spiritual leader, fled with some 100,000 supporters to Dharamsala, northern India, where a government-in-exile was established. The Chinese ended the former dominance of the lamas (Buddhist monks) and destroyed many monasteries. Tibet became an 'Autonomous Region' of China in September 1965, but the majority of Tibetans have continued to regard the Dalai Lama as their 'god-king', and to resent the Chinese presence. In October 1987 violent clashes occurred in Lhasa (the regional capital) between the Chinese authorities and Tibetans seeking independence. Further demonstrations during a religious festival in March 1988 resulted in a riot and several deaths, and a number of Tibetan separatists were arrested and detained without trial. The Dalai Lama, however, renounced demands for complete independence, and in 1988 proposed that Tibet become a self-governing Chinese territory, in all respects except foreign affairs. In December 1988 an offer from the Dalai Lama to meet Chinese representatives in Geneva was rejected, and later that month two more demonstrators were killed by security forces during a march to commemorate the 40th anniversary of the UN General Assembly's adoption of the Universal Declaration of Human Rights.

On 7 March 1989 martial law was imposed in Lhasa for the first time since 1959, after further violent clashes between separatists and the Chinese police, which resulted in the deaths of 16 protesters. In October the Chinese Government condemned as an interference in its internal affairs the award of the Nobel Peace Prize to the Dalai Lama. In November several Tibetan Buddhist nuns claimed to have been severely tortured for their part in the demonstrations in March 1989. In May 1990 martial law was lifted in Lhasa. Human rights groups claimed that during the last six months of the period of martial law as many as 2,000 persons had been executed. Furthermore, political and religious repression and torture were reported to be continuing throughout 1990. Renewed anti-Chinese protests were reported in October 1991 and in March 1992. In May a report issued by Amnesty International was critical of the Chinese authorities' violations of the human rights of the monks and nuns of Tibet. A document entitled *Tibet—Its Ownership and Human Rights Situation* was published by the Chinese Government in September, attempting to prove that historically the region was part of China. In May 1993 several thousand Tibetans were reported to have demonstrated in Lhasa against Chinese rule. A number of protesters were believed to have been killed by the security forces. In January 1994 two prominent Tibetan activists were released from detention. In July, however, five secessionists were found guilty of counter-revolutionary acts and received prison sentences of up to 15 years.

In April 1994 China condemned the Dalai Lama's meeting with President Clinton during the former's lecture tour of the USA. In September the Dalai Lama warned China that Tibet might resort to armed uprising if oppression continued to worsen. In late 1994 the construction of new monasteries and temples in Tibet was banned. In March 1995 regulations restricting the number of Buddhist monks were announced, and in the same month the Dalai Lama's proposal that a referendum be held on the future of Tibet was dismissed by China. In May the Dalai Lama's nomination of the 11th incarnation of the Panchen Lama (the second position in the spiritual hierarchy, the 10th incumbent having died in 1989) was condemned by the Chinese authorities, which banned the six-year old boy from travelling to Dharamsala. In September 1995, as the 30th anniversary of the imposition of Chinese rule approached, it was reported that independence activists had carried out two bombings in Lhasa.

In September 1995, during the UN World Conference on Women and the Non-Governmental Organizations' Forum held concurrently in China, a silent protest by a group of female Tibetan exiles attracted much attention. Following an informal meeting between the Dalai Lama and President Clinton in Washington in mid-September, China lodged a strong protest. In November the Chinese Government announced its own nomination of a new Panchen Lama. The boy was enthroned at a ceremony in Lhasa in December, the whereabouts of the Dalai Lama's choice remaining unknown until mid-1996, when China's ambassador to the UN in Geneva admitted that the boy was in detention in Beijing. There were violent confrontations in Tibet in May 1996, following the banning of any public display of images of the Dalai Lama. During the latter part of 1996 visits by the Dalai Lama to the United Kingdom and Australia aroused further protests from the Chinese Government. A series of minor explosions during 1996 culminated in late December with the detonation of a powerful bomb outside a government office in Lhasa, which injured several people. The attack was denounced by the Dalai Lama. In an unprecedented admission, the Chinese Government acknowledged the existence of a terrorist problem in Tibet.

The Chinese leadership condemned the Dalai Lama's visit to Taiwan in March 1997, despite assurances that he was visiting in his capacity as a spiritual leader. In May it was reported that Chatral Rinpoche, an official in the Tibetan administration and one of Tibet's most senior monks, had been sentenced to six years' imprisonment for allegedly revealing information to the Dalai Lama about Beijing's search for the new Panchen Lama. The USA's decision in mid-1997 to appoint a special co-ordinator for Tibet was criticized by the Chinese authorities. In October the Dalai Lama appealed to the Chinese Government to reopen negotiations over the status of Tibet, confirming that he did not seek full independence for the region. In December the Geneva-based International Commission of Jurists (see p. 322) published a report accusing China of suppressing nationalist dissent in Tibet and attempting to extinguish Tibetan culture, and appealed for a referendum, under the auspices of the UN, to decide the territory's future status.

In April 1998 China agreed to allow envoys of the European Union (EU) to make a one-week investigatory visit to Tibet. Later that month in New Delhi, India, Thupten Ngodup, one of six Tibetan exiles who had been engaged in a hunger strike for 49 days, died after setting himself alight as security forces attempted forcibly to transport the protesters to hospital to end their hunger strike. The hunger strikers had declared their intention of starving themselves to death unless the UN agreed to debate the issue of Tibet in the General Assembly, to appoint a special rapporteur to investigate human rights violations and to oversee a referendum on independence. The protest was arranged by the Tibetan Youth Congress (TYC), a movement advocating independence for Tibet. In May 1998 the EU adopted two resolutions relating to China, condemning the sale of organs of executed prisoners and calling for a UN committee to investigate the transactions and, furthermore, urging the UN to appoint a rapporteur for Tibet issues.

During his visit to China and Hong Kong in late June 1998 (see below), the US President, Bill Clinton, discussed Tibet with Chinese leaders, with the Dalai Lama's support. Beijing proclaimed its readiness to open negotiations if the Dalai Lama first declared both Tibet and Taiwan to be inalienable parts of China. This statement was repeated regularly during 1998. In October the Dalai Lama admitted that since the 1960s he had received US $1.7m. annually from the Central Intelligence Agency (CIA) to support the Tibetan separatist movement. Whilst visiting the USA in early November, the Dalai Lama had an unofficial meeting with Bill Clinton, thereby angering the Chinese authorities. Later that month the Dalai Lama requested informal talks with the Chinese leadership before he would make any unilateral statement. In December, in Paris, he was presented with a human rights prize by the French Prime Minister.

In January 1999 a new US special co-ordinator for Tibetan affairs was appointed, amid opposition from China. Earlier in the month TYC activists had attempted to storm the Chinese embassy in New Delhi and had burnt Chinese flags outside the building to protest against China's occupation of Tibet. In May the Dalai Lama visited the United Kingdom and met the British Prime Minister, Tony Blair. In order to avoid criticism from Beijing, it was reported that Blair had received the religious leader in a spiritual capacity. The World Bank provoked US anger in the following month, when it approved a loan to settle 58,000 Chinese farmers on land in western China considered by Tibetans to be their own. Tibetan support groups feared that the project would aid China's policy of diminishing the minority Tibetan population living in the region. It was agreed that no funds would be disbursed until an independent panel had ensured that the plan conformed to World Bank rules. In August Sino-US relations deteriorated further following the injury in police custody of a US academic and human rights activist who had been detained whilst conducting an unofficial investigation into the project; he was reportedly released and repatriated in September. The project was abandoned in July 2000, owing to the perceived excessively demanding nature of the World Bank's conditions.

In January 2000 the Chinese Government was embarrassed by the flight of Tibet's second most important Lama, the Karmapa, from Tibet to Dharamsala. Frequent requests by him to be permitted to visit his guru in India had been ignored. The Karmapa, who had, unusually, been recognized both by the Dalai Lama and by Beijing, had previously been rewarded by the latter for his perceived loyalty to the Chinese regime. Reports that the Karmapa's parents had been detained by the Tibetan authorities, following anti-China remarks by their son, were denied. The Karmapa's request for political asylum placed the Indian authorities in a difficult position; India maintained close contact with both the Dalai Lama and with Beijing, but by the end of 2000 no decision had been reached. Meanwhile, there was some discord between followers of the Karmapa and other Tibetans, the former proclaiming their leader to be the Dalai Lama's equal. Furthermore, three other people staked their claim to be the real Karmapa. In January 2000 in Lhasa, Soinam Puncog, a two-year-old boy selected by the Chinese authorities but rejected by followers of the Dalai Lama, was ordained as the new Reting Lama.

China continued to exert great influence over the Dalai Lama's movements in 2000. Following the UN's decision to exclude him from a summit meeting of world religious leaders in August, in October the Republic of Korea refused to grant a visa to the Dalai Lama, on the grounds that it would be 'inappropriate'. Reports confirmed that Beijing had expressed strong opposition to a trip planned by the Dalai Lama for the following month. In April, however, despite warnings from Beijing, Japan had granted the Dalai Lama a visa to lecture at a Buddhist college. He also made his first-ever visit to Northern Ireland, to promote peace, in October 2000. In December contact was resumed between the Dalai Lama and the Chinese authorities, following a visit to Beijing by the former's brother. Meanwhile, in October in Lhasa, following a bomb explosion attributed to the continuing campaign of resistance to Chinese rule, security was increased, and foreign tourists were confined to their hotels.

Anti-Chinese sentiment in the Xinjiang Uygur Autonomous Region intensified in the early 1990s, resulting in the initiation of a new, often brutal, campaign by the authorities to repress the Islamic separatist movement. Suppression of separatism increased in 1996, following a number of violent incidents. Hundreds of people were detained for their part in rioting and bomb attacks, and many were subsequently executed or imprisoned. Reports in late 1997 indicated that there had been a renewal of armed separatist activity, in which more than 300 people had been killed. In January 1998 13 people were executed in Xinjiang, allegedly for robbery and murder, although unofficial reports suggested that those executed were Muslim separatist demonstrators. Muslim separatists were believed to be responsible for an incendiary device on a bus in Wuhan in February, which killed 16 people. Two leading activists, Yibulayin Simayi and Abudureyimu Aisha, were executed in January 1999. Detentions continued during the year, and a further 10 separatists were reportedly executed at the end of May. Three Muslims were sentenced to death in September for participating in the separatist campaign, whilst six others received long prison sentences. In October 2000 Abduhelil Abdulmejit, a leading organizer of resistance to Chinese rule in Xinjiang who had been imprisoned three years previously, was reported to have died of pneumonia while in custody; international groups alleged that he had been tortured and murdered.

In September 1984, following protracted negotiations, China reached agreement with the British Government over the terms of the future administration of Hong Kong upon the territory's return to Chinese sovereignty, scheduled for 1 July 1997. In

1985 a Basic Law Drafting Committee (BLDC), including 25 representatives from Hong Kong, was established in Beijing to prepare a new Basic Law (Constitution) for Hong Kong, which was duly approved by the NPC in April 1990. In September 1991, during a visit to China by the British Prime Minister, a Memorandum of Understanding on the construction of a new airport in Hong Kong was signed. Relations between China and the United Kingdom were strained in 1992 by the announcement of ambitious plans for democratic reform in Hong Kong prior to 1997. In December 1993 China declared that it would regard as null and void any laws enacted by the territory's Legislative Council (which, it was subsequently confirmed, would be disbanded in 1997). In July 1995 the Chief Secretary of Hong Kong, Anson Chan, confirmed that she had had clandestine meetings with Chinese officials during a three-day visit to Beijing. In October Qian Qichen, the Chinese Vice-Premier and Minister of Foreign Affairs, visited London for discussions with the British Prime Minister and his Foreign Secretary. In January 1996 the 150-member Preparatory Committee of the Hong Kong Special Administrative Region (SAR) was formally established in Beijing, in succession to the Preliminary Working Committee (PWC), which had been formed in July 1993 to study issues relating to the transfer of sovereignty. The new body duly appointed a 400-member Selection Committee, responsible for the choice of Hong Kong's future Chief Executive. In December 1996 the Selection Committee chose Tung Chee-hwa as the SAR's first Chief Executive and elected the 60 members of the Provisional Legislative Council (PLC), which held its first meeting in January 1997. Objections from the United Kingdom and the USA to Chinese proposals to abolish the Legislative Council, and to repeal human rights legislation, were dismissed by China.

The transfer of Hong Kong from British to Chinese sovereignty was effected at midnight on 30 June 1997, whereupon some 4,000 PLA troops were deployed in the territory. In December 1997 36 deputies from Hong Kong were directly elected to the Ninth NPC in Beijing. Elections for the SAR's new Legislative Council took place in May 1998. The question of the right of abode in the territory for mainland-born children and the ultimate referral of the matter to the Standing Committee of the NPC caused tensions during 1999. Meanwhile, following the NATO bombing of the Chinese embassy in Yugoslavia in May 1999 (see below), US military aircraft and ships were temporarily denied access to Hong Kong. In April 2000 there were fears for the freedom of the Hong Kong media following a warning by Beijing against reporting any remarks advocating Taiwanese independence. (See p. 1069 for further information on Hong Kong.)

In June 1986 China and Portugal opened negotiations for the return of the Portuguese overseas territory of Macau to full Chinese sovereignty. In January 1987 it was agreed that this would take place in December 1999. The agreement was based upon the 'one country, two systems' principle, which had formed the basis of China's negotiated settlement regarding the return of Hong Kong. In March 1993 the final draft of the Basic Law for Macau was approved by the NPC. In May 1995 China proposed the swift establishment of a preparatory working committee to facilitate the transfer of sovereignty. Cordial relations were maintained, and the Portuguese Minister of Foreign Affairs visited Beijing in February 1996. The two sides agreed to accelerate the pace of work of the Sino-Portuguese Joint Liaison Group (JLG). In January 1997 the Chinese Vice-Premier and Minister of Foreign Affairs, Qian Qichen, travelled to Portugal for discussions. Confidence in the future of Macau was reiterated. Following a series of murders, bombings and arson attacks in Macau, Qian Qichen announced that China would station an 'appropriate' number of troops in the territory to help combat organized crime and ensure public security upon its resumption of sovereignty in December 1999.

In April 1999 the 200-member Selection Committee, which was comprised entirely of residents of the territory and which was to be responsible for the appointment of members of Macau's post-1999 government, was established in Beijing. In the following month Edmund Ho, a banker and a member of the legislature since 1988, was elected the first Chief Executive of Macau. China resumed sovereignty of the territory at midnight on 19 December 1999, whereupon Ho was duly inaugurated and the PLA garrison was established. In general, local reaction was favourable, as it was hoped that China would succeed, where Portugal had failed, in restoring public security. (See p. 1090 for further information on Macau.)

Taiwan has repeatedly rejected China's proposals for reunification, whereby the island would become a 'special administrative region' along the lines of Hong Kong and Macau, and has sought reunification under its own terms. China threatened military intervention, should Taiwan declare itself independent of the mainland. Trade and reciprocal visits greatly increased in 1988, as relations improved. Reconciliation initiatives were abruptly halted, however, by the violent suppression of the pro-democracy movement in Beijing in June 1989. In May 1990 President Lee of Taiwan suggested the opening of direct dialogue on a government-to-government basis with the People's Republic. Beijing, however, maintained that it would negotiate only on a party-to-party basis with the ruling KMT. In April 1991 a delegation from the Straits Exchange Foundation (SEF) of Taiwan, established in late 1990 to handle bilateral issues, travelled to China for discussions, the first such delegation ever to visit the People's Republic. The Association for Relations across the Taiwan Straits (ARATS) was established in Beijing in December 1991. In April 1993 historic talks between the Chairmen of the ARATS and SEF took place in Singapore, where a formal structure for future negotiations on economic and social issues was agreed. In August, however, the People's Republic issued a document entitled *The Taiwan Question and the Reunification of China*, reaffirming its claim to sovereignty over the island. Relations were further strained by a series of aircraft hijackings from the mainland to Taiwan, and they deteriorated sharply in April 1994, when 24 Taiwanese tourists were among those robbed and murdered on board a pleasure boat in China. In June three men were convicted of the murders and promptly executed. In August Tang Shubei, the Vice-Chairman and Secretary-General of the ARATS, travelled to Taipei for discussions, the most senior CCP official ever to visit the island. Despite tensions earlier in the month, in late November a further round of ARATS-SEF talks took place in Nanjing, at which agreement in principle on the procedure for the repatriation of hijackers and illegal immigrants was confirmed.

Discussions were resumed in Beijing in January 1995. At the end of that month President Jiang Zemin announced an 'eight-point' policy for Taiwan's peaceful reunification with the mainland. In response, in April, President Lee proposed a 'six-point' programme for cross-Straits relations. Following President Lee's controversial visit to the USA in June, however, the ARATS postponed the forthcoming second session of SEF discussions at senior level. Cross-Straits relations deteriorated further in July upon the People's Republic's announcement that it was to conduct a series of guided missile and artillery-firing tests off the northern coast of Taiwan. In the following month President Jiang Zemin confirmed that the People's Republic would not renounce the use of force against Taiwan.

In early 1996 unconfirmed reports of the mobilization of mainland troops, and the commencement of new missile tests aroused international concern. Live artillery exercises were conducted in the Taiwan Strait. Tension subsequently eased, however, and a number of mainland business executives travelled to Taiwan. In January 1997, as the reversion of the entrepôt of Hong Kong to Chinese sovereignty approached, representatives of the People's Republic and Taiwan reached a preliminary consensus on the issue of direct shipping links. Limited services resumed in April, thus ending a ban of 48 years. In August the deputy secretary-general of the ARATS, the highest-ranking Chinese official to visit Taiwan since 1995, held talks with members of the SEF.

Following preliminary visits by members of the ARATS and SEF, Koo Chen-fu, Chairman of the SEF, visited China for cross-Straits talks in October 1998. He held several meetings with his ARATS counterpart, Wang Daohan, as well as an historic meeting with Jiang Zemin and Qian Qichen. A four-point agreement was reached, allowing for increased bilateral communications. In January 1999 the ARATS invited the SEF Deputy Secretary-General to visit the People's Republic for talks in order to prepare for the forthcoming visit of Wang Daohan. The SEF, however, proposed that ARATS officials visit Taiwan to discuss preparations. In February, during a flight to the island of Kinmen, an SEF official was attacked by four Chinese convicted aircraft hijackers, who were part of a group being transferred to the nearby island prior to their repatriation to the mainland. During the following months Taiwan repatriated several hundred Chinese illegal immigrants. In March an ARATS delegation visited Taiwan, and in the same month an SEF group travelled to Beijing. In April President Lee reaffirmed that Beijing should recognize Taiwan as being of equal status. In August the ARATS suspended contacts with the SEF, following President Lee's insistence on the 'two-state theory' (which in the same month was incorporated into the party resolution of the ruling KMT). It was confirmed in October that, while Taiwan continued to adhere to this theory, Wang Daohan would not visit the island as previously agreed.

Meanwhile, China was becoming increasingly demonstrative in its opposition to Taiwan's inclusion in the US-led Theater Missile Defence anti-missile system. Ballistic missiles were deployed in mainland coastal regions facing Taiwan, and in July 1999 the People's Republic announced that it had developed a neutron bomb, after declaring itself ready for war should Taiwan attempt to gain independence. Chinese military exercises took place in the Taiwan Strait later that month. In August the USA reaffirmed its readiness to defend Taiwan against any Chinese military action. The Taiwanese Government refused a request by Beijing that it retract the 'state-to-state' theory with regard to cross-Straits relations. In September, however, following a severe earthquake in Taiwan that killed or injured several thousand people, China was among the many countries to offer emergency assistance to the island, although Taiwan accused the People's Republic of contravening humanitarian principles by trying to compel other countries to seek its approval before offering help.

In February 2000 the People's Republic threatened to attack Taiwan if it indefinitely postponed reunification talks. There was some trepidation in Beijing in March, following the election of Taiwan's first non-KMT President, Chen Shui-bian of the pro-independence Democratic Progressive Party (DPP). The approval by the Taiwanese legislature in that month of a law providing for the first direct transport links between Taiwan's outlying islands and mainland China for 50 years did not substantially improve matters, and when the first voyage took place in January 2001 it was largely disregarded by the People's Republic. Meanwhile, in April 2000 the Taiwanese Vice President-elect, Annette Lu, was denounced by the Chinese media after she made 'separatist' remarks televised in Hong Kong, declaring that Taiwan was only a 'remote relative and close neighbour' of China. In an attempt to improve relations with Beijing, President Chen offered to compromise and to reopen negotiations on the basis that each side was free to interpret the 'one China' formula as it saw fit. Chinese Premier Zhu Rongji rejected the suggestion, and questioned Taiwan's motives, effectively ending hopes of restarting negotiations in the near future. In July the Chinese authorities responded angrily when the United Kingdom issued a visa to former President Lee Teng-hui, who continued to be regarded as a dissident by the People's Republic. Despite the fact that Lee's visa was for the purposes of a private visit by an individual, and specified as a condition that no public statements would be made during the trip, China took action against British governmental and trade interests, to register its displeasure.

In October 2000 China published a policy document on its national defence, which confirmed that the People's Republic would use force to prevent Taiwanese secession, to stop any occupation of the island, and also in the event of Taiwan indefinitely postponing reunification with the mainland. In November, however, there were signs of an improvement in relations when Wu Po-hsiung, the Vice-Chairman of the KMT, travelled to Beijing and met unofficially with Qian Qichen. Wu was the most senior KMT official to visit mainland China for more than 50 years, and it was thought that Beijing was attempting to isolate Chen Shui-bian by currying favour with his political rivals. During the meeting both sides agreed to hold important academic forums to discuss cross-Straits relations and to attempt to devise common positions. Qian stressed, however, the importance of Taiwan's recognition of the 'One China' principle before official negotiations could resume. (See p. 1102 for further information on Taiwan.)

In the early years of the People's Republic, China was dependent on the USSR for economic and military aid, and Chinese planning was based on the Soviet model, with highly centralized control. From 1955, however, Mao Zedong set out to develop a distinctively Chinese form of socialism. As a result, the USSR withdrew all technical aid to China in August 1960. Chinese hostility to the USSR increased, and was aggravated by territorial disputes, and by the Soviet invasion of Afghanistan and the Soviet-supported Vietnamese invasion of Cambodia. Sino-Soviet relations remained strained until 1987, when representatives of the two countries signed a partial agreement concerning the exact demarcation of the disputed common border at the Amur River. The withdrawal of Soviet troops from Afghanistan (completed in February 1989) and Viet Nam's assurance that it would end its military presence in Cambodia by September 1989 resulted in a further *rapprochement*. In May 1989 a full summit meeting was held in Beijing, at which normal state and party relations between China and the USSR were formally restored. During the next two years senior Chinese officials visited the USSR. In December 1991, upon the dissolution of the USSR, China recognized the newly-independent states of the former union. The President of Russia, Boris Yeltsin, visited China in December 1992. In May 1994, in Beijing, Premier Li Peng and his Russian counterpart signed various co-operation agreements. In September President Jiang Zemin travelled to Moscow, the first visit to Russia by a Chinese Head of State since 1957. The two sides reached agreement on the formal demarcation of the western section of the border (the eastern section having been delimited in May 1991), and each pledged not to aim nuclear missiles at the other. In June 1995 the Chinese Premier paid an official visit to Russia, where several bilateral agreements were signed.

Sino-Russian relations continued to improve, and in April 1996 in Beijing Presidents Jiang and Yeltsin signed a series of agreements, envisaging the development of closer co-operation in areas such as energy, space research, environmental protection, and the combating of organized crime. Together with their counterparts from Kazakhstan, Kyrgyzstan and Tajikistan, the two Presidents also signed a treaty aimed at reducing tension along their respective borders. Progress on the Sino-Russian border question, and also on matters such as trade, was made during the Chinese Premier's visit to Moscow in December 1996. A further treaty on military co-operation and border demilitarization was signed by the Presidents of China, Russia, Kazakhstan, Kyrgyzstan and Tajikistan in April 1997, during a visit by President Jiang Zemin to Russia. Presidents Jiang and Yeltsin affirmed their commitment to building a strategic, co-operative partnership, and a Sino-Russian committee on friendship, peace and development was established. Progress on the Sino-Russian border issue culminated in the signing of an agreement, during President Yeltsin's visit to Beijing in November, which formally ended the territorial dispute.

In May 1998 a direct telephone link was established between Jiang Zemin and President Yeltsin of Russia. In November, in Moscow, representatives from Russia, China and the Democratic People's Republic of Korea signed an inter-governmental agreement on the delimitation of their borders along the Tumannaya River. Relations continued to improve between China and Russia in 1999. In February 11 agreements on bilateral economic and trade co-operation were signed during a visit to Russia by Zhu Rongji. In June, following a visit to China by the Russian Minister of Foreign Affairs, it was announced that a final accord on the demarcation of a common border between the two countries had been agreed after seven years of negotiations. The relevant legal documents were signed in December. During a summit meeting of China, Russia, Kazakhstan, Kyrgyzstan and Tajikistan in the Kyrgyz capital, Bishkek, agreements were signed on the China-Kazakhstan-Kyrgyzstan and the Chinese-Kyrgyz borders. In November it was announced that all Chinese-Kazakh border issues had been completely resolved.

Following the resignation of Boris Yeltsin as Russian President in December 1999, his successor, Vladimir Putin, confirmed his commitment to maintaining and improving links with China. A 'significant upgrading' in Sino-Russian relations occurred during Putin's visit to Beijing in July 2000, when the two countries issued a joint statement condemning US plans for the deployment of a missile defence system (see above). Presidents Jiang and Putin expressed fears of a new nuclear arms race, should installation of the system be implemented. A number of bilateral agreements were also signed during the summit meeting.

During the 1970s there was an improvement in China's relations with the West and Japan. Almost all Western countries had recognized the Government of the People's Republic as the sole legitimate government of China, and had consequently withdrawn recognition from the 'Republic of China', which had been confined to Taiwan since 1949. For many years, however, the USA refused to recognize the People's Republic, regarding the Taiwan administration as the legitimate Chinese government. In February 1972 President Richard Nixon of the USA visited the People's Republic and acknowledged that 'Taiwan is a part of China'. In January 1979 the USA recognized the People's Republic and severed diplomatic relations with Taiwan.

China's relations with the USA improved steadily throughout the 1980s. Following the suppression of the pro-democracy movement in 1989, however, all high-level government exchanges were suspended, and the export of weapons to China was prohibited. In November 1990 President Bush received the Chinese Minister of Foreign Affairs in Washington, thereby resuming contact at the most senior level. In August 1993 the USA imposed sanctions on China, in response to the latter's sales of technology for nuclear-capable missiles to Pakistan, in alleged violation of international non-proliferation guidelines. The sanctions remained in force until October 1994. In October 1995 Sino-US relations appeared to improve when, at a meeting in New York, Presidents Jiang Zemin and Bill Clinton agreed to resume dialogue on various issues, the USA reaffirming its commitment to the 'one China' policy. In November the two countries reached agreement on the resumption of bilateral military contacts. During 1996 there were several causes of renewed Sino-US tension, mainly related to various trade issues, including China's prospective membership of the World Trade Organization (WTO).

Another obstacle to good relations between China and the USA is the question of Taiwan, and, in particular, the continued sale of US armaments to Taiwan. Sino-US relations deteriorated in September 1992, upon President Bush's announcement of the sale of fighter aircraft to Taiwan. China condemned the USA's decision, in September 1994, to expand its official links with Taiwan. In June 1995, following President Clinton's highly controversial decision to grant him a visa, President Lee of Taiwan embarked upon an unofficial visit to the USA, where he met members of the US Congress. The visit so outraged Beijing that the Chinese ambassador to Washington was withdrawn. In March 1996, as China began a new series of missile tests, the USA stationed two naval convoys east of Taiwan, its largest deployment in Asia since 1975. President Clinton's decision to sell anti-aircraft missiles and other defensive weapons to Taiwan was condemned by China.

In October 1999 the Taiwan Security Enhancement Act (TSEA), establishing direct military ties between the USA and Taiwan, was adopted, albeit in modified form, by the International Relations Committee of the US House of Representatives, despite opposition from the Clinton administration. Reaction from the People's Republic was unfavourable, and its displeasure increased in February 2000 when the House of Representatives overwhelmingly approved the Act, the consideration of which was postponed by the US Senate in April 2000 at the behest of Taiwanese President-elect Chen Shui-bian (in order not to antagonize Beijing during the sensitive period preceding his inauguration). In the same month the US Government announced that it had decided to defer the sale of four naval destroyers to Taiwan, although it was prepared to supply long-range radar and medium-range air-to-air missiles.

Negotiations on the issue of human rights, the USA's growing trade deficit with China, and China's proposed entry into the WTO were the focus of Sino-US relations in 1997. President Jiang Zemin visited the USA in October 1997, the first such visit by a Chinese Head of State since 1985. Vocal public criticism of China's failure to observe human rights, particularly with regard to Tibet, was widespread in the USA, but the Clinton administration defended its policy of engagement with China, warning of the dangers of isolation. Measures to reduce the trade deficit with China and to accelerate China's entry into the WTO were negotiated. In addition, the Chinese Government agreed to control the export of nuclear-related materials, in return for the removal of sanctions on the sale of nuclear-reactor technology to the People's Republic. Increased military co-operation and the holding of annual summit meetings were also agreed.

In April 1998 the US Secretary of State, Madeleine Albright, visited China to prepare for an official visit by President Clinton in late June and early July. Prior to his visit it was announced that China's most favoured nation (subsequently restyled normal trading relations) status would be renewed for a further year. Clinton continued to be criticized for his constructive engagement policy, and it was also alleged that the PLA had illegally funded Clinton's re-election campaign in 1996. The visit was a diplomatic success, notable for an unprecedented live broadcast in which Clinton and Jiang debated such issues as human rights, freedom of speech and the 1989 events in Tiananmen Square. In response to China's pledge in March

1998 to sign the International Covenant on Civil and Political Rights, the USA announced that it would abandon its sponsorship of an annual resolution of the UN Commission on Human Rights condemning China for human rights abuses. The decision, which followed a similar commitment by the EU in February, was deplored by human rights organizations.

Sino-US relations deteriorated significantly during 1999, owing to continued differences over China's human rights record, Tibet, trade relations, espionage and US plans for a missile defence system for Asia. During an official visit by Albright to the People's Republic at the end of February, she reiterated US disapproval at the suppression of organized dissent in China and urged the release of a number of political prisoners (although emphasizing that the USA would continue its policy of separating human rights issues from trade relations). Further acrimonious exchanges took place concerning demands from the US Congress that the proposed US theater missile defence system, which was principally designed to protect Japan and the Republic of Korea, be extended to include Taiwan. During a visit to the USA by Zhu Rongji in April, despite the Chinese Premier's offer of a number of economic concessions in return for a bilateral trade agreement to facilitate WTO entry, no agreement was reached. At a final press conference, however, the two sides affirmed their commitment to signing an agreement by the end of 1999. Although China suspended bilateral negotiations in May, following the NATO bombing of the Chinese embassy in Yugoslavia (see below), China's normal trade relations status was renewed in July. China agreed to resume talks in September, and in November (following 13 years of negotiations) a bilateral trade agreement was concluded, which would allow for China's eventual accession to the WTO. The agreement with the USA facilitated the conclusion of bilateral trade agreements with the EU and other WTO members during 2000, and China was expected to accede to the Organization in 2001.

It was widely believed that the failure to reach a trade agreement in April 1999 was, in part, due to popular US anti-Chinese sentiment, which had been exacerbated by US claims in March that a Chinese spy had stolen important nuclear data during the 1980s. A further disclosure of Chinese espionage (which had allegedly taken place in 1995), involving information relevant to the construction of a 'neutron' bomb emerged during Zhu's visit to the USA. Beijing dismissed the reports as unfounded. The findings of a select committee of the US House of Representatives, which were released in May, confirmed that Chinese spies had systematically stolen US nuclear technology from the late 1970s until the mid-1990s. China denounced the document as a plot to encourage anti-Chinese sentiment and to deflect attention from the bombing of the Chinese embassy in Yugoslavia, which had occurred earlier that month. China had vigorously opposed the NATO bombing of Yugoslavia, during which the Chinese embassy had been severely damaged, leading to the deaths of three people and injuring 20 others. US apologies and explanations were rejected, and violent popular attacks on the US and British diplomatic missions in Beijing, allegedly encouraged by the Government, ensued. Bilateral relations improved slightly in July, when the USA agreed to pay US \$4.5m. in compensation to the families of those killed and injured by the bombing, leading to the lifting of a ban on US military access to Hong Kong. In December compensation of US \$28m. was agreed for damage caused to the Chinese embassy building, and in April 2000 the CIA dismissed one intelligence officer and reprimanded six managers for errors that had led to the bombing.

In June 2000 the US Secretary of State, Madeleine Albright, visited China, the most senior US official to do so since the events of May 1999. She criticized the People's Republic's human rights record and urged Beijing to increase its efforts for peace with Taiwan. In retaliation, the Chinese Government insisted that US military aid to Taiwan be immediately suspended. In October the situation improved upon the signature of a law granting China the status of Permanent Normal Trading Relations. In the following month Bill Clinton announced the waiving of penalties against China for supplying missile parts to Iran and Pakistan. Despite an agreement to resume discussions on human rights, tensions relating to China's treatment of dissidents persisted in late 2000. Although there were fears that the election of the Republican administration, led by George W. Bush, would lead to the termination of the US policy of engagement of recent years, Jiang Zemin pronounced himself optimistic that relations would continue to develop positively.

China's relations with Japan began to deteriorate in 1982, after China complained that passages in Japanese school textbooks sought to justify the Japanese invasion of China in 1937. In June 1989 the Japanese Government criticized the Chinese Government's suppression of the pro-democracy movement and suspended (until late 1990) a five-year aid programme to China. In April 1992 Jiang Zemin travelled to Japan, the first visit by the General Secretary of the CCP for nine years. In October Emperor Akihito made the first ever imperial visit to the People's Republic. Japan was one of many countries to criticize China's resumption of underground nuclear testing, at Lop Nor in Xinjiang Province, in October 1993. Relations were seriously strained in May 1994, when the Japanese Minister of Justice referred to the 1937 Nanjing massacre (in which more than 300,000 Chinese citizens were killed by Japanese soldiers) as a 'fabrication', and again in August, when a second Japanese minister was obliged to resign, following further controversial remarks about his country's war record. In May 1995, during a visit to Beijing, the Japanese Prime Minister expressed his deep remorse for the wartime atrocities, but offered no formal apology.

China's continuation of its nuclear-testing programme, in defiance of international opinion, prompted Japan to announce a reduction in financial aid to China. In August 1995 Japan suspended most of its grant aid to China. Following China's conduct of its 'final' nuclear test in July 1996, and its declaration of a moratorium, Japan resumed grant aid in March 1997. (China signed the Comprehensive Nuclear Test Ban Treaty in September 1996.) In July 1996, however, Sino-Japanese relations were affected by a territorial dispute relating to the Diaoyu (or Senkaku) Islands, a group of uninhabited islets in the East China Sea, to which Taiwan also laid claim. The construction of a lighthouse on one of the islands by a group of Japanese nationalists led to strong protests from the Governments of both the People's Republic and Taiwan. The Japanese Government sought to defuse the tension by withholding recognition of the lighthouse, but did not condemn the right-wing activists responsible. A further incursion in September prompted China to warn of damage to bilateral relations if Japan failed to take action.

At a meeting with President Jiang Zemin during the Asia-Pacific Economic Co-operation (APEC) conference, in November 1996, the Japanese Prime Minister apologized for Japanese aggression during the Second World War, and emphasized his desire to resolve the dispute over the Diaoyu Islands. In May 1997, following the landing on one of the Islands by a member of the Japanese Diet, the Japanese Government distanced itself from the incident. The US-Japanese agreement on expanded military co-operation caused further tension in Sino-Japanese relations. Nevertheless, Japan's support for China's entry into the WTO remained firm, while China backed Japanese proposals for a permanent seat on the UN Security Council.

Following the normalization of ties between the Japanese Communist Party (JCP) and its Chinese equivalent after a period of more than 30 years, the Chairman of the JCP, Tetsuzo Fuwa, paid an official visit to China in July 1998. During a visit by Jiang Zemin to Japan in November, the first of its kind by a Chinese Head of State, relations were strained when Japan failed to issue an unequivocal apology for its invasion and occupation of China during 1937–45. The summit meeting between Jiang and the Japanese Prime Minister, Keizo Obuchi, was, nevertheless, deemed to have been successful. Keizo Obuchi paid a reciprocal visit to the People's Republic, intended to repair ties, in July 1999, during which he held summit talks with Zhu Rongji and Jiang Zemin. Tensions remained, but a number of co-operation agreements were reached, including a bilateral accord on terms for China's WTO entry. The People's Republic, however, opposed the new US-Japan defence co-operation guidelines, as it suspected that they could be invoked to defend Taiwan. Obuchi refused to guarantee that Taiwan be excluded from the security arrangements.

In August 2000 China withdrew permission for the Japanese Minister of Transport, Hajime Morita, to visit the People's Republic in September, owing to scheduling difficulties with Chinese officials. The Japanese media, however, attributed the Chinese change of attitude to a recent visit by Morita to a shrine honouring Japan's war dead, including those convicted of war crimes. Zhu Rongji visited Japan in October, and admitted that his failure to demand an apology for the host country's wartime conduct had attracted criticism in China.

The long-standing border dispute with India, which gave rise to a short military conflict in 1962, remained unresolved (see chapter on India). Discussions on the issue were held in 1988 and in 1991, and in September 1993 the two countries signed an agreement to reduce their troops along the frontier and to resolve the dispute by peaceful means. Discussions continued in 1994. In December China and India agreed to hold joint military exercises in mid-1995. In August 1995 it was confirmed that the two countries were to disengage their troops from four border posts in Arunachal Pradesh. Further progress was made at the ninth round of Sino-Indian border discussions, held in October 1996, and during the visit of President Jiang Zemin to India (the first by a Chinese Head of State) in November. Negotiations continued in August 1997. Li Peng visited India in January 2001, and discussions were held with a view to the restoration of normal relations. Outstanding Indian concerns included the increasing levels of imports of cheap Chinese goods and the question of China's nuclear co-operation with Pakistan.

The question of the sovereignty of the Spratly (Nansha) Islands, situated in the South China Sea and claimed by six countries (including China and Viet Nam), remained unresolved. By 1994 both China and Viet Nam had awarded petroleum exploration concessions to US companies, leading to increased tension among the claimants. In February 1995 it emerged that Chinese forces had occupied a reef to which the Philippines laid claim, resulting in a formal diplomatic protest from Manila. More than 60 Chinese fishermen and several vessels were subsequently detained by the Philippine authorities. Following consultations in August, China and the Philippines declared their intention to resolve peacefully their claims to the Spratly Islands. In January 1996 the Chinese Government denied any involvement in a naval skirmish in Philippine waters, during which a ship flying the Chinese flag and a Philippine patrol boat exchanged gunfire. In March China and the Philippines agreed to co-operate in combating piracy in the region. In November 1998 China angered the Philippine Government by building permanent structures on the disputed Mischief Reef. In late November 20 Chinese fishermen were arrested near Mischief Reef by the Philippine navy. Following Chinese protests, the men were released. In December China reiterated both its claim to sovereignty over the Spratly Islands and surrounding waters and its commitment to pursuing a peaceful solution through negotiation. Discussions between the two countries in April 1999 were unsuccessful, and relations deteriorated further in May when a Chinese fishing vessel sank following a collision with a Philippine navy boat, which was claimed to be accidental by the Philippines but deliberate by the People's Republic. A further Chinese fishing vessel sank in a collision with a Philippine navy vessel in July. A code of conduct for claimants of the Spratly Islands, drafted by members of the Association of South East Asian Nations (ASEAN, see p. 134) in late 1999, had neither been fully agreed by the organization nor signed by China in early 2001.

In 1996 China's application to become a full dialogue partner of the ASEAN Regional Forum (ARF, see p. 136) was approved. It was hoped that this would facilitate discussions on the question of the Spratly Islands. A similar territorial dispute relating to the Paracel (Xisha) Islands, which had been seized by China from South Vietnamese forces in 1974, also remained unresolved. In May 1996, despite having agreed to abide by the UN Convention on the Law of the Sea, China declared an extension of its maritime boundaries in the South China Sea. Other claimants to the Paracel Islands, in particular Indonesia, the Philippines and Viet Nam, expressed grave concern at China's apparent expansionism.

In August and October 1990 diplomatic relations were established with Indonesia and Singapore respectively. During 1992 China established diplomatic relations with Israel and with the Republic of Korea. China remained committed to the achievement of peace on the Korean peninsula, and in June 1996 it was reported that secret discussions between representatives of the Republic and of the Democratic People's Republic of Korea had been held in Beijing. In late 1997 China participated in quadripartite negotiations, together with the USA, the Democratic People's Republic of Korea and the Republic of Korea, to resolve the Korean issue. The Republic of Korea remained a major trading partner, and was one of the largest investors in China. Further quadripartite negotiations took place throughout 1999. In May 2000 the North Korean leader, Kim Jong Il, visited China, on his first trip abroad for 17 years. China was delighted in the following month by the holding of the first ever-inter-Korean presidential summit meeting in the Democratic People's Republic of Korea. Regular inter-Korean meetings followed. Premier Zhu Rongji made his first trip to the Republic of Korea in October. In November President Jiang Zemin toured Laos, Cambodia and Brunei, culminating in his attendance at the APEC conference convened in Brunei. His visit to Cambodia was the first by a Chinese Head of State for more than 30 years. Local security forces suppressed protests at China's support for the Khmer Rouge regime in the late 1970s.

Relations between China and the United Kingdom improved significantly in 1998. The British Secretary of State for Foreign and Commonwealth Affairs, Robin Cook, paid a visit to China and Hong Kong in January. The first China-EU summit, which was scheduled to become an annual event, took place in London in April, prior to the Asia-Europe Meeting (ASEM). China and the EU, presided over at the time by the United Kingdom, committed themselves to greater mutual co-operation in the area of trade and economic relations. The Chinese Premier also had talks with his British counterpart, Tony Blair, on Sino-British relations, apparently consolidating an improved relationship between the two countries, following the disagreements surrounding the return of Hong Kong to Chinese sovereignty (see above). Blair visited China and Hong Kong in October 1998. He declared his intention to broach the issue of human rights through 'persuasion and dialogue' rather than 'confrontation and empty rhetoric'. Following the visit, the two sides pledged to increase co-operation in a number of areas, and it was announced that in 1999 Jiang Zemin would become the first Chinese Head of State to visit the United Kingdom. This visit took place in October 1999, as part of a six-nation tour, which also included France, Portugal, Morocco, Algeria and Saudi Arabia. In the United Kingdom and France Jiang's visit prompted protests by supporters of human rights, resulting in complaints from the Chinese authorities that more should have been done to suppress demonstrations in London. In December, during a China-EU summit in Beijing, the Chinese Government rejected criticism of human rights abuses, reiterating its previous position that economic development would precede an improvement in human rights and defending its use of the death penalty, citing social stability. In November 2000 further criticism, by a British parliamentary committee, was dismissed by the People's Republic. Meanwhile, in October China concluded bilateral trade agreements with the EU necessary for WTO accession.

The USA exerted pressure on Israel to cancel a lucrative contract to supply military equipment to China in early 2000. Initially, Israel refused to comply, particularly after Jiang Zemin had made the first official trip to the country by a Chinese Head of State, in April. In July, however, Israel was obliged to yield to pressure, as it could not risk losing the USA as a major ally. In October 2000 China improved its relations with African nations when, during a Sino-African forum in Beijing, the People's Republic announced its decision to reduce or exempt outstanding debt totalling US $1,200m.

Government

China is a unitary state. Directly under the Central Government there are 22 provinces, five autonomous regions, including Xizang (Tibet), and four municipalities (Beijing, Chongqing, Shanghai and Tianjin). The highest organ of state power is the National People's Congress (NPC). In March 1993 the first session of the Eighth NPC was attended by 2,921 deputies, indirectly elected for five years by the people's congresses of the provinces, autonomous regions, municipalities directly under the Central Government, and the People's Liberation Army. The NPC elects a Standing Committee to be its permanent organ. The current Constitution, adopted by the NPC in December 1982 and amended in 1993, was China's fourth since 1949. It restored the office of Head of State (President of the Republic). Executive power is exercised by the State Council (Cabinet), comprising the Premier, Vice-Premiers and other ministers heading ministries and commissions. The State Council is appointed by, and accountable to, the NPC.

Political power is held by the Chinese Communist Party (CCP). The CCP's highest authority is the Party Congress, convened every five years. In September 1997 the CCP's 15th National Congress elected a Central Committee of 193 full members and 151 alternate members. To direct policy, the Central Committee elected a 22-member Politburo.

Provincial people's congresses are the local organs of state power. Local revolutionary committees, created during the Cul-

tural Revolution, were abolished in January 1980 and replaced by provincial people's governments.

Defence

China is divided into seven major military units. All armed services are grouped in the People's Liberation Army (PLA). In August 2000, according to Western estimates, the regular forces totalled 2,470,000, of whom 1,000,000 were conscripts: the army numbered 1,700,000, the navy 220,000 (including a naval air force of 26,000), and the air force 420,000 (including 220,000 air defence personnel). Reserves number some 600,000, and the People's Armed Police comprises an estimated 1.3m. Military service is by selective conscription, and lasts for three years in the army and marines, and for four years in the air force and navy. In September 1997 it was announced that the number of forces in the PLA was to be reduced by some 500,000 over the next three years. This reduction was in progress in 2000. Defence expenditure for 2000 was budgeted at 120,500m. yuan.

Economic Affairs

In 1998, according to estimates by the World Bank, China's gross national product (GNP), measured at average 1996–98 prices, was US $923,560m., equivalent to some $750 per head (or $3,051 on an international purchasing-power parity basis). During 1990–98, it was estimated, GNP per head increased, in real terms, at an average annual rate of 9.6%, one of the highest growth rates in the world. Over the same period, the population grew at an average annual rate of 1.2%. GNP in 1999 was $980,200m., equivalent to $780 per head. China's gross domestic product (GDP) increased, in real terms, at an average annual rate of 10.7% in 1990–99. According to official sources, GDP increased by 7.8% in 1998 and by 7.1% in 1999.

Agriculture (including forestry and fishing) contributed 17.6% of GDP in 1999, and employed 53.6% of the working population in that year. China's principal crops are rice (production of which accounted for about 33% of the total world harvest in 1999), sweet potatoes, wheat, maize, soybeans, sugar cane, tobacco, cotton and jute. Devastating floods in July and August 1998 had a significant adverse effect on agricultural production in that year. The floods were partly attributed to massive deforestation and prompted the introduction of a forest conservation programme and restrictions on logging. According to the World Bank, agricultural GDP increased at an average annual rate of 4.3%, in real terms, in 1990–99. According to the Asian Development Bank (ADB), growth in agricultural GDP was an estimated 2.8% in 1999.

Industry (including mining, manufacturing, construction and power) contributed 49.3% of GDP and engaged 20.0% of the employed labour force in 1999. According to the World Bank, industrial GDP increased at an average annual rate of 14.4%, in real terms, in 1990–99. According to the ADB, growth in industrial GDP was an estimated 8.5% in 1999.

The mining sector accounted for 1.1% of total employment in 1999, and output in the sector accounted for some 6% of total industrial output in 1996. China has enormous mineral reserves and is the world's largest producer of coal, natural graphite, antimony, tungsten, iron ore and zinc. Other important minerals include molybdenum, tin, lead, mercury, bauxite, phosphate rock, diamonds, gold, manganese, crude petroleum and natural gas. A move to increase competitiveness, and to reduce air pollution caused by the burning of coal, resulted in the closure of some 14 major coal mines in 1999, with the loss of 400,000 jobs. The discovery of significant copper deposits in Xinjiang in September 2000 would, it was hoped, alleviate China's reliance on imports of that metal.

The manufacturing sector contributed an estimated 37.6% of GDP in 1995, and the sector accounted for 13.0% of total employment in 1999. China is the world's leading producer of chemical fertilizers and cement, with output in 1999 totalling an estimated 32.5m. and 573.0m. metric tons, respectively. With output of more than 101m. metric tons in 1996, China also became the world's largest producer of steel; production increased to more than 124m. metric tons in 1999. The GDP of the manufacturing sector increased at an average annual rate of 14.7%, in real terms, during 1990–98, according to the World Bank.

Energy is derived principally from coal (68.2% in 1999); other sources are petroleum, hydroelectric power and natural gas. China became a net importer of crude petroleum in 1993. By December 1999 the People's Republic's largest hydroelectric power station, at Ertan, was fully functioning. The 18,200-MW Three Gorges hydropower scheme on the Changjiang (River

Yangtze), the world's largest civil engineering project, is scheduled for completion in 2009 and will have a potential annual output of 84,700m. kWh. China's national grid was also scheduled for completion in that year. Imports of mineral fuels comprised 4.9% of the cost of total imports in 1998.

Services contributed 33.0% of GDP in 1999 and engaged 26.4% of the employed labour force in that year. Tourism and retail and wholesale trade are expanding rapidly. During 1990–99, according to the World Bank, the GDP of the services sector increased at an average annual rate of 9.2% in real terms. According to the ADB, growth in the GDP of the services sector was an estimated 6.9% in 1999.

In 1999 China recorded a trade surplus of US $36,207m., and there was a surplus of $15,667m. on the current account of the balance of payments. In 1999 the principal source of imports was Japan (which provided 20.4% of total imports). Other important suppliers were the USA (11.8%), Taiwan (11.8%), and the Republic of Korea (10.4%). The principal markets for exports in 1999 were the USA (21.5% of total exports), Hong Kong (18.9%) and Japan (16.6%). Most of the goods exported to Hong Kong are subsequently re-exported. The principal imports in 1999 were machinery and transport equipment, chemicals and related products, and textiles and textile articles. The principal exports in that year were machinery and transport equipment, textiles and clothing, and footwear, headgear and umbrellas.

In 1999 China's overall budget deficit was 174,359m. yuan, equivalent to 2.1% of GDP. China's total external debt at the end of 1998 was estimated to be US $154,599m., of which $126,667m. was long-term public debt. In 1998 the cost of debt-servicing was equivalent to 8.6% of the value of exports of goods and services. The annual rate of inflation averaged 8.6% in 1990–99. The average rise in consumer prices was 2.8% in 1997, but prices declined by 0.8% in 1998, and by 4.2% in 1999. According to a sample survey, the number of unemployed persons in December 1999 was officially estimated at 14.0m. (2.0% of the total labour force). The scale of rural surplus labour in May 1997, however, was estimated at 130m., equivalent to 25% of the total rural labour force; unofficial estimates put the total as high as 300m. In December 1999 the total number of registered unemployed in urban areas was some 5,750,000 (3.1% of the urban labour force).

China joined the Asian Development Bank (ADB, see p. 131) in 1986 and the Asia-Pacific Economic Co-operation forum (APEC, see p. 128) in 1991. In 1994 China became a member of the Association of Tin Producing Countries (ATPC, see p. 303). In July 1995 China was granted observer status at the World Trade Organization (WTO, see p. 292), which had succeeded the General Agreement on Tariffs and Trade (GATT) in January of that year. Negotiations on full membership continued, and by late 2000 substantial progress had been made towards entry in 2001. China joined the Bank for International Settlements (BIS, see p. 140) in 1996. In the same year the secretariat of the Tumen River Economic Development Area (TREDA) was established in Beijing by the Governments of China, North and South Korea, Mongolia and Russia.

In 1978 Deng Xiaoping introduced the 'open door' reform policy, which aimed to decentralize the economic system and to attract overseas investment to China. The state monopoly on foreign trade was gradually relinquished, commercial links with foreign countries were diversified, several Special Economic Zones were established, and the planned economy was combined with market regulation. In 1997, following several years of high economic growth, the Government announced a three-year plan for the revitalization of the state-owned enterprises (SOEs) and the reform of the weak banking sector. The performance of the SOEs had suffered a significant decline in the 1990s, and failing SOEs were often supported by credit from the banking sector; around 25% of all bank loans were believed to be non-performing. In 1999–2000, however, SOE reform was constrained by the necessity to minimize the number of workers being made redundant, amid concerns about possible social unrest. Lack of job security kept domestic consumption at a low level, and consumer prices continued to fall. The creation of new employment opportunities and the improvement of social welfare provision were identified as official priorities, and it was recognized that very high growth rates would have to be maintained if sufficient expansion of the economy were to enable the financing of such improvements. In recent years, although remaining at relatively high levels, economic growth had gradually decelerated. In 2000, however, there was some evidence of acceleration, as structural reforms gained pace and exports performed

strongly. It was anticipated that China's accession to the WTO, which was expected to take place in 2001, would help to overcome the political obstacles to the restructuring of the SOEs and banks, as these institutions would henceforth be obliged to become competitive in external markets. In the longer term, WTO entry was expected to generate increased investment in China. In 2000, however, the weakness of China's institutions continued to deter overseas investment. Although exports increased in that year, rising by almost 28% compared with 1999, to reach $249,000m., imports rose at a faster rate, expanding by 36% to total $225,000m. The deceleration in the economy of the USA, one of the People's Republic's major trading partners, and the possible repercussions for other Asia-Pacific economies were expected adversely to affect China's trade balance in 2001. Also, in the short term, accession to the WTO was likely to cause a consolidation of domestic industries, which would exert negative pressures on the economy. The objectives of the Tenth Five-Year Plan, for the period 2001–06, included China's scientific and technological advancement, the intensification of infrastructure projects, and improved environmental protection, as well as the completion of the transition to a socialist market economy.

Social Welfare

In mid-1997 five extrabudgetary funds (pension, unemployment, medical, injury and maternity) financed social welfare provisions in China. Large enterprises also provided social services for their employees. However, a programme of comprehensive social security reforms was being devised, in recognition of the increasing levels of expenditure required to provide for an ageing population (it was estimated that by 2050 the number of people aged over 65 will have reached 300m., compared with 76m. in 1995) and the rising rate of unemployment. The Chinese authorities have implemented a variety of social welfare schemes, in order to determine how best to structure and finance the new social security system. These include a health care programme in several cities, where medical costs are financed by the State, the employer and the employee. A medical insurance system, announced in 1996, reportedly covered all urban employees by the year 2000. Western and traditional medical care, for which a fee is charged, is available in the cities and, to a lesser extent, in rural areas. Semi-professional peasant physicians assist with simple cures, treatment and the distribution of contraceptives. In December 1999 there were over 2.0m. physicians, more than 1.2m. nurses and over 2.9m. hospital beds. In that year there were 310,996 health establishments, including 66,935 hospitals. Budgetary expenditure on pensions and social welfare in 1999 was 17,988m. yuan (1.4% of total government spending). A unified, nation-wide pension scheme, to provide pensions to all categories of worker, which was announced in 1996, had not been implemented by 2000 (the current pension system is limited to urban areas and state-owned enterprises). Individual pension accounts, financed by contributions from the State, the employer and the employee, were to be established by 2006. The provision of social insurance for the rural population was also to be expanded.

Unemployment-insurance funds, established in cities in 1986, were also undergoing revision. It was reported that by September 2000 some 99.3m. people had registered with an unemployment insurance system. The ageing population meant that by 2000 the pension funds in many areas had already been exhausted, and in September state lottery tickets went on sale, a proportion of the revenue from which was destined for social welfare funds for the elderly.

Education

The education system expanded rapidly after 1949. Fees are charged at all levels. Much importance is attached to kindergartens. Primary education begins for most children at seven years of age and lasts for five years. Secondary education usually begins at 12 years of age and lasts for a further five years, comprising a first cycle of three years and a second cycle of two years. Free higher education was abolished in 1985; instead, college students have to compete for scholarships, which are awarded according to academic ability. As a result of the student disturbances in 1989, college students were required to complete one year's political education, prior to entering college. In November 1989 it was announced that postgraduate students were to be selected on the basis of assessments of moral and physical fitness, as well as academic ability. Since 1979 education has been included as one of the main priorities for modernization. The whole educational system was to be reformed, with the aim of introducing nine-year compulsory education in 85% of the country by the year 2000. The establishment of private schools has been permitted since the early 1980s. As a proportion of the total school-age population, enrolment at primary and secondary schools in 1997 was equivalent to 98% (boys 99%; girls 96%). In that year 100% of both boys and girls in the relevant age-group were enrolled at primary schools. Total enrolment at secondary schools in 1997 was equivalent to 70% of the total school-age population (males 74%; females 66%). In 1996 enrolment at tertiary level schools was equivalent to 5.7% of the relevant age-group (males 7.3%; females 3.9%). According to census results, the average rate of adult illiteracy in 1990 was 22.2% (males 13.0%; females 31.9%). In 1999, according to a sample survey, the rate had declined to 13.4% (males 8.0%, females 18.8%). Budgetary expenditure on education by all levels of government was 135,770m. yuan in 1997.

Public Holidays

2001: 1 January (Solar New Year), 24–27 January* (Lunar New Year), 8 March (International Women's Day, women only), 1 May (Labour Day), 1 August (Army Day), 9 September (Teachers' Day), 1–2 October (National Days).

2002: 1 January (Solar New Year), 12–15 February* (Lunar New Year), 8 March (International Women's Day, women only), 1 May (Labour Day), 1 August (Army Day), 9 September (Teachers' Day), 1–2 October (National Days).

* From the first to the fourth day of the first moon of the lunar calendar.

Weights and Measures

The metric system is officially in force, but some traditional Chinese units are still used.

Statistical Survey

Source (unless otherwise stated): State Statistical Bureau, 38 Yuetan Nan Jie, Sanlihe, Beijing 100826; tel. (10) 68515074; fax (10) 68515078; e-mail service@stats.gov.cn; internet www.stats.gov.cn.

Note: Wherever possible, figures in this Survey exclude Taiwan. In the case of unofficial estimates for China, it is not always clear if Taiwan is included or excluded. Where a Taiwan component is known, either it has been deducted from the all-China figure or its inclusion is noted. Figures for the Hong Kong Special Administrative Region (SAR — incorporated into the People's Republic of China on 1 July 1997) and for the Macau SAR (incorporated on 20 December 1999) are listed separately (pp. 1076–1080 and p. 1096 respectively). Transactions between the SARs and the rest of the People's Republic continue to be treated as external transactions.

Area and Population

AREA, POPULATION AND DENSITY

Area (sq km)	9,571,300*
Population (census results)	
1 July 1990	1,130,510,638
1 November 2000 (provisional)	
Males	653,550,000
Females	612,280,000
Total	1,265,830,000
Population (official estimates at 31 December)	
1997	1,236,260,000
1998	1,248,100,000
1999	1,259,090,000
Density (per sq km) at 1 November 2000	132.3

* 3,695,500 sq miles.

PRINCIPAL ETHNIC GROUPS (at census of 1 July 1990)

	Number	%
Han (Chinese)	1,039,187,548	91.92
Zhuang	15,555,820	1.38
Manchu	9,846,776	0.87
Hui	8,612,001	0.76
Miao	7,383,622	0.65
Uygur (Uigur)	7,207,024	0.64
Yi	6,578,524	0.58
Tujia	5,725,049	0.51
Mongolian	4,802,407	0.42
Tibetan	4,593,072	0.41
Bouyei	2,548,294	0.23
Dong	2,508,624	0.22
Yao	2,137,033	0.19
Korean	1,923,361	0.17
Bai	1,598,052	0.14
Hani	1,254,800	0.11
Li	1,112,498	0.10
Kazakh	1,110,758	0.10
Dai	1,025,402	0.09
She	634,700	0.06
Lisu	574,589	0.05
Others	3,838,337	0.34
Unknown	752,347	0.07
Total	1,130,510,638	100.00

BIRTHS AND DEATHS (sample surveys)

	1997	1998	1999
Birth rate (per 1,000) . . .	16.57	16.03	15.23
Death rate (per 1,000) . . .	6.51	6.50	6.46

Marriages (number registered): 9,090,571 in 1997, 8,866,593 in 1998; 8,799,079 in 1999.

Expectation of life (official estimates, years at birth, 1996): 70.80 (males 68.71; females 73.04).

PRINCIPAL TOWNS
(Wade-Giles or other spellings in brackets)

Population at 31 December 1990 (official estimates in '000)*

Shanghai (Shang-hai)	7,830
Beijing (Pei-ching or Peking, the capital)	7,000
Tianjin (T'ien-chin or Tientsin)	5,770
Shenyang (Shen-yang or Mukden)	4,540
Wuhan (Wu-han or Hankow)	3,750
Guangzhou (Kuang-chou or Canton)	3,580
Chongqing (Ch'ung-ch'ing or Chungking)	2,980
Harbin (Ha-erh-pin)	2,830
Chengdu (Ch'eng-tu)	2,810
Xian (Hsi-an or Sian)	2,760
Nanjing (Nan-ching or Nanking)	2,500
Zibo (Tzu-po or Tzepo)	2,460
Dalian (Ta-lien or Dairen)	2,400
Jinan (Chi-nan or Tsinan)	2,320
Changchun (Ch'ang-ch'un)	2,110
Qingdao (Ch'ing-tao or Tsingtao)	2,060
Taiyuan (T'ai-yüan)	1,960
Zhengzhou (Cheng-chou or Chengchow)	1,710
Guiyang (Kuei-yang or Kweiyang)	1,530
Kunming (K'un-ming)	1,520
Lanzhou (Lan-chou or Lanchow)	1,510
Tangshan (T'ang-shan)	1,500
Anshan (An-shan)	1,390
Qiqihar (Ch'i-ch'i-ha-erh or Tsitsihar)	1,380
Fushun (F'u-shun)	1,350
Nanchang (Nan-ch'ang)	1,350
Hangzhou (Hang-chou or Hangchow)	1,340
Changsha (Chang-sha)	1,330
Shijiazhuang (Shih-chia-chuang or Shihkiachwang)	1,320
Fuzhou (Fu-chou or Foochow)	1,290
Jilin (Chi-lin or Kirin)	1,270
Baotau (Pao-t'ou or Paotow)	1,200
Huainan (Huai-nan or Hwainan)	1,200
Luoyang (Lo-yang)	1,190
Urumqi (Urumchi)	1,160
Datong (Ta-t'ung or Tatung)	1,110
Handan (Han-tan)	1,110
Ningbo (Ning-po)	1,090
Nanning (Nan-ning)	1,070
Hefei (Hofei)	1,000

* Data refer to municipalities, which may include large rural areas as well as an urban centre. The listed towns comprise those with a total population of more than 1,000,000 and a non-agricultural population of more than 500,000.

ADMINISTRATIVE DIVISIONS (previous or other spelling given in brackets)

	Area ('000 sq km)	Estimated population at 31 December 1999		Capital of province or region	Estimated population ('000) at 31 Dec. 1990*
		Total ('000)	Density (per sq km)		
Provinces					
Sichuan (Szechwan)	485	85,500	176	Chengdu (Chengtu)	2,810
Henan (Honan)	167	93,870	562	Zhengzhou (Chengchow)	1,710
Shandong (Shantung)	153	88,830	581	Jinan (Tsinan)	2,320
Jiangsu (Kiangsu)	103	72,130	700	Nanjing (Nanking)	2,500
Guangdong (Kwangtung)	178	72,700	408	Guangzhou (Canton)	3,580
Hebei (Hopei)	188	66,140	352	Shijiazhuang (Shihkiachwang)	1,320
Hunan (Hunan)	210	65,320	311	Changsha (Changsha)	1,330
Anhui (Anhwei)	139	62,370	449	Hefei (Hofei)	1,000
Hubei (Hupeh)	186	59,380	319	Wuhan (Wuhan)	3,750
Zhejiang (Chekiang)	102	44,750	439	Hangzhou (Hangchow)	1,340
Liaoning (Liaoning)	146	41,700	286	Shenyang (Shenyang)	4,540
Jiangxi (Kiangsi)	169	42,310	250	Nanchang (Nanchang)	1,350
Yunnan (Yunnan)	394	41,920	109	Kunming (Kunming)	1,520
Heilongjiang (Heilungkiang)	469	37,920	81	Harbin (Harbin)	2,830
Guizhou (Kweichow)	176	37,100	211	Guiyang (Kweiyang)	1,530
Shaanxi (Shensi)	206	36,180	176	Xian (Sian)	2,760
Fujian (Fukien)	121	33,160†	274	Fuzhou (Foochow)	1,290
Shanxi (Shansi)	156	32,040	205	Taiyuan (Taiyuan)	1,960
Jilin (Kirin)	187	26,580	142	Changchun (Changchun)	2,110
Gansu (Kansu)	454	25,430	56	Lanzhou (Lanchow)	1,510
Hainan	34	7,620	224	Haikou	n.a.
Qinghai (Tsinghai)	721	5,100	7	Xining (Hsining)	650
Autonomous regions					
Guangxi Zhuang (Kwangsi Chuang)	236	47,130	200	Nanning (Nanning)	1,070
Nei Mongol (Inner Mongolia)	1,183	23,620	20	Hohhot (Huhehot)	890
Xinjiang Uygur (Sinkiang Uighur)	1,600	17,740	11	Urumuqi (Urumchi)	1,160
Ningxia Hui (Ninghsia Hui)	66	5,430	82	Yinchuan (Yinchuen)	576‡
Tibet (Xizang)	1,228	2,560	2	Lhasa (Lhasa)	105‡
Municipalities					
Shanghai	6	14,740	2,457	—	7,830
Beijing (Peking)	17	12,570	739	—	7,000
Tianjin (Tientsin)	11	9,590	872	—	5,770
Chongqing (Chungking)	82	30,750	375	—	2,980
Total	9,571	1,242,180§	130		

* Excluding population in counties under cities' administration.

† Excluding islands administered by Taiwan, mainly Jinmen (Quemoy) and Mazu (Matsu), with 49,050 inhabitants according to figures released by the Taiwan authorities at the end of March 1990.

‡ 1982 figure.

§ This is the sum of the official estimates provided by the administrative divisions, whereas the estimated national total was 1,259,090,000. The difference of 16,910,000 includes military personnel, excluded from regional population figures.

EMPLOYMENT*

(official estimates, '000 persons at 31 December)

	1997	1998	1999
Agriculture, forestry and fishing	330,950	332,320	334,930
Mining	8,680	7,210	6,670
Manufacturing	96,120	83,190	81,090
Electricity, gas and water	2,830	2,830	2,850
Construction	34,490	33,270	34,120
Transport, storage and communications	20,620	20,000	20,220
Wholesale and retail trade and catering	47,950	46,450	47,510
Banking and insurance	3,080	3,140	3,280
Social services	8,100	8,680	9,230
Health care, sports and social welfare	4,710	4,780	4,820
Education, culture, art, radio, film and television broadcasting	15,570	15,730	15,680
Government agencies, etc.	10,930	10,970	11,020
Others	52,640	55,060	53,490
Total	636,670	623,630	624,910

* In addition to employment statistics, sample surveys of the economically active population are conducted. On the basis of these surveys, the total labour force ('000 persons at 31 December) was: 705,800 in 1997; 714,070 in 1998; 719,830 in 1999. Of these totals, the number of employed persons ('000 at 31 December) was: 696,000 (agriculture, etc. 347,300; industry 164,950; services 183,750) in 1997; 699,570 (agriculture, etc. 348,380; industry 164,400; services 186,790) in 1998; 705,860 (agriculture, etc. 353,640; industry 162,350; services 189,870) in 1999.

Agriculture

PRINCIPAL CROPS

(official figures, unless otherwise indicated; '000 metric tons)

	1997	1998	1999
Wheat	123,289	109,726	113,880
Rice (paddy)	198,713	198,487	198,487
Barley*	4,313	3,400	3,300
Maize	104,309	132,954	128,086
Rye*	850	700	628
Oats*	850	756	600
Millet	2,313	3,113	2,319†
Sorghum	3,638	4,086	3,242†
Potatoes	57,207†	64,579	65,025†
Sweet potatoes	102,367	115,585	117,000†
Cassava (Manioc)*	3,650	3,700	3,750
Taro (Coco yam)*‡	1,408	1,468	1,468
Dry beans†‡	1,312	1,577	1,668
Dry broad beans†‡	1,520	1,832	1,860
Dry peas†‡	1,000	1,207	1,270
Soybeans (Soyabeans)	14,731	15,152†	13,900†
Groundnuts (in shell)	9,648	11,886	12,639
Castor beans†	180	210	215
Sunflower seed	1,176	1,465	1,680†
Rapeseed	9,578	8,301	10,132
Sesame seed	566	656	743
Linseed‡	393	523	550†
Flax fibre and tow‡	154	101	121*
Coconuts‡	191	207	182*
Vegetables and melons‡	242,560	251,335	259,550*
Grapes	2,033	2,358	2,708
Apples	17,219	19,481	20,802
Pears	6,415	7,275	7,742
Citrus fruits	10,102	8,590	10,787
Bananas	2,892	3,518	4,194
Other fruits (excl. melons)	12,233	13,306	16,143
Walnuts	250	265	274
Sugar cane	78,897	83,438	74,703
Sugar beet	14,968	14,466	8,639
Tea (made)	613	665	676
Tobacco (leaves)	4,251	2,364	2,469
Jute and jute substitutes	430	248	164
Cotton (lint)	4,603	4,501	3,829
Natural rubber	452	462	490

* FAO estimate(s).   † Unofficial figure(s).
‡ Including Taiwan.

Source: partly FAO.

LIVESTOCK ('000 head at 31 December)

	1997	1998	1999
Horses	8,912	8,981	8,914
Mules	4,806	4,739	4,673
Asses	9,528	9,558	9,348
Cattle and buffaloes	121,757	124,419	126,983
Camels	350	335	330
Pigs	400,348	422,563	430,198
Sheep	120,956	127,352	131,095
Goats	134,801	141,683	148,163
Chickens	3,000,000*	3,300,000*	n.a.
Ducks	500,000*	550,000*	n.a.

* FAO estimate.

Source: FAO.

LIVESTOCK PRODUCTS

(FAO estimates, unless otherwise indicated; '000 metric tons)

	1997	1998	1999
Beef and buffalo meat*	4,409	4,799	5,054
Mutton and goat meat*	2,128	2,346	2,513
Pig meat*	35,963	38,837	40,056
Other meat*	10,188	11,256	11,867
Cows' milk*	6,011	6,629	7,176
Buffaloes' milk†	2,450	2,450	2,450
Sheep's milk*	1,074	824	893
Goats' milk†	213	218	223
Butter*†	77	79	79
Cheese*†	191	174	185
Poultry eggs*	18,971	20,213	21,347
Honey*	211	207	230
Raw silk (incl. waste)*	51	68	70
Wool: greasy*	255	278	283
Cattle and buffalo hides†	1,048*	1,140*	1,141
Sheepskins*†	220*	235*	235
Goatskins*†	209	241	253

* Official figure(s).   † Including Taiwan.

Sources: FAO; State Statistical Bureau, *China Statistical Yearbook*.

Forestry

ROUNDWOOD REMOVALS*

('000 cubic metres, excl. bark)

	1996	1997	1998
Sawlogs, veneer logs and logs for sleepers	60,423	60,423	56,043
Pulpwood	7,751	7,751	7,264
Other industrial wood	40,544	40,544	37,611
Fuel wood	204,019	204,020	190,968
Total	312,737	312,738	291,886

* Including Taiwan.

Source: FAO, *Yearbook of Forest Products*.

Timber production (official figures, '000 cubic metres): 67,103 in 1996; 63,948 in 1997; 59,662 in 1998; 52,368 in 1999..

SAWNWOOD PRODUCTION*

('000 cubic metres, incl. railway sleepers)

	1996	1997	1998
Coniferous (softwood)	16,613	12,346	10,997
Broadleaved (hardwood)	10,797102	8,636	7,736
Total	27,410	20,982	18,733

* Including Taiwan.

Source: FAO, *Yearbook of Forest Products*.

Fishing

('000 metric tons, live weight)

	1996	19976	1998
Capture .	14,182.1	15,722.3	17,230.0
Freshwater fishes .	995.0	1,032.9	1,218.2
Japanese anchovy .	671.4	1,202.0	1,373.3
Largehead hairtail .	1,071.9	1,041.6	1,223.4
Aquaculture .	17,714.6	19,315.6	20,795.4
Common carp .	1,591.5	1,761.3	1,928.0
Crucian carp .	689.9	858.5	1,032.0
Bighead carp .	1,400.2	1,535.2	1,566.5
Grass carp (White amur) .	2,407.9	2,632.4	2,807.5
Silver carp .	2,800.4	3,070.5	3,133.0
Pacific cupped oyster .	2,284.7	2,328.6	2,833.2
Yesso scallop .	999.6	1,001.5	629.4
Japanese carpet shell .	1,093.9	1,257.5	1,404.4
Total catch .	31,896.7	35,038.0	38,025.3

Note: Figures exclude aquatic plants ('000 metric tons, wet weight): 4,645.6 (Capture 151.6, Aquaculture 4,493.9) in 1996; 4,899.0 (Capture 184.3, Aquaculture 4,714.7) in 1997; 6,447.1 (Capture 170.5, Aquaculture 6,276.6) in 1998.

Source: FAO, *Yearbook of Fishery Statistics*.

Aquatic products (official figures, '000 metric tons): 32,880.9 (marine 20,128.8, freshwater 12,752.2) in 1996; 36,017.8 (marine 21,764.2, freshwater 14,253.5) in 1997; 39,065.1 (marine 23,567.2, freshwater 15,497.9) in 1998; 41,224.1 (marine 24,719.2, freshwater 16,504.9) in 1999; 42,900 (provisional) in 2000. The totals include artificially cultured products ('000 metric tons): 18,628.5 (marine 7,639.0, freshwater 10,989.5) in 1996; 20,277.5 (marine 7,910.4 freshwater 12,367.1) in 1997; 21,814.7 (marine 8,600.4, freshwater 13,214.3) in 1998; 23,970.1 (marine 9,743.0, freshwater 14,227.1) in 1999. Figures include aquatic plants on a dry-weight basis ('000 metric tons): 929.1 in 1996; 979.8 in 1997; 1,041.2 in 1998; 1,194.4 in 1999. Freshwater plants are not included.

Mining

('000 metric tons, unless otherwise indicated; unofficial figures)

	1995	1996	1997
Coal* .	1,360,731	1,396,699	1,372,820
Crude petroleum* .	150,050	157,334	160,741
Iron ore† .	133,475	118,920	139,701
Bauxite .	1,585	1,755	2,201
Copper ore† .	441.9	436.4	494.0
Lead ore† .	514.2	643.4	711.9
Magnesite‡ .	2,050.0	2,100.0	2,000.0
Manganese ore†‡ .	4,707.0	4,417.3	3,706.2
Zinc ore† .	1,000.6	1,161.0	1,209.7
Salt (unrefined)* .	29,777	29,036	30,827
Phosphate rock‡ .	19,300	21,000	20,000
Potash‡‖ .	80§	110§	115
Sulphur (native)‡ .	160§	170§	170
Natural graphite‡ .	204.0	185.0	190.0
Antimony ore (metric tons)†¶ .	69,385	58,161	60,000
Mercury (metric tons)‡§ .	780	510	500
Molybdenum ore (metric tons)†‡ .	33,000	29,600	32,000
Silver (metric tons)†‡ .	910§	1,140	1,300§
Tin concentrates (metric tons)† .	61,913	69,700	67,500
Tungsten concentrates (metric tons)†‡ .	27,400§	26,500§	25,000
Gold (kg)†§ .	140,000	145,000‡	175,000‡
Natural gas (million cu m)* .	17,947	20,114	22,703

1998*: Coal ('000 metric tons) 1,250,000; Crude petroleum ('000 metric tons) 161,000; Salt (unrefined, '000 metric tons) 22,425; Natural gas (million cu m) 23,279.

1999*: Coal ('000 metric tons) 1,045,000; Crude petroleum ('000 metric tons) 160,000; Salt (unrefined, '000 metric tons) 28,124; Natural gas (million cu m) 25,198.

2000*: (provisional, '000 metric tons): Coal 880,100; Crude petroleum 162,620.

* Official figures. Figures for coal include brown coal and waste. Figures for petroleum include oil from shale and coal.
† Figures refer to the metal content of ores and concentrates.
‡ Data from the US Bureau of Mines.
§ Provisional or estimated figure(s).
‖ Potassium oxide (K_2O) content of potash salts mined.
¶ Data from *World Metal Statistics* (London).

Source: mainly UN, *Industrial Commodity Statistics Yearbook*.

Industry

SELECTED PRODUCTS

Unofficial Figures ('000 metric tons, unless otherwise indicated)

	1995	1996	1997
Rayon and acetate continuous filaments* .	70.2	73.0	72.0
Rayon and acetate discontinuous fibres* .	365.2	359.0	378.0
Non-cellulosic continuous filaments* .	1,168.7	1,286.3	1,446.7
Plywood ('000 cu m)†‡ .	8,103	5,413	8,093
Mechanical wood pulp†‡ .	640	540	440
Chemical wood pulp†‡ .	1,725	1,195	1,755
Other fibre pulp†‡ .	22,206	12,566	15,986
Sulphur§‖ (a) .	700	700	700
(b) .	5,930	5,990	5,880
Kerosene .	4,458	5,385	n.a.
Residual fuel oil .	29,607	29,000	n.a.
Lubricating oils .	3,936	4,000	n.a.
Paraffin wax¶ .	750	780	n.a.
Petroleum coke .	1,435¶	1,450	n.a.
Petroleum bitumen (asphalt) .	2,800¶	2,850	n.a.
Liquefied petroleum gas .	5,408	5,600	n.a.
Aluminium (unwrought) .	1,869.7	1,896.2	2,180.1
Refined copper (unwrought) .	1,079.7	1,120.5	1,152.9
Lead (unwrought) .	607.9	715.5	707.5
Tin (unwrought) .	67.7	71.5	67.7
Zinc (unwrought) .	1,076.7	1,163.8	1,434.4

* Data from the Fiber Economics Bureau, Inc, USA.
† Data from the FAO.
‡ Including Taiwan.
§ Data from the US Bureau of Mines.
‖ Figures refer to (a) sulphur recovered as a by-product in the purification of coal-gas, in petroleum refineries, gas plants and from copper, lead and zinc sulphide ores; and (b) the sulphur content of iron and copper pyrites, including pyrite concentrates obtained from copper, lead and zinc ores.
¶ Provisional or estimated figure(s).
** Data from *World Metal Statistics* (London).

Source: UN, *Industrial Commodity Statistics Yearbook*.

Official Figures ('000 metric tons, unless otherwise indicated)

	1997	1998	1999
Edible vegetable oils .	8,937.3	6,024.8	7,337.9
Raw sugar .	7,025.8	8,260.0	8,610.0
Beer .	18,889.4	19,876.7	20,987.7
Cigarettes ('000 cases) .	33,774.2	33,740.0	33,400.0
Cotton yarn (pure and mixed) .	5,598.3	5,420.0	5,670.0
Woven cotton fabrics—pure and mixed (million metres) .	24,879	24,100	25,000
Woollen fabrics ('000 metres) .	387,913.0	267,767.2	273,173.9
Silk fabrics (metric tons) .	82,500	67,700	70,200
Chemical fibres .	4,716.2	5,100.0	6,000.0
Paper and paperboard .	27,332.0	21,256.3	21,593.0
Rubber tyres ('000) .	95,989.9	95,134.6	109,698.4
Ethylene (Ethene) .	3,586.2	n.a.	n.a.
Sulphuric acid .	20,368.7	21,710.0	23,560.0
Caustic soda (Sodium hydroxide) .	5,744.0	5,393.7	5,801.4
Soda ash (Sodium carbonate) .	7,257.6	7,440.0	7,660.0
Insecticides .	526.7	559.0	625.0
Nitrogenous fertilizers (a)* .	20,749.3	22,256.7	24,719.6
Phosphate fertilizers (b)* .	7,145.6	6,667.9	6,360.7
Potash fertilizers (c)* .	314.7	1,175.4	1,429.7
Synthetic rubber .	642.3	589.0	732.8
Plastics .	6,857.6	6,925.8	8,711.0
Motor spirit (gasoline) .	35,178.2	34,654.0	37,412.7
Distillate fuel oil (diesel oil) .	49,244.5	48,841.1	63,026.8
Coke .	137,311.7	128,059.9	120,737.4
Cement .	511,738.0	536,000.0	573,000.0
Pig-iron .	115,114.1	118,636.7	125,392.4
Crude steel .	108,941.7	115,590.0	124,260.0
Internal combustion engines ('000 horse-power)† .	206,418.5	160,343.0	178,016.2
Tractors—over 20 horse-power (number) .	82,400	67,800	65,400

— continued	1997	1998	1999
Sewing machines ('000) . . .	7,026.4	n.a.	n.a.
Railway locomotives (number) .	1,069	n.a.	n.a.
Railway freight wagons (number) .	31,200	23,500	18,600
Road motor vehicles ('000) . .	1,582.5	1,630.0	1,832.0
Bicycles ('000)	29,992.9	23,124.9	23,975.7
Watches ('000)	295,046.1	n.a.	n.a.
Electric fans ('000) . . .	81,714.2	67,244.9	61,581.4
Floppy disks ('000) . . .	538,000	404,000	460,000
Microcomputers ('000) . .	2,065.5	2,914.0	4,050.0
Large Semiconductor integrated circuits ('000) . . .	1,030,000	556,000	1,400,000
Recorders ('000) . . .	82,738.6	n.a.	n.a.
Radio receivers ('000)‡ . .	46,242.1	n.a.	n.a.
Colour television receivers ('000)	27,113.3	34,970.0	42,620.0
Cameras ('000)	46,868.9	55,218.7	48,322.9
Electric energy (million kWh) .	1,135,553	1,167,000	1,239,300

* Production in terms of (a) nitrogen; (b) phosphoric acid; or (c) potassium oxide.
† Sales.
‡ Portable battery sets only.

Finance

CURRENCY AND EXCHANGE RATES

Monetary Units

100 fen (cents) = 10 jiao (chiao) = 1 renminbiao (People's Bank Dollar), usually called a yuan.

Sterling, Dollar and Euro Equivalents (29 December 2000)
£1 sterling = 12.352 yuan;
US $1 = 8.277 yuan;
€1 = 7.702 yuan;
1,000 yuan = £80.96 = $120.81 = €129.83.

Average Exchange Rate (yuan per US $)
1998   8.2790
1999   8.2783
2000   8.2785

Note: Since 1 January 1994 the official rate has been based on the prevailing rate in the interbank market for foreign exchange.

STATE BUDGET (million yuan)*

Revenue	1997	1998	1999
Taxes	823,404	926,280	1,068,258
Industrial and commercial taxes	662,704	762,542	888,544
Tariffs	31,949	31,304	56,223
Agricultural and animal husbandry taxes . . .	39,748	39,880	42,350
Taxes on income of state-owned enterprises	72,128	74,393	63,900
Taxes on income of collectively-owned enterprises . . .	16,875	18,161	17,410
Other receipts	78,559	94,664	105,153
Sub-total	901,963	1,020,944	1,173,411
Less Subsidies for losses by enterprises	36,849	33,349	29,003
Total	865,114	987,595	1,144,408
Central Government . . .	422,692	489,200	584,921
Local authorities	442,422	498,395	559,487

Expenditure†	1997	1998	1999
Capital construction . . .	101,950	138,774	211,657
Agriculture, forestry and water conservancy	56,077	62,602	67,746
Culture, education, science and health care‡ . . .	190,359	215,438	240,806
National defence	81,257	93,470	107,640
Administration	113,716	132,677	152,568
Pensions and social welfare . .	14,214	17,126	17,988
Subsidies to compensate price increases	55,196	71,212	69,764
Development of enterprises . .	64,320	64,118	76,605
Other purposes	246,267	284,401	373,993
Total	923,356	1,079,818	1,318,767
Central Government	253,250	312,560	415,233
Local authorities	670,106	767,258	903,534

* Figures represent a consolidation of the regular (current) and construction (capital) budgets of the central Government and local administrative organs. The data exclude extrabudgetary transactions, totalling (in million yuan): Revenue, 282,600 (central 14,508, local 268,092) in 1997, 308,229 (central 16,415, local 291,814) in 1998; Expenditure 268,554 (central 14,391, local 254,163) in 1997, 291,831 (central 13,974, local 277,857) in 1998.
† Excluding payments of debt interest.
‡ Current expenditure only.

INTERNATIONAL RESERVES (US $ million at 31 December)

	1998	1999	2000
Gold*	624	608	578
IMF special drawing rights . .	676	741	798
Reserve position in IMF . .	3,553	2,312	1,905
Foreign exchange† . . .	144,959	154,675	165,574
Total†	149,812	158,336	168,856

* Valued at SDR 35 per troy ounce.
† Excluding the Bank of China's holdings of foreign exchange.

Source: IMF, *International Financial Statistics*.

MONEY SUPPLY (million yuan at 31 December)*

	1997	1998	1999
Currency outside banking institutions	1,017,460	1,120,070	1,345,210
Demand deposits at banking institutions	2,381,030	2,648,570	3,235,620
Total money (incl. others) . .	3,480,650	3,869,050	4,697,640

* Figures are rounded to the nearest 10 million yuan.

Source: IMF, *International Financial Statistics*.

COST OF LIVING
(General Consumer Price Index; base: previous year = 100)

	1997	1998	1999
Food	99.9	96.8	95.8
Clothing	103.0	99.2	97.3
Housing*	108.3	101.7	101.7
All items (incl. others) . . .	102.8	99.2	98.6

* Including water, electricity and fuels.

NATIONAL ACCOUNTS
(million yuan at current prices)

Expenditure on the Gross Domestic Product*

	1997	1998	1999
Government final consumption expenditure	872,480	948,480	1,028,600
Private final consumption expenditure	3,485,460	3,692,110	3,939,860
Increase in stocks	330,340	191,510	102,080
Gross fixed capital formation	2,515,420	2,763,080	2,947,550
Total domestic expenditure	7,203,700	7,595,180	8,018,090
Exports of goods and services . } Less Imports of goods and services }	285,720	305,150	224,880
Sub-total	7,489,420	7,900,330	8,242,970
Statistical discrepancy†	−43,160	−65,810	−51,880
GDP in purchasers' values	7,446,260	7,834,520	8,191,090

* Figures are rounded to the nearest 10 million yuan.
† Referring to the difference between the sum of the expenditure components and official estimates of GDP, compiled from the production approach.

2000 (provisional, million yuan at current prices): GDP in purchasers' values 8,940,400.

Gross Domestic Product by Economic Activity*

	1997	1998	1999
Agriculture, forestry and fishing	1,421,120	1,455,240	1,445,720
Industry†	3,241,210	3,338,790	3,497,520
Construction	481,060	523,140	544,270
Transport, storage and communications	379,720	412,130	445,950
Wholesale and retail trade and catering	615,990	675,910	684,230
Other services	1,307,160	1,429,310	1,573,400
Total	7,446,260	7,834,520	8,191,090

* Figures are rounded to the nearest 10 million yuan.
† Includes mining, manufacturing, electricity, gas and water.

BALANCE OF PAYMENTS (US $ million)

	1997	1998	1999
Exports of goods f.o.b.	182,670	183,529	194,716
Imports of goods f.o.b.	−136,448	−136,915	−158,509
Trade balance	46,222	46,614	36,207
Exports of services	24,569	23,895	23,778
Imports of services	−27,967	−26,672	−31,288
Balance on goods and services	42,824	43,837	28,697
Other income received	5,710	5,584	10,571
Other income paid	−16,715	−22,228	−28,545
Balance on goods, services and income	31,819	27,193	10,723
Current transfers received	5,477	4,661	5,368
Current transfers paid	−333	−382	−424
Current balance	36,963	31,472	15,667
Capital account (net)	−21	−47	−26
Direct investment abroad	−2,563	−2,634	−1,775
Direct investment from abroad	44,237	43,751	38,753
Portfolio investment assets	−899	−3,830	−10,535
Portfolio investment liabilities	7,842	98	555
Other investment assets	−39,608	−35,041	−24,394
Other investment liabilities	12,028	−8,619	6,317
Net errors and omissions	−22,122	−18,902	−14,656
Overall balance	35,857	6,248	8,652

Source: IMF, *International Financial Statistics*.

External Trade

PRINCIPAL COMMODITIES (distribution by SITC, US $ million)

Imports c.i.f.	1996	1997	1998
Food and live animals	5,648.9	4,288.2	3,763.2
Crude materials (inedible) except fuels	10,447.2	11,727.6	10,536.2
Textile fibres (excl. wool-tops) and waste	3,528.1	3,691.7	2,225.2
Metalliferous ores and metal scrap	3,069.8	3,430.3	3,290.6
Mineral fuels, lubricants, etc.	6,930.4	10,364.3	6,834.6
Petroleum, petroleum products, etc.	5,974.0	9,389.1	5,941.5
Crude petroleum oils, etc.	3,406.6	5,456.3	3,274.5
Refined petroleum products	2,437.5	3,740.7	2,466.7
Chemicals and related products	17,898.8	19,046.8	19,907.2
Organic chemicals	3,057.9	3,013.6	3,512.4
Manufactured fertilizers	3,538.9	2,989.3	2,503.5
Artificial resins, plastic materials, etc.	7,918.2	9,210.4	9,504.2
Products of polymerization, etc.	6,681.5	7,648.2	7,798.9
Basic manufactures	32,065.1	32,909.0	31,616.3
Paper, paperboard and manufactures	2,846.1	3,334.4	3,534.4
Paper and paperboard (not cut to size or shape)	2,423.8	2,955.9	3,176.5
Textile yarn, fabrics, etc.	12,207.0	12,527.5	11,248.7
Textile yarn	2,881.3	3,095.4	2,738.6
Woven fabrics of man-made fibres*	3,960.6	3,873.2	3,398.1
Iron and steel	7,309.9	6,737.8	6,563.2
Universals, plates and sheets	3,700.6	3,708.7	3,548.8
Non-ferrous metals	3,001.6	3,183.2	3,471.3
Machinery and transport equipment	54,705.2	52,722.9	56,774.8
Power-generating machinery and equipment	3,211.6	3,717.9	4,099.5
Machinery specialized for particular industries	14,218.9	9,704.9	8,152.4
Textile and leather machinery	3,294.8	2,227.8	1,436.6
Metalworking machinery	3,637.7	2,474.6	2,513.0
General industrial machinery, equipment and parts	7,781.1	6,798.2	6,062.7
Office machines and automatic data-processing equipment	3,421.0	4,475.3	5,892.5
Telecommunications and sound equipment	5,833.4	5,966.9	7,817.9
Other electrical machinery, apparatus, etc.	11,274.2	14,057.0	16,671.0
Switchgear, resistors, printed circuits, switchboards, etc.	2,093.2	2,689.4	3,036.9
Thermionic valves, tubes, etc.	4,685.5	6,253.9	8,331.7
Electronic microcircuits	2,605.1	3,482.2	4,602.7
Transport equipment and parts†	5,327.8	5,528.5	5,566.3
Aircraft, associated equipment and parts†	2,648.6	3,234.3	3,174.2
Miscellaneous manufactured articles	8,164.9	8,352.3	8,348.6
Total (incl. others)	138,832.8	142,370.4	140,236.9

* Excluding narrow or special fabrics.
† Data on parts exclude tyres, engines and electrical parts.

Exports f.o.b.	1996	1997	1998
Food and live animals	10,206.8	11,050.8	10,599.6
Vegetables and fruit	3,178.7	3,138.0	3,041.8
Crude materials (inedible) except fuels	4,019.7	4,151.6	3,487.5
Mineral fuels, lubricants, etc.	5,937.6	6,992.5	5,178.8
Petroleum, petroleum products, etc.	3,920.5	4,252.9	2,661.3
Chemicals and related products	8,771.3	10,102.4	10,206.0
Basic manufactures	29,209.7	35,158.4	33,067.6
Textile yarn, fabrics, etc.	12,317.6	14,028.9	12,967.7
Non-metallic mineral manufactures	3,297.1	4,011.0	3,788.1
Iron and steel	4,068.0	5,003.8	3,836.7
Machinery and transport equipment	35,239.2	43,614.4	50,143.0
Office machines and automatic data-processing equipment	6,716.8	9,243.9	11,846.4
Automatic data-processing machines and units	3,690.4	5,361.8	7,066.7
Telecommunications and sound equipment	9,004.1	10,303.8	11,111.0
Other electrical machinery, apparatus, etc.	10,335.9	13,016.5	14,599.3
Miscellaneous manufactured articles	55,723.6	69,636.4	69,585.9
Clothing and accessories (excl. footwear)	25,101.0	31,875.5	30,121.2
Men's and boys' outer garments of non-knitted textile fabrics	5,476.5	6,321.3	5,639.1
Women's, girls' and infants' outer garments of non-knitted textile fabrics	6,269.5	6,880.9	6,318.1
Knitted or crocheted outer garments and accessories (excl. gloves, stockings, etc.), non-elastic	4,252.1	6,398.7	6,968.2
Knitted or crocheted undergarments (incl. foundation garments of non-knitted fabrics	3,290.2	5,295.1	4,546.7
Cotton undergarments, non-elastic	2,813.1	4,656.0	3,829.5
Footwear	6,704.9	8,149.4	8,055.0
Leather footwear	3,969.9	4,720.2	4,709.9
Photographic apparatus, optical goods, watches and clocks	3,055.9	3,489.8	3,619.0
Articles of plastic materials	2,791.1	3,616.5	3,945.0
Baby carriages, toys, games and sporting goods	6,444.8	8,045.2	8,412.5
Children's toys, indoor games, etc.	5,578.7	6,984.0	7,258.5
Total (incl. others)	151,047.6	182,791.7	183,809.1

Source: UN, *International Trade Statistics Yearbook*.

PRINCIPAL TRADING PARTNERS (US $ million)*

Imports c.i.f.	1997	1998	1999
Australia	3,247.6	2,682.5	3,607.2
Brazil	1,489.0	1,133.1	968.6
Canada	2,007.1	2,237.2	2,433.0
Finland	687.0	1,260.0	1,831.9
France	3,246.7	3,204.9	3,784.8
Germany	6,181.3	7,020.7	8,335.4
Hong Kong	6,990.3	6,658.0	6,891.9
Indonesia	2,673.6	2,460.9	3,050.9
Italy	2,452.1	2,279.0	2,679.9
Japan	28,994.8	28,275.1	33,763.4
Korea, Republic	14,929.7	15,014.4	17,226.2
Malaysia	2,495.1	2,673.9	3,605.6
Russia	4,085.7	3,640.0	4,222.6
Singapore	4,464.7	4,235.4	4,061.1
Sweden	1,297.5	2,046.4	2,151.8
Taiwan	16,441.2	16,631.1	19,526.8
Thailand	2,013.9	2,414.0	2,780.4
United Kingdom	1,978.5	1,952.6	2,994.8
USA	16,301.3	16,883.2	19,478.3
Total (incl. others)	142,370.4	140,236.8	1651,699 1

Exports f.o.b.	1997	1998	1999
Australia	2,056.2	2,365.0	2,704.4
Canada	1,906.5	2,126.9	2,433.0
France	2,230.0	2,822.8	2,921.1
Germany	6,496.9	7,354.3	7,779.6
Hong Kong†	43,782.9	38,741.8	36,862.8
Indonesia	1,841.0	1,170.2	1.779.1
Italy	2,238.9	2,577.4	2,929.5
Japan	31,838.6	29,660.1	32,410.6
Korea, Republic	9,126.9	6,251.5	7,807.6
Malaysia	1,921.9	1,596.4	1,673.8
Netherlands	4,406.0	5,161.8	5,413.0
Russia	2,038.1	1,839.9	1,497.3
Singapore	4,323.3	3,943.9	4,502.2
Taiwan	3,396.7	3,868.9	3,949.9
United Kingdom	3,815.2	4,631.8	4,880.0
USA	32,715.1	37,947.7	41,946.9
Total (incl. others)	182,791.7	183,809.1	194,930.9

* Imports by country of origin; exports by country of consumption.
† The majority of China's exports to Hong Kong are re-exported.
2000 (provisional, US $ million): Totall imports c.i.f. 225,100; Total exports f.o.b. 249,200.

Transport

	1997	1998	1999
Freight (million ton-km):			
Railways	1,325,330	1,251,707	1,283,840
Roads	527,150	548,338	572,430
Waterways	1,923,500	1,940,580	2,126,300
Air	2,910	3,345	4,230
Passenger-km (million):			
Railways	358,486	377,342	413,593
Roads	554,140	594,281	619,920
Waterways	15,570	12,027	10,730
Air	77,352	80,024	85,730

ROAD TRAFFIC ('000 motor vehicles in use)*

	1997	1998	1999
Passenger cars and buses	5,805.6	6,548.3	7,402.3
Goods vehicles	6,012.3	6,278.9	6,769.5
Total (incl. others)	12,190.9	13,193.0	14,529.4

* Excluding military vehicles.

SHIPPING

Merchant Fleet (registered at 31 December)

	1996	1997	1998
Number of vessels	3,121	3,175	3,214
Total displacement ('000 grt)	16,992.9	16,338.6	16,503.4

Source: Lloyd's Register of Shipping, *World Fleet Statistics*.

Sea-borne Shipping (freight traffic, '000 metric tons)

	1997	1998	1999
Goods loaded and unloaded	908,220	922,370	1,051,620

Tourism

FOREIGN VISITORS (arrivals, '000)

Country of origin	1997	1998	1999
Hong Kong and Macau . . .	47,943.3	54,075.4	61,670.6
Taiwan	2,117.6	2,174.6	2,584.6
Australia	156.8	186.4	203.5
Canada	174.1	196.0	213.7
France	131.3	138.0	155.6
Germany	184.7	191.9	217.6
Indonesia	147.3	104.6	182.9
Japan	1,581.7	1,572.1	1,855.2
Korea, Republic . . .	781.1	632.8	992.0
Malaysia	361.3	300.1	372.9
Mongolia	342.9	264.8	354.5
Philippines	276.7	256.5	298.3
Russia	813.7	692.0	833.0
Singapore	316.8	316.4	352.5
Thailand	168.5	144.3	206.4
United Kingdom . . .	227.9	242.9	258.9
USA	616.4	224.8	736.4
Total (incl. others) . . .	57,587.9	63,478.4	72,795.6

Total tourism receipts (US $ million): 12,074 in 1997; 12,602 in 1998; 14,990 (estimate) in 1999.

Communications Media

	1997	1998	1999
Radio receivers ('000 in use)* . .	417,000	n.a.	n.a.
Television receivers ('000 in use)* .	400,000	n.a.	n.a.
Telephones ('000 in use) . .	101,111	131,234	175,674
Mobile cellular telephones ('000 subscribers)	13,232.9	23,862.9	43,296.0
Telefax stations ('000 in use)† . .	2,000	n.a.	n.a.
Book production:			
Titles	120,106	130,613	141,831
Copies (million) . . .	7,305.3	7,238.6	7,316.3
Newspapers:			
Number	2,149	2,053	2,038
Average circulation ('000 copies)	182,590	182,110	186,320
Magazines:			
Number	7,918	7,999	8,187
Average circulation ('000 copies)	200,460	209,280	218,450

* Source: UNESCO, *Statistical Yearbook*.

† Source: UN, *Statistical Yearbook*.

Education

(1999)

	Institutions	Full-time Teachers ('000)	Students ('000)
Kindergartens	181,136	872	23,263
Primary schools	582,291	5,861	135,480
General secondary schools. .	77,213	3,841	67,713
Secondary technical schools .	3,147	212	4,250
Teacher-training schools . .	815	62	905
Agricultural and vocational schools	9,636	336	5,339
Special schools	1,520	31	372
Higher education	1,071	426	4,134

Directory

The Constitution

A new Constitution was adopted on 4 December 1982 by the Fifth Session of the Fifth National People's Congress. Its principal provisions, including amendments made in 1993 and 1999, are detailed below. The Preamble, which is not included here, states that 'Taiwan is part of the sacred territory of the People's Republic of China'.

GENERAL PRINCIPLES

Article 1: The People's Republic of China is a socialist state under the people's democratic dictatorship led by the working class and based on the alliance of workers and peasants.

The socialist system is the basic system of the People's Republic of China. Sabotage of the socialist system by any organization or individual is prohibited.

Article 2: All power in the People's Republic of China belongs to the people.

The organs through which the people exercise state power are the National People's Congress and the local people's congresses at different levels.

The people administer state affairs and manage economic, cultural and social affairs through various channels and in various ways in accordance with the law.

Article 3: The state organs of the People's Republic of China apply the principle of democratic centralism.

The National People's Congress and the local people's congresses at different levels are instituted through democratic election. They are responsible to the people and subject to their supervision.

All administrative, judicial and procuratorial organs of the State are created by the people's congresses to which they are responsible and under whose supervision they operate.

The division of functions and powers between the central and local state organs is guided by the principle of giving full play to the initiative and enthusiasm of the local authorities under the unified leadership of the central authorities.

Article 4: All nationalities in the People's Republic of China are equal. The State protects the lawful rights and interests of the minority nationalities and upholds and develops the relationship of equality, unity and mutual assistance among all of China's nationalities. Discrimination against and oppression of any nationality are prohibited; any acts that undermine the unity of the nationalities or instigate their secession are prohibited.

The State helps the areas inhabited by minority nationalities speed up their economic and cultural development in accordance with the peculiarities and needs of the different minority nationalities.

Regional autonomy is practised in areas where people of minority nationalities live in compact communities; in these areas organs of self-government are established for the exercise of the right of autonomy. All the national autonomous areas are inalienable parts of the People's Republic of China.

The people of all nationalities have the freedom to use and develop their own spoken and written languages, and to preserve or reform their own ways and customs.

Article 5: The People's Republic of China shall be governed according to law and shall be built into a socialist country based on the rule of law.

The State upholds the uniformity and dignity of the socialist legal system.

No law or administrative or local rules and regulations shall contravene the Constitution.

All state organs, the armed forces, all political parties and public organizations and all enterprises and undertakings must abide by the Constitution and the law. All acts in violation of the Constitution and the law must be looked into.

No organization or individual may enjoy the privilege of being above the Constitution and the law.

Article 6: The basis of the socialist economic system of the People's Republic of China is socialist public ownership of the means of production, namely, ownership by the whole people and collective ownership by the working people.

The system of socialist public ownership supersedes the system of exploitation of man by man; it applies the principle of 'from each according to his ability, to each according to his work.'

In the initial stage of socialism, the country shall uphold the basic economic system in which the public ownership is dominant and diverse forms of ownership develop side by side, and it shall uphold the distribution system with distribution according to work remaining dominant and a variety of modes of distribution coexisting.

Article 7: The state-owned economy, namely the socialist economy under the ownership of the whole people, is the leading force in the national economy. The State ensures the consolidation and growth of the state-owned economy.

Article 8: The rural collective economic organizations shall implement a two-tier operations system that combines unified operations with independent operations on the basis of household contract operations and different co-operative economic forms in the rural areas—the producers', supply and marketing, credit, and consumers' co-operatives—are part of the socialist economy collectively owned by the working people. Working people who are all members of rural economic collectives have the right, within the limits prescribed by law, to farm plots of cropland and hilly land allotted for their private use, engage in household sideline production and raise privately-owned livestock.

The various forms of co-operative economy in the cities and towns, such as those in the handicraft, industrial, building, transport, commercial and service trades, all belong to the sector of socialist economy under collective ownership by the working people.

The State protects the lawful rights and interests of the urban and rural economic collectives and encourages, guides and helps the growth of the collective economy.

Article 9: Mineral resources, waters, forests, mountains, grassland, unreclaimed land, beaches and other natural resources are owned by the State, that is, by the whole people, with the exception of the forests, mountains, grassland, unreclaimed land and beaches that are owned by collectives in accordance with the law.

The State ensures the rational use of natural resources and protects rare animals and plants. The appropriation or damage of natural resources by any organization or individual by whatever means is prohibited.

Article 10: Land in the cities is owned by the State.

Land in the rural and suburban areas is owned by collectives except for those portions which belong to the State in accordance with the law; house sites and private plots of cropland and hilly land are also owned by collectives.

The State may in the public interest take over land for its use in accordance with the law.

No organization or individual may appropriate, buy, sell or lease land, or unlawfully transfer land in other ways.

All organizations and individuals who use land must make rational use of the land.

Article 11: The non-public sector of the economy comprising the individual and private sectors, operating within the limits prescribed by law, is an important component of the socialist market economy.

The State protects the lawful rights and interests of the non-public sector comprising the individual and private sectors. The State exercises guidance, supervision, and control over the individual and private sectors of the economy.

Article 12: Socialist public property is sacred and inviolable.

The State protects socialist public property. Appropriation or damage of state or collective property by any organization or individual by whatever means is prohibited.

Article 13: The State protects the right of citizens to own lawfully earned income, savings, houses and other lawful property.

The State protects by law the right of citizens to inherit private property.

Article 14: The State continuously raises labour productivity, improves economic results and develops the productive forces by enhancing the enthusiasm of the working people, raising the level of their technical skill, disseminating advanced science and technology, improving the systems of economic administration and enterprise operation and management, instituting the socialist system of responsibility in various forms and improving organization of work.

The State practises strict economy and combats waste.

The State properly apportions accumulation and consumption, pays attention to the interests of the collective and the individual as well as of the State and, on the basis of expanded production, gradually improves the material and cultural life of the people.

Article 15: The State practises a socialist market economy. The State strengthens economic legislation and perfects macro-control. The State prohibits, according to the law, disturbance of society's economic order by any organization or individual.

Article 16: State-owned enterprises have decision-making power in operations within the limits prescribed by law.

State-owned enterprises practise democratic management through congresses of workers and staff and in other ways in accordance with the law.

Article 17: Collective economic organizations have decision-making power in conducting economic activities on the condition that they abide by the relevant laws. Collective economic organizations practise democratic management, elect and remove managerial personnel, and decide on major issues in accordance with the law.

Article 18: The People's Republic of China permits foreign enterprises, other foreign economic organizations and individual foreigners to invest in China and to enter into various forms of economic co-operation with Chinese enterprises and other economic organizations in accordance with the law of the People's Republic of China.

All foreign enterprises and other foreign economic organizations in China, as well as joint ventures with Chinese and foreign investment located in China, shall abide by the law of the People's Republic of China. Their lawful rights and interests are protected by the law of the People's Republic of China.

Article 19: The State develops socialist educational undertakings and works to raise the scientific and cultural level of the whole nation.

The State runs schools of various types, makes primary education compulsory and universal, develops secondary, vocational and higher education and promotes pre-school education.

The State develops educational facilities of various types in order to wipe out illiteracy and provide political, cultural, scientific, technical and professional education for workers, peasants, state functionaries and other working people. It encourages people to become educated through self-study.

The State encourages the collective economic organizations, state enterprises and undertakings and other social forces to set up educational institutions of various types in accordance with the law.

The State promotes the nation-wide use of Putonghua (common speech based on Beijing pronunciation).

Article 20: The State promotes the development of the natural and social sciences, disseminates scientific and technical knowledge, and commends and rewards achievements in scientific research as well as technological discoveries and inventions.

Article 21: The State develops medical and health services, promotes modern medicine and traditional Chinese medicine, encourages and supports the setting up of various medical and health facilities by the rural economic collectives, state enterprises and undertakings and neighbourhood organizations, and promotes sanitation activities of a mass character, all to protect the people's health.

The State develops physical culture and promotes mass sports activities to build up the people's physique.

Article 22: The State promotes the development of literature and art, the press, broadcasting and television undertakings, publishing and distribution services, libraries, museums, cultural centres and other cultural undertakings, that serve the people and socialism, and sponsors mass cultural activities.

The State protects places of scenic and historical interest, valuable cultural monuments and relics and other important items of China's historical and cultural heritage.

Article 23: The State trains specialized personnel in all fields who serve socialism, increases the number of intellectuals and creates conditions to give full scope to their role in socialist modernization.

Article 24: The State strengthens the building of socialist spiritual civilization through spreading education in high ideals and morality, general education and education in discipline and the legal system, and through promoting the formulation and observance of rules of conduct and common pledges by different sections of the people in urban and rural areas.

The State advocates the civic virtues of love for the motherland, for the people, for labour, for science and for socialism; it educates the people in patriotism, collectivism, internationalism and communism and in dialectical and historical materialism; it combats capitalist, feudalist and other decadent ideas.

Article 25: The State promotes family planning so that population growth may fit the plans for economic and social development.

Article 26: The State protects and improves the living environment and the ecological environment, and prevents and remedies pollution and other public hazards.

The State organizes and encourages afforestation and the protection of forests.

Article 27: All state organs carry out the principle of simple and efficient administration, the system of responsibility for work and the system of training functionaries and appraising their work in order constantly to improve quality of work and efficiency and combat bureaucratism.

All state organs and functionaries must rely on the support of the people, keep in close touch with them, heed their opinions and suggestions, accept their supervision and work hard to serve them.

Article 28: The State maintains public order and suppresses treasonable and other criminal activities that endanger national security; it penalizes activities that endanger public security and disrupt the socialist economy as well as other criminal activities; and it punishes and reforms criminals.

Article 29: The armed forces of the People's Republic of China belong to the people. Their tasks are to strengthen national defence, resist aggression, defend the motherland, safeguard the people's peaceful labour, participate in national reconstruction, and work hard to serve the people.

The State strengthens the revolutionization, modernization and regularization of the armed forces in order to increase the national defence capability.

Article 30: The administrative division of the People's Republic of China is as follows:

(1) The country is divided into provinces, autonomous regions and municipalities directly under the central government;

(2) Provinces and autonomous regions are divided into autonomous prefectures, counties, autonomous counties and cities;

(3) Counties and autonomous counties are divided into townships, nationality townships and towns.

Municipalities directly under the central government and other large cities are divided into districts and counties. Autonomous prefectures are divided into counties, autonomous counties, and cities.

All autonomous regions, autonomous prefectures and autonomous counties are national autonomous areas.

Article 31: The State may establish special administrative regions when necessary. The systems to be instituted in special administrative regions shall be prescribed by law enacted by the National People's Congress in the light of the specific conditions.

Article 32: The People's Republic of China protects the lawful rights and interests of foreigners within Chinese territory, and while on Chinese territory foreigners must abide by the law of the People's Republic of China.

The People's Republic of China may grant asylum to foreigners who request it for political reasons.

FUNDAMENTAL RIGHTS AND DUTIES OF CITIZENS

Article 33: All persons holding the nationality of the People's Republic of China are citizens of the People's Republic of China.

All citizens of the People's Republic of China are equal before the law.

Every citizen enjoys the rights and at the same time must perform the duties prescribed by the Constitution and the law.

Article 34: All citizens of the People's Republic of China who have reached the age of 18 have the right to vote and stand for election, regardless of nationality, race, sex, occupation, family background, religious belief, education, property status, or length of residence, except persons deprived of political rights according to law.

Article 35: Citizens of the People's Republic of China enjoy freedom of speech, of the press, of assembly, of association, of procession and of demonstration.

Article 36: Citizens of the People's Republic of China enjoy freedom of religious belief.

No state organ, public organization or individual may compel citizens to believe in, or not to believe in, any religion; nor may they discriminate against citizens who believe in, or do not believe in, any religion.

The State protects normal religious activities. No one may make use of religion to engage in activities that disrupt public order, impair the health of citizens or interfere with the educational system of the state.

Religious bodies and religious affairs are not subject to any foreign domination.

Article 37: The freedom of person of citizens of the People's Republic of China is inviolable.

No citizen may be arrested except with the approval or by decision of a people's procuratorate or by decision of a people's court, and arrests must be made by a public security organ.

Unlawful deprivation or restriction of citizens' freedom of person by detention or other means is prohibited; and unlawful search of the person of citizens is prohibited.

Article 38: The personal dignity of citizens of the People's Republic of China is inviolable. Insult, libel, false charge or frame-up directed against citizens by any means is prohibited.

Article 39: The home of citizens of the People's Republic of China is inviolable. Unlawful search of, or intrusion into, a citizen's home is prohibited.

Article 40: The freedom and privacy of correspondence of citizens of the People's Republic of China are protected by law. No organization or individual may, on any ground, infringe upon the freedom and privacy of citizens' correspondence except in cases where, to meet the needs of state security or of investigation into criminal offences, public security or procuratorial organs are permitted to censor correspondence in accordance with procedures prescribed by law.

Article 41: Citizens of the People's Republic of China have the right to criticize and make suggestions to any state organ or functionary. Citizens have the right to make to relevant state organs complaints and charges against, or exposures of, violation of the law or dereliction of duty by any state organ or functionary; but fabrication or distortion of facts with the intention of libel or frame-up is prohibited.

In case of complaints, charges or exposures made by citizens, the state organ concerned must deal with them in a responsible manner after ascertaining the facts. No one may suppress such complaints, charges and exposures, or retaliate against the citizen making them.

Citizens who have suffered losses through infringement of their civic rights by any state organ or functionary have the right to compensation in accordance with the law.

Article 42: Citizens of the People's Republic of China have the right as well as the duty to work.

Using various channels, the State creates conditions for employment, strengthens labour protection, improves working conditions and, on the basis of expanded production, increases remuneration for work and social benefits.

Work is the glorious duty of every able-bodied citizen. All working people in state-owned enterprises and in urban and rural economic collectives should perform their tasks with an attitude consonant with their status as masters of the country. The State promotes socialist labour emulation, and commends and rewards model and advanced workers. The State encourages citizens to take part in voluntary labour.

The State provides necessary vocational training to citizens before they are employed.

Article 43: Working people in the People's Republic of China have the right to rest.

The State expands facilities for rest and recuperation of working people, and prescribes working hours and vacations for workers and staff.

Article 44: The State prescribes by law the system of retirement for workers and staff in enterprises and undertakings and for functionaries of organs of state. The livelihood of retired personnel is ensured by the State and society.

Article 45: Citizens of the People's Republic of China have the right to material assistance from the State and society when they are old, ill or disabled. The State develops the social insurance, social relief and medical and health services that are required to enable citizens to enjoy this right.

The State and society ensure the livelihood of disabled members of the armed forces, provide pensions to the families of martyrs and give preferential treatment to the families of military personnel.

The State and society help make arrangements for the work, livelihood and education of the blind, deaf-mute and other handicapped citizens.

Article 46: Citizens of the People's Republic of China have the duty as well as the right to receive education.

The State promotes the all-round moral, intellectual and physical development of children and young people.

Article 47: Citizens of the People's Republic of China have the freedom to engage in scientific research, literary and artistic creation and other cultural pursuits. The State encourages and assists creative endeavours conducive to the interests of the people that are made by citizens engaged in education, science, technology, literature, art and other cultural work.

Article 48: Women in the People's Republic of China enjoy equal rights with men in all spheres of life, political, economic, cultural and social, including family life.

The State protects the rights and interests of women, applies the principle of equal pay for equal work for men and women alike and trains and selects cadres from among women.

Article 49: Marriage, the family and mother and child are protected by the State.

Both husband and wife have the duty to practise family planning.

Parents have the duty to rear and educate their minor children, and children who have come of age have the duty to support and assist their parents.

Violation of the freedom of marriage is prohibited. Maltreatment of old people, women and children is prohibited.

Article 50: The People's Republic of China protects the legitimate rights and interests of Chinese nationals residing abroad and protects the lawful rights and interests of returned overseas Chinese and of the family members of Chinese nationals residing abroad.

Article 51: The exercise by citizens of the People's Republic of China of their freedoms and rights may not infringe upon the interests of the State, of society and of the collective, or upon the lawful freedoms and rights of other citizens.

Article 52: It is the duty of citizens of the People's Republic of China to safeguard the unity of the country and the unity of all its nationalities.

Article 53: Citizens of the People's Republic of China must abide by the Constitution and the law, keep state secrets, protect public property and observe labour discipline and public order and respect social ethics.

Article 54: It is the duty of citizens of the People's Republic of China to safeguard the security, honour and interests of the motherland; they must not commit acts detrimental to the security, honour and interests of the motherland.

Article 55: It is the sacred obligation of every citizen of the People's Republic of China to defend the motherland and resist aggression.

It is the honourable duty of citizens of the People's Republic of China to perform military service and join the militia in accordance with the law.

Article 56: It is the duty of citizens of the People's Republic of China to pay taxes in accordance with the law.

STRUCTURE OF THE STATE

The National People's Congress

Article 57: The National People's Congress of the People's Republic of China is the highest organ of state power. Its permanent body is the Standing Committee of the National People's Congress.

Article 58: The National People's Congress and its Standing Committee exercise the legislative power of the State.

Article 59: The National People's Congress is composed of deputies elected by the provinces, autonomous regions and municipalities directly under the Central Government, and by the armed forces. All the minority nationalities are entitled to appropriate representation.

Election of deputies to the National People's Congress is conducted by the Standing Committee of the National People's Congress.

The number of deputies to the National People's Congress and the manner of their election are prescribed by law.

Article 60: The National People's Congress is elected for a term of five years.

Two months before the expiration of the term of office of a National People's Congress, its Standing Committee must ensure that the election of deputies to the succeeding National People's Congress is completed. Should exceptional circumstances prevent such an election, it may be postponed by decision of a majority vote of more than two-thirds of all those on the Standing Committee of the incumbent National People's Congress, and the term of office of the incumbent National People's Congress may be extended. The election of deputies to the succeeding National People's Congress must be completed within one year after the termination of such exceptional circumstances.

Article 61: The National People's Congress meets in session once a year and is convened by its Standing Committee. A session of the National People's Congress may be convened at any time the Standing Committee deems this necessary, or when more than one-fifth of the deputies to the National People's Congress so propose.

When the National People's Congress meets, it elects a presidium to conduct its session.

Article 62: The National People's Congress exercises the following functions and powers:

(1) to amend the Constitution;

(2) to supervise the enforcement of the Constitution;

(3) to enact and amend basic statutes concerning criminal offences, civil affairs, the state organs and other matters;

(4) to elect the President and the Vice-President of the People's Republic of China;

(5) to decide on the choice of the Premier of the State Council upon nomination by the President of the People's Republic of China, and to decide on the choice of the Vice-Premiers, State Councillors, Ministers in charge of Ministries or Commissions and the Auditor-General and the Secretary-General of the State Council upon nomination by the Premier;

(6) to elect the Chairman of the Central Military Commission and, upon his nomination, to decide on the choice of all the others on the Central Military Commission;

(7) to elect the President of the Supreme People's Court;

(8) to elect the Procurator-General of the Supreme People's Procuratorate;

(9) to examine and approve the plan for national economic and social development and the reports on its implementation;

(10) to examine and approve the state budget and the report on its implementation;

(11) to alter or annul inappropriate decisions of the Standing Committee of the National People's Congress;

(12) to approve the establishment of provinces, autonomous regions, and municipalities directly under the Central Government;

(13) to decide on the establishment of special administrative regions and the systems to be instituted there;

(14) to decide on questions of war and peace; and

(15) to exercise such other functions and powers as the highest organ of state power should exercise.

Article 63: The National People's Congress has the power to recall or remove from office the following persons:

(1) the President and the Vice-President of the People's Republic of China;

(2) the Premier, Vice-Premiers, State Councillors, Ministers in charge of Ministries or Commissions and the Auditor-General and the Secretary-General of the State Council;

(3) the Chairman of the Central Military Commission and others on the Commission;

(4) the President of the Supreme People's Court; and

(5) the Procurator-General of the Supreme People's Procuratorate.

Article 64: Amendments to the Constitution are to be proposed by the Standing Committee of the National People's Congress or by more than one-fifth of the deputies to the National People's Congress and adopted by a majority vote of more than two-thirds of all the deputies to the Congress.

Statutes and resolutions are adopted by a majority vote of more than one-half of all the deputies to the National People's Congress.

Article 65: The Standing Committee of the National People's Congress is composed of the following:

the Chairman;

the Vice-Chairmen;

the Secretary-General; and

members.

Minority nationalities are entitled to appropriate representation on the Standing Committee of the National People's Congress.

The National People's Congress elects, and has the power to recall, all those on its Standing Committee.

No one on the Standing Committee of the National People's Congress shall hold any post in any of the administrative, judicial or procuratorial organs of the State.

Article 66: The Standing Committee of the National People's Congress is elected for the same term as the National People's Congress; it exercises its functions and powers until a new Standing Committee is elected by the succeeding National People's Congress.

The Chairman and Vice-Chairmen of the Standing Committee shall serve no more than two consecutive terms.

Article 67: The Standing Committee of the National People's Congress exercises the following functions and powers:

(1) to interpret the Constitution and supervise its enforcement;

(2) to enact and amend statutes with the exception of those which should be enacted by the National People's Congress;

(3) to enact, when the National People's Congress is not in session, partial supplements and amendments to statutes enacted by the National People's Congress provided that they do not contravene the basic principles of these statutes;

(4) to interpret statutes;

(5) to examine and approve, when the National People's Congress is not in session, partial adjustments to the plan for national economic and social development and to the state budget that prove necessary in the course of their implementation;

(6) to supervise the work of the State Council, the Central Military Commission, the Supreme People's Court and the Supreme People's Procuratorate;

(7) to annul those administrative rules and regulations, decisions or orders of the State Council that contravene the Constitution or the statutes;

(8) to annul those local regulations or decisions of the organs of state power of provinces, autonomous regions and municipalities directly under the Central Government that contravene the Constitution, the statutes or the administrative rules and regulations;

(9) to decide, when the National People's Congress is not in session, on the choice of Ministers in charge of Ministries or Commissions or the Auditor-General and the Secretary-General of the State Council upon nomination by the Premier of the State Council;

(10) to decide, upon nomination by the Chairman of the Central Military Commission, on the choice of others on the Commission, when the National People's Congress is not in session;

(11) to appoint and remove the Vice-Presidents and judges of the Supreme People's Court, members of its Judicial Committee and the President of the Military Court at the suggestion of the President of the Supreme People's Court;

(12) to appoint and remove the Deputy Procurators-General and Procurators of the Supreme People's Procuratorate, members of its Procuratorial Committee and the Chief Procurator of the Military Procuratorate at the request of the Procurator-General of the Supreme People's Procuratorate, and to approve the appointment and removal of the Chief Procurators of the People's Procuratorates of provinces, autonomous regions and municipalities directly under the Central Government;

(13) to decide on the appointment and recall of plenipotentiary representatives abroad;

(14) to decide on the ratification and abrogation of treaties and important agreements concluded with foreign states;

(15) to institute systems of titles and ranks for military and diplomatic personnel and of other specific titles and ranks;

(16) to institute state medals and titles of honour and decide on their conferment;

(17) to decide on the granting of special pardons;

(18) to decide, when the National People's Congress is not in session, on the proclamation of a state of war in the event of an armed attack on the country or in fulfilment of international treaty obligations concerning common defence against aggression;

(19) to decide on general mobilization or partial mobilization;

(20) to decide on the enforcement of martial law throughout the country or in particular provinces, autonomous regions or municipalities directly under the Central Government; and

(21) to exercise such other functions and powers as the National People's Congress may assign to it.

Article 68: The Chairman of the Standing Committee of the National People's Congress presides over the work of the Standing Committee and convenes its meetings. The Vice-Chairmen and the Secretary-General assist the Chairman in his work.

Chairmanship meetings with the participation of the Chairman, Vice-Chairmen and Secretary-General handle the important day-to-day work of the Standing Committee of the National People's Congress.

Article 69: The Standing Committee of the National People's Congress is responsible to the National People's Congress and reports on its work to the Congress.

Article 70: The National People's Congress establishes a Nationalities Committee, a Law Committee, a Finance and Economic Committee, an Education, Science, Culture and Public Health Committee, a Foreign Affairs Committee, an Overseas Chinese Committee and such other special committees as are necessary. These special committees work under the direction of the Standing Committee of the National People's Congress when the Congress is not in session.

The special committees examine, discuss and draw up relevant bills and draft resolutions under the direction of the National People's Congress and its Standing Committee.

Article 71: The National People's Congress and its Standing Committee may, when they deem it necessary, appoint committees of inquiry into specific questions and adopt relevant resolutions in the light of their reports.

All organs of State, public organizations and citizens concerned are obliged to supply the necessary information to those committees of inquiry when they conduct investigations.

Article 72: Deputies to the National People's Congress and all those on its Standing Committee have the right, in accordance with procedures prescribed by law, to submit bills and proposals within the scope of the respective functions and powers of the National People's Congress and its Standing Committee.

Article 73: Deputies to the National People's Congress during its sessions, and all those on its Standing Committee during its meetings, have the right to address questions, in accordance with procedures prescribed by law, to the State Council or the Ministries or Commissions under the State Council, which must answer the questions in a responsible manner.

Article 74: No deputy to the National People's Congress may be arrested or placed on criminal trial without the consent of the presidium of the current session of the National People's Congress or, when the National People's Congress is not in session, without the consent of its Standing Committee.

Article 75: Deputies to the National People's Congress may not be called to legal account for their speeches or votes at its meetings.

Article 76: Deputies to the National People's Congress must play an exemplary role in abiding by the Constitution and the law and keeping state secrets and, in production and other work and their public activities, assist in the enforcement of the Constitution and the law.

Deputies to the National People's Congress should maintain close contact with the units which elected them and with the people, listen to and convey the opinions and demands of the people and work hard to serve them.

Article 77: Deputies to the National People's Congress are subject to the supervision of the units which elected them. The electoral units have the power, through procedures prescribed by law, to recall the deputies whom they elected.

Article 78: The organization and working procedures of the National People's Congress and its Standing Committee are prescribed by law.

The President of the People's Republic of China

Article 79: The President and Vice-President of the People's Republic of China are elected by the National People's Congress.

Citizens of the People's Republic of China who have the right to vote and to stand for election and who have reached the age of 45 are eligible for election as President or Vice-President of the People's Republic of China.

The term of office of the President and Vice-President of the People's Republic of China is the same as that of the National People's Congress, and they shall serve no more than two consecutive terms.

Article 80: The President of the People's Republic of China, in pursuance of decisions of the National People's Congress and its Standing Committee, promulgates statutes; appoints and removes the Premier, Vice-Premiers, State Councillors, Ministers in charge of Ministries or Commissions, and the Auditor-General and the Secretary-General of the State Council; confers state medals and titles of honour; issues orders of special pardons; proclaims martial law; proclaims a state of war; and issues mobilization orders.

Article 81: The President of the People's Republic of China receives foreign diplomatic representatives on behalf of the People's Republic of China and, in pursuance of decisions of the Standing Committee of the National People's Congress, appoints and recalls plenipotentiary representatives abroad, and ratifies and abrogates treaties and important agreements concluded with foreign states.

Article 82: The Vice-President of the People's Republic of China assists the President in his work.

The Vice-President of the People's Republic of China may exercise such parts of the functions and powers of the President as the President may entrust to him.

Article 83: The President and Vice-President of the People's Republic of China exercise their functions and powers until the new President and Vice-President elected by the succeeding National People's Congress assume office.

Article 84: In case the office of the President of the People's Republic of China falls vacant, the Vice-President succeeds to the office of President.

In case the office of the Vice-President of the People's Republic of China falls vacant, the National People's Congress shall elect a new Vice-President to fill the vacancy.

In the event that the offices of both the President and the Vice-President of the People's Republic of China fall vacant, the National People's Congress shall elect a new President and a new Vice-President. Prior to such election, the Chairman of the Standing Committee of the National People's Congress shall temporarily act as the President of the People's Republic of China.

The State Council

Article 85: The State Council, that is, the Central People's Government, of the People's Republic of China is the executive body of the highest organ of state power; it is the highest organ of state administration.

Article 86: The State Council is composed of the following: the Premier; the Vice-Premiers; the State Councillors; the Ministers in charge of ministries; the Ministers in charge of commissions; the Auditor-General; and the Secretary-General.

The Premier has overall responsibility for the State Council. The Ministers have overall responsibility for the respective ministries or commissions under their charge.

The organization of the State Council is prescribed by law.

Article 87: The term of office of the State Council is the same as that of the National People's Congress.

The Premier, Vice-Premiers and State Councillors shall serve no more than two consecutive terms.

Article 88: The Premier directs the work of the State Council. The Vice-Premiers and State Councillors assist the Premier in his work.

Executive meetings of the State Council are composed of the Premier, the Vice-Premiers, the State Councillors and the Secretary-General of the State Council.

The Premier convenes and presides over the executive meetings and plenary meetings of the State Council.

Article 89: The State Council exercises the following functions and powers:

(1) to adopt administrative measures, enact administrative rules and regulations and issue decisions and orders in accordance with the Constitution and the statutes;

(2) to submit proposals to the National People's Congress or its Standing Committee;

(3) to lay down the tasks and responsibilities of the ministries and commissions of the State Council, to exercise unified leadership over the work of the ministries and commissions and to direct all other administrative work of a national character that does not fall within the jurisdiction of the ministries and commissions;

(4) to exercise unified leadership over the work of local organs of state administration at different levels throughout the country, and to lay down the detailed division of functions and powers between the Central Government and the organs of state administration of provinces, autonomous regions and municipalities directly under the Central Government;

(5) to draw up and implement the plan for national economic and social development and the state budget;

(6) to direct and administer economic work and urban and rural development;

(7) to direct and administer the work concerning education, science, culture, public health, physical culture and family planning;

(8) to direct and administer the work concerning civil affairs, public security, judicial administration, supervision and other related matters;

(9) to conduct foreign affairs and conclude treaties and agreements with foreign states;

(10) to direct and administer the building of national defence;

(11) to direct and administer affairs concerning the nationalities, and to safeguard the equal rights of minority nationalities and the right of autonomy of the national autonomous areas;

(12) to protect the legitimate rights and interests of Chinese nationals residing abroad and protect the lawful rights and interests of returned overseas Chinese and of the family members of Chinese nationals residing abroad;

(13) to alter or annul inappropriate orders, directives and regulations issued by the ministries or commissions;

(14) to alter or annul inappropriate decisions and orders issued by local organs of state administration at different levels;

(15) to approve the geographic division of provinces, autonomous regions and municipalities directly under the Central Government, and to approve the establishment and geographic division of autonomous prefectures, counties, autonomous counties and cities;

(16) to decide on the enforcement of martial law in parts of provinces, autonomous regions and municipalities directly under the Central Government;

(17) to examine and decide on the size of administrative organs and, in accordance with the law, to appoint, remove and train administrative officers, appraise their work and reward or punish them; and

(18) to exercise such other functions and powers as the National People's Congress or its Standing Committee may assign it.

Article 90: The Ministers in charge of ministries or commissions of the State Council are responsible for the work of their respective departments and convene and preside over their ministerial meetings or commission meetings that discuss and decide on major issues in the work of their respective departments.

The ministries and commissions issue orders, directives and regulations within the jurisdiction of their respective departments and in accordance with the statutes and the administrative rules and regulations, decisions and orders issued by the State Council.

Article 91: The State Council establishes an auditing body to supervise through auditing the revenue and expenditure of all departments under the State Council and of the local government at different levels, and those of the state financial and monetary organizations and of enterprises and undertakings.

Under the direction of the Premier of the State Council, the auditing body independently exercises its power to supervise through auditing in accordance with the law, subject to no interference by any other administrative organ or any public organization or individual.

Article 92: The State Council is responsible, and reports on its work, to the National People's Congress or, when the National People's Congress is not in session, to its Standing Committee.

The Central Military Commission

Article 93: The Central Military Commission of the People's Republic of China directs the armed forces of the country.

The Central Military Commission is composed of the following: the Chairman; the Vice-Chairmen; and members.

The Chairman of the Central Military Commission has overall responsibility for the Commission.

The term of office of the Central Military Commission is the same as that of the National People's Congress.

Article 94: The Chairman of the Central Military Commission is responsible to the National People's Congress and its Standing Committee.

(Two further sections, not included here, deal with the Local People's Congresses and Government and with the Organs of Self-Government of National Autonomous Areas, respectively.)

The People's Courts and the People's Procuratorates

Article 123: The people's courts in the People's Republic of China are the judicial organs of the State.

Article 124: The People's Republic of China establishes the Supreme People's Court and the local people's courts at different levels, military courts and other special people's courts.

The term of office of the President of the Supreme People's Court is the same as that of the National People's Congress; he shall serve no more than two consecutive terms.

The organization of people's courts is prescribed by law.

Article 125: All cases handled by the people's courts, except for those involving special circumstances as specified by law, shall be heard in public. The accused has the right of defence.

Article 126: The people's courts shall, in accordance with the law, exercise judicial power independently and are not subject to interference by administrative organs, public organizations or individuals.

Article 127: The Supreme People's Court is the highest judicial organ.

The Supreme People's Court supervises the administration of justice by the local people's courts at different levels and by the special people's courts; people's courts at higher levels supervise the administration of justice by those at lower levels.

Article 128: The Supreme People's Court is responsible to the National People's Congress and its Standing Committee. Local people's courts at different levels are responsible to the organs of state power which created them.

Article 129: The people's procuratorates of the People's Republic of China are state organs for legal supervision.

Article 130: The People's Republic of China establishes the Supreme People's Procuratorate and the local people's procuratorates at different levels, military procuratorates and other special people's procuratorates.

The term of office of the Procurator-General of the Supreme People's Procuratorate is the same as that of the National People's Congress; he shall serve no more than two consecutive terms.

The organization of people's procuratorates is prescribed by law.

Article 131: People's procuratorates shall, in accordance with the law, exercise procuratorial power independently and are not subject to interference by administrative organs, public organizations or individuals.

Article 132: The Supreme People's Procuratorate is the highest procuratorial organ.

The Supreme People's Procuratorate directs the work of the local people's procuratorates at different levels and of the special people's procuratorates; people's procuratorates at higher levels direct the work of those at lower levels.

Article 133: The Supreme People's Procuratorate is responsible to the National People's Congress and its Standing Committee. Local people's procuratorates at different levels are responsible to the organs of state power at the corresponding levels which created them and to the people's procuratorates at the higher level.

Article 134: Citizens of all nationalities have the right to use the spoken and written languages of their own nationalities in court proceedings. The people's courts and people's procuratorates should provide translation for any party to the court proceedings who is not familiar with the spoken or written languages in common use in the locality.

In an area where people of a minority nationality live in a compact community or where a number of nationalities live together, hearings should be conducted in the language or languages in common use in the locality; indictments, judgments, notices and other documents should be written, according to actual needs, in the language or languages in common use in the locality.

Article 135: The people's courts, people's procuratorates and public security organs shall, in handling criminal cases, divide their functions, each taking responsibility for its own work, and they shall co-ordinate their efforts and check each other to ensure correct and effective enforcement of law.

THE NATIONAL FLAG, THE NATIONAL EMBLEM AND THE CAPITAL

Article 136: The national flag of the People's Republic of China is a red flag with five stars.

Article 137: The national emblem of the People's Republic of China is the Tiananmen (Gate of Heavenly Peace) in the centre, illuminated by five stars and encircled by ears of grain and a cogwheel.

Article 138: The capital of the People's Republic of China is Beijing (Peking).

The Government

HEAD OF STATE

President: JIANG ZEMIN (elected by the Eighth National People's Congress on 27 March 1993; re-elected by the Ninth National People's Congress on 16 March 1998).

Vice-President: HU JINTAO.

STATE COUNCIL
(March 2001)

Premier: ZHU RONGJI.

Vice-Premiers: QIAN QICHEN, LI LANQING, WU BANGGUO, WEN JIABAO.

State Councillors:

Gen. CHI HAOTIAN   ISMAIL AMAT
WANG ZHONGYU   LUO GAN
WU YI

Secretary-General: WANG ZHONGYU.

Minister of Foreign Affairs: TANG JIAXUAN.

Minister of National Defence: Gen. CHI HAOTIAN.

Minister of State Economic and Trade Commission: LI RONGRONG.

Minister of State Development and Planning Commission: ZENG PEIYAN.

Minister of Education: CHEN ZHILI.

Minister of Science and Technology: XU GUANHUA.

Minister of State Commission of Science, Technology and Industry for National Defence: LIU JIBIN.

Minister of State Nationalities Affairs Commission: LI DEZHU.

Minister of Public Security: JIA CHUNWANG.

Minister of State Security: XU YONGYUE.

Minister of Civil Affairs: DOJI CERING.

Minister of Justice: ZHANG FUSEN.

Minister of Supervision: HE YONG.

Minister of Finance: XIANG HUAICHENG.

Minister of Foreign Trade and Economic Co-operation: SHI GUANGSHENG.

Minister of Agriculture: CHEN YAOBANG.

Minister of Water Resources: WANG SHUCHENG.

Minister of Construction: YU ZHENGSHENG.

Minister of Land and Natural Resources: TIAN FENGSHAN.

Minister of Railways: FU ZHIHUAN.

Minister of Communications: HUANG ZHENDONG.

Minister of Information Industry: WU JICHUAN.

Minister of Personnel: ZHANG XUEZHANG.

Minister of Labour and Social Security: ZHANG ZUOJI.

Minister of Culture: SUN JIAZHENG.

Minister of Public Health: ZHANG WENKANG.

Minister of State Family Planning Commission: ZHANG WEIQING.

Governor of the People's Bank of China: DAI XIANGLONG.

Auditor-General of Auditing Administration: LI JINHUA.

MINISTRIES

Ministry of Agriculture: 11 Nongzhanguan Nanli, Chaoyang Qu, Beijing 100026; tel. (10) 64192293; fax (10) 64192468; e-mail webmaster@agri.gov.cn; internet www.agri.gov.cn.

Ministry of Civil Affairs: 147 Beiheyan Dajie, Dongcheng Qu, Beijing 100721; tel. (10) 65135333; fax (10) 65135332.

Ministry of Communications: 11 Jianguomennei Dajie, Dongcheng Qu. Beijing 100736; tel. (10) 65292114; fax (10) 65292345; internet www.moc.gov.cn.

Ministry of Construction: 9 Sanlihe Dajie, Xicheng Qu, Beijing 100835; tel. (10) 68394215; fax (10) 68393333; e-mail webmaster@mail.cin.gov.cn; internet www.cin.gov.cn.

Ministry of Culture: 10 Chaoyangmen Bei Jie, Dongcheng Qu, Beijing 100020; tel. (10) 65551432; fax (10) 65551433; e-mail webmaster@whb1.ccnt.com.cn; internet www.ccnt.com.cn.

Ministry of Education: 37 Damucang Hutong, Xicheng Qu, Beijing 100816; tel. (10) 66096114; fax (10) 66011049; e-mail webmaster@moe.edu.cn; internet www.moe.edu.cn.

Ministry of Finance: 3 Nansanxiang, Sanlihe, Xicheng Qu, Beijing 100820; tel. (10) 68551888; fax (10) 68533635; e-mail webmaster@mof.gov.cn; internet www.mof.gov.cn.

Ministries

Ministry of Foreign Affairs: 225 Chaoyangmennei Dajie, Dongsi, Beijing 100701; tel. (10) 65961114; fax (10) 65962146; e-mail webmaster@fmprc.gov.cn; internet www.fmprc.gov.cn.

Ministry of Foreign Trade and Economic Co-operation: 2 Dongchangan Jie, Dongcheng Qu, Beijing 100731; tel. (10) 67081526; fax (10) 67081513; e-mail webmaster@moftec.gov.cn; internet www.moftec.gov.cn.

Ministry of Information Industry: 13 Xichangan Jie, Beijing 100804; tel. (10) 66014249; fax (10) 66034248; e-mail webmaster@ mii.gov.cn; internet www.mii.gov.cn.

Ministry of Justice: 10 Chaoyangmennan Dajie, Chaoyang Qu, Beijing 100020; tel. (10) 65205114; fax (10) 65205316.

Ministry of Labour and Social Security: 12 Hepinglizhong Jie, Dongcheng Qu, Beijing 100716; tel. (10) 84201235; fax (10) 64218350.

Ministry of Land and Natural Resources: 3 Guanyingyuanxiqu, Xicheng Qu, Beijing 100035; tel. (10) 66127001; fax (10) 66175348; internet www.mlr.gov.cn.

Ministry of National Defence: 20 Jingshanqian Jie, Beijing 100009; tel. (10) 66730000; fax (10) 65962146.

Ministry of Personnel: 12 Hepinglizhong Jie, Dongcheng Qu, Beijing 100716; tel. (10) 84223240; fax (10) 64211417.

Ministry of Public Health: 1 Xizhinenwai Bei Lu, Xicheng Qu, Beijing 100044; tel. (10) 68792114; fax (10) 64012369; e-mail zhou@chsi.moh.gov.cn; internet www.moh.gov.cn.

Ministry of Public Security: 14 Dongchangan Jie, Dongcheng Qu, Beijing 100741; tel. (10) 65122831; fax (10) 65136577.

Ministry of Railways: 10 Fuxing Lu, Haidian Qu, Beijing 100844; tel. (10) 63244150; fax (10) 63242150; e-mail webmaster@ns .chinamor.cn.net; internet www.chinamor.cn.net.

Ministry of Science and Technology: 15B Fuxing Lu, Haidian Qu, Beijing 100862; tel. (10) 68515050; fax (10) 68515006; e-mail officemail@mail.most.gov.cn; internet www.most.gov.cn.

Ministry of State Security: 14 Dongchangan Jie, Dongcheng Qu, Beijing 100741; tel. (10) 65244702.

Ministry of Supervision: 4 Zaojunmiao, Haidian Qu, Beijing 100081; tel. (10) 62256677; fax (10) 62254181.

Ministry of Water Resources: 2 Baiguang Lu, Ertiao, Xuanwu Qu, Beijing 100053; tel. (10) 63203069; fax (10) 63202650.

STATE COMMISSIONS

State Commission of Science, Technology and Industry for National Defence: 2a Guang'anmennan Jie, Xuanwu Qu, Beijing 100053; tel. (10) 63571397; fax (10) 63571398; internet www.cost ind.gov.cn.

State Development and Planning Commission: 38 Yuetannan Jie, Xicheng Qu, Beijing 100824; tel. (10) 68504409; fax (10) 68512929; e-mail news@sdpc.gov.cn; internet www.sdpc.gov.cn.

State Economic and Trade Commission: 26 Xuanwumenxi Dajie, Xuanwumen Qu, Beijing 100053; tel. (10) 63192334; fax (10) 63192348; e-mail webmaster@setc.gov.cn; internet www.setc.gov.cn.

State Family Planning Commission: 14 Zhichun Lu, Haidian Qu, Beijing 100088; tel. (10) 62046622; fax (10) 62051865; e-mail sfpcdfa@public.bta.net.cn; internet www.sfpc.gov.cn.

State Nationalities Affairs Commission: 252 Taipingqiao Dajie, Xicheng Qu, Beijing 100800; tel. and fax (10) 66017375.

Legislature

QUANGUO RENMIN DAIBIAO DAHUI
(National People's Congress)

The National People's Congress (NPC) is the highest organ of state power, and is indirectly elected for a five-year term. The first plenary session of the Ninth NPC was convened in Beijing in March 1998, and was attended by 2,979 deputies. The first session of the Ninth National Committee of the Chinese People's Political Consultative Conference (CPPCC, Chair. LI RUIHUAN), a revolutionary united front organization led by the Communist Party, took place simultaneously. The CPPCC holds discussions and consultations on the important affairs in the nation's political life. Members of the CPPCC National Committee or of its Standing Committee may be invited to attend the NPC or its Standing Committee as observers.

Standing Committee

In March 1998 134 members were elected to the Standing Committee, in addition to the following:

Chairman: LI PENG.

Vice-Chairmen:

TIAN JIYUN	JIANG ZHENGHUA
JIANG CHUNYUN	ZOU JIAHUA
PAGBALHA GELEG NAMGYAI	WANG GUANGYING
PENG PEIYUN	CHENG SIYUAN
HE LULI	ZHOU GUANGZHAO
CAO ZHI	BUHE
DING SHISUN	TOMUR DAWAMAT
CHENG SIWEI	WU JIEPING
	XU JIALU

Secretary-General: HE CHUNLIN.

Provincial People's Congresses

Province	Chairman of Standing Committee of People's Congress
Anhui	MENG FULIN
Fujian	YUAN QITONG
Gansu	LU KEJIAN
Guangdong	ZHU SENLIN
Guizhou	LIU FANGREN
Hainan	DU QINGLIN
Hebei	CHENG WEIGAO
Heilongjiang	XU YOUFANG
Henan	REN KELI
Hubei	GUAN GUANGFU
Hunan	YANG ZHENGWU
Jiangsu	CHEN HUANYOU
Jiangxi	SHU HUIGUO
Jilin	WANG YUNKUN
Liaoning	WANG HUAIYUAN
Qinghai	BAI ENPEI
Shaanxi	LI JIANGUO
Shandong	ZHAO ZHIHAO
Shanxi	LU GONGXUN
Sichuan	XIE SHIJIE
Yunnan	YIN JUN
Zhejiang	LI ZEMIN

Special Municipalities	
Beijing	ZHANG JIANMIN
Chongqing	WANG YUNLONG
Shanghai	CHEN TIEDI
Tianjin	ZHANG LICHANG

Autonomous Regions	
Guangxi Zhuang	ZHAO FULIN
Nei Monggol	LIU MINGZU
Ningxia Hui	MAO RUBAI
Tibet (Xizang)	RAIDI
Xinjiang Uygur	AMUDUN NIYAZ

People's Governments

Province	Governor
Anhui	XU ZHONGLIN
Fujian	XI JINPING
Gansu	SONG ZHAOSU
Guangdong	LU RUIHUA
Guizhou	SHI XIUSHI (acting)
Hainan	WANG XIAOFENG
Hebei	NIU MAOSHENG
Heilongjiang	SONG FATANG
Henan	LI KEQIANG
Hubei	ZHANG GUOGUANG
Hunan	CHU BO
Jiangsu	JI YUNSHI
Jiangxi	SHU SHENGYOU
Jilin	HONG HU
Liaoning	BO XILAI
Qinghai	ZHAO LEJI
Shaanxi	CHENG ANDONG
Shandong	LI CHUNTING
Shanxi	LIU ZHENHUA
Sichuan	ZHANG ZHONGWEI
Yunnan	LI JIATING
Zhejiang	CHAI SONGYUE

Special Municipalities	Mayor
Beijing	LIU QI
Chongqing	BAO XUDING
Shanghai	XU KUANGDI
Tianjin	LI SHENGLIN

Autonomous Regions	Chairman
Guangxi Zhuang	Li Zhaozhuo
Nei Monggol	Uyunqimg (acting)
Ningxia Hui	Ma Qizhi
Tibet (Xizang)	Legqog
Xinjiang Uygur	Abdulahat Abdurixit

Political Organizations

COMMUNIST PARTY

Zhongguo Gongchan Dang (Chinese Communist Party—CCP): Beijing; f. 1921; 61m. mems in Dec. 1998; at the 15th Nat. Congress of the CCP, in September 1997, a new Cen. Cttee of 193 full mems and 151 alternate mems was elected; at its first plenary session the 15th Cen. Cttee appointed a new Politburo.

Fifteenth Central Committee

General Secretary: Jiang Zemin.

Politburo

Members of the Standing Committee:

Jiang Zemin	Hu Jintao
Li Peng	Wei Jianxing
Zhu Rongji	Li Lanqing
Li Ruihuan	

Other Full Members:

Ding Guangen	Gen. Zhang Wannian
Tian Jiyun	Luo Gan
Li Changchun	Jiang Chunyun
Li Tieying	Jia Qinglin
Wu Bangguo	Qian Qichen
Wu Guanzheng	Huang Ju
Gen. Chi Haotian	Wen Jiabao

Alternate Members: Zeng Qinghong, Wu Yi.

Secretariat

Hu Jintao	Luo Gan
Wei Jianxing	Wen Jiabao
Ding Guangen	Zeng Qinghong
Gen. Zhang Wannian	

OTHER POLITICAL ORGANIZATIONS

China Association for Promoting Democracy: 98 Xinanli Guloufangzhuangchang, Beijing 100009; tel. (10) 64033452; f. 1945; mems drawn mainly from literary, cultural and educational circles; Chair. Xu Jialu; Sec.-Gen. Chen Yiqun.

China Democratic League: 1 Beixing Dongchang Hutong, Beijing 100006; tel. (10) 65137983; fax (10) 65125090; f. 1941; formed from reorganization of League of Democratic Parties and Organizations of China; 131,300 mems, mainly intellectuals active in education, science and culture; Chair. Ding Shisun; Sec.-Gen. Zhang Baowen.

China National Democratic Construction Association: 208 Jixiangli, Chaowai Lu, Beijing 100020; tel. (10) 65523229; fax (10) 65523518; internet www.cndca.org.cn; f. 1945; 81,686 mems, mainly industrialists and business executives; Chair. Cheng Siwei; Sec.-Gen. Chen Mingde.

China Zhi Gong Dang (Party for Public Interests): Beijing; e-mail zhigong@public2.east.net.cn; f. 1925; reorg. 1947; mems are mainly returned overseas Chinese and scholars; Chair. Luo Haocai; Sec.-Gen. Qiu Guoyi.

Chinese Communist Youth League: 10 Qianmen Dongdajie, Beijing 100051; tel. (10) 67018132; fax (10) 67018131; f. 1922; 68.5m. mems; First Sec. of Cen. Cttee Zhou Qiang.

Chinese Peasants' and Workers' Democratic Party: f. 1930 as the Provisional Action Cttee of the Kuomintang; took present name in 1947; more than 65,000 mems, active mainly in public health and medicine; Chair. Jiang Zhenghua; Sec.-Gen. Yu Shenlong.

Jiu San (3 September) Society: f. 1946; fmrly Democratic and Science Soc.; 68,400 mems, mainly scientists and technologists; Chair. Wu Jieping; Sec.-Gen. Liu Ronghan.

Revolutionary Committee of the Chinese Kuomintang: tel. (10) 6550388; f. 1948; mainly fmr Kuomintang mems, and those in cultural, educational, health and financial fields; Chair. He Luli.

Taiwan Democratic Self-Government League: f. 1947; recruits Taiwanese living on the mainland; Chair. Zhang Kehui; Sec.-Gen. Li Minkuan.

During 1998 there were repeated failed attempts by pro-democracy activists to register an opposition party, the Chinese Democratic Party. The leaders of the party (Wang Youcai, Xu Wenli and Qin Yongmin) were sentenced to lengthy terms of imprisonment, and many other members of the party were detained.

Diplomatic Representation

EMBASSIES IN THE PEOPLE'S REPUBLIC OF CHINA

Afghanistan: 8 Dong Zhi Men Wai Dajie, Chao Yang Qu, Beijing 100600; tel. (10) 65321582; fax (10) 65321710; Chargé d'affaires: Abdolbasir Hotek.

Albania: 28 Guang Hua Lu, Jian Guo Men Wai, Beijing 100600; tel. (10) 65321120; fax (10) 65325451; Ambassador: Kujtim Xhani.

Algeria: 2 Dong Zhi Men Wai Dajie, Chao Yang Qu, Beijing 100600; tel. (10) 65321231; fax (10) 65321648; Ambassador: Ahmed Amine Kherbi.

Angola: 1-13-1 Tayuan Diplomatic Office Bldg, Beijing 100600; tel. (10) 65326968; Ambassador: Manuel Bernardo de Sousa.

Argentina: Bldg 11, 5 Dong Wu Jie, San Li Tun, Beijing 100600; tel. (10) 65322090; fax (10) 65322319; Ambassador: Federico Carlos Barttfeld.

Australia: 21 Dong Zhi Men Wai Dajie, San Li Tun, Beijing 100600; tel. (10) 65322331; fax (10) 65326718; e-mail webmaster@austemb .org.cn; Ambassador: David Irvine.

Austria: 5 Xiu Shui Nan Jie, Jian Guo Men Wai, Beijing 100600; tel. (10) 65322061; fax (10) 65321505; e-mail oebpekin@public.bta .net.cn; Ambassador: Erich Buttenhauser.

Azerbaijan: 3-2-31 San Li Tun Diplomatic Compound, Beijing 100600; tel. (10) 65324614; fax (10) 65324615; e-mail safirprc@ public.fhnet.cn.net; Ambassador: Tamerlan Garayev.

Bahrain: 2-9-1 Tayuan Diplomatic Office Bldg, Beijing 100600; tel. (10) 65325025; fax (10) 65325016; Ambassador: Mohammed Hamad al-Mahmeed.

Bangladesh: 42 Guang Hua Lu, Beijing 100600; tel. (10) 65321819; fax (10) 65324346; e-mail embbd@public.intercom.com.cn; Ambassador: Humayun A. Kamal.

Belarus: 2-10-1 Tayuan Diplomatic Office Bldg, Xin Dong Lu, Chao Yang Qu, Beijing 100600; tel. (10) 65326426; fax (10) 65326417; Ambassador: Uladzimir Rusakevich.

Belgium: 6 San Li Tun Lu, Beijing 100600; tel. (10) 65321736; fax (10) 65325097; e-mail Beijing@diplobel.org; Ambassador: Johan Maricou.

Benin: 38 Guang Hua Lu, Jian Guo Men Wai, Beijing 100600; tel. (10) 65323054; fax (10) 65325103; Ambassador: Michel Adechian.

Bolivia: 2-3-2 Tayuan Diplomatic Office Bldg, Beijing 100600; tel. (10) 65323074; fax (10) 65324686; e-mail embolch@ public3.bta.net.cn; Ambassador: Oscar D. Z. Medinaceli.

Botswana: 1-8-1/2 Tayuan Diplomatic Office Bldg, Beijing 100600; tel. (10) 65325751; fax (10) 65325713; Ambassador: Alfred Uyapo Majaye Dube.

Brazil: 27 Guang Hua Lu, Jian Guo Men Wai, Beijing 100600; tel. (10) 65322881; fax (10) 65322751; Ambassador: Affonso Celso de Ouro-Preto.

Brunei: 1-91 San Li Tun Diplomatic Office Bldg, Chao Yang Qu, Beijing 100600; tel. (10) 65324094; fax (10) 65324097; Ambassador: Pehin Dato' H. J. Mahdini.

Bulgaria: 4 Xiu Shui Bei Jie, Jian Guo Men Wai, Beijing 100600; tel. (10) 65321946; fax (10) 65324502; Ambassador: Dimitar Tzanev.

Burundi: 25 Guang Hua Lu, Jian Guo Men Wai, Beijing 100600; tel. (10) 65321801; fax (10) 65322381; Ambassador: Alfred Nkurunziza.

Cambodia: 9 Dong Zhi Men Wai Dajie, Beijing 100600; tel. (10) 65321889; fax (10) 65323507; Ambassador: Khek Sysoda.

Cameroon: 7 San Li Tun, Dong Wu Jie, Beijing 100600; tel. (10) 65321771; fax (10) 65321761; Ambassador: Eleih-Elle Etian.

Canada: 19 Dong Zhi Men Wai Dajie, Chao Yang Qu, Beijing 100600; tel. (10) 65323536; fax (10) 65324311; Ambassador: Howard Balloch.

Chile: 1 Dong Si Jie, San Li Tun, Beijing 100600; tel. (10) 65321641; fax (10) 65323170; e-mail echilecn@public3.bta.net.cn; Ambassador: Jorge Tarud Daccarett.

Colombia: 34 Guang Hua Lu, Jian Guo Men Wai, Beijing 100600; tel. (10) 65321713; fax (10) 65321969; Ambassador: Rodrigo Querubin Londoño.

Congo, Democratic Republic: 6 Dong Wu Jie, San Li Tun, Beijing 100600; tel. (10) 65321995; fax (10) 65321360; Ambassador: Lombo Lo Mangamanga.

Congo, Republic: 7 Dong Si Jie, San Li Tun, Beijing 100600; tel. (10) 65321658; Ambassador: Pierre Passi.

Côte d'Ivoire: 9 San Li Tun, Bei Xiao Jie, Beijing 100600; tel. (10) 65321223; fax (10) 65322407; Ambassador: Konan Kramo.

Croatia: 2-72 San Li Tun Diplomatic Office Bldg, Beijing 100600; tel. (10) 65326241; fax (10) 65326257; e-mail vrhpek@public.bta .net.cn; Ambassador: Zeljko Kirinčić.

Cuba: 1 Xiu Shui Nan Jie, Jian Guo Men Wai, Beijing 100600; tel. (10) 65321714; fax (10) 65322870; Ambassador: ALBERTO RODRÍGUEZ ARUFE.

Cyprus: 2-13-2 Tayuan Diplomatic Office Bldg, Liang Ma He Nan Lu, Chao Yang Qu, Beijing 100600; tel. (10) 65325057; fax (10) 65325060; e-mail cybjemb@info.iuol.cn.net; Ambassador: LORIA MARKIDES.

Czech Republic: Ri Tan Lu, Jian Guo Men Wai, Beijing 100600; tel. (10) 65326902; fax (10) 65325653; Ambassador: ALEXANDR KARYCH.

Denmark: 1 Dong Wu Jie, San Li Tun, Beijing 100600; tel. (10) 65322431; fax (10) 65322439; e-mail ambadan@public .bta.net.cn; internet www.dk-embassy-cn.org/; Ambassador: CHRISTOPHER BO BRAMSEN.

Ecuador: 11-2-1 Diplomatic Apartments, Jian Guo Men Wai, Beijing 100600; tel. (10) 65322264; fax (10) 65323158; Ambassador: FERNANDO CÓRDOVA BOSSANO.

Egypt: 2 Ri Tan Dong Lu, Jian Guo Men Wai, Beijing 100600; tel. (10) 65321825; fax (10) 65325365; Ambassador: MOHAMED NOMAN GALAL.

Equatorial Guinea: 2 Dong Si Jie, San Li Tun, Beijing; tel. (10) 65323709; fax (10) 65323805; Ambassador: MANUEL MOTO TOMO.

Eritrea: Tayuan Diplomatic Office Bldg, Beijing 100600; tel. (10) 56326534; fax (10) 65326532; Ambassador: TEWOLDEBRHAN WOLDEMIKAEL.

Ethiopia: 3 Xiu Shui Nan Jie, Jian Guo Men Wai, Beijing 100600; tel. (10) 65325258; fax (10) 65325591; e-mail ethembcn@public .bta.net.cn; Ambassador: ADDIS ALEM BALEMA.

Finland: Beijing Kerry Centre, 26/F South Tower, 1 Guanghua Lu, Beijing 100020; tel. (10) 85298541; fax (10) 85298547; e-mail sanomat.pek@formin.fi; internet www.finland-in-china.com; Ambassador: PASI RUTANEN.

France: 3 Dong San Jie, San Li Tun, Chao Yang Qu, Beijing 100600; tel. (10) 65321331; fax (10) 65324841; e-mail ambafra@public3.bta .net.cn; internet www.lotus.ia.ac.cn/ambafra; Ambassador: PIERRE MOREL.

Gabon: 36 Guang Hua Lu, Jian Guo Men Wai, Beijing 100600; tel. (10) 65322810; fax (10) 65322621; Ambassador: M. OBIANG-NDOUDUM.

Germany: 17 Dong Zhi Men Wai Dajie, San Li Tun, Beijing 100600; tel. (10) 65322161; fax (10) 65325336; Ambassador: Dr HANS-CHRISTIAN UEBETSCHAET.

Ghana: 8 San Li Tun Lu, Beijing 100600; tel. (10) 65321319; fax (10) 65323602; Ambassador: EMMANUEL OSCAR AMEYEDOWO.

Greece: 19 Guang Hua Lu, Jian Guo Men Wai, Beijing 100600; tel. (10) 65321588; fax (10) 65321277; Ambassador: IOANNIS THEOPHANOPOULOS.

Guinea: 2 Xi Liu Jie, San Li Tun, Beijing 100600; tel. (10) 65323649; fax (10) 65324957; Ambassador: MAMADY CONDÉ.

Guinea-Bissau: Diplomatic relations re-established April 1998.

Guyana: 1 Xiu Shui Dong Jie, Jian Guo Men Wai, Beijing 100600; tel. (10) 65321601; fax (10) 65325741; Ambassador: RONALD MORTIMER AUSTIN.

Hungary: 10 Dong Zhi Men Wai Dajie, San Li Tun, Beijing 100600; tel. (10) 65321431; fax (10) 65325053; Ambassador: OTTO JUHASZ.

Iceland: Landmark Tower 1, 802, 8 North Dongsanhuan Lu, Beijing 100600; tel. (10) 65907795; fax (10) 65907801; e-mail icemb.beijing @utn.stjr.is; Ambassador: OLAFUR EGILSSON.

India: 1 Ri Tan Dong Lu, Jian Guo Men Wai, Beijing 100600; tel. (10) 65321927; fax (10) 65324684; Ambassador: SHIVSHANKAR MENON.

Indonesia: Diplomatic Office Bldg B, San Li Tun, Beijing 100600; tel. (10) 65325486; fax (10) 65325368; e-mail kombei@public3.bta .net.cn; Ambassador: KUNTARA.

Iran: 13 Dong Liu Jie, San Li Tun, Beijing 100600; tel. (10) 65322040; fax (10) 65321403; Ambassador: MOHAMMAD HOSSEIN MALAEK.

Iraq: 25 Xiu Shui Bei Jie, Jian Guo Men Wai, Beijing 100600; tel. (10) 65321950; fax (10) 65321596; Ambassador: BASSAM SALIH KUBBA.

Ireland: 3 Ri Tan Dong Lu, Jian Guo Men Wai, Beijing 100600; tel. (10) 65322691; fax (10) 65322168; Ambassador: DECLAN CONNOLLY.

Israel: Room 405, West Wing Office, 1 Jian Guo Men Wai Dajie, Beijing 100004; tel. (10) 65052970; fax (10) 65050328; e-mail israemb@public.bta.net.cn; Ambassador: ITZHAK SHELEF.

Italy: 2 Dong Er Jie, San Li Tun, Beijing 100600; tel. (10) 65322131; fax (10) 65324676; Ambassador: PAOLO BRUNI.

Japan: 7 Ri Tan Lu, Jian Guo Men Wai, Beijing 100600; tel. (10) 65322361; fax (10) 65324625; Ambassador: SAKUTARO TANINO.

Jordan: 5 Dong Liu Jie, San Li Tun, Beijing 100600; tel. (10) 65323906; fax (10) 65323283; Ambassador: SAMIR I. AL-NAOURI.

Kazakhstan: 9 Dong Liu Jie, San Li Tun, Beijing 100600; tel. (10) 65326182; fax (10) 65326183; e-mail kazconscan@on.aibn.com; Ambassador: KUANYSH SULTANOVICH SULTANOV.

Kenya: 4 Xi Liu Jie, San Li Tun, Beijing 100600; tel. (10) 65323381; fax (10) 65321770; Ambassador: MATTHEW KATHURIMA MITHIRI.

Korea, Democratic People's Republic: Ri Tan Bei Lu, Jian Guo Men Wai, Beijing 100600; tel. (10) 65321186; fax (10) 65326056; Ambassador: CHO JIN SU.

Korea, Republic: 3rd–4th Floors, China World Trade Centre, 1 Jian Guo Men Wai Dajie, Beijing 100600; tel. (10) 65053171; fax (10) 65053458; Ambassador: HONG SOON-YOUNG.

Kuwait: 23 Guang Hua Lu, Jian Guo Men Wai, Beijing 100600; tel. (10) 65322216; fax (10) 65321607; Ambassador: ABDUL-MUHSEN NASIR A. GEAN.

Kyrgyzstan: 2-4-1 Tayuan Diplomatic Office Bldg, Beijing 100600; tel. (10) 65326458; fax (10) 65326459; e-mail kyrgyzch@public2 .east.net.cn; Ambassador: MARAT SARALINOV.

Laos: 11 Dong Si Jie, San Li Tun, Chao Yang Qu, Beijing 100600; tel. (10) 65321224; fax (10) 65326748; e-mail laoemcn@public .east.cn.net; Ambassador: SOUKTHAVONE KEOLA.

Latvia: 3-2-21 San Li Tun Diplomatic Compound, Beijing 100600; tel. (10) 65320106; fax (10) 65320107; e-mail kinas@163bj.com; Ambassador: Dr EINARS SEMANIS.

Lebanon: 51 Dong Liu Jie, San Li Tun, Beijing; tel. (10) 65322197; fax (10) 65322770; Ambassador: ZEIDAN AL-SAGHIR.

Lesotho: 2-3-13 San Li Tun Diplomatic Apartment, Beijing 100600; tel. (10) 65326842; fax (10) 65326845; e-mail doemli@public.bta .net.cn; Ambassador: LEBOHANG K. MOLEKO.

Libya: 3 Dong Liu Jie, San Li Tun, Beijing 100600; tel. (10) 65323666; fax (10) 65323391; Secretary of the People's Bureau: MUFTAH OTMAN MADI.

Lithuania: 8-2-12 Tayuan Diplomatic Office Bldg, Beijing 100600; tel. (10) 65324421; fax (10) 65324451; Ambassador: DAINIUS VOVERIS.

Luxembourg: 21 Nei Wu Bu Jie, Beijing 100600; tel. (10) 65135937; fax (10) 65137268; e-mail ambluxcn@public.bta.net.cn; Ambassador: MARTINE SCHOMMER.

Madagascar: 3 Dong Jie, San Li Tun, Beijing 100600; tel. (10) 65321353; fax (10) 65322102; Ambassador: JEAN-JACQUES MAURICE.

Malaysia: 13 Dong Zhi Men Wai Dajie, San Li Tun, Beijing; tel. (10) 65322531; fax (10) 65325032; Ambassador: Dato' ABDUL MAJID.

Mali: 8 Dong Si Jie, San Li Tun, Beijing 100600; tel. (10) 65321704; fax (10) 65321618; Ambassador: KAFOUGOUNA KONE.

Malta: 5-2-22 San Li Tun Diplomatic Compound, Beijing 100600; tel. (10) 65323114; fax (10) 65326125; e-mail savfborg@public3 .bta.net.cn; Ambassador: SAVIOUR F. BORG.

Mauritania: 9 Dong San Jie, San Li Tun, Beijing 100600; tel. (10) 65321346; fax (10) 65321685; Ambassador: ABDELLAHI OULD ABDI.

Mexico: 5 Dong Wu Jie, San Li Tun, Beijing 100600; tel. (10) 65321947; fax (10) 65323744; e-mail embmxchn@public.bta.net.cn; Ambassador: LUIS WYBO ALFARO.

Moldova: 3-1-152 Tayuan Diplomatic Office Bldg, Beijing 100600; tel. (10) 65325379; Ambassador: VASILE SOVA.

Mongolia: 2 Xiu Shui Bei Jie, Jian Guo Men Wai, Beijing 100600; tel. (10) 65321203; fax (10) 65325045; e-mail monembbj@public3 .bta.net.cn; Ambassador: L. TSAHILGAAN.

Morocco: 16 San Li Tun Lu, Beijing 100600; tel. (10) 65321489; fax (10) 65321453; e-mail embmor@public.bta.net.cn; Ambassador: MIMOUN MEHDI.

Mozambique: 1-7-2 Tayuan Diplomatic Office Bldg, Beijing 100600; tel. (10) 65323664; fax (10) 65325189; e-mail embamoc@public .bta.net.cn; Ambassador: JOSÉ MARIA DA SILVA DE MORAIS.

Myanmar: 6 Dong Zhi Men Wai Dajie, Chao Yang Qu, Beijing 100600; tel. (10) 65321584; fax (10) 65321344; Ambassador: U BA HTAY CHIT.

Namibia: 1-13-2 Tayuan Diplomatic Office Bldg, Beijing 100600; tel. (10) 65324810; fax (10) 65324549; e-mail namemb@eastnet.com.cn; Ambassador: H.U. IPINGE.

Nepal: 1 Xi Liu Jie, San Li Tun Lu, Beijing 100600; tel. (10) 65322739; fax (10) 65323251; Ambassador: RAJESHWAR ACHARYA.

Netherlands: 4 Liang Ma He Nan Lu, Beijing 100600; tel. (10) 65321131; fax (10) 65324689; Ambassador: ATE OOSTRA.

New Zealand: 1 Ri Tan, Dong Er Jie, Chao Yang Qu, Beijing 100600; tel. (10) 65322731; fax (10) 65324317; e-mail nzemb@ eastnet.com.cn; Ambassador: JOHN McKINNON.

Niger: 3-2-12 San Li Tun, Beijing 100600; tel. (10) 65324279; mail nigerbj@public.bta.net.cn; Ambassador: BOZARI SEYDOU.

Nigeria: 2 Dong Wu Jie, San Li Tun, Beijing; tel. (10) 65323631; fax (10) 65321650; Ambassador: OLAGUNJU ADESAKIN.

Norway: 1 Dong Yi Jie, San Li Tun, Beijing; tel. (10) 65322261; fax (10) 65322392; e-mail emb.beijing@mfa.no; Ambassador: HAAKON B. HJELDE.

Oman: 6 Liang Ma He Nan Lu, San Li Tun, Beijing 100600; tel. (10) 65323956; fax (10) 65325030; Ambassador: ABDULLAH BIN MOHAMMED BIN ABDULLAH AL-FARISY.

Pakistan: 1 Dong Zhi Men Wai Dajie, San Li Tun, Beijing 100600; tel. (10) 65322504; fax (10) 65322715; e-mail pak@public.bta.net.cn; Ambassador: RIAZ KHOKHAR.

Papua New Guinea: 2-11-2 Tayuan Diplomatic Office Bldg, Beijing 100600; tel. (10) 65324312; fax (10) 65325483; Ambassador: BARNEY RONGAP.

Peru: 1-91 San Li Tun, Bangonglou, Beijing 100600; tel. (10) 65323477; fax (10) 65322178; e-mail embperu@public.bta.net.cn; internet www.embperu.cn.net; Ambassador: LUZMILA ZANABRIA ISHI-KAWA.

Philippines: 23 Xiu Shui Bei Jie, Jian Guo Men Wai, Beijing 100600; tel. (10) 65321872; fax (10) 65323761; Ambassador: ROMUALDO A. ONG.

Poland: 1 Ri Tan Lu, Jian Guo Men Wai, Beijing 100600; tel. (10) 65321235; fax (10) 65321745; Ambassador: KSAWERY BURSKI.

Portugal: 8 San Li Tun Dong Wu Jie, Beijing 100600; tel. (10) 65323497; fax (10) 65324637; Ambassador: PEDRO CATARINO.

Qatar: 2-9-2 Tayuan Diplomatic Office Bldg, 14 Liang Ma He Nan Lu, Beijing 100600; tel. (10) 65322231; fax (10) 65325274; Ambassador: SALEH ABDULLA AL-BOUANIN.

Romania: Ri Tan Lu, Dong Er Jie, Beijing 100600; tel. (10) 65323442; fax (10) 65325728; e-mail roamb@ht.rol.cn.net; Ambassador: IOAN DONCA.

Russia: 4 Dong Zhi Men Nei, Bei Zhong Jie, Beijing 100600; tel. (10) 65321291; fax (10) 65324853; e-mail rusemb@public3.bta.net.cn; Ambassador: IGOR ROGACHEV.

Rwanda: 30 Xiu Shui Bei Jie, Jian Guo Men Wai, Beijing 100600; tel. (10) 65322193; fax (10) 65322006; Ambassador: VALENS MUNYABAGISHA.

Saudi Arabia: 1 Bei Xiao Jie, San Li Tun, Beijing 100600; tel. (10) 65324825; fax (10) 65325324; Ambassador: Mr YUSEF.

Sierra Leone: 7 Dong Zhi Men Wai Dajie, Beijing 100600; tel. (10) 65321222; fax (10) 65323752; Ambassador: ALHUSIN DEEN.

Singapore: 1 Xiu Shui Bei Jie, Jian Guo Men Wai, Beijing 100600; tel. (10) 65323926; fax (10) 65322215; Ambassador: CHIN SIAT YOON.

Slovakia: Ri Tan Lu, Jian Guo Men Wai, Beijing 100600; tel. (10) 65321531; fax (10) 65324814; Ambassador: PETER PAULEN.

Slovenia: Block F, 57 Ya Qu Yuan, King's Garden Villas, 18 Xiao Yun Lu, Chaoyang Qu, Beijing 100016; tel. (10) 64681030; fax (10) 64681040; Ambassador: VLADIMIR GASPARIČ.

Somalia: 2 San Li Tun Lu, Beijing 100600; tel. (10) 65321752; Ambassador: MOHAMED HASSAN SAID.

South Africa: 5 Dongzhimen Wai Dajie, Chaoyang Qu, Beijing 100016; tel. (10) 65320175; fax (10) 65320177; e-mail safrican@homeway.com.cn; Ambassador: CHRISTOPHER DLAMINI.

Spain: 9 San Li Tun Lu, Beijing 100600; tel. (10) 65321986; fax (10) 65323401; Ambassador: EUGENIO BREGOLAT.

Sri Lanka: 3 Jian Hua Lu, Jian Guo Men Wai, Beijing 100600; tel. (10) 65321861; fax (10) 65325426; e-mail lkembj@public.east.cn.net; Ambassador: B. A. B. GOONETILLEKE.

Sudan: Bldg 27, San Li Tun, Beijing 100600; tel. (10) 65323715; fax (10) 65321280; e-mail mission.sudan@itu.cn; Ambassador: ABDEL-HAMEED ABDEEN MOHAMMED.

Sweden: 3 Dong Zhi Men Wai Dajie, San Li Tun, Beijing 100600; tel. (10) 65323331; fax (10) 65325008; Ambassador: KJELL ANNELING.

Switzerland: 3 Dong Wu Jie, San Li Tun, Beijing 100600; tel. (10) 65322736; fax (10) 65324353; Ambassador: DOMINIQUE DREYER.

Syria: 6 Dong Si Jie, San Li Tun, Beijing 100600; tel. (10) 65321563; fax (10) 65321575; Ambassador: LOUTOF ALLAH HAYDAR.

Tanzania: 8 Liang Ma He Nan Lu, San Li Tun, Beijing 100600; tel. (10) 65321408; fax (10) 65324985; Ambassador: CHARLES ASILIA SANGA.

Thailand: 40 Guang Hua Lu, Jian Guo Men Wai, Beijing 100600; tel. (10) 65321903; fax (10) 65321748; Ambassador: NIKHOM TANTEMSAPYA.

Togo: 11 Dong Zhi Men Wai Dajie, Beijing 100600; tel. (10) 65322202; Ambassador: NOLANA TA-AMA.

Tunisia: 1 Dong Jie, San Li Tun, Beijing 100600; tel. (10) 65322435; fax (10) 65325818; e-mail ambtun@public.netchina.com.cn; Ambassador: MOHAMED MONGI LAHBIB.

Turkey: 9 Dong Wu Jie, San Li Tun, Beijing 100600; tel. (10) 65322490; fax (10) 65325480; e-mail trkelcn@public.bta.net.cn; Ambassador: RAFET AKGUNAY.

Turkmenistan: 5-2-131/5-2-132 Tayuan Diplomatic Compound, Beijing 100600; tel. (10) 65326975; fax (10) 65326976; Ambassador: AMANGELDY RAKHMANOV.

Uganda: 5 Dong Jie, San Li Tun, Beijing 100600; tel. (10) 65322370; fax (10) 65322242; e-mail ugembssy@public.bta.net.cn; internet www.uganda.cn777.com.cn; Ambassador: PHILIP IDRO.

Ukraine: 11 Dong Liu Jie, San Li Tun, Beijing 100600; tel. (10) 65324014; fax (10) 65326765; e-mail ukrembcn@public3.bta.net.cn; internet www.ukrembcn.gov; Ambassador: IHOR LYTVYN.

United Arab Emirates: 1-9-1 Tayuan Diplomatic Office Bldg, Beijing 100600; tel. (10) 65322112; fax (10) 65325089; Ambassador: JUMA RASHED JASSIM.

United Kingdom: 11 Guang Hua Lu, Jian Guo Men Wai, Beijing 100600; tel. (10) 65321961; fax (10) 65321937; internet www.britishembassy.org.cn; Ambassador: Sir ANTHONY GALSWORTHY.

USA: 3 Xiu Shui Bei Jie, Beijing 100600; tel. (10) 65323831; fax (10) 65323178; internet www.usembassy-china.org.cn; Ambassador: Adm. JOSEPH PRUEHER.

Uruguay: 2-7-2 Tayuan Diplomatic Office Bldg, Beijing 100600; tel. (10) 65324445; fax (10) 65324357; e-mail urubei@public.bta.net.cn; Ambassador: ALVARO ALVAREZ.

Uzbekistan: 11 Bei Xiao Jie, San Li Tun, Beijing 100600; tel. (10) 65326305; fax (10) 65326304; Ambassador: IZMATILLA R. IRGASHEV.

Venezuela: 14 San Li Tun Lu, Beijing 100600; tel. (10) 65321295; fax (10) 65323817; e-mail embvenez@public.bta.net.cn; Ambassador: JOCELYN HENRÍQUEZ.

Viet Nam: 32 Guang Hua Lu, Jian Guo Men Wai, Beijing 100600; tel. (10) 65321155; fax (10) 65325720; Ambassador: BUI HONG PHUC.

Yemen: 5 Dong San Jie, San Li Tun, Beijing 100600; tel. (10) 65321558; fax (10) 65324305; Ambassador: MOHAMMED HADI AWAD.

Yugoslavia: 1 Dong Liu Jie, San Li Tun, Beijing 100600; tel. (10) 65323516; fax (10) 65321207; Ambassador: Dr SLOBODAN UNKOVIĆ.

Zambia: 5 Dong Si Jie, San Li Tun, Beijing 100600; tel. (10) 65321554; fax (10) 65321891; Ambassador: MWENYA LWATULA.

Zimbabwe: 7 Dong San Jie, San Li Tun, Beijing 100600; tel. (10) 65323795; fax (10) 65325383; Ambassador: LUCAS PANDE TAVAYA.

Judicial System

The general principles of the Chinese judicial system are laid down in Articles 123–135 of the December 1982 Constitution (q.v.).

PEOPLE'S COURTS

Supreme People's Court: 27 Dongjiaomin Xiang, Beijing 100745; tel. (10) 65136195; f. 1949; the highest judicial organ of the State; handles first instance cases of national importance; handles cases of appeals and protests lodged against judgments and orders of higher people's courts and special people's courts, and cases of protests lodged by the Supreme People's Procuratorate in accordance with the procedures of judicial supervision; reviews death sentences meted out by local courts, supervises the administration of justice by local people's courts; interprets issues concerning specific applications of laws in judicial proceedings; its judgments and rulings are final; Pres. XIAO YANG (five-year term of office coincides with that of National People's Congress, by which the President is elected).

Local People's Courts: comprise higher courts, intermediate courts and basic courts.

Special People's Courts: include military courts, maritime courts and railway transport courts.

PEOPLE'S PROCURATORATES

Supreme People's Procuratorate: 147 Beiheyan Dajie, Beijing 100726; tel. (10) 65126655; acts for the National People's Congress in examining govt depts, civil servants and citizens, to ensure observance of the law; prosecutes in criminal cases. Procurator-Gen. HAN ZHUBIN (elected by the National People's Congress for five years).

Local People's Procuratorates: undertake the same duties at the local level. Ensure that the judicial activities of the people's courts, the execution of sentences in criminal cases and the activities of departments in charge of reform through labour conform to the law; institute, or intervene in, important civil cases which affect the interest of the State and the people.

Religion

During the 'Cultural Revolution' places of worship were closed. After 1977 the Government adopted a policy of religious tolerance, and the 1982 Constitution states that citizens enjoy freedom of religious belief and that legitimate religious activities are protected. Many temples, churches and mosques subsequently reopened. Since 1994 all religious organizations have been required to register with the Bureau of Religious Affairs.

Bureau of Religious Affairs: Beijing; tel. (10) 652625; Dir YE XIAOWEN.

ANCESTOR WORSHIP

Ancestor worship is believed to have originated with the deification and worship of all important natural phenomena. The divine and human were not clearly defined; all the dead became gods and were worshipped by their descendants. The practice has no code or dogma and the ritual is limited to sacrifices made during festivals and on birth and death anniversaries.

BUDDHISM

Buddhism was introduced into China from India in AD 67, and flourished during the Sui and Tang dynasties (6th–8th century), when eight sects were established. The Chan and Pure Land sects are the most popular. According to official sources, in 1998 there were 9,500 Buddhist temples in China. There were 100m. believers in 1997.

Buddhist Association of China (BAC): f. 1953; Pres. ZHAO PUCHU; Sec.-Gen. DAO SHUREN.

Tibetan Institute of Lamaism: Pres. BUMI JANGBALUOZHU; Vice-Pres. CEMOLIN DANZENGCHILIE.

14th Dalai Lama: His Holiness the Dalai Lama TENZIN GYATSO, Thekchen Choeling, McLeod Ganj, Dharamsala 176 219, Himachal Pradesh, India; tel. (91) 1892-21343; fax (91) 1892-21813; e-mail ohhdl@cta.unv.ernet.ind; spiritual and temporal leader of Tibet; fled to India after failure of Tibetan national uprising in 1959.

CHRISTIANITY

During the 19th century and the first half of the 20th century large numbers of foreign Christian missionaries worked in China. According to official sources, there were 10m. Protestants and more than 4m. Catholics in China in 2000, although unofficial sources estimate that the Christian total could be as high as 90m. The Catholic Church in China operates independently of the Vatican.

Three-Self Patriotic Movement Committee of Protestant Churches of China: Chair. LUO GUANZONG; Sec.-Gen. DENG FUCUN.

China Christian Council: 169 Yuan Ming Yuan Lu, Shanghai 200002; tel. (21) 63210806; fax (21) 63232605; e-mail ban9sb@online.sh.cn; f. 1980; comprises provincial Christian councils; Pres. Dr HAN WENZAO; Sec.-Gen. Rev. SU DECI.

The Roman Catholic Church: Catholic Mission, Si-She-Ku, Beijing; Bishop of Beijing MICHAEL FU TIESHAN (not recognized by the Vatican).

Chinese Patriotic Catholic Association: Chair. MICHAEL FU TIESHAN; Sec.-Gen. LIU BAINIAN; c. 3m. mems (1988).

CONFUCIANISM

Confucianism is a philosophy and a system of ethics, without ritual or priesthood. The respects that adherents accord to Confucius are not bestowed on a prophet or god, but on a great sage whose teachings promote peace and good order in society and whose philosophy encourages moral living.

DAOISM

Daoism was founded by Zhang Daoling during the Eastern Han dynasty (AD 125–144). Lao Zi, a philosopher of the Zhou dynasty (born 604 BC), is its principal inspiration, and is honoured as Lord the Most High by Daoists. According to official sources, there were 600 Daoist temples in China in 1998.

China Daoist Association: Temple of the White Cloud, Xi Bian Men, Beijing 100045; tel. (10) 6367179; f. 1957; Pres. (vacant); Sec.-Gen. LI WENCHENG.

ISLAM

According to Muslim history, Islam was introduced into China in AD 651. There were some 18m. adherents in China in 1997, chiefly among the Wei Wuer (Uygur) and Hui people.

Beijing Islamic Association: Dongsi Mosque, Beijing; f. 1979; Chair. Imam Al-Hadji SALAH AN SHIWEI.

China Islamic Association: Beijing 100053; tel. (10) 63546384; fax (10) 63529483; f. 1953; Chair. Imam Al-Hadji SALAH AN SHIWEI; Sec.-Gen. WAN YAOBIN.

The Press

In December 1999 China had 2,038 newspaper titles (including those below provincial level) and 8,187 periodicals. Each province publishes its own daily. Only the major newspapers and periodicals are listed below. In late 1999 the Government announced its intention to merge or close down a number of newspapers, leaving a single publication in each province.

PRINCIPAL NEWSPAPERS

Anhui Ribao (Anhui Daily): 206 Jinzhai Lu, Hefei, Anhui 230061; tel. (551) 2827842; fax (551) 2847302; Editor-in-Chief QIAN YUSUI.

Beijing Ribao (Beijing Daily): 34 Xi Biaobei Hutong, Dongdan, Beijing 100743; tel. (10) 65131071; fax (10) 65136522; f. 1952; organ

of the Beijing municipal cttee of the CCP; Dir WAN YUNLAI; Editor-in-Chief LIU ZONGMING; circ. 700,000.

Beijing Wanbao (Beijing Evening News): 34 Xi Biaobei Hutong, Dongdan, Beijing 100743; tel. (10) 65132233; fax (10) 65126581; f. 1958; Editor LI BINGREN; circ. 800,000.

Beijing Youth Daily: Beijing; national and local news; promotes ethics and social service; circ. 3m.–4m.

Changsha Wanbao (Changsha Evening News): 161 Caie Zhong Lu, Changsha, Hunan 410005; tel. (731) 4424457; fax (731) 4445167.

Chengdu Wanbao (Chengdu Evening News): Qingyun Nan Jie, Chengdu 610017; tel. (28) 664501; fax (28) 666597; circ. 700,000.

China Business Times: Beijing; f. 1989; Editor HUANG WENFU; circ. 500,000.

Chungcheng Wanbao (Chungcheng Evening News): 51 Xinwen Lu, Kunming, Yunnan 650032; tel. (871) 4144642; fax (871) 4154192.

Dazhong Ribao (Dazhong Daily): 46 Jinshi Lu, Jinan, Shandong 250014; tel. (531) 2968989; fax (531) 2962450; internet www.dzdaily.com.cn; f. 1939; Dir XU XIYU; Editor-in-Chief LIU GUANGDONG; circ. 2,100,000.

Economic News: Editor-in-Chief DU ZULIANG.

Fujian Ribao (Fujian Daily): Hualin Lu, Fuzhou, Fujian; tel. (591) 57756; daily; Dir HUANG SHIYUN; Editor-in-Chief HUANG ZHONGSHENG.

Gongren Ribao (Workers' Daily): Liupukang, Andingmen Wai, Beijing 100718; tel. (10) 64211561; fax (10) 64214890; f. 1949; trade union activities and workers' lives; also major home and overseas news; Dir LIU YUMING; Editor-in-Chief SHENG MINGFU; circ. 2.5m.

Guangming Ribao (Guangming Daily): 106 Yongan Lu, Beijing 100050; tel. (10) 63017788; fax (10) 63039387; f. 1949; literature, art, science, education, history, economics, philosophy; Editor-in-Chief YUAN ZHIFA; circ. 920,000.

Guangxi Ribao (Guangxi Daily): Guangxi Region; Dir and Editor-in-Chief LI MINGDE.

Guangzhou Ribao (Canton Daily): 10 Dongle Lu, Renmin Zhonglu, Guangzhou, Guangdong; tel. (20) 81887294; fax (20) 81862022; f. 1952; daily; social, economic and current affairs; Editor-in-Chief LI YUANJIANG; circ. 600,000.

Guizhou Ribao (Guizhou Daily): Guiyang, Guizhou; tel. (851) 627779; f. 1949; Dir and Editor-in-Chief GAO ZONGWEN; circ. 300,000.

Hainan Ribao (Hainan Daily): 7 Xinhua Nan Lu, Haikou, Hainan 570001; tel. (898) 6222021; Editor-in-Chief ZUO AIGUO.

Hebei Ribao (Hebei Daily): 210 Yuhuazhong Lu, Shijiazhuang, Hebei 050013; tel. (311) 6048901; fax (311) 6046969; f. 1949; Dir PAN GUILIANG; Editor-in-Chief YE ZHEN; circ. 500,000.

Heilongjiang Ribao (Heilongjiang Daily): Heilongjiang Province; Editor-in-Chief JIA SHIXIANG.

Henan Ribao (Henan Daily): 1 Weiyi Lu, Zhengzhou, Henan; tel. (371) 5958319; fax (371) 5955636; f. 1949; Editor-in-Chief GUO ZHENGLING; circ. 390,000.

Huadong Xinwen (Eastern China News): f. 1995; published by Renmin Ribao.

Huanan Xinwen (South China News): Guangzhou; f. 1997; published by Renmin Ribao.

Hubei Ribao (Hubei Daily): 65 Huangli Lu, Wuhan, Hubei 430077; tel. (27) 6833522; fax (27) 6813989; f. 1949; Dir ZHOU NIANFENG; Editor-in-Chief SONG HANYAN; circ. 800,000.

Hunan Ribao (Hunan Daily): 18 Furong Zhong Lu, Changsha, Hunan 410071; tel. (731) 4312999; fax (731) 4314029; Dir and Editor-in-Chief JIANG XIANLI.

Jiangxi Ribao (Jiangxi Daily): 175 Yangming Jie, Nanchang, Jiangxi; tel. (791) 6849888; fax (791) 6772590; f. 1949; Dir ZHOU JINGUANG; Editor-in-Chief DUAN FURUI; circ. 300,000.

Jiefang Ribao (Liberation Daily): 300 Han Kou Lu, Shanghai 200001; tel. (21) 63521111; fax (21) 63516517; f. 1949; Editor-in-Chief JIA SHUMEI; circ. 1m.

Jiefangjun Bao (Liberation Army Daily): Beijing; f. 1956; official organ of the Central Military Comm.; Dir Maj.-Gen. SUN ZHONGTONG; Editor-in-Chief YU SHUNCHANG; circ. 800,000.

Jilin Ribao (Jilin Daily): Jilin Province; Dir and Editor-in-Chief YI HONGBIN.

Jingji Ribao (Economic Daily): 2 Bai Zhi Fang Dong Jie, Beijing 100054; tel. (10) 63559988; fax (10) 63539408; f. 1983; financial affairs, domestic and foreign trade; administered by the State Council; Editor-in-Chief WU CHUNHE; circ. 1.2m.

Jinrong Shibao (Financial News): 44 Taipingqiao Fengtaiqu, Beijing 100073; tel. (10) 63269233; fax (10) 68424931.

Liaoning Ribao (Liaoning Daily): Liaoning Province; Dir ZHU SHILIANG; Editor-in-Chief XIE ZHENGQIAN.

Nanfang Ribao (Nanfang Daily): 289 Guangzhou Da Lu, Guangzhou, Guangdong 510601; tel. (20) 87373998; fax (20) 87375203; f. 1949; Dir LI MENGYU; Editor-in-Chief FAN YIJIN; circ. 1m.

Nanjing Ribao (Nanjing Daily): 53 Jiefang Lu, Nanjing, Jiangsu 210016; tel. (25) 4496564; fax (25) 4496544.

Nongmin Ribao (Peasants' Daily): Shilipu Beili, Chao Yang Qu, Beijing 100025; tel. (10) 65005522; fax (10) 65071154; f. 1980; 6 a week; circulates in rural areas nation-wide; Dir and Editor-in-Chief ZHANG DEXIU; circ. 1m.

Renmin Ribao (People's Daily): 2 Jin Tai Xi Lu, Chao Yang Men Wai, Beijing 100733; tel. (10) 65092121; fax (10) 65091982; f. 1948; organ of the CCP; also publishes overseas edn; Dir SHAO HUAZE; Editor-in-Chief XU ZHONGTIAN; circ. 2.15m.

Shaanxi Ribao (Shaanxi Daily): Shaanxi Province; Dir YIN WEIZU; Editor-in-Chief DU YAOFENG.

Shanxi Ribao (Shanxi Daily): 24 Shuangtasi Jie, Taiyuan, Shanxi; tel. (351) 446561; fax (351) 441771; Dir ZHAO WENBIN; Editor-in-Chief LI DONGXI; circ. 300,000.

Shenzhen Commercial Press: Shenzhen; Editor-in-Chief GAO XINGLIE.

Shenzhen Tequ Bao (Shenzhen Special Economic Zone Daily): 4 Shennan Zhonglu, Shenzhen 518009; tel. (755) 3902688; fax (755) 3906900; f. 1982; reports on special economic zones, as well as mainland, Hong Kong and Macau; Pres. and Editor-in-Chief WU SONGYING.

Sichuan Ribao (Sichuan Daily): 70 Hongxing Zhong Lu, Erduan, Chengdu, Sichuan 610012; tel. (28) 6758900; fax (28) 6745035; internet www.sichuandaily.com.cn; f. 1952; Dir LI ZHIXIA; Editor-in-Chief TANG XIAOQIANG; circ. 8m.

Tianjin Ribao (Tianjin Daily): 873 Dagu Nan Lu, Heri Qu, Tianjin 300211; tel. (22) 7301024; fax (22) 7305803; f. 1949; Dir and Editor-in-Chief QIU YUNSHENG; circ. 600,000.

Wenhui Bao (Wenhui Daily): 50 Huqiu Lu, Shanghai 200002; tel. (21) 63211410; fax (21) 63230198; f. 1938; Editor-in-Chief SHI JUNSHENG; circ. 500,000m.

Xin Min Wan Bao (Xin Min Evening News): 839 Yan An Zhong Lu, Shanghai 200040; tel. (21) 62791234; fax (21) 62473220; f. 1929; specializes in public policy, education and social affairs; Editor-in-Chief JIN FUAN; circ. 1.8m.

Xinhua Ribao (New China Daily): 55 Zhongshan Lu, Nanjing, Jiangsu 210005; tel. (21) 741757; fax (21) 741023; Editor-in-Chief ZHOU ZHENGRONG; circ. 900,000.

Xinjiang Ribao (Xinjiang Daily): Xinjiang Region; Dir TIAN YUMIAN; Editor-in-Chief HUANG YANCAI.

Xizang Ribao (Tibet Daily): Tibet; Editor-in-Chief LI CHANGWEN.

Yangcheng Wanbao (Yangcheng Evening News): 733 Dongfeng Dong Lu, Guangzhou, Guangdong 510085; tel. (20) 87776211; fax (20) 87765103; e-mail ycwbic@ycwb.com.cn; internet www.ycwb.com.cn; f. 1957; Pres. CAO CHUNLIANG; Editor-in-Chief PAN WEI WEN; circ. 1.3m.

Yunnan Ribao (Yunnan Daily): Yunnan Province; Editor-in-Chief SUN GUANSHENG.

Zhejiang Ribao (Zhejiang Daily): Zhejiang Province; Editor-in-Chief YANG DAJIN.

Zhongguo Qingnian Bao (China Youth News): 2 Haiyuncang, Dong Zhi Men Nei, Beijing 100702; tel. (10) 64032233; fax (10) 64033792; f. 1951; daily; aimed at 14–40 age-group; Dir XU ZHUQING; Editor-in-Chief LI XUEQIAN; circ. 1.0m.

Zhongguo Ribao (China Daily): 15 Huixin Dongjie, Chao Yang Qu, Beijing 100029; tel. (10) 64918633; fax (10) 64918377; internet www.chinadaily.com.cn; f. 1981; English; China's political, economic and cultural developments; world, financial and sports news; also publishes *Business Weekly* (f. 1985), *Beijing Weekend* (f. 1991), *Shanghai Star* (f. 1992), *Reports from China* (f. 1992), *21st Century* (f. 1993); Editor-in-Chief ZHU YINGHUANG; circ. 300,000.

Zhongguo Xinwen (China News): 12 Baiwanzhuang Nanjie, Beijing; tel. (10) 68315012; f. 1952; daily; Editor-in-Chief WANG XIJIN; current affairs.

SELECTED PERIODICALS

Ban Yue Tan (Fortnightly Review): Beijing; tel. (10) 6668521; f. 1980; in Chinese and Wei Wuer (Uygur); Editor-in-Chief WANG QIXING; circ. 6m.

Beijing Review: 24 Baiwanzhuang Lu, Beijing 100037; tel. (10) 68328115; fax (10) 68326628; e-mail bjreview@public3 .bta.net.cn; internet www.china.org.cn/beijingreview; f. 1958; weekly; edns in English, French, Spanish, Japanese and German; also **Chinafrica** (monthly in English and French); Publr and Editor-in-Chief LIN LIANGQI; Man. Editor LI HAIBO.

BJ TV Weekly: 2 Fu Xing Men Wai Zhenwumiao Jie, Beijing 100045; tel. (10) 6366036; fax (10) 63262388; circ. 1m.

China TV Weekly: 15 Huixin Dong Jie, Chao Yang Qu, Beijing 100013; tel. (10) 64214197; circ. 1.7m.

Chinese Literature Press: 24 Baiwanzhuang Lu, Beijing 100037; tel. (10) 68326010; fax (10) 68326678; e-mail chinalit@public .east.cn.net; f. 1951; monthly (bilingual in English); quarterly (bilingual in French); contemporary and classical writing, poetry, literary criticism and arts; Exec. Editor LING YUAN.

Chinese Science Abstracts: Science Press, 16 Donghuangchenggen Beijie, Beijing 100717; tel. (10) 64018833, ext. 391; fax (10) 64019810; f. 1982; monthly; in English; science and technology; Chief Editor LI RUIXU.

Dianying Xinzuo (New Films): 796 Huaihai Zhong Lu, Shanghai; tel. (21) 64379710; f. 1979; bi-monthly; introduces new films.

Dianzi yu Diannao (Electronics and Computers): Beijing; f. 1985; popularized information on computers and microcomputers.

Elle (China): 14 Lane 955, Yan'an Zhong Lu, Shanghai; tel. (21) 62790974; fax (21) 62479056; f. 1988; monthly; fashion; Pres. YANG XINCI; Chief Editor WU YING; circ. 300,000.

Family Magazine: 14 Siheng Lu, Xinhepu, Dongshan Qu, Guangzhou 510080; tel. (20) 7777718; fax (20) 7185670; monthly; circ. 2.5m.

Feitian (Fly Skywards): 50 Donggan Xilu, Lanzhou, Gansu; tel. (931) 25803; f. 1961; monthly.

Guoji Xin Jishu (New International Technology): Zhanwang Publishing House, Beijing; f. 1984; also publ. in Hong Kong; international technology, scientific and technical information.

Guowai Keji Dongtai (Recent Developments in Science and Technology Abroad): Institute of Scientific and Technical Information of China, 15 Fuxing Lu, Beijing 100038; tel. (10) 68515544, ext. 2954; fax (10) 68514027; e-mail baiyr@istic.ac.cn; internet www .chinainfo.gov.cn/periodical; f. 1962; monthly; scientific journal; Editor-in-Chief LI YANYAN; circ. 100,100.

Hai Xia (The Strait): 27 De Gui Xiang, Fuzhou, Fujian; tel. (10) 33656; f. 1981; quarterly; literary journal; CEOs YANG YU, JWO JONG LIN.

Huasheng Monthly (Voice for Overseas Chinese): 12 Bai Wan Zhuang Nan Jie, Beijing 100037; tel. (10) 68311578; fax (10) 68315039; f. 1995; monthly; intended mainly for overseas Chinese and Chinese nationals resident abroad; Editor-in-Chief FAN DONGSHENG.

Jianzhu (Construction): Baiwanzhuang, Beijing; tel. (10) 68992849; f. 1956; monthly; Editor FANG YUEGUANG; circ. 500,000.

Jinri Zhongguo (China Today): 24 Baiwanzhuang Lu, Beijing 100037; tel. (10) 68326037; fax (10) 68328338; internet www .china.org.cn; f. 1952; fmrly *China Reconstructs*; monthly; edns in English, Spanish, French, Arabic, German, Chinese and English braille; economic, social and cultural affairs; illustrated; Pres. and Editor-in-Chief HUANG ZU'AN.

Liaowang (Outlook): 57 Xuanwumen Xijie, Beijing; tel. (10) 63073049; f. 1981; weekly; current affairs; Gen. Man. ZHOU YICHANG; Editor-in-Chief JI BIN; circ. 500,000.

Luxingjia (Traveller): Beijing; tel. (10) 6552631; f. 1955; monthly; Chinese scenery, customs, culture.

Meishu Zhi You (Friends of Art): 32 Beizongbu Hutong, East City Region, Beijing; tel. (10) 65122583. 1982; every 2 months; art review journal, also providing information on fine arts publs in China and abroad; Editors PENG SHEN, BAOLUN WU.

Nianqingren (Young People): 169 Mayuanlin, Changsha, Hunan; tel. (731) 23610; f. 1981; monthly; general interest for young people.

Nongye Zhishi (Agricultural Knowledge): 21 Ming Zi Qian Lu, Jinan, Shandong 250100; tel. (531) 8932238; e-mail sdnyzs@ jn-public.sd.cninfo.net; internet www.sdny.com.cn; f. 1950; fortnightly; popular agricultural science; Dir YANG LIJIAN; circ. 410,000.

Qiushi (Seeking Truth): 2 Shatan Beijie, Beijing 100727; tel. (10) 64037005; fax (10) 64018174; f. 1988 to succeed *Hong Qi* (Red Flag); 2 a month; theoretical journal of the CCP; Editor-in-Chief DAI ZHOU; circ. 1.83m.

Renmin Huabao (China Pictorial): Huayuancun, West Suburbs, Beijing 100044; tel. (10) 68411144; fax (10) 68413023; f. 1950; monthly; edns: 2 in Chinese, 1 in Tibetan and 12 in foreign languages; Dir and Editor-in-Chief ZHANG JIAHUA.

Shichang Zhoubao (Market Weekly): 2 Duan, Sanhao Jie, Heping Qu, Shenyang, Liaoning; tel. (24) 482983; f. 1979; weekly in Chinese; trade, commodities, and financial and economic affairs; circ. 1m.

Shufa (Calligraphy): 81 Qingzhou Nan Lu, Shanghai 200233; tel. (21) 64519008; fax (21) 64519015; f. 1977; every 2 months; journal on ancient and modern calligraphy; Chief Editor LU FUSHENG.

Tiyu Kexue (Sports Science): 8 Tiyuguan Lu, Beijing 100763; tel. (10) 67112233. 1981; sponsored by the China Sports Science Soc.; every 2 months; summary in English; Chief Officer YUAN WEIMIN; in Chinese; circ. 20,000.

Wenxue Qingnian (Youth Literature Journal): 27 Mu Tse Fang, Wenzhou, Zhejiang; tel. (577) 3578; f. 1981; monthly; Editor-in-Chief CHEN YUSHEN; circ. 80,000.

Xian Dai Faxue (Modern Law Science): Chongqing, Sichuan 630031; tel. (811) 961671; f. 1979; bi-monthly; with summaries in English; Dirs Xu JINGCUN, XIE XOUPING.

Yinyue Aihaozhe (Music Lovers): 74 Shaoxing Lu, Shanghai 200020; tel. (21) 64372608; fax (21) 64332019; f. 1979; every 2 months; music knowledge; illustrated; Editor-in-Chief CHEN XUEYA; circ. 50,000.

Zhongguo Duiwai Maoyi Ming Lu (Directory of China's Foreign Trade): CCPIT Bldg, 1 Fuxingmen Wai Da Jie, Beijing 100860; tel. (10) 68022948; fax (10) 68510201; e-mail inform@press-media.com; f. 1974; monthly; edns in Chinese and English; information on Chinese imports and exports, foreign trade and economic policies; Editor-in-Chief YANG HAIQING.

Zhongguo Ertong (Chinese Children): 21 Xiang 12, Dongsi, Beijing; tel. (10) 6444761. 1980; monthly; illustrated journal for elementary school pupils.

Zhongguo Funu (Women of China): 15 Jian Guo Men Dajie, Beijing 100730; tel. (10) 65134616; fax (10) 65225380; f. 1956; monthly; in English; administered by All-China Women's Federation; women's rights and status, marriage and family, education, family planning, arts, cookery, etc.; Editor-in-Chief Ms WANG XIULIN.

Zhongguo Guangbo Dianshi (China Radio and Television): 12 Fucheng Lu, Beijing; tel. (10) 6896217; f. 1982; monthly; reports and comments.

Zhongguo Jin Rong Xin Xi: Beijing; f. 1991; monthly; economic news.

Zhongguo Sheying (Chinese Photography): 61 Hongxing Hutong, Dongdan, Beijing 100005; tel. (10) 65252277; fax (10) 65253197; e-mail cphoto@public.bta.net.cn; internet www.cphoto.com.cn; f. 1957; monthly; photographs and comments; Editor LIU BANG.

Zhongguo Zhenjiu (Chinese Acupuncture and Moxibustion): China Academy of Traditional Chinese Medicine, Dongzhimen Nei, Beijing 100700; tel. (10) 84014607; fax (10) 64013968; e-mail weihongliu@263.net; f. 1981; monthly; publ. by Chinese Soc. of Acupuncture and Moxibustion; abstract in English; Editor-in-Chief Prof. DENG LIANGYUE.

Zijing (Bauhinia): Pres. and Editor-in-Chief CHEN HONG.

Other popular magazines include **Gongchandang Yuan** (Communists, circ. 1.63m.) and **Nongmin Wenzhai** (Peasants' Digest, circ. 3.54m.).

NEWS AGENCIES

Xinhua (New China) News Agency: 57 Xuanwumen Xidajie, Beijing 100803; tel. (10) 63071114; fax (10) 63071210; internet www.xinhuanet.com; f. 1931; offices in all Chinese provincial capitals, and about 100 overseas bureaux; news service in Chinese, English, French, Spanish, Portuguese, Arabic and Russian, feature and photographic services; Pres. TIAN CONGMING; Editor-in-Chief NAN ZHENZHONG.

Zhongguo Xinwen She (China News Agency): POB 1114, Beijing; f. 1952; office in Hong Kong; supplies news features, special articles and photographs for newspapers and magazines in Chinese printed overseas; services in Chinese; Dir WANG SHIGU.

Foreign Bureaux

Agence France-Presse (AFP) (France): 11-11 Jian Guo Men Wai, Diplomatic Apts, Beijing 100600; tel. (10) 65321409; fax (10) 65322371; e-mail afppek@afp.com; Bureau Chief ELIZABETH ZINGO.

Agencia EFE (Spain): 2-2-132 Jian Guo Men Wai, Beijing 100600; tel. (10) 65323449; fax (10) 65323688; Rep. CARLOS REDONDO.

Agenzia Nazionale Stampa Associata (ANSA) (Italy): 1-11 Ban Gong Lu, San Li Tun, Beijing 100600; tel. (10) 65323651; fax (10) 65321954; e-mail barbara@public3.bta.net.cn; Bureau Chief BARBARA ALIGHIERO.

Allgemeiner Deutscher Nachrichtendienst (ADN) (Germany): 7-2-61, Jian Guo Men Wai, Qi Jia Yuan Gong Yu, Beijing 100600; tel. and fax (10) 65321115; Correspondent Dr LUTZ POHLE.

Associated Press (AP) (USA): 6-2-22 Jian Guo Men Wai, Diplomatic Quarters, Beijing 100600; tel. (10) 65326650; fax (10) 65323419; Bureau Chief ELAINE KURTENBACH.

Deutsche Presse-Agentur (dpa) (Germany): Ban Gong Lou, Apt 1-31, San Li Tun, Beijing 100600; tel. (10) 65321473; fax (10) 65321615; e-mail dpa@public3.bta.net.cn; Bureau Chief ANDREAS LANDWEHR.

Informatsionnoye Telegrafnoye Agentstvo Rossii—Telegrafnoye Agentstvo Suverennykh Stran (ITAR—TASS) (Russia): 6-1-41 Tayuan Diplomatic Office Bldg, Beijing 100600; tel. (10) 65324821; fax (10) 65324820; Bureau Chief GRIGORII KURBANOVICH ARSLANOV.

Inter Press Service (TIPS) (Italy): 15 Fuxing Lu, POB 3811, Beijing 100038; tel. (10) 68514046; fax (10) 68518210; e-mail tipscn@istic.ac.cn; internet www.tips.org.cn; Dir WANG XIAOYING.

Jiji Tsushin (Japan): 9-1-13 Jian Guo Men Wai, Waijiao, Beijing; tel. (10) 65322924; fax (10) 65323413; Correspondents YOSHIHISA MURAYAMA, TETSUYA NISHIMURA.

Korean Central News Agency (Democratic People's Republic of Korea): Beijing; Bureau Chief SONG YONG SONG.

Kyodo News Service (Japan): 3-91 Jian Guo Men Wai, Beijing; tel. (10) 6532680; fax (10) 65322273; e-mail kyodob@ccnet.cn.net; Bureau Chief YASUHIRO MORI.

Magyar Táviroti Iroda (MTI) (Hungary): 1-42 Ban Gong Lu, San Li Tun, Beijing 100600; tel. (10) 65321744; Correspondent GYÖRGY BARTA.

Prensa Latina (Cuba): 4-1-23 Jianguomenwai, Beijing 100600; tel. and fax (10) 65321914; e-mail prelatin@public.bta.net.cn; Correspondent ILSA RODRÍGUEZ SANTANA.

Press Trust of India: 5-131 Diplomatic Apts, Jian Guo Men Wai, Beijing 100600; tel. and fax (10) 65322221.

Reuters (UK): Hilton Beijing, 1 Dong Fang Lu/Bei Dong Sanhuan Lu, Chaoyang Qu, Beijing; tel. (10) 64662288; fax (10) 64653052; e-mail hilton@hiltonbeijing.com.cn; internet www.hilton.com; Bureau Man. RICHARD PASCOE.

Tanjug News Agency (Yugoslavia): Qijayuan Diplomatic Apt, Beijing 100600; tel. (10) 65324821.

United Press International (UPI) (USA): 7-1-11 Qi Jia Yuan, Beijing; tel. (10) 65323271; Bureau Chief CHRISTIAAN VIRANT.

The following are also represented: Rompres (Romania) and VNA (Viet Nam).

PRESS ORGANIZATIONS

All China Journalists' Association: Xijiaominxiang, Beijing 100031; tel. (10) 66023981; fax (10) 66014658; Exec. Chair. WU LENGXI.

China Newspapers Association: Beijing; Chair. XU ZHONGTIAN.

The Press and Publication Administration of the People's Republic of China: 85 Dongsi Nan Dajie, East District, Beijing 100703; tel. (10) 65124433; fax (10) 65127875; Dir YU YOUXIAN.

Publishers

In 1999 there were 530 publishing houses in China. A total of 141,831 titles (and 7,316.3m. copies) were published in that year.

Beijing Chubanshe (Beijing Publishing House): 6 Bei Sanhuan Zhong Lu, Beijing 100011; tel. (10) 62016699; fax (10) 62012339; e-mail geo@bph.com.cn; f. 1956; politics, history, law, economics, geography, science, literature, art, etc.; Dir ZHU SHUXIN; Editor-in-Chief TAO XINCHENG.

Beijing Daxue Chubanshe (Beijing University Publishing House): Beijing University, Haidian Qu, Beijing 100871; tel. (10) 62502024; fax (10) 62556201; f. 1979; academic and general.

China International Book Trading Corpn: POB 399, 35 Chegongzhuang Xilu, Beijing 100044; tel. (10) 68412255; fax (10) 68412023; e-mail cibtc@www.cibtc.co.cn; internet www.cibtc.com.cn; f. 1949; foreign trade org. specializing in publs, including books, periodicals, art and crafts, microfilms, etc.; import and export distributors; Pres. LIU ZHIBIN.

CITIC Publishing House: Capital Mansion, 9/F, 6 Xinyuannan Lu, Chaoyang Qu, Beijing 100004; tel. (10) 64661093; fax (10) 64661098; e-mail citicph@mx.cei.gov.cn; internet www.citicpublish.com.cn; f. 1988; finance, investment, economics and business; Pres. LUO WEIYAO.

Dianzi Gongye Chubanshe (Publishing House of the Electronics Industry—PHEI): POB 173, Wan Shou Lu, Beijing 100036; tel. (10) 68159028; fax (10) 68159025; f. 1982; electronic sciences and technology; Pres. LIANG XIANGFENG; Vice-Pres. WANG MINGJUN.

Dolphin Books: 24 Baiwanzhuang Lu, Beijing 100037; tel. (10) 68326332; fax (10) 68326642; f. 1986; children's books in Chinese and foreign languages; Dir WANG YANRONG.

Falü Chubanshe (Law Publishing House): POB 111, Beijing 100036; tel. (10) 6815325; f. 1980; current laws and decrees, legal textbooks, translations of important foreign legal works; Dir LAN MINGLIANG.

Foreign Languages Press: 19 Chegongzhuang Xi Lu, Fu Xing Men Wai, Beijing 100044; tel. (10) 68413344; fax (10) 68424931; e-mail info@flp.com.cn; internet www.flp.com.cn; f. 1952; books in 20 foreign languages reflecting political and economic developments in People's Republic of China and features of Chinese culture; Dir GUO JIEXIN; Editor-in-Chief XU MINGQIANG.

Gaodeng Jiaoyu Chubanshe (Higher Education Press): 55 Shatan Houjie, Beijing 100009; tel. (10) 64014043; fax (10) 64054602; e-mail linm@public.bta.net.cn; internet www.hep.edu.cn; f. 1954; academic, textbooks; Pres. YU GUOHUA; Editor-in-Chief ZHANG ZENGSHUN.

Gongren Chubanshe (Workers' Publishing House): Liupukeng, Andingmen Wai, Beijing; tel. (10) 64215278; f. 1949; labour movement, trade unions, science and technology related to industrial production.

Guangdong Keji Chubanshe (Guangdong Science and Technology Press): 11 Shuiyin Lu, Huanshidong Lu, Guangzhou, Guangdong 510075; tel. (20) 87768688; fax (20) 87769412; f. 1978; natural sciences, technology, agriculture, medicine, computing, English language teaching; Dir OUYANG LIAN.

Heilongjiang Kexue Jishu Chubanshe (Heilongjiang Science and Technology Press): 41 Jianshe Jie, Nangang Qu, Harbin 150001, Heilongjiang; tel. and fax (451) 3642127; f. 1979; industrial and agricultural technology, natural sciences, economics and management, popular science, children's and general.

Huashan Wenyi Chubanshe (Huashan Literature and Art Publishing House): 45 Bei Malu, Shijiazhuang, Hebei; tel. 22501; f. 1982; novels, poetry, drama, etc.

Kexue Chubanshe (Science Press): 16 Donghuangchenggen Beijie, Beijing 100717; tel. (10) 64034205; fax (10) 64010642; f. 1954; books and journals on science and technology; Dir of Int. Sales & Marketing ZHAO SHIXIONG.

Lingnan Meishu Chubanshe (Lingnan Art Publishing House): 11 Shuiyin Lu, Guangzhou, Guangdong 510075; tel. (20) 87771044; fax (20) 87771049; f. 1981; works on classical and modern painting, picture albums, photographic, painting techniques; Pres. CAO LIXIANG.

Minzu Chubanshe (Nationalities Publishing House): 14 Hepingli Beijie, Beijing 100013; tel. (10) 64211261; f. 1953; books and periodicals in minority languages, e.g. Mongolian, Tibetan, Uygur, Korean, Kazakh, etc.; Editor-in-Chief ZHU YINGWU.

Qunzhong Chubanshe (Masses Publishing House): Bldg 15, Part 3, Fangxingyuan, Fangzhuan Lu, Beijing 100078; tel. (10) 67633344; f. 1956; politics, law, judicial affairs, criminology, public security, etc.

Renmin Chubanshe (People's Publishing House): 8 Hepinglidongjie, Andingmenwai, Beijing; tel. (10) 4213713; managed by the Ministry of Communications; science and technology, textbooks, laws and specifications of communications; Dir and Editor-in-Chief XUE DEZHEN.

Renmin Jiaoyu Chubanshe (People's Education Press): 55 Sha Tan Hou Jie, Beijing 100009; tel. (10) 64035745; fax (10) 64010370; f. 1950; school textbooks, guidebooks, teaching materials, etc.

Renmin Meishu Chubanshe (People's Fine Arts Publishing House): Beijing; tel. (10) 65122371; fax (10) 65122370; f. 1951; works by Chinese and foreign painters, sculptors and other artists, picture albums, photographic, painting techniques; Dir CHEN YUNHE; Editor-in-Chief LIU YUSHAN.

Renmin Weisheng Chubanshe (People's Medical Publishing House): Beijing; tel. (01) 67617283; fax (01) 645143; f. 1953; medicine (Western and traditional Chinese), pharmacology, dentistry, public health; Pres. LIU YIQING.

Renmin Wenxue Chubanshe (People's Literature Publishing House): 166 Chaoyangmen Nei Dajie, Beijing 100705; tel. (10) 65138394; f. 1951; largest publr of literary works and translations into Chinese; Dir NIE ZHENNING; Editor-in-Chief CHEN ZAOCHUN.

Shanghai Guji Chubanshe (Shanghai Classics Publishing House): 272 Ruijin Erlu, Shanghai 200020; tel. (21) 64370011; fax (21) 64339287; f. 1956; classical Chinese literature, history, philosophy, geography, linguistics, science and technology.

Shanghai Jiaoyu Chubanshe (Shanghai Educational Publishing House): 123 Yongfu Lu, Shanghai 200031; tel. (21) 64377165; fax (21) 64339995; f. 1958; academic; Dir and Editor-in-Chief CHEN HE.

Shanghai Yiwen Chubanshe (Shanghai Translation Publishing House): 14 Xiang 955, Yanan Zhonglu, Shanghai 200040; tel. (21) 62472890; fax (21) 62475100; e-mail cpbq@bj.cal.com.cn; internet www.cp.com.cn; f. 1978; translations of foreign classic and modern literature; philosophy, social sciences, dictionaries, etc.

Shangwu Yinshuguan (The Commercial Press): 36 Wangfujing Dajie, Beijing; tel. (10) 65252026; fax (10) 65135899; f. 1897; dictionaries and reference books in Chinese and foreign languages, translations of foreign works on social sciences; Pres. YANG DEYAN.

Shaonian Ertong Chubanshe (Juvenile and Children's Publishing House): 1538 Yan An Xi Lu, Shanghai 200052; tel. (21) 62823025; fax (21) 62821726; e-mail forwardz@public4.sta.net.cn; f. 1952; children's educational and literary works, teaching aids and periodicals; Gen. Man. ZHOU SHUNPEI.

Shijie Wenhua Chubanshe (World Culture Publishing House): Dir ZHU LIE.

Wenwu Chubanshe (Cultural Relics Publishing House): 29 Wusi Dajie, Beijing 100009; tel. (10) 64048057; fax (10) 64010698; e-mail web@wenwu.com; internet www.wenwu.com; f. 1956; books and catalogues of Chinese relics in museums and those recently discovered; Dir SU SHISHU.

Wuhan Daxue Chubanshe (Wuhan University Press): Suojia Hill, Wuhan, Hubei; tel. (27) 7820651; fax (27) 7812661; f. 1981; reference books, academic works, etc.; Pres. and Editor-in-Chief Prof. NIU TAICHEN.

Xiandai Chubanshe (Modern Press): 504 Anhua Li, Andingmenwai, Beijing 100011; tel. (10) 64263515; fax (10) 64214540; f. 1981; directories, reference books, etc.; Dir ZHOU HONGLI.

Xinhua Chubanshe (Xinhua Publishing House): 57 Xuanwumen Xidajie, Beijing 100803; tel. (10) 63074022; fax (10) 63073880; e-mail xhpub@xinhua.org; f. 1979; social sciences, economy, politics, history, geography, directories, dictionaries, etc.; Dir WANG CHUNRONG Editor-in-Chief ZHANG SHOUDI.

Xuelin Chubanshe (Scholar Books Publishing House): 120 Wenmiao Lu, Shanghai 200010; tel. and fax (21) 63768540; f. 1981; academic, including personal academic works at authors' own expense; Dir LEI QUNMING.

Zhongguo Caizheng Jingji Chubanshe (China Financial and Economic Publishing House): 8 Dafosi Dongjie, Dongcheng Qu, Beijing; tel. (10) 64011805; f. 1961; finance, economics, commerce and accounting.

Zhongguo Dabaike Quanshu Chubanshe (Encyclopaedia of China Publishing House): 17 Fu Cheng Men Bei Dajie, Beijing 100037; tel. (10) 68315610; fax (10) 68316510; e-mail ygh@bj.col.com.cn; f. 1978; specializes in encyclopaedias; Dir SHAN JIFU.

Zhongguo Ditu Chubanshe (China Cartographic Publishing House): 3 Baizhifang Xijie, Beijing 100054; tel. (10) 63530808; fax (10) 63531961; e-mail infa@chinamap.com; internet www.chinamap.com; f. 1954; cartographic publr; Dir WANG JIXIAN.

Zhongguo Funü Chubanshe (China Women Publishing House): 24A Shijia Hutong, 100010 Beijing; tel. (10) 65126986; f. 1981; women's movement, marriage and family, child-care, etc.; Dir LI ZHONGXIU.

Zhongguo Qingnian Chubanshe (China Youth Press): 21 Dongsi Shiertiao, Beijing 100708; tel. (10) 84015396; fax (10) 64031803; e-mail cyph@eastnet.com.cn; internet www.cyp.com.cn; f. 1950; literature, social and natural sciences, youth work, autobiography; also periodicals; Editor-in-Chief CHEN HAOZENG.

Zhongguo Shehui Kexue Chubanshe (China Social Sciences Publishing House): 158A Gulou Xidajie, Beijing 100720; tel. (10) 64073837; fax (10) 64074509; f. 1978; Dir ZHENG WENLIN.

Zhongguo Xiju Chubanshe (China Theatrical Publishing House): 52 Dongsi Batiao Hutong, Beijing; tel. (10) 64015815. 1957; traditional and modern Chinese drama.

Zhongguo Youyi Chuban Gongsi (China Friendship Publishing Corpn): e-mail tmdoxu@public.east.cn.net; Dir YANG WEI.

Zhonghua Shuju (Zhonghua Book Co): 38 Taipingqiao Xili, Fenglai Qu, Beijing; tel. (10) 63458226; f. 1912; general; Pres. SONG YIFU.

PUBLISHERS' ASSOCIATION

Publishers' Association of China: Beijing; f. 1979; arranges academic exchanges with foreign publrs; Chair. SONG MUWEN; Sec.-Gen. FANG ZHENJIANG.

Broadcasting and Communications

TELECOMMUNICATIONS

Ministry of Information Industry: 13 Xichangan Jie, Beijing 100804; tel. (10) 66014249; fax (10) 66034248; e-mail webmaster@mii.gov.cn; internet www.mii.gov.cn; regulates all issues concerning the telecommunications sector.

China Telecom: internet www.chinatelecom.com.cn; f. 1997 as a vehicle for foreign investment in telecommunications sector; Dir.-Gen. LI LIGUI.

China Netcom Corpn: Beijing; f. 1999; internet telephone service provider; CEO EDWARD TIAN.

China United Telecommunications Corpn (UNICOM): 1/F, Hongji Centre Office Bldg, 18 Jianguomenei Dajie, Beijing; tel. (10) 65181800; fax (10) 65183405; internet www.chinaunicom.com.cn; f. 1994; cellular telecommunications; Chair. and Pres. YANG XIANZU.

BROADCASTING

At the end of 1998 there were 298 radio broadcasting stations, 748 medium- and short-wave radio transmitting and relay stations (covering 88.3% of the population), 347 television stations and 41,252 television transmitting and relay stations with a capacity of over 1,000 watts (covering 89.0% of the population).

Regulatory Authorities

State Administration of Radio, Film and Television (SARFT): 2 Fu Xing Men Wai Dajie, POB 4501, Beijing 100866; tel. (10) 68513409; fax (10) 68512174; internet www.dns.incmrft.gov.cn; controls the Central People's Broadcasting Station, the Central TV Station, Radio Beijing, China Record Co., Beijing Broadcasting Institute, Broadcasting Research Institute, the China Broadcasting Art Troupe, etc.; Chair. TIAN CONGMING.

State Radio Regulatory Authority: Beijing; operates under the State Council; Chair. ZOU JIAHUA.

Radio

China National Radio (CNR): 2 Fu Xing Men Wai Dajie, Beijing 100866; tel. (10) 68045630; fax (10) 68045631; internet www.cnradio .com; f. 1945; domestic service in Chinese, Zang Wen (Tibetan), Min Nan Hua (Amoy), Ke Jia (Hakka), Hasaka (Kazakh), Wei Wuer (Uygur), Menggu Hua (Mongolian) and Chaoxian (Korean); Dir-Gen. YANG BO.

Zhongguo Guoji Guangbo Diantai (China Radio International): 16A Shijingshan Lu, Beijing 100039; tel. (10) 68891001; fax (10) 68891582; e-mail crieng@public.bta.net.cn; internet www.cri .com.cn; f. 1941; fmrly Radio Beijing; foreign service in 38 languages incl. Arabic, Burmese, Czech, English, Esperanto, French, German, Indonesian, Italian, Japanese, Lao, Polish, Portuguese, Russian, Spanish, Turkish and Vietnamese; Dir ZHANG ZHENHUA.

Television

China Central Television (CCTV): 11 Fuxing Lu, Haidian, Beijing 100859; tel. (10) 8500000; fax (10) 8513025; internet www.wtdb.com/CCTV/about.htm; operates under Bureau of Broadcasting Affairs of the State Council, Beijing; f. 1958; operates eight networks; 24-hour global satellite service commenced in 1996; Pres. YANG WEIGWANG.

In April 1994 foreign companies were prohibited from establishing or operating cable TV stations in China. By mid-1996 there were more than 3,000 cable television stations in operation, with networks covering 45m. households. The largest subscriber service is Beijing Cable TV (Dir GUO JUNJIN). Satellite services are available in some areas: millions of satellite receivers are in use. In October 1993 the Government approved new regulations, attempting to restrict access to foreign satellite broadcasts.

Finance

(cap. = capital; auth. = authorized; p.u. = paid up; res = reserves; dep. = deposits; m. = million; amounts in yuan unless otherwise stated)

BANKING

Radical economic reforms, introduced in 1994, included the strengthening of the role of the central bank and the establishment of new commercial banks. The Commercial Bank Law took effect in July 1995. The establishment of private banks was to be permitted.

Central Bank

People's Bank of China: 32 Chengfang Jie, Xicheng Qu, Beijing 100800; tel. (10) 66194114; fax (10) 66015346; e-mail master@ pbc.gov.cn; internet www.pbc.gov.cn; f. 1948; bank of issue; decides and implements China's monetary policies; Gov. DAI XIANGLONG; 2,204 brs.

Other Banks

Agricultural Bank of China: 23A Fuxing Lu, Haidian Qu, Beijing 100036; tel. (10) 68216807; fax (10) 68297160; e-mail webmaster@ intl.abocn.com; internet www.abocn.com; f. 1951; serves mainly China's rural financial operations, providing services for agriculture, industry, commerce, transport, etc. in rural areas; cap. 132,011m., res 3,196m., dep. 1,660,933m. (Dec. 1999); Pres. SHANG FULIN; 2,500 brs.

Agricultural Development Bank of China: 2A Yuetanbei Jie, Xicheng Qu, Beijing 100045; tel. (10) 68081557; fax (10) 68081773; f. 1994; cap. 20,000m.; Pres. HE LINXIANG.

Bank of China: Bank of China Bldg, 410 Fu Cheng Men Nei Dajie, Beijing 100818; tel. (10) 66016688; fax (10) 66016869; e-mail webmaster@bank-of-china.com; internet www.bank-of-china.com; f. 1912; handles foreign exchange and international settlements; cap. 104,500m., res 39,458m., dep. 2,355,926m. (Dec. 1999); Chair. and Pres. LIU MINGKANG; 116 domestic, 74 overseas brs.

Bank of Communications Ltd: 18 Xian Xia Lu, Shanghai 200335; tel. (21) 62756784; fax (21) 62756874; internet www.bankcomm.com; f. 1908; commercial bank; cap. 13,791.9m., res 11,276.3m., dep. 318,146.8m. (Dec. 1999); Chair. YIN JIEYAN; Pres. FANG CHENGGUO; 90 brs.

Beijing City Co-op Bank: 65 You An Men Nei Lu, Xuanwu Qu, Beijing 100054; tel. and fax (10) 63520159; f. 1996; cap. 1,000m., res 3,466m., dep. 26,660m. (Dec. 1996); 90 brs.

Bengbu House Saving Bank: 85 Zhong Rong Jie, Bengbu 233000; tel. (552) 2042069.

China and South Sea Bank Ltd: 410 Fu Cheng Men Nei Dajie, Beijing; internet www.cssb.com; f. 1921; cap. 1,200.0m., res 3,735.1m., dep. 38,850.2m. (Dec. 1999); Chair. HUA QINGSHAN.

China Construction Bank (CCB): 25 Jinrong Jie, Beijing 100032; tel. (10) 67597114; fax (10) 66212863; e-mail ccb@bj.china.com; internet www.ccb.com.cn; f. 1954; fmrly People's Construction Bank of China; makes payments for capital construction projects in accordance with state plans and budgets; issues medium- and long-term loans to enterprises and short-term loans to construction enterprises and others; also handles foreign exchange business; housing loans; cap. 85,119m., res 16,792m., dep. 1,942,674m. (Dec. 1999); Pres. WANG XUEBING; 49 brs.

China International Capital Corporation (CICC): 23rd Floor, Everbright Bldg, 6 Fu Xing Men Wai Dajie, Beijing 100045; tel. (10) 68561166; fax (10) 68561145; f. 1995; international investment bank; 42.5% owned by China Construction Bank; registered cap. US $100m.; CEO EDWIN LIM.

China International Trust and Investment Corporation (CITIC): Capital Mansion, 6 Xianyuannan Lu, Chaoyang Qu, Beijing 100004; tel. (10) 64661105; fax (10) 64662137; f. 1979; economic and technological co-operation; finance, banking, investment and trade; registered cap. 3,000m.; Chair. WANG JUN; Pres. QIN XIAO.

China Merchants Bank: News Centre Bldg, 2 Shennan Lu, Shenzhen 518001; tel. (755) 2090000; fax (755) 2090066; internet www.cmbchina.com; f. 1987; cap. 4,207m., res 6,603m., dep. 132,080m. (Dec. 1999); Chair. LIU SONGJIN; Pres. MA WEIHUA; 19 brs.

China Minsheng Banking Corporation: 4 Zhengyi Lu, Dongcheng Qu, Beijing 100006; tel. (10) 65269610; fax (10) 68588570; e-mail msbgs@cmbc.com.cn; internet www.cmbc.com.cn; first non-state national commercial bank, opened Jan. 1996; registered cap. 1,380m., res 112m., dep. 22,477m. (Dec. 1998); Chair. JING SHUPING; Pres. DONG WENBIAO; 5 brs.

China State Bank Ltd: 17 Xi Jiao Min Xiang, Beijing 100031; f. 1927; cap. 1,100m., res 3,850m., dep. 41,861m. (Dec. 1999); Gen. Man. LI PINZHOU.

Chinese Mercantile Bank: Ground and 23rd Floors, Dongfeng Bldg, 2 Yannan Lu, Futian Qu, Shenzhen 518031; tel. (755) 3257880; fax (755) 3257801; e-mail szcmbank@public.szptt.net.cn; f. 1993; cap. US $55.3m., res US $3.2m., dep. US $227.0m. (Dec. 1998); Pres. HUANG MINGXIANG.

CITIC Industrial Bank: Block C, Fuhua Bldg, 8 Chao Yang Men Bei Dajie, Dongcheng Qu, Beijing 100027; f. 1987; tel. (10) 65541658; fax (10) 65541671; internet www.citicib.com.cn; f. 1987; cap. 5,307m., res 282m., dep. 102,174m. (Dec. 1997); Chair. QIN YIAO; Pres. DOU JIANZHONG; 17 brs.

Everbright Bank of China: Everbright Tower, 6 Fu Xing Men Wai Lu, Beijing 100045; tel. (10) 58565577; fax (10) 68561260; e-mail EBBC@public.bta.net.cn; internet www.ebeb.com.cn/bank/ index.html; f. 1992; acquired China Investment Bank in 1999; cap. 2,800m., res 2,179.6m., dep. 65,343.8m. (Dec. 1998); Chair. ZHU XIAOHUA; Pres. XU BIN; 10 brs.

Export and Import Bank of China: 1 Dingandongli, Yongdingmenwai, Beijing; tel. (10) 67626688; fax (10) 67638940; f. 1994; provides trade credits for export of large machinery, electronics, ships, etc.; Chair. and Pres. YANG ZILIN.

Fujian Asia Bank Ltd: 2nd Floor, Yuan Hong Bldg, 32 Wuyi Lu, Fuzhou, Fujian 350005; tel. (591) 3330788; fax (591) 3330843; f. 1993; cap. US $27.0m., res US $1.6m., dep. US $3.5m. (Dec. 1998); Chair. YAN JIANGUO; Gen. Man. DENNIS H. LAM.

Fujian Industrial Bank: Zhong Shang Bldg, 154 Hudong Lu, Hualin, Fuzhou, Fujian 350003; tel. (591) 7844196; fax (591) 7841932; internet www.fujian-window.com/Fujian_w/ad/xy/xy.html; f. 1982; cap. 1,500m., res 1,658m., dep. 29,912m. (Dec. 1998); Chair. and Pres. CHEN YI; 11 brs.

Guangdong Development Bank: 83 Nonglinxia Lu, Dongshan Qu, Guangzhou, Guangdong 510080; tel. (20) 87310888; fax (20) 87310799; internet www.gdb.com.cn; f. 1988; cap. 3,500m., res 3,724.3m., dep. 75,029.1m. (Dec. 1999); Pres. LIU ZHIQIANG; Chair. LI RUOHONG; 32 brs.

Guangdong (Kwangtung) Provincial Bank: 410 Fu Cheng Men Nei Dajie, Beijing 100818; internet www.kpb-hk.com; f. 1924; cap. 1,500.0m., res 5,696.3m., dep. 71,468.1m. (Dec. 1998).

Hua Xia Bank: 9th–12th Floors, Xidan International Mansion, 111 Xidan Bei Dajie, Beijing 100032; tel. (10) 66151199; fax (10) 66188484; internet www.serve.cei.gov/so1/007/huaxia; f. 1992 as part of Shougang Corpn; registered cap. 2,500m., res 332m., dep. 32,242m. (Dec. 1999); Chair. LU YUCHENG; Pres. DUAN XIAOXING.

Industrial and Commercial Bank of China: 55 Fuxingmennai Dajie, Xicheng Qu, Beijing 100031; tel. (10) 66106114; fax (10) 66106053; e-mail webmaster@icbc.com.cn; internet www.icbc

.com.cn; f. 1984; handles industrial and commercial credits and international business; cap. 167,417m., res 11,301m., dep. 3,170,459m. (Dec. 1999); Chair. LIU TINGHUAN; Pres. JIANG JIANQING; 38,219 brs.

International Bank of Paris and Shanghai: 13th Floor, North Tower, Shanghai Stock Exchange Bldg, 528 Pudong Nan Lu, Shanghai 200120; tel. (21) 58405500; fax (21) 58889232; f. 1992; cap. US $33.6m., res US $824,000, dep. US $111m. (Dec. 1998); Chair. and Dir JIANG JIANQING.

Kincheng Banking Corporation: 410 Fu Cheng Men Nei Dajie, Beijing; internet kincheng.bocgroup.com; f. 1917; cap. 2,200.0m., res 6,520.9m., dep. 54,358.3m. (Dec. 1999); Chair. ZHANG GUOWEN.

National Commercial Bank Ltd: 410 Fu Cheng Men Nei Dajie, Beijing; e-mail hkbrmain@natcombank.com; internet www. natcombank.com; f. 1907; cap. 1,200.0m., res 4,754.2m., dep. 44,124.8m. (Dec. 1999); 26 brs.

Qingdao International Bank: Full Hope Mansion C, 12 Hong Kong Middle Rd, Qingdao, Shandong 266071; tel. (532) 5026211; fax (532) 5026221; e-mail qibankc@public.qd.sd.cn; f. 1996; joint venture between Industrial and Commercial Bank of China and Korea First Bank; cap. US $166m., res US $5.6m., dep. US $61.4m. (Dec. 1998); Pres. DUCK SUNG YUN.

Shanghai Pudong Development Bank: 12 Zongshan Lu, Shanghai 200002; tel. (21) 63296188; fax (21) 63232036; internet www.spdb.com.cn; f. 1993; cap. 2,410.0m., res 5,328.5m., dep. 91,646.5m. (Dec. 1999); Chair. ZHUANG XIAOTIAN; Pres. JIN YUN.

Shenzhen Development Bank Co Ltd: Shenzhen Development Bank Tower, 178 Shen Nan Dong Lu, Shenzhen 518001; tel. (755) 2080387; fax (755) 2080386; e-mail shudi@sdb.com.cn; f. 1987; cap. 1,552m., res 1,139m., dep. 32,482m. (Dec. 1998); Chair. CHEN ZHAOMIN; Pres. ZHOU LIN.

Sin Hua Bank Ltd: 17 Xi Jiao Min Xiang, Beijing 100031; subsidiary of Bank of China; cap. 2,200.0m., res 7,723.2m., dep. 90,021.3m. (Dec. 1998); Chair. JIANG ZUQI.

State Development Bank (SDB): 29 Fuchengmenwai Lu, Xicheng Qu, Beijing 100037; tel. (10) 68306557; fax (10) 68306541; f. 1994; merged with China Investment Bank 1998; handles low-interest loans for infrastructural projects and basic industries; Gov. CHEN YUAN.

Xiamen International Bank: 10 Hu Bin Bei Lu, Xiamen, Fujian 361012; tel. (592) 5310686; fax (592) 5310685; e-mail xib@public.xm.fi.cn; f. 1985; cap. HK $620m., res HK $477m., dep. HK $7,543m. (Dec. 1999); Chair. LI LIHUI; 3 brs.

Yantai House Saving Bank: 248 Nan Da Jie, Yantai 264001; tel. (535) 6207047.

Yien Yieh Commercial Bank Ltd: 17 Xi Jiao Min Xiang, Beijing 100031; f. 1915; cap. 800m., res 4,129m., dep. 40,248m. (Dec. 1999); Chair. ZHAO ANGE; Gen. Man. WU GUORUI; 29 brs.

Zhejiang Commercial Bank Ltd: 88 Xi Zhongshan Lu, Ningbo 315010; tel. (574) 7245678; fax (574) 7245409; f. 1993; cap. US $40m., dep. US $86m. (Dec. 1997); Pres. and Chair. SHEN SONGJUN.

Zhongxin Shiye Bank is a nation-wide commercial bank. Other commercial banks include the Fujian Commercial Bank and Zhaoshang Bank.

Foreign Banks

Before mid-1995 foreign banks were permitted only to open representative offices in China. The first foreign bank established a full branch in Beijing in mid-1995, and by March 1998 there were 51 foreign banks in China. In March 1997 foreign banks were allowed for the first time to conduct business in yuan. However, they are only entitled to accept yuan deposits from joint-venture companies. Representative offices totalled 519 in December 1996. In March 1999 the Government announced that foreign banks, hitherto restricted to 23 cities and Hainan Province, were to be permitted to open branches in all major cities.

STOCK EXCHANGES

Several stock exchanges were in the process of development in the mid-1990s, and by early 1995 the number of shareholders had reached 38m. By 1995 a total of 15 futures exchanges were in operation, dealing in various commodities, building materials and currencies. By the end of 1997 the number of companies listed on the Shanghai and Shenzhen Stock Exchanges had reached 745. In August 1997, in response to unruly conditions, the Government ordered the China Securities Regulatory Commission (see below) to assume direct control of the Shanghai and Shenzhen exchanges.

Stock Exchange Executive Council (SEEC): Beijing; tel. (10) 64935210; f. 1989 to oversee the development of financial markets in China; mems comprise leading non-bank financial institutions authorized to handle securities; Vice-Pres. WANG BOMING.

Securities Association of China (SAC): Olympic Hotel, 52 Baishiqiao Lu, Beijing 100081; tel. (10) 68316688; fax (10) 68318390; f. 1991; non-governmental organization comprising 122 mems (stock exchanges and securities cos) and 35 individual mems; Pres. GUO ZHENQIAN.

Beijing Securities Exchange: 5 Anding Lu, Chao Yang Qu, Beijing 100029; tel. (10) 64939366; fax (10) 64936233.

Shanghai Stock Exchange: 528 Pudong Nan Lu, Shanghai 200120; f. 1990; tel. (21) 68808888; fax (21) 68807813; e-mail webmaster@sse.com.cn; internet www.sse.com.cn; Chair. MAO YINGLIANG; Pres. TU GUANGSHAO.

Shenzhen Stock Exchange: 5045 Shennan Dong Lu, Shenzhen, Guangdong 518010; tel. (755) 20833333; fax (755) 2083117; internet www.sse.org.cn; f. 1991; Chair. ZHENG KELIN; Pres. GUI MINJIE.

Regulatory Authorities

Operations are regulated by the State Council Securities Policy Committee and by the following:

China Securities Regulatory Commission (CSRC): Bldg 3, Area 3, Fangqunyuan, Fangzhuang, Beijing 100078; tel. (10) 67617343; fax (10) 67653117; f. 1993; Chair. ZHOU XIAOCHUAN; Sec.-Gen. WANG YI.

INSURANCE

A new Insurance Law, formulated to standardize activities and to strengthen the supervision and administration of the industry, took effect in October 1995. Changes included the separation of life insurance and property insurance businesses. By late 1998 the number of insurance companies totalled 25. Total premiums rose from 44,000m. yuan in 1994 to some 139,000m. yuan in Dec. 1999.

AXA-Minmetals Assurance Co: f. 1999; joint venture by Groupe AXA (France) and China Minmetals Group; Gen. Man. JOSEPH SIN.

China Insurance Co Ltd: 22 Xi Jiao Min Xiang, POB 20, Beijing 100032; tel. (10) 6654231; fax (10) 66011869; f. 1931; cargo, hull, freight, fire, life, personal accident, industrial injury, motor insurance, reinsurance, etc.; Chair. YANG CHAO; Pres. WANG XIANGZHANG.

China Insurance Group: 410 Fu Cheng Men Nei Dajie, Beijing; tel. (10) 66016688; fax (10) 66011869; f. 1996 (fmrly People's Insurance Co of China (PICC), f. 1949); hull, marine cargo, aviation, motor, life, fire, accident, liability and reinsurance, etc.; in process of division into three subsidiaries (life insurance (China Life Insurance Co—CLIC), property-casualty insurance and reinsurance) by mid-1996, in preparation for transformation into joint-stock cos; 1996 300m. policy-holders; Chair. and Pres. MA YONGWEI.

China Pacific Insurance Co Ltd (CPIC): 12 Zhongshan Lu (Dong 1), Shanghai 200001; tel. (21) 63232488; fax (21) 63218398; internet www.cpic.com.cn.; f. 1991; joint-stock co; Chair. WANG MINGQUAN; Pres. WANG GUOLIANG.

China Ping An Insurance Co: Ping An Bldg, Bagua San Lu, Bagualing, Shenzhen 518029; tel. (755) 2262888; fax (755) 2431019; f. 1988.

Hua Tai Insurance Co of China Ltd: Beijing; tel. (10) 68565588; fax (10) 68561750; f. 1996 by 63 industrial cos.

Pacific-Aetna Life Insurance Co: Shanghai; f. 1998 by CPIC and Aetna Life Insurance Co.; China's first Sino-US insurance co.

Tai Ping Insurance Co Ltd: 410 Fu Cheng Men Nei Dajie, Beijing 100034; tel. (10) 66016688; fax (10) 66011869; marine freight, hull, cargo, fire, personal accident, industrial injury, motor insurance, reinsurance, etc.; Pres. SUN XIYUE.

Taikang Life Insurance Co Ltd: Beijing; f. 1996; Chair. CHEN DONGSHENG.

Joint-stock companies include the Xinhua (New China) Life Insurance Co Ltd (Gen. Man. SUN BING). By April 1998 a total of 84 foreign insurance companies had established some 150 offices in China, being permitted to operate in Shanghai and Guangzhou only.

Regulatory Authority

China Insurance Regulatory Commission (CIRC): Beijing; f. 1998; Chair. MA YONGWEI.

Trade and Industry

GOVERNMENT AGENCIES

China Council for the Promotion of International Trade (CCPIT): 1 Fuxingmenwai Dajie, Beijing 100860; tel. (10) 68013344; fax (10) 68011370; e-mail ccpitweb@public.bta.net.cn; internet www.ccpit.org; f. 1952; encourages foreign trade and economic co-operation; sponsors and arranges Chinese exhbns abroad and foreign exhbns in China; helps foreigners to apply for patent rights and trade-mark registration in China; promotes foreign investment and organizes tech. exchanges with other countries; provides legal services; publishes trade periodicals; Chair. Yu Xiaosong; Sec.-Gen. Zhong Min.

Chinese General Association of Light Industry: 22B Fuwai Dajie, Beijing 100833; tel. (10) 68396114; under supervision of State Council; Chair. Yu Chen.

Chinese General Association of Textile Industry: 12 Dong Chang An Jie, Beijing 100742; tel. (10) 65129545; under supervision of State Council; Chair. Shi Wanpeng.

Ministry of Foreign Trade and Economic Co-operation: (see under Ministries).

National Administration of State Property: Dir Zhang Youcai.

State Administration for Industry and Commerce: 8 San Li He Dong Lu, Xicheng Qu, Beijing 100820; tel. (10) 68010463; fax (10) 68020848; responsible for market supervision and administrative execution of industrial and commercial laws; functions under the direct supervision of the State Council; Dir Wang Zhongfu.

Takeover Office for Military, Armed Police, Government and Judiciary Businesses: Beijing; f. 1998 to assume control of enterprises formerly operated by the People's Liberation Army.

CHAMBERS OF COMMERCE

All-China Federation of Industry and Commerce: 93 Beiheyan Dajie, Beijing 100006; tel. (10) 65136677; fax (10) 65122631; f. 1953; promotes overseas trade relations; Chair. Jing Shuping; Sec.-Gen. Cheng Lu.

China Chamber of International Commerce—Shanghai: Jinling Mansions, 28 Jinling Lu, Shanghai 200021; tel. (21) 53060228; fax (21) 63869915; e-mail ccpitllb@online.sh.cn; Chair. Yang Zhihua.

China Chamber of International Commerce—Zhuhai: 127 Xinguangli, Zhuhai, Guangdong 519000; tel. (756) 2218954; fax (756) 2228640.

TRADE AND INDUSTRIAL ORGANIZATIONS

Anshan Iron and Steel Co: Huangang Lu, Tiexi Qu, Anshan 114021; tel. and fax(412) 6723090; Pres. Liu Jie.

Aviation Industries of China: 67 Nan Dajie, Jiaodaokou, Dongcheng Qu, Beijing; tel. (10) 64013322; fax (10) 64013648; Pres. Zhu Yuli.

Baoshan Iron and Steel Complex Corpn (Group): 2 Mudangjiang Lu, Shanghai 201900; tel. (21) 5646944; fax (21) 56600260; proposals for merger with Shanghai Metallurgical announced late 1997; registered cap. 100m. yuan; Chair. Li Ming; Pres. Xie Qihua.

Baotou Iron and Steel Co: Gangtie Dajie, Kundulun Qu, Baotou 014010, Inner Mongolia; tel. (472) 2125619; fax (472) 2183708; Pres. Zeng Guoan.

China Aviation Supplies Corpn: 155 Xi Dongsi Jie, Beijing 100013; tel. (10) 64012233; fax (10) 64016392; f.1980; Pres. Liu Yuanfan.

China Civil Engineering Construction Corpn (CCECC): 4 Beifeng Wo, Haidian Qu, Beijing 100038; tel. (10) 63263392; fax (10) 63263864; e-mail zongban@ccecc.com.cn; f. 1953; general contracting, provision of technical and labour services, consulting and design, etc.; Pres. Qian Wuyun.

China Construction International Inc: 9 Sanlihe Lu, Haidian Qu, Beijing; tel. (10) 68394086; fax (10) 68394097; Pres. Fu Renzhang.

China Electronics Corpn: 27 Wanshou Lu, Haidian Qu, Beijing 100846; tel. (10) 68218529; fax (10) 68213745; e-mail cec@public .gb.com.cn; internet www.cec.com.cn; Pres. Wang Jincheng.

China Garment Industry Corpn: 9A Taiyanggong Beisanhuandong Lu, Chao Yang Qu, Beijing 100028; tel. (10) 64216660; fax (10) 64239134; Pres. Dong Binggen.

China General Technology (Group) Holding Ltd: f. 1998 through merger of China National Technical Import and Export Corpn, China National Machinery Import and Export Corpn, China National Instruments Import and Export Corpn and China National Corpn for Overseas Economic Co-operation; total assets 16,000m. yuan; Chair. and Pres. Tong Changyin.

China Gold Co: 1 Bei Jie, Qingnianhu, Andingmenwai, Beijing; tel. (10) 64214831; Pres. Cui Lan.

China Great Wall Computer Group: 38A Xueyuan Lu, Haidian Qu, Beijing 100083; tel. (10) 68342714; fax (10) 62011240; internet www.gwssi.com.cn; Chair. Wang Zhi; Pres. Lu Ming.

China Great Wall Industry Corpn: Hangtian Changcheng Bldg, 30 Haidian Nanlu, Haidian Qu, Beijing 100080; tel. (10) 68748737; fax (10) 68748865; e-mail cgwic@cgwic.com; internet www.cgwic .com.cn; registered cap. 200m. yuan; Pres. Zhang Xinxia.

China International Book Trading Corpn: (see under Publishers).

China International Contractors Association: 28 Donghouxiang, Andingmenwai, Beijing 100710; tel. (10) 64211159; fax (10) 64213959; Chair. Li Rongmin.

China International Futures Trading Corpn: 24th Floor, Capital Mansion, 6 Xinyuan Nan Lu, Chao Yang Qu, Beijing 100004; tel. (10) 64665388; fax (10) 64665140; Chair. Tian Yuan; Pres. Lu Jian.

China International Telecommunications Construction Corpn (CITCC): 22 Yuyou Lane, Xicheng Qu, Beijing 100035; tel. (10) 66012244; fax (10) 66024103; Pres. Qi Fusheng.

China International Water and Electric Corpn: 3 Liupukang Yiqu Zhongjie, Xicheng Qu, Beijing 100011; tel. (10) 64015511; fax (10) 64014075; e-mail cwe@mx.cei.go.cn; f. 1956 as China Water and Electric International Corpn, name changed 1983; imports and exports equipment for projects in the field of water and electrical engineering; undertakes such projects; provides technical and labour services; Pres. Wang Shuohao.

China Iron and Steel Industry and Trade Group Corpn: 17B Xichangan Jie, Beijing 100031; tel. (10) 66067733; fax (10) 66078450; e-mail support@sinosteel.com.cn; internet www.sinosteel. com; f. 1999 by merger of China National Metallurgical Import and Export Corpn, China Materials Corpn and China Metallurgical Steel Products Processing Corpn.; Chair. Weng Yuqing; Pres. Bai Baohua.

China National Aerotechnology Import and Export Corpn: 5 Liangguochang, Dongcheng Qu, Beijing 100010; tel. (10) 64017722; fax (10) 64015381; f.1952; exports signal flares, electric detonators, tachometers, parachutes, general purpose aircraft, etc.; Pres. Yang Chunshu; Gen. Man. Liu Guomin.

China National Animal Breeding Stock Import and Export Corpn (CABS): 10 Yangyi Hutong Jia, Dongdan, Beijing 100005; tel. (10) 65131107; fax (10) 65128694; sole agency for import and export of stud animals including cattle, sheep, goats, swine, horses, donkeys, camels, rabbits, poultry, etc., as well as pasture and turf grass seeds, feed additives, medicines, etc.; Pres. Yang Chengshan.

China National Arts and Crafts Import and Export Corpn: Arts and Crafts Bldg, 103 Jixiangli, Chao Yang Men Wai, Chao Yang Qu, Beijing 100020; tel. (10) 65931075; fax (10) 65931036; e-mail po@mbox.cnart.com.cn; internet www.cnart-group.com; deals in jewellery, ceramics, handicrafts, embroidery, pottery, wicker, bamboo, etc.; Pres. Chen Kun.

China National Automotive Industry Corpn (CNAIC): 46 Fucheng Lu, Haidian Qu, Beijing 100036; tel. (10) 88123968; fax (10) 68125556; Pres. Gu Yaotian.

China National Automotive Industry Import and Export Corpn (CAIEC): 5 Beishihuan Xi Lu, Beijing 100083; tel. (10) 62310650; fax (10) 62310688; e-mail info@chinacaiec.com; internet www.chinacaiec.com; sales US $540m. (1995); Pres. Zhang Fusheng; 1,100 employees.

China National Cereals, Oils and Foodstuffs Import and Export Corpn: 7th–13th Floors, Tower A, COFCO Plaza, Jian Guo Men Wai Dajie, Beijing 100005; tel. (10) 65268888; fax (10) 65278612; e-mail minnie@cofco.com.cn; internet www.cofco .com.cn; imports and exports grains, etc.; Pres. Zhou Mingchen.

China National Chartering Corpn (SINOCHART): Rm 1601/ 1602, 1607/1608, Jiu Ling Bldg, 21 Xisanhuan Bei Lu, Beijing 100081; tel. (10) 68405601; fax (10) 68405628; e-mail sinochrt@ public.intercom.co.cn; f. 1950; functions under Ministry of Foreign Trade and Economic Co-operation; subsidiary of SINOTRANS (see below); arranges chartering of ships, reservation of space, managing and operating chartered vessels; Pres. Liu Shunlong; Gen. Man. Zhang Jianwei.

China National Chemical Construction Corpn: Block 7, 16 Hepingli, Dongcheng Qu, Beijing 100013; tel. (10) 64214043; fax (10) 64215982; e-mail infolegal@cnccc.cnnet.sic.gov.cn; internet www.cnccc.com; registered cap. 50m.; Pres. Chen Lihua.

China National Chemicals Import and Export Corpn (SINO-CHEM): Sinochem Tower, 2A Fuxingmenwai Jie, Beijing 100045; tel. (10) 68568888; fax (10) 685868890; internet www.sinochem.com; deals in rubber products, crude petroleum, petroleum products, chemicals, etc.; Pres. Liu Deshu.

China National Coal Industry Import and Export Corpn (CNCIEC): 88B Andingmenwai, Dongcheng Qu, Beijing 100011; tel. (10) 64287188; fax (10) 64287166; e-mail cnciec@chinacoal.com; internet www.chinacoal.com; f. 1982; sales US $800m. (1992); imports and exports coal and tech. equipment for coal industry, joint coal development and compensation trade; Chair. and Pres. Wang Changchun.

China National Coal Mine Corpn: 21 Bei Jie, Heipingli, Beijing 100013; tel. (10) 64217766; Pres. Wang Senhao.

China National Complete Plant Import and Export Corpn (Group): 9 Xi Bin He Lu, An Ding Men, Beijing; tel. (10) 64253388; fax (10) 64211382; Chair. Hu Zhaoqing; Pres. Li Zhimin.

China National Electronics Import and Export Corpn: 8th Floor, Electronics Bldg, 23A Fuxing Lu, Beijing 100036; tel. (10) 68219550; fax (10) 68212352; e-mail ceiec@ceiec.com.cn; internet www.ceiec.com.cn; imports and exports electronics equipment, light industrial products, ferrous and non-ferrous metals; advertising; consultancy; Chair. and Pres. QIAN BENYUAN.

China National Export Bases Development Corpn: Bldg 16–17, District 3, Fang Xing Yuan, Fang Zhuang Xiaoqu, Fengtai Qu, Beijing 100078; tel. (10) 67628899; fax (10) 67628803; Pres. XUE ZHAO.

China National Foreign Trade Transportation Corpn (Group) (SINOTRANS): Sinotrans Plaza, A43, Xizhimen Beidajie, Beijing 100044; tel. (10) 62295900; fax (10) 62295901; e-mail office@sinotrans.com; internet www.sinotrans.com; f. 1950; agents for Ministry's import and export corpns; arranges customs clearance, deliveries, forwarding and insurance for sea, land and air transportation; registered cap. 150m. yuan; Chair. and Pres. LUO KAIFU.

China National Import and Export Commodities Inspection Corpn: 15 Fanghuadi Xi Jie, Chaoyang Qu, Beijing 100020; tel. (10) 65013951; fax (10) 65004625; internet www.ccic.com.cn; inspects, tests and surveys import and export commodities for overseas trade, transport, insurance and manufacturing firms; Pres. ZHOU WENHUI.

China National Instruments Import and Export Corpn (Instrimpex): Instrimpex bldg, 6 Xizhimenwai Jie, Beijing 100044; tel. (10) 68330618; fax (10) 68330528; e-mail zcb@instrimpex.com.cn; internet www.instrimpex.com.cn; f. 1955; imports and exports; technical service, real estate, manufacturing, information service, etc.; Pres. ZHANG RUEN.

China National Light Industrial Products Import and Export Corpn: 910, 9th Section, Jin Song, Chao Yang Qu, Beijing 100021; tel. (10) 67766688; fax (10) 67747246; e-mail info@chinalight.com.cn; internet www.chinalight.com.cn; imports and exports household electrical appliances, audio equipment, photographic equipment, films, paper goods, building materials, bicycles, sewing machines, enamelware, glassware, stainless steel goods, footwear, leather goods, watches and clocks, cosmetics, stationery, sporting goods, etc.; Pres. XU LIEJUN.

China National Machine Tool Corpn: 19 Fang Jia Xiaoxiang, An Nei, Beijing 100007; tel. (10) 64033767; fax (10) 64015657; f. 1979; imports and exports machine tools and tool products, components and equipment; supplies apparatus for machine building industry; Pres. QUAN YILU.

China National Machinery and Equipment Import and Export Corpn (Group): 6 Xisanhuannan Lu, Liuliqiao, Beijing 100073; tel. (10) 63271392; fax (10) 63261865; f. 1978; imports and exports machine tools, all kinds of machinery, automobiles, hoisting and transport equipment, electric motors, photographic equipment, etc.; Pres. HU GUIXIANG.

China National Machinery Import and Export Corpn: Sichuan Mansion, West Wing, 1 Fu Xing Men Wai Jie, Xicheng Qu, Beijing 100037; tel. (10) 68991188; fax (10) 68991000; e-mail cmc@cmc.com.cn; internet www.cmc.com.cn; f. 1950; imports and exports machine tools, diesel engines and boilers and all kinds of machinery; imports aeroplanes, ships, etc.; Chair and Pres. CHEN WEIGUN.

China National Medicine and Health Products Import and Export Corpn: Meheco Plaza, 18 Guangming Zhong Jie, Chongwen Qu, Beijing 100061; tel. (10) 67116688; fax (10) 67021579; e-mail webmaster@meheco.com.cn; internet www.meheco.com.cn; Pres. LIU GUOSHENG.

China National Metals and Minerals Import and Export Corpn: Bldg 15, Block 4, Anhuili, Chao Yang Qu, Beijing 100101; tel. (10) 64916666; fax (10) 64916421; e-mail support@minmetals.com.cn; internet www.minmetals.com.cn; f. 1950; principal imports and exports include steel, antimony, tungsten concentrates and ferrotungsten, zinc ingots, tin, mercury, pig iron, cement, etc.; Pres. MIAO GENGSHU.

China National Native Produce and Animal By-Products Import and Export Corpn (TUHSU): Sanli Bldg, 208 Andingmenwai Jie, Beijing 100011; tel. (10) 64248899; fax (10) 64204099; e-mail info@china-tuhsu.com; internet www.china-tuhsu.com; f. 1949; imports and exports include tea, coffee, cocoa, fibres, etc.; 13 subsidiary enterprises; 18 tea brs; 19 overseas subsidiaries; Pres. ZHANG ZHENMING.

China National Non-Ferrous Metals Import and Export Corpn (CNIEC): 12B Fuxing Lu, Beijing 100814; tel. (10) 63975588; fax (10) 63964424; Chair. WU JIANCHANG; Pres. XIAO JUNQING.

China National Nuclear Corpn: 1 Nansanxiang, Sanlihe, Beijing; tel. (10) 68512211; fax (10) 68533989; internet www.cnnc.com.cn; Pres. LI DINGFAN.

China National Offshore Oil Corpn (CNOOC): PO Box 4705, Jingxin Bldg, 2A North Dongsanhuan Lu, Chao Yang Qu, Beijing 100027; tel. (10) 64662993; fax (10) 64669007; e-mail webinfo@cnooc.com.cn; internet www.cnooc.com.cn; sales 2,039m.; Pres. WEN LIUCHENG.

China National Oil Development Corpn: Liupukang, Beijing 100006; tel. (10) 6444313; Pres. CHENG SHOULI.

China National Packaging Import and Export Corpn: Xinfu Bldg B, 3 Dong San Huan Bei Lu, Chao Yang Qu, Beijing 100027; tel. (10) 64611166; fax (10) 64616437; e-mail info@chinapack.net; internet www.chinapack.net; handles import and export of packaging materials, containers, machines and tools; contracts for the processing and converting of packaging machines and materials supplied by foreign customers; registered cap. US $30m.; Pres. ZHENG CHONGXIANG.

China National Petro-Chemical Corpn (SINOPEC): Jia 6, Dong Huixin Lu, Chao Yang Qu, Beijing 100029; tel. (10) 64225533; fax (10) 64212429; f. 1983; restructured mid-1998; responsible for petroleum extraction and refining in northern and western China, and for setting retail prices of petroleum products; Pres. LI YIZHONG.

China National Petroleum Corpn: 6 Liupukang Jie, Xicheng Qu, Beijing 100724; tel. (10) 62094538; fax (10) 62094806; e-mail admin@hq.cnpc.com.cn; internet www.cnpc.com.cn; restructured mid-1998; responsible for petroleum extraction and refining in southern and eastern China, and for setting retail prices of petroleum products; Pres. MA FUCAI.

China National Publications Import and Export Corpn: 16 Gongrentiyuguandong Lu, Chao Yang Qu, Beijing; tel. (10) 65066688; fax (10) 65063101; e-mail cnpiec@cnpiec.com.cn; internet www.cnpiec.com.cn; imports and exports books, newspapers and periodicals, records, CD-ROMs, etc. Pres. SONG XIAOHONG.

China National Publishing Industry Trading Corpn: POB 782, 504 An Hua Li, Andingmenwai, Beijing 100011; tel. (10) 64215031; fax (10) 64214540; f. 1981; imports and exports publications, printing equipment technology; holds book fairs abroad; undertakes joint publication; Pres. ZHOU HONGLI.

China National Seed Group Corpn: 16A Xibahe, Chao Yang Qu, Beijing 100028; tel. (10) 64201817; fax (10) 64201820; imports and exports crop seeds, including cereals, cotton, oil-bearing crops, teas, flowers and vegetables; seed production for foreign seed companies etc.; Pres. HE ZHONGHUA.

China National Silk Import and Export Corpn: 105 Bei He Yan Jie, Dongcheng Qu, Beijing 100006; tel. (10) 65123338; fax (10) 65125125; e-mail cnsiec@public.bta.net.cn; internet www.chinasilk.com; Pres. XU HONGXIN.

China National Star Petroleum Corpn: Beijing; e-mail jf@mail.cnspc.com.cn; internet www.cnspc.com.cn; f. 1997; Pres. ZHU JIAZHEN.

China National Technical Import and Export Corpn: Jiuling Bldg, 21 Xisanhuan Beilu, Beijing 100081; tel. (10) 68404000; fax (10) 68414877; e-mail info@cntic.com.cn; internet www.cntic.com.cn; f. 1952; imports all kinds of complete plant and equipment, acquires modern technology and expertise from abroad, undertakes co-production and jt ventures, and technical consultation and updating of existing enterprises; registered cap. 200m.; Pres. WANG HUIHENG.

China National Textiles Import and Export Corpn: 82 Donganmen Jie, Beijing 100747; tel. (10) 65123844; fax (10) 65124711; e-mail webmaster@chinatex.com; internet www.chinatex-group.com; imports synthetic fibres, raw cotton, wool, garment accessories, etc.; exports cotton yarn, cotton fabric, knitwear, woven garments, etc.; Pres. ZHAO BOYA.

China National Tobacco Import and Export Corpn: 11 Hufang Lu, Xuanwu Qu, Beijing 100052; tel. (10) 63533399; fax (10) 63015331; Pres. XUN XINGHUA.

China National United Oil Corpn: 57 Wangfujing Jie, Dongcheng Qu, Beijing 100006; tel. (10) 65223828; fax (10) 65223817; Chair. ZHANG JIAREN; Pres. ZHU YAOBIN.

China No. 1 Automobile Group: 63 Dongfeng Jie, Chao Yang Qu, Changchun, Jilin; tel. (431) 5003030; fax (431) 5001309; f. 1953; mfr of passenger cars; Gen. Man. GENG ZHAOJIE.

China North Industries Group: 46 Sanlihe Lu, Beijing 100821; tel. (10) 68594210; fax (10) 68594232; internet www.corincogroup.com.cn; exports vehicles and mechanical products, light industrial products, chemical products, opto-electronic products, building materials, military products, etc.; Pres. MA ZHIGENG.

China Nuclear Energy Industry Corpn (CNEIC): 1A Yuetan Bei Jie, Xicheng Qu, Beijing 100037; tel. (10) 68013395; fax (10) 68512393; internet www.cnnc.com.cn; exports air filters, vacuum valves, dosimeters, radioactive detection elements and optical instruments; Pres. ZHANG ZHIFENG.

China Petro-Chemical International Co: 2 Ofc Bldg, 6A Huixin Dongjie, Chao Yang Qu, Beijing 100029; tel. (10) 64916672; fax (10) 64218351; f. 1983; registered cap. 120m.; Pres. YANG SHUSHAN.

China Road and Bridge Corpn: Zhonglu Bldg, 88C, An Ding Men Wai Dajie, Beijing 100011; tel. (10) 64285616; fax (10) 64285686; e-mail crbc@crbc.com; internet www.crbc.com; overseas and domestic building of highways, urban roads, bridges, tunnels, industrial and residential buildings, airport runways and parking areas; contracts to do surveying, designing, pipe-laying, water supply and sewerage, building, etc., and/or to provide technical or labour services; Chair. ZHOU JICHANG.

China Shipbuilding Trading Corpn Ltd: 10 Yue Tan Bei Xiao Jie, Beijing 100861; tel. (10) 68032560; fax (10) 68033380; e-mail webmaster@cstc.com.cn; internet www.ctsc.com.cn; Pres. LI ZHUSHI.

China State Construction Engineering Corpn: Baiwanzhuang, Xicheng Qu, Beijing 100835; tel. (10) 68347766; fax (10) 68314326; e-mail cscec-us@worldnet.att.net; internet www.cscec.com; Pres. MA TINGGUI.

China State Shipbuilding Corpn: 5 Yuetan Beijie, Beijing; tel. (10) 68030208; fax (10) 68031579; Pres. CHEN XIAOJIN; Gen. Man. XU PENGHANG.

China Tea Import and Export Corpn: Zhongtuchu Bldg, 208 Andingmenwai Jie, Beijing 100011; tel. (10) 64204123; fax (10) 64204101; e-mail info@teachina.com; internet www.chinatea.com .cn; Pres. LI JIAZHI.

China Xinshidai (New Era) Corpn: 40 Xie Zuo Hu Tong, Dongcheng Qu, Beijing 100007; tel. (10) 64017384; fax (10) 64032935; Pres. QIN ZHONGXING.

China Xinxing Corpn (Group): 17 Xisanhuan Zhong Lu, Beijing 100036; tel. (10) 685166688; fax (10) 68514669; e-mail black-lily@ nihao.com; internet www.black-lily.com; Pres. FAN YINGJUN.

Chinese General Co of Astronautics Industry (State Aerospace Bureau): 8 Fucheng Lu, Haidian Qu, Beijing 100712; tel. (10) 68586047; fax (10) 68370080; Pres. LIU JIYUAN.

Daqing Petroleum Administration Bureau: Sartu Qu, Daqing, Heilongjiang; tel. (459) 814649; fax (459) 322845; Gen. Man. WANG ZHIWU.

Maanshan Iron and Steel Co: 8 Hongqibei Lu, Maanshan 243003, Anhui; tel. (555) 2883492; fax (555) 2324350; Chair. HANG YONGYI; Pres. LI ZONGBI.

Shanghai Automobile Industry Sales Corpn: 548 Caoyang Lu, Shanghai 200063; tel. and fax (21) 62443223; Gen. Man. XU JIANYU.

Shanghai Foreign Trade Corpn: 27 Zhongshan Dong Yi Lu, Shanghai 200002; tel. (21) 63217350; fax (21) 63290044; f. 1988; handles import-export trade, foreign trade transportation, chartering, export commodity packaging, storage and advertising for Shanghai municipality; Gen. Man. WANG MEIJUN.

Shanghai International Trust Trading Corpn: 201 Zhaojiabang Lu, Shanghai 200032; tel. (21) 64033866; fax (21) 64034722; f. 1979, present name adopted 1988; handles import and export business, international mail orders, processing, assembling, compensation trade etc.

Shougang Corpn: Shijingshan, Beijing 100041; tel. and fax (10) 68293532; e-mail webmaster@shougang.com.cn; internet www .shougang.com.cn; Chair. BI QUN; Gen. Man. LUO BINGSHENG.

State Bureau of Non-Ferrous Metals Industry: 12B Fuxing Lu, Beijing 100814; tel. (10) 68514477; fax (10) 68515360; under supervision of State Economic and Trade Commission; Dir ZHANG WULE.

Wuhan Iron and Steel (Group) Co: Qingshan Qu, Wuhan, Hubei Province; tel. (27) 6892004; fax (27) 6862325; proposals for merger with two other steel producers in Hubei announced late 1997; Pres. LIU BENREN.

Xinxing Oil Co (XOC): Beijing; f. 1997; exploration, development and production of domestic and overseas petroleum and gas resources; Gen. Man. ZHU JIAZHEN.

Yuxi Cigarette Factory: Yujiang Lu, Yuxi, Yunnan Province; tel. and fax (877) 2052343; Gen. Man. CHU SHIJIAN.

Zhongjiang Group: Nanjing, Jiansu; f. 1998; multi-national operation mainly in imports and exports, contract projects and real estate; group consists of 126 subsidiaries incl. 25 foreign ventures.

UTILITIES
Electricity

Beijing Power Supply Co: Qianmen Xidajie, Beijing 100031; tel. (10) 63129201.

Beijing Datang Power Generation: 33 Nanbinhe Lu, Xuanwu Qu, Beijing; one of China's largest independent power producers; Chair. JIAO YIAN.

Central China Electric Power Group Co: 47 Xudong Lu, Wuchang, Wuhan 430077; tel. (27) 6813398.

Changsha Electric Power Bureau: 162 Jiefang Sicun, Changsha 410002; tel. (731) 5912121; fax (731) 5523240.

China Atomic Energy Authority: Chair. ZHANG HUAZHU.

China Northwest Electric Power Group Co: 57 Shangde Lu, Xian 710004; tel. (29) 7275061; fax (29) 7212451; Chair. LIU HONG.

China Power Grid Development (CPG): f. to manage transmission and transformation lines for the Three Gorges hydroelectric scheme; Pres. ZHOU XIAOQIAN.

China Yangtze Three Gorges Project Development Corpn: 1 Jianshe Dajie, Yichang, Hubei Province; tel. (717) 6762212; fax (717) 6731787; Pres. LU YOUMEI.

Dalian Power Supply Co: 102 Zhongshan Lu, Dalian 116001; tel. (411) 2637560; fax (411) 2634430; Chief Gen. Man. LIU ZONGXIANG.

Fujian Electric Industry Bureau: 4 Xingang Dao, Taijrang Qu, Fuzhou 350009; tel. and fax (591) 3268514; Dir WANG CHAOXU.

Gansu Bureau of Electric Power: 306 Xijin Dong Lu, Qilihe Qu, Lanzhou 730050; tel. (931) 2334311; fax (93) 2331042; Dir ZHANG MINGXI.

Guangdong Electric Power Bureau: 757 Dongfeng Dong Lu, Guangzhou 510600; tel. (20) 87767888; fax (20) 87770307.

Guangdong Shantou Electric Power Bureau: Jinsha Zhong Lu, Shantou 515041; tel. (754) 8257606.

Guangxi Electric Power Bureau: 6 Minzhu Lu, Nanning 530023; tel. (771) 2801123; fax (771) 2803414.

Guangzhou Electric Power Co: 9th Floor, Huale Bldg, 53 Huale Lu, Guangzhou 510060; tel. (20) 83821111; fax (20) 83808559.

Hainan Electric Power Industry Bureau: 34 Haifu Dadao, Haikou 570203; tel. (898) 5334777; fax (898) 5333230.

Heilongjiang Electric Power Co: B12Fl High Tech Development Zone, Harbin 150001; tel. (451) 2308810; fax (451) 2525878; Chair. XUE YANG.

Huadong Electric Power Group Corpn: 201 Nanjing Dong Lu, Shanghai; tel. (21) 63290000; fax (21) 63290727; power supply.

Huazhong Electric Power Group Corpn: Liyuan, Donghu, Wuhan, Hubei Province; tel. (27) 6813398; fax (27) 6813143; electrical engineering; Gen. Man. LIN KONGXING.

Inner Mongolia Electric Power Co: 28 Xilin Nan Lu, Huhehaose 010021; tel. (471) 6942222; fax (471) 6924863

Jiangmen Electric Power Supply Bureau: 87 Gangkou Lu, Jiangmen 529030; tel. and fax (750) 3360133.

Jiangxi Electric Power Bureau: 13 Yongwai Zheng Jie, Nanchang 330006; tel. (791) 6224701; fax (791) 6224830.

National Grid Construction Co: established to oversee completion of the National Grid by 2009.

North China Electric Power Group Corpn: 32 Zulinqianjie, Xuanwu Qu, Beijing 100053; tel. and fax (10) 63263377; Pres. JIAO YIAN.

Northeast China Electric Power Group: 11 Shiyiwei Lu, Heping Qu, Shenyang 110003; tel. (24) 3114382; fax (24)3872665.

Shandong Electric Power Group Corpn: 150 Jinger Lu, Jinan 250001; tel. (531) 6911919.

Shandong Rizhao Power Co Ltd: 1st Floor, Bldg 29, 30 Northern Section, Shunyu Xiaoqu, Jinan 250002; tel. (531) 2952462; fax (531) 2942561.

Shanghai Electric Power Co: 181 Nanjing Dong Lu, Huangpu Qu, Shanghai 200002; tel. (21) 63291010; fax (21) 63248586; Dir GU YINZHANG.

Shenzhen Power Supply Co: 2 Yanhe Xi Lu, Luohu Qu, Shenzhen 518000; tel. (755) 5561920.

Sichuan Electric Power Co: Room 1, Waishi Bldg, Dongfeng Lu, Chengdu 610061; tel. (28) 444321; fax (28) 6661888.

State Power Corpn: Pres. GAO YAN.

Tianjin Electric Power Industry Bureau: 29 Jinbu Dao, Hebei Qu, Tianjin 300010; tel. (22) 24406326; fax (22) 22346965.

Wenergy Co Ltd: 81 Wuhu Lu, Hefei 230001; tel. (551) 2626906; fax (551) 2648061.

Wuhan Power Supply Bureau: 981 Jiefang Dadao, Hankou, Wuhan 430013; tel. (27) 2426455; fax (27) 2415605.

Wuxi Power Supply Bureau: 8 Houxixi, Wuxi 214001; tel. (510) 2717678; fax (510) 2719182.

Xiamen Power Transformation and Transmission Engineering Co: 67 Wenyuan Lu, Xiamen 361004; tel. (592) 2046763.

Xian Power Supply Bureau: Huancheng Dong Lu, Xian 710032; tel. (29) 7271483.

Gas

Beijing Gas Co: 30 Dongsanhuan Zhong Lu, Beijing 100020; tel. (10) 65024131; fax (10) 65023815; Dir LIU BINGIUN.

Beijing Natural Gas Co: Bldg 5, Dixingju, An Ding Men wai, Beijing 100011; tel. (10) 64262244.

Changchun Gas Co: 30 Tongzhi Jie, Changchun 130021; tel. (431) 8926479.

Changsha Gas Co: 18 Shoshan Lu, Changsha 410011; tel. (731) 4427246.

Qingdao Gas Co: 399A Renmin Lu, Qingdao 266032; tel. (532) 4851461; fax (532) 4858653.

Shanghai Gas Supply Co: 656 Xizang Zhong Lu, Shanghai 200003; tel. (21) 63222333; fax (21) 63528600; Gen. Man. LI LONGLING.

Wuhan Gas Co: Qingnian Lu, Hankou, Wuhan 430015; tel. (27) 5866223.

Xiamen Gas Corpn: Ming Gong Bldg, Douxi Lukou, Hubin Nan Lu, Xiamen 361004; tel. (592) 2025937; fax (592) 2033290.

Water

Beijing District Heating Co: 1 Xidawang Lu, Hongmiao, Chao Yang Qu, Beijing 100026; tel. (10) 65060066; fax (10) 65678891.

Beijing Municipal Water Works Co: 19 Yangrou Hutong, Xicheng Qu, Beijing 100034; tel. (10) 66167744; fax (10) 66168028.

Changchun Water Co: 53 Dajing Lu, Changchun 130000; tel. (431) 8968366.

Chengdu Water Co: 16 Shierqiao Jie, Shudu Dadao, Chengdu 610072; tel. (28) 77663122; fax (28) 7776876.

The China Water Company: f. to develop investment opportunities for water projects.

Guangzhou Water Supply Co: 5 Huanshi Xi Lu, Guangzhou 510010; tel. (20) 81816951.

Haikou Water Co: 31 Datong Lu, Haikou 570001; tel.(898) 6774412.

Harbin Water Co: 49 Xi Shidao Jie, Daoli Qu, Harbin 150010; tel. (451) 4610522; fax (451) 4611726.

Jiangmen Water Co: 44 Jianshe Lu, Jiangmen 529000; tel. (750) 3300138; fax (750) 3353704.

Qinhuangdao Pacific Water Co: Hebei; Sino-US water supply project; f. 1998.

Shanghai Municipal Waterworks Co: 484 Jiangxi Zhong Lu, Shanghai 200002; tel. (21) 63215577; fax (21) 63231346; service provider for municipality of Shanghai.

Shenzhen Water Supply Group Co: Water Bldg, 1019 M. Shennan Lu, Shenzhen 518031; tel. (755) 2137888; fax (755) 2137882, internet www.waterchina.com.

Tianjin Waterworks Group: 54 Jianshe Lu, Heping Qu, Tianjin 300040; tel. (22) 3393887; fax (22) 3306720.

Xian Water Co: Huancheng Xi Lu, Xian 710082; tel. (29) 4244881.

Zhanjiang Water Co: 20 Renmin Dadaonan, Zhanjiang 524001; tel. (759) 2286394.

Zhongshan Water Supply Co: 23 Yinzhu Jie, Zhuyuan Lu, Zhongshan 528403; tel. (760) 8312969; fax (760) 6326429.

Zhuhai Water Supply General Corpn: Yuehai Zhong Lu, Gongbei, Zhuhai 519020; tel. (756) 8881160; fax (756) 8884405

TRADE UNIONS

All-China Federation of Trade Unions (ACFTU): 10 Fu Xing Men Wai Jie, Beijing 100865; tel. (10) 68592114; fax (10) 68562030; f. 1925; organized on an industrial basis; 15 affiliated national industrial unions, 30 affiliated local trade union councils; membership is voluntary; trade unionists enjoy extensive benefits; 103,996,000m. mems (1995); Pres. WEI JIANXING; First Sec. ZHANG JUNJIU.

Principal affiliated unions:

All-China Federation of Railway Workers' Unions: Chair. HUANG SICHUAN.

Architectural Workers' Trade Union: Sec. SONG ANRU.

China Self-Employed Workers' Association: Pres. REN ZHONGLIN.

Educational Workers' Trade Union: Chair. JIANG WENLIANG.

Light Industrial Workers' Trade Union: Chair. LI SHUYING.

Machinery Metallurgical Workers' Union: Chair. ZHANG CUNEN.

National Defence Workers' Union: Chair. GUAN HENGCAI.

Postal and Telecommunications Workers' Trade Union of China: Chair. LUO SHUZHEN.

Seamen's Trade Union of China: Chair. ZHANG SHIHUI.

Water Resources and Electric Power Workers' Trade Union: Chair. DONG YUNQI.

Workers' Autonomous Federation (WAF): f. 1989; aims to create new trade union movement in China, independent of the All-China Federation of Trade Unions.

Transport

RAILWAYS

Ministry of Railways: 10 Fuxing Lu, Haidian Qu, Beijing 100844; tel. (10) 63244150; fax (10) 63242150; e-mail webmaster@ns.chinamor.cn.net; internet www.chinamor.cn.net; controls all railways through regional divisions. The railway network has been extended to all provinces and regions except Tibet (Xizang), where construction is in progress. Total length in operation in December 1999 was 57,923 km, of which 14,025 km were electrified. The major routes include Beijing–Guangzhou, Tianjin–Shanghai, Manzhouli–Vladivostok, Jiaozuo–Zhicheng and Lanzhou–Badou. In addition, special railways serve factories and mines. A new 2,536-km line from Beijing to Kowloon (Hong Kong) was completed in late 1995. Plans for a 1,300-km high-speed link between Beijing and Shanghai, to be completed by the year 2000, were announced in 1994. China's first high-speed service, linking Guangzhou and Shenzhen, commenced in December 1994. A direct service between Shanghai and Hong Kong commenced in 1997.

An extensive programme to develop the rail network was announced in early 1998, which aimed to increase the total network to 68,000 km by the year 2000, and to more than 70,000 km by 2002. Railways were to be constructed along the Changjiang valley, starting at Sichuan, and along China's east coast, originating at Harbin. In December 1999 plans were announced for a railway to Kazakhstan.

City Underground Railways

Beijing Metro Corpn: 2 Beiheyan Lu, Xicheng, Beijing 100044; tel. (10) 68024566; f. 1969; total length 54 km, with 64 km of further lines to be built by the year 2010; Gen. Man. FENG SHUANGSHENG.

Guangzhou Metro: 204 Huanshi Lu, Guangzhou 510010; tel. (20) 6665287; fax (20) 6678232; opened June 1997; total network of 35.9 km planned; Gen. Man. CHEN QINGQUAN.

Shanghai Metro Corpn: 12 Heng Shan Lu, Shanghai 200031; tel. (21) 64312460; fax (21) 64339598; f. 1995; 21 km open, with a further 41.1 km under construction; Pres. SHI LIAN.

Tianjin Metro: 97 Jiefangbei Lu, Heping, Tianjin 300041; tel. (22) 23395410; fax (22) 23396194; f. 1984; total planned network 154 km; Gen. Man. WANG YUJI.

Underground systems were planned for Chongqing and Qingdao.

ROADS

At the end of 1999 China had 1,351,691 km of highways (of which at least 1,268,393 km were paved). Four major highways link Lhasa (Tibet) with Sichuan, Xinjiang, Qinghai Hu and Kathmandu (Nepal). A programme of expressway construction began in the mid-1980s. By 1999 there were 11,605 km of expressways (1,313 km of which were constructed in 1997), routes including the following: Shenyang–Dalian, Beijing–Tanggu, Shanghai–Jiading, Guangzhou–Foshan and Xian–Lintong. A new 123-km highway linking Shenzhen (near the border with Hong Kong) to Guangzhou opened in 1994. A 58-km road between Guangzhou and Zhongshan connects with Zhuhai, near the border with Macau. Construction of a bridge, linking Zhuhai with Macau, began in June 1998 and was scheduled for completion by late 1999. A bridge connecting the mainland with Hong Kong was to be built, with completion scheduled for the year 2004. In 1997 some 20% of villages in China were not connected to the road infrastructure.

INLAND WATERWAYS

At the end of 1999 there were some 116,504 km of navigable inland waterways in China. The main navigable rivers are the Changjiang (Yangtze River), the Zhujiang (Pearl River), the Heilongjiang, the Grand Canal and the Xiangjiang. The Changjiang is navigable by vessels of 10,000 tons as far as Wuhan, more than 1,000 km from the coast. Vessels of 1,000 tons can continue to Chongqing upstream. There were 5,142 river ports at the end of 1996. In 1997 there were some 5,100 companies involved in inland waterway shipping.

SHIPPING

China has a network of more than 2,000 ports, of which more than 130 are open to foreign vessels. The main ports include Dalian, Qinhuangdao, Tianjin, Yantai, Qingdao, Rizhao, Lianyungang, Shanghai, Ningbo, Guangzhou and Zhanjiang. In 1999 the main coastal ports handled 1,052m. tons of cargo. In December 1998 China's merchant fleet comprised 3,214 ships, totalling 16.5m. grt.

Bureau of Water Transportation: Beijing; controls rivers and coastal traffic.

China National Chartering Corpn (SINOCHART): see p. 1064.

China Ocean Shipping (Group) Co (COSCO): 3 Dongsanhuan Bei Lu, Chaoyang Qu, Beijing 100027; tel. (10) 64661188; fax (10) 64669859; reorg. 1993, re-established 1997; head office transferred to Tianjin late 1997; br. offices: Shanghai, Guangzhou, Tianjin, Qingdao, Dalian; 200 subsidiaries (incl. China Ocean Shipping Agency—PENAVIC) and joint ventures in China and abroad, engaged in ship-repair, container-manufacturing, warehousing, insurance, etc.; merchant fleet of 600 vessels; 47 routes; Pres. CHEN ZHONGBIAO.

China Shipping Group: f. 1997; Pres. LI KELIN.

Minsheng Shipping Co Ltd: Minsheng Bldg, 83 Xinhua Lu, Chongqing 400011; tel. (23) 63833121 fax (23) 63832359; f. 1984; Gen. Man. LU GUOJI.

CIVIL AVIATION

Air travel is expanding very rapidly. In 1999 120 airports were equipped to handle Boeing-737 and larger aircraft. Chinese airlines carried a total of 60.9m. passengers in 1999. In 1998 there were 34 airlines, including numerous private companies, operating in China.

General Administration of Civil Aviation of China (CAAC): POB 644, 155 Dongsixi Jie, Beijing 100710; tel. (10) 64014104; fax (10) 64016918; f. 1949 as Civil Aviation Administration of China; restructured in 1988 as a purely supervisory agency, its operational functions being transferred to new, semi-autonomous airlines (see below; also China United Airlines (division of Air Force) and China Capital Helicopter Service); domestic flights throughout China; external services are mostly operated by **Air China, China Eastern** and **China Southern Airlines**; Dir LIU JIANFENG.

Air China: Beijing International Airport, POB 644, Beijing 100621; tel. (10) 64663366; fax (10) 64563831; e-mail webmaster@airchina.com.cn; internet www.airchina.com.cn; international and domestic scheduled passenger and cargo services; Pres. WANG LIAN.

China Eastern Airlines: 2550 Hongqiao Rd, Hongqiao Airport, Shanghai 200335; tel. (21) 62688558; fax (21) 62688107; e-mail webmaster@cea.online.sh.cn; internet www.cea.online.sh.cn; f. 1987; domestic services; overseas destinations include USA, Europe, Japan, Singapore, Seoul and Bangkok; Pres. LI ZHONGMING.

China Northern Airlines: 3-1 Xiaoheyan Lu, Dadong Qu, Shenyang, Liaoning 110043; tel. (24) 23198405; fax (24) 23198410; e-mail northern_air@163.net; internet www.cna.ln.cninfo.net; f. 1990; scheduled flights to the Democratic People's Republic of Korea, the Republic of Korea, Russia, Hong Kong, Macau and Japan; Pres. JIANG LIANYING.

China Northwest Airlines: Laodong Nan Lu, Xian, Shaanxi 710082; tel. (29) 8702021; fax (29) 4207040; e-mail cnwadzz@pub.xa-online.sn.cn; internet www.cnwa.com; f. 1992; domestic services and flights to Macau, Singapore and Nagoya; Pres. NIE SHENGLI.

China Southern Airlines: Baiyuan International Airport, Guangzhou, Guangdong 510406; tel. (20) 86122528; fax (20) 86644623; e-mail webmaster@cs-air.com; internet www.csair.com; f. 1991; merged with Zhong Yuan Airlines, 2000; domestic services; overseas destinations include Bangkok, Hanoi, Ho Chi Minh City, Kuala Lumpur, Penang, Singapore, Manila, Vientiane, Jakarta and Surabaya; Chair. YU YANEN; Pres. YAN SHIQING.

China Southwest Airlines: Shuangliu Airport, Chengdu, Sichuan 610202; tel. (28) 5814466; fax (28) 5582630; e-mail szmaster@cswa.com; internet www.cswa.com; f. 1987; 70 domestic routes; international services to Singapore and Bangkok; also Lhasa (Tibet) to Kathmandu (Nepal); Pres. WANG SHIXIANG.

Changan Airlines: 6 Dong Feng Hao Lu, Xian, Shaanxi 710077; tel. (29) 4257662; fax (29) 4263432; e-mail caair@pub.xaonline; internet www.changanair.com; f. 1992; local passenger and cargo services; Pres. SHE YINING.

China General Aviation Corpn: Wusu Airport, Taiyuan, Shanxi 030031; tel. (351) 7040600; fax (351) 7040094; f. 1989; 34 domestic routes; Pres. ZHANG CHANGJING.

China Xinhua Airlines: 1 Jinsong Nan Lu, Chaoyang Qu, Beijing 100021; tel. (10) 67739754; fax (10) 67740126; e-mail infoxh@

homeway.com.cn; internet www.chinaxinhuaair.com; f. 1992; Pres. LAN SHILIANG.

Fujian Airlines: 228A Fuxing East Road, Fuzhou 350014; tel. (591) 3674504; fax (591) 3674304; f. 1993; domestic services; Man. Dir HU JIANNAN.

Guizhou Airlines: 20 Shengfu Lu, Guiyang, Guizhou 550001; tel. (851) 525626; f. 1991; regional passenger and cargo services; Pres. MA YONGXING.

Hainan Airlines: Haihang Devt Bldg, 29 Haixiu Lu, Haikou, Hainan 570206; tel. (898) 6709602; fax (898) 6798976; f. 1993; domestic services; Chair. CHENG FENG.

Nanjing Airlines: Dajiaochang Airport, Nanjing 210000; tel. (25) 4602629; fax (25) 4494461; f. 1994; local services; Pres. JIANG HEPING.

Shandong Airlines: Yaoqiang Airport, Jinan, Shandong 250011; tel. (531) 7966043; fax (531) 7966020; f. 1991; domestic services; Pres. SUN DEHAN.

Shanghai Air Lines: North Gate of Hongqiao International Airport, Shanghai 200335; tel. (21) 62688558; fax (21) 62688107; internet www.shanghai-air.com; f. 1985; domestic services; Chair. YANG XIONG; Pres. ZHOU CHI.

Shanxi Airlines: 36 Yingze Jie, Taiyun 030001; tel. and fax (351) 447178; f. 1991; domestic services; Pres. QIN JIANMING.

Shenzhen Airlines: Lingtian Tian, Lingxiao Garden, Shenzhen Airport, Shenzhen, Guangdong 518128; tel. (755) 7777243; fax (755) 7777242; f. 1993; domestic services; Pres. DUAN DAYANG.

Sichuan Airlines: Chengdu Shuangliu International Airport, Chengdu, Sichuan 610202; tel. (28) 5393114; fax (28) 5393888; e-mail scaloffice@mail.sc.cninfo.net; f. 1986; domestic services; Pres. LAN XINGLIO.

Wuhan Air Lines: 435 Jianshe Dajie, Wuhan 430030; tel. (87) 63603888; fax (87) 83625693; e-mail wuhanair@public.wh.hb.cn; f. 1986; domestic services; Pres. CHENG YAOKUN.

Xiamen Airlines: Gaoqi Airport, Xiamen, Fujian 361009; tel. (592) 6022961; fax (592) 6028263; f. 1992; domestic services; Pres. WU RONGNAN.

Zhejiang Airlines: Jian Qiao Airport, 78 Shiqiao Lu, Hangzhou, Zhejiang 310021; tel. (571) 6400888; fax (571) 6400777; e-mail zjair@public.hz.zj.cn; f. 1990; domestic services; Pres. LUO QIANG.

Tourism

China has enormous potential for tourism, and the sector is developing rapidly. Attractions include dramatic scenery and places of historical interest such as the Temple of Heaven and the Forbidden City in Beijing, the Great Wall, the Ming Tombs, and also the terracotta warriors at Xian. Tibet (Xizang), with its monasteries and temples, has also been opened to tourists. Tours of China are organized for groups of visitors, and Western-style hotels have been built as joint ventures in many areas. By 1999 7,035 tourist hotels were in operation. A total of 72.8m. tourists visited China in 1999. In that year receipts from tourism totalled an estimated US $14,990m.

China International Travel Service (CITS): 103 Fu Xing Men Nei Dajie, Beijing 100800; tel. (10) 66011122; fax (10) 66039331; e-mail mktng@cits.com.cn; internet www.cits.net; f. 1954; makes travel arrangements for foreign tourists; subsidiary overseas companies in 10 countries and regions; Pres. LI LUAN.

China National Tourism Administration (CNTA): 9A Jian Guo Men Nei Dajie, Beijing 100740; tel. (10) 65138866; fax (10) 65122096; Dir HE GUANGWEI.

Chinese People's Association for Friendship with Foreign Countries: 1 Tai Ji Chang Dajie, Beijing 100740; tel. (10) 65122474; fax (10) 65128354; f. 1954; Pres. QI HUAIYUAN; Sec.-Gen. BIAN QINGZU.

State Bureau of Tourism: Jie 3, Jian Guo Men Nei Dajie, Beijing 100740; tel. (10) 65122847; fax (10) 65122095; Dir LIU YI.

CHINESE SPECIAL ADMINISTRATIVE REGIONS

HONG KONG

Introductory Survey

Location, Climate, Language, Religion, Flag, Capital

The Special Administrative Region (SAR) of Hong Kong, as the territory became on 1 July 1997, lies in eastern Asia, off the south coast of the People's Republic of China. The SAR consists of the island of Hong Kong, Stonecutters Island, the Kowloon Peninsula and the New Territories, which are partly on the mainland. The climate is sunny and dry in winter, and hot and humid in summer. The average annual rainfall is 2,214 mm (87 ins), of which about 80% falls between May and September. The official languages are Chinese and English. Cantonese is spoken by the majority of the Chinese community, while Putonghua (Mandarin) is widely understood and of increasing significance. The main religion is Buddhism. Confucianism, Islam, Hinduism and Daoism are also practised, and there are about 500,000 Christians. The flag of the Hong Kong SAR (proportions 3 by 2), flown subordinate to the flag of the People's Republic of China, displays a bauhinia flower consisting of five white petals, each bearing a red line and a red five-pointed star, at the centre of a red field. The capital is Victoria.

Recent History

Hong Kong Island was ceded to the United Kingdom under the terms of the Treaty of Nanking (Nanjing) in 1842. The Kowloon Peninsula was acquired by the Convention of Peking (Beijing) in 1860. The New Territories were leased from China in 1898 for a period of 99 years. From the establishment of the People's Republic in 1949, the Chinese Government asserted that the 'unequal' treaties giving Britain control over Hong Kong were no longer valid.

Japanese forces invaded Hong Kong in December 1941, forcing the British administration to surrender. In August 1945, at the end of the Second World War, the territory was recaptured by British forces. Colonial rule was restored, with a British military administration until May 1946. Upon the restoration of civilian rule, the territory was again administered in accordance with the 1917 Constitution, which vested full powers in the British-appointed Governor. In 1946 the returning Governor promised a greater measure of self-government but, after the communist revolution in China in 1949, plans for constitutional reform were abandoned. Thus, unlike most other British colonies, Hong Kong did not proceed, through stages, to democratic rule. The essential features of the colonial regime remained unaltered until 1985, when, following the Sino-British Joint Declaration (see below), the first changes were introduced into the administrative system. Prior to 1985 the Executive and Legislative Councils consisted entirely of nominated members, including many civil servants in the colonial administration. There were, however, direct elections for one-half of the seats on the Urban Council, responsible for public health and other amenities, but participation was low.

Between 1949 and 1964 an estimated 1m. refugees crossed from the People's Republic of China to Hong Kong, imposing serious strains on Hong Kong's housing and other social services. More than 460,000 Chinese immigrants arrived, many of them illegally, between 1975 and 1980. Strict measures, introduced in October 1980, reduced the continuous flow of refugees from China, but the number of legal immigrants remained at a high level.

During the 1980s the influx of large numbers of refugees from Viet Nam, most of whom lived for substantial periods in detention camps, was problematic. The Hong Kong authorities, meanwhile, exerted pressure on the British Government to end its policy of granting first asylum to these refugees. In response, legislation was introduced in June 1988 to distinguish between political refugees and 'economic migrants'. The latter were to be denied refugee status, and in October the British and Vietnamese Governments agreed terms for their voluntary repatriation. In March 1989 the first group of co-operative 'economic migrants' flew back to Viet Nam. The number of Vietnamese arrivals increased sharply in the late 1980s, despite the unpleasant conditions in the camps where they were confined on arrival, and the restricting of the definition of refugee status. The relative paucity of those who agreed to return to Viet Nam (totalling 1,225 by February 1990) prompted the British Government to attempt, unsuccessfully, to gain general international endorsement for a policy of compulsory repatriation (which, it was claimed, would discourage further large-scale immigration). The Vietnamese Government announced in December 1989 that an agreement had been concluded between the United Kingdom and Viet Nam on a programme of 'involuntary' repatriation, whereby 'economic migrants' could be returned to Viet Nam against their will, on condition that no physical force were used. Reports of forcible repatriation caused violent disturbances in many of the camps. The programme was subsequently halted. At a meeting in January 1990, the UN steering committee for the Comprehensive Plan of Action on Indo-Chinese refugees failed to agree upon a policy. By May 1990 no further cases of the involuntary repatriation of Vietnamese had been reported. At an international conference held in that month, Hong Kong and the member countries of the Association of South East Asian Nations (ASEAN) threatened to refuse asylum to Vietnamese refugees altogether, unless the USA and Viet Nam gave approval to the policy of involuntary repatriation. In September Hong Kong, Viet Nam and the United Kingdom reached an agreement, supported by the UN High Commissioner for Refugees (UNHCR), to allow the repatriation of a new category of refugees—those who were not volunteering to return but who had indicated that they would not actively resist repatriation. This policy had little success, and the number of refugees increased. In October 1991, following protracted negotiations, it was announced that Viet Nam had agreed to the mandatory repatriation of refugees from Hong Kong. The first forcible deportation (mainly of recent arrivals) under the agreement was carried out in November. Tension and violence in the camps continued. In May 1992 an agreement between the United Kingdom and Viet Nam provided for the forcible repatriation of all economic migrants. By the end of 1995 the detention camp population had been greatly reduced, with only 1,479 being classified as refugees. Unrest in the camps continued intermittently. The People's Republic of China, meanwhile, continued to insist that all camps be cleared prior to the transfer of sovereignty in mid-1997. The Whitehead Detention Centre was closed in January 1997, and the refugees were transferred to other camps. Despite an acceleration in the repatriation programme, some 1,200 Vietnamese migrants remained in Hong Kong in December 1997. In January 1998 the SAR administration (see below) announced that it was abolishing the 'port of asylum' policy which had been applied to Vietnamese refugees. Those arriving illegally would no longer be given time to apply for asylum. At the end of May 2000 the last Vietnamese refugee camp, at Pillar Point, was closed. Most of the refugees were granted residency in the SAR.

Meanwhile, following a visit to Hong Kong by the British Prime Minister in September 1982, discussions between the United Kingdom and China were held regarding the territory's future status. In 1984 the United Kingdom conceded that in mid-1997, upon the expiry of the lease on the New Territories, China would regain sovereignty over the whole of Hong Kong. In September 1984 British and Chinese representatives met in Beijing and initialled a legally-binding agreement, the Sino-British Joint Declaration, containing detailed assurances on the future of Hong Kong. China guaranteed the continuation of the territory's capitalist economy and life-style for 50 years after 1997. The territory, as a Special Administrative Region of the People's Republic, would be designated 'Hong Kong, China', and would continue to enjoy a high degree of autonomy, except in matters of defence and foreign affairs. It was agreed that Hong Kong would retain its identity as a free port and separate customs territory, and its citizens would be guaranteed freedom of speech, of assembly, of association, of travel and of religious belief. In December 1984, after being approved by the National People's Congress (NPC—the Chinese legislature) and the British Parliament, the agreement was signed in Beijing by the British and Chinese Prime Ministers, and in May 1985 the two Governments exchanged documents ratifying the agreement. A Joint Liaison Group (JLG), comprising British and Chinese representatives, was established to monitor the provisions of the agreement, and this group held its first meeting in July 1985. A 58-member Basic Law Drafting Committee (BLDC), including 23 representatives from Hong Kong, was formed in Beijing in June, with the aim of drawing up a new Basic Law (Constitution) for Hong Kong, in accordance with Article 31 of the Chinese Constitution, which provides for special administrative regions within the People's Republic.

The majority of the population reportedly accepted the terms of the Joint Declaration, but the sensitive issue of the future nationality of Hong Kong residents proved controversial. The 1981 British Nationality Act had already caused alarm in the territory, where the reclassification of 2.3m. citizens was perceived as a downgrading of their status. As holders of Hong Kong residents' permits, they had no citizenship status under British laws. Following the approval of the Hong Kong agreement, the British Government announced a new form of nationality, to be effective from 1997, designated 'British National (Overseas)', which would not be transferable to descendants and would confer no right of abode in the United Kingdom.

In September 1985 indirect elections were held for 24 new members of an expanded Legislative Council, to replace the former appointees and government officials. The participation rate among the very small proportion of the population eligible to vote in the elections was low. In March 1986 municipal elections were held for the urban and regional councils, which were thus, for the first time, wholly directly-elected. A new Governor, Sir David Wilson (who had played a prominent part in the Sino-British negotiations on the territory's future), formally assumed office in April 1987, following the death of his predecessor, Sir Edward Youde, in December 1986. In May 1987 the Hong Kong Government published proposals regarding the development of representative government during the final decade of British rule. Among the options that it proposed was the introduction, in 1988, of direct elections to the Legislative Council, based upon universal adult suffrage. In spite of the disapproval of the Chinese Government, in February 1988 the Hong Kong Government published, with the support of the majority of the population, a policy document on the development of representative government; the principal proposal was the introduction, in 1991, of 10 (subsequently increased) directly-elected members of the Legislative Council.

In April 1988 the first draft of the Basic Law for Hong Kong was published, and a Basic Law Consultative Committee (BLCC) was established in Hong Kong, initially with 176 members, to collect public comments on its provisions, over a five-month period; the draft was to be debated by the Legislative Council and by the Parliament of the United Kingdom, but no referendum was to be held in Hong Kong, and final approval of the Basic Law rested with the NPC of China. The draft offered five options for the election of a chief executive and four regarding the composition of the future Legislative Council, none of which, however, proposed that the Council should be elected entirely by universal suffrage. Although the legislature would be empowered to impeach the chief executive for wrongdoing, the Chinese Government would have final responsibility for his removal. Critics of the draft Basic Law complained that it failed to offer democratic representation or to guarantee basic human rights; they argued that Hong Kong's autonomy was not clearly defined, and would be threatened by the fact that power to interpret those parts of the Basic Law relating to defence, foreign affairs and China's 'executive acts' would be granted to the NPC in Beijing and not to the Hong Kong judiciary.

In November 1988 the UN Commission on Human Rights criticized the British attitude to the transfer of Hong Kong, with particular reference to the lack of direct elections. A second draft of the Basic Law was approved by the Chinese NPC in February 1989, which ignored all five options previously proposed for the election of a chief executive. In May there were massive demonstrations in Hong Kong in support of the anti-Government protests taking place in China. In June, following the killing of thousands of protesters by the Chinese armed forces in Tiananmen Square in Beijing, further demonstrations

and a general strike took place in Hong Kong, expressing the inhabitants' revulsion at the massacres and their doubts as to whether the Basic Law would, in practice, be honoured by the Chinese Government after 1997. The British Government refused to consider renegotiating the Sino-British Joint Declaration but, in response to demands that the British nationality laws should be changed to allow Hong Kong residents the right to settle in the United Kingdom after 1997, it announced in December 1989 that the British Parliament would be asked to enact legislation enabling as many as 50,000 Hong Kong residents (chosen on a 'points system', which was expected to favour leading civil servants, business executives and professional workers), and an estimated 175,000 dependants, to be given the right of abode in the United Kingdom. The measure was intended to 'maintain confidence' in the colony during the transition to Chinese sovereignty, by curbing the emigration of skilled personnel. The Hong Kong authorities cautiously welcomed the announcement, but China warned prospective applicants that it would not recognize their British nationality after 1997. Widespread popular protests took place in Hong Kong itself over the unfairness of a scheme which was perceived as elitist. The bill containing the measures was approved in the United Kingdom's House of Commons in April 1990.

Among other recommendations made by the parliamentary select committee were the introduction of a Bill of Rights for Hong Kong and an increase in the number of seats subject to direct election in the Hong Kong Legislative Council, to one-half of the total in 1991, leading to full direct elections in 1995. A draft Bill of Rights, based on the UN International Covenant on Civil and Political Rights, was published by the Hong Kong Government in March 1990. The draft was criticized in principle because its provisions would have been subordinate, in the case of conflict, to the provisions of the Basic Law. Nevertheless, the Bill of Rights entered into law in June 1991, its enactment immediately being deemed unnecessary by the Government of China.

China's NPC approved a final draft of the Basic Law for Hong Kong in April 1990. In this version, 24 of the 60 seats in the Legislative Council would be subject to direct election from 1999, and 30 seats from 2003; a referendum, to be held after 2007, would consult public opinion on the future composition of the Council, although the ultimate authority to make any changes would rest with the NPC. The British Government had agreed to co-operate with these measures by offering 18 seats for direct election in 1991 and 20 seats in 1995. Under the Basic Law, the Chief Executive of the Hong Kong Special Administrative Region (SAR), as the territory was to be designated in 1997, would initially be elected for a five-year term by a special 800-member election committee; a referendum was to be held during the third term of office in order to help to determine whether the post should be subject to a general election. However, no person with the right of residence in another country would be permitted to hold an important government post. Particular concern was expressed over a clause in the Law that would 'prohibit political organizations and groups in the Hong Kong SAR from establishing contacts with foreign political organizations or groups'. The British Government and the Hong Kong authorities expressed disappointment that the Basic Law did not allow the development of democratic government at a more rapid pace.

In April 1990 liberal groups founded Hong Kong's first formal political party, the United Democrats of Hong Kong (UDHK), with Martin Lee as its Chairman. The party subsequently became the main opposition to the conservatives, and achieved considerable success in local elections in March and May 1991, and in the territory's first direct legislative elections in September. Of the 18 seats in the Legislative Council subject to election by universal suffrage, 17 were won by members of the UDHK and like-minded liberal and independent candidates. Only 39% of registered electors, however, reportedly voted. Despite the party's electoral success, the Governor nominated only one of the UDHK's 20 suggested candidates when selecting his direct appointees to the Legislative Council. Changes in the membership of the Executive Council were announced in October, liberal citizens again being excluded by the Governor.

In April 1992 Christopher Patten, hitherto Chairman of the Conservative Party in the United Kingdom, was appointed Governor to replace Sir David Wilson upon his retirement. Patten took office in July. Plans for democratic reform in the territory, announced by the Governor in October, included the separation of the Executive Council from the Legislative

Council. The former was reorganized to include prominent lawyers and academics. At the 1995 elections to the latter, the number of directly-elected members was to be increased to the maximum permissible of 20; the franchise for the existing 21 'functional constituencies', representing occupational and professional groups, was to be widened and nine additional constituencies were to be established, in order to encompass all categories of workers. Various social and economic reforms were also announced. In the same month Patten paid his first visit to China.

The proposed electoral changes were denounced by China as a contravention of the Basic Law and of the 1984 Joint Declaration. Although Patten's programme received the general support of the Legislative Council, many conservative business leaders were opposed to the proposals. In November 1992, following Hong Kong's announcement that it was to proceed with the next stage of preparations for the disputed construction of a new airport (without, as yet, the Chinese Government's agreement to the revised financing of the project), China threatened to cancel, in 1997, all commercial contracts, leases and agreements between the Hong Kong Government and the private sector that had been signed without its full approval. The dispute continued in early 1993, China's criticism of the territory's Governor becoming increasingly acrimonious. In February China announced plans to establish a 'second stove', or alternative administration for Hong Kong, if the Governor's proposed reforms were implemented. In April, however, the impasse was broken when the United Kingdom and China agreed to resume negotiations. In July the 57-member Preliminary Working Committee (PWC), established to study issues relating to the forthcoming transfer of sovereignty and chaired by the Chinese Minister of Foreign Affairs, held its inaugural meeting in Beijing. Negotiations between the United Kingdom and China continued intermittently throughout 1993. In December, however, no progress having been made, proposed electoral reforms were submitted to the Legislative Council. The Governor's decision to proceed unilaterally was denounced by China, which declared that it would regard as null and void any laws enacted in Hong Kong.

In February 1994 the Legislative Council approved the first stage of the reform programme, which included the lowering of the voting age from 21 to 18 years. China confirmed that all recently-elected bodies would be disbanded in 1997. The second stage was presented to the Legislative Council in March. Relations with China deteriorated further in April, upon the publication of a British parliamentary report endorsing Patten's democratic reforms. In the same month the UDHK and Meeting Point, a smaller party, merged and formed the Democratic Party of Hong Kong. In April the trial in camera of a Beijing journalist (who worked for a respected Hong Kong newspaper) on imprecise charges of 'stealing state secrets' and his subsequent severe prison sentence aroused widespread concern in the territory over future press freedom. Hundreds of journalists took part in a protest march through the streets of Hong Kong.

In June 1994, in an unprecedented development that reflected growing unease with Patten's style of government, the Legislative Council passed a motion of censure formally rebuking the Governor for refusing to permit a debate on an amendment to the budget. Nevertheless, at the end of the month the Legislative Council approved further constitutional reforms, entailing an increase in the number of its directly-elected members and an extension of the franchise. Despite China's strong opposition to these reforms, shortly afterwards the People's Republic and the United Kingdom concluded an agreement on the transfer of defence sites, some of which were to be retained for military purposes and upgraded prior to 1997, while others were to be released for redevelopment. At the end of August, following the issuing of a report by the PWC in the previous month, the Standing Committee of the NPC in Beijing approved a decision on the abolition, in 1997, of the current political structure of Hong Kong.

In September 1994, at elections to the 18 District Boards (the first to be held on a fully democratic basis), 75 of the 346 seats were won by the Democratic Party. The pro-Beijing Democratic Alliance for the Betterment of Hong Kong (DAB) won 37 seats, the progressive Association for Democracy and People's Livelihood (ADPL) 29 seats, and the pro-Beijing Liberal Party and Liberal Democratic Foundation 18 seats and 11 seats, respectively. Independent candidates secured 167 seats. The level of voter participation was a record 33.1%. In December 1994 the director of the State Council's Hong Kong and Macau Affairs

Office and secretary-general of the PWC, Lu Ping, formally confirmed that the Legislative Council would be disbanded in 1997.

Elections for the 32 seats on the Urban Council and the 27 seats on the Regional Council took place in March 1995. The Democratic Party took 23 seats, the DAB eight seats and the ADPL also eight seats. Fewer than 26% of those eligible voted in the polls. In the same month Donald Tsang was nominated as Financial Secretary; his predecessor, along with other expatriate senior officials, had been requested to take early retirement to allow for the appointment of a local civil servant. Tsang took office in September.

Following a redrafting of the legislation, in June 1995 the United Kingdom and China reached agreement on the establishment of the Court of Final Appeal. Contrary to the Governor's original wishes, this new body would not now be constituted until after the transfer of sovereignty in mid-1997. The agreement was approved by the Legislative Council in July 1995. In the same month an unprecedented motion of 'no confidence' in the Governor was defeated at a session of the Legislative Council. Also in July the territory's Chief Secretary, Anson Chan, confirmed that she had had clandestine meetings with senior Chinese officials during a three-day visit to Beijing.

At elections to the Legislative Council in September 1995, for the first time all 60 seats were determined by election. The Democratic Party won 19 seats in total, including 12 of the 20 seats open to direct election on the basis of geographical constituencies and two of the 10 chosen by an electoral committee. The Liberal Party took nine of the 60 seats, the pro-Beijing DAB six, and the ADPL four. Independent candidates won 17 seats.

The Governor aroused much controversy in September 1995, when he urged the United Kingdom to grant the right of abode to more than 3m. citizens of Hong Kong. The proposals were rebuffed by the British Home Secretary. In October, however, an improvement in Sino-British relations was confirmed by the visit of the Chinese Minister of Foreign Affairs to London. The two sides reached agreement on the establishment of a liaison office to improve bilateral contacts between civil servants. China's disclosure of a plan to establish a parallel administration six months prior to the transfer of sovereignty provoked outrage in Hong Kong.

In January 1996 the 150-member Preparatory Committee of the Hong Kong SAR was formally established in Beijing to succeed the PWC. The 94 Hong Kong delegates included representatives of the territory's business and academic communities. The Democratic Party was excluded from the new body, which was to appoint a 400-member Selection Committee responsible for the choice of the territory's future Chief Executive.

In March 1996, during a visit to the territory, the British Prime Minister announced that more than 2m. holders of the forthcoming Hong Kong SAR passports would be granted visa-free access to (but not residency in) the United Kingdom. He also declared that China had a legal obligation to maintain the Legislative Council and to uphold basic rights in the territory. The Preparatory Committee in Beijing, however, approved a resolution to appoint a provisional body to replace the Legislative Council. Towards the end of March, as the final deadline approached, thousands of Hong Kong residents rushed to submit applications for British Dependent Territories Citizenship (BDTC) which, although conferring no right of abode in the United Kingdom, would provide an alternative travel document to the new SAR passports. As tension continued to rise, in April Anson Chan travelled to Beijing for discussions with Lu Ping. A visit to Hong Kong by Lu Ping earlier in the month had been disrupted by pro-democracy demonstrators. In early July eight pro-democracy politicians from Hong Kong, including five members of the Legislative Council, were refused entry to China to deliver a petition of 60,000 signatures against the proposed establishment of a provisional legislative body for Hong Kong. In mid-August nominations opened for candidacy for the 400-member Selection Committee. In the same month a new pro-democracy movement, The Frontier, comprising teachers, students and trade unionists, was established. In October 1996 the Chinese Minister of Foreign Affairs declared that from mid-1997 the annual protests against the Tiananmen Square massacre of 1989 (and similar demonstrations) would not be tolerated in Hong Kong; furthermore, criticism of the Chinese leadership by the territory's press would not be permitted.

In December 1996 the second ballot for the selection of Hong Kong's Chief Executive (the first having been held in November)

resulted in the choice of Tung Chee-hwa, a shipping magnate and former member of the territory's Executive Council, who obtained 320 of the 400 votes. Later in the month the Selection Committee chose the 60 members of the SAR's controversial Provisional Legislative Council (PLC). More than 30 of the new appointees were members of the existing Legislative Council, belonging mainly to the DAB and to the Liberal Party. Despite much criticism of the PLC's establishment, the new body held its inaugural meeting in Shenzhen in January 1997, and elected Rita Fan as its President.

In early 1997 the Chief Executive-designate announced the composition of the Executive Council, which was to comprise three ex-officio members (as previously) and initially 11 non-official members. Anson Chan was to remain as Chief Secretary, while Donald Tsang was to continue as Financial Secretary; Elsie Leung was to become Justice Secretary, replacing the incumbent Attorney General. China's approval of Tung Chee-hwa's recommendations that senior civil servants be retained did much to enhance confidence in the territory's future. In February, however, relations with the outgoing administration deteriorated when the Preparatory Committee voted overwhelmingly in favour of proposals to repeal or amend 25 laws, thereby reducing the territory's civil liberties.

Meanwhile, Lawrence Leung had abruptly resigned as Director of Immigration in July 1996 for 'personal reasons'. In January 1997 he cast doubt on the integrity of the Hong Kong Government when he appeared before a hearing of the Legislative Council and claimed that he had in fact been dismissed, thus denying the official version of his departure from office. The scandal deepened with the revelation that Leung had been found to possess undisclosed business interests. Newspaper reports alleged that Leung had been involved in espionage activities on behalf of China. The Government finally admitted that Leung had indeed been dismissed, but denied the reports of espionage.

In May 1997 the PLC approved its first legislation (a bill on public holidays), despite protests from the British Government and pro-democracy groups in Hong Kong that the PLC was not entitled to pass laws during the transition period. The PLC declared, however, that the legislation would come into effect only on 1 July. Following the circulation in April of a public consultation document on proposed legislation governing civil liberties and social order, a series of amendments, relating to the holding of public demonstrations and the funding of political organizations, was announced in May. Pro-democracy groups and the outgoing administration remained dissatisfied with the legislation.

Shortly after the transfer of Hong Kong from British to Chinese sovereignty at midnight on 30 June 1997, the inauguration of the SAR Executive Council, the PLC and members of the judiciary was held. Some 4,000 dignitaries attended the ceremonies, although the British Prime Minister and Foreign Secretary, and the US Secretary of State, did not attend the inauguration of the PLC, to register their disapproval at the undemocratic nature of its formation. Pro-democracy groups and members of the former legislature staged peaceful demonstrations in protest at the abolition of the Legislative Council. More than 4,000 Chinese troops of the People's Liberation Army entered Hong Kong shortly after the handover ceremony, joining the small number of Chinese military personnel that had been deployed in the territory in April, following protracted negotiations with the British Government; a further 500 had entered the territory on 30 June, immediately prior to the handover.

Details of the procedure for elections to a new Legislative Council, which would replace the PLC, were announced by the SAR Government in early July 1997. The elections were scheduled to take place in May 1998, and were to be conducted under a new system of voting. Of the 60 seats in the legislature, 20 were to be directly elected by means of a revised system of proportional representation, 30 were to be elected by 'functional constituencies' (comprising professional and special interest groups) and 10 by an 800-member electoral college. Legislative amendments governing the electoral arrangements were approved by the PLC in late September 1997. The significant reduction of the franchise, by comparison with the 1995 legislative elections, was condemned by the Democratic Party. The appointment by indirect election of 36 Hong Kong delegates to the Chinese NPC, in December 1997, also attracted criticism from pro-democracy activists. Nevertheless, the Government maintained that democracy and the rule of law were being upheld in Hong Kong.

Following the transfer of sovereignty to China, concerns continued about freedom of expression in the SAR. In March 1998 a prominent publisher and a member of the Chinese People's Political Consultative Conference (CPPCC), Xu Simin, challenged the right of the public broadcaster, Radio Television Hong Kong, to criticize government policy, while Tung stated on the same day that government policies should be positively presented by the media. Following expressions of popular discontent, Tung issued a denial that Xu's position reflected government policy. In the same month the Secretary of Justice, Elsie Leung, was criticized following the Government's decision not to prosecute another prominent publisher, CPPCC member and a friend of Tung's, Sally Aw Sian, for corruption, despite a ruling against her by the Independent Commission Against Corruption. Pro-democracy groups expressed fears regarding the independence of the Justice Department. This occurred two weeks after Leung had declined to prosecute the official Chinese news agency, Xinhua, for an alleged breach of privacy laws, after it took 10 months (despite a legal 40-day limit) to issue a denial that it possessed information pertaining to Emily Lau, the leader of The Frontier. (In March 1999 a motion of 'no confidence' in Elsie Leung, prompted by these controversial legal decisions, was defeated in the Legislative Council.) In May 1998 two pro-democracy activists were found guilty of defacing flags of China and the Hong Kong SAR at a rally in January, the first such conviction since Hong Kong's transfer to Chinese sovereignty. In March 1999 the Court of Final Appeal ruled that the law prohibiting the defacing of the SAR flag was an unconstitutional restriction of freedom of expression. In December, however, under pressure from Beijing, the Court rescinded its own decision, and the conviction was confirmed, provoking protests from civil rights organizations. In January 1998 a demonstration was staged to coincide with the visit of the former Chinese President, Yang Shangkun, who was regarded as one of those responsible for the Tiananmen Square massacre in 1989. Similar protests were conducted during a visit by Qiao Shi, the Chairman of the Standing Committee of the Eighth Chinese NPC, in February 1998, and in June a commemoration of the 1989 massacre took place without incident. In the following year, the 10th anniversary of the massacre was marked by a peaceful demonstration, attended by 70,000 protesters. On the second anniversary of the resumption of Chinese sovereignty, on 1 July 1999, more than 2,000 pro-democracy demonstrators protested against Chinese control. Tung Chee-hwa's unpopular policies were the subject of similar demonstrations on 1 July 2000.

In October 1999 the SAR administration announced the sudden transfer of Cheung Man-yee, Director of Broadcasting of the government-owned Radio Television Hong Kong, to a post as senior economic and trade representative in Tokyo, Japan. It was suspected that Cheung's defence of the broadcaster's editorial independence had made her unpopular with the pro-China establishment, resulting in her removal for political reasons. Shortly afterwards Emily Lau announced that she would report the transfer to the UN Committee on Human Rights, citing it as an example of the erosion of freedom of expression in Hong Kong.

In April 2000 there were renewed fears for the freedom of the Hong Kong media after a warning by Beijing against the reporting of any remarks advocating Taiwanese independence. The statement was issued following the broadcast in Hong Kong of an interview with Taiwanese Vice President-elect Annette Lu, during which she made 'separatist' remarks. China's interference was widely condemned, prompting an assurance by Tung Chee-hwa that freedom of the press and freedom of speech continued to be guaranteed under the provisions of the Basic Law. In October, in Beijing, relations between the Hong Kong media and the People's Republic were further damaged when Hong Kong reporters were accused by Jiang Zemin of being 'naïve' for implying that Beijing's support for the Chief Executive would lead to Tung Chee-hwa's reappointment without election. A number of unprecedented personal attacks on the Chinese President subsequently appeared in the Hong Kong media, and in the following month journalists from the SAR were banned from attending celebrations in China to mark the 20th anniversary of the establishment of the Shenzhen Special Economic Zone. Those who attempted to contravene the ban were detained until after the ceremony. Concerns over press freedom had increased earlier in November when Willy Wo-Lap Lam, a prominent journalist and critic of mainland policy, resigned from the *South China Morning Post*. His work had been subject to 'pre-screening' for any material likely to anger the People's Republic.

Also in November 2000, students held the latest in a series of protests against the Public Order Ordinance (POO), which stipulated that permission for demonstrations had to be obtained from the security forces at least seven days in advance. Earlier in the month the Government had postponed until December a debate on POO in the Legislative Council, after opposition politicians protested that the administration was trying to enact the law by forcible means.

Fears concerning the SAR's autonomy were exacerbated by the rapid adoption by the PLC in April 1998 of the Adaptation of Laws Bill. The Bill was ostensibly simply to replace references to the British crown in existing legislation but in practice it exempted Xinhua, the office of the Chinese Ministry of Foreign Affairs and the garrison of the People's Liberation Army from all laws unless otherwise stated. Concerns about the territory's legal autonomy were also raised by the conviction and execution, in November and December respectively, of five criminals from Hong Kong in the People's Republic.

At the elections to the first Legislative Council (Legco) of the SAR on 24 May 1998, participation (53.3% of registered voters) was the highest since the introduction of direct elections in Hong Kong. The Democratic Party and other pro-democracy parties suffered a reduction in their overall political strength in the legislature, despite the fact that they won 14 of the 20 directly elective seats. A total of 19 seats were secured by pro-democracy candidates, including 13 by the Democratic Party (nine directly-elected), led by Martin Lee, which became the largest party in the Legislative Council. Lee advocated direct elections by universal suffrage for all 60 seats in the next poll, to be held in 2000. Pro-Beijing supporters dominated the functional constituencies and the election committee ballot. The pro-business Liberal Party, led by Allen Lee, failed to win a single seat in the direct elections but obtained nine in the other constituencies. The DAB also won nine seats, five of which were directly elective.

The powers of the new legislature were curbed by the Basic Law. Legislative Councillors were not permitted to introduce bills related to political expenditure, the political structure or the operation of the government. The passage of private members' bills or motions also required a majority of votes of both groups of councillors—those elected directly and those returned through functional constituencies and the election committee. At its first session in July 1998 the Legislative Council elected Rita Fan as its President. The division between the Chief Executive, who rarely consulted the legislature, and the Legislative Council became more apparent after Tung Chee-hwa's second annual policy address in October. He announced the abolition of urban and regional councils, a move opposed by many members of the legislature, who also criticized the Executive Council for failing to stimulate the territory's ailing economy.

In March 1999 Anson Chan agreed to continue serving as Chief Secretary for two years beyond her normal retirement age, until 2002, when Tung Chee-hwa's term of office was to end. In April 1999 the administration decided to abolish the municipal and regional councils, while existing district boards were to be replaced by district councils. Although the public had been dissatisfied with the performance of the municipal councils, there was resentment at the restructuring of local democracy, which was perceived as a regressive step. In November the Democratic Party threatened legal action if the plan was not abandoned, as it contravened the Basic Law. The first district elections in the Hong Kong SAR took place on 28 November. The Democratic Party won the largest number of elected seats (86), but the pro-Beijing DAB substantially increased its representation, from 37 seats to 83.

Popular support for the SAR Government declined substantially throughout 2000, and public unrest increased. In February Tung Chee-hwa effected a reshuffle of senior officials following the retirement of three officials from the civil service. In May Elsie Leung was reappointed Secretary of Justice for an additional two years. The reappointment was contentious as Leung was regarded as unpopular, having been responsible for some controversial decisions (see above). In June Tung Chee-hwa's administration was embarrassed by the resignation of Rosanna Wong as Secretary for Housing. Three days later the Legislative Council passed a vote of 'no confidence' in Wong and one of her senior officials, holding them responsible for a series of scandals relating to sub-standard construction works. Wong, however,

remained a member of the Executive Council. This affair appeared to justify the resignation in April of the prominent opposition politician, Christine Loh, from the Legislative Council. Loh had cited her frustration with the Government's reluctance to share power with the legislature. According to a public opinion poll conducted in July, only 20% of those surveyed were satisfied with the Government's performance. This was the lowest level of approval recorded in these surveys, which had been conducted regularly since the transfer of sovereignty to China. In September one of Tung Chee-hwa's aides and two officials of Hong Kong University resigned after an independent inquiry found them guilty of attempting to suppress the results of public opinion polls conducted by a university researcher. The Government suffered a further reverse in January 2001, when Anson Chan unexpectedly announced that she was to resign in April, for 'personal reasons'. While visiting Beijing in September 2000, she had been publicly reprimanded by China for her perceived lack of support for the Chief Executive. Chan was widely respected by the international community, and there were fears that Hong Kong might lose some credibility as a result of her resignation. Anson Chan was to be succeeded by Donald Tsang, and the latter was to be replaced as Financial Secretary by Antony Leung.

Meanwhile, the second elections to the Legislative Council took place on 10 September 2000. Twenty-four (increased from 20 in the previous legislature) of the seats were directly elective, with 30 seats elected by 'functional constituencies' and six (reduced from 10) by an 800-member electoral college. The level of voter participation was 43.6%. The Democratic Party won the highest number of seats, with 12 (of which nine were directly elected), just ahead of the DAB, which obtained 11 seats. The Democratic Party's share of the votes cast, however, was inferior to that obtained in the 1998 elections. Public apathy was attributed to dissatisfaction with the Government and to the main political parties' failure to publicize coherent manifestos. Nine days later the DAB legislator-elect, Gary Cheng, resigned from the Legislative Council following a scandal over his failure to declare business interests. (A by-election held in December was won by an independent candidate.) At the first session of the new Legislative Council, Rita Fan was re-elected President.

Legislation approved by the PLC in July 1997, meanwhile, included the introduction of measures to restrict the immigration into the territory of mainland-born children of Hong Kong residents. However, in January 1998 a judge ruled that this new legislation contravened the Basic Law. The Court of Final Appeal ruled against the SAR Government in January 1999, upholding the judgment that the legislation was unconstitutional, prompting condemnation of the Court by the People's Republic of China. Fearing that the ruling on the right of abode by the Court of Final Appeal would result in an influx of more than 1.6m. mainland Chinese, the SAR administration asked the Court in February to clarify its judgment, which apparently asserted the Court's right to overrule decisions relating to the Basic Law made by the NPC in Beijing. The Court of Final Appeal declared that it recognized the authority of the Standing Committee of the Chinese NPC. In May the Legislative Council voted to request the Standing Committee of the NPC to interpret the relevant articles of the Basic Law, to the dissatisfaction of lawyers and democrats, who protested that the SAR's autonomy was being undermined. The NPC published its interpretation, which was not retroactive, in June, stating that the Court of Final Appeal had failed to adhere to the Basic Law in not requesting an interpretation before delivering its judgment. The NPC stipulated that mainlanders were to be granted the right of abode in Hong Kong only if at least one parent had been permanently resident in the territory at the time of their birth and that mainland children of Hong Kong parents who wished to settle in the territory had to apply for mainland approval before entering the SAR. These changes to the interpretation of the Basic Law were estimated to reduce the number of successful applicants to 200,000. In December 17 immigrants with parents resident in Hong Kong were denied the right of abode by the Court of Final Appeal, which recognized China's unrestricted powers to interpret the Basic Law (three subsequently obtained permission to reside in the territory). Violent clashes between demonstrators and the security forces followed the ruling. In August 2000 disaffected mainland Chinese immigrants seeking the right of abode in Hong Kong firebombed the Immigration Department building. Two people were killed, including one immigration officer; 22 people were subsequently arrested and charged with murder.

In August 1999 the People's Republic banned the Pope from visiting Hong Kong later in the year, citing the Vatican's diplomatic relations with Taiwan. The decision was widely criticized as an infringement of the territory's autonomy. Later that month a former adviser to the Taiwanese President was denied a visa to enter Hong Kong to attend an academic conference, a decision widely regarded as indicative of deteriorating relations between China and Taiwan.

In September 1998 the Sino-British JLG met in Hong Kong, for the first time since Hong Kong's transfer to China, to resolve outstanding issues. The most significant problem was that of the 1,100 Vietnamese refugees remaining in Hong Kong; China requested funds from the United Kingdom to facilitate their repatriation. At the final meeting of the JLG before its dissolution (on 1 January 2000), in December 1999 there was a disagreement over the treatment of a Hong Kong resident who had reportedly been arrested in Thailand and deported to the People's Republic of China without any formal extradition proceedings. The man, who had a British National Overseas passport, was entitled to British consular protection. The Chinese authorities, however, maintained that, as he was a Chinese national suspected of perpetrating crimes in the mainland, their jurisdiction applied.

Despite the tensions surrounding the transfer of sovereignty, many citizens of Hong Kong supported the Government of the People's Republic of China in its territorial dispute with Japan regarding the Diaoyu (or Senkaku) Islands (see p. 1036). In September 1996 a Hong Kong activist, David Chan, was accidentally drowned during a protest against Japan's claim to the islands. As issues of patriotism assumed greater significance in Hong Kong, more than 10,000 people attended a demonstration to mourn the death of David Chan and to denounce Japan. In October protesters from Hong Kong joined a flotilla of small boats from Taiwan and Macau, which successfully evaded Japanese patrol vessels and raised the flags of China and Taiwan on the disputed islands.

The European Union (EU, see p. 181) agreed in principle in December 2000 to grant residents of Hong Kong and Macau visa-free access to member states, subject to final approval by the European Parliament.

Government

Since 1 July 1997 the Hong Kong SAR has been administered by a Chief Executive, chosen by a 400-member Selection Committee in December 1996. The Chief Executive is accountable to the State Council of the People's Republic of China, and serves a five-year term, there being a limit of two consecutive terms. In early 2001 14-member Executive Council comprised the Chief Executive, three ex-officio members and 10 non-official members. Elections to the second four-year term of the 60-member Legislative Council took place on 10 September 2000; 24 (compared with 20 in the previous legislature) of the seats were directly elective (under a system of proportional representation), with 30 seats elected by 'functional constituencies' (comprising professional and special interest groups) and six (reduced from 10) by an 800-member electoral college. At the 2004 elections the number of directly-elective seats on the Legislative Council was to be increased to from 24 to 30.

Defence

The British army, navy and air force completed their final withdrawal on 30 June 1997. In December 1996 the Standing Committee of the National People's Congress in Beijing adopted the Hong Kong Garrison Law, which provided for the stationing in Hong Kong of troops of the People's Liberation Army (PLA). The Garrison Law defined the duties and obligations of the troops, jurisdiction over them and also the relationship between the troops and the Government of the Hong Kong SAR. The legislation took effect on 1 July 1997. Almost 200 unarmed members of the PLA were permitted to enter Hong Kong (in three stages) prior to the transfer of sovereignty. In July 1997 a garrison of 4,800 PLA troops was established in Hong Kong. The garrison can intervene in local matters only at the request of the Hong Kong Government, which remains responsible for internal security.

Economic Affairs

In 1998, according to estimates by the World Bank, Hong Kong's gross domestic product (GDP), measured at average 1996–98 prices, was US $158,238m., equivalent to US $23,660 per head (or US $20,763 on an international purchasing-power parity basis). During 1990–98, it was estimated, GDP per head in-

creased, in real terms, at an average annual rate of 2.4%. Over the same period, the population increased by an average of 2.3% per year. GDP was estimated at US $161,700m. in 1999, equivalent to US $23,520 per head. During 1990–99 GDP increased, in real terms, at an average rate of 3.9% per year. Real GDP increased by 5.0% in 1997, but declined by 5.1% in 1998. Positive growth of 2.9% was recorded in 1999.

Agriculture and fishing together employed only 0.3% of the working population in 1999, and contributed an estimated 0.1% of GDP in 1998. Crop production is largely restricted to flowers, vegetables and some fruit and nuts, while pigs and poultry are the principal livestock. A virulent strain of avian influenza led to the slaughter of the territory's entire stock of 1.4m. chickens in January 1998. In March and April toxic algae killed 1,500 metric tons of farmed fish in Hong Kong (about one-half of the total farmed fish production in 1997). Hong Kong relies heavily on imports for its food supplies.

Industry (including mining, manufacturing, construction and power) provided an estimated 14.0% of GDP in 1998. In 1999 the sector employed 21.3% of the working population.

Manufacturing employed 11.5% of the working population in 1999, and contributed an estimated 5.7% of GDP in 1998. Measured by the value of output, the principal branches of manufacturing are textiles and clothing, plastic products, metal products and electrical machinery (particularly radio and television sets).

The services sector plays the most important role in the economy, accounting for an estimated 85.9% of GDP in 1998 and employing 78.5% of the working population in 1999. The value of Hong Kong's invisible exports (financial services, tourism, shipping, etc.) was HK $291,030m. in 1995. Revenue from tourism (including expenditure by visitors from mainland China) was HK $53,000m. in 1999, when 10.7m. people visited the territory. This represented an increase of 1.1m. compared with 1998. A new Disney theme park, to be opened in 2005, was expected further to increase the number of visitors to Hong Kong. The SAR's banking and mercantile houses have branches throughout the region, and Hong Kong is regarded as a major financial centre, owing partly to the existence of an excellent international telecommunications network and to the absence of restrictions on capital inflows.

In 1999 Hong Kong recorded a visible trade deficit of US $3,159m. and there was a surplus of $9,281m. on the current account of the balance of payments. Re-exports constituted 87.4% of total exports in 1999. The principal sources of Hong Kong's imports in 1999 were the People's Republic of China (43.6%) and Japan (11.7%); the principal markets for exports (including re-exports) were the People's Republic of China (33.3%) and the USA (23.8%). Other major trading partners included Taiwan, Germany and the United Kingdom. In 1998 the principal domestic exports were clothing, textiles, electrical machinery, data-processing equipment, and photographic apparatus. The principal imports in that year were foodstuffs, chemicals, textiles, machinery, transport equipment, and other manufactured articles.

By early 2001 the 2000/01 budget deficit was projected at HK $85,800m. The annual rate of inflation averaged 6.4% in 1990–99. The composite consumer price index rose by by 2.8% in 1998. In 1999, however, a decline of 4.0% in consumer prices was recorded. An estimated 4.6% of the labour force were unemployed, according to seasonally-adjusted figures, in the three months to November 2000. The shortage of skilled labour continued.

Hong Kong is a member of the Asian Development Bank (ADB, see p. 131) and an associate member of the UN's Economic and Social Commission for Asia and the Pacific (ESCAP, see p. 28). The territory became a member of Asia-Pacific Economic Co-operation (APEC, see p. 128) in 1991. Hong Kong joined the Bank for International Settlements (see p. 140) in 1996, and in early 1997 announced its participation in the IMF's New Arrangements to Borrow scheme (NAB, see p. 94). After mid-1997 Hong Kong remained a separate customs territory, within the World Trade Organization (WTO, see p. 292).

Under the terms of the Basic Law, Hong Kong's financial system remained unchanged following the transfer to Chinese sovereignty in mid-1997. The territory continued as a free port, and the Hong Kong dollar was retained, remaining freely convertible and linked to the US currency. Hong Kong's economy declined into recession in 1998, owing to the regional financial crisis of 1997. Real GDP contracted, domestic demand declined and unemployment increased sharply. Recovery began slowly in 1999 and accelerated in 2000. As the regional economies continued to revive, Hong Kong benefited from a growth in its re-exports to Asian countries. Renewed external demand led to strong GDP growth, estimated at more than 10% for 2000 as a whole. Such a high growth rate was not expected to be sustainable, however, given that private consumption had not increased substantially and investment remained relatively weak. Furthermore, in early 2001 the deceleration in the economy of the USA (a major export market) began to cause some concern. Despite Hong Kong's recovery in other areas, consumer prices continued to fall, albeit at a slower pace, and the property market remained depressed. By late 2000, although unemployment had declined to its lowest level for several months, there were concerns that a lack of relevant qualifications was preventing many people from finding work. The Government consequently announced increased spending on education, and the creation of 15,000 new jobs, which would generate opportunities for lower income groups. The economic outlook for 2001 was favourable, especially as China's prospects of joining the WTO in the near future had improved. In the short term many Hong Kong companies operating in China would benefit from better access to global markets, and in the longer term Hong Kong was likely to profit from increased trade and investment flows into the People's Republic. The progress of reforms in the banking and telecommunications sectors was also encouraging.

Social Welfare

Social welfare is administered by the Social Welfare Department. Expansion of social welfare services in the 1990s was to continue in accordance with the objectives formulated in the 1991 White Paper on social welfare. The establishment of a government-administered pension scheme for the elderly was proposed in 1994. In December 1999 there were 9,818 registered physicians, 38,960 nurses (not all resident and working in Hong Kong) and 28,602 hospital beds in the territory. Of total estimated expenditure by the public sector in the year ending 31 March 2000, HK $32,319m. (11.6 %) was for health services, while a further HK $28,389m. (10.2%) was for social services.

Education

In September 1999 an estimated 169,130 children attended kindergarten. Full-time education is compulsory between the ages of six and 15. Primary education has been free in all government schools and in nearly all aided schools since 1971 and junior secondary education since 1978. There are three main types of secondary school: grammar, technical and pre-vocational. The four government-run teacher-training colleges merged to form the Hong Kong Institute of Education in 1994. The Hong Kong Institute of Vocational Education (IVE), which was founded in 1999, incorporates seven government-funded technical institutes and two colleges. In 1995 total enrolment at primary and secondary schools was equivalent to 82% of the school-age population (males 80%, females 84%). Primary enrolment in that year included 91% of children in the relevant age-group (males 90%, females 92%), while the comparable ratio for secondary enrolment was 71% (males 69%, females 73%). In September 1999 the seven universities, (including Lingnan University, formerly Lingnan College, renamed in July 1999) and the Hong Kong Institute of Education had an estimated combined enrolment of 83,840 full-time and part-time students. The Open Learning Institute of Hong Kong, founded in 1989, had 25,654 students in September 1999. The adult illiteracy rate in 1995 was estimated by UNESCO at 8.2% (males 4.0%; females 12.6%). Budgetary expenditure (capital and recurrent) on education was HK $52,252m. for the financial year 1999/2000.

Public Holidays

2001: 1 January (first weekday in January), 24–26 January (Chinese New Year), 5 April (day following Ching Ming), 13–16 April (Easter), 30 April (the Buddha's Birthday), 1 May (Labour Day), 25 June (Tuen Ng, Dragon Boat Festival), 1, 2 July (SAR Establishment Day and weekday following), 1 October (National Day), 2 October (Day following Chinese Mid-Autumn Festival), 25 October (day following Chung Yeung Festival), 25–26 December (Christmas).

2002 (provisional): 1 January (first weekday in January), 12–15 February (Chinese New Year), 29 March–1 April (Easter), 5 April (Ching Ming), April/May (the Buddha's birthday), May/June (Tuen Ng, Dragon Boat Festival), 1 July (SAR Establishment Day), 21 September (Chinese Mid-Autumn Festival), 1 October (National Day), 14 October (Chung Yeung Festival), 25–26 December (Christmas).

Weights and Measures

The metric system is in force. Chinese units include: tsün (37.147 mm), chek or ch'ih (37.147 cm); kan or catty (604.8 grams), tam or picul (60.479 kg).

Statistical Survey

Source (unless otherwise stated): Census and Statistics Department, 19/F Wanchai Tower, 12 Harbour Rd, Hong Kong; tel. 25825073; fax 28271708; e-mail genenq@censtatd.gcn.gov.hk; internet www.info.gov.hk/censtatd/eng/hkstat/index.html/.

Area and Population

AREA, POPULATION AND DENSITY

Land area (sq km)	1,098*
Population (census results)†	
15 March 1991	5,674,114
15 March 1996	
Males	3,108,107
Females	3,109,449
Total	6,217,556
Population (official estimates at mid-year)‡	
1998	6,645,600
1999	6,720,700
2000	6,796,700
Density (per sq km) at mid-2000	6,190

* 423.9 sq miles.
† All residents on the census date, including those who were temporarily absent from Hong Kong.
‡ Revised figures, referring to resident population.

DISTRIBUTION OF RESIDENT POPULATION
(1991 census)

Hong Kong Island	Kowloon and New Kowloon	Marine	New Territories
1,250,993	2,030,683	17,620	2,374,818

PRINCIPAL TOWNS (population at 1996 census)

Kowloon* . . .	1,988,515	Tai Po . . .	271,661
Victoria (capital) .	1,011,433	Tseun Wan . .	268,659
Tuen Mun . . .	445,771	Sheung Shui . .	192,321
Sha Tin . . .	445,383	Tsing Yu . .	185,495
Kwai Chung . .	285,231	Aberdeen . . .	164,439

* Including New Kowloon.

BIRTHS, MARRIAGES AND DEATHS*

	Known live births		Registered marriages		Known deaths	
	Number	Rate (per '000)	Number	Rate (per '000)	Number	Rate (per '000)
1991 . .	68,281	12.0	42,568	7.5	28,429	5.0
1992 . .	70,949	12.3	45,702	7.9	30,550	5.3
1993 . .	70,451	12.0	41,681	7.1	30,571	5.2
1994 . .	71,646	11.9	38,264	6.3	29,905	5.0
1995 . .	68,836	11.2	38,786	6.3	31,183	5.1
1996 . .	64,559†	10.2	37,045	5.9	32,049†	5.1
1997‡. .	60,379†	9.3	37,593	5.8	32,079†	4.9
1998‡. .	53,356†	7.9	31,673	4.7	32,680†	4.8
1999‡. .	50,513	7.5	31,287	4.6	33,387	4.8

* Excluding Vietnamese migrants.
† Figure calculated by year of registration.
‡ Provisional.
Expectation of life (years at birth, 1999, provisional): Males 77.2; Females 82.6.

ECONOMICALLY ACTIVE POPULATION
('000 persons aged 15 years and over, excl. armed forces)

	1997	1998	1999
Agriculture and fishing . . .	10.5	9.4	9.4
Mining and quarrying . . .	0.5	0.2	0.3
Manufacturing	450.7	385.6	359.4
Electricity, gas and water. . .	19.4	17.9	17.1
Construction.	308.4	309.5	289.2
Wholesale, retail and import/ export trades, restaurants and hotels	968.0	961.6	941.3
Transport, storage and communications	349.7	353.0	342.7
Financing, insurance, real estate and business services . . .	405.0	411.6	437.6
Community, social and personal services	679.5	701.3	736.3
Total employed	**3,191.5**	**3,150.1**	**3,133.0**
Unemployed	72.6	155.4	209.4
Total labour force	**3,264.2**	**3,305.5**	**3,342.5**
Males	1,974.4	1,971.4	1,963.7
Females	1,289.8	1,334.1	1,378.8

Source: ILO, *Yearbook of Labour Statistics.*

Agriculture

PRINCIPAL CROPS

	1997	1998	1999
Field crops* (metric tons) . . .	799	1,120	540
Vegetables† (metric tons) . . .	64,000	59,500	48,000
Fresh fruit and nuts (metric tons) .	4,611	3,873	3,770
Flowers (HK $'000) . . .	175,924	283,780	278,626

* Includes yam, groundnut, sugar cane, sweet potato and water chestnut.
† Fresh, frozen or preserved.

Source: Agriculture, Fisheries and Conservation Department, Hong Kong.

LIVESTOCK (estimates—head)

	1995	1996	1997
Cattle	1,950	1,550	1,600
Water buffaloes . . .	220	170	200
Pigs.	106,700	166,200	175,900
Goats	200	150	200
Chickens . . .	3,290,000	3,184,500	2,678,500
Ducks	106,500	28,500	18,300
Quail	35,000	28,800	34,800
Pigeons (pairs) . . .	365,813	412,210	412,700

Source: Agriculture, Fisheries and Conservation Department, Hong Kong.

LIVESTOCK PRODUCTS

	1997	1998	1999
Milk (metric tons)	215	246	241
Poultry eggs ('000) . . .	33,450	3,550	3,530

Fishing

('000 metric tons, live weight)

	1996	1997	1998
Capture .	183.9	186.0	180.0
Lizardfishes	9.0	8.1	6.6
Threadfin breams	19.6	20.0	19.4
Other marine fishes (incl. unspecified) .	136.2	134.9	138.0
Shrimps and prawns	6.6	6.2	5.3
Squids	8.6	13.6	8.3
Aquaculture .	8.4	8.3	6.4
Total catch .	192.3	194.3	186.4

Source: FAO, *Yearbook of Fishery Statistics.*

Industry

SELECTED PRODUCTS
('000 metric tons, unless otherwise indicated)

	1994	1995	1996
Crude groundnut oil .	22	16	24
Uncooked macaroni and noodle products .	75	126	76
Soft drinks ('000 hectolitres) .	3,435	3,273	3,356
Cigarettes (million) .	24,747	22,767	21,386
Cotton yarn (pure and mixed).	169.6	147.9	125.2
Cotton woven fabrics (million sq m)	691.7	655.0	540
Knitted sweaters ('000) .	166,935	166,467	151,502
Men's and boys' jackets ('000) .	13,708	13,552	14,843
Men's and boys' trousers ('000) .	61,788	49,499	n.a.
Women's and girls' blouses ('000) .	152,823	119,258	124,535
Women's and girls' dresses ('000) .	8,103	10,433	6,585
Women's and girls' skirts, slacks and shorts ('000) .	74,286	70,013	74,502
Men's and boys' shirts ('000) .	119,456	96,323	82,157
Telephones ('000) .	n.a.	1,053	830
Watches ('000) .	133,651	131,431	67,352
Electric energy (million kWh) .	34,994	35,461	36,819

Finance

CURRENCY AND EXCHANGE RATES

Monetary Units
100 cents = 1 Hong Kong dollar (HK $).

Sterling, US Dollar and Euro Equivalents (29 December 2000)
£1 sterling = HK $11.633;
US $1 = HK $7.796;
€1 = HK $7.254;
HK $1,000 = £85.96 = US $128.27 = €137.85.

Average Exchange Rate (HK $ per US $)
1998   7.7453
1999   7.7575
2000   7.7912

BUDGET (HK $ million, year ending 31 March)

Revenue	1997/98	1998/99	1999/2000*
Direct taxes:			
Earnings and profits tax .	91,524	75,746	65,350
Estate duty .	1,588	1,237	1,250
Indirect taxes:			
Duties on petroleum products, beverages, tobacco and cosmetics .	8,465	7,698	7,413
General rates (property tax) .	6,258	3,614	6,855
Motor vehicle taxes .	4,246	2,237	2,554
Royalties and concessions .	1,889	1,286	1,557
Others .	44,263	23,404	22,403
Fines, forfeitures and penalties .	1,566	1,333	1,084
Receipts from properties and investments .	7,159	8,335	6,817
Reimbursements and contributions	6,042	6,517	5,454
Operating revenue from utilities:			
Airport and air services .	3,968	1,087	—
Postal services .	53	—	—
Water .	2,450	2,415	2,385
Others .	264	898	877
Fees and charges .	11,279	10,565	10,823
Interest receipts (operating revenue) .	8,976	21,568	15,664
Capital Works Reserve Fund (land sales and interest) .	48,067	25,686	38,387
Capital Investment Fund .	3,888	6,329	2,669
Loan funds .	2,475	2,533	11,585
Other capital revenue .	26,806	13,627	26,195
Total government revenue .	281,226	216,115	229,322

Expenditure†	1997/98	1998/99	1999/2000*
Economic affairs and services .	17,064	21,421	13,033
Internal security .	18,834	19,534	21,054
Immigration .	1,935	2,034	2,162
Other security services .	2,995	3,547	3,755
Social welfare .	21,710	26,377	28,389
Health services .	27,982	31,400	32,319
Education .	47,027	48,479	52,252
Environmental services .	13,077	13,346	12,676
Recreation, culture and amenities .	6,622	7,109	7,975
Other community and external affairs .	1,490	1,523	1,767
Transport .	7,212	6,656	6,919
Land and buildings .	7,588	8,261	8,826
Water supply .	6,366	8,215	8,576
Support .	30,227	26,696	31,685
Housing .	24,651	38,850	47,028
Total .	234,780	266,448	278,416
Recurrent .	172,419	187,857	199,672
Capital .	62,361	78,591	78,744

* Revised estimates.
† Figures refer to consolidated expenditure by the public sector. Of the total, government expenditure, after deducting grants, debt repayments and equity injections, was (in HK $ million): 194,241 in 1997/98; 218,811 in 1998/99; 222,325 (estimate) in 1999/2000. Expenditure by other public-sector bodies (in HK $ million) was: 40,539 in 1997/98; 47,637 in 1998/99; 56,091 (estimate) in 1999/2000.

INTERNATIONAL RESERVES (US $ '000 million at 31 December)

	1998	1999	2000
Gold* .	0.02	0.02	0.02
Reserve position in the IMF .	0.04	—	—
Foreign exchange† .	89.60	96.24	107.54
Total .	89.67	96.26	107.56

* National valuation.
† Including the foreign exchange reserves of the Hong Kong Special Administrative Region Government's Land Fund.

Source: IMF, *International Financial Statistics.*

MONEY SUPPLY (HK $ '000 million at 31 December)

	1997	1998	1999
Currency outside banks . .	80.34	80.92	99.27
Demand deposits at banking institutions	87.44	79.07	85.35
Total money	167.78	159.99	184.62

Source: IMF, *International Financial Statistics*.

COST OF LIVING
(Consumer price index; base: October 1994–September 1995 = 100)

	1997	1998	1999
Foodstuffs	109.3	111.4	109.4
Housing	123.7	129.4	122.9
Fuel and light . . .	112.8	114.6	114.1
Alcoholic drinks and tobacco . .	113.3	120.8	122.3
Clothing and footwear . .	119.4	118.5	94.1
Durable goods . . .	105.1	105.3	98.7
Miscellaneous goods . .	109.2	112.0	111.2
Transport	112.3	116.6	117.2
Miscellaneous services . .	112.7	115.7	114.2
All items	114.7	117.9	113.2

NATIONAL ACCOUNTS
(HK $ million at current market prices)
Expenditure on the Gross Domestic Product

	1997	1998*	1999*
Government final consumption expenditure	113,749	117,863	121,339
Private final consumption expenditure	798,450	766,887	742,349
Change in stocks . . .	12,313	−11,271	−3,628
Gross domestic fixed capital formation	444,963	387,241	316,196
Total domestic expenditure	1,369,475	1,260,720	1,176,256
Exports of goods and services	1,754,125	1,615,042	1,623,704
Less Imports of goods and services	1,799,738	1,608,922	1,569,533
GDP in purchasers' values .	1,323,862	1,266,840	1,230,427
GDP at constant 1990 prices .	829,017	786,426	809,326

Gross Domestic Product by Economic Activity

	1996	1997	1998*
Agriculture and fishing . .	1,444	1,464	1,530
Mining and quarrying . .	311	272	303
Manufacturing . . .	82,769	80,049	73,080
Electricity, gas and water . .	26,989	29,212	33,548
Construction	65,058	71,650	72,459
Wholesale, retail and import/ export trades, restaurants and hotels	301,277	313,270	283,919
Transport, storage and communications . . .	111,087	112,829	109,452
Financing, insurance, real estate and business services . .	284,119	322,618	302,491
Community, social and personal services	198,967	220,451	234,990
Ownership of premises . .	147,547	171,383	170,974
Sub-total	1,219,568	1,323,198	1,282,746
Less Imputed bank service charges	89,356	90,164	100,319
GDP at factor cost . . .	1,130,212	1,233,034	1,182,427
Indirect taxes, *less* subsidies . .	62,443	85,001	62,538
GDP in purchasers' values .	1,192,656	1,318,035	1,244,965

* Preliminary estimates.

BALANCE OF PAYMENTS (US $ million)

	1998	1999
Exports of goods f.o.b.	175,833	174,719
Imports of goods f.o.b.	−183,666	−177,878
Trade balance	−7,833	−3,159
Exports of services	33,653	34,850
Imports of services	−25,036	−24,456
Balance on goods and services . . .	784	7,235
Other income received	46,831	47,296
Other income paid	−43,117	−43,780
Balance on goods, services and income .	4,498	10,751
Current transfers received	669	708
Current transfers paid	−2,265	−2,178
Current balance	2,901	9,281
Capital account (net)	−2,382	−1,774
Direct investment abroad	−16,973	−19,905
Direct investment from abroad . . .	14,776	23,068
Portfolio investment assets	25,492	−25,467
Portfolio investment liabilities . . .	−3,407	57,734
Financial derivatives assets	10,799	24,037
Financial derivatives liabilities . . .	−7,523	−11,729
Other investment assets	119,830	42,236
Other investment liabilities	−151,470	−88,477
Net errors and omissions	1,061	500
Overall balance	−6,896	9,505

Source: IMF, *International Financial Statistics*.

External Trade

PRINCIPAL COMMODITIES (HK $ million, excl. gold)

Imports	1996	1997	1998
Food and live animals . .	61,972	65,993	57,483
Mineral fuels, lubricants and related materials . . .	34,644	31,803	24,795
Chemicals and related products	105,461	104,598	91,219
Plastic in primary forms . .	37,811	38,138	33,668
Basic manufactures . .	308,694	311,903	264,148
Textile yarn, fabrics, made-up articles, etc.	127,730	125,460	104,439
Non-metallic mineral manufactures	43,391	44,679	35,496
Machinery and transport equipment . . .	568,856	623,665	562,814
Office machines and automatic data-processing equipment .	81,382	100,029	103,145
Telecommunications and sound recording and reproducing apparatus and equipment . .	141,033	152,377	130,886
Electrical machinery, apparatus and appliances n.e.s., and electrical parts thereof . .	195,942	219,701	195,561
Miscellaneous manufactured articles	394,582	416,788	378,286
Clothing (excl. footwear) . .	105,419	116,277	110,744
Footwear	56,734	57,243	44,982
Photographic apparatus, equipment and supplies, optical goods, watches and clocks . .	62,745	62,937	54,627
Total (incl. others) . . .	1,535,582	1,615,090	1,429,092

Domestic exports	1996	1997	1998
Chemicals and related products	8,691	8,077	6,753
Basic manufactures	24,538	22,350	18,164
Textile yarn, fabrics, made-up articles, etc.	13,693	12,655	10,767
Machinery and transport equipment	59,360	58,707	46,471
Office machines and automatic data-processing equipment	13,090	10,425	8,922
Telecommunications and sound recording and reproducing apparatus and equipment	8,586	9,251	6,304
Electrical machinery, apparatus and appliances n.e.s., and electrical parts thereof	30,357	32,958	26,688
Miscellaneous manufactured articles	107,193	109,749	108,770
Clothing (excl. footwear)	69,447	72,228	74,874
Photographic apparatus, equipment and supplies, optical goods, watches and clocks	15,084	14,488	12,535
Total (incl. others)	212,160	211,410	188,454

Re-exports	1996	1997	1998
Chemicals and related products	74,143	74,046	66,565
Plastic in primary forms	28,819	30,047	27,798
Basic manufactures	208,518	215,918	197,442
Textile yarn, fabrics, made-up articles, etc.	95,719	100,395	90,234
Machinery and transport equipment	391,071	419,976	407,400
General industrial machinery, equipment and parts	29,134	25,110	21,891
Office machines and automatic data-processing equipment	70,757	86,253	92,902
Telecommunications and sound recording and reproducing apparatus and equipment	115,959	116,801	114,348
Electrical machinery, apparatus and appliances n.e.s., and electrical parts thereof	123,764	136,784	132,040
Miscellaneous manufactured articles	434,522	459,074	426,262
Clothing (excl. footwear)	100,524	106,669	96,799
Footwear	65,233	65,619	51,913
Photographic apparatus, equipment and supplies, optical goods, watches and clocks	55,519	58,838	58,379
Total (incl. others)	1,185,758	1,244,539	1,159,195

PRINCIPAL TRADING PARTNERS (HK $ million, excl. gold)

Imports	1998	1999	2000
China, People's Repub.	580,614	607,546	714,987
Germany	32,639	28,114	32,215
Japan	179,947	162,652	198,976
Korea, Repub.	68,836	65,432	80,600
Malaysia	32,479	30,010	37,906
Singapore	61,457	60,017	74,998
Taiwan	104,075	100,426	124,172
Thailand	22,234	22,798	28,001
United Kingdom	29,671	26,961	30,797
USA	106,537	98,572	112,801
Total (incl. others)	1,429,092	1,392,718	1,657,962

Domestic exports	1998	1999	2000
Canada	3,598	3,151	3,210
China, People's Repub.	56,066	50,414	54,158
France	3,171	3,081	2,730
Germany	9,805	8,543	9,294
Japan	6,435	5,459	5,084
Netherlands	4,736	4,119	3,910
Singapore	5,103	3,682	4,716
Taiwan	6,505	5,101	6,104
United Kingdom	10,058	10,392	10,681
USA	54,842	51,358	54,438
Total (incl. others)	188,454	170,600	180,967

Re-exports	1998	1999	2000
China, People's Repub.	407,366	399,188	488,823
France	21,316	22,837	25,205
Germany	42,161	44,122	50,599
Japan	64,194	67,506	82,050
Korea, Repub.	12,241	19,793	26,978
Netherlands	20,332	19,422	20,373
Singapore	25,625	28,716	32,028
Taiwan	27,368	27,859	33,696
United Kingdom	42,259	45,541	52,356
USA	259,856	269,444	311,047
Total (incl. others)	1,159,195	1,178,400	1,391,722

Transport

RAILWAYS (traffic)

	1997	1998	1999
Passenger trains:			
Arrivals	2,108	2,376	2,595
Departures	2,108	2,376	2,596
Freight (in metric tons):			
Loaded	174,272	137,918	173,415
Unloaded	537,046	323,654	293,061

ROAD TRAFFIC (registered motor vehicles at 31 December)

	1997	1998	1999
Private cars	348,450	359,694	365,533
Private buses	423	437	447
Public buses	10,984	11,886	12,173
Private light buses	2,392	2,297	2,228
Public light buses	4,350	4,350	4,350
Taxis	18,136	18,138	18,138
Goods vehicles	134,861	132,785	130,374
Motor cycles	31,212	32,004	33,079
Government vehicles (excl. military vehicles)	7,689	7,363	7,368
Total (incl. others)	558,903	569,411	574,193

Note: Figures do not include tramcars.

SHIPPING
Merchant Fleet (registered at 31 December)

	1996	1997	1998
Number of vessels	398	375	391
Total displacement ('000 grt)	7,863.0	5,770.6	6,170.7

Source: Lloyd's Register of Shipping, *World Fleet Statistics*.

Traffic (1999)

	Ocean-going Vessels	River Vessels
Vessels entered (number)	37,205	175,265
Vessels cleared (number)	37,275	175,193
Passengers landed ('000)	8,543*	—
Passengers embarked ('000) . . .	8,898*	—
Cargo landed ('000 metric tons) . . .	88,621	17,684
Cargo loaded ('000 metric tons) . . .	39,601	22,932

* Includes helicopter passengers to/from Macau.

CIVIL AVIATION

	1997	1998	1999
Passengers:			
Arrivals	10,841,000	10,284,000	10,699,000
Departures . . .	10,933,000	10,209,000	10,623,000
Freight (in metric tons):			
Landed	839,872	774,544	841,856*
Loaded	946,615	854,198	1,135,676*

* Provisional.

Tourism

VISITOR ARRIVALS BY COUNTRY OF RESIDENCE

	1997	1998	1999
Australia	293,974	272,454	281,151
Canada	178,046	194,351	210,899
China, People's Repub. . . .	2,297,128	2,597,442	3,083,859
Germany	235,006	170,716	172,166
Indonesia	174,947	104,885	188,069
Japan	1,368,988	945,334	1,020,307
Korea, Repub. . . .	357,538	179,499	259,549
Macau	526,858	441,523	416,839
Malaysia	269,337	235,928	262,940
Philippines	326,418	214,556	259,858
Singapore	339,689	331,610	351,175
Taiwan	1,782,580	1,812,634	2,000,180
Thailand	214,782	130,406	176,437
United Kingdom	340,263	325,738	308,754
USA and Guam	800,539	773,309	802,705
Total (incl. others) . . .	10,406,261	9,574,711	10,678,460

Receipts from tourism: HK $69,900m. in 1997; HK $55,251m. in 1998; HK $53,000m. in 1999.

Source: Hong Kong Tourist Association, Hong Kong.

Communications Media

	1996	1997	1998
Radio receivers (number in use)	4,300,000	4,450,000	n.a.
Television receivers (number in use)	1,790,000	1,840,000	n.a.
Telephones	4,446,000*	4,685,000*	4,763,000*
Telefax stations (number in use) .	308,000	343,000	360,000
Mobile cellular telephones (subscribers)†	1,361,861	2,229,862	n.a.
Daily newspapers	58	50	45
Periodicals	625	693	684

* Estimate.
† Year beginning 1 April.

Sources: partly UNESCO, *Statistical Yearbook*; UN, *Statistical Yearbook*.

Education

(1999)

	Institutions	Full-time Teachers*	Students†
Kindergartens	756†	9,057	171,138
Primary schools	822†	21,364	491,851
Secondary schools	519†	24,016	465,250
Special schools	74†	1,614	9,687
Institute of Vocational Education .	1‡	1,167	57,735
Approved post-secondary college .	1†	116	2,361
Other post-secondary colleges . .	19†	—	4,624
UGC-funded institutions . . .	8§	5,776	83,840
Open University Institute . .	1	85	25,654
Adult education institutions . .	859†	—	130,028

* 1998 figures.
† Provisional figure(s). Revised figures for kindergartens: 763 institutions; 169,130 students.
‡ Formed by merger of two technical colleges and seven technical institutes in 1999.
§ Funded by the University Grants Committee.

Directory

The Constitution

Under the terms of the Basic Law of the Hong Kong Special Adminis-trative Region, the Government comprises the Chief Executive, the Executive Council and the Legislative Council. The Chief Executive must be a Chinese citizen of at least 40 years of age; he is appointed by a 400-member Selection Committee for a five-year term, with a limit of two consecutive terms; he is accountable to the State Council of the People's Republic of China, and has no military authority; he appoints the Executive Council (which has a total of 13 members—the Chief Executive, three ex-officio members and 9 non-official members), judges and the principal government officials; he makes laws with the advice and consent of the legislature; he has a veto over legislation, but can be overruled by a two-thirds' majority; he may dissolve the legislature once in a term, but must resign if the legislative impasse continues with the new body. The Legislative Council has 60 members; 24 seats are directly elected under a system of proportional representation, 30 seats are elected by 'functional constituencies' (comprising professional and special interest groups) and six by an 800-member electoral college. The Legislative Council is responsible for enacting, revising and abrogating laws, for approving the budget, taxation and public expenditure, for debating the policy address of the Chief Executive and for approving the appointment of the judges of the Court of Final Appeal and of the Chief Justice of the High Court.

The Government

Chief Executive: TUNG CHEE-HWA (assumed office 1 July 1997).

EXECUTIVE COUNCIL
(April 2001)

Chairman: The Chief Executive.

Ex-Officio Members:

Chief Secretary for Administration: DONALD TSANG.

Financial Secretary: ANTONY LEUNG KAM-CHUNG.

Secretary for Justice: ELSIE LEUNG.

Non-Official Members:

LEUNG CHUN-YING
YANG TI-LIANG
NELLIE FONG WONG KUT-MAN
Dr. ROSANNA WONG YICK-MING
TAM YIU-CHUNG

Dr RAYMOND CH'IEN KUO-FUNG
LEE YEH-KWONG
HENRY TANG YING-YEN
CHUNG SHUI-MING

LEGISLATIVE COUNCIL

The second Legislative Council to follow Hong Kong's transfer to Chinese sovereignty was elected on 10 September 2000. The Legislative Council comprises 60 members—30 chosen by functional constituencies, 24 (increased from 20 in the previous legislature) by direct election in five geographical constituencies and six (reduced from 10) by an 800-member Election Committee. The term of office of the Legislative Council commenced on 1 October 2000 and was to last for four years.

President: RITA FAN.

Election, 10 September 2000

Party	Directly-elective seats	Func-tional Constitu-uency seats	Election Com-mittee seats	Total seats
Democratic Party of Hong Kong	9	3	—	12
Democratic Alliance for the Betterment of Hong Kong	8	3	—	11
Liberal Party	—	8	—	8
Hong Kong Progressive Alliance	—	1	3	4
The Frontier	3	—	—	3
Association for Democracy and People's Livelihood	1	—	—	1
New Century Forum	—	1	1	2
Independents and others	3	14	2	19
Total	**24**	**30**	**6**	**60**

GOVERNMENT OFFICES

Executive Council: Central Government Offices, Lower Albert Rd, Central; tel. 28102545; fax 28450176.

Office of the Chief Executive: 5/F Main Wing, Central Government Offices, Lower Albert Rd, Central; tel. 28783300; fax 25090577.

Government Secretariat: Central Government Offices, Lower Albert Rd, Central; tel. 28102900; fax 28457895.

Government Information Services: Murray Bldg, Garden Rd, Central; tel. 28428777; fax 28459078; internet www.info.gov.hk.

Political Organizations

Association for Democracy and People's Livelihood (ADPL): Sun Beam Commercial Bldg, Room 1104, 469–471 Nathan Rd, Kowloon; tel. 27822699; fax 27823137; e-mail adpl@netvigator.com; internet www.adpl.org.hk; advocates democracy; Chair. FREDERICK FUNG KIN-KEE; Gen. Sec. TAM KWOK-KIU.

Citizens' Party: 1203 Dominion Centre, 43 Queen's Rd East, Wan-chai; tel. 28930029; fax 21475796; e-mail enquiry@citizensparty.org; internet www.citizensparty.org; f. 1997; urges mass participation in politics; Leader CHRISTINE LOH.

Democratic Alliance for the Betterment of Hong Kong (DAB): SUP Tower, 12/F, 83 King's Rd, North Point; tel. 25280136; fax 25284339; e-mail info@dab.org.hk; internet www.dab.org.hk; f. 1992; pro-Beijing; supported return of Hong Kong to the mother-land and implementation of the Basic Law; Chair. TSANG YOK-SING; Sec.-Gen. MA LIK.

Democratic Party of Hong Kong: Central Government Offices, Rooms 401–410, West Wing, 11 Ice House St, Central; tel. 25371469; fax 25374874; f. 1994 by merger of United Democrats of Hong Kong (UDHK—declared a formal political party in 1990) and Meeting Point; liberal grouping; advocates democracy; Chair. MARTIN LEE; Sec.-Gen. LAW CHI-KWONG.

The Frontier: Hong Kong House, Room 301, 11–19 Wellington St, Central; tel. 25372482; fax 28456203; f. 1996; pro-democracy movement, comprising teachers, students and trade unionists; Spokesperson EMILY LAU.

Hong Kong Democratic Foundation: Hong Kong House, Room 301, 17–19 Wellington St, Central; GPOB 12287; tel. 28696443; fax 28696318; advocates democracy; Chair. ALAN LUNG.

Hong Kong Progressive Alliance: c/o The Legislative Council, Hong Kong; tel. 25262316; fax 28450127; f. 1994; advocates close relationship with mainland China; 52-mem. organizing cttee drawn from business and professional community; Spokesman AMBROSE LAU.

Hong Kong Voice of Democracy: 7/F, 57 Peking Rd, Tsimshatsui; tel. 92676489; fax 27915801; internet www.democracy.org.hk; pro-democracy movement; Dir LAU SAN-CHING.

Liberal Democratic Foundation (LDF): Hong Kong; pro-Beijing.

Liberal Party: Shun Ho Tower, 2/F, 24–30 Ice House St, Central; tel. 28696833; fax 28453671; f. 1993 by mems of Co-operative Resources Centre (CRC); business-orientated; pro-Beijing; Leader ALLEN LEE PENG-FEI; Chair. JAMES TIEN.

New Hong Kong Alliance: 4/F, 14–15 Wo On Lane, Central; fax 28691110; pro-China.

The **Chinese Communist Party** (based in the People's Republic) and the **Kuomintang** (Nationalist Party of China, based in Taiwan) also maintain organizations.

Judicial System

The Court of Final Appeal was established on 1 July 1997 upon the commencement of the Hong Kong Court of Final Appeal Ordinance. It replaced the Privy Council in London as the highest appellate court in Hong Kong to safeguard the rule of law. The Court comprises five judges—the Chief Justice, three permanent judges and one non-permanent Hong Kong judge or one judge from another common-law jurisdiction.

The High Court consists of a Court of Appeal and a Court of First Instance. The Court of First Instance has unlimited jurisdiction in civil and criminal cases, while the District Court has limited jurisdiction. Appeals from these courts lie to the Court of Appeal, presided over by the Chief Judge or a Vice-President of the Court of Appeal with one or two Justices of Appeal. Appeals from Magistrates' Courts are heard by a Court of First Instance judge.

HIGH COURT

38 Queensway; tel. 28690869; fax 28690640; internet www.info.gov.hk/jud.

Chief Justice of the Court of Final Appeal: ANDREW K. N. LI.

Permanent Judges of the Court of Final Appeal: R. A. V. RIBEIRO, PATRICK S. O. CHAN, K. BOKHARY.

Chief Judge of the High Court: (vacant).

Justices of Appeal: K. H. WOO, M. STUART-MOORE, F. STOCK, Mrs D. LE PICHON, S. H. MAYO, A. S. C. LEONG, A. G. ROGERS, M. K. C. WONG, B. R. KEITH.

Judges of the Court of First Instance: C. G. JACKSON, G. J. LUGAR-MAWSON, A. O. T. CHUNG, T. M. GALL, T. LONG, D. Y. K. YAM, P. C. Y. CHEUNG, W. S. Y. WAUNG, C. SEAGROATT, W. C. K. YEUNG, M. P. BURRELL, Ms C. CHU, Mrs V. S. BOKHARY, K. K. PANG, W. D. STONE, Ms C. M. BEESON, Ms M. K. N. YUEN, P. V. T. NGUYEN, M. J. HARTMANN, A. R. SUFFIAD, A. H. SAKHRANI.

OTHER COURTS

District Courts: There are 34 District Judges.

Magistrates' Courts: There are 59 Magistrates and 11 Special Magistrates, sitting in 9 magistracies.

Religion

The Chinese population is predominantly Buddhist. In 1994 the number of active Buddhists was estimated at between 650,000 and 700,000. Confucianism and Daoism are widely practised. The three religions are frequently found in the same temple. In 1999 there were some 527,000 Christians, approximately 80,000 Muslims, 12,000 Hindus, 1,000 Jews and 1,200 Sikhs. The Bahá'í faith and Zoroastrianism are also represented.

BUDDHISM

Hong Kong Buddhist Association: 1/F, 338 Lockhart Rd; tel. 25749371; fax 28340789; internet www.hkbuddhist.org; Pres. Ven. KOK KWONG.

CHRISTIANITY

Hong Kong Christian Council: 9/F, 33 Granville Rd, Kowloon; tel. 23687123; fax 27242131; e-mail hkcc@hkcc.org.hk; internet www.hkcc.org.hk; f. 1954; 21 mem. orgs; Chair. Rev. LI PING-KWONG; Gen. Sec. Rev. ERIC SO SHING-YIT.

The Anglican Communion

Primate of Hong Kong Sheng Kung Hui and Bishop of Hong Kong Island and Macau: Most Rev. PETER K. K. KWONG, Bishop's House, 1 Lower Albert Rd, Central; tel. 25265355; fax 25212199; e-mail office1@hkskh.org.

Bishop of Eastern Kowloon: Rt Rev. LOUIS TSUI, Holy Trinity Bradbury Centre, 4/F, 139 Ma Tau Chung Rd, Kowloon; tel. 27139983; fax 27111609; e-mail ekoffice@ekhkskh.org.hk.

Bishop of Western Kowloon: Rt Rev. THOMAS SOO, Ultra Grace Commercial Bldg, 15/F, 5 Jordan Rd, Kowloon; tel. 27830811; fax 27830799; e-mail hkskhdwk@netvigator.com.

The Lutheran Church

Evangelical Lutheran Church of Hong Kong: 50A Waterloo Rd, Kowloon; tel. 23885847; fax 23887539; e-mail info@elchk.org.hk; internet www.elchk.org.hk; 12,400 mems; Pres. Rev. TSO SHUI-WAN.

The Roman Catholic Church

For ecclesiastical purposes, Hong Kong forms a single diocese, nominally suffragan to the archdiocese of Canton (Guangzhou), China. In 1999 there were an estimated 227,000 adherents in the territory, representing more than 3% of the total population.

Bishop of Hong Kong: Cardinal JOHN BAPTIST WU CHENG-CHUNG, Catholic Diocese Centre, 12/F, 16 Caine Rd; tel. 25241633; fax 28104619; e-mail bishophk@hk.super.net.

The Press

Hong Kong has a thriving press. In 1999, according to government figures, there were 44 daily newspapers, including 24 Chinese-language and 9 English-language dailies, and 724 periodicals.

PRINCIPAL DAILY NEWSPAPERS
English Language

Asian Wall Street Journal: GPOB 9825; tel. 25737121; fax 28345291; f. 1976; business; Editor REGINALD CHUA; circ. 65,378.

China Daily: Hong Kong edition of China's official English-language newspaper; launched 1997; Editor LIU DIZHONG; circ. 11,000.

Hong Kong Standard: Sing Tao Bldg, 4/F, 1 Wang Kwong Rd, Kowloon Bay, Kowloon; tel. 27982798; fax 27953009; e-mail imail@hk-imail.com; internet www.hk-imail.com; f. 1949; Editor ANDREW LYNCH; circ. 45,000.

International Herald Tribune: 1201 K Wah Centre, 191 Java Rd, North Point; tel. 29221188; fax 29221190; internet www.iht.com; Correspondent KEVIN MURPHY.

South China Morning Post: Morning Post Centre, Dai Fat St, Tai Po Industrial Centre, Tai Po, New Territories; tel. 26808888; fax 26616984; internet www.scmp.com; f. 1903; CEO OWEN JONATHAN; Editor ROBERT KEATLEY; circ. 118,000.

Target Intelligent Report: Suite 2901, Bank of America Tower, 12 Harcourd Rd, Central; tel. 25730379; fax 28381597; e-mail info@targetnewspapers.com; internet www.targetnewspaper.com; f. 1972; financial news, commentary, politics, property, litigations, etc.

Chinese Language

Ching Pao: 3/F, 141 Queen's Rd East; tel. 25273836; f. 1956; Editor MOK KONG; circ. 120,000.

Hong Kong Commercial Daily: 1/F, 499 King's Rd, North Point; tel. 25905322; fax 25658947.

Hong Kong Daily News: All Flats, Hong Kong Industrial Bldg, 17/F, 444–452 Des Voeux Rd West; tel. 28555111; fax 28198717; f. 1958; morning; CEO PETER S. W. FUNG; Chief Editor W. T. CHEUNG; circ. 120,000.

Hong Kong Economic Journal: North Point Industrial Bldg, 22/F, 499 King's Rd; tel. 28567567; fax 28111070; e-mail info@hkej.com; Editor-in-Chief H. C. CHIU; circ. 70,000.

Hong Kong Economic Times: Kodak House, Block 2, Room 808, 321 Java Rd, North Point; tel. 28802888; fax 28111926; f. 1988; Publr PERRY MAK; Chief Editor ERIC CHAN; circ. 64,565.

Hong Kong Sheung Po (Hong Kong Commercial Daily): 499 King's Rd, North Point; tel. 25640788; f. 1952; morning; Editor-in-Chief H. CHEUNG; circ. 110,000.

Hsin Wan Pao (New Evening Post): 342 Hennessy Rd, Wanchai; tel. 28911604; fax 28382307; f. 1950; Editor-in-Chief CHAO TSE-LUNG; circ. 90,000.

Ming Pao Daily News: Block A, Ming Pao Industrial Centre, 15/F, 18 Ka Yip St, Chai Wan; tel. 25953111; fax 28982534; e-mail mingpao@mingpao.com; internet www.mingpao.com; f. 1959; morning; Chief Editor PAUL CHEUNG; circ. 84,217.

Oriental Daily News: Oriental Press Centre, Wang Tai Rd, Kowloon Bay, Kowloon; tel. 27951111; fax 27955599; Chair. C. F. MA; Editor-in-Chief MA KAI LUN; circ. 650,000.

Ping Kuo Jih Pao (Apple Daily): Hong Kong; tel. 29908685; fax 23708908; f. 1995; Propr JIMMY LAI; Publr LOH CHAN; circ. 400,000.

Seng Weng Evening News: f. 1957; Editor WONG LONG-CHAU; circ. 60,000.

Sing Pao Daily News: Sing Pao Bldg, 101 King's Rd, North Point; tel. 25702201; fax 28870348; f. 1939; morning; Chief Editor HON CHUNG-SUEN; circ. 229,250.

Sing Tao Daily: Sing Tao Bldg, 3/F, 1 Wang Kwong Rd, Kowloon Bay, Kowloon; tel. 27982575; fax 27953022; f. 1938; morning; Editor-in-Chief LUK KAM WING; circ. 60,000.

Ta Kung Pao: 342 Hennessy Rd, Wanchai; tel. 25757181; fax 28345104; e-mail tkp@takungpao.com; internet www.takungpao.com; f. 1902; morning; supports People's Republic of China; Editor T. S. TSANG; circ. 150,000.

Tin Tin Yat Pao: Culturecom Centre, 10/F, 47 Hung To Rd, Kwun Tong, Kowloon; tel. 29507300; fax 23452285; f. 1960; Chief Editor IP KAI-WING; circ. 199,258.

Wen Wei Po: Hing Wai Centre, 2–4/F, 7 Tin Wan Praya Rd, Aberdeen; tel. 28738288; fax 28730657; f. 1948; morning; communist; Dir CHANG YUN-FENG; Editor-in-Chief LIU ZAI-MING; circ. 180,000.

SELECTED PERIODICALS
English Language

Asian Business: c/o TPL Corporation (HK) Ltd, Block C, 10/F, Seaview Estate, 2–8 Watson Rd, North Point; tel. 25668381; fax 25080197; monthly; Publr and Executive Editor JAMES LEUNG; circ. 100,000.

Asian Medical News: Pacific Plaza, 8/F, 410 Des Voeux Rd West; tel. 25595888; fax 25596910; e-mail amn@medimedia.com.hk; internet www.amn.com; f. 1979; monthly; Man. Editor ROSS GARBETT; circ. 28,300.

Asian Profile: Asian Research Service, GPOB 2232; tel. 25707227; fax 25128050; f. 1973; 6 a year; multi-disciplinary study of Asian affairs.

Asiaweek: Oxford House, 30/F, Taikoo Place, 979 King's Rd, Quarry Bay; tel. 31283333; fax 31285013; e-mail editors@asiaweek.com; internet www.asiaweek.com; f. 1975; Asian news weekly; Editor DORINDA ELLIOTT; circ. 131,780.

Business Traveller Asia/Pacific: Unit 404, Printing Hse, 6 Duddell St, Central; tel. 25119317; fax 25196846; e-mail enquiry@

businesstravellerasia.com; f. 1982; consumer business travel; 12 a year; Publr PEGGY TEO; Editor JONATHAN WALL; circ. 23,320.

Far East Business: POB 9765; tel. 25721116; fax 28650844; f. 1967; business, government and industry; 12 a year; Editor LEWIS H. YOUNG; circ. 70,000.

Far Eastern Economic Review: Citicorp Centre, 25/F, 18 Whitfield Rd, Causeway Bay, GPOB 160; tel. 25084338; fax 25031537; e-mail review@feer.com; internet www.feer.com; f. 1946; weekly; Editor PHILIP REVZIN; circ. 95,570.

Hong Kong Electronics: Office Tower, Convention Plaza, 38/F, 1 Harbour Rd; tel. 25844333; fax 28240249; e-mail hktdc@tdc.org.ht; internet www.tdctrade.com; f. 1985; monthly; publ. by the Hong Kong Trade Development Council; Editor JOHN CAIRNS; circ. 90,000.

Hong Kong Enterprise: Office Tower, Convention Plaza, 38/F, 1 Harbour Rd; tel. 25844333; fax 28240249; e-mail hktdc@tdc.org.hk; internet www.tdctrade.com; f. 1967; monthly; publ. by the Hong Kong Trade Development Council; Editor TESS LUGOS; circ. 150,000.

Hong Kong Government Gazette: Govt Printing Dept, Cornwall House, Taikoo Trading Estate, 28 Tong Chong St, Quarry Bay; tel. 25649500; weekly.

Hong Kong Household: Office Tower, Convention Plaza, 38/F, 1 Harbour Rd, Wanchai; tel. 25844333; fax 28240249; e-mail hktdc@tdc.org.hk; internet www.tdctrade.com; f. 1983; publ. by the Hong Kong Trade Development Council; household and hardware products; 2 a year; Editor TESS LUGOS; circ. 90,000.

Hong Kong Industrialist: Federation of Hong Kong Industries, Hankow Centre, 4/F, 5–15 Hankow Rd, Tsimshatsui, Kowloon; tel. 27323188; fax 27213494; e-mail fhki@fhki.org.hk; monthly; publ. by the Federation of Hong Kong Industries; Editor JAMES MANNING; circ. 6,000.

Hong Kong Trader: Office Tower, Convention Plaza, 38/F, 1 Harbour Rd, Wanchai; tel. 25844333; fax 28243485; e-mail trader@tdc.org.hk; internet www.tdc.org.hk/hktrader; f. 1983; publ. by the Hong Kong Trade Development Council; trade, economics, financial and general business news; monthly; Man. Editor SOPHY FISHER; circ. 70,000.

Official Hong Kong Guide: Wilson House, 3/F, 19–27 Wyndham St, Central; tel. 25215392; fax 25218638; f. 1982; monthly; information on sightseeing, shopping, dining, etc. for overseas visitors; Editor-in-Chief DEREK DAVIES; circ. 9,300.

Orientations: 17/F, 200 Lockhart Rd; tel. 25111368; fax 25074620; e-mail orientations@iohk.com; internet www.orientations.com.hk; f. 1970; 10 a year; arts of East Asia, the Indian subcontinent and South-East Asia; Publr and Editorial Dir ELIZABETH KNIGHT.

Reader's Digest (Asia Edn): 3 Ah Kung Ngam Village Rd, Shaukiwan; tel. 96906381; fax 96906389; e-mail friends@rdasia.com.hk; f. 1963; general topics; monthly; Editor PETER DOCKRILL; circ. 332,000.

Sunday Examiner: Catholic Diocese Centre, 11/F, 16 Caine Rd; tel. 25220487; fax 25213095; e-mail sundayex@catholic.org.hk; f. 1946; religious; weekly; Editor Fr JOHN J. CASEY; circ. 2,300.

Textile Asia: c/o Business Press Ltd, California Tower, 11/F, 30–32 D'Aguilar St, GPOB 185, Central; tel. 25233744; fax 28106966; e-mail texasia@netvigator.com; f. 1970; monthly; textile and clothing industry; Publr and Editor-in-Chief KAYSER W. SUNG; circ. 17,000.

Tradefinance Asia: Hong Kong; Editor RICHARD TOURRET.

Travel Business Analyst: GPOB 12761; tel. 25072310; fax 94490949; e-mail tba@asiaonline.net; internet www.travelbusinessanalyst.com; f. 1982; travel trade; monthly; Editor MURRAY BAILEY.

Chinese Language

Affairs Weekly: Hong Kong; tel. 28950801; fax 25767842; f. 1980; general interest; Editor WONG WAI MAN; circ. 130,000.

Cheng Ming Monthly: Hennessy Rd, POB 20370; tel. 25740664; Chief Editor WAN FAI.

City Magazine: Hang Seng Bldg, 7/F, 200 Hennessy Rd, Wanchai; tel. 28931393; fax 28388761; f. 1976; monthly; fashion, wine, cars, society, etc.; Publr JOHN K. C. CHAN; Chief Editor PETER WONG; circ. 30,000.

Contemporary Monthly: Unit 705, Westlands Centre, 20 Westlands Rd, Quarry Bay; tel. 25638122; fax 25632984; f. 1989; monthly; current affairs; 'China-watch'; Editor-in-Chief CHING CHEONG; circ. 50,000.

Disc Jockey: Fuk Keung Ind. Bldg, B2, 14/F, 66–68 Tong Mei Rd, Taikoktsui, Kowloon; tel. 23905461; fax 27893869; e-mail vinpres@netvigator.com; f. 1990; monthly; music; Publr VINCENT LEUNG; Editor ALGE CHEUNG; circ. 32,000.

Eastweek: Oriental Press Centre, Wang Tai Rd, Kowloon Bay, Kowloon; tel. 27951111; fax 27955599; f. 1992; weekly; general interest; Chair. C. F. MA; circ. 238,000.

Elegance HK: Aik San Bldg, 14/F, 14 Westlands Rd, Quarry Bay; tel. 2963011; fax 25658217; f. 1977; monthly; for thinking women; Chief Editor WINNIE YUEN; circ. 75,000.

Kung Kao Po (Catholic Chinese Weekly): 16 Caine Rd; tel. 25220487; fax 25213095; e-mail kungkopo@catholic.org.hk; f. 1928; religious; weekly; Editor-in-Chief Fr LOUIS HA.

Lisa's Kitchen Bi-Weekly: Fuk Keung Ind. Bldg, B2, 14/F, 66–68 Tong Mei Rd, Taikoktsui, Kowloon; tel. 23910668; fax 27893869; f. 1984; recipes; Publr VINCENT LEUNG; circ. 50,000.

Metropolitan Weekly: f. 1983; weekly; entertainment, social news; Chief Editor CHARLES YOU; circ. 130,000.

Ming Pao Monthly: Ming Pao Industrial Centre, 15/F, Block A, 18 Ka Yip St, Chai Wan; tel. 25155107; fax 28982566; Chief Editor KOO SIU-SUN.

Motor Magazine: Prospect Mansion, Flat D, 1/F, 66–72 Paterson St, Causeway Bay; tel. 28822230; fax 28823949; f. 1990; Publr and Editor-in-Chief KENNETH LI; circ. 32,000.

Next Magazine: 8 Chun Ying St, T. K. O. Industrial Estate West, Tseung Kwan O, Hong Kong; tel. 27442733; fax 29907210; internet www.nextmedia.com; f. 1989; weekly; news, business, lifestyle, entertainment; Editor-in-Chief CHEUNG KIM HUNG; circ. 172,708.

Open Magazine: Causeway Bay, POB 31429; tel. 28939197; fax 28915591; e-mail open@open.com.hk; internet www.open.com.hk; f. 1990; monthly; Chief Editor JIN CHONG; circ. 15,000.

Oriental Sunday: Oriental Press Centre, Wang Tai Rd, Kowloon Bay, Kowloon; tel. 27951111; fax 27952299; f. 1991; weekly; leisure magazine; Chair. C. F. MA; circ. 120,000.

Reader's Digest (Chinese Edn): Reader's Digest Association Far East Ltd, 3 Ah Kung Ngam Village Rd, Shaukiwan; tel. 28845590; fax 25671479; e-mail chrd@netvigator.com; f. 1965; monthly; Editor-in-Chief VICTOR FUNG KEUNG; circ. 295,000.

Today's Living: Prospect Mansion, Flat D, 1/F, 66–72 Paterson St, Causeway Bay; tel. 28822230; fax 28823949; e-mail magazine@todayliving.com; f. 1987; monthly; interior design; Publr and Editor-in-Chief KENNETH LI; circ. 35,000.

TV Week: 1 Leighton Rd, Causeway Bay; tel. 28366147; fax 28346717; f. 1967; weekly; Publr PETER CHOW; circ. 59,082.

Yazhou Zhoukan: Block A, Ming Pao Industrial Centre, 15/F, 18 Ka Yip St, Chai Wan; tel. 25155358; fax 25059662; e-mil loppoon@mingpao.com; internet www.yzzk.com; f. 1987; international Chinese news weekly; Chief Editor YAU LOP-POON; circ. 110,000.

Young Girl Magazine: Fuk Keung Ind. Bldg, B2, 14/F, 66–68 Tong Mei Rd, Taikoktsui, Kowloon; tel. 23910668; fax 27893869; f. 1987; biweekly; Publr VINCENT LEUNG; circ. 65,000.

Yuk Long TV Weekly: Hong Kong; tel. 25657883; fax 25659958; f. 1977; entertainment, fashion, etc.; Publr TONY WONG; circ. 82,508.

NEWS AGENCIES

International News Service: 2E Cheong Shing Mansion, 33–39 Wing Hing St, Causeway Bay; tel. 25665668; Rep. AU KIT MING.

Xinhua (New China) News Agency, Hong Kong SAR Bureau: 387 Queen's Rd East, Wanchai; tel. 28314126; f. 2000 from fmr news dept of branch office of Xinhua (responsibility for other activities being assumed by Liaison Office of the Central People's Government in the Hong Kong SAR); Dir ZHANG GUOLIANG.

Foreign Bureaux

Agence France-Presse (AFP): Telecom House, Room 1840, 18/F, 3 Gloucester Rd, Wanchai, GPOB 5613; tel. 28020224; fax 28027292; Regional Dir YVAN CHEMLA.

Agencia EFE (Spain): 10A Benny View House, 63–65 Wong Nai Chung Rd, Happy Valley; tel. 28080199; fax 28823101; Correspondent MIREN GUTIÉRREZ.

Associated Press (AP) (USA): 1282 New Mercury House, Waterfront Rd; tel. 25274324; Bureau Chief ROBERT LIU.

Central News Agency (CNA) Inc (Taiwan): Hong Kong Bureau Chief CONRAD LU.

Jiji Tsushin-Sha (Japan): 3503 Far East Finance Centre, 16 Harcourt Rd; tel. 25237112; fax 28459013; Bureau Man. KATSUHIKO KABASAWA.

Kyodo News Service (Japan): Unit 1303, 13/F, 9 Queen's Rd, Central; tel. 25249750; fax 28105591; e-mail tyoko@po.iijnet.or.jp; Correspondent TSUKASA YOKOYAMA.

Reuters Asia Ltd (United Kingdom): Hong Kong; tel. 258436363; Bureau Man. GEOFF WEETMAN.

United Press International (UPI) (USA): 1287 Telecom House, 3 Gloucester Rd, POB 5692; tel. 28020221; fax 28024972; Vice-Pres. (Asia) ARNOLD ZEITLIN; Editor (Asia) PAUL H. ANDERSON.

PRESS ASSOCIATIONS

Chinese Language Press Institute: Hong Kong; tel. 25616211.

Hong Kong Chinese Press Association: Cheong K Bldg, Rm 404, 4/F, 84–86 Des Voeux Rd, Central; tel. 28613622; fax 28661933; 13 mems; Chair. HUE PUE-YING; Pres. WINSTON CHOU.

Hong Kong Journalists Association: GPOB 11726; tel. 25910692; fax 25727329; e-mail hkja@hk.super.net; internet www.hkja.org.hk; f. 1968; 549 mems; Chair. MAK YIN-TING.

Newspaper Society of Hong Kong: Culturecom Centre, 12/F, 47 Hung To Rd, Kwun Tong, Kowloon; tel. 29507129; fax 27639691; f. 1954; Chair. L. Y. TANG; Vice-Chair. PAUL HUI.

Publishers

Art House of Collectors HK Ltd: 37 Lyndhurst Terrace, Ground Floor, Central; tel. 28818026; fax 28904304; Dir. LI LAP FONG.

Asia 2000 Ltd: 302 Seabird House, 22–28 Wyndham St, Central; tel. 25301409; fax 25261107; e-mail info@asia2000.com.hk; internet www.asia2000.com.hk; Asian studies, politics, photography, fiction; Man. Dir MICHAEL MORROW.

Asian Research Service: GPOB 2232; tel. 25707227; fax 25128050; f. 1972; maps, atlases, monographs on Asian studies and journals; Dir NELSON LEUNG.

Business Press Ltd: California Tower, 11/F, 30–32 D'Aguilar St, GPOB 185, Central; tel. 25233744; fax 28106966; e-mail texasia@netvigator.com; f. 1970; textile magazine; Man. Dir KAYSER W. SUNG.

Chinese University Press: Chinese University of Hong Kong, Sha Tin, New Territories; tel. 26096508; fax 26036692; e-mail cup@cuhk.edu.hk; internet www.cuhk.edu.hk/cupress; f. 1977; studies on China and Hong Kong and other academic works; Dir Dr STEVEN K. LUK.

Commercial Press (Hong Kong) Ltd: Eastern Central Plaza, 8/F, 3 Yiu Hing Rd, Shau Kei Wan; tel. 25651371; fax 25645277; e-mail enquiry@commercialpress.com.hk; internet www.commercialpress.com.hk; f. 1897; trade books, dictionaries, textbooks, Chinese classics, art, etc.; Man. Dir and Chief Editor CHAN MAN HUNG.

Excerpta Medica Asia Ltd: 8/F, 67 Wyndham St; tel. 25243118; fax 28100687; f. 1980; sponsored medical publications, abstracts, journals etc.

Hoi Fung Publisher Co: 125 Lockhart Rd, 2/F, Wanchai; tel. 25286246; fax 25286249; Dir. K. K. TSE.

Hong Kong University Press: Hing Wai Centre, 14/F, 7 Tin Wan Praya Rd, Aberdeen; tel. 25502703; fax 28750734; e-mail hkupress@hkucc.hku.hk; internet www.hkupress.org; f. 1956; Publr COLIN DAY.

International Publishing Co: Rm 213–215, HK Industrial Technology Centre, 72 Tat Chee Ave, Kowloon Tong, Kowloon; tel. 23148882; fax 23192208; Admin. Man. KAREN CHOW.

Ismay Publications Ltd: C. C. Wu Building; tel. 25752270; Man. Dir MINNIE YEUNG.

Ling Kee Publishing Co Ltd: Zung Fu Industrial Bldg, 1067 King's Rd, Quarry Bay; tel. 25616151; fax 28111980; f. 1956; educational and reference; Chair. B. L. AU; Man. Dir K. W. AU.

Oxford University Press (China) Ltd: Warwick House, 18/F, 979 King's Rd, Taikoo Place, Quarry Bay; tel. 25163222; fax 25658491; e-mail oupchina@oupchina.com.hk; internet www.oupchina.com.hk; f. 1961; school textbooks, reference, academic and general works relating to Hong Kong, Taiwan and China; Regional Dir SIMON LI.

Taosheng Publishing House: Luther House, 3/F, 50A Waterloo Rd, Mong Kok, Kowloon; tel. 27802206; fax 23852592; Dir CHAN PUI TAK.

The Woods Publishing Co: Li Yuen Building, 2/F, 7 Li Yuen St West, Central; tel. 25233002; fax 28453296; e-mail tybook@netvigator.com; Production Man. TONG SZE HONG.

TPL Corporation (HK) Ltd: Seaview Estate, Block C, 10/F, 2–8 Watson Rd, North Point; tel. 25668381; fax 25080197; trade magazines and directories; Executive Editor JAMES LEUNG.

Government Publishing House

Government Information Services: see p. 1081.

PUBLISHERS' ASSOCIATIONS

Hong Kong Publishers' and Distributors' Association: National Bldg, 4/F, 240–246 Nathan Rd, Kowloon; tel. 23674412; 45 mems; Chair. HO KAM-LING; Sec. HO NAI-CHI.

Society of Publishers in Asia: c/o Worldcom Hong Kong, 502–503 Admiralty Centre, Tower I, 18 Harcourt Rd, Admiralty; tel. 28654007; fax 28652559; e-mail worldcom@hkstar.com.

Broadcasting and Communications

TELECOMMUNICATIONS

Asia Satellite Telecommunications Co Ltd (AsiaSat): East Exchange Tower, 23–24/F, 38–40 Leighton Rd; tel. 28056666; fax 25043875; e-mail wpang@asiasat.com; internet www.asiasat.com; CEO PETER JACKSON.

Cable and Wireless HKT Ltd: Hongkong Telecom Tower, 39/F, Taikoo Place, 979 King's Rd, Quarry Bay; tel. 28882888; fax 28778877; e-mail info@cwhkt.com; internet www.cwhkt.com; fmrly Hong Kong Telecommunications; in 1998 acquired Pacific Link Communications to become largest mobile telephone operator in Hong Kong; monopoly on provision of international lines expired March 1998; full competition began Jan. 1999; CEO LINUS CHEUNG.

Regulatory Authority

Telecommunications Authority: statutory regulator, responsible for implementation of the Govt's pro-competition and pro-consumer policies; Dir.Gen. ANTHONY S. K. WONG.

Hutchison Telecom, New T and T Hong Kong Ltd, and New World Telecom also operate local services. In 1999 six companies were licensed to provide mobile telecommunications services, serving over 3.8m. customers.

BROADCASTING
Regulatory Authority

Broadcasting Authority: regulatory body; administers and issues broadcasting licences.

Radio

Hong Kong Commercial Broadcasting Co Ltd: 3 Broadcast Drive, KCPOB 73000; tel. 23365111; fax 23380021; e-mail comradio@crhk.com.hk; internet www.crhk.com.hk; f. 1959; broadcasts in English and Chinese on three radio frequencies; Chair. G. J. HO; Dir and CEO WINNIE YU.

Metro Broadcast Corpn Ltd (Metro Broadcast): Hong Kong; tel. 23649333; fax 23646577; e-mail tech@metroradio.com.hk; internet www.metroradio.com.hk; f. 1991; broadcasts on three channels in English, Cantonese and Mandarin; Gen. Man. CRAIG B. QUICK.

Radio Television Hong Kong: Broadcasting House, 30 Broadcast Drive, POB 70200, Kowloon Central PO; tel. 23396300; fax 23380279; e-mail rthk@hk.super.net; internet www.rthk.org.hk; f. 1928; govt-funded; 24-hour service in English and Chinese on seven radio channels; service in Putonghua inaugurated in 1997; Dir CHU PUI-HING.

Star Radio: Hutchison House, 12/F, 10 Harcourt Rd, Central; f. 1995; satellite broadcasts in Mandarin and English; Gen. Man. MIKE MACKAY.

Television

Asia Television Ltd (ATV): Television House, 81 Broadcast Drive, Kowloon; tel. 29928888; fax 23380438; e-mail atv@hkatv.com; internet www.hkatv.com; f. 1973; operates two commercial television services (English and Chinese) and produces television programmes; Dir and CEO FENG XIAO PING.

Satellite Television Asian Region Ltd—STAR TV: One Harbourfront, 8/F, 18 Tak Fung St, Hunghom, Kowloon; tel. 26218888; fax 26218000; internet www.startv.com; f. 1990; subsidiary of the News Corpn Ltd; broadcasts programming services via satellite to 300m. viewers in 53 countries across Asia, the Indian subcontinent and the Middle East; music, news, sport and entertainment broadcasts in English, Mandarin, Hindi, Japanese, Tagalog, Arabic, and Thai; subscription and free-to-air services on several channels; Chair. and CEO Exec. JAMES MURDOCH.

Radio Television Hong Kong: (see Radio); produces drama, documentary and public affairs programmes; also operates an educational service for transmission by two local commercial stations; Dir CHU PUI-HING (acting).

Television Broadcasts Ltd (TVB): TV City, Clearwater Bay Rd, Kowloon; tel. 23352288; fax 23581300; e-mail external.affairs@tvb.com.hk; internet www.tvb.com.hk; f. 1967; operates Chinese and English language services; two colour networks; Exec. Chair. Sir RUN RUN SHAW; Man. Dir LOUIS PAGE.

Wharf Cable Ltd: Wharf Cable Tower, 4/F, 9 Hoi Shing Rd, Tsuen Wan; tel. 26115533; fax 24171511; f. 1993; 24-hour subscription service of news, sport and entertainment on 35 channels; carries BBC World Service Television; Chair. PETER WOO; Man. Dir STEPHEN NG.

Finance

(cap. = capital; res = reserves; dep. = deposits; m. = million; brs = branches; amounts in Hong Kong dollars unless otherwise stated)

BANKING

In December 1999 there were 165 licensed banks, of which 31 were locally incorporated, operating in Hong Kong. There were also 58 restricted licence banks (formerly known as licensed deposit-taking companies), 71 deposit-taking companies, and 128 foreign banks' representative offices.

Hong Kong Monetary Authority (HKMA): 30/F, 3 Garden Rd, Central; tel. 28788196; fax 28788197; e-mail hkma@hkma.gov.hk; internet www.hkma.gov.hk; f. 1993 by merger of Office of the Commissioner of Banking and Office of the Exchange Fund; carries out central banking functions; maintains Hong Kong dollar stability within the framework of the linked exchange rate system; supervises licensed banks, restricted licence banks and deposit-taking cos, their overseas brs and representative offices; manages foreign currency reserves; Chief Exec. JOSEPH YAM; Deputy Chief Execs DAVID CARSE, TONY LATTER, NORMAN CHAN.

Banks of Issue

Bank of China (People's Repub. of China): Bank of China Tower, 1 Garden Rd, Central; tel. 28266888; fax 28105963; f. 1917; became third bank of issue in May 1994; Gen. Man. LIU JINBAO; 44 brs.

The Hongkong and Shanghai Banking Corporation Ltd: 1 Queen's Rd, Central; tel. 28221111; fax 28101112; internet www.asiapacific.hsbc.com; f. 1865; personal and commercial banking; cap. 16,258m., res 63,228m., dep. 1,387,551m. (Dec. 1999); Chair. DAVID ELDON; CEO AMAN MEHTA; more than 600 offices world-wide.

Standard Chartered Bank: Standard Chartered Bank Bldg, 4–4A Des Voeux Rd, Central; tel. 28203333; fax 28569129; internet www.standardchartered.com.hk; f. 1859; Group Exec. Dir MERVYN DAVIES.

Other Commercial Banks

Asia Commercial Bank Ltd: Asia Financial Centre, 120–122 Des Voeux Rd, Central; tel. 25419222; fax 25410009; f. 1934; fmrly Commercial Bank of Hong Kong; cap. 800.0m., res 448.1m., dep. 11,591.9m. (Dec. 1999); Chair. and CEO ROBIN Y. H. CHAN; Gen. Man. and Exec. Dir STEPHEN TAN; 15 domestic, 2 overseas brs.

Bank of East Asia Ltd: GPOB 31, 10 Des Voeux Rd, Central; tel. 28423200; fax 28459333; internet www.hkbea.com; inc in Hong Kong in 1918; cap. 3,436.8m., res 10,609.7m., dep. etc. 117,291.2m. (Dec. 1998); Chair. and Chief Exec. DAVID K. P. LI; 105 brs in Hong Kong and 15 overseas brs.

Chekiang First Bank Ltd: Chekiang First Bank Centre, 1 Duddell St, Central; tel. 29221222; fax 28669133; e-mail contact@cfb.com.hk; internet www.cfb.com.hk; f. 1950; cap. 1,650m., res 1,595.2m., dep. 22,530.8m. (Dec. 1999); Chair. JAMES Z. M. KUNG; 18 brs.

Chiyu Banking Corpn Ltd: 78 Des Voeux Rd, Central; tel. 28430111; fax 25267420; f. 1947; cap. 300m., res 3,488m., dep. 24,033.5m. (Dec. 1998); Chair. TAN KONG PIAT; 15 brs.

CITIC Ka Wah Bank Ltd: 232 Des Voeux Rd, Central; tel. 25457131; fax 25417029; e-mail info@citickawahbank.com; internet://www.citickawahbank.com; f. 1922; cap. 2,595m., res 2,765m., dep. 41,705m. (Dec. 1999); Chair. HONG YUNCHENG; Pres. and CEO CAI ZHONGZHI; 30 domestic brs, 2 overseas brs.

Dah Sing Bank Ltd: Dah Sing Financial Centre, 36/F, 108 Gloucester Rd, Central; tel. 25078866; fax 25985052; e-mail ops@dahsing.com.hk; internet www.dahsing.com; f. 1947; cap. 800.0m., res 1,024.3m., dep. 36,981.5m. (Dec. 1999); Chair. DAVID S. Y. WONG; Man. Dir DEREK H. H. WONG; 39 domestic brs, 1 overseas br.

Dao Heng Bank Ltd: The Centre, 11/F, 99 Queen's Rd, Central; tel. 22188822; fax 22853822; e-mail webmaster@daoheng.com; internet www.daoheng.com; f. 1921; cap. 5,200m., res 6,307.7m., dep. 105,127.3m. (June 1999); Chair. QUEK LENG-CHAN; CEO KWEK LENG-HAI; 48 domestic brs, 4 overseas brs.

DBS Kwong On Bank Ltd: 139 Queen's Rd, Central; tel. 28153636; fax 28506129; e-mail dbskob@dbs.com; internet www.dbs.com.hk; f. 1938, inc 1954 as Kwong On Bank, name changed 2000; subsidiary of the Development Bank of Singapore; cap. 750.0m., res 3,338.9m., dep. 24,412.2m. (Dec. 1998); Chair. RONALD LEUNG DING-BONG; Sr Man. Dir KENNETH T. M. LEUNG; 32 brs.

First Pacific Bank Ltd: First Pacific Bank Centre, 22/F, 56 Gloucester Rd, Wanchai; tel. 28239823; fax 28655151; e-mail info@firstpacbank.com; internet www.firstpacbank.com; f. 1922; fmrly The Hong Nin Savings Bank Ltd; merged with Far East Bank in 1989; cap. 1,248m., res 1,597.8m., dep. 21,380m. (Dec. 1998); Chair. MANUEL PANGILINAN; Man. Dir JAMES C. NG; 23 brs.

Hang Seng Bank Ltd: 83 Des Voeux Rd, Central; tel. 21981111; fax 28459301; e-mail ccd@hangseng.com; internet www.hangseng.com; f. 1933; cap. 9,559m., res 30,015m., dep. 382,600m. (Dec. 1999); Chair. DAVID ELDON; Vice-Chair. and CEO VINCENT CHENG; 156 domestic brs, 4 overseas brs.

Hongkong Chinese Bank Ltd: Lippo Centre, Floor Mezz. 1, 89 Queensway, Central; tel. 28676833; fax 28459221; internet www.hkcb.com.hk; f. 1954; cap. 2,393.3m., res 814.1m., dep. 21,579.2m. (Dec. 1999); Chair. MOCHTAR RIADY; Man. Dir and Chief Exec. DAVID P. L. CHAN; 24 domestic, 2 overseas brs.

Hua Chiao Commercial Bank Ltd: Hua Chiao Commercial Bldg, 88–98 Des Voeux Rd, Central; tel. 25429888; fax 25434035; internet hccb.bocgroup.com; f. 1962; cap. 400m., res 5,410.4m., dep. 34,044m. (Dec. 1999); Chair. KHOE BOEN TJOEN; 24 domestic brs, 1 overseas br.

ICBC (Asia): Union Bank Tower, 122–126 Queen's Rd, Central; tel. 25343333; fax 28051166; f. 1964; fmrly Union Bank of Hong Kong; cap. 901.4m., res 1,528m., dep. 15,433m. (Dec. 1999); Chair. FU YUNING; 23 brs.

International Bank of Asia Ltd: International Bank of Asia Bldg, 38 Des Voeux Rd, Central; tel. 28426222; fax 28101483; e-mail corpcomm@iba.com.hk; internet www.iba.com.hk; f. 1982 as Sun Hung Kai Bank Ltd, name changed 1986; subsidiary of Arab Banking Corpn; cap. 1,172.2m., res 1,121.8m., dep. 19,399.5m. (Dec. 1999); Chair. Sheikh ALI JARRAH AL-SABAH; Man. Dir and CEO MIKE M. MURAD; 28 brs.

Liu Chong Hing Bank Ltd: POB 2535, 24 Des Voeux Rd, Central; tel. 28417417; fax 28459134; e-mail intlcorrbankhk@lchbhk.com; internet www.lchbank.com; f. 1948; cap. 217.5m., res. 5,055.0m., dep. 29,685.6m. (Dec. 1999); Chair. and Man. Dir LIU LIT-MAN; 35 domestic brs, 3 overseas brs.

Nanyang Commercial Bank Ltd: Nanyang Commercial Bank Bldg, 151 Des Voeux Rd, Central; tel. 28520888; fax 28153333; internet www.nanyang.bocgroup.com; f. 1949; cap. p.u. 600m., res 9,296m., dep. 74,226.6m. (Dec. 1999); Chair. ZHANG HONG-YI; 42 brs, 6 mainland brs, 1 overseas br.

Overseas Trust Bank Ltd: The Centre, 11/F, 99 Queen's Rd, Central; tel. 22188822; fax 22853822; e-mail webmaster@daoheng.com; internet www.daoheng.com; f. 1955; under govt control 1985–93; cap. 2,000m. (Dec. 1998), res 2,458.7m., dep. 27,297.8m. (Jun. 1999); Chair. QUEK LENG-CHAN; Man. Dir R. G. SULLIVAN; 28 domestic brs, 4 overseas brs.

Po Sang Bank Ltd: 71 Des Voeux Rd, Central; tel. 28436111; fax 28101126; f. 1949; cap. 400m., res 8,121.8m., dep. 39,047.3m. (Dec. 1999); Chair. LAM KWONG-SUI; Gen. Man. GAO JI-LU; 20 brs.

Shanghai Commercial Bank Ltd: 12 Queen's Rd, Central; tel. 28415415; fax 28104623; e-mail contact@shacombank.com.hk; internet www.shacombank.com.hk; f. 1950; cap. 1,600m., res 5,855.8m., dep. 48,366m. (Dec. 1999); Chair. SHIH PAO-CHU; Man. Dir and Gen. Man. JOHN KAM-PAK YAN; 39 domestic brs, 4 overseas brs.

Sin Hua Bank Ltd: 2A Des Voeux Rd, Central; tel. 21608888; fax 28542596; f. 1914; cap. 2,200m. yuan, res 8,254.4m. yuan, dep. 79,609.0m. yuan (Dec. 1998); Chair JIANG ZU-QI; Gen. Man. WU JUN SHENG; 43 brs.

Wing Hang Bank Ltd: POB 514, 161 Queen's Rd, Central; tel. 28525111; fax 25410036; e-mail whbpsd@whbhk.com; internet www.whbhk.com; f. 1937; cap. 294.0m., res 4,546.6m., dep. 44,644.9m. (Dec. 1999); Chair. and Chief Exec. PATRICK Y. FUNG; 27 domestic brs, 14 overseas brs.

Wing Lung Bank Ltd: 45 Des Voeux Rd, Central; tel. 28268333; fax 28100592; e-mail wlb@winglungbank.com.hk; internet www.bankwinglung.com; f. 1933; cap. 1,161.0m., res 2,276.0m., dep. 49,453.1m. (Dec. 1999); Chair. MICHAEL PO-KO WU; Exec. Dir and Gen. Man. CHE-SHUM CHUNG; 35 domestic brs, 2 overseas brs.

Principal Mainland Chinese and Foreign Banks

ABN AMRO Bank NV (Netherlands): Edinburgh Tower, 3–4/F, Landmark, 15 Queen's Rd, Central; tel. 28429211; fax 28459049; CEO (China) SERGIO RIAL; 10 brs.

American Express Bank Ltd (USA): One Pacific Place, 36/F, 88 Queensway, Central; tel. 28440688; fax 28453637; Senior Country Exec. DOUGLAS H. SHORT III; 4 brs.

Australia and New Zealand Banking Group Ltd: 27/F, One Exchange Square, 8 Connaught Place, Central; tel. 28437111; fax 28680089; Gen. Man. DAVID MORGAN.

Bangkok Bank Public Co Ltd (Thailand): Bangkok Bank Bldg, 28 Des Voeux Rd, Central; tel. 28016688; fax 28105679; Gen. Man. AMNUAY LILAONITKUL; 4 brs.

Bank of America (Asia) Ltd (USA): Devon House, 17/F, 979 King's Rd, Quarry Bay; tel. 28052383; fax 25973300; internet www.bankofamerica.com.hk; Chair. JOHN RINDLAUB; Pres. and CEO SAMUEL TSIEN; 17 brs.

Bank of Communications, Hong Kong Branch: 20 Pedder St, Central; tel. 28419611; fax 28106993; f. 1934; Gen. Man. FANG LIANKUI; 1 br, 36 sub-brs..

Bank of India: Ruttonjee House, 2/F, 11 Duddell St, Central; tel. 25240186; fax 28106149; e-mail boihk@netvigator.com; Chief Exec. O. P. GUPTA; 2 brs.

Bank Negara Indonesia (Persero) Tbk: Far East Finance Centre, 16 Harcourt Rd, Central; tel. 25299871; fax 28656500; Gen. Man. AGUS SULAKSONO; 1 br.

Bank of Scotland: Jardine House, 11/F, 1 Connaught Place, Central; tel. 25212155; fax 28459007; Sr Man. I. A. McKINNEY; 1 br.

Bank of Tokyo-Mitsubishi Ltd (Japan): Far East Finance Centre, 1/F, 16 Harcourt Rd, Central; tel. 28627888; fax 25293821; 3 brs.

Bank of Yokohama Ltd (Japan): Edinburgh Tower, 36/F, 15 Queen's Rd, Central; tel. 25236041; fax 28459022; Gen. Man. SUSUMU YAMADA; 1 br.

Banque Worms (France): Central Plaza, 39/F, 18 Harbour Rd, Wanchai; tel. 28028382; fax 28028065; Gen. Man. JEAN-FRANÇOIS FERRACHAT; 1 br.

Barclays Capital Asia Ltd: Citibank Tower, 42/F, 3 Garden Rd, Central; tel. 29032000; fax 29032999; internet www.barclayscapital .com; f. 1972; Chair. and CEO ROGER DAVIS.

Belgian Bank (Belgium): Belgian Bank Tower, G/F, 77–79 Gloucester Rd, Wanchai; tel. 28230566; fax 25297966; Man. Dir GEORGES LEGROS; 33 brs.

BNP Paribas (France): Central Tower, 4–14/F, 28 Queen's Rd, Central; tel. 29098888; fax 28652523; e-mail didier.balme@ bnpgroup.com; internet www.bnpparibas.com.hk; f. 1958; Man. DIDIER BALME; 6 brs.

Chase Manhattan Bank (USA): Chase Manhattan Tower, 18/F, Shatin, Central; tel. 26855111; fax 26855099; Sr Vice-Pres. EDWARD J. COOPER, Jr; 4 brs.

China and South Sea Bank Ltd (People's Repub. of China): 136 Des Voeux Rd, Central; tel. 21386008; fax 21386009; Chair. HUA QING SHAN; Gen. Man. WANG ZHEN JUN.

China State Bank Ltd (People's Repub. of China): China State Bank Bldg, 39–41 Des Voeux Rd, Central; tel. 28419333; fax 28450584; Gen. Man. CHAN SHUE BIU.

Chung Khiaw Bank Ltd (Singapore): Edinburgh Tower, Room 2508, 25/F, The Landmark, 15 Queen's Rd, Central; tel. 25250318; fax 28684598; Man. LIEW CHAN HARN; 2 brs.

Citibank, NA (USA): Citibank Tower, 39–40/F and 44–50/F, Citibank Plaza, 3 Garden Rd, Central; tel. 28688888; 27 brs.

Commerzbank AG (Germany): Hong Kong Club Bldg, 21/F, 3A Chater Rd, Central; tel. 28429666; fax 28681414; 1 br.

Crédit Agricole Indosuez (France): One Exchange Square, 44/F, 8 Connaught Rd, Central; tel. 28489000; fax 28681406; Sr Country Officer FRANÇOIS BEYLER; 1 br.

Dai-Ichi Kangyo Bank Ltd (Japan): Gloucester Tower, 31/F, 11 Pedder St, Central; tel. 25266591; fax 28681421; Gen. Man. TAKESHI TANIMURA; 1 br.

Deutsche Bank AG (Germany): New World Tower, 37/F, 16–18 Queen's Rd, Central, POB 3193; tel. 28430400; fax 28459056; Gen. Mans Dr MICHAEL THOMAS, REINER RUSCH; 1 br.

Equitable Banking Corpn (Philippines): 4 Duddell St, Central; tel. 28680323; fax 28100050; Vice-Pres. PAUL LANG; 1 br.

Indian Overseas Bank: Ruttonjee House, 3/F, 11 Duddell St, Central; tel. 25227249; fax 28451549; 2 brs.

Kincheng Banking Corpn (People's Repub. of China): Kincheng Bank Bldg, 55 Des Voeux Rd, Central; tel. 28430222; fax 28450116; internet kincheng.bocgroup.com; f. 1917; Gen. Man. SUN HUNG-KAY; 34 brs.

Kwangtung Provincial Bank (People's Repub. of China): Euro Trade Centre, G–3/F, 13–14 Connaught Rd, Central; tel. 28410410; fax 28459302; Gen. Man. ZHENG BAILIN; 30 brs.

Malayan Banking Berhad (Malaysia): Entertainment Bldg, 18–19/F, 30 Queen's Rd, Central; tel. 25227141; fax 28106013; trades in Hong Kong as Maybank; Man. AMOS ONG; 2 brs.

National Bank of Pakistan: Central Bldg, Room 324, 21–27 Queen's Rd, Central; tel. 25217321; fax 28451703; Sr Vice-Pres. M. IQBAL SHEIKH; 2 brs.

National Commercial Bank Ltd (People's Repub. of China): 1–3 Wyndham St, Central; tel. 28432888; fax 28104634; e-mail hkbrmain@natcombank.com; internet www.natcombank.com; Gen. Man. M. L. LAM; 27 brs.

National Westminster Bank PLC (UK): Natwest Tower, Times Square, 43/F, 1 Matheson St, Causeway Bay; tel. 29662800; fax 29660966; Chair. JOHN HOWLAND-JACKSON; 2 brs.

Oversea-Chinese Banking Corpn Ltd (Singapore): 9/F, 9 Queen's Rd, Central; tel. 28682086; fax 28453439; Man. NA WU BENG; 3 brs.

Overseas Union Bank Ltd (Singapore): Edinburgh Tower, 5/F, 15 Queen's Rd, The Landmark, Central; tel. 25211521; fax 28105506; Vice-Pres. and Gen. Man. KWIK SAM AIK; 2 brs.

Philippine National Bank: Wing's Bldg, 2/F, 110–116 Queen's Rd, Central; tel. 25439555; fax 25253107; Sr Vice-Pres. and Gen. Man. ARTICER O. QUEBAL; 1 br.

Royal Bank of Canada: Gloucester Tower, 18/F, 11 Pedder St, The Landmark, Central; tel. 28430888; fax 28681871; Vice-Pres. T. P. GIBBS; 1 br.

Sanwa Bank Ltd (Japan): Fairmont House, 8 Cotton Tree Drive, Central; tel. 28433888; fax 28400730; Gen. Man. Y. KIDA; 6 brs.

Sumitomo Bank Ltd (Japan): 2601 Edinburgh Tower, 15 Queen's Rd, Central; tel. 28421700; fax 28106452; Gen. Man. TOSIO MORIKAWA; 1 br.

Toyo Trust and Banking Co Ltd (Japan): Gloucester Tower, 15/F, The Landmark, 11 Pedder St, Central; tel. 25265657; fax 28459247; Gen. Man. KOICHI KUBOYAMA; 1 br.

United Overseas Bank Ltd (Singapore): United Overseas Bank Bldg, 54–58 Des Voeux Rd, Central; tel. 25257171; fax 28105773; Sr Vice-Pres. and CEO ROBERT CHAN TZE LEUNG; 4 brs.

Yien Yieh Commercial Bank Ltd (People's Repub. of China): 242–252 Des Voeux Rd, Central; tel. 25411601; fax 25414037; Gen. Man. WU GUO RUI; 26 sub-brs.

Banking Associations

The Chinese Banks' Association: South China Bldg, 5/F, 1–3 Wyndham St, Central; tel. 25224789; fax 28775102; 1,666 mems; Chair. Bank of East Asia (represented by DAVID K. P. LI).

The DTC Association (The Hong Kong Association of Restricted Licence Banks and Deposit-Taking Companies): Suite 3738, 37/F, Sun Hung Kai Centre, 30 Harbour Rd; tel. 25264079; fax 25230180.

The Hong Kong Association of Banks: GPOB 11391; tel. 25211169; fax 28685035; e-mail hkab@pacific.net.hk; f. 1981 to succeed The Exchange Banks' Asscn of Hong Kong; all licensed banks in Hong Kong are required by law to be mems of this statutory body, whose function is to represent and further the interests of the banking sector; 154 mems; Chair. HSBC (represented by RAYMOND C. F. OR; Sec. DAVID MAY.

STOCK EXCHANGE

Honk Kong Exchanges and Clearing Ltd: 1 International Finance Centre, 12/F, 1 Harbour View St, Central; tel. 25221122; fax 22953106; e-mail info@hkex.com.hk; internet www.hkex.com.hk; f. 2000 by unification of the Stock Exchange of Hong Kong, the Hong Kong Futures Exchange and the Hong Kong Securities Clearing Co; 572 mems; Chair. LEE YEH KWONG; CEO KWONG KI CHI.

In 1998 **Exchange Fund Investment Ltd** was established by the Government to manage its stock portfolio acquired during the intervention of August (Chair. YANG TI-LIANG).

SUPERVISORY BODY

Securities and Futures Commission (SFC): Edinburgh Tower, 12/F, The Landmark, 15 Queen's Rd, Central; tel. 28409222; fax 28459553; e-mail enquiry@hksfc.org.hk; internet www.hksfc.org.hk; f. 1989 to supervise the stock and futures markets; Chair. ANDREW SHENG; Dep. Chair. LAURA CHA.

INSURANCE

In June 1999 there were 208 authorized insurance companies, including 106 overseas companies. The following are among the principal companies:

Asia Insurance Co Ltd: World-Wide House, 16/F, 19 Des Voeux Rd, Central; tel. 28677988; fax 28100218; Chair. SEBASTIAN KI CHIT LAU.

CGU International Insurance plc: Cityplaza One, 9/F, Taikoo Shing; tel. 28940555; fax 28905741; e-mail cguasia.com; Gen. Man. ANDREW LO.

Hong Kong Export Credit Insurance Corpn: South Seas Centre, Tower I, 2/F, 75 Mody Rd, Tsim Sha Tsui East, Kowloon; fax 27226277; Commr D. K. DOWDING.

Mercantile and General Reinsurance Co PLC: 13C On Hing Bldg, 1 On Hing Terrace, Central; tel. 28106160; fax 25217353; Man. T. W. HO.

Ming An Insurance Co (HK) Ltd: Ming An Plaza, 22/F, 8 Sunning Rd, Causeway Bay; tel. 28151551; fax 25416567; e-mail mai@ mingan.com.hk; internet www.mingan.com; Dir and Gen. Man. K. P. CHENG.

National Mutual Insurance Co (Bermuda) Ltd: 151 Gloucester Rd, Wanchai; tel. 25191111; fax 25987204; life and general insurance; Chair. Sir DAVID AKERS-JONES; CEO TERRY SMITH.

Prudential Assurance Co Ltd: Cityplaza 4, 10/F, 12 Taikoo Wan Rd, Taikoo Shing; tel. 29773888; fax 28776994; life and general; Gen. Man. EDDIE K. F. FONG.

Royal and Sun Alliance (Hong Kong) Ltd: Dorset House, 32/F, Taikoo Place, 979 King's Road, Quarry Bay; tel. 29683000; fax 29685111; Man. Dir KEITH LAND.

Summit Insurance (Asia) Ltd: Sunshine Plaza, 25/F, 253 Lockhart Rd, Wanchai; tel. 21059000; fax 25166992; e-mail psi@hcg.com.hk; internet www.hsinchong.com/summit; CEO IU PO SING.

Taikoo Royal Insurance Co Ltd: Dorset House, 32/F, Taikoo Place, 979 King's Rd, Quarry Bay; tel. 29683000; fax 29685111; Man. Dir ANDREW LEUNG.

Willis China (Hong Kong) Ltd: 17/F, AIA Plaza, 18 Hysan Ave, Causeway Bay; tel. 28270111; fax 28270966; e-mail wongm@willis.com; internet www.willis.com; CEO HOWARD H. K. TSANG; Man. Dir MICHAEL WONG.

Winterthur Swiss Insurance (Asia) Ltd: Dah Sing Financial Centre, 19/F, 108 Gloucester Rd, Wanchai; tel. 25986282; fax 25985838; Man. Dir ALLAN YU.

Insurance Associations

Hong Kong Federation of Insurers (HKFI): First Pacific Bank Centre, Room 902, 9/F, 56 Gloucester Rd, Wanchai; tel. 25201868; fax 25201967; e-mail hkfi@hkfi.org.hk; internet www.hkfi.org.hk; f. 1988; 117 general insurance and 42 life insurance mems; Chair. CHOY CHUNG FOO; Exec. Dir LOUISA FONG.

Insurance Institute of Hong Kong: GPO Box 6747; tel. 25825601; fax 28276033; internet www.iihk.org.hk; f. 1967; Pres. STEPHEN LAW.

Trade and Industry

Hong Kong Trade Development Council: Office Tower, 38/F, Convention Plaza, 1 Harbour Rd, Wanchai; tel. 25844333; fax 28240249; e-mail hktdc@tdc.org.hk; internet www.tdctrade.com; f. 1966; Chair. Dr VICTOR K. FUNG; Exec. Dir MICHAEL SZE.

Trade and Industry Department: Trade and Industry Department Tower, 700 Nathan Rd, Kowloon; tel. 23985333; fax 27892491; e-mail enqtid@tid.gcn.gov.hk; internet www.info.gov.hk/tid; Dir-Gen. JOSHUA LAW.

DEVELOPMENT ORGANIZATIONS

Hong Kong Housing Authority: 33 Fat Kwong St, Homantin, Kowloon; tel. 27615002; fax 27621110; f. 1973; plans, builds and manages public housing; Chair. DOMINIC WONG; Dir of Housing J. A. MILLER.

Hong Kong Productivity Council: HKPC Bldg, 78 Tat Chee Ave, Yau Yat Chuen, Kowloon Tong, Kowloon; tel. 27885678; fax 27885900; e-mail bettylee@hkpc.org; internet www.hkpc.org; f. 1967 to promote increased productivity of industry and to encourage optimum utilization of resources; council of 23 mems appointed by the Government, representing management, labour, academic and professional interests, and govt depts associated with productivity matters; Chair. KENNETH FANG; Exec. Dir THOMAS TANG.

Kadoorie Agricultural Aid Loan Fund: c/o Director of Agriculture, Fisheries and Conservation, Cheung Sha Wan Govt Offices, 5/F, 303 Cheung Sha Wan Rd, Kowloon; tel. 21506666; fax 23113731; e-mail afcdenq@afcd.gcn.gov.hk; f. 1955; provides low-interest loans to farmers; HK $8,890,000 was loaned in 1999/2000.

J. E. Joseph Trust Fund: c/o Director of Agriculture, Fisheries and Conservation, Cheung Sha Wan Govt Offices, 5/F, 303 Cheung Sha Wan Rd, Kowloon; tel. 21506666; fax 23113731; e-mail afcdenq@afcd.gcn.gov.hk; f. 1954; grants low-interest credit facilities to farmers and farmers' co-operative socs; HK $4,373,000 was loaned in 1999/2000.

CHAMBERS OF COMMERCE

Chinese Chamber of Commerce, Kowloon: 2/F, 8–10 Nga Tsin Long Rd, Kowloon; tel. 23822309; f. 1936; 234 mems; Chair. and Exec. Dir YEUNG CHOR-HANG.

Chinese General Chamber of Commerce: 4/F, 24–25 Connaught Rd, Central; tel. 25256385; fax 28452610; e-mail cgcc@cgcc.org.hk; internet www.cgcc.org.hk; f. 1900; 6,000 mems; Chair. Dr CHAN YAU-HING.

Hong Kong General Chamber of Commerce: United Centre, 22/F, 95 Queensway, POB 852; tel. 25299229; fax 25279843; e-mail chamber@chamber.org.hk; internet www.chamber.org.hk; f. 1861; 4,000 mems; Chair. C. C. TUNG; Dir EDEN WOON.

Kowloon Chamber of Commerce: KCC Bldg, 3/F, 2 Liberty Ave, Homantin, Kowloon; tel. 27600393; fax 27610166; internet www.hkkcc.org.hk; f. 1938; 1,640 mems; Chair. TONG KWOK-WAH; Exec. Dir CHENG PO-WO.

FOREIGN TRADE ORGANIZATIONS

Hong Kong Chinese Importers' and Exporters' Association: Champion Bldg, 7–8/F, 287–291 Des Voeux Rd, Central; tel. 25448474; fax 25444677; f. 1954; 3,000 mems; Pres. HUI CHEUNG-CHING.

Hong Kong Exporters' Association: Room 824–825, Star House, 3 Salisbury Rd, Tsimshatsui, Kowloon; tel. 27309851; fax 27301869; e-mail exporter@exporters.org.hk; internet www.exporters.org.hk; f. 1955; 630 mems comprising leading merchants and manufacturing exporters; Pres. JEFFREY K. F. LAM; Exec. Dir JOANNA KWOK.

INDUSTRIAL AND TRADE ASSOCIATIONS

Chinese Manufacturers' Association of Hong Kong: CMA Bldg, 64 Connaught Rd, Central; tel. 25456166; fax 25414541; e-mail info@cma.org.hk; internet www.cma.org.hk; f. 1934 to promote and protect industrial and trading interests; operates testing and certification laboratories; 3,700 mems; Pres. CHAN WING KEE; Exec. Dir FRANCIS T. M. LAU.

Federation of Hong Kong Garment Manufacturers: Cheung Lee Commercial Bldg, Room 401–3, 25 Kimberley Rd, Tsimshatsui, Kowloon; tel. 27211383; fax 23111062; f. 1964; 200 mems; Pres. CHOI HIN-TO; Sec.-Gen. ANTHONY K. K. TANG.

Federation of Hong Kong Industries (FKHI): Hankow Centre, 4/F, 5–15 Hankow Rd, Tsimshatsui, Kowloon; tel. 27323188; fax 27213494; e-mail fhki@fhki.org.hk; internet www.fhki.org.hk; f. 1960; 3,000 mems; Chair. HENRY Y. Y. TANG.

Federation of Hong Kong Watch Trades and Industries Ltd: Peter Bldg, Room 604, 58–62 Queen's Rd, Central; tel. 25233232; fax 28684485; e-mail hkwatch@netvigator.com; f. 1947; 700 mems; Chair. FRANK CHAU.

Hong Kong Chinese Enterprises Association: Harbour Center, Room 2104–6, 25 Harbour Rd; tel. 28272831; fax 28272606; f. 1991; 1,000 mems; Chair. ZHU YUENING; Exec. Dir SUN WENJIE.

Hong Kong Chinese Textile Mills Association: 11/F, 38–40 Tai Po Rd, Sham Shui Po, Kowloon; tel. 27778236; fax 27881836; f. 1931; 150 mems; Pres. LEE CHUNG-CHIU.

Hong Kong Construction Association Ltd: 3/F, 180–182 Hennessy Rd, Wanchai; tel. 25724414; fax 25727104; e-mail hkca@hingenet.com; internet www.hkca.hingenet.com; f. 1920; 372 mems; Pres. JIMMY TSE; Sec.-Gen. PATRICK CHAN.

Hong Kong Electronic Industries Association Ltd: Units 208–9, HK Industrial Technology Centre, 72 Tat Chee Ave, Kowloon; tel. 27788328; fax 27882200; e-mail hkeia@hkeia.org.; internet www.hkeia.org; 370 mems; Chair. SAMSON TAM.

Hong Kong Garment Manufacturers Association: 3/F, 63 Tai Yip St, Kowloon Bay, Kowloon; tel. 23052893; fax 23052493; e-mail textclhk@netvigator.com; f. 1987; 40 mems; Chair. Dr HARRY N. S. LEE.

Hong Kong Information Technology Federation Ltd: Wyndham Mansion, 2/F, 30–32 Wyndham St, Central; tel. 25228118; fax 28682083; e-mail edward@abc.com.hk; internet www.hkitf.org.hk; 250 mems; f. 1980; Pres. ANTHONY AU.

Hong Kong Jewellery and Jade Manufacturers' Association: Flat A, 12/F, 41 Man Yue St, Kaiser Estate Phase 1, Hunghom, Kowloon; tel. 25430543; fax 28150164; e-mail hkjja@hkstar.com; internet www.jewellery-hk.org; f. 1965; 216 mems; Chair. CHARLES CHAN SING-CHUK; Gen. Man. CATHERINE CHAN.

Hong Kong Jewelry Manufacturers' Association: Unit G, 2/F, 51 Man Yue St, Kaiser Estate Phase 2, Hunghom, Kowloon; tel. 27663002; fax 23623647; e-mail hkjma@jewelry.org.hk; internet www.jewelry.org.hk; f. 1988; 260 mems; Chair. DENNIS NG.

Hong Kong Knitwear Exporters and Manufacturers Association: Clothing Industry Training Authority, 3/F, Kowloon Bay Training Centre, 63 Tai Yip St, Kowloon; tel. 27552621; fax 27565672; f. 1966; 108 mems; Chair. WILLY LIN; Exec. Sec. SHIRLEY LIU.

Hong Kong and Kowloon Footwear Manufacturers' Association: Kam Fung Bldg, 3/F, Flat D, 8 Cleverly St, Sheung Wan; tel. and fax 25414499; 88 mems; Pres. LOK WAI-TO; Sec. LEE SUM-HUNG.

Hong Kong Optical Manufacturers' Association Ltd: 2/F, 11 Fa Yuen St, Mongkok, Kowloon; tel. 23326505; fax 27705786; f. 1982; 114 mems; Pres. HUI LEUNG-WAH.

Hong Kong Plastics Manufacturers Association Ltd: Fu Yuen Bldg, 1/F, Flat B, 39–49 Wanchai Rd; tel. 25742230; fax 25742843; f. 1957; 200 mems; Chair. KENNETH W. S. TING; Pres. DENNIS H. S. TING.

Hong Kong Printers Association: 1/F, 48–50 Johnston Rd, Wanchai; tel. 25275050; fax 28610463; f. 1939; 437 mems; Chair. HO KA-HUN; Exec. Dir LEE SHUN-HAY.

Hong Kong Rubber and Footwear Manufacturers' Association: Kar Tseuk Bldg, Block A, 2/F, 185 Prince Edward Rd, Kowloon; tel. 23812297; fax 23976927; f. 1948; 180 mems; Chair. PATRICK TANG KIM-KWAN; Gen. Sec. LAI YUEN-MAN.

Hong Kong Sze Yap Commercial and Industrial Association: Cosco Tower, Unit 1205–6, 183 Queen's Rd, Central; tel. 25438095; fax 25449495; f. 1909; 1,082 mems; Chair. NG YUEN-KWOK; Exec. Dir and Sec. CHIU KING-WAN.

Hong Kong Toys Council: Hankow Centre, 4/F, 5–15 Hankow Rd, Tsimshatsui, Kowloon; tel. 27323188; fax 27213494; e-mail fhki@fhki.org.hk; f. 1986; 200 mems; Chair. WONG TIT-SHING.

Hong Kong Watch Manufacturers' Association: Yu Wing Bldg, 3/F and 11/F, Unit A, 64–66 Wellington St, Central; tel. 25225238;

fax 28106614; e-mail hkwma@netvigator.com; internet www.hkwma.org; 682 mems; Pres. Tom H. K. Lee; Sec.-Gen. Wong Hung-fai.

New Territories Commercial and Industrial General Association Ltd: Cheong Hay Bldg, 2/F, 107 Hoi Pa St, Tsuen Wan; tel. 24145316; fax 24934130; f. 1973; 4,000 mems; Pres. H. L. Wan; Sec.-Gen. K. C. Ngan.

Real Estate Developers Association of Hong Kong: Worldwide House, Room 1403, 19 Des Voeux Rd, Central; tel. 28260111; fax 28452521; f. 1965; 750 mems; Pres. Dr Stanley Ho; Exec. Vice-Pres. Thomas Kwok.

Telecom Association of Hong Kong: GPOB 13461; tel. 25042732; fax 25042752; e-mail tahk@glink.net.hk; internet www.tahk.org.hk; 130 mems; Chair. Tony Hau; Vice-Chair. Hubert Chan.

Textile Council of Hong Kong Ltd: 3/F, 63 Tai Yip St, Kowloon Bay, Kowloon; tel. 23052893; fax 23052493; e-mail textelhk@netvigator.com; f. 1989; 10 mems; Chan Wing-kee; Exec. Dir John Yung.

Toys Manufacturers' Association of Hong Kong Ltd: Room 1302, Metroplaza, Tower 2, 223 Hing Fong Rd, Kwai Chung, New Territories; tel 24221209; fax 24221639; e-mail tmhk@harbourring.com.hk; 250 mems; Pres. Danny K. F. Ngai; Sec. Becky To.

EMPLOYERS' ORGANIZATIONS

Employers' Federation of Hong Kong: United Centre, Unit C3, 12/F, 95 Queensway; tel. 25280536; fax 28655285; e-mail empfedhk@netvigator.com; f. 1947; 446 mems; Chair. Ross Sayers; Exec. Dir May Chow.

Hong Kong Factory Owners' Association Ltd: Wing Wong Bldg, 11/F, 557–559 Nathan Rd, Kowloon; tel. 23882372; fax 23857184; f. 1982;1,179 mems; Pres. Hwang Jen; Sec. Cheng Mo-ching.

UTILITIES
Electricity

CLP Power Ltd: 147 Argyle St, Kowloon; tel. 26788111; fax 27604448; internet www.clpgroup.com; f. 1918; fmrly China Light and Power Co Ltd; generation and supply of electricity to Kowloon and the New Territories; Chair. Michael D. Kadoorie; Man. Dir Ross Sayers.

Hongkong Electric Co Ltd: Electric Centre, 28 City Garden Rd, North Point; tel. 28433111; fax 28100506; e-mail mail@hec.com.hk; internet www.hec.com.hk; generation and supply of electricity to Hong Kong Island, and the islands of Ap Lei Chau and Lamma; Chair. George C. Magnus; Man. Dir K. S. Tso.

Gas

Gas Authority: all gas supply cos, gas installers and contractors are required to be registered with the Gas Authority. In 1997 there were eight gas supply cos registered.

Hong Kong and China Gas Co Ltd: 23/F, 363 Java Rd, North Point; tel. 29633388; fax 25632233; internet www.towngas.com; production, distribution and marketing of town gas and gas appliances; operates two plants; Chair. Lee Shau-kee; Man. Dir Alfred W. K. Chan.

Water

Drainage Services Department: responsible for planning, designing, constructing, operating and maintaining the sewerage, sewage treatment and stormwater drainage infrastructures.

Water Supplies Department: tel. 28294709; responsible for water supplies; approx. 2.2m. customers (1997).

TRADE UNIONS

In December 1999 there were 626 trade unions in Hong Kong, comprising 583 employees' unions, 25 employers' associations and 18 mixed organizations.

Hong Kong and Kowloon Trades Union Council (TUC): Labour Bldg, 11 Chang Sha St, Kowloon; tel. 23845150; f. 1949; 66 affiliated unions, mostly covering the catering and building trades; 28,200 mems; supports Taiwan; affiliated to ICFTU; Officer-in-Charge Wong Yiu Kam.

Hong Kong Confederation of Trade Unions: Wing Wong Commercial Bldg, 19/F, 557–559 Nathan Rd, Kowloon; tel. 27708668; fax 27707388; e-mail hkctu@hkctu.org.hk; internet www.hkctu.org.hk; registered Feb. 1990; 53 affiliated independent unions; 150,000 mems; Chair. Lau Chin-shek.

Hong Kong Federation of Trade Unions (FTU): 7/F, 50 Ma Tau Chung Rd, Tokwawan, Kowloon; tel. 27120231; fax 27608477; f. 1948; 120 member unions, mostly concentrated in shipyards, public transport, textile mills, construction, department stores, printing and public utilities; supports the People's Republic of China;

280,000 mems; Chair. Cheng Yiu-tong; Pres. Lee Chark-tim; Gen. Sec. Chan Jik-kwei.

Also active are the **Federation of Hong Kong and Kowloon Labour Unions** (31 affiliated unions with 21,700 mems) and the **Federation of Civil Service Unions** (29 affiliated unions with 12,000 mems).

Transport

Transport Department: Immigration Tower, 41/F, 7 Gloucester Rd, Wanchai; tel. 28295258; fax 28240433; internet www.info.gov.hk/td.

RAILWAYS

Kowloon–Canton Railway Corpn: KCRC House, 9 Lok King St, Fo Tan, Sha Tin, New Territories; tel. 26881333; fax 26880983; internet www.kcrc.com; operated by the Kowloon–Canton Railway Corpn, a public statutory body f. 1983; operates both heavy and light rail systems; the 34-km East Rail runs from the terminus at Hung Hom to the frontier at Lo Wu; through passenger services to Guangzhou (Canton), suspended in 1949, were resumed in 1979; the electrification and double-tracking of the entire length and redevelopment of all stations has been completed, and full electric train service came into operation in 1983; in 1988 a light railway network serving Tuen Mun, Yuen Long and Tin Shui Wai in the north-western New Territories was opened; passenger service extended to Foshan in 1993, Dongguan in 1994, Zhaoqing in 1995 and Shanghai in 1997; direct Kowloon–Beijing service commenced in May 1997; also freight services to several destinations in China; West Rail, a domestic passenger line linking Tuen Mun and Yuen Long with Kowloon, was scheduled to begin services in late 2003; three East Rail extensions due for completion in 2004; Chair. and CEO Yueng Kai-yin.

MTR Corporation: MTR Tower, Telford Plaza, Kowloon Bay; tel. 29932111; fax 27988822; f. 1975; plans for privatization announced in 1999; network of 77 km of railway lines and 44 stations; the first section of the underground mass transit railway (MTR) system opened in 1979; a 15.6-km line from Kwun Tong to Central opened in 1980; a 10.5-km Tsuen Wan extension opened in 1982; the 12.5-km Island Line opened in 1985–86; in 1989 a second harbour crossing between Cha Kwo Ling and Quarry Bay, known as the Eastern Harbour Crossing, commenced operation, adding 4.6 km to the railway system; 34-km link to new airport at Chek Lap Kok and to Tung Chung New Town opened in mid-1998; an additional line, the Tseung Kwan O Extension, was under construction and was scheduled for completion by 2002; Chair. and Chief Exec. Jack C. K. So.

TRAMWAYS

Hong Kong Tramways Ltd: Whitty Street Tram Depot, Connaught Rd West, Western District; tel. 21186338; fax 21186038; f. 1904; operates six routes and 161 double-deck trams between Kennedy Town and Shaukeiwan; Gen. Man. T. K. Wong.

ROADS

In March 2000 there were 1,888 km of roads. Almost all of them are concrete or asphalt surfaced. Owing to the hilly terrain, and the density of building development, the scope for substantial increase in the road network is limited.

Highways Department: Ho Man Tin Government Offices, 5/F, 88 Chung Hau St, Ho Man Tin, Kowloon; tel. 27623333; fax 27145216; f. 1986; planning, design, construction and maintenance of the public road system; co-ordination of major highway projects; Dir. K. S. Leung.

FERRIES

Conventional ferries, hoverferries and catamarans operate between Hong Kong, China and Macau. There is also an extensive network of ferry services to outlying districts.

Hongkong and Yaumati Ferry Co Ltd: 98 Tam Kon Shan Rd, Ngau Kok Wan, North Tsing Yi, New Territories; tel. 23944294; fax 27869001; e-mail hkferry@hkf.com; internet www.hkf.com; licensed routes on ferry services, incl. cross-harbour, to outlying islands, excursion, vehicular and dangerous goods; fleet of 50 vessels (passenger ferries, vehicular ferries, hoverferries, catamarans, oil barges and floating pontoons); also operates hoverferry services between Hong Kong and Shekou and catamaran service to Macau; Gen. Man. David C. S. Ho.

Hongkong Macao Hydrofoil Co Ltd: Turbojet Ferry Services (Guangzhou) Ltd, 83 Hing Wah St West, Lai Chi Kok, Kowloon; operates services to Macau, Fu Yong (Shenzhen airport) and East River Guangzhou.

'Star' Ferry Co Ltd: Kowloon Point Pier, Tsimshatsui, Kowloon; tel. 21186223; fax 21186028; f. 1898; operates 13 passenger ferries between the Kowloon Peninsula and Central, the main business district of Hong Kong; between Central and Hung Hom; between Tsimshatsui and Wanchai; between Tsimshatsui and Central; and between Wanchai and Hung Hom; Man. JOHNNY LEUNG.

SHIPPING

Hong Kong is one of the world's largest shipping centres and was the world's busiest container port in 1999. Hong Kong was a British port of registry until the inauguration of a new and independent shipping register in December 1990. Following Hong Kong's reunification with the People's Republic of China, Hong Kong maintains full autonomy in its maritime policy. At the end of 1999 the register comprised a fleet of 521 vessels, totalling 8.3m. grt. The eight container terminals at Kwai Chung, which are privately-owned and operated, comprised 18 berths in 1998. The construction of a ninth terminal (CT9) commenced in 1998 and was expected to be operational by 2001. Lantau Island has been designated as the site for any future expansion.

Hong Kong Government Marine Department: Harbour Bldg, 22/F, 38 Pier Rd, Central, GPOB 4155; tel. 28523001; fax 25449241; e-mail webmaster@mardep.gcn.gov.hk; internet www.info.gov.hk/mardep; Dir of Marine S. Y. TSUI.

Shipping Companies

Anglo-Eastern Ship Management Ltd: Universal Trade Centre, 14/F, 3 Arbuthnot Rd, Central, POB 11400; tel. 28636111; fax 28612419; e-mail allhx470@gncomtext.com; internet www.webhk.com/angloeastern/; Chair. PETER CREMERS; Man. Dir MARCEL LIEDTS.

Chung Gai Ship Management Co Ltd: Admiralty Centre Tower 1, 31/F, 18 Harcourt Rd; tel. 25295541; fax 28656206; Chair. S. KODA; Man. Dir K. ICHIHARA.

Fairmont Shipping (HK) Ltd: Fairmont House, 21/F, 8 Cotton Tree Drive; tel. 25218338; fax 28104560; Man. CHARLES LEUNG.

Far East Enterprising Co (HK) Ltd: China Resources Bldg, 18–19/F, 26 Harbour Rd, Wanchai; tel. 28283668; fax 28275584; f. 1949; shipping, chartering, brokering; Gen. Man. WEI KUAN.

Gulfeast Shipmanagement Ltd: Great Eagle Centre, 9/F, 23 Harbour Rd, Wanchai; tel. 28313344; Finance Dir A. T. MIRMOHAMMADI.

Hong Kong Borneo Shipping Co Ltd: 815 International Bldg, 141 Des Voeux Rd, Central; tel. 25413797; fax 28153473; Pres. Datuk LAI FOOK KIM.

Hong Kong Ming Wah Shipping Co: Unit 3701, China Merchants Tower, 37/F, Shun Tak Centre, 168–200 Connaught Rd, Central; tel. 25172128; fax 25473482; e-mail mwins@cmhk.com; Chair. CHEUNG KING WA; Man. Dir and Vice-Chair. Capt. MAO SHI JIAN.

Island Navigation Corpn International Ltd: Harbour Centre, 28–29/F, 25 Harbour Rd, Wanchai; tel. 28333222; fax 28270001; Man. Dir F. S. SHIH.

Jardine Ship Management Ltd: Jardine Engineering House, 11/F, 260 King's Rd, North Point; tel. 28074101; fax 28073351; e-mail jsmhk@ibm.net; Man. Dir Capt. PAUL UNDERHILL.

Oak Maritime (HK) Inc Ltd: 2301 China Resources Bldg, 26 Harbour Rd, Wanchai; tel. 25063866; fax 25063563; Chair. STEVE G. K. HSU; Pres. FRED C. P. TSAI.

Ocean Tramping Co Ltd: Hong Kong; tel. 25892645; fax 25461041; Chair. Z. M. GAO.

Orient Overseas Container Line Ltd: Harbour Centre, 31/F, 25 Harbour Rd, Wanchai; tel. 28333888; fax 25318122; internet www.oocl.com; member of the Grand Alliance of shipping cos (five partners); Chair. C. C. TUNG.

Teh-Hu Cargocean Management Co Ltd: Unit B, Fortis Bank Tower, 15/F, 77–79 Gloucester Rd, Wanchai; tel. 25988688; fax 28249339; e-mail tehhuhk@netvigator.com; f. 1974; Man. Dir KENNETH K. W. LO.

Wah Kwong Shipping Agency Co Ltd: Shanghai Industrial Investment Bldg, 26/F, 48–62 Hennessy Rd, POB 283; tel. 25279227; fax 28656544; e-mail wk@wahkwong.com.hk; Chair. GEORGE S. K. CHAO.

Wah Tung Shipping Agency Co Ltd: China Resources Bldg, Rooms 2101–5, 21/F, 26 Harbour Rd, Wanchai; tel. 28272818; fax 28275361; e-mail mgr@watunship.com.hk; f. 1981; Dir and Gen. Man. B. L. LIU.

Wallem Shipmanagement Ltd: Hopewell Centre, 46/F, 183 Queen's Rd East; tel. 28768200; fax 28761234; e-mail rgb@wallem.com; Man. Dir R. G. BUCHANAN.

Worldwide Shipping Agency Ltd: Wheelock House, 6–7/F, 20 Pedder St; tel. 28423888; fax 28100617; Man. J. WONG.

Associations

Hong Kong Cargo-Vessel Traders' Association: 21–23 Man Wai Bldg, 2/F, Ferry Point, Kowloon; tel. 23847102; fax 27820342; 978 mems; Chair. CHOW YAT-TAK; Sec. CHAN BAK.

Hong Kong Shipowners' Association: Queen's Centre, 12/F, 58–64 Queen's Rd East, Wanchai; tel. 25200206; fax 25298246; e-mail hksoa@hksoa.org.hk; internet www.hksoa.org.hk; 220 mems; Chair. ANDREW Y. CHEN; Dir ARTHUR BOWRING.

Hong Kong Shippers' Council: Rm 2407, Hopewell Centre, 183 Queen's Rd East; tel. 28340010; fax 28919787; e-mail shippers@hkshippers.org.hk; internet www.hkshippers.org.hk; 63 mems; Chair. WILLY LIN; Exec. Dir SUNNY HO.

CIVIL AVIATION

By the end of 1999 Hong Kong was served by 62 foreign airlines. Opening of a new international airport, on the island of Chek Lap Kok, near Lantau Island, to replace that at Kai Tak and initially scheduled for April 1998, was postponed to July, following delays in the construction of a connecting high-speed rail-link. The airport has two runways, with the capacity to handle 35m. passengers and 3m. metric tons of cargo per year. The second runway commenced operations in May 1999. A helicopter link with Macau was established in 1990.

Airport Authority of Hong Kong: Cheong Yip Rd, Hong Kong International Airport, Lantau; tel. 21887111; fax 28240717; f. 1995; Chair. Dr VICTOR FUNG KWOK-KING; CEO Dr DAVID J. PANG.

Civil Aviation Department: Queensway Government Offices, 46/F, 66 Queensway; tel. 28674332; fax 28690093; e-mail enquiry@cad.gov.hk; internet www.info.gov.hk/cad/; Dir-Gen. ALBERT K. Y. LAM.

AHK Air Hong Kong Ltd: Units 3601–8, 36/F, Tower 1, Millennium City, 388 Kwun Tong Rd, Kowloon; tel. 27618588; fax 27618586; e-mail ahk.hq@airhongkong.com.hk; f. 1986; international cargo carrier; Chief Operating Officer HUNTER CRAWFORD.

Cathay Pacific Airways Ltd: South Tower, 5/F, Cathay Pacific City, 8 Scenic Rd, Hong Kong International Airport, Lantau; tel. 27471888; fax 25601411; internet www.cathaypacific.com/hk; f. 1946; services to more than 40 major cities in the Far East, Middle East, North America, Europe, South Africa, Australia and New Zealand; Chair. PETER D. A. SUTCH; Man. Dir DAVID TURNBULL.

Hong Kong Dragon Airlines Ltd (Dragonair): Devon House, 22/F, Taikoo Place, 979 King's Rd, Quarry Bay; tel. 25901328; fax 25901333; internet www.dragonair.com; f. 1985; scheduled and charter flights to 25 destinations in Asia, 16 of which are in mainland China; scheduled regional services include Phuket (Thailand), Hiroshima and Sendai (Japan), Kaohsiung (Taiwan), Phnom-Penh (Cambodia), Dhaka (Bangladesh), Bandar Seri Begawan (Brunei), and Kota Kinabalu (Malaysia); Chair. WANG GUIXIANG; Dir and CEO STANLEY HUI.

Tourism

Tourism is a major source of foreign exchange, tourist receipts reaching HK $53,000m. (including receipts from visitors from mainland China) in 1999. Some 10.7m. people visited Hong Kong in 1999. In December 1999 there were some 91 hotels, and the number of rooms available totalled 35,420. The number of rooms was to be increased to 38,550 in 97 hotels by December 2000. In November 1999 it was agreed that a new Disneyland theme park would be constructed in Hong Kong, to be opened in 2005. The Government expected the park to create a huge influx of tourists to the territory.

Hong Kong Tourist Association: Citicorp Centre, 9–11/F, 18 Whitfield Rd, North Point; tel. 28076543; fax 28076595; e-mail dm@hkta.org; internet www.hkta.org; f. 1957; co-ordinates and promotes the tourist industry; has govt support and financial assistance; 11 mems of the Board represent the Govt, the private sector and the tourism industry; Chair. Y. S. LO; Exec. Dir AMY CHAN.

MACAU

Introductory Survey

Location, Climate, Language, Religion, Flag, Capital

The Special Administrative Region (SAR) of Macau comprises the peninsula of Macau, an enclave on the mainland of southern China, and two nearby islands, Taipa, which is linked to the mainland by two bridges, and Coloane, which is connected to Taipa by a causeway and by an area of reclaimed land. The territory lies opposite Hong Kong on the western side of the mouth of the Xijiang (Sikiang) River. The climate is subtropical, with temperatures averaging 15°C in January and 29°C in July. There are two official languages, Chinese (Cantonese being the principal dialect) and Portuguese. English is also widely spoken. The predominant religions are Roman Catholicism, Chinese Buddhism, Daoism and Confucianism. The flag of the Macau SAR (proportions 3 by 2), introduced upon the territory's reversion to Chinese sovereignty in December 1999 and flown subordinate to the flag of the People's Republic of China, displays a stylized white flower below an arc of one large and four small yellow stars, above five white lines, on a green background. The capital, the city of Macau, is situated on the peninsula.

Recent History

Established by Portugal in 1557 as a permanent trading post with China, Macau became a Portuguese Overseas Province in 1951. After the military coup in Portugal in April 1974, Col José Garcia Leandro was appointed Governor of the province. A new statute, promulgated in February 1976, redefined Macau as a 'Special Territory' under Portuguese jurisdiction, but with a great measure of administrative and economic independence. Proposals to enlarge the Legislative Assembly from 17 to 21 members, thus giving the Chinese population an increased role in the administration of Macau, were abandoned when they did not receive the approval of the Government of the People's Republic of China in March 1980. China and Portugal established diplomatic relations in February 1979. In the same month Col Leandro was replaced as Governor by Gen. Nuno de Melo Egídio, deputy chief of staff of Portugal's armed forces. In June 1981 Gen. Egídio was, in turn, replaced by Cdre (later Rear-Adm.) Vasco Almeida e Costa, a Portuguese former minister and naval commander. Following a constitutional dispute in March 1984 over the Governor's plans for electoral reform (extending the franchise to the ethnic Chinese majority), the Legislative Assembly was dissolved. Elections for a new Assembly were held in August, at which the Chinese majority were allowed to vote for the first time, regardless of their length of residence in the territory. Following the elections, the Assembly was for the first time dominated by ethnic Chinese deputies.

In January 1986 Governor Almeida e Costa resigned. In May he was replaced by Joaquim Pinto Machado, whose appointment represented a break in the tradition of military governors for Macau. His political inexperience, however, placed him at a disadvantage. In May 1987 he resigned, citing 'reasons of institutional dignity' (apparently referring to the problem of corruption in the Macau administration). He was replaced in August by Carlos Melancia, a former Socialist deputy in the Portuguese legislature, who had held ministerial posts in several Portuguese governments.

The first round of negotiations between the Portuguese and Chinese Governments on the future of Macau took place in June 1986 in Beijing. Portugal's acceptance of China's sovereignty greatly simplified the issue. On 13 April 1987, following the conclusion of the fourth round of negotiations, a joint declaration was formally signed in Beijing by the Portuguese and Chinese Governments, during an official visit to China by the Prime Minister of Portugal. According to the agreement (which was formally ratified in January 1988), Macau was to become a 'special administrative region' (SAR) of the People's Republic (to be known as Macau, China) on 20 December 1999. Macau was thus to have the same status as that agreed (with effect from 1997) for Hong Kong, and was to enjoy autonomy in most matters except defence and foreign policy. A Sino-Portuguese Joint Liaison Group (JLG), established to oversee the transfer of power, held its inaugural meeting in Lisbon in April 1988. In

1999 a Chief Executive for Macau was to be appointed by the Chinese Government, following 'elections or consultations to be held in Macau', and the territory's legislature was to contain 'a majority of elected members'. The inhabitants of Macau were to become citizens of the People's Republic of China. The Chinese Government refused to allow the possibility of dual Sino-Portuguese citizenship, although Macau residents in possession of Portuguese passports were apparently to be permitted to retain them for travel purposes. The agreement guaranteed a 50-year period during which Macau would be permitted to retain its free capitalist economy, and to be financially independent of China.

In August 1988 a Macau Basic Law Drafting Committee was formed. Comprising 30 Chinese members and 19 representatives from Macau, the Committee was to draft a law determining the territory's future constitutional status within the People's Republic of China. Elections to the Legislative Assembly were held in October 1988. Low participation (fewer than 30% of the electorate) was recorded, and a 'liberal' grouping secured three of the seats reserved for directly-elected candidates, while the Electoral Union, a coalition of pro-Beijing and conservative Macanese (lusophone Eurasian) groups, won the other three.

In January 1989 it was announced that Portuguese passports were to be issued to about 100,000 ethnic Chinese inhabitants, born in Macau before October 1981, and it was anticipated that as many as a further 100,000 would be granted before 1999. Unlike their counterparts in the neighbouring British dependent territory of Hong Kong, therefore, these Macau residents (but not all) were to be granted the full rights of a citizen of the European Community (EC, now European Union—EU, see p. 181). In February 1989 President Mário Soares of Portugal visited Macau, in order to discuss the transfer of the territory's administration to China.

Following the violent suppression of the pro-democracy movement in China in June 1989, as many as 100,000 residents of Macau participated in demonstrations in the enclave to protest against the Chinese Government's action. The events in the People's Republic caused great concern in Macau. In August, however, China assured Portugal that it would honour the agreement to maintain the capitalist system of the territory after 1999.

In March 1990 the implementation of a programme to grant permanent registration to parents of 4,200 Chinese residents, the latter having already secured the right of abode in Macau, developed into chaos when other illegal immigrants demanded a similar concession. The authorities decided to declare a general amnesty, but were unprepared for the numbers of illegal residents, some 50,000 in total, who rushed to take advantage of the scheme, thereby revealing the true extent of previous immigration from China. Border security was subsequently increased, in an effort to prevent any further illegal immigration.

In late March 1990 the Legislative Assembly approved the final draft of the territory's revised Organic Law. The Law was approved by the Portuguese Assembly of the Republic in mid-April, and granted Macau greater administrative, economic, financial and legislative autonomy, in advance of 1999. The powers of the Governor and of the Legislative Assembly, where six additional seats were to be created, were therefore increased. The post of military commander of the security forces was abolished, responsibility for the territory's security being assumed by a civilian Under-Secretary.

Meanwhile, in February 1990, it was alleged that Carlos Melancia had accepted a substantial bribe from a foreign company in connection with a contract for the construction of the new airport in Macau. In September Melancia was served with a summons relating to the alleged bribery. Although he denied any involvement in the affair, the Governor resigned, and was replaced on an acting basis by the Under-Secretary for Economic Affairs, Dr Francisco Murteira Nabo. In September 1991 it was announced that Melancia and five others were to stand trial on charges of corruption. Melancia's trial opened in April 1993. In August the former Governor was acquitted on the grounds of insufficient evidence. In February 1994, however, it was announced that Melancia was to be retried, owing to irregularities in his defence case.

Meanwhile, many observers believed that the enclave was being adversely affected by the political situation in Lisbon, as differences between the socialist President and centre-right Prime Minister were being reflected in rivalries between officials in Macau. In an attempt to restore confidence, therefore, President Soares visited the territory in November 1990. In January 1991, upon his re-election as Head of State, the President appointed Gen. Vasco Rocha Vieira (who had previously served as the territory's Chief of Staff and as Under-Secretary for Public Works and Transport) Governor of Macau. In March 1991 the Legislative Assembly was expanded from 17 to 23 members. All seven Under-Secretaries were replaced in May.

Following his arrival in Macau, Gen. Rocha Vieira announced that China would be consulted on all future developments in the territory. The 10th meeting of the Sino-Portuguese JLG took place in Beijing in April 1991. Topics under regular discussion included the participation of Macau in international organizations, progress towards an increase in the number of local officials employed in the civil service (hitherto dominated by Portuguese and Macanese personnel) and the status of the Chinese language. The progress of the working group on the translation of local laws from Portuguese into Chinese was also examined, a particular problem being the lack of suitably-qualified bilingual legal personnel. It was agreed that Portuguese was to remain an official language after 1999. The two sides also reached agreement on the exchange of identity cards for those Macau residents who would require them in 1999. Regular meetings of the JLG continued.

In July 1991 the Macau Draft Basic Law was published by the People's Republic of China. Confidence in the territory's future was enhanced by China's apparent flexibility on a number of issues. Unlike the Hong Kong Basic Law, that of Macau did not impose restrictions on holders of foreign passports assuming senior posts in the territory's administration after 1999, the only exception being the future Chief Executive. Furthermore, the draft contained no provision for the stationing of troops from China in Macau after the territory's return to Chinese administration.

In November 1991 the Governor of Macau visited the People's Republic of China, where it was confirmed that the 'one country, two systems' policy would operate in Macau from 1999. In March 1993 the final draft of the Basic Law of the Macau SAR was ratified by the National People's Congress (NPC) in Beijing, which also approved the design of the future SAR's flag. The adoption of the legislation was welcomed by the Governor of Macau, who reiterated his desire for a smooth transfer of power in 1999. The Chief Executive of the SAR was to be selected by local representatives. The SAR's first Legislative Council was to comprise 23 members, of whom eight would be directly elected. Its term of office would expire in October 2001, when it would be expanded to 27 members, of whom 10 would be directly elected.

Meanwhile, elections to the Legislative Assembly were held in September 1992. The level of participation was higher than on previous occasions, with 59% of the registered electorate (albeit only 13.5% of the population) attending the polls. Fifty candidates contested the eight directly-elective seats, four of which were won by members of the main pro-Beijing parties, the União Promotora para o Progresso and the União para o Desenvolvimento.

Relations between Portugal and China remained cordial. In June 1993 the two countries reached agreement on all outstanding issues regarding the construction of the territory's airport and the future use of Chinese air space. Furthermore, Macau was to be permitted to negotiate air traffic agreements with other countries. Later in the year visits by President Soares of Portugal to Macau and by the Chinese President, Jiang Zemin, to Lisbon took place. In February 1994 the Chinese Minister of Communications visited Macau to discuss with the Governor the progress of the airport project.

In April 1994, during a visit to China, the Portuguese Prime Minister received an assurance that Chinese nationality would not be imposed on Macanese people of Portuguese descent, who would be able to retain their Portuguese passports. Speaking in Macau itself, the Prime Minister expressed confidence in the territory's future. Regarding the issue as increasingly one of foreign policy, he stated his desire to transfer jurisdiction over Macau from the Presidency of the Republic to the Government, despite the necessity for a constitutional amendment.

In July 1994 a group of local journalists dispatched a letter, alleging intimidation and persecution in Macau, to President Soares, urging him to intervene to defend the territory's press freedom. The journalists' appeal followed an incident involving

the director of the daily *Gazeta Macaense*, who had been fined for reproducing an article from a Lisbon weekly newspaper, and now faced trial. The territory's press had been critical of the Macau Supreme Court's decision to extradite ethnic Chinese to the mainland (despite the absence of any extradition treaty) to face criminal charges and a possible death sentence.

The draft of the new penal code for Macau did not incorporate the death penalty. In January 1995, during a visit to Portugal, Vice-Premier Zhu Rongji of China confirmed that the People's Republic would not impose the death penalty in Macau after 1999, regarding the question as a matter for the authorities of the future SAR. The new penal code, prohibiting capital punishment, took effect in January 1996.

On another visit to the territory in April 1995, President Soares emphasized the need for Macau to assert its identity, and stressed the importance of three issues: the modification of the territory's legislation; the rights of the individual; and the preservation of the Portuguese language. Travelling on to Beijing, accompanied by Gen. Rocha Vieira, the Portuguese President had successful discussions with his Chinese counterpart on various matters relating to the transition.

In May 1995, during a four-day visit to the territory, Lu Ping, the director of the mainland Hong Kong and Macau Affairs Office, proposed the swift establishment of a preparatory working committee (PWC) to facilitate the transfer of sovereignty. He urged that faster progress be made on the issues of the localization of civil servants and of the law, and on the use of Chinese as the official language. Lu Ping also expressed his desire that the reorganized legislative and municipal bodies to be elected in 1996–97 conform with the Basic Law.

In December 1995, while attending the celebrations to mark the inauguration of the territory's new airport, President Soares had discussions with the Chinese Vice-President, Rong Yiren. During a four-day visit to Beijing in February 1996, the Portuguese Minister of Foreign Affairs, Jaime Gama (who urged that the rights and aspirations of the people of Macau be protected), met President Jiang Zemin and other senior officials, describing the discussions as positive. While acknowledging the sound progress of recent years, Gama and the Chinese Minister of Foreign Affairs agreed on an acceleration in the pace of work of the Sino-Portuguese JLG. In the same month Gen. Rocha Vieira was reappointed Governor of Macau by the newly-elected President of Portugal, Jorge Sampaio. António Guterres, the new Portuguese Prime Minister, confirmed his desire for constitutional consensus regarding the transition of Macau.

At elections to the Legislative Assembly in September 1996 the pro-Beijing União Promotora para o Progresso received 15.2% of the votes and won two of the eight directly-elective seats, while the União para o Desenvolvimento won 14.5% and retained one of its two seats. The business-orientated groups were more successful: the Associação Promotora para a Economia de Macau took 16.6% of the votes and secured two seats; the Convergência para o Desenvolvimento and the União Geral para o Desenvolvimento de Macau each won one seat. The pro-democracy Associação de Novo Macau Democrático also won one seat. The level of voter participation was 64%. The 23-member legislature was to remain in place beyond the transfer of sovereignty in 1999.

In October 1996 Portugal and China announced the establishment of a mechanism for regular consultation on matters pertaining to international relations. In the same month citizens of Macau joined a flotilla of small boats carrying activists from Taiwan and Hong Kong to protest against a right-wing Japanese group's construction of a lighthouse on the disputed Diaoyu (or Senkaku) Islands, situated in the East China Sea (see People's Republic of China, p. 1036). Having successfully evaded Japanese patrol vessels, the protesters raised the flags of China and Taiwan on the disputed islands. In November activists from around the world attended a three-day conference in Macau, in order to discuss their strategy for the protection of the islands.

Meanwhile, the rising level of violent criminal activity had become a cause of increasing concern. During 1996 there were numerous bomb attacks and brutal assaults, including several serious attacks on local casino staff. Violent incidents continued in 1997, giving rise to fears for the future of the territory's vital tourism industry. Many attributed the alarming increase in organized crime to the opening of the airport in Macau, which was believed to have facilitated the entry of rival gangsters from mainland China, Taiwan and Hong Kong. In May, following the murder of three men believed to have associations with one such group of gangsters, the Chinese Government expressed its concern at the deterioration of public order in Macau and urged Portugal to observe its responsibility, as undertaken in the Sino-Portuguese joint declaration of 1987, to maintain the enclave's social stability during the transitional period, whilst pledging the enhanced co-operation of the Chinese security forces in the effort to curb organized crime in Macau.

The freedom of Macau's press was jeopardized in June 1997, when several Chinese-language newspapers, along with a television station, received threats instructing them to cease reporting on the activities of the notorious 14K triad, a 10,000-member secret society to which much of the violence had been attributed. In July an explosive device was detonated in the grounds of the Governor's palace, although it caused no serious damage. In the following month China deployed 500 armed police-officers to reinforce the border with Macau in order to intensify its efforts to combat illegal immigration, contraband and the smuggling of arms into the enclave. Despite the approval in July of a law further to restrict activities such as extortion and 'protection rackets', organized crime continued unabated. In early October the police forces of Macau and China initiated a joint campaign against illegal immigration.

Meanwhile, the slow progress of the 'three localizations' (civil service, laws and the implementation of Chinese as an official language) continued to concern the Government of China. In mid-1996 almost 50% of senior government posts were still held by Portuguese expatriates. In January 1997 the Governor pledged to accelerate the process with regard to local legislation, the priority being the training of the requisite personnel. In February President Sampaio travelled to both Macau and China, where he urged respect for Macau's identity and for the Luso-Chinese declaration regarding the transfer of sovereignty. In December 1997 details of the establishment in Macau of the office of the Chinese Ministry of Foreign Affairs, which was to commence operations in December 1999, were announced. In January 1998 the Macau Government declared that the vast majority of senior civil service posts were now held by local officials.

In March 1998 the Chinese authorities reiterated their concern at the deteriorating situation in Macau. In April, by which month none of the 34 triad-related murders committed since January 1997 had been solved, the Portuguese and Chinese Governments agreed to co-operate in the exchange of information about organized criminal activities. Also in April 1998 the trial, on charges of breaching the gaming laws, of the head of the 14K triad, Wan Kuok-koi ('Broken Tooth'), was adjourned for two months, owing to the apparent reluctance of witnesses to appear in court. In early May Wan Kuok-koi was rearrested and charged with the attempted murder of Macau's chief of police, António Marques Baptista, in a car-bomb attack. The case was dismissed by a judge three days later on the grounds of insufficient evidence. Wan Kuok-koi remained in prison, charged with other serious offences. His renewed detention led to a spate of arson attacks. The Portuguese Government was reported to have dispatched intelligence officers to the enclave to reinforce the local security forces. In June Marques Baptista travelled to Beijing and Guangzhou for discussions on the problems of cross-border criminal activity and drugs-trafficking.

The Preparatory Committee for the Establishment of the Macau SAR, which was to oversee the territory's transfer to Chinese sovereignty and was to comprise representatives from both the People's Republic and Macau, was inaugurated in Beijing in May 1998. Four subordinate working groups (supervising administrative, legal, economic, and social and cultural affairs) were subsequently established. The second plenary session of the Preparatory Committee was convened in July 1998, discussions encompassing issues such as the 'localization' of civil servants, public security and the drafting of the territory's fiscal budget for the year 2000. In July 1998, during a meeting with the Chinese Premier, the Governor of Macau requested an increase in the mainland's investment in the territory prior to the 1999 transfer of sovereignty.

In July 1998, as abductions continued and as it was revealed, furthermore, that the victims had included two serving members of the Legislative Assembly, President Jiang Zemin of China urged the triads of Macau to cease their campaign of intimidation. The police forces of Macau, Hong Kong and Guangdong Province launched 'S Plan', an operation aiming to curb the activities of rival criminal gangs. In August, in an apparent attempt to intimidate the judiciary, the territory's Attorney-General and his wife were shot and slightly wounded. In the following month five police-officers and 10 journalists who were investigating a bomb attack were injured when a second bomb exploded.

In August 1998 representatives of the JLG agreed to intensify Luso-Chinese consultations on matters relating to the transitional period. In September, in response to the increasing security problems, China unexpectedly announced that, upon the transfer of sovereignty, it was to station troops in the territory. This abandonment of a previous assurance to the contrary caused much disquiet in Portugal, where the proposed deployment was deemed unnecessary. Although the Basic Law made no specific provision for the stationing of a mainland garrison, China asserted that it was to be ultimately responsible for the enclave's defence. By October, furthermore, about 4,000 soldiers of the People's Liberation Army (PLA) were on duty at various Chinese border posts adjacent to Macau. During a one-week visit to Beijing, the territory's Under-Secretary for Public Security had discussions with senior officials, including the Chinese Minister of Public Security. In mid-October four alleged members of the 14K triad were detained without bail in connection with the May car-bombing and other incidents.

In November 1998 procedures for the election of the 200 members of the Selection Committee were established by the Preparatory Committee. Responsible for the appointment of the members of Macau's post-1999 Government, the delegates of the Selection Committee were required to be permanent residents of the territory: 60 members were to be drawn from the business and financial communities, 50 from cultural, educational and professional spheres, 50 from labour, social service and religious circles and the remaining 40 were to be former political personages.

In November 1998 raids on casinos believed to be engaged in illegal activities, conducted by the authorities, resulted in several arrests. Further violence took place in December. At the end of that month it was confirmed that Macau residents of wholly Chinese origin would be entitled to full mainland citizenship, while those of mixed Chinese and Portuguese descent would be obliged to decide between the two nationalities. In January 1999 several protesters were arrested during demonstrations to draw attention to the plight of numerous immigrant children, who had been brought illegally from China to Macau to join their legitimately-resident parents. The problem had first emerged in 1996 when, owing to inadequate conditions, the authorities had closed down an unofficial school attended by 200 children, who because of their irregular status were not entitled to the territory's education, health and social services.

In January 1999 details of the composition of the future PLA garrison were disclosed. The troops were to comprise solely ground forces, totalling fewer than 1,000 soldiers and directly responsible to the Commander of the Guangzhou Military Unit. They would be permitted to intervene to maintain social order in the enclave only if the local police were unable to control major triad-related violence or if street demonstrations posed a threat of serious unrest. In March, during a trip to Macau (where he had discussions with the visiting Portuguese President), Qian Qichen, a Chinese Vice-Premier, indicated that an advance contingent of PLA soldiers would be deployed in Macau prior to the transfer of sovereignty. Other sources of contention between China and Portugal remained the unresolved question of the post-1999 status of those Macau residents who had been granted Portuguese nationality and also the issue of the court of final appeal.

In April 1999, at the first plenary meeting of the Selection Committee, candidates for the post of the SAR's Chief Executive were elected. Edmund Ho received 125 of the 200 votes, while Stanley Au garnered 65 votes. Three other candidates failed to secure the requisite minimum of 20 votes. Edmund Ho and Stanley Au, both bankers and regarded as moderate pro-business candidates, thus proceeded to the second round of voting by secret ballot, held in May. Edmund Ho received 163 of the 199 votes cast, and confirmed his intention to address the problems of law and order, security and the economy. The Chief Executive-designate also fully endorsed China's decision to deploy troops in Macau.

During 1999, in co-operation with the Macau authorities, the police forces of Guangdong Province, and of Zhuhai in particular, initiated a new offensive against the criminal activities of the triads, which had been in regular evidence with further murders throughout the year. China's desire to deploy an advance contingent of troops prior to December 1999, however, reportedly continued to be obstructed by Portugal. Furthermore, the announcement that, subject to certain conditions, the future garrison was to be granted law-enforcement powers raised various constitutional issues. Some observers feared the imposition of martial law, if organized crime were to continue unabated. Many Macau residents, however, appeared to welcome the mainland's decision to station troops in the enclave. In a further effort to address the deteriorating security situation, from December 1999 Macau's 5,800-member police force was to be restructured.

In July 1999 the penultimate meeting of the JLG took place in Lisbon. In August, in accordance with the nominations of the Chief Executive-designate, the composition of the Government of the future SAR was announced by the State Council in Beijing. Appointments included that of Florinda da Rosa Silva Chan as Secretary for Administration and Justice. Also in August an outspoken pro-Chinese member of the Legislative Assembly was attacked and injured by a group of unidentified assailants. This apparently random assault on a serving politician again focused attention on the decline in law and order in the enclave. In September the Governor urged improved co-operation with the authorities of Guangdong Province in order to combat organized crime, revealing that the majority of the inmates of Macau's prisons were not residents of the territory. In the same month it was reported that 90 former Gurkhas of the British army were being drafted in as prison warders, following the intimidation of local officers. In September the Chief Executive-designate announced the appointment of seven new members of the Legislative Council, which was to succeed the Legislative Assembly in December 1999. While the seven nominees of the Governor in the existing Legislative Assembly were thus to be replaced, 15 of the 16 elected members (one having resigned) were to remain in office as members of the successor Legislative Council. The composition of the 10-member Executive Council was also announced.

In October 1999 President Jiang Zemin paid a two-day visit to Portugal, following which it was declared that the outstanding question of the deployment of an advance contingent of Chinese troops in Macau had been resolved. The advance party was to be restricted to a technical mission, which entered the territory in early December. In November the 37th and last session of the JLG took place in Beijing, where in the same month the Governor of Macau held final discussions with President Jiang Zemin.

Meanwhile, in April 1999 Wan Kuok-koi had been acquitted of charges of coercing croupiers. In November his trial on other serious charges concluded: he was found guilty of criminal association and other illegal gambling-related activities and sentenced to 15 years' imprisonment. Eight co-defendants received lesser sentences. In a separate trial Artur Chiang Calderon, a former police officer alleged to be Wan Kuok-koi's military adviser, received a prison sentence of 10 years and six months for involvement in organized crime. While two other defendants were also imprisoned, 19 were released on the grounds of insufficient evidence. As the transfer of the territory's sovereignty approached, by mid-December almost 40 people had been murdered in triad-related violence in Macau since January 1999.

In late November 1999 representatives of the JLG reached agreement on details regarding the deployment of Chinese troops in Macau and on the retention of Portuguese as an official language. At midnight on 19 December 1999, therefore, in a ceremony attended by the Presidents and heads of government of Portugal and China, the sovereignty of Macau was duly transferred; 12 hours later (only after the departure from the newly-inaugurated SAR of the Portuguese delegation), 500 soldiers of the 1,000-strong force of the PLA, in a convoy of armoured vehicles, crossed the border into Macau, where they were installed in a makeshift barracks. Prior to the ceremony, however, it was reported that the authorities of Guangdong Province had detained almost 3,000 persons, including 15 residents of Macau, suspected of association with criminal gangs. The celebrations in Macau were also marred by the authorities' handling of demonstrations by members of Falun Gong, a religious movement recently outlawed in China. The expulsion from Macau of several members of the sect in the days preceding the territory's transfer and the arrest of 30 adherents on the final day of Portuguese sovereignty prompted strong criticism from President Jorge Sampaio of Portugal. Nevertheless, in an effort to consolidate relations with the EU, in May 2000 the first official overseas visit of the SAR's Chief Executive was to Europe, his itinerary including Portugal. The EU agreed in principle in December 2000 to grant residents of Hong Kong and Macau visa-free access to member states, subject to final approval by the European Parliament.

Meanwhile, a spate of arson attacks on vehicles in February 2000 was followed by the fatal shooting, in a residential district of Macau, of a Hong Kong citizen believed to have triad connections. In March, in an important change to the immigration rules, it was announced that children of Chinese nationality whose parents were permanent residents of Macau would shortly be allowed to apply for residency permits. A monthly quota of 420 successful applicants was established, while the youngest children were to receive priority.

In May 2000 hundreds of demonstrators participated in a march to protest against Macau's high level of unemployment. This shortage of jobs was attributed to the territory's use of immigrant workers, mainly from mainland China and South-East Asia, who were estimated to total 28,000. During the ensuing clashes several police officers and one demonstrator were reportedly injured. Trade unions continued to organize protests, and in July (for the first time since the unrest arising from the Chinese Cultural Revolution of 1966) tear gas and water cannon were used to disperse about 200 demonstrators who were demanding that the immigration of foreign workers be halted by the Government. In the same month it was announced that, in early 2001, an office of the Macau SAR was to be established in Beijing, in order to promote links between the two Governments. In Guangzhou in August 2000, as cross-border crime continued to increase, senior officials of Macau's criminal investigation unit met with their counterparts from China and Hong Kong for discussions on methods of improving co-operation. It was agreed that further meetings were henceforth to be held twice a year, alternately in Beijing and Macau.

Celebrations to mark the first anniversary of the reversion to Chinese sovereignty were attended by Jiang Zemin, who made a speech praising Macau's local administration, but warning strongly against those seeking to use either of the SARs as a base for subversion. A number of Falun Gong adherents from Hong Kong who had attempted to enter Macau for the celebrations were expelled. The same fate befell two Hong Kong human rights activists who had hoped to petition Jiang Zemin during his stay in Macau about the human rights situation in the People's Republic. A group of Falun Gong members in Macau, who held a protest the day before the Chinese President's arrival, were detained in custody and subsequently alleged that they had suffered police brutality.

In January 2001 China urged the USA to cease interfering in its internal affairs, following the signature by President Bill Clinton of the US Macau Policy Act, which related to the control of Macau's exports and the monitoring of its autonomy. In the same month voter registration began in Macau, in preparation for the expiry of the first Legislative Council's term of office in October and the election of a new assembly.

Government

The Macau Special Administrative Region (SAR) is governed by a Chief Executive, who was chosen by a 200-member Selection Committee in May 1999. The Chief Executive is assisted by a number of Secretaries and is accountable to the State Council of China, the term of office being five years, with a limit of two consecutive terms. Upon the territory's transfer to Chinese sovereignty in December 1999, a 10-member Executive Council, appointed by the Chief Executive to assist in policy-making, assumed office. The 23-member Legislative Assembly, which included eight deputies elected by direct, universal suffrage and eight chosen by indirect election, was superseded by the Legislative Council: 15 of the 16 elected deputies remained in office (one representative having failed to request continued membership), while the seven members appointed by the Governor were replaced by nominees of the new Chief Executive. The term of office of the SAR's transitional Legislative Council (commonly referred to as the Legislative Assembly) was to expire in October 2001, when it was to be expanded to 27 members, of whom 10 would be directly elected, 10 indirectly elected and seven appointed, all with a mandate of four years. In 2005 the membership of the Legislative Council was to be increased to 29, to incorporate two additional deputies to be chosen by direct election. For the purposes of local government, the islands of Taipa and Colane are administered separately.

Defence

The 1998 budget allocated 1,200m. patacas to Macau's security. Upon the territory's transfer of sovereignty in December 1999, troops of the People's Liberation Army (PLA) were stationed in

Macau. The force comprises around 1,000 troops: a maximum of 500 soldiers are stationed in Macau, the remainder being positioned in China, on the border with the SAR. The unit is directly responsible to the Commander of the Guangzhou Military Region and to the Central Military Commission. The Macau garrison is composed mainly of ground troops. Naval and air defence tasks are performed by the naval vessel unit of the PLA garrison in Hong Kong and by the airforce unit in Huizhou. Subject to certain conditions, the garrison was granted law-enforcement powers, to assist the maintenance of public security.

Economic Affairs

In 1999, according to official estimates, Macau's gross domestic product (GDP), measured at current prices, was 49,210m. patacas (about US $6,159m.), equivalent to 113,387 patacas ($14,191) per head. During 1990–95 the territory's GDP increased, in real terms, at an average annual rate of 6.0%. Between 1996 and 1999, however, GDP contracted at an average annual rate of 0.8%. In 1998 and 1999, in real terms, negative growth rates of 4.6% and 2.9% respectively were recorded. Between 1990 and 1998 the population increased at an average annual rate of 3.0%.

Agriculture is of minor importance. In 1989 only 0.6% of the economically active population were employed in agriculture and fishing. The main crops are rice and vegetables. Cattle, buffaloes and pigs are reared.

Industry (including manufacturing, construction and public utilities) employed 30.6% of the economically active population in 1999. Mining is negligible.

The manufacturing sector engaged 22.0% of the economically active population in 1999. The most important manufacturing industry is the production of textiles and garments. Exports of textiles and garments in 1999 reached 14,728.2m. patacas, compared with 14,441.6m. in 1998. Other industries include toys, footwear, furniture and electronics.

Macau possesses few natural resources. Energy is derived principally from imported petroleum. Imports of fuels and lubricants accounted for 6.2% of total import costs in 1999. The territory receives some electricity and water supplies from the People's Republic of China.

The services sector employed 69.2% of the economically active population in 1999. Tourism makes a substantial contribution to the territory's economy, the licensed casinos' gambling receipts totalling US $2,300m. in 1997. In 1997 the tourism and gambling industries employed an estimated 25% of the labour force and contributed an estimated 43% of GDP. The number of visitor arrivals, however, declined from 7.0m. in 1997, when arrivals from Hong Kong accounted for almost 63% of the total, to 6.9m. in 1998. In 1999 total visitor arrivals increased to 7.4m. In 1999 the number of visitors from the People's Republic of China increased to 1,645,193, compared with 816,816 in 1998 (the latter figure excluding visitors using a double-entry visa between January and July of that year). Visitors from China and those from Hong Kong accounted for 22.1% and 56.8% of the total, respectively, in 1999. The number of tourists also increased markedly in 2000, exceeding 9m. In 1996 the Government's receipts from gambling decreased to 4,954m. patacas, before rising to 6,013m. in 1997. In 1998, however, direct taxes from gambling yielded only 5,100m. patacas, contributing nevertheless more than 50% to the Government's revenue. Legislation regulating 'offshore' banking was introduced in 1987. It was hoped that the territory would develop as an international financial centre. The Financial System Act, which took effect in September 1993, aimed to improve the reputation of Macau's banks by curbing the unauthorized acceptance of deposits. A law enacted in April 1995 aimed to attract overseas investment by offering the right of abode in Macau to entrepreneurs with substantial funds (at least US $250,000) at their disposal.

In 1999 Macau recorded a trade surplus of 1,279.8m. patacas, compared with a surplus of 1,487.2m. patacas in 1998. In 2000 exports rose to an estimated 20,400m. patacas, and imports reached 18,100m. patacas. The principal sources of imports in 1999 were the People's Republic of China (which supplied 35.6% of the total), Hong Kong (18.1%), and Japan (6.7%). The principal market for exports was the USA (which purchased 46.9%), followed by the People's Republic of China, Germany, Hong Kong and France. The main exports were textiles and garments (which accounted for 83.8% of the total), machines and apparatus, and footwear. The principal imports were raw materials for industry, fuels, foodstuffs and other consumer goods. Following the territory's reversion to Chinese sovereignty in

December 1999, Macau retained its status as a free port, and remained a separate customs territory. The pataca was retained, remaining freely convertible.

In 1999 a budgetary surplus of 306.4m. patacas was projected. The draft budget for 2000 envisaged a substantial reduction in expenditure, although it aimed to increase spending on anti-corruption measures. The average annual rate of inflation (excluding rents) between 1990 and 1998 was 5.9%. The rate of inflation declined to only 0.2% in 1998 and to a negative rate of 3.2% in 1999. According to official figures, the level of unemployment increased from 6.4% of the labour force in 1999 to 6.6% in the final quarter of 2000. There is a shortage of skilled labour in Macau.

In 1991 Macau became a party to the General Agreement on Tariffs and Trade (GATT, now superseded by the World Trade Organization—WTO, see p. 292) and an associate member of the Economic and Social Commission for Asia and the Pacific (ESCAP, see p. 28). In June 1992 Macau and the European Community (now the European Union) signed a five-year trade and economic co-operation agreement, granting mutual preferential treatment on tariffs and other commercial matters. The agreement was extended in December 1997. Macau remained a 'privileged partner' of the EU after December 1999. Macau also retained its membership of WTO after December 1999.

The opening of an airport in 1995 afforded the enclave access to international transport networks. In the airport's first year of operation, however, passenger numbers proved disappointing. Furthermore, tourist arrivals decreased in 1997 and 1998 as a result of the Asian economic crisis and the worsening security situation in the territory. In 1999, however, public security began to improve and, as the regional economies began to recover, the number of visitors to Macau increased by 7.1% compared with 1998. During 1998 the territory's trade was also adversely affected by neighbouring countries' financial difficulties. In 1999 and 2000 exports increased, although not as rapidly as imports. Macau's position had been considerably weakened by the relative appreciation of the pataca against the currencies of its South-East Asian competitors. Attempts to diversify the economy, in order to reduce dependence on tourism and the textile industry, have been made. During the 1990s, however, many non-textile operations were relocated to China and to South-East Asia, where labour costs were lower. A major land-reclamation programme continued to progress. The completion of the Nam Van Lakes project, scheduled for 2001, will enlarge the territory's peninsular area by 20%. The development was to incorporate residential and business accommodation for 60,000 people. Owing to a sharp decline in the property market, however, by late 1996 the number of unsold apartments (mainly on the island of Taipa) was estimated at 30,000–50,000, thus casting some doubt on the viability of the Nam Van Lakes scheme. Competition between Macau and the neighbouring Chinese Special Economic Zone of Zhuhai continued to increase, the latter's lower labour costs having encouraged many factories to relocate from Macau. The property market remained depressed in 1999. Following the transfer of sovereignty to China in December of that year, doubts surrounded the forthcoming renewal of the franchise of the gambling and entertainment syndicate, STDM (see p. 1101). In his 2000 policy address, the SAR's Chief Executive announced that upon the expiry of the company's concession in late 2001, STDM would indeed lose its long-standing monopoly. Further development of the hotel and tourism sector was envisaged. The Chinese authorities also planned greater integration of Macau within the Zhujiang (Pearl River) Delta region, particularly with regard to infrastructural development. Prospects for 2000 were good, as the Macau economy recovered from recession and the Government gave priority to rapid economic reform.

Social Welfare

In addition to the network of health centres, Macau has two major hospitals (one public and one private). In 1999 there were 488 inhabitants per physician and also 488 per nurse. There were 415 inhabitants per hospital bed. The elderly have access to free medicines. Certain others receive subsidized medicines. In 1998 the sum of 1,400m. patacas, or 13% of the territory's total budget, was allocated to public health and social affairs.

Education

The education system in Macau comprises: pre-school education (lasting two years); primary preparatory year (one year); primary education (six years); secondary education (five–six years, divided into junior secondary of three years and senior secondary of two–three years). Schooling normally lasts from the ages of three to 17. In 1998/99 schools enrolled a total of 97,899 pupils (kindergarten 17,354; primary 48,269; secondary 31,782 (including 3,239 technical and vocational students; and special education 494). From 1995/96 free education was extended from government schools to private schools. Private schools provide education for more than 90% of children. Of these schools 77% have joined the free education system, and together with the government schools they form the public school system, in which all pupils from primary preparatory year up to the junior secondary level (10 years) receive free tuition. Based on the four years of free education, compulsory education was implemented from 1999/2000. In 1998/99 the enrolment rate was as follows: pre-school education and primary preparatory year 92.2% (some families leave their children in China); primary education 103.2%; and secondary education 77.5%. In higher learning, there are nine public and private universities, polytechnic institutes and research centres. Around 10,000 students attended courses offered by those institutions in the academic year 1998/99, ranging from the bacharelato (three-year courses) to doctorate programmes. The University of Macau was inaugurated, as the University of East Asia, in 1981 (passing from private to government control in 1988), and had 3,314 students, with 231 teachers, in 1999/2000. The languages of instruction are primarily English, Cantonese and Portuguese. The rate of literacy in Macau was 93.7% in 1996. The 1998 budget allocated 1,910.8m. patacas to education and training (13.7% of total government expenditure).

Public Holidays

2001: 1 January (New Year), 24–26 January (Chinese Lunar New Year), 5 April (Ching Ming), 13–14 April (Easter), 30 April (Feast of Buddha), 1 May (Labour Day), 25 June (Dragon Boat Festival), 1–2 October (National Day of the People's Republic of China and day following), 2 October (day following Chinese Mid-Autumn Festival), 25 October (Festival of Ancestors—Chung Yeung), 2 November (All Souls' Day), 8 December (Immaculate Conception), 20 December (SAR Establishment Day), 22 December (Winter Solstice), 24–25 December (Christmas).

2002 (provisional): 1 January (New Year), 12–15 February (Chinese Lunar New Year), 5 April (Ching Ming), 29–30 March (Easter), 1 May (Labour Day), May (Feast of Buddha), May/June (Dragon Boat Festival), September/October (day following Chinese Mid-Autumn Festival), 1–2 October (National Day of the People's Republic of China and day following), October (Festival of Ancestors—Chung Yeung), 2 November (All Souls' Day), 8 December (Immaculate Conception), 20 December (SAR Establishment Day), 22 December (Winter Solstice), 24–25 December (Christmas).

Weights and Measures

The metric system is in force.

Statistical Survey

Source (unless otherwise indicated): Direcção dos Serviços de Estatística e Censos, Alameda Dr Carlos d'Assumpção 411–417, Dynasty Plaza, 17° andar, Macau; tel. 728188; fax 561884; e-mail info@dsec.gov.mo; internet www.dsec.gov.mo.

AREA AND POPULATION

Area (1999): 23.80 sq km (9.18 sq miles).

Population: 414,128 (males 199,257, females 214,871) at by-census of 30 August 1996; 112,706 inhabitants were of Portuguese nationality; 437,455 at 31 December 1999 (estimate).

Density (at 31 December 1999): 18,380 per sq km.

Births, Marriages and Deaths (1999): Registered live births 4,148 (birth rate 9.5 per 1,000); Registered marriages 1,367 (marriage rate 3.1 per 1,000); Registered deaths 1,374 (death rate 3.1 per 1,000).

Expectation of Life (years at birth, 1994–97): 76.79 (males 75.32; females 79.89).

Economically Active Population (1999): Manufacturing 44,507; Production and distribution of electricity, gas and water 1,200; Construction 16,300; Wholesale and retail trade; repair of motor vehicles, motorcycles and personal and household goods 31,269; Hotels, restaurants and similar activities 21,692; Transport, storage and communications 15,016; Financial activities 6,011; Real estate, renting and services to companies 9,686; Public administration, defence and compulsory social security 16,730; Education 9,153; Health and social work 5,164; Other community, social and personal service activities 19,779; Private households with employed persons 5,607; Others 366; Total employed 202,480.

AGRICULTURE, ETC.

Meat Production (1996, metric tons, slaughter weight): Buffaloes 1,246.5, Pigs 10,938.5.

Fishing (FAO estimates, metric tons, live weight, 1998): Marine fishes 1,020; Shrimps and prawns 230; Other marine crustaceans 210; Total catch (incl. others) 1,500. Source: FAO, *Yearbook of Fishery Statistics*.

INDUSTRY

Production (1999): Wine 582,972 litres; Knitwear 30.56m. units; Footwear 8.94m. pairs; Clothing 182.02m. units; Furniture 14,606 units; Electric energy 1,526.10m. kWh.

FINANCE

Currency and Exchange Rates: 100 avos = 1 pataca. *Sterling, Dollar and Euro Equivalents* (29 December 2000): £1 sterling = 11.982 patacas; US $1 = 8.030 patacas; €1 = 7.472 patacas; 1,000 patacas = £83.46 = $124.53 = €133.84. *Average Exchange Rate* (patacas per US dollar): 7.978 in 1998; 7.990 in 1999; 8.025 in 2000. Note: The pataca has a fixed link with the value of the Hong Kong dollar (HK $1 = 1.030 patacas).

Budget (million patacas, 1999, provisional): *Total revenue:* 10,111.8 (direct taxes 5,987.4; indirect taxes 495.9; others 3,628.5). *Total expenditure:* 9,805.4.

Money Supply (million patacas at 31 December): *Total money:* 18,953.1 in 1997; 20,171.1 in 1998; 21,045.4 in 1999.

Cost of Living (Consumer Price Index; base: July 1995/June 1996 = 100): 102.82 in 1997; 103.00 in 1998; 99.7 in 1999.

Gross Domestic Product (million patacas at current prices): 55,894 in 1997; 51,902 in 1998; 49,210 (provisional) in 1999.

EXTERNAL TRADE

Principal Commodities (million patacas, 1999): *Imports:* Foodstuffs, beverages and tobacco 1,469.3; Raw materials 8,781.1; Fuels and lubricants 1,012.1; Capital goods 2,166.6; Other consumer goods 2,871.1; Total 16,300.2. *Exports:* Textiles and garments 14,728.2; Machines and apparatus, parts and accessories thereof 658.9; Footwear 503.0; Total (incl. others) 17,580.0.

Principal Trading Partners (million patacas, 1999): *Imports:* China, People's Republic 5,808.9; EU 2,102.8 (France 281.5, Germany 864.2); Hong Kong 2,945.0; Japan 1,084.2; Total (incl. others) 16,300.2. *Exports:* China, People's Republic 1,616.5; EU 5,303.7 (France 919.5, Germany 1,546.5); Hong Kong 1,195.2; Japan 111.6; USA 8,249.1; Total (incl. others) 17,580.0.

TRANSPORT

Road Traffic (motor vehicles in use, Dec. 1999): Light vehicles 50,552; Heavy vehicles 4,592; Motor cycles 58,116.

Shipping (international sea-borne freight traffic, '000 metric tons, 1990): Goods loaded 755; Goods unloaded 3,935. Source: UN, *Monthly Bulletin of Statistics*.

COMMUNICATIONS MEDIA

Radio Receivers (1997): 160,000 in use.

Television Receivers (1997): 49,000 in use.

Source: UNESCO, *Statistical Yearbook*.

Daily newspapers (1999): 11.

Telephones (Dec. 1999): 270,526 in use.

TOURISM

Visitor Arrivals by Country of Residence (1999): China, People's Republic 1,645,193; Hong Kong 4,229,833; Japan 145,284; Philippines 36,614; Taiwan 984,820; Thailand 25,706; United Kingdom 47,449; USA 67,552; Total (incl. others) 7,443,924.

EDUCATION
(1998/99)

Kindergarten: 62 schools; 644 teachers; 17,354 pupils.

Primary: 83 schools; 1,728 teachers; 48,269 pupils.

Secondary (incl. technical colleges): 41 schools; 1,394 teachers; 28,543 pupils.

Higher: 26 institutes; 766 teachers; 10,014 students (of which Teacher-Training: 2 institutes; 54 teachers; 717 students; Nurse-Training: 2 institutes; 78 teachers; 207 students).

Notes: Figures for schools and teachers refer to all those for which the category is applicable. Some schools and teachers provide education at more than one level.

Directory

The Constitution

Under the terms of the Basic Law of the Macau Special Administrative Region (SAR), which took effect on 20 December 1999, the Macau SAR is an inalienable part of the People's Republic of China. The Macau SAR, which comprises the Macau peninsula and the islands of Taipa and Coloane, exercises a high degree of autonomy and enjoys executive, legislative and independent judicial power, including that of final adjudication. The executive authorities and legislature are composed of permanent residents of Macau. The socialist system and policies shall not be practised in the Macau SAR, and the existing capitalist system and way of life shall not be changed for 50 years. In addition to the Chinese language, the Portuguese language may also be used by the executive, legislative and judicial organs.

The central people's Government is responsible for foreign affairs and for defence. The Government of Macau is responsible for maintaining social order in the SAR. The central people's Government appoints and dismisses the Chief Executive, principal executive officials and Procurator-General.

The Chief Executive of the Macau SAR is accountable to the central people's Government. The Chief Executive shall be a Chinese national of no less than 40 years of age, who is a permanent resident of the region and who has resided in Macau for a continuous period of 20 years. He or she is elected locally by a broadly-representative Selection Committee and appointed by the central people's Government.

The Basic Law provides for a 300-member Selection Committee, which serves a four-year term. The Selection Committee responsible for the choice of the Chief Executive in 1999 comprised 200 members; 60 representatives of business and financial circles; 50 from cultural, educational and professional circles; 50 from labour, social welfare and religious circles; and 40 former politicians. The term of office of the Chief Executive of the Macau SAR is five years; he or she may serve two consecutive terms. The Chief Executive's functions include the appointment of a portion of the legislative councillors and the appointment or removal of members of the Executive Council.

With the exception of the first term (which was to expire on 15 October 2001), the term of office of members of the Legislative Council (commonly known as the Legislative Assembly) shall be four years. The second Legislative Council shall be composed of 27 members, of whom 10 shall be returned by direct election, 10 by indirect election and seven by appointment. The third and subsequent Legislative Councils shall comprise 29 members, of whom 12 shall be returned by direct election, 10 by indirect election and seven by appointment.

The Macau SAR shall maintain independent finances. The central people's Government shall not levy taxes in the SAR, which shall practise an independent taxation system. The Macau pataca will remain the legal currency. The Macau SAR shall retain its status as a free port and as a separate customs territory.

The Government

(April 2001)

Chief Executive: EDMUND H. W. HO.

Secretary for Administration and Justice: FLORINDA DA ROSA SILVA CHAN.

Secretary for Economy and Finance: FRANCIS TAM PAK YUEN.

Secretary for Security: CHEONG KUOK VA.

Secretary for Social and Cultural Affairs: FERNANDO CHUI SAI ON.

Secretary for Transport and Public Works: AO MAN LONG.

GOVERNMENT OFFICES

Office of the Chief Executive: Palácio do Governo, Rua da Praia Grande; tel. 726886; fax 725468; internet www.macau.gov.mo.

Office of the Secretary for Administration and Justice: Rua de S. Lourenço 28, Edif. dos Secretários; tel. 9895178; fax 726880; internet www.macau.gov.mo.

Office of the Secretary for Economy and Finance: Rua de S. Lourenço 28, Edif. dos Secretários; tel. 7978160; fax 726665.

Office of the Secretary for Security: Calçada dos Quartéis, Quartel de S. Francisco; tel. 7997510; fax 580702.

Office of the Secretary for Social and Cultural Affairs: Rua de S. Lourenço 28, Edif. dos Secretários; tel. 7978197; fax 725778.

Office of the Secretary for Transport and Public Works: Rua de S. Lourenço 28, Edif. dos Secretários, 1° andar; tel. 9895124; fax 727566.

Macau Government Information Services: Gabinete de Comunicação Social do Governo de Macau, Rua de S. Domingos 1, POB 706; tel. 332886; fax 336372; e-mail info@macau.gov.mo; internet www.macau.gov.mo; Dir AFONSO CAMÕES.

Economic Services: Direcção dos Serviços de Economia, Rua Dr Pedro José Lobo 1–3, Edif. Luso Internacional, 25/F; tel. 386937; fax 590310; e-mail cdidse@economia.gov.mo; internet www.economia.gov.mo.

EXECUTIVE COUNCIL

VICTOR NG, MA IAO LAI, TONG CHI KIN, LEONG HENG TENG, FERNANDO CHUI SAI ON, FLORINDA DA ROSA SILVA CHAN, CHEONG KUOC VA, LIU CHAK WAN, AO MAN LONG, FRANCIS TAM PAK YUEN.

Legislature

LEGISLATIVE COUNCIL (LEGISLATIVE ASSEMBLY)

Alameda Dr Carlos d'Assumpção 411–417, Edif. Dynasty Plaza, 8° andar; tel. 728377; fax 727857.

Following the revision of Macau's Organic Law in 1990, the Legislative Assembly comprised 23 members: seven appointed by the Governor, eight elected directly and eight indirectly. Members served for four years. The Assembly chose its President from among its members, by secret vote. The most recent elections were held in September 1996. The business-orientated Associação Promotora para a Economia de Macau won two of the eight directly-elective seats, while the Convergência para o Desenvolvimento and União Geral para o Desenvolvimento de Macau each won one seat. The pro-Beijing candidates of the União Promotora para o Progresso and of the União para o Desenvolvimento won two seats and one seat respectively. The pro-democracy Associação de Novo Macau Democrático took one seat. Fifteen of the 16 elected members of the above Legislative Assembly remained in office beyond Macau's transfer of sovereignty in December 1999 (one deputy having resigned). Vacancies were to be filled by nominees chosen by the 200-member Selection Committee. The seven members appointed by the Governor were replaced by nominees of the new Chief Executive, the Legislative Assembly being superseded, under the terms of the Basic Law, by the Legislative Council. In practice, however, the legislature continues to be referred to as the Legislative Assembly.

President: SUSANA CHOU.

Political Organizations

There are no formal political parties, but a number of civic associations exist. Those contesting the 1996 Legislative Assembly elections included the União Promotora para o Progresso (UNIPRO), Associação Promotora para a Economia de Macau (APPEM), União para o Desenvolvimento (UPD), Associação de Novo Macau Democrático (ANMD), Convergência para o Desenvolvimento (CODEM), União para o Desenvolvimento (UPD), União Geral para o Desenvolvimento de Macau (UDM), Associação de Amizade (AMI), Aliança para o Desenvolvimento da Economia (ADE), Associação dos Empregados e Assalariados (AEA) and Associação pela Democracia e Bem-Estar Social de Macau (ADBSM).

Judicial System

Formal autonomy was granted to the territory's judiciary in 1993. A new penal code took effect in January 1996. Macau operates its own five major codes, namely the Penal Code, the Code of Criminal Procedure, the Civil Code, the Code of Civil Procedure and the Commercial Code. In March 1999 the authority of final appeal was granted to the supreme court of Macau, effective from June. The judicial system operates independently of the mainland Chinese system.

Court of Final Appeal: Praçeta 25 de Abril, Edif. dos Tribunais de Segunda Instância e Ultima Instância; tel. 3984391; fax 963967; Pres. SAM HOU FAI.

Procurator-General: HO CHIO MENG.

Religion

The majority of the Chinese residents profess Buddhism, and there are numerous Chinese places of worship, Daoism and Confucianism also being widely practised. The Protestant community numbers about 2,500. There are small Muslim and Hindu communities.

CHRISTIANITY
The Roman Catholic Church

Macau forms a single diocese, directly responsible to the Holy See. At 31 December 1998 there were 28,015 adherents in the territory.

Bishop of Macau: Rt Rev. DOMINGOS LAM KA TSEUNG, Paço Episcopal, Largo da Sé s/n, POB 324; tel. 309954; fax 309861; e-mail mdiocese@ macau.ctm.net.

The Anglican Communion

Macau forms part of the Anglican diocese of Hong Kong (q.v.).

The Press

A new Press Law, prescribing journalists' rights and obligations, was enacted in August 1990.

PORTUGUESE LANGUAGE

Boletim Oficial: Rua da Imprensa Nacional, POB 33; tel. 573822; fax 596802; e-mail iom@macau.ctm.net; internet www.imprensa .macau.gov.mo; f. 1838; weekly govt gazette; Dir Dr ANTÓNIO GOMES MARTINS.

O Clarim: Rua Central 26-A; tel. 573860; fax 307867; e-mail clarim @macau.ctm.net; f. 1948; weekly; Editor ALBINO BENTO PAIS; circ. 1,500.

Jornal Tribuna de Macau: Calçada do Tronco Velho 4–6, POB 945; tel. 329270; fax 573277; f. 1998 through merger of Jornal de Macau (f. 1982) and Tribuna de Macau (f. 1982); daily; Dir JOÃO DRAGO; circ. 1,000.

MacaU: Livros do Oriente, Av. Amizade 876, Edif. Marina Gardens, 15E; tel. 700320; fax 700423; e-mail relilau@macau.ctm.net; internet www.books.macau.com; f. 1992; monthly magazine.

Macau Hoje: Rua do Chunambeiro, Edif. Keng Fai 5° D; tel. 371950; fax 976575; e-mail hoje@macau.ctm.net; internet www.macauhoje .ctm.net/; daily; Dir JOÃO SEVERINO; circ. 1,000.

Ponto Final: Rua da Praia Grande 763, Edif. Lun Pon, 11/F–D; tel. 339566; fax 339563; e-mail pontofin@macau.ctm.net; internet www.unitel.net/pontofinal; Dir RICARDO PINTO; circ. 1,500.

CHINESE LANGUAGE

Boletim Oficial: see above; Chinese edn.

Cheng Pou: Rua da Praia Grande 57–63, Edif. Hang Cheong, E–F; tel. 965972; fax 965741; daily; Dir KUNG SU KAN; Editor-in-Chief CHENG PUI; circ. 5,000.

Correio Sino-Macaense: Av. Venseslau de Morais 221, Edif. Ind. Nam Fong, 2a Fase, 15°, Bloco E; tel. 717569; fax 717572; daily; Dir LAM CHONG; circ. 1,500.

Jornal 'Si-Si': Rua do Padre António 26, R/C; tel. 974354; weekly; Dir and Editor-in-Chief CHEANG VENG PENG; circ. 3,000.

Jornal Son Pou: Rua de Fran António 22, 1° C, Edif. Mei Fun; tel. 561557; fax 566575; weekly; Dir CHAO CHONG PENG; circ. 8,000.

Ou Mun Iat Pou (Macau Daily News): Rua Pedro Nolasco da Silva 37; tel. 371688; fax 331998; f. 1958; daily; Dir LEI SENG CHUN; Editor-in-Chief LEI PANG CHU; circ. 100,000.

Semanário Desportivo: Estrada D. Maria II, Edif. Kin Chit Garden, 2 G–H; tel. 718259; fax 718285; weekly; sport; Dir FONG SIO LON; Editor-in-Chief FONG LIN LAM; circ. 2,000.

Seng Pou (Star): Travessa da Caldeira 9; tel. 938387; fax 388192; f. 1963; daily; Dir KUOK KAM SENG; Deputy Editor-in-Chief TOU MAN KAM; circ. 6,000.

Si Man Pou (Jornal do Cidadão): Rua dos Pescadores, Edif. Ind. Oceano, Bl. 11, 2/F–B; tel. 722111; fax 722133; f. 1944; daily; Dir and Editor-in-Chief KONG MAN; circ. 8,000.

Tai Chung Pou: Rua Dr Lourenço P. Marques 7A, 2/F; tel. 939888; fax 934114; f. 1933; daily; Dir VONG U. KONG; Editor-in-Chief SOU KIM KEONG; circ. 8,000.

Today Macau Journal: Pátio da Barca 20, R/C; tel. 215050; fax 210478; daily; Dir LAM VO I; circ. 6,000.

Va Kio Pou: Rua da Alfândega 7–9; tel. 345888; fax 580638; f. 1937; daily; Dir CHIANG SAU MENG; Editor-in-Chief TANG CHOU KEI; circ. 21,000.

NEWS AGENCIES

Associated Press (AP) (USA): POB 221; tel. 361204; fax 343220; Correspondent ADAM LEE.

LUSA—Agência de Notícias de Portugal: Av. Conselheiro Ferreira de Almeida 95-A; tel. 967601; fax 967605; e-mail lusa2@ macau.ctm.net; internet www.lusamacau.com; Dir GONÇALO CÉSAR DE SÁ.

Reuters (United Kingdom): Rua da Alfândega 69; tel. 345888; fax 930076; Correspondent HARALD BRUNING.

Xinhua (New China) News Agency Macau SAR Bureau: Av. Gov. Jaime Silvério Marques, Edif. Zhu Kuan, 13 andar-V; tel. 7911802; fax 700548; Dir CHEN BOLIANG.

PRESS ASSOCIATION

Associação dos Jornalistas de Macau: Plum Court, 12/F, J, Ocean Garden, Taipa; tel. 921395; fax 921315; f. 1999.

Associação dos Trabalhadores da Imprensa de Macau: Travessa do Auto Novo 301–303, Edif. Cheng Peng; tel. 375245; Pres. TANG CHOU KEI.

Clube de Jornalistas de Macau: Travessa dos Alfaiates 8–10; tel. 921395; fax 921315; Pres. CHAN CHI WA.

Publishers

Instituto Cultural de Macau: see under Tourism; publishes literature, social sciences and history.

Livros do Oriente: Av. Amizade 876, Edif. Marina Gardens, 15 E; tel. 700320; fax 700423; e-mail relilau@macau.ctm.net; internet www.loriente.com; f. 1990; publishes in Portuguese, English and Chinese on regional history, culture, etc.; Gen. Man. ROGÉRIO BELTRÃO COELHO; Exec. Man. CECÍLIA JORGE.

Universidade de Macau—Centro de Publicações: POB 3001; tel. 3974506; fax 831694; e-mail PUB_GRP@umac.mo; internet www.umac.mo.pc; f. 1993; art, economics, education, political science, history, literature, management, social sciences, etc.; Head Dr ZHENG DEHUA.

GOVERNMENT PUBLISHER

Imprensa Oficial: Rua da Imprensa Nacional s/n; tel. 573822; fax 596802; e-mail helpdesk@imprensa.macau.gov.mo.

Broadcasting and Communications

TELECOMMUNICATIONS

Companhia de Telecomunicações de Macau, SARL (CTM): Rua de Lagos, Edif. Telecentro, Taipa; tel. 833833; fax 8913031; e-mail mktg@macau.ctm.net; internet www.ctm.com.mo; holds local telecommunications monopoly; shareholders include Cable and Wireless (51%) and Portugal Telecom (28%); Chair. LINUS CHEUNG; CEO JOHN LINDFIELD; 1,000 employees.

BROADCASTING

Radio

Rádio Comercial Vila Verde: Rua Francisco Xavier Pereira 133H, 13/F; tel. 573355; fax 311668; private radio station; programmes in Chinese; Man. KOK HOI.

Television

Teledifusão de Macau, SARL (TDM): Rua Francisco Xavier Pereira 157-A, POB 446; tel. 335888 (Radio), 519188 (TV); fax 520208; privately-owned; two radio channels: **Rádio Macau** (Av. Dr Rodrigo Rodrigues, Edif. Nam Kwong, 7/F; fax 343220) in Portuguese, broadcasting 24 hours per day, and **Ou Mun Tin Toi** in Chinese, 24 hours per day; also 12.5 hours per day of TV broadcasting in Portuguese on **TDM Channel 1** and 11.5 hours in Chinese on **TDM Channel 2**; Chair. STANLEY HO; Exec. Vice-Chair. Dr MANUEL GONÇALVES.

Macao Five-star Satellite TV: Macau; commenced transmissions in 2000; domestic and international broadcasts in Chinese aimed at Chinese-speaking audiences worldwide.

Macau is within transmission range of the Hong Kong television stations.

Cosmos Televisão por Satélite: Macau; commenced trial satellite transmissions in 1999, initially for three hours per day; by the year 2003 the company planned to provide up to six channels; Chair. NG FOK.

Finance

(cap. = capital; res = reserves; dep. = deposits; m. = million;
brs = branches;
amounts in patacas unless otherwise indicated)

BANKING

Macau has no foreign-exchange controls, its external payments system being fully liberalized on current and capital transactions. The Financial System Act, aiming to improve the reputation of the territory's banks and to comply with international standards, took effect in September 1993.

Issuing Authority

Autoridade Monetária de Macau—AMCM (Monetary Authority of Macau): Calçada do Gaio 24–26, POB 3017; tel. 568288; fax 325433; e-mail amcm@macau.ctm.net; internet www.amcm.macau

.gov.mo; f. 1989 as Autoridade Monetária e Cambial de Macau (AMCM), to replace the Instituto Emissor de Macau; govt-owned; Pres. ANSELMO L. S. TENG.

Banks of Issue

Banco Nacional Ultramarino (BNU), SA: Av. Almeida Ribeiro 2, POB 465; tel. 376644; fax 355653; e-mail jmorgado@bnu.com.mo; internet www.bnu.com.mo; f. 1864, est. in Macau 1902; Head Office in Lisbon; agent of Macau Government; Gen. Man. Dr HERCULANO J. SOUSA; 11 brs.

Bank of China: Bank of China Bldg, Av. Dr Mário Soares; tel. 781828; fax 781833; e-mail bocmacau@ctm.net; f. 1950 as Nan Tung Bank, name changed 1987; authorized to issue banknotes from Oct. 1995; Gen. Man. ZHU CHI; 23 brs.

Other Commercial Banks

Banco da América (Macau), SARL: Av. Almeida Ribeiro 70–76, POB 165; tel. 568821; fax 570386; f. 1937; fmrly Security Pacific Asian Bank (Banco de Cantão); Chair. SAMUEL NG TSIEN; Vice-Pres. and Man. Dir KENNETH CHEONG.

Banco Comercial de Macau, SA: Av. da Praia Grande 572, POB 545; tel. 7910000; fax 595817; f. 1995; cap. 225m., res 187m., dep. 5,500m. (March 2000); Chair. JORGE JARDIM GONÇALVES; CEO Dr MANUEL MARECOS DUARTE; 18 brs.

Banco Delta Asia, SARL: Av. Conselheiro Ferreira de Almeida 79; tel. 559898; fax 570068; e-mail deltasia@deltasia.com; internet www.deltasia.com; f. 1935; fmrly Banco Hang Sang; cap. 150.0m., res 30.4m., dep. 2,794.3m. (Dec. 1998); Chair. STANLEY AU; Gen. Man. DAVID LAM; 9 brs.

Banco Seng Heng, SARL: Seng Heng Bank Tower, Macau Landmark, Av. da Amizade; tel. 555222; fax 338064; e-mail sengheng@macau.ctm.net; internet www.senghengbank.com; f. 1972; cap. 150.0m., res 514.7m., dep. 8,714.1m. (Dec. 1999); Gen. Man. ALEX LI; 6 brs.

Banco Tai Fung, SARL: Tai Fung Bank Bldg, Av. Alameda Dr Carlos d'Assumpção 418; tel. 322323; fax 570737; e-mail tfbsecr@taifungbank.com; internet www.taifungbank.com; f. 1971; cap. 1,000m., dep. 16,743m. (Dec. 1999); Chair. FUNG KA YORK; Gen. Man. LONG RONGSHEN; 20 brs.

Banco Totta e Açores, SA (Portugal): Av. da Praia Grande 429, 21/F, POB 912; tel. 573299; fax 563852; e-mail totta@macau.ctm.net; f. 1843; est. in Macau 1982; Gen. Man. Dr CARLOS DE CASTRO.

Banco Weng Hang, SA: Av. Almeida Ribeiro 241; tel. 335678; fax 576527; e-mail wenghang@macau.ctm.net; internet www.whbmac.com; f. 1973; subsidiary of Wing Hang Bank Ltd, Hong Kong; cap. 120m., dep. 6,412m. (Dec. 1999); Chair. PATRICK FUNG YUK-BUN; Gen. Man. and Dir TAM MAN-KUEN; 11 brs.

Finibanco (Macau), SARL: Av. da Praia Grande 111–111B, Edif. Centro Comercial Talento, R/C; tel. 3226789; fax 322680; Gen. Man. JÚLIO CEIRÃO.

Guangdong Development Bank: Av. da Praia Grande 269; tel. 323628; fax 323668; Gen. Man. LI RUO-HONG.

Luso International Banking Ltd: Av. Dr Mário Soares 47; tel. 378977; fax 578517; e-mail lusobank@lusobank.com.mo; internet www.lusobank.com.mo; f. 1974; cap. 151.5m., res 224.1m., dep. 6,172m. (Dec. 1999); Chair. EUGENE HO; Gen. Man. IP KAI MING; 13 brs.

Foreign Banks

Banco Comercial Português (Portugal): Av. Dr Mário Soares, BOC Bldg, 21/F; tel. 786769; fax 786772; Gen. Man. Dr MANUEL MARECOS DUARTE.

Banco Espírito Santo do Oriente (Portugal): Av. Dr Mário Soares 323, Bank of China Bldg, 28/F, E–F; tel. 785222; fax 785228; e-mail besor@macau.ctm.net; f. 1996; subsidiary of Banco Espírito Santo, SA (Portugal); Exec. Dir Dr LUÍS DE ALMEIDA CAPELA; Man. JOÃO MANUEL AMBRÓSIO.

BNP Paribas (France): Av. Central Plaza, 10F, Almeida Ribeiro 61; tel. 562777; fax 560626; f. 1979; Man. SANCO SZE.

Citibank NA (USA): Rua da Praia Grande 31B–C; tel. 378188; fax 578451; Asst Vice-Pres. ALEX LI.

The Hongkong and Shanghai Banking Corporation Ltd (Hong Kong): Av. da Praia Grande 639, POB 476; tel. 553669; fax 322716; f. 1972; CEO THOMAS YAM.

International Bank of Taipei (Taiwan): Av. Infante D. Henrique 52–58; tel. 715175; fax 715035; e-mail tpbbmomx@macau.ctm.net; f. 1996; fmrly Taipei Business Bank; Gen. Man. KEVIN CHIOU.

Liu Chong Hing Bank Ltd (Hong Kong): Av. da Praia Grande 693, Edif. Tai Wah, R/C; tel. 339982; fax 339990; Gen. Man. LAM MAN KING.

Overseas Trust Bank Limited (Hong Kong): Rua de Santa Clara 5–7E, Edif. Ribeiro, Loja C e D; tel. 329338; fax 323711; Senior Man. KENNETH LAU.

Standard Chartered Bank (UK): Av. Infante D. Henrique 60–64, Edif. Centro Comercial Central, 16/F–17/F; tel. 378271; fax 594134; f. 1982; Man. ABRAHAM WONG.

Banking Association

Associação de Bancos de Macau—ABM (The Macau Association of Banks): Av. da Praia Grande 575, Edif. 'Finanças', 15/F; tel. 511921; fax 346049; Chair. ZHU CHI.

INSURANCE

AIA Co (Bermuda) Ltd: Central Plaza, 13/F, Av. Almeida Ribeiro 61; tel. 9881888; fax 315900; Rep. ALEXANDRA FOO.

American Home Assurance Co: Av. Almeida Ribeiro 61, Central Plaza, 15/F; tel. 355602; fax 355299; Man. ALICE K. I. MAK.

Asia Insurance Co Ltd: Rua do Dr Pedro José Lobo 1–3, Luso International Bank Bldg, 11/F; tel. 563166; fax 570438; Rep. S. T. CHAN.

AXA Insurance: Rua de Xangai 175, Edif. da Associação Comercial de Macau; tel. 781188; fax 780022; Rep. KANE CHOW.

CGU International Insurance plc: Av. da Praia Grande 693, Edif. Tai Wah A & B, 13/F; tel. 923329; fax 923349; Man. VICTOR WU.

China Insurance Co Ltd: Av. Dr Rodrigo Rodrigues 338, Edif. do Grupo de Seguros da China, 18–19/F; tel. 785578; fax 787216; e-mail cic@macau.ctm.net; Rep. JIANG JIDONG.

China Life Insurance Co Ltd: Av. Dr Rodrigo Rodrigues, Edif. do Grupo de Seguros da China, 15/F; tel. 787288; fax 787215; Rep. CHAN MAN LONG.

Companhia de Seguros Fidelidade: Av. Almeida Ribeiro 22 & 38 (BNU); tel. 374072; fax 338549; Man. LEONEL RODRIGUES.

Companhia de Seguros de Macau, SARL: Av. da Praia Grande 57, Centro Comercial Praia Grande, 18/F; tel. 555078; fax 551074; Gen. Man. IVAN CHEUNG.

Crown Life Insurance Co: Av. da Praia Grande 51, Nam Yue Commercial Centre, Bl. B, 8/F; tel. 570828; fax 570844; Rep. STEVEN SIU.

East Asia Aetna Insurance (Macau) Ltd: Av. Almeida Ribeiro 61, POB 1212; tel. 9886060; fax 9886100; Man. STEVEN CHIK.

Forex Insurance Co Ltd: Av. da Praia Grande 51, Edif. Keng Ou, 13/F–D, tel. 337036; fax 337037; Rep. STUART LUI.

HSBC Insurance Co Ltd: Av. Horta e Costa 122–124, 4/F, Rm A; tel. 212323; fax 217162; Rep. JOHNNY HO.

Insurance Co of North America: Av. Almeida Ribeiro 32, Tai Fung Bank Bldg, Rm 806–7; tel. 557191; fax 570188; Rep. JOSEPH LO.

Luen Fung Hang Insurance Co Ltd: Rua de Pequim 202A–246, Macau Finance Centre, 6/F–A; tel. 700033; fax 700088; Rep. SI CHI HOK.

Macau Life Insurance: Av. da Praia Grande 57, Centro Comercial Praia Grande, 18/F; tel. 555078; fax 551074; Rep. MANUEL BALCÃO REIS.

Manulife (International) Ltd: Av. Almeida Ribeiro 61, Central Plaza D & E, 12/F; tel. 3980388; fax 323312; internet www.manulife.com.hk; Rep. CARMEN LEONG.

Min Xin Insurance Co Ltd: Rua do Dr Pedro José Lobo 1–3, Luso International Bank Bldg, 27/F, Rm 2704; tel. 305684; fax 305600.

QBE Insurance (International) Ltd: Av. da Praia Grande 51, Edif. Keng On 'B', 9/F; tel. 323909; fax 323911; Rep. SALLY SIU.

Sumitomo Marine and Fire Insurance Co, Ltd: Av. Almeida Ribeiro 32, Tai Fung Bank Bldg, Rm 802; tel. 385917; fax 596667; Rep. CARMEN PANG.

The Wing On Fire & Marine Insurance Co Ltd: Central Plaza, 7/F, Block E7; tel. 356688; fax 333710; Rep. HAZEL AO.

Winterthur Swiss Insurance (Macau) Ltd: Av. da Praia Grande 599, Edif. Rodrigues, 10/F, C; tel. 356618; fax 356800; Man. ALLAN YU.

Insurers' Association

Macau Insurers' Association: Av. da Praia Grande 575, Edif. 'Finanças', 15/F; tel. 511923; fax 337531; Pres. VICTOR WU.

Trade and Industry

CHAMBER OF COMMERCE

Associação Comercial de Macau: Rua de Xangai 175, Edif. ACM, 5/F; tel. 576833; fax 594513; Pres. MA MAN KEI.

INDUSTRIAL AND TRADE ASSOCIATIONS

Associação dos Construtores Civis (Association of Building Development Cos): Rua do Campo 9–11; tel. 323854; fax 345710; Pres. CHUI TAK KEI.

Associação dos Exportadores e Importadores de Macau: Av. Infante D. Henrique 60–62, Centro Comercial 'Central', 3/F; tel. 375859; fax 512174; e-mail aeim@macau.ctm.net; exporters' and importers' asscn; Pres. VÍTOR NG.

Associação dos Industriais de Tecelagem e Fiação de Lã de Macau (Macau Weaving and Spinning of Wool Manufacturers' Asscn): Av. da Amizade 271, Edif. Kam Wa Kok, 6/F–A; tel. 553378; fax 511105; Pres. WONG SHOO KEE.

Associação Industrial de Macau: Rua Dr Pedro José Lobo 34–36, Edif. AIM, 17/F, POB 70; tel. 574125; fax 578305; e-mail aim@macau.ctm.net; f. 1959; Pres. PETER PAN.

Centro de Produtividade e Transferência de Tecnologia de Macau (Macau Productivity and Technology Transfer Centre): Rua de Xangai 175, Edif. ACM, 6/F; tel. 781313; fax 788233; e-mail cpttm@cpttm.org.mo; internet www.cpttm.org.mo; Dir ERIC YEUNG.

Euro-Info Centre Macau: Av. Sidónio Pais 1-A, Edif. Tung Hei Kok, R/C; tel. 713338; fax 713339; e-mail eic@macau.ctm.net; internet www.ieem.org.mo/eic/eicmacau.html; promotes trade with EU; Man. SAM LEI.

Instituto de Promocão do Comércio e do Investimento de Macau—IPIM (Macau Trade and Investment Promotion Institute): Av. da Amizade 918, World Trade Center Bldg, 3/F–4/F; tel. 710300; fax 590309; e-mail ipim@ipim.gov.mo; internet www.ipim.gov.mo; Pres. LEE PENG HONG.

World Trade Center Macau, SARL: Av. da Amizade 918, Edif. World Trade Center, 16/F–19/F; tel. 727666; fax 727633; e-mail wtcmc@macau.ctm.net; internet www.wtc-macau.com; f. 1995; trade information and business services, office rentals, exhibition and conference facilities; Man. Dir Dr ANTÓNIO LEÇA DA VEIGA PAZ.

UTILITIES

Electricity

Companhia de Electricidade de Macau, SARL—CEM: Estrada D. Maria II 32–36, Edif. CEM; tel. 339933; fax 719760; f. 1972; sole distributor; Pres. Eng. CUSTÓDIO MIGUENS.

Water

Sociedade de Abastecimento de Aguas de Macau, SARL—SAAM: Av. do Conselheiro Borja 718; tel. 233332; fax 234658; f. 1984 as jt venture with Suez Lyonnaise des Eaux; Dir-Gen. JIM CONLON.

TRADE UNIONS

Macau Federation of Trade Unions: Rua Ribeira do Patane 2; tel. 576231; fax 553110; Pres. TONG SENG CHUN.

Transport

RAILWAYS

There are no railways in Macau. A plan to connect Macau with Zhuhai and Guangzhou (People's Republic of China) is under consideration. Construction of the Zhuhai–Guangzhou section was under way in 2000.

ROADS

In 1999 the public road network extended to 321.2 km. The peninsula of Macau is linked to the islands of Taipa and Coloane by two bridges and by a 2.2-km causeway respectively. The first bridge (2.6 km) opened in 1974. In conjunction with the construction of an airport on Taipa (see below), a new 4.4-km four-lane bridge to the mainland was opened in April 1994. A second connection to the mainland, the 1.5-km six-lane road bridge (the Lotus Bridge) linking Macau with Hengqin Island (in Zhuhai, Guangdong Province), opened to traffic in December 1999.

SHIPPING

There are representatives of shipping agencies for international lines in Macau. There are passenger and cargo services to the People's Republic of China. Catamarans, jetfoils and high-speed ferries operate regular services between Macau and Hong Kong. The principal services carried 7.4m. passengers in 1997. A new terminal opened in late 1993. The new port of Kao-ho (on the island of Coloane), which handles cargo and operates container services, entered into service in 1991.

CTS Parkview Holdings Ltd: Av. Amizade, Porto Exterior, Terminal Marítimo de Macau, Sala 2006B; tel. 726789; fax 727112; purchased by STDM in 1998.

Hongkong Macao Hydrofoil Co Ltd: Av. Amizade Porto Exterior, Terminal Marítimo de Macau, 2/F, Sala 2011B; tel. 726266; fax 726277.

STDM Shipping Dept: Av. da Amizade Terminal Marítimo do Porto Exterior; tel. 726111; fax 726234; affiliated to Sociedade de Turismo e Diversões de Macau; Gen. Man. ALAN HO; Exec. Man. Capt. AUGUSTO LIZARDO.

Association

Associação de Agências de Navegação e Congêneres de Macau: Av. Horta e Costa 7D–E, POB 6133; tel. 528207; fax 302667; Pres. VONG KOK SENG.

Port Authority

Capitania dos Portos de Macau: Calçada da Barra, Quartel dos Mouros, POB 47; tel. 559922; fax 511986; e-mail cpm@macau.ctm.net; internet www.cpm.gov.mo.

CIVIL AVIATION

In August 1987 plans were approved for the construction of an international airport, on reclaimed land near the island of Taipa, and work began in 1989. The final cost of the project was 8,900m. patacas. Macau International Airport was officially opened in December 1995. In 1999 the airport handled a total of 2,640,166 passengers. The terminal has the capacity to handle 6m. passengers a year. Between January and December 1999 53,117.5 tons of cargo were processed. By 2000 a total of 16 airlines operated more than 400 scheduled flights weekly. A helicopter service between Hong Kong and Macau commenced in 1990: East Asia Airlines transported a total of 72,579 helicopter passengers in 1999.

AACM—Macau Civil Aviation Authority: Rua Dr Pedro José Lobo 1–3, Luso International Bldg, 26/F; tel. 511213; fax 338089; e-mail aacm@macau.ctm.net; internet www.macau-airport.gov.mo; f. 1991; Pres. RUI ALFREDO BALACÓ MOREIRA.

Administração de Aeroportos, Lda—ADA: Av. de João IV, Centro Comercial Iat Teng Hou, 5/F; tel. 711808; fax 711803; e-mail adamkt@macau.ctm.net; internet www.ada.com.mo; airport administration; Chair. DUNG JUN; Dir CARLOS SERUCA SALGADO.

CAM—Sociedade do Aeroporto Internacional de Macau, SARL: Av. Dr Mário Soares, Bank of China Bldg, 29/F; tel. 785448; fax 785465; e-mail cam@macau.ctm.net; internet www.macau-airport.gov.mo; f. 1989; airport owner, responsible for design, construction, development and international marketing of Macau International Airport; Chair. Eng. JOÃO MANUEL DE SOUZA MOREIRA.

Air Macau: Av. da Praia Grande 693, Edif. Tai Wah, 9/F–12/F, POB 1910; tel. 3966888; fax 3966866; e-mail airmacau@airmacau.com.mo; internet www.airmacau.com.mo; f. 1994; controlled by China National Aviation Corporation (Group) Macau Co Ltd; services to several cities in the People's Republic of China, the Republic of Korea, the Philippines, Taiwan and Thailand; other destinations planned; Chair. GU TIEFEI; Pres. ZHANG HONGYING.

Tourism

Tourism is now a major industry, a substantial portion of the Government's revenue being derived from the territory's casinos. The other attractions are the cultural heritage and museums, dog-racing, horse-racing, and annual events such as Chinese New Year (January/February), the Macau Arts Festival (February/March), Dragon Boat Festival (May/June), the Macau International Fireworks Festival (September/October), the International Music Festival, (October) the Macau Grand Prix for racing cars and motorcycles (November) and the Macau International Marathon (December). At the end of 1999 there were 40 hotels, and capacity totalled 8,886 rooms. In 1999 total visitor arrivals reached 7.44m., of whom 4.23m. were arrivals from Hong Kong. Average per caput visitor spending (excluding expenditure by mainland Chinese visitors) decreased by 1.38% to US $171.63 in 1999. In the same year per caput expenditure by visitors from the People's Republic of China decreased by 5.07% to US $332.63. Total visitor arrivals exceeded 9m. in 2000.

Macau Government Tourist Office (MGTO): Direcção dos Serviços de Turismo, Largo do Senado 9, Edif. Ritz, POB 3006; tel. 315566; fax 510104; e-mail mgto@macautourism.gov.mo; internet www.macautourism.gov.mo; Dir Eng. João Manuel Costa Antunes.

Instituto Cultural de Macau: Praçeta de Miramar 87U, Edif. San On; tel. 700391; fax 700405; e-mail postoffice@icm.gov.mo; internet www.icm.gov.mo; f. 1982; organizes performances, concerts, exhibitions, festivals, etc.; library facilities; Pres. Wang Zeng Yang.

Macau Hotels Association: Rua Luís Gonzaga Gomes s/n, Bl. IV, r/c, Centro de Actividades Turísticas, Cabinet A; tel. 703416; fax 703415.

Sociedade de Turismo e Diversões de Macau (STDM), SARL: Hotel Lisboa, 9F, Old Wing, POB 3036; tel. 566065; fax 371981; e-mail stdmmdof@macau.ctm.net; operates 10 casinos, five hotels, tour companies, helicopter and jetfoil services from Hong Kong, etc.; Man. Dir Dr Stanley Ho.

CHINA (TAIWAN)

Introductory Survey

Location, Climate, Language, Religion, Flag, Capital

The Republic of China has, since 1949, been confined mainly to the province of Taiwan (comprising one large island and several much smaller ones), which lies off the south-east coast of the Chinese mainland. The territory under the Republic's effective jurisdiction consists of the island of Taiwan (also known as Formosa) and nearby islands, including the P'enghu (Pescadores) group, together with a few other islands which lie just off the mainland and form part of the province of Fujian (Fukien), west of Taiwan. The largest of these is Kinmen (Jinmen), also known as Quemoy, which (with three smaller islands) is about 10 km from the port of Xiamen (Amoy), while five other islands under Taiwan's control, mainly Matsu (Mazu), lie further north, near Fuzhou. Taiwan itself is separated from the mainland by the Taiwan (Formosa) Strait, which is about 130 km (80 miles) wide at its narrowest point. The island's climate is one of rainy summers and mild winters. Average temperatures are about 15°C (59°F) in the winter and 26°C (79°F) in the summer. The average annual rainfall is 2,580 mm (102 in). The official language is Northern Chinese (Mandarin), but Taiwanese, a dialect based on the language of Fujian Province, is widely spoken. The predominant religions are Buddhism and Daoism (Taoism), but there are also adherents of I-kuan Tao, Christianity (mainly Roman Catholics and Protestants) and Islam. The philosophy of Confucianism has a large following. The national flag (proportions 3 by 2) is red, with a dark blue rectangular canton, containing a white sun, in the upper hoist. The capital is Taipei.

Recent History

China ceded Taiwan to Japan in 1895. The island remained under Japanese rule until the end of the Second World War in 1945, when it was returned to Chinese control, becoming a province of the Republic of China, then ruled by the Kuomintang (KMT, Nationalist Party). The leader of the KMT was Gen. Chiang Kai-shek, President of the Republic since 1928. The KMT Government's forces were defeated in 1949 by the Communist revolution in China. President Chiang and many of his supporters withdrew from the Chinese mainland to Taiwan, where they established a KMT regime in succession to their previous all-China administration. This regime continued to assert that it was the rightful Chinese Government, in opposition to the People's Republic of China, proclaimed by the victorious Communists in 1949. The Nationalists successfully resisted attacks by their Communist rivals, and declared that they intended to recover control of mainland China.

Although its effective control was limited to Taiwan, the KMT regime continued to be dominated by politicians who had formerly been in power on the mainland. Unable to replenish their mainland representation, the National Assembly (last elected fully in 1947) and other legislative organs extended their terms of office indefinitely, although fewer than half of the original members were alive on Taiwan by the 1980s. The political domination of the island by immigrants from the mainland caused some resentment among native Taiwanese, and led to demands for increased democratization and for the recognition of Taiwan as a state independent of China. The KMT, however, consistently rejected demands for independence, restating the party's long-standing policy of seeking political reunification, although under KMT terms, with the mainland.

The KMT regime continued to represent China at the United Nations (and as a permanent member of the UN Security Council) until 1971, when it was replaced by the People's Republic. Nationalist China was subsequently expelled from several other international organizations. In November 1991, however, as 'Chinese Taipei', Taiwan joined the Asia-Pacific Economic Co-operation forum (APEC). In September 1992, under the name of the 'Separate Customs Territory of Taiwan, P'enghu, Kinmen and Matsu', Taiwan was granted observer status at the General Agreement on Tariffs and Trade (GATT), and by 2000 the island's application for full membership of the successor World Trade Organization (WTO) was well advanced. In June 1995 Taiwan offered to make a donation of US $1,000m.,

to be used for the establishment of an international development fund, if the island were permitted to rejoin the UN. In September 2000, for the eighth consecutive year, the General Committee of the UN General Assembly rejected a proposal urging Taiwan's participation in the UN. After 1971 a number of countries broke off diplomatic relations with Taiwan and recognized the People's Republic, and in late 2000, the Taiwan Government was recognized by some 29 countries.

In 1973 the Government of Taiwan rejected an offer from the People's Republic to hold secret discussions on the reunification of China. In October 1981 Taiwan rejected China's suggested terms for reunification, whereby Taiwan would become a 'special administrative region' and would have a substantial degree of autonomy, including the retention of its own armed forces. In 1983 China renewed its offer, including a guarantee to maintain the status quo in Taiwan for 100 years if the province agreed to reunification. In 1984, following the agreement between the People's Republic of China and the United Kingdom that China would regain sovereignty over the British colony of Hong Kong in 1997, mainland Chinese leaders urged Taiwan to accept similar proposals for reunification on the basis of 'one country—two systems'. The Taipei Government insisted that Taiwan would never negotiate with Beijing until the mainland regime renounced communism. In May 1986, however, the Government was forced to make direct contact with the Beijing Government for the first time, over the issue of a Taiwanese pilot who had defected to the mainland. In October 1987 the Government announced the repeal of the 38-year ban on visits to the mainland by Taiwanese citizens, with the exception of civil servants and military personnel. These regulations were relaxed in November 1998.

In April 1989 the Government announced that it was considering a 'one China, two governments' formula, whereby China would be a single country under two administrations, one in Beijing and one in Taipei. In May a delegation led by the Minister of Finance attended a meeting of the Asian Development Bank (ADB) in Beijing, as representatives of 'Taipei, China', demonstrating a considerable relaxation in Taiwan's stance. Reconciliation initiatives were abruptly halted, however, by the violent suppression of the pro-democracy movement in Beijing in June. In May 1990 a proposal by the President of Taiwan to open direct dialogue on a government-to-government basis with the People's Republic was rejected by Beijing, which continued to maintain that it would negotiate only on a party-to-party basis with the KMT. In December Taiwan announced that the state of war with the People's Republic would be formally ended by May 1991 (see below).

In February 1991 the recently-formed National Unification Council, under the chairmanship of the President of Taiwan, put forward radical new proposals, whereby Taiwan and the People's Republic of China might recognize each other as separate political entities. In March a national unification programme, which incorporated the demand that Taiwan be acknowledged as an independent and equal entity, was approved by the Central Standing Committee of the KMT. The programme also included a proposal for direct postal, commercial and shipping links with the mainland.

In April 1991 a delegation from the Straits Exchange Foundation (SEF), established in late 1990 to deal with bilateral issues, travelled to Beijing for discussions, the first such delegation ever to visit the People's Republic. In August 1991 a Beijing magazine published an informal 10-point plan for the eventual reunification of China, whereby Taiwan would become a special administrative region and retain its own legislative, administrative and judicial authority. Two senior envoys of the mainland Chinese Red Cross were allowed to enter Taiwan in August on a humanitarian mission.

As the Beijing Government continued to warn against independence for Taiwan, in September 1991 the island's President asserted that conditions were not appropriate for reunification with the mainland and that Taiwan was a *de facto* sovereign and autonomous country. The President of the People's Republic indicated that force might be used to prevent the separation of

Taiwan. In December the non-governmental Association for Relations across the Taiwan Straits (ARATS) was established in Beijing. In January 1992 the SEF protested to the People's Republic over the detention of a former pilot of the mainland air force who had defected to Taiwan in 1965 and, upon returning to his homeland for a family reunion in December 1991, had been arrested. He subsequently received a 15-year prison sentence. In May 1992 the National Unification Council's proposal for a non-aggression pact between Taiwan and the People's Republic was rejected.

In July 1992 the Taiwanese Government reiterated that it would not consider party-to-party talks with Beijing. In the same month President Lee urged the establishment of 'one country, one good system'. In mid-July statutes to permit the further expansion of economic and political links with the People's Republic were adopted by the Legislative Yuan. In August the vice-president of the mainland Red Cross travelled to the island, thus becoming the most senior representative of the People's Republic to visit Taiwan since 1949. Delegates from the SEF and ARATS met in Hong Kong in October 1992 for discussions. The Chairman of the Mainland Affairs Council, however, insisted upon the People's Republic's renunciation of the use of military force prior to any dialogue on the reunification question. Upon taking office in February 1993, the new Premier of Taiwan confirmed the continuation of the 'One China' policy.

In 1993 divisions between Taiwan's business sector and political groupings (the former advocating much closer links with the People's Republic, the latter urging greater caution) became evident. In January, and again later in the year, the Secretary-General of the SEF resigned, following disagreement with the Mainland Affairs Council. Historic talks between the Chairmen of the SEF and of the ARATS were held in Singapore in April. Engaging in the highest level of contact since 1949, Taiwan and the People's Republic agreed on the establishment of a formal structure for future negotiations on economic and social issues.

In August 1993 the People's Republic issued a document entitled *The Taiwan Question and the Reunification of China*, reiterating its claim to sovereignty over the island. Relations were further strained by a series of aircraft hijackings to Taiwan from the mainland. A SEF-ARATS meeting, held in Taiwan in December, attempted to address the issue of the repatriation of hijackers. Incidents of air piracy continued in 1994, substantial prison sentences being imposed on the hijackers by the Taiwanese authorities.

Further meetings between delegates of the SEF and ARATS were held in early 1994. Relations between Taiwan and the mainland deteriorated sharply in April, however, when 24 Taiwanese tourists were among those robbed and killed on board a pleasure boat plying Qiandao Lake, in the People's Republic. Taiwan suspended all commercial and cultural exchanges with the People's Republic. In June three men were convicted of the murders and promptly executed. In February 1995 compensation totalling 1.2m. yuan was awarded to the victims' families by the People's Republic.

In July 1994 the Taiwanese Government released a White Paper on mainland affairs, urging that the division be acknowledged and the island accepted as a separate political entity. In August the SEF-ARATS talks were resumed when Tang Shubei, Vice-Chairman and Secretary-General of the ARATS, flew to Taipei for discussions with his Taiwanese counterpart, Chiao Jen-ho. Tang thus became the most senior Communist Chinese official ever to visit the island. Although the visit was marred by opposition protesters, the two sides reached tentative agreement on several issues, including the repatriation of hijackers and illegal immigrants from Taiwan to the mainland. Procedures for the settlement of cross-Straits fishing disputes were also established. In mid-November relations were strained once again when, in an apparent accident during a training exercise, Taiwanese anti-aircraft shells landed on a mainland village, injuring several people. Nevertheless, in late November a further round of SEF-ARATS talks took place in Nanjing, at which agreement in principle on the procedure for the repatriation of hijackers and illegal immigrants was confirmed. Further progress was made at meetings in Beijing in January 1995, although no accord was signed. It was announced in March that the functions of the SEF were to be enhanced. To improve co-ordination, the SEF board of directors would henceforth include government officials, while meetings of the Mainland Affairs Council would be attended by officials of the SEF. In the same month the Mainland Affairs Council approved a resolution providing for the relaxation of restrictions on visits by mainland officials and civilians.

President Jiang Zemin's Lunar New Year address, incorporating the mainland's 'eight-point' policy on Taiwan, was regarded as more conciliatory than hitherto. In April 1995, in response, President Lee proposed a 'six-point' programme for cross-Straits relations: unification according to the reality of separate rules; increased exchanges on the basis of Chinese culture; increased economic and trade relations; admission to international organizations on an equal footing; the renunciation of the use of force against each other; and joint participation in Hong Kong and Macau affairs. In late April, however, the eighth round of working-level SEF-ARATS discussions was postponed, owing to disagreement over the agenda.

In May 1995 the SEF Chairman, Koo Chen-fu, and his mainland counterpart, Wang Daohan, formally agreed to meet in Beijing in July. In June, however, this proposed second session of senior-level negotiations was postponed by the ARATS, in protest at President Lee's recent visit to the USA. Tension between the two sides increased in July, when the People's Republic unexpectedly announced that it was about to conduct an eight-day programme of guided missile and artillery-firing tests off the northern coast of Taiwan. A second series of exercises took place in August, again arousing much anxiety on the island. In mid-August President Jiang Zemin confirmed that the People's Republic would not renounce the use of force against Taiwan. Nevertheless, at the end of that month President Lee reaffirmed the KMT's commitment to reunification. In October President Jiang Zemin's offer to visit Taiwan in person was cautiously received on the island. President Lee confirmed his Government's anti-independence stance in November.

In January 1996 the Taiwanese Premier again urged the early resumption of cross-Straits dialogue. In February there were unconfirmed reports of the extensive mobilization of mainland troops. In the same month, upon his appointment as Chairman of the Mainland Affairs Council, Chang King-yuh pledged to attempt to improve relations with the mainland. In March the People's Republic began a new series of missile tests, including the firing of surface-to-surface missiles into coastal areas around Taiwan. Live artillery exercises continued in the Taiwan Strait until after the island's presidential election, arousing international concern. The USA deployed two naval task forces in the area (see below).

In April 1996, as tension eased, the Mainland Affairs Council removed the ban on visits to Taiwan by officials of the People's Republic. The Ministry of Transportation and Communications announced that mainland container traffic was to be permitted direct entry to Taiwanese ports. At the end of April the SEF, which had lodged a strong protest with the ARATS during the missile tests of March, urged the resumption of bilateral discussions. In July President Lee re-affirmed his commitment to peaceful reunification. In the same month a number of business delegations from the mainland made visits to Taiwan.

In November 1996 the Mainland Affairs Council announced that the permanent stationing of mainland media representatives in Taiwan was to be permitted. President Lee's renewed offer to travel to the People's Republic was rejected and, despite repeated SEF requests, Tang Shubei of the ARATS continued to assert that Taiwan's pursuit of its 'two Chinas' policy (a reference to President Lee's attempts to raise the diplomatic profile of the island) prevented the resumption of cross-Straits discussions. In January 1997, however, as the reversion of the entrepôt of Hong Kong to Chinese sovereignty approached, shipping representatives of Taiwan and of the People's Republic reached a preliminary consensus on the establishment of direct sea links. Limited services resumed in April, thus ending a ban of 48 years. In March 1998 it was reported that Taiwan had agreed to allow a mainland Chinese shipping company to operate a direct shipping link between Shanghai and the northern Taiwanese port of Keelung.

In July 1997, upon the reversion to Chinese sovereignty of the British colony of Hong Kong, President Lee firmly rejected the concept of 'one country, two systems' and any parallel with Taiwan, and strenuously refuted a suggestion by President Jiang Zemin that Taiwan would eventually follow the example of Hong Kong. In September the Taiwanese Minister of Finance and the Governor of the central bank were obliged to cancel a visit to Hong Kong, where they had planned to have informal discussions with delegates to the forthcoming IMF/World Bank meeting, owing to Hong Kong's failure to issue them with visas.

The affair compounded fears that Taiwan's business dealings with Hong Kong might be jeopardized.

A call for the opening of political negotiations, made by the Minister of Foreign Affairs of the People's Republic in September 1997, was welcomed by the Mainland Affairs Council. However, the Taiwanese authorities continued to insist that Beijing remove all preconditions before the opening of dialogue. In November the Secretary-General of the SEF was invited by the ARATS to attend a seminar on the mainland in the following month. The SEF proposed instead that its Chairman head a delegation to the People's Republic.

The declaration by an ARATS official in January 1998 that Taiwan did not need to recognize the Government of the People's Republic as the central Government as a precondition for dialogue was regarded as a significant concession on the part of the mainland authorities. However, Taiwan continued to insist that China abandon its demand that talks be conducted under its 'One China' principle. In February the ARATS sent a letter to the SEF requesting the resumption of political and economic dialogue between the two sides, and inviting a senior SEF official to visit the mainland. The SEF responded positively to the invitation in March, and proposed that a delegation be sent to the People's Republic to discuss procedural details, prior to a visit to the mainland by the SEF Chairman.

In April 1998 a delegation of the SEF visited the People's Republic. Following negotiations with the ARATS, it was announced that the Chairman of the SEF would visit the People's Republic later in 1998 formally to resume the dialogue, which had been suspended since 1995. The arrest on the mainland in May 1998 of four Taiwanese business executives on charges of espionage, and their subsequent conviction, and the visit to Malaysia by the Taiwanese Premier, in April, threatened to reverse the recent improvement in relations. However, in July the Chinese Minister of Science and Technology visited Taiwan, the first such visit by a mainland Minister since the civil war. This was followed later in the month by a formal visit to Taiwan by the Deputy Secretary-General of the ARATS. The kidnap and murder in August in the People's Republic of a Taiwanese local government official caused serious concern for the Taiwanese authorities. In October Koo Chen-fu, the SEF Chairman, duly travelled to the People's Republic, where he held several meetings with his ARATS counterpart, Wang Daohan, and met with President Jiang Zemin (the highest level of bilateral contact since 1949) and had discussions with other senior officials. A four-point agreement was reached, allowing for increased communications between the two sides, but little was achieved in terms of a substantive breakthrough. However, the talks were considered to mark an important improvement in cross-Straits relations, and Wang Daohan accepted an invitation to visit Taiwan in March 1999.

In January 1999 the ARATS invited the SEF Deputy Secretary-General to visit the People's Republic for talks in order to prepare for Wang Daohan's visit. The SEF made a counter-proposal that ARATS officials visit Taiwan to discuss preparations. In March the Government announced that it was to establish a supra-ministerial task force to examine the suitability of trips by certain former government officials to the People's Republic of China, owing to security concerns. In the same month an ARATS delegation visited Taiwan. In April President Lee reaffirmed that Beijing should recognize Taiwan as being of equal status, that cross-Straits negotiations should concentrate on practical issues and that reunification could take place only if the mainland were to become a democracy. An SEF group went to Beijing in March, and preliminary agreement was reached that the ARATS Chairman would visit Taiwan in either mid-September or mid-October. In August, however, the ARATS suspended contacts with the SEF, following President Lee's insistence on the 'two-state theory' (see below), and it was confirmed in October that Wang Daohan would not visit Taiwan while the island continued to adhere to the theory.

Meanwhile, China was becoming increasingly demonstrative in its opposition to Taiwan's inclusion in the US-led Theater Missile Defence (TMD) anti-missile system. Ballistic missiles were deployed in mainland coastal regions facing Taiwan, and fears were heightened within the international community in July 1999, when the People's Republic announced that it had developed a neutron bomb, after declaring itself ready for war should Taiwan attempt to gain independence. This declaration was prompted by a radio interview given by President Lee, during which he asserted that relations with the People's Republic were 'state-to-state'. Chinese military exercises took

place in the Taiwan Strait later that month, allegedly to intimidate Taiwan. Faced with this aggression and a lack of US support, Taiwan promised that it would not amend its Constitution to enshrine its claim to statehood in law. In August the USA reaffirmed its readiness to defend Taiwan against Chinese military action. Shortly afterwards the Taiwanese Government refused a request by Beijing that it retract the 'state-to-state' theory with regard to cross-Straits relations, and tension increased in late August when the KMT incorporated the 'two-state theory' into the party resolution, claiming that this would henceforth become the administrative guideline and priority of the Taiwanese authorities. Later that month the Mainland Affairs Council announced that former Taiwan government officials involved in affairs related to national intelligence or secrets were not to be permitted to travel to China within three years of leaving their posts. In September, following a severe earthquake in Taiwan that killed or injured several thousand people, China was among the many countries to offer emergency assistance to the island. Taiwan, however, accused the People's Republic of contravening humanitarian principles by trying to force other countries to seek its approval before offering help. Relations became increasingly strained following the reversion of Macau to Chinese sovereignty in December 1999. The People's Republic announced that reunification of the two sides of the Taiwan Strait would also be on the basis of 'one country, two systems'. Taiwan, however, insisted that its stance on the issue remained unchanged, and that the system was inapplicable in this case. By early 2000 it was clear that reunification was a mainland priority, by military means if necessary.

In February 2000 the People's Republic threatened to attack Taiwan if it indefinitely postponed reunification talks. The approval in the Legislative Yuan in March of a law providing for the first direct transport links between Taiwan's outlying islands and mainland China for 50 years did not substantially improve matters, and in April the Vice President-elect, Annette Lu, was denounced by the Chinese media after she made 'separatist' remarks, televised in Hong Kong, declaring that Taiwan was only a 'remote relative and close neighbour' of China. A Taiwanese opposition group subsequently endorsed a motion to dismiss Lu for putting the island at risk by provoking China. In an attempt to improve relations with the People's Republic, President Chen offered to compromise and to reopen negotiations on the basis that each side was free to interpret the 'one China' formula as it saw fit. Chinese Premier Zhu Rongji rejected the suggestion, and questioned Taiwan's motives, effectively dispelling all hopes of restarting negotiations in the near future. In July 2000 the Chinese authorities responded angrily when the United Kingdom issued a visa to former President Lee Teng-hui, who continued to be perceived as a dissident by the People's Republic. Despite the fact that Lee's visa was for the purpose of a private visit by an individual, and specified as a condition that no public statements would be made during the trip, China took action against British governmental and trade interests to register its displeasure.

In October 2000 Beijing published a policy document on its national defence, which confirmed that the People's Republic would use force to prevent Taiwanese secession, to stop occupation of the island, and also in the event of Taiwan indefinitely postponing reunification with the mainland. In November, however, there were signs of an improvement in relations when Wu Po-hsiung, the Vice-Chairman of the KMT, travelled to Beijing and met unofficially with Chinese Vice-Premier Qian Qichen. Wu was the most senior KMT official to visit mainland China for more than 50 years, and it was thought that Beijing was attempting to isolate Chen Shui-bian by consorting with his political rivals. During the meeting both sides agreed to hold important academic forums to discuss cross-Straits relations and to attempt to devise common positions. Qian stressed, however, the importance of Taiwan's recognition of the 'One China' principle before official negotiations could resume.

Also in November 2000, Taiwan announced that journalists from the People's Republic were to be granted permission to stay in Taiwan for periods of up to one month, during which time they would be invited to attend any press conferences called by the President's office and the Executive Yuan, in order to enhance cross-Straits exchanges and understanding. In the following month plans were announced for 'mini three links' with China, providing for direct trade, transport and postal links between Kinmen and Matsu islands and the mainland. The Taiwanese Government stressed, however, that any future direct links with Taiwan itself would be subject to rigorous security checks. In early January 2001 groups sailed from Kinmen and Matsu to Xiamen and Fuzhou, respectively, in the People's Republic. Beijing's response toward the initiative was guarded.

In December 1972, meanwhile, legislative elections were held, for the first time in 24 years, to fill 53 seats in the National Assembly. The new members, elected for a fixed term of six years, joined 1,376 surviving 'life-term' members of the Assembly. President Chiang Kai-shek remained in office until his death in April 1975. He was succeeded as leader of the ruling KMT by his son, Gen. Chiang Ching-kuo, who had hitherto been Premier. Dr Yen Chia-kan, Vice-President since 1966, became the new President. In 1978 President Yen retired and was succeeded by Gen. Chiang. At elections for 71 seats in the Legislative Yuan in December 1983, the KMT won an overwhelming victory, confirming its dominance over the independent 'Tangwai' (non-party) candidates. In March 1984 President Chiang was re-elected for a second six-year term, and Lee Teng-hui, a former Mayor of Taipei and a native Taiwanese, became Vice-President. President Chiang died in January 1988 and was succeeded by Lee Teng-hui.

In September 1986 135 leading opposition politicians formed the Democratic Progressive Party (DPP), in defiance of the KMT's ban on the formation of new political parties. Partial elections to the National Assembly and the Legislative Yuan were held in December. The KMT achieved a decisive victory, but the DPP received about one-quarter of the total votes, and more than doubled the non-KMT representation. In February 1987 the KMT began to implement a programme of political reform. Martial law (in force since 1949) was replaced by the National Security Law in July and, under the terms of the new legislation, political parties other than the KMT were permitted, and civilians were removed from the jurisdiction of military courts. In April seven major posts in a reorganization of the Executive Yuan were allocated to reformist members of the KMT. In November 1987 the second annual Congress of the DPP approved a resolution declaring that Taiwanese citizens had the right to advocate independence. In January 1988, however, two opposition activists were imprisoned, on charges of sedition, for voicing such demands.

In February 1988 a plan to restructure the legislative bodies was approved by the Central Standing Committee of the KMT. Voluntary resignations were to be sought from 'life-term' members of the Legislative Yuan and National Assembly, and seats were no longer to be reserved for representatives of mainland constituencies. The 13th national Congress of the KMT was held in July. Following a decision to hold free elections for two-thirds of the members of the KMT's Central Committee, numerous new members were elected, and the proportion of native Taiwanese increased sharply. In January 1989 three legislative measures were enacted: a revision of regulations concerning the registration of political parties; a retirement plan for those members of the three legislative assemblies who had been elected by mainland constituencies in 1947; and a new law aiming to give greater autonomy to the Taiwan Provincial Government and its assembly, and in the following month the KMT became the first political party to register under the new legislation. Despite objections to the new laws, regarding the size of the retirement pensions being offered and the terms of the Civic Organizations Law (under which political parties were obliged to reject communism and any notion of official political independence for Taiwan), the DPP applied for official registration in April.

Partial elections to the Legislative Yuan and the Taiwan Provincial Assembly were held on 2 December 1989. A total of 101 seats in the Legislative Yuan were contested, with the KMT obtaining 72 seats and the DPP winning 21, thus securing the prerogative to propose legislation in the Legislative Yuan. In February 1990 the opening of the National Assembly's 35-day plenary session, convened every six years to elect the country's President, was disrupted by DPP members' violent action in a protest against the continuing domination of the Assembly by elderly KMT politicians, who had been elected on the Chinese mainland prior to 1949 and who had never been obliged to seek re-election. Many injuries resulted from clashes between riot police and demonstrators. In March 1990 DPP members were barred from the National Assembly for refusing to swear allegiance to 'The Republic of China', attempting instead to substitute 'Taiwan' upon taking the oath. Various amendments to the Temporary Provisions, which for more than 40 years had permitted the effective suspension of the Constitution, were approved

by the National Assembly in mid-March. Revisions included measures to strengthen the position of the mainland-elected KMT members, who were granted new powers to initiate and veto legislation, and also an amendment to permit the National Assembly to meet annually. The revisions were opposed not only by the DPP but also by more moderate members of the KMT, and led to a large protest rally in Taipei, demanding the abolition of the National Assembly and the holding of direct presidential elections. Nevertheless, President Lee was duly re-elected, unopposed, by the National Assembly for a six-year term, two rival KMT candidates having withdrawn from the contest.

The National Affairs Conference (NAC) convened in June 1990 to discuss proposals for reform. A Constitutional Reform Planning Group was subsequently established. The NAC reached consensus on the issue of direct presidential elections, which would permit the citizens of Taiwan, rather than the members of the National Assembly, to select the Head of State. Meanwhile, the Council of Grand Justices had ruled that elderly members of the National Assembly and of the Legislative Yuan should step down by the end of 1991.

In October 1990 the National Unification Council, chaired by President Lee, was formed. In the same month the Mainland Affairs Council, comprising heads of government departments and led by the Vice-Premier of the Executive Yuan, was founded. In December President Lee announced that Taiwan would formally end the state of war with the mainland; the declaration of emergency was to be rescinded by May 1991. Plans were announced for gradual constitutional reform, to be implemented in 1991–93. Meanwhile, in early December 1990 Huang Hwa, the leader of a faction of the DPP and independence activist, had received a 10-year prison sentence upon being found guilty of 'preparing to commit sedition'.

In April 1991 the National Assembly was convened, the session again being marred by violent clashes between KMT and DPP members. The DPP subsequently boycotted the session, arguing that a completely new constitution should be introduced and that elderly KMT delegates, who did not represent Taiwan constituencies, should not have the right to make amendments to the existing Constitution. Some 20,000 demonstrators attended a DPP-organized protest march. Nevertheless, the National Assembly duly approved the constitutional amendments, and at midnight on 30 April the 'period of mobilization for the suppression of the Communist rebellion' and the Temporary Provisions were formally terminated. The existence, but not the legitimacy, of the Government of the People's Republic was officially acknowledged by President Lee. Furthermore, Taiwan remained committed to its 'one China' policy. In May 1991 widespread protests following the arrest of four advocates of independence for Taiwan led to the abolition of the Statute of Punishment for Sedition. The law had been adopted in 1949 and had been frequently employed by the KMT to suppress political dissent.

A senior UN official visited the island in August 1991, the first trip by such a representative since Taiwan's withdrawal from the organization in 1971. Large-scale rallies calling for a referendum to be held on the issue of Taiwan's readmission to the UN as an independent state, resulting in clashes between demonstrators and the security forces, took place in September and October.

In August 1991 the opposition DPP officially announced its alternative draft constitution for 'Taiwan', rather than for 'the Republic of China', thus acknowledging the *de facto* position regarding sovereignty. In September, after being reinstated in the Legislative Yuan, Huang Hsin-chieh, the Chairman of the DPP, relinquished his seat in the legislature and urged other senior deputies to do likewise. Huang had been deprived of his seat and imprisoned in 1980, following his conviction on charges of sedition. At the party congress in October 1991, Huang was replaced as DPP Chairman by Hsu Hsin-liang. Risking prosecution by the authorities, the DPP congress adopted a resolution henceforth to advocate the establishment of 'the Republic of Taiwan', and urged the Government to declare the island's independence.

Elections to the new 405-member National Assembly, which was to be responsible for amending the Constitution, were held in December 1991. The 225 seats open to direct election were widely contested. The campaign was dominated by the issue of Taiwan's possible independence. The opposition's independence proposal was overwhelmingly rejected by the electorate, the DPP suffering a humiliating defeat. The KMT secured a total of 318 seats (179 of which were won by direct election), while the DPP won 75 seats (41 by direct election). All elderly mainland-elected delegates were obliged to relinquish their seats. In February 1992 20,000 demonstrators protested against the sedition laws and demanded a referendum on the issue of independence.

In March 1992, at a plenary session of the KMT Central Committee, it was agreed to reduce the President's term of office from six to four years. The principal question of arrangements for future presidential elections, however, remained unresolved. In April street demonstrations were organized by the DPP to support demands for direct presidential elections. In May the National Assembly adopted eight amendments to the Constitution, one of which empowered the President to appoint members of the Control Yuan.

Meanwhile, the radical dissident, (Stella) Chen Wan-chen, who had established the pro-independence Organization for Taiwan Nation-Building upon her return from the USA in 1991, was sentenced to 46 months' imprisonment in March 1992, having been found guilty of 'preparing to commit sedition'. In May, however, Taiwan's severe sedition law was amended, non-violent acts ceasing to be a criminal offence. Several independence activists were released from prison and other dissidents were able to return from overseas exile. Nevertheless, in June (George) Chang Tsang-hung, the chairman of the banned, US-based World United Formosans for Independence (WUFI), who had returned from exile in the USA in December 1991, received a prison sentence of five (commuted from 10) years upon conviction on charges of sedition and attempted murder, involving the dispatch of letter-bombs to government officials in 1976. Chang was released for medical treatment in October 1992. In March 1993 he was acquitted of the sedition charges, on the grounds of insufficient evidence.

Taiwan's first full elections since the establishment of Nationalist rule in 1949 were held in December 1992. The KMT retained 102 of the 161 seats in the Legislative Yuan. The DPP, however, garnered 31% of the votes and more than doubled its representation in the legislature, winning 50 seats. Following this set-back, the Premier and the KMT Secretary-General resigned. In February 1993 Lien Chan, hitherto Governor of Taiwan Province, became the island's first Premier of Taiwanese descent.

In May 1993 about 30 conservative rebels resigned from the KMT, and formed the New Alliance Nationalist Party. Furthermore, in June the Government was defeated in the Legislative Yuan, when a group of KMT deputies voted with the opposition to approve legislation on financial disclosure requirements for elected and appointed public officials. The unity of the KMT was further undermined in August, when six dissident legislators belonging to the New Kuomintang Alliance, which had registered as a political group in March, announced their decision to leave the ruling party in order to establish the New Party. Nevertheless, in August 1993, at the 14th KMT Congress, Lee Teng-hui was re-elected Chairman of the party. A new 31-member Central Standing Committee and 210-member Central Committee, comprising mainly Lee's supporters, were selected. In a conciliatory gesture by the KMT Chairman, four vice-chairmanships were created, the new positions being filled by representatives of different factions of the party.

In September 1993, following a series of bribery scandals, the Executive Yuan approved measures to combat corruption. The administrative reform plan included stricter supervision of public officials and harsher penalties for those found guilty of misconduct. In the same month a KMT member of the Legislative Yuan was sentenced to 14 years' imprisonment for bribery of voters during the 1992 election campaign; similar convictions followed. At local government elections held in November 1993, although its share of the votes declined, the KMT secured 15 of the 23 posts at stake. The DPP, which accused the KMT of malpractice, won only six posts, despite receiving a substantial proportion of the votes; it retained control of Taipei County. Following allegations of extensive bribery at further local polls in early 1994 (at which the DPP and independent candidates made strong gains), the Ministry of Justice intensified its campaign against corruption. Proposals for constitutional amendments to permit the direct election in 1996 of the Taiwanese President by popular vote (rather than by electoral college) and to limit the powers of the Premier were approved by the National Assembly in July 1994.

At gubernatorial and mayoral elections in December 1994 the DPP took control of the Taipei mayoralty, in the first such direct

polls for 30 years, while the KMT succeeded in retaining the provincial governorship of Taiwan, in the first ever popular election for the post, and the mayoralty of Kaohsiung. The New Party established itself as a major political force, its candidate for the mayoralty of Taipei receiving more votes than the KMT incumbent.

In March 1995, following the President's formal apology at a ceremony of commemoration in February, the Legislative Yuan approved a law granting compensation to the relatives of the victims of a massacre by Nationalist troops in 1947 (the 'February 28 Incident'), in which an estimated 18,000 native Taiwanese had been killed.

Elections to the Legislative Yuan were held on 2 December 1995. A major campaign issue was that of corruption, allegations of malpractice and indictments and having reached alarming levels. The KMT's strength declined to 84 of the 164 seats, faring particularly badly in Taipei. The DPP increased its representation to 53 seats. The New Party, which favoured reconciliation with the mainland, secured 21 seats. The first direct presidential election was scheduled for March 1996, to coincide with the National Assembly polls. President Lee had declared his intention to stand for re-election in August 1995. There were a number of other candidates for the presidency. The campaign was dominated by the issue of reunification with the mainland. In mid-March a DPP demonstration on the streets of Taipei, in support of demands for Taiwan's independence, was attended by 50,000 protesters. At the presidential election, held on 23 March 1996, the incumbent President Lee received 54.0% of the votes cast, thus securing his re-election for a four-year term. At the concurrent elections for the National Assembly, the KMT took 183 of the 334 seats. The DPP won 99 seats and the New Party 46 seats. The Chairman of the DPP, Shih Ming-teh, resigned and Hsu Hsin-liang, who had resigned in November 1993, subsequently returned to the post.

In June 1996 the President's announcement of the composition of the new Executive Yuan aroused much controversy. Although several members retained their previous portfolios, the President (apparently under pressure from within the KMT and disregarding public concern at the rising levels of corruption and organized crime) demoted the popular Ministers of Justice, and of Transportation and Communications, who had exposed malpractice and initiated campaigns against corruption. Other changes included the replacement of the Minister of Foreign Affairs by John Chang, the grandson of Chiang Kai-shek. The most controversial nomination, however, was the reappointment as Premier of Lien Chan, despite his recent election as the island's Vice-President. As fears of a constitutional crisis grew, opposition members of the Legislative Yuan, along with a number of KMT delegates, demanded that the President submit the membership of the Executive Yuan to the legislature for approval, and threatened to boycott the chamber.

In December 1996 the multi-party National Development Conference (NDC), established to review the island's political system, held its inaugural meeting. The convention approved KMT proposals to abolish the Legislative Yuan's right to confirm the President's choice of Premier, to permit the legislature to introduce motions of no confidence in the Premier and to empower the President to dismiss the legislature. The Provincial Governor, (James) Soong Chu-yu, subsequently tendered his resignation in protest at the NDC's recommendations that elections for the provincial governorship and assembly be abolished, as the first stage of the dissolution of the provincial apparatus. The Provincial Government was responsible for the entire island, with the exception of the cities of Taipei and Kaohsiung. In January 1997 President Lee refused to accept the Governor's resignation, but the affair drew attention to the uneasy relationship between the island's President and its Governor, and brought to the fore the question of reunification with the mainland. In July the National Assembly approved a series of constitutional reforms, implementing the NDC's recommendations.

In early May 1997 more than 50,000 demonstrators, protesting against the problem of increasing crime (particularly crimes of violence), demanded the resignation of President Lee. Three members of the Executive Yuan subsequently resigned. The appointment of Yeh Chin-feng as Minister of the Interior (the first woman to oversee Taiwan's police force) did little to appease the public, which remained highly suspicious of the alleged connections between senior politicians and the perpetrators of organized crime. In mid-May thousands of protesters, despairing of the rapid deterioration in social order, again took to the streets of Taipei, renewing their challenge to President

Lee's leadership and demanding the immediate resignation of Premier Lien Chan. In late June a 'Say No to China' rally attracted as many as 70,000 supporters.

In August 1997 Vincent Siew, former Chairman of the Council for Economic Planning and Development and also of the Mainland Affairs Council, replaced Lien Chan as Premier (Lien Chan retained the post of Vice-President), and John Chang was appointed Vice-Premier. In the same month President Lee was re-elected unopposed as Chairman of the ruling KMT. The KMT experienced a serious set-back in elections at mayoral and magistrate levels, held in November 1997. The DPP, which had campaigned on a platform of more open government, won 12 of the 23 constituency posts contested, while the KMT achieved only eight posts. Consequently, more than 70% of Taiwan's population was to come under DPP administration. Following the KMT's poor performance in the ballot, the Secretary-General of the party resigned, and was replaced by John Chang. A major reorganization of the party followed.

At local elections, held in January 1998, the KMT won an overwhelming majority of the seats contested, while the DPP, in a reversal of fortune, performed badly. In April the Minister of Justice tendered, and then subsequently withdrew, his resignation, claiming that lawmakers with connections to organized crime were exerting pressure on the Government to dismiss him. However, in July he was forced to resign, following his mishandling of an alleged scandal concerning the acting head of the Investigation Bureau.

In June 1998 the first-ever direct election for the leadership of the DPP was held. Lin Yi-hsiung won a convincing victory, assuming the chairmanship of the party in August. Meanwhile, in local elections in June, the KMT suffered a set-back, winning fewer than 50% of the seats contested. Independent candidates performed well. In August 17 new members were elected to the KMT Central Standing Committee, the 16 others being appointed by President Lee.

Elections to the newly-expanded 225-member Legislative Yuan took place on 5 December 1998. The KMT won 46.4% of the votes cast, securing 125 seats, the DPP received 29.6% of the votes and won 72 seats, while the pro-unification New Party secured only 7.1% of the votes and 11 seats. The New Nation Alliance, a breakaway group from the DPP (formed in September), won only one seat (with 1.6% of the votes cast). The KMT's victory was widely attributed to its management of the economy, in view of the Asian financial crisis, the developments in cross-Straits dialogue and a decline in factionalism within the party in 1998. In the election (held simultaneously) to select the mayor of Taipei, the KMT candidate, Ma Ying-jeou, a popular former Minister of Justice, defeated the DPP incumbent, Chen Shui-bian. However, Frank Hsieh, the DPP candidate, won the office of mayor of Kaohsiung. The KMT retained control of both city councils.

Chiou I-jen resigned as Secretary-General of the DPP in December 1998 and was replaced by You Hsi-kun. Later that month Chao Shu-po, a Minister without Portfolio, was appointed Governor of Taiwan Province, replacing the elected incumbent, James Soong, as part of the plans to dismantle the provincial government, agreed in 1997. In March 1999 an unprecedented vote of 'no confidence' in the leadership of Premier Vincent Siew was defeated in the Legislative Yuan. The motion was presented by the opposition following Siew's reversal of his earlier position and his decision to reduce the tax on share transactions, apparently as a result of pressure from President Lee. The National Assembly passed a controversial constitutional amendment on 4 September, which, *inter alia*, extended the terms of the deputies from May 2000 to June 2002. Election to the Assembly was henceforth to be on the basis of party proportional representation. Several politicians and critical citizens condemned the move as being 'against the public will'. Shortly afterwards, the KMT leadership expelled the Speaker of the National Assembly, Su Nan-cheng, from the party on the grounds that he had violated its policy on the tenure extension, thereby also removing him from his parliamentary seat and the post of Speaker. There was widespread dissatisfaction regarding the National Assembly's action, and in March 2000 the Council of Grand Justices of the Judicial Yuan ruled it to be unconstitutional. Later that month the DPP and the KMT reached an agreement on the abolition of the body and the cancellation of elections scheduled for early May. In April the National Assembly convened, and approved a series of constitutional amendments, which effectively deprived the body of most of its powers, and reduced it to an *ad hoc* institution. The powers to initiate

constitutional amendments, to impeach the President or Vice-President and to approve the appointment of senior officials were transferred to the Legislative Yuan. The National Assembly was to retain the functions of ratifying constitutional amendments and impeachment proceedings, in which case 300 delegates, appointed by political parties according to a system of proportional representation, would convene for a session of a maximum duration of one month.

Meanwhile, in September 1999, following the earthquake (see above), the Legislative Yuan approved an emergency decree, which was to remain in effect for six months, permitting the use of police and troops to maintain order in stricken areas, the punishment of those engaging in 'black market' activities and the raising of relief bonds.

In November 1999 it was announced that a presidential election was to be held in March 2000. Five candidates registered: Lien Chan (with Vincent Siew as candidate for Vice-President) was the KMT nominee, while Chen Shui-bian, a former mayor of Taipei, was to stand for the DPP (with the feminist Annette Lu as vice-presidential candidate), and Li Ao was to represent the New Party; the former DPP Chairman, Hsu Hsin-liang, qualified as an independent candidate, as did James Soong, who was consequently expelled from the KMT, along with a number of his supporters. It became evident in December 1999, when Soong was publicly accused of embezzlement, that the election would be bitterly contested. Although Soong denied the charges, his popularity was affected. In January 2000 Lien Chan, in an attempt to regain the support of disillusioned voters, proposed that the KMT's extensive business holdings be placed in trust and that the party terminate its direct role in the management of the numerous companies in which it owned shares. The KMT adopted the proposal shortly afterwards. In a reflection of the tense political situation between Taiwan and China, Chen Shui-bian of the DPP modified the party's stance and pledged not to declare formal independence for the island unless Beijing attacked.

The presidential election, held on 18 March 2000, was won by Chen Shui-bian, who obtained 39.3% of the votes cast. James Soong, his closest rival, received 36.8% of the votes. (On the day after the election he founded the People First Party, in an attempt to take advantage of his popularity.) Lien Chan of the KMT secured only 23.1% of the votes. The remaining candidates obtained less than 1%. The poll attracted a high level of participation, 82.7% of the electorate taking part. (Upon his inauguration in May, Chen would thus become Taiwan's first non-KMT President since 1945.) Violence erupted as disappointed KMT supporters besieged the party's headquarters, attributing the KMT's defeat to the leadership's expulsion of James Soong and the resultant division of the party. Lee Teng-hui subsequently accepted responsibility for the defeat and resigned from the chairmanship of the Party. Lien Chan assumed the leadership. As the KMT continued to dominate the Legislative Yuan, however, the party did not entirely relinquish its influence, and in early April gave permission for Tang Fei, a KMT member and hitherto Minister of National Defense, to serve as Premier, although he was to be suspended from party activities while in the post. Following protracted negotiations, the membership of the new Executive Yuan, which incorporated 11 DPP members and 13 KMT members, was approved in early May. The incoming Government largely lacked ministerial experience. Furthermore, the DPP's lack of a legislative majority impeded the passage of favourable legislation. The size of the budget deficit also made it difficult for the DPP to fulfil specific electoral pledges on health, housing and education. In July Frank Hsieh replaced Lin Yi-hsiung as Chairman of the DPP.

In July 2000 the Government was heavily criticized after a river accident in which four workers, stranded by a flash flood, drowned as a result of the authorities' failure to provide a rescue helicopter. While the various government departments deliberated over the allocation of responsibility, the victims' final hours were broadcast live on national television. The Vice-Premier and Chairman of the Consumer Protection Commission, You Hsi-kun, subsequently resigned, as did senior officials of the emergency services. The Premier's offer of resignation was refused by President Chen Shui-bian. In October 2000, however, Tang Fei resigned as Premier, ostensibly owing to ill-health. It was suggested his departure from the post was due to the Government's failure to agree upon the fate of Taiwan's fourth nuclear power plant, the DPP being opposed to the project. Vice-Premier Chang Chun-hsiung was appointed Premier, and a minor cabinet reorganization was effected. Changes included the appointment of Yen Ching-chang as Minister of Finance, his predecessor having resigned following a sharp decline in the stock market.

Political disputes over the construction of Taiwan's fourth nuclear power plant intensified later in October 2000. The Minister of Economic Affairs, Lin Hsin-yi, was expelled from the KMT for 'seriously opposing KMT policies and impairing the people's interests' after he had demonstrated his support for the cancellation of the project. At the end of the month Chang Chun-hsiung announced that the Executive Yuan had decided to halt construction of the plant for financial and economic reasons. Although environmentalists were pleased, citing Taiwan's inability to process nuclear waste and to cope with accidents, the KMT reacted furiously, rejecting the Government's right to cancel a project approved by the legislature, and, together with the New Party and the People First Party, immediately began collecting legislators' signatures for the recall (dismissal) of Chen Shui-bian. The opposition was not mollified by a subsequent apology from Chen, and shortly afterwards the Legislative Yuan passed revised legislation on the process for presidential impeachment. Owing to the controversy, KMT member Vincent Siew refused to act as the President's representative to the annual APEC forum in Brunei in November and was replaced by Perng Fai-nan, the Governor of the Central Bank. The dispute became so serious that the business community issued an unprecedented public message that economic recovery should take priority over political differences, but in December some 10,000 protesters in Taipei demanded that Chen resign. In November the Government requested a constitutional interpretation on the issue from the Council of Grand Justices, which it agreed to be bound by. The Council ruled in mid-January 2001 that the Government should have sought the legislature's approval before halting construction of the plant, and in mid-February 2001 the Government decided immediately to resume construction of the plant. In March 2001 a minor government reorganization was effected. The most notable change was the appointment of Hu Ching-piao, hitherto a Minister without Portfolio, as Chairman of the Atomic Energy Council, replacing Hsia Der-yu. It was rumoured that Hsia had disagreed with Chang Chun-hsiung over the future of the nuclear plant.

Meanwhile, in September 2000 four retired naval officers and one still serving were arrested in connection with the suspected murder in 1993 of a naval captain to prevent him from revealing a scandal surrounding Taiwan's 1991 purchase of French-built frigates. It was alleged that bribery had influenced the award of the contract, which had been abruptly withdrawn from a South Korean firm. In October the Control Yuan impeached three former naval admirals, including the former Commander-in-Chief of the Navy Adm. (retd) Yeh Chang-tung, for their involvement in the affair. In December the Taiwanese authorities appealed to the French Government for information to assist their investigations.

In foreign relations, meanwhile, in January 1979 Taiwan suffered a serious set-back when the USA established full diplomatic relations with the People's Republic of China and severed relations with Taiwan. The USA also terminated the 1954 mutual security treaty with Taiwan. Commercial links are still maintained, however, and Taiwan's purchase of armaments from the USA has remained a controversial issue. In August 1982 a joint Sino-US communiqué was published, in which the USA pledged to reduce gradually its sale of armaments to Taiwan. In September 1992 President Bush announced the sale of up to 150 F-16 fighter aircraft to Taiwan. The announcement was condemned by the People's Republic. In December the US trade representative became the first senior US government official to visit the island since 1979. In September 1994 the USA announced a modification of its policy towards Taiwan, henceforth permitting senior-level bilateral meetings to be held in US government offices. In December the US Secretary of Transportation visited the Ministry of Foreign Affairs in Taipei, the first US official of cabinet rank to visit Taiwan for more than 15 years. In June 1995 President Lee was permitted to make a four-day unofficial visit to the USA, where he gave a speech at Cornell University, and met members of the US Congress. This visit provoked outrage in Beijing, and the Chinese ambassador to Washington was recalled. During 1996 the Taiwanese Vice-President was granted transit visas permitting him to disembark in the USA on a number of occasions.

In March 1996, as the mainland began a new series of missile tests off the Taiwanese coast (see above), the USA stationed two naval convoys in waters east of the island, representing the largest US deployment in Asia since 1975. The sale of defensive weapons to Taiwan was agreed. In September 1996 President Lee and the US Deputy Treasury Secretary met in Taipei for discussions, the most senior-level contact between the two sides since 1994. In late 1996, however, Taiwanese donors were implicated in reported irregularities in the financing of President Clinton's re-election campaign, and in a large illicit contribution to the US Democratic Party. In early 1997 the first of the Patriot anti-missile air defence systems, purchased from the USA under an arrangement made in 1993, were reported to have been deployed on the island. The first of the F-16s were delivered to Taiwan in April 1997. The Taiwanese Government expressed satisfaction at the USA's continued commitment to Taiwan's security, confirmed following the visit to the USA of the President of the People's Republic, Jiang Zemin, in October and again in June 1998, during President Clinton's visit to the People's Republic. However, a statement by Clinton affirming that the USA would not support Taiwan's membership of the UN was sharply criticized in Taiwan. In late October 1998 the Taiwanese Chief of Staff, Gen. Tang Fei, made a secret two-week visit to the USA. This was regarded as an extremely sensitive matter, in light of the fact that Koo Chen-fu had recently met with Jiang Zemin. In the following month the People's Republic complained to the USA following the US Energy Secretary's visit to Taiwan.

In January 1999 the People's Republic was angered by Taiwan's proposed inclusion in the US-led TMD system (see above). Tensions continued throughout the year, and in August the USA reaffirmed its commitment to defend Taiwan against Chinese military action. In the following month, however, the USA again refused to support Taiwan's application for UN membership. In October of that year the island welcomed the adoption, albeit in modified form, of the Taiwan Security Enhancement Act (TSEA), establishing direct military ties, by the International Relations Committee of the US House of Representatives, despite opposition from the Clinton administration. Reaction from the People's Republic was unfavourable, and its displeasure increased in early February 2000 when the House of Representatives overwhelmingly approved the Act. In April of that year the US Senate postponed consideration of the Act at the behest of the Taiwanese President-elect, Chen Shui-bian, in order not to antagonize Beijing during the sensitive period preceding his inauguration. In the same month the US Government announced that it had decided to defer the sale of four naval destroyers to Taiwan, although it was prepared to supply long-range radar and medium-range air-to-air missiles. In September the USA granted a transit visa to Taiwanese Vice-President Annette Lu to stay in New York *en route* to Central America. Lu subsequently declared that the stopover had marked a breakthrough in talks between the USA and Taiwan. In October China was angered by a resolution passed by the US Congress supporting Taiwan's participation in the UN and other international organizations.

In January 1993 the official confirmation of Taiwan's purchase of 60 fighter aircraft from France again provoked strong protest from Beijing. In January 1994 Taiwan suffered a reverse when (following pressure from the People's Republic) France recognized Taiwan as an integral part of Chinese territory, and the French Prime Minister agreed not to sell weapons to the island. In March 1995, however, it was reported that Taiwan was to purchase anti-aircraft missiles from a French company. The sale of these missiles, as well as the delivery of the aircraft and six frigates, was confirmed in 1996. Deliveries commenced in 1997.

Taiwan severed diplomatic relations with Japan in 1972, following Tokyo's *rapprochement* with Beijing. Mainland displeasure was compounded in February 1993, however, when, for the first time in two decades, the Taiwanese Minister of Foreign Affairs paid a visit to Japan. In September 1994 pressure from Beijing resulted in the withdrawal of President Lee's invitation to attend the forthcoming Asian Games in Hiroshima. Instead, however, the Taiwanese Vice-Premier was permitted to visit Japan. Similarly, in July 1995 Japan announced that the Taiwanese Vice-Premier would not be permitted to attend a meeting of APEC members to be held in Osaka in November. Instead, President Lee was represented by Koo Chen-fu, the SEF Chairman. The latter also attended the APEC meeting in the Philippines in November 1996. At the Kuala Lumpur APEC summit in November 1998 President Lee was represented by a Minister without Portfolio, Chiang Pin-kung, who also attended the 1999 APEC conference, held in September in Auckland, New Zealand. Perng Fai-nan, the Governor of the Central Bank, represented President Chen Shui-bian at the APEC meeting in Brunei in November 2000. In 1996 Taiwan's relations with Japan continued to be strained by the issue of adequate compensation for the thousands of Asian (mostly Korean) women used by Japanese troops for sexual purposes during the Second World War. In October Taiwan rejected a Japanese offer of nominal compensation for Taiwanese women. Relations deteriorated further in 1996 on account of a dispute relating to a group of uninhabited islets in the East China Sea: known as the Tiaoyutai (Diaoyu Dao) in Chinese, or Senkaku in Japanese, the islands were claimed by Taiwan, China and Japan. In July, following the construction of a lighthouse on one of the islands by a Japanese right-wing group, the Taiwanese Ministry of Foreign Affairs lodged a strong protest over Japan's decision to incorporate the islands within its 200-mile (370-km) exclusive economic zone. In early October further discussions with Japan on the question of Taiwanese fishing rights within the disputed waters ended without agreement. In the same month a flotilla of small boats, operated by activists from Taiwan, Hong Kong and Macau, succeeded in evading Japanese patrol vessels. Having reached the disputed islands, protesters raised the flags of Taiwan and of China. In May 1997 the Taiwanese Minister of Foreign Affairs expressed grave concern, following the landing and planting of their national flag on one of the disputed islands by a Japanese politician. A number of protesters and journalists from Taiwan and Hong Kong set sail from the port of Shenao, ostensibly to participate in an international fishing contest. They were intercepted by Japanese coastguard vessels and failed to gain access to the islands. Reports in October that Japanese patrol boats were forcibly intercepting Taiwanese fishing vessels were a further cause for concern for the Taiwanese authorities. There was a significant development in relations between the two countries in November 1999, when the Governor of Tokyo paid an official visit to Taiwan, the most senior Japanese official to do so since the severing of diplomatic relations. The People's Republic condemned the visit, claiming that it undermined Sino-Japanese relations.

In March 1989, meanwhile, President Lee paid a state visit to Singapore, the first official visit overseas by a President of Taiwan for 12 years. In February 1994 President Lee embarked upon an eight-day tour of South-East Asia. Although the tour was described as informal, President Lee had meetings with the Heads of State of the Philippines, Indonesia and Thailand, leading to protests from Beijing. In May the Taiwanese President visited Central American and Southern African states. In 1995 President Lee made a number of what were described as private visits (Taiwan having no diplomatic relations with the countries visited). The visits provoked strong protest from China. In August 1996 Beijing continued to urge Pretoria to sever its diplomatic links with Taipei. In September the Taiwanese Minister of Foreign Affairs was obliged to curtail an ostensibly private visit to Jakarta, following protests from the People's Republic of China. In January 1997 the Vice-President was received by the Pope during a visit to the Holy See, the only European state that continued to recognize Taiwan. In the same month the Minister of Foreign Affairs embarked upon a tour of seven African nations, in order to consolidate relations. His itinerary included South Africa, despite that country's recent announcement of its intention to sever diplomatic relations with Taiwan (a major set-back to the island's campaign to gain wider international recognition). In March a visit to Taiwan by the Dalai Lama, during which he met with President Lee, was strongly condemned by the People's Republic of China. A second visit by the Dalai Lama, scheduled for July 1998, was indefinitely postponed, following mainland China's criticism of the opening of a representative office of the Dalai Lama's religious foundation in Taiwan.

In July 1997 the Taiwanese Minister of Foreign Affairs undertook an extensive tour of the countries of Central America and the Caribbean, in an effort to maintain their support. In September, during a tour of Central America, President Lee attended an international conference on the development of the Panama Canal. The USA granted a transit visa to the Taiwanese President. A visit to Europe in October by Vice-President Lien Chan was curtailed when pressure from Beijing forced the Spanish Government to withdraw an invitation. The Malaysian and Singaporean Prime Ministers met their Taiwanese counterpart in Taiwan in November, on their return from the APEC

forum in Canada. The People's Republic expressed concern at the meetings.

In January 1998 the Taiwanese Premier, Vincent Siew, met senior officials during a visit to the Philippines and Singapore. It was believed that discussions had focused on the possibility of Taiwan extending economic assistance to those countries. Moreover, the Taiwanese Government expressed its intention to pursue the creation of a multilateral Asian fund, under the auspices of APEC, to support the ailing Asian economies. Relations with Taiwan's Asian neighbours were further strengthened in February, when a leading member of the KMT visited the Republic of Korea, again, it was understood, to discuss financial assistance in the wake of the Asian economic crisis. Negotiations between the Malaysian Deputy Prime Minister and Finance Minster and the Taiwanese Premier, held in Taiwan in February, also concentrated on economic and financial issues. Vincent Siew made a return visit to Malaysia in April. China was highly critical of these visits, accusing Taiwan of seeking to gain political advantage from the regional economic crisis. In August 1999 the Taiwanese Government threatened to refuse entry to the island to Philippine labourers in retaliation for Manila's unilateral termination of its aviation agreement with Taipei. In October the Philippine authorities decided to close the country to Taiwanese aircraft. Access was, however, temporarily granted in November during talks on the renewal of the agreement. Negotiations faltered in December, but reached a successful conclusion in early 2000, thus permitting flights to the Philippines to resume. In March, however, the agreement collapsed, and flights were suspended again. In June the Taiwanese Government imposed a three-month ban on new work permits for Philippine nationals, citing interference by the Philippines' representative office in Taiwan concerning labour disputes. Any connection with the aviation dispute was denied. In September a new aviation agreement, enabling flights between Manila and Taipei to restart, was signed.

Taiwanese officials made extensive efforts to maintain relations with Taiwan's diplomatic allies in Africa and Central America in 1998. The Minister of Foreign Affairs visited eight African countries in February, and in April it was announced that Taiwan's overseas aid budget was to be substantially increased in an attempt to retain diplomatic support. In May the Vice-President, Lien Chan, visited Taiwan's Central American and Caribbean allies. China expressed serious concern in November at New Zealand's decision to grant Taiwanese officials in Wellington privileges accorded to accredited diplomats. In January 1999 diplomatic relations were established with the former Yugoslav republic of Macedonia, which received substantial financial aid from Taiwan throughout the year. In December Taiwan denied offering financial inducements to Albania in return for recognition.

Amid allegations of 'cash diplomacy', the Prime Minister of Papua New Guinea initiated diplomatic relations with Taiwan in July 1999. Following his resignation later that month, recognition was withdrawn from Taiwan, allegedly because of a failure to adhere to correct procedures for the establishment of relations. Full diplomatic relations were established with Palau in December of that year, and Taiwan opened an embassy in the capital of the Pacific nation in March 2000. In August 2000 the new Taiwanese President, Chen Shui-bian, embarked upon a tour of diplomatic allies in Central America and West Africa. In October Taiwan was concerned that it might lose a diplomatic ally when the Minister of Foreign Affairs of Solomon Islands unexpectedly cancelled a visit to Taipei and travelled instead to Beijing. The Premier of Solomon Islands did not attend a regional forum, instead visiting Taipei to make amends and to reiterate his commitment to maintaining relations. There was speculation that this commitment arose from a need for substantial financial assistance from Taiwan.

In November 2000, after eight years' suspension, the 25th Joint Conference of Korea-Taiwan Business Councils took place in Seoul. It was agreed that henceforth conferences would be held annually alternately in Taipei and Seoul, and Taiwan ultimately hoped for a resumption of ministerial-level discussions on the establishment of bilateral air links. In the same month the European Parliament passed a resolution on strengthening relations with Taiwan, and in December Taiwan and Egypt agreed to exchange representative offices. Also in December, France refused to grant a visa to the Taiwanese Minister of Justice.

The question of the sovereignty of the Spratly Islands, situated in the South China Sea and believed to possess petroleum resources, to which Taiwan and five other countries laid claim, remained unresolved in 2000. In December 1998 the Legislative Yuan approved the first legal definition of Taiwan's sea borders, with 21- and 24-nautical mile zones. The Spratly islands were included within Taiwan's borders. A contingent of Taiwanese marines is maintained on Taiping Island, the largest of the disputed islands, located some 1,574 km south-west of Taiwan. A satellite telecommunications link between Taiping and Kaohsiung was inaugurated in October 1995.

Government

Under the provisions of the amended 1947 Constitution, the Head of State is the President, who is elected by popular vote for a four-year term. There are five Yuans (governing bodies), the highest legislative organ being the Legislative Yuan, to which the Executive Yuan (the Council of Ministers) is responsible. Following elections in December 1998, the Legislative Yuan comprised 225 members; 176 chosen by direct election, most of the remainder being appointed from separate lists of candidates on the basis of proportional representation. The Legislative Yuan serves a three-year term. There are also Control, Judicial and Examination Yuans. Their respective functions are: to investigate the work of the executive; to interpret the Constitution and national laws; and to supervise examinations for entry into public offices. In April 2000 the role of the National Assembly was revised. The powers to initiate constitutional amendments, to impeach the President or Vice-President, and to approve the appointment of senior officials were transferred to the Legislative Yuan. The National Assembly retained the functions of ratifying constitutional amendments and responsibility for impeachment proceedings, in which case 300 delegates appointed by political parties according to a system of proportional representation were to convene for a session of a maximum duration of one month. The Taiwan Provincial Government handles the general administrative affairs of the island (excluding the cities of Taipei and Kaohsiung). Its policy-making body is the Taiwan Provincial Government Council. In July 1997 the National Assembly approved a series of constitutional amendments, including the suspension of elections at local government level, as the first stage of the dissolution of the provincial apparatus. Accordingly, the elected Governor of Taiwan was replaced by an appointed Governor in December 1998. The Taiwan Provincial Assembly exercises the province's legislative power. The Fukien (Fujian) Provincial Government is responsible for the administration of Quemoy and Matsu.

Defence

In August 2000 the armed forces totalled an estimated 370,000: army 240,000 (with deployments of 35,000–40,000 and 8,000–10,000, respectively, on the islands of Quemoy and Matsu), air force 68,000 and navy 62,000 (including 30,000 marines). Paramilitary forces numbered 26,650. Reserves totalled 1,657,500. Military service lasts for two years. Projected budgetary defence expenditure for 1999/2000 was estimated at NT $353,770m. (equivalent to 15.8% of total projected expenditure).

Economic Affairs

In 1998 Taiwan's gross national product (GNP), at current prices, totalled US $269,176m., having increased, in real terms, by 4.3% compared with 1997. GNP per head reached US $12,360 in 1998. In 1990–99 the population increased at an average annual rate of 0.9%. Between 1990 and 1999 real gross domestic product (GDP) expanded at an average annual rate of 6.5%. In 1999 GDP increased by 5.7%, in real terms, to total US $287,881m. GDP growth was estimated at 6.3% in 2000.

Agriculture (including hunting, forestry and fishing) contributed 2.5% of GDP, and employed 8.3% of the working population, in 1999. The principal crops are rice, sugar cane, maize, sweet potatoes and pineapples. Agricultural GDP decreased at an average annual rate of 0.4%, in real terms, during 1990–99. Compared with the previous year, agricultural GDP increased by 1.8% in 1999.

Industry (comprising mining, manufacturing, construction and utilities) employed 37.2% of the working population, and provided 31.9% of GDP, in 1999. Industrial GDP increased, in real terms, at an average rate of 5.1% per year between 1990 and 1999. Compared with the previous year, industrial GDP rose by 4.7% in 1999.

Mining contributed 0.5% of GDP, and employed 0.1% of the working population, in 1999. Coal, marble and dolomite are the principal minerals extracted. Taiwan also has substantial reserves of natural gas. The GDP of the mining sector increased at an average rate of 0.2% per year between 1990 and 1999. Mining GDP decreased by 4.3% in 1999, compared with 1998.

Manufacturing contributed 25.5% of GDP, and employed 27.7% of the working population, in 1999. The most important branches, measured by gross value of output, are electronics (particularly personal computers), plastic goods, synthetic yarns and the motor vehicle industry. The sector's GDP grew at an average annual rate of 5.1%, in real terms, in 1990–99. Growth in manufacturing GDP in 1999 was 6.4%, compared with the previous year.

In 1999 51.5% of Taiwan's energy supply was derived from imported petroleum. Imports of crude petroleum accounted for 4.1% of total import expenditure in 1999. In that year nuclear power supplied 9.7% of Taiwan's energy requirements.

The services sector contributed 65.7% of GDP in 1999, while engaging 54.5% of the employed labour force. In 1990–99 the GDP of this sector increased at an average annual rate of 7.8%. In 1999 services GDP increased by 6.4%, compared with the previous year.

In 1999 Taiwan recorded a visible trade surplus of US $15,042m., and there was a surplus of US $8,384m. on the current account of the balance of payments. In 1999 the principal sources of imports were Japan (accounting for 27.6%) and the USA (17.8%). The principal markets for exports in that year were the USA (25.4%), Hong Kong (21.4%) and Japan (9.8%). Trade with the People's Republic of China (mainly via Hong Kong) is of increasing significance. Taiwan's principal imports in 1999 were machinery and transport equipment, manufactured goods and chemical and related products. The principal exports in that year were valves and tubes, textiles and toys.

In the 18 months ending 31 December 2000 (from 2001 the financial year was to correspond to the calendar year) there was a projected budgetary deficit of NT $249,124m. The 2001 budget proposals envisaged revenue of NT $1,458,500m. and expenditure of NT $1,608,200m. (excluding special procurements). At mid-2000 Taiwan's external public debt was US $36.0m. In the second quarter of that year the cost of debt-servicing was equivalent to 0.01% of the value of exports of goods and services. The annual rate of inflation averaged 2.7% during the period 1990–99. Consumer prices rose by 0.2% in 1999 and by an estimated 1.3% in 2000. Some 3.2% of the labour force were unemployed in October 2000. There is a shortage of labour in certain sectors.

Taiwan became a member of the Asian Development Bank (ADB, see p. 131) in 1966, and of the Asia-Pacific Economic Co-operation forum (APEC, see p. 128) in late 1991. In September 1992 Taiwan was granted observer status at the General Agreement on Tariffs and Trade (GATT), and in early 2001 continued to await approval of its application for full membership of the successor World Trade Organization (WTO, see p. 292).

Taiwan's economic growth since 1949 has been substantial, with its economy proving to be very resilient to world recession, owing to the versatility of its manufacturing base and its large reserves of foreign exchange (estimated at US $106,700m. at the end of 2000). A privatization programme, introduced in 1989, was accelerated from the late 1990s in support of Taiwan's application to join the WTO. In 2000 the reconstruction work that followed the earthquake of September 1999 and the concomitant rapid recovery led to strong economic growth. During 2000, however, investigations into corruption in the financial sector damaged investor confidence. Between May 2000 and January 2001 the stock market lost about 40% of its value. The tense political situation that arose from the Government's decision to halt construction of a fourth nuclear power plant in October 2000 (see Recent History) did not improve matters. Construction of the plant was to resume in February 2001, partly as a concession to encourage economic development. Exports increased strongly in 2000, growth being assisted by the depreciation of the currency. In 2001, however, the economic deceleration in the USA (Taiwan's major export market) was expected adversely to affect the island's economic growth. Furthermore, global demand for high-technology and electronic products was declining, and Taiwanese businesses faced increasing competition from other Asian nations. Lower production costs and easier access to capital prompted many companies to relocate their operations to South-East Asia or mainland China. In the short term, it was anticipated that Taiwan's accession to the WTO (which was expected to take place in 2001) would have a negative impact on the island's economy, as domestic markets would henceforth be subjected to an influx of cheap foreign imports. In late 2000 the Government announced an extensive employment-creation programme, in an attempt to minimize the negative effects of industrial reorganization In February 2001, in response to the changing global situation and in an effort to improve domestic investment conditions, the Premier announced an eight-point programme of measures to stimulate the Taiwanese economy. Proposals included improvements in the island's electricity and water supplies and a relaxation of restrictions on the employment of foreign professional workers, while domestic demand for mainland Chinese technicians and engineers was to be evaluated.

Social Welfare

At the end of 1999 the Labour Insurance programme covered around 7,740,000 workers, providing benefits for injury, disability, birth, death and old age. At the same time, 623,016 government employees and their dependants were covered by a separate scheme. In 1978 a system of supplementary benefits for those with low incomes was introduced. An unemployment insurance scheme began in July 1994. A universal health insurance scheme took effect in March 1995. In 1999 Taiwan had a total of 17,770 medical institutions, hospitals and clinics, with a total of 122,937 beds. There were 28,216 physicians, 3,546 doctors of traditional Chinese medicine, 75,603 nurses and 8,240 dentists working in the country. Of total projected government budgetary expenditure in 1999/2000, 16.4% (NT $366,965m.) was allocated to social welfare.

Education

Education at primary schools and junior high schools is free and compulsory between the ages of six and 15 years. Secondary schools consist of junior and senior middle schools, normal schools for teacher-training and vocational schools. There are also a number of private schools. Higher education is provided in universities, colleges, junior colleges and graduate schools. Total projected budgetary expenditure on education, science and culture in 1999/2000 was estimated at NT $360,369m. (equivalent to 16.1% of total projected expenditure). In that year there were over 1.9m. pupils enrolled in state primary schools. There were almost 1.8m. children in secondary schools. There were 141 universities and other institutes of higher education. The adult literacy rate in 1999 was 95.3%.

Public Holidays

2001: 1–2 January (Founding of the Republic/New Year), 24–26 January (Chinese New Year), 5 April (Ching Ming/Tomb-Sweeping Day and Death of President Chiang Kai-shek), 25 June (Dragon Boat Festival), 28 September (Teachers' Day/Birthday of Confucius), 1 October (Mid-Autumn Moon Festival), 10 October (Double Tenth Day, anniversary of 1911 revolution), 25 October (Retrocession Day, anniversary of end of Japanese occupation), 12 November (Birthday of Sun Yat-sen), 25 December (Constitution Day).

2002 (provisional): 1–2 January (Founding of the Republic/New Year), 12–15 February (Chinese New Year), 5 April (Ching Ming/Tomb-Sweeping Day and Death of President Chiang Kai-shek), May/June (Dragon Boat Festival), September/October (Mid-Autumn Moon Festival), 28 September (Teachers' Day/Birthday of Confucius), 10 October (Double Tenth Day, anniversary of 1911 revolution), 25 October (Retrocession Day, anniversary of end of Japanese occupation), 12 November (Birthday of Sun Yat-sen), 25 December (Constitution Day).

Weights and Measures

The metric system is officially in force, but some traditional Chinese units are still used.

Statistical Survey

Source (unless otherwise stated): Bureau of Statistics, Directorate-General of Budget, Accounting and Statistics (DGBAS), Executive Yuan, 2 Kwang Chow St, Taipei 10729; tel. (2) 23710208; fax (2) 23319925; e-mail edp@emc.dgbasey.gov.tw; internet www.dgbasey.gov.tw.

Area and Population

AREA, POPULATION AND DENSITY

Area (sq km)	36,006*
Population (census results)	
28 December 1980	17,968,797
16 December 1990	
Males	10,533,921
Females	9,751,705
Total	20,285,626
Population (official figures at 31 December)	
1997	21,683,316
1998	21,870,876
1999	22,034,096
Density (per sq km) at 31 December 1999 . . .	612.0

* 13,902 sq miles.

PRINCIPAL TOWNS
(population at 31 December 1999)

Taipei (capital).	.	2,641,312	Hsinchu	. . .	361,958
Kaohsiung.	. .	1,475,505	Chungli	. . .	318,649
Taichung	. .	940,589	Fengshan	. . .	318,562
Tainan	. .	728,060	Taoyuan	. . .	316,438
Panchiao	. .	523,850	Chiayi.	. . .	265,109
Chungho	. .	392,176	Hsintien	. . .	263,603
Keelung	. .	385,201	Changhwa	. . .	227,715
Shanchung	. .	380,084	Yungho	. . .	227,700
Hsinchuang	. .	365,048	Pingtung	. . .	214,727

BIRTHS, MARRIAGES AND DEATHS (registered)

	Live births		Marriages		Deaths	
	Number	Rate (per 1,000)	Number	Rate (per 1,000)	Number	Rate (per 1,000)
1992 . .	320,963	15.54	169,234	8.19	110,140	5.33
1993 . .	324,944	15.59	157,539	7.56	110,563	5.30
1994 . .	322,263	15.32	170,580	8.11	113,486	5.40
1995 . .	328,904	15.50	159,943	7.54	118,737	5.60
1996 . .	324,874	15.19	169,106	7.91	122,152	5.71
1997 . .	325,263	15.07	165,842	7.69	120,610	5.59
1998 . .	270,779	12.43	145,678	6.69	122,806	5.64
1999 . .	282,936	12.89	172,786	7.87	125,704	5.73

Expectation of life (years at birth, 1998): Males 72.26; Females 78.04.

ECONOMICALLY ACTIVE POPULATION
(annual averages, '000 persons aged 15 years and over*)

	1997	1998	1999
Agriculture, forestry and fishing .	878	822	776
Mining and quarrying . .	13	12	11
Manufacturing	2,570	2,611	2,603
Construction.	885	865	843
Electricity, gas and water. . .	35	35	35
Commerce	1,995	2,047	2,130
Transport, storage and communications . . .	465	477	476
Finance, insurance and real estate	351	385	406
Business services . . .	240	260	284
Social, personal and related community services . . .	1,421	1,461	1,502
Public administration . . .	323	315	318
Total employed	9,176	9,289	9,385
Unemployed	256	257	283
Total labour force . . .	9,432	9,546	9,668
Males	5,731	5,780	5,812
Females	3,701	3,767	3,856

* Excluding members of the armed forces and persons in institutional households.

Agriculture

PRINCIPAL CROPS ('000 metric tons)

	1997	1998	1999
Potatoes.	52.5	39.2	36.1
Rice*	1,662.7	1,489.4	1,558.6
Sweet potatoes	207.8	187.2	218.6
Asparagus	7.3	6.3	7.5
Soybeans	4.7	1.5	0.4
Sorghum	57.2	43.8	33.6
Maize	337.6	243.6	201.2
Tea	23.5	22.6	21.1
Tobacco	10.3	10.0	9.3
Groundnuts	84.2	68.3	67.2
Sugar cane	4,112.4	3,559.8	3,255.8
Bananas	204.7	215.6	212.5
Pineapples	300.7	316.1	348.5
Citrus fruit	494.7	481.7	486.5
Vegetables	3,003.8	2,892.5	3,470.3
Mushrooms	12.2	9.6	8.0

* Figures are in terms of brown rice. The equivalent in paddy rice (in '000 metric tons) was: 2,041.8 in 1997; 1,859.2 in 1998; 1,916.3 in 1999.

LIVESTOCK ('000 head at 31 December)

	1996	1997	1998
Cattle	151.9	156.8	156.8
Buffaloes	11.2	9.6	8.6
Pigs.	10,698.4	7,966.9	6,538.6
Sheep and goats . . .	309.1	315.2	273.4
Chickens	110,535	117,565	120,510
Ducks	12,977	11,863	11,513
Geese	3,021	3,180	3,225
Turkeys	180	211	229

LIVESTOCK PRODUCTS

	1997	1998	1999
Beef (metric tons) . . .	5,898	5,288	5,168
Pig meat (metric tons) . .	1,248,300	1,080,940	996,780
Goat meat (metric tons) . .	9,882	8,871	8,916
Chickens ('000 head)* . .	389,966	389,524	385,563
Ducks ('000 head)* . . .	41,156	35,719	35,208
Geese ('000 head)* . . .	7,503	7,955	7,464
Turkeys ('000 head)* . .	429	432	488
Milk (metric tons) . . .	330,469	338,368	338,005
Duck eggs ('000)	531,669	520,188	485,629
Hen eggs ('000)	7,104,433	7,157,707	7,274,451

* Figures refer to numbers slaughtered.

Forestry

ROUNDWOOD REMOVALS ('000 cubic metres)

	1997	1998	1999
Industrial wood	32.8	29.2	23.3
Fuel wood	4.7	5.0	4.3
Total	37.5	34.2	27.6

Fishing*

('000 metric tons, live weight)

	1996	1997	1998
Tilapias	44.9	42.3	36.3
Other freshwater fishes . .	26.1	25.4	22.8
Japanese eel. . . .	25.1	22.3	17.2
Milkfish	58.5	62.7	58.3
Pacific saury	8.2	21.9	12.8
Skipjack tuna	173.5	119.8	197.3
Albacore	55.4	55.2	59.9
Yellowfin tuna	78.6	101.4	122.5
Bigeye tuna	55.3	74.2	76.3
Chub mackerel	53.9	47.3	35.5
Sharks, rays, skates, etc. .	41.2	40.1	40.0
Other fishes (incl. unspecified) .	304.0	307.8	301.6
Total fish	924.7	920.4	980.5
Marine shrimps and prawns .	57.8	47.1	37.0
Other crustaceans . . .	8.1	6.5	6.6
Pacific cupped oyster . . .	28.1	24.1	19.4
Common squids . . .	24.7	28.4	26.9
Argentine shortfin squid . .	138.9	213.2	202.9
Flying squids	7.2	8.6	7.2
Other molluscs . . .	1.3	0.8	1.0
Other aquatic animals . .	38.6	46.5	49.8
Total catch	1,229.4	1,295.6	1,331.3

* Figures include products of fish-farming.

Mining

(metric tons, unless otherwise indicated)

	1997	1998	1999
Coal	98,203	79,310	91,673
Crude petroleum ('000 litres)	50,669	53,978	47,106
Natural gas ('000 cu m) . .	849,287	870,294	848,353
Salt	62,484	7,425	76,916
Sulphur	163,964	184,324	194,812
Marble	18,071,024	17,519,017	n.a.
Dolomite	197,716	180,635	200,595

Industry

SELECTED PRODUCTS
('000 metric tons, unless otherwise indicated)

	1997	1998	1999
Wheat flour	761.6	745.9	738.2
Granulated sugar . . .	355.1	286.5	286.0
Carbonated beverages ('000 litres)	477,450	511,572	461,032
Alcoholic beverages—excl. beer			
('000 hectolitres) . .	2,377.2	2,204.7	2,482.0
Cigarettes (million) . . .	27,102	24,961	22,735
Cotton yarn	365.1	363.9	353.6
Man-made fibres	3,036.8	3,181.4	3,227.9
Paper	1,180	1,175	1,246
Paperboard	3,254	2,975	3,074
Sulphuric acid	917.6	885.7	848.2
Spun yarn	533.5	502.9	485.9
Cement	21,522.4	19,651.5	18,283.2
Steel ingots	15,824.2	17,192.2	16,026.7
Sewing machines ('000 units) .	3,449	3,290	2,778
Electric fans ('000 units) . .	21,325	20,347	23,800
Personal computers ('000 units)	9,898	11,708	12,959
Monitors ('000 units) . . .	20,461	16,406	10,942
Radio cassette recorders ('000			
units)	6,044	5,361	4,621
Radio receivers ('000 units) .	2,434	2,837	2,157
Television receivers ('000 units)	1,021	988	1,022
Picture tubes ('000 units) . .	15,372	15,217	23,344
Integrated circuits (million units) .	3,949	3,071	2,718
Electronic condensers (million			
units)	5,667	6,421	7,191
Telephone sets ('000 units) .	8,584	7,737	6,629
Passenger motor cars (units) .	369,795	397,188	341,133
Trucks and buses (units) . .	5,843	5,154	4,227
Bicycles ('000 units) . . .	7,672	9,043	7,228
Ships ('000 dwt)* . . .	742	852	270
Electric energy (million kWh) .	143,661	155,450	160,570
Liquefied petroleum gas . .	727.2	733.6	746.3

* Excluding motor yachts.

Finance

CURRENCY AND EXCHANGE RATES

Monetary Units
100 cents = 1 New Taiwan dollar (NT $).

Sterling, US Dollar and Euro Equivalents (29 December 2000)
£1 sterling = NT $49.23;
US $1 = NT $32.99;
€1 = NT $30.70;
NT $1,000 = £20.31 = US $30.31 = €32.57.

Average Exchange Rate (NT $ per US $)
1998   33.456
1999   32.270
2000   31.235

BUDGET
(central government accounts, NT $ million, year ending 30 June)

Revenue	1997/98	1998/99	1999/2000*
Taxes	858,799	772,881	1,300,177
Monopoly profits	37,341	35,959	86,313
Non-tax revenue from other sources	355,384	419,808	599,155
Total	1,251,524	1,228,649	1,985,645

Expenditure	1997/98	1998/99	1999/2000*
General administration . .	112,717	134,569	243,424
National defence . . .	257,125	263,166	353,770
Education, science and culture .	184,816	202,669	360,369
Economic development . .	126,478	172,552	348,083
Social welfare . . .	150,152	157,588	366,965
Community development and environmental protection . .	15,758	19,260	37,877
Pensions and survivors' benefits .	139,832	129,272	213,856
Obligations	167,417	198,269	259,409
Subsidies to provincial and municipal governments . .	29,663	1,773	25,980
Other expenditure . . .	3,052	2,879	25,037
Total	1,187,011	1,281,996	2,234,769

* Projections for 18 months ending 31 December 2000. From 2001 the financial year will correspond to the calendar year.

INTERNATIONAL RESERVES (US $ million at 31 December)

	1997	1998	1999
Gold*	4,684	4,743	4,861
Foreign exchange . . .	83,502	90,341	106,200
Total	88,186	95,084	111,061

* National valuation.

MONEY SUPPLY (NT $ million at 31 December)

	1997	1998	1999
Currency outside banks . . .	510,364	513,745	611,167
Demand deposits at deposit money banks	3,204,888	3,341,039	3,896,013
Total money	3,715,252	3,854,784	4,507,180

COST OF LIVING
(Consumer Price Index; base: 1996 = 100)

	1997	1998	1999
Food	99.10	103.49	102.97
Clothing	100.73	95.59	94.28
Housing	101.15	102.44	102.54
Transport and communications .	102.21	100.10	99.33
Medicines and medical care .	102.36	103.32	106.91
Education and entertainment . .	103.36	106.51	108.60
All items (incl. others) . .	100.90	102.60	102.78

NATIONAL ACCOUNTS (NT $ million in current prices)
National Income and Product

	1997	1998	1999
Compensation of employees . .	4,149,844	4,501,506	4,687,235
Operating surplus . . .	2,755,161	2,967,013	3,106,004
Domestic factor incomes .	6,905,005	7,468,519	7,793,239
Consumption of fixed capital .	703,404	748,699	804,144
Gross domestic product (GDP) at factor cost . . .	7,608,409	8,217,218	8,597,383
Indirect taxes . . .	746,017	766,430	726,810
Less Subsidies	25,646	44,681	34,264
GDP in purchasers' values .	8,328,780	8,938,967	9,289,929
Factor income from abroad . .	198,537	216,501	224,468
Less Factor income paid abroad .	109,925	148,843	138,556
Gross national product (GNP) .	8,417,392	9,006,625	9,375,841
Less Consumption of fixed capital .	703,404	748,699	804,144
National income in market prices	7,713,988	8,257,926	8,571,697
Other current transfers from abroad	83,571	98,398	100,750
Less Other current transfers paid abroad	146,145	149,600	171,150
National disposable income .	7,651,414	8,206,724	8,501,297

Expenditure on the Gross Domestic Product

	1997	1998	1999
Government final consumption expenditure	1,197,631	1,279,698	1,221,717
Private final consumption expenditure	4,936,084	5,334,143	5,641,313
Increase in stocks . . .	121,089	122,572	130,621
Gross fixed capital formation .	1,895,357	2,103,919	2,124,744
Total domestic expenditure .	8,150,161	8,840,332	9,118,395
Exports of goods and services .	4,019,880	4,274,219	4,402,101
Less Imports of goods and services	3,841,261	4,175,584	4,230,567
GDP in purchasers' values	8,328,780	8,938,967	9,289,929
GDP at constant 1991 prices .	8,190,783	8,565,134	9,029,704

Gross Domestic Product by Economic Activity

	1997	1998	1999
Agriculture, hunting, forestry and fishing	212,100	220,605	237,531
Mining and quarrying . .	38,631	46,777	46,391
Manufacturing	2,315,420	2,448,395	2,470,012
Construction	391,785	389,255	358,300
Electricity, gas and water .	195,779	205,575	207,749
Transport, storage and communications . . .	530,916	588,555	625,637
Trade, restaurants and hotels . .	1,434,915	1,588,691	1,717,692
Finance, insurance and real estate*	1,711,972	1,819,990	1,890,388
Business services . . .	189,279	212,428	237,144
Community, social and personal services	676,642	761,170	835,631
Government services . . .	848,859	895,887	946,549
Other services . . .	82,945	101,908	96,514
Sub-total	8,629,243	9,279,236	9,669,538
Value-added tax	164,897	170,554	173,642
Import duties	158,030	153,416	139,348
Less Imputed bank service charge .	623,390	664,239	692,599
GDP in purchasers' values .	8,328,780	8,938,967	9,289,929

* Including imputed rents of owner-occupied dwellings.

BALANCE OF PAYMENTS (US $ million)

	1997	1998	1999
Exports of goods f.o.b. . .	121,725	110,178	121,119
Imports of goods f.o.b. . . .	−107,843	−99,862	−106,077
Trade balance	13,882	10,316	15,042
Exports of services . . .	17,144	16,768	17,259
Imports of services . . .	−24,888	−24,169	−24,405
Balance on goods and services	6,138	2,915	7,896
Other income received . .	6,919	6,481	6,965
Other income paid . . .	−3,797	−4,432	−4,294
Balance on goods, services and income	9,260	4,964	10,567
Current transfers received .	2,898	2,943	3,126
Current transfers paid . .	−5,107	−4,470	−5,309
Current balance . . .	7,051	3,437	8,384
Capital account (net) . .	−314	−181	−173
Direct investment abroad .	−5,243	−3,836	−4,420
Direct investment from abroad .	2,248	222	2,926
Portfolio investment assets .	−6,749	−4,220	−4,835
Portfolio investment liabilities .	−1,204	1,808	13,914
Other investment assets . .	−1,291	3,494	2,334
Other investment liabilities .	4,948	5,027	−699
Net errors and omissions . .	−174	−924	1,162
Overall balance . . .	−728	4,827	18,593

External Trade

PRINCIPAL COMMODITIES (US $ million)

Imports c.i.f.	1997	1998	1999
Vegetable products	2,823.0	2,142.4	2,022.4
Prepared foodstuffs; beverages, spirits and vinegar; tobacco and manufactured substitutes	2,398.8	1,988.3	2,048.2
Mineral products	10,304.1	7,809.6	9,145.6
Products of chemical or allied industries	11,440.0	9,950.0	10,596.4
Plastics, rubber and articles thereof	3,081.3	2,724.6	3,006.5
Paper-making material; paper and paperboard and articles thereof	2,081.1	1,806.8	1,895.7
Textiles and textile articles	3,654.5	3,163.6	2,873.8
Base metals and articles thereof	11,674.3	9,502.0	9,511.2
Machinery and mechanical appliances; electrical equipment; sound and television apparatus	41,115.6	42,925.8	50,598.4
Vehicles, aircraft, vessels and associated transport equipment	5,360.6	5,593.7	4,022.0
Optical, photographic, cinematographic, measuring, precision and medical apparatus; clocks and watches; musical instruments	6,375.4	5,180.8	6,186.2
Total (incl. others)	114,424.7	104,665.3	110,689.9

Exports f.o.b.	1997	1998	1999
Live animals and animal products	1,593.1	1,184.9	1,117.6
Products of chemical or allied industries	3,277.6	2,857.0	3,266.9
Plastics, rubber and articles thereof	7,716.3	6,870.1	7,524.3
Textiles and textile articles	16,660.5	14,545.9	14,172.7
Base metals and articles thereof	11,530.6	10,870.1	11,606.9
Machinery and mechanical appliances; electrical equipment; sound and television apparatus	58,990.8	55,274.0	64,161.9
Vehicles, aircraft, vessels and associated transport equipment	5,587.7	5,216.2	5,151.9
Optical, photographic, cinematographic, measuring, precision and medical apparatus; clocks and watches; musical instruments	2,751.8	2,462.8	2,966.9
Toys, games and sports requisites; parts and accessories thereof	2,382.8	1,901.3	1,781.2
Total (incl. others)	122,080.7	110,582.3	121,590.9

PRINCIPAL TRADING PARTNERS (US $ million)

Imports c.i.f.	1997	1998	1999
Australia	3,217.3	2,913.0	2,957.1
Canada	1,586.7	1,159.9	1,124.6
China, People's Republic	3,915.3	4,110.5	4,526.3
France	4,726.0	5,328.5	1,887.3
Germany	5,369.2	5,149.0	5,312.6
Hong Kong	1,996.1	1,952.3	2,092.9
Indonesia	2,184.7	2,101.1	2,291.4
Italy	1,604.8	1,481.8	1,308.5
Japan	29,021.7	27,000.9	30,591.0
Korea, Republic	5,024.5	5,669.4	7,192.8
Malaysia	4,228.3	3,623.0	3,882.0
Netherlands	1,638.3	1,565.5	1,705.7
Philippines	1,374.6	1,823.0	2,172.5
Russia	1,236.8	844.0	1,183.2
Saudi Arabia	1,904.4	1,204.2	1,383.6
Singapore	3,150.4	2,696.9	3,312.2
Switzerland	1,112.3	1,115.1	1,105.5
Thailand	1,926.9	1,967.7	2,383.4
United Kingdom	1,952.8	1,683.6	1,720.5
USA	23,233.8	19,678.9	19,693.1
Total (incl. others)	114,424.7	104,665.3	110,689.9

Exports f.o.b.	1997	1998	1999
Australia	1,873.0	1,631.7	1,847.4
Canada	1,598.2	1,572.9	1,750.5
China, People's Republic	626.5	834.7	2,536.9
France	1,394.3	1,376.1	1,584.1
Germany	3,690.6	4,084.5	4,076.6
Hong Kong*	28,688.1	24,819.7	26,012.1
Indonesia	2,133.8	1,048.9	1,298.6
Italy	1,130.4	1,344.0	1,326.5
Japan	11,691.0	9,324.0	11,900.3
Korea, Republic	2,365.9	1,485.6	2,604.9
Malaysia	3,035.5	2,285.9	2,848.1
Netherlands	4,298.0	4,369.0	4,214.3
Philippines	2,242.5	1,934.3	2,611.4
Singapore	4,894.6	3,255.6	3,818.3
Thailand	2,562.1	1,925.8	2,104.5
United Kingdom	3,278.2	3,279.8	3,830.3
USA	29,551.8	29,376.4	30,901.5
Viet Nam	1,297.0	1,213.4	1,341.6
Total (incl. others)	122,080.7	110,582.3	121,590.9

* The majority of Taiwan's exports to Hong Kong are re-exported.

Transport

RAILWAYS (traffic)

	1997	1998	1999
Passengers ('000)	166,033	172,560	182,862
Passenger-km ('000)	9,263,252	9,793,173	9,989,026
Freight ('000 metric tons)	26,569	26,540	25,993
Freight ton-km ('000)	1,513,847	1,404,321	1,313,727

ROAD TRAFFIC (motor vehicles in use at 31 December)

	1997	1998	1999
Passenger cars	4,403,966	4,536,605	4,509,430
Buses and coaches	22,522	22,652	23,798
Goods vehicles	811,023	811,506	779,912
Motorcycles and scooters	10,027,471	10,503,877	10,958,469

SHIPPING

Merchant Fleet (at 31 December)

	1996	1997	1998
Number of vessels	681	692	686
Total displacement ('000 grt)	6,174.5	5,931.3	5,491.7

Source: Lloyd's Register of Shipping, *World Fleet Statistics*.

Sea-borne freight traffic ('000 metric tons)

	1997	1998	1999
Goods loaded	182,127	188,050	209.518
Goods unloaded	301,275	305,968	324,567

CIVIL AVIATION (traffic on scheduled services)

	1997	1998	1999
Passengers carried ('000) . . .	54,448.3	49,734.3	50,342.2
Passenger-km (million) . . .	39,878.0	39,217.4	41,698.8
Freight carried ('000 metric tons) .	1,307.6	1,299.3	1,445.6
Freight ton-km (million) . . .	3,936.3	4,129.1	5,449.9

Tourism

TOURIST ARRIVALS BY COUNTRY OF ORIGIN

	1997	1998	1999
Hong Kong	50,557	54,574	63,323
Indonesia	54,092	47,415	76,424
Korea, Republic	94,632	59,766	74,411
Malaysia	54,022	48,904	52,358
Philippines	112,844	120,543	120,319
Singapore	81,356	86,695	85,569
Thailand	121,534	127,987	137,664
USA	293,681	300,753	311,955
Overseas Chinese* . . .	256,591	266,895	295,595
Total (incl. others) . . .	2,372,232	2,298,706	2,411,248

* i.e. those bearing Taiwan passports.

Tourism receipts (US $ million): 3,403 in 1997; 3,372 in 1998; 3,571 in 1999.

Communications Media

	1997	1998	1999
Book production (titles) . .	23,801	30,868	30,871
Newspapers	344	360	367
Magazines	5,676	5,884	5,884
Telephone subscribers ('000) .	10,862	11,500	12,044
Mobile telephones ('000 in use) .	1,492	4,727	11,541

Radio receivers (1994): more than 16 million in use.
Television receivers (1994): 5,050,000 in use.

Education

(1999/2000)

	Schools	Full-time teachers	Pupils/ Students
Pre-school	3,005	19,168	232,610
Primary	2,583	98,745	1,927,179
Secondary (incl. vocational) . .	1,171	98,709	1,756,034
Higher	141	41,949	994,283
Special	23	1,629	5,697
Supplementary	992	3,341	323,581
Total (incl. others) . . .	7,915	263,541	5,239,384

Directory

The Constitution

On 1 January 1947 a new Constitution was promulgated for the Republic of China (confined to Taiwan since 1949). The form of government that was incorporated in the Constitution is based on a five-power system and has the major features of both cabinet and presidential government. A process of constitutional reform, initiated in 1991, continued in 2000. The following is a summary of the Constitution, as subsequently amended:

PRESIDENT

The President shall be directly elected by popular vote for a term of four years. Both the President and Vice-President are eligible for re-election to a second term. The President represents the country at all state functions, including foreign relations; commands land, sea and air forces, promulgates laws, issues mandates, concludes treaties, declares war, makes peace, declares martial law, grants amnesties, appoints and removes civil and military officers, and confers honours and decorations. The President convenes the National Assembly and, subject to certain limitations, may issue emergency orders to deal with national calamities and ensure national security; may dissolve the Legislative Yuan; also nominates the Premier (who may be appointed without the Legislative Yuan's confirmation), and the officials of the Judicial Yuan, the Examination Yuan and the Control Yuan.

NATIONAL ASSEMBLY

Three hundred delegates shall be elected by proportional representation to the National Assembly within three months of the expiration of a six-month period following the public announcement of a proposal by the Legislative Yuan to amend the Constitution or alter the national territory, or within three months of a petition initiated by the Legislative Yuan for the impeachment of the President or the Vice-President. Delegates to the National Assembly shall convene their own accord within 10 days after the election results have been confirmed and shall remain in session for no more than one month. The term of office of the delegates to the National Assembly shall terminate on the last day of the convention. The powers of the National Assembly are: to vote on the Legislative Yuan's proposals to amend the Contitution or alter the National territory; to deliberate a petition for the impeachment of the President or the Vice-President initiated by the Legislative Yuan.

EXECUTIVE YUAN

The Executive Yuan is the highest administrative organ of the nation and is responsible to the Legislative Yuan; has three categories of subordinate organization:

  Executive Yuan Council (policy-making organization)
  Ministries and Commissions (executive organization)
  Subordinate organization (19 bodies, including the Secretariat, Government Information Office, Directorate-General of Budget, Accounting and Statistics, Council for Economic Planning and Development, and Environmental Protection Administration).

LEGISLATIVE YUAN

The Legislative Yuan is the highest legislative organ of the State, empowered to hear administrative reports of the Executive Yuan, and to change government policy. It may hold a binding vote of 'no confidence' in the Executive Yuan. It comprises 225 members, 176 chosen by direct election, the remaining delegates being appointed on the basis of proportional representation. Members serve for three years and are eligible for re-election.

JUDICIAL YUAN

The Judicial Yuan is the highest judicial organ of state and has charge of civil, criminal and administrative cases, and of cases concerning disciplinary measures against public functionaries (see Judicial System).

EXAMINATION YUAN

The Examination Yuan supervises examinations for entry into public offices, and deals with personnel questions of the civil service.

CONTROL YUAN

The Control Yuan is the highest control organ of the State, exercising powers of impeachment, censure and audit. Comprising 29 members serving a six-year term, nominated and (with the consent of the National Assembly) appointed by the President, the Control Yuan may impeach or censure a public functionary at central or local level, who is deemed guilty of violation of law or dereliction of duty, and shall refer the matter to the law courts for action in cases involving a criminal offence; may propose corrective measures to the Executive Yuan or to its subordinate organs.

The Government

HEAD OF STATE

President: CHEN SHUI-BIAN (inaugurated 20 May 2000).
Vice-President: HSU-LIEN ANNETTE LU.
Secretary-General: YU HSI-KUN.

THE EXECUTIVE YUAN

(March 2001)

Premier: CHANG CHUN-HSIUNG.
Vice-Premier and Chairman of the Consumer Protection Commission: LAI YING-CHAO.
Ministers without Portfolio: HU SHENG-CHENG, TSAY CHING-YEN, CHANG YU-HUEI, HUANG JONG-TSUN, CHEN CHIN-HUANG, CHUNG CHIN.
Secretary-General: CHIOU I-JEN.
Minister of the Interior: CHANG PO-YA.
Minister of Foreign Affairs: TIEN HUNG-MAO.
Minister of National Defense: WU SHIH-WEN.
Minister of Finance: YEN CHING-CHANG.
Minister of Education: OVID J. L. TZENG.
Minister of Economic Affairs: LIN HSIN-I.
Minister of Justice: CHEN DING-NAN.
Minister of Transportation and Communications: YEH CHU-LAN.
Chairman of the Mainland Affairs Council: TSAI ING-WEN.
Chairman of the Overseas Chinese Affairs Commission: CHANG FU-MEI.
Chairman of the Mongolian and Tibetan Affairs Commission: HSU CHENG-KUANG.
Chairman of the Council for Economic Planning and Development: CHEN PO-CHIH.
Director-General of the Government Information Office: SU CHENG-PING.
Director-General of Directorate-General of Budget, Accounting and Statistics: LIN CHUAN.
Director-General of Central Personnel Administration: CHU WU-HSIEN.
Director-General of the Department of Health: LEE MING-LIANG.
Director-General of the Environmental Protection Administration: LIN JUN-YI.
Chairman of the National Science Council: WEI CHE-HO.
Chairman of the Council of Agriculture: CHEN HSI-HUANG.
Chairwoman of the Council for Cultural Affairs: TCHEN YU-CHIOU.
Chairman of the Research, Development and Evaluation Commission: LIN CHIA-CHENG.
Chairman of Veterans' Affairs Commission: YANG TE-CHIH.
Chairwoman of the National Youth Commission: LIN FANG-MEI.
Chairman of the Atomic Energy Council: HU CHING-PIAO.
Chairman of the Council of Labor Affairs: CHEN CHU.
Chairman of the Fair Trade Commission: CHAO YANG-CHING.
Chairman of the Public Construction Commission: LIN NENG-PAI.
Chairman of the Council of Aboriginal Affairs: ISQAQAVUT YOHANI.
Chairman of the National Council on Physical Fitness and Sports: HSU I-HSIUNG.

MINISTRIES, COMMISSIONS, ETC.

Office of the President: Chiehshou Hall, 122 Chungking South Rd, Sec. 1, Taipei 100; tel. (2) 23718889; fax (2) 23611604; e-mail public@mail.oop.gov.tw; internet www.oop.gov.tw.

Ministry of Economic Affairs: 15 Foo Chou St, Taipei; tel. (2) 23212200; fax (2) 23919398; e-mail service@moea.gov.tw; internet www.moea.gov.tw.

Ministry of Education: 5 Chung Shan South Rd, Taipei 10040; tel. (2) 23566051; fax (2) 23976978; internet www.moe.gov.tw.

Ministry of Finance: 2 Ai Kuo West Rd, Taipei; tel. (2) 23228000; fax (2) 23965829; e-mail root@www.mof.gov.tw; internet www.mof .gov.tw.

Ministry of Foreign Affairs: 2 Chiehshou Rd, Taipei 10016; tel. (2) 23119292; fax (2) 23144972; internet www.mofa.gov.tw.

Ministry of the Interior: 5th–9th Floors, 5 Hsu Chou Rd, Taipei; tel. (2) 23565005; fax (2) 23566201; e-mail gethics@mail.moi.gov.tw; internet www.moi.gov.tw.

Ministry of Justice: 130 Chungking South Rd, Sec. 1, Taipei 100 10036; tel. (2) 23146871; fax (2) 23896759; internet www.moj.gov.tw.

Ministry of National Defense: 2nd Floor, 164 PoAi Rd, Taipei; tel. (2) 23116117; fax (2) 23144221; internet www.ndmc.edu.tw.

Ministry of Transportation and Communications: 2 Chang Sha St, Sec. 1, Taipei; tel. (2) 23492900; fax (2) 23118587; e-mail motceyes@motc.gov.tw; internet www.motc.gov.tw.

Mongolian and Tibetan Affairs Commission: 4th Floor, 5 Hsu Chou Rd, Sec. 1, Taipei; tel. (2) 23566166; fax (2) 23566432; internet gopher://serv.hinet.net/11/government/department/EY/mtac.

Overseas Chinese Affairs Commission: 4th Floor, 5 Hsu Chou Rd, Taipei; tel. (2) 23566166; fax (2) 23566323; e-mail ocacinfo@mail .ocac.gov.tw; internet www.ocac.gov.tw.

Directorate-General of Budget, Accounting and Statistics: 2 Kwang Chow St, Taipei 100; tel. (2) 23823899; fax (2) 23319925; e-mail sicbs@emc.dgbasey.gov.tw; internet www.dgbasey.gov.tw.

Government Information Office: 2 Tientsin St, Taipei; tel. (2) 33568888; fax (2) 23568733; e-mail service@mail.gio.gov.tw; internet www.gio.gov.tw.

Council of Aboriginal Affairs: 16-17th Floors, 4 Chung Hsiao West Rd, Sec. 1, Taipei; tel. (2) 23882122; fax (2) 23891967.

Council of Agriculture: see p. 1125.

Atomic Energy Council: 67 Lane 144, Kee Lung Rd, Sec. 4, Taipei; tel. (2) 23634180; fax (2) 23635377; internet www.aec.gov.tw.

Central Personnel Administration: 109 Huai Ning St, Taipei; tel. (2) 23111720; fax (2) 23715252; internet www.cpa.gov.tw.

Consumer Protection Commission: 1 Chung Hsiao East Rd, Sec. 1, Taipei; tel. (2) 23566600; fax (2) 23214538; e-mail tcpc@ms1 .hinet.net; internet www.cpc.gov.tw.

Council for Cultural Affairs: 102 Ai Kuo East Rd, Taipei; tel. (2) 25225300; fax (2) 25519011; e-mail wwwadm@ccpdunx.ccpd.gov.tw; internet expo96.gov.tw/cca/welcome_c.html.

Council for Economic Planning and Development: 9th Floor, 87 Nanking East Rd, Sec. 2, Taipei; tel. (2) 25225300; fax (2) 25519011; internet www.cepd.gov.tw.

Environmental Protection Administration: 41 Chung Hua Rd, Sec. 1, Taipei; tel. (2) 23228751; fax (2) 23516227; e-mail www@sun .epa.gov.tw; internet www.epa.gov.tw.

Fair Trade Commission: 12–14th Floor, 2-2 Chi Nan Rd, Sec. 2, Taipei; tel. (2) 23517588; fax (2) 23974997; e-mail ftcse@ftc.gov.tw; internet www.ftc.gov.tw.

Department of Health: 100 Ai Kuo East Rd, Taipei; tel. (2) 23210151; fax (2) 23122907; internet www.doh.gov.tw.

Council of Labor Affairs: 5th–15th Floors, 132 Min Sheng East Rd, Sec. 3, Taipei; tel. (2) 27182512; fax (2) 25149240; internet gopher://192.192.46.131.

Mainland Affairs Council: 5th–13th Floors, 2-2 Chi-nan Rd, Sec. 1, Taipei; tel. (2) 23975589; fax (2) 23975700; e-mail macst@mac .gov.tw; internet www.mac.gov.tw.

National Science Council: 17th–22nd Floors, 106 Ho Ping East Rd, Sec. 2, Taipei; tel. (2) 27377501; fax (2) 27377668; e-mail nsc@nsc.gov.tw; internet www.nsc.gov.tw.

National Youth Commission: 14th Floor, 5 Hsu Chou Rd, Taipei; tel. (2) 23566271; fax (2) 23566290; internet www.nyc.gov.tw.

Research, Development and Evaluation Commission: 7th Floor, 2-2 Chi-nan Rd, Sec. 1, Taipei; tel. (2) 23419066; fax (2) 23928133; e-mail service@rdec.gov.tw; internet rdec.gov.tw.

Veterans' Affairs Commission: 222 Chung Hsiao East Rd, Sec. 5, Taipei; tel. (2) 27255700; fax (2) 27253578; e-mail hsc@www.vac .gov.tw; internet vac.gov.tw.

President and Legislature

PRESIDENT

Election, 18 March 2000

Candidate	Votes	% of votes
CHEN SHUI-BIAN (Democratic Progressive Party—DPP)	4,977,737	39.3
JAMES C. Y. SOONG (Independent)	4,664,932	36.8
LIEN CHAN (Kuomintang—KMT)	2,925,513	23.1
HSU HSIN-LIAN (Independent)	79,429	0.6
LI AO (New Party—NP)	16,782	0.1
Total	.12,664,393*	100.0

* Not including invalid or spoiled ballot papers, which numbered 122,278.

LI-FA YUAN
(Legislative Yuan)

The Legislative Yuan is the highest legislative organ of the State. It comprises 225 seats. The 176 directly-elected members include eight representatives of aboriginal communities. The remaining delegates are appointed on a proportional basis according to the parties' share of the popular vote, with eight seats reserved for overseas Chinese communities. Members serve a three-year term.

President: WANG JIN-PYNG.

General Election, 5 December 1998

Party	% of votes	Seats
Kuomintang (KMT)	46.4	125
Democratic Progressive Party (DPP)	29.6	72
New Party (NP)	7.1	11
Democratic Union of Taiwan (DUT)	3.7	4
Nationwide Democratic Non-Partisan Union (NDNU)	0.7	2
New Nation Alliance (NNA)	1.6	1
Jiann Gwo (Taiwan Independence) Party (TAIP)	1.5	1
Independents	9.4	9
Total	100.0	225

Political Organizations

Legislation adopted in 1989 permitted political parties other than the KMT to function. By mid-2000 a total of 90 parties had registered with the Ministry of the Interior.

China Democratic Socialist Party (CDSP): 5 Alley 10, Lane 1, Ho Ping East Rd, Sec. 3, Taipei; tel. (2) 27072883; f. 1932 by merger of National Socialists and Democratic Constitutionalists; aims to promote democracy, to protect fundamental freedoms, and to improve public welfare and social security; Chair. SHIEH HANN-RU; Sec.-Gen. KAO SHAO-CHUNG.

China Young Party: 12th Floor, 2 Shin Sheng South Rd, Sec. 3, Taipei; tel. (2) 23626715; f. 1923; aims to recover sovereignty over mainland China, to safeguard the Constitution and democracy, and to foster understanding between Taiwan and the non-communist world; Chair. JAW CHWEN-SHIAW.

Chinese Republican Party (CRP): 3rd Floor, 26 Lane 90, Jong Shuenn St, Sec. 2, Taipei; tel. (2) 29366572; f. 1988; advocates peaceful struggle for the salvation of China and the promotion of world peace; Chair. WANG YING-CHYUN.

Democratic Liberal Party (DLP): 4th Floor, 20 Lane 5, Ching Tyan, Taipei; tel. (2) 23121595; f. 1989; aims to promote political democracy and economic liberty for the people of Taiwan; Chair. HER WEI-KANG.

Democratic Progressive Party (DPP): 10th Floor, 30 Pei Ping East Rd, Taipei; tel. and fax (2) 23929989; f. 1986; advocates 'self-determination' for the people of Taiwan and UN membership; supports establishment of independent Taiwan following plebiscite; 140,000 mems; Chair. FRANK HSIEH; Sec.-Gen. YU HSI-KUN.

Democratic Union of Taiwan (DUT): 16th Floor, 15-1 Harng Joe South Rd, Sec. 1, Taipei; tel. (2) 23211531; f. 1998; Chair. HSU CHERNG-KUEN.

Green Party: 11/F-1, 273 Roosevelt Rd, Sec. 3, Taipei; tel. (2) 23621362; f. 1996 by breakaway faction of the DPP; Chair. CHEN GUANG-YEU.

Jiann Gwo Party (Taiwan Independence Party—TAIP): 6/F-4, 1 Ching-Tao East Rd, Taipei; tel. (2) 23958545; f. 1996 by dissident mems of DPP; Chair. JENG BANG-JENN; Sec.-Gen. LI SHENG-HSIUNG.

Kungtang (KT) (Labour Party): 2nd Floor, 22 Kai Feng St, Sec. 2, Taipei; tel. (2) 23121472; fax (2) 23719687; e-mail no1hsieh@eagle .seed.net.tw; f. 1987; aims to become the main political movement of Taiwan's industrial work-force; 10,000 mems; Chair. JENG JAU-MING; Sec.-Gen. HSIEH CHENG-YI.

Kuomintang (KMT) (Nationalist Party of China): 11 Chung Shan South Rd, Taipei 100; tel. (2) 23121472; fax (2) 23434524; f. 1894; ruling party; aims to supplant communist rule in mainland China; supports democratic, constitutional government, and advocates the unification of China under the 'Three Principles of the People'; aims to promote market economy and equitable distribution of wealth; 2,523,984 mems; Chair. LIEN CHAN; Sec.-Gen. LIN FONG-CHENG.

Nationwide Democratic Non-Partisan Union (NDNU): c/o The Legislative Yuan, Taipei.

New Nation Alliance: 14th Floor, 9 Song Jiang Rd, Taipei; tel. (2) 23585643; f. 1998; promotes independence for Taiwan and the establishment of a 'new nation, new society and new culture'; Chair. PERNG BAE-SHEAN.

New Party (NP): 4th Floor, 65 Guang Fuh South Rd, Taipei; tel. (2) 27562222; fax (2) 27565750; e-mail npncs@ms2.hinet.net; f. 1993 by dissident KMT legislators (hitherto mems of New Kuomintang Alliance faction); merged with China Social Democratic Party in late 1993; advocates co-operation with the KMT and DPP in negotiations with the People's Republic, the maintenance of security in the Taiwan Straits, the modernization of the island's defence systems, measures to combat government corruption, the support of small and medium businesses and the establishment of a universal social security system; 80,000 mems; Chair. HAO LONG-BIN; Sec.-Gen. LI BING-NAN.

People First Party: Taipei; f. 2000; Chair. JAMES C. Y. SOONG.

Workers' Party: 2nd Floor, 181 Fu-hsing South Rd, Taipei; tel. (2) 27555868; f. 1989 by breakaway faction of the Kungtang; radical; Leader LOU MEIWEN.

Various pro-independence groups (some based overseas and, until 1992, banned in Taiwan) are in operation. These include the **World United Formosans for Independence** (WUFI—4,000 mems world-wide; Chair. GEORGE CHANG) and the **Organization for Taiwan Nation-Building**.

Diplomatic Representation

EMBASSIES IN THE REPUBLIC OF CHINA

Burkina Faso: 6/F, 9-1, Lane 62, Tien Mou West Rd, Taipei 111; tel. (2) 28733096; fax (2) 28733071; Ambassador: JACQUES Y. SAWADOGO.

Chad: 8/F, 9 Lane 62, Tien Mou West Rd, Taipei; tel. (2) 28742943; fax (2) 28742971; e-mail amchadtp@ms23.hinet.net; Ambassador: SALIM ABDERAMAN TAHA.

Costa Rica: 5/F, 9-1, Lane 62, Tien Mou West Rd, Taipei 111; tel. (2) 28752964; fax (2) 28753151; e-mail oscaralv@pichet.net; Ambassador: OSCAR ALVAREZ.

Dominican Republic: 6/F, 9 Lane 62, Tien Mou West Rd, Taipei 111; tel. (2) 28751357; fax (2) 28752661; Ambassador: VÍCTOR MANUEL SÁNCHEZ PEÑA.

El Salvador: 2/F, 9 Lane 62, Tien Mou West Rd, Shih Lin, Taipei 111; tel. (2) 28763509; fax (2) 28763514; e-mail embasal.taipei@ msa.hinet.net; Ambassador: FRANCISCO RICARDO SANTANA BERRÍOS.

The Gambia: 9/F, 9-1 Lane 62, Tien Mou West Rd, Taipei 111; tel. (2) 28753911; fax (2) 28752775; Ambassador: MAMBURY NJIE.

Guatemala: 3/F, 9-1 Lane 62, Tien Mou West Rd, Taipei 111; tel. (2) 28756952; fax (2) 28740699; Ambassador: JULIO ROBERTO PALOMO SILVA.

Haiti: 8/F, 9-1 Lane 62, Tien Mou West Rd, Taipei 111; tel. (2) 28766718; fax (2) 28766719; Ambassador: FRANCEL SAINT-HILLIEN.

Holy See: 87 Ai Kuo East Rd, Taipei 106 (Apostolic Nunciature); tel. (2) 23216847; fax (2) 23911926; e-mail aposnunc@tptsl.seed.net.tw; Chargé d'affaires a.i.: Mgr ADOLFO TITO C. YLLANA.

Honduras: 9/F, 9 Lane 62, Tien Mou West Rd, Taipei 111; tel. (2) 28755507; fax (2) 28755726; e-mail honduras@msa.hinet.net; internet www.hondurasinfo.hn; Ambassador: MARGARITA DURÓN DE GÁLVEZ.

Liberia: 11/F, 9-1 Lane 62, Tien Mou West Rd, Taipei 111; tel. (2) 28766387; fax (2) 28751313; e-mail libemb@tpts5.seed.net.tw; Ambassador: JOHN CUMMINGS.

Macedonia, former Yugoslav republic: 5/F, 9 Lane 62, Tien Mou West Road, Taipei 111; tel. (2) 28760189; fax (2) 28729159; e-mail embmktpe@ms36.hinet.net; Envoy: VERA MODANU.

Nicaragua: 3/F, 9 Lane 62, Tien Mou West Rd, Taipei 111; tel. (2) 28749034; fax (2) 28749080; Ambassador: LUISA WONG.

Panama: 6th Floor, 111 Sung Kiang Rd, Taipei 104; tel. (2) 25099189; fax (2) 25099801; Ambassador: JOSÉ ANTONIO DOMÍNGUEZ.

Paraguay: 7/F, 9-1 Lane 62, Tien Mou West Rd, Taipei 111; tel. (2) 28736310; fax (2) 28736312; Ambassador: CEFERINO ADRIÁN VÁLDEZ PERALTA.

Senegal: 10/F, 9-1 Lane 62, Tien Mou West Rd, Taipei 111, tel. (2) 28766519; fax (2) 28734909; Ambassador: AHMED TIJANE KANE.

Judicial System

The power of judicial review is exercised by the Judicial Yuan's 16 Grand Justices nominated and appointed for nine years by the President of Taiwan with the consent of the National Assembly. From 2003 the Judicial Yuan was to have 15 Grand Justices, one of whom was to serve as its President and another as Vice-President, nominated and appointed by the President of Taiwan with the consent of the Legislative Yuan. The President of the Judicial Yuan is also the *ex-officio* chairman for the Plenary Session of the Grand Justices. The Ministry of Justice is under the jurisdiction of the Executive Yuan.

Judicial Yuan: 124 Chungking South Rd, Sec. 1, Taipei; tel. (2) 23618577; fax (2) 23821739; Pres. WENG YUEH-SHENG; Vice-Pres. CHENG CHUNG-MO; Sec.-Gen. YANG JEN-SHOU; the highest judicial organ, and the interpreter of the constitution and national laws and ordinances; supervises the following:

Supreme Court: 6 Chang Sha St, Sec. 1, Taipei; tel. (2) 23141160; fax (2) 23114246; Court of third and final instance for civil and criminal cases; Pres. LIN MING-TEH.

High Courts: Courts of second instance for appeals of civil and criminal cases.

District Courts: Courts of first instance in civil, criminal and non-contentious cases.

Supreme Administrative Court: 1 Lane 126, Chungking South Rd, Sec. 1, Taipei; tel. (2) 23113691; fax (2) 23111791; e-mail jessie@judicial.gov.tw; Court of final resort in cases brought against govt agencies; Pres. JONG YAW-TANG.

High Administrative Courts: Courts of first instance in cases brought against government agencies.

Commission on Disciplinary Sanctions Against Functionaries: 124 Chungking South Rd, 3rd Floor, Sec. 1, Taipei 10036; tel. (2) 23619375; fax (2) 23311934; decides on disciplinary measures against public functionaries impeached by the Control Yuan; Chief Commissioner LIN KUO-HSIEN.

Religion

According to the Ministry of the Interior, in 1999 34% of the population were adherents of Buddhism, 42% of Daoism (Taoism), 7.8% of I-Kuan Tao and 3.6% of Christianity.

BUDDHISM

Buddhist Association of Taiwan: Mahayana and Theravada schools; 1,613 group mems and more than 9.61m. adherents; Leader Ven. CHIN-HSIN.

CHRISTIANITY

The Roman Catholic Church

Taiwan comprises one archdiocese, six dioceses and one apostolic administrative area. In December 1999 there were 304,000 adherents.

Bishops' Conference: Regional Episcopal Conference of China, 34 Lane 32, Kuangfu South Rd, Taipei 10552; tel. (2) 25782355; fax (2) 25773874; f. 1967; Pres. Cardinal PAUL SHAN KUO-HSI, Bishop of Kaohsiung.

Archbishop of Taipei: Most Rev. JOSEPH TI-KANG, Archbishop's House, 94 Loli Rd, Taipei 10668; tel. (2) 27371311; fax (2) 27373710.

The Anglican Communion

Anglicans in Taiwan are adherents of the Protestant Episcopal Church. In 1999 the Church had 2,000 members.

Bishop of Taiwan: Rt Rev. JOHN CHIH-TSUNG CHIEN, 7 Lane 105, Hangchow South Rd, Sec. 1, Taipei 100; tel. (2) 23411265; fax (2) 23962014; e-mail skhtpe@ms12.hinet.net; internet www.dfms.org/ taiwan.

Presbyterian Church

Tai-oan Ki-tok Tiu-Lo Kau-Hoe (Presbyterian Church in Taiwan): No. 3, Lane 269, Roosevelt Rd, Sec. 3, Taipei 106; tel. (2) 23625282; fax (2) 23632669; f. 1865; Gen. Sec. Rev. L. K. LO; 224,819 mems (1997).

DAOISM (TAOISM)

In 1999 there were about 4.54m. adherents. Temples numbered 8,604, and clergy totalled 33,850.

I-KUAN TAO

Introduced to Taiwan in the 1950s, this 'Religion of One Unity' is a modern, syncretic religion, drawn mainly from Confucian, Buddhist and Daoist principles and incorporating ancestor worship. In 1998 there were 87 temples and 18,000 family shrines. Adherents totalled 845,000.

ISLAM

Leader MOHAMMED MA CHA-JENG; 53,000 adherents in 1999.

The Press

In 1999 the number of registered newspapers stood at 367. The majority of newspapers are privately owned.

PRINCIPAL DAILIES

Taipei

Central Daily News: 260 Pa Teh Rd, Sec. 2, Taipei; tel. (2) 27765368; fax (2) 27775835; f. 1928; morning; Chinese; official Kuomintang organ; Publr and Editor-in-Chief CHAN TIEN-SHING; circ. 600,000.

The China Post: 8 Fu Shun St, Taipei 104; tel. (2) 25969971; fax (2) 25957962; e-mail cpost@msl.hinet.net; internet www.chinapost.com.tw; f. 1952; morning; English; Publr and Editor JACK HUANG; circ. 250,000.

China Times: 132 Da Li St, Taipei; tel. (2) 23087111; fax (2) 23063312; f. 1950; morning; Chinese; Chair. YU CHI-CHUNG; Publr YU ALBERT CHIEN-HSIN; circ. 1.2m.

China Times Express: 132 Da Li St, Taipei; tel. (2) 23087111; fax (2) 23048138; e-mail chinaexpress@mail.chinatimes.com.tw; f. 1988; evening; Chinese; Publr S. F. LIN; Editor C. L. HUANG; circ. 400,000.

Commercial Times: 132 Da Li St, Taipei; tel. (2) 23087111; fax (2) 23069456; e-mail commercialtimes@mail.chinatimes.com.tw; f. 1978; morning; Chinese; Publr PENG CHWEI-MING; Editor-in-Chief PHILLIP CHEN; circ. 300,000.

Economic Daily News: 555 Chung Hsiao East Rd, Sec. 4, Taipei; tel. (2) 27627632; fax (2) 27463550; f. 1967; morning; Chinese; Publr WANG PI-LY.

The Great News: 216 Chen Teh Rd, Sec. 3, Taipei; tel. (2) 25973111; f. 1988; morning; also *The Great News Daily-Entertainment* (circ. 460,000) and *The Great News Daily-Sport* (circ. 410,000); Publr CHEN CHI-CHIA.

Independence Evening Post: 15 Chi Nan Rd, Sec. 2, Taipei; tel. (2) 23519621; fax (2) 23215211; f. 1947; afternoon; Chinese; Publr CHEN TSEN-HUEI; Editor LEE SEN-HONG; circ. 307,071.

Liberty Times: 137 Nanking East Rd, 11th Floor, Sec. 2, Taipei; tel. (2) 25042828; fax (2) 25042212; f. 1988; Publr WU A-MING; Editor-in-Chief ROGER CHEN.

Mandarin Daily News: 4 Foo Chou St, Taipei; tel. (2) 23213479; fax (2) 23410203; f. 1948; morning; Publr LIN LIANG.

Min Sheng Daily: 555 Chung Hsiao East Rd, Sec. 4, Taipei; tel. (2) 27681234; fax (2) 27560955; f. 1978; sport and leisure; Publr WANG SHAW-LAN.

Taiwan Hsin Sheng Pao: 12th Floor, 110 Yengping South Rd, Taipei; tel. (2) 23117000; fax (2) 23825093; f. 1945; morning; Chinese; also southern edn publ. in Kaohsiung; Publr LU I-MING.

Taiwan News: 10th Floor, 41 Tung Hsing St, Shinyi Chiu, Taipei 110; tel. (2) 87683456; fax (2) 87682908; f. 1949; morning; English; Chair. and Publr LUIS KO.

United Daily News: 555 Chung Hsiao East Rd, Sec. 4, Taipei; tel. (2) 27681234; fax (2) 27632303; e-mail udnid@eagle.seed.net.tw; f. 1951; morning; Publr WANG SHAW-LAN; Editor-in-Chief SHUANG KUO-NING; circ. 1.2m.

Youth Daily News: 3 Hsinyi Rd, Sec. 1, Taipei; tel. (2) 23222722; fax (2) 2322245; f. 1984; morning; Chinese; armed forces; Publr HUANG SUEY-SHENG.

Provincial

China Daily News (Southern Edn): 57 Hsi Hwa St, Tainan; tel. (6) 2296381; fax (6) 2201804; f. 1946; morning; Publr CHAN TIEN-SHING; circ. 670,000.

Keng Sheng Daily News: 36 Wuchuan St, Hualien; tel. (38) 340131; fax (38) 329664; f. 1947; morning; Publr HSIEH YING-YIN; circ. 50,000.

The Commons Daily: 180 Min Chuan 2 Rd, Kaohsiung; tel. (7) 3363131; fax (7) 3363604; f. 1950; frmrly Min Chung Daily News; morning; Publr TSAI HAU; Editor LEE WANG-TAI; circ. 148,000.

Taiwan Daily News: 361 Wen Shin Rd, Sec. 3, Taichung; tel. (4) 2958511; fax (4) 2958950; f. 1964; morning; Publr ANTONIO CHIANG; Editor-in-Chief LIU CHIH TSUNG; circ. 250,000.

Taiwan Hsin Wen Daily News: 249 Chung Cheng 4 Rd, Kaohsiung; tel. (7) 2958951; f. 1949; morning; southern edn of *Hsin Sheng Pao*; Publr CHAO LI-NIEN.

Taiwan Times: 110 Chung Shan 1 Rd, Kaohsiung; tel. (7) 2155666; fax (7) 2150264; f. 1971; Publr WANG YUH-CHEN.

SELECTED PERIODICALS

Artist Magazine: 6th Floor, 147 Chung Ching South Rd, Sec. 1, Taipei; tel. (2) 23719692; fax (2) 23317096; f. 1975; monthly; Publr HO CHENG KUANG; circ. 28,000.

Better Life Monthly: 11 Lane 199, Hsin-yih Rd, Sec. 4, Taipei; tel. (2) 27549588; fax (2) 27016068; f. 1987; Publr JACK S. LIN.

Brain: 9th Floor, 47 Nanking East Rd, Sec. 4, Taipei; tel. (2) 27132644; fax (2) 27137318; f. 1977; f. 1977; monthly; Publr JOHNSON WU.

Business Weekly: 5th Floor, 62 Tun Hwa North Rd, Taipei; tel. (2) 27736611; fax (2) 27110833; f. 1987; Publr JIN WEI-TSUN.

Car Magazine: 1st Floor, 3 Lane 3, Tung-Shan St, Taipei; tel. (2) 23218128; fax (2) 23935614; e-mail carguide@ms13.hinet.net; f. 1982; monthly; Publr H. K. LIN; Editor-in-Chief TA-WEI LIN; circ. 85,000.

Central Monthly: 7th Floor, 11 Chung Shan South Rd, Taipei; tel. (2) 23433140; fax (2) 23433139; f. 1950; Publr HUANG HUI-TSEN.

China Times Weekly: 5th Floor, 25 Min Chuan East Rd, Sec. 6, Taipei; tel. (2) 27929688; fax (2) 27929568; f. 1978; weekly; Chinese; Editor CHANG KUO-LI; Publr CHUANG SHU-MING; circ. 180,000.

Commonwealth Monthly: 4th Floor, 87 Sung Chiang Rd, Taipei; tel. (2) 25078627; fax (2) 25079011; f. 1981; monthly; business; Pres. CHARLES H. C. KAO; Publr and Editor DIANE YING; circ. 83,000.

Continent Magazine: 3rd Floor, 11-6 Foo Chou St, Taipei; tel. (2) 23518310; f. 1950; monthly; archaeology, history and literature; Publr HSU CHO-YU.

Cosmopolitan: 5th Floor, 8 Lane 181, Jiou-Tzung Rd, Nei Hu Area, Sec. 2, Taipei 114; tel. (2) 287978900; fax (2) 287978990; e-mail hwaker@ms13.hinet.net; f. 1992; monthly; Publr MINCHUN CHANG.

Country Road: 14 Wenchow St, Taipei; tel. (2) 23628148; fax (2) 23636724; e-mail h3628148@ms15.hinet.net; internet www.coa.gov.tw/magazine/fst/road.htm; f. 1975; monthly; Editor CHRISTINE S. L. YU; Publr KAO YU-HSIN.

Crown Magazine: 50 Lane 120, Tun Hua North Rd, Taipei; tel. (2) 27168888; fax (2) 27133422; f. 1954; monthly; literature and arts; Publr PING HSIN TAO; Editor CHEN LIH-HWA; circ. 76,000.

Defense Technology Monthly: 10th Floor, 74 Song Der Rd, Taipei; tel. (2) 27204568; fax (2) 27581335; f. 1894; Publr J. D. BIH.

Earth Geographic Monthly: 2nd Floor, 130 Min Chuan Rd, Hsin-Tien, Taipei; tel. (2) 22182218; fax (2) 22185418; f. 1988; Publr HSU CHEN ERH-HONG.

Elle-Taipei: 9/F, 9 Lane 30, Sec. 3, Minsheng East Rd, Taipei; tel. (2) 27522425; fax (2) 27514583; e-mail jdewitt@hft.com.tw; f. 1991; monthly; women's magazine; Publr JEAN DE WITT; Editor-in-Chief LENA YANG; circ. 50,000.

Evergreen Monthly: 11th Floor, 2 Pa Teh Rd, Sec. 3, Taipei; tel. (2) 25785078; fax (2) 25786838; f. 1983; health care knowledge; Publr LIANG GUANG-MING; circ. 50,000.

Excellence Magazine: 2nd Floor, 15 Lane 3, Sec. 2, Chien Kuo North Rd, Taipei; tel. (2) 25093578; fax (2) 25173607; f. 1984; monthly; business; Man. WU SHIEN-ER; Editor-in-Chief LIU JEN; circ. 70,000.

Families Monthly: 11th Floor, 2 Pa Teh Rd, Sec. 3, Taipei; tel. (2) 25785078; fax (2) 25786838; f. 1976; family life; Editor-in-Chief THELMA KU; circ. 155,000.

Foresight Investment Weekly: 7th Floor, 52 Nanking East Rd, Sec. 1, Taipei; tel. (2) 25512561; fax (2) 25681999; f. 1980; weekly; Dir and Publr SUN WUN HSIUNG; Editor-in-Chief WU WEN SHIN; circ. 55,000.

The Gleaner: 7th Floor, 7 Chung Ching South Rd, Sec. 1, Taipei; tel. (2) 23813781; fax (2) 23899801; Publr CHIN KAI-YIN.

Global Views Monthly: 7th Floor, 87 Sung Chiang Rd, Taipei; tel. (2) 25078627; fax (2) 25079011; f. 1986; Pres. CHARLES H. C. KAO; Publr and Editor-in-Chief WANG LI-HSING.

Gourmet World: 4th Floor, 52 Hang Chou South Rd, Taipei; tel. (2) 23972215; fax (2) 23412184; f. 1990; Publr HSU TANG-JEN.

Harvest Farm Magazine: 14 Wenchow St, Taipei; tel. (2) 23628148; fax (2) 23636724; e-mail h3628148@ms15.hinet.net; internet www.coa.gov.tw/magazine/fst/road.htm; f. 1951; every 2 weeks; Publr KAO YU-HSIN; Editor KAO MING-TANG.

Information and Computer: 6th Floor, 153 Hsinyi Rd, Sec. 3, Taipei; tel. (2) 23255750; fax (2) 23255749; f. 1980; monthly; Chinese; Publr FANG HSIEN-CHI; Editor JENNIFER CHIU; circ. 28,000.

Issues and Studies: Institute of International Relations, 64 Wan Shou Rd, Wenshan, Taipei 116; tel. (2) 29394921; fax (2) 29397352; e-mail scchang@nccu.edu.tw; f. 1965; bimonthly; English; Chinese studies and international affairs; Publr Ho SZU-YIN; Editor JAUSHIEH JOSEPH WU.

Jade Biweekly Magazine: 7th Floor, 222 Sung Chiang Rd, Taipei; tel. (2) 25811665; fax (2) 25210586; f. 1982; economics, social affairs, leisure; Publr HSU CHIA-CHUNG; circ. 98,000.

Journalist: 4th Floor-6, 79 Hsin Tai Wu Rd, Hsi Chin, Taipei; tel. (2) 26981898; fax (2) 26981086; f. 1987; weekly; Publr WANG SHIN-CHING.

Ladies Magazine: 11F-3, 187 Shin Yi Rd, Sec. 4, Taipei; tel. (2) 27026908; fax (2) 27014090; f. 1978; monthly; Publr CHENG CHIN-SHAN; Editor-in-Chief THERESA LEE; circ. 60,000.

Living: 7th Floor, 2531-1 Chung Cheng Rd, Hsin Tien, Taipei; tel. (2) 21181828; fax (2) 22181081; f. 1997; monthly; Publr LISA WU.

Madame Figaro: 5th Floor, 25 Min Chuan East Rd, Sec. 6, Taipei; tel. (2) 27929868; fax (2) 27928838; e-mail tina@mail.chinatimes .com.tw; f. 1993; fmrly *Marie Claire*; Publr CHANG SHU-MING.

Management Magazine: 3rd Floor, 143 Sim-Yi Rd, Sec. 4, Hsichih, Taipei; tel. (2) 26485828; fax (2) 26484666; e-mail flhung@email.gcn .net.tw; internet www.harment.com; monthly; Chinese; Publr and Editor FRANK L. HUNG; circ. 65,000.

Money Monthly: 12th Floor, 102 Tun Hua North Rd, Taipei; tel. (2) 25149822; fax (2) 27154657; f. 1986; monthly; personal financial management; Publr PATRICK SUN; Man. Editor JENNIE SHUE; circ. 55,000.

Music and Audiophile: 2nd Floor, 2 Kingshan South Rd, Sec. 1, Taipei; tel. (2) 25684607; fax (2) 23958654; f. 1973; Publr CHANG KUO-CHING; Editor-in-Chief CHARLES HUANG.

National Palace Museum Bulletin: 211 Chih-shan Rd, Wai Shuang Hsi, Sec. 2, Taipei 11102; tel. (2) 28812021; fax (2) 28821440; e-mail service@npm.gov.tw; internet www.npm.gov.tw; f. 1965; every 2 months; Chinese art history research in English; Publr and Dir TU CHENG-SHENG; Editor-in-Chief WANG YAO-TING; circ. 1,000.

National Palace Museum Monthly of Chinese Art: Wai Shuang Hsi, Shih Lin, Taipei 11102; tel. (2) 28821230; fax (2) 28821440; f. 1983; monthly in Chinese; Publr and Editor-in-Chief TU CHENG-SHENG; circ. 10,000.

Nong Nong Magazine: 7th Floor, 531-1 Chung Cheng Rd, Hsin Tien, Taipei; tel. (2) 22181828; fax (2) 22181081; e-mail group@ nongnong.com.tw; f. 1984; monthly; women's interest; Publr LISA WU; Editor DIANA LIU; circ. 70,000.

PC Home: 3rd Floor-1, 64 Tun Hwa North Rd, Taipei; tel. (2) 27739858; fax (2) 27116527; f. 1996; monthly; Publr HUNG-TZE JANG.

PC Office: 11th Floor, 8 Tun Hwa North Rd, Taipei; tel. (2) 27815390; fax (2) 27780899; f. 1997; monthly; Publr HUNG-TZE JANG.

Power News: 51 Tung-Hsing Rd, Taipei; tel. (2) 87681568; fax (2) 87681628; f. 1999; evening; Publr CHEN WEN CHINE.

Reader's Digest (Chinese Edn): 2nd Floor, 2 Ming Sheng East Rd, Taipei; tel. (2) 27607262; fax (2) 27461588; monthly; Editor-in-Chief ANNIE CHENG.

Sinorama: 8th Floor, 15-1 Hangchow South Rd, Sec. 1, Taipei 100; tel. (2) 23922256; fax (2) 23970655; f. 1976; monthly; cultural; bilingual magazine with edns in Chinese with Japanese, Spanish and English; Publr CHIEN-JEN CHEN; Editor-in-Chief ANNA Y. WANG; circ. 110,000.

Sinwen Tienti (Newsdom): 10th Floor, 207 Fuh Hsing North Rd, Taipei; tel. (2) 27139668; fax (2) 27131763; f. 1945; weekly; Chinese; Dir PU SHAO-FU.

Star: 555 Chung Hsiao East Rd, Sec. 4, Taipei; tel. (2) 27681234; Publr WANG SHAW-LAN.

Studio Classroom: 10 Lane 62, Ta-Chih St, Taipei; tel. (2) 25339123; fax (2) 25331811; f. 1962; monthly; Publr DORIS BROUGHAM.

Taipei Journal: 2 Tientsin St, Taipei 10041; tel. (2) 23970180; fax (2) 23568233; f. 1964 (fmrly Free China Journal); weekly; English; news review; Publr SU TZEN-PING; Exec. Editor VANCE CHANG; circ. 32,000.

Taipei Review: 2 Tientsin St, Taipei 100; tel. (2) 23510829; e-mail tr@gio.gov.tw; f. 1951; monthly; English; illustrated; Publr SU TZEN-PING; Editor-in-Chief JASON JAN-CHUN CHERNG.

Taipei Times: 5th Floor, 137 Nanking East Rd, Sec. 4, Taipei; tel. (2) 25182728; fax (2) 25162313; f. 1999; Publr ANTONIO CHIANG.

Time Express: 7th Floor-2, 76 Tun Hwa South Rd, Sec. 2, Taipei; tel. (2) 27084410; fax (2) 27084420; f. 1973; monthly; Publr RICHARD C. C. HUANG.

TV Weekly: 11th Floor, 2 Pa Teh Rd, Taipei; tel. (2) 25785078; fax (2) 25786838; f. 1962; Publr LIANG GUANG-MING; circ. 160,000.

Unitas: 10th Floor, 180 Keelung Rd, Sec. 1, Taipei; tel. (2) 27666759; fax (2) 27567914; e-mail unitas@udngroup.com.tw; monthly; Chi-

nese; literary journal; Publr CHANG PAO-CHING; Editor-in-Chief CHU AN-MIN.

Vi Vi Magazine: 7th Floor, 550 Chung Hsiao East Rd, Sec. 5, Taipei; tel. (2) 27275336; fax (2) 27592031; f. 1984; monthly; women's interest; Pres. TSENG CHING-TANG; circ. 60,000.

Vogue: 5th Floor, 232 Tun Hwa North Rd, Taipei; tel. (2) 27172000; fax (2) 27172004; f. 1996; monthly; Publr BENTHAM LIU.

Wealth Magazine: 7th Floor, 52 Nanking East Rd, Sec. 1, Taipei; tel. (2) 25512561; fax (2) 25816196; f. 1974; monthly; finance; Pres. TSHAI YEN-KUEN; Editor ANDY LIAN; circ. 75,000.

Win Win Weekly: 7th Floor, 52 Nanking East Rd, Taipei; tel. (2) 25816196; fax (2) 25119596; f. 1996; Publr GIN-HO HSHIE.

Youth Literary: 3rd Floor, 66-1 Chung Cheng South Rd, Sec. 1, Taipei; tel. (2) 23146181; fax (2) 23612239; f. 1954; Publr LEE CHUNG-GUAI.

NEWS AGENCIES

Central News Agency (CNA): 209 Sung Chiang Rd, Taipei; tel. (2) 25051180; fax (2) 25014806; e-mail cnamark@ms9.hinet.net; internet www.cna.com.tw; f. 1924; news service in Chinese, English and Spanish; feature and photographic services; 12 domestic and 30 overseas bureaux; Pres. BILL WANG.

Chiao Kwang News Agency: 4th Floor, 58 Chinsan South Rd, Sec. 1, Taipei; tel. (2) 23214803; fax (2) 23516416; Dir HUANG HER.

Foreign Bureaux

Agence France-Presse (AFP): Room 617, 6th Floor, 209 Sung Chiang Rd, Taipei; tel. (2) 25016395; fax (2) 25011881; Bureau Chief YANG HSIN-HSIN.

Associated Press (AP) (USA): Room 630, 6th Floor, 209 Sung Chiang Rd, Taipei; tel. (2) 25036651; fax (2) 25007133; Bureau Chief WILLIAM FOREMAN.

Reuters (UK): 8th Floor, 196 Chien Kuo North Rd, Sec. 2, Taipei; tel. (2) 25004881; fax (2) 25080204; Bureau Chief BENJAMIN KANG LIM.

Publishers

There are 6,388 publishing houses. In 1999 a total of 30,871 titles were published.

Art Book Co: 4th Floor, 18 Lane 283, Roosevelt Rd, Sec. 3, Taipei; tel. (2) 23620578; fax (2) 23623594; Publr HO KUNG SHANG.

Cheng Wen Publishing Co: 3rd Floor, 277 Roosevelt Rd, Sec. 3, Taipei; tel. (2) 23628032; fax (2) 23660806; e-mail ccicncwp@ms17 .hinet.net; Publr LARRY C. HUANG.

China Economic News Service (CENS): 555 Chung Hsiao East Rd, Sec. 4, Taipei 110; tel. (2) 26422629; fax (2) 26496311; e-mail webmaster@www.cens.com; internet www.cens.com; f. 1974; trade magazines.

China Times Publishing Co: 5th Floor, 240 Hoping West Rd, Sec. 3, Taipei; tel. (2) 23027845; fax (2) 23027844; e-mail ctpc@mse .hinet.net; internet www.publish.chinatimes.com.tw; f. 1975; Pres. MO CHAO-PING.

Chinese Culture University Press: 55 Hua Kang Rd, Yangming-shan, Taipei; tel. (2) 28611861; fax (2) 28617164; e-mail ccup@ ccuo16.pccu.edu.tw; Publr LEE FU-CHEN.

Chung Hwa Book Co Ltd: 14th Floor, 51 Keelung Rd, Sec. 2, Taipei; tel. (2) 23780215; fax (2) 27355887; e-mail du13@ms29 .hinet.net; humanities, social sciences, medicine, fine arts, school books, reference books; Publr LIN WIN-RONG.

The Commercial Press Ltd: 37 Chungking South Rd, Sec. 1, Taipei; tel. (2) 23614739; fax (2) 23710274; e-mail cptw@ms12 .hinet.net; Man.-Editor TANG HAO-CHUAN.

Crown Publishing Co: 50 Lane 120, Tun Hua North Rd, Taipei; tel. (2) 27168888; fax (2) 27161793; e-mail magazine@crown.com.tw; internet www.crown.com.tw; Publr PHILIP PING.

The Eastern Publishing Co Ltd: 121 Chungking South Rd, Sec. 1, Taipei; tel. (2) 23114514; fax (2) 23317402; Publr CHENG LI-TSU.

Elite Publishing Co: 1st Floor, 33-1 Lane 113, Hsiamen St, Taipei 100; tel. (2) 23671021; fax (2) 23657047; e-mail elite113@ms12 .hinet.net; f. 1975; Publr KO CHING-HWA.

Far East Book Co: 10th Floor, 66-1 Chungking South Rd, Sec. 1, Taipei; tel. (2) 23118740; fax (2) 23114184; e-mail webmaster@mail .fareast.com.tw; internet www.fareast.com.tw; art, education, history, physics, mathematics, law, literature, dictionaries, textbooks, language tapes, Chinese-English dictionary; Publr GEORGE C. L. PU.

Hilit Publishing Co Ltd: 11th Floor, 79 Hsin Tai Wu Rd, Sec. 1, Hsichih Town, Taipei County; tel. (2) 26984565; fax (2) 26984980; e-mail hilit@tpts5.seed.net.tw; internet www.ptri.org.tw/hilit/; Publr DIXON D. S. SUNG.

Hua Hsin Culture and Publications Center: 2nd Floor, 133 Kuang Fu North Rd, Taipei; tel. (2) 27658190; fax (2) 27694980; f. 1960; Dir CHENG CHI.

International Cultural Enterprises: 5th Floor, 25 Po Ai Rd, Taipei 100; tel. (2) 23318080; fax (2) 23318090; e-mail itstpeh@ MS8.hinet.net; internet www.itstpeh.com.tw; Publr LAKE HU.

Kwang Fu Book Enterprises Co Ltd: 5th Floor, 54 Chunghsiao East Rd, Sec. 1, Taipei; tel. (2) 23922256; fax (2) 23970655; e-mail service@mail.sinorama.com.tw; internet www.sinorama.com.tw; Publr CHUNG CHIN.

Kwang Hwa Publishing Co: 8th Floor, 15-1 Hangchow South Rd, Sec. 1, Taipei; tel. (2) 23516419; fax (2) 23510821; e-mail fcr@mail .gio.gov.tw; Publr CHEN CHIEN-JEN.

Li-Ming Cultural Enterprise Co: 3rd Floor, 49 Chungking South Rd, Sec. 1, Taipei 100; tel. (2) 23821233; fax (2) 23821244; e-mail liming2f@ms15.hinet.net; internet www.limingco.com.tw; Pres. HSU MING-SHIUNG.

Linking Publishing Co Ltd: 555 Chung Hsiao East Rd, Sec. 4, Taipei; tel. (2) 27683708; fax (2) 27634590; e-mail linkingp@ms9 .hinet.net; internet www.udngroup.com.tw/linkingp; Publr LIU KUO-JUEI.

San Min Book Co Ltd: 5th Floor, 386 Fushing North Rd, Taipei; tel. (2) 25006600; fax (2) 25064000; e-mail sanmin@ms2.hinet.net; internet www.sanmin.com.tw; f. 1953; literature, history, philosophy, social sciences, dictionaries, art, politics, law; Publr LIU CHEN-CHIANG.

Senseio Business Group: 259 Tun Hwa South Rd, Sec. 1, Taipei; tel. (2) 27037777; fax (2) 27049948; f. 1966; Publr LIAW SUSHI-IGU.

Sitak Publishing Group: 10th Floor, 15 Lane 174, Hsin Ming Rd, Neihu Dist, Taipei; tel. (2) 27911197; fax (2) 27955824; e-mail cryco@ms27.hinet.net; Publr CHU PAO-LOUNG; Dir KELLY CHU.

Taiwan Kaiming Book Co: 77 Chung Shan North Rd, Sec. 1, Taipei; tel. (2) 25415369; fax (2) 25212894; Publr LUCY CHOH LIU.

Tung Hua Book Co Ltd: 105 Ermei St, Taipei; tel. (2) 23114027; fax (2) 23116615; Publr CHARLES CHOH.

The World Book Co: 99 Chungking South Rd, Sec. 1, Taipei; tel. (2) 23311616; fax (2) 23317963; e-mail wbc@ms2.hinet.net; internet www.worldbook.com.tw; f. 1921; literature, textbooks; Chair. YEN FENG-CHANG; Publr YEN ANGELA CHU.

Youth Cultural Enterprise Co Ltd: 3rd Floor, 66-1 Chungking South Rd, Sec. 1, Taipei; tel. (2) 23112837; fax (2) 23711736; e-mail youth@ms2.hinet.net; internet www.youth.com.tw; Publr LEE CHUNG-KUEI.

Yuan Liou Publishing Co Ltd: 7F/5, 184 Ding Chou Rd, Sec. 3, Taipei 100; tel. (2) 23651212; fax (2) 23657979; e-mail ylib@yuanliou .ylib.com.tw; internet www.ylib.com.tw; f. 1975; fiction, non-fiction, children's; Publr WANG JUNG-WEN.

Broadcasting and Communications

TELECOMMUNICATIONS

Directorate-General of Telecommunications: Taipei; regulatory authority.

Chunghwa Telecommunications Co Ltd: 21 Hsinyi Rd, Sec. 1, Taipei; tel. (2) 23445385; fax (2) 23972254; internet www.cht.com.tw; f. 1996; state-controlled company, privatization commenced 2000; Chair. MAO CHI-KUO.

Far EasTone Telecom: 334 Sze Chuan Rd, Sec. 1, Taipei; tel. (2) 29505478; internet www.fareastone.com.tw; mobile telephone services.

KG Telecom: 43 Kuan Chien Rd, Taipei; tel. (2) 23888800; e-mail kgtweb@kgt.com.tw; internet www.kgt.com.tw; mobile telephone services.

Taiwan Cellular Corpn: internet www.twngsm.com.tw; f. 1998 as Pacific Cellular Corpn; mobile telephone and internet services; Pres. JOSEPH FAN.

BROADCASTING

Broadcasting stations are mostly commercial. The Ministry of Transportation and Communications determines power and frequencies, and the Government Information Office supervises the operation of all stations, whether private or governmental.

Radio

In June 2000 there were 135 radio broadcasting corporations in operation, and permission for the establishment of a further 65 radio stations was to be given by the end of that year.

Broadcasting Corpn of China (BCC): 375 Sung Chiang Rd, Taipei 104; tel. (2) 25019688; fax (2) 25018793; e-mail ls@mail.bcc.com.tw; internet www.bcc.com.tw; f. 1928; domestic (6

networks and 1 channel) services; 9 local stations, 133 transmitters; Pres. LEE CHING-PING; Chair. HUANG KUN-HUEI.

Central Broadcasting System (CBS): 55 Pei An Rd, Tachih, Taipei 104; tel. (2) 25918161; fax (2) 25850741; e-mail rtm@cbs.org.tw; internet www.cbs.org.tw; domestic and international service; Dir. HUANG SZE-CHUAN.

Cheng Sheng Broadcasting Corpn Ltd: 7th Floor, 66-1 Chungking South Rd, Sec. 1, Taipei; tel. (2) 23617231; fax (2) 23715665; f. 1950; 6 stations, 3 relay stations; Chair. YANG HSUEH-YENN; Pres. CHEN SHENG-CHUAN.

International Community Radio Taipei (ICRT): 8-1 Chungyung 2 Rd, Shantzehou, Yangmingshan, Taipei; tel. (2) 28612280; fax (2) 28613863; internet www.icrt.com.tw; predominantly English-language broadcaster; Station Man. GEORGE CHU.

Kiss Radio: 34th Floor, 6 Min Chuan 2 Rd, Kaohsiung; tel. (7) 3365888; fax (7) 3364931; Chair. IVAN YUAN; Pres. HELENA YUAN.

M-radio Broadcasting Corpn: 8th Floor, 1-18 Taichung Kang Rd, Sec. 2, Taichung City; tel. (4) 23235656; fax (4) 23231199; e-mail jason@mradio.com.tw; internet www.mradio.com.tw; Pres. SHEN CHIN-HWEI; Gen. Man. JASON C. LIN.

UFO Broadcasting Co Ltd: 25th Floor, 102 Roosevelt Rd, Sec. 2, Taipei; tel. (2) 23636600; fax (2) 23673083; Pres. JAW SHAU-KONG.

Voice of Taipei Broadcasting Co Ltd: 10th Floor, B Rm, 15-1 Han Chou South Rd, Sec. 1, Taipei; tel. (2) 23957255; fax (2) 27724370; Pres. WEI-CHUNG WANG; Man. HSU LU.

Television

Legislation to place cable broadcasting on a legal basis was adopted in mid-1993, and by June 2000 42 cable television companies were in operation. A non-commercial station, Public Television (PTV), went on air in July 1998. Legislation to place satellite broadcasting on a legal basis was adopted in February 1999, and by June 2000 132 satellite broadcasting channels (including 36 foreign satellite channels) were in operation.

China Television Co (CTV): 120 Chung Yang Rd, Nan Kang District, Taipei; tel. (2) 27838308; fax (2) 27826007; e-mail pubr@mail.chinatv.com.tw; internet www.chinatv.com.tw; f. 1969; Pres. JIANG FENG-CHYI; Chair. SUMING CHENG.

Chinese Television System (CTS): 100 Kuang Fu South Rd, Taipei 10658; tel. (2) 27510321; fax (2) 27775414; e-mail public@ mail.cts.com.tw; internet www.cts.com.tw; f. 1971; cultural and educational; Chair. YEE CHIEN-CHIU; Pres. WU SHIH-SHUNG.

Formosa Television Co (FTV): 14th Floor, 30 Pa Teh Rd, Sec. 3, Taipei; tel. (2) 25702570; fax (2) 25773170; internet www.ftv.com.tw; f. 1997; Chair. TSAI TUNG-RONG; Pres. LEE GUANG-HUEI.

Public Television Service Foundation (PTS): 90, Lane 95, Sec. 9, Kang Ning Rd, Neihu, Taipei; tel. (2) 26349122; fax (2) 26338124; e-mail pts@mail.pts.org.tw; internet www.pts.org.tw; Chair. FRANK WU; Pres. YUNG-PE LEE.

Taiwan Television Enterprise (TTV): 10 Pa Teh Rd, Sec. 3, Taipei 10560; tel. (2) 25781515; fax (2) 25799626; internet www.ttv.com.tw; f. 1962; Chair. HSU CHING-TEH; Pres. WALTER C. H. YANG.

Finance

(cap. = capital; dep. = deposits; m. = million; brs = branches; amounts in New Taiwan dollars unless otherwise stated)

BANKING

In June 1991 the Ministry of Finance granted 15 new banking licences to private banks. A 16th bank was authorized in May 1992; further authorizations followed. Restrictions on the establishment of offshore banking units were relaxed in 1994.

Central Bank

Central Bank of China: 2 Roosevelt Rd, Sec. 1, Taipei 100; tel. (2) 23936161; fax (2) 23571974; e-mail adminrol@mail.cbc.gov.tw; internet www.cbc.gov.tw; f. 1928; bank of issue; cap. 80,000m., dep. 3,189,597m. (May 2000); Gov. PERNG FAI-NAN.

Domestic Banks

Bank of Taiwan: 120 Chungking South Rd, Sec. 1, Taipei 10036; tel. (2) 23493456; fax (2) 23613203; e-mail bot076@mail.bot.com.tw; internet www.bot.com.tw; f. 1899; cap. 32,000m., dep. 1,678,523m. (Dec. 1999); Chair. M. T. CHEN; Pres. HO KUO-HWA; 117 brs, incl. 6 overseas.

Chiao Tung Bank: 91 Heng Yang Rd, Taipei 100; tel. (2) 23613000; fax (2) 23612046; e-mail dp092@ctnbank.com.tw; internet www .ctnbank.com.tw; f. 1907; fmrly Bank of Communications; cap.

22,200m., dep. 231,149m. (June 2000); Chair. PATRICK C. J. LIANG; Pres. KUO HSIUNG-CHUANG (acting); 34 brs, incl. 3 overseas.

Export-Import Bank: 7th Floor, 3 Nan Hai Rd, Taipei 100; tel. (2) 23210511; fax (2) 23940630; e-mail eximbank@eximbank.com.tw; internet www.eximbank.com.tw; f. 1979; cap. 10,000m., dep. 8,487m. (Dec. 1999); Chair. PAULINE FU; Pres. HERBERT S. S. CHUNG; 3 brs.

Farmers Bank of China: 85 Nanking East Rd, Sec. 2, Taipei 10408; tel. (2) 25517141; fax (2) 25622162; internet www .farmerbank.com.tw; f. 1933; cap. 11,800m., dep. 403,245m. (Dec. 1999); Chair. MU-TSAI CHEN; Pres. C. C. HUANG; 74 brs.

International Commercial Bank of China: 100 Chi Lin Rd, Taipei 10424; tel. (2) 25633156; fax (2) 25632614; e-mail service@ icbc.com.tw; internet www.icbc.com.tw/; f. 1912; cap. 30,108m., dep. 625,984m. (Dec. 1999); Chair. LEE YUNG-SAM; Pres. SHUE-SHENG WANG; 82 brs, incl. 18 overseas.

Land Bank of Taiwan: 46 Kuan Chien Rd, Taipei 10038; tel. (2) 23483456; fax (2) 23819548; e-mail lbot@mail.landbank.com.tw; internet www.landbank.com.tw; f. 1946; cap. 25,000m., dep. 1,235,073m. (June 1999); Chair. DONALD T. CHEN; Pres. LIN PONG-LONG; 108 brs.

Taiwan Co-operative Bank: POB 33, 77 Kuan Chien Rd, Taipei 10038; tel. (2) 23118811; fax (2) 23316567; e-mail tacbid01@14 .hinet.net; internet www.tcb-bank.com.tw; f. 1946; acts as central bank for co-operatives, and as major agricultural credit institution; cap. 20,034m., dep. 1,414,949m. (June 2000); Chair. W. H. LEE; Pres. MCKINNEY Y. C. TSAI; 140 brs.

Commercial Banks

Asia Pacific Bank: 66 Minchuan Rd, Taichung; tel. (4) 2272458; fax (4) 2265110; e-mail service@apacbank.com.tw; internet www .apacbank.com.tw; f. 1992; cap. 11,608m., dep. 134,050m. (Dec. 1999); Chair. CHIOU JIA-SHYONG; Pres. WU WEN KE; 35 brs.

Bank of Kaohsiung: 168 Po Ai 2nd Rd, Kaohsiung; tel. (7) 5570535; fax (7) 3478392; e-mail service@mail.bok.com.tw; internet www .bok.com.tw; f. 1982; cap. 4,487m., dep. 139,862m. (Dec. 1999); Chair. JEROME J. CHEN; Pres. S. H. CHUANG; 31 brs.

Bank of Overseas Chinese: 8 Hsiang Yang Rd, Taipei 10014; tel. (2) 23715181; fax (2) 23814056; e-mail plan@mail.booc.com.tw; internet www.booc.com.tw; f. 1961; cap. 16,752m., dep. 254,050m. (Dec. 1999); Chair. LININ DAY; Pres. CHING PANG CHANG; 52 brs.

Bank of Panhsin: 18 Cheng Tu St, Pan Chiao City, Taipei; tel. (2) 29629170; fax (2) 29572011; f. 1997; cap. 6,000m., dep. 77,602m. (Dec. 1999); Chair. L. P. HUI; Pres. JAMES J. C. CHEN; 28 brs.

Bank SinoPac: 9-1, Chien Kuo North Rd, Sec. 2, Taipei; tel. (2) 25082288; fax (2) 25083456; internet www.banksinopac.com.tw; f. 1992; cap. 15,846m., dep. 164,060m. (Dec. 1999); Chair. L. S. LIN; Pres. PAUL C. Y. LO; 35 brs.

Bao-Dao Commercial Bank: 10 Chung King S. Rd, Sec. 1, Taipei; tel. (2) 23119888; fax (2) 23613988; internet www.baodaobank .com.tw; f. 1992; cap. 10,815m., dep. 148,405m. (May 2000); Chair. EDWARD K. H. CHEN; Pres. JAU-SONG CHEN; 24 brs.

Central Trust of China: 49 Wu Chang St, Sec. 1, Taipei 10006; tel. (2) 23111511; fax (2) 23118107; e-mail ctc17001@ctc.com.tw; internet www.ctoc.com.tw; f. 1935; cap. 4,530m., dep. 156,636m. (Dec. 1999); Chair. WANG RONG-JOU; Pres. HUANG JACK-H; 19 brs.

Chang Hwa Commercial Bank Ltd: 38 Tsuyu Rd, Sec. 2, Taichung 40010; tel. (4) 2222001; fax (4) 2231170; e-mail customers@ms1.chb.com.tw; internet www.ccb.com.tw; f. 1905; cap. 29,492m., dep. 823,940m. (Dec. 1999); Chair. PO-SHIN CHANG; Pres. CHIUNG SHIN-WU; 153 brs, 7 overseas.

Chinatrust Commercial Bank: 3 Sung Shou Rd, Taipei; tel. (2) 27222002; fax (2) 27233872; internet www.chinatrust.com.tw; f. 1966; cap. 34,002m., dep. 435,137m. (Sept. 1999); Chair. JEFFREY L. S. KOO; 46 brs, 8 overseas.

The Chinese Bank: 68 Nanking East Rd, Sec. 3, Taipei; tel. (2) 25168686; fax (2) 25170797; internet www.chinesebank.com.tw; f. 1992; cap. 15,171m., dep. 169,238m. (Dec. 1999); Chair. WANG YOU-THENG; Pres. CHEN FEN; 30 brs.

Chinfon Commercial Bank: 1 Nanyang St, Taipei 100; tel. (2) 23114881; fax (2) 23141068; e-mail ibd@chinfonbank.com.tw; internet www.chinfonbank.com.tw; f. 1971; cap 11,128m., dep. 155,386m. (Dec. 1999); Chair. HUANG SHI-HUI; Pres HOWARD J. S. LIN; 34 brs, 2 overseas.

Chung Shing Bank: 228–230 Sung Chiang Rd, Taipei; tel. (2) 25616601; fax (2) 25114389; internet www.csbank.com.tw; f. 1992; cap. 15,076m., dep. 186,529m. (Dec. 1999); Chair. Y. Y. WANG; Pres. ABEL S. WANG; 25 brs.

Cosmos Bank: 39 Tun Hua South Rd, Sec. 2, Taipei; tel. (2) 27011777; fax (2) 27541742; e-mail ibd@cosmosbank.com.tw; internet www.cosmosbank.com.tw; f. 1992; cap. 14,009m., dep. 162,840m. (May 1999); Chair. HSUI SHENG-FA; Pres. C. C. HU; 35 brs.

COTA Commercial Bank: 32-1 Kung Yuan Rd, Taichung; tel. (4) 2245161; fax (4) 2275237; f. 1995; cap. 3,184m., dep. 49,939m. (Dec. 1999); Chair. CHUN TZE-LIAO; Pres JUN-CHUN WANG; 15 brs.

Ta Chong Bank: 58 Chungcheng 2nd Rd, Kaohsiung; tel. and fax (7) 2241620; f. 1992; cap. 13,563m., dep. 144,953m. (Dec. 1999); Chair. CHEN TIEN-MAO; Pres. HENRY LIN; 38 brs.

Dah An Commercial Bank: 41 Chung Hwa Rd, Sec. 1, Taipei; tel. (2) 23893456; fax (2) 23894567; e-mail A001@mail.dab .com.tw; internet www.dab.com.tw; f. 1992; cap. 15,712m., dep. 153,306m. (Dec. 1999); Chair. HENRY KAO; Pres. Y. C. CHAO; 33 brs.

E. Sun Commercial Bank: 77 Wuchang St, Sec. 1, Taipei; tel. (2) 23891313; fax (2) 23125182; e-mail esbintl@email.esunbank.com.tw; internet www.esunbank.com.tw; f. 1992; cap. 15,610m., dep. 188,749m. (Dec. 1999); Chair. LIN JONG-SHONG; Pres. HUANG YUNG-JEN; 36 brs.

En Tie Commercial Bank: 3rd Floor, 158 Ming Sheng East Rd, Sec. 3, Taipei; tel. (2) 27189999; fax (2) 27175940; f. 1993; cap. 13,551m., dep. 159,169m. (Dec. 1999); Chair. YU-LIN LIN; Pres. CHENG-DER LIU; 39 brs.

Far Eastern International Bank: 27th Floor, 207 Tun Hua South Rd, Sec. 2, Taipei; tel. (2) 23786868; fax (2) 23765691; e-mail 800@mail.feib.com.tw; internet www.feib.com.tw; f. 1992; cap. 14,797m., dep. 143,423m. (Dec. 1999); Chair. DOUGLAS T. HSU; Pres. ELI HONG; 28 brs.

First Commercial Bank: POB 395, 30 Chungking South Rd, Sec. 1, Taipei; tel. (2) 23481111; fax (2) 23610036; e-mail fcb@mail .firstbank.com.tw; internet www.firstbank.com.tw; f. 1899; cap. 32,746m., dep. 1,083,942m. (Dec. 1999); Chair. GERRY Y. G. LEE; Pres. A. C. CHEN; 159 brs, 11 overseas.

Fubon Commercial Bank: 2nd Floor, 169 Jen Ai Rd, Sec. 4, Taipei; tel. (2) 27716699; fax (2) 27730763; e-mail 014.mgr@ fubonbank.com.tw; internet www.fubonbank.com.tw; f. 1992; cap. 20,255m., dep. 191,596m. (Dec. 1999); Chair. CHEN S. YU; Pres. WANG CHUAN-HSI; 35 brs.

Grand Commercial Bank: 17 Chengteh Rd, Sec. 1, Taipei; tel. (2) 25562088; fax (2) 25561579; e-mail service@grandbank.com.tw; internet www.grandbank.com.tw; f. 1991; cap. 14,933m., dep. 162,475m. (Dec. 1999); Chair. KAO CHIH-YEN; Pres. and Man. Dir ALEXANDER T. Y. DEAN; 38 brs.

Hsinchu International Bank: 106 Chung Yang Rd, Hsinchu 300; tel. (3) 5245131; fax (3) 5250977; f. 1948; cap. 12,665m., dep. 245,378m. (Dec. 1999); Chair. S. Y. CHAN; Pres C. W. WU; 73 brs.

Hua Nan Commercial Bank Ltd: POB 989, 38 Chungking South Rd, Sec. 1, Taipei; tel. (2) 23713111; fax (2) 23711972; e-mail service@ms.hncb.com.tw; internet www.hncb.com.tw; f. 1919; cap. 31,775m., dep. 1,088,699m. (Dec. 1999); Chair. EDWARD H. T. CHIEN; Pres. BSU THE-NAN; 138 brs, 5 overseas.

Hwa Tai Commercial Bank: 246 Chang An E. Rd, Sec. 2, Taipei; tel. (2) 27525252; fax (2) 27711495; f. 1999; cap. 3,300m., dep. 50,111m. (Dec. 1999); Chair. M. H. LIN; Pres. S. Y. WU; 18 brs.

International Bank of Taipei: 36 Nanking East Rd, Sec. 3, Taipei; tel. (2) 25063333; fax (2) 25062462; e-mail 630@ibtpe.com.tw; internet www.ibtpe.com.tw; f. 1948; cap. 15,593m., dep. 249,331m. (Dec. 1999); Chair. S. C. HO; Pres. K. C. YU; 82 brs.

Kao Shin Commercial Bank: 75 Lih Wen Rd, Kaohsiung; tel. (7) 3460711; fax (7) 3502980; f. 1997; cap. 2,300m., dep. 48,244m. (Dec. 1999); Chair. C. N. HUANG; Pres. F. T. CHAO; 27 brs.

Lucky Bank: 35 Chung Hua Rd, Sec. 1, Taichung 403; tel. (4) 2259111; fax (4) 2232652; f. 1997; cap. 3,146m., dep. 74,753m. (Dec. 1999); Chair. C. C. CHANG; Pres. T. Y. SU; 27 brs.

Makoto Bank: 134 Hsi Chang St, Taipei; tel. (2) 23812160; fax (2) 23880828; e-mail master@makoto.com.tw; internet www .makotobank.com.tw; f. 1997; cap. 6,029m., dep. 122,744m. (Dec. 1999); Chair. C. I. LIN; Pres. SHERMAN CHUANG; 49 brs.

Pan Asia Bank: 3rd–4th Floors, 60-8 Chungkang Rd, Taichung; tel. (02) 23279998; fax (02) 33931581; e-mail pabkdbu@ms4.hinet.net; internet www.panasiabank.com.tw; f. 1992; cap. 14,700m., dep. 147,690m. (Dec. 1999); Chair. KOH FEI-LO; Pres. YIN YI-NA; 35 brs.

Shanghai Commercial and Savings Bank Ltd: 2 Min Chuan East Rd, Sec. 1, Taipei 104; tel. (2) 25817111; fax (2) 25671921; internet www.scsb.com.tw; f. 1915; cap. 11,718m., dep. 264,555m. (Dec. 1999); Chair. H. C. YUNG; Pres. Y. P. CHEN; 47 brs.

Sunny Bank: 88 Shin Pai Rd, Sec. 1, Taipei 112; tel. (2) 28208166; fax (2) 28233414; f. 1997; cap. 3,800m., dep. 82,129m. (Dec. 1999); Chair. S. H. CHEN; Pres. C. W. CHEN; 22 brs.

Taichung Commercial Bank: 45 Min Tsu Rd, POB 108, Taichung 400; tel. (4) 22360021; fax (4) 2240748; e-mail webmaster@ ms1.tcbbank.com.tw; internet www.tcbbank.com.tw; f. 1953; cap. 15,380m., dep. 185,162m. (Dec. 1999); Chair. Y. F. TSAI; Pres. Y. C. TSAI; 76 brs.

Taipeibank: 50 Chung Shan North Rd, Sec. 2, Taipei 10419; tel. (2) 25425656; fax (2) 25428870; e-mail 0180@mail.taipeibank.com.tw;

internet www.taipeibank.com.tw; f. 1969; fmrly City Bank of Taipei; cap. 15,400m., dep. 467,890m. (Dec. 1999); Chair. C. C. LIAO; Pres. JESSE Y. DING ; 73 brs, 2 overseas.

Taishin International Bank: 44 Chung Shan North Rd, Sec. 2, Taipei; tel. (2) 25683988; fax (2) 25234564; e-mail pr@taishinbank .com.tw; internet www.taishinbank.com.tw; f. 1992; cap. 18,322m., dep. 281,579m. (Dec. 1999); Chair. THOMAS T. L. WU; Pres. CHARLES W. Y. WANG; 39 brs.

Union Bank of Taiwan: 109 Ming Sheng East Rd, Sec. 3, Taipei; tel. (2) 27180001; fax (2) 27137515; e-mail 014_0199@email.ubot .com.tw; internet www.ubot.com.tw; f. 1992; cap. 14,187m., dep. 171,745m. (Dec. 1999); Chair. C. C. HUANG; Pres. S. C. LEE; 31 brs.

United World Chinese Commercial Bank: 65 Kuan Chien Rd, POB 1670, Taipei 10038; tel. (2) 23125555; fax (2) 23311093; e-mail yinglin@uwccb.com.tw; internet www.uwccb.com.tw; f. 1975; cap. 30,408m., dep. 554,896m. (Dec. 1999); Chair. GREGORY K. H. WANG; Pres. C. C. TUNG; 75 brs, incl. 5 overseas.

There are also a number of Medium Business Banks throughout the country.

Community Financial System

The community financial institutions include both credit co-operatives and credit departments of farmers' and fishermen's associations. These local financial institutions focus upon providing savings and loan services for the community. At the end of 1999 there were 50 credit co-operatives, 287 credit departments of farmers' associations and 27 credit departments of fishermen's associations, with a combined total deposit balance of NT $2,339,000m., while outstanding loans amounted to NT $1,340,200m.

Foreign Banks

In December 1998 41 foreign banks maintained 72 branches in Taiwan.

STOCK EXCHANGE

In January 1991 the stock exchange was opened to direct investment by foreign institutions, and in March 1996 it was also opened to direct investment by foreign individuals. By the end of June 2000 463 foreign institutional investors had been approved to invest in the local securities market. Various liberalization measures have been introduced since 1994. In March 1999 the limits on both single and aggregate foreign investment in domestic shares were raised to 50% of the outstanding shares of a listed company. In November of that year the 'ceiling' of investment amount for each qualified foreign institutional investor in domestic securities markets was increased from US $600m. to US $1,200m.

Taiwan Stock Exchange Corpn: 13th Floor, 17 Po Ai Rd, Taipei 100; tel. (2) 23485678; fax (2) 23485324; f. 1962; Chair. C. Y. LEE.

Supervisory Body

Securities and Futures Commission: 85 Hsin Sheng South Rd, Sec. 1, Taipei; tel. (2) 87734202; fax (2) 8734134; Chair. CHU JAW-CHYUAN; Sec.-Gen. CHEN WEI-LUNG.

INSURANCE

In 1993 the Ministry of Finance issued eight new insurance licences, the first for more than 30 years. Two more were issued in 1994.

Allianz President General Insurance Co Ltd: 11/F, 69 Ming-Sheng East Rd, Sec. 3, Taipei; tel. (2) 25157177; fax (2) 25077506; e-mail azpl@ms2.seeder.net; internet www.allianz.com.tw; f. 1995; Chair. NAN-TEN CHUNG; Gen. Man. NICHOLAS CHANG.

Cathay Life Insurance Co Ltd: 296 Jen Ai Rd, Sec. 4, Taipei 10650; tel. (2) 27551399; fax (2) 27551322; e-mail master@cathlife .com.tw; internet www.cathlife.com.tw; f. 1962; Chair. TSAI HONG-TU; Gen. Man. LIU CHIU-TE.

Central Insurance Co Ltd: 6 Chung Hsiao West Rd, Sec. 1, Taipei; tel. (2) 23819910; fax (2) 23116901; internet www.cins.com.tw; f. 1962; Chair. H. K. SHE; Gen. Man. C. C. HUANG.

Central Reinsurance Corpn: 53 Nanking East Rd, Sec. 2, Taipei; tel. (2) 25115211; fax (2) 25235350; e-mail chlin@crc.com.tw; internet www.crc.com.tw; f. 1968; Chair. CHING-HSIEN LIN; Pres. C. T. YANG.

Central Trust of China, Life Insurance Dept: 3rd–8th Floors, 69 Tun Hua South Rd, Sec. 2, Taipei; tel. (2) 27849151; fax (2) 27052214; e-mail sectrl@ctclife.com.tw; internet www.ctclife.com.tw; f. 1941; life insurance; Pres. EDWARD LO; Gen. Man. MAN-HSIUNG TSAI.

China Life Insurance Co Ltd: 122 Tun Hwa North Rd, Taipei; tel. (2) 27196678; fax (2) 27125966; e-mail services@mail.chinalife .com.tw; internet www.chinalife.com.tw; f. 1963; Chair. C. F. KOO; Gen. Man. CHESTER C. Y. KOO.

China Mariners' Assurance Corpn Ltd: 11th Floor, 2 Kuan Chien Rd, Taipei; tel. (2) 23757676; fax (2) 23756363; internet www.cmac.com.tw; f. 1948; Chair. VINCENT M. S. FAN; Pres. W. H. HUNG.

Chung Kuo Insurance Co Ltd: 10th–12th Floors, ICBC Bldg, 100 Chilin Rd, Taipei 10424; tel. (2) 25513345; fax (2) 25414046; f. 1931; fmrly China Insurance Co Ltd; Chair. S. Y. LIU; Pres. C. Y. LIU.

Chung Shing Life Insurance Co Ltd: 18th Floor, 200 Keelung Rd, Sec. 1, Taipei 110; tel. (2) 27583099; fax (2) 23451635; f. 1993; Chair. T. S. CHAO; Gen. Man. DAH-WEI CHEN.

The First Insurance Co Ltd: 54 Chung Hsiao East Rd, Sec. 1, Taipei; tel. (2) 23913271; fax (2) 23930685; f. 1962; Chair. C. H. LEE; Gen. Man. M. C. CHEN.

Fubon Insurance Co Ltd: 237 Chien Kuo South Rd, Sec. 1, Taipei; tel. (2) 27067890; fax (2) 27042915; internet www.fubon-ins.com.tw; f. 1961; Chair. TSAI MING-CHUNG; Gen. Man. T. M. SHIH.

Fubon Life Insurance Co Ltd: 14th Floor, 108 Tun Hwa South Rd, Sec. 1, Taipei; tel. (2) 87716699; fax (2) 87715919; f. 1993; Chair. RICHARD M. TSAI; Gen. Man. CHIAO PEN TIAN.

Global Life Insurance Co Ltd: 18 Chung Yang South Rd, Sec. 2, Peitou, Taipei 11235; tel. (2) 28967899; fax (2) 28958312; f. 1993; Chair. JOHN TSENG; Gen. Man. ROBERT KUO.

Hontai Life Insurance Co Ltd: 7th Floor, 70 Cheng Teh Rd, Sec. 1, Taipei; tel. (2) 25595151; fax (2) 25562840; internet www.hontai .com.tw; f. 1994; frmrly Hung Fu Life Insurance Co; Chair. TONY SHE; Gen. Man. YU-CHIEH YANG.

Kuo Hua Insurance Co Ltd: 166 Chang An East Rd, Sec. 2, Taipei; tel. (2) 27514225; fax (2) 27819388; e-mail kh11601@kuohua.com.tw; internet www.kuohua.com.tw; f. 1962; Chair. and Gen. Man. J. B. WANG.

Kuo Hua Life Insurance Co Ltd: 42 Chung Shan North Rd, Sec. 2, Taipei; tel. (2) 25621101; fax (2) 25423832; internet www.khl.com.tw; f. 1963; Chair. JASON CHANG; Gen. Man. CHEN TUNG-CHENG.

Mercuries Life Insurance Co Ltd: 6th Floor, 2 Lane 150, Hsin-Yi North Rd, Sec. 5, Taipei; tel. (2) 23455511; fax (2) 23456616; internet www.mli.com.tw; f. 1993; Chair. HARVEY TANG; Gen. Man. CHUNG-SHIN LU.

Mingtai Fire and Marine Insurance Co Ltd: 1 Jen Ai Rd, Sec. 4, Taipei; tel. (2) 27725678; fax (2) 27729932; internet www .mingtai.com.tw; f. 1961; Chair. LARRY P. C. LIN; Gen. Man. H. T. CHEN.

Nan Shan Life Insurance Co Ltd: 144 Min Chuan East Rd, Sec. 2, Taipei 104; tel. (2) 25013333; fax (2) 25012555; internet www.nanshanlife.com.tw; f. 1963; Chair. EDMUND TSE; Pres. SUNNY LIN.

Prudential Life Assurance Co Ltd: 12th Floor, 550 Chung Hsiao East Rd, Sec. 4, Taipei; tel. (2) 27582727; fax (2) 27086758; internet www.prudential-uk.com.tw; f. 1999; Chair. MARK TUCKER; Man. Dir DOMINIC LEUNG KA KUI.

Shin Fu Life Insurance Co Ltd: 8th Floor, 6 Chung Hsiao West Rd, Sec. 1, Taipei; tel. (2) 23817172; fax (2) 23817162; f. 1993; Chair. and Gen. Man. SONG CHI CHIENG.

Shin Kong Insurance Co Ltd: 15 Chien Kuo North Rd, Sec. 2, Taipei; tel. (2) 25075335; fax (2) 25074580; internet www.shinkon .com.tw; f. 1963; Chair. ANTHONY T. S. WU; Pres. YIH HSIUNG LEE.

Shin Kong Life Insurance Co Ltd: 66 Chung Hsiao West Rd, Sec. 1, Taipei; tel. (2) 23895858; fax (2) 23758688; internet www.skl.com.tw; f. 1963; Chair. EUGENE T. C. WU; Gen. Man. HONG-CHI CHENG.

Sinon Life Insurance Co Ltd: 11-2F, 155 Tsu Chih St, Taichung; tel. (4) 3721653; fax (4) 3722008; e-mail sinonlife@mail.sinonlife .com.tw; internet www.sinonlife.com.tw; f. 1993; Chair. PO-YEN HORNG; Gen. Man. P. T. LAI.

South China Insurance Co Ltd: 5th Floor, 560 Chung Hsiao East Rd, Sec. 4, Taipei; tel. and fax (2) 27298022; internet www.south-china.com.tw; f. 1963; Chair. C. F. LIAO; Pres. ALLAN I. R. HUANG.

Tai Ping Insurance Co Ltd: 3rd–5th Floors, 550 Chung Hsiao East Rd, Sec. 4, Taipei; tel. (2) 27582700; fax (2) 27295681; f. 1929; Chair. T. C. CHEN; Gen. Man. T. Y. TUNG.

Taian Insurance Co Ltd: 59 Kwantsien Rd, Taipei; tel. (2) 23819678; fax (2) 23315332; e-mail taian@mail.taian.com.tw; f. 1961; Chair. C. H. CHEN; Gen. Man. PATRICK S. LEE.

Taiwan Fire and Marine Insurance Co Ltd: 49 Kuan Chien Rd, Taipei; tel. (2) 23317261; fax (2) 23145287; f. 1946; Chair. W. Y. LEE; Gen. Man. JOHN F. KAO.

Taiwan Life Insurance Co Ltd: 16th–19th Floors, 17 Hsu Chang St, Taipei; tel. (2) 23116411; fax (2) 23759714; e-mail service1@twlife .com.tw; internet www.twlife.com.tw; f. 1947; Chair. PING-YU CHU; Pres. CHENG-TAO LIN.

Union Insurance Co Ltd: 12th Floor, 219 Chung Hsiao East Rd, Sec. 4, Taipei; tel. (2) 27765567; fax (2) 27737199; internet www.unionins.com.tw; f. 1963; Chair. S. H. CHIN; Gen. Man. FRANK S. WANG.

Zurich Insurance Taiwan Ltd: 56 Tun Hua North Rd, Taipei; tel. (2) 27752888; fax (2) 27416004; internet www.zurich.com.tw; f. 1961; Chair. DEAN T. CHIANG; Gen. Man. JUNG H. CHEN.

Trade and Industry

GOVERNMENT AGENCIES

Board of Foreign Trade (Ministry of Economic Affairs): 1 Houkow St, Taipei; tel. (2) 23510271; fax (2) 23513603; Dir-Gen. WU WEN-YEA.

Council of Agriculture (COA): 37 Nan Hai Rd, Taipei 100; tel. (2) 23812991; fax (2) 23310341; e-mail webmaster@www.coa.gov.tw; f. 1984; govt agency directly under the Executive Yuan, with ministerial status; a policy-making body in charge of national agriculture, forestry, fisheries, the animal industry and food administration; promotes technology and provides external assistance; Chair. Dr CHEN HSI-HUANG; Sec.-Gen. Dr HUANG CHIN-RONG.

Industrial Development Bureau (Ministry of Economic Affairs): 41-3 Hsin Yi Rd, Sec. 3, Taipei; tel. (2) 27541255; fax (2) 27030160; Dir-Gen. SHIH YEN-SHIANG.

Industrial Development and Investment Center (Ministry of Economic Affairs): 19th Floor, 4 Chung Hsiao West Rd, Sec. 1, Taipei; tel. (2) 23892111; fax (2) 23820497; e-mail njlin@mail.idic .gov.tw; internet www.idic.gov.tw; f. 1959 to assist investment and planning; Dir-Gen. HUANG CHIH-PENG.

CHAMBER OF COMMERCE

General Chamber of Commerce of the Republic of China: 6th Floor, 390 Fu Hsing South Rd, Sec. 1, Taipei; tel. (2) 27012671; fax (2) 27542107; f. 1946; 39 mems, incl. 14 nat. feds of trade asscns, 22 district export asscns and 3 district chambers of commerce; Chair. Dr Y. T. WANG; Sec.-Gen. CHIU JAW-SHIN.

INDUSTRIAL AND TRADE ASSOCIATIONS

China External Trade Development Council: 4th–8th Floors, CETRA Tower, 333 Keelung Rd, Sec. 1, Taipei 110; tel. (2) 27255200; fax (2) 27576653; trade promotion body; Sec.-Gen. RICKY Y. S. KAO.

China Productivity Center: 2nd Floor, 79 Hsin Tai 5 Rd, Sec. 1, Hsichih, Taipei County; tel. (2) 26982989; fax (2) 26982976; f. 1956; management, technology, training, etc.; Pres. CHEN MING-CHANG.

Chinese National Association of Industry and Commerce: 13th Floor, 390 Fu Hsing South Rd, Sec. 1, Taipei; tel. (2) 27070111; fax (2) 27017601; Chair. JEFFREY L. S. KOO.

Chinese National Federation of Industries (CNFI): 12th Floor, 390 Fu Hsing South Rd, Sec. 1, Taipei; tel. (2) 27033500; fax (2) 27033982; f. 1948; 136 mem. asscns; Chair. KAO CHIN-YUAN; Sec.-Gen. HO CHUN-YIH.

Taiwan Handicraft Promotion Centre: 1 Hsu Chou Rd, Taipei; tel. (2) 23933655; fax (2) 23937330; f. 1956; Pres. Y. C. WANG.

Trading Department of Central Trust of China: 49 Wuchang St, Sec. 1, Taipei 10006; tel. (2) 23111511; fax (2) 23821047; f. 1935; export and import agent for private and govt-owned enterprises.

UTILITIES

Electricity

Taiwan Power Co (Taipower): 242 Roosevelt Rd, Sec. 3, Taipei 100; tel. (2) 3967777; fax (2) 3968593; e-mail service@ taipower.com.tw; internet www.taipower.com.tw; f. 1946; electricity generation; scheduled for privatization from 2001; Chair. S. C. HSI; Pres. J. H. KUO.

Gas

The Great Taipei Gas Corpn: 5th Floor, 35 Kwang Fu North Rd, Taipei; tel. (2) 27684999; fax (2) 27630480; supply of gas and gas equipment.

Water

Taipei Water Dept: 131 Changxing St, Taipei; tel. (2) 7352141; fax (2) 7353185; f. 1907; responsible for water supply in Taipei and suburban areas; Commr LIN WEN-YUAN.

CO-OPERATIVES

In December 1999 there were 5,375 co-operatives, with a total membership of 5,679,976 and total capital of NT $46,000m. Of the specialized co-operatives the most important was the consumers' co-operative (4,440 co-ops).

The Co-operative League (f. 1940) is a national organization responsible for co-ordination, education and training and the movement's national and international interests (Chair. K. L. CHEN).

TRADE UNIONS

Chinese Federation of Labour: 11th Floor, Back Bldg, 201–18 Tun Hua North Rd, Taipei; tel. (2) 27135111; fax (2) 27135116; e-mail cfllabor@ms10.hinet.net; f. 1958; mems: c. 3,691 unions representing 2,950,000 workers; Pres. LEE CHENG-CHONG.

National Federations

Chinese Federation of Postal Workers: 9th Floor, 45 Chungking South Rd, Sec. 2, Taipei 100; tel. (2) 23921380; fax (2) 23414510; e-mail cfpw@ms16.hinet.net; f. 1930; 27,957 mems; Pres. CHEN SHIAN-JUH.

Chinese Federation of Railway Workers Union: Room 6048, 6th Floor, 3 Peiping West Rd, Taipei; tel. (2) 23611149; fax (2) 23881395; f. 1947; 17,129 mems; Pres. LIN HUI-KUAN.

National Chinese Seamen's Union: 8th Floor, 25 Nanking East Rd, Sec. 3, Taipei; tel. (2) 25150265; fax (2) 25078211; f. 1913; 22,278 mems; Pres. FANG FU-LIANG.

Regional Federations

Taiwan Federation of Textile and Dyeing Industry Workers' Unions (TFTDWU): 2 Lane 64, Chung Hsiao East Rd, Sec. 2, Taipei; tel. (2) 23415627; f. 1958; 11,906 mems; Chair. CHANG MING-KEN.

Taiwan Provincial Federation of Labour: 11th Floor, 44 Roosevelt Rd, Sec. 2, Taipei; tel. and fax (2) 23938080; f. 1948; 81 mem. unions and 1,571,826 mems; Pres. WU HAI-RAY; Sec.-Gen. HUANG YAO-TUNG.

Transport

RAILWAYS

Taiwan Railway Administration (TRA): 3 Peiping West Rd, Taipei 10026; tel. (2) 23815226; fax (2) 23831367; f. 1891; a public utility under the Ministry of Communications and Transportation; operates both the west line and east line systems, with a route length of 1,103.7 km, of which 510.8 km are electrified; the west line is the main trunk line from Keelung, in the north, to Fangliao, in the south, with several branches; electrification of the main trunk line was completed in 1979; the east line runs along the east coast, linking Hualien with Taitung; the north link line, with a length of 79.2 km from Suao Sing to Hualien, connecting Suao and Hualien, was opened in 1980; the south link line, with a length of 98.2 km from Taitung Shin to Fangliao, opened in late 1991, completing the round-the-island system; construction of a high-speed link between Taipei and Kaohsiung (345 km) was scheduled for completion in 2005; Man. Dir T. P. CHEN.

There are also 1,440 km of private narrow-gauge track, operated by the Taiwan Sugar Corpn in conjunction with the Taiwan Forestry Bureau and other organizations. These railroads are mostly used for freight.

Construction of a five-line, 86.8-km, mass rapid-transit system (MRTS) in Taipei, incorporating links to the airport, began in 1987. The first 10.9km section of the Mucha line opened in March 1996 and the Tamshui line (22.8 km) opened in December 1997. The Chungho and Hsintien lines, and part of the Nannkang line, were in operation by 1999. The remainder of the network was scheduled for completion by 2005. A 42.7-km system is planned for Kaohsiung, scheduled for completion in the year 2006. MRT systems are also projected for Taoyuan, Hsinchu, Taichung and Tainan.

ROADS

There were 20,222 km of highways in 1999, most of them asphalt-paved. The Sun Yat-sen (North–South) Freeway was completed in 1978. Construction of a 505-km Second Freeway, which is to extend to Pingtung, in southern Taiwan, began in July 1987 and was scheduled to be completed by the end of 2003. Work on the Taipei–Ilan freeway began in 1991.

Taiwan Area National Expressway Bureau: 1 Lane 1, Hoping East Rd, Sec. 3, Taipei; tel. (2) 27078808; fax (2) 27017818; e-mail neebeyes@taneeb.gov.tw; internet www.taneeb.gov.tw; f. 1946; responsible for planning, design, construction and maintenance of provincial and county highways; Dir-Gen. CHENG WEN-LON.

Taiwan Area National Freeway Bureau: POB 75, Sinchwang, Taipei 242; tel. (2) 29096141; fax (2) 29093218; internet www.freeway.gov.tw; f. 1970; Dir-Gen. HO NUAN-HSUAN.

Taiwan Motor Transport Co Ltd: 5th Floor, 17 Hsu Chang St, Taipei; tel. (2) 23715364; fax (2) 23820634; f. 1980; operates national bus service; Gen. Man. CHEN WU-SHIUNG.

SHIPPING

Taiwan has five international ports: Kaohsiung, Keelung, Taichung, Hualien and Suao. In 1998 the merchant fleet comprised 686 vessels, with a total displacement of 5,491,718 grt.

Evergreen Marine Corpn: 166 Ming Sheng East Rd, Sec. 2, Taipei 104; tel. (2) 25057766; fax (2) 25055256; f. 1968; world-wide container liner services; Indian subcontinent feeder service; two-way round-the-world services; Chair. LING SENG-SAN; Pres. CHAN MING BO.

Taiwan Navigation Co Ltd: 29, Chi Nan Rd, Sec. 2, Taipei 104; tel. (2) 23941769; Chair. J. M. MA; Pres. I. Y. CHANG.

U-Ming Marine Transport Corpn: 29th Floor, Taipei Metro Tower, 207 Tun Hua South Rd, Sec. 2, Taipei; tel. (2) 27338000; fax (2) 27359900; world-wide tramp services; Chair. DOUGLAS HSU; Pres. C. K. ONG.

Uniglory Marine Corpn: 6th Floor, 172 Ming Sheng East Rd, Sec. 2, Taipei; tel. (2) 25016711; fax (2) 25017592; Chair. LOH YAO-FON; Pres. DAVID YONG PO CHEN.

Wan Hai Lines Ltd: 10th Floor, 136 Sung Chiang Rd, Taipei; tel. (2) 25677961; fax (2) 25216000; f. 1965; regional container liner services; Chair. CHEN CHAO HON; Pres. CHEN PO TING.

Yang Ming Marine Transport Corpn (Yang Ming Line): 271 Ming de 1st Rd, Chidu, Keelung 206; tel. (2) 24559988; fax (2) 24559958; e-mail winsor@imail.yml.com.tw; internet www.yml.com.tw; f. 1972; world-wide container liner services, bulk carrier and supertanker services; Chair. T. H. CHEN; Pres. FRANK F. H. LU.

CIVIL AVIATION

There are two international airports, Chiang Kai-shek at Taoyuan, near Taipei, which opened in 1979 (a second passenger terminal and expansion of freight facilities being completed in 2000), and Hsiaokang, in Kaohsiung (where an international terminal building was inaugurated in 1997). There are also 14 domestic airports.

Civil Aeronautics Administration: 340 Tun Hua North Rd, Taipei; tel. (2) 23496000; fax (2) 23496277; e-mail gencaa@ms31.hinet.net; internet www.caa.gov.tw; Dir-Gen. Dr CHANG YU-HERN.

China Air Lines Ltd (CAL): 131 Nanking East Rd, Sec. 3, Taipei; tel. (2) 25062345; fax (2) 25145786; internet www.chinaairlines.com.tw; f. 1959; international services to destinations in the Far East, Europe, the Middle East and the USA; Chair. Capt. Y. L. LEE.

EVA Airways: Eva Air Bldg, 376 Hsin-nan Rd, Sec. 1, Luchu, Taoyuan Hsien; tel. (3) 3515151; fax (3) 3510005; internet www.evaair.com.tw; f. 1989; subsidiary of Evergreen Group; commenced flights in 1991; services to destinations in Asia (incl. Hong Kong and Macau), the Middle East, Europe, North America, Australia and New Zealand; Pres. FRANK HSU.

Far Eastern Air Transport Corpn (FAT): 5, Alley 123, Lane 405, Tun Hua North Rd, Taipei 10592; tel. (2) 7121555; fax (2) 7122428; f. 1957; domestic services and international services to Palau and Subic Bay (Philippines); Chair. and Pres. STEPHEN J. TSUEI.

Mandarin Airlines (AE): 13th Floor, 134 Ming Sheng East Rd, Sec. 3, Taipei; tel. (2) 7171188; fax (2) 7170716; e-mail mandarin@mandarin-airlines.com; internet www.mandarin-airlines.com; f. 1991; subsidiary of CAL; merged with Formosa Airlines 1998; domestic and regional international services; Chair. CHIANG HUNG-I; Pres. MICHAEL LO.

TransAsia Airways: 9th Floor, 139 Chengchou Rd, Taipei; tel. (2) 25575767; fax (2) 25570643; internet www.tna.com.tw; f. 1951; fmrly Foshing Airlines; domestic flights and international services; Chair. CHARLES C. LIN; Pres. EDWIN LEE.

U-Land Airlines: 340 Tun Hua North Rd, Taipei; tel. (2) 26981280; fax (2) 26982890; fmrly China Asia Airlines; domestic services; Chair. WANG KER-GER; Pres. TING ZEAN.

UNI Airways Corpn: 9/F, 260 Pah-Teh Rd, Sec. 2, Taipei; tel. (2) 27768576; fax (2) 87722029; internet www.uniair.com.tw; f. 1989; fmrly Makung Airlines; merged with Great China Airlines and Taiwan Airlines 1998; domestic flights and international services (to Kota Kinabalu, Malaysia; Bali, Indonesia; Phuket, Thailand; Yangon, Myanmar); Pres. DANIEL WU.

Tourism

The principal tourist attractions are the cuisine, the cultural artefacts and the island scenery. In 1999 there were 2,411,248 visitor arrivals (including 295,595 overseas Chinese) in Taiwan. Receipts from tourism in that year totalled US $3,571m.

Tourism Bureau, Ministry of Transportation and Communications: 9th Floor, 290 Chung Hsiao East Rd, Sec. 4, Taipei 106; tel. (2) 23491635; fax (2) 27735487; e-mail tbroc@tbroc.gov.tw; internet www.tbroc.gov.tw; f. 1972; Dir-Gen. CHANG SHUO-LAO.

Taiwan Visitors' Association: 5th Floor, 9 Min Chuan East Rd, Sec. 2, Taipei; tel. (2) 25943261; fax (2) 25943265; f. 1956; promotes domestic and international tourism; Chair. STANLEY C. YEN.

COLOMBIA

Introductory Survey

Location, Climate, Language, Religion, Flag, Capital

The Republic of Colombia lies in the north-west of South America, with the Caribbean Sea to the north and the Pacific Ocean to the west. Its continental neighbours are Venezuela and Brazil to the east, and Peru and Ecuador to the south, while Panama connects it with Central America. The coastal areas have a tropical rain forest climate, the plateaux are temperate, and in the Andes mountains there are areas of permanent snow. The language is Spanish. Almost all of the inhabitants profess Christianity, and about 95% are Roman Catholics. There are small Protestant and Jewish minorities. The national flag (proportions 3 by 2) has three horizontal stripes, of yellow (one-half of the depth) over dark blue over red. The capital is Santafé de Bogotá (formerly Bogotá).

Recent History

Colombia was under Spanish rule from the 16th century until 1819, when it achieved independence as part of Gran Colombia, which included Ecuador, Panama and Venezuela. Ecuador and Venezuela seceded in 1830, when Colombia (then including Panama) became a separate republic. In 1903 the province of Panama successfully rebelled and became an independent country. For more than a century, ruling power in Colombia has been shared between two political parties, the Conservatives (Partido Conservador Colombiano, PCC) and the Liberals (Partido Liberal Colombiano, PL), whose rivalry has often led to violence. President Laureano Gómez of the PCC, who was elected 'unopposed' in November 1949, ruled as a dictator until his overthrow by a coup in June 1953, when power was seized by Gen. Gustavo Rojas Pinilla. President Rojas established a right-wing dictatorship but, following widespread rioting, he was deposed in May 1957, when a five-man military junta took power. According to official estimates, lawlessness during 1949–58, known as 'La Violencia', caused the deaths of about 280,000 people.

In an attempt to restore peace and stability, the PCC and the PL agreed to co-operate in a National Front. Under this arrangement, the presidency was to be held by the PCC and the PL in rotation, while cabinet portfolios would be divided equally between the two parties and both would have an equal number of seats in each house of the bicameral Congress. In December 1957, in Colombia's first vote on the basis of universal adult suffrage, this agreement was overwhelmingly approved by a referendum and was subsequently incorporated in Colombia's Constitution, dating from 1886.

In May 1958 the first presidential election under the amended Constitution was won by the National Front candidate, Dr Alberto Lleras Camargo, a PL member who had been President in 1945–46. He took office in August 1958, when the ruling junta relinquished power. As provided by the 1957 agreement, he was succeeded by a member of the PCC, Dr Guillermo León Valencia, who was, in turn, succeeded by a PL candidate, Dr Carlos Lleras Restrepo, in 1966.

At the presidential election in April 1970, the National Front candidate, Dr Misael Pastrana Borrero (PCC) narrowly defeated Gen. Rojas, the former dictator, who campaigned as leader of the Alianza Nacional Popular (ANAPO), with policies that had considerable appeal for the poorer sections of the population. At elections to Congress, held simultaneously, the National Front lost its majority in each of the two houses, while ANAPO became the main opposition group in each. The result of the presidential election was challenged by supporters of ANAPO, and an armed wing of the party, the Movimiento 19 de Abril (M-19), began to organize guerrilla activity against the Government. It was joined by dissident members of a pro-Soviet guerrilla group, the Fuerzas Armadas Revolucionarias de Colombia (FARC), established in 1966.

The bipartisan form of government ended formally with the presidential and legislative elections of April 1974, although the 1974–78 Cabinet remained subject to the parity agreement. The PCC and the PL together won an overwhelming majority of seats in Congress, and support for ANAPO was greatly reduced. The presidential election was won by the PL candidate, Dr Alfonso López Michelsen.

At elections to Congress in February 1978, the PL won a clear majority in both houses, and in June the PL candidate, Dr Julio César Turbay Ayala, won the presidential election. President Turbay continued to observe the National Front agreement, and attempted to address the problems of urban terrorism and drugs-trafficking. In 1982 the guerrillas suffered heavy losses after successful counter-insurgency operations, combined with the activities of a new anti-guerrilla group which was associated with drugs-smuggling enterprises, the Muerte a Secuestradores (MAS, Death to Kidnappers), whose targets later became trade union leaders, academics and human rights activists.

At congressional elections in March 1982, the PL maintained its majority in both houses. In May the PCC candidate, Dr Belisario Betancur Cuartas, won the presidential election, benefiting from a division within the PL. President Betancur, who took office in August, declared a broad amnesty for guerrillas in November, reconvened the Peace Commission (first established in 1981) and ordered an investigation into the MAS. An internal pacification campaign, which was begun in November, met with only moderate success. Despite the Peace Commission's successful negotiation of cease-fire agreements with the FARC, the M-19 (now operating as a left-wing guerrilla movement) and the Ejército Popular de Liberación (EPL) during 1984, factions of all three groups which were opposed to the truce continued to conduct guerrilla warfare against the authorities. In May 1984 the Government's campaign for internal peace was severely hampered by the assassination of the Minister of Justice. His murder was regarded as a consequence of his energetic attempts to eradicate the flourishing drugs industry, and Colombia's leading drugs dealers were implicated in the killing. The Government declared a nation-wide state of siege and announced its intention to enforce its hitherto unobserved extradition treaty with the USA.

Relations between the M-19 and the armed forces deteriorated during 1985, and in June the M-19 formally withdrew from the cease-fire agreement. In November a dramatic siege by the M-19 at the Palace of Justice in the capital, during which more than 100 people were killed, resulted in severe public criticism of the Government and the armed forces for their handling of events. Negotiations with the M-19 were suspended indefinitely.

At congressional elections in March 1986, the traditional wing of the PL secured a clear victory over the PCC and obtained 49% of the votes cast. The Unión Patriótica (UP), formed by the FARC in 1985, won seats in both houses. At the presidential election in May, Dr Virgilio Barco Vargas of the PL was elected President, with 58% of the votes cast. The large majority secured by the PL at both elections obliged the PCC to form the first formal opposition to a government for 30 years.

Attempts by the new administration to address the problems of political violence and the cultivation and trafficking of illicit drugs enjoyed little success during 1986–87. Hopes that an indefinite cease-fire agreement, concluded between the FARC and the Government in March 1986, would facilitate the full participation of the UP in the political process were largely frustrated by the Government's failure to respond effectively to a campaign of assassinations of UP members, conducted by paramilitary 'death squads' during 1985–87, which resulted in an estimated 450 deaths. The crisis was compounded in October 1987 by the decision of six guerrilla groups, including the FARC, the Ejército de Liberación Nacional (ELN) and the M-19, to form a joint front, the Coordinadora Guerrillera Simón Bolívar (CGSB). Although in 1987 the Government extended police powers against drugs dealers, its efforts were severely hampered by the Supreme Court's rulings that Colombia's extradition treaty with the USA was unconstitutional.

In 1988 the Comisión de Convivencia Democrática (Commission of Democratic Cohabitation) was established, with the aim of holding further meetings between all sides in the internal conflict in Colombia. Moreover, in September President Barco announced a peace initiative, composed of three phases: pacification; transition; and definitive reintegration into the democratic system. Under the plan, the Government was committed to entering into a dialogue with those guerrilla groups that renounced violence and intended to resume civilian life. However, violence continued to escalate, and in December it was estimated that some 18,000 murders had occurred in Colombia in 1988, of which at least 3,600 were attributed to political motives or related to drugs-trafficking.

In January 1989 the Government and the M-19 concluded an agreement to initiate direct dialogue between the Government, all political parties in Congress and the CGSB. In March the M-19 and the Government signed a document providing for the reintegration of the guerrillas into society. In the same month, the ELN, the EPL and the FARC publicly confirmed their willingness to participate in peace talks with the Government; in July the leading guerrilla groups (including the M-19) held a summit meeting, at which they agreed to the formation of a commission, which was to draft proposals for a peace dialogue with the Government. In September the M-19 announced that it had reached agreement with the Government on a peace treaty, under which its members were to demobilize and disarm in exchange for a full pardon. In addition, the movement was to enter the political mainstream; in October the M-19 was formally constituted as a political party, and its leader, Carlos Pizarro León Gómez, was named presidential candidate for the movement. By March 1990 all M-19 guerrilla forces had surrendered their weapons. In exchange for firm commitments from the Barco administration that a referendum would be held to decide the question of constitutional reform and that proposals for comprehensive changes to the electoral law would be introduced in Congress, members of the M-19 were guaranteed a general amnesty, reintegration into civilian life and full political participation in forthcoming elections.

The increasingly destabilizing influence of the drugs cartels, meanwhile, continued to undermine government initiatives. The murder, in August 1989, of a popular PL politician who had been an outspoken critic of the drugs-traffickers, was the latest in a series of assassinations of prominent citizens, ascribed to the drugs cartels of Cali and Medellín, and was widely deplored, prompting President Barco to introduce emergency measures, including the reactivation of Colombia's extradition treaty with the USA. The US administration requested the arrest by the Colombian authorities of 12 leading drugs-traffickers, popularly known as the 'Extraditables', who responded to the USA's request by issuing a declaration of 'total war' against the Government and all journalists, judges and trade unionists opposed to their activities.

At the congressional and municipal elections in March 1990 the PL won 72 of the 114 seats in the Senate and an estimated 60% of the 199 contested seats in the House of Representatives. Ballot papers had also presented the opportunity to vote for the convening of a National Constituent Assembly (a measure which was heavily endorsed) and the selection procedure for the PL's presidential candidate, from which César Gaviria Trujillo emerged as a clear winner.

Bernardo Jaramillo, the presidential candidate of the UP (who had secured the only left-wing seat in the Senate), was assassinated later in March 1990, and in April Carlos Pizarro became the third presidential candidate to be killed by hired assassins since August 1989. Pizarro was replaced by Antonio Navarro Wolff as presidential candidate for the M-19, in conjunction with the recently established Convergencia Democrática (later Alianza Democrática—AD), an alliance of 13 (mainly left-wing) groups and factions. Responsibility for the murder of Pizarro was officially ascribed to the Medellín drugs cartels (as in the case of Jaramillo), in spite of speculation that both men had been the victims of political extremists.

A presidential election was held on 27 May 1990. César Gaviria Trujillo of the PL was proclaimed the winner, with 47% of the votes cast. Some 90% of voters indicated their approval of proposals for the creation of a National Constituent Assembly in a *de facto* referendum held simultaneously.

Gaviria's Cabinet was described as a cabinet of 'national unity' and comprised seven members of the PL, four of the PCC and, most surprisingly, Navarro Wolff, the AD—M-19 presidential nominee, who was appointed Minister of Public Health. President Gaviria emphasized, however, that the diversity in composition of the Cabinet did not represent the installation of a coalition government. In his inaugural address, Gaviria confirmed his commitment to continuing the strenuous efforts to combat drugs-trafficking, having previously made comprehensive changes to police and military personnel in an

apparent attempt to strengthen the Government's resistance to infiltration by the cartels. In October the Government proposed an initiative by which some articles of law would be relaxed and others not invoked (including the extradition treaty) for suspected drugs-traffickers who were prepared to surrender to the authorities. By early 1991 Jorge Luis Ochoa (who narrowly avoided extradition in 1987) and two brothers, members of one of Medellín's most notorious cartels and all sought by US courts for drugs-related offences, had surrendered.

In October 1990 the creation of the National Constituent Assembly was declared constitutionally acceptable by the Supreme Court, and later in the month Navarro Wolff resigned the health portfolio in order to head the list of candidates representing the AD—M-19 in elections to the Assembly, which took place in December. Candidates for the AD—M-19 secured 19 of the 70 contested Assembly seats, forcing the ruling PL and the Conservatives to seek support from them and seven elected independents for the successful enactment of reform proposals.

In February 1991 the five-month session of the National Constituent Assembly was inaugurated. The composition of the Assembly had been expanded from 70 to 73 members in order to incorporate three invited members of former guerrilla groupings (two from the EPL and one from the Partido Revolucionario de Trabajadores—PRT) and was later expanded further to accommodate a representative of the Comando Quintín Lame. By June a political pact had been negotiated between President Gaviria and representatives of the PL, the AD—M-19 and the MSN, and an agreement was reached that, in order to facilitate the process of political and constitutional renovation, Congress should be dissolved prematurely. The Assembly subsequently voted to dismiss Congress, pending new congressional and gubernatorial elections, to be conducted in October 1991 (although congressional elections had not been scheduled to take place until 1994). Incumbent government ministers and members of the National Constituent Assembly were declared to be ineligible for congressional office.

The new Constitution became effective on 6 July 1991. At the same time, the state of siege, imposed in 1984 in response to the escalation in political and drugs-related violence, was ended. The new Constitution placed considerable emphasis was placed upon provisions to encourage greater political participation and to restrict electoral corruption and misrepresentation. It also identified and sought to protect a comprehensive list of civil liberties, among which, controversially, was the prohibition of the extradition of Colombian nationals (see below). While the Constitution was welcomed enthusiastically by the majority of the population, reservations were expressed that clauses relating to the armed forces remained largely unchanged and that provisions which recognized the democratic rights of indigenous groups did not extend to their territorial claims.

Relations with the Medellín cartel improved considerably following the release, in May 1991, of two remaining hostages, and in June, following the decision to prohibit constitutionally the practice of extradition, the Government's efforts were rewarded with the surrender of Pablo Escobar, the supposed head of the Medellín cartel. Charges later brought against Escobar included several of murder, kidnapping and terrorism. In July spokesmen for the Medellín drugs cartel announced that its military operations were to be suspended and that the 'Extraditables' were to be disbanded. Hopes that Escobar's surrender might precipitate a decline in drugs-related violence were frustrated by reports that Escobar was continuing to direct the operations of the Medellín cocaine cartels from his purpose-built prison at Envigado, and by the emergence of the powerful Cali drugs cartel, which was expected to compensate for any shortfall in the supply of illicit drugs resulting from the demise of the Medellín cartel.

Congressional and gubernatorial elections, conducted in October 1991, were distinguished by a high level of voter apathy, attributed to the busy electoral schedule of the previous 18 months. The Liberals were most successful, with a clear majority of seats in both chambers. The traditional Conservative opposition suffered from a division in their support between the PCC, the MSN and the Nueva Fuerza Democrática, securing around one-quarter of the seats in both houses between them. The AD—M-19 received only 10% of the votes cast, equivalent to nine seats in the Senate and 15 seats in the House of Representatives.

Meanwhile, in February 1990 the Government had established the National Council for Normalization, in an attempt to repeat the success of recent peace initiatives with the M-19 in negotiations with other revolutionary groups. The EPL announced the end of its armed struggle in August and joined the political mainstream (retaining the Spanish acronym EPL as the Partido de Esperanza, Paz y Libertad), along with the Comando Quintín Lame and the PRT, in 1991. Attempts to negotiate with the FARC and the ELN, however, proved fruitless, and violent clashes between the remaining guerrilla groups (now co-ordinating actions as the Coordinadora Nacional Guerrillera Simón Bolívar—CNGSB) and security forces persisted.

An escalation in guerrilla activity in 1992 prompted the Government to intensify anti-insurgency measures. In October Congress approved government proposals for an increased counterinsurgency budget and for the creation of new armed units to combat terrorism. The Government's rejection of any agenda for renewed negotiations provoked an intensification of the conflict, and this, together with a resurgence of drugs-related violent incidents following the death of the supposed military commander of the Medellín cartel, prompted Gaviria, in November, to declare a 90-day state of emergency, thereby extending wide-ranging powers to the security forces and imposing restrictions on media coverage. As a result, in November the M-19 announced that it was to withdraw from the Government and resume an active opposition role.

The security situation continued to deteriorate in 1993, leading the Government to announce, in February, a significant increase in its budget allocation for security, and in April, to double the length of prison terms for terrorist acts. The state of internal disturbance was also extended twice. Attempts by the Government and the ELN to negotiate a truce were frustrated by a perceived lack of commitment to compromise on both sides, and the prospects for future successful discussions were severely undermined by the insistence of security forces that ELN members were responsible for the murder of the Vice-President of the Senate in November. In December negotiations with the Corriente de Renovación Socialista (CRS), a dissident faction of the ELN more disposed to political assimilation, produced a tentative agreement for the guerrillas' reincorporation into civilian life and transformation into a legitimate political force. In April 1994, under the supervision of international observers, the CRS duly surrendered its weapons, and was subsequently awarded two seats in the newly-elected House of Representatives (see below).

An intensification of drugs-related violence in the capital during early 1993 was attributed to an attempt by Pablo Escobar (who had escaped from prison in mid-1992) to force the Government to negotiate more favourable conditions for his surrender, and prompted the formation of a vigilante group, Pepe (Perseguidos por Pablo Escobar—those Persecuted by Pablo Escobar), which launched a campaign of retaliatory violence against Escobar's family, associates and property. Pepe was thought to number among its members several of Escobar's disgruntled rivals from the Medellín cartel. A simultaneous and sustained assault by Pepe and by the security forces against the remnants of the Medellín cartel resulted in the death and surrender of many notable cartel members, culminating in the death of Escobar himself, in December, during an exchange of fire with security forces attempting to effect his arrest.

The dispatch of a contingent of US troops to the Valle del Cauca region in December 1993, described as a humanitarian mission to improve communications and health and education facilities, aroused widespread political outrage from the Government's opponents, who interpreted the accommodation of the troops as capitulation to US demands for military participation in the region, in order to ensure the destruction of the Cali cartel. By late February 1994, however, the troops had been withdrawn, the Council of State having ruled earlier in the month that President Gaviria had abused his authority by endorsing their deployment prior to consultation with the Senate. Relations with the USA deteriorated further in March following US criticism of the lenient terms of surrender being offered to leaders of the Cali cartel. A suspension of co-operation with regard to the exchange of evidence relating to drugs offences ensued. The situation was exacerbated in May following a Constitutional Court ruling which recognized the legal right of the individual to possess small quantities of drugs (including cocaine) for personal use. An unsuccessful attempt by Gaviria to amend the ruling by emergency decree, together with his statement of intent to revoke the decision by means of a referendum, did little to allay US fears that the Colombian judiciary was attempting to destroy the wealth of the cartels by legalizing the trade in illicit drugs.

The results of congressional and local elections conducted in March 1994 represented a serious reversal for the political left in Colombia and re-established the traditional two-party dominance of the PL and the PCC. The elections were particularly disappointing for the AD—M-19, whose representation was reduced from 13 seats to two in the House of Representatives and from nine seats to just one in the Senate. The PL retained a comfortable congressional majority. Following a second round of voting in the presidential election on 19 June between the two leading candidates, Ernesto Samper Pizano (PL) and Andrés Pastrana Arango (PCC), Samper was eventually declared the winner, with 50.9% of the valid votes cast. He was inaugurated on 7 August and a new Cabinet was installed simultaneously.

Shortly after President Samper's inauguration, allegations emerged that his election campaign had been partly funded by contributions from the Cali cartel. Tape-recordings of conversations which appeared to provide evidence that contact had at least been made with the cartels were subsequently dismissed by the Prosecutor-General as insufficient proof of such contributions actually having been made. In July 1994 a similar recording, which appeared to implicate the Colombian Chief of National Police in the payment of a bribe by the Cali cartel, prompted the US Senate to vote to make the disbursement of future aid to Colombia dependent on an assessment of the level of its co-operation in anti-drugs programmes. The existence of the tape-recordings was widely attributed to the US Drugs Enforcement Agency (DEA), which the Colombian media accused of fomenting mistrust in an attempt to ensure that the new administration would pursue an uncompromising anti-drugs policy. Restrictions were subsequently imposed on DEA operations and access to information in Colombia. However, it was hoped that bilateral relations would improve following the appointment of a new Prosecutor-General and a new Chief of the National Police in late 1994, and the House of Representatives' rejection, in December, of the 'narco bill', which sought to limit the powers of the authorities to confiscate funds and assets proceeding from illicit activities.

CNGSB offensives during 1994 were launched to coincide with campaigning for the March legislative elections, and to disrupt the weeks preceding the transfer of power from Gaviria to Samper in early August. Fighting between guerrillas and the security forces resulted in numerous deaths on both sides and considerable damage was inflicted on power installations and the transport infrastructure. Prospects for the swift negotiation of a peace agreement between the new administration and the CNGSB were immediately undermined by the murder of the UP's Manuel Cepeda Vargas (the only left-wing member of the Senate) and deteriorated as guerrilla activities intensified. However, in November Samper complied with a guerrilla request that imprisoned rebel leaders should be moved from military installations to civilian prisons, and also declared the Government's willingness to enter into unconditional dialogue with the guerrillas.

During 1994 the Government was subject to intense international pressure to formalize a greater commitment to respect for human rights, following a series of revelations in which the security forces were implicated in abuses of human rights, and the publication of a report by Amnesty International which claimed that the vast majority of infringements of human rights in Colombia were perpetrated by the armed forces and associated paramilitary groups. In September the Minister of the Interior, Horacio Serpa Uribe, announced an initiative to address the human rights crisis, including plans to reform the National Police and to disband all paramilitary units. In September 1995 Brig.-Gen. Alvaro Velandia Hurtado was removed from active duty by the Government, after a report by the office of the Prosecutor for Human Rights had pronounced him responsible for the detention and murder of a prominent M-19 member in 1987. Velandia's dismissal marked the first such action undertaken by the Government against senior army personnel in response to abuses of human rights.

In February 1995, in the context of the US Government's persistence in attaching preconditions to the disbursement of financial aid to Colombia, President Samper reiterated his commitment to the eradication of all illegal drugs-related activities in the country. A number of initiatives to address the problem were launched in Cali, resulting in the capture of the head of the Cali drugs cartel, Gilberto Rodríguez Orejuela, and four other cartel leaders in mid-1995. Meanwhile, in April nine prominent PL politicians were suspended from the party pending their investigation by the office of the Prosecutor-

General, following allegations of their maintaining links with the Cali cartel. In the following months it was confirmed that the Comptroller-General and the Attorney-General were also to be the subject of investigation as a result of similar allegations, while Samper's former election campaign treasurer, Santiago Medina, was arrested on charges related to the processing of drugs cartel contributions through Samper's election fund. In August the Minister of National Defence, Fernando Botero Zea, resigned, having been implicated in the affair by evidence submitted to the authorities by Medina. Medina also insisted that Samper had been fully aware of the origin of the funds. The President's former campaign manager was arrested in September, in which month Samper protested his own innocence before a congressional accusations committee. In October the Constitutional Court confirmed the jurisdiction of the congressional committee to conduct further investigations into the allegations.

In May 1995 the Government extended an offer of participation in legislative and consultative processes to the FARC, in the hope of securing their commitment to surrender arms. While the FARC responded positively to the initial proposal, further progress was to be dependent on the Government's successful execution of its stated intention to demilitarize the sensitive north-eastern region of La Uribe. A Government proposal for the exchange of armed struggle for a political agenda, issued to the ELN and dissident groups of the EPL and the M-19 at the same time, received a more cautious response from the guerrillas. However, all negotiations were severely hampered by renewed FARC and ELN offensives in late May. An escalation in the number of acts of violence perpetrated by guerrilla forces and by paramilitary defence groups in the north-western Urabá region prompted Samper to declare a state of internal disturbance for a 90-day period. In October, however, the Constitutional Court rejected the terms of the state of emergency, forcing the President to seek immediate congressional approval for alternative powers to extend the period of detention of some 3,500 suspected insurgents. Following the assassination, in November, of a prominent Conservative politician, the President declared a new 90-day state of internal disturbance. Responsibility for the assassination was claimed by the little-known Movimiento por la Dignidad de Colombia. (In April 1996 the group kidnapped the brother of former President Gaviria and demanded that the latter resign as Secretary-General of the Organization of American States—OAS; the hostage was released in June, even though the demand was not met.) However, negotiations between the President and Andrés Pastrana of the PCC, for a 'national agreement against violence', were frustrated by the latter's insistence that the establishment of an independent commission of inquiry into the allegations of Samper's campaign funding by the Cali cartel should be a precondition to any political negotiation.

In December 1995 the congressional accusations committee voted against the initiation of a full-scale inquiry into allegations of Samper's impropriety in the use of funds proceeding from drugs cartels, on the grounds of insufficient evidence at that time. The repercussions of the scandal, however, were considered to have severely undermined the political integrity of the Government, both at home and abroad. Relations between the US Government and the Samper administration deteriorated dramatically during 1995, culminating in allegations—made by official sources in Colombia—that the US Government was attempting to destabilize the administration through the covert actions of the DEA.

In January 1996 Botero reiterated Medina's claim that Samper had been in full possession of the facts regarding the cartel's funding of his election campaign, prompting the PCC to announce an immediate suspension of co-operation with the Government and the resignation of two of the four incumbent PCC members of the Cabinet. Samper subsequently urged Congress to reopen investigations into his involvement in the affair, seeking to demonstrate his innocence. Evidence collected by the Prosecutor-General was submitted to the accusations committee in February, together with four formal charges to be brought against the President, including that of illegal enrichment. Later in the month congressional commissions of both parliamentary chambers decided to launch a new and public investigation into the funding of Samper's election campaign. In March Samper testified before the accusations committee and denied allegations that he had contrived the plan to solicit funding from the Cali cartel; however, he did concede that the cartel had part-financed the campaign, albeit without his knowledge.

In March 1996, in the context of the Supreme Court's investigation into the financing of Samper's election campaign, the Ministers of the Interior, Foreign Affairs and Communications were summoned to face charges of illegal enrichment. In the following month Rodrigo Pardo García-Peña (who had since announced his temporary retirement as Minister of Foreign Affairs) admitted that he had been aware of the Cali cartel's role in the financing of the campaign. In May the charges of illegal enrichment against the three ministers were abandoned, although they were formally accused of the lesser charge of deliberately concealing the use of illicit funds in the campaign. Meanwhile, in April the Supreme Court took the unprecedented step of requesting that the Senate suspend the Attorney-General, Orlando Vásquez Velásquez, in order that he face charges of obstructing the course of justice (he had allegedly fabricated evidence to discredit the Prosecutor-General). In October Vásquez Velásquez was found guilty of the charges; he was dismissed as Attorney-General and banned from holding public office for a five-year period. Moreover, in December 1997 he was sentenced to eight years' imprisonment on drugs charges. During 1996 Botero, Medina and María Izquierdo, a former PL senator, were all sentenced to terms of imprisonment for their involvement in the Samper affair.

In June 1996 Congress voted to acquit Samper of charges of having been aware of the part-financing of his election campaign by drugs-traffickers. The US administration condemned the result and threatened to impose trade sanctions against Colombia. (In March the US Congress had refused to 'certify' Colombia as a co-operating nation with regard to US anti-drugs activities after a leading Cali cartel member escaped from prison.) In July, following the release of a prominent Medellín cartel member after only five-and-a-half years in prison, the US Government accused Samper of failing to take appropriate measures to deter drugs-trafficking and revoked his visa to travel to the USA.

Meanwhile, civil unrest and guerrilla activity continued during 1996. The state of internal disturbance was extended for a further 90 days in January, and then again in April following a CNGSB-organized nation-wide 'armed industrial strike', which had resulted in as many as 40 deaths. In March a FARC attack on a drugs-control police unit had renewed speculation of links between guerrilla groups and the drugs cartels. Moreover, it was suggested that a major offensive launched in August by FARC and ELN rebels (resulting in as many as 100 fatalities) had been deliberately timed to coincide with large-scale protests by coca growers demanding a review of the coca eradication programme, particularly the use of aerial spraying. In September the continuing unrest prompted the Government to announce the imminent mobilization of thousands of reserves. Although 26 members of the FARC and some 250 dissident EPL rebels surrendered to the authorities during September and October, violent skirmishes continued unabated, and disaffected members of the ELN were reported to have regrouped as the Ejército Revolucionario del Pueblo.

In September 1996 Samper's credibility was undermined by the resignation of the Vice-President, Humberto de la Calle, who appealed to the President to renounce his office in order to prevent the country from descending into 'total chaos'. (Congress subsequently elected Carlos Lemos-Simmonds as the new Vice-President.) Later in the same month Samper was again humiliated by the discovery of 3.7 kg of heroin aboard the aircraft in which he had been scheduled to fly to the USA (using a diplomat visa) to attend a meeting of the UN General Assembly. (A subsequent investigation into the drugs seizure did not implicate the President in any way.) In an apparent attempt to appease the US administration, Samper announced that Colombia's Congress would debate whether to amend the Constitution in order to permit the extradition of Colombian nationals. Moreover, in December Congress approved controversial legislation to allow for the confiscation of drugs-traffickers' assets. (Many members of the congressional constitutional committees had been reluctant to adopt or even debate the law for fear of reprisals from the drugs cartels.) In addition, the authorities arrested six prominent Cali cartel members during 1996.

In early 1997 the Samper administration encountered increasing pressure from the USA to address the issues of drugs-trafficking and corruption. The appointment of Guillermo Alberto González as Colombia's Minister of National Defence was condemned by the USA, which alleged that he had maintained links with drugs-traffickers; González resigned as a result of the allegations in March. In February, meanwhile, the

USA again refused to 'certify' Colombia, claiming that there had been a substantial increase in the production of illicit drugs in that country during 1996. In response, Samper announced the temporary suspension of Colombia's drugs-crop eradication programme. The programme was resumed shortly afterwards, but relations with the USA remained strained. Although legislation permitting the extradition of Colombian nationals sought for criminal offences abroad was approved in November, it was strongly criticized by the US administration as it would not have retroactive effect. Nevertheless, in February 1998 the USA waived sanctions on Colombia, although it did not fully 'certify' the country.

Meanwhile, in January 1997 President Samper risked civil unrest by decreeing a state of economic emergency. In the following month, after an eight-day nation-wide strike, the Government agreed to substantial pay awards for public-sector employees and to the establishment of a joint commission with labour unions to analyse the effects of its privatization plans. In March the Constitutional Court legally annulled the economic emergency, obliging Samper to seek congressional approval for the measures announced in January.

The activities of guerrilla and paramilitary groups in Colombia intensified during 1997. In May the Government agreed to the temporary demilitarization of part of the Caquetá department in order to secure the release of 70 members of the armed forces captured by the FARC. Notably, President Samper acknowledged that paramilitary groups had increasingly instigated violent attacks (sometimes with the tacit support of the security forces) and agreed that they should be included in peace negotiations. In July, after a series of assaults on the security forces by FARC and ELN rebels, Samper reorganized the military and police command, replacing the Commander-in-Chief of the Armed Forces, Gen. Harold Bedoya Pizarro, who had vehemently opposed negotiating with the guerrillas. In addition, Samper presented legislation to Congress that would lead to the establishment of a national peace commission.

In mid-1997 there was a marked increase in violent attacks by guerrilla and paramilitary groups, apparently intent on sabotaging departmental and municipal elections, scheduled to be held in October. In the months preceding the elections more than 40 candidates were killed, some 200 were kidnapped and as many as 1,900 were persuaded to withdraw after receiving death threats. Voting was cancelled in numerous municipalities, while in August the vulnerability of the Government to rebel attacks was emphasized by the assassination (most probably by the ELN) of a PL senator who was a close ally of Samper. Meanwhile, reports of secret preliminary peace negotiations between government representatives and the FARC were undermined by a major military offensive in September, in which 652 FARC guerrillas were killed and a further 1,600 were captured. The Government's subsequent conciliatory gestures to the guerrillas, including a promise by the President to submit legislation to Congress granting an amnesty in return for the signing of a peace accord, were met with little enthusiasm by the FARC and the ELN. In early November 1997 the ELN secured significant concessions from the Government in return for the release of two OAS election observers abducted in October. In the same month there was a sharp increase in attacks by paramilitary groups; some 47 people were killed in an eight-day period.

Changes to the Cabinet took place on numerous occasions during 1997 and early 1998, affecting most of the principal ministries. Horacio Serpa Uribe, a close ally of President Samper, resigned as Minister of the Interior in May 1997 and was selected as the official PL presidential candidate in January 1998. His candidature was strongly opposed by the US administration as he was alleged to have links with drugs-traffickers and was implicated in the affair regarding the illegal funding of Samper's 1994 election campaign. (In December 1997 Serpa was cleared of criminal charges relating to the affair.) Also in May 1997, Alfonso Valdivieso, whose vigorous investigations into corruption and drugs-trafficking had bolstered his popularity, resigned as Prosecutor-General in order to contest the presidency. In March 1998, however, Valdivieso withdrew his candidacy and pledged support for Pastrana, who had been selected again as the PCC nominee.

At congressional elections, conducted on 8 March 1998, the PL retained a narrow overall majority in the legislature, obtaining 53 of the 102 seats in the Senate, and 84 of the 161 seats in the House of Representatives. The PCC secured 27 and 28 seats in each chamber, respectively. An estimated 54% of the electorate participated in the elections, which were preceded by a period of violent attacks on the security forces by the FARC and the ELN; in one incident 80 counter-insurgency troops were killed by the FARC, and a further 43 were taken prisoner. In May tens of thousands of Colombians staged a demonstration to protest at the escalation of violence by guerrillas and paramilitary groups.

In the first round of the presidential election, held on 31 May 1998, Serpa secured 34.6% of the valid votes cast, followed by Pastrana (34.3%), Noemí Sanín Posada—an independent candidate who performed particularly well in Medellín, Cali and the capital—(26.9%), and Gen. (retd) Bedoya (1.8%). Nine other candidates contested the election. A second ballot was held on 21 June, at which Pastrana defeated Serpa, winning 50.4% of the valid votes cast. Pastrana was inaugurated as President on 7 August and a new Cabinet was installed simultaneously. Shortly afterwards the military leadership was reorganized and Gen. Fernando Tapias Stahelín, a moderate, was appointed Commander-in-Chief of the Armed Forces. Pastrana's immediate declared priorities included reaching a peace settlement with the guerrillas, eliminating corruption and strengthening the ailing economy.

In July 1998 President-elect Pastrana announced that he had held secret talks with Manuel Marulanda Vélez (alias 'Tirofijo'), the FARC leader, and that he had agreed to demilitarize five southern municipalities for a 90-day period (commencing in November) in order to facilitate negotiations with the guerrillas. Pastrana subsequently recognized the political status of the FARC, thereby allowing the Government to negotiate with an outlawed group. Notwithstanding, FARC attacks on the security forces continued, increasing significantly in August, before Pastrana's inauguration, and also in November, prior to the completion of the demilitarization of the five districts in the departments of Caquetá and Meta. Despite the demilitarization, negotiations with the FARC were stalled owing to the group's objection to the continued presence of some 100 soldiers in a barracks in San Vicente del Caguán, Caquetá. The soldiers were evacuated in December, and in January 1999 peace negotiations between the Government and the FARC began in San Vicente. Shortly before the negotiations began, it was revealed that in December the FARC had held informal talks in Costa Rica with government officials from the USA and Colombia. The FARC was reported to have invited the US officials to visit illegal crop plantations in Colombia and to consider possible substitution programmes. (Relations between Colombia and the USA had improved notably under the Pastrana administration: in October Pastrana made an official visit to the USA—the first by a Colombian Head of State in 23 years—and in December the two countries agreed on measures to improve military co-operation in the fight against the drugs trade.) In mid-January 1999 the FARC suspended talks with the Government until the authorities provided evidence that they were taking action against paramilitary groups, which claimed responsibility for the massacre of more than 130 civilians earlier in the month. In February Pastrana announced the extension of the period of demilitarization by three months, in order to facilitate negotiations.

The ELN, meanwhile, made tentative moves to negotiate a peace settlement during 1998. In February the group signed an accord with government peace negotiators in Madrid, Spain, on the holding of preliminary peace talks. In April the ELN disclosed that its leader, Gregorio Manuel Pérez Martínez, had died shortly afterwards; a collective leadership was appointed subsequently, with José Nicolás Rodríguez Bautista as the group's political commander. In July, at a meeting in Mainz, Germany, between the ELN and representatives of Colombian 'civil society' (grouped in the National Peace Council—Consejo Nacional de Paz—CNP), the ELN made concessions on the 'humanization' of the war and agreed to facilitate talks between its members and the Government. The guerrillas subsequently postponed a meeting with the CNP in protest at its signing of an agreement with the Autodefensas Unidas de Colombia (AUC), an organization representing most of Colombia's paramilitary groups, to hold parallel peace talks. Nevertheless, in October representatives of the ELN, the CNP and the Government agreed on a timetable for preliminary peace talks, beginning in February 1999, which would culminate in the assembling of a national convention. The Government recognized the political status of the ELN, but the group did not cease hostilities. Later in October 1998 an ELN attack on an oil pipeline in the department of Antioquia resulted in the deaths of at least 66 civilians. The planned peace negotiations failed to begin in

February 1999, not least because of the Government's refusal to agree to the ELN's request that four districts in the department of Bolívar be demilitarized. The ELN subsequently intensified its operations, in an apparent attempt to increase pressure on the Government to accede to its demands. The guerrillas hijacked a domestic flight in April, kidnapping all 46 people on board, and abducted some 140 members of the congregation of a church in Cali in May. In June Pastrana withdrew political recognition of the ELN and made the release of hostages a precondition for future peace talks. A civilian commission was subsequently appointed by the Government to negotiate towards this end. The ELN gradually freed hostages throughout 1999 and 2000, although by early 2001 the guerrillas still held four hostages from the seizure of the aircraft.

Little progress was achieved in negotiations with the FARC until April 1999, as the guerrillas continued to insist that the Government demonstrate some success in its actions against paramilitary groups prior to a resumption of talks. The enforced resignation in that month of two senior army officers, alleged to have collaborated with paramilitary groups, appeared to appease the FARC, however, and in early May talks between Marulanda and Pastrana resulted in an agreement on a comprehensive agenda for future peace negotiations; the period of demilitarization was again extended. Shortly afterwards a police offensive against a cocaine-production complex operated by paramilitaries in the central department of Magdalena was perceived as further evidence of a change in the attitude of the authorities towards paramilitary groups. However, Pastrana's strategy was not entirely supported by his administration, and at the end of May Rodrigo Lloreda, the Minister of National Defence, resigned in protest at concessions granted to the FARC. Meanwhile, the AUC was demanding to be granted political status and included in the peace negotiations. Pastrana's position was further undermined by Congress's rejection of legislation aimed at increasing the President's power concerning the peace process, as independent deputies voted with the opposition PL for the first time. Furthermore, the FARC continued to pursue its military campaign. The postponement of talks in early July, owing to a failure to agree on the role of international observers, was followed by a nation-wide guerrilla offensive that resulted in more than 200 deaths. The talks were subsequently postponed indefinitely, with the Government insisting that international monitors be allowed to investigate abuses allegedly committed by the FARC in the demilitarized zone. As negotiations resumed on October in La Uribe, after Pastrana had apparently withdrawn his demand for international observers, demonstrations for peace were attended by some 10m. people throughout the country. At further talks in November it was agreed that public hearings on the peace process would be held from late December. However, the FARC's commitment to the process was questioned by the military when, prior to the second round of November talks, the guerrillas launched attacks against 13 towns in several departments, amid renewed claims that they were using the demilitarized zone as a recruitment and training base from which to mount offensives. Guerrilla violence continued until, on 19 December, the FARC declared a 22-day unilateral cease-fire.

Relations between the US Government and the Pastrana administration continued to improve in 1999 and 2000, most notably regarding anti-drugs activities. In March 1999 the USA decided to 'certify' Colombia's efforts to combat drugs-trafficking. In September Pastrana announced the establishment of a new anti-narcotics battalion, to be trained and financed by the USA. Furthermore, collaboration between the Colombian and US authorities led to the arrest of more than 60 suspected drugs-traffickers in two major operations conducted in October and December. A car bomb that exploded in northern Santafé de Bogotá, in November, killing at least eight people and injuring some 45, was believed to have been a reaction to the Government's decision to resume the extradition of suspected drugs-traffickers to stand trial in the USA. However, the most important progress in Colombian–US relations came in 2000 with the development of President Pastrana's so-called 'Plan Colombia'. This was an ambitious, US $7,500m. project intended to strengthen the Colombian state by increasing the efficiency of both the security forces and the judicial system, eliminating drugs production through both eradication and crop substitution, and reducing unemployment. In July 2000 the US Congress approved a contribution to the Plan of $1,300m., which included a military component of $1,000m., but also significant sums for judicial reform and human-rights education. However, human-

rights organizations warned of an escalation of human-rights abuses following the Plan's implementation, as the main aid component was allocated to strengthening the security forces, whose links to paramilitary groups were, allegedly, yet to be severed. At the same time, Colombia's Andean neighbours feared that an escalation in violence would force thousands of refugees on to their territory and subsequently strengthened their borders. During US President Bill Clinton's visit to Colombia in August, some 2,000 students and trade-union members demonstrated outside the US embassy in protest at his country's involvement in Colombia. Earlier that month President Clinton had waived the human-rights conditions on which the disbursement of US aid to Colombia was dependent, in the interests of national security. In October the European Union announced aid disbursements to Colombia totalling $321m., intended to support social and economic development projects, although it was subsequently specified that the aid would not be given directly to the Colombian Government but distributed through non-governmental organizations. In May 2000 a so-called 'necklace' bomb killed a woman and four others in an abortive extortion scheme. The FARC was initially assumed to be responsible for the atrocity and peace talks were temporarily suspended. Negotiations were resumed in September. However, the FARC threatened to halt the peace process if plans for the US military component of Plan Colombia, to be directed against coca-growing areas of the Putamayo, were implemented. The FARC effectively blockaded Putamayo from the end of September to retain control of the province and it succeeded in delaying the aerial spraying of coca plantations, which were scheduled to begin in November. (The military offensive against coca plantations, as stipulated in Plan Colombia, was officially initiated in January 2001.) In October the Government dismissed 388 members of the armed forces in a move designed to improve military efficiency as well as to allay accusations of corruption and violations of human rights. However, the dismissals did not prevent the FARC from withdrawing from peace talks in November in order to demand greater government action in combating the AUC, which was posing a greater threat to the guerrilla groups in their strongholds. The Government's ombudsman reported that, in the first six months of 2000, 512 unarmed civilians were killed by the AUC, compared with 120 killed by guerrilla groups. The FARC was particularly angered by the decision of Minister of the Interior, Humberto de la Calle, to meet the AUC leader, Carlos Castaño. By the end of the year Pastrana was under increasing pressure to take back by force control of the demilitarized zone; a report released in December estimated a 30% increase in FARC military capacity since the zone was created. The murder in late December of Diego Turbay Cote, President of the congressional peace commission, allegedly by members of the FARC, further heightened tensions. However, following threats by the FARC that failure to prolong the demilitarized zone would lead to 'total war', Pastrana extended the deadline until the end of January 2001. Following a further extension in early February, in an attempt to encourage the FARC to resume peace talks, the FARC leadership met the President in the demilitarized zone and agreed to revive the stalled negotiations.

In April 2000 an agreement was reached with the ELN on the establishment of a demilitarized zone, similar to that granted to the FARC, in southern Bolívar. However, the Government faced much local opposition to the proposed zone, including roadblocks and demonstrations. In July informal discussions on a national convention, as demanded by the guerrilla movement as a precursor to peace talks, were held with the ELN in Geneva, Switzerland, with envoys from Cuba, France, Norway, Spain and Switzerland present, but they ended without agreement. In response, the ELN continued to sabotage Colombia's oil industry by attacking pipeline transport. Tentative moves towards peace recommenced in December after the ELN released 42 hostages. Negotiations in Havana, Cuba, at the end of the year resulted in a preliminary agreement on the terms and conditions of the demilitarized zone in Bolívar, though it was conditional on the acceptance by the ELN of the presence of an international verification committee in the region, as well as representatives from local and judicial institutions and one civilian police agency. The agreement was strongly opposed by residents of the proposed region and in February 2001 more than 10,000 people in Bolívar participated in a peaceful demonstration against the establishment of the zone.

In March 2000 Armando Pomarico Ramos, the President of the House of Representatives and a close ally of President

Pastrana, resigned after it was revealed that tenders for congressional contracts had been awarded to friends of legislative officials. The corruption scandal prompted the President to propose that a referendum on legislative reform be held; however, the offer was withdrawn in May after legislators suggested that Pastrana himself should also face elections. In the same month several ministers were forced to resign after being implicated in the corruption scandal, prompting a cabinet reshuffle which saw an increase in the number of Liberals and independents represented in the Government. The entire economic team was replaced and Juan Manuel Santos Calderón was appointed Minister of Finance and Public Credit. In July Congress approved legislation that codified forced disappearances and displacements as crimes and increased the punishment for torture. In local elections, held in October, independent candidates won mayoral races in four of Colombia's five largest cities (including Santafé de Bogotá). The election campaign was overshadowed by an unprecedented number of kidnappings and murders of candidates. The results were interpreted as a sign of voters' frustration with the Government.

In May 2001 the Ministers of National Defence and of Economic Development resigned, amid speculation that they would seek the PCC nomination for the presidential election, to be held in 2002. The Vice-President, Gustavo Bell, was assigned the defence portfolio.

Colombia has a long-standing border dispute with Venezuela. However, relations between the countries improved following the signing, in October 1989, of a border integration agreement, which included a provision on joint co-operation in the campaign to eradicate drugs-trafficking. (A permanent reconciliation commission to investigate the border dispute had been established in March 1989.) In March 1990 the San Pedro Alejandrino agreement, signed by the two countries, sought to initiate the implementation of recommendations made by existing bilateral border commissions and to establish a number of new commissions, including one to examine the territorial claims of both sides. Colombia's efforts to improve relations with Venezuela were hampered by the activities of FARC guerrillas in the border region, leading the two countries to sign an agreement to improve border co-operation in February 1997; however, in April Venezuela deployed 5,000 troops along its frontier with Colombia in an attempt to halt repeated incursions by Colombian guerrillas. Agreements were subsequently signed by the two countries to strengthen military co-operation and intelligence sharing. However, in 2000 relations deteriorated, owing to Venezuelan President Hugo Chávez's opposition to the Plan Colombia and accusations by Colombia that Venezuela was covertly aiding the guerrilla forces. In November 2000 Colombia recalled its ambassador to Venezuela after a FARC representative was allowed to speak in the Venezuelan National Assembly. In an attempt to normalize relations, the ambassador was authorized to return in January 2001.

In June 1997 Panama also announced its intention to station 1,200 soldiers along its border with Colombia to counter an increase in the activities of Colombian guerrilla and paramilitary groups in the country, and, following the death of a member of Panama's security forces during an attack by the FARC in November, the Heads of State of the two countries agreed to improve border co-operation. In 1999 increasing concern regarding the threat posed to regional stability by Colombia's internal conflict prompted neighbouring countries to increase security measures on the common border. Further measures were implemented in 2000 after renewed concerns that the implementation of the Plan Colombia would prompt an increase in conflict.

In 1980 Nicaragua laid claim to the Colombian-controlled islands of Providencia and San Andrés. Colombia has a territorial dispute with Honduras over cays in the San Andrés and Providencia archipelago. In October 1986 the Colombian Senate approved a delimitation treaty of marine and submarine waters in the Caribbean Sea, which had been signed by the Governments of Colombia and Honduras in August. In late 1999 the Honduran National Assembly finally ratified the treaty, strengthening Colombia's claim to the islands of Providencia and San Andrés, and thus angering Nicaragua, which filed a complaint with the International Court of Justice.

In December 1991 the leaders of the countries of the Andean Pact agreed to remove trade barriers between their countries in early 1992 and to adopt unified external tariffs by 1993. However, subsequent negotiations failed to produce agreement on a common external tariff. In February 1995 a three-level tariff system was implemented to cover 90% of imports (the remainder to be incorporated by 1999). In March 1996 the Presidents of the member nations of the Pact signed the Reform Protocol of the Cartagena Agreement, whereby the Pact was superseded by the Andean Community.

In October 1993 the ministers with responsibility for foreign affairs of Colombia, Mexico and Venezuela (known as the Group of Three) announced the implementation, as of 1 January 1994, of a 10-year trade liberalization programme. A free trade agreement, the Acuerdo de Complementación Económica (ACE), concluded with Chile in December 1993, took effect from 1 January 1994, and was expected to have eliminated tariffs on most goods by the time of its full implementation on 1 January 1999.

Government

Executive power is exercised by the President (assisted by a Cabinet), who is elected for a four-year term by universal adult suffrage. Legislative power is vested in the bicameral Congress, consisting of the Senate (102 members elected for four years) and the House of Representatives (161 members elected for four years). The country is divided into 32 Departments and one Capital District.

Defence

At 18 years of age, every male (with the exception of students) must present himself as a candidate for military service of between one and two years. In August 2000 the strength of the army was 130,000 (including 63,800 conscripts), the navy 15,000 (including 8,500 marines) and the air force 8,000. The paramilitary police force numbers about 95,000 men. Some 4,000,000m. pesos were allocated to defence expenditure as part of the state budget for 2000.

Economic Affairs

In 1998, according to estimates by the World Bank, Colombia's gross national product (GNP), measured at average 1996–98 prices, was US $100,667m., equivalent to $2,470 per head (or $5,861 per head on an international purchasing-power parity basis). During 1990–98, it was estimated, GNP per head increased, in real terms, by an average of 1.7% per year. Over the same period, the population increased at an average annual rate of 2.2%. Estimated GNP in 1999 was $93,600m. ($2,250 per head). Colombia's gross domestic product (GDP) increased, in real terms, by an average of 3.3% per year in 1990–99; GDP increased by 0.5% in 1998, but decreased by 4.3% in 1999.

Agriculture (including hunting, forestry and fishing) contributed 12.2% of GDP in 1999, and employed some 21.6% of the labour force in 1998. The principal cash crops are coffee (which accounted for 11.4% of official export earnings in 1999), cocoa, sugar cane, bananas, tobacco, cotton and cut flowers. Rice, cassava, plantains and potatoes are the principal food crops. Timber and beef production are also important. During 1990–99 agricultural GDP decreased at an average annual rate of 2.6%. Growth in agricultural GDP was 0.8% in 1998.

Industry (including mining, manufacturing, construction and power) employed 19.9% of the labour force in 1997, and contributed 24.8% of GDP in 1999. During 1990–99 industrial GDP increased at an average annual rate of 2.3%. Industrial GDP declined by 2.7% in 1996, but increased by 1.3% in 1997.

Mining contributed 3.6% of GDP in 1997, and employed 0.7% of the labour force in that year. Petroleum, natural gas, coal, nickel, emeralds and gold are the principal minerals exploited. Silver, platinum, iron, lead, zinc, copper, mercury, limestone and phosphates are also mined. Growth in mining GDP was 3.7% in 1997 and 10.0% in 1998.

Manufacturing contributed 12.9% of GDP in 1999, and employed 13.1% of the labour force in 1997. During 1990–97 manufacturing GDP increased at an average annual rate of 1.5%. Manufacturing GDP increased by 0.4% in 1997, although it declined by 0.5% in 1998. Based on the value of output, the most important branches of manufacturing in 1995 were food products (accounting for 25.3% of the total), chemical products (14.8%), beverages, textiles and transport equipment.

In the late 1990s hydroelectricity provided about 75% of Colombia's electricity requirements. In the early 1990s a rapid expansion programme of thermal power-stations was undertaken in order to increase electricity output in line with demand, which increased by 4.5% per year in the 1990s, and to reduce reliance on hydroelectric power. The country is self-sufficient in petroleum and coal, and minerals accounted for 39.8% of export revenues in 1999.

The services sector contributed 62.9% of GDP in 1999, and engaged 56.7% of the labour force in 1997. During 1990–99 the combined GDP of the service sectors increased, in real terms, at an estimated average rate of 6.3% per year. Growth in services GDP was 5.1% in 1997.

In 1999 Colombia recorded a visible trade surplus of US $1,776m. and there was a deficit of $61m. on the current account of the balance of payments. The country's principal trading partner in 1999 was the USA, which provided 38.5% of imports and took 48.5% of exports. Other important trading partners in that year were Venezuela and Germany. The principal exports in 1998 were minerals (particularly petroleum and its derivatives and coal), coffee, other agricultural products (chiefly cut flowers and bananas), chemicals, textiles and leather products, and foodstuffs, beverages and tobacco. The principal imports in 1997 were machinery and transport equipment, chemicals, vegetables and vegetable products, minerals, metals, and foodstuffs, beverages and tobacco. A significant amount of foreign exchange is believed to be obtained from illegal trade in gold, emeralds and, particularly, the drug cocaine: in 1995 it was estimated that some $3,500m. (equivalent to around 4% of GDP) was entering Colombia each year as the proceeds of drugs-trafficking activities.

In 1998 there was a budgetary deficit of 6,940,600m. pesos in central government spending, equivalent to 5.3% of GDP. Colombia's external debt amounted to US $34,428m. at the end of 1999. In 1998 the cost of debt-servicing was equivalent to 30.7% of the value of exports of goods and services. In 1990–99 the average annual rate of inflation was 21.5%; consumer prices increased by an annual average of 20.4% in 1998, by 11.2% in 1999 and by 9.5% in 2000. Some 20.4% of the labour force were unemployed in June 2000.

Colombia is a member of ALADI (see p. 230) and of the Andean Community (see p. 122). Both organizations attempt to increase trade and economic co-operation within the region.

A programme of structural reform was adopted in 1990–94, resulting in the liberalization of trade and the reorganization of the public sector. Strong economic growth was recorded during this period, not least because of the discovery of significant petroleum reserves. However, during the Samper administration (1994–98) GDP slowed, unemployment soared and the fiscal deficit widened. In the late 1990s economic problems in Colombia were compounded by a fall in the international price of the country's principal export commodities, petroleum and coffee, and by high interest rates, which had led to a rise in the cost of debt-servicing. Despite the attempts of newly-inaugurated President Pastrana to prevent further decline, the economy continued to contract in late 1998 and throughout 1999. Domestic demand fell substantially, largely as a result of fiscal adjustments, and the rate of unemployment continued to increase. Meanwhile, efforts were made to attract foreign investment to the country, although the continued sabotage of petroleum installations by guerrilla groups did little to inspire investor confidence. In September 1999 the central bank allowed the flotation of the peso, the value of which had depreciated by 23% since the beginning of the year. Also in September the Government secured some US $6,900m. in financial assistance from international donors, including an IMF credit worth some $2,700m. (which was approved in December) in support of its economic programme for 1999–2002, which emphasized further fiscal reform, the restructuring of the financial sector and a reduction in public spending, as well as the introduction of new social welfare programmes to alleviate the effects of austerity measures. GDP growth was an estimated 3.2% in 2000, but the problems of high levels of unemployment and low investment spending still needed to be addressed. The privatization prog-

ramme planned for 2000 failed to get underway, with the sale of electrical companies delayed as a result of guerrilla attacks on power installations and low investor interest in the public banks. Furthermore, Colombia was unable to take full advantage of the high price of petroleum during the year because of guerrilla attacks on pipelines. In September 2000 Pastrana submitted tax reform legislation to Congress, which included measures to raise an extra $1,600m. in order to balance the budget in 2001.

Social Welfare

There is compulsory social security, paid for by the Government, employers and employees, and administered by the Institute of Social Security. It provides benefits for disability, old age, death, sickness, maternity, industrial accidents and unemployment. Large enterprises are required to provide life insurance schemes for their employees, and there is a comprehensive system of pensions. Implementation of a system of private pension funds (modelled on the AFP system in Chile) was under consideration at the end of the 1990s. In 1997 there were 116 physicians per 100,000 people and, in 1994, there were 48 nurses per 100,000 people working in Colombia. Of total expenditure by the central Government in 1998, 1,862,700m. pesos (9.3%) was for health.

Education

Primary education is free and compulsory for five years, to be undertaken by children between six and 12 years of age. No child may be admitted to secondary school unless these five years have been successfully completed. Secondary education, beginning at the age of 11, lasts for up to six years. Following completion of a first cycle of four years, pupils may pursue a further two years of vocational study, leading to the Bachiller examination. In 1996 the total enrolment at primary schools included 89% of pupils in the relevant age-group, while the comparable ratio for secondary education in 1995 was 50%. In the late 1990s there were 25 public universities in Colombia. Government expenditure on education in the 1998 budget was 4,706,900m. pesos, representing 23.6% of total spending. The rate of adult illiteracy averaged 19.2% in 1973, but, according to estimates by UNESCO, had declined to 8.7% (males 8.8%; females 8.6%) by 1995.

Public Holidays

2001: 1 January (New Year's Day), 8 January (for Epiphany), 19 March (St Joseph's Day), 12 April (Maundy Thursday), 13 April (Good Friday), 1 May (Labour Day), 28 May (for Ascension Day), 18 June (for Corpus Christi), 25 June (for SS Peter and Paul), 2 July (for Sacred Heart of Jesus), 20 July (Independence), 7 August (Battle of Boyacá), 20 August (for Assumption), 15 October (for Discovery of America), 5 November (for All Saints' Day), 12 November (for Independence of Cartagena), 8 December (Immaculate Conception), 25 December (Christmas Day).

2002: 1 January (New Year's Day), 6 January (Epiphany), 25 March (for St Joseph's Day), 28 March (Maundy Thursday), 29 March (Good Friday), 1 May (Labour Day), 13 May (for Ascension Day), 3 June (for Corpus Christi), 1 July (for SS Peter and Paul and Sacred Heart of Jesus), 20 July (Independence), 7 August (Battle of Boyacá), 19 August (for Assumption), 14 October (for Discovery of America), 4 November (for All Saints' Day), 11 November (Independence of Cartagena), 8 December (Immaculate Conception), 25 December (Christmas Day).

Weights and Measures

The metric system is in force.

Statistical Survey

Sources (unless otherwise stated): Departamento Administrativo Nacional de Estadística (DANE), Centro Administrativo Nacional (CAN), Avda El Dorado, Apdo Aéreo 80043, Santafé de Bogotá, DC; tel. (1) 222-1100; fax (1) 222-2107; internet www.dane.gov.co; Banco de la República, Carrera 7, No 14-78, Apdo Aéreo 3531, Santafé de Bogotá, DC; tel. (1) 343-1090; fax (1) 286-1731; internet www.banrep.gov.co.

Area and Population

AREA, POPULATION AND DENSITY

Area (sq km)		
Total		1,141,748*
Population (census results)†		
15 October 1985		
Males		14,642,835
Females		14,838,160
Total		29,480,995
24 October 1993		37,664,711
Population (official estimates at mid-year)		
1997		40,064,092
1998		40,826,815
1999		41,589,018
Density (per sq km) at mid-1999		36.4

* 440,831 sq miles.
† Revised figures, including adjustment for underenumeration. The enumerated total was 27,853,436 (males 13,785,523; females 14,067,913) in 1985 and 33,109,840 (males 16,296,539; females 16,813,301) in 1993.

DEPARTMENTS (census of 24 October 1993)

Department	Area (sq km)	Population	Capital (with population)
Amazonas	109,665	56,399	Leticia (30,045)
Antioquia	63,612	4,919,619	Medellín (1,834,881)
Arauca	23,818	185,882	Arauca (59,805)
Atlántico	3,388	1,837,468	Barranquilla (1,090,618)
Bolívar	25,978	1,702,188	Cartagena (747,390)
Boyacá	23,189	1,315,579	Tunja (112,807)
Caldas	7,888	1,055,577	Manizales (345,539)
Caquetá	88,965	367,898	Florencia (107,620)
Casanare	44,640	211,329	Yopal (57,279)
Cauca	29,308	1,127,678	Popayán (207,700)
César	22,905	827,219	Valledupar (278,216)
Chocó	46,530	406,199	Quibdó (122,371)
Córdoba	25,020	1,275,623	Montería (308,506)
Cundinamarca	22,623	1,875,337	Santafé de Bogotá*
Guainía	72,238	28,478	Puerto Inírida (18,270)
La Guajira	20,848	433,361	Riohacha (109,474)
Guaviare	42,327	97,602	San José del Guaviare (48,237)
Huila	19,890	843,798	Neiva (278,350)
Magdalena	23,188	1,127,691	Santa Marta (313,072)
Meta	85,635	618,427	Villavicencio (272,118)
Nariño	33,268	1,443,671	Pasto (331,866)
Norte de Santander	21,658	1,162,031	Cúcuta (538,126)
Putumayo	24,885	264,291	Mocoa (25,910)
Quindío	1,845	495,212	Armenia (258,990)
Risaralda	4,140	844,184	Pereira (401,909)
San Andrés y Providencia Islands	44	61,040	San Andrés (56,361)
Santander del Sur	30,537	1,811,740	Bucaramanga (472,461)
Sucre	10,917	701,105	Sincelejo (194,962)
Tolima	23,562	1,286,078	Ibagué (399,838)
Valle del Cauca	22,140	3,736,090	Cali (1,847,176)
Vaupés	65,268	24,671	Mitú (13,177)
Vichada	100,242	62,073	Puerto Carreño (11,452)

Capital District

Santafé de Bogotá, DC	1,587	5,484,244	Bogotá*
Total	1,141,748	37,664,711	

* The capital city, Santafé de Bogotá, exists as the capital of a department as well as the Capital District. The city's population is included only in Santafé de Bogotá, DC.

PRINCIPAL TOWNS
(estimated population at mid-1999)

Santafé de Bogotá, DC (capital)	6,260,862	Neiva	300,052
Cali	2,077,386	Soledad	295,058
Medellín	1,861,265	Armenia	281,422
Barranquilla	1,223,260	Villavicencio	273,140
Cartagena	805,757	Soacha	272,058
Cúcuta	606,932	Valledupar	263,247
Bucaramanga	515,555	Montería	248,245
Ibagué	393,664	Itagüí	228,985
Pereira	381,725	Palmira	226,509
Santa Marta	359,147	Buenaventura	224,336
Manizales	337,580	Floridablanca	221,913
Bello	333,470	Sincelejo	220,704
Pasto	332,396	Popayán	200,719

BIRTHS, MARRIAGES AND DEATHS*

	Registered live births	Registered deaths
1983	829,348	140,292
1984	825,842	137,189
1985	835,922	153,947
1986	931,956	146,346
1987	937,426	151,957

Registered live births: 989,071 in 1998; 989,117 in 1999.
Registered deaths: 173,506 in 1996; 167,172 in 1997; 171,210 in 1998.
Registered marriages: 102,448 in 1980; 95,845 in 1981; 70,350 in 1986.

* Data are tabulated by year of registration rather than by year of occurrence, although registration is incomplete. According to UN estimates, the average annual rates in 1985–90 were: births 27.8 per 1,000; deaths 6.5 per 1,000; and in 1990–95: births 27.0 per 1,000; deaths 6.4 per 1,000 (Source: UN, *World Population Prospects: The 1998 Revision*).

Expectation of life (UN estimates, years at birth, 1990–95): 68.2 (males 64.3; females 73.0) (Source: UN, *World Population Prospects: The 1998 Revision*).

ECONOMICALLY ACTIVE POPULATION
(household survey, September 1997)

Agriculture, hunting, forestry and fishing	3,478,832
Mining and quarrying	110,969
Manufacturing	1,996,470
Electricity, gas and water	132,999
Construction	798,739
Trade, restaurants and hotels	3,330,221
Transport, storage and communications	831,591
Financing, insurance, real estate and business services	753,572
Community, social and personal services	3,744,301
Activities not adequately described	81,777
Total labour force	15,259,471

Agriculture

PRINCIPAL CROPS ('000 metric tons)

	1997	1998	1999
Wheat	50	39	36
Rice (paddy)	1,830	1,898	2,059
Barley	19	12	15
Maize	978	755	975
Sorghum	338	189	201
Potatoes	2,717	2,547	2,705
Cassava (Manioc)	1,677	1,597	1,956
Soybeans	90	72	44
Seed cotton	109	97	109
Cabbages*	320	210	250
Tomatoes*	350	347	390
Onions (dry)*	210	200	248
Carrots*	225	185	210
Sugar cane*	36,000	34,000	36,900
Oranges	450*	470*	509
Pineapples	330*	360*	408
Bananas	1,607	1,517	1,570
Plantains	2,776	2,559	2,689
Coffee (green)	642	767	547
Cocoa beans	50	51	52
Tobacco (blond and black)	23	30	33

* FAO estimate(s).

Source: FAO.

LIVESTOCK ('000 head, year ending September)

	1997	1998	1999
Horses*	2,450	2,450	2,450
Mules*	590	590	590
Asses*	710	710	710
Cattle	25,673	25,764	25,614
Pigs	2,480	2,452	2,765
Sheep	2,325	1,994	2,196
Goats	1,006	1,050	1,115
Poultry*	85,000	95,000	98,000

* FAO estimates.

Source: FAO.

LIVESTOCK PRODUCTS ('000 metric tons)

	1997	1998	1999
Beef and veal	763	766	724*
Mutton and lamb†	11	11	11
Goat meat	6	6	6
Pig meat†	135	135	150
Horse meat	5	5	5
Poultry meat	433	507	504
Cows' milk	5,492	5,712	5,710†
Cheese	51	51	51†
Butter and ghee	17	18	18
Poultry eggs	316	323	339
Cattle hides	81	81	85

* Unofficial figure.
† FAO estimate(s).

Source: FAO.

Forestry

ROUNDWOOD REMOVALS ('000 cu metres, excl. bark)

	1996	1997	1998
Sawlogs, veneer logs and logs for sleepers*	1,706	1,706	1,706
Pulpwood	589†	589†	21
Other industrial wood	100	66	62
Fuel wood	16,092	16,401	16,712
Total	18,487	18,762	18,439

* Assumed to be unchanged from 1994.
† Assumed to be unchanged from 1986.

Source: FAO, *Yearbook of Forest Products*.

SAWNWOOD PRODUCTION ('000 cu metres, incl. railway sleepers)

	1996	1997	1998
Coniferous (softwood)	100	139	131
Broadleaved (hardwood)	1,034	946	888
Total	1,134	1,085	1,019

Source: FAO, *Yearbook of Forest Products*.

Fishing

('000 metric tons, live weight)

	1996	1997	1998
Capture*	131.1	149.4	167.5
Characins	5.5	3.7	6.4
Other freshwater fishes	17.6	16.9	15.2
Pacific anchoveta	26.3	28.7	28.5
Skipjack tuna	15.7	24.3	30.0
Yellowfin tuna	18.3	42.3	14.5
Other tuna-like fishes	26.3	12.1	59.5
Aquaculture	30.0	43.7	45.9
Tilapias and other cichlids	14.0	16.1	17.7
Cachama blanca	6.2	11.6	11.8
Rainbow trout	4.5	7.8	6.2
Whiteleg shrimp	5.2	6.9	7.5
Total catch	161.1	193.1	213.4

* Data refer to landings.

Note: Figures exclude crocodiles, recorded by number rather than by weight. The number of spectacled caimans caught was: 656,522 in 1996; 452,707 in 1997; 670,389 in 1998.

Source: FAO, *Yearbook of Fishery Statistics*.

Mining

('000 metric tons, unless otherwise indicated)

	1996	1997	1998
Gold ('000 troy oz)	690.1	521.8	598.0
Silver ('000 troy oz)	190.0	109.5	167.7
Salt (refined)	560.3	n.a.	n.a.
Hard coal*	30,065	n.a.	n.a.
Iron ore†	595.6	754.9	525.9
Crude petroleum ('000 barrels)	228,748	238,046	275,475

* Source: UN, *Industrial Commodity Statistics Yearbook*.

† Figures refer to the gross weight of ore. The estimated iron content is 46%.

Industry

SELECTED PRODUCTS ('000 metric tons, unless otherwise indicated)

	1996	1997	1998
Sugar	2,149.2	2,136.2	2,125.6
Cement	8,590.1	8,870.4	8,464.0
Steel ingots	298.4	344.9	264.5
Diesel oil ('000 barrels) . .	24,552	24,266	23,210
Fuel oil ('000 barrels) . .	19,453	19,700	18,758
Motor fuel ('000 barrels) . .	41,160	34,445	38,354

Finance

CURRENCY AND EXCHANGE RATES

Monetary Units
100 centavos = 1 Colombian peso.

Sterling, Dollar and Euro Equivalents (29 December 2000)
£1 sterling = 3,263.5 pesos;
US $1 = 2,187.0 pesos;
€1 = 2,035.0 pesos;
10,000 Colombian pesos = £3.064 = $4.572 = €4.914.

Average Exchange Rate (pesos per US $)
1998   1,426.04
1999   1,756.23
2000   2,087.90

CENTRAL GOVERNMENT BUDGET ('000 million pesos)

Revenue	1996	1997	1998
Direct taxation	4,804.9	5,038.7	7,280.7
Indirect taxation	7,720.1	8,247.9	8,285.5
Rates and fines	102.7	399.7	104.6
Revenue under contracts . .	290.8	30.3	—
Credit resources	5,380.2	8,721.9	10,527.9
Other	2,387.4	4,386.4	2,047.6
Total	20,686.1	26,824.9	28,246.3

Expenditure*	1996	1997	1998
Congress and comptrollership . .	186.4	238.9	281.0
General administration . .	879.7	856.0	742.0
Home office and foreign affairs .	123.2	127.7	147.8
Finance and public credit . .	3,184.6	3,509.1	3,263.7
Public works and transportation .	1,370.6	1,519.6	1,207.4
Defence	2,039.5	2,466.6	2,605.4
Police	973.0	1,237.4	1,471.4
Agriculture	811.8	622.3	425.0
Health	1,309.4	1,597.9	1,862.7
Education	2,950.3	3,656.9	4,706.9
Development, labour, mines and communications	1,411.4	1,674.5	1,765.3
Justice and legal affairs . . .	947.7	1,118.2	1,234.8
Trade	31.1	26.2	21.2
Environment	139.0	167.5	138.7
Culture	—	12.4	64.3
Total	16,357.7	18,831.1	19,937.4

* Excluding public debt.

INTERNATIONAL RESERVES (US $ million at 31 December)

	1998	1999	2000
Gold*	103	95	89
IMF special drawing rights . .	196	131	135
Reserve position in IMF . .	575	392	372
Foreign exchange . . .	7,983	7,580	8,498
Total	8,857	8,198	9,094

* Valued at market-related prices.

Source: IMF, *International Financial Statistics*.

MONEY SUPPLY ('000 million pesos at 31 December)

	1998	1999	2000
Currency outside banks . . .	4,997.3	6,507.4	7,676.2
Demand deposits at commercial banks	5,673.3	6,533.1	8,845.0
Total money (incl. others) . .	10,785.7	13,404.5	16,859.7

Source: IMF, *International Financial Statistics*.

COST OF LIVING
(Consumer price index for low-income families; base: 1990 = 100)

	1997	1998	1999
Food and beverages . . .	379.4	465.5	491.1
Clothing and footwear . . .	295.0	320.2	336.6
Rent, fuel and light* . . .	525.4	617.3	680.7
All items (incl. others) . . .	432.1	520.2	578.5

* Including certain household equipment.

Source: ILO, *Yearbook of Labour Statistics*.

NATIONAL ACCOUNTS ('000 million pesos at current prices)
Composition of the Gross National Product

	1995	1996	1997
Compensation of employees . .	29,558.6	37,367.1	45,299.5
Operating surplus . . . .⎫ Consumption of fixed capital . .⎭	46,803.3	54,250.6	64,472.3
Gross domestic product (GDP) at factor cost	76,361.9	91,617.7	109,771.8
Indirect taxes	8,518.1	9,766.5	12,598.9
Less Subsidies	440.9	672.8	663.2
GDP in purchasers' values . .	84,439.1	100,711.4	121,707.5
Net factor income from abroad .	−1,441.7	−2,128.3	−2,705.7
Gross national product (GNP) .	82,997.4	98,583.1	119,001.8

Expenditure on the Gross Domestic Product

	1997	1998	1999
Government final consumption expenditure . . .	24,245.7	28,887.2	36,634.4
Private final consumption expenditure	79,193.8	94,680.3	98,524.8
Increase in stocks	874.0	1,328.1	563.9
Gross fixed capital formation .	24,591.8	24,445.4	18,197.7
Total domestic expenditure .	128,905.3	149,341.0	153,920.8
Exports of goods and services .	18,063.3	21,331.5	27,500.4
Less Imports of goods and services	25,261.0	29,623.1	29,601.3
GDP in purchasers' values . .	121,707.5	141,295.2*	152,165.8*

* Including adjustment.

Source: IMF, *International Financial Statistics*.

Gross Domestic Product by Economic Activity

	1995	1996	1997
Agriculture, hunting and forestry	11,528.5	12,546.9	14,937.1
Fishing.	308.2	312.7	405.9
Mining and quarrying	3,273.8	4,178.8	4,260.6
Manufacturing	12,464.5	14,511.7	16,782.0
Electricity, gas and water	2,623.6	3,419.7	4,190.6
Construction	6,318.7	6,611.7	7,723.5
Wholesale and retail trade; repair of motor vehicles, motorcycles and personal and household goods	7,960.4	9,277.3	11,153.4
Hotels and restaurants	2,233.0	2,637.9	2,706.7
Transport, storage and communications	6,067.2	6,957.7	8,539.8
Financial intermediation	5,125.0	6,625.8	8,172.2
Real estate, renting and business activities	9,850.8	12,135.9	14,939.1
Public administration and defence; compulsory social security	5,716.9	8,606.4	10,890.7
Education	3,626.9	5,365.8	7,300.9
Health and social work	3,103.2	3,790.1	4,717.1
Other community, social and personal service activities	1,433.4	1,732.0	2,082.0
Private households with employed persons	424.0	494.2	568.5
Sub-total	82,058.3	99,204.6	119,370.2
Less Imputed bank service charge	4,610.9	6,157.4	7,451.1
GDP in basic prices	77,447.4	93,047.2	111,919.1
Taxes on products	7,113.7	7,792.3	9,847.9
Less Subsidies on products	122.0	128.1	59.5
GDP in purchasers' values	84,439.1	100,711.4	121,707.5

BALANCE OF PAYMENTS (US $ million)

	1997	1998	1999
Exports of goods f.o.b.	12,064	11,480	12,030
Imports of goods f.o.b.	−14,705	−13,932	−10,254
Trade balance	−2,641	−2,452	1,776
Exports of services	2,135	1,925	1,835
Imports of services	−3,650	−3,394	−3,097
Balance on goods and services	−4,156	−3,921	514
Other income received	891	912	796
Other income paid	−3,213	−2,627	−2,217
Balance on goods, services and income	−6,478	−5,636	−907
Current transfers received	831	596	1,103
Current transfers paid	−217	−169	−257
Current balance	−5,864	−5,209	−61
Direct investment abroad.	−810	−529	6
Direct investment from abroad	5,638	2,961	1,109
Portfolio investment assets	−762	801	−1,419
Portfolio investment liabilities	1,673	1,008	650
Other investment assets	−1,112	−326	−114
Financial derivatives liabilities	290	−39	100
Other investment liabilities	2,100	381	−428
Net errors and omissions	−876	−445	−155
Overall balance	277	−1,397	−312

Source: IMF, *International Financial Statistics*.

External Trade

PRINCIPAL COMMODITIES (US $ million)

Imports c.i.f.	1998	1999
Vegetables and vegetable products	849.2	652.3
Prepared foodstuffs, beverages and tobacco	953.8	788.3
Textiles and leather products	689.9	580.8
Paper and paper products	494.8	422.9
Chemical products	2,737.2	2,352.5
Petroleum and its derivatives	371.8	302.6
Metals	755.7	379.8
Mechanical, electrical and transport equipment	6,898.5	4,488.0
Total (incl. others)	14,634.7	10,659.1

Source: Dirección de Impuestos y Aduanas Nacionales.

Exports f.o.b.	1998	1999
Vegetables and vegetable products	1,157.6	1,187.8
Coffee	1,893.1	1,323.7
Coal	935.7	847.9
Petroleum and its derivatives	2,328.9	3,757.0
Prepared foodstuffs, beverages and tobacco	945.7	799.5
Textiles and leather products	932.8	872.9
Paper and publishing	272.8	259.3
Chemicals	1,021.5	1,103.0
Mechanical, electrical and transport equipment	601.5	477.6
Total (incl. others)	10,865.6	11,568.7

PRINCIPAL TRADING PARTNERS (US $ million)

Imports c.i.f.	1998	1999
Argentina	243.1	177.0
Belgium-Luxembourg	228.9	188.8
Brazil	520.0	428.5
Canada	406.4	212.2
Chile	238.8	272.7
Ecuador	318.5	262.4
France	376.9	273.3
Germany	749.3	452.7
Italy	357.9	213.0
Japan	844.7	417.3
Korea, Republic	273.9	159.6
Mexico	620.0	475.2
Netherlands	226.1	151.4
Panama	204.3	282.4
Peru	155.7	111.6
Spain	416.6	257.0
Sweden	153.8	82.1
United Kingdom	301.7	155.1
USA	5,092.3	4,099.9
Venezuela	1,399.4	888.1
Total (incl. others)	14,634.7	10,659.1

Source: Dirección de Impuestos y Aduanas Nacionales.

Exports f.o.b.	1998	1999
Belgium-Luxembourg	318.1	261.0
Brazil	101.6	166.2
Canada	136.9	120.1
Chile	159.3	152.2
Costa Rica	102.1	115.8
Ecuador	581.5	323.8
France	231.0	140.5
Germany	684.5	485.5
Italy	214.6	198.8
Japan	268.5	245.0
Mexico	128.5	201.6
Netherlands	288.7	169.5
Panama	106.1	144.0
Peru	370.1	357.3
Puerto Rico	101.7	167.3
Spain	151.0	149.3
United Kingdom	236.6	212.5
USA	4,048.5	5,615.4
Venezuela	1,154.6	915.6
Total (incl. others)	10,865.6	11,568.7

Transport

RAILWAYS (traffic)

	1996	1997	1998
Freight ('000 metric tons) . .	321	348	281
Freight ton-km ('000) . .	746,544	736,427	657,585

Source: Sociedad de Transporte Ferroviario, SA.

ROAD TRAFFIC (motor vehicles in use)

	1986	1987	1988
Passenger cars	611,978	655,201	706,922
Buses	52,136	53,354	55,111
Goods vehicles . . .	282,386	291,070	300,254
Heavy-duty vehicles . . .	230,034	233,555	239,524
Total (incl. others) . . .	1,242,650	1,301,802	1,375,405

1996 (vehicles in use at 31 December, estimates): Passenger cars 762,000; Goods vehicles (incl. vans) 672,000; Total 1,434,000 (Source: IRF, *World Road Statistics*).

SHIPPING

Merchant Fleet (registered at 31 December)

	1996	1997	1998
Number of vessels . . .	118	118	112
Total displacement ('000 grt) .	121.7	117.7	111.7

Source: Lloyd's Register of Shipping, *World Fleet Statistics*.

Domestic Sea-borne Freight Traffic ('000 metric tons)

	1987	1988	1989
Goods loaded and unloaded . .	772.1	944.8	464.6

International Sea-borne Freight Traffic ('000 metric tons)

	1996	1997	1998
Goods loaded	38,053	47,567	40,965
Goods unloaded	13,257	27,097	19,732

CIVIL AVIATION (traffic)

	1997	1998	1999
Domestic			
Passengers carried ('000) . .	8,027	7,947	7,545
Freight carried (metric tons) .	135,154	113,790	129,806
International			
Passengers ('000):			
arrivals	1,311	1,373	1,337
departures	1,355	1,407	1,480
Freight (metric tons):			
loaded.	198,572	205,866	145,596
unloaded	226,875	232,979	233,015

Source: Departamento Administrativo de Aeronáutica Civil.

Tourism

TOURIST ARRIVALS ('000)

Country of origin	1995	1996	1997
Argentina	32.0	29.9	20.2
Aruba	38.5	30.3	24.8
Brazil	24.3	22.0	16.8
Canada	20.8	16.3	18.0
Chile	22.1	19.5	13.4
Costa Rica	33.6	25.2	12.9
Cuba	18.7	24.6	17.1
Ecuador	79.8	77.5	57.4
France	34.0	31.2	23.3
Germany	36.7	32.1	18.2
Mexico	35.6	32.9	25.8
Panama	146.6	137.7	105.0
Peru	41.1	35.0	31.1
Spain	63.9	61.9	54.1
United Kingdom	21.8	18.8	18.2
USA	537.4	477.4	386.5
Venezuela	163.4	142.5	99.3
Total (incl. others) . . .	1,399.0	1,254.0	969.0

Tourism receipts (US $ million): 859 in 1995; 905 in 1996; 955 in 1997.

Source: World Tourism Organization, *Yearbook of Tourism Statistics*.

Communications Media

	1995	1996	1997
Telephones ('000 main lines in use)	3,873	4,645	5,334
Telefax stations ('000 in use) . .	100	141	173
Mobile cellular telephones ('000 subscribers)	275	523	1,265
Radio receivers ('000 in use) . .	20,200	20,600	21,000
Television receivers ('000 in use) .	4,200	4,500	4,590
Daily newspapers: number . .	34	37	n.a.

Book production: 1,481 titles in 1991.

Sources: UN, *Statistical Yearbook*; UNESCO, *Statistical Yearbook*.

Education

(1999)

	Institutions	Teachers	Pupils
Nursery	30,138	58,524	1,034,182
Primary	60,183	214,911	5,162,260
Secondary	13,421	200,337	3,594,083
Higher (incl. universities)* . .	266	75,568	673,353

* 1996 figures.

Source: partly Ministerio de Educación Nacional.

Directory

The Constitution

A new, 380-article Constitution, drafted by a 74-member National Constituent Assembly, took effect from 6 July 1991. The new Constitution retained the institutional framework of a directly-elected President with a non-renewable four-year term of office, together with a bicameral legislature composed of an upper house or Senate (with 102 directly-elected members) and a lower house or House of Representatives (with 161 members, to include at least two representatives of each national department). A Vice-President is elected at the same time as the President, and also holds office for a term of four years.

The new Constitution also contained comprehensive provisions for the recognition and protection of civil rights, and for the reform of the structures and procedures of political participation and of the judiciary.

The fundamental principles upon which the new Constitution is based are embodied in articles 1–10.

Article 1: Colombia is a lawful state, organized as a single Republic, decentralized, with autonomous territorial entities, democratic, participatory and pluralist, founded on respect for human dignity, on the labour and solidarity of its people and on the prevalence of the general interest.

Article 2: The essential aims of the State are: to serve the community, to promote general prosperity and to guarantee the effectiveness of the principles, rights and obligations embodied in the Constitution, to facilitate the participation of all in the decisions which affect them and in the economic, political, administrative and cultural life of the nation; to defend national independence, to maintain territorial integrity and to ensure peaceful coexistence and the validity of the law.

The authorities of the Republic are instituted to protect the residents of Colombia, in regard to their life, honour, goods, beliefs and other rights and liberties, and to ensure the fulfilment of the obligations of the State and of the individual.

Article 3: Sovereignty rests exclusively with the people, from whom public power emanates. The people exercise power directly or through their representatives in the manner established by the Constitution.

Article 4: The Constitution is the highest authority. In all cases of incompatability between the Constitution and the law or other juridical rules, constitutional dispositions will apply.

It is the duty of nationals and foreigners in Colombia to observe the Constitution and the law, and to respect and obey the authorities.

Article 5: The State recognizes, without discrimination, the primacy of the inalienable rights of the individual and protects the family as the basic institution of society.

Article 6: Individuals are solely responsible to the authorities for infringements of the Constitution and of the law. Public servants are equally accountable and are responsible to the authorities for failure to fulfil their function or abuse of their position.

Article 7: The State recognizes and protects the ethnic diversity of the Colombian nation.

Article 8: It is an obligation of the State and of the people to protect the cultural and natural riches of the nation.

Article 9: The foreign relations of the State are based on national sovereignty, with respect for self-determination of people and with recognition of the principles of international law accepted by Colombia.

Similarly, Colombia's external politics will be directed towards Caribbean and Latin American integration.

Article 10: Spanish (Castellano) is the official language of Colombia. The languages and dialects of ethnic groups are officially recognized within their territories. Education in communities with their own linguistic traditions will be bilingual.

The Government

HEAD OF STATE

President: ANDRÉS PASTRANA ARANGO (took office 7 August 1998).
Vice-President and Minister of National Defence: GUSTAVO BELL LEMUS.

CABINET
(May 2001)

A coalition of the Partido Conservador Colombiano (PCC), the Partido Liberal Colombiano (PL) and independents (Ind.).

Minister of the Interior: ARMANDO ESTRADA VILLA.
Minister of Foreign Affairs: GUILLERMO FERNÁNDEZ DE SOTO (PCC).
Minister of Justice and Law: RÓMULO GONZÁLEZ TRUJILLO (PCC).
Minister of Finance and Public Credit: JUAN MANUEL SANTOS CALDERÓN (PL).
Minister of Agriculture and Rural Development: RODRIGO VILLALBA MOSQUERA (PCC).
Minister of Labour and Social Security: ANGELINO GARZÓN (Ind.).
Minister of Foreign Trade: MARTA LUCÍA RAMÍREZ DE RINCÓN (Ind.).
Minister of Public Health: SARA ORDÓNEZ (PCC).
Minister of Economic Development: EDUARDO PIZANO (PCC).
Minister of Mines and Energy: LUIS RAMIRO VALENCIA COSSIO (PCC).
Minister of National Education: FRANCISCO JOSÉ LLOREDA MERA (PCC).
Minister of Communications: ANGELA MONTOYA HOLGUÍN (PCC).
Minister of Transport: GUSTAVO CANAL MORA (PCC).
Minister of the Environment: JUAN MAYR MALDONADO (Ind.).
Minister of Culture: ARACELY MORALES LÓPEZ (Ind.).

MINISTRIES

Office of the President: Palacio de Nariño, Carrera 8A, No 7-26, Santafé de Bogotá, DC; tel. (1) 562-9300; fax (1) 286-8063.

Ministry of Agriculture and Rural Development: Avda Jiménez, No 7-65, Santafé de Bogotá, DC; tel. (1) 334-1199; fax (1) 284-1775; e-mail minagric@colomsat.net.co; internet www.minagricultura.gov.co.

Ministry of Communications: Edif. Murillo Toro, Carrera 7 y 8, Calle 12 y 13, Apdo Aéreo 14515, Santafé de Bogotá, DC; tel. (1) 286-6911; fax (1) 344-3434; internet www.mincomunicaciones.gov.co.

Ministry of Culture: Calle 8, No 6-97, Santafé de Bogotá, DC; tel. (1) 342-4100; fax (1) 342-1721; e-mail fvasquez@mincultura.gov.co; internet www.mincultura.gov.co.

Ministry of Economic Development: Carrera 13, No 28-01, 5°–9°, Apdo Aéreo 99412, Santafé de Bogotá, DC; tel. (1) 320-0077; fax (1) 350-5791; internet www.mindesa.gov.co.

Ministry of the Environment: Calle 37, No 8-40, Santafé de Bogotá, DC; tel. (1) 288-6877; fax (1) 288-9788; internet www.minambienle.gov.co.

Ministry of Finance and Public Credit: Carrera 8A, No 6-64, Of. 308, Santafé de Bogotá, DC; tel. (1) 284-5400; fax (1) 286-3858; internet www.minhacienda.gov.co.

Ministry of Foreign Affairs: Palacio de San Carlos, Calle 10A, No 5-51, Santafé de Bogotá, DC; tel. (1) 282-7811; fax (1) 341-6777; internet www.minrelext.gov.co.

Ministry of Foreign Trade: Calle 28, No 13A-15, 5°, 7° y 9°, Santafé de Bogotá, DC; tel. (1) 286-9111; fax (1) 336-3690; internet www.mincomex.gov.co.

Ministry of the Interior: Palacio Echeverry, Carrera 8A, No 8-09, Santafé de Bogotá, DC; tel. (1) 334-0630; fax (1) 341-9583; internet www.presidencia.gov.co/mininterior.

Ministry of Justice and Law: Avda Jiménez, No 8-89, Santafé de Bogotá, DC; tel. (1) 286-0211; fax (1) 281-6384; internet www.minjusticia.gov.co.

Ministry of Labour and Social Security: Carrera 7A, No 34-50, Santafé de Bogotá, DC; tel. (1) 287-3434; fax (1) 285-7091; e-mail oaai@tutopia.com.

Ministry of Mines and Energy: Centro Administrativo Nacional (CAN), Avda El Dorado, Santafé de Bogotá, DC; tel. (1) 222-4555; fax (1) 222-3651; internet www.minminas.gov.co.

Ministry of National Defence: Centro Administrativo Nacional (CAN), 2°, Avda El Dorado, Santafé de Bogotá, DC; tel. (1) 220-4999; fax (1) 222-1874; internet www.mindefensa.gov.co.

Ministry of National Education: Centro Administrativo Nacional (CAN), Of. 501, Avda El Dorado, Santafé de Bogotá, DC; tel. (1) 222-2800; fax (1) 222-4578; internet www.icfes.gov.co/men.html.

Ministry of Public Health: Carrera 13, No 32-76, Santafé de Bogotá, DC; tel. (1) 336-5066; fax (1) 336-0296; internet www.minsalud.gov.co.

Ministry of Transport: Centro Administrativo Nacional (CAN), Of. 409, Avda El Dorado, Santafé de Bogotá, DC; tel. (1) 222-4411; fax (1) 222-1647; internet www.mintransporte.gov.co.

President and Legislature

PRESIDENT

Presidential Elections, 31 May and 21 June 1998

	First ballot (votes)	Second ballot %
	Votes	
ANDRÉS PASTRANA ARANGO (PCC) . . .	3,607,945	50.4
HORACIO SERPA URIBE (PL)	3,634,823	46.5
NOEMÍ SANÍN POSADA	2,824,735	—
Gen. (retd) HAROLD BEDOYA PIZARRO .	191,981	—
Others	125,822	—

CONGRESO

Senado
(Senate)

President: MARIO URIBE ESCOBAR.

General Election, 8 March 1998

	Seats
Partido Liberal Colombiano (PL)	53
Partido Conservador Colombiano (PCC) . . .	27
Independent groups	20
Indigenous groups*	2
Total	**102**

* Under the reforms of the Constitution in 1991, at least two Senate seats are reserved for indigenous groups.

Cámara de Representantes
(House of Representatives)

President: BASILIO VILLAMIZAR.

General Election, 8 March 1998

	Seats	% of votes cast
Partido Liberal Colombiano (PL) . .	84	52.2
Independent groups	30	18.6
Partido Conservador Colombiano (PCC) .	28	17.4
Coalitions	16	9.9
Others	3	1.9
Total	**161**	**100.0**

Political Organizations

Alianza Democrática—M-19 (AD—M-19): Transversal 28, No 37-78, Santafé de Bogotá, DC; tel. (1) 368-9436; f. 1990; alliance of centre-left groups (including factions of Unión Patriótica, Colombia Unida, Frente Popular and Socialismo Democrático) which supported the M-19 campaign for elections to the National Constituent Assembly in December 1990; Leader DIEGO MONTAÑA CUÉLLAR.

Alianza Nacional Popular (ANAPO): Carrera 18, No 33-95, Santafé de Bogotá, DC; tel. (1) 287-7050; fax (1) 245-3138; f. 1971 by supporters of Gen. Gustavo Rojas Pinilla; populist party; Leader MARÍA EUGENIA ROJAS DE MORENO DÍAZ.

Democracia Cristiana: Avda 42, No 18-08, Apdo 25867, Santafé de Bogotá, DC; tel. (1) 285-6639; f. 1964; Christian Democrat party; 10,000 mems; Pres. JUAN A. POLO FIGUEROA; Sec.-Gen. DIEGO ARANGO OSORIO.

Frente por la Unidad del Pueblo (FUP): Santafé de Bogotá, DC; extreme left-wing front comprising socialists and Maoists.

Movimiento 19 de Abril (M-19): Calle 26, No 13B-09, Of. 1401, Santafé de Bogotá, DC; tel. (1) 282-7891; fax (1) 282-8129; f. 1970 by followers of Gen. Gustavo Rojas Pinilla and dissident factions from the FARC (see below); left-wing urban guerrilla group, until formally constituted as a political party in Oct. 1989; Leaders ANTONIO NAVARRO WOLFF, OTTY PATIÑO.

Movimiento Colombia Unida (CU): Santafé de Bogotá, DC; left-wing group allied to the UP; Leader ADALBERTO CARVAJAL.

Movimiento Nacional Conservador (MNC): Carrera 16, No 33-24, Santafé de Bogotá, DC; tel. (1) 245-4418; fax (1) 284-8529; Sec.-Gen. JUAN PABLO CEPERA MÁRQUEZ.

Movimiento Nacional Progresista (MNP): Carrera 10, No 19-45, Of. 708, Santafé de Bogotá, DC; tel. (1) 286-7517; fax (1) 341-9368; Sec.-Gen. EDUARDO AISAMAK LEÓN BELTRÁN.

Movimiento Obrero Independiente Revolucionario (MOIR): Calle 52A, No 20-09, Santafé de Bogotá, DC; tel. (1) 249-4312; e-mail moir@moir.org.co; internet www.moir.org.co; left-wing workers' movement; Maoist; Leader HÉCTOR VALENGA.

Movimiento de Salvación Nacional (MSN): Carrera 7A, No 58-00, Santafé de Bogotá, DC; tel. (1) 249-0209; fax (1) 310-1991; f. 1990; split from the Partido Conservador Colombiano.

Movimiento Unitario Metapolítico (MUM): Calle 13, No 68D-40, Santafé de Bogotá, DC; tel. (1) 292-1330; fax (1) 292-5502; f. 1985; populist-occultist party; Leader REGINA BETANCOURT DE LISKA.

Mujeres para la Democracia: Santafé de Bogotá, DC; f. 1991; women's party; Leader ANGELA CUEVAS DE DOLMETSCH.

Partido Conservador Colombiano (PCC): Avda 22, No 37-09, Santafé de Bogotá, DC; tel. (1) 369-0011; fax (1) 369-0187; f. 1849; 2.9m. mems; Leader OMAR YEPES-ALZATE; Sec.-Gen. HUMBERTO ZULUAGA MONEDERO.

Partido Liberal Colombiano (PL): Avda Caracas, No 36-01, Santafé de Bogotá, DC; tel. (1) 287-9311; fax (1) 287-9540; f. 1815; divided into two factions, the official group (HERNANDO DURÁN LUSSÁN, MIGUEL PINEDO) and the independent group, Nuevo Liberalismo (New Liberalism, led by Dr ALBERTO SANTOFIMIO BOTERO, ERNESTO SAMPER PIZANO, EDUARDO MESTRE); Pres. LUIS FERNANDO JARAMILLO.

Partido Nacional Cristiano (PNC): Calle 22C, No 31-01, Santafé de Bogotá, DC; tel. (1) 337-9211; fax (1) 269-3621; e-mail mision2@latino.net.co; Pres. LIÑO LEAL COLLAZOS.

Unidad Democrática de la Izquierda (Democratic Unity of the Left): Santafé de Bogotá, DC; f. 1982; left-wing coalition incorporating the following parties:

Firmes: Santafé de Bogotá, DC; democratic party.

Partido Comunista Colombiano (PC): Calle 18A, No 14-56, Apdo Aéreo 2523, Santafé de Bogotá, DC; tel. (1) 334-1947; fax (1) 281-8259; f. 1930; Marxist-Leninist party; Sec.-Gen. ALVARO VÁSQUEZ DEL REAL.

Partido Socialista de los Trabajadores (PST): Santafé de Bogotá, DC; workers' socialist party; Leader MARÍA SOCORRO RAMÍREZ.

Unión Patriótica (UP): Carrera 13A, No 38-32, Of. 204, Santafé de Bogota, DC; fax (1) 570-4400; f. 1985; Marxist party formed by the FARC (see below); obtained legal status in 1986; Pres. ERNÁN PASTRANA; Exec. Sec. OVIDIO SALINAS.

The following guerrilla groups and illegal organizations were active in the late 1980s and in the 1990s:

Autodefensas Unidas de Colombia (AUC): right-wing paramilitary org.; 2,000 mems; Leader CARLOS CASTAÑO.

Comando Ricardo Franco-Frente Sur: f. 1984; common front formed by dissident factions from the FARC and M-19 (see below); Leader JAVIER DELGADO.

Ejército de Liberación Nacional (ELN): Castroite guerrilla movement; f. 1965; 930 mems; political status recognized by the Govt in 1998; Leaders NICOLÁS ROGRÍGUEZ BAUTISTA, VÁSQUEZ CASTAÑO; factions include:

Corriente de Renovación Socialista (CRS): (ceased hostilities in December 1993).

Frente Simón Bolívar: (ceased hostilities in December 1985).

Frente Antonio Nariño: (ceased hostilities in December 1985).

Frente Domingo Laín: formed splinter group in October 1993; armed wing.

Ejército Popular de Liberación (EPL): Maoist guerrilla movement; f. 1969; splinter group from Communist Party; abandoned armed struggle in March 1991; joined the political mainstream as the **Partido de Esperanza, Paz y Libertad (EPL)**; Leader FRANCISCO CARABALLO.

Frente Popular de Liberación Nacional (FPLN): f. 1994 by dissident members of the ELN and the EPL.

Fuerzas Armadas Revolucionarias de Colombia (FARC): fmrly military wing of the Communist Party; composed of 39 armed fronts; political status recognized by the Govt in 1998; Leader MANUEL MARULANDA VÉLEZ (alias TIROFIJO).

Movimiento de Autodefensa Obrera (MAO): workers' self-defence movement; Trotskyite; Leader ADELAIDA ABADIA REY.

Movimiento de Restauración Nacional (MORENA): right-wing; Leader ARMANDO VALENZUELA RUIZ.

Muerte a Secuestradores (MAS) (Death to Kidnappers): right-wing paramilitary org.; funded by drugs dealers.

Nuevo Frente Revolucionario del Pueblo: f. 1986; faction of M-19; active in Cundinamarca region.

Partido Revolucionario de Trabajadores (PRT): left-wing; abandoned its armed struggle in 1991 and announced its intention to join the political mainstream as part of the Alianza Democrática.

Patria Libre: f. 1985; left-wing guerrilla movement.

In late 1985 the M-19, the Comando Ricardo Franco-Frente Sur and the **Comando Quintín Lame** (an indigenous organization active in the department of Cauca) announced the formation of a united front, the **Coordinadora Guerrillera Nacional (CGN)**. In 1986 the CGN participated in joint campaigns with the Movimiento Revolucionario Tupac Amarú (Peru) and the Alfaro Vive ¡Carajo! (Ecuador). The alliance operated under the name of **Batallón América**. In late 1987 six guerrilla groups, including the ELN, the FARC and the M-19, formed a joint front, to be known as the **Coordinadora Guerrillera Simón Bolívar (CGSB)** and subsequently as the **Coordinadora Nacional Guerrillera Simón Bolívar (CNGSB)**.

Diplomatic Representation

EMBASSIES IN COLOMBIA

Argentina: Avda 40A, No 13-09, 16°, Santafé de Bogotá, DC; tel. (1) 288-0900; Ambassador: CARLOS CARRASCO.

Austria: Carrera 11, No 75-29, Santafé de Bogotá, DC; tel. (1) 235-6628; Ambassador: MARIANNE DA COSTA DE MORAES.

Belgium: Calle 26, No 4A-45, 7°, Santafé de Bogotá, DC; tel. (1) 282-8881; fax (1) 282-8862; Ambassador: FRANCOIS RONSE.

Bolivia: Carrera 9, No 114-96, Santafé de Bogotá, DC; tel. (1) 629-8237; fax (1) 612-9325; e-mail embolivia-bogota@rree.gov.bo; Ambassador: GUIDO RIVEROS FRANCK.

Bosnia and Herzegovina: Carrera 13A, No 89-38, Of. 607, Santafé de Bogotá, DC; tel. (1) 618-4869; fax (1) 618-4847; Chargé d'affaires: NARCISA ABDULAGIĆ.

Brazil: Calle 93, No 14-20, 8°, Santafé de Bogotá, DC; tel. (1) 218-0800; Ambassador: MARCOS CAMACHO DE VINCENZI.

Canada: Calle 7, No 115-33, Apdo Aéreo 53531, Santafé de Bogotá, DC; tel. (1) 657-9800; fax (1) 657-9912; internet www.dfait-maeci.gc.ca/bogota; Ambassador: C. GUILLERMO E. RISHCHYNSKI.

Chile: Calle 100, No 11B-44, Santafé de Bogotá, DC; tel. (1) 214-7926; Ambassador: OSCAR PIZARRO ROMERO.

China, People's Republic: Calle 16, No 98-30A-41, Santafé de Bogotá, DC; tel. (1) 622-3215; fax (1) 622-3114; e-mail embchina@andinet.com; Ambassador: JU YIJIE.

Costa Rica: Carrera 15, No 102-25, Santafé de Bogotá, DC; tel. (1) 622-8830; fax (1) 623-0205; Ambassador: Dr FERNANDO DEL CASTILLO RIGGIONI.

Cuba: Carrera 9, No 92-54, Santafé de Bogotá, DC; tel. (1) 257-3353; fax (1) 611-4382; Ambassador: LUIS HERNÁNDEZ ÓJEDA.

Czech Republic: Carrera 7, No 113-16, 4°, Santafé de Bogotá, DC; tel. (1) 215-0633; fax (1) 612-8205.

Dominican Republic: Carrera 16A, No 86A-33, Santafé de Bogotá, DC; tel. (1) 621-1925; fax (1) 236-2588; Ambassador: MIGUEL A. FERSOBE PICHARDO.

Ecuador: Calle 89, No 13-07, Santafé de Bogotá, DC; tel. (1) 257-0066; fax (1) 257-9799; Ambassador: Dr FERNANDO RIBADENEIRA.

Egypt: Carrera 19A, No 98-17, Santafé de Bogotá, DC; tel. (1) 236-4832; Ambassador: AHMED FATHI ABULKHEIR.

El Salvador: Carrera 9A, No 80-15, Of. 503, Edif. El Nogal, Santafé de Bogotá, DC; tel. (1) 211-0012; fax (1) 255-9482; Ambassador: GUILLERMO RUBIO FUNES.

France: Carrera 11, No 93-12, Santafé de Bogotá, DC; tel. (1) 285-4311; Ambassador: DANIEL PARFAIT.

Germany: Edif. Sisky, 6°, Carrera 4, No 72-35, Apdo Aéreo 91808, Santafé de Bogotá, DC; tel. (1) 348-4040; fax (1) 210-4256; Ambassador: PETER VON JAGOW.

Guatemala: Transversal 29A, No 139A-41, Santafé de Bogotá, DC; tel. (1) 259-1496; fax (1) 274-5365; e-mail emguacol@colomsat.net.co; Ambassador: DANTE MARINELLI GOLOM.

Haiti: Carrera 11A, No 96-63, Santafé de Bogotá, DC; tel. (1) 256-6236; fax (1) 218-0326; Chargé d'affaires: CARLO TOUSSAINT.

Holy See: Carrera 15, No 36-33, Apdo Aéreo 3740, Santafé de Bogotá, DC (Apostolic Nunciature); tel. (1) 320-0289; fax (1) 285-1817; e-mail nunciocol@col1.telecom.com.co; Apostolic Nuncio: Most Rev. BENIAMINO STELLA, Titular Archbishop of Midila.

Honduras: Carrera 16, No 85-15, Of. 302, Santafé de Bogotá, DC; tel. (1) 236-0357; fax (1) 616-0774; Ambassador: HERNÁN ANTONIO BERMÚDEZ.

Hungary: Carrera 6A, No 77-46, Santafé de Bogotá, DC; tel. (1) 347-1467; fax (1) 347-1469; e-mail huembog1@netsoft.net.co; Ambassador: JÓZSEF NAGY.

India: Calle 71A, No 6-30, Of. 501, Santafé de Bogotá, DC; tel. (1) 217-5143; fax (1) 212-7648; e-mail indembog@colomsat.net.co; Ambassador: PRAMATHESH RATH.

Iran: Calle 96, No 11A-16/20, Santafé de Bogotá, DC; tel. (1) 218-6205; fax (1) 610-2556; Ambassador: HOSSEIN SHEIKH ZEINEDDIN.

Indonesia: Carrera 9, No 76-27, Santafé de Bogotá; tel. (1) 217-6738; fax (1) 210-3507.

Israel: Calle 35, No 7-25, 14°, Santafé de Bogotá, DC; tel. (1) 287-7808; fax (1) 287-7783; Ambassador: AVRAHAM HADAD.

Italy: Calle 93B, No 9-92, Apdo Aéreo 50901, Santafé de Bogotá, DC; tel. (1) 218-6680; fax (1) 610-5886; e-mail ambitbog@internet.co; internet www.ambitaliabogota.org; Ambassador: FELICE SCAUSO.

Japan: Carrera 9A, No 99-02, 6°, Edif. Latinoamericano de Seguros, Santafé de Bogotá, DC; tel. (1) 618-2800; fax (1) 618-2828; Ambassador: GUNKATSU KANO.

Korea, Democratic People's Republic: Santafé de Bogotá, DC; Ambassador: JI YONG HO.

Korea, Republic: Calle 94, No 9-39, Santafé de Bogotá, DC; tel. (1) 616-7200; fax (1) 610-0338; e-mail embcorea@cable.net.co; Ambassador: WON JONG-CHAN.

Lebanon: Calle 74, No 12-44, Santafé de Bogotá, DC; tel. (1) 212-8360; fax (1) 347-9106; Ambassador: MOUNIR KHREICH.

Mexico: Calle 99, No 12-08, Santafé de Bogotá, DC; tel. (1) 256-6121; internet www.sre.gob.mx/colombia; Ambassador: LUIS ORTIZ MONASTERIO.

Morocco: Carrera 13A, No 98-33, Santafé de Bogotá, DC; tel. (1) 218-7147; fax (1) 218-8068; Ambassador: MOHAMED AYACHI.

Netherlands: Carrera 13, No 93-40, 5°, Apdo Aéreo 43585, Santafé de Bogotá, DC; tel. (1) 611-5080; fax (1) 623-3020; e-mail nlgovbog@trauco.colomsat.net.co; Ambassador: TEUNIS KAMPER.

Nicaragua: Transversal 19A, No 108-77, Santafé de Bogotá, DC; tel. (1) 214-1445; fax (1) 215-9582; Ambassador: DONALD CASTILLO RIVAS.

Panama: Calle 92, No 7-70, Santafé de Bogotá, DC; tel. (1) 257-5068; Ambassador: ALFREDO ANTONIO MONTANER.

Paraguay: Calle 57, No 7-11, Of. 702, Apdo Aéreo 20085, Santafé de Bogotá, DC; tel. (1) 255-4160; Ambassador: GERARDO FOGEL.

Peru: Carrera 10, No 93-48, Santafé de Bogotá, DC; tel. (1) 257-6292; fax (1) 623-5102; Ambassador: ALEJANDRO GORDILLO FERNÁNDEZ.

Poland: Calle 104A, No 23-48, Santafé de Bogotá, DC; tel. (1) 214-0143; fax (1) 218-0854; e-mail epolonia@col1.telecom.com.co; Ambassador: PAWEL KULKA KULPIOWSKI.

Portugal: Calle 71, No 11-10, Of. 703, Santafé de Bogotá, DC; tel. (1) 212-4223; Ambassador: AUGUSTO MARTINS GONÇALVES P.

Romania: Carrera 7, No 92-58, Santafé de Bogotá, DC; tel. (1) 256-6438; Ambassador CRISTIAN LAZARESCU.

Russia: Carrera 4, No 75-00, Apdo Aéreo 90600, Santafé de Bogotá, DC; tel. (1) 212-1881; fax (1) 210-4694; e-mail embrusia@impsat.net.co; Ambassador: EDNAN AGAYEV.

Slovakia: Avda 13, No 104A-30, Santafé de Bogotá, DC; tel. (1) 214-2240.

Spain: Calle 92, No 12-68, Santafé de Bogotá, DC; tel. (1) 618-1888; fax (1) 616-6104; Ambassador: YAGO PICO DE COAÑA.

Sweden: Calle 72, No 5-83, 9°, Santafé de Bogotá, DC; tel. (1) 325-2165; fax (1) 325-2166; Ambassador: BJÖRN STERNBY.

Switzerland: Carrera 9, No 74-08/1101, 11°, Santafé de Bogotá, DC; tel. (1) 349-7230; fax (1) 349-7195; Ambassador: VIKTOR CHRISTEN.

United Kingdom: Carrera 9, No 76-49, 9°, Santafé de Bogotá, DC; tel. (1) 317-6690; fax (1) 317-6265; e-mail britain@cable.net.co; internet www.britain.gov.co; Ambassador: JEREMY W. THORP.

USA: Calle 22D-bis, No 47-51, Apdo Aéreo 3831, Santafé de Bogotá, DC; tel. (1) 315-0811; fax (1) 315-2197; internet usembassy.state.gov/posts/co1/wwwhmane.html; Ambassador: ANNE W. PATTERSON.

Uruguay: Carrera 9A, No 80-15, 11°, Apdo Aéreo 101466, Santafé de Bogotá, DC; tel. (1) 235-2748; fax (1) 248-3734; e-mail urucolom@impsat.com.co; Ambassador: DOMINGO SCHIPANI.

Venezuela: Carrera 11, No 87-51, 5°, Santafé de Bogotá, DC; tel. (1) 640-1213; fax (1) 640-1242; e-mail embajada@embaven.org.co; Ambassador: ROY CHADERTON.

Yugoslavia: Calle 93A, No 9A-22, Apdo Aéreo 91074, Santafé de Bogotá, DC; tel. (1) 257-0290; Ambassador: RADOMIR ZECEVIĆ.

Judicial System

The constitutional integrity of the State is ensured by the Constitutional Court. The Constitutional Court is composed of nine judges who are elected by the Senate for eight years. Judges of the Constitutional Court are not eligible for re-election.

President of the Constitutional Court: FABIO MORÓN DÍAZ.

Judges of the Constitutional Court: ALEJANDRO MARTÍNEZ CABALLERO, VLADIMIRO NARANJO MESA, ANTONIO BARRERO CARBONELL, CARLOS GAVIRIA DÍAZ, ALVARO TAFUR GALVIS, JOSÉ GREGORIO HERNÁNDEZ, EDUARDO CIFUENTES MUÑOZ, ALFREDO BELTRAN SIERRA.

The ordinary judicial integrity of the State is ensured by the Supreme Court of Justice. The Supreme Court of Justice is composed of the Courts of Civil and Agrarian, Penal and Laboral Cassation. Judges of the Supreme Court of Justice are selected from the nominees of the Higher Council of Justice and serve an eight-year term of office which is not renewable.

Prosecutor-General: ALFONSO GÓMEZ MÉNDEZ.

Attorney-General: EDGARDO JOSÉ MAYA VILLAZON.

SUPREME COURT OF JUSTICE

Supreme Court of Justice: Carrera 7A, No 27-18, Santafé de Bogotá, DC; fax (1) 334-8745; internet www.fij.edu.co.

President: Dr JORGE ANTONIO CASTILLO RUGECES.

Vice-President: FERNANDO ARBOLEDA RIPOLL.

Court of Civil and Agrarian Cassation (seven judges): President: JORGE ANTONIO CASTILLO RUGELES.

Court of Penal Cassation (nine judges): President: JORGE ANIBAL GÓMEZ GALLEGO.

Court of Laboral Cassation (seven judges): President: JOSÉ ROBERTO HERRERA VERGARA.

Religion

Roman Catholicism is the religion of 95% of the population.

CHRISTIANITY

The Roman Catholic Church

Colombia comprises 12 archdioceses, 48 dioceses, four Apostolic Vicariates and five Apostolic Prefectures.

Bishops' Conference: Conferencia Episcopal de Colombia, Carrera 47, No 84-87, Apdo Aéreo 7448, Santafé de Bogotá, DC; tel. (1) 311-4277; fax (1) 311-5575; e-mail colcec@net.co; f. 1978; Pres. ALBERTO GIRALDO JARAMILLO, Archbishop of Medellín.

Archbishop of Barranquilla: RUBÉN SALAZAR GÓMEZ, Carrera 45, No 53-122, Apdo Aéreo 1160, Barranquilla 4, Atlántico; tel. (5) 340-1648; fax (5) 340-6239.

Archbishop of Bucaramanga: VÍCTOR MANUEL LÓPEZ FORERO, Calle 33, No 21-18, Bucaramanga, Santander; tel. (7) 642-4387; fax (7) 642-1361.

Archbishop of Cali: ISAÍAS DUARTE CANCINO, Carrera 4, No 7-17, Apdo Aéreo 8924, Cali, Valle del Cauca; tel. (2) 889-0562; fax (2) 83-7980.

Archbishop of Cartagena: CARLOS JOSÉ RUISECO VIEIRA, Apdo Aéreo 400, Cartagena; tel. (5) 664-5308; fax (5) 664-4974; e-mail arzoctg@telecartagena.com.

Archbishop of Ibagué: JUAN FRANCISCO SARASTI JARAMILLO, Calle 10, No 2-58, Ibagué, Tolima; tel. (82) 61-1680; fax (82) 63-2681.

Archbishop of Manizales: FABIO BETANCUR TIRADO, Carrera 23, No 19-22, Manizales, Caldas; tel. (68) 84-0114; fax (68) 82-1853.

Archbishop of Medellín: ALBERTO GIRALDO JARAMILLO, Calle 57, No 49-44, 3°, Medellín; tel. (4) 251-7700; fax (4) 251-8306.

Archbishop of Nueva Pamplona: GUSTAVO MARTÍNEZ FRÍAS, Carrera 5, No 4-87, Nueva Pamplona; tel. (4) 68-2886; fax (4) 68-4540.

Archbishop of Popayán: IVÁN MARÍN-LÓPEZ, Calle 5, No 6-71, Apdo Aéreo 593, Popayán; tel. (928) 24-1710; fax (928) 24-0101.

Archbishop of Santa Fe de Antioquia: IGNACIO GÓMEZ ARISTIZÁBAL, Plazuela Martínez Pardo, No 12-11, Santa Fe de Antioquia; tel. (94) 853-1155; fax (94) 853-1596.

Archbishop of Santafé de Bogotá: Cardinal PEDRO RUBIANO SÁENZ, Carrera 7A, No 10-20, Santafé de Bogotá, DC; tel. (1) 334-5500; fax (1) 334-7867.

Archbishop of Tunja: LUIS AUGUSTO CASTRO QUIROGA; Calle 17, No 9-85, Apdo Aéreo 1019, Tunja, Boyacá; tel. (987) 42-2094; fax (987) 42-2096.

The Anglican Communion

Anglicans in Colombia are members of the Episcopal Church in the USA.

Bishop of Colombia: Rt Rev. BERNARDO MERINO BOTERO, Carrera 6, No 49-85, Apdo Aéreo 52964, Santafé de Bogotá, DC; tel. (1) 288-3167; fax (1) 288-3248; there are 3,500 baptized mems, 2,000 communicant mems, 29 parishes, missions and preaching stations; 5 schools and 1 orphanage; 8 clergy.

Protestant Churches

The Baptist Convention: Apdo Aéreo 51988, Medellín; tel. (4) 38-9623; Pres. RAMÓN MEDINA IBÁÑEZ; Exec. Sec. Rev. RAMIRO PÉREZ HOYOS.

Iglesia Evangélica Luterana de Colombia: Calle 75, No 20-54, Apdo Aéreo 51538, Santafé de Bogotá, DC; tel. (1) 212-5735; fax (1) 212-5714; e-mail ielco@yahoo.com; 3,000 mems; Pres. Bishop NEHEMÍAS PARADA.

BAHÁ'Í FAITH

National Spiritual Assembly: Apdo Aéreo 51387, Santafé de Bogotá, DC; tel. (1) 268-1658; fax (1) 268-1665; e-mail bahaicol@colombianet.net; adherents in 1,013 localities.

JUDAISM

There is a community of about 25,000 with 66 synagogues.

The Press

DAILIES
Santafé de Bogotá, DC

El Espacio: Carrera 61, No 45-35, Apdo Aéreo 80111, Avda El Dorado, Santafé de Bogotá, DC; tel. (1) 410-5066; fax (1) 410-4595; f. 1965; evening; Dir JAIME ARDILA CASAMITJANA; circ. 159,000.

El Espectador: Carrera 68, No 23-71, Apdo Aéreo 3441, Santafé de Bogotá, DC; tel. (1) 294-5555; fax (1) 260-2323; e-mail redactor@elespectador.com; internet www.elespectador.com; f. 1887; morning; Dir CARLOS LLERAS; Editor LUIS CAÑÓN; circ. 200,000.

El Nuevo Siglo: Calle 45A, No 102-02, Apdo Aéreo 5452, Santafé de Bogotá, DC; tel. (1) 413-9200; fax (1) 413-8547; f. 1925; Conservative; Dirs JUAN PABLO URIBE, JUAN GABRIEL URIBE; circ. 68,000.

La República: Calle 46, No 103-59, Santafé de Bogotá, DC; tel. (1) 413-5077; fax (1) 413-3725; f. 1953; morning; economics; Dir RODRIGO OSPINA HERNÁNDEZ; Editor JORGE EMILIO SIERRA M.; circ. 55,000.

El Tiempo: Avda El Dorado, No 59-70, Apdo Aéreo 3633, Santafé de Bogotá, DC; tel. (1) 294-0100; fax (1) 410-5088; internet www.eltiempo.com; f. 1911; morning; Liberal; Dir ENRIQUE SANTOS CALDERÓN; Editor FRANCISCO SANTOS; circ. 265,118 (weekdays), 536,377 (Sundays).

Barranquilla, Atlántico

El Heraldo: Calle 53B, No 46-25, Barranquilla, Atlántico; tel. (5) 41-1090; fax (5) 41-6918; e-mail elheraldo@metrotel.net.co; internet www.elheraldo.com.co; f. 1933; morning; Liberal; Dir JUAN B. FERNÁNDEZ; circ. 70,000.

La Libertad: Carrera 53, No 55-166, Barranquilla, Atlántico; tel. (5) 31-1517; Liberal; Dir ROBERTO ESPER REBAJE; circ. 25,000.

El Tiempo Caribe: Carrera 50B No 41-18, Barranquilla, Atlántico; tel. (5) 379-1510; fax (5) 341-7715; e-mail orlgam@eltiempo.com.co; internet www.eltiempo.com; f. 1956; daily; Liberal; Dir ORLANDA GAMBOA; circ. 45,000.

Bucaramanga, Santander del Sur

El Frente: Calle 35, No 12-22, Apdo Aéreo 665, Bucaramanga, Santander del Sur; tel. (7) 42-5369; fax (7) 33-4541; f. 1942; morning; Conservative; Dir RAFAEL SERRANO PRADA; circ. 10,000.

Vanguardia Liberal: Calle 34, No 13-42, Bucaramanga, Santander del Sur; tel. (7) 33-4000; fax (7) 30-2443; e-mail vanglibe@colomsat.net.co; f. 1919; morning; Liberal; Sunday illustrated literary supplement and women's supplement; Dir and Man. ALEJANDRO GALVIS RAMÍREZ; circ. 48,000.

Cali, Valle del Cauca

Occidente: Calle 12, No 5-22, Cali, Valle del Cauca; tel. (2) 895-9756; fax (2) 884-6572; e-mail occidente@cali.cercol.net.co; f. 1961; morning; Conservative; Dir ALVARO H. CAICEDO GONZÁLEZ; circ. 25,000.

El País: Carrera 2A, No 24-46, Apdo Aéreo 4766, Cali, Valle del Cauca; tel. (2) 883-5011; fax (2) 883-5014; e-mail diario@elpais-cali.com; internet www.elpais-cali.com; f. 1950; Conservative; Dir FRANCISCO JOSÉ LLOREDA MERA; circ. 60,000 (weekdays), 120,000 (Saturdays), 108,304 (Sundays).

El Pueblo: Avda 3A, Norte 35-N-10, Cali, Valle del Cauca; tel. (2) 68-8110; morning; Liberal; Dir LUIS FERNANDO LONDOÑO CAPURRO; circ. 50,000.

Cartagena, Bolívar

El Universal: Calle 30, No 17-36, Cartagena, Bolívar; fax (5) 666-1964; e-mail eluniversal@ctgred.net.co; internet www.eluniversal.com.co; f. 1948; daily; Liberal; Dir PEDRO LUIS MOGOLLÓN; Man. GERARDO ARAÚJO; circ. 30,000.

Cúcuta, Norte de Santander

Diario La Frontera: Calle 14, No 3-44, Cúcuta, Norte de Santander; tel. and fax (75) 71-0505; f. 1951; morning; Dir MARIO JAVIER PACHECO GARCÍA; circ. 25,000.

La Opinión: Avda 4, No 16-12, Cúcuta, Norte de Santander; tel. (75) 71-9999; fax (75) 71-7869; e-mail laopinion@coll.telecom.com.co; f. 1960; morning; Liberal; Dir Dr José Eustorgio Colmenares Ossa; circ. 26,000.

Manizales, Caldas

La Patria: Carrera 20, No 21-51, Apdo Aéreo 70, Manizales, Caldas; tel. (68) 84-2460; fax (68) 84-7158; e-mail lapatria@lapatria.com; f. 1921; morning; Independent; Dir Dr Luis José Restrepo Restrepo; circ. 22,000.

Medellín, Antioquia

El Colombiano: Carrera 48, No 30 sur-119, Apdo Aéreo 80636, Medellín, Antioquia; tel. (4) 331-5252; fax (4) 331-4858; e-mail elcolombiano@elcolombiano.com.co; internet www.elcolombiano .com; f. 1912; morning; Conservative; Dir Ana Mercedes Gómez Martínez; circ. 90,000.

El Mundo: Calle 53, No 74-50, Apdo Aéreo 53874, Medellín, Antioquia; tel. (4) 264-2800; fax (4) 264-3729; e-mail elmundo@elmundo .com; internet www.elmundo.com; f. 1979; Dir Guillermo Gaviria; Man. Aníbal Gaviria Correa; circ. 25,000.

Montería, Córdoba

El Meridiano de Córdoba: Avda Circunvalar, No 38-30, Montería, Córdoba; tel. (47) 82-6888; fax (47) 82-1981; e-mail meridiano@ monteria.cetcol.net.co; internet www.elmeridianodecordoba.com; f. 1995; morning; Dir William Enrique Salleg Taboada; circ. 17,000.

Neiva

Diario del Huila: Calle 8A, No 6-30, Neiva; tel. (88) 71-2458; fax (88) 71-2446; f. 1966; Dir María M. Rengifo de D.; circ. 12,000.

Pasto, Nariño

El Derecho: Calle 20, No 26-20, Pasto, Nariño; tel. (277) 2170; f. 1928; Conservative; Pres. Dr José Elías del Hierro; Dir Eduardo F. Mazuera; circ. 12,000.

Pereira, Risaralda

Diario del Otún: Carrera 8A, No 22-75, Apdo Aéreo 2533, Pereira, Risaralda; tel. (63) 51313; fax (1) 324-1900; e-mail eldiario@ interco.net.co; internet www.eldiario.com.co; f. 1982; Financial Dir Javier Ignacio Ramírez Múnera; circ. 30,000.

El Imparcial: km 11 vía Pereira-Armenia, El Jordán, Pereira, Risaralda; tel. (63) 25-9935; fax (63) 25-9934; f. 1948; morning; Dir Zahur Klemath Zapata; circ. 15,000.

La Tarde: Carrera 9A, No 20-54, Pereira, Risaralda; tel. (63) 35-7976; fax (63) 35-5187; f. 1975; evening; Man. Luis Fernando Baena Mejía; circ. 15,000.

Popayán, Cauca

El Liberal: Carrera 3, No 2-60, Apdo Aéreo 538, Popayán, Cauca; tel. (28) 24-2418; fax (28) 23-3888; f. 1938; Man. Carlos Alberto Cabal Jiménez; circ. 6,500.

Santa Marta, Magdalena

El Informador: Calle 21, No 5-06, Santa Marta, Magdalena; f. 1921; Liberal; Dir José B. Vives; circ. 9,000.

Tunja, Boyacá

Diario de Boyacá: Tunja, Boyacá; Dir-Gen. Dr Carlos H. Mojica; circ. 3,000.

Villavicencio, Meta

Clarín del Llano: Villavicencio, Meta; tel. (866) 23207; Conservative; Dir Elías Matus Torres; circ. 5,000.

PERIODICALS

Santafé de Bogotá, DC

Antena: Santafé de Bogotá, DC; television, cinema and show business; circ. 10,000.

Arco: Carrera 6, No 35-39, Apdo Aéreo 8624, Santafé de Bogotá, DC; tel. (1) 285-1500; f. 1959; monthly; history, philosophy, literature and humanities; Dir Alvaro Valencia Tovar; circ. 10,000.

ART NEXUS/Arte en Colombia: Carrera 5, No 67-19, Apdo Aéreo 90193, Santafé de Bogotá, DC; tel. (1) 312-9435; fax (1) 312-9252; e-mail artnex@impsat.net.co; f. 1976; quarterly; Latin American art, architecture, films and photography; editions in English and Spanish; Dir Celia Sredni de Birbragher; Exec. Editor Ivonne Pini; circ. 15,000.

El Campesino: Carrera 39A, No 15-11, Santafé de Bogotá, DC; f. 1958; weekly; cultural; Dir Joaquín Gutiérrez Macías; circ. 70,000.

Consigna: Diagonal 34, No 5-11, Santafé de Bogotá, DC; tel. (1) 287-1157; fortnightly; Turbayista; Dir (vacant); circ. 10,000.

Coyuntura Económica: Calle 78, No 9-91, Apdo Aéreo 75074, Santafé de Bogotá, DC; tel. (1) 312-5300; fax (1) 212-6073; e-mail bibliote@fedesarrollo.org.co; f. 1970; quarterly; economics; published by Fundación para Educación Superior y el Desarrollo (FEDESARROLLO); Editor María Angélica Arbelaez; circ. 1,500.

Cromos Magazine: Calle 70A, No 7-81, Apdo Aéreo 59317, Santafé de Bogotá, DC; f. 1916; weekly; illustrated; general news; Dir Alberto Zalamea; circ. 102,000.

As Deportes: Calle 20, No 4-55, Santafé de Bogotá, DC; f. 1978; sports; circ. 25,000.

Economía Colombiana: Edif. de los Ministerios, Of. 126A, No 6-40, Santafé de Bogotá, DC; f. 1984; published by Contraloría General de la República; monthly; economics.

Escala: Calle 30, No 17-70, Santafé de Bogotá, DC; tel. (1) 287-8200; fax (1) 232-5148; e-mail escala@col-online.com; f. 1962; fortnightly; architecture; Dir David Serna Cárdenas; circ. 16,000.

Estrategia: Carrera 4A, 25A–12B, Santafé de Bogotá, DC; monthly; economics; Dir Rodrigo Otero.

Guión: Carrera 16, No 36-89, Apdo Aéreo 19857; Santafé de Bogotá, DC; tel. (1) 232-2660; f. 1977; weekly; general; Conservative; Dir Juan Carlos Pastrana; circ. 35,000.

Hit: Calle 20, No 4-55, Santafé de Bogotá, DC; cinema and show business; circ. 20,000.

Hoy Por Hoy: Santafé de Bogotá, DC; weekly; Dir Diana Turbay de Uribe.

Menorah: Apdo Aéreo 9081, Santafé de Bogotá, DC; tel. (1) 611-2014; f. 1950; independent monthly review for the Jewish community; Dir Eliécer Celnik; circ. 10,000.

Nueva Frontera: Carrera 7A, No 17-01, 5°, Santafé de Bogotá, DC; tel. (1) 334-3763; f. 1974; weekly; politics, society, arts and culture; Liberal; Dir Carlos Lleras Restrepo; circ. 23,000.

Pluma: Apdo Aéreo 12190, Santafé de Bogotá, DC; monthly; art and literature; Dir (vacant); circ. 70,000.

Que Hubo: Santafé de Bogotá, DC; weekly; general; Editor Consuelo Montejo; circ. 15,000.

Revista Diners: Calle 85, No 18-32, 6°, Santafé de Bogotá, DC; tel. (1) 636-0508; fax (1) 623-1762; e-mail diners@cable.net.co; f. 1963; monthly; Dir Germán Santamaría; circ. 110,000.

Semana: Calle 93B, No 13-47, Santafé de Bogotá, DC; tel. (1) 622-2277; fax (1) 621-0475; general; Pres. Felipe López Caballero.

Síntesis Económica: Calle 70A, No 10-52, Santafé de Bogotá, DC; tel. (1) 212-5121; fax (1) 212-8365; f. 1975; weekly; economics; Dir Félix Lafaurie Rivera; circ. 16,000.

Teorema: Calle 70A, No 8-17, Santafé de Bogotá, DC; tel. (1) 217-2266; fax (1) 212-0639; f. 1983; computer technology; Dir Dionisio Ibáñez; circ. 5,000.

Tribuna Médica: Calle 8B, No 68A-41 y Calle 123, No 8-20, Santafé de Bogotá, DC; tel. (1) 262-6085; fax (1) 262-4459; f. 1961; monthly; medical and scientific; Editor Jack Alberto Grimberg; circ. 50,000.

Tribuna Roja: Apdo Aéreo 19042, Santafé de Bogotá, DC; tel. (1) 243-0371; f. 1971; quarterly; organ of the MOIR (pro-Maoist Communist party); Dir Carlos Naranjo; circ. 300,000.

Vea: Calle 20, No 4-55, Santafé de Bogotá, DC; weekly; popular; circ. 90,000.

Voz La Verdad del Pueblo: Carrera 8, No 19-34, Of. 310–311, Santafé de Bogotá, DC; tel. (1) 284-5209; fax (1) 342-5041; weekly; left-wing; Dir Carlos A. Lozano G.; circ. 45,000.

NEWS AGENCIES

Ciep—El País: Carrera 16, No 36-35, Santafé de Bogotá, DC; tel. (1) 232-6816; fax (1) 288-0236; Dir Jorge Téllez.

Colprensa: Diagonal 34, No 5-63, Apdo Aéreo 20333, Santafé de Bogotá, DC; tel. (1) 287-2200; fax (1) 285-5915; e-mail colpre@ elsitio.net.co; f. 1980; Dir Roberto Vargas Galvis.

Foreign Bureaux

Agence France-Presse (AFP): Carrera 5, No 16-14, Of. 807, Apdo Aéreo 4654, Santafé de Bogotá, DC; tel. (1) 281-8613; Dir Marie Sanz.

Agencia EFE (Spain): Carrera 16, No 39A-69, Apdo Aéreo 16038, Santafé de Bogotá, DC; tel. (1) 285-1576; fax (1) 285-1598; Bureau Chief Antonio Martínez Martín.

Agenzia Nazionale Stampa Associata (ANSA) (Italy): Carrera 4, No 67-30, Apdo Aéreo 16077, Santafé de Bogotá, DC; tel. (1) 211-9617; fax (1) 212-5409; Bureau Chief Alberto Rojas Morales.

Associated Press (AP) (USA): Transversal 14, No 122-36, Apdo Aéreo 093643, Santafé de Bogotá, DC; tel. (1) 619-3487; fax (1) 213-8467; e-mail apbogota@bigfoot.com; Bureau Chief Frank Bajak.

Central News Agency Inc. (Taiwan): Carrera 13A, No 98-34, Santafé de Bogotá, DC; tel. (1) 25-6342; Correspondent Christina Chow.

Deutsche Presse-Agentur (dpa) (Germany): Carrera 7A, No 17-01, Of. 909, Santafé de Bogotá, DC; tel. (1) 284-7481; fax (1) 281-8065; Correspondent RODRIGO RUIZ TOVAR.

Informatsionnoye Telegrafnoye Agentstvo Rossii—Telegrafnoye Agentstvo Suverennykh Stran (ITAR—TASS) (Russia): Calle 20, No 7-17, Of. 901, Santafé de Bogotá, DC; tel. (1) 243-6720; Correspondent GENNADII KOCHUK.

Inter Press Service (IPS) (Italy): Calle 19, No 3-50, Of. 602, Apdo Aéreo 7739, Santafé de Bogotá, DC; tel. (1) 341-8841; fax (1) 334-2249; Correspondent MARÍA ISABEL GARCÍA NAVARRETE.

Prensa Latina: Carrera 3, No 21-46, Apdo Aéreo 30372, Santafé de Bogotá, DC; tel. (1) 282-4527; fax (1) 281-7286; Bureau Chief FAUSTO TRIANA.

Reuters (United Kingdom): Calle 94A, No 13-34, 4°, Apdo Aéreo 29848, Santafé de Bogotá, DC; tel. (1) 610-7633; fax (1) 610-7733; Correspondent MICHAEL STOTT.

United Press International (UPI) (USA): Carrera 4A, No 67-30, 4°, Apdo Aéreo 57570, Santafé de Bogotá, DC; tel. (1) 211-9106; Correspondent FEDERICO FULLEDA.

Xinhua (New China) News Agency (People's Republic of China): Calle 74, No 4-26, Apdo Aéreo 501, Santafé de Bogotá, DC; tel (1) 211-5347; Dir HOU YAOQI.

PRESS ASSOCIATIONS

Asociación Colombiana de Periodistas: Avda Jiménez, No 8-74, Of. 510, Santafé de Bogotá, DC; tel. (1) 243-6056.

Asociación Nacional de Diarios Colombianos (ANDIARIOS): Calle 61, No 5-20, Apdo Aéreo 13663, Santafé de Bogotá, DC; tel. (1) 212-8694; fax (1) 212-7894; f. 1962; 30 affiliated newspapers; Pres. LUIS MIGUEL DE BEDOUT; Vice-Pres. LUIS FERNANDO BAENA.

Asociación de la Prensa Extranjera: Pedro Meléndez, No 87-93, Santafé de Bogotá, DC; tel. (1) 288-3011.

Círculo de Periodistas de Santafé de Bogotá, DC (CPB): Calle 26, No 13A-23, 23°, Santafé de Bogotá, DC; tel. (1) 282-4217; Pres. MARÍA TERESA HERRÁN.

Publishers

Santafé de Bogotá, DC

Comunicadores Técnicos Ltda: Carrera 18, No 46-58, Apdo Aéreo 28797, Santafé de Bogotá, DC; technical; Dir PEDRO P. MORCILLO.

Ediciones Cultural Colombiana Ltda: Calle 72, No 16-15 y 16-21, Apdo Aéreo 6307, Santafé de Bogotá, DC; tel. (1) 217-6529; fax (1) 217-6570; f. 1951; textbooks; Dir JOSÉ PORTO VÁSQUEZ.

Ediciones Lerner Ltda: Calle 8A, No 68A-41, Apdo Aéreo 8304, Santafé de Bogotá, DC; tel. (1) 420-0650; fax (1) 262-4459; f. 1959; general; Commercial Man. FABIO CAICEDO GÓMEZ.

Editora Cinco, SA: Calle 61, No 13-23, 7°, Apdo Aéreo 15188, Santafé de Bogotá, DC; tel. (1) 285-6200; recreation, culture, textbooks, general; Man. PEDRO VARGAS G.

Editorial El Globo, SA: Calle 16, No 4-96, Apdo Aéreo 6806, Santafé de Bogotá, DC.

Editorial Presencia, Ltda: Calle 23, No 24-20, Apdo Aéreo 41500, Santafé de Bogotá, DC; tel. (1) 269-2188; fax (1) 269-6830; textbooks, tradebooks; Gen. Man. MARÍA UMAÑA DE TANCO.

Editorial San Pablo: Carrera 46, No 22A–90, Quintaparedes, Apdo Aéreo 080152, Santafé de Bogotá, DC; tel. (1) 368-2099; fax (1) 244-4383; f. 1951; religion, culture, humanism; Editorial Dir JOHN FREDY ECHAVARRÍA A.

Editorial Temis SA: Calle 13, No 6-45, Apdo Aéreo 5941, Santafé de Bogotá, DC; tel. (1) 269-0713; fax (1) 292-5801; f. 1951; law, sociology, politics; Man. Dir JORGE GUERRERO.

Editorial Voluntad, SA: Carrera 7A, No 24-89, 24°, Santafé de Bogotá, DC; tel. (1) 286-0666; fax (1) 286-5540; e-mail voluntad@colomsat.net.co; f. 1930; school books; Pres. GASTÓN DE BEDOUT.

Fundación Centro de Investigación y Educación Popular (CINEP): Carrera 5A, No 33A-08, Apdo Aéreo 25916, Santafé de Bogotá, DC; tel. (1) 285-8977; fax (1) 287-9089; f. 1977; education and social sciences; Man. Dir FRANCISCO DE ROUX.

Instituto Caro y Cuervo: Carrera 11, No 64-37, Apdo Aéreo 51502, Santafé de Bogotá, DC; tel. (1) 255-8289; fax (1) 217-0243; e-mail carocuer@gaitana.interred.net.co; internet www.caroycuervo.edu.co; f. 1942; philology, general linguistics and reference; Man. Dir IGNACIO CHAVES CUEVAS; Gen. Sec. CARLOS JULIO LUQUE CAGUA.

Inversiones Cromos SA: Calle 70A, No 7-81, Apdo Aéreo 59317, Santafé de Bogotá, DC; tel. (1) 217-1754; fax (1) 211-2642; f. 1916; Dir ALBERTO ZALAMEA; Gen. Man. JORGE EDUARDO CORREA ROBLEDO.

Legis, SA: Avda El Dorado, No 81-10, Apdo Aéreo 98888, Santafé de Bogotá, DC; tel. (1) 263-4100; fax (1) 295-2650; f. 1952; economics, law, general; Man. MAURICIO SERNA MELÉNDEZ.

McGraw Hill Interamericana, SA: Avda Américas, No 46-41, Apdo Aéreo 81078, Santafé de Bogotá, DC; tel. (1) 337-7800; fax (1) 245-4786; e-mail cmarquez@mcgraw-hill.com; university textbooks; Dir-Gen. CARLOS G. MÁRQUEZ.

Publicar, SA: Avda 68, No 75A-50, 4°, Centro Comercial Metrópolis, Apdo Aéreo 8010, Santafé de Bogotá, DC; tel. (1) 225-5555; fax (1) 225-4015; e-mail m-navia@publicar.com; internet www.publicar.com; f. 1954; directories; CEO MARÍA SOL NAVIA.

Siglo del Hombre Editores Ltda: Carrera 32, No 25-46, Santafé de Bogotá, DC; tel. (1) 337-7700; fax (1) 337-7665; e-mail siglodelhombre@sky.net.co; f. 1992; arts, politics, anthropology, history, fiction, etc.; Gen. Man. EMILIA FRANCO DE ARCILA.

Tercer Mundo Editores SA: Transversal 2A, No 67-27, Apdo Aéreo 4817, Santafé de Bogotá, DC; tel. (1) 255-1539; fax (1) 212-5976; e-mail tmundoed@polcola.com.co; f. 1963; social sciences; Pres. SANTIAGO POMBO VEJARANO.

ASSOCIATIONS

Cámara Colombiana del Libro: Carrera 17A, No 37-27, Apdo Aéreo 8998, Santafé de Bogotá, DC; tel. (1) 288-6188; fax (1) 287-3320; e-mail camlibro@camlibro.com.co; internet www.camlibro.com.co; f. 1951; Pres. GONZALO ARBOLEDA; Exec. Dir RICHARD URIBE SCHROEDER; 120 mems.

Colcultura: Calle 8, No 6-97, 2°, Santafé de Bogotá, DC; tel. (1) 282-8656; fax (1) 282-5104; Dir ISADORA DE NORDEN.

Fundalectura: Avda 40, No 16-46, Santafé de Bogotá, DC; tel. (1) 320-1511; fax (1) 287-7071; e-mail fundalec@cable.net.co; internet www.fundalectura.org.co; Exec. Dir SILVIA CASTRILLÓN.

Broadcasting and Communications

Ministerio de Comunicaciones, Dirección de Telecomunicaciones: Edif. Murillo Toro, Carreras 7A y 8A, Calle 12A y 13, Apdo Aéreo 14515, Santafé de Bogotá, DC; tel. (1) 286-6911; fax (1) 286-1185; broadcasting authority; Dir Minister of Communications.

Instituto Nacional de Radio y Televisión—INRAVISION: Centro Administrativo Nacional (CAN), Avda El Dorado, Santafé de Bogotá, DC; tel. (1) 222-0700; fax (1) 222-0080; e-mail inras@col1.telecom.com.co; f. 1954; govt-run TV and radio broadcasting network; educational and commercial broadcasting; Dir GUSTAVO SAMPER RODRÍGUEZ.

TELECOMMUNICATIONS

Celumóvil SA: Calle 71A, No 6-30, 18°, Santafé de Bogotá, DC; tel. (1) 346-1666; fax (1) 211-2031; Sec.-Gen. CARLOS BERNARDO CARREÑO R.

Empresa Nacional de Telecomunicaciones (TELECOM): Calle 23, No 13-49, Santafé de Bogotá, DC; tel. (1) 286-0077; fax (1) 282-8768; e-mail jblackbu@bogota.telecom.net.co; internet www.telecom.com.co; f. 1947; national telecommunications enterprise; Pres. JULIO MOLANO GONZÁLEZ.

Empresa de Telecomunicaciones de Santafé de Bogotá (ETB): Carrera 7A, No 20–37, Santafé de Bogotá, DC; tel. (1) 341-4233; fax (1) 342-3550; e-mail sugeetb@axesnet.com; internet www.etb.com.co; Bogotá telephone co; scheduled for privatization in 2000; Pres. SERGIO REGUEROS.

BROADCASTING

Radio

In 1988 there were 516 radio stations officially registered with the Ministry of Communications. Most radio stations belong to ASOMEDIOS. The principal radio networks are as follows:

Cadena Radial Auténtica: Calle 32, No 16-12, Apdo Aéreo 18350, Santafé de Bogotá, DC; tel. (1) 285-3360; fax (1) 285-2505; f. 1983; stations include Radio Auténtica and Radio Mundial; Pres. JORGE ENRIQUE GÓMEZ MONTEALEGRE.

Cadena Radial La Libertad Ltda: Carrera 53, No 55-166, Apdo Aéreo 3143, Barranquilla; tel. (5) 31-1517; fax (5) 32-1279; news and music programmes for Barranquilla, Cartagena and Santa Marta; stations include Emisora Ondas del Caribe (youth programmes), Radio Libertad (classical music programmes) and Emisora Fuentes.

Cadena Super: Calle 16A, No 86A-78, Santafé de Bogotá, DC; tel. (1) 618-1371; fax (1) 618-1360; internet www.889.com.co; f. 1971; stations include Radio Super and Super Stereo FM; Pres. JAIME PAVA NAVARRO.

Cadena Melodía de Colombia: Calle 45, No 13-70, Santafé de Bogotá, DC; tel. (1) 323-1500; fax (1) 288-4020; Pres. EFRAÍN PÁEZ ESPITIA.

CARACOL, SA (Primera Cadena Radial Colombiana, SA): Carretera 39A, No 15-81, Apdo Aéreo 9291, Santafé de Bogotá, DC;

tel. (1) 337-8866; fax (1) 337-7126; internet www.caracol.com.co; f. 1948; 126 stations; Pres. JOSÉ MANUEL RESTREPO FERNÁNDEZ DE SOTO.

Circuito Todelar de Colombia: Avda 13, No 84-42, Apdo Aéreo 27344, Santafé de Bogotá, DC; tel. (1) 616-1011; fax (1) 616-0056; f. 1953; 74 stations; Pres. BERNARDO TOBÓN DE LA ROCHE.

Colmundo Radio, SA ('La Cadena de la Paz'): Diagonal 58, 26A-29, Apdo Aéreo 36750, Santafé de Bogotá, DC; tel. (1) 217-8911; fax (1) 217-9358; f. 1989; Pres. Dr NÉSTOR CHAMORRO P.

Organización Radial Olímpica, SA (ORO, SA): Calle 72, No 48-37, 2°, Apdo Aéreo 51266, Barranquilla; tel. (5) 358-0500; fax (5) 345-9080; programmes for the Antioquia and Atlantic coast regions.

Radio Cadena Nacional, SA (RCN Radio): Carrera 13A, No 37-32, Santafé de Bogotá, DC; tel. (1) 288-2288; fax (1) 288-6130; e-mail rcn@impsat.net.co; internet www.rcn.com.co; 116 stations; official network; Pres. RICARDO LONDOÑO LONDOÑO.

Radiodifusora Nacional de Colombia: Centro Administrativo Nacional (CAN), Avda El Dorado, Santafé de Bogotá, DC; tel. (1) 222-0415; fax (1) 222-0409; e-mail radiodifusora@hotmail.com; f. 1940; national public radio; Dir ATHALA MORRIS.

Radiodifusores Unidos, SA (RAU): Carrera 13, No 85-51, Of. 705, Santafé de Bogotá, DC; tel. (1) 617-0584; commercial network of independent local and regional stations throughout the country.

TELEVISION

Television services began in 1954, and the NTSC colour television system was adopted in 1979. The government-run broadcasting network, INRAVISION, controls two national commercial stations and one national educational station. There are also three regional stations. Broadcasting time is distributed among competing programmers through a public tender. The first two privately-run stations began test transmissions in mid-1998.

Cadena Uno: Centro Administrativo Nacional (CAN), Avda El Dorado, Santafé de Bogotá, DC; tel. (1) 342-3777; fax (1) 341-6198; e-mail cadena1@latino.net.co; internet www.cadena1.com.co; f. 1992; Dir FERNANDO BARRERO CHÁVEZ.

Canal 3: Centro Administrativo Nacional (CAN), Avda El Dorado, Santafé de Bogotá, DC; tel. (1) 222-1640; fax (1) 222-1514; f. 1970; Exec. Dir RODRIGO ANTONIO DURÁN BUSTOS.

Canal A: Calle 35, No 7-51, CENPRO, Santafé de Bogotá, DC; tel. (1) 232-3196; fax (1) 245-7526; f. 1966; Gen. Man. ROCÍO FERNÁNDEZ DEL CASTILLO.

Caracol Televisión, SA: Calle 76, No 11-35, Apdo Aéreo 26484, Santafé de Bogotá, DC; tel. (1) 319-0860; fax (1) 321-1720; f. 1969; Pres. RICARDO ALARCÓN GAVIRIA.

Teleantioquia: Carrera 41, No 52-28, Edif. EDA, 3°, Apdo Aéreo 8183, Medellín, Antioquia; tel. (4) 262-0311; fax (4) 262-0832; f. 1985; Pres. ALVARO URIBE VÉLEZ.

Telecafé: Carrera 24, No 19-51, Apdo Aéreo 770, Manizales, Caldas; tel. (68) 84-5678; fax (68) 84-4623; e-mail telecafe@col2.telecom.com.co; f. 1986; Gen. Man. JUAN MANUEL LENIS LARA.

Telecaribe: Carrera 54, No 72-142, 11°, Barranquilla, Atlántico; tel. (5) 358-2297; fax (5) 356-0924; e-mail ealviz@canal.telecaribe.com.co; internet www.telecaribe.com.co; f. 1986; Gen. Man. IVÁN OVALLE POVEDA.

Telepacífico: Calle 5A, No 38A-14, 3°, esq. Centro Comercial Imbanaco, Cali, Valle del Cauca; tel. (2) 589-933; fax (2) 588-281; Gen. Man. LUIS GUILLERMO RESTREPO.

TV Cúcuta: Calle 4, No 11E-41, Quinta Oriental Cúcuta, Norte de Santander; tel. (75) 74-7874; fax (75) 75-2922; f. 1992; Pres. JOSÉ A. ARMELLA.

ASSOCIATIONS

Asociación Nacional de Medios de Comunicación (ASOME-DIOS): Carrera 22, No 85-72, Santafé de Bogotá, DC; tel. (1) 611-1300; fax (1) 621-6292; f. 1978 and merged with ANRADIO (Asociación Nacional de Radio, Televisión y Cine de Colombia) in 1980; Pres. Dr SERGIO ARBOLEDA CASAS.

Federación Nacional de Radio (FEDERADIO): Santafé de Bogotá, DC; Dir LIBARDO TABORDA BOLÍVAR.

Finance

(cap. = capital; res = reserves; dep. = deposits; m. = million; amounts in pesos, unless otherwise indicated)

Contraloría General de la República: Carrera 10, No 17-18, Torre Colseguros, 27°, Santafé de Bogotá, DC; tel. (1) 282-7905; fax (1) 282-3549; Controller-General Dr MANUEL FRANCISCO BECERRA.

BANKING

In August 1989 the Government authorized plans to return to private ownership 65% of the assets of all financial institutions nationalized after the financial crisis of 1982.

Supervisory Authority

Superintendencia Bancaria: Carrera 7A, No 4-49, 11°, Apdo Aéreo 3460, Santafé de Bogotá, DC; tel. (1) 350-8166; fax (1) 350-7999; e-mail superban@superbancaria.gov.co; internet www.superbancaria.gov.co; Banking Supt PATRICIA CORREA BONILLA.

Central Bank

Banco de la República: Carrera 7A, No 14-78, 5°, Apdo Aéreo 3531, Santafé de Bogotá, DC; tel. (1) 343-0190; fax (1) 286-1731; f. 1923; internet www.banrep.gov.co; sole bank of issue; cap. 12.7m.; res 11,238.6m.; dep. 4,570.0m. (Dec 1999); Gov. MIGUEL URRUTIA MONTOYA; 28 brs.

Commercial Banks

Santafé de Bogotá, DC

ABN AMRO Bank (Colombia), SA (fmrly Banco Real de Colombia): Carrera 7A, No 33-80, Apdo Aéreo 34262, Santafé de Bogotá, DC; tel. (1) 285-0763; fax (1) 285-5671; f. 1975; cap. 8,110.5m., res 6,217.7m., dep. 56,787.7m. (Dec. 1993); Pres. CARLOS EDUARDO ARRUDA PENTEADO; 17 brs.

Banco Agrario de Colombia: Carrera 6, No 14-98, Santafé de Bogotá, DC; tel. (1) 212-3404; fax (1) 345-2279; f. 1999; Pres. JUAN BAUTISTA PÉREZ RUBIANO.

Banco America Colombia (fmrly Banco Colombo-Americano): Carrera 7, No 71-52, Torre B, 4°, Apdo Aéreo 12327, Santafé de Bogotá, DC; tel. (1) 312-2020; fax (1) 312-1645; cap. 3,268m., res 6,205m., dep. 14,475m. (Dec. 1993); wholly-owned subsidiary of Bank of America; Pres. EDUARDO ROMERO JARAMILLO; 1 br.

Banco Andino Colombia, SA (fmrly Banco de Crédito y Comercio): Carrera 7A, No 71-52, Torre B, 1°, 18° y 19°, Apdo Aéreo 6826, Santafé de Bogotá, DC; tel. (1) 312-3666; fax (1) 312-3273; e-mail geraldo@latino.net.co; f. 1954; cap. 7,206.5m., res 10,705.9m., dep. 121,367.4m. (Dec. 1993); Pres. CARLOS CUEVAS; 21 brs.

Banco Anglo-Colombiano (Lloyds Bank): Carrera 7, No 71-21, 16°, Apdo Aéreo 3532, Santafé de Bogotá, DC; tel. (1) 334-5088; fax (1) 341-9433; e-mail anglomer@impsat.net.co; internet www.bancoanglocolombiano.com; f. 1976; cap. 14,990.7m., res 24,983.8m., dep. 229,629.3. (Dec. 1996); Pres. DAVID HUTCHINSON; 52 brs.

Banco de Bogotá: Calle 36, No 7-47, 15°, Apdo Aéreo 3436, Santafé de Bogotá, DC; tel. (1) 332-0032; fax (1) 338-3375; internet www.bancodebogota.com.co; f. 1870; acquired Banco del Comercio in 1992; cap. 876.6m.; res 572.4m.; dep. 3,103.0m. (June 2000); Pres. Dr ALEJANDRO FIGUEROA JARAMILLO; 274 brs.

Banco Cafetero (Bancafe): Calle 28, No 13A-15, Apdo Aéreo 240332, Santafé de Bogotá, DC; tel. (1) 341-1511; fax (1) 284-6516; f.1953; cap. US $45,288.4m., res 598,622.2m., dep. 3,330,281.8m. (Dec. 1999); Pres. GILBERTO GÓMEZ ARANGO; 301 brs.

Banco Caja Social: Carrera 7, No 77-65, 11°, Santafé de Bogotá, DC; tel. (1) 310-0099; fax (1) 313-0809; e-mail bancaj_vjuridica@fundacion-social; f. 1911; savings bank; cap. 93,077m., res 13,543m., dep. 559,729m. (Dec. 1996); Pres. EULALIA ARBOLEDA DE MONTES; 135 brs.

Banco Central Hipotecario: Carrera 6, No 15-32, 11°, Apdo Aéreo 3637, Santafé de Bogotá, DC; tel. (1) 336-0055; fax (1) 282-2802; f. 1932; Pres. MARÍA JOSÉ GARCÍA JARAMILLO; 132 brs.

Banco Colpatria, SA: Carrera 7A, No 24-89, 12°, Apdo Aéreo 30241, Santafé de Bogotá, DC; tel. (1) 286-8277; fax (1) 334-0867; internet www.banco.colpatria.com; f. 1955; cap. 1,002m., res 15,575m., dep. 197,390m. (Dec. 1994); Pres. SANTIAGO PERDOMO MALDONADO; 26 brs.

Banco de Comercio Exterior de Colombia, SA—BANCOLDEX: Calle 28, No 13A-15, 38°, Apdo Aéreo 240092, Santafé de Bogotá, DC; tel. (1) 341-0677; fax (1) 284-5087; internet www.bancoldex.com; f. 1992; provides financing alternatives for Colombian exporters; affiliate trust company FIDUCOLDEX, SA manages PROEXPORT (Export Promotion Trust); Pres. MIGUEL GÓMEZ MARTÍNEZ.

Banco de Crédito: Carrera 7, No 27-18, Santafé de Bogotá, DC; tel. (1) 286-8400; fax (1) 286-7236; e-mail loginter@impsat.net.co; internet www.bancodecredito.com; f. 1963; cap. 60,000.0m., res 61,880.0m., dep. 870,537.5m. (Dec. 1998); Pres. JAMES P. FENTON; 24 brs.

Banco Mercantil de Colombia, SA (fmrly Banco de los Trabajadores): Avda 82, No 12-18, 8°, Santafé de Bogotá, DC; tel. (1) 635-0035; fax (1) 623-7669; e-mail bmjuridi@impsat.net.co; internet www.bancomercantil.com; f.1974; wholly-owned subsidiary of Banco Mercantil (Venezuela); cap. 19,409.9m., res 24,459.5m., dep. 98,699.7m. (Dec. 1997); Pres. GUSTAVO SINTES ULLOA; 10 brs.

Banco del Pacífico, SA: Calle 100, 19-05, Santafé de Bogotá, DC; tel. (1) 416-5945; fax (1) 611-2339; e-mail cbernal@banpacifico.com.co; f. 1994; wholly-owned by Banco del Pacífico, SA, Guayaquil (Ecuador); cap. 12,000.0m., res 6,120.2m., dep. 196,873.3m. (Dec. 1996); Pres. JUAN CARLOS BERNAL 3 brs.

Banco Popular, SA: Calle 17, 7-43, 4°, Apdo Aéreo 6796, Santafé de Bogotá, DC; tel. (1) 283-3964; fax (1) 281-9448; e-mail upinternacional@bancopopular.com.co; internet www.bancopopular .com.co; f. 1951; cap. 68,486m., res 331,363m., dep. 2,043,749m. (Dec. 1998); Pres. JOSÉ HERNÁN RINCÓN GÓMEZ; 158 brs.

Banco Santander: Carrera 10A, No 28-49, Edif. Bavaria, 9°, Santafé de Bogotá, DC; tel. (1) 282-5266; fax (1) 281-0311; internet www.bancosantander.com.co; f. 1961; Pres. MONICA IÑES MARÍA APARICIO; 30 brs.

Banco Standard Chartered: Calle 74, No 6-65, Santafé de Bogotá, DC; tel. (1) 217-7200; fax (1) 212-5786; f. 1982; cap. 10,312m., res 5,574m., dep. 84,200m. (Dec. 1996); Pres. HANS JUERGUEN HEILKUHL OCHOA; 11 brs.

Banco Sudameris Colombia (fmrly Banco Francés e Italiano): Carrera 11, No 94A-03, 5°, Apdo Aéreo 3440, Santafé de Bogotá, DC; tel. (1) 636-8729; fax (1) 636-7702; internet www.banco-sudameris .com.co; cap. 14,113.6m., res 60,949.3m., dep. 528,588.2m. (Dec. 1997); Pres. GIANCARLO PANICUCCI; 7 brs.

Banco Tequendama, SA: Diagonal 27, No 6-70, 2°, Santafé de Bogotá, DC; tel. (1) 320-2100; fax (1) 287-7020; f. 1976; wholly-owned subsidiary of Banco Construcción (Venezuela); cap. 12,049m., dep. 53,522m. (Dec. 1992); Pres. HÉCTOR MUÑOZ ARJUELA; 11 brs.

Banco Unión Colombiano (fmrly Banco Royal Colombiano): Torre Banco Unión Colombiano, Carrera 7A, No 71-52, 2°, Apdo Aéreo 3438, Santafé de Bogotá, DC; tel. (1) 312-0411; fax (1) 312-0843; e-mail bcounion@impsat.net.co; f. 1925; cap. 12,350.3m. res 27,667.2m., dep. 131,063.0m. (Dec. 1995); Pres. ALBERTO GUILLERMO VILLAVECES MEDINA; 26 brs.

BBV-Banco Ganadero: Carrera 9A, No 72-21, 11°, Apdo Aéreo 53859, Santafé de Bogotá, DC; tel. (1) 347-1600; fax (1) 235-1248; f. 1956 as Banco Ganadero; name changed as above 1998; cap. 879,467.8m., dep. 2,989,659.8m. (Dec. 1998); Exec.-Pres. JOSÉ MARÍA AYALA VARGAS; 286 brs.

Citibank Colombia, SA: Carrera 9A, No 99-02, 3°, Santafé de Bogotá, DC; tel. (1) 618-4455; fax (1) 621-0259; internet www .citibank.com/colombia; wholly-owned subsidiary of Citibank (USA); cap. 483m., res 9,399m., dep. 152,139m. (Dec. 1992); Pres. ANTONIO URIBE; 23 brs.

Cali

Banco de Occidente: Carrera 4, No 7-61, 12°, Apdo Aéreo 4400, Cali, Valle del Cauca; tel. (2) 886-1117; fax (2) 886-1297; e-mail banoccdi@col2.telecom.com.co; internet www.bancooccidente.com .co; cap. 2,790,400m.; res 281,808m., dep. 1,795,245m. (Dec. 1998); Pres. EFRAIN OTERO ÁLVAREZ; 116 brs.

Medellín

Bancolombia, SA (fmrly Banco Industrial de Colombia): Carrera 52, No 50-20, Medellín, Antioquia; tel. (4) 251-5474; fax (4) 513-4827; e-mail mfranco@bancolombia.com.co; internet www .bancolombia.com.co; f. 1945; renamed 1998 following merger with Banco de Colombia; cap. 169,524m., res 768,382m., dep. 4,386,515m. (Dec. 1999); Pres. JORGE LONDOÑO SALDARRIAGA; 341 brs.

Banking Associations

Asociación Bancaria y de Entidades Financieras de Colombia: Carrera 9A, No 74-08, 9°, Santafé de Bogotá, DC; tel. (1) 249-6411; fax (1) 211-9915; e-mail info@asobancaria.com; internet www.asobancaria.com; f. 1936; 56 mem. banks; Pres. PATRICIA CÁRDENAS SANTA MARÍA.

Asociación Nacional de Instituciones Financieras (ANIF): Calle 70A, No 7-86, Santafé de Bogotá, DC; tel. (1) 310-1500; fax (1) 235-5947; Pres. ARMANDO MONTENEGRO TRUJILLO.

STOCK EXCHANGES

Superintendencia de Valores: Avda El Dorado, Calle 26, No 68-85, Torre Suramericana, 2° y 3°, Santafé de Bogotá, DC; tel. (1) 427-0222; fax (1) 427-0870; f. 1979 to regulate the securities market; Supt JORGE GABRIEL TABOADA HOYOS.

Bolsa de Bogotá: Carrera 8A, No 13-82, 4°-8°, Apdo Aéreo 3584, Santafé de Bogotá, DC; tel. (1) 243-6501; fax (1) 281-3170; f. 1928; Pres. AUGUSTO ACOSTA TORRES; Sec.-Gen. MARÍA FERNANDA TORRES.

Bolsa de Medellín, SA: Carrera 50, No 50-48, 2°, Apdo Aéreo 3535, Medellín, Antioquia; tel. (4) 260-3000; fax (4) 251-1981; e-mail info@medellin.impsat.net.co; f. 1961; Pres. CRISTIÁN TORO LUDEKE.

Bolsa de Occidente, SA: Calle 10, No 4-40, 13°, Apdo Aéreo 11718, Santiago de Cali; tel. (2) 889-8400; fax (2) 889-9435; e-mail bolsaocc@cali.cetcol.net.co; internet www.bolsadeoccidente.com.co; f. 1983; Pres. JOSÉ RICARDO CAICEDO PEÑA.

INSURANCE
Principal National Companies

ACE Seguros, SA: Calle 72, No 10-51, 6°, 7° y 8°, Apdo Aéreo 29782, Santafé de Bogotá, DC; tel. (1) 319-0300; fax (1) 319-0304; internet www.ace-ina.com; fmrly Cigna Seguros de Colombia, SA; Pres. ALVARO A. ROZO PALOU.

Aseguradora Colseguros, SA: Carrera 13A, No 29-24, Parque Central Bavaria, Apdo Aéreo 3537, Santafé de Bogotá, DC; tel. (1) 561-6392; fax (1) 561-6427; e-mail thiermoo@colseguros.com; internet www.colseguros.com; f. 1874; Pres. MAX THIERMANN.

Aseguradora El Libertador, SA: Carrera 13, No 26-45, 9°, Apdo Aéreo 10285, Santafé de Bogotá, DC; tel. (1) 281-2427; fax (1) 286-0662; e-mail aselib@impsat.net.co; Pres. FERNANDO ROJAS CÁRDENAS.

Aseguradora Solidaria de Colombia: Carrera 12, No 93-30, Apdo Aéreo 252030, Santafé de Bogotá, DC; tel. (1) 621-4330; fax (1) 621-4321; e-mail eguzman@solidaria.com.co; Pres. CARLOS GUZMÁN.

Chubb de Colombia Cía de Seguros, SA: Carrera 7A, No 71-52, Torre B, 10°, Apdo Aéreo 26931, Santafé de Bogotá, DC; tel. (1) 312-3700; fax (1) 312-2401; e-mail jvelandia@chubb.com.co; Pres. LUIS FERNANDO MATHIEU.

Cía Agrícola de Seguros, SA: Carrera 11, No 93-46, Apdo Aéreo 7212, Santafé de Bogotá, DC; tel. (1) 635-5827; fax (1) 635-5876; e-mail agricola@impsat.net.co; f. 1952; Pres. Dr JOSÉ F. JARAMILLO HOYOS.

Cía Aseguradora de Fianzas, SA (Confianza): Calle 82, No 11-37, 7°, Apdo Aéreo 056965, Santafé de Bogotá, DC; tel. (1) 617-0899; fax (1) 610-8866; e-mail rjaramillo@confianza.com; Pres. RODRIGO JARAMILLO ARANGO.

Cía Central de Seguros, SA: Carrera 7A, No 76-07, 9°, Apdo Aéreo 5764, Santafé de Bogotá, DC; tel. (1) 319-0700; fax (1) 640-5553; e-mail recursos@centralseguros.com.co; internet www.central seguros.com.co; f. 1956; Pres. SYLVIA LUZ RINCÓN LEMA.

Cía de Seguros Atlas, SA: Calle 21, No 23-22, 3°-11°, Apdo Aéreo 413, Manizales, Caldas; tel. (68) 84-1500; fax (168) 84-1447; e-mail satlas@andi.org.co; internet www.andi.org.co/seguros_atlas.htm; Pres. JORGE HOYOS MAYA.

Cía de Seguros Bolívar, SA: Carrera 10A, No 16-39, Apdo Aéreo 4421, Santafé de Bogotá, DC; tel. (1) 341-0077; fax (1) 281-8262; e-mail maria.cristina.zuluga@bolnet.com.co; f. 1939; Pres. JORGE E. URIBE MONTAÑO.

Cía de Seguros Colmena, SA: Calle 72, No 10-07, 7° y 8°, Apdo Aéreo 6774, Santafé de Bogotá, DC; tel. (1) 211-9111; fax (1) 211-4952; e-mail juand@colmena-seguros.com.co; Pres. JUAN MANUEL DÍAZ-GRANADOS.

Cía de Seguros Generales Aurora, SA: Edif. Seguros Aurora, 1°, 2° y 3°, Carrera 7, No 74-21, Apdo Aéreo 8006, Santafé de Bogotá, DC; tel. (1) 212-2800; fax (1) 212-2138; e-mail aurosis@colomsat .net.co; Pres. GERMÁN ESPINOSA.

Cía Mundial de Seguros: Calle 33, No 6-94, 2° y 3°, Santafé de Bogotá, DC; tel. (1) 285-5600; fax (1) 285-1220; e-mail mundial@ impsat.net.co; Dir-Gen. CAMILO FERNÁNDEZ ESCOVAR.

Cía Suramericana de Seguros, SA: Centro Suramericana, Carrera 64B, No 49A-30, Apdo Aéreo 780, Medellín, Antioquia; tel. (4) 260-2100; fax (4) 260-3194; e-mail contactenos@suramericana .com.co; internet www.suramericana.com.co; f. 1944; Pres. Dr NICANOR RESTREPO SANTAMARÍA.

Condor SA, Cía de Seguros Generales: Calle 119, No 16-59, Apdo Aéreo 57018, Santafé de Bogotá, DC; tel. (1) 612-0666; fax (1) 215-6121; Pres. EUDORO CARVAJAL IBÁÑEZ.

Generali Colombia—Seguros Generales, SA: Carrera 7A, No 72-13, 1°, 7° y 8°, Apdo Aéreo 076478, Santafé de Bogotá, DC; tel. (1) 217-8411; fax (1) 255-1164; Pres. MARCO PAPINI.

La Ganadera Cía de Seguros, SA: Carrera 7, No 71-52, Torre B, 11°, Apdo Aéreo 052347, Santafé de Bogotá, DC; tel. (1) 312-2630; fax (1) 312-2599; e-mail ganadera@impsat.net.co; internet www .laganadera.com.co; Pres. CARLOS VERGARA GÓMEZ.

La Interamericana Cía de Seguros Generales, SA: Calle 78, No 9-57, 4° y 5°, Apdo Aéreo 92381, Santafé de Bogotá, DC; tel. (1) 210-2200; fax (1) 210-2021; e-mail interb1@ibm.net; Pres. DIDIER SERRANO.

La Previsora, SA, Cía de Seguros: Calle 57, No 8-93, Apdo Aéreo 52946, Santafé de Bogotá, DC; tel. (1) 211-2880; fax (1) 211-8717; e-mail previpr@andinet.com; Pres. ALVARO ESCALLÓN EMILIANI.

Liberty Seguros, SA: Calle 71A, No 6-30, 2°, 3°, 4° y 14°, Apdo Aéreo 100327, Santafé de Bogotá, DC; tel. (1) 212-4900; fax (1) 212-7706; e-mail lhernandez@impsat.net.co; f. 1954; fmrly Latino-americana de Seguros, SA; Pres. MAURICIO GARCÍA ORTIZ.

Mapfre Seguros Generales de Colombia, SA: Carrera 7A, No 74-36, 2°, Apdo Aéreo 28525, Santafé de Bogotá, DC; tel. (1) 346-8702; fax (1) 346-8793; e-mail jmincha@mapfre.com.co; Pres. JOSÉ MANUEL INCHAUSTI.

Pan American de Colombia Cía de Seguros de Vida, SA: Carrera 7A, No 75-09, Apdo Aéreo 76000, Santafé de Bogotá, DC; tel. (1) 212-1300; fax (1) 217-8799; e-mail aponton@reymoreno .net.co; Pres. ALFONSO PONTÓN.

Real Seguros, SA: Carrera 7A, No 115-33, 10°, Apdo Aéreo 7412, Santafé de Bogotá, DC; tel. (1) 523-1400; fax (1) 523-4010; e-mail realseg@colomsat.net.co; Gen. Man. JOSÉ LUIZ TOMAZINI.

Royal and Sun Alliance Seguros (Colombia), SA: Carrera 7A, No 32-33, 6°, 7°, 11° y 12°, Santafé de Bogotá, DC; tel. (1) 561-0380; fax (1) 320-3726; e-mail meradeo@royal-sunalliance-col.com; internet www.royal-sunalliance-col.com; fmrly Seguros Fénix, SA; Pres. DINAND BLOM.

Segurexpo de Colombia, SA: Calle 72, No 6-44, 12°, Apdo Aéreo 75140, Santafé de Bogotá, DC; tel. (1) 217-0900; fax (1) 211-0218; e-mail segurexp@col1.telecom.co; Pres. JUAN PABLO LUQUE LUQUE.

Seguros Alfa, SA: Carrera 13, No 27-47, 22° y 23°, Apdo Aéreo 27718, Santafé de Bogotá, DC; tel. (1) 344-4720; fax (1) 344-6770; e-mail sistemas@andinet.lat.net; Pres. JESÚS HERNANDO GÓMEZ.

Seguros Colpatria, SA: Carrera 7A, No 24-89, 9°, Apdo Aéreo 7762, Santafé de Bogotá, DC; tel. (1) 616-6655; fax (1) 281-5053; e-mail capicolc@openway.com.co; Pres. Dr FERNANDO QUINTERO.

Seguros La Equidad, OC: Calle 19, No 6-68, 10°, 11° y 12°, Apdo Aéreo 30261, Santafé de Bogotá, DC; tel. (1) 284-1910; fax (1) 286-5124; e-mail equidad@colomsat.net.co; Pres. Dr JULIO ENRIQUE MEDRANO LEÓN.

Seguros del Estado, SA: Carrera 11, No 90-20, Apdo Aéreo 6810, Santafé de Bogotá, DC; tel. (1) 218-6977; fax (1) 218-0971; e-mail seguros2@latino.net.co; Pres. Dr JORGE MORA SÁNCHEZ.

Skandia Seguros de Vida, SA: Avda 19, No 113-30, Apdo Aéreo 100327, Santafé de Bogotá, DC; tel. (1) 214-1200; fax (1) 214-0038; Pres. RAFAEL JARAMILLO SAMPER.

Insurance Association

Federación de Aseguradores Colombianos—FASECOLDA: Carrera 7A, No 26-20, 11° y 12°, Apdo Aéreo 5233, Santafé de Bogotá, DC; tel. (1) 210-8080; fax (1) 210-7090; e-mail fasecolda@fasecolda .com; internet www.fasecolda.com; f. 1976; 33 mems; Pres. Dr WILLIAM R. FADUL VERGARA.

Trade and Industry

GOVERNMENT AGENCIES

Departamento Nacional de Planeación: Calle 26, No 13-19, 14°, Santafé de Bogotá, DC; tel. (1) 336-1600; fax (1) 281-3348; f. 1958; supervises and administers devt projects; approves foreign investments; Dir JOSÉ ANTONIO OCAMPO GAVIRIA.

Instituto Colombiano de Comercio Exterior—INCOMEX: Calle 28, No 13A-15, 5°, Apdo Aéreo 240193, Santafé de Bogotá, DC; tel. (1) 283-3284; fax (1) 281-2560; sets and executes foreign trade policy; Dir. MARÍA URIZA PARDO.

Instituto Colombiano de la Reforma Agraria—INCORA: Centro Administrativo Nacional (CAN), Avda El Dorado, Apdo Aéreo 151046, Santafé de Bogotá, DC; tel. (1) 222-0963; f. 1962; a public institution which, on behalf of the govt, administers public lands and those it acquires; reclaims land by irrigation and drainage facilities, roads, etc. to increase productivity in agriculture and stock-breeding; provides technical assistance and loans; supervises the distribution of land throughout the country; Dir GERMÁN BULA E.

Superintendencia de Industria y Comercio—SUPERINDUSTRIA: Carrera 13, No 27-00, 5°, Santafé de Bogotá, DC; tel. (1) 234-2035; fax (1) 281-3125; supervises chambers of commerce; controls standards and prices; Supt MARCO AURELIO ZULUAGA GIRALDO.

Superintendencia de Sociedades—SUPERSOCIEDADES: Avda El Dorado, No 46-80, Apdo Aéreo 4188, Santafé de Bogotá, DC; tel. (1) 222-0566; fax (1) 221-1027; e-mail supersoc1@sinpro.gov.co; f. 1931; oversees activities of local and foreign corpns; Supt DARÍO LAGUADO MONSALVE.

DEVELOPMENT ORGANIZATIONS

Fondo Nacional de Proyectos de Desarrollo—FONADE: Calle 26, No 13-19, 19°-22°, Apdo Aéreo 24110, Santafé de Bogotá, DC; tel. (1) 594-0407; fax (1) 282-6018; e-mail fonade@colomsat.net.co; f. 1968; responsible for channelling loans towards economic devt projects; administered by a committee under the head of the Departamento Nacional de Planeación; FONADE works in close association with other official planning orgs; Gen. Man. Dr AGUSTÍN MEJÍA JARAMILLO.

Fundación para el Desarrollo Integral del Valle del Cauca—FDI: Calle 8, No 3-14, 17°, Apdo Aéreo 7482, Cali, Valle del Cauca; tel. (2) 80-6660; fax (2) 82-4627; f. 1969; industrial devt org.; Pres. GUNNAR LINDAHL HELLBERG; Exec. Pres. FABIO RODRÍGUEZ GONZÁLEZ.

CHAMBERS OF COMMERCE

Confederación Colombiana de Cámaras de Comercio—CONFECAMARAS: Carrera 13, No 27-47, Of. 502, Apdo Aéreo 29750, Santafé de Bogotá, DC; tel. (1) 288-1200; fax (1) 288-4228; e-mail confecamaras@inter.net.co; internet www.confecamaras.org.co; f. 1969; 56 mem. orgs; Exec.-Pres. EUGENIO MARULANDA GÓMEZ.

Cámara de Comercio de Bogotá: Carrera 9A, No 16-21, Santafé de Bogotá, DC; tel. (1) 334-7900; fax (1) 284-8506; internet www.ccb.org.co; f. 1878; 3,650 mem. orgs; Dir ARIEL JARAMILLO JARAMILLO; Exec.-Pres. GUILLERMO FERNÁNDEZ DE SOTO.

There are also local Chambers of Commerce in the capital towns of all the Departments and in many of the other trading centres.

INDUSTRIAL AND TRADE ASSOCIATIONS

Colombiana de Minería—COLMINAS: Santafé de Bogotá, DC; state mining concern; Man. ALFONSO RODRÍGUEZ KILBER.

Corporación de la Industria Aeronáutica Colombiana, SA (CIAC SA): Aeropuerto Internacional El Dorado, Entrada 1 y 2, Apdo Aéreo 14446, Santafé de Bogotá, DC; tel. (1) 413-9735; fax (1) 413-8673; Gen. Man. ALBERTO MELÉNDEZ.

Empresa Colombia de Niquel—ECONIQUEL: Santafé de Bogotá, DC; tel. (1) 232-3839; administers state nickel resources; Dir JAVIER RESTREPO TORO.

Empresa Colombiana de Uranio—COLURANIO: Centro Administrativo Nacional (CAN), 4°, Ministerio de Minas y Energía, Santafé de Bogotá, DC; tel. (1) 244-5440; f. 1977 to further the exploration, processing and marketing of radio-active minerals; initial cap. US $750,000; Dir JAIME GARCÍA.

Empresa de Comercialización de Productos Perecederos—EMCOPER: Santafé de Bogotá, DC; tel. (1) 235-5507; attached to Ministry of Agriculture; Dir LUIS FERNANDO LONDOÑO RUIZ.

Industria Militar—INDUMIL: Diagonal 40, No 47-75, Apdo Aéreo 7272, Santafé de Bogotá, DC; tel. (1) 222-3001; fax (1) 222-4889; attached to Ministry of National Defence; Man. Adm. (retd) MANUEL F. AVENDAÑO.

Instituto Colombiano Agropecuario (ICA): Calle 37, No 8-43, 4° y 5°, Apdo Aéreo 7984, Santafé de Bogotá, DC; tel. (1) 285-5520; fax (1) 285-4351; f. 1962; institute for promotion, co-ordination and implementation of research into and teaching and devt of agriculture and animal husbandry; Dir Dr HERNÁN MARIN GUTIÉRREZ.

Instituto de Crédito Territorial (ICT): Carrera 13, No 18-51, Apdo Aéreo 4037, Santafé de Bogotá, DC; tel. (1) 234-3560; Gen. Man. GABRIEL GIRALDO.

Instituto de Fomento Industrial (IFI): Calle 16, No 6-66, Edif. Avianca, 7°-15°, Apdo Aéreo 4222, Santafé de Bogotá, DC; tel. (1) 336-0377; fax (1) 286-4166; f. 1940; state finance corpn for enterprise devt; cap. 469,808m. pesos, total assets 2,246,480m. pesos (Dec. 1998); Pres. ENRIQUE CAMACHO MATAMOROS.

Instituto de Hidrología, Meteorología y Estudios Ambientales IDEAM: Diagonal 97, No 17-60, 1°, 2°, 3° y 7°, Santafé de Bogotá, DC; tel. (1) 283-6927; fax (1) 635-6218; f. 1995; responsible for irrigation, flood control, drainage, hydrology and meteorology; Dir PABLO LEYVA.

Instituto de Investigaciones en Geociencias, Minería y Química—INGEOMINAS: Diagonal 53, No 34-53, Apdo Aéreo 4865, Santafé de Bogotá, DC; tel. (1) 222-1811; fax (1) 222-3597; f. 1968; responsible for mineral research, geological mapping and research including hydrogeology, remote sensing, geochemistry and geophysics; Dir Dr ADOLFO ALARCÓN GUZMÁN.

Instituto de Mercadeo Agropecuario—IDEMA: Carrera 10A, No 16-82, Of. 1006, Santafé de Bogotá, DC; tel. (1) 342-2596; fax (1) 283-1838; state enterprise for the marketing of agricultural products; Dir-Gen. ENRIQUE CARLOS RUIZ RAAD.

Instituto Nacional de Fomento Municipal—INSFOPAL: Centro Administrativo Nacional (CAN), Avda El Dorado, Santafé de Bogotá, DC; tel. (1) 222-3177; Gen. Man. JAIME MARIO SALAZAR VELÁSQUEZ.

Instituto Nacional de los Recursos Naturales Renovables y del Ambiente—INDERENA: Diagonal 34, No 5-18, 3°, Santafé de Bogotá, DC; tel. (1) 285-4417. 1968; govt agency regulating the devt of natural resources.

Minerales de Colombia, SA (MINERALCO): Calle 32, No 13-07, Apdo Aéreo 17878, Santafé de Bogotá, DC; tel. (1) 287-7136; fax (1) 87-4606; administers state resources of emerald, copper, gold, sulphur, gypsum, phosphate rock and other minerals except coal, petroleum and uranium; Gen. Man. ORLANDO ALVAREZ PÉREZ.

Sociedad Minera del Guainía (SMG): Santafé de Bogotá, DC; f. 1987; state enterprise for exploration, mining and marketing of gold; Pres. Dr JORGE BENDECK OLIVELLA.

There are several other agricultural and regional development organizations.

EMPLOYERS' AND PRODUCERS' ORGANIZATIONS

Asociación Colombiana Popular de Industriales (ACOPI): Carrera 23, No 41-94, Apdo Aéreo 16451, Santafé de Bogotá, DC;

tel. (1) 244-2741; fax (1) 268-8965; f. 1951; asscn of small industrialists; Pres. Juan A. Pinto Saavedra; Man. Miguel Carrillo M.

Asociación de Cultivadores de Caña de Azúcar de Colombia (ASOCAÑA): Calle 58n, No 3n-15, Apdo Aéreo 4448, Cali, Valle del Cauca; tel. (2) 64-7902; fax (2) 64-5888; f. 1959; sugar planters' asscn; Pres. Dr Ricardo Villaveces Pardo.

Asociación Nacional de Exportadores (ANALDEX): Carrera 10, No 27, Int. 137, Of. 902, Apdo Aéreo 29812, Santafé de Bogotá, DC; tel. (1) 342-0788; fax (1) 284-6911; exporters' asscn; Pres. Jorge Ramírez Ocampo.

Asociación Nacional de Exportadores de Café de Colombia: Calle 72, No 10-07, Of. 1101, Santafé de Bogotá, DC; tel. (1) 347-8419; fax (1) 347-9523; f. 1938; private asscn of coffee exporters; Pres. Jorge E. Lozano Mancera.

Asociación Nacional de Industriales (ANDI) (National Asscn of Manufacturers): Calle 52, No 47-48, Apdo Aéreo 997, Medellín, Antioquia; tel. (4) 511-1177; fax (4) 251-8830; f. 1944; Pres. Luis Carlos Villegas Echeverri; 9 brs; 756 mems.

Expocafé Ltda: Edif. Seguros Caribe, Carrera 7A, No 74-36, 3°, Apdo Aéreo 41244, Santafé de Bogotá, DC; tel. (1) 217-8900; fax (1) 217-3554; f. 1985; coffee exporting org.; Gen. Man. Luis José Alvarez L.

Federación Colombiana de Ganaderos (FEDEGAN): Carrera 14, No 36-65, Apdo Aéreo 9709, Santafé de Bogotá, DC; tel. (1) 245-3041; fax (1) 232-7153; f. 1963; cattle raisers' asscn; about 350,000 affiliates; Pres. José Raimundo Sojo Zambrano.

Federación Nacional de Cacaoteros: Carrera 17, No 30-39, Apdo Aéreo 17736, Santafé de Bogotá, DC; tel. (1) 288-7188; fax (1) 288-4424; fed. of cocoa growers; Gen. Man. Dr Miguel Uribe.

Federación Nacional de Cafeteros de Colombia (National Federation of Coffee Growers): Calle 73, No 8-13, Apdo Aéreo 57534, Santafé de Bogotá, DC; tel. (1) 345-6600; fax (1) 217-1021; f. 1927; totally responsible for fostering and regulating the coffee economy; Gen. Man. Jorge Cárdenas Gutiérrez; 203,000 mems.

Federación Nacional de Cultivadores de Cereales (FENALCE): Carrera 14, No 97-62, Apdo Aéreo 8694, Santafé de Bogotá, DC; tel. (1) 218-9366; fax (1) 218-9463; f. 1960; fed. of grain growers; Gen. Man. Adriano Quintana Silva; 12,000 mems.

Federación Nacional de Comerciantes (FENALCO): Carrera 4, No 19-85, 7°, Santafé de Bogotá, DC; tel. (1) 286-0600; fax (1) 282-7573; fed. of businessmen; Pres. Sabas Pretelt de la Vega.

Sociedad de Agricultores de Colombia (SAC) (Colombian Farmers' Society): Carrera 7A, No 24-89, 44°, Apdo Aéreo 3638, Santafé de Bogotá, DC; tel. (1) 281-0263; fax (1) 284-4572; e-mail socdeagr @impsat.net.co; f. 1871; Pres. Juan Manuel Ospina Restrepo; Sec.-Gen. Dr Gabriel Martínez Teláez.

There are several other organizations, including those for rice growers, engineers and financiers.

UTILITIES

Electricity

Corporación Eléctrica de la Costa Atlántica (Corelca): Calle 55, No 72-109, 9°, Barranquilla, Atlántico; tel. (5) 356-0200; fax (5) 356-2370; responsible for supplying electricity to the Atlantic departments; generates more than 2,000m. kWh annually from thermal power-stations; Man. Dir Hernán Correa Noguera.

Empresa de Energía Eléctrica de Bogotá, SA (EEB): Avda El Dorado, No 55-51, Santafé de Bogotá, DC; tel. (1) 221-1665; fax (1) 221-6858; internet www.eeb.com.co; provides electricity for Bogotá area by generating capacity of 680 MW, mainly hydroelectric; Man. Dir Paulo Orozco Días.

Instituto Colombiano de Energía Eléctrica (ICEL): Carrera 13, No 27-00, 3°, Apdo Aéreo 16243, Santafé de Bogotá, DC; tel. (1) 342-0181; fax (1) 286-2934; formulates policy for the devt of electrical energy; constructs systems for the generation, transmission and distribution of electrical energy; Man. Douglas Velásquez Jacome; Sec.-Gen. Patricia Oliveros Laverde.

Interconexión Eléctrica, SA (ISA): Calle 12 Sur, No 18-168, Apdo Aéreo 8915, Medellín, Antioquia; tel. (4) 317-1331; fax (4) 823-970; e-mail isa@isa.com.co; internet www.isa.com.co; f. 1967; created by Colombia's principal electricity production and distribution cos to form a national network; installed capacity of 2,641m. kWh; operates major power-stations at Chivor and San Carlos; scheduled for privatization in 2001; Man. Dir Javier Gutiérrez.

Isagen: Medellín, Antioquia; e-mail isagen@isagen.com.co; internet www.isagen.com.co; state-owned, scheduled for privatization in late 2000; generates electricity from three hydraulic and two thermal power plants.

Gas

Gas Natural ESP: Avda 40A, No 13-09, 9°, Santafé de Bogotá, DC; tel. (1) 338-1199; fax (1) 288-0807; f. 1987; private gas corpn; Pres. Antoni Peris Mingot.

Gasoriente: distributes gas to 8 municipalities in north-eastern Colombia.

TRADE UNIONS

According to official figures, an estimated 900 of Colombia's 2,000 trade unions are independent.

Central Unitaria de Trabajadores (CUT): Calle 35, No 7-25, 9°, Apdo Aéreo 221, Santafé de Bogotá, DC; tel. (1) 288-8577; fax (1) 287-5769; f. 1986; comprises 50 feds and 80% of all trade union members; Pres. Luis Eduardo Garzón; Sec.-Gen. Miguel Antonio Caro.

Frente Sindical Democrática (FSD): f. 1984; centre-right trade union alliance; comprises:

Confederación de Trabajadores de Colombia (CTC) (Colombian Confederation of Workers): Calle 39, No 26A-23, 5°, Apdo Aéreo 4780, Santafé de Bogotá, DC; tel. (1) 269-7119; f. 1934; mainly Liberal; 600 affiliates, including 6 national orgs and 20 regional feds; admitted to ICFTU; Pres. Alvis Fernández; 400,000 mems.

Confederación de Trabajadores Democráticos de Colombia (CTDC): Carrera 13, No 59-52, Of. 303, Santafé de Bogotá, DC; tel. (1) 255-3146; fax (1) 484-581; f. 1988; comprises 23 industrial feds and 22 national unions; Pres. Mario de J. Valderrama.

Confederación General de Trabajadores Democráticos (CGTD): Calle 39A, No 14-48, Apdo Aéreo 5415, Santafé de Bogotá, DC; tel. (1) 288-1560; fax (1) 288-1504; Christian Democrat; Sec.-Gen. Julio Roberto Gómez Esguerra.

Transport

Land transport in Colombia is rendered difficult by high mountains, so the principal means of long-distance transport is by air. As a result of the development of the El Cerrejón coal field, Colombia's first deep-water port was constructed at Bahía de Portete and a 150 km rail link between El Cerrejón and the port became operational in 1989.

Instituto Nacional del Transporte (INTRA): Edif. Minobras (CAN), 6°, Apdo Aéreo 24990, Santafé de Bogotá, DC; tel. (1) 222-4100; govt body; Dir Dr Guillermo Anzola Lizarazo.

RAILWAYS

In 1989, following the entry into liquidation of the Ferrocarriles Nacionales de Colombia (FNC), the Government created three new companies, which assumed responsibility for the rail network in 1992. However, the new companies were beset by financial difficulties, and many rail services were subsequently suspended.

Empresa Colombiana de Vías Férreas (Ferrovías): Calle 31, No 6-41, 20°, Santafé de Bogotá, DC; tel. (1) 636-9673; fax (1) 287-2515; responsible for the maintenance and devt of the national rail network; Dir Juan Gonzalo Jaramillo.

Ferroviario Atlántico, SA: Calle 72, No 13-23, 2°, Santafé de Bogotá, DC; tel. (1) 255-8684; fax (1) 255-8704; operated on a 30-year concession, awarded in 1998 to Asociación Futura Ferrocarriles de la Paz (Fepaz); 1,490 km (1993).

Fondo de Pasivo Social de Ferrocarriles Nacionales de Colombia: Santafé de Bogotá, DC; administers welfare services for existing and former employees of the FNC.

El Cerrejón Mine Railway: International Colombia Resources Corpn, Carrera 54, No 72-80, Apdo Aéreo 52499, Barranquilla, Atlántico; tel. (5) 350-5389; fax (5) 350-2249; f. 1989 to link the mine and the port at Bahía de Portete; 150 km (1996); Supt M. Mendoza.

Metro de Medellín Ltda: Calle 44, No 46-001, Apdo Aéreo 9128, Medellín, Antioquia; tel. (4) 452-6000; fax (4) 452-4450; e-mail emetro@col3.telecom.com.co; two-line metro with 25 stations opened in stages in 1995–96; 29 km; Gen. Man. Luis Guillermo Gómez A.

ROADS

In 1997 there were an estimated 115,564 km of roads, of which 13,200 km were highways and main roads and 13,364 km were secondary roads. About 12% of the total road network was paved in the same year. The country's main highways are the Caribbean Trunk Highway, the Eastern and Western Trunk Highways, the Central Trunk Highway and there are also roads into the interior. There are plans to construct a Jungle Edge highway to give access to the interior, a link road between Turbo, Bahía Solano and Medellín, a highway between Bogotá and Villavicencio and to complete the short section of the Pan-American highway between Panama and Colombia. In 1992 the World Bank granted a loan of US $266m. to Colombia for the construction of 400 km of new roads and the completion of 2,000 km of roads begun under an earlier programme.

There are a number of national bus companies and road haulage companies.

Instituto Nacional de Vías: Transversal 45, Entrada 2, Santafé de Bogotá, DC; tel. (1) 428-0400; fax (1) 315-6713; e-mail director@latino.net.co; f. 1966, reorganized 1994; wholly state-owned; responsible to the Ministry of Transport; maintenance and construction of national road network; Gen. Man. LUIS E. TOBON CARDONA.

INLAND WATERWAYS

The Magdalena–Cauca river system is the centre of river traffic and is navigable for 1,500 km, while the Atrato is navigable for 687 km. The Orinoco system has more than five navigable rivers, which total more than 4,000 km of potential navigation (mainly through Venezuela); the Amazonas system has four main rivers, which total 3,000 navigable km (mainly through Brazil). There are plans to connect the Arauca with the Meta, and the Putamayo with the Amazon, and also to construct an Atrato–Truandó inter-oceanic canal.

Dirección de Navegación y Puertos: Edif. Minobras (CAN), Of. 562, Santafé de Bogotá, DC; tel. (1) 222-1248; responsible for river works and transport; the waterways system is divided into four sectors: Magdalena, Atrato, Orinoquia, and Amazonia; Dir ALBERTO RODRÍGUEZ ROJAS.

SHIPPING

The four most important ocean terminals are Buenaventura on the Pacific coast and Santa Marta, Barranquilla and Cartagena on the Atlantic coast. The port of Tumaco on the Pacific coast is gaining in importance and there are plans for construction of a deep-water port at Bahía Solano.

In 1998 Colombia's merchant fleet totalled 111,686 grt.

Port Authorities

Port of Barranquilla: Sociedad Portuaria Regional de Barranquilla, Carrera 38, Calle 1A, Barranquilla, Atlántico; tel. (5) 379-9555; fax (5) 379-9557; e-mail sprbbaq@latino.net.co; internet www.sprb.com.co; privatized in 1993; Port Man. ANÍBAL DAU.

Port of Buenaventura: Empresa Puertos de Colombia, Edif. El Café, Of. 1, Buenaventura; tel. (224) 22543; fax (224) 34447; Port Man. VÍCTOR GONZÁLEZ.

Port of Cartagena: Sociedad Portuaria Regional de Cartagena, SA, Manga, Terminal Marítimo, Cartagena, Bolívar; tel. (5) 660-7781; fax (5) 650-2239; e-mail comercial@sprc.com.co; internet www.sprc.com.co; f. 1959; Port Man. ALFONSO SALAS TRUJILLO; Harbour Master Capt. GONZALO PARRA.

Port of Santa Marta: Empresa Puertos de Colombia, Calle 15, No 3-25, 11°, Santa Marta, Magdalena; tel. (54) 210739; fax (54) 210711; Port Man. JULIÁN PALACIOS.

Principal Shipping Companies

Flota Mercante Grancolombiana, SA: Edif. Grancolombiana, Carrera 13, No 27-75, Apdo Aéreo 4482, Santafé de Bogotá, DC; tel. (1) 286-0200; fax (1) 286-9028; f. 1946; owned by the Colombian Coffee Growers' Federation (80%) and Ecuador Development Bank (20%); f. 1946; one of Latin America's leading cargo carriers serving 45 countries world-wide; Pres. LUIS FERNANDO ALARCÓN MANTILLA.

Colombiana Internacional de Vapores, Ltda (Colvapores): Avda Caracas, No 35-02, Apdo Aéreo 17227, Santafé de Bogotá, DC; cargo services mainly to the USA.

Líneas Agromar, Ltda: Calle 73, Vía 40-350, Apdo Aéreo 3256, Barranquilla, Atlántico; tel. (5) 345-1874; fax (5) 345-9634; Pres. MANUEL DEL DAGO FERNÁNDEZ.

Petromar Ltda: Bosque, Diagonal 23, No 56-152, Apdo Aéreo 505, Cartagena, Bolívar; tel. (5) 662-7208; fax (5) 662-7592; Chair. SAVERIO MINERVINI S.

Transportadora Colombiana de Graneles, SA (NAVESCO, SA): Avda 19, No 118-95, Of. 214-301, Santafé de Bogotá, DC; tel. (1) 620-9035; fax (1) 620-8801; e-mail navesco@colomsat.net.co; Gen. Man. GUILLERMO SOLANO VARELA.

Several foreign shipping lines call at Colombian ports.

CIVIL AVIATION

Colombia has more than 100 airports, including 11 international airports: Santafé de Bogotá, DC (El Dorado International Airport),

Medellín, Cali, Barranquilla, Bucaramanga, Cartagena, Cúcuta, Leticia, Pereira, San Andrés and Santa Marta.

Airports Authority

Unidad Administrativa Especial de Aeronáutica Civil: Aeropuerto Internacional El Dorado, 4°, Santafé de Bogotá, DC; tel. (1) 413-9500; fax (1) 413-9878; f. 1967 as Departamento Administrativo de Aeronáutica Civil, reorganized 1993; wholly state-owned; Dir ERNESTO HUERTAS ESACALLÓN.

National Airlines

Aerolíneas Centrales de Colombia, SA (ACES): Edif. del Café, Calle 49, No 50-21, 34°, Apdo Aéreo 6503, Medellín, Antioquia; tel. (4) 251-7500; fax (4) 251-1677; e-mail gusuga@acescolombia.com.co; internet www.acescolombia.com; f. 1971; operates scheduled domestic passenger services throughout Colombia, and charter and scheduled flights to the USA and the Caribbean; Pres. JUAN E. POSADA.

Aerotaca, SA (Aerotransportes Casanare): Avda El Dorado, Entrada 1, Interior 20, Santafé de Bogotá, DC; tel. (1) 413-9884; fax (1) 413-5256; f. 1965; scheduled regional and domestic passenger services; Gen. Man. RAFAEL URDANETA.

AVIANCA (Aerovías Nacionales de Colombia, SA): Avda El Dorado, No 93-30, 5°, Santafé de Bogotá, DC; tel. (1) 413-9511; fax (1) 413-8716; internet www.avianca.com; f. 1940; operates domestic services to all cities in Colombia and international services to the USA, France, Spain and throughout Central and Southern America; Chair. ANDRÉS OBREGÓN SANTO DOMINGO; Pres. GUSTAVO A. LENIS.

Intercontinental de Aviación: Avda El Dorado, Entrada 2, Interior 6, Santafé de Bogotá, DC; tel. (1) 413-9700; fax (1) 413-8458; internet www.insite-network.com/inter; f. 1965 as Aeropesca Colombia (Aerovías de Pesca y Colonización del Suroeste Colombiano): operates scheduled domestic, regional and international passenger and cargo services: Pres. Capt. LUIS HERNÁNDEZ ZIA.

Servicio de Aeronavegación a Territorios Nacionales (Satena): Avda El Dorado, Entrada 1, Interior 11, Apdo Aéreo 11163, Santafé de Bogotá, DC; tel. (1) 413-8438; fax (1) 413-8178; f. 1962; commercial enterprise attached to the Ministry of National Defence; internal services; CEO and Gen. Man. Brig.-Gen. ALFREDO GARCÍA ROJAS.

Sociedad Aeronáutica de Medellín Consolidada, SA (SAM): Edif. SAM, Calle 53, No 45-211, 21°, Apdo Aéreo 1085, Medellín, Antioquia; tel. (4) 251-5544; fax (4) 251-0711; f. 1945; subsidiary of AVIANCA; internal services; and international cargo services to Central America and the Caribbean; Pres JULIO MARIO SANTO DOMINGO, GUSTAVO LENIS.

Transportes Aéreos Mercantiles Panamericanos (Tampa): Carrera 76, No 34A-61, Apdo Aéreo 494, Medellín, Antioquia; tel. (4) 250-2939; fax (4) 250-5639; e-mail tampa@ticsanet.net; f. 1973; operates international cargo services to destinations throughout South America, also to Puerto Rico and the USA; Chair. GUSTAVO MORENO; Pres. FREDERICK JACOBSEN.

In addition, the following airlines operate international and domestic charter cargo services: Aerosucre Colombia, Aero Transcolombiana de Carga (ATC), Aerovías Colombianas (ARCA), Líneas Aéreas del Caribe (LAC Airlines Colombia), and Líneas Aéreas Suramericanas (LAS).

Tourism

The principal tourist attractions are the Caribbean coast (including the island of San Andrés), the 16th-century walled city of Cartagena, the Amazonian town of Leticia, the Andes mountains rising to 5,700 m above sea-level, the extensive forests and jungles, pre-Columbian relics and monuments of colonial art. In 1997 there were 968,999 visitors (compared with 1,253,999 in 1996), most of whom came from Venezuela, Ecuador and the USA. Tourism receipts in 1997 were estimated to be US $955m.

Viceministerio de Turismo: Calle 28, No 13A-15, 17°, Edif. Centro de Comercio Internacional, Santafé de Bogotá, DC; tel. (1) 283-9558; fax (1) 286-4492; Vice-Minister of Tourism MARÍA PAULINA ESPINOSA DE LÓPEZ.

Asociación Colombiana de Agencias de Viajes y Turismo—ANATO: Carrera 21, No 83-63/71, Santafé de Bogotá, DC; tel. (1) 610-7099; fax (1) 218-7103; e-mail presidencia@anato.com.co; internet www.anato.com.co; f. 1949; Pres. Dr OSCAR RUEDA GARCÍA.

THE COMOROS*

Introductory Survey

Location, Climate, Language, Religion, Flag, Capital

The Federal Islamic Republic of the Comoros is an archipelago in the Mozambique Channel, between the island of Madagascar and the east coast of the African mainland. The group comprises four main islands (Ngazidja, Nzwani and Mwali, formerly Grande-Comore, Anjouan and Mohéli respectively, and Mayotte) and numerous islets and coral reefs. The climate is tropical, with average temperatures ranging from 23°C (73.4°F) to 28°C (82.4°F). Average annual rainfall is between 1,500 mm (59 ins) and 5,000 mm (197 ins). The official languages are Comorian (a blend of Swahili and Arabic), French and Arabic. Islam is the state religion. The flag is green, with a white crescent moon and four five-pointed white stars in the centre; the white Arabic inscriptions 'Allah' and 'Muhammad' appear respectively in the upper fly and lower hoist corners of the obverse and in the upper hoist and lower fly of the reverse. The capital, which is situated on Ngazidja, is Moroni.

Recent History

Formerly attached to Madagascar, the Comoros became a separate French Overseas Territory in 1947. The islands achieved internal self-government in December 1961, with a Chamber of Deputies and a Government Council responsible for local administration.

Elections in December 1972 resulted in a large majority for parties advocating independence, and Ahmed Abdallah became President of the Government Council. In June 1973 he was restyled President of the Government. At a referendum in December 1974 96% of the voters expressed support for independence, despite the opposition of the Mayotte Party, which sought the status of a French Department for the island of Mayotte. On 6 July 1975, despite French insistence that any constitutional settlement should be ratified by all the islands voting separately, the Chamber of Deputies voted for immediate independence, elected Abdallah to be first President of the Comoros and reconstituted itself as the National Assembly. Although France made no attempt to intervene, it maintained control of Mayotte. Abdallah was deposed in August, and the National Assembly was abolished. A National Executive Council was established, with Prince Saïd Mohammed Jaffar, leader of the opposition party, the Front national uni, as its head, and Ali Soilih, leader of the coup, among its members. In November the Comoros was admitted to the UN, as a unified state comprising the whole archipelago. In December France officially recognized the independence of Ngazidja, Nzwani and Mwali, but all relations between France and the Comoros were effectively suspended. In February 1976 Mayotte voted overwhelmingly to retain its links with France.

In January 1976 Ali Soilih was elected Head of State, and adopted extended powers under the terms of a new Constitution. In May 1978 Soilih was killed, following a coup by a group of European mercenaries, led by a Frenchman, Bob Denard, on behalf of the exiled former President, Ahmed Abdallah, and the Comoros was proclaimed a Federal Islamic Republic. Shortly afterwards, diplomatic relations with France were restored. In July the Comoran delegation was expelled from the Organization of African Unity (OAU, see p. 256) as a result of the continued presence of the mercenaries (but was readmitted in February 1979).

In October 1978 a new Constitution was approved in a referendum, on the three islands excluding Mayotte, by 99.3% of the votes cast. Abdallah was elected President in the same month, and in December elections for a new legislature, the Federal Assembly, took place. In January 1979 the Federal Assembly approved the formation of a one-party state (unofficial opposition groups, however, continued to exist). Ali Mroudjae, hitherto

Minister of Foreign Affairs and Co-operation, was appointed Prime Minister in February 1982, and legislative elections took place in March. Constitutional amendments adopted in October vested additional powers in the President. Abdallah was the sole candidate at a presidential election in September 1984. Despite appeals by the opposition for voters to boycott the election, 98% of the electorate participated. Abdallah was re-elected President by 99.4% of the votes cast. In January 1985, following further amendments to the Constitution, the position of Prime Minister was abolished, and Abdallah assumed the office of Head of Government.

In March 1985 an attempt by members of the presidential guard to overthrow Abdallah, while he was in France, failed; in November 17 people, including Moustoifa Saïd Cheikh, the Secretary-General of the banned opposition movement, Front démocratique (FD), were sentenced to forced labour for life for their involvement. In February 1987 Abdallah indicated that independent opposition candidates would be permitted to contest legislative elections scheduled for March. In the event, however, opposition candidates were only allowed to contest 20 seats on Ngazidja, where they received 35% of the total votes, and pro-Government candidates retained full control of the 42-seat Federal Assembly. There were allegations of widespread fraud and intimidation of opposition candidates. In November a further coup attempt by a left-wing group was suppressed by the authorities.

In November 1989 a constitutional amendment, which permitted Abdallah to remain in office for a third six-year term, was approved by 92.5% of votes cast in a popular referendum. The result of the referendum, however, was disputed by the President's opponents. Violent demonstrations followed, and opposition leaders were detained.

On the night of 26–27 November 1989 Abdallah was assassinated by members of the presidential guard, under the command of Bob Denard. Under the terms of the Constitution, the President of the Supreme Court, Saïd Mohamed Djohar, was appointed interim Head of State, pending a presidential election. Denard, however, staged a coup, in which 27 members of the security forces were reportedly killed, and the regular army was defeated by Denard and his supporters. The mercenaries' action provoked international condemnation, despite denials by Denard of complicity in Abdallah's death. (In May 1999 Denard stood trial in Paris, France, in connection with the assassination. Both Denard and his co-defendant, Dominique Malacrino, were acquitted of the murder charge.) In mid-December Denard finally agreed to relinquish power, and, following the arrival of French paratroops in Moroni, was transported to South Africa, together with the remaining mercenaries. Djohar subsequently announced that the French Government's troops were to remain in the Comoros for up to two years in order to train local security forces.

At the end of December 1989 the main political groups formed a provisional Government of National Unity. An amnesty for all political prisoners was proclaimed, and an inquiry into the death of Abdallah was instigated. It was announced that a multi-candidate presidential election, which was to end the system of single-party rule, was to take place in January 1990. Following delays caused by alleged widespread irregularities and after an inconclusive first round held on 4 March, Djohar, the official candidate for the Union comorienne pour le progrès (Udzima), was elected President on 11 March, with 55.3% of the votes cast, while Mohamed Taki Abdulkarim, the leader of the Union nationale pour la démocratie aux Comores (UNDC), secured 44.7% of the votes. Djohar appointed a new Government, in which the eight political parties that had supported his presidential candidacy were represented. In April Djohar announced plans for the formal constitutional restoration of a multi-party political system.

In August 1990 an attempted coup was staged by armed rebels, who attacked various French installations on Ngazidja. The revolt was allegedly organized by a small group of European mercenaries, who intended to provoke Djohar's resignation through the enforced removal of French forces from the islands;

---

* Some of the information contained in this chapter refers to the whole Comoros archipelago, which the independent Comoran state claims as its national territory. However, the island of Mayotte (Mahoré) is, in fact, administered by France. Separate information on Mayotte may be found in the chapter on French Overseas Possessions.

supporters of Mohamed Taki were also implicated in the conspiracy. In September the Minister of the Interior and Administrative Reforms was dismissed for his alleged involvement in the attempted coup, and more than 20 arrests were made. In October it was reported that the leader of the conspirators had been killed by Comoran security forces. In the same month Djohar implemented an extensive ministerial reorganization.

In May 1991 a conference, which was to comprise three representatives of each political association, was convened to discuss constitutional reform, although several principal opposition parties, which objected to arrangements whereby Djohar reserved the right to modify the conference's recommendations, refused to attend. However, the conference presented draft constitutional amendments, which were to be submitted to a national referendum.

In August 1991 the President of the Supreme Court, Ibrahim Ahmed Halidi, announced the dismissal of Djohar, on the grounds of negligence, and proclaimed himself interim President with the support of the Supreme Court. Opposition leaders declared the seizure of power to be legitimate under the terms of the Constitution. However, the Government condemned the coup attempt, and Halidi and several other members of the Supreme Court were arrested. A state of emergency was imposed, and remained in force until early September. A number of demonstrations in favour of Djohar took place in early August, although members of Udzima did not express support for the Government. Later that month, however, the Government banned all public demonstrations, following clashes between opposition members and pro-Government demonstrators.

In August 1991 Djohar established a new coalition Government, which included two members of the FD and, in an attempt to appease increasing discontent on Mwali, two members of the Mwalian opposition. However, the two leading political associations represented in the coalition Government, Udzima and the Parti comorien pour la démocratie et le progrès (PCDP), objected to the reshuffle, and accused Djohar of attempting to reduce their power; shortly afterwards the ministers belonging to the two parties resigned. In November Udzima (which had been officially renamed Parti Udzima—Udzima) withdrew its support for Djohar and joined the opposition. The party also condemned the proposed constitutional amendments that had been drafted in May. Opposition leaders demanded the dissolution of the Federal Assembly, which was declared to be invalid on the grounds that it had been elected under the former one-party system. In the same month, despite efforts at appeasement by Djohar, Mwali announced plans to conduct a referendum on self-determination for the island. Later in November, agreement was reached between Djohar and the principal opposition leaders to initiate a process of national reconciliation, which would include the formation of a government of national unity and the convening of a constitutional conference. The accord also guaranteed the legitimacy of Djohar's election as President. In January 1992 a new transitional Government of National Unity was formed, under the leadership of Mohamed Taki as its Co-ordinator, pending legislative elections, which were originally scheduled for April. A national conference, comprising representatives of political parties and other organizations, was convened to draft a new constitution, although Mwalian representatives refused to attend.

In May 1992 opposition parties demanded the resignation of Djohar's son-in-law, Mohamed Saïd Abdallah M'Changama, as Minister of Finance, Commerce and Planning, following allegations of irregularities in the negotiation of government contracts. Djohar subsequently formed a new interim Council of Ministers, in which, however, M'Changama retained his portfolio. At a constitutional referendum, held on 7 June, the reform proposals, which had been submitted in April, were approved by 74.3% of the votes cast, despite opposition from eight parties, notably Udzima and the FD. The new Constitution limited the presidential tenure to a maximum of two five-year terms of office, and provided for a bicameral legislature, comprising a Federal Assembly, elected for a term of four years, and a 15-member Senate, selected for a six-year term by the regional Councils. In early July Djohar dismissed Mohamed Taki, following the latter's appointment of a former mercenary to a financial advisory post in the Government. Later that month Djohar formed a new Government, although the post of Co-ordinator remained vacant.

In mid-1992 social and economic conditions on the Comoros deteriorated, following renewed strikes in a number of sectors. In September Djohar announced that legislative elections were to commence in the following month, contrary to the recommendation of an electoral commission that they take place in December. Opposition parties claimed that the schedule allowed insufficient time for preparation, and indicated that they would boycott the elections. Later that month a demonstration, organized by Udzima, the UNDC and the FD, in support of demands for Djohar's resignation, was suppressed by security forces. In an apparent attempt to restore order, Djohar subsequently announced that legislative elections would take place in early November and local government elections in December.

In September 1992 an abortive coup attempt was staged by disaffected members of the armed forces, who seized the radio station at Moroni and announced that the Government had been overthrown. Six opposition leaders and six members of the armed forces, including two sons of the former President, Ahmed Abdallah, were subsequently charged with involvement in the attempted coup. In October some 100 rebel troops, led by a former member of Abdallah's presidential guard, attacked the military garrison of Kandani, in an attempt to release the detainees. Government forces attacked the rebels at Mbeni, to the north-east of Moroni; fighting was also reported on Nzwani. Later in October a demonstration was staged in protest at the French Government's support of Djohar, following French consignments of food rations to government forces, which prompted speculation that armaments had also been dispatched. By the end of October some 25 people had been killed in clashes between rebels and government forces in Moroni.

In October 1992 Djohar agreed to reschedule the legislative elections for late November, although opposition parties demanded a further postponement, and Udzima and the UNDC continued to support an electoral boycott. The first round of the legislative elections, which took place on 22 November, was contested by some 320 candidates representing 21 political parties. Numerous electoral irregularities and violent incidents were reported, however, and several opposition parties demanded that the results be declared invalid, and joined the boycott. Election results in six constituencies were subsequently annulled, while the second round of voting on 29 November took place in only 34 of the 42 constituencies. Following partial elections on 13 and 30 December, reports indicated that candidates supporting Djohar—including seven members of the Union des démocrates pour la démocratie (UDD), a pro-Government organization based on Nzwani—had secured a narrow majority in the Federal Assembly. The leader of the UDD, Ibrahim Abdérémane Halidi, was appointed Prime Minister on 1 January 1993, and formed a new Council of Ministers. Later in January a Mwalian, Amir Attoumane, was elected as Speaker of the Federal Assembly in response to demands by Mwalian deputies.

Shortly after the new Government took office, however, disagreement between Djohar and Halidi was reported, while the presidential majority in the Federal Assembly fragmented into three dissenting factions. In mid-February 1993 a vote of censure against the Government, which was proposed by representatives of several pro-Djohar parties, was rejected. Later that month Halidi effected an extensive reorganization of the Council of Ministers, although the political parties that supported Djohar remained dissatisfied with its composition.

In April 1993 nine people, including Abdallah's sons and two prominent members of Udzima, were convicted on charges of involvement in the coup attempt of September 1992, and sentenced to death. Following considerable domestic and international pressure, however, Djohar commuted the sentences to terms of imprisonment. In May 1993 eight supporters of M'Changama, allied with a number of opposition deputies, proposed a motion of 'no confidence' in the Government (apparently with the tacit support of Djohar), which was approved by 23 of the 42 deputies. Shortly afterwards, Djohar appointed an associate of M'Changama, Saïd Ali Mohamed, as Prime Minister and a new Council of Ministers was formed. In June an alliance of pro-Halidi deputies proposed a motion of censure against the new Government, on the grounds that the Prime Minister had not been appointed from a party that commanded a majority in the Federal Assembly. Djohar, however, declared the motion to be unconstitutional and, in view of the continued absence of a viable parliamentary majority, dissolved the Federal Assembly and announced legislative elections. He subsequently dismissed Mohamed and appointed a former presidential adviser, Ahmed Ben Cheikh Attoumane, as Prime Minister. Shortly afterwards, an interim Council of Ministers was formed (although two of the newly-appointed ministers immediately resigned).

Following the dissolution of the Federal Assembly, opposition parties declared Djohar unfit to hold office, in view of the increasing political confusion, and demanded that legislative elections take place within the period of 40 days stipulated in the Constitution. In July 1993, however, Djohar announced that the legislative elections (which were to take place concurrently with local government elections) were to be postponed until October. In response, opposition parties organized a one-day strike, in support of demands that Djohar bring forward the date of the legislative elections or resign. In September a number of opposition movements, notably Udzima and the UNDC, established an informal electoral alliance, known as the Union pour la République et le progrès, while the FD, the PCDP, CHUMA (Islands' Fraternity and Unity Party), and the Mouvement pour la démocratie et le progrès (MDP) agreed to present joint candidates. Later in September Djohar postponed the legislative elections until November, officially on financial grounds. In October Djohar (who had failed to induce the political parties that supported him to form an electoral alliance, owing to their hostility towards M'Changama) established a political organization, the Rassemblement pour la démocratie et le renouveau (RDR), principally comprising supporters of M'Changama and several prominent members of the Government. In November the legislative elections were rescheduled for December, while the local government elections were postponed indefinitely. Later in November Djohar reorganized the Council of Ministers, and established a new National Electoral Commission (NEC), in compliance with the demands of the opposition (which had objected to the composition of the former commission).

In the first round of the legislative elections, which took place on 12 December 1993, four opposition candidates secured seats in the Federal Assembly, apparently prompting concern in the Government. Following the second round of the polls on 20 December, it was reported that three people had been killed in violent incidents in Nzwani, where the authorities had assumed control of the electoral process. The NEC subsequently declared the results in several constituencies to be invalid. Opposition candidates refused to participate in further elections in these constituencies, on the grounds that voting was again to be conducted under the supervision of the authorities, rather than that of the NEC; RDR candidates consequently won all 10 contested seats, and 22 seats overall, thereby securing a narrow majority in the Federal Assembly. In January 1994 Djohar appointed the Secretary-General of the RDR, Mohamed Abdou Madi, as Prime Minister. The new Council of Ministers included several supporters of M'Changama, who was elected Speaker of the Federal Assembly. Later in January 12 principal opposition parties, which claimed that the RDR had assumed power illegally, formed a new alliance, the Forum pour le redressement national (FRN).

In April 1994 pressure increased from both the Comoran opposition and the French Government in support of an amnesty for political prisoners. In the same month division emerged between M'Changama and Abdou Madi regarding the appointment of a number of prominent government officials. In May teachers initiated strike action (which was later joined by health workers) in support of demands for an increase in salaries and the reorganization of the public sector. In mid-June it was reported that five people had been killed on Mwali, following an opposition demonstration in support of the public-sector strike, which was violently suppressed by the security forces. Later that month legislation (which had been approved by Djohar) providing for the sale of the state-owned airline, Air Comores, to an alleged international financier, known as Rowland Ashley, was rescinded, following protests from both opposition and government supporters in the Federal Assembly. Under a compromise arrangement, Ashley's privately-owned company was granted management of the airline's operations. In August, however, Ashley's background was proved to be fraudulent, and the existence of his company fabricated. Ashley subsequently claimed that prominent members of the Government had accepted financial inducements in connection with the proposed sale of the airline. Later that month the political management committee of the RDR, which was headed by M'Changama, criticized Abdou Madi's involvement in the affair.

In September 1994 public-sector workers initiated further strike action; union officials refused to enter into negotiations with the authorities while Abdou Madi's Government remained in power. Despite previous expressions of support for Abdou Madi, in October Djohar dismissed him from the office of Prime Minister (apparently owing to his involvement in the Air Comores affair), and appointed Halifa Houmadi to the post. A new Council of Ministers included only two members of the former administration.

In December 1994 Djohar failed to accede to a request by the Federal Assembly that political prisoners who had been implicated in the abortive coup attempt in September 1992 be granted amnesty. In January 1995 public-sector workers suspended strike action, after the Government agreed to a number of union demands. In the same month Djohar condemned a decision by the French Government to reimpose visa requirements for Comoran nationals entering Mayotte (which further undermined the Comoros' claim of sovereignty over the territory). A demonstration at the French embassy in Moroni, which was staged in protest at the measure, was suppressed by security forces, after degenerating into violence. It was subsequently reported that threats had been issued against French nationals resident in the Comoros. Later in January division emerged within the RDR, after both the party's Chairman and its Secretary-General (Abdou Madi) criticized the Government's failure to contain the hostility towards French citizens. At a congress of the RDR in February the two officials were removed from the party, and Houmadi became Chairman. In the same month the Government announced that elections to the regional councils were to take place in April (later postponed until July), and were to be followed by the establishment of a Senate and a Constitutional Council. The opposition, however, accused Djohar of acting unconstitutionally in the preparation for elections, and claimed that he planned to assume control of the electoral process.

In April 1995 reports emerged of a widening rift between Djohar and Houmadi, after the Prime Minister apparently claimed that Djohar and M'Changama had engaged in financial malpractice. At the end of that month Djohar dismissed Houmadi from the premiership and appointed a former Minister of Finance, Mohamed Caabi El Yachroutu, as his successor. A 13-member Council of Ministers, which included only five members of the previous administration, was established. In May three former Prime Ministers (Mohamed, Abdou Madi and Houmadi) conducted a series of political meetings urging public support for the removal of M'Changama (who, they claimed, exerted undue influence over Djohar), and demanded the dissolution of the Federal Assembly. In July further tension developed within the Government over an agreement whereby Air Comores was to be transferred to the joint management of an airline based in the United Arab Emirates; M'Changama and the Minister of Transport and Tourism, Ahmed Saïd Issilame, claimed that the agreement was technically invalid on the grounds that it had been signed by Djohar before legislation providing for the privatization of Air Comores had been approved in the Federal Assembly. Meanwhile, it was feared that the further postponement of elections to the regional councils would delay the presidential election. In an effort to facilitate the organization of the presidential election, the Government introduced minor constitutional amendments, including the relaxation of regulations governing the registration of political candidates and a provision empowering the Prime Minister to act as interim Head of State. At the end of July Djohar removed Issilame and a further three associates of M'Changama from the Council of Ministers.

In September 1995 about 30 European mercenaries, led by Denard, staged a military coup, seizing control of the garrison at Kandani and capturing Djohar. The mercenaries, who were joined by some 300 members of the Comoran armed forces, released a number of prisoners (including those detained for involvement in the failed coup attempt in September 1992), and installed a former associate of Denard, Capt. Ayouba Combo, as leader of a Transitional Military Committee. The French Government denounced the coup and suspended economic aid to the Comoros, but initially refused to take military action, despite requests for assistance from El Yachroutu, who had taken refuge in the French embassy. In October Combo announced that he had transferred authority to Mohamed Taki and the leader of CHUMA, Saïd Ali Kemal (who had both welcomed the coup), as joint civilian Presidents, apparently in an attempt to avert military repercussions by the French Government. The FRN, however, rejected the new leadership and entered into negotiations with El Yachroutu. Following a further appeal for intervention from El Yachroutu, who invoked a defence co-operation agreement that had been established between the two countries in 1978, some 900 French military personnel landed on the Comoros and surrounded the mercenaries at Kandani. Shortly afterwards, Denard and his associates, together with the disaffected members of the Comoran armed forces, surrendered to the French troops. The mercenaries were subsequently placed under arrest and transported to France. (In October 1996, following his release from imprisonment in France in July, Denard claimed that the coup attempt had been planned at the request of several Comoran officials, including Mohamed Taki.)

Following the French military intervention, El Yachroutu declared himself interim President in accordance with the Constitution and announced the formation of a Government of National Unity, which included members of the constituent parties of the FRN. Djohar (who had been transported to Réunion by the French in order to receive medical treatment) rejected El Yachroutu's assumption of power and announced the reappointment of Saïd Ali Mohamed as Prime Minister. Later in October 1995 a National Reconciliation Conference decided that El Yachroutu would remain interim President, pending the forthcoming election, which was provisionally scheduled for early 1996. The incumbent administration opposed Djohar's stated intention to return to the Comoros and announced that measures would be taken to prevent him from entering the country. At the end of October El Yachroutu granted an amnesty to all Comorans involved in the coup attempt and appointed representatives of the UNDC and Udzima (which had supported the coup) to the new Council of Ministers. In November Djohar announced the formation of a rival Government, headed by Mohamed. El Yachroutu, who was supported by the Comoran armed forces, refused to recognize the legitimacy of Djohar's appointments, while opposition parties equally opposed his return to power; only elements of the RDR continued to support Djohar's authority. It was reported that representatives of the OAU, who visited the Comoros and Réunion in November in an effort to resolve the situation, had unofficially concluded that only El Yachroutu's administration was capable of governing. There was also widespread speculation that the French Government had believed Djohar's authority to be untenable and had tacitly supported his removal from power. Later that month, however, supporters of Djohar, including M'Changama, organized a political gathering to demand the resignation of El Yachroutu's administration. Meanwhile, political leaders on Mwali rejected the authority of both rival Governments, urged a campaign of civil disobedience and established a 'citizens' committee' to govern the island; discontent with the central administration also emerged on Nzwani.

In January 1995 Djohar returned to the Comoros, after apparently signing an agreement stipulating that he would retain only symbolic presidential powers. In February it was reported that the island of Mwali had unilaterally proclaimed itself a democratic republic. Presidential elections took place, in two rounds, on 6 and 16 March. In the first round, which was contested by some 15 candidates, Mohamed Taki obtained the highest number of votes, with 21%, while the leader of the FRN, Abbas Djoussouf, secured about 15% of votes. According to reports, 12 of the 13 unsuccessful candidates urged support for Mohamed Taki in the second round of the election, and Taki was duly elected to the presidency on 16 March, obtaining 64% of the vote. International observers, including delegates from the UN and OAU, were satisfied with the electoral process; officials reported that 62% of the electorate had participated in the second round. The new Head of State was sworn in on 25 March. Taki appointed a new Council of Ministers, which included five of the presidential candidates who had supported him in the second round of the election.

In April 1996 Taki dissolved the Federal Assembly and announced that legislative elections would take place in October, despite the constitutional requirement that elections be held within a period of 40 days following the dissolution of the legislature. New Governors, all belonging to the UNDC, were appointed to each of the three islands. In August Taki issued a decree awarding himself absolute powers. This measure was widely criticized in the media, and by opposition groups, notably CHUMA, the Forces pour l'action républicaine (FAR) and the FRN, as being in violation of the Constitution. In a government reorganization later in the month, Saïd Ali Kemal and a representative of the FAR were dismissed, following their parties' refusal to disband in order to join the single pro-presidential party that Taki intended to establish.

In September 1996 Taki established a constitutional consultative committee, comprising 42 representatives of political parties and other organizations, which was to provide advice concerning the drafting of a new constitution; the FRN refused to participate in the committee. Also in that month the forthcoming legislative elections were postponed until November. At the beginning of October a national referendum to endorse a new draft Constitution was scheduled for 20 October. In order to comply with a constitutional proposal, which effectively restricted the number of political parties to a maximum of three, 24 pro-Taki political organizations merged to form one presidential party, the Rassemblement national pour le développement (RND). The opposition condemned the extensive powers that the draft Constitution vested in the President, and the rapidity with which it was to be installed, and urged a boycott of the constitutional referendum. On 20 October, however, the new Constitution was approved by 85% of votes cast; according to official estimates, about 64% of the electorate voted. The new Constitution vested legislative power in a unicameral parliament, the Federal Assembly (thereby abolishing the Senate), and extended the presidential term to six years, with an unrestricted number of consecutive mandates. Political parties were required to have two parliamentary deputies from each island (following legislative elections) to be considered legal; organizations that did not fulfil these stipulations were to be dissolved. Extensive executive powers were vested in the President, who was to appoint the Governors of the islands, and gained the right to initiate constitutional amendments. The opposition parties disputed the official result of the referendum, insisting that only about 20% of the electorate had voted.

Following unsuccessful negotiations with the Government, which rejected demands for the creation of an independent electoral commission and the revision of electoral lists, the opposition parties (having formed a new alliance) refused to participate in the electoral process. Consequently, the legislative elections, which took place after a further delay, in two rounds, in December 1996, were only contested by the RND and the Front national pour la justice (FNJ), a fundamentalist Islamic organization, together with 23 independent candidates (in apparent contravention of a stipulation in the new Constitution that only legally-created political parties were entitled to participate in national elections). The RND secured 36 of the 43 seats in the Federal Assembly, while the FNJ won three, with four seats taken by independent candidates. Taki nominated Ahmed Abdou, who had served in the administration of the former President Ahmed Abdallah, as Prime Minister to head a new Council of Ministers.

In December 1996 industrial action in the public sector in support of demands by civil servants for the payment of salary arrears resulted in severe disruption in government services. A grouping of teachers' and hospital workers' unions joined the strike action in January 1997, and up to 30 people were injured when the security forces violently suppressed a demonstration organized by trade unions in Moroni. Civil unrest, exacerbated by severe shortages of water and electricity, continued, and in February a one-day general strike, organized by the opposition, was widely supported. Meanwhile, discontent with the Government intensified on Nzwani; in March a general strike escalated into riots, during which four people were killed, when some 3,000 demonstrators (reported to be secessionists) clashed with the security forces in Mutsamudu, the main town. Taki replaced the Governor of Nzwani and other senior island officials and carried out a government reshuffle. In May it was reported that, in an attempt to alleviate the crisis, Taki and Djoussouf had agreed to establish a joint commission to define terms for the participation of the FRN in the governing of internal affairs. However, sympathy for the separatist movements on both Nzwani and Mwali continued to increase, amid claims that the Government had consistently ignored their political and economic interests, and on 14 July (France's national day) two people were killed in skirmishes between the security forces and demonstrators. Separatist leaders declared their intention to seek the restoration of French rule and established a 'political directorate' on Nzwani, chaired by Abdallah Ibrahim, the leader of the Mouvement populaire anjouanais, a grouping of separatist movements on Nzwani. (The relative prosperity of neighbouring Mayotte appeared to have prompted the demand for a return to French rule; it was reported that up to 200 illegal migrants a day attempted to enter Mayotte from Nzwani.) Military reinforcements were sent to Nzwani and the Governor of the island was replaced once again.

On 3 August 1997 the 'political directorate' unilaterally declared Nzwani's secession from the Comoros. The separatists subsequently elected Ibrahim as president of a 13-member 'politico-administrative co-ordination', which included Abdou Madi, a former Prime Minister during Djohar's presidency, as spokesperson. The declaration of independence was condemned by Djoussouf, who appealed for French mediation in the crisis. However, France, while denouncing the secession, declared itself in favour of the intervention of the OAU. The OAU responded by sending a special envoy, Pierre Yéré, to the Comoros. Meanwhile, separatist agitation intensified on Mwali, culminating on 11 August, when secessionists declared Mwali's independence from the Comoros, appointed a president and a prime minister to head a 12-member government, and called for reattachment to France.

As OAU mediation efforts continued, it was announced in mid-August 1997 that secessionist leaders on Mwali and Nzwani had agreed to negotiate with the authorities in Moroni, although those on Nzwani had insisted on the immediate withdrawal of the military reinforcements that had been sent to the island in July. By late August the Government had complied with this demand, and the OAU announced its intention to hold a reconciliation conference in September in Addis Ababa, Ethiopia, while maintaining that secession was unacceptable. Nzwani's Governor resigned and was not replaced. At the end of August Yéré returned to the Comoros in order to prepare for the forthcoming conference. However, in early September, despite OAU and French opposition to military intervention, Taki despatched some 300 troops to Nzwani in an attempt forcibly to suppress the separatist insurrection. After two days of heavy fighting between secessionist and government forces, the OAU declared that the government troops had failed to quash the rebellion. The Government claimed that the separatists had been aided by foreign elements and expressed regret at France's refusal to support the military operation. As it emerged that some 40 Comoran soldiers and 16 Nzwani residents had been killed in the fighting, with many more injured, demonstrators demanding Taki's resignation clashed violently with the security forces in Moroni. The separatists on Nzwani reaffirmed their independence and empowered Ibrahim to rule by decree. Taki subsequently declared a state of emergency, assumed absolute power and dismissed the Government of Ahmed Abdou and his military and civilian advisers. (Abdou, from Mutsamudu, had reportedly resigned his position in late August, although this had not been announced publicly.) Shortly afterwards, Taki established a State Transition Commission, which included representatives from Nzwani and Mwali. The reconciliation conference was postponed indefinitely by the OAU. The League of Arab States (Arab League) agreed to a request from Taki for assistance, and following talks with the OAU regarding the co-ordination of the mediation effort, all three islands hosted discussions in late September, which were convened by envoys from both organizations. The opposition continued to call for Taki's resignation, the decentralization of power through constitutional reform and the organization of new elections.

In September 1997, despite the misgivings of some members of the 'politico-administrative co-ordination', notably Abdou Madi, Ibrahim announced his decision to hold a referendum on self-determination for Nzwani on 26 October, prior to a reconciliation conference sponsored by both the OAU and the Arab League, which all parties had agreed to attend. Despite international opposition, the referendum was conducted as scheduled; according to separatist officials, 99.9% of the electorate voted in favour of independence for Nzwani, with a turn-out of 94%. The following day Ibrahim dissolved the 'politico-administrative co-ordination' and appointed a temporary government, which was charged with preparing a constitution and organizing a presidential election, although it did not receive international recognition. Taki responded by severing Nzwani's telephone lines, suspending air and maritime links and establishing a commission to liaise with opposition leaders prior to the appointment of a government of national unity. However, the opposition refused to participate in such a government before the reconciliation conference had taken place. The conference had been postponed several times, largely owing to disagreements regarding the composition and strength of the delegations. In November the OAU announced plans to deploy a force of military observers in the Comoros, despite the separatists' insistence that the force would not be allowed to land on Nzwani; an initial eight-member contingent, which arrived that month, was subsequently to be increased to 25 and was to receive logistical

support from France. Meanwhile, amid reports of dissension within the separatist government, it was reported that Abdou Madi (believed to hold more moderate views than Ibrahim) was in Moroni, having fled Nzwani.

In early December 1997 Taki formed a new Council of Ministers, appointing Nourdine Bourhane as Prime Minister. The inter-Comoran reconciliation conference was held later that month; some agreement was reached on proposals for the establishment of an international commission of inquiry to investigate September's military intervention and on the holding of a Comoran inter-island conference to discuss institutional reform. In January 1998, following the first meeting in Fomboni, Mwali, of a committee charged with pursuing negotiations on the crisis, the OAU announced that both the Comoran Government and the Nzwani separatists had agreed to a number of conciliatory measures, including the restoration of air and maritime links and the release of 18 federal soldiers still detained on Nzwani. However, Ibrahim subsequently rejected all the agreements that his delegation had signed in Fomboni, with the exception of the release of detainees.

In February 1998 tension increased further on Nzwani, where several rival separatist factions had emerged; fighting broke out between Ibrahim's supporters and followers of Abdou Madi, who had returned to the island, with the apparent support of both Taki and the OAU, in an abortive attempt to mount resistance to the secessionists. Later in February a separatist constitution was approved by a reported 99.5% of voters in a referendum on Nzwani. Ibrahim subsequently appointed a new separatist government. OAU mediation efforts effectively broke down in March, following an unsuccessful visit to Nzwani by a ministerial delegation.

In Moroni public discontent intensified in May 1998, when a 48-hour strike was widely supported by civil servants (who claimed to be owed some 15 months of salary); at least three people were reported to have been killed in violent anti-Government protests. Later that month Taki, who appeared to be moderating his stance, acted to break the political deadlock, forming a committee to re-establish dialogue with the opposition, appointing a new Council of Ministers, and releasing a prominent separatist from detention in Moroni. Abdou Madi returned to federal government and, seemingly as a conciliatory gesture to the secessionists, the premiership (a position traditionally held by a Nzwanian) was left vacant. In June Taki held discussions with a number of opposition leaders, although the FRN refused to participate.

In July 1998, as social unrest on Nzwani escalated, a dispute over the future aims of the secessionist movement led to the dismissal of the island's government, provoking violent clashes between islanders loyal to Ibrahim, who favoured independence within the framework of an association of the Comoran islands, and supporters of the outgoing prime minister of the island, Chamassi Saïd Omar, who continued to advocate reattachment to France.

Meanwhile, as social and economic conditions deteriorated further, with salaries still unpaid and strike action ongoing, Taki sought overseas assistance in resolving the crisis. In August 1998 the Government provisionally suspended transport links with both Nzwani and Mayotte. France later refused the Government's request for a suspension of links between Mayotte and Nzwani, thus worsening the already fragile relations between the two countries. As industrial action continued into September, it was reported that the Government had banned news broadcasts by privately-owned radio and television stations. In October, in a renewed effort to find a solution to the crisis, the OAU suggested that a meeting be held in South Africa between Taki and Ibrahim, and also encouraged dialogue between Taki and opposition leaders. At subsequent meetings with Djoussouf and the leadership of his own party, Taki proposed the establishment of a government of public salvation, an idea opposed by many members of the RND and several government ministers.

On 6 November 1998 President Taki died unexpectedly, reportedly having suffered a heart attack, although several senior officials expressed serious doubts about the cause of death. Tadjidine Ben Saïd Massoundi, the President of the High Council of the Republic and a former Prime Minister (March–December 1996), was designated acting President, in accordance with the Constitution, pending an election, which would be held after 30–90 days. Massoundi immediately revoked the ban on the movement of people and goods to Nzwani and, despite the continued opposition of several government ministers, proceeded with Taki's project for the formation of a government of public salvation. Djoussouf, the main opposition leader, was subsequently appointed Prime Minister, to head a Council of Ministers composed of members of the FRN and the RND. Divisions within the RND over its participation in the new Government led to a split in the party. In late January 1999 Massoundi extended his presidential mandate, which was soon to expire, pending a resolution of the crisis dividing the islands. In February an agreement was signed by Massoundi and political parties opposed to the FRN-RND Government, which provided for the formation of a new federal administration to be supported by up to three technical commissions. However, the FRN refused to endorse the agreement, declaring its intention to remain in power until a Comoran inter-island conference had been held.

Meanwhile, renewed tension within the separatist administration on Nzwani escalated in December 1998, provoking eight days of armed clashes between rival militias, which reportedly resulted in at least 60 deaths before a cease-fire agreement was signed. In January 1999 Ibrahim agreed to relinquish some of his powers to a five-member 'politico-administrative directorate', as meetings commenced between the rival separatist factions. No consensus was reached in the following months, however, and when Ibrahim replaced the directorate with a 'committee of national security' in March, the new administration was immediately rejected by rival leaders. In Moroni there were further protests against the ruling federal administration, during which President Massoundi was vehemently denounced. Several anti-Government demonstrators were injured in clashes with the security forces.

At an OAU-sponsored inter-island conference, held in Antananarivo, Madagascar, on 19–23 April 1999, an agreement was reached which envisaged substantial autonomy for Nzwani and Mwali, the changing of the country's name to the Union of the Comoran Islands and the rotation of the presidency among the three islands, and which also provided for a transitional period of one year until the new presidential and legislative structures were fully implemented. However, the delegates from Nzwani refused to sign the agreement, insisting on the need to consult the Nzwani population prior to a full endorsement. There followed several days of rioting in Moroni, as demonstrators protested against Nzwani's failure to ratify the accord, and more than 1,000 Nzwanians were reportedly forced from their homes before order was restored. On 30 April the Chief of Staff of the Comoran armed forces, Col Assoumani Azali, seized power in a bloodless coup, deposing Massoundi and dissolving the Government, the Federal Assembly and all other constitutional institutions. Azali promulgated a new constitutional charter, in which he proclaimed himself head of state and of government and Commander-in-Chief of the armed forces, and sought to justify the coup by claiming that the authorities had not taken the political measures necessary to control the security situation in the Comoros. Full legislative functions were also vested in Azali, who announced his intention to stay in power for one year only, during which time he pledged to oversee the creation of the new institutions envisaged in the Antananarivo accord. The appointment of a State Committee (composed of six members from Ngazidja, four from Mwali and two from Nzwani) was followed by that of a State Council, which was to supervise the activities of the State Committee and comprised eight civilians and 11 army officers. The coup was condemned by the OAU, which withdrew its military observers from the Comoros and urged the international community not to recognize the new regime; the UN, however, sent representatives to Azali's inauguration.

In June 1999 Azali created five technical commissions, which were charged with directing the implementation of the Antananarivo accord, including the drafting of new constitutions for the proposed union and its component parts. However, amid increasing discontent with the new administration, the main political parties boycotted a meeting at which they were to have nominated representatives to serve on the new commissions. Lt-Col Saïd Abeid Abdérémane, who had previously held the role of 'national mediator' on Nzwani, formed a government of national unity on the island and assumed the role of 'national co-ordinator'. In July delegates from the three islands, including Azali and Abeid, met on Mwali for talks aimed at resolving the political crisis. The negotiations represented the most senior-level contact between the islands since the secessions of August 1997.

In August 1999 elections to establish a 25-member national assembly on Nzwani were held. No official results were released, but reports indicated that the most staunch separatists won the majority of seats. In the same month the OAU Secretary-General's newly-appointed special envoy for the Comoros, Francisco Caetano José Madeira, visited the islands in an attempt to persuade the separatists on Nzwani to sign the Antananarivo accord. At the end of August the growing divisions between Ngazidja and Nzwani became more apparent when Azali refused to allow 500 Nzwanian secondary-school students to sit an exam on Ngazidja. Furthermore, several senior civil servants from Nzwani were dismissed from their jobs in Moroni and many more were threatened with transfers back to their island. In September the Nzwani executive council announced its decision not to sign the Antananarivo peace agreement; Abeid stated that the signature of the accord would not be in accordance with the aspirations of the island's population. In October Madeira again visited the Comoros in an attempt to convince the separatists to sign the peace agreement. The separatist leaders, however, refused to relent, citing their fear of social unrest if they signed the agreement. In response, Madeira suggested that an OAU peace-keeping force be dispatched to Nzwani to prevent possible trouble; the separatist leaders requested further time to reconsider their position. In December the OAU adopted a tougher stance towards the Nzwani separatists by threatening the imposition of sanctions on the island should its leaders not have signed the peace accord by 1 February 2000. In retaliation, Abeid announced that a referendum would be held on Nzwani on 23 January 2000 regarding the signing of the Antananarivo accord. According to the separatist authorities of Nzwani, the results of the referendum revealed an overwhelming majority (94.47%) in favour of full independence for the island; the OAU, however, announced that it did not recognize the outcome of the ballot, following allegations of intimidation and repression of those in favour of reconciliation.

Meanwhile, following a series of meetings between Azali and a number of political parties from all three islands regarding the establishment of a more representative and decentralized government in Moroni, the State Committee underwent an extensive reorganization in December 1999, including the appointment of a Prime Minister, namely Bianrifi Tarmidi (from Mwali). Although Mwali was well represented in the new executive, only one Nzwanian minister was appointed.

On 1 February 2000, as threatened, the OAU imposed economic sanctions on Nzwani and demanded the co-operation of all countries in the region in implementing the sanctions; the overseas assets of the separatist leaders were 'frozen' and they themselves were confined to the island. Furthermore, as part of the OAU sanctions, the federal Government suspended sea and air transport links, as well as telephone communications with Nzwani.

In March 2000 army units, led by Capt. Abderamane Ahmed Abdallah (the son of former President Ahmed Abdallah), reportedly attempted, unsuccessfully, to overthrow Azali; Abdallah was subsequently arrested. In the following month demonstrations were organized by a number of political parties in protest at Azali's failure to transfer the country to civilian rule by 14 April, as he had promised following the April 1999 coup (see above). Azali later claimed that the conditions set for the holding of elections, namely the signing of the Antananarivo accord by the Nzwanian separatists, had not been met.

In May 2000 the OAU announced that the lifting of sanctions against Nzwanian separatists was connected to the return to constitutional order on the Comoros; it advocated the restoration of the October 1996 Constitution, the reinstatement of Tajidine Ben Saïd Massoundi as Head of State, as well as the appointment of an interim government and Prime Minister. The following month an OAU delegation, led by Madeira, arrived in Moroni in an attempt to revive peace talks. However, Abeid reiterated his rejection of the Antananarivo accord. In response, the OAU announced the possibility of armed intervention on Nzwani. However, this was rejected at the OAU summit, held in July, although it was agreed to establish a total maritime blockade of Nzwani.

On 26 August 2000 an agreement, known as the Fomboni Accord, was reached by Azali and Abeid, following negotiations on Mwali. The agreement provided for the establishment of a new Comoran entity and granted the three islands considerable control over internal matters. A new constitution was to be drafted and approved, by referendum, within 12 months. Moreover, Abeid and Azali called for the sanctions imposed on

Nzwani to be lifted. The declaration was rejected by the OAU, however, on the grounds that it did not conform with the Antananarivo accord, and that it threatened the integrity of the Comoros. Demonstrations, during which a number of people were reportedly injured, arrested and imprisoned, took place on Nzwani following the signing of the declaration. The protests had been organized by opposition members displeased with the new settlement. Nevertheless, a tripartite commission, comprising delegates from Ngazidja, Nzwani and Mwali, was established in November to define the terms of the new constitution. In late November Bianrifi Tarmidi was replaced as Prime Minister by Hamada Madi 'Boléro', who subsequently formed a new Government, appointing seven new ministers. Despite attempts to include them in the new Government and the tripartite commission, opposition members refused to participate, instead presenting to international mediators their own proposals for a resolution to the crisis.

With the mediation of the OAU and the Organisation internationale de la francophonie (OIF), negotiations between opposition and government members continued throughout late 2000 and early 2001, in an attempt to find a solution acceptable to all parties. On 17 February an agreement on national reconciliation was signed in Fomboni by representatives of the Comoran Government, the Nzwani administration, opposition parties and civil society. The OAU, the OIF and the EU were to be guarantors of the peace accord, which provided for the establishment of a new Comoran entity. The OAU subsequently lifted sanctions against Nzwani. Under the provisions of the agreement, an independent tripartite commission (comprising equal numbers of delegates from all the islands, representing all the signatory groups) was to draft a new constitution, which would be subject to approval in a national referendum scheduled for June 2001. The new constitution was to define the areas of jurisdiction of the new entity and the individual islands, although the central administration would retain control over religion, nationality, currency, foreign affairs and defence. An independent national electoral commission was also to be created. Following the constitutional referendum, a transitional government of national union was to be formed and charged with creating the new institutions by 31 December. The Head of State (Azali) was to act as President during the transitional period. The agreement also envisaged the formation of a 'follow-up' committee to monitor the implementation of the accord. However, in mid-March the opposition suspended its involvement in this committee, following disagreements regarding its composition and the appointment of a co-ordinator.

Diplomatic relations between the Comoros and France, suspended in December 1975, were restored in July 1978; in November of that year the two countries signed agreements on military and economic co-operation, apparently deferring any decision on the future of Mayotte. In subsequent years, however, member countries of the UN General Assembly repeatedly voted in favour of a resolution affirming the Comoros' sovereignty over Mayotte, with only France dissenting. Following Djohar's accession to power, diplomatic relations were established with the USA in June 1990. In September 1993 the Arab League (see p. 232) accepted an application for membership from the Comoros. In mid-1999, following the military coup headed by Col Azali, France and the USA suspended all military co-operation with the Comoros.

Government

Under the Constitution of 20 October 1996, each of the islands in the Comoros has a Council and Governor, who is appointed by the President. The Head of State is the President, who is elected by direct universal suffrage for an unlimited number of six-year terms. The President appoints the Prime Minister, who heads the Council of Ministers. The Constitution provides for a unicameral legislature, a 43-member Federal Assembly, which is directly-elected for a term of five years.

On 6 May 1999, following the coup of 30 April, Col Assoumani Azali promulgated a new constitutional charter, pending the introduction of new constitutional arrangements, which were to take effect within one year. According to the charter, Col Azali was the Head of State and held full legislative and executive power. He also appointed and headed an executive body known as the State Committee. On 17 February 2001 an agreement on national reconciliation, providing for the creation of a new Comoran entity, was signed by representatives of Azali's administration, the separatist authorities on Nzwani, opposition parties and civil society. Under the terms of the accord, a tripartite commission was to draft a new constitution, which was to be

subject to approval by referendum by June 2001. A transitional government of national union was subsequently to be formed.

Defence

In mid-1997 the national army, the Force Comorienne de Défense (FCD), numbered about 1,500 men. Government expenditure on defence in 1994 was an estimated US $3m. In December 1996 an agreement was ratified with France, which provided for the permanent presence of a French military contingent in the Comoros, which was to be renewed by rotation. In July 1997, however, it was reported that the rotations had ceased several months previously.

Economic Affairs

In 1998, according to estimates from the World Bank, the gross national product (GNP) of the Comoros (excluding Mayotte), measured at average 1996–98 prices, was US $197m., equivalent to $370 per head (or $1,400 per head on an international purchasing-power parity basis). During 1990–98, it was estimated, GNP per head declined, in real terms, at an average rate of 3.1% per year. Over the same period, the population increased at an average annual rate of 2.9%. Estimated GNP in 1999 was $189m. ($350 per head). According to IMF estimates, the Comoros' gross domestic product (GDP) declined, in real terms, at an average annual rate of 0.6% in 1990–99; real GDP declined by 0.5% in 1998, and by 1.4% in 1999. According to provisional figures released by the central bank, however, real GDP increased by 1.2% in 1998, and by 1.1% in 1999.

Agriculture (including hunting, forestry and fishing) contributed an estimated 39.9% of GDP in 1999. Approximately 74.1% of the labour force were employed in the agricultural sector in that year. In 1989 the sector accounted for more than 98% of total export earnings. The principal cash crops are vanilla, ylang-ylang, cloves and basil. Cassava, taro, rice, maize, pulses, coconuts and bananas are also cultivated. According to IMF estimates, the real GDP of the agricultural sector declined at an average annual rate of 1.3% in 1990–99; agricultural GDP declined by 0.1% in 1998 and by 1.8% in 1999.

Industry (including manufacturing, construction and power) contributed an estimated 11.1% of GDP in 1999. About 6% of the labour force were employed in the industrial sector at mid-1980. According to IMF estimates, the Comoros' industrial GDP increased at an average annual rate of 3.5% in 1990–99 (owing mainly to a sharp rise in construction activity); industrial GDP increased by 3.1% in 1998 and by 0.6% in 1999.

The manufacturing sector contributed an estimated 3.7% of GDP in 1999. The sector consists primarily of the processing of agricultural produce, particularly of vanilla and essential oils. According to IMF estimates, manufacturing GDP declined at an average annual rate of 0.8% in 1990–99; it declined by 3.7% in 1998 and by 2.1% in 1999.

Electrical energy is derived from wood (78%), and from thermal installations. Imports of fuel and energy comprised an estimated 11.8% of the total cost of imports in 1995.

The services sector contributed 48.9% of GDP in 1999. Strong growth in tourism from 1991 led to a significant expansion in trade, restaurant and hotel activities, although political instability has inhibited subsequent growth. According to IMF estimates, the GDP of the services sector declined at an average rate of 1.6% per year in 1990–99; it declined by 0.9% in 1998 and by 1.2% in 1999.

In 1999 the Comoros recorded an estimated visible trade deficit of US $35.3m., and there was a surplus of $0.1m. on the current account of the balance of payments. In that year the principal source of imports was France (accounting for some 32.0% of the total). The USA was the principal market for exports (26.8%). Germany, Singapore, South Africa and Réunion were also major trading partners. The leading exports in 1999 were vanilla (providing 43.2% of the total), clove buds (27.7%) and ylang-ylang (13.3%). The principal imports in that year were rice (18.9%), petroleum products (13.5%) and vehicles (13.4%).

The overall budget surplus in 1999 was estimated at 258m. Comoros francs (equivalent to 0.3% of GDP). The Comoros' external public debt at the end of 1998 totalled US $203.1m., of which $188.1m. was long-term public debt. In that year the cost of debt-servicing was equivalent to 13.4% of the value of exports of goods and services. The annual rate of inflation averaged 4.6% during 1990–98. The rate rose to 25.3% in 1994, following the 33.3% devaluation of the Comoros franc in January 1994, but slowed thereafter, reaching 0.8% in 1999. An estimated 20% of the labour force were unemployed in 1996.

In 1985 the Comoros joined the Indian Ocean Commission (IOC, see p. 308). The country is also a member of the Common Market for Eastern and Southern Africa (COMESA, see p. 148) and of the Franc Zone (see p. 210).

The Comoros has a relatively undeveloped economy, with high unemployment, a limited transport system, a severe shortage of natural resources and heavy dependence on foreign aid, particularly from France. In 1994 the devaluation of the Comoros franc by 33.3% in relation to the French franc resulted in a dramatic increase in the price of imported goods. In February 1997 the Government agreed a six-month surveillance programme with the IMF and the World Bank, however, following a six-month extension of the programme, the IMF concluded that insufficient progress had been achieved. Furthermore, mounting arrears on loan repayments led the World Bank to suspend the disbursement of funds to the Comoros in August 1998. The European Union (EU) suspended all aid to the islands in early 1999. An intensification of political instability on the islands, following the seizure of power by the army in April 1999, had a particularly adverse effect on maritime trade and tourism. In January 2000, following the required repayment of arrears by the Comoran authorities, the World Bank resumed the disbursement of funds to the Comoros. Moreover, measures aimed at reducing the Comoros' state deficit were proposed, in March, by a joint delegation of the World Bank and the IMF; suggested measures included cuts in government spending and the possibility of a reduction of, or moratorium on, the Comoran foreign debt. Also in 2000 customs duties were reduced by 80% on products from member countries of the IOC, as part of efforts to comply with an integrated regional programme for trade development. Concerns were expressed that this could lead to a significant shortfall in customs revenue, which usually represents up to three-quarters of the state budget. In March the OAU suspended telephone communications and restricted petroleum deliveries to Nzwani; serious fuel shortages ensued, and petroleum prices increased significantly. However, in September the Comoros Government lifted sanctions on Nzwani (despite opposition from the OAU). Budgetary estimates for 2000 envisaged receipts totalling 14,141 Comoros francs and expenditure of 16,258 Comoros francs. Following the conclusion of an agreement on national reconciliation in February 2001 (see above) and the subsequent suspension of all OAU sanctions against Nzwani, it was hoped that international aid to the Comoros would be forthcoming.

Social Welfare

In 1978 the Government administered six hospital establishments, with a total of 698 beds, and in 1984 there were 31 physicians working in the country. In 1989 it was estimated that there was one hospital bed per 342 inhabitants, and in 1997, according to estimates by the World Health Organization, there were 7.4 physicians per 100,000 inhabitants in the country and 34.1 nurses per 100,000 inhabitants.

Education

Education is officially compulsory for nine years between seven and 16 years of age. Primary education begins at the age of six and lasts for six years. Secondary education, beginning at 13 years of age, lasts for seven years, comprising a first cycle of four years and a second of three years. Enrolment at primary schools in 1995 was equivalent to 75% of children in the relevant age-group. Children may also receive a basic education through traditional Koranic schools, which are staffed by Comoran teachers. Enrolment at secondary schools in 1995 was equivalent to 21% of children in the relevant age-group (males 24%; females 19%). Current expenditure by the Ministry of Education in 1995 was 3,381m. Comoros francs, representing 21.1% of total current government expenditure. In 1995, according to estimates by UNESCO, the average rate of adult illiteracy was 45.0% (males 37.5%; females 52.4%).

Public Holidays

2001: 6 March* (Id al-Adha, Feast of the Sacrifice), 26 March* (Muharram, Islamic New Year), 4 April* (Ashoura), 4 June* (Mouloud, Birth of the Prophet), 6 July (Independence Day), 15 October* (Leilat al-Meiraj, Ascension of the Prophet), 27 November (Anniversary of President Abdallah's assassination), 17 November* (Ramadan begins), 17 December* (Id al-Fitr, end of Ramadan).

2002: 23 February* (Id al-Adha, Feast of the Sacrifice), 15 March* (Muharram, Islamic New Year), 24 March* (Ashoura), 24 May* (Mouloud, Birth of the Prophet), 6 July (Independence Day), 4 October* (Leilat al-Meiraj, Ascension of the Prophet), 6 November* (Ramadan begins), 27 November (Anniversary of President Abdallah's assassination), 6 December* (Id al-Fitr, end of Ramadan).

* Religious holidays, which are dependent on the Islamic lunar calendar, may differ by one or two days from the dates given.

Weights and Measures

The metric system is in force.

Statistical Survey

Source (unless otherwise stated): Ministry of Finance, the Budget and Privatization, BP 324, Moroni; tel. (74) 4145; fax (74) 4140.
Note: Unless otherwise indicated, figures in this Statistical Survey exclude data for Mayotte.

AREA AND POPULATION

Area: 1,862 sq km (719 sq miles). *By island:* Ngazidja (Grande-Comore) 1,146 sq km, Nzwani (Anjouan) 424 sq km, Mwali (Mohéli) 290 sq km.

Population: 335,150 (males 167,089; females 168,061), excluding Mayotte (estimated population 50,740), at census of 15 September 1980; 446,817 (males 221,152; females 225,665), excluding Mayotte, at census of 15 September 1991; 527,900 in 1998. *By island* (1991 census): Ngazidja (Grande-Comore) 233,533, Nzwani (Anjouan) 188,953, Mwali (Mohéli) 24,331.

Density (per sq km, 1998): 283.5.

Principal Towns (population at 1980 census): Moroni (capital) 17,267; Mutsamudu 13,000; Fomboni 5,400.

Births and Deaths (including figures for Mayotte, UN estimates): Average annual birth rate 48.5 per 1,000 in 1980–85, 42.4 per 1,000 in 1985–90, 38.2 per 1,000 in 1990–95; average annual death rate 13.8 per 1,000 in 1980–85, 11.9 per 1,000 in 1985–90, 10.2 per 1,000 in 1990–95. Source: UN, *World Population Prospects: The 1998 Revision.*

Expectation of Life (UN estimates, years at birth, including Mayotte, 1990–95): 57.2 (males 55.4; females 59.2). Source: UN, *World Population Prospects: The 1998 Revision.*

Economically Active Population (ILO estimates, '000 persons at mid-1980, including figures for Mayotte): Agriculture, forestry and fishing 150; Industry 10; Services 20; Total 181 (males 104, females 77). Source: ILO, *Economically Active Population Estimates and Projections, 1950–2025.*

1991 census (persons aged 12 years and over, excluding Mayotte): Total labour force 126,510 (males 88,034; females 38,476). Source: UN, *Demographic Yearbook.*

AGRICULTURE, ETC.

Principal Crops (estimates, '000 metric tons, unless otherwise indicated, 1999): Rice (paddy) 3.0; Maize 4.0; Potatoes 1.3; Cassava (Manioc) 51.9; Taro 9.0; Other tubers 6.1; Pulses 0.8; Groundnuts 0.2; Coconuts (million) 75; Tomatoes 0.6; Other vegetables 5.6; Bananas 59.0; Other fruits 3.3; Vanilla (dried, metric tons) 140; Clove buds (metric tons) 2,500; Ylang-ylang essence (metric tons) 50. Source: Banque Centrale des Comores, *Rapport Annuel.*

Livestock (FAO estimates, '000 head, year ending September 1999): Asses 5, Cattle 50, Sheep 20, Goats 140. Source: FAO.

Livestock Products (estimates, metric tons, unless otherwise indicated, 1999): Beef and veal 971; Mutton, lamb and goat meat 175; Poultry meat 215; Milk ('000 litres) 1,977; Eggs ('000) 5,601. Source: Banque Centrale des Comores, *Rapport Annuel.*

Fishing (FAO estimates, '000 metric tons, live weight, 1998): Total catch 12.5 (Carangids 0.5, Sardinellas 1.0, Anchovies, etc. 0.9, Skipjack tuna 2.1, Yellowfin tuna 5.3, Other tuna-like fishes 1.3). Source: FAO, *Yearbook of Fishery Statistics.*

1999 ('000 metric tons): Total catch 12.0. Source: Banque Centrale des Comores, *Rapport Annuel.*

INDUSTRY

Electric Energy (million kWh): 12.3 in 1997; 28.5 in 1998; 34.4 in 1999. Source: Banque Centrale des Comores, *Rapport Annuel.*

FINANCE

Currency and Exchange Rates: 100 centimes = 1 Comoros franc. *Sterling, Dollar and Euro Equivalents* (29 December 2000): £1 sterling = 788.95 Comoros francs; US $1 = 528.71 Comoros francs; €1 = 491.97 Comoros francs; 1,000 Comoros francs = £1.268 = $1.891 = €2.033. *Average Exchange Rate* (Comoros francs per US $): 442.46 in 1998; 461.77 in 1999; 533.98 in 2000. Note: The Comoros franc was introduced in 1981, replacing (at par) the CFA franc. The fixed link to French currency was retained, with the exchange rate set at 1 French franc = 50 Comoros francs. This remained in effect until January 1994, when the Comoros franc was devalued by 33.3%, with the exchange rate adjusted to 1 French franc = 75 Comoros francs. This relationship to French currency remained in effect with the introduction of the euro on 1 January 1999. From that date, accordingly, a fixed exchange rate of €1 = 491.968 Comoros francs has been in operation.

Budget (provisional, million Comoros francs, 1999): *Revenue:* Tax revenue 10,741; Other revenue 813; Total 11,554, excluding grants received (6,806). *Expenditure:* Budgetary current expenditure 11,223 (Wages and salaries 6,307; Goods and services 3,486; Transfers 522; Interest payments 908); Current expenditure under technical assistance programmes 1,083; Other current expenditure 265; Budgetary capital expenditure 192; Capital expenditure financed with external resources 5,339; Total 18,102. Source: Banque Centrale des Comores, *Rapport Annuel.*

International Reserves (US $ million at 31 December 1999): Gold n.a.; IMF special drawing rights 0.16; Reserve position in IMF 0.74; Foreign exchange 36.24; Total (excl. gold) 37.15. Source: IMF, *International Financial Statistics.*

Money Supply (million Comoros francs at 31 December 1999): Currency outside deposit money banks 6,310; Demand deposits at deposit money banks 4,386; Total money (incl. others) 11,662. Source: IMF, *International Financial Statistics.*

Cost of Living (Consumer Price Index; base: 1993 = 100): All items 137 in 1997; 139 in 1998; 140 in 1999. Source: Banque Centrale des Comores, *Rapport Annuel.*

Expenditure on the Gross Domestic Product (million Comoros francs at current prices, 1999, estimates): Government final consumption expenditure 11,072; Private final consumption expenditure 77,759; Increase in stocks 700; Gross fixed capital formation 12,426; *Total domestic expenditure* 101,957; Exports of goods and services 23,226; *Less* Imports of goods and services 36,178; *GDP in purchasers' values* 89,005. Source: IMF, *Comoros: Statistical Annex* (August 2000).

Gross Domestic Product by Economic Activity (million Comoros francs at current prices, 1999, estimates): Agriculture, hunting, forestry and fishing 35,557; Manufacturing 3,311; Electricity, gas and water 1,333; Construction 5,264; Trade, restaurants and hotels 22,119; Transport and communications 4,505; Finance, insurance, real estate and business services 4,378; Government services 12,111; Other services 428; *GDP in purchasers' values* 89,005. Source: IMF, *Comoros: Statistical Annex* (August 2000).

Balance of Payments (US $ million, 1999, estimates): Exports of goods f.o.b. 8.1; Imports of goods f.o.b. –43.4; *Trade balance* –35.3; Services (net) 7.3; *Balance on goods and services* –27.9; Other income (net) –0.1; *Balance on goods, services and income* –28.0; Private transfers (net) 12.8; Official transfers (net) 15.3; *Current balance* 0.1; Direct investment from abroad (net) 0.3; Other long-term capital (net) –6.1; Short-term capital (incl. net errors and omissions) –0.2; *Overall balance* –5.9. Source: IMF, *Comoros: Statistical Annex* (August 2000).

EXTERNAL TRADE

Principal Commodities (million Comoros francs, 1999, estimates): *Imports c.i.f.:* Rice 4,721; Meat and fish 1,528; Flour 641; Sugar 808; Dairy products 551; Petroleum products 3,374; Cement 1,370; Vehicles 3,333; Iron and steel 708; Total (incl. others) 24,929. *Exports f.o.b.:* Vanilla 1,835; Cloves 1,177; Ylang-ylang 563; Total (incl. others) 4,248. Source: Banque Centrale des Comores, *Rapport Annuel.*

Principal Trading Partners (US $'000, 1995): *Imports:* France 20,040; India 10,834; Saudi Arabia 5,887; Total (incl. others) 62,625. *Exports:* France 4,150; Germany 913; USA 3,222; Total (incl. others) 11,361. Source: UN, *International Trade Statistics Yearbook.*

1999 (percentage of trade): *Imports:* France 32%; South Africa 8%; Réunion 8%; Kenya 6%; United Arab Emirates 6%. *Exports:* USA 26.8%; France 25.4%; Germany 12.2%; Singapore 8.6%.

TRANSPORT

Road Traffic (estimates, motor vehicles in use, 1996): Passenger cars 9,100; Lorries and vans 4,950. Source: International Road Federation, *World Road Statistics.*

International Shipping (estimated sea-borne freight traffic, '000 metric tons, 1991): Goods loaded 12; Goods unloaded 107. Source: UN Economic Commission for Africa, *African Statistical Yearbook.*

Civil Aviation (traffic on scheduled services, 1996): Passengers carried ('000) 27; Passenger-km (million) 3. Source: UN, *Statistical Yearbook.*

TOURISM

Tourist Arrivals: 26,219 in 1997; 28,840 in 1998; 24,479 in 1999. Source: Banque Centrale des Comores, *Rapport Annuel.*

Tourist Arrivals by Country (1997): France 7,870, Germany 729, Madagascar 877, Réunion 1,728, South Africa 9,452, United Kingdom 1,016; Total (incl. others) 26,219.

Receipts from Tourism (US $ million): 21 in 1995; 23 in 1996; 26 in 1997. Source: World Tourism Organization, *Yearbook of Tourism Statistics*.

COMMUNICATIONS MEDIA

Radio Receivers (1997): 90,000 in use. Source: UNESCO, *Statistical Yearbook*.

Television Receivers (1997): 1,000 in use. Source: UNESCO, *Statistical Yearbook*.

Telephones (1998): 6,226 main lines in use. Source: Banque Centrale des Comores, *Rapport Annuel*.

Telefax Stations (1993): 98 in use. Source: UN, *Statistical Yearbook*.

EDUCATION

Pre-primary (1980/81): 600 teachers; 17,778 pupils.

Primary (1995/96): 327 schools; 1,508 teachers (public education only); 78,527 pupils.

Secondary: Teachers: general education 591 (1995/96, public education only); teacher training 11 (1991/92); vocational 31 (1986/87). Pupils: general education 21,192 (1995/96); teacher training 37 (1993/94); vocational 126 (1993/94).

Higher: 32 teachers (1989/90); 348 pupils (1995/96).

Source: UNESCO, *Statistical Yearbook*.

Directory

The Constitution

On 6 May 1999, following the coup of 30 April, Col Assoumani Azali promulgated a new constitutional charter, pending the introduction of new constitutional arrangements which were to take effect within one year. According to the charter, Col Azali is the Head of State and leader of a State Committee and the Armed Forces, and holds full legislative and executive power. Under the terms of an agreement on national reconciliation, which was signed on 17 February 2001 by representatives of the Government, the separatist administration on Nzwani, opposition parties and civil society, a new constitution was to be drafted and approved by June 2001. Prior to their revocation, the following constitutional provisions had been in effect since their approval by referendum on 20 October 1996.

PREAMBLE

The preamble affirms the will of the Comoran people to derive from the state religion, Islam, inspiration for the principles and laws that the State and its institutions govern, to adhere to the principles laid down by the Charters of the UN, the Organization of African Unity and the Organization of the Islamic Conference and by the Treaty of the League of Arab States, and to guarantee the rights of all citizens, without discrimination, in accordance with the UN Declaration of Human Rights and the African Charter of Human Rights.

GENERAL PROVISIONS

The Comoros archipelago constitutes a federal Islamic republic. Sovereignty belongs to the people, and is exercised through their elected representatives or by the process of referendum. There is universal secret suffrage, which can be direct or indirect, for all citizens who are over the age of 18 and in full possession of their civil and political rights. Political parties and groups operate freely, respecting national sovereignty, democracy and territorial integrity. However, political parties which are not represented by at least two deputies from each island, as a result of the first legislative election to follow the adoption of the Constitution, will be dissolved, unless those parties merge with others which are legitimately represented in the Federal Assembly. If only one political party has representation in the Federal Assembly, the party which has obtained the second highest number of votes will continue to operate freely. Only political parties and groups active throughout the Republic may participate in national elections. Political parties must be democratic both in their internal structure and their activities.

PRESIDENT OF THE REPUBLIC

The President is the Head of State and is elected by direct universal suffrage for a six-year term, which is renewable for an unrestricted number of mandates. He is also Head of the Armed Forces and ensures the legitimate functioning of public powers and the continuation of the State. He is the guarantor of national independence, the unity of the Republic, the autonomy of the islands, territorial integrity and adherence to international agreements. Candidates for the presidency must be aged between 40 and 75 years, of Comoran nationality by birth, and resident in the archipelago for at least 12 consecutive months prior to elections. The President presides over the Council of Ministers. He is empowered to ask the Federal Assembly to reconsider a Bill. The President can, having consulted with the Prime Minister and the Presidents of the Federal Assembly and the High Council of the Republic in writing, dissolve the Federal Assembly. The President determines and implements the Republic's foreign policy.

THE GOVERNMENT

The President appoints the Prime Minister, and on his recommendations, the other members of the Government. Under the authority of the President of the Republic, the Council of Ministers determines and implements domestic policy.

LEGISLATIVE POWER

Legislative power is vested in the Federal Assembly, which represents the Comoran nation. Deputies in the Federal Assembly are elected for five years by direct suffrage. Legislative elections take place between 30 and 90 days after the expiry of the mandate of the incumbent Federal Assembly. The electoral law dictates the number of members of the Federal Assembly, but there is a minimum of five deputies from each island. The deputies elect the President of the Federal Assembly at the beginning of their mandate. The Federal Assembly sits for two sessions each year and, if necessary, for extraordinary sessions. Matters covered by federal legislation include constitutional institutions, defence, posts and telecommunications, transport, civil and penal law, public finance, external trade, federal taxation, long-term economic planning, education and health.

JUDICIAL POWER

Judicial power is independent of executive and legislative power. The President is the guarantor of the independence of the judicial system and chairs the Higher Council of the Magistracy (Conseil Supérieur de la Magistrature), of which the Minister of Justice is Vice-President.

HIGH COUNCIL OF THE REPUBLIC

The High Council of the Republic considers constitutional matters and the control of public finance, and acts as a High Court of Justice. It has a renewable mandate of seven years and is composed of four members appointed by the President, three members elected by the Federal Assembly and one member elected by the Council of each island. The High Council oversees and proclaims the results of presidential and legislative elections and referendums.

COUNCIL OF THE ULÉMAS

The Council of the Ulémas offers opinions on projects for laws, ordinances and decrees. The President of the Republic, the Prime Minister, the President of the Federal Assembly, the Presidents of the Councils and the Governors of the islands may consult the Council of the Ulémas on any religious issue. The Council of the Ulémas may submit recommendations to the Federal Assembly, the Government or the Governors of the islands if it considers legislation to be in contravention of the principles of Islam.

ISLAND INSTITUTIONS

While respecting the unity of the Republic, each island is an autonomous territorial entity which freely controls its own administration through a Governor and a Council. The Governor of each island is appointed by the President of the Republic, from three candidates proposed by the Council of the island. The Council of each island is composed of the mayors of the communes and sits for not more than 15 days at a time, in March and December, and, if necessary, for extraordinary sessions. The Council is responsible for such matters as the budget of the island, taxes, culture, health, primary education and the environment.

REVISION OF THE CONSTITUTION

The power to initiate constitutional revision is vested in the President of the Republic. However, one-third of the members of the Federal Assembly may propose amendments to the President. Constitutional revision must be approved by a majority of two-thirds of the deputies in the Federal Assembly, and is subject to approval by national referendum. However, the President of the Republic may decide to promulgate a constitutional project, without submitting it to a referendum, if it has been adopted at a congress of deputies and the councillors of the islands, by a majority of two-thirds. The Republican and Islamic nature of the State cannot be revised.

The Government

HEAD OF STATE

Head of State and Minister of Defence: Col Assoumani Azali (assumed power 30 April 1999, inaugurated 6 May 1999).

STATE COMMITTEE
(April 2001)

Head of State and Minister of Defence: Col Assoumani Azali.

Prime Minister: Hamada Madi 'Boléro'.

Minister of Foreign Affairs and Co-operation: Mohamed El-Amine Souef.

Minister of Finance, the Budget and Privatization: Assoumani Aboudou.

Minister of Production and the Environment: Boina Ali Saïd Ali.

Minister of Justice and Islamic Affairs: Yahaya Mohamed Iliasse.

Minister of Transport, Tourism and Posts and Telecommunications: Mohamed Ali Athoumani.

Minister of Facilities, Energy and Town Planning: ABDALLAH CHARIF.

Minister of Culture, Youth and Sports: MADI AHAMADA.

Minister of National Education, Professional and Vocational Training, and Human Rights: SAÏD ABDALLAH CHEIKH SOILIHI.

Minister of the Interior and Decentralization: AHMED ALI DJALIM.

Minister of Public Health, Population and the Status of Women: ATTOUMANE JAFFAR ABBAS.

Minister of the Economy, Trade, Crafts, and Investments: BACAR HARITHI.

Minister of the Civil Service, Employment and Labour: MMADI DJAFFAR.

Minister-delegate to the Prime Minister, with responsibility for Communication and National Reconciliation: MOHAMED ABDOU SOIMADOU.

MINISTRIES

Office of the Head of State: BP 521, Moroni; tel. (74) 4814; fax (74) 4829, internet www.presidence-rfic.com.

Office of the Prime Minister: Moroni; tel. 74-44-00; fax 74-44-32; internet www.primature-rficomores.com.

Ministry of the Civil Service, Employment and Labour: Moroni; tel. (74) 4277.

Ministry of Culture, Youth and Sports: BP 421, Moroni.

Ministry of Defence: Moroni; tel. (74) 4862.

Ministry of the Economy, Trade, Crafts and Investments: Moroni; tel. (74) 4235.

Ministry of Facilities, Energy and Town Planning: Moroni.

Ministry of Finance, the Budget and Privatization: BP 324, Moroni; tel. (74) 4145; fax (74) 4140.

Ministry of Foreign Affairs and Co-operation: BP 482, Moroni; tel. (74) 4100; fax (74) 4111.

Ministry of the Interior and Decentralization: BP 520, Moroni; tel. (74) 4666.

Ministry of Justice and Islamic Affairs: Moroni; tel. (74) 4200.

Ministry of National Education, Professional and Vocational Training, and Human Rights: BP 421, Moroni; tel. (74) 4185; fax (74) 4180.

Ministry of Production and the Environment: Moroni.

Ministry of Public Health, Population and the Status of Women: Moroni.

Ministry of Transport, Tourism, and Posts and Telecommunications: Moroni; tel. (73) 2098.

President and Legislature

PRESIDENT

In the first round of voting, which took place on 6 March 1996, none of the 15 candidates received 50% of the total votes cast. A second round of voting took place on 16 March, when voters chose between the two leading candidates. MOHAMED TAKI ABDOULKARIM received 64.3% of the votes, while ABBAS DJOUSSOUF obtained 35.7%. Following the death of MOHAMED TAKI ABDOULKARIM on 6 November 1998, TADJIDINE BEN SAÏD MASSOUNDI was designated acting President, pending the holding of an election. Col ASSOUMANI AZALI was sworn in as Head of State on 6 May 1999, having seized power in a military coup on 30 April.

ASSEMBLÉE FÉDÉRALE

Following the coup of 30 April 1999, the Federal Assembly (Assemblée Fédérale) was dissolved.

Political Organizations

Chawiri: Leader MAHAMOUD MRADABI.

CHUMA (Islands' Fraternity and Unity Party): Moroni; Leader ASSOUMANI ABDOU.

Comité de suivi et d'orientation pour l'autonomie de Mohéli.

Congazi (Co-ordination for Ngazidja Party): Moroni; Leader SAÏD HABIB.

Forces pour l'action républicaine (FAR): Leader Col ABDOURAZAK ABDULHAMID.

Forum pour le redressement national (FRN): f. 1994; alliance of 12 parties.

Front démocratique (FD): BP 758, Moroni; tel. (73) 3603; e-mail idriss@snpt.km; f. 1982; Leader MOUSTOIFA SAÏD CHEIKH.

Front national pour la justice (FNJ): Islamic fundamentalist orientation; Leader AHMED RACHID.

Front populaire comorien (FPC): Mwali; Leader MOHAMED HASSANALY.

Groupe d'initiative pour le redressement du mouvement anjouanais (GIRMA): f. 1999; separatist group on Nzwani (Anjouan); Leader AHMED CHARIKAN.

Mkoutrouo: principal separatist group on Mwali (Mohéli); Leader SAÏD MOHAMED SOUEF.

Mouvement des citoyens pour la République (MCR): f. 1998; Leader MAHAMOUD MRADABI.

Mouvement mohélien pour l'égalité des îles: f.1995.

Mouvement populaire anjouanais (MPA): f. 1997 by merger of Organisation pour l'indépendance d'Anjouan and Mouvement séparatiste anjouanais; principal separatist movement on Nzwani (Anjouan).

Mouvement pour la démocratie et le progrès (MDP-NGDC): Moroni; founder-mem. of the FRN (see above), from which it withdrew in May 1999; leader ABBAS DJOUSSOUF.

Mouvement pour la rénovation et l'action démocratique (MOURAD): Moroni; f. 1990; aims to promote economic and financial rehabilitation; Leader ABDOY ISSA.

Mouvement pour le socialisme et la démocratie (MSD): Moroni; f. 2000 by splinter group of the FD; Leader ABDOU SOEFOU.

Nguzo: Moroni; Leader TAKI MBOREHA.

Parti comorien pour la démocratie et le progrès (PCDP): Route Djivani, BP 179, Moroni; tel. (73) 1733; fax (73) 0650; Leader ALI MROUDJAE.

Parti républicain des Comores: f. 1998; Leader MOHAMED M'CHANGAMA.

Parti socialiste des Comores (PASOCO): POB 720, Moroni; tel. (73) 1328; Leader ALI IDAROUSSE.

Parti du salut national (PSN): f. 1993; breakaway faction of PCDP; Islamic orientation; Leader SAÏD ALI MOHAMED.

Rassemblement national pour le développement (RND): f. 1996; Chair. OMAR TAMOU; Sec. Gen. ABDOULHAMID AFFRAITANE.

Diplomatic Representation

EMBASSIES IN THE COMOROS

China, People's Republic: BP 442, Moroni; tel. (73) 2721; fax (73) 2866; Ambassador: XU DAIJIE.

France: blvd de Strasbourg, BP 465, Moroni; tel. (73) 0753; fax (73) 1727; Ambassador: JEAN PIERRE LAJAUNIE.

Korea, Democratic People's Republic: Moroni; Ambassador: KIM RYONG YONG.

Libya: BP 1787, Moroni; tel. (73) 2819.

Mauritius: Moroni.

Seychelles: Moroni.

Judicial System

Under the terms of the Constitution of October 1996, the President is the guarantor of the independence of the judicial system, and chairs the Higher Council of the Magistracy (Conseil Supérieur de la Magistrature), of which the Minister of Justice is Vice-President. The High Council of the Republic, which comprises four members appointed by the President, three members elected by the Federal Assembly and one member elected by the Council of each island, acts as a High Court of Justice. The judicial system was to be reorganized under new constitutional arrangements under consideration in mid-1999.

Religion

The majority of the population are Muslims. At 31 December 1998 there were an estimated 2,000 adherents of the Roman Catholic Church, equivalent to 0.3% of the total population.

CHRISTIANITY

The Roman Catholic Church

Office of Apostolic Administrator of the Comoros: Mission Catholique, BP 46, Moroni; tel. (73) 0570; fax (73) 0503; Apostolic Pro-Admin. Fr JAN SZPILKA.

The Press

Al Watwan: Nagoudjou, BP 984, Moroni-Coulée; tel. and fax (74) 4047; e-mail alwatwan@snpt.km; internet www.comoros

-online.com/al-watwan; f. 1985; weekly; state-owned; Dir-Gen. AMAD MDAHOMA; Editor-in-Chief AHMED ALIAMIR; circ. 1,500.

L'Archipel: BP 1327, Moroni; f. 1988; monthly; independent; Publrs ABOUBACAR MCHANGAMA, SAINDOU KAMAL; circ. 300.

La Gazette des Comores: BP 2216, Moroni; tel. (73) 5234; e-mail la_gazette@snpt.km; weekly.

NEWS AGENCIES

Agence Comores Presse (ACP): Moroni.

Foreign Bureau

Agence France-Presse (AFP): BP 1327, Moroni. ABOUBACAR MICH-ANGAMA.

Broadcasting and Communications

TELECOMMUNICATIONS

Société Nationale des Postes et des Télécommunications: BP 5000, Moroni; tel. (73) 0610; fax (73) 1079; e-mail snpt@snpt.km; internet www.snpt.km; operates post and telecommunications services; Dir-Gen. SAÏD ABASSE DAHLANI.

RADIO

Transmissions to the Comoros from Radio France Internationale commenced in early 1994. By 1998 a number of privately-owned radio stations were broadcasting in the Comoros.

Radio-Comoro: BP 452, Moroni; tel. (73) 2531; fax (73) 0303; govt-controlled; domestic programmes in Comoran and French; international broadcasts in Swahili, Arabic and French; Dir-Gen. ISMAIL IBOUROI; Tech. Dir ABDULLAH RADJAB.

Finance

BANKING

(cap. = capital; res = reserves; dep. = deposits; m. = million; brs = branches; amounts in Comoros francs)

Central Bank

Banque Centrale des Comores: place de France, BP 405, Moroni; tel. (73) 1814; fax (73) 0349; e-mail bcc@snpt.km; f. 1981; bank of issue; cap. 1,100m., res 7,260m., dep. 5,640m. (Dec. 1999); Pres. SALIM AHMED ABDALLAH; Gov. SAÏD AHMED SAÏD ALI.

Commercial Bank

Banque pour l'Industrie et le Commerce—Comores (BIC): place de France, BP 175, Moroni; tel. (73) 0243; fax (73) 1229; e-mail bic@snpt.km; f. 1990; 51% owned by Banque Nationale de Paris Intercontinentale; 34% state-owned; total assets 22,364m. (Dec. 1999); Pres. MRADABI MAHAMOUD; Dir-Gen. GUY CAZENAVE; 6 brs.

Development Bank

Banque de Développement des Comores: place de France, BP 298, Moroni; tel. (73) 0818; fax (73) 0397; e-mail bdcmoroni@snpt.km; f. 1982; provides loans, guarantees and equity participation for small- and medium-scale projects; 50% state-owned; cap. and res 1,165.6m., total assets 3,206.4m. (Dec. 1999); Pres. MZE CHEI OUBEIDI; Gen. Man. SAÏD ABDILLAHI.

Trade and Industry

GOVERNMENT AGENCIES

Office National du Commerce: Moroni; state-operated agency for the promotion and development of domestic and external trade.

Société de Développement de la Pêche Artisanale des Comores (SODEPAC): Moroni; state-operated agency overseeing fisheries development programme.

DEVELOPMENT ORGANIZATIONS

CEFADER: a rural design, co-ordination and support centre, with brs on each island.

Mission de Coopération et d'Action Culturelle: BP 85, Moroni; tel. (73) 0391; fax (73) 1274; f. 1978; centre for administering bilateral aid from France; Dir JEAN-FRANCIS GOSPODAROWICZ.

CHAMBER OF COMMERCE

Chambre de Commerce, d'Industrie et d'Agriculture: BP 763, Moroni; privatized in 1995.

EMPLOYERS' ORGANIZATION

Club d'Actions des Promoteurs Economiques: Moroni; f. 1999; Head SAID HASSANE DINI.

UTILITIES

Comorienne de l'Eau et de l'Electricité (CEE): BP 1762, Moroni; tel. (73) 3130; fax (73) 2359; e-mail cee@snpt.km; fmrly Electricité et Eau des Comores; state-controlled enterprise responsible for the production and distribution of electricity and water; transferred to private management in 1997; Dir-Gen. PAUL-EMILE ROBLEL.

TRADE UNION

Union des Syndicats Autonomes des Travailleurs des Comores: BP 1199, Moroni; tel. and fax (73) 5143; f. 1996; Sec.-Gen. IBOUROI ALI TABIBOU.

Transport

ROADS

In 1996 there were an estimated 900 km of classified roads, of which 440 km were principal roads and 230 km secondary roads. About 76.5% of the network was paved in 1995.

SHIPPING

The port of Mutsamudu, on Ngazidja, can accommodate vessels of up to 11 m draught. Goods from Europe are routed via Madagascar, and coastal vessels connect the Comoros with the east coast of Africa. The development of the port of Moroni, with support from the European Community (EC, now European Union), was completed in mid-1991. In 1993 the EC pledged US $4m. to finance the construction of a port at Fomboni, on Mwali, to improve shipping access to the island.

Société Comorienne de Navigation: Moroni; services to Madagascar.

CIVIL AVIATION

The international airport is at Moroni-Hahaya on Ngazidja. Each of the three other islands has a small airfield. At the end of 1995 it was announced that Air Comores, the national airline, was to be liquidated. In October 1999 Yemen Airways (Yemenia), following negotiations with the Comoran Government, was granted the status of the national airline of the Comoros and the use of the Comoran air traffic rights between Moroni and Paris, France. In September 2000 it was announced that an agreement had been signed with Air Gulf Falcon (based in the United Arab Emirates) to create a new Comoran airline, Comores Air International (CAI), which would service the Moroni–Paris route.

Comores Aviation: Moroni; f. 1999; twice-weekly charter flights between Moroni and Mayotte; Dir JEAN MARC HEINTZ.

Tourism

The principal tourist attractions are the beaches, underwater fishing and mountain scenery. In 1991 hotel capacity increased from 112 to 294 rooms, following the implementation of a number of hotel development projects. In 1997 receipts from tourism totalled US $26m.; tourist arrivals increased to 28,840 in 1998, but decreased to 24,479 in 1999, mainly as a result of the unstable political situation.

Société Comorienne de Tourisme et d'Hôtellerie (COM-OTEL): Itsandra Hotel, BP 1027, Moroni; tel. (73) 2365; national tourist agency: Dir-Gen. SITTI ATTOMANE.

THE DEMOCRATIC REPUBLIC OF THE CONGO

Introductory Survey

Location, Climate, Language, Religion, Flag, Capital

The Democratic Republic of the Congo (formerly Zaire) lies in central Africa, bordered by the Republic of the Congo to the north-west, by the Central African Republic and Sudan to the north, by Uganda, Rwanda, Burundi and Tanzania to the east and by Zambia and Angola to the south. There is a short coastline at the outlet of the River Congo. The climate is tropical, with an average temperature of 27°C (80°F) and an annual rainfall of 150cm–200cm (59ins–97ins). French is the official language. More than 400 Sudanese and Bantu dialects are spoken; Kiswahili, Kiluba, Kikongo and Lingala being the most widespread. An estimated 50% of the population is Roman Catholic, and there is a smaller Protestant community. Many inhabitants follow traditional (mostly animist) beliefs. The national flag (proportions 3 by 2) is blue with a large central yellow star and six smaller yellow stars arranged vertically at the hoist. The capital is Kinshasa.

Recent History

The Democratic Republic of the Congo, formerly the Belgian Congo, became independent from Belgium as the Republic of the Congo on 30 June 1960. Five days later the armed forces mutinied, and the UN subsequently dispatched troops to the region to maintain order. In September the Head of State, Joseph Kasavubu, dismissed the Prime Minister, Patrice Lumumba. Later in that month government was assumed temporarily by Col (subsequently Marshal) Joseph-Désiré Mobutu. Mobutu returned power to President Kasavubu in February 1961. In August a new Government was formed, with Cyrille Adoula as Prime Minister. In July 1964 Kasavubu appointed Moïse Tshombe, the former leader of a group supporting the secession of the Katangan region, as interim Prime Minister, pending elections, and in August the country was renamed Democratic Republic of the Congo. Following elections in March and April 1965, a power struggle developed between Tshombe and Kasavubu; in November Mobutu intervened, seizing power and proclaiming himself head of the 'Second Republic'. In late 1970 Mobutu, as sole candidate, was elected President. (From January 1972, as part of a national policy of 'authenticity', he became known as Mobutu Sese Seko.) In November 1970 elections took place to a new National Assembly (subsequently renamed the National Legislative Council, NLC). In October 1971 the Democratic Republic of the Congo was redesignated the Republic of Zaire, and a year later the Government of Zaire and the Executive Committee of the Mouvement populaire de la révolution (MPR), the sole legal political party, merged into the National Executive Council (NEC).

In March 1977 and May 1978 Katangan separatists invaded Zaire from Angola, taking much of Shaba (formerly Katanga) region; however, the separatists were repulsed on both occasions by the Zairean army, with armed support from a number of Western Governments. The invasion of 1977 prompted Mobutu to introduce a number of political reforms, including the introduction of a new electoral code. Legislative elections took place in October and, at a presidential election held in December, Mobutu (again the sole candidate) was re-elected for a further seven-year term. In August 1980 Mobutu assumed the new post of Chairman of the MPR, thus consolidating his control of power. In early 1982 opponents of Zaire's one-party system of government formed the Union pour la démocratie et le progrès social (UDPS). This was followed by the formation, later in that year, of the Front congolais pour le rétablissement de la démocratie (FCD), a coalition of opposition parties, for which Nguza Karl-I-Bond, the First State Commissioner (Prime Minister) from August 1980 until April 1981, was the spokesman. Léon Kengo Wa Dondo was appointed First State Commissioner in a ministerial reshuffle in November 1982. Mobutu was re-elected President in July 1984. Elections to the NLC were held in September 1987. In November 1988 Mobutu replaced about one-third of the members of the NEC and reappointed Kengo

Wa Dondo to the post of First State Commissioner, from which he had been removed in October 1986.

The organization of opposition demonstrations (violently suppressed by the security forces) during 1989 and early 1990, prompted Mobutu's announcement, in April 1990, that a plural political system, initially to comprise three parties, would be introduced after a transitional period of one year; the UDPS was immediately legalized. At the same time Mobutu declared the inauguration of the 'Third Republic' and relinquished the posts of Chairman of the MPR and State Commissioner for National Defence in the NEC, although remaining Head of State. N'Singa Udjuu Ongwakebi Untube, who had been First State Commissioner in 1981–82, was subsequently appointed the new Chairman of the MPR. The NEC was dissolved and Kengo Wa Dondo was replaced as First State Commissioner by Prof. Lunda Bululu, a distinguished international civil servant. In May 1990 a new, smaller, transitional NEC was formed, and Mobutu announced the imminent 'depoliticization' of the security forces and of the administration in general. In June Mobutu relinquished presidential control over the NEC and over foreign policy, and authorized the formation of independent trade unions. In October it was announced that a full multi-party political system would be established, and in November the necessary legislation was introduced. In the same month the USA announced that it was to suspend military and economic aid to Zaire. This development followed renewed allegations of abuses of human rights by the Mobutu regime, and also reflected speculation that Mobutu had misappropriated large amounts of foreign economic aid for his personal enrichment.

By February 1991 a large number of new parties had emerged. Prominent among them was the Union des fédéralistes et républicains indépendants (UFERI), led by Nguza Karl-I-Bond. An enlarged transitional Government, appointed in March and reshuffled in April, included members of minor opposition groups. None of the major opposition parties, including the UDPS and the UFERI, agreed to join the new Government. Prof. Mulumba Lukoji, an economist who had served in previous administrations, was appointed First State Commissioner.

In early April 1991 Mobutu announced that a national conference would be convened at the end of that month, at which members of the Government and of opposition organizations would draft a new constitution. However, the Conference was postponed, owing to widespread disturbances and anti-Government demonstrations in several parts of the country. In late April Mobutu resumed the chairmanship of the MPR. In July some 130 opposition movements formed a united front, the Union sacrée. Later in July Mulumba Lukoji resigned as First State Commissioner. Etienne Tshisekedi Wa Mulumba, leader of the UDPS, was appointed in his place, but refused the post following threats to his life, and Mulumba Lukoji was subsequently reappointed. The National Conference was convened at the beginning of August, but was repeatedly suspended, initially owing to the dissatisfaction of the Union sacrée with the composition of its participants, and eventually by the Government, prompting renewed civil unrest, and the dispatch of French and Belgian troops to Zaire to evacuate nationals of those countries. Although Tshisekedi finally accepted the post of First State Commissioner in September, he later refused to swear allegiance to the President and the Constitution; shortly afterwards he was replaced as First State Commissioner by Bernardin Mungul Diaka, also a member of the opposition. In November Mobutu dismissed Mungul and appointed Nguza Karl-I-Bond to the premiership. The Union sacrée denounced the appointment, and expelled UFERI members from its ranks. Despite the expiry of his mandate as President in early December, Mobutu remained in office. In mid-December the Roman Catholic Archbishop of Kisangani, Laurent Monsengwo Pasinya, was elected President of the National Conference.

In early April 1992 the National Conference reopened, and in mid-April it declared its status to be sovereign and its decisions to be binding. Mobutu reacted with cautious opposition to the erosion of his powers, anxious to secure confirmation of his position as Head of State. In mid-August the National Conference asserted its new sovereign powers by electing Tshisekedi as First State Commissioner, following the resignation of Nguza Karl-I-Bond. A 'transition act', adopted by the Conference in early August, afforded Tshisekedi a mandate to govern for 24 months, pending the promulgation of a new constitution that would curtail the powers of the President. On 30 August Tshisekedi appointed a transitional 'Government of National Union', which included opponents of Mobutu.

The political interests of Tshisekedi and Mobutu clashed almost immediately when the President declared his intention to promote the adoption of a 'semi-presidential constitution', in opposition to the parliamentary system favoured by the Conference. On 14 November 1992 the National Conference (without the participation of Mobutu's supporters) adopted a draft Constitution providing for the establishment of a 'Federal Republic of the Congo', the introduction of a bicameral legislature and the election of the President, by universal suffrage, to fulfil a largely ceremonial function. (Executive and military power was to be exercised by the Prime Minister.) The draft document was vigorously opposed by Mobutu, who unsuccessfully attempted in early December to remove the Tshisekedi Government. On 6 December the National Conference dissolved itself and was succeeded by a 453-member High Council of the Republic (HCR), headed by Archbishop Monsengwo, which, as the supreme interim executive and legislative authority, was empowered to amend and adopt the new Constitution and to organize legislative and presidential elections. At the same time, Monsengwo declared that the report of a special commission, established by the Conference in order to examine allegations of corruption brought against Mobutu and his associates, would be considered by the HCR. Mobutu responded by ordering the suspension of the HCR and the Government. Attempts by the presidential guard to obstruct the convening of the HCR ended, following the organization of a public rally in Kinshasa, undertaken by Monsengwo and other members of the HCR. With support from the USA, Belgium and France, Monsengwo reiterated the HCR's recognition of Tshisekedi as head of Zaire's Government.

In mid-January 1993 the HCR declared Mobutu to be guilty of treason, on account of his mismanagement of state affairs, and threatened impeachment proceedings unless he recognized the legitimacy of the 'Government of National Union'. At the end of the month an attempt by the President to pay army units with discredited banknotes provoked a mutiny that resulted in 65 deaths (including that of the French ambassador to Zaire) and necessitated the intervention of French troops. In early March, in an attempt to reassert his political authority, Mobutu convened a special 'conclave' of political forces to debate the country's future. The HCR and the Union sacrée refused to attend. In mid-March the 'conclave' appointed Faustin Birindwa, a former UDPS member and adviser to Tshisekedi, as Prime Minister, charged with the formation of a 'Government of National Salvation'. The somewhat perfunctory NLC was also revived to rival the HCR, and was reconvened to operate within the terms of reference of the old Mobutu-inspired Constitution. In early April Birindwa appointed a Cabinet that included Nguza Karl-I-Bond (as First Deputy Prime Minister in charge of Defence) and three members of the Union sacrée, who were immediately expelled from that organization. While the Birindwa administration was denied widespread official international recognition, Tshisekedi became increasingly frustrated at the impotence of his own Government (the armed forces recommenced blocking access to the HCR), and the deteriorating stability of the country. During April the army embarked upon a campaign of intimidation of opposition members, while tribal warfare re-emerged in Shaba and also erupted in the northeastern region of Kivu. Tshisekedi urged the intervention of the UN to address these problems, and in July the Secretary-General of the UN appointed a Special Envoy to Zaire. Meanwhile, in late June six of Birindwa's ministers, all former activists in the Union sacrée, had announced the formation of the Union sacrée rénovée (USR), claiming that the Union sacrée had abandoned its political objectives in the pursuit of extremist policies.

At the end of September 1993 an agreement was concluded between representatives of President Mobutu and of the principal opposition groups, providing for the adoption of a single constitutional text for the transitional period, which would be subject to approval by a national referendum. Under the provisions of the agreement, national transitional institutions would include the President of the Republic, a reorganized transitional parliament (a unicameral legislature to include all existing members of the HCR and most members of the NLC, as well as independent legislators, to be co-opted in order to ensure full national representation), the transitional Government and the national judiciary. As previously agreed, the organization of presidential and legislative elections would provide for the establishment of a new republic in January 1995. During October 1993, however, attempts to finalize the terms of the agreement were complicated by the insistence of Tshisekedi's supporters that he should continue in the office of Prime Minister, despite the objections of Mobutu's representatives that Tshisekedi's mandate had been superseded by the September agreement. The opposing positions of the principal political parties (largely polarized as the pro-Tshisekedi Union sacrée de l'opposition radicale—USOR and the pro-Mobutu Forces politiques du conclave—FPC) became more firmly entrenched during November and December.

An ultimatum, issued to all political parties by President Mobutu in early January 1994, in an attempt to end the political impasse, resulted in the conclusion of an agreement to form a government of national reconciliation, signed by all major constituent parties of the FPC and the USOR (with the notable exception of Tshisekedi's own UDPS). Encouraged by the unexpected level of political support for the initiative, on 14 January Mobutu announced the dissolution of the HCR and the NLC, the dismissal of the Government of National Salvation, headed by Birindwa, and the candidacy for the premiership of two contestants, Tshisekedi and Mulumba Lukoji, to be decided by the transitional legislature (to be known as the Haut Conseil de la République-Parlement de Transition, HCR-PT). Despite condemnation of Mobutu's procedural circumvention of the HCR's authority, and a well-supported 24-hour general strike, organized in Kinshasa on 19 January in protest at Mobutu's unilateral declarations, the HCR-PT convened for the first time on 23 January. The HCR-PT promptly rejected Mobutu's procedure for the selection of a new Prime Minister. Subsequent attempts by the legislature to formulate a new procedure were frustrated by the increasingly divergent interests of the member parties of the USOR, and by Tshisekedi's insistence of his legitimate claim to the office.

On 8 April 1994 the HCR-PT endorsed a new Transitional Constitution Act, reiterating the provisions of previous accords for the organization of a constitutional referendum and presidential and legislative elections, and defining the functions of and relationship between the President of the Republic, the transitional Government and the HCR-PT, during a 15-month transitional period. The Government, to be accountable to the HCR-PT, was to assume some former powers of the President, including the control of the Central Bank and the security forces and the nomination of candidates for important civil service posts. A new Prime Minister was to be appointed from opposition candidates, to be nominated within 10 days of the President's promulgation of the Act (on 9 April). Widening divisions within the USOR frustrated attempts to unite the opposition behind Tshisekedi as sole candidate, prompting the expulsion, in May, of 10 dissident parties from the USOR.

In June 1994 the HCR-PT ratified the candidature of seven opposition representatives for the premiership, rejecting that of Tshisekedi for having failed to attend a parliamentary commission in order to explain the promotion of his position as 'Prime Minister awaiting rehabilitation', rather than candidate for the office. On 14 June it was reported that Léon Kengo Wa Dondo had been elected Prime Minister by 322 votes to 133 in the HCR-PT. However, Kengo Wa Dondo's election was immediately denounced as illegitimate, under the terms of the April Constitution Act, by the opposition and by the Speaker of the HCR-PT, Monsengwo Pasinya (who refused to endorse the actions of the legislature). A new transitional Government, announced on 6 July, was similarly rejected by the radical opposition, despite the offer of two cabinet posts to the UDPS. On 11 July, during a motion of confidence, the Government received overwhelming support from the HCR-PT. In early October an expanded radical opposition grouping (the Union sacrée de l'opposition radicale et ses alliés, USORAL) resumed its participation in the HCR-PT, having boycotted proceedings since the election of Kengo Wa Dondo in June. A reallocation of portfolios, carried out in mid-November, included the appointment of two ministers and two deputy ministers who were (or had previously been) members of the UDPS.

Despite the successful adoption, in May 1995, of the electoral law establishing the National Electoral Commission, a shortage of government funds and the logistical problems presented by the presence in Zaire of as many as 2.5m. refugees seemed likely to force the extension of the 15-month period of transitional government beyond the 9 July deadline. In late June political consensus between the FPC and the USORAL resulted in the HCR–PT's adoption of a constitutional amendment (approved by Mobutu) whereby the period of national transition was to be extended by two years. On 1 July deputies from both groups voted to remove Monsengwo Pasinya from the post of President of the transitional legislature. Meanwhile, opposition frustration at the Government's failure to publish an electoral timetable continued to escalate. In late July an anti-Government demonstration in the capital, organized by the Parti lumumbiste unifié (a group supporting the aims of the murdered former Prime Minister, Patrice Lumumba), led to violent clashes that resulted in 10 fatalities. A subsequent anti-Government protest in Kinshasa, organized by the USORAL in August, denounced international endorsement of Prime Minister Kengo Wa Dondo and urged his removal. In December opposition groups unanimously rejected a government offer to participate in a national coalition government, and reiterated their demands for the prompt announcement of a timetable for multi-party elections. The National Electoral Commission, composed of 44 members (22 from both of the major political groupings) and headed by Bayona Bameya (a close political associate of President Mobutu), was formally installed in April 1996.

In mid-April 1996 it was announced that multi-party presidential and legislative elections would be conducted in May 1997. Regional and municipal elections would be organized for June and July of the same year. All elections would be preceded by a referendum on a new constitution, to be conducted in December 1996. President Mobutu announced that he was to contest the presidential poll. (However, neither the elections nor the referendum took place, as the security situation in the country worsened—see below.) A draft of the new Constitution, which provided for a federal state with a semi-presidential parliamentary system of government, was adopted by the Government in late May.

In the mid-1990s existing ethnic tensions in eastern Zaire were heightened by the inflow of an estimated 1m. Hutu refugees from Rwanda (see below). The plight of the region's Zairean Tutsis (Banyamulenge) aroused international concern in late 1996, following reports of the organized persecution of Banyamulenge communities by elements of the Zairean security forces and by extremist Hutu refugees. (Legislation enacted by the Government in 1981 had sought to undermine Banyamulenge claims to citizenship, and aroused concerns regarding their increasingly precarious circumstances.) In October 1996 the Sud-Kivu regional administration ordered all Banyamulenge to leave the area within one week or risk internment or forced expulsion. Although the order was subsequently rescinded, this threat provoked the mobilization of armed Banyamulenge rebels, who launched a violent counter-offensive, allegedly supported by the Tutsi-dominated authorities in Rwanda and Burundi. Support for the rebels from dissidents of diverse ethnic origin (including Shaba and Kasaï secessionists, and local Mai-Mai warriors) increased during the month, and later in October the rebels announced the formation of the Alliance des forces démocratiques pour la libération du Congo-Zaïre (AFDL), under the leadership of Laurent-Désiré Kabila (hitherto leader of the Parti de la révolution populaire, and a known opponent of the Mobutu regime since the 1960s). AFDL forces made rapid territorial gains and the movement soon gathered momentum and emerged as a national rebellion aiming to overthrow Mobutu. In late January 1997 a counter-offensive by Zairean troops, reportedly assisted by foreign mercenaries, failed to recapture any significant area of territory. In March the AFDL entered the strategically-important northern town of Kisangani (which had served as the centre of military operations for the Government), and in early April Mbuji-Mayi fell to the rebels. Nguza Karl-I-Bond, now leader of the pro-Mobutu FPC, urged his followers (for the most part Shaba secessionists) to support the AFDL. AFDL troops, entering Lubumbashi on 9 April, were welcomed as liberators, while government troops withdrew from the city. The Zairean Government continued to make allegations that the AFDL offensive was being supported by government troops from Rwanda, Uganda, Burundi and Angola, while the

AFDL, in turn, claimed that the Zairean army was being augmented by white mercenary soldiers and by forces of the União Nacional para a Independência Total de Angola (UNITA). Several attempts at mediation between the two sides, undertaken by various foreign governments (most notably South Africa) and international organizations, during February–April, failed to halt the escalation of the conflict.

Meanwhile, in August 1996 Mobutu had travelled to Switzerland to receive treatment for cancer. His absence, and uncertainties as to the state of his health, contributed to the poor co-ordination of the Zairean Government's response to the AFDL, which by the end of November was in control of most of Kivu. In that month the HCR–PT urged the expulsion of all Tutsis from Zairean territory; following attacks on Tutsis and their property, many Tutsi residents of Kinshasa fled to Brazzaville (Republic of the Congo). In the same month repeated public demonstrations demanded the resignation of Kengo Wa Dondo (himself part-Tutsi in origin) for having failed to respond effectively to the insurrection. In December Mobutu returned to Zaire, appointed Gen. Mahele Bokungu as Chief of General Staff, and re-organized the Government, retaining Kengo Wa Dondo as Prime Minister.

The continued exclusion of Tshisekedi from the Government prompted his supporters to mount a campaign of civil disobedience, and in January 1997 his faction of the UDPS announced its support for the AFDL. In February, following a highly effective general strike in Kinshasa, Mobutu banned all demonstrations and industrial action. In March, following the capture of Kisangani, the HCR–PT voted to dismiss Kengo Wa Dondo, who tendered his resignation as Prime Minister towards the end of the month. He was replaced at the beginning of April by Tshisekedi, who, having offered government posts to members of the AFDL (which they refused), announced that he was dissolving the HCR–PT. Parliament, in turn, voted to dismiss Tshisekedi, whose supporters organized a demonstration of support in Kinshasa, only to come under attack from the security forces. On 8 April Mobutu declared a national state of emergency, dissolving the Government and ordering the deployment of security forces throughout Kinshasa. Gen. Likulia Bolongo was appointed Prime Minister at the head of a new 28-member 'Government of National Salvation', in which the USORAL refused to participate. An arrest warrant was subsequently issued for Kengo Wa Dondo, who was alleged to have fled to Switzerland with funds from the national treasury.

Following inconclusive peace talks between Mobutu and Kabila, mediated by the South African President, Nelson Mandela, in early May 1997, Mobutu refused to resign and Kabila reiterated his intention to take the capital by force. A hastily-assembled regional initiative to transfer interim executive power to Monsengwo Pasinya (recently re-elected Speaker of the HCR–PT) was rejected by the rebels, and was widely dismissed as a procedural device designed to afford Mobutu a dignified withdrawal from office.

On 16 May 1997 Mobutu left Kinshasa (travelling to Togo, and then to Morocco, where he died in September), whilst many of his supporters and family fled across the border to Brazzaville. On 17 May AFDL troops entered Kinshasa (encountering no resistance), and Kabila, speaking from Lubumbashi, declared himself President of the Democratic Republic of the Congo (DRC, the name in use during 1964–71), which swiftly gained international recognition. He immediately announced plans to form a provisional government within 72 hours and a commission to draft a new constitution within 60 days; presidential and parliamentary elections were to be held in April 1999. On 20 May 1997 Kabila arrived in Kinshasa, and by 22 May the AFDL was in control of most of the country. On 23 May Kabila announced the formation of a transitional Government, which, while dominated by members of the AFDL, also included members of the UDPS and of the Front patriotique, and avoided a potentially unpopular preponderance of ethnic Tutsis. No Prime Minister was appointed, and Tshisekedi was not offered a cabinet post; he refused to recognize the new Government, and advocated public protest against the administration, but failed to raise the mass support that he had previously enjoyed. On 26 May, following a number of protest demonstrations, Kabila issued a decree indefinitely banning all political parties and public demonstrations. On 28 May Kabila issued a constitutional decree (which was to remain in force pending the adoption of a new constitution), investing the President with virtually absolute legislative and executive power, as well as control over the armed forces and the treasury. Of the previously existing state institutions, only the judiciary was not dissolved.

On 29 May 1997 Kabila was sworn in as President of the DRC, assuming full executive, legislative and military powers. Despite the concerns of a number of humanitarian organizations regarding the new administration's treatment of refugees (see below), Kabila's assumption of power was well received internationally. In early June it was announced that a number of high-ranking officials from the Mobutu period, including the Secretary-General of the MPR and the Governor of the Central Bank, had been arrested, and that the directors of all parastatal companies had been suspended, pending further investigations. Later in the month, the detention overnight of Tshisekedi, following a political address to students, prompted renewed scepticism regarding the Kabila Government's commitment to future political pluralism. In late July it was reported that the Minister of Finance, Ferdinand Mawapanga Mwana Nanga, had been arrested following accusations of fraud. Although any wrongdoing on the part of the minister (who was obliged to relinquish his post) was swiftly denied by the Government, it aroused fears of high-level corruption. Instability persisted for the remainder of 1997; in July a protest march against the ban on political activity was reported to have resulted in three civilian deaths following clashes between troops and demonstrators.

In mid-1997 the Government blocked attempts by a UN investigation team to enquire into the alleged massacre of thousands of Rwandan Hutu refugees by Kabila's troops and his Rwandan Tutsi allies during the rebellion against Mobutu. In October, however, following intensive negotiations, Kabila, while professing his army's innocence, agreed to permit the UN team to carry out its investigations between November 1997 and the end of February 1998.

Meanwhile, in late August 1997 a military Court of Justice was established by decree, and at the end of October two statutory orders were signed by Kabila; one updated and defined the new designation of administrative areas and local authorities of the DRC (the nine former regions were reorganized into 11 provinces) and the other created a paramilitary force (the Service national) which, under the control of the President, was to monitor and facilitate activities to rebuild the country. In late October Kabila appointed a 42-member Constitutional Commission (originally due to be appointed in June), which was to draft a new constitution by March 1998. In the following month Kabila reaffirmed that the activities of political parties were suspended, pending presidential and legislative elections, scheduled to take place in 1999. At the end of November 1997 Kabila's Special Adviser for Security and the acting Army Chief of Staff, Gen. Masasu Nindanga, was arrested by troops in Kinshasa and accused of maintaining a private militia and of fraternizing with state enemies; he was later sentenced to 20 years' imprisonment. It was subsequently reported that up to 20 people had been killed in clashes between rival army factions. By late 1997 Kabila had yet to gain full military control over the Eastern Province, where ethnic violence continued between the Tutsi and Bantu groups.

On 8 December 1997 the UN investigation team was given permission to visit Mbandaka in the north-west of the country; on 15 December, however, following unrest in the area, the team was forced to return to Kinshasa. As a result, the investigations exceeded their original deadline of February 1998; the team was subsequently obstructed in its work by the Government, and in April the UN Secretary-General, Kofi Annan, announced that investigative activities were being suspended in the DRC but would continue from other countries in the Great Lakes region.

On 3 January 1998 Kabila reorganized the Cabinet, creating two new ministerial posts. On 20 January Joseph Olenghankoy, the chairman of the opposition Forces novatrices pour l'union et la solidarité (FONUS), was arrested for reasons believed to be related to a complaint he had made against two government ministers. He was later sentenced by a military court to 15 years' imprisonment for violating the ban on political activity, although he was released from prison in June 1999. In February 1998 Tshisekedi was banished to his native village and placed under house arrest for his continued political activity on behalf of the UDPS. In March the new draft Constitution was presented to Kabila. In May Arthur Z'Ahidi Ngoma, a UNESCO official and political activist who had been arrested in November 1997, was given a 12-month suspended sentence for breaking the ban on political activity. In April 1998 UNESCO had suspended co-

operation with the DRC Government pending his release; in June he was released. In July Tshisekedi was returned to Kinshasa and announced that he was willing to co-operate with Kabila.

During 1998 there were problems with security on many of the DRC's borders and agreements to increase border security were negotiated with Uganda, Burundi and the Central African Republic; talks were also held with Rwanda. In May a summit meeting of Great Lakes countries, which was to take place in the DRC on the first anniversary of Kabila's accession to power, was cancelled after only three of the 16 invited countries sent delegates to Kinshasa. This was widely interpreted as an indication of worsening relations between the DRC and its neighbours. On 1 June, following continued fighting in the east of the DRC, the military authorities announced the capture of 500 Mai-Mai insurgents in Kivu. Human rights organizations accused the Government of killing more than 1,000 civilians during its operation to suppress the Mai-Mai, and a report, published in Canada in late June, claimed that 20,000 people had died or disappeared in the eastern DRC.

Following accusations of financial impropriety against several members of the Cabinet and the subsequent arrest of the Minister of Information and the Minister without Portfolio, on 6 June 1998 Kabila announced a cabinet reorganization, in which five ministers suspected of fraud or corruption were dismissed. Eight new posts were created, increasing the number of ministers from 29 to 37. In July the UN investigation team published its report, in which it was alleged that the AFDL had massacred a large number of Rwandan Hutu refugees in 1996 and 1997; these findings were rejected by the Government on the grounds that they were based on an incomplete investigation.

On 27 July 1998 Kabila issued a decree expelling Rwandan troops from the country. He had earlier replaced the DRC Chief of Staff, James Kabereke, a Rwandan national, with Céléstin Kifwa, a DRC citizen. In early August a rebellion was launched in Nord-Kivu province, in the east of the DRC, which was reported to have Rwandan and French support. The Minister of State for the Presidency, Deogratias Bugera, and the Minister of Foreign Affairs, Bizima Karaha, defected from the Government and joined the rebellion. Karaha was subsequently replaced by Jean-Charles Okoto, formerly deputy Governor of Kasaï Oriental province. Western Governments advised their citizens to leave the country, and several diplomatic missions were closed. The rebels advanced quickly in the east of the country and were soon reported to have captured Bukavu and Goma. Shortly afterwards, a second front was opened from Kitona, in the west of the country, where further advances placed the rebels in control of Boma, Banana and Matadi. The Inga Dam, which supplies both electricity and water to Kinshasa and the Katanga mining region, was also captured, enabling the rebels to interrupt power supplies. At that time the rebel forces announced that they had formed a political organization, the Rassemblement congolais démocratique (RCD), with the aim of introducing political democracy in the DRC. The RCD leadership included Arthur Z'Ahidi Ngoma, together with a former Prime Minister, Lunda Bululu, and Ernest Wamba dia Wamba. In mid-August Kabila was reported to have left Kinshasa for Lubumbashi, the former base of the AFDL insurgency. Kabila returned to Kinshasa at the end of the month, by which time he had installed his son, Joseph, as Chief of Staff, leading to renewed accusations of nepotism. In late August a number of human rights organizations expressed their concern over alleged incitement to violence by the DRC Government and the media, following reports that government troops were detaining and killing Tutsis and Rwandans and that rebels, retreating from the west, were victims of mob attacks.

Other countries in the region were, meanwhile, becoming involved in the conflict. While Rwanda had initially denied accusations that it was supporting the rebels, it quickly became evident that the anti-Kabila insurgents had the support of both Rwanda and Uganda, and that Kabila was receiving support from Angola, Namibia and Zimbabwe. Angolan troops, in particular, were instrumental in recapturing rebel-held towns in the western DRC, and in early September 1998 Angolan forces had expelled the rebels from that part of the country. Regional divisions were clearly evident at a meeting of Ministers of Defence of the Southern African Development Community (SADC, see p. 280), convened by President Mugabe of Zimbabwe on 18–19 August, to mobilize support for Kabila; only half of the participating delegates favoured intervention in the conflict. Regional efforts to reach a political solution to the civil conflict continued in September. The RCD and MLC, however, were excluded from these discussions, since the Government maintained that their activities were supported by Rwanda and Uganda, and consequently refused to negotiate with the rebels.

In mid-September 1998 an Institutional Reform Commission (IRC) was established by Kabila to examine the draft Constitution. The IRC comprised 12 members, appointed by Kabila, with the Minister of Justice as Chairman. Kabila still maintained that elections would be held in April 1999, and, as part of the electoral preparations, a census was to be conducted in October 1998. At the end of that month the IRC presented the revised draft Constitution to Kabila.

Although their advance had been halted in the west, the rebels continued to make progress in the east, capturing towns in Kasaï Oriental and Katanga. Despite their continued military successes, however, the rebels lacked popular support and the movement was widely perceived as a Rwandan-backed Tutsi invasion. In mid-October the rebels shot down a passenger plane, which, they claimed, was transporting troops to the front; the Government denied this and stated that a number of civilians had been on board. In late October the Minister of Finance and the Budget, Ferdinand Tala Ngai, was arrested; his duties were assumed by the Minister of Agriculture. (In August 1999 Tala Ngai was found guilty of embezzlement and sentenced to seven months' hard labour.)

In early November 1998 rebel leaders conceded that the insurgency was receiving support from Rwanda and Uganda, but insisted that the rebellion was internally driven. At that time, Maj.-Gen. Paul Kagame, the Vice-President of Rwanda, officially admitted that Rwandan troops were present in the DRC. In mid-November the various rebel forces denied reports of internal divisions, although it was later reported that a new rebel grouping, the Mouvement pour la libération du Congo (MLC), had been founded in that month.

In January 1999 the ongoing civil war led to the declaration of a state of siege in six of the 11 provinces of the DRC. On 29 January Kabila issued a decree lifting the ban on political parties. There were, however, many conditions attached to the formation and registration of a party, most of which appeared to exclude those parties that were already active; the decree was widely criticized for preventing many existing parties from registering. Kabila also announced that the AFDL was to be transformed into People's Power Committees to encourage involvement in the political process at a local level. In mid-March Kabila announced the initial appointments to his new Government (he had dismissed the previous administration on 20 February); it was further enlarged on 19 March and on 2 April, and eventually contained 37 members. Yerodia Abdoulaye Ndombasi was appointed Minister of State for Foreign Affairs and International Co-operation, and Bemba Saolona (father of the MLC rebel leader, Jean-Pierre Bemba) was appointed Minister of the Economy and Industry. During March Kabila proposed that a national debate be held with representatives from all the major political parties, although it subsequently emerged that the Government would decide who would be allowed to attend. However, the debate was twice postponed.

In May 1999 the RCD announced changes to its executive committee; Wamba dia Wamba was replaced as President by Dr Emile Ilunga (Arthur Z'Ahidi Ngoma had resigned in February). However, a number of the RCD's founding members opposed this move, and Wamba dia Wamba denounced it as a coup. Following clashes in Kisangani between supporters of Wamba dia Wamba and those of Ilunga, two factions emerged; one led by Ilunga, based in Goma with the support of Rwanda, the other led by Wamba dia Wamba, based in Kisangani and supported by Uganda. In June the DRC began proceedings at the International Court of Justice (ICJ) against Burundi, Rwanda and Uganda for acts of armed aggression, which it claimed to have been in contravention of both the charters of the OAU and the UN. (In February 2001 the DRC abandoned the proceedings against Burundi and Rwanda.)

Despite a number of regional initiatives to end the civil war in late 1998 and early 1999, no lasting cease-fire agreement was negotiated, largely owing to Kabila's continued insistence that the rebels were supported by Rwanda and Uganda, and that they, therefore, be excluded from any talks. Although Col Muammar al-Qaddafi, the Libyan leader, hosted two rounds of regional talks in Sirte (Libya), it was in Lusaka, Zambia, under the mediation of Zambia's President Chiluba, that the rebels were first accorded a place at the negotiations, during a summit held in late June. Following this meeting, a cease-fire agreement

was signed by the Heads of State of the DRC, Angola, Namibia, Zimbabwe, Rwanda and Uganda on 10 July (witnessed by the OAU, the SADC, the UN and Zambia), by the leader of the MLC on 1 August, and, following the resolution of a dispute (owing to the divisions within the RCD), by all 50 founding members of the RCD on 31 August. The agreement provided for an immediate cease-fire, the establishment of a Joint Military Commission (JMC), which was to investigate cease-fire violations, disarm militia groups and monitor the withdrawal of foreign troops, the deployment of a UN peace-keeping force and the organization of a national debate within the DRC. However, the UN stressed that authorization for a full peace-keeping force would have to be preceded by a 90-strong military liaison mission and a subsequent 500-strong military observer mission. In July a general amnesty for rebels within the DRC was announced, and in that month the JMC was formed, comprising representatives of the rebel groups and the six Lusaka signatory states (the DRC, Angola, Namibia, Rwanda, Uganda and Zimbabwe). In mid-August the UN military liaison mission received official approval.

In August 1999 further fighting erupted in Kisangani between forces from Rwanda and Uganda and their respective factions of the RCD. A cease-fire was negotiated in late August, and at the end of the month the Ilunga faction of the RCD announced a new executive committee. An investigation into the causes of the fighting recommended that all fighting forces be removed from Kisangani; as a result, the Ugandan forces moved their headquarters to Gbadolite and the Wamba dia Wamba faction of the RCD left for Bunia. Ugandan and Rwandan troops withdrew from Kisangani in September. Following an earlier decree dividing the country into eight military regions, military commanders were announced for each of the new regions in September; Kabila also appointed new chiefs of staff at that time. In October the Wamba dia Wamba faction of the RCD announced that it was henceforth to be known as the RCD—mouvement de libération (RCD—ML).

In early September 1999 the rebels raised objections to the composition of the cease-fire commission and voiced doubts over the neutrality of the mediators. At the end of the month, however, the rebels and the Government agreed that the national debate would be facilitated by the Italian Sant'Egidio Roman Catholic Community, although differences remained over the location for the conference and over OAU involvement. In October the rebels denied that they had violated the cease-fire in Katanga province, and at the end of the month the discovery of evidence of mass graves in rebel-held territory was reported. During the civil war both the rebels and the Government were accused of a number of massacres; both sides denied the accusations.

In late October 1999 the Government criticized UN demands that the military liaison officers be deployed throughout the DRC, and authorized them to visit only certain areas of the country; they remain banned from parts of the DRC. In early November the Ilunga faction of the RCD held talks with Uganda's President Museveni in Kampala. At that time the Government threatened to abandon the peace process unless Rwanda and Uganda withdrew their troops from the DRC.

Unrest became increasingly evident in late 1999. In November both factions of the RCD announced that they no longer respected the cease-fire, and the Ilunga faction of the movement accused the Government of openly violating the agreement. On 5 November the UN Security Council voted to extend the mandate of the military liaison mission until 15 January 2000, owing to the difficulties experienced in obtaining security assurances and permission to deploy throughout the DRC. At the end of the month the Council approved the establishment of the Mission de l'organisation des nations unies en République démocratique du Congo (MONUC, see p. 63), with an initial mandate until 1 March 2000. It was principally to comprise liaison and technical assessment officers, although the Council requested that up to 500 military observers be equipped ready for deployment pending further recommendations on the security situation. Their deployment, together with a protective force of up to 5,037 troops, was approved on 24 February; at the same time, the mandate of the mission was extended until 31 August.

At a meeting of the UN Security Council concerning the conflict in the DRC, which took place in New York, USA, in January 2000, regional Heads of State expressed support for the rapid deployment of MONUC forces to support the Lusaka peace accord. In February the UN Security Council adopted a subsequent proposal extending the mandate of MONUC to the end of August and expanding the force to number 5,537. In late February the national debate was convened in Kinshasa, but was boycotted by opposition politicians, as well as by representatives of the rebel groups. Participants in the discussions subsequently submitted a final report, urging the establishment of a new national assembly and the revision of the Lusaka accord. The rebel groups rejected an offer by Kabila of a general amnesty in return for the cessation of hostilities, and fierce fighting between government and rebel forces continued in the east of the country, particularly in Kasaï Occidental. In early April participants at a meeting of the JMC signed a new cease-fire agreement, whereby all the forces involved in the conflict were to suspend hostilities and remain in position for a period of three months, pending the deployment of MONUC personnel to form a neutral zone between them. In early May, however, Ugandan and Rwandan forces again clashed in Kisangani, in violation of the cease-fire. After meeting a UN Security Council delegation, the Rwandan and Ugandan contingents agreed to the demilitarization of the town, and its transfer to the control of MONUC. Later that month RCD, Rwandan and Ugandan forces commenced withdrawal to a certain distance from the town. In June, however, it was reported that some 400 civilians had been killed in further hostilities between Rwandan and Ugandan troops in Kisangani. At the end of the month UN military personnel confirmed that Rwandan and Ugandan forces had withdrawn from the town, although some RCD members remained.

In June three ministers, responsible, respectively, for the portfolios of energy, the economy, commerce and industry, and mines, were arrested in connection with fraudulent activities, and subsequently removed from office. In early July the Government withdrew the DRC ambassador in Belgium, in protest at an international arrest warrant issued by a Belgian magistrate against the Minister of State for Foreign Affairs and International Co-operation, Abdoulaye Yérodia Ndombasi, for crimes against humanity. (DRC refugees in Belgium had submitted a legal appeal accusing Ndombasi of inciting violence against the Tutsi ethnic group.) In the same month 240 deputies of a new 300-member Legislative and Constituent Assembly–Transitional Parliament were elected by a commission under the supervision of the Ministry of Internal Affairs, while the remaining 60 were nominated by Kabila. A presidential decree, adopted in that month, provided for the decentralization of the Government, with the transferral of the legislature to Lubumbashi and the Supreme Court to Kisangani. On 22 August the new Transitional Parliament was inaugurated in Lubumbashi, despite criticism from the international community, which accused Kabila of acting in contravention of the Lusaka accord.

In August 2000 the UN Security Council adopted a resolution extending the mandate of MONUC until mid-October to allow further time for the implementation of the cease-fire agreement. Kabila subsequently informed the UN that he authorized the immediate deployment of MONUC troops throughout the DRC (thereby removing a major impediment to their arrival). In early September the Cabinet was extensively reorganized, following the dismissal of the ministers in June. (A further government reshuffle was effected in November.) Later in September it was reported that, after the resumption of hostilities between government and MLC forces, the MLC had recaptured the north-western town of Dongo. In October Ilunga was replaced in a reorganization of the leadership of the main RCD faction. In the same month an attempt to oust Wamba dia Wamba from the leadership of the RCD—ML was reported to have been suppressed. In early December, following renewed fierce fighting, the RCD, supported by Rwandan troops, succeeded in gaining control of the significant town of Pweto, in the south-eastern province of Katanga. The six countries and three rebel groups involved in the conflict subsequently signed an agreement in Harare, Zimbabwe, pledging to withdraw forces 15 km from positions of military engagement, prior to the deployment of MONUC troops (which was scheduled to take place within 45 days). Nevertheless, hostilities subsequently continued at Pweto, and in other eastern regions, while the RCD refused to withdraw its forces in accordance with the agreement until the Government entered into bilateral discussions with the rebels and permitted the complete deployment of MONUC troops. In mid-December the UN Security Council adopted a resolution in favour of extending the mandate of MONUC to mid-June 2001.

On 16 January 2001 Kabila was fatally injured by one of his bodyguards at his private residence in Kinshasa. (The circumstances of his assassination remained unclear, and a committee

of investigation was established in early February.) The Transitional Parliament approved the nomination by the political leadership of his son, Joseph (hitherto Chief of Staff), as interim President. Following his inauguration on 26 January, Maj.-Gen. Joseph Kabila immediately engaged in international diplomatic efforts to resolve the conflict, and urged rebel leaders to attend peace discussions with him. Following a meeting with Kabila in early February, the President of Rwanda, Maj.-Gen. Paul Kagame, announced that Rwandan troops would be withdrawn from Pweto on condition that control of the town was transferred to MONUC. However, the UN Security Council continued to demand that the DRC Government demonstrate its commitment to peace prior to the deployment of MONUC troops, and insisted that the implementation of the disengagement plan agreed in December was essential to this end. At a meeting of the UN Security Council in mid-February Kabila accepted the former Botswanan President, Sir Quett Ketumile Masire, as mediator to the conflict. (Laurent Kabila had previously opposed Masire's nomination to the post.) Following a further meeting of the UN Security Council, attended by representatives of the six countries and three rebel factions involved in the conflict, later that month, it was agreed that the 15 km withdrawal of forces was to commence by mid-March; it was further envisaged that a complete withdrawal of foreign troops, which was to be monitored by MONUC troops, would take place by mid-May. In April Kabila appointed a new enlarged Cabinet, which included only four members of the previous administration.

Zaire's relations with its neighbours have been complicated by the presence of large numbers of refugees in the border areas. From mid-1994 the credibility of Mobutu's Transitional Government was somewhat enhanced by its support for French and US initiatives to address the humanitarian crisis presented by the flight to Zaire of more than 2m. Rwandan refugees fleeing violence after the death of President Habyarimana. By mid-August 1995, however, the security situation in refugee camps along the Zairean border had deteriorated to such an extent that the Zairean Government initiated a programme of forcible repatriation. Some 15,000 Rwandans were deported in a number of days, prompting widespread international concern for their welfare. Later in the month in Geneva, at a meeting with the office of the UN High Commissioner for Refugees (UNHCR), the Zairean Prime Minister, Kengo Wa Dondo, agreed to entrust the repatriation process to UNHCR officials until the end of the year, after which time the Zairean Government would resume the forcible return of all remaining refugees. In early September a formal agreement was concluded between UNHCR and the Zairean Government for a more regulated and bilateral approach to the refugee crisis, and later in the month further commitments were made by the Zairean and Rwandan Governments to improve security conditions on both sides of the border. In December President Mobutu confirmed that the forcible return of remaining refugees in early 1996 was no longer a realistic objective.

By October 1996 little progress had been made in repatriating displaced Rwandans in Zaire. In that month UNHCR warned that the distribution of food to the refugees was being prevented by the prevailing instability in eastern Zaire. Hundreds of thousands of Rwandan Hutus fled in advance of the arrival of AFDL troops (see above), who, in early November, declared a cease-fire for returning refugees, and later in the month announced the creation of a humanitarian corridor to the Rwandan border, in the hope that the estimated 700,000 Rwandan refugees now seeking shelter at the Mugunga camp, west of Goma, would return to Rwanda. (An additional 300,000 refugees were believed to have scattered into the surrounding hills.) However, the large-scale return of refugees was finally prompted by an AFDL attack on extremist Hutu units operating from the camp. In mid-November UNHCR reported the return of some 400,000 refugees in recent weeks, which did much to reassure the international aid community that the immediate humanitarian crisis had abated (a number of initiatives for multinational intervention were cancelled), but failed to allay continuing concern as to the whereabouts and welfare of a vast number of refugees who could not be accounted for. As the AFDL advance continued as far west as Kisangani, reports began to emerge that relief supplies for the estimated 200,000 remaining refugees were being intercepted by the rebels, who were also accused of forcing refugees to flee nearby camps, and of refusing to allow aid workers and journalists to enter the camps. In late April 1997 the AFDL leader, Laurent Kabila, demanded that the UN complete full repatriation of the refugees within 60 days, after which time their return would be undertaken unilaterally by the rebels. By early May the AFDL had initiated an organized repatriation programme which encountered almost immediate condemnation from the UN, owing to the overcrowded conditions in which the refugees were being transported. Allegations continued to emerge during 1997 that elements of the AFDL had committed massacres of Hutu refugees, and in May the EU Commissioner for Humanitarian Affairs accused the AFDL of complicity in the death of refugees from disease and starvation. By March 1998 more than 40,000 DRC refugees had been repatriated from Tanzania, and in May UNHCR announced the repatriation of DRC refugees from Uganda. The outbreak of civil war in the DRC, however, caused further refugee movement in the region. Many Rwandan and Burundian refugees were evacuated to Burundi, while other groups of displaced people arrived in Tanzania from the DRC. During 1998 some 31,000 refugees fled the DRC, and at the end of the year the total number of DRC refugees in neighbouring countries was 141,730, of whom 115,530 were being assisted by UNHCR. At that time there were 240,200 refugees in the DRC, including 137,000 from Angola. Despite the continuing conflict in the DRC, the influx of Angolans continued; by mid-2000 some 166,500 Angolan refugees had fled to the DRC. At that time some 20,000 Burundian refugees, 60,000 Rwandan refugees, and 2,800 Ugandan refugees remained in the country. The improved humanitarian situation in the Republic of the Congo had prompted most of the Congolese refugees in the DRC to return to that country. Meanwhile, continuing hostilities in the DRC, particularly in the province of Equateur, had prompted a further 20,000 civilians to seek refuge in the Republic of the Congo and 5,000 to flee to Zambia by mid-2000.

Government

Under the terms of a constitutional decree, which was promulgated in May 1997, executive power is exercised by the President, in consultation with the Government. In October 1997 a 42-member Constitutional Commission was appointed to draft a new constitution. The resultant draft Constitution was referred, in March 1988, to a 300-member Constituent Assembly, which was to review the document and submit it to a national referendum. The Assembly was, however, unable to convene, owing to the outbreak of civil war, and the work was completed in October by a 12-member Institutional Reform Commission, appointed by Kabila. In mid-2000 a new 300-member Legislative and Constituent Assembly–Transitional Parliament was established; 240 deputies were elected by a commission under the supervision of the Ministry of Internal Affairs, while the remaining 60 were nominated by Kabila. The new transitional legislature was inaugurated on 22 August.

Defence

Following the overthrow of Mobutu's regime in May 1997, the former Zairean armed forces were disbanded. In August 2000 government forces, known as the Alliance des forces démocratiques pour la libération du Congo-Zaire (AFDL), were estimated to number 55,900, and the navy an estimated 900. A civil war began in August 1998 in the east of the country. In early 2001 rebel forces were estimated to number 48,000. At that time it was reported that a number of other African troops (1,000 Angolan, 1,000 Namibian and 12,000 Zimbabwean) were deployed in the country supporting the Government; some 1,000 Burundian, 15,000–20,000 Rwandan and 15,000 Ugandan troops supported the opposition. At 1 January 2001 the Mission de l'organisation des nations unies en République démocratique du Congo (MONUC) comprised 183 military observers, 24 troops, and 216 international and 142 local civilian personnel; MONUC had a total authorized strength of 5,537 personnel (including 500 military observers). A number of troops belonging to the Burundian rebel movement, Force pour la défence de la démocratie, were also in the country. The UN Security Council envisaged a complete withdrawal of all foreign troops by mid-May 2001, under the supervision of MONUC troops. The defence budget for 1999 was US $400m.

Economic Affairs

In 1998, according to estimates by the World Bank, the gross national product (GNP) of the DRC (formerly Zaire), measured at average 1996–98 prices, was US $5,433m., equivalent to $110 per head (or $733 per head on an international purchasing-power parity basis). During 1990–98, it was estimated, GNP per head decreased, in real terms, at an average annual rate of 8.5%. Over the same period the population increased by an

average of 3.6% per year. The DRC's gross domestic product (GDP) decreased, in real terms, by an average of 5.1% per year in 1990–98.

Agriculture (including forestry and fishing) contributed an estimated 58% of GDP in 1997. About 63.7% of the working population were employed in agriculture at mid-1999. The principal cash crops are coffee (which accounted for 12.5% of export earnings in 1994), palm oil and palm kernels, sugar, tea, cocoa, rubber and cotton. During 1990–98 agricultural GDP increased at an average annual rate of 2.9%.

Industry (including mining, processing of minerals, manufacturing, power and construction) contributed an estimated 17% of GDP in 1997. Some 15.9% of the working population were employed in industry in 1991. During 1990–97 industrial GDP decreased at an average annual rate of 11.7%.

Mining and metallurgy contributed about 10% of GDP in 1990, but the proportion declined to an estimated 4.4% of GDP in 1995. Mineral products accounted for about 92% of export earnings in 1993. The most important minerals are copper and cobalt (of which the country has 65% of the world's reserves). Manganese, zinc, tin and gold are also mined. There are rich diamond deposits, and in the late 1980s Zaire was the world's second largest producer of industrial diamonds. (Diamonds became Zaire's principal source of foreign exchange—US $532m.—in 1993.) There are also extensive offshore reserves of petroleum (revenue from petroleum accounts for about 20% of total government income). The mining sector was significantly affected following the outbreak of civil conflict in 1998 (see below). During 1987–95 the sector's GDP (including the processing of minerals) decreased, in real terms, by an estimated average of 17.6% per year.

Manufacturing contributed an estimated 6.5% of GDP in 1995. The most important sectors are textiles, cement, engineering and agro-industries producing consumer goods. During 1987–95 manufacturing GDP declined, in real terms, by an estimated average of 10.5% per year; the sector's GDP increased, in real terms, by 19.4% in 1995.

Energy is derived principally from hydroelectric power. In 1994 an estimated 99.9% of electric energy was generated by hydroelectric plants. In 1995 imports of fuel and energy comprised 6.0% of the value of total merchandise imports.

The services sector contributed an estimated 25% of GDP in 1997, and employed some 19.0% of the working population in 1991. During 1990–97 the GDP of the services sector decreased by an average of 15.2% per year.

In 1996 Zaire recorded an estimated trade surplus of US $830m., while there was a deficit of $545m. on the current account of the balance of payments. In 1995 the principal source of imports (an estimated 16.6%) was Belgium-Luxembourg; other major suppliers were South Africa, Nigeria, Ecuador, the United Kingdom and Germany. In that year South Africa was the principal market for exports (taking an estimated 29.6% of the total); the USA, Belgium-Luxembourg and Angola were also important markets for exports. In 1994 the principal exports were mineral products (mainly copper, cobalt, industrial diamonds and petroleum) and agricultural products (primarily coffee). The principal imports are manufactured goods, food and raw materials.

In 1997 there was an estimated budgetary deficit of 6,291,000m. new zaires. At the end of 1998 external debt totalled US $12,929m., of which $8,949m. was long-term public debt. In that year the cost of debt-servicing was equivalent to 1.2% of the value of exports of goods and services. Annual inflation averaged 1,710% in 1990–97. Consumer prices increased by 175.5% in 1997.

The DRC maintains economic co-operation agreements with its neighbours, Burundi and Rwanda, through the Economic Community of the Great Lakes Countries (see p. 307). The DRC is also a member of the International Coffee Organization (see p. 304) and of the Common Market for Eastern and Southern Africa—COMESA (see p. 148). In September 1997 the DRC became a member of the Southern African Development Community (SADC, see p. 280).

Potentially one of Africa's richest states, the DRC has extensive agricultural, mineral and energy resources. During the early 1990s, however, most foreign investment in the country was withdrawn, and by February 1994 government revenues had declined to such an extent (by 84% between 1989 and 1994) that the World Bank closed its office in the capital, Kinshasa, having declared the country 'insolvent'; in June 1994 Zaire was suspended from the IMF. The Kabila administration, which came to power in May 1997, secured foreign investment to revive the highly lucrative mining sector, and subsequently succeeded in reducing inflation. It was announced that a new currency, the Congolese franc, would gradually replace the new zaire from June 1998. However, the outbreak of civil war in August adversely affected the economic reform measures already introduced; the new currency was repeatedly devalued, inflation increased rapidly, and the rebels' advance in the east of the country severely curtailed economic activity in the region. A ban on foreign currency transactions in early 1999 led to difficulties in financing imports and a consequent shortage of supplies. External debt arrears had increased dramatically by the end of that year. Rebel groups continued to exploit mineral resources; the rival administration of one of them, the Mouvement pour la libération du Congo, had commenced organized economic activities in the northern province of Equateur. Ugandan and Rwandan forces supporting the rebels had benefited from gaining control of mineral concessions in the east, while Zimbabwe had become involved in the conflict on behalf of the DRC Government in return for significant control of the mining industry and the awarding of a number of contracts to Zimbabwean state-owned enterprises. A diamond export monopoly, granted in July 2000 to an Israeli-owned company, with the aim of maximizing government revenue and preventing illicit trafficking in diamonds from 'conflict regions', contributed to a severe shortage in foreign exchange. In October the central bank devalued the Congolese franc by more than 100%, as part of continuing efforts to narrow the difference between the official and 'black market' exchange rates. It was reported that, with an increase in the internally-displaced population resulting from the conflict, the humanitarian situation had reached a critical level by the end of the year, compounded by severe fuel shortages and a dramatically high rate of inflation. The succession to the presidency of Joseph Kabila, following the death of his father in January 2001 (see Recent History), prompted renewed hopes for the restoration of peace, and the initiation of economic recovery in the country.

Social Welfare

There is an Institut National de la Sécurité Sociale, guaranteeing insurance coverage for sickness, pensions and family allowances under an obligatory scheme of national insurance. In 1997, of total expenditure by the central Government, 17,000m. new zaires (0.02%) were allocated to public health, and 10,000m. new zaires (0.01%) to social security and welfare. In 1996 the DRC had 6.9 physicians, 44.2 nurses and 1.1 dentists per 100,000 inhabitants. The introduction of a new health insurance plan, announced in early 2001, was designed to enable a greater number of people to gain access to health care.

Education

Primary education, beginning at six years of age and lasting for six years, is officially compulsory. Secondary education, which is not compulsory, begins at 12 years of age and lasts for up to six years, comprising a first cycle of two years and a second of four years. In 1994 the total enrolment at primary and secondary schools was equivalent to 52% of the school-age population (males 62%; females 41%). In that year primary enrolment was equivalent to 72% of students in the relevant age-group (boys 86%; girls 59%). The comparable ratio for secondary enrolment in 1994 was 26% (boys 32%; girls 19%). The country has four universities, situated at Kinshasa, Kinshasa/Limete, Kisangani and Lubumbashi. According to estimates by UNESCO, the average rate of adult illiteracy in 1995 was 22.7% (males 13.4%; females 32.3%). In the budget for 1997 a total of 144,000m. new zaires (0.2% of total expenditure by the central Government) was allocated to education.

Public Holidays

2001: 1 January (New Year's Day), 4 January (Commemoration of the Martyrs of Independence), 1 May (Labour Day), 24 June (Promulgation of the 1967 Constitution and Day of the Fishermen), 30 June (Independence Day), 1 August (Parents' Day), 14 October (Youth Day), 27 October (Naming Day), 17 November (Army Day), 24 November (Anniversary of the Second Republic), 25 December (Christmas Day).

2002: 1 January (New Year's Day), 4 January (Commemoration of the Martyrs of Independence), 1 May (Labour Day), 24 June (Promulgation of the 1967 Constitution and Day of the Fishermen), 30 June (Independence Day), 1 August (Parents' Day), 14 October (Youth Day), 27 October (Naming Day), 17 November (Army Day), 24 November (Anniversary of the Second Republic), 25 December (Christmas Day).

Weights and Measures

The metric system is in force.

Statistical Survey

Sources (unless otherwise stated): Département de l'Economie Nationale, Kinshasa; Institut National de la Statistique, Office Nationale de la Recherche et du Développement, BP 20, Kinshasa; tel. (12) 31401.

Area and Population

AREA, POPULATION AND DENSITY

Area (sq km)	2,344,885*
Population (census result)	
1 July 1984	
Males	14,543,800
Females	15,373,000
Total	29,916,800
Population (UN estimates at mid-year)†	
1997	47,987,000
1998	49,139,000
1999	50,335,000
Density (per sq km) at mid-1999	21.5

* 905,365 sq miles.

† Source: UN *World Population Prospects: The 1998 Revision*. Figures are based on a UN-estimated mid-year population of 37,363,000 in 1990; according to official estimates, however, the population at mid-1990 was 35,562,000.

REGIONS*

	Area (sq km)	Population (31 Dec. 1985)†
Bandundu	295,658	4,644,758
Bas-Zaïre	53,920	2,158,595
Equateur	403,293	3,960,187
Haut-Zaïre	503,239	5,119,750
Kasaï Occidental . . .	156,967	3,465,756
Kasaï Oriental. . . .	168,216	2,859,220
Kivu	256,662	5,232,442
Shaba (formerly Katanga) . .	496,965	4,452,618
Kinshasa (city)‡ . . .	9,965	2,778,281
Total	**2,344,885**	**34,671,607**

* In October 1997 a statutory order redesignated the regions as provinces. Kivu was divided into three separate provinces, and several of the other provinces were renamed. There are now 11 provinces: Bandundu, Bas-Congo, Equateur, Kasaï Occidental, Kasaï Oriental, Katanga (formerly Shaba), Kivu-Maniema, Nord-Kivu, Province Orientale (formerly Haut-Zaïre), Sud-Kivu, Kinshasa (city).

† Provisional.   ‡ Including the commune of Maluku.

Source: Département de l'Administration du Territoire.

PRINCIPAL TOWNS (population at census of July 1984)

Kinshasa	2,664,309
Lubumbashi	564,830
Mbuji-Mayi	486,235
Kolwezi	416,122
Kisangani	317,581
Kananga	298,693
Likasi	213,862
Boma	197,617
Bukavu	167,950
Kikwit	149,296
Matadi	138,798
Mbandaka	137,291

Source: UN, *Demographic Yearbook*.

BIRTHS AND DEATHS (UN estimates, annual averages)

	1980–85	1985–90	1990–95
Birth rate (per 1,000) . . .	48.3	47.9	48.2
Death rate (per 1,000) . . .	16.4	15.2	14.7

Expectation of life (UN estimates, years at birth, 1990–95): 51.7 (males 50.0; females 53.5).

Source: UN, *World Population Prospects: The 1998 Revision*.

ECONOMICALLY ACTIVE POPULATION

Mid-1999 (estimates in '000): Agriculture, etc. 13,182; Total labour force 20,696 (Source: FAO, *Production Yearbook*).

Agriculture

PRINCIPAL CROPS ('000 metric tons)

	1997	1998	1999
Rice (paddy)	355	363	350
Maize	1,167	1,215	1,199
Millet	48	50	40*
Sorghum	52	54	50*
Potatoes.	62	55*	50*
Sweet potatoes	404	390*	370*
Cassava (Manioc) . . .	16,973	17,060	16,500
Yams*	270	260	255
Taro (Coco yam) . . .	60	50*	45*
Dry beans	135	138	130
Dry peas	48	45	40
Groundnuts (in shell). . .	400	412	396
Palm kernels* . . .	66	63	63
Cabbages*	27	25	23
Tomatoes	43	41	38*
Onions (dry)	59	57	53*
Pumpkins	42	40	38
Sugar cane	1,726	1,731	1,700
Oranges.	198	199	192
Grapefruit*	12	11	10
Avocados	30	30	27*
Mangoes	213	214	210
Pineapples	203	204	200
Bananas	318	318	315
Plantains	1,889	1,850*	1,800*
Papayas.	226	227	220
Coffee (green) . . .	70	57	46
Cocoa beans	7	7	7*
Tea (made)	3	3	3*
Tobacco (leaves) . . .	4	4	4*
Cotton (lint)	9	8*	8*
Natural rubber (dry weight) . .	5	9†	8*

* FAO estimate(s).   † Unofficial figure.

Source: FAO.

LIVESTOCK ('000 head, year ending September)

	1997	1998	1999*
Cattle	982	909	900
Sheep	955	941	930
Goats	4,448	4,584	4,400
Pigs	1,144	1,170	1,100
Poultry	22,027	21,863	21,000

* FAO estimates.

Source: FAO.

LIVESTOCK PRODUCTS ('000 metric tons)

	1997	1998	1999
Beef and veal	16	14	14
Mutton and lamb . . .	3	3	3
Goat meat	21	22	19
Pig meat*	43	43	41
Poultry meat* . . .	19	20	19
Other meat* . . .	161	165	164
Cows' milk*	6	5	5
Hen eggs*	7	7	7

* FAO estimates.

Source: FAO.

Forestry

ROUNDWOOD REMOVALS ('000 cubic metres, excl. bark)

	1996	1997	1998
Sawlogs, veneer logs and logs for sleepers	274	218	224
Other industrial wood . .	3,236	3,320	3,400
Fuel wood	43,699	44,834	45,910
Total	47,209	48,372	49,534

Source: FAO, *Yearbook of Forest Products*.

SAWNWOOD PRODUCTION ('000 cubic metres, incl. railway sleepers)

	1996	1997	1998
Total (all broadleaved) . . .	85	90	80

Source: FAO, *Yearbook of Forest Products*.

Fishing

(metric tons, live weight)

	1996	1997	1998
Capture	163,010	162,211	178,041
Aquaculture*	750	750	750
Total catch	163,760	162,961	178,791

* FAO estimates.

Source: FAO, *Yearbook of Fishery Statistics*.

Mining

('000 metric tons, unless otherwise indicated)

	1994	1995	1996
Hard coal*	94	95	95
Copper ore†‡	30.0	30.0	42.2
Cobalt ore†§	0.8	1.6	2.0
Zinc ore†§	0.6	0.8	1.2
Gold ore (kg)*†§ . . .	800	600	1,000
Tin ore†§	1.0	0*	0*
Crude petroleum . .	1,124	1,146*	1,148*
Diamonds ('000 carats)§ . .	17,000	17,000	18,000*

* Provisional figures.

† Figures refer to the metal content of ores.

‡ Source: *World Metal Statistics*.

§ Source: US Bureau of Mines.

Source: UN, *Industrial Commodity Statistics Yearbook*.

1997 ('000 metric tons, unless otherwise indicated): Copper 39.7; Cobalt 4.0; Zinc 1.7; Gold (kg) 394; Diamonds ('000 carats) 21.0.

1998 ('000 metric tons, unless otherwise indicated): Copper 35.0; Cobalt 3.9; Zinc 1.2; Gold (kg) 134; Diamonds ('000 carats) 24.5.

Source: Banque Centrale du Congo in *Mining Annual Review 1999*.

Industry

SELECTED PRODUCTS

('000 metric tons, unless otherwise indicated)

	1992	1993	1994
Maize flour	13.0	12.8	10.3
Sugar	81.7	82.3	79.0
Cigarettes ('000 cartons) . .	2,682.1	2,472.5	2,535.0
Beer (million litres) . .	165.4	148.8	160.7
Soft drinks (million litres) . .	85.3	71.1	75.9
Soaps	38.7	38.6	37.4
Acetylene	39.2	54.3	62.0
Tyres	41.0	26.0	35.6
Cement	208.0	161.7	165.7
Glassware	10.9	12.5	12.9
Diesel and gas oil . .	52.6	30.7	20.7
Fuel oil	34.3	32.8	9.1
Jet fuel and kerosene. .	31.4	31.2	1.1
Butane	0.1	10.2	0.2
Premium gasoline . . .	28.3	30.8	8.3
Cotton fabrics ('000 sq metres) .	20,510	15,099	17,804
Printed fabrics ('000 sq metres) .	30,994	28,400	25,900
Footwear ('000 pairs). . .	934	1,661	1,061
Blankets ('000 units) . .	54	177	94
Metallic furniture ('000 pieces) .	9.0	6.0	7.5
Sheet metal ('000 pieces) . .	144.6	163.4	151.0
Motor cars (units) . . .	131	150	140
Electric energy (million kWh). .	5,883	5,351	5,006

Source: IMF, *Zaire—Background Information and Statistical Data* (April 1996).

1995 (estimates, '000 metric tons, unless otherwise indicated): Cement 100; Jet fuel 3; Motor gasoline (petrol) 9; Kerosene 10; Gas-diesel (distillate fuel) oils 19; Residual fuel oils 7; Electric energy (million kWh) 5,920.

1996 (estimates, '000 metric tons, unless otherwise indicated): Jet fuel 3; Motor gasoline (petrol) 9; Kerosene 10; Gas-diesel (distillate fuel) oils 18; Residual fuel oils 8; Electric energy (million kWh) 5,408.

Source (for 1995 and 1996): UN, *Industrial Commodity Statistics Yearbook*.

Finance

CURRENCY AND EXCHANGE RATES

Monetary Units

100 centimes = 1 new Congolese franc.

Sterling, Dollar and Euro Equivalents (29 December 2000)

£1 sterling = 74.61 new Congolese francs;
US $1 = 50.00 new Congolese francs;
€1 = 46.53 new Congolese francs;
1,000 new Congolese francs = £13.40 = $20.00 = €21.49.

Average Exchange Rate (new Congolese francs per US $)

1998	1.61
1999	4.02
2000	21.82

Note: In June 1967 the zaire was introduced, replacing the Congolese franc (CF) at an exchange rate of 1 zaire = CF 1,000. In October 1993 the zaire was replaced by the new zaire (NZ), equivalent to 3m. old zaires. On 30 June 1998 a new Congolese franc, equivalent to NZ 100,000, was introduced. The NZ was withdrawn from circulation on 30 June 1999. Some of the figures in this Survey are still in terms of old or new zaires.

BUDGET ('000 million new zaires, unless otherwise indicated)

Revenue*	1995	1996	1997
Taxation	1,955	13,787	32,430
Taxes on income, profits, etc. .	700	5,552	10,068
Taxes on payroll and workforce .	27	203	479
Turnover tax	109	1,603	3,931
Excises	286	917	3,475
Import duties	642	4,163	10,534
Export duties	50	453	624
Other tax revenue . . .	140	896	3,293
Administrative fees and charges, etc. .	48	619	5,781
Other current revenue . .	117	1,282	2,153
Total†	2,120	15,688	40,364

Expenditure	1995	1996	1997
General public services‡ . . .	1,646	7,777	26,962
Defence	122	4,482	13,911
Education	27	136	144
Health	25	64	17
Social security and welfare . .	n.a.	11	10
Housing and community amenities	1	12	155
Recreational, cultural and			
religious affairs and services .	19	142	6
Economic affairs and services . .	1,194	18,472	37,588
Fuel and energy	8	113	321
Agriculture, forestry and fishing	1,183	17,105	287
Mining, manufacturing and			
construction.	1	1,253	36,921
Transport and communications .	2	1	59
Other purposes	255	2,617	80
Interest payments . . .	21	1,009	80
Total†	**3,289**	**33,713**	**78,953**

* Excluding grants received (million new zaires): 1,177,000 in 1995; 17,091,000 in 1996; 32,298,000 in 1997.
† Excluding the operations of the social security system.
‡ Including public order and safety.

Source: IMF, *Government Finance Statistics Yearbook*.

INTERNATIONAL RESERVES (US $ million at 31 December)

	1993	1994	1995
Gold	8.59	10.71	10.83
Foreign exchange . . .	46.20	120.69	146.60
Total	**54.79**	**131.40**	**157.43**

1996 (US $ million at 31 December): Foreign exchange 82.50.
1997 (US $ million at 31 December): Gold 15.80.

Source: IMF, *International Financial Statistics*.

MONEY SUPPLY (million new zaires at 31 December)

	1993	1994	1995
Currency outside banks . .	4,693	277,000	1,684,000
Demand deposits at deposit			
money banks . . .	1,618	92,000	187,000
Total money (incl. others) . .	**6,495**	**373,000**	**1,889,000**

Source: IMF, *International Financial Statistics*.

COST OF LIVING
(Consumer Price Index for Kinshasa; base: 1988 = 100)

	1990	1991	1992
Food	785.2	33,900	1,002,187
Rent	771.6	29,658	973,432
Health	1,046.7	50,004	1,881,696
Clothing	488.1	21,019	689,652
Transport and other . . .	930.7	44,134	797,283
All items	**782.4**	**33,867**	**958,367**

All items (base: 1995 = 100): 0.1 in 1993; 15.6 in 1994; 100.0 in 1995; 758.8 in 1996; 2,090.7 in 1997. (Source: IMF, *International Financial Statistics*.)

NATIONAL ACCOUNTS
Expenditure on the Gross Domestic Product
('000 million old zaires at current prices, unless otherwise indicated)

	1993	1994*	1995*†
Government final consumption			
expenditure	12,462,186	522.2	3,356.1
Private final consumption			
expenditure	64,305,274	5,417.7	31,924.1
Gross capital formation . .	1,817,933	162.1	982.4
Total domestic expenditure .	**78,585,393**	**6,102.0**	**36,262.6**
Exports of goods and services .	10,648,434	825.6	5,527.2
Less Imports of goods and services	8,462,269	627.7	5,167.5
GDP in purchasers' values . .	**80,771,558**	**6,300.0**	**36,622.3**

* Figures in '000 million new zaires (1 new zaire = 3m. old zaires).
† Estimates.

Source: IMF, *Zaire — Background Information and Statistical Data* (April 1996).

Gross Domestic Product by Economic Activity
('000 million old zaires at current prices, unless otherwise indicated)

	1993	1994*	1995*†
Agriculture, forestry, livestock,			
hunting, and fishing . .	41,443,328	3,631.2	21,247.6
Mining‡	5,111,950	296.1	1,590.7
Manufacturing	5,523,985	338.6	2,364.8
Construction and public works .	797,646	126.2	845.1
Electricity and water . . .	1,793,098	106.8	603.6
Transportation and			
telecommunications . .	2,833,538	176.0	1,022.6
Trade and commerce . . .	17,074,694	1,021.9	6,114.4
Public administration . .	2,743,993	195.4	482.9
Other services	2,796,040	349.5	2,038.1
GDP at factor cost . . .	**80,118,272**	**6,241.7**	**36,309.8**
Import duties	653,286	58.3	312.5
GDP at market prices . . .	**80,771,558**	**6,300.0**	**36,622.3**

* Figures in '000 million new zaires (1 new zaire = 3m. old zaires).
† Estimates.
‡ Including processing.

Source: IMF, *Zaire — Background Information and Statistical Data* (April 1996).

BALANCE OF PAYMENTS (US $ million)

	1994	1995*	1996†
Exports of goods f.o.b. . . .	1,255	1,632	1,944
Imports of goods f.o.b. . . .	−667	−951	−1,114
Trade balance	**589**	**681**	**830**
Services (net)	−309	−393	−536
Balance on goods and services .	**280**	**288**	**294**
Income (net)	−773	−849	−837
Balance on goods, services and			
income	**−493**	**−561**	**−543**
Current transfers (net) . . .	0	0	−2
Current balance	**−493**	**−561**	**−545**
Capital account (net) . . .	41	51	−11
Financial account (net) . . .	−801	−740	−469
Net errors and omissions . . .	−94	−88	—
Overall balance	**−1,347**	**−1,337**	**−1,025**

*Provisional.   †Estimated.

Source: IMF, *Zaire's Hyperinflation 1990–96* (April 1997).

External Trade

PRINCIPAL COMMODITIES (UN estimates, million old zaires)

Imports c.i.f.	1989	1990	1991
Food and live animals	63,380	121,824	2,172,956
Beverages and tobacco	3,436	6,605	117,812
Crude materials (inedible) except fuels	9,545	18,347	327,252
Mineral fuels, lubricants, etc.	24,436	46,968	837,761
Chemicals	33,217	63,848	1,138,847
Basic manufactures	68,343	131,365	2,343,137
Machinery and transport equipment	102,706	197,414	3,521,243
Miscellaneous manufactured articles	16,418	31,557	562,877
Other commodities and transactions	2,673	5,137	91,628
Total	324,154	623,066	11,113,531

Exports f.o.b.	1989	1990	1991
Food and live animals	93,541	148,201	2,535,635
Beverages and tobacco	5,071	8,035	137,474
Crude materials (inedible) except fuels	14,087	22,319	381,865
Mineral fuels, lubricants, etc.	36,064	57,138	977,599
Chemicals	49,024	77,672	1,328,924
Basic manufactures	100,866	159,807	2,734,207
Machinery and transport equipment	151,581	240,157	4,108,950
Miscellaneous manufactured articles	24,230	38,389	656,814
Other commodities and transactions	3,944	6,249	106,917
Total	478,409	757,967	12,968,384

Source: UN Economic Commission for Africa, *African Statistical Yearbook*.

1994 (US $ million): *Imports c.i.f.:* Mineral fuels 45.4; Total 628.8. *Exports f.o.b.:* Copper 42.8; Cobalt 140.3; Zinc 0.5; Diamonds 293.6; Crude petroleum 123.5; Coffee 158.6; Total 1,271.6. (Source: IMF, *Zaire — Background Information and Statistical Data*, April 1996).

1996 (US $ million): Total imports 921; Total exports 1,629 (Source: *African Economic Digest*).

SELECTED TRADING PARTNERS (US $ million)

Imports c.i.f.	1995
Belgium-Luxembourg.	147.2
Canada	9.8
China, People's Repub.	26.8
Côte d'Ivoire.	35.5
Ecuador.	65.1
Germany	48.2
India	9.9
Iran.	10.3
Italy	26.5
Japan	11.8
Kenya	22.5
Morocco.	9.2
Netherlands.	36.5
Nigeria.	72.5
South Africa.	89.3
Togo	22.5
United Kingdom.	50.2
Zambia.	9.4
Total (incl. others)	889.2

Exports f.o.b.	1995
Angola	51.0
Belgium-Luxembourg.	90.9
Canada	11.6
Germany	8.7
Irael	17.2
Italy	29.6
Philippines	30.2
Senegal.	9.5
South Africa.	219.7
Switzerland.	29.7
United Kingdom.	29.7
USA	107.6
Total (incl. others)	742.8

Source: UN, *International Trade Statistics Yearbook*.

Transport

RAILWAYS (Total traffic, million)

	1988	1989	1990
Passenger-km	465	467	469
Freight (net ton-km)	1,670	1,687	1,655

Source: UN, *Statistical Yearbook*.

ROAD TRAFFIC (motor vehicles in use at 31 December)

	1994	1995*	1996*
Passenger cars	698,672	762,000	787,000
Buses and coaches	51,578	55,000	60,000
Lorries and vans.	464,205	495,000	538,000
Total vehicles	1,214,455	1,312,000	1,384,000

* Estimates.

Source: International Road Federation, *World Road Statistics*.

SHIPPING

Merchant Fleet (registered at 31 December)

	1996	1997	1998
Number of vessels	27	27	20
Total displacement ('000 grt)	14.9	14.9	12.9

Source: Lloyd's Register of Shipping, *World Fleet Statistics*.

International Sea-borne Freight Traffic (estimates, '000 metric tons)

	1988	1989	1990
Goods loaded	2,500	2,440	2,395
Goods unloaded	1,400	1,483	1,453

Source: UN, *Monthly Bulletin of Statistics*.

CIVIL AVIATION (traffic on scheduled services)

	1992	1993	1994
Kilometres flown (million) . .	4	4	6
Passengers carried ('000) . .	116	84	178
Passenger-km (million) . .	295	218	480
Total ton-km (million) . .	56	42	87

Source: UN, *Statistical Yearbook*.

Tourism

	1995	1996	1997
Tourist arrivals ('000) . .	35	37	30
Tourism receipts (US $ million) .	5	5	2

Tourist arrivals: 53,139 in 1998.

Source: World Tourism Organization, *Yearbook of Tourism Statistics*.

Communications Media

	1995	1996	1997
Radio receivers ('000 in use) . .	14,103	15,970	18,030
Television receivers ('000 in use) .	3,679	5,051	6,478
Telephones ('000 main lines in use)*	36	36	21
Telefax stations (number in use)* .	5,000	5,000	n.a.
Mobile cellular telephones (subscribers)	8,500*	7,200	8,900
Daily newspapers	9	9	n.a.

Book production (titles published): 64 in 1992.

* Provisional or estimated figure(s).

Sources: UNESCO, *Statistical Yearbook*; UN Economic Commission for Africa, *African Statistical Yearbook*.

Education

(1994/95)

	Insti-tutions	Teachers	Students Males	Females	Total
Pre-primary* . .	429	768	15,956	17,279	33,235
Primary . .	14,885	121,054	3,218,822	2,198,684	5,417,506
Secondary. .	n.a.	n.a.	943,059	571,264	1,514,323
Higher . .	n.a.	n.a.	n.a.	n.a.	52,501

* Figures refer to 1992/93.

Source: UNESCO, *Statistical Yearbook*.

Directory

The Constitution

Following the proclamation of the Democratic Republic of the Congo, a 15-point constitutional decree was promulgated on 28 May 1997, which abrogated all previous constitutional dispositions. The decree declared the institutions of the Republic to be the President, the Government and the courts and tribunals; all institutions of the previous regime were suspended, except for the judiciary. All power was to be vested in the Head of State, pending the adoption of a new Constitution. In October 1997 President Kabila appointed a 42-member Constitutional Commission, which was to draft a new constitution by March 1998. The resultant draft Constitution was subsequently referred to a 300-member Constituent Assembly, which was to review the document and submit it to a national referendum. The Assembly was, however, unable to convene, owing to the outbreak of civil war, and the work was undertaken in October by a 12-member Institutional Reform Commission, appointed by Kabila.

EXECUTIVE POWER

The President of the Republic exercises legislative power by decree, following consultation with the Cabinet; he is chief of the executive and of the armed forces and has the authority to issue currency; he has the power to appoint and dismiss members of the Government, ambassadors, provincial governors, senior army officers, senior civil servants and magistrates.

POLITICAL PARTIES

All political parties, with the exception of the Alliance des forces démocratiques pour la libération du Congo-Zaïre (AFDL), were banned by decree on 26 May 1997. In January 1999, however, President Kabila issued a decree legalizing the formation of political parties (see Recent History).

PROVINCIAL GOVERNMENTS

Local government in each province is administered by a provincial governor and deputy governor, who are appointed and dismissed by the President.

The Government

HEAD OF STATE

President: Maj.-Gen. JOSEPH KABILA (inaugurated 23 January 2001).

CABINET
(May 2001)

President and Minister of Defence: Maj.-Gen. JOSEPH KABILA.

Minister of Agriculture: ANDRÉ PHILLIPE FUTA.

Minister of the Civil Service: CÉLESTIN LWANGHY.

Minister of Communications and the Press: KIKAYA BIN KARUBI.

Minister of Culture and the Arts: MARTHE NGALULA WAFWANA.

Minister of the Economy: MATUNGULU MBUYAMU.

Minister of Education: AUGUSTIN RWAKAIKARA KAMARA.

Minister of Energy: GEORGES BUSE FALAY.

Minister of Enterprises: NORBERT LIKULIA BOLONGO.

Minister of Finance and the Budget: JEAN AMISI KALONDAYA.

Minister of Fisheries and Livestock: MWANA NANGA MAWAMPANGA.

Minister of Foreign Affairs and International Co-operation: LÉONARD SHE OKITUNDU.

Minister of Health: MASHAKO MAMBA.

Minister of Housing, the Environment and Tourism Development: HENRI MOVA SAKANYA.

Minister of Human Rights: NTUMBA LUABA.

Minister of Industry and Commerce: HÉLÈNE MATEYIBO.

Minister of Information and Tourism: SAKOMBI ILONGO.

Minister of Internal Affairs: MIRA NDJOKOU MANYANGA.

Minister of Justice: NGELE MASUDI.

Minister of Labour and Social Security: MARIE ANGE LUKIANA MUFWANKOL.

Minister of Land Registration: SALOMON BANAMUHERE.

Minister of Mining and Petroleum: SIMON TUMAWAKO BAVANGU.

Minister of National Education: KUTAMISA KIOTA.

Minister of National Security and Public Order: MWENZE KONGOLO.

Minister of Petroleum Resources: ANATOLE BISHIKWABO CHUBAKA.

Minister of Planning and Reconstruction: DENIS KALUME NUMBI.

Minister of Posts, Telephones and Telecommunications: PHILLIPE KUWUTAMA.

Minister in the Office of the Presidency: AUGUSTIN KATUMBA MWANKE.

Minister of Public Administration: BENJAMIN MUKULUNGU.

Minister of Public Works: NKONDI MBAKI.

Minister of Regional Co-operation: ODELIVE META MUTOMBO MUDIAY.

Minister of Social Affairs: JEANNE EBAMBA.

Minister of Transport: DAKARUDINO WAKALE MINADA.

Minister of Youth and Sports: THIMOTHÉE MOLEKA NZULAMA.

Minister of State for Education: ABDOULAYE YERODIA NDOMBASI.

Minister of State for Internal Affairs: GAËTAN KAKUDJI.

Minister of State without Portfolio: PIERRE-VICTOR MPOYO.

Minister-delegate for Defence: IRUNG ILUNGA AWAN.

MINISTRIES

All ministries are in Kinshasa.

Office of the President: Hôtel du Conseil Exécutif, ave de Lemera, Kinshasa-Gombé; tel. (12) 30892.

Ministry of Agriculture: Immeuble Sozacom, 3rd floor, blvd du 30 juin, BP 8722 KIN I, Kinshasa-Gombé; tel. (12) 31821.

Ministry of Communications and the Press: ave du 24 novembre, BP 3171, KIN 1, Kinshasa-Kabinda; tel. (12) 23171.

Ministry of Culture and the Arts: BP 8541, Kinshasa 1; tel. (12) 31005.

Ministry of Defence: BP 4111, Kinshasa-Gombé; tel. (12) 59375.

Ministry of the Economy: Immeuble Onatra, blvd du 30 juin, BP 8500 KIN I, Kinshasa-Gombé.

Ministry of Energy: Immeuble Snel, 239 ave de la Justice, BP 5137 KIN I, Kinshasa-Gombé; tel. (12) 22570.

Ministry of Finance and the Budget: blvd du 30 juin, BP 12998 KIN I, Kinshasa-Gombé; tel. (12) 31197.

Ministry of Foreign Affairs and International Co-operation: place de l'Indépendance, BP 7100, Kinshasa-Gombé; tel. (12) 32450.

Ministry of Health: blvd du 30 juin, BP 3088 KIN I, Kinshasa-Gombé; tel. (12) 31750.

Ministry of Housing, the Environment and Tourism Development: 15 ave des Cliniques, BP 12348 KIN I, Kinshasa-Gombé; tel. (12) 31252.

Ministry of Internal Affairs: ave de Lemera, Kinshasa-Gombé; tel. (12) 23171.

Ministry of Justice: 228 ave de Lemera, BP 3137, Kinshasa-Gombé; tel. (12) 32432.

Ministry of Labour and Social Security: blvd du 30 juin, BP 3840, Kinshasa.

Ministry of National Education: Enceinte de l'Institut de la Gombé, BP 3163, Kinshasa-Gombé; tel. (12) 30098.

Ministry of Planning and Reconstruction: 4155 ave des Côteaux, BP 9378, Kinshasa-Gombé 1; tel. (12) 31346.

Ministry of Posts, Telephones and Telecommunications: Immeuble Kilou, 4484 ave des Huiles, BP 800 KIN I, Kinshasa-Gombé; tel. (12) 24854.

Ministry of Public Works: Immeuble Travaux Publics, Kinshasa-Gombé.

Ministry of Transport: Immeuble Onatra, blvd du 30 juin, BP 3304, Kinshasa-Gombé; tel. (12) 23660.

Ministry of Youth and Sports: 77 ave de la Justice, BP 8541 KIN I, Kinshasa-Gombé.

President

Following the assassination of President Laurent-Désiré Kabila on 16 January 2001, his son, Maj.-Gen. Joseph Kabila, was inaugurated as interim President on 26 January.

Legislature

The Head of State legislates by decree. In mid-2000 a 300-member transitional Parliament was formed; a selection committee, supervised by the Ministry of Internal Affairs, nominated candidates, who were subsequently approved by the President. Under a further presidential decree, signed in July, the Government was to be decentralized, with the legislature relocating to Lubumbashi. The new Parliament was inaugurated on 22 August in Lubumbashi.

Political Organizations

Comités du pouvoir populaire (CPP): f. 1999 as successor to **Alliance des forces démocratiques pour la libération du Congo-Zaïre** (AFDL); committees formed in each village to devolve power to the people; to debate political policy.

Political movements reported to be active in early 2001 included:

Forces novatrices pour l'union et la solidarité (FONUS): Kinshasa; advocates political pluralism; Pres. JOSEPH OLENGHANKOY; Sec.-Gen. JOHN KWET.

Forces politiques du conclave (FPC): Kinshasa; f. 1993; alliance of pro-Mobutu groups, incl the UFERI, led by MPR; Chair. JEAN NGUZA KARL-I-BOND.

Forces pour le salut du Congo (FSC): f. June 2000 by fmr supporters of Pres. Mobutu; Leader JÉRÔME TSHISHIMBI.

Mouvement national du Congo—Lumumba (MNC—Lumumba): Kinshasa; f. 1994; coalition of seven parties, incl. the Parti lumumbiste unifié (PALU), led by ANTOINE GIZENGA; supports the aims of the late Patrice Lumumba; Co-ordinating Cttee PASCAL TABU, MBALO MEKA, OTOKO OKITASOMBO.

Mouvement populaire de la révolution (MPR): f. 1966 by Pres. Mobutu; sole legal political party until Nov. 1990; advocates national unity and opposes tribalism; Leader (vacant); Sec.-Gen. KITHIMA BIN RAMAZANI.

Mouvement pour la libération du Congo (MLC): Equateur; f. 1998; rebel movement; Head JEAN-PIERRE BEMBA; Sec.-Gen. OLIVIER KAMITATU.

Parti démocrate et social chrétien (PDSC): 32B ave Tombalbaye, Kinshasa-Gombé; tel. (12) 21211; f. 1990; centrist; Pres. ANDRÉ BO-BOLIKO; Sec. Gen. TUYABA LEWULA.

Rassemblement congolais pour la démocratie (RCD): e-mail congorcd@congorcd.org; internet www.congorcd.org; f. 1998; advocates introduction of a democratic political system; split into two factions in 1999: Ilunga faction: Goma; supported by Rwanda; Pres. ADOLPHE ONUSUMBA.

Rassemblement congolais pour la démocratie—mouvement de libération (RCD—ML): Bunia; broke away from main RCD in 1999; supported by Uganda; Pres. ERNEST WAMBA DIA WAMBA.

Rassemblement congolais pour la démocratie—national (RCD—N): Bafwasende; broke away from RCD—ML in Oct. 2000; Leader ROGER LUMBALA.

Union des fédéralistes et républicains indépendants (UFERI): Kinshasa; f. 1990; seeks autonomy for province of Katanga; dominant party in the USOR; Pres. JEAN NGUZA KARL-I-BOND; Leader KOUYOUMBA MUCHULI MULEMBE.

Union pour la démocratie et le progrès social (UDPS): Twelfth St, Limete Zone, Kinshasa; e-mail udps@globalserve.net; internet www.udps.org/udps.html; f. 1982; Leader ETIENNE TSHISEKEDI WA MULUMBA; Sec.-Gen. Dr ADRIEN PHONGO KUNDA.

Union pour la République (UPR): Kinshasa; f. 1997 by fmr mems of the MPR; Leader CHARLES NDAYWEL.

Union sacrée de l'opposition radicale (USOR): Kinshasa; f. 1991, comprising c. 130 movements and factions opposed to Pres. Mobutu, in which the UDPS was the dominant party; a radical internal faction, known as the **Union sacrée de l'opposition radicale et ses alliés** (USORAL) (Pres. FRÉDÉRIC KIBASSA MALIBA), emerged in 1994.

Union sacrée rénovée (USR): Kinshasa; f. 1993 by several ministers in fmr Govt of Nat. Salvation; Leader KIRO KIMATE.

Diplomatic Representation

EMBASSIES IN THE DEMOCRATIC REPUBLIC OF THE CONGO

Angola: 4413–4429 blvd du 30 juin, BP 8625, Kinshasa; tel. (12) 32415; Ambassador: MAWETE JOÃO BAPTISTA.

Belgium: Immeuble Le Cinquantenaire, place du 27 octobre, BP 899, Kinshasa; tel. (12) 20110; fax 22120; Ambassador: FRANK DE CONINCK.

Benin: 3990 ave des Cliniques, BP 3265, Kinshasa-Gombé; tel. (12) 33156; Ambassador: GEORGES S. WHANNOU DE DRAVO.

Cameroon: 171 blvd du 30 juin, BP 10998, Kinshasa; tel. (12) 34787; Chargé d'affaires a.i.: DOMINIQUE AWONO ESSAMA.

Canada: BP 8341, Kinshasa 1; tel. (12) 8841277; e-mail knsha@dfait-maeci.gc.ca; Ambassador ROLAND GOULET.

Central African Republic: 11 ave Pumbu, BP 7769, Kinshasa; tel. (12) 30417; Ambassador: SISSA LE BERNARD.

Chad: 67–69 ave du Cercle, BP 9097, Kinshasa; tel. (12) 22358; Ambassador: MAITINE DJOUMBE.

China, People's Republic: 49 ave du Commerce, BP 9098, Kinshasa; tel. (12) 21207; Ambassador: SUN KUNSHAN.

Congo, Republic: 179 blvd du 30 juin, BP 9516, Kinshasa; tel. (12) 30220; Ambassador: MAURICE OGNAMY.

Côte d'Ivoire: 68 ave de la Justice, BP 9197, Kinshasa; tel. (12) 30440; Ambassador: GILBERT DOH.

Cuba: 4660 ave Cateam, BP 10699, Kinshasa; Ambassador: ENRIQUE MONTERO.

Egypt: 519 ave de l'Ouganda, BP 8838, Kinshasa; tel. (12) 34368; Ambassador: AZIZ ABDEL HAMID HAMZA.

Ethiopia: BP 8435, Kinshasa; tel. (12) 23327; Ambassador: DIEUDEONNE A. GANGA.

France: 97 ave de la République du Tchad, BP 3093, Kinshasa; tel. (12) 30513; Ambassador: GILDAS LE LIDEC.

Gabon: ave du 24 novembre, BP 9592, Kinshasa; tel. (12) 68325; Ambassador: MICHEL MADOUNGOU.

Germany: 82 ave de Lemera, BP 8400, Kinshasa-Gombé; tel. (12) 33399; fax (satellite) 871-112-0323; Ambassador: HELMUT OHBRAUN.

Greece: Immeuble de la Communauté Hellénique, 3éme étage, blvd du 30 juin, BP 478, Kinshasa; tel. (12) 8844862; fax (12) 8801002; e-mail grembkin@ic.cd; Ambassador: SPYROS THEOCHAROPOULOS.

Holy See: 81 ave Goma, BP 3091, Kinshasa; tel. (12) 33128; fax (12) 33346; Apostolic Nuncio: Most Rev. FAUSTINO SAINZ MUÑOZ, Titular Archbishop of Novaliciana.

Iran: 76 blvd du 30 juin, BP 16599, Kinshasa; tel. (12) 31052.

Israel: 12 ave des Aviateurs, BP 8343, Kinshasa; tel. (12) 21955; Ambassador: JAMAR F. GOLAN.

Italy: 8 ave de la Mongala, BP 1000, Kinshasa; tel. (88) 46106; e-mail ambitalykin@raga.net; Ambassador: PIETRO BALLERO.

Japan: Immeuble Citibank, 2e étage, ave Colonel Lukusa, BP 1810, Kinshasa; tel. (88) 45305; fax (satellite) 871-761-21-41-42; e-mail ambj@ic.cd; Ambassador YASUO TAKANO.

Kenya: 4002 ave de l'Ouganda, BP 9667, Kinshasa; tel. (12) 8806834; Chargé d'affaires J. K. CHUMBA.

Korea, Democratic People's Republic: 168 ave de l'Ouganda, BP 16597, Kinshasa; tel. (12) 31566; Ambassador: HAN PON CHUN.

Korea, Republic: 2A ave des Orangers, BP 628, Kinshasa; tel. (88) 20722; Ambassador: CHUN SOON-KYU.

Lebanon: 3 ave de l'Ouganda, BP 8940, Kinshasa; tel. (12) 82469; Chargé d'affaires a.i.: CHEHADE MOUALLEM.

Liberia: 3 ave de l'Okapi, BP 8940, Kinshasa; tel. (12) 82289; Ambassador: JALLA D. LANSANAH.

Mauritania: BP 16397, Kinshasa; tel. (12) 59575; Ambassador: Lt-Col M'BARECK OULD BOUNA MOKHTAR.

Morocco: 4497 ave Lubefu, BP 912, Kinshasa; tel. (12) 34794; Ambassador: ABDELAZIZ BENNIS.

Namibia: Kinshasa; Ambassador EDDIE AMKONGO.

Netherlands: 11 ave Zongo Ntolo, BP 10299, Kinshasa; tel (12) 30733; Ambassador: F. RACKE.

Nigeria: 141 blvd du 30 juin, BP 1700, Kinshasa; tel. (12) 43272; Ambassador: AHMED MOHAMMED KELE.

Portugal: 270 ave des Aviateurs, BP 7775, Kinshasa; tel. (12) 21335; Ambassador: LUÍS DE VASCONCELOS PIMENTEL QUARTIN BASTOS.

Russia: 80 ave de la Justice, BP 1143, Kinshasa 1; tel. (12) 33157; fax (12) 45575; Ambassador: VALERII GAMAIVNE.

South Africa: 17 ave Pumbu, BP 7829, Kinshasa-Gombé; tel. (88) 48287; fax (satellite) 1-212-3723510; Ambassador: (vacant).

Sudan: 83 ave des Treis, BP 7347, Kinshasa; tel. (12) 33200; Ambassador: MUBARAK ADAM HADI.

Sweden: 89 ave de Lemera, BP 11096, Kinshasa; tel. (12) 34084; fax (12) 33683; e-mail ambasuede@ic.cd; Chargé d'affaires a.i.: EVA EMNÉUS.

Togo: 3 ave de la Vallée, BP 10117, Kinshasa; tel. (12) 30666; Ambassador: MAMA GNOFAM.

Tunisia: 67–69 ave du Cercle, BP 1498, Kinshasa; tel. and fax (88) 03901; Chargé d'affaires a.i.: FARHAT BAROUN.

Turkey: 18 ave Pumbu, BP 7817, Kinshasa; tel. (88) 01207; fax (88) 04740; Ambassador: DENIZ UZMEN.

United Kingdom: ave de Lemera, BP 8049, Kinshasa; tel. (88) 46102; fax (satellite) 871-144-7753; e-mail ambrit@ic.cd; Ambassador: JAMES ATKINSON.

USA: 310 ave des Aviateurs, BP 697, Kinshasa; tel. (12) 21523; fax 21232; Ambassador: WILLIAM L. SWING.

Zambia: 54–58 ave de l'Ecole, BP 1144, Kinshasa; tel. (12) 23038; Ambassador: IAN SIKAZWE.

Judicial System

The Minister of Justice is responsible for the organization and definition of competence of the judiciary; civil, penal and commercial law and civil and penal procedures; the status of persons and property; the system of obligations and questions pertaining to nationality; international private law; status of magistrates; organization of the legal profession, counsels for the defence, notaries and of judicial auxiliaries; supervision of cemeteries, non-profit-making organizations, cults and institutions working in the public interest; the operation of prisons; confiscated property.

There is a Supreme Court in Kinshasa, and there are also nine Courts of Appeal and 36 County Courts. A presidential decree, signed in July 2000, provided for government decentralization, with the Supreme Court relocating to Kisangani.

The Head of State is empowered to appoint and dismiss magistrates.

Supreme Court: cnr ave de la Justice and ave de Lemera, BP 3382, Kinshasa-Gombé; tel. (12) 25104.

President of the Supreme Court: BIYANGO KETESE.

Procurator-General of the Republic: MONGULU T'APANGANE.

Religion

Many of the country's inhabitants follow traditional beliefs, which are mostly animistic. A large proportion of the population is Christian, predominantly Roman Catholic, and there are small Muslim, Jewish and Greek Orthodox communities.

CHRISTIANITY

The Roman Catholic Church

The Democratic Republic of the Congo comprises six archdioceses and 41 dioceses. An estimated 51% of the population are Roman Catholics.

Bishops' Conference: Conférence Episcopale de la République Démocratique du Congo, BP 3258, Kinshasa-Gombé; tel. (12) 30082; f. 1981; Pres. Rt Rev. FAUSTIN NGABU, Bishop of Goma.

Archbishop of Bukavu: Most Rev. EMMANUEL KATALIKO, Archevêché, BP 3324, Bukavu; tel. 2707; fax (16) 82060067.

Archbishop of Kananga: Most Rev. GODEFROID MUKENG'A KALOND, Archevêché, BP 70, Kananga; tel. 2477.

Archbishop of Kinshasa: Cardinal FRÉDÉRIC ETSOU-NZABI-BAMUNGWABI, Archevêché, ave de l'Université, BP 8431, Kinshasa 1; tel. (12) 3723-546.

Archbishop of Kisangani: Most Rev. LAURENT MONSENGWO PASINYA, Archevêché, ave Mpolo 10B, BP 505, Kisangani; tel. (761) 608334; fax (761) 3132898.

Archbishop of Lubumbashi: Most Rev. FLORIBERT SONGASONGA MWITWA, Archevêché, BP 72, Lubumbashi; tel. (2) 34-1442.

Archbishop of Mbandaka-Bikoro: Most Rev. JOSEPH KUMUONDALA MBIMBA, Archevêché, BP 1064, Mbandaka; tel. 2234.

The Anglican Communion

The Church of the Province of the Congo comprises six dioceses.

Archbishop of the Province of the Congo and Bishop of Boga: Most Rev. PATRICE BYANKYA NJOJO, CAC-Boga, POB 21285, Nairobi, Kenya.

Bishop of Bukavu: Rt Rev. FIDÈLE BALUFUGA DIROKPA, CAC-Bukavu, POB 53435, Nairobi, Kenya.

Bishop of Katanga: Rt Rev. ISINGOMA KAHWA, BP 16482, Kinshasa; tel. 8806533; peac_isingoma@yahoo.fr.

Bishop of Kindu: Rt Rev. ZACHARIA MASIMANGE KATANDA, CAC-Kindu, POB 53435, Nairobi, Kenya; e-mail angkindu@antenna.nl.

Bishop of Kisangani: Rt Rev. SYLVESTRE MUGERA TIBAFA, CAC-Kisangani, BP 861, Kisangani.

Bishop of Nord Kivu: Rt Rev. METHUSELA MUNZENDA MUSUBAHO, CAC-Butembo, POB 21285, Nairobi, Kenya; fax (satellite) 871-166-1121.

Kimbanguist

Eglise de Jésus Christ sur la Terre par le Prophète Simon Kimbangu: BP 7069, Kinshasa; tel. (12) 68944; f. 1921 (officially est. 1959); c. 5m. mems (1985); Spiritual Head HE SALOMON DIALUNGANA KIANGANI; Sec.-Gen. Rev. LUNTADILLA.

Protestant Churches

Eglise du Christ au Congo (ECC): ave de la Justice (face no. 75), BP 4938, Kinshasa-Gombe; f. 1902; a co-ordinating agency for all the Protestant churches, with the exception of the Kimbanguist

Church; 62 mem. communities and a provincial org. in each province; c. 10m. mems (1982); Pres. Bishop MARINI BODHO; includes:

Communauté Baptiste du Congo-Ouest: BP 4728, Kinshasa 2; f. 1970; 450 parishes; 170,000 mems (1985); Gen. Sec. Rev. LUSAKWENO-VANGU.

Communauté des Disciples du Christ: BP 178, Mbandaka; tel. 31062; f. 1964; 250 parishes; 650,000 mems (1985); Gen. Sec. Rev. Dr ELONDA EFEFE.

Communauté Episcopale Baptiste en Afrique: 2 ave Jason Sendwe, BP 3866, Lubumbashi 1; tel. (2) 24724; f. 1956; 1,300 episcopal communions and parishes; 150,000 mems (1993); Pres. Bishop KITOBO KABWEKA-LEZA.

Communauté Evangélique: BP 36, Luozi; f. 1961; 50 parishes; 33,750 mems (1985); Pres. Rev. K. LUKOMBO NTONTOLO.

Communauté Lumière: BP 10498, Kinshasa 1; f. 1931; 150 parishes; 220,000 mems (1985); Patriarch KAYUWA TSHIBUMBU WA KAHINGA.

Communauté Mennonite: BP 18, Tshikapa; f. 1960; 40,000 mems (1985); Gen. Sec. Rev. KABANGY DJEKE SHAPASA.

Communauté Presbytérienne: BP 117, Kananga; f. 1959; 150,000 mems (1985); Gen. Sec. Dr M. L. TSHIHAMBA.

Eglise Missionaire Apostolique: 375 ave Commerciale, BP 15859, Kinshasa 1; tel. (12) 8804569; f. 1986; 5 parishes; 2,500 mems.; Apostle for Africa LUFANGA-AYIMOU NANANDANA.

The Press

DAILIES

L'Analyste: 129 ave du Bas-Congo, BP 91, Kinshasa-Gombé; tel. (12) 80987; Dir and Editor-in-Chief BONGOMA KONI BOTAHE.

Boyoma: 31 blvd Mobutu, BP 982, Kisangani, Dir and Editor BADRIYO ROVA ROVATU.

Elima: 1 ave de la Révolution, BP 11498, Kinshasa; tel. (12) 77332; f. 1928; evening; Dir and Editor-in-Chief ESSOLOMWA NKOY EA LINGANGA.

Mjumbe: BP 2474, Lubumbashi; tel. (2) 25348; f. 1963; Dir and Editor TSHIMANGA KOYA KAKONA.

Le Palmarès: 220 ave Mpolo, BP 63, Kinshasa-Gombé; supports Union pour la démocratie et le progrès social; Editor MICHEL LADELUYA.

Le Phare: BP 15662, Kinshasa 1; tel. (12) 45896; f. 1983; Editor POLYDOR MUBOYAYI MUBANGA; circ 4,000.

Le Potentiel: Immeuble Ruzizi, 873 ave du Bas-Congo, BP 11338, Kinshasa; tel. (2) 44456; f. 1982; Editor MODESTE MUTINGA MUTUISHAYI; circ. 8,000.

La Référence Plus: BP 22520, Kinshasa; tel. (2) 45783; f. 1989; Dir ANDRÉ IPAKALA.

Le Soft: Kinshasa; Man. KINKIEY MALUMBA; Chief Editor AWASI KHAROMON.

PERIODICALS

Allo Kinshasa: 3 rue Kayange, BP 20271, Kinshasa-Lemba; monthly; Editor MBUYU WA KABILA.

L'Aurore Protestante: Eglise du Christ au Congo, BP 4938, Kinshasa-Gombe; French; religion; monthly; circ. 1,000.

BEA Magazine de la Femme: 2 ave Masimanimba, BP 113380, Kinshasa 1; every 2 weeks; Editor MUTINGA MUTWISHAYI.

Bingwa: ave du 30 juin, zone Lubumbashi no 4334; weekly; sport; Dir and Editor MATEKE WA MULAMBA.

Cahiers Economiques et Sociaux: BP 257, Kinshasa XI, (National University of the Congo); sociological, political and economic review; quarterly; Dir Prof. NDONGALA TADI LEWA; circ. 2,000.

Cahiers des Religions Africaines: Faculté de Théologie Catholique de Kinshasa, BP 712, Kinshasa/Limete; tel. (12) 78476; f. 1967; English and French; religion; 2 a year; circ. 1,000.

Le Canard Libre: Kinshasa; f. 1991; Editor JOSEPH CASTRO MULEBE.

Circulaire d'Information: Association Nationale des Entreprises du Congo, 10 ave des Aviateurs, BP 7247, Kinshasa 1; tel. (12) 22565; f. 1959; French; legal and statutory texts for the business community; monthly.

La Colombe: 32B ave Tombalbaye, Kinshasa-Gombé; tel. (12) 21211; organ of Parti démocrate et social chrétien; circ. 5,000.

Congo-Afrique: Centre d'Etudes pour l'Action Sociale, 9 ave Père Boka, BP 3375, Kinshasa-Gombé; tel. (12) 34682; f. 1961; economic, social and cultural; monthly; Editors FRANCIS KIKASSA MWANALESSA, RENÉ BEECKMANS; circ. 2,500.

Le Conseiller Comptable: 51 rue du Grand Séminaire, Quartier Nganda, BP 308, Kinshasa; tel. (88) 01216; fax (88) 00075; f 1974; French; public finance and taxation; quarterly; Editor TOMENA FOKO; circ. 2,000.

Le Courrier du Zaïre: aut. no 04/DIMOPAP 0018/84, 101 Lukolela, Kinshasa; weekly; Editor NZONZILA NDONZUAU.

Cultures au Zaïre et en Afrique: BP 16706, Kinshasa; f. 1973; French and English; quarterly.

Dionga: Immeuble Amassio, 2 rue Dirna, BP 8031, Kinshasa; monthly.

Documentation et Information Protestante (DIP): Eglise du Christ au Congo, BP 4938, Kinshasa-Gombé; tel. and fax (88) 46387; e-mail eccm@ic.cd; French and English; religion.

Documentation et Informations Africaines (DIA): BP 2598, Kinshasa 1; tel. (12) 33197; fax (12) 33196; Roman Catholic news agency reports; 3 a week; Dir Rev. Père VATA DIAMBANZA.

L'Entrepreneur Flash: Association Nationale des Entreprises du Congo, 10 ave des Aviateurs, BP 7247, Kinshasa 1; tel. (12) 22565; f. 1978; business news; monthly; circ. 1,000.

Etudes d'Histoire Africaine: National University of the Congo, BP 1825, Lubumbashi; f. 1970; French and English; history; annually; circ. 1,000.

Horizons 80: Société Congolaise d'Edition et d'Information, BP 9839, Kinshasa; economic affairs; weekly.

JuriCongo: coin des aves commerce et plateau, Galerie du 24 Novembre, Kinshasa; fax (12) 20320; e-mail cavas@ic.cd; guide to judicial affairs; Pres. EMERY MUKENDI WAFWANA.

Les Kasaï: 161 9e rue, BP 575, Kinshasa/Limete; weekly; Editor NSENGA NDOMBA.

Kin-Média: BP 15808, Kinshasa 1; monthly; Editor ILUNGA KASAMBAY.

KYA: 24 ave de l'Equateur, BP 7853, Kinshasa-Gombé; tel. (12) 27502; f. 1984; weekly for Bas-Congo; Editor SASSA KASSA YI KIBOBA.

Libération: Kinshasa; f. 1997; politics; supports the AFDL; weekly; Man. NGOYI KABUYA DIKATETA M'MIANA.

Mambenga 2000: BP 477, Mbandaka; Editor BOSANGE YEMA BOF.

Le Moniteur de l'Economie (Economic Monitor): Kinshasa; Man. Ed. FÉLIX NZUZI.

Mwana Shaba: Générale des Carrières et des Mines, BP 450, Lubumbashi; monthly; circ. 25,000.

Ngabu: Société Nationale d'Assurances, Immeuble Sonas Sankuru, blvd du 30 juin, BP 3443, Kinshasa-Gombé; tel. (12) 23051; f. 1973; insurance news; quarterly.

Njanja: Société Nationale des Chemins de Fer Congolais, 115 place de la Gare, BP 297, Lubumbashi; tel. (2) 23430; fax (2) 61321; railways and transportation; annually; circ. 10,000.

NUKTA: 14 chaussée de Kasenga, BP 3805, Lubumbashi; weekly; agriculture; Editor NGOY BUNDUKI.

L'Opinion: BP 15394, Kinshasa; weekly; Editor SABLE FWAMBA KIEPENDA.

Problèmes Sociaux Zaïrois: Centre d'Exécution de Programmes Sociaux et Economiques, Université de Lubumbashi, 208 ave Kasavubu, BP 1873, Lubumbashi; f. 1946; quarterly; Editor N'KASHAMA KADIMA.

Promoteur Congolais: Centre du Commerce International du Congo, 119 ave Colonel Tshatshi, BP 13, Kinshasa; f. 1979; international trade news; six a year.

Sciences, Techniques, Informations: Centre de Recherches Industrielles en Afrique Centrale (CRIAC), BP 54, Lubumbashi.

Le Sport Africain: 13è niveau Tour adm., Cité de la Voix du Congo, BP 3356, Kinshasa-Gombé; monthly; Pres. TSHIMPUMPU WA TSHIMPUMPU.

Taifa: 536 ave Lubumba, BP 884, Lubumbashi; weekly; Editor LWAMBWA MILAMBU.

Telema: Faculté Canisius, Kimwenza, BP 3724, Kinshasa-Gombé; f. 1974; religious; quarterly; edited by the Central Africa Jesuits; circ. 1,200.

Umoja: 23 Bunkeye Matonge, Kinshasa; weekly; Publr LÉON MOUKANDA LUNYAMA.

Vision: Kinshasa; 2 a week; independent; Man. Editor XAVIER BONANE YANGANZI.

Zaïre Business: Immeuble Amasco, 3968 rue ex-Belgika, BP 9839, Kinshasa; f. 1973; French; weekly.

Zaïre Informatique: Conseil Permanent de l'Informatique au Zaïre, Kinshasa 1; f. 1978; quarterly.

Zaïre Ya Sita: Direction Générale et Administration, 1 rue Luozi Kasavubu, BP 8246, Kinshasa; f. 1968; Lingala; political science; 6 a year.

NEWS AGENCIES

Agence Congolaise de Presse (ACP): 44–48 ave Tombalbaye, BP 1595, Kinshasa 1; tel. (12) 22035; f. 1957; state-controlled; Dir-Gen. ALI KALONGA.

Documentation et Informations Africaines (DIA): BP 2598, Kinshasa 1; tel. (12) 34528; f. 1957; Roman Catholic news agency; Dir Rev. Père VATA DIAMBANZA.

Foreign Bureaux

Agence France-Presse (AFP): Immeuble Wenge 3227, ave Wenge, Zone de la Gombé, BP 726, Kinshasa 1; tel. (12) 27009; Bureau Chief JEAN-PIERRE REJETTE.

Agencia EFE (Spain): BP 2653, Lubumbashi; Correspondent KANKU SANGA.

Agência Lusa de Informação (Portugal): BP 4941, Kinshasa; tel. (12) 24437.

Agenzia Nazionale Stampa Associata (ANSA) (Italy): BP 2790, Kinshasa 15; tel. (12) 30315; Bureau Chief (vacant).

Pan-African News Agency (PANA) (Senegal): BP 1400, Kinshasa; tel. (12) 23290; f. 1983; Bureau Chief ADRIEN HONORÉ MBEYET.

Xinhua (New China) News Agency (People's Republic of China): 293 ave Mfumu Lutunu, BP 8939, Kinshasa; tel. (12) 25647; Correspondent CHEN WEIBIN.

PRESS ASSOCIATIONS

Médias Libres—Médias pour Tous: Kinshasa; org. representing Kinshasa newspapers.

Union de la Presse du Congo: BP 4941, Kinshasa 1; tel. (12) 24437.

Publishers

Aequatoria Centre: BP 276, Mbandaka; f. 1980; anthropology, biography, ethnicity, history, language and linguistics, social sciences; Dir HONORÉ VINCK.

CEEBA Publications: BP 246, Bandundu; f. 1965; humanities, languages, fiction; Man. Dir (Editorial) Dr HERMANN HOCHEGGER.

CELTA (Centre de Linguistique Théorique et Appliquée): BP 4956, Kinshasa-Gombé; tel. (2) 30503; fax (2) 21394; f 1971; language arts and linguistics; Gen. Man. N. KIKO; Dir NTITA NYEMBWE.

Centre de Documentation Agricole: BP 7537, Kinshasa 1; tel. (12) 32498; agriculture, science; Dir PIERTE MBAYAKABUYI; Chief Editor J. MARCELLIN KAPUKUNGESA.

Centre de Recherches Pédagogiques: BP 8815, Kinshasa 1; f. 1959; accounting, education, geography, language, science; Dir P. DETIENNE.

Centre de Vulgarisation Agricole: BP 4008, Kinshasa 2; tel. (12) 71165; fax (12) 21351; agriculture, environment, health; Dir-Gen. KIMPIANGA MAHANIAH.

Centre International de Semiologie: 109 ave Pruniers, BP 1825, Lubumbashi.

Centre Protestant d'Editions et de Diffusion (CEDI): 209 ave Kalémie, BP 11398, Kinshasa 1; tel. (12) 22202; fax (12) 26730; f. 1935; fiction, poetry, biography, religious, juvenile; Christian tracts, works in French, Lingala, Kikongo, etc.; Dir-Gen. HENRY DIRKS.

Commission de l'Education Chrétienne: BP 3258, Kinshasa-Gombé; tel. (12) 30086; education, religion; Man. Dir Abbé MUGADJA LEHANI.

Connaissance et Pratique du Droit Congolais Editions (CDPC): BP 5502, Kinshasa-Gombé; f. 1987; law; Editor DIBUNDA KABUINJI.

Facultés Catholiques de Kinshasa: BP 1534, Kinshasa-Limete; tel. and fax (12) 46965; f. 1957; anthropology, art, economics, history, politics, computer science; five titles in 1994; Dir Mgr LUDIONGO NDOMBASI.

Editions Lokole: BP 5085, Kinshasa 10; state org. for the promotion of literature; Dir BOKEME SHANE MOLOBAY.

Editions Saint Paul: BP 8505, Kinshasa; tel. (12) 77726; fiction, general non-fiction, poetry, religion; Dir Sister FRANKA PERONA.

Les Editions du Trottoir: BP 629, Kinshasa; f. 1989; communications, fiction, literature, drama; Pres. CHARLES DJUNJU-SIMBA.

Librarie les Volcans: 22 ave Pres. Mobutu, BP 400, Goma, Nord-Kivu; f. 1995; social sciences; Man. Dir RUHAMA MUKANDOLI.

Presses Universitaires du Congo (PUC): 290 rue d'Aketi, BP 1682, Kinshasa 1; tel. (12) 30652; f. 1972; scientific publs; Dir Prof. MUMBANZA MWA BAWELE.

Government Publishing House

Imprimerie du Gouvernement Central: BP 3021, Kinshasa-Kalina.

Broadcasting and Communications

TELECOMMUNICATIONS

Comcell: Kinshasa; provides satellite communications network; 4,000 subscribers.

Office Congolais des Postes et des Télécommunications (OCPT): Hôtel des postes, blvd du 30 juin, BP 13798, Kinshasa; tel. (12) 21871; fax (88) 45010; state-owned; 13,000 lines; 40,000 subscribers; Dir-Gen. KAPITAO MAMBWENI.

Telecel-Congo: Kinshasa; provides satellite communications network; largest private operator; 45% nationalized in 1998; 12,000 subscribers.

BROADCASTING

Radio-Télévision Nationale Congolaise (RTNC): BP 3171, Kinshasa-Gombé; tel. (12) 23171; state radio terrestrial and satellite television broadcasts; Dir-Gen. JOSE KAJANGUA.

Radio

Several private radio broadcasters operate in Kinshasa.

Radio Candip: Centre d'Animation et de Diffusion Pedagogique, BP 373, Bunia; state-controlled; under rebel control in late 1998.

La Voix du Congo: Station Nationale, BP 3164, Kinshasa-Gombé; tel. (12) 23175; state-controlled; operated by RTNC; broadcasts in French, Swahili, Lingala, Tshiluba, Kikongo; regional stations at Kisangani, Lubumbashi, Bukavu, Bandundu, Kananga, Mbuji-Mayi, Matadi, Mbandaka and Bunia.

Television

Several private television broadcasters operate in Kinshasa.

Antenne A: Immeuble Forescom, 2e étage, ave du Port 4, POB 2581, Kinshasa 1; tel. (243) 21736; private and commercial station; Dir-Gen. IGAL AVIVI NEIRSON.

Canal Z: ave du Port 6, POB 614, Kinshasa 1; tel. (243) 20239; commercial station; Dir-Gen. FRÉDÉRIC FLASSE.

Tele Kin Malebo (TKM): Kinshasa; private television station; nationalization announced 1997; Dir-Gen. NGONGO LUWOWO.

Télévision Congolais: BP 3171, Kinshasa-Gombé: tel. (12) 23171; govt commercial station; operated by RTNC; broadcasts for 5 hours daily on weekdays and 10 hours daily at weekends.

Finance

(cap. = capital; res = reserves; dep. = deposits; m. = million; brs = branches; amounts in old zaires unless otherwise indicated)

BANKING

A reorganization of the banking sector was expected to follow the introduction as legal tender of a new currency unit, the Congolese franc (CF), which was completed on 30 June 1999.

Central Bank

Banque Centrale du Congo: blvd Colonel Tshatshi au nord, BP 2697, Kinshasa; tel. (12) 20701; f. 1964; cap. and res 50,088.4m. (Dec. 1988); Gov. JEAN-CLAUDE MASANGU MULONGO; 8 brs.

Commercial Banks

African Trade Bank (ATB): ave Lemarinel, BP 3459, Kinshasa-Gombé; tel. (12) 33845; fax (12) 8846991; cap. and res NZ 67,893.3m., total assets NZ 406,946.6m. (Dec. 1996); Pres. ABDALLAH HASSAN WAZNI; Gen. Man. GHAZI ABDALLAH WAZNI.

BANCOR SARL: Immeuble Régidesco-DG, BP 7997, Kinshasa; tel. (12) 20635; fax (satellite) 1-212-3769207; f. 1998.

Banque de Commerce et de Développement (BCD): 87 blvd du 30 juin, Kinshasa; tel. (12) 20106; fax (satellite) 1-703-3902716; e-mail bcd-kin@ic.cd; cap. and res CF 5.2m., total assets CF 29.1m. (Dec. 1998).

Banque Commerciale du Congo SARL (BCDC): blvd du 30 juin, BP 488, Kinshasa; tel. (12) 21693; fax (12) 21770; e-mail bcdc@raga.cd; f. 1909 as Banque du Congo Belge, name changed as above 1997; cap. and res CF 249.0m., dep. 238.4m. (Dec. 1999); Pres. NKEMA LILOO; Gen. Man. KASONGO TAIBU; 29 brs.

Banque Congolaise du Commerce Extérieur SARL: blvd du 30 juin, BP 400, Kinshasa 1; tel. (12) 20393; fax (12) 27947; f. 1947, reorg. 1987; state-owned; in liquidation in 1999; cap. and res NZ 19,303.1m., dep. NZ 27,419.9m. (Dec. 1994); Chair. and Gen. Man. GBENDO NDEWA TETE; Dirs MAKUMA NDESEKE, ZIKONDOLO BIWABEKI; 31 brs.

Banque Continentale Africaine (Congo) SCARL: 4 ave de la Justice, BP 7613, Kinshasa-Gombé; tel. (12) 24388; fax (12) 21237; f. 1983; total assets 28,786.5m. (Dec. 1994); Pres. NASIR ABID; Dir-Gen. M. A. DOCHY.

Banque de Crédit Agricole: angle ave Kasa-Vubu et ave M'Polo, BP 8837, Kinshasa-Gombé; tel. (12) 21800; fax (12) 27221; f. 1982 to expand and modernize enterprises in agriculture, livestock and fishing, and generally to improve the quality of rural life; state-

owned; in liquidation in 1999; cap. 5m. (Dec. 1991); Pres. MOLOTO MWA LOPANZA.

Banque Internationale de Crédit SCARL (BIC): 191 ave de l'Equateur, BP 1299, Kinshasa 1; tel. (88) 41940; fax (12) 123769600; f. 1994; cap. and res NZ 8,355.4m., total assets NZ 35,077.9m. (Dec. 1995); Pres. PASCAL KINDUELO LUMBU; Man. Dir THARCISSE K. M. MILEMBWE.

Banque Internationale pour l'Afrique au Congo (BIAC): Immeuble Nioki, ave de la Douane, Kinshasa 1; tel. (88) 20612; fax (12) 20120; e-mail biac-rj@raga.net; cap. and res US $1.4m., total assets US $17.4m. (Dec. 1998); Pres. ROBERT JONCHERAY.

Caisse Générale d'Epargne du Congo: 38 ave de la Caisse d'Epargne, BP 8147, Kinshasa-Gombé; tel. (12) 33701; f. 1950; state-owned; Chair. and Man. Dir NSIMBA M'VUEDI; 45 brs.

Citibank NA Congo: Immeuble Citibank Congo, angle aves Col Lukusa et Ngongo Lutete, BP 9999, Kinshasa 1; tel. (12) 20554; fax (12) 21064; f. 1971; cap. and res NZ 199,425.2m., total assets NZ 1,928,804.9m. (Dec. 1996); Pres. ROBERT THORNTON; 1 br.

Fransabank (Congo) SARL: Immeuble Flavica 14/16, ave du Port, BP 9497, Kinshasa 1; tel. (88) 00445376; fax (88) 0046423; f. 1989; cap. and res NZ 7,351.7m., total assets NZ 174,809.7m. (Dec. 1996); Pres. ADNAN WAFIC KASSAR.

Nouvelle Banque de Kinshasa: 1 place du Marché, BP 8033, Kinshasa 1; tel. (12) 26361; fax (12) 20587; f. 1969, nationalized 1975; control transferred to National Union of Congolese Workers in 1989; in liquidation in 1999; cap. NZ 2,000 (1990), res NZ 92,179.4m., dep. NZ 25,396.8m. (Dec. 1994); Pres. MANTOMINA KIALA; 15 brs.

Société Financière de Développement SCARL (SOFIDE): Immeuble SOFIDE, 9–11 angle aves Ngabu et Kisangani, BP 1148, Kinshasa 1; tel. (12) 20676; fax (12) 20788; f. 1970; partly state-owned; provides tech. and financial aid, primarily for agricultural devt; cap. and res NZ 44,610.4m., total assets NZ 519,789.7m. (Dec. 1997); Pres. and Dir-Gen. KIYANGA KI-N'LOMBI; 4 brs.

Stanbic Bank Congo SARL: 12 ave de Mongala, BP 16297, Kinshasa 1; tel. (12) 20028; fax (12) 46216; f. 1973; subsidiary of Standard Bank Investment Corpn (South Africa); cap. and res CF 1.2m., total assets CF 21.3m. (Dec. 1998); Chair. J. N. LEGGETT; Man. Dir NICOLAS CLAVEL; 1 br.

Union de Banques Congolaises (UBC) SARL: angle ave de la Nation et ave des Aviateurs 19, BP 197, Kinshasa 1; tel. (88) 41333; fax (88) 46628; e-mail ubc@ic.cd; f. 1929, renamed as above in 1997; total assets US $ 59.3m. (Dec. 1997); Man. Dir LUC DELVA; 8 brs.

INSURANCE

Société Nationale d'Assurances (SONAS): 3473 blvd du 30 juin, Kinshasa-Gombé; tel. (12) 23051; f. 1966; state-owned; cap. 23m.; 9 brs.

Trade and Industry

At November 1994 the Government's portfolio of state enterprises numbered 116, of which 56 were wholly owned by the Government. The heads of all state-owned enterprises were suspended by decree in June 1997.

DEVELOPMENT ORGANIZATIONS

Caisse de Stabilisation Cotonnière (CSCo): BP 3058, Kinshasa-Gombé; tel. (12) 31206; f. 1978 to replace Office National des Fibres Textiles; acts as an intermediary between the Govt, cotton ginners and textile factories, and co-ordinates international financing of cotton sector.

La Générale des Carrières et des Mines (GÉCAMINES): BP 450, Lubumbashi; tel. (2) 6768105; fax (2) 6768041; f. 1967 to acquire assets of Union Minière du Haut-Katanga; state-owned corpn engaged in mining and marketing of copper, cobalt, zinc and coal; also has interests in agriculture; privatization announced in 1994, subsequently delayed; Exec. Chair. GEORGE FORREST; operates the following enterprise:

GÉCAMINES—Exploitation: mining operations.

Institut National pour l'Etude et la Recherche Agronomiques: BP 1513, Kisangani; f. 1933; agricultural research.

Office National du Café: ave Général Bobozo, BP 8931, Kinshasa 1; tel. (12) 77144; f. 1979; state agency for coffee and also cocoa, tea, quinquina and pyrethrum.

Pêcherie Maritime Congolaise: Kinshasa; DRC's only sea-fishing enterprise.

CHAMBERS OF COMMERCE

Chambre de Commerce, d'Industrie et d'Agriculture du Congo: 10 ave des Aviateurs, BP 7247, Kinshasa 1; tel. (12) 22286.

INDUSTRIAL AND TRADE ASSOCIATIONS

Association Nationale des Entreprises du Congo: 10 ave des Aviateurs, BP 7247, Kinshasa; tel. (12) 24623; f. 1972; represents business interests for both domestic and foreign institutions; Man. Dir EDOUARD LUBOYA DIYOKA; Gen. Sec. ATHANASE MATENDA KYELU.

EMPLOYERS' ASSOCIATION

Fédération des Entreprises du Congo (FEC): Kinshasa; Head JOSE ENDUNDO.

UTILITIES

Electricity

Société Nationale d'Electricité (SNEL): 2831 ave de la Justice, BP 500, Kinshasa; tel. (12) 26893; fax (12) 33735; f. 1970; state-owned; Dir-Gen. PASCAL KUNDA PAKA (acting).

Water

Régie de Distribution d'Eau (REGIDESCO): 65 blvd du 30 juin, BP 12599, Kinshasa; tel. (12) 22792; water supply admin; Dir-Gen. EALE BOMBOLE (acting).

TRADE UNIONS

The Union Nationale des Travailleurs was founded in 1967 as the sole trade union organization. In 1990 the establishment of independent trade unions was legalized, and by early 1991 there were 12 officially recognized trade union organizations.

Union Nationale des Travailleurs du Congo: BP 8814, Kinshasa; f. 1967; comprises 16 unions; Pres. KATALAY MOLELI SANGOL.

Transport

Office National des Transports (ONATRA): BP 98, Kinshasa 1; tel. (12) 21457; fax (12) 1398632; operates 12,174 km of waterways, 366 km of railways and road and air transport; administers ports of Kinshasa, Matadi, Boma and Banana; Pres. and Gen. Man. JEAN PHILIBERT MABAYA GIZI AMINE.

RAILWAYS

The main line runs from Lubumbashi to Ilebo. International services run to Dar es Salaam (Tanzania) and Lobito (Angola), and also connect with the Zambian, Zimbabwean, Mozambican and South African systems. In May 1997 the railway system was nationalized.

Kinshasa–Matadi Railway: BP 98, Kinshasa 1; 366 km operated by ONATRA; Pres. JACQUES MBELOLO BITWEMI.

Société Nationale des Chemins de Fer du Congo (SNCC): 115 place de la Gare, BP 297, Lubumbashi; tel. (2) 46306; fax (2) 342254; e-mail sncc01aie-lubum-cd; f. 1974; 3,606 km (including 858 km electrified); administers all internal railway sections as well as river transport and transport on Lakes Tanganyika and Kivu; man. contract concluded with a Belgian-South African corpn, Sizarail, in 1995 for the man. of the Office des Chemins de Fer du Sud (OCS) and the Société des Chemins de Fer de l'Est (SFE) subsidiaries, with rail networks of 2,835 km and 1,286 km respectively; assets of Sizarail nationalized and returned to SNCC control in May 1997; Pres. and Gen. Man. KIBWE MIBUYA KAKUDJI.

ROADS

In 1996 there were approximately 157,000 km of roads, of which some 33,100 km were main roads. In general road conditions are poor, owing to inadequate maintenance. In August 1997 a rehabilitation plan was announced by the Government under which 28,664 km of roads were to be built or repaired. The project was to be partly financed by external sources.

Office des Routes: Direction Générale, ave Ex-Descamp, BP 10899, Kinshasa-Gombé; tel. (12) 32036; construction and maintenance of roads.

INLAND WATERWAYS

The River Congo is navigable for more than 1,600 km. Above the Stanley Falls the Congo becomes the Lualaba, and is navigable along a 965-km stretch from Ubundu to Kindu and Kongolo to Bukama. The River Kasai, a tributary of the River Congo, is navigable by shipping as far as Ilebo, at which the line from Lubumbashi terminates. The total length of inland waterways is 14,935 km.

Régie des voies fluviales: 109 ave Lumpungu, Kinshasa-Gombé, BP 11697, Kinshasa 1; tel. (12) 26526; fax (12) 42580; administers river navigation; Gen. Man. NGIAM KIPOY.

Société Congolaise des Chemins de Fer des Grands Lacs: River Lualaba services: Bubundu–Kindu and Kongolo–Malemba N'kula; Lake Tanganyika services: Kamina–Kigoma–Kalundu–Moba–Mpulungu; Pres. and Gen. Man. KIBWE MBUYU KAKUDJI.

SHIPPING

The principal seaports are Matadi, Boma and Banana on the lower Congo. The port of Matadi has more than 1.6 km of quays and can accommodate up to 10 deep-water vessels. Matadi is linked by rail with Kinshasa. The country's merchant fleet numbered 20 vessels and amounted to 12,918 gross registered tons at 31 December 1998.

Compagnie Maritime du Congo SARL: USB Centre, place de la Poste, BP 9496, Kinshasa; tel. (12) 21031; fax (12) 26234; f. 1946; services: North Africa, Europe, North America and Asia to West Africa, East Africa to North Africa; Gen. Man. ALEX MUKENDI KAMAMA.

CIVIL AVIATION

International airports are located at Ndjili (for Kinshasa), Luano (for Lubumbashi), Bukavu, Goma and Kisangani. There are smaller airports and airstrips dispersed throughout the country.

Blue Airlines: BP 1115, Kinshasa 1; tel. (12) 20455; f. 1991; regional and domestic charter services for passengers and cargo; Man. T. MAYANI.

Compagnie Africaine d'Aviation: Edifice du GAP, blvd du 30 juin, Kinshasa; f. 1992.

Congo Airlines: 1928 ave Kabambare, N'dolo-Kinshasa, BP 12847, Kinshasa; tel. (88) 43947; fax (88) 00235; e-mail cal-fih-dg@ic.cd; f.1994 as Express Cargo, assumed present name in 1997; international, regional and domestic scheduled services for passengers and cargo; Pres. JOSE ENDUNO; CEO STAVROS PAPAIOANNOU.

Eastern Congo Airlines: Bukavu; f. 1997; 60% state-owned, 40% by Belgian interests; Chair. Chief NAKAZIBA CIMANYE.

Filair: BP 14671, Kinshasa; tel. (88) 45702; fax (88) 45702; f. 1987; regional and domestic charter services; Pres. DANY PHILEMOTTE.

Lignes Aériennes du Congo (LAC): Air Terminus 4, ave du Port, Kinshasa-Gombé, BP 8552, Kinshasa 1; tel. (12) 20874; Pres. and Gen. Man. PAUL MUKANDILA MBAYABU.

Scibe Airlift: BP 614, Kinshasa; tel. (12) 26237; fax (12) 24386; f. 1979; domestic and international passenger and cargo charter services between Kinshasa, Lubumbashi, Bujumbura (Burundi) and Brussels; Pres. BEMBA SAOLONA; Dir-Gen. BEMBA GOMBO.

Zairean Airlines (Congo): 3555–3560 blvd du 30 juin, BP 2111, Kinshasa; tel. (88) 48103; f. 1981; international, regional and domestic services for passengers and cargo; Dir-Gen. Capt. ALFRED SOMMERAUER.

Local charter services are also provided by Trans Service Airlift, Transair Cargo and Wetrafa Airlift.

Tourism

The country offers extensive lake and mountain scenery, although tourism remains largely undeveloped. In 1998 tourist arrivals totalled 53,139, and receipts from tourism amounted to an estimated US $5m. in 1996.

Office National du Tourisme: 2A/2B ave des Orangers, BP 9502, Kinshasa-Gombé; tel. (12) 30070; f. 1959; Man. Dir BOTOLO MAGOZA.

Société Congolaise de l'Hôtellerie: Immeuble Memling, BP 1076, Kinshasa; tel. (12) 23260; Man. N'JOLI BALANGA.

THE REPUBLIC OF THE CONGO

Introductory Survey

Location, Climate, Language, Religion, Flag, Capital

The Republic of the Congo is an equatorial country on the west coast of Africa. It has a coastline of about 170 km on the Atlantic Ocean, from which the country extends northward to Cameroon and the Central African Republic. The Republic of the Congo is bordered by Gabon to the west and the Democratic Republic of the Congo (formerly Zaire) to the east, while in the south there is a short frontier with the Cabinda exclave of Angola. The climate is tropical, with temperatures averaging 21°C–27°C (70°F–80°F) throughout the year. The average annual rainfall is about 1,200 mm (47 ins). The official language is French; Kikongo, Lingala and other African languages are also used. At least one-half of the population follow traditional animist beliefs and about 45% are Roman Catholics. There are small Protestant and Muslim minorities. The national flag (proportions 3 by 2) comprises a yellow stripe running diagonally from lower hoist to upper fly, separating a green triangle at the hoist from a red triangle in the fly. The capital is Brazzaville.

Recent History

Formerly part of French Equatorial Africa, Middle Congo became the autonomous Republic of the Congo, within the French Community, in November 1958, with Abbé Fulbert Youlou as the first Prime Minister, and subsequently as President when the Congo became fully independent on 15 August 1960. Youlou was compelled to relinquish office in August 1963, following a period of ethnic tensions and internal unrest, and was succeeded by Alphonse Massamba-Débat, initially as Prime Minister, and from December as President. In July 1964 the Mouvement national de la révolution (MNR) was established as the sole political party. In August 1968 Massamba-Débat was overthrown in a military coup, led by Capt. (later Maj.) Marien Ngouabi, who was proclaimed President in January 1969. A new Marxist-Leninist party, the Parti congolais du travail (PCT), replaced the MNR, and in January 1970 the country was renamed the People's Republic of the Congo. In March 1977 Ngouabi was assassinated by supporters of ex-President Massamba-Débat, and in the following month Col (later Brig.-Gen.) Jacques-Joachim Yhombi-Opango, the head of the armed forces, became the new Head of State. In February 1979, faced with a collapse in support, Yhombi-Opango surrendered his powers to a Provisional Committee appointed by the PCT. In the following month the head of the Provisional Committee, Col (later Gen.) Denis Sassou-Nguesso, became Chairman of the PCT Central Committee and President of the Republic.

Persistent ethnic rivalries, together with disillusionment with the Government's response to the country's worsening economic situation, resulted in increased opposition to the Sassou-Nguesso regime during the late 1980s. In July 1987 some 20 army officers were arrested for alleged complicity in a coup plot. Shortly afterwards fighting broke out in the north between government forces and troops led by Pierre Anga, a supporter of Yhombi-Opango. In September government troops suppressed the rebellion with French military assistance. Yhombi-Opango was transferred from house arrest to prison. Anga was subsequently killed by Congolese security forces.

At the PCT Congress in July 1989 Sassou-Nguesso, the sole candidate, was re-elected Chairman of the party and President of the Republic for a third five-year term. In August Alphonse Mouissou Poaty-Souchalaty, formerly the Minister of Trade and Small- and Medium-sized Enterprises, was appointed Prime Minister. At legislative elections in September the PCT-approved single list of 133 candidates was endorsed by 99.2% of voters. The list included, for the first time, candidates who were not members of the party. In November Sassou-Nguesso announced plans for economic reform, signifying a departure from socialist policies.

Progress towards political reform dominated the latter half of 1990. In July the Government announced that an extraordinary Congress of the PCT would be convened to formulate legislation enabling the introduction of a multi-party system. The regime also approved measures that would limit the role of the ruling party in the country's mass and social organizations. In August, on the occasion of the 30th anniversary of the country's independence, several political prisoners were released, among them Yhombi-Opango. In September the Confederation of Congolese Trade Unions (CSC), which had demanded the immediate implementation of a multi-party system and increased salaries for workers in the public sector, was refused permission by the Government to disaffiliate itself from the ruling PCT. Following a two-day general strike, Sassou-Nguesso assented to free elections to the leadership of the CSC, and in late September the Central Committee of the PCT agreed to the immediate registration of new political parties. In early December Poaty-Souchalaty resigned. On the following day the extraordinary Congress of the PCT commenced. The party abandoned Marxism-Leninism as its official ideology and formulated constitutional amendments legalizing a multi-party system, which took effect in January 1991. Gen. Louis Sylvain Goma was appointed Prime Minister (a position he had previously held between December 1975 and August 1984), and shortly afterwards an interim Government was installed.

A National Conference on the country's future was convened in February 1991. Opposition movements were allocated seven of the 11 seats on the Conference's governing body, and were represented by 700 of the 1,100 delegates attending the Conference. The Roman Catholic Bishop of Owando, Ernest N'Kombo, was elected as Chairman. The Conference voted to establish itself as a sovereign body, the decisions of which were to be binding and not subject to approval by the transitional Government. In April the Conference announced proposals to draft legislation providing for the abrogation of the Constitution and the abolition of the National People's Assembly, several national institutions and regional councils. In June, prior to the dissolution of the Conference, a 153-member legislative Higher Council of the Republic was established, under the chairmanship of N'Kombo; this was empowered to supervise the implementation of the resolutions made by the National Conference, pending the adoption of a new constitution and the holding of legislative and presidential elections in 1992. From June 1991 the President was replaced as Chairman of the Council of Ministers by the Prime Minister, and the country reverted to its previous official name, the Republic of the Congo. A new Prime Minister, André Milongo (a former World Bank official), was appointed in June, and during that month the Government agreed to permit workers to form independent trade unions. In December the Higher Council of the Republic adopted a draft Constitution, which provided for legislative power to be vested in an elected Assemblée nationale and Senate and for executive power to be held by an elected President.

In January 1992 a reallocation of senior army posts by the Prime Minister led to a mutiny by military personnel who demanded the reinstatement of military personnel who had allegedly been dismissed because of their ethnic allegiances, the removal of the newly-appointed Secretary of State for Defence and the payment of overdue salaries. Although Milongo refused to comply with these demands, the crisis was eventually resolved by the resignation of the Secretary of State for Defence and the installation of a candidate acceptable to the army as Minister of Defence. Milongo appointed himself Chief of the Armed Forces.

The draft Constitution was approved by 96.3% of voters at a national referendum in March 1992. In May Milongo appointed a new Council of Ministers, membership of which was drawn from each of the country's regions, in order to avoid accusations of domination by any one ethnic group. Following two rounds of elections to the new Assemblée nationale, in late June and mid-July, the Union panafricaine pour la démocratie social (UPADS) became the major party, winning 39 of the 125 seats; the Mouvement congolais pour la démocratie et le développement intégral (MCDDI) took 29 seats and the PCT secured 18 seats. At elections to the Senate, held in late July, the UPADS again won the largest share (23) of the 60 seats, followed by the MCDDI, with 13 seats. At the first round of presidential voting, in early August, Pascal Lissouba, the leader of the UPADS (who had been Prime Minister in 1963–66), won the largest share of the votes cast (35.9%); of the 15 other candidates, his closest rival was Bernard Kolelas of the MCDDI (22.9%). Sassou-Nguesso took 16.9% of the votes cast. Lissouba and Kolelas thus proceeded to a second round of voting, held two weeks later, at which Lissouba won 61.3% of the votes cast.

Lissouba took office as President at the end of August 1992. Maurice-Stéphane Bongho-Nouarra (a member of the UPADS) was appointed as Prime Minister at the head of a new Council of Ministers. Meanwhile, the Union pour le renouveau démocratique (URD), a new alliance of seven parties, including the MCDDI, formed a coalition with the PCT (thereby establishing a parliamentary majority), which succeeded in winning a vote of 'no confidence' against the Government in October. In November Bongho-Nouarra's Government resigned, and shortly afterwards Lissouba dissolved the Assemblée nationale and announced that fresh legislative elections would be held in 1993. The URD-PCT coalition, which demanded the right to form the Government, commenced a protest campaign of civil disobedience. In December Claude Antoine Dacosta, a former FAO and World Bank official, was appointed Prime Minister and formed a transitional Government, comprising members of all the main political parties.

At the first round of legislative elections, which took place in early May 1993, the Mouvance présidentielle (MP), an electoral coalition of the UPADS and its allies, won 62 of the 125 seats in the Assemblée nationale, while the URD-PCT coalition secured 49. Protesting that serious electoral irregularities had occurred, the URD-PCT refused to contest the second round of elections in early June (for seats where a clear majority had not been achieved in the first round) and demanded that some of the first-round polls should be repeated. At the second round the MP secured an absolute majority (69) of seats in the Assemblée nationale. In late June President Lissouba appointed a new Council of Ministers, with ex-President Yhombi-Opango as Prime Minister. During June Bernard Kolelas, the leader of the MCDDI and of the URD-PCT coalition, instigated a campaign of civil disobedience in an attempt to compel the Government to organize new elections. Violent conflict ensued between armed militiamen, representing party political and ethnic interests, and the security forces. At the end of June the Supreme Court ruled that electoral irregularities had occurred at the first round of elections. In mid-July Lissouba declared a state of emergency, but by the end of the month the Government and the opposition had negotiated a truce, and in early August, following mediation by the Organization of African Unity (OAU—see p. 256), France and President Bongo of Gabon, the two sides agreed to refer the disputed first-round election results to impartial international arbitration and to rerun the second round of elections. The state of emergency was repealed in mid-August.

In the repeated second round of legislative elections, which took place in October 1993, the MP secured 65 seats, retaining its overall majority in the Assemblée nationale; no changes were made to the Council of Ministers. The URD-PCT coalition, which had taken 57 seats, agreed to participate in the new Assemblée. However, further confrontations between armed militia affiliated to political parties and the security forces reportedly resulted in at least 2,000 deaths in the second half of 1993. Although a cease-fire was agreed at the end of January 1994, sporadic fighting continued.

In February 1994 the committee of international arbitrators that had been investigating the conduct of the first round of the legislative elections ruled that the results in eight constituencies were unlawful. In September 1994 six opposition parties formed an alliance, the Forces démocratiques unies (FDU), headed by the leader of the PCT, Sassou-Nguesso, and affiliated with the URD. In December the Government announced its intention to re-form as a coalition administration, including members of the opposition. In that month a co-ordinating body was established to oversee the disarmament of the party militia and the restoration of judicial authority. Meanwhile, Lissouba and the two main opposition leaders—Sassou-Nguesso and Kolelas—signed an agreement seeking a permanent end to hostilities between their supporters. In January 1995 it was announced that 2,000 places in the national army would be set aside for former militiamen once their units had disbanded.

In January 1995 the Government resigned, and a new coalition Council of Ministers was appointed, including members of the MCDDI and headed by Yhombi-Opango. The FDU, however, refused to participate in the new administration. Some 12 deputies defected from the majority UPADS in protest at the lack of representation for south-western Congolese in the newly-appointed Council of Ministers, subsequently establishing a new party, the Union pour la République, which affiliated itself with the MP.

In March 1995 the Government announced the introduction of measures to restrain state expenditure, including significant reductions in the number of civil service personnel, in order to secure continued assistance from the IMF. The Lissouba administration banned all public demonstrations in August, in order to restrict protests by trade unions. In the following month the Assemblée nationale approved legislation to restrict the freedom of the press.

In October 1995 the Government announced the impending restructuring of the armed forces, with the aim of achieving a more balanced representation of ethnic and regional interests. During 1994–96 some 4,000 militiamen were integrated into the defence and security forces. Nevertheless, activities by armed militia groups continued to be reported.

In August 1996 Yhombi-Opango resigned as Prime Minister and was replaced by David Charles Ganao, the leader of the Union des forces démocratiques and a former Minister of Foreign Affairs. In September Ganao appointed an expanded Council of Ministers, including representatives of the URD. The Ganao administration undertook to continue with the implementation of the economic reform programme agreed with the IMF. In October elections were held for 23 of the 60 seats in the Senate. The MP retained its majority, winning 12 of the seats, while opposition organizations took 10 seats and one seat was secured by an independent candidate.

Factional divisions remained apparent in early 1997. Opposition politicians accused Lissouba of political and ethnic partiality when he was perceived to grant preferential treatment to army members from his native southern Congo, while dismissing several high-ranking northern officers installed under the Sassou-Nguesso administration. In February 19 opposition parties demanded the expedited establishment of republican institutions, the free movement of people and goods, and more equitable access to the media and to public funds, in addition to the creation of an independent electoral commission, the disarmament of civilians and the deployment of a multinational peace-keeping force to counteract the continued existence of militia groups. In May further inter-militia unrest erupted, and in June an attempt by the Government, in preparation for legislative and presidential elections scheduled for July and August, to disarm the militia group associated with Sassou-Nguesso's Forces démocratiques et patriotiques (as the FDU had been renamed) precipitated a fierce national conflict along ethnic and political lines, involving the militias and opposing factions within the regular armed forces. Barricades were erected in Brazzaville, which was divided into three zones, controlled by supporters of Lissouba, Sassou-Nguesso and Kolelas. The conflict soon became polarized between troops loyal to the Lissouba administration and the rebel forces of Sassou-Nguesso; both sides were allegedly reinforced by mercenaries and by foreign troops. Despite efforts to mediate—led by Kolelas at a national level and, on behalf of the international community, by President Bongo of Gabon and Muhammad Sahnoun, the joint UN-OAU special representative to the Great Lakes region—none of the numerous cease-fires signed during mid-1997 led to more than a brief lull in hostilities. An attempt by Lissouba to postpone the impending elections and prolong his presidential mandate beyond the end of August was strongly opposed by Sassou-Nguesso, and both sides were unable to agree on the nature or composition of a proposed government of national unity. In early June French troops assisted in the evacuation of foreign residents from Brazzaville; in mid-June they themselves departed, despite mediators' requests that they remain. Fighting intensified in August and spread to the north. In early September Lissouba appointed a Government of National Unity, under the premiership of Kolelas, thereby compromising the latter's role as a national mediator. Sassou-Nguesso refused the offer of five seats for his allies in the Council of Ministers. In September political organizations loyal to Lissouba formed the Espace républicain pour la défense de la démocratie et l'unité nationale.

In October 1997 Sassou-Nguesso's forces, assisted by Angolan government troops, won control of Brazzaville and the strategic port of Pointe-Noire. Lissouba was ousted from the presidential palace, and, with Kolelas, found refuge in Burkina Faso. In late October Sassou-Nguesso was inaugurated as President, having retaken by force the office that he lost at the 1992 presidential election. He appointed a new transitional Government in November.

It was reported that some 10,000 people were killed during the civil war and that about 800,000 people were displaced. Brazzaville was severely damaged, while the national infrastructure and institutions were severely disrupted.

A Forum for Unity and National Reconciliation was established in January 1998. Subsequently a National Transitional Council (NTC) was to hold legislative power, pending the creation of a new constitution, to be approved by a referendum scheduled for 2001, and the organization of legislative elections. Upon his accession to power, President Sassou-Nguesso decreed that party militias would be disarmed and outlawed as a matter of priority. This proved difficult to enforce. In January 1998 the Director-General of the judicial police was assassinated during arms seizures in Gambona, and in February members of Sassou-Nguesso's militia looted businesses in Brazzaville, in protest at their exclusion from the armed forces. In April militiamen loyal to former President Lissouba temporarily took control of the Moukoukoulou hydroelectric dam. In the same month Sassou-Nguesso rejected an appeal from the country's Roman Catholic bishops for the removal of political and civil rights from the leaders of private militias, declaring that this would further jeopardize the reconciliation process. Throughout 1998 clashes continued in the southern Pool region, a stronghold of the militia loyal to Kolelas, causing thousands to flee the area. Warrants were issued in November for the arrests of Lissouba, Kolelas and Yhombi-Opango, on charges of genocide and crimes against humanity, allegedly committed during 1997.

In November 1998 President Sassou-Nguesso appointed a constitutional committee to draft proposals for a new constitution, to be submitted to a national forum and subsequently to a public referendum later in 1999. These plans were stalled, however, by the spread of violence in December 1998 from the Pool region to the outskirts of Brazzaville. In late December a full-scale battle for control of Brazzaville broke out between pro-Kolelas forces, reputedly supported by Angolan rebel groups, and Congolese government forces, augmented by Sassou-Nguesso's militia and Angolan government troops. Both sides claimed victory; Kolelas, speaking from the USA, suggested that he might return to take power, while the Congolese authorities denied that there had been a concerted attack on the city, blaming looters and bandits for the eruption of violence. More than 8,000 refugees were reported to have fled into the neighbouring Democratic Republic of the Congo (DRC). In late December government forces, aided by Angolan troops, launched offensives against Kolelas' forces in the south and west of the country.

On 12 January 1999 Sassou-Nguesso appointed a new Council of Ministers, with the responsibility of restoring security and peace in the south. Itihi Ossetoumba Lekoundzou, the former Minister of State for Reconstruction and Urban Development, was appointed Minister of Defence, a portfolio previously held by Sassou-Nguesso. In mid-January rebels again seized the Moukoukoulou hydroelectric dam, while in Brazzaville sporadic fighting continued as government forces sought to suppress insurgents in the southern districts. Fighting was also reported in the south-west of the country, particularly around the strategically important city of Dolisie, where an attack by militia loyal to Lissouba led to the killing of the military commander of the region in February; the struggle for control of the city continued into March.

In late February 1999 the conflict in the area immediately south of Brazzaville intensified, and a further 10,000 people were estimated to have taken refuge in the DRC. By early March, however, the rebel militias had been obliged to withdraw to the Pool region, where clashes continued, and residents began to return to the south of Brazzaville, and also to Dolisie by early April. In May the army secured the city of Kinkala, capital of the Pool region, and captured the main rebel base in the south-west, while an insurgent attack to the north of Brazzaville was also repulsed. During mid-1999 government forces continued their advances in the south and west of the country, and in late August it was announced that they had regained control of the railway line between Brazzaville and Pointe-Noire.

In August 1999 Sassou-Nguesso offered to grant an amnesty to any militiamen prepared to renounce violence and to surrender their weapons. In September it was reported that some 600 militiamen loyal to Kolelas had surrendered to the authorities under these terms. In the same month several prominent opposition members, including four former ministers, volunta-

rily returned to the Congo from exile, following an announcement that the Government had begun talks with the exiled opposition, and in October 12 senior officers, who had been imprisoned for supporting Lissouba, were released and were apparently to be reintegrated into the armed forces. In early October, however, the Government rejected an appeal for a cease-fire made by Congolese bishops, suggesting that the refusal of Lissouba and Kolelas to renounce violence excluded them from participation in any negotiations. In the same month the authorities announced that the armed forces had regained control of all the towns in the Pool region.

On 17 November 1999, following intensive negotiations with local militia leaders, the Government announced that it had reached agreement with the militias loyal to Lissouba and Kolelas. The agreement, which included provision for a cease-fire and for a general amnesty, was, however, rejected by Lissouba and Kolelas. In December the NTC adopted legislation providing for an amnesty for those militiamen who surrendered their weapons to the authorities before 15 January 2000. The amnesty excluded the opposition leaders in exile, notably Lissouba and Kolelas, and the Government announced its intention to continue to seek their prosecution for alleged war crimes.

In December 1999 President Bongo of Gabon was designated the official mediator between the Government and the militias, and at the end of the month he hosted further discussions in Libreville, Gabon. These discussions led to the signing of a second peace agreement, in the presence of Presidents Bongo and Sassou-Nguesso, by representatives of the armed forces and of the rebel militias. The new agreement provided for further dialogue, for the integration of militiamen into the armed forces and for the opening of a humanitarian 'corridor' to enable displaced persons to return to their homes. Militia leaders continued, however, to demand the withdrawal of Angolan troops from the Congo. None the less, in late December a ceremony of reconciliation was held in Brazzaville between senior government figures and members of the previous Lissouba administration.

By mid-February 2000 it was estimated that some 2,000 former militiamen had surrendered to the authorities, although some sources indicated that up to a further 16,000 militiamen remained at large, principally in the Pool region. The Government was forced to acknowledge that it would not be possible to integrate all of the former rebels into the armed forces or the police force, although further job-creation schemes were promised. In the same month the committee in charge of observing the implementation of the peace process announced, at a meeting with Bongo, that the civil war was definitively over. The Congolese Government subsequently appealed for funds from the international community in order to begin the process of reconstruction. In the same month it was estimated that around one-half of the estimated 810,000 people displaced by the conflict had returned to their homes.

In May 2000 Kolelas and his nephew, Col Philippe Bikinkita, the Minister of the Interior in the previous Lissouba administration, were convicted *in absentia* of operating personal prisons in the southern districts of Brazzaville and of mistreating prisoners and causing their deaths during the 1997 civil war. Both men were sentenced to death and ordered to pay compensation to their victims. Kolelas, who denied the charges, later demanded that an international team investigate the allegations. In late May the Chairman of the NTC, Justin Koumba, announced that in either late 2000 or early 2001 a referendum would be held on the future form of government for the Republic, and that presidential, legislative and local government elections would follow. In mid-July, during a visit to Brazzaville, Bongo expressed satisfaction at the implementation of the peace process, although he urged the authorities to continue to engage in dialogue with all elements of society in order to establish a permanent settlement.

In late July the Government approved legislation that was intended to allow greater freedom of expression in the media. In August Sassou-Nguesso announced an intensification of the 'all-inclusive' national reconciliation talks, which Bongo would continue to co-ordinate, although the Congolese Government sought to exclude Lissouba and Kolelas. In the same month rail traffic on the main line from Brazzaville to Pointe-Noire resumed after some two years of suspension. In September a section of the UPADS reportedly criticized the continued participation in Sassou-Nguesso's Government of the party's General- Secretary, Martin Mberi, as Minister of Construction, Urban Development, Housing and Land Reform. Meanwhile, a newly-formed opposition group, based in Paris, France, the Front patriotique pour le dialogue et la réconciliation nationale (FPDRN), chaired by Augustin Poignet, a former Speaker of the Senate, announced that it would seek to represent the opposition in exile, including Lissouba and Kolelas, in discussions with Sassou-Nguesso, although it was not initially evident that the President would be willing to meet with the group.

In mid-November 2000 the Government adopted a draft Constitution, which had been prepared by a commission established in 1999 and amended by the Government. The draft Constitution, which was to be presented to a referendum in early 2001, following national debate, included provisions for a presidential and democratic system of government, with a bicameral legislature and independent judiciary. It was proposed that the Head of State, the sole holder of executive power, be elected for a term of seven years, which would be renewable only once. In early December, during a conference in Pointe-Noire, it was announced that some 13,000 weapons had been surrendered and 12,000 militiamen disarmed in the past year, although UN sources suggested that this represented less than one-half of the total number of militiamen in the Congo. Also in December, the PCT rejected demands by the MCDDI for an amnesty for Lissouba and Kolelas. Later that month government radio announced that 11 of the 14 urban centres in Niari region remained under the control of rebel forces.

In February 2001 the Government established a commission to prepare for a period of 'national dialogue', which was to commence in mid-March. The commission proposed that regional debates be followed by a national convention in Brazzaville. However, internal and exiled opposition groups, displeased by their exclusion from this commission, and also citing security concerns, boycotted both the opening ceremony of the 'national dialogue' on 17 March and the regional debates, which took place on 22–26 March. An estimated 2,200 delegates from public institutions, civic associations, political parties loyal to the Government and independent parties attended the debates throughout the country, reportedly reaching a consensus on the draft Constitution, despite some concerns regarding the extent of presidential power envisaged. Earlier attempts by Bongo to secure the participation of opposition groups, during talks in Libreville, were unsuccessful, although it was agreed to create a technical committee to monitor the dialogue process, which was to include opposition representatives and have equal status with the government commission. None the less, opposition groups announced their intention to boycott the national convention, scheduled to take place in Brazzaville on 11–14 April, unless they received assurances regarding the security of exiled opposition members convicted of crimes *in absentia* by Congolese courts.

Since the 1997 civil war, the principal aim of Congolese foreign policy has been to gain international recognition for the legitimacy of the Sassou-Nguesso Government, and to ensure the continued support of the country's bilateral and multilateral donors. Sassou-Nguesso's exiled political opponents have, however, appealed for international support for their efforts to overthrow the regime.

During the 1997 civil war President Lissouba accused France of favouring the rebel forces of Sassou-Nguesso (who was reported to have allied himself with French petroleum interests) over the elected administration. In April 1998 Lissouba and Kolelas unsuccessfully sought to prosecute a French petroleum company, Elf Aquitaine, claiming that it had provided support for Sassou-Nguesso. In May France extended its formal recognition to the Sassou-Nguesso Government, and in the following month resumed aid payments that had been suspended since the 1997 conflict. France granted further economic assistance in July, and in September French military advisers were sent to Brazzaville to train the Congolese gendarmerie. Further reconstruction assistance was promised in January 2000.

In the 1997 conflict Angolan government troops facilitated Sassou-Nguesso's victory by providing tactical support, including the occupation of Pointe-Noire, the Congo's main seaport and focus of the petroleum industry. Angola had accused the Lissouba Government of providing assistance both to rebels of the União Nacional para a Independência Total de Angola and to Cabindan separatist guerrillas. In response to international criticism of his role, President dos Santos of Angola announced in early 1998 that the majority of his forces had departed the Congo, and that the role of the remaining troops was merely to help rebuild and train the Congolese army. However, Angolan troops played an important role in the defeat of the rebel attack

on Brazzaville in December 1998. In January 1999 the Heads of State of Angola, the Congo, and the DRC met to agree a common policy on the conflicts in their countries. In December the Ministers of the Interior of the three countries met in Luanda, Angola, and signed a co-operation accord. The accord created a tripartite commission to ensure border security, the free movement of people and goods, the training of personnel, and the provision of assistance to displaced persons. In April 2000 further meetings were held in Kinshasa, DRC, in order to discuss the implementation of the Luanda accord, which was expected to include the formation of joint military patrols. In the same month it was announced that the Angolan and Congolese Governments were to investigate the joint exploitation of off-shore petroleum resources.

Relations between the Republic of the Congo and the DRC steadily improved during 1998. In May a bilateral meeting was held to discuss the prevention of the clandestine movement of armed groups across the two countries' common border, and in August Sassou-Nguesso agreed to extradite rebels to the DRC. A further bilateral meeting was held in September. Relations were, however, undermined later that month when the DRC alleged that the Congo had turned back a DRC naval vessel seeking to enlist some of the thousands of Rwandan Hutu refugees in the Congo into forces loyal to President Kabila. In December relations were further strained by Congolese claims that a training camp for anti-Government militiamen existed in the DRC. This accusation was strongly denied by the DRC, and later in the month the two countries signed a non-aggression pact and agreed to establish a joint force to guarantee border security. In December 1999 Sassou-Nguesso paid a brief visit to President Kabila in order to discuss bilateral co-operation and the implementation of the tripartite Luanda accord. Further discussion on issues of common interest, including notably border security and the rehabilitation of refugees and displaced persons, took place in October 2000, when a delegation from the DRC visited Brazzaville.

Government

The 1992 Constitution, providing for an elected President, Assemblée nationale and Senate, was suspended following the assumption of power by Gen. Denis Sassou-Nguesso on 15 October 1997. A Forum for Unity and National Reconciliation was established in January 1998. Subsequently a National Transitional Council was appointed, with 75 designated members, to act as a legislative body pending the organization of national elections in 2001. In November 2000 the Government adopted a draft Constitution, based on the proposals of a commission established in 1999. The draft Constitution, which provided for a presidential system of government, with a bicameral legislature, was to be presented to a referendum in 2001, following a period of national debate. It was proposed that the President would be elected for a term of seven years, renewable only once.

For administrative purposes the country is divided into 10 regions and six municipalities (communes).

Defence

In August 1999 the army numbered 8,000, the navy about 800 and the air force 1,200. There were 5,000 men in paramilitary forces, comprising 2,000 members of the Gendarmerie and 3,000 of the People's Militia. The latter was to be absorbed into the national army. National service is voluntary for men and women, and lasts for two years. The estimated defence budget for 2000 was 52,000m. francs CFA.

Economic Affairs

In 1998, according to estimates by the World Bank, the Congo's gross national product (GNP), measured at average 1996–98 prices, was US $1,899m., equivalent to $680 per head (or $846 on an international purchasing-power parity basis). During 1990–98, it was estimated, GNP per head declined, in real terms, at an average rate of 2.6% annually. Over the same period, the population increased at an average annual rate of 3.2%. GNP in 1999 was estimated at $1,900m., equivalent to $670 per head. The Congo's gross domestic product (GDP) increased, in real terms, at an average annual rate of 0.9% in 1990–99. GDP increased by 3.7% in 1998, but declined by 3.0% in 1999.

Agriculture (including forestry and fishing) contributed 9.0% of GDP in 1999, according to preliminary figures, and employed about 41.5% of the total labour force in that year. The staple crops are cassava and plantains, while the major cash crops are sugar cane, oil palm, cocoa and coffee. Forests cover about 57% of the country's total land area, and forestry is a major economic activity. Sales of timber provided an estimated 8.4% of export earnings in 1995, but in February 1998, to encourage local processing of wood, forestry companies were banned from exporting rough timber. During 1990–99 agricultural GDP increased at an average annual rate of 1.7%; agricultural GDP increased by 1.7% in 1998, but declined by an estimated 2.8% in 1999.

Industry (including mining, manufacturing, construction and power) contributed 60.7% of GDP in 1999, and employed an estimated 12.7% of the labour force in 1984. During 1990–99 industrial GDP declined at an average annual rate of 0.2%; industrial GDP increased by 5.6% in 1998 and by an estimated 2.4% in 1999.

Mining contributed 28.6% of GDP in 1989. The hydrocarbons sector is the only significant mining activity. In 1995 sales of petroleum and petroleum products provided an estimated 84.6% of export earnings. The real GDP of the petroleum sector (extraction and refining) increased by 6.1% in 1998 and by an estimated 4.3% in 1999. Annual petroleum production (13.6m. metric tons in 1998, according to the Banque des Etats de l'Afrique Centrale—BEAC) was expected to continue to grow, as a result of major exploration and development planned at various offshore deposits. Deposits of natural gas are also exploited. Lead, zinc, gold and copper are produced in small quantities, and the large-scale mining of magnesium was expected to commence by 2004. There are also exploitable reserves of diamonds, phosphate, iron ore, bauxite and potash.

Manufacturing contributed an estimated 6.5% of GDP in 1999, according to the World Bank. The most important industries are the processing of agricultural and forest products. The textile, chemical and construction materials industries are also important. During 1990–98 manufacturing GDP decreased at an average annual rate of 2.5%.

Energy is derived principally from hydroelectric power. Imports of fuel and energy comprised an estimated 26.1% of the value of total imports in 1995.

The services sector contributed an estimated 30.3% of GDP in 1999, according to preliminary figures. During 1990–99, it was estimated, the GDP of the services sector increased at an average annual rate of 1.5%. The sector's GDP declined by 0.9% in 1998 and by an estimated 9.3% in 1999.

In 1999, according to IMF preliminary estimates, the Congo recorded a visible trade surplus of 644,100m. francs CFA, but there was a deficit of 241,600m. francs CFA on the current account of the balance of payments. In 1995 the principal source of imports (32.0%) was France, while the USA was the principal market for exports (22.6%). Italy and the Netherlands are also important trading partners. The principal exports in 1996 were petroleum and petroleum products. The principal imports were machinery, chemical products, iron and steel and transport equipment.

The budget surplus for 1999 was estimated at 209,799m. francs CFA (equivalent to 15.4% of GDP). The country's external debt totalled US $5,119m. at the end of 1998, of which $4,250m. was long-term public debt. In that year the cost of debt-servicing was equivalent to 3.3% of the value of exports of goods and services. The annual rate of inflation averaged 8.1% in 1990–99. The rate rose to 41.1% in 1994, following the 50% devaluation of the currency in January of that year, but declined to 9.0% in 1995. Consumer prices increased by an average of 10.2% in 1996 and by 19.4% in 1997, but declined by only 4.2% in 1998, before increasing by an average of 4.2% in 1999.

The Republic of the Congo is a member of the Central African organs of the Franc Zone (see p. 210) and of the Communauté économique des Etats de l'Afrique centrale (CEEAC, see p. 307).

From 1985 the decline in international petroleum prices significantly reduced government revenue, leading to a decline in industrial investment and growth, and to unsustainable levels of external borrowing. In January 1994 the devaluation by 50% of the CFA franc resulted in an immediate sharp increase in

consumer prices. In May the Government agreed a programme of economic measures with the IMF, and in July the Government obtained an agreement on debt rescheduling with the 'Paris Club' of official creditors. An economic reform programme for 1996–99, supported by the IMF, and agreed in June 1996, was halted by the 1997 civil war. In November 1997 the World Bank suspended relations with the Congo in protest at the non-payment of debt arrears. In June 1998 Congo's international creditors agreed to co-ordinate action to support reconstruction. The World Bank subsequently approved an emergency post-conflict loan and also agreed to negotiate a new three-year programme. However, the outbreak in December 1998 of further hostilities led to the suspension of all donor activity, and in June 1999 the World Bank suspended the disbursement of the remaining funds accorded to the Congo under the June 1998 agreement. Following the signing of peace agreements between the Government and rebel militias in late 1999, economic objectives for 2000–01 included the creation of sustainable economic growth, the continued rehabilitation of state infrastructure, the normalization of relations with external creditors and the strengthening of the non-petroleum sector, the real GDP of which had declined by 19% in 1997–99. The restructuring and privatization of the Congo's three commercial banks and the privatization of the five largest state enterprises were also envisaged. In November 2000 the IMF approved a credit of some US $14m. for the Congo in emergency post-conflict assistance.

Social Welfare

There is a state pension scheme and a system of family allowances and other welfare services. Both social welfare and health provision have, however, been seriously impeded by a lack of government funds and by the devastating effects of the 1997 civil war. The breakdown in water supplies and sanitation, caused by the civil war, was blamed for the 1998 cholera epidemic in Pointe-Noire. In 1987 there were 43 hospitals, providing a total of 7,917 hospital beds. In the early 1990s there were an estimated 27 physicians per 100,000 inhabitants, and 49 nurses per 100,000 inhabitants, working in the country. Since the late 1980s rising numbers of AIDS cases have placed considerable strain on resources. Average annual health expenditure per caput was estimated at US $77 during 1990–97.

Education

Education is officially compulsory for 10 years between six and 16 years of age. Primary education begins at the age of six and lasts for six years. Secondary education, from 12 years of age, lasts for seven years, comprising a first cycle of four years and a second of three years. In 1996 there were 489,546 pupils enrolled at primary schools, while 190,409 pupils were receiving general secondary education. In addition, 23,606 students were attending vocational institutions. The Marien Ngouabi University, at Brazzaville, was founded in 1971. In 1999 there were some 16,000 students at university level, with 1,100 lecturers. The provision of education has been severely disrupted by the ongoing conflict in the Congo. In 1995, according to estimates by UNESCO, the average rate of adult illiteracy was 25.6% (males 17.3%, females 33.2%), one of the lowest in Africa. Expenditure on education by all levels of government was 52,274m. francs CFA in 1995, equivalent to 6.2% of GNP.

Public Holidays

2001: 1 January (New Year's Day), 13 April (Good Friday), 16 April (Easter Monday), 1 May (Labour Day), 4 June (Whit Monday), 15 August (Independence Day), 25 December (Christmas).

2002: 1 January (New Year's Day), 29 March (Good Friday), 1 April (Easter Monday), 1 May (Labour Day), 20 May (Whit Monday), 15 August (Independence Day), 25 December (Christmas).

Weights and Measures

The metric system is in force.

Statistical Survey

Source (unless otherwise stated): Direction Générale, Centre National de la Statistique et des Etudes Economiques, BP 2031, Brazzaville; tel. and fax 81-59-09.

Area and Population

AREA, POPULATION AND DENSITY

Area (sq km)	342,000*
Population (census results)	
7 February 1974	1,319,790
22 December 1984	1,843,421
Population (UN estimates at mid-year)†	
1997	2,709,000
1998	2,785,000
1999	2,864,000
Density (per sq km) at mid-1999	8.4

* 132,047 sq miles.
† Source: UN, *World Population Prospects: The 1998 Revision.*

PRINCIPAL TOWNS (estimated population in 1997)

Brazzaville (capital)	950,000
Pointe-Noire	500,000
Loubomo (Dolisie)	83,000

Source: La Zone Franc, *Rapport Annuel.*

BIRTHS AND DEATHS (UN estimates, annual averages)

	1980–85	1985–90	1990–95
Birth rate (per 1,000) . . .	43.9	44.3	44.7
Death rate (per 1,000) . . .	15.7	15.6	16.1

Expectation of life (UN estimates, years at birth, 1990-95): 48.9 (males 46.6; females 51.3).
Source: UN, *World Population Prospects: The 1998 Revision.*

EMPLOYMENT ('000 persons at 1984 census)

	Males	Females	Total
Agriculture, etc.	105	186	291
Industry	61	8	69
Services	123	60	183
Total	**289**	**254**	**543**

Mid-1999 (FAO estimates, '000 persons): Agriculture, etc. 486; Total labour force 1,170 (Source: FAO).

Agriculture

PRINCIPAL CROPS
('000 metric tons)

	1997	1998	1999*
Maize	4†	2†	2
Sugar cane	420	454	460
Potatoes*	3	3	3
Sweet potatoes*	23	24	25
Cassava (Manioc)	780	791	800
Yams*	12	13	14
Other roots and tubers* . . .	40	41	42
Dry beans	3	3	3
Tomatoes*	10	10	10
Other vegetables (incl. melons)* .	31	32	33
Oranges*	3	4	4
Avocados*	24	25	25
Pineapples*	12	13	13
Bananas	50	51	52
Plantains	76	77*	78
Palm kernels*	3	3	3
Palm oil*	16	16	17
Groundnuts (in shell). . . .	23	22*	23
Coffee (green)	1	1*	1
Cocoa beans	2	2*	2
Natural rubber*	1	1	1

* FAO estimate(s).   † Unofficial figure.
Source: FAO.

LIVESTOCK ('000 head, year ending September)

	1997	1998	1999*
Cattle	75	72	75
Pigs	45	44*	45
Sheep	115	114	115
Goats	286	280*	285
Poultry*	1,900	1,850	1,900

* FAO estimate(s).
Source: FAO.

LIVESTOCK PRODUCTS ('000 metric tons)

	1997	1998	1999
Beef and veal	2	2	2
Pig meat	2	2	2
Poultry meat	6	6	6
Other meat	14	16	17
Cows' milk	1	1	1
Hen eggs	1	1	1

Source: FAO.

Forestry

ROUNDWOOD REMOVALS ('000 cubic metres, excluding bark)

	1996	1997	1998
Sawlogs, veneer logs and logs for			
sleepers	704	911	1,057
Pulpwood	120	373	373
Other industrial wood	340	350	359
Fuel wood	2,388	2,456	2,525
Total	**3,552**	**4,090**	**4,314**

Source: FAO, *Yearbook of Forest Products.*

SAWNWOOD PRODUCTION
('000 cubic metres, including railway sleepers)

	1996	1997	1998
Total (all broadleaved) . . .	59	64	78

Source: FAO, *Yearbook of Forest Products.*

Fishing

('000 metric tons, live weight)

	1996	1997	1998*
Capture	45.5	38.1	40.0
Nile tilapia . . .	25.9	19.0	20.0
Sardinellas . . .	12.1*	11.8*	12.3
Other clupeoids . . .	1.7*	1.7*	1.8
Aquaculture	0.1	0.1	0.1
Total catch . . .	45.6	38.2	40.1

* FAO estimate(s).

Source: FAO, *Yearbook of Fishery Statistics.*

Mining

('000 metric tons, unless otherwise indicated)

	1996	1997	1998
Crude petroleum	10,359	11,586	13,599
Gold (kg)*	10	10	10

* Estimated metal content of ores.

Sources: US Geological Survey; Banque des Etats de l'Afrique Centrale, *Etudes et Statistiques.*

Industry

SELECTED PRODUCTS ('000 metric tons, unless otherwise indicated)

	1994	1995	1996
Raw sugar*	28	41	42
Veneer sheets ('000 cu metres)* .	47	49	50
Jet fuels†	15	16	16
Motor spirit (petrol)† . . .	55	55	56
Kerosene†	50	48	50
Distillate fuel oils† . . .	92	90	92
Residual fuel oils† . . .	268	258	260
Cement	87‡	97	43
Electric energy (million kWh)† .	431	435	438

1997: Raw sugar ('000 metric tons) 45*; Veneer sheets ('000 cu metres) 50*; Cement ('000 metric tons) 20.
1998: Raw sugar ('000 metric tons) 44*.
* Data from the FAO.
† Provisional figures.
‡ Data from the US Geological Survey.

Source: mainly UN, *Industrial Commodity Statistics Yearbook.*

Finance

CURRENCY AND EXCHANGE RATES
Monetary Units
100 centimes = 1 franc de la Coopération financière en Afrique centrale (CFA).

Sterling, Dollar and Euro Equivalents (29 December 2000)
£1 sterling = 1,051.93 francs CFA;
US $1 = 704.95 francs CFA;
€1 = 655.96 francs CFA;
10,000 francs CFA = £9.506 = $14.185 = €15.245.

Average Exchange Rate (francs CFA per US $)
1998   589.95
1999   615.70
2000   711.98

Note: The exchange rate of 1 French franc = 50 francs CFA, established in 1948, remained in force until January 1994, when the CFA franc was devalued by 50%, with the exchange rate adjusted to 1 French franc = 100 francs CFA. The relationship to French currency remained in effect with the introduction of the euro on 1 January 1999. From that date, accordingly, a fixed exchange rate of €1 = 655.957 francs CFA has been in operation.

BUDGET ('000 million francs CFA)

Revenue*	1998	1999	2000†
Petroleum revenue . . .	137.8	275.6	445.6
Other revenue . . .	121.7	108.7	151.7
Domestic taxes . . .	78.0	76.4	102.0
Customs receipts . . .	34.8	21.7	33.8
Domestic petroleum taxes .	8.4	7.8	10.0
Total	259.4	384.3	597.3

Expenditure	1998	1999	2000†
Current expenditure . . .	438.3	386.3	367.9
Wages and salaries . .	102.4	100.7	106.0
Local authority subsidies .	0.9	6.5	11.0
Interest payments . . .	160.0	168.1	152.5
Other current expenditure .	175.0	111.0	98.5
Capital expenditure . . .	54.6	89.1	156.7
Sub-total . . .	492.9	475.4	524.6
Less Adjustment for payment arrears	354.2	294.6	73.5
Total (cash basis) . . .	138.7	180.8	451.1

* Excluding grants received ('000 million francs CFA): 3.6 in 1998; 6.3 in 1999; 11.0† in 2000.
† Forecast(s).

Source: IMF, *Republic of Congo: Statistical Annex* (January 2001) and Republic of Congo, *Letter of Intent* (November 2000).

CENTRAL BANK RESERVES (US $ million at 31 December)

	1997	1998	1999
Gold*	3.24	3.21	2.10
IMF special drawing rights . .	0.01	0.01	0.11
Reserve position in IMF . .	0.72	0.75	0.74
Foreign exchange . . .	59.19	0.08	38.51
Total	63.16	4.05	41.46

* National valuation.

Source: IMF, *International Financial Statistics.*

MONEY SUPPLY ('000 million francs CFA at 31 December)

	1997	1998	1999
Currency outside banks . .	93.26	73.26	102.34
Demand deposits at commercial and development banks .	68.85	68.39	76.68
Total money (incl. others) . .	166.56	143.98	184.03

Source: IMF, *International Financial Statistics.*

COST OF LIVING
(Consumer Price Index for Africans in Brazzaville; base: 1990 = 100)

	1997	1998	1999
All items	202.4	194.0	202.1

Source: UN, *Monthly Bulletin of Statistics*.

NATIONAL ACCOUNTS
('000 million francs CFA at current prices)
Expenditure on the Gross Domestic Product

	1997	1998	1999
Government final consumption expenditure . . .	270.7	245.6	228.5
Private final consumption expenditure . . .	611.1	807.2	597.5
Increase in stocks	8.6	27.0	17.2
Gross fixed capital formation . .	294.5	279.9	287.7
Total domestic expenditure .	1,184.9	1,359.7	1,130.9
Exports of goods and services . .	974.6	741.7	1,087.6
Less Imports of goods and services	803.8	951.4	853.2
GDP in purchasers' values .	1,355.7	1,150.1	1,365.3

Source: IMF, *International Financial Statistics*.

Gross Domestic Product by Economic Activity

	1997	1998	1999*
Agriculture, hunting, forestry and fishing	123.9	126.0	119.8
Mining and quarrying† . . .}	740.7	499.6	771.6
Manufacturing† . . . .}			
Electricity, gas and water . .	13.6	14.9	9.3
Construction	16.6	15.2	26.2
Trade, restaurants and hotels. .	132.9	139.3	116.7
Transport, storage and communication . . .	77.5	77.7	72.0
Government services . . .	122.0	119.2	122.2
Other services	98.3	108.3	91.1
GDP at factor cost . . .	1,325.5	1,100.2	1,328.9
Import duties	30.2	49.9	36.4
GDP in purchasers' values .	1,355.7	1,150.1	1,365.3

* Preliminary figures.

† Including petroleum sector ('000 million francs CFA): 666.7 in 1997; 419.6 in 1998; 692.3 (preliminary figure) in 1999.

Source: IMF, *Republic of Congo: Statistical Annex* (January 2001).

BALANCE OF PAYMENTS (US $ million)

	1995	1996	1997
Exports of goods f.o.b. . . .	1,167.0	1,554.5	1,744.1
Imports of goods f.o.b. . . .	−650.7	−1,361.0	−802.9
Trade balance	516.3	193.5	941.3
Exports of services . . .	76.3	91.1	55.7
Imports of services . . .	−778.5	−721.1	−565.2
Balance on goods and services	−185.9	−436.5	431.8
Other income received . . .	3.0	11.7	5.1
Other income paid	−459.4	−670.1	−668.9
Balance on goods, services and income	−642.3	−1,094.9	−232.0
Current transfers received . .	30.9	29.9	24.7
Current transfers paid . . .	−38.3	−44.0	−44.5
Current balance . . .	−649.7	−1,109.0	−251.9
Investment assets . . .	−10.4	0.4	−3.6
Investment liabilities . . .	−69.9	656.8	−170.1
Net errors and omissions . .	120.7	102.1	−122.1
Overall balance . . .	−609.3	−349.7	−547.7

Source: IMF, *International Financial Statistics*.

External Trade

PRINCIPAL COMMODITIES (distribution by SITC, US $ million)

Imports c.i.f.	1993	1994	1995
Food and live animals . . .	59.6	87.9	108.6
Meat and meat preparations . .	15.9	23.8	28.2
Fresh, chilled or frozen meat and edible offals	15.1	21.7	26.8
Meat of bovine animals . .	0.4	11.8	14.8
Poultry (dead) and edible poultry offals (except liver) .	12.4	7.0	8.8
Dairy products and birds' eggs .	10.1	8.7	13.4
Milk and cream	7.7	7.2	12.0
Preserved, concentrated or sweetened milk and cream .	7.3	6.8	11.4
Fish and fish preparations . .	0.2	21.8	16.5
Fresh, chilled or frozen fish . .	0.1	10.0	9.3
Frozen fish (excl. fillets) . .	0.1	10.0	9.3
Dried, salted or smoked fish .	0.1	11.1	6.4
Cereals and cereal preparations .	27.6	23.8	36.8
Rice	5.1	7.0	12.4
Milled or semi-milled rice . .	5.1	7.0	12.4
Flour of wheat or meslin . .	18.1	8.2	13.8
Mineral fuels, lubricants, etc. .	2.9	5.0	108.7
Petroleum, petroleum products, etc.	2.8	4.9	106.1
Refined petroleum products . .	2.8	3.1	105.5
Motor spirit (gasoline) and other light oils	−	−	38.5
Motor spirit (incl. aviation spirit)	−	−	30.8
Kerosene and other medium oils	−	−	19.3
Gas oils	−	−	44.5
Animal and vegetable oils, fats and waxes	8.3	10.7	1.2
Fixed vegetable oils and fats . .	8.3	10.5	1.2
'Soft' fixed vegetable oils . .	0.6	8.5	0.5
Chemicals and related products .	54.7	54.8	77.0
Medicinal and pharmaceutical products	39.3	24.6	38.9
Medicaments (incl. veterinary) .	38.5	24.0	38.0
Basic manufactures . . .	61.6	76.7	69.5
Paper, paperboard and manufactures	8.0	4.8	7.7
Iron and steel	17.8	20.6	15.6
Tubes, pipes and fittings . .	14.7	17.7	9.8
'Seamless' tubes and pipes; blanks for tubes and pipes .	13.3	15.9	6.5
Iron, steel or aluminium structures and parts . . .	0.3	21.7	1.1
Iron or steel structures, etc.. .	0.2	21.6	1.0
Machinery and transport equipment	127.1	112.6	112.6
Machinery specialized for particular industries . .	10.8	17.4	17.3
Civil engineering and contractors' plant and equipment	7.3	12.0	10.0
General industrial machinery, equipment and parts . . .	24.9	30.4	32.1
Pumps (except for liquids), compressors, fans, centrifuges, etc..	5.1	9.2	4.4
Electrical machinery, apparatus, etc.	11.8	23.8	19.1
Switchgear, resistors, printed circuits, switchboards, etc. .	5.9	11.4	5.8
Switchgear, switchboards, control panels and parts .	5.9	11.3	5.6
Road vehicles and parts* . .	20.4	20.7	21.2
Passenger motor cars (excl. buses)	8.1	8.4	6.0
Other transport equipment and parts*	47.1	6.5	3.8
Ships, boats and floating structures	46.9	3.0	0.4
Tugs, special-purpose vessels and floating structures .	46.7	2.9	0.4
Light-vessels, fire-floats, dredgers, floating cranes, etc.	45.7	−	0.1

Imports c.i.f. — *continued*	1993	1994	1995
Miscellaneous manufactured articles . . .	24.2	36.4	65.2
Professional, scientific and controlling instruments, etc.	8.2	13.3	29.2
Measuring, checking, analysing and controlling instruments, etc. . .	7.6	11.7	26.4
Total (incl. others) . . .	347.1	395.2	556.0

* Data on parts exclude tyres, engines and electrical parts.

Exports f.o.b.	1993	1994	1995
Crude materials (inedible) except fuels	18.4	124.6	94.2
Cork and wood	17.8	114.6	90.7
Non-coniferous sawlogs and veneer logs . . .	8.7	105.9	80.3
Mineral fuels, lubricants, etc.	911.2	765.3	955.2
Petroleum, petroleum products, etc.	911.2	765.3	955.2
Crude petroleum oils, etc. . .	890.9	746.8	936.3
Refined petroleum products . .	20.4	18.6	18.9
Total (incl. others) . . .	965.3	917.9	1,089.8

Source: UN, *International Trade Statistics Yearbook*

1996 (million francs CFA): Imports c.i.f. 716,160; Exports f.o.b. 795,300.
1997 (million francs CFA): Imports c.i.f. 540,650; Exports f.o.b. 973,700.
1998 (million francs CFA): Imports c.i.f. 401,290; Exports f.o.b. 806,900.
1999 (million francs CFA): Imports c.i.f. 505,220; Exports f.o.b. 960,500.
Source: IMF, *International Financial Statistics*.

PRINCIPAL TRADING PARTNERS (US $ million)

Imports c.i.f.	1993	1994	1995*
Belgium-Luxembourg . .	9.7	14.9	19.4
France (incl. Monaco) . . .	114.0	127.5	145.2
Germany	8.4	9.2	15.8
Hong Kong	4.5	4.0	3.7
Italy	66.2	17.1	20.8
Japan	11.1	10.2	12.3
Mauritania	—	0.7	5.9
Netherlands	27.5	24.6	30.7
Norway	1.7	4.0	2.4
Senegal	1.8	6.0	7.2
South Africa† . . .	2.8	8.2	0.0
United Kingdom	9.0	12.7	16.6
USA	16.1	39.5	44.6
Total (incl. others) . . .	347.1	395.2	555.9

* Figures for individual countries exclude imports from free zones ($56.4 million) and stores and bunkers for ships and aircraft ($50.8 million).
† Including Botswana, Lesotho, Namibia and Swaziland.

Exports f.o.b.	1993	1994	1995
Angola	10.2	5.1	6.5
Brazil	0.1	14.0	—
Chile	—	15.6	—
France (incl. Monaco) . .	79.5	56.3	107.3
Germany	2.6	8.1	11.5
Israel	12.8	11.8	—
Italy	226.3	191.8	189.6
Japan	14.4	3.2	3.4
Malta	—	—	31.3
Netherlands	16.6	11.0	130.7
Portugal	1.6	21.9	0.4
Spain	17.3	28.1	0.1
Switzerland-Liechtenstein .	12.3	—	—
USA	503.4	386.3	311.1
Total (incl others) . . .	965.3	917.8	1,089.8

Source: UN, *International Trade Statistics Yearbook*.

Transport

RAILWAYS (traffic)

	1996	1997	1998
Passenger-km (million) . . .	360	235	242
Freight ton-km (million) . . .	289	139	135

Source: IMF, *Republic of Congo: Statistical Annex* (January 2001).

ROAD TRAFFIC (estimates, '000 motor vehicles in use at 31 December)

	1994	1995	1996
Passenger cars	33.7	36.3	37.2
Goods vehicles	14.6	15.7	15.5

Source: IRF, *World Road Statistics*.

SHIPPING
Merchant Fleet (registered at 31 December)

	1996	1997	1998
Number of vessels . . .	20	21	20
Total displacement ('000 grt) . .	6.3	6.7	3.8

Source: Lloyd's Register of Shipping, *World Fleet Statistics*.

Freight Traffic at Pointe-Noire (metric tons)

	1996	1997	1998*
Goods loaded	670,150	708,203	663,480
Goods unloaded	584,376	533,170	486,525

* Figures cover 11 months, excluding December.
Source: Banque des Etats de l'Afrique Centrale, *Etudes et Statistiques*.

Inland Waterways (freight traffic, '000 metric tons)

Port of Brazzaville	1985	1986	1987
Goods loaded	77	77	62
Goods unloaded	407	309	331

CIVIL AVIATION (traffic on scheduled services)*

	1995	1996	1997
Kilometres flown (million) . .	4	4	5
Passengers carried ('000) . .	267	253	245
Passenger-km (million) . .	283	279	305
Total ton-km (million) . .	43	42	44

* Including an apportionment of the traffic of Air Afrique.
Source: UN, *Statistical Yearbook*.

Tourism

	1996	1997	1998
Foreign tourist arrivals . . .	39,111	25,811	25,082
Tourism receipts (US $ million) .	8	3	n.a.

Source: World Tourism Organization, *Yearbook of Tourism Statistics*.

Communications Media

	1995	1996	1997
Radio receivers ('000 in use) . .	300	330	341
Television receivers ('000 in use) .	20	30	33
Telephones ('000 main lines in use)	21	22*	22*
Mobile cellular telephones			
(subscribers)	n.a.	1,000	n.a.
Daily newspapers . . .	6	6	n.a.
Non-daily newspapers . . .	15	n.a.	n.a.

* Estimate.

Sources: UNESCO, *Statistical Yearbook*; UN, *Statistical Yearbook*.

Education

(1996)

	Teachers	Pupils
Pre-primary*	619	4,415
Primary	6,926	489,546
Secondary		
General	5,466	190,409
Vocational	1,746	23,606
Higher†	1,341	16,602

* 1993/94 figures.   † 1995 figures.

Source: mainly Ministry of Education, Brazzaville.

Directory

The Constitution

The 1992 Constitution, which provided for legislative power to be exercised by a directly-elected Assemblée nationale and Senate and for executive power to be held by a directly-elected President, was suspended following the assumption of power by Gen. Denis Sassou-Nguesso on 15 October 1997. A Forum for Unity and National Reconciliation was convened in January 1998. Subsequently a 75-member National Transitional Council, elected by delegates at the Forum, was appointed to act as a legislative body pending the organization of national elections in 2001. In November 2000 the Government adopted a draft Constitution, which was to be submitted to a public referendum in 2001, following a period of national debate.

The Government

HEAD OF STATE

President: Gen. DENIS SASSOU-NGUESSO (assumed power 15 October 1997; inaugurated 25 October 1997).

COUNCIL OF MINISTERS
(May 2001)

Minister at the Presidency responsible for the Cabinet of the Head of State and State Control: GÉRARD BITSINDOU.

Minister at the Presidency responsible for National Defence: ITIHI OSSETOUMBA LEKOUNDZOU.

Minister of State for Agriculture and Livestock: AUGUSTE-CÉLESTIN GONGARAD-NKOUA.

Minister of State for Justice and Keeper of the Seals: JEAN-MARTIN MBEMBA.

Minister of the Economy, Finance and the Budget: MATHIAS DZON.

Minister of Foreign Affairs, Co-operation and Francophone Affairs: RODOLPHE ADADA.

Minister for Transport and Civil Aviation, in charge of the Merchant Navy: ISIDORE MVOUBA.

Minister of Territorial and Regional Development: PIERRE MOUSSA.

Minister of Equipment, Public Works, Construction, Urban Development, Housing and Land Reform: Brig.-Gen. FLORENT NTSIBA.

Minister of the Interior, Security and Territorial Administration: Brig.-Gen. PIERRE OBA.

Minister of Hydrocarbons: JEAN-BAPTISTE TATI LOUTARD.

Minister of Energy and Water Resources: JEAN-MARIE TASSOUA.

Minister of Culture, the Arts and Tourism: MAMBOU AIMÉE GNALI.

Minister of Health, Solidarity and Humanitarian Action: LÉON-ALFRED OPIMBAT.

Minister of Industry, Mines and the Environment: MICHEL MAMPOUYA.

Minister of Forestry and Fishing: HENRI DJOMBO.

Minister of Commerce, Supplies and Small- and Medium-sized Enterprises, in charge of Handicrafts: PIERRE-DAMIEN BOUSSOUKOU-BOUMBA.

Minister of the Civil Service, Administrative Reforms, and the Promotion of Women: JEANNE DAMBENDZET.

Minister of Communication and Government Spokesman, in charge of Relations with the National Assembly: FRANÇOIS IBOVI.

Minister of Primary, Secondary and Tertiary Education, in charge of Scientific Research: PIERRE NZILA.

Minister of Technical Education and Vocational Training, in charge of Youth Redeployment, Civic Education and Sports: ANDRÉ OKOMBI SALISSA.

Minister of Posts and Telecommunications: JEAN DELLO.

Minister of Labour and Social Security: DAMBERT NDOUANE.

Minister of Industrial Development, in charge of the Promotion of the Private Sector: ALPHONSE MBAMA.

MINISTRIES

All Ministries are in Brazzaville.

Office of the President: Palais du Peuple, Brazzaville; e-mail collgros@altranet.fr; internet www.congo-site.com.

Ministry of Commerce, Supplies and Small- and Medium-sized Enterprises: BP 2098, Brazzaville; tel. 83-19-79.

Ministry of the Economy, Finance and the Budget: Centre Administratif, Quartier Plateau, BP 2083, Brazzaville; tel. 81-41-43; fax 81-43-45.

Ministry of Education: BP 169, Brazzaville; tel. 83-24-60.

Ministry of Foreign Affairs, Co-operation and Francophone Affairs: BP 2070, Brazzaville; tel. 83-20-28.

Ministry of Health, Solidarity and Humanitarian Action: Palais du Peuple, Brazzaville; tel. 83-33-65.

Ministry of Industrial Development and the Promotion of the Private Sector: Centre Administratif, Quartier Plateau, BP 2093, Brazzaville; tel. 81-06-20.

Ministry of Industry, Mines and the Environment: Brazzaville; tel. 83-18-27.

Ministry of the Interior, Security and Territorial Administration: Brazzaville; tel. 83-12-94.

Ministry of Transport and Civil Aviation: POB 2148, Brazzaville; tel. 81-43-34; fax 83-09-16.

President and Legislature

Gen. Denis Sassou-Nguesso assumed power on 15 October 1997, deposing the elected Government of President Pascal Lissouba. Sassou-Nguesso was formally installed as President on 25 October 1997. A Forum for Unity and National Reconciliation was convened in January 1998. Immediately afterwards a 75-member National Transitional Council, elected by delegates at the Forum, was appointed to act as a legislative body pending the organization of national elections. In November 2000 the Government adopted a draft Constitution, which was to be submitted to a public referendum in the first half of 2001, prior to the organization of presidential and legislative elections.

Political Organizations

Alliance pour la citoyenneté et la démocratie (ACD): f. 2000; Pres. GODEFROY MAVUNGU.

Espace républicain pour la défense de la démocratie et l'unité nationale (ERDDUN); f. 1997; coalition of political organizations opposed to Pres. Sassou-Nguesso; Pres. BERNARD KOLELAS.

Forces démocratiques et patriotiques (FDP): Brazzaville; f. 1994 as an alliance of six political parties; fmrly Forces démocratiques unies; Leader Gen. DENIS SASSOU-NGUESSO; Deputy Leader PIERRE NZE.

> **Convention pour l'alternative démocratique:** Leader ALFRED OPIMBA.

> **Parti congolais du travail (PCT):** Brazzaville; f. 1969; sole legal political party 1969–90; Pres. Gen. DENIS SASSOU-NGUESSO; Sec.-Gen. AMBROISE NOUMAZALAY.

> **Parti libéral républicain:** Leader NICÉPHORE FYLA.

> **Union nationale pour la démocratie et le progrès (UNDP):** f. 1990; Leader PIERRE NZE.

> **Union patriotique pour la réconstruction nationale:** Leader MATHIAS DZON.

> **Union pour le renouveau nationale:** Leader GABRIEL BOKILO.

Front uni des républicains congolais (FURC): e-mail furc@multimedia.com; f. 1994; seeks national development on a non-ethnic and non-regional basis; Chair. RAYMOND TIMOTHÉE MACKITA.

Horizon 2000: Brazzaville; f. 1997; coalition of independent republican parties.

Mouvement national pour la libération du Congo rénové: Brazzaville; Pres. MPIKA MPIKA NIANGUI (PAUL MOULÉRY).

Mouvement pour l'unité et la réconstruction du Congo (MURC): f. 1997 as an alliance of three political parties:

> **Mouvement pour la démocratie et la solidarité (MDS):** Pres. PAUL KAYA.

> **Rassemblement pour la démocratie et le progrès social (RDPS):** Pointe-Noire; f. 1990; Pres. JEAN-PIERRE THYSTÈRE-TCHICAYA; Sec.-Gen. JEAN-FÉLIX DEMBA DELO.

> **Union pour la République (UR):** Brazzaville; f. 1995 by dissident mems of UPADS; Leader BENJAMIN BOUNKOULOU.

Parti du renouvellement et du progrès: Leader HENRI MARCEL DOUMANGUELE.

Parti pour l'unité, le travail et le progrès (PUTP): f. 1995 by fmr mems of the MCDDI; Leader DIDIER SENGHA.

Rassemblement des citoyens (RC): f. 1998 to promote solidarity and tolerance; Leader CLAUDE ALPHONSE SILOU.

Rassemblement pour la démocratie et le développement (RDD): f. 1990; advocates a mixed economy; Chair. SATURNIN OKABE.

Rassemblement démocratique et populaire du Congo: Leader JEAN-MARIE TASSOUA.

Rassemblement pour la démocratie et la République (RDR): f. 1996; Leader Gen. RAYMOND DAMASSE NGOLLO.

Union pour la démocratie congolaise (UDC): f. 1989; advocates economic liberalization; Chair. FÉLIX MAKOSSO.

Union pour la démocratie et la République–Mouinda (UDR–Mouinda): f. 1992; Leader ANDRÉ MILONGO.

Union pour la démocratie et le progrès social (UDPS): f. 1994 by merger of the Union pour le développement et le progrès social and the Parti populaire pour la démocratie sociale et la défense de la République; Leader JEAN-MICHEL BOUKAMBA-YANGOUMA.

Union des forces démocratiques (UFD): Chair. SÉBASTIEN EBAO.

Union panafricaine pour la démocratie sociale (UPADS): Sec.-Gen. MARTIN MBERI.

Union patriotique pour la démocratie et le progrès: Sec.-Gen. CÉLESTIN NKOUA.

Union patriotique des forces Ninjas: f. 1999; political wing of the Ninja militia loyal to fmr prime minister Bernard Kolelas.

Union pour le progrès du peuple congolais: f. 1991; advocates democracy and national unity; Leader ALPHONSE NBIHOULA.

Union pour le progrès social et la démocratie (UPSD): Brazzaville; f. 1991; Pres. ANGE-EDOUARD POUNGUI.

Union pour le renouveau démocratique (URD): f. 1992 as an alliance of seven political parties; Chair. BERNARD KOLELAS; prin. mems:

> **Mouvement congolais pour la démocratie et le développement intégral (MCDDI):** Brazzaville; f. 1990; Sec.-Gen. MICHEL MAMPOUYA.

Diplomatic Representation

EMBASSIES IN THE REPUBLIC OF THE CONGO

Following the 1997 conflict and subsequent unrest in Brazzaville, many diplomatic missions have remained closed, or operate with only essential staff.

Algeria: BP 2100, Brazzaville; tel. 83-40-11.

Angola: BP 388, Brazzaville; tel. 81-14-71.

Belgium: BP 225, Brazzaville; tel. 66-26-14; fax 81-37-04.

Cameroon: BP 2136, Brazzaville; tel. 83-34-04.

Central African Republic: BP 10, Brazzaville; tel. 83-40-14.

Chad: BP 386, Brazzaville; tel. 81-22-22.

China, People's Republic: BP 213, Brazzaville; tel. 83-11-20; fax 83-77-06; Ambassador QU FUJUN.

Congo, Democratic Republic: BP 2450, Brazzaville; tel. 83-29-38; Ambassador FÉLIX MUMENGUI OTTHUW.

Cuba: BP 80, Brazzaville; tel. 81-29-80.

Egypt: BP 917, Brazzaville; tel. 83-44-28; Ambassador MOHAMED HASSAN EL KHADRAWY.

France: rue Alfassa, BP 2089, Brazzaville; tel. 81-55-41; fax 87-13-82; Ambassador: HERVÉ BOLOT.

Guinea: Brazzaville; tel. 81-24-66.

Holy See: rue Colonel Brisset, BP 1168, Brazzaville; tel. 81-55-80; fax 81-55-81; e-mail nonapcg@yahoo.com; Apostolic Nuncio: Most Rev. MARIO ROBERTO CASSARI, Titular Archbishop of Tronto.

Italy: 2 blvd Lyauté, BP 2484, Brazzaville; tel. and fax 81-11-52; e-mail ambitbra@congonet.cg; Ambassador ANNA FEDELE RUBENS.

Korea, Democratic People's Republic: Brazzaville; tel. 83-41-98; Ambassador: HAN PONG CHUN.

Libya: BP 920, Brazzaville.

Nigeria: BP 790, Brazzaville; tel. 83-13-16; Ambassador GREG MBADIWE.

Russia: BP 2132, Brazzaville; tel. 81-19-23; fax 81-50-85; Ambassador: SERGEI NENASHEV.

USA: BP 1015, Brazzaville; tel. 81-14-72; Ambassador: DAVID H. KAEUPER.

Judicial System

The _Acte fondamental_ of October 1997 confirmed the independence of the judiciary. The constituent bodies of the judiciary are the Cour suprême (Supreme Court), the Haute cour de la justice (High Court) and the Conseil supérieur de la magistrature (Supreme Council of Magistrates).

Cour suprême: Brazzaville; Pres. GASTON MAMBOUANA.

Religion

At least one-half of the population follow traditional animist beliefs. Most of the remainder are Christians (mainly Roman Catholics).

CHRISTIANITY

The Roman Catholic Church

The Congo comprises one archdiocese and five dioceses. According to Church figures, at 31 December 1998 an estimated 47.8% of the population were adherents.

Bishops' Conference: Conférence Episcopale du Congo, BP 200, Brazzaville; tel. 83-06-29; fax 83-79-08; f. 1992; Pres. Rt Rev. ANATOLE MILANDOU, Bishop of Kinkala.

Archbishop of Brazzaville: Most Rev. BARTHÉLÉMY BATANTU, Archevêché, BP 2301, Brazzaville; tel. 83-17-93; fax 83-17-98.

Protestant Church

Eglise Evangélique du Congo: BP 3205, Bacongo-Brazzaville; tel. 81-43-64; fax 83-77-33; internet www.chez.com/ngouedippc/page3.html; f. 1909; Presbyterian; autonomous since 1961; 135,811 mems (1993); 105 parishes (1998); Pres. Rev. ALPHONSE MBAMA.

ISLAM

In 1997 an estimated 2% of the population were Muslims. There were 49 mosques in the Congo in 1991.

Comité Islamique du Congo: 77 Makotipoko Moungali, BP 55, Brazzaville; tel. 82-87-45; f. 1988; Leaders HABIBOU SOUMARE, BACHIR GATSONGO, BOUILLA GUIBIDANESI.

The Press

In July 2000 legislation was adopted on the freedom of information and communication. The legislation, which confirmed the abolition of censorship and reduced the penalty for defamation from imprisonment to a fine, specified three types of punishable offence: the encouragement of social tension (including incitement to ethnic conflict), attacks on the authorities (including libels on the head of state or on the judiciary), and libels against private individuals. The terms of the legislation were to be guaranteed by a regulatory body, the Conseil de la liberté de la communication.

DAILIES

Aujourd'hui: BP 1171, Brazzaville; tel. and fax 83-77-44; f. 1991; Man. Dir and Chief Editor FYLLA DI FUA DI SASSA.

L'Eveil de Pointe-Noire: Pointe-Noire.

Journal de Brazzaville: BP 132, Brazzaville.

Mweti: BP 991, Brazzaville; tel. 81-10-87; national news; Dir MATONGO AVELEY; Chief Editor HUBERT MADOUABA; circ. 7,000.

PERIODICALS

Bakento Ya Congo: BP 309, Brazzaville; tel. 83-27-44; quarterly; Dir MARIE LOUISE MAGANGA; Chief Editor CHARLOTTE BOUSSE; circ. 3,000.

Bulletin Mensuel de la Chambre de Commerce de Brazzaville: BP 92, Brazzaville; monthly.

Bulletin de Statistique: Centre Nationale de la Statistique et des Etudes Economiques, BP 2031, Brazzaville; tel. and fax 81-59-09; f. 1977; quarterly; Dir-Gen. DOROTHÉE OUISSIKA.

Le Choc: BP 1314, Brazzaville; weekly; satirical; Chief Editor: JEAN-BAPTISTE BAKOUVOUKA.

Combattant Rouge: Brazzaville; tel. 83-02-53; monthly; Dir SYLVIO GEORGES ONKA; Chief Editor GILLES OMER BOUSSI.

Congo-Magazine: BP 114, Brazzaville; tel. 83-43-81; monthly; Dir GASPARD MPAN; Chief Editor THÉODORE KIAMOSSI; circ. 3,000.

Les Dépêches de Brazzaville: Résidence Méridien, BP 15457, Brazzaville; tel. and fax 81-28-13; e-mail belie@congonet.cg; internet www.brazzaville-adiac.com; monthly; published by Agence d'Information de l'Afrique Centrale (ADIAC); Man. Dir JEAN-PAUL PIGASSE; Editor-in-Chief BELINDA AYESSA.

Effort: BP 64, Brazzaville; monthly; general interest.

Le Flambeau: Brazzaville; weekly; independent; Man. Editor RICHARD NTSANA.

Le Forum: BP 3232, Brazzaville; f. 1992; weekly; Publr MAURICE MASSENGO TIASSE.

Le Gardien: 39 rue Bouenza Talangai, Brazzaville; f. 1993; fortnightly; Publr GILLES ANDAH-LEYET; circ. 2,500.

Jeunesse et Révolution: BP 885, Brazzaville; tel. 83-44-13; weekly; Dir JEAN-ENOCH GOMA-KENGUE; Chief Editor PIERRE MAKITA.

Le Madukutsekele: Brazzaville; f. 1991; weekly; satirical; Editor MATHIEU BAKIMA-BALIELE; circ. 5,000.

La Nouvelle République: Brazzaville; pro-government; weekly.

L'Opinion: Brazzaville; monthly.

Paris-Brazzaville: Brazzaville; weekly; general interest.

Le Pays: f. 1991; weekly; Dir ANTOINE MALONGA.

La Rue Meurt: BP 1258, Brazzaville; f. 1991; satirical weekly magazine; Publr JEAN-PAUL BAFOUIRI; circ. 3,000.

La Semaine Africaine: BP 2080, Brazzaville; tel. 81-03-28; f. 1952; weekly; Roman Catholic; general news and social comment; circulates widely in francophone equatorial Africa; Dir JEAN-PIERRE GALLET; Chief Editor JOACHIM MBANZA; circ. 7,500.

Le Soleil: f. 1991; weekly; organ of the Rassemblement pour la démocratie et le développement.

Le Stade: BP 114, Brazzaville; tel. 81-47-18; f. 1985; weekly; sports; Dir HUBERT-TRÉSOR MADOUABA-NTOUALANI; Chief Editor LELAS PAUL NZOLANI; circ. 6,500.

Le Temps: Brazzaville; weekly; owned by supporters of former Pres. Lissouba.

Voix de la Classe Ouvrière (Voco): BP 2311, Brazzaville; tel. 83-36-66; six a year; Dir MICHEL JOSEPH MAYOUNGOU; Chief Editor MARIE-JOSEPH TSENGOU; circ. 4,500.

NEWS AGENCIES

Agence Congolaise d'Information (ACI): ave E. P. Lumumba, BP 2144, Brazzaville; tel. 81-17-96; Gen. Man. THÉODORE KIAMOSSI.

Agence d'Information d'Afrique Centrale (ADIAC): Hôtel Méridien, BP 15457, Brazzaville; tel. and fax 81-28-13; e-mail belie@congonet.cg; internet www.brazzaville-adiac.com; f. 1997; Dirs JEAN-PAUL PIGASSE, BELINDA AYESSA; br. in Paris.

Foreign Bureaux

Agence France-Presse (AFP): c/o Agence Congolaise d'Information, BP 2144, Brazzaville; tel. 83-46-76.

Associated Press (AP) (USA): BP 2144, Brazzaville.

Inter Press Service (IPS) (Italy): POB 964, Brazzaville; tel. 810565.

Pan-African News Agency (PANA) (Senegal): BP 2144, Brazzaville; tel. 83-11-40; fax 83-70-15.

Reuters (United Kingdom): BP 2144, Brazzaville.

Xinhua (New China) News Agency (People's Republic of China): 40 ave Maréchal Lyauté, BP 373, Brazzaville; tel. 83-44-01.

Publishers

Editions ADIAC: Hôtel Méridien, BP 15457, Brazzaville; tel. and fax 81-28-13; f. 1997; publishes chronicles of current affairs; Dirs JEAN-PAUL PIGASSE, BELINDA AYESSA.

Editions 'Héros dans l'Ombre': BP 1678, Brazzaville; tel. 82-23-03; fax 83-50-51; f. 1980; literature, criticism, poetry, essays; President LÉOPOLD PINDY-MAMONSONO.

Imprimerie Centrale d'Afrique (ICA): BP 162, Pointe-Noire; f. 1949; Man. Dir M. SCHNEIDER.

Government Publishing House

Imprimerie Nationale: BP 58, Brazzaville; Man. KIALA MATOUBA.

Broadcasting and Communications

TELECOMMUNICATIONS

Office National des Postes et Télécommunications (ONPT): ave Patrice Lumumba, BP 39, Brazzaville; tel. 81-16-86; operates national telecommunications network; mobile cellular telephone system introduced in 1996; division into separate postal and telecommunications companies pending, with the latter (SOTEL CO) scheduled for privatization in June 2001; Man. Dir BERNARD OKIEMOU.

Celtel Congo: Celtel House, BP 1267, Pointe-Noire; tel. 94-86-02; fax 94-88-75; e-mail celtelcongo@yahoo.fr; internet www.msi-cellular.com; Brazzaville; f. 1999; mobile cellular telephone operator and internet access provider; network covers Brazzaville and Pointe-Noire; subsid. of MSI Cellular; Man. Dir ROB GELDERLOOS; 30,000 subscribers (Dec. 2000).

Cyrus International (CYRTEL): Brazzaville; mobile cellular telephone operator; operates as a jt venture between Nexus International (70%), a subsidiary of France Telecom, and the ONPT.

Libertis: ave Amílcar Cabral, Brazzaville; tel. 81-37-70; fax 81-47-20; internet www.orascomtelecom.com; f. 2000; mobile cellular telephone operator; subsid. of Orascom Telecom (Egypt).

RADIO AND TELEVISION

Radio Brazzaville: face Direction Générale, ONPT, Brazzaville; tel. 51-60-73; f. 1999; official station: Man. JEAN PASCAL MONGO SLYM.

Radio Congo Liberté: Brazzaville; f. 1997; operated by supporters of Pres. Sassou-Nguesso.

Radiodiffusion-Télévision Congolaise: BP 2241, Brazzaville; tel. 81-24-73; state-owned; Pres. JEAN-GILBERT FOUTOU; Dir-Gen. GILBERT-DAVID MUTAKALA.

Radio Congo: BP 2241, Brazzaville; tel. 81-50-60; radio programmes in French, Lingala, Kikongo, Subia, English and Portuguese; transmitters at Brazzaville and Pointe-Noire; Gen. Man. ALPHONSE BOUYA DIMI; Dir of Broadcasting THÉOPHILE MIETE LIKIBI.

Télé-Congo: BP 975, Brazzaville; tel. 81-01-16; began transmission in 1963; operates for 46 hours per week, with most programmes in French but some in Lingala and Kikongo; Gen. Man. WAMENE EKIAYE-ACKOLI.

Radio Rurale: BP 60, Brazzaville; tel. 83-03-09; community stations established by the Agence de coopération culturelle et technique (ACCT); transmitters in Sembé, Nkayi, Etoumbi and Mossendjo.

Télédiffusion du Congo: BP 2912, Brazzaville; tel. 81-06-08; Gen. Man. MÉDARD BOKATOLA.

The Republic of the Congo also receives broadcasts from Radio France International and Radio Africa No. 1.

Finance

(cap. = capital; res = reserves; dep. = deposits; m. = million; br. = branch; amounts in francs CFA)

BANKING
Central Bank

Banque des Etats de l'Afrique Centrale (BEAC): BP 126, Brazzaville; tel. 81-10-73; fax 81-10-94; HQ in Yaoundé, Cameroon; f. 1973; bank of issue for mem. states of the Communauté économique et monétaire en Afrique centrale (CEMAC, fmrly Union douanière et économique de l'Afrique centrale); comprising Cameroon, the Central African Repub., Chad, the Repub. of the Congo, Equatorial Guinea and Gabon; cap. 45,000m., res 172,198m., total assets 1,407,908m. (Dec. 1999); Gov. JEAN-FÉLIX MAMALEPOT; Dir in Repub. of the Congo PACIFIQUE ISSOIBEKA; br. at Pointe-Noire.

Commercial Banks

Banque Française Intercontinentale du Congo (FIBA): BP 14579, Brazzaville; tel. 81-40-50; fax 81-50-89; Dir HENRI-JEAN RESCA.

Banque Internationale de Développement du Congo (BIDC): ave Amílcar Cabral, BP 33, Brazzaville; tel. 81-07-14; fax 81-16-69; f. 1983; state-owned; privatization pending; total assets 51,980m. (Dec. 1997); Pres. EDOUARD EBOUKA BABACKAS; Gen. Man. FRANÇOIS BOUMANDOUKI; 1 br.

Crédit pour l'Agriculture, l'Industrie et le Commerce (CAIC): ave Amílcar Cabral, BP 2889, Brazzaville; tel. 81-09-78; fax 81-09-77; fmrly Caisse de Crédit Agricole; 50% state-owned; transfer to private sector pending; Man. Dir DELPHINE MBOUYOU.

Union Congolaise de Banques SARL (UCB): ave Amílcar Cabral, BP 147, Brazzaville; tel. 81-58-33; fax 81-47-34; f. 1974; state-owned; transfer pending to private sector; total assets 104,400m. (Dec. 1997); Dir-Gen. GERVAIS BOUITI-VIAUDO; 8 brs.

Co-operative Banking Institution

Mutuelles Congolaises de l'Epargne et de Crédit (MUCODEC): BP 13237, Brazzaville; tel. 81-07-57; fax 81-01-68; f. 1994; Dir. JEAN-CLAUDE GARCIA.

Development Bank

Banque de Développement des États de l'Afrique Centrale: Head Office, place du Gouvernement, BP 1177, Brazzaville; tel. 81-17-61; fax 81-18-80; Chair. ZACHARIE PEREVET; Gen. Man. JEAN-MARIE MBIOKA.

Financial Institution

Caisse Congolaise d'Amortissement: ave Foch Beltrando, BP 2090, Brazzaville; tel. 81-57-35; fax 81-52-36; f. 1971; management of state funds; Dir-Gen. ROGER GOSSAKI.

INSURANCE

Assurances et Réassurances du Congo (ARC): ave Amílcar Cabral, BP 977, Brazzaville; tel. 83-01-71; f. 1973; 50% state-owned;

to be restructured prior to pending privatization; Dir-Gen. RAYMOND IBATA; brs at Pointe-Noire, Loubomo and Ouesso.

Gras Savoye Congo: BP 1901, Pointe Noire; tel. 94-79-72; fax 94-79-74; e-mail grassavoyecongo1@aol.com; internet www.grassavoye .com; insurance brokers and risk managers; Man. ERIC MANTOT.

Trade and Industry

DEVELOPMENT ORGANIZATIONS

Agence Française de Développement: BP 96, Brazzaville; tel. 81-53-30; fax 81-29-42; e-mail mahes@afd.fr; internet www.afd.fr; French fund for economic co-operation; Dir ANDRÉ MEYER.

Mission Française de Coopération: BP 2175, Brazzaville; tel. 83-15-03; f. 1959; administers bilateral aid from France; Dir JEAN-BERNARD THIANT.

Office des Cultures Vivrières (OCV): Brazzaville; tel. 82-11-03; f. 1979; state-owned; food-crop development; Dir-Gen. GILBERT PANA.

Société Nationale d'Elevage (SONEL): BP 81, Loutété, Massangui; f. 1964; development of semi-intensive stock-rearing; exploitation of cattle by-products; Man. Dir THÉOPHILE BIKAWA.

CHAMBERS OF COMMERCE

Chambre de Commerce, d'Agriculture et d'Industrie de Brazzaville: BP 92, Brazzaville; tel. 83-21-15; Pres. MAURICE OGNAOY; Sec.-Gen. FRANÇOIS DILOU-YOULOU.

Chambre de Commerce, d'Agriculture et d'Industrie de Loubomo: BP 78, Loubomo.

Chambre de Commerce, d'Industrie et d'Agriculture et des Métiers de Pointe-Noire: 8 ave Charles de Gaulle, BP 665, Pointe-Noire; tel. 94-12-80; fax 94-07-13; f. 1948; Chair. NARCISSE POATY PACKA; Sec.-Gen. JEAN-BAPTISTE SOUMBOU.

INDUSTRIAL AND TRADE ASSOCIATIONS

Office Congolais des Bois (OCB): 2 ave Moe Vangoula, BP 1229, Pointe-Noire; tel. 94-22-38; f. 1974; purchase and marketing of timber products; Man. Dir ALEXANDRE DENGUET-ATTIKI.

Office National de Commercialisation des Produits Agricoles (ONCPA): Brazzaville; tel. 83-24-01; f. 1964; marketing of all agricultural products except sugar; promotion of rural co-operatives; Dir JEAN-PAUL BOCKONDAS.

Office National du Commerce (OFNACOM): Brazzaville; tel. 83-43-99; f. 1964; importer and distributor of general merchandise; monopoly importer of salted and dried fish, cooking salt, rice, tomato purée, buckets, enamelled goods and blankets; Dir-Gen. VALENTIN ENOUSSA NCONGO.

EMPLOYERS' ORGANIZATIONS

Union Nationale des Opérateurs du Congo (UNOC): Brazzaville; employers' assn; operates a professional training centre; Pres. El Hadj DJIBRIL ABDOULAYE BOPAKA.

Union Patronale et Interprofessionnelle du Congo (UNI-CONGO): BP 42, Brazzaville; tel. 81-47-65; fax 81-47-66; f. 1960; employers' asscn; Pres. G. BOUR; Sec.-Gen. J. FUMEY.

UTILITIES

Electricity

Société Nationale d'Electricité (SNE): 95 ave Paul Doumer, BP 95, Brazzaville; tel. 81-38-58; f. 1967; transfer pending to private management; operates hydroelectric plants at Bouenza and Djoué; Dir-Gen. ALPHONSE BOUDONESA.

Water

Société Nationale de Distribution d'Eau (SNDE): rue du Sergent Malamine, BP 229 and 365, Brazzaville; tel. 83-73-26; fax 83-38-91; f. 1967; transfer pending to private-sector management; water supply and sewerage; holds monopoly over wells and import of mineral water; Chair. and Man. Dir S. MPINOU.

TRADE UNIONS

Independent trade unions were legalized in 1991.

Confédération Générale des Travailleurs du Congo (CGTC): Brazzaville; f. 1995; Chair. PAUL DOUNA.

Confédération Nationale des Syndicats Libres (CNASYL): Brazzaville; f. 1994; Sec.-Gen. MICHEL KABOUL MAOUTA.

Confédération Syndicale Congolaise (CSC): BP 2311, Brazzaville; tel. 83-19-23; f. 1964; 80,000 mems.

Confédération Syndicale des Travailleurs Congolais (CSTC): Brazzaville; f. 1993; fed. of 13 trade unions; Chair. DAMAS KIKONI; Sec.-Gen. LOUIS GOUNDOU; 40,000 mems.

Confédération des Syndicats Libres et Autonomes du Congo (COSYLAC): Brazzaville; Pres. RENÉ BLANCHARD SERGE OBA.

Transport

Agence Transcongolaise des Communications (ATC): BP 711, Pointe-Noire; tel. 94-15-32; f. 1969; transfer pending to private-sector ownership; three divisions: Congo-Océan Railways, inland waterways and Brazzaville inland port, and the Atlantic port of Pointe-Noire; Man. Dir Col JEAN-FÉLIX ONGOUYA.

RAILWAYS

There are 515 km of track from Brazzaville to Pointe-Noire. A 286-km section of privately-owned line was used until 1991 to link the manganese mines at Moanda (in Gabon) with the main line to Pointe-Noire. Rail traffic has been severely disrupted since the 1997 civil war. The main line to Pointe-Noire reopened briefly in November 1998 for freight traffic, but was subsequently closed following further unrest and sabotage. In early 2000 the Government signed two agreements with SNCF of France relating to the repair of the line and associated infrastructure, and to the management of the network. Freight services resumed in August 2000, followed by passenger services in January 2001.

ATC—Chemin de Fer Congo-Océan (CFCO): BP 651, Pointe-Noire; tel. 94-11-84; fax 94-12-30; f. 1969; entered partnership with Rail Afrique International in June 1998; transfer pending to private ownership; Exec. Vice Pres. ROBERT LAMPARNESSE; Man. Dir Adm. PIERRE NGOMBE.

INLAND WATERWAYS

The Congo and Oubangui rivers form two axes of a highly developed inland waterway system. The Congo river and seven tributaries in the Congo basin provide 2,300 km of navigable river, and the Oubangui river, developed in co-operation with the Central African Republic, an additional 2,085 km.

ATC—Direction des Voies Navigables, Ports et Transports Fluviaux: BP 2048, Brazzaville; tel. 83-06-27; waterways authority; Dir MÉDARD OKOUMOU.

Compagnie Congolaise de Transports: Loubomo; f. 1960; Pres. and Dir-Gen. ROBERT BARBIER.

Société Congolaise de Transports (SOCOTRANS): BP 617, Pointe-Noire; tel. 94-23-31; fax 94-45-02; e-mail soco10@calva.com; f. 1977; transport; handling; consignments; Man. HENRI BENATOUIL.

Transcap—Congo: BP 1154, Pointe-Noire; tel. 94-01-46; f. 1962; Chair. J. DROUAULT.

SHIPPING

The deep-water Atlantic seaport at Pointe-Noire is the most important port in Central Africa and Brazzaville is one of the principal ports on the Congo river. A major rehabilitation programme began in October 1999, with the aim of establishing Pointe-Noire as a regional centre for container traffic and as a logistics centre for offshore oil exploration. In 1997 708,203 metric tons of goods were loaded at the port of Pointe-Noire, and 533,170 tons were unloaded.

ATC—Direction du Port de Brazzaville: BP 2048, Brazzaville; tel. 83-00-42; port authority; Dir JEAN-PAUL BOCKONDAS.

ATC—Direction du Port de Pointe-Noire: BP 711, Pointe-Noire; tel. 94-00-52; fax 94-20-42; port authority; Dir DOMINIQUE BEMBA.

La Congolaise de Transport Maritime (COTRAM): f. 1984; national shipping co; state-owned.

SAGA Congo: 18 rue du Prophète Lasse Zephirin, BP 674, Pointe Noire; tel. 94-10-16; fax 94-34-04.

ROADS

In 1996 there were an estimated 12,800 km of roads and tracks, including 3,440 km of main roads and 4,150 km of secondary roads. Only about 9.7% of the total network was paved. The principal routes link Brazzaville with Pointe-Noire, in the south, and with Ouesso, in the north. The proposed privatization of national road maintenance services was announced in late 1999.

Régie Nationale des Transports et des Travaux Publics: BP 2073, Brazzaville; tel. 83-35-58; f. 1965; civil engineering, maintenance of roads and public works; Man. Dir HECTOR BIENVENU OUAMBA.

CIVIL AVIATION

There are international airports at Brazzaville (Maya-Maya) and Pointe-Noire (Agostinho Neto). There are also five regional airports, at Dolisie, Nkaye, Owando, Ouesso and Impfondo, as well as 12 smaller airfields. In 1994 the state monopoly on internal flights was terminated, and in 1999 there were 10 airline companies operating in the Congo.

Aéro-Service: ave Charles de Gaulle, BP 1138, Brazzaville; tel. 81-34-88; fax 83-09-47; f. 1967; scheduled and charter services; operates nationally and to regional destinations; Pres. and Dir-Gen. C. GRIES-BAUM.

Air Afrique: BP 1126, Pointe-Noire; tel. 94-17-00; see under Côte d'Ivoire; Dir at Pointe-Noire GUY C. CODIJA; Dir at Brazzaville AHMED LAMINE-ALI.

Congo-Aviation: Brazzaville; f. 1994.

Lina Congo (Lignes Nationales Aériennes Congolaises): ave Amílcar Cabral, BP 2203, Brazzaville; tel. 81-30-65; fax 82-80-34; f. 1965; 33% state-owned; operates an extensive internal network; international flights to Gabon and Angola; Man. Dir RAOUL MAIXANT ODZOTO.

Trans Air Congo: ave Amílcar Cabral, BP 2422, Brazzaville; tel. 81-10-57; fax 94-44-36; e-mail TAC10@calva.com; f. 1994; Lebanese-owned private airline operating internal scheduled and international charter flights; Dir BASSAM ELHAGE.

Tourism

The tourism sector has been severely disrupted by political instability and internal unrest. Tourist visitors numbered 25,000 in 1998 (compared with tourist arrivals of 36,072 in 1992). In 1997 earnings from tourism were estimated at US $3m.

Direction Générale du Tourisme et des Loisirs: BP 456, Brazzaville; tel. 83-09-53; f. 1980; Dir-Gen. ANTOINE KOUNKOU-KIBOUILOU.

COSTA RICA

Introductory Survey

Location, Climate, Language, Religion, Flag, Capital

The Republic of Costa Rica lies in the Central American isthmus, with Nicaragua to the north, Panama to the south, the Caribbean Sea to the east and the Pacific Ocean to the west. The climate is warm and damp in the lowlands (average temperature 27°C (81°F)) and cooler on the Central Plateau (average temperature 22°C (72°F)), where two-thirds of the population live. The language spoken is Spanish. Almost all of the inhabitants profess Christianity, and the majority adhere to the Roman Catholic Church, the state religion. The national flag (proportions 5 by 3) has five horizontal stripes, of blue, white, red, white and blue, the red stripe being twice the width of the others. The state flag, in addition, has on the red stripe (to the left of centre) a white oval enclosing the national coat of arms, showing three volcanic peaks between the Caribbean and the Pacific. The capital is San José.

Recent History

Costa Rica was ruled by Spain from the 16th century until 1821, when independence was declared. The only significant interruption in the country's constitutional government since 1920 occurred in February 1948, when the victory of the opposition candidate, Otilio Ulate Blanco, in the presidential election was disputed. The legislature annulled the election in March but a civil war ensued. The anti-Government forces, led by José Figueres Ferrer, were successful, and a revolutionary junta took power in April. Costa Rica's army was abolished in December. After the preparation of a new Constitution, Ulate took office as President in January 1949.

Figueres, who founded the socialist Partido de Liberación Nacional (PLN), dominated national politics for decades, holding presidential office in 1953–58 and 1970–74. Under his leadership, Costa Rica became one of the most democratic countries in Latin America. Since the 1948 revolution, there have been frequent changes of power, all achieved by constitutional means. Figueres's first Government nationalized the banks and instituted a comprehensive social security system. The presidential election of 1958, however, was won by a conservative, Mario Echandi Jiménez, who reversed many PLN policies. His successor, Francisco Orlich Bolmarich (President from 1962 to 1966), was supported by the PLN but continued the encouragement of private enterprise. Another conservative, José Joaquín Trejos Fernández, held power in 1966–70. In 1974 the PLN candidate, Daniel Oduber Quirós, was elected President. He continued the policies of extending the welfare state and of establishing amicable relations with communist states. Communist and other left-wing parties were legalized in 1975. In 1978 Rodrigo Carazo Odio of the conservative Partido Unidad Opositora (PUO) coalition (subsequently the Coalición Unidad) was elected President. During Carazo's term of office increasing instability in Central America led to diplomatic tension, and in 1981 the President was criticized for his alleged involvement in illegal arms trafficking between Cuba and El Salvador.

At presidential and legislative elections in February 1982, Luis Alberto Monge Alvarez of the PLN gained a comfortable majority when his party won 33 of the 57 seats in the Legislative Assembly. Following his inauguration in May, President Monge announced a series of emergency economic measures, in an attempt to rescue the country from near-bankruptcy. A policy of neutrality towards the left-wing Sandinista Government of Nicaragua was continued. However, following a number of cross-border raids, a national alert was declared in May. The rebel Nicaraguan leader, Edén Pastora Gómez, was expelled in order to reduce Costa Rican involvement in the Nicaraguan conflict. Relations with Nicaragua deteriorated as guerrilla activity spread to San José.

Throughout 1983 Monge came under increasing pressure from liberal members of the Cabinet and PLN supporters to adopt a more neutral stance in foreign policy. Three leading members of the anti-Sandinista (Contra) movement were expelled from Costa Rica in May, and 80 of Pastora's supporters were arrested in September. In addition, some 82 guerrilla camps were dismantled by the Civil Guard. In November Monge declared Costa Rica's neutrality in an attempt to elicit foreign support for his country. This declaration was opposed by the USA and led to the resignation of the Costa Rican Minister of Foreign Affairs.

In early 1984 there were increasing reports of incursions into Costa Rica by the Sandinista forces. Public opposition to any renunciation of neutrality was emphasized by a demonstration in support of peace and neutrality, held in San José and attended by over 20,000 people. An attempt was made to defuse the tension with the establishment of a commission, supported by the Contadora group (Colombia, Mexico, Panama and Venezuela), to monitor events in the border area. In late May, however, the attempted assassination of Pastora near the Costa Rican border exacerbated the rift within the Cabinet concerning government policy towards Nicaragua. In December, following an incident involving a Nicaraguan refugee at the Costa Rican embassy in Managua, diplomatic relations with Nicaragua were reduced to a minimal level. Reports of clashes between Costa Rican Civil Guardsmen and Sandinista forces along the joint border became increasingly frequent. In 1985 the Government's commitment to neutrality was disputed when it decided to establish an anti-guerrilla battalion, trained by US military advisers.

During 1983 there were signs of increasing urban unrest in response to the Government's austerity measures and to the agrarian crisis, which had produced high levels of unemployment, principally among workers on banana plantations. By August 1984 the Government's position was regarded as unstable. The division within the Cabinet over policy towards Nicaragua, coupled with the effects of the unpopular austerity programme and a protracted strike by banana plantation workers, which had resulted in two deaths, led to fears of a coup. At Monge's request, the Cabinet resigned, and in the subsequent reshuffle four ministers were replaced.

At presidential and legislative elections in February 1986 Oscar Arias Sánchez, the candidate of the PLN, was elected President, with 52% of the votes cast. The PLN also obtained a clear majority in the Legislative Assembly. The new Government was committed to the development of a welfare state, the renegotiation of the country's external debt, and the conclusion of a social pact with the trade unions. Furthermore, Arias was resolved to maintain and reinforce Costa Rica's policy of neutrality.

In February 1986 diplomatic relations with Nicaragua were fully restored, and it was decided to establish a permanent inspection and vigilance commission at the common border. In accordance with the Government's pledge to protect neutrality, Costa Rica objected to the allocation of US $100m. in US aid to the Contra forces in mid-1986. In addition, the Government embarked on a series of arrests and expulsions of Contras resident in Costa Rica. A degree of Costa Rican complicity in anti-Sandinista activity became apparent, however, in 1986, when the existence of a secret airstrip in Costa Rica, which was used as a supply base for the Contras, was made public. The airstrip had been constructed by the USA during President Monge's administration but had been closed on Arias's accession to power.

Throughout 1986 and 1987 Arias became increasingly involved in the quest for peace in Central America. In August 1987 the Presidents of El Salvador, Nicaragua, Guatemala, Honduras and Costa Rica signed a peace agreement based on proposals presented by Arias, who was subsequently awarded the Nobel Peace Prize. In January 1988 Arias brought Nicaraguan government officials and Contra leaders together in San José for their first discussions concerning the implementation of a cease-fire. Prior to this meeting, Arias ordered three Contra leaders to leave Costa Rica or cease their military activities. Arias maintained his independent position by supporting discussions between the Contras and Sandinistas, held in Nicaragua in March, and by condemning any continuation of aid to the Contras. In November a border agreement was signed with Nicaragua.

In 1988 there were renewed indications of internal unrest as a result of the Government's economic policies. In March there were stoppages by public employees, to protest against concessions made to the International Monetary Fund (IMF, see p. 92) and the World Bank (see p. 79). In August there were strikes by farmers aggrieved at the Government's 'Agriculture for Change' policy of promoting the cultivation of cash crops, and thereby sacrificing the interests of many smallholders, to appease the IMF. Labour unrest increased throughout the country during 1989.

In September 1989 the Legislative Assembly's commission of enquiry into the extent of drugs-trafficking and related activities published its findings. As a result, a number of high-ranking public figures were asked to resign, including the former President (then a senior PLN official), Daniel Oduber Quirós.

At presidential and legislative elections in February 1990, Rafael Angel Calderón Fournier, the candidate of the Partido Unidad Social Cristiana (PUSC), was elected President, with 51.3% of the votes cast. The PUSC obtained a clear majority in the Legislative Assembly, with 29 seats. On assuming office in May, Calderón inherited a large fiscal deficit and was therefore forced to renege on his pre-election promise of improvements in welfare and income distribution. In an attempt to reduce the deficit, the Government introduced an adjustment programme of austerity measures. In October 70,000–100,000 public- and private-sector employees participated in a one-day national strike to protest against the Government's economic policies. Later that month the Minister of Labour resigned, stating that his decision to do so reflected the rift between 'economic and social groups' within the Cabinet.

In August 1991 the Minister of Public Security and the Minister of National Planning and Economic Policy resigned, following disagreements with President Calderón. The Minister of the Interior and Police, Luis Fishman, was subsequently appointed acting Minister of Public Security. The Civil Guard and the Rural Guard (which had previously been responsible to the Ministry of Public Security and the Ministry of the Interior and Police, respectively) therefore came under the sole charge of Fishman. Opposition groups expressed concern at this concentration of power, in view of the continuing decline in popular support for Calderón and the level of public unrest. In November, in response to pressure from student and public-sector unions, Calderón abandoned austerity measures involving a reduction in the education budget and the dismissal of thousands of public employees. This decision prompted the resignation of the Minister of Finance, who claimed that the President's action would make it impossible to curb the rapidly increasing fiscal deficit and thus attain IMF-agreed targets.

In January 1992 Calderón was summoned before the Legislative Assembly's commission on drugs-trafficking to answer allegations that the PUSC had been the recipient of the proceeds of illegal drugs-trafficking during its election campaign in 1990. Calderón denied any knowledge of such payments. Following the decision made by the Government in March 1992 to remove foreign-exchange controls, there was mounting concern that Costa Rican banking institutions were being increasingly used for the purposes of laundering money obtained from illegal drugs-trafficking.

In March 1993 some 25 people, including the Nicaraguan Ambassador to Costa Rica, were taken hostage at the Nicaraguan embassy in San José by three armed men whose demands included the dismissals of the head of the Nicaraguan armed forces and the Nicaraguan President's chief adviser. The hostages were later released unharmed in return for a ransom and safe passage out of the country. A similar incident, which took place in April and involved members of the Supreme Court being taken hostage, served to heighten concern about the security situation in Costa Rica.

Presidential and legislative elections were held in February 1994. The presidential ballot was narrowly won by José María Figueres Olsen, the PLN candidate. The PLN failed to obtain an outright majority in the Legislative Assembly, securing only 28 of the 57 seats, while the PUSC won 25 seats and the Fuerza Democrática (FD) gained two seats. The remaining two seats were won by independent candidates. Figueres assumed office in early May.

In May 1994 industrial action by employees of the Geest banana company resulted in violent clashes with the security forces. The strike was organized in protest at the dismissal of some 400 workers for attempting to join a union. The dispute, which was resolved following government intervention, came in the wake of allegations by a US trade union body, the American Federation of Labor and Congress of Industrial Organizations,

of violations of labour rights in Costa Rica. In late 1993 the Costa Rican authorities avoided an investigation into the country's labour practices by the US trade representative office and the possible loss of trading benefits enjoyed under the Generalized System of Preferences by introducing legislation reforming the labour code.

In July 1995 some 50,000 teachers began strike action in protest at proposed reforms to the state pension system. Growing dissatisfaction among other public-sector employees at government economic policy, in particular proposals for the deregulation and privatization of state enterprises, resulted in an escalation of the unrest, which culminated, in August, in a 100,000-strong demonstration in the capital. Following the protest, the Government reached an accord with the teachers, under which it agreed to establish a commission, to include representatives of the teachers' unions, to debate the proposed reform of the pension system and to review certain other of the Government's economic policies.

In January 1996, in an incident that had serious repercussions for the country's important tourism sector, two European women were abducted from a hotel in San Carlos in northern Costa Rica, close to the border with Nicaragua. An insurgent group, the Viviana Gallardo Commando, claimed responsibility for the abduction and reportedly demanded a ransom of US $1m. The women were released unharmed in March. In November the Minister of Security resigned, following an investigation by the Comptroller General's Office into allegations that he had been involved in corrupt practices.

Presidential and legislative elections were held in February 1998. Miguel Angel Rodríguez Echeverría, again the candidate of the PUSC, received 46.9% of the votes cast in the presidential contest, thus securing a narrow victory over the PLN candidate, José Miguel Corrales Bolaños, who obtained 44.4% of the votes. The PUSC failed to obtain an outright majority in the legislature, securing only 27 of the 57 seats, while the PLN won 23, the FD obtained three, the Partido Movimiento Libertario (PML) won two, and the Partido Integración Nacional (PIN) and the Partido Acción Laborista Agrícola (PALA) each secured one seat. In April the Minister of Labour and Social Security in the outgoing administration resigned in order to answer embezzlement charges. On 8 May Rodríguez was sworn in as President, and the new Cabinet was inaugurated.

The new President's attempts to alleviate the budget deficit through economic reform met with considerable opposition in 2000. In May of that year the Government was forced to withdraw proposed legislation on the privatization of the telecommunications and energy sectors, after the largest popular protests in the country in 30 years. In the same month a commission, comprising government, private-sector and trade-union representatives, was established to draft new proposals.

In December 1998 a 10-year co-operation agreement was signed with the USA, allowing for US troops to enter Costa Rican territory in order to conduct joint operations with Costa Rican security forces against drugs-traffickers. An amended version of the agreement was finally approved by the Costa Rican legislature in August 1999, despite the efforts of opponents to the measure, who claimed that it would lead to the establishment of a US military base in Costa Rica. In the following month the legislature approved the creation of a coastguard to participate in joint patrols with US forces.

In February 1989 the Presidents of Costa Rica, El Salvador, Guatemala, Honduras and Nicaragua met and agreed to draft a plan to remove the Contra forces from base camps in Honduras, in exchange for the introduction of political reforms and the holding of free elections in Nicaragua. The plan was ratified at a second summit meeting, held in August in Honduras, with the signing of the Tela Agreement. Peace proposals for El Salvador and Guatemala were also elaborated, as was an agreement on co-operation in the campaign against the trafficking and use of illicit drugs. In November, however, the conflicts in Nicaragua and El Salvador intensified. In December the deadline for the disbanding of Contra forces, agreed at Tela, passed unfulfilled, and the Presidents of the five Central American countries, meeting in Costa Rica, agreed on measures to revive the regional peace process. In February 1990, after being defeated in elections, Nicaragua's Sandinista Government decreed an immediate cease-fire. The Contras accepted this, and a cease-fire agreement was concluded in April.

In early 1995 relations with Nicaragua became strained, following a series of incidents concerning immigration and the policing of the countries' joint border. In February the Nicaraguan Government issued a formal protest at the allegedly violent manner in which a group of illegal Nicaraguan immigrants had been expelled from Costa Rica. A tightening of immigration policy in Costa Rica had led to the automatic expulsion of illegal immigrants who had previously been tolerated (providing, as they did, a source of cheap labour for agriculture and the construction industry). The change in government policy had been prompted by the excessive burden placed on Costa Rica's social services by a recent rapid increase in immigrant arrivals, and by a downturn in the country's economy. In 1998 the Costa Rican Government estimated the number of Nicaraguan immigrants living in the country at 400,000–500,000, of whom some 250,000 were residing illegally. In January of that year bilateral discussions were held regarding the continuing expulsion of Nicaraguan immigrants. Costa Rica demanded, as a condition for agreement on the issue, that Nicaragua grant concessions allowing Costa Rican artisan fishermen to operate in Nicaraguan territorial waters. Nicaragua, however, rejected the demand, and no agreement was reached. In July further antagonism developed between the two countries when Nicaragua prohibited Costa Rican civil guards from carrying arms while navigating the San Juan river, which forms the border between the two countries. According to a long-standing treaty, the river, which is Nicaraguan territory, was only to be used by Costa Rica for commercial purposes. Following protests by Costa Rica, the two sides reached an agreement allowing Costa Rican civil guards to carry arms on the river while under escort by the Nicaraguan authorities. However, in August Nicaragua annulled the accord and dismissed the possibility of international mediation on the issue, asserting that Nicaraguan sovereignty over the river was not open to dispute. In June 2000, however, both Governments agreed a procedure that would allow armed Costa Rican police officers to patrol the river. On 1 February 1999 Costa Rica declared a six-month amnesty for all illegal Nicaraguan immigrants who had entered Costa Rica before 9 November 1998. All those who registered were to be issued with one-year renewable residence permits. However, by the expiry of the amnesty, on 31 July, only 160,000 immigrants had registered. While the Costa Rican authorities assured Nicaragua that the amnesty period would not be followed by mass deportations, they insisted that the law would be firmly applied.

The first inter-American summit meeting for 22 years, which was attended by 17 heads of state, was held in San José in October 1989, to celebrate a centenary of democracy in Costa Rica. In April 1990 an extradition treaty between Costa Rica and the USA was approved by the Legislative Assembly. The treaty, which does not apply to Costa Rican citizens, was aimed at combating crime, particularly international drugs-trafficking.

Government

Under the Constitution of 1949, executive power is vested in the President, assisted by two Vice-Presidents (or, in exceptional circumstances, one Vice-President) and an appointed Cabinet. The President is elected for a four-year term by compulsory adult suffrage, and a successful candidate must receive at least 40% of the votes. The legislative organ is the unicameral Asamblea Legislativa (Legislative Assembly), with 57 members who are similarly elected for four years.

Defence

There have been no Costa Rican armed forces since 1948. In August 2000 Rural and Civil Guards totalled 2,000 and 4,400 men, respectively. In addition, there were 2,000 Border Security Police. In 1985 an anti-terrorist battalion was formed, composed of 750 Civil Guards; in 1994 it was superseded by the Immediate Action Unit. In September 1999 legislation was approved providing for the establishment of a coastguard to participate in joint anti-drugs patrols with units of the US coastguard, under the terms of a co-operation agreement with the USA, which had received legislative approval in the previous month. Expenditure on the security forces was budgeted at 25,600m. colones in 2000.

Economic Affairs

In 1998, according to estimates by the World Bank, Costa Rica's gross national product (GNP), measured at average 1996–98 prices, was US $9,771m., equivalent to $2,770 per head (or $5,812 per head on an international purchasing-power parity basis). During 1990–98, it was estimated, GNP per head increased, in real terms, at an average annual rate of 2.0%. Over the same period, the population increased by an average of 2.3% per year. Costa Rica's gross domestic product (GDP) increased,

in real terms, by an average of 4.1% per year in 1990–99. Real GDP increased by 8.0% in 1998 and by 8.3% in 1999. GDP increased by only 1.4% in 2000, but was expected to increase by 3.2% in 2001.

Agriculture (including hunting, forestry and fishing) contributed an estimated 10.2% of GDP in 1999 and employed 20.4% of the economically active population in 2000. The principal cash crops are bananas (which accounted for an estimated 9.0% of general export earnings in 2000), coffee (4.7% of general export earnings), flowers and tropical fruit. Seafood exports were also significant. Sugar cane, rice, maize and beans are also cultivated. The GDP of the agricultural sector increased at an average annual rate of 2.5% during 1990–99. It increased by 6.0% in 1998 and by an estimated 3.6% in 1999.

Industry (including mining, manufacturing, construction and power) employed 22.3% of the economically active population in 2000, and provided an estimated 34.1% of GDP in 1999. Industrial GDP increased at an average annual rate of 3.7% during 1990–99. It increased by 11.3% in 1998 and by an estimated 21.1% in 1999. Mining employed only 0.2% of the economically active population in 2000. The manufacturing sector employed 14.4% of the employed work-force in 2000 and contributed an estimated 28.1% of GDP in 1999. In terms of the value of output, the principal branches of manufacturing in 1996, according to provisional figures, were food products (39.1%), chemical products (14.0%), beverages (8.6%) and electrical machinery (6.0%). Production of computer components by the US manufacturer Intel began in 1998.

Energy is derived principally from petroleum and hydroelectric power. The Arenal hydroelectricity project was inaugurated in 1979, and, at its full generating capacity of 1,974 MW, was expected to fulfil Costa Rica's entire electricity requirements. In 1992 hydroelectric power accounted for 75.6% of total electrical energy consumption. In 1993, as part of an electricity development programme, work began on a US $300m. hydroelectric power project on the Río Reventazón. Imports of fuels and lubricants accounted for an estimated 7.4% of the total value of imports in 2000.

The services sector employed 56.7% of the economically active population in 2000, and provided an estimated 55.7% of GDP in 1999. The GDP of this sector increased at an average annual rate of 4.9% during 1990–99 It increased by 6.7% in 1998 and by an estimated 3.1% in 1999. Tourism is the country's most important source of foreign-exchange earnings, accounting for an estimated 24.7% of total export revenue in 1997. The tourism sector experienced a downturn in growth in 1996 as a result of concerns about security following the abduction of two Europeans early in that year, before recovering in 1997. In 1998 receipts from tourism totalled US $830m.

In 1999 Costa Rica recorded a visible trade surplus of US $659.6m., but there was a deficit of $649.5m. on the current account of the balance of payments. In 2000 the principal source of imports (53.2%) was the USA; other major suppliers were Mexico, Venezuela and Japan. The USA was also the principal market for exports (51.8%) in that year; other significant purchasers were the Netherlands, the United Kingdom and Guatemala. The principal exports in 2000 were electrical components for microprocessors, textiles and bananas. The principal imports in 2000 were raw materials for industry, capital goods for industry and consumer non-durables.

In 1999 there was an estimated budgetary deficit of 99,851m. colones (equivalent to some 2.2% of GDP). Costa Rica's estimated total external debt at the end of 1999 was US $4,182m. The cost of debt-servicing in that year was $528m. The annual rate of inflation averaged 16.4% in 1990–99. Consumer prices increased by an annual average of 11.7% in 1998, falling to an estimated 10.1% in 1999. Some 5.2% of the labour force (including those seeking work for the first time) were unemployed in 2000.

Costa Rica is a member of the Central American Common Market (CACM, see p. 147) and the Inter-American Development Bank (IDB, see p. 212). In May 2000 legislation was passed enhancing the Caribbean Basin Initiative, first introduced in 1983, granting North American Free Trade Agreement (NAFTA) parity to products from 24 states, including Costa Rica.

During the 1990s successive Governments adopted austerity measures aimed at addressing the country's high public-sector deficit. Measures promoting increased foreign investment and enabling private-sector participation in activities formerly confined to the state sector, including the deregulation of the banking system, were implemented in 1996. In early 1998 the IMF urged the incoming Rodríguez administration to expedite the divestment of public assets, initiated by the previous Government, and to use the proceeds to reduce the country's public domestic debt, which was equivalent to 27.6% of GDP in 1997. However, the Government's efforts to end the state's monopoly in the telecommunications, energy and insurance sectors proved unsuccessful in 1999, owing to legislative opposition. A similar attempt in 2000 resulted in public protests and in May a commission was established to draft new privatization proposals. In its draft budget for 1999 the Government proposed to allocate 38% of total expenditure to servicing the domestic debt. In March 1998 the US microprocessor manufacturer Intel began production at the first of four plants under construction in Costa Rica. Exports from the Intel plants, situated in a free-trade zone close to the capital, contributed some 3%–4% of GDP in 1999, superseding the traditional exports of bananas and coffee. However, despite expectations that it would remain the country's principal source of exports, in 2000 there was a significant decrease in microchip exports, owing to plant restructuring. In January 1999 Rodríguez announced a three-year economic programme, which aimed to reduce the rate of inflation to 7% by 2001. In 1999, for the first time in four decades, Costa Rica achieved a trade surplus, led by manufacturing exports. In the same year total exports from free-trade zones increased to \$3,609m. (54% of all exports).

In the late 1990s the agricultural sector was affected by fluctuations in the prices of coffee and bananas. In early 2000 the Instituto del Café de Costa Rica (Costa Rica Coffee Institute) announced a slightly improved 1999/2000 harvest of 152,000 metric tons. However, in late 2000 the situation in the banana industry became critical, with the three principal exporters, Chiquita Brands, Banana Development Corporation and Standard Fruits Company, cancelling contracts. This set-back was exacerbated by the ongoing dispute with the EU over its banana-import regime. At the beginning of the 21st century bananas provided the country's third largest income, employing some 40,000 people directly and a further 100,000 indirectly.

Social Welfare

Costa Rica possesses an advanced social welfare system, which provides a comprehensive programme of care and assistance for all wage-earners and their dependants.

All social services are co-ordinated by the National Development Plan, administered by the Ministry of Planning, and are organized by state institutions. The Social Security Fund (CCSS) provides health services and general social insurance, the National Insurance Institute provides professional insurance, and the Ministry of Public Health operates a preventive health programme through a network of health units throughout the country. Benefits include disability and retirement pensions, workers' compensation and family assistance. During 1995–96, in order to ensure the future viability of its pension scheme, the CCSS raised the minimum age for retirement and restricted eligibility requirements for disability benefits.

In 1998 there were 3,178 physicians and in 1997 there were 109.1 nursing personnel per 100,000 inhabitants working in the country. In 1998 there were 5,922 hospital beds. Of total expenditure by the central Government in 1996, about 126,690m. colones (22.1%) was for health services, and a further 117,310m. colones (20.5%) for social security and welfare.

Education

Education at all levels is available free of charge, and is officially compulsory for children between six and 15 years of age. Primary education begins at six years of age and lasts for six years. Secondary education consists of a three-year basic course, followed by a more highly specialized course of two years. In 1997 total enrolment at primary and secondary schools was equivalent to 65.5% of the school-age population (males 66%; females 65%). In that year primary enrolment included an estimated 91.8% of children in the relevant age-group (males 91.1%; females 92.5%), while the comparable ratio for secondary enrolment was 55.8% (males 54.7%; females 56.9%). There are six universities, one of which is an open university. Costa Rica has the highest adult literacy rate in Central America. In 1998, according to estimates by the World Bank, the average rate of adult illiteracy was only 4.7% (males 4.7%; females 4.6%). Government expenditure on education in 1996 was 99,631m. colones (22.8% of total spending).

Public Holidays

2001: 1 January (New Year's Day), 19 March (Feast of St Joseph, San José only), 11 April (Anniversary of the Battle of Rivas), 12 April (Maundy Thursday), 13 April (Good Friday), 1 May (Labour Day), 14 June (Corpus Christi), 29 June (St Peter and St Paul), 25 July (Anniversary of the Annexation of Guanacaste Province), 2 August (Our Lady of the Angels), 15 August (Assumption), 15 September (Independence Day), 12 October (Columbus Day), 1 December (Abolition of the Armed Forces Day), 8 December (Immaculate Conception), 25 December (Christmas Day), 28–31 December (San José only).

2002: 1 January (New Year's Day), 19 March (Feast of St Joseph, San José only), 28 March (Maundy Thursday), 29 March (Good Friday), 11 April (Anniversary of the Battle of Rivas), 1 May (Labour Day), 30 May (Corpus Christi), 29 June (St Peter and St Paul), 25 July (Anniversary of the Annexation of Guanacaste Province), 2 August (Our Lady of the Angels), 15 August (Assumption), 15 September (Independence Day), 12 October (Columbus Day), 1 December (Abolition of the Armed Forces Day), 8 December (Immaculate Conception), 25 December (Christmas Day), 28–31 December (San José only).

Weights and Measures

The metric system is in force.

Statistical Survey

Sources (unless otherwise stated): Dirección General de Estadística y Censos, Ministry of the Economy, Industry and Commerce, Apdo 10.163, 1000 San José; tel. 221-0983; fax 223-0813; Banco Central de Costa Rica, Avdas Central y Primera, Calles 2 y 4, Apdo 10.058, 1000 San José; tel. 233-4233; fax 223-4658.

Area and Population

AREA, POPULATION AND DENSITY

Area (sq km)	
Land	51,060
Inland water	40
Total	51,100*
Population (census results)†	
14 May 1973	1,871,780
11 June 1984	
Males	1,208,216
Females	1,208,593
Total	2,416,809
Population (official estimates at mid-year)	
1998	3,525,701
1999	3,589,163
2000	3,651,803
Density (per sq km) at mid-2000	71.5

* 19,730 sq miles.

† Excluding adjustment for underenumeration.

Census of 28 June 2000 (provisional results): Total population 3,824,593 (males 1,913,910; females 1,910,683).

PROVINCES (mid-2000)

	Area (sq km)	Population (estimates)	Density (per sq km)	Capital (with population)
Alajuela	9,757.5	655,944	67.2	Alajuela (189,981)
Cartago	3,124.7	408,571	130.8	Cartago (129,910)
Guanacaste	10,140.7	285,388	28.1	Liberia (44,979)
Heredia	2,657.0	293,939	110.6	Heredia (81,947)
Limón	9,188.5	286,221	31.1	Limón (84,986)
Puntarenas	11,265.7	406,448	36.1	Puntarenas (110,190)
San José	4,965.9	1,315,292	264.9	San José (345,599)
Total	**51,100.0**	**3,651,803**	**71.5**	—

BIRTHS, MARRIAGES AND DEATHS

	Registered live births		Registered marriages		Registered deaths	
	Number	Rate (per 1,000)	Number	Rate (per 1,000)	Number	Rate (per 1,000)
1992	80,164	25.6	20,888	6.7	12,253	3.9
1993	79,714	24.6	21,715	6.7	12,543	3.8
1994	80,391	24.6	21,520	6.5	13,313	4.0
1995	80,306	24.1	24,274	7.3	14,061	4.2
1996	79,203	23.3	23,574	6.9	13,993	4.1
1997	78,018	22.5	n.a.	n.a.	14,260	4.1
1998	76,982	21.8	24,831	7.0	14,708	4.2
1999	78,526	21.9	25,613	7.1	15,052	4.2

Expectation of life (estimates, years at birth, 1998): 76.2 (males 74.4; females 79.1) (Source: UN Development Programme, *Human Development Report*).

ECONOMICALLY ACTIVE POPULATION*

(persons aged 12 years and over, household survey, '000 persons, July 1999)

	Males	Females	Total
Agriculture, hunting and forestry	230.47	19.72	250.19
Fishing	6.16	0.11	6.27
Mining and quarrying	1.91	0.22	2.13
Manufacturing	133.36	70.64	204.00
Electricity, gas and water supply	11.84	1.41	13.25
Construction	81.59	1.04	82.62
Wholesale and retail trade	126.11	77.75	203.86
Hotels and restaurants	30.35	34.37	64.72
Transport, storage and communications	66.92	7.69	74.61
Financial intermediation	12.87	7.50	20.37
Real estate, renting and business activities	3.81	1.64	5.45
Education	21.16	44.23	65.39
Health and social work	24.70	31.11	55.80
Other community, social and personal service activities	115.13	43.74	158.86
Private households with employed persons	6.94	76.55	83.50
Extra-territorial organizations and bodies	1.40	0.82	2.21
Not classifiable by economic activity	4.92	2.01	6.93
Total employed	**879.63**	**420.52**	**1,300.15**
Unemployed	45.60	37,71	83.31
Total labour force	**925.22**	**458.23**	**1,383.45**

* Figures for activities are rounded to the nearest 10 persons.

Source: ILO, *Yearbook of Labour Statistics*.

2000 ('000 persons): Agriculture, etc. 269.21; Mining and quarrying 2.61; Manufacturing 190.26; Electricity, gas and water supply 10.88; Construction 89.72; Wholesale and retail trade 266.83; Transport, storage and communications 78.83; Finance 64.26; Services 337.09; Activities not adequately defined 8.95; Total employed 1,318.63; Unemployed 71.94; Total labour force 1,390.56 (males 943.70; females 446.86).

Agriculture

PRINCIPAL CROPS ('000 metric tons)

	1997	1998	1999
Rice (paddy)	216.6	287.1	262.2
Maize	33.1	29.1	30.0*
Beans (dry)	13.3	17.6	16.9
Palm kernels†	26.0	25.0	24.0
Palm oil	101.0	108.6	110.0†
Sugar cane*	3,350.0	3,850.0	3,950.0
Bananas	2,300.0*	2,098.3	2,101.4
Coffee (green)	142.6†	138.0	147.5†
Cocoa beans†	4.0	4.1	4.0

* FAO estimate(s). † Unofficial figure(s).

Source: FAO.

LIVESTOCK ('000 head, year ending September)

	1997	1998	1999
Horses*	114.5	114.5	114.5
Mules*	5.0	5.0	5.0
Asses*	7.6	7.6	7.6
Cattle†	1,529.0	1,527.0	1,617.0
Pigs*	300.0	280.0	290.0
Sheep*	2.5	2.5	2.5
Goats*	1.6	1.7	1.7
Chickens*	16,500.0	17,000.0	17,000.0

* FAO estimates.   † Unofficial figures.

Source: FAO.

LIVESTOCK PRODUCTS ('000 metric tons)

	1997	1998	1999
Beef and veal*	86.0	78.0	86.0
Pig meat†	20.3	18.8	18.8
Poultry meat	70.0*	80.0†	80.0†
Cows' milk	595.0*	600.0†	600.0†
Cheese	5.3	5.6	5.6†
Butter and ghee . . .	3.5	3.5	3.5†
Hen eggs†	27.2	27.2	27.2
Cattle hides (fresh)† .	14.7	10.7	11.7

* Unofficial figure.   † FAO estimate(s).

Source: FAO.

Forestry

ROUNDWOOD REMOVALS
('000 cubic metres, excluding bark)

	1996	1997	1998
Sawlogs, veneer logs and logs for sleepers	1,400	1,400	1,400
Pulpwood	8	8	8
Other industrial wood . .	253	260	266
Fuel wood	3,458	3,548	3,637
Total	**5,119**	**5,216**	**5,311**

Source: FAO, *Yearbook of Forest Products.*

SAWNWOOD PRODUCTION (FAO estimates, '000 cubic metres)

	1996	1997	1998
Coniferous (softwood). . .	12	12	12
Broadleaved (hardwood) . .	768	768	768
Total	**780**	**780**	**780**

Source: FAO, *Yearbook of Forest Products.*

Fishing

('000 metric tons, live weight)

	1996	1997	1998
Capture	24.2	24.2	20.6
Freshwater fishes . .	1.9	0.8	0.8
Clupeoids	0.9	1.6	1.0
Tuna-like fishes . . .	3.9	1.0	1.2
Sharks, rays, skates, etc. .	2.5	2.8	3.3
Other marine fishes . .	10.1	14.1	11.1
Penaeus shrimps . .	2.3	2.0	1.4
Natantian decapods . .	1.4	1.0	0.7
Aquaculture	7.0	7.0	8.7
Tilapias	4.1	4.1	5.4
Whiteleg shrimp . . .	2.4	2.4	2.3
Total catch	**31.2**	**31.2**	**29.3**

Source: FAO, *Yearbook of Fishery Statistics.*

Industry

SELECTED PRODUCTS
('000 metric tons, unless otherwise indicated)

	1995	1996	1997
Cigarettes (million units) . . .	16	16	n.a.
Non-cellulosic continuous fibres	7.7	7.8	7.9
Jet fuels	37	30	35
Motor spirit (gasoline) . .	100	77	81
Naphthas	5	12	7
Kerosene	3	3	6
Distillate fuel oils . .	203	175	176
Residual fuel oils . . .	369	310	325
Bitumen.	25	23	26
Liquefied petroleum gas (refined)	2	2	2
Cement	990	n.a.	n.a.
Electric energy (million kWh) . .	4,840	4,894	5,589

Source: UN, *Industrial Commodity Statistics Yearbook.*

1999: Electric energy 6,198 million kWh.

Finance

CURRENCY AND EXCHANGE RATES

Monetary Units
  100 céntimos =1 Costa Rican colón.

Sterling, Dollar and Euro Equivalents (29 December 2000)
  £1 sterling = 474.5 colones;
  US $1 = 318.0 colones;
  €1 = 295.9 colones;
  1,000 Costa Rican colones = £2.107 = $3.144 = €3.379.

Average Exchange Rate (colones per US $)
  1998   257.23
  1999   285.68
  2000   308.19

GENERAL BUDGET (million colones)

Revenue	1997	1998	1999
Taxation	373,776	455,522	538,867
Income tax	66,268	88,588	131,932
Social security contributions .	14,454	15,500	17,694
Taxes on property . . .	2,705	2,619	2,422
Taxes on goods and services .	237,596	291,473	339,891
Taxes on international trade .	52,753	57,341	46,928
Other current revenue . .	2,356	3,152	1,866
Current transfers . . .	1,368	1,031	2,237
Capital transfers. . . .	—	—	20,257
Total	**377,500**	**459,704**	**563,227**

Expenditure	1997	1998	1999
Current expenditure . . .	416,329	498,236	603,110
Wages and salaries. . .	128,256	155,541	191,193
Social security contributions .	14,427	21,031	21,906
Other purchases of goods and services	16,944	21,121	21,883
Interest payments . . .	113,579	116,026	164,226
Internal	103,024	103,577	142,840
External	10,555	12,449	21,386
Current transfers . . .	143,124	184,517	203,901
Capital expenditure . . .	49,153	50,701	59,968
Investment	20,339	20,491	24,457
Capital transfers . . .	28,814	30,210	35,511
Total	**465,482**	**548,936**	**663,078**

INTERNATIONAL RESERVES (US $ million at 31 December)

	1998	1999	2000
Gold*	0.02	0.02	0.02
IMF special drawing rights . .	0.07	0.81	0.43
Reserve position in IMF . .	12.29	27.45	26.06
Foreign exchange . . .	1,051.04	1,432.14	926.07
Total	1,063.41	1,460.42	952.58

* National valuation.

Source: IMF, *International Financial Statistics*.

MONEY SUPPLY ('000 million colones at 31 December)

	1998	1999	2000
Currency outside banks . . .	124.2	154.9	143.0
Demand deposits at commercial banks . .	279.6	330.7	456.0
Total money (incl. others) . .	415.4	516.6	617.7

Source: IMF, *International Financial Statistics*.

COST OF LIVING
(Consumer Price Index; base: January 1995 = 100)

	1998	1999	2000
Food, beverages and tobacco . .	165.0	181.0	198.7
Clothing and footwear . .	135.8	145.2	152.4
Housing . .	138.2	153.8	173.9
All items (incl. others) . .	159.6	175.7	194.9

NATIONAL ACCOUNTS (million colones at current prices)
Expenditure on the Gross Domestic Product

	1998	1999*	2000*
Government final consumption expenditure	469,316	565,217	656,330
Private final consumption expenditure	2,540,540	2,890,647	3,247,697
Increase in stocks . . .	−22,033	−8,762	−25,371
Gross fixed capital formation .	731,353	788,938	835,571
Total domestic expenditure	3,719,176	4,236,040	4,714,228
Exports of goods and services	1,714,312	2,296,597	2,353,963
Less Imports of goods and services	1,809,169	2,065,454	2,276,170
GDP in purchasers' values .	3,624,318	4,467,184	4,792,021
GDP at constant 1991 prices .	1,285,243	1,391,827	1,411,882

* Figures are provisional.

Gross Domestic Product by Economic Activity

	1997	1998	1999*
Agriculture, hunting, forestry and fishing . . .	351,464	424,803	431,192
Mining and quarrying . .	3,758	4,796	6,172
Manufacturing . .	608,919	764,384	1,186,814
Electricity, gas and water. .	82,167	90,497	94,733
Construction. .	102,443	136,781	152,459
Trade, restaurants and hotels. .	542,225	667,778	765,956
Transport, storage and communications . . .	242,761	285,962	315,207
Finance and insurance . .	127,475	145,662	178,810
Real estate . . .	136,352	156,534	178,336
Other business services . .	72,539	85,828	105,229
Public administration . .	104,827	121,874	146,113
Other community, social and personal services . .	425,836	530,774	660,781
Sub-total	2,800,766	3,415,673	4,221,801
Less Imputed bank service charge	83,176	99,427	128,908
GDP at basic prices . .	2,717,590	3,316,246	4,092,893
Taxes, less subsidies, on products	264,850	308,073	374,291
GDP in purchasers' values .	2,982,440	3,624,318	4,467,184

* Figures are provisional.

BALANCE OF PAYMENTS (US $ million)

	1997	1998	1999
Exports of goods f.o.b. . . .	4,220.6	5,538.3	6,667.7
Imports of goods f.o.b. . . .	−4,718.2	−5,937.4	−6,008.1
Trade balance	−497.6	−399.0	659.6
Exports of services . . .	1,128.6	1,343.4	1,525.6
Imports of services . . .	−988.4	−1,109.8	−1,173.7
Balance on goods and services	−357.4	−165.5	1,011.6
Other income received . .	185.4	182.7	198.2
Other income paid . . .	−434.4	−651.2	−1,961.4
Balance on goods, services and income . .	−606.4	−634.0	−751.6
Current transfers received .	191.2	190.5	190.7
Current transfers paid . .	−65.7	−77.3	−88.6
Current balance . . .	−480.9	−520.8	−649.5
Direct investment abroad. .	−4.4	−4.8	−5.0
Direct investment from abroad	408.2	613.1	669.3
Portfolio investment assets .	−22.5	−33.9	−28.1
Portfolio investment liabilities	−190.8	−296.0	−239.7
Other investment assets . .	−267.4	−95.6	106.8
Other investment liabilities .	206.7	16.2	73.3
Net errors and omissions . .	157.8	−182.6	224.2
Overall balance . . .	−193.3	−504.3	151.3

Source: IMF, *International Financial Statistics*.

External Trade

PRINCIPAL COMMODITIES (US $ million)

Imports c.i.f.	1998	1999	2000
Raw materials for industry and mining	3,137.8	3,411.5	3,335.4
Raw materials for agriculture. .	156.9	151.7	141.7
Consumer non-durables . .	743.3	770.7	807.7
Consumer durables . . .	540.0	371.9	371.8
Capital goods for industry and mining	963.9	900.7	851.2
Capital goods for transport .	205.4	195.5	178.7
Building materials . . .	172.6	174.1	173.4
Fuels and lubricants . . .	260.8	320.2	472.1
Total (incl. others) . . .	6,238.4	6,350.7	6,379.8

Exports f.o.b.	1998	1999	2000
Livestock and fishing products .	350.8	168.5	159.7
Agricultural products (unprocessed) . . .	1,588.9	1,422.2	1,270.9
Bananas	634.5	632.2	531.3
Coffee.	409.4	289.5	277.8
Pineapples . . .	112.4	133.1	121.1
Industrial products . .	3,569.1	5,129.4	4,466.8
Textiles . . .	812.1	804.4	772.6
Electrical components for microprocessors . .	959.7	2,526.0	1,653.3
Products of food industry . .	378.4	387.3	382.3
Other products of Free Zone .	344.3	668.3	886.3
Infusion equipment . .	64.8	79.6	169.3
Total	5,508.8	6,720.1	5,897.4

Source: Promotora del Comercio Exterior de Costa Rica.

PRINCIPAL TRADING PARTNERS (US $ million)

Imports c.i.f.	1998	1999	2000
Brazil	88.6	99.9	113.7
Canada	84.8	74.1	72.7
China, People's Republic	58.1	60.5	78.4
Colombia	98.4	97.5	120.9
El Salvador	115.3	106.8	91.0
France	72.0	74.6	93.4
Germany	131.0	124.8	124.6
Guatemala	144.8	142.2	139.9
Italy	88.1	79.3	73.4
Japan	385.1	300.7	214.7
Korea, Republic	93.6	108.2	117.5
Mexico	328.2	345.6	392.7
Netherlands	53.4	45.0	96.0
Panama	92.7	86.0	91.1
Spain	100.2	89.1	143.9
Taiwan	71.0	68.7	65.4
USA	3,464.2	3,581.4	3,388.0
Venezuela	186.3	248.8	337.3
Total (incl. others)	6,238.7	6,350.7	6,373.3

Exports f.o.b.	1998	1999	2000
Belgium-Luxembourg	93.8	66.5	115.2
Canada	87.3	40.2	35.1
El Salvador	111.8	115.4	135.2
France	85.0	40.6	35.5
Germany	216.3	183.7	137.5
Guatemala	171.9	179.5	193.4
Honduras	90.5	102.4	115.8
Hong Kong	55.8	35.7	17.4
Italy	137.6	105.2	99.9
Japan	64.2	128.2	50.9
Malaysia	114.9	63.4	52.5
Mexico	82.6	144.2	98.2
Netherlands	204.2	452.3	394.9
Nicaragua	141.6	177.4	179.1
Panama	119.7	126.3	129.0
Puerto Rico	136.8	175.4	163.2
Singapore	40.1	75.0	43.7
Spain	98.7	68.6	24.2
United Kingdom	219.3	387.8	300.0
USA	2,551.3	3,452.1	3,056.7
Total (incl. others)	5,478.5	6,719.0	5,897.3

Source: Ministry of Foreign Commerce.

Transport

RAILWAYS

	1992	1993	1994
Passenger journeys	11,580	367,803	335,276
Freight ton-km (million)	845.2	833.2	729.3

Source: Ministry of Public Works and Transport.

ROAD TRAFFIC (motor vehicles in use at 31 December)

	1996	1997	1998
Private cars	277,888	294,083	316,844
Buses and coaches	9,476	10,317	11,102
Goods vehicles	141,941	153,111	164,796
Motorcycles and mopeds	51,433	n.a.	79,446

Source: mainly IRF, *World Road Statistics*.

SHIPPING

Merchant Fleet (registered at 31 December)

	1996	1997	1998
Number of vessels	14	14	14
Total displacement ('000 grt)	5.9	5.9	5.6

Source: Lloyd's Register of Shipping, *World Fleet Statistics*.

International Sea-borne Freight Traffic ('000 metric tons)

	1996	1997	1998
Goods loaded	3,017	3,421	3,721
Goods unloaded	3,972	4,522	5,188

Source: Ministry of Public Works and Transport.

CIVIL AVIATION (traffic on scheduled services)

	1996	1997	1998
Passengers carried ('000)	918	992	1,170
Air freight ton-km (million)	45	55	96

Sources: International Civil Aviation Organization; UN, *Statistical Yearbook*; World Bank, *World Development Indicators*.

Tourism

FOREIGN TOURIST ARRIVALS BY COUNTRY OF ORIGIN

	1997	1998	1999
Canada	37,032	42,097	43,662
Colombia	19,357	22,013	26,449
El Salvador	24,166	24,741	28,752
Germany	27,406	23,366	24,034
Guatemala	26,360	30,982	34,064
Honduras	18,319	19,380	26,762
Italy	18,878	17,079	16,827
Mexico	25,347	30,109	31,972
Nicaragua	129,333	170,059	166,511
Panama	48,861	48,648	53,249
Spain	20,461	24,453	27,833
USA	285,361	347,442	392,217
Total (incl. others)	811,490	942,853	1,027,462

Tourism receipts (US $ million): 689 in 1996; 731 in 1997; 830 in 1998.

Communications Media

	1995	1996	1997
Radio receivers ('000 in use) . .	900	950	980
Television receivers ('000 in use) .	490	510	525
Telephones ('000 main lines in use)	479	526	584
Telefax stations (number in use) .	6,600	7,500	8,500
Mobile cellular telephones			
(subscribers)	18,704	46,531	64,387
Daily newspapers:			
Number	5*	6	6
Circulation	300*	320	n.a.

Non-daily newspapers: 12 in 1991 (average circulation 106,000 copies).
Book production: 1,034 titles (excluding pamphlets) in 1995.

* Estimate.

Sources: UNESCO, *Statistical Yearbook*, and UN, *Statistical Yearbook*.

Education

(1999)

	Institu-tions	Tea-chers	Students		
			Males	Females	Total
Pre-primary . . .	1,821	3,604	40,015	37,952	77,967
Primary. . . .	3,768	20,185	275,976	259,081	535,057
Secondary . . .	468	11,891	115,443	119,982	235,425
General . . .	386	8,908	92,202	96,895	189,097
Vocational. . .	82	2,983	23,241	23,087	46,328
Tertiary. . . .	52	n.a.	n.a.	n.a.	59,947

Directory

The Constitution

The present Constitution of Costa Rica was promulgated in November 1949. Its main provisions are summarized below:

GOVERNMENT

The government is unitary: provincial and local bodies derive their authority from the national Government. The country is divided into seven Provinces, each administered by a Governor who is appointed by the President. The Provinces are divided into Cantons, and each Canton into Districts. There is an elected Municipal Council in the chief city of each Canton, the number of its members being related to the population of the Canton. The Municipal Council supervises the affairs of the Canton. Municipal government is closely regulated by national law, particularly in matters of finance.

LEGISLATURE

The government consists of three branches: legislative, executive and judicial. Legislative power is vested in a single chamber, the Legislative Assembly, which meets in regular session twice a year—from 1 May to 31 July, and from 1 September to 30 November. Special sessions may be convoked by the President to consider specified business. The Assembly is composed of 57 deputies elected for four years. The chief powers of the Assembly are to enact laws, levy taxes, authorize declarations of war and, by a two-thirds' majority, suspend, in cases of civil disorder, certain civil liberties guaranteed in the Constitution.

Bills may be initiated by the Assembly or by the Executive and must have three readings, in at least two different legislative periods, before they become law. The Assembly may override the presidential vote by a two-thirds' majority.

EXECUTIVE

The executive branch is headed by the President, who is assisted by the Cabinet. If the President should resign or be incapacitated, the executive power is entrusted to the First Vice-President; next in line to succeed to executive power are the Second Vice-President and the President of the Legislative Assembly.

The President sees that the laws and the provisions of the Constitution are carried out, and maintains order; has power to appoint and remove cabinet ministers and diplomatic representatives, and to negotiate treaties with foreign nations (which are, however, subject to ratification by the Legislative Assembly). The President is assisted in these duties by a Cabinet, each member of which is head of an executive department.

ELECTORATE

Suffrage is universal, compulsory and secret for persons over the age of 18 years.

DEFENCE

A novel feature of the Costa Rican Constitution is the clause outlawing a national army. Only by a continental convention or for the purpose of national defence may a military force be organized.

The Government

HEAD OF STATE

President: MIGUEL ANGEL RODRÍGUEZ ECHEVERRÍA (took office 8 May 1998).

First Vice-President and Minister of Culture: ASTRID FISCHEL VOLIO.

Second Vice-President and Minister of the Environment and Energy: ELIZABETH ODIO BENITO.

THE CABINET
(April 2001)

Minister of Agriculture and Livestock: ALBERTO DENT-ZELEDON.

Minister of Economy, Industry and Commerce: GILBERTO BARRANTES RODRÍGUEZ.

Minister of Finance: LEONEL BARUCH GOLDBERG.

Minister of Foreign Commerce: TOMÁS DUEÑAS LEIVA.

Minister of Foreign Relations: ROBERTO ROJAS LÓPEZ.

Minister of Housing: DONALD MONROE.

Minister of the Interior: JUAN RAFAEL LIZANO SÁENZ.

Minister of Justice: MÓNICA NÁGEL BERGER.

Minister of Labour and Social Security: (vacant).

Minister of Police and Public Security: ROGELIO RAMOS MARTÍNEZ.

Minister of the Presidency and of Planning: DANILO CHAVERRI SOTO.

Minister of Public Education: GUILLERMO VARGAS SALAZAR.

Minister of Public Health: ROGELIO PARDO EVANS.

Minister of Public Works and Transport: RODOLFO MÉNDEZ MATA.

Minister of Science and Technology: GUY DE TARAMOND.

Minister of Tourism: WALTER NIEHOUS.

Minister of Women's Affairs: GLORIA VALERÍN RODRÍGUEZ.

MINISTRIES

Ministry of Agriculture and Livestock: Apdo 10.094, 1000 San José; tel. 290-5463; fax 231-2062; internet www.mag.go.cr.

Ministry of Culture: Apdo 10.227, 1000 San José; tel. 223-1658; fax 233-7066.

Ministry of the Economy, Industry and Commerce: Edificio Antiguo CODESA, Calles 1 y 3, Avda Central, 1000 San José; tel. 222-1016; fax 222-2305; internet www.meic.go.cr.

Ministry of the Environment and Energy: Avdas 8 y 10, Calle 25, Apdo 10.104, 1000 San José; tel. 257-1417; fax 257-0697; e-mail root@ns.minae.go.cr; internet www.minae.go.cr.

Ministry of Finance: Apdo 5.016, San José; tel. 222-2481; fax 255-4874; internet www.impuestos.go.cr .

Ministry of Foreign Commerce: Montes de Oca, Apdo 96, 2050 San José; tel. 256-7111; fax 255-3281; e-mail info@comex.go.cr; internet www.comex.go.cr.

Ministry of Foreign Relations: Apdo 10.027, 1000 San José; tel. 223-7555; fax 223-9328; internet www.rree.go.cr.

Ministry of Housing: Paseo de los Estudiantes, Apdo 222, 1002 San José; tel. 257-9166; fax 255-1976.

Ministry of the Interior: Apdo 10.006, 1000 San José; tel. 223-8354; fax 222-7726.

Ministry of Justice: Apdo 5.685, 1000 San José; tel. 223-9739; fax 223-3879; e-mail mnagel@gobnet.go.cr.

Ministry of Labour and Social Security: Apdo 10.133, 1000 San José; tel. 221-0238.

Ministry of Planning: Avdas 3 y 5, Calle 4, Apdo 10.127, 1000 San José; tel. 221-9524; fax 253-6243; internet www.mideplan.go.cr.

Ministry of Police and Public Security: Apdo 55, 4874 San José; tel. 226-0093; fax 226-6581.

Ministry of the Presidency: 2010 Zapote, Apdo 520, San José; tel. 224-4092; fax 253-6984.

Ministry of Public Education: Apdo 10.087, 1000 San José; tel. 222-0229; fax 233-0390; internet www.mep.go.cr.

Ministry of Public Health: Apdo 10.123, 1000 San José; tel. 233-0683; fax 255-4997; internet www.netsalud.sa.cr.

Ministry of Public Works and Transport: Apdo 10.176, 1000 San José; tel. 226-7311; fax 227-1434.

Ministry of Science and Technology: San José; internet www.micit.go.cr.

Ministry of Tourism: San José.

Ministry of Women's Affairs: San José.

President and Legislature

PRESIDENT

Presidential Election, 1 February 1998

Candidate	Votes	% of votes cast
MIGUEL ANGEL RODRÍGUEZ ECHEVERRÍA (PUSC)	650,399	46.9
JOSÉ MIGUEL CORRALES BOLAÑOS (PLN)	616,600	44.4
VLADIMIR DE LA CRUZ DE LEMOS (FD)	41,922	3.0
WÁLTER MUÑOZ CÉSPEDES (PIN)	20,226	1.5
SHERMAN THOMAS JACKSON (PRC)	19,103	1.4
ALVARO GONZÁLEZ ESPINOZA (PD)	13,559	1.0
Total (incl. others)*	**1,387,287**	**100.0**

* Excluding 6,080 blank ballots.

ASAMBLEA LEGISLATIVA

General Election, 1 February 1998

Party	Seats
Partido Unidad Social Cristiana (PUSC)	27
Partido de Liberación Nacional (PLN)	23
Fuerza Democrática (FD)	3
Partido Movimiento Libertario (PML)	2
Partido Integración Nacional (PIN)	1
Partido Acción Laborista Agrícola (PALA)	1
Total	**57**

Political Organizations

Acción del Pueblo (AP): San José; Pres. ANGEL RUIZ ZÚÑIGA; Sec. HENRY MORA JIMÉNEZ.

Acción Agrícola Cartaginesa: Cartago; provincial party; Pres. JUAN BRENES CASTILLO; Sec. RODRIGO FALLAS BONILLA.

Acción Democrática Alajuelense: Alajuela; provincial party; Pres. FRANCISCO ALFARO FERNÁNDEZ; Sec. JUAN BAUTISTA CHACÓN SOTO.

Alianza Nacional Cristiana (ANC): Pres. VÍCTOR HUGO GONZÁLEZ MONTERO; Sec. JUAN RODRÍGUEZ VENEGAS.

Fuerza Democrática (FD): Pres. ISAAC FELIPE AZOFEIFA; coalition comprising:

Movimiento Humanista Ecologista.

Partido del Progreso.

Partido Unión Patriótica.

Pueblo Unido (PU): Calle 4, Avdas 7 y 9, San José; tel. 223-0032; Sec. ALBERTO SALOM ECHEVERRÍA; left-wing coalition comprising:

    Partido del Pueblo Costarricense: Apdo 6.613, 1000 San José; tel. 225-9024; fax 253-2628; f. 1931; communist; Sec.-Gen. LENIN CHACÓN VARGAS.

    Partido Socialista Costarricense: San José; socialist; Pres. ALVARO MONTERO MEJÍA; Sec. ALBERTO SALOM ECHEVERRÍA.

    Partido de los Trabajadores: San José; Maoist; Pres. JOHNNY FRANCISCO ARAYA MONGE; Sec. ILSE ACOSTA POLONIO.

Movimiento Nacional (MN): San José; Pres. MARIO ECHANDI JIMÉNEZ; Sec. RODRIGO SANCHO ROBLES.

Partido Acción Laborista Agrícola (PALA): San José; f. 1987.

Partido Alajuelita Nueva: Alajuelita Centro, 100W Escuela Abraham Lincoln, San José; tel. 254-3879; fax 254-6072; f. 1981; Pres. ANNIE BADILLA CALDERÓN; Sec. CARLOS RETANA RETANA.

Partido Auténtico Limonense: Limón; provincial party; Pres. MARVIN WRIGHT LINDO; Sec. GUILLERMO JOSEPH WIGNALL.

Partido Concordia Costarricense: Calles 2 y 4, Avda 10, San José; tel. 223-2497; Pres. EMILIO PIEDRA JIMÉNEZ; Sec. ROBERTO FRANCISCO SALAZAR MADRIZ.

Partido Demócrata (PD): San José.

Partido Independiente (PI): San José; Pres. EUGENIO JIMÉNEZ SANCHO; Sec. GONZALO JIMÉNEZ CHAVES.

Partido Integración Nacional (PIN): San José; tel. 243-2583; fax 255-0834; e-mail wmunoz@congreso.aleg.go.cr; internet www.pin.freeservers.com; Pres. Dr WALTER MUÑOZ CÉSPEDES.

Partido de Liberación Nacional (PLN): Sabana Oeste, San José; tel. 232-5133; fax 296-0916; e-mail palina@sol.racsa.co.cr; internet www.pln.org; f. 1948; social democratic party; affiliated to the Socialist International; 500,000 mems; Pres. SONIA PICADO SOTELA; Sec.-Gen. ROLANDO GONZÁLEZ ULLOA.

Partido Movimiento Libertario (PML): San José; e-mail otto@libertario.org; internet www.libertario.org; f. 1994; Pres. OTTO GUEVARA GUTH; Sec.-Gen. RAÚL COSTALES DOMÍNGUEZ.

Partido Nacional Democrático: San José; Pres. RODOLFO CERDAS CRUZ; Sec. ELADIO JARA JIMÉNEZ.

Partido Renovación Costarricense (PRC): San José; f. 1994.

Partido Revolucionario de los Trabajadores (PRT): San José; worker's revolutionary party.

Partido Radical Demócrata: San José; Pres. JUAN JOSÉ ECHEVERRÍA BREALEY; Sec. RODRIGO ESQUIVEL RODRÍGUEZ.

Partido Republicano Nacional: San José; Pres. ROLANDO RODRÍGUEZ VARELA; Sec. FERNANDO PEÑA HERRERA.

Partido Unidad Social Cristiana (PUSC): San José; internet www.pusc.or.cr; Pres. ABEL PACHECO; Sec. LORENA VÁSQUEZ.

Partido Unión General (PUGEN): Pérez Zeledón, Apdo 440-8.000, San José; tel. 771-0524; fax 771-0737; f. 1980; e-mail pugen@apc.c.co.cr; Pres. Dr CARLOS A. FERNÁNDEZ VEGA; Sec. LOURDES RODRÍGUEZ.

Partido Unión Nacional: San José; Pres. OLGA MARTA ULATE ROJAS; Sec. RODRIGO GONZÁLEZ SABORÍO.

Diplomatic Representation

EMBASSIES IN COSTA RICA

Argentina: Apdo 1.963, San José; tel. 234-6520; fax 283-9983; Ambassador: MANUEL MARIA PINTO.

Belgium: Los Yoses, 4a entrada, 25 metros sur, Apdo 3.725, 1000 San José; tel. 225-6255; fax 225-0351; Ambassador: WILLY J. STEVENS.

Belize: Marschu International Realty, San José; tel. 256-0542; fax 222-5523; e-mail marschu@sol.racsa.co.cr; Chargé d'affaires a.i.: FEDERICO A. MARIN-SCHUMACHER.

Bolivia: Barrio Rohrmoser 669, 1000 San José; tel. 232-9455; fax 231-4454; e-mail embocr@sol.racsa.co.cr; Ambassador: OSCAR DAZA.

Brazil: Paseo Colón frente a Nissan Lachner y Sáenz, San José; tel. 233-1544; fax 223-4325; Ambassador: LUIZ JORGE RANGEL DE CASTRO.

Bulgaria: Edif. Delcoré, 3°, 100 metros sur Hotel Balmoral, Apdo 4.752, San José; Ambassador: KIRIL ZLATKOV NIKOLOV.

Canada: Oficentro Ejecutivo La Sabana, Edif. 5, 3°, detrás de la Contracoría, Centro Colón, Apdo 351, 1007 San José; tel. 296-4149; fax 296-4270; Ambassador: DAN GOODLEAF.

Chile: De la Pulpería La Luz 125 metros norte, Casa 116, Apdo 10.102, San José; tel. 224-4243; Ambassador: PEDRO PALACIOS CAMERÓN.

China (Taiwan): 300 metros al norte y 150 al este de la Iglesia Sta Teresita, Barrio Escalante, Apdo 676-2010, San José; tel. 224-8180; fax 253-8333; Ambassador: KAO-WEN MAO.

Colombia: Apdo 3.154, 1000 San José; tel. 221-0725; fax 255-1705; Ambassador: MARÍA CRISTINA ZULETA DE PATÍN.

Czech Republic: 75 metros oeste de la entrada principal del Colegio Humboldt, Apdo 12041, 1000 San José; tel. 296-5671; fax 296-5595; Ambassador: Ing. VÍT KORSELT.

Dominican Republic: Lomas de Ayarco, Curridabat, de la Embajada de Rusia 100 metros oeste, 300 metros sur, 300 metros oeste y 150 metros norte, Apdo 4.746, San José; tel. and fax 272-2398; Ambassador: ALFONSO ARIA JIMÉNEZ.

Ecuador: Edif. de la esquina sureste del Museo Nacional, 125 metros al este, Avda 2, Calles 19 y 21, Apdo 1.374, 1000 San José; tel. 223-6281; Ambassador: Lic. ANDRÉS CÓRDOVA GALARZA.

El Salvador: Edif. Trianón, 3°, Avda Central y Calle 5, Apdo 1.378, San José; tel. 222-5536; Ambassador: HUGO ROBERTO CARRILLO CORLETO.

France: Carretera a Curridabat, del Indoor Club 200 metros sur y 25 metros oeste, Apdo 10.177, San José; tel. 234-4187; fax 234-4197; e-mail sjfrance@sol.racsa.co.cr; Ambassador: NICOLE TRAMOND.

Germany: Barrio Rohrmoser, de la Casa de Oscar Arias 200 metros norte, 50 metros este, Apdo 4.017, 1000 San José; tel. 232-5533; fax 231-6403; e-mail info@embajada-alemana.org; internet www.embajada-alemana.org; Ambassador FRIEDRICH GRÖNING.

Guatemala: De Pops Curridabat 500 metros sur y 30 metros este, 2a Casa Izquierda, Apdo 328, 1000 San José; tel. 283-2290; fax 231-6645; Ambassador: JORGE MARIO GARCÍA LaGUARDIA.

Holy See: Urbanización Rohrmoser, Sabana Oeste, Centro Colón, Apdo 992, 1007 San José (Apostolic Nunciature); tel. 232-2128; fax 231-2557; e-mail nuapcr@sol.racsa.co.cr; Apostolic Nuncio: Most Rev. ANTONIO SOZZO, Titular Archbishop of Concordia.

Honduras: Los Yoses sur, del ITAN hacia la Presidencia la primera entrada a la izquierda, 200 metros norte y 100 metros este, Apdo 2.239, San José; tel. 234-9502; fax 253-2209; Ambassador: EDGARDO SEVILLA IDIÁQUEZ.

Hungary: Los Yoses, 5a entrada, 50 metros sur, No 1099, Apdo 765, 2010 San José; tel. 225-0908; fax 225-9741; Ambassador: Dr ZSOLT HORVÁTH.

India: 1000 San José; tel. 223-2341; fax 223-2231.

Israel: Edif. Centro Colón, 11°, Calle 2, Avdas 2 y 4, Apdo 5.147, San José; tel. 221-6444; fax 257-0867; Ambassador: YAACOV BRAKHA.

Italy: Los Yoses, 5a entrada, Apdo 1.729, San José; tel. 224-6574; fax 225-8200; e-mail ambiter@sol.racsa.co.cr; internet www.ambitcr.com; Ambassador: GIAN B. CAMPAGNOLA.

Japan: De la primera entrada del Barrio Rohrmoser (Sabana Oeste) 500 metros oeste y 100 metros norte, Apdos 501 y 10.145, San José; tel. 232-1255; fax 231-3140; Ambassador: YASUO MATSUI.

Korea, Republic: Calle 28, Avda 2, Barrio San Bosco, Apdo 3.150, San José; tel. 221-2398; Ambassador: JAE HOON KIM.

Mexico: Avda 7, No 1371, Apdo 10.107, San José; tel. 257-0633; fax 222-6080; Ambassador: ENRIQUE BERRUGA FILLOY.

Netherlands: Los Yoses, Avda 8, Calles 35 y 37, Apdo 10.285, 1000 San José; tel. 296-1490; fax 296-2933; Ambassador: F. B. A. M. VAN HAREN.

Nicaragua: Edif. Trianón, Avda Central 250, Barrio la California, San José; tel. 222-2373; fax 221-5481; e-mail embanic@sol.racsa .co.cr; Ambassador: Dr ENRIQUE PAGUAGA FERNÁNDEZ.

Panama: 200 metros sur, 25 metros este de Higuerón, La Granja, San Pedro, Montes de Oca, San José; tel. 225-3401; Ambassador: WALTER MYERS.

Peru: Barrio Pops de Curridabat, del Indoor Club 100 metros sur y 75 metros oeste, Apdo 4.248, 1000 San José; tel. 225-9145; fax 253-0457; Ambassador: ALBERTO VARILLAS MONTENEGRO.

Romania: Urbanización Rohrmoser, al costado norte de la Nunciatura Apostólica, Sabana Oeste, Centro Colón, Apdo 10.321, San José; tel. 231-0741; fax 232-6461; Ambassador: NICOLAE TURTUREA.

Russia: Apdo 6.340, San José; tel. 272-1021; Ambassador: VLADIMIR N. KAZIMIROV.

Spain: Calle 32, Paseo Colón, Avda 2, Apdo 10.150, San José; tel. 222-1933; fax 222-4180; e-mail embaes@racsa.co.cr; Ambassador: VICTOR IBÁÑEZ-MARTIN MELLADO.

Switzerland: Paseo Colón, Centro Colón, Apdo 895, San José; tel. 221-4829; Ambassador: Dr JOHANN BUCHER.

United Kingdom: Edif. Centro Colón, 11°, Apdo 815, 1007 San José; tel. 258-2025; fax 233-9938; e-mail britemb@sol.racsa.co.cr; Ambassador: PETER SPICELEY.

USA: Apdo 920-1200, Pavas San José; tel. 220-3939; fax 232-7944; e-mail hdssjo@usia.gov; internet usembassy.or.cr/; Ambassador: PETER JON DE VOS.

Venezuela: Avda Central, Los Yoses, 5a entrada, Apdo 10.230, San José; tel. 225-5813; Ambassador: Dr FRANCISCO SALAZAR MARTÍNEZ.

Judicial System

Ultimate judicial power is vested in the Supreme Court, the 22 justices of which are elected by the Assembly for a term of eight years, and are automatically re-elected for an equal period, unless the Assembly decides to the contrary by a two-thirds vote. Judges of the lower courts are appointed by the Supreme Court's five-member Supreme Council.

The Supreme Court may also meet as the Corte Plena, with power to declare laws and decrees unconstitutional. There are, in addition, four appellate courts, criminal courts, civil courts and special courts. The jury system is not used.

La Corte Suprema: San José; tel. 295-3000; fax 257-0801.

President of the Supreme Court: EDGAR CERVANTES VILLALTA.

Religion

Under the Constitution, all forms of worship are tolerated. Roman Catholicism is the official religion of the country. Various Protestant Churches are represented. There are an estimated 7,000 members of the Methodist Church.

CHRISTIANITY

The Roman Catholic Church

Costa Rica comprises one archdiocese and six dioceses. At 31 December 1998 Roman Catholics represented some 88% of the total population.

Bishops' Conference: Conferencia Episcopal de Costa Rica, Arzobispado, Apdo 497, 1000 San José; tel. 221-3053; fax 221-6662; f. 1977; Pres. Most Rev. ROMÁN ARRIETA VILLALOBOS, Archbishop of San José de Costa Rica.

Archbishop of San José de Costa Rica: Most Rev. ROMÁN ARRIETA VILLALOBOS, Arzobispado, Apdo 497, 1000 San José; tel. 258-1015; fax 221-2427; e-mail curiam@sol.racsa.co.cr.

The Anglican Communion

Costa Rica comprises one of the five dioceses of the Iglesia Anglicana de la Región Central de América.

Bishop of Costa Rica: Rt Rev. CORNELIUS JOSHUA WILSON, Apdo 2.773, 1000 San José; tel. 225-0209; fax 253-8331; e-mail amiecr@sol .racsa.co.cr.

Other Churches

Federación de Asociaciones Bautistas de Costa Rica: Apdo 1.631, 2100 Guadalupe; tel. 253-5820; fax 253-4723; f. 1946; represents Baptist churches; Pres. CARLOS MANUEL UMAÑA ROJAS.

Iglesia Evangélica Metodista de Costa Rica (Evangelical Methodist Church of Costa Rica): Apdo 5.481, 1000 San José; tel. 236-2171; fax 236-5921; autonomous since 1973; 6,000 mems; Pres. Bishop LUIS F. PALOMO.

BAHÁ'Í FAITH

Bahá'í Information Centre: Apdo 553, 1150 San José; tel. 231-0647; fax 296-1033; adherents resident in 242 localities.

National Spiritual Assembly of the Bahá'ís of Costa Rica: Apdo 553, 1150 La Uruca; tel. 231-0647; fax 296-1033; e-mail bahaiscr@sol.racsa.co.cr.

The Press

DAILIES

Al Día: Llorente de Tibás, Apdo 7.0270, San José; tel. 247-4647; fax 247-4665; e-mail aldia@nacion.co.cr; f. 1992; morning; independent; Dir ARMANDO M. GONZÁLEZ RODICIO; circ. 60,000.

Boletín Judicial: La Uruca, Apdo 5.024, San José; tel. 231-5222; f. 1878; journal of the judiciary; Dir ISAÍAS CASTRO VARGAS; circ. 2,500.

Diario Extra: Edif. Borrasé, 2°, Calle 4, Avda 4, Apdo 177, 1009 San José; tel. 223-9505; fax 223-5921; internet www.diarioextra.com; f. 1978; morning; independent; Dir WILLIAM GÓMEZ VARGAS; circ. 120,000.

La Gaceta: La Uruca, Apdo 5.024, San José; tel. 231-5222; internet www.imprenal.go.cr; f. 1878; official gazette; Dir ISAÍAS CASTRO VARGAS; circ. 5,300.

El Heraldo: 400 metros al este de las oficinas centrales, Apdo 1500, San José; tel. 222-6665; fax 222-3039; e-mail info@elheraldo.net; internet www.elheraldo.net; f. 1994; morning; independent; Dir ERWIN KNOHR R.; circ. 30,000.

La Nación: Llorente de Tibás, Apdo 10.138, San José; tel. 247-4747; fax 247-5022; e-mail webmaster@nacion.co.cr; internet www.nacion.co.cr; f. 1946; morning; independent; Dir EDUARDO ULIBARRI BILBAO; circ. 118,000.

La Prensa Libre: Calle 4, Avda 4, Apdo 10.121, San José; tel. 223-6666; fax 233-6831; e-mail plibre@prensalibre.co.cr; internet www.prensalibre.co.cr; f. 1889; evening; independent; Dir ANDRÉS BORRASÉ SANOU; circ. 56,000.

La República: Barrio Tournón, Guadalupe, Apdo 2.130, San José; tel. 223-0266; fax 255-3950; e-mail larazon@sol.racsa.co.cr; internet www.larepublica.net; f. 1950, reorganized 1967; morning; independent; Dir JULIO SUÑOL; circ. 60,000.

PERIODICALS

Abanico: Calle 4, esq. Avda 4, Apdo 10.121, San José; tel. 223-6666; fax 223-4671; weekly supplement of *La Prensa Libre*; women's interests; Editor MARÍA DEL CARMEN POZO C.; circ. 50,000.

Acta Médica: Sabana Sur, Apdo 548, San José; tel. 232-3433; f. 1954; organ of the Colegio de Médicos; 3 issues per year; Editor Dr BAUDILIO MORA MORA; circ. 2,000.

El Cafetalero: Calle 1, Avdas 18 y 20, Apdo 37, 1000 San José; tel. 222-6411; fax 223-6025; e-mail evilla@icafe.go.cr; f. 1964 as Noticiero del Café; changed name in 2000; bi-monthly; coffee journal; owned by the Instituto del Café de Costa Rica; Editor ERNESTO VILLALOBOS; circ. 10,000.

Contrapunto: La Uruca, Apdo 7-1.980, San José; tel. 231-3333; f. 1978; fortnightly; publication of Sistema Nacional de Radio y Televisión; Dir FABIO MUÑOZ CAMPOS; circ. 10,000.

Eco Católico: Calle 22, Avdas 3 y 5, Apdo 1.064, San José; tel. 222-6156; fax 256-0407; f. 1931; Catholic weekly; Dir ARMANDO ALFARO; circ. 20,000.

Mujer y Hogar: San José; tel. 236-3128; f. 1943; weekly; women's journal; Editor and Gen. Man. CARMEN CORNEJO MÉNDEZ; circ. 15,000.

Perfil: Llorente de Tibás, Apdo 1517-1100, San José, 1000; tel. 247-4345; fax 247-5110; e-mail perfil@nacion.co.cr; f. 1984; fortnightly; women's interest; Dir CAROLINA CARAZO BARRANTES; circ. 16,000.

Polémica: Icadis, Paseo de los Estudiantes, Apdo 1.006, San José; tel. 233-3964; f. 1981; every 4 months; left-wing; Dir GABRIEL AGUILERA PERALTA.

Primera Plana: Sabana Este, San José; tel. 255-1590.

Rumbo: Llorente de Tibás, Apdo 10.138, 1000 San José; tel. 240-4848; fax 240-6480; f. 1984; weekly; general; Dir ROXANA ZÚNIGA; circ. 15,000.

San José News: Apdo 7-2.730, San José; 2 a week; Dir CHRISTIAN RODRÍGUEZ.

Semanario Libertad: Calle 4, Avdas 8 y 10, Apdo 6.613, 1000 San José; tel. 225-5857; f. 1962; weekly; organ of the Partido del Pueblo Costarricense; Dir RODOLFO ULLOA B.; Editor JOSÉ A. ZÚNIGA; circ. 10,000.

Semanario Universidad: Ciudad Universitaria Rodrigo Facio, San Pedro, Montes de Oca, Apdo 21, San José; tel. 207-5355; fax 207-4774; internet cariari.ucr.ac.cr; f. 1970; weekly; general; Dir CARLOS MORALES; circ. 15,000.

The Tico Times: Calle 15, Avda 8, Apdo 4.632, 1000 San José; tel. 258-1558; fax 223-6378; e-mail ttimes@sol.racsa.co.cr; internet www .ticotimes.net; weekly; in English; Dir DERY DYER; circ. 15,210.

Tiempos de Costa Rica: Casa 3372 Barrio Escalante, Avda 9, 480 Metros al este, San José; tel. 280-2332; fax 280-6840; internet www.tdm.com; f. 1996; Costa Rican edition of the international *Tiempos de Mundo*.

PRESS ASSOCIATIONS

Colegio de Periodistas de Costa Rica: Sabana Este, Calle 42, Avda 4, Apdo 5.416, San José; tel. 233-5850; fax 223-8669; f. 1969; 550 mems; Exec. Dir Licda ADRIANA NÚÑEZ.

Sindicato Nacional de Periodistas: Sabana Este, Calle 42, Avda 4, Apdo 5.416, San José; tel. 222-7589; f. 1970; 200 mems; Sec.-Gen. ADRIÁN ROJAS JAÉN.

FOREIGN NEWS BUREAUX

ACAN-EFE (Central America): Costado Sur, Casa Matute Gómez, Casa 1912, Apdo 84.930, San José; tel. 222-6785; Correspondent WILFREDO CHACÓN SERRANO.

Agence France-Presse (France): Calle 13, Avdas 9 y 11 bis, Apdo 5.276, San José; tel. 233-0757; Correspondent DOMINIQUE PETTIT.

Agencia EFE (Spain): Avda 10, Calles 19 y 21, No 1912, Apdo 84.930, San José; tel. 222-6785.

Agenzia Nazionale Stampa Associata (ANSA) (Italy): c/o Diario La República, Barrio Tournón, Guadalupe, Apdo 545-1200, San José; tel. 231-1140; fax 231-1140; Correspondent LUIS CARTÍN S.

Associated Press (AP) (USA): San José; tel. 221-6146; Correspondent REID MILLER.

Deutsche Presse-Agentur (dpa) (Germany): Edif. 152, 3°, Calle 11, Avdas 1 y 3, Apdo 7.156, San José; tel. 233-0604; fax 233-0604; Correspondent ERNESTO RAMÍREZ.

Informatsionnoye Telegrafnoye Agentstvo Rossii—Telegrafnoye Agentstvo Suverennykh Stran (ITAR—TASS) (Russia): De la Casa Italia 1000 metros este, 50 metros norte, Casa 675, Apdo 1.011, San José; tel. 224-1560; Correspondent ENRIQUE MORA.

Inter Press Service (IPS) (Italy): Latin American Regional Center, Calle 11, Avdas 1 y 3, No 152, Paseo de los Estudiantes, Apdo 70, 1002 San José; tel. 255-3861; fax 233-8583; Regional Dir GONZALO ORTIZ-CRESPO.

Prensa Latina (Cuba): Avda 11, No 3185, Calles 31 y 33, Barrio Escalante (de la parrillada 25 metros al oeste), San José; tel. 253-1457; Correspondent FRANCISCO A. URIZARRI TAMAYO.

Rossiyskoye Informatsionnoye Agentstvo—Novosti (RIA—Novosti) (Russia): De la Casa Italiana 100 metros este, 50 metros norte, San José; tel. 224-1560.

United Press International (UPI) (USA): Calle 15, Avda 2, Radioperiódicos Reloj, Apdo 4.334, San José; tel. 222-2644; Correspondent WILLIAM CESPEDES CHAVARRÍA.

Xinhua (New China) News Agency (People's Republic of China): Apdo 4.774, San José; tel. 231-3497; Correspondent XU BIHUA.

Publishers

Alfalit Internacional: Apdo 292, 4050 Alajuela; f. 1961; educational; Dirs GILBERTO BERNAL, OSMUNDO PONCE.

Antonio Lehmann Librería, Imprenta y Litografía, Ltda: Calles 1 y 3, Avda Central, Apdo 10.011, San José; tel. 223-1212; f. 1896; general fiction, educational, textbooks; Man. Dir ANTONIO LEHMANN STRUVE.

Editorial Caribe: Apdo 1.307, San José; tel. 222-7244; f. 1949; religious textbooks; Dir JOHN STROWEL.

Editorial Costa Rica: 100 metros sur y 50 metros este del Supermercado Periféricos en San Francisco de Dos Ríos, Apdo 10.010, San José; tel. 286-1817; f. 1959; government-owned; cultural; Gen. Man. SHEILA DI PALMA GAMBOA.

Editorial Fernández Arce: Apdo 6.523, 1000 San José; tel. 224-5201; fax 225-6109; f. 1967; textbooks for primary, secondary and university education; Dir Dr MARIO FERNÁNDEZ LOBO.

Editorial de la Universidad Autónoma de Centroamérica (UACA): Apdo 7.637, 1000 San José; tel. 234-0701; fax 224-0391; e-mail lauaca@sol.racsa.co.cr; f. 1981; Editor ALBERTO DI MARE.

Editorial de la Universidad Estatal a Distancia (EUNED): Paseo de los Estudiantes, Apdo 597, 1002 San José; tel. 223-5430; fax 257-5042; f. 1979; Dir AUXILIADORA PROTTI QUESADA.

Editorial Universitaria Centroamericana (EDUCA): Ciudad Universitaria Rodrigo Facio, San Pedro, Apdo 64, 2060 San José; tel. 224-3727; fax 253-9141; e-mail educacr@sol .racsa.co.cr; f. 1969; organ of the CSUCA; science, literature, philosophy; Dir ANITA DE FORMOSO.

Mesén Editores: Urbanización El Cedral, 52, Cedros de Montes de Oca, Apdo 6.306, 1000 San José; tel. 253-5203; fax 283-0681; f. 1978; general; Dir DENNIS MESÉN SEGURA.

Trejos Hermanos Sucs, SA: Curridabat, Apdo 10.096, San José; tel. 224-2411; f. 1912; general and reference; Man. ALVARO TREJOS.

PUBLISHING ASSOCIATION

Cámara Costarricense del Libro: San José; Pres. LUIS FERNANDO CALVO FALLAS.

Broadcasting and Communications

TELECOMMUNICATIONS

Cámara Costarricense de Telecomunicaciones: Edif. Centro Colón, Apdo 591-1007, 1000 San José; tel. and fax 255-3422; Pres. EVITA ARGUEDAS MAKLOUF.

Cámara Nacional de Medios de Comunicación Colectiva (CANAMECC): Apdo 6.574, 1000 San José; tel. 222-4820; f. 1954; Pres. ANDRÉS QUINTANA CAVALLINI.

Instituto Costarricense de Electricidad (ICE): govt agency for power and telecommunications (see Trade and Industry: Utilities, below).

Radiográfica Costarricense, SA (RACSA): Avda 5, Calle 1, Frente al Edif. Numar, Apdo 54, 1000 San José; tel. 287-0087; fax 287-0379; e-mail mcruz@sol.sacsa.co.cr; f. 1921; state telecommunications co.; Dir-Gen. MARCO A. CRUZ MIRANDA.

RADIO

Asociación Costarricense de Información y Cultura (ACIC): Apdo 365, 1009 San José; f. 1983; independent body; controls private radio stations; Pres. JUAN FCO. MONTEALEGRE MARTÍN.

Cámara Nacional de Radio (CANARA): Paseo de los Estudiantes, Apdo 1.583, 1002 San José; tel. 233-1845; fax 255-4483; e-mail canara@sol.racsa.co.cr; internet www.canara.org; f. 1947; Exec. Dir LUZMILDA VARGAS GONZÁLEZ.

Control Nacional de Radio (CNR): Dirección Nacional de Comunicaciones, Ministerio de Gobernación y Policia, Apdo 10.006, 1000 San José; tel. 221-0992; fax 283-0741; f. 1954; governmental supervisory department; Dir MELVIN MURILLO ALVAREZ.

Non-commercial

Faro del Caribe: Apdo 2.710, 1000 San José; tel. 226-2573; fax 227-1725; f. 1948; religious and cultural programmes in Spanish and English; Man. CARLOS ROZOTTO PIEDRASANTA.

Radio Costa Rica: De Autos Bohío, en barrio Córdoba, 100 metros sur y 100 metros este, Apdo 6.462, 1000 San José; tel. 227-4690; fax 231-3408; e-mail canalcr@sol.racsa.co.cr; f. 1988; broadcasts Voice of America news bulletins (in Spanish) and locally-produced educational and entertainment programmes; Gen. Man. ANTONIO ALEXANDRE GARCÍA.

Radio Fides: Avda 4, Curia Metropolitana, Apdo 5.079, 1000 San José; tel. 233-4546; fax 233-2387; f. 1952; Roman Catholic station; Dir Rev. ROMÁN ARRIETA VILLALOBOS.

Radio Nacional: 1km oeste del Parque Nacional de Diversiones, La Uruca, Apdo 7-1980, San José; tel. 231-7983; fax 220-0070; e-mail sinart@sol.racsa.co.cr; f. 1978; Dir RODOLFO RODRÍGUEZ.

Radio Santa Clara: Santa Clara, San Carlos, Apdo 221, Ciudad Quesada, Alajuela; tel. 479-1264; f. 1986; Roman Catholic station; Dir Rev. MARCO A. SOLÍS V.

Radio Universidad: Ciudad Universitaria Rodrigo Facio, San Pedro, Montes de Oca, Apdo 2060, 1000 San José; tel. 207-5356; fax 207-5459; f. 1949; classical music; Dir CARLOS MORALES.

Commercial

There are about 40 commercial radio stations, including:

89 Ya!: Costado sur del Parque Desamparados, Apdo 301, San José; tel. 259-3657; fax 250-2376; f. 1995; Dir ALEXANDER RAMOS RODRÍGUEZ.

Cadena de Emisoras Columbia: San José; tel. 234-0355; fax 225-9275; operates Radio Columbia, Radio Uno, Radio Sabrosa, Radio Puntarenas; Dir C. ARNOLDO ALFARO CHAVARRA.

Cadena Musical: Apdo 854, 1000, San José; tel. 257-2789; fax 233-9975; f. 1954; operates Radio Musical, Radio Emperador; Gen. Man. JORGE JAVIER CASTRO.

Grupo Centro: Apdo 6.133, San José; tel. 240-7591; fax 236-3672; operates Radio Centro 96.3 FM, Radio 820 AM, Televisora Guanacasteca Channels 16 and 28; Dir ROBERTO HERNÁNDEZ RAMÍREZ.

Radio Chorotega: Apdo 92, 5175 Santa Cruz de Guanacaste; tel. 663-2757; fax 663-0183; f. 1983; Roman Catholic station; Dir Rev. EMILIO MONTES DE OCA CORDERO.

Radio Emaus: San Vito de Coto Brus; tel. and fax 773-3101; f. 1962; Roman Catholic station; Dir Rev. LUIS PAULINO CABRERA SOTO.

Radio Monumental: Avda Central y 2, Calle 2, Apdo 800, 1000 San José; tel. 222-0000; fax 222-8237; e-mail monument@sol.racsa.co.cr; internet www.novanet.co.cr/monumental; f. 1929; all news station; Gen. Man. TERESA MARÍA CHÁVES ZAMORA.

Radio Sinaí: Apdo 262, 8000 San Isidro de El General; tel. 771-0367; f. 1957; Roman Catholic station; Dir Mgr ALVARO COTO OROZCO.

Sistema Radiofónico: Edif. Galería La Paz, 3°, Avda 2, Calles 2 y 4, Apdo 341, 1000 San José; tel. 222-4344; fax 255-0587; operates Radio Reloj; Dir Dr HERNÁN BARQUERO MONTES DE OCA.

TELEVISION
Government-owned

Sistema Nacional de Radio y Televisión Cultural (SINART): 1 km al oeste del Parque Nacional de Diversiones La Uruca, Apdo 7-1.980, San José; tel. 231-0839; fax 231-6604; e-mail sinart@racsa .co.cr; f. 1977; cultural; Dir-Gen. GUIDO SÁENZ GONZÁLEZ.

Commercial

Alphavisión (Canal 19): Detrás Iglesia de Santa María y Griega, Carretera a Desamparados, Apdo 1490, San José; tel. 226-9333; fax 226-9095; f. 1987; Gen. Man. CECILIA RAMÍREZ.

Canal 2: Del Hospital México 300 metros oeste, Antiguo Hotel Cristal, Apdo 2.860, San José; tel. 231-2222; fax 231-0791; f. 1983; Pres. RAMÓN COLL MONTERO.

Canal 54: De Plaza Mayot, en Rohrmoser, 50 metros oeste, 50 metros sur, Apdo 640, San José; tel. 232-6337; fax 231-3408; e-mail canalcr@sol.racsa.co.cr; f. 1996; Pres. ANTONIO ALEXANDRE GARCÍA.

Corporación Costarricense de Televisión, SA (Canal 6): Apdo 2.860, 1000 San José; tel. 232-9255; fax 232-6087; Gen. Man. MARIO SOTELA BLEN.

Multivisión de Costa Rica, Ltda (Canales 4 y 9): 150 metros oeste del Centro Comercial de Guadelupe, Apdo 4.666, 1000 San José; tel. 233-4444; fax 221-1734; f. 1961; operates Radio Sistema Universal A.M. (f. 1956), Channel 9 (f. 1962) and Channel 4 (f. 1964) and FM (f. 1980); Gen. Man. ARNOLD VARGAS V.

Televisora de Costa Rica (Canal 7), SA (Teletica): Costado oeste Estadio Nacional, Apdo 3.876, San José; tel. 232-2222; fax 231-6258; f. 1960; operates Channel 7; Pres. OLGA COZZA DE PICADO; Gen. Man. RENÉ PICADO COZZA.

Televisora Sur y Norte (Canal 11): Apdo 99, 1000 San José; tel. 233-4988; Gen. Man. FEDERICO ZAMORA.

Finance

(cap. = capital; p.u. = paid up; res = reserves; dep. = deposits; m. = million; brs = branches; amounts in colones, unless otherwise indicated)

BANKING

Banco Central de Costa Rica: Avdas Central y Primera, Calles 2 y 4, Apdo 10.058, 1000 San José; tel. 233-4233; fax 233-5930; internet www.bccr.fi.cr; f. 1950; cap. 5.0m., res 10.0m., total resources 1,078,058.4m. (Dec. 1997); scheduled for privatization in 2001; Pres. EDUARDO LIZANO FAIT; Man. CARLOS MUÑOZ V.

State-owned Banks

Banco de Costa Rica: Avdas Central y 2, Calles 4 y 6, Apdo 10.035, 1000 San José; tel. 255-1100; fax 255-0911; internet www.bancosta.fi.cr; f. 1877; responsible for industry; total assets 10,353m. (1999); Pres. JORGE ELÍAS RAMÍREZ R.; Gen. Man. MARIO BARRENECHEA; 44 brs and agencies.

Banco Crédito Agrícola de Cartago: Avda 2, Calles 3 y 5, Apdo 297, Cartago; tel. 550-0202; fax 552-0364; f. 1918; responsible for housing; total assets 5,731m. (1999); Pres. BERNARDO GARCÍA UMAÑA; Gen. Man. VALENTÍN FONSECA MENA; 10 brs.

Banco Nacional de Costa Rica: Calles 2 y 4, Avda Primera, Apdo 10.015, 1000 San José; tel. 221-2223; fax 233-3875; internet www.bncr.fi.cr; f. 1914; responsible for the agricultural sector; total assets 5,829m. (1999); Gen. Man. Lic. OMAR GARRO V.; 125 brs and agencies.

Banco Popular y de Desarrollo Comunal: Calle 1, Avdas 2 y 4, Apdo 10.190, San José; tel. 257-5797; fax 255-1966; f. 1969; total assets 29,450m. (1999); Pres. Ing. RODOLFO NAVAS ALVARADO; Gen. Man. ALVARO UREÑA ALVAREZ.

Private Banks

Banco BANEX, SA: Barrio Tournón, Diagonal a Ulacit, Apdo 8983, 1000 San José; tel. 257-0522; fax 257-5967; e-mail interna@banex .co.cr; internet www.banex.co.cr; f. 1981 as Banco Agroindustrial y de Exportaciones, SA; adopted present name 1987; cap. 13,929.0m.,

res. 3,738.3m., dep. 183.1m. (Dec. 1999); Pres. ALBERTO VALLARINO; Gen. Man. JAVIER LEJÁRRAGA; 9 brs.

Banco BCT, SA: Calle Central No. 160, Apdo 7.698, San José; tel. 257-0544; fax 233-6833; f. 1984; total assets 13,794m. (1999); Pres. ANTONIO BURGUÉS; Gen. Man. Lic. LEONEL BARUCH.

Banco BFA, SA: Centro Comercial CAFESA, La Uruca, Apdo 6.531, 1000 San José; tel. 231-4444; fax 232-7476; f. 1984 as Banco de Fomento Agrícola; present name adopted 1994; cap. US $3.9m.; res $4.5m.; dep. $16.0m. (Dec. 1996); Pres. ERNESTO ROHRMOSER; Gen. Man. and CEO MANUEL PÉREZ LARA.

Banco de COFISA, SA: Barrio Tournón, San Francisco de Goicoechea, Apdo 10.067, San José; tel. 257-6363; fax 223-4594; f. 1986; cap. and res 378m. (Aug. 1991); Pres. Lic. OMAR DENGO; Gen. Man. WILLIAM J. PHELPS.

Banco del Comercio, SA: 150 metros norte de la Catedral Metropolitana, Apdo 1.106, 1000 San José; tel. 257-6010; fax 222-3706; e-mail bancomer@bancomer.fi.cr; internet www.bancomer.fi.cr; f. 1978; cap. 1,216.3m., res 191.3m., dep. 9,426.0m. (Dec. 1997); Pres. JAVIER QUIRÓS RAMOS DE ANAYA; Gen. Man. RAFAEL ANGEL MORA BADILLA.

Banco Continental, SA: Edif. LAICA, Barrio Tournón, Apdo 7.969, San José; tel. 257-1155; fax 257-1169; f. 1984; cap. and res 782m. (Oct. 1993); Pres. RODOLFO SALAS; Gen. Man. Ing. JUAN J. FLÓREZ.

Banco Cooperativo Costarricense, RL: Avda 7, Calles 3 y 5, Apdo 8.593, 1000 San José; tel. 233-5044; fax 233-9661; f. 1982; cap. 602.7m., res 104.1m., dep. 4,000.9m. (Dec. 1997); Pres. MARIO CARVAJAL HERRERA; Gen. Man. Dr DENNIS MELÉNDEZ HOWELL.

Banco de Crédito Centroamericano, SA (Bancentro): Calles 26 y 38, Paseo Colón, de la Mercedes Benz 200 metros norte y 150 metros oeste, Apdo 5.099, 1000 San José; tel. 280-5555; fax 280-5090; f. 1974; cap. 492m. (1996); Pres. ROBERTO J. ZAMORA LLANES; Gen. Man GILBERTO SERRANO GUTIÉRREZ.

Banco Federado, RL: 200 metros sur Autos Subarú, Los Yoses, San Pedro, Apdo 806, 1000 San José; tel. 283-5050; fax 253-4803; f. 1987; cap. and res 505m. (Aug. 1991); Pres. CARLOS BONILLA AYUB; Gen. Man. PABLO CRUZ MONGE.

Banco de la Industria, SA: Calle 9, Avdas Central y Primera, Apdo 4.254, 1000 San José; tel. 221-3355; fax 233-8383; f. 1985; cap. and res 200m. (Aug. 1993); Pres. Lic. ALBÁN BRENES IBARRA; Gen. Man. Dr ABELARDO BRENES IBARRA.

Banco Interfin, SA: Calle 3, Avdas 2 y 4, Apdo 6.899, San José; tel. 287-4000; fax 233-4823; f. 1982; total assets 11,139m. (1999); Pres. Ing. LUIS LUKOWIECKI; Gen. Man. Dr LUIS LIBERMAN.

Banco Internacional de Costa Rica, SA: Edif. Inmobiliaria BICSA, Barrio Tournón, Apdo 6.116, San José; tel. 243-1000; fax 257-2378; f. 1987; cap. and res 1,625m. (Nov. 1994); Pres. Lic. FERNANDO SUÑOL PREGO; Gen. Man. MARCO ALFARO CHAVARRÍA.

Banco Internacional de Exportación, SA: Calle Central, Avda 3, Apdo 5.384, San José; tel. 222-3033; f. 1981; Pres. HOJABAR YAZDANI; Gen. Man. HERNÁN VOLIO.

Banco del Istmo, SA: Calle 2, Avdas Primera y Central, Apdo 10.184, 1000 San José; tel. 257-9011; fax 221-6795; f. 1871; frmly Banco Lyon, SA, name changed as above 1996; cap. 592.5m., res 78.4m., dep. 636.5m. (Dec. 1993); Pres. ALBERTO VALLARINO CLEMENT; Gen. Man. MARCIAL DÍAZ DEL VALLE.

Banco Latinoamericano (Costa Rica), SA: San José; f. 1974; cap. 5m.; Pres. FERNANDO BERROCAL S.; Man. FRED O'NEILL G.

Banco Metropolitano, SA: Calle Central, Avda 2, Apdo 6.714, 1000 San José; tel. 290-6900; fax 296-9665; f. 1985; cap. 386.0m., res 610.1m., dep. 3,828.9m. (Dec. 1996); Pres. ABRAHAM MELTZER SPIGEL; Gen. Man. FRANCISCO LAY SOLANO; 3 brs.

Banco de San José, SA: Calle Central, Avdas 3 y 5, Apdo 5.445, 1000 San José; tel. 256-9911; fax 223-3063; f. 1968; fmrly Bank of America, SA; total assets 10,616m. (1999); Pres. ERNESTO CASTEGNARO ODIO; Gen. Man. MARIO MONTEALEGRE-SABORÍO.

Banco de Santander (Costa Rica), SA: Avda 2, Calle Central, Apdo 6.714, San José; tel. 222-8066; fax 222-8840; f. 1977; cap. 60m. (1986); Pres. ABRAHAM WAIESLEDER; Gen. Man. LUIS MIER ABANS.

Citibank (Costa Rica), SA: Oficentro ejecutivo la Sabana, distrito Mata Redonda, Apdo 10.277, San José; tel. 296-1494; fax 296-2458.

Scotiabank Costa Rica: Avda Primera, Calles Central y 2, Apdo 5.395, 1000, San José; tel. 287-8700; fax 255-3076; f. 1995; Gen. Man. BRIAN W. BRADY; 11 brs.

Credit Co-operatives

Federación Nacional de Cooperativas de Ahorro y Crédito (Fedecrédito, RL): Calle 20, Avdas 8 y 10, Apdo 4.748, 1000 San José; tel. 233-5666; fax 257-1724; f. 1963; 55 co-operatives, with 150,000 mems; combined cap. US $82m.; Pres. Lic. CARLOS BONILLA AYUB; Gen. Man. Lic. MARIO VARGAS ALVARADO.

STOCK EXCHANGE

Bolsa Nacional de Valores, SA: Edif. Cartagena, 4°, Calle Central, Avda Primera, Santa Ana, Apdo 03-6155, 1000 San José; tel. 204-

4848; fax 204-4802; e-mail bnv@bnv.co.cr; f. 1976; Chair. RODRIGO ARIAS SÁNCHEZ; CEO FEDERICO CARRILLO ZÜRCHER.

INSURANCE

In mid-1998 the Legislative Assembly approved legislative reform effectively terminating the state monopoly of all insurance activities.

Instituto Nacional de Seguros: Calles 9 y 9 bis, Avda 7, Apdo 10.061, 1000 San José; tel. 223-5800; fax 255-3381; internet www.ins.go.cr; f. 1924; administers the state monopoly of insurance; services of foreign insurance companies may be used only by authorization of the Ministry of the Economy, Industry and Commerce, and only after the Instituto has certified that it will not accept the risk; Exec. Pres. JORGE A. HERNÁNDEZ CASTAÑEDA; Gen. Man. ANA ROSS SALAZAR.

Trade and Industry

GOVERNMENT AGENCIES

Instituto Nacional de Vivienda y Urbanismo (INVU): Apdo 2.534, San José; tel. 221-5266; fax 223-4006; housing and town planning institute; Exec. Pres. Ing. Lic. VICTOR EVELIO CASTRO; Gen. Man. Lic. PEDRO HERNÁNDEZ RUIZ.

Ministry of Planning: Avdas 3 y 5, Calle 4, Apdo 10.127, 1000 San José; tel. 221-9524; fax 253-6243; f. 1963; formulates and supervises execution of the National Development Plan; main aims: to increase national productivity; to improve distribution of income and social services; to increase citizen participation in solution of socio-economic problems; Pres. Dr LEONARDO GARNIER.

Promotora del Comercio Exterior de Costa Rica (PROC-OMER): Calle 40, Avdas Central y 3, Centro Colón, Apdo 1.278, 1007 San José; tel. 256-7111; fax 233-5755; e-mail info@procomer.com; internet www.procomer.com; f. 1968 to improve international competitiveness by providing services aimed at increasing, diversifying and expediting international trade.

DEVELOPMENT ORGANIZATIONS

Cámara de Azucareros: Calle 3, Avda Fernández Güell, Apdo 1.577, 1000 San José; tel. 221-2103; fax 222-1358; f. 1949; sugar growers; Pres. RODRIGO ARIAS SÁNCHEZ.

Cámara Nacional de Bananeros: Edif. Urcha, 3°, Calle 11, Avda 6, Apdo 10.273, 1000 San José; tel. 222-7891; fax 233-1268; f. 1967; banana growers; Pres. Lic. JOSÉ ALVARO SANDOVAL; Exec. Dir Lic. JORGE MADRIGAL.

Cámara Nacional de Cafetaleros: Calle 3, Avdas 6 y 8, No. 652, Apdo 1.310, San José; tel. 221-8207; fax 257-5381; f. 1948; 70 mems; coffee millers and growers; Pres. CARLOS R. AUBERT Z.; Exec. Dir JOAQUÍN VALVERDE B.

Cámara Nacional de Ganaderos: Edif. Ilifilán, 4°, Calles 4 y 6, Avda Central, Apdo 5.539, 1000 San José; tel. 222-1652; cattle farmers; Pres. Ing. ALBERTO JOSÉ AMADOR ZAMORA.

Cámara Nacional de Artesanía y Pequeña Industria de Costa Rica (CANAPI): Calle 17, Avda 10, detrás estatua de San Martín, Apdo 1.783-2.100 Goicoechea, San José; tel. 223-2763; fax 255-4873; f. 1963; development, marketing and export of small-scale industries and handicrafts; Pres. and Exec. Dir RODRIGO GONZÁLEZ.

Costa Rican Investment and Development Board (CINDE): Apdo 7.170, 1000 San José; tel. 220-0366; fax 220-4750; e-mail cindes.m@sol.racsa.co.cr; internet www.cinde.co.cr; f. 1983; coalition for development of initiatives to attract foreign investment for production and export of new products; Chair. EMILIO BRUCE; CEO ENRIQUE EGLOFF.

Instituto del Café de Costa Rica: Calle 1, Avdas 18 y 20, Apdo 37, San José; tel. 222-6411; fax 222-2838; www.icafe.go.cr/homepage .nsf; f. 1948 to develop the coffee industry, to control production and to regulate marketing; Pres. Lic. LUIS DIEGO ESCALANTE; Exec. Dir GUILLERMO CANET.

CHAMBERS OF COMMERCE

Cámara de Comercio de Costa Rica: Urbanización Tournón, 150 metros noroeste del parqueo del Centro Comercial El Pueblo, Apdo 1.114, 1000 San José; tel. 221-0005; fax 233-7091; e-mail biofair@sol .racsa.co.cr; f. 1915; 900 mems; Pres. EMILIO BRUCE JIMÉNEZ; Exec. Dir Lic. EUGENIO PIGNATARO PACHECO.

Cámara de Industrias de Costa Rica: 350 metros sur de la Fuente de la Hispanidad, San Pedro de Montes de Oca, Apdo 10.003, San José; tel. 281-0006; fax 234-6163; e-mail cicr@cicr.com; internet www.cicr.com; Pres. Ing. MARCO VINICIO RUIZ; Exec. Dir MAYI ANTILLON GUERRERO.

Unión Costarricense de Cámaras y Asociaciones de la Empresa Privada (UCCAEP): 1002 Paseo de los Estudiantes, Apdo 539, San José; tel. 290-5595; fax 290-5596; f. 1974; business

federation; Pres. Ing. SAMUEL YANKELEWITZ BERGER; Exec. Dir ALVARO RAMÍREZ BOGANTES.

INDUSTRIAL AND TRADE ASSOCIATIONS

Cámara Nacional de Agricultura: Avda 10-10 bis, Cv. 23, Apdo 1.671, 1000 San José; tel. 221-6864; fax 233-8658; f. 1947; Pres. Ing. LEONEL PERALTA; Exec. Dir Lic. JOSÉ CARLOS BARQUERO ARCE.

Consejo Nacional de Producción: Calle 36 a 12, Apdo 2.205, San José; tel. 223-6033; fax 233-9660; f. 1948 to encourage agricultural and fish production and to regulate production and distribution of basic commodities; Pres. Ing. JAVIER FLORES GALAGARZA; Man. Lic. VIRGINIA VALVERDE DE MOLINA.

Instituto de Desarrollo Agrícola (IDA): Apdo 5.054, 1000 San José; tel. 224-6066; Exec. Pres. Ing. ROBERTO SOLÓRZANO SANABRIA; Gen. Man. Ing. JORGE ANGEL JIMÉNEZ CALDERÓN.

Instituto Mixto de Ayuda Social (IMAS): Calle 29, Avdas 2 y 4, Apdo 6.213, San José; tel. 225-5555; fax 224-8783; Pres. CLOTILDE FONSECA QUESADA.

Instituto Nacional de Fomento Cooperativo: Apdo 10.103, 1000 San José; tel. 223-4355; fax 255-3835; f. 1973; to encourage the establishment of co-operatives and to provide technical assistance and credit facilities; Pres. Lic. RAFAEL ANGEL ROJAS JIMÉNEZ; Exec. Dir Lic. LUIS ANTONIO MONGE ROMÁN.

UTILITIES

Electricity

Instituto Costarricense de Electricidad—ICE (Costa Rican Electricity Institute): Apdo 10.032, 1000 San José; tel. 220-7720; fax 220-1555; internet www.ice.co.cr; govt agency for power and telecommunications; Exec. Pres. PABLO COB; Gen. Man. INGRID HERRMAN.

Servicio Nacional de Electricidad: Apdo 936, 1000 San José; tel. 220-0102; fax 220-0374; co-ordinates the development of the electricity industry; Chair. LEONEL FONSECA.

Water

Instituto Costarricense de Acueductos y Alcantarillados: Avda Central, Calle 5, Apdo 5.120, 1000 San José; tel. 233-2155; fax 222-2259; water and sewerage; Pres. MARIO FERNÁNDEZ ORTIZ.

TRADE UNIONS

Central del Movimiento de Trabajadores Costarricenses—CMTC (Costa Rican Workers' Union): Calle 20, Avdas 3 y 5, Apdo 4.137, 1000 San José; tel. 221-7701; fax 221-3353; e-mail cmtccr@ solracsa.co.cr; Pres. DENNIS CABEZAS BADILLA.

Confederación Auténtica de Trabajadores Democráticos (Democratic Workers' Union): Calle 13, Avdas 10 y 12, Solera; tel. 253-2971; Pres. LUIS ARMANDO GUTIÉRREZ; Sec.-Gen. Prof. CARLOS VARGAS.

Confederación Costarricense de Trabajadores Democráticos (Costa Rican Confederation of Democratic Workers): Calles 3 y 5, Avda 12, Apdo 2.167, San José; tel. 222-1981; f. 1966; mem. ICFTU and ORIT; Sec.-Gen. LUIS ARMANDO GUTIÉRREZ R.; 50,000 mems.

Confederación Unitaria de Trabajadores—CUT: Calles 1 y 3, Avda 12, Casa 142, Apdo 186, 1009 San José; tel. 233-4188; f. 1980 from a merger of the Federación Nacional de Trabajadores Públicos and the Confederación General de Trabajadores; 53 affiliated unions; Sec.-Gen. GILBER BERMÚDEZ UMAÑA; c. 75,000 mems.

Federación Sindical Agraria Nacional—FESIAN (National Agrarian Confederation): Apdo 2.167, 1000 San José; tel. 233-5897; 20,000 member families; Sec.-Gen. JUAN MEJÍA VILLALOBOS.

The **Consejo Permanente de los Trabajadores,** formed in 1986, comprises six union organizations and two teachers' unions.

Transport

Ministry of Public Works and Transport: Apdo 10.176, 1000 San José; tel. 226-7311; fax 227-1434; the Ministry is responsible for setting tariffs, allocating funds, maintaining existing systems and constructing new ones.

Cámara Nacional de Transportes: San José; national chamber of transport.

RAILWAYS

In 1998 there were 581.0 km of railway track.

Instituto Costarricense de Ferrocarriles (INCOFER): Calle 2, Avda 20, Apdo 1-1009, San José; tel. 221-0777; fax 222-3458; e-mail incofer@sol.racsa.co.cr; f. 1985; government-owned; 471 km, of which 388 km are electrified.

INCOFER comprised:

División I: Atlantic sector running between Limón, Río Frío, Valle la Estrella and Siquirres. Main line of 109 km, with additional 120 km of branch lines, almost exclusively for transport of bananas; services resumed in 1999.

División II: Pacific sector running from San José to Puntarenas and Caldera; 116 km of track, principally for transport of cargo.

Note: In 1995 INCOFER suspended most operations, pending privatization; in 2000 plans were proposed to re-open INCOFER for cargo transport only.

ROADS

In 1997 there were 35,597 km of roads, of which 7,405 km were main roads and 28,192 km were secondary roads. An estimated 21% of the total road network was paved in 1998.

SHIPPING

Local services operate between the Costa Rican ports of Puntarenas and Limón and those of Colón and Cristóbal in Panama and other Central American ports. The multi-million dollar project at Caldera on the Gulf of Nicoya is now in operation as the main Pacific port; Puntarenas is being used as the second port. The Caribbean coast is served by the port complex of Limón/Moín. International services are operated by various foreign shipping lines. In 2000 plans were announced to open up the ports to private investment and operation from 2002.

Junta de Administración Portuaria y de Desarrollo Económico de la Vertiente Atlántica (JAPDEVA): Calle 17, Avda 7, Apdo 8-5.330, 1000 San José; tel. 233-5301; state agency for the development of Atlantic ports; Exec. Pres. Ing. JORGE ARTURO CASTRO HERRERA.

Instituto Costarricense de Puertos del Pacífico (INCOP): Calle 36, Avda 3, Apdo 543, 1000 San José; tel. 223-7111; fax 223-9685; state agency for the development of Pacific ports; Exec. Pres. GERARDO MEDINA MADRIZ.

CIVIL AVIATION

Costa Rica's main international airport is the Juan Santamaría Airport, 16 km from San José at El Coco. Following a report by the US Federal Aviation Administration, the Government began negotiating a contract of expansion and modernization, to begin in 2001. There is a second international airport, the Daniel Oduber Quirós Airport, at Liberia and there are regional airports at Limón and Pavas (Tobías Bolaños Airport).

Aero Costa Rica: San Pedro, Montes de Oca, Apdo 1.328, San José; tel. 296-1111; fax 232-1815; regional carrier; Chair. CALIXTO CHAVEL; Gen. Man. JUAN FERNÁNDEZ.

Líneas Aéreas Costarricenses, SA—LACSA (Costa Rican Airlines): Edif. Lacsa, La Uruca, Apdo 1.531, San José; tel. 290-2727; fax 232-4178; internet www.flylatinamerica.com; f. 1945; operates international services within Latin America and to North America; Chair. ALONSO LARA; Pres. JOSÉ G. ROJAS.

Servicios Aéreos Nacionales, SA (SANSA): Paseo Colón, Centro Colón, Apdo 999, 1.007 San José; tel. 233-2714; fax 255-2176; subsidiary of LACSA; international, regional and domestic scheduled passenger and cargo services; Man. Dir CARLOS MANUEL DELGADO AGUILAR.

Servicios de Carga Aérea (SERCA): Aeropuerto Internacional Juan Santamaría, Apdo 6.855, San José; f. 1982; operates cargo service from San José.

Tourism

Costa Rica boasts a system of nature reserves and national parks unique in the world, which cover one-third of the country. The main tourist features are the Irazú and Poás volcanoes, the Orosí valley and the ruins of the colonial church at Ujarras. Tourists also visit San José, the capital, the Pacific beaches of Guanacaste and Puntarenas, and the Caribbean beaches of Limón. In 2001 there were numerous hotel and resort construction projects underway in the Guanacaste province. The project was being undertaken by the Instituto Costarricense de Turismo. Some 942,853 tourists visited Costa Rica in 1998, when tourism receipts totalled an estimated US $830m. In this year most visitors came from the USA (36.9% of the total) and Nicaragua (18.0%). There were 27,103 hotel rooms in Costa Rica in 1998.

Cámara Nacional de Turismo (Canatur): tel. 234-6222; fax 253-8102; e-mail info@tourism.co.cr; internet www.costarica.tourism .co.cr.

Instituto Costarricense de Turismo: Edif. Genaro Valverde, Calles 5 y 7, Avda 4, Apdo 777, 1000 San José; tel. 223-1733; fax 223-5107; internet www.tourism-costarica.com; f. 1955; Exec. Pres. Ing. CARLOS ROESCH CARRANZA.

CÔTE D'IVOIRE

(THE IVORY COAST)

Introductory Survey

Location, Climate, Language, Religion, Flag, Capital

The Republic of Côte d'Ivoire lies on the west coast of Africa, between Ghana to the east and Liberia to the west, with Guinea, Mali and Burkina Faso to the north. Average temperatures vary between 21°C and 30°C (70°F and 86°F). The main rainy season, from May to July, is followed by a shorter wet season in October–November. The official language is French, and a large number of African languages are also spoken. At the time of the 1988 census some 39% of the population were Muslims, 26% Christians (mainly Roman Catholics), and about 17% followed traditional beliefs. The national flag (proportions 3 by 2) has three equal vertical stripes, of orange, white and green. The political and administrative capital is Yamoussoukro, although most government ministries and offices remain in the former capital, Abidjan, which is the major centre for economic activity.

Recent History

Formerly a province of French West Africa, Côte d'Ivoire achieved self-government, within the French Community, in December 1958. Dr Félix Houphouët-Boigny, leader of the Parti démocratique de la Côte d'Ivoire–Rassemblement démocratique africain (PDCI–RDA), became Prime Minister in 1959. The country became fully independent on 7 August 1960; a new Constitution was adopted in October 1960, and Houphouët-Boigny became President in November.

Until 1990 the PDCI–RDA, founded in 1946, was Côte d'Ivoire's only legal political party. Despite constitutional provision for the existence of other political organizations, no opposition party was granted official recognition (although from November 1980 more than one candidate was permitted to contest each seat in the legislature, the Assemblée nationale), since Houphouët-Boigny maintained that a multi-party system would impede progress towards national unity. A high rate of economic growth (particularly during the 1970s), together with strong support from France, contributed, until the late 1980s, to the stability of the regime, and sporadic political unrest was without strong leadership. (A number of plots against the Government in the 1960s were later admitted by Houphouët-Boigny to have been fabricated as a means of strengthening support for the regime and removing potential rivals from positions of influence.)

In October 1985 the PDCI–RDA approved constitutional amendments abolishing the post of Vice-President of the Republic and allowing for the President of the Assemblée nationale to succeed the Head of State, on an interim basis, in the event of a vacancy. Later that month Houphouët-Boigny was re-elected President for a sixth five-year term. Municipal and legislative elections took place in November, and in January 1986 Henri Konan Bédié was re-elected to the presidency of the legislature.

In April 1986 it was announced that the country wished to be known internationally by its French name of Côte d'Ivoire, rather than by translations of it. The request was subsequently endorsed by the UN.

The announcement in early 1990 of austerity measures, in compliance with an IMF-sponsored programme, precipitated an unprecedented level of unrest. In April, as it became clear that the measures would fail to generate sufficient revenue to reduce Côte d'Ivoire's increasingly burdensome foreign debt, Houphouët-Boigny appointed Alassane Ouattara, the Governor of the Banque centrale des états de l'Afrique de l'ouest (the regional central bank), to chair a special commission whose task would be to formulate measures that would be both economically effective and politically acceptable. From May it was announced that hitherto unofficial political organizations were to be formally recognized, and many new parties were formed. A new Minister of the Economy and Finance, Daniel Kablan Duncan, was appointed in July.

Côte d'Ivoire's first contested presidential election was held on 28 October 1990. During the campaign the intervention of the security forces at several opposition rallies prompted accusations that the Government was seeking to impede democratization. Houphouët-Boigny—challenged by Laurent Gbagbo, the candidate of the Front populaire ivoirien (FPI)—was re-elected for a seventh term with the support of 81.7% of votes cast. The FPI alleged malpractice, and appealed unsuccessfully to the Supreme Court to declare the election invalid. In November the legislature approved two constitutional amendments. The first concerned the procedure to be adopted should the presidency become vacant, to the effect that the President of the Assemblée nationale would assume the functions of the President of the Republic until the expiry of the previous incumbent's mandate. Secondly, provision was made for the appointment of a Prime Minister, who would be accountable to the President; Ouattara was subsequently designated premier.

Almost 500 candidates, representing some 17 political parties, contested legislative elections on 25 November 1990. Opposition parties again accused the PDCI–RDA of electoral fraud. The PDCI–RDA returned 163 deputies to the 175-member Assemblée nationale; Gbagbo and eight other members of the FPI were elected, along with the leader of the Parti ivoirien des travailleurs (PIT), Francis Wodié, and two independent candidates. Bédié was re-elected President of the legislature. Ouattara's first Council of Ministers was named following the elections, in which the Prime Minister—assisted by Duncan—assumed personal responsibility for the economy.

Tensions between the authorities and the education sector were revived in May 1991, after security forces used violent methods to disperse a students' meeting at the University of Abidjan. In June the death of a student who had defied an order to boycott classes, following an attack by members of the Fédération estudiantine et scolaire de Côte d'Ivoire (FESCI), prompted the Government to order that FESCI be disbanded, and that the security forces be deployed at the campus. The situation deteriorated, however, as student unrest continued and academic staff began an indefinite strike. The Government's response to the report of a commission of inquiry into the disturbances, published in January 1992, provoked renewed violence. Houphouët-Boigny refused to subject the armed forces Chief of the General Staff, Brig.-Gen. Robert Gueï, or any member of the security forces to disciplinary proceedings, despite the commission's conclusion that Gueï was ultimately responsible for violent acts perpetrated by forces under his command. In February Gbagbo was among more than 100 people arrested during a violent anti-Government demonstration in Abidjan, and in March was one of nine opposition leaders sentenced to two-year prison sentences under a new presidential ordinance that rendered political leaders responsible for violent acts committed by their supporters. In late February the leader of FESCI was fined and sentenced to three years' imprisonment, convicted of reconstituting a banned organization and of responsibility for offences committed by students.

In July Houphouët-Boigny proclaimed an amnesty for all those convicted of political offences committed since 1990. However, the opposition protested that the amnesty nullified the right of appeal and exempted members of the security forces from charges relating to alleged offences committed during this period.

Houphouët-Boigny left Côte d'Ivoire in May 1993, and spent the following six months receiving medical treatment in France and Switzerland. As the President's health failed, controversy intensified concerning the issue of succession. Many senior politicians, including Ouattara and Gbagbo (both of whom were known to have presidential aspirations), asserted that the process defined in the Constitution effectively endorsed a 'hereditary presidency', since Bédié, like Houphouët-Boigny, was a member of the Baoulé ethnic group. Houphouët-Boigny died on 7 December. Later the same day Bédié announced that, in accordance with the Constitution, he was assuming the duties of President of the Republic with immediate effect. Ouattara initially refused to recognize Bédié's right of succession, but tendered his resignation two days later. Duncan was appointed as Prime Minister.

Several months of labour unrest were brought to an end by Houphouët-Boigny's death. In subsequent months Bédié appointed close associates to positions of influence in government, the judiciary and in the state-owned media. The new regime also used legislation, introduced under Houphouët-Boigny, to bring charges against several journalists deemed to have been disrespectful to Bédié or to other state officials. Bédié's position was further consolidated by his election to the chairmanship of the PDCI—RDA in April 1994, and by Ouattara's departure for the USA following his appointment to the post of Deputy Managing Director of the IMF. Disaffected members of the PDCI—RDA left the party in June to form what they termed a moderate, centrist organization, the Rassemblement des républicains (RDR); Ouattara formally announced his membership of the RDR in early 1995.

A new electoral code, adopted in December 1994, imposed new restrictions on eligibility for public office, notably stipulating that candidates for the presidency or for the Assemblée nationale be of direct Ivorian descent. The RDR protested that these restrictions might prevent Ouattara from contesting the presidency, since the former Prime Minister was of Burkinabè descent and would also be affected by the code's requirement that candidates have been continuously resident in Côte d'Ivoire for five years prior to seeking election. Opposition parties, grouped in a Front républicain (FR), organized a series of mass demonstrations in Abidjan to demand the withdrawal of the electoral code, the establishment of an independent electoral commission and a revision of voters' lists. Ouattara, who had been invited by the RDR to be the party's presidential candidate, subsequently announced that he would not contest the presidency in violation of the law. In September the Government imposed a three-month ban on political demonstrations. The FR countered that the ban violated the constitutional right to demonstrate, and protests persisted.

In October 1995 the FPI (which was to have been represented by Gbagbo) and the RDR (whose Secretary-General, Djény Kobina, was to have replaced Ouattara as the party's candidate) stated that they would not contest the election as long as the conditions were not 'clear and open'. Subsequent negotiations involving Bédié and opposition groups made no effective progress, as the FR refused to accept an offer to include opposition representatives on the commission responsible for scrutinizing voters' lists and election results as sufficient guarantee of the commission's autonomy, while the Government rejected the opposition's demand that the elections be postponed.

The presidential election took place on 22 October 1995, following a week of violence in several towns. The FR claimed that its campaign for an 'active boycott' of the poll had been largely successful (despite appeals by Wodié, Bédié's sole challenger, for the support of opposition sympathizers), while the Government claimed that voters had participated peacefully and in large numbers. Troops were deployed, ostensibly to prevent the disruption of voting by the opposition, although it was reported that polling had proceeded in only one of 60 designated centres in the FPI stronghold of Gagnoa, in the Centre-Ouest region. Bédié, with 95.25% of the valid votes cast, secured an overwhelming victory. While most areas remained calm following the election, there were reports of the persecution of Baoulé around Gagnoa by members of the local majority Bété ethnic group.

Prior to the legislative elections of 26 November 1995, representatives of both the FPI and the RDR were appointed to the electoral commission; both parties abandoned their threatened boycott of the poll, which proceeded generally without incident. However, disruption resulting from recent disturbances was cited as the reason for the postponement of polling in three of Gagnoa's four constituencies (including the constituency that was to have been contested by Gbagbo); moreover, Kobina's candidacy was disallowed, on the grounds that he had been unable to prove direct Ivorian descent. In December the Constitutional Council annulled the results of the elections in three constituencies, including the one seat in Gagnoa for which voting had been permitted. The PDCI—RDA thus held 146 seats, the RDR 14, and the FPI nine, indicating a notable loss of support for the PDCI—RDA in the Nord region in favour of the RDR.

In October 1995, shortly before the presidential election, Brig.-Gen. Guéï was replaced in his armed forces command and appointed as Minister of Employment and the Civil Service. In January 1996, as part of a ministerial reshuffle, Guéï became Minister of Sports, and the former Minister of Defence, Léon Konan Koffi, was appointed Minister of State responsible for Religious Affairs and Dialogue with the Opposition. Reports emerged in May 1996 of a coup attempt by members of the armed forces at the time of the civil unrest that preceded the 1995 presidential election. Guéï's apparent demotion to these posts and a further reorganization of government portfolios in August 1996, in which Guéï and Koffi left the Government, were interpreted as an indication of Bédié's desire to remove from positions of influence figures connected with the insecurity prior to the 1995 elections. In November the Government announced the dismissal or suspension of several members of the military, in accordance with investigations into what was now seemingly confirmed as a coup plot. In January 1997 Guéï was dismissed from the army, having been found to have committed 'serious disciplinary offences' in the discharge of his duties.

A commission of inquiry into the 1995 pre-election unrest was inaugurated in December 1996. The RDR and the FPI refused to take up their allotted seats, however, protesting that the opposition had been judged responsible in advance of the inquiry. By-elections for eight parliamentary seats, including those for which voting did not take place or was cancelled in 1995, took place in December 1996; the FPI won five seats, and the PDCI—RDA three.

From December 1996 the higher education sector was severely disrupted, as university students protested against the late payment of grants and demanded changes to the examinations system. The arrest of several members of FESCI (which remained outlawed) provoked further disturbances in early 1997. An order by Bédié to release all detained student activists in February, briefly restored calm, but student unrest resumed in April. National consultations on higher education began in September, apparently at Bédié's instigation, as a result of which the ban on FESCI was revoked.

Adama Coulibaly's acceptance of the post of Minister of Transport in a reorganization of the Council of Ministers in March 1998 was denounced by the RDR, of which he had been Deputy Secretary-General, and he was subsequently expelled from the party. Further government changes in August included the appointment of Wodié as Minister of Higher Education and Scientific Research.

In June 1998 RDR and FPI deputies boycotted a vote in the Assemblée nationale that approved substantial amendments to the Constitution. The opposition objected, in particular, to provisions conferring wider powers on the Head of State, including the right to delay elections, or the proclamation of election results, on the grounds of 'events, serious troubles or *force majeure*'. The presidential mandate was, furthermore, to be extended to seven years. Moreover, candidates for public office were henceforth constitutionally required to be Ivorian by birth, of direct Ivorian descent, and to have been continuously resident in Côte d'Ivoire for 10 years. The amendments included provisions for the establishment of an upper legislative chamber, the Sénat; two-thirds of its members were to be indirectly elected and the remainder appointed by the Head of State. In September 1998 Gbagbo and Kobina led a demonstration in Abidjan to denounce the amendments. Kobina died in October and Henrietta Dagba Diabaté assumed the post of Secretary-General of the RDR. Attending Kobina's funeral, Ouattara (who earlier in the year had announced that he would return to Côte d'Ivoire in 1999, upon the expiry of his contract with the IMF) announced his intention to contest the presidential election due in 2000. Ouattara expressed confidence that laws of filiation, nationality and residency which might prevent his candidacy would be altered.

In December 1998 the PDCI—RDA and the FPI reached an agreement on democracy and good governance, whereby the authorities agreed to an amnesty in respect of the 1995 'active boycott', together with new legislation relating to the funding of political parties during elections and the establishment of a national electoral commission.

There was renewed unrest involving FESCI from April 1999, as students and school pupils boycotted classes in support of demands regarding tuition fees and the disbursement of scholarships and other allowances. In May the Government ordered the closure of all university campuses, asserting that accommodation was, with the collusion of FESCI, being occupied by non-students, and that stockpiles of weapons had been found on campus. FESCI denied these allegations, and strike action proceeded in June. The boycott of classes was suspended later in the month following a meeting between Bédié and FESCI, pending efforts to secure a lasting settlement of the education crisis. However, tensions escalated following the arrest, in August, of Charles Blé Goudé, the FESCI leader, on charges arising from the murder of a trader, forced entry into the Prime Minister's residence, destruction of property and looting. It was reported that more than 200 students had hitherto been given custodial sentences in connection with these events. In October, however, Bédié granted amnesty to students detained in relation to the FESCI boycott.

The Council of Ministers was reorganized in August 1999, following the dismissal of a number of ministers, including, the Minister of Public Health, Maurice Kakou Guikahue, whose departure was apparently connected to the misappropriation of aid, from the European Union (EU, see p. 181), allocated for health care projects. The discovery of the apparent fraud led to the suspension of much EU assistance, which, combined with the withholding of IMF funding as a result, *inter alia*, of suspicions of fraud at the state marketing body for cocoa and coffee, resulted in a loss of much external budgetary support and a depletion of the country's capital reserves.

Alassane Ouattara returned to Côte d'Ivoire in July 1999 and, in August, was appointed to the newly created post of Chairman of the RDR; Ouattara again announced his intention to contest the 2000 presidential election. However, the authorities disputed the validity of documents submitted by Ouattara as proof of his Ivorian citizenship, and in October, following an investigation by the office of the public prosecutor, it was announced that Ouattara's nationality certificate (which had been issued in the previous month by a court in Dimbokro) had been annulled. The announcement provoked violent demonstrations in Abidjan, after which a number of senior RDR leaders were arrested. Diabaté was among several party activists found guilty of inciting violence and given custodial sentences. In December a warrant was issued for Ouattara's arrest on charges of fraud and use of fraud in the procurement of identity papers, following the announcement that he would not, as previously intended, shortly return to Côte d'Ivoire from France, where he had spent much of the previous two months.

Bédié was overthrown in late December 1999, after a mutiny by soldiers demanding salary increases and the payment of outstanding arrears rapidly escalated into a *coup d'état*. President Bédié had initially sought to appease the soldiers by promising an amelioration of pay and conditions, but the protesters had extended their demands to include the reinstatement of Brig.-Gen. Robert Gueï to the position of armed forces Chief of General Staff, which he had held prior to the 1995 presidential election. The soldiers seized control of many public buildings in Abidjan, and on 24 December Gueï announced that he had assumed power at the head of a Comité national de salut public (CNSP), and that the Constitution and its institutions had been suspended. Constitutional review and fresh legislative elections were promised, and the country's opposition parties were invited to submit nominations for an interim government, pending the restoration of constitutional order. Bédié sought refuge in his native town of Daoukro, leaving in early January 2000 for Togo and subsequently for France.

The unexpected coup was, initially, condemned internationally, but apparently largely welcomed within Côte d'Ivoire, where the Bédié regime had been increasingly regarded as authoritarian and corrupt. None the less, Gueï encountered considerable difficulty in achieving his early objective of constituting a broadly-based government, as the CNSP, having released the imprisoned RDR leaders, was at first perceived as being strongly supportive of Ouattara, particularly as one prominent member, Intendant-General Lassana Palenfo, had previously served in Ouattara's Government. Consequently, the FPI withdrew its nominees from the coalition Government appointed in early January 2000, although subsequent negotiations between the CNSP and the FPI resulted in the party attaining a larger number of ministerial posts than any other. The PDCI—RDA had declined to propose ministers, and the appointment of two representatives of the former ruling party by Gueï was not officially approved by the party.

In late January a constitutional review body was inaugurated and Gueï announced that presidential and legislative elections would be held by 31 October, following a constitutional referendum in July. While the response of the international community to the military takeover had become increasingly positive in the weeks following the coup, both the Organization

of African Unity and the Economic Community of West African States (ECOWAS, see p. 170) continued to demand a return to constitutional government by the end of June. Political parties proceeded to confirm their presidential candidates, while the CNSP prohibited political gatherings until after the referendum. Elements within the PDCI—RDA campaigned for Gueï to stand as the party's candidate, although no announcement was forthcoming.

The draft Constitution was presented in May 2000, provoking considerable controversy, as it demanded that presidential candidates be of only Ivorian nationality and be born of Ivorian parents. Allegations persisted that Ouattara had previously held a Burkinabè passport and had a Burkinabè mother. Following protests from the RDR, Gueï dismissed all ministers of that party, with the exception of Diabaté, in a government reshuffle. Seydou Elimane Diarra, hitherto President of the Chambre de Commerce et d'Industrie de Côte d'Ivoire, was appointed Prime Minister. Also in May the authorities in Côte d'Ivoire issued an international warrant for the arrest of Bédié (in exile in France) on charges of embezzlement.

In early July soldiers led two days of disturbances in Abidjan and Bouaké to demand bonus payments in recognition of their role in the December coup. The authorities arrested 35 soldiers, accusing them of attempting to overthrow the CNSP, and briefly detained four members of the RDR on charges of complicity in the mutiny. A number of soldiers subsequently received custodial sentences. The revised Constitution was endorsed by 86.5% of votes cast in a referendum on 23 and 24 July, with turn-out estimated at 56%. Notably, the Constitution granted immunity from prosecution to members of the CNSP and all those involved in the *coup d'état*.

During mid-2000 19 candidates presented themselves as candidates for the presidential election, which was scheduled for 17 September. Among them was Ouattara, who asserted that he complied fully with all of the conditions of eligibility for the election. In August Gueï refuted earlier reports that he would stand as the candidate for the PDCI—RDA and announced that he would contest the election as an independent, reportedly with the support of the country's traditional chiefs. France and the USA expressed concern that Gueï's participation would be liable to render the election less free and fair. Meanwhile, the PDCI—RDA selected former Minister of the Interior Emile Constant Bombet as their presidential candidate, in preference to Bédié among others. In late August the election was postponed until 22 October, owing to organizational difficulties.

In mid-September 2000 an attack on Gueï's residence, in which two members of the presidential guard were killed, was repelled by troops loyal to the President. On 22 September Gueï effected a government reshuffle, dismissing three ministers, including Palenfo and Abdoulaye Coulibaly, both leading members of Gueï's regime. Believed to be allies of Ouattara, they were accused of involvement in the attack on Gueï's residence and subsequently sought refuge in the Nigerian Embassy in Abidjan. A further minor cabinet reshuffle, on 27 September, ensured that the FPI was now the only political party represented in the transitional Government, with six ministers.

In early October 2000 the Supreme Court announced that only five of the 19 presidential candidates complied with the conditions of eligibility. Rejected candidates included Ouattara, as had been widely anticipated, Bombet, who was to be investigated for alleged embezzlement, and several unofficial representatives of the PDCI—RDA, most notably Bédié. Of the five candidates permitted to stand, only Gueï and Gbagbo were regarded as capable of eliciting popular support; allegations that the two men had undertaken a private agreement of co-operation had been encouraged by the increasingly prominent role of the FPI in Gueï's Government and by Gbagbo's subsequent refusal to comment on the exclusion of other candidates from the presidential election. The remaining approved three candidates were Nicolas Dioulo, an independent, Wodié, for the PIT, and Théodore Eg Mel, the leader of the Union démocratique de la Côte d'Ivoire (UDCI). Leaders of the PDCI—RDA and the RDR urged an electoral boycott in protest at the Supreme Court's decision, with supporters of the RDR further calling for a two-day general strike. Dissent within the PDCI—RDA, which had been apparent since the December coup, was emphasized by reports that between 30 and 75 of the party's 145 deputies supported Gueï's presidential candidacy.

The two weeks preceding the presidential election were characterized by heightened unrest, particularly in Abidjan, leading to the imposition of curfews and a state of emergency. Nevertheless, voting proceeded generally without incident on 22 October 2000. Preliminary results indicated that Gbagbo had received a greater percentage of votes cast than Gueï. However, on 24 October the Ministry of the Interior announced the dissolution of the national electoral commission, on the grounds of inefficiency, and declared Gueï the winner of the presidential election. The Government claimed that certain, unspecified, political parties had instigated campaigns of fraudulent voting and obstruction, and announced that, following the readjustment of the results, to exclude the allegedly fraudulent votes, Gueï, with 52.7% of the votes cast, had defeated Gbagbo, with 41.0%. These results were widely condemned as fraudulent, both domestically and internationally. Prime Minister Seydou Elimane Diarra had resigned in protest on 23 October, and demonstrations in Abidjan, Bouaké and San Pedro were held to demand that Gueï step down in favour of Gbagbo, who had gained a majority of votes, according to the unadjusted results held by the electoral commission. Although Gueï declared a renewed state of emergency on 24 October, on the following day soldiers joined the demonstrators, and the head of the presidential guard declared that he would no longer support Gueï. Following the outbreak of heavy fighting between rival army factions in the military barracks in Abidjan, and a declaration of support for Gbagbo by the Chief of Staff of the Armed Forces, Gueï fled and Gbagbo declared himself President.

According to the official figures released by the electoral commission, and confirmed by the Supreme Court, Gbagbo had secured 59.36% of the valid votes cast, while Gueï had received only 32.72%; turn-out was estimated at 33.2%. Participation was notably low in the Muslim and RDR-supporting regions in the north of the country, as well as in Yamoussoukro and other strongholds of the PDCI—RDA, casting further doubt on the legitimacy of Gbagbo's win. Additionally, concern was raised that Gbagbo had voiced support, during his campaign, for the notion of strengthening national identity, or 'ivoirité', in similar terms to those used previously by Bédié and Gueï. It was feared that this might inflame inter-ethnic tensions within the country. Gbagbo was inaugurated as President on 26 October.

Although the PDCI—RDA accepted Gbagbo's victory, the RDR continued to demand the annulment and re-organization of the election. In the three days following Gbagbo's accession to the presidency violent clashes between the security forces and RDR demonstrators reportedly resulted in more than 170 deaths. The majority of those killed were believed to be Muslims and members of the northern Dioula ethnic group. The discovery of a mass grave, which contained the bodies of some 57 people who had been shot dead in Yopougon, a primarily Islamic suburb of Abidjan, prompted the Government to announce an investigation into the violence. The RDR demanded the establishment of an international commission of inquiry to condemn the perpetrators of the killings.

On 27 October Gbagbo appointed a new Council of Ministers, including members of the FPI, the PDCI—RDA and the PIT. (The RDR stated that it would await legislative elections in December before participating in any coalition government.) Affi N'Guessan, the manager of Gbagbo's election campaign and Minister of Industry and Tourism in the outgoing Government, was named as Prime Minister. Gbagbo also appointed a new military Chief of Staff and a new Supreme Commander for the Gendarmerie. In mid-November Gueï announced his recognition of Gbagbo as President, and Gbagbo stated that he regarded both Gueï and Bédié as worthy recipients of the honours due to any former Head of State.

In early November 2000 legislative elections were scheduled for 10 December. The PDCI—RDA announced that it would seek closer co-operation with the FPI. At the beginning of December the Supreme Court ruled that the candidacy of Ouattara, who was to have represented the RDR in Kong, his native town, was ineligible. The RDR urged an 'active boycott' of the elections in protest, and also withdrew its members from the Comité de médiation pour la réconciliation nationale (CMRN), which had been established by Gbagbo in November. However, a minority grouping within the RDR, the Mouvement des militants et candidats modérés (MMCM—RDR), announced that it would participate in the elections. The decision again to exclude Ouattara from seeking election provoked further unrest, particularly in Kong, prompting the Government to announce that the RDR was intending to instigate a *coup d'état*. At least 30 people were estimated to have died in clashes between supporters of Ouattara and the police in the first week of December, and several senior RDR officials were detained. The press made

allegations of harassment of residents of Burkinabè origin and human rights abuses by the security forces. Subsequent estimates suggested that more than 200 people had died in the intermittent clashes in the last three months of 2000, following the presidential election. Meanwhile, Ouattara fled to France, following the death of his personal secretary, who had been beaten by police officers, according to opposition sources. A recommendation by the CMRN that the elections be postponed for one week nation-wide, and indefinitely in Kong was rejected by the Government and the PDCI—RDA. The UN, the Organization of African Unity (OAU) and the EU announced that they would withdraw their observers from the legislative elections in response to the unrest and the exclusion of Ouattara.

Legislative elections proceeded in relatively peaceful circumstances on 10 December 2000, although clashes between RDR supporters and the security forces prevented voting in 28 northern constituencies. Electoral turn-out was low, at 31.5%. The FPI secured 96 of the 225 seats in the Assemblée nationale, thus becoming the largest legislative party. The PDCI—RDA won 77 seats, the PIT four and independent candidates 17, while the MMCM—RDR, the Mouvement des forces d'avenir and the UDCI all obtained one seat each. Elections in the constituencies where voting had been disrupted were to take place on 14 January 2001.

One week before the remaining elections dissident soldiers seized control of the state radio and television station in Abidjan, amid incidences of explosions and heavy gunfire across the city, in what was widely regarded as a further coup attempt. Troops loyal to the Government suppressed the uprising within several hours. More than 30 people, mainly from the north of the country, were subsequently arrested in connection with the insurgency. A number of the detainees were apparently members of a traditional northern hunting militia, known as the Dozos, which was regarded as being sympathetic to the RDR, although the RDR denied any involvement. The Government also accused unspecified neighbouring countries of having encouraged the failed coup, prompting attacks on properties owned by foreigners, particularly Guineans. During early 2001 a number of RDR members, including senior officials such as Diabaté, were arrested and accused of involvement in the coup attempt. In February Palenfo and Coulibaly, who had been arrested in November 2000 on charges related to the attack on Gueï's residence in September, were further charged with the embezzlement of funds and, in the case of Palenfo, with the illegal distribution of weapons. In January 2001 Gbagbo announced that a warrant had been issued for the arrest of Gueï, although his whereabouts remained unknown. The security forces raided the offices of the independent newspaper, *Le Jour*, in February, reportedly acting on suspicions that the newspaper was harbouring mercenaries and weapons to be used against the Government.

Meanwhile, the remaining legislative elections took place, as scheduled, on 14 January, largely without incident. The PDCI—RDA gained 17 of the 26 contested seats, increasing their overall representation in the Assemblée nationale to 94 seats, only two less than the FPI, which significantly won no new seats. Of the remaining nine seats, independent candidates won five, and the MMCM—RDR four. Two seats in Kong remained uncontested, in the absence of presiding officials. Only 13.3% of the electorate participated in the elections, with the turn-out below 4% in some regions. This reduced the nation-wide rate of participation in the legislative elections to 31.5%, suggesting that the RDR's campaign for a boycott of the elections in the had been widely supported.

The legislative balance of power remained unclear as the new parliamentary session opened on 22 January. Mamadou Koulibaly, hitherto Minister of the Economy and Finance, was elected President of the Assemblée nationale, with the support of both his own party, the FPI, and the PDCI—RDA. It soon emerged that seven of the 22 independents elected had been financed by the PDCI—RDA and were to return to the party. A further 14 independents, PDCI—RDA dissidents who had left the party to support Gueï, formed a parliamentary alliance with the FPI, having previously announced their intention to form a new party together with some 50 former members of the PDCI—RDA. This new centre-right party, the Union pour la démocratie et la paix, was established in February.

N'Guessan was retained as Prime Minister in a new Council of Ministers appointed on 24 January; some 18 of the 28 ministers were members of the FPI, while six were from the PDCI—RDA, two from the PIT and two were independents.

The RDR performed well in municipal elections on 25 March 2001, securing control of 64 of Côte d'Ivoire's 197 communes, compared with 59 for the PDCI—RDA, 38 for independents, 34 for the FPI and one for the PIT. (Voting in the remaining commune, Zouan-Hounien, was abandoned, following violent clashes between rival groups.) In April, however, the leaders of 21 of the independently-held communes announced their decision to join the PDCI—RDA, thereby giving that party control of 80 communes overall.

President Houphouët-Boigny was widely respected as an active participant in regional and international affairs, although his commitment to a policy of dialogue between black Africa and the apartheid regime in South Africa prompted frequent criticism. In April 1992 (once the process of dismantling apartheid had begun) Côte d'Ivoire became the first black African country to establish diplomatic relations with South Africa. Moreover, in the final years of his life Houphouët-Boigny's role in the civil conflict in Liberia (see below) was a focus of considerable external scrutiny.

Côte d'Ivoire's foreign policy orientation remained largely unaltered under Bédié. Relations with France, the country's principal trading partner and provider of bilateral assistance, which have been close since independence, were apparently enhanced following the election of the Gaullist Jacques Chirac to the presidency in May 1995—Chirac's predecessor, François Mitterrand, having latterly shown considerable support for Gbagbo and the FPI. French reaction to Gbagbo's election as President in October 2000 was divided, largely along party lines. Chirac and one of the minor parties in the governing coalition, Les Verts, demanded that the elections be rerun, incorporating those candidates who had been excluded from participating. The leading party in the Government, the Parti socialiste, while critical of these exclusions, welcomed Gbagbo's accession to power as a positive move towards democracy. Following meetings between Gbagbo and Chirac at the Franco-African summit in Yaoundé, Cameroon, in January 2001, France announced that full co-operation with Côte d'Ivoire, which had been suspended following the *coup d'état* of December 1999, would be restored. Co-operation in matters pertaining to the military and the police would, however, remain suspended, pending further consideration.

The importance of '*ivoirité*', or national identity, in the domestic policies of Bédié, Guëi and Gbagbo, has been a cause for concern in international relations, particularly with other West African states. Notably, relations with Burkina Faso have deteriorated, as Burkinabè migrants in Côte d'Ivoire have increasingly suffered from discrimination. In February 2001 Burkinabè officials estimated that about 10,000 natives of Burkina and of Mali were leaving Côte d'Ivoire for their countries of origin every week. Relations with Senegal were also strained as a result of widely-publicized comments by the Senegalese President, Abdoulaye Wade, in January 2001, to the effect that Burkinabè residents in Côte d'Ivoire experienced greater racial discrimination than African residents in Europe. The Senegalese Government subsequently apologized for any 'misunderstanding' caused by Wade's remarks, which had provoked violent anti-Senegalese protests in Abidjan.

Despite evidence to the contrary, Houphouët-Boigny consistently denied suggestions that his Government was supporting Charles Taylor's rebel National Patriotic Front of Liberia (NPFL), which was instrumental in the overthrow of President Samuel Doe of that country in mid-1990 (q.v.). The presence in Côte d'Ivoire of a large number of refugees from Liberia was increasingly cited by the Ivorian authorities as a cause of the perceived escalation in insecurity in the country, and periodic incursions on to Ivorian territory by members of armed factions in the Liberian conflict provoked considerable disquiet. In July 1995 Côte d'Ivoire, which had hitherto promoted the full integration of refugees into Ivorian society, announced the establishment of the first reception centre for Liberian refugees at Guiglo. The installation of elected institutions in Liberia in 1997 facilitated the repatriation of refugees. The office of the UN High Commissioner for Refugees put the total number of refugees in Côte d'Ivoire at 135,600 at the end of 1999, compared with 327,300 at the end of 1996. Liberia rejected an appeal for asylum from Guëi following Gbagbo's election as President in October 2000; in December Taylor refuted a declaration by Gbagbo that Guëi was in Liberia, recruiting mercenaries. In January 2001 it was announced that 13 suspected Liberian dissidents were to be tried in Danane, Côte d'Ivoire, on charges of illegally entering Côte d'Ivoire from Liberia with weapons.

Government

Under the terms of the Constitution of July 2000, executive power is vested in the President, as Head of State, who is appointed by direct universal suffrage for a term of five years, renewable only once. The President appoints a Prime Minister, and on the latter's recommendation, a Council of Ministers. Legislative power is held by the Assemblée nationale, which is elected for a term of five years. The country is divided into 16 Regions, and further sub-divided into 49 Departments, each with its own elected Council.

Defence

In August 2000 Côte d'Ivoire's active armed forces comprised an army of 6,800 men, a navy of about 900, an air force of 700, a presidential guard of 1,100 and a gendarmerie of 4,400. There was also a 1,500-strong militia. Reserve forces numbered 12,000 men. Military service is by selective conscription and lasts for six months. France supplies equipment and training, and maintains a military presence in Côte d'Ivoire (500 men in 2000). The defence budget for 1999 was 95,000m. francs CFA.

Economic Affairs

In 1998, according to estimates by the World Bank, Côte d'Ivoire's gross national product (GNP), measured at average 1996–98 prices, was US $10,196m., equivalent to $700 per head (or $1,484 on an international purchasing-power parity basis). During 1990–98, it was estimated, GNP per head increased at an average annual rate of 1.4% in real terms, while the population increased by an average of 3.1% per year. GNP in 1999 was estimated at $10,400m., equivalent to $710 per head. During 1990–99 Côte d'Ivoire's gross domestic product (GDP) increased by an average of 3.7% per year, in real terms. According to the IMF, real GDP increased by 4.5% in 1998 and by an estimated 2.8% in 1999.

Agriculture (including forestry and fishing) contributed an estimated 27.0% of GDP in 1999, and employed about 50.3% of the labour force in that year. Côte d'Ivoire is the world's foremost producer of cocoa, and exports of cocoa and related products contributed an estimated 35.5% of total export earnings in 1999. Côte d'Ivoire is also among the world's largest producers and exporters of coffee, although the value of exports of coffee beans in 1999 was some 46.1% lower than in 1998. Other major cash crops include cotton, rubber, bananas and pineapples. The principal subsistence crops are maize, yams, cassava, plantains and, increasingly, rice (although large quantities of the last are still imported). Excessive exploitation of the country's forest resources has led to a decline in the importance of this sector, although measures have now been instigated to preserve remaining forests. Abidjan is among sub-Saharan Africa's principal fishing ports; however, the participation of Ivorian fishing fleets is minimal. During 1990–99 agricultural GDP increased by an average of 1.8% per year.

Industry (including mining, manufacturing, construction and power) contributed an estimated 27.4% of GDP in 1999. According to UN estimates, 11.5% of the labour force were employed in the sector in 1994. During 1990–99 industrial GDP increased by an average of 5.9% per year.

Mining contributed only an estimated 0.3% of GDP in 1999. The sector's contribution was, however, expected to increase considerably following the commencement, in the mid-1990s, of commercial exploitation of important offshore reserves of petroleum and natural gas. Gold and diamonds are also mined, although illicit production of the latter has greatly exceeded commercial output. There is believed to be significant potential for the development of nickel deposits, and there are also notable reserves of manganese, iron ore and bauxite.

The manufacturing sector, which contributed an estimated 15.9% of GDP in 1999, is dominated by agro-industrial activities (such as the processing of cocoa, coffee, cotton, palm kernels, pineapples and fish). Crude petroleum is refined at Abidjan, while the tobacco industry uses mostly imported tobacco. During 1990–98 manufacturing GDP increased by an average of 3.7% per year.

Almost two-thirds of Côte d'Ivoire's electricity generation in 1999 was derived from thermal sources, the remainder being derived mainly from hydroelectric installations. Through the exploitation, from 1995, of indigenous reserves of natural gas, the country expected to generate sufficient energy for its own requirements by 2000, and for regional export thereafter. Imports of petroleum products (including crude oil for refining) accounted for 18.9% of the value of total imports in 1999.

An important aim of economic policy in the late 1990s was the expansion of the services sector, which contributed an estimated 45.7% of GDP in 1999, and (according to UN estimates) employed 37.4% of the labour force in 1994. The transformation of Abidjan's stock market into a regional exchange for the member states of the Union économique et monétaire ouest-africaine (UEMOA, see p. 211) was expected to enhance the city's status as a centre for financial services. In addition, emphasis was placed on the revival of tourism as a major source of foreign exchange. Abidjan is also central to regional communications and trade. The GDP of the sector increased by an average of 3.9% per year in 1990–99.

In 1998 Côte d'Ivoire recorded a visible trade surplus of US $1,870.0m., although there was a deficit of $312.6m. on the current account of the balance of payments. In 1999 the principal source of imports was France (which supplied 25.9% of total imports); Italy and the USA were also notable suppliers. France was the principal market for exports in 1999 (taking 14.4% of total exports), followed by the Netherlands, the USA and Mali. The principal exports in 1999 were cocoa and related products, petroleum products, fish products, sawnwood, and coffee and related products. The principal imports in the same year were petroleum products, mechanical capital goods, electrical capital goods, fish and shellfish, and cereals.

Côte d'Ivoire's overall budget deficit in 1999 was estimated at 202,300m. francs CFA (equivalent to 2.9% of GDP). The country's total external debt was US $14,852m. at the end of 1998, of which $12,362m. was long-term public debt. In that year the cost of debt-servicing was equivalent to 26.1% of the value of exports of goods and services. The annual rate of inflation averaged 2.7% in 1990–93. Consumer prices increased by an average of 26.1% in 1994 (following the devaluation of the currency at the beginning of the year); the inflation rate slowed to an annual average of 14.3% in 1995, and averaged 3.2% in 1996–99. Consumer prices increased by 2.4% in 2000. Some 114,880 persons were registered as unemployed at the end of 1992.

Côte d'Ivoire is a member of numerous regional and international organizations, including the Economic Community of West African States (ECOWAS, see p. 170), the West African organs of the Franc Zone (see p. 210), the African Petroleum Producers' Association (APPA, see p. 303), the Association of Coffee Producing Countries (ACPC, see p. 303), the International Cocoa Organization (ICCO, see p. 304), the International Coffee Organization (see p. 304) and the Conseil de l'Entente (see p. 307). The African Development Bank (see p. 120) has its headquarters in Abidjan.

In 1995–98 Côte d'Ivoire enjoyed annual GDP growth in excess of the rate of population increase. This was in large part attributable to the 50% devaluation of the CFA franc in 1994, which had increased demand for traditional exports and stimulated growth. The liberalization of the cocoa and coffee sector in the late 1990s, with IMF support, under its Enhanced Structural Adjustment Facility (ESAF), had been intended to reduce vulnerability to fluctuations in world prices. However, full liberalization and the restructuring of the former state marketing body for the sector coincided with a sharp fall in international prices for cocoa. Furthermore, IMF funding was suspended from late 1998, as a result of Côte d'Ivoire's failure to comply with ESAF targets. This, compounded by the suspension of assistance by the European Union (EU), following revelations of the misappropriation of aid, meant that actual receipts of foreign budgetary assistance for 1999 stood at about 10% of the level originally forecast. Thus, by the time of the *coup d'état* of December 1999, Côte d'Ivoire's financial situation was precarious. Under Guëi the economy deteriorated further. A low level of direct investment reflected a continued absence of support from Côte d'Ivoire's principal external creditors, while there was a steep decline in the market value of cocoa and coffee. In October 2000 the World Bank suspended payment of all outstanding credits to Côte d'Ivoire and announced that it would finance no further projects, following a failure to repay debt totalling US $39.8m.

In January 2001 the Government announced its intention to seek aid from the EU and from France to help repay its debts to the World Bank. None the less, in the same month Côte d'Ivoire was notably omitted from a list of 19 African states that were to benefit from the cancellation of bilateral debt by France. Political uncertainty and growing inter-ethnic tensions are among significant factors inhibiting the rate of economic growth. In late 2000 it was announced that the port of Abidjan was losing some 30% of its trade to neighbouring countries, owing to instability. Disputes over land tenure between Ivorians and Malian and Burkinabè residents in the cocoa-growing regions of south-western Côte d'Ivoire, coupled with the prospect of large-scale emigration prompted by inter-ethnic hostility, further threatened the stability of an agricultural economy historically largely dependant on an immigrant work-force.

Social Welfare

Medical services are organized by the State. In 1996, according to estimates by the World Health Organization, there were 9.0 physicians, 31.2 nurses and 15.0 midwives per 100,000 population. There is a minimum wage for workers in industry and commerce. Draft legislation, which would guarantee a degree of free health care to all, was to be considered by the Assemblée nationale during 2001. Total government expenditure on health in 1999 was estimated at 66,100m. francs CFA, equivalent to 5.5% of total spending (excluding expenditure on the external debt). Expenditure by the Caisse nationale de prévoyance sociale and the Caisse générale de retraite des agents de l'Etat was estimated at 90,400m. francs CFA in 1999.

Education

At the time of the 1988 census adult illiteracy averaged 65.9% (males 55.6%; females 76.6%); UNESCO estimated the average in 1995 to be 60.0% (males 51.3%; females 69.4%). Education at all levels is available free of charge. Primary education, which is officially compulsory for six years between the ages of seven and 13 years, begins at six years of age and lasts for six years. Total enrolment at primary schools in 1996/97 included 55% of children in the relevant age-group (males 63%; females 47%). The Ivorian Government's long-term objective is to provide primary education for all children by 2010. Secondary education, from the age of 12, lasts for up to seven years, comprising a first cycle of four years and a second cycle of three years. In 1996/97 total enrolment at secondary schools was equivalent to 24% of children in the relevant age-group (males 33%; females 16%). The National University at Abidjan has six faculties, and university-level facilities have been constructed in Yamoussoukro. Some 43,147 students were enrolled at university-level institutions in 1994/95. Expenditure on education in 1999 was estimated at 303,700m. francs CFA, equivalent to 25.3% of total government expenditure (excluding spending on the public debt).

Public Holidays

2001: 1 January (New Year's Day), 6 March* (Id al-Adha, Feast of the Sacrifice), 13 April (Good Friday), 16 April (Easter Monday), 1 May (Labour Day), 24 May (Ascension Day), 4 June (Whit Monday), 7 August (National Day), 15 August (Assumption), 1 November (All Saints' Day), 7 December (Félix Houphouët-Boigny Remembrance Day), 17 December (Id al-Fitr, end of Ramadan), 25 December (Christmas).

2002: 1 January (New Year's Day), 23 February* (Id al-Adha, Feast of the Sacrifice), 29 March (Good Friday), 1 April (Easter Monday), 1 May (Labour Day), 9 May (Ascension Day), 20 May (Whit Monday), 7 August (National Day), 15 August (Assumption), 1 November (All Saints' Day), 6 December (Id al-Fitr, end of Ramadan), 7 December (Félix Houphouët-Boigny Remembrance Day), 25 December (Christmas).

* These holidays are dependent on the Islamic lunar calendar and may vary by one or two days from the dates given.

Weights and Measures

The metric system is in force.

Statistical Survey

Source (unless otherwise stated): Institut National de la Statistique, BP V55, Abidjan; tel. 20-21-05-38.

Area and Population

AREA, POPULATION AND DENSITY

Area (sq km)	322,462*
Population (census results)	
30 April 1975	6,702,866
1 March 1988	
Males	5,527,343
Females	5,288,351
Total	10,815,694
Population (UN estimates at mid-year)	
1997	14,064,000
1998	14,292,000
1999	14,526,000
Density (per sq km) at mid-1999	45.0

* 124,503 sq miles.

POPULATION BY ETHNIC GROUP (1988 census)

Ethnic group	Number	%
Akan	3,251,227	30.1
Voltaïque	1,266,235	11.7
Mane Nord	1,236,129	11.4
Krou	1,136,291	10.5
Mane Sud	831,840	7.7
Naturalized Ivorians	51,146	0.5
Others	3,039,035	28.1
Unknown	3,791	0.0
Total	**10,815,694**	**100.0**

Source: UN, *Demographic Yearbook.*

POPULATION BY REGION (1988 census)

Region	Population
Centre	815,664
Centre-Est	300,407
Centre-Nord	915,269
Centre-Ouest	1,542,945
Nord	745,816
Nord-Est	514,134
Nord-Ouest	522,247
Ouest	968,267
Sud	3,843,249
Sud-Ouest	647,696
Total	**10,815,694**

Source: UN, *Demographic Yearbook.*

Note: In January 1997 the Government adopted legislation whereby Côte d'Ivoire's regions were to be renamed. The new regions (with their regional capitals) were to be: Lagoon (Abidjan), Sassandra supérieur (Daloa), Savannah (Korhogo), Vallée de Bandama (Bouaké), Lacs (Yamoussoukro), Comoé central (Abengourou), Montagnes (Man), Zanzan (Bondoukou), Cavally inférieur (San Pedro), Denguélé (Odienné), Marahoué (Bouaflé), Nzi Comoé (Dimbroko), Comoé sud (Aboisso), Worodougou (Seguéla), Bandama sud (Divo), Agneby (Agboville).

PRINCIPAL TOWNS (population at 1988 census)

Abidjan*	1,929,079	Korhogo	109,445
Bouaké	329,850	Yamoussoukro*	106,786
Daloa	121,842		

* The process of transferring the official capital from Abidjan to Yamoussoukro began in 1983.

Source: UN, *Demographic Yearbook.*

BIRTHS AND DEATHS (UN estimates, annual averages)

	1980–85	1985–90	1990–95
Birth rate (per 1,000)	50.1	45.6	38.9
Death rate (per 1,000)	16.0	14.8	14.9

Expectation of life (UN estimates, years at birth, 1990–95): 48.9 (males 47.9; females 50.2).

Source: UN, *World Population Prospects: The 1998 Revision.*

ECONOMICALLY ACTIVE POPULATION

Mid-1999 (estimates in '000): Agriculture, etc. 2,891; Total 5,742 (Source: FAO).

Agriculture

PRINCIPAL CROPS ('000 metric tons)

	1997	1998	1999
Maize	576	573	571
Millet	65	65*	65*
Sorghum	19	19*	19*
Rice (paddy)	1,287	1,197	1,162
Sweet potatoes	36	36*	36*
Cassava (Manioc)	1,699	1,692	1,673
Yams	2,986	2,921	2,923
Taro (Coco yam)	374	368	365
Pulses*	8	8	8
Tree nuts	27	34*	34*
Sugar cane*	1,350	1,155	1,155
Palm kernels*	32	39	35
Groundnuts (in shell)	147	145	144
Coconuts*	221	193	193
Tomatoes	137	130	130*
Aubergines (Eggplants)*	40	40	40
Chillies and peppers (green)	21	21*	21*
Other vegetables*	343	343	343
Oranges	29	29*	29*
Other citrus fruit*	28	28	28
Bananas	227	234	241
Plantains	1,441	1,410	1,405
Mangoes	9	9*	9*
Pineapples	261	198	226
Other fruit*	14	14	14
Coffee (green)	279	332	365
Cocoa beans	1,119	1,120	1,153
Tobacco (leaves)*	10	10	10
Cotton (lint)	114	130	130*
Natural rubber (dry weight)	113	116	119

* FAO estimate(s).

Source: FAO.

LIVESTOCK ('000 head, year ending September)

	1997	1998*	1999*
Cattle	1,312	1,330	1,330
Pigs	271	275	275
Sheep	1,347	1,370	1,370
Goats	1,053	1,070	1,070
Poultry	31,059	29,000	29,000

* FAO estimates.

Source: FAO.

LIVESTOCK PRODUCTS ('000 metric tons)

	1997	1998	1999
Beef and veal	38	46	46
Mutton and lamb	5	6	6
Goat meat	5	5	5
Pig meat	13	13	13
Poultry meat	55	51	51
Other meat	28	28	28
Cows' milk	23	24	24
Poultry eggs*	16	16	16
Cattle hides	5	6	6
Sheepskins	1	1	1
Goatskins	1	1	1

* FAO estimates.

Source: FAO.

Forestry

ROUNDWOOD REMOVALS ('000 cubic metres, excluding bark)

	1996	1997	1998
Sawlogs, veneer logs and logs for sleepers	2,081	2,054	2,245
Other industrial wood	871	887	901
Fuel wood	9,799	9,975	10,137
Total	12,751	12,916	13,283

Source: FAO, *Yearbook of Forest Products.*

SAWNWOOD PRODUCTION

('000 cubic metres, including railway sleepers)

	1996	1997	1998
Total (all broadleaved)	596	613	623

Source: FAO, *Yearbook of Forest Products.*

Fishing

('000 metric tons, live weight)

	1996	1997	1998
Freshwater fishes	11.5	11.5	11.5*
Bigeye grunt	4.6	4.7	1.6
Sardinellas*	20.7	12.1	13.1
Bonga shad*	9.5	9.3	9.5
Total catch* (incl. others)	69.1	67.7	67.5

* FAO estimate(s).

Source: FAO, *Yearbook of Fishery Statistics.*

Mining

	1997	1998	1999
Gold (kg)	2,485	1,995	2,706
Crude petroleum (barrels)	5,266	3,806	3,547

Source: Banque centrale des états de l'Afrique de l'ouest.

Diamonds ('000 carats): 117.3 in 1992; 98.4 in 1993; 84.3 in 1994.

Industry

SELECTED PRODUCTS ('000 metric tons, unless otherwise indicated)

	1994	1995	1996
Salted, dried or smoked fish*	15.0	—	n.a.
Canned fish*	43.6	49.9	n.a.
Palm oil—unrefined*	259	249	n.a.
Raw sugar*	125	119	121
Plywood ('000 cubic metres)	41	58	57
Jet fuel†	61	62	62
Motor gasolene (Petrol)†	425	428	432
Kerosene†	488	490	491
Gas-diesel (Distillate fuel) oils†	685	705	710
Residual fuel oils†	474	477	479
Cement†‡	500	500	n.a.

Cocoa powder (exports, '000 metric tons): 22.1*† in 1988.
Cocoa butter (exports, '000 metric tons): 28.2*† in 1988.
Cotton yarn (pure and mixed, '000 metric tons): 24.7† in 1989.

* Data from FAO.
† Provisional or estimated figure(s).
‡ Data from the US Bureau of Mines.

Source: UN, *Industrial Commodity Statistics Yearbook.*

Electric energy (million kWh): 2,757 in 1997; 3,984 in 1998; 4,785 in 1999 (Source: Banque centrale des états de l'Afrique de l'ouest).

Finance

CURRENCY AND EXCHANGE RATES

Monetary Units
100 centimes = 1 franc de la Communauté financière africaine (CFA).

Sterling, Dollar and Euro Equivalents (29 December 2000)
£1 sterling = 1,051.93 francs CFA;
US $1 = 704.95 francs CFA;
€1 = 655.96 francs CFA;
10,000 francs CFA = £9.506 = $14.185 = €15.245.

Average Exchange Rate (francs CFA per US $)
1998   589.95
1999   615.70
2000   711.98

Note: An exchange rate of 1 French franc = 50 francs CFA, established in 1948, remained in force until January 1994, when the CFA franc was devalued by 50%, with the exchange rate adjusted to 1 French franc = 100 francs CFA. This relationship to French currency remained in effect with the introduction of the euro on 1 January 1999. From that date, accordingly, a fixed exchange rate of €1 = 655.957 francs CFA has been in operation.

BUDGET ('000 million francs CFA)

Revenue*	1997	1998	1999
Tax revenue	1,112.9	1,142.0	1,149.1
Direct taxes	303.5	327.7	322.3
Taxes on profits	147.2	166.2	143.6
Individual income taxes	97.8	104.8	115.8
Employers' contributions	22.4	26.0	27.8
Taxes on petroleum products	96.9	96.2	96.9
Excise taxes	61.2	62.8	62.3
Value-added tax (VAT)	30.5	28.3	29.3
Other indirect taxes	227.3	240.0	241.2
VAT and withholding tax	145.6	146.8	132.5
Registration and stamp taxes	30.6	33.5	47.9
Other taxes on imports	311.9	320.2	311.8
Customs, fiscal and statistical duties	153.0	162.2	143.5
Other import charges	20.6	14.1	21.8
VAT	138.4	143.9	146.5
Taxes on exports	173.2	158.0	176.9
Coffee and cocoa	165.9	150.2	169.9
Other revenue	215.1	246.5	122.5
Stabilization fund surplus	84.0	131.6	1.0
Social security contributions	83.1	79.2	83.7
Petroleum revenue	29.1	17.3	—
Total	1,328.0	1,388.5	1,271.6

Expenditure	1997	1998	1999†
Wages and salaries . . .	408.1	415.2	425.3
Social security benefits . .	73.6	76.5	76.0
Subsidies and other current			
transfers	54.9	55.9	59.5
Other current expenditure . .	301.8	309.9	326.9
Investment expenditure . .	372.3	455.9	327.6
Interest due on public debt . .	303.2	286.3	298.6
Total	1,513.9	1,599.7	1,513.9

* Excluding grants received ('000 million francs CFA): 44.1 in 1997; 50.5 in 1998; 40.0 in 1999.
† Estimates.

Source: IMF, *Côte d'Ivoire: Selected Issues and Statistical Appendix* (August 2000).

INTERNATIONAL RESERVES (US $ million at 31 December)

	1997	1998	1999
Gold*	13.6	13.1	13.1
IMF special drawing rights .	—	0.2	3.4
Reserve position in IMF . .	0.2	0.3	0.3
Foreign exchange . . .	618.1	855.0	626.6
Total	632.0	868.6	643.4

* Valued at market-related prices.
Source: IMF, *International Financial Statistics*.

MONEY SUPPLY ('000 million francs CFA at 31 December)

	1997	1998	1999
Currency outside banks . .	571.8	652.1	615.5
Demand deposits at deposit money			
banks*	502.8	562.0	576.7
Checking deposits at post office .	3.6	2.0	3.0
Total money (incl. others) . .	1,080.0	1,219.3	1,198.0

* Excluding the deposits of public establishments of an administrative or social nature.
Source: IMF, *International Financial Statistics*.

COST OF LIVING (Consumer Price Index for African households in Abidjan; base: 1995 = 100)

	1998	1999	2000
All items	111.6	112.5	115.2

Source: IMF, *International Financial Statistics*.

NATIONAL ACCOUNTS ('000 million francs CFA at current prices)
Expenditure on the Gross Domestic Product

	1997	1998	1999*
Government final consumption			
expenditure	697.5	733.3	803.5
Private final consumption			
expenditure	3,950.7	4,228.6	4,534.7
Increase in stocks . . .	165.0	165.5	−37.2
Gross fixed capital formation .	959.4	1,062.1	1,124.6
Total domestic expenditure .	5,772.6	6,189.5	6,425.6
Exports of goods and services .	2,788.4	2,891.4	3,058.3
Less Imports of goods and			
services	2,384.8	2,452.7	2,584.3
GDP in purchasers' values .	6,176.2	6,628.2	6,899.7

* Estimates.

Gross Domestic Product by Economic Activity

	1997	1998	1999*
Agriculture, livestock-rearing,			
forestry and fishing . .	1,650.9	1,831.5	1,795.2
Mining and quarrying . .	19.4	16.6	20.4
Manufacturing	868.0	1,002.9	1,054.7
Electricity, gas and water. .	329.0	342.9	391.5
Construction and public works .	285.0	319.8	352.6
Transport, storage and			
communications . . .	536.6	555.5	592.8
Trade	960.0	993.9	1,042.6
Public administration . .	478.7	498.0	525.8
Other services	788.7	816.5	875.5
Sub-total	5,916.3	6,377.6	6,651.1
Import duties and taxes . .	259.9	251.1	248.6
GDP in purchasers' values .	6,176.2	6,628.8	6,899.7

* Estimates.
Source: IMF, *Côte d'Ivoire: Selected Issues and Statistical Appendix* (August 2000).

BALANCE OF PAYMENTS (US $ million)

	1996	1997	1998
Exports of goods f.o.b. . .	4,446.1	4,298.7	4,575.1
Imports of goods f.o.b. . . .	−2,622.4	−2,479.5	−2,705.1
Trade balance	1,823.7	1,819.2	1,870.0
Exports of services . . .	565.9	532.3	549.9
Imports of services . . .	−1,443.4	−1,367.7	−1,474.4
Balance on goods and services	946.1	983.8	945.5
Other income received . .	171.0	167.4	169.8
Other income paid . . .	−939.5	−895.4	−879.6
Balance on goods, services and			
income	177.7	255.8	235.8
Current transfers received .	55.5	50.0	50.9
Current transfers paid . .	−546.6	−547.6	−599.2
Current balance . . .	−313.4	−241.7	−312.6
Capital account (net) . . .	49.8	39.7	36.3
Direct investment abroad . .	−0.4	—	—
Direct investment from abroad .	269.2	341.3	435.3
Portfolio investment assets .	−15.8	−15.4	−14.2
Portfolio investment liabilities .	26.6	30.7	38.5
Financial derivatives assets .	−3.3	n.a.	n.a.
Other investment assets . .	−254.1	−278.4	−324.3
Other investment liabilities .	−719.4	−533.7	−669.2
Net errors and omissions . .	−36.2	64.8	171.3
Overall balance	−997.0	−592.8	−638.9

Source: IMF, *International Financial Statistics*.

External Trade

PRINCIPAL COMMODITIES ('000 million francs CFA)

Imports c.i.f.	1997	1998	1999*
Foodstuffs, beverages and tobacco .	311.3	371.2	344.2
Dairy products .	28.1	32.3	29.5
Fish and shellfish (fresh) .	90.5	112.6	106.6
Cereals .	104.4	119.9	94.5
Rice .	64.6	81.9	68.5
Wheat .	29.7	36.2	25.3
Other consumer goods .	346.4	380.1	338.2
Pharmaceutical products .	63.3	67.6	68.9
Plastic products .	73.1	84.9	71.0
Passenger cars .	59.4	55.0	51.1
Raw materials and semi-finished products .	547.3	543.5	595.2
Petroleum products .	296.1	262.5	328.7
Crude petroleum .	254.1	195.0	240.4
Chemical products .	45.5	45.3	45.1
Fertilizers .	30.9	41.5	26.6
Construction materials .	35.7	36.6	38.8
Paper and paperboard .	43.6	48.2	48.7
Capital goods .	393.0	470.4	461.9
Mechanical .	156.2	160.6	162.7
Electrical .	75.7	116.9	136.6
Transport equipment .	66.2	78.3	61.9
Iron and steel products .	69.9	94.6	79.0
Total (incl. others) .	1,598.1	1,765.2	1,739.5

Exports f.o.b.	1997	1998	1999*
Coffee beans .	174.3	176.9	95.4
Cocoa beans .	707.8	740.5	776.4
Cotton fibre .	76.9	67.1	58.8
Natural rubber .	63.2	48.5	46.2
Processed cocoa .	120.0	162.9	137.1
Processed coffee .	33.7	45.3	57.2
Sawnwood .	152.3	119.6	157.2
Fish products .	126.0	148.6	160.0
Crude petroleum .	98.0	82.3	96.9
Petroleum products .	215.8	155.3	225.7
Total (incl. others) .	2,378.9	2,439.2	2,572.1

* Estimates.

Source: IMF, *Côte d'Ivoire: Selected Issues and Statistical Appendix* (August 2000).

PRINCIPAL TRADING PARTNERS (percentage of trade)

Imports	1997	1998	1999*
Belgium-Luxembourg .	3.3	3.1	3.8
Brazil .	0.8	1.2	0.8
China, People's Repub. .	2.4	2.2	2.5
France .	26.7	28.6	25.9
Germany .	4.7	4.6	4.3
Italy .	4.3	5.2	5.6
Japan .	4.3	3.4	4.3
Netherlands .	3.7	3.7	3.5
Pakistan .	1.1	0.6	0.6
Spain .	3.2	3.6	3.5
United Kingdom .	2.9	2.7	2.4
USA .	6.1	5.0	5.2

Exports	1997	1998	1999*
Belgium-Luxembourg .	4.2	2.6	2.1
Brazil .	0.3	0.4	7.7
Benin .	1.2	1.2	1.2
Burkina Faso .	3.0	3.7	4.3
Cameroon .	1.2	0.8	0.8
France .	17.3	17.4	14.4
Germany .	4.8	5.0	3.2
Ghana .	3.7	3.6	3.2
Italy .	5.3	6.0	4.3
Mali .	4.9	5.0	4.7
Netherlands .	13.2	12.5	13.1
Niger .	1.0	1.2	1.3
Senegal .	1.1	1.1	1.6
Spain .	4.0	3.8	3.7
Taiwan .	0.6	1.3	1.3
Togo .	1.6	1.5	1.7
United Kingdom .	2.6	2.4	2.9
USA .	7.5	9.0	8.5

* Estimates.

Source: IMF, *Côte d'Ivoire: Selected Issues and Statistical Appendix* (August 2000).

Transport

RAILWAYS (traffic)

	1996	1997	1998
Passenger-km (million) .	157.5	154.6	118.8
Freight ton-km (million) .	451.0	504.8	529.8

Source: Banque centrale des états de l'Afrique de l'ouest.

ROAD TRAFFIC (estimates, '000 motor vehicles in use)

	1994	1995	1996
Passenger cars .	255	271	293
Lorries and vans .	140	150	163

Source: IRF, *World Road Statistics*.

SHIPPING
Merchant Fleet (registered at 31 December)

	1996	1997	1998
Number of vessels .	45	43	35
Total displacement ('000 grt) .	12.7	11.4	9.5

Source: Lloyd's Register of Shipping, *World Fleet Statistics*.

International Sea-borne Freight Traffic
(freight traffic at Abidjan, '000 metric tons)

	1996	1997	1998
Goods loaded .	5,466	5,040	5,102
Goods unloaded .	7,895	87,140	9,972

Freight traffic at San Pedro ('000 metric tons, 1998): Goods loaded 763; Goods unloaded 306.

Source: Banque centrale des états de l'Afrique de l'ouest.

CIVIL AVIATION (traffic on scheduled services)*

			1995	1996	1997
Kilometres flown (million)	.	.	4	5	4
Passengers carried ('000)	.	.	175	179	158
Passenger-km (million)	.	.	302	307	302
Total ton-km (million)	.	.	44	44	44

* Including an apportionment of the traffic of Air Afrique.

Source: UN, *Statistical Yearbook*.

Tourism

ARRIVALS BY COUNTRY OF RESIDENCE ('000)

						1996	1997	1998
Belgium	.	.	.	.	.	4.3	4.2	4.5
Benin	.	.	.	.	.	12.5	11.1	14.3
Burkina Faso	.	.	.	.	.	11.0	11.9	17.1
Congo, Repub.	.	.	.	.	.	6.0	n.a.	7.6
France	.	.	.	.	.	66.7	69.0	73.2
Gabon	.	.	.	.	.	3.0	n.a.	5.4
Germany	.	.	.	.	.	3.2	3.8	3.9
Ghana	.	.	.	.	.	5.4	n.a.	6.7
Guinea	.	.	.	.	.	8.1	n.a.	12.5
Italy	.	.	.	.	.	5.0	14.0	7.6
Mali	.	.	.	.	.	10.7	n.a.	15.2
Niger	.	.	.	.	.	5.0	n.a.	5.4
Nigeria	.	.	.	.	.	7.9	n.a.	14.1
Senegal	.	.	.	.	.	13.0	12.1	16.6
Togo	.	.	.	.	.	8.7	8.2	10.8
United Kingdom	.	.	.	.	.	5.1	4.5	5.6
USA	.	.	.	.	.	15.3	17.0	18.8
Total (incl. others)						236.9	274.1	301.0

Tourism receipts (US $ million): 75 in 1996; 88 in 1997.

Source: World Tourism Organization: *Yearbook of Tourism Statistics*.

Communications Media

	1995	1996	1997
Radio receivers ('000 in use) . .	2,100	2,200	2,260
Television receivers ('000 in use) .	850	870	900
Telephones ('000 main lines in use)	116	130	142
Mobile cellular telephones			
(subscribers)	n.a.	13,549	36,000
Daily newspapers			
Number	9	12	n.a.
Average circulation ('000 copies)	235	251	n.a.
Non-daily newspapers			
Number	13	15	n.a.
Average circulation ('000 copies)	235	251	n.a.

Sources: UNESCO, *Statistical Yearbook*; UN, *Statistical Yearbook*.

Education

(1994/95, unless otherwise indicated)

	Institu-tions	Teach-ers	Students		
			Males	Females	Total
Pre-primary	281	1,192	13,315	12,323	25,638
Primary	7,185	36,058	930,386	679,543	1,609,929
Secondary					
General	n.a.	9,505*	313,445	150,365	463,810
Teacher					
training†‡	13	538	n.a.	n.a.	2,821
Vocational‡	n.a.	1,424	8,588	2,449	11,037
University level	n.a.	1,657	34,069	9,078	43,147

* Public education only.

† 1993/94 figures.

‡ Data refer only to schools attached to the Ministry of National Education and Basic Training.

1995/96: *Primary:* Institutions 7,401; Students 1,662,265 (males 959,419; females 702,846). *General Secondary:* Students 489,740 (males 327,779; females 161,961).

1996/97: *Pre-primary:* Students 32,141 (males 16,590; females 15,551). *Primary:* Institutions 7,599; Students 1,734,416 (males 993,157; females 741,259). *General Secondary:* Students 534,214 (males 365,201; females 169,013).

Directory

The Constitution

Following the *coup d'état* of 24 December 1999, the Constitution that had been in force, with amendments, since 1960 was suspended. A new Constitution (below) was subsequently prepared by a consultative committee, and was approved by referendum in July 2000.

PREAMBLE

The people of Côte d'Ivoire recognize their diverse ethnic, cultural and religious backgrounds, and desire to build a single, unified and prosperous nation based on constitutional legality and democratic institutions, the rights of the individual, cultural and spiritual values, transparency in public affairs, and the promotion of sub-regional, regional and African unity.

FREEDOMS, RIGHTS AND DUTIES

Articles 1–28: The State guarantees the implementation of the Constitution and guarantees to protect the rights of each citizen. The State guarantees its citizens equal access to health, education, culture, information, professional training, employment and justice. Freedom of thought and expression are guaranteed to all, although the encouragement of social, ethnic and religious discord is not permitted. Freedom of association and demonstration are guaranteed. Political parties may act freely within the law, however, parties must not be created solely on a regional, ethnic or religious basis. The rights of free enterprise, the right to a union and the right to strike are guaranteed.

NATIONAL SOVEREIGNTY

Articles 29–33: Côte d'Ivoire is an independent and sovereign republic. The official language is French. Legislation regulates the promotion and development of national languages. The Republic of Côte d'Ivoire is single and indivisible, secular, democratic and social. All its citizens are equal. Sovereignty belongs to the people, and is exercised through referendums and the election of representatives. The right to vote freely and in secret is guaranteed to all citizens over 18 years of age.

HEAD OF STATE

Articles 34–57: The President of the Republic is the Head of State. The President is elected for a five-year mandate (renewable once only) by direct universal suffrage. Candidates must be aged between 40 and 65, and be Ivorian citizens holding no other nationality, and resident in the country, with Ivorian parents. If one candidate does not receive a simple majority of votes cast, a second round of voting takes place between the two most successful candidates. The President holds executive power, and appoints a Prime Minister to co-ordinate government action. The President appoints the Government on the recommendation of the Prime Minister. The President presides over the Council of Ministers, is the head of the civil service and the supreme head of the armed forces. The President may initiate legislation and call referendums. The President may not hold any other office or be a leader of a political party.

NATIONAL ASSEMBLY

Articles 58–83: The National Assembly holds legislative power. The National Assembly votes on the budget and scrutinizes the accounts of the nation. Deputies are elected for periods of five years by direct universal suffrage. Except in exceptional cases, deputies have legal immunity during the period of their mandate.

INTERNATIONAL AGREEMENTS

Articles 84–87: The President negotiates and ratifies treaties and international agreements. International agreements, which modify internal legislation, must be ratified by further legislation. The Constitution must be amended prior to the ratification of certain agreements if the Constitutional Council deems this necessary.

CONSTITUTIONAL COUNCIL

Articles 88–100: The Constitutional Council rules on the constitutionality of legislation. It also regulates the functioning of government. It is composed of a President, of the former Presidents of Côte d'Ivoire and of six councillors named by the President and by the President of the National Assembly for mandates of six years. The Council supervises referendums and announces referendum and election results. It also examines the eligibility of candidates to the presidency and the legislature. There is no appeal against the Council's decisions.

JUDICIAL POWER

Articles 101–112: The judiciary is independent, and is composed of the Haute cour de justice, the Cour de cassation, the Conseil d'Etat, the Cour des comptes, and regional tribunals and appeals courts. The Conseil supérieur de la magistrature examines questions relating to judicial independence and nominates and disciplines senior magistrates. The Haute cour de justice judges members of the Government in cases relating to the execution of their duties. The Haute cour, which is composed of deputies elected by the National Assembly, may only judge the President in cases of high treason.

ECONOMIC AND SOCIAL COUNCIL

Articles 113–114: The Economic and Social Council gives its opinion on proposed legislation or decrees relating to its sphere of competence. The President may consult the council on any economic or social matter.

THE MEDIATOR OF THE REPUBLIC

Articles 115–118: The Mediator is an independent mediating figure, appointed for a non-renewable six-year mandate by the President, in consultation with the President of the National Assembly. The Mediator, who may not hold any other office or position, receives immunity from prosecution during the term of office.

OTHER ISSUES

Articles 119–133: Only the President or the National Assembly, of whom a two-thirds majority must be in favour, may propose amending the Constitution. Amendments relating to the nature of the presidency or the mechanism whereby the Constitution is amended must be approved by referendum; all other amendments may be enacted with the agreement of the President and of a four-fifths majority of the National Assembly. The form and the secular nature of the republic may not be amended. Immunity from prosecution is granted to members of the Comité national de salut public (CNSP) and to all those involved in the change of government of December 1999.

The Government

HEAD OF STATE

President of the Republic: LAURENT GBAGBO (took office 26 October 2000).

COUNCIL OF MINISTERS

(April 2001)

A coalition of the Front populaire ivorien (FPI), the Parti démocratique de la Côte d'Ivoire—Rassemblement démocratique africain (PDCI—RDA), the Parti ivorien des travailleurs (PIT) and Independents.

Prime Minister, responsible for Planning and Development: AFFI N'GUESSAN (FPI).

Minister of State, responsible for Foreign Relations: ABOUDRAMANE SANGARÉ (FPI).

Minister of State, responsible for the Interior and Decentralization: EMILE BOGA DOUDOU (FPI).

Minister of State, responsible for Defence and Civil Protection: MOÏSE LIDA KOUASSI (FPI).

Keeper of the Seals, Minister of Justice and Public Liberty: SIENE OULAÏ (FPI).

Minister of the Economy and Finance: BOHOUN BOUABRÉ (FPI).

Minister responsible for Relations with Parliament and the Institutions: DANON SEBASTIEN DJÉDJÉ (FPI).

Minister of Higher Education and Scientific Research: SERY BAILLY (FPI).

Minister of Employment, the Civil Service and Administrative Reform: HUBERT OULAÏ (FPI).

Minister of National Education: MICHEL NGUESSAN AMANI (FPI).

Minister of Tourism and Handicrafts: BAKO ODETTE LIKOUKOUET (FPI).

Minister of Mines and Energy: LÉON EMMANUEL MONNET (FPI).

Minister of Public Health: RAYMOND ABOUO N'DORI (FPI).

Minister of Agriculture and Animal Husbandry: ALPHONSE DOUATY (FPI).

Minister of Economic Infrastructure: PATRICK ACHI (PDCI—RDA).

Minister of Construction and Town Planning: ASSOA ADOU (FPI).

Minister of Transport: AIMÉ KABRAN APPIAH (PIT).

Minister of the Environment: GILBERT BLEU-LAINE (Ind.).

Minister of Social Security and National Unity: CLOTILDE OHOU-OUCHI (PDCI—RDA).

Minister of Culture and Francophone Affairs: DRAMANE KONÉ (FPI).

Minister of Industry and the Promotion of the Private Sector: ALAIN COCAUTHREY (PDCI—RDA).

Minister of the Family, Women and Children: HENRIETTE LAGOU (PDCI—RDA).

Minister of Youth, Employment and Professional Training: KOFFI LAZARE KOFFI (FPI).

Minister of Water and Forestry: ANGELE BOKA (PIT).

Minister of Sports and Leisure: GENEVIEVE BRO GREBE (PDCI—RDA).

Minister of Communications and New Information Technologies: LIA-BI DOUAYOUA (FPI).

Minister of Trade: KAHE ERIC VICTOR KPLOHOUROU (Ind.).

Minister-delegate to the Prime Minister, responsible for the Fight against AIDS and other Pandemics: ASSANA SANGARÉ (PDCI—RDA).

MINISTRIES

Office of the President: 01 BP 1354, Abidjan; tel. 20-22-02-22; fax 20-21-14-25; internet www.pr.ci.

Office of the Prime Minister: blvd Angoulvant, 01 BP 1533, Abidjan 01; tel. 20-21-11-00; fax 20-21-70-41.

Office of the Minister of State with responsibility for Defence and Civil Protection: Abidjan.

Office of the Minister of State with responsibility for Foreign Relations: BP V109, Abidjan; tel. 20-22-71-50; fax 20-33-23-08.

Office of the Minister of State with responsibility for the Interior and Decentralization: BP V121, Abidjan; tel. 20-32-23-43.

Ministry of Agriculture and Animal Husbandry: BP V82, Abidjan; tel. 20-21-08-33; fax 20-21-46-18.

Ministry of Communications and New Information Technologies: Abidjan.

Ministry of Construction and Town Planning: BP V153, Abidjan; tel. 20-21-94-06; fax 20-21-45-61.

Ministry of Culture and Francophone Affairs: Tour E, 22e étape, BP V39, Abidjan; tel. 20-21-40-34; fax 20-21-33-59; e-mail culture.ci@ci.refer.org.

Ministry of Economic Infrastructure: Immeuble POSTEL, 23e étape, BP V6, Abidjan; tel. 20-34-73-15; fax 20-21-30-37.

Ministry of the Economy and Finance: Immeuble SCIAM, 16e étage, ave Marchand, BP V163, Abidjan; tel. 20-21-05-66; fax 20-21-16-90.

Ministry of Employment, the Civil Service and Administrative Reform: BP V193, Abidjan; tel. 20-21-42-90; fax 20-22-84-15.

Ministry of the Environment: BP V06, Abidjan; tel. 20-34-60-00.

Ministry of the Family, Women and Children: BP V200, Abidjan; tel. 20-21-76-26; fax 20-21-44-61.

Ministry of Higher Education and Scientific Research: BP V151, Abidjan; tel. 20-21-78-70; fax 20-21-22-25.

Ministry of Industry and the Promotion of the Private Sector: Immeuble CCI, 15e étage, BP V65, Abidjan; tel. 20-21-30-88.

Ministry of Justice and Public Liberty: BP V107, Abidjan; tel. 20-32-08-88; fax 20-33-12-59.

Ministry of Mines and Energy: BP V50, Abidjan; tel. 20-21-50-03; fax 20-21-53-20.

Ministry of National Education: BP V120, Abidjan; tel. 20-21-02-75; fax 20-21-83-93; e-mail menfb@ci.refer.org; internet www.refer.org/ivoir_ct/edu/c_nation/accueil.htm.

Ministry of Public Health: Cité Administrative, Tour C, 16e étage, BP V4, Abidjan; tel. 20-21-08-71; fax 20-21-10-85.

Ministry of Social Security and National Unity: BP V241, Abidjan; tel. 20-21-19-50.

Ministry of Sports and Leisure: Abidjan.

Ministry of Tourism and Handicrafts: 01 BP 8538, Abidjan 01; tel. 20-20-65-00; fax 20-20-65-31; e-mail oith@africaonline.co.ci; internet www.tourisme.ci.

Ministry of Trade: Immeuble CCIA, 23e étage, BP V142, Abidjan; tel. 20-21-24-35; fax 20-21-23-24.

Ministry of Transport: BP V06, Abidjan; tel. 20-34-60-00.

Ministry of Water and Forestry: Abidjan.

Ministry of Youth, Employment and Professional Training: BP V136, Abidjan; tel. 20-21-52-51; fax 20-22-48-21.

President and Legislature

PRESIDENT

Presidential Election, 22 October 2000

Candidate	Votes	% of votes
LAURENT GBAGBO (FPI)	1,065,597	59.36
ROBERT GUEÏ (Independent)	587,267	32.72
FRANCIS WODIÉ (PIT)	102,253	5.70
THÉODORE EG MEL (UDCI)	26,331	1.47
NICOLAS DIOULO (Independent) . . .	13,558	0.76
Total*	1,795,006	100.00

* Excluding invalid votes (25,413).

ASSEMBLÉE NATIONALE

President: MAMADOU KOULIBALY.

General Election, 10 December 2000*

Party	Seats
Front populaire ivorien (FPI)	96
Parti démocratique de la Côte d'Ivoire—Rassemblement démocratique africain (PDCI—RDA) . . .	94
Mouvement des militants et candidats modérés—Rassemblement des républicains (MMCM—RDR) .	5
Parti ivorien des travailleurs (PIT)	4
Union démocratique de la Côte d'Ivoire (UDCI) .	1
Mouvement des forces d'avenir (MFA) . . .	1
Independents	22
Total†	223

* These figures include the results of voting in 26 constituencies where elections were postponed until 14 January 2001, owing to unrest.

† Voting for the remaining two seats was postponed indefinitely.

Advisory Councils

Conseil Constitutionnel: Abidjan; f. 1994; Pres. TIA KONÉ.

Conseil Economique et Social: 04 BP 301, Abidjan 04; tel. 20-21-14-54; Pres. (vacant); Vice-Pres BEDA YAO, GLADYS ANOMA, AUGUSTE DAUBREY, MARTIN KOUAKOU KOUADIO, BERNARD ANO BOA; 120 mems.

Political Organizations

In mid-2000 there were around 100 registered political organizations, of which the following were among the most important:

Front populaire ivorien (FPI): 22 BP 302, Abidjan 22; tel. 21-24-36-76; fax 21-35-35-50; e-mail fpi@africaonline.co.ci; internet www.fpi.ci; f. 1983 in France; social-democratic; Chair. LAURENT GBAGBO; Sec.-Gen. ABOU DRAHAMANE SANGARÉ.

Mouvement des forces d'avenir (MFA): Abidjan; f. 2000; Sec.-Gen. KOBENAN ANAKY.

Mouvement des militants et candidats modérés—Rassemblement des républicains (MMCM—RDR): 18 BP 3120, Abidjan 18; f. Dec. 2000 as a grouping of c. 60 candidates within the RDR to compete in legislative elections that the main party was boycotting; Pres. ALPHONSE OULAÏ TOUSSÉA.

Parti démocratique de la Côte d'Ivoire—Rassemblement démocratique africain (PDCI—RDA): Maison du parti, Cocody, Abidjan; f. 1946 as the local section of the Rassemblement démocratique africain; e-mail information@pdci-rda.org; internet www.pdci-rda.org; Pres. (acting) and Sec.-Gen. LAURENT DONA FOLOGO.

Parti ivorien des travailleurs (PIT): Abidjan; internet www.wodie.ci; social-democratic; f. 1990; Sec.-Gen. FRANCIS WODIÉ.

Rassemblement des républicains (RDR): 06 BP 111, Abidjan 06; tel. 22-44-33-51; e-mail hdiaby@rdrci.com; internet www.rdrci.com; f. 1994, following split from PDCI—RDA; officially boycotted the general election of Dec. 2000, except for MMCM—RDR, q.v.; Pres. ALASSANE DRAMANE OUATTARA; Sec.-Gen. HENRIETTE DAGBA DIABATÉ.

Union démocratique de la Côte d'Ivoire (UDCI): Abidjan; f. 2000, following split from PDCI—RDA; Sec.-Gen. THÉODORE EG MEL.

Other registered parties include:

The **Alliance nationale de la Côte d'Ivoire (ANACI)**: Sec.-Gen. MAMADOU DOUKOURÉ; the **Groupement pour la solidarité (GPS)**: Pres. ACHI KOMAN; the **Mouvement démocratique et social (MDS)**: First Nat. Sec.-Gen. SIAKA TOURÉ; the **Mouvement indépendantiste ivoirien (MII)**: Pres. ADOU YAPI; the **Organisation populaire de la jeunesse (OPJ)**: Sec.-Gen. DENIS LATTA; the **Parti africain pour la renaissance ivoirienne (PARI)**: Sec.-Gen. DANIEL ANIKPO; the **Parti communiste ivoirien (PCI)**: Sec.-Gen. DENIS GUEU DRO; the **Parti ivoirien des forces démocrates (PIFD)**: Sec.-Gen SÉRI PAMPHILE GUIE; the **Parti ivoirien pour la démocratie (PID)**: Sec.-Gen. FAUSTIN BOTOKO LÉKA; the **Parti libéral de Côte d'Ivoire (PLCI)**: Sec.-Gen. YADY SOUMAH; the **Parti pour les libertés et la démocratie (PLD)**: Pres. JEAN-PIERRE OUYA; the **Parti pour le progrès et la solidarité (PPS)**: Sec.-Gen. BAMBA MORIFÉRÉ; the **Parti progressiste ivoirien (PPI)**: Pres. SOUMAHORO KASSINDOU; the **Parti pour la protection de l'environnement (PPE)**: Sec.-Gen. DIOBA COULIBALY; the **Parti réformiste démocratique ivoirien (PRDI)**: Sec.-Gen. RAPHAËL BEUGRÉ KOAUMÉ; the **Parti républicain de Côte d'Ivoire (PRCI)**: Sec.-Gen. ROBERT GBAI TAGRO; the **Parti social democrate (PSD)**: Sec-Gen. VINCENT AKADJE; the **Parti socialiste ivoirien (PSI)**: First Nat. Sec. MANDOUADJOA KOUAKOU; the **Rassemblement des forces démocratiques (RFD)**: Pres. FAKOUROU TOURÉ; the **Rassemblement pour le progrès social (RPS)**: Pres. MAMADOU KONÉ; the **Rassemblement des sociaux-démocrates (RSD)**: Sec.-Gen. MAHI GUINA; the **Union pour la cause du peuple (UCP)**: Sec.-Gen JEAN-BAPTISTE OMOUI-GBA; the **Union nationale des démocrates (UND)**: Sec.-Gen. AMADOU KONÉ; the **Union des paysans, des ouvriers et des salariés de Côte d'Ivoire (UPOSCI)**: Sec.-Gen. COA KIÉMOKO; the **Union pour le progrès social (UPS)**: Sec.-Gen. CLIMANLO JÉRÔME; the **Union des sociaux-démocrates (USD)**: Sec.-Gen. KOUADIO KONAN DIEUDONNÉ.

Diplomatic Representation

EMBASSIES IN CÔTE D'IVOIRE

Algeria: 53 blvd Clozel, 01 BP 1015, Abidjan 01; tel. 20-32-32-40; fax 20-22-37-12; Ambassador: BOUKADOUM SABRI.

Angola: Lot 2461, rue des Jardins, Cocody-Deux-Plateaux, 16 BP 1734, Abidjan 16; tel. 22-41-38-79; fax 22-41-28-89; Ambassador: (vacant).

Austria: Immeuble N'Zarama, blvd Lagunaire, Plateau, 01 BP 1837, Abidjan 01; tel. 20-21-25-00; fax 20-22-19-23; Ambassador: FERDINAND MAULTASCH.

Belgium: Immeuble Alliance, angle rue Lecoeur, 01 BP 1800, Abidjan 01; tel. 20-21-00-88; fax 20-22-41-77; Ambassador: GREGOIRE VARDAKIS.

Benin: rue des Jasmins, Lot 1610, Cocody-Deux-Plateaux, 09 BP 283, Abidjan 09; tel. 22-41-44-13; fax 22-41-27-89; Ambassador: AUGUSTE COMLAN ALAVO.

Brazil: Immeuble Alpha 2000, rue Gourgas, 01 BP 3820, Abidjan 01; tel. 20-22-23-41; fax 22-22-64-01; Ambassador: LUIZ BRUN DE ALMEIDA E SUZA.

Burkina Faso: 2 ave Terrasson de Fougères, 01 BP 908, Abidjan 01; tel. 20-21-14-93; fax 20-21-66-41; Ambassador: EMILE ILBOUDO.

Cameroon: Immeuble le Général, blvd Botreau Roussel, 06 BP 326, Abidjan 06; tel. 20-21-20-86; fax 20-21-66-11; Ambassador: DJOBO SAMUEL.

Canada: Immeuble Trade Centre, ave Nogues, 01 BP 4104, Abidjan 01; tel. 20-21-20-09; fax 20-21-77-28; Ambassador: DONALD MCMASTER.

Cape Verde: Immeuble Neuilly, 16 BP 1941, Abidjan 16; tel. 20-22-80-67; fax 20-33-43-28; Chargé d'Affaires a.i.: CARLOS F. SEMEDO.

Central African Republic: 9 rue des Jasmins, Cocody Danga Nord, 01 BP 3387, Abidjan 01; tel. 22-44-86-29; fax 22-44-85-16; Ambassador: JOB ISIMA.

China, People's Republic: 01 BP 3691, Abidjan 01; tel. 22-44-59-00; fax 22-44-67-81; Ambassador: ZHAO BAOZHEN.

Colombia: Tour BIAO, ave Lamblin, 01 BP 3874, Abidjan 01; tel. 20-33-15-15; fax 20-32-47-31; e-mail emcoci@africaonline.co.ci; Chargé d'affaires a.i.: SANTIAGO SALCEDO BUITRAGO.

Congo, Democratic Republic: 29 blvd Clozel, 01 BP 3961, Abidjan 01; tel. 20-21-70-46; fax 20-21-07-08; Ambassador: WAMU W'EKUNDA ANTOINE.

Czech Republic: Immeuble Tropique III, 01 BP 1349, Abidjan 01; tel. 20-21-20-30; fax 20-22-19-06; e-mail ambassade.tcheque@globeaccess.net; Ambassador: PETR LOM.

Egypt: Immeuble El Nasr, 01 BP 2104, Abidjan 01; tel. 20-32-79-25; fax 20-22-30-53; Ambassador: SAMI YASSA ABDEL SHAHID YASSA.

Ethiopia: Immeuble Nour Al-Hayat, 01 BP 3712, Abidjan 01; tel. 20-21-33-65; fax 20-21-37-09; Chargé d'Affaires: WESHI TAMRAT.

France: rue Lecoeur, 01 BP 175, Abidjan 01; tel. 20-20-04-04; fax 20-22-42-54; e-mail presse@ambafrance-abidjan.org; internet www.ambafrance-abidjan.org; Ambassador: FRANCIS LOTT.

Gabon: Cocody Danga Nord, 01 BP 3765, Abidjan 01; tel. 22-41-51-54; fax 22-44-75-05; Ambassador: TCHIBOTA SOUAMY ROGER.

Germany: 39 blvd Hassan II, Cocody, 01 BP 1900, Abidjan 01; tel. 22-44-20-30; fax 22-44-20-41; e-mail d.bo.adj@africaonline.co.ci; internet www.allemagne.ci; Ambassador: KARIN ELSA BLUMBERGER-SAUERTEIG.

Ghana: rue J 95, Cocody-Deux-Plateaux, 01 BP 1871, Abidjan 01; tel. 20-41-02-88; fax 22-41-03-99; Ambassador: AKUNFI AMEYAW MUN-IFIE.

Guinea: Immeuble Duplessis, 08 BP 2288, Abidjan 08; tel. 20-22-25-20; fax 20-32-82-45; Ambassador: FODE CISSE.

Holy See: Apostolic Nunciature, 08 BP 1347, Abidjan 08; tel. 22-44-38-05; fax 22-44-72-40; e-mail nuntius@comete.ci; Apostolic Nuncio: Most Rev. MARIO ZENARI, Titular Archbishop of Zuglio.

India: Cocody Danga Nord, 06 BP 318, Abidjan 06; tel. 22-42-37-69; fax 22-42-66-49; e-mail indeamadj@africaonline.co.ci; Ambassador: NEELAM DEO.

Iran: 08 BP 44, Abidjan 08; tel. 22-48-75-48; fax 22-48-75-47; Ambassador: ABDI ABYANEH HOSSEIN.

Israel: Immeuble Nour Al-Hayat, 01 BP 1877, Abidjan 01; tel. 20-21-31-78; fax 20-21-87-04; Ambassador: YOEL BARNEA.

Italy: 16 rue de la Canebière, Cocody, 01 BP 1905, Abidjan 01; tel. 22-44-61-70; fax 22-44-35-87; e-mail ambitali@aviso.ci; Ambassador: LUIGI COSTA SANSEVERINO DI BISIGNANO.

Japan: Immeuble Alpha 2000, 01 BP 1329, Abidjan 01; tel. 20-21-28-63; fax 20-21-30-51; Ambassador: MITSUHIRO NAKAMURA.

Korea, Democratic People's Republic: Abidjan; Ambassador: RI JAE RIM.

Korea, Republic: Immeuble le Mans, 01 BP 3950, Abidjan 01; tel. 20-32-22-90; fax 20-22-22-74; Chargé d'Affaires: CHO WON-HO.

Lebanon: Immeuble Trade Centre, ave Nogues, 01 BP 2222, Abidjan 01; tel. 20-33-28-24; fax 20-32-11-37; Ambassador: MUSTAPHA ISSAM.

Liberia: Immeuble Taleb, 20 ave Delafosse, 01 BP 2514, Abidjan 01; tel. 20-33-12-28; fax 20-21-85-29; Ambassador: KRONYANH M. WEEFUR.

Libya: Immeuble Shell, 01 BP 5725, Abidjan 01; tel. 20-22-01-27; fax 20-22-01-30; Ambassador: FATHI NASHAD.

Mali: Maison du Mali, 01 BP 2746, Abidjan 01; tel. 20-32-30-71; fax 20-21-55-14; Ambassador: AMIDOU OUMAR SY.

Malta: 38 rue de la Canebière, Cocody, Abidjan; tel. 22-44-63-62; fax 22-44-19-78; Ambassador: MARTHE BLOHORN.

Mauritania: blvd Latrille, rue Eglise St Jacques, 01 BP 2275, Abidjan 01; tel. 22-41-16-43; fax 22-41-05-77; Ambassador: TIJANI OULD KERIM.

Morocco: 24 rue de la Canebière, Cocody, 01 BP 146, Abidjan 01; tel. 22-44-58-73; fax 22-44-60-58; Ambassador: MOHAMED HAMA.

Netherlands: Immeuble Les Harmonies, blvd Carde, 01 BP 1086, Abidjan 01; tel. 20-22-77-12; fax 20-21-17-61; e-mail nlgovabi@africaonline.co.ci; Ambassador: PETER VAN LEEUWEN.

Niger: 6 blvd Achalme, Marcory, 01 BP 2743, Abidjan 01; tel. 21-26-28-14; fax 21-26-41-88; Ambassador: DAN MARADI ADAM ABDOULAYE.

Nigeria: blvd de la République, 01 BP 1906, Abidjan 01; tel. 20-22-30-82; fax 20-21-38-17; Ambassador: KEHINDE ONWAZU OLISEMEKA.

Norway: Immeuble N'Zarama, 01 BP 607, Abidjan 01; tel. 20-22-25-34; fax 20-21-91-99; Ambassador: LARS TANGERAAS.

Poland: 04 BP 308, Abidjan 08; tel. 22-44-10-67; fax 22-44-12-25; e-mail polska@globeaccess.net; Chargé d'affaires a.i.: PIOTR MYSLIWIEC.

Portugal: Immeuble N'Zarama, 01 BP 3669, Abidjan 01; tel. 20-21-92-41; fax 20-22-57-05; Ambassador: FRANCISCO MANUEL GUIMARĀES HENRIQUES DA SILVA.

Russia: Riviera Sud 1, 01 BP 7646, Abidjan 01; tel. 22-43-09-59; fax 22-43-11-66; Ambassador: ALEKSANDR MIKHAILOVICH TROFIMOV.

Senegal: Résidence Nabil, 08 BP 2163, Abidjan 08; tel. 20-33-28-76; fax 20-32-50-39; Ambassador: OUSMANE CAMARA.

South Africa: Villa Marc André, rue Mgr René Kouassi, Cocody, 08 BP 1806, Abidjan 08; tel. 22-44-59-63; fax 22-44-74-50; Chargé d'affaires: ANDRÉ-FRANÇOIS JACOBS.

Spain: impasse Abla Pokou Cocody, Danga Nord, 08 BP 876, Abidjan 08; tel. 22-44-48-50; fax 22-44-71-22; e-mail embespan@aviso.ci; Ambassador: MARÍA ROSA BOCETA OSTOS.

Sweden: Immeuble N'Zarama, blvd Lagunaire, 04 BP 992, Abidjan 04; tel. 20-21-24-10; fax 20-21-21-07; e-mail ambsuede@aviso.ci; Ambassador: GÖRAN ANKARBERG.

Switzerland: Immeuble Alpha 2000, 01 BP 1914, Abidjan 01; tel. 20-21-17-21; fax 20-21-27-70; Ambassador: FRANÇOIS CHAPPUIS.

Tunisia: 01 BP 6586, Abidjan 01; tel. 20-22-61-23; fax 20-22-61-24; Ambassador: ZINE EL ABIDINE TERRAS.

United Kingdom: Immeuble Les Harmonies, ave du Dr Jamot, 01 BP 2581, Abidjan 01; tel. 20-22-68-50; fax 20-22-32-21; e-mail britemb.a@aviso.ci; internet www.cahro.co.uk/embassy; Ambassador: HAYDON WARREN-GASH.

USA: 5 rue Jesse Owens, 01 BP 1712, Abidjan 01; tel. 20-21-09-79; fax 20-22-15-45; Ambassador: GEORGE MU.

Judicial System

Since 1964 all civil, criminal, commercial and administrative cases have come under the jurisdiction of the Tribunaux de première instance (magistrates' courts), the assize courts and the Court of Appeal, with the Cour de cassation as the highest court of appeal.

Cour de cassation (Supreme Court): rue Gourgas, BP V30, Abidjan; has four chambers: constitutional, judicial, administrative and auditing; Pres. TIA KONÉ.

Courts of Appeal: Abidjan and Bouaké; hear appeals from courts of first instance; Abidjan.

Haute cour de justice (High Court of Justice): composed of Deputies elected from and by the National Assembly; has jurisdiction to impeach the President or other member of the Government.

Courts of First Instance: Abidjan: Pres. ANTOINETTE MARSOUIN; Bouaké: Pres. KABLAN AKA EDOUKOU; Daloa: Pres. WOUNE BLEKA; there are a further 25 courts in the principal centres.

Religion

The Constitution guarantees religious freedom, and this right is generally respected. Religious groups are required to register with the authorities, although no penalties are imposed on a group that fails to register. At the 1988 census it was estimated that about 25.1% of the population were Muslims, 22.8% followed traditional indigenous beliefs, 22.7% were Catholics, 6.6% were Protestants, 1.9% were Harrists, 4.0% practised other religions, while 16.9% had no religious affiliation. It is, however, estimated that the proportion of Muslims is in fact significantly higher, as the majority of unregistered foreign workers are Muslims. Muslims are found in greatest numbers in the north of the country, while Catholics and Protestants are found mostly in the southern, central, western and eastern regions. Traditional indigenous beliefs are generally prevalent in rural areas.

ISLAM

Confédération Islamique du Développement de la Côte d'Ivoire: Abidjan; Chair. El Hadj BABILY DEMBÉLÉ.

Conseil National Islamique (CNI): BP 174 Cidex 03, Abidjan 08; tel. and fax 22-42-67-79; e-mail cni@africaonline.co.ci; internet www.cni.ci; f. 1993; Chair. El Hadj IDRISS KOUDOUSS KONÉ.

Conseil Supérieur Islamique (CSI): f. 1978; Chair. El Hadj MOUSTAPHA KOWEÏT DIABY.

Front de la Oumma Islamique: Abidjan.

CHRISTIANITY
The Roman Catholic Church

Côte d'Ivoire comprises four archdioceses and 10 dioceses. At 31 December 1998 Roman Catholics comprised about 12.6% of the total population.

Bishops' Conference: Conférence Episcopale de la Côte d'Ivoire, 01 BP 1287, Abidjan 01; tel. 20-33-22-56; f. 1973; Pres. Most Rev. VITAL KOMENAN YAO, Archbishop of Bouaké.

Archbishop of Abidjan: Cardinal BERNARD AGRÉ, Archevêché, ave Jean Paul II, 01 BP 1287, Abidjan 01; tel. 20-21-23-08; fax 20-21-40-22.

Archbishop of Bouaké: Most Rev. VITAL KOMENAN YAO, Archevêché, 01 BP 649, Bouaké 01; tel. and fax 63-24-59.

Archbishop of Gagnoa: Most Rev. NOËL KOKORA-TEKRY, Archevêché, BP 527, Gagnoa; tel. 77-25-68; fax 77-20-96.

Archbishop of Korhogo: Most Rev. AUGUSTE NOBOU, Archevêché, BP 12, Korhogo; tel. 86-01-18; fax 86-05-26.

Protestant Churches

CB International: BP 109, Korhogo; tel. 86-01-07; fax 86-11-50; f. 1947; fmrly Conservative Baptist Foreign Mission Society; active in evangelism, medical work, translation, literacy and theological education in the northern area and in Abidjan.

Christian and Missionary Alliance: BP 585, Bouaké 01; tel. 63-23-12; fax 63-54-12; f. 1929; 13 mission stations; Dir Rev. DAVID W. ARNOLD.

Eglise du Nazaréen (Church of the Nazarene): 22 BP 623, Abidjan 22; tel. 22-41-07-80; fax 22-41-07-81; e-mail awfcon@compuserve.com; f. 1987; active in evangelism, ministerial training and medical work; Dir JOHN SEAMAN.

Eglise Evangélique des Assemblées de Dieu de Côte d'Ivoire: 04 BP 266, Abidjan 04; tel. 20-37-05-79; fax 20-24-94-65; f. 1960; Pres. JEAN-BAPTISTE NIELBIEN.

Eglise Protestante Baptiste Oeuvres et Mission: 03 BP 1032, Abidjan 03; tel. 23-45-20-18; fax 23-45-56-41; f. 1975; active in evangelism, teaching and social work; medical centre, 677 places of worship, 285 missionaries and 100,000 mems; Pres. YAYE ROBERT DION.

Eglise Protestante Méthodiste de Côte d'Ivoire: 41 blvd de la République, 01 BP 1282, Abidjan 01; tel. 20-21-17-97; fax 20-22-52-03; c. 650,000 mems; Pres. BENJAMIN BONI.

Harrist Church: Abidjan; f. 1913 by William Wade Harris; African Protestant denomination; affiliated to World Council of Churches 1998; allows polygamous new converts; 100,000 mems, 1,400 preachers, 7,000 apostles.

Mission Evangélique de l'Afrique Occidentale: BP 822, Bouaflé; e-mail 105344.2207@compuserve.com; f. 1934; 11 mission centres, 59 missionaries; Field Dirs LINDA NAGEL, MARRY SCHOTTE; affiliated church: Alliance des Eglises Evangéliques de Côte d'Ivoire; 254 churches, 65 full-time pastors; Pres. BOAN BI ZRÈ EMMANUEL.

Mission Evangélique Luthérienne en Côte d'Ivoire (MELCI): BP 196, Touba; tel. 33-70-77-11; e-mail melci@aviso.ci; f. 1984; active in evangelism and social work; Dir KAI OVE BERG.

Union des Eglises Evangéliques du Sud-Ouest de la Côte d'Ivoire and **Mission Biblique:** 08 BP 20, Abidjan 08; f. 1927; c. 250 places of worship.

Other religious groups in Côte d'Ivoire include the Adventist Church, Bossonism (the traditional religious practices of the Akan ethnic group), the Autonomous Church of Celestial Christianity of Oschoffa, the Union of the Evangelical Church of Services and Works of Côte d'Ivoire, the Church of Jesus Christ of the Latter-Day Saints, the Yoruba First Church, the Church of God International Missions, the Church of the Prophet Papa Nouveau, the Pentecostal Church of Côte d'Ivoire, the Messianic Church, the Limoudim of Rabbi Jesus, the Unification Church, Jehovah's Witnesses, and the Interdenominational Church.

The Press
DAILIES

Actuel: Cocody-les-Deux-Plateaux, 06 BP 2868, Abidjan 06; tel. 22-42-83-27; fax 22-42-63-32; f. 1996; organ of the FPI; Dir MARTIN SOUKOURI BOHOUI.

L'Aurore: Abidjan; Editor-in-Chief VENANCE KONAN (EHOUMAN KASSY).

Douze (Sport): rue Louis Lumière, zone 4C, 10 BP 2462, Abidjan 10; tel. 21-25-54-00; fax 21-35-85-66; e-mail olympe@afnet.net; internet www.presseci.com/douze/; f. 1994; Dir RAYES NADY.

Fraternité Matin: blvd du Général de Gaulle, 01 BP 1807, Abidjan 01; tel. 20-37-06-66; e-mail fratmat@africanonline.co.ci; internet www.fratmat.co.ci; f. 1964; official newspaper; Man. Dir MICHEL KOUAMÉ; circ. 80,000.

L'Inter: rue Louis Lumière, Zone 4C, 10 BP 2462, Abidjan 10; tel. 21-25-32-77; fax 21-35-85-66; e-mail olympe@afnet.net; internet www.presseci.com/inter/; f. 1998; Dir RAYES NADY.

Ivoir 'Soir: blvd du Général de Gaulle, 01 BP 1807, Abidjan 01; tel. 20-21-95-78; fax 20-37-25-45; internet www.ivoirsoir.ci; f. 1987; organ of the PDCI–RDA; Dir-Gen. EMMANUEL KOUASSI KOKORÉ; circ. 52,000.

Le JD (Jeune Démocrate): 23 BP 3842, Abidjan 23; tel. 23-51-62-45; fax 23-51-63-75; e-mail lejd@africaonline.co.ci; internet ibs.africaonline.co.ci/jd/; f. 1999; Dir IGNACE DASSOHIRI; Editor-in-Chief OCTAVE BOYOU.

Le Jour: 26 ave Chardy, Plateau, 01 BP 2432, Abidjan 01; tel. 20-21-95-78; fax 20-21-95-80; e-mail lejour@africaonline.co.ci; internet www.lejour.ci; f. 1994; Dirs DIEGOU BAILLY, ABDOULAYE SANGARÉ; circ. 16,000.

Le Libéral: 01 BP 6938, Abidjan 01; tel. and fax 22-52-21-41; e-mail leliberal@leliberal.com; internet leliberal.com; f. 1997; Dir YORO KONÉ; Editor-in-Chief BAKARY NIMAG.

Le National: 16 BP 465, Abidjan 16; tel. 22-52-27-42; e-mail national@africanonline.co.ci; internet www.africaonline.co.ci/africaonline/infos/national/; f. 1999; Dir TAPÉ KOULOU LAURENT; Editor-in-Chief ASSÉ ALAFÉ.

Notre Voie: Cocody-les-Deux-Plateaux, 06 BP 2868, Abidjan 06; tel. 22-42-63-31; fax 22-42-63-32; e-mail gnh@africaonline.co.ci; internet www.notrevoie.ci; f. 1978; organ of the FPI; Dir WANYOU EUGÈNE ALLOU; Editor-in-chief DIABATÉ A. SIDICK.

La Nouvelle République: face Théâtre de la Cité, impasse P. L. Clouzet, Cocody Danga, 09 BP 960, Abidjan 09; tel. 22-41-15-89; fax 22-44-97-10; f. 1994; Dir NOËL YAO.

Le Patriote: rue Marconi prologée, Zone 4C, 22 BP 509, Abidjan 22; tel. 07-83-72-47; fax 20-22-59-26; e-mail info@patriote.ci; internet www.lepatriote.ci; organ of the RDR; Dir PATRICE G. LENONHIN; Editor-in-Chief SINDOU METTE.

Le Populaire–Nouvelle Formule: 19 blvd Angoulvant, résidence Neuilly, Plateau, 01 BP 5496, Abidjan 01; tel. 21-36-34-15; fax 21-36-43-28; Dir RAPHAËL ORE LAKPE.

Soir Info: rue Louis Lumière, zone 4C, 10 BP 2462, Abidjan 10; tel. 21-25-32-77; fax 21-35-85-66; e-mail olympe@afnet.net; internet www.presseci.com/soirinfo/; f. 1994; Dir MAURICE FERRO B. BALLY; circ. 10,000–15,000.

La Voie: face Institut Marie-Thérèse Houphouët-Boigny, 17 BP 656, Abidjan 17; tel. 20-37-68-23; fax 20-37-74-76; organ of the FPI; Dir ABOU DRAHAMANE SANGARÉ; Man. MAURICE LURIGNAN.

SELECTED WEEKLIES

Agora: Immeuble Nana Yamoussou, ave 13, rue 38, Treichville, 01 BP 5326, Abidjan 01; tel. 21-25-12-43; f. 1997; Dir FERNAND DÉDÉ; Editor-in-Chief BAMBA ALEX SOULEYMANE.

Argument: 09 BP 3328, Abidjan 09; tel. 20-37-63-96; f. 1998; Dir GUY-BADIETO LIALY.

Le Changement: Abidjan; tel. 21-25-52-52; f. 1991; weekly; Dir BELIWA DAVID GOGBÉ; circ. 10,000.

Citypoche: Immeuble Nour al-Ayat, 18 BP 3136, Abidjan 18; tel. 20-21-91-89; f. 1997; Dir ELIANE STROEHLIN.

Le Démocrate: Maison du Congrès, ave 2, Treichville, 01 BP 1212, Abidjan 01; tel. 21-24-45-88; fax 21-24-25-61; f. 1991; organ of the PDCI–RDA; Dir NOËL YAO.

Mousso: zone 4C, prolongement blvd du 7 décembre, Abidjan; fax 21-35-19-06; f. 1993; Dir MOUSSA SIDIBE.

Notre chance: Immeuble SICOGI, 1er étage, porte escalier E, blvd du Gabon (Marcory), 10 BP 654, Abidjan 10; tel. 21-26-44-28; Dir MICHEL NAHOUA LEPREGNON.

Le Nouvel Horizon: 220 Logements, blvd du Général de Gaulle, Adjamé, 17 BP 656, Abidjan 17; tel. 20-37-68-23; f. 1990; organ of the FPI; Dir ABOU DRAHAMANE SANGARÉ; circ. 15,000.

La Nouvelle Presse: rue des Jardins, Cocody-les-deux-Plateaux, 01 BP 8534, Abidjan 01; tel. 22-41-04-76; fax 22-41-04-15; e-mail jvieyra@africaonline.co.ci; f. 1992; publ. by Centre Africain de Presse et d'Edition; current affairs; Editors JUSTIN VIEYRA, JÉRÔME CARLOS; circ. 10,000.

Le Réveil-Hebdo: face Théâtre de la Cité, impasse P. L. Clouzet, Cocody Danga, 09 BP 960, Abidjan 09; tel. 22-44-90-96; fax 22-44-97-10; f. 1993; Dir NOËL YAO.

Sports Magazine: Yopougon-SOGEFIHA, 01 BP 4030, Abidjan 01; tel. 23-45-14-02; f. 1997; Dir JOSEPH ABLE.

Téré: 220 Lgts, blvd du Général de Gaulle, Adjamé Liberté, 20 BP 43, Abidjan 20; tel. and fax 20-37-79-42; organ of the PIT; weekly; Dir ANGÈLE GNONSOA.

La Voie du Compatriote: Adjamé St-Michel; 09 BP 2008, Abidjan 09; tel. 20-37-50-13; f. 1998; Dir SINARI KAL.

SELECTED PERIODICALS

Côte d'Ivoire Magazine: Présidence de la République, 01 BP 1354, Abidjan 01; tel. 20-22-02-22; f. 1998; quarterly; Dir JEAN-NOËL LOUKO.

La Lettre de l'Afrique de l'Ouest: rue des Jardins, Cocody-les-Deux-Plateaux, 01 BP 8534, Abidjan 01; tel. 22-41-04-76; fax 22-41-04-15; e-mail jvieyra@africaonline.co.ci; f. 1995; publ. by Centre Africain de Presse et d'Edition; six a year; politics, economics, regional integration; Editors JUSTIN VIEYRA, JÉRÔME CARLOS.

La Lettre de la Communication: Cité Administrative, BP V138, Abidjan; tel. 20-21-11-16; Dir PIERRE AYOUN N'DAH.

Maisons et Matériaux: 08 BP 2150, Abidjan 08; tel. 22-42-92-17; monthly; Dir THIAM T. DJENEBOU.

Roots-Rock Magazine: 01 BP 1418, Abidjan 01; tel. 22-42-84-74; f. 1998; monthly; music; Dir DIOMANDÉ DAVID.

RTI-Mag: 08 BP 663, Abidjan 08; tel. 20-33-14-46; fax 20-32-12-06; publ. by Radiodiffusion-Télévision Ivoirienne; listings magazine.

Stades d'Afrique: blvd du Général de Gaulle, 01 BP 1807, Abidjan 01; tel. 20-37-06-66; fax 20-37-25-45; e-mail fratmat@africaonline.co.ci; f. 2000; sports magazine; monthly; Dir-Gen. EMMANUEL KOUASSI KOKORÉ.

Le Succès: 21 BP 3748, Abidjan 21; tel. 20-37-71-64; monthly; Dir AKPLA PLAKATOU.

Univers jeunes: 01 BP 3713, Abidjan 01; tel. 21-35-35-35; fax 21-35-35-45; e-mail univers@africaonline.co.ci; monthly; Dir MARIAM SY DIAWARA.

La Voix d'Afrique: rue des Jardins, Cocody-les-Deux-Plateaux, 01 BP 8534, Abidjan 01; tel. 22-41-04-76; fax 22-41-04-15; e-mail jvieyra@africaonline.co.ci; publ. by Centre Africain de Presse et d'Edition; monthly; Editor-in-Chief GAOUSSOU KAMISSOKO.

NEWS AGENCIES

Agence Ivoirienne de Presse (AIP): ave Chardy, 04 BP 312, Abidjan 04; tel. 20-22-71-89; fax 20-21-73-39; e-mail aip@ci.refer.org; f. 1961; 12 perm. bureaux; Dir KONÉ SEMGUÉ SAMBA.

Foreign Bureaux

Agence France-Presse (AFP): 18 ave du Docteur Crozet, 01 BP 726, Abidjan 01; tel. 20-21-90-17; fax 20-21-10-36; e-mail afp@aviso.ci; Dir SERGE ARNOLD.

Associated Press (AP) (USA): 01 BP 5843, Abidjan 01; tel. 22-41-37-49.

Reuters West Africa (United Kingdom): Résidence Les Acacias, 2e étage, appt 203–205, 20 blvd Clozel, 01 BP 2338, Abidjan 01; tel. 20-21-12-22; fax 20-21-30-77; e-mail abidjan.newsroom@reuters .com; West Africa Man. MICHEL CLÉMENT; Bureau Chief NICHOLAS PHYTHIAN.

Xinhua (New China) News Agency (People's Republic of China): Cocody Danga Nord, Lot 46, Abidjan; tel. 22-44-01-24.

PRESS ASSOCIATIONS

Association de la Presse Démocratique Ivoirienne (APDI): Abidjan; f. 1994; tel. 37-06-66; Chair. JEAN-BAPTISTE AKROU.

Union nationale des journalistes de Côte d'Ivoire (UNJCI): 06 BP 1675, Abidjan 06; tel. 20-21-61-07; e-mail unjci@globeaccess.net; internet www.unjci.ci; f. 1991; Pres. NDJOMOU YÉDAGNE HONORAT; 200 mems.

Publishers

Centre Africain de Presse et d'Edition (CAPE): rue des Jardins, Cocody-les-Deux-Plateaux, 01 BP 8534, Abidjan 01; tel. 22-41-04-76; fax 22-41-04-15; e-mail jvieyra@africaonline.co.ci; Man. JUSTIN VIEYRA.

Centre d'Edition et de Diffusion Africaines (CEDA): 04 BP 541, Abidjan 04; tel. 20-22-22-42; fax 20-32-72-62; f. 1961; general non-fiction; Chair. and Man. Dir VENANCE KACOU.

Centre de Publications Evangéliques: 08 BP 900, Abidjan 08; tel. 22-44-48-05; fax 22-44-58-17; e-mail jules_ouoba@crosswalkmail.com; f. 1970; religious; Dir JULES OUOBA.

Nouvelles Editions Ivoiriennes: 01 BP 1818, Abidjan 01; tel. 21-24-07-66; fax 21-24-24-56; e-mail info@nei.co.ci; internet www .nei.co.ci; f. 1972; literature, criticism, essays, drama, religion, art, history; Dir G. LAMBIN.

Université Nationale de Côte d'Ivoire: 01 BP V34, Abidjan 01; tel. 22-44-08-59. f. 1964; academic and general non-fiction and periodicals; Publications Dir GILLES VILASCO.

Government Publishing House

Imprimerie Nationale: BP V87, Abidjan; tel. 20-21-76-11; fax 20-21-68-68.

Broadcasting and Communications

TELECOMMUNICATIONS

Regulatory Authorities

Agence des Télécommunications de Côte d'Ivoire: Immeuble POSTEL 2001, 2e étage, 18 BP 2203, Abidjan 18; tel. 20-34-42-54; fax 20-34-42-58; e-mail atci@africaonline.co.ci; f. 1995; Man. Dir KOUATCHI EBOU.

Conseil des Télécommunications de Côte d'Ivoire: 17 BP 110, Abidjan 17; tel. 20-34-43-04; f. 1995; deals with issues of arbitration.

Service Providers

Côte d'Ivoire-Télécom (CI-Télécom): Immeuble Postel 2000, rue Lecoeur, 17 BP 275, Abidjan 17; tel. 34-34-40-00; fax 34-34-48-28; e-mail info@telecomci.com; internet www.telecomci.com; f. 1991; 51% owned by France Câble Radio; 49% state-owned; Pres. LÉON AKA BONNY; Man. Dir ALAIN PETIT.

Comstar Wireless: Immeuble Alpha 2000, 11e étage, Plateau, Abidjan; tel. 20-22-81-01; fax 20-22-81-05; f. 1996; mobile cellular telephone operator; owned by International Wireless Inc.

Loteny Télécom SA: 12 rue Crossons Duplessis, 01 BP 3685, Abidjan 01; tel. 20-32-32-32; fax 20-32-27-25; e-mail info@telecel.net; internet www.telecel.net; f. 1996; mobile cellular telephone operator; partnership between Telecel International, Access Télécom and Loteny Electronics; Pres. MIKO RWAYITARE.

Société Ivoirienne de Mobiles (SIM): Immeuble Le Quartz, 5e étage, blvd Valery Giscard d'Estaing, Zone 4C, 11 BP 202, Abidjan 11; tel. 21-23-90-10; fax 21-23-90-11; f. 1996; mobile cellular telephone operator; 85% owned by France Télécom; Man. Dir BERNARD CLIVET; 220,000 subscribers (January 2001).

BROADCASTING
Radio

Radiodiffusion-Télévision Ivoirienne (RTI): BP V 191, Abidjan 01; tel. 20-21-48-00; e-mail rti@rti.ci; internet www.rti.ci; f. 1962; state-owned; Pres. JOACHIM BONY; Dir-Gen. GEORGES ABOKE.

La Chaîne Nationale: general FM broadcasts; 280 hrs of programmes weekly; also broadcasts regional news in national languages; 10 studios (eight in Abidjan and two in Bouaké).

Fréquence 2: themed FM broadcasts; entertainment, youth and relaxation; 147 hrs of programming weekly.

Africa N° 1 Côte d'Ivoire: Abidjan; internet www.africa1.com; FM station; Dir NOËL YAO.

BBC Afrique: Abidjan; broadcasts commenced 1994; FM station operated by British Broadcasting Corpn.

Radio Espoir: 12 BP 27, Abidjan 12; tel. 21-27-60-01; fax 21-27-69-70; e-mail respoir@globeaccess.net; internet www.multimania.com/radioespoir; f. 1990; broadcasts from Port-Bouët by Roman Catholic Church; Dir Fr BASILE DIANÉ KOGNAN.

RFI Internationale: Abidjan; operated by Radio France Internationale.

Television

Radiodiffusion-Télévision Ivoirienne (RTI): see above.

La Première Chaîne: 08 BP 883, Abidjan 08; tel. 22-44-90-39; general national and regional broadcasting; French and national languages; Dir KOFFI YOUBOUÉ.

TV 2: 08 BP 883, Abidjan 08; tel. 22-44-90-39; f. 1991; operates in Abidjan and the southern region; local news and current affairs; Dir MAIXENT DEGNEY.

Canal Horizon: Abidjan; e-mail abo.canal@aviso.ci; internet www.canalhorizons.com; broadcasts commenced 1994; subsidiary of Canal Plus (France); 15,000 subscribers (1995).

Côte d'Ivoire also receives international broadcasts from TVS, CNN, MCM Africa and Euronews.

Finance

(cap. = capital; res = reserves; m. = million; br. = branch; amounts in francs CFA)

BANKING
Central Bank

Banque Centrale des Etats de l'Afrique de l'Ouest (BCEAO): ave Terrasson-de-Fougères, 01 BP 1769, Abidjan 01; tel. 20-21-04-66; fax 20-22-28-52; internet www.bceao.int; f. 1962; HQ in Dakar, Senegal; bank of issue for the mem. states of the Union économique et monétaire ouest-africaine (UEMOA, comprising Benin, Burkina Faso, Côte d'Ivoire, Guinea-Bissau, Mali, Niger, Senegal and Togo); cap. and res 806,918m., total assets 4,084,464m. (Dec. 1998); Gov. CHARLES KONAN BANNY; Dir in Côte d'Ivoire LANSINA BAKARY; 5 brs.

Commercial Banks

Bank of Africa–Côte d'Ivoire (BOA–CI): Immeuble ex-BNDA, 11 rue Joseph Anoma, 01 BP 4132, Abidjan 01; tel. 20-33-15-36; fax 20-32-89-93; e-mail c.i.boa@globeaccess.net; 52% owned by Groupe African Financial Holding; cap. and res 4,355m., total assets 31,965m. (Dec. 1998); Chair. PAUL DERREUMAUX; Man. Dir JEAN-PIERRE GALIBERT.

Banque Atlantique–Côte d'Ivoire: Immeuble Atlantique, ave Nogues, 04 BP 1036, Abidjan 04; tel. 20-31-59-50; fax 20-21-68-52; f. 1979; cap. and res 7,189m., total assets 59,713m. (Dec. 1998); Pres. SERGE GUETTA; Dir-Gen. JACKY VASSEUR; 2 brs.

Banque de l'Habitat de Côte d'Ivoire (BHCI): 22 ave Joseph Anoma, 01 BP 2325, Abidjan 01; tel. 20-22-60-00; fax 20-22-58-18; f. 1993; cap. and res 1,108m., total assets 14,407m. (Dec. 1998); Chair. DAVID AMUAH; Man. Dir LACINA COULIBALY.

Banque Internationale pour le Commerce et l'Industrie de la Côte d'Ivoire SA (BICICI): Tour BICICI, ave Franchet d'Espérey, 01 BP 1298, Abidjan 01; tel. 20-20-16-00; fax 20-20-17-00; f. 1962; 28% owned by Société Financière pour les Pays d'Outre-Mer (Switzerland), 21% by BNP Paribas, SA (France), 20% state-owned; cap. 15,000.0m., res 15,633.4m., dep. 282,101.5m. (Dec. 1999); Chair. ANGE KOFFY; Man. Dir PATRICK MATHIEU; 39 brs.

Banque Paribas Côte d'Ivoire: Immeuble Alliance, 6e étage, 17 ave Terrasson de Fougères, 17 BP 09, Abidjan 17; tel. 20-21-86-86; fax 20-21-88-23; f. 1984; 84% owned by BNP Paribas, SA (France); cap. and res 2,856m., total assets 26,632m. (Dec. 1998); Chair. FRANÇOIS DAUGE; Man. Dir FRANÇOIS DU PEUTY.

BIAO–Côte d'Ivoire SA (BIAO–CI): 8–10 ave Joseph Anoma, 01 BP 1274, Abidjan 01; tel. 20-20-07-20; fax 20-20-07-00; e-mail biaosq@africaonline.co.ci; internet www.biao.co.ci; f. 1980; 80% owned by Banque Belgolaise; cap. and res 6,022m., total assets 219,989m. (Dec. 1999); Chair. SEYDOU DIARRA; 31 brs.

Citibank NA: Immeuble Botreau Roussel, 28 ave Delafosse, 01 BP 3698, Abidjan 01; tel. 20-20-90-00; ; fax 20-21-76-85; e-mail citibank@odaci.net; Dir-Gen. MARC H. WIESSING.

Compagnie Bancaire de l'Atlantique Côte d'Ivoire (COBACI): Immeuble Alpha 2000, rue Gourgas, Plateau, 01 BP 522, Abidjan 01; tel. 20-21-28-04; fax 20-21-07-98; e-mail cobaci@africaonline.co.ci; 65% owned by Banque Atlantique–Côte d'Ivoire; cap. 1,500.0m., res 288.0m., dep. 9,525.0m. (Dec. 1999); Chair SERGE GUETTA; Man. Dir MICHEL FRANÇOIS KAHN.

Compagnie Financière de la Côte d'Ivoire (COFINCI): Tour BICICI, 15e étage, ave Franchet d'Espérey, 01 BP 1566, Abidjan 01; tel. 20-21-27-32; fax 20-21-26-43; f. 1974; subsidiary of Banque Internationale pour le Commerce et l'Industrie de la Côte d'Ivoire; 34.5% owned by BNP Paribas, SA (France); cap. and res 2,337m., total assets 10,183m. (Dec. 1998); Chair. ANGE KOFFY; Man. Dir PATRICK MATHIEU.

Ecobank–Côte d'Ivoire, SA: Immeuble Alliance, 17 ave Terrasson de Fougères, 01 BP 4107, Abidjan 01; tel. 20-21-10-41; fax 20-21-88-16; e-mail ecobankci@ecobank.com.; internet www.ecobank.com; f. 1989; 92% owned by Ecobank Transnational Inc and subsids (operating under the auspices of the Economic Community of West African States); cap. 3,226.0m., res 272.3m., dep. 80,433.7m. (Dec. 1999); Chair. ABDOULAYE KONÉ; Man. Dir AMIN UDDIN; 1 br.

Société Générale de Banques en Côte d'Ivoire SA (SGBCI): 25 ave Joseph Anoma, Plateau, 01 BP 1355, Abidjan 01; tel. 20-20-12-34; fax 20-20-14-82; e-mail sgbci@globeaccess.net; f. 1962; 39% owned by Société Générale (France); cap. and res 33,990m., total assets 452,208m. (Dec. 1998); Chair. and Man. Dir TIÉMOKO YADÉ COULIBALY; Man. Dir MICHEL MIAILLE; 55 brs.

Société Générale de Financement et de Participations en Côte d'Ivoire (SOGEFINANCE): 25 ave Joseph Anoma, 01 BP 3904, Abidjan 01; tel. 20-22-55-30; fax 20-32-67-60; f. 1978; 58% owned by SGBCI; cap. and res 1,788m., total assets 6,633m. (Dec. 1998); Chair. and Man. Dir TIÉMOKO YADÉ COULIBALY; Man. Dir ANTOINE YAO CASSAIGNAN.

Société Ivoirienne de Banque (SIB): Immeuble Alpha 2000, 34 blvd de la République, 01 BP 1300, Abidjan 01; tel. 20-20-00-00; fax 20-21-97-41; e-mail cob.infprod@aviso.ci; f. 1962; 51% owned by Crédit Lyonnais (France); 49% state-owned; reduction of state holding to 19% pending; cap. and res 10,955m., total assets 224,308m. (Dec. 1998); Man. Dir JEAN-PIERRE GREYFIE DE BELLECOMBE; 14 brs.

Credit Institutions

Afribail Côte d'Ivoire (Afribail–CI): 01 BP 1274, Abidjan 01; tel. 20-20-07-25; fax 20-20-07-26; 95% owned by (BIAO–CI); cap. and res 623m., total assets 7,375m. (Dec. 1996); Chair. RENÉ AMANY; Man. Dir JACOB AHIWA.

BICI Bail de Côte d'Ivoire: Tour BICICI, 5e étage, ave Franchet d'Espérey, 01 BP 6495, Abidjan 01; tel. 20-22-24-31; fax 20-20-17-00; internet www.bicibail.com; 75% owned by BICICI; cap. and res 1,792m., total assets 13,977m. (Dec. 1997); Pres. ANGE KOFFY; Man. Dir PATRICK MATHIEU.

Compagnie Ivoirienne de Vente à Crédit et Acquisition (CIVECA): 04 BP 2084, Abidjan 04; tel. 20-22-77-13; fax 20-22-77-35; 87.8% owned by Mutuelle d'Assurance des Taxis Compteur d'Abidjan; cap. and res 826m., total assets 2,343m. (Dec. 1997); Pres. O. YOU TIDJANI; Dir-Gen. DOMINIQUE KONAN KOUAME.

Société Africaine de Crédit Automobilière (SAFCA): Immeuble SAFCA, 1 rue des Carrossiers, Zone 3, 04 BP 27, Abidjan 04; tel. 20-24-91-77; fax 21-35-77-90; e-mail safca@africaonline.co.ci; cap. and res 5,417m., total assets 27,660m. (Dec. 1998); Pres. and Dir-Gen. DIACK DIAWAR.

Société Africaine de Crédit-Bail (SAFBAIL): Immeuble SAFCA, 1 rue des Carrossiers, Zone 3, 04 BP 27, Abidjan 04; tel. 21-24-91-77; fax 21-35-77-90; e-mail safbail@africaonline.co.ci; cap. and res 2,456m., total assets 10,743m. (Dec. 1998); Chair. and Man. Dir DIACK DIAWAR.

SOGEFIBAIL–CI: 26 ave Delafosse, 01 BP 1355, Abidjan 01; tel. 20-32-85-15; fax 20-33-14-93; 35% owned by GENEFITEC, 35% by

SOGEFINANCE, 25% by SGBCI; cap. and res 2,145m., total assets 9,515m. (June 1999); Dir Pierre Gabriel Siby.

Financial Institution

Caisse Autonome d'Amortissement: Immeuble SCIAM, ave Marchand, 01 BP 670, Abidjan 01; tel. 20-21-06-11; fax 20-21-35-78; f. 1959; management of state funds; Chair. Abdoulaye Koné; Man. Dir Victor Kouamé.

Bankers' Association

Association Professionnelle des Banques et Etablissements Financiers de Côte d'Ivoire (APBEFCI): 01 BP 3810, Abidjan 01; tel. 20-21-20-08; Pres. Jean-Pierre Meyer.

STOCK EXCHANGE

Bourse Régionale des Valeurs Mobilières (BRVM): 18 ave Joseph Anoma, 01 BP 3802, Abidjan 01; tel. 20-32-66-85; fax 20-32-66-84; e-mail brvm@brvm.org; internet www.brvm.org; f. 1998 to succeed Bourse des Valeurs d'Abidjan; regional stock exchange serving mem. states of UEMOA; Dir-Gen. Jean-Paul Gillet.

BRVM (Antenne Nationale de Côte d'Ivoire): 18 ave Joseph Anoma, 01 BP 1541, Abidjan 01; tel. 20-31-55-50; fax 20-32-47-77; e-mail tbah@brvm.org; Man. Tidiane Amadou Bah.

INSURANCE

Abidjanaise d'Assurances: Immeuble Woodin Center, ave Noguès, 01 BP 2909, Abidjan 01; tel. 20-22-46-96; fax 20-22-64-81; e-mail abjassur@africaonline.co.ci.

AFRAM: Immeuble ex-Monopris, 2 ave Noguès, 01 BP 7124, Abidjan 01; tel. 20-32-30-44; fax 20-32-69-72.

AFRICASSUR: blvd Giscard d'Estaing, 01 BP 4092, Abidjan 01; tel. 21-26-05-83.

Assurances Générales de Côte d'Ivoire (AGCI): Immeuble AGCI, ave Noguès, 01 BP 4092, Abidjan 01; tel. 20-32-10-52; fax 20-33-25-79; e-mail agci@africaonline.co.ci; f. 1979; mem. of Groupe NSIA–AGCI since 1996; Chair. and Man. Dir Jean Kacou Diagou.

Assurances Générales de Côte d'Ivoire–Vie (AGCI–Vie): Immeuble AGCI, ave Nogues, 01 BP 4092, Abidjan 01; tel. 20-33-11-31; fax 20-33-25-79; f. 1988; mem. of Groupe NSIA–AGCI since 1996; life; Chair. and Man. Dir Jean Kacou Diagou.

AXA Assurances Côte d'Ivoire: ave Delafosse Prolongée, 01 BP 378, Abidjan 01; tel. 20-21-73-81; fax 20-22-12-43; f. 1981; fmrly l'Union Africaine–IARD; insurance and reinsurance; Chair. Joachim Richmond; Dir Alexandre Ahui Atte.

AXA Vie Côte d'Ivoire: 9 ave Houdaille, 01 BP 2016, Abidjan 01; tel. 20-22-25-15; fax 20-22-37-60; f. 1985; fmrly Union Africaine Vie; life assurance and capitalization; Chair. Joachim Richmond; Dir Patrice Desgranges.

Colina SA: Immeuble Colina, blvd Roume, 01 BP 3832, Abidjan 01; tel. 20-21-65-05; fax 20-22-59-05; f. 1980; e-mail c-dg@colina-sa.com; internet www.colina-sa.com; Chair. Michel Pharaon; Dir-Gen. Raymond Farhat.

Mutuelle Centrale d'Assurances: 15 Immeuble Ebrien, 01 BP 1217, Abidjan 01; tel. 20-21-11-24; fax 20-33-18-37.

La Nationale d'Assurances (CNA): Immeuble Symphonie, 30 ave du Général de Gaulle, 01 BP 1333, Abidjan 01; tel. 20-21-49-19; fax 20-22-49-06; f. 1972; cap. 400m.; insurance and reinsurance; Chair. Sounkalo Djibo; Man. Dir Richard Coulibaly.

Nouvelle Société Interafricaine d'Assurances (NSIA): 01 BP 1571, Abidjan 01; tel. 20-22-76-22; fax 20-22-76-20; e-mail nsia@africaonline.co.ci; f. 1995; mem. of Groupe NSIA–AGCI; Chair. and Man. Dir Jean Kacou Diagou.

La Sécurité Ivoirienne: Immeuble La Sécurité Ivoirienne, blvd Roume, Abidjan; tel. 20-21-50-63; fax 20-21-05-67; f. 1971; general; Dir-Gen. Jacques Bardoux.

Société Africaine d'Assurances et de Réassurances en République de Côte d'Ivoire (SAFARRIV): 01 BP 1741, Abidjan 01; tel. 20-21-91-57; fax 20-21-82-72; e-mail groupe-safarriv@safarriv.ci; internet www.safarriv.ci; f. 1975; Pres. Tiémoko Yadé Coulibaly; Man. Dir Christian Arrault.

Société Ivoirienne d'Assurances Mutuelles–Mutuelle d'Assurances Transports (SIDAM–MAT): Immeuble SIDAM, ave Houdaille, 01 BP 1217, Abidjan 01; tel. 20-21-97-82; fax 20-32-94-39; f. 1970; Chair. Abou Doumbia; Dir-Gen. Souleymane Meite.

Trade and Industry

GOVERNMENT AGENCIES

Bureau Nationale d'Etudes Techniques et de Développement (BNETD): ancien hôtel 'Le Relais', blvd Hassan II, Cocody, 04 BP 945, Abidjan 04; tel. 22-44-28-05; fax 22-44-56-66; e-mail info@bnetd.sita.net; internet www.bnetd.sita.net; f. 1978 as Direction et Controle des Grands Travaux; management and supervision of major public works projects; Man. Dir Don-Mello Ahoua.

Comité de Privatisation: 6 blvd de l'Indénié, 01 BP 1141, Abidjan 01; tel. 20-22-22-31; fax 20-22-22-35; e-mail cpct@africaonline.co.ci; state privatization authority; Pres. Jean-Claude Brou; Dir Nazaire Gounongbe.

Compagnie Ivoirienne pour le Développement des Cultures Vivrières (CIDV): 01 BP 2049, Abidjan 01; tel. 20-21-00-79. 1988; production of food crops; Man. Dir Benoît N'Dri Brou.

PETROCI Exploration Production SA: Immeuble les Hévéas, 05 BP 2954, Abidjan 01; tel. 20-20-25-00; fax 20-21-68-24; f. 1975; f. 1998 to succeed Société Nationale d'Opérations Pétrolières de la Côte d'Ivoire (PETROCI); transfer to private ownership pending; all aspects of hydrocarbons development; Pres and Man. Dir (vacant).

Société pour le Développement Minier de la Côte d'Ivoire (SODEMI): 31 blvd André Latrille, 01 BP 2816, Abidjan 01; tel. 22-44-29-94; fax 22-44-08-21; internet www.sodemi.ci; f. 1962; geological and mineral research; Pres. Nicolas Kouandi Angba; Man. Dir Joseph N'Zi.

Société de Développement des Plantations Forestières (SODEFOR): blvd François Mitterrand, 01 BP 3770, Abidjan 01; tel. 22-44-46-16; fax 22-44-02-40; f. 1966; establishment and management of tree plantations, management of state forests, marketing of timber products; Pres. Minister of Agriculture and Animal Resources; Man. Dir Jean-Claude Aneh.

Société pour le Développement des Productions Animales (SODEPRA): 01 BP 1249, Abidjan 01; tel. 20-21-13-10; f 1970; rearing of livestock; Man. Dir Paul Lamizana.

DEVELOPMENT AGENCIES

Agence Française de Développement (AFD): 01 BP 1814, Abidjan 01; tel. 22-44-53-05; fax 22-44-21-78; e-mail afd.ci@globeaccess.net; internet www.ambafrance-abidjan.org/menu_afd.htm; fmrly Caisse Française de Développement; Dir in Côte d'Ivoire Guy Terracol.

Centre pour la Promotion des Investissements en Côte d'Ivoire (CEPICI): BP V152, Abidjan 01; tel. 20-21-40-70; fax 20-21-40-71; e-mail info@cepici.go.ci; internet www.cepici.go.ci; f. 1993 investment promotion authority; Dir Jean-Claude Kouassi; Gen. Man. M. Koffivi.

CHAMBERS OF COMMERCE

Chambre d'Agriculture de la Côte d'Ivoire: 11 ave Lamblin, 01 BP 1291, Abidjan 01; tel. 20-32-92-13; fax 20-32-92-20; Sec.-Gen. Gauthier N'Zi.

Chambre de Commerce et d'Industrie de Côte d'Ivoire: 6 ave Joseph Anoma, 01 BP 1399, Abidjan 01; tel. 20-33-16-00; fax 20-32-39-46; internet www.africaonline.co.ci/africaonline/societes/ccic/ccic.html; f.1992; Pres. Seydou Elimane Diarra; Dir-Gen. Konan Koffi.

TRADE ASSOCIATIONS

Bureau Ivoirien du Café-cacao (BICC): Abidjan; f. 2000 to replace La Nouvelle Caistab (Caisse de Stabilisation et de Soutien des Prix des Productions Agricoles); fmrly govt agency responsible for controlling price, quality and export of cocoa and coffee; restructured 1995–98 prior to liberalization in 1999; offices in Paris, London and New York.

Fédération Ivoirienne des Producteurs de Café et de Cacao (FIPCC): Yamoussoukro; f. 1998; coffee and cocoa growers' assoc.; Chair. Cissé Lociné; c. 3,000 mems.

Organisation de Commercialisation de l'Ananas et de la Banane (OCAB): Abidjan; pineapple and banana growers' assoc.

EMPLOYERS' ASSOCIATIONS

Fédération Maritime de la Côte d'Ivoire (FEDERMAR): 04 BP 723, Abidjan 04; tel. 20-21-25-83; f. 1958; Sec.-Gen. Vacaba Touré de Movaly.

Fédération Nationale des Industries de la Côte d'Ivoire: 01 BP 1340, Abidjan 01; tel. 20-21-71-42; fax 20-21-72-56; f. 1993; Pres. Pierre Magne; Sec.-Gen. Daniel Teurquetil; 280 mems.

Groupement Interprofessionnel de l'Automobile (GIPA): 01 BP 1340, Abidjan 01; tel. 20-21-71-42; fax 20-21-72-56; f. 1953; Pres. Bouaké Fofana; Sec.-Gen. Daniel Teurquetil; 32 mems.

Syndicat des Commerçants Importateurs, Exportateurs et Distributeurs de la Côte d'Ivoire (SCIMPEX): 01 BP 3792, Abidjan 01; tel. 20-21-54-27; Pres. Jacques Rossignol; Sec.-Gen. M. Koffi.

Syndicat des Entrepreneurs et des Industriels de la Côte d'Ivoire (SEICI): Immeuble Jean Lefèbvre, 14 blvd de Marseille, 01 BP 464, Abidjan 01; tel. 20-21-83-85; f. 1934; Pres. Abdel Aziz Thiam.

Syndicat des Exportateurs et Négociants en Bois de Côte d'Ivoire: Immeuble CCIA, 11e étage, 01 BP 1979, Abidjan 01; tel. 20-21-12-39; fax 20-21-26-42; Pres. JEAN-CLAUDE BERNARD.

Syndicat des Producteurs Industriels du Bois (SPIB): Immeuble CCIA, 11e étage, 01 BP 318, Abidjan 01; tel. 20-21-12-39; fax 20-21-26-42; f. 1943; Pres. BRUNO FINOCCHIARO.

Union des Entreprises Agricoles et Forestières: Immeuble CCIA, 11e étage, 01 BP 2300, Abidjan 01; tel. 20-21-12-39; fax 20-21-26-42; f. 1952; Pres. FULGENCE KOFFY.

UTILITIES
Electricity

Compagnie Ivoirienne d'Electricité (CIE): ave Christiani, 01 BP 6932, Abidjan 01; tel. 21-23-33-00; fax 21-75-00-50; e-mail info@cie.ci; internet www.cie.ci; f. 1990 to assume electricity distribution network fmrly operated by Energie Electrique de la Côte d'Ivoire; 70% controlled by Société Bouygues group (France); Pres. MARCEL ZADI KESSY; Dir GÉRARD THEURIAU.

Compagnie Ivoirienne de Production d'Electricité (CIPREL): Tour Sidom, 12e étage, ave Houdaille, 01 BP 4039, Abidjan 01; tel. 20-22-60-97; independent power production.

Gas

Gaz de Côte d'Ivoire (GDCI): 01 BP 1351, Abidjan; tel. 22-44-49-55; f. 1961; transfer to majority private ownership pending; gas distributor; Man. Dir LAMBERT KONAN.

Water

Société de Distribution d'Eau de la Côte d'Ivoire (SODECI): 1 ave Christiani-Treichville, 01 BP 1843, Abidjan 01; tel. 21-23-30-00; fax 21-24-20-33; f. 1959; production, treatment and distribution of drinking water; 46% owned by SAUR, 51% owned by employees, 3% state-owned; Chair. MARCEL ZADI KESSY; Man. Dir. PIERRE LE TAREAU.

TRADE UNIONS

Fédération des Syndicats Autonomes de la Côte d'Ivoire (FESACI): Abidjan; breakaway group from the Union Générale des Travailleurs de Côte d'Ivoire; Sec. Gen. MARCEL ETTÉ.

Union Générale des Travailleurs de Côte d'Ivoire (UGTCI): 05 BP 1203, Abidjan 05; tel. 20-21-26-65; f. 1962; Sec.-Gen. HYACINTHE ADIKO NIAMKEY; 100,000 individual mems; 190 affiliated unions.

Transport

RAILWAYS

The 660 km of track in Côte d'Ivoire run from Abidjan to Niangoloko, on the border with Burkina Faso; from there, the railway extends to Kaya, via the Burkinabè capital, Ouagadougou.

SITARAIL–Transport Ferroviaire de Personnel et de Marchandises: Résidence Memanou, blvd Clozel, Plateau, 16 BP 1216, Abidjan 16; tel. 20-21-06-36; fax 20-22-48-47; f. 1995 to operate services on Abidjan–Kaya (Burkina Faso) line; Man. Dir ABDEL AZIZ THIAM.

ROADS

There are about 68,000 km of roads, of which some 6,000 km are paved. Some 68,000m. francs CFA was invested in the road network in 1994–98; projects included the upgrading of 3,000 km of roads and 30,000 km of tracks. Tolls were introduced on some roads in the mid-1990s, to assist in funding the maintenance of the network.

Société des Transports Abidjanais (SOTRA): 01 BP 2009, Abidjan 01; tel. 21-75-71-00; fax 21-25-97-21; e-mail sotra@access.net; f. 1960; 60% state-owned; urban transport; Man. Dir PHILIPPE ATTEY.

SHIPPING

Côte d'Ivoire has two major ports, Abidjan and San Pedro, both of which are industrial and commercial establishments with financial autonomy. Abidjan, which handled some 15.2m. metric tons of goods in 1998, is the largest container and trading port in west Africa. Access to the port is via the 2.7-km Vridi Canal. The port at San Pedro, which handled 1.1m. tons of goods in 1994, remains the main gateway to the south-western region of Côte d'Ivoire.

Port Autonome d'Abidjan (PAA): BP V85, Abidjan; tel. 21-23-80-00; fax 21-23-80-80; e-mail info@paa-ci.org; internet www.paa-ci.org; f. 1950; public undertaking supervised by the Govt; Man. Dir JEAN-MICHEL MOULOD.

Port Autonome de San Pedro (PASP): BP 339/340, San Pedro; tel. 71-20-80; fax 71-27-85; internet ibs.africaonline.co.ci/pasp; f. 1971; Man. Dir OGOU ATTEMENE.

AMICI: Km 1, blvd de Marseille, 16 BP 643, Abidjan 16; tel. 21-35-28-50; fax 21-35-28-54; e-mail amici.abj@aviso.ci; f. 1998.

Compagnie Maritime Africaine–Côte d'Ivoire (COMAF–CI): rond-point du Nouveau Port, 08 BP 867, Abidjan 08; tel. 20-32-40-77; f. 1973; navigation and management of ships; Dir FRANCO BERNARDINI.

Nouvelle SITRAM: rue des Pétroliers, 01 BP 1546, Abidjan 01; tel. 21-36-92-00; fax 21-35-73-93; f. 1967, nationalized in 1976 as Société Ivoirienne de Transport Maritime; returned to private ownership in 1995; services between Europe and west Africa and the USA; Chair. BONIFACE PEGAWAGNABA; Dir Commdt FAKO KONÉ.

SAGA–CI: Immeuble SAGA–CI, rond-point du Nouveau Port, 01 BP 1727, Abidjan 01; tel. 21-23-23-23; fax 21-24-25-06; merchandise handling, transit and storage; Chair. CHARLES BENITAL; Dir DANIEL CHARRIER.

Société Agence Maritime de l'Ouest Africain–Côte d'Ivoire (SAMOA–CI): rue des Gallions, 01 BP 1611, Abidjan 01; tel. 20-21-29-65; f. 1955; shipping agents; Man. Dir CLAUDE PERDRIAUD.

Société Ivoirienne de Navigation Maritime (SIVOMAR): 5 rue Charpentier, zone 2b, Treichville, 01 BP 1395, Abidjan 01; tel. 20-21-73-23; fax 20-32-38-53; f. 1977; shipments to ports in Africa, the Mediterranean and the Far East; Dir SIMPLISSE DE MESSE ZINSOU.

Société Ouest-Africaine d'Entreprises Maritimes en Côte d'Ivoire (SOAEM–CI): 01 BP 1727, Abidjan 01; tel. 20-21-59-69; fax 20-32-24-67; f. 1978; merchandise handling, transit and storage; Chair. JACQUES PELTIER; Dir JACQUES COLOMBANI.

SOCOPAO–Côte d'Ivoire: Km 1, blvd de la République, 01 BP 1297, Abidjan 01; tel. 21-24-13-14; fax 21-24-21-30; e-mail socopao@africaonline.co.ci; shipping agents; Shipping Dir OLIVIER RANJARD.

CIVIL AVIATION

There are three international airports: Abidjan–Félix Houphouët-Boigny, Bouaké and Yamoussoukro. Work to expand and modernize Abidjan's airport began in mid-1996: the project, costing an estimated 14,000m. francs CFA, was scheduled for completion in late 2000. In addition, there are 25 domestic and regional airports, including those at Bouna, Korhogo, Man, Odienné and San Pedro.

Agence Nationale de l'Aviation Civile: 07 BP 148, Abidjan 07; tel. 21-27-74-24; fax 21-27-63-46; civil aviation authority; Dir JEAN KOUASSI ABONOUAN.

Air Afrique (Société Aérienne Africaine Multinationale): 3 ave Joseph Anoma, 01 BP 3927, Abidjan 01; tel. 20-20-30-00; fax 20-20-30-08; internet www.airafrique.com; f. 1961; 33% owned jtly by the Govts of Benin, Burkina Faso, the Central African Repub., Chad, the Repub. of the Congo, Côte d'Ivoire, Mali, Mauritania, Niger, Senegal and Togo; extensive regional flights and services to Europe, North America and the Middle East; Chair. ABDOULAYE SOULE; Chief Exec. PAPE SOW THIAM.

Société Nouvelle Air Ivoire: place de la République, 01 BP 1027, Abidjan 01; tel. 20-20-66-66; fax 20-33-26-26; f. 2000 to replace Air Ivoire (f. 1960); 49% state-owned, 34% owned by Air France, 17% owned by Air Afrique; Man. Dir VASSIRIKE SAVANÉ.

Tourism

The game reserves, forests, lagoons, coastal resorts, rich ethnic folklore and the lively city of Abidjan are tourist attractions; Côte d'Ivoire also has well-developed facilities for business visitors, including golfing centres. Some 301,000 tourists visited Côte d'Ivoire in 1998; receipts from tourism in 1997 totalled US $88m.

Office Ivoirien du Tourisme et de l'Hôtellerie: Immeuble ex-EECI, place de la République, 01 BP 8538, Abidjan 01; tel. 20-20-65-00; fax 20-20-65-31; e-mail oith@africaonline.co.ci; internet www.tourisme.ci; f. 1992; Dir CAMILLE KOUASSI.

CROATIA

Introductory Survey

Location, Climate, Language, Religion, Flag, Capital

The Republic of Croatia is situated in south-eastern Europe and has a long western coastline on the Adriatic Sea. It is bordered to the north-west by Slovenia, to the north-east by Hungary and to the east by the Vojvodina area of Serbia, part of the Federal Republic of Yugoslavia (FRY). Bosnia and Herzegovina abuts into Croatia, forming a southern border along the Sava river. The Croatian territory of Dubrovnik (formerly known as Ragusa), which is situated at the southern tip of the narrowing stretch of Croatia (beyond a short coastal strip of Bosnia and Herzegovina), has a short border with Montenegro, also part of the FRY. The climate is continental in the hilly interior and Mediterranean on the coast. There is steady rainfall throughout the year, although summer is the wettest season. The average annual rainfall in Zagreb is 890 mm (35 ins). Both the ethnic Croats (who comprised 78.1% of the total population according to the 1991 census) and the Serb minority (12.2%) speak versions of Serbo-Croat, but the largely Roman Catholic Croats use the Latin script and the Eastern Orthodox Serbs use the Cyrillic script. Since 1991 the ethnic Croats have rejected the 1954 Novi Sad Agreement (which proclaimed Serbo-Croat to be one language with two scripts), and now claim the distinctness of a Croatian language (Croat). There are, in addition, a number of small minority communities in Croatia, notably the Muslim community (which comprised 0.9% of the total population in 1991). The national flag (proportions 2 by 1) consists of three horizontal stripes, of red, white and dark blue, with the arms of Croatia (a shield of 25 squares, alternately red and white, below a blue crown composed of five shields) fimbriated in red and white and set in the centre of the flag, overlapping all three stripes. The capital is Zagreb.

Recent History

From the 16th century the territory of what is now the Republic of Croatia was divided between the Ottoman (Turkish) and Habsburg (Austrian) empires (although Dalmatia and Istria were dominated at different times by Venice and by France). After the Hungarian revolution of 1848–49, Croatia and Slavonia were made Austrian crown-lands. The Habsburg Empire became the Dual Monarchy of Austria-Hungary in 1867, and the territories were restored to the Hungarian Crown in the following year. Croatia gained its autonomy and was formally joined with Slavonia in 1881. However, Hungarian nationalism transformed traditional Croat-Serb rivalries into Southern Slav ('Yugoslav') solidarity. Following the collapse of the Austro-Hungarian Empire at the end of the First World War in October 1918, a Kingdom of Serbs, Croats and Slovenes (under the Serbian monarchy) was proclaimed on 4 December. The new Kingdom united Serbia, including Macedonia and Kosovo, with Montenegro and the Habsburg lands (modern Croatia, Slovenia and Vojvodina).

The new Kingdom, however, was dominated by the Serbs, and the Croats, as the second-largest ethnic group, sought a greater share of power. There was increasing unrest within the Kingdom, culminating in the meeting of a separatist assembly in Zagreb in 1928, which led King Aleksandar (Alexander) to impose a royal dictatorship in 1929, when he formally changed the country's name to Yugoslavia. In 1934 the King was assassinated in France by Croatian extremists.

Meanwhile, the Fascist Ustaša movement was gaining support among the discontented Croat peasantry. When German and Italian forces invaded Yugoslavia in 1941, many Croats welcomed the Axis powers' support for the establishment of an Independent State of Croatia. The new Croatian state, which included most of Bosnia and Herzegovina and parts of Serbia as well as modern-day Croatia, was proclaimed on 9 April 1941 and was led by the leader of the Ustaša, the 'Poglavnik' Ante Pavelić. During the Ustaša regime a vast number of Jews, Serbs, Roma (Gypsies) and political dissidents were murdered in extermination camps. At the same time fierce armed resistance was being waged by the Partisans, who were led by Josip Broz, known as Tito, the leader of the Communist Party of Yugoslavia (CPY). By 1943 the Fascist regime was beginning to lose control, and Tito's forces were able to proclaim a provisional government in a number of areas. The Ustaša state collapsed in 1944, and Croatia was restored to Yugoslavia as one unit of a federal Communist republic.

During the 1960s there was an increase in nationalism in Croatia. This 'mass movement' (*Maspok*) was supported by Croatian members of the ruling League of Communists (as the CPY had been renamed), as well as by non-Communists. The movement encouraged the local Communist leadership, which was associated with the reform wing of the party, to defy central policy in certain areas. In December 1971 Tito committed himself to opposing the nationalist movement, and the Croatian Communist leaders were obliged to resign. Together with others prominent in *Maspok*, they were arrested, and a purge of the League of Communists of Croatia (LCC) followed. In 1974, however, Tito introduced a new Constitution, which enshrined the federal (almost confederal) and collective nature of the Yugoslav state. Any manifestations of Croatian nationalism continued to be prosecuted, even after the death of Tito in 1980.

When the power of the LCC (which contained a high proportion of Serbs) began to decline, particularly from 1989, Croatian nationalism re-emerged as a significant force. Dissidents of the 1970s and 1980s were the main beneficiaries. Dr Franjo Tudjman, who had twice been imprisoned for publicly criticizing repression in Croatia, formed the Croatian Democratic Union (CDU) in 1990. This rapidly became the main challenger to the ruling party, which had changed its name to the League of Communists of Croatia—Party of Democratic Reform (LCC–PDR). The Communists introduced a plurality ('first-past-the-post') voting system for the multi-party elections to the republican legislature in April–May 1990. Tudjman campaigned as a nationalist, prompting considerable concern among the Serbs by advocating a 'Greater Croatia' (that is, including Bosnia) and complaining of Serb domination.

At the elections to the tricameral republican Assembly (Sabor), which took place on 24 April and 6–7 May 1990, the CDU benefited from the new voting system, taking a majority of the seats, despite winning only about 42% of the votes cast in the second round (in both the Socio-Political Chamber and the Chamber of Counties). The CDU obtained 54 of the 80 seats in the Socio-Political Chamber, 68 of the 115 seats filled in the Chamber of Counties, and 83 of the 156 seats filled in the Chamber of Associated Labour; thus, of the 351 seats of all three chambers of the Sabor (a maximum of 356 could have been filled), the CDU won 205. The next-largest party was the LCC–PDR, with a total of 73 seats. Both the leading parties won further seats in alliance with other parties. Tudjman was elected President of Croatia, but he attempted to allay Serb fears by offering the vice-presidency of the Sabor to Dr Jovan Rašković, the leader of the Serbian Democratic Party (SDP). Although Rašković eventually refused the post, another Serb was appointed to it. However, Serb-dominated areas remained alienated by Tudjman's Croat nationalism. A 'Serb National Council', based at Knin (in Krajina), was formed in July and organized a referendum on autonomy for the Croatian Serbs. Despite attempts by the Croatian authorities to prohibit the referendum, it took place, amid virtual insurrection in some areas, in late August and early September. The result was an overwhelming endorsement of the proposal for Serbian autonomy. By December Serbian areas were issuing declarations of autonomy, the extent of which expanded as Croatia moved further from acceptance of the federal Yugoslav state. By October 1991 three 'Serbian Autonomous Regions' (SARs) had been established in Croatia: Krajina, with its headquarters at Knin (which had declared its unification with the self-proclaimed Serb 'Municipal Community of Bosanska Krajina' in neighbouring Bosnia and Herzegovina in June); Eastern Slavonia, Baranja and Western Srem (Sirmium), with its temporary headquarters in Dalj (transferred to Vukovar in November, following the surrender of the Croatian resistance); and Western Slavonia, most of which was held by the Croats. The three regions, none of which was officially recognized by the Croatian Government, stated their determination to remain in a federal

Yugoslavia or in a 'Greater Serbian' state. In December the three SARs announced their union as a 'Republic of Serbian Krajina' (RSK).

Meanwhile, the new Croatian Government was intent on dismantling the structures of Communist power. In August 1990 the Socialist Republic of Croatia became the Republic of Croatia. In the same month the Sabor voted to dismiss the republican member of the federal State Presidency, Dr Stipe Šuvar, and replace him with Stipe Mesić, then President of the Government (premier) of Croatia. His appointment was confirmed in October. In December the Sabor enacted a new republican Constitution, which declared Croatia's sovereignty, its authority over its own armed forces and its right to secede from the federation. Tensions increased when, in January 1991, the federal State Presidency ordered the disarming of all paramilitary groups, and the Croatian authorities refused to comply. The Croatian Minister of Defence was indicted on a charge of plotting armed rebellion, but the Croatian Government refused to arrest him and boycotted negotiations on the future of the federation. In March the Sabor resolved that republican legislation take precedence over federal legislation. In April the Croatian National Guard was formed, replacing the Territorial Defence Force, which had been under the jurisdiction of the Jugoslovenska Narodna Armija (JNA—Yugoslav People's Army). On 19 May some 94% of the voters participating in a referendum favoured Croatia's becoming a sovereign entity, possibly within a confederal Yugoslavia, and 92% rejected a federal Yugoslavia. Some 84% of the registered electorate participated in the referendum, which was largely boycotted by the Serb population.

On 25 June 1991 Croatia and Slovenia declared their independence and began the process of dissociation from the Yugoslav federation. However, the federal and Serbian authorities were less prepared to accept the loss of Croatia than that of Slovenia, since Croatia contained a significant Serb minority. During July, despite European Community (EC) peace efforts, civil war effectively began in Croatia. In September the UN placed an embargo on the delivery of all weapons and other military equipment to the territories of the former Yugoslavia. By November the JNA, supported by Serbian irregular troops, had secured about one-third of Croatian territory. The main area of conflict was Slavonia, in eastern Croatia, although Serbian and JNA attacks were also concentrated on the port of Zadar, in central Dalmatia. In October the JNA attacked and besieged the coastal city of Dubrovnik, despite the fact that it contained neither a JNA barracks nor a significant Serb minority. There were accusations that the JNA was attempting to secure the borders of a 'Greater Serbian' state by linking the RSK territories to Serbia; among the main obstacles to this alleged goal, however, were the eastern Slavonian cities of Osijek, Vinkovci and Vukovar, the last of which finally surrendered on 18 November, after the 13th cease-fire agreement negotiated by the EC, which supervised the subsequent civilian evacuation. Both Croatia and Serbia indicated readiness to accept a UN peace-keeping force; military action continued, however, while negotiations on the terms for such a force were conducted. The 14th cease-fire agreement, therefore, involved the UN, although it did not bring an end to all the fighting. In mid-December the UN Security Council's Resolution 724 provided for observers to be sent to Yugoslavia, in addition to a small team of civilian and military personnel to prepare for a possible peace-keeping force.

In August 1991 Tudjman appointed a coalition Government, dominated by the CDU, but containing members of almost all the parties in the legislature. The SDP was not included. The new Government continued to seek international recognition and to pursue negotiations at the EC-sponsored peace conference in The Hague (the Netherlands). However, in October the Croatian Government refused to extend the three-month moratorium on the process of dissociation from the Yugoslav federation (which had been agreed during the first round of EC peace negotiations in July). In November, in accordance with the principles formulated at The Hague, the Sabor declared its readiness to enact legislation guaranteeing minority rights, to allay the anxieties of the Serbs. However, there were increasing allegations of atrocities on both sides. The CDU came under increasing pressure from its own right-wing and more extreme groups to make no concessions to the Serbs. One of the most prominent of the nationalist parties was the Croatian Party of Rights (CPR), of which the armed wing, the Croatian Defence Association, was actively involved in the fighting and was implicated in other anti-Serb incidents.

Despite such domestic and military pressures, the Croatian Government continued the process of dissociation, and in November 1991 the Supreme Council (a special war cabinet, chaired by the President of the Republic, which had been established in Croatia following the outbreak of civil conflict) ordered all Croatians to vacate any federal posts that they held and to place their services at the disposal of the Croatian state. On 5 December Stipe Mesić, Yugoslavia's nominal Head of State, resigned, as did Ante Marković, the federal Prime Minister, on 19 December. On 23 December Germany recognized Croatia, and on 15 January 1992 the other members of the EC initiated general international recognition of Croatia, which culminated in its accession to the UN in May.

With more than 6,000 dead, 23,000 wounded and 400,000 internally displaced in Croatia, a UN-sponsored unconditional cease-fire was signed by the Croatian National Guard and the JNA on 2 January 1992. In late February a 14,000-strong UN Protection Force (UNPROFOR, see p. 62) was entrusted with ensuring the withdrawal of the JNA from Croatia and the complete demilitarization of three Serbian-held enclaves, which were designated UN Protected Areas (UNPAs). In the same month UNPROFOR's mandate in Croatia was extended to cover the so-called 'pink zones' (areas occupied by JNA troops and with majority Serb populations, but outside the official UNPAs).

In mid-May 1992 the JNA began to withdraw from Croatia, in accordance with the UN demilitarization of Serb areas, and the siege of Dubrovnik ended on 28 May. Sporadic shelling continued, however, and UNPROFOR proved unable to prevent the expulsion of more than 1,000 non-Serbs by Serbian forces from Eastern Slavonia, and had only limited success in its enforcement of the demilitarization of the UNPAs. In June Croatian forces launched a series of offensives in Serbian areas, beginning with the shelling of Knin. This development provoked UN Security Council Resolution 762, adopted on 30 June, which required the Croats to withdraw to the positions that they had held prior to 21 June and to refrain from entering Serbian areas. Relations between Croatia and the UN remained strained.

In late July 1992 a military court in Split convicted 19 leading figures from the RSK for 'threatening the territorial integrity' of the Republic of Croatia. Shortly afterwards, however, as a precondition of their participation in the EC/UN peace conference on the former Yugoslavia, to be held in August, in London (the United Kingdom), the leaders of the RSK renounced their claims to independence. In early September the Prime Minister of the Federal Republic of Yugoslavia (FRY, comprising Serbia and Montenegro), Milan Panić, announced Yugoslavia's willingness to recognize Croatia within the borders existing prior to the outbreak of civil war in mid-1991, on the condition that the Serbian enclaves be granted special status. During the London peace talks, agreement was reached on economic co-operation between representatives of the Croatian Government and of the RSK, and at the end of September Presidents Tudjman of Croatia and Dobrica Ćosić of the FRY agreed to work towards a normalization of relations between their respective countries.

Presidential and legislative elections were held in Croatia on 2 August 1992. These were the first elections to be held under the new Constitution (promulgated in December 1990), which provided for a bicameral legislature composed of a Chamber of Representatives and a Chamber of Counties; however, the legislative election was to the former house only. The elections were contested by eight presidential candidates and 37 political parties. President Tudjman was re-elected, with 56% of the presidential votes cast, more than twice that of his nearest rival, Dražen Budiša of the Croatian Social-Liberal Party (CSLP), while the ruling CDU obtained an outright majority in the Chamber of Representatives, winning 85 of the 138 seats contested. The new Government, under the premiership of Hrvoje Šarinić (hitherto head of the President's office), was appointed shortly thereafter.

In late November 1992 the Chamber of Representatives approved legislation providing for the internal reorganization of Croatia, for electoral purposes, into 21 counties, 420 municipalities and 61 towns, and in early January 1993 proportional representation was introduced to replace the former plurality electoral system. An election to the Chamber of Counties was held on 7 February. The CDU won 37 of the elective 63 seats, while the CSLP, together with allied parties, obtained 16 seats. The CPR boycotted the election.

Meanwhile, in October 1992 one of the co-Chairmen of the EC/UN peace talks, Lord (David) Owen (a British politician), threatened to impose EC sanctions on Croatia if it did not withdraw its troops from Bosnia and Herzegovina, where Croatia was supporting the self-styled breakaway Croat state, the 'Croatian Union of Herzeg-Bosna', which proclaimed its independence, with Mostar as its capital and the Croatian National Guard as sole authority, on 24 October. He also accused the Croats of 'ethnic cleansing' (involving the expulsion by one ethnic group of other ethnic groups in an attempt to create a homogenous population) in Bosnia and Herzegovina. The accusation was strenuously denied by the Croatian authorities. Croatia continued its military involvement in Bosnia and Herzegovina throughout 1993 and into 1994, despite EC threats of economic sanctions.

In late January 1993 Croatian troops launched an offensive across the UN peace-keeping lines into Serb-held Krajina, an action that was provoked, they claimed, by the failure of the UN to restore the Maslenica bridge, a vital communications link between northern Croatia and the Dalmatian coast, to Croatian control. The Serbian forces in Krajina reclaimed weapons that they had earlier surrendered to UNPROFOR, in order to defend themselves. The UN responded by ordering Croatia to withdraw its troops and the Serbian forces to return their weapons. As Croatian forces advanced towards the coastal town of Zadar on 26 January, President Ćosić of Yugoslavia warned the UN that, if UNPROFOR did not intervene, Yugoslavia would dispatch troops to defend the Serbs in Croatia. Eight French UN troops were wounded, and two were killed, in fighting around Zadar on the following day; consequently the French Government dispatched an aircraft-carrier to the Adriatic Sea. The Croats regained control of the Maslenica bridge and Zemunik airport, and by the end of January the peace process in both Croatia and Bosnia and Herzegovina appeared to be in serious jeopardy, with President Tudjman openly promising to repulse the Serbs and to aid the Bosnian Croats.

There was extensive political unrest in Croatia throughout 1993. The issues of continuing civil strife in Krajina and of the quest for autonomy in the Istrian peninsula in the north-west of Croatia (see below) proved increasingly problematic for the Government and added to domestic dissatisfaction with the country's desperate economic circumstances and concern regarding Croatian involvement in the Bosnian conflict. In late March Šarinić's Government resigned, following a series of financial scandals and a rapid deterioration in the economic situation. A former executive of the Croatian state petroleum company, Nikica Valentić, was appointed Prime Minister. The new Government, which consisted only of members of the CDU, won a vote of confidence in the Chamber of Representatives in late April. Despite growing opposition to his policies within the party, Tudjman was re-elected Chairman of the CDU in October.

Meanwhile, the problem of war refugees escalated rapidly and in January 1993 the Croatian authorities appealed to the international community for humanitarian and financial aid to provide for the large number of those seeking asylum in Croatia. (The number of refugees from Bosnia and Herzegovina totalled more than 800,000 in early 1993.) A state committee for the normalization of Serb-Croat relations within Croatia was established in Zagreb in May, but tensions between the two ethnic communities were exacerbated by repeated allegations of abuses of Serbian human rights.

At local elections in Istria in early February 1993, the Istrian Democratic Assembly (IDA), a party advocating Istrian autonomy, obtained 72% of the total votes cast. The Croatian Government and the IDA were subsequently in conflict throughout 1993. The IDA proposed that Istria become a transborder region comprising Croatian, Slovenian and Italian areas. Tudjman and his Government, however, strongly opposed any suggestion of Istrian autonomy, fearing the destabilization of Croatia and renewed support for the reconstitution of a Yugoslav federation.

In early April 1993 a UN-sponsored agreement guaranteed the reconstruction and reopening of the Maslenica bridge, Zemunik airport and the Peruca hydroelectric plant (all situated in Krajina) under UNPROFOR supervision. The Croats decided to reconstruct the bridge themselves, however, and it was duly reopened by President Tudjman in July. In the same month the Serbs, frustrated by the continued Croatian military presence in the area, launched an attack on Croatian forces. In mid-July the UN successfully negotiated the Erdut Agreement between the leaders of Croatia and Serbia, whereby Croat forces were to leave the Maslenica area (which would again be placed under the administration of UNPROFOR) and return captured villages

to the Serbs; in return, President Milošević of Serbia was to dissuade Serbian troops from attacking the bridge. However, the Croats did not withdraw from Maslenica by the deadline of 31 July; the Croatian Government claimed that Serbian weapons had not been surrendered to UNPROFOR, and fighting resumed. In August the Croatian Minister of Foreign Affairs, Dr Mate Granić, declared the Erdut Agreement redundant. In the following month a full-scale mobilization was undertaken among the Serbs living in the SAR of Eastern Slavonia, Baranja and Western Sirmium, in response to the Croatian offensives in Krajina. Serb-Croat hostilities extended to Zagreb by mid-September. By this time most of the JNA had withdrawn from Croatia, and some Serb artillery had been placed under UN control, but UNPROFOR forces were not yet in effective control of Croatian borders. The Serbs still occupied approximately 30% of the territory of Croatia.

In late September 1993 the UN Secretary-General recommended the extension of the UNPROFOR mandate in the former Yugoslavia for a further six months; the Croatian Council of Defence and National Security, however, rejected the recommendation. A few days later a special commission for relations with UNPROFOR was established in Croatia, but anti-UNPROFOR demonstrations took place across the country. On 4 October the UN Security Council voted unanimously to extend UNPROFOR's mandate in Croatia by Resolution 871. This Resolution also required the return to Croatian sovereignty of all 'pink zones', the restoration of all communications links between these regions and the remainder of Croatia, and the disarmament of Serb paramilitary groups. The UNPROFOR forces were empowered by the Resolution to act in self-defence while implementing the mandate. The Croat administration accepted the Resolution, but it was rejected by the assembly of the RSK, based in Beli Menastir, which proceeded to order the mobilization of all Serb conscripts in Krajina. Multi-party elections were held in the RSK in December, but these were declared illegal by the Constitutional Court of Croatia. In January 1994 Milan Martić, a candidate supported by President Milošević of Serbia, was elected to the post of 'President' of the RSK.

In mid-January 1994 Croatia and the FRY announced their intention to begin the normalization of relations, including the establishment of representative offices in Zagreb and Belgrade. A parallel agreement was also signed between representatives of the Bosnian Croats and the Bosnian Serbs. The question of Serb-occupied territories in Croatia was, however, not specifically addressed. The declarations prompted much criticism in Croatia, where opposition parties and elements within the CDU protested that the Muslims, and not the Serbs, were the natural allies of the Croats. In the same month President Tudjman and senior government officials indicated the possibility of direct Croatian intervention in central Bosnia and Herzegovina in support of Bosnian Croat forces encircled by Bosnian government troops, prompting the USA's Permanent Representative to the UN, Madeleine Albright, to warn Croatia that international economic sanctions could be imposed in the event of Croatian military intervention in the Bosnian conflict.

In an apparent reversal of policy, in late February 1994 President Tudjman approved US proposals for a Muslim-Croat federation within Bosnia and Herzegovina, which would ultimately seek formal association with Croatia within a loose confederation (see chapter on Bosnia and Herzegovina). In the RSK, meanwhile, a cease-fire, which had been agreed between Croatia and the rebel Serbs in December 1993, was extended for a third time, until 31 March 1994. On 30 March a further cease-fire, negotiated by the Russian Special Envoy to the Former Yugoslavia, Vitalii Churkin, was agreed in Zagreb; a 'buffer' zone, monitored by UNPROFOR, was to be created between the front lines.

In April 1994 a long-standing public dispute between President Tudjman and Josip Manolić, the President of the Chamber of Municipalities and a leading member of the CDU, led to a division in the party. Manolić and other prominent liberals in the CDU (and in other parties) were displeased with Tudjman's perceived anti-Muslim views and his collusion with Gojko Šušak, the Minister of Defence, who was widely considered responsible for Croatia's involvement against the Muslims in the Bosnian conflict. Manolić demanded Šušak's resignation on the grounds that Tudjman could not hope to adhere to the Muslim-Croat federation accords with Šušak as Minister of Defence. Tudjman responded by suspending Manolić from his position within the CDU (also attempting, unsuccessfully, to dismiss him from his legislative office). On 5 April it was announced that Manolić, together with Stipe Mesić (now the President of the Chamber of Representatives), had left the CDU to form a new party, the Croatian Independent Democrats (CID). Formally established in late April, with Mesić as Chairman, the CID became the largest opposition party in the Sabor, with some 18 deputies.

There was further internal controversy in May 1994, when a new currency, the kuna, was introduced (the kuna had been the official tender of the Ustaša regime). From June the principal opposition parties staged a boycott of the Sabor in protest at the appointment of two CDU deputies as Presidents of the parliamentary Chambers (Manolić and Mesić having agreed to resign from their posts in mid-May); opposition deputies only returned to the Sabor in September.

Meanwhile, the cease-fire in the RSK continued precariously, as Croatian officials threatened to terminate the UN peace-keeping mandate in the area and forcibly reclaim Serb-held territory, unless the Krajina Serbs co-operated more fully in international peace negotiations. In late September 1994 the Chamber of Representatives voted to end the existing mandate of UNPROFOR in Croatia, offering a renewed mandate, on the condition that UNPROFOR disarm Serb troops in Krajina, facilitate the return of Croatian refugees to Krajina and protect Croatia's official borders. On 30 September, however, the Government reversed its opposition to the continued presence of UN forces in Croatia, and on the same day the UN Security Council adopted a resolution renewing the UNPROFOR mandate in Croatia for a further six months.

In mid-October 1994 a new negotiating forum was established in Zagreb with the aim of resolving the Krajina question; known as the 'Zagreb Group', it comprised two representatives of the European Union (EU, as the EC had been restructured) and the US and Russian ambassadors to Croatia. The group initially proposed that the RSK be reintegrated into Croatia while receiving extensive autonomy. In late October, however, the RSK 'Prime Minister', Borislav Mikelić, rejected any notion of Krajina's reintegration. Nevertheless, in December the two sides concluded an economic accord, which provided for the re-establishment of basic infrastructural links between the RSK and Croatia.

On 12 January 1995 President Tudjman, encountering pressure from nationalist factions of the CDU and public dissatisfaction at the Government's perceived failure to assert control over Croatian territory, announced that the Government would not renew the UNPROFOR mandate in Croatia upon its expiry at the end of March, claiming that the UN presence had merely reinforced the Serbs' position. In late January, amid growing fears of the outbreak of war throughout the former Yugoslavia, the 'Zagreb Group' presented a fresh peace plan to President Tudjman and the Krajina Serbs. The plan, which emphasized Croatia's territorial integrity, while affording rights to the Serb minority, envisaged the return of one-half of Serb-controlled territory to Croatia, in exchange for extensive regional autonomy for the Krajina Serbs. (The areas to be reintegrated into Croatia would be demilitarized, and administered by the UN for a minimum of five years.) The Krajina Serbs initially refused to consider the plan, but on 3 February Martić announced that the RSK would be willing to consider peace proposals if the UNPROFOR mandate were renewed and the RSK received guarantees of protection against Croatian aggression. A few days later the RSK suspended the economic accord concluded with Croatia in December 1994, following Croatia's decision to terminate UNPROFOR's mandate.

On 12 March 1995, in response to international pressure, President Tudjman reversed his decision to expel UNPROFOR from Croatian territory, two weeks before the UN troops were due to begin their withdrawal from the area. Croatia had agreed to a revised peace-keeping plan, following intensive diplomatic negotiations conducted by the international community (in particular, the USA), as a result of which a compromise UN mandate was to provide for a reduced peace-keeping force (to be known as the UN Confidence Restoration Operation—UNCRO), including several hundred troops to be posted along Croatia's official frontiers with Bosnia and Herzegovina and the FRY (effectively isolating Serb-occupied territory in Croatia from sources of military aid). In April the UN Security Council authorized UNCRO's strength at 8,750.

In early March 1995, following talks in Zagreb, a formal military alliance was announced between the Croatian, Bosnian Croat and Bosnian government armies amid general prepara-

tion for new offensive campaigns in Bosnia and Herzegovina. (A similar agreement establishing a military alliance between the Croatian Serbs and the Bosnian Serbs had been drawn up in Banja Luka, Bosnia and Herzegovina, in February.) UN relief supplies to Serb-held enclaves in Croatia were halted in March, following the disruption of aid convoys by Croatian Serbs and their rebel Muslim allies in Bosnia and Herzegovina. It was subsequently announced that the relief operations would not be resumed until the Serb and rebel Muslim blockade of the Bihać enclave in north-western Bosnia and Herzegovina was lifted.

In early April 1995 President Tudjman warned of Croatia's determination to 'liberate' Serb-held territories within its borders. Three days later the Croatian Minister of Defence, Gojko Šušak, announced the demobilization of some 30,000 government troops (but denied that, in doing so, he was hoping to draw the Croatian Serbs into taking offensive military action against Croatia). On 13 April the town and airport of Dubrovnik were attacked by Bosnian Serb artillery, resulting in one death and prompting Mate Granić to lodge a formal protest with the UN.

On 1–2 May 1995 Croatian government forces seized the SAR of Western Slavonia; large numbers of Serb troops fled the area during the offensive. Government sources claimed that the attack was necessary in order to restore the Zagreb-Belgrade motorway (which was re-opened to civilian traffic on 3 May). The Croatian Serbs retaliated almost immediately with artillery attacks on Zagreb (where six civilians were killed), Karlovak and Sisak. The international community immediately intensified its efforts to achieve peace in Croatia, and on 3 May, under the mediation of the UN Special Envoy, Yasushi Akashi, the warring parties agreed a cease-fire, according to which Serb artillery was to be surrendered to the UN, in exchange for the safe passage of all Serb civilians and troops from Western Slavonia into Bosnia and Herzegovina (an evacuation was to be organized by the UN). Sporadic fighting continued in the enclave despite the cease-fire, however, and there were allegations of Croatian human-rights abuses.

On 21 May 1995 a vote in the 'Assembly' of the RSK in favour of the unification of Bosnian Serb and Croatian Serb territories exposed differences within the RSK leadership; 'President' Martić voted in favour of unification, while 'Prime Minister' Borislav Mikelić remained strongly opposed to the idea.

In early June 1995 President Tudjman aroused international controversy when he threatened further offensive campaigns to seize Serb-held territories, following the expiry date of UNCRO's mandate in Croatia on 31 October, unless the Croatian Serbs accepted Croatian sovereignty and a peace agreement. In late July a joint offensive campaign by Croatian government forces and Bosnian Croat troops resulted in the seizure of the strategic Serb-held town of Bosansko Grahovo, in south-western Bosnia and Herzegovina, thus blocking the principal supply route from Serb-held areas of Bosnia to Serb-held Krajina. On 4 August Croatian government troops launched a massive military operation and rapidly recaptured the Krajina enclave from the Croatian Serbs, prompting the largest exodus of refugees since the Yugoslav crisis began in 1991; about 150,000 Croatian Serbs either fled or were forcibly expelled from Krajina and took refuge in Serb-held areas in Bosnia or in Serbia itself. Following the capture of Krajina, it was reported that Serbian troops had been stationed along the Serbian border with Croatia (thus strengthening the position of the Serb-held enclave of Eastern Slavonia against possible Croatian attack). In early September the UN announced that some 10,500 peace-keeping troops were to be withdrawn from Croatia, in view of the reoccupation of Krajina. On 20 September the Croatian Chamber of Representatives voted to suspend sections of the law on minorities, which had provided the Krajina Serbs with special rights in areas where they had been a majority; this decision had been preceded two days earlier by a new electoral law reducing the representation of the Serb minority in the Croatian legislature from 13 seats to three. The law also provided for 12 seats in the Chamber of Representatives to represent some 470,000 Croatian emigrés, thus giving the right to vote to some 291,000 Bosnian Croats (many of whom supported the CDU's associated party in Bosnia and Herzegovina). At the end of September the Croatian Government, despite UN criticism, was reported to have resettled some 100,000 Bosnian refugees (both Croat and Muslim) in Krajina. In late September it was announced that an election to the Chamber of Representatives would take place on 29 October. A few days later seven opposition parties formed an informal electoral alliance and agreed to present joint candidates in a number of constituencies.

During October 1995 fighting continued in parts of Croatia despite the UN-brokered cease-fire. Heavy clashes were reported between Croatian troops and Serb forces in Eastern Slavonia, and President Tudjman continued to threaten the recapture of the Eastern Slavonian enclave by force, as part of the CDU's electoral manifesto. On 3 October, however, an 'agreement on basic principles' was signed between Croatian government officials and Serb leaders in Eastern Slavonia, following talks in the Serb-held town of Erdut, conducted under the mediation of the US ambassador to Croatia, Peter Galbraith, and UN negotiator Thorvald Stoltenberg. The 11-point agreement provided for a 'transitional period', during which authority over the enclave would be invested in an interim administration established by the UN. The area would be demilitarized and a joint Serb-Croat police force would be created; the agreement also provided for the safe return of refugees.

The Croatian electoral campaign was marred by widespread allegations of media bias, since the Government only allowed very limited access to television for opposition parties; in early October 1995 the state-owned television network banned opposition broadcasts. The election duly took place on 29 October; the CDU secured about 45% of the votes cast (although the party failed to gain sufficient votes to achieve the two-thirds parliamentary majority required to make constitutional amendments). A new Government was appointed in early November, under the premiership of the erstwhile Minister of the Economy, Zlatko Matesa.

On 12 November 1995 representatives of the Croatian Government and Eastern Slavonian Serbs signed an agreement in Erdut on the reintegration of the Eastern Slavonian enclave into Croatia. The signature of this accord followed peace negotiations between Tudjman, Milošević and the President of the Presidency of Bosnia and Herzegovina, Dr Alija Izetbegović, conducted in Dayton, the USA (where the three leaders signed a comprehensive peace agreement, providing for the division of Bosnia and Herzegovina between a Muslim-Croat Federation and a Serb Republic—see chapter on Bosnia and Herzegovina). Under the terms of the accord, Eastern Slavonia was to be administered by a transitional administration appointed by the UN for a period of up to two years prior to its complete reintegration into Croatia. The interim administration and UN peace-keeping forces would supervise the demilitarization of the area and the return of refugees and displaced persons. Long-standing Serbian demands for a referendum to be held at the end of the transitional period, in which citizens would vote for the region's integration into either Croatia or Serbia, were not included in the agreement. On 15 January 1996, by Resolution 1037, the UN Security Council established the UN Transitional Administration for Eastern Slavonia, Baranja and Western Sirmium (UNTAES), with an initial one-year mandate; UNTAES, comprising some 5,000 troops, replaced UNCRO, the mandate of which expired on that day. A US diplomat, Jacques Paul Klein, was subsequently appointed Transitional Administrator of the region. The UN Security Council also authorized the UN Mission of Observers in Prevlaka (UNMOP, see p. 64) to assume responsibility for monitoring the demilitarization of the Prevlaka peninsula, south-east of Dubrovnik.

In February 1996 Tudjman, Izetbegović and Milošević attended a meeting in Rome, Italy, where the Croat and Muslim delegations reached an agreement regarding the administration of Mostar, in Bosnia and Herzegovina. (In November 1995 Tudjman and Izetbegović, the Bosnian Muslim leader, signed an agreement providing for the unification of Mostar as the capital of the Muslim-Croat Federation—see chapter on Bosnia and Herzegovina.) In March a FRY delegation, headed by the Minister of Foreign Affairs, Milan Milutinović, visited Croatia; a number of co-operation agreements were signed. On 19 April the Regional Executive Council of Eastern Slavonia appointed a former RSK 'President' (1992–94), Goran Hadžić, as President of the region. A new Regional Assembly (comprising representatives of Krajina and the five Eastern Slavonian municipalities) and Regional Executive Council were subsequently established. In the same month the Chamber of Representatives approved legislation on co-operation between Croatia and the UN International Criminal Tribunal for the Former Yugoslavia (ICTY—based in the Hague, the Netherlands), which provided for the transfer of authority to conduct criminal proceedings to the Tribunal and the extradition of the accused.

In early May 1996 Tudjman dissolved the Zagreb City Assembly and appointed a Government Commissioner in its place (on the grounds that the Assembly had approved unconstitutional legislation), following a protracted dispute with an alliance of opposition parties that had won the local elections and held a majority in the Assembly. Also in May the Ministers of Foreign Affairs of the member states of the Council of Europe (see p. 165) refused to endorse Croatia's admission to the organization (despite a favourable vote by the Council's Parliamentary Assembly in April), on the grounds that the Government had failed to meet EU democratic standards

In May 1996 the Croatian Chamber of Representatives adopted legislation granting amnesty for crimes committed during the civil conflict in Eastern Slavonia from August 1990, excepting 'war crimes'; the legislation was designed to expedite the return of displaced persons to the region. Later that month the demilitarization of Eastern Slavonia commenced; the process was completed within 30 days, as scheduled. In early July an international security force was installed in Eastern Slavonia for the transitional period. Later that month the Regional Assembly of Eastern Slavonia submitted an official request to the UN Security Council that the mandate of UNTAES, which was officially due to expire in January 1997, be extended for one further year. (The Croatian Government opposed the extension of the mandate for more than three months.)

In August 1996 Tudjman met the US President, Bill Clinton, for discussions in Washington, DC, the USA. It was subsequently reported that Tudjman influenced the Bosnian Croats to abandon a boycott of Mostar city council, which they had staged in protest at the results of municipal elections. Later in August, following a meeting between Tudjman and Milošević in Athens, Greece, an agreement was signed, providing for the establishment of full diplomatic relations between Croatia and the FRY; remaining issues of contention, most notably the territorial dispute over the Prevlaka peninsula (which, under the terms of the Dayton agreement, was to be ceded to Bosnian Serb control), were to be resolved by further negotiations. In October the Council of Europe agreed to accept Croatia's application for membership, after the Government undertook to ratify the European Convention on Human Rights within one year of admission.

In November 1996 the UN Security Council announced that the mandate of UNTAES had been extended for an additional six months, to mid-July 1997. At the end of December, following a meeting between Tudjman and Klein, it was announced that local government elections in Eastern Slavonia were to take place in March 1997, at the same time as an election to the upper house (Chamber of Counties) in Croatia. Serbs in Eastern Slavonia subsequently objected to elections taking place concurrently in Croatia and Eastern Slavonia (on the grounds that this pre-empted the reintegration of the region). In January 1997 it was reported that the Croatian Government had submitted to the UN proposals for the reintegration of Eastern Slavonia, whereby the Serb community would be allocated two seats in the Chamber of Counties and Serbs would be exempt from serving in the Croatian army for the first two years. In early February Tudjman announced that the election to the Chamber of Counties, which had been scheduled to take place in mid-March, had been postponed until 13 April, apparently owing to difficulties in the organization of the concurrent local government elections in Eastern Slavonia. In March the Independent Democratic Serb Party (SDSS), headed by Vojislav Stanimirović (the President of the Regional Council of Eastern Slavonia), was established to contest the elections in the enclave.

In early April 1997 Serb officials in Eastern Slavonia conducted a referendum (which, however, the Croatian Government and UN officials declared to be illegitimate) regarding the future of the enclave; about 99.5% of the participating electorate voted in favour of Eastern Slavonia remaining a single administrative unit under Serb control after its return to Croatia. On 13 April elections to the Chamber of Counties and to a number of municipal and regional councils took place. Voting in the concurrent local government elections in Eastern Slavonia was extended for two days, owing to administrative irregularities (which, it was reported, resulted from the Government's failure to provide sufficient ballot papers for voters in the enclave). Nevertheless, representatives of the Organization for Security and Co-operation in Europe (OSCE, see p. 252) who monitored the elections declared that they had been largely 'free and fair'. The CDU secured 42 of the 63 elective seats in the Chamber of Counties, while the Croatian Peasants' Party took nine, the

CSLP six, the Social Democratic Party (which had been reconstituted from the former LCC–PDR) four, and the IDA two seats. (A further five deputies were to be nominated by Tudjman, of whom two were to be members of the Serb community in Eastern Slavonia.) The SDSS gained control of 11 of the 28 municipalities contested in the enclave. In May the CDU secured a narrow majority in the Zagreb City Assembly, following protracted negotiations, which resulted in the defection of two councillors from the Croatian Peasants' Party to the CDU. Marina Dropulić-Matulović (who had been appointed to act as Mayor of Zagreb following the controversy between the Government and opposition parties in May 1996) was subsequently elected to the office by CDU councillors.

In May 1997 the Government announced that the forthcoming presidential election was to take place on 15 June. Tudjman had been formally nominated as the presidential candidate of the CDU earlier that year (despite persistent reports, denied by government officials, that he was seriously ill). During a visit to Eastern Slavonia in early June Tudjman publicly offered reconciliation to all Serbs who were willing to accept Croatian citizenship, following continued pressure from Madeleine Albright, who had met Tudjman in late May. The presidential election took place on 15 June as scheduled. Tudjman was re-elected with 61.4% of the votes cast; the Social Democratic Party candidate, Zdravko Tomac, secured 21.0% of the votes cast and the CSLP leader, Vlado Gotovac, 17.6%. However, OSCE monitors declared that the election had not been conducted fairly, on the grounds that opposition parties had not been permitted coverage in the state-controlled media during the electoral campaign. Later in June the Constitutional Court endorsed the results of the election.

At the end of June 1997 a former Serb mayor of Vukovar, Slavko Dokmanović, who had been indicted by the ICTY, was arrested for his alleged involvement in the killing of some 260 civilians in Vukovar in November 1991. (In June 1998, following the conclusion of his trial, Dokmanović committed suicide in detention, while awaiting the verdict of the ICTY.) In early July 1997 the Government announced that the programme for the return of some 80,000 Croatian refugees to Eastern Slavonia had commenced; it was planned that about 40,000 displaced civilians would resettle in the region by the end of that year. Despite previous objections from the Croatian Government, the UN Security Council adopted a resolution to extend the mandate of UNTAES (which had been due to expire in mid-July) until mid-January 1998, owing to UN concern over the continued stability of Eastern Slavonia, in view of the planned return of refugees to the enclave. (However, a number of UN troops withdrew from the region, reducing the size of the contingent from about 5,000 to 2,800.) Later in July the Croatian Government refused to comply with instructions from the ICTY to release official documents (which would be used as evidence in the trial of a former Bosnian Croat army officer) on the grounds of national security. In the same month the Bretton Woods institutions postponed the disbursement of financial assistance to Croatia, as a result of pressure from the Governments of the USA, the United Kingdom and Germany, which continued to criticize, in particular, the slow progress in the resettlement of refugees, the Croatian administration's failure to comply with extradition orders on suspects issued by the ICTY and continued state control of the media.

On 5 August 1997 Tudjman was officially inaugurated for a second presidential term. In the same month the President of the CPR, Dobroslav Paraga, submitted a proposal at the ICTY that Tudjman, Šušak and a number of Bosnian Croats be officially charged in connection with the former conflict in Bosnia and Herzegovina. Paraga and a human-rights activist, Ivan Zvonimir Čičak, were subsequently charged by the Croatian authorities with disseminating false information, after publishing claims in a national newspaper that Tudjman had been actively involved in initiating the Bosnian conflict. In October the IMF approved the resumption of credit payments to Croatia. In November the legislature approved constitutional amendments, proposed by Tudjman, which, notably, prohibited the re-establishment of a union of Yugoslav states. In December Gotovac left the CSLP and formed a breakaway faction of the Party.

In mid-January 1998 the mandate of UNTAES ended and Eastern Slavonia was officially returned to Croatian authority. An increase in the number of ethnic Serbs leaving the former enclave was subsequently reported. In the same month the UN Security Council voted to extend the mandate of the UNMOP

contingent (at this time comprising 28 military observers) deployed in the Prevlaka peninsula until mid-July.

In February 1998 Tudjman was re-elected Chairman of the CDU at a party convention. In the same month trade unions, together with opposition political parties, organized a demonstration in Zagreb, in protest at poor social and economic conditions, despite a ban imposed by the Government; a number of demonstrators were injured in clashes with members of the security forces. In March a government advisory council proposed that the authorities prohibit demonstrations in Eastern Slavonia, in order to maintain public security, following an attempt by ethnic Serbs to stage an unauthorized rally in the former enclave earlier that month. At the end of March the OSCE criticized the Government's promulgation of legal provisions for the return of refugees to Eastern Slavonia, stating that the right to repatriation should be unconditional. In April the Government adopted legislation regulating public gatherings and demonstrations, which, it claimed, was in accordance with the standards of Western authorities. In May the Government proposed a draft programme that relaxed conditions for the return of Serbian refugees to Croatia, following pressure from the international community (which had threatened to impose sanctions if the Croatian Government failed to allow the return of refugees); it was envisaged that some 220,000 displaced persons would be repatriated by 2003. Legislation providing for the new programme for the return of refugees was officially adopted by the Sabor in late June.

In early May 1998 Šušak died of cancer; Dr Andrija Hebrang (hitherto Minister of Health) was subsequently allocated the defence portfolio. In the same month the former Prime Minister, Hrvoje Sarinić, resigned from the post of head of the Office of the President, prompting speculation regarding increasing division within the CDU between moderates, who favoured cordial relations with Western governments, and nationalists.

In June 1998 Croatia submitted to the UN a proposal for a permanent settlement to the dispute over the Prevlaka peninsula; it was envisaged that a joint Croatian-Yugoslav commission would demarcate the borders between the two countries and that a demilitarized zone would be established for a period of five years. In mid-July the UN Security Council extended UNMOP's mandate to remain in the region for a further six months. In August Granić and the Yugoslav Minister of Foreign Affairs, meeting in Zagreb, agreed to conduct discussions on the issue of the Prevlaka peninsula. In September, following a meeting between Granić and the US ambassador in Croatia, it was agreed that joint Croatian-US commissions were to be established to further progress in the implementation of the Dayton peace agreement and Croatia's admission to the NATO 'Partnership for Peace' programme.

In September 1998 the trial of three Croats, who were charged, together with a further six Croats *in absentia*, with the massacre of hundreds of ethnic Serbs in 1991, commenced in Zagreb (the first trial of Croats accused of perpetrating human-rights violations against Serbs to take place in Croatia). In early October Sarinić tendered his resignation from his remaining government and party offices, including the post of presidential Chief of Staff, claiming that Tudjman had failed to support his allegations that CDU nationalists, with connections to members of the intelligence service, were campaigning against him and other moderate members of the party. In the same month Hebrang resigned from his posts of Minister of Defence and Vice-President of the CDU, also as a result of disagreement with Tudjman. Gen. Pavao Miljavac, hitherto Chief of Staff of the army, was subsequently appointed Minister of Defence.

In January 1999 the UN Security Council adopted a resolution on UNMOP, stating that violations of the demilitarized zone in the Prevlaka peninsula had continued and that negotiations on the normalization of relations between the FRY and Croatia had not resulted in any significant progress. Following the commencement of the NATO bombardment of the FRY in March (see chapter on Yugoslavia), the Croatian Government protested to the UN in April at Yugoslav forces entering the demilitarized zone from Montenegro. During the conflict in the FRY it was reported that the security situation in Eastern Slavonia had become increasingly unstable.

In February 1999 the Minister of Agriculture and Forestry was replaced in a government reorganization, after farmers attributed the failure of the agriculture sector to his policies. In March a US government report criticized the human-rights situation in Croatia, citing, in particular, the state control of the media, the Government's lack of co-operation with the ICTY and the failure to reintegrate displaced ethnic Serbs. In April Milan Ramljak resigned from the posts of Deputy Prime Minister and Minister of Justice, in protest at the Government's increasingly authoritarian stance; the Government was subsequently reorganized.

In July 1999 Croatia submitted an application at the ICTY to institute legal proceedings against the FRY for crimes of genocide committed by Yugoslav forces in Croatia in 1991–95. In August the Croatian Government complied with a request by the ICTY for the extradition of Vinko Martinović, who had been indicted for crimes committed during the Croatian–Muslim conflict in 1993–94. However, the Croatian authorities' reluctance to extradite Mladen Naletilić, who had also been indicted for crimes committed during the Croatian–Muslim conflict, prompted severe criticism from the Tribunal; the US Government threatened to initiate sanctions against Croatia, in response to its continued failure to comply with the ICTY. In early September the County Court in Zagreb ruled that there were no legal impediments to the extradition of Naletilić (following an earlier decision that he was unable to stand trial, on grounds of ill health). In mid-October the Supreme Court rejected an appeal by Naletilić against the ruling in favour of his extradition. (Naletilić was finally extradited in March 2000, following a delay to allow him to recover from surgery.)

In late October 1999 Tudjman announced that the election to the Chamber of Representatives would take place on 22 December. In early November, however, it was announced that Tudjman had undergone emergency medical treatment, after becoming seriously ill. He was consequently unable to confirm the election date, and on 26 November the Sabor declared him to be 'temporarily incapacitated' and provisionally transferred the powers of Head of State to the incumbent parliamentary Speaker, Vlatko Pavletić. On the following day the mandate of the Chamber of Representatives expired, and Pavletić rescheduled the election to take place on 3 January 2000. An alliance of six principal opposition parties, known as Opposition Six, signed an agreement, whereby they pledged to establish a coalition government in the event of winning the parliamentary election; of the Opposition Six parties, the SDP and CSLP were to present one joint candidate, while the Croatian Peasants' Party, the Liberal Party (LP), the Croatian People's Party (CPP) and the IDA were to submit a second joint candidate to contest the elections. Meanwhile, Tudjman's medical condition deteriorated, and he died on 10 December. Later that month the Government announced that the election for his successor would take place on 24 January 2000 (in accordance with the Constitution, whereby an election was to be conducted within 60 days of the death of the President).

The election to the Chamber of Representatives, which took place on 3 January 2000 as scheduled, was contested by some 55 political associations. The coalition of the SDP and the CSLP (together with two minor parties) secured 47.0% of the votes cast and 71 of the 151 seats, defeating the CDU, with 30.5% of the votes cast and 45 seats; the alliance of the four other principal opposition parties, together with the Croatian Social Democrats' Action, won 15.9% of the total votes cast and 25 seats. The Chairman of the SDP, Ivica Račan, was subsequently designated as Prime Minister. Later in January nine candidates emerged to contest the forthcoming presidential election, including the CSLP leader, Dražen Budiša (who was to represent the SDP/CSLP alliance), and the former Yugoslav President Stipe Mesić, who was the joint candidate of the four other principal opposition parties. The CDU elected Mate Granić, hitherto Deputy Prime Minister and Minister of Foreign Affairs, as its presidential candidate, while Vladimir Seks (who was reported to be a traditional party member) became acting leader, pending a party congress. In the event that none of the candidates received more than 50% of the votes cast, a second round of voting, between the two candidates who received the most votes in the first ballot, was to take place within 15 days. In the first round of the election, which took place on 24 January, Mesić secured 41.1% of the votes cast, while Budiša won 27.7% and Granić 22.5%. Mesić and Budiša were consequently to contest a second round of voting, which was scheduled for 7 February. On 27 January Pavletić formally appointed Račan to the office of Prime Minister. Račan announced the establishment of a new coalition Government, comprising members of the Opposition Six parties. In the second presidential ballot, Mesić achieved an outright majority, with 56.2% of the votes cast; Budiša secured 43.8% of the votes. On 9 February the Sabor adopted a motion expressing confidence in the new Government

headed by Račan. Following his inauguration as President on 18 February, Mesić pledged to support the return of ethnic Serbian refugees to Croatia.

In March 2000 the Government established a council for co-operation with the ICTY. In May, however, nationalists who had participated in the conflict of 1991–95 organized mass demonstrations in protest at the Government's policy of co-operation with the Tribunal. Meanwhile, in early April Granić left the CDU to form a new party, which became known as the Croatian Democratic Centre. Later that month the head of the Croatian Intelligence Service resigned, in protest at what he claimed to be government obstruction of reforms to the Service. (A dispute between Mesić and Račan over whether control of the service be vested in the President or the Government was ongoing in 2000.) In May a coalition of the SDP and the Croatian Pensioners' Party won the largest number of seats in the election to Zagreb City Assembly, and an SDP member, Milan Bandić, became the new Mayor of Zagreb. In the same month the Chamber of Representatives approved constitutional amendments that guaranteed the educational and linguistic rights of minority groups, and representation in the legislature for those groups that constituted more than 8% of the total population. Later in May Croatia was officially admitted to NATO's 'Partnership for Peace' programme.

In early August 2000 it was reported in the Croatian media that Gen. Petar Stipetić, the Chief of General Staff appointed in March, was under investigation over human-rights abuses perpetrated against Serbs in August 1995. In the same month a Croat military officer, Milan Levar, who had testified at the ICTY in 1997 regarding the mass execution of Serbs in Gospić, in central Croatia, was killed in a bomb explosion at his private residence. In September the Croatian authorities detained 10 people on suspicion of involvement in Levar's murder; a further four suspects were arrested in connection with the massacre of some 100 Muslim civilians in the Bosnian village of Ahmici in 1993. Members of the armed forces and former supporters of Tudjman continued to condemn the Government's policy of co-operation with the ICTY, and in late September Mesić dismissed seven senior military officials who had publicly criticized the detention of war-crimes suspects. In early November the Chamber of Representatives adopted constitutional amendments that reduced the powers of the President and increased those of the legislature (which, henceforth, was to appoint the Government).

In January 2001 the UN Security Council extended the mandate of UNMOP for a further six-month period, until mid-July. In February a mass demonstration was organized by non-governmental and human-rights groups, in opposition to continuing nationalist protests against the arrest of war-crimes suspects by the Croatian authorities. In the same month the Government announced that it planned to abolish the opposition-controlled Chamber of Counties, following the expiry of its mandate in April; the proposal was to be referred to the Chamber of Representatives.

Government

According to the 1990 Constitution, legislative power is vested in the bicameral Assembly (Sabor), comprising a Chamber of Representatives (Zastupnički dom), with up to 151 seats, and a 68-member Chamber of Counties (Županijski dom). Both chambers are elected for a four-year term by universal adult suffrage. (Five of the 68 deputies in the Chamber of Counties are appointed by the President.) Executive power is held by the President, who is elected by universal adult suffrage for a period of five years. The Assembly appoints the Prime Minister, and (upon the recommendation of the Prime Minister) the ministers. The country is divided, for electoral purposes, into 21 counties, 420 municipalities and 61 towns.

Defence

Military service is compulsory for men and lasts for a period of 10 months. In August 2000 the estimated total strength of the armed forces was 61,000 (the number of reservists totalled 220,000), including an army of 53,000, a navy of 3,000 and an air force of 5,000. There were, in addition, 40,000 armed military police. The UN Mission of Observers in Prevlaka (UNMOP) was deployed in Croatia from 1996, with responsibility for supervising the demilitarization of the Prevlaka peninsula; at 1 January 2001 UNMOP comprised 27 military observers, supported by seven civilian personnel. Projected budgetary expenditure on defence by the central Government was estimated at 4,744.9m. kuna (9.5% of total spending) in 2000.

Economic Affairs

In 1998, according to estimates by the World Bank, Croatia's gross national product (GNP), measured at average 1996–98 prices, was US $20,786m., equivalent to $4,620 per head (or $6,698 per head on an international purchasing-power parity basis). During 1990–98, according to estimates by the World Bank, Croatia's population declined by 0.9% per year. In 1999 estimated GNP was $20,400m. ($4,580 per head). Croatia's gross domestic product (GDP) declined, in real terms, at an average annual rate of 0.4% during 1990–99; however, GDP increased by 6.8% in 1997 and by 2.5% in 1998, before declining by an estimated 0.3% in 1999.

Agriculture (including forestry and fishing) contributed 9.4% of GDP in 1998. About 16.7% of the employed labour force were engaged in the sector in that year. The principal crops are maize, wheat, potatoes and sugar beet. (However, the civil conflict, which began in 1991, destroyed much arable land.) The GDP of the agricultural sector declined, in real terms, at an average annual rate of 6.5% in 1990–95. However, agricultural production increased by 1.8% in 1997 and by 6.3% in 1998.

Industry (including mining, manufacturing, construction and power) contributed 31.6% of GDP and engaged 30.1% of the employed labour force in 1998. In real terms, industrial GDP declined at an average rate of 13.3% per year during 1990–95. Industrial production (excluding construction) increased by 6.8% in 1997 and by 3.7% in 1998, but declined by 1.4% in 1999.

The mining sector contributed 5.5% of GDP and engaged only 0.6% of the employed labour force in 1998. Croatia has many exploitable mineral resources, including petroleum, coal and natural gas. The GDP of the mining sector declined by 3.0% in 1996; it increased by 0.1% in 1997, but declined once again, by 2.4%, in 1998. Mining production increased by 1.9% in 1999.

The manufacturing sector contributed 21.2% of GDP and engaged 21.3% of the employed labour force in 1998. In 1992 the principal branches of the manufacturing sector, measured by the value of output, were food products (accounting for 19.2% of the total), chemicals (12.8%), textiles and clothing (8.5%), transport equipment and electrical machinery. The output of the manufacturing sector declined at an average rate of 6.6% per year during 1990–98. However, it increased by 3.9% in 1997 and by 3.2% in 1998. Manufacturing production declined by 2.9% in 1999.

Approximately 30% of Croatia's electricity-generating capacity was destroyed in the civil conflict. Production of electricity increased by 11.6% in 1999, but declined by 10.0% in 2000. However, the country remains dependent on imported fuel, which accounted for some 11.0% of total imports in 1999.

Services provided 59.0% of GDP and engaged 53.2% of the employed labour force in 1998. The virtual elimination of tourism in Croatia (which in the late 1980s accounted for some 82% of Yugoslavia's total tourism trade) represented the largest war-related economic loss for Croatia. There was a significant recovery in the tourism sector in the 1990s; however, the conflict in the Federal Republic of Yugoslavia in March–June 1999 severely disrupted regional tourism. In 2000 tourist arrivals were estimated to have increased by 30%, compared with 1999. In real terms, the GDP of services decreased at an average annual rate of 3.3% in 1990–95.

In 1999 Croatia recorded a visible trade deficit of US $3,298.6m., while there was a deficit of $1,522.6m. on the current account of the balance of payments. In 1999 the principal source of imports was Germany (18.5%); other major sources were Italy, Russia, Slovenia and Austria. The principal market for exports in that year was Italy (18.0%); other important purchasers were Germany, Bosnia and Herzegovina and Slovenia. The principal exports in 1999 were machinery and transport equipment, miscellaneous manufactured articles (particularly clothing and accessories), basic manufactures, and chemical products. The main imports in that year were machinery and transport equipment (most notably road vehicles), basic manufactures, chemical products, miscellaneous manufactured articles, fuels (particularly petroleum and petroleum products) and foodstuffs.

Croatia's overall budget deficit for 1999 was 2,522.0m. kuna. The country's total external debt was US $8,297m. at the end of 1998, of which $4,910m. was long-term public debt. In that year the cost of debt-servicing was equivalent to 8.9% of the value of exports of goods and services. Total outstanding external debt was estimated at $9,853.6m. at the end of 1999. Consumer prices increased by an average of 124.7% per year in 1990–98. However, the average rate of inflation was only 6.4%

in 1998, 3.5% in 1999 and 5.3% in 2000. At mid-2000 the rate of unemployment was estimated at 15.1%.

Croatia was admitted to the IMF in January 1993, and became a member of the European Bank for Reconstruction and Development (EBRD, see p. 176) in April of that year.

The outbreak of civil conflict in Croatia in the early 1990s resulted in a rapid deterioration of the economy. In 1993 the Government initiated an economic programme, which achieved some success in slowing the rate of inflation and controlling public expenditure. The introduction of a new national currency, the kuna, in May 1994 rapidly restrained the rate of inflation. In October of that year the IMF extended its first stand-by loan to Croatia. The Government subsequently received reconstruction loans from other official creditors and concluded a rescheduling agreement with the 'Paris Club' of donor nations. In April 1996 an agreement was reached with the 'London Club' of commercial creditor banks, establishing Croatia's share of the foreign commercial bank debt incurred by the former Yugoslavia. In March 1997 the IMF approved a further three-year credit arrangement to support the Government's programme of economic reform. The conflict in Yugoslavia in March–June 1999 adversely affected Croatia's economy, particularly trade and tourism, and impeded efforts to attract foreign investment. Despite an acceleration of the privatization process, in an attempt to increase budgetary revenue, industrial production declined in 1999, while external debt remained high. Following the death of President Tudjman in December, a new coalition Government was elected (see Recent History), which resulted in improved relations with the US and western European Governments (and consequently increased financial aid). In July 2000 Croatia was formally admitted to the World Trade Organization (see p. 292). Later that year negotiations commenced regarding Croatia's prospective signature of a stabilization and association agreement with the European Union (EU, see p. 181); together with other regional states, Croatia was to be offered financial assistance for reconstruction under an EU assistance programme. As a result of fraudulent practices committed during the previous administration's term of office, however, both Croatia's domestic and external debt had reached unprecedented levels. Planned economic reforms, including the initiation of bankruptcy proceedings against numerous insolvent enterprises and the privatization of the banking sector, were expected to increase further the high rate of unemployment (and, consequently, prove unpopular). Following a 0.3% increase in GDP in 1999, GDP growth was estimated at some 4% in the first six months of 2000, although it slowed in the second half of the year.

Social Welfare

A state health service is available to all citizens. In 1998 there were 229.0 physicians, 474.0 nurses and 65.7 dentists per 100,000 of the population. Of total projected expenditure by the central Government in 2000, 13,724.3m. kuna (27.5%) was for health, social security and welfare. Most government spending on social services is disbursed through extra-budgetary funds, principally the Health Insurance Fund and the Pension Fund. From 1998 retirement pensions represented around 50% of the average monthly wage. The retirement age for men was 65 years from January 1999; women retired at the age of 60. In January 2000 the Government introduced a private-pension scheme, in an attempt to reduce state expenditure on pensions.

Education

Pre-school education, for children aged from three to six years, is available free of charge. Education is officially compulsory for eight years, between seven and 15 years of age. Primary education, which is provided free, begins at the age of seven and continues for four years. Enrolment at primary schools in 1997 was equivalent to 87% of children in the appropriate age-group. Special education in foreign languages is provided for children of non-Croat ethnic origin, since all national minorities in Croatia have the right to learn their minority language. Secondary education is available free (although private schools also exist) and lasts for up to eight years, comprising two cycles of four years each. There are various types of secondary school: grammar, technical and specialized schools and mixed-curriculum schools. Enrolment at secondary schools in 1997 was equivalent to 82% of the relevant age-group. In 1999/2000 there were four universities in Croatia—in Zagreb, Rijeka, Osijek and Split, and seven polytechnics. In 1999/2000 a total of 96,798 students were enrolled in higher education establishments. Projected budgetary expenditure on education by the central

Government in 2000 was 6,406.3m. kuna (12.8% of total spending).

Public Holidays

2001: 1 January (New Year's Day), 6 January (Epiphany), 13 April (Good Friday), 16 April (Easter Monday), 1 May (Labour Day), 30 May (Independence Day), 22 June (Anti-Fascism Day), 5 August (National Day), 15 August (Assumption), 1 November (All Saints' Day), 25–26 December (Christmas).

2002: 1 January (New Year's Day), 6 January (Epiphany), 29 March (Good Friday), 1 April (Easter Monday), 1 May (Labour Day), 30 May (Independence Day), 22 June (Anti-Fascism Day), 5 August (National Day), 15 August (Assumption), 1 November (All Saints' Day), 25–26 December (Christmas).

Weights and Measures

The metric system is in force.

Statistical Survey

Source (unless otherwise stated): Central Bureau of Statistics of the Republic of Croatia, 10000 Zagreb, Ilica 3; tel. (1) 4806111; fax (1) 4806148; e-mail ured@dzs.hr; internet www.dzs.hr.

Area and Population

AREA, POPULATION AND DENSITY

Area (sq km)	56,542*
Population (census results)	
31 March 1981	4,601,469
31 March 1991	
Males	2,318,623
Females	2,465,642
Total	4,784,265
Population (official estimates at mid-year)	
1997	4,572,000
1998	4,501,000
1999	4,554,000
Density (per sq km) at mid-1999	80.5

* 21,831 sq miles.

POPULATION BY ETHNIC GROUP (census of 31 March 1991)

	Number ('000)	%
Croat	3,736.4	78.1
Serb	581.7	12.2
Muslim	43.5	0.9
Slovene	22.4	0.5
Hungarian	22.3	0.5
Italian	21.3	0.4
Czech	13.1	0.3
Albanian	12.0	0.3
Montenegrin	9.7	0.2
Gypsy	6.7	0.1
Macedonian	6.3	0.1
Slovak	5.6	0.1
Others*	303.3	6.3
Total	**4,784.3**	**100.0**

* Including (in '000) persons who declared themselves to be Yugoslav (106.0), persons with a regional affiliation (45.5), persons of unknown nationality (62.9) and persons who refused to reply (73.4).

PRINCIPAL TOWNS (population at 1991 census)

Zagreb (capital) .	.	706,770	Vukovar .	.	44,639
Split . . .	.	189,388	Varaždin .	.	41,846
Rijeka . .	.	167,964	Šibenik .	.	41,012
Osijek . .	.	104,761	Vinkovci .	.	35,347
Zadar . .	.	76,343	Sesvete .	.	35,337
Pula . .	.	62,378	Velika Gorica .	.	31,614
Karlovac .	.	59,999	Bjelovar .	.	26,926
Slavonski Brod . .	.	55,683	Koprivnica .	.	24,238
Dubrovnik .	.	49,728	Požega .	.	21,046
Sisak . .	.	45,792	Djakovo .	.	20,317

BIRTHS, MARRIAGES AND DEATHS

	Registered live births		Registered marriages		Registered deaths	
	Number	Rate (per 1,000)	Number	Rate (per 1,000)	Number	Rate (per 1,000)
1992 . .	46,970	10.5	22,169	4.9	51,800	11.6
1993 . .	48,535	10.8	23,021	5.1	50,846	11.4
1994 . .	48,584	10.9	23,966	5.3	49,482	11.1
1995 . .	50,182	11.2	24,385	5.1	50,536	11.3
1996 . .	53,811	12.0	24,596	5.5	50,636	11.3
1997 . .	55,501	12.1	24,517	5.4	51,964	11.4
1998 . .	47,068	10.5	24,243	5.4	52,311	11.6
1999 . .	45,179	9.9	23,778	5.2	51,953	11.4

Expectation of life (years at birth, 1998): 73.

Source: World Bank, *World Development Indicators*.

EMPLOYMENT (labour force surveys, '000 persons)

	1997*	1998†	1999
Agriculture, hunting and forestry	280.0	255.0	243.5
Fishing	3.1	2.7	3.9
Mining and quarrying . . .	7.2	8.6	8.8
Manufacturing	343.1	329.3	325.0
Electricity, gas and water supply	29.8	28.6	26.2
Construction	90.5	98.9	97.1
Wholesale and retail trade; repair of motor vehicles, motorcycles and personal and household goods	210.5	206.1	197.2
Hotels and restaurants . .	81.3	82.4	74.0
Transport, storage and communications . . .	108.1	110.5	101.1
Financial intermediation . .	32.5	32.8	34.6
Real estate, renting and business activities	55.2	60.5	56.6
Public administration and defence; compulsory social security	123.2	108.4	105.4
Education	78.6	75.3	80.8
Health and social work . .	89.3	92.5	89.1
Other community, social and personal service activities .	49.8	52.0	44.9
Private households with employed persons	4.6	—	3.4
Extra-territorial organizations and bodies	6.2	—	—
Total employed . . .	**1,593.0**	**1,543.7**	**1,491.6**
Males	863.6	832.2	802.2
Females	729.4	711.6	689.5

* June. † Annual average.

Source: partly ILO, *Yearbook of Labour Statistics*.

Unemployed (sample surveys, '000 persons): 175.2 in June 1997; 193.5 in January–June 1998; 203.4 in July–December 1998; 216.8 in January–June 1999; 251.1 in July–December 1999.

Registered unemployed (annual averages, '000 persons): 277.7 in 1997; 287.8 in 1998; 321.9 in 1999; 357.9 in 2000.

Agriculture

PRINCIPAL CROPS ('000 metric tons)

	1997	1998	1999
Wheat	834	1,020	558
Barley	108	144	125
Maize	2,183	1,983	2,135
Rye	5	6	6
Oats	47	56	57
Potatoes	620	665	729
Dry beans	21	21	22
Soybeans (Soya beans) . .	39	77	116
Sunflower seed . . .	36	62	72
Rapeseed	11	22	33
Cabbages	134	130	144
Tomatoes	48	62	71
Cucumbers and gherkins . .	29	37	37*
Onions (fresh) . . .	44	52	56
Garlic	9	11	10
Carrots	20	28	30
Watermelons and melons . .	25	60	53
Grapes	406	421	394
Sugar beets	931	1,233	1,114
Apples	58	72	67
Pears	10	12	10
Peaches and nectarines . .	7	9	10
Plums	47	83	38
Tobacco (leaves) . . .	11	12	10

* FAO estimate.

LIVESTOCK ('000 head, year ending September)

	1997	1998	1999
Horses	19	16	13
Asses and mules* . . .	4	4	4
Cattle	451	443	438
Pigs	1,175	1,166	1,362
Sheep	453	427	489
Goats	100	84	78
Chickens†	10,945	9,959	10,871
Ducks*	170	140	140
Geese*	200	150	150
Turkeys	691†	630†	630*

* FAO estimate(s).   † Unofficial figure(s).

LIVESTOCK PRODUCTS ('000 metric tons)

	1997	1998	1999
Beef and veal	43*	50*	19
Mutton and lamb . . .	2†	2†	2*
Pigmeat	68*	68*	37
Poultry meat . . .	46*	46	32
Cows' milk	622	635	635*
Butter	3	2	2
Cheese (all kinds) . . .	22	19	19
Hen eggs	48	49	49*
Honey	1	1	1*

* FAO estimate.   † Unofficial figure.

Source: FAO.

Forestry

ROUNDWOOD REMOVALS ('000 cubic metres)

	1997	1998	1999*
Sawlogs and veneer logs . . .	1,693	1,901	
Pulpwood	—	285	2,261
Other industrial wood . . .	92	105	
Fuel wood	1,006	1,107	802
Total	3,050	3,398	3,063

* From state-owned forests only.

SAWNWOOD PRODUCTION ('000 cubic metres)

	1996	1997	1998
Coniferous (softwood) . .	114	99	106
Broadleaved (hardwood) . .	483	462	424
Total . . .	597	561	530

Fishing

('000 metric tons, live weight)

	1997	1998	1999
Freshwater fishes . . .	3.6	3.2	3.3
Marine fishes	14.5	26.6	19.3
Crustaceans and molluscs . .	2.2	3.1	2.5
Total catch	20.3	27.9	25.1

Mining

('000 metric tons, unless otherwise indicated)

	1998	1999	2000
Coal	51	15	n.a.
Crude petroleum . . .	1,389	1,292	1,214
Natural gas (million cu m) . .	1,570	1,567	1,768

Industry

SELECTED PRODUCTS ('000 metric tons, unless otherwise indicated)

	1998	1999	2000
Beer ('000 hectolitres) . . .	3,759	3,663	3,847
Spirits ('000 hectolitres) . . .	241	208	177
Cigarettes (million) . . .	11,987	12,785	13,692
Cotton fabric blankets ('000 sq metres)	16,749	13,179	13,873
Household linen ('000 sq metres) .	8,088	6,928	7,229
Ready-to-wear clothing ('000 sq metres)	26,640	24,704	24,397
Leather footwear ('000 pairs) . .	5,685	5,428	5,430
Paper and cardboard . . .	158	181	228
Cardboard packaging . . .	156	167	174
Motor spirit (petrol) . . .	1,117	1,212	1,333
Gas oil (distillate fuels) . . .	906	1,006	1,050
Compound fertilizers . . .	458	459	492
Synthetic materials and resin . .	123	92	57
Cement	2,294	2,712	2,852
Tractors (number) . . .	3,755	2,325	1,751
Tankers ('000 gross registered tons)	209	203	144
Cargo ships ('000 gross registered tons)	53	131	147
Chairs ('000)	675	937	1,502
Electric energy (million kWh) . .	10,244	11,435	10,293

Finance

CURRENCY AND EXCHANGE RATES

Monetary Unit
100 lipa = 1 kuna.

Sterling, Dollar and Euro Equivalents (29 December 2000)
£1 sterling = 12.169 kuna;
US $1 = 8.155 kuna;
€1 = 7.589 kuna;
1,000 kuna = £82.17 = $122.62 = €131.78.

Average Exchange Rate (kuna per US $)
1998   6.362
1999   7.112
2000   8.277

Note: The Croatian dinar was introduced on 23 December 1991, replacing (and initially at par with) the Yugoslav dinar. On 30 May 1994 the kuna, equivalent to 1,000 dinars, was introduced.

STATE BUDGET (million kuna)

Revenue	1998	1999	2000*
Tax revenue	40,327.5	38,317.6	38,918.5
Taxes on personal income .	4,915.1	4,571.1	4,142.0
Taxes on corporate income .	2,461.1	2,366.0	1,713.4
General sales, turnover or value-added taxes . .	22,200.3	20,217.9	20,880.8
Excises	5,768.0	6,011.3	7,495.3
Excises on petroleum products	3,169.8	3,433.0	4,446.3
Excises on tobacco products .	1,983.4	1,969.9	2,174.6
Customs duties . . .	4,256.3	4,437.3	3,952.5
Other current revenue . .	1,691.9	1,728.2	1,592.1
Capital revenue	1,789.2	6,310.9	3,507.1
Total	**43,808.6**	**46,356.7**	**44,017.7**

Expenditure	1998	1999	2000*
General public services . .	3,382.4	3,047.1	2,782.1
Defence	7,373.2	5,617.3	4,744.9
Public order and safety . .	4,251.5	4,628.1	4,983.5
Education	4,668.8	5,718.2	6,406.3
Health	816.8	476.6	420.8
Social security and welfare .	8,024.6	11,300.7	13,303.5
Housing and community amenities	2,620.4	2,025.7	1,525.7
Recreational, cultural and religious affairs	576.6	842.0	899.0
Agriculture, forestry and fisheries	1,103.2	1,245.7	1,369.6
Mining and mineral resources, manufacturing and construction	728.9	2,819.5	585.5
Transport and communications .	4,073.1	5,304.0	4,778.7
Other economic affairs and services	548.4	659.2	717.3
Other purposes	3,222.4	3,694.7	7,413.1
Total	**41,390.4**	**47,379.6**	**49,930.5**

* Projected figures.
† Excluding lending minus repayments (million kuna): 1,161.5 in 1998; 1,499.2 in 1999; 733.1 in 2000 (projected figure).

Source: Ministry of Finance.

INTERNATIONAL RESERVES (US $ million at 31 December)

	1997	1998	1999
IMF special drawing rights . .	147.1	231.2	189.5
Reserve position in IMF . .	0.1	0.2	0.2
Foreign exchange . . .	2,391.9	2,584.4	2,835.3
Total	**2,539.1**	**2,815.7**	**3,025.0**

Source: IMF, *International Financial Statistics.*

MONEY SUPPLY (million kuna at 31 December)

	1997	1998	1999
Currency outside banks . .	5,319.6	5,730.1	5,958.9
Demand deposits at deposit money banks. .	8,423.8	7,808.9	7,891.5
Total (incl. others) . . .	**13,814.3**	**13,621.1**	**13,858.9**

Source: IMF, *International Financial Statistics.*

COST OF LIVING (Consumer price index; base: 1990 = 100)

	1998	1999	2000
Food	62,296.9	62,359.2	62,608.6
Fuel and light	56,646.9	58,798.1	60,209.3
Clothing (incl. footwear) . .	64,525.7	69,816.8	74,424.7
Housing.	54,669.3	56,473.4	60,426.5
All items (incl. others) . .	**64,984.5**	**67,259.0**	**70,823.7**

NATIONAL ACCOUNTS

Gross Domestic Product by Economic Activity
(million kuna at current prices)

	1996	1997	1998
Agriculture, hunting and forestry	8,887.4	9,471.2	10,661.6
Fishing	171.4	216.5	238.9
Mining and quarrying . .	234.9	645.9	642.5
Manufacturing	19,660.2	22,791.4	24,661.2
Electricity, gas and water supply	3,411.3	3,675.5	3,770.4
Construction. . . .	5,965.1	7,437.0	7,732.1
Wholesale and retail trade; repair of motor vehicles, motorcycles and personal and household goods	11,121.6	13,050.9	13,787.8
Hotels and restaurants . .	2,731.8	3,266.3	3,581.2
Transport, storage and communications . . .	8,022.3	9,091.7	9,777.2
Financial intermediation . .	3,952.3	4,043.7	4,901.7
Real estate, renting and business activities	9,362.5	10,649.9	11,485.8
Public administration and defence; compulsory social security	8,241.9	9,548.7	11,684.0
Education	3,433.8	3,864.6	4,944.7
Health and social work . .	3,522.2	4,441.4	5,702.4
Other community, social and personal service activities . .	2,140.8	2,487.9	2,685.3
Private households with employed persons	20.7	24.7	36.6
Sub-total	**90,880.4**	**104,707.2**	**116,293.4**
Less Financial intermediation services indirectly measured	2,793.7	3,788.2	5,232.4
GDP at basic prices . .	**88,086.7**	**100,918.9**	**111,061.0**
Taxes, *less* subsidies, on products .	19,893.9	22,891.8	26,542.7
GDP in purchasers' values . .	**107,980.6**	**123,810.7**	**137,603.7**

BALANCE OF PAYMENTS (US $ million)

	1997	1998	1999
Exports of goods f.o.b. . .	4,210.3	4,604.5	4,394.7
Imports of goods f.o.b. . .	−9,406.5	−8,751.9	−7,693.3
Trade balance	**−5,196.2**	**−4,147.4**	**−3,298.6**
Exports of services . . .	4,004.3	3,964.1	3,723.0
Imports of services . . .	−1,980.1	−1,889.3	−2,097.8
Balance on goods and services	**−3,172.0**	**−2,072.6**	**−1,673.4**
Other income received . .	363.8	394.9	252.2
Other income paid . . .	−386.2	−558.7	−601.7
Balance on goods, services and income	**−3,194.4**	**−2,236.4**	**−2,022.9**
Current transfers received . .	964.0	919.1	835.2
Current transfers paid . .	−94.6	−213.1	−335.0
Current balance	**−2,325.1**	**−1,530.4**	**−1,522.6**
Capital account (net) . . .	21.5	19.1	24.9
Direct investment abroad. .	−186.1	−97.5	−34.1
Direct investment from abroad .	529.9	898.1	1,408.0
Portfolio investment assets .	11.1	−0.1	−0.3
Portfolio investment liabilities .	565.8	15.0	574.3
Other investment assets . .	171.3	348.8	−588.4
Other investment liabilities .	1,963.2	402.9	457.7
Net errors and omissions . .	−323.5	95.9	109.1
Overall balance	**428.0**	**151.5**	**428.5**

Source: IMF, *International Financial Statistics.*

External Trade

PRINCIPAL COMMODITIES (distribution by SITC, US $ million)

Imports c.i.f.	1997	1998	1999
Food and live animals	832	675	560
Crude materials (inedible) except fuels	274	223	172
Mineral fuels, lubricants, etc.	850	596	859
Petroleum and petroleum products	672	394	673
Chemicals and related products	965	961	940
Medicinal and pharmaceutical products	185	200	214
Basic manufactures	1,515	1,398	1,252
Paper, paperboard, etc.	251	242	231
Textile yarn, fabrics, etc.	212	194	160
Non-metallic mineral manufactures	188	173	174
Iron and steel	285	247	211
Machinery and transport equipment	3,062	2,952	2,732
Machinery specialized for particular industries	381	324	257
General industrial machinery, equipment and parts	455	393	373
Office machines and automatic data-processing equipment	247	175	176
Telecommunications and sound equipment	251	171	155
Other electrical machinery, apparatus, etc.	427	380	339
Road vehicles and parts (excl. tyres, engines and electrical parts)	947	853	816
Miscellaneous manufactured articles	1,178	1,068	924
Clothing and accessories (excl. footwear)	271	257	213
Footwear	246	208	181
Total (incl. others)	9,104	8,383	7,799

Exports f.o.b.	1997	1998	1999
Food and live animals	385	385	291
Beverages and tobacco	121	111	101
Crude materials (inedible) except fuels	261	231	243
Wood, lumber and cork	168	157	164
Mineral fuels, lubricants, etc.	426	264	338
Petroleum and petroleum products	385	232	287
Chemicals and related products	570	545	515
Medicinal and pharmaceutical products	157	149	169
Fertilizers (other than crude)	87	76	73
Plastics in primary forms	171	176	135
Basic manufactures	589	584	573
Textile yarn, fabrics, etc.	91	89	83
Non-metallic mineral manufactures	133	131	153
Machinery and transport equipment	752	1,380	1,262
Telecommunications and sound equipment	93	80	38
Other electrical machinery, apparatus, etc.	227	234	230
Transport equipment (excl. road vehicles)	165	771	713
Miscellaneous manufactured articles	1,049	1,023	966
Furniture and parts	125	107	105
Clothing and accessories (excl. footwear)	555	556	525
Footwear	226	199	174
Total (incl. others)	4,171	4,541	4,302

PRINCIPAL TRADING PARTNERS (US $ million)

Imports c.i.f.	1997	1998	1999
Austria	709	612	558
Belgium	96	110	114
Bosnia and Herzegovina	137	156	117
Czech Republic	208	181	148
France	293	401	393
Germany	1,841	1,616	1,441
Hungary	239	212	174
Italy	1,705	1,500	1,240
Japan	139	146	138
Libya	133	64	26
Netherlands	170	161	142
Russia	457	364	668
Slovenia	756	722	616
Spain	94	110	83
Sweden	147	109	116
Switzerland	213	181	158
United Kingdom	189	176	187
USA	266	278	241
Total (incl. others)	9,104	8,383	7,799

Exports f.o.b.	1997	1998	1999
Austria	223	247	276
Bosnia and Herzegovina	649	654	546
France	79	102	108
Germany	746	767	676
Hungary	48	52	40
Italy	787	802	775
Liberia	124	336	169
Macedonia, former Yugoslav republic	77	64	64
Netherlands	62	53	50
Norway	n.a.	36	113
Poland	47	46	40
Russia	164	164	71
Slovenia	506	432	454
United Kingdom	67	71	80
USA	97	89	87
Total (incl. others)	4,171	4,541	4,302

Transport

RAILWAYS (traffic)

	1997	1998	1999
Passenger journeys ('000)	17,003	17,102	17,537
Passenger-kilometres (million)	981	921	943
Freight carried ('000 metric tons)	12,168	12,643	11,491
Freight net ton-km (million)	1,876	2,001	1,849

ROAD TRAFFIC (registered motor vehicles at 31 December)

	1997	1998	1999
Passenger cars	932,278	1,000,052	1,063,546
Buses	4,771	4,814	4,743
Lorries	101,051	106,634	109,387
Special vehicles }			
Motorcycles and mopeds	42,178	50,538	58,109

INLAND WATERWAYS (vessels and traffic)

	1997	1998	1999
Tugs	25	27	27
Motor barges	3	3	3
Barges	101	101	95
Goods unloaded (million metric tons)	1	1	1

SHIPPING
Merchant Fleet (registered at 31 December)

	1996	1997	1998
Number of vessels . . .	232	245	260
Total displacement ('000 grt) . .	579.8	871.0	896.4

Source: Lloyd's Register of Shipping, *World Fleet Statistics*.

International Sea-borne Freight Traffic

	1997	1998	1999
Vessels entered (million gross reg. tons)	21.5	24.4	20.8
Goods loaded ('000 metric tons) .	2,458	2,373	3,728
Goods unloaded ('000 metric tons)	6,782	6,666	6,739
Goods in transit ('000 metric tons)	3,180	3,578	2,680

CIVIL AVIATION

	1997	1998	1999
Kilometres flown ('000) . . .	11,083	12,100	11,434
Passengers carried ('000) . . .	866	920	926
Passenger-kilometres (million) .	546	624	643
Freight carried (metric tons) . .	4,696	5,215	4,858
Ton-kilometres ('000) . . .	2,997	3,374	3,219

Tourism

FOREIGN TOURIST ARRIVALS BY COUNTRY OF ORIGIN ('000)

	1997	1998	1999
Austria	447	457	374
Czech Republic	579	499	415
France	35	42	32
Germany	640	721	531
Hungary	127	138	141
Italy	688	751	538
Netherlands	65	88	73
Slovakia	154	162	108
Slovenia	578	638	690
United Kingdom	51	68	51
Total (incl. others) . . .	3,834	4,112	3,443

Receipts from tourism (US $ million): 2,014 in 1996; 2,530 in 1997; 2,733 in 1998.

Communications Media

	1997	1998	1999
Radio licences ('000) . . .	1,032	1,098	1,110
Television licences ('000) . . .	989	1,056	1,083
Telephone subscribers ('000) . .	1,477	1,573	1,641
Book production: titles . . .	3,277	3,626	2,768
Daily newspapers:			
Number	10	11	16

Non-daily newspapers (1996): 767 (average circulation 584,000 copies).
Other periodicals (1990): 352 (average circulation 6,357,000 copies).
Telefax stations (number in use): 28,350 in 1994; 39,072 in 1995; 45,259 in 1996 (Source: UN, *Statistical Yearbook*).
Mobile cellular telephones (subscribers): 21,664 in 1994; 33,688 in 1995; 64,943 in 1996 (Source: UN, *Statistical Yearbook*).

Education

(1999/2000)

	Institu-tions	Teach-ers	Students		
			Males	Females	Total
Pre-primary . . .	1,034	6,372	37,381	34,000	71,381
Primary . . .	2,144	10,605	102,437	96,647	199,084
Secondary: general .	1,131	20,420	128,542	135,466	264,008
Secondary: vocational .	484	14,231	79,083	67,316	146,399
University level* . .	84	7,563	45,777	51,021	96,798

* Excluding post-graduate students.

Directory

The Constitution

The Constitution of the Republic of Croatia was promulgated on 21 December 1990. Croatia issued a declaration of dissociation from the Socialist Federal Republic of Yugoslavia in June 1991, and formal independence was proclaimed on 8 October 1991. Constitutional amendments, which were adopted in November 1997, included a prohibition on the re-establishment of a union of Yugoslav states.

The following is a summary of the main provisions of the Constitution:

GENERAL PROVISIONS

The Republic of Croatia is a democratic, constitutional state where power belongs to the people and is exercised directly and through the elected representatives of popular sovereignty.

The Republic of Croatia is an integral state, while its sovereignty is inalienable, indivisible and non-transferable. State power in the Republic of Croatia is divided into legislative, executive and judicial power.

All citizens of the Republic of Croatia over the age of 18 years have the right to vote and to be candidates for election to public office. The right to vote is realized through direct elections, by secret ballot. Citizens of the Republic living outside its borders have the right to vote in elections for the Assembly and the President of the Republic.

In a state of war or when there is a direct threat to the independence and unity of the Republic, as well as in the case of serious natural disasters, some freedoms and rights that are guaranteed by the Constitution may be restricted. This is decided by the Assembly of the Republic of Croatia by a two-thirds majority of its deputies and, if the Assembly cannot be convened, by the President of the Republic.

BASIC RIGHTS

The following rights are guaranteed and protected in the Republic: the right to life (the death sentence has been abolished), fundamental freedoms and privacy, equality before the law, the right to be presumed innocent until proven guilty and the principle of legality, the right to receive legal aid, the right to freedom of movement and residence, the right to seek asylum, inviolability of the home, freedom and secrecy of correspondence, safety and secrecy of personal data, freedom of thought and expression of opinion, freedom of conscience and religion (all religious communities are equal before the law and are separated from the State), the right of assembly and peaceful association, the right of ownership, entrepreneurship and free trade (monopolies are forbidden), the right to work and freedom of labour, the right to a nationality, the right to strike, and the right to a healthy environment.

Members of all peoples and minorities in the Republic enjoy equal rights. They are guaranteed the freedom to express their nationality, to use their language and alphabet and to enjoy cultural autonomy.

GOVERNMENT

Legislature

Legislative power resides with the Assembly (Sabor), which consists of the 151-member Chamber of Representatives (Zastupnički dom), and the 68-member Chamber of Counties (Županijski dom).

The Chamber of Representatives decides on the adoption and amendment of the Constitution, approves laws, adopts the state budgets, decides on war and peace, decides on the alteration of the borders of the Republic, calls referendums, supervises the work of the Government and other public officials responsible to the Assembly, in accordance with the Constitution and the law, and deals with other matters determined by the Constitution.

The Chamber of Counties proposes laws and gives opinions on issues within the competence of the Chamber of Representatives; however, after the adoption of a law in the Chamber of Representatives, the Chamber of Counties may return the same law to the former for reconsideration. The citizens of each district elect, by direct and secret ballot, three deputies to the Chamber of Counties. A further five deputies are appointed by the President.

Members of the Chambers of the Assembly are elected by universal, direct and secret ballot for a term of four years, and their term is not mandatory. The Chambers of the Assembly may be dissolved, if the majority of all the deputies decides so. The Assembly has the power to appoint and dismiss the Prime Minister and (upon his recommendation) the ministers.

President of the Republic

The President of the Republic is the Head of State of Croatia. The President represents the country at home and abroad and is responsible for ensuring respect for the Constitution, guaranteeing the existence and unity of the Republic and the regular functioning of state power. The President is elected directly for a term of five years.

The President is the Supreme Commander of the Armed Forces of the Republic of Croatia. In the event of war or immediate danger, the President issues decrees having the force of law. The President may convene a meeting of the Government and place on its agenda items which, in his opinion, should be discussed. The President attends the Government's meetings and presides over them.

Ministers

Executive power in the Republic resides with the President, the Prime Minister and the Ministers. The Government of the Republic consists of the Ministers and the Prime Minister. The Government issues decrees, proposes laws and the budget, and implements laws and regulations that have been adopted by the Assembly. In its work, the Government is responsible to the President of the Republic and the Chamber of Representatives.

JUDICATURE

Judicial power is vested in the courts and is autonomous and independent. The courts issue judgments on the basis of the Constitution and the law. The Supreme Court is the highest court and is responsible for the uniform implementation of laws and equal rights of citizens. Judges and state public prosecutors are appointed and relieved of duty by the Judicial Council of the Republic, which is elected, from among distinguished lawyers, by the Chamber of Representatives for a term of eight years.

The Government

HEAD OF STATE

President of the Republic: STIPE MESIĆ (elected 7 February 2000; inaugurated 18 February 2000).

Office of the President: 10000 Zagreb, Banski Dvori.

GOVERNMENT

(March 2001)

A coalition of the Social Democratic Party (SDP), the Croatian Social-Liberal Party (CSLP), the Croatian People's Party (CPP), the Liberal Party (LP), the Croatian Peasants' Party and the Istrian Democratic Assembly (IDA).

Prime Minister: IVICA RAČAN (SDP).

First Deputy Prime Minister: GORAN GRANIĆ (CSLP).

Deputy Prime Minister (Economy): SLAVKO LINIĆ (SDP).

Deputy Prime Minister (Social Affairs): ZELJKA ANTUNOVIĆ (SDP).

Minister of Finance: MATO CRKVENAC (SDP).

Minister of Defence: JOZO RADOS (CSLP).

Minister of the Interior: SIME LUCIN (SDP).

Minister of Foreign Affairs: TONINO PICULA (SDP).

Minister of Public Works, Reconstruction and Construction: RADIMIR ČAČIĆ (CPP).

Minister of the Economy: GORANKO FIZULIĆ (CSLP).

Minister of Croatian Homeland War Defenders: IVICA PANČIĆ.

Minister of Agriculture and Forestry: BOZIDAR PANKRETIĆ (Croatian Peasants' Party).

Minister of Transport and Telecommunications: ALOJZ TUSEK (CSLP).

Minister of Justice, Administration and Local Self-Government: STJEPAN IVANISEVIĆ (SDP).

Minister of Environmental Protection and Physical Planning: BOZO KOVACEVIĆ (LP).

Minister of Education and Sport: VLADIMIR STRUGAR (Croatian Peasants' Party).

Minister of Labour and Social Welfare: DAVORKO VIDOVIĆ (SDP).

Minister of Tourism: PAVE ZUPAN RUSKOVIĆ (Independent).

Minister of Health: MAJA STAVLJEVIĆ-RUKAVINA (Independent).

Minister of Science and Technology: HRVOJE KRALJEVIĆ (CSLP).

Minister of Culture: ANTUN VUJIĆ (SDP).

Minister of European Integration: Ivan Jakovčić (IDA).

Minister of Trades, Small and Medium Businesses: Željko Pecek (CSLP).

MINISTRIES

Office of the Prime Minister: Govt of the Republic of Croatia, 10000 Zagreb, trg sv. Marka 2; tel. (1) 4569201; fax (1) 432041.

Ministry of Agriculture and Forestry: 10000 Zagreb, Ave. Vukovar 78; tel. (1) 6133444; fax (1) 442070; internet www.mps.hr.

Ministry of Croatian Homeland War Defenders: Park Stara Trešnjevka 4, Zagreb; tel. (1) 3657800; fax (1) 3657852; e-mail pommin4@mhbdr.tel.hr.

Ministry of Culture: 10000 Zagreb, trg Burze 6; tel. (1) 4569000; fax (1) 410487; internet www.mini-kulture.hr.

Ministry of Defence: 10000 Zagreb, trg kralja Petra Krešimira IV 1; tel. (1) 4567111; e-mail infor@morh.hr; internet www.morh.hr.

Ministry of the Economy: 10000 Zagreb, trg sv. Marka 2; tel. (1) 4569207; fax (1) 4550606; e-mail info@mingo.hr; internet www.mingo.hr.

Ministry of Education and Sport: 10000 Zagreb, trg Burze 6; tel. (1) 4569000; fax (1) 4569087; e-mail office@mps.hr; internet www.mips.hr.

Ministry of Environmental Protection and Physical Planning: 10000 Zagreb, Republike Austrije 20; tel. (1) 3782444; fax (1) 3772822; e-mail kabinet.ministra@zg.tel.hr; internet www.mzopu.hr.

Ministry of European Integration: 10000 Zagreb, ul. grada Vukovara 62; tel. (1) 4569335; fax (1) 6303182; e-mail info@mei.hr; internet www.mei.hr.

Ministry of Finance: 10000 Zagreb, ul. Katančićeva 5; tel. (1) 4591333; fax (1) 4922583; e-mail kabinet@mfin.hr; internet www.mfin.hr.

Ministry of Foreign Affairs: 10000 Zagreb, trg Nikole Šubića Zrinskog 7-8; tel. (1) 4569964; fax (1) 4569977; e-mail mvp@mvp.hr; internet www.mvp.hr.

Ministry of Health: 10000 Zagreb, ul. Baruna Tranka 6; tel. (1) 431068; fax (1) 431067; internet www.tel.hr/mzrh.

Ministry of the Interior: 10000 Zagreb, Savska cesta 39; tel. (1) 6122129; fax (1) 6122299; e-mail webinfo@vlada.hr; internet www.vlada.hr.

Ministry of Justice, Administration and Local Self-Government: 10000 Zagreb, Savska cesta 41; tel. (1) 535935; fax (1) 536321.

Ministry of Labour and Social Welfare: 10000 Zagreb, Prisavlje 14; tel. (1) 6169111; fax (1) 6169206; e-mail info@mrss.hr; internet www.mrss.hr.

Ministry of Public Works, Reconstruction and Construction: Zagreb, Savska cesta 41/12; tel. (1) 6176011; fax (1) 6176161; e-mail mpu@mpu.hr.

Ministry of Tourism: 10000 Zagreb, Ave. Vukovar 78; tel. (1) 6106300; fax (1) 6109300; e-mail mthcei@mint.hr; internet www.mint.hr.

Ministry of Trades, Small and Medium Businesses: 10000 Zagreb, Ksaver 200; tel. (1) 4698300; fax (1) 4698307; e-mail momsp@momsp.hr; internet www.momsp.hr.

Ministry of Transport and Telecommunications: 10000 Zagreb, Prisavlje 14; tel. (1) 6169100; fax (1) 6196519.

President and Legislature

PRESIDENT

Presidential Election, First Ballot, 24 January 2000

	Votes	% of votes
Stipe Mesić*	1,100,671	41.11
Dražen Budiša†	741,837	27.71
Dr Mate Granić (Croatian Democratic Union)	601,588	22.47
Slaven Letica (Independent)	110,782	4.14
Ante Djapić (Croatian Party of Rights)	49,288	1.84
Ante Ledić (Independent)	22,875	0.85
Tomislav Mercep (Croatian People's Party)	22,672	0.85
Ante Prkacin (New Croatia)	7,401	0.28
Dr Zvonimir Šeparović (Independent)	7,235	0.27
Total	**2,664,349‡**	**100.00**

* Candidate of the Croatian Peasants' Party, the Liberal Party, the Croatian People's Party and the Istrian Democratic Assembly.

† Candidate of the Social Democratic Party and the Croatian Social-Liberal Party.

‡ Excluding 13,212 invalid votes (0.49% of the total votes).

Presidential Election, Second Ballot, 7 February 2000*

	% of votes
Stipe Mesić†	56.21
Dražen Budiša‡	43.79
Total	**100.00**

* Preliminary results.

† Candidate of the Croatian Peasants' Party, the Liberal Party, the Croatian People's Party and the Istrian Democratic Assembly.

‡ Candidate of the Social Democratic Party and the Croatian Social-Liberal Party.

SABOR
(Assembly)

President: Zlatko Tomčić; 10000 Zagreb, trg sv. Marka 617; tel. (1) 4569222; fax (1) 276483.

Vice-Presidents: Mato Arlović, Zdravko Tomac, Baltazar Jalsovec, Vlatko Pavletić, Ivić Pasalić.

Zastupnički dom
(Chamber of Representatives)

President: Zlatko Tomčić.

Election, 3 January 2000

	% of votes	Seats
Social Democratic Party		44
Croatian Social-Liberal Party	47.0	24
Primorian-Goranian Union		2
Slavonian-Baranian Croatian Party		1
Croatian Democratic Union	30.5	45
Croatian Peasants' Party		16
Istrian Democratic Assembly		4
Liberal Party	15.9	2
Croatian People's Party		2
Croatian Social Democrats' Action		1
Croatian Party of Rights	3.3	5
Croatian Christian Democratic Union		1
Total*	**100.0**	**151**

* Includes one representative of the Serbian National Party, one representative of the Hungarian Democratic Community of Croatia and two independent representatives of minorities.

Županijski dom
(Chamber of Counties)

President: Katica Ivanešević.

Election, 13 April 1997

Party	Seats
Croatian Democratic Union (CDU)	41
Croatian Peasants' Party (HSS)	9
Croatian Social-Liberal Party (CSLP)	7
Social Democratic Party (SDP)	4
Istrian Democratic Assembly (IDA)	2
Total	**63***

* An additional five deputies, of whom two were members of the Serb community, were appointed by the President.

Political Organizations

Christian People's Party (CPP) (Kršćanska Narodna Stranka—KNS): 10000 Zagreb, Degenova 7; tel. (1) 427258; fax (1) 273595; Pres. Zdravko Mršić.

Croatian Christian Democratic Union (CCDU) (Hrvatska Kršćanska Demokratska Unija—HKDU): 10000 Zagreb; tel. (1) 327233; fax (1) 325190; e-mail bihdem@posluh.hr; internet www.posluh.hr; Pres. Ivan Cesar.

Croatian Democratic Centre: 10000 Zagreb; f. March 2000 by a breakaway faction of the Croatian Democratic Union; pro-European, moderate; Pres. Mate Granić.

Croatian Democratic Party (CDP) (Hrvatska Demokratska Stranka—HDS): 10000 Zagreb; tel. (1) 431837; Pres. Marko Veselica.

Croatian Democratic Republican Party: f. Oct. 2000 by merger of Croatian Spring, National Democratic Party and Croatian Peasants' National Party; Leader Josko Kovac.

Croatian Democratic Union (CDU) (Hrvatska Demokratska Zajednica—HDZ): 10000 Zagreb, trg hrvatskih velikana 4; tel. (1) 4553000; fax (1) 4552600; e-mail hdz@hdz.hr; internet www.hdz.hr; f. 1989; Christian Democrat; Chair. Ivo SANADER; Sec.-Gen. JOSO SKARA.

Croatian Independent Democrats (CID) (Hrvatski Nezavisni Demokrati—HND): 10000 Zagreb; f. 1994 by a faction from the CDU.

Croatian Muslim Democratic Party (CMDP) (Hrvatska Muslimanska Demokratska Stranka—HMDS): 10000 Zagreb; tel. (1) 421562.

Croatian Party of Rights (CPR) (Hrvatska Stranka Prava—HSP): 10000 Zagreb, ul. Šenoina 13; tel. and fax (1) 4839938; e-mail hsp1861@hsp1861.hr; internet www.hsp1861.hr; f. 1861, re-established 1990; right-wing, nationalist; armed br. was the Croatian Defence Asscn or Hrvatske Obrambene Snage (HOS); Pres. DOBROSLAV PARAGA.

Croatian Party of Slavonia and Baranja (CPSB) (Slavonsko–Baranjska Hrvatska Stranka—SBHS): Osijek.

Croatian Peasants' Party (Hrvatska Seljačka Stranka—HSS): 10000 Zagreb, ul. Kralja Zvonimira 17; tel. and fax (1) 4553624; e-mail hss-sredisnjica@hss.hr; internet www.hss.hr; Pres. ZLATKO TOMČIĆ.

Croatian Pensioners' Party: 10000 Zagreb; contested local elections in 2000 in a coalition with the SDP.

Croatian People's Party (CPP) (Hrvatska Narodna Stranka—HNS): 10000 Zagreb, Tomićeva 2; tel. (1) 4877000; fax (1) 4877009; e-mail webmaster@hns.hr; internet www.hns.hr; Pres. VESNA PUSIĆ.

Croatian Republican Community (CRC) (Hrvatska Republikanska Zajednica—HRZ): 10000 Zagreb, Nalješkovićeva 11; tel. and fax (1) 4666740; e-mail hrz@zg.tel.hr; internet www.hrz.hr; Pres. BORKO JURIN.

Croatian Social Democrats' Action (Akcija socijaldemokrata Hrvatske—ASH): Zagreb.

Croatian Social-Liberal Party (CSLP) (Hryatska Socijalno-Liberalna Stranka—HSLS): 10000 Zagreb, trg N. Š. Zrinskog 17; tel. (1) 4810401; fax (1) 4810404; e-mail hsls@hsls.hr; internet www.hsls.hr; f. 1989; Pres. DRAŽEN BUDIŠA; Gen. Sec. JOZO RADOŠ.

Dalmatian Action (DA) (Dalmatinska Akcija): 21000 Split, ul. bana Jelačića 4/I; tel. (21) 344322; f. 1990; Pres. Dr MIRA LJUBIĆ-LORGER.

Independent Democratic Serb Party (Samostalne Demokratska Srpska Stranka—SDSS): 32000 Vukovar, Radnički dom 1–3; tel. and fax (32) 665116; f. 1997 by Serbs in Eastern Slavonia; Pres. Dr VOJISLAV STANIMIROVIĆ.

Istrian Democratic Assembly (IDA) (Istarski Demokratski Sabor—IDS): Pula, Splitska 3; tel. (52) 223316; fax (52) 213702; e-mail ids-ddi@pu.tel.hr; internet www.ids-ddi.com; Pres. IVAN JAKOVČIĆ.

Istrian People's Party (IPP) (Istarska Pučka Stranka—IPS): Pula, trg revolucije 3; tel. (52) 23863; fax (52) 23832; Pres. JOSIP FABRIS.

Liberal Party (Liberalna Stranka): 10000 Zagreb; e-mail liberaliebbm.hr; internet www.liberali.hr; f. 1998 by a breakaway faction of the Croatian Social-Liberal Party; Pres. VLADO GOTOVAC.

New Croatia: Zagreb; Pres. ANTE PRKACIN.

Party of Serbs: 10000 Zagreb; f. 1993 by mems of Serb cultural asscn Prosveta (Enlightenment) and Serb Democratic Forum; promotes liberal, democratic values; Leader MILORAD PUPOVAĆ.

Primorian-Goranian Union (Primorski-Goranski Savez): Zagreb; regionalist.

Programme for Croatian Identity and Prosperity: f. Nov. 2000 by former supporters of Pres. Dr Franjo Tudjman; Leader MIROSLAV TUDJMAN.

Rijeka Democratic Alliance (RDA) (Riječki Demokratski Savez—RDS): 51000 Rijeka, Žrtava fašizma 29; tel. (51) 423713; Pres. NIKOLA IVANIŠ; Sec. FRANJO BUTORAC.

Serb People's Party (SPP) (Srpska Narodna Stranka—SNS): 10000 Zagreb, trg Mažuranića 3; tel. and fax (1) 451090; promotes cultural and individual rights for ethnic Serbs in Croatia; 4,500–5,000 mems; Pres. MILAN DUKIĆ.

Slavonian-Baranian Croatian Party (Slavonsko-baranjska hrvatska stranka): Zagreb.

Social Democratic Party (SDP) (Socijaldemokratska Partija Hrvatske SPH): 10000 Zagreb, trg Iblerov 9; tel. (1) 4552658; fax (1) 4552842; e-mail sdp@sdp.tel.hr; internet www.sdp.hr; formerly the ruling League of Communists of Croatia (Party of Democratic Reform), renamed as above in 1993; 20,000 mems; Chair. IVICA RAČAN.

Social Democratic Union of Croatia (SDUC) (Socijalno Demokratska Unija Hrvatske—SDUH): 10000 Zagreb, Tratinska 27; tel. and fax (1) 394055; f. 1992; Pres. VLADIMIR BEBIĆ.

Socialist Party of Croatia (SPC) (Socijalistička Stranka Hrvatske—SSH): 10000 Zagreb, Prisavlje 14; tel. (1) 517835; fax (1) 510235; Pres. ŽELJKO MAŽAR.

Socialist Workers' Party of Croatia (SRPH) (Socijalističke Radničke Partije Hrvatske): 10000 Zagreb; tel. (1) 483958; e-mail srp@srp.hr; internet www.srp.hr; f. 1997; Leader STIPE SUVAR.

Diplomatic Representation

EMBASSIES IN CROATIA

Albania: 10000 Zagreb, Jurišićeva 2A; tel. (1) 4810679; fax (1) 4810682; Ambassador: ARBEN CICI.

Australia: 10000 Zagreb, Isidora Kršnjavoga; tel. (1) 4891200; fax (1) 4836606; Ambassador: FRANCES NEIL.

Austria: 10000 Zagreb, Jabukovać 39; tel. (1) 4834457; fax (1) 4834461; e-mail austrijsko-veleposlanstvo@alf.tel.hr; Ambassador: HANS KNITEL.

Belgium: 10000 Zagreb, Pantovčak 125; tel. (1) 4578901; fax (1) 4578902; Ambassador: LUC LIEBAUT.

Bosnia and Herzegovina: 10001 Zagreb, Torbarova 9; tel. (1) 4683761; fax (1) 4683764; e-mail ambasada-bh-zg@zg.tel.hr; Ambassador: Dr HASAN MURATOVIĆ.

Bulgaria: 10000 Zagreb, Novi Gajeva 25; tel. (1) 4823336; fax (1) 4823338; Ambassador: ENČEV VELIZAR.

Canada: 10000 Zagreb, Prilaz Gjure Deželića; tel. (1) 4881200; fax (1) 4881230; e-mail zagreb@dfait-maeci.gc.ca; Ambassador: D. A. SNIDER.

China, People's Republic: 10000 Zagreb, Mlinovi 132; tel. (1) 4637011; fax (1) 4637012; Ambassador: ŽHI ZHAOLIN.

Czech Republic: 10000 Zagreb, Savska cesta 41; tel. (1) 6177246; fax (1) 6176630; Ambassador: JIRI KUDELA.

Finland: 10000 Zagreb, Berislavićeva 2/II; tel. (1) 4811662; fax (1) 4819946; Ambassador: OSMO LIPPONEN.

France: 10000 Zagreb, Schlosserove stube 5; tel. (1) 4557767; fax (1) 4557765; e-mail presse@ambafrance.hr; internet www .ambafrance.hr; Ambassador: ALBERT TUROT.

Germany: 10000 Zagreb, Ulica grada Vukovara 64; tel. (1) 6158105; fax (1) 6158103; Ambassador: WEISS GEBHARDT.

Greece: 10000 Zagreb, Babukićeva 3A; tel. (1) 4810444; fax (1) 4810419; Ambassador: CHRISTIAN GEORGES-STAVROS VASSILOPOULOS.

Holy See: 10000 Zagreb, Ksaverska cesta bb; tel. (1) 4554995; fax (1) 4554997; Apostolic Delegate: Most Rev. GIULIO EINAUDI, Titular Archbishop of Villamagna in Tripolitania.

Hungary: 10000 Zagreb, Krležin gvozd 11A; tel. (1) 4834990; fax (1) 4834998; e-mail hungemb-tajnica@hungemb.tel.hr; Ambassador: GYÖRGY CSÓTI.

India: 10000 Zagreb, ul. Boškovićeva 7A; tel. (1) 4873240; fax (1) 4817907; e-mail embassy.india@zg.tel.hr; Ambassador: UDAI SINGH.

Iran: 10000 Zagreb, Pantovčak 125C; tel. (1) 4578981; fax (1) 4578987; Ambassador: KEYVAN IMANI.

Italy: 10000 Zagreb, Medulićeva 22; tel. (1) 4846386; fax (1) 4846384; e-mail veleposlanstvo_italije@zg.tel.hr; Ambassador: FABIO PIGLIAPOCO.

Japan: 10000 Zagreb, Ksaver 211; tel. (1) 4677755; fax (1) 4677766; Ambassador: OBA KEISUKE.

Macedonia, former Yugoslav republic: 10000 Zagreb, Petrinjska 29/I; tel. (1) 4922903; fax (1) 4922902; Ambassador: SERVET AVZIU.

Malaysia: 10000 Zagreb, Slavujevac 4A; tel. (1) 483436; fax (1) 4834348; Ambassador: MOHAMAD BIN SANI.

Netherlands: 10000 Zagreb, Medvešćak 56; tel. (1) 4684582; fax (1) 4819583; internet www.nlgovzag@zg.tel.hr; Chargé d'affaires: IDA L. VAN VELDHUIZEN ROTHENBÜCHER.

Norway: 10000 Zagreb, Petrinjska 9; tel. (1) 4922829; fax (1) 4922828; Ambassador: KNUT MØRKVED.

Poland: 10000 Zagreb, Krležin Gvozd 3; tel. (1) 4834575; fax (1) 4834576; Ambassador: JERZY CHMIELEWSKI.

Portugal: 10000 Zagreb, trg ban J. Jelačića 5/II; tel. (1) 4882210; fax (1) 4920663; Ambassador: ANA BARATA.

Romania: 10000 Zagreb, Srebrnjak 150A; tel. (1) 2430137; Ambassador: Dr CONSTANTIN GHIRDĂ.

Russia: 10000 Zagreb, Bosanska 44; tel. (1) 3755038; fax (1) 3755040; Ambassador: EDUARD LEONIDOVIĆ-KUZMIN.

Slovakia: 10000 Zagreb, Prilaz Djure Deželića 10; tel. (1) 4848941; fax (1) 4848942; e-mail velep-rep-slovacke-u-rh@zg.tel.hr; Ambassador: JÁN PETRÍK.

Slovenia: 10000 Zagreb, Savska cesta 41/II; tel. (1) 6311000; fax (1) 6177236; Ambassador: BOŠTJAN KOVAČIĆ.

Spain: 10000 Zagreb, Medulićeva 5; tel. (1) 4848603; fax (1) 4848605; Ambassador: ANTONIO PEDAUYE Y GONZALEZ.

Sweden: 10000 Zagreb, Frankopanska 22; tel. (1) 4849322; fax (1) 4849244; e-mail swedish.embassy@zg.tel.hr; Ambassador: INGEMAR BÖRJESSON.

Switzerland: 10000 Zagreb, Bogovićeva 3; tel. (1) 4810891; fax (1) 4810890; e-mail swiemzag@zg.tel.hr; Ambassador: PAUL WIDMER.

Turkey: 10000 Zagreb, Masarykova 3/II; tel. (1) 4855200; fax (1) 4855606; e-mail turembzag@zg.tel.hr; Ambassador: SELAHATTIN ALPAR.

Ukraine: 10000 Zagreb, Voćarska 52; tel. (1) 4616296; fax (1) 4556128; Ambassador: ANATOLIY SHOSTAK.

United Kingdom: 10000 Zagreb, Vlaska 121; tel. (1) 4555310; fax (1) 4551685; e-mail british-embassy@zg.tel.hr; Ambassador: NICHOLAS JARROLD.

USA: 10000 Zagreb, Andrije Hebranga 2; tel. (1) 4555500; fax (1) 4558585; internet www.usembassy.hr; Ambassador: LAWRENCE ROSSIN.

Yugoslavia: 10000 Zagreb, Mesićeva 19; tel. (1) 4680552; fax (1) 4680770; Chargé d'affaires: VELJKO KNEZEVIĆ.

Judicial System

The judicial system of Croatia is administered by the Ministry of Justice. The Supreme Court is the highest judicial body in the country, comprising 26 judges who are elected for a period of eight years by the Chamber of Municipalities at the proposal of the Chamber of Representatives. The Constitutional Court consists of 11 judges, elected for a period of eight years by the House of Representatives, on the proposal of the House of Counties.

Public Prosecutor: PETAR ŠALE.

Public Attorney: (vacant).

Ombudsman: 10000 Zagreb, Opatička 4; tel. (1) 4814893.

Constitutional Court of Croatia: 10000 Zagreb, Marka trg 4; tel. (1) 4851276; fax (1) 4550908; internet www.usud.hr; Pres. SMILJO SOKOL.

Supreme Court: 10000 Zagreb, trg Nikole Zrinskog 3; tel. (1) 4810036; fax (1) 4810035; Pres. MARIJAN HRANJSKI.

Office of the Public Prosecutor: 10000 Zagreb, ul. Vinogradska 25; tel. (1) 3712700; fax (1) 3769302; e-mail dorh@zg.hinet.hr.

Religion

Most of the population are Christian, the largest denomination being the Roman Catholic Church, of which most ethnic Croats are adherents. The Archbishop of Zagreb is the most senior Roman Catholic prelate in Croatia. The Croatian Old Catholic Church does not acknowledge the authority of Rome or the papal reforms of the 19th century. There is a significant Serbian Orthodox minority. According to the 1991 census, 76.5% of the population of Croatia were Roman Catholics, 11.1% were Serbian Orthodox, 1.2% Muslims and there were small communities of Protestants and Jews.

CHRISTIANITY
The Roman Catholic Church

For ecclesiastical purposes, Croatia comprises four archdioceses (including one, Zadar, directly responsible to the Holy See) and nine dioceses (including one for Catholics of the Byzantine rite). At 31 December 1997 there were an estimated 3.8m. adherents.

Latin Rite

Bishops' Conference: 10000 Zagreb, Kaptol 22; tel. (1) 4811893; fax (1) 4811894; f. 1993; Pres. Mgr JOSIP BOZANIĆ, Archbishop of Zagreb.

Archbishop of Rijeka: Dr ANTON TAMARUT, Nadbiskupski Ordinarijat, 51000 Rijeka, Slaviše Vajnera Čiče 2; tel. (51) 337999; fax (51) 215287; e-mail rijecka-nadbiskupija@ri.hinet.hr.

Archbishop of Split-Makarska: ANTE JURIĆ, 21001 Split, pp 328, ul. Zrinjsko-Frankopanska 14; tel. (21) 319515; fax (21) 319522.

Archbishop of Zadar: IVAN PRENDJA, Nadbiskupski Ordinarijat, 23000 Zadar, trg Zeleni 1; tel. (23) 315712; fax (23) 316299.

Archbishop of Zagreb: JOSIP BOZANIĆ, 10001 Zagreb, pp 553, Kaptol 31; tel. (1) 4894802; fax (1) 4816094.

Byzantine Rite

Bishop of Križevci: SLAVOMIR MIKLOVŠ, Ordinarijat Križevačke Eparhije, 10000 Zagreb, Kaptol 20; tel. (1) 270767; 48,975 adherents (1993).

Old Catholic Church

Croatian Catholic Church: Hrvatska Katolička Crkva Ordinariat, 10000 Zagreb, ul. Kneza Branimira 11; tel. (1) 4841361; f. 894, re-established 1923; Archbishop MIHOVIL DUBRAVČIĆ.

Serbian Orthodox Church

Metropolitan of Zagreb and Ljubljana: Bishop JOVAN, Srpska Biskupija, 10000 Zagreb.

The Press
PRINCIPAL DAILIES
Osijek

Glas Slavonije: 31000 Osijek, Hrvatske Republike 20; tel. (31) 223200; fax (31) 223203; e-mail glas@glas-slavonije.tel.hr; morning; independent; Editor SANJA MARKETIĆ; circ. 25,000.

Pula

Glas Istre: 52100 Pula, Riva 10; tel. (52) 212969; fax (52) 211434; morning; Dir ŽELJKO ŽMAK; circ. 20,000.

Rijeka

Novi List: 51000 Rijeka, POB 130, Zvonimirova 20A; tel. (51) 32122; fax (51) 213654; morning; Editor VELJKO VICEVIĆ; circ. 60,000.

La Voce del Popolo: 51000 Rijeka, Zvonimirova 20A; tel. (51) 211154; fax (51) 213528; f. 1944; morning; Italian; Editor RODOLFO SEGNAN; circ. 4,000.

Split

Nedjeljna Dalmacija: 21000 Split, Gundulićeva 23; tel. (21) 362821; fax (21) 362526; f. 1972; weekly; politics and culture; Editor DRAŽEN GUDIĆ; circ. 45,000.

Slobodna Dalmacija: 21000 Split, ul. Hrvatske mornarice 4; tel. (21) 513888; fax (21) 551220; internet www.slobodnadalmacija.com; morning; Editor JOSIP JOVIĆ; circ. 102,000.

Zagreb

Imperijal: 10000 Zagreb; weekly; Editor-in-Chief VELIMIR BUJANEC.

Nedjeljna Dalmacija: 10000 Zagreb, Ilica 24/II; tel. (1) 433716; fax (1) 433916; f. 1972; weekly; politics and culture; Editor-in-Chief DUBRAVKO GRAKALIĆ; circ. 45,000.

Novi Vjesnik: 10000 Zagreb, Slavonska Ave. 4; tel. (1) 333333; fax (1) 341650; f. 1940; morning; Editor RADOVAN STIPETIĆ; circ. 45,000.

Sportske novosti: 10000 Zagreb, Slavonska Ave. 4; tel. (1) 341920; fax (1) 341950; morning; Editor DARKO TIRONI; circ. 55,000.

Večernji list: 10000 Zagreb, Slavonska Ave. 4; tel. (1) 6500600; fax (1) 6500676; internet www.vecernji-list.hr; evening; Editor BRANKO TUDEN; circ. 200,000.

Vjesnik: 10000 Zagreb, Slavonska Ave. 4, POB 104; tel. (1) 342760; fax (1) 341602; internet www.vjesnik.com; morning; Editor IGOR MANDIĆ; circ. 50,000.

PERIODICALS

Arena: 10000 Zagreb, Slavonska Ave. 4; tel. (1) 6162795; fax (1) 6161572; e-mail arena@eph.hr; f. 1957; illustrated weekly; Editor MLADEN GEROVAĆ; circ. 135,000.

Feral Tribune: 21000 Split; weekly; satirical; Editor VIKTOR IVANCIĆ.

Glasnik: 10000 Zagreb, trg hrvatskih velikana 4; tel. (1) 453000; fax (1) 453752; fortnightly; Editor ZDRAVKO GAVRAN; circ. 9,000.

Globus: 10000 Zagreb, Slavonska Ave. 4; tel. (1) 6162057; fax (1) 6162058; e-mail globus@eph.hr; f. 1990; political weekly; Editor MIRKO GALIĆ; circ. 110,000.

Gloria: 10000 Zagreb, Slavonska Ave. 4; tel. (1) 6161288; fax (1) 6182042; e-mail gloria@eph.hr; weekly; Editor DUBRAVKA TOMEKOVIĆ-ARALICA; circ. 110,000.

Informator: 10000 Zagreb, Zelinska 3; tel. (1) 611150; fax 6111446; f. 1950; economic and legal matters; Dir Dr IVO BURIĆ.

Mila: 10000 Zagreb, Slavonska Ave. 4; tel. (1) 6161982; fax (1) 6162021; e-mail mila@eph.hr; weekly; Editor ZOJA PADOVAN; circ. 110,000.

Nacionalni Oglasnik: 10000 Zagreb, Slavonska Ave. 4; tel. (1) 6162061; fax (1) 6161541; weekly; Editor IVO PUKANIĆ; circ. 55,000.

OK: Croatia: 10000 Zagreb, Slavonska Ave. 4; tel. (1) 6162127; fax (1) 6162125; e-mail ok@eph.hr; f. 1989; illustrated monthly; Editor NEVEN KEPESKI; circ. 55,000.

Privredni vjesnik: 10000 Zagreb, Kačićeva 9A; tel. (1) 422182; fax (1) 422100; f. 1953; weekly; economic; Man. ANTE GAVRANOVIĆ; Editor-in-Chief FRANJO ŽILIĆ; circ. 10,000.

Republika: 10000 Zagreb, trg bana Josipa Jelačića; tel. (1) 274211; fax (1) 434790; f. 1945; monthly; published by Društvo hrvatskih književnika; literary review; Editor-in-Chief VELIMIR VISKOVIĆ.

Studio: 10000 Zagreb, Slavonska Ave. 4; tel. (1) 6162085; fax (1) 6162031; e-mail studio@eph.hr; f.1964; illustrated weekly; Editor ROBERT NAPRTA; circ. 45,000.

Vikend: 10000 Zagreb, Slavonska Ave. 4; tel. and fax (1) 6162064; 2 a week; Editor Josip Mušnjak; circ. 50,000.

NEWS AGENCIES

HINA News Agency: 10000 Zagreb, trg Marulićev 16; tel. (1) 4808700; fax (1) 4808820; e-mail newsline@hina.hr; internet www.hina.hr; f. 1990; Man. Mirko Bolfek.

IKA (Catholic Information Agency): 10000 Zagreb, Kaptol 4; tel. (1) 4814951; fax (1) 4814957; e-mail ika-zg@zg.tel.hr; internet www.ika.hr; Man. Editor Anton Šuljić.

Publishers

AGM Publisher: 10000 Zagreb, Mihanovićeva 28; tel. (1) 4856307; fax (1) 4856316; Croatian and foreign literature, arts, economics, science; Gen. Dir Bože Čović.

Algoritam: 10000 Zagreb, Gajeva 12; tel. (1) 4803333; fax (1) 271541; e-mail mm@algoritam.hr; international bestsellers; Pres. Neven Antičević.

August Cesarec: 10000 Zagreb, Prilaz Gjure Deželića 57; tel. (1) 171071; fax (1) 573695; Croatian and foreign literature.

Books Trade and Services (BTS) Knjiga Trgovina: 10000 Zagreb, Donji prečac 19; tel. (1) 2421754; fax (1) 2421831; e-mail info@btsltd.com; internet www.btsltd.com; imports and exports publications; Gen. Man. Branko Vuković.

Ceres: 10000 Zagreb, Tomašićeva 13; tel. (1) 4558501; fax (1) 4550387; e-mail ceres@zg.tel.hr; internet www.ceres.hr; poetry, fiction, and philosophical and scientific writings; Gen. Dir Dragutin Dumančič.

Erasmus Publishing: 10000 Zagreb, Rakušina 4; tel. and fax (1) 433114; Croatian literature; Gen. Dir Srećko Lipovčan.

Europa Press: 10000 Zagreb, Slavonska Ave. 4; tel. (1) 6190011; fax (1) 6190033; Dir Marjan Jurleka.

Hena Com: 10000 Zagreb, Horvaćanska 65; tel. and fax (1) 3750206; e-mail hena-com@hena-com.hr; internet www.hena-com.hr; childrens' books; Gen. Man. Uzeir Husković.

Hrvatska Akademija Znanosti i Umjetnosti: 10000 Zagreb, trg Zrinski 11; tel. (1) 4819983; fax (1) 4819979; e-mail kabpred@mahazu.hazu.hr; f. 1861; publishing dept of the Croatian Academy of Sciences and Arts; Pres. Dr Ivo Padovan.

Izvori: 10000 Zagreb, Trnjanska 64; tel. and fax (1) 6112576; e-mail izvori@iname.com; internet www.bakal.hr/izvori; scientific journalism, literature, comic books.

Kršćanska Sadašnjost: 10001 Zagreb, trg Marulićev 14, POB 434; tel. (1) 4828219; fax (1) 4828227; e-mail ks@zg.tel.hr; internet www.ks.hr; theological publications.

Leksikografski zavod 'Miroslav Krleža' (Miroslav Krleža Lexicographic Institute): 10000 Zagreb, Frankopanska 26; tel. (1) 4800333; fax (1) 4800399; f. 1951; encyclopedias, bibliographies and dictionaries; Pres. Dalibor Brozović.

Masmedia: 10000 Zagreb, ul. baruna Trenka 13; tel. (1) 4577400; fax (1) 4577769; e-mail masmedia@zg.tel.hr; business and professional literature; Gen. Dir Stjepan Andrašić.

Matica Hrvatska (Matrix Croatica): 10000 Zagreb, trg Strossmayerov 2; tel. (1) 4819310; fax (1) 4819319; arts and science; Pres. Prof. Josip Bratulić.

Mladost: 10000 Zagreb, Ilica 30; tel. (1) 453222; fax (1) 434878; f. 1947; fiction, science, art, children's books; Gen. Dir Branko Vuković.

Mosta: 10000 Zagreb, Majevička 12a; tel. (1) 325196; fax (1) 327898; popular fiction; Gen. Dir Nladimir Vučur.

Mozaik Knjiga: 10000 Zagreb, Tomićeva 5a; tel. (1) 425011; fax (11) 431291; educational books; Gen. Dir Nives Tomašević.

Nakladni zavod Matice hrvatske: 10000 Zagreb, Nova ves 5; tel. (1) 4812422; fax (1) 4819317; e-mail nzm@zg.tel.hr; f. 1960; fiction, popular science, politics, economics, sociology, history; Dir Niko Vidović.

Naprijed: 10000 Zagreb, POB 1029, trg bana Jelacica 17; tel. (1) 432026; fax (1) 426897; e-mail naklada-napried@zg.tel.hr; f. 1946; philosophy, psychology, religion, sociology, medicine, dictionaries, children's books, art, politics, economics, tourist guides; Dir Zdenko Ljevak.

Naša Djeca: 10000 Zagreb, Gundulićeva 40; tel. (1) 423046; fax (1) 430613; picture books, postcards, etc.; Dir Prof. Drago Kozina.

Nip Školske Novine: 10000 Zagreb, Hebranga 40; tel. (1) 4855709; fax (1) 4855712; education, religion, poetry, textbooks; Gen. Man. Ivan Rodić.

Sims: 10000 Zagreb, Ive Tijardovića 4; tel. (1) 3880500; fax (1) 3880731; e-mail info@sims-hr.com; internet www.simshr.com; exports Croatian and foreign language books; Gen. Man. Ivan Matijević.

Školska Knjiga: 10001 Zagreb, POB 1039, Masarykova 28; tel. (1) 420784; fax (1) 430260; e-mail skolska@skolskaknjiga.hr; education, textbooks, art; Dir Dr Dragomir Maderić.

Tehnička Knjiga: 10000 Zagreb, Jurišićeva 10; tel. (1) 278172; fax (1) 423611; f. 1947; technical literature, popular science, reference books; Gen. Man. Zvonimir Vistrička.

Verbum: 21000 Split, Kraj zlatnih vrata 1; tel. and fax (21) 356770; e-mail verbum@st.tel.hr; religion, philosophy and humanism; Gen. Man. Miro Radalj.

Znanje: 10000 Zagreb, Zvonimirova 17; tel. (1) 4556000; fax (1) 4553652; e-mail znanje@zg.tel.hr; f. 1946; popular science, agriculture, fiction, poetry, essays; Pres. Žarko Šepetavić; Dir Branko Jazbec.

PUBLISHERS' ASSOCIATION

Croatian Publishers' and Authors' Business Union (Poslovna Zajednica Izdavača i Knjižara Hrvatske): 10000 Zagreb, Klaićeva 7; fax (1) 171624.

Broadcasting and Communications

TELECOMMUNICATIONS

Croatian Telecommunications (Hrvatske Telekomunikacije—HT): 10000 Zagreb, Jurišićeva 13; tel. (1) 435435; fax (1) 429000; f. 1987; 35% owned by Deutsche Telekom (Germany), remainder of shares were scheduled to be sold off by mid-2001; Pres. Ivica Mudrinić.

BROADCASTING

Croatian Radio and Television (Hrvatska Radiotelevizija—HRT): 10000 Zagreb, Dezmanova 10; tel. (1) 276338; fax (1) 424654; govt-owned; Editor-in-Chief Neda Ritz; Chair. Zacko Canjuga.

Radio

Croatian Radio: 10000 Zagreb, HRT House, Prisavlje 3; tel. (1) 6163280; fax (1) 6163285; f. 1926; 3 radio stations; 7 regional stations (Sljeme, Osijek, Pula, Rijeka, Split, Zadar and Dubrovnik); broadcasts in Serbo-Croat; Dir Tomislav Bakarić.

Radio 101: Zagreb; independent radio station; Editor-in-Chief Zrinka Vrabec-Mojzes.

Radio Baranja: Beli Manastir; independent radio station; Dir Karolj Janesi.

Vaš Otvoreni Radio: 10000 Zagreb, Radnička cesta 27; tel. (1) 6154805; fax (1) 6154802; broadcasts nation-wide.

Television

Croatian Television: 10000 Zagreb, Prisavlje bb; tel. (1) 6163366; fax (1) 6163692; internet www.hrt.hr; f. 1956; 3 channels; broadcasts in Serbo-Croat; Head of TV Ivan Vrkić; Editor-in-Chief Obrad Kosovac.

Finance

A new currency, the kuna (equivalent to 1,000 Croatian dinars), was introduced on 30 May 1994.

(d.d. = dioničko društvo (joint-stock company); cap. = capital; res = reserves; dep. = deposits; m. = million; amounts in kuna, unless otherwise indicated; HRD = Croatian dinars; brs = branches)

BANKING

Central Bank

National Bank of Croatia: 10000 Zagreb, trg burze 3; tel. (1) 4564555; fax (1) 4610551; e-mail webmaster@hnb.hr; internet www.hnb.hr; in 1991 it assumed the responsibilities of a central bank empowered as the republic's bank of issue; cap. 10,953.7m., res 2,215.1m., dep. 8,535.6m. (Dec. 1999); Gov. Zeljko Rohatinski.

Selected Banks

Erste and Steiermärkische Bank d.d.: 10000 Zagreb, Varšavska 3–5; tel. (1) 4561999; fax (1) 4561900; internet www.esb.hr; f. Sept. 2000 by merger of Bjelovarska Banka d.d., Cakoveka Banka d.d. and Trgovačka Banka d.d.; Pres. Petar Radaković.

Croatia Banka d.d.: 10000 Zagreb, Kvaternikov trg 9; tel. (1) 2391111; fax (1) 2332470; internet www.open.hr/com/crobanka/; f. 1989; cap. 204.6m., res 9.8m., dep. 622.3m. (Dec. 1999); Chair. Ivan Tarle; 29 brs.

Croatian Bank for Reconstruction and Development (Hrvatska Banka za Obnovu i Razvoj—HBOR): 10000 Zagreb, Gajeva 30a; tel. (1) 4569106; fax (1) 4591666; e-mail dstimac@hbor.hr; internet www.hbor.hr; f. 1995; cap. 2,734.6m., res 1.2m., dep. 168.1m. (Dec. 1999); Dir Anton Kovačev.

Dalmatinska Banka d.d., Zadar: 23000 Zadar, trg sv. Stošije 3; tel. (23) 311311; fax (23) 437867; e-mail dbz@dbz.hr; internet www.dbz.hr; f. 1957; 79% privately owned; cap. 208.0m., res 71.1m., dep. 1,328.0m. (Dec. 1999); Chair. ZDRAVKO BUBALO; 2 brs.

Dubrovačka Banka d.d., Dubrovnik (Bank of Dubrovnik): 20000 Dubrovnik, put Republike 9; tel. (20) 356333; fax (20) 356778; e-mail dubank@dubank.hr; internet www.dubank.hr; f. 1955; cap. 185.0m., dep. 1,883.3m. (Dec. 1999); Pres. VLAHO SUTIĆ.

Hrvatska Poštanska Banka d.d.: 10000 Zagreb, Jurišićeva 4; tel. (1) 4804400; fax (1) 4810773; internet www.hpb.hr; cap. 384.8m., res 47.2m., dep. 1,127.5m. (Dec. 1999); Chair. JOSIP SLADE.

Hypo Alpe-Adria-Bank d.d.: 10000 Zagreb, Koturaška 47; tel. (1) 6103500; fax (1) 6103555; e-mail hypo@hypo.hr; internet www .hypo.hr; cap. 145.1m., res 72.9m., dep. 848.4m. (Dec. 1998); Chair. MAG GUENTER STRIEDINGER.

Istarska Kreditna Banka Umag d.d.: 52470 Umag, Ernesta Miloša 1; tel. (52) 741622; fax (52) 741275; e-mail ikb-marketing@ ikb-umag.tel.hr; f. 1956; commercial and joint-stock bank; cap. 64.9m., res 16.6m., dep. 458.7m. (Dec. 1999); Chair. MIRO DODIĆ; 14 brs.

Kreditna Banka Zagreb d.d.: 10000 Zagreb, Ulica grada Vukovara 74; tel. (1) 6167333; fax (1) 6116466; e-mail kbz-forex@kbz.hr; internet www.kbz.hr/kbz; f. 1994; cap. 156.5m., res 25.7m., dep. 359.8m. (Dec. 1999); Pres. ANTE TODORIĆ.

Medimurska Banka d.d., Čakovec; 40000 Čakovec, Valenta Morandinija 37; tel. (40) 370676; fax (40) 314610; e-mail ljhorvst@ open.hr; internet www.open.hr/com.mb; f. 1954; cap. 125.1m., res 24.9m., dep. 893.9m. (June 1999); Gen. Man MAŠAN SREDANOVIĆ.

Podravska Banka dd: 48000 Koprivnica, Opaticka 1a; tel. (48) 622193; fax (48) 622542; e-mail podravska-banka1@podravska-banka.tel.hr; cap. 62.9m., res 49.9m., dep. 342.8m. (Dec. 1998); Pres. JULIO KURAC.

Privredna Banka Zagreb d.d.: 10000 Zagreb, POB 1032, Račkoga 6; tel. (1) 4723344; fax (1) 4723131; e-mail pbz@pbz.hr; internet www.pbz.hr; f. 1966; commercial bank; cap. 1,666m., res 169m., dep. 12,328m. (Dec. 1999); CEO BOZO PRKA; 28 brs.

Raiffeisenbank Austria d.d.: 10000 Zagreb, POB 651, Petrinjska ulica 59; tel. (1) 4566466; fax (1) 4811624; e-mail ihrakud@ rbazagreb.raiffeisen.at; internet www.tel.hr/ba; cap. 240.0m., res 19.0m., dep. 1,517.4m. (Dec. 1999); Chair. ZDENKO ADROVIĆ.

Riječka Banka d.d.: 51000 Rijeka, POB 300, trg Jadranski 3A; tel. (51) 208211; fax (51) 330525; e-mail drazen.kurpisl@rbri.tel.hr; internet www.multilink.hr/ribri; f. 1954 as Komunalna banka i štedionica, renamed 1967; cap. 306.0m., res 211.8m., dep. 4,523.7m. (Dec. 1999); Chair. IVAN ŠTOKIĆ; 18 brs.

Sisačka Banka d.d.: 44000 Sisak, trg Ljudevita Posavskog 1; tel. (44) 549100; fax (44) 549101; e-mail savia@sibank.hr; internet www.sibank.hr/sibank; f. 1957; cap. 93.1m., res 23.4m., dep. 341.5m. (Dec. 1998); Pres. DINKO PINTARIĆ.

Slavonska Banka d.d., Osijek (Bank of Slavonia): 31000 Osijek, POB 108, Kapucinska 29; tel. (31) 231231; fax (31) 127125; e-mail sbo@slavonska-banka.tel.hr; internet www.slbo.hr; f. 1989; cap. 149.2m., res 110.4m., dep. 1,011.9m. (Dec. 1998); Pres. IVAN MIHALJEVIĆ; 9 brs.

Splitska Banka dd. Split: 21000 Split, Boškovića 16; tel. (21) 312569; fax (21) 312586; e-mail info@splitskabanka.hr; internet www.splitskabanka.hr; f. 1966; cap. 320.0m., res 99.1m., dep. 5,002.9m. (Dec. 1999); Man. Dir TOMO BOLOTIN.

Varaždinska Banka d.d.: 42000 Varaždin, POB 95, trg Kapucinski 5; tel. (42) 400000; fax (42) 400742; internet www.banka.hr; f. 1869, adopted current name 1981; cap. 168.8m., res 23.5m., dep. 1,749.8m. (Dec. 1999); Pres. MATO LUKINIĆ; 17 brs.

Zagrebačka Banka Zagreb d.d. (Bank of Zagreb): 10000 Zagreb, Paromlinska 2; tel. (1) 6104000; fax (1) 6110555; e-mail zaba@ zaba.hr; internet www.zaba.hr; f. 1913; 1,096.2m., res 395.3m., dep. 19,055.9m. (Dec. 1999); Chair. FRANJO LUKOVIĆ; 139 brs.

STOCK EXCHANGE

Zagreb Stock Exchange: 10000 Zagreb, Ksaver 208; tel. (1) 428455; fax (1) 420293; f. 1990; Gen. Man. MARINKO PAPUGA.

INSURANCE

Croatia Osiguranje: 10000 Zagreb; f. 1884; state-owned; scheduled for privatization.

Trade and Industry

GOVERNMENT AGENCY

Croatian Privatization Fund: 10000 Zagreb, Gajeva 30A; tel. (1) 469168; fax (1) 469138; internet www.hfp.hr; f. 1994 by merger of the Croatian Fund for Development and the Restructuring and Development Agency; Chair. TOMISLAV DRUZAK.

CHAMBERS OF COMMERCE

Croatian Chamber of Economy (Hrvatska Gospodarska Komora): 10000 Zagreb, trg Rooseveltov 2; tel. (1) 4561555; fax (1) 4828380; e-mail hgk@alf.hr; internet www.hgk.hr; Pres. NADAN VIDOŠEVIĆ.

Zagreb Chamber of Commerce: 10000 Zagreb, Draškovićeva 45; tel. (1) 4606777; fax (1) 4606813; e-mail hgk-zagreb@hgk.hr; internet www.hgk.hr; f. 1852.

UTILITIES
Electricity

HEP—Hrvatska Elektroprivreda d.d.: 10000 Zagreb, Ave. Vukovar 37; tel. (1) 6322111; fax (1) 6170430; e-mail ivo.covic@ hep.hr; internet www.hep.hr; f. 1990; production and distribution of electricity; scheduled for privatization in 2002; Dir IVO COVIĆ.

Gas

Gradska Plinara: 10000 Zagreb, Radnička 1; tel. (1) 6302333; fax (1) 6184653; f. 1862; municipal and regional distribution of natural gas; Dir IVAN VULAS.

INA—Naftaplin: 10000 Zagreb, Subičeva 29; tel. (1) 418011; fax (1) 440604; subsidiary of Industrija Nafte d.d.; exploration of petroleum, natural-gas and geothermal energy; scheduled for privatization.

Water

Hrvatske Vode: 10000 Zagreb, Vukovara 220; tel. (1) 6151820; fax (1) 6151821; e-mail du.vode@zg.hinet.hr; f. 1995; state water management organization; Dir ZORISLAV BALIAE.

TRADE UNIONS

Association of Autonomous Trade Unions of Croatia: 10000 Zagreb; f. 1990; 26 branch unions with some 500,000 mems; Pres. DRAGUTIN LESAR.

Confederation of Independent Trade Unions of Croatia: 10000 Zagreb; f. 1990; 40,000 mems; Pres. DAVOR JURIĆ.

Croatian Association of Trade Unions: Zagreb; f. 1990; 200,000 mems; Pres. BERISLAV BELEC.

Croatian Union of Posts and Telecommunications: Zagreb; Pres. JOSIP PUPIĆ.

Transport
RAILWAYS

In 1995 there were 2,452 km of railway lines in Croatia, of which 36% were electrified. In mid-1996 railway links between Croatia and Serbia, via Eastern Slavonia, were reopened. In May 2000 the Government announced plans for the modernization of the Rijeka–Budapest (Hungary) railroad.

Croatian Railways Ltd (Hrvatske Željeznice p.o.): 10000 Zagreb, Mihanovićeva 12; tel. (1) 4577111; fax (1) 4577730; f. 1990 as Hrvatsko željezničko poduzeće, renamed 1992; state-owned; public railway transport, construction, modernization and maintenance of railway vehicles; Pres. DAVOR STERN; Gen. Dir DRAGUTIN ŠUBAT.

ROADS

The Road Fund was responsible for the planning, construction, maintenance and rehabilitation of all interurban roads in Croatia. As of 1 January 1995 the Fund was under the control of the budgetary central Government. In late 1995 a US $705m.-project was announced to build a 75-km motorway linking Dragonje, near the Slovenian border, with Pula in southern Istria. The construction of the road was to be undertaken by a French company, Bouygues, and was to be financed by World Bank loans, tolls and a domestic debt. In 1996 plans were announced to build a further 1,200 km of new roads over a period of 10 years. In May 1996 the motorway between Zagreb and Belgrade (Yugoslavia) was reopened. In 1998 there were 27,840 km of roads in Croatia, of which 330 km were motorways, 7,378 km were main roads and 10,193 km were secondary roads. In April 2000 the Regional Funding Conference of the Stability Pact for South-East Europe allocated Croatia resources to implement five infrastructure projects, including the construction of a 23 km section of the Zagreb–Gorican highway. In May the Croatian and Hungarian Governments agreed to draft a joint agreement on the construction, by 2003, of a highway connecting Rijeka with the Hungarian capital, Budapest. In June Croatia and Bosnia and Herzegovina signed a statement on the construction of the Ploče–Budapest transport corridor, to link Croatia with Hungary, via Bosnia and Herzegovina. The construction of this 'C5' corridor was to end the isolation of Croatia's southern areas and ensure the optimal use of Ploče's port capacity.

Croatian Roads Authority (Hrvatske Ceste): 10000 Zagreb, Vončinina 3; tel. (1) 445422; fax (1) 445215; f. 1991; state-owned; maintenance, construction and reconstruction of public roads; Pres. J. ZAVOREO; Man. Dir ALEKSANDAR ČAKLOVIĆ.

SHIPPING

Atlantska Plovidba d.d.: 20000 Dubrovnik, od sv. Mihajla 1; tel. (20) 412666; fax (20) 20384; f. 1974; Dir ANTE JERKOVIĆ.

Croatia Line: 51000 Rijeka, POB 379, Riva 18; tel. (51) 205111; fax (51) 331915; f. 1986; cargo and passenger services; chartering and tramp service; Gen. Man. DARIO VUKIĆ; 377 employees.

Jadrolinija (Adriatic Shipping Line): 51000 Rijeka, Riva 16; tel. (51) 330899; fax (51) 213116; f. 1872; regular passenger and carferry services between Italian, Greek and Croatian ports; Pres. M. RUŽIĆ.

Jadroplov: 21000 Split, Obala kneza Branimira 16; tel. (21) 302666; fax (21) 342198; f. 1984; fleet of 17 vessels and 1,500 containers engaged in linear and tramp service; Gen. Man. NIKŠA GIOVANELLI.

Lošinjska Plovidba—Brodarstvo: 51550 Mali Lošinj, Privlaka bb; tel. (51) 231832; fax (51) 231811; f. 1980; Dir DUMANČIĆ MARINKO.

Slobodna Plovidba: 22000 Šibenik, Drage 2; tel. (22) 23755; fax (22) 27860; f. 1976; transport of goods by sea; tourism services; Dir VITOMIR JURAGA.

Tankerska Plovidba d.d.: 23000 Zadar, Božidara Petranovića 4; tel. (23) 311132; fax (23) 314375; f. 1976; Dir STANKO BANIĆ; 1,283 employees.

CIVIL AVIATION

There are 10 international airports in Croatia.

Croatia Airlines: 10000 Zagreb, Savska 41; tel. (1) 6160066; fax (1) 6176845; internet www.ctn.tel.hr/ctn; f. 1989 as Zagreb Airlines; name changed 1990; operates domestic services and 16 international routes to European destinations; Pres. IVAN HIŠETIĆ.

Anić Airways: Zagreb; tel. (1) 200200; fax (1) 204253; f. 1992; first private airline company in Croatia; domestic and international flights; Pres. DAMIR ANIĆ.

Tourism

The attractive Adriatic coast and the country's 1,185 islands made Croatia a very popular tourist destination before the 1990s. However, the civil conflict of the early 1990s greatly reduced tourist activity in the country. The industry showed signs of recovery after 1992, with foreign tourist arrivals reaching some 4.1m. in 1998. Revenue generated by tourism in 1998 reached US $2,733m. In 1999, however, foreign tourist arrivals declined to 3.4m., owing to the conflict in Kosovo, the Federal Republic of Yugoslavia, in March–June. In that year income from tourism declined to $2,502m.

Croatian National Tourist Board: 10000 Zagreb, Ilica 1A; tel. (1) 4556455; fax (1) 4816757; e-mail info@htz.hr; internet www.htz.hr/text_e/htz.htm.

Generalturist: 10000 Zagreb, Praška 5; tel. (1) 4805555; fax (1) 4810420; e-mail generalturist@generalturist.com; f. 1923; renamed 1963; 17 brs.

Jadran-Turist d.d.: 55210 Rovinj, V. Nazora 6; tel. (52) 800300; fax (52) 800376; e-mail jadrantur-rovinj@pu.tel.hr; internet www.istra.com/rovinj/jadranturist; f. 1954; Dir IVAN SORIĆ.

CUBA

Introductory Survey

Location, Climate, Language, Religion, Flag, Capital

The Republic of Cuba is an archipelago of two main islands, Cuba and the Isla de la Juventud (Isle of Youth), formerly the Isla de Pinos (Isle of Pines), and about 1,600 keys and islets. It lies in the Caribbean Sea, 145 km (90 miles) south of Florida, USA. Other nearby countries are the Bahamas, Mexico, Jamaica and Haiti. The climate is tropical, with the annual rainy season from May to October. The average annual temperature is 25°C (77°F) and hurricanes are frequent. The language spoken is Spanish. Most of the inhabitants are Christians, of whom the great majority are Roman Catholics. The national flag (proportions 2 by 1) has five equal horizontal stripes, of blue, white, blue, white and blue, with a red triangle, enclosing a five-pointed white star, at the hoist. The capital is Havana (La Habana).

Recent History

Cuba was ruled by Spain from the 16th century until 1898, when the island was ceded to the USA following Spain's defeat in the Spanish–American War. Cuba became an independent republic on 20 May 1902, but the USA retained its naval bases on the island and, until 1934, reserved the right to intervene in Cuba's internal affairs. In 1933 an army sergeant, Fulgencio Batista Zaldivar, came to power at the head of a military revolt. Batista ruled the country, directly or indirectly, until 1944, when he retired after serving a four-year term as elected President.

In March 1952, however, Gen. Batista (as he had become) seized power again, deposing President Carlos Prío Socarrás in a bloodless coup. Batista's new regime soon proved to be unpopular and became harshly repressive. In July 1953 a radical opposition group, led by Dr Fidel Castro Ruz, attacked the Moncada army barracks in Santiago de Cuba. Castro was captured, with many of his supporters, but was later released. He went into exile and formed a revolutionary movement which was committed to Batista's overthrow. In December 1956 Castro landed in Cuba with a small group of followers, most of whom were captured or killed. However, 12 survivors, including Castro and the Argentine-born Dr Ernesto ('Che') Guevara, escaped into the hills of the Sierra Maestra, where they formed the nucleus of the guerrilla forces which, after a prolonged struggle, forced Batista to flee from Cuba on 1 January 1959. The Batista regime collapsed, and Castro's forces occupied Havana.

The assumption of power by the victorious rebels was initially met with great popular acclaim. The 1940 Constitution was suspended in January 1959 and replaced by a new 'Fundamental Law'. Executive and legislative power was vested in the Council of Ministers, with Fidel Castro as Prime Minister and his brother Raúl as his deputy. Guevara reportedly ranked third in importance. The new regime ruled by decree but promised to hold elections within 18 months. When it was firmly established, the Castro Government adopted a radical economic programme, including agrarian reform and the nationalization of industrial and commercial enterprises. These drastic reforms, combined with the regime's authoritarian nature, provoked opposition from some sectors of the population, including former supporters of Castro, and many Cubans went into exile.

All US business interests in Cuba were expropriated, without compensation, in October 1960, and the USA severed diplomatic relations in January 1961. A US-sponsored force of anti-Castro Cuban émigrés landed in April 1961 at the Bahía de Cochinos (Bay of Pigs), in southern Cuba, but the invasion was thwarted by Castro's troops. Later in the year, all pro-Government groups were merged to form the Organizaciones Revolucionarias Integradas (ORI). In December 1961 Fidel Castro publicly announced that Cuba had become a communist state, and he proclaimed a 'Marxist-Leninist' programme for the country's future development. In January 1962 Cuba was excluded from active participation in the Organization of American States (OAS). The USA instituted a full economic and political blockade of Cuba. Hostility to the USA was accompanied by increasingly close relations between Cuba and the USSR. In October 1962 the USA revealed the presence of Soviet missiles in Cuba but, after the imposition of a US naval blockade, the weapons were withdrawn. The missile bases, capable of launching nuclear weapons against the USA, were dismantled, thus resolving one of the most serious international crises since the Second World War. In 1964 the OAS imposed diplomatic and commercial sanctions against Cuba.

The ORI was replaced in 1962 by a new Partido Unido de la Revolución Socialista Cubana (PURSC), which was established, under Fidel Castro's leadership, as the country's sole legal party. Guevara resigned his military and government posts in April 1965, subsequently leaving Cuba to pursue revolutionary activities abroad. In October 1965 the PURSC was renamed the Partido Comunista de Cuba (PCC). Although ostracized by most other Latin American countries, the PCC Government maintained and consolidated its internal authority, with little effective opposition. Supported by considerable aid from the USSR, the regime made significant progress in social and economic development, including improvements in education and public health. At the same time, Cuba continued to give active support to left-wing revolutionary movements in Latin America and in many other parts of the world. Guevara was killed in Bolivia, following an unsuccessful guerrilla uprising under his leadership, in October 1967.

In July 1972 Cuba's links with the Eastern bloc were strengthened when the country became a full member of the Council for Mutual Economic Assistance (CMEA—dissolved in 1991), a Moscow-based organization linking the USSR and other communist states. As a result of its admission to the CMEA, Cuba received preferential trade terms and more technical advisers from the USSR and East European countries.

In June 1974 the country's first elections since the revolution were held for municipal offices in Matanzas province. Cuba's first 'socialist' Constitution was submitted to the First Congress of the PCC, held in December 1975, and came into force in February 1976, after being approved by popular referendum. As envisaged by the new Constitution, elections for 169 municipal assemblies were held in October 1976. These assemblies later elected delegates to provincial assemblies and deputies to the National Assembly of People's Power, inaugurated in December 1976 as 'the supreme organ of state'. The National Assembly chose the members of a new Council of State, with Fidel Castro as President. The Second Congress of the PCC was held in December 1980, when Fidel and Raúl Castro were re-elected First and Second Secretaries, respectively. In December 1981 Fidel Castro was re-elected by the Assembly as President of the Council of State, and Raúl Castro re-elected as First Vice-President.

Cuba continued to be excluded from the activities of the OAS, although the Organization voted in favour of allowing members to normalize their relations with Cuba in 1975. Relations with the USA deteriorated because of Cuban involvement in Angola in 1976 and in Ethiopia in 1977. The relaxation of restrictions on emigration in April 1980 resulted in the departure of more than 125,000 Cubans for Florida, USA. Antagonism continued as Cuba's military and political presence abroad increased, threatening US spheres of influence.

In 1981 Cuba expressed interest in discussing foreign policy with the USA, and declared that the shipment of arms to guerrilla groups in Central America had ceased. High-level talks between the two countries took place in November 1981 but US hostility increased. Economic sanctions were strengthened, the major air link was closed, and tourism and investment by US nationals was prohibited in April 1982. Cuba's support of Argentina during the 1982 crisis concerning the Falkland Islands improved relations with the rest of Latin America, and the country's legitimacy was finally acknowledged when it was elected to the chair of the UN General Assembly Committee on Decolonization in September 1982, while continuing to play a leading role in the Non-Aligned Movement (despite its firm alliance with the Soviet bloc).

An increase in US military activity in Honduras and the Caribbean region led President Castro to declare a 'state of national alert' in August 1983. The US invasion of Grenada in October, and the ensuing short-lived confrontation between US forces and Cuban personnel on the island, severely damaged hopes that the two countries might reach an agreement over the problems in Central America, and left Cuba isolated in the Caribbean, following the weakening of its diplomatic and military ties with Suriname in November.

In July 1984 official negotiations were begun with the USA on the issues of immigration and repatriation. In December agreement was reached on the resumption of Cuban immigration to the USA and the repatriation of 2,746 Cuban 'undesirables', who had accompanied other Cuban refugees to the USA in 1980. The repatriation of Cuban 'undesirables' began in February 1985, but, following the inauguration of Radio Martí (a radio station sponsored by the 'Voice of America' radio network, which began to broadcast Western-style news and other programmes to Cuba from Florida, USA), the Cuban Government suspended its immigration accord with the USA. Subsequently, all visits to Cuba by US residents of Cuban origin were banned. The US Government responded by restricting visits to the USA by PCC members and Cuban government officials. In September 1986, as a result of mediation by the Roman Catholic Church, more than 100 political prisoners and their families were permitted to leave Cuba for the USA.

In 1987 relations with the USA continued to deteriorate when, in February, the US Government launched a campaign to direct public attention to violations of human rights in Cuba. A resolution to condemn Cuba's record on human rights was narrowly defeated at a meeting of the UN Commission on Human Rights in March. The Cuban Government subsequently allowed 348 current and former political prisoners to return to the USA. The restoration of the 1984 immigration accord, in October 1987, provoked rioting by Cuban exiles detained in US prisons lasting several days until the US Government assured the exiles that their return to Cuba would be suspended indefinitely and that their cases would be studied individually. The accord allowed for the repatriation of 2,500 Cuban 'undesirables' in exchange for a US agreement to allow 23,000 Cubans to enter the USA annually. In 1988 the Government released some 250 political prisoners, and in the following January President Castro pledged to release the remaining 225 political prisoners acknowledged by the regime. In 1989 human rights activists formed a co-ordinating body and increased their operations. The Government responded in August by imprisoning leading activists for up to two years for having published allegedly false information. In September 1991 eight Cuban dissident organizations united to form a single democratic opposition group, the Concertación Democrática Cubana—CDC (Cuban Democratic Convergence), to campaign for political pluralism and economic reform.

At the Third Congress of the PCC in February 1986 drastic changes were made within the Central Committee; almost one-third of the 146 full members were replaced. A new Council of State was elected in December.

In June 1989 President Castro was confronted by Cuba's most serious political crisis since the 1959 Revolution. It was discovered that a number of senior military personnel were not only involved in smuggling operations in Angola but were also aiding Colombian drugs-traffickers from the infamous Medellín cartel, by enabling them to use Cuban airstrips as refuelling points (en route from Colombia to the USA) in return for bribes. Following court-martial proceedings, Gen. Arnaldo Ochoa Sánchez, who had led the military campaign in Angola, was found guilty of high treason and was executed. Three other officers were also executed. A further purge led to the imposition of harsh sentences on 14 senior officials, including the head of civil aviation and the Ministers of the Interior and of Transport, who had been found guilty of corruption. President Castro insisted that the bureaucracy in Cuba needed to undergo a process of 'purification', but not reform. However, the scandal had clearly undermined the regime's credibility at the international, as well as the domestic, level.

In Angola, where Cuban troops numbered an estimated 50,000, the peace process gathered momentum in 1988. In May a large Cuban offensive almost succeeded in expelling South African forces from Angola and lent new impetus to the peace negotiations. A cease-fire was implemented, and at discussions held in New York, USA, in October, agreement was reached on a phased withdrawal of Cuban troops over a period of 24–30 months. By December a timetable had been agreed, and withdrawal began in April 1989 and was completed in May 1991.

In April 1989 President Gorbachev of the USSR undertook the first official visit to Cuba by a Soviet leader since 1974. The two Heads of State discussed ways in which Cuba's dependence

on Soviet aid might be reduced and Central American issues, and the talks culminated in the signing of a treaty of friendship and economic co-operation. Although, ostensibly, relations remained good, tensions had arisen, owing to Castro's resistance to Soviet-style reforms. Gorbachev made it clear that, in future, general financial aid would be replaced by assistance for specific projects, thus giving the USSR greater power to influence policy decisions in Cuba. In July President Castro strongly attacked the ideas of *perestroika* and *glasnost*, which he blamed for the 'crisis in socialism'. He pledged to eradicate all market forms of economic activity, despite the fact that Cuba's failure to integrate into the new supply-and-demand system of many Eastern European factories had led to delays in imports and acute shortages.

In early October 1990 President Castro announced plans to reduce the PCC's bureaucracy by as much as 50%, including the reassignment of thousands of employees to more productive sectors. In November rationing was extended to all products. Cubans were told to prepare for the possibility of a 'special wartime period' by the Minister of the Revolutionary Armed Forces, Gen. Raúl Castro, who warned of a possible US military attack if the currently intensified US economic blockade should fail. In spite of the gravity of Cuba's political and economic situation, President Castro was defiant in his rejection of recommendations that, as a condition for the removal of the blockade, Cuba should adopt a market economy and political pluralism.

In September 1991 the USSR announced that it intended to withdraw the majority of its military personnel (some 3,000 troops and advisers) from Cuba. The decision, which was condemned by Cuba as presenting a major threat to its national security, came as the result of US demands that the USSR reduce its aid to Cuba as a precondition to the provision of US aid to the USSR. Cuba's subsequent demands that the USA withdraw its troops from the naval base at Guantánamo were rejected. The Soviet withdrawal was completed in June 1993.

In early 1992 President Castro's efforts to quiet internal dissent and bolster the country against the perceived US threat revealed an increasingly militant attitude, as several death sentences were imposed on Cuban dissidents. In the same year the USA began to implement a series of measures tightening its economic blockade against Cuba. In April US President Bush issued an executive order barring ships that were engaged in trade with Cuba from entering US ports. In October the Cuban Democracy Act, also known as the 'Torricelli Law', was adopted, making it illegal for foreign subsidiaries of US companies to trade with Cuba. These measures encountered widespread international criticism, including protests by the European Community (EC, later European Union—EU) that they violated international law. In November the UN General Assembly adopted a non-binding resolution demanding the cessation of the trade embargo.

In July 1992 the National Assembly approved a number of amendments to the Constitution. Under the reforms, President Castro was granted the authority to declare a state of emergency and, in such an event, to assume full control of the armed forces at the head of a National Defence Council. An electoral reform, which had originally been proposed at the Fourth Congress of the PCC in October 1991, was formally adopted, providing for elections to the National Assembly to be conducted by direct vote. The constitutional revisions also included an updating of the business law, legitimizing foreign investment in approved state enterprises and recognizing foreign ownership of property in joint ventures.

On 24 February 1993 elections to the National Assembly and the 14 provincial assemblies were, for the first time, conducted by direct secret ballot. Only candidates nominated by the PCC were permitted to contest the elections. According to official results, there was an abstention rate of only 1.2%, and 87.3% of the electorate cast a 'united' ballot (a vote for the entire list of candidates). Only 7.2% of votes cast were blank or spoilt. All 589 deputies of the National Assembly were elected with more than the requisite 50% of the votes. In the following month Fidel Castro and Gen. Raúl Castro were unanimously re-elected by the National Assembly to their respective posts as President and First Vice-President of the Council of State.

In July 1993, with the economic crisis deepening and international reserves exhausted, Castro announced that a 30-year ban on Cuban citizens' possessing foreign currency was to be lifted. The measure, which represented a significant departure from the country's centrally-planned socialist economy, was intended to attract the large sums of foreign currency (principally US dollars) in circulation on the black market into the economy, and to encourage remittances from Cuban exiles. Restrictions on Cuban exiles travelling to Cuba were also to be relaxed. Concerns that the measures were socially divisive, affording privileges to those receiving currency from relatives abroad, were acknowledged by the Government. In September, in a further move away from traditional economic policy, the Government authorized limited individual private enterprise in a range of 117 occupations. In the same month plans were announced for the introduction of agricultural reforms allowing for the decentralization and reorganization of state farms into 'Units of Basic Co-operative Production', to be managed and financed by the workers themselves.

In April 1994, in a reorganization of the Government, four new ministries were created and a number of state committees and institutes dissolved. The creation of the new ministries (of economy and planning, finance and prices, foreign investment and economic co-operation, and tourism) reflected a significant change in the economic management of the country. In early August, however, increasing discontent at deteriorating economic conditions resulted in rioting in the capital, precipitated by a confrontation between police and a large number of Cubans attempting to commandeer a ferry in order to take the vessel to the USA. In a public speech broadcast on the following day Castro indicated that, if the USA failed to halt the promotion of such illegal departures, Cuba would suspend its travel restrictions. The resultant surge of Cubans attempting to reach the USA by sea reached crisis proportions, and the US President, Bill Clinton, was forced to adopt measures to deter them. The automatic refugee status conferred on Cubans under the 1966 Cuban Adjustment Act was revoked, and Cubans were warned that those intercepted by the US Coast Guard would be transported to Guantánamo naval base and would not be allowed entry into the USA. Further measures imposed included the halting of cash remittances from Cuban exiles in the USA. However, these measures failed to stem the flow of Cubans seeking refuge in the USA, and in September the US and Cuban Governments held bilateral talks to resolve the crisis. As a result of the talks, the USA promised to grant visas allowing for the migration of a minimum of 20,000 Cubans annually (despite the 1984 immigration accord, a total of only 11,222 US entry visas had been granted to Cubans between December 1984 and July 1994). An additional 4,000–6,000 Cubans already on waiting lists for US visas would be granted them. In return, Cuba reintroduced border restrictions. More than 30,000 Cubans were estimated to have left the country during the period when travel restrictions were suspended, although the majority of these were detained by the US authorities and transported to camps in Guantánamo and the Panama Canal Zone. Talks continued with the USA throughout 1995. In May a further immigration accord was signed, bringing to an official end the automatic refugee status that had been revoked in August 1994. The accord also stated that all Cuban refugees intercepted at sea by the USA would thenceforth be repatriated. In addition, the USA agreed to grant visas to the majority of the approximately 20,000 Cuban refugees detained at Guantánamo, although the figure was to be deducted, over a period of four years, from the annual quota of visas granted under the September 1994 accord.

In early 1995 legislative proposals seeking to tighten the US embargo against Cuba were introduced to the US Congress by the Chairman of the Senate Foreign Relations Committee, Jesse Helms, and the Chairman of the House of Representatives Sub-Committee on the Western Hemisphere, Dan Burton. The proposals, referred to as the Helms-Burton bill, sought to impose sanctions on countries trading with or investing in Cuba, and threatened to reduce US aid to countries providing Cuba with financial assistance, notably Russia. The bill provoked international criticism, and a formal complaint was registered by the EU, which claimed that the legislation would be in violation of international law and the rules of the World Trade Organization (WTO, see p. 292). The legislation was approved by the House of Representatives in September but was considerably modified by the Senate.

In February 1996 Cuban MiG fighters shot down two US light aircraft piloted by members of the Cuban-American exile group, Brothers to the Rescue, killing all four crew members. The action was vigorously condemned by the USA, which rejected Cuban claims that the aircraft had violated Cuban airspace. Further US sanctions were immediately implemented, including the indefinite suspension of charter flights to Cuba. In June,

following an investigation, the International Civil Aviation Organization issued a report confirming US claims that the aircraft had been shot down over international waters. As a result of the incident, President Clinton reversed his previous opposition to certain controversial elements of the Helms-Burton bill, and on 12 March he signed the legislation, officially entitled the Cuban Liberty and Solidarity Act, thus making it law. However, Clinton was empowered to issue executive orders, at six-monthly intervals, postponing the implementation of a section of the law, Title III, which allowed US citizens, including naturalized Cuban exiles, to prosecute through US courts any foreign corporation or investor with business dealings involving property that had been expropriated during the Castro regime. Approval of the Helms-Burton bill prompted strenuous criticism from Cuba's major trading partners. The EU announced its intention to challenge the extra-territorial provisions of the Act through the WTO, while Mexico and Canada sought to dispute the law under the provisions of the North American Free Trade Agreement. International opposition to the Helms-Burton bill increased following the issue, in May, by the US State Department of letters to companies in Canada, Mexico and Italy, warning of possible prosecution. In June Canada initiated a series of legal measures to protect Canadian companies against the Act. Similar legislation was subsequently adopted by Mexico and the EU. In July Clinton imposed a six-month moratorium on Title III of the Act, which had been due to come into force in August. In November, in its annual vote on the US embargo, the UN General Assembly voted for its repeal with the largest majority to date. Notably, the United Kingdom, Germany and the Netherlands, which had all previously abstained on this question, voted in favour of a repeal. In the same month the WTO adopted a resolution to establish a disputes panel to rule on the legality of the Helms-Burton-sponsored Act.

In December 1996 agreement was reached by the members of the EU to make the extent of economic co-operation with Cuba contingent upon progress towards democracy in the country. In that month the Cuban Government adopted legislation to counteract the application of the Cuban Liberty and Solidarity (Helms-Burton) Act in an attempt to protect foreign investment in the country. The Government also expressed its readiness to negotiate with the USA regarding the compensation of US citizens with property claims in Cuba. In early February 1997 the EU requested that the WTO postpone the appointment of a disputes panel in order that further discussions be conducted with the USA in an effort to reach a negotiated settlement. However, these efforts were not successful, and on 20 February a disputes panel was appointed and given six months to reach a decision on whether the extra-territorial provisions of the Act contravened WTO rules on multilateral trade, or whether, as the USA maintained, the Act was a matter of national security and therefore not within the jurisdiction of the WTO. In March, in a further attempt to avoid confrontation, the EU and the USA resumed discussions concerning the Act, and in the following month agreement was reached in principle on a resolution of the dispute. Under the terms of the agreement, the USA was to continue deferring the implementation of Title III indefinitely, while the EU was to withdraw its petition to the WTO until October. In the interim, negotiations were to continue towards a multilateral accord defining investment principles, with particular emphasis on expropriated foreign assets. In a move widely interpreted as a concession to mounting domestic pressure to end restrictions on exports of food and medicines from the USA to Cuba, in March 1998 it was agreed that shipments of both commodities, via non-governmental organizations, were to be permitted. In addition, President Clinton announced an end to the ban on direct flights between the USA and Cuba (imposed in 1996) and on the transfer of cash remittances from the USA to Cuba. Henceforth, Cuban residents in the USA were to be permitted to send up to US $300 quarterly to relatives in Cuba. The process whereby applications for licences to sell medicines to Cuba were considered was also to be examined, with a view to accelerating procedures. However, the Cuban Government was extremely critical of a further outline agreement on extraterritorial legislation drafted by the US Government and the EU in May, which it considered to be highly concessionary on the part of the EU, at the expense of Cuban interests. Under the terms of the agreement, in return for a commitment from President Clinton to seek congressional consensus for a relaxation of the application of the Cuban Liberty and Solidarity Act, EU member states would participate in the compilation of a register of former US assets in Cuba (considered to have been illegally expropriated) and would observe firm US recommendations regarding their exclusivity.

Support for the annual UN General Assembly resolution urging an end to the US embargo against Cuba increased once again in October 1998. The resolution received the support of 157 member nations. Twelve members abstained from the vote, while only two (the USA and Israel) voted against the resolution.

Despite a further easing of restrictions relating to the US embargo in August 1999, and well-publicized visits to Cuba by the head of the US Chamber of Commerce in July, by two prominent US senators in August and by George Ryan, Governor of the US State of Illinois in October, attempts by the US Government to appease the increasingly influential anti-embargo lobby were largely frustrated by an exchange of legal challenges. In March a US judge ruled that payments owed to the Cuban national telecommunications company, which were currently being withheld by a number of US telecommunications companies by judicial request, could be used to help honour a compensation award of US $187m. against the Cuban authorities, made in the USA in 1997 to benefit relatives of four pilots shot down by the Cuban air force in 1996 (see above). The US Government had made known its objection to the ruling, claiming that the decision amounted to interference in foreign policy. In response, in early June a new lawsuit was brought to the Cuban courts by a number of government-sponsored organizations, which were seeking some $181,100m. in compensation for more than 3,000 deaths and more than 2,000 injuries allegedly inflicted on Cuban nationals since the 1959 Revolution by the 'aggressive' policies of the US Government. In September a unanimous declaration of the National Assembly condemned the US trade embargo as an act of 'genocide'. In October 2000 legislation was passed by the US Congress easing some aspects of the trade embargo, including the export of food and medicine. However, the Cuban Government declared that the conditions attached to the lifting of the restrictions were such that the legislation would tighten, rather than ease, the US embargo. In response, Cuba imposed a 10% tax on all telephone calls between the two countries and, in December, suspended telephone links with the USA, following the refusal of US telecommunications companies to pay the levy.

In the first six months of 2000 Cuban–US relations were dominated by the case of Elián González. In November 1999 Elián, a five-year-old Cuban boy, was rescued from the Atlantic Ocean off the coast of Florida (USA), the sole survivor of a shipwrecked attempt to reach the USA, in which his mother had died. A dispute resulted between the boy's Miami-based relatives, who attempted to have him granted US citizenship, and his father in Cuba, who wanted his son repatriated. The ensuing custody battle dominated Cuban–US relations in the first six months of 2000. The US Department of Justice granted custody to Elián's father, but his Miami relatives refused to relinquish charge of the boy. In April armed Federal Bureau of Investigation agents seized Elián from his Miami relatives. He eventually returned to Cuba on 28 June, after the US Supreme Court had declined to hear further appeals from his US-based family. In Cuba the case prompted public demonstrations in protest at the USA's 'abduction' of the child.

In May 1995, following the first visit to Cuba by an international human rights mission since the 1959 Revolution, the Government authorized the release of six political prisoners. The mission had been co-ordinated by the human rights organization France-Libertés. According to Cuban human rights groups, however, more than 1,000 political prisoners remained in detention in the country.

During 21–25 January 1998 Cuba received its first ever papal visit. Pope John Paul II conducted four large-scale open-air masses throughout Cuba, and attended a private meeting with President Castro. During the visit the Pope was critical of the 'unjust and ethically unacceptable' US embargo against Cuba, and urged the reintegration of Cuba into the international community. In response, in late January, the Guatemalan Government announced that diplomatic relations were to be restored with Cuba, prompting a rebuke from the US Department of State. During February, moreover, it was announced that almost 300 Cuban prisoners were to be released, many as a result of a petition for clemency made by the papal delegation. In April, at a meeting of the UN Commission on Human Rights the annual US-sponsored vote of censure against the Cuban Government for alleged abuses of human rights was defeated for the first time since 1991; the motion was supported by 16 countries and opposed by 19, while 18 abstained.

In mid-March 1999 the Provincial Court in Havana sentenced four prominent political dissidents to prison terms of between three and a half and five years' duration. The decision followed the introduction, in February, of uncompromising new legislation to combat increasing criminal activity and to curb subversion and dissent. The incarceration of the dissidents, together with the imposition of death sentences in March on two Salvadorean nationals (see below), drew criticism of Cuba's respect for human rights from the international community in general, and resulted in a significant deterioration in relations with Canada (Cuba's largest trading partner) and Spain in particular.

In mid-1997 a spate of bombings, designed to undermine the country's vital tourism industry and allegedly organized by the anti-Castro Cuban-American National Foundation (CANF, based in Florida, USA), began in the capital. In March 1999 two Salvadorean nationals were convicted (and subsequently sentenced to death) on terrorism charges relating to the bomb attacks. In December 1999 the US Department of Justice acquitted five Cuban exiles, including a member of the CANF executive, accused of plotting to assassinate President Castro in Venezuela in 1997. Following an announcement by the US Government that 10 Cubans had been arrested on charges of spying, in October 1998 Castro admitted that Cuban nationals had been deployed in the USA on espionage duties, charged with infiltrating counter-revolutionary organizations there.

On 11 January 1998 elections to the National Assembly (enlarged from 589 to 601 seats) and to the 14 provincial assemblies were conducted. All 601 candidates who contested the legislative ballot were elected. Of the 7.8m. registered voters, 98.35% participated in the elections. Only 5% of votes cast were blank or spoilt. At the first meeting of the newly-constituted National Assembly on 24 February, the new Council of State was announced, confirming Fidel and Raúl Castro, and the five incumbent Vice-Presidents in their positions for a further five-year term. Of the remaining 23 ordinary members of the Council, 14 were new appointments. In November 2000, during a visit to Panama to attend the Ibero-American Summit, an alleged plot to assassinate President Castro was uncovered. In the same month the leaders of some 50 Cuban organizations opposed to the regime requested the aid of the leaders of 21 Ibero-American countries in achieving a peaceful transition to democracy.

In January 2001 a former Czech finance minister and current member of the Czech parliament, Ivan Pilip, and a Czech political activist, Jan Bubenik, were arrested in Cuba after meeting with anti-Castro dissidents. They were charged with counter-revolutionary plotting on behalf of anti-Castro groups and committed to stand trial.

Since 1985 Cuba has succeeded in establishing strong ties throughout Latin America and the Caribbean. Full diplomatic relations were restored with Colombia (suspended in 1981) in 1993, with Chile in 1995 and with Guatemala in 1998. Diplomatic relations were also re-established with the Dominican Republic in 1998. In August of that year, during President Castro's first visit to the Dominican Republic, he attended a summit meeting of the Cariforum grouping of CARICOM (see p. 142) states and the Dominican Republic, at which the Statement of Santo Domingo was endorsed, envisaging full Cuban participation in any successor arrangement to Lomé IV (see p. 206). (Recent statements by the US and British Governments had indicated that pressure might be applied to EU member states to attach preconditions relating to human rights and democratic processes to Cuban participation in such an arrangement.) Cuba was afforded observer status at a meeting of the Council of Ministers of the Africa, Caribbean and Pacific (ACP) signatory nations to the Lomé Convention (which expired in February 2000 and was replaced by the Cotonou Agreement in June—see p. 208) convened in Barbados in May 1998, and was admitted as a full member in December 2000. In November 1998 Cuba became the 12th full member of the Latin American Integration Association (LAIA, see p. 230), having enjoyed observer status since 1986.

In September 1988 diplomatic relations were established with the EC (restyled the European Union—EU—in late 1993). In the mid-1990s Spain played a significant role in advising Cuba on economic affairs and mediating in negotiations with the International Monetary Fund (IMF, see p. 92), with a view to future co-operation. In 1994 Cuba and Spain concluded an agreement providing for the compensation of Spanish citizens whose property was expropriated during the Cuban Revolution of 1959. In 1996, however, following the transfer of power in Spain from a socialist government to the centre-right administration of José María Aznar, relations between the two countries became more strained. In November 2000 Cuba refused to support a special declaration condemning terrorism by the Basque separatist organization, Euskadi ta Askatasuna (ETA).

In 1992 Cuba signed a number of accords and protocols establishing diplomatic relations with republics of the former USSR, including Belarus, Georgia, Kyrgyzstan and Ukraine. In October 1989 Cuba was elected to the UN Security Council (for a two-year term from January 1990) for the first time in the 30 years of President Castro's rule. In April 2000 Cuba hosted the South G77 Summit of Developing Countries.

Government

Under the 1976 Constitution (the first since the 1959 Revolution, amended in July 1992), the supreme organ of state, and the sole legislative authority, is the National Assembly of People's Power (Asamblea Nacional del Poder Popular), with 601 deputies elected for five years by direct vote. The National Assembly elects 31 of its members to form the Council of State, the Assembly's permanent organ. The Council of State is the highest representative of the State, and its President is both Head of State and Head of Government. Executive and administrative authority is vested in the Council of Ministers, appointed by the National Assembly on the proposal of the Head of State. Municipal, regional and provincial assemblies have also been established. The Partido Comunista de Cuba (PCC), the only authorized political party, is 'the leading force of society and the State'. The PCC's highest authority is the Party Congress, which elects a Central Committee (150 members in December 1997) to supervise the Party's work. To direct its policy, the Central Committee elects a Politburo (24 members in 1997).

Defence

Conscription for military service is for a two-year period, and conscripts also work on the land. In August 2000, according to Western estimates, the armed forces totalled 58,000 (including ready reserves serving 45 days per year to complete active and reserve units): the army numbered 45,000, the navy 3,000 and the air force 10,000. Army reserves were estimated to total 39,000. Paramilitary forces include 20,000 State Security troops, 6,500 border guards, a civil defence force of 50,000 and a Youth Labour Army of 65,000. A local militia organization (Milicias de Tropas Territoriales—MTT), comprising an estimated 1m. men and women, was formed in 1980. Expenditure on defence and internal security for 1999 was estimated at US $750m. Despite Cuban hostility, the USA maintains a base at Guantánamo Bay, with 590 naval and 490 marine personnel in 2000. In June 1993, in accordance with the unilateral decision of the USSR in September 1991, the 3,000-strong military unit of the former USSR, which had been stationed in Cuba since 1962, was withdrawn. A number of Russian military personnel remained to operate military intelligence facilities. Following the political changes in eastern Europe, previously high levels of military aid to Cuba were dramatically reduced in the early 1990s, and the size of the army has been reduced by some 60,000 personnel.

Economic Affairs

In 1999 Cuba's gross domestic product (GDP), measured at constant 1981 prices, was an estimated 15,674m. pesos. During 1990–99, it was estimated, GDP declined, in real terms, at an average annual rate of 2.1%. However, GDP increased by 2.5% in 1997, by 1.2% in 1998 and by an estimated 6.2% in 1999. In 2000, according to government figures, GDP grew by 5.6%. During 1990–98 the population increased by an average of 0.6% per year.

Agriculture (including hunting, forestry and fishing) contributed 6.9% of GDP in 1998 and employed about 14.9% of the labour force. The principal cash crop is sugar cane, with sugar and its derivatives accounting for 52.8% of export earnings in 1996. The sugar crop in 1998/99 was the worst in 50 years, reaching only some 32.8m. metric tons. However, it recovered slightly in 1999/2000, amounting to 35.0m. tons. In 1999/2000 Cuba produced some 37,900 tons of tobacco and exported a record 160m. cigars. Other important crops are rice, citrus fruits (382,500 tons in 1998/99), plantains and bananas. Fishing exports in 1997 reached US $180m. Cuba's principal seafood export markets were Japan, France, Spain, Italy and Canada. In real terms, the GDP of the agricultural sector declined at an average rate of 6.6% per year during 1990–98. Agricultural GDP decreased by 0.2% in 1997 and by 5.2% in 1998. In 2000 severe drought caused a reduction in the sugar and tobacco harvests.

Industry (including mining, manufacturing, construction and power) contributed 37.2% of GDP in 1998. The sector employed 27.7% of the labour force in 1981. Industrial GDP decreased, in real terms, at an average rate of 2.5% per year in 1990–98. The sector's GDP increased by 7.4% in 1997 and by 3.3% in 1998.

Mining contributed 1.2% of GDP in 1998, an increase of 1.2% compared with the previous year. Nickel is the principal mineral export. In 1998 nickel output reached a record level of 68,000 metric tons, an increase of some 10.6% compared with the previous year. Cuba also produces considerable amounts of chromium, cobalt and copper, some iron and manganese, and there are workable deposits of gold and silver.

Manufacturing contributed 29.1% of GDP in 1998. The principal branches of manufacturing were food products, beverages and tobacco, machinery and industrial chemicals. During 1990–98 manufacturing GDP declined, in real terms, at an average annual rate of 1.0%. The sector's GDP increased by 8.3% in 1997, and by 3.3% in 1998. The biomedical industry continued to expand in the 1990s and in July 1999 a joint venture was agreed with the pharmaceutical manufacturer SmithKline Beecham to market the Cuban meningitis vaccine.

Energy is derived principally from petroleum and natural gas. Current levels of production of crude petroleum satisfy approximately 20% of domestic demand. In the late 1990s Cuba produced approximately 30,000 b/d of crude petroleum and in 1998 total production was 1.7m. metric tons. Imports of mineral fuels accounted for 27.9% of the total cost of imports in 1996. Formerly, some 13m. tons of petroleum were imported annually from the USSR, with 2m. tons being re-exported, but in 1990 imports were dramatically reduced. In 2000 two oil-processing plants were planned for Santiago de Cuba and Cienfuegos and two power-generation plants were being built by Sherritt Power of Canada.

Services employed 46.3% of the total labour force in 1981 and accounted for 55.9% of GDP in 1998. Tourism is one of the country's principal sources of foreign exchange, earning an estimated US $1,626m. in 1998, and development of the sector remains a priority of the Government. In 1998 the industry employed some 150,000 people directly and indirectly. In real terms, the GDP of the service sectors decreased at an average rate of 3.0% per year during 1990–98. The GDP of services increased by 0.1% in 1997 and in 1998.

In 1999 Cuba recorded a trade deficit of US $600m., and a deficit of $350m. on the current account of the balance of payments. In 1998 the principal source of imports was Spain (22.3%) and the principal market for exports was Russia (21.7%). Other major trading partners were France and Canada. The principal imports in 1996 were mineral fuels, machinery and transport equipment. The principal exports in the same year were sugar, minerals and concentrates, and agricultural produce.

In 1999 Cuba recorded an estimated budget deficit of 612m. pesos. According to the Central Bank, the country's external debt to Western creditor nations was US $11,208.9m. in 1998. Cuba's debt to the former USSR was estimated to be $20,000m. in 2000. In December of this year the Russian Government proposed writing off 70% of this debt and renegotiating the remainder through the 'Paris Club' of Western government creditors. However, the Cuban Government refused to negotiate with the Paris Club and disputed the size of the debt owed to Russia. According to official figures, some 5.5% of the labour force were unemployed at the end of 2000. Although no index of consumer prices is published, official estimates put inflation at 2.9% in 1998 and at 0.3% in 1999.

Cuba is a member of the Latin American Economic System (see p. 308) and of the Group of Latin American and Caribbean Sugar Exporting Countries (see p. 304).

In the early 1990s Cuba suffered severe economic decline, prompted by the collapse of the USSR and by the consequent termination of the favourable aid and trade arrangements that had supported the Cuban economy. Resultant shortages, particularly of petroleum and basic raw materials, seriously affected production in all sectors and necessitated wide-ranging austerity measures. In 1994, in a significant departure from the country's traditional command economy, a series of adjustment measures was introduced. The measures included the introduction of new taxes and the drastic reduction (by some 40%) of subsidies to loss-making state enterprises. In December 1994 a new 'convertible peso' was introduced to regulate the circulation of foreign currency. A new investment law, approved in September 1995, opened all sectors of the economy, with the exception of defence, health and education, to foreign participation and introduced the possibility of 100% foreign ownership. In February 1999 an investment project for a Panamanian-Lebanese diesel-electric power-station was approved; however, by 2000 this remained the only such project.

In 1996 the USA intensified its sanctions against Cuba with the introduction of the Cuban Liberty and Solidarity (Helms-Burton) Act. Denied access to medium- and long-term loans, Cuba's indebtedness increased substantially as high-interest short-term loans were contracted in order to finance production, most notably in the sugar industry. Despite reports of a shortage of foreign exchange in mid-1998 resulting from a poor sugar harvest and a decline in world prices for nickel, other sectors of the economy performed sufficiently well to encourage economic growth of 6.2% in 1999, and forecasted growth of 4.5% for 2000. In 1997 three free-trade zones were opened to attract foreign investment. By the end of 1998, however, only 34 of the 243 companies located in the zones were in production. During 1999 the Central Bank made known its intention henceforth to prefer to conduct international transactions in euros, hoping thus to weaken the stranglehold of the US dollar on the Cuban economy. In September the Central Bank announced a debt-rescheduling agreement involving £17m. of short-term debt with the United Kingdom Government's export credits guarantee department. It was hoped that the move would signal a reactivation of British investor interest in Cuba. In 1999 the largest investments were in mining (specifically nickel), tourism and telecommunications sectors. In December a 50% stake in Habanos, the state-owned cigar distributor, was sold for US $500m.

Social Welfare

Through the State Social Security System, employees receive benefits for sickness, accidents, maternity, disability, retirement and unemployment. Health services are available free of charge. In 1999 there were 276 hospitals and 607 clinics in Cuba and in 1997 there were 82,037 hospital beds. In 1999 there were 64,863 physicians working in the country and in 1997 there were an estimated 677.6 nurses per 100,000 inhabitants. In 1999 the infant mortality rate was only 6.4 per 1,000 live births. The 1999 budget allocation for public health, was some 1,600m. pesos, equivalent to 11.4% of total expenditure.

Education

Education is universal and free at all levels. Education is based on Marxist-Leninist principles and combines study with manual work. Day nurseries are available for all children after their 45th day, and national schools at the pre-primary level are operated by the State for children of five years of age. Primary education, from six to 11 years of age, is compulsory, and secondary education lasts from 12 to 17 years of age, comprising two cycles of three years each. In 1997 total enrolment at primary and secondary schools was equivalent to 71.5% of the school-age population(males 70%; females 73%). In that year primary enrolment included almost 100% of children in the relevant age-group (males 99.9%; females 99.9%), while secondary enrolment was equivalent to 69.9% of the population in the appropriate age-group (males 67.2%; females 72.6%). In 1999/2000 there were an estimated 106,800 students in higher education. Workers attending university courses receive a state subsidy to provide for their dependants. Courses at intermediate and higher levels lay an emphasis on technology, agriculture and teacher training. In 1998, according to estimates by the World Bank, the illiteracy rate among persons aged 15 years and over was 3.6% (males 3.5%; females 3.7%). In 1999 budgetary expenditure on education was estimated at 1,865m. pesos (13.3% of total spending).

Public Holidays

2001: 1 January (Liberation Day), 1 May (Labour Day), 25–27 July (Anniversary of the 1953 Revolution), 10 October (Wars of Independence Day), 25 December (Christmas Day).

2002: 1 January (Liberation Day), 1 May (Labour Day), 25–27 July (Anniversary of the 1953 Revolution), 10 October (Wars of Independence Day), 25 December (Christmas Day).

Weights and Measures

The metric system is in force.

Statistical Survey

Source (unless otherwise stated): Cámara de Comercio de la República de Cuba, Calle 21, No 661/701, esq. Calle A, Apdo 4237, Vedado, Havana; tel. (7) 30-3356; fax (7) 33-3042; internet www.camaracuba.cubaweb.cu; Oficina Nacional de Estadísticas, Calle Paseo 60, entre 3 y 5, Vedado, Havana; tel. (7) 30-0005; fax (7) 33-3083; internet www.cubagob.cu/otras_info/estadisticas.htm.

Area and Population

AREA, POPULATION AND DENSITY

Area (sq km)	110,860*
Population (census results)	
6 September 1970	8,569,121
11 September 1981	
Males	4,914,873
Females	4,808,732
Total	9,723,605
Population (official estimates at mid-year)	
1997	11,065,900
1998	11,116,500
1999	11,160,200
Density (per sq km) at mid-1999	100.7

* 42,803 sq miles.

PRINCIPAL TOWNS
(estimated population at 31 December 1999)

La Habana			Santa Clara . .	210,100
(Havana, the			Guantánamo . .	208,030
capital) . . .	2,189,716		Pinar del Río . .	148,500
Santiago de Cuba .	441,524		Bayamo . . .	143,600
Camagüey . . .	306,049		Cienfuegos. . .	137,513
Holguín . . .	259,300		Las Tunas . . .	137,331
			Matanzas . . .	124,754

BIRTHS, MARRIAGES AND DEATHS*

	Registered live births†		Registered marriages‡		Registered deaths	
	Number	Rate (per 1,000)	Number	Rate (per 1,000)	Number	Rate (per 1,000)
1992 . .	157,349	14.5	191,837	17.7	75,457	7.0
1993 . .	152,238	14.0	135,138	12.4	78,531	7.2
1994 . .	147,265	13.4	116,935	10.7	78,648	7.2
1995 . .	147,170	13.4	70,413	6.4	77,937	7.1
1996 . .	148,276	13.5	65,009	5.9	79,654	7.2
1997 . .	152,681	13.8	60,900§	5.5	77,316	7.0
1998 . .	151,080	13.6	64,900§	5.8	77,565	7.0
1999§ . .	150,900	13.5	57,300	5.1	79,300	7.1

* Data are tabulated by year of registration rather than by year of occurrence.
† Births registered in the National Consumers Register, established on 31 December 1964.
‡ Including consensual unions formalized in response to special legislation.
§ Provisional.

Expectation of life (UNDP estimates, years at birth, 1998): 76.3 (males 74.3; females 78.2). Source: UN Development Programme, *Human Development Report*.

ECONOMICALLY ACTIVE POPULATION (1981 census)

	Males	Females	Total
Agriculture, hunting, forestry and fishing	677,565	113,304	790,869
Mining and quarrying . . .			
Manufacturing	472,399	195,941	668,340
Electricity, gas and water . .			
Construction	279,327	33,913	313,240
Trade, restaurants and hotels .	170,192	135,438	305,630
Transport, storage and communications . . .	205,421	43,223	248,644
Financing, insurance, real estate and business services . . .			
	541,387	544,665	1,086,052
Community, social and personal services . . .			
Activities not adequately defined .	87,778	40,139	127,917
Total labour force	2,434,069	1,106,623	3,540,692

Source: ILO, *Yearbook of Labour Statistics*.

1998 (persons aged 15 years and over): Total employed 3,753,600; Unemployment rate 6.6%.

CIVILIAN EMPLOYMENT IN THE STATE SECTOR
(annual averages, '000 persons)

	1987	1988	1989
Industry*	726.9	742.8	767.5
Construction	314.1	339.4	344.3
Agriculture	602.7	653.2	690.3
Forestry	30.1	26.8	30.8
Transport	196.9	199.9	204.4
Communications . . .	28.4	30.1	31.5
Trade	376.2	387.3	395.3
Social services . . .	116.5	121.5	124.5
Science and technology . .	28.7	27.5	27.4
Education	383.0	388.2	396.4
Arts and culture	42.2	42.1	43.9
Public health . . .	222.4	232.5	243.5
Finance and insurance . .	20.6	20.9	21.7
Administration	161.4	155.1	151.7
Total (incl. others) . . .	3,299.2	3,408.4	3,526.6

* Fishing, mining, manufacturing, electricity, gas and water.

Agriculture

PRINCIPAL CROPS ('000 metric tons)

	1997	1998	1999
Rice (paddy) .	418.8	280.4	280.4*
Maize .	126.0	110.8	110.8*
Potatoes .	329.9	206.2	206.2*
Sweet potatoes .	145.6	157.5	157.5*
Cassava (Manioc) .	189.4	205.8	205.8*
Dry beans .	15.8	18.5	18.5*
Groundnuts (in shell)* .	15.0	15.0	15.0
Coconuts* .	26.0	26.0	26.0
Cabbages* .	26.0	28.0	28.0
Tomatoes .	146.2	112.2	112.2*
Pumpkins, squash and gourds* .	45.0	47.0	47.0
Cucumbers and gherkins* .	35.0	37.0	37.0
Other vegetables* .	65.0	68.0	68.0
Melons* .	25.0	23.0	23.0
Sugar cane .	38,900.0	32,800.0	35,000.0*
Oranges .	482.3	358.7	358.7*
Tangerines, mandarins, clementines and satsumas .	6.1†	6.5*	6.5*
Lemons and limes .	21.0	17.3	17.3*
Grapefruit and pomelos .	296.3	324.1	300.0*
Mangoes .	52.6	43.0	43.0*
Pineapples* .	19.0	19.0	19.0
Bananas .	118.9	153.5	153.5*
Plantains .	263.4	308.7	308.7*
Coffee (green)† .	20.0	13.5	22.0
Tobacco (leaves) .	30.9	37.9	37.9*

* FAO estimate(s).   † Unofficial figure(s).

Source: FAO.

LIVESTOCK ('000 head, year ending September)

	1997	1998	1999
Cattle .	4,606.0	4,643.7	4,650.0*
Horses .	525.3	433.6	620.0*
Mules .	27.5	24.3	24.3*
Pigs* .	2,400.0	2,400.0	2,400.0
Sheep* .	310.0	310.0	310.0
Goats .	138.5	162.1	140.0*
Poultry .	13,667	13,118	13,118*

* FAO estimate(s).

Source: FAO.

LIVESTOCK PRODUCTS ('000 metric tons)

	1997	1998	1999
Beef and veal .	67.6	70.0*	70.0*
Pig meat .	73.4	80.0*	80.0*
Poultry meat .	63.2	59.6	59.6*
Cows' milk .	650.8	655.3	655.3*
Butter* .	7.5	7.5	7.5
Cheese* .	14.5	14.5	14.5
Hen eggs .	60.2	59.3	59.3*

* FAO estimate(s).

Source: FAO.

Forestry

ROUNDWOOD REMOVALS ('000 cubic metres, excl. bark)

	1996	1997	1998
Sawlogs, veneer logs and logs for sleepers .	193	193	193
Other industrial wood .	418	418	418
Fuel wood .	2,145	2,145	2,145
Total .	2,756	2,756	2,756

Source: FAO, *Yearbook of Forest Products*.

SAWNWOOD PRODUCTION
('000 cubic metres, incl. railway sleepers)

	1996	1997	1998
Coniferous (softwood) .	59	59	59
Broadleaved (hardwood) .	72	72	72
Total .	130	130	130

Source: FAO, *Yearbook of Forest Products*.

Fishing

('000 metric tons, live weight)

	1996	1997	1998
Capture .	75.8	77.3	62.2
Silver hake .	22.3	12.7	6.3
Caribbean spiny lobster .	9.4	9.0	9.4
Aquaculture .	33.9	46.2	38.0
Silver carp .	15.5	22.6	25.2
Blue tilapia .	11.9	11.1	5.8
Total catch .	109.7	123.6	100.2

Note: Figures exclude crocodiles, recorded by number rather than by weight. The number of spectacled caimans caught was: 302 in 1996; 506 in 1997; 5 in 1998. Also excluded are sponges (metric tons): 56.8 in 1996; 81.5 in 1997; 72.1 in 1998.

Source: FAO, *Yearbook of Fishery Statistics*.

Mining

('000 metric tons, unless otherwise indicated)

	1996	1997	1998
Crude petroleum .	1,275.9	1,461.5	1,678.2
Natural gas (million cu metres) .	19.3	37.2	124.1
Copper concentrates (metric tons) .	2,362.3	2,208.2	1,351.4
Nickel and cobalt (metal content) .	53.7	61.6	67.7
Refractory chromium .	37.3	44.1	46.0
Salt (unrefined) .	159.8	163.6	134.6
Silica and sand ('000 cu metres) .	1,828.2	1,949.1	1,861.2
Crushed stone ('000 cu metres) .	2,899.9	2,919.6	2,860.0

1999: Crude petroleum ('000 metric tons) 2,104.3; Natural gas (million cubic metres) 460.0; Nickel and cobalt ('000 metric tons, metal content) 66.5.

Industry

SELECTED PRODUCTS
('000 metric tons, unless otherwise indicated)

	1996	1997	1998
Crude steel .	223.6	334.6	278.0
Corrugated steel bars .	82.9	94.8	106.1
Grey cement .	1,437.9	1,700.6	1,713.4
Mosaics ('000 sq metres) .	1,236.4	1,225.8	1,208.0
Motor spirit (gasoline) .	359.1	320.8	273.7
Kerosene .	222.2	167.6	75.9
Sulphuric acid (98%) .	359.7	428.8	411.9
Fertilizers .	241.5	183.5	156.7
Tyres ('000) .	212.3	233.4	164.7
Woven textile fabrics (million sq metres) .	47.9	53.7	54.0
Cigarettes ('000 million) .	10.7	10.7	11.7
Cigars (million) .	193.7	214.5	263.5
Raw sugar .	4,367.2	4,154.8	3,158.9
Leather footwear (million pairs) .	5.0	5.7	6.3
Electric energy (million kWh) .	13,236.5	14,145.6	14,145.1

1999: ('000 metric tons, unless otherwise indicated): Crude steel 302.7; Grey cement 1,781.9; Fertilizers 138.3; Tyres ('000) 156.6; Woven textile fabrics (million sq metres) 51.0; Cigarettes ('000 million) 12.3; Electric energy (million kWh) 14,487.5.

Finance

CURRENCY AND EXCHANGE RATES

Monetary Units:

100 centavos = 1 Cuban peso.

Sterling, Dollar and Euro Equivalents (29 December 2000)

£1 sterling = 1.4922 pesos;

US $1 = 1.0000 pesos;

€1 = 93.05 centavos;

100 Cuban pesos = £67.02 = $100.00 = €107.47.

Note: The foregoing information relates to official exchange rates. For the purposes of foreign trade, the peso was at par with the US dollar during each of the 10 years 1987–96. A 'convertible peso' was introduced in December 1994. The free market rate of exchange in September 1998 was US $1 = 23 Cuban pesos.

STATE BUDGET (million pesos)

	1997	1998*	1999*
Total revenue	12,242.8	12,502.0	13,400.0
Total expenditure . . .	12,813.5	13,061.7	14,012.0
Productive sector	2,605.7	2,588.4	2,893.0
Housing and community services	1,630.2	1,705.1	1,758.0
Education	1,421.3	1,509.7	1,865.0
Public health	1,190.3	1,344.9	1,600.0
Government administration and judicial bodies . .	397.5	437.8	476.0
Defence and public order . .	496.7	537.1	851.0

Source: Ministry of Finance and Prices.

INTERNATIONAL RESERVES (million pesos at 31 December)

	1987	1988
Gold and other precious metals	17.5	19.5
Cash and deposits in foreign banks (convertible currency)	36.5	78.0
Sub-total	54.0	97.5
Deposits in foreign banks (in transferable roubles)	142.5	137.0
Total	196.5	234.5

NATIONAL ACCOUNTS

Composition of Gross National Product

(million pesos at current prices)

	1995	1996	1997
Compensation of employees . .	9,860.7	10,181.9	10,291.9
Operating surplus . . . . }	4,283.6	5,671.2	6,085.4
Consumption of fixed capital . . }			
Gross domestic product (GDP) at factor cost	14,144.3	15,853.1	16,377.3
Indirect taxes *less* subsidies . .	7,592.8	6,961.6	6,574.5
GDP in purchasers' values .	21,737.1	22,814.7	22,951.8
Less Factor income from abroad (net)	524.8	492.6	482.9
Gross national product . .	21,212.3	22,322.1	22,468.9

Source: UN Economic Commission for Latin America and the Caribbean, *Statistical Yearbook*.

1998 (million pesos at current prices): GDP in purchasers' values 23,900.8.
1999 (million pesos at current prices): GDP in purchasers' values 25,503.6.

Expenditure on the Gross Domestic Product

(million pesos at current prices)

	1995	1996	1997
Government final consumption expenditure	5,302.5	5,521.8	5,513.8
Private final consumption expenditure	16,281.7	16,281.7	16,347.0
Increase in stocks	−160.8	−637.4	−513.6
Gross fixed capital formation . .	1,685.5	2,258.2	2,274.7
Total domestic expenditure .	22,281.7	23,424.3	23,621.9
Exports of goods and services . .	2,913.1	3,563.6	3,785.5
Less Imports of goods and services	3,457.7	4,173.2	4,455.6
GDP in purchasers' values .	21,737.1	22,814.7	22,951.8
GDP at constant 1981 prices .	13,184.5	14,218.0	14,572.4

Source: UN Economic Commission for Latin America and the Caribbean, *Statistical Yearbook*.

Gross Domestic Product by Economic Activity

(million pesos at constant 1981 prices)

	1997	1998	1999
Agriculture, hunting, forestry and fishing	1,073.7	1,017.5	1,122.9
Mining and quarrying . . .	181.9	184.1	186.0
Manufacturing	4,154.5	4,290.7	4,594.9
Electricity, gas and water . .	421.8	426.8	430.2
Construction	556.0	587.9	632.0
Wholesale and retail trade, restaurants and hotels . .	3,175.8	3,089.6	3,370.2
Transport, storage and communications . . .	845.4	855.4	911.7
Finance, insurance, real estate and business services . .	544.5	599.3	637.0
Community, social and personal services	3,618.8	3,702.8	3,789.5
Total	14,572.4	14,754.1	15,674.4

BALANCE OF PAYMENTS (million pesos)

	1996	1997	1998
Exports of goods	1,866.2	1,823.1	1,444.4
Imports of goods	−3,656.5	−4,087.6	−4,229.7
Trade balance	−1,790.3	−2,264.5	−2,785.3
Services (net)	1,372.4	1,519.0	2,168.2
Balance on goods and services.	−417.9	−745.5	−617.1
Other income (net) . . .	−492.6	−482.9	−599.2
Balance on goods, services and income	−910.5	−1,228.4	−1,216.3
Current transfers (net) . . .	743.7	791.7	820.0
Current balance	−166.8	−436.7	−396.3
Direct investment (net) . . .	82.1	442.0	206.6
Other long-term capital (net) . .	225.8	344.9	426.1
Other capital (net) . . .	−133.5	−329.5	−219.4
Overall balance	7.6	20.7	17.0

External Trade

PRINCIPAL COMMODITIES (US $ million)

Imports c.i.f.	1994	1995	1996
Food and live animals	467.4	610.9	689.2
Dairy products and birds' eggs	72.1	90.4	84.9
Cereals and cereal preparations	237.1	331.6	396.9
Wheat and meslin (unmilled)	119.7	132.8	158.4
Rice	72.5	107.3	126.5
Vegetables and fruit	60.6	57.2	61.1
Dried beans, peas, lentils, etc. (shelled)	56.0	49.8	49.3
Bran sharps, etc.	49.1	49.9	60.6
Crude materials (inedible) except fuels	79.9	113.7	98.3
Mineral fuels, lubricants, etc.	766.7	871.9	971.6
Petroleum and petroleum products	742.6	849.6	953.1
Crude petroleum oils, etc.	170.3	156.2	250.2
Kerosene and other medium oils	245.1	330.7	333.1
Gas oils	216.4	256.9	299.4
Chemicals and related products	172.9	309.2	302.6
Disinfectants, insecticides, fungicides, weed-killers, etc.	44.6	64.7	55.7
Basic manufactures	198.4	374.6	520.1
Rubber manufactures	42.5	74.4	54.2
Iron and steel	43.9	90.5	125.1
Machinery and transport equipment	196.3	426.7	561.6
Power-generating machinery and equipment	96.7	197.5	256.1
Miscellaneous manufactured articles	32.1	93.0	177.2
Total (incl. others)	2,016.9	2,882.6	3,480.7

Exports f.o.b.	1994	1995	1996
Food and live animals	914.6	899.6	1,159.5
Fish, crustaceans, molluscs and preparations	99.3	121.8	125.0
Fresh, chilled or frozen fish	98.2	120.6	124.6
Vegetables and fruit	30.3	31.3	38.5
Sugar, sugar preparations and honey	763.3	718.1	976.5
Raw beet and cane sugars (solid)	748.1	704.5	951.7
Beverages and tobacco	78.8	112.1	120.0
Tobacco and tobacco manufactures	71.4	102.1	108.4
Manufactured tobacco	55.2	75.5	79.4
Crude materials (inedible) except fuels	208.9	351.8	437.6
Metalliferous ores and metal scrap	206.6	347.8	433.9
Nickel ores, concentrates, etc.	196.1	323.7	417.1
Chemicals and related products	77.6	53.2	57.7
Medicaments	76.3	48.3	51.7
Basic manufactures	42.5	60.3	57.0
Iron and steel	21.4	30.5	32.7
Total (incl. others)	1,330.8	1,491.7	1,848.9

Source: UN, *International Trade Statistics Yearbook*.

PRINCIPAL TRADING PARTNERS (US $ million)

Imports c.i.f.	1996	1997	1998
Argentina	137	131	78
Brazil	47	55	66
Canada	187	266	263
China, People's Republic	111	172	140
France	217	233	285
Germany	77	66	83
Italy	124	134	213
Mexico	350	n.a.	n.a.
Netherlands Antilles	40	44	50
Spain	513	522	584
Russia	508	314	77
United Kingdom	42	34	61
Venezuela	126	140	145
Total (incl. others)	3,007	2,846	2,613

Source: IMF, *Direction of Trade Statistics Yearbook*.

Exports f.o.b.	1996	1997	1998
Algeria	35	41	44
Belarus	25	77	25
Canada	294	255	227
China, People's Republic	125	91	85
Colombia	19	25	29
Egypt	15	69	79
France	48	50	55
Germany	24	28	26
Japan	61	99	56
Netherlands	204	240	230
Russia	369	320	374
Spain	119	112	130
United Kingdom	27	22	24
Total (incl. others)	1,855	1,755	1,721

Source: IMF, *Direction of Trade Statistics Yearbook*.

Transport

RAILWAYS

	1995	1996	1997
Passenger-kilometres (million)	2,188.2	2,159.5	1,962.2
Freight ton-kilometres (million)	886.4	1,054.5	1,074.8

Source: UN Economic Commission for Latin America and the Caribbean, *Statistical Yearbook*.

Passengers ('000): 19,600 in 1997; 16,000 in 1998; 16,000 in 1999.
Freight carried ('000 metric tons): 6,721.9 in 1997; 6,491.2 in 1998; 6,037.8 in 1999.

ROAD TRAFFIC (motor vehicles in use at 31 December)

	1996	1997
Passenger cars	216,575	172,574
Buses and coaches	28,089	28,861
Lorries and vans	246,105	156,634

Source: IRF, *World Road Statistics*.

SHIPPING
Merchant Fleet (registered at 31 December)

	1996	1997	1998
Number of vessels	324	148	105
Total displacement ('000 grt)	291	203	158

Source: Lloyd's Register of Shipping, *World Fleet Statistics*.

International Sea-borne Freight Traffic ('000 metric tons)

	1988	1989	1990
Goods loaded	8,600	8,517	8,092
Goods unloaded	15,500	15,595	15,440

Source: UN, *Monthly Bulletin of Statistics.*

CIVIL AVIATION (traffic on scheduled services)

	1995	1996	1997
Kilometres flown (million) . .	16	20	26
Passengers carried ('000) . .	824	929	1,117
Passenger-kilometres (million) . .	2,006	2,649	3,543
Total ton-kilometres (million) .	219	292	388

Source: UN, *Statistical Yearbook.*

Tourism

ARRIVALS BY NATIONALITY*

	1996	1997	1998
Argentina	31,331	41,511	47,579
Canada	162,766	169,686	215,644
Colombia	25,251	28,745	20,702
France	62,742	93,897	101,604
Germany	80,185	86,509	148,987
Italy	192,297	200,238	186,688
Mexico	37,229	52,712	61,589
Spain	117,957	116,606	140,435
United Kingdom	28,077	46,215	64,276
USA	27,113	34,956	46,778
Total (incl. others) . . .	1,004,336	1,170,083	1,415,832

* Figures include same-day visitors (excursionists).

Source: World Tourism Organization, *Yearbook of Tourism Statistics.*

Tourism receipts (US $ million): 1,350 in 1996; 1,338 in 1997; 1,626 in 1998.

Communications Media

	1995	1996	1997
Radio receivers ('000 in use) . .	3,850	3,870	3,900
Television receivers ('000 in use) .	2,500	2,600	2,640
Telephones ('000 main lines in use)	353	356	371
Mobile cellular telephones (subscribers)	1,939	2,427	2,994
Book production (titles) . .	698	679	625

Telefax stations (number in use): 392 in 1992.

Sources: mainly UNESCO, *Statistical Yearbook,* and UN, *Statistical Yearbook.*

Book production (titles): 621 in 1998; 708 in 1999.

Education

(1999/2000)

	Institutions	Teachers	Students
Pre-primary	1,114	19,600	149,100
Primary	9,375	76,300	987,900
Secondary	2,018	70,900	857,700
Universities	37	23,500	106,800

Directory

The Constitution

Following the assumption of power by the Castro regime, on 1 January 1959, the Constitution was suspended and a Fundamental Law of the Republic was instituted, with effect from 7 February 1959. In February 1976 Cuba's first socialist Constitution came into force after being submitted to the first Congress of the Communist Party of Cuba, in December 1975, and to popular referendum, in February 1976; it was amended in July 1992. The main provisions of the Constitution, as amended, are summarized below:

POLITICAL, SOCIAL AND ECONOMIC PRINCIPLES

The Republic of Cuba is a socialist, independent, and sovereign state, organized with all and for the sake of all as a unitary and democratic republic for the enjoyment of political freedom, social justice, collective and individual well-being and human solidarity. Sovereignty rests with the people, from whom originates the power of the State. The Communist Party of Cuba is the leading force of society and the State. The State recognizes, respects and guarantees freedom of religion. Religious institutions are separate from the State. The socialist State carries out the will of the working people and guarantees work, medical care, education, food, clothing and housing. The Republic of Cuba bases its relations with other socialist countries on socialist internationalism, friendship, co-operation and mutual assistance. It reaffirms its willingness to integrate with and co-operate with the countries of Latin America and the Caribbean.

The State organizes and directs the economic life of the nation in accordance with a central social and economic development plan. The State directs and controls foreign trade. The State recognizes the right of small farmers to own their lands and other means of production and to sell that land. The State guarantees the right of citizens to ownership of personal property in the form of earnings, savings, place of residence and other possessions and objects which serve to satisfy their material and cultural needs. The State also guarantees the right of inheritance.

Cuban citizenship is acquired by birth or through naturalization.

The State protects the family, motherhood and matrimony.

The State directs and encourages all aspects of education, culture and science.

All citizens have equal rights and are subject to equal duties.

The State guarantees the right to medical care, education, freedom of speech and press, assembly, demonstration, association and privacy. In the socialist society work is the right and duty, and a source of pride for every citizen.

GOVERNMENT

National Assembly of People's Power

The National Assembly of People's Power (Asamblea Nacional del Poder Popular) is the supreme organ of the State and is the only organ with constituent and legislative authority. It is composed of deputies, over the age of 18, elected by free, direct and secret ballot, for a period of five years. All Cuban citizens aged 16 years or more, except those who are mentally incapacitated or who have committed a crime, are eligible to vote. The National Assembly of People's Power holds two ordinary sessions a year and a special session when requested by one-third of the deputies or by the Council of State. More than one-half of the total number of deputies must be present for a session to be held.

All decisions made by the Assembly, except those relating to constitutional reforms, are adopted by a simple majority of votes. The deputies may be recalled by their electors at any time.

The National Assembly of People's Power has the following functions:

to reform the Constitution;

to approve, modify and annul laws;

to supervise all organs of the State and government;

to decide on the constitutionality of laws and decrees;

to revoke decree-laws issued by the Council of State and the Council of Ministers;

to discuss and approve economic and social development plans, the state budget, monetary and credit systems;

to approve the general outlines of foreign and domestic policy, to ratify and annul international treaties, to declare war and approve peace treaties;

to approve the administrative division of the country;

to elect the President, First Vice-President, the Vice-Presidents and other members of the Council of State;

to elect the President, Vice-President and Secretary of the National Assembly;

to appoint the members of the Council of Ministers on the proposal of the President of the Council of State;

to elect the President, Vice-President and other judges of the People's Supreme Court;

to elect the Attorney-General and the Deputy Attorney-Generals;

to grant amnesty;

to call referendums.

The President of the National Assembly presides over sessions of the Assembly, calls ordinary sessions, proposes the draft agenda, signs the Official Gazette, organizes the work of the commissions appointed by the Assembly and attends the meetings of the Council of State.

Council of State

The Council of State is elected from the members of the National Assembly and represents that Assembly in the period between sessions. It comprises a President, one First Vice-President, five Vice-Presidents, one Secretary and 23 other members. Its mandate ends when a new Assembly meets. All decisions are adopted by a simple majority of votes. It is accountable for its actions to the National Assembly.

The Council of State has the following functions:

to call special sessions of the National Assembly;

to set the date for the election of a new Assembly;

to issue decree-laws in the period between the sessions of the National Assembly;

to decree mobilization in the event of war and to approve peace treaties when the Assembly is in recess;

to issue instructions to the courts and the Office of the Attorney-General of the Republic;

to appoint and remove ambassadors of Cuba abroad on the proposal of its President, to grant or refuse recognition to diplomatic representatives of other countries to Cuba;

to suspend those provisions of the Council of Ministers that are not in accordance with the Constitution;

to revoke the resolutions of the Executive Committee of the local organs of People's Power which are contrary to the Constitution or laws and decrees formulated by other higher organs.

The President of the Council of State is Head of State and Head of Government and for all purposes the Council of State is the highest representative of the Cuban state.

Head of State

The President of the Council of State is the Head of State and the Head of Government and has the following powers:

to represent the State and Government and conduct general policy;

to convene and preside over the sessions of the Council of State and the Council of Ministers;

to supervise the ministries and other administrative bodies;

to propose the members of the Council of Ministers to the National Assembly of People's Power;

to receive the credentials of the heads of foreign diplomatic missions;

to sign the decree-laws and other resolutions of the Council of State;

to exercise the Supreme Command of all armed institutions and determine their general organization;

to preside over the National Defence Council;

to declare a state of emergency in the cases outlined in the Constitution.

In the case of absence, illness or death of the President of the Council of State, the First Vice-President assumes the President's duties.

The Council of Ministers

The Council of Ministers is the highest-ranking executive and administrative organ. It is composed of the Head of State and Government, as its President, the First Vice-President, the Vice-Presidents, the Ministers, the Secretary and other members determined by law. Its Executive Committee is composed of the President, the First Vice-President, the Vice-Presidents and other members of the Council of Ministers determined by the President.

The Council of Ministers has the following powers:

to conduct political, economic, cultural, scientific, social and defence policy as outlined by the National Assembly;

to approve international treaties;

to propose projects for the general development plan and, if they are approved by the National Assembly, to supervise their implementation;

to conduct foreign policy and trade;

to draw up bills and submit them to the National Assembly;

to draw up the draft state budget;

to conduct general administration, implement laws, issue decrees and supervise defence and national security.

The Council of Ministers is accountable to the National Assembly of People's Power.

LOCAL GOVERNMENT

The country is divided into 14 provinces and 169 municipalities. The provinces are: Pinar del Río, Habana, Ciudad de la Habana, Matanzas, Villa Clara, Cienfuegos, Sancti Spíritus, Ciego de Avila, Camagüey, Las Tunas, Holguín, Granma, Santiago de Cuba and Guantánamo.

Voting for delegates to the municipal assemblies is direct, secret and voluntary. All citizens over 16 years of age are eligible to vote. The number of delegates to each assembly is proportionate to the number of people living in that area. A delegate must obtain more than one-half of the total number of votes cast in the constituency in order to be elected. The Municipal and Provincial Assemblies of People's Power are elected by free, direct and secret ballot. Nominations for Municipal and Provincial Executive Committees of People's Power are submitted to the relevant assembly by a commission presided over by a representative of the Communist Party's leading organ and consisting of representatives of youth, workers', farmers', revolutionary and women's organizations. The President and Secretary of each of the regional and the provincial assemblies are the only full-time members, the other delegates carrying out their functions in addition to their normal employment.

The regular and extraordinary sessions of the local Assemblies of People's Power are public. More than one-half of the total number of members must be present in order for agreements made to be valid. Agreements are adopted by simple majority.

JUDICIARY

Judicial power is exercised by the People's Supreme Court and all other competent tribunals and courts. The People's Supreme Court is the supreme judicial authority and is accountable only to the National Assembly of People's Power. It can propose laws and issue regulations through its Council of Government. Judges are independent but the courts must inform the electorate of their activities at least once a year. Every accused person has the right to a defence and can be tried only by a tribunal.

The Office of the Attorney-General is subordinate only to the National Assembly and the Council of State and is responsible for ensuring that the law is properly obeyed.

The Constitution may be totally or partially modified only by a two-thirds majority vote in the National Assembly of People's Power. If the modification is total, or if it concerns the composition and powers of the National Assembly of People's Power or the Council of State, or the rights and duties contained in the Constitution, it also requires a positive vote by referendum.

The Government
(May 2001)

Head of State: Dr FIDEL CASTRO RUZ (took office 2 December 1976; re-elected December 1981, December 1986, March 1993 and February 1998).

COUNCIL OF STATE

President: Dr FIDEL CASTRO RUZ.

First Vice-President: Gen. RAÚL CASTRO RUZ.

Vice-Presidents:
JUAN ALMEIDA BOSQUE.
Gen. ABELARDO COLOMÉ IBARRA.
CARLOS LAGE DÁVILA.
JUAN ESTEBAN LAZO HERNÁNDEZ.
JOSÉ RAMÓN MACHADO VENTURA.

Secretary: Dr JOSÉ M. MIYAR BARRUECOS.

Members:
JOSÉ RAMÓN BALAGUER CABRERA.
VILMA ESPÍN GUILLOIS DE CASTRO.
Dr ARMANDO HART DÁVALOS.

ORLANDO LUGO FONTE.
REGLA MARTÍNEZ HERRERA.
MAÍA CARIDAD ABREUS RUIZ.
CONRADO MARTÍNEZ CORONA.
Gen. JULIO CASAS REGUEIRO.
MARCOS RAÚL AGUILERA GUETÓN.
JOSÉ LUIS RODRÍGUEZ GARCÍA.
SALVADOR VALDÉS MESA.
PEDRO MIRET PRIETO.
ROBERTO T. DÍAZ SOTOLONGO.
SERGIO CORRIERI HERNÁNDEZ.
ROBERTO FERNÁNDEZ RETAMAR.
FELIPE RAMÓN PÉREZ ROQUE.
MARCOS J. PORTAL LEÓN.
CARIDAD DIEGO BELLO.
JUAN CONTINO ASLÁN.
PEDRO ROSS LEAL.
OTTO RIVERO TORRES.
CARLOS MANUEL VALENCIAGA DÍAZ.
Dra ROSA ELENA SIMEÓN NEGRÍN.

COUNCIL OF MINISTERS

President: Dr FIDEL CASTRO RUZ.

First Vice-President: Gen. RAÚL CASTRO RUZ.

Secretary: CARLOS LAGE DÁVILA.

Vice-Presidents:
OSMANY CIENFUEGOS GORRIARÁN.
JOSÉ RAMÓN FERNÁNDEZ ALVAREZ.
PEDRO MIRET PRIETO.
JOSÉ LUIS RODRÍGUEZ GARCÍA.

Minister of Agriculture: ALFREDO JORDÁN MORALES.

Minister of Foreign Trade: RAÚL DE LA NUEZ RAMÍREZ.

Minister of Internal Trade: BÁRBARA CASTILLO CUESTA.

Minister of Information and Communications: Gen. ROBERTO IGNACIO GONZÁLEZ PLANAS.

Minister of Construction: JUAN MARIO JUNCO DEL PINO.

Minister of Culture: ABEL ENRIQUE PRIETO JIMÉNEZ.

Minister of Economy and Planning: JOSÉ LUIS RODRÍGUEZ GARCÍA.

Minister of Education: LUIS IGNACIO GÓMEZ GUTIÉRREZ.

Minister of Higher Education: FERNANDO VECINO ALEGRET.

Minister of the Revolutionary Armed Forces: Gen. RAÚL CASTRO RUZ.

Minister of Finance and Prices: JOSÉ MANUEL MILLARES RODRÍGUEZ.

Minister of the Food Industry: ALEJANDRO ROCA IGLESIAS.

Minister of Foreign Investment and Economic Co-operation: MARTHA LOMAS MORALES.

Minister of Sugar: Gen. ULISES ROSALES DEL TORO.

Minister of the Construction Materials Industry: (vacant).

Minister of Light Industry: JESÚS D. PÉREZ OTHÓN.

Minister of the Fishing Industry: ALFREDO LÓPEZ VALDÉS.

Minister of the Iron and Steel, Metallurgical and Electronic Industries: FERNANDO ACOSTA SANTANA.

Minister of Basic Industries: MARCOS J. PORTAL LEÓN.

Minister of the Interior: Gen. ABELARDO COLOMÉ IBARRA.

Minister of Justice: ROBERTO T. DÍAZ SOTOLONGO.

Minister of Foreign Affairs: FELIPE RAMÓN PÉREZ ROQUE.

Minister of Labour and Social Security: ALFREDO MORALES CARTAYA.

Minister of Public Health: CARLOS DOTRES MARTÍNEZ.

Minister of Science, Technology and the Environment: Dra ROSA ELENA SIMEÓN NEGRÍN.

Minister of Transport: ALVARO PÉREZ MORALES.

Minister of Tourism: IBRAHÍM FERRADAZ GARCÍA.

Minister of Auditing and Control: LINA PEDRAZA RODRÍGUEZ.

Minister, President of the State Committee for Technical and Material Supplies: SONIA RODRÍGUEZ CARDONA.

Minister, President of the State Committee for Statistics: FIDEL EMILIO VASCOS GONZÁLEZ.

Minister, President of the State Committee for Standardization: RAMÓN DARIAS RODÉS.

Minister, President of the Banco Central de Cuba: FRANCISCO SOBERÓN VALDÉS.

Ministers without Portfolio: RICARDO CABRISAS RUIZ, WILFREDO LÓPEZ RODRÍGUEZ.

MINISTRIES

Ministry of Agriculture: Avda Independencia, entre Conill y Sta Ana, Havana; tel. (7) 84-5770; fax (7) 33-5086.

Ministry of Auditing and Control: Havana.

Ministry of Basic Industries: Avda Salvador Allende 666, Havana; tel. (7) 70-7711.

Ministry of Construction: Avda Carlos M. de Céspedes y Calle 35, Havana; tel. (7) 81-8385; fax (7) 33-5585; e-mail dirinter@ceniai .inf.cu.

Ministry of the Construction Materials Industry: Calle 17, esq. 0, Vedado, Havana; tel. (7) 32-2541; fax (7) 33-3176.

Ministry of Culture: Calle 2, No 258, entre 11 y 13, Vedado, Havana; tel. (7) 55-2228; fax (7) 66-2053; e-mail rinter@min.cult.cu; internet www.cubarte.cult.cu.

Ministry of Economy and Planning: 20 de Mayo y Ayestarán, Plaza de la Revolución, Havana; fax (7) 33-3387.

Ministry of Education: Obispo 160, Havana; tel. (7) 61-4888.

Ministry of Finance and Prices: Obispo 211, esq. Cuba, Havana; tel. (7) 57-3280; fax (7) 33-8050; internet www2.cuba.cu/economia/ finanzas.

Ministry of the Fishing Industry: Avda 5 y 248 Jaimanitas, Santa Fé, Havana; tel. (7) 29-7034; fax (7) 24-9168; e-mail alvarez@ fishery.inf.cu.

Ministry of the Food Industry: Avda 41, No 4455, Playa, Havana; tel. (7) 23-6801; fax (7) 23-4052; e-mail minalvm1@ceniai.inf.cu.

Ministry of Foreign Affairs: Calzada 360, esq. G, Vedado, Havana; tel. (7) 55-3537; fax (7) 33-3460; e-mail cubaminrex@ minrex.gov.cu; internet www.cubaminrex.cu.

Ministry of Foreign Investment and Economic Co-operation: Primera No 2203, entre 22 y 24, Miramar, Havana; tel. (7) 22-3873; fax (7) 24-2105; e-mail epinv@minuce.cu.

Ministry of Foreign Trade: Infanta 16, esquina 23, Vedado, Havana; tel. (7) 55-0428; fax (7) 55-0376; e-mail cepecdir@infocex.cu; internet www.infocex.cu/cepec/.

Ministry of Higher Education: Calle 23, No 565, esq. a F, Vedado, Havana; tel. (7) 3-6655; fax (7) 33-3090; e-mail dri@reduniv .edu.cu.

Ministry of Information and Communications: Plaza de la Revolución 'José Martí', CP 10600, Havana; tel. (7) 81-7654.

Ministry of the Interior: Plaza de la Revolución, Havana.

Ministry of Internal Trade: Calle Habana 258, Havana; tel. (7) 62-5790.

Ministry of the Iron and Steel, Metallurgical and Electronic Industries: Avda Rancho Boyeros y Calle 100, Havana; tel. (7) 20-4861.

Ministry of Justice: Calle 0, No 216, entre 23 y Humboldt, Vedado, CP 10400, Havana 4; tel. (7) 32-6319.

Ministry of Labour and Social Security: Calle 23, esq. Calle P, Vedado, Havana; tel. (7) 70-4571; fax (7) 33-5816.

Ministry of Light Industry: Empedrado 302, Havana; tel. (7) 62-4041.

Ministry of Public Health: Calle 23, No 301, Vedado, Havana; tel. (7) 32-2561.

Ministry of the Revolutionary Armed Forces: Plaza de la Revolución, Havana.

Ministry of Science, Technology and the Environment: Havana.

Ministry of Sugar: Calle 23, No 171, Vedado, Havana; tel. (7) 30-5061.

Ministry of Tourism: Havana; internet www.cubatravel.cu.

Ministry of Transport: Avda Independencia y Tulipán, Havana; tel. (7) 81-2076.

Legislature

ASAMBLEA NACIONAL DEL PODER POPULAR

The National Assembly of People's Power was constituted on 2 December 1976. In July 1992 the National Assembly adopted a constitutional amendment providing for legislative elections by direct vote. Only candidates nominated by the PCC were permitted to contest the elections. At elections to the National Assembly conducted on 11 January 1998 all 601 candidates were elected. Of the 7.8m. registered voters, 98.35% participated in the elections. Only 5% of votes cast were blank or spoilt.

President: Ricardo Alarcón de Quesada.

Vice-President: Jaime Crombet Hernández Maurell.

Secretary: Dr Ernesto Suárez Méndez.

Political Organizations

Partido Comunista de Cuba (PCC) (Communist Party of Cuba): Havana; internet www2.cuba.cu/politica/webpcc; f. 1961 as the

Organizaciones Revolucionarias Integradas (ORI) from a fusion of the Partido Socialista Popular (Communist), Fidel Castro's Movimiento 26 de Julio and the Directorio Revolucionario 13 de Marzo; became the Partido Unido de la Revolución Socialista Cubana (PURSC) in 1962; renamed as the Partido Comunista de Cuba in 1965; 150-member Central Committee, Political Bureau (24 mems in 1997), and five Commissions; 706,132 mems (1994).

Political Bureau: Dr Fidel Castro Ruz, Gen. Raúl Castro Ruz, Juan Almeida Bosque, José Ramón Machado Ventura, Juan Esteban Lazo Hernández, Gen. Abelardo Colomé Ibarra, Pedro Ross Leal, Carlos Lage Dávila, Roberto Robaína González, Alfredo Jordán Morales, Gen. Ulises Rosales del Toro, Concepción Campa Huergo, Yadira García Vera, Abel Enrique Prieto Jiménez, Gen. Julio Casas Regueiro, Gen. Leopoldo Cintra Frías, Ricardo Alarcón de Quesada, José Ramón Balaguer Cabrera, Misael Enamorado Dager, Gen. Ramón Espinosa Martín, Marcos J. Portal León, Juan Carlos Robinson Agramonte, Pedro Sáez Montejo, Jorge Luis Sierra Cruz.

There are a number of dissident groups operating in Cuba. These include:

Concertación Democrática Cubana—CDC: f. 1991; alliance of 11 dissident organizations campaigning for political pluralism and economic reform; Leader Elizardo Sánchez Santa Cruz.

Cuban Democratic Platform: f. 1990; alliance comprising three dissident organizations:

Coordinadora Social Demócrata.

Partido Demócrata Cristiano de Cuba—PDC: POB 558987, Miami, FL 33155, USA; tel. (305) 264-9411; fax (954) 489-1572; e-mail amayawarry@aol.com; internet www.pdc-cuba.org.

Unión Liberal Cubana: Menéndez y Pelayo 83, 28007 Madrid, Spain; fax (91) 5011342; e-mail cubaliberal@mercuryin.es; internet www.cubaliberal.org; mem. of Liberal International; Founder and Chair. Carlos Alberto Montaner.

Partido Cubano Ortodoxo: f. 1999; Leader Nelson Aguiar.

Partido Liberal Democrático de Cuba: Chair. Osvaldo Alfonso Valdés.

Partido pro-Derechos Humanos: f. 1988 to defend human rights in Cuba; Pres. Hiram Abi Cobas; Sec.-Gen. Tania Díaz.

Partido Social Revolucionario Democrático de Cuba: POB 351081, Miami, FL 33135, USA; tel. and fax (305) 649-2886; e-mail soreb123@aol.com; Pres. Jorge Valls.

Partido Solidaridad Democrática—PSD: POB 310063, Miami, FL 33131, USA; tel. (305) 408-2659; e-mail gladyperez@aol.com; internet www.ccsi.com/~ams/psd; Pres. Fernando Sánchez López.

Solidaridad Cubana: Leader Fernando Sánchez López.

Diplomatic Representation

EMBASSIES IN CUBA

Algeria: Avda 5, No 2802, esq. 28, Miramar, Havana; tel. (7) 24-2835; fax (7) 24-2702; Ambassador: Rabah Kerouaz.

Angola: Avda 5, No 1012, entre 10 y 12, Miramar, Havana; tel. (7) 24-2474; fax (7) 24-2117; Ambassador: Joao Manuel Bernardo.

Argentina: Calle 36, No 511, entre 5 y 7, Miramar, Havana; tel. (7) 24-2972; fax (7) 24-2140; Ambassador: Oscar Torres Avalos (recalled February 2001).

Austria: Calle 4, No 101, entre 1 y 3, Miramar, Havana; tel. (7) 24-2824; fax (7) 24-1235; Ambassador: Dra Helga Konrad.

Belarus: Avda 5, No 3802, entre 38 y 40, Miramar, Havana; tel. (7) 33-0341; fax (7) 33-0340; Chargé d'affaires a.i.: Vladimir Pischaco.

Belgium: Avda 5, No 7408, esq. 76, Miramar, Havana; tel. (7) 24-2410; fax (7) 24-1318; Ambassador: Patrick de Beyter.

Belize: Avda 5, No 3608, entre 36 y 36A, Miramar, Havana; tel. (7) 24-3504; fax (7) 24-3506; e-mail belize.embassy@tip.etecsa.cu; Ambassador: Amalia Mai-Rancharan.

Benin: Calle 20, No 119, entre 1 y 3, Miramar, Havana; tel. (7) 24-2179; fax (7) 24-2334; Ambassador: Simplice Gnanguessy.

Bolivia: Calle 26, No 113, entre 1 y 3, Miramar, Havana; tel. (7) 24-2426; fax (7) 24-2127; Ambassador: Maria Eugenia Salinas Inarra.

Brazil: Calle Lamparilla, No 2, 4°K, Miramar, Havana; tel. (7) 66-9052; fax (7) 66-2912; Ambassador: Luciano Martins de Almeida.

Bulgaria: Calle B, No 252, entre 11 y 13, Vedado, Havana; tel. (7) 33-3125; fax (7) 33-3297; Chargé d'affaires a.i.: Emilia Stefanova.

Burkina Faso: Calle 40, No 516, entre 5 y 7A, Miramar, Havana; tel. (7) 24-2217; fax (7) 24-1942; e-mail ambfaso@cenia.inf.cu; Ambassador: Salif Nébié.

Cambodia: Avda 5, No 7001, esq. 70, Miramar, Havana; tel. (7) 24-1496; fax (7) 24-6400; Ambassador: Chim Prorng.

Canada: Calle 30, No 518, entre 5 y 7, Miramar, Havana; tel. (7) 24-2516; fax (7) 24-2044; e-mail havan@dfait-maeci.gc.ca; Chargé d'affaires a.i.: JENNIFER IRISH.

Cape Verde: Calle 20, No 2001, esq. 7, Miramar, Havana; tel. (7) 24-2979; fax (7) 24-1072; e-mail ecvc@ceniai.inf.cu; Ambassador: FATIMA LIMA VEIGA.

Chile: Avda 33, No 1423, entre 16 y 18, Mitamar, Havana; tel. (7) 24-1222; fax (7) 24-1694; Ambassador: GERMÁN GUERRERO PAVEZ.

China, People's Republic: Calle 13, No 551, Vedado, Havana; tel. (7) 33-3005; fax (7) 33-3092; Ambassador: WANG CHENGJIA.

Colombia: Calle 14, No 515, entre 5 y 7, Miramar, Havana; tel. (7) 24-1246; fax (7) 24-1249; Ambassador: JULIO LONDOÑO PAREDES.

Congo, Republic: Avda 5, No 1003, Miramar, Havana; tel. and fax 24-9055; Ambassador: PASCAL ONGUEMBY.

Czech Republic: Avda Kohly 259, entre 41 y 43, Nuevo Vedado, Havana; tel. (7) 33-3201; fax (7) 33-3596; Chargé d'affaires a.i.: JOSEF MARSICEK.

Dominican Republic: Avda 5, No 9202, entre 92 y 94, Miramar, Havana; tel. (7) 24-8429; fax (7) 24-8431; Ambassador: Dr DANIEL GUERRERO TAVERAS.

Ecuador: Avda 5A, No 4407, entre 44 y 46, Miramar, Havana; tel. (7) 24-2034; fax (7) 24-2868; Ambassador: JOSÉ EDUARDO TOBAR FIERRO.

Egypt: Avda 5, No 1801, esq. 18, Miramar, Havana; tel. (7) 24-2441; fax (7) 24-0905; Ambassador: HAZEM MUHAMMAD TAHER.

Ethiopia: Calle 6, No 318, Miramar, Havana; tel. (7) 22-1260; Ambassador: ABEBE BELAYNEH.

Finland: Havana; tel. (7) 33-2698; Ambassador: HEIKKI PUURUNEN.

France: Calle 14, No 312, entre 3 y 5, Miramar, Havana; tel. (7) 24-2132; fax (7) 24-1439; Ambassador: JEAN DÉVY.

Germany: Calle B, No 652, esq. 13, Vedado, Havana; tel. (7) 33-2539; fax (7) 33-1586; Ambassador: Dr REINHOLD HUBER.

Ghana: Avda 5, No 1808, esq. 20, Miramar, Havana; tel. (7) 24-2153; fax (7) 24-2317; Ambassador: Dr KWAKU DANSO-BOAFO.

Greece: Avda 5, No 7802, esq. 78, Miramar, Havana; tel. (7) 24-2995; fax (7) 24-1784; Ambassador: GEORGE COSTOULAS.

Guatemala: Calle 16, No 505, entre 3 y 5, Miramar, Havana; tel. 24-3417; fax 24-3200; Ambassador: HUGO RENÉ GUZMÁN MALDONADO.

Guinea: Calle 20, No 504, entre 5 y 7, Miramar, Havana; tel. (7) 24-2003; fax (7) 24-2380; Ambassador: CHEICK ALIOUNE CONDÉ.

Guinea-Bissau: Calle 14, No 313, entre 3 y 5, Miramar, Havana; tel. (7) 24-2689; fax (7) 24-2794; Chargé d'affaires a.i.: LIBERATO GOMES.

Guyana: Calle 18, No 506, entre 5 y 7, Miramar, Havana; tel. (7) 24-2094; fax (7) 24-2867; Chargé d'affaires: TIMOTHY N. CRICHLOW.

Haiti: No 6804, entre 68 y 70, Miramar, Havana; tel. (7) 24-5421; fax (7) 24-5423; Chargé d'affaires a.i.: JEAN WILLIAM EXANTUS.

Holy See: Calle 12, No 514, entre 5 y 7, Miramar, Havana (Apostolic Nunciature); tel. (7) 24-2700; fax (7) 24-2257; e-mail csa@pcn.net; Apostolic Nuncio: Most Rev. LUIS ROBLES DÍAZ, Titular Archbishop of Stefaniaco.

Hungary: Calle G, No 458, entre 19 y 21, Vedado, Havana; tel. (7) 33-3365; fax (7) 33-3286; e-mail embhuncu@ceniai.inf.cu; Ambassador: VILMOS KOPÁNYI.

India: Calle 21, No 202, esq. a K, Vedado, Havana; tel. (7) 33-3777; fax (7) 33-3287; e-mail eoihav@ceniai.inf.cu; Ambassador: RAMIAH RAJAGOPALAN.

Indonesia: Avda 5, No 1607, esq. 18, Miramar, Havana; tel. (7) 24-9618; fax (7) 24-9617; Ambassador: Dr R. HARIDADI SUDJONO.

Iran: Avda 5, No 3002, esq. 30, Miramar, Havana; tel. (7) 24-2675; fax (7) 24-2770; Ambassador: SEYED DAVOOD MOHSENI SALEHI MONFARED.

Iraq: Avda 5, No 8201, entre 82 y 84, Miramar, Havana; tel. (7) 24-1607; fax (7) 24-2157; Ambassador: MUHAMMED MAHMOUD K. H. AL-AMILI.

Italy: Paseo 606, No 54, entre 25 y 27, Vedado, Havana; tel. (7) 33-3334; fax (7) 33-3416; e-mail ambitcub@ip.etecsa.cu; Ambassador: GIUSEPPE MOSCATO.

Jamaica: Avda 5, No 3608, entre 36 y 36A, Miramar, Havana; tel. (7) 24-2908; fax (7) 24-2531; e-mail embjmcub@mail.infocom.etecsa.cu; Ambassador: CARLYLE DUNKLEY.

Japan: Centro de Negocios Miramar, Avda 3, No 1, 5°, esq. 80, Miramar, Havana; tel. (7) 24-3508; fax (7) 24-8902; Ambassador: MUTSUO MABUCHI.

Korea, Democratic People's Republic: Calle 17, No 752, Vedado, Havana; tel. (7) 66-2313; fax (7) 33-3073; Ambassador: PAK TONG-CHUN.

Laos: Avda 5, No 2808, esq. 30, Miramar, Havana; tel. (7) 24-1056; fax (7) 24-9622; Ambassador: CHANPHENG SIHAPHOM.

Lebanon: Calle 17A, No 16403, entre 164 y 174, Siboney, Havana; tel. (7) 28-6220; fax (7) 28-6432; e-mail lbcunet@ceniai.inf.cu; Ambassador: SLEIMAN C. RASSI.

Libya: Avda 7, No 1402, esq. 14, Miramar, Havana; tel. (7) 24-2192; fax (7) 24-2991; Chargé d'affaires a.i.: ABDULLATIF H. EL-KHAZMI.

Mexico: Calle 12, No 518, Miramar, Playa, Havana; tel. (7) 24-2553; fax (7) 24-2717; Ambassador: RICARDO PASCOE.

Mongolia: Calle 66, No 505, esq. 5, Miramar, Havana; tel. (7) 24-2763; fax (7) 24-0639; Ambassador: BALJIN NYAMAA.

Mozambique: Avda 7, No 2203, entre 22 y 24, Miramar, Havana; tel. (7) 24-2443; fax (7) 24-2232; Ambassador: JULIO GONCALO BRAGA.

Namibia: Avda 5, No 4406, entre 44 y 46, Miramar, Havana; tel. (7) 24-1430; fax (7) 24-1431; e-mail embnamib@ceniai.inf.cu; Ambassador: ELÍA AKWAAKE.

Netherlands: Calle 8, No 307, entre 3 y 5, Miramar, Havana; tel. (7) 24-2511; fax (7) 24-2059; Ambassador: CORNELIA MINDERHOUD.

Nicaragua: Calle 20, No 709, entre 7 y 9, Miramar, Havana; tel. (7) 24-1025; fax (7) 24-6323; Chargé d'affaires a.i.: Dr LUIS NAPOLEÓN GADEA ARÓSTEGUI.

Nigeria: Avda 5, No 1401, entre 14 y 16, Miramar, Havana; tel. (7) 24-2898; fax (7) 24-2202; Ambassador: NGAM NWACHUKWU.

Panama: Calle 26, No 109, entre 1 y 3, Miramar, Havana; tel. (7) 24-1673; fax (7) 24-1674; Ambassador: MARCO ANTONIO ALARCÓN PALOMINO.

Paraguay: Calle 34, No 503, entre 5 y 7, Miramar, Havana; tel. (7) 24-0884; fax (7) 24-0883; Chargé d'affaires a.i.: ANASTACIO MEDINA ARMOA.

Peru: Calle 30, No 107, entre 1 y 3, Miramar, Havana; tel. (7) 24-2477; fax (7) 24-2636; Ambassador: JUAN CASTILLA MEZA.

Philippines: Avda 5, No 2207, esq. 24, Miramar, Havana; tel. (7) 24-1372; fax (7) 24-2915; e-mail philhav@ip.etecsa.cu; Ambassador: WENCESLAO JOSÉ O. QUIROLGICO.

Poland: Cale G, No 452, esq. 19, Vedado, Havana; tel. (7) 66-2439; fax (7) 66-2442; Ambassador: JAN JANISZEWSKI.

Portugal: Avda 5, No 6604, entre 66 y 68, Miramar, Havana; tel. (7) 24-2871; fax (7) 24-2593; Ambassador: MANUEL SILVA DUARTE COSTA.

Romania: Calle 21, No 307, Vedado, Havana; tel. (7) 33-3325; fax (7) 33-3324; Chargé d'affaires a.i.: CONSTANTIN RUSEI.

Russia: Avda 5, No 6402, entre 62 y 66, Miramar, Havana; tel. (7) 24-2686; fax (7) 24-1038; Ambassador: ANDREI VICTOROVICH DIMITRIEV.

Slovakia: Calle 66, No 521, entre 5B y 7, Miramar, Havana; tel. (7) 24-1884; fax (7) 24-1883; Chargé d'affaires a.i.: JÁN GÁBOR.

South Africa: Avda 5, No 4201, esq. 42, Miramar, Havana; tel. (7) 24-9658; fax (7) 24-1101; Ambassador: NOEL MAKHAYA NDLOU JOHN MOSIA.

Spain: Cárcel No 51, esq. Zulueta, Havana; tel. (7) 33-8025; fax (7) 33-8006; Ambassador: EDUARDO JUNCO BONET.

Sri Lanka: Calle 32, No 307, entre 3 y 5, Miramar, Havana; tel. (7) 24-2562; fax (7) 24-2183; e-mail sri.lanka@ip.etecsa.cu; Chargé d'affaires a.i. JAYANTHA DISSANAYAKE.

Sweden: Calle 34, No 510, entre 5 y 7, Miramar, Havana; tel. (7) 24-2831; fax (7) 24-1194; e-mail ambassaden.havanna@foreign.ministry.se; Ambassador: EIVOR HALKJAER.

Switzerland: Avda 5, No 2005, entre 20 y 22, Miramar, Havana; tel. (7) 24-2611; fax (7) 24-1148; e-mail swissem@ip.etecsa.cu; Ambassador: JEAN-CAUDE RICHARD.

Syria: Avda 5, No 7402, entre 74 y 76, Miramar, Havana; tel. (7) 24-2266; fax (7) 24-2829; Chargé d'affaires: Dr CHAHIN FARAH.

Turkey: Avda 5A, No 3805, entre 36 y 40, Miramar, Havana; tel. (7) 24-1205; fax (7) 24-2899; e-mail turkemb@ip.etecsa.cu; Ambassador: ATAMAN YALGIN.

Uganda: Calle 20, No 713, entre 7 y 9, Miramar, Havana; tel. (7) 24-0469; fax (7) 33-6668; Ambassador: ELIZABETH PAULA NAPEYOK.

Ukraine: Avda 5, No 4405, entre 44 y 46, Miramar, Havana; tel. (7) 24-2586; fax (7) 24-2341; Ambassador: EVGEN G. SVINARCHUK.

United Kingdom: Calle 34, No 702/4, esq. 7, Miramar, Havana; tel. (7) 24-1771; fax (7) 24-8104; e-mail embrit@ceniai.inf.cu; Ambassador: DAVID RIDGWAY.

USA (Relations broken off in 1961): Interests Section: Calzada, entre L y M, Vedado, Havana; tel. (7) 33-3543; fax (7) 66-2095; Counsellor and Principal Officer: VICKY HUDDLESTON.

Uruguay: Calle 14, No 506, entre 5 y 7, Miramar, Havana; tel. (7) 24-2311; fax (7) 24-2246; e-mail urucub@ceniai.inf.cu; Ambassador: ENRIQUE ESTRÁZULAS.

Venezuela: Calle 36A, No 704, entre 7 y 42, Miramar, Havana; tel. (7) 24-2662; fax (7) 24-2773; e-mail vencuba@ceniai.cu; Chargé d'affaires a.i.: ROCÍO MANEIRO.

Viet Nam: Avda 5, No 1802, Miramar, Havana; tel. (7) 24-1502; fax (7) 24-1041; Ambassador: THAI VAN LUNG.

Yemen: Calle 16, No 503, entre 5 y 7, Miramar, Havana; tel. (7) 24-1506; fax (7) 24-1131; Ambassador: Dr AHMED ABDULLA ABDUL ELAH.

Yugoslavia: Calle 42, No 115, entre 1 y 3, Miramar, Havana; tel. (7) 24-2488; fax (7) 24-2982; Ambassador: VELIMIR LALEVIC.

Zimbabwe: Avda 3, No 1001, esq. a 10, Miramar, Havana; tel. (7) 24-2857; fax (7) 24-2720; Ambassador: JEVANA BEN MASEKO.

Judicial System

The judicial system comprises the People's Supreme Court, the People's Provincial Courts and the People's Municipal Courts. The People's Supreme Court exercises the highest judicial authority.

PEOPLE'S SUPREME COURT

The People's Supreme Court comprises the Plenum, the six Courts of Justice in joint session and the Council of Government. When the Courts of Justice are in joint session they comprise all the professional and lay judges, the Attorney-General and the Minister of Justice. The Council of Government comprises the President and Vice-President of the People's Supreme Court, the Presidents of each Court of Justice and the Attorney-General of the Republic. The Minister of Justice may participate in its meetings.

President: Dr RUBÉN REMIGIO FERRO.

Vice-Presidents: Dr MANUEL DE JESÚS PÉREZ PÉREZ, Dra GRACIELA PRIETO MARTÍN.

Criminal Court:
President: Dr JORGE L. BODES TORRES.

Civil and Administrative Court:
President: ANDRÉS BOLAÑOS GASSÓ.

Labour Court:
President: Dr ANTONIO R. MARTÍN SÁNCHEZ.

Court for State Security:
President: Dr GUILLERMO HERNÁNDEZ INFANTE.

Economic Court:
President: Dr ELPIDIO PÉREZ SUÁREZ.

Military Court:
President: Col JUAN MARINO FUENTES CALZADO.

Attorney-General: JUAN ESCALONA REGUERA.

Religion

There is no established Church, and all religions are permitted, though Roman Catholicism predominates. The Afro-Cuban religions of Regla de Ocha (Santéria) and Regla Conga (Palo Monte) also have numerous adherents.

CHRISTIANITY

Consejo Ecuménico de Cuba (Ecumenical Council of Cuba): Calle 14, No 304, entre 3 y 5, Miramar, Playa, Havana; tel. (7) 33-1792; fax (7) 33-178820; f. 1941; 11 mem. churches; Pres. Rev. ORESTES GONZÁLEZ; Exec. Sec. Rev. JOSÉ LÓPEZ.

The Roman Catholic Church

Cuba comprises three archdioceses and eight dioceses. At 31 December 1998 there were 5,907,600 adherents, representing about 50% of the total population.

Conferencia de Obispos Católicos de Cuba—COCC (Bishops' Conference): Calle 26, No 314, entre 3 y 5, Miramar, Apdo 594, Havana; tel. (7) 29-2395; fax (7) 24-2168; e-mail dei@cocc.co.cu; f. 1983; Pres. ADOLFO RODRÍGUEZ HERRERA, Archbishop of Camagüey.

Archbishop of Camagüey: ADOLFO RODRÍGUEZ HERRERA, Calle Luaces, No 55, Apdo 105, Camagüey 70100; tel. (322) 92268; fax (322) 87143.

Archbishop of San Cristóbal de la Habana: Cardinal JAIME LUCAS ORTEGA Y ALAMINO, Calle Habana 152, esq. a Chacón, Apdo 594, Havana 10100; tel. (7) 62-4000; fax (7) 33-8109; e-mail cocc@ brigadoon.com.

Archbishop of Santiago de Cuba: PEDRO CLARO MEURICE ESTIÚ, Sánchez Hechevarría 607, Apdo 26, Santiago de Cuba 90100; tel. (226) 25480; fax (226) 86186.

The Anglican Communion

Anglicans are adherents of the Iglesia Episcopal de Cuba (Episcopal Church of Cuba).

Bishop of Cuba: Rt Rev. JORGE PERERA HURTADO, Calle 6, No 273, Vedado, Havana 10400; fax (7) 33-3293.

Protestant Churches

Convención Bautista de Cuba Oriental (Baptist Convention of Eastern Cuba): San Jerónimo, No 467, entre Calvario y Carnicería, Santiago; tel. 2-0173; f. 1905; Pres. Rev. Dr ROY ACOSTA; Sec. RAFAEL MUSTELIER.

Iglesia Metodista en Cuba (Methodist Church in Cuba): Calle K, No 502, 25 y 27, Vedado, Apdo 10400, Havana; tel. (7) 32-2991; fax (7) 33-3135; e-mail imecu@ip.etecsa.cu; autonomous since 1968; 6,000 mems; Bishop RICARDO PEREIRA DÍAZ.

Iglesia Presbiteriana-Reformada en Cuba (Presbyterian-Reformed Church in Cuba): Apdo 154, Matanzas; autonomous since 1967; 8,000 mems; Gen. Sec. Rev. Dr SERGIO ARCE.

Other denominations active in Cuba include the Apostolic Church of Jesus Christ, the Bethel Evangelical Church, the Christian Pentecostal Church, the Church of God, the Church of the Nazarene, the Free Baptist Convention, the Holy Pentecost Church, the Pentecostal Congregational Church and the Salvation Army.

The Press

DAILY

In October 1990 President Castro announced that, in accordance with other wide-ranging economic austerity measures, only one newspaper, *Granma*, would henceforth be published as a nationwide daily. The other national dailies were to become weeklies or were to cease publication.

Granma: Avda Gen. Suárez y Territorial, Plaza de la Revolución, Apdo 6187, Havana; tel. (7) 81-3333; fax (7) 33-5176; e-mail redac@ granmai.get.cma.net; internet www.granma.cubaweb.cu; f. 1965 to replace *Hoy* and *Revolución*; official Communist Party organ; Dir FRANK AGÜERO GÓMEZ; circ. 400,000.

PERIODICALS

Adelante: Avda A, Rpto Jayamá, Camagüey; f. 1959; morning; Dir EVARISTO SARDIÑAS VERA; circ. 42,000.

Ahora: Salida a San Germán y Circunvalación, Holguín; f. 1962; Dir RADOBALDO MARTÍNEZ PÉREZ; circ. 50,000.

ANAP: Línea 206, entre H e I, Vedado, Havana; f. 1961; monthly; information for small farmers; Dir LEONEL VÁLDEZ ALONSO; circ. 30,000.

Bastión: Territorial esq. a Gen. Suárez, Plaza de la Revolución, Havana; tel. (7) 79-3361; organ of the Revolutionary Armed Forces; Dir FRANK AGÜERO GÓMEZ; circ. 65,000.

Bohemia: Avda Independencia y San Pedro, Apdo 6000, Havana; tel. (7) 81-9213; fax (7) 33-5511; e-mail bohemia@bohemia.get.tor.cu; f. 1908; weekly; politics; Dir JOSÉ FERNÁNDEZ VEGA; circ. 100,000.

Boletín Alimentaria de Cuba: Amargura 103, 10100 Havana; tel. (7) 62-9245; f. 1996; quarterly; food industry; Dir ANTONIO CAMPOS; circ. 10,000.

El Caimán Barbudo: Paseo 613, Vedado, Havana; f. 1966; monthly; cultural; Dir ALEX PAUSIDES; circ. 47,000.

Cinco de Septiembre: Calle 35, No 5609, entre 56 y 58, Cienfuegos; f. 1980; Dir FRANCISCO VALDÉS PETITÓN; circ. 18,000.

Cómicos: Calle 28, No 112, entre 1 y 3, Miramar, Havana; tel. (7) 22-5892; monthly; humorous; circ. 70,000.

Con la Guardia en Alto: Havana; f. 1961; monthly; for mems of the Committees for the Defence of the Revolution; Dir OMELIA GUERRA PÉREZ; circ. 60,000.

Cuba Internacional: Calle 21, No 406, Vedado, Havana 4, Apdo 3603 Havana 3; tel. (7) 32-3578; fax (7) 32-3268; f. 1959; monthly; political; Dir FÉLIX ALBISÚ; circ. 30,000.

Dedeté: Territorial y Gen. Suárez, Plaza de la Revolución, Apdo 6344, Havana; tel. (7) 82-0134; fax (7) 81-8621; e-mail jrebelde@ teleda.get.cma.net; f. 1969; monthly; Dir ALEN LAUZÁN; circ. 70,000.

La Demajagua: Amado Estévez, esq. Calle 10, Rpto R. Reyes, Bayamo; f. 1977; Dir PEDRO MORA ESTRADA; circ. 21,000.

El Deporte, Derecho del Pueblo: Vía Blanca y Boyeros, Havana; tel. (7) 40-6838; f. 1968; monthly; sport; Dir MANUEL VAILLANT CARPENTE; circ. 15,000.

Escambray: Adolfo del Castillo 10, Sancti Spíritus; tel. (41) 23003; e-mail escambray@esiss.colombus.cu; internet www.escambray .islagrande.cu; f. 1979; Dir JUAN ANTONIO BORREGO DÍAZ; circ. 21,000.

Girón: Avda Camilo Cienfuegos No 10505, P. Nuero, Matanzas; f. 1960; Dir OTHONIEL GONZÁLEZ QUEVEDO; circ. 25,000.

Guerrillero: Colón esq. Delicias y Adela Azcuy, Pinar del Río; f. 1969; Dir RONALD SUÁREZ; circ. 33,000.

El Habanero: Gen. Suárez y Territorial, Plaza de la Revolución, Apdo 6269, Havana; tel. (7) 6160; f. 1987; Dir TUBAL PÁEZ HERNÁNDEZ; circ. 21,000.

Invasor: Marcial Gómez 401, esq. Estrada Palma, Ciego de Avila; f. 1979; Dir Migdalia Utrera Peña; circ. 10,500.

Juventud Rebelde: Territorial esq. Gen. Suárez, Plaza de la Revolución, Apdo 6344, Havana; tel. (7) 82-0155; fax (7) 33-8959; e-mail cida@jrebelde.cip.cu; internet www.jrebelde.cubaweb.cu; f. 1965; organ of the Young Communist League; Dir Rogelio Polanco Fuentes; circ. 250,000.

Juventud Técnica: Prado 553, esq. Teniente Rey, Habana Vieja, Havana; tel. (7) 31-1825; e-mail eabril@jcce.org.cu; f. 1965; monthly; scientific-technical; Dir Miriam Zito Valdés; circ. 20,000.

Mar y Pesca: San Ignacio 303, Havana; tel. (7) 61-5518; fax 33-8438; f. 1965; quarterly; fishing; Dir Gustavo López; circ. 20,000.

El Militante Comunista: Calle 11, No 160, Vedado, Havana; tel. (7) 32-7581; f. 1967; monthly; Communist Party publication; Dir Manuel Menéndez; circ. 200,000.

Moncada: Belascoaín esq. Zanja, Havana; tel. (7) 79-7109; f. 1966; monthly; Dir Ricardo Martínez; circ. 70,000.

Muchacha: Galiano 264, esq. Neptuno, Havana; tel. (7) 61-5919; f. 1980; monthly; young women's magazine; Dir Silvia Martínez; circ. 120,000.

Mujeres: Galiano 264, esq. Neptuno, Havana; tel. (7) 61-5919; f. 1961; monthly; women's magazine; Dir Regla Zulueta; circ. 270,000.

El Muñe: Calle 28, No 112, entre 1 y 3, Mirimar, Havana; tel. (7) 22-5892; weekly; circ. 50,000.

Opciones: Territorial esq. Gen. Suárez, Plaza de la Revolucíon, Havana; e-mail jrebelde@teleda.get.cma.net; internet www .cubaweb.cu/jrebelde/index.html; weekly; finance, commerce and tourism.

Opina: Edif. Focsa, M entre 17 y 19, Havana; f. 1979; 2 a month; consumer-orientated; published by Institute of Internal Demand; Dir Eugenio Rodríguez Balari; circ. 250,000.

Pablo: Calle 28, No 112, entre 1 y 3, Mirimar, Havana; tel. (7) 22-5892; 16 a year; circ. 53,000.

Palante: Calle 21, No 954, entre 8 y 10, Vedado, Havana; tel. (7) 3-5098; f. 1961; weekly; humorous; Dir Rosendo Gutiérrez Román; circ. 235,000.

Pionero: Calle 17, No 354, Havana 4; tel. (7) 32-4571; f. 1961; weekly; children's magazine; Dir Pedro González (Péglez); circ. 210,000.

Prisma: Calle 21 y Avda G, No 406, Vedado, Havana; tel. (7) 8-7995; f. 1979; bimonthly; international news; Man. Dir Luis Manuel Arce; circ. 15,000 (Spanish), 10,000 (English).

RIL: O'Reilly 358, Havana; tel. (7) 62-0777; f. 1972; 2 a month; technical; Dir Exec. Council of Publicity Dept, Ministry of Light Industry; Chief Officer Mireya Crespo; circ. 8,000.

Sierra Maestra: Avda de Los Desfiles, Santiago de Cuba; tel. (7) 2-2813; f. 1957; weekly; Dir Arnaldo Clavel Carmenaty; circ. 45,000.

Sol de Cuba: Calle 19, No 60, entre M y N, Vedado, Havana 4; tel. (7) 32-9881; f. 1983; every 3 months; Spanish, English and French editions; Gen. Dir Alcides Giro Mitjans; Editorial Dir Doris Vélez; circ. 200,000.

Somos Jóvenes: Calle 17, No 354, esq. H, Vedado, Havana; tel. (7) 32-4571; f. 1977; monthly; Dir Guillermo Cabrera; circ. 200,000.

Trabajadores: Territorial esq. Gen. Suárez, Plaza de la Revolución, Havana; tel. (7) 79-0819; f. 1970; organ of the trade-union movement; Dir Jorge Luis Canela Ciurana; circ. 150,000.

Tribuna de la Habana: Territorial esq. Gen. Suárez, Plaza de la Revolución, Havana; tel. (7) 81-5932; f. 1980; weekly; Dir Angel Zúñiga Suárez; circ. 90,000.

Vanguardia: Céspedes 5 (altos), Santa Clara, Matanzas; f. 1962; Dir Pedro Hernández Soto; circ. 24,000.

Venceremos: Carretera Jamaica, Km 1½, Guantánamo; tel. (7) 35980; f. 1962; Dir Haydée León Moya; circ. 28,000.

Ventiseis: Avda Carlos J. Finley, Las Tunas; f. 1977; Dir José Infantes Reyes; circ. 21,000.

Verde Olivo: Avda de Rancho Boyeros y San Pedro, Havana; tel. (7) 79-8373; f. 1959; monthly; organ of the Revolutionary Armed Forces; Dir Eugenio Suárez Pérez; circ. 100,000.

Victoria: Carretera de la Fe, Km 1½, Plaza de la Revolución, Nueva Gerona, Isla de la Juventud; f. 1967; Dir Nieve Varona Puente; circ. 9,200.

PRESS ASSOCIATIONS

Unión de Periodistas de Cuba: Calle 23, No 452, esq. I, Vedado, 10400 Havana; tel. (7) 32-7098; fax (7) 33-3079; e-mail upec@jcce.org.cu; f. 1963; Pres. Tubal Páez Hernández.

Unión de Escritores y Artistas de Cuba: Calle 17, No 351, Vedado, Havana; tel. (7) 32-4571; fax (7) 33-3158; Pres. Abel E. Prieto Jiménez; Exec. Vice-Pres. Lisandro Otero.

NEWS AGENCIES

Agencia de Información Nacional (AIN): Calle 23, No 358, esq. a J, Vedado, Havana; tel. (7) 32-5541; fax (7) 66-2049; e-mail RPT@ain.sld.cu; national news agency; Dir Roberto Pavón Tamayo.

Prensa Latina (Agencia Informativa Latinoamericana, SA): Calle 23, No 201, esq. a N, Vedado, Havana; tel. (7) 32-5561; fax (7) 33-3069; e-mail dirdifu@prensa-latina.cu; internet www .prensa-latina.cu; f. 1959; Dir Pedro Margolles Villanueva.

Foreign Bureaux

Agence France-Presse (AFP): Calle 17, No 4, 13°, entre N y 0, Vedado, Havana; tel. (7) 33-3503; fax (7) 33-3034; e-mail mlsanz@ip .etecsa.cu; Bureau Chief Marie Sanz.

Agencia EFE (Spain): Calle 36, No 110, entre 1 y 3, Miramar, Apdo 5, Havana; tel. (7) 33-2293; fax (7) 33-2272; Bureau Chief Soledad Marín Martín.

Agenzia Nazionale Stampa Associata (ANSA) (Italy): Edif. Fomeillán, Línea 5, Dpt 12, Vedado, Havana; tel. (7) 33-3542; Correspondent Katty Salerno.

Associated Press (AP) (USA): Havana.

Bulgarska Telegrafna Agentsia (BTA) (Bulgaria): Edif. Focsa, Calle 17, esq. M, Vedado, Apdo 22e, Havana; tel. (7) 32-4779; Bureau Chief Vasil Mikoulach.

Česká tisková kancelář (ČTK) (Czech Republic): Edif. Fajardo, Calle 17 y M, Vedado, Apdo 3a, Vedado, Havana; tel. (7) 32-6101; Bureau Chief Pavel Zovadil.

Deutsche Presse-Agentur (dpa) (Germany): Edif. Focsa, Calle 17 y M, Vedado, Apdo 2k, Havana; tel. (7) 33-3501; Bureau Chief Victorio Copa.

Informatsionnoye Telegrafnoye Agentstvo Rossii–Telegrafnoye Agentstvo Suverennykh Stran (ITAR–TASS) (Russia): Calle 96, No 317, entre 3 y 5, Miramar, Havana; tel. (7) 29-2528; Bureau Chief Aleksandr Kanichev.

Inter Press Service (IPS) (Italy): Calle 36a, No 121 Bajos, esq. a 3, Miramar, Apdo 1, Havana; tel. (7) 22-1981; Bureau Chief Claude Joseph Hackin; Correspondent Carlos Bastista Moreno.

Korean Central News Agency (Democratic People's Republic of Korea): Calle 10, No 613, esq. 25, Vedado, Apdo 6, Havana; tel. (7) 31-4201; Bureau Chief Chang Yon Chol.

Magyar Távirati Iroda (MTI) (Hungary): Edif. Fajardo, Calle 17 y M, Apdo 2c, Havana; tel. (7) 32-8353; Bureau Chief: Zoltán Takacs; Correspondent Tibor Császár.

Novinska Agencija Tanjug (Yugoslavia): Calle 5f, No 9801, esq. 98, Miramar, Havana; tel. (7) 22-7671; Bureau Chief Dušan Daković.

Polska Agencja Prasowa (PAP) (Poland): Calle 6, No 702, Apdo 5, entre 7 y 9, Miramar; Havana; tel. (7) 20-7067; Bureau Chief Piotr Sommerfed.

Reuters (United Kingdom): Edif. Someillán, Linea 5, 9°, Vedado, Havana 4; tel. (7) 33-3145; Bureau Chief Frances Kerry.

Rossiyskoye Informatsionnoye Agentstvo–Novosti (RIA–Novosti) (Russia): Calle 28, No 510, entre 5 y 7, Miramar, Havana; tel. (7) 22-4129; Bureau Chief Yurii Goloviatenko.

Viet Nam Agency (VNA): Calle 16, No 514, 1°, entre 5 y 7, Miramar, Havana; tel. (7) 2-4455; Bureau Chief Pham Dinh Loi.

Xinhua (New China) News Agency (People's Republic of China): Calle G, No 259, esq. 13, Vedado, Havana; tel. (7) 32-4616; Bureau Chief Gao Yonghua.

Publishers

Casa de las Américas: Calle 3 y Avda G, Vedado, Havana; tel. (7) 32-3587; fax (7) 32-7272; e-mail casa@arsoft.cult.cu; f. 1960; Latin American literature and social sciences; Dir Roberto Fernández Retamar.

Ediciones Unión: Calle 17, No 354 esq. a H, Vedado, Havana; tel. (7) 55-3112; fax (7) 33-3158; e-mail uneac@artsoft.cult.cu; f.1962; publishing arm of the Unión de Escritores y Artistas de Cuba; Cuban literature, art; Dir Mercy Ruiz.

Editora Abril: Prado 553, esq. Teniente Rey, Habana Vieja, Havana; tel. (7) 62-7871; fax (7) 62-7871; e-mail eabril@tinored.cu; f. 1980; attached to the Union of Young Communists; children's literature; Dir Iroel Sánchez Espinosa.

Editora Política: Belascoaín No 864, esq. a Desagüe y Peñalver, Havana; tel. (7) 79-8553; fax (7) 81-1084; e-mail editors@epol .cipcc.get.cma.net; f. 1963; publishing institution of the Communist Party of Cuba; Dir Santiago Dórquez Pérez.

Editorial Academia: Industria No 452, esq. a San José, Habana Vieja, Havana; tel. (7) 62-9501; f. 1963; attached to the Ministry of Science, Technology and the Environment; scientific and technical; Dir Miriam Raya Hernández.

Editorial de Ciencias Médicas y Centro Nacional de Información de Ciencias Médicas: Calle E, No 452, entre 19 y 21, Vedado, Apdo 6520, Havana 10400; tel. (7) 32-4519; fax (7) 32-5008; attached to the Ministry of Public Health; books and magazines specializing in the medical sciences; Dir Augusto Hernández Batista.

Editorial Ciencias Sociales: Calle 14, No 4104, entre 41 y 43, Miramar, Playa, Havana; tel. (7) 23-3959; f. 1967; attached to the Cuban Book Institute; social and political literature, history, philosophy, juridical sciences and economics; Dir Ricardo García Pampín.

Editorial Científico-Técnica: Calle 2, No 58, entre 3 y 5, Vedado, Havana; tel. (7) 3-9417; f. 1967; attached to the Ministry of Culture; technical and scientific literature; Dir Isidro Fernández Rodríguez.

Editorial Gente Nueva: Palacio del Segundo Cabo, Calle O'Reilly, No 4, esq. a Tacón, Havana; tel. (7) 62-4753; f. 1967; books for children; Dir Rubén del Valle Lantarón.

Editorial José Martí/Arte y Literatura: Calzada 259, entre I y J, Apdo 4208, Havana; tel. (7) 33-3541; fax (7) 33-8187; f. 1983; attached to the Ministry of Culture; foreign-language publishing; Dir Cecilia Infante Guerrero.

Editorial Letras Cubanas: Calle O'Reilly, No 4, esq. Tacón, Habana Vieja, Havana; tel. (7) 62-4378; fax (7) 33-8187; e-mail elc@ilc.cult.cu; f. 1977; attached to the Ministry of Culture; general, particularly classic and contemporary Cuban literature and arts; Dir Daniel García Santos.

Editorial Oriente: Santa Lucía 356, Santiago de Cuba; tel. (226) 22496; fax (226) 23715; e-mail edoriente@cultstgo.cult.cu; f. 1971; publishes works from the Eastern provinces; literature, art and culture and practical books (cookery, house and home, crafts and games); Dir Aida Bahr.

Editorial Pueblo y Educación: Avda 3A, No 4601, entre 46 y 60, Playa, Havana; tel. (7) 22-1490; fax (7) 24-0844; e-mail epe@ceniai.inf.cu; f. 1971; textbooks and educational publications; publishes Revista Educación three times a year (circ. 2,200); Dir Catalina Lajud Herrero.

Government Publishing Houses

Instituto Cubano del Libro: Palacio del Segundo Cabo, Calle O'Reilly, No 4, esq. a Tacón, Havana; tel. (7) 62-4789; fax (7) 33-8187; e-mail cclfilh@artsoft.cult.cu; printing and publishing organization attached to the Ministry of Culture which combines several publishing houses and has direct links with others; presides over the National Editorial Council (CEN); Pres. Omar González Jiménez.

Oficina de Publicaciones: Calle 17, No 552, esq. a D, Vedado, Havana; tel. (7) 32-1883; fax (7) 33-5106; attached to the Council of State; books, pamphlets and other printed media on historical and political matters; Dir Pedro Alvarez Tabío.

Broadcasting and Communications

TELECOMMUNICATIONS

Empresa de Telecomunicaciones de Cuba, SA (ETECSA): Calle Egido, No 610, entre Gloria y Apodaca, Habana Vieja, Havana; tel. (7) 33-4848; fax (7) 33-5144; Exec. Pres. Rafael Marrero Gómez.

Empresa de Telecomunicaciones Internacionales (EMTEL-CUBA): Zanja, No 855, 6°, Havana; tel. (7) 70-8794; fax (7) 78-3722; 50% sold to Mexico's Grupo Domor in 1994; Dir Regino González Toledo.

Instituto de Investigación y Desarrollo de las Telecomunicaciones (LACETEL): Rancho Boyeros, Km 14½, Santiago de las Vegas, Rancho Boyeros, Havana; tel. (7) 20-2929; fax (7) 33-5812; Dir Eduardo Truffín Triana.

Ministerio de Comunicaciones (Dirección General de Telecomunicaciones): Plaza de la Revolución, Havana: Dir Carlos Martínez Albuerne.

Teléfonos Celulares de Cuba, SA (CUBACEL): Calle 28, No 10, entre 5 y 7, Playa, Havana; tel. (7) 33-2222; fax (7) 33-1737; Dir-Gen. Rafael Galindo Mier.

BROADCASTING

Ministerio de la Informática y las Comunicaciones (Dirección de Frecuencias Radioeléctricas): Plaza de la Revolución, CP 10600, Havana; tel. (7) 70-6932; Dir Carlos Martínez Albuerne.

Empresa Cubana de Radio y Televisión (INTERTV): Avda 23, No 156, entre N y O, Vedado, Havana; tel. (7) 32-7571; fax (7) 33-3939; Dir Andrés Salcedo Gancedo.

Instituto Cubano de Radio y Televisión (ICRT): Edif. Radiocentro, Avda 23, No 258, entre L y M, Vedado, Havana 4; tel. (7) 32-1568; fax (7) 33-3107; e-mail icrt@cecm.get.tur.cu; f. 1962; Pres. Ernesto López Domínguez.

Radio

In 1997 there were 5 national networks and 1 international network, 14 provincial radio stations and 31 municipal radio stations, with a total of some 170 transmitters.

Radio Enciclopedia: Calle N, No 266, entre 21 y 23, Vedado, Havana; tel. (7) 81-2809; national network; instrumental music programmes; 24 hours daily; Dir Edelsa Palacios Gordo.

Radio Habana Cuba: Infanta 105 esq. a 25, 6°, Apdo 6240, Havana; tel. (7) 57-6533; fax (7) 79-5810; e-mail cartas@radiohc.org; f. 1961; shortwave station; broadcasts in Spanish, English, French, Portuguese, Arabic, Esperanto, Quechua, Guaraní and Creole; Dir Milagro Hernández Cuba.

CMBF—Radio Musical Nacional: Edif. ENE, Calle N, entre 23 y 21, Vedado, Havana; tel. (7) 57-5527; f. 1948; national network; classical music programmes; 17 hours daily; Dir Luiz López-Quintana.

Radio Progreso: Infanta 105, Apdo 3042, Havana; tel. (7) 70-4561; f. 1929; national network; mainly entertainment and music; 24 hours daily; Dir Manuel E. Andrés Mazorra.

Radio Rebelde: Edif. ICRT, Avda 23, No 258, entre L y M, Vedado, Apdo 6277, Havana; tel. (7) 31-3514; fax (7) 33-4270; e-mail rebelde @ceniai.inf.cu; internet www.cuba.cu/RRebelde; f. 1958 (merged with Radio Liberación in 1984); national network; 24-hour news programmes, music and sports; Dir Gen. Pedro P. Figueredo Rodríguez.

Radio Reloj: Edif. Radiocentro, Avda 23, No 258, entre L y M, Vedado, Havana; tel. (7) 32-9689; f. 1947; national network; 24-hour news service; Dir Osvaldo Rodríguez Martínez.

Television

Instituto Cubano de Radiodifusión (Televisión Nacional): Calle M, No 313, entre 21 y 23, Vedado, Havana; tel. (7) 32-5000; broadcasts in colour on channel 2 and channel 6; Vice-Pres. Josefa Bracero Torres, Ovidio Cabrera, Ernesto López.

Cubavisión: Calle M, No 313, Vedado, Havana.

Tele Rebelde: Mazón, No 52, Vedado, Havana; tel. (7) 32-3369; Vice-Pres. Gary González.

CHTV: Habana Libre Hotel, Havana; f. 1990; subsidiary station of Tele-Rebelde.

Finance

BANKING

All banks were nationalized in 1960. Legislation establishing the national banking system was approved by the Council of State in 1984. A restructuring of the banking system, initiated in 1995, to accommodate Cuba's transformation to a more market-orientated economy was proceeding in 2001. A new central bank, the Banco Central de Cuba (BCC), was created in 1997 to supersede the Banco Nacional de Cuba (BNC). The BCC was to be responsible for issuing currency, proposing and implementing monetary policy and the regulation of financial institutions. The BNC was to continue functioning as a commercial bank and servicing the country's foreign debt. Also envisaged in the restructuring of the banking system was the creation of an investment bank, the Banco de Inversiones, to provide medium- and long-term financing for investment, and the Banco Financiero Internacional, SA, to offer short-term financing. A new agro-industrial and commercial bank was also to be created to provide services for farmers and co-operatives. The new banking system is under the control of Grupo Nueva Banca, which holds a majority share in each institution.

Central Bank

Banco Central de Cuba (BCC): Havana; f. 1997; sole bank of issue; Pres. Francisco Soberón Valdez.

Commercial Banks

Banco Financiero Internacional, SA: Edif. Someillán, Calle Línea, y 0, Vedado, Havana; tel. (7) 32-1518; fax (7) 33-3006; f. 1984; autonomous; capital US $10m. (1985); finances Cuba's foreign trade; Chair. Eduardo Bencomo Zurdos; Gen. Man. Arnaldo Alayón.

Banco Internacional de Comercio, SA: 20 de Mayo y Ayestarán, Apdo 6113, Havana; tel. (7) 55-5482; fax (7) 33-5112; e-mail bicsa@bicsa.colombus.cu; f. 1993; cap. and res US $45.5m., dep. $212.7m. (Dec. 1997); Chair. Ernesto Medina.

Banco Metropolitano: Avda 5 y Calle 112, Playa, Havana; tel. (7) 24-3869; fax (7) 24-9193; e-mail banmetcm@nbbcm.colombus.cu; internet www.banco-metropolitano.com; f. 1996; offers foreign currency and deposit account facilities; Pres. Ivaniosky Matos Torres; Dir Pedro de la Rosa Gonzalez.

Banco Nacional de Cuba (BNC): Aguiar 456, entre Amargura y Lamparillla, Havana; tel. (7) 62-8896; fax (7) 66-9514; e-mail postmaster@bnc.cu; f. 1950, reorganized 1997; Chair. DIANA AMELIA FERNÁNDEZ VILA.

Foreign Banks

There are 13 foreign banks represented in Cuba, including Banco Bilbao Vizcaya (Spain), Banco de Comercio Exterior de México, Banco Exterior de España, Banco Sabadell (Spain), ING Bank (Netherlands) and Société General de France.

Savings Bank

Banco Popular del Ahorro: Calle 16, No 306, entre 3 y 5, Playa, Havana; tel. (7) 22-2545; f. 1983; savings bank; cap. 30m. pesos; dep. 5,363.7m. pesos; Pres. MARISELA FERREYRA DE LA GÁNDARA; 520 brs.

INSURANCE
State Organizations

Empresa del Seguro Estatal Nacional (ESEN): Obispo No 211, 3°, Apdo 109, 10100 Havana; tel. (7) 60-4111; f. 1978; motor and agricultural insurance; Man. Dir PEDRO MANUEL ROCHE ALVAREZ.

Seguros Internacionales de Cuba, SA—Esicuba: Cuba No 314, Apdo 79, Havana; tel. (7) 62-5051; fax (7) 33-8038; f. 1963, reorganized 1986; all classes of insurance except life; Pres. RAMÓN MARTÍNEZ CARRERA.

Trade and Industry

GOVERNMENT AGENCIES

Ministry of Foreign Investment and Economic Co-operation: Primera No 1404, entre 14 y 16, Miramar, Havana; tel. (7) 22-3873; fax (7) 24-0797; e-mail cecupi@ceniai.cu.

Free-Trade Zones National Office: Calie 22, No 528, entre 3 y 5, Miramar, Havana; tel. (7) 24-7636; fax (7) 24-7637.

CHAMBER OF COMMERCE

Cámara de Comercio de la República de Cuba: Calle 21, No 661/701, esq. Calle A, Apdo 4237, Vedado, Havana; tel. (7) 30-3356; fax (7) 33-3042; f. 1963; mems include all Cuban foreign trade enterprises and the most important agricultural and industrial enterprises; Pres. CARLOS MARTÍNEZ SALSAMENDI; Sec.-Gen. MARTA CAMACHO FUNDORA.

AGRICULTURAL ORGANIZATION

Asociación Nacional de Agricultores Pequeños—ANAP (National Association of Small Farmers): Calle I, No 206, entre Linea y 13, Vedado, Havana; tel. (7) 32-4541; fax (7) 33-4244; f. 1961; 220,000 mems; Pres. ORLANDO LUGO FONTE; Vice-Pres. EVELIO PAUSA BELLO.

STATE IMPORT-EXPORT BOARDS

Alimport (Empresa Cubana Importadora de Alimentos): Infanta 16, 3°, Apdo 7006, Havana; tel. (7) 54-2501; fax (7) 33-3151; e-mail precios@alimport.com.cu; controls import of foodstuffs and liquors; Man. Dir PEDRO ALVAREZ.

Autoimport (Empresa Central de Abastecimiento y Venta de Equipos de Transporte Ligero): Galiano 213, entre Concordia y Virtudes, Havana; tel. (7) 62-8180; imports cars, light vehicles, motor cycles and spare parts; Man. Dir EDELIO VERA RODRÍGUEZ.

Aviaimport (Empresa Cubana Importadora y Exportadora de Aviación): Calle 182, No 126, entre 1 y 5, Reparto Flores, Playa, Havana; tel. (7) 21-7687; fax (7) 33-6234; import and export of aircraft and components; Man. Dir MARCOS LAGO MARTÍNEZ.

Caribex (Empresa Exportadora del Caribe): Aparthotel Las Brisas, Apdo 3C 41, Villa Panamericana, Havana; tel. (7) 95-1140; fax (7) 95-1142; e-mail acepex@fishnavy.inf.cu; import and export of seafood and marine products; Dir PEDRO SUÁREZ GAMBE.

Construimport (Empresa Central de Abastecimiento y Venta de Equipos de Construcción y sus Piezas): Carretera de Varona, Km 1½, Capdevila, Havana; tel. (7) 45-2567; fax (7) 66-6180; e-mail construimport@colombus.cu; f. 1969; controls the import and export of construction machinery and equipment; Man. Dir JESÚS SERRANO RODRÍGUEZ.

Consumimport (Empresa Cubana Importadora de Artículos de Consumo General): Calle 23, No 55, 9°, Apdo 6427, Vedado, Havana; tel. (7) 54-3110; fax (7) 54-2142; e-mail comer@consumimport .infocex.cu; f. 1962; imports and exports general consumer goods; Dir MERCEDES REY HECHAVARRÍA.

Copextel (Corporación Productora y Exportadora de Tecnología Electrónica): Calle 194 y 7A, Siboney, Havana; tel. (7) 21-8400; fax (7) 33-1414; f. 1986; exports LTEL personal computers and microcomputer software; Man. Dir LUIS J. CARRASCO.

Coprefil (Empresa Comercial y de Producciones Filatélicas): Zanja No 855, 2°, esq. San Francisco e Infanta, Havana 1; tel. (7) 7-8812; fax (7) 33-5077; imports and exports postage stamps, postcards, calendars, handicrafts, communications equipment, electronics, watches, etc.; Dir NELSON IGLESIAS FERNÁNDEZ.

Cubaelectrónica (Empresa Importadora y Exportadora de Productos de la Electrónica): Calle 22, No 510, entre 5 y 7, Miramar, Havana; tel. (7) 22-7316; fax (7) 33-1233; f. 1986; imports and exports electronic equipment and devices; Man. LUIS BLANCA.

Cubaexport (Empresa Cubana Exportadora de Alimentos y Productos Varios): Calle 23, No 55, entre Infanta y P, 8°, Vedado, Apdo 6719, Havana; tel. (7) 54-3130; fax (7) 33-3587; e-mail cexport@ infocex.cu; export of foodstuffs and industrial products; Man. Dir MILDA PICOS RIVERS.

Cubafrutas (Empresa Cubana Exportadora de Frutas Tropicales): Calle 23, No 55, Apdo 6683, Vedado, Havana; tel. and fax (7) 79-5653; f. 1979; controls export of fruits, vegetables and canned foodstuffs; Dir JORGE AMARO MOREJÓN.

Cubalse (Empresa para Prestación de Servicios al Cuerpo Diplomático): Avda 3 y Final, Miramar, Havana; tel. (7) 24-2284; fax (7) 24-2282; e-mail cubalse@ceniai.inf.cu; f. 1974; imports consumer goods for the diplomatic corps and foreign technicians residing in Cuba; exports beverages and tobacco, leather goods and foodstuffs; other operations include real estate, retail trade, restaurants, clubs, automobile business, state-of-the-art equipment and household appliances, construction, investments, wholesale, road transport, freight transit, shipping, publicity, photography and video, financing, legal matters; Pres. REIDAL RONCOURT FONT.

Cubametales (Empresa Cubana Importadora de Metales, Combustibles y Lubricantes): Infanta 16, 4°, Apdo 6917, Vedado, Havana; tel. (7) 70-4225; fax (7) 33-3477; controls import of metals (ferrous and non-ferrous), crude petroleum and petroleum products; also engaged in the export of petroleum products and ferrous and non-ferrous scrap; Dir RAFAEL PRIEDE GONZÁLEZ.

Cubaniquel (Empresa Cubana Exportadora de Minerales y Metales): Calle 23, No 55, 8°, Apdo 6128, Havana; tel. (7) 33-5334; fax (7) 33-3332; f. 1961; sole exporter of minerals and metals; Man. Dir ARIEL MASÓ MARZAL.

Cubatabaco (Empresa Cubana del Tabaco): Calle O'Reilly, No 104, Apdo 6557, Havana; tel. (7) 61-5759; fax (7) 33-8214; f. 1962; controls export of leaf tobacco, cigars and cigarettes to France; Dir JUAN MANUEL DÍAZ TENORIO.

Cubatécnica (Empresa de Contratación de Asistencia Técnica): Calle 12, No 513, entre 5 y 7, Miramar, Havana; tel. (7) 22-3270; fax (7) 24-0923; e-mail cubatec@ceniai.inf.cu; f. 1976; controls export and import of technical assistance; Dir FÉLIX GONZÁLEZ NAVERÁN.

Cubatex (Empresa Cubana Importadora de Fibras, Tejidos, Cueros y sus Productos): Calle 23, No 55, Apdo 7115, Vedado, Havana; tel. (7) 70-3269; fax (7) 33-3321; controls import of fibres, textiles, hides and by-products and export of fabric and clothing; Dir LUISA AMPARO SESÍN VIDAL.

Cubazúcar (Empresa Cubana Exportadora de Azúcar y sus Derivados): Calle 23, No 55, 7°, Vedado, Apdo 6647, Havana; tel. (7) 54-2175; fax (7) 33-3482; e-mail cubazucar@cbz.infocex.cu; f. 1962; controls export of sugar, molasses and alcohol; Dir ALEJANDRO GUTIÉRREZ MAIRIGAL.

Ecimact (Empresa Comercial de Industrias de Materiales, Construcción y Turismo): Calle 1C, entre 152 y 154, Miramar, Havana; tel. (7) 21-9783; controls import and export of engineering services and plant for industrial construction and tourist complexes; Dir OCTAVIO CASTILLA CANGAS.

Ecimetal (Empresa Importadora y Exportadora de Objetivos Industriales): Calle 23, No 55, esq. Plaza, Vedado, Havana; tel. (7) 55-0548; fax (7) 33-4737; e-mail ecimetal@infocex.cu; f. 1977; controls import and export of plant, equipment and raw materials for all major industrial sectors; Dir ADALBERTO DUMÉNIGO CABRERA.

Ediciones Cubanas (Empresa de Comercio Exterior de Publicaciones): Obispo 527, Apdo 43, Havana; tel. (7) 63-1989; fax (7) 33-8943; e-mail edicuba@artsoft.cult.cu; controls import and export of books and periodicals; Dir ADALBERTO DUMÉNIGO CABRERA.

Egrem (Estudios de Grabaciones y Ediciones Musicales): San Miguel 410, Havana; tel. (7) 62-9762; fax (7) 33-8043; f. 1964; controls the import and export of records, tapes, printed music and musical instruments; Dir Gen. JULIO BALLESTER GUZMÁN.

Emexcon (Empresa Importadora y Exportadora de la Construcción): Calle 25, No 2602, Miramar, Havana; tel. (7) 22-3694; f. 1978; consulting engineer services, contracting, import and export of building materials and equipment; Dir ELEODORO PÉREZ.

Emiat (Empresa Importadora y Exportadora de Suministros Técnicos): Calle 20, No 519, entre 5 y 7, Miramar, Havana; tel. (7) 22-1163; fax (7) 22-5176; f. 1983; imports technical materials, equipment and special products; exports furniture, kitchen utensils and accessories; Dir MARTA ALFONSO SÁNCHEZ.

Emidict (Empresa Especializada Importadora, Exportadora y Distribuidora para la Ciencia y la Técnica): Calle 16, No 102, esq. Avda 1, Miramar, Playa, 13000 Havana; tel. (7) 22-8452; fax (7) 24-1768; e-mail emidict@ceniai.inf.cu; f. 1982; controls import and export of scientific and technical products and equipment, live animals; scientific information; Dir MIGUEL JULIO PÉREZ FLEITAS.

Energoimport (Empresa Importadora de Objetivos Electro-energéticos): Calle 7, No 2602, esq. a 26, Miramar, Havana; tel. (7) 23-8156; fax (7) 33-0147; f. 1977; controls import of equipment for electricity generation; Man. LÁZARO HERNÁNDEZ

Eprob (Empresa de Proyectos para las Industrias de la Básica): Avda 31A, entre 18 y 20, Miramar, Playa, Apdo 12100, Havana; tel. (7) 33-2146; fax (7) 33-2146; f. 1967; exports consulting services and processing of engineering construction projects, consulting services and supplies of complete industrial plants and turn-key projects; Man. Dir RAÚL RIVERO MARTÍNEZ.

Eproyiv (Empresa de Proyectos para Industrias Varias): Calle 33, No 1815, entre 18 y 20, Playa, Havana; tel. (7) 24-2149; e-mail eproyiv@ceniai.inf.cu; f. 1967; consulting services, feasibility studies, development of basic and detailed engineering models, project management and turn-key projects; Dir MARTA ELENA HERNÁNDEZ DÍAZ.

Esi (Empresa de Suministros Industriales): Calle Aguiar, No 556, entre Teniente Rey y Muralla, Havana; tel. (7) 62-0696; fax (7) 33-8951; f. 1985; imports machinery, equipment and components for industrial plants; Dir-Gen. FRANCISCO DÍAZ CABRERA.

Fecuimport (Empresa Cubana Importadora y Exportadora de Ferrocarriles): Avda 7, No 6209, entre 62 y 66, Miramar, Apdo 6003, Havana; tel. (7) 79-7678; f. 1968; imports and exports railway equipment; Pres. DOMINGO HERRERA.

Ferrimport (Empresa Cubana Importadora de Artículos de Ferretería): Calle 23, No 55, 2°, Vedado, Apdo 6258, Havana; tel. (7) 70-6678; fax (7) 79-4417; importers of industrial hardware; Dir.-Gen. ALEJANDRO MUSTELIER.

Fondo Cubano de Bienes Culturales: Calle 36, esq. 47, Reparto Kohly, Playa, Havana; tel. (7) 23-6523; fax (7) 24-0391; f. 1978; controls export of fine handicraft and works of art; Dir ANGEL ARCOS.

Habanos, S.A.: Mercaderes 21, Havana; tel. 33-8998; fax 33-8946; e-mail habanos@infocex.cu; f. 1994; controls export of leaf tobacco, cigars and cigarettes (except to France—see Cubatabaco).

ICAIC (Instituto Cubano del Arte e Industria Cinematográficos): Calle 23, No 1155, Vedado, Havana 4; tel. (7) 55-3128; fax (7) 33-3032; f. 1959; production, import and export of films and newsreel; Dir ANTONIO RODRÍGUEZ RODRÍGUEZ.

Imexin (Empresa Importadora y Exportadora de Infraestructura): Avda 5, No 1007, esq. a 12, Miramar, Havana; tel. (7) 23-9293; f. 1977; controls import and export of infrastructure; Man. Dir RAÚL BENCE VIJANDE.

Imexpal (Empresa Importadora y Exportadora de Plantas Alimentarias, sus Complementos y Derivados): Calle 22, No 313, entre 3 y 5, Miramar, Havana; tel. (7) 29-1671; controls import and export of food-processing plants and related items; Man. Dir Ing. CONCEPCIÓN BUENO CAMPOS.

Maprinter (Empresa Cubana Importadora y Exportadora de Materias Primas y Productos Intermedios): Infanta 16, 2A, Apdo 2110, Havana; tel. (7) 74-2971; fax (7) 33-3535; f. 1962; controls import and export of raw materials and intermediate products; Dir ENRIQUE DÍAZ DE VILLEGAS OTERO.

Maquimport (Empresa Cubana Importadora de Maquinarias y Equipos): Calle 23, No 55, 6°, Vedado, Apdo 6052, Havana; tel. (7) 55-0639; fax (7) 33-5443; e-mail maquimport@infocex.cu; imports industrial goods and equipment; Dir JORGE MIGUEL HERNÁNDEZ.

Marpesca (Empresa Cubana Importadora y Exportadora de Buques Mercantes y de Pesca): Conill No 580, esq. Avda 26, Nuevo Vedado, Havana; tel. (7) 81-1300; f. 1978; imports and exports ships and port and fishing equipment; Dir JOSÉ CEREIJO CASAS.

Medicuba (Empresa Cubana Importadora y Exportadora de Productos Médicos): Máximo Gómez 1, esq. a Egido, Havana; tel. (7) 62-3983; fax (7) 61-7995; e-mail medicuba@infomed.sld.cu; enterprise for the export and import of medical and pharmaceutical products; Dir ALFONSO SÁNCHEZ DÍAZ.

Produimport (Empresa Central de Abastecimiento y Venta de Productos Químicos y de la Goma): Calle Consulado 262, entre Animas y Virtudes, Havana; tel. (7) 62-0581; fax (7) 62-9588; f. 1977; imports and exports spare parts for motor vehicles; Dir JOSÉ GUERRA MATOS.

Quimimport (Empresa Cubana Importadora y Exportadora de Productos Químicos): Calle 23, No 55, Apdo 6088, Vedado, Havana; tel. (7) 33-3394; fax (7) 33-3190; controls import and export of chemical products; Dir ARMANDO BARRERA MARTÍNEZ.

Suchel (Empresa de Jabonería y Perfumería): Calzada de Buenos Aires 353, esq. a Durege, Apdo 6359, Havana; tel. (7) 33-8008; fax (7) 33-5311; f. 1985; exports and imports materials for the detergent, perfumery and cosmetics industry, exports cosmetics, perfumes, hotel amenities and household products; Dir JOSÉ GARCÍA DÍAZ.

Tecnoazúcar (Empresa de Servicios Técnicos e Ingeniería para la Agro-industria Azucarera): Calle 12, No 310, entre 3 y 5, Miramar, Playa, Havana; tel. (7) 29-5441; fax (7) 33-1218; imports machinery and equipment for the sugar industry, provides technical and engineering assistance for the sugar industry; exports sugar-machinery equipment and spare parts; provides engineering and technical assistance services for sugar-cane by-product industry; Gen. Man. VICTOR R. HERNÁNDEZ MARTÍNEZ.

Tecnoimport (Empresa Importadora y Exportadora de Productos Técnicos): Edif. La Marina, Avda del Puerto 102, entre Justiz y Obrapía, Habana Vieja, Havana; tel. (7) 61-5552; fax (7) 66-9777; f. 1968; imports technical products; Dir ADEL IZQUIERDO RODRÍGUEZ.

Tecnotex (Empresa Cubana Exportadora e Importadora de Servicios, Artículos y Productos Técnicos Especializados): Avda 47, No 3419, Playa, Havana; tel. (7) 81-3989; fax (7) 33-1682; f. 1983; imports specialized technical and radiocommunications equipment, exports outdoor equipment and geodetic networks; Dir ADEL IZQUIERDO RODRÍGUEZ.

Tractoimport (Empresa Central de Abastecimiento y Venta de Maquinaria Agrícola y sus Piezas de Repuesto): Avda Rancho Boyeros y Calle 100, Apdo 7007, Havana; tel. (7) 45-1044; fax (7) 27-0896; f. 1960 for the import of tractors and agricultural equipment; also exports pumps and agricultural implements; Dir MANUEL CASTRO DEL AGUILA.

Transimport (Empresa Central de Abastecimiento y Venta de Equipos de Transporte Pesados y sus Piezas): Calle 20 y Avda 63, Marianao, Apdo 6665, 11500 Havana; tel. (7) 20-0325; fax (7) 33-5338; f. 1962; controls import and export of vehicles and transportation equipment; Dir JESÚS DINIS RIVERO.

UTILITIES

Electricity

Empresa Consolidada de Electricidad: Avda Salvador Allende 666, Havana; public utility.

TRADE UNIONS

All workers have the right to become members of a national trade union according to their industry and economic branch.

The following industries and labour branches have their own unions: Agriculture, Chemistry and Energetics, Civil Workers of the Revolutionary Armed Forces, Commerce and Gastronomy, Communications, Construction, Culture, Education and Science, Food, Forestry, Health, Light Industry, Merchant Marine, Mining and Metallurgy, Ports and Fishing, Public Administration, Sugar, Tobacco and Transport.

Central de Tradajadores de Cuba—CTC (Confederation of Cuban Workers): Palacio de los Trabajadores, San Carlos y Peñalver, Havana; tel. (7) 78-4901; f. 1939; affiliated to WFTU and CPUSTAL; 19 national trade unions affiliated; Gen. Sec. PEDRO ROSS LEAL; 2,767,806 mems (1996).

Transport

The Ministry of Transport controls all public transport.

RAILWAYS

The total length of railways in 1998 was 14,331 km, of which 9,638 km were used by the sugar industry. The remaining 4,520 km were public service railways operated by Ferrocarriles de Cuba. All railways were nationalized in 1960.

Ferrocarriles de Cuba: Edif. Estación Central, Egido y Arsenal, Havana; tel. (7) 62-1530; fax (7) 33-8628; f. 1960; operates public services; Dir Gen. P. PÉREZ FLEITES; divided as follows:

División Occidente: serves Pinar del Río, Ciudad de la Habana, Havana Province and Matanzas.

División Centro: serves Villa Clara, Cienfuegos and Sancti Spíritus.

División Centro-Este: serves Camagüey, Ciego de Avila and Tunas.

División Oriente: serves Santiago de Cuba, Granma, Guantánamo and Holguín.

División Camilo Cienfuegos: serves part of Havana Province and Matanzas.

ROADS

In 1997 there were an estimated 60,858 km of roads, of which 4,353 km were highways or main roads. The Central Highway runs from Pinar del Río in the west to Santiago, for a length of 1,144 km. In addition to this paved highway, there are a number of secondary and 'farm-to-market' roads. A small proportion of these secondary roads is paved but many can be used by motor vehicles only during the dry season.

SHIPPING

Cuba's principal ports are Havana (which handles 60% of all cargo), Santiago de Cuba, Cienfuegos, Nuevitas, Matanzas, Antilla, Guayabal and Mariel. Maritime transport has developed rapidly since 1959, and at 31 December 1998 Cuba had a merchant fleet of 105 ships (with a total displacement of 157,847 grt). In 2000 a US $100m. renovation and enlargement project for the port of Mariel was announced.

Coral Container Lines, SA: Oficios 170, 1°, Habana Vieja, Havana; tel. (7) 67-0854; fax (7) 67-0850; e-mail bfdez@coral.com.cu; f. 1994; liner services to Europe, Canada, Brazil and Mexico; 11 containers; Chair. and Man. Dir EVELIO GONZÁLEZ GONZÁLEZ.

Empresa Consignataria Mambisa: San José No 65, entre Prado y Zulueta, Habana Vieja, Havana; tel. (7) 62-2061; fax (7) 33-8111; e-mail denis@mambisas.transnet.cu; shipping agent, bunker suppliers; Man. Dir EDUARDO DENIS VALCÁRCEL; Commercial Operations Man. MERCEDES PÉREZ NEWHALL.

Empresa Cubana de Fletes (Cuflet): Calle Oficios No 170, entre Teniente Rey y Amargura, Apdo 6755, Havana; tel. (7) 61-2604; freight agents for Cuban cargo; Man. Dir CARLOS SÁNCHEZ PERDOMO.

Empresa de Navegación Caribe (Navecaribe): San Martín, 4°, Agramonte y Pasco de Martí, Habana Vieja, Havana; tel. (7) 62-5878; fax (7) 33-8564; f. 1966; operates Cuban coastal fleet; Dir RAMÓN DURÁN SUÁREZ.

Empresa de Navegación Mambisa: San Ignacio No 104, Apdo 543, Havana; tel. (7) 62-7031; fax (7) 61-0044; operates dry cargo, reefer and bulk carrier vessels; Gen. Man. GUMERSINDO GONZÁLEZ FELIÚ.

Naviera Frigorífica Marítima: Havana; tel. (7) 35743; fax (7) 33-5185.

Naviera Mar América: 5a Avda y 246, Barlovento, Playa; tel. (59) 24-9053; fax (59) 24-8889; e-mail nubia@maramerica.fishnavy.inf.eu.

Naviera Poseidon: Altos de la Aduana, San Pedro 1, Habana Vieja, Havana; tel. (7) 29-8073; fax (7) 24-8627; e-mail ccom@poseidon.fishnavy.inf.cu.

Nexus Reefer: Avda de la Pesquera y Atarés, Puerto Pesquero de la Habana, Habana Vieja, Havana 1; tel. (7) 33-8478; fax (7) 33-8046; merchant reefer ships; Gen. Dir QUIRINO L. GUTIÉRREZ LÓPEZ.

CIVIL AVIATION

There are a total of 16 civilian airports, with nine international airports, including Havana, Santiago de Cuba, Camagüey, Varadero and Holguín.

Aerocaribbean: Calle 23, No 64 esq. a P. Vedado, Havana; tel. (7) 33-4543; fax (7) 33-5016; e-mail aerocarvpcr@iacc3.6ct.cma.net; f. 1982; international and domestic charter services; Chair. JULIÁN INFIESTA.

Aerogaviota: Avda 47, No 2814, Reparto Kolhy, Havana; tel. (7) 81-3068; fax (7) 33-2621; f. 1994; operated by Cuban air force.

Empresa Consolidada Cubana de Aviación (Cubana): Calle 23, Pt 64 Vedado, La Rampa, Havana 4; tel. (7) 78-4961; fax (7) 79-3333; internet www.cubana.cu; f. 1929; international services to North America, Central America, the Caribbean, South America and Europe; internal services from Havana to 14 other cities; Gen. Dir HERIBERTO PRIETO.

Instituto de Aeronáutica Civil de Cuba (IACC): Calle 23, No 64, La Rampa, Vedado, Havana; tel. (7) 33-4471; fax (7) 33-3082; f. 1985; Pres. ROGELIO ACEVEDO GONZÁLEZ.

Tourism

Tourism began to develop after 1977, with the easing of travel restrictions by the USA, and Cuba subsequently attracted European tourists. At the Fourth Congress of the PCC, held in 1991, emphasis was placed on the importance of expanding the tourism industry, and, in particular, on its promotion within Latin America. Receipts totalled an estimated US $1,338m. in 1997, when there were some 1,170,000 visitors. In 2000 there were an estimated 1,774,000 arrivals. The number of hotel rooms increased to 34,000 in 2000. In that year there were 189 hotels.

Cubanacán: Calle 148, entre 11 y 13, Playa, Apdo 16046, Havana; tel. (7) 22-5512; fax (7) 22-8382; f. 1987; Pres. ABRAHAM MACIQUES MACIQUES.

Empresa de Turismo Internacional (Cubatur): Calle 23, No 156, entre N y O, Apdo 6560, Vedado, Havana; tel. (7) 35-4521; fax (7) 32-3157; f. 1968; Dir JOSÉ PADILLA.

Empresa de Turismo Nacional (Viajes Cuba): Calle 20, No 352, entre 21 y 23, Vedado, Havana; tel. (7) 30-0587; f. 1981; Dir ANA ELIS DE LA CRUZ GARCÍA.

CYPRUS

Introductory Survey

Location, Climate, Language, Religion, Flag, Capital

The Republic of Cyprus is an island in the eastern Mediterranean Sea, about 100 km south of Turkey. The climate is mild, although snow falls in the mountainous south-west between December and March. Temperatures in Nicosia are generally between 5°C (41°F) and 36°C (97°F). About 75% of the population speak Greek and almost all of the remainder Turkish. The Greek-speaking community is overwhelmingly Christian, and nearly all Greek Cypriots adhere to the Orthodox Church of Cyprus, while most of the Turkish Cypriots are Muslims. The national flag (proportions 5 by 3) is white, with a gold map of Cyprus, above two crossed green olive branches, in the centre. The capital is Nicosia.

Recent History

A guerrilla war against British rule in Cyprus was begun in 1955 by Greek Cypriots seeking unification (*Enosis*) with Greece. Their movement, the National Organization of Cypriot Combatants (EOKA), was led politically by Archbishop Makarios III, head of the Greek Orthodox Church in Cyprus, and militarily by Gen. George Grivas. Archbishop Makarios was suspected by the British authorities of being involved in EOKA's campaign of violence, and in March 1956 he and three other leaders of the *Enosis* movement were deported. After a compromise agreement between the Greek and Turkish communities, a Constitution for an independent Cyprus was finalized in 1959. Makarios returned from exile and was elected the country's first President in December 1959. Cyprus became independent on 16 August 1960, although the United Kingdom retained sovereignty over two military base areas.

A constitutional dispute resulted in the withdrawal of the Turks from the central Government in December 1963, and there was serious inter-communal violence. In March 1964 a UN Peace-keeping Force in Cyprus (UNFICYP, see p. 64) was established to prevent a recurrence of fighting between the Greek and Turkish Cypriot communities. The effective exclusion of the Turks from political power led to the creation of separate administrative, judicial and legislative organs for the Turkish community. Discussions with a view to establishing a more equitable constitutional arrangement began in 1968 and continued intermittently for six years without achieving any agreement, as the Turks favoured some form of federation, while the Greeks advocated a unitary state. Each community received military aid from its mother country, and the Greek Cypriot National Guard was controlled by officers of the Greek Army.

In 1971 Gen. Grivas returned to Cyprus, revived EOKA, and began a terrorist campaign for *Enosis*, directed against the Makarios Government and apparently supported by the military regime in Greece. Grivas died in January 1974, and in June Makarios ordered a purge of EOKA sympathizers from the police, National Guard and civil service, accusing the Greek regime of subversion. On 15 July Makarios was deposed in a military coup led by Greek officers of the National Guard, who appointed as President Nikos Sampson, an extremist Greek Cypriot politician and former EOKA militant. Makarios escaped from the island the following day and travelled to the United Kingdom. At the request of Rauf Denktaş, the Turkish Cypriot leader, the Turkish army intervened to protect the Turkish community and to prevent Greece from using its control of the National Guard to take over Cyprus. Turkish troops landed on 20 July and rapidly occupied the northern third of Cyprus, dividing the island along what became the Attila Line, which runs from Morphou through Nicosia to Famagusta. Sampson resigned on 23 July, and Glavkos Klerides, the President of the House of Representatives, became acting Head of State. The military regime in Greece collapsed on the same day. In December Makarios returned to Cyprus and resumed the presidency. However, the Turkish Cypriots established a *de facto* Government in the north, and in February 1975 declared a 'Turkish Federated State of Cyprus' ('TFSC'), with Denktaş as President.

Makarios died in August 1977. He was succeeded as President by Spyros Kyprianou, a former Minister of Foreign Affairs and the President of the House of Representatives since 1976. Following a government reorganization in September 1980 the powerful communist party, the Anorthotiko Komma Ergazomenou Laou (AKEL—Progressive Party of the Working People), withdrew its support from the ruling Dimokratiko Komma (DIKO—Democratic Party), and Kyprianou lost his overall majority in the legislature. At the next general election, held in May 1981, AKEL and the Dimokratikos Synagermos (DISY—Democratic Rally) each won 12 seats in the House. DIKO, however, won only eight seats, so the President remained dependent on the support of AKEL.

In the 'TFSC' a new Council of Ministers was formed in December 1978 under Mustafa Çağatay, a former minister belonging to the Ulusal Bırlık Partisi (UBP—National Unity Party). At elections held in June 1981 President Denktaş was returned to office, but his party, the UBP, lost its legislative majority, and the Government that was subsequently formed by Çağatay was defeated in December. In March 1982 Çağatay formed a coalition Government, comprising the UBP, the Demokratik Halk Partisi (Democratic People's Party) and the Türkiye Bırlık Partisi (Turkish Unity Party).

In September 1980 UN-sponsored intercommunal peace talks were resumed. The constitutional issue remained the main problem: the Turkish Cypriots demanded equal status for the two communities, with equal representation in government and strong links with the mother country, while the Greeks, although accepting the principle of an alternating presidency, favoured a strong central government and objected to any disproportionate representation for the Turkish community, who constituted less than 20% of the population. Discussions on a UN plan involving a federal council, an alternating presidency and the allocation of 70% of the island to the Greek community faltered in February 1982, when the Greek Prime Minister, Andreas Papandreou, proposed the withdrawal of all Greek and Turkish troops and the convening of an international conference rather than the continuation of intercommunal talks. Meanwhile, in April 1981 it was agreed to establish a Committee on Missing Persons in Cyprus, comprising one representative of each community and a representative of the International Committee of the Red Cross (ICRC), to investigate the fate of 1,619 Greek Cypriots and 803 Turkish Cypriots listed as missing since the 1974 invasion. In May 1983 the UN General Assembly voted in favour of the withdrawal of Turkish troops from Cyprus, whereupon Denktaş threatened to boycott any further intercommunal talks and to seek recognition for the 'TFSC' as a sovereign state; simultaneously it was announced that the Turkish lira was to replace the Cyprus pound as legal tender in the 'TFSC'.

On 15 November 1983 the 'TFSC' made a unilateral declaration of independence as the 'Turkish Republic of Northern Cyprus' ('TRNC'), with Denktaş as President. Çağatay subsequently resigned the premiership and as leader of the UBP, and an interim Government was formed in December, led by Nejat Konuk (Prime Minister of the 'TFSC' from 1976 to 1978 and President of the Legislative Assembly from 1981), pending elections in 1984. Like the 'TFSC', the 'TRNC' was recognized only by Turkey, and the declaration of independence was condemned by the UN Security Council. The 'TRNC' and Turkey established diplomatic relations in April 1984, and the 'TRNC' formally rejected UN proposals for a suspension of its declaration of independence prior to further talks.

During 1984 a 'TRNC' Constituent Assembly, comprising the members of the Legislative Assembly and 30 nominated members, drafted a new Constitution, which was approved by 70% of voters at a referendum in May 1985. At a presidential election in the 'TRNC' on 9 June Denktaş was returned to office with more than 70% of the vote. A general election followed on 23 June, at which the UBP, led by Dr Derviş Eroğlu, won 24 of the 50 seats in the Legislative Assembly. In July Eroğlu became 'TRNC' Prime Minister, leading a coalition Government formed by the UBP and the Toplumcu Kurtuluş Partisi (TKP—Communal Liberation Party).

At elections held in February 1983 Kyprianou was returned to the presidency for a further five-year term, taking 56.5% of the votes. In November 1985, however, following a debate on his leadership, the House of Representatives was dissolved. A general election for an enlarged legislature proceeded in December, at which Kyprianou's DIKO secured 16 seats. DISY, which won 19 seats, and AKEL, with 15, failed to secure the two-thirds' majority required to amend the Constitution and thus challenge the President's tenure of power. Kyprianou failed to secure a third presidential term in February 1988; the election was won at a second round of voting by Georghios Vassiliou, an economist who presented himself as an independent but who was unofficially supported by AKEL and the Socialistiko Komma Kyprou EDEK (EDEK—EDEK Socialist Party of Cyprus). Vassiliou undertook to restore the National Council (originally convened by President Makarios), which was to include representatives of all the main Greek Cypriot political parties, to address the Cyprus issue. Settlement plans proposed by the UN Secretary-General in July 1985 and in April 1986 were rejected by the Turkish Cypriots and the Greek Cypriots, respectively. Further measures concerning the demilitarization of the island, reportedly proposed by the Greek Cypriot Government, were rejected by Denktaş, who maintained that negotiations on the establishment of a two-zone, federal republic should precede any demilitarization.

In March 1988 the new Greek Cypriot President rejected various proposals submitted by Denktaş, via the UN, including a plan to form committees to study the possibilities of intercommunal co-operation. Following a meeting with the revived National Council in June, however, Vassiliou agreed to a proposal by the UN Secretary-General that he and Denktaş should resume intercommunal talks, without pre-conditions, in their capacity as the leaders of two communities. Denktaş also approved the proposal, and a summit meeting took place, under UN auspices, in Geneva, Switzerland, in August; this was the first such meeting between Greek and Turkish Cypriot leaders since January 1985. Vassiliou and Denktaş subsequently began direct negotiations, under UN auspices, in September 1988. No real progress was made and, although Vassiliou and Denktaş resumed negotiations at the UN in February 1990, the talks were abandoned in March, chiefly because Denktaş demanded recognition of the right to self-determination for Turkish Cypriots.

In April 1988 Eroğlu resigned as 'TRNC' Prime Minister, following a disagreement between the UBP and its coalition partner (since September 1986), the Yeni Doğuş Partisi (New Dawn Party), which was demanding greater representation in the Government. At the request of Denktaş, Eroğlu formed a new Council of Ministers in May, comprising mainly UBP members but also including independents. In April 1990 Denktaş was the successful candidate in an early presidential election, securing nearly 67% of the votes cast. Eroğlu retained the office of Prime Minister after the UBP won 34 of the 50 seats in the 'TRNC' Legislative Assembly at elections in May. (Following by-elections for 12 seats in October 1991, the UBP increased its representation in the Assembly to 45 members.)

In July 1990 the Government of Cyprus formally applied to join the European Community (EC, now European Union—EU—see p. 181). Denktaş condemned the application, on the grounds that the Turkish Cypriots had not been consulted, and stated that the action would prevent the resumption of intercommunal talks. In June 1993, none the less, the European Commission approved the eligibility of Cyprus for EC membership, although it insisted that the application should be linked to progress in the latest UN-sponsored talks concerning the island. The Commission's recommendation was endorsed by the EC Council of Ministers in October.

At the Greek Cypriot general election held on 19 May 1991, the conservative DISY, in alliance with the Komma Phileleftheron (Liberal Party), received 35.8% of the votes cast, thereby securing 20 of the 56 seats in the House of Representatives. AKEL, contrary to pre-election predictions, made the most significant gains, obtaining 30.6% of the votes and 18 seats.

Following unsuccessful attempts to promote the resumption of discussions between Vassiliou and Denktaş by the UN, the EC and the USA during 1990–91, the new UN Secretary-General, Dr Boutros Boutros-Ghali, made the resolution of the Cyprus problem one of his priorities in 1992. UN envoys visited Cyprus, Turkey and Greece in February, and in January and March Boutros-Ghali himself held separate meetings in New York, USA, with Vassiliou and Denktaş. However, no progress was achieved on the fundamental differences between the two sides concerning territory and displaced persons. In mid-1992

the UN Secretary-General conducted a second round of talks in New York with Vassiliou and Denktaş, initially separately but subsequently involving direct discussions between the two leaders. The talks aimed to arrive at a draft settlement based on a 'set of ideas', compiled by Boutros-Ghali and endorsed by a UN Security Council resolution (No. 750), advocating 'uninterrupted negotiations' until a settlement was reached. Discussions centred on UN proposals for the demarcation of Greek Cypriot and Turkish Cypriot areas of administration under a federal structure. However, following the publication of what was described as a 'non-map' in the Turkish Cypriot press, which showed the proposed area of Turkish administration as being about 25% smaller than the 'TRNC', Denktaş asserted that the UN's territorial proposals were totally unacceptable to the 'TRNC' Government, while political opinion in the Greek Cypriot area was divided. The five weeks of talks came to an end in August, again without having achieved significant progress. A third round of UN-sponsored talks opened in New York in late October, but were suspended in the following month with no discernible progress having been made in the main areas of discussion, i.e. refugees, constitutional and territorial issues. The UN Security Council held Denktaş responsible for the lack of progress, and adjourned the talks.

At the election for the Greek Cypriot presidency held in February 1993 the DISY leader, Glavkos Klerides, defeated the incumbent Vassiliou by a margin of less than 1% at a second round of voting. Vassiliou subsequently formed a new party, the Kinema ton Eleftheron Dimokraton (KED—Movement of Free Democrats).

UN-sponsored negotiations were reconvened in New York in May 1993, focusing on the Secretary-General's plan to introduce a series of what were termed 'confidence-building measures' (CBMs). These included the proposed reopening, under UN administration, of the international airport at Nicosia, and the resettlement, also under UN directives, of a fenced suburb of Famagusta. Denktaş presented separate demands at the talks, among them the removal of the embargo against 'TRNC' airports, ports and sporting activities. The talks were abandoned in June, when the Turkish Cypriot negotiators declined to respond to the UN proposals. In December the EU decided to appoint an observer to monitor and report on the UN talks.

In November 1993 Klerides and Andreas Papandreou, who had recently resumed the Greek premiership, agreed at a meeting in Athens that their countries would take joint decisions in negotiations for the settlement of the Cyprus problem. The two leaders also agreed on a common defence doctrine, whereby Greece was to provide Cyprus with a guarantee of air, land and naval protection. In October 1994 the Greek air force participated for the first time in an exercise of the Cypriot National Guard.

An early general election was held in the 'TRNC' in December 1993, partly in response to increasing conflict between President Denktaş and Prime Minister Eroğlu over the handling of the UN-sponsored peace talks. The UBP lost its majority in the Legislative Assembly, retaining only 17 of the 50 seats, and at the end of the month a coalition Government was formed by the Demokrat Parti (DP—Democrat Party), which had been supported by Denktaş, and the left-wing Cumhuriyetçi Türk Partisi (CTP—Republican Turkish Party). Together the DP and the CTP won 53.4% of the votes cast and 28 seats. The leader of the DP, Hakkı Atun (hitherto the Speaker of the Assembly), was appointed as Prime Minister of the new administration.

In February 1994, following the confirmation by both authorities of their acceptance, in principle, of the CBMs, UN officials undertook what were designated 'proximity talks' separately with the Greek and Turkish Cypriot leaders. However, Denktaş considered that the proposals under discussion differed from the intention of the measures that had originally been agreed upon, and therefore refused to accept the document that was presented to both sides in March. A report issued at the end of May by Boutros-Ghali for consideration by the UN Security Council held the 'TRNC' authorities responsible for the breakdown of the process. In the following month the UN conducted negotiations to reclarify the CBMs. Denktaş accepted certain UN requests on the implementation of the measures, including the withdrawal of Turkish Cypriot troops from the access road to Nicosia international airport, but no substantive progress was made.

In July 1994 the UN Security Council adopted a resolution (No. 939), advocating a new initiative on the part of the Secretary-General to formulate a solution for peace, based on a single nationality, international identity and sovereignty. In response, in the following month the 'TRNC' Legislative Assembly approved measures seeking to co-ordinate future foreign and defence policies with those of Turkey, asserting that no peace solution based on the concept of a federation would be acceptable, and demanding political and sovereign status equal to that of Greek Cyprus. No substantive progress was made at informal UN-sponsored meetings between Klerides and Denktaş during October.

The issue of Cyprus's bid to accede to the EU had, furthermore, greatly unsettled the progress of negotiations. In June 1994 EU heads of government, meeting in Corfu, Greece, confirmed that Cyprus would be included in the next round of expansion of the Union. Denktaş remained adamant that any approach by the Greek Cypriots to the EU would prompt the 'TRNC' to seek further integration with Turkey. In early 1995 US officials commenced discussions with the two sides in an attempt to break the existing deadlock: while Denktaş insisted that the 'TRNC' would oppose Cyprus's EU membership application until a settlement for the island had been reached, the Greek Cypriot Government demanded 'TRNC' acceptance of the application as a pre-condition to pursuing the talks. In March the EU agreed to consider Cyprus's membership application without discrimination based on the progress (or otherwise) of settlement talks. This was ratified in June by a meeting of the EU-Cyprus Association Council, at which it was agreed to commence pre-accession 'structured dialogue' talks. In late June Klerides attended for the first time a summit meeting of EU heads of government.

Meanwhile, in February 1995 Hakkı Atun and the 'TRNC' Government resigned, following serious disagreements with Denktaş regarding the redistribution of Greek Cypriot-owned housing and land. However, the UBP failed to negotiate the formation of a new coalition, and in the following month Atun was reappointed Prime Minister. At a presidential election held in April Denktaş secured a conclusive victory only at a second round of voting (having taken 40.4% of votes cast in the first poll), winning 62.5% of the votes in a run-off contest with Eroğlu. Following protracted inter-party negotiations, a new coalition of the DP and CTP, under Atun's premiership, took office in June.

So-called 'secret' negotiations between representatives of the two Cypriot communities, held in May 1995 in London, United Kingdom, on a joint US-British initiative, achieved little in furthering agreement on the island's future or in securing agreement for direct talks between Denktaş and Klerides. Allegations which emerged in July that Turkish Cypriot construction work in the capital was, in fact, part of efforts to fortify the buffer zone presented a new political obstacle to inter-communal negotiations.

In August 1995 the 'TRNC' Legislative Assembly adopted legislation concerning compensation for Greek-owned property in the north (the issue which had provoked Atun's resignation earlier in the year). At the end of October Özker Özgür resigned as Deputy Prime Minister, reportedly owing to his disapproval of Denktaş's uncompromising attitude regarding the Cyprus issue. In the following month Atun submitted the resignation of his entire Government, after Denktaş rejected a new list of CTP ministers which had been approved by both parties in the coalition administration. A new DP-CTP coalition, again under Atun's leadership and with Mehmet Ali Talat (of the CTP) replacing Özgür as Deputy Prime Minister, took office in December.

In late 1995 the US administration declared its intention to strengthen efforts in Cyprus, led by Richard Holbrooke, the Assistant Secretary of State with responsibility for Europe, with the aim of achieving significant progress towards a final settlement during 1996. Early in the new year, however, Holbrooke postponed a visit to the region, owing to renewed tension between Greece and Turkey in the Aegean and the effective absence of a Turkish Government following elections in that country in December 1995. Representatives of the British Government and of the EU did, however, hold discussions with Greek and Turkish Cypriot representatives in February 1996 to assess the potential success of a new political initiative to achieve a peaceful settlement.

Elections to the Greek Cypriot House of Representatives in May 1996 produced little change in the composition of the legislature. DISY retained its 20 seats, with 34.5% of the votes cast; AKEL took 19 seats, an increase of one, with 33.0% of the votes, while DIKO held 10 seats, a loss of one compared with the 1991 election, with 16.4.

Also in May 1996 the Turkish Cypriot DP elected Serdar Denktaş, the President's son, as its new leader. Atun, now honorary party leader, was to continue to serve as Prime Minister. However, persistent policy differences between the two coalition parties caused the Government to resign in July. Negotiations to establish a new administration were undertaken by the DP and the UBP. A coalition agreement whereby UBP leader Eroğlu would become Prime Minister was signed by the leaders of the two parties in August, and the new Government was endorsed by a confidence motion in the Legislative Assembly later that month.

In April 1996 the UN Security Council endorsed a US initiative to promote a federal-based settlement for Cyprus. In the following month the United Kingdom appointed Sir David Hannay, a former Permanent Representative to the UN, as its first special representative to Cyprus. In June Boutros-Ghali held discussions, separately, with Denktaş and Klerides, with the intention of generating support for future direct bilateral negotiations. The meetings preceded a visit to the island by the UN Secretary-General's newly-appointed Special Representative in Cyprus, Han Sung-Joo. However, all efforts towards international mediation were diminished by a sharp escalation in intercommunal hostilities. At the end of October a military dialogue, involving senior commanders of the Greek and Turkish Cypriot armed forces, did commence with UN mediation to consider UN proposals for reducing intercommunal tension. Further mediation efforts were undermined in November by alleged of violations of Greek Cypriot airspace by Turkish military aircraft, as well as by efforts by the Greek Cypriot community to prevent tourists from visiting the 'TRNC' and the continued opposition of the 'TRNC' to the Cypriot application to join the EU.

In December 1996 the European Court of Human Rights ruled that Turkey was in breach of the European Convention on Human Rights by, as a result of its occupation in the north, denying a woman access to her property. The ruling implicated Turkey as fully responsible for activities in the 'TRNC' and for the consequences of the military action in 1974.

In January 1997 an agreement signed by the Greek Cypriot Government and Russia regarding the purchase of an advanced anti-aircraft missile system became the focus of political hostilities between the Greek and Turkish Cypriots, and the cause of considerable international concern. The purchase agreement was condemned by the 'TRNC' as an 'act of aggression', and the potential for conflict over the issue increased when Turkey declared its willingness to use military force to prevent the deployment of the system—which would have the effect of challenging the air superiority that Turkish forces had enjoyed since 1974. Greece in turn insisted that it would defend Cyprus against any Turkish attack. US mediators sought urgent meetings with the Cypriot leaders, and were assured by the Greek Cypriot Government that the system would not be deployed until May 1998 at the earliest, and that its deployment would be dependent upon the progress made in talks. In addition, both sides approved measures, supported by the UN, to reduce tension in the border area, although a US proposal for a ban on all military flights over the island was rejected by the Greek Cypriots. Later in January Turkey threatened to establish air and naval bases in the 'TRNC' if Greece continued to promote plans for the establishment of military facilities in the Greek Cypriot zone, and at the end of the month Turkish military vessels arrived in the 'TRNC' port of Famagusta. Turkey and the 'TRNC' also declared their commitment to a joint military concept whereby any attack on the 'TRNC' would be deemed a violation against Turkey.

In June 1997, following proximity talks between Klerides and Denktaş that had begun in March, the Cypriot leaders agreed to take part in direct UN-sponsored negotiations in the USA in July, under the chairmanship of the UN Special Envoy for Cyprus, Dr Diego Córdovez. The talks took place under the auspices of the UN Secretary-General, Kofi Annan, and with the participation of Richard Holbrooke, whose appointment in June as US Special Envoy to Cyprus had been welcomed by both Klerides and Denktaş. Further private direct talks took place in Nicosia at the end of July, when agreement was reached to co-operate in efforts to trace persons missing since the hostilities in 1974. However, a second formal round of UN-sponsored negotiations, convened in Switzerland in August 1997, collapsed without agreement, as Denktaş demanded the suspension of Cyprus's application for EU membership—to which the Turkish Cypriot leader remained opposed on the grounds that accession negotiations, scheduled to begin in 1998, were to be conducted with the Greek Cypriot Government, ignoring the issue of Turkish Cypriot sovereignty. (The EU had in the previous month formally agreed that Cyprus would be included in the next phase of the organization's enlargement.) An agreement by the 'TRNC' and Turkey, prior to the latest round of UN-sponsored talks, to create a joint committee to co-ordinate the partial integration of the 'TRNC' into Turkey was widely regarded as a response to the EU's decision to negotiate future membership with the Greek Cypriot Government while excluding Turkey from EU expansion. Although negotiations concerning security issues were held under UN auspices in Nicosia in September, US and UN efforts during October and November to promote progress in the talks, including visits to Cyprus by both Holbrooke and Córdovez, achieved little success, partly owing to the imminence of the Greek Cypriot presidential election. Denktaş rejected Holbrooke's attempts to persuade the 'TRNC' to join the Greek Cypriot Government at EU accession talks in 1998, insisting on EU recognition of the 'TRNC' and the simultaneous admission of Turkey to EU membership. Meanwhile, tension remained high, as Turkish fighter aircraft violated Greek Cypriot airspace in October 1997 in retaliation for Greek participation in Greek Cypriot military manoeuvres.

In November 1997 DIKO voted to leave the Greek Cypriot ruling coalition in advance of the presidential election, and the party's five government members resigned their posts. On 15 February 1998, at the second round of voting in the presidential election, Klerides defeated Georghios Iacovou, an independent candidate supported by AKEL and DIKO, taking 50.8% of the votes cast and thus retaining the presidency. A new coalition Government, composed of members of DISY, EDEK, the Enomeni Dimokrates (EDE—United Democrats—formed in 1996 by a merger of Vassiliou's KED and the Ananeotiko Dimokratiko Socialistiko Kinema) and independents, was sworn in at the end of the month.

The Greek Cypriot Government began accession talks with the EU in March 1998, and in the following month Cyprus confirmed its application for associate membership of Western European Union (WEU, see p. 286). In May Holbrooke visited Cyprus and held discussions with Klerides and Denktaş, with the aim of relaunching formal negotiations. However, no progress was made; Holbrooke cited the principal obstacles as Denktaş' demands for recognition of the 'TRNC' and for the withdrawal of the Cypriot application to join the EU, and the decision of the EU to delay further Turkey's application for membership. Russian efforts to facilitate the peace process at that time were also unsuccessful. In August Denktaş rejected a UN plan for the reunification of Cyprus, proposing instead, in a letter to the UN, a confederation of equal status; this was deemed unacceptable by Klerides on the grounds that it would legitimize the status of the 'TRNC'. In October Holbrooke held a meeting in New York with the Greek Cypriot Deputy Minister of Foreign Affairs, Ioannis Kranidhiotis, to discuss the peace process. The UN Special Envoy also held individual meetings with Klerides and Denktaş in Cyprus that month, but no progress was made.

In June 1998 a number of Greek military aircraft landed at the Paphos airfield in southern Cyprus for the first time since the airfield's completion in January. Shortly afterwards Turkish military aircraft made reciprocal landings in the 'TRNC'. In July the Greek Cypriot Government condemned the arrival of Turkish military naval vessels and aircraft in the 'TRNC' for the celebrations of the anniversary of the Turkish invasion of the island. During the course of the year Turkish aircraft were accused of violating Greek Cypriot airspace on a number of occasions, and in October Turkish fighter planes allegedly harassed Greek military aircraft that were participating in joint exercises with Greek-Cypriot forces. Earlier in the month, however, Denktaş had proposed a non-aggression treaty between the two sides. Joint Turkish-'TRNC' military exercises were held in November. During a visit to Cyprus in that month the Israeli President, Ezer Weizman, sought to assure Klerides that Israel's close military co-operation with Turkey was not directed against Cyprus. Shortly afterwards two Israelis were arrested in Cyprus on suspicion of espionage; Israel denied that the two men (who were subsequently sentenced to three years' imprisonment for approaching a prohibited military area (although they were pardoned in August 1999), had acted either against Cyprus or on behalf of Turkey.

At the end of December 1998 it was formally announced that the contentious Russian missile system would not be deployed in Cyprus, and that negotiations would instead be held with a view to their installation on the Greek island of Crete. This decision followed diplomatic pressure from Greece, the EU (which threatened to suspend Cypriot accession talks if the deployment proceeded in Cyprus), the USA and the UN, and was influenced by the adoption earlier in the month of two resolutions by the UN Security Council (both of which were dismissed by Denktaş): the first renewed the UNFICYP mandate and appealed for the resumption of negotiations on reunification as a single sovereign state (apparently rejecting the 'TRNC' Government's proposed confederation), and the second expressed concern at the lack of progress towards a political settlement and advocated a phased reduction of military personnel and armaments on the island. Both the 'TRNC' and Turkey welcomed the Greek Cypriot decision regarding the Russian system, although Turkey warned that the deployment of the missiles in Greece would still be regarded as a threat to its security. The missiles were reportedly deployed in Crete in March 1999, following the signature in February of an agreement by the Greek and Greek Cypriot Government to the effect that Cyprus would own the missiles although they would be under Greek operational control.

There was intense domestic criticism of Klerides' reversal of policy regarding the missiles' deployment; EDEK's withdrawal, in protest, from the Greek Cypriot governing coalition entailed the resignation of the Ministers of Defence and of Education and Culture. The Minister of the Interior, Dinos Michaelides, resigned in March 1999 in response to allegations of corruption (which he strenuously denied). A further government reorganization in August involved the reallocation of the defence, health and communications and works portfolios.

Meanwhile, at legislative elections held in the 'TRNC' on 6 December 1998, the UBP increased its representation to 24 seats (from 16 in 1993), while the DP held only 13 seats. The TKP won seven of the 50 seats and the CTP the remaining six. At the end of the month a new UBP-TKP Council of Ministers received presidential approval. Eroğlu remained as Prime Minister, and the TKP leader, Mustafa Akıncı, became Minister of State and Deputy Prime Minister.

In June 1999 the UN Security Council, extending the mandate of UNFICYP for a further six months, adopted a resolution urging the Greek and Turkish Cypriot authorities to participate in UN-sponsored negotiations in late 1999 without preconditions or proscribed issues. In November, despite his earlier reluctance to attend the proposed meeting, Denktaş confirmed that he would attend proximity talks with Klerides in New York under the auspices of the UN. The UN Secretary-General acted as a mediator in the indirect talks in the first half of December, which aimed to facilitate meaningful negotiations leading to a comprehensive settlement in Cyprus. The talks were, however, undermined by a decision of that month's summit meeting of EU Heads of State and Government in Helsinki, Finland, that a political settlement for Cyprus was not a precondition to the accession of the Greek Cypriot Government to the EU. This decision was widely acknowledged to be a response to Greece's reversal of its opposition to Turkey's EU membership application, and the summit thus accorded Turkey formal status as a candidate for EU membership. Although Denktaş criticized the EU decision on Cyprus's accession, a second round of UN-sponsored proximity talks began in Geneva at the end of January 2000. The UN Secretary-General and his Special Adviser on Cyprus, Alvaro de Soto, held separate meetings with Klerides and Denktaş, but again there were no direct exchanges between the two Cypriot leaders, and the talks ended without any substantive progress. Meanwhile, after an interval of more than three years, the Committee on Missing Persons in Cyprus met from November 1999 to discuss resuming its investigative work; however, following the death, in January 2000, of the ICRC representative, it was emphasized that the appointment of a successor was contingent upon assurances that obstacles impeding investigations had been removed and that both the Greek and Turkish Cypriot parties were committed to the committee's task.

A first round of presidential voting in the 'TRNC' was held on 15 April 2000, contested by eight candidates. Denktaş took 43.7% of the votes cast, thus failing to secure the majority necessary for outright victory. A second round was scheduled for 22 April, to be contested by Denktaş and his closest rival, Eroğlu (who had polled 30.1% at the first round), but this was cancelled following Erğolu's withdrawal on 19 April and Denktaş was thus declared elected for a fourth term as President.

In mid-June 2000 the UN Security Council adopted a resolution (No. 1303) extending the mandate of UNFICYP for a further six months. The resolution notably excluded any reference to the authority of the 'TRNC', citing only the Government of Cyprus, and at the end of the month the 'TRNC' instituted a number of retaliatory measures against UNFICYP including measures to impede the movement of UN forces and new tariffs for UN vehicles and for the use of utilities supplied by the north. 'TRNC' and Turkish forces also crossed into the buffer zone and established a check-point at a village inhabited by Greek Cypriots. Meanwhile, the newly-installed Turkish President, Ahmet Necdet Sezer, visited the 'TRNC' in late June in an apparent demonstration of his country's support for the state.

In mid-2000 remarks by the 'TRNC' deputy premier, Mustafa Akıncı, that the Constitution of the 'republic' should be amended to the effect that the local police force and fire service would be placed under the authority of the Ministry of the Interior and Rural Affairs, rather than that of the Turkish Cypriot security forces, provoked accusations of treason from the forces' commander, Maj.-Gen. Ali Nihat Ozayranli (a Turkish officer). The issue of the Turkish military's role in the islands assumed wider dimensions in July as the editor and three journalists of a left-wing newspaper, *Avrupa*, which had openly criticized the general were among six people arrested on charges of spying for the Greek Cypriot authorities. The arrests, made on apparently scant evidence, were condemned not only by the 'TRNC' media but also by the Turkish press, and in the 'TRNC' liberal political parties, trade unions and non-governmental organizations formed a 'platform against oppression' to denounce the arrests and demand the replacement of Ozeyranli; some 8,000 protesters joined a rally organized by the group in mid-July. Meanwhile, the six were released pending further investigations. Ozeyranli returned to Turkey in August to take up a new military command.

Preparations were made for a third round of proximity talks to be held in New York in May 2000, but the sessions were delayed to enable Klerides to recuperate after surgery. The talks—mediated by Alvaro de Soto and focusing on what were termed 'core' issues of territory, constitutional arrangements, property rights and guarantees—were eventually convened in Geneva in early July; they were adjourned after a week but reconvened later in the month, continuing into early August. Again, there were no direct exchanges between the Greek and Turkish Cypriot representatives and the talks ended without progress.

A further round of indirect negotiations began in New York in mid-September 2000. Klerides boycotted the early stages of the talks, in protest at a statement in which the UN Secretary-General had, in the view of the Greek Cypriots, implied that the 'TRNC' was equal in authority to the internationally-recognized Cypriot Government, but the Greek Cypriot leader resumed attendance after he received assurances that the UN would act in accordance with earlier Security Council resolutions on the Cyprus issue. Although de Soto expressed cautious optimism regarding the outcome of the talks, the Greek and Turkish Cypriots remained apparently irreconcilable on the issue of a future structure for Cyprus: with the former advocating a reunified, bi-communal federation and the latter a looser confederation based on equal sovereignty. A fifth round of UN-sponsored proximity talks was convened in Geneva at the beginning of November. After separate meetings with both Klerides and Denktaş, Kofi Annan expressed his view that the negotiations had moved beyond procedure into substance, and both leaders were invited to a further round of contacts in January 2001. Later in November 2000, however, Denktaş condemned the process as 'a waste of time', stating that he would not return to the talks until such time as the 'TRNC' was accorded international recognition. His decision, taken with the support of the Government of Turkey, apparently reflected anger in the 'TRNC' that the UN Secretary-General had emphasized that any agreement on Cyprus must be based on the premise of a single sovereign entity, and in Turkey that the European Commission had, in a draft partnership agreement published earlier in November 2000, stipulated among preconditions for Turkish admission to the EU Turkey's willingness to promote a settlement for Cyprus based on UN resolutions. Alvaro de Soto visited Cyprus in early December in an effort to foster a resumption of contacts, but Denktaş reiterated that the 'TRNC' would not take part in any further talks unless its sovereignty was recognized; he warned, furthermore, that in the absence of such recognition UNFICYP would no longer be welcome in the 'TRNC'. In mid-

December the UN Security Council adopted a resolution extending the mandate of the force for a further six-month period; the resolution urged the 'TRNC' to revoke restrictive measures imposed against UNFICYP in June (see above), noting that these had undermined the operational effectiveness of the peace-keeping force. Meanwhile, it was reported in late 2000 that Turkey had strengthened its military personnel in the 'TRNC' to a record number of 36,000.

The European Commission's Progress Towards Accession report on Cyprus, published in November 2000, assessed Cyprus as being among the candidate countries best equipped to join the union; the report also reiterated the EU's invitation to the Turkish Cypriot community to participate in the accession negotiations.

At elections to the Greek Cypriot House of Representatives, held on 27 May 2001, AKEL secured a narrow victory over DISY, taking 20 seats compared with the latter's 19. A few days earlier the governing coalition of the 'TRNC' collapsed, following disagreement between the UBP and TKP on the issue of whether to rejoin talks on the future status of the island.

Government

The 1960 Constitution provided for a system of government in which power would be shared by the Greek and Turkish communities in proportion to their numbers. This Constitution officially remains in force, but since the ending of Turkish participation in the Government in 1963, and particularly since the creation of a separate Turkish area in northern Cyprus in 1974, each community has administered its own affairs, refusing to recognize the authority of the other's Government. The Greek Cypriot administration claims to be the Government of all Cyprus, and is generally recognized as such, although it has no Turkish participation. The northern area is under the *de facto* control of the 'Turkish Republic of Northern Cyprus' (for which a new Constitution was approved by a referendum in May 1985). Each community has its own President, Council of Ministers, legislature and judicial system.

Defence

The formation of the National Guard was authorized by the House of Representatives in 1964, after the withdrawal of the Turkish members. Men between 18 and 50 years of age are liable to 26 months' conscription. At 1 August 2000 the National Guard comprised an army of 10,000 regulars, mainly composed of Cypriot conscripts (some 8,700) but with an estimated 200 seconded Greek Army officers and NCOs, and 60,000 reserves. A further 1,250 Greek army personnel were stationed in Cyprus at that time. There is also a Greek Cypriot paramilitary police force of 750. In 2000 the defence budget for the Greek Cypriot area was C£330m.

At 1 August 2000 the 'TRNC' had an army of about 5,000 regulars and 26,000 reserves. Men between 18 and 50 years of age are liable to 24 months' conscription. The 'TRNC' forces were being supported by an estimated 36,000 Turkish troops. In 1999 the defence expenditure of the 'TRNC' was TL 17,300,000m.

The UN Peace-keeping Force in Cyprus (UNFICYP—see p. 64) consisted of 1,247 military and police personnel at 31 January 2001. There are British military bases (with personnel numbering 3,200 in August 2000) at Akrotiri, Episkopi and Dhekelia.

Economic Affairs

In 1998, according to estimates by the World Bank, Cyprus's gross national product (GNP), measured at average 1996–98 prices, was US $8,983m., equivalent to $11,920 per head (or $17,599 per head on an international purchasing-power parity basis). During 1990–98, it was estimated, GNP per head increased, in real terms, by an average of 2.7% per year. Over the same period the population increased at an average annual rate of 1.4%. GNP was estimated at $9,086m. in 1999, equivalent to $11,960 per head. Cyprus's gross domestic product (GDP) increased, in real terms, by an estimated annual average of 3.4% in 1990–95; according to provisional data, GDP increased by 5.0% in 1998 and by 4.5% in 1999. In the 'TRNC' GNP was officially estimated at $940.7m., or $5,584 per head, in 1999. In 1991–97 real GDP increased at an average annual rate of 3.3%. Economic growth of 5.1% and 4.9% was recorded in 1998 and 1999, respectively. However, GDP per head in the 'TRNC' remains only about one-third of that of the remainder of the island.

According to provisional figures, agriculture (including forestry and fishing) contributed 4.2% of GDP in 1999. In the government-controlled area 9.3% of the employed labour force were engaged in the sector in 1999. The principal export crops of the government-controlled area are potatoes (which accounted for 8.9% of domestic export earnings in 1998), citrus fruit and vegetables; grapes are cultivated notably for the wine industry, and barley is the principal cereal crop. In an effort to offset the island's vulnerability to drought, during the 1990s the Greek Cypriot authorities granted concessions for the construction and operation of several desalination plants. The GDP of the area's agricultural sector declined by an average of 0.3% per year in 1995–99; agricultural GDP fell by 12.4% in 1997 but, as the sector began to recover from drought, was estimated to have increased by 6.1% in 1998 and by 7.1% in 1999. In the 'TRNC' 22.7% of the working population were employed in agriculture (mainly in the production of citrus fruit), forestry and fishing in 1995, and the sector contributed an estimated 8.6% of GDP in 1998. The principal crops of the 'TRNC' are wheat, barley, potatoes and citrus fruit. The 'TRNC' imports water from Turkey in order to address the problem of drought. Construction of a water pipeline from Turkey was scheduled to begin in late 2000.

Industry (comprising mining, manufacturing, construction and utilities) engaged 22.4% of the employed labour force in the government-controlled area in 1999, and accounted for 21.2% of GDP in that year. Industrial GDP increased by an average of 0.2% per year in 1995–99; the sector's GDP declined by 1.1% in 1997, but expanded by a projected 1.5% in 1998 and by 0.5% in 1999. In the 'TRNC' the industrial sector contributed 18.1% of GDP in 1998, and engaged 23.5% of the working labour force in 1995.

Mining, principally the extraction of material for the construction industry, provided only 0.3% of GDP, and engaged just 0.2% of the employed labour force, in the government-controlled area in 1999. Minerals accounted for 5.6% of domestic exports (by value) from the government-controlled sector in 1999. The GDP of the mining sector increased at an average annual rate of 6.1% in 1995–99; according to provisional data, mining GDP increased by 16.1% in 1998, although growth slowed to 3.6% in 1999. In the 'TRNC' mining and quarrying contributed 0.7% of GDP in 1998.

Manufacturing accounted for 10.9% of GDP in the government-controlled area in 1999, and engaged 13.3% of the employed labour force in that year. Clothing represents the southern sector's main export commodity, providing 11.0% of domestic export earnings in 1999. The GDP of the manufacturing sector increased by an average of less that 0.1% per year in 1995–99; manufacturing GDP increased by 1.1% and 0.2%, respectively, in 1998 and 1999. In the 'TRNC' the manufacturing sector provided 7.5% of GDP in 1998.

Energy is derived principally from imported petroleum, and mineral fuels and lubricants comprised 7.6% of total imports (including goods for re-export) in the government-controlled area in 1999. The Greek Cypriot Government is encouraging the development of sustainable energy sources, including solar and wind power. Mineral fuels, lubricants, etc. comprised 6.7% of total imports in the 'TRNC' in 1998.

The services sector in the government-controlled area contributed an estimated 74.6% of GDP, and engaged 68.4% of the employed labour force in 1999. Within the sector, financial and business services provided an estimated 21.2% of overall GDP and generated 9.8% of employment in that year. In 1999 there were 29 'offshore' banking units in the government-controlled area, and the number of registered 'offshore' enterprises was estimated to total more than 40,000. In the 'TRNC' the services sector contributed 73.3% of GDP in 1997, and engaged 53.8% of the employed labour force in 1995. Both Cypriot communities have undertaken measures to expand their tourism industries, which are important generators of revenue and employment. Tourist arrivals to the government-controlled area increased from 2,222,706 in 1998 to 2,434,300 in 1999. Receipts from tourism in 1999 amounted to an estimated C£1,022m. In 1998 a total of 393,027 tourists (315,797 of whom were from Turkey) visited the 'TRNC'. Net tourism receipts in the 'TRNC' totalled US $192.2m. in 1997. The Greek Cypriot authorities are also attempting to enhance the island's status as an entrepôt for shipping and trade throughout the Eastern Mediterranean, while Cyprus's shipping registry has developed rapidly, to become the world's sixth largest by the end of 1998. In the government-controlled area the GDP of the services sector increased at an average annual rate of 4.7% in 1995–99; according

to provisional figures, services GDP expanded by 6.0% and 5.6%, respectively, in 1998 and 1999.

In 1999 the government-controlled area recorded a visible trade deficit of US $2,309.2m. and a deficit of $233.7m. on the current account of the balance of payments. The 'TRNC' recorded a visible trade deficit in 1998 of $336.7m., while there was a deficit of $62.7m. on the current account of the balance of payments. In 1999 the principal sources of imports to the government-controlled area were the United Kingdom (which supplied 11.4% of merchandise imports) and the USA (10.8%); Italy, Greece, Germany, Japan and France were also important suppliers. The United Kingdom was also the principal purchaser of Greek Cypriot exports in 1999, taking 16.1% of the total; Greece and Russia were also important markets. The principal domestic exports from the government-controlled area in 1998 were clothing, pharmaceutical products, potatoes, citrus fruit and cigarettes. The principal imports in that year were machinery and electrical equipment, foodstuffs, beverages and tobacco, vehicles, chemical products, textiles, base metals and minerals. In 1998 the principal imports to the 'TRNC' were machinery and transport equipment, basic manufactures, food and live animals, chemicals, mineral fuels and beverages; the principal exports were clothing, citrus fruit and beverages and tobacco. Turkey is by far the principal trading partner of the 'TRNC', supplying 59.2% of imports and taking 50.6% of exports in 1998, although the United Kingdom purchased 30.9% of exports in that year.

In 1998 the government-controlled area recorded a budget deficit of an estimated C£201.3m., equivalent to 4.1% of GDP. External debt totalled C£1,796.0m. at the end of 1999, of which C£1,142.3m. was medium- and long-term public debt. In that year the cost of debt-servicing was equivalent to 5.8% of the value of exports of goods and services. The annual rate of inflation averaged 3.8% in 1990–99. Consumer prices increased by an average of 1.6% in 1999. The average level of unemployment in the government-controlled area was 3.6% of the labour force in 1999. The 1998 budget of the 'TRNC' recorded expenditure of TL 105,910,719.5m. and revenue of TL 98,140,537.4m. (with aid from Turkey contributing TL 35,280,831.8m. to revenue), resulting in a deficit of TL 7,770,182.1m. (equivalent to 3.4% of GDP). The annual average rate of inflation in the 'TRNC' was 81.7% in 1997 and 66.5% in 1998. According to census figures, 6.5% of the labour force were unemployed in December 1996.

In 1972 Cyprus concluded an association agreement with the European Community (EC, now European Union—EU—see p. 181), and in 1987 an agreement was signed on the progressive establishment of a customs union with the EC, with effect from 1 January 1988. An application to become a full member of the EC was submitted by the Greek Cypriot Government in July 1990; accession negotiations commenced in March 1998. The 'TRNC' has guest status at the Economic Co-operation Organization (ECO, see p. 175).

By the end of the 1990s the Greek Cypriot economy was enjoying strong growth, owing in large part to continued advances in the services sector, notably in tourism; a further expansion in GDP of some 4.8% was forecast for 2000. However, the steady decline in the rate of inflation was expected to be reversed, as a period of enhanced consumer demand (reflecting in particular an increase of some 700% in the value of the Cyprus Stock Exchange in late 1999, following a period of intense trading activity), together with sustained increases in world petroleum prices, coincided with the depreciation in the value of the euro (to which the Cyprus pound has been linked since January 1999) in relation to the US dollar. Furthermore, while the budget deficit was reduced to 4.1% of GDP in 1999, from 5.5% in 1998 (mainly by means of small increases in indirect taxes and by the postponement of defence-related outlays), consolidated government debt widened from less than 52% of GDP in 1998 to 61% in 1999. The Government has frequently been restricted in its efforts at redressing such imbalances by the need to command the support of its coalition partners in the legislature: thus, enhanced revenues arising from an increase in the rate of value-added tax from mid-2000 were expected to be more than offset by compensatory increases in pensions and welfare expenditure. The Klerides administration none the less remained committed to reducing the fiscal deficit to the equivalent of 2% of GDP in 2002, notably by means of countering tax evasion and curbing overall expenditure on public sector salaries. A review of tax arrangements for 'offshore' banks and other enterprises has been necessitated by accession procedures, and the Government has pledged full compliance with efforts by the Organisation for Economic Co-operation and Development (of which Cyprus is not a member) to combat tax evasion and money-laundering. Following the partial sale of the state holding in Cyprus Airways, and the removal (with effect from January 2001) of a 'ceiling' on bank interest rates, increased liberalization of the telecommunications and energy sectors was anticipated. Economic policy thus continued to be governed by efforts to achieve the criteria necessary for EU membership—a process that was accelerated by the union's decision in late 1999 to dissociate Cypriot accession from the achievement of a political settlement for the island—and confidence was enhanced by a report published by the European Commission in late 1999 that judged Cyprus to be among the applicant countries best equipped for admission to the EU at the next round of enlargement.

The economy of the 'TRNC', although substantially less prosperous and affected by diplomatic isolation, has also achieved significant growth since the 1980s, with considerable assistance from Turkey. By the late 1990s higher education had become one of the territory's most significant economic sectors, with some 20,000 students, mostly from Turkey, attending private universities in the 'TRNC'; revenue from this sector was projected at US $250m. in 1999. The tourism sector was also expanding, although the development of the north as an international tourist destination remained hampered by the embargo on direct flights to the 'TRNC' (visitors must first land in Turkey). The close linkage with the Turkish economy, including the use of the Turkish lira as currency in the 'TRNC', has resulted in persistently high levels of inflation, and has rendered northern Cyprus particularly vulnerable to adverse economic developments in Turkey. In late 1999 the take-over by the Turkish authorities of several ailing banks precipitated a 'run' on several banks in the 'TRNC', necessitating their being placed under central control, and in October it was announced that four of the banks in question were to be liquidated. Furthermore, there was considerable concern that the severe financial crisis affecting the Turkish economy in early 2001 (q.v.) would be detrimental to the 'TRNC', where the Government was obliged in late February to revise its budget for that year to include a 20% reduction in current expenditure. The crisis was likely to further the economic divergence of the Turkish and Greek Cypriot communities, notably clear disparities in wealth between north and south, and to exacerbate long-term weaknesses in the 'TRNC' such as the comparative lack of diversification of the manufacturing sector and a high rate of emigration, while the potential loss of income in the form of essential grants and subsidies from Turkey would adversely affect the public sector, which remains the largest employer in the 'TRNC'.

Social Welfare

A comprehensive social insurance scheme, covering every working male and female and their dependants, is in operation in the government-controlled area. It includes provisions for protection against arbitrary and unjustified dismissal, for industrial welfare and for tripartite co-operation in the formulation and implementation of labour policies and objectives. Benefits and pensions from the social insurance scheme cover unemployment, sickness, maternity, widows, orphans, injury at work, old age and death. According to WHO data, in 1996, in the government-controlled area, there were 255 doctors, and 447 nurses for every 100,000 inhabitants. Of total expenditure by the central Government in the Greek Cypriot area in 1997, C£101.3m. (6.9%) was for health services, and a further C£392.7m. (26.6%) for social security and welfare. In 1997 the state health service in the Turkish Cypriot zone included nine hospital establishments, with a total of 814 beds, while there were 287 private establishments, with 263 beds. In that year there were 467 physicians and dentists, of whom 178 worked in the state health service.

Education

In the Greek Cypriot sector elementary education, which is compulsory and available free of charge, is provided in six grades for children between five-and-a-half and 12 years of age.

Enrolment at primary level in 1996 was equivalent to 100% of children in the relevant age-group in 1996. Secondary education is free for all years of study and lasts six years, with three compulsory years at the Gymnasium being followed by three non-compulsory years at a technical school or a Lyceum. Comprehensive secondary schools were introduced in 1995. There are five options of specialization at the Lyceums: classical, science, economics, commercial/secretarial and foreign languages. In 1996 enrolment in secondary education was equivalent to 97% of the relevant age-group (males 95%; females 99%). There are 11 three-year technical schools. Higher education for teachers, technicians, engineers, hoteliers and caterers, foresters, nurses and health inspectors is provided by technical and vocational colleges. The University of Cyprus was inaugurated in September 1992, and there were a further 33 post-secondary institutions in 1997/98. In that year the university had 2,311 enrolled students, while a total of 10,815 students from the Greek Cypriot area were studying at universities abroad. Budgetary expenditure on education by the central Government in the Greek Cypriot area was C£190.3m. (12.9% of total spending) in 1997. In 1992, according to census results, 5.6%. of the adult population (males 2.2%; females 8.9%) were illiterate.

Education in the Turkish Cypriot zone is controlled by the 'TRNC'. Pre-primary education is provided by kindergartens for children of 5 and 6 years of age. Primary education is free and compulsory: it comprises elementary schools for the 7–11 age-group, and secondary-junior schools for the 12–14 age-group. Secondary education, for the 15–17 age-group, is provided by high schools (Lycées) and vocational schools, including colleges of agriculture, nursing and hotel management. It is free, but not compulsory. In 1998/99 21,912 students were enrolled at eight higher education establishments in the 'TRNC', including five international universities. In 1996, according to census figures, the rate of adult illiteracy in the 'TRNC' was 6.5%.

Public Holidays

2001: 1 January (New Year's Day), 6 January (Epiphany)*, 26 February (Green Monday)*, 5–7 March (Kurban Bayram—Feast of the Sacrifice)†, 25 March (Greek Independence Day)*, 1 April (Anniversary of Cyprus Liberation Struggle), 13–16 April (Easter)*, 23 April (National Sovereignty and Children's Day)†, 1 May (May Day), 19 May (Youth and Sports Day)†, 4 June (Pentecost* and Birth of the Prophet†), 20 July (Peace and Freedom Day, anniversary of the Turkish invasion in 1974)†, 1 August (Communal Resistance Day)†, 15 August (Assumption)*. 30 August (Victory Day)†, 1 October (Independence Day)*, 28 October (Greek National Day)*, 29 October (Turkish Republic Day)†, 15 November (TRNC Day)†, 16–18 December (Ramazam Bayram—end of Ramadan)†, 25–26 December (Christmas)*.

2002: 1 January (New Year's Day), 6 January (Epiphany)*, 22–24 February (Kurban Bayram—Feast of the Sacrifice)†, 18 March (Green Monday)*, 25 March (Greek Independence Day)*, 1 April (Anniversary of Cyprus Liberation Struggle), 23 April (National Sovereignty and Children's Day)†, 1 May (May Day), 3–6 May (Easter)*, 19 May (Youth and Sports Day)†, 24 May (Birth of the Prophet)†, 24 June (Pentecost)*, 20 July (Peace and Freedom Day, anniversary of the Turkish invasion in 1974)†, 1 August (Communal Resistance Day)†, 15 August (Assumption)*, 30 August (Victory Day)†, 1 October (Independence Day)*, 28 October (Greek National Day)*, 29 October (Turkish Republic Day)†, 15 November (TRNC Day)†, 5–7 December (Ramazam Bayram—end of Ramadan)†, 25–26 December (Christmas)*.

* Greek and Greek Orthodox.

† Turkish and Turkish Muslim.

Weights and Measures

Although the imperial and the metric systems are understood, Cyprus has a special internal system:

Weights: 400 drams = 1 oke = 2.8 lb (1.27 kg.).
        44 okes = 1 Cyprus kantar.
        180 okes = 1 Aleppo kantar.
Capacity: 1 liquid oke = 2.25 pints (1.28 litres).
        1 Cyprus litre = 5.6 pints (3.18 litres).
Length and Area: 1 pic = 2 feet (61 cm).
Area: 1 donum = 14,400 sq ft (1,338 sq m).

Statistical Survey

Source (unless otherwise indicated): Department of Statistics and Research, Ministry of Finance, Nicosia; tel. (2) 309301; fax (2) 374830; internet www.pio.gov.cy/dsr/index.htm.

Note: Since July 1974 the northern part of Cyprus has been under Turkish occupation. As a result, some of the statistics relating to subsequent periods do not cover the whole island. Some separate figures for the 'TRNC' are given on p. 0000.

AREA AND POPULATION

Area: 9,251 sq km (3,572 sq miles), incl. Turkish-occupied region.

Population: 602,025 (males 299,614; females 302,411), excl. Turkish-occupied region, at census of 1 October 1992; 754,800, incl. 88,000 in Turkish-occupied region, at 31 December 1999 (official estimate). Note: Figures for the Turkish-occupied region exclude settlers from Turkey, estimated at 114,000 in 1998.

Ethnic Groups (estimates, 31 December 1998): Greeks 639,200 (85.1%), Turks 88,200 (11.7%), others 24,100 (3.2%); Total 751,500.

Principal Towns (population at 1 October 1992): Nicosia (capital) 181,234 (excl. Turkish-occupied portion); Limassol 139,424; Larnaca 62,178; Famagusta (Gazi Magusa) 39,500 (mid-1974); Paphos 33,246; (estimated population at 31 December 1998: Nicosia 195,000 (excl. Turkish-occupied portion); Limassol 154,400; Larnaca 68,500; Paphos 38,800.

Births, Marriages and Deaths (government-controlled area, 1999): Registered live births 8,505 (birth rate 12.8 per 1,000); Registered marriages 9,080 (marriage rate 13.7 per 1,000); Registered deaths 5,070 (death rate 7.6 per 1,000).

Expectation of Life (government-controlled area, years at birth, 1999): Males 75.3; Females 80.4.

Employment (government-controlled area, provisional figures, '000 persons aged 15 years and over, excl. armed forces, 1999): Agriculture, hunting, forestry and fishing 26.9; Mining and quarrying 0.6; Manufacturing 38.6; Electricity, gas and water 1.5; Construction 24.2; Trade, restaurants and hotels 83.6; Transport, storage and communications 19.4; Financing, insurance, real estate and business services 28.5; Community, social and other services 66.9; *Total* 290.2. Figures exclude employment on British sovereign bases. Source: IMF, *Cyprus: Selected Issues and Statistical Appendix* (September 2000).

AGRICULTURE, ETC.

Principal Crops (government-controlled area, '000 metric tons, 1999): Wheat 14.0; Barley 112.7; Potatoes 161.5; Olives 14.0; Cabbages 5.9; Tomatoes 40.0; Cucumbers and gherkins 18.5; Onions (dry) 7.6; Watermelons 40.5; Melons 10.4; Grapes 107.3; Apples 11.5; Oranges 52.8; Tangerines, mandarins, etc. 24.3; Lemons and limes 22.1; Grapefruit and pomelos 44.2; Bananas 13.5. Source: FAO.

Livestock (government-controlled area, '000 head, 1999): Cattle 54.0; Sheep 233.0; Goats 346.0; Pigs 418.5; Chickens (1998) 3,600.

Livestock Products (government-controlled area, '000 metric tons, 1999): Beef and veal 4.0; Mutton and lamb 4.5; Goat meat 6.3; Pig meat 49.2; Poultry meat 34.5; Cows' milk 132.5; Sheep's milk 17.0; Goats' milk 28.5; Cheese 4.5; Hen eggs 10.6. Source: FAO.

Forestry (government-controlled area, '000 cubic metres, 1998): Roundwood removals (excl. bark) 29; Sawnwood production (incl. railway sleepers) 11.

Fishing (metric tons, live weight, government-controlled area, 1998): Capture 2,491 (Bogue 233, Picarels 709, Red mullet 176, Striped mullet 115, Common cuttlefish 146, Octopuses, etc. 228); Aquaculture 1,178 (European seabass 205, Gilthead seabream 827); Total catch 3,669. Source: FAO, *Yearbook of Fishery Statistics*.

MINING AND QUARRYING

Selected Products (metric tons, government-controlled area, 1999): Sand and gravel 9,150,000*; Marble 6,750 (1998); Gypsum 181,446*; Bentonite 140,182*; Umber 9,169*. *Provisional figure.

INDUSTRY

Selected Products (government-controlled area, 1998): Cement 1,206,674 metric tons; Bricks 44.4 million; Mosaic tiles 1.0 million sq metres; Cigarettes 4,362 million; Footwear (excluding plastic and semi-finished shoes) 2.1 million pairs; Beer 35.1 million litres; Wines 31.6 million litres; Carbonated soft drinks 58.9 million litres.

FINANCE

Currency and Exchange Rates: 100 cents = 1 Cyprus pound (Cyprus £). *Sterling, Dollar and Euro Equivalents* (29 December 2000): £1 sterling = 92.03 Cyprus cents; US $1 = 61.68 Cyprus cents; €1 = 57.39 Cyprus cents; Cyprus £100 = £108.66 sterling = $162.14

= €174.25. *Average Exchange Rate* (US $ per Cyprus £): 1.9342 in 1998; 1.8440 in 1999; 1.6107 in 2000.

Budget (Cyprus £ million, government-controlled area, 1999): *Revenue:* Taxation 1,283.8 (Income tax 334.0, Other direct taxes 160.1, Import duty 56.5, Excises 128.5, Value-added tax 236.1, Other indirect taxes 141.7, Social security contributions 226.9); Other current revenue 305.7 (Sales of goods and services 52.3, Interest, rents and dividends 171.5, Transfers 70.4); Capital revenue 0.6; Total 1,590.1, excl. grants from abroad (0.9). *Expenditure:* Current expenditure 1,594.9 (Wages and salaries 482.7, Other goods and services 205.3, Pensions and gratuities 94.6, Other current transfers 208.0, Social security payments 280.3, Subsidies 39.0, Interest payments 285.0); Capital expenditure 192.8 (Investments 131.0, Capital transfers 61.8); Total 1,787.7, excl. net lending (4.6). Source: Central Bank of Cyprus.

International Reserves (US $ million at 31 December 1999): Gold (national valuation) 142.6; IMF special drawing rights 0.5; Reserve position in IMF 48.5; Foreign exchange 1,783.8; Total 1,975.5. Source: IMF, *International Financial Statistics*.

Money Supply (Cyprus £ million at 31 December 1999, government-controlled area): Currency outside banks 313.8, Demand deposits at deposit money banks 724.0; Total money (incl. others) 1,038.3. Source: IMF, *International Financial Statistics*.

Cost of Living (Retail Price Index, government-controlled area; base: 1992 = 100): 120.2 in 1997; 122.9 in 1998; 125.0 in 1999.

Gross Domestic Product in Purchasers' Values (Cyprus £ million, government-controlled area): *GDP at current prices:* 4,356.6 in 1997; 4,679.6 (provisional) in 1998; 4,942.6 (provisional) in 1999. *GDP at constant 1995 prices:* 4,177.9 in 1997; 4,385.7 (provisional) in 1998; 4,583.1 (provisional) in 1999. Source: IMF, *Cyprus: Selected Issues and Statistical Appendix* (September 2000).

Expenditure on the Gross Domestic Product (provisional, Cyprus £ million at current prices, government-controlled area, 1999): Government final consumption expenditure 889.0; Private final consumption expenditure 3,308.5; Increase in stocks 65.0; Gross fixed capital formation 880.5; Statistical discrepancy 31.9; *Total domestic expenditure* 5,174.9; Exports of goods and services 2,204.3; *Less* Imports of goods and services 2,436.6; *GDP in purchasers' values* 4,942.6.

Gross Domestic Product by Economic Activity (provisional, Cyprus £ million at current prices, government-controlled area, 1999): Agriculture and hunting 190.6; Fishing 11.3; Mining and quarrying 14.7; Manufacturing 522.6; Electricity, gas and water supply 103.2; Construction 369.3; Wholesale and retail trade 607.0; Restaurants and hotels 433.0; Transport, storage and communications 419.5; Financial intermediation 337.5; Real estate, renting and business activities 672.6; Public administration and defence 446.7; Education 250.3; Health and social work 167.8; Other community, social and personal services 198.5; Private households with employed persons 29.0; *Sub-total* 4,773.6; Import duties 129.0; Value-added tax 230.0; *Less* Imputed bank service charges 190.0; *GDP in purchasers' values* 4,942.6.

Balance of Payments (US $ million, government-controlled area, 1999): Exports of goods f.o.b. 1,000.3, Imports of goods f.o.b. –3,309.5; *Trade balance* –2,309.2; Exports of services 3,184.7; Imports of services –1,157.2; *Balance on goods and services* –281.8; Other income received 330.4; Other income paid –369.3; *Balance on goods, services and income* –320.7; Current transfers received 194.7; Current transfers paid –107.7; *Current balance* –233.7; Direct investment abroad –158.2; Direct investment from abroad 65.4; Portfolio investment assets –474.8; Portfolio investment liabilities 476.5; Other investment assets –385.1; Other investment liabilities 1,406.0; Net errors and omissions –57.0; *Overall balance* 639.0. Source: IMF, *International Financial Statistics*.

EXTERNAL TRADE

Total Trade (Cyprus £ '000, government-controlled area): *Imports c.i.f.:* 1,899,339 in 1997; 1,904,738 in 1998; 1,970,905 in 1999. *Exports f.o.b.* (incl. re-exports): 640,015 in 1997; 551,134 in 1998; 542,919 in 1999.

Principal Commodities (Cyprus £ '000, government-controlled area, 1998): *Imports c.i.f.:* Prepared foodstuffs, beverages, spirits and tobacco 287,297; Mineral products 129,397; Products of chemical or allied industries 144,617; Textiles and textile articles 143,540; Base metal and articles of base metal 132,726; Machinery and electrical equipment (incl. household appliances) 343,579; Vehicles and associated transport equipment 213,881; Total (incl. others) 1,904,738. *Exports f.o.b.*: Potatoes 18,998; Citrus fruit 12,731; Cheese 6,712; Wine 6,786; Cigarettes 12,179; Cement 8,970; Pharmaceutical products 20,281; Articles of paper or paperboard 4,974; Clothing 29,031; Footwear 8,357; Furniture 7,388; Total (incl. others) 213,162. Figures for exports exclude re-exports (Cyprus £ '000): 306,596. Also excluded are exports of stores and bunkers for ships and aircraft (Cyprus £ '000): 31,376.

Principal Trading Partners (Cyprus £ million, government-controlled area, 1999): *Imports c.i.f.*: China, People's Repub. 54.5; Egypt 47.7; France 103.9; Germany 135.2; Greece 163.6; Israel 58.5; Italy 176.6; Japan 132.7; Korea, Repub. 24.2; Netherlands 42.2; Russia 58.9; Spain 60.5; Syria 22.4; Taiwan 32.5; Thailand 29.4; United Kingdom 225.2; USA 212.5; Total (incl. others) 1,970.9. *Exports f.o.b.* (incl. re-exports): Bulgaria 14.5; Egypt 13.2; France 6.2; Germany 22.8; Greece 48.9; Israel 20.3; Italy 9.2; Lebanon 26.4; Netherlands 13.3; Russia 35.3; Saudi Arabia 6.6; Syria 22.9; United Arab Emirates 22.0; United Kingdom 87.2; USA 21.8; Total (incl. others) 542.9.

TRANSPORT

Road Traffic (licensed motor vehicles, government-controlled area, 31 December 1999): Private passenger cars 249,752; Taxis and self-drive cars 7,237; Buses and coaches 2,835; Lorries and vans 111,125; Motorcycles 44,756; Total (incl. others) 430,974.

Shipping (freight traffic, '000 metric tons, government-controlled area, 1998): Goods loaded 1,418, Goods unloaded 5,080. At 31 December 1998 a total of 1,602 merchant vessels (combined displacement 23,301,517 grt) were registered in Cyprus (Source: Lloyd's Register of Shipping, *World Fleet Statistics*).

Civil Aviation (government-controlled area, 1998): Overall passenger traffic 5,091,990; Total freight transported 35,614 metric tons.

TOURISM

Tourist Arrivals (government-controlled area): 2,088,000 in 1997; 2,222,706 in 1998; 2,434,300 in 1999.

Arrivals by Country of Residence (government-controlled area, 1998): Germany 208,349; Greece 70,762; Israel 53,614; Netherlands 48,206; Norway 46,481; Russia 175,705; Sweden 112,668; Switzerland 83,715; United Kingdom 1,015,228; Total (incl. others) 2,222,706. Source: World Tourism Organization, *Yearbook of Tourism Statistics*.

Tourism Receipts (Cyprus £ million, government-controlled area): 843 in 1997; 878 in 1998; 1,022 (provisional) in 1999.

COMMUNICATIONS MEDIA

Radio Receivers (government-controlled area, 1997): 310,000 in use.

Television Receivers (government-controlled area, 1997): 248,000 in use.

Telephones (main lines in use, 1998): 404,710.

Telefax Stations (provisional or estimated figure, number in use, 1996): 7,000.

Mobile Telephones (subscribers, 1997): 90,968.

Book Production (government-controlled area, 1996): 930 titles and 1,776,000 copies.

Newspapers (1996): 9 daily (circulation 84,000 copies); 31 non-daily (circulation 185,000 copies).

Sources: mainly UNESCO, *Statistical Yearbook*, and UN, *Statistical Yearbook*.

EDUCATION

1997/98 (government-controlled area): Kindergarten: 665 institutions, 1,461 teachers, 26,517 pupils; Primary schools: 372 institutions, 3,521 teachers, 64,592 pupils; Secondary schools (Gymnasia and Lyceums): 114 institutions, 4,438 teachers, 56,872 pupils; Technical colleges: 11 institutions, 594 teachers, 4,831 pupils; University of Cyprus: 196 teachers, 2,311 students; Other post-secondary: 33 institutions, 639 teachers, 8,216 students.

'Turkish Republic of Northern Cyprus'

Sources: Statistics and Research Dept, State Planning Organization, Prime Ministry, Lefkoşa (Nicosia), Mersin 10, Turkey; tel. (22) 83141; fax (22) 85988; Office of the London Representative of the 'Turkish Republic of Northern Cyprus', 29 Bedford Sq., London WC1B 3EG; tel. (20) 7631-1920; fax (20) 7631-1948.

AREA AND POPULATION

Area: 3,355 sq km (1,295 sq miles).

Population (census, 15 December 1996): 200,587 (males 105,978; females 94,609).

Ethnic Groups (census, 15 December 1996): Turks 197,264, English 627, Greeks 384, Maronites 173, Russians 130, Germans 106, Others 1,903; Total 200,587.

Principal Towns (population within the municipal boundary, census, 15 December 1996): Lefkoşa (Nicosia) 39,176 (Turkish-occupied area only); Gazi Mağusa (Famagusta) 27,637; Girne (Kyrenia) 14,205.

Births, Marriages and Deaths (registered, 1998): Live births 2,433 (birth rate 11.8 per 1,000); Marriages 1,108 (marriage rate 5.4 per 1,000); Deaths 717 (death rate 3.5 per 1,000).

Expectation of life (years at birth, 1990–95): Males 72.1; Females 76.9.

Employment (1995): Agriculture, forestry and fishing 17,383; Industry 8,348; Construction 9,584; Trade and tourism 8,367; Transport and communications 6,510; Financial institutions 2,397; Business and personal services 7,276; Public Services 16,589; *Total employed* 76,454. Total unemployed 567; *Total labour force* 77,021.

AGRICULTURE, ETC.

Principal Crops ('000 metric tons, 1998): Wheat 16.7; Barley 37.6; Potatoes 8.8; Legumes 2.2; Tomatoes 2.0; Onions 2.0; Artichokes 0.7; Watermelons 4.3; Melons 1.6; Cucumbers 1.1; Carobs 3.3; Olives 0.4; Lemons 7.7; Grapefruit 36.0; Oranges 92.8; Tangerines 1.0.

Livestock ('000 head, 1998): Cattle 26.1; Sheep 220.5; Goats 59.4; Chickens 3,916.1.

Livestock Products ('000 metric tons, unless otherwise indicated, 1998): Sheep's and goats' milk 12.2; Cows' milk 47.1; Mutton and lamb 3.2; Goat meat 0.8; Beef 1.8; Poultry meat 5.3; Wool 0.3; Eggs (million) 26.1.

Fishing (metric tons, 1994): Total catch 400.

FINANCE

Currency and Exchange Rates: Turkish currency: 100 kuruş = 1 Turkish lira (TL) or pound. *Sterling, Dollar and Euro Equivalents* (29 December 2000): £1 sterling = 1,004,825 liras; US $1 = 673,385 liras; €1 = 626,585 liras; 10,000,000 Turkish liras = £9.952 = $14.850 = €15.960. *Average Exchange Rate* (liras per US dollar): 260,724 in 1998; 418,783 in 1999; 625,219 in 2000.

Budget (million Turkish liras, 1998): *Revenue:* Internal revenue 62,798,381.2 (Direct taxes 26,699,107.9, Indirect taxes 21,005,724.4, Non-tax revenue 12,400,201.6); Aid from Turkey 35,280,831.8; Aid from other countries 61,324.4; Loans 7,770,182.1; Total 105,910,719.5. *Expenditure:* Personnel 34,074,324.2; Other goods and services 5,298,414.3; Transfers 41,169,950.9; Investments 14,368,030.1; Defence 11,000,000.0; Total 105,910,719.5.

Cost of Living (Retail Price Index at December; base: December of previous year = 100): 187.5 in 1996; 181.7 in 1997; 166.5 in 1998.

Expenditure on the Gross Domestic Product (provisional, '000 million Turkish liras at current prices, 1998): Government final consumption expenditure 59,100.1; Private final consumption expenditure 146,053.2; Increase in stocks 4,211.4; Gross fixed capital formation 38,854.7; *Total domestic expenditure* 248,219.4; Exports of goods and services, *less* Imports of goods and services −18,735.4; *GDP in purchasers' values* 229,484.0; *GDP at constant 1977 prices* (million liras) 8,313.0.

Gross Domestic Product by Economic Activity (million Turkish liras, 1998): Agriculture, forestry and fishing 18,075,858.1; Industry 28,038,334.1 (Mining and quarrying 1,492,631.8; Manufacturing 15,710,065.3; Electricity and water 10,835,637.0); Construction 10,131,978.4; Wholesale and retail trade 25,469,159.2; Restaurants and hotels 11,154,957.1; Transport and communications 22,712,786.8; Finance 18,702,391.5; Ownership of dwellings 6,375,054.6; Business and personal services 20,514,511.0; Government services 49,485,813.4; *Sub-total* 210,660,884.1; Import duties 18,823,123.7; *GDP in purchasers' values* 229,483,967.8.

Balance of Payments (US $ million, 1998): Merchandise exports f.o.b. 53.4; Merchandise imports c.i.f. –390.1; *Trade balance* –336.7; Services and unrequited transfers (net) 274.0; *Current balance* –62.7; Capital movements (net) 171.7; Net errors and omissions –6.3; *Total* (net monetary movements) –102.7.

EXTERNAL TRADE

Principal Commodities (US $ million, 1998): *Imports c.i.f.:* Food and live animals 53.2; Beverages and tobacco 24.0; Mineral fuels, lubricants, etc. 26.1; Chemicals 31.5; Basic manufactures 87.0; Machinery and transport equipment 128.0; Miscellaneous manufactured articles 31.2; Total (incl. others) 390.1. *Exports f.o.b.:* Food and live animals 20.9 (Citrus fruit 12.8, Concentrated citrus 2.3); Beverages and tobacco 6.6; Crude materials (inedible) except fuels 2.3; Chemicals 1.6; Clothing 21.4; Total (incl. others) 53.4.

Principal Trading Partners (US $ million, 1998): *Imports c.i.f:* Belgium 4.5; Germany 13.2; Hong Kong 6.4; Italy 16.7; Japan 21.5; Netherlands 6.8; Sri Lanka 5.9; Turkey 231.1; United Kingdom 49.9; USA 6.4; Total (incl. others) 390.1. *Exports f.o.b.:* Germany 4.5; Kuwait 1.2; Netherlands 1.2; Russia 1.1; Turkey 27.0; United Kingdom 16.5; Total (incl. others) 53.4.

TRANSPORT

Road Traffic (registered motor vehicles, 1998): Saloon cars 64,940; Estate cars 8,688; Pick-ups 3,375; Vans 7,798; Buses 1,781; Trucks 775; Lorries 5,335; Motor cycles 14,830; Agricultural tractors 6,125; Total (incl. others) 115,574.

Shipping (1998): Freight traffic ('000 metric tons): Goods loaded 298.7, Goods unloaded 1,036.4; Vessels entered 3,483.

Civil Aviation: Kilometres flown (Turkish Cypriot Airlines) 1,126,848 (1985); Passenger arrivals and departures 624,189 (1994); Freight landed and cleared (metric tons) 6,868 (1998).

TOURISM

Visitors (1998): 393,027 (including 315,797 Turkish); **Accommodation** (1998): Hotels 47, Tourist beds (in all tourist accommodation, including pensions and hotel-apartments) 9,365; **Net Receipts** (US $ million, 1997): 192.2.

COMMUNICATIONS MEDIA

Radio Receivers (1994, provisional): 56,450 in use.

Television Receivers (1994, provisional): 52,300 in use.

Telephones (31 December 1998): 83,162 subscribers.

EDUCATION

1998/99: *Primary and pre-primary education:* 113 institutions, 1,825 teachers, 27,440 pupils; *High schools:* 14 institutions, 744 teachers, 5,341 students; *Vocational schools:* 10 institutions, 363 teachers, 1,890 students; *Higher education:* 8 institutions, 21,912 students.

Directory

The Constitution

The Constitution, summarized below, entered into force on 16 August 1960, when Cyprus became an independent republic.

THE STATE OF CYPRUS

The State of Cyprus is an independent and sovereign Republic with a presidential regime.

The Greek Community comprises all citizens of the Republic who are of Greek origin and whose mother tongue is Greek or who share the Greek cultural traditions or who are members of the Greek Orthodox Church.

The Turkish Community comprises all citizens of the Republic who are of Turkish origin and whose mother tongue is Turkish or who share the Turkish cultural traditions or who are Muslims.

The official languages of the Republic are Greek and Turkish.

The Republic shall have its own flag of neutral design and colour, chosen jointly by the President and the Vice-President of the Republic.

The Greek and the Turkish Communities shall have the right to celebrate respectively the Greek and the Turkish national holidays.

THE PRESIDENT AND VICE-PRESIDENT

Executive power is vested in the President and the Vice-President, who are members of the Greek and Turkish Communities respectively, and are elected by their respective communities to hold office for five years.

The President of the Republic as Head of the State represents the Republic in all its official functions; signs the credentials of diplomatic envoys and receives the credentials of foreign diplomatic envoys; signs the credentials of delegates for the negotiation of international treaties, conventions or other agreements; signs the letter relating to the transmission of the instruments of ratification of any international treaties, conventions or agreements; confers the honours of the Republic.

The Vice-President of the Republic, as Vice-Head of the State, has the right to be present at all official functions; at the presentation of the credentials of foreign diplomatic envoys; to recommend to the President the conferment of honours on members of the Turkish Community, which recommendation the President shall accept unless there are grave reasons to the contrary.

The election of the President and the Vice-President of the Republic shall be direct, by universal suffrage and secret ballot, and shall, except in the case of a by-election, take place on the same day but separately.

The office of the President and of the Vice-President shall be incompatible with that of a Minister or of a Representative or of a member of a Communal Chamber or of a member of any municipal council including a Mayor or of a member of the armed or security forces of the Republic or with a public or municipal office.

The President and Vice-President of the Republic are invested by the House of Representatives.

The President and the Vice-President of the Republic in order to ensure the executive power shall have a Council of Ministers composed of seven Greek Ministers and three Turkish Ministers. The Ministers shall be designated respectively by the President and the Vice-President of the Republic who shall appoint them by an instrument signed by them both. The President convenes and presides over the meetings of the Council of Ministers, while the Vice-President may ask the President to convene the Council and may take part in the discussions.

The decisions of the Council of Ministers shall be taken by an absolute majority and shall, unless the right of final veto or return is exercised by the President or the Vice-President of the Republic or both, be promulgated immediately by them.

The executive power exercised by the President and the Vice-President of the Republic conjointly consists of:

Determining the design and colour of the flag.

Creation or establishment of honours.

Appointment of the members of the Council of Ministers.

Promulgation by publication of the decisions of the Council of Ministers.

Promulgation by publication of any law or decision passed by the House of Representatives.

Appointments and termination of appointments as in Articles provided.

Institution of compulsory military service.

Reduction or increase of the security forces.

Exercise of the prerogative of mercy in capital cases.

Remission, suspension and commutation of sentences.

Right of references to the Supreme Constitutional Court and publication of Court decisions.

Address of messages to the House of Representatives.

The executive powers which may be exercised separately by the President and Vice-President include: designation and termination of appointment of Greek and Turkish Ministers respectively; the right of final veto on Council decisions and on laws concerning foreign affairs, defence or security; the publication of the communal laws and decisions of the Greek and Turkish Communal Chambers respectively; the right of recourse to the Supreme Constitutional Court; the prerogative of mercy in capital cases; and addressing messages to the House of Representatives.

THE COUNCIL OF MINISTERS

The Council of Ministers shall exercise executive power in all matters, other than those which are within the competence of a Communal Chamber, including the following:

General direction and control of the government of the Republic and the direction of general policy.

Foreign affairs, defence and security.

Co-ordination and supervision of all public services.

Supervision and disposition of property belonging to the Republic.

Consideration of Bills to be introduced to the House of Representatives by a Minister.

Making of any order or regulation for the carrying into effect of any law as provided by such law.

Consideration of the Budget of the Republic to be introduced to the House of Representatives.

THE HOUSE OF REPRESENTATIVES

The legislative power of the Republic shall be exercised by the House of Representatives in all matters except those expressly reserved to the Communal Chambers.

The number of Representatives shall be 50, subject to alteration by a resolution of the House of Representatives carried by a majority comprising two-thirds of the Representatives elected by the Greek Community and two-thirds of the Representatives elected by the Turkish Community.

Out of the number of Representatives 70% shall be elected by the Greek Community and 30% by the Turkish Community separately from amongst their members respectively, and, in the case of a contested election, by universal suffrage and by direct and secret ballot held on the same day.

The term of office of the House of Representatives shall be for a period of five years.

The President of the House of Representatives shall be a Greek, and shall be elected by the Representatives elected by the Greek Community, and the Vice-President shall be a Turk and shall be elected by the Representatives elected by the Turkish Community.

THE COMMUNAL CHAMBERS

The Greek and the Turkish Communities respectively shall elect from amongst their own members a Communal Chamber.

The Communal Chambers shall, in relation to their respective Community, have competence to exercise legislative power solely with regard to the following:

All religious, educational, cultural and teaching matters.

Personal status; composition and instances of courts dealing with civil disputes relating to personal status and to religious matters.

Imposition of personal taxes and fees on members of their respective Community in order to provide for their respective needs.

THE PUBLIC SERVICE AND THE ARMED FORCES

The public service shall be composed as to 70% of Greeks and as to 30% of Turks.

The Republic shall have an army of 2,000 men, of whom 60% shall be Greeks and 40% shall be Turks.

The security forces of the Republic shall consist of the police and gendarmerie and shall have a contingent of 2,000 men. The forces shall be composed as to 70% of Greeks and as to 30% of Turks.

OTHER PROVISIONS

The following measures have been passed by the House of Representatives since January 1964, when the Turkish members withdrew:

The amalgamation of the High Court and the Supreme Constitutional Court (see Judicial System section).

The abolition of the Greek Communal Chamber and the creation of a Ministry of Education.

The unification of the Municipalities.

The unification of the Police and the Gendarmerie.

The creation of a military force by providing that persons between the ages of 18 and 50 years can be called upon to serve in the National Guard.

The extension of the term of office of the President and the House of Representatives by one year intervals from July 1965 until elections in February 1968 and July 1970 respectively.

New electoral provisions; abolition of separate Greek and Turkish rolls; abolition of post of Vice-President, which was re-established in 1973.

The Government*

HEAD OF STATE

President: GLAVKOS KLERIDES (took office 28 February 1993; re-elected 15 February 1998).

COUNCIL OF MINISTERS

A coalition Government, comprising DISY, EDE (United Democrats) and Independents (Ind.).

(May 2001)

Minister of Foreign Affairs: YIANNAKIS KASOULIDES (DISY).

Minister of Defence: SOKRATIS HASIKOS (DISY).

Minister of Finance: TAKIS KLERIDES (Ind.).

Minister of the Interior: CHRISTODOULOS CHRISTODOULOU (DISY).

Minister of Justice and Public Order: NIKOS KOSHIS (DISY).

Minister of Commerce, Industry and Tourism: NIKOS ROLANDIS (DISY).

Minister of Education and Culture: OURANIOS IOANNIDES (DISY).

Minister of Health: FRIXOS SAVVIDHIS (Ind.).

Minister of Labour and Social Insurance: ANDREAS MOUSH-ATTAS (Ind.).

Minister of Communications and Works: AVEROF NEOPHITOU (DISY).

Minister of Agriculture, Natural Resources and the Environment: KOSTAS THEMISTOKLEOUS (EDE).

* Under the Constitution of 1960, the vice-presidency and three posts in the Council of Ministers are reserved for Turkish Cypriots. However, there has been no Turkish participation in the Government since December 1963. In 1968 President Makarios announced that he considered the office of Vice-President in abeyance until Turkish participation in the Government is resumed, but the Turkish community elected Rauf Denktaş Vice-President in February 1973.

MINISTRIES

Office of the President: Presidential Palace, Dem. Severis Ave, 1400 Nicosia; tel. (2) 661333; fax (2) 665016.

Ministry of Agriculture, Natural Resources and the Environment: Loukis Akritas Ave, 1411 Nicosia; tel. (2) 300807; fax (2) 781156.

Ministry of Commerce, Industry and Tourism: 6 Andreas Araouzos St, 1424 Nicosia; tel. (2) 867100; fax (2) 375120; e-mail mcitrade@cytanet.com.cy.

Ministry of Communications and Works: 28 Achaion St, 1101, Nicosia; tel. (2) 800203; fax (2) 776254; e-mail airtelecom@mcw.gov.cy.

Ministry of Defence: 4 Emmanuel Roides Ave, 1432 Nicosia; tel. (2) 807622; fax (2) 675289.

Ministry of Education and Culture: Kimonos & Thoukydidou, Akropolis, 1434 Nicosia; tel. (2) 800600; fax (2) 305974; e-mail roc1@cytanet.com.cy.

Ministry of Finance: Ex Secretariat Compound, 1439 Nicosia; tel. (2) 803660; fax (2) 676080.

Ministry of Foreign Affairs: 18–19 Dem. Severis Ave, 1447 Nicosia; tel. (2) 300600; fax (2) 665778; e-mail minforeign1@cytanet .com.cy.

Ministry of Health: Byron Ave, 1448 Nicosia; tel. (2) 309526; fax (2) 305803.

Ministry of the Interior: Dem. Severis Ave, Ex Secretariat Compound, 1453 Nicosia; tel. (2) 302423; fax (2) 671465.

Ministry of Justice and Public Order: 125 Athalassa Ave, 1461 Nicosia; tel. (2) 805955; fax (2) 518356.

Ministry of Labour and Social Insurance: Byron Ave, 1463 Nicosia; tel. (2) 303481; fax (2) 670993.

President and Legislature

PRESIDENT

Election, First round, 8 February 1998

Candidate	Votes	%
GLAVKOS KLERIDES (Democratic Rally)	158,763	40.1
GEORGHIOS IACOVOU (Independent, with AKEL-DIKO support)	160,918	40.6
VASSOS LYSSARIDES (EDEK—Socialist Party*)	41,978	10.6
ALEXIS GALANOS (Independent)	16,003	4.0
GEORGHIOS VASSILIOU (United Democrats)	11,908	3.0
NIKOS KOUTSOU (New Horizons)	3,625	0.9
NIKOS ROLANDIS (Liberal Party†)	3,104	0.8
Total	396,299	100.0

* Became Kinima Sosialdimokraton (KISOS) in 2000.
† Subsequently merged with DISY.

Second round, 15 February 1998

Candidate	Votes	%
GLAVKOS KLERIDES (Democratic Rally)	206,879	50.8
GEORGHIOS IACOVOU (Independent, with AKEL-DIKO support)	200,222	49.2
Total	407,101	100.0

HOUSE OF REPRESENTATIVES

The House of Representatives originally consisted of 50 members, 35 from the Greek community and 15 from the Turkish community, elected for a term of five years. In January 1964 the Turkish members withdrew and set up the 'Turkish Legislative Assembly of the Turkish Cypriot Administration' (see p. 1288). At the 1985 elections the membership of the House was expanded to 80 members, of whom 56 were to be from the Greek community and 24 from the Turkish community (according to the ratio of representation specified in the Constitution).

President: SPYROS KYPRIANOU.

Elections for the Greek Representatives, 27 May 2001

Party	Votes	% of Votes	Seats
AKEL (Progressive Party of the Working People)	142,648	34.7	20
DISY (Democratic Rally)	139,721	34.0	19
DIKO (Democratic Party)	60,986	14.8	9
KISOS (Movement of Social Democrats)	26,767	6.5	4
NEO (New Horizons)	12,333	3.0	1
EDE (United Democrats)	10,635	2.6	1
ADIK (Fighting Democratic Movement)	8,860	2.2	1
Movement of Ecologist and Environmentalists	8,129	2.0	1
Independents	908	0.1	—
Total	410,987	100.0	56

Political Organizations

Agnostiko Dimokratiko Kinima (ADIK) (Fighting Democratic Movement): POB 16095, 80 Arch. Makariou III St, Flat 401, 1077 Nicosia; tel. (2) 765353; fax (2) 375737; e-mail adhk@spidernet .com.cy; f. 1999; centre-right; supports independent and united Cyprus and a settlement based on UN resolutions; advocates accession of Cyprus to the European Union; Pres. DINOS MICHAELIDES; Gen. Sec. PANIKOS LEONIDOU.

Anorthotiko Komma Ergazomenou Laou (AKEL) (Progressive Party of the Working People): POB 21827, 4 E. Papaioannou St, 1513 Nicosia; tel. (2) 761121; fax (2) 761574; e-mail k.e.akel@cytanet .com.cy; internet www.akel.org.cy; f. 1941; successor to the Communist Party of Cyprus (f. 1926); Marxist-Leninist; supports demilitarized, non-aligned and independent Cyprus; over 14,000 mems; Sec.-Gen. DEMETRIS CHRISTOFIAS.

Dimokratiko Komma (DIKO) (Democratic Party): POB 23979, 50 Grivas Dhigenis Ave, 1080 Nicosia; tel. (2) 666002; fax (2) 666488; e-mail diko@diko.org.cy; internet www.diko.org.cy; f. 1976; absorbed Enosi Kentrou (Centre Union, f. 1981) in 1989; supports settlement of the Cyprus problem based on UN resolutions; Pres. TASSOS PAPADO-POULOS; Gen. Sec. ANDREAS ANGELIDES.

Dimokratikos Synagermos (DISY) (Democratic Rally): POB 25303, 25 Pindarou St, 1061 Nicosia; tel. (2) 883164; fax (2) 753821; e-mail disy@disy.org.cy; internet www.disy.org.cy; f. 1976; absorbed Democratic National Party (DEK) in 1977, New Democratic Front (NEDIPA) in 1988 and Liberal Party in 1998; advocates entry of Cyprus into the European Union and greater active involvement by the EU in the settlement of the Cyprus problem; advocates market economy with restricted state intervention and increased state social role; 27,000 mems; Pres. NIKOS ANASTASIADES; Dir-Gen. GEORGE LIVERAS.

Enomeni Dimokrates (EDE) (United Democrats): POB 23494, 8 Iassonos St, 1683 Nicosia; tel. (2) 663030; fax (2) 664747; e-mail edicy@spidernet.com.cy; f. 1996 by merger of Ananeotiko Dimokratiko Socialistiko Kinema (ADISOK—Democratic Socialist Reform Movement) and Kinema ton Eleftheron Dimokraton (KED—Movement of Free Democrats); Pres. GEORGHIOS VASSILIOU; Gen. Sec. KOSTAS THEMISTOKLEOUS.

Epalxi Anasygrotisis Kentrou (EAK) (Political Forum for the Restructuring of the Centre): POB 22119, Lambousa St, 1095 Nicosia; tel. (2) 773564; fax (2) 779939; e-mail kchrysos@logos.cy.net; f. 1998; aims to achieve a wider grouping of all centrist social-democratic movements; supports a settlement to the Cyprus problem based on the principles of the Rule of Law, international law and respect for human rights for all citizens, and the establishment of a democratic federal system of government.

Kinima Ekologon-Perivallontiston (Movement of Ecologists and Environmentalists): POB 29682, 3 Nikos Kazantzakis St, 2007 Nicosia; tel. (2) 778820; fax (2) 772417; e-mail cyprusgreens@hotmail.com; internet cycentral.com/greens; f. 1996; opposed to any geographical division of the island; supports entry into the European Union; Gen. Co-ordinator KYRIACOS TSIMILLIS.

Kinima Sosialdimokraton (KISOS) Movement of Social Democrats): POB 21064, 40 Byron Avenue, 1096 Nicosia; tel. (2) 670121; fax (2) 678894; f. 2000 as successor to Socialistico Komma Kyprou (EDEK—Socialist Party of Cyprus); supports independent, non-aligned, unitary, demilitarized Cyprus; advocates accession of Cyprus to the European Union; Pres. Dr VASSOS LYSSARIDES; Dep. Pres. YIANNAKIS OMIROU.

Kinisi Politikou Eksychronismou (Movement for Political Reforms): 22 Stasikratous St, 1065 Nicosia; tel. (2) 668894; fax (2) 6698892; f. 1995; aims to contribute to realignment of the parties of the Centre; supports settlement of the Cyprus problem based on UN resolutions; supports accession of Cyprus to the European Union.

Komma Evrodimokratikis Ananeosis (KEA) (Eurodemocratic Renewal Party): 176 Athalassa Ave, Office 402, 2025 Nicosia; tel. (2) 514551; fax (2) 513565; f. 1998; supports entry into the European Union and federal settlement to the Cyprus problem based on UN resolutions; Pres. ANTONIS PASCHALIDES; Gen. Sec. TAKIS HADJIOANNOU.

Neoi Orizontes (NEO) (New Horizons): POB 22496, 3 Trikoupi St, 1522 Nicosia; tel. (2) 761476; fax (2) 761144; e-mail neo@logos.cy.net; internet www.neoiorizontes.org; f. 1996; supports settlement of the Cyprus problem through political means and the establishment of a non-federal unitary state with single sovereignty throughout the whole territory of the island; Pres. NIKOS KOUTSOU; Gen. Sec. MARIA ROSSIDOU.

Diplomatic Representation

EMBASSIES AND HIGH COMMISSIONS IN CYPRUS

Australia: 4 Annis Komninis St, 2nd Floor, 1060 Nicosia; tel. (2) 473001; fax (2) 366486; High Commissioner: FRANZ JOHANN INGRUBER.

Bulgaria: POB 24029, 13 Konst. Paleologos St, 2406 Engomi, Nicosia; tel. (2) 672486; fax (2) 676598; e-mail bulgaria@cytanet.com.cy; Ambassador: ALEXEI IVANOV.

China, People's Republic: POB 4531, 28 Archimedes St, 2411 Engomi, Nicosia; tel. (2) 352182; fax (2) 353530; Ambassador: YIN ZUOJIN.

Cuba: 7 Yiannis Taliotis St, Strovolos 2014, Nicosia; tel. (2) 512332; fax (2) 512331; e-mail embacuba@spidernet.com.cy; Ambassador: MANUEL PARDIÑAS AJENO.

Czech Republic: POB 5202, 48 Arsinois St, 1307 Nicosia; tel. (2) 421118; fax (2) 421059; e-mail nicosia@embassy.mzv.cz; Ambassador: VEŘA JEŘÁBIKOVÁ.

Egypt: POB 1752, 3 Egypt Ave, 1097 Nicosia; tel. (2) 465144; fax (2) 462287; Ambassador: OMAR METWALLY.

France: POB 1671, 12 Ploutarchou St, Engomi, Nicosia; tel. (2) 779910; fax (2) 781052; e-mail ambachyp@spidernet.com.cy; internet www.ambafrancechypre.org; Ambassador: JEAN BERNARD DE VAIVRE.

Germany: POB 25705, 10 Nikitaras St, Ay. Omoloyitae, 1311 Nicosia; tel. (2) 451145; fax (2) 665694; e-mail germanembassy@cytanet.com.cy; Ambassador: Dr PETER WITTIG.

Greece: POB 1799, 8/10 Byron Ave, Nicosia; tel. (2) 680670; fax (2) 680649; Ambassador: KYRIAKOS RODOUSSAKIS.

Holy See: POB 21964, Holy Cross Catholic Church, Paphos Gate, 1010 Nicosia (Apostolic Nunciature); tel. (2) 662132; fax (2) 660767; Apostolic Nuncio: Most Rev. PIETRO SAMBI, Titular Archbishop of Belcastro (with residence in Jerusalem).

India: POB 25544, 3 Indira Gandhi St, Engomi, 2413 Nicosia; tel. (2) 351741; fax (2) 350402; e-mail india@spidernet.com.cy; High Commissioner: SHYAMALA B. COWSIK.

Iran: POB 8145, 42 Armenias St, Akropolis, Nicosia; tel. (2) 314459; fax (2) 315446; Ambassador: BAHMAN AGHA-RAZI.

Israel: POB 1049, 4 I. Gryparis St, Nicosia; tel. (2) 445195; fax (2) 453486; Ambassador: MICHAEL ELIGAL.

Italy: POB 27695, 11 25th March St, Engomi 2432, Nicosia; tel. (2) 357635; fax (2) 358112; e-mail italian.embassy@cytanet.com.cy; internet italian.embassy.cyprus.homepage.com; Ambassador: FRANCESCO BASCONE.

Lebanon: POB 21924, 1 Vasilissis Olgas St, Nicosia; tel. (2) 776845; fax (2) 776662; Ambassador: SAMIRA HANNA-ED-DAHER.

Libya: POB 3669, 14 Estias St, 1041 Nicosia; tel. (2) 317366; fax (2) 316152; Ambassador: KHALIFA AHMAD BAZELYA.

Poland: 11 Acharnon St, Strovolos, Nicosia; tel. (2) 427077; fax (2) 510611; Ambassador: TOMASZ LIS.

Romania: POB 2210, 83 Kennedy Ave, 1077 Nicosia; tel. (2) 379303; fax (2) 379121; Chargé d'affaires: FLORIAN UNCHIASU.

Russia: Ay. Prokopias St and Archbishop Makarios III Ave, Engomi, Nicosia; tel. (2) 772141; fax (2) 774854; Ambassador: VLADIMIR PRYGIN.

Slovakia: POB 21165, 4 Kalamatas St, 2002 Strovolos, Nicosia; tel. (2) 311683; fax (2) 311715; Ambassador: DUŠAN ROZBORA.

Switzerland: POB 20729, MEDCON Bldg, 6th Floor, 46 Themistoklis Dervis St, 1663 Nicosia; tel. (2) 766261; fax (2) 766008; e-mail swiemnic@spidernet.com.cy; Chargé d'affaires a.i.: MARGRITH BIERI.

Syria: POB 21891, 24 Nikodimos Mylona St, Ay. Antonios, 1071 Nicosia; tel. (2) 764481; fax (2) 756963; Chargé d'affaires a.i.: Dr AHMAD HAJ-IBRAHIM.

United Kingdom: POB 21978, Alexander Pallis St, Nicosia; tel. (2) 861100; fax (2) 861125; e-mail infobhc@cylink.com.cy; internet www.britain.org.cy; High Commissioner: EDWARD CLAY.

USA: 7 Ploutarchou, 2406 Engomi, Nicosia; tel. (2) 776400; fax (2) 780944; e-mail amembass@spidernet.com.cy; internet www.americanembassy.org.cy; Ambassador: DONALD K. BANDLER.

Yugoslavia: 2 Vasilissis Olgas St, Nicosia; tel. (2) 445511; fax (2) 445910; Ambassador: PERO JANCOVIC.

Judicial System

Supreme Council of Judicature: Nicosia. The Supreme Council of Judicature is composed of the President and Judges of the Supreme Court. It is responsible for the appointment, promotion, transfer, etc., of the judges exercising civil and criminal jurisdiction in the District Courts, the Assize Courts, the Family Courts, the Military Court, the Rent Control Courts and the Industrial Dispute Court.

SUPREME COURT

Supreme Court: Char. Mouskos St, 1404 Nicosia; tel. (2) 865716; fax (2) 304500. The Constitution of 1960 provided for a separate Supreme Constitutional Court and High Court but in 1964, in view of the resignation of their neutral presidents, these were amalgamated to form a single Supreme Court.

The Supreme Court is the final appellate court in the Republic and the final adjudicator in matters of constitutional and administrative law, including recourses on conflict of competence between state organs on questions of the constitutionality of laws, etc. It deals with appeals from Assize Courts, District Courts and other inferior Courts as well as from the decisions of its own judges when exercising original jurisdiction in certain matters such as prerogative orders of *habeas corpus, mandamus, certiorari,* etc., and in admiralty cases.

President: GEORGHIOS M. PIKIS.

Judges: I. C. CONSTANTINIDES, T. ELIADES, CHR. C. ARTEMIDES, G. NIKO-LAOU, P. KALLIS, FR. G. NIKOLAIDES, S. NIKITAS, P. CH. ARTEMIS, M. KRONIDES, A. KRAMVIS, R. GAVRIELIDES, Y. CHRYSOSTOMIS.

Attorney-General: ALEKOS MARKIDES.

OTHER COURTS

As required by the Constitution a law was passed in 1960 providing for the establishment, jurisdiction and powers of courts of civil and criminal jurisdiction, i.e. of six District Courts and six Assize Courts. In accordance with the provisions of new legislation, approved in 1991, a permanent Assize Court, with powers of jurisdiction in all districts, was established.

In addition to a single Military Court, there are specialized Courts concerned with cases relating to industrial disputes, rent control and family law.

'Turkish Republic of Northern Cyprus'

The Turkish intervention in Cyprus in July 1974 resulted in the establishment of a separate area in northern Cyprus under the control of the Autonomous Turkish Cypriot Administration, with a Council of Ministers and separate judicial, financial, police, military and educational machinery serving the Turkish community.

On 13 February 1975 the Turkish-occupied zone of Cyprus was declared the 'Turkish Federated State of Cyprus', and Rauf Denktaş declared President. At the second joint meeting held by the Executive Council and Legislative Assembly of the Autonomous Turkish Cypriot Administration, it was decided to set up a Constituent Assembly which would prepare a constitution for the 'Turkish Federated State of Cyprus' within 45 days. This Constitution, which was approved by the Turkish Cypriot population in a referendum held on 8 June 1975, was regarded by the Turkish Cypriots as a first step towards a federal republic of Cyprus. The main provisions of the Constitution are summarized below:

The 'Turkish Federated State of Cyprus' is a democratic, secular republic based on the principles of social justice and the rule of law. It shall exercise only those functions which fall outside the powers and functions expressly given to the (proposed) Federal Republic of Cyprus. Necessary amendments shall be made to the Constitution of the 'Turkish Federated State of Cyprus' when the Constitution of the Federal Republic comes into force. The official language is Turkish.

Legislative power is vested in a Legislative Assembly, composed of 40 deputies, elected by universal suffrage for a period of five years. The President is Head of State and is elected by universal suffrage for a period of five years. No person may be elected President for more than two consecutive terms. The Council of Ministers shall be composed of a prime minister and 10 ministers. Judicial power is exercised through independent courts.

Other provisions cover such matters as the rehabilitation of refugees, property rights outside the 'Turkish Federated State', protection of coasts, social insurance, the rights and duties of citizens, etc.

On 15 November 1983 a unilateral declaration of independence brought into being the 'Turkish Republic of Northern Cyprus', which, like the 'Turkish Federated State of Cyprus', was not granted international recognition.

The Constituent Assembly, established after the declaration of independence, prepared a new constitution, which was approved by the Turkish Cypriot electorate on 5 May 1985. The new Constitution is very similar to the old one, but the number of deputies in the Legislative Assembly was increased to 50.

HEAD OF STATE

President of the 'Turkish Republic of Northern Cyprus': RAUF R. DENKTAŞ (assumed office as President of the 'Turkish Federated State of Cyprus' 13 February 1975; became President of the 'TRNC' 15 November 1983; re-elected 1985, 1990, 1995 and 15 April 2000).

COUNCIL OF MINISTERS*
(May 2001)

A coalition of the Ulusal Bırlık Partisi (UBP) and the Toplumcu Kurtuluş Partisi (TKP).

Prime Minister: Dr DERVİŞ EROĞLU (UBP).

Minister of State and Deputy Prime Minister: MUSTAFA AKINCI (TKP).

Minister of Foreign Affairs and Defence: TAHSIN ERTUĞRULOGLU (UBP).

Minister of the Interior and Rural Affairs: İLKAY KAMIL (UBP).

Minister of the Economy and Finance: MEHMET BAYRAM (UBP).

Minister of National Education and Culture: MEHMET ALTINAY (TKP).

Minister of Agriculture and Forestry: İRSEN KÜÇÜK (UBP).

Minister of Communications and Works: SALİH MİROĞLU (UBP).

Minister of Labour and Housing: MEHMET ALBAYRAK (UBP).

Minister of Health and the Environment: GÜLSEN BOZKURT (TKP).

Minister of Youth Affairs and Sports: TANSEL DORATH (UBP).

* Derviş Eroğlu resigned as Prime Minister in late May 2001, following the collapse of the governing coalition. All ministers were to remain in office in an acting capacity pending the formation of a new government.

MINISTRIES

Prime Minister's Office: Lefkoşa (Nicosia), Mersin 10, Turkey; tel. (22) 83141; fax (22) 75281; e-mail pressdpt@brimnet.com.

Ministry of State and Deputy Prime Minister's Office: Lefkoşa (Nicosia), Mersin 10, Turkey; tel. (22) 77283; fax (22) 73976.

Ministry of Agriculture and Forestry: Lefkoşa (Nicosia), Mersin 10, Turkey; tel. (22) 83735; fax (22) 86945.

Ministry of Communications, Works and Tourism: Lefkoşa (Nicosia), Mersin 10, Turkey; tel. (22) 83666; fax (22) 81891.

Ministry of the Economy and Finance: Lefkoşa (Nicosia), Mersin 10, Turkey; tel. (22) 83116; fax (22) 85204; e-mail ekonomi@ebim .com.tr.

Ministry of Education, Culture, Youth and Sports: Lefkoşa (Nicosia), Mersin 10, Turkey; tel. (22) 83136; fax (22) 82334.

Ministry of Foreign Affairs and Defence: Lefkoşa (Nicosia), Mersin 10, Turkey; tel. (22) 83241; fax (22) 84290.

Ministry of Health and the Environment: Lefkoşa (Nicosia), Mersin 10, Turkey; tel. (22) 83173; fax (22) 83893.

Ministry of the Interior and Rural Affairs: Lefkoşa (Nicosia), Mersin 10, Turkey; tel. (22) 85453; fax (22) 83043.

Ministry of Social Welfare and Rehabilitation: Lefkoşa (Nicosia), Mersin 10, Turkey; tel. (22) 78765; fax (22) 76349.

PRESIDENT

Election, 15 April 2000*

Candidates	Votes	%
RAUF R. DENKTAŞ (Independent) . . .	42,819	43.67
Dr DERVİŞ EROĞLU (UBP)	29,505	30.14
MUSTAFA AKINCI (TKP)	11,469	11.70
MEHMET ALI TALAT (CTP)	9,834	10.03
ARIF HASAN TAHSIN (YBH)	2,545	2.60
ŞENER LEVET (Independent)	899	0.92
TURGUT AFSAROGLU (Independent) . .	553	0.56
AYHAN KAYMAK (Independent) . . .	369	0.38
Total	97,993†	100.00

* Although Denktaş did not gain the 50% of the votes necesary to be elected in the first round, he was declared the winner after Eroğlu withdrew from a second round of voting, scheduled for 22 April 2000.

† Excluding invalid votes.

LEGISLATIVE ASSEMBLY

Speaker: ERTUĞRUL HASIPOĞLU (UBP).

Deputy Speaker: SALİH COSAR (DP).

General Election, 6 December 1998

Party	% of votes	Seats
Ulusal Bırlık Partisi	40.3	24
Demokrat Parti	22.6	13
Toplumcu Kurtuluş Partisi	15.4	7
Cumhuriyetçi Türk Partisi	13.4	6
Others*	8.3	—
Total	100.0	50

* The other parties that contested the election were the National Revival Party, which won 4.6% of the votes; the Patriotic Unity Movement, which obtained 2.5%; and Our Party, which won 1.2%.

POLITICAL ORGANIZATIONS

Cumhuriyetçi Türk Partisi (CTP) (Republican Turkish Party): 99A Şehit Salahi, Şevket Sok., Lefkoşa (Nicosia), Mersin 10, Turkey; tel. (22) 73300; fax (22) 81914; e-mail ctp@cypronet.net; f. 1970 by members of the Turkish community in Cyprus; socialist principles with anti-imperialist stand; district organizations at Gazi Mağusa (Famagusta), Girne (Kyrenia), Güzelyurt (Morphou) and Lefkoşa (Nicosia); Leader MEHMET ALI TALAT; Gen. Sec. MUSTAFA FERDİ SOYER.

Demokrat Parti (DP) (Democrat Party): Lefkoşa (Nicosia), Mersin 10, Turkey; tel. (22) 83795; fax (22) 87130; e-mail yenidem@kktc.net; f. 1992 by disaffected UBP representatives; merged with the Yeni Doğuş Partisi (New Dawn Party; f. 1984) and Sosyal Demokrat

Partisi (Social Democrat Party) in May 1993; Leader SERDAR DENKTAŞ; Sec.-Gen. HURSIT EMINER.

Hür Demokrat Parti (Free Democrat Party): Lefkoşa (Nicosia), Mersin 10, Turkey; f. 1991. Leader ÖZEL TAHSIN.

Toplumcu Kurtuluş Partisi (TKP) (Communal Liberation Party): 44 İkinci Selim Sok., Lefkoşa (Nicosia), Mersin 10, Turkey; tel. (22) 72555; f. 1976; merged with the Atılımcı Halk Partisi (Progressive People's Party, f. 1979) in 1989; democratic left party; wants a solution of Cyprus problem as an independent, non-aligned, bi-zonal and bi-communal federal state; Leader MUSTAFA AKINCI; Gen. Sec. HÜSEYIN ANGOLEMLİ.

Ulusal Bırlık Partisi (UBP) (National Unity Party): 9 Atatürk Meydanı, Lefkoşa (Nicosia), Mersin 10, Turkey; tel. (22) 73972; f. 1975; right of centre; based on Atatürk's reforms, social justice, political equality and peaceful co-existence in an independent, bi-zonal, bi-communal, federal state of Cyprus; Leader Dr DERVIŞ EROĞLU; Sec.-Gen. Dr VEIIBI ZEKI SERTER.

Ulusal Dirilis Partisi (UDP) (National Revival Party): Lefkoşa (Nicosia), Mersin 10, Turkey; f. 1997; Leader ENVER EMIN.

Unity and Sovereignty Party (BEP): Lefkoşa (Nicosia), Mersin 10, Turkey; Leader ARIF SALIH KIRDAĞ.

Yeni Doğus Partisi (New Dawn Party): Lefkoşa (Nicosia); f. 1984; merged with DP in May 1993, revived 1997.

Yurtsever Bırlık Hareketi (YBH) (Patriotic Unity Movement): Lefkoşa (Nicosia), Mersin 10, Turkey; tel. (22) 74917; fax (22) 88931; e-mail ybh@north-cyprus.net; f. 1989; Leader RASIH KESKINER.

DIPLOMATIC REPRESENTATION
Embassy in the 'TRNC'

Turkey: Bedrettin Demirel Cad., T.C. Lefkoşa Büyükelçisi, Lefkoşa (Nicosia), Mersin 10, Turkey; tel. (22) 72314; fax (22) 85118; e-mail tclefkbe@cc.emu.edu.tr; Ambassador: HAYATI GÜVEN.

Turkey is the only country officially to have recognized the 'Turkish Republic of Northern Cyprus'.

JUDICIAL SYSTEM

Supreme Court: Lefkoşa (Nicosia), Mersin 10, Turkey; tel. (22) 87535; fax (22) 85265; e-mail mahkeme@kktc.net. The highest court in the 'TRNC' is the Supreme Court. The Supreme Court functions as the Constitutional Court, the Court of Appeal and the High Administrative Court. The Supreme Court, sitting as the Constitutional Court, has exclusive jurisdiction to adjudicate finally on all matters prescribed by the Constitution. The Supreme Court, sitting as the Court of Appeal, is the highest appellate court in the 'TRNC'. It also has original jurisdiction in certain matters of judicial review. The Supreme Court, sitting as the High Administrative Court, has exclusive jurisdiction on matters relating to administrative law.

The Supreme Court is composed of a president and seven judges.

President: SALIH S. DAYIOĞLU.

Judges: CELÂL KARABACAK, TANER ERGINEL, METIN A. HAKKI, NEVVAR NOLAN, MUSTAFA ÖZKÖK, GÖNÜL ERÖNEN, SEYIT A. BENSEN.

Subordinate Courts: Judicial power other than that exercised by the Supreme Court is exercised by the Assize Courts, District Courts and Family Courts.

Supreme Council of Judicature: The Supreme Council of Judicature, composed of the president and judges of the Supreme Court, a member appointed by the President of the 'TRNC', a member appointed by the Legislative Assembly, the Attorney-General and a member elected by the Bar Association, is responsible for the appointment, promotion, transfer and matters relating to the discipline of all judges. The appointments of the president and judges of the Supreme Court are subject to the approval of the President of the 'TRNC'.

Attorney-General: SAİT AKIN.

Religion

Greeks form 77% of the population and most of them belong to the Orthodox Church, although there are also adherents of the Armenian Apostolic Church, the Anglican Communion and the Roman Catholic Church (including Maronites). Most Turks (about 18% of the population) are Muslims.

CHRISTIANITY
The Orthodox Church of Cyprus

The Autocephalous Orthodox Church of Cyprus, founded in AD 45, is part of the Eastern Orthodox Church; the Church is independent, and the Archbishop, who is also the Ethnarch (national leader of the Greek community), is elected by representatives of the towns and villages of Cyprus. The Church comprises six dioceses, and in 1995 had an estimated 600,000 members.

Archbishop of Nova Justiniana and all Cyprus: Archbishop CHRYSOSTOMOS, POB 1130, Archbishop Kyprianos St, Nicosia; tel. (2) 430696; fax (2) 432470.

Metropolitan of Paphos: Bishop CHRYSOSTOMOS.

Metropolitan of Kitium: Bishop CHRYSOSTOMOS, Dem. Lipertis St, Larnaca; fax (41) 55588.

Metropolitan of Kyrenia: Bishop PAULUS.

Metropolitan of Limassol: Bishop ATHANASIOS.

Metropolitan of Morphou: Bishop NEOPHYTIOS.

The Roman Catholic Church

Latin Rite

The Patriarchate of Jerusalem covers Israel, Jordan and Cyprus. The Patriarch is resident in Jerusalem (see the chapter on Israel).

Vicar Patriarchal for Cyprus: Father UMBERTO BARATO, Holy Cross Catholic Church, Paphos Gate, POB 3751, 1515 Nicosia; tel. (2) 662132; fax (2) 660767.

Maronite Rite

Most of the Roman Catholics in Cyprus are adherents of the Maronite rite. Prior to June 1988 the Archdiocese of Cyprus included part of Lebanon. At December 1998 the archdiocese contained an estimated 10,000 Maronite Catholics.

Archbishop of Cyprus: Most Rev. BOUTROS GEMAYEL, POB 22249, Maronite Archbishop's House, 8 Ayios Maronas St, Nicosia; tel. (2) 678877; fax (2) 668260.

The Anglican Communion

Anglicans in Cyprus are adherents of the Episcopal Church in Jerusalem and the Middle East, officially inaugurated in January 1976. The Church has four dioceses. The diocese of Cyprus and the Gulf includes Cyprus, Iraq and the countries of the Arabian peninsula.

Bishop in Cyprus and the Gulf: Rt Rev. CLIVE HANDFORD, c/o POB 22075, Diocesan Office, 2 Grigoris Afxentiou St, 1517 Nicosia; tel. (2) 671220; fax (2) 674553; e-mail georgia@spidernet.com.cy.

Other Christian Churches

Among other denominations active in Cyprus are the Armenian Apostolic Church and the Greek Evangelical Church.

ISLAM

Most adherents of Islam in Cyprus are Sunni Muslims of the Hanafi sect. The religious head of the Muslim community is the Mufti.

Mufti of Cyprus: AHMET CEMAL İLKTAÇ (acting), PK 142, Lefkoşa (Nicosia), Mersin 10, Turkey.

The Press

GREEK CYPRIOT DAILIES

Alithia (Truth): POB 21695, 26A Pindaros and Androklis St, 1060 Nicosia; tel. (2) 763040; fax (2) 763945; e-mail alithia@spidernet .com.cy; f. 1952 as a weekly, 1982 as a daily; morning; Greek; right-wing; Dir SOCRATIS HASIKOS; Chief Editor ALEKOS KONSTANTINIDES; circ. 11,000.

Apogevmatini (Afternoon): POB 25603, 5 Aegaleo St, Strovolos, Nicosia; tel. (2) 353603; fax (2) 353223; f. 1972; afternoon; Greek; independent, Dirs EFTHYMIOS HADJIEFTHIMIOU, ANTONIS STAVRIDES; Chief Editor COSTAKIS ANTONIOY; circ. 8,000.

Cyprus Mail: POB 21144, 24 Vassilios Voulgaroktonos St, Nicosia; tel. (2) 462074; fax (2) 366385; e-mail cyprus.mail@cytanet.com.cy; internet www.cynews.com; f. 1945; morning; English; independent; Dir. KYRIACOS IAKOVIDES; Editor STEVEN MYLES; circ. 4,000.

Epilogi: 19 Nikitara St, Ay. Omologiles, Nicosia; tel. (2) 367345; fax (2) 367511; f. 1997; Greek; Chief Editor COSTAS ZACHARIADES.

Haravghi (Dawn): POB 21556, ETAK Bldg, 6 Akamantos St, Nicosia; tel. (2) 766666; fax (2) 765154; f. 1956; morning; Greek; organ of AKEL (Communist Party); Dir NIKOS KATSOURIDES; Chief Editor ANDREAS ROUSOS: circ. 9,000.

Machi (Combat): POB 27628, 4A Danaes, Engomi, Nicosia; tel. (2) 356676; fax (2) 356701; f. 1961; morning; Greek; right-wing; Dir SOTIRIS SAMPSON; Chief Editor MINA SAMPSON; circ. 4,750.

Phileleftheros (Liberal): POB 21094, Commercial Centre, 1 Diogenous St, 3rd, 6th–7th Floor, Engomi, 1501 Nicosia; tel. (2) 744000; fax (2) 590122; e-mail artemiou@phileleftheros.com; internet www.in.cy.com; f. 1955; morning; Greek; independent, moderate; Dir N. PATTICHIS; Editorial Dir A. LYKAVGIS; Chief Editor T. KOUNNAFIS; circ. 26,000.

Politis (Citizen): 12 Makhera St, Engomi, Nicosia; tel. (2) 861861; fax (2) 861871; e-mail info@politis-news.com; internet www

.politis-news.com; f. 1999; morning; Greek; independent; Chief Editor ARISTOS MICHAELIDES.

Simerini (Today): POB 21836, 31 Archangelos Ave, Strovolos, Nicosia; tel. (2) 353532; fax (2) 352298; internet www.odyssey .com.cy/simerini; f. 1976; morning; Greek; right-wing; supports DISY party; Dir KOSTAS HADJIKOSTIS; Chief Editor SAVVAS IAKOVIDES; circ. 17,000.

TURKISH CYPRIOT DAILIES

Avrupa (Europe): Lefkoşa (Nicosia), Mersin 10, Turkey; tel. (22) 71338; fax (22) 74585; e-mail avrupa@cc.emu.edu.tr; independent; Editor ŞENER LEVENT; circ. 3,000.

Bırlık (Unity): 43 Yediler Sok., PK 841, Lefkoşa (Nicosia), Mersin 10, Turkey; tel. (22) 72959; fax (22) 83959; f. 1980; Turkish; organ of UBP; Editor LÜTFI ÖZTER.

Halkın Sesi (Voice of the People): 172 Kyrenia Sok., Lefkoşa (Nicosia), Mersin 10, Turkey; tel. (22) 73141; f. 1942; morning; Turkish; independent Turkish nationalist; Editor AKAY CEMAL; circ. 6,000.

Kıbrıs: Dr Fazil Küçük Bul., Lefkoşa (Nicosia), Mersin 10, Turkey; tel. (22) 52555; fax 52934; e-mail kibris@cypronet.net; Editor MEHMET ALI AKPINAR; circ. 13,000.

Ortam (Political Conditions): 158A Girne Cad., Lefkoşa (Nicosia), Mersin 10, Turkey; tel. (22) 74872; Turkish; organ of the TKP; Editor ÖZAL ZIYA; circ. 1,250.

Vatan (Homeland): 46 Mufti Ziyai Sok., PK 842, Lefkoşa (Nicosia), Mersin 10, Turkey; tel. (22) 77557; fax (22) 77558; e-mail vatan@ kktc.net; f. 1991; Editor ERTEN KASIMOĞLU.

Yeni Demokrat (New Democrat): 1 Cengiz Han Cad., Kösklüçiftlik, Lefkoşa (Nicosia), Mersin 10, Turkey; tel. (22) 81485; fax (22) 72558; Turkish; organ of the DP; Editor MUSTAFA OKAN; circ. 450.

Yeni Düzen (New System): Yeni Sanayi Sok., Lefkoşa (Nicosia), Mersin 10, Turkey; tel. (22) 56658; fax (22) 53240; e-mail yeniduze@ north-cyprus.net; Turkish; organ of the CTP; Editor ÖZKAN YORGANCI-OĞLU; circ. 1,000.

GREEK CYPRIOT WEEKLIES

Athlitiki tis Kyriakis: 5 Epias, Engomi, Nicosia; tel. (2) 352966; fax (2) 348835; f. 1996; Greek; athletic; Dir PANAYIOTIS FELLOUKAS; Chief Editor SAWAS KOSHARIS; circ. 4,000.

Cyprus Financial Mirror: POB 24280, 80B Thermopylon St, 2007 Nicosia; tel. (2) 495790; fax (2) 495907; e-mail shavasb@ financialmirror.com; internet www.financialmirror.com; f. 1993; English (with Greek-language supplement); independent; Dirs MASIS DER PARTHOGH, SHAVASB BOHDJALIAN; circ. 3,500.

Cyprus Weekly: POB 24977, Suite 102, Trust House, Gryparis St, 1306 Nicosia; tel. (2) 666047; fax (2) 668665; e-mail weekly@ spidernet.com.cy; internet www.cyprusweekly.com.cy; f. 1979; English; independent; Dirs GEORGES DER PARTHOGH, ALEX EFTHYVOULOS, A. HADJIPAPAS; Chief Editor MARTYN HENRY; circ. 18,000.

Ergatiki Phoni (Workers' Voice): POB 25018, SEK Bldg, 23 Alkeou St, Engomi, Nicosia; tel. (2) 441142; fax (2) 476360; f. 1947; Greek; organ of SEK trade union; Dir MICHALAKIS IOANNOU; Chief Editor XENIS XENOFONTOS; circ. 10,000.

Ergatiko Vima (Workers' Tribune): POB 21185, 31-35 Archemos St, Nicosia; tel. (2) 349400; fax (2) 349382; f. 1956; Greek; organ of the PEO trade union; Chief Editor KOSTAS GREKOS; circ. 14,000.

Official Gazette: Printing Office of the Republic of Cyprus, Nicosia; tel. (2) 302202; fax (2) 303175; f. 1960; Greek; published by the Government of the Republic of Cyprus; circ. 5,000.

Paraskinio (Behind the Scenes): 6 Psichikou St, Strovolos, Nicosia; tel. (2) 322959; fax (2) 322940; f. 1987; Greek; Dir and Chief Editor D. MICHAEL; cir. 3,000.

Selides (Pages): POB 21094, 1501 Nicosia; tel. (2) 590000; fax (2) 590122; e-mail selides@phileleftheros.com; internet www .phileleftheros.com; f. 1991; Greek; Dir N. PATTICHIS; Chief Editor STAVROS CHRISTODOLOU; circ. 16,500.

Super Flash: POB 23647, 11 Kolokotronis St, Kaimakli, Nicosia; tel. (2) 316674; fax (2) 316582; f. 1979; youth magazine; Greek; Dir DEMETRIS ALONEFTIS; circ. 4,000.

Ta Nea (News): POB 4349, 40 Vyronos Ave, Nicosia; tel. (2) 476575; fax (2) 476512; f. 1968; Greek; organ of EDEK (Socialist Party); Chief Editor PHYTOS SOCRATOUS; circ. 3,000.

Tharros (Courage): POB 27628, 4A Danaes, Engomi, Nicosia; tel. (2) 356676; fax (2) 356701; f. 1961; Greek; right-wing; Dir SOTIRIS SAMPSON; Chief Editor MINA SAMPSON; circ. 5,500.

To Periodiko: POB 21836, Dias Bldg, 31 Archangelos Ave, Strovolos, Nicosia; tel. (2) 353646; fax (2) 352268; f. 1986; Greek; Dir KOSTAS HADJIKOSTIS; Chief Editor ANDREAS DEMETROPOULOS; circ. 16,000.

TURKISH CYPRIOT WEEKLIES

Cyprus Today: Dr Fazil Küçük Bul., PK 831, Lefkoşa (Nicosia), Mersin 10, Turkey; tel. (22) 52555; fax (22) 52934; e-mail cyprustoday@yahoo.com; f. 1991; English; political, social, cultural and economic; Editor GILL FRASER; circ. 5,000.

Ekonomi (The Economy): Bedrettin Demirel Cad. No.90, Lefkoşa (Nicosia), Mersin 10, Turkey; tel. (22) 83760; fax (22) 83089; f. 1958; Turkish; published by the Turkish Cypriot Chamber of Commerce; Editor-in-Chief SAMI TAŞARKAN; circ. 3,000.

Safak: PK 228, Lefkoşa (Nicosia), Mersin 10, Turkey; tel. (22) 71472; fax (22) 87910; f. 1992; Turkish; circ. 1,000.

Yeni Çağ: 28 Ramadan Cad., Lefkoşa (Nicosia), Mersin 10, Turkey; tel. (22) 74917; fax (22) 71476; e-mail yenicag@8m.com; internet www.north-cyprus.net/ybh; f. 1990; Turkish; publ. of the YBH; circ. 500.

OTHER WEEKLIES

The Blue Beret: POB 21642, HQ UNFICYP, 1590 Nicosia; tel. (2) 864550; fax (2) 864461; e-mail blueberetcyprus@hotmail.com; internet www.unficyp.org; English, Spanish, Hungarian, German; circ. 1,500.

Lion: 55 AEC Episkopi, British Forces Post Office 53; tel. (5) 262445; fax (5) 263181; e-mail wolves1@cytanet.com.cy; distributed to British Sovereign Base Areas, United Nations Forces and principal Cypriot towns; weekly; includes British Forces Broadcasting Services programme guide; Editor SARA WOOTTON; circ. 5,000.

Middle East Economic Survey: Middle East Petroleum and Economic Publications (Cyprus), POB 24940, 1355 Nicosia; tel. (2) 665431; fax (2) 671988; e-mail mees@spidernet.com.cy; internet www.mees.com; f. 1957 (in Beirut); weekly review and analysis of petroleum, finance and banking, and political developments; Publr BASIM W. ITAYIM; Editor WALID KHADDURI.

GREEK CYPRIOT PERIODICALS

Cool: POB 8205, 86 Iphigenias St, 2091 Nicosia; tel. (2) 378900; fax (2) 378916; f. 1994; Greek; youth magazine; Chief Editor: PROMETHEAS CHRISTOPHIDES; circ. 4,000.

Cypria (Cypriot Woman): POB 28506, 56 Kennedy Ave, 11th Floor, 1076 Nicosia; tel. (2) 494907; fax (2) 427051; f. 1983; every 2 months; Greek; Owner MARO KARAYIANNI; circ. 7,000.

Cyprus Bulletin: 1465 Nicosia; tel. (2) 801183; fax (2) 666123; e-mail pioxx@cytanet.com.cy; internet www.pio.gov.cy; f. 1964; fortnightly; Arabic, Greek; published by the Cyprus Press and Information Office; Principal Officers M. CHARALAMPIDES, A. LANITIS; circ. 1,500 (Arabic), 4,000 (Greek).

Cyprus P.C.: POB 24989, 53 Kyrakou Matsi St, 1306 Nicosia; tel. (2) 514008; fax (2) 515017; e-mail peri@infomedia.cy.net; internet www.infomedia.cy.net; f. 1990; monthly; Greek; computing magazine; Dir LAKIS VARNAVA; circ. 5,000.

Cyprus Time Out: POB 3697, 4 Pygmalionos St, 1010 Nicosia; tel. (2) 472949; fax (2) 360668; f. 1978; monthly; English; Dir ELLADA SOPHOCLEOUS; Chief Editor LYN HAVILAND; circ. 8,000.

Cyprus Today: c/o Ministry of Education and Culture, Nicosia; tel. (2) 303337; fax (2) 673565; f. 1963; quarterly; English; cultural and information review; published and distributed by Press and Information Office; Principal Officer STELIOS HADJISTYLLIS; circ. 15,000.

Cyprus Tourism: POB 51697, Limassol; tel. (5) 337377; fax (5) 337374; f. 1989; bimonthly; Greek; English; tourism and travel; Man. Dir G. EROTOKRITOU; circ. 250,000.

Dimosios Ypallilos (Civil Servant): 3 Dem. Severis Ave, 1066 Nicosia; tel. (2) 667260; fax (2) 665189; fortnightly; published by the Cyprus Civil Servants' Association (PASYDY); circ. 14,000.

Enosis (Union): 71 Piraeus & Tombazis, Nicosia; tel. (2) 756862; fax (2) 757268; f. 1996; monthly; Greek; satirical; Chief Editor VASOS FTOCHOPOLILOS; circ. 2,000.

Eso-Etimos (Ever Ready): POB 4544, Nicosia; tel. (2) 443587; f. 1913; quarterly; Greek; publ. by Cyprus Scouts' Asscn; Editor TAKIS NEOPHYTOU; circ. 2,500.

Eva: 6 Psichikou St, Strovolos, Nicosia; tel. (2) 322959; fax (2) 322940; f. 1996; Greek; Dir DINOS MICHAEL; Chief Editors CHARIS PONTIKIS, KATIA SAVVIDOU; circ. 4,000.

Hermes International: POB 24512, Nicosia; tel. (2) 570570; fax (2) 581617; f. 1992; quarterly; English; lifestyle, business, finance, management; Chief Editor JOHN VICKERS; circ. 8,000.

Nicosia This Month: POB 21015, Nikoklis Publishing House, Ledras and Pygmalionos St, Nicosia; tel. (2) 673124; fax (2) 663363; f. 1984; monthly; English; Chief Editor ELLADA SOPHOCLEOUS; circ. 4,000.

Omicron: POB 25211, 1 Commercial Centre Diogenous, 2nd Floor, 1307 Nicosia; tel. (2) 590110; fax (2) 590410; f. 1996; Greek; Dir NIKOS CHR. PATTICHIS; Chief Editor STAVROS CHRISTODOULOU; circ. 8,000.

Paediki Chara (Children's Joy): POB 136, 18 Archbishop Makarios III Ave, 1065 Nicosia; tel. (2) 752638; fax (2) 760410; e-mail poed@logos.cy.net; f. 1962; monthly; for pupils; publ. by the Pancyprian Union of Greek Teachers; Editor SOFOCLES CHARALAMBIDES; circ. 15,000.

Synergatiko Vima (The Co-operative Tribune): Kosti Palama 5, 1096 Nicosia; tel. (2) 680757; fax (2) 660833; e-mail coop.confeder@cytanet.com.cy; f. 1983; monthly; Greek; official organ of the Pancyprian Co-operative Confederation Ltd; circ. 5,000.

Synthesis (Composition): 6 Psichikou St, Strovolos, Nicosia; tel. (2) 322759; fax (2) 322940; f. 1988; every 2 months; Greek; interior decorating; Dir DINOS MICHAEL; circ. 6,000.

Tele Ores: POB 28205, 4 Acropoleos St, 1st Floor, 2091 Nicosia; tel. (2) 513300; fax (2) 513363; f. 1993; Greek; fortnightly; television guide; Chief Editor PROMETHEAS CHRISTOPHIDES; circ. 17,000.

TV Kanali (TV Channel): POB 25603, 5 Aegaleo St, Strovolos, Nicosia; tel. (2) 353603; fax (2) 353223; f. 1993; Greek; Dirs A. STAVRIDES, E. HADJIEFTHYMIOU; Chief Editor CHARIS TOMAZOS; circ. 13,000.

TURKISH CYPRIOT PERIODICALS

Güvenlik Kuvvetleri Magazine: Lefkoşa (Nicosia), Mersin 10, Turkey; tel. (22) 75880; publ. by the Security Forces of the 'TRNC'.

Halkbilimi: Has-Der, PK 199, Lefkoşa (Nicosia), Mersin 10, Turkey; tel. (22) 83146; fax (22) 84125; internet www.cypnet.com/.ncyprus/gifs/halkbil.gif; f. 1986; 1 a year; publ. of Folk Arts Assoc.; academic; Turkish; Chief Editor KANI KANOL; circ. (2000) 1,500.

Kıbrıs—Northern Cyprus Monthly: Ministry of Foreign Affairs and Defence, Lefkoşa (Nicosia), Mersin 10, Turkey; tel. (22) 83241; fax (22) 84290; f. 1963; Editor GÖNÜL ATANER.

Kıbrıslı Türkün Sesi: 44 Mecidiye St, Lefkoşa (Nicosia), Mersin 10, Turkey; tel. (22) 78520; fax (22) 87966; internet www.medyatext.com/kibrisli/; monthly; political; Exec. Dir DOGAN HARMAN; Gen. Co-ordinator CEVDET ALPARSLAN.

Kültür Sanat Dergisi: Girne Cad. 92, Lefkoşa (Nicosia), Mersin 10, Turkey; tel. (22) 83313; e-mail info@turkishbank.com; internet www.turkishbank.com; publ. of Türk Bankası; circ. 1,000.

Kuzey Kıbrıs Kültür Dergisi (North Cyprus Cultural Journal): PK 157, Lefkoşa (Nicosia), Mersin 10, Turkey; tel. (22) 31298; f. 1987; monthly; Turkish; Chief Editor GÜNSEL DOĞASAL.

New Cyprus: PK 327, Lefkoşa (Nicosia), Mersin 10, Turkey; tel. (22) 78914; fax (22) 72592; English; publ. by the North Cyprus Research and Publishing Centre; also Turkish edition *Yeni Kıbrıs*; Editor AHMET C. GAZIOĞLU.

OTHER PERIODICAL

International Crude Oil and Product Prices: Middle East Petroleum and Economic Publications (Cyprus), POB 24940, 1355 Nicosia; tel. (2) 665431; fax (2) 671988; e-mail mees@spidernet.com.cy; internet www.mees.com; f. 1971 (in Beirut); 2 a year; review and analysis of petroleum price trends in world markets; Publisher BASIM W. ITAYIM.

NEWS AGENCIES

Cyprus News Agency: POB 23947, 7 Kastorias St, 2002 Strovolos, 1687 Nicosia; tel. (2) 319009; fax (2) 319006; e-mail cna@cytanet.com.cy; internet www.cyna.org.cy; f. 1976; English and Greek; Dir THEMIS THEMISTOCLEOUS.

Kuzey Kıbrıs Haber Ajansı (Northern Cyprus News Agency): Alirizin Efendi Cad., Vakiflar Işhani, Kat 2, No. 3, Ortaköy, Lefkoşa (Nicosia), Mersin 10, Turkey; tel. (22) 81922; fax (22) 81934; f. 1977; Dir-Gen. M. ALI AKPINAR.

Papyrus General Press Distribution Agency: POB 12669, 5 Arch. Kyprianou, Latsia, Nicosia; tel. (2) 488855; fax (2) 488883; e-mail papyrus@spidernet.com.cy.

TürkAjansı-Kıbrıs (TAK) (Turkish News Agency of Cyprus): POB 355, 30 Mehmet Akif Cad., Lefkoşa (Nicosia), Mersin 10, Turkey; tel. (22) 71818; fax (22) 71213; e-mail tak@cc.emu.edu.tr; internet www.emu.edu.tr/Tak; f. 1973; Dir EMIR HÜSEYIN ERSOY.

Foreign Bureaux

Agence France-Presse (AFP) (France): POB 7242, Loizides Centre, 7th Floor, 36 Kypranoros St, Nicosia; tel. (2) 754050; fax (2) 768977; e-mail nicosie.redaction@afp.com; Bureau Chief MICHEL GARIN.

Agencia EFE (Spain): 64 Metochiou St, Office 401, Nicosia; tel. (2) 775725; fax (2) 781662; Correspondent DOMINGO DEL PINO.

Agenzia Nazionale Stampa Associata (ANSA) (Italy): Middle East Office, 10 Katsonis St, Ayii Omoloyites, Nicosia; tel. (2) 491699; fax (2) 492732; Rep. VITTORIO FRENQUELLUCCI.

Associated Press (AP) (USA): POB 4853, Neoelen Marina, 10 Katsonis St, Nicosia; tel. (2) 492599; fax (2) 491617; Correspondent ALEX EFTY.

Athinaikon Praktorion Eidiseon (Greece): Flat 64, Tryfonos Bldg, Eleftherias Sq., 1011 Nicosia; tel. (2) 441110; fax (2) 457418; Rep. GEORGE LEONIDAS.

Informatsionnoye Telegrafnoye Agentstvo Rossii—Telegrafnoye Agentstvo Suverennykh Stran (ITAR—TASS) (Russia): POB 2235, 5–6 Evangelias St, Archangelos, Nicosia; tel. (2) 382486; Rep. ALEXEI YEROVTCHENKOV.

Iraqi News Agency: POB 1098, Flat 201, 11 Ippocratous St, Nicosia; tel. (2) 472095; fax (2) 472096; Correspondent AHMAD SULEYMAN.

Jamahiriya News Agency (JANA) (Libya): Flat 203, 12 Kypranoros, Nicosia; tel. (2) 361129; Rep. MUHAMMAD ALI ESHOWEIHIDI.

Reuters: POB 25725, 5th Floor, George and Thelma Paraskevaides Foundation Bldg, 36 Grivas Dhigenis Ave, Nicosia; tel. (2) 469607; fax (2) 662487; Correspondent MICHELE KAMBAS.

Sofia-Press Agency (Bulgaria): 9 Roumeli St, Droshia, Larnaca; tel. (4) 494484; Rep. IONKA VERESIE.

United Press International (UPI) (USA): 24A Heroes Ave, Nicosia 171; tel. (2) 456643; fax (2) 455998; Rep. GEORGES DER PARTHOGH.

Xinhua (New China) News Agency (People's Republic of China): 12 Byzantiou St, Flat 201, Ayios Dhometios, Nicosia; tel. (2) 590133; fax (2) 590146; Rep. HUANG JIANMING.

Publishers

GREEK CYPRIOT PUBLISHERS

Action Publications: POB 4676, 35 Ayiou Nicolaou St, Engomi, 1302 Nicosia; tel. (2) 590555; fax (2) 590048; e-mail actionpr@spidernet.com.cy; f. 1971; travel; Pres. TONY CHRISTODOULOU.

Andreou Chr. Publications: POB 22298, 67a Regenis St, 1520 Nicosia; tel. (2) 666877; fax (2) 666878; e-mail andreou2@cytanet.com.cy; f. 1979; biography, literature, history, regional interest.

James Bendon Ltd: POB 56484, 3307 Limasol; tel. (5) 633181; fax (5) 632352; e-mail jbendon@attglobal.net; internet www.jamesbendon.com; philately; Pres. JAMES BENDON: Vice-Pres. RIDA BENDON.

Chrysopolitissa: 27 Al. Papadiamantis St, 2400 Nicosia; tel. (2) 353929; f. 1973; theatre, literature.

Costas Epiphaniou: Ekdoseis Antiprosopies Ltd, POB 2451, 1521 Nicosia; tel. (2) 750873; fax (2) 759266; f. 1973; Dir COSTAS EPIPHANIOU.

Foundation 'Anastasios G. Leventis': 40 Gladstonos St, POB 22543, 1095 Nicosia; tel. (2) 667706; fax (2) 675002; e-mail leventcy@zenon.logos.cy.net; internet www.leventisfoundation.org.

KY KE M: POB 4108, Nicosia; tel. (2) 450302; fax (2) 463624; Pres. NIKOS KOUTSOU.

MAM (The House of Cyprus Publications): POB 21722, Phaneromeni Library Building, 46 Phaneromeni St, 1512 Nicosia; tel. (2) 664698; fax (2) 669411; e-mail mam@mam.cy.net; internet www.mam.cy.net; f. 1965.

Nikoklis Publishing House: POB 23697, Nicosia; tel. (2) 672949; fax (2) 330218; ethnicity, travel; Man. ELLADA SOPHOCLEOUS.

Omilos Pnevmatikis Ananeoseos: 1 Omirou St, 2407 Engomi, Nicosia; tel. (2) 775854; literature.

Pierides Foundation: Larnaca; tel. (4) 651345; fax (4) 657227.

POLTE (Pancyprian Organization of Tertiary Education): c/o Higher Technical Institute, Nicosia; tel. (2) 305030; fax (2) 494953; Pres. KOSTAS NEOKLEOUS.

TURKISH CYPRIOT PUBLISHERS

Birlik Gazetesi: Yediler Sok., Lefkoşa (Nicosia), Mersin 10, Turkey; tel. (22) 72959; f. 1980; Dir MEHMET AKAR.

Bolan Matbaasi: 35 Pencizade Sok., Lefkoşa (Nicosia), Mersin 10, Turkey; tel. (22) 74802.

Devlet Basımevi (Turkish Cypriot Government Printing House): Şerif Arzik Sok., Lefkoşa (Nicosia), Mersin 10, Turkey; tel. (22) 72010; Dir S. KÜRŞAD.

Halkın Sesi Ltd: 172 Girne Cad., Lefkoşa (Nicosia), Mersin 10, Turkey; tel. (22) 73141.

Kema Matbaasi: 1 Tabak Hilmi Sok., Lefkoşa (Nicosia), Mersin 10, Turkey; tel. (22) 72785.

K. Rüstem & Bro.: 22–24 Girne Cad., Lefkoşa (Nicosia), Mersin 10, Turkey; tel. (22) 71418.

Sebil International Press: 59 Atatürk Ave, Gönyeli, PK 7, Lefkoşa (Nicosia), Mersin 10, Turkey; tel. (22) 46805; fax (22) 310804;

e-mail ics@analiz.net; f. 1985; technical and scientific; Principal Officer E. BAŞARAN.

Tezel Matbaası: 35 Şinasi Sok., Lefkoşa (Nicosia), Mersin 10, Turkey; tel. (22) 71022.

Broadcasting and Communications

TELECOMMUNICATIONS

Cyprus Telecommunications Authority (CYTA): POB 24929, 1396 Nicosia; tel. (2) 701000; fax (2) 494940; e-mail pr@cyta.cytanet .com.cy; internet www.cyta.com.cy; provides national, international and cellular services in Cyprus.

Telekomünikasyon Diaresi Müdürlügü (Directorate of Telecommunications): Lefkoşa (Nicosia), Mersin 10, Turkey; tel. (22) 81888; fax (22) 88666; f. 1963; state-owned; responsible to Ministry of Communications, Works and Tourism; admin. and operation of telecommunications services; Gen. Man. SALIH KARA.

BROADCASTING
Radio

British Forces Broadcasting Service, Cyprus: Akrotiri, British Forces Post Office 57; tel. (5) 252009; fax (5) 268580; e-mail patricke@bfbs_com; f. 1948; broadcasts a two-channel 24-hour radio service in English on VHF; Station Man. PATRICK EADE; Engineering Man. DAVE RAMSAY.

Cyprus Broadcasting Corporation (CyBC): POB 24824, Broadcasting House, 1397 Nicosia; tel. (2) 422231; fax (2) 314050; e-mail rik@cybc.com.cy; internet www.cybc.com.cy; radio f. 1952; Programme I in Greek, Programme II in Greek, Turkish, English and Armenian, Programme III in Greek; two medium wave transmitters of 100 kW in Nicosia with relay stations at Paphos and Limassol; three 10-kW ERP VHF FM stereo transmitters on Mount Olympus; and three relay stations; Chair. ANTONIS DRAKOS; Dir-Gen. MICHAEL STYLIANOU; Head of Radio ELLI KORAI-YEROLEMOU.

Logos: Church of Cyprus, POB 27400, 1644 Nicosia; tel. (2) 355444; fax (2) 355737; e-mail director@logos.cy.net; Chair. ANDREAS PHIL-IPPOU; Dir Gen. CHRISTODOULOS PROTOPAPAS.

Radio Astra: 145 Athalassas Ave, Strovolos, 2045 Nicosia; tel. (2) 313200; fax (2) 319261; e-mail info@astra.com.cy; internet www .astra.com.cy; Dir TAKIS HADJIGEORGIOU.

Radio Proto: POB 21836, 31 Archangelos St, Parissinos, 2054 Nicosia; tel. (2) 353545; fax (2) 352266; internet www .radioproto.com.cy; Chair. KOSTAS HADJIKOSTIS; Gen. Man. PAVLOS PAPACHRISTODOULOU.

Bayrak Radio and TV Corpn (BRTK): Atatürk Sq., Lefkoşa (Nicosia), Mersin 10, Turkey; tel. (22) 85555; fax (22) 81991; e-mail brt@cc.emu.edu.tr; internet www.brt.emu.edu.tr; in July 1983 it became an independent Turkish Cypriot corpn, partly financed by the Govt; Radio Bayrak f. 1963; home service in Turkish, overseas service in Turkish, Greek, English, Arabic and German; broadcasts 52.5 hours per day; Chair. GÜNAY YORGANCIOGLU; Dir. ISMET KOTAK; Head of Radio ŞIFA NESIM.

First FM and Interfirst FM: Lefkoşa (Nicosia), Mersin 10, Turkey; f. 1996.

Kıbrıs FM: Dr Fazil Küçük Blvd, Yeni Sanayi Bolgesi, Lefkoşa (Nicosia), Mersin 10, Turkey; tel. (22) 81922; fax (22) 81934; Dir MEHMET ALI AKPINAR.

Radio Emu: Gazi Mağusa (Famagusta), Mersin 10, Turkey; e-mail radioemu@cc.emu.edu.tr; internet www.emu.edu.tr/~radioemu.

Television

In 1991, under an agreement between Cyprus and Greece, Cypriot viewers were to be given access to Greek television channels for several hours daily via satellite. Several Turkish channels are transmitted to the 'TRNC'.

Antenna T.V.: POB 20923, 1655 Nicosia: tel. (2) 311111; fax (2) 314959; Chair. LOUKIS PAPAPHILIPPOU; Man. Dir STELIOS MALEKOS.

British Forces Broadcasting Service, Cyprus: Akrotiri, British Forces Post Office 57; tel. (5) 252009; fax (5) 268580; e-mail patrick@bfbs.com; f. 1948; broadcasts a daily TV service; Station Man. PATRICK EADE; Engineering Man. DAVE RAMSAY.

Cyprus Broadcasting Corporation (CyBC): POB 4824, Broadcasting House, 1397 Nicosia; tel. (2) 422231; fax (2) 314050; e-mail rik@cybc.com.cy; internet www.cybc.com.cy; television f. 1957;
Channel 1: one Band III 100/10-kW transmitter on Mount Olympus.
Channel 2: one Band IV 100/10-kW ERP transmitter on Mount Olympus. **ET 1:** one Band IV 100/10-kW ERP transmitter on Mount Olympus for transmission of the ETI Programme received, via satellite, from Greece. The above three TV channels are also transmitted from 77 transposer stations; Chair. ANTONIS DRAKOS; Dir-Gen. MICHAEL STYLIANOU.

Lumier TV Ltd: POB 25614, 2063 Nicosia; tel. (2) 357272; fax (2) 354638; e-mail administration@ltv.com.cy; internet www .lumiertv.com; encoded signal; Chair. and Man. Dir AKIS AVRAAMIDES; Gen. Man. GEORGE XINARIS.

O Logos: POB 27400, 1644 Nicosia; tel. (2) 355444; fax (2) 355737; e-mail director@logos.cy.net; Chair. ANDREAS PHILIPPOU; Dir CHRISTODOULOS PROTOPAPAS.

Sigma: POB 21836, 1513 Nicosia; tel. (2) 357070; fax (2) 352237; island-wide coverage; Chair. and Dir KOSTAS HADJIKOSTIS; Man. DINOS MENELAOU; New Business Devt Dir VIVIEN LADOMATOS.

Bayrak Radio and TV Corpn (BRTK): Atatürk Sq., Lefkoşa (Nicosia), Mersin 10, Turkey; tel. (22) 85555; fax (22) 81991; e-mail brt@cc.emu.edu.tr; internet www.cc.emu.edu.tr/press/brt/brt.htm; in July 1983 it became an independent Turkish Cypriot corpn, partly financed by the Govt; Bayrak TV f. 1976; transmits programmes in Turkish, Greek, English and Arabic on nine channels; Chair. GÜNAY YORGANCIOGLU; Dir. ISMET KOTAK; Head of Television TÜLIN URAL.

Gene TV: Bevel Yusuf Cad. 8, Yenişehir, Lefkoşa (Nicosia), Mersin 10, Turkey; tel. (22) 80790; fax (22) 76363; Dir ERTAN BIRINCI.

Kanal T: Dr Fazıl Küçük Cad. Foto Filiz Binaları, Göçmenköy, Lefkoşa (Nicosia), Mersin 10, Turkey; tel. (22) 37678; fax (22) 34257; Owner ERSIN FATAR.

Finance

(brs = branches; cap. = capital; dep. = deposits; res = reserves; m. = million; amounts in Cyprus pounds, except for Turkish Cypriot banks)

BANKING
Central Bank

Central Bank of Cyprus: POB 25529, 80 Kennedy Ave, 1395 Nicosia; tel. (2) 379800; fax (2) 378153; e-mail cbcinfo@ centralbank.gov.cy; internet www.centralbank.gov.cy; f. 1963; cap. p.u. 15m., res 15m., dep. 1,004m. (Dec. 1999); Gov. AFXENTIOS C. AFXENTIOU.

Greek Cypriot Banks

Alpha Bank Ltd: POB 21661, Yiorkion Bldg, 1 Prodromou St, 1596 Nicosia; tel. (2) 888888; fax (2) 773766; e-mail secretariat@ alphabank.com; internet www.alphabank.com; f. 1960 as Lombard Banking (Cyprus) Ltd; name changed to Lombard NatWest Banking Ltd in 1989 and as above in 1998; locally incorporated although foreign-controlled; cap. 12.0m., res 20.0m., dep. 585.2m. (Dec. 1999); Chair. M. G. KOLOKASSIDES; Man. Dir A. DEMETRIADES; 25 brs.

Bank of Cyprus Group: POB 21472, 51 Stassinos St, Ayia Paraskevi, 2002 Strovolos 140, 1599 Nicosia; tel. (2) 378000; fax (2) 378111; e-mail info@cy.bankofcyprus.com; internet www .bankofcyprus.com; f. 1899, reconstituted 1943 by the amalgamation of Bank of Cyprus, Larnaca Bank Ltd and Famagusta Bank Ltd; cap. 159.6m., res 206.6m., dep. 4,412.8m. (Dec. 1999); Chair. SOLON A. TRIANTAFYLLIDES; Group Chief Exec. CHR. PANTZARIS; 187 brs.

Co-operative Central Bank Ltd: POB 24537, 8 Gregoris Afxentiou St, 1389 Nicosia; tel. (2) 743000; fax (2) 670261; e-mail coopbank.gm@cytanet.com.cy; f. 1937 under the Co-operative Societies Law; banking and credit facilities to member societies, importer and distributor of agricultural requisites, insurance agent; cap. 3.6m., dep. 599.0m. (Dec. 2000); Chair. D. STAVROU; Sec.-Gen. D. PITSILLIDES; 4 brs.

The Cyprus Popular Bank Ltd: POB 22032, Laiki Bank Bldg, 154 Limassol Ave, 1598 Nicosia; tel. (2) 752000; fax (2) 811491; e-mail laiki.teleservice@laiki.com; internet www.laiki.com; f. 1901; full commercial banking; cap. 76.0m., res 104.7m. dep. 2,445.8m. (Dec. 1998); Chair. KIKIS N. LAZARIDES; Group Man. Dir MARIOS LANITIS; 145 brs.

Hellenic Bank Ltd: POB 24747, 1394 Nicosia; tel. (2) 860000; fax (2) 754074; e-mail hellenic@hellenicbank.com; internet www .hellenicbank.com; f. 1974; financial services group; cap. p.u. 35.6m., res 64.0m., dep. 1,268.0m. (Dec. 1999); Chair. and Chief Exec. PANOS CHR. GHALANOS; 101 brs.

Housing Finance Corpn: POB 23898, 41 Themistoklis Dervis St, Hawaii Tower, Nicosia; tel. (2) 761777; fax (2) 762870; f. 1980; provides long-term loans for home-buying; cap. 12m., dep. 213m. (June 2000); Gen. Man. CH. SHAMBARTAS; 6 brs.

National Bank of Greece (Cyprus) Ltd: POB 21191, Galaxias Centre, 2nd Floor, 36 Ayias Elenis St, 1597 Nicosia; tel. (2) 840000; fax (2) 762080; f. 1994 by incorporating all local business of the National Bank of Greece SA; full commercial banking; cap. p.u. 15m. (Jan. 1997); Chair. TH. KARATZAS; Man. Dir M. TAGAROULIAS; 29 brs.

Universal Bank: POB 28510, 12–14 Kennedy Ave, 2080 Nicosia; tel. (2) 777333; fax (2) 358702; e-mail unimail@usb.com.cy; internet www.universalbank.com.cy; f. 1925 as Yialousa Savings Ltd (closed 1974, reopened 1990), renamed as above 1996; cap. p.u. 8.8m., res 3.8m., dep. 62.2m. (Dec. 1999); Chair. GEORGE SYRIMIS; Gen. Man. GEORGE MAKARIOU; 11 brs.

Turkish Cypriot Banks
(amounts in Turkish liras unless otherwise indicated)

Akdeniz Garanti Bankası Ltd: PK 149, 2–4 Celaliye Sok. İnönu Meydan, Lefkoşa (Nicosia), Mersin 10, Turkey; tel. (22) 86742; fax (22) 86741; f. 1989 as Mediterranean Guarantee Bank; cap. and res 605,600m., dep. 22,867,000m. (Dec. 1999); Chair. ERDOĞAN NAİM.

Asbank Ltd: 8 Mecidiye Sok., PK 448, Lefkoşa (Nicosia), Mersin 10, Turkey; tel. (22) 83023; fax (22) 81244; internet www.asbank.com.tr; f. 1986; cap. and res 1,910,117m., dep. 26,121,207m. (Dec. 1999); Pres. M. Y. ALTUNER; Dep. Gen. Man. T. M. ALTUNER; 7 brs.

Cyprus Altınbaş Bank Ltd: PK 843, 2 Müftü Ziyai Efendi Sok., Lefkoşa (Nicosia), Mersin 10, Turkey; tel. (22) 88222; fax (22) 71623; f. 1993; cap. 748,100m., res 81,330m., dep. 7,822,563m. (Dec. 2000); Chair. VAKKAS ALTINBAŞ; Gen. Man. MEHMET ŞENER.

First Merchant Bank OSH Ltd.: 25 Serif Arzik Sok., Lefkoşa (Nicosia), Mersin 10, Turkey; tel. (22) 75373; fax (22) 75377; e-mail fmb@firstmerchantbank.com; internet www.firstmerchantbank.com; f. 1993; also provides offshore services; cap. US $10m., res US $3.7m., dep. US $2,073.5m. (March 1999); Chair. and Gen. Man. Dr H. YAMAN.

Kıbrıs Endüstri Bankası Ltd: (Industrial Bank of Cyprus Ltd): Bedrettin Demirel Cad., Başbakanlık Kavşağı, Lefkoşa (Nicosia), Mersin 10, Turkey; tel. (22) 83770; fax (22) 71830; administrators appointed in May 2000.

Kıbrıs Eurobank Ltd: PK 35, 18 Mecidiye Sok., Lefkoşa (Nicosia), Mersin 10, Turkey; tel. (22) 87550; fax (22) 87670; e-mail eurobank@kktc.net; f. 1993; cap. 60,000m., dep. 521,264m. (Dec. 1998); Pres. and Chair. BEDI TUNASOY; Gen. Man. N. SENLET SELHEP.

Kıbrıs İktisat Bankası Ltd (Cyprus Economy Bank Ltd): 151 Bedrettin Demirel Cad., Lefkoşa (Nicosia), Mersin 10, Turkey; tel. (22) 85300; fax (22) 81311; e-mail info@iktisatbank.cc; internet www.iktisatbank.cc; f. 1990; cap. 450,000m., res 1,816,724m., dep. 13,739,207m. (Dec. 2000); Chair. and Gen. Man. METE ÖZMERTER; 7 brs.

Kıbrıs Kredi Bankası Ltd (Cyprus Credit Bank Ltd): 5–7 İplik Pazarı Sok., Lefkoşa (Nicosia), Mersin 10, Turkey; tel. (22) 83667; fax (22) 76999; f. 1978; administrators appointed in May 2000; cap. 30,930m., res 164,131m., dep. 2,628,193m. (Dec. 1994); Chair. SALIH BOYACI; Gen. Man. YÜKSEL YAZGIN; 12 local brs.

Kıbrıs Ticaret Bankası Ltd (Cyprus Commercial Bank Ltd): 111 Bedrettin Demirel Ave, Lefkoşa (Nicosia), Mersin 10, Turkey; tel. (22) 83180; fax (22) 82278; f. 1982; cap. 500,000m., res 833,934m., dep. 10,679,115m. (Dec. 1998); Chair. YÜKSEL AHMET RAŞIT; Gen. Man. HÜCEYIN HARMANCI; 9 brs.

Kıbrıs Türk Kooperatif Merkez Bankası Ltd (Cyprus Turkish Co-operative Central Bank): 49–55 Mahmut Paşa Sok., PK 823, Lefkoşa (Nicosia), Mersin 10, Turkey; tel. (22) 73398; fax (22) 76787; e-mail info@koopcb.com; internet www.koopbank.com; f. 1959; cap. and res 1,061,488m., dep. 88,595,553m. (Dec. 1999); banking and credit facilities to member societies and individuals; Chair. AHMET ALPER; Gen. Man. TAŞKENT ATASAYAN; 10 brs.

Kıbrıs Vakıflar Bankası Ltd: 58 Yediler Sok., PK 212, Lefkoşa (Nicosia), Mersin 10, Turkey; tel. (22) 75109; fax (22) 75169; f. 1982; cap. 100,000m., res 281,238m., dep. 9,605,905m. (Dec. 1998); Chair. Dr TUNCER ARIFOĞLU; Gen. Man. ALPAY R. ADANIR; 7 brs.

Limassol Turkish Co-operative Bank Ltd: 10 Orhaneli Sok., Kyrenia, PK 247, Mersin 10, Turkey; tel. (2) 8156786; fax (2) 8156959; e-mail fordept@kktc.net; f. 1939; cap. 11,261m., res 489,433m, dep. 15,786,573m. (Dec. 1998); Chair. GÜZEL HALIM; Gen. Man. TANER EKDAL.

Türk Bankası Ltd (Turkish Bank Ltd): 92 Girne Cad., PK 242, Lefkoşa (Nicosia), Mersin 10, Turkey; tel. (22) 83313; fax (22) 82432; e-mail info@turkishbank.com; internet www.turkishbank.com; f. 1901; cap. 12,600,245m., res 5,438,241m., dep. 175,361,031m. (Dec. 2000); Chair. M. TANJU ÖZYOL; Gen. Man. C. YENAL MUSANNIF; 12 brs.

Turkish Cypriot Bankers' Association
Northern Cyprus Bankers' Association: Lefkoşa (Nicosia), Mersin 10, Turkey; f. 1987; tel. (22) 83180; fax (22) 82278; e-mail info@turkishbank.com; internet www.turkishbank.com; 31 mems (1998).

Investment Organization
Cyprus Investment and Securities Corpn: POB 597, Ghinis Bldg, 4th Floor, 58–60 Dhigenis Akritas Ave, Nicosia; tel. (2) 451535; fax (2) 445481; f. 1982 to promote development of capital market; member of Bank of Cyprus Group; issued cap. 1m. (1990); Chair. J. CL. CHRISTOPHIDES; Gen. Man. SOKRATES R. SOLOMIDES.

Development Bank
The Cyprus Development Bank Ltd: POB 21415, Alpha House, 50 Archbishop Makarios III Ave, 1508 Nicosia; tel. (2) 846500; fax (2) 846603; e-mail info@cdb.com.cy; f. 1963; cap. 12.4m., res 40.0m., dep. 167.8m. (Dec. 2000); aims to accelerate the economic development of Cyprus by providing medium- and long-term loans for productive projects, developing the capital market, encouraging joint ventures and providing technical and managerial advice to productive private enterprises; Chair. J. CHR. STRONGYLOS; Gen. Man. JOHN G. JOANNIDES; 1 br.

Foreign Banks
Arab Bank PLC: POB 25700, 1 Santaroza Ave, 1393 Nicosia; tel. (2) 899100; fax (2) 760890; e-mail info@arabbank.com.cy; f. 1984; commercial; Area Exec. TOUFIC J. DAJANI; 15 brs.

Commercial Bank of Greece SA: POB 25151, 4 Ionos St, 2015 Nicosia; tel. (2) 363646; fax (2) 663923; f. 1992; Country Man. G. KANTIANIS; 3 brs.

Türkiye Cumhuriyeti Ziraat Bankası: Girnekapi Cad., Ibrahimpaşa Sok. 105, Lefkoşa (Nicosia), Mersin 10, Turkey; tel. (22) 83050; fax (22) 82041.

Türkiye Halk Bankası AŞ: Osman Paşa Cad., Ümit Office, Lefkoşa (Nicosia), Mersin 10, Turkey; tel. (22) 72145; fax (22) 72146.

Türkiye İş Bankası AŞ: Girne Cad. 9, Lefkoşa (Nicosia), Mersin 10, Turkey; tel. (22) 83133; fax (22) 78315; f. 1924; Man. KEMAL AĞANOĞLU.

Offshore (International) Banking Units
Cyprus-based Offshore Banking Units (OBUs) are fully-staffed units which conduct all forms of banking business from within Cyprus with other offshore or foreign entities and non-resident persons. (OBUs are not permitted to accept deposits from persons of Cypriot origin who have emigrated to the United Kingdom and taken up permanent residence there.) Although exempt from most of the restrictions and regulatory measures applicable to onshore banks, OBUs are subject to supervision and inspection by the Central Bank of Cyprus. OBUs may conduct business with onshore and domestic banks in all banking matters which the latter are allowed to undertake with banks abroad. OBUs are permitted to grant loans or guarantees in foreign currencies to residents of Cyprus (conditional on obtaining an exchange control permit from the Central Bank of Cyprus). Interest and other income earned from transactions with residents is subject to the full rate of income tax (20%), but the Minister of Finance is empowered by law to exempt an OBU from the above tax liability if satisfied that a specific transaction substantially contributes towards the economic development of the Republic. In 1999 there were 29 OBUs operating in Cyprus.

Agropromstroybank: POB 55297, Maximos Court B, 17 Leontiou St, Limassol; tel. (5) 384747; fax (5) 384858; Man. ALEXANDER MOKHONKO.

Allied Business Bank SAL: POB 54232, 3rd Floor, Flat 31, Lara Court, 276 Archbishop Makarios III Ave, Limassol; tel. (5) 363759; fax (5) 372711; Local Man. NAJIBA HAWILLA.

Arab Bank PLC: POB 25700, 1 Santaroza Ave, 1393 Nicosia; tel. (2) 899100; fax (2) 760890; e-mail arabbank@spidernet.com.cy; OBU licence granted 1997; Area Exec. TOUFIC J. DAJAN.

Arab Jordan Investment Bank SA: POB 54384, Libra Tower, 23 Olympion St, Limassol; tel. (5) 351351; fax (5) 360151; e-mail ajib@.cy.net; internet www.ajib.com; f. 1978; cap. and dep. US $388m., total assets US$410m. (Dec. 1999); Man. ABED ABU-DAYEH.

AVTOVAZBANK: POB 22025, Office 201, Stefanie Court, 301A Saint-Andrews, 3035 Limassol; tel. (5) 354594; fax (5) 362582; Local Man. A. TSELOUNOV.

Banca Română de Comerţ Exterior (Bancorex) SA: POB 22538, Margarita House, 5th Floor, 15 Them. Dervis St, 1309 Nicosia; tel. (2) 677992; fax (2) 677945; Local Man. GRIGORE IOAN BUDISAN.

Bank of Beirut and the Arab Countries SAL: POB 56201, Emelle Bldg, 1st Floor, 135 Archbishop Makarios III Ave, Limassol; tel. (5) 381290; fax (5) 381584; Man. O. S. SAAB.

Banque du Liban et d'Outre-Mer SAL: POB 53243, P. Lordos Centre Roundabout, Byron St, Limassol; tel. (5) 376433; fax (5) 376292; Local Man. S. FARAH.

Banque Nationale de Paris Intercontinentale SA: POB 50058, Kanika Business Centre, 319 28th October St, 3600 Limassol; tel. (5) 840840; fax (5) 840698; Local Man. YANNIK CHAUVIN.

Banque SBA: POB 54405, Iris House, Kanika Enaerios Complex, 8c Kennedy St, Limassol; tel. (5) 588650; fax (5) 581643; branch of Banque SBA (fmrly Société Bancaire Arabe), Paris; Local Man. ADNAN NUWAYHED.

Barclays Bank PLC International Banking Unit: POB 27320, 88 Dhigenis Akritas Ave, 1644 Nicosia; tel. (2) 764777; fax (2) 754233; Head of IBU JONATHAN PINE.

BEMO—Banque Européenne pour le Moyen-Orient SAL: POB 6232, Doma Court, 1st-2nd Floors, 227 Archbishop Makarios III Ave, Limassol; tel. (5) 583628; fax (5) 588611; e-mail bemolobu@ spidernet.com.cy; Local Man. N. A. HCHAIME.

Byblos Bank SAL: POB 50218, Loucaides Bldg, 1 Archbishop Kyprianou St/St Andrew St, 3602 Limassol; tel. (5) 341433; fax (5) 367139; e-mail byblos@spidernet.com.cy; internet www.byblosbank .com.lb; Man. ANTOINE SMAIRA.

Commercial Bank of Greece SA: 1 Iona Nicolaou, POB 27587, Engomi, 2431 Nicosia, tel. (2) 663686; fax (2) 663688; Man. G. KANTIANIS.

Crédit Libanais SAL: POB 53492, Chrysalia Court, 1st Floor, 206 Archbishop Makarios III Ave, 3030 Limassol; tel. (5) 376444; fax (5) 376807; e-mail credub@inco.com.lb; Local Man. HAYAT HARFOUCHE.

Crédit Suisse First Boston (Cyprus) Ltd: POB 57530, 199 Christodolou Hadsipavlou Ave, 3316 Limassol; tel. (5) 341244; fax (5) 817424; f. 1996, OBU status granted 1997; cap. US $2.0m., dep. US $171.3m., total assets US $180.5m. (Dec. 1996); Gen. Man. ANTONIS ROUVAS.

DePfa Investment Bank Ltd: POB 20909, 2nd Floor, 178 Athalassa Ave, 1665 Nicosia, tel. (2) 879300; fax (2) 318978; e-mail mail@depfacy.com; internet www.depfa.com; IBU licence granted 1998; Gen. Mans FRANK OTTERSBACH, LAMBROS CHARIDEMOU.

Federal Bank of the Middle East Ltd: POB 25566, J&P Bldg, 90 Archbishop Makarios III Ave, 1391 Nicosia; tel. (2) 888444; fax (2) 888555; e-mail mail@fbme.com; internet www.fbme.com; f. 1983; cap. US $40.0m., dep. US $243.2m. (Dec. 1999); Chair. A. F. M. SAAB; Chief Exec. MICHAEL ROWIBAB.

First Investment Bank Ltd: POB 16023, corner of Kennedy Ave & 39 Demoforitos St, 4th Floor, Flat 401, 2085 Nicosia; tel. (2) 760150; fax (2) 376560; Gen. Man. ENU NEDELE.

HSBC Investment Bank Cyprus Ltd: POB 25718, Para Bldg, Block C, 7 Dositheou St, 1311 Nicosia; tel. (2) 376116; fax (2) 376121; f. 1984, as Wardley Cyprus Ltd; Man. Dir T. TAOUSHANIS.

Karić Banka: POB 26522, Flat 22, Cronos Court, 66 Archbishop Makarios III Ave, Nicosia; tel. (2) 374980; fax (2) 374151; Man. Dir O. ERDELIJANOVIĆ.

Lebanon and Gulf Bank SAL: POB 40337, Akamia Court, 3rd Floor, corner of G. Afxentiou and Archbishop Makarios III Ave, Larnaca; tel. (4) 620500; fax (4) 620708; Local Man. M. HAMMOUD.

Marcuard Cook & Cie S.A.: Lophitis Business Centre, Cnr 28 October & Emiliou Chourmouziou, 4th Floor, 3035 Limassol; tel. (5) 747129; fax (5) 344940; Local Man. CHRISTINE SPYROU CATRAS.

Mega Euro Banka A.D.: Nicosia; OBU licence granted 1998.

Russian Commercial Bank (Cyprus) Ltd: POB 56868, 2 Amathuntos St, 3310 Limassol; tel. (5) 342190; fax (5) 342192; cap. US $10.8m., dep. US $256.3m. (Dec. 1998); Gen. Man. YURI V. BABKIN.

Société Générale Cyprus Ltd: POB 25400, 7–9 Grivas Dhigenis Ave, 1309 Nicosia; tel. (2) 817777; fax (2) 764471; cap. US $2.0m., res US $2.0m., dep. US $70.6m. (Dec. 1998); Gen. Man. GÉRARD MALHAME.

Vojvodjanska Bank AD: POB 20872, Xenios Commercial Centre, 5th floor, Suite 502, Archbishop Makarios III Ave, 1664 Nicosia; tel. (2) 374920; fax (2) 374937; Local CEO MILAN BORKOVIĆ.

STOCK EXCHANGE

Cyprus Stock Exchange: POB 5427, 54 Grivas Dhigenis Ave, 1309 Nicosia; tel. (2) 668782; fax (2) 668790; e-mail cyse@zenon .logos.cy.net; internet www.cse.com.cy; official trading commenced in March 1996; 60 companies listed in 1999; Chair. DINOS PAPADOPOULOS; Gen. Man. NONDAS METAXAS.

INSURANCE

Service for the Control of Insurance Companies: Ministry of Finance, POB 23364, 1682 Nicosia; tel. (2) 303256; fax (2) 302938; f. 1969 to control insurance companies, insurance agents, brokers and agents for brokers in Cyprus.

Greek Cypriot Insurance Companies

Aegis Insurance Co Ltd: POB 23450, 7 Klimentos St, Ayios Antonios, 1061 Nicosia; tel. (2) 343644; fax (2) 343866; Chair. ARISTOS KAISIDES; Principal Officer PANTELAKIS SOUGLIDES.

Aetna Insurance Co Ltd: POB 8909, 19 Stavrou St, 2035 Strovolos; tel. (2) 510933; fax (2) 510934; f. 1966; Chair. KONSTANTINOS L. PRODROMOU; Principal Officer KONSTANTINOS TSANGARIS.

Agrostroy Insurance Co Ltd: POB 6624, 89 Kennedy Ave, Office 201, 1077 Nicosia; tel. (2) 379210; fax (2) 379212; f. 1996; offshore captive company operating outside Cyprus; Chair. VALERIE V. USHAKOV; Principal Officer IOANNIS ELIA.

Akelius Insurance Ltd: POB 23415, 36 Laodikias St, 1683 Nicosia; tel. (2) 318883; fax (2) 318925; f. 1989; offshore company operating outside Cyprus; Chair. ROGER AKELIOUS; Principal Officer IOANNIS LOIZOU.

Allied Assurance & Reinsurance Co Ltd: POB 5509, 66 Grivas Dhigenis Ave, 1310 Nicosia; tel. (2) 672235; fax (2) 677656; f. 1982; offshore company operating outside Cyprus; Chair. HENRI J. G. CHALHOUB; Principal Officer DEMETRIOS DEMETRIOU.

Alpha Insurance Ltd: POB 26516, cnr Kennedy Ave and Stasinou St, 1640 Nicosia; tel. (2) 379999; fax (2) 379097; e-mail metropolitan @cytanet.com.cy; f. 1993; Chair. DOUKAS PALEOLOGOS; Principal Officer EVANGELOS ANASTASIADES.

AMI Alpha Marine Insurance Cyprus Co. Ltd: POB 53250, 8 Alasias St, 3095 Limassol; tel. (5) 373279; fax (5) 355869; f. 1995; offshore captive company operating outside Cyprus; Principal Officer CHRIS GEORGHIADES.

Antarctic Insurance Co Ltd: POB 613, 199 Archbishop Makarios III Ave, Neokleou Bldg, 3030 Limassol; tel. (5) 362818; fax (5) 359262; offshore captive company operating outside Cyprus; Principal Officer ANDREAS NEOKLEOUS.

Apac Ltd: POB 25403, 5 Mourouzi St, Apt 1, 1055 Nicosia; tel. (2) 343086; fax (2) 343146; f. 1983; captive offshore company operating outside Cyprus; Chair. KYPROS CHRYSOSTOMIDES; Principal Officer GEORGHIOS POYATZIS.

APOL Insurance Ltd: 24 Perea St, Mocassino Centre, 3rd Floor, 2023 Strovolos, Nicosia; tel. (2) 513533; fax (2) 513330; offshore company operating outside Cyprus; Chair. M. ARBOUZOV; Principal Officer STELIOS MICHAEL.

Asfalistiki Eteria I 'Kentriki' Ltd: POB 25131, Greg Tower, 3rd Floor, 7 Florinis St, Nicosia 136; tel. (2) 473931; fax (2) 366276; f. 1985; Chair. ARISTOS CHRYSOSTOMOU; Principal Officer GEORGHIOS GEORGALLIDES.

Aspis Pronia Insurance Co Ltd: POB 25183, 101 Acropolis Ave, 2012 Strovolos; tel. (2) 871087; fax (2) 492402; f. 1996; Chair. P. PSOMIADES; Principal Officer CHRISTAKIS ELEFTHERIOU.

Atlantic Insurance Co Ltd: POB 24579, 37 Prodromou St, 2nd Floor, 1090 Strovolos; tel. (2) 664052; fax (2) 661100; f. 1983; Chair. and Man. Dir ZENIOS PYRISHIS; Principal Officer EMILIOS PYRISHIS.

Axioma Insurance (Cyprus) Ltd: POB 24881, 2 Ionni Klerides St, Demokritos No. 2 Bldg, Flat 83, 1070 Nicosia; tel. (2) 374197; fax (2) 374972; offshore company operating outside Cyprus; Principal Officer KONSTANTINOS KYAMIDES.

B & B Marine Insurance Ltd: POB 22545, 46 Gladstonos St, 1095 Nicosia; tel. (2) 666599; fax (2) 676476; f. 1996; offshore company operating outside Cyprus; Chair. DMITGRI MOLTCHANOV; Principal Officer GEORGHIOS YIANGOU.

Berytus Marine Insurance Ltd: POB 50132, 284 Archbishop Makarios III Ave, 3105 Limassol; tel. (5) 369404; fax (5) 377871; f. 1997; offshore company operating outside Cyprus; Principal Officer CHRIS GEORGHIADES.

Cathay Insurance Co Ltd: POB 54708, 21 Vasili Michailidi, 3727 Limassol; f. 1997; offshore captive company operating outside Cyprus; Principal Officer ARETI CHARIDEMOU.

Commercial Union Assurance (Cyprus) Ltd: POB 21312, Commercial Union House, 101 Archbishop Makarios III Ave, 1071 Nicosia; tel. (2) 377373; fax (2) 376155; e-mail mailbox@commercial-union .com.cy; f. 1974; Chair. J. CHRISTOPHIDES; Dir and Gen. Man. KONSTANTINOS P. DEKATRIS.

Cosmos (Cyprus) Insurance Co Ltd: POB 21770, 1st Floor, Flat 12, 6 Ayia Eleni St, 1060 Nicosia; tel. (2) 441235; fax (2) 457925; f. 1982; Chair. and Gen. Man. ANDREAS K. TYLLIS.

Crown Insurance Co Ltd: POB 24690, Royal Crown House, 20 Mnasiadou St, Nicosia 136; tel. (2) 673333; fax (2) 670757; f. 1992; Chair. W. R. ROWLAND; Principal Officer PHILIOS ZACHARIADES.

Cygnet Insurance Ltd: POB 58482, 56 Grivas Dhigenis Ave, Anna Tower, 4th floor, Office 42, 3101 Limassol; tel. (5) 583253; fax (5) 584514; e-mail tcsl@logos.cy.net; f. 1997; offshore captive company operating outside Cyprus; Principal Officer MARIOS LOUKAIDES.

Cyprialife Ltd: POB 20819, 64 Archbishop Makarios III Ave and 1 Karpenisiou St, 1077 Nicosia; tel. (2) 887300; fax (2) 374450; e-mail cyprialife@cytanet.com.cy; f. 1995; Chair. KIKIS LAZARIDES; Principal Officer DIMIS MICHAELIDES.

Direct Insurance Company Ltd: POB 22274, 35–37 Byzantium St, 1585 Nicosia; tel. (2) 664433; fax (2) 665139; Chair. STAVROS DAVERONAS.

E.F.U. General Insurance Ltd: POB 1612, 3 Themistoklis Dervis St, Julia House, Nicosia; tel. (2) 453053; fax (2) 475194; offshore company; Chair. ROSHEN ALI BHIMJEE; Principal Officer CHARALAMBOS ZAVALLIS.

Emergency Market Insurance Ltd: POB 613, 199 Archbishop Makarios Ave, Neokleou Bldg, 3030 Limassol; tel. (5) 362818; fax

(5) 359262; f. 1997; offshore captive company operating outside Cyprus; Principal Officer ANDREAS NEOKLEOUS.

Eurolife Ltd: POB 21655, 40 Them. Dervis St, Eurolife House, 1655 Nicosia; tel. (2) 670067; fax (2) 671040; internet www .bankofcyprus.com/eurolife; Chair. E. XENOPHONTOS; Principal Officer ANDREAS KRITOTIS.

Eurosure Insurance Co Ltd: POB 21961, Eurosure Tower, 5 Limassol Ave, 2112 Aglantzia, 1515 Nicosia; tel. (2) 882500; fax (2) 882599; e-mail info@eurosure.com; internet www.eurosure.com; Chair. STELIOS IOANNOU.

Excelsior General Insurance Co Ltd: POB 6106, 339 Ayiou Andreou St, Andrea Chambers, Of. 303, Limassol; tel. (5) 427021; fax (5) 312446; f. 1995; Chair. CLIVE E. K. LEWIS; Principal Officer MARIA HADJIANTONIOU.

FAM Financial and Mercantile Insurance Co Ltd: POB 50132, 284 Archbishop Makarios III Ave, Fortuna Bldg, Block 'B', 2nd Floor, 4007 Limassol; tel. (5) 362424; fax (5) 370055; f. 1993; offshore captive company operating outside Cyprus; Chair. VLADIMIR MOISSEEV; Principal Officer CHR. GEORGHIADES.

General Insurance of Cyprus Ltd: POB 21668, 2–4 Themistoklis Dervis St, 1066 Nicosia; tel. (2) 848700; fax (2) 676682; e-mail gic-boc@logos.cy.net; f. 1951; Chair. V. ROLOGIS; Gen. Man. A. STYLIANOU.

Geopolis Insurance Ltd: POB 8530, 6 Neoptolemou St, 2045 Strovolos; tel. (2) 490094; fax (2) 490494; f. 1993; Chair. MARIOS PROIOS; Principal Officer NIKOS DRYMIOTIS.

Granite Insurance Co Ltd: POB 613, 199 Archbishop Makarios III Ave, Neokleou Bldg, 3030 Limassol; tel. (5) 362818; fax (5) 359262; captive offshore company operating outside Cyprus; Chair. and Gen. Man. KOSTAS KOUTSOKOUMNIS; Principal Officer ANDREAS NEOKLEOUS.

Greene Insurances Ltd: POB 132, 4th Floor, Vereggaria Bldg, 25 Spyrou Araouzou St, 3036 Limassol; tel. (5) 362424; fax (5) 363842; f. 1987; Chair. GEORGHIOS CHRISTODOULOU; Principal Officer JOSIF CHRISTOU.

Hermes Insurance Co Ltd: POB 24828, 1st Floor, Office 101–103, Anemomylos Bldg, 8 Michalakis Karaolis St, 1095 Nicosia; tel. (2) 669888; fax (2) 661888; f. 1980; Chair. and Man. Dir P. VOGAZIANOS.

I.G.R. Co Ltd: POB 21343, 20 Vasilissias Friderikis St, El Greco House, Office 104, 1066 Nicosia; tel. (2) 473688; fax (2) 455259; f. 1996; offshore company operating outside Cyprus; Principal Officer CHRISTODOULOS VASSILIADES.

Marketrends Insurance Ltd: POB 24841, corner Kennedy Ave and 7 Epaninonda St, 1076 Nicosia; tel. (2) 796600; fax (2) 768065; e-mail markins@cytanet.com.cy; Man. Dir PANOS JOAHNOU.

Laiki Insurance Co Ltd: POB 22069, 45 Vyzantiou St, Strovolos, 1517 Nicosia; tel. (2) 887600; fax (2) 662026; e-mail laiki.telebank@ laiki.com; internet www.laiki.com; f. 1981; Chair. K. N. LAZARIDES; Gen. Man. A. PISSIRIS.

LCF Reinsurance Co Ltd: POB 60479, Abacus House, 58 Grivas Dhigenis Ave, 8103 Paphos, Nicosia; tel. (2) 555000; fax (2) 555001; f. 1984; Chair. ALAIN COPINE; Principal Officer SOPHIA XINARI.

Ledra Insurance Ltd: POB 23942, 93 Kennedy Ave, 1077 Nicosia; tel. (2) 378200; fax (2) 378330; f. 1994; Chair. KONSTANTINOS KITTIS; Principal Officer ALEKOS PULCHERIOS.

Liberty Life Insurance Ltd: POB 26070, 75 Limassol Ave, 5th Floor, Nicosia; tel. (2) 319300; fax (2) 429134; f. 1994; Chair. KONSTANTINOS KITTIS; Principal Officer EURIPIDES NEOKLEOUS.

Medlife Insurance Ltd: POB 21675, Themistoklis Dervis-Florinis St, 1512 Nicosia; tel. (2) 675181; fax (2) 671889; e-mail office@ medlife.net; internet www.medlife.net; f. 1995; Chair. Dr WOLFGANG GOSHNIK.

Minerva Insurance Co Ltd: POB 20866, 8 Epaminondas St, 1684 Nicosia 137; tel. (2) 445134; fax (2) 455528; f. 1970; Chair. and Gen. Man. K. KOUTSOKOUMNIS.

Pancyprian Insurance Ltd: POB 21352, Mepa Tower, 66 Grivas Dhigenis Ave, 1080 Nicosia; tel. (2) 672235; fax (2) 677656; f. 1993; Chair. HENRI CHALHOUB; Principal Officer SOCRATES DEMETRIOU.

Paneuropean Insurance Co Ltd: POB 553, 88 Archbishop Makarios III Ave, 1660 Nicosia; tel. (2) 377960; fax (2) 377396; f. 1980; Chair. N. K. SHACOLAS; Gen. Man. POLIS MICHAELIDES.

Philiki Insurance Co Ltd: POB 22274, 35–37 Byzantium St, 2026 Strovolos, 1585 Nicosia; tel. (2) 664433; fax (2) 665139; f. 1982; Chair. NIKOS SHAKOLAS; Principal Officer DOROS ORPHANIDES.

Progressive Insurance Co Ltd: POB 22111, 44 Kallipoleos St, 1071 Nicosia; tel. (2) 758585; fax (2) 754747; e-mail progressive@ cytanet.com.cy; Chair. ANDREAS HADJIANDREOU; Principal Officer TAKIS HADJIANDREOU.

Saviour Insurance Co Ltd: POB 23957, 8 Michalakis Karaolis St, Anemomylos Bldg, Flat 204, 1687 Nicosia; tel. (2) 675085; fax (2) 676097; f. 1987; Chair. ROBERT SINCLAIR; Principal Officer KONSTANTINOS KITTIS.

Sunlink Insurance Co Ltd: POB 3585, 3 Themistoklis Dervis St, Julia House, 1066 Nicosia, tel. (2) 453053; fax (2) 475194; f. 1995; offshore captive company operating outside Cyprus; Chair. ANDREAS STYLIANOU; Principal Officer MARIA LAMBROU.

Technolink Insurance Services Ltd: POB 7007, 70 Kennedy Ave, Papavasiliou House, 1076 Nicosia; tel. (2) 496000; fax (2) 493000; f. 1996; offshore captive company operating outside Cyprus; Principal Officer GEORGHIOS YIALLOURIDES.

Tercet Insurance Ltd: POB 2545, 46 Gladstones St, 1095 Nicosia; tel. (2) 466456; fax (2) 466476; f. 1994; Chair. ANDREAS STYLIANOU; Principal Officer MARIA PIPINGA.

Triada Insurance Ltd: POB 21675, corner Themistoklis Dervis & Florinis St, Stadyl Bldg, 6th Floor, 1512 Nicosia; tel. (2) 675182; fax (2) 675926; f. 1996; offshore captive company operating outside Cyprus; Principal Officer ANDREAS STYLIANOU.

Trust International Insurance Co (Cyprus) Ltd: POB 54857, 284 Archbishop Makarios III Ave, Fortuna Bldg, 2nd Floor, 4007 Limassol; tel. (5) 369404; fax (5) 377871; f. 1992; Chair. GHAZI K. ABU NAHL; Principal Officer CHR. GEORGHIADES.

Universal Life Insurance Company Ltd: POB 21270, Universal Tower, 85 Dhigenis Akritas Ave, 1505 Nicosia; tel. (2) 882222; fax (2) 882200; e-mail unilife@unilife.com.cy; internet www .universallife.com.cy; f. 1970; Chair. J. CHRISTOPHIDES; Principal Officer ANDREAS GEORGHIOU.

UPIC Ltd: POB 57237, Nicolaou Pentadromos Centre, 10th Floor, Ayias Zonis St, 3314 Limassol; tel. (5) 347664; fax (5) 347081; e-mail upic@spidernet.com.cy; f. 1992; Principal Officer POLAKIS SARRIS.

Veritima Insurance Ltd: POB 956, 2B Orpheus St, Office 104, 1070 Nicosia; tel. (2) 375646; fax (2) 375620; f. 1996; offshore captive company operating outside Cyprus; Principal Officer SANDROS DIKEOS.

VTI Insurance Co Ltd: POB 50613, 199 Archbishop Makarios III Ave, Neokleou Bldg, 4004 Limassol; tel. (5) 362818; fax (5) 359262; f. 1994; Chair. SOTERIS PITTAS; Principal Officer ANDREAS NEOKLEOUS.

Turkish Cypriot Insurance Companies

Akfinans Sigorta Insurance AŞ: 16 Osman Paşa Cad., Lefkoşa (Nicosia), Mersin 10, Turkey; tel. (22) 84506; fax (22) 85713; e-mail info@akfinans.com; internet www.akfinans.com.

Altınbaş Sigorta Ltd: Müftü Ziya Sok. 2, Lefkoşa (Nicosia), Mersin 10, Turkey; tel. (22) 88222; fax (22) 76648.

Anadolu Anonim: 1-7-9 Girne Cad., Lefkoşa (Nicosia), Mersin 10, Turkey; tel. (22) 83133; fax (22) 79596.

Ankara Sigorta: PK 551, Bedrettin Demirel Cad., Lefkoşa (Nicosia), Mersin 10, Turkey; tel. (22) 85815; fax (22) 83099.

Başak Sigorta AŞ: Mehmet Akif Cad. 95, Lefkoşa (Nicosia), Mersin 10, Turkey; tel. (22) 80208; fax (22) 86160.

Bey Sigorta Ltd: Atatürk Cad. 5, Yenişehir, Lefkoşa (Nicosia), Mersin 10, Turkey; tel. (22) 88241; fax (22) 87362.

Birinci Sigorta Ltd: Tekin Yurdabak Cad., Tekin Birinci Binaları, Göçmenköy, Lefkoşa (Nicosia), Mersin 10, Turkey; tel. (22) 83200; fax (22) 83498.

Gold Insurance Ltd: Salih Mecit Sok. 12/B, Lefkoşa (Nicosia), Mersin 10, Turkey; tel. (22) 86500; fax (22) 86300.

Güneş Sigorta AŞ: Vakıflar İş Hanı 1C Girne Cad., Lefkoşa (Nicosia), Mersin 10, Turkey; tel. (22) 87333; fax (22) 81585.

Güven Sigorta (Kıbrıs) Sirketi AŞ: Mecidiye Sok. 8, Lefkoşa (Nicosia), Mersin 10, Turkey; tel. (22) 83023; fax (22) 81431.

İnan Sigorta TAŞ: Mehmet Akif Cad. 98, Kumsal, Lefkoşa (Nicosia), Mersin 10, Turkey; tel. (22) 83333; fax (22) 81976.

İşlek Sigorta: Bahçelievler Bul., Güzelyurt (Morphou), Mersin 10, Turkey; tel. (71) 42473; fax (71) 45507.

İsviçre Sigorta AŞ: Arkom Ltd, PK 693, Lefkoşa (Nicosia), Mersin 10, Turkey; tel. (22) 82125; fax (22) 88236.

Kıbrıs Sigorta: Osman Paşa Cad., Yağcıoğlu Işhanı 4, Lefkoşa (Nicosia), Mersin 10, Turkey; tel. (22) 83022; fax (22) 79277.

Limassol Sigorta Ltd: PK 267, Orhaneli Sok., Girne, Mersin 10, Turkey; tel. (81) 56786; fax (81) 58773.

Middle East Sigorta: 2 Selim Cad. No 56, Lefkoşa (Nicosia), Mersin 10, Turkey; tel. (22) 86522; fax (22) 86395.

Ray Sigorta AŞ: Bedrettin Demirel Cad. Arabacıoğlu Apt. 7, Lefkoşa (Nicosia), Mersin 10, Turkey; tel. (22) 70380; fax (22) 70383.

Saray Sigorta: 182 Girne Cad., Lefkoşa (Nicosia), Mersin 10, Turkey; tel. (22) 72976; fax (22) 79001.

Şeker Sigorta (Kıbrıs) Ltd: Mahmut Paşa Sok. 14/A, PK 664, Lefkoşa (Nicosia), Mersin 10, Turkey; tel. (22) 85883; fax (22) 74074.

Zirve Sigorta Ltd: Gültekin Şengör Sok., Abahorlu Türk Apt. 9, Lefkoşa (Nicosia), Mersin 10, Turkey; tel. (22) 75633; fax (22) 83600.

Trade and Industry

GREEK CYPRIOT CHAMBERS OF COMMERCE AND INDUSTRY

Cyprus Chamber of Commerce and Industry: POB 21455, 38 Grivas Dhigenis Ave, 1509 Nicosia; tel. (2) 889800; fax (2) 669048; e-mail chamber@ccci.org.cy; internet www.ccci.org.cy; f. 1927; Pres. VASSILIS ROLOGIS; Sec.-Gen. PANAYIOTIS LOIZIDES; 8,000 mems, 100 affiliated trade asscns.

Famagusta Chamber of Commerce and Industry: POB 53124, 339 Ayiou Andreou St, Andrea Chambers Bldg, 2nd Floor, Office No 201–202, 3300 Limassol; tel. (5) 370165; fax (5) 370291; e-mail chamberf@cytanet.com.cy; f. 1952; Pres. PHOTIS PAPATHOMAS; Sec. IACOVOS HADJIVARNAVAS; 450 mems.

Larnaca Chamber of Commerce and Industry: POB 287, 12 Gregoriou Afxentiou St, Skouros Bldg, Apt 43, 4th Floor, 6302 Larnaca; tel. (4) 655051; fax (4) 628281; Pres. IACOVOS DEMETRIOU; Sec. OTHON THEODOULOU; 450 mems.

Limassol Chamber of Commerce and Industry: POB 347, 25 Spyrou Araouzou St, Veregaria Bldg, 3rd Floor, 3603 Limassol; tel. (5) 362556; fax (5) 371655; e-mail chamberl@dial.cylink.com.cy; f. 1962; Pres. TONY ANTONIOU; Sec. CHRISTOS NICOLAOU; 770 mems.

Nicosia Chamber of Commerce and Industry: POB 21455, 38 Grivas Dhigenis Ave, Chamber Bldg, 1509 Nicosia; tel. (2) 889600; fax (2) 667433; e-mail ncci@ccci.org.cy; f. 1962; Pres. MANTHOS MAVROMATIS; Sec. SOCRATES HERACLEOUS; 1,200 mems.

Paphos Chamber of Commerce and Industry: POB 82, Athinon Ave & corner Alexandrou Papayou Ave, 8100 Paphos; tel. (6) 235115; fax (6) 244602; Pres. THEODOROS ARISTODEMOU; Sec. KENDEAS ZAMPIRINIS; 450 mems.

TURKISH CYPRIOT CHAMBERS OF COMMERCE AND INDUSTRY

Turkish Cypriot Chamber of Industry: 14 Osman Paşa Cad., PK 563, Köşklüçiftlik, Lefkoşa (Nicosia), Mersin 10, Turkey; tel. (22) 84596; fax (22) 84595; Pres. EREN ERTANIN.

Turkish Cypriot Chamber of Commerce: Bedrettin Demirel Cad., PK 718, Lefkoşa (Nicosia), Mersin 10, Turkey; tel. (22) 83645; fax (22) 83089; f. 1958; more than 6,000 regd mems; Chair. SALIH BOYACI; Sec.-Gen. JANEL BURCAN.

GREEK CYPRIOT EMPLOYERS' ORGANIZATION

Cyprus Employers' & Industrialists' Federation: POB 21657, 30 Grivas Dhigenis Ave, 1511 Nicosia; tel. (2) 665102; fax (2) 669459; e-mail oeb@dial.cylink.com.cy; internet www.oeb-eif.org; f. 1960; 41 member trade associations, 400 direct and 3,000 indirect members; Dir-Gen. ANTONIS PIERIDES; Chair. MICHAEL ZIVANARIS. The largest of the trade association members are: Cyprus Building Contractors' Association; Land and Building Developers' Association; Association of Cyprus Tourist Enterprises; Cyprus Shipping Association; Cyprus Footwear Manufacturers' Association; Cyprus Metal Industries Association; Cyprus Bankers Employers' Association.

TURKISH CYPRIOT EMPLOYERS' ORGANIZATION

Kıbrıs Türk İşverenler Sendikası (Turkish Cypriot Employers' Association): PK 674, Lefkoşa (Nicosia), Mersin 10, Turkey; tel. (22) 76173; Chair. ALPAY ALİ RIZA GÖRGÜNER.

GREEK CYPRIOT UTILITIES

Electricity

Electricity Authority of Cyprus (EAC): POB 24506, 1399 Nicosia; tel. (2) 845000; fax (2) 767658; e-mail eac@eac.com.cy; internet www.eac.com.cy; generation, transmission and distribution of electric energy in government-controlled area; total installed capacity 728 MW in 1999.

Water

Water Development Department: Dem. Severis Ave, 1413 Nicosia; tel. (2) 803100; fax (2) 675019; e-mail waterdep@cytanet .com.cy; dam storage capacity 300m. cu m; Dir CHR. MARCOULLIS.

TURKISH CYPRIOT UTILITIES

Electricity

Cyprus Turkish Electricity Corpn: Lefkoşa (Nicosia), Mersin 10, Turkey; tel. (22) 83648; fax (22) 83851.

TRADE UNIONS

Greek Cypriot Trade Unions

Cyprus Civil Servants' Trade Union: 3 Dem. Severis Ave, Nicosia; tel. (2) 662337; fax (2) 665199; e-mail pasydy@spidernet .com.cy; f. 1949, registered 1966; restricted to persons in the civil

employment of the Government and public authorities; 6 brs with a total membership of 15,383; Pres. ANDREAS PAPAPOLYUIOU; Gen. Sec. GLAFKOS HADJIPETROU.

Dimokratiki Ergatiki Omospondia Kyprou (Democratic Labour Federation of Cyprus): POB 21625, 40 Byron Ave, Nicosia; tel. (2) 676506; fax (2) 670494; e-mail deok@cytanet.com.cy; f. 1962; 5 workers' unions with a total membership of 7,316; Gen. Sec. DIOMEDES DIOMEDOUS.

Pankypria Ergatiki Omospondia—PEO (Pancyprian Federation of Labour): POB 1885, 31–35 Archermos St, Nicosia; tel. (2) 886400; fax (2) 349382; e-mail peo@cytanet.com.cy; internet www .cytanet.com.cy/peo; f. 1946, registered 1947; previously the Pancyprian Trade Union Committee f. 1941, dissolved 1946; 8 unions and 176 brs with a total membership of 75,000; affiliated to the WFTU; Gen. Sec. PAMBIS KYRITSIS.

Pankyprios Omospondia Anexartition Syntechnion (Pancyprian Federation of Independent Trade Unions): 4B Dayaes St, 2369 Ay. Dhometios; POB 7521, 2430 Nicosia; tel. (2) 356414; fax (2) 354216; f. 1956, registered 1957; has no political orientations; 8 unions with a total membership of 798; Gen. Sec. KYRIACOS NATHANAEL.

Synomospondia Ergaton Kyprou (Cyprus Workers' Confederation): POB 25018, 11 Strovolos Ave, 2018 Strovolos, 1306 Nicosia; tel. (2) 849849; fax (2) 849850; e-mail sek@org.cy.net; f. 1944, registered 1950; 7 federations, 5 labour centres, 47 unions, 12 brs with a total membership of 62,559; affiliated to the ICFTU and the ETUC; Gen. Sec. DEMETRIS KITTENIS; Deputy Gen. Sec. NIKOS MOESEOS.

Union of Cyprus Journalists: POB 23495, 2 Kratinos St, Strovolos, 1683 Nicosia; tel. (2) 664680; fax (2) 664598; e-mail cyjourun@ logosnet.cy.net; f. 1959; Chair. ANDREAS KANNAOUROS.

Turkish Cypriot Trade Unions

In 1998 trade union membership totalled 24,864.

Devrimci İşçi Sendikaları Federasyonu (Dev-İş) (Revolutionary Trade Unions' Federation): 8 Serabioğlu Sok., Lefkoşa (Nicosia), Mersin 10, Turkey; tel. (22) 72640; f. 1976; two unions with a total membership of 2,274 (1998); affiliated to WFTU; Pres. (acting) and Gen. Sec. BAYRAM ÇELİK.

Kıbrıs Türk İşçi Sendikaları Federasyonu (TÜRK-SEN) (Turkish Cypriot Trade Union Federation): POB 829, 7–7A Şehit Mehmet R. Hüseyin Sok., Lefkoşa (Nicosia), Mersin 10, Turkey; tel. (22) 72444; fax (22) 87831; f. 1954, regd 1955; 12 unions with a total membership of 5,250 (1998); affiliated to ICFTU, ETUC, CTUC and the Confederation of Trade Unions of Turkey (Türk-İş); Pres. ÖNDER KONULOĞLU; Gen. Sec. ASLAN BIÇAKLI.

Transport

RAILWAYS

There are no railways in Cyprus.

ROADS

In December 1995 there were 25,378 km of roads in the government-controlled areas, of which 5,942 km were paved and the remainder were earth or gravel roads. The Nicosia–Limassol four-lane dual carriageway, which was completed in 1985, was subsequently extended with the completion of the Limassol and Larnaca bypasses. New highways between Nicosia and Larnaca, and Larnaca and Kophinou have been completed, as well as the Aradippo–Dhekelia and Larnaca Airport bypasses. The Nicosia–Anthoupolis–Kokkinotrimithia highway was completed in 1994. At December 1995 the total extent of the highway network was 178.4 km., which was expected to be increased further with the construction of a Limassol–Paphos highway (the first section of which opened in 1997; work was scheduled to be completed in 2000). In 1997 work began on a Dhekelia–Ammochostos (Famagusta) highway. The north and south are now served by separate transport systems, and there are no services linking the two sectors.

SHIPPING

Until 1974 Famagusta, a natural port, was the island's most important harbour, handling about 83% of the country's cargo. Since its capture by the Turkish army in August 1974 the port has been officially declared closed to international traffic. However, it continues to serve the Turkish-occupied region.

The main ports which serve the island's maritime trade at present are Larnaca and Limassol, which were constructed in 1973 and 1974 respectively. Both ports have since been expanded and improved. There is also an industrial port at Vassiliko and there are three specialized petroleum terminals, at Larnaca, Dhekelia and Moni. A second container terminal became operational at Limassol in 1995.

In 1998 4,475 vessels, with a total net registered tonnage of 15,963,000, visited Cyprus, carrying 7,017,000 metric tons of cargo to and from Cyprus. In addition to serving local traffic, Limassol and Larnaca ports act as transhipment load centres for the Eastern Mediterranean, North Adriatic and Black Sea markets and as regional warehouse and assembly bases for the Middle East, North Africa and the Persian (Arabian) Gulf. Containerized cargo handled at Cypriot ports amounted to 1,722,300 metric tons in 1998.

Both Kyrenia and Karavostassi are under Turkish occupation and have been declared closed to international traffic. Karavostassi used to be the country's major mineral port, dealing with 76% of the total mineral exports. However, since the war minerals have been passed through Vassiliko which is a specified industrial port. A hydrofoil service operates between Kyrenia and Mersin on the Turkish mainland. Car ferries sail from Kyrenia to Taşucu and Mersin, in Turkey.

Department of Merchant Shipping: POB 6193, Kyllinis St, Mesk Geitonia, 4405 Limassol; tel. (5) 848100; fax (5) 848200; e-mail dms@cytanet.com.cy; Dir. SERGHIOS SERGHIOU.

Cyprus Ports Authority: POB 22007, 23 Crete St, 1516 Nicosia; tel. (2) 756100; fax (2) 765420; e-mail cpa@cpa.gov.cy; internet www.cpa.gov.cy; f. 1973; Chair. CHRISTOS HADJIMANOLIS; Gen. Man. Dr ANTONIS TOUMAZIS.

Cyprus Shipping Council: POB 56607, 3309 Limassol; tel. (5) 360717; fax (5) 358642; e-mail csc@csc-cy.org; internet www .csc-cy.org; Gen. Sec. THOMAS A. KAZAKOS.

Greek Cypriot Shipping Companies

Amer Shipping Ltd: POB 27363, 6th Floor, Ghinis Bldg, 58–60 Dhigenis Akritas Ave, 1061 Nicosia; tel. (2) 751707; fax (2) 751460; e-mail amer@spidernet.com.cy; internet www.amershipping.com; Man. Dir ANIL DESHPANDE.

C. F. Ahrenkiel Shipmanagement (Cyprus) Ltd: POB 53594, 4th Floor, O & A Tower, 25 Olympion St, 3033 Limassol; tel. (5) 854000; fax (5) 854001; Man. Dir VASSOS STAVROU.

Columbia Shipmanagement Ltd: POB 51624, Columbia House, Dodekanissou and Kolonakiou Corner, 3507 Limassol; tel. (5) 320900; fax (5) 320325; e-mail shipmanagement@csmcy.com; internet www.columbia.com.cy; f. 1978; Chair. H. SCHOELLER, Man. Dir D. FRY.

Hanseatic Shipping Co Ltd: POB 127, 111 Spyrou Araouzou St, Limassol; tel. (5) 345111; fax (5) 342879; f. 1972; Man. Dirs A. J. DROUSSIOTIS, R. GROOL.

Interorient Navigation Co Ltd: POB 51309, 3 Thalia St, 3504 Limassol; tel. (5) 840300; fax (5) 575895; e-mail management@ interorient.com.cy; internet www.interorient.com; Man. Dir JAN LISSOW.

Louis Cruise Lines: POB 21301, 54-58 Evagoras I Ave, Nicosia; tel. (2) 678000; fax (2) 679800; Exec. Chair. KOSTAKIS LOIZOU; Man. Dir STELIOS KILIARIS.

Marlow Navigation Co Ltd: POB 4077, Marlow Bldg, cnr 28th October St and Sotiris Michaelides St, Limassol; tel. (5) 348888; fax (5) 748222; e-mail marlow@marlow.com.cy; Gen. Man. ANDREAS NEOPHYTOU.

Oldendorff Ltd, Reederei Nord Klaus E: POB 56345, Libra Tower, 23 Olympion St, 3306 Limassol; tel. (5) 841400; fax (5) 345077; e-mail rnkeo@spidernet.com.cy; Chair. and Man. Dir KLAUS E. OLDENDORFF.

Seatankers Management Co Ltd: POB 3562, Flat 411, Deana Beach Apartments, Promachon Eleftherias St, 4103 Limassol; tel. (5) 326111; fax (5) 323770; Man. Dir DANIEL IONNIDES; Gen. Man. DEMETRIS HANNAS.

Turkish Cypriot Shipping Companies

Armen Shipping Ltd: Altun Tabya Yolu No. 10–11, Gazi Mağusa (Famagusta), Mersin 10, Turkey; tel. (36) 64086; fax (36) 65860; e-mail armen@birimnet.com; Dir VARGIN VARER.

Compass Shipping Ltd: Seagate Court, Gazi Mağusa (Famagusta), Mersin 10, Turkey; tel. (36) 66393; fax (36) 66394.

Denko Koop Marine Cargo Department: PK 4, 12 Canbulat St, Gazi Mağusa (Famagusta), Mersin 10, Turkey; tel. (36) 65419; fax (36) 62773; e-mail info@koopbank.com; internet www .koopbank.com; Dir MEHMET EFE.

Ertürk Ltd: Kyrenia (Girne), Mersin 10, Turkey; tel. (81) 55834; fax (81) 51808; Dir KEMAL ERTÜRK.

Fergun Maritime Co: Kyrenia (Girne), Mersin 10, Turkey; tel. (81) 54993; ferries to Turkish ports; Owner FEHIM KÜÇÜK.

Kıbrıs Türk Denizcilik Ltd, Şti (Turkish Cypriot Maritime Co Ltd): 3 Bülent Ecevit Bul., Gazi Mağusa (Famagusta), Mersin 10, Turkey; tel. (36) 65995; fax (36) 67840.

Medusa Marine Shipping Ltd: Aycan Apt, Gazi Mağusa (Famagusta), Mersin 10, Turkey; tel. (36) 63945; fax (36) 67800; Dir ERGÜN TOLAY.

Orion Navigation Ltd: Seagate Court, Gazi Mağusa (Famagusta), Mersin 10, Turkey; tel. (36) 62643; fax (36) 64773; e-mail orion@ analiz.net; f. 1976; shipping agents; Dir O. LAMA; Shipping Man. L. LAMA.

Özari Shipping Ltd: Seagate Court, Gazi Mağusa (Famagusta), Mersin 10, Turkey; tel. (36) 66555; fax (36) 67098; Dir YALÇIN RUHI.

Tahsin Transtürk ve Oğlu Ltd: 11 Kizilkule Yolu, Gazi Mağusa (Famagusta), Mersin 10, Turkey; tel. (36) 65409.

CIVIL AVIATION

There is an international airport at Nicosia, which can accommodate all types of aircraft, including jet-engined airliners. It has been closed since 1974, following the Turkish invasion. A new international airport was constructed at Larnaca, from which flights operate to Europe, the USA, the Middle East and the Gulf. Another international airport at Paphos began operations in 1983.

Avistar: POB 5532, Nicosia; tel. (2) 459533; fax (2) 477367; f. 1990; freight; Chief Exec. Dr WALDEMAR HAAS.

Cyprus Airways: 21 Alkeou St, Engomi 2404, POB 21903, 1514 Nicosia; tel. (2) 663054; fax (2) 663167; internet www.cyprusair .com.cy; f. 1947; jointly owned by Cyprus Government (66%) and local interests; wholly-owned subsidiaries Cyprair Tours Ltd, Eurocypria Airlines Ltd, Duty Free Shops Ltd and Zenon NDC Ltd; Chair. HARIS LOIZIDES; Gen. Man. CHRISTOS KYRIAKIDES; services throughout Europe and the Middle East.

Eurocypria Airlines (ECA): POB 970, 97 Artemidos Ave, Artemis Bldg, Larnaca; tel. (4) 658000; fax (4) 658000; services to European destinations from Larnaca and Paphos; Chair. VASSILIS ROLOGIS; Gen. Man. CHARALAMBOS HADJIPANAYIOTOU.

In 1975 the Turkish authorities opened Ercan (formerly Tymbou) airport, and a second airport was opened at Geçitkale (Lefkoniko) in 1986.

Kıbrıs Türk Hava Yolları (Cyprus Turkish Airlines): Bedrettin Demirel Cad., PK 793, Lefkoşa (Nicosia), Mersin 10, Turkey; tel. (22) 83901; fax (22) 81468; e-mail info@kthy.net; internet www .cathy.net; f. 1974; jointly owned by the Turkish Cypriot Community Assembly Consolidated Improvement Fund and Turkish Airlines Inc; services to Turkey and five European countries; Gen. Man. Dr FERDA ÖNEŞ.

Tourism

In 1999 a total of 2,434,300 foreign tourists visited the Greek Cypriot area, and receipts from tourism amounted to C£1,022m. In 1998 an estimated 393,027 tourists visited the Turkish Cypriot area, and in 1997 revenue from tourism reached US $192.2m.

Cyprus Tourism Organization (CTO): POB 24535, 19 Limassol Ave, 1390 Nicosia; tel. (2) 337715; fax (2) 331644; e-mail cytour@cto.org.cy; internet www.cyprustourism.org; Chair. ADONIS PAPADOPOULOS; Dir-Gen. PHRYNE MICHAEL.

THE CZECH REPUBLIC

Introductory Survey

Location, Climate, Language, Religion, Flag, Capital

The Czech Republic lies in central Europe and comprises the Czech Lands of Bohemia and Moravia and part of Silesia. Its neighbours are Poland to the north, Germany to the north-west and west, Austria to the south and Slovakia to the east. The climate is continental, with warm summers and cold winters. The average mean temperature is 9°C (49°F). Czech, a member of the west Slavonic group, is the official language. There is a sizeable Slovak minority and also small Polish, German, Silesian, Romany, Hungarian and other minorities. The major religion is Christianity (about 39% of the population are Roman Catholics). The national flag (proportions 3 by 2) has two equal horizontal stripes, of white and red, on which is superimposed a blue triangle (half the length) at the hoist. The capital is Prague (Praha).

Recent History

In October 1918, following the collapse of the Austro-Hungarian Empire at the end of the First World War, the Republic of Czechoslovakia was established. The new state united the Czech Lands of Bohemia and Moravia, which had been incorporated into the Austrian Empire in the 16th and 17th centuries, and Slovakia, which had been under Hungarian rule for almost 1,000 years. After the Nazis came to power in Germany in 1933, there was increased agitation in the Sudetenland (an area in northern Bohemia that was inhabited by about 3m. German-speaking people) for autonomy within, and later secession from, Czechoslovakia. In 1938, to appease German demands, the British, French and Italian Prime Ministers concluded an agreement with the German leader, Adolf Hitler, whereby the Sudetenland was ceded to Germany, while other parts of Czechoslovakia were transferred to Hungary and Poland. The remainder of Czechoslovakia was invaded and occupied by Nazi armed forces in March 1939, and a German protectorate was established in Bohemia and Moravia. In Slovakia, which had been granted self-government in late 1938, a separate Slovak state was formed, under the pro-Nazi regime of Jozef Tiso.

After Germany's defeat in the Second World War (1939–45), the pre-1938 frontiers of Czechoslovakia were restored, although a small area in the east was ceded to the USSR in June 1945. Almost all of the German-speaking inhabitants of Czechoslovakia were expelled, and the Sudetenland was settled by Czechs from other parts of Bohemia. In response to Slovak demands for greater autonomy, a legislature (the Slovak National Council) and an executive Board of Commissioners were established in Bratislava, the Slovak capital. At elections in 1946 the Communist Party of Czechoslovakia (CPCz) emerged as the leading party, winning 38% of the votes cast. The CPCz's leader, Klement Gottwald, became Prime Minister in a coalition Government. After ministers of other parties resigned, Communist control became complete on 25 February 1948. A People's Republic was established on 9 June 1948. Gottwald replaced Edvard Beneš as President, a position that he held until his death in 1953. The country aligned itself with the Soviet-led Eastern European bloc, joining the Council for Mutual Economic Assistance (CMEA) and the Warsaw Pact.

Government followed a rigid Stalinist pattern, and in the early 1950s there were many political trials. Although these ended under Gottwald's successors, Antonín Zápotocký and, from 1956, Antonín Novotný, there was no relaxation of policy until 1963, when a new Government, with Jozef Lenárt as Prime Minister, was formed. Meanwhile, the country was renamed the Czechoslovak Socialist Republic, under a new Constitution, proclaimed in July 1960.

In January 1968 Alexander Dubček succeeded Novotný as CPCz Secretary, and in March Gen. Ludvík Svoboda succeeded Novotný as President. Oldřich Černík became Prime Minister in April. The new Government envisaged widespread reforms, including the introduction of more democratic elections, greater freedom of expression and a greater degree of separation between party and state. A federal system of government was also to be introduced. The Government's reformist policies were regarded by other members of the Eastern European bloc as

endangering their unity and in August Warsaw Pact forces (numbering an estimated 600,000 men) invaded Czechoslovakia, occupying Prague and other major cities. Mass demonstrations in protest at the invasion were held throughout the country, and many people were killed in clashes with occupation troops. The Soviet Government exerted heavy pressure on the Czechoslovak leaders to suppress their reformist policies and in April 1969 Dubček was replaced by a fellow Slovak, Dr Gustáv Husák, as First (subsequently General) Secretary of the Central Committee of the CPCz. Under Husák's leadership, there was a severe purge of CPCz membership and most of Dubček's supporters were removed from the Government. All the reforms of 1968 were duly abandoned, with the exception of the federalization programme. This was implemented in January 1969, when the unitary Czechoslovak state was transformed into a federation, with separate Czech and Slovak Republics, each having its own National Council (legislature) and Government. A Federal Government was established as the supreme executive organ of state power, while the country's existing legislature, the National Assembly, was transformed into a bicameral Federal Assembly. The first legislative election since 1964 was held in November 1971 and 99.81% of the votes cast were in favour of candidates of the National Front (the Communist-dominated organization embracing all the legal political parties in Czechoslovakia).

In May 1975 Husák was appointed to the largely ceremonial post of President of Czechoslovakia, retaining his positions of Chairman of the National Front and General Secretary of the CPCz. He held the latter post until December 1987, when he was replaced by Miloš Jakeš, an economist and member of the Presidium of the Party's Central Committee. However, Husák remained as President of the Republic.

Although Jakeš affirmed his commitment to the moderate programme of reform initiated by his predecessor, repressive measures against the Roman Catholic Church and dissident groups continued. Of the latter, the most influential was Charter 77, which had been established in January 1977 by intellectuals, former politicians and others to campaign for the observance of civil and political rights. Despite the regime's continued attempts to suppress the movement, its sphere of influence broadened and it played a leading role in anti-Government demonstrations, which began in 1988. In February 1989, following one such demonstration, the Czech playwright, Václav Havel (a leader of Charter 77), was sentenced to nine months' imprisonment. (He was released in May, following international condemnation.) Anti-Government demonstrations followed in May, August and October 1989.

In November 1989 the protest actions of preceding months evolved into a process of dramatic, yet largely peaceful, political change, which subsequently became known as the 'velvet revolution'. On 17 November some 50,000 people, mainly students, participated in an anti-Government demonstration in Prague, the largest public protest for 20 years. The demonstration was violently dispersed by the police and more than 500 people were injured. Following reports (which later proved to be unfounded) that a student had been killed, a series of demonstrations culminated in gatherings of as many as 500,000 people in Prague, while large-scale protests took place in other towns throughout the country.

A new opposition group, Civic Forum, was established in November 1989 as an informal alliance embracing several existing opposition and human-rights organizations, including Charter 77, and rapidly gained widespread popular support. Meanwhile, Alexander Dubček addressed mass rallies in Bratislava and Prague, expressing his support for the opposition's demands for reform. On 24 November it was announced that Jakeš and the entire membership of the Presidium of the Central Committee had resigned. Karel Urbánek, a member of the Presidium, replaced Jakeš as General Secretary of the party, and a new Presidium was elected.

The increasing strength of Civic Forum and its Slovak counterpart, Public Against Violence (PAV), was demonstrated during discussions on reform with the Federal Prime Minister,

Ladislav Adamec. The opposition's demands for the ending of censorship and the release of all political prisoners were fulfilled and, in late November 1989, the articles guaranteeing the CPCz's predominance were deleted from the Constitution. In the following month the CPCz condemned the invasion of Czechoslovakia by Warsaw Pact forces in 1968 as 'unjustified and mistaken'. Shortly afterwards, the Governments of the five countries that had invaded Czechoslovakia issued a joint statement condemning their action.

In early December 1989 a reshuffle of the Federal Government took place. Civic Forum and PAV denounced the new Government, as the majority of its ministers had been members of the previous administration, and it included only five non-communists. Adamec subsequently resigned as Prime Minister, and was replaced by Marián Čalfa, the newly appointed First Deputy Prime Minister. In the following week a new, interim Federal Government was formed, with a majority of non-Communist members, including seven non-party supporters of Civic Forum. Husák resigned from the office of President of the Republic and at the end of December was replaced by Václav Havel. Alexander Dubček was elected Chairman of the Federal Assembly. At an emergency congress of the CPCz, held in December, Urbánek was dismissed from the post of General Secretary of the Central Committee and this position was abolished. Adamec was appointed to the new post of Chairman of the Party.

In April 1990 the Federal Assembly voted to rename the country the Czech and Slovak Federative Republic (CzSFR). The decision, which followed intense controversy, satisfied Slovak demands that the new title should reflect the equal status of Slovakia within the federation.

On 8–9 June 1990 the first free legislative elections since 1946 were held in Czechoslovakia. About 97% of the electorate voted for a total of 27 parties and movements for representation in the Federal Assembly (now numbering 300 seats) and in the National Councils of each republic. In the elections at federal level, the largest proportion of the total votes cast (about 46%) was won by Civic Forum, in the Czech Lands, and by PAV, in Slovakia. The CPCz won a larger proportion of the total votes (about 14%) than had been expected, obtaining the second-largest representation in the Federal Assembly. The Christian Democratic Union—a coalition of the Czechoslovak People's Party, the Christian Democratic Party (Chr.DP) and the Slovak-based Christian Democratic Movement (CDM)—obtained approximately 12% of the total votes cast. Contrary to expectations, two parties that had campaigned for regional autonomy or secession secured more than the 5% of the votes required for representation in the legislature: the Movement for Autonomous Democracy–Society for Moravia and Silesia (MAD–SMS) and the separatist Slovak National Party (SNP). The newly elected Federal Assembly was to serve a transitional two-year term, during which period it was to draft new federal and republican constitutions and elect a new President of the Republic. In late June Alexander Dubček was re-elected Chairman of the Federal Assembly. A new Federal Government, announced in that month, comprised 16 members: four from Civic Forum, three from PAV, one from the CDM and eight independents. In early July Václav Havel was re-elected to the post of President.

In the latter half of 1990 there was increasing unrest in Slovakia, as several newly established parties and groups, most prominently the SNP, organized demonstrations and rallies as part of a campaign for Slovak autonomy. In an attempt to alleviate the increasing ethnic tension in the country, in December the Federal Assembly voted overwhelmingly to transfer broader powers to the Czech and Slovak Governments, while the Federal Government was to retain jurisdiction over defence, foreign affairs and monetary policy. None the less, the Slovak question remained the dominant topic of political debate during 1991 and 1992. A widening division appeared between the more moderate Slovak movements, such as PAV and the CDM (which advocated the preservation of the federation, albeit in a looser form), and a minority of more radical parties, which campaigned for full independence. In early March 1991 Vladimír Mečiar, the Slovak Prime Minister and a founding member of PAV, announced the formation of a minority faction within PAV—the Movement for a Democratic Slovakia (MDS)—in support of greater Slovak autonomy. However, leading officials in PAV and some of its representatives in the Slovak Government viewed Mečiar's policies and aggressive style of leadership as detrimental to the future of Czech–Slovak relations, and in April the Slovak National Council voted to remove Mečiar from

the Slovak premiership. He was replaced by Ján Čarnogurský, the Chairman of the CDM. In response, Mečiar and his supporters left PAV, and the MDS was established as a separate political group.

Meanwhile, disagreement over the direction of post-communist politics and economic management had led to a split within Civic Forum. Two main groups emerged in February 1991—the conservative Civic Democratic Party (CDP), led by Václav Klaus, and the liberal Civic Movement (CM), led by Jiří Dienstbier. However, it was announced that, in the interests of national unity, the two new groups were to remain as coalition partners in the Federal Government, pending the next legislative election, due to take place in June 1992.

In March 1991 representatives of all political forces in Czechoslovakia reached agreement on the framework of a new federal Constitution. This stipulated, *inter alia*, that the country would remain a federative state comprising two 'sovereign and equal republics, linked voluntarily and by the free will of their citizens'. However, by late 1991 the Federal Assembly's discussions on the new Constitution had reached an impasse, as deputies failed to agree on the status of the two republics within any future federation. President Havel repeatedly proposed the holding of a referendum on the possible division of Czechoslovakia into two separate states, as the only democratic means of resolving the issue. His proposals, however, were rejected by the Federal Assembly. The constitutional debate continued in the first half of 1992, with increasing Slovak support for the loosest possible confederation, comprising two nominally independent states. The majority of Czech politicians, however, were in favour of preserving the existing state structure, and rejected Slovak proposals as impracticable. In March it was agreed to postpone the constitutional talks until after the legislative election in June.

The legislative elections of 5–6 June 1992 proved to be decisive in the eventual dismantling of Czechoslovakia, particularly as the MDS, led by Mečiar, emerged clearly as the dominant political force in Slovakia. With about 34% of the total Slovak votes cast, the party obtained 57 seats (the second-largest representation) in the 300-member Federal Assembly. The leading party in the Slovak Government, the CDM (which advocated a continued federation), won only 9% of the Slovak votes cast, securing 14 seats in the Federal Assembly, one seat less than the separatist SNP. As had been expected, Václav Klaus's party, the CDP (in coalition with the Chr.DP), won the largest proportion (about 34%) of the total votes cast in the Czech Lands. The CDP was one of only two parties to contest the election in both republics, and in Slovakia it received 4% of the votes cast. In total, the CDP won 85 seats in the Federal Assembly, thus becoming the largest party in the legislature. Two other splinter groups of the former Civic Forum—Dienstbier's CM and the Civic Democratic Alliance (CDA)—failed to win representation in the Federal Assembly, as did the Civic Democratic Union (formerly PAV), in Slovakia. The successor organizations to the Communist parties of the two republics achieved considerable success: the Left Bloc (which included the Communist Party of Bohemia and Moravia, CPBM) won a total of 34 seats in the Federal Assembly, while the Slovak-based Party of the Democratic Left secured 23 seats. The representation of parties in the new republican legislatures did not differ greatly from that of the Federal Assembly, although the CDA and the MAD–SMS succeeded in winning seats in the Czech National Council.

Negotiations on the formation of a new federal government were initiated forthwith by the CDP and the MDS, but only served to emphasize the two leading parties' fundamental divergence of opinion on the future of the CzSFR. Nevertheless, a transitional Federal Government, dominated by members of the CDP and the MDS, was appointed in early July 1992. The new Prime Minister was Jan Stráský of the CDP, who had served as a Deputy Prime Minister in the outgoing Czech Government. There was increasing recognition by Czech politicians that the constitutional talks on the future of Czechoslovakia were no longer viable and that a complete separation was preferable to the compromise measures that most Slovak parties favoured. The principal task of the new Federal Government, it was acknowledged, was to supervise the eventual dissolution of the CzSFR. Meanwhile, in late June, the new Slovak Government was announced, with Mečiar as Prime Minister. All but one of the ministers were members of the MDS. A new coalition Czech Government, dominated by the CDP and with Klaus as Prime Minister, was appointed in early July. In three rounds of presidential elections, held in the same month, the Federal

Assembly failed to elect any of the candidates. Havel's re-election as President had effectively been blocked by the MDS and the SNP, and in mid-July he resigned from the post. Further rounds of voting in August and October were aborted, as no candidates presented themselves.

The events of June and July 1992 had ensured that the emergence of two independent states was now inevitable. On 17 July the Slovak National Council overwhelmingly approved a (symbolic) declaration of Slovak sovereignty, and in the following week the Czech and Slovak Prime Ministers agreed, in principle, to the dissolution of the CzSFR. In the following months extensive negotiations were conducted to determine the modalities of the division, which was to take effect from 1 January 1993. International observers expressed surprise not only that the dissolution of Czechoslovakia should be effected in so short a time, but also that the majority of Czechs and Slovaks (more than 60%, according to the results of public opinion polls) were still opposed to the country's division. Moreover, it appeared that Slovak leaders were less intent to leave the federation. Indeed, the Federal Assembly's failure, in early October 1992 and again in mid-November, to adopt legislation permitting the dissolution of the CzSFR was the result of opposition by (mainly) MDS deputies. However, the two republican Prime Ministers, supported by their respective governments, stressed that the process of partition was now irreversible. In late October the Czech and Slovak Governments ratified a number of accords, including a customs union treaty to abolish trade restrictions between the two republics following their independence. Finally, on 25 November the Federal Assembly adopted legislation providing for the constitutional disbanding of the federation, having secured the necessary three-fifths majority by a margin of only three votes. Accordingly, the Federal Government accelerated the process of dividing the country's assets and liabilities as well as its armed forces. In most cases federal property was divided territorially (according to its location in either of the republics). It was agreed, however, that the two states would continue to share some federal infrastructure and would retain a single currency for the immediate future, although respective central banks were established. (Two separate currencies, the Czech and the Slovak koruna, were introduced in February 1993.)

On 17 December 1992 a treaty pledging cordial relations and co-operation was signed, followed by the establishment of diplomatic relations between the two republics. At midnight on 31 December all federal structures were dissolved and the Czech Republic and the Slovak Republic came into being. The dissolution of the CzSFR had thus been effected in an entirely peaceful fashion. As legal successors to Czechoslovakia, the two republics were quickly recognized by the states that had maintained diplomatic relations with the CzSFR, as well as by those international bodies of which the CzSFR had been a member. Existing treaties and agreements, to which the CzSFR had been a party, were to be honoured by both republics.

In anticipation of the establishment of the Czech Republic as an independent state, the existing legislature was replaced by a bicameral body, in accordance with the Czech Constitution (adopted in mid-December 1992); the Czech National Council was transformed into a Chamber of Deputies (lower house), which retained the Council's 200 members, while an upper house, or Senate, was to be elected at a later date. In late January 1993 the Chamber of Deputies elected Václav Havel to be the Czech Republic's first President. The composition of the Government remained largely unchanged. It included among its principal objectives the pursuance of the former Federal Government's economic reforms, including its programme of large-scale privatization. Another of its priorities was to curb the rise in organized crime.

Relations between the Czech Republic and Slovakia were troubled in early 1993 by disagreements over former Czechoslovak assets and property that still remained to be divided. In late 1993 the Czech Government was divided over the issue of the restitution of property that had been expropriated from Czech Jews during the period of Nazi occupation (1938–45). There were fears that any such restitution would lead to claims for compensation by those surviving Sudeten Germans who were expelled from Czechoslovakia in 1945 (see below). Nevertheless, in April 1994 the Chamber of Deputies adopted legislation permitting the restitution of Jewish property. In November local elections were held, at which the CDP was confirmed as the party with the broadest support (receiving some 31% of

the total votes cast), followed by the CPBM (with 13%); voter participation was about 60%.

There was renewed controversy in 1995 over the so-called 'lustration' or screening law, which had been adopted by the Czechoslovak Federal Assembly in October 1991. The law effectively banned former Communist functionaries as well as members of the former state security service and the People's Militia (the CPCz's paramilitary force) from holding senior political, economic and judicial posts. In September 1995 the Chamber of Deputies voted to extend until 2000 the legislation on screening (which had been due to expire in late 1996). In the following month President Havel rejected the decision, but the Chamber approved it for a second time, and the extension of the law entered into force.

The first general election to be held since the dissolution of the CzSFR took place on 31 May and 1 June 1996. The CDP (which had merged with the Chr.DP in April) won 68 of the 200 seats in the Chamber of Deputies (with 29.6% of the total votes cast), while the Czech Social Democratic Party (CSDP), which had become a major force of the centre-left under the leadership of Miloš Zeman, almost quadrupled its parliamentary representation, winning 61 seats (26.4%). As a result, the coalition of the CDP, the Christian Democratic Union–Czechoslovak People's Party (CDU–CPP, which obtained 18 seats) and the CDA (13 seats) lost its overall majority, achieving a total of 99 seats. The CPBM and the Association for the Republic–Republican Party of Czechoslovakia were the only other parties to exceed the 5% threshold required for representation in the legislature, securing 22 seats and 18 seats, respectively. Despite losing its parliamentary majority, the governing coalition remained intact. The CSDP ruled out the possibility of joining the coalition, but agreed to give tacit support on most issues to a minority government. In early July Václav Klaus formed a new Government; in a major concession to the CSDP, Miloš Zeman was appointed Chairman of the Chamber of Deputies. The Government survived a vote of confidence in late July, despite CSDP opposition to government proposals to return some 175,000 ha of land, confiscated by the Communists, to the Catholic Church, without seeking the approval of the legislature.

Voter participation in the election to the 81-seat Senate, which was held in mid-November 1996, was low (35%), but the ruling coalition gained a majority of the votes, winning 52 seats. The CSDP won 25 seats, and the CPBM won two, while the remaining two seats went to the Democratic Union (DU) and an independent candidate. At the first meeting of the Senate (the main role of which would be to scrutinize legislation), held in December, Petr Pithart was elected Chairman.

As a result of economic problems and growing divisions within the ruling coalition in May 1997, three ministers resigned, although the resignation of Jan Ruml, the Minister of the Interior, was rejected by Havel. In June the Government narrowly won a vote of confidence in the Chamber of Deputies, relying on the vote of one independent deputy.

In August 1997 the Government was forced to address the problems of the Romany population (unofficially estimated at some 300,000), as hundreds of Romanies, claiming to have suffered persecution in the Czech Republic, attempted to gain political asylum in Canada (which subsequently reimposed visa requirements for Czech visitors) and the United Kingdom. The Government established an interministerial commission for Romany community affairs in October and outlined further measures aimed at improving the situation of Romanies in the Czech Republic. In early 1998 the Government formed a second commission, headed by Romanies, to address issues affecting the Romany population, and a 40-year law restricting their nomadic way of life was revoked. None the less, large number of Romanies continued to seek political asylum abroad during 1998–99.

Tension within the CDP and between the coalition parties intensified in October 1997. Josef Zieleniec resigned from his position as Minister of Foreign Relations and as Deputy Chairman of the CDP, citing a lack of consultation on important party decisions as the reason for his departure. In early November, while coalition leaders failed to reach agreement on a solution to the political and economic situation, at least 60,000 trade-union members demonstrated in Prague against the Government's social-welfare and economic policies. At the end of that month allegations of impropriety in the funding of the CDP led to the resignation of the Klaus administration, following the withdrawal of the CDU–CPP and the CDA from the coalition, and appeals from both the President and senior members of the

CDP for the Government to stand down. Klaus denied all allegations of corruption. In December Josef Lux, the Chairman of the CDU–CPP, was asked to lead talks on the formation of a new government. Klaus was re-elected Chairman of the CDP at the Party's national conference later that month, defeating Jan Ruml, who subsequently formed a new faction within the party. Josef Tošovský, hitherto Governor of the Czech National Bank, was designated Prime Minister in December, and a new temporary Government, comprising seven non-political ministers, four CDP members, three CDU–CPP members and three CDA members, was appointed in January 1998. The CDP was divided over its participation in the new administration, and the Party's four ministers subsequently defected to the Freedom Union (FU), a newly established breakaway party, which had 31 seats in the Chamber of Deputies by mid-February.

In the presidential election, which took place on 20 January 1998, Havel was narrowly re-elected in a second round of voting. At the end of that month the Government won a vote of confidence when its policy statement was adopted in the Chamber of Deputies. In February Jiří Skalický resigned from the posts of Deputy Prime Minister and Minister of the Environment, and from the chairmanship of the CDA, after admitting that, prior to the 1996 elections (when the CDA controlled the ministries responsible for privatization and industry), the party had received donations from a number of companies. A further two ministers were among a number of CDA deputies who subsequently resigned from the party, although they retained their positions in the Government. In April 1998 the Czech Republic's proposed membership of NATO was formally approved by the legislature; the CSDP had earlier withdrawn its demand for a referendum on the issue.

Early elections to the Chamber of Deputies were held on 19–20 June 1998. The CSDP retained its position (held since the defection of the CDP deputies to the FU earlier in the year) as the largest party in the Chamber of Deputies, winning 74 seats (with 32.3% of the votes cast), while the CDP secured 63 seats (with 27.7%). The remaining seats were divided between the CPBM (with 24 seats), the CDU−CPP (20 seats) and the FU (19 seats). The rate of voter participation was 74%. As leader of the CSDP, Zeman was given the task of attempting to form a government. The parliamentary parties failed to reach agreement on a coalition grouping. In July Zeman and Klaus signed an agreement whereby the CDP pledged not to initiate or support a motion expressing 'no confidence' in a minority CSDP government, in exchange for a number of senior parliamentary posts, including the chairmanship of the Chamber of Deputies (to which Klaus was later elected), and a commitment to early constitutional reform. On 17 July Zeman was formally appointed Prime Minister, and a new Council of Ministers was subsequently named. Political observers doubted the ability of the new Government to survive a full electoral term, reliant as it was on the co-operation of the CDP in order to implement its policies. Later that year the new administration encountered strong opposition, particularly from the CDP, regarding its plan for a large budgetary deficit for 1999, a proposal that had already caused some dissent within the Government. In late September Josef Lux resigned from the post of Chairman of the CDU−CPP, owing to serious health problems.

Elections to renew one-third of the seats in the Senate were held in two rounds in November 1998. The CSDP performed poorly, winning only three of the 27 seats contested, while the CDP secured nine seats, and a four-party informal alliance, comprising the CDUCPP, the CDA, the DU and the FU, won 13 seats. The CPBM doubled its representation to four seats. Voter participation was very low, reaching only 20.4% in the second round. In local elections, also held in November, independent candidates, followed by the CDU−CPP, gained the largest number of seats on municipal councils, owing to strong support in smaller, rural communities. In terms of votes, however, the CDP received the greatest endorsement, with 24.3% of the total votes cast, although the Party secured only 9.2% of seats, mainly in urban areas. The CSDP won 17.5% of the total votes (6.8% of seats). Observers largely attributed the CSDP's poor performance to its agreement with the CDP, which was deemed to be unpopular with the electorate.

In May 1999 a decision by the Council of Ministers to complete the construction of the controversial Temelín nuclear power plant in southern Bohemia, despite a resolution by the European Parliament opposing its completion, provoked international concern and was strong criticism from President Havel and environmental groups. In June the Chamber of Deputies rejected a government proposal for constitutional amendments that would have enabled the Council of Ministers to issue decrees with the effect of law, but without the approval of the legislature. As anticipated, the CSDP Government had encountered difficulties in enacting new legislation, owing to its minority status. In July Ivo Svoboda was dismissed from the post of Minister of Finance after it was announced that he was to be prosecuted for allegedly harming creditors of a bankrupt company of which he had been on the management board. In September the Council of Ministers approved a number of proposals for constitutional change that had been drafted by a joint CSDP-CDP commission. The amendments aimed to restrict presidential powers, including the right to appoint the Prime Minister and the heads of principal state institutions, and the right to grant amnesty. (The Chamber of Deputies approved the changes in January 2000, despite an opposition boycott of the vote.)

On 17 November 1999 celebrations held to commemorate the 10th anniversary of the 'velvet revolution' were attended by Western leaders who had been in power at the time. On the same day, however, a group of former student leaders who had participated in the events of November 1989 staged a protest initiative against the current political system, urging the leaders of all the main parties to withdraw from political life. Their appeal had been signed by some 150,000 people by early December 1999, when more than 50,000 demonstrators attended a rally in Prague. Jan Ruml subsequently resigned from the chairmanship of the FU, explaining that he felt a sense of responsibility for the political situation. Meanwhile, Egon Lánský resigned from the post of Deputy Prime Minister for European Integration in December, citing ill health, although opposition parties had been demanding his resignation for several months, principally owing to dissatisfaction with preparations for EU entry. The Minister of Foreign Affairs, Jan Kavan, was subsequently elevated to the position of Deputy Prime Minister. In late January 2000 the CSDP and the CDP extended their agreement on bilateral co-operation; the CSDP promised to reshuffle the Council of Ministers and to propose electoral reform measures in return for the CDP's continued tolerance of the CSDP minority Government and its budgetary proposals for 2000.

In accordance with the co-operation agreement between the CDP and the CSDP, the Council of Ministers was reorganized in March–April 2000 and four ministers were replaced. In May the Chamber of Deputies endorsed a series of amendments to electoral legislation, stipulating that parties belonging to an electoral alliance secure a minimum of 5% of the votes cast in order to achieve representation in the legislature and increasing the number of local government districts to 35. (In January 2001, however, the Constitutional Court upheld an appeal by President Havel and a number of Senators against the latter provision.) In early August 2000, following the country's admission to NATO (see below), the Senate adopted a constitutional amendment permitting the Government to deploy peace-keeping forces abroad and to authorize the deployment of foreign troops on Czech territory without the prior approval of the legislature.

In September 2000 mass demonstrations were staged in Prague, where annual IMF and World Bank meetings were taking place, as part of an international campaign of protests against global financial institutions. In the same month, on a number of occasions, Austrian environmental protesters blockaded crossings at the Austrian-Czech border, following a decision by the Czech authorities that the nuclear-power installation at Temelín was to commence operations; the demonstrations continued until mid-October. Despite pressure from the Austrian Government, which threatened to veto the Czech Republic's accession to the EU and suspended the import of Czech electricity, the nuclear power plant commenced production in early October, after receiving authorization from the state nuclear-safety office. In early November border protests were temporarily resumed, after discussions between Prime Minister Zeman and the Federal Chancellor of Austria, Dr Wolfgang Schüssel, failed to resolve the ongoing dispute. In December, following further negotiations, the Czech Republic and Austria signed an agreement, whereby the plant was not to operate at commercial capacity until its safety and its environmental impact had been fully evaluated, under the supervision of the European Commission. (In early 2001 production at the installation was repeatedly suspended, owing to technical difficulties.)

In October 2000 the Minister of Justice, Otakar Motejl, tendered his resignation, as a result of his failure to implement planned judicial reforms. In elections to one-third of seats in the Senate in November, the alliance of the CDU−CPP, the CDA, the DU and the FU secured 16 seats, thereby increasing its overall representation to 39 seats (although narrowly failing to obtain a majority in the chamber). The CDP won eight seats, reducing its total number of seats held to 22, and the CSDP won only one seat, reducing its representation to 15.

In December 2000 employees of the state-owned Czech Television service began a strike, in protest at the appointment of the new Director-General, Jiri Hodac, who, it was feared, might influence editorial independence, owing to his affiliation to the CDP. Mass protests were staged in Prague in support of the striking journalists, who occupied part of the station's headquarters and initiated rival news broadcasts. At the end of the month the dismissal of 20 of the station's employees further increased tension. The dispute also prompted dissension between Havel, who expressed support for the protesters, and Zeman, who condemned their action. At the beginning of 2001 a mass demonstration (the largest since the fall of Communism) was staged in support of the striking employees. Although the Council of Czech Television refused to comply with a ruling by the Chamber of Deputies that Hodac be removed from his post, he resigned in early January on the grounds of ill health. The Chamber of Deputies subsequently voted to dissolve the nine-member Council and approved a legislative amendment whereby the Council would, henceforth, comprise 15 members, selected by the Chamber from nominees of civic and professional organizations (rather than political parties). Later that month the Chamber of Deputies overruled a veto of the proposal by the Senate (which had demanded that part of the Council be elected by the upper house) and the amended legislation was formally approved by Havel. The striking television-station employees announced that, despite some objections to the new legislation, they would end their protest and co-operate with a new Council.

An important focus of the Czech Republic's foreign policy is to maintain close relations with Slovakia and other neighbouring Eastern European states. It is a member, with Slovakia, Hungary and Poland, of the Visegrad Group (established, following the collapse of Communist rule, to promote economic, defence and other co-operation in the region). The Governments of the Czech Republic, Hungary and Poland have agreed to co-ordinate preparations for accession to NATO and the EU (see below). Relations with Slovakia have been strained, mainly because of disagreements over the division of former federal property. In mid-September 1998, however, following talks between Miloš Zeman and Vladimír Mečiar, the Slovak Prime Minister, it was announced that a joint Czech-Slovak committee would meet shortly in an attempt to further discussions on unresolved issues. The success of opposition parties in Slovak elections held at the end of that month, and the subsequent change of government, led to a further improvement in bilateral relations. Measures providing for dual Czech-Slovak citizenship became fully effective in October 1999, and in November an agreement on the division of former federal property was signed in Bratislava by Zeman and Mikuláš Dzurinda, the Slovak Prime Minister. The agreement provided for the exchange of shares between the Czech Republic's Komerční banka and Slovakia's Všeobecná úverová banka and the restitution of gold reserves to Slovakia. The gold had been held by the Czech Central Bank as collateral for debts owed by Slovakia to the Czech Republic. These debts, totalling some 26,000m. koruny, had proved to be a major obstacle during negotiations, as they had never been recognized by Slovakia. The Czech Government consequently opted effectively to relieve Slovakia of its debts by buying the Central Bank's claim for a symbolic one koruna, despite the opposition of several Czech politicians. In May 2000 Zeman and Dzurinda signed an agreement resolving remaining problems associated with the division of jointly held assets.

The Czech Republic actively pursues a policy of European integration and co-operation, and envisages early full membership of the EU (for which it officially applied in January 1996). In this connection, the Czech Government has emphasized the importance of close ties with western European states, particularly neighbouring Germany (the Czech Republic's most important trading partner). The Czech Republic was one of a number of Central and Eastern European states invited to begin negotiations in March 1998 on possible entry to the EU. In November more substantive talks commenced regarding the compliance of potential EU entrants with membership regulations. Earlier that month, however, the European Commission had criticized the slow pace of legislative reform in the Czech Republic. Preparations for accession to the EU continued to advance very slowly during 1999, and in October the Commission was again critical of the Czech Republic's lack of progress in adopting necessary EU legislation and expressed concern regarding the situation of the country's Romany minority. Formal admittance to the EU was envisaged for 2003.

Since the end of the Second World War Czech-German relations have been dominated by two issues: the question of compensation for Czech victims of Nazism, and demands for the restitution of property to the Sudeten Germans who were driven from Czechoslovakia in 1945. From 1993 negotiations were held to formulate a declaration on bilateral relations, but progress was hampered by these unresolved issues. However, a joint declaration was finally signed by both Ministers of Foreign Affairs on 20 December 1996, and by Václav Klaus of the Czech Republic and Chancellor Kohl of Germany on 21 January 1997. In the declaration, Germany admitted that it was to blame for the Nazi occupation and the partition of Czechoslovakia in 1939, while the Czech Republic apologized for the abuses of human rights that were committed during the deportation of ethnic Germans in 1945–46. The declaration did not, however, condemn the expulsion of the Sudeten Germans as a crime, which would have meant that those people expelled could have made claims for compensation. A joint Czech-German fund was established in January 1998 to finance joint projects, in particular benefiting victims of the Nazis. Relations were strained somewhat in February and August 1998, however, when the nomination of Sudeten Germans to a Czech-German advisory council was rejected by Miloš Zeman, who claimed that the nominees had opposed the January 1997 declaration that had provided for the establishment of the council.

In August 1993 the Czech Republic and the Russian Federation signed a treaty of friendship and co-operation (replacing the Russian-Czechoslovak treaty of 1992). In March 1994, despite Russia's apparent opposition, the Czech Republic joined NATO's 'Partnership for Peace' programme of military co-operation. In 1996 the Chamber of Deputies approved legislation prohibiting the storage of nuclear weapons on Czech territory, except where international treaties are concerned, thereby allowing for full membership of NATO. In July 1997 the Czech Republic, together with Hungary and Poland, was invited to commence membership negotiations. A protocol providing for the accession of the three states to NATO was signed in December 1997 and was subsequently ratified by the legislatures of member states. In March 1999 the Czech Republic, Hungary and Poland became full members of NATO. Associate membership of the Western European Union (see p. 286) was subsequently granted. The Czech Republic is a member of the Council of Europe (see p. 165) and the Organization for Security and Co-operation in Europe (OSCE, see p. 252).

Government

Legislative power is held by two chambers, the 200-member Chamber of Deputies (lower house) and the 81-member Senate. Members of the Chamber of Deputies and the Senate are elected for four and six years, respectively, by universal adult suffrage. The President of the Republic (Head of State) is elected for a term of five years by a joint session of the legislature. The President, who is also Commander of the Armed Forces, may be re-elected for a second consecutive term. He appoints the Prime Minister and, on the latter's recommendation, the other members of the Council of Ministers (the highest organ of executive power). For administrative purposes, the Czech Republic is divided into 72 districts.

Defence

In August 2000 total armed forces numbered 57,700 (including 25,000 conscripts): an army of 25,100 and an air force of 13,400; there were also some 19,200 troops attached to the Ministry of Defence and centrally-controlled formations. In addition, there were 4,000 border guards and 1,600 internal security forces. Military service is compulsory and lasts for 12 months. Of total expenditure by the central Government in 1999, 33,682m. koruny (5.0%) was allocated to defence. In March 1994 the Czech Republic joined NATO's 'Partnership for Peace' programme of military co-operation (see p. 243), and in March 1999 it was formally admitted to NATO.

Economic Affairs

In 1998, according to estimates by the World Bank, the Czech Republic's gross national product (GNP), measured at average 1996–98 prices, was US $53,034m., equivalent to $5,150 per head (or $12,197 per head on an international purchasing-power parity basis). During 1990–98, it was estimated, GNP per head declined, in real terms, at an average annual rate of 0.2%. Over the same period the population was estimated to have decreased by an average of 0.1% per year. In 1999 GNP was estimated at $52,000m., equivalent to $5,060 per head. Gross domestic product (GDP) declined, in real terms, by an average of 2.6% annually during 1990–95. Real GDP declined by 1.6% per year in 1996–99, falling by 0.8% in 1999, but increased by an estimated 2.5% in 2000.

Agriculture (including forestry and fishing) contributed 3.7% of GDP in 1999, and, according to preliminary figures, engaged 5.2% of the employed labour force in that year. The principal crops are wheat, sugar beets, barley, potatoes and hops (the Czech Republic is a major beer producer and exporter). Agricultural GDP increased by 4.5% per year in 1996–99, increasing by 5.0% in 1999.

Industry (including manufacturing, mining, construction and power) contributed 41.8% of GDP in 1999, and, according to preliminary figures, engaged 40.7% of the employed labour force in that year. Industrial GDP declined by 2.0% per year in 1996–99, declining by 5.7% in 1999.

The principal minerals extracted are coal and lignite. In 1999 the mining sector engaged 1.4% of the employed labour force, according to preliminary figures. Production of mining and quarrying increased by 1.4% in 1996, but declined by 2.9% in 1997, by 5.7% in 1998 and by 12.1% in 1999.

The manufacturing sector engaged 30.0% of the employed labour force in 1999, according to preliminary figures. Based on the value of output, the most important branches of manufacturing in 1996 were food products and beverages (accounting for 16.3% of the total), basic metals (12.7%), non-electric machinery and domestic appliances (9.0%), and metal products (7.6%). Manufacturing production increased by 1.7% in 1996, by 6.4% in 1997 and by 2.6% in 1998, but declined by 2.7% in 1999.

In 1998 thermal power provided 76.9% of total electricity production, nuclear power 20.2% and hydroelectric power 2.9%. Imports of mineral fuels comprised 6.5% of the value of total imports in 1999, according to preliminary figures.

The services sector contributed 54.4% of GDP in 1999 and, according to preliminary figures, engaged 54.1% of the employed labour force in that year. Tourism is an important source of revenue, providing receipts of US $3,792m. in 1998; tourist arrivals totalled 5.6m. in 1999. The GDP of the services sector declined by 1.0% per year in 1996–99, but increased by 3.4% in 1999.

In 1999 the Czech Republic recorded a visible trade deficit of US $1,902m., and there was a deficit of US $1,032m. on the current account of the balance of payments. In 1999, according to preliminary figures, the principal source of imports (33.9%) was Germany; other major sources were Slovakia, Austria, France and Italy. Germany was also the principal market for exports (42.1%) in that year; other important purchasers were Slovakia, Austria and Poland. The principal exports in 1999 were machinery and transport equipment, basic manufactures and miscellaneous manufactured articles. The principal imports in that year were machinery and transport equipment, basic manufactures, chemicals and related products, and miscellaneous manufactured articles.

In 1999 there was a budgetary deficit of 29,712m. koruny (equivalent to 1.6% of GDP). The Czech Republic's total external debt was US $25,301m. at the end of 1998, of which $12,901m. was long-term public debt. In that year the cost of debt-servicing was equivalent to 15.3% of the value of exports of goods and services. The annual rate of inflation averaged 16.1% in 1990–98; consumer prices increased by 2.1% in 1999 and by an estimated 3.9% in 2000. The rate of unemployment at the end of 2000 was estimated at 8.8%.

The Czech Republic is a member of the IMF and the World Bank and an associate member of the European Union (EU, see p. 181). It is also a member of the European Bank for Reconstruction and Development (EBRD, see p. 176), and in late 1995 became the first post-Communist state in Eastern Europe to be admitted to the Organisation for Economic Co-operation and Development (OECD, see p. 247).

Of all the post-Communist states of Eastern Europe, for much of the 1990s the Czech Republic was considered to have undertaken the transition to a market economic system with greatest success. The country's programme of rapid privatization, price and currency stabilization and the establishment of a new banking system, while preserving a low level of unemployment, won strong popular support during 1992–95, attracting widespread foreign investment. In 1996, however, economic growth decelerated and the first budgetary deficit since the transition to a market economy was recorded. Difficulties were experienced in the banking sector, with several banks forced to cease operations. Economic performance deteriorated in 1997 and investor confidence was weakened by cases of embezzlement of investment funds. In May the Central Bank devalued the koruna, owing to concern that the deficit on the current account had become unsustainable. The imposition of tighter monetary policies contributed to a worsening of the recession, however. In the second quarter of 1999 the economy finally began to recover, following the Government's relaxation of monetary policies in late 1998 and significant progress in the restructuring of banks and state enterprises. The country subsequently benefited from a strong export performance, stimulated by buoyant activity in the EU, and from a dramatic increase in foreign direct investment. After three years of decline, GDP growth was estimated at 2.5% in 2000. The Government continued to achieve considerable progress in privatization, with the sale of most of the large banks and the two major telecommunications companies undertaken by 2000. Nevertheless, a large number of enterprises continued to suffer from financial difficulties. The restructuring process resulted in a further increase in the rate of unemployment (which had risen significantly during the period of recession). Furthermore, the high overall fiscal deficit continued to increase, principally as a consequence of financing the structural reforms and the rising cost of social security.

Social Welfare

Following the dissolution of Czechoslovakia in January 1993, the two successor states announced plans to introduce changes to the existing social-welfare system. In the Czech Republic the privatization programme extended to the health-care system, although at a slower rate than in many other parts of the economy. In 1998 there were 303 physicians, 886 nurses and 62 dentists per 100,000 inhabitants. Of total expenditure by the central Government in 1999, 117,031m. koruny (17.5%) was allocated to health, and a further 248,723m. koruny (37.1%) to social security and welfare. A new pensions insurance law came into effect in 1996, which was gradually to increase the retirement age for men to 65 years (from 60) and for women to 57–61 (from 53–57, according to the number of children born) by 2007.

Education

Almost 90% of children between the ages of three and six years attend kindergarten. From the age of six children attend basic school, which covers both primary (grades 1–5) and lower secondary (grades 6–9) levels, and is attended by almost 97% of pupils aged between six and 15, when education is compulsory. Most children (almost 97%) continue their education at an upper secondary school, of which there were three types in 1999: gymnasia (providing general education and preparing students mainly for university entry), secondary vocational schools and secondary technical schools. Students follow three- to four-year courses. Tertiary education consists of non-university schools, which offer three-year courses, and universities, at which most courses last from five to six years. Since 1990 many private schools, particularly at upper secondary level, have been established.

In 1999/2000 1,071,318 students attended basic schools, while 463,349 attended the different types of upper secondary school. In the same year 215,027 students were enrolled in higher education. Of total expenditure by the central Government in 1999, 66,576m. koruny (9.9%) was allocated to education.

Public Holidays

2001: 1 January (New Year's Day), 16 April (Easter Monday), 1 May (Labour Day), 8 May (Liberation Day), 5 July (Day of the Apostles St Cyril and St Methodius), 6 July (Anniversary of the Martyrdom of Jan Hus), 28 October (Independence Day), 24–25 December (Christmas), 26 December (St Stephen's Day).

2002: 1 January (New Year's Day), 1 April (Easter Monday), 1 May (Labour Day), 8 May (Liberation Day), 5 July (Day of the Apostles St Cyril and St Methodius), 6 July (Anniversary of the Martyrdom of Jan Hus), 28 October (Independence Day), 24–25 December (Christmas), 26 December (St Stephen's Day).

Weights and Measures

The metric system is in force.

Statistical Survey

Source: mainly Czech Statistical Office, Sokolovská 142, 186 04 Prague 8; tel. (2) 66042451; fax (2) 66310429; e-mail bondyova@gw.czso.cz; internet www.czso.cz.

Area and Population

AREA, POPULATION AND DENSITY

Area (sq km)	78,866*
Population (census results)	
1 November 1980	10,291,927
3 March 1991	
Males	4,999,935
Females	5,302,280
Total	10,302,215
Population (official estimates at 31 December)	
1997	10,299,125
1998	10,289,621
1999	10,278,098
Density (per sq km) at 31 December 1999	130.3

* 30,450 sq miles.

POPULATION BY NATIONALITY (census of 3 March 1991)

	Number	%
Czech (Bohemian)	8,363,768	81.2
Moravian	1,362,313	13.2
Slovak	314,877	3.1
Polish	59,383	0.6
German	48,556	0.5
Silesian	44,446	0.4
Roma (Gypsy)	32,903	0.3
Hungarian	19,932	0.2
Others	34,020	0.3
Unknown	22,017	0.2
Total	10,302,215	100.0

REGIONS (estimates, 1 January 2000)

	Population	Density (per sq km)
Středočeský kraj	1,111,354	101
Budějovický kraj	626,112	62
Plzeňský kraj	551,870	73
Karlovarský kraj	304,823	92
Ustecký kraj	827,151	155
Liberecký kraj	429,012	136
Královéhradecký kraj	551,651	116
Pardubický kraj	508,744	113
Jihlavský kraj	521,472	75
Brněnský kraj	1,137,289	161
Olomoucký kraj	642,016	125
Zlínský kraj	598,339	151
Ostravský kraj	1,281,410	231
Praha (Prague, capital)	1,186,855	2,394
Total	10,278,098	130

PRINCIPAL TOWNS (estimated population, 1 January 1999)

Praha (Prague,		Hradec Králové . .	98,700
capital) . . .	1,186,855	Ústí nad Labem . .	96,070
Brno . . .	383,569	Pardubice . . .	92,069
Ostrava . . .	321,263	Havířov . . .	87,113
Plzeň (Pilsen) . .	167,534	Zlín	81,400
Olomouc . . .	103,015	Kladno . . .	71,508
Liberec . . .	99,588	Most	69,852
České Budějovice		Karviná . . .	65,585
(Budweis) . .	98,926		

BIRTHS, MARRIAGES AND DEATHS

	Registered live births		Registered marriages		Registered deaths	
	Number	Rate (per 1,000)	Number	Rate (per 1,000)	Number	Rate (per 1,000)
1992 . .	121,705	11.8	74,060	7.2	120,337	11.7
1993 . .	121,025	11.7	66,033	6.4	118,185	11.4
1994 . .	106,579	10.3	58,440	5.7	117,373	11.4
1995 . .	96,097	9.3	54,956	5.3	117,913	11.4
1996 . .	90,446	8.8	53,896	5.2	112,782	10.9
1997 . .	90,657	8.8	57,804	5.6	112,744	10.9
1998 . .	90,535	8.8	55,027	5.3	109,527	10.6
1999 . .	89,471	8.7	53,523	5.2	109,768	10.7

Expectation of life: (UN estimates, years at birth, 1990–95): 71.4 (males 67.3; females 75.7) (Source: UN, *World Population Prospects: The 1998 Revision*).

EMPLOYMENT (annual averages)*

	1997	1998†	1999†
Agriculture, forestry and fishing .	282,785	269,567	243,991
Mining and quarrying . . .	79,671	73,592	64,586
Manufacturing	1,444,539	1,448,608	1,408,079
Electricity, gas and water. . .	84,553	80,433	78,192
Construction.	435,401	404,458	360,380
Trade, restaurants and hotels. .	884,830	867,598	832,126
Transport, storage and communications . . .	352,938	343,808	341,618
Finance, insurance, real estate and business services . .	481,753	488,529	486,254
Public administration, defence and compulsory social security .	175,478	176,959	177,770
Education	308,612	304,097	298,272
Health and social welfare. . .	267,173	262,741	259,985
Other community, social and personal services . . .	148,841	148,832	141,843
Total	4,946,574	4,869,222	4,693,096

* Excluding women on maternity leave.
† Preliminary figures.

Agriculture

PRINCIPAL CROPS ('000 metric tons)

	1997	1998	1999
Wheat	3,640	3,845	4,028
Barley	2,485	2,093	2,137
Maize	285	201	261
Rye*	259	261	202
Oats	247	180	179
Potatoes	1,402	1,520	1,408
Peas (dry)	93	122	105
Rapeseed	561	680	931
Cabbages	154	157	151
Tomatoes	23	30	34
Cauliflowers	34	35	34
Cucumbers and gherkins	56	49	52
Onions (dry)	83	88	99
Carrots	74	76	79
Other vegetables	112	101	n.a.
Grapes	36	55	67
Sugar beets	3,722	3,479	2,691
Apples	291	283	264
Pears	20	25	23
Peaches and nectarines	7	7	7
Plums	39	24	21
Hops	7	5	6

* Including mixed crops of wheat and rye.

LIVESTOCK ('000 head at 1 March)

	1997	1998	1999
Horses	21	23	24
Cattle	1,701	1,657	1,574
Pigs	4,013	4,001	3,688
Sheep	94	86	84
Goats	35	34	32
Poultry	29,035	30,222	30,784

LIVESTOCK PRODUCTS
('000 metric tons, unless otherwise indicated)

	1997	1998	1999
Beef and veal*	293.6	246.6	237.4
Pig meat*	679.9	669.9	638.8
Poultry meat*	206.1	240.9	271.2
Milk (million litres)	2,703	2,716	2,700†
Eggs (million)	3,322	3,615	3,300†

* Slaughter weight.
† Rounded.

Forestry

LOGGING ('000 cubic metres)

	1997	1998	1999
Coniferous (softwood)	11,942.1	12,250.1	12,422.0
Broadleaved (hardwood)	1,548.9	1,741.2	1,781.0
Total	13,491.0	13,991.3	14,203.0

Fishing*

(metric tons)

	1997	1998	1999
Common carp	17,482	17,960	19,454
Others	3,339	3,223	3,511
Total catch	20,881	21,183	22,965

* Figures refer only to fish caught by the Fishing Association (formerly State Fisheries) and members of the Czech and Moravian Fishing Union.

Mining

('000 metric tons)

	1997	1998	1999
Hard coal	16,069	16,112	14,342
Brown coal and lignite	57,446	51,419	44,790
Kaolin	822	879	n.a.

Crude petroleum ('000 metric tons): 350 in 1997; 415 in 1998 (Source: Institute of Petroleum, London).

Industry

SELECTED PRODUCTS
('000 metric tons, unless otherwise indicated)

	1997	1998	1999
Wheat flour and meal	858	837	797
Refined sugar	598	492	420
Wine ('000 hectolitres)	564.8	554.0	562.8
Beer ('000 hectolitres)	18,558.3	18,289.2	17,946.0
Cotton yarn (metric tons)	62,373	66,460	56,374
Woven cotton fabrics ('000 metres)	345,605	331,009	267,020
Woollen fabrics ('000 metres)	28,454	27,787	20,146
Linen fabrics ('000 metres)	27,504	23,577	20,938
Paper and paperboard	171.2	193.5	184.5
Footwear ('000 pairs)	15,682	11,110	11,553.0
Nitrogenous fertilizers*	245	247	220
Soap	34.0	30.7	26.9
Motor spirit (petrol)	1,204	1,057	956
Gas-diesel (distillate fuel) oil	2,455	2,481	2,172
Residual fuel oils	1,523	1,512	1,128
Coke	4,290	4,007	3,320
Cement	4,874	4,599	4,241
Pig-iron	5,276	5,165	n.a.
Crude steel	6,749†	6,525†	n.a.
Trucks (number)	39,537	39,098	23,113
Motorcycles and mopeds (number)	9,645	4,398	4,828
Bicycles (number)	473,505	395,059	181,988
Electric energy (million kWh)	64,598	65,112	64,692

* Production in terms of nitrogen.
† Source: UN, *Monthly Bulletin of Statistics*.

Finance

CURRENCY AND EXCHANGE RATES

Monetary Units
100 haléřů (singular: haléř—heller) = 1 Czech koruna (Czech crown or Kč.; plural: koruny).

Sterling, Dollar and Euro Equivalents (29 December 2000)
£1 sterling = 56.42 koruny;
US $1 = 37.81 koruny;
€1 = 35.18 koruny;
1,000 koruny = £17.72 = $26.45 = €28.42.

Average Exchange Rate (koruny per US $)
1998   32.281
1999   34.569
2000   38.598

Note: In February 1993 the Czech Republic introduced its own currency, the Czech koruna, to replace (at par) the Czechoslovak koruna.

BUDGET (million koruny)*

Revenue†	1997	1998	1999
Taxation	538,887	573,746	606,320
Taxes on income, profits and			
capital gains	75,580	87,663	86,567
Individual	33,378	36,339	35,224
Corporate	42,202	51,324	51,343
Social security contributions .	251,110	267,566	276,424
From employees . . .	67,247	69,399	72,716
From employers . . .	170,819	180,521	185,896
Domestic taxes on goods and			
services	192,104	198,523	224,309
Value-added tax . . .	117,656	119,395	138,330
Excises	64,171	67,801	78,143
Taxes on international trade and			
transactions	14,931	13,621	12,050
Import duties . . .	14,931	13,621	12,050
Other current revenue . . .	20,890	20,021	18,013
Entrepreneurial and property			
income	10,109	9,551	6,462
Administrative fees and			
charges, non-industrial and			
incidental sales . . .	6,160	5,307	6,852
Capital revenue	369	260	297
Total	560,146	594,027	624,630

Expenditure‡	1997	1998	1999
General public services . .	15,136	16,898	20,198
Defence	26,655	30,481	33,682
Public order and safety . .	27,989	28,791	31,118
Education	62,815	61,539	66,576
Health	103,911	113,281	117,031
Social security and welfare .	214,980	231,976	248,723
Housing and community amenities	16,452	12,649	12,539
Recreational, cultural and			
religious affairs and services .	5,701	5,754	6,983
Economic affairs and services . .	68,119	83,428	79,492
Fuel and energy . . .	3,154	3,132	2,897
Agriculture, forestry, fishing and			
hunting	13,163	14,166	16,947
Mining and mineral resources,			
manufacturing and			
construction . . .	1,343	2,301	2,556
Transport and communications	29,639	26,780	31,812
Other purposes . . .	54,646	57,217	58,830
Transfers to other levels of			
government	35,839	37,355	41,374
Interest payments . . .	18,351	19,028	17,272
Sub-total . . .	596,404	642,014	675,172
Adjustment§	−4,565	−4,601	−5,095
Total	591,839	637,413	670,077
Current	538,266	582,935	607,724
Capital	53,573	54,478	62,353

* Figures represent a consolidation of transactions by the central Government, including the operations of the Central Budget, social security funds (controlled by the General Health Insurance Organization) and extrabudgetary accounts.
† Excluding grants received (million koruny): 1,416 in 1997; 883 in 1998; 1,033 in 1999.
‡ Excluding lending minus repayments (million koruny): 12,582 in 1997; −12,196 in 1998; −14,704 in 1999.
§ Relating to employer's contributions to social security schemes at the same level of government.

Source: Ministry of Finance, Prague.

INTERNATIONAL RESERVES (US $ million at 31 December)

	1997	1998	1999
Gold*	57	18	23
Foreign exchange . . .	9,734	12,542	12,806
Total	9,791	12,560	12,829

* Valued at 60.61 koruny per gram.

Source: IMF, *International Financial Statistics*.

MONEY SUPPLY ('000 million koruny at 31 December)

	1997	1998	1999
Currency outside banks . .	118.74	127.16	157.90
Demand deposits at deposit money			
banks	297.24	275.68	288.88
Total money (incl. others) . .	418.39	404.00	447.81

Source: IMF, *International Financial Statistics*.

COST OF LIVING
(Consumer Price Index; base: 1994 = 100)

	1997	1998	1999
Food, beverages and tobacco . .	125.2	132.0	127.5
Clothing and footwear . . .	132.4	140.6	140.8
Housing, water, fuel and light .	146.6	190.9	208.2
Furnishings, household			
equipment and maintenance	116.0	123.0	125.3
All items (incl. others) . .	128.8	142.6	145.6

NATIONAL ACCOUNTS ('000 million koruny at current prices)
Expenditure on the Gross Domestic Product

	1997	1998	1999
Government final consumption			
expenditure	331.8	340.9	362.5
Private final consumption			
expenditure	889.6	949.3	975.7
Increase in stocks . . .	33.0	25.6	31.8
Gross fixed capital formation . .	514.4	508.1	490.8
Total domestic expenditure .	1,768.8	1,823.6*	1,860.8
Exports of goods and services .	949.7	1,092.1	1,148.5
Less Imports of goods and services	1,049.7	1,117.7	1,176.3
GDP in purchasers' values .	1,668.8	1,798.3	1,833.0
GDP at constant 1995 prices .	1,432.8	1,401.3	1,390.6

* Including adjustment.

Gross Domestic Product by Economic Activity

	1997	1998	1999
Agriculture, hunting, forestry and			
fishing	73.5	76.9	62.7
Mining and quarrying . .			
Manufacturing	531.4	590.0	575.1
Electricity, gas and water . .			
Construction	132.6	134.6	126.4
Trade, restaurants and hotels .	217.4	230.7	242.0
Transport, storage and			
communications . . .	120.9	155.0	163.0
Financial services . . .	64.2	78.9	68.5
Business services* . . .	191.2	183.2	196.5
Public administration, education			
and health	217.7	222.8	243.4
Sub-total	1,548.9	1,672.1	1,677.6
Less Imputed bank service charge	69.4	73.6	56.6
GDP at basic prices . .	1,479.5	1,598.5	1,617.7
Taxes on products . .	189.3	199.8	215.3
Less Subsidies on products .			
GDP in purchasers' values .	1,668.8	1,798.3	1,833.0

* Including real estate, renting and business activities.

Source: IMF, *Czech Republic: Statistical Appendix* (September 2000).

BALANCE OF PAYMENTS (US $ million)

	1997	1998	1999
Exports of goods f.o.b.	22,737	26,395	26,259
Imports of goods f.o.b.	−27,325	−28,989	−28,161
Trade balance	−4,588	−2,595	−1,902
Exports of services	7,132	7,513	6,929
Imports of services	−5,389	−5,724	−5,828
Balance on goods and services	−2,845	−806	−801
Other income received	1,405	1,428	1,669
Other income paid	−2,197	−2,417	−2,408
Balance on goods, services and income	−3,636	−1,795	−1,541
Current transfers received	866	781	1,072
Current transfers paid	−501	−373	−563
Current balance	−3,271	−1,387	−1,032
Capital account (net)	11	2	−2
Direct investment abroad	−28	−77	−196
Direct investment from abroad	1,286	2,734	5,093
Portfolio investment assets	−159	−44	−1,882
Portfolio investment liabilities	1,152	1,146	500
Other investment assets	−4,427	−1,600	−2,703
Other investment liabilities	3,298	749	1,687
Net errors and omissions	379	367	173
Overall balance	−1,758	1,890	1,639

Source: IMF, *International Financial Statistics*.

External Trade

COMMODITY GROUPS (distribution by SITC, million koruny)

Imports f.o.b.	1997	1998	1999*
Food and live animals	44,584	45,876	45,973
Crude materials (inedible) except fuels	32,112	36,199	31,068
Mineral fuels, lubricants, etc.	74,493	60,233	65,321
Chemicals and related products	105,340	112,648	119,804
Basic manufactures	166,551	193,805	205,332
Machinery and transport equipment	327,496	366,285	402,315
Miscellaneous manufactured articles	99,698	102,578	116,783
Total (incl. others)	861,770	928,939	997,320

* Preliminary figures.

Exports f.o.b.	1997	1998	1999*
Food and live animals	26,417	28,382	26,275
Crude materials (inedible) except fuels	29,137	29,419	34,298
Mineral fuels, lubricants, etc.	27,137	27,079	26,470
Chemicals and related products	63,593	65,515	66,915
Basic manufactures	193,380	225,048	236,756
Machinery and transport equipment	272,501	350,863	401,598
Miscellaneous manufactured articles	99,176	112,333	127,128
Total (incl. others)	722,501	850,308	929,196

* Preliminary figures.

SELECTED TRADING PARTNERS (million koruny)

Imports f.o.b.	1997	1998	1999*
Austria	52,238	54,438	55,917
China, People's Republic	11,971	16,088	19,533
France	35,505	41,607	53,318
Germany	274,908	320,782	337,694
Hungary	11,255	12,780	15,806
Italy	47,390	48,640	52,987
Japan	16,613	17,019	19,748
Netherlands	20,786	22,237	23,475
Poland	27,609	31,278	35,069
Russia	57,435	51,199	48,235
Slovakia	72,081	66,866	60,987
Switzerland	14,251	16,568	17,553
United Kingdom	33,439	35,358	37,783
USA	32,637	34,749	40,695
Total (incl. others)	861,770	928,939	997,320

* Preliminary figures.

Exports f.o.b.	1997	1998	1999*
Austria	46,420	53,504	59,662
France	22,980	28,734	36,155
Germany	258,251	327,610	391,094
Hungary	13,564	16,181	16,281
Italy	26,454	31,965	33,452
Netherlands	17,481	19,236	22,620
Poland	41,447	48,075	50,868
Russia	24,498	21,196	13,310
Slovakia	93,304	90,547	76,480
Switzerland	8,761	11,494	11,018
United Kingdom	21,876	28,886	31,301
USA	18,602	18,992	22,621
Total (incl. others)	722,501	850,308	929,196

* Preliminary figures.

Transport

RAILWAYS (traffic)

	1997	1998	1999
Passenger-km (million)	7,710	7,001	6,957
Freight net ton-km (million)	22,173	19,529	16,713

ROAD TRAFFIC (motor vehicles in use at 31 December)

	1997	1998	1999
Passenger cars*	3,547,745	3,687,451	3,695,792
Buses and coaches	20,916	20,505	20,013
Goods vehicles†	265,598	312,404	302,487
Motorcycles	438,484	446,350	401,463

* Including vans.
† Excluding special-purpose lorries.

INLAND WATERWAYS (freight carried, '000 metric tons)

	1997	1998	1999
Imports	488	583	574
Exports	834	717	721
Internal	428	223	407
Total (incl. others)	1,828	1,678	1,877

AIR TRANSPORT

	1997	1998	1999
Kilometres flown ('000)	41,473	45,842	52,743
Passengers carried ('000)	2,166	2,377	2,904
Freight carried (metric tons)	13,585	13,168	17,359
Passenger-km ('000)	3,522,649	3,680,215	4,353,602
Freight ton-km ('000)	27,233	55,782	30,326

Tourism

FOREIGN TOURIST ARRIVALS*

Country of origin	1997	1998	1999
Austria	197,358	203,723	198,717
Denmark	106,631	133,600	160,189
France	161,427	178,772	171,669
Germany	1,753,858	1,731,103	1,654,400
Italy	282,220	287,183	320,505
Netherlands	267,240	296,100	285,164
Poland	247,030	346,843	379,417
Russia	211,639	273,658	235,807
Slovakia	243,308	266,425	242,396
Spain	139,742	139,581	169,277
United Kingdom	234,212	256,553	286,947
USA	201,827	246,392	240,830
Total (incl. others)	4,975,658	5,482,080	5,609,700

* Figures refer to visitors staying for at least one night at registered accommodation facilities.

Tourism receipts (US $ million): 4,075 in 1996; 3,647 in 1997; 3,792 in 1998 (Source: partly IMF, *Czech Republic: Statistical Appendix*, August 1999).

Communications Media

	1997	1998	1999
Radio receivers (subscribers)	3,259,006	3,223,195	3,201,931
Television receivers (subscribers)	3,500,983	3,447,118	3,438,304
Telephones (main lines in use)	3,806,112	4,710,252	5,750,690
Mobile cellular telephones (subscribers)	524,641	968,760	1,944,553
Book production: titles	11,519	11,738	12,551
Daily newspapers (number)	99	103	208
Other periodicals (number)	5,164	5,337	3,686

Telefax stations: 73,552 in use in 1995.
Source: partly UNESCO, *Statistical Yearbook*, and UN, *Statistical Yearbook*.

Education

(1999/2000)

	Institutions	Teachers	Students
Pre-primary	5,901	24,484	290,192
Basic:			
Primary	} 4,068	57,202	1,071,318
Lower secondary			
Upper secondary:			
General	345	10,749	126,797
Technical	826	17,296	164,640
Vocational	583	9,751	171,912
Tertiary:			
Higher professional schools	165	2,917	31,073
Universities	23	13,260	183,954

Directory

The Constitution

The following is a summary of the main provisions of the Constitution of the Czech Republic, which was adopted on 16 December 1992 and entered into force on 1 January 1993:

GENERAL PROVISIONS

The Czech Republic is a sovereign, unified and democratic law-abiding state, founded on the respect for the rights and freedoms of the individual and citizen. All state power belongs to the people, who exercise this power through the intermediary of legislative, executive and judicial bodies. The fundamental rights and freedoms of the people are under the protection of the judiciary.

The political system is founded on the free and voluntary operation of political parties respecting fundamental democratic principles and rejecting force as a means to assert their interests. Political decisions derive from the will of the majority, expressed through the free ballot. Minorities are protected in decision-making by the majority.

The territory of the Czech Republic encompasses an indivisible whole, whose state border may be changed only by constitutional law. Procedures covering the acquisition and loss of Czech citizenship are determined by law. No one may be deprived of his or her citizenship against his or her will.

GOVERNMENT

Legislative Power

Legislative power in the Czech Republic is vested in two chambers, the Chamber of Deputies and the Senate. The Chamber of Deputies has 200 members, elected for a term of four years. The Senate has 81 members, elected for a term of six years. Every two years one-third of the senators are elected. Both chambers elect their respective Chairman and Deputy Chairmen from among their members. Members of both chambers of the legislature are elected on the basis of universal, equal and direct suffrage by secret ballot. All citizens of 18 years and over are eligible to vote.

The legislature enacts the Constitution and laws; approves the state budget and the state final account; and approves the electoral law and international agreements. It elects the President of the Republic (at a joint session of both chambers), supervises the activities of the Government, and decides upon the declaration of war.

President of the Republic

The President of the Republic is Head of State. He/she is elected for a term of five years by a joint session of both chambers of the legislature. The President may not be elected for more than two consecutive terms.

The President appoints, dismisses and accepts the resignation of the Prime Minister and other members of the Government, dismisses the Government and accepts its resignation; convenes sessions of the Chamber of Deputies; may dissolve the Chamber of Deputies; names the judges of the Constitutional Court, its Chairman and Deputy Chairmen; appoints the Chairman and Deputy Chairmen of the Supreme Court; has the right to return adopted constitutional laws to the legislature; initials laws; and appoints members of the Council of the Czech National Bank. The President also represents the State in external affairs; is the Supreme Commander of the Armed Forces; receives heads of diplomatic missions; calls elections to the Chamber of Deputies and to the Senate; and has the right to grant amnesty.

Council of Ministers

The Council of Ministers is the highest organ of executive power. It is composed of the Prime Minister, the Deputy Prime Ministers and Ministers. It is answerable to the Chamber of Deputies. The President of the Republic appoints the Prime Minister, on whose recommendation he/she appoints the remaining members of the Council of Ministers and entrusts them with directing the ministries or other offices.

JUDICIAL SYSTEM

Judicial power is exercised on behalf of the Republic by independent courts. Judges are independent in the exercise of their function. The judiciary consists of the Supreme Court, the Supreme Administrative Court, high, regional and district courts.

The Constitutional Court is a judicial body protecting constitutionality. It consists of 15 judges appointed for a 10-year term by the President of the Republic with the consent of the Senate.

The Government

HEAD OF STATE

President: Václav Havel (elected 26 January 1993; re-elected 20 January 1998).

COUNCIL OF MINISTERS
(May 2001)

A minority Government of the Czech Social Democratic Party (CSDP).

Prime Minister: Miloš Zeman.

Deputy Prime Minister and Minister of Industry and Trade: Miroslav Grégr.

Deputy Prime Minister responsible for Legislation: Pavel Rychetský.

Deputy Prime Minister and Minister of Labour and Social Affairs: Vladimir Špidla.

Deputy Prime Minister and Minister of Foreign Affairs: Jan Kavan.

Minister of Defence: Jaroslav Tvrdik.

Minister of the Interior: Stanislav Gross.

Minister of Agriculture: Jan Fencl.

Minister of the Environment: Miloš Kužvart.

Minister of Finance: Jiři Rusnok.

Minister of Health: Bohumil Fišer.

Minister of Education, Youth and Sport: Eduard Zeman.

Minister of Transport and Communications: Jaromír Schling.

Minister of Justice: Jaroslav Bures.

Minister of Culture: Pavel Dostál.

Minister for Local Development: Petr Lachnit.

Minister without Portfolio: Karel Brezina.

MINISTRIES

Office of the Government of the Czech Republic: nábř. E. Beneše 4, 118 01 Prague 1; tel. (2) 24002111; fax (2) 24810231; e-mail www@vlada.cz; internet www.vlada.cz.

Ministry of Agriculture: Těšnov 17, 117 05 Prague 1; tel. (2) 2181111; fax (2) 24810478; e-mail vicenova@mze.cz; internet www.mze.cz.

Ministry of Culture: Milady Horákové 139, 160 41 Prague 6; tel. (2) 57085294; fax (2) 24324282; internet www.mkcr.cz.

Ministry of Defence: Tychonova 1, 160 01 Prague 6; tel. (2) 20201111; fax (2) 3116238.

Ministry of Education, Youth and Sport: Karmelitská 8, 118 12 Prague 1; tel. (2) 57193111; fax (2) 57193790; e-mail kastan @msmt.cz; internet www.msmt.cz.

Ministry of the Environment: Vršovická 65, 100 10 Prague 10; tel. (2) 67121111; fax (2) 67310308; e-mail info@env.cz; internet www.env.cz.

Ministry of Finance: Lětenská 15, 118 00 Prague 1; tel. (2) 57041111; fax (2) 57042788; e-mail podatelna@mfcr.cz; internet www.mfcr.cz.

Ministry of Foreign Affairs: Loretánské nám. 5, 118 00 Prague 1; tel. (2) 24181111; fax (2) 24310017; internet www.czech.cz.

Ministry of Health: Palackého nám. 4, POB 81, 128 01 Prague 2; tel. (2) 24971111; fax (2) 24972111; e-mail mzcr@mzcr.cz; internet www.mzcr.cz.

Ministry of Industry and Trade: Na Františku 32, 110 15 Prague 1; tel. (2) 24851111; fax (2) 24811089; internet www.mpo.cz.

Ministry of the Interior: Nad štolou 3, 170 34 Prague 7; tel. (2) 61432972; fax (2) 61433552; e-mail public@mvcr.cz; internet www.mvcr.cz.

Ministry of Justice: Vyšehradská 16, 128 10 Prague 2; tel. (2) 219977111; fax (2) 24919927; e-mail msp@msp.justice.cz; internet www.justice.cz.

Ministry of Labour and Social Affairs: Na poříčním právu 1, 128 01 Prague 2; tel. (2) 24918391; fax (2) 21922664; e-mail webmaster@mpsv.cz; internet www.mpsv.cz.

Ministry of Local Development: Staroměstské nám. 6, 110 15 Prague 1; tel. (2) 24861111; fax (2) 24861333; internet www.mmr.cz.

Ministry of Transport and Communications: nábř. L. Svobody 12, 110 15 Prague 1; tel. (2) 51431111; fax (2) 24810596; internet www.mdcr.cz.

Legislature

The Czech Constitution, which was adopted in December 1992, provided for the creation of a bicameral legislature as the highest organ of state authority in the Czech Republic (which was established as an independent state on 1 January 1993, following the dissolution of the Czech and Slovak Federative Republic). The lower house, the Chamber of Deputies, retained the structure of the Czech National Council (the former republican legislature). The upper chamber, or Senate, was first elected in November 1996.

CHAMBER OF DEPUTIES
(Poslanecká sněmovna)

Chairman: Václav Klaus.

General election, 19–20 June 1998

Party	% of votes	Seats
Czech Social Democratic Party . . .	32.3	74
Civic Democratic Party	27.7	63
Communist Party of Bohemia and Moravia .	11.0	24
Christian Democratic Union—Czechoslovak People's Party	9.0	20
Freedom Union	8.6	19
Others	11.4	—
Total	**100.0**	**200**

SENATE
(Senát)

Chairman: Libuse Benesova.

Party	Seats after elections* Nov. 1996	Nov. 1998	Nov. 2000
Civic Democratic Party	32	27	22
Christian Democratic Union—Czechoslovak People's Party† . .	13	12	21
Civic Democratic Alliance† . . .	7	5 }	18
Freedom Union†	—	1 }	
Czech Social Democratic Party . .	25	20	15
Communist Party of Bohemia and Moravia	2	4	3
Independents	—	12	2
Others	2	—	—
Total	**81**	**81**	**81**

* One-third of the 81 seats are renewable every two years.
† Contested the 1998 and 2000 elections as an informal electoral alliance, together with the Democratic Union.

Political Organizations

Alternative 2000 (Alternativa 2000): POB 154, 718 00 Ostrava 18; e-mail kvazar@telecom.cz; f. 1998.

Association for the Republic—Republican Party of Czechoslovakia (Sdružení pro republiku–Republikánská strana Československa): Gerstnerova 5, 170 00 Prague 7; tel. (2) 20571450; fax (2) 20570075; f. 1989; extreme right-wing; Chair. Miroslav Sládek; Vice-Chair. Martin Smetana.

Christian Democratic Union—Czechoslovak People's Party (CDU–CPP) (Křestanská a demokratická uniei—Československá strana lidová): Revoluční 5, 110 15 Prague 1; tel. (2) 2328086; fax (2) 24812114; internet www.kdu.cz; f. 1992; Chair. Jan Kasal.

Civic Democratic Alliance (CDA) (Občanská demokratická aliance): Štefánikova 21, 150 00 Prague 5; tel. (2) 57329855; fax (2) 57327072; e-mail usek@oda.cz; internet www.oda.cz; f. 1991 as a formal political party, following a split in Civic Forum (f. 1989); fmrly an informal group within Civic Forum; conservative; Chair. Daniel Kroupa.

Civic Democratic Party (CDP) (Občanská demokratická strana): Sněmovní 3, 110 00 Prague 1; tel. (2) 3114809; fax (2) 24510731; e-mail info@ods.cz; internet www.ods.cz; f. 1991 following a split in Civic Forum (f. 1989); merged with Christian Democratic Party in 1996; liberal-conservative; c. 17,000 mems (March 1998); Chair. Václav Klaus.

Communist Party of Bohemia and Moravia (Komunistická strana Čech a Moravy): Politických věznů 9, 111 21 Prague 1; tel. (2) 24210172; fax (2) 24264572; e-mail leftnews@kscm.cz; internet www.ksm.cz; f. 1991 as a result of the reorganization of the fmr Communist Party of Czechoslovakia; c. 200,000 mems; Leader Miroslav Grebeníček.

Communist Party of Czechoslovakia: f. 1995 as Party of Czechoslovak Communists; renamed as above 1999; 19,980 mems; Sec.-Gen. Miroslav Stepan.

Conservative Consensus Party (Strana konzervativní smlouvy): Čímská 26, 120 00 Prague 2; tel. (2) 250223; fax (2) 259424; e-mail skos@skos.cz; internet www.skos.cz; f. 1998 by fmr mems of right-wing faction in CDA.

Countryside Party: f. 1996 to promote interests of rural areas; c. 3,000 mems; Chair. Jan Veleba.

Czech Right (Česká pravice): Pod Divínem 34, 150 00 Prague 5; e-mail cp-praha@ceskapravice.cz; internet www.ceskapravice.cz; f. 1994; conservative.

Czech Social Democratic Party (CSDP) (Česká strana sociálně demokratická): Lidový dům, Hybernská 7, 110 00 Prague 1; tel. and fax (2) 24219911; e-mail info@socdem.cz; internet www.cssd.cz; f. 1878; prohibited 1948; re-established 1989; formerly the Czechoslovak Social Democratic Party; Chair. Ing. Miloš Zeman.

Democratic Left (Strana demokratická levice): Čitná 49, 110 00 Prague 1; tel. (2) 24221313; fax (2) 24221506; Chair. Josef Meěl.

Democratic Socialist Party (Strana demokratického socialismu): e-mail mailto:secret@sds.cz; f. 1997 by merger of Left Bloc and Party of the Democratic Left; c. 9,000 mems; Chair. Marie Stiborova.

Democratic Union (DU) (Demokratická unie): Revoluční 5, POB 3, 110 15 Prague 1; tel. and fax (2) 2323996; e-mail deu@login.cz; internet www.deu.cz; right-wing; c. 2,000 mems; Chair. Ratibor Majzlík.

Free Democrats—Liberal National Social Party (Svobodní demokraté—Liberální strana národně sociální): Republiky nám. 7, 111 49 Prague 1; tel. (2) 24223443; fax (2) 21618554; e-mail sdlsns@mbox.vol.cz; f. 1995 by merger of Free Democrats (fmrly Civic Movement) and Liberal National Social Party (fmrly Czechoslovak Socialist Party); Chair. Jiří Dienstbier.

Freedom Union (FU) (Unie svobody): Legerova 72, 120 00 Prague 2; tel. (2) 24221291; fax (2) 24221215; e-mail info@unie.cz; internet www.uniesvobody.cz; f. 1998, following a split in the Civic Democratic Party; c. 2,500 mems (March 1998); Chair. Karel Kühnl.

Green Party (Strana zelených): Murmanská 13, Prague 10; tel. and fax (2) 736580; f. 1989; Chair. Jaroslav Vlček.

Moravian Democratic Party: Joštova 4, 68200 Brno; tel. (5) 42215276; e-mail modestr@seznam.cz; internet www.mujweb.cz/www/modestr; f. 1997 by merger of Bohemian-Moravian Union of the Centre and Moravian National Party; Chair. Ivan Drimal.

Union for Europe (Unie pro Evropu): Plzeň; f. 2000; c. 6,000 mems.

Diplomatic Representation

EMBASSIES IN THE CZECH REPUBLIC

Afghanistan: V tišině 6, 160 00 Prague 6; tel. and fax (2) 372417; Chargé d'affaires a.i.: Wazir Ahmad Faizi.

Albania: Pod kaštany 22, 160 00 Prague 6; tel. (2) 379329; fax (2) 371742; Ambassador: Piro Mibicani.

Algeria: V tišině 10/483, POB 021, 225 21 Prague 025; tel. (2) 33371142; fax (2) 33371144; internet www.algeria.cz; Ambassador: Abderrahmane Meziane-Cherif.

Argentina: Washingtonova 25, 225 22 Prague 1; tel. (2) 24212448; fax (2) 22241246; Ambassador: Horacio Adolfo Basabe.

Austria: Viktora Huga 10, 151 15 Prague 5; tel. (2) 57090511; fax (2) 57316045; e-mail austria@mbox.vol.cz; internet www.vol.cz/austria; Ambassador: Peter Niesner.

Belarus: Sádky 626, 171 00 Prague 7; tel. (2) 6888216; fax (2) 6888217; Ambassador: Uladzimir Petrovič Belsky.

Belgium: Valdštejnská 6, 118 01 Prague 1; tel. (2) 57320389; fax (2) 57320753; Ambassador: Bernard Pierre.

Brazil: Sušická 12, POB 79, 160 41 Prague 6; tel. (2) 3116694; fax (2) 3118274; Ambassador: Sergio Paulo Rouanet.

Bulgaria: Krakovská 6, 125 25 Prague 1; tel. (2) 22211259; fax (2) 22211728; e-mail bulvelv@mbox.vol.cz; Ambassador: Martin Tomov.

Cambodia: Na Hubálce 1, 169 00 Prague 6; tel. (2) 352603; fax (2) 351078; Chargé d'affaires a.i.: Makana Yous.

Canada: Mickiewiczova 6, 125 33 Prague 6; tel. (2) 24311108; fax (2) 24310294; internet www.dfait-maeci.gc.ca/~prague/; Ambassador: Ronald Halpin.

Chile: U Vorlíků 4/623, 160 00 Prague 6; tel. (2) 24315064; fax (2) 24316069; e-mail echilecz@mbox.vol.cz; internet www.eol.cz/CHILE; Ambassador: RICARDO CONCHA GAZMURI.

China, People's Republic: Pelléova 22, 160 00 Prague 6; tel. (2) 24311323; fax (2) 324902; Ambassador: YAN PENG.

Colombia: Washingtonova 25, 110 00 Prague 1; tel. (2) 21674200; fax (2) 24225538; Ambassador: ENRIQUE GAVIRIA LIEVANO.

Costa Rica: Eliášova 21, 160 00 Prague 6; tel. and fax (2) 3123750; Chargé d'affaires a.i.: JOHNNY JOSÉ SUÁREZ SANDÍ.

Croatia: V Průhledu 9, 162 00 Prague 6; tel. (2) 3120479; fax (2) 3123464; Ambassador: ZORAN PIČULJAN.

Cuba: Na Kazance 7/634, apts. 18 až 19, 177 00 Prague 7; tel. (2) 8544228; fax (2) 8544227; Chargé d'affaires a.i.: ALCIDES DE LA ROSA DEL TORO.

Cyprus: Sibirske nam. 6, 160 00 Prague 6; tel. (2) 3114622; fax (2) 3115751; e-mail cyprusembass@mbox.vol.cz; Ambassador: GEORGE L. VYRIDES.

Denmark: Maltézské nám. č. 5, POB 25, 118 01 Prague 1; tel. (2) 57316630; fax (2) 57316640; e-mail danemb@terminal.cz; internet www.denmark.cz; Ambassador: ULRIK HELWEG-LARSEN.

Egypt: Pelléova 14, 160 00 Prague 6; tel. (2) 24311516; fax (2) 24311157; Ambassador: ASSEM A. MEGAHED.

Estonia: Na Kampě 1, 118 00 Prague 1; tel. (2) 57530512; fax (2) 57530513; e-mail sekretar@estemb.cz; Chargé d'affaires a.i.: JAAN HEIN.

Finland: Hellichova 1, Chotkův palác, 110 00 Prague 1; tel. (2) 57007130; fax (2) 57007132; e-mail sanomat.pra@formin.fi; Ambassador: RISTO RÄNNÄLI.

France: Velkopřevorské nám. 2, POB 102, 118 01 Prague 1; tel. (2) 57532756; fax (2) 57532757; e-mail ambafrcz@vol.cz; internet www.france.cz; Ambassador: PHILIPPE COSTE.

Germany: Vlašská 19, 118 01 Prague 1; tel. (2) 57113111; fax (2) 57534056; e-mail d_botschaft@vdny.cz; internet www .german-embassy.cz; Ambassador: Count HAGEN LAMBSDORFF.

Ghana: V tišině 4, 160 00 Prague 6; tel. (2) 33377236; fax (2) 33375647; e-mail ghanaemb@mbox.vol.cz; Ambassador: S. VALIS-AKYIANU.

Greece: Na Ořechovce 19, 162 00 Prague 6; tel. (2) 3121702; fax (2) 24311235; Ambassador: GEORGES LINARDOS.

Holy See: Voršilská 12, 110 00 Prague 1; tel. (2) 24912192; fax (2) 24914160; e-mail nunciatgc@mbox.vol.cz; Apostolic Nuncio: Most Rev. GIOVANNI COPPA, Titular Archbishop of Serta.

Hungary: Badeniho 1, 225 37 Prague 6; tel. (2) 365041; fax (2) 329425; Ambassador: ZOLTÁN VEZÉR.

India: Valdštejnska 6, Malastrana, 118 00 Prague 1; tel. (2) 57533490; fax (2) 57533285; e-mail Indembprague@bohem-net.cz; Ambassador: Dr S. JAISBANKAR.

Indonesia: Nad Buď'ánkami II/7, 150 00 Prague 5; tel. (2) 57214388; fax (2) 57212105; e-mail informace@indoneske-velvyslanectvi.cz; internet www.indoneske-velvyslanectvi.cz; Ambassador: SOENARTO SOEDARNO.

Iran: Na Zátorce 18, 160 00 Prague 6; tel. (2) 20570454; fax (2) 371468; Ambassador: SEYED-JAFAR HASHEMI (recalled Nov. 1998).

Iraq: Na Zátorce 10, 160 00 Prague 6; tel. (2) 24321715; fax (2) 24315748; Ambassador: SADIQ KH. R. AHMED.

Ireland: Tržiště 13, 118 00 Prague 1; tel. (2) 57530061; fax (2) 57311492; Ambassador: MICHAEL COLLINS.

Israel: Badeniho 2, 170 06 Prague 7; tel. (2) 33325109; fax (2) 33320092; e-mail israemb@bohem-net.cz; Ambassador: ERELLA HADAR.

Italy: Nerudova 20, 118 00 Prague 1; tel. (2) 33080111; fax (2) 57531522; e-mail italemba@mbox.vol.cz; internet www .italianembassy.cz; Ambassador: PAOLO FAIOLA.

Japan: Maltézské nám. 6, 118 01 Prague 1; tel. (2) 57320561; fax (2) 539997; Ambassador: SHUNJI MARUYAMA.

Kazakhstan: Fetrovská 15, 160 00 Prague 6; tel. (2) 3114596; fax (2) 3112124; Ambassador: TULEUTAI SULEIMENOV.

Korea, Democratic People's Republic: Na Zátorce 6, 160 00 Prague 6; tel. (2) 24320783; fax (2) 24318817; Chargé d'affaires a.i.: KIM JONG NAM.

Korea, Republic: Slavíčkova 5, 160 00 Prague 6; tel. (2) 24318100; fax (2) 24320538; Ambassador: CHO CHANG-BEOM.

Kuwait: Pod kaštany 2, 160 00 Prague 6; tel. (2) 24311966; fax (2) 24311972; Ambassador: AHMAD BU-ZUOBAR.

Latvia: Hradešínská 3, POB 54, 101 00 Prague 10; tel. (2) 24252454; fax (2) 24255099; Ambassador: AIJA ODINA.

Lebanon: Masarykovo nábřeží 14, 110 00 Prague 1; tel. (2) 293633; fax (2) 293406; Ambassador: SLEIMAN YOUNES.

Libya: Na baště sv. Jiří 5–7, 160 00 Prague 6; tel. (2) 323410; fax (2) 329119; Chargé d'affaires a.i.: MILUD MOHAMED JADID.

Lithuania: Pod Klikovkou 1916/2, 150 00 Prague 5; tel. (2) 57210122; fax (2) 57210124; e-mail ltembcz@mbox.vol.cz; internet www.ltembassycz.urrn.lt; Ambassador: VYGINTAS GRINIS.

Mexico: Nad Kazankou 8, 171 00 Prague 7; tel. (2) 8555554; fax (2) 8550477; Ambassador: GONZALO AGUIRRE ENRILE.

Mongolia: Na Marně 5, 160 00 Prague 6; tel. (2) 24311198; fax (2) 24314827; Chargé d'affaires: NAIDANSUREN JARGALSAIKHAN.

Morocco: Ke starému Bubenči 4, 160 00 Prague 6; tel. (2) 329404; fax (2) 321758; Ambassador: ABDESSELEM OUAZZANI.

Netherlands: Gotthardská 6/27, 225 40 Prague 6; tel. (2) 24312190; fax (2) 24312160; e-mail nlgovpra@ti.cz; Ambassador: ROBERT JAN VAN HOUTOM.

Nigeria: Před bateriemi 18, 162 01 Prague 6; tel. (2) 24312065; fax (2) 24312072; e-mail embassy@nigeria.cz; Chargé d'affaires a.i.: ABBA A. TIJJANT.

Norway: Na Ořechovce 69, 162 00 Prague 6; tel. (2) 3111411; fax (2) 3123797; e-mail noramb@noramb.cz; Ambassador: LASSE SEIM.

Pakistan: Šmolíkova 1009, 161 00 Prague 6; tel. (2) 33312421; fax (2) 33311369; Ambassador: SAMUEL THOMAS JOSHUA.

Peru: Muchova 9, 160 00 Prague 6; tel. (2) 24316210; fax (2) 24314749; e-mail emba.peru.praga@ms.anat.cz; Ambassador: A. RAÚL PATIÑO-ALVÍSTUR

Philippines: Karolíny Světlé 34, 110 00 Prague 1; tel. (2) 21635301; fax (2) 21635302; Ambassador: CARMELITA RODRÍGUEZ SALAS.

Poland: Valdštejnská 8, 118 01 Prague 1; tel. (2) 5732068; fax (2) 57320764; e-mail ambpolcz@mbox.vol.cz; Ambassador: MAREK PERNAL.

Portugal: Kinských nám. 7, 150 00 Prague 5; tel. (2) 57311230; fax (2) 57311234; e-mail embport@mbox.vol.cz; Ambassador: ANTÓNIO CASCAIS.

Romania: Nerudova 5, POB 87, 118 10 Prague 1; tel. (2) 57320494; fax (2) 534393; Ambassador: NICOLAE VULPAŠIN.

Russia: Pod kaštany 1, 160 00 Prague 6; tel. (2) 33374100; fax (2) 373800; e-mail rusembas@bohem-net.cz; Ambassador: NIKOLAI T. RYABOV.

Slovakia: Pod hradbami 1, 160 00 Prague 6; tel. (2) 321441; fax (2) 324289; e-mail skembassy@pha.inecnet.cz; Ambassador: LADISLAV BALLEK.

Slovenia: Pod hradbami 15, 160 41 Prague 6; tel. (2) 24315106; fax (2) 24314106; Ambassador: DAMJAN PRELOVŠEK.

South Africa: Ruská 65, POB 133, 100 00 Prague 10; tel. (2) 67311114; fax (2) 67311395; e-mail saprague@terminal.cz; Ambassador: THOMAS LANGLEY.

Spain: Pevnostní 9, 162 00 Prague 6; tel. (2) 24311222; fax (2) 3121770; Ambassador: CABANAS ANSORENA.

Sweden: Úvoz 13-Hradčany, POB 35, 160 12 Prague 612; tel. (2) 20313200; fax (2) 20313240; e-mail ambassaden.prag@foreign .ministry.se; Ambassador: INGMAR KARLSSON.

Switzerland: Pevnostní 7, POB 84, 162 01 Prague 6; tel. (2) 24311228; fax (2) 24311312; Ambassador: WALTER FETSCHERIN.

Syria: Pod kaštany 16, 160 00 Prague 6; tel. (2) 24310952; fax (2) 24317911; Chargé d'affaires a.i.: HAYSSAM MASHFEJ.

Thailand: Romaina Rollanda 3, 160 00 Prague 6; tel. (2) 20571435; fax (2) 20570049; e-mail thai@thaiemb.cz; internet www.thaiemb.cz; Ambassador: MANN PONTHAM.

Tunisia: Nad Kostelem 8, 147 00 Prague 4; tel. (2) 44460652; fax (2) 44460825; e-mail atprague@vol.cz; Ambassador: MONDHER MAMI.

Turkey: Pevnostní 3, 162 00 Prague 6; tel. (2) 24311402; fax (2) 24311279; Ambassador: TEMEL ISKIT.

Ukraine: Charlese de Gaulla 29, 160 00 Prague 6; tel. (2) 3122000; fax (2) 3124366; e-mail kosak@mbox.vol.cz; Ambassador: SERHII USTYCH.

United Kingdom: Thunovská 14, 118 00 Prague 1; tel. (2) 57530278; fax (2) 57530285; e-mail info@britain.cz; internet www.britain.cz; Ambassador: DAVID BROUCHER.

USA: Tržiště 15, 118 01 Prague 1; tel. (2) 57530663; fax (2) 57530583; internet www.usembassy.cz; Chargé d'affaires a.i.: STEVEN J. COFFEY.

Uruguay: Malátova 12, 150 00 Prague 5; tel. (2) 545455; fax (2) 548852; Ambassador: Dr PEDRO VIDAL SELBERRY.

Venezuela: Jánský vršek 2/350, 118 00 Prague 1; tel. (2) 57313740; fax (2) 57313742; e-mail embaven@mbox.vol.cz; internet www.vol.cz/embavenezuela; Chargé d'affaires a.i.: OSWALDO A. NIÑO H.

Viet Nam: Plzeňská 214, 150 00 Prague 5; tel. (2) 57211540; fax (2) 57211792; Ambassador: NGUYEN VAN KHIEU.

Yemen: Pod hradbami 5, 160 00 Prague 6; tel. (2) 3111598; Ambassador: ALI ABDULLAH ABO-LOHOM.

Yugoslavia: Mostecká 15, 118 00 Prague 1; tel. (2) 57320031; fax (2) 57320491; Ambassador: DJOKO STOJIČIĆ.

Judicial System

The judicial system comprises the Supreme Court, the Supreme Administrative Court, chief, regional and district courts. There is also a 15-member Constitutional Court.

Supreme Court: Buresova 20, 657 37 Brno; tel. (5) 41213293; fax (5) 41212917; e-mail sekretariat@nsoud.cz; internet www.nsoud.cz; Chair. ELISKA WAGNEROVA.

Office of the Attorney-General: Jezuitska 4, 660 55 Brno; tel. (5) 42512111; fax (5) 42219621; Attorney-Gen. MARIE BENESOVA.

Constitutional Court: Jostova 8, 660 83 Brno; tel. (5) 42161111; fax (5) 42218326; e-mail ivan@concourt.cz; internet www.concourt .cz; Chair. ZDENĚK KESSLER.

Religion

The principal religion in the Czech Republic is Christianity. The largest denomination in 1995 was the Roman Catholic Church. About 30% of the population profess no religious belief.

CHRISTIANITY

Ecumenical Council of Churches in the Czech Republic (Ekumenická rada církví v České republice): Donská 5/370, 101 00 Prague 10; tel. and fax (2) 71742326; e-mail ekumrada@iol.cz; f. 1955; 11 mem. churches; Pres. Bishop VLADISLAV VOLNÝ; Gen. Sec. NADĚJE MANDYSOVÁ.

The Roman Catholic Church

Latin Rite

The Czech Republic comprises two archdioceses and six dioceses. At 31 December 1997 there were 4.1m. adherents in the country, representing about 39% of the population.

Czech Bishops' Conference (Česká biskupská konference): Thákurova 3, 160 00 Prague 6; tel. (2) 20181421; fax (2) 24310144; e-mail cbk2@ktf.cuni.cz; f. 1990; Pres. Cardinal Dr MILOSLAV VLK, Archbishop of Prague.

Archbishop of Olomouc: Most Rev. JAN GRAUBNER, Wurmova 9, 771 01 Olomouc; tel. (68) 5500211; fax (68) 5224840.

Archbishop of Prague: Cardinal Dr MILOSLAV VLK, Hradčanské nám. 16, 119 02 Prague 1; tel. (2) 20510615; fax (2) 20514647.

Byzantine Rite

Apostolic Exarch in the Czech Republic: Rt Rev. IVAN LJAVINEC (Titular Bishop of Acalissus), Haštalské nám. 4, 110 00 Prague 1; tel. and fax (2) 2312817.

The Eastern Orthodox Church

Orthodox Church (Pravoslavná církev): V jámě 6, 111 21 Prague 1; divided into two eparchies: Prague and Olomouc; Head of the Orthodox Church, Metropolitan of Prague and of all Czechoslovakia His Holiness Patriarch DOROTEJ.

Protestant Churches

Baptist Union in the Czech Republic: Na Topolce 14, 140 00 Prague 4; tel. and fax (2) 41434256; e-mail czechbaptist@iol.cz; f. 1994; 2,395 mems; Pres. Rev. MILOŠ SOLA; Sec. Rev. JAN TITERA.

Brethren Church: Soukenická 15, 110 00 Prague 1; tel. and fax (2) 2318131; e-mail pavel.cerny@cb.cz; internet www.cbchurch.cz; f. 1880; 8,331 mems, 46 churches; Pres. PAVEL ČERNÝ; Sec. KAREL FOJTÍK.

Christian Corps: nám. Konečného 5, 602 00 Brno; tel. (5) 756365; 3,200 mems; 123 brs; Rep. Ing. PETR ŽEMAN.

Evangelical Church of Czech Brethren (Presbyterian): Jungmannova 9, 111 21 Prague 1; tel. (2) 24947503; fax (2) 24948556; f. 1781; united since 1918; activities extend over Bohemia, Moravia and Silesia; 138,616 adherents (1997) and 264 parishes (1995); Pres. Rev. PAVEL SMETANA; Synodal Curator Dr LYDIE ROSKOVCOVÁ.

Silesian Evangelical Church of the Augsburg Confession in the Czech Republic (Silesian Lutheran Church): Na nivách 7, 737 01 Český Těšín; tel. (659) 731804; fax (659) 731815; e-mail sceav@silesnet.cz; internet www.sceav.silesnet.cz; founded in the 16th century during the Lutheran Reformation, reorganized in 1948; 40,000 mems; Bishop VLADISLAV VOLNÝ.

United Methodist Church: Ječná 19, 120 00 Prague 2; tel. (2) 290623; fax (2) 290167; e-mail ecmradacz@mbox.vol.cz; 1,890 mems; 17 parishes; Supt JOSEF ČERVEŇÁK.

Unity of Brethren (Moravian Church): Kollárova 456, 509 01 Nová Paka; tel. and fax (434) 621258; e-mail jbmb@iol.cz; internet www.moravian.cz; f. 1457; 2,447 mems; 21 parishes; Pres. Rev. JAROSLAV PLEVA.

Other Christian Churches

Apostolic Church in the Czech Republic: V Zídkách 402, 280 02 Kolín; tel. (321) 720457; fax (321) 727668; e-mail hqbishopac@ clever.cz; f. 1989; 4,277 mems; Bishop RUDOLF BUBIK.

Church of the Seventh-day Adventists: Zálesí 50, 142 00 Prague 4; tel. (2) 4723745; fax (2) 44471863; e-mail unie@casd.cz; internet www.casd.cz; f. 1919; 10,000 mems; 183 churches; Pres. KAREL NOWAK.

Czechoslovak Hussite Church: Wuchterlova 5, 166 26 Prague 6; tel. (2) 20398109; fax (2) 24320308; f. 1920; 131,000 mems; five dioceses, divided into 310 parishes; Bishop-Patriarch JOSEF ŠPAK.

Old Catholic Church: Hládkov 3, 169 00 Prague 6; tel. and fax (2) 33353547; e-mail stkat@comp.cz; 4,150 mems, 12 parishes; Bishop Mgr DUŠAN HEJBAL.

JUDAISM

Federation of Jewish Communities in the Czech Republic (Federace židovských obcí v České republice): Maiselova 18, 110 01 Prague 1; tel. (2) 24811090; fax (2) 24810912; 3,000 mems; Pres. Dr JAN MUNK; Chief Rabbi KAROL SIDON.

The Press

PRINCIPAL DAILIES

Brno

Brněnský večerník (Brno Evening Paper): Jakubské nám. 7, 658 44 Brno; tel. (5) 42321227; fax (5) 45215150; f. 1968; Editor-in-Chief PETR HOSKOVEC; circ. 16,000.

Rovnost (Equality): M. Horákové 9, 658 22 Brno; tel. (5) 45321121; fax (5) 45212873; f. 1885; morning; Editor-in-Chief LUBOMÍR SELINGER; circ. 62,000.

České Budějovice

Jihočeské listy (South Bohemia Paper): Vrbenská 23, 370 45 České Budějovice; tel. (38) 22081; f. 1991; morning; Editor-in-Chief VLADIMÍR MAJER; circ. 53,000.

Hradec Králové

Hradecké noviny (Hradec News): Škroupova 695, 501 72 Hradec Králové; tel. (49) 613511; fax (49) 615681; Editor-in-Chief JAROMÍR FRIDRICH; circ. 30,000.

Karlovy Vary

Karlovarské noviny (Karlovy Vary News): třída TGM 32, 360 21 Karlovy Vary; tel. (17) 3224496; fax (17) 3225115; f. 1991; Editor-in-Chief JIŘÍ LINHART ; circ. 15,000.

Ostrava

Moravskoslezský den (Moravia-Silesia Daily): Novinářská 7, 700 00 Ostrava 1; tel. (69) 55134; fax (69) 57021; f. 1991; Editor-in-Chief VLADIMÍR VAVRDA; circ. 130,000.

Svoboda (Freedom): Mlýnská 10, 701 11 Ostrava; tel. (69) 2472311; fax (69) 2472312; f. 1991; morning; Editor-in-Chief JOSEF LYS; circ. 100,000.

Pardubice

Pardubické noviny (Pardubice News): Tříd Míru 60, 530 02 Pardubice; tel. (40) 517366; fax (40) 517156; f. 1991; Editor-in-Chief ROMAN MARČÁK; circ. 15,000.

Plzeň

Plzeňský deník (Plzeň Daily): Husova 15, 304 83 Plzeň; tel. (19) 551111; fax (19) 551234; f. 1991 (fmrly *Pravda*, f. 1919); Editor-in-Chief JAN PERTL; circ. 50,000.

Prague

Hospodářské noviny (Economic News): Dobrovského 25, 170 55 Prague 7; tel. (2) 33071111; fax (2) 33072307; e-mail data@hn .economia.cz; f. 1957; morning; Editor-in-Chief PETR ŠTĚPÁNEK; circ. 130,000.

Lidové noviny (People's News): Pobřežni 20/224, 186 21 Prague 8; tel. (2) 67098700; fax (2) 67098799; e-mail inzerce@lidovky.cz; internet www.lidovenoyiny.cz; f. 1893, re-established 1988; morning; Editor-in-Chief PAVEL SAFR; circ. 83,728.

Mladá fronta Dnes (Youth Front Today): Senovážná 4, 110 00 Prague 1; tel. (2) 22062111; fax (2) 22062229; e-mail mfdnes@ mafra.cz; f. 1990; morning; independent; Editor-in-Chief PETR ŠABATA; circ. 350,000.

Právo (Right): Slezská 13, 120 00 Prague 2; tel. (2) 21001111; fax (2) 21001361; f. 1920, as *Rudé právo*: name changed as above 1995; morning; Editor-in-Chief ZDENĚK PORYBNÝ; circ. 250,000.

Slovo (Word): Václavské nám. 36, 112 12 Prague 1; tel. (2) 24227258; fax (2) 24229477; f. 1945; Editor-in-Chief LIBOR ŠEVČÍK; circ. 95,000.

Večerník Praha (Evening Prague): Na Florenci 19, 111 21 Prague 1; tel. (2) 24227625; fax (2) 2327361; f. 1991 (fmrly *Večerní Praha*, f. 1955); evening; Editor-in-Chief IVAN ČERVENKA; circ. 130,000.

Ústí nad Labem

Severočeský deník (North Bohemia Daily): Ústí nad Labem; tel. (47) 5220525; fax (47) 5220587; f. 1920; Editor-in-Chief MARIE SRPOVÁ; circ. 95,000.

PRINCIPAL PERIODICALS
Czech Language

100+1 ZZ: Karlovo nám. 5, 120 00 Prague 2; tel. (2) 293291; fax (2) 299824; f. 1964; fortnightly foreign press digest; Editor-in-Chief VÁCLAV DUŠEK; circ. 85,000.

Ateliér (Studio): Masarykovo nábř. 250, 110 00 Prague 1; tel. and fax (2) 24930232; e-mail atelier@auclionsarl.cz; f. 1988; visual arts; fortnightly; Editor-in-Chief BLANKA JIRÁČKOVÁ.

Auto Tip: Střelničina 1680/8, 182 21 Prague 8; tel. (2) 66193173; fax (2) 66193172; e-mail autotip@automedia.cz; f. 1990; fortnightly for motorists; Editor-in-Chief VLADIMÍR ŠULC; circ. 60,000.

Českomoravský profit (Czech–Moravia Profit): Domažlická 3, 130 00 Prague 3; tel. (2) 277084; fax (2) 278514; weekly; Editor-in-Chief JAN BALTUS.

Divadelní noviny (Theatre News): c/o Divadelní ústav, Celetná 17, 110 00 Prague 1; tel. and fax (2) 2315912; e-mail divadelni .noviny@czech-theatre.cz; internet www.divadlo.cz/noviny; fortnightly; Editor-in-Chief JAN KOLÁŘ.

Ekonom (Economist): Dobrovského 25, 170 55 Prague 7; tel. (2) 33071301; fax (2) 33072002; e-mail ekonom@economia.cz; weekly; Editor-in-Chief EVA KLVAČOVÁ.

Katolický týdeník (Catholic Weekly): Londýnská 44, 120 00 Prague 2; tel. (2) 24250385; fax (2) 24257041; e-mail tydenik@mbox .vol.cz; f. 1989; weekly; Editor-in-Chief NORBERT BADAL; circ. 70,000.

Květy (Flowers): Na Florenci 3, 117 14 Prague 1; tel. and fax (2) 24219549; f. 1834; illustrated family weekly; Editor-in-Chief JINDŘICH MAŘAN; circ. 320,000.

Mladý svět (Young World): Na Poříčí 30, 112 86 Prague 1; tel. (2) 24229087; fax (2) 24210211; f. 1956; illustrated weekly; Editor-in-Chief OLGA DOUBRAVOVÁ; circ. 110,000.

Obchod-Kontakt-Marketing (Trade-Contact-Marketing): Korunní 87, 130 00 Prague 3; tel. and fax (2) 255440; monthly; Editor-in-Chief MARCELA NOVÁKOVÁ.

Reflex: Jeseniova 51, 130 00 Prague 3; tel. (2) 67097542; fax (2) 61216239; f. 1990; social weekly; Editor-in-Chief PETR BÍLEK; circ. 220,000.

Respekt: Sokolská 66, 120 00 Prague 2; tel. (2) 24941962; fax (2) 24941965; e-mail redakce@respekt.cz; f. 1990; political weekly; Editor-in-Chief MARTIN FENDRYCH; circ. 30,000.

Romano Hangos (Romany Voice): f. 1999; fortnightly; Editor-in-Chief KAREL HOLOMEK.

Romano Kurko (Romany Week): Černovické nábř. 7, 618 00 Brno; tel. and fax (5) 330785; f. 1991; weekly; in Czech with Romany vocabulary; Dir M. SMOLEŇ; circ. 8,000.

Sondy (Soundings): W. Churchilla 2, 130 00 Prague 3; tel. (2) 24462328; fax (2) 24462313; f. 1990; weekly; Editor-in-Chief JANA KAŠPAROVÁ; circ. 40,000.

Týdeník Rozhlas (Radio Weekly): Na Florenci 3, 112 86 Prague 1; tel. and fax (2) 2323261; f. 1923; Editor-in-Chief AGÁTA PILÁTOVÁ; circ. 170,000.

Vesmír (Universe): Národní 3, 111 42 Prague 1; tel. (2) 24229181; fax (2) 24240513; e-mail vesmir@mbox.cesnet.cz; f. 1871; monthly; popular science magazine; Editor IVAN M. HAVEL; circ. 8,000–10,000.

Vlasta: Žitná 18, 120 00 Prague 2; tel. (2) 298641; fax (2) 294535; f. 1947; weekly; illustrated magazine for women; Editor-in-Chief MARIE FORMÁČKOVÁ; circ. 380,000.

Zahrádkář (Gardener): Prague; tel. (2) 766346; fax (2) 768042; monthly; Editor-in-Chief ANTONÍN DOLEJŠÍ; circ. 200,000.

Zora: Krakovská 21, 115 17 Prague 1; tel. (2) 24228126; fax (2) 24228120; f. 1917; every two months; for the visually handicapped; Editor-in-Chief JIŘÍ REICHEL.

Other Languages

Amaro Lav (Our Word): Černovické nábř. 7, 618 00 Brno; tel. and fax (5) 330785; f. 1990; monthly; in Romany and Czech; Dir M. SMOLEŇ; circ. 3,000.

Czech Business and Trade: V jirchářích 8, 110 00 Prague 1; tel. (2) 24912185; fax (2) 24912355; e-mail journal@ppagency.cz; internet www.ppagency.cz; f. 1960; monthly; publ. in English, German, Spanish, Russian and French; Editor-in-Chief Dr PAVLA PODSKALSKÁ; circ. 15,000.

Prager Wochenblatt (Prague Weekly): Vítkovická 373, 199 00 Prague 9; tel. (2) 6282029; weekly; politics, culture, economy; in German; Editor-in-Chief FELIX SEEBAUER; circ. 30,000.

Prague Post: Štěpánská 20 Prague 1; tel. (2) 96334400; fax (2) 96334450; e-mail office@praguepost.cz; f. 1991; political, economic and cultural weekly; in English; Editor-in-Chief ALAN LEVY; circ. 15,000.

Prognosis: Prague; tel. (2) 3167007; fax (2) 368139; f. 1991; political, economic and cultural fortnightly; in English; Editor-in-Chief BEN SULLIVAN; circ. 10,000.

NEWS AGENCIES

Česká tisková kancelář (ČTK) (Czech News Agency): Opletalova 5–7, 111 44 Prague 1; tel. (2) 22098111; fax (2) 24220553; e-mail ctk@mail.ctk.cz; internet www.ctk.cz; f. Nov. 1992, assuming control of all property and activities (in the Czech Lands) of the former Czechoslovak News Agency; news and photo-exchange service with all international and many national news agencies; maintains network of foreign correspondents; Czech and English general and economic news service; publishes daily bulletins in English; Gen. Dir Dr MILAN STIBRAL.

Foreign Bureaux

Agence France-Presse (AFP): Ječná 15, 120 00 Prague 2; tel. (2) 24921155; fax (2) 24919155; e-mail afp@mbox.vol.cz; Bureau Chief RENÉ PASCAL BIAGI.

Agencia EFE (Spain): Uhrineveska 65, 100 00 Prague 1; tel. (2) 67313620; fax (2) 67313975; Bureau Chief MIGUEL FERNÁNDEZ.

Agenzia Nazionale Stampa Associata (ANSA) (Italy): Prague; tel. (2) 71735816; fax (2) 74782319; e-mail efe@iol.cz; internet www.efe.es; Bureau Chief MIGUEL FERNÁNDEZ.

Allgemeiner Deutscher Nachrichtendienst (ADN) (Germany): Milevská 835, 140 00 Prague 4; tel. (2) 6921911; fax (2) 6921627; Bureau Chief STEFFI GENSICKE.

Associated Press (AP) (USA): Prague; tel. (2) 24224346; fax (2) 24227445; Correspondent ONDŘEJ HEJMA.

Deutsche Presse-Agentur (dpa) (Germany): Petrské nám. 1, 110 00 Prague 1; tel. (2) 24810290; fax (2) 2315196; Bureau Chief WOLFGANG JUNG.

Informatsionnoye Telegrafnoye Agentstvo Rossii—Telegrafnoye Agentstvo Suverennykh Stran (ITAR–TASS) (Russia): Pevnostní 5, 162 00 Prague 6; tel. (2) 328307; fax (2) 327527; Bureau Chief ALEKSANDR YAKOVLEV.

Magyar Távirati Iroda (MTI) (Hungary): Prague; tel. and fax (2) 66710131; Bureau Chief GYÖRGY HARSÁNYI.

Novinska Agencija Tanjug (Yugoslavia): Prague; tel. (2) 2674401; Correspondent BRANKO STOŠIĆ.

Polska Agencja Prasowa (PAP) (Poland): Petrské nám. 1, 110 00 Prague 1; tel. and fax (2) 24812205; Correspondent ZBYGNIEW KRZYSTYNJAK.

Rossiiskoye Informatsionnoye Agentstvo—Novosti (RIA–Novosti) (Russia): Italská 36, 130 00 Prague 3; tel. (2) 22253088; fax (2) 22253084; e-mail riapraha@bohem-net.cz; Bureau Chief VALERIJ ENIN.

Tlačová agentúra Slovenskej republiky (TASR) (Slovakia): Šmeralova 7, 170 00 Prague 7; tel. (2) 33372617; fax (2) 33379663; e-mail bkopcak@iol.cz; internet www.tasr.sk; Correspondent BOHDAN KOPČÁK.

Xinhua (New China) News Agency (People's Republic of China): Pelléova 22, 169 00 Prague 6; tel. and fax (2) 24311325; Correspondent SAN XI-YOU.

PRESS ASSOCIATION

Syndicate of Journalists of the Czech Republic: Pařížská 9, 116 30 Prague 1; tel. (2) 2325109; fax (2) 2327782; e-mail sncr@mbox .vol.cz; f. 1877; reorganized in 1990; 5,000 mems; Chair. IRENA VÁLOVÁ.

Publishers

Academia: Legerova 61, 120 00 Prague 2; tel. (2) 24942584; fax (2) 24941982; f. 1953; scientific books, periodicals; Dir ALEXANDER TOMSKÝ.

AkcentiBlok: Rooseveltova 4, 657 00 Brno; tel. and fax (5) 42214516; f. 1957; regional literature, fiction, general; Dir JAROSLAV NOVÁK.

Albatros: Truhlářská 9, 110 01 Prague 1; tel. (2) 24810704; fax (2) 24810850; internet www.albatros.cz; f. 1949; literature for children and young people; Dir MARTIN SLAVÍK.

Kalich, evangelické nakladatelství (Evangelical Publishing House): Jungmannova 9, 111 21 Prague 1; tel. (2) 2350342; fax (2) 2357594; f. 1920; Dir Ing. JAN RYBÁŘ.

Kartografie Praha, a.s.: Fr. Křížka 1, 170 30 Prague 7; tel. (2) 375541; fax (2) 375555; f. 1954; cartographic publishing and printing house; Dir Ing. JIŘÍ KUČERA.

Kruh (Circle): Dlouhá 108, 500 21 Hradec Králové; tel. (49) 22076; f. 1966; regional literature, fiction and general; Dir Dr JAN DVOŘÁK.

Melantrich: Václavské nám. 36, 112 12 Prague 1; tel. (2) 22093215; fax (2) 24213176; f. 1919; general, fiction, humanities, newspapers and magazines; Dir MILAN HORSKÝ.

Mladá fronta (Young Front): Radlická 61, 150 02 Prague 5; tel. (2) 51550008; fax (2) 51554014; e-mail prodej@mfnakl.cz; f. 1945; fiction, history, poetry, popular science, magazines; Dir VLADIMÍR PISTORIUS.

Nakladatelství dopravy a spojů (Transport and Communications): Hybernská 5, 115 78 Prague 1; tel. (2) 2365774; fax (2) 2356772; Dir Ing. ALOIS HOUDEK.

Nakladatelství Svoboda (Freedom): Na Florenci 3, POB 704, 113 03 Prague 1; tel. (2) 24224705; fax (2) 24226026; f. 1945 as the publishing house of the Communist Party; restructured in 1992–94 as a limited company; in voluntary liquidation since Sept. 1997; politics, history, philosophy, fiction, general; Dir STEFAN SZERYŃSKI.

Odeon: Prague; tel. (2) 24225248; fax (2) 24225262; f. 1953; literature, poetry, fiction (classical and modern), literary theory, art books, reproductions; Dir MILUŠE SLAPNIČKOVÁ.

Olympia: Klimentská 1, 110 15 Prague 1; tel. (2) 24810146; fax (2) 2315192; e-mail olympia@mbox.vol.cz; f. 1954; sports, tourism, encyclopaedias, fiction, illustrated books; Dir Ing. KAREL ZELNÍČEK.

Panton: Radlická 99, 150 00 Prague 5; tel. and fax (2) 548627; f. 1958; publishing house of the Czech Musical Fund; books on music, sheet music, records; Dir KAREL ČERNÝ.

Práce (Labour): Václavské nám. 17, 112 58 Prague 1; tel. (2) 24009100; fax (2) 2320989; f. 1945; trade-union movement, fiction, general, periodicals; Dir JANA SCHMIDTOVÁ.

Rapid, a.s.: 28. října 13, 112 79 Prague 1; tel. (2) 24195111; fax (2) 2327520; advertising; Dir-Gen. ČESTMÍR ČEJKA.

Severočeské nakladatelství (North Bohemian Publishing House): Ústí nad Labem; tel. (47) 28581; regional literature, fiction and general; Dir JIŘÍ SVEJDA.

Státní pedagogické nakladatelství: Ostrovní 30, 113 01 Prague 1; tel. and fax (2) 24912206; f. 1775; state publishing house; school and university textbooks, dictionaries, literature; Dir MILAN KOVÁŘ.

Vyšehrad: Bartolomějská 9, 110 00 Prague 1; tel. (2) 2326851; fax (2) 268390; e-mail vysehrad@login.cz; f. 1934; religion, philosophy, history, fiction; Dir PRAVOMIL NOVÁK; Chief Editor VLASTA HESOUNOVÁ.

PUBLISHERS' ASSOCIATION

Association of Czech Booksellers and Publishers: Jana Masaryka 56, 120 00 Prague 2; tel. (2) 90030150; fax (2) 22513198; e-mail sckn@mbox.vol.cz; internet www.sckn.cz; f. 1879; Chair. JAROSLAV CÍSAŘ.

WRITERS' UNION

Society of Writers (Obec spisovatelů): POB 669, 111 21 Prague 1; tel. and fax (2) 22220106; e-mail obecspis@volny.cz; f. 1989; 700 mems; Dir ANTONÍN JELÍNEK.

Broadcasting and Communications

TELECOMMUNICATIONS

Český Telecom: Olsanska 5, 130 00 Prague 3; tel. (2) 67142500; fax (2) 67142526; e-mail jindrich.trpisovsky@ct.cz; fmrly SPT Telecom, renamed 2000; partially privatized 1995; 33%-owned by Dutch/Swiss consortium; privatization completed in 2000; monopoly operator of long-distance and international services; Chair. of Bd ANDRÉ FRANS BESSEL KOK.

EuroTel: Sokolovská 225, POB 49, 190 00 Prague 9; tel. (2) 67011111; fax (2) 2327383; f. 1991; mobile telephone communications; launched GSM service July 1996; owned by SPT Telecom (51%) and West Atlantic (49%—consortium of US West and Bell Atlantic); Chief Exec. and Man. Dir EDWARD KINGMAN.

Český Mobil: Prague; 51% owned by Telesystem International Wireless (Canada); awarded licence to operate mobile telephone network in October 1999; Dir-Gen. ALEXANDER TOLSLTOY.

České Radiokomunikace, a.s.: U nákladového nádraži 4, 130 00 Prague 3; tel. (2) 67005119; fax (2) 6919292; e-mail l.stary@cra.cz;

internet www.cra.cz; f. 1994; privatized 2000; Dir-Gen. MIROSLAV CURÍN.

Contactel: Vinohradská 174, 130 19 Prague 3; tel. (2) 33011111; fax (2) 33011112; e-mail press@contact.cz; internet www.contactel .cz; f. 1999; owned by České Radiokomunikace, a.s. (50%) and Tele Danmark A/S (50%); internet, data and voice services; Chief Exec. MICHAL ČUPA.

Czech RadioMobil, a.s.: Prague; owned by České Radiokomunikace, a.s. (51%) and an international consortium, C-Mobil (49%); awarded 20-year licence to operate mobile telephone network in April 1996; launched GSM service Sept. 1996; Gen. Dir KLAUS TEBBE.

RADIO

The national networks include Radio Prague (medium wave and VHF), Radio Vltava (VHF from Prague—programmes on Czech and world culture), Radio Regina (medium and VHF—programme of regional studios), and Interprogramme (medium and VHF—for foreign visitors to the Czech Republic, in English, German and French).

Local stations broadcast from Prague (Central Bohemian Studio), Brno, České Budějovice, Hradec Králové, Ostrava, Plzeň, Ústí nad Labem and other towns. By August 1993 44 private stations had been licensed, 37 of which were in operation (14 in Prague).

Český rozhlas (Czech Radio): Vinohradská 12, 120 99 Prague 2; tel. (2) 24094111; fax (2) 24222223; e-mail cr@radio.cz; internet www.radio.cz; 4 nation-wide stations; Dir-Gen. VÁCLAV KASÍK.

Country Radio: Zenklova 34, 180 00 Prague 8; tel. (2) 5102411; fax (2) 51024224; e-mail country@ecn.cz; internet www.ecn.cz/country; commercial station; Man. Dir ZDENĚK PETERA.

Evropa 2: Nádrazní 56, 150 05 Prague 5, tel. (2) 57001808; fax (2) 57001807; e-mail info@evropa2.cz; internet www.evropa2.cz; commercial station; Pres. MICHAEL FLEISCHMANN.

Frekvence 1: Nádrazní 56, 150 05 Prague 5; tel. (2) 57001900; fax (2) 57314186; e-mail info@frekvence1.cz; internet www .frekvence1.cz; commercial station; Pres. MICHAEL FLEISCHMANN.

Radio Alfa: Na Poříčí 12, 110 00 Prague 1; tel. (2) 24872822; fax (2) 24872823; commercial station; Man. Dir V. KASÍK.

Radio FM Plus: POB 40, 320 90 Plzeň; tel. (19) 276666; fax (19) 7422221; e-mail info@fmplus.cz; internet www.fmplus.cz; commercial station; Dir ZBYNĚK SUCHÝ.

Radio Free Europe/Radio Liberty: Vinohradská 1, 110 00 Prague 1; fax (2) 21123420; internet www.rferl.org; broadcasts in 23 languages.

TELEVISION

In 2000 there were five main television stations: the two state-run channels, ČT1 and ČT2, reached 98% and 71% of the population, respectively, while two private commercial stations, Nova TV and Prima TV, were received by 99% and approximately 50%, respectively. TV3, which began broadcasting in May 2000, was initially received by some 30% of the population and aimed to reach 45% by the end of that year.

Česká televize (Czech Television): Kavčí hory, 140 70 Prague 4; tel. (2) 61131111; fax (2) 6927202; e-mail jakub.puchalsky@ czech-tv.cz; internet www.czech-tv.cz; f. 1992; state-owned; two channels; studios in Prague, Brno and Ostrava; Dir-Gen. JIRI BALVIN (acting).

Nova TV: Vladislavova 20, 113 13 Prague 1; tel. (2) 21100111; fax (2) 21100565; f. 1994; 93.5%-owned by Central European Media Enterprises; the first independent commercial station.

Prima TV: Na Žertvách 24, 180 00 Prague 8; tel. (2) 66100111; fax (2) 66100201; e-mail kvizova@prima-televize.cz; internet www .prima-televize.cz; f. 1993; Gen. Dir. KATEŘINA FRIČOVÁ.

TV3: Prague; e-mail info@tv3.cz; internet www.tv3.cz; f. 2000; independent commercial station; Dir JAN OBERMAN.

Finance

(cap. = capital; res = reserves; dep. = deposits; m. = million;
brs = branches; amounts in Czech koruny)

BANKING

With the establishment of independent Czech and Slovak Republics on 1 January 1993, the State Bank of Czechoslovakia was divided and its functions were transferred to the newly-created Czech National Bank and National Bank of Slovakia. The Czech National Bank is independent of the Government.

At 31 December 1998 there were 45 banks actively operating in the Czech Republic, with combined total assets of 2,437,915m. Czech koruny.

Central Bank

Czech National Bank (Česká národní banka): Na Příkopě 28, 115 03 Prague 1; tel. (2) 24411111; fax (2) 24413708; e-mail pavel .zubek@cnb.cz; internet www.cnb.cz; f. 1993; bank of issue, the central authority of the Czech Republic in the monetary sphere, legislation and foreign exchange permission; central bank for directing and securing monetary policy, supervision of activities of other banks and savings banks; cap. 1,400m., res 8,935m., dep. 339,552m. (Dec. 1999); Gov. ZDENĚK TŮMA; 7 brs.

Commercial Banks

Banka Haná, a.s.: Prikop 8, POB 58, 602 00 Brno; tel. (5) 42219549; fax (5) 45215969; internet www.bhan.cz; f. 1990; cap. 5,101.2m., res 3,177.9m., dep. 17,506.7m. (Dec. 1998); Chair. STANSLAV ZALMANEK; 2 brs.

Československá obchodní banka, a.s. (CSOB) (Czechoslovak Commercial Bank): Na Příkopě 14, 115 20 Prague 1; tel. (2) 24111111; fax (2) 24225049; e-mail webmaster@csob.cz; internet www.csob.cz; f. 1965; 66% state holding purchased by KBC Bank (Belgium) May 1999; commercial and foreign-trade transactions; cap. 5,105m., res 19,591m., dep. 210,611m. (Dec. 1999); Chair. and Gen. Man. PAVEL KAVÁNEK; 34 brs.

Investiční a Poštovní banka, a.s.: Senovážné nám. 32, POB 819, 114 03 Prague 1; tel. (2) 22041111; fax (2) 24244035; e-mail info@ipb.cz; internet www.ipb.cz; f. 1990; 36% state holding purchased by Nomura (Japan) March 1998; placed under central-bank administration and subsequently transferred to ownership of CSOB in June 2000; cap. 13,383m., res 1,755m., dep. 231,135m. (Dec. 1998); Chair. and Gen. Man. JAN KLACEK; 157 brs.

Komerční banka, a.s.: Na Příkopě 33, POB 839, 114 07 Prague 1; tel. (2) 22433020; fax (2) 24243020; e-mail group_strategy@koba.cz; internet www.koba.cz; f. 1990; 49% state-owned; scheduled for privatization in 2000; cap. 16,604m., res 1,172m., dep. 345,327m. (Dec. 1999); Chair. and Chief Exec. RADOVAN VÁVRA; 354 brs.

Konsolidační banka Praha, s.p.ú.: Janovského 438/2, 170 06 Prague 7; tel. (2) 20141111; fax (2) 33370033; e-mail kobp@ms.aned.cz; internet www.kopb.cz; f. 1991; cap. 5,950m., res 942.9m., dep. 106,661.5m. (Dec. 1998); Chair. KAMIL ZIEGLER.

Union banka, a.s.: ul. 30. dubna č. 35, 702 00 Ostrava; tel. (69) 6108111; fax (69) 211586; e-mail union@union.cz; internet www.union.cz; f. 1991; cap. 2,444m., dep. 21,591m. (Dec. 1999); Pres., Chair. and Gen. Man. JIŘÍ BABIS; 101 brs.

Volksbank CZ, a.s.: M-Palác Herspická 5, POB 226, 658 26 Brno; tel. (5) 43525111; fax (5) 43525555; e-mail mail@volksbank.cz; cap. 650.0m., res 15.2m., dep. 6,636.1m. (Dec. 1999); Chair. JOHANN LURF.

Foreign and Joint-Venture Banks

Bank Austria Creditanstalt Czech Republic, a.s.: Revoluční 7, 110 15 Prague 1; tel. (2) 22853111; fax (2) 24827337; e-mail cabra@creditanstalt.co.at; internet www.ba-ca.cz; f. 1998 by merger of Bank Austria, a.s. and Creditanstalt, a.s.; shareholders: Bank Austria Creditanstalt International AG, Vienna (89.1%), CARIPLO SpA, Milan (10.9%); cap. 1,997m., res 1,145.5m., dep. 50,745.0m. (Dec. 1999); Chair. of Bd MANFRED MEIER; 15 brs.

BNP—Dresdner Bank (ČR), a.s.: Vítězná 1, POB 229, 150 00 Prague 5; tel. (2) 57006111; fax (2) 57006200; internet www .bnp-dresdner-bank.cz; f. 1991; ownership: Banque Nationale de Paris (50%), Dresdner Bank (50%); cap. and res 1,448m., dep. 5,479m. (Dec. 1997); Chair. and Gen. Man. ROLF D. BECK.

Citibank, a.s.: Evropská 178, 166 40 Prague 6; tel. (2) 24304111; fax (2) 24304613; f. 1991; wholly-owned subsidiary of Citibank Overseas Investment Corpn (Delaware, USA); cap. 1,825m., res 1,597m., dep. 31,149m. (Dec. 1998); Gen. Man. AKSHAYA BHARGAVA; 6 brs.

Crédit Lyonnais Bank Praha, a.s.: Ovocný trh 8, 117 19 Prague 1; tel. (2) 22076111; fax (2) 22076119; wholly-owned subsidiary of Crédit Lyonnais Global Banking, Paris; cap. 500m., res 416m., dep. 32,495m. (Dec. 1997); Chair. and Gen. Man. HEINRICH SITTLER.

Erste Bank Sparkassen (ČR), a.s.: Václavské nám. 56, POB 749, 110 00 Prague 1; tel. (2) 21010202; fax (2) 21010406; e-mail erste@erstebank.cz; internet www.erstebank.cz; f. 1993; fmrly Girocredit-Sparkassen Banka Praha, a.s.; cap. 700m., res 105m., dep. 23,784m. (Dec. 1999); Chair. and Gen. Man. Dr WILHELM REICHMANN; 6 brs.

GE Capital bank, a.s.: Vyskočilova 1422, BB Centrum, 140 28 Prague 4; tel. (2) 24441111; fax (2) 24441500; internet www.gecb.cz; f. 1998 from purchase of Agrobanka Praha, a.s.; wholly-owned by GE Capital International Holdings Corpn, Wilmington; cap. 510m., res. 5,150.9m., dep. 33,082.8m. (Dec. 1999); Chair. and Gen. Man. PETR ŠMÍDA; 81 brs.

HypoVereinsbank CZ, a.s.: Italská 24, POB 70, Prague 2; tel. (2) 22091111; fax (2) 22251158; f. 1999 by merger of HYPO-BANK CZ, as and Vereinsbank CZ, as; wholly-owned subsidiary of Bayerische Hypo-und Vereinsbank AG, Munich; cap. 5,047.0m., res 1,544.4m.,

dep. 42,954.5m.; Exec. Mems of Bd HANS-PETER HORSTER, Dr KAREL KRATINA, DAVID SVOJITKA.

Interbanka, a.s.: Václavské nám. 40, 110 00 Prague 1; tel. (2) 24406215; fax (2) 24227333; e-mail fi@interbanka.cz; f. 1991; cap. 1,709m., res 21m., dep. 1,864m. (Dec. 2000); Chair. and Chief Exec. VLADIMÍR KOLMAN.

Raiffeisenbank, as: Vodičkova 38, 111 21 Prague 1; tel. (2) 24231270; fax (2) 24231278; e-mail raiffeisenbank@rb.cz; internet www.rb.cz; f. 1993; cap. 1,000m., res 69.5m., dep. 28,003.5m. (Dec. 1999); Chair. and Gen. Man. JAN VLACHÝ.

Živnostenská banka, a.s.: Na Příkopě 20, POB 421, 113 80 Prague 1; tel. (2) 24121111; fax (2) 24125555; e-mail info@ziba.cz; internet www.ziba.cz; f. 1868; cap. 362m., dep. 26,637m. (Dec. 1999); Chair. of Bd and Gen. Man. JIŘÍ KUNERT; 8 brs.

Savings Bank

Czech Savings Bank (Česká spořitelna, a.s.): Olbrachtova 62, POB 838, 140 00 Prague 4; tel. (2) 61073492; fax (2) 61073006; e-mail csas@csas.cz; internet www.csas.cz; f. 1825; 52% holding purchased by Erste Bank AG (Austria) in February 2000; accepts deposits and issues loans; 12,374,657 depositors (Sept. 1998); cap. 15,200m., res 7,644m., dep. 333,400m. (Dec. 1999); Chair. and Chief Exec. JOHN JACK STACK; 876 brs.

Bankers' Organization

Association of Banks, Prague: Vodičkova 30, 110 00 Prague 1; tel. (2) 24225926; fax (2) 24225957; e-mail bank.asociace@mbox.vol.cz.

STOCK EXCHANGE

Prague Stock Exchange (Burza cenných papírů Praha, a.s.): Rybná 14, 110 00 Prague 1; tel. (2) 21832116; fax (2) 21833040; f. 1992; Man. Dir JIŘÍ HUEBNER.

Regulatory Authority

Czech Securities Commission: Prague; f. 1998; Chair. FRANTIŠEK JAKUB.

INSURANCE

Czech Association of Insurers: f. 1994; 27 members.

Co-operative Insurance Company (Kooperativa, pojišťovna, a.s.): Templová 5, 110 01 Prague 1; tel. (2) 21000111; fax (2) 2322633; e-mail info@koop.cz; internet www.koop.cz; f. 1993; Chair. and Gen. Man. Ing. VLADIMÍR MRÁZ.

Czech Insurance and Reinsurance Corporation (Česká pojišťovna, a.s.): Spálená 16, 113 04 Prague 1; tel. (2) 24051111; fax (2) 24052200; e-mail murban@cpoj.cz; internet www.cpoj.cz; f. 1827; many home brs and some agencies abroad; issues life, accident, fire, aviation, industrial and marine policies, all classes of reinsurance; Lloyd's agency; Chair. of Bd. IVAN KOČÁRNÍK; Gen. Man. LADISLAV BARTONÍČEK.

Trade and Industry

GOVERNMENT AGENCIES

Czech Trade Promotion Agency (Česká agentura na podporu obchodu): Vittrichova 21, POB 76, 128 01 Prague 2; tel. (2) 24907500; fax (2) 24907503; e-mail info@czechtrade.cz; internet www .czechtrade.cz; Gen. Dir MARTIN TLAPA.

Česká agentura pro zahraniční investice (CzechInvest): Štěpánská 15, 120 00 Prague 2; tel. (2) 96342500; fax (2) 96342501; e-mail marketing@czechinvest.com; internet www.czechinvest.com; f. 1992; foreign investment agency; Dir Ing. MARTIN JAHN.

National Property Fund: Rašínovo nábřeží 42, 128 00 Prague 2; tel. (2) 24991285; fax (2) 24991379; responsible for state property and state-owned companies in the period up to their privatization; Chair. JAN STIESS.

CHAMBER OF COMMERCE

Economic Chamber of the Czech Republic (Hospodářská komora České republiky): Argentinská 38, 170 05 Prague 7; tel. (2) 66794939; fax (2) 875438; f. 1850; has almost 20,000 members (trading corporations, industrial enterprises, banks and private enterprises); Chair. Dr ZDENĚK SOMR.

EMPLOYERS' ORGANIZATIONS

Association of Entrepreneurs of the Czech Republic (Sdružení podnikatelů České republiky): Škrétova 6/44, 120 59 Prague 2; tel. and fax (2) 24230572; Chair. RUDOLF BARÁNEK.

Confederation of Industry of the Czech Republic (Svaz průmyslu a dopravy České republiky): Mikulandská 7, 113 61 Prague 1; tel. (2) 24915679; fax (2) 24919311; e-mail spcr@spcr.cz; internet www.spcr.cz; f. 1990; Dir-Gen. ZDENĚK LIŠKA.

UTILITIES

Electricity

Central Bohemian Electricity Distribution Company (Středočeská Energetická—STE a.s.): Na Přikopě 15, 113 20 Prague 1; tel. (2) 24224469; fax (2) 24216424; e-mail ste-ucebna@ste.cz.

ČEZ (České Energeticke Zavody): Hlavni Sprava, Jungmannova 29, 111 48 Prague 1; tel. (2) 24081111; fax (2) 24082440; 68% state-owned, privatization planned for 2000–02; production co; Gen. Man. JAVOSLAV MILMBA; 8,800 employees.

Dukovany Nuclear Power Plant: ČEZ, a.s., JE Dukovany, 675 50, Dukovany; tel. (618) 811111; fax (618) 866360; e-mail sedlaj2.edu@mail.cez.cz; Dir JOSEF SEDLAK.

East Bohemian Electricity Company (Východočeská Energetika—VCE): Sladovského 215, 501 03 Hradec Králové; tel. (49) 5841111; fax (49) 30150; Chair. and Chief Exec. PETR ZEMAN.

North Bohemian Electricity (Severočeská Energetika—SČE a.s.): Teplická 8, 405 49 Děčín IV; tel. (412) 571111; fax (412) 572977; Chair. JIŘÍ ŠTASTNÝ.

North Moravian Electricity (Severomoravská Energetika—SME a.s.): 709 02 Ostrava; tel. (69) 6671111; fax (69) 6611187; distribution co; Dir Gen. TOMÁŠ HÜNER.

Opatovice Electricity (Elektrarny Opatovice a.s.): Pardubice 0, 532 13 Opatovice nad Labem; tel. (40) 6841111; fax (40) 6536010; f. 1905; generation and distribution co; 48% owned by National Power (United Kingdom); Chair. and Man. Dir ARNOŠT POUL.

South Bohemian Electricity (Jihočeská Energetika—JČE a.s.): Lannova 16, 370 49 České Budějovice; tel. (38) 7312682; fax (38) 59803; e-mail kan@jee.anet.cz; majority-owned by Bayernwerk (Germany) and Raiffesenlandesbank (Austria); Pres. and Gen. Dir JAN ŠPIKA.

South Moravian Electricity (Jihomoravska Energetika—JME): Lidicka 36, POB 344, 659 44 Brno; tel. (5) 45141111; fax (5) 45142551; e-mail jme@jme.cz; internet www.jme.cz; f. 1994; Man. Dir ZDENĚK MACHALA.

State Office for Nuclear Safety (Státni úřad pro jadernou bezpečnost): Senovážné nám. 9, 110 00 Prague 1; tel. (2) 21624111; fax (2) 21624396; internet www.sujb.cz; state supervision of nuclear safety, co-ordination of international relations in the sphere of nuclear safety; Chair. DANA DRÁBOVÁ.

Gas

North Moravian Gas (Severomoravsjká Plynárenská—SMP): distribution co; Man. Dir LIBOR JURICEK.

South Moravian Gas Company (Jihomoravská plynárenská—JMP a.s.): Plynárenská 1, 657 02 Brno; tel. (5) 45548111; fax (5) 578571; e-mail jmpbrno@jmpbrno.cz; internet www.jmpbrno.cz; distribution co; Chair. LIBOR MARTÍNEK.

Transgas/Český Plynárensky Podnik: Limuzská 12, 100 98 Prague 10; tel. (2) 70771111; fax (2) 70776930; f. 1971; state-owned, privatization planned for 2000–02; import and distribution co; Man. Dir MIROSLAV GREC.

Water

Prazske Vodovody a Kanalizace a.s.: Narodni 13, 112 65 Prague; tel. (2) 57320132; fax (2) 57535011; e-mail info@pvk.cz; internet www.pvk.cz; f. 1998; water supply and sewerage co; privatized in 2000.

TRADE UNIONS

Czech-Moravian Confederation of Trade Unions (Českomoravská konfederace odborových svazů): nám. W. Churchilla 2, 113 59 Prague 3; tel. (2) 24461111; fax (2) 22718994; f. 1990; 30 affiliated unions (1999); Pres. RICHARD FALBR.

Affiliated unions include the following:

Czech-Moravian Trade Union of Workers in Education (Českomoravský odborový svaz školství): nám. W. Churchilla 2, 113 59 Prague 3; tel. (2) 24226491; fax (2) 24218010; Pres. JAROSLAV RÖSSLER; 164,000 mems.

Trade Union of the Health Service and Social Care of the Czech Republic (Odborový svaz zdravotnictví a sociální péče ČR): Koněvova 54, 130 00 Prague 3; tel. (2) 22714629; fax (2) 22718211; e-mail osz_cr@cmkos.cz; internet www.osz.cmkos.cz; Pres. JIŘÍ SCHLANGER; 65,000 mems.

Trade Union of Workers in Textile, Clothing and Leather Industry of Bohemia and Moravia (Odborový svaz pracovníků textilního, oděvního a kožedělného průmyslu Čech a Moravy): nám. W. Churchilla 2, 113 59 Prague 3; tel. (2) 24222123; fax (2) 273589; Pres. KAREL NOCOTNY; 79,600 mems.

Trade Union of Workers in Woodworking Industry, Forestry and Management of Water Supplies in the Czech Republic (Odborový svaz pracovníků dřevozpracujícího odvětví, lesního a vodního hospodářství v České republice): nám. W. Churchilla 2, 113 59 Prague 3; tel. (2) 24462659; fax (2) 22716373; e-mail kyncl.rudolf@cmkos.cz; Pres. RUDOLF KYNCL; 43,000 mems.

TU UNIOS: nám. W. Churchilla 2, 113 59 Prague 3; tel. (2) 24463172; fax (2) 24463185; f. 1994 to succeed Czech-Moravian Trade Union of Workers in Services (f. 1990); Pres. KAREL SLADKOVSKÝ; 38,000 mems.

Transport

RAILWAYS

In 1998 the total length of the Czech railway network was 9,430 km.

České dráhy (Czech Railways): nábř. L. Svobody 12, 110 15 Prague 1; tel. (2) 51431111; fax (2) 24812569; internet www.cdrail.cz; f. 1993, as successor to Czechoslovak State Railways; Gen. Dir Ing. DALIBOR ZELENÝ.

Prague Metropolitan Railway: Dopravní podnik hlavního města Prahy, a.s.-Metro, o.z., Sliačská 1, 141 41 Prague 4; tel. (2) 71763657; fax (2) 764762; e-mail pavlicar@dp-praha.cz; the Prague underground railway opened in 1974, and in 1998 50km were operational; 50 stations; Chair. M. HEJL; Gen. Dir Ing. LADISLAV HOUDEK.

ROADS

In 1998 there were an estimated 54,895 km of roads (not including local roads) in the Czech Republic, including 498 km of motorways.

INLAND WATERWAYS

The total length of navigable waterways in the Czech Republic is 663.6 km. The Elbe (Labe) and its tributary, the Vltava, connect the Czech Republic with the North Sea via the port of Hamburg (Germany). The Oder provides a connection with the Baltic Sea and the port of Szczecin (Poland). The Czech Republic's river ports are Prague Holešovice, Prague Radotín, Kolín, Mělník, Ústí nad Labem and Děčín, on the Vltava and Elbe.

Czechoslovak Elbe Navigation Ltd (Československá plavba labská, a.s.): K. Čapka 1, 405 91 Děčín; tel. (412) 561111; fax (412) 510140; f. 1922; river transport of goods to Germany, Poland, the Netherlands, Belgium, Luxembourg, France and Switzerland; Man. Dir KAREL HORYNA.

SHIPPING

Since August 1997 no ships have operated under the Czech flag. All Czech-owned ships operate under the Maltese and Cypriot flags.

Czech Ocean Shipping, Joint-Stock Company (Česká námořní plavba, akciová společnost): Počernická 168, 100 99 Prague 10; tel. (2) 778941; fax (2) 773962; e-mail coscompu@login.cz; internet www.cos.cz; f. 1959; six ships totalling 199,331 dwt; Man. Dir Capt. PAVEL TRNKA.

CIVIL AVIATION

There are main civil airports at Prague (Ruzyně), Brno, Karlovy Vary and Ostrava, operated by the Czech Airport Administration. The opening of a new terminal at Ruzyně in November 1997 increased the airport's capacity from 2.3m. passengers to 4.8m.

Air Ostrava: Ostrava International Airport, 742 51 Mosnov; tel. (69) 6659401; fax (69) 6659402; e-mail air.ostrava@ova.prtnet.cz; internet www.airostrava.cz; f. 1994; services to international, regional and domestic destinations; Pres. MILAN ROUSÁN; Man. Dir PAVEL HRADEC.

ČSA (České aerolinie, a.s.) (Czech Airlines): Ruzyně Airport, 160 08 Prague 6; tel. (2) 20111111; fax (2) 20562266; e-mail info@uit.csa.cz; internet www.csa.cz; f. 1923; external services to most European capitals, the Near, Middle and Far East, North Africa and North America; scheduled for privatization; Pres. MIROSLAV KULA.

Tourism

The Czech Republic has magnificent scenery, with summer and winter sports facilities. Prague, Kutna Hora, Olomouc, Český Krumlov and Telč are among the best known of the historic towns, and there are famous castles and cathedrals and numerous resorts, as well as spas with natural mineral springs at Karlovy Vary (Carlsbad) and Mariánské Lázně (Marienbad). Registered accommodation establishments recorded some 5.6m. stays of at least one night by foreigners in 1999. In 1998 tourism receipts totalled US $3,792m.

Czech Tourist Authority: Vinohradská 46, POB 32, 120 41 Prague 2; tel. (2) 22515078; fax (2) 24257145; e-mail kejvalova@cccr-cta.cz; internet www.visitczech.cz; f. 1993; Dir KAREL NEJDL.

Čedok Travel Corpn: Na Příkopě 18, 111 35 Prague 1; tel. (2) 24197111; fax (2) 2321656; internet www.cedok.cz; f. 1920; 80 domestic travel offices; eight branches throughout Europe; Pres. ČESTMÍR SAJDA.

DENMARK

Introductory Survey

Location, Climate, Language, Religion, Flag, Capital

The Kingdom of Denmark is situated in northern Europe. It consists of the peninsula of Jutland, the islands of Zealand, Funen, Lolland, Falster and Bornholm, and 401 smaller islands. The country lies between the North Sea, to the west, and the Baltic Sea, to the east. Denmark's only land frontier is with Germany, to the south. Norway lies to the north of Denmark, across the Skagerrak, while Sweden, whose most southerly region is separated from Zealand by a narrow strait, lies to the north-east. Outlying territories of Denmark are Greenland and the Faroe Islands in the North Atlantic Ocean. Denmark is low-lying and the climate is temperate, with mild summers and cold, rainy winters. The language is Danish. Almost all of the inhabitants profess Christianity: the Evangelical Lutheran Church, to which some 85% of the population belong, is the established Church, and there are also small communities of other Protestant groups and of Roman Catholics. The national flag (proportions 37 by 28) displays a white cross on a red background, the upright of the cross being to the left of centre. The capital is Copenhagen (København).

Recent History

In 1945, following the end of German wartime occupation, Denmark recognized the independence of Iceland, which had been declared in the previous year. Home rule was granted to the Faroe Islands in 1948 and to Greenland in 1979. Denmark was a founder member of the North Atlantic Treaty Organization (NATO, see p. 241) in 1949 and of the Nordic Council (see p. 237) in 1952. In January 1973, following a referendum, Denmark entered the European Communities (including the EEC), later more commonly referred to as simply the European Community (EC), and from 1993 restyled as the European Union (EU, see p. 181).

In 1947 King Frederik IX succeeded to the throne on the death of his father, Christian X. Denmark's Constitution was radically revised in 1953: new provisions allowed for female succession to the throne, abolished the upper house of Parliament and amended the franchise. King Frederik died in January 1972, and his eldest daughter, Margrethe, became the first queen to rule Denmark for nearly 600 years.

The system of proportional representation which is embodied in the 1953 Constitution makes it difficult for a single party to gain a majority in the Folketing (Parliament). The Liberal Party's minority Government, led by Poul Hartling and formed in 1973, was followed in 1975 by a minority Social Democratic Government under Anker Jørgensen. Jørgensen led various coalitions and minority Governments until 1982. General elections in 1977, 1979 and 1981 were held against a background of growing unemployment and attempts to tighten control of the economy. By September 1982 Jørgensen's economic policy, including attempts to reduce the budget deficit by introducing new taxes, had once more led to disagreements within the Cabinet, and the Government resigned.

The Conservative People's Party, which had been absent from Danish coalitions since 1971, formed a centre-right four-party Government (with the Liberals, the Centre Democrats and the Christian People's Party), led by Poul Schlüter, who became Denmark's first Conservative Prime Minister since 1894. Holding only 66 of the Folketing's 179 seats, the coalition narrowly avoided defeat in October 1982, when it introduced stringent economic measures, and again in September 1983, when larger reductions in public spending were proposed. In December the right-wing Progress Party withdrew its support for further cuts in expenditure, and the Government was defeated. A general election to the Folketing was held in January 1984, and Schlüter's Government remained in office, with its component parties holding a total of 77 seats, and relying on the support of the Social Liberal members.

In January 1986 the left-wing parties in the Folketing combined to reject the ratification by Denmark of the Single European Act (which amended the Treaty of Rome—the agreement that founded the EC—so as to establish the EC's single market and allow the EC Council of Ministers to take decisions by a qualified majority vote if a unanimous one was not achieved). Opponents of ratification, led by the Social Democrats, argued that it would lead to a diminution of Denmark's power to maintain strict environmental controls. In a national referendum in February, however, 56.2% of the votes cast were in favour of ratification, and the Folketing formally approved it in May.

At a general election held in September 1987 Schlüter's coalition retained only 70 seats in the Folketing while the opposition Social Democrats lost two of their 56 seats. Jørgensen later resigned as leader of the latter party. Several of the smaller and extremist parties made considerable gains, with the result that the outgoing coalition was weakened, while the main opposition parties were unable to command a working majority. Schlüter eventually formed a new Cabinet comprising representatives of the former four-party governing coalition. However, the Social Liberals had earlier declared that they would not support any administration that depended on the support of the Progress Party. This therefore left a precarious balance of power within the Folketing.

In April 1988 the Folketing adopted an opposition-sponsored resolution requiring the Government to inform visiting warships of the country's ban on nuclear weapons. The British and US Governments were highly critical of the resolution. Schlüter therefore announced an early general election for May 1988, on the issue of Denmark's membership of NATO and defence policy. For the main parties the election result was inconclusive, and negotiations lasting three weeks were necessary before Schlüter was appointed to seek a basis for viable government. At the beginning of June a new minority coalition, comprising members of the Conservative People's Party, Liberals and Social Liberals, formed a Cabinet under Schlüter. The new Government restored good relations with its NATO allies by adopting a formula that requested all visiting warships to respect Danish law in its territorial waters, while making no specific reference to nuclear weapons.

The Government proposed large reductions in social welfare provision for 1989, and attacked Progress Party demands for less taxation as unrealistic. The Progress Party, however, continued to increase in popularity, and in November 1989 its share of the vote rose significantly in municipal elections, while the Conservative People's Party lost support. The Government therefore proposed to reduce the rates of taxation in 1990, despite Social Democratic opposition to the accompanying decreases in welfare expenditure. An early general election was organized for December 1990. Although the Social Democrats retained the largest share of the vote (winning an additional 14 seats to bring their total to 69), Schlüter formed a minority coalition Government, comprising the Conservative People's Party, which had lost five seats in the election, and the Liberals, who had gained an additional seven seats. As expected, the Social Liberals, while no longer part of the Government, continued to support the majority of the new coalition Government's policies.

In May 1992 the Folketing voted, by 130 votes to 25, to approve the Treaty on European Union (the Maastricht Treaty), which further expanded the scope of the Treaty of Rome. In a referendum held in Denmark in June, however, 50.7% of those who participated voted against ratification of the Treaty, compared with 49.3% in favour. This unexpected result caused consternation among Denmark's European partners, and during the rest of the year discussions took place among representatives of EC countries, who sought to establish a formula that, without necessitating the renegotiation of the Treaty, would allow the Danish Government to conduct a second referendum with some hope of success. In December EC heads of government agreed that Denmark should be allowed exemption from certain provisions of the Treaty, namely the final stage of European monetary union (including the adoption of a single currency); participation in a common defence policy; common European citizenship; and co-operation in legal and home affairs: all provisions that had been regarded as a threat to national sovereignty by Danish opponents of ratification. Despite uncertainty as to how far these exemptions were legally binding, the agreement was endorsed by seven of the eight parties represented in the Folketing (the exception being the Progress Party), and in a second referendum, held in May 1993, 56.7% of the votes were cast in favour of ratification and 43.3% against. In June 1994 the Government announced that it would seek an amendment to the Maastricht Treaty to ensure that environmental safety took precedence over European free-trade initiatives.

Meanwhile, in January 1993 Schlüter resigned from the premiership after a judicial inquiry disclosed that he had misled the Folketing in April 1989 over a scandal that had its origin in 1987, when the then Minister of Justice, Erik Ninn-Hansen, had illegally ordered civil servants to delay issuing entry visas to the families of Tamil refugees from Sri Lanka. In subsequent negotiations between political parties, Poul Nyrup Rasmussen, the leader of the Social Democrats, obtained enough support to form a new government, and in late January 1993 a majority coalition Government (the first majority Government in Denmark for 11 years, controlling 90 of the 179 seats in the legislature) took office: it comprised members of the Social Democrats and three small centre parties (the Social Liberals, the Centre Democrats and the Christian People's Party). The new Government gave priority to securing an affirmative vote for the Maastricht Treaty (see above).

In a general election in September 1994, three months earlier than scheduled, the Social Democrats won a reduced number of seats, although they retained the largest share of the vote. The Liberals, led by Uffe Ellemann-Jensen, gained an additional 13 seats, but the Christian People's Party, a member of the outgoing coalition, failed to secure representation in the new legislature. Rasmussen, however, was able to form a minority Government with his two remaining coalition partners, the Social Liberals and the Centre Democrats, and denied that the Government would be dependent for support on the left-wing Socialist People's Party. In December 1996, however, the Centre Democrats withdrew from the coalition, following the Government's decision to seek support from left-wing parties in order to achieve parliamentary approval for legislation relating to the 1997 budget.

In late October 1997 Thorkild Simonsen was appointed as the new Minister of the Interior and of Health, following mounting public concern at reports of increasingly high levels of immigration. As expected, a new government initiative was launched in December, enforcing stricter immigration policies.

The results of local elections conducted in November 1997 indicated that the Social Democrats, who received some 33% of the votes, were continuing to attract the largest share of popular support. In February 1998 Prime Minister Rasmussen announced that an early general election would be conducted on 11 March, six months before the expiry of the mandate of the incumbent Government and in advance of a referendum on the Amsterdam Treaty on European integration (drafted at a meeting of EU members in the Netherlands in June 1997), which was scheduled to be held in late May. Despite the fact that the Centre Democrats supported an electoral alliance comprising the Conservative People's Party and the Liberals in the election, Rasmussen's Government was returned to office with a narrow majority in the Folketing: the Social Democrats, together with their coalition partner the Social Liberals and other informal allies, secured a total of 90 seats, compared with 89 seats won by the centre-right opposition (led by Ellemann-Jensen). The right-wing Danish People's Party, which campaigned for stricter immigration controls, performed strongly in its first general election, winning 7.4% of the total votes (13 seats). Following his defeat in the general election, Ellemann-Jensen resigned as leader of the Liberals. Later in March a cabinet reshuffle was announced; a number of new ministers were appointed, although the most important portfolios remained unchanged.

On 28 May 1998 Danish voters narrowly endorsed the ratification of the Amsterdam Treaty by a margin of 55.1% votes in favour to 44.9% against. The referendum followed the rejection by the Danish Supreme Court early in the previous month of a legal challenge to the constitutional validity of the Maastricht Treaty, which had been brought by a group of private individuals who were opposed to further European integration.

Elections to the European Parliament were held in June 1999. The rate of voter participation in Denmark, at 50.5%, was marginally greater than the EU average of 49.4% but significantly lower than the rate of voter participation at the elections to the Folketing held in March 1998. The Liberals won the largest share of the votes in the European parliamentary elections, and increased their level of representation in the Parliament from four seats to five, while the Conservative People's Party performed badly (partly owing to the success of the extreme right-wing Danish People's Party, which won its first seat in the European Parliament) and lost two of its previously-held three seats. The Social Democrats retained their three seats in the Parliament, and the two anti-EU parties—the Danish People's Movement Against the European Union and the June Movement—together held on to four seats. The formal nomination by the European Commission's President-designate, Romano Prodi, in July 1999 of the Danish Minister of Development Co-operation, Poul Nielson, as the European Commissioner for Development and Humanitarian Aid prompted a reshuffle of the Cabinet later in the same month. Nielson was formally appointed to the European Commission post in September.

In early November 1999 serious rioting erupted in a district of Copenhagen which housed a high concentration of immigrants. The rioting, which was the most serious to occur in Denmark for six years, was reportedly provoked by the earlier announcement of a controversial judicial ruling, in accordance with which a man of Turkish origin became the first Danish-born person to receive an expulsion order from the country. (The man, convicted on charges of theft, had failed to apply for the Danish citizenship to which he was entitled.) The court decision was announced just days after the readmittance to the membership of the right-wing Progress Party of the party's founder, Mogens Glistrup, who was renowned for his vociferous opposition to immigration; Glistrup's extreme racist sentiments, expressed following the court ruling, led, later in November, to the resignation from the party of all four of its representatives in the Folketing, leaving the Progress Party with no parliamentary representation. (The four legislators subsequently founded a new political organization, Freedom 2000.)

In September 2000 the Government held a referendum to ascertain whether the population supported the adoption of the single European currency, the euro. Approval for the euro was strong when the referendum was called in May, but declined throughout the months preceding the vote, despite the support of the Government, most major political parties, the industrial sector, banks, trade unions, and the media. Opposition to the single currency came mainly from the far right, socialists in Copenhagen (mostly women working in the public sector), farmers, fishermen and monarchists from rural Jutland, with the support of old age pensioners throughout the country.

Campaigning in support of the single currency focused mainly on the possible economic disadvantages of rejecting the euro. These were expected to be lower economic growth, higher interest rates and rising unemployment. However, following a decline in the value of the euro during August and September 2000, opponents of the new currency adopted the same economic arguments with better effect. The currency's weakness, they claimed, could bring higher inflation, higher interest rates and lower real wages; with oil prices rising it could also lead to reductions in welfare benefits, particularly pensions. Shortly before the referendum, Rasmussen disclosed that the central bank had spent 10,000m. kroner (about £1,000m.) to maintain the value of the krone. The Minister of Finance, Mogens Lykketoft, announced that a vote to reject the euro would ultimately cost the country roughly 5,600m. kroner per year in extra borrowing costs (the krone is part of the exchange rate mechanism (ERM) and thus the Government is forced to intervene to keep its value within certain limits). However opponents of the euro claimed that Lykketoft was playing on public fears and cited a study by the Ministry of Finance admitting that such a vote would have no significant long-term effect. The Government also stressed the potential repercussions for Denmark should the country's rejection of the euro lead to the establishment of a so-called 'two-speed' Europe, where countries ready for further economic and political integration progressed independently of the rest.

The campaign against adoption of the single currency concentrated mainly on popular concerns that adopting the euro would diminish national identity and restrict Denmark's self-determination, which would adversely affect the generous Danish welfare system, notably its pension provision. In an attempt to refute these accusations, the Government pledged to guarantee the level of state pensions until 2045. Fears of interference from abroad in Danish affairs were exemplified for many by the imposition of EU sanctions against Austria, in protest at the presence of the far-right Freedom Party in Austria's Government. In late September, as popular support for the adoption of the euro dwindled, largely owing to the decline in value of the euro, it emerged that Rasmussen had been considering sending a letter to the 14 other EU Governments urging them to confirm that they would not interfere with Denmark's welfare system. He claimed that he had decided not to proceed because of resistance from other pro-euro parties, who thought such a letter would be counter-productive. The news that Rasmussen was even considering such action attracted adverse attention from the public, as did disagreements between various members of the campaign in favour of adopting the euro.

On 28 September 2000 Danish voters rejected membership of the single currency, with 53.1% opposed to the euro and 46.9% in favour; the rate of participation was 87.5%. The central bank raised interest rates by 0.5% to defend the krone; opposition parties claimed the move was politically motivated in order to vindicate scaremongering by supporters of the euro prior to the referendum. Rasmussen underlined the significance of the setback by arguing that Europe now needed to develop a new and clearer delineation between policies to be decided nationally and those to be determined at a community level. Indications of a shift in Denmark's European policy became apparent when the Minister of Foreign Affairs, Niels Helveg Petersen, intimated that Denmark was no longer opposed to the creation of a 'two-speed' Europe. Observers noted that the right-wing Danish People's Party, led by Pia Kjaersgaard, was the principal beneficiary of the referendum, which propelled the anti-immigration movement to the forefront of Danish politics.

A government reorganization took place in December 2000, prompted by the resignation of Petersen from the foreign affairs portfolio in protest at the result of the referendum on the euro and by the need to replace the Minister of Defence, Hans Hækkerup, who was appointed as head of the UN Mission in Kosovo. Five new ministers were appointed, some of whom were relatively inexperienced, in an attempt to revitalize the Government.

In March 2000 Svend Auken, the Minister of the Environment and Energy, called for a moratorium on the reprocessing of spent nuclear fuel after safety fears at the Sellafield nuclear reprocessing plant in the United Kingdom. Together with ministers from other Nordic countries and from Ireland, he put proposals before the Oslo Paris Convention (Ospar—an international convention signed in July 1998, which controls marine pollution in the Irish sea, north-east Atlantic and North Sea) at the beginning of June, calling for the end of nuclear reprocessing in Europe.

In August 1988 the Danish Government submitted a dispute with Norway, concerning maritime economic zones between Greenland and Jan Mayen island, to the International Court of Justice (ICJ) at The Hague. A delimitation line was fixed by the ICJ in June 1993. In 1991 the construction of a bridge across the Great Belt, between the Danish islands of Zealand and Funen, was the subject of an objection presented by Finland to the ICJ that the proposed bridge's clearance would not allow Finland to move oil-drilling rigs through the strait and would, therefore, be in contravention of Denmark's international treaty obligations to permit the free passage of shipping through the Great Belt. In September 1992, however, the ICJ was informed by the parties that the dispute had been settled, and construction of the bridge was completed in mid-1998.

In August 1991 Denmark and Sweden signed an agreement on the proposed construction of a 15.9-km road and rail system across the Oresund strait between Copenhagen and Malmö. Although construction was initially delayed, owing to objections raised by environmentalists in Sweden and Germany, the agreement was finally ratified by the Swedish Government in 1994 and the project was completed in July 2000 at a total cost of approximately 23,400m. kroner.

In May 1999 the Danish Government signed a maritime boundary agreement with representatives of the Faroese Landsstýri and the British Government, thus ending a 30-year dispute over the location of the boundaries of a 42,000 sq km-area in the North Sea, which was potentially rich in petroleum reserves.

Following the dissolution of the USSR at the end of 1991, Denmark rapidly established diplomatic relations with (and began investing in) the former Soviet Baltic states of Estonia, Latvia and Lithuania, and was a founder member of the Council of Baltic Sea States (see p. 164), established in 1992.

Government

Denmark is a constitutional monarchy. Under the 1953 constitutional charter, legislative power is held jointly by the hereditary monarch (who has no personal political power) and the unicameral Folketing (Parliament), with 179 members, including 175 from metropolitan Denmark and two each from the Faroe Islands and Greenland. Members are elected for four years (subject to dissolution) on the basis of proportional representation. Executive power is exercised by the monarch through a Cabinet, which is led by the Prime Minister and is responsible to the Folketing. Denmark comprises 14 counties (amtskommuner), one city and one borough, all with elected councils.

Defence

In August 2000 Denmark maintained an army of some 12,850 (including about 4,400 conscripts), a navy of 4,060 (500 conscripts) and an air force of 4,900 (125 conscripts). There were, in total, 64,900 reservists, and a volunteer Home Guard numbering 58,680. Military service is for four–12 months, although some ranks are required to serve for 24 months. Denmark abandoned its neutrality after the Second World War and has been a member of NATO since 1949. In 1992 Denmark assumed observer status in Western European Union (WEU, see p. 286). The defence budget for 2001 was estimated at 18,500m. kroner.

Economic Affairs

In 1998, according to estimates by the World Bank, Denmark's gross national product (GNP), measured at average 1996–98 prices, was US $175,160m., equivalent to $33,040 per head (or $23,855 per head on an international purchasing-power parity basis). Denmark's level of GNP per head is one of the highest among industrialized countries. It was estimated that GNP per head increased, in real terms, at an average rate of 2.7% per year between 1990 and 1998. Over the same period, Denmark's population grew at an average annual rate of 0.4%. Denmark's gross domestic product (GDP) increased, in real terms, at an average annual rate of 2.2% in 1990–99. Real GDP growth was 2.5% in 1998, but decreased to 1.7% in 1999.

Agriculture (including forestry and fishing) employed 3.6% of the economically active population in 1998 and contributed 3.7% of GDP, measured in 1995 prices, in 1999. In 1997 about 56% of Denmark's land area was used for agriculture. The principal activities are pig-farming (Denmark is a major exporter of pork products and pig meat accounted for 4.0% of total exports in 1999) and dairy farming. Most of Denmark's agricultural production is exported, and the sector accounted for 19.3% of total exports in 1999. The fishing industry accounted for 4.3% of total export earnings in that year. Agricultural GDP increased, in real terms, at an average annual rate of 2.9% in 1990–99; the GDP of the sector increased by 3.9% in 1998 and by 2.4% in 1999.

Industry (including mining, manufacturing, construction, power and water) employed 26.6% of the working population in 1998, and provided 22.7% of GDP in that year. Industrial GDP increased, in real terms, at an average annual rate of 0.9% in 1990–99; it rose by 1.3% in 1998 and by 1.0% in 1999.

Mining accounted for only 0.1% of employment in 1998, and provided 1.2% of GDP in 1999. Denmark has few natural resources, but exploration for petroleum reserves in the Danish sector of the North Sea in the 1970s proved successful. Natural gas has also been extensively exploited. In 1989, in northwestern Jutland, it was established that there was a significant reserve of sand which could be exploited for rich yields of titanium, zirconium and yttrium. The GDP of the mining sector increased, in real terms, at an average annual rate of 8.2%, in 1990–1999; the sector's GDP declined by 2.7% in 1998 but increased by 13.7% in 1999.

Manufacturing employed 19.2% of the working population in 1999, and contributed 15.1% of GDP in that year. In 1998 the most important manufacturing industries were food products, non-electric machinery and domestic appliances, metal products, pharmaceuticals and furniture. Manufacturing GDP increased, in real terms, at an average annual rate of 0.6% in 1990–99; it rose 2.5% in 1998, but decreased by 3.3% in 1999.

Energy is derived principally from petroleum and natural gas. In 1997 output of crude petroleum reached 11.4m. metric tons, and in 1993 oil equivalents of gas amounted to 4m. metric tons, enough to satisfy Denmark's own energy requirements. In 1999 mineral fuels comprised about 3.9% of the total cost of imports. The use of renewable sources of energy (including wind power) has been encouraged. In 2000 Denmark derived 15% of its energy from wind power, and planned to increase the share to 50% by 2030.

Services engaged 69.8% of the employed population in 1998, and provided 73.6% of GDP in the same year. In real terms, the combined GDP of the service sectors increased at an average rate of 2.1% per year in 1990–99; rises of 2.6% and 3.81% were recorded in 1998 and 1999, respectively.

In 1999 Denmark recorded a visible trade surplus of US $6,757m., and a surplus of US $2,580m. on the current account of the balance of payments. Most Danish trade is with the other member states of the European Union (EU, see p. 181), which accounted for 66.4% of imports and 61.7% of exports in 1999). The principal source of imports in 1999 was Germany (21.6%); other major sources were Sweden (12.1%), the Netherlands (8.1%), the United Kingdom (7.8%) and France (5.8%). Germany was also the principal market for exports (19.9%); other major purchasers included Sweden (11.2%), the United Kingdom (9.5%), Norway (6.0%) and the USA (5.6%). The principal exports are manufactures such as industrial machinery, food and food products, and chemicals. The principal imports are machinery, basic manufactures such as iron, steel and paper, chemicals, and food and live animals.

In 1999 there was an actual budget surplus of some 6,296m. kroner (equivalent to 0.5% of GDP). Denmark has one of the highest levels of debt per head of population among industrialized nations. By the end of 1995 Denmark's net external debt stood at an estimated 266,000m. kroner (equivalent to about 27% of annual GDP). The average annual rate of inflation was 2.1% in 1990–99. Consumer prices increased by 1.8% in 1998, 2.5% in 1999 and by 2.9% in 2000. The rate of unemployment decreased from an average of 10.2% of the labour force in 1995 to 5.6% in 1999.

Denmark is a member of the EU (see p. 181), the Nordic Council (p. 237) and the Nordic Council of Ministers (p. 237).

Following a period of stagnation and declining employment, Denmark began a strong economic recovery in 1994, with average real growth in GDP at 3.3% per year in 1994–98 and a return to previous high employment levels. The recovery was fuelled by an increase in domestic demand, with growth in both consumption and investment. Although domestic demand remained strong in 1998 exports were adversely affected by a general strike and the effects of economic crises in Asia and Russia. With domestic demand increasing at an unacceptable rate, and high wage settlements affecting the competitiveness of Danish businesses, there was a deficit on the current account of the balance of payments in 1998—the first since 1989. A series of measures intended to eliminate excess domestic demand and strengthen Denmark's external position were adopted in mid-1998, and were to be phased in during 1999–2002. A sharp decline in domestic demand produced a surplus on the current account of the balance of payments, instead of the expected narrowing of the previous year's deficit. In an improved international climate, Denmark's competitiveness was enhanced by a decline in the effective exchange rate for the krone, which led to a significant trade surplus. Inflation increased in 1999 and 2000 in relation to other EU member states, following a level of under 2% during 1994–98. Analysts predicted GDP growth of 1.8% in 2000, and later revised that figure to 2.4%, attributing it to unexpectedly high activity in the investment sector. As a result the central government deficit was expected to be 57,200m. kroner, 10,100m. kroner less than the previous year, despite the comprehensive nature of welfare in Denmark and the size of the national debt. A budget surplus of 12,600m. kroner was forecast for 2001. Proposals in the budget included

the allocation of up to 1,000m. kroner for pension provision, as well as pledges for increased funds for the health service and education. The Government intended to recover this sum from industry; measures included a reduction of 1,300m. kroner in existing subsidies for ship-building, agriculture and fisheries. The rejection of the single European currency by Danish voters in September 2000 necessitated a rise of 0.5% in Denmark's interest rates; the Danish central bank was also forced to intervene directly to preserve the value of the krone. However, no long-term adverse effects were expected, especially since the krone (as part of the European exchange rate mechanism—ERM) closely shadows the euro irrespective of Danish adoption of the single currency.

Social Welfare

Denmark was one of the first countries to introduce state social welfare schemes. The principal benefits cover unemployment, sickness, old age and disability, and are financed largely by state subventions. The Government introduced a new system in 1984, whereby social benefits are regulated according to the individual's means. In 1997 Denmark had 94 hospital establishments; in the same year there were 24,538 hospital beds. In 1998 there were 16,688 physicians, 2,153 dentists and 48,536 qualified nurses working in Denmark. In 2000 98,008m. kroner, an estimated 24.5% of proposed budget expenditure, was allocated to social services.

Education

Education is compulsory for nine years between seven and 16 years of age. The State is obliged to offer a pre-school class and a 10th voluntary year. In 1995 enrolment at pre-primary level was equivalent to 83% of children in the relevant age-group (males 83%; females 83%). State-subsidized private schools are available, but about 90% of pupils attend municipal schools. Primary and lower secondary education begins at seven years of age and lasts for nine (optionally 10) years. This includes at least six years at primary school. Enrolment at primary level included 99% of those in the relevant age-group in 1995 (males 99%; females 99%). Secondary education is divided into two cycles of three years the first beginning at 13 years of age, the second at the age of 16 or 17. Students may transfer to vocational courses at this stage. Total enrolment at secondary level included 88% of those in the relevant age-group in 1995 (males 87%; females 89%). There are eight universities and many other institutions of further and higher education. The traditional folk high schools offer a wide range of further education opportunities, which do not confer any professional qualification. In 1995 enrolment at tertiary level was equivalent to 48% of those in the relevant age-group (males 43%; females 53%). In 2000 proposed government expenditure on education totalled an estimated 26,596m. kroner, representing 6.9% of total budget spending.

Public Holidays

2001: 1 January (New Year's Day), 12–16 April (Easter), 11 May (General Prayer Day), 24 May (Ascension Day), 4 June (Whit Monday), 5 June (Constitution Day), 24–26 December (Christmas), 31 December (New Year's Eve).

2002: 1 January (New Year's Day), 28 March–1 April (Easter), 26 April (General Prayer Day), 9 May (Ascension Day), 20 May (Whit Monday), 5 June (Constitution Day), 24–26 December (Christmas), 31 December (New Year's Eve).

Weights and Measures

The metric system is in force.

Statistical Survey

Note: The figures in this survey relate only to metropolitan Denmark, excluding the Faroe Islands and Greenland, which are dealt with in separate chapters. (see pp. 1343 and 1347 respectively).

Source (unless otherwise stated): Danmarks Statistik, Sejrøgade 11, POB 2550, 2100 Copenhagen Ø; tel. 39-17-39-17; fax 39-17-39-99; e-mail dst@dst.dk; internet www.dst.dk.

Area and Population

AREA, POPULATION AND DENSITY

Area (sq km) .	43,096*
Population (census results)	
1 January 1981.	5,123,989
1 January 1991	
Males	2,536,391
Females .	2,610,078
Total	5,146,469
Population (official estimates at 1 January)	
1998	5,294,860
1999	5,313,577
2000	5,330,020
Density (per sq km) at 1 January 2000 .	123.7

* 16,640 sq miles.

PRINCIPAL TOWNS (population at 1 January 2000)

København		Kolding	. .	53,447
(Copenhagen,		Horsens	. .	48,730
the capital) .	1,075,851*	Vejle .	. .	47,930
Århus (Aarhus)	217,260	Roskilde	. .	43,100
Odense	145,062	Greve Strand	.	41,376
Ålborg (Aalborg)	119,617	Naestved	. .	39,408
Esbjerg	73,341	Sikeborg	. .	37,088
Randers	55,761			

* Copenhagen metropolitan area, including Frederiksberg and 11 suburb municipalities. The estimated population of the Copenhagen municipality was 495,699 at 1 January 2000.

BIRTHS, MARRIAGES AND DEATHS

	Registered live births		Registered marriages		Registered deaths	
	Number	Rate (per 1,000)	Number	Rate (per 1,000)	Number	Rate (per 1,000)
1992 .	67,726	13.1	32,188	6.2	60,821	11.8
1993 .	67,369	13.0	31,638	6.1	62,809	12.1
1994 .	69,666	13.4	35,321	6.8	61,099	11.7
1995 .	69,771	13.3	34,736	6.6	63,127	12.1
1996 .	67,638	12.9	35,953	6.8	61,043	11.6
1997 .	67,636	12.8	34,244	6.5	59,898	11.3
1998 .	66,170	12.5	34,733	6.6	58,442	11.0
1999 .	66,232	12.5	35,459	6.7	59,156	11.1

Expectation of life (years at birth, 1998/99): Males 74.0; Females 78.8.

ECONOMICALLY ACTIVE POPULATION

(sample surveys, '000 persons aged 15 to 66 years, April–June)

	1996	1997	1998
Agriculture, hunting and forestry	98.1	93.6	91.9
Fishing .	5.4	5.3	4.7
Mining and quarrying	3.5	3.0	3.2
Manufacturing	510.5	512.7	516.0
Electricity, gas and water supply	16.7	16.6	20.5
Construction.	170.2	176.1	177.5
Wholesale and retail trade; repair of motor vehicles, motorcycles and personal and household goods	359.2	365.8	367.7
Hotels and restaurants .	69.2	74.0	71.3
Transport, storage and communications	184.5	185.4	181.9
Financial intermediation .	83.3	79.8	79.2
Real estate, renting and business activities	189.1	209.1	227.9
Public administration and defence; compulsory social security	167.5	168.3	168.3
Education	193.3	199.4	198.8
Health and social work .	444.1	457.4	458.8
Other community, social and personal service activities .	119.5	125.0	118.5
Private households with employed persons	7.2	4.7	5.4
Extra-territorial organizations and bodies.	1.1	0.7	0.9
Activities not adequately defined	5.0	5.1	5.2
Total employed	2,627.3	2,682.0	2,692.4
Unemployed.	194.5	174.2	155.3
Total labour force	2,821.8	2,856.2	2,847.7
Males	1,528.3	1,539.5	1,528.5
Females.	1,293.5	1,316.7	1,319.1

Source: ILO, *Yearbook of Labour Statistics*.

Agriculture

PRINCIPAL CROPS ('000 metric tons)

	1997	1998	1999
Wheat	4,965	4,928	4,471
Barley	3,887	3,565	3,675
Rye .	453	538	248
Oats	154	161	150
Potatoes.	1,545	1,546	1,502
Pulses .	384	386	193
Rapeseed	291	359	411
Sugar beet	3,367	3,486	3,545

LIVESTOCK ('000 head at May)

	1997	1998	1999
Horses .	38.9	38.2	40.5
Cattle .	2,004.2	1,977.4	1,887.1
Pigs.	11,383.2	12,096.1	11,626.0
Sheep .	142.4	156.0	142.9
Chickens	18,155.5	18,023.3	19,967.9
Turkeys.	469.0	312.3	615.8
Ducks .	347.6	328.9	410.0
Geese	21.4	9.3	16.2

LIVESTOCK PRODUCTS ('000 metric tons)

	1997	1998	1999
Beef and veal	179	164	159
Pig meat	1,572	1,698	1,709
Poultry meat	185	193	205
Cows' milk	4,632	4,668	4,655
Butter	50	49	48
Cheese	291	292	290
Eggs	85	84	78

Forestry

ROUNDWOOD REMOVALS ('000 cu m, excl. bark)

	1996	1997	1998
Sawlogs, veneer logs and logs for sleepers	875	621	621
Pulpwood*	571	571	521
Other industrial wood	325	318	318
Fuel wood	485	485	485
Total	2,256	1,995	1,945

* FAO estimates.

Source: FAO, *Yearbook of Forest Products*.

SAWNWOOD PRODUCTION ('000 cu m, incl. railway sleepers)

	1996	1997	1998
Coniferous (softwood)*	338	338	338
Broadleaved (hardwood)*	245	245	245
Total	583	583	583

* FAO estimates.

Source: FAO, *Yearbook of Forest Products*.

Fishing*

('000 metric tons, live weight)

	1996	1997	1998
Capture	1,681.5	1,826.9	1,557.3
Atlantic cod	90.7	80.5	69.0
Norway pout	162.9	153.0	63.7
Blue whiting (Poutassou)	52.7	33.5	69.3
Sandeels (Sandlances)	669.0	840.8	646.9
Capelin	60.9	48.5	40.3
Atlantic horse mackerel	63.9	63.4	32.6
Atlantic herring	153.0	125.3	139.7
European sprat	226.1	284.5	270.4
Blue mussel	86.0	90.8	108.3
Aquaculture	41.4	38.9	42.4
Total catch	1,722.9	1,865.5	1,599.7

* Data include quantities landed by Danish fishing craft in foreign ports and exclude quantities landed by foreign fishing craft in Danish ports. Aquatic plants and mammals are excluded.

Source: FAO, *Yearbook of Fishery Statistics*.

Mining

('000 metric tons)

	1993	1994	1995
Crude petroleum	8,265	9,118	9,169
Salt (unrefined)	591	634	603
Sulphur*	10	7	8
Limestone flux and calcareous stone	803	955	1,092

* Sulphur of all kinds, other than sublimed sulphur, precipitated sulphur and colloidal sulphur.

Natural gas ('000 terajoules): 210 in 1995; 238 in 1996; 292 in 1997.

Crude petroleum ('000 metric tons, including condensate production): 10,121 in 1996; 11,360 in 1997.

Source: UN, *Industrial Commodity Statistics Yearbook*.

Industry

SELECTED PRODUCTS ('000 metric tons, unless otherwise indicated)

	1997	1998	1999
Pig meat:			
Fresh, chilled or frozen	1,031	1,072	1,183
Salted, dried or smoked	128	135	112
Poultry meat and offals	154	176	195
Fish fillets: fresh, chilled, frozen	48	37	37
Salami, sausages, etc.	100	94	89
Meat in airtight containers:			
Hams	45	42	37
Other meat	145	143	137
Beet and cane sugar (solid)	509	573	654
Beer ('000 hectolitres)	9,181	8,044	8,205
Flours, meals and pastes of fish	393	352	305
Oil cake and meal	82	81	101
Cigarettes (million)	12,262	12,392	11,749
Cement	2,683	2,667	2,534
Motor spirit (Petrol)	2,932	2,636	2,571
Motor and fuel oils	1,672	1,921	1,780
Powder asphalt	1,184	907	816
Washing powders, etc	34	26	38
Refrigerators for household use ('000)	127	128	107

Finance

CURRENCY AND EXCHANGE RATES

Monetary Units

100 øre = 1 Danish krone (plural: kroner).

Sterling, Dollar and Euro Equivalents (29 December 2000)
£1 sterling = 11.9682 kroner;
US $1 = 8.0205 kroner;
€1 = 7.4631 kroner;
1,000 Danish kroner = £83.55 = $124.68 = €133.99.

Average Exchange Rate (kroner per US $)
1998 6.701
1999 6.976
2000 8.083

BUDGET (million kroner)

Revenue	1998*	1999*	2000†
Income and property taxes	124,575	133,471	122,013
Customs and excise duties	189,531	199,435	215,656
Other revenue	107,236	74,422	86,285
Interest (net)			
Total	421,342	407,328	423,954

Expenditure			1998*	1999*	2000†
Ministry of Social Affairs	.	.	95,057	95,718	98,008
Ministry of Education	.	.	26,426	26,445	26,596
Ministry of Defence	.	.	17,689	16,944	16,474
Public corporations	.	.	2,341	1,346	998
Ministry of Agriculture and Fisheries	.	.	2,713	2,774	2,731
Ministry of Justice	.	.	8,968	8,704	9,220
Ministry of Finance	.	.	6,232	5,168	7,349
Other expenditure	.	.	224,747	236,844	238,277
Total	.	.	**384,173**	**393,943**	**399,653**

* Approved.   † Estimates.

2001 (budget proposals, million kroner): Revenue 422,996; Expenditure 406,709.

INTERNATIONAL RESERVES (US $ million at 31 December)*

			1997	1998	1999
Gold†	.	.	545	677	531
IMF special drawing rights	.	.	336	346	343
Reserve position in IMF	.	.	631	1,165	799
Foreign exchange	.	.	18,157	13,753	21,145
Total	.	.	**19,669**	**15,941**	**22,818**

* Data referring to holdings of gold and foreign exchange exclude deposits made with the European Monetary Institute.
† Valued at market-related prices.

Source: IMF, *International Financial Statistics*.

MONEY SUPPLY ('000 million kroner at 31 December)

			1997	1998	1999
Currency outside banks	.	.	33.3	34.5	36.7
Demand deposits at banks	.	.	304.5	321.4	336.3
Total money (incl. others)	.	.	**334.0**	**360.7**	**381.8**

COST OF LIVING (Consumer Price Index; base: 1980 = 100)

			1997	1998	1999
Food	.	.	187.5	191.4	192.7
Fuel and power	.	.	201.9	207.9	218.2
Clothing and footwear	.	.	181.0	182.6	185.3
Rent	.	.	236.3	242.1	248.6
All items (incl. others)	.	.	**204.1**	**207.9**	**213.0**

NATIONAL ACCOUNTS
(million kroner)

National Income and Product (at current prices)

			1997	1998*	1999*
Compensation of employees	.	.	590,122	623,044	656,014
Operating surplus	.	.	198,866	194,149	205,976
Domestic factor incomes	.	.	**788,988**	**817,193**	**861,990**
Consumption of fixed capital	.	.	165,865	174,431	184,874
Gross domestic product at factor cost	.	.	**954,853**	**991,624**	**1,046,864**
Indirect taxes	.	.	197,766	213,070	221,342
Less Subsidies	.	.	36,295	35,697	38,621
GDP in purchasers' values	.	.	**1,116,324**	**1,168,997**	**1,229,585**
Factor income from abroad	.	.	90,274	80,311	76,742
Less Factor income paid abroad	.	.	106,294	93,021	81,929
Gross national product	.	.	**1,100,304**	**1,156,287**	**1,224,398**
Less Consumption of fixed capital	.	.	165,865	174,431	184,874
National income in market prices	.	.	**934,439**	**981,856**	**1,039,524**
Other current transfers from abroad	.	.	14,764	14,481	13,838
Less Other current transfers paid abroad	.	.	33,509	34,305	40,148
National disposable income	.	.	**915,694**	**962,032**	**1,013,214**

* Provisional figures.

Expenditure on the Gross Domestic Product
(at current prices)

			1997	1998*	1999*
Government final consumption expenditure	.	.	284,529	300,452	313,280
Private final consumption expenditure	.	.	560,854	591,521	609,727
Increase in stocks	.	.	11,220	13,173	−2,009
Gross fixed capital formation	.	.	220,516	240,971	250,138
Total domestic expenditure	.	.	**1,077,119**	**1,146,117**	**1,171,136**
Exports of goods and services	.	.	406,891	413,352	460,081
Less Imports of goods and services	.	.	367,685	390,473	401,633
GDP in purchasers' values	.	.	**1,116,324**	**1,168,996**	**1,229,585**
GDP at constant 1990 prices	.	.	**1,067,667**	**1,094,796**	**1,113,193**

* Provisional figures.

Gross Domestic Product by Economic Activity
(provisional, at constant 1995 prices)

	1997	1998	1999
Agriculture and forestry . . .	31,978	33,075	34,308
Fishing	2,097	2,324	1,950
Mining and quarrying . . .	10,338	10,056	11,430
Manufacturing	151,200	154,945	149,842
Electricity, gas and water. . .	22,951	21,545	20,022
Construction.	44,672	45,680	43,598
Wholesale and retail trade . .	134,497	133,443	140,773
Restaurants and hotels . .	13,372	15,675	15,262
Transport, storage and communication . . .	73,638	77,607	79,561
Finance and insurance . .	44,081	44,890	46,724
Real estate and renting activities	109,957	112,106	116,328
Business services . . .	57,373	62,087	72,842
Public administration and defence; compulsory social security	68,179	69,573	69,559
Education	49,726	51,039	51,274
Health care activities. . .	39,915	41,860	41,903
Social work activities. . .	53,094	54,661	54,977
Other community, social and personal service activities .	31,219	39,623	39,803
Sub-total	940,287	970,189	990,156
Less Imputed bank service charges	31,128	31,461	32,503
GDP at basic prices . .	909,159	938,728	957,653
Taxes on products . . .⎱ *Less* subsidies on products . .⎰	208,545	212,972	213,250
GDP in purchasers' values . .	1,117,704	1,151,700	1,170,903

BALANCE OF PAYMENTS (US $ million)

	1997	1998	1999
Exports of goods f.o.b. . . .	48,103	47,908	49,845
Imports of goods f.o.b. . . .	−42,734	−44,021	−43,087
Trade balance . . .	5,369	3,886	6,757
Exports of services . . .	14,044	15,212	15,842
Imports of services . . .	−13,727	−15,779	−14,993
Balance on goods and services	5,685	3,319	7,607
Other income received . .	18,774	10,401	8,536
Other income paid . . .	−22,203	−14,247	−11,439
Balance on goods, services and income	2,256	−527	4,703
Current transfers received . .	3,633	3,443	3,431
Current transfers paid . .	−4,968	−4,924	−5,554
Current balance . . .	921	−2,008	2,580
Capital account (net). . .	128	50	128
Direct investment abroad. .	−4,355	−4,215	−9,784
Direct investment from abroad	2,792	6,675	8,482
Portfolio investment assets .	−6,239	−7,563	−9,748
Portfolio investment liabilities .	11,186	−2,598	6,938
Financial derivatives liabilities	n.a.	n.a.	384
Other investment assets . .	−8,033	−1,797	717
Other investment liabilities . .	13,146	8,010	11,010
Net errors and omissions . .	−3,013	−793	−1,270
Overall balance . . .	6,532	−4,239	9,437

Source: IMF, *International Financial Statistics.*

External Trade

PRINCIPAL COMMODITIES (distribution by SITC, million kroner)

Imports c.i.f.	1997	1998	1999
Food and live animals . . .	30,226.8	30,853.2	30,595.4
Fish (not marine mammals), crustaceans, molluscs and aquatic invertebrates . .	7,556.6	8,214.2	8,200.4
Crude materials (inedible) except fuels	11,522.5	11,898.1	10,914.0
Mineral fuels, lubricants, etc.	15,250.3	10,919.8	12,303.6
Petroleum, petroleum products, etc	10,974.1	8,257.0	10,170.0
Chemicals and related products	31,312.4	31,655.0	33,017.8
Medicinal and pharmaceutical products	5,585.8	6,069.7	6,730.4
Plastics in primary forms. . .	5,945.6	5,970.7	5,833.9
Basic manufactures . . .	50,947.1	54,307.6	51,735.1
Paper, paperboard and manufactures . . .	9,388.3	9,663.5	9,458.5
Textile yarn, fabrics, etc. . .	7,357.6	8,026.2	7,863.7
Iron and steel	10,402.8	11,291.7	8,832.9
Machinery and transport equipment	100,031.3	109,056.2	113,894.5
Machinery specialized for particular industries . . .	9,525.9	9,907.8	10,316.8
General industrial machinery, equipment and parts . .	12,775.9	14,300.2	14,460.1
Office machines and automatic data-processing equipment .	16,243.5	14,597.6	18,294.6
Telecommunications and sound equipment	12,638.6	13,927.9	15,263.4
Other electrical machinery, apparatus, etc. . .	15,339.2	16,543.4	17,421.6
Road vehicles (incl. air-cushion vehicles) and parts* . .	23,136.4	25,923.2	25,260.6
Other transport equipment* . .	4,346.2	6,789.7	6,067.6
Miscellaneous manufactured articles	43,098.6	47,580.6	47,415.0
Clothing and accessories (excl. footwear)	14,189.2	15,656.0	15,572.5
Total (incl. others) . . .	293,522.1	308,816.7	311,789.8

* Data on parts exclude tyres, engines and electrical parts.

Exports f.o.b.	1997	1998	1999
Food and live animals . . .	70,701.0	66,655.3	66,974.5
Meat and meat preparations . .	27,151.6	23,171.6	23,444.1
Dairy products and birds' eggs .	10,434.0	9,961.3	10,337.0
Fish (not marine mammals), crustaceans, molluscs and aquatic invertebrates . .	13,658.4	13,869.7	14,999.8
Crude materials (inedible) except fuels	13,655.9	12,967.5	13,001.0
Mineral fuels, lubricants, etc.	14,694.8	10,894.4	15,247.9
Petroleum, petroleum products, etc.	10,500.7	7,687.8	12,478.5
Chemicals and related products	35,277.1	36,575.7	42,309.7
Medicinal and pharmaceutical products . . .	15,593.9	16,853.6	21,110.0
Basic manufactures . .	35,997.9	37,136.5	38,876.6
Machinery and transport equipment	89,070.5	92,951.2	99,737.4
Power-generating machinery and equipment	6,686.4	7,670.4	10,151.7
Machinery specialized for particular industries . .	12,662.0	12,980.4	12,893.8
General industrial machinery, equipment and parts . .	23,990.9	24,916.4	24,386.2
Office machines and automatic data-processing equipment .	6,545.0	6,141.6	6,764.0
Telecommunications and sound equipment. . . .	11,816.9	13,427.6	15,543.8
Other electrical machinery, apparatus, etc.. . .	12,142.7	12,334.7	12,397.0
Road vehicles (incl. air-cushion vehicles) and parts* . .	6,899.1	7,454.5	7,836.9
Other transport equipment* . .	7,275.3	6,968.1	8,677.3

Exports f.o.b. — *continued*	1997	1998	1999
Miscellaneous manufactured			
articles	53,590.0	56,657.7	60,514.5
Furniture and parts . . .	12,903.0	13,335.6	13,594.0
Clothing and accessories (excl.			
footwear)	10,050.6	11,444.9	12,366.5
Professional, scientific and			
controlling instruments, etc. .	7,192.6	7,424.4	7,860.8
Total (incl. others) . . .	321,185.4	322,796.9	346,756.5

* Data on parts exclude tyres, engines and electrical parts.

PRINCIPAL TRADING PARTNERS (million kroner)

Imports c.i.f.	1997	1998	1999
Austria	2,814.7	3,116.0	3,386.8
Belgium-Luxembourg . . .	10,502.3	11,150.3	11,084.9
China, People's Republic . .	6,004.5	6,396.5	8,237.7
Finland	8,586.2	8,193.1	8,556.0
France (incl. Monaco) . .	15,656.2	17,405.4	18,303.7
Germany	63,203.3	67,822.5	67,353.6
Ireland	3,468.0	3,361.2	3,853.4
Italy	12,770.6	14,549.1	14,455.7
Japan	5,887.8	5,967.8	6,231.7
Netherlands	22,832.1	23,098.2	25,220.4
Norway	15,657.9	14,545.8	13,788.3
Poland	5,022.3	5,308.3	5,543.9
Portugal	3,019.1	2,852.3	2,481.5
Spain	3,952.0	4,430.4	4,652.2
Sweden	37,411.3	39,286.3	37,700.1
Switzerland	3,966.0	4,042.2	3,947.5
United Kingdom	21,894.6	23,900.2	24,463.4
USA	14,938.9	15,292.9	14,871.4
Total (incl. others) . . .	293,522.1	308,816.7	311,789.8

Exports f.o.b.	1997	1998	1999
Austria	3,066.1	3,380.1	3,501.0
Belgium-Luxembourg . . .	6,395.4	6,700.9	7,001.5
Finland	8,462.9	9,772.9	11,066.5
France (incl. Monaco) . .	16,964.5	16,702.1	18,227.9
Germany	68,130.7	66,971.1	68,869.7
Italy	11,522.8	12,666.0	12,749.6
Japan	10,776.4	9,428.2	11,805.6
Netherlands	14,168.5	14,948.9	15,986.9
Norway	20,064.9	19,875.9	20,943.5
Poland	5,936.6	6,392.3	6,192.7
Russia	6,142.5	4,856.9	2,939.6
Spain	6,229.7	7,183.5	8,244.0
Sweden	36,400.5	34,509.9	38,918.3
Switzerland	4,575.4	4,615.9	5,042.0
United Kingdom	31,076.0	30,567.2	32,909.2
USA	14,863.1	16,063.9	19,360.9
Total (incl. others) . . .	321,185.4	322,796.9	346,756.5

Transport

RAILWAYS (traffic)

	1997	1998	1999
Number of journeys ('000) .	144,414	149,800	149,300
Passenger-kilometres (million) .	4,988	5,365	5,318
Ton-kilometres (million) . .	1,992	2,066	1,949

ROAD TRAFFIC (motor vehicles in use at 31 December)

	1997	1998	1999
Private cars	1,777,209	1,811,211	1,837,285
Taxis	5,889	5,936	5,969
Buses, coaches . . .	13,779	13,911	13,909
Vans, lorries	336,011	347,136	362,002
Tractors	123,809	122,291	130,779
Trailers	443,550	473,357	502,616
Motor cycles	59,889	64,013	69,231

SHIPPING
Merchant Fleet (registered at 31 December)

	1997	1998	1999
Number of vessels . . .	935	915	1,057
Total displacement ('000 grt) . .	5,753.8	5,686.7	5,912.3

Source: Lloyd's Register of Shipping, *World Fleet Statistics*.

Sea-borne Freight Traffic at Danish Ports*
('000 metric tons loaded and unloaded)

	1997	1998	1999
Ålborg	2,634	2,408	2,542
Århus	6,120	6,452	7,077
Copenhagen	8,100	8,713	6,068
Fredericia	13,113	13,619	14,539
Kalundborg	8,747	8,593	8,822
Skaelskør	1,261	783	964
Others	44,483	32,568	31,752
Total	84,459	73,136	71,764

* Including domestic traffic, excluding ferry traffic.

International Sea-borne Shipping* (freight traffic, '000 metric tons)

	1997	1998	1999
Goods loaded	21,060	21,237	22,949
Goods unloaded	38,291	33,997	31,982

* Excluding international ferry traffic.

CIVIL AVIATION (Scandinavian Airlines System)

	1993	1994	1995
Kilometres flown ('000) . .	225,583	217,185	218,483
Passengers carried ('000) . .	18,584	18,775	18,704
Passenger-kilometres (million) .	18,137	18,466	18,506
Cargo and mail ton-kilometres			
(million)	470	496	502

Tourism

(income from visitors, million kroner)

	1997	1998	1999
Scandinavian visitors . . .	4,129	4,160	5,308
German visitors . . .	5,670	5,142	4,804
All other visitors	11,222	12,202	15,876
Total	21,021	21,504	25,989

OVERNIGHT STAYS (foreign visitors)

	1997	1998	1999
In hotels	6,224,952	6,083,964	5,774,557
At camping sites	4,246,537	3,763,600	3,768,205
Total	10,471,489	9,847,564	9,542,766

Communications Media

	1996	1997	1998
Radio licences	2,173,000	2,208,000	2,216,000
Television licences (black and white)	51,000	43,000	36,000
Television licences (colour) . .	2,030,000	2,072,000	2,085,000
Number of daily newspapers . .	37	37	36
Total circulation (weekdays) .	1,628,000	1,615,000	1,613,000
Books published (titles)* . .	12,352	13,450	13,175

* Including pamphlets (4,144 titles in 1996; 4,330 titles in 1997; 4,274 titles in 1998).

Telephones ('000 main lines in use): 3,060 in 1993; 3,123 in 1994; 3,203 in 1995.

Telefax stations ('000 in use): 185 in 1993; 210 in 1994; 250 in 1995.

Mobile cellular telephones (subscribers): 361,366 in 1993; 503,500 in 1994; 822,264 in 1995.

(Source: UN, *Statistical Yearbook*).

Education

(1994/95)

	Institutions	Teachers	Students
Pre-primary	4,395	19,200	201,571
Primary	n.a.	33,100	328,875
Secondary			
General	n.a.	37,000	321,448
Vocational	n.a.	13,100	123,234
Higher	n.a.	9,600	169,783

1995/96: *Students*: Pre-primary 209,005; Primary 336,690; Secondary (General) 438,809; Secondary (Vocational) 122,059; Higher 174,975.

Source: UNESCO, *Statistical Yearbook*.

Directory

The Constitution

The constitutional charter (*Grundlov*), summarized below, was adopted on 5 June 1953.

GOVERNMENT

The form of government is a limited (constitutional) monarchy. The legislative authority rests jointly with the Crown and Parliament. Executive power is vested in the Crown, and the administration of justice is exercised by the courts. The Monarch can constitutionally 'do no wrong'. She exercises her authority through the Ministers appointed by her. The Ministers are responsible for the government of the country. The Constitution establishes the principle of Parliamentarism under which individual Ministers or the whole Cabinet must retire when defeated in Parliament by a vote of 'no confidence'.

MONARCH

The Monarch acts on behalf of the State in international affairs. Except with the consent of the Parliament, she cannot, however, take any action that increases or reduces the area of the Realm or undertake any obligation, the fulfilment of which requires the co-operation of the Parliament or which is of major importance. Nor can the Monarch, without the consent of the Parliament, terminate any international agreement that has been concluded with the consent of the Parliament.

Apart from defence against armed attack on the Realm or on Danish forces, the Monarch cannot, without the consent of the Parliament, employ military force against any foreign power.

PARLIAMENT

The Parliament (Folketing) is an assembly consisting of not more than 179 members, two of whom are elected in the Faroe Islands and two in Greenland. Danish nationals, having attained 18 years of age, with permanent residence in Denmark, have the franchise and are eligible for election. The members of the Folketing are elected for four years. Election is by a system of proportional representation, with direct and secret ballot on lists in large constituencies. A bill adopted by the Folketing may be submitted to referendum, when such referendum is claimed by not less than one-third of the members of the Folketing and not later than three days after the adoption. The bill is void if rejected by a majority of the votes cast, representing not less than 30% of all electors.

The Government

HEAD OF STATE

Queen of Denmark: HM Queen MARGRETHE II (succeeded to the throne 14 January 1972).

THE CABINET
(April 2001)

A coalition of the Social Democrats (SD) and the Social Liberals (SL).

Prime Minister: POUL NYRUP RASMUSSEN (SD).

Deputy Prime Minister and Minister of Economic Affairs and of Nordic Co-operation: MARIANNE JELVED (SL).

Minister of Foreign Affairs: MOGENS LYKKETOFT (SD).

Minister of Finance: PIA GJELLERUP (SD).

Minister of the Environment and Energy: SVEND AUKEN (SD).

Minister of Information Technology and Research: BIRTE WEISS (SD).

Minister of Education: MARGRETHE VESTAGER (SL).

Minister of Defence: JAN TRØJBORG (SD).

Minister of the Interior: KAREN JESPERSEN (SD).

Minister of Food, Agriculture and Fisheries: RITT BJERRE-GAARD (SD).

Minister of Justice: FRANK JENSEN (SD).

Minister of Social Affairs: HENRIK DAM KRISTENSEN (SD).

Minister of Trade and Industry: OLE STAUAD (SD).

Minister of Culture: ELSEBETH GERNER NIELSEN (SL).

Minister of Labour: OVE HYGUM (SD).

Minister of Transport: JACOB BUKSTI (SD).

Minister of Housing and Urban Affairs and of Gender Equality: LOTTE BUNDSGAARD (SD).

Minister of Taxation: FRODE SØRENSEN (SD).

Minister of Ecclesiastical Affairs: NIELS JOHANNES LEBECH (SL).

Minister of Health: ARNE ROLIGHED (SD).

Minister of Development Co-operation: ANITA BAY BUNDEGAARD (SL).

MINISTRIES

Office of the Prime Minister: Christiansborg, Prins Jørgens Gård 11, 1218 Copenhagen K; tel. 33-92-33-00; fax 33-11-16-65; e-mail stm@stm.dk; internet www.stm.dk.

Ministry of Trade and Industry: Slotsholmsgade 10–12, 1216 Copenhagen K; tel. 33-92-33-50; fax 33-12-37-78; e-mail em@em.dk; internet www.em.dk.

Ministry of Culture: Nybrogade 2, POB 2140, 1015 Copenhagen K; tel. 33-92-33-70; fax 33-91-33-88; e-mail kum@kum.dk; internet www.kum.dk.

Ministry of Defence: Holmens Kanal 42, 1060 Copenhagen K; tel. 33-92-33-20; fax 33-32-06-55; e-mail fmn@fmn.dk; internet www.fmn.dk.

Ministry of Ecclesiastical Affairs: Frederiksholms Kanal 21, 1220 Copenhagen K; tel. 33-92-33-90; fax 33-92-39-13; e-mail km@km.dk; internet www.km.dk.

Ministry of Economic Affairs: Ved Stranden 8, 1061 Copenhagen K; tel. 33-92-33-22; fax 33-93-60-20; e-mail oem@oem.dk; internet www.oem.dk.

Ministry of Education: Frederiksholms Kanal 21–25, 1220 Copenhagen K; tel. 33-92-50-00; fax 33-92-55-47; e-mail uvm@uvm.dk; internet www.uvm.dk.

Ministry of the Environment and Energy: Højbro Plads 4, 1200 Copenhagen K; tel. 33-92-76-00; fax 33-32-22-27; e-mail mem@mem.dk; internet www.mem.dk.

Ministry of Finance: Christiansborg Slotsplads 1, 1218 Copenhagen K; tel. 33-92-33-33; fax 33-32-80-30; e-mail fm@fm.dk; internet www.fm.dk.

Ministry of Food, Agriculture and Fisheries: Holbergsgade 2, 1057 Copenhagen K; tel. 33-92-33-01; fax 33-14-50-42; e-mail fvm@fvm.dk; internet www.fvm.dk.

Ministry of Foreign Affairs: Asiatisk Plads 2, 1448 Copenhagen K; tel. 33-92-00-00; fax 31-54-05-33; e-mail um@um.dk; internet www.um.dk.

Ministry of Health: Holbergsgade 6, 1057 Copenhagen K; tel. 33-92-33-60; fax 33-93-15-63; e-mail sum@sum.dk; internet www.sum.dk.

Ministry of Housing and Urban Affairs: Slotsholmsgade 1, 1216 Copenhagen K; tel. 33-92-61-00; fax 33-92-61-04; e-mail bm@bm.dk; internet www.bm.dk.

Ministry of the Interior: Slotsholmsgade 6, 1216 Copenhagen K; tel. 33-92-33-80; fax 33-11-12-39; e-mail inm@inm.dk; internet www.inm.dk.

Ministry of Justice: Slotsholmsgade 10, 1216 Copenhagen K; tel. 33-92-33-40; fax 33-93-35-10; e-mail jm@jm.dk; internet www.jm.dk.

Ministry of Labour: Holmens Kanal 20, 1060 Copenhagen K; tel. 33-92-59-00; fax 33-12-13-78; e-mail am@am.dk; internet www.am.dk.

Ministry of Information Technology and Research: Bredgade 43, 1260 Copenhagen K; tel. 33-92-97-00; fax 33-32-35-01; e-mail fsk@fsk.dk; internet www.fsk.dk.

Ministry of Social Affairs: Holmens Kanal 22, 1060 Copenhagen K; tel. 33-92-93-00; fax 33-93-25-18; e-mail sm@sm.dk; internet www.sm.dk.

Ministry of Taxation: Slotsholmsgade 12, 1216 Copenhagen K; tel. 33-92-33-92; fax 33-14-91-05; e-mail skm@skm.dk; internet www.skm.dk.

Ministry of Transport: Frederiksholms Kanal 27, 1220 Copenhagen K; tel. 33-92-33-55; fax 33-12-38-93; e-mail trm@trm.dk; internet www.trm.dk.

Legislature

FOLKETING

Christiansborg, 1240 Copenhagen K; tel. 33-37-55-00; fax 33-32-85-36.

President of the Folketing: IVAR HANSEN.

Secretary-General: OLE STIG ANDERSEN.

General Election, 11 March 1998
(metropolitan Denmark only)

	Votes ('000)	% of votes	Seats
Social Democrats	1,223.6	35.9	63
Liberals	817.9	24.0	42
Conservative People's Party . .	304.0	8.9	16
Socialist People's Party . .	257.4	7.6	13
Danish People's Party . .	252.4	7.4	13
Centre Democrats . . .	146.8	4.3	8
Social Liberals	131.3	3.9	7
Red–Green Alliance . . .	91.9	2.7	5
Christian People's Party . .	85.7	2.5	4
Progress Party	82.4	2.4	4*
Democratic Renewal Party . .	10.8	0.3	—
Independents	1.8	0.1	—
Total	**3,406.0**	**100.0**	**175**

The Folketing also includes two members from Greenland and two from the Faroe Islands.

* The four Progress Party legislators resigned from the party in November 1999 and subsequently founded a new political organization known as Freedom 2000.

Political Organizations

Centrum-Demokraterne (Centre Democrats): Christiansborg, 1240 Copenhagen K; tel. 33-37-48-77; fax 33-37-48-56; e-mail cd@ft.dk; internet www.centrumdemokraterne.dk; f. 1973; opposes extreme ideologies, supports EU and NATO; Leader MIMI JAKOBSEN; Nat. Chair. INGER BORIIS.

Danmarks Kommunistiske Parti (Danish Communist Party): Studiestræde 24, 1455 Copenhagen K; tel. 33-91-66-44; fax 33-32-03-72; f. 1919; Chair. MOGENS HØVER.

Danmarks kommunistiske Parti/Marxister Leninister (Marxist-Leninist Party): Griffenfeldsgade 26, 2200 Copenhagen N; tel. 35-35-60-69; fax 35-37-20-39; e-mail dkp-ml@dkp-ml.dk; internet www.dkp-ml.dk; Sec.-Gen. JØRGEN PETERSEN.

Danmarks Retsforbund (Justice Party): Landssekretariatet, Lyngbyvej 42, 2100 Copenhagen Ø; tel. 39-20-44-88; fax 39-20-44-50; internet www.retsforbundet.dk; f. 1919; programme is closely allied to Henry George's teachings (single tax, free trade); Chair. METTE LANGDAL.

Dansk Folkeparti (Danish People's Party): Christiansborg, 1240 Copenhagen K; tel. 33-37-51-99; fax 33-37-51-91; e-mail df@ft.dk; internet www.danskfolkparti.dk; f. 1995 by defectors from the Progress Party; right-wing; Leader PIA KJAERSGAARD.

Enhedslisten—De Rød-Grønne (Red–Green Alliance): Studiestraede 24, 1455 Copenhagen K; tel. 33-93-33-24; fax 33-32-03-72; e-mail enhedslisten@enhedslisten.dk; internet www. enhedslisten.dk; f. 1989 by three left-wing parties; membership of individual socialists; 21-mem. collective leadership.

Fælles Kurs (Common Course): Copenhagen; tel. 33-14-44-18; fax 33-32-40-16; f. 1986; socialist; Chair. PREBEN MØLLER HANSEN.

Folkebevægelsen mod EU (Danish People's Movement Against the European Union): Sigurdsgade 39A, 2200 Copenhagen N; tel. 35-82-18-00; fax 35-82-18-06; e-mail katte-ud@post1.tele.dk; internet www.folkebevaegelsen.dk; opposes membership of the EU, in favour of self-determination for Denmark and all European countries; 21-mem. collective leadership.

Fremskridtspartiet (Progress Party): POB 180, 2630 Taastrup; tel. 70-26-20-27; fax 70-26-23-27; e-mail frp@frp.dk; internet www.frp.dk; f. 1972; right-wing; advocates gradual abolition of income tax, disbandment of most of the civil service, and abolition of diplomatic service and about 90% of legislation; Chair. JOHANNES SØRENSEN; Leader KIRSTEN JACOBSEN; Sec.-Gen. MARTIN IPSEN.

Frihed 2000 (Freedom 2000): Christiansborg, 1240 Copenhagen K; tel. 33-37-38-60; fax 33-15-13-99; e-mail frihed@folketinget.dk; internet www.frihed-2000.dk; f. 1999 by four former Progress Party MPs; right-wing; Chair. KIM BEHNKE.

De Grønne/Økologisk-realistisk Alternativ (Green Party/The Realistic Ecological Alternative): Copenhagen; tel. 31-38-00-97; f. 1983, reformed 1991.

Det Humanistiske Parti (The Humanist Party): Skt Jorgens Alle 7, 1615 Copenhagen V; tel. 31-24-70-60; pro-democratic, non-violent; Chair. CHRISTIAN ADAMSEN.

JuniBevægelsen (June Movement): Copenhagen; tel. 33-93-00-46; fax 33-93-30-67; e-mail jb@junibevaegelsen.dk; internet www .junibevaegelsen.dk. f. 1992; opposes the EU; Leader JENS-PETER BONDE.

Kommunistisk Arbejderparti (Communist Workers' Party): Studiestræde 24, 1455 Copenhagen K; tel. 33-15-21-33; fax 33-33-86-56; f. 1968.

Det Konservative Folkeparti (Conservative People's Party): Nyhavn 4, POB 1515, 1020 Copenhagen K; tel. 33-13-41-40; fax 33-93-37-73; e-mail konservative@konservative.dk; internet www .konservative.dk; f. 1916; advocates free initiative and the maintenance of private property, but recognizes the right of the State to take action to keep the economic and social balance; Leader POUL ANDREASSEN; Sec.-Gen. IAN HØGSKILDE.

Kristeligt Folkeparti (Christian People's Party): Allégade 24A, I., 2000 Frederiksberg; tel. 33-27-78-10; fax 33-21-31-16; e-mail krf@krf.dk; internet www.krf.dk; f. 1970; emphasizes the need for political decisions based on Christian ethics; Chair. JANN SJURSEN; Sec.-Gen. IB ALGOT NIELSEN.

Det Radikale Venstre (Social Liberals): Christiansborg, 1240 Copenhagen K; tel. 33-37-47-47; fax 33-13-72-51; e-mail radikale@ radikale.dk; internet www.radikale.dk; f. 1905; supports international *détente* and co-operation within regional and world organizations, social reforms without socialism, incomes policy, workers' participation in industry, state intervention in industrial disputes, state control of trusts and monopolies, strengthening private enterprise; Chair. JOHANNES LEBECH; Leader MARIANNE JELVED; Gen. Sec. ANDERS KLOPPENBORG.

Schleswigsche Partei (Schleswig Party): Vestergade 30, 6200 Abenrå; tel. 74-62-38-33; fax 74-62-79-39; e-mail sp@bdn.dk; internet www.nordschleswig.dk; f. 1920; represents the German minority in North Schleswig; Chair. GERHARD D. MAMMEN.

Socialdemokratiet (Social Democrats): Thorvaldsensvej 2, 1780 Copenhagen V; tel. 35-39-15-22; fax 35-39-40-30; e-mail socialdemokratiet@net.dialog.dk; internet www.socialdemokratiet .dk; f. 1871; finds its chief adherents among workers, employees and public servants; 60,000 mems; Leader POUL NYRUP RASMUSSEN; Gen. Sec. WILLY STIG ANDERSEN.

Socialistisk Arbejderparti (Socialist Workers' Party): Norre Allé 11A, POB 547, 2200 Copenhagen N; tel. 35-39-79-48; fax 35-37-32-17; e-mail sap@sap-fi.dk; internet www.sap-fi.dk.

Socialistisk Folkeparti (Socialist People's Party): Christiansborg, 1240 Copenhagen K; tel. 33-12-70-11; fax 33-14-70-10; e-mail sf@sf.dk; internet www.sf.dk; f. 1959; socialist; Chair. HOLGER K. NIELSEN; Parliamentary Leader JES LUNDE; Sec. OLE HVAS KRISTIANSEN.

Venstre (Liberals): Søllerødvej 30, 2840 Holte; tel. 45-80-22-33; fax 45-80-38-30; e-mail venstre@venstre.dk; internet www.venstre.dk; f. 1870; supports free trade, a minimum of state interference, and the adoption, in matters of social expenditure, of a modern general social security system; 79,182 mems; Pres. ANDERS FOGH RASMUSSEN; Sec.-Gen. CLAUS HJORT FREDERIKSEN.

Diplomatic Representation

EMBASSIES IN DENMARK

Agleria: Amaliegade 36, 1256 Copenhagen K; tel. 33-11-94-40; fax 33-11-58-50; e-mail ambalda@post10.tele.dk; Ambassador MOHAMOD BENHACINE.

Argentina: Borgergade 16, I., 1300 Copenhagen K; tel. 33-15-80-82; fax 33-15-55-74; e-mail embardin@post1.tele.dk; Ambassador: ABEL PARENTINI POSSE.

Austria: Sølundsvej 1, 2100 Copenhagen Ø; tel. 39-29-41-41; fax 39-29-20-86; e-mail austria@post7.tele.dk; Ambassador: HELMUT WESSLY.

Belgium: Øster Allé 7, 2100 Copenhagen Ø; tel. 35-25-02-00; fax 35-25-02-11; e-mail ambelcph@inet.uni2.dk; Ambassador: BAUDOUIN DE LA KETHULLE DE RYHOVE.

Bolivia: Amaliegade 16C, 2nd Floor, 1256 Copenhagen K; tel. 33-12-49-00; fax 33-12-49-03; e-mail embodk-1@inet.uni2.dk; Chargé d'affaires a.i. JORGE HEREDIA.

Bosnia and Herzegovina: Nytorv 3, 1450 Copenhagen K; tel. 33-33-80-40; fax 33-33-80-17; e-mail ba-emb-dk-cph@mobilxnet.dk; Chargé d'affaires a.i.: Prof. Dr LAMIJA TANOVIĆ.

Brazil: Ryvangs Allé 24, 2100 Copenhagen Ø; tel. 39-20-64-78; fax 39-27-36-07; e-mail ambassade@denmark.dk; Ambassador: CARLOS LUIA COUTINHO PEREZ.

Bulgaria: Gamlehave Allé 7, 2920 Charlottenlund; tel. 39-64-24-84; fax 39-63-49-23; e-mail bbb25387@vip.cybercity.dk; Ambassador: KROUM DIMITROV SLAVOV.

Burkina Faso: Svanemøllevej 20, 2100 Copenhagen Ø; tel. 39-18-40-22; fax 39-27-18-86; e-mail amba@burkina.dk; Ambassador: ANNE KONATÉ.

Canada: Kr. Bernikowsgade 1, 1105 Copenhagen K; tel. 33-48-32-00; fax 33-48-32-20; internet www.canada.dk; Ambassador: MARY M. SIMON.

Chile: Kastelsvej 15, 3rd Floor, 2100 Copenhagen Ø; tel. 35-38-58-34; fax 35-38-42-01; e-mail chiledk@inet.uni2.dk; Ambassador: RAÚL SCHMIDT.

China, People's Republic: Øregårds Allé 25, 2900 Hellerup; tel. 39-46-08-89; fax 39-62-54-84; Ambassador: YANG HEXIONG.

Colombia: Kastelsvej 15, 2100 Copenhagen Ø; tel. 35-26-30-26; fax 35-26-22-97; e-mail emdinamarca@colombia.dk; internet www.colombia.dk; Ambassador: TERESA IVARS.

Côte d'Ivoire: Gersonsvej 8, 2900 Hellerup; tel. 39-62-88-22; fax 39-62-01-62; Ambassador: LILIANE MARIE-LAURE BOA.

Croatia: Dronningens Tværgade 5, 1st Floor, 1302 Copenhagen K; tel. 33-91-90-95; fax 33-91-71-31; e-mail vpdk@koebenhavn.mail.telia.com; Ambassador: ANA MARI BESKEŘ.

Cuba: Carolinevej 12, Ground Floor left, 2900 Hellerup; tel. and fax 39-40-15-10; e-mail embadin@hotmail.com; Chargé d'affaires a.i.: CARLOS A. AMORES.

Czech Republic: Ryvangs Allé 14–16, 2100 Copenhagen Ø; tel. 39-29-18-88; fax 39-29-09-30; e-mail copenhagen@embassy.mzv.cz; Ambassador: ALOIS BUCHTA.

Egypt: Kristianiagade 19, 2100 Copenhagen Ø; tel. 35-43-70-70; fax 35-43-36-49; Ambassador: Dr MUHAMMAD SHAABAN.

Estonia: Aurehøjvej 19, 2900 Hellerup; tel. 39-46-30-70; fax 39-46-30-76; e-mail sekretar@estemb.dk; Ambassador: JÜRI KAHN.

Finland: Skt Annæ Plads 24, 1250 Copenhagen K; tel. 33-13-42-14; fax 33-32-47-10; e-mail webmaster@finamb.dk; internet www.finamb.dk; Ambassador: RALF FRIBERG.

France: Kongens Nytorv 4, 1050 Copenhagen K; tel. 33-67-01-00; fax 33-93-97-52; e-mail presse@amba-france.dk; internet www.amba-france.dk; Ambassador: JEAN-PIERRE MASSET.

Germany: Stockholmsgade 57, POB 2712, 2100 Copenhagen Ø; tel. 35-45-99-00; fax 35-26-71-05; e-mail tyskeamba@email.dk; internet www.tyskeambasssade.dk; Ambassador: JOHANN DREHER.

Ghana: Egebjerg Allé 13, 2900 Hellerup; tel. 39-62-82-22; fax 39-62-16-52; e-mail ghanaemb@post7.tele.dk; Ambassador: (vacant).

Greece: Borgergade 16, 1300 Copenhagen K; tel. 33-11-45-33; fax 33-93-16-46; e-mail greekembcop@post.tele.dk; Ambassador: ANDONIOS NICOLAIDIS.

Holy See: Immortellevej 11, 2950 Vedbæk (Apostolic Nunciature); tel. 45-89-35-36; fax 45-66-17-71; e-mail nunciature@inet.zitech.dk; Apostolic Nuncio: Most Rev. PIERO BIGGIO, Titular Archbishop of Otricoli.

Hungary: Strandvejen 170, 2920 Charlottenlund; tel. 39-63-16-88; fax 39-63-00-52; e-mail ambassador.cph@humfa.kum.hu; Ambassador: LÁSZLÓ DESEÖ.

Iceland: Dantes Plads 3, 1556 Copenhagen V; tel. 33-18-10-50; fax 33-18-10-59; e-mail coph@um.stjr.is; Ambassador: HELGI AGUSTSSON.

India: Vangehusvej 15, 2100 Copenhagen Ø; tel. 39-18-28-88; fax 39-27-02-18; e-mail indemb@euroconnect.dk; Ambassador: Mr SHASHANK.

Indonesia: Ørehøj Allé 1, 2900 Hellerup; tel. 39-62-44-22; fax 39-62-44-83; e-mail indon-dkocybernet.dk; internet www.cybernet.dk/users/indon.dk; Ambassador: ANDJAR SOEDJITO MANGKOEWIJOTO.

Iran: Engskiftevej 6, 2100 Copenhagen Ø; tel. 39-16-00-71; fax 39-16-00-75; Chargé d'affaires a.i.: NASSER JASBI.

Ireland: Østbanegade 21, 2100 Copenhagen Ø; tel. 35-42-32-33; fax 35-43-18-58; e-mail irlemb_dk@yahoo.com; Ambassador: JAMES ANTHONY SHARKEY.

Israel: Lundevangsvej 4, 2900 Hellerup; tel. 39-62-62-88; fax 39-62-19-38; e-mail info@embassy-of-israel.dk; Ambassador: YITZHAK ELPAN.

Italy: Gammel Vartov Vej 7, 2900 Hellerup; tel. 39-62-68-77; fax 39-62-25-99; e-mail italambcph@get2net.dk; Ambassador: ANTONIO CATALANO DI MELLI.

Japan: Pilestræde 61, 1112 Copenhagen K; tel. 33-11-33-44; fax 33-11-33-77; e-mail info@embjapan.dk; internet www.embjapan.dk; Ambassador: MASAKI ORITA.

Korea, Republic: Svanemøllevej 104, 2900 Hellerup; tel. 39-46-04-00; fax 39-46-04-22; Ambassador: KIE-OK CHUNG.

Latvia: Rosbæksvej 17, 2100 Copenhagen Ø; tel. 39-27-60-00; fax 39-27-61-73; e-mail letambas@pip.dknet.dk; Ambassador: AIVARS BAUMANIS.

Lesotho: Tuborg Nord, Strandvejen 64H, 2900 Hellerup; tel. 39-62-43-43; fax 39-62-15-38; e-mail ccc23925@vip.cybercity.dk; Ambassador: RALECHATE LINCOLN MOKOSE.

Libya: Rosenvængets Hovedvej 4, 2100 Copenhagen Ø; tel. 35-26-36-11; fax 35-26-56-06; Ambassador: AHMED ABDULSSALAM BEN KHAYAL.

Lithuania: Bernstorffsvej 214, 2920 Charlottenlund; tel. 39-63-62-07; fax 39-63-65-32; e-mail lrambdan@inet.uni2.dk; internet inet.uni2.dk/home/ltembassy.dk; Ambassador: Dr RAIMUNDAS JASINEVIČIUS.

Luxembourg: Fridtjof Nansens Plads 5, 1st Floor, 2100 Copenhagen Ø; tel. 35-26-82-00; fax 35-26-82-08; Ambassador: FRANÇOIS BREMER.

Macedonia, former Yugoslav republic: Vestagervej 7, 2100 Copenhagen Ø; tel. 39-27-43-14; fax 39-27-43-15; Ambassador: MUHAMED HALILI.

Mexico: Strandvejen 64E, 2900 Hellerup; tel. 39-61-05-00; fax 39-61-05-12; e-mail info@mexican-embassy.dk; internet www.mexican-embassy.dk; Ambassador: EVERARDO SUÁREZ AMEZCUA.

Morocco: Øregårds Allé 19, 2900 Hellerup; tel. 39-62-45-11; fax 39-62-24-49; Ambassador: MENOUAR ALEM.

Netherlands: Toldbodgade 33, 1253 Copenhagen K; tel. 33-70-72-00; fax 33-14-03-50; e-mail nlgovkop@euroconnect.dk; internet www.nlembassy.dk; Ambassador: HANS A. F. M. FÖRSTER.

Norway: Amaliegade 39, 1256 Copenhagen K; tel. 33-14-01-24; fax 33-14-06-24; e-mail emb.copenhagen@mfa.no; internet www.norsk.dk; Ambassador: DAGFINN STENSETH.

Pakistan: Valeursvej 17, 2900 Hellerup; tel. 39-62-11-88; fax 39-40-10-70; e-mail parepcopenhagen@hotmail.com; Ambassador: SALMAN BASHIR.

Peru: Rosenvængets Allé 20, 2100 Copenhagen Ø; tel. 35-26-58-48; fax 35-26-84-06; e-mail embaperu@worldonline.dk; internet www.peruembassy.dk; Ambassador: LILIANA CINO DE SILVA.

Poland: Richelieus Allé 12, 2900 Hellerup; tel. 39-46-77-00; fax 39-46-77-66; e-mail mail@ambpol.dk; internet www.ambpol.dk; Ambassador: JAN GÓRECKI.

Portugal: Hovedvagtsgade 6, 1103 Copenhagen K; tel. 33-13-13-01; fax 33-14-92-14; e-mail embport@get2met.dk; Ambassador: JOSÉ ANTÓNIO MOYA RIBERA.

Romania: Strandagervej 27, 2900 Hellerup; tel. 39-40-71-77; fax 39-62-78-99; Ambassador: Dr GRETE TARTLER TĂBĂRAŞI.

Russia: Kristianiagade 5, 2100 Copenhagen Ø; tel. 35-42-55-85; fax 35-42-37-41; e-mail emb.ru@get2net.dk; Ambassador: NICOLAJ BORDJUSJA.

Saudi Arabia: Lille Strandvej 27, 2900 Hellerup; tel. 39-62-12-00; fax 39-62-60-09; Ambassador: (vacant).

Slovakia: Vesterled 26–28, 2100 Copenhagen Ø; tel. 39-20-99-11; fax 39-20-99-13; e-mail slovakiskamb@vip.cybercity.dk; internet slovakiskamb.homepage.dk; Chargé d'affaires a.i.: IVAN SURKOŠ.

South Africa: Gammel Vartov Vej 8, POB 128, 2900 Hellerup; tel. 39-18-01-55; fax 39-18-40-06; e-mail sa.embassy@inform-bbs.dk; Ambassador: THEMBA MUZIWAKHE NICHOLAS KUBHEKA.

Spain: Kristianiagade 21, 2100 Copenhagen Ø; tel. 35-42-47-00; fax 35-26-30-99; Ambassador: JOSÉ LUIS PARDOS PÉREZ.

Swaziland: Kastelsvej 19, 2100 Copenhagen Ø; tel. 35-42-61-11; fax 35-42-63-00; Ambassador: Prince DAVID DLAMINI.

Sweden: Skt Annæ Plads 15A, 1250 Copenhagen K; tel. 33-36-03-70; fax 33-36-03-95; e-mail ambassaden.kopenhamn@foreign.ministry.se; Ambassador: HÅKAN BERGGREN.

Switzerland: Amaliegade 14, 1256 Copenhagen K; tel. 33-14-17-96; fax 33-33-75-51; e-mail vertretung@cop.rep.admin.ch; Ambassador: JEAN-MARC BOULGARIS.

Thailand: Norgesmindevej 18, 2900 Hellerup; tel. 39-62-50-10; fax 39-62-50-59; e-mail thai-dk@inet.uni2.dk; Ambassador: APIPHONG JAYANAMA.

Turkey: Rosbæksvej 15, 2100 Copenhagen Ø; tel. 39-20-27-88; fax 30-20-51-66; e-mail turkembassy@internet.dk; internet www.turkembassy.dk; Ambassador: GÜN GÜR.

Uganda: Sofievej 15, 2900 Hellerup; tel. 39-62-09-66; fax 39-61-01-48; Ambassador: OMAR MIGADDE LUBULWA.

Ukraine: Toldbodgade 37A, 1st Floor, 1253 Copenhagen K; tel. 33-16-16-35; fax 33-16-00-74; Ambassador: OLEKSANDR SLIPCHENKO.

United Kingdom: Kastelsvej 36–40, 2100 Copenhagen Ø; tel. 35-44-52-00; fax 35-44-52-93; e-mail info@britishembassy.dk; internet www.britishembassy.dk; Ambassador: PHILIP S. ASTLEY.

USA: Dag Hammarskjölds Allé 24, 2100 Copenhagen Ø; tel. 35-55-31-44; fax 35-43-02-23; Ambassador: RICHARD NELSON SWETT.

Venezuela: Holbergsgade 14, 3rd Floor, 1057 Copenhagen K; tel. 33-93-63-11; fax 33-15-69-11; e-mail emvendk@post5.tele.dk; internet home7.inet.tele.dk/emvendk; Ambassador: HUGO ALVAREZ PIFANO.

Yugoslavia: Svanevænget 36–38, 2100 Copenhagen Ø; tel. 39-29-71-61; fax 39-29-79-19; Ambassador: LJUBISA IGLIC.

Judicial System

In Denmark the judiciary is independent of the Government. Judges are appointed by the Crown on the recommendation of the Minister of Justice and cannot be dismissed except by judicial sentence.

The ordinary courts are divided into three instances, the Lower Courts, the High Courts and the Supreme Court. There is one Lower Court for each of the 82 judicial districts in the country. These courts must have at least one judge trained in law and they hear the majority of minor cases. The two High Courts serve Jutland and the islands respectively. They serve as appeal courts for cases from the lower courts, but are also used to give first hearing to the more important cases. Each case must be heard by at least three judges. The Supreme Court, at which at least five judges must sit, is the court of appeal for cases from the Higher Courts. Usually only one appeal is allowed from either court, but in special instances the Board of Appeal may give leave for a second appeal, to the Supreme Court, from a case which started in a lower court. Furthermore, in certain minor cases, appeal from the Lower Courts to the High Courts is allowed only by leave of appeal from the Board of Appeal.

There is a special Maritime and Commercial Court in Copenhagen, consisting of a President and two Vice-Presidents with legal training and a number of commercial and nautical assessors; and also a Labour Court, which deals with labour disputes.

An Ombudsman is appointed by Parliament, after each general election, and is concerned with the quality and legality of the administration of the laws and administrative provisions. Although the Ombudsman holds no formal power to change decisions taken by the administration, he may, on a legal basis, express criticism of acts and decisions of administrative bodies. He must present an annual report to Parliament.

Supreme Court: Prins Jørgens Gård 13, 1218 Copenhagen K; tel. 33-63-27-50; fax 33-15-00-10.

President of the Supreme Court: NIELS ERIK PONTOPPIDAN.

President of the East High Court: SVEN ZIEGLER.

President of the West High Court: BJARNE CHRISTENSEN.

President of the Maritime and Commercial Court: JENS FEILBERG.

President of the Labour Court: MOGENS HORNSLET.

Ombudsman: HANS GAMMELTOFT-HANSEN.

Religion

CHRISTIANITY

Det Økumeniske Fællesraad i Danmark (Ecumenical Council of Denmark): Dag Hammarskjölds Allé 17/3, 2100 Copenhagen Ø; tel. 35-43-29-43; fax 35-43-29-44; e-mail oikoumene@oikoumene.dk; internet www.oikoumene.dk; f. 1939; associate council of the World Council of Churches; six mem. churches, one observer; Chair. Bishop KARSTEN NISSEN; Gen. Sec. HOLGER LAM.

The National Church

Den evangelisk-lutherske Folkekirke i Danmark (Evangelical Lutheran Church in Denmark): Nørregade 11, 1165 Copenhagen K; tel. 33-13-35-08; fax 33-14-39-69; the established Church of Denmark, supported by the State; no bishop exercises a presiding role, but the Bishop of Copenhagen is responsible for certain co-ordinating questions. The Church of Denmark Council on Inter-Church Relations (Vestergade 8, 1456 Copenhagen K; tel. 33-11-44-88; fax 33-11-95-88; e-mail interchurch@folkekirken.dk; internet www .folkekirken.dk) is responsible for ecumenical relations. Membership in 1999 was 4,539,857 (85% of the population).

Bishop of Copenhagen: ERIK NORMAN SVENDSEN.

Bishop of Helsingør: LISE LOTTE REBEL.

Bishop of Roskilde: B. WIBERG.

Bishop of Lolland-Falster: HOLGER JEPSEN.

Bishop of Odense: KRESTEN DREJERGAARD.

Bishop of Ålborg: SØREN LODBERG HVAS.

Bishop of Viborg: KARSTEN NISSEN.

Bishop of Århus: KJELD HOLM.

Bishop of Ribe: NIELS HOLM.

Bishop of Haderslev: NIELS HENRIK ARENDT.

The Roman Catholic Church

Denmark comprises a single diocese, directly responsible to the Holy See. At 31 December 1997 there were an estimated 34,818 adherents in the country. The Bishop participates in the Scandinavian Episcopal Conference (based in Sweden).

Bishop of Copenhagen: CZESLAW KOZON, Katolsk Bispekontor, Bredgade 69A, 1260 Copenhagen K; tel. 33-11-60-80; fax 33-14-60-86; e-mail kozon@katolsk.dk.

Other Churches

Apostolic Church in Denmark: Lykkegaardsvej 100, 6000 Kolding; tel. 75-54-12-01; fax 75-52-11-64; e-mail akd@apostolic.dk; internet www.apostolic.dk; Nat. Leader JOHANNES HANSEN.

Church of England: St Alban's Church, Churchillparken 11, 1263 Copenhagen K; tel. and fax 39-62-77-35; e-mail chaplain@ paradis.dk; f. 1728; Chaplain Rev. T. O. MENDEL.

Church of Jesus Christ of Latter-day Saints (Mormons): Rødovre; tel. 31-70-90-43; f. in Denmark 1850; 4,500 mems.

Danish Mission Covenant Church: Rosenlunden 17, 5000 Odense C; tel. 66-14-83-31; fax 66-14-83-00; e-mail ddm@email.dk; Rev. LEO HANSEN.

Det Danske Baptistsamfund (Baptist Union of Denmark): Købnerhus, Lærdalsgade 7, 2300 Copenhagen S; tel. 32-59-07-08; fax 32-59-01-33; e-mail Sekretariat@baptistkirken.dk; internet www.baptistkirken.dk; f. 1839; 5,400 mems; Pres. Rev. OLE JØRGENSEN.

First Church of Christ, Scientist, Copenhagen: Nyvej 7, 1851 Frederiksberg C; tel. 33-13-08-91; also in Århus; tel. 86-16-22-78.

German Lutheran Church: Skt Petri Church Office, Larslejsstræde 11, 1451 Copenhagen K; tel. 33-13-38-33; fax 33-13-38-35; e-mail stpetri@post10.tele.dk.

Methodist Church: Metodistkirkens Social Arbejde, Rigensgade 21A, 1316 Copenhagen K; f. 1910; tel. 33-93-25-96; e-mail msac@ image.dk; Chair. FINN UTH.

Moravian Brethren: The Moravian Church, 6070 Christiansfeld; f. in Denmark 1773; Pastor JØRGEN BØYTLER, Lindegade 26, 6070 Christiansfeld; tel. 74-56-14-20; fax 74-56-14-21; e-mail boeytler@ post7.tele.dk.

Norwegian Seamen's Church: Kong Håkons Kirke, Ved Mønten 9, 2300 Copenhagen S; tel. 32-57-11-03; fax 32-57-40-05; e-mail kobenhavn@sifh.no; f. 1958.

Reformed Church: Reformed Synod of Denmark, Nørrebrogade 32A, 7000 Fredericia; tel. 75-92-05-51; Rev. SABINE HOFMEISTER.

Russian Orthodox Church: Alexander Nevski Church, Bredgade 53, 1260 Copenhagen K; tel. 33-13-60-46; fax 33-13-28-85; e-mail russiske-kirke@get2net.dk; f. 1883.

Seventh-day Adventists: Adventistsamfundet, Concordiavej 16, 2850 Nærum; tel. 45-58-77-77; fax 45-58-77-78; internet www .adventist.dk; f. 1863; Pres. PAUL BIRCH PETERSEN; Sec. JOHN PEDERSEN.

Society of Friends: Danish Quaker Centre, Vendersgade 29, 4., 1363 Copenhagen K; tel. and fax 35-83-09-76; internet www .kvaekerne.dk.

Swedish Lutheran Church: Svenska Gustafskyrkan, Folke Bernadottes Allé, 2100 Copenhagen Ø; tel. 33-15-54-58; fax 33-15-02-94.

Unitarians: Unitarernes Hus, Dag Hammarskjølds Allé 30, 2100 Copenhagen Ø; e-mail unitar@postlo.tele.dk; internet www.homelo .inet.tele.dk/unitar/; Chair. P. BOVIN; mems: 100 families.

The Salvation Army is also active in the country (Frederiksberg Allé 9, 1621 Copenhagen V; tel. 31-31-41-92).

BAHÁ'Í FAITH

Bahá'í: Det Nationale Åndelige Råd, Sofievej 28, 2900 Hellerup; tel. 39-62-35-18; e-mail sekretariat@bahai.dk; internet www.bahai.dk; National Centre for the Bahá'í faith in Denmark.

ISLAM

The Muslim Community: Nusrat Djahan Mosque (and Ahmadiyya Mission), Eriksminde Allé 2, 2650 Hvidovre; tel. 36-75-35-02; fax 36-75-00-07.

JUDAISM

Jewish Community: Mosaisk Trossamfund, Ny Kongensgade 6, 1472 Copenhagen K; tel. 33-12-88-68; fax 33-12-33-57; e-mail bent_lexner@hotmail.com; 5,000 mems; Chief Rabbi BENT LEXNER.

The Press

There are more than 220 separate newspapers, including some 37 principal dailies. The average total circulation of daily newspapers in 1997 was 1,615,000 on weekdays.

Most newspapers and magazines are privately owned and published by joint concerns, co-operatives or limited liability companies. The main concentration of papers is held by the Berlingske Group, which owns *Berlingske Tidende, Weekendavisen Berlingske,* and *B.T.,* and the provincial *Jydske Vestkysten* and *Århus Stiftstidende.*

There is no truly national press. Copenhagen accounts for 20% of the national dailies and about one-half of the total circulation. No paper is directly owned by a political party, although all papers show a fairly pronounced political leaning.

PRINCIPAL DAILIES

Ålborg

Nordjyske Stiftstidende: Langagervej 1, POB 8000, 9220 Ålborg Ø; tel. 99-35-35-35; fax 99-35-32-24; e-mail nordjyske@nordjyske.dk;

internet www.nordjyske.dk; f. 1767; adopted present name in 1999, following the merger of six regional dailies; mornings; Liberal independent; Publr and Editor-in-Chief PER LYNGBY; approx. circ. weekdays 100,000, Sundays 114,000.

Århus

Århus Stiftstidende: Olof Palmes Allé 39, POB 1, 8200 Århus N; tel. 87-40-10-10; fax 87-40-14-04; f. 1794; evening and weekend mornings; Liberal independent; Editors AGE LUNDGÅRD, HANS PETERSEN; circ. 176,000.

Copenhagen

Aktuelt: Kalvebod Brygge 35–37, 1595 Copenhagen V; tel. 33-18-40-00; fax 33-18-40-04; f. 1871; morning; Social Democratic; Editor-in-Chief ANDERS JERICHOW; circ. weekdays 156,000.

Berlingske Tidende: Pilestræde 34, 1147 Copenhagen K; tel. 33-75-75-75; fax 33-75-20-20; internet www.berlingske.dk; f. 1749; morning; Conservative independent; Editor-in-Chief PETER WIVEL; circ. weekdays 160,000, Sundays 250,000.

Børsen: Møntergade 19, 1140 Copenhagen K; tel. 33-32-01-02; fax 33-12-24-45; e-mail redaktionen@borsen.dk; internet www.borsen.dk; f. 1896; morning; independent; business news; Editor-in-Chief LEIF BECK FALLESEN; circ. 56,020.

B.T.: Kr. Bernikowsgade 6, 1147 Copenhagen K; tel. 33-75-75-33; fax 33-75-20-33; e-mail bt@bt.dk; f. 1916; morning; Conservative independent; Editor-in-Chief ERIK BISTRUP; circ. weekdays 144,910, Sundays 190,053.

Ekstra Bladet: Rådhuspladsen 37, 1785 Copenhagen V; tel. 33-11-13-13; fax 33-14-10-00; e-mail post@ekstrabladet.dk; internet www.ekstrabladet.dk; f. 1904; evening; Liberal independent; Editor-in-Chief S. O. GADE; Man. Dir LARS HENRIK MUNCH; circ. weekdays 159,500, Sundays 192,900.

Information: Store Kongensgade 40C, 1264 Copenhagen K; tel. 33-69-60-00; fax 33-69-60-79; e-mail inf-dk@information.dk; internet www.information.dk; f. 1943 (underground during occupation), legally 1945; morning; independent; Editors JACOB MOLLERUP, JØRGAN STEEN NIELSEN; circ. 22,380.

Kristeligt Dagblad: Rosengården 14, 1174 Copenhagen K; tel. 33-48-05-00; fax 33-48-05-01; f. 1896; morning; independent; Editor ERIK BJERAGER; circ. 17,000.

Politiken: Politikens Hus, Rådhuspladsen 37, 1585 Copenhagen V; tel. 33-11-85-11; fax 33-15-41-17; e-mail pol_hid@online.pol.dk; internet www.pol.dk; f. 1884; morning; Liberal independent; Editor-in-Chief TOEGER SEIDENFADEN; circ. 571,000.

Esbjerg

Jydske Vestkysten: Banegårdspladsen, 6700 Esbjerg; tel. 75-12-45-00; fax 75-13-62-62; e-mail jydskevestkysten@jv.dk; internet www.jv.dk; f. 1917 as *Vestkysten,* merged with *Jydske Tidende* in 1991 to form present daily; morning; Liberal; Editors NILS THOSTRUP, JÖRGEN BAUUGAARD; circ. weekdays 94,234, Sundays 106,157.

Herning

Herning Folkeblad: Østergade 25, 7400 Herning; tel. 96-26-37-00; fax 97-22-36-00; e-mail hf@herningfolkeblad.dk; f. 1869; evening; Liberal; Editor-in-Chief GORM ALBRECHTSEN; circ. 15,360 (Wednesday 55,000).

Hillerød

Frederiksborg Amts Avis: Milnersvej 44–46, 3400 Hillerød; tel. 48-24-41-00; fax 42-25-48-40; f. 1874; morning; Liberal; Editor TORBEN DALLEY LARSEN; circ. weekdays 38,000, Sundays 35,800.

Holbæk

Holbæk Amts Venstreblad: Ahlgade 1, 4300 Holbæk; tel. 59-48-02-00; fax 59-44-28-10; f. 1905; evening; Social Liberal; Editor-in-Chief MOGENS FLYVHOLM; circ. 53,000.

Holstebro

Dagbladet Holstebro-Struer: Lægårdvej 86, 7500 Holstebro; tel. 99-12-83-00; fax 97-41-03-20; evening; Liberal independent; Editor ERIK MØLLER; circ. 13,500.

Horsens

Horsens Folkeblad: Søndergade 47, 8700 Horsens; tel. 76-27-20-00; fax 75-61-07-97; e-mail redaktionen@horsens-folkeblad.dk; f. 1866; evening; Liberal; Editor JENS BEBE; circ. 23,277.

Næstved

Næstved Tidende: Ringstedgade 13, 4700 Næstved; tel. 55-72-45-11; fax 55-77-01-57; e-mail red@sj-dagblade.dk; internet www.sj-dagblade.dk; f. 1866; Liberal; 6 days a week; Editor SØREN BAUMANN; circ. 19,240.

Nykøbing

Folketidende: Tværgade 14, 4800 Nykøbing F; tel. 54-88-02-00; fax 54-85-38-52; f. 1873; evening; Liberal; Editor BO BISCHOFF; circ. 27,245.

Odense

Fyens Stiftstidende: Blangstedgårdsvej 2–6, 5220 Odense Sø; tel. 66-11-11-11; fax 65-93-25-74; internet www.fyensdl.dk; f. 1772; morning; independent; Editor-in-Chief HANS DAM; circ. 93,000.

Randers

Amtsavisen: Narregade 7, 8900 Randers; tel. 86-42-75-11; fax 86-41-92-11; f. 1810; evening; independent; Editor-in-Chief OLE C. JØRGENSEN; circ. 81,000.

Ringkøbing

Ringkøbing Amts Dagblad: Skt Blichersvej 5, 6950 Ringkøbing; tel. 99-75-73-00; fax 97-32-05-46; evening; Editor KRISTIAN SAND; circ. 46,000.

Rønne

Bornholms Tidende: Nørregade 11–13, 3700 Rønne; tel. 56-95-14-00; fax 56-95-31-19; f. 1866; evening; Liberal; Editor-in-Chief BJARNE PEDERSEN; circ. 14,300.

Silkeborg

Midtjyllands Avis: Vestergade 30, 8600 Silkeborg; tel. 86-82-13-00; fax 86-81-35-77; f. 1857; daily except Sundays; Editor-in-Chief STEFFEN LANGE; circ. 30,000.

Skive

Skive Folkeblad: Gemsevej 7–9, 7800 Skive; tel. 97-51-34-11; fax 97-51-28-35; f. 1880; Social Liberal; Editor OLE DALL; circ. 40,000.

Slagelse

Sjællands Tidende: Korsgade 4, 4200 Slagelse; tel. 53-52-37-00; fax 53-52-34-97; f. 1815; evening; Liberal; for western part of Zealand; Editor SØREN BAUMANN; circ. 15,247.

Svendborg

Fyns Amts Avis: Skt Nicolaigade 3, 5700 Svendborg; tel. 62-21-46-21; fax 62-22-06-10; e-mail post@fynsamtsavis.dk; f. 1863; Liberal; Editor OLE C. JØRGENSEN; circ. 69,000.

Thisted

Thisted Dagblad: Jernbanegade 15–17, 7700 Thisted; tel. 99-19-93-00; fax 97-91-07-20; Liberal independent; Editor HANS PETER KRAGH; circ. 29,000.

Vejle

Vejle Amts Folkeblad: Bugattivej 8, 7100 Vejle; tel. 75-85-77-88; fax 75-85-74-76; f. 1865; evening; Liberal; Editor ARNE MARIAGER; circ. 32,626.

Viborg

Viborg Stifts Folkeblad: Skt Mathiasgade 7, 8800 Viborg; tel. 89-27-63-00; fax 89-27-63-70; f. 1877; evening; Liberal Democrat; also published: *Viborg Nyt* (weekly); Editor PER SUNESEN; circ. 13,131.

Viby

Jyllands-Posten Morgenavisen: Grøndalsvej 3, 8260 Viby J; tel. 87-38-38-38; fax 86-11-26-29; e-mail jp@jp.dk; internet www.jp.dk; independent; Editor-in-Chief JØRGEN EJBØL; circ. 817,000.

OTHER NEWSPAPERS

Den Blå Avis (East edition): Generatorvej 8D, 2730 Herlev; tel. 44-85-44-44; internet www.dba.dk; 2 a week; circ. 73,000.

Den Blå Avis (West edition): Marelisborg Havnevej 26, POB 180, 8100 Århus C; tel. 87-31-31-31; fax 86-20-20-02; internet www.dba.dk; Thursday; circ. 46,160.

Weekendavisen Berlingske: Pilestræde 34, 1147 Copenhagen K; tel. 33-75-75-75; fax 33-75-20-50; e-mail weekendavisen@berlingske.dk; f. 1749; independent Conservative; Friday; Editor-in-Chief ANNE KNUDSEN; circ. 60,000.

POPULAR PERIODICALS

Ældre Sagen: Vester Farimagsgade 15, 1606 Copenhagen V; tel. 33-96-86-86; fax 33-96-86-87; internet www.aeldresagen.dk; 6 a year; for senior citizens; Editor JESPER HALLER; circ. 330,000.

ALT for damerne: Hellerupvej 51, 2900 Hellerup; tel. 39-45-74-00; fax 39-45-74-80; e-mail alt@altfordamerne.dk; internet www.altfordamerne.dk; f. 1946; weekly; women's magazine; Editor-in-Chief HANNE HØIBERG; circ. 96,040.

Anders And & Co: Vognmagergade 11, 1148 Copenhagen K; tel. 33-30-50-00; fax 33-30-55-10; internet www.andeby.dk; weekly; children's magazine; Editor TOMMY MELLE; circ. 99,826.

Arte-Nyt: Hvidkildevej 64, 2400 Copenhagen NV; tel. 38-88-49-00; fax 38-33-20-83; 3 a year; arts; Editor MOGENS HJORTH; circ. 50,000.

Basserne: Hellerupvej 51, 2900 Hellerup; tel. 33-33-75-35; fax 33-33-75-05; fortnightly; children and youth; circ. 49,000.

Det Bedste fra Reader's Digest A/S: Jagtvej 169B, 2100 Copenhagen Ø; tel. 39-18-12-13; fax 39-18-12-36; e-mail det-bedste@internet.dk; monthly; Danish *Reader's Digest*; Editor YNGVE SKOVMAND; circ. 69,556.

Billed-Bladet: Vesterbrogade 16, 1620 Copenhagen V; tel. 31-23-16-11; fax 31-24-10-08; f. 1938; weekly; family picture magazine; Editor ANDERS THISTED; circ. 222,951.

Bo Bedre: Strandboulevarden 130, 2100 Copenhagen Ø; tel. 39-17-20-00; fax 39-17-23-02; e-mail bobedre@bp.bonnier.dk; monthly; homes and gardens; Editor-in-Chief ERIK RIMMER; circ. 99,894.

Camping: Lillehøjvej 10, 8600 Silkeborg; tel. 86-82-55-00; fax 86-81-63-02; monthly; circ. 44,107.

Familie Journalen: Vigerslev Allé 18, 2500 Valby, Copenhagen; tel. 36-15-22-22; fax 36-15-22-99; e-mail redaklion@famaliejournalen.dk; f. 1877; weekly; Editor-in-Chief ANKER SVENDSEN-TUNE; circ. 243,000.

Femina: Vigerslev Allé 18, 2500 Valby, Copenhagen; tel. 36-30-33-33; fax 36-44-19-79; f. 1873; weekly; Editor JUTTA LARSEN; circ. 93,866.

Gør Det Selv: Strandboulevarden 130, 2100 Copenhagen Ø; tel. 39-17-20-00; fax 39-29-01-99; e-mail gds@isa.dknet.dk; f. 1975; 14 a year; do-it-yourself; Editor KÅRE OLOFSEN; circ. 150,000.

Helse—Familiens Lægemagasin: Classensgade 36, 2100 Copenhagen Ø; tel. 35-25-05-25; fax 35-26-87-60; monthly; family health; circ. 300,000.

Hendes Verden: Hellerupvej 51, 2900 Hellerup; tel. 39-45-75-50; fax 39-45-75-99; f. 1937; weekly; for women; Editor IBEN NIELSEN; circ. 58,302.

Hjemmet (The Home): Vognmagergade 10, 1145 Copenhagen K; tel. 39-45-76-00; fax 39-45-76-60; weekly; Editor-in-Chief BJARNE RAUNSTED; circ. 207,087.

I form: Strandboulevarden 130, 2100 Copenhagen Ø; tel. 39-17-20-00; fax 39-17-23-11; e-mail iform@bp.bonnier.dk; monthly; sport, health, nutrition, sex, psychology; Editor KAREN LYAGER HORVE; circ. 70,766.

idé-nyt: Gl. Klausdalsbrovej 480, 2730 Herlev; tel. 44-53-40-00; fax 44-92-11-21; e-mail idenyt@idenyt.dk; internet www.idenyt.dk; f. 1973; 5 a year; free magazine (regional editions); homes and gardens; circ. 2,500,000.

Illustreret Videnskab: Strandboulevarden 130, 2100 Copenhagen Ø; tel. 39-17-20-00; fax 39-17-23-12; 16 a year; popular science; Editor JENS E. MATTHIESEN; circ. 88,132.

Mad og Bolig: Skt Annæ Plads 8, 1250 Copenhagen K; tel. 33-14-44-22; fax 33-17-60-68; f. 1991; 8 a year; gastronomy, wine, interiors and travel; Editor JETTE ØSTERLUND; circ. 70,107.

Månedsmagasinet Bilen: Eckersbergsvej 5, 3000 Elsinore; tel. 49-26-30-04; fax 39-17-23-02; e-mail bilen@bp.bonnier.dk; monthly; cars, motor sport; Editor FLEMMING HASLUND; circ. 37,500.

Månedsmagasinet IN: Skt Annæ Plads 8, 1250 Copenhagen K; fashion magazine; tel. 33-11-29-29; fax 33-14-60-67; e-mail in@in.dk; internet www.in.dk; Editor CAMILLA LINDEMANN; circ. 49,582.

Motor: Firskovvej 32, POB 500, 2800 Lyngby; tel. 45-27-07-07; fax 45-27-09-89; e-mail motor@fdm.dk; internet www.fdm.dk; monthly; cars and motoring; circ. 210,000.

Penny: Vognmagergade 11, 1148 Copenhagen K; tel. 33-15-19-25; fax 33-91-05-85; monthly; children's magazine; circ. 43,000.

Rapport: Vigerslev Allé 18, 2500 Valby; tel. 44-85-88-66; fax 44-85-88-67; e-mail rap@rapport.dk; internet www.rapport.dk; f. 1971; men's weekly; Editor-in-Chief JAN SCHIWE NIELSEN; circ. 36,964.

Samvirke: Roskildevej 65, 2620 Albertslund; tel. 43-86-43-86; fax 43-86-44-89; f. 1928; consumer monthly; Publr and Editor-in-Chief POUL DINES; circ. 500,000.

Se og Hør: Vigerslev Allé 18, 2500 Valby; tel. 36-15-24-00; fax 36-15-24-99; e-mail redaktionen@sh-online.dk; internet www.sh-online.dk; f. 1940; news and TV; Editor PETER SALSKOV; circ. 315,083.

Sofus' Lillebror: Copenhagen; tel. 33-33-75-35; fax 33-33-75-05; monthly; children and youth; circ. 44,000.

TIPS-bladet: Alsgarde Centret 2, 3140 Alsgarde; tel. 49-70-89-00; fax 49-70-88-30; weekly; sport; circ. 39,467.

Ud og Se: Allégade 8F, 2000 Frederiksberg; tel. 31-22-20-20; fax 31-22-99-59; travel monthly; circ. 290,000.

Ude og Hjemme: Vigerslev Allé 18, 2500 Valby, Copenhagen; tel. 36-15-25-25; fax 36-15-25-99; e-mail redaktionen@udeoghjemme.dk; internet www.udeoghjemme.dk; f. 1926; family weekly; Editor JØRN BAUENMAND; circ. 181,000.

Ugebladet Søndag: Otto Mønsteds Gade 3, 1505 Copenhagen V; tel. 36-15-34-00; fax 36-15-34-01; e-mail soendag@soendag.dk; f. 1921; weekly; family magazine; Editor JOHNNY JOHANSEN; circ. 129,700.

Wendy: Vognmagergade 9, 1148 Copenhagen K; tel. 33-30-50-00; fax 33-30-55-10; fortnightly; children's comics; circ. 30,000.

SPECIALIST PERIODICALS

ABF-Nyt: Carsten Ekström, Bagsværdhovedgade 296–298, 2880 Bagsværd; tel. 44-44-77-47; fax 44-44-67-47; e-mail abfnyt@announce-service.dk; 4 a year; Editor JAN HANSEN; circ. 60,185.

Aktive Kvinder: Niels Hemmingsensgade 10, 2. sal, 1153 Copenhagen K; tel. 33-13-12-22; fax 33-33-03-28; e-mail ddh@ddh-aktive-kvinder.dk; internet www.ddh-aktive-kvinder.dk; f. 1920; 6 a year; home management; Editor KIRSTEN WULFF; circ. 25,000.

Aktuel Elektronik: Skelbækgade 4, 1780 Copenhagen V; tel. 31-21-68-01; fax 31-21-23-96; 22 a year; computing and information technology; circ. 21,642.

Alt om Data: St. Kongensgade 72, 1264 Copenhagen K; tel. 33-91-28-33; fax 33-91-01-21; e-mail redaktion@aod.dk; internet www.aod.dk/aod; f. 1983; monthly; Editor-in-Chief TORBEN OKHOLM; circ. 35,000.

Automatik: Algade 10, POB 80, 4500 Nykøbing; tel. 53-41-23-10; engineering; monthly; circ. 39,250.

Bådnyt (Boats): Marielundvej 46E, 2730 Herlev; tel. 44-85-89-55; fax 44-85-89-56; e-mail redaktionen@baadnyt.dk; monthly; Editor KNUT IVERSEN; circ. 18,500.

Beboerbladet: Allégade 8F, 2000 Frederiksberg; tel. 31-22-20-20; fax 31-22-99-59; quarterly; for tenants in public housing; circ. 475,000.

Beredskab: Nørrebrogade 66D, 2200 Copenhagen N; tel. 35-37-75-00; fax 35-37-73-95; e-mail beredskab@euroconnect.dk; internet www.beredskabsforbundet.dk; f. 1934; 6 a year; civil protection and preparedness; publ. by the Danish Civil Protection League; circ. 20,500.

Bilsnak: Park Allé 355, 2605 Brøndby; tel. 43-28-82-00; fax 43-63-27-22; internet www.volkswagen.dk; quarterly; cars; circ. 181,400.

Boligen: Studiestræde 50, 1554 Copenhagen V; tel. 33-76-20-21; fax 33-76-20-01; monthly; housing associations, architects; Editor HELGE MØLLER; circ. 30,000.

BygTek: Stationsparken 25, 2600 Glostrup; tel. 43-43-29-00; fax 43-43-13-28; e-mail odsgard@odsgard.dk; internet www.byggeri.dk; monthly; building and construction; circ. 25,000.

Computerworld: Carl Jacobsensvej 25, 2500 Valby; tel. 36-19-91-00; fax 36-44-25-69; e-mail computerworld.dk@idg.com; internet www.computerworld.dk; f. 1981; weekly; computing; Chief Officers PETER HVIDTFELDT, JENS JØRGEN KRAG HANSEN, KIM MARQUART; circ. 26,000.

Cyklister: Dansk Cyklist Forbund, Rømersgade 7, 1362 Copenhagen K; tel. 33-32-31-21; fax 33-32-76-83; e-mail dcf@dcf.dk; internet www.dcf.dk; f. 1905; 6 a year; organ of Danish Cyclist Federation; Editor INGRID E. PETERSEN; circ. 19,000.

Effektivt Landbrug: Skelbækgade 4, 1780 Copenhagen V; tel. 31-21-68-01; fax 31-21-53-50; 21 a year; farming; circ. 31,407.

FINANS: Langebrogade 5, 1411 Copenhagen K; tel. 32-96-46-00; internet www.finansforbundet.dk; 16 a year; for employees in the financial sector; circ. 53,000.

Folkeskolen: Vandkunsten 12, POB 2139, 1015 Copenhagen K; tel. 33-69-63-00; fax 33-69-64-26; e-mail folkeskolen@dlf.org; internet www.folkeskolen.dk; 43 a year; teaching; Editor THORKILD THEJSEN; circ. 84,461.

Forbrugsforeningsbladet: Knabrostræde 12, 1210 Copenhagen K; tel. 33-15-88-26; monthly; for civil servants and doctors; circ. 60,000.

Foto Guiden: POB 239, 9900 Frederikshavn; tel. 98-42-90-60; fax 98-42-90-61; f. 1960; 2 a year; photography; Editor E. STEEN SØRENSEN; circ. 24,000.

Havebladet: Hvidehusv 24, POB 173, 3450 Allerød; tel. 42-27-14-09; fax 42-27-72-88; 6 a year; gardening; circ. 47,000.

High Fidelity: Blegdamsvej 112A, 2100 Copenhagen Ø; tel. 70-23-70-01; fax 70-23-70-02; e-mail hifired@hifi.dk; f. 1968; 11 a year; Editor-in-Chief MICHAEL MADSEN; circ. 24,833.

Hunden: Parkvej 1, 2680 Solrød Strand; tel. 53-14-74-00; fax 53-14-30-03; internet www.dansk-kennel-klub.dk; 10 a year; organ of the kennel club; circ. 25,000.

Ingeniøren: POB 373, Skelbækgade 4, 1503 Copenhagen V; tel. 33-26-53-00; fax 33-26-53-05; e-mail ing@ing.dk; internet www.ing.dk;

f. 1892; weekly engineers' magazine; Editor PER WESTERGÅRD; circ. 74,500.

Jaeger: Hojnæsvej 56, 2610 Rødovre; tel. 36-72-42-00; fax 36-72-09-11; monthly except July; circ. 89,000.

Jern- og Maskinindustrien: Falkoner Allé 90, 2000 Frederiksberg; tel. 35-36-37-00; fax 35-36-37-90; e-mail jm@df-jm.dk; 22 a year; iron and metallic industries; circ. 25,295.

Jyllands Ringens program: Vilvordevej 102, 2920 Charlottenlund; tel. 31-64-46-92; 5 a year; cars and motor cycles; circ. 280,000.

Kommunalbladet: Park Allé 9, 8000 Aarhus C; tel. 86-76-13-22; fax 86-76-13-10; e-mail redaktionen@kommunalbladet.dk; internet www.kommunalbladet.dk; 22 a year; municipal administration, civil servants; Editor ULLA KRAG JESPERSEN; circ. 75,000.

Kontor & IT: Sydvestvej 49, 2600 Glostrup; tel. 43-22-50-00; fax 43-22-50-99; e-mail kontorogit@visholm.dk; internet www .kontorogit.dk; monthly; management in trade and industry; Editor BO LYNGJAA; circ. 28,747.

Landsbladet Kvæg: Vester Farimagsgade 6, 1606 Copenhagen V; tel. 33-11-22-22; fax 33-11-31-48; monthly; for cattle-breeders and dairy-farmers; (related titles *Landsbladet Mark* for arable farmers, *Landsbladet Svin* for pig-farmers); circ. 15,000.

Lederne: Vermlandsgade 65, 2300 Copenhagen S; tel. 32-83-32-83; fax 32-83-32-84; e-mail lh@lederne.dk; internet www.lederne.dk; 12 a year; for managers; circ. 80,136.

Metal: Nyropsgade 38, 1602 Copenhagen V; tel. 33-63-20-00; fax 33-63-21-00; 16 a year; metal industries; circ. 150,571.

Produktion: Axelborg, Vesterbrogade 4A, 1503 Copenhagen; tel. 33-69-87-00; fax 33-69-87-07; internet www.dlg.dk; 6 a year; farming; Editor ELSE DAMSGAARD; circ. 63,000.

Spejd: The Danish Guide and Scout Association, Arsenalvej 10, 1436 Copenhagen K; tel. 32-64-00-50; fax 32-64-00-75; e-mail dds@dds.dk; internet www.dds.dk; 7 a year; organ of the Scout Movement; circ. 38,900.

Stat, Amt og KommuneInformation: 2600 Glostrup; tel. 43-43-31-21; fax 43-43-15-13; e-mail saki@post4.tele.dk; monthly; public works and administration; circ. 21,000.

Sundhedsbladet: Concordiavej 16, 2850 Noerum; tel. 45-80-43-00; fax 45-80-70-75; 6 a year; health; Editor TUE WESTING; circ. 27,000.

Sygeplejersken: Vimmelskaftet 38, POB 1084, 1008 Copenhagen K; tel. 33-15-15-55; e-mail redaktionen@dansk-sygeplejeraad.dk; internet www.tfs.dk; 50 a year; nursing; circ. 72,000.

Tidsskrift for Sukkersyge—Diabetes: Filosofgangen 24, 5000 Odense C; tel. 66-12-90-06; fax 65-91-49-08; e-mail df@ diabetesforeningen.dk; internet www.diabetesforeningen.dk; f. 1940; 6 a year; diabetes; Dir FLEMMING KJERSGAARD JOHANSEN; circ. 50,000.

Ugeskrift for Læger: Trondhjemsgade 9, 2100 Copenhagen Ø; tel. 35-44-85-00; e-mail ufl-vidensvab-praksis@dadl.dk; weekly; medical; Editor L. HØJGAARD; circ. 21,000.

NEWS AGENCY

Ritzaus Bureau I/S: St. Kongensgade 14, 1264 Copenhagen K; tel. 33-30-00-00; fax 33-30-00-01; e-mail ritzau@ritzau.dk; internet www.ritzau.dk; f. 1866; general, financial and commercial news; owned by all Danish newspapers; Chair. of Board of Dirs TORBEN DALBY LARSEN; Gen. Man. and Editor-in-Chief UFFE RIIS SØRENSEN.

Foreign Bureaux

Agence France-Presse (AFP): Store Kongensgade 14, 3rd floor, 1264 Copenhagen K; tel. 33-13-23-31; fax 33-14-32-06; e-mail afp@nitzau.dk; Bureau Chief SLIM ALLAGUI.

Agencia EFE (Spain): Copenhagen; Correspondent MARÍA CAMINO SÁNCHEZ.

Agenzia Nazionale Stampa Associata (ANSA) (Italy): Vestergade 2, 1456 Copenhagen K; tel. 33-32-03-59; fax 33-32-03-69; Correspondent DANIELA ROMITI.

Allgemeiner Deutscher Nachrichtendienst (ADN) (Germany): 2660 Brøndbystrand, Kisumparken 65 st. th., Copenhagen; Bureau Chief HERBERT HANSCH.

Associated Press (AP) (USA): Bremerholm 1, 1069 Copenhagen K; tel. 33-11-15-04; fax 33-32-36-60; Bureau Chief ED McCULLOUGH.

Deutsche Presse-Agentur (dpa) (Germany): Store Kongensgade 14, 3rd floor, 1264 Copenhagen K; tel. 33-14-22-19; fax 33-14-66-72; e-mail dpa@ritzau.dk; Chief Correspondent THOMAS BORCHERT.

Informatsionnoye Telegrafnoye Agentstvo Rossii-Telegrafnoye Agentstvo Suverennykh Stran (ITAR-TASS) (Russia): Uraniavej 9B, 1878 Frederiksberg C; tel. 31-31-88-48; Correspondent TARAS B. LARIOKHIN.

Reuters (UK): Badstuestræde 18, 1209 Copenhagen K; tel. 33-96-96-96; fax 33-12-32-72; e-mail copenhagen.newsroom@ reuters.com; Bureau Chief PER BECH THOMSEN.

PRESS ASSOCIATIONS

Dansk Fagpresse (Danish Periodical Press Association): Vesterbrogade 24, 2. sal, 1620 Copenhagen V; tel. 33-86-31-00; fax 31-23-43-10; e-mail df@danskfagpresse.dk; internet www.danskfagpresse .dk; Man. Dir PAUL KRESTENSEN.

Dansk Magasinpresses Udgiverforening (Danish Magazine Publishers' Association): Hammerensgade 6, 1267 Copenhagen K; tel. 33-11-88-44; fax 33-15-01-86; e-mail dmu-mags@internet.dk; internet www.dmu-mags.dk; Chair. NILS PRIEMÉ; Dir FINN SKOVSGAARD.

Danske Dagblades Forening (Danish Newspaper Publishers' Association): Pressens Hus, Skindergade 7, 1159 Copenhagen K; tel. 33-97-40-00; fax 33-14-23-25; e-mail ddf@danskedagblade.dk; comprises managers and editors-in-chief of all newspapers; general spokesbody for the Danish press; Man. Dir EBBE DAL.

Publishers

Aarhus Universitetsforlag: Langelandsgade 177, 8200 Aarhus N; tel. 89-42-53-70; fax 89-42-53-80; e-mail unipress@au.dk; internet www.unipress.dk; reference, non-fiction and educational; Man. Dir CLAES HVIDBAK.

Forlaget åløkke A/S: Porskærvej 15, Nim, 8700 Horsens; tel. 75-67-11-19; fax 75-67-10-74; e-mail alokke@get2net.dk; internet www.alokke.dk; f. 1977; educational, children's books, audio-visual and other study aids; Pres. BERTIL TOFT HANSEN; Man. Dir EVA B. HANSEN.

Akademisk Forlag A/S (Danish University Press): Adelgade 15, 4., POB 54, 1304 Copenhagen K; tel. 33-11-98-26; fax 33-32-05-70; e-mail akademisk@akademisk.dk; f. 1962; history, health, linguistics, university textbooks, educational materials; Dir KELD LUND JENSEN.

Forlaget Amanda: 7 Rathsacksvej, 1862 Frederiksberg C; tel. 33-79-00-10; fax 33-79-00-11; e-mail forlag@dansklf.dk; art, culture, school books, non-fiction; Editorial Dir GERT EMBORG.

Forlaget Apostrof ApS: Berggreensgade 24, 2100 Copenhagen Ø; tel. 39-20-84-20; fax 39-20-84-53; e-mail info@apostrof.dk; internet www.apostrof.dk; f. 1980; psychotherapy and contemporary psychology, fiction and non-fiction for children; Publrs MIA THESTRUP, OLE THESTRUP.

Arkitektens Forlag: Strandgade 27A, 1401 Copenhagen K; tel. 32-83-69-00; fax 32-83-69-41; e-mail eksp@arkfo.dk; architecture, planning; Dir KIM DIRCKINCK-HOLMFELD.

Forlaget Artia (Ars Audiendi ApS); Vognmagergade 9, 1120 Copenhagen K; tel. 33-12-28-98; fax 33-14-12-63; fiction, non-fiction, science fiction, music, horror; Publr ERIK LÆSSØE STILLING; Dir PETER SCHANTZ.

Aschehoug Dansk Forlag A/S: Landemærket 8, POB 2179, 1017 Copenhagen K; tel. 33-30-55-22; fax 33-30-58-22; e-mail info@ash .egmont.com; internet www.aschehoug.dk; imprints: Aschehoug (fiction), Aschehoug Fakta (non-fiction, reference, children's books), Sesam (educational, children's books, history); Man. Dir (Aschehoug) ANETTE WAD.

Peter Asschenfeldt's nye Forlag A/S: Ny Adelgade 8–10, 1104 Copenhagen K; tel. 33-37-07-60; fax 33-91-03-04; fiction; Publr PETER ASSCHENFELDT.

Thomas Bloms Forlag ApS: Skovenggaardsvej 8, 9490 Pandrup; tel. 98-24-85-25; fax 98-24-80-60; fiction, non-fiction, children's books, talking books; Publrs CONNIE BLOM, THOMAS BLOM.

Bogans Forlag: Kastaniebakken 8, POB 39, 3540 Lynge; tel. 48-18-80-55; fax 48-18-87-69; f. 1974; general paperbacks, popular science, non-fiction, humour, health; Publr EVAN BOGAN.

Borgens Forlag A/S: Valbygårdsvej 33, 2500 Valby; tel. 36-15-36-15; fax 36-15-36-16; e-mail post@borgen.dk; internet www.borgen .dk; f. 1948; fiction, poetry, children's books, humour, general nonfiction; Man. Dir NIELS BORGEN.

Bøornegudstjeneste-Forlaget: Korskærvej 25, 7000 Fredericia; tel. 75-93-44-55; fax 75-92-42-75; religion, children's books; Dir FINN ANDERSEN; Editorial Dir JØRGEN HEDAGER.

Carit Andersens Forlag A/S: Upsalagade 18, 2100 Copenhagen Ø; tel. 35-43-62-22; fax 35-43-51-51; e-mail info@mercantila.dk; internet www.caritandersen.dk; illustrated books, non-fiction, fiction, science fiction; Publr ERIK ALBRECHTSEN.

Forlaget Carlsen A/S: Krogshøjvej 32, 2880 Bagsværd; tel. 44-44-32-33; fax 44-44-36-33; e-mail carlsen@carlsen.dk; internet www.carlsen.dk; children's books; Man. Dir JESPER HOLM.

Forlaget Centrum: St. Kongensgade 10, 3TV, 1264 Copenhagen K; tel. 33-32-12-06; fax 33-32-12-07; e-mail lmm@forlaget-centrum.dk; fiction, non-fiction, travel guides, management; Man. Dir CLAES HVIDBAK.

Cicero (Chr. Erichsens Forlag A/S): Vester Voldgade 83, 1552 Copenhagen V; tel. 33-16-03-08; fax 33-16-03-07; e-mail info@

cicero.dk; internet www.cicero.dk; f. 1902; fiction, non-fiction, art, culture; Publrs NIELS GUDBERGSEN, ALIS CASPERSEN.

DA-Forlag/Dansk Arbejdsgiverforening: Vester Voldgade 113, 1552 Copenhagen V; tel. 33-38-94-63; fax 33-91-09-32; e-mail smh@da.dk; non-fiction and reference; Publishing Dir SØREN MELDORF HANSEN.

Dafolo A/S: Suderbovej 22–24, 9900 Frederikshavn; tel. 96-20-66-66; fax 98-42-97-11; e-mail dafolo@dafolo.dk; internet www .dafolo.dk; educational books; Publr MICHAEL SCHELDE.

Dansk BiblioteksCenter A/S: Tempovej 7–11, 2750 Ballerup; tel. 44-86-77-77; fax 44-86-78-91; e-mail dbc@dbc.dk; internet www.dbc.dk; bibliographies, library literature, talking books; Man. Dir MOGENS BRABRAND JENSEN.

Dansk Historisk Håndbogsforlag A/S: Buddingevej 87A, 2800 Lyngby; tel. 45-93-48-00; fax 45-93-47-47; e-mail mrjensen@ image.dk; f. 1976; genealogy, heraldry, law, culture and local history, facsimile editions, microfiches produced by subsidiary co; Owners and Man. Dirs RITA JENSEN, HENNING JENSEN.

Dansk psykologisk Forlag: Stockholmsgade 29, 2100 Copenhagen Ø; tel. 35-38-16-55; fax 35-38-16-65; e-mail dk-psych@dpf.dk; internet www.dpf.dk; educational books, health, psychology; Man. Dir HANS GERHARDT.

Det Danske Bibelselskabs Forlag/Det Kongelige Vajsenshus' Forlag: Frederiksborggade 50, 1360 Copenhagen K; tel. 33-12-78-35; fax 33-93-21-50; e-mail bibelselskabet@bibelselskabet.dk; internet www.bibelselskabet.dk; religious and liturgical books, children's books; Dir PETER BIRCH.

Christian Ejlers' Forlag ApS: Brolæggerstræde 4, POB 2228, 1018 Copenhagen K; tel. 33-12-21-14; fax 33-12-28-84; e-mail liber@ce-publishers.dk; internet www.ejlers.dk; f. 1967; art, cultural, educational and academic; Publr CHRISTIAN EJLERS.

Forlaget for Faglitteratur A/S: Vandkunsten 6, 1467 Copenhagen K; tel. 33-13-79-00; fax 33-14-51-56; medicine, technology.

FinansSupport: Hovedvejen 9, POB 70, 2600 Glostrup; tel. 43-44-04-44; fax 43-44-07-44; educational books; Pres. ERLING JENSEN.

Flachs: Øverødvej 98, 2840 Holte; tel. 45-42-48-30; fax 45-42-48-29; e-mail flachs@flachs.dk; internet www.flachs.dk; fiction, non-fiction, reference, educational and children's books; Publrs ALLAN FLACHS, ANETTE FLACHS.

Palle Fogtdal A/S: Østergade 22, 1100 Copenhagen K; tel. 33-15-39-15; fax 33-93-35-05; Danish history; Man. Dir PALLE FOGTDAL.

Forum: Købmagergade 62, 1019 Copenhagen K; tel. 33-41-18-30; fax 33-41-18-31; f. 1940; history, fiction, biographies, quality paperbacks and children's books; Man. Dir OLE KNUDSEN.

Fremad: Købmagergade 62, POB 2252, 1019 Copenhagen K; tel. 33-41-18-10; fax 33-41-18-11; f. 1912; general trade, fiction, non-fiction, juveniles, reference, children's books; Man. Dir NIELS KØLLE.

Forlaget FSR: Nytorv 5, 1450 Copenhagen K; tel. 33-74-07-74; fax 33-93-30-77; textbooks, legal, economic, financial, management, business, accounting; Editorial Dir VIBEKE CHRISTIANSEN.

G.E.C. Gad Publishers Ltd: Vimmelskaftet 32, 1161 Copenhagen K; tel. 33-15-05-58; fax 33-11-08-00; e-mail sekr@gads-forlag.dk; internet www.gads-forlag.dk; biographies, natural science, history, reference, fiction, educational materials, food and drink, travel guides; Man. Dir AXEL KIELLAND.

Gyldendalske Boghandel, Nordisk Forlag A/S: Klareboderne 3, 1001 Copenhagen K; tel. 33-11-07-75; fax 33-11-03-23; e-mail gyldendal@gyldendal.dk; internet www.gyldendal.dk; f. 1770; fiction, non-fiction, reference books, paperbacks, children's books, textbooks; Man. Dir STIG ANDERSEN.

P. Haase & Søns Forlag A/S: Løvstræde 8, 1152 Copenhagen K; tel. 33-14-41-75; fax 33-11-59-59; e-mail haase@haase.dk; internet www.haase.dk; f. 1877; educational books, audio-visual aids, children's books, humour, fiction, non-fiction; imprints: Natur og Harmoni, Rasmus Navers Forlag; Man. Dir MICHAEL HAASE.

Edition Wilhelm Hansen A/S: Bornholmsgade 1, 1266 Copenhagen K; tel. 33-11-78-88; fax 33-14-81-78; e-mail ewh@ewh.dk; internet www.ewh.dk; f. 1857; music books, school and educational books; Man. Dir TINE BIRGER CHRISTENSEN.

Hernovs Forlag: Siljangade 6, 4, 2300 Copenhagen S; tel. 32-96-33-14; fax 32-96-04-46; e-mail admin@hernov.dk; internet www.her nov.dk; f. 1941; fiction, non-fiction, children's; Man. Dir PETER HERNOV.

Holkenfeldt 3: Fuglevadsvej 71, 2800 Lyngby; tel. 45-93-12-21; fax 45-93-82-41; fiction, non-fiction, reference, sport, humour; Publr KAY HOLKENFELDT.

Høst & Søns Forlag: Købmagergade 62, POB 2212, 1018 Copenhagen K; tel. 33-15-30-31; fax 33-15-51-55; e-mail host@ euroconnect.dk; f. 1836; crafts and hobbies, languages, books on Denmark, children's books; Skarv imprint (travel, ecology, etc.); Man. Dir ERIK C. LINDGREN.

Forlaget Hovedland: Stenvej 21, 8270 Højbjerg; tel. 86-27-65-00; fax 86-27-65-37; e-mail mail@hovedland.dk; internet www .hovedland.dk; fiction, non-fiction, environment, sport, health, crafts; Publr STEEN PIPER.

Forlaget Klematis A/S: Østre Skovvej 1, 8240 Risskov; tel. 86-17-54-55; fax 86-17-59-59; fiction, non-fiction, crafts, children's books; Dir CLAUS DALBY.

Forlaget Per Kofod ApS: Kompagnistræde 4B, 1208 Copenhagen K; tel. 33-32-70-27; fax 33-32-60-27; fiction, non-fiction, art and culture; Publr PER KOFOD.

Krak: Virumgaardsvej 21, 2830 Virum; tel. 45-95-65-00; fax 45-95-65-65; e-mail krak@krak.dk; internet www.krak.dk; f. 1770; reference works, maps and yearbooks; Dir IB LE ROY TOPHOLM.

Egmont Lademann A/S: Gerdasgade 37, 2500 Valby; tel. 36-15-66-00; fax 36-44-11-62; internet www.lademann.dk; f. 1954; non-fiction, reference; Man. Dir SØREN FOGTDAL; Editor-in-Chief LISELOTTE NELSON.

Lindhardt og Ringhof A/S: Frederiksborggade 1, 1360 Copenhagen K; tel. 33-69-50-00; fax 33-69-50-01; e-mail lr@lindhardt -og-ringhof.dk; internet www.lindhardt-og-ringhof.dk; general fiction and non-fiction; Dir TRINE LICHT.

L & R FAKTA/Møntergården: Larsbjørnstræde 3, 1454 Copenhagen K; tel. 33-32-18-96; fax 33-37-71-38; e-mail montergarden@ borsen.dk; f. 1997; non-fiction, reference; Man. Dir HENRIK HJORTH; Publr ANNEMARIE ELKJÆR.

Lohses Forlag (incl. Forlaget Korskaer): Korskærvej 25, 7000 Fredericia; tel. 75-93-44-55; fax 75-92-42-75; e-mail finn@lohse .imh.dk; f. 1868; religion, children's, biographies, devotional novels; Man. Dir FINN ANDERSEN.

Forlaget Lotus: Industrikrogen 4, 2635 Ishøj; tel. 43-45-78-74; fax 43-45-97-71; e-mail fiolotus@post7.tele.dk; management, health, religion, the occult, educational; Publr FINN ANDERSEN.

Forlaget Magnus A/S Skattekartoteket: Informationskontor, Palægade 4, 1261 Copenhagen K; tel. 33-11-78-74; fax 33-93-80-09; e-mail magnus@cddk.dk; internet www.cddk.dk; f. 1962; guidebooks, journals, law; Man. Dir MORTEN ARNBERG.

Medicinsk Forlag ApS: Tranevej 2, 3650 Ølstykke; tel. and fax 47-17-65-92; astrology, medical and scientific books; Man. Dir ANNI LINDELØV.

Modtryk AmbA: Anholtsgade 4, 8000 Århus C; tel. 87-31-76-00; fax 87-13-76-01; e-mail modtryk@ibm.net; internet www.modtryk.dk; f. 1972; children's and school books, fiction, thrillers and non-fiction; Man. Dir ILSE NØRR.

Munksgaard International Publishers Ltd: Nørre Søgade 35, POB 2148, 1016 Copenhagen K; tel. 77-33-33-33; fax 77-33-33-77; e-mail headoffice@munksgaard.dk; internet www.munksgaard.dk; f. 1917; medicine, nursing, dentistry, social science, psychology, scientific journals; Man. Dir ANDERS GEERTSEN.

Nyt Nordisk Forlag-Arnold Busck A/S: Købmagergade 49, 1150 Copenhagen K; tel. 33-73-35-75; fax 33-73-35-76; e-mail nnf@ nytnordiskforlag.dk; internet www.nytnordiskforlag.dk; f. 1896; textbooks, school books, guidebooks, fiction and non-fiction; Man. Dir OLE ARNOLD BUSCK.

Jørgen Paludans Forlag ApS: 4 Straedet, 3100 Hornbæk; tel. 49-75-15-36; fax 49-75-15-37; language teaching, non-fiction, psychology, history, politics, economics, reference; Man. Dir JØRGEN PALUDAN.

Politikens Forlag A/S: Vestergade 26, 1456 Copenhagen K; tel. 33-47-07-07; fax 33-47-07-08; internet www.polforlag.dk; f. 1946; non-fiction, reference, history, family, health, biography, travel; Ekstra Bladets imprint; Man. Dir KARSTEN BLAUERT.

C.A. Reitzels Boghandel og Forlag A/S: Nørregade 20, 1165 Copenhagen K; tel. 33-12-24-00; fax 33-14-02-70; f. 1819; reference books, philosophy, educational and academic books, Hans Christian Andersen, Kierkegaard; Dir SVEND OLUFSEN.

Hans Reitzels Forlag A/S: Købmagergade 62, POB 1073, 1008 Copenhagen K; tel. 33-38-28-00; fax 33-38-28-08; e-mail hrf@ hansreitzel.dk; internet www.hansreitzel.dk; f. 1949; education, philosophy, psychology, sociology, Hans Christian Andersen; Man. Dir ERIK C. LINDGREN.

Rhodos, International Science and Art Publishers: Niels Brocks Gård, Strandgade 36, 1401 Copenhagen K; tel. 32-54-30-20; fax 32-95-47-42; e-mail rhodos@rhodos.dk; internet www .rhodos.dk; f. 1959; university books, art, science, fiction, poetry; Man. Dir NIELS BLAEDEL; Dir RUBEN BLAEDEL.

Samlerens Forlag A/S: POB 2252, Købmagergade 62, 1019 Copenhagen K; tel. 33-41-18-00; fax 33-41-18-01; e-mail torben_madsen@jamleren.dk; Danish and foreign fiction, contemporary history and politics, biographies; Man. Dir TORBEN MADSEN.

Scandinavia Publishing House: Drejervej 11–12, 2400 Copenhagen NV; tel. 33-14-00-91; fax 33-32-00-91; e-mail jvo@ scanpublishing.dk; internet www.scanpublishing.dk; f. 1973; children's books, religion, Hans Christian Andersen; Dir Jørgen Vium Olesen.

Det Schønbergske Forlag A/S: Landemærket 5, 1119 Copenhagen K; tel. 33-73-35-85; fax 33-73-35-86; f. 1857; fiction, humour, psychology, biography, children's books, paperbacks, textbooks; Dir Joakim Werner; Editor Arvid Honoré.

Spektrum: Købmagergade 62, POB 2252, 1019 Copenhagen K; tel. 33-41-18-30; fax 33-41-18-31; non-fiction, history, biographies, science, psychology, religion, philosophy, arts; Man. Dir Ole Knudsen.

Strandbergs Forlag ApS: Vedbæk Strandvej 475, 2950 Vedbæk; tel. 42-89-47-60; fax 42-89-47-01; cultural history, travel; Publr Hans Jørgen Strandberg.

Strubes Forlag og Boghandel ApS: Damhus Blvd 65, 2610 Rødovre; ; tel. 36-72-17-50; fax 36-72-17-52; health, astrology, philosophy, the occult; Man. Dir Jonna Strube.

Teknisk Forlag A/S: Skelbækgade 4, 1780 Copenhagen V; tel. 33-43-65-00; fax 33-43-66-77; e-mail bogredaktion@tekniskforlag.dk; internet www.tekniskforlag.dk; f. 1948; computing, technical books, reference, business, educational, science; Man. Dir Ole Skals Pedersen.

Tiderne Skifter: Købmagergade 62, 1., 1019 Copenhagen K; tel. 33-41-18-20; fax 33-41-18-21; e-mail tiderneskifte@tiderneskifte.dk; fiction, sexual and cultural politics, psychology, science, religion, arts; Man. Dir Claus Clausen.

Unitas Forlag: Valby Langgade 19, 2500 Valby; tel. 36-16-64-81; fax 36-16-08-18; e-mail forlag@unitas.dk; internet forlag .unitas.dk; religion, fiction, education, children's books; Man. Peder Gundersen.

Forlaget Vindrose A/S: Valbygaardsvej 33, 2500 Valby; tel. 36-15-36-15; fax 36-15-36-16; f. 1980; general trade, fiction and non-fiction; Man. Dir Niels Borgen.

Vitafakta ApS: Kohavevej 28, 2950 Vedbæk; tel. and fax 45-16-11-50; health books, nutrition, school books; Dir Inger Marie Haut.

Wisby & Wilkens: Vestergade 6, POB 98, 8464 Galten; tel. 86-94-46-22; fax 86-94-47-22; e-mail mail@bogshop.dk; internet www .bogshop.dk; f. 1986; children's books, crafts, fiction, health, humour, science, religion; imprints: Mikro (drama, poetry, humour) ; Publr Jacob Wisby.

Government Publishing House

Statens Information (State Information Service): Nørre Farimagsgade 65, POB 1103, 1009 Copenhagen K; tel. 33-37-92-00; fax 33-37-92-99; e-mail si@si.dk; f. 1975; acts under the purview of the Ministry of Research and Information Technology, as public relations and information body for the public sector; publishes Statstidende (Official Gazette), etc.; Dir Leon Østergaard.

PUBLISHERS' ASSOCIATION

Den danske Forlæggerforening: Kømpagnistræde 18, 1208 Copenhagen K; tel. 33-15-66-88; fax 33-15-65-88; e-mail publassn@ webpartner.dk; f. 1837; 75 mems; Chair. Erik C. Lindgren; Man. Dir Ib Tune Olsen.

Broadcasting and Communications

TELECOMMUNICATIONS

Telecommunications services are administered by the National Telecom Agency, Telestyrelsen.

Telecommunications links with the Faroe Islands are provided by satellite ground stations at Tórshavn and Herstedvester. The latter also provides international data communication links via the EUTELSAT system and the French Telecom 1 satellite system, while a station at Blåvand receives signals from INTELSAT.

Regulatory Organization

National Telecom Agency: Holsteinsgade 63, 2100 Copenhagen Ø; tel. 45-35-00-00; fax 45-35-00-10; e-mail tst@tst.dk; internet www.tst.dk; f. 1991; under the Ministry of Research and Information Technology, in charge of administration and regulation of the telecommunications sector as laid down in telecommunications legislation; works on legislation; government centre of expertise in telecommunications; Dir-Gen. Jørgan Abild Andersen; Deputy Dir-Generals Finn Petersen, Michael Henneberg Pedersen.

Major Service Providers

GN Store Nordiske Telegraf-Selskab as (GN Great Northern Telegraph Co Ltd): Kongens Nytorv 26, POB 2167, 1016 Copenhagen; tel. 33-95-09-09; fax 33-95-09-09; e-mail info@gn.dk; Pres. and CEO Jorgen Lindegaard.

LASAT Networks A/S: Skalhuse 13, 9240 Nibe; tel. 96-71-10-00; fax 96-71-10-99; e-mail lasat@lasat.com; internet www.lasat.com; f. 1982; CEO Claus Christensen.

Telecom A/S: Telegade 2, 2630 Tåstrup; tel. 42-52-91-11; fax 42-52-93-31; Man. Dir Gregers Mogensen.

Tele Danmark A/S: Norregade 21, 0900 Copenhagen; tel. 33-43-77-77; fax 33-43-73-89; e-mail teledanmark@tdk.dk; internet www.teledanmark.dk; fmrly state-owned telecommunications company; transferred to private ownership in 1998; CEO Henning Dyremose.

RADIO

DR RADIO: Radio House, Rosenørns Alle 22, 1999 Frederiksberg C; tel. 35-20-30-40; fax 35-20-26-44; e-mail webmaster@dr.dk; internet www.dr.dk; fmrly Danmarks Radio; independent statutory corpn; Dir-Gen. Chr. S. Nissen; Dir of Radio Programmes Leif Lønsmann; operates a foreign service (Radio Denmark), nine regional stations and four national channels:

Channel 1 broadcasts for 110 hours per week on FM, in Danish (Greenlandic programmes weekly); Head Finn Slumstrup.

Channel 2, a music channel, broadcasts on FM, for 45 hours per week nationally, in Danish, as well as regional and special (for foreign workers) programmes; Head Steen Frederiksen.

Channel 3 broadcasts on FM for 24 hours per day, in Danish; primarily a popular music channel, there is news in Greenlandic, Faroese and in English; Head Jesper Grunwald.

Channel 4 broadcasts on FM for about 97 hours per week; news, entertainment and regional progs.

There are also some 250 operators licensed for low-power FM transmissions of local and community radio, etc.

TELEVISION

DR TV: TV-Byen, 2860 Søborg; tel. 35-20-30-40; fax 35-20-26-44; e-mail dr-kontakten@dr.dk; internet www.dr.dk; operates two services, DR 1 and DR 2; Dir-Gen. Chr. S. Nissen; Man. Dir Bjørn Erichsen; Dir (News) Lisbeth Kmudsen.

DR 1: terrestrial television channel; Controller Jørgen Ramskov.

DR 2: satellite television channel; Controller Torben Frølich.

TV 2/DANMARK: Rugaardsvej 25, 5100 Odense C; tel. 65-91-12-44; fax 65-91-33-22; e-mail tv2@tv2;.dk; internet www.tv2.dk; began broadcasts in 1988; Denmark's first national commercial and public service TV station; 20% of its finances come from licence fees, the rest from advertising and sponsorship; CEO Cristina Lage.

Viasat Broadcasting/TV 3: Wildersgade 8, 1408 Copenhagen K; tel. 35-25-90-00; fax 35-25-90-10; e-mail viasat@viasat.dk; internet www.tv3.dk; reaches 71% of the country via cable and satellite; Man. Dir Lars Bo Andersen; Dir of Programmes Henrik Ravn.

There are some 50 operators licensed for local television transmission.

Finance

The first Danish commercial bank was founded in 1846. In 1975 restrictions on savings banks were lifted, giving commercial and savings banks equal rights and status, and restrictions on the establishment of full branches of foreign banks were removed. In 1988 all remaining restrictions on capital movements were ended. In 1998 there were some 187 banks and savings banks in operation. All banks are under government supervision, and public representation is obligatory on all bank supervisory boards.

BANKING

(cap. = capital; p.u. = paid up; res = reserves; dep. = deposits; m. = million; brs = branches; amounts in kroner)

Supervisory Authority

Finanstilsynet (Danish Financial Supervisory Authority): Gammel Kongevej 74A, 1850 Frederiksberg C; tel. 33-55-82-82; fax 33-55-82-00; e-mail finanstilsynet@ftnet.dk; internet www.ftnet.dk; agency of the Ministry of Economic Affairs; Man. Dir Henrik Bjerre-Nielsen.

Central Bank

Danmarks Nationalbank: Havnegade 5, 1093 Copenhagen K; tel. 33-63-63-63; fax 33-63-71-06; internet www.nationalbanken.dk; f. 1818; self-governing; sole right of issue; conducts monetary policy; administers reserves of foreign exchange; cap. 50m., res 43,424m., dep. 93,114m. (Dec. 1998); Govs Bodil Nyboe Andersen (Chair.), Torben Nielsen, Jens Thomsen.

Commercial Banks

Alm. Brand Bank: Jarmers Plads 7, 1551 Copenhagen V; tel. 33-30-70-30; fax 33-93-15-88; internet www.almbrand-bank.dk; f. 1988; cap. 350m., res 25m., dep. 9,688m. (Dec. 1998); Chair. Christian N. B. Ulrich; Man. Dir Henrik Nordam; 24 brs.

Amagerbanken A/S: Amagerbrogade 25, 2300 Copenhagen S; tel. 32-66-66-66; fax 32-54-45-34; e-mail info@amagerbanken.dk; internet www.amagerbanken.dk; f. 1903; cap.195m., res 45m., dep. 7,555m. (Dec. 1998); Chair. N. E. NIELSEN; Man. Dirs KNUD CHRISTENSEN, BENT SCHØN HANSEN; 26 brs.

Arbejdernes Landsbank A/S: Vesterbrogade 5, 1502 Copenhagen V; tel. 33-38-80-00; fax 33-38-89-60; e-mail info@al-bank.dk; internet www.albank.dk; f. 1919; cap. 300m., res 78m., dep. 12,005m. (Dec. 1998); Chair. ANTON JOHANNSEN; Gen. Mans E. MIDTGAARD, P. E. LETH, E. CASTELLA; 14 brs.

Bikuben Girobank A/S: Højbro Plads 10, 1200 Copenhagen K; tel. 43-30-30-30; fax 33-15-90-33; e-mail info@bgbank.dk; internet www.bgbank.dk; f. 1996 by merger of Sparekassen Bikuben A/S (f. 1857) and Girobank A/S (f. 1990); cap. 3,000m., res 4,722m., dep. 150,844m. (Dec. 1998); Chair. HENRIK THUFASON; Vice-Chair. BJARNE WIND; 256 brs.

Codan Bank A/S: Borgergade 24, 1790 Copenhagen V; tel. 33-66-66-66; fax 33-66-66-67; e-mail codanbank@codanbank.dk; internet www.codanbank.dk; f. 1993 by merger of Alliance Bank of Copenhagen, Hafnia Bank A/S and Hafnia Börs-Börsmaeglerselskab; cap. 500m., res 127m., dep. 4,865m. (Dec. 1998); CEO JENS OLE PEDERSEN; Gen. Man. THORKILD KOKHOLM.

Danske Bank A/S: Holmens Kanal 2–12, 1092 Copenhagen K; tel. 33-44-00-00; fax 39-18-58-73; internet www.danskebank.dk; f. 1871 as Danske Landmandsbank; merged with Copenhagen Handelsbank and Provinsbanken in 1990 to form Den Danske Bank A/S; present name adopted 2000; the bank acquired the insurance group, Danica, in 1995, the Norwegian Fokus Bank in 1999, and Real Denmark in 2000; cap. 5,293m., res 52m., dep. 266,095m. (Dec. 1999); Chair. PETER STRAARUP; 650 brs.

Egnsbank Nord A/S: Jernbanegade 4–6, POB 701, 9900 Frederikshavn; tel. 99-21-22-23; fax 99-21-22-67; e-mail email@nordbank.dk; internet www.nordbank.dk; f. 1979; cap. 48m., res 371m., dep. 2,607m. (Dec. 1999); Chair. HANS JOERGEN KAPTAIN; Man. Dirs JENS OLE JENSEN, OLE KRISTENSEN; 66 brs.

Forstædernes Bank A/S: Malervangen 1, 2600 Glostrup; tel. 43-96-17-20; fax 43-63-32-36; e-mail finans@forbank.dk; internet www.forbank.dk; f. 1902; cap. 250m., res 3m., dep. 3,992m. (Dec. 1998); subsidiary, Den Fri Bank, f. 1994, provides telephone banking service to individual customers; Chair. HELMER OLSEN; Chief Exec. KJELD MOSEBO CHRISTENSEN; 19 brs.

A/S Jyske Bank: Vestergade 8–16, 8600 Silkeborg; tel. 89-22-22-22; fax 89-22-24-96; e-mail jyskebank@jyskebank.dk; internet www.jyskebank.dk; f. 1855, established in 1967; cap. 900m., res 4,208m., dep. 57,539m. (Dec. 1998); Chair. ANDERS DAM; Chief Exec. LEIF E. LARSEN; 133 brs.

Midtbank A/S: Østergade 2, 7400 Herning; tel. 96-26-26-26; fax 96-26-28-98; e-mail udland@midtbank.dk; internet www.midtbank.dk; f. 1965; cap. 260m., res 552m., dep. 6,240m. (Dec. 2000); Chair. IB SCHMIDT HANSEN; Gen. Man. STEEN HOVE; 23 brs.

Nørresundby Bank A/S: Torvet 4, 9400 Nørresundby; tel. 98-17-33-33; fax 98-19-18-78; e-mail nbcentral@nrsbank.dk; internet www.nrsbank.dk; f. 1898; cap. 50m., res 11m., dep. 3,734m. (Dec. 1998); Chair. KJELD KOLIND JENSEN; Gen. Mans ANDREAS RASMUSSEN, FINN ØST ANDERSSON; 16 brs.

Nykredit Bank A/S: Bredgade 40, POB 3033, 1021 Copenhagen K; tel. 33-42-18-00; fax 33-42-18-01; e-mail nykredit-bank@nykredit.dk; internet www.nykredit.dk/bank;f. 1986; cap. 1,300m., res 915m., dep. 26,168m. (Dec. 1998); Chair. HENNING KRUSE PETERSEN; Chief Exec., Man. Dir HANS MØLLER CHRISTENSEN.

Ringkjøbing Landbobank A/S: Torvet 1, 6950 Ringkøbing; tel. 97-32-11-66; fax 97-32-18-18; e-mail post@landbobanken.dk; internet www.landbobanken.dk; f. 1886; res 612m., dep. 2,808m. (Dec. 1999); Chair. KR. OLE KRISTENSEN; Gen. Mans BENT NAUR KRISTENSEN, JOHN BULL FISKER; 12 brs.

Roskilde Bank A/S: Algade 14, POB 39, 4000 Roskilde; tel. 46-35-17-00; fax 46-34-83-52; f. 1884; cap. 100m., res 455m., dep. 2,896m. (Dec. 1999); Chair. JENS WINTHER; Man. NIELS VALENTIN HANSEN; 17 brs.

Sparbank Vest: Adelgade 8, POB 505, 7800 Skive; tel. 97-52-33-11; fax 97-52-73-11; e-mail sparbank@inet.uni-c.dk; internet www.sparbankvest.dk; f. 1857; cap. 121m., res 576m., dep. 4,758m. (Dec. 1998); Chair. OLE BROENDUM JENSEN; CEO PREBEN RASMUSSEN; 35 brs.

Sydbank A/S: Peberlyk 4, POB 169, 6200 Åbenrå; tel. 74-36-36-36; fax 74-36-35-49; e-mail info@sydbank.dk; internet www.sydbank.com; f. 1970; cap. 825m., res 958m., dep. 47,150m. (Dec. 1999); Chair. VAGN JACOBSEN; CEO CARSTEN ANDERSEN; 115 brs.

Unibank A/S: Strandegade 3, 1401 Copenhagen V; tel. 33-33-33-33; fax 33-33-63-63; internet www.unibank.dk; f. 1990 by merger of Andelsbanken, Privatbanken and SDS; in June 1999 the bank merged with Tryg-Baltica Forsikring A/S, the insurance company, but remained part of the Unidanmark A/S group; res 14,057m., dep. 377,437m. (Dec. 1998); Man. Dir THORLEIF KRARUP; 369 brs.

Savings Banks

Amtssparekassen Fyn A/S: Vestre Stationsvej 7, POB 189, 5100 Odense C; tel. 66-14-04-74; fax 65-91-01-10; e-mail udland@amtssparekassen.dk; f. 1974; cap. 196m., res 743m., dep. 11,247m. (Dec. 1999); Chair. CLAUS HANSEN; Man. Dirs POUL BALLE, FINN B. SORENSEN; 39 brs.

Lån & Spar Bank: Højbro Plads 9–11, POB 2117, 1014 Copenhagen K; tel. 33-14-87-48; fax 33-14-18-48; e-mail laan.spar@laan-spar.dk; internet www.laan-spar.dk; f. 1880 (present name 1990); cap. 281m., res 264m., dep. 6,099m. (Dec. 1998); Chair. TOMMY AGERSKOV THOMSEN; Man. Dir, CEO PETER SCHOU; 12 brs.

Spar Nord Bankaktieselskab: Karlskogavej 4, POB 162, 9100 Alborg; tel. 96-34-40-00; fax 96-34-45-75; e-mail int_div@sparnord.dk; internet www.sparnordbank.com; f. 1967; cap. 519m., res 1,103m., dep. 21,927m. (Dec. 1999); CEO LASSE NYBY; Man. Dirs LARS MØLLER, JOHN LUNDSGAARD; 68 brs.

Sparekassen Kronjylland: Middelgade 1, POB 162, 8900 Randers; tel. 89-12-12-12; fax 86-41-00-23; Dir JAKOB LETH; 30 brs.

Sparekassen Vestsjælland: POB 70, Ahlgade 51, 4300 Holboek; tel. 59-43-15-15; fax 59-44-25-15; e-mail sv@sparekassen-vestsjaelland.dk; f. 1825; cap. 91m., res 289m., dep. 2,294m. (Dec. 1998); Pres. FLEMMING HANSEN; 15 brs.

Bankers' Organization

Finansrådet: Finansrådets Hus, Amaliegade 7, 1256 Copenhagen K; tel. 33-12-02-00; fax 33-93-02-60; e-mail f@finansraadet.dk; internet www.finansraadet.dk; f. 1990; 173 mems; Chair. PETER STRAARUP; Man. Dir LARS BARFOED.

STOCK EXCHANGE

Københavns Fondsbørs (Copenhagen Stock Exchange): Nikolaj Plads 6, POB 1040, 1007 Copenhagen K; tel. 33-93-33-66; fax 33-12-86-13; e-mail xcse@xcse.dk; internet www.xcse.dk; f. 1861; part of the Norex Alliance (launched June 1999) with direct access to the Stockholm Stock Exchange in Sweden; Pres. HANS-OLE JOCHUMSEN; Chair. HANS EJVIND HANSEN.

INSURANCE
Principal Companies

Alm. Brand af 1792: Lyngby Hovedgade 4, POB 1792, 2800 Lyngby; tel. 45-96-70-00; fax 45-93-05-46; f. 1792; subsidiaries: finance, life, non-life and reinsurance; Chief Gen. Man. BENT KNIE-ANDERSEN.

Codan Forsikring A/S: Codanhus, Gl. Kongevej 60, 1790 Copenhagen V; tel. 31-21-21-21; fax 31-21-21-22; f. 1915 as Forsikringsselskabet Codan A/S; adopted present name 2000; controlled by Royal and Sun Alliance Group Ltd (UK); acquired insurance operations of Hafnia Holdings in 1993; accident, life; CEO JENS ERIK CHRISTENSEN.

Danica Liv I, Livsforsikringsaktieselskab: Parallelvej 17, 2800 Lyngby; tel. 45-23-23-23; fax 45-23-20-20; e-mail servicecentre@danica.dk; internet www.danica.dk; f. 1842 as state insurance co; privatized in 1990; pensions, life and non-life.

GE Frankona Reinsurance S/S: Grønningen 25, 1270 Copenhagen K; tel. 33-97-95-93; fax 33-97-94-41; f. 1894 as ERC Frankona Reinsurance A/S; present name adopted 2000; reinsurance, life and non-life, international; Gen. Mans WALTHER HAMMERSTROEM, ANNETTE SADOLIN.

A/S Det Kjøbenhavnske Reassurance-Compagni: Midtermolen 7, POB 325, 21000 Copenhagen Ø; tel. 35-47-45-45; fax 35-47-72-72; e-mail copre@copre.com; internet www.copre.com; f. 1915; reinsurance; CEO JAN HORNSBERG; Gen. Man. HENRIK HAUGAARD-JENSEN.

Købstædernes almindelige Brandforsikring: Grønningen 1, 1270 Copenhagen K; tel. 33-14-37-48; fax 33-32-06-66; e-mail kab@kab.dk; f. 1761; fire; Chair. SVEND E. CHRISTENSEN; CEO MOGENS N. SKOV.

Kompas Rejseforsikring A/S: Klausdalsbrovej 601, 2750 Ballerup; tel. 44-68-81-00; fax 44-68-84-00; e-mail kompas@kompas.dk; internet www.kompas.dk; travel, health; Chief Gen. Man. PETER BOESEN.

Max Levig & Cos Eft. A/S: Klausdalsbrovej BO1, 2750 Ballerup; tel. 44-20-39-60; fax 44-20-66-70; f. 1890; Gen. Man. HUGO ANDERSEN.

PFA Pension: Marina Park, Sundkrogsgade 4, 2100 Copenhagen Ø; tel. 39-17-50-00; fax 39-17-59-50; f. 1917; life; non-life, property; Gen. Mans ANDRÉ LUBLIN, A. KÜHLE.

Skandia Forsikring A/S: Stamholmen 159, 2650 Hvidovre; tel. 36-87-47-47; fax 36-87-47-87; f. 1798 as Kgl. Brand A/S; adopted present name 2000; all branches; subsidiaries: workers' liability, life; Gen. Man. JAN SVENSSON.

Topdanmark Forsikring A/S: Borupvang 4, 2750 Ballerup; tel. 44-68-33-11; fax 44-68-12-64; e-mail topdanmark.dk; internet www.topdanmark.dk; f. 1985; all classes, with subsidiaries; CEO MICHAEL PRAM RASMUSSEN.

Tryg-Baltica Forsikring A/S: Klausdalsbrovej 601, 2750 Ballerup; tel. 44-20-20-20; fax 44-20-66-00; f. 1995 by merger of Tryg Forsikring A/S and Baltica Forsikring A/S; in June 1999 merged with Unibank A/S under the Unidanmark group; all classes, with subsidiaries; Group Chief Exec. HUGO ANDERSEN.

Insurance Association

Forsikring & Pension: Amaliegade 10, 1256 Copenhagen K; tel. 33-43-55-00; fax 33-43-55-01; e-mail fp@forsikringenshus.dk; internet www.forsikringenshus.dk; f. 1918 as Raadet for Dansk Forsikring og Pension; present name adopted 2000; Chair. HOLGER DOCK; Dir STEEN LETH JEPPESEN; 200 mems.

Trade and Industry

GOVERNMENT AGENCY

Dansk Industri (Confederation of Danish Industries): 1787 Copenhagen V; tel. 33-77-33-77; fax 33-77-33-00; e-mail di@di.dk; f. 1992; Dir HANS SKOV CHRISTENSEN.

DEVELOPMENT ORGANIZATION

Det Økonomiske Råd (Danish Economic Council): Adelgade 13, 1304 Copenhagen K; tel. 33-13-51-28; fax 33-32-90-29; e-mail dors@dors.dk; f. 1962 to supervise national economic development and help to co-ordinate the actions of economic interest groups; 26 members representing both sides of industry, the Government and independent economic experts; Co-Chairs Prof. NIELS KIERGAARD, Prof. PETER BIRCH SØRENSEN, Prof. JØRGEN BIRK MORTENSEN; Sec.-Gen. PEDER ANDERSEN.

CHAMBER OF COMMERCE

Det Danske Handelskammer (Danish Chamber of Commerce): Børsen, 1217 Copenhagen K; tel. 33-95-05-00; fax 33-32-52-16; e-mail handelskammeret@commerce.dk; internet www.commerce.dk; f. 1742; approx. 2,000 mems; Man. Dir LARS KROBAEK; Pres. BENT LARSEN.

INDUSTRIAL AND TRADE ASSOCIATIONS

Dansk Elvaerkers Forening (Association of Danish Electric Utilities): Rosenørns Allé 9, 1970 Frederiksberg C; tel. 31-39-01-11; f. 1923; promotes the interests of Danish producers and suppliers of electricity; 105 mem. companies.

Det Kgl. Danske Landhusholdningsselskab (The Royal Danish Agricultural Society): Mariendalsvej 27, 2, 2000 Frederiksberg; tel. 38-88-66-88; fax 38-88-66-11; e-mail jordbrugsforlaget@bogpost.dk; internet www.jordbrugsforlaget.dk; f. 1769 to promote agricultural progress; Pres. JON KRABBE, SCHALL HOLBERG, NIELS KÆRGÅRD, KIRSTEN JAKOBSEN, IVER TESDORPF; Dir GRETHE ERSKOV; 1,400 mems.

Landbrugsradet (Agricultural Council): Axelborg, Axeltorv 3, 1609 Copenhagen V; tel. 33-14-56-72; fax 33-14-95-74; e-mail agriculture@agriculture.dk; internet www.agriculture.dk; f. 1919; Pres. PETER GAEMELKE; Dir KLAUS BUSTRUP; 41 mems.

Mejeriforeningen (Danish Dairy Board): Frederiks Allé 22, 8000 Århus; tel. 87-31-20-00; fax 87-31-20-01; e-mail ddb@mejeri.dk; f. 1912; Chair. KAJ OLE PEDERSEN; Man. Dir K. THAYSEN; 30 mems.

Oliebranchens Fællesrepræsentation—OFR (Danish Petroleum Industry Association): Vognmagergade 7, POB 120, 1004 Copenhagen K; tel. (01) 33-11-30-77; fax (01) 33-32-16-18; e-mail ofr@oil-forum.dk; internet www.oil-forum.dk; representative organization for petroleum industry; Chair. K. M. OLESEN; Sec.-Gen. PER THORKILDSEN.

EMPLOYERS' ORGANIZATIONS

Bryggeriforeningen (Danish Brewers' Association): Frederiksberggade 11, 1459 Copenhagen K; tel. 33-12-62-41; fax 33-14-25-13; e-mail info@bryggeriforeningen.dk; internet www.bryggeriforeningen.dk; f. 1899; Chair. FLEMMING LINDELØV; Dir NIELS HALD; 10 mems.

Dansk Arbejdsgiverforening (Danish Employers' Confederation): Vester Voldgade 113, 1790 Copenhagen V; tel. 33-93-40-00; fax 33-12-29-76; e-mail da@da.dk; internet www.da.dk; f. 1896; Chair. NIELS FOG; Dir-Gen. JØRN NEERGAARD LARSEN; 18 mem. orgs.

Dansk Pelsdyravlerforening (DPF) (Danish Fur Breeders' Association): Langagervej 60, POB 1479, 2600 Glostrup; tel. 43-26-10-00; fax 43-26-11-26; e-mail cfc@cfc.dk; internet www.cfc.dk; co-operative of 2,700 mems.

Danske Husmandsforeninger (Danish Family Farmers' Association): Landbrugsmagasinet, Vester Farimagsgade 6, 1606 Copenhagen V; tel. 33-12-99-50; fax 33-93-63-62; f. 1906; Chair. CHR. SØRENSEN; Sec.-Gen. OLAV POVLSGÅRD; 30,000 mems.

Danske Landboforeninger (Danish Farmers' Union): Axelborg, Vesterbrogade 4A, 1620 Copenhagen V; tel. 33-12-75-61; fax 33-32-

76-62; e-mail ddl@ddl.dk; internet www.ddl.dk; f. 1893; Pres. PETER GÆMELKE; Dir CARL AAGE DAHL; 59,000 mems.

Håndværksrådet (Danish Federation of Small- and Medium-Sized Enterprises): Amaliegade 31, 1256 Copenhagen K; tel. 33-93-20-00; fax 33-32-01-74; e-mail hvr@hvr.dk; internet www.hvr.dk; f. 1879; Chair. POUL ULSØE; Man. LARS JØRGEN NIELSEN; 110 asscns with 26,000 mems.

Industriens Arbejdsgivere i København (The Copenhagen Employers' Federation): 1787 Copenhagen V; tel. 33-77-33-77; fax 33-77-33-00; e-mail di@di.dk; internet www.di.dk; Chair. GERHARD ALBRECHTSEN; Sec. H. ENGELHARDT; 475 mems.

Provinsindustriens Arbejdsgiverforening (Federation of Employers in the Provincial Industry): 1787 Copenhagen V; tel. 33-77-33-77; fax 33-77-33-00; e-mail di@di.dk; internet www.di.dk; f. 1895; Chair. SVEND-AAGE NIELSEN; Sec. GLENN SØGÅARD.

Sammenslutningen af Landbrugets Arbejdsgiverforeninger (SALA) (Danish Confederation of Employers' Associations in Agriculture): Vester Farimagsgade 1, 1606 Copenhagen V; tel. 33-13-46-55; fax 33-11-89-53.

Skibsværftsforeningen (Association of Danish Shipbuilders): St. Kongensgade 128, 1264 Copenhagen K; tel. 33-13-24-16; fax 33-11-10-96; e-mail association@shipbuilders.dk; internet www.shipbuilders.dk.

UTILITIES

Danish Energy Agency: Amaliegade 44, 1256 Copenhagen K; tel. 33-92-67-00; fax 33-11-47-43; e-mail ens@ens.dk; internet www.ens.dk; f. 1976; department of the Ministry of the Environment and Energy; Dir IB LARSEN.

Electricity

Elektricitetsrådet (Electricity Council): Gothersgade 160, 1123 Copenhagen K; tel. 33-73-20-00; fax 33-73-20-99; e-mail er@elraadet.dk; internet www.elraadet.dk; f. 1907; responsible for the general planning, operation and safety of the electricity-supply industry in Denmark; Pres. TAGE DRAEBYE; Man. Dir HR. JARBY.

Elkraft Power Company Ltd: Lautruphøj 5, 2750 Ballerup; tel. 44-66-00-22; fax 44-65-61-04; e-mail elkraft@elkraft.dk; f. 1978; co-ordinates supply of electricity and co-generated heat to eastern Denmark; Man. Dir BENT AGERHOLM.

Københavns Belysningsvaesen (The Copenhagen Energy Department): Vognmagergade 8, 1149 Copenhagen K; tel. 33-12-72-90; fax 33-12-72-91; one of the largest distributors of electricity in Denmark; also supplier of gas, district-heating and public-lighting systems.

NESA A/S: Strandvejen 102, 2900 Hellerup; tel. 72-10-10-10; fax 72-10-10-11; e-mail nesa@nesa.dk; internet www.nesa.dk; f. 1902; largest distributor of electricity in Denmark; Man. Dir PAUL LIND.

SK Power Company, Denmark: Strandvejen 102, 2900 Hellerup; tel. 39-47-39-47; fax 39-47-35-33; e-mail skpower@skpower.dk; internet www.skpower.dk; f. 1992; power production; owns and operates Asnæs, Avedøre, Kyndby, Masnedø and Stigsnæs power stations and a number of local stations.

Gas

Dansk Gasteknisk Forening (Danish Technical Gas Association): Rønnehaven 12, 5320 Agedrup; f. 1911; promotes the use of gas; 680 mems.

DONG (Dansk Olie og Naturgas A/S): Agern Allé 24-26, 2970 Hørsholm; tel. 45-57-10-22; fax 45-17-10-44; e-maildong@dong.dk; internet www.dong.dk; f. 1972; petroleum and natural gas exploration, production and distribution; acts as consultant in other countries; Chair. SVEN RISKÆR.

CO-OPERATIVE

Fællesforeningen for Danmarks Brugsforeninger (Co-operative of Denmark): Roskildevej 65, 2620 Albertslund; f. 1896; Chair. EBBE LUNDGAARD; 1,113,506 mems.

TRADE UNIONS

Landsorganisationen i Danmark (LO) (Danish Confederation of Trade Unions): Rosenørns Allé 12, 1634 Copenhagen V; tel. 35-24-60-00; fax 35-24-63-00; e-mail lo@lo.dk; internet www.lo.dk; Pres. HANS JENSEN; Vice-Pres. TINE A. BRØNDUM; 1,483,828 mems (Jan. 1998); 1,031 brs.

Principal Affiliated Unions

Blik- og Rørarbejderforbundet i Danmark (Metal and Steel Workers): Alholmvej 55, 2500 Valby; tel. 38-71-30-22; fax 38-71-29-97; Pres. PER FREDERIKSEN; 9,237 mems.

Dansk Artist Forbund: Vendersgade 24, 1363 Copenhagen K; tel. 33-32-66-77; fax 33-33-73-30; e-mail artisten@artisten.dk; internet www.artisten.dk; f. 1918; Pres. NICK OLANDER; Gen. Sec. ANDY FIL-IPSEN; 1,600 mems.

Dansk Beklædnings- og Textilarbejderforbund (Textile and Garment Workers): Copenhagen; tel. 33-11-67-65; fax 33-32-99-94; Pres. ANNE M. PEDERSEN; 18,450 mems.

Dansk El-Forbund (Electricians' Union): Vodroffsvej 26, 1900 Frederiksberg C; tel. 33-29-70-00; fax 33-29-70-70; e-mail def@def.dk; internet www.def.dk; Pres. ERIK ANDERSSON; 30,000 mems.

Dansk Funktionærforbund—Serviceforbundet (Danish Federation of Salaried Employees): Upsalagade 20, 2100 Copenhagen Ø; tel. 70-15-04-00; fax 70-15-04-05; Pres. KARSTEN HANSEN; 22,071 mems.

Dansk Jernbaneforbund (Railway Workers): Svanemøllevej 65, 2900 Hellerup; tel. 39-40-11-66; fax 39-40-17-71; f. 1899; Pres. KURT CHRISTIANSEN; 8,567 mems.

Dansk Metalarbejderforbund (Metalworkers): Nyropsgade 38, 1780 Copenhagen V; tel. 33-63-20-00; fax 33-63-21-50; f. 1888; Pres. MAX BAHRING; 143,808 mems.

Dansk Postforbund (Postal Workers): Vodroffsvej 13A, Frederiksberg C; tel. 33-21-41-24; fax 33-21-06-42; e-mail dpf@postforbundet.dk; f. 1908; Pres. JAN SVENDSEN; 11,916 mems.

Forbundet af Offentligt Ansatte (Public Employees): POB 11, Staunings Plads 1–3, 1790 Copenhagen V; tel. 33-13-40-00; fax 33-13-40-42; Pres. POUL WINCKLER; 202,479 mems.

Forbundet Trae-Industri-Byg i Danmark (Timber Industry and Construction Workers): Mimersgade 41, 2200 Copenhagen N; tel. 35-31-95-99; fax 35-31-94-52; Pres. ARNE JOHANSEN; 72,000 mems.

Frisør- og Kosmetiker Forbund (Hairdressers and Beauticians): Lersø Park Allé 21, 2100 Copenhagen Ø; tel. 31-83-18-80; fax 35-82-14-62; Pres. POUL MONGGAARD; 5,288 mems.

Grafisk Forbund (Printing Workers): Lygten 16, 2400 Copenhagen NV; tel. 31-81-44-89; fax 31-81-24-25; f. 1993 by merger; Pres. TOM DURBING; 24,025 mems.

Hærens Konstabel- og Korporal-Forening: Kronprinsensgade 8, 1114 Copenhagen K; tel. 33-93-65-22; fax 33-93-65-23; e-mail hkkf@hkkf.dk; internet www.hkkf.dk; Pres. SVEND-ERIK LARSEN; 4,586 mems.

Handels- og Kontorfunktionærernes Forbund i Danmark (Commercial and Clerical Employees): H. C. Andersens Blvd 50, POB 268, 1780 Copenhagen V; tel. 33-30-43-43; fax 33-30-40-99; f. 1900; Pres. JOHN DAHL; 370,000 mems.

Kvindeligt Arbejderforbund i Danmark (Female Workers): Applebys Plads 5, 1411 Copenhagen K; tel. 32-83-83-83; fax 32-83-86-67; f. 1901; Pres. LILLIAN KNUDSEN; 90,000 mems.

Malerforbundet i Danmark (Housepainters): Copenhagen; tel. 38-34-75-22; fax 38-33-75-22; f. 1890; Pres. JØRN ERIK NIELSEN; 14,042 mems.

Nærings- og Nydelsesmiddelarbejder Forbundet (Food, Sugar Confectionery, Chocolate, Dairy Produce and Tobacco Workers): C.F. Richsvej 103, POB 1479, 2000 Frederiksberg; tel. 38-18-72-72; fax 38-18-72-00; Pres. ANTON JOHANNSEN; 43,307 mems.

Pædagogisk Medhjælper Forbund (Nursery and Child-care Assistants): St. Kongensgade 79, 1017 Copenhagen K; tel. 33-11-03-43; fax 33-11-31-36; f. 1974; Pres. JAKOB BANG; 32,162 mems.

Restaurations Branchens Forbund (Restaurant Workers): Thoravej 29-33, 2400 Copenhagen NV; tel. 38-33-89-00; fax 38-33-67-91; e-mail postmaster@rbf.dk; Chair. PREBEN RASMUSSEN; 30,770 mems.

Socialpædagogernes Landsforbund (National Federation of Social Educators in Denmark): Brolæggerstræde 9, 1211 Copenhagen K; tel. 33-96-28-00; fax 33-96-29-96; e-mail sl@sl-dk.dk; Pres. KIRSTEN NISSEN; 21,864 mems.

Specialarbejderforbundet i Danmark (General Workers' Union in Denmark): Kampmannsgade 4, POB 392, 1790 Copenhagen V; tel. 33-14-21-40; fax 33-97-24-60; e-mail sid@sid.dk; internet www.sid.dk; Pres. POUL ERIK SKOV CHRISTENSEN; Int. Sec. SUNE BOEGH; 336,110 mems.

Teknisk Landsforbund (Technical Workers): Nørre Voldgade 12, 1358 Copenhagen K; tel. 33-12-22-00; fax 33-11-42-72; f. 1919; Pres. ESKE PEDERSEN; 33,915 mems.

Telekommunikations Forbundet (Telecommunications): Rolfsvej 37, 2000 Frederiksberg; tel. 38-88-00-55; fax 38-88-15-11; Pres. BO STENØR LARSEN; 11,500 mems.

Other Unions

Akademikernes Centralorganisation (Danish Confederation of Professional Associations): Nørre Voldgade 29, 1358 Copenhagen K; tel. 33-69-40-40; fax 33-93-85-40; e-mail ac@ac.dk.

Den Almindelige Danske Lægeforening (Danish Medical Association): Trondhjemsgade 9, 2100 Copenhagen Ø; tel. 35-44-85-00; fax 35-44-85-05; e-mail dadl@dadl.dk.

Dansk Journalistforbund (Journalists): Gammel Strand 46, 1202 Copenhagen K; tel. 33-42-80-00; fax 33-42-80-03; e-mail dj@journalistforbundet.dk; internet www.journalistforbundet.dk; f. 1961; Pres. MOGENS BLICHER BJERREGAARD; 13,000 mems.

Funktionærernes og Tjenestemændenes Fællesråd (Civil Servants' and Salaried Employees' Confederation): Niels Hemmingsens Gade 12, POB 1169, 1010 Copenhagen K; tel. 33-36-88-00; fax 33-36-88-80; f. 1952; Chair. ANKER CHRISTOFFERSEN; 400,000 mems.

Transport

In June 1998 an 18-km combined tunnel-and-bridge road and rail link across the Great Belt, linking the islands of Zealand and Funen, was completed, at a cost of US $6,500m.; the project incorporated the world's second longest suspension bridge. A 15.9-km road and rail link across the Oresund strait, between Copenhagen and Malmö was completed in July 2000 at a total cost of about 23,400m. kroner. In October 1992 the Danish, German and Swedish state railways announced a plan to develop a high-speed rail system linking Stockholm and Oslo with Copenhagen, and Copenhagen with Berlin, Hamburg and Köln. The plan, which was estimated to cost 40,000m.–50,000m. kroner, would include the bridge over the Oresund and would require new track between Copenhagen and Hamburg and the construction of a tunnel under the Fehmern Belt. In 1996 contracts were signed for the construction of a 22-km underground light railway system in Copenhagen.

RAILWAYS

Banestyrelsen (Danish National Railway Agency): Solvgade 40, 1349 Copenhagen; tel. 33-14-04-00; fax 33-11-20-38; f. 1997 to assume, from the DSB (see below), responsibility for the maintenance and development of the national rail network; controls 2,349 km of line, of which 602 km are electrified; also manages signalling and train control; CEO E. ELSBORG.

DSB (Danish State Railways): Sølvgade 40, 1349 Copenhagen K; tel. 33-14-04-00; fax 33-14-04-40; e-mail dsb@dsb.dk; internet www.dsb.dk; became an independent public corporation in Jan. 1999; operates passenger and freight services; Man. Dir HENRIK HASSENKAM.

A total of 526 km, mostly branch lines, is run by 15 private companies.

ROADS

At 31 December 1998 Denmark had an estimated 71,437 km of paved roads, including 843 km of motorways, 780 km of national roads and 9,953 km of secondary roads.

SHIPPING

The Port of Copenhagen is the largest port in Denmark and the only one including a Free Port Zone. The other major ports are Århus, Fredericia, Alborg and Esbjerg, all situated in Jutland. There are oil terminals, with adjacent refineries, at Kalundborg, Stigsnæs and Fredericia. Ferry services are provided by DSB (see above) and by private companies.

Farvandsvæsenet (Royal Danish Administration of Navigation and Hydrography): Overgaden oven Vandet 62B, POB 1919, 1023 Copenhagen K; tel. 32-68-95-00; fax 31-57-43-41.

Port Authorities

Århus: Port Authority of Århus, Mindet 2, POB 130, 8100 Århus; tel. 86-13-32-66; fax 86-12-76-62; e-mail port@aarhus.dk; Gen. Man. KAJ SCHMIDT.

Associated Danish Ports A/S—ADP: Vesthavnsvej 33, 7000 Fredericia ; tel. 79-21-50-00; fax 79-21-50-05; e-mail post@adp-as.dk; internet www.adp-as.dk; has authority for ports of Fredericia and Nyborg; Man. Dir JENS PETER PETERS.

Copenhagen: Port of Copenhagen Authority, Nordre Tolbod 7, POB 2083, 1013 Copenhagen K; tel. 33-47-99-99; fax 33-47-99-33; e-mail cphport@cphport.dk; internet www.cphport.dk; Gen. Man. H. HUMMELMOSE; Port captain S. ANDERSEN.

Esbjerg: Port of Esbjerg Authority, Hulvejen 1, POB 2, 6701 Esbjerg; tel. 75-12-41-44; fax 75-13-40-50; e-mail adm@portesbjerg.dk; internet www.portesbjerg.dk; Habour Dir PER WISTOFT; Harbour Captain IB MOLLER NIELSEN.

Frederikshavn: Frederikshavn Havnekontor, Oliepieren 7, POB 129, 9900 Frederikshavn; tel. 98-42-19-88; fax 96-20-09-88; e-mail info@frederikshavnhavn.dk; internet www.frederikshavnhavn.dk; Man. BOERGE MORTENSEN; Harbour Master JESPER THOMSEN.

Kalundborg: Kalundborg Port Authority, POB 50, 4400 Kalundborg; tel. 53-51-33-11; fax 53-51-00-89.

Sønderborg: Sønderborg Havn, Norrebro 1, 6400 Sønderborg; tel. 74-42-27-65; fax 74-43-30-19; internet www.sonderborg.dk; Harbour Master LASS ANDERSEN.

Principal Shipping Companies

Rederiet Otto Danielsen: Kongevejen 272A, 2830 Virum; tel. 45-83-25-55; fax 45-83-50-55; f. 1944; 6 general cargo vessels, totalling 16,400 grt, under foreign flags; general tramp trade, chartering, ship sales; Fleet Man. JØRN STAUREBY.

Dannebrog Rederi A/S: Rungsted Strandvej 113, 2960 Rungsted Kyst; tel. 45-17-77-77; fax 45-17-77-70; e-mail dbrog@dannebrog.com; f. 1883; 3 ro-ro vessels, product chemical tanker services; liner service US–Europe, US Gulf–Caribbean, Mediterranean–Caribbean; CEO DITLEV WEDELL-WEDELLSBORG.

DFDS A/S: Skt Annæ Plads 30, 1295 Copenhagen K; tel. 33-42-33-42; fax 33-42-33-41; e-mail dfds@dfds.dk; internet www.dfds.com; f. 1866; 7 car/passenger ships of 166,233 grt and 21 ro-ro vessels of 390,812 grt (incl. Swedish and German subsidiaries); passenger and car ferry services between Denmark, Sweden, the UK, the Netherlands, Germany and Norway, liner trade between Denmark, Sweden, Norway, the UK, the Netherlands, eastern Europe and Belgium; J. Lauritzen Holding owns majority share; Man. Dir OLE FRIE.

The East Asiatic Co Ltd A/S: Nikolai Plads 34, 1067 Copenhagen K; tel. 33-75-00-00; fax 33-75-00-11; e-mail eac@eac.dk; f. 1897; trading, industry, food processing, plantations, shipping; totally owned and managed tonnage: 4 bulk/log carriers of 94,400 grt and 2 tankers of 33,700 grt under foreign flags; world-wide services; Chair. JAN ERLUND; Man. Dir MICHAEL FIORINI.

Elite Shipping A/S: H.C. Andersens Blvd 12, 3rd floor, 1553 Copenhagen V; tel. 33-15-32-33; fax 33-15-32-06; internet www.elite-shipping.dk; 29 dry cargo vessels of 80,200 grt; tramp, world-wide; Man. Dirs RINO LANGE, TORBEN PALLE HANSEN.

H. Folmer & Co: Fredericiagade 57, 1310 Copenhagen K; tel. 33-13-25-10; fax 33-13-54-64; f. 1955; 14 general cargo vessels of 14,100 grt; world-wide tramping; Man. Owners J. J. FOLMER, UFFE MARTIN JENSEN.

KIL Shipping A/S: 8 Smakkedalen, 2820 Gentofte; tel. 39-77-03-00; fax 39-76-03-99; e-mail kil@kil.dk; f. 1998; 13 container vessels totalling 121,800 dwt, 4 under the Danish Flag and 9 under a foreign flag, 16 chemical carriers totalling 130,400 dwt under foreign flags, and 6 gas carriers totalling 18,056 dwt under foreign flags; Man. Dir BJARNE TUILDE.

J. Lauritzen A/S: Skt Annæ Plads 28, POB 2147, 1291 Copenhagen K; tel. 33-11-12-22; fax 33-11-85-13; e-mail info@j-lauritzen.com; internet www.j-lauritzen.com; f. 1884; operates reefer ships, LPG/C Carriers and bulk ships; Pres. TORBEN JANHOLT.

Lauritzen Kosan Tankers: Skt Annæ Plads 28, 1291 Copenhagen K; tel. 33-14-34-00; fax 33-91-00-39; e-mail cphkos@j-lauritzen.com; internet www.j-lauritzen.com; f. 1951; 26 gas carriers of 94,546 grt; Man. Dir TORBEN MEJNERTSEN.

Mercandia Rederierne: Prags Blvd 92–94, 2300 Copenhagen S; tel. 32-83-01-55; fax 32-83-01-50; e-mail mercandia@vip.cybercity.dk; internet www.mercandia.dk; f. 1964; 24 ro-ro vessels and car ferries totalling 238,200 grt; tramp and liner services; Man. Owner PER HENRIKSEN.

A. P. Møller: Esplanaden 50, 1098 Copenhagen K; tel. 33-63-33-63; fax 33-14-15-15; internet www.maersk.com; f. 1904; fleet of 38 container vessels, 13 products tankers, 5 crude oil tankers, 13 gas carriers, 26 offshore vessels and 7 drilling rigs, totalling 3,081,900 grt under the Danish flag; further tonnage owned by subsidiary cos in Singapore and the UK; world-wide liner and feeder services under the name of **Maersk Line**, and world-wide tanker, bulk, offshore and rig services; Man. Owner JESS SØDERBERG.

A/S Em. Z. Svitzer: Park Allé 350B, 2605 Brøndby; tel. 43-43-43-71; fax 43-43-60-22; f. 1833; wholly-owned subsidiary of A. P. Møller; 22 tugs and salvage vessels and a barge fleet; salvage, towage and barge services; Gen. Man. KELD BALLE-MORTENSEN.

Mortensen & Lange A/S: Kongevejen 2, 2480 Fredensborg; tel. 48-40-85-85; fax 42-28-00-57; f. 1961; general cargo vessels of 13,800 grt and 6 reefer vessels of 8,000 grt; world-wide tramping; Man. Dir (vacant).

Dampskibsselskabet Norden A/S: Amaliegade 49, 1256 Copenhagen K; tel. 33-15-04-51; fax 33-15-61-99; e-mail mail@ds-norden.dk; internet www.ds-norden.com; f. 1871; 5 bulk carriers of 224,600 grt, 1 product tanker of 43,700 grt and 1 oil tanker of 55,000 grt; world-wide tramping; Man. Dir STEEN KRABBE.

Sønderborg Rederiaktieselskab: Havnevej 18, POB 20, 6320 Egernsund; tel. 74-44-14-35; fax 74-44-14-75; 6 livestock carriers of

5,700 grt; shipowners, managers, chartering agents; world-wide; Chair. B. CLAUSEN.

Terkol-Rederierne: Jægergårdsvej 107, 8000 Århus C; tel. 86-13-36-88; fax 86-18-15-10; 2 container vessels of 21,100 grt and 17 chemical tankers of 42,400 grt; world-wide tanker services; Gen. Man. N. B. TERKILDSEN.

A/S D/S Torm: Marina Park, Sundkrogsgade 10, 2100 Copenhagen Ø; tel. 39-17-92-00; fax 39-17-93-93; f. 1889; 16 product carriers of 617,772 grt, 7 bulk carriers of 199,507 grt, 2 multipurpose vessels of 27,376 grt and 2 AHTs (1999); operator of a time-chartered fleet; liner services USA–West Africa; Man. Dir KLAUS KJÆRULFF.

Shipping Association

Danmarks Rederiforening (Danish Shipowners' Asscn): Amaliegade 33, 1256 Copenhagen K; tel. 33-11-40-88; fax 33-11-62-10; e-mail info@danmarksrederiforening.dk; internet www.danmarksrederiforening.dk; f. 1884; 21 members, representing 4,841,000 grt (July 1998); Chair. of the Board STEEN R. KRABBE; Man. Dir PETER BJERREGAARD.

CIVIL AVIATION

The main international airport is Copenhagen Airport, situated about 10 km from the centre of the capital. The following domestic airports have scheduled flights to European and Scandinavian destinations: Ålborg, Århus and Billund in Jutland. Other domestic airports include Roskilde (30 km south-west of Copenhagen); Esbjerg, Karup, Skrydstrup, Stauning, Sønderborg and Thisted in Jutland; Odense in Funen; and Bornholm Airport on the island of Bornholm.

Statens Luftfartsvæsen (Civil Aviation Administration): Luftfartshuset, POB 744, 2450 Copenhagen SV; tel. 36-18-60-00; fax 36-18-60-01; e-mail dcaa@slv.dk; Dir-Gen. OLE ASMUSSEN.

Det Danske Luftfartselskab A/S—DDL (Danish Airlines): Industriens Hus, H. C. Andersens Blvd 18, 1553 Copenhagen V; tel. 33-14-13-33; fax 33-14-28-28; f. 1918; 50% govt-owned; Danish parent company of the designated national carrier, Scandinavian Airlines System—SAS (see under Sweden), SAS Commuter; Chair. HUGO SCHRØDER; Man. Dir GUNNAR TIETZ.

National Airlines

Cimber Air Denmark: Sønderborg Airport, Lufthavnsvej 2, 6400 Sønderborg; tel. 74-42-22-77; fax 74-42-65-11; f. 1950; operates domestic service in co-operation with Lufthansa and SAS; operates charter flights and total route systems for other cos throughout Europe; markets electronic data systems for airlines and industry; Pres., CEO JORGEN NIELSEN; Vice-Pres. (Airline Division) HANS I. NIELSEN.

Maersk Air: Copenhagen Airport South, 2791 Dragør; tel. 32-31-44-44; fax 32-31-44-90; e-mail mail@maersk-air.dk; internet www.maersk-air.com; f. 1969; provides charter flights for Scandinavian tour operators, operates domestic services and international flights to Belgium, Germany, Sweden, the Netherlands, Norway, Italy, Greece and the UK; owned by Møller Group (see under Shipping); subsidiary: Maersk Air Cargo; Chair. BJARNE HANSEN; Pres. OLE DIETZ.

Muk Air: Copenhagen Airport South, 2791 Dragør; tel. 32-82-00-00; fax 32-82-00-78; f. 1979; operates scheduled services to destinations in Scandinavia and Germany; Pres. Capt. KNUT LINDAU; Vice-Pres. FRANK HOLTON.

Premiair: Copenhagen Airport South, Hangar 276, 2791 Dragør; tel. 32-47-72-00; fax 32-45-12-20; f. 1994 by merger of Conair A/S (Denmark) and Scanair (Sweden); controlling stake acquired by Airtours (United Kingdom) in 1996; flights to major destinations in Europe; Pres. TOM CLAUSEN.

Star Air: Copenhagen Airport South, 2791 Dragør; tel. 32-31-43-43; fax 32-31-43-90; f. 1987; operates cargo services in Europe; Pres. OLE DIETZ.

Tourism

There were 9.5m. overnight stays in all types of accommodation in 1999 made by foreign visitors.

Danmarks Turistråd (The Danish Tourist Board): Vesterbrogade 6D, 1620 Copenhagen V; tel. 33-11-14-15; fax 33-93-14-16; e-mail dt@dt.dk; internet www.visitdenmark.com; f. 1967; Dir BJARNE EKLUND.

DANISH EXTERNAL TERRITORIES
THE FAROE ISLANDS

Introductory Survey

Location, Climate, Language, Religion, Flag, Capital

The Faroe Islands are a group of 18 islands (of which 17 are inhabited) in the Atlantic Ocean, between Scotland and Iceland. The main island is Streymoy, where more than one-third of the population resides. The climate is mild in winter and cool in summer, with a mean temperature of 7°C (45°F). Most of the inhabitants profess Christianity: the majority of Faroese belong to the Evangelical Lutheran Church of Denmark. The principal language is Faroese, but Danish is a compulsory subject in all schools. The flag (proportions 22 by 16) displays a red cross, bordered with blue, on a white background, the upright of the cross being to the left of centre. The capital is Tórshavn, which is situated on Streymoy.

History and Government

The Faroe Islands have been under Danish administration since Queen Margrethe I of Denmark inherited Norway in 1380. The islands were occupied by the United Kingdom while Denmark was under German occupation during the Second World War, but they were restored to Danish control immediately after the war. The Home Rule Act of 1948 gave the Faroese control over all their internal affairs. The Faroe Islands did not join the European Community (EC, now European Union, EU, see p. 181) with Denmark in 1973. There is a local parliament (the Løgting), but the Danish legislature, the Folketing, to which the Faroese send two members, is responsible for defence and foreign policy, constitutional matters and the judicial and monetary systems. The Faroes control fishing resources within their fisheries zone, and in September 1992 a long-standing dispute between Denmark and the Faroes was settled when the Danish Government agreed to give the Faroese authorities legislative and administrative power over mineral resources, including those beneath the bed of the sea in the area adjacent to the islands. This agreement removed one of the major obstacles to exploration for hydrocarbons off the Faroe Islands, where geologists consider that prospects for discovering reserves of petroleum and natural gas are favourable. In 1994 the Faroe Islands accordingly awarded a US company a licence to begin exploratory surveys, despite the existence of a long-standing dispute between Denmark and the United Kingdom over the demarcation of the continental shelf west of the Shetland Islands and south-east of the Faroe Islands, which had threatened to delay prospecting. This dispute was resolved in May 1999, however, when representatives of the Faroese Government signed an agreement with the Danish and British Governments regarding the location of the boundaries of the area concerned. The area, known as the 'golden corner' (formerly the White Zone), was believed to be potentially rich in petroleum reserves. In mid-August 2000 the Faroese Government issued seven licences in the 'golden corner' to 12 oil companies; drilling was expected to commence in 2001.

The centre-left coalition Government of the Social Democratic Party (SDP), Republicans and the People's Party, formed in 1975, collapsed in 1980 over a plan, opposed by the conservative People's Party, to extend through the winter months a government-owned ferry service linking the islands with Denmark, Norway and Scotland. At a general election, held in November, conservative political groups slightly increased their share of the popular vote. Although there was no material change in the balance of party representation in the Løgting, the Union Party formed a centre-right coalition with the People's Party and the Home Rule Party in January 1981. A general election was held in November 1984, and in December a four-party, centre-left coalition Government was formed under the premiership of Atli Dam, comprising his SDP, the Home Rule Party, the Republican Party and the Christian People's Party combined with the Progressive and Fishing Industry Party (CPP-PFIP).

Elections in 1988 demonstrated a shift to the right in the Faroes, to the benefit of the People's Party. Its one member in the Danish Folketing increased his support in the national elections of September 1987 and May 1988. At a Faroese general election in November 1988 the incumbent Government lost its majority, and the People's Party became the largest party in the Løgting. In January 1989, after 10 weeks of negotiations, a centre-right coalition comprising the People's Party, the Republican Party, the Home Rule Party and the CPP-PFIP, and led by Jógvan Sundstein (Chairman of the People's Party), was formed. The coalition was committed to economic austerity and support for the fishing industry. In June 1989, however, the CPP-PFIP and the Home Rule Party withdrew their support for the Government. After three weeks a new coalition was formed. Sundstein remained Løgmadur (Prime Minister), and his People's Party was supported by the Republican and Union Parties. In October 1990, however, these two parties withdrew their support for the coalition Government. As a result, an early general election was held in November. The SDP obtained the largest share of the vote, winning 10 seats (an increase of three), while the People's Party, which led the outgoing coalition, won seven seats (a loss of one seat).

In January 1991 a coalition between the SDP and the People's Party was formed, under the leadership of Atli Dam. He was replaced in January 1993 by Marita Petersen (also of the SDP). In April the People's Party withdrew from the coalition, and was replaced by the Republican Party and the Home Rule Party. At a general election, held in July 1994, the Union Party became the largest party in the Løgting, winning eight seats (an increase of two), while the SDP's allocation of seats was reduced from 10 to five. In September a coalition of the Union Party, the SDP, the Home Rule Party and the newly-formed Labour Front took office. Edmund Joensen replaced Petersen as Prime Minister. In 1996 the People's Party replaced the SDP in the governing coalition. Joensen remained Prime Minister, while Anfinn Kallsberg succeeded Jóannes Eidesgaard as Minister of Finance and Economics. A general election was held on 30 April 1998, at which both the Republican Party and the People's Party each increased their allocation of seats to eight, while the number of seats secured by the SDP rose from five to seven; the parliamentary representation of the Union Party was reduced from eight seats to six. In mid-May a coalition Government was formed by members of the People's Party, the Republican Party and the Home Rule Party, under the premiership of Anfinn Kallsberg.

Tensions with the Danish Government in the early 1990s, the nationalist persuasion of the new Government and the prospect of offshore petroleum discoveries revived Faroese ambitions for political and economic independence. (The Faroese had narrowly favoured independence from Denmark in a referendum in 1946 but the decision had been overturned by the Danish Folketing.) In October 1998 the Løgting adopted a resolution in support of the Government's intention (announced earlier that year) to seek status for the Faroe Islands as a 'sovereign nation' under the Danish monarchy, having a common monetary system with Denmark; it was envisaged by the Faroese Government that sovereignty for the islands would be most appropriately achieved through continued co-operation with Denmark within a new constitutional framework, based on a bilateral treaty between the two countries as equal, independent partners. A commission charged with the development of a proposal for a Faroese constitution was established by the Government in February 1999, and submitted its conclusions to the Løgting in June 2000. The Faroese envisaged retaining the Danish Queen Margrethe II as their Head of State and maintaining the link between their local currency and the Danish krone. The islands would seek to continue to co-operate with Denmark in social affairs, justice, health and air traffic control, and would also maintain present arrangements such as mutual rights of residence, employment and education. The Faroes would also seek to join NATO (see p. 241) and the UN.

Negotiations between the Danish and Faroese administrations concerning the future independence of the Faroe Islands began in March 2000 but swiftly stalled after the Danish Government confirmed that it would not oppose Faroese independence but would terminate annual subsidies (of about 1,000m. kroner) to the Faroes in four years, compared with the 15 envisaged by the Faroese. The Danish Prime Minister, Poul Nyrup Rasmussen, rejected an offer of mediation from the Icelandic premier, David Oddson. Discussions were resumed later in the year but finally collapsed in late October, prompting Anfinn Kallsberg to announce a plan to hold a referendum on independence in 2001. The Faroese had initially envisaged the successful negotiation of a treaty with the Danish Government prior to a referendum. The referendum, which in February was scheduled for 26 May, was to include four issues; the full transfer of authority to the Faroese by 2012; the establishment of an economic fund to guarantee financial security during the transitional period; the gradual elimination of subsidies from Denmark; and the holding of a further referendum establishing the Faroe Islands as an independent state by 2012. The Danish Government reacted strongly to plans for a plebiscite, claiming that Denmark would regard it as a *de facto* referendum on sovereignty and that a vote in favour of the proposals for independence would result in the halting of Danish aid within four years. The reluctance of the Faroese population to lose Danish subsidies and disagreement within the Faroese coalition Government resulted in the cancellation of the referendum in early March. Shortly afterwards agreement was reached within the Faroese Government on a plan for independence that was submitted to the Danish authorities.

The Minister for Industry, Transport and Communications, Finnbogi Arge, resigned in August 2000 citing personal reasons and was replaced by another member of the Folkaflokkurin Party, Bjarni Djurholm. The Minister for Education and Cultural Affairs, Sigar Á Brúnni, resigned in March 2000 over his decision the previous year to allocate 1.6m. kroner to the Faroese broadcast company, Sjónvarp Føroya, without the approval of the Government or the Løgting. He was temporarily replaced by Høgni Hoydal, the Minister for Home Rule Affairs.

In international affairs, the Faroe Islanders earned opprobrium for their traditional slaughter of pilot whales, an important source of food. After foreign journalists publicized the whaling in 1986, stricter regulations were imposed on whaling operations. In July 1992 the Faroese Government threatened to leave the International Whaling Commission (IWC, see p. 300), following the latter's criticism of whaling methods practised in the Faroe Islands. It was, however, claimed that the Faroese did not have the legal right to withdraw from the Commission independently of Denmark. In September the Faroe Islands, Greenland, Norway and Iceland agreed to establish the North Atlantic Marine Mammal Commission, in protest at what they viewed as the IWC's preoccupation with conservation.

Economic Affairs

In 1995 gross national product (GNP), estimated at 1990 prices, was US $829m., equivalent to $19,000 per head. Between 1973 and 1988, it was estimated, GNP increased, in real terms, at an average rate of 4.5% per year, with real GNP per head rising by 3.3% annually. Between 1989 and 1993, however, real GNP decreased dramatically, at an average rate of 9.4% per year. During 1994–95 real GNP increased by 4.2%. The population declined at an average annual rate of 1.6% in 1989–95, but increased by 1.1% per year in 1995–1999. Gross domestic product (GDP) increased, in real terms, by about 5% in 1997, 8% in 1998 and 3% in 1999.

Agriculture (principally sheep-farming) and fishing contributed 20.2% of gross domestic product (GDP) in 1999. Potatoes and other vegetables are the main crops. Only about 6% of the land surface is cultivated.

Fishing is the dominant industry. In 1999 fishing, aquaculture and fish-processing accounted for 25.1% of GDP; it employed 23% of the labour force in 1994. The sector accounted for 95.2% of exports in 1999. Most fishing takes place within the 200-nautical-mile (370-km) fisheries zone imposed around the Faroes in 1977. In the 1980s fish farming began to be encouraged. The traditional hunting of whales (see Recent History) is an important source of meat.

Industry (including mining, manufacturing, construction and power) contributed 17.8% of GDP in 1999.

Mining contributed only 0.3% of GDP in 1999. Coal is mined on Suduroy. The potential for petroleum production around the islands is believed to be significant. Following the resolution of a boundary dispute with the United Kingdom in May 1999, in mid-August 2000 the Ministry of Petroleum issued seven licences (of six to nine years' duration) to 12 oil companies, organized into five groups, in the 'golden corner' (formerly the White Zone), an area south-east of the Faroe Islands. Drilling by two licencees was expected to begin in 2001. In December 2000 the Faroes Oil and Gas Company (FOGC), known locally as Føroya Kolvetni, announced plans to float on the London stock exchange.

Manufacturing contributed 10.8% of GDP in 1999. The dominant sector is fish-processing, which accounted for 5.7% of GDP in that year. Technical repairs and shipyards contributed 2.1% of GDP, while exports of vessels accounted for 3.6% of exports in 1999. A small textile industry exports traditional Faroese woollens.

The energy sector contributed 2.2% of GDP in 1999. About 48% of the islands' energy requirements are provided by a hydroelectric power plant. Imports of fuels and related products accounted for 0.8% of imports in 1999.

The services sector accounted for 62.0% of GDP in 1999.

In 1999 the Faroe Islands recorded a trade deficit of 316m. kroner, and there was a surplus of 695m. kroner on the current account of the balance of payments. Denmark was the Faroes' principal source of imports (27.8%) in 1999; other major suppliers were Norway (26.1%), Germany (7.2%) and the United Kingdom (5.9%). Denmark was also the principal market for exports (32.1%) in that year; other major purchasers were the United Kingdom (21.2%), France (9.4%), Spain (6.7%) and Germany (6.6%). In 1999 the European Union (EU, see p. 181) as a whole took 82.3% of exports and supplied 54.8% of imports. The principal imports in 1999 were products for household consumption, products for industry and machinery and capital goods. Principal exports in that year were chilled and frozen fish fillets, chilled and frozen salmon and trout, other fish and fish products and vessels.

Danish subsidies are an important source of income to the islands, and accounted for about 24% of total government revenue in 1996. In that year, including the central government grant of 867m. kroner as revenue, the Faroese Government recorded a budget surplus of 926m. kroner. At the end of 1999 the net foreign debt was estimated at 447m. kroner. The annual rate of inflation was 2.8% in 1997, 4.7% in 1998 and 5.1% in 1999. In the 1980s there was an acute labour shortage in the Faroes, but by mid-1995 unemployment had increased to some 16% of the labour force. By August 2000, however, unemployment had declined to some 4% of the labour force.

The Faroe Islands did not join the European Community (now EU) with Denmark in 1973, but did secure favourable terms of trade with Community members and special concessions in Denmark and the United Kingdom. Agreements on free trade were concluded between the Faroe Islands and Iceland, Norway, Sweden, Finland and Austria in 1992 and 1993. In international fisheries organizations, where Denmark is represented by the EU, the Kingdom maintains separate membership in respect of the Faroe Islands (and Greenland). The Faroe Islands is also a member of the Nordic Council (see p. 237).

During the 1980s the Faroes' principal source of income, the fishing industry, was expanded with the help of substantial investment and official subsidies, financed by external borrowing. However, depletion of stocks and the resulting decline in catches, together with a fall in export prices, led to a reduction in export earnings and a financial crisis in the early 1990s (GDP was estimated to have declined by some 20% in 1993). The Danish Government attempted to stabilize the economy by restructuring the banking sector and by extending significant loans (by the end of 1997 it was estimated that the Faroes owed some 5,500m. kroner to the Danish Government, equivalent to 140,000 kroner per head). The report of an independent commission of inquiry into Denmark's response to the crisis in the Faroes, which had been established by the islanders in 1995, was published in early 1998 and levelled accusations of serious mismanagement at Danish government officials, and at the Danish Den Danske Bank. In June 1998 an agreement was reached by the Faroese and Danish Governments regarding a reduction of Faroese debt to Denmark as a form of compensation. Denmark's annual subsidy of (1,000m. kroner) provides nearly one-third of the Faroes budget. However, oil companies are expected to start exploratory offshore drilling during 2001. A discovery of reserves of natural gas and petroleum would enable the Faroese economy to diversify, reducing its overwhelming dependence on the fisheries sector.

Education and Social Welfare

The education system is similar to that of Denmark, except that Faroese is the language of instruction. Danish is, however, a compulsory subject in all schools. The Faroese Academy was upgraded to the University of the Faroe Islands in May 1990.

In 2000 government medical services included three hospitals. In 1999 there were 0.58 physicians and 0.85 dentist for every 1,000 of the population.

In 1995 government expenditure on social welfare represented 28% of total budget spending, while education received a further 13% of the total.

Statistical Survey

Sources (unless otherwise stated): Statistical Bureau of the Faroe Islands, POB 355, 110 Tórshavn; tel. 314636; fax 318696; e-mail farostat@olivant.fo; Statistics Faroe Islands, Traðagøta 39, POB 2068, 165 Argir; tel 352028; fax 352038; e-mail hagstova@hagstova.fo; internet www.hagstova.fo; Faroese Government Office, Hovedvagtsgade 8, 2, 1103 Copenhagen K; tel. 33-14-08-66; fax 33-93-85-75; *Yearbook of Nordic Statistics.*

AREA AND POPULATION

Area: 1,398.9 sq km (540.1 sq miles).

Population: 44,806 at 31 December 1998; 45,412 at 31 December 1999; 46,122 (provisional) at 31 December 2000.

Density (2000, provisional): 33.0 per sq km.

Principal Town: Tórshavn (capital), population 16,673 at 31 July 2000.

Births and Deaths (1998): Registered live births 627 (birth rate 13.9 per 1,000); Deaths 377 (death rate 8.4 per 1,000). *1999:* Registered live births 627 (birth rate 13.9 per 1,000); Deaths 402 (death rate 8.9 per 1,000). *2000* (provisional): Registered live births 660 (birth rate 14.3 per 1,000); Deaths 350 (death rate 7.6 per 1,000).

Expectation of Life (years at birth, 1998): Males 74.1; Females 80.8.

Employed Labour Force (at 31 August, 2000): Total 23,556.

AGRICULTURE AND FISHING

Principal Crop (FAO estimate, 2000): Potatoes 1,500 metric tons. Source: FAO.

Livestock (FAO estimates, '000 head, 2000): Cattle 2; Sheep 68. Source: FAO.

Fishing ('000 metric tons, live weight, 1998): Capture 376.2 (Atlantic cod 42.2, Haddock 24.0, Saithe (Pollock) 28.7, Blue whiting (Poutassou) 71.2, Atlantic herring 70.9, Capelin 45.2, Northern prawn 13.0, Argentines 17.6); Aquaculture 20.6 (Atlantic salmon 18.1); Total catch 396.8. Figures exclude aquatic mammals, recorded by number rather than by weight. The number of long-finned pilot whales caught was 1,162 in 1997. Source: FAO, *Yearbook of Fishery Statistics.*

INDUSTRY

Selected Products ('000 metric tons, unless otherwise indicated, 1996): Frozen or chilled fish 123; Salted and processed fish products 15; Aquamarine products 13; Oils, fats and meal of aquatic animals 124; Electric energy (million kWh) 182.

FINANCE

Danish currency is in use.

Government Accounts ('000 kroner, 1996): Revenue 2,781,000; Danish state subsidy 867,000; Expenditure 2,722,000.

Cost of Living (Consumer Price Index; base: 1983 = 100): *2000:* Food 242.8; Fuel and power 133,0; Clothing 152.1; Dwellings 142; Other 138.7; All items 183.9.

Gross Domestic Product by Economic Activity (million kroner at current factor cost, 1999): Agriculture, fishing, etc. 1,397; Mining and quarrying 18; Manufacturing 744; Electricity, gas and water 150; Construction 321; Trade, restaurants and hotels 768; Transport, storage and communications 552; Financing 403; Dwellings 742; Business services 187; Domestic services, etc. 80; Government services 1,556; Sub-total (incl. adjustment) 6,918; *Less* imputed bank service charges 373; Gross domestic product at factor cost 6,546.

Balance of Payments (US $ million, 1995): Merchandise exports f.o.b. 362; Merchandise imports c.i.f. –315; *Trade balance* 46; Services, other income and private unrequited transfers (net) –114; Official unrequited transfers (net) 193; *Current balance* 125.

EXTERNAL TRADE

Principal Commodities (million kroner, 1999): *Imports c.i.f.:* Products for agriculture 264 (Animal fodder 242); Products for the construction industry 240; products for other industries 554; Fuels and related products 265; Machinery and other capital goods 329; Vehicles 201; Products for household consumption 841; Vessels 418; Fish 119; Total (incl. others) 3,276. *Exports f.o.b.:* Chilled or frozen fish fillets 1,035; Chilled or frozen salmon and trout 685; Other chilled or frozen fish 438; Salted fish 450; Crustaceans and molluscs 274; Fish for reduction 158; Vessels 117; Total (incl. others) 3,252.

Principal Trading Partners (million kroner, 1999): *Imports c.i.f.:* Denmark 911; Germany 235; Iceland 122; Japan 79; Norway 856; Sweden 148; United Kingdom 194; USA 42; Total (incl. others) 3,276. *Exports f.o.b.:* Denmark 1,044; France (incl. Monaco) 306; Germany 216; Italy 101; Japan 38; Spain 219; United Kingdom 690; USA 151; Total (incl. others) 3,252.

TRANSPORT

Road Traffic (registered motor vehicles, 31 December 1997): Private motor cars 12,748; Goods vehicles 2,867; Buses 111; Coaches 107; Trailers 1,078; Motor cycles 148.

Shipping: Merchant fleet (31 December 1998): 141 vessels (fishing vessels 113), Total displacemet 103,478 grt (fishing vessels 70,789 grt); International sea-borne freight traffic (1996, '000 metric tons): Goods loaded 223, Goods unloaded 443.

COMMUNICATIONS MEDIA

Radio Receivers (1996): 24,000 registered.

Television Receivers (1997): 13,000 registered.

Book Production (1999): 121 titles.

Newspapers (1996): 5 titles (average circulation 7,000 copies per issue).

Telephones ('000 main lines in use, 1995): 22 (Source: UN, *Statistical Yearbook*).

Telefax Stations (1993): 1,400 in use (Source: UN, *Statistical Yearbook*).

Mobile Cellular Telephones (subscribers, 1995): 2,558 (Source: UN, *Statistical Yearbook*).

Directory

The Government

The legislative body is the Løgting (Lagting in Danish) which consists of 27 members, elected on a basis of proportional representation in seven constituencies, with up to five supplementary seats dependent upon the discrepancy between the distribution of seats among the parties and the numbers of people voting. All Faroese over the age of 18 years have the right to vote. Based on the strength of the parties in the Løgting, a Government, the Landsstýri, is formed. This is the administrative body in certain spheres, chiefly relating to Faroese economic affairs. The Løgmaður (Prime Minister) has to ratify all Løgting laws. Power is decentralized and there are about 50 local authorities. The Ríkisumboðsmaður, or High Commissioner, represents the Danish Government, and has the right to address the Løgting and to advise on joint affairs. All Danish legislation must be submitted to the Landsstýri before becoming law in the Faroe Islands.

The Danish Folketing (Parliament), to which the Faroese send two members, is responsible for defence and foreign policy, constitutional matters and the judicial and monetary systems.

LANDSSTÝRI
(March 2001)

A coalition of the People's Party (PP), the Republican Party (RP) and the Home Rule Party (HRP).

Prime Minister (with responsibility for Constitutional Affairs, Foreign Affairs and Municipal Affairs): ANFINN KALLSBERG (PP).

Deputy Prime Minister and Minister of Self-governmental and Judicial Affairs and of Nordic Affairs: HØGNI HOYDAL (RP).

Minister of Education and Cultural Affairs: TORBJØRN JACOBSEN (RP).

Minister of Finance: KARSTIN HANSEN (RP).

Minister of Industry, Transport and Communications: BJARNI DJURHOLM (PP).

Minister of Oil-related Matters and Environmental Affairs: EYÐUN ELTTØR (HRP).

Minister of Health and Social Affairs: HELENA DAM Á NEYSTABØ (HRP).

Minister of Fisheries: JØRGEN NICLASEN (PP).

Government Offices

Ríkisumboðsmaðurin (Danish High Commission): POB 12, Amtmansbrekkan 4, 110 Tórshavn; tel. 351200; fax 310864; e-mail riomfr@fo.stm.dk; High Commissioner VIBEKE LARSEN.

Løgtingsskrivstovan (Parliament Office): POB 208, Erling Jalsgøtu 6, 110 Tórshavn; tel. 310850; fax 310686; e-mail logting@ logting.fo; Leader SÚSANNA DANIELSEN.

Faroese Government Office: Hovedvagtsgade 8, 2, 1103 Copenhagen K; tel. 33-14-08-66; fax 33-93-85-75; e-mail focph@faroff.dk.

Løgmansskrivstovan (Prime Minister's Office): Tinganes, POB 64, 110 Tórshavn; tel. 351010; fax 351015; e-mail fl@fl.fo; internet www.fl.fo.

Ministry of Finance: Traðagøta 39, POB 2039, 165 Argir; tel. 352020; fax 352030; e-mail fms@fms.fo.

Ministry of Fisheries and Maritime Affairs: Yviri við Strond 17, POB 87, 110 Tórshavn; tel. 353035; e-mail fisk@fisk.fl.fo.

Ministry of Education and Culture: Hoyvíksvegur 72, 110 Tórshavn; tel. 355050; fax 355055; e-mail umms@umms.fo.

Ministry of Health and Social Affairs: Eirargarður 2, 110 Tórshavn; tel. 354040; fax 354045; e-mail ash@ahs.fo.

Ministry of Petroleum: Brekkutún 1, POB 3050, 110 Tórshavn; tel. 357070; fax 357075; e-mail oms@oms.fo; internet www.oms.fo.

Ministry of Trade and Industry: Tinganes, POB 377, 110 Tórshavn; tel. 356060; fax 356065; e-mail vms@vms.fo; internet www.vms.fo.

LØGTING

The Løgting has between 27 and 32 members, elected by universal adult suffrage.

Speaker: FINNBOGI ISAKSON (Republican Party).

Election, 30 April 1998

	Votes	% of votes	Seats
Tjóðveldisflokkurin (Republican Party) .	6,583	23.8	8
Fólkaflokkurin (People's Party) . .	5,887	21.3	8
Javnaðarflokkurin (Social Democratic Party)	6,062	21.9	7
Sambandsflokkurin (Union Party) . .	4,992	18.0	6
Sjálvstýrisflokkurin (Home Rule Party) .	2,116	7.7	2
Miðflokkurin (Centre Party)	1,123	4.1	1
Kristiligi Fólkaflokkurin (Christian People's Party).	682	2.5	–
Verkmannafylkingin (Labour Front) .	215	0.8	–
Total	27,660	100.0	32

Political Organizations

Unless otherwise indicated, the address of each of the following organizations is: Aarvegur, POB 208, 110 Tórshavn; tel. 310850; fax 310686.

Fólkaflokkurin (People's Party): f. 1940; conservative-liberal party, favours free enterprise and wider political and economic autonomy for the Faroes; Chair. ÓLI BRECKMANN.

Hin Føroyski Flokkurin (The Faroese Party): f. 1994; seeks to abolish Home Rule and fully to re-integrate the Faroes into the Kingdom of Denmark; Chair. ÓLAVUR CHRISTIANSEN.

Javnaðarflokkurin (Social Democratic Party—SDP): POB 208, Aarvegur 2, 110 Tórshavn; tel. 312493; fax 319397; e-mail javnadarflokkarin@logting.fo; internet www.javnadarflokkarin.fo; f. 1928; Chair. JÓANNES EIDESGAARD.

Kristiligi Fólkaflokkurin, Føroya Framburðs- og Fiskivinnuflokkurin (Christian People's Party, Progressive and Fishing Industry Party—CPP-PFIP): à Brekku 5, 700 Klaksvík; tel. 457580; fax 457581; f. 1954; centre party; Chair. NIELS PAULI DANIELSEN; Parliamentary Chair. LASSE KLEIN.

Miðflokkurin (Centre Party): POB 3237, 110 Tórshavn; f. 1991; Chair. TORDUR NICLASEN.

Sambandsflokkurin (Union Party): Lucas Debersargøta 3, POB 1340, 110 Tórshavn; tel. 318870; fax 318910; e-mail samband@ post.divant.fo; internet www.samband.fo; f. 1906; favours the maintenance of close relations between the Faroes and the Kingdom of Denmark; conservative in internal affairs; Chair. EDMUND JOENSEN.

Sjálvstýrisflokkurin (Home Rule Party): f. 1906; social-liberal party advocating eventual political independence for the Faroes within the Kingdom of Denmark; Chair. HELENA DAM Á NEYSTABØ.

Tjóðveldisflokkurin (Republican Party): Kongagøta 11, POB 143, 100 Tórshavn; tel. 312200; e-mail logsing@post.alivant.fo; internet www.tjodveldi.fo; f. 1948; left-wing party, advocates the secession of the Faroes from Denmark; Chair. FINNBOGI ISAKSON.

Verkmannafylkingin (Labour Front): f. 1994 by Union leaders and former members of the SDP.

Religion

CHRISTIANITY

The Faroes Church (Evangelical Lutheran Church of Denmark) regained its diocese in November 1990, and the suffragan bishop became Bishop of the Faroe Islands. The largest independent group is the 'Plymouth Brethren'. There is also a small Roman Catholic community.

Evangelical Lutheran Church

Føroya Biskupur (Bishop of the Faroe Islands): HANS J. JOENSEN, J. Paturssonargøta 20, POB 8, 110 Tórshavn; tel. 311995; fax 315889.

The Press

In 1996 there were six general interest newspapers in the Faroe Islands.

Dagblaðið: Reynagøta 9, 100 Tórshavn; tel. 319833; fax 319823; weekly; People's Party.

Dimmalætting: Smyrilsvegur 13, POB 3019, 110 Tórshavn; tel. 341200; fax 341201; e-mail post@dimma.fo; internet www.dimma.fo; f. 1878; 5 a week; Union Party; circ. 11,000.

FF/FA-Blaðið: Vágsbotnur, POB 58, 110 Tórshavn; tel. 312169; fax 318769; weekly; Editor VILMUND JACOBSEN; circ. 2,500.

Norðlýsið: á Hædd, POB 58, 700 Klaksvík; tel. 456285; fax 456498; weekly; circ. 1,200.

Oyggjatíðindið: R. C. Effersøesgøta 7, POB 3312, 110 Tórshavn; tel. 314411; fax 316410; 2 a week; circ. 4,500.

Tíðindablaðið Sosialurin: POB 76, 110 Tórshavn; tel. 311820; fax 314720; e-mail post@sosialurin.fo; internet www.sosialurin.fo; f. 1927; 5 a week; Editor JAN MÜLLER; Social Democratic Party; circ. 7,000.

NEWS AGENCY

Ritzaus Bureau: Gamli Vegur 3; tel. 316366; f. 1980; Man. RANDI MOHR.

Broadcasting and Communications

RADIO

Útvarp Føroya (Radio Faroe Islands): Norðari Ringvegur, POB 328, 110 Tórshavn; tel. 316566; fax 310471; e-mail uf@uf.fo; internet www.uf.fo; f. 1957; Man. JÓGVAN JESPERSEN.

TELEVISION

Sjónvarp Føroya (Faroese Television): M. A. Winthersgøta 2, POB 21, 110 Tórshavn; tel. 317780; fax 318815; e-mail svf@svf.fo; internet www.svf.fo; f. 1984; Gen. Man. TRÓNDUR DJURHUUS.

Finance

BANKS

(cap. = capital; res = reserves; dep. = deposits; m. = million; amounts in kroner; brs = branches)

Føroya Banki P/f: Húsagøta 3, POB 3048, 110 Tórshavn; tel. 311350; fax 315850; e-mail fbk@post.olivant.fo; internet www .foroyabanki.fo; f. 1994 following merger of Føroya Banki (f. 1906) and Sjóvinnubankin (f. 1932); cap. 100m., res 1.2m., dep. 3,435.6m. (Dec. 1999); Chair. JÓHAN PÁLL JOENSEN; Mans JØRN ASTRUP HANSEN, JANUS PETERSEN; 25 brs.

Føroya Sparikassi (Faroese Savings Bank): POB 34, Yviri við Strond 2, 110 Tórshavn; tel. 348000; fax 348348; e-mail spak@ sparikassin.fo; internet www.sparikassin.fo; f. 1832; cap. 10.6m., res 6.7m., dep. 2,937.8m. (Dec. 1998); Chair. PETER ZACHARIASSEN; Chief Man. Dir MARNER JACOBSEN.

Landsbanki Føroya: Müllers Hús—Gongin, POB 229, 110 Tórshavn; tel. 318305; fax 318537; e-mail landsbank@landsbank.fo; internet landsbank.fo; Man. SIGURD POULSEN.

Norðoya Sparikassi: Ósávegur 1, POB 149, 700 Klaksvík; tel. 456366; fax 456761.

Suðuroya Sparikassi: POB 2, 900 Vágur; tel. 373064; fax 373340; e-mail sparsu@post.olivant.fo.

INSURANCE

Tryggingarfelagio Føroyar: Kongabrúgvin, POB 329, 110 Tórshavn; tel. 314590; fax 315590; marine, fire, accident and life; sole insurance co in islands; Man. JENS PETUR ARGE.

Trade and Industry

GOVERNMENT AGENCY

Fiskivinnuumsitingin (Fisheries Administration): POB 87, 110 Tórshavn; tel. 313068; fax 314942.

INDUSTRIAL AND TRADE ASSOCIATIONS

L/F Føroya Fiskasøla—Faroe Seafood P/F: POB 68, 110 Tórshavn; tel. 345345; fax 345300; e-mail faroe@faroe.com; f. 1948, restructured 1995; joint stock company of fish producers; exports all seafood products; Man. Dir POUL MICHELSEN.

Føroya Reiðarafelag (Faroe Fishing Vessel-Owners' Association): R.C. Effersøesgøta, POB 179, 110 Tórshavn; tel. 311864; fax 317278.

Menningarstovan (Faroe Islands Trade Council): Bryggjubakki 12, POB 259, 110 Tórshavn; tel. 313028; fax 310459; e-mail trade@trade.fo; internet www.trade.fo; Man. KJARTAN KRISTIANSEN.

TRADE UNION

Føroya Arbeiðarafelag (Faroese Labour Organization): Tjarnðeild 5, POB 56, 110 Tórshavn; tel. 312101; fax 315374.

Transport

There are about 458 km of roads in the Faroe Islands. In August 2000 construction began on a 4.9-km-tunnel running under the sea, linking Vágar to Streymoy. The tunnel was projected to cost 240m. kroner and was expected to open within three years.

The main harbour is at Tórshavn; the other ports are at Fuglafjorður, Klaksvík, Skálafjorður, Tvøroyri, Vágur and Vestmanna. Between mid-May and mid-September, a summer roll-on, roll-off ferry service links the Faroe Islands with Iceland, Shetland (United Kingdom), Denmark and Norway.

There is an airport on Vágar.

Atlantic Airways Faroe Islands: Vágar Airport, 380 Sørvágur; tel. 333700; fax 333380; e-mail info@atlantic.fo; internet www .atlanticairways.fo; f. 1987; owned by Faroese Govt; scheduled and charter passenger and cargo services to Copenhagen, Reykjavík and Aberdeen; Man. Dir MAGNI ARGE.

Smyril Line: Jonas Broncks gøta 37, POB 370, 110 Tórshavn; tel. 345900; fax 345707; e-mail office@smyril-line.fo; internet www.smyril-line.fo; ferry service.

Tourism

Ferðaráð Føroya (Faroe Islands Tourist Board): Gongin, POB 118, 100 Tórshavn; tel. 316055; fax 310858; e-mail tourist@tourist.fo; internet www.tourist.fo; f. 1984; Man. ANNIKA W. JOENSEN.

GREENLAND

Introductory Survey

Location, Climate, Language, Religion, Flag, Capital

Greenland (Kalaallit Nunaat) is the world's largest island, with a total area of 2,166,086 sq km, and lies in the North Atlantic Ocean, east of Canada. Most of it is permanently covered by ice, but 410,449 sq km of coastland are habitable. Greenlandic, an Inuit (Eskimo) language, and Danish are the official languages. The majority of the population profess Christianity and belong mainly to the Evangelical Lutheran Church of Denmark. There are also small communities of other Protestant groups and of Roman Catholics. The flag (proportions 3 by 2) consists of two equal horizontal stripes (white above red), on which is superimposed a representation of the rising sun (a disc divided horizontally, red above white) to the left of centre. Nuuk (Godthåb) is the capital.

Recent History

Greenland first came under Danish rule in 1380. In the revision of the Danish Constitution in 1953, Greenland became part of the Kingdom and acquired the representation of two members in the Danish Folketing. In October 1972 the Greenlanders voted, by 9,658 to 3,990, against joining the European Community (EC, now European Union, EU, see p. 181) but, as part of Denmark, were bound by the Danish decision to join. Resentment of Danish domination of the economy, education and the professions continued, taking expression when, in 1977, the nationalist Siumut movement formed a left-wing party. In 1975 the Minister for Greenland appointed a commission to devise terms for Greenland home rule, and its proposals were approved, by 73.1% to 26.9%, in a referendum among the Greenland electorate in January 1979. Siumut, led by a Lutheran pastor, Jonathan Motzfeldt, secured 13 seats in the 21-member Landsting (the local legislature) at a general election in April, and a five-member Landsstyre (Home Rule Government), with Motzfeldt as Prime Minister, took office in May. From 1979 the island gradually assumed full administration of its internal affairs.

In February 1982 a referendum was held to decide Greenland's continued membership of the EC. This resulted in a 53% majority in favour of withdrawal. Negotiations were begun in May, with the Danish Government acting on Greenland's behalf, and were concluded in March 1984 (with effect from 1 February 1985): Greenland was accorded the status of an overseas territory in association with the Community, with preferential access to EC markets.

At the April 1983 general election to the Landsting (enlarged, by measures adopted in 1982, to between 23 and 26 seats, depending on the proportion of votes cast), Siumut and the conservative Atassut party won 12 seats each, while the Inuit Ataqatigiit (IA) won two seats. Siumut once again formed a Government, led by Motzfeldt, dependent on the support of the IA members in the Landsting: this support was withdrawn in March 1984, when the IA members voted against the terms of withdrawal from the EC, and Motzfeldt resigned. In the ensuing general election, held in June, Siumut and Atassut won 11 seats each, while the IA won three. Motzfeldt again formed a coalition Government, comprising Siumut and the IA.

In March 1987 the coalition Government collapsed, following a dispute between Siumut and the IA over policy towards the modernization of the US radar facility at Thule, which was claimed by the IA to be in breach of the 1972 US-Soviet Anti-Ballistic Missile Treaty. A general election was held in May. Siumut and Atassut retained 11 seats each in the Landsting (which had been enlarged in 1986, to 27 seats—23 of which were to be obtained by election in multi-member constituencies, while four were to be supplementary seats); the IA won four seats, and the remaining seat was won by the newly-formed Issittup Partiia, which was demanding the privatization of the trawler fleet. Motzfeldt eventually formed a new coalition Government with the IA. In May 1988, at elections to the Danish Folketing, Siumut was the most successful party. In June the coalition between Siumut and the IA collapsed, and Motzfeldt formed a new Siumut Government, with support from Atassut. In December 1990, when Atassut withdrew its support for the

Siumut administration (following allegations that government ministers had misused public funds), Motzfeldt organized an early general election for March 1991, at which both Siumut and Atassut obtained a reduced share of the vote, while the IA's share rose. Accordingly, Siumut retained 11 seats in the Landsting, while Atassut's representation decreased to eight seats and the IA's increased to five. A new party, the liberal Akulliit Partiiat, won two seats, and the remaining place was taken by the Issittup Partiia. Siumut and the IA formed a coalition Government and elected the Chairman of Siumut, Lars Emil Johansen, as Prime Minister.

At the general election held in March 1995 Siumut increased its representation in the Landsting (enlarged to 31 seats) to 12 seats, while Atassut won 10 seats and the IA obtained six seats. A coalition Government was formed between Siumut and Atassut, following the withdrawal from negotiations of the IA, which failed to reach agreement with Siumut on the question of independence. Johansen retained the premiership, while Daniel Skifte, the leader of Atassut, was appointed Minister of Finance and Housing. In early 1997 Johansen asserted that Greenland could achieve economic independence from Denmark on the basis of its unexploited mineral resources. In September Motzfeldt replaced Johansen as Prime Minister at the head of the coalition. Johansen was reported to have taken a senior position with the Royal Greenland fishing group.

At the general election held on 16 February 1999 Siumut received 35.3% of the votes cast, securing 11 seats in the Landsting. Atassut obtained 25.3% of the votes (eight seats), while the IA received 22.1% (seven seats). On 22 February a coalition Government was formed between Siumut and the IA; the two parties were to be represented in the Landsstyre by five and two ministers respectively. Jonathan Motzfeldt retained the premiership, while Josef Motzfeldt, the Chairman of the IA, was appointed Minister of Economy and Trade and of Taxation.

Denmark remains responsible for Greenland's foreign relations. Greenland does, however, have separate representation on the Nordic Council (see p. 237), and is a member of the Inuit Circumpolar Conference (see p. 317). Denmark, a member of NATO (see p. 241), retains its responsibility for defence, and Danish-US military co-operation in Greenland began in 1951. Under a 1981 agreement on the defence of Greenland, two US radar bases were established on the island, at Thule and at Kangerlussuaq (Søndre Strømfjord). An agreement between the USA and Denmark for the reduction of the bases from 325,000 ha to 160,000 ha took effect from October 1986, and the land thus available was returned to the Inuit. In March 1991 the USA agreed to transfer ownership and control of the base at Kangerlussuaq to the Greenland Government in September 1992, in exchange for the right to use it again in the future. In July 1996 it was announced that the base at Thule would be opened to aircraft. In August 1999 it was reported that the Danish Court of Appeal had ordered the Danish Government to pay compensation to Inuits who had been forced to leave their land in 1953 to allow for the expansion of the base at Thule.

Jonathan Motzfeldt and the Danish Minister for Foreign Affairs, Mogens Lykketoft, agreed in February 2001 not to adopt an official policy on the proposed US missile defence system, which would involve the upgrading of the early-warning radar station in the Thule base, pending an official request by the USA. Motzfeldt did, however, express personal concern at the plans, and called on the USA to discuss the proposals with its NATO allies. He added that Greenland would not accept the plans if they proved to be in breach of the 1972 Anti-Ballistic Missile Treaty, or if Russia opposed them. Josef Motzfeldt and the opposition parties of the Danish Folketing were already expressing strong opposition to the proposals, claiming that they risked provoking another arms race. Public opinion in Greenland was also strongly opposed to the plans; many feared that they would make Greenland a target for nuclear strikes. Reports that a nuclear bomb could still be lying on the sea-bed south-west of the Thule base, following a crash involving a US B-52 aircraft in 1968, although unconfirmed and denied by both the USA and Denmark, did little to bolster public support for the US plans.

In January 2001 the newly-inaugurated US President, George W. Bush, stated in a letter to Prime Minister Motzfeldt that Greenland 'should be open for dialogue' on the future of the Thule base. That the letter was sent directly to Motzfeldt rather than to Copenhagen caused consternation in Denmark, which still has control over Greenland's foreign policy. Motzfeldt, who had for years been seeking greater influence in foreign policy matters, was heartened by the development.

In June 1980 the Danish Government declared an economic zone extending 200 nautical miles (370 km) off the east coast of Greenland. This, however, caused a dispute with Norway over territorial waters, owing to the existence of the small Norwegian island of Jan Mayen, 460 km off the east coast of Greenland. In 1988 Denmark requested the International Court of Justice (ICJ), based in The Hague, the Netherlands, to arbitrate on the issue of conflicting economic zones. A delimitation line was established by the ICJ in June 1993. A subsequent accord on maritime delimitation, agreed between the Governments of Norway, Greenland and Iceland in November 1997, established the boundaries of a 1,934-sq km area of Arctic sea that had been excluded from the terms of the 1993 settlement.

Government

Greenland is part of the Kingdom of Denmark, and the Danish Government, which remains responsible for foreign affairs, defence and justice, is represented by the Rigsombudsmand, or High Commissioner, in Nuuk (Godthåb). Most functions of government are administered by the 'Home Rule Government', the Landsstyre. The formation of this executive is dependent upon support in the local legislature, the Landsting. The Landsting has 31 members elected for a maximum term of four years, on a basis of proportional representation. Greenland also elects two members to the Danish Folketing. For administration purposes, Greenland is divided into 18 municipalities, of which the largest is Nuuk.

Defence

The Danish Government, which is responsible for Greenland's defence, co-ordinates military activities through its Greenland Command. The Greenland Command, which also undertakes fisheries control and sea rescues, is based at the Grønnedal naval base, in south-west Greenland. Greenlanders are not liable for military service. As part of the Kingdom of Denmark, Greenland belongs to NATO (see p. 241). The USA operates an air base, at Pituffik in Thule (see Recent History). In 1998 the Danish Government spent 353m. kroner (11.1% of total central government expenditure on Greenland) on the territory's defence (including the Fisheries Inspectorate).

Economic Affairs

In 1994, according to preliminary official estimates, Greenland's gross national product (GNP) was 6,381m. kroner, equivalent to some 114,800 kroner per head. The population increased at an average annual rate of 0.1% in 1990–2000. The economy enjoyed overall growth during the 1970s and 1980s, but gross domestic product (GDP) declined by 9%, in real terms, in 1990, and continued to decline significantly (owing to depleted fish stocks and the discontinuation of lead and zinc mining) until 1994 and 1995, when real growth rates of 5% and 3%, respectively, were recorded. GDP increased, in real terms, by 1.5% in 1996, 1.4% in 1997 and by 7.8% in 1998.

Fishing dominates the commercial economy, as well as being important to the traditional way of life. In 1999 the fishing industry accounted for 93.9% of Greenland's total export revenue. It was estimated that the industry, including the processing of the catch, employed about one-sixth of the paid labour force in the late 1980s. The cod catch has declined substantially, however, since 1989. The traditional occupation of the Greenlanders is seal-hunting, which remains important in the north. The only feasible agricultural activity in the harsh climate is livestock-rearing, and only sheep-farming has proved to be of any commercial significance. There are also herds of domesticated reindeer.

Industry (including mining, manufacturing, construction and public works) employed some 25% of those in paid employment in March 1987. Mining earned 13.0% of total export revenue in 1990. A Swedish company extracted lead, zinc and some silver at the important mine at Marmorilik in the north-west. The mine was closed, however, in 1990. In recent years there have been several discoveries of petroleum, natural gas and other mineral deposits (including gold), which, it is hoped, can be exploited.

Manufacturing is mainly dependent upon the fishing industry. Water power (meltwater from the ice-cap and glaciers) is an important potential source of electricity. All mineral fuels are imported. Mineral fuels accounted for 8.7% of total imports in 1999.

In 1999 Greenland recorded a trade deficit of 924m. kroner. The principal trading partner remains Denmark, although its monopoly on trade ceased in 1950. Denmark supplied 68.8% of imports and received 83.7% of exports in 1999. Trade is still dominated by companies owned by the Home Rule Government. The principal exports are fish and fish products, and the principal imports are machinery and transport equipment.

Greenland is dependent upon large grants from the central Danish Government. In 1998 central government expenditure on Greenland included some 2,575m. kroner in the form of a direct grant to the Home Rule Government. Greenland has few debts, and also receives valuable revenue from the European Union (EU, see p. 181) for fishing licences. The annual rate of inflation averaged 0.9% in 1995–99, and stood at 0.7% in 1999. In August 1997 8.4% of the urban labour force were unemployed.

Greenland, although a part of the Kingdom of Denmark, withdrew from the European Community (now EU) in 1985 (see Recent History). It remains a territory in association with the EU, however, and has preferential access to European markets. The loss of EU development aid has been offset by the annual payment (ECU 37.7m. during 1995–2000) for member countries to retain fishing rights in Greenlandic waters.

Greenland's economy is dominated by the fishing industry, but remains a subsistence, barter economy for a large part of the population. Migration to the towns and the rejection of a traditional life-style by many young people have, however, created new social and economic problems. Dependence on a single commodity leaves the economy vulnerable to the effects of depletion of fish stocks and fluctuating international prices. Any development or progress is possible only with Danish aid, which is already fundamental to Greenlandic finances. In an effort to generate revenue from the tourist industry, the Home Rule Government undertook, in 1990, to achieve a target of 35,000 tourist arrivals (equivalent to 500m. kroner) annually by 2005; by 1994 the campaign was showing positive results and tourist arrivals had doubled compared with levels in previous years.

Education and Social Welfare

The educational system is based on that of Denmark, except that the main language of instruction is Greenlandic. Danish is, however, widely used. There is a school in every settlement. In 1999/2000 there were 86 pre-primary and primary schools, with 11,164 pupils and 1,109 teachers. In the same year there were also three secondary schools with 571 pupils. There is a teacher-training college in Nuuk, and a university centre opened in 1987. In 1998 current expenditure on education by the Home Rule Government represented 9.9% of total current budget spending (including allocations to the municipalities).

There is a free health service for all residents, comprising examination, treatment and nursing, and dental services. In 1999 there were 83 physicians, and the territory had 17 regional health centres and one central hospital, Queen Ingrid's Hospital. The Home Rule Government assumed control of health services in January 1992 (and Denmark's annual subsidy to Greenland was increased accordingly thereafter). In 1998 the Home Rule Government allocated some 658m. kroner (14.6% of total current budgetary spending) to health services.

The social welfare system is based on the Scandinavian welfare model. In 1998 16.1% of total current budget expenditure by the Home Rule Government was allocated to social security and welfare. Public aid for the unemployed is administered locally, and trade union members also have a system of unemployment insurance. Old age pensions (beginning at the age of 60), disability pensions, housing benefits and maternity and child benefits are also provided.

Statistical Survey

Sources: Statistics Greenland, *Statistical Yearbook*; Greenland Home Rule Government—Denmark Bureau, Pilestræde 52, POB 2151, 1122 Copenhagen K; tel. 33-13-42-24; fax 33-13-49-71; Statistics Greenland, POB 1025, 3900 Nuuk; tel. 345000; fax 322954; e-mail stat@gs.gh.gl; internet www.statgreen.gl.

AREA, POPULATION AND DENSITY

Area: Total 2,166,086 sq km (836,330 sq miles); Ice-free portion 410,449 sq km (158,475 sq miles).

Population: 56,307 (males 30,053; females 26,254) at 1 January 2001 (incl. 49,681 born in Greenland).

Density (2001): 0.026 per sq km.

Capital: Nuuk (Godthåb), population 14,058 at 1 January 2000.

Births, Marriages and Deaths (1999): Registered live births 947 (birth rate 16.9 per 1,000); Registered marriages 253 (marriage rate 4.5 per 1,000); Registered deaths 482 (death rate 8.6 per 1,000).

Labour Force (census of 26 October 1976): Males 14,234; Females 7,144; Total 21,378. **1996:** Total 29,130 (incl. 25,170 employed).

AGRICULTURE AND FISHING

Livestock (1998): Sheep 21,195, Reindeer 2,600.

Hunting (1998): Fox skins 53, Polar bears 71, Seals 86,131, Whales 184.

Fishing ('000 metric tons, live weight, 1998): Greenland halibut 22.8, Atlantic cod 5.6, Capelin 16.9; Other fishes 9.5, Crabs 1.9, Northern prawn 69.5, Clams 2.2; Total catch 128.4. The total excludes seals and whales, which are recorded by number rather than by weight (see Hunting, above).

MINING

Production (concentrates, '000 metric tons, 1989): Lead 36; Zinc 131. The estimated metal content ('000 metric tons) was: Lead 20.0; Zinc 71.5 (Source: US Bureau of Mines). Note: The mine producing lead and zinc closed in 1990.

INDUSTRY

Selected Products: Frozen fish (1994) 11,000 metric tons; Salted, dried or smoked fish (1993) 300 metric tons; Electric energy (1998) 281 million kWh. Source: partly UN, *Industrial Commodity Statistics Yearbook*.

FINANCE
Danish currency is in use.

Central Government Expenditure (by Ministry, million kroner, 1998): *Current:* Finance 2,575 (Grant to Home Rule Government 2,575), Defence (incl. Fisheries Inspection) 353, Justice 131, Environment and Energy 54, Transport 36, Research 8, Prime Minister's Office 7, Labour 4, Agriculture and Fisheries 3, Business and Industry 2, Total 3,173. *Capital:* 7. *Total:* 3,180.

Home Rule Government Accounts (million kroner, 1998): *Revenue:* Current 4,726 (Income tax 753, Import and production duties 628, Interests 239, Fishing licences 286, Danish central govt grant 2,575); Capital 0; Total 4,726. *Expenditure:* Current 4,218 (Administration 252, Education 446, Church and culture 155, Social security and welfare 727, Health 658, Housing 130, Business and Trade 150, Industry 149, Transport and communication 322, Energy 26, Fisheries, hunting and agriculture 95; Other (incl. Grants to municipalities) 1,068); Capital 304; Total 4,522.

Cost of Living (consumer price index; at July each year; base: July 1995 = 100): 101.7 in 1997; 102.8 in 1998; 103.5 in 1999.

Gross Domestic Product (provisional, million kroner at current market prices): 7,263 in 1996; 7,080 in 1997; 7,706 in 1998.

Gross National Product by Economic Activity (million kroner at factor cost, 1988): Agriculture and fisheries 971; Mineral resources 328; Manufacturing 171; Electricity, gas and heating 195; Construction 1,063, Other private services 1,989; Public sector 1,648; Total 6,365.

EXTERNAL TRADE

Principal Commodities (provisional, million kroner, 1998): *Imports c.i.f.:* Food and live animals 378.6 (Meat and meat preparations 98.3); Beverages and tobacco 104.3 (Beverages 75.8); Mineral fuels, lubricants etc. 232.5 (Petroleum products 232.3); Chemicals 110.3; Basic manufactures 458.5; Machinery and transport equipment 655.2 (Machinery 483.2, Transport equipment 172.0); Miscellaneous manufactured articles 326.8; Total (incl. others) 2,740.3. *Exports f.o.b.:* Prawns 1,146.6; Greenland halibut 310.4; Cod 18.8; Other fish products 112.5; Total (incl. others) 1,702.1.

Principal Trading Partners (million kroner, 1999): *Imports c.i.f.:* Denmark 1,616.9; Cyprus 64.0; France 126.4; Germany 56.8; Japan 90.2; Norway 153.7; USA 59.9; Total (incl. others) 2,856.2. *Exports f.o.b.:* Denmark 1,616.9, Japan 160.8; Thailand 36.4; USA 33.1; Total (incl. others) 1,932.4.

TRANSPORT

Road Traffic (registered vehicles, 1999): Passenger cars 2,226, Lorries and trucks 1,409, Total (incl. others) 4,026.

Shipping (1999): Number of vessels 153 (passenger ships 8, dry cargo ships 37, fishing vessels 102, others 6); Total displacement 51,759 grt (passenger ships 3,966 grt, dry cargo ships 5,035 grt, fishing vessels 42,057 grt, others 701 grt).

International Sea-borne Freight Traffic ('000 cubic metres, 1999): Goods loaded 175; Goods unloaded 332.

International Transport (passengers conveyed between Greenland and Denmark): Ship (1983) 94; Aircraft (1999) 93,200.

TOURISM

Registered Hotel Accommodations (nights, 1999): 205,047 (incl. 69,946 by Danish visitors).

COMMUNICATIONS MEDIA

Radio Receivers (1996): 30,000 in use.

Television Receivers (1996): 21,000 in use.

Telephones ('000 subscribers 1999): 25.6.

Telefax Stations (1992): 1,153 in use.

Mobile Cellular Telephones (subscribers, 1999): 12,676.

Sources: partly UNESCO, *Statistical Yearbook*, and UN, *Statistical Yearbook*.

EDUCATION
(1998/99)

Pre-primary and Primary: 86 schools; 1,109 teachers; 11,164 pupils.

Secondary: 3 schools; 571 pupils (244 new pupils).

Directory
The Government

The legislative body is the Landsting, with 31 members elected for four years, on a basis of proportional representation. Greenlanders and Danes resident in Greenland for at least six months prior to an election and over the age of 18 years have the right to vote. Based on the strength of the parties in the Landsting, an executive, the Landsstyre, is formed. Since 1979 the Landsstyre has gradually assumed control of the administration of Greenland's internal affairs. Jurisdiction in constitutional matters, foreign affairs and defence remains with the Danish Government, the highest representative of which, in Greenland, is the Rigsombudsmand or High Commissioner. Greenland sends two representatives to the Danish legislature, the Folketing.

LANDSSTYRE
(March 2001)

A coalition of Siumut (S) and Inuit Ataqatigiit (IA).

Prime Minister: JONATHAN MOTZFELDT (S).

Minister of Economy and Trade and of Taxation: JOSEF MOTZFELDT (IA).

Minister of Fisheries, Business, Hunting and Agriculture: SIMON OLSEN (S).

Minister of Social Affairs and Labour Market: JØRGEN WAVER JOHANSEN.

Minister of Education, Culture and Research: LISE LENNERT (S).*

Minister of Infrastructure and Housing: STEFFEN-ULRICH LYNGE (S).*

Minister of Health and the Church and of the Environment and Nature: ALFRED JAKOBSEN (IA).*

* Not members of the Landsting.

Government Offices

Rigsombudsmanden i Grønland (High Commission for Greenland): POB 1030, 3900 Nuuk; tel. 321001; fax 324171; e-mail riomgr@gl.stm.dk; internet www.rigsombudsmanden.gl.; High Commissioner GUNNAR MARTENS.

Grønlands Hjemmestyre (Greenland Home Rule Government): POB 1015, 3900 Nuuk; tel. 345000; fax 325002; Denmark Bureau, Pilestræde 52, POB 2151, 1016 Copenhagen K; tel. 33-69-34-00; fax 33-69-34-01.

LANDSTING

Chairman: OLE LYNGE (IA).

Election, 16 February 1999

	Votes	%	Seats
Siumut (Forward)	9,897	35.3	11
Atassut (Solidarity)	7,100	25.3	8
Inuit Ataqatigiit (Inuit Brotherhood)	6,194	22.1	7
Kandidatforbundet (Alliance of Candidates).	3,454	12.3	4
Independents	1,409	5.0	1*
Total	**28,054**	**100.0**	**31**

* The Independent representative subsequently joined Siumut.

Political Organizations

Akulliit Partiiat (Centre Party): POB 456, 3900 Nuuk; f. 1991; liberal, supports open-sea fishing industry; Chair. BJARNE KREUTZ-MANN.

Atassut (Solidarity): POB 399, 3900 Nuuk; tel. 323366; fax 325840; e-mail atassut.landsorganisation@partiit.centadm.gh.gl; f. 1978 and became political party in 1981; supports close links with Denmark and favours EU membership for Greenland; part of Venstre (Liberal) party in the Danish legislature, and of Liberal group in the Nordic Council; Leader DANIEL SKIFTE.

Inuit Ataqatigiit (Inuit Brotherhood): POB 321, 3900 Nuuk; f. 1978; socialist organization, demanding that Greenland citizenship be restricted to those of Inuit parentage; advocates Greenland's eventual independence from Denmark; Chair. JOSEF MOTZFELDT.

Siumut (Forward): POB 357, 3900 Nuuk; tel. 322077; fax 322319; e-mail siumut@greennet.gl; f. 1971 and became political party in 1977; aims to promote collective ownership and co-operation, and to develop greater reliance on Greenland's own resources; favours greatest possible autonomy within the Kingdom of Denmark; social democratic party; Chair. MICHAEL PETERSEN.

Judicial System

The island is divided into 18 court districts and these courts all use lay assessors. For most cases these lower courts are for the first instance and appeal is to the Landsret, the higher court in Nuuk, which is the only one with a professional judge. This court hears the more serious cases in the first instance and appeal in these cases is to the High Court (Østre Landsret) in Copenhagen.

Religion

CHRISTIANITY

The Greenlandic Church, of which most of the population are adherents, forms an independent diocese of the Evangelical Lutheran Church in Denmark and comes under the jurisdiction of the Landsstyre and of the Bishop of Greenland. There are 17 parishes and in 1995 there were 23 ministers serving in Greenland.

Biskoppen over Grønlands Stift (Bishop of Greenland): SOFIE PETERSEN, Evangelical Lutheran Church, POB 90, 3900 Nuuk; tel. 321134; fax 321061; e-mail bispekontor@gh.gl.

There are also small groups of other Protestant churches and of Roman Catholics.

The Press

There are no daily newspapers in Greenland.

Atuagagdliutit/Grønlandsposten: POB 39, 3900 Nuuk; tel. 321083; fax 323147; e-mail redaktion@ag.gl; 2 a week; Editor JENS BRØNDEN.

Niviarsiaq: POB 357, 3900 Nuuk; tel. 322077; fax 322319; e-mail siumut@greennet.gl; organ of Siumut; monthly; Editor J. WAEVER JOHANSEN.

Sermitsiaq: Spindlers Bakke 10B, POB 150, 3900 Nuuk; tel. 321903; fax 322499; weekly; Editor POUL KRARUP.

Publisher

Atuakkiorfik/Greenland Publishers: Hans Egedesvej 3, POB 840, 3900 Nuuk; tel. 322122; fax 322500; e-mail greenpub@greennet.gl; f. 1956; general fiction and non-fiction, children's and textbooks, public relations; Man. NUKAARAQ EUGENIUS.

Broadcasting and Communications

TELECOMMUNICATIONS

TELE Greenland A/S: Nuuk; f. 1994; owned by Home Rule Govt.

BROADCASTING

Radio

Kalaallit Nunaata Radioa (KNR)—Grønlands Radio: POB 1007, 3900 Nuuk; tel. 325333; fax 325042; internet www.knr.gl; 5 AM stations, 45 FM stations; bilingual programmes in Greenlandic and Danish, 17 hours a day; Man. Dir PETER FREDERIK ROSING.

Kujataata Radioa: POB 158, 3920 Qaqortoq; regional station in south Greenland.

Avannaata Radioa: POB 223, 3952 Ilulissat; tel. 943633; fax 943618; e-mail avannaata@radio.knr.gl; regional station in north Greenland.

Thule Air Base Radio—50Z20: DAC POB 1117, 3970 Dundas; FM, non-commercial station; broadcasts 24 hours a day; news, music, etc.; Station Man. KURT CHRISTENSEN.

Television

Kalaallit Nunaata Radioa TV: POB 1007, 3900 Nuuk; tel. 325333; fax 325042; internet www.knr.gl; broadcasts by VHF transmitter to all Greenland; commercial; most programmes in Danish; Man. Dir JENS LYBERTH.

Finance

BANK

(cap. = capital; dep. = deposits; m. = million; amounts in kroner; br. = branch)

The BANK of Greenland—GrønlandsBANKEN A/S: POB 1033, 3900 Nuuk; tel. 347700; fax 347706; e-mail banken@banken.gl; internet www.banken.gl; f. 1967 as The Bank of Greenland A/S; name changed as above following merger with Nuna Bank A/S in 1997; cap. 191.8m., res 314.0m., dep. 2,195.9m. (Dec. 1999); Pres. SVEND-ERIK DANIELSEN; Man. JESPER FLENSTED NIELSEN; 5 brs.

Trade and Industry

GOVERNMENT AGENCY

Government of Greenland, Bureau of Minerals and Petroleum: POB 930, 3900 Nuuk; tel. 346800; fax 324302; e-mail bmp@gh.gl; internet www.bmp.gl; f. 1998; performs the central administrative co-ordinating and regulatory tasks regarding exploration and production of mineral resources in Greenland; Dep. Min. HANS KRISTIAN SCHØNWANDT.

STATE-OWNED COMPANIES

KNI Udvikling A/S: POB 1008, 3900 Nuuk; tel. 325211; fax 324431; f. 1774; Home Rule Govt assumed control 1986, reorganized 1993; Chair. JONATHAN MOTZFELDT; Man. Dir STIG BENDTSEN.

Kalaallit Pilersuisoq A/S (KNI Service A/S)—Greenland Trade Service Ltd: POB 193, 3912 Maniitsoq; tel. 813844; fax 813814; f. 1993; statutory wholesale and retail trading co, mail service, petroleum and fuel supply; Chair. JONATHAN MOTZFELDT; Pres. KELD ASKÆR; Mans HANS THOMSEN, GERHARDT PETERSEN.

Pisiffik A/S Greenland TRADE RETAIL Ltd: POB 1009, 3911 Sisimiut; tel. 864911; fax 864175; e-mail mos@mail.kni.gl; f. 1993; statutory wholesale and retail trading co.; Chair. KELD ASKÆR; Man. MICHAEL ØSTERGAARD.

Royal Greenland A/S: POB 1073, 3900 Nuuk; tel. 324422; fax 323349; internet www.royalgreenland.com; f. 1774; trade monopoly ended 1950; Home Rule Govt assumed control 1986; established as share company 1990 (all shares owned by Home Rule Govt); fishing group based in Greenland with subsidiaries in Japan, the United Kingdom, Scandinavia, the USA, Italy, France and Germany; main products are coldwater prawns and halibut; five trawlers; factories in Greenland, Denmark and Germany; Chair. SØREN HALD MOELLER; Pres. and CEO OLE RAMLAU-HANSEN.

Transport

Domestic traffic is mainly by aircraft (fixed-wing and helicopter), boat and dog-sled. There are airports or heliports in all towns for domestic flights.

The main port is at Nuuk; there are also all-year ports at Paamiut (Frederikshåb), Maniitsoq (Sukkertoppen) and Sisimiut (Holsteinsborg). In addition, there are shipyards at Nuuk, Qaqortoq, Paamiut, Maniitsoq, Sisimiut and Aasiaat. Coastal motor vessels operate passenger services along the west coast from Upernavik to Nanortalik.

Shipping Company

Royal Arctic Line A/S: POB 1580, 3900 Nuuk; tel. 322420; fax 322450; e-mail info@ral.dk; internet www.ral.gl; f. 1993; owned by Home Rule Govt; four container vessels of 38,922 grt and one general cargo vessel of 4,209 grt; Pres. KARSTEN STOCK ANDRESEN.

Airline

Grønlandsfly A/S (Greenlandair Inc.): POB 1012, Nuuk Airport, 3900 Nuuk; tel. 343434; fax 327288; e-mail glahq@greenlandair.gl; internet www.greenlandair.gl; f. 1960; air services to the 19 principal centres in Greenland, and to Copenhagen (Denmark), Reykjavík and Keflavík (Iceland) and Ottawa (Canada); supply, survey, ice-reconnaissance services and helicopter/fixed-wing charters; owned by Danish and Greenland Home Rule Govts and SAS; Chair. PETER GRØNVOLD SAMUELSEN; Pres. FINN ØELUNO.

Tourism

Tourist arrivals traditionally did not exceed 5,000–7,000 per year. In order to stimulate increased revenue, it was decided in 1990 to set a target of 30,000–35,000 tourist arrivals per year (generating income of some 500m. kroner) to be achieved by 2005. The national tourist board of Greenland, Greenland Tourism, was established in 1992 in order to develop tourism in Greenland, and concentrates primarily on developing sustainable tourism projects. Some 13,000 tourist arrivals were registered in 1994.

Greenland Tourism: POB 1552, 3900 Nuuk; tel. 322888; fax 322877; e-mail info@visitgreenland.com; internet www .greenland-guide.gl; f. 1992; Chair. NILS WILHJELM; Man. Dir STIG RØMER WINTHER.

DJIBOUTI

Introductory Survey

Location, Climate, Language, Religion, Flag, Capital

The Republic of Djibouti is in the Horn of Africa, at the southern entrance to the Red Sea. It is bounded on the north by Eritrea, on the north, west and south-west by Ethiopia, and on the south-east by Somalia. The land is mainly volcanic desert, and the climate hot and arid. There are two main ethnic groups, the Issa, who are of Somali origin and comprise 50% of the population, and the Afar, who comprise 40% of the population and are of Ethiopian origin. Both groups are Muslims, and they speak related Cushitic languages. The official languages are Arabic and French. The flag has two equal horizontal stripes, of light blue and light green, with a white triangle, enclosing a five-pointed red star, at the hoist. The capital is Djibouti.

Recent History

In 1945 the area now comprising the Republic of Djibouti (then known as French Somaliland) was proclaimed an overseas territory of France, and in 1967 was renamed the French Territory of the Afars and the Issas. The Afar and the Issa have strong connections with Ethiopia and Somalia respectively. Until the 1960s ethnic divisions were not marked; subsequently, however, conflicting international tensions in the Horn of Africa, together with France's policy of favouring the minority Afar community, combined to create internal tensions. Demands for independence were led by the Issa community, and, under pressure from the Organization of African Unity (OAU) to grant full independence to the territory, France acted to improve relations between the two communities. A unified political movement, the Ligue populaire africaine pour l'indépendance (LPAI), was formed, and, following an overwhelming vote favouring independence at a referendum held in May 1977, the territory became independent on 27 June. Hassan Gouled Aptidon, a senior Issa politician and leader of the LPAI, became the first President of the Republic of Djibouti.

Initial intentions to maintain an ethnic balance in government were not sustained. In March 1979 Gouled replaced the LPAI with a new political party, the Rassemblement populaire pour le progrès (RPP). Afar opposition groups, led by the Mouvement populaire pour la libération de Djibouti (MPLD), responded by forming a clandestine movement, the Front démocratique pour la libération de Djibouti, based in Ethiopia. In June 1981 Gouled, as sole candidate, was elected to a further six-year term as President, and in October the RPP was declared the sole legal party. Legislative elections were held in May 1982, when candidates were chosen from a single list approved by the RPP. At the next presidential and legislative elections, held in April 1987, President Gouled, the sole candidate, was re-elected, while RPP-sponsored candidates for all 65 seats in the Chamber of Deputies were elected unopposed. Successive government reorganizations failed, however, to achieve national unity.

Until the mid-1980s there was little overt opposition to the RPP under Gouled's leadership. In May 1986 Aden Robleh Awalleh, a former political associate of President Gouled, fled to Ethiopia and announced the formation of an opposition group, the Mouvement national djiboutien pour l'instauration de la démocratie (MNDID), with the stated aim of restoring a multi-party parliamentary democracy. Within Djibouti, political tensions began to escalate during 1987, prompting Gouled to reorganize the Government. In April 1989 inter-tribal hostilities erupted in the capital and the Afar town of Tadjourah. Inter-ethnic tensions persisted, and in May 1990 fighting broke out between the Issa and the Gadabursi communities in the capital. In June units of the Djibouti armed forces raided Tadjourah and arrested Afars who were suspected of involvement in the MPLD.

In April 1991 a new and powerful armed opposition group, the Front pour la restauration de l'unité et de la démocratie (FRUD), was formed by a merger of three insurgent Afar movements. In November the FRUD launched a full-scale insurrection against the Government. By late November the FRUD controlled many towns and villages in the north of the country, and was besieging the northern towns of Tadjourah and Obock, which were held by the national army. The Government introduced mass conscription, and requested military assistance from France (see below) to repel what it described as 'external aggression' by soldiers loyal to the deposed President Mengistu of Ethiopia. The FRUD denied that it constituted a foreign aggressor (although many of its officers had received training in Ethiopian military camps), claiming that its aim was to secure fair political representation for all ethnic groups in Djibouti.

In December 1991 Gouled announced that a national referendum regarding proposed changes in the system of government would be held, but only when the 'external aggressors' had been expelled from the country. At the end of the month 14 Afar deputies resigned from the RPP (and, therefore, from the Chamber of Deputies), claiming that its leaders were seeking to protect their privileges rather than the national interest.

In early 1992, under pressure from the French Government to accommodate opposition demands for democratic reform, President Gouled appointed a commission to draft a new constitution, which was to restore the multi-party system and provide for free elections. The FRUD stated its willingness to negotiate with Gouled, and undertook to observe a cease-fire, subject to satisfactory progress on democratic reforms. Gouled, however, reasserted that the FRUD was controlled by 'foreign interests', and accused France of failing to honour its defence agreement. By late January, most of northern Djibouti was under FRUD control. In the following month, after further mediation by France, a cease-fire was implemented under the supervision of a French peace-keeping force. These arrangements collapsed in March, however, and armed conflict between the FRUD and the Government was resumed. In June Ahmed Dini, who had been Djibouti's first Prime Minister after independence, assumed the leadership of the FRUD.

President Gouled's constitutional plan, which was announced in April 1992, conceded the principle of political pluralism, but proposed few other changes and retained a strong executive presidency. The plan was rejected by the opposition parties and by the FRUD, although cautiously welcomed by France. However, Gouled's intention that a constitutional referendum should take place in June, with legislative elections to follow in July, was recognized as unrealistic, especially with large areas of the country no longer under government control. The referendum, which was held in September, was boycotted by all the opposition groups; the Government, however, stated that, with 75% of the electorate participating, 97% of voters had endorsed the new Constitution. At the 30 September deadline for party registration, only the RPP and the Parti du renouveau démocratique (PRD), an opposition group formed earlier in 1992 under the leadership of Mohamed Djama Elabe (a former minister), were granted legal status. The application for registration by the opposition Parti national démocratique (PND) was initially rejected, although it was allowed in October. Parliamentary elections were held on 18 December, and all 65 seats were won by the RPP. Elabe accused the Government of electoral irregularities. More than 51% of the electorate abstained from voting, leading to charges from the PND that the chamber was unrepresentative.

Gouled reshuffled the Council of Ministers in February 1993, preserving the traditional ethnic balance, with Issa ministers receiving eight portfolios, and Afar representatives seven, and one portfolio each being given to members of the Arab, Issaq and Gadabursi minorities. However, the Government maintained its refusal to negotiate with the FRUD. Five candidates stood in Djibouti's first contested presidential election, which was held on 7 May: Gouled himself, Elabe (for the PRD), Aden Robleh Awalleh (PND) and two independents. The election was again notable for a low level of participation (49.9% of the electorate), suggesting an Afar boycott, but resulted in a clear victory for Gouled, who, according to official results, obtained 60.8% of the valid votes cast, compared with 22.0% for Elabe and 12.3% for Awalleh. The opposition alleged that there had been widespread electoral fraud.

Following his re-election, Gouled appealed to the FRUD to negotiate with the Government. His appeal was rejected, as he proposed that discussions should take place in Djibouti, while the FRUD insisted that it would only meet the Government abroad, in the presence of foreign mediators. In July 1993 the army launched a successful offensive on FRUD positions in the centre and north of the country, capturing the FRUD's headquarters, as well as other towns and areas held by the rebel group. As a result of the hostilities, thousands of the inhabitants of these largely Afar-populated areas fled towards the Ethiopian border. Many of the rebels retreated into the mountains in the far north of the country. The FRUD continued its struggle, however, and began launching armed attacks on government forces. By July an estimated 80,000 civilians had been displaced by the fighting. In September the Gouled administration was strongly criticized by Amnesty International for alleged abuses of human rights by the army.

The extent of the military reverses inflicted on the FRUD was reflected in the intensification of political activity during late 1993. In October the PRD and the FRUD issued joint proposals for a cease-fire, to be followed by negotiations aimed at forming a transitional 'government of national unity' to supervise the implementation of democratic reforms. These objectives were also defined by two new parties formed in the same month: the Organisation des masses Afars and the Parti centriste et des reformes démocratiques (PCRD). The PCRD, whose leadership comprised former members of the FRUD, announced that it was to seek legal recognition. In December the PRD and the PND launched a co-ordinated campaign to persuade the Government to hold new parliamentary elections under the supervision of an independent electoral commission. In early 1994, again under economic pressure from France, the Government agreed to reduce its military expenditure, although operations against the FRUD continued in February.

During March 1994 serious divisions emerged within the FRUD leadership. It was reported that the political bureau, led by Ahmed Dini, had been dissolved and that dissident members had formed an 'executive council' under the leadership of Ougoureh Kifleh Ahmed. This dissident leadership (Ali Mohamed Daoud was subsequently declared President) sought support within the movement for a negotiated political settlement of the conflict. In June Kifleh Ahmed and the Government agreed terms for a cease-fire, and formal negotiations for a peace settlement began in July. Executive bodies of both FRUD factions continued to operate during the latter half of 1994, and parallel national congresses rejected the legitimacy of the opposing faction's leadership. In December an agreement signed by Kifleh Ahmed and the Minister of the Interior, Idris Harbi Farah, provided for a permanent cessation of hostilities, the incorporation of FRUD armed forces into the national force, the recognition of the FRUD as a legal political party, the multi-ethnic composition of a new council of ministers and the reform of electoral procedures prior to the next general election. In accordance with the peace agreement, 300 members of the FRUD armed forces were integrated into the national army in March 1995. However, there was little further implementation of the accord, and there was considerable criticism of the agreement by the radical faction of the FRUD (which, under the leadership of Ahmed Dini, favoured a continuation of military operations and launched a number of small-scale attacks against government targets in late 1995) and other opposition groups. Nevertheless, Ali Mohamed Daoud and Kifleh Ahmed were appointed to posts in the Government in June. In March 1996 the Government granted legal recognition to the FRUD, which became the country's fourth and largest political party. However, at approximately the same time, Ibrahim Chehem Daoud, a former high-ranking official in the FRUD, rejected the reconciliation between the Government and the group, and formed a new group, called FRUD-Renaissance.

In September 1995 trade unions organized a widely-observed one-day general strike. In October a demonstration organized by the PND, to protest at the Government's economic austerity policy, resulted in the arrest of several protesters, including the PND leader, Awalleh. In November he was released, but subsequently was reported to have begun a hunger strike in support of other demonstrators who remained in prison. In January 1996, after demonstrations organized by school teachers against the economic reforms, some 500 protesters were reported to have been arrested. They were released later in the month and further strikes were staged in April and May.

In December 1995 President Gouled received medical treatment in France, where he remained in convalescence until March 1996. His prolonged absence from Djibouti prompted a succession crisis within the RPP, between the President's nephew and principal adviser, Ismael Omar Gelleh, and his private secretary, Ismael Gedi Hared. In February a prison riot in the capital provoked a confrontation between the Minister of Justice and Islamic Affairs, Moumin Bahdon Farah (who suggested that the incident had occurred because the cost of maintaining a sizeable army had resulted in poor staffing levels at the prison), and the Minister of the Interior, Idris Harbi Farah, who attributed the uprising to inadequate prison food supplies. Bahdon Farah's remarks reflected his opposition to Gelleh (whom Harbi Farah supported), who was known to favour a large standing army. In March Bahdon Farah was dismissed from the Council of Ministers, together with Ahmed Bulaleh Barreh, the Minister of Defence. Both ministers had openly opposed the December 1994 peace agreement with the FRUD, on the grounds that it strengthened the position of Gelleh and his followers. In April 1996 Bahdon Farah established a splinter group of the RPP, the Groupe pour la démocratie de la république (RPP–GDR), which included 13 of the 65 members of the Chamber of Deputies. The President of the Chamber subsequently claimed that the RPP–GDR would remain banned while Bahdon Farah continued to hold his position as Secretary-General of the RPP. In May Gouled expelled Gedi Hared from the RPP's executive committee, together with Bahdon Farah and former ministers Barreh and Ali Mahamade Houmed, all of whom opposed Gelleh. In June Gedi Hared formed an opposition alliance, the Coordination de l'opposition djiboutienne, embracing the PND, the Front uni de l'opposition djiboutienne (a coalition of internal opposition groups) and the RPP–GDR. In August Gedi Hared, Bahdon Farah and Barreh were among five people sentenced to six months' imprisonment, and the suspension of their civil rights for five years, for 'insulting the Head of State'. The accused reportedly signed a document in May alleging that President Gouled ruled by force and terror. The detainees were released from prison in January 1997, following a presidential pardon, although their civil rights were not restored.

In September 1996 an internal dispute arose in the RPP when Gelleh began a discreet campaign against the holding of several positions concurrently, which was aimed at the Prime Minister and Deputy Chairman of the RPP, Barkad Gourad Hamadou. In an apparent attempt to end these internecine disputes, President Gouled announced his intention to remain as Head of State until the expiry of his term of office in 1999, and in March 1997 was re-elected President of the RPP.

In April 1997 the FRUD faction led by Ali Mohamed Daoud announced its intention to participate in the forthcoming legislative elections (scheduled to be held in December) and to present joint electoral lists with the RPP. Meanwhile, in September an attack on an army division in northern Djibouti (during which 11 soldiers were killed and 16 were wounded) was attributed to the armed wing of the FRUD, under the leadership of Ahmed Dini. In the following month the armed forces of Djibouti and Ethiopia launched a joint offensive against FRUD rebels, and in February 1998 the Djiboutian security forces killed 12 members of the armed faction and arrested another 20. In March Dini appealed to the Intergovernmental Authority on Development (IGAD) to mediate an end to the conflict. Shortly afterwards FRUD insurgents attacked several southern towns, and in November, following further FRUD assaults on the armed forces in the north, the authorities announced the creation of military zones around Tadjourah and Obock.

At the legislative elections, held on 19 December 1997, the RPP–FRUD alliance won all the seats in the Chamber of Deputies. According to official results, 63.8% of the electorate participated nation-wide, but only 47.8% voted in the capital and 32.9% in Ali-Sabieh. The PRD and the PND presented candidates in some districts, but neither succeeded in gaining representation. The PRD had suffered a split in May when Abdillahi Hamareiteh was elected as the party's new President (to succeed Elabe, who died in late 1996). A rival faction, led by Kaireh Allaleh Hared, was refused legal recognition. In late December President Gouled announced the formation of a new Council of Ministers; minor reshuffles had been effected in April and November.

In October 1998 some 20 human rights activists temporarily occupied the Djiboutian embassy in France to protest at the imprisonment of opposition politicians in Djibouti and at alleged abuses by the country's armed forces. In September Bahdon Farah and Barreh had been given 12-month suspended sentences and fined for preparing a 'civil disobedience movement' in the armed forces. Sixteen soldiers (including three officers and a retired gendarme) were also sentenced to suspended prison terms. In October 12 people were arrested following the alleged discovery of a large armaments cache in a village some 40 km south-west of the capital.

In February 1999 President Gouled confirmed that he would not stand in the forthcoming presidential election; the RPP named Ismael Omar Gelleh, Gouled's principal adviser, as its presidential candidate. At the election, held on 9 April, Gelleh won 74.4% of the votes cast, convincingly defeating his sole opponent, Moussa Ahmed Idris, who represented an opposition coalition, the Opposition djiboutienne unifiée (ODU), including the PND, the PRD and the Dini wing of the FRUD. Electoral participation was estimated at 60% of eligible voters. Following his inauguration as President on 7 May, Gelleh reappointed Hamadou as Prime Minister, at the head of a new Council of Ministers. Also in May, in response to considerable international pressure, Gelleh decreed the release of some 40 prisoners, among whom was a prominent lawyer and long-term opponent of the Government, Aref Mohammed Aref.

In September 1999 Idris, the defeated presidential candidate, was arrested on charges of violating press laws, after publishing a number of articles in his newspaper, *Le Temps*, which allegedly criticized the Government and undermined the morale of the armed forces. During the arrest, clashes took place between police and Idris's supporters; his wife was injured and a relative shot dead. Idris was later sentenced to four months' imprisonment. In December Idris was one of some 250 detainees to benefit from an amnesty granted by Gelleh, to celebrate the start of the Islamic month of Ramadan, and was released.

In early February 2000 the Government and the Dini wing of the FRUD signed a peace agreement in Paris, France. The accord provided for an end to hostilities; the reciprocal release of prisoners; the return of military units to positions held before the conflict; freedom of movement for persons and goods; the reintegration of FRUD insurgents into their previous positions of employment; and an amnesty for the rebels. In late March Dini returned to Djibouti from a self-imposed nine-year exile and announced his intention to assist in the implementation of the peace agreement. Meanwhile, earlier that month the RPP had convened its eighth congress, at which Gouled officially announced his retirement from active politics. Gelleh was elected to succeed him as President of the party. In April the commission for the implementation of the peace agreement between the Government and the Dini wing of the FRUD held its first meeting, during which four subcommissions were established to organize disarmament and compensation, the rehabilitation of former combatants, the implementation of the decentralization programme and the strengthening of the democratic process. Meetings between the two sides continued during 2000, however, in October the FRUD demanded the revision of the Constitution, in order to curb the powers of the executive, the introduction of legislation to guarantee the independence of the magistrature, and the tribal rebalancing of the civil service. Furthermore, the FRUD leadership criticized Gelleh's apparent preoccupation with the Somali national reconciliation conference and reports circulated that FRUD members were preparing to resume their armed struggle, if negotiations continued to be stalled.

In early December 2000 President Gelleh demoted General Yacine Yabeh Galeb, who had held the position of chief of staff of the national police force since 1977, to an advisory role at the Ministry of the Interior. The decision prompted police protesters, led by Galeb, to occupy the national broadcasting company and surround the presidential palace. Gunshots were fired during a stand-off between the protestors and the army and, according to official sources, two people were killed and six others injured before order was restored. Later that month Galeb and 12 police officers were charged with conspiracy and breaching state security.

In early February 2001 Barkad Gourad Hamadou resigned as Prime Minister on the grounds of ill health, after some 22 years in office. Dileita Mohamed Dileita, hitherto ambassador to Ethiopia, was appointed as Hamadou's replacement in March.

Separate treaties of friendship and co-operation were signed in 1981 with Ethiopia, Somalia, Kenya and Sudan, with the aim of resolving regional conflicts. In August 1984 the Minister of Foreign Affairs reaffirmed Djibouti's policy of maintaining a neutral stance in the conflict between its neighbours in the Horn of Africa, and expressed his Government's willingness to act as a mediator. A joint ministerial committee, which held its first session in mid-1985, was formed between Djibouti and Ethiopia, to strengthen existing relations and co-operation

between the two countries. These relations, however, were overshadowed in 1986 by Ethiopia's support for the MNDID.

Djibouti's interest in promoting regional co-operation was exemplified by the creation, in February 1985, of the Intergovernmental Authority on Drought and Development (IGADD, now the IGAD, see p. 214), with six (now seven) member states; Djibouti was chosen as the site of its permanent secretariat, and President Gouled became the first Chairman. Under the auspices of IGADD, the Heads of State of Ethiopia and Somalia met in January 1986 for the first time in 10 years, and in March 1988 they held a further meeting. In the following month the two countries agreed to re-establish diplomatic relations, to withdraw troops from their common border and to exchange prisoners of war.

Following the overthrow of the Ethiopian President, Mengistu Haile Mariam, in May 1991, Djibouti established good relations with the successor transitional Government in that country. In June Djibouti hosted a preliminary conference of groups from southern Somalia, aimed at forming a transitional Somali government. In October the borders between Djibouti and Somalia were reopened for the first time since May 1989, when they had been closed as a result of civil unrest in Somalia. Relations with the self-proclaimed 'Republic of Somaliland', which declared independence in 1991, were increasingly strained during 1995. In August there were reports of clashes along the border, apparently between local militia groups from Djibouti and 'Somaliland' troops. In June 1996, however, Djibouti and 'Somaliland' concluded an agreement, which included provisions for co-operation on border security and the establishment of trade relations. Moreover, in November 1997 Djibouti granted official recognition to 'Somaliland'. In late 1999 President Gelleh drafted a peace plan aimed at reunifying Somali territory, to which the leaders of 'Somaliland' expressed their vehement opposition. In December of that year the border between Djibouti and 'Somaliland', which had temporarily been closed in the previous month, was reopened. However, relations deteriorated again in mid-April 2000 when the 'Somaliland' authorities again closed the common border with Djibouti. This followed an incident in which a Djiboutian delegation, led by the President of the Djibouti legislature, was refused permission to leave its aircraft after landing at Hargeisa airport in 'Somaliland'. 'Somaliland' officials claimed that Djibouti was encouraging ethnic violence and had been responsible for a series of bomb attacks in Hargeisa. In response, Djibouti expelled three 'Somaliland' diplomats and closed the 'Somaliland' liaison office in Djibouti town. Furthermore, in May the 'Somaliland' authorities issued a ban on all flights from Djibouti to its territory; the Djibouti Government responded by prohibiting all flights to and from 'Somaliland'. Also in May the Djibouti-sponsored Somali national reconciliation conference, presided over by President Gelleh, opened in Arta, about 40 km south of Djibouti town. The conference was attended by some 900 representatives of Somali clans and political and armed groups and in August, following three months of extensive negotiations, the newly-created Somali Transitional National Assembly elected Abdulkasim Salad Hasan President of Somalia.

In December 1995 the Djibouti Government protested to the Eritrean authorities about alleged incursions by Eritrean troops into north-eastern Djibouti. These allegations were vehemently denied by Eritrea. Relations between the two countries were strained in April 1996, when President Gouled rejected a map of Eritrea submitted by the Eritrean Minister of Foreign Affairs, which reportedly included a 20-km strip of territory belonging to Djibouti. Concurrently, reports emerged of exchanges of artillery fire at a frontier post in northern Djibouti; Eritrea denied the incident. Relations between the two countries subsequently improved, but in November 1998 Djibouti suspended diplomatic relations with Eritrea, following accusations by that country that it was supporting Ethiopia in the Eritrea–Ethiopia border dispute. Gouled had been actively involved in an OAU committee mediating on the dispute, which earlier in the month had proposed a peace plan that was accepted by Ethiopia, but not by Eritrea. In 1999 relations between Djibouti and Ethiopia continued to improve, while those between Djibouti and Eritrea deteriorated further. In November President Gelleh visited Ethiopia and was praised by the Ethiopian President, Negasso Gidada, for his efforts in promoting a peace settlement in Somalia. Gidada pledged his country's continuing support for these endeavours. The two countries also undertook to strengthen their bilateral relations. However, Gelleh criticized the Eritrean Government for its aggressive attitude towards Ethiopia, and there were reports that French troops based in Djibouti were being stationed along the Eritrea–Djibouti border. In December the Djibouti and Ethiopian Governments signed a protocol of understanding on military co-operation, with the aim of establishing a further mutual defence pact. In March 2000, following Libyan mediation, Djibouti and Eritrea announced that they had resumed diplomatic relations.

In August 1986 a new scheme for repatriating Ethiopian refugees, under the auspices of the UN High Commissioner for Refugees (UNHCR), was begun. The burden that 'official' refugees imposed on the economy was exacerbated by an influx of illegal immigrants from Somalia and Ethiopia, and in June 1987 the Djibouti Government announced tighter controls on border crossings and identity papers. Following discussions in February 1988, Djibouti and Ethiopia agreed to control movements across their common border and to curb the influx of refugees into Djibouti. In January 1989 illegal immigrants were alleged to have taken part in a violent confrontation between the security forces and inhabitants of Balbala, a densely-populated shanty-town close to the capital, in which four people died and 100 were injured. In response, President Gouled announced that measures were to be taken against illegal refugees, who, he claimed, were not only an economic burden on the country, but also a source of instability. Although the Government maintained that by early 1993 the number of Somali refugees in Djibouti had reached 120,000, UNHCR argued that many of these were economic migrants. In September 1994 UNHCR initiated a programme of voluntary repatriation for Ethiopian refugees in Djibouti. According to UNHCR, some 35,000 Ethiopians returned voluntarily to their homes between early 1995 and April 1996. UNHCR estimated that at 31 December 1999 there were 21,600 Somali and 1,500 Ethiopian refugees in Djibouti. There were also some 1,600 Djiboutian refugees in Ethiopia.

President Gouled consistently fostered cordial relations with France, and encouraged the maintenance of French troops in Djibouti. However, the French military presence became more controversial following Iraq's invasion of Kuwait in August 1990 and the onset of the 'Gulf crisis', during which Djibouti became the base of operations connected with France's participation in the multinational force deployed in Saudi Arabia. By supporting the UN resolutions that were formulated against Iraq, Djibouti jeopardized its future relations with that country, which was emerging as an important supplier of economic and military aid. However, Djibouti's stance during the Gulf War of January–February 1991 strengthened its ties with France, and in February the Djibouti and French Governments signed defence treaties, extending military co-operation, although France refused to intervene militarily in the conflict between the Government and the FRUD. The failure of the Government to conclude a peace agreement with the FRUD strained relations with France in 1993–94. Relations improved as a result of the peace accord of December 1994, but tensions remained between the two countries, largely owing to Djibouti's reluctance to adopt a strict programme of economic reform. In April 1998, during a visit to Djibouti by the French Minister of Defence, it was announced that France planned to reduce its military presence in the country from 3,200 troops to 2,600 by 2000. However, following a visit to Djibouti by the French army chief of staff, Gen. Jean-Pierre Kelche, in October 1999, the suspension of the troop reduction programme was announced. Furthermore, Gen. Kelche confirmed France's guarantees of Djibouti's territorial integrity.

Government

Executive power is vested in the President, who is directly elected by universal adult suffrage for a six-year term. Legislative power is held by the Chamber of Deputies, consisting of 65 members elected for five years. The Council of Ministers, presided over by a Prime Minister, is responsible to the President. The Republic forms a single electoral district.

Defence

Since independence, a large portion of the annual budget has been allocated to military expenditure, and defence (excluding demobilization) absorbed an estimated 12.9% of total governmental budgetary expenditure in 1998. In August 2000 there were about 3,200 French troops stationed in Djibouti. The total armed forces of Djibouti itself, in which all services form part of the army, was estimated at 9,600 (including 200 naval and 200 air force personnel, and 1,200 gendarmes), and there was

a 3,000-strong national security force. The defence budget for 2000 was expected to amount to 4,000m. Djibouti francs.

Economic Affairs

In 1999, according to estimates by the World Bank, Djibouti's gross national product (GNP), measured at average 1997–99 prices, was US $511m., equivalent to $790 per head. Djibouti's overall gross domestic product (GDP) expanded, in real terms, at an average annual rate of 2.0% in 1985–89, although, as a result of rapid population increase, GDP per head declined, in real terms, during 1980–86. According to estimates by the IMF, GDP declined, in real terms, in each of the five years 1992–96. Real GDP fell by 1.5% in 1996, but remained at a constant level in 1997, before provisionally increasing by 1.7% in 1998. According to official estimates, real GDP growth of 1.5% was recorded in 1999. During 1990–98 the population increased by an average of 3.0% per year (according to World Bank estimates), owing partly to the influx of refugees from neighbouring Ethiopia and Somalia.

Agriculture (including hunting, forestry and fishing) provided an estimated 3.6% of GDP in 1998, although some 75.2% of the labour force were engaged in the sector in 1991. There is little arable farming, owing to Djibouti's unproductive terrain, and the country is able to produce only about 3% of its total food requirements. More than one-half of the population are pastoral nomads, herding goats, sheep and camels.

Industry (comprising manufacturing, construction and utilities) provided an estimated 19.9% of GDP in 1998 and engaged 11.0% of the employed labour force in 1991. Industrial activity is mainly limited to a few small-scale enterprises.

The manufacturing sector contributed an estimated 5.2% of GDP in 1998. Almost all consumer goods have to be imported.

In 1986 work commenced on a major geothermal exploration project, funded by the World Bank and foreign aid. In that year Saudi Arabia granted Djibouti US $21.4m. for the purchase and installation of three electricity generators, with a combined capacity of 15 MW. Total electricity generating capacity rose from 40 MW to 80 MW in 1988, when the second part of the Boulaos power station became operative. Imported fuels satisfy 90% of Djibouti's energy requirements.

Djibouti's economic viability is based on trade through the international port of Djibouti, and on the developing service sector, which accounted for an estimated 76.5% of GDP in 1998, and engaged 13.8% of the employed labour force in 1991. In May 2000 the Government and Dubai Ports International (DPI) signed an agreement providing DPI with a 20-year contract to manage the port of Djibouti.

In 1998, according to provisional figures, Djibouti recorded a visible trade deficit of US $179.7m., and there was a deficit of $14.4m. on the current account of the balance of payments. According to the IMF, the principal sources of imports in 1998 were France (12.5%), Ethiopia (12.0%) and the United Kingdom (6.2%). The principal markets for exports in that year were Somalia (53.0%) and Yemen (22.5%). The principal imports in 1998 were food and beverages, qat (a narcotic leaf), petroleum products, and machinery and electrical appliances. Most exports are unclassified.

According to provisional figures, Djibouti recorded a budget surplus of 83m. Djibouti francs in 1998 (equivalent to 0.1% of GDP). The country's total external debt was US $287.8m. at the end of 1998, of which $263.8m. was long-term public debt. In 1997 the cost of debt-servicing was equivalent to 3.4% of revenue from exports of goods and services. The annual rate of inflation averaged 4.8% during 1989–97. Consumer prices increased by an estimated 2.0% in 1997. In 1996 unemployment was estimated to affect some 58% of the labour force.

Djibouti is a member of the Intergovernmental Authority on Development (see p. 214) and numerous other international organizations, including the African Development Bank (see p. 120), the Arab Fund for Economic and Social Development (see p. 125) and the Islamic Development Bank (see p. 229). In 1995 Djibouti became a member of the World Trade Organization (see p. 292).

Djibouti is heavily dependent on foreign assistance, and the decline in foreign aid since 1986 has led to financial problems. The high level of military expenditure in 1991–94, in response to internal insurgency, caused a substantial deficit in the government budget. Attempts by aid donors, notably France, to insist on structural reforms to the economy were initially resisted by the Government, but in mid-1995 considerable reductions in government spending were announced, and in April 1996 the IMF approved Djibouti's first stand-by credit, equivalent to US $6.7m. Djibouti agreed to implement a programme of austerity measures, concentrating on budgetary adjustment and structural reform. In October 1999 the IMF agreed a $26.5m.-loan to support the Government's three-year economic reform programme. An initial payment of $3.8m. was released immediately. However, the payment of the balance was conditional on Djibouti fulfilling its promised programme of economic and financial reform for the period 1999–2002: this included reforms to tax, revenue administration and budget management; the completion of the army demobilization programme by the end of 2000; the reform of the civil service, thus lowering the wage bill; and the publication of a privatization programme for the six principal state-owned enterprises. Following the announcement of a supplementary budget in July 2000, the second tranche of the IMF loan, amounting to $3.6m., was released, despite delays in the army demobilization programme and the reform of the civil service. Furthermore, Djibouti was also successful in negotiating the rescheduling of its obligations to its 'Paris Club' creditors. In order to finance the Somali national reconciliation conference, which was held in Djibouti between May and August, the Djibouti Government imposed additional taxes on alcohol, tobacco and qat. Meanwhile, GDP growth for 2000 was predicted to reach 2% and the Government forecast that inflation would remain at around 2%. The Government's major priority, however, remained the reduction of poverty and, in contrast to other sectors, increased expenditure on health, social security and education was planned for 2001.

Social Welfare

The social insurance scheme in Djibouti is divided into three categories, according to whether the worker is employed in the private sector, the civil service or the army. Employees receive benefits in case of accidents at work, and are allocated retirement pensions after the age of 55 years. In 1990 there were 20 hospital establishments, with a total of 1,369 beds, and more than 660 medical personnel, including 73 physicians and four dentists. Budgetary current expenditure on health for 1998 was provisionally estimated at 1,641m. Djibouti francs (equivalent to 5.3% of total spending).

Education

The Government has overall responsibility for education. Primary education generally begins at six years of age and lasts for six years. Secondary education, usually starting at the age of 12, lasts for seven years, comprising a first cycle of four years and a second of three years. In 1996 the total enrolment at primary and secondary schools was equivalent to 26% of the school-age population (31% of boys; 22% of girls), while primary enrolment was equivalent to 39% of pupils in the relevant age-group (44% of boys; 33% of girls) and secondary enrolment was equivalent to 14% of pupils in the relevant age-group (17% of boys; 12% of girls). Budgetary current expenditure on education in 1998 was provisionally estimated at 2,645m. Djibouti francs, equivalent to 8.5% of total government expenditure. In 1996/97 there were 36,896 primary school pupils and 13,311 pupils receiving general secondary and vocational education (including teacher training). As Djibouti has no university, students seeking further education travel abroad to study, mainly to France. In 1995, according to UNESCO estimates, the rate of illiteracy among the population aged 15 years and over was 53.7% (males 39.6%; females 67.2%).

Public Holidays

2001: 1 January (New Year's Day), 6 March* (Id al-Adha, Feast of the Sacrifice), 26 March* (Muharram, Islamic New Year), 1 May (Workers' Day), 4 June* (Mouloud, Birth of the Prophet), 27 June (Independence Day), 17 December* (Id al-Fitr, end of Ramadan), 25 December (Christmas Day).

2002: 1 January (New Year's Day), 23 February* (Id al-Adha, Feast of the Sacrifice), 15 March* (Muharram, Islamic New Year), 1 May (Workers' Day), 24 May* (Mouloud, Birth of the Prophet), 27 June (Independence Day), 6 December* (Id al-Fitr, end of Ramadan), 25 December (Christmas Day).

* These holidays are dependent on the Islamic lunar calendar and may vary by one or two days from the dates given.

Weights and Measures

The metric system is in force.

Statistical Survey

Source (unless otherwise stated): the former Ministère de l'Economie et du Commerce, BP 1846, Djibouti; tel. 351682.

AREA AND POPULATION

Area: 23,200 sq km (8,958 sq miles).

Population: 220,000 (1976 estimate), including Afars 70,000, Issas and other Somalis 80,000, Arabs 12,000, Europeans 15,000, other foreigners 40,000; 519,900 (including refugees and resident foreigners) at 31 December 1990 (official estimate); 629,000 (UN estimate) at mid-1999 (Source: UN, *World Population Prospects: The 1998 Revision*).

Density (mid-1999): 27.1 per sq km.

Principal Towns: Djibouti (capital), population 200,000 (1981); Dikhil; Ali-Sabieh; Tadjourah; Obock.

Births and Deaths (UN estimates, 1990–95): Average annual birth rate 39.0 per 1,000; Average annual death rate 16.2 per 1,000. Source: UN, *World Population Prospects: The 1998 Revision*.

Expectation of Life (UN estimates, years at birth, 1990–95): 48.3 (males 46.7; females 50.0). Source: UN, *World Population Prospects: The 1998 Revision*.

Economically Active Population (estimates, '000 persons, 1991): Agriculture, etc. 212; Industries 31; Services 39; *Total* 282 (males 167, females 115). Source: UN Economic Commission for Africa, *African Statistical Yearbook*.

AGRICULTURE, ETC.

Principal Crops (FAO estimates, '000 metric tons, 1999): Tomatoes 1.0; Other vegetables 23.2. Source: FAO.

Livestock (FAO estimates, '000 head, year ending September 1999): Cattle 269; Sheep 465; Goats 512; Asses 9; Camels 66. Source: FAO.

Livestock Products: ('000 metric tons, 1999): Beef and veal 3.6; Mutton and lamb 2.1; Goat meat 2.3; Camel meat 0.6; Cows' milk 7.7; Camels' milk 5.7; Cattle hides 0.7; Sheepskins 0.4; Goatskins 0.5. Source: FAO.

Fishing (FAO estimates, metric tons, live weight, 1998): Groupers 105; Snappers and jobfishes 80; Porgies and seabreams 40; Barracudas 20; Carangids 20; Seerfishes 60; Other tuna-like fishes 15; Total catch (incl. others) 350. Source: FAO, *Yearbook of Fishery Statistics*.

INDUSTRY

Electric energy (million kWh): 202.5 in 1996; 200.7 in 1997; 133.0 in 1998. Source: IMF, *Djibouti: Statistical Annex* (December 1999).

FINANCE

Currency and Exchange Rates: 100 centimes = 1 Djibouti franc. *Sterling, Dollar and Euro Equivalents* (29 December 2000): £1 sterling = 265.20 Djibouti francs; US $1 = 177.72 Djibouti francs; €1 = 165.37 Djibouti francs; 1,000 Djibouti francs = £3.771 = $5.627 = € 6.074. *Exchange Rate:* Fixed at US $1 = 177.721 Djibouti francs since February 1973.

Budget (provisional, million Djibouti francs, 1998): *Revenue:* Tax revenue 20,258 (Taxes on incomes and profits 4,574, Other direct taxes 4,499, Indirect taxes 10,335; Registration fees, etc. 850); Other revenue (incl. property sales) 2,896; Total 23,154, excl. grants received from abroad (8,079). *Expenditure:* Current expenditure 24,350 (General administration 8,116, Defence 4,013, Mobilization and demobilization 2,083, Education 2,645, Health 1,641, Economic services 931, Transfers 2,534); Capital expenditure 6,077; Sub-total 30,427; Reduction in payment arrears 723; Total 31,150. Source: IMF, *Djibouti: Statistical Annex* (December 1999).

International Reserves (US $ million at 31 December 2000): IMF special drawing rights 0.36; Reserve position in IMF 1.43; Foreign exchange 66.01; Total 67.80. Source: IMF, *International Financial Statistics*.

Money Supply (million Djibouti francs at 31 December 2000): Currency outside banks 9,207; Demand deposits at commercial banks 18,704; Total money 27,911. Source: IMF, *International Financial Statistics*.

Cost of Living: (Consumer Price Index for expatriates; base: 1989 = 100): All items 137.2 in 1995; 142.9 in 1996; 145.8 (estimate) in 1997. Source: IMF, *Djibouti: Statistical Annex* (August 1998).

Expenditure on the Gross Domestic Product (provisional, million Djibouti francs at current purchasers' values, 1998): Government final consumption expenditure 21,497; Private final consumption expenditure 72,466; Gross capital formation 13,958;

Total domestic expenditure 107,921; Exports of goods and services 41,449; *Less* Imports of goods and services 58,172; *GDP in purchasers' values* 91,198. Source: IMF, *Djibouti: Statistical Annex* (December 1999).

Gross Domestic Product by Economic Activity (provisional, million Djibouti francs at current factor cost, 1998): Agriculture, hunting, forestry and fishing 2,917; Manufacturing 4,239; Electricity, gas and water 4,850; Construction 6,971; Trade, restaurants and hotels 14,481; Transport, storage and communications 15,824; Finance, insurance, real estate and business services 8,772; Public administration 18,469; Other services 4,340; *GDP at factor cost* 80,863; Indirect taxes *less* subsidies 10,335; *GDP in purchasers' values* 91,198. Source: IMF, *Djibouti: Statistical Annex* (December 1999).

Balance of Payments (provisional, US $ million, 1998): Exports of goods f.o.b. 59.1; Imports of goods f.o.b. −238.8; *Trade balance* −179.7; Exports of services and other income 195.6; Imports of services and other income −98.2; *Balance on goods, services and income* −82.3; Official transfers (net) 72.2; Private transfers (net) −4.3; *Current balance* −14.4; Foreign direct investment 3.5; Public sector (net) 19.1; Private capital (net) and net errors and omissions −19.5; *Overall balance* −11.4. Source: IMF, *Djibouti: Statistical Annex* (December 1999).

EXTERNAL TRADE

Principal Commodities: *Imports c.i.f.* (provisional, million Djibouti francs, 1998): Food and beverages 9,379; Qat 3,049; Petroleum products 2,976; Chemical products 1,114; Clothing and footwear 882; Metals and metal products 1,182; Machinery and electrical appliances 2,613; Vehicles and transport equipment 1,036; Total (incl. others) 24,067. Note: figures refer only to imports for domestic use. Source: IMF, *Djibouti: Statistical Annex* (December 1999). *Exports f.o.b.* (distribution by SITC, US $'000, 1992): Food and live animals 3,292 (Rice 726, Coffee and coffee substitutes 1,773); Crude materials (inedible) except fuels 867; Basic manufactures 771; Machinery and transport equipment 1,260 (Road vehicles and parts 585, Other transport equipment 501); Commodities not classified according to kind 9,481; Total (incl. others) 15,919. Source: UN, *International Trade Statistics Yearbook*.

Principal Trading Partners (percentage of total trade, 1998): *Imports c.i.f.:* Bahrain 3.2; Ethiopia 12.0; France 12.5; India 1.9; Italy 9.2; Japan 4.2; Netherlands 3.1; Saudi Arabia 5.7; Singapore 2.0; Taiwan 1.6; Thailand 3.0; United Kingdom 6.2; Yemen 2.3. *Exports f.o.b.:* Ethiopia 5.0; Somalia 53.0; Yemen 22.5. Source: IMF, *Direction of Trade Statistics* in *Djibouti: Statistical Annex* (December 1999).

TRANSPORT

Railways (traffic, 1997): Passenger-km ('000) 762; Freight ton-km (million) 232. Source: IMF, *Djibouti: Statistical Annex* (December 1999).

Road Traffic (estimates, motor vehicles in use, 1996): Passenger cars 9,200; Lorries and vans 2,040. Source: International Road Federation, *World Road Statistics*.

Shipping: *Merchant Fleet* (registered at 31 December 1998): 12 vessels (displacement 3,967 grt). Source: Lloyd's Register of Shipping. *Freight Traffic* ('000 metric tons, 1998): Goods loaded and unloaded 808. Source: IMF, *Djibouti: Statistical Annex* (December 1999).

Civil Aviation (1998): Passengers arriving and departing 107,369; Freight loaded and unloaded 7,290 metric tons. Source: IMF, *Djibouti: Statistical Annex* (December 1999).

TOURISM

Tourist Arrivals ('000): 21 in 1995; 20 in 1996; 19 in 1997.

Receipts from Tourism (US $ million): 4 in 1995; 4 in 1996; 4 in 1997.

Source: World Tourism Organization, *Yearbook of Tourism Statistics*.

COMMUNICATIONS MEDIA

Newspapers (1995): 1 non-daily (estimated circulation 1,000).

Periodicals (1989): 7 (estimated combined circulation 6,000).

Radio Receivers (1997): 52,000 in use.

Television Receivers (1997): 28,000 in use.

Telephones (1997): 8,257 main lines in use.

Telefax Stations (1997): 345 in use.

Mobile Cellular Telephones (1997): 203 subscribers.

Sources: mainly UNESCO, *Statistical Yearbook*, and UN, *Statistical Yearbook*.

EDUCATION

Pre-primary (1996/97): 2 schools; 247 pupils.

Primary (1996/97): 72 schools; 36,896 pupils; 1,096 teachers.

Secondary (1996/97): 13,311 pupils (general 11,367, teacher-training 103, vocational 1,841); 628 teachers (1995/96).

Higher (1996/97): 161 students.

Source: UNESCO, *Statistical Yearbook*.

Directory

The Constitution

In February 1981 the National Assembly approved the first constitutional laws controlling the election and terms of office of the President, who is elected by universal adult suffrage for six years and may serve for no more than two terms. Candidates for the presidency must be presented by a regularly constituted political party and represented by at least 25 members of the Chamber of Deputies. The Chamber, comprising 65 members, is elected for a five-year term.

In October 1984 a new constitutional law was proposed, specifying that, when the office of President falls vacant, the President of the Supreme Court will assume the power of Head of State for a minimum of 20 days and a maximum of 35 days, during which period a new President shall be elected.

Laws approving the establishment of a single-party system were adopted in October 1981. A new Constitution, providing for the establishment of a maximum of four political parties, was approved by national referendum on 4 September 1992 and entered into force on 15 September.

The Government

HEAD OF STATE

President and Commander-in-Chief of the Armed Forces: ISMAEL OMAR GELLEH (inaugurated 7 May 1999).

COUNCIL OF MINISTERS
(March 2001)

Prime Minister: DILEITA MOHAMED DILEITA.

Minister of Justice, Muslim and Penal Affairs, and Human Rights: IBRAHIM IDRISS DJIBRIL.

Minister of the Interior: ABDALLAH ABDILLAHI MIGUIL.

Minister of Defence: OUGOUREH KIFLEH AHMED.

Minister of Foreign Affairs, International Co-operation and Parliamentary Relations: ALI ABDI FARAH.

Minister of Economy, Finance and Privatization: YACIN ELMI BOUH.

Minister of Trade, Industry and Handicrafts: ELMI OBSIEH WA'AYS.

Minister of Agriculture, Livestock and Fishing: ALI MOHAMED DAOUD.

Minister of Communication and Culture, in charge of Post and Telecommunications, and Government Spokesman: RIFKI ABDULKADER BAMAKHRAMA.

Minister of Education: ABDI IBRAHIM ABSIEH.

Minister of Employment and National Solidarity: MOHAMED BARKAT ABDILLAHI.

Minister of Energy and Natural Resources: MOHAMED ALI MOHAMED.

Minister of Equipment and Transportation: OSMAN IDRISS DJAMA.

Minister of Health: MOHAMED DINI FARAH.

Minister of Presidential Affairs, in charge of Investment Promotion: OSMAN AHMED MOUSSA.

Minister of Urban Planning, Housing, the Environment, and National and Regional Development: SOULEIMAN OMAR OUDINE.

Minister of Youth, Sports, Leisure and Tourism: DINI ABDALLAH BILILIS.

Minister-delegate to the Prime Minister in charge of Decentralization: AHMED GUIRREH WABERI.

Minister-delegate to the Prime Minister in charge of Mosque Properties and Muslim Affairs: CHEIK MOGUEH DIRIR.

Minister-delegate to the Prime Minister in charge of the Promotion of Women's, Family and Social Affairs: HAWA AHMED YOUSSOUF.

MINISTRIES

Office of the Prime Minister: BP 2086, Djibouti; tel. 351494; fax 355049.

Ministry of Agriculture, Livestock and Fishing: BP 453, Djibouti; tel. 351297.

Ministry of the Civil Service and Administrative Reform: BP 155, Djibouti; tel. 351464.

Ministry of Defence: BP 42, Djibouti; tel. 352034.

Ministry of the Economy, Finance and Privatization: BP 13, Djibouti; tel. 350297; fax 35601.

Ministry of Education: BP 2102, Djibouti; tel. 350850; internet www.education.dj.

Ministry of Employment and National Solidarity: Djibouti.

Ministry of Energy and Natural Resources: BP 175, Djibouti; tel. 350340.

Ministry of Foreign Affairs and International Co-operation: BP 1863, Djibouti; tel. 352471.

Ministry of Health: BP 296, Djibouti; tel. 353331; fax 356300.

Ministry of the Interior: BP 33, Djibouti; tel. 350791.

Ministry of Justice, Muslim and Penal Affairs and Human Rights: BP 12, Djibouti; tel. 351506; fax 354012.

Ministry of Labour and Vocational Training: BP 170, Djibouti; tel. 350497.

Ministry of Trade, Industry and Handicrafts: BP 1846, Djibouti; tel. 351682.

Ministry of Transport and Communications: BP 2501, Djibouti; tel. 350971.

Ministry of Urban Planning, Housing, the Environment and National and Regional Development: Djibouti.

Ministry of Youth, Sports, Leisure and Tourism: BP 2506, Djibouti; tel. 355886; fax 356830.

President and Legislature

PRESIDENT

Presidential Election, 9 April 1999

Candidates		Votes	%
ISMAEL OMAR GELLEH (RPP) .	. . . .	70,993	74.44
MOUSSA AHMED IDRIS (ODU)*	. . . .	24,375	25.56
Total .	. . . . . .	**95,368**	**100.00**

* Opposition djiboutienne unifiée, an electoral coalition including the PND, the PRD and the Dini faction of the FRUD.

CHAMBRE DES DÉPUTÉS

Elections for the 65-seat Chamber of Deputies were held on 19 December 1997. The election was contested by the governing Rassemblement populaire pour le progrès (RPP), in alliance with the Front pour la restauration de l'unité et de la démocratie (FRUD), and by the Parti national démocratique (PND) and the Parti du renouveau démocratique (PRD). All 65 seats were won by the RPP-FRUD alliance.

President of the Chamber: SAID IBRAHIM BADOUL.

Political Organizations

Constitutional reforms permitting a maximum of four political parties took effect in September 1992. By late 1999 the following parties were legally recognized:

Front pour la restauration de l'unité et de la démocratie (FRUD): f. 1991 by merger of three militant Afar groups; advocates fair representation in govt for all ethnic groups; commenced armed insurgency in Nov. 1991; split into two factions in March 1994; the dissident group, which negotiated a settlement with the Govt, obtained legal recognition in March 1996 and recognizes the following leaders: Pres. ALI MOHAMED DAOUD; Sec.-Gen. OUGOUREH KIFLEH AHMED; the faction favouring a continuation of mil. operations is led by AHMED DINI AHMED; another dissident group, FRUD–Renaissance (led by IBRAHIM CHEHEM DAOUD), was formed in 1996.

Parti national démocratique (PND): f. 1992; seeks formation of a 'govt of national unity' to supervise implementation of democratic reforms; Chair. ADEN ROBLEH AWALLEH.

Parti du renouveau démocratique (PRD): BP 2198, Djibouti; tel. 356235; fax 351474; f. 1992; seeks to establish democratic parliamentary govt; Pres. ABDILLAHI HAMAREITEH; Sec.-Gen. MAKI HOUMED GABA.

Rassemblement populaire pour le progrès (RPP): Djibouti; f. 1979; sole legal party 1981–92; Pres. ISMAEL OMAR GELLEH; Sec.-Gen. MOHAMED ALI MOHAMED.

The following organizations are banned:

Coordination de l'opposition djiboutienne: f. 1996; alliance of the PND, the FUOD and the RPP–GDR; Leader ISMAEL GEDI HARED.

Front des forces démocratiques (FFD): Leader OMAR ELMI KHAIREH.

Front de libération de la côte des Somalis (FLCS): f. 1963; Issa-supported; has operated from Somalia; Chair. ABDALLAH WABERI KHALIF; Vice-Chair. OMAR OSMAN RABEH.

Front uni de l'opposition djiboutienne (FUOD): f. 1992; based in Ethiopia; united front of internal opposition groups, incl. some fmr mems of the RPP; Leader MAHDI IBRAHIM A. GOD.

Groupe pour la démocratie de la république (RPP–GDR): f. 1996 by a dissident faction of the RPP; Leader MOUMIN BAHDON FARAH.

Mouvement de la jeunesse djiboutienne (MJD): Leader ABDOUL-KARIM ALI AMARKAK.

Mouvement pour l'unité et la démocratie (MUD): advocates political pluralism; Leader MOHAMED MOUSSA ALI ('TOURTOUR').

Organisation des masses Afar (OMA): f. 1993 by mems of the fmr Mouvement populaire de libération; Chair. AHMED MALCO.

Parti centriste et des reformes démocratiques (PCRD): f. 1993 in Addis Ababa, Ethiopia, by a breakaway faction of the FRUD; seeks official registration as an opposition party; Chair. HASSAN ABDALLAH WATTA.

Parti populaire djiboutien (PPD): f. 1981; mainly Afar-supported; Leader MOUSSA AHMED IDRIS.

Union des démocrates djiboutiens (UDD): affiliated to the FUOD; Chair. MAHDI IBRAHIM AHMED.

Union démocratique pour le progrès (UDP): f. 1992; advocates democratic reforms; Leader FARAH WABERI.

Union des mouvements démocratiques (UMD): f. 1990 by merger of two militant external opposition groups; Pres. MOHAMED ADOYTA.

Diplomatic Representation

EMBASSIES IN DJIBOUTI

China, People's Republic: Djibouti; tel. 352246; Ambassador: GUAN JINDI.

Egypt: BP 1989, Djibouti; tel. 351231; Ambassador: IBRAHIM EL-CHOUMI.

Eritrea: BP 1944, Djibouti; tel. 354961; fax 351831; Ambassador: MOHAMED ALI JABRA.

Ethiopia: rue Clochette, BP 230, Djibouti; tel. 350718; fax 354803; Ambassador: SAHLEWORK ZEWDIE.

France: 45 blvd du Maréchal Foch, BP 2039, Djibouti; tel. 350963; fax 350272; e-mail ambfrdj@intnet.dj; Ambassador: PATRICK ROUSSEL.

Iraq: BP 1983, Djibouti; tel. 353469; Ambassador: ABDEL AZIZ AL-GAILANI.

Libya: BP 2073, Djibouti; tel. 350202; Ambassador: KAMEL AL-HADI ALMARASH.

Oman: Djibouti; tel. 350852; Ambassador: SAOUD SALEM HASSAN AL-ANSI.

Russia: BP 1913, Djibouti; tel. 352051; fax 355990; Ambassador: MIKHAIL TSVIGOUN.

Saudi Arabia: BP 1921, Djibouti; tel. 351645; fax 352284; Chargé d'affaires a.i.: MOWAFFAK AL-DOLIGANE.

Somalia: BP 549, Djibouti; tel. 353521; Ambassador: MOHAMED SHEK MOHAMED MALINGUR.

Sudan: BP 4259, Djibouti; tel. 356404; fax 356662; Ambassador: ABELWAHAB EL SAWI KHALAFALLA.

USA: Villa Plateau du Serpent, blvd du Maréchal Joffre, BP 185, Djibouti; tel. 353995; fax 353940; e-mail amembadm@bow.intnet.dj; Ambassador: LANGE SCHERMERHORN.

Yemen: BP 194, Djibouti; tel. 352975; Ambassador: MUHAMMAD ABDOUL WASSI HAMID.

Judicial System

The Supreme Court was established in 1979. There is a high court of appeal and a court of first instance in Djibouti; each of the five administrative districts has a 'tribunal coutumier'.

President of the Court of Appeal: KADIDJA ABEBA.

Religion

ISLAM

Almost the entire population are Muslims.

Qadi of Djibouti: MOGUE HASSAN DIRIR, BP 168, Djibouti; tel. 352669.

CHRISTIANITY

The Roman Catholic Church

Djibouti comprises a single diocese, directly responsible to the Holy See. There were an estimated 7,000 adherents in the country at 31 December 1998.

Bishop of Djibouti: (vacant), Evêché, blvd de la République, BP 94, Djibouti; tel. 350140; fax 354831: e-mail evecheat@intnet.dj.

The Anglican Communion

Within the Episcopal Church in Jerusalem and the Middle East, Djibouti lies within the jurisdiction of the Bishop in Egypt.

Other Christian Churches

Eglise Protestante: blvd de la République, BP 416, Djibouti; tel. 351820; fax 350706; e-mail eped@intnet.dj; f. 1957; Pastor FRANCIS MULLER.

Greek Orthodox Church: blvd de la République, Djibouti; tel. 351325; c. 350 adherents; Archimandrite STAVROS GEORGANAS.

The Ethiopian Orthodox Church is also active in Djibouti.

The Press

L'Atout: Palais du peuple, Djibouti; twice a year; publ. by the Centre National de la Promotion Culturelle et Artistique.

Carrefour Africain: BP 393, Djibouti; fax 354916; fortnightly; publ. by the Roman Catholic mission; circ. 500.

La Nation de Djibouti: place du 27 juin, BP 32, Djibouti; tel. 352201; fax 353937; weekly; Dir ISMAEL H. TANI; circ. 4,300.

Le Progrès: Djibouti; weekly; publ. by the RPP; Publr ALI MOHAMED HUMAD.

Le Renouveau: Djibouti; weekly; independent; Editor-in-Chief DAHER AHMED FARAH.

La Republique: Djibouti; weekly; independent; Editor-in-Chief AMIR ADAWEH.

Revue de l'ISERT: BP 486, Djibouti; tel. 352795; twice a year; publ. by the Institut Supérieur d'Etudes et de Recherches Scientifiques et Techniques (ISERT).

Le Temps: Djibouti; opposition newspaper; Owners MOUSSA AHMED IDRIS, ALI MEIDAL WAIS.

NEWS AGENCIES

Agence Djiboutienne d'Information (ADJI): place du 27 juin, BP 32, Djibouti; tel. 355672; fax 353957; internet www.intnet.dj; f. 1978.

Foreign Bureau

Agence France-Presse (AFP): BP 97, Djibouti; tel. 352294; Correspondent KHALID HAIDAR ABDALLAH.

Broadcasting and Communications

TELECOMMUNICATIONS

Djibouti Telecom: Djibouti; f. 2000 to replace Société des Télécommunications Internationales; 100% state-owned; Dir-Gen. ABDU-RAHMAN MOHAMED HASSAN.

BROADCASTING

Radio and Television

Radiodiffusion-Télévision de Djibouti (RTD): BP 97, Djibouti; tel. 352294; fax 356502; f. 1957; state-controlled; programmes in French, Afar, Somali and Arabic; 17 hours radio and 5 hours television daily; Dir-Gen. (Radio) ABDI ATTEYEH ABDI; Dir-Gen. (Television) MOHAMED DJAMA ADEN.

Finance

(cap. = capital; res = reserves; dep. = deposits; m. = million; brs = branches; amounts in Djibouti francs)

BANKING

Central Bank

Banque Nationale de Djibouti: BP 2118, Djibouti; tel. 352751; fax 356288; e-mail bndj@intnet.dj; f. 1977; bank of issue; cap. and res 1,078.4m., dep. 2,327m. (Dec. 1998); Gov. DJAMA MAHAMOUD HAID; Dirs HOUMED ABDOU DAOUD, AHMED OSMAN ALI.

Commercial Banks

Bank of Africa: Djibouti; f. 2000; subsidiary of AFH Holding (Luxembourg); cap. 300m.

Banque Indosuez–Mer Rouge (BIS–MR): 10 place Lagarde, BP 88, Djibouti; tel. 353016; fax 351638; e-mail indomr@intnet.dj; f. 1908; owned by Crédit Agricole Indosuez (France); cap. 1,500m., res 290.3m., dep. 19,903m. (Dec. 1998); Chair. and CEO JEAN-BERNARD ANGLADA.

Banque pour le Commerce et l'Industrie–Mer Rouge (BCI–MR): place Lagarde, BP 2122, Djibouti; tel. 350857; fax 354260; e-mail nespoux@intnet.dj; f. 1954; 51% owned by Banque Nationale de Paris Intercontinentale; cap. 3,000m., res 1,540m., dep. 25,483.3m. (Dec. 1998); Pres. MOHAMED ADEN; Vice-Pres. VINCENT DEROUX; Gen. Man. JOSEPH DETRAUX; 8 brs.

Development Bank

Banque de Développement de Djibouti: angle ave Georges Clemenceau et rue Pierre Curie, BP 520, Djibouti; tel. 353391; fax 355022; f. 1983; 39.2% govt-owned; total assets 3,081m., cap. and res 1,233m. (Dec. 1997); Dir-Gen. ABDOURAHMAN ISMAEL GELLEH.

Banking Association

Association Professionnelle des Banques: c/o Banque pour le Commerce et l'Industrie–Mer Rouge, place Lagarde, BP 2122, Djibouti; tel. 350857; fax 354260; Pres. MOHAMED ADEN.

INSURANCE

Boucher Assurances: AGF–Assurances Générales de France, rue Marchand, BP 200, Djibouti; tel. 353636; fax 353056; Country Man. CHRISTIAN BOUCHER.

Ethiopian Insurance Corporation: rue de Marseille, BP 2047, Djibouti; tel. 352306.

Les Assureurs de la Mer Rouge et du Golfe Arabe (AMERGA): Djibouti; f. 2000; Dirs THIERRY MARILL, LUC MARILL, ABDURAHMAN BARKAT ABDILLAHI, MOHAMED ADEN ABUBAKER.

Trade and Industry

CHAMBER OF COMMERCE

Chambre Internationale de Commerce et d'Industrie: BP 84, Djibouti; tel. 351070; fax 350096; internet www.intnet.dj/public/cicid/index.html; f. 1906; 24 mems, 12 assoc. mems; Pres. SAID ALI COUBECHE; First Vice-Pres. ABDOURAHMAN MAHAMOUD BOREH.

TRADE ASSOCIATION

Office National d'Approvisionnement et de Commercialisation (ONAC): BP 119, Djibouti; tel. 350327; Chair. MOHAMED ABDULKADER.

UTILITIES

Electricity

Electricité de Djibouti (EdD): c/o Ministry of Trade and Industry, BP 1846, Djibouti; tel. 351682; Dir-Gen. DJAMA ALI GELLEH.

Water

Office National des Eaux de Djibouti (ONED): c/o Ministry of Trade and Industry, BP 1846, Djibouti; tel. 351682.

Société des Eaux de Tadjourah: c/o Ministry of Trade and Industry, BP 1846, Djibouti; tel. 351682.

TRADE UNION

Union Générale du Travail: Djibouti; f. 1992 to succeed Union Générale des Travailleurs de Djibouti; confed. of 22 unions; Chair. YUSSUF MOHAMED; Sec.-Gen. ADEN MOHAMED ARDOU.

Transport

RAILWAYS

Chemin de Fer Djibouti–Ethiopien (CDE): BP 2116, Djibouti; tel. 350280; fax 351256; POB 1051, Addis Ababa; tel. 517250; fax 513533; f. 1909, adopted present name in 1981; jtly-owned by Govts of Djibouti and Ethiopia; 781 km of track (121 km in Djibouti)

linking Djibouti with Addis Ababa; Pres. SALEH OMAR HILDID; Dir-Gen. ALI ABDALLAH GADID.

ROADS

In 1996 there were an estimated 2,890 km of roads, comprising 1,090 km of main roads and 1,800 km of regional roads; some 12.6% of the roads were paved. Of the remainder, 1,000 km are serviceable throughout the year, the rest only during the dry season. About one-half of the roads are usable only by heavy vehicles. In 1981 the 40-km Grand Bara road was opened, linking the capital with the south. In 1986 the Djibouti–Tadjourah road, the construction of which was financed by Saudi Arabia, was opened, linking the capital with the north. In 1996 the Islamic Development Bank granted Djibouti a loan of US $3.6m. to finance road construction projects.

SHIPPING

Djibouti, which was established as a free port in 1981, handled 720,000 metric tons of freight in 1997.

Port Autonome International de Djibouti: BP 2107, Djibouti; tel. 352331; fax 356187; e-mail port@intnet.dj; internet www.port.dj; Dir ADEN AHMED DOUALE.

Maritime and Transit Service: rue de Marseille, BP 680, Djibouti; tel. 353204; fax 354149.

Principal Shipping Agents

Almis Shipping Line & Transport Co: BP 85, Djibouti; tel. 356996; fax 356998; Man. Dir MOHAMED NOOR.

Cie Générale Maritime: 3 rue Marchand, BP 182, Djibouti; tel. 353825; fax 354778; Gen. Man. HENRI FERRAND.

Cie Maritime et de Manutention de Djibouti: ave des Messageries Maritimes, BP 89, Djibouti; tel. 351028; fax 350466; e-mail comad@intnet.dj; internet www.intnet.dj/comad/index.htm; shipping agents and freight forwarders; Man. Dir ALI A. HETTAM.

Inchcape Shipping Services & Co (Djibouti) SA: 9–11 rue de Genève, BP 81, Djibouti; tel. 353844; fax 353294; e-mail iss@intnet.dj; f. 1942; Dir-Gen. AHMED OSMAN GELLEH.

J. J. Kothari & Co Ltd: rue d'Athens, BP 171, Djibouti; tel. 350219; fax 351778; e-mail kothari@intnet.dj; shipping agents; also ship managers, stevedores, freight forwarders; Dirs S. J. KOTHARI, NALIN KOTHARI.

Mitchell Cotts Djibouti SARL: blvd de la République, BP 85, Djibouti; tel. 351204; fax 355851; Dir FAHMY SAID CASSIM.

Société Maritime L. Savon et Ries: blvd Cheikh Osman, BP 2125, Djibouti; tel. 352351; fax 351103; Gen. Man. J. P. DELARUE.

CIVIL AVIATION

The international airport is at Ambouli, 6 km from Djibouti. There are six other airports providing domestic services.

Air Djibouti (Red Sea Airlines): BP 499, rue Marchand, Djibouti; tel. 356723; fax 356734; f. 1971; fmrly govt-owned, transferred to private ownership in 1997; internal flights and international services to points in Africa, the Middle East and Europe; Chair. SAAD BEN MOUSSA AL-JANAIBI.

Daallo Airlines: BP 2565, Djibouti; tel. 353401; fax 351765; internet www.daallo.com; f. 1992; regional carrier operating services to Somalia, Saudi Arabia and the United Arab Emirates; Man. Dir MOHAMED IBRAHIM YASSIN.

Djibouti Airlines (Puntavia Airline de Djibouti): BP 2240, place Lagarde, Djibouti; tel. 351006; fax 352429; f. 1996; scheduled and charter regional and domestic flights; Man. Dir Mr VABERI.

Tourism

Djibouti offers desert scenery in its interior and watersport facilities on its coast. A casino operates in the capital. There were about 20,000 tourist arrivals in 1996, when receipts from tourism totalled US $4m.

Office National du Tourisme de Djibouti (ONTD): place du 27 juin, BP 1938, Djibouti; tel. 353790; fax 356322; e-mail onta@intnet.dj; Dir MOHAMED ABDILLAHI WAIS.

DOMINICA

Introductory Survey

Location, Climate, Language, Religion, Flag, Capital

The Commonwealth of Dominica is situated in the Windward Islands group of the West Indies, lying between Guadeloupe, to the north, and Martinique, to the south. The climate is tropical, though tempered by sea winds which sometimes reach hurricane force, especially from July to September. The average temperature is about 27°C (80°F), with little seasonal variation. Rainfall is heavy, especially in the mountainous areas, where the annual average is 6,350 mm (250 ins), compared with 1,800 mm (70 ins) along the coast. English is the official language, but a local French patois, or Creole, is widely spoken. In parts of the northeast an English dialect, known as Cocoy, is spoken by the descendents of Antiguan settlers. There is a small community of Carib Indians on the east coast. Almost all of the inhabitants profess Christianity, and about 80% are Roman Catholics. The national flag (proportions 2 by 1) has a green field, with equal stripes of yellow, white and black forming an upright cross, on the centre of which is superimposed a red disc containing a parrot surrounded by ten five-pointed green stars (one for each of the island's parishes). The capital is Roseau.

Recent History

Dominica was first settled by Arawaks and then Caribs. Control of the island was fiercely contested by the Caribs, British and French during the 17th and 18th centuries. The British eventually prevailed and Dominica formed part of the Leeward Islands federation until 1939. In 1940 it was transferred to the Windward Islands and remained attached to that group until the federal arrangement was ended in December 1959. Under a new Constitution, effective from January 1960, Dominica (like each other member of the group) achieved a separate status, with its own Administrator and an enlarged Legislative Council.

At the January 1961 elections to the Legislative Council, the ruling Dominica United People's Party was defeated by the Dominica Labour Party (DLP), formed from the People's National Movement and other groups. Edward LeBlanc, leader of the DLP, became Chief Minister. In March 1967 Dominica became one of the West Indies Associated States, gaining full autonomy in internal affairs, with the United Kingdom retaining responsibility for defence and foreign relations. The Legislative Council was replaced by the House of Assembly, the Administrator became Governor and the Chief Minister was restyled Premier. At elections to the House in October 1970, LeBlanc was returned to power as Premier.

In July 1974 LeBlanc retired, and was replaced as DLP leader and Premier by Patrick John, formerly Deputy Premier and Minister of Finance. At elections to the enlarged House of Assembly in March 1975 the DLP was returned to power. Following a decision in 1975 by the Associated States to seek independence separately, Dominica became an independent republic within the Commonwealth on 3 November 1978. John became Prime Minister, and Frederick Degazon, formerly Speaker of the House of Assembly, was eventually elected President.

In May 1979 two people were killed by the Defence Force at a demonstration against the Government's attempts to introduce legislation that would restrict the freedom of the trade unions and the press. The deaths fuelled increasing popular opposition to the Government, and a pressure group, the Committee for National Salvation (CNS), was formed to campaign for John's resignation. Government opponents organized a general strike which lasted 25 days, with John relinquishing power only after all his cabinet ministers had resigned and President Degazon had gone into hiding abroad (there was a succession of Acting Presidents; Degazon finally resigned in February 1980). Oliver Seraphin, the candidate proposed by the CNS, was elected Prime Minister, and an interim Government was formed to prepare for a general election after six months.

A general election was eventually held in July 1980, when the Dominica Freedom Party (DFP) achieved a convincing victory, winning 17 of the 21 elective seats in the House of Assembly. Eugenia Charles, the party's leader, became the Caribbean's first female Prime Minister. Both John, who contested the

election as leader of the DLP, and Seraphin, who stood as leader of the newly-formed Democratic Labour Party (DEMLAB), lost their seats. The DLP and DEMLAB had both suffered from major political scandals prior to the election.

Fears for the island's security dominated 1981. In January the Government disarmed the Defence Force (which was officially disbanded in April), following reports that weapons were being traded for marijuana. Against a background of increasing violence and the declaration of a state of emergency, however, there were two coup attempts involving former Defence Force members. John, the former Prime Minister, was also implicated and imprisoned. In June 1982 John and his fellow prisoners were tried and acquitted, but the Government secured a retrial in October 1985. John and the former Deputy Commander of the Defence Force each received a prison sentence of 12 years (they were released in May 1990). In 1986 the former Commander of the Defence Force was hanged for the murder of a police officer during the second coup attempt. The death sentences on five other soldiers were commuted to life imprisonment.

After his release in June 1982, John attempted to form a new left-wing coalition party. By 1985 the DLP, DEMLAB, the United Dominica Labour Party and the Dominica Liberation Movement had united to form a left-wing grouping, known as the Labour Party of Dominica (LPD). The new leader, however, was Michael Douglas, a former Minister of Finance. At a general election in July 1985 the DFP was returned to power, winning 15 of the 21 elective seats in the House of Assembly. The opposition LPD won five seats, with the remaining seat being won by Roosevelt (Rosie) Douglas, the brother of the LPD leader, whose candidature was not officially endorsed by the LPD. Following the election, the LPD began an 18-month boycott of the House, in protest at the Government's decision to curtail live broadcasts of parliamentary proceedings. By July 1987, the DFP's strength in the House had increased to 17 seats, with four seats still being held by the LPD.

Dissatisfaction at continued government austerity measures was offset by the success of the land reform programme. Since independence, the Government had acquired nearly all the large estates, often in an attempt to forestall violence. In 1986 the first of the estates was divided, and tenure granted to the former workers. Despite the success of this programme, the opposition LPD and the Dominica United Workers' Party (UWP—formed in 1988) bitterly denounced many other government policies and criticized Charles's style of leadership. The two opposition parties failed to agree on the formation of an electoral alliance, however, and the DFP was returned for a third term in government at a general election in May 1990. The DFP won a total of 11 seats, the UWP became the official opposition (with six seats) and the LPD won four seats. The results were reported to indicate the electorate's disenchantment with the traditional parties; participation and voting preferences were determined by personality rather than policy.

A programme, introduced in August 1991, granting Dominican citizenship to foreigners in return for a minimum investment of US $35,000 in the country caused considerable controversy during 1992. The UWP expressed opposition to the policy, and a pressure group, 'Concerned Citizens', organized protests demanding that the programme be modified. In response to such pressure, the Government announced in July that the minimum investment was to be increased substantially, the number of applications was to be limited to 800 and restrictions were to be placed on the investors' right to vote in Dominica. By early 1995 some 615 people (mainly Taiwanese) had been granted citizenship under the scheme, and about US $7.1m. had been invested in the country.

In 1993, following the retirement of President Clarence Seignoret, Crispin Sorhaindo, formerly the Speaker of the House of Assembly, was appointed to the presidency. He assumed office in October.

At a general election in June 1995 the DFP's 15-year tenure was finally ended, with the party winning only five seats. The LPD also won five seats, while the UWP secured a narrow victory, with 11 seats and 34.5% of total votes cast (compared with 35.8% for the DFP). Some observers attributed the DFP's poor performance in the election to Charles's failure to give full support to her successor, Brian Alleyne, upon her retirement. The leader of the UWP, Edison James, was subsequently appointed as Prime Minister, and the LPD and DFP leaders agreed to occupy the position of Leader of the Opposition in alternate years, commencing with Alleyne. In July a legal dispute arose concerning the eligibility to serve in the House of Assembly of one of the DFP's members, Charles Savarin, owing to a potential conflict of interests. As a result of the dispute, the position of Leader of the Opposition was transferred to the LPD leader, Rosie Douglas. In April 1996, however, Savarin was elected leader of the DFP following Alleyne's resignation, which had been prompted by his appointment as a judge in Grenada. In August a by-election for Alleyne's seat was won by the UWP candidate, thus increasing the Government's representation in the House of Assembly to 12 seats. Government support for a long-term programme to privatize several state-owned enterprises and to implement structural adjustment measures (recommended by the International Monetary Fund—IMF) attracted criticism from the opposition in 1996–97, as well as from the Civil Service Association, which pledged its resistance to any retrenchment in the sector.

In April 1997 an investigation of the police force was conducted, following allegations of corruption. In November the Prime Minister announced that the Police Commissioner, Desmond Blanchard, his deputy and five other officers had been sent on leave, owing to the findings of the report. In April 1998 Rosie Douglas announced that he was taking legal action against the Government, on the grounds that it had acted unconstitutionally by failing to give him a copy of the report. Meanwhile, in 1997 the Government established a Constitutional Commission to examine several issues, including civil rights, standards in public service, the responsibility of politicians and public involvement in government.

In December 1997 the Government's citizenship programme (see above) again provoked controversy. *The Independent Newspaper* reported that, under the scheme, passports were being sold by agents for between US $15,000 and $20,000, and claimed that about 400 people (including 80 Russians and 50 Chinese) had acquired citizenship in 1997. The opposition LPD accused the Government of undermining the credibility of Dominican citizenship, and in August 1998 Rosie Douglas demanded an inquiry into the programme, following an administrative error which had allowed an Australian, who was sought by investigators in connection with a business collapse, to acquire citizenship. In late 1999 it was announced that the Dominican Government had stopped granting citizenship to Russians, following reports that up to 300 Russians had paid US $50,000 each to obtain a Dominican passport. In addition, there were complaints from the US Government that the trade in passports had increased 'suspicions of money laundering' in Dominica.

In early 1998 the LPD complained to the Electoral Boundaries Commission, accusing the Government of proposing changes to the boundaries of six electoral constituencies (four of which were regarded as LPD strongholds) purely for political gain. In November the High Court upheld the opposition's complaint, ruling that the proposed alterations were unconstitutional. (This judgment was endorsed by the Eastern Caribbean Court of Appeal in May 1999.)

In early October 1998 President Sorhaindo's five-year term in office ended. Following the failure of the Prime Minister and the Leader of the Opposition to agree on a joint nominee, the House of Assembly held a secret ballot to elect the new President. Vernon Shaw, a former cabinet secretary in the previous administration of Eugenia Charles, was duly elected and assumed the presidency on 6 October.

On 1 January 2000 the Prime Minister unexpectedly called a general election, to be held on 31 January. The DFP accused James of breaking a 1995 undertaking to give at least 90 days' notice of an election (which was not due constitutionally until June), and formed an electoral alliance with the LPD. The UWP suffered a narrow electoral defeat, while the LPD was returned to power after two decades in opposition, winning 10 of the 21 elective seats in the House of Assembly and receiving 42.9% of total votes cast. The UWP secured nine seats (with 43.4% of the votes), and the DFP won two. The leader of the LPD, Rosie Douglas, was named as Prime Minister and formed a coalition Government with the DFP (which was allocated two ministerial portfolios).

On taking office, the new Government immediately suspended the controversial citizenship programme. However, following a review, in April 2000 the Government announced that the programme should be resumed, claiming that changes had been made to ensure that passports would not be granted to those with a criminal record.

In July 2000 Atherton Martin, the Minister for Agriculture, Planning and the Environment, resigned from his post after the Government voted against the establishment of a South Pacific whaling sanctuary at a meeting of the International Whaling Commission in Australia. The vote was reported to be contrary to a cabinet agreement to abstain. Martin claimed that Japan had threatened to withdraw funding for two fish processing plants in Dominica if the Government abstained, and accused the Japanese Government of 'international extortion'. Martin was replaced by Lloyd Pascal, hitherto Dominica's whaling commissioner.

On 1 October 2000 the Prime Minister, Rosie Douglas, died suddenly of a heart attack. Two days later, following a vote in the House of Assembly, Pierre Charles, previously the Minister of Communications and Works, was sworn in as premier. Reginald Austrie succeeded him as Minister of Communications and Works. On 11 December a by-election for Douglas's seat was won by his nephew, Ian Douglas, the candidate of the LPD, thus maintaining the Government's narrow parliamentary majority.

In December 2000 legislation was passed in the House of Assembly making the crime of money laundering punishable by up to seven years' imprisonment and a fine of EC $1m. At the same time, the Government introduced stricter regulations governing its 'offshore' banking sector, following Dominica's inclusion on blacklists published by the Organisation for Economic Co-operation and Development and the Financial Action Task Force earlier in the year.

In foreign policy, Dominica has close links with France and the USA. France helped in suppressing the coup attempts against the DFP Government in 1981, and Dominica was the first Commonwealth country to benefit from the French aid agency FAC. In October 1983 Dominica, as a member of the Organisation of Eastern Caribbean States (OECS—see p. 309), contributed forces to the US-backed invasion of Grenada. In 1988 four countries of the Windward group (Dominica, Grenada, Saint Lucia and Saint Vincent and the Grenadines) decided to proceed with plans for the formation of a political union. In 1990 the four countries decided to convene a constituent assembly, which in early 1992 agreed a draft constitution, including provision for the election of an executive president by universal suffrage. Following its election in mid-1995, the Government of Edison James stated its commitment to further economic integration of the Windward Islands, leading to political union.

Government

Legislative power is vested in the unicameral House of Assembly, comprising 30 members (nine nominated and 21 elected for five years by universal adult suffrage). Executive authority is vested in the President, who is elected by the House, but in most matters the President is guided by the advice of the Cabinet and acts as the constitutional Head of State. He appoints the Prime Minister, who must be able to command a majority in the House, and (on the Prime Minister's recommendation) other ministers. The Cabinet is responsible to the House. The island is divided into 10 administrative divisions, known as parishes, and there is limited local government in Roseau, the capital, and in the Carib Territory.

Defence

The Dominican Defence Force was officially disbanded in 1981. There is a police force of about 300, which includes a coastguard service. The country participates in the US-sponsored Regional Security System.

Economic Affairs

In 1999, according to estimates by the World Bank, Dominica's gross national product (GNP), measured at average 1997–99 prices, was US $231m., equivalent to US $3,170 per head (or $4,825 per head on an international purchasing-power parity basis). Between 1990 and 1998, it was estimated, GNP per head increased, in real terms, at an average rate of 1.1% per year. Between 1990 and 1998 the population increased by an average of 0.1% per year. Gross domestic product (GDP), in real terms, increased by an average of 2.2% per year in 1990–97. Real GDP growth was 2.0% in 1997, 3.5% in 1998 and an estimated 0.4%

in 1999. In 1999 GDP stood at EC $601.3m. The slowdown in economic growth in this year was largely attributable to the weak performance of the major productive sectors.

Agriculture (including forestry and fishing) is the principal economic activity, accounting for an estimated 16.9% of GDP in 1999. In 1997 the sector engaged 23.7% of the employed labour force. The principal cash crop is bananas. The banana industry, which was already experiencing difficulties (owing to a decline in prices), was adversely affected by a September 1997 ruling of the World Trade Organization (WTO—see p. 292) against Dominica's preferential access to the European (particularly the British) market. In 1998 banana production decreased by some 27%, to some 30,000 metric tons, while receipts from banana exports fell by 8.9% to EC $42.2m. (some 24.8% of total domestic exports). In 1999, according to the FAO, banana output remained at the same level. Other important crops include coconuts (which provide copra for export as well as edible oil and soap), mangoes, avocados, papayas, ginger, citrus fruits and, mainly for domestic consumption, vegetables. Livestock-rearing and fishing are also practised for local purposes. In mid-1997 construction of a fishing port and market in Roseau was completed. Dominica has extensive timber reserves (more than 40% of the island's total land area is forest and woodland), and international aid agencies are encouraging the development of a balanced timber industry. The GDP of the agricultural sector decreased at an average annual rate of 1.0% in 1990–99. In real terms, agricultural GDP declined by 1.5% in 1997, by 2.0% in 1998 and by 0.4% in 1999.

Industry (comprising mining, manufacturing, construction and utilities) provided 20.6% of GDP in 1999, and employed 18.2% of the employed labour force in 1997. Industrial GDP increased at an average rate of 2.4% per year during 1990–99; however, industrial GDP contracted by 4.3% in 1999, owing to a decline in the manufacturing sector. Manufacturing activity is mainly small-scale and dependent upon agriculture. The mining sector contributed only 0.7% of GDP in 1999. There is some quarrying of pumice, and there are extensive reserves of limestone and clay. In 1996 an Australian mining company began investigations into the possible exploitation of extensive copper deposits in north-eastern Dominica. Pumice is useful to the construction industry, which accounted for 7.0% of GDP in 1999, and employed 8.4% of the employed labour force in 1997. Extensive infrastructure development by the Government has maintained high levels of activity in the construction sector in recent years. The GDP of the construction sector increased at an average annual rate of 2.1% in 1990–99; however, the sector's GDP contracted by 1.7% in 1997 and by 8.0% in 1998, but increased by 5.0% in 1999. The Government has also encouraged the manufacturing sector in an attempt to diversify the economy. In 1999 manufacturing contributed 7.8% of GDP and, in 1997, employed 8.8% of the employed work-force. Manufacturing GDP increased at an average rate of 0.9% per year during 1990–9; it rose by 16.8% in 1998, largely owing to an 18.8% increase in the output of soap products, but also to the production of toothpaste, which began in November 1997. However, in 1999, a significant decline in soap production resulted in a 19% contraction in the sector's GDP. There is a banana-packaging plant and factories for the manufacturing and refining of crude and edible vegetable oils and for the production of soap, canned juices and cigarettes. A brewery was established in 1995 to supply domestic requirements. Furniture, paint, cardboard boxes and candles are also significant manufactures.

In 2000 70% of Dominica's energy requirements were supplied by hydroelectric power. Investment in a hydroelectric development scheme and in the water supply system has been partially financed by the export of water, from Dominica's extensive reserves, to drier Caribbean islands such as Aruba. A hydroelectric power-station, with a generating capacity of 1.24 MW, began operation at Laudat in 1990. By 1997 Dominica had reduced imports of mineral fuels to 6.8% of the cost of total imports. In 1995 a US company announced that it would invest EC $25m. in a geothermal energy project in Soufrière, which began producing electricity in 1998. In December 1996 the state-owned Dominica Electricity Services (DOMLEC) was privatized, with the British Government's overseas private finance institution, the Commonwealth Development Corporation (CDC), buying 72% of the company. The CDC outlined plans to increase electricity generation by 80% by 2000. Construction of a new 20-MW electric power plant, at an estimated cost of EC $80m., was scheduled to begin in mid-1999 and was due for completion by early 2001. However, in November 2000 a demonstration took

place outside DOMLEC's headquarters in protest at the company's failure to improve efficiency following its transfer to the private sector.

Services engaged 53.8% of the employed labour force in 1997, and provided 62.5% of GDP in 1999. The combined GDP of the service sectors increased at an average rate of 3.6% per year during 1990–99; in 1999 the growth rate was 3.8%. The tourist industry is of increasing importance to the economy and exploits Dominica's natural history and scenery. Since 1998 the Government has placed considerable emphasis on the country's potential as an 'eco-tourism' destination, pursuing a development programme funded by the European Union (EU). The majority of tourists are cruise-ship passengers. Arrivals from cruise ships increased from 6,777 in 1990 to 64,762 in the following year, and by 1998 totalled 240,905. In 1999, however, cruise ship arrivals fell to 202,003. In 1999 tourism receipts totalled EC $131.8m. In 1990 the Government decided to proceed with the construction of an international airport. However, in 2000 the administration was still experiencing problems in securing the necessary finance for the project, although the Republic of China (Taiwan) had pledged US $35m. The 1999/2000 budget proposals allocated capital expenditure of US $28m. to the construction of the airport and related infrastructure, estimated to cost a total of US $110m. In early 2001 a study of the proposed sites for the airport was due to begin.

In 1999 Dominica recorded a visible trade deficit of EC $185.60m. and a deficit of EC $103.58m. on the current account of the balance of payments. The principal source of imports in 1999 was the USA, which accounted for 38.3% of total imports, followed by Trinidad and Tobago (13.9%) and the United Kingdom (10.4%). The principal market for exports is Jamaica, which, in 1999, received 26.5% of total exports. The United Kingdom, which receives virtually all Dominica's banana production, received 25.1% of total domestic exports in 1999. The principal imports are food and live animals, basic manufactures (such as paper), and machinery and transport equipment. The principal exports are bananas and soap.

In 1999 there was an estimated budget deficit of EC $74.0m. Recurrent expenditure for the financial year ending 30 June 2000 was projected to increase by 8.1%, to EC $223.3m., while capital expenditure was forecast to increase to EC $322.0m. At the end of 1998 Dominica's total external debt was US $108.9m., of which US $90.9m. was long-term public debt. In that year the cost of debt-servicing was equivalent to 6.7% of the value of exports of goods and services. The annual rate of inflation averaged 2.4% in 1990–98; consumer prices increased by an average of 2.5% in 1997, but by only 1.0% in 1998 and by 1.1% in 1999. An estimated 23.1% of the labour force were unemployed in 1997.

Dominica is a member of the Organization of American States (OAS—see p. 261), the Caribbean Community and Common Market (CARICOM, see p. 142), the OECS, and is a signatory of the Lomé Conventions with the EU (see p. 206). Under the Charles administration, the island received considerable aid from the United Kingdom, France, the USA and various international aid agencies.

The Dominican economy is heavily dependent on the production of coconut-based products and bananas, and their export to a limited market, and is thus vulnerable to adverse weather conditions, price fluctuations and economic conditions in its principal markets. In the 1990s growth in the economy slowed, owing to the uncertainty surrounding Dominica's preferential access to the European market and the devastation of the 1995 banana crop by a hurricane. Efforts to expand the country's economic base have been impeded by poor infrastructure and, in terms of tourism, a paucity of desirable beaches. However, by the late 1990s the tourist sector was expanding steadily, aided by an 'eco-tourism' development programme with EU funding. In 1998 the pace of economic activity increased, largely owing to strong growth in the manufacturing and services sectors, but slowed down again in 1999. Banana exports decreased in both 1998 and 1999, owing to drought, a fall in producer prices and uncertainties caused by the WTO's ruling in September 1997 against the EU's banana import regime. Many marginal farmers were unable to attain the new stringent quality standards of the industry, another contributing factor in the decline in banana output. However, the banana sector was expected to recover in 2000. In the 1998/99 budget, in an effort to make the tax system more efficient, the Government announced the implementation of value-added tax (VAT), which was to be introduced over two years, and changes to income tax. Budget proposals for 1999/2000 focused on the planned construction of an international airport, which was expected to expedite further expansion of the tourism industry. The likely expansion of the construction industry in 2000, however, was expected to widen the current account deficit, as imports increased.

Social Welfare

There are main hospitals at Roseau and Portsmouth, with 136 and 50 beds respectively, and two cottage hospitals, at Marigot and Grand Bay. There is a polyclinic at the Princess Margaret Hospital, Roseau. There are 51 health centres, located throughout the island. In 1996 Dominica had one hospital bed for every 88 citizens, and one physician for every 225 inhabitants.

Education

Education is free and is provided by both government and denominational schools. There are also a number of schools for the mentally and physically handicapped. Education is compulsory for 10 years between five and 15 years of age. Primary education begins at the age of five and lasts for seven years. Enrolment of children in the primary age-group was 70.7% in 1992. Secondary education, beginning at 12 years of age, lasts

for five years. A teacher-training college and nursing school provide further education, and there is also a branch of the University of the West Indies on the island. In 1997 the Government announced plans to invest EC $17.9m. in a Basic Education Reform project. The rate of adult illiteracy was 6.0% in 1996.

Public Holidays

2001: 1 January (New Year's Day), 26–27 February (Masquerade, Carnival), 13 April (Good Friday), 16 April (Easter Monday), 1 May (May or Labour Day), 4 June (Whit Monday), 6 August (Emancipation, August Monday), 3 November (Independence Day), 4 November (Community Service Day), 25–26 December (Christmas).

2002: 1 January (New Year's Day), 11–12 February (Masquerade, Carnival), 29 March (Good Friday), 1 April (Easter Monday), 1 May (May or Labour Day), 20 May (Whit Monday), 5 August (Emancipation, August Monday), 3 November (Independence Day), 4 November (Community Service Day), 25–26 December (Christmas).

Weights and Measures

The metric system is replacing the imperial system of weights and measures.

Statistical Survey

Sources (unless otherwise stated): Ministry of Finance, Roseau; OECS Economic Affairs Secretariat, *Annual Digest of Statistics*.

AREA AND POPULATION

Area: 751 sq km (290 sq miles).

Population: 69,548 at census of 7 April 1970; 73,795 at census of 7 April 1981; 71,183 (males 35,471, females 35,712) at census of 12 May 1991; 75,871 (official estimate) at mid-1998.

Density (mid-1998): 101.0 per sq km.

Population by Ethnic Group (*de jure* population, excl. those resident in institutions, 1981): Negro 67,272; Mixed race 4,433; Amerindian (Carib) 1,111; White 341; Total (incl. others) 73,795 (males 36,754, females 37,041). Source: UN, *Demographic Yearbook*.

Principal Town (population at 1991 census): Roseau (capital) 15,853.

Births, Marriages and Deaths (registrations, 1998): Live births 1,230 (birth rate 16.2 per 1,000); Marriages (1996) 230 (marriage rate 3.1 per 1,000); Deaths 595 (death rate 7.8 per 1,000). Source: UN *Demographic Yearbook* and *Vital Statistics Report*.

Expectation of Life (UN estimates, years at birth, 1990–95): 67.8 (males 64.1; females 71.4). Source: ECLAC Demography Unit.

Economically Active Population (rounded estimates, persons aged 15 years and over, 1997): Agriculture, hunting, forestry and fishing 6,000; Fishing 100; Manufacturing 2,250; Electricity, gas and water supply 280; Construction 2,150; Wholesale and retail trade 4,050; Hotels and restaurants 980; Transport, storage and communications 1,500; Financial intermediation 540; Real estate, renting and business activities 850; Public administration, defence and social security 1,530; Education 1,260; Health and social work 1,110; Other community, social and personal service activities 930; Private households with employed persons 1,080; Not classifiable by economic activity 1,090; Total employed 25,690; Unemployed 7,720; Total labour force 33,420 (males 18,120; females 15,300). Source: ILO.

AGRICULTURE, ETC.

Principal Crops (FAO estimates, '000 metric tons, 1999): Sweet potatoes 1.8; Cassava 0.9; Yams 7.8; Taro (Dasheen) 11.0; Other roots and tubers 5.5; Coconuts 1.0; Cabbages 0.6; Pumpkins 0.8; Cucumbers 1.6; Carrots 0.5; Other vegetables 2.8; Sugar cane 4.3; Oranges 8.4; Lemons and limes 1.0; Grapefruit 0.5; Mangoes 1.8; Bananas 30; Plantains 10.0. Source: FAO.

Livestock (FAO estimates, '000 head, year ending September 1999): Cattle 13; Pigs 5; Sheep 8; Goats 10. Source: FAO.

Livestock Products (FAO estimates, '000 metric tons, 1999): Beef and veal 1; Cows' milk 6. Source: FAO.

Fishing (metric tons, live weight, 1998): Capture 1,212 (Marine fishes 1,212); Aquaculture 5; Total catch 1,217. Source: FAO, *Yearbook of Fishery Statistics*.

MINING

Pumice ('000 metric tons, incl. volcanic ash): Estimated production 100 per year in 1988–99 (Source: US Geological Survey).

INDUSTRY

Production (1996, metric tons, unless otherwise indicated): Soap 14,815; Crude coconut oil 753 (estimate); Edible coconut oil 82 (estimate); Coconut meal 350 (estimate); Electricity 37 million kWh*.

* Source: UN, *Industrial Commodity Statistics Yearbook*.

FINANCE

Currency and Exchange Rates: 100 cents = 1 Eastern Caribbean dollar (EC $). *Sterling, US Dollar and Euro Equivalents* (29 December 2000): £1 sterling = EC $4.029; US $1 = EC $2.700; €1 = EC $2.512; EC $100 = £24.82 = US $37.04 = €39.80. *Exchange Rate:* Fixed at US $1 = EC $2.70 since July 1976.

Budget (estimates, EC $ million, 1999): *Revenue:* Tax revenue 168.4; Other current revenue 32.1; Capital revenue 3.1; Total 203.6, excl. grants received (11.6). *Expenditure:* Current expenditure 206.5 (Wages and salaries 116.5); Capital expenditure and net lending 82.7; Total 289.2. Source: Eastern Caribbean Central Bank, *Report and Statement of Accounts* (2000).

International Reserves (US $ million at 31 December 1999): Reserve position in IMF 0.01; Foreign exchange 31.55; Total 31.57. Source: IMF, *International Financial Statistics*.

Money Supply (EC $ million at 31 December 1999): Currency outside banks 34.09; Demand deposits at commercial banks 95.00; Total money (incl. others) 130.18. Source: IMF, *International Financial Statistics*.

Cost of Living (Retail Price Index, base: 1995 = 100): All items 104.2 in 1997; 105.2 in 1998; 106.4 in 1999. Source: IMF, *International Financial Statistics*.

National Accounts (EC $ million at current prices): Gross domestic product in purchasers' values 638.4 in 1996; 660.0 in 1997; 693.6 in 1998. Source: IMF, *International Financial Statistics*.

Expenditure on the Gross Domestic Product (EC $ million at current prices, 1998): Government final consumption expenditure 162.9; Private final consumption expenditure 403.7; Gross fixed capital formation (incl. increase in stocks) 204.0; *Total domestic expenditure* 729.5; Exports of goods and services 374.0; *Less* Imports of goods and services 451.1; GDP in purchasers' values 693.6. Source: IMF, *International Financial Statistics*.

Gross Domestic Product by Economic Activity (EC $ million at current prices, 1999): Agriculture, hunting, forestry and fishing 111.4; Mining and quarrying 4.9; Manufacturing 51.0; Electricity and water 33.4; Construction 46.0; Wholesale and retail trade 70.6; Restaurants and hotels 16.2; Transport 56.4; Communications 51.7; Finance and insurance 69.3; Real estate and housing 20.3; Government services 116.5; Other services 9.7; Sub-total 657.4; *Less* imputed bank service charge 56.1; GDP at factor cost 601.3. Source: Eastern Caribbean Central Bank, *Statistical Digest* (December 2000).

Balance of Payments (EC $ million, 1999): Exports of goods f.o.b. 147.44; Imports of goods f.o.b. –333.04; *Trade balance* –185.60; Exports of services 265.13; Imports of services –164.17; *Balance on goods and services* –84.64; Other income received 12.49; Other income paid –78.51; *Balance on goods, services and income* –150.66; Current transfers received 62.02; Current transfers paid –14.94; *Current balance* –103.58; Capital account (net) 34.07; Direct investment from abroad 48.48; Portfolio investment liabilities 102.39; Portfolio investment assets –26.22; Other investment liabilities 27.03; Other investment assets –55.30; Net errors and omissions –15.33; *Overall balance* –11.54. Source: Eastern Caribbean Central Bank, *Balance of Payments* (2000).

EXTERNAL TRADE

Principal Commodities (EC $ '000, 1997): *Imports c.i.f.*: Meat and meat preparation 15,379; Butter, milk and cheese 10,213; Alcoholic beverages 7,582; Wood and lumber 11,171; Motor spirit (petrol) 9,449; Diesel oil 8,656; Metals and metal products 22,038; Machinery (non-electric) 33,738; Electric machinery 24,364; Transport equipment 24,734; Total (incl. others) 363,142. *Exports f.o.b.*: Bananas 46,331; Plantains 5,111; Paints, varnishes and lacquers 3,949; Toothpaste 2,947; Soap 44,289; Disinfectant 3,985; Total (incl. others) 138,652, excl. re-exports (2,606).

Principal Trading Partners (EC $ million, estimates, 1999): *Imports c.i.f.*: Barbados 14,558; Canada 7,865; France 9,880; Germany 5,085; Guadeloupe 4,545; Jamaica 5,589; Netherlands 5,772; Saint Lucia 6,903; Saint Vincent and the Grenadines 7,746; Trinidad and Tobago 52,999; United Kingdom 39,745; USA 145,922; Total (incl. others) 381,300. *Exports f.o.b.*: Antigua and Barbuda 11,152; Barbados 8,272; France 9,810; Grenada 1,443; Guadeloupe 8,671; Guyana 10,019; Jamaica 43,689; Saint Christopher and Nevis 3,367; Saint Lucia 6,238; Saint Vincent and the Grenadines 2,840; Trinidad and Tobago 9,580; United Kingdom 41,424; USA 5,679; Total (incl. others) 164,972.

TRANSPORT

Road Traffic (motor vehicles licensed in 1994): Private cars 6,491; Taxis 90; Buses 559; Motorcycles 94; Trucks 2,266; Jeeps 461; Tractors 24; Total 9,985.

Shipping: *Merchant Fleet* (registered at 31 December 1998): 8 vessels (total displacement 2,522 grt) (Source: Lloyd's Register of Shipping, *World Fleet Statistics*); *International freight traffic* ('000 metric tons, estimates, 1993): Goods loaded 103.2; Goods unloaded 181.2.

Civil Aviation (1997): Aircraft arrivals and departures 18,672; Freight loaded 363 metric tons; Freight unloaded 575 metric tons.

TOURISM

Tourist Arrivals: *Stop-overs:* 65,446 in 1997; 65,501 in 1998; 70,791 in 1999. *Cruise-ship passengers:* 230,581 in 1997; 240,905 in 1998;

202,003 in 1999. *Excursionists:* 3,310 in 1997; 1,447 in 1998; 3,924 in 1999. Source: Eastern Caribbean Central Bank, *Balance of Payments* (2000).

Tourism Receipts (EC $ million): 106.8 in 1997; 125.6 in 1998; 131.8 in 1999. Source: Eastern Caribbean Central Bank, *Balance of Payments* (2000).

COMMUNICATIONS MEDIA

Radio Receivers (1997): 45,000 in use.

Television Receivers (1997): 6,000 in use.

Telephones (1996): 19,000 main lines in use.

Telefax Stations (1996): 396 in use.

Non-daily Newspapers (1996): 1.

Source: mainly UNESCO, *Statistical Yearbook*.

EDUCATION

Institutions (1994/95): Pre-primary 72 (1992/93); Primary 64; Secondary 14; Tertiary 2.

Teachers: Pre-primary 131 (1992/93); Primary 628 (1994/95); Secondary 269 (1994/95); Tertiary 34 (1992/93).

Pupils (1997/98): Pre-primary 3,000 (1992/93); Primary 13,418; Secondary 5,772; Tertiary 461 (1995/96).

Sources: UNESCO, *Statistical Yearbook*; Caribbean Development Bank, *Selected Indicators of Development*; UN Economic Commission for Latin America and the Caribbean, *Statistical Yearbook*.

Directory

The Constitution

The Constitution came into effect at the independence of Dominica on 3 November 1978. Its main provisions are summarized below:

FUNDAMENTAL RIGHTS AND FREEDOMS

The Constitution guarantees the rights of life, liberty, security of the person, the protection of the law and respect for private property. The individual is entitled to freedom of conscience, of expression and assembly and has the right to an existence free from slavery, forced labour and torture. Protection against discrimination on the grounds of sex, race, place of origin, political opinion, colour or creed is assured.

THE PRESIDENT

The President is elected by the House of Assembly for a term of five years. A presidential candidate is nominated jointly by the Prime Minister and the Leader of the Opposition and on their concurrence is declared elected without any vote being taken; in the case of disagreement the choice will be made by secret ballot in the House of Assembly. Candidates must be citizens of Dominica aged at least 40 who have been resident in Dominica for five years prior to their nomination. A President may not hold office for more than two terms.

PARLIAMENT

Parliament consists of the President and the House of Assembly, composed of 21 elected Representatives and nine Senators. According to the wishes of Parliament, the latter may be appointed by the President—five on the advice of the Prime Minister and four on the advice of the Leader of the Opposition—or elected. The life of Parliament is five years.

Parliament has the power to amend the Constitution. Each constituency returns one Representative to the House who is directly elected in accordance with the Constitution. Every citizen over the age of 18 is eligible to vote.

THE EXECUTIVE

Executive authority is vested in the President. The President appoints as Prime Minister the elected member of the House who commands the support of a majority of its elected members, and other ministers on the advice of the Prime Minister. Not more than three ministers may be from among the appointed Senators. The President has the power to remove the Prime Minister from office if a resolution expressing 'no confidence' in the Government is adopted by the House and the Prime Minister does not resign within three days or advise the President to dissolve Parliament.

The Cabinet consists of the Prime Minister, other ministers and the Attorney-General in an ex officio capacity.

The Leader of the Opposition is appointed by the President as that elected member of the House who, in the President's judgement, is best able to command the support of a majority of the elected members who do not support the Government.

The Government

HEAD OF STATE

President: VERNON LORDEN SHAW (assumed office 6 October 1998).

CABINET
(April 2001)

A coalition of the Labour Party of Dominica (LPD) and the Dominica Freedom Party (DFP).

Prime Minister and Minister of Foreign Affairs, Legal Affairs, Labour and Carib Affairs: PIERRE CHARLES (LPD).

Minister of Communications and Works: REGINALD AUSTRIE (LPD).

Minister of Finance: AMBROSE GEORGE (LPD).

Minister of Trade, Industry and Marketing: OSBORNE RIVIERE (LPD).

Minister of Community Development and Women's Affairs: MATTHEW WALTER (LPD).

Minister of Housing and Planning: VINCE HENDERSON (LPD).

Minister of Sports and Youth Affairs: ROOSEVELT SKERRIT (LPD).

Minister of Tourism: CHARLES SAVARIN (DFP).

Minister of Health and Social Security: Sen. JOHN TOUSSAINT (LPD).

Minister of Education, Science and Technology: Sen. HERBERT SABROACHE (DFP).

Minister of Agriculture and the Environment: Sen. LLOYD PASCAL (LPD).

Attorney-General: BERNARD WILTSHIRE (LPD) (acting).

Minister of State: LOREEN BANNIS-ROBERTS.

MINISTRIES

Office of the President: Morne Bruce, Roseau; tel. 4482054; fax 4498366.

Office of the Prime Minister: Government Headquarters, Kennedy Ave, Roseau; tel. 4482401; fax 4485200.

All other ministries are at Government Headquarters, Kennedy Ave, Roseau; tel. 4482401.

CARIB TERRITORY

This reserve of the remaining Amerindian population is located on the central east coast of the island. The Caribs enjoy a measure of local government and elect their chief.

Chief: GARNET JOSEPH.

Waitukubuli Karifuna Development Committee: Salybia, Carib Territory; tel. 4457336.

Legislature

HOUSE OF ASSEMBLY

Speaker: F. OSBORNE G. SYMES.

Clerk: Mrs ALEX F. PHILLIP.

Senators: 9.

Elected Members: 21.

General Election, 31 January 2000

Party	Votes cast	%	Seats
Labour Party of Dominica . .	15,362	42.9	10
Dominica United Workers' Party . .	15,555	43.4	9
Dominica Freedom Party . .	4,858	13.6	2
Independents	29	0.1	—
Total	35,804	100.0	21

Political Organizations

Dominica Freedom Party (DFP): Great George St, Roseau; tel. 4482104; Leader CHARLES SAVARIN.

Dominica United Workers' Party (UWP): 37 Cork St, Roseau; tel. 4485051; f. 1988; Leader EDISON JAMES; Chair. GARNET L. DIDIER.

Labour Party of Dominica (LPD): Cork St, Roseau; tel. 4488511; f. 1985 as a merger and reunification of left-wing groups, incl. the Dominica Labour Party (DLP; f. 1961); Leader PIERRE CHARLES.

Diplomatic Representation

EMBASSIES IN DOMINICA

China (Taiwan): Checkhall, Massacre, POB 56, Roseau; tel. 4491385; fax 4492085; e-mail rocemb@cwdom.dom; Chargé d'affaires: R. C. WU.

Venezuela: 37 Cork St, 3rd Floor, POB 770, Roseau; tel. 4483348; fax 4486198; Ambassador: HERNANI ESCOBAR.

Judicial System

Justice is administered by the Eastern Caribbean Supreme Court (based in Saint Lucia), consisting of the Court of Appeal and the High Court. One of the six puisne judges of the High Court is resident in Dominica and presides over the Court of Summary Jurisdiction. The District Magistrate Courts deal with summary offences and civil offences involving limited sums of money (specified by law).

Religion

Most of the population profess Christianity, but there are some Muslims, Bahá'ís and Jews. The largest denomination is the Roman Catholic Church (with some 80% of the inhabitants in 1991).

CHRISTIANITY
The Roman Catholic Church

Dominica comprises the single diocese of Roseau, suffragan to the archdiocese of Castries (Saint Lucia). At 31 December 1998 there were an estimated 59,707 adherents in the country, representing a large majority of the inhabitants. The Bishop participates in the Antilles Episcopal Conference (currently based in Port of Spain, Trinidad).

Bishop of Roseau: Rt Rev. EDWARD J. GILBERT; Bishop's House, 20 Virgin Lane, POB 790, Roseau; tel. 4482837; fax 4483404; e-mail bishop@cwdom.dm.

The Anglican Communion

Anglicans in Dominica are adherents of the Church in the Province of the West Indies. The country forms part of the diocese of the North Eastern Caribbean and Aruba. The Bishop is resident in Antigua, and Archbishop of the Province is the Bishop of the Bahamas and the Turks and Caicos Islands.

Other Christian Churches

Christian Union Church of the West Indies: District 1, Rose St, Goodwill; tel. 4482725.

Other denominations include Methodist, Pentecostal, Baptist, Church of God, Presbyterian, the Assemblies of Brethren, Moravian and Seventh-day Adventist groups, and the Jehovah's Witnesses.

BAHÁ'Í FAITH

National Spiritual Assembly: 9 James Lane, POB 136, Roseau; tel. 4484269; fax 4483881; e-mail coolesp@cwdom.dm.

The Press

The Chronicle: Wallhouse, POB 1724, Roseau; tel. 4487887; fax 4480047; e-mail thechronicle@cwdom.dm; internet www.delphis.dm .chron.htm; f. 1996; Friday; progressive independent; Editor CHARLES HARDING; Gen. Man. J. ANTHONY WHITE; circ. 3,500.

The Independent Newspaper: POB 462, 9 Great Marlborough St, Roseau; tel. 4480221; fax 4484368; internet www.delphis.dm/ indpub; weekly.

Official Gazette: Government Printery, Roseau; tel. 4482401, ext. 330; weekly; circ. 550.

The Sun: Sun Inc., POB 2255, Roseau; tel. 4484744; fax 4484764; e-mail acsun@cwdom.dm; f. 1998; Editor CHARLES JAMES.

The Tropical Star: POB 1998, Roseau; tel. 4484634; fax 4485984; e-mail tpl@cwdom.dm; weekly; circ. 3,000.

Broadcasting and Communications

TELECOMMUNICATIONS

Cable & Wireless Dominica: Hanover St, POB 6, Roseau; tel. 448100; fax 4481111; internet www.tod.dm/index.htm; Gen. Man. CARL ROBERTS.

Telecommunications of Dominica (TOD): Mercury House, Hanover St, Roseau; tel. 4481024.

BROADCASTING
Radio

Dominica Broadcasting Corporation: Victoria St, POB 1, Roseau; tel. 4483283; fax 4482918; e-mail dbsradio@dbsradio.com; internet www.dbsradio.com; government station; daily broadcasts in English; 2 hrs daily in French patois; 10 kW transmitter on the medium wave band; FM service; programmes received throughout Caribbean excluding Jamaica and Guyana; Gen. Man. DENNIS JOSEPH; Programme Dir SHERMAINE GREEN-BROWN.

Kairi FM: Island Communications Corporation, Great George St, POB 931, Roseau; tel. 4487330; fax 4487332; e-mail kairfm@tod.dm; internet www.delphis.dm/kairi.htm; f. 1994.

Radio Enba Mango: Grand Bay; tel. 4463207.

Voice of Life Radio—ZGBC: Gospel Broadcasting Corpn, Loubiere, POB 205, Roseau; tel. 4487017; fax 4487094; e-mail volradio @tod.dm; linked to the US Christian Reformed Church; 112 hrs weekly AM, 24 hrs daily FM; Man. Dir GRANT HOEPPNER.

Television

There is no national television service, although there is a cable television network serving one-third of the island.

Marpin Telecom and Broadcasting: POB 2381, Roseau; tel. 4484107; fax 4482965; e-mail manager@marpin.dm; internet www.marpin.dm; commercial; cable service; Programme Man. RON ABRAHAM.

Finance

(cap. = capital; res = reserves; dep. = deposits; m. = million; amounts in East Caribbean dollars)

The Eastern Caribbean Central Bank (see p. XXX), based in Saint Christopher, is the central issuing and monetary authority for Dominica.

BANKS

Agricultural, Industrial and Development (AID) Bank: cnr Charles Avenue and Rawles Lane, Goodwill, POB 215, Roseau; tel. 4482853; fax 4484903; e-mail aidbank@cwdom.dm; f. 1971; responsible to Ministry of Finance; planned privatization suspended in 1997; cap. 9.5m. (1991); Chair. CRISPIN SORHAINDO; Man. PATRICIA CHARLES.

Bank of Nova Scotia—Scotiabank (Canada): 28 Hillsborough St, POB 520, Roseau; tel. 4485800; fax 4485805; Man. C. M. SMITH.

Banque Française Commerciale (France): Queen Mary St, Roseau; tel. 4484040; fax 4485335; e-mail bfc@cwd.dom.dm; Man. THIERRY FREY.

Barclays Bank PLC (United Kingdom): 2 Old St, POB 4, Roseau; tel. 4482571; fax 4483471; Man. LEROY L. DANGLAR; sub-br. in Portsmouth.

National Commercial Bank of Dominica: 64 Hillsborough St, POB 271, Roseau; tel. 4482571; fax 4483982; e-mail ncbdom@cwdom.dm; f. 1976; cap. 10.0m., res 10.0m., dep. 247.0m. (June 1999); 51% govt-owned; Chair. NICHOLAS WALDRON; Gen. Man. JULIUS CORBETT; 2 brs.

Royal Bank of Canada: Dame Mary Eugenia Charles Blvd, POB 19, Roseau; tel. 4482771; fax 4485398; Man. H. PINARD.

INSURANCE

Several British, regional and US companies have agents in Roseau. Local companies include the following:

First Domestic Insurance Co Ltd. 19–21 King George V St, POB 1931, Roseau; tel. 4488337; fax 4485778; e-mail: insurance@ cwdom.dm.

Insurance Specialists and Consultants: 19–21 King George V St, POB 20, Roseau; tel. 4482022; fax 4485778.

J. B. Charles and Co Ltd: Old St, POB 121, Roseau; tel. 4482876.

Tonge Inc Ltd: 19–21 King George V St, POB 20, Roseau; tel. 4484027; fax 4485778.

Windward Islands Crop Insurance Co (Wincrop): Vanoulst House, Goodwill, POB 469, Roseau; tel. 4483955; fax 4484197; f. 1987; regional; coverage for weather destruction of, mainly, banana crops; Man. KERWIN FERREIRA; brs in Grenada, Saint Lucia and Saint Vincent.

Trade and Industry

DEVELOPMENT ORGANIZATIONS

National Development Corporation (NDC): Valley Rd, POB 293, Roseau; tel. 4482045; fax 4485840; e-mail ndc@cwdom.dm; internet www.dominica.dm; f. 1988 by merger of Industrial Development Corpn (f. 1974) and Tourist Board; promotes local and foreign investment to increase employment, production and exports; promotes and co-ordinates tourism development; Chair. ISAAC BAPTISTE; Gen. Man. SHERIDAN G. GREGOIRE.

Eastern Caribbean States Export Development and Agricultural Diversification Unit (EDADU): POB 769, Roseau; tel. 4486655; fax 4485554; e-mail oecsundp@cwdom.dm; internet www.oecs-edadu.org; f. 1990 as Eastern Caribbean States Export Development Agency; reformed as above in 1997; OECS regional development.; Exec. Dir COLIN BULLY.

INDUSTRIAL AND TRADE ASSOCIATIONS

Dominica Association of Industry and Commerce (DAIC): POB 85, cnr Old St and Fields Lane, Roseau; tel. 4482874; fax 4486868; e-mail daic@marpin.dm; internet www.delphis.dm/ daic.htm; f. 1972 by a merger of the Manufacturers' Association and the Chamber of Commerce; represents the business sector, liaises with the Government, and stimulates commerce and industry; 100 mems; Pres. MICHAEL ASTAPHAN; CEO JEANILIA R. V. DE SMET.

Dominica Banana Marketing Corporation (DBMC): Vanoulst House, POB 1620, Roseau; tel. 4482671; fax 4486445; internet www.delphis.dm/dbmc.htm; f. 1934 as Dominica Banana Growers' Association; restructured 1984; state-supported; Chair. Dr BERNARD YANKEY; Gen. Man. GREGORY SHILLINGFORD.

Dominica Export-Import Agency (Dexia): Bay Front, POB 173, Roseau; tel. 4483494; fax 4486308; e-mail dexia@cwdom.dm; internet www.delphis.dm/dexia/trade.htm; f. 1986; replaced the Dominica Agricultural Marketing Board and the External Trade Bureau; exporter of Dominican agricultural products, trade facilitator and importer of bulk rice, sugar and other essential commodities; Gen. Man. GREGOIRE THOMAS (acting).

EMPLOYERS' ORGANIZATION

Dominica Employers' Federation: 14 Church St, POB 1783, Roseau; tel. 4482314; fax 4484474; e-mail def@cwdom.dm; Pres. LAMBERT LEWIS.

UTILITIES

Electricity

Dominica Electricity Services Ltd (DOMLEC): 18 Castle St, POB 1593, Roseau; tel. 4482681; fax 4485397; e-mail mandomlec@cwdom.dm; national electricity service; 72%-owned by the Commonwealth Development Corporation (United Kingdom); Gen. Man. MURRAY ROGERS.

Water

Dominica Water and Sewerage Co Ltd (DOWASCO): 3 High St, POB 185, Roseau; tel. 4484811; fax 4485813; Chair. DON CHRISTOPHER; Gen. Man. DAMIEN SHILLINGFORD.

TRADE UNIONS

Dominica Amalgamated Workers' Union (DAWU): 18 King George V St, POB 137, Roseau; tel. 4483048; fax 4485787; f. 1960; Gen. Sec. FEDELINE MOULON; 500 mems (1996).

Dominica Association of Teachers: 7 Boyd's Ave, Roseau; tel. 4488177; fax 4488177; e-mail DAT@cwdom.dm; Pres. CELIA NICHOLAS; 630 mems (1996).

Dominica Trade Union: 70–71 Independence St, Roseau; tel. 4498139; fax 4499060; f. 1945; Pres. HAROLD SEALEY; Gen. Sec. LEO J. BERNARD NICHOLAS; 400 mems (1995).

Media Workers' Association: Roseau; Pres. MATTHIAS PELTIER.

National Workers' Union: 69 Queen Mary St, Roseau; tel. 4484465; f. 1977; Pres. RAWLINS JERMOTT; Gen. Sec. PATRICK JOHN; 450 mems (1996).

Public Service Union: cnr Valley Rd and Windsor Lane, Roseau; tel. 4482102; fax 4488060; f. 1940 and registered as a trade union in 1960; representing all grades of civil servants, including firemen, prison officers, nurses, teachers and postal workers; Pres. SONIA D. WILLIAMS; Gen. Sec. THOMAS LETANG; 1,400 mems.

Waterfront and Allied Workers' Union: 43 Hillsborough St, Roseau; tel. 4482343; f. 1965; Pres. LOUIS BENOIT; Gen. Sec. NEVILLE LEE; 1,500 mems.

Transport

ROADS

In 1996 there were an estimated 780 km (485 miles) of roads, of which about 50.4% was paved; there were also numerous tracks. A road and bridge reconstruction project, costing an estimated EC $33m., was announced by the Government in 1997.

SHIPPING

A deep-water harbour at Woodbridge Bay serves Roseau, which is the principal port. Several foreign shipping lines call at Roseau, and there is a high-speed ferry service between Martinique and Guadeloupe which calls at Roseau eight times a week. Ships of the Geest Line call at Prince Rupert's Bay, Portsmouth, to collect bananas, and cruise-ship facilities were constructed there during 1990. There are other specialized berthing facilities on the west coast.

Dominica Ports Authority: POB 243, Roseau; tel. 4484431; fax 4486131; f. 1972; responsible to the Ministry of Communications and Works; pilotage and cargo handling.

CIVIL AVIATION

Melville Hall Airport, 64 km (40 miles) from Roseau, and Canefield Airport, 5 km (3 miles) from Roseau, are the two airports on the island. In 2001 proposals for the construction of an international airport were under review. Construction of the new airport was to be funded by the European Union. A feasibility study on the expansion and upgrading of Melville Hall Airport was completed in 1998. The construction of a new runway at the nearby village of Wesley was chosen in preference to an earlier plan to realign Melville Hall's existing runway. The EC $78m.-project was due to begin in late 1998. Canefield Airport was also to be improved. The regional airline, LIAT (based in Antigua and Barbuda, and in which Dominica is a shareholder), provides daily services and, with Air Caraibe, Air Guadeloupe and Air BVI, connects Dominica with all the islands of the Eastern Caribbean, including the international airports of Puerto Rico, Antigua, Guadeloupe and Martinique.

Tourism

The Government has designated areas of the island as nature reserves, to preserve the beautiful, lush scenery and the rich, natural heritage that constitute Dominica's main tourist attractions. Birdlife is particularly prolific, and includes several rare and endangered species, such as the Imperial parrot. There are also two marine reserves. Tourism is not as developed as it is among Dominica's neighbours, but the country is being promoted as an 'eco-tourism' and cruise destination. There were an estimated 276,718 visitors in 1999 (of whom 202,003 were cruise-ship passengers), and in 1996 there were 764 hotel rooms. Receipts from tourism increased by 4.9% from EC $125.64m. in 1998 to EC $131.77m. in 1999.

National Development Corporation (NDC)—Division of Tourism: Valley Rd, POB 73, Roseau; tel. 4482045; fax 4485840; e-mail ndc@cwdom.dm; internet www.dominica.dm; f. 1988, when Tourist Board merged with Industrial Development Corpn; Dir of Tourism SOBERS ESPRIT.

Dominica Hotel and Tourism Association: POB 384, Roseau; tel. 4486565; fax 4480299; Pres. ATHERTON MARTIN.

THE DOMINICAN REPUBLIC

Introductory Survey

Location, Climate, Language, Religion, Flag, Capital

The Dominican Republic occupies the eastern part of the island of Hispaniola, which lies between Cuba and Puerto Rico in the Caribbean Sea. The country's only international frontier is with Haiti, to the west. The climate is sub-tropical, with an average annual temperature of 27°C (80°F). In Santo Domingo, temperatures are generally between 19°C (66°F) and 31°C (88°F). The west and south-west of the country are arid. Hispaniola lies in the path of tropical cyclones. The official language is Spanish. Almost all of the inhabitants profess Christianity, and some 88% are Roman Catholics. There are small Protestant and Jewish communities. The national flag (proportions 8 by 5) is blue (upper hoist and lower fly) and red (lower hoist and upper fly), quartered by a white cross. The state flag has, in addition, the national coat of arms, showing a quartered shield in the colours of the flag (on which are superimposed national banners, a cross and an open Bible) between scrolls above and below, at the centre of the cross. The capital is Santo Domingo.

Recent History

The Dominican Republic became independent in 1844, although it was occupied by US military forces between 1916 and 1924. General Rafael Leónidas Trujillo Molina overthrew the elected President, Horacio Vázquez, in 1930 and dominated the country until his assassination in May 1961. The dictator ruled personally from 1930 to 1947 and indirectly thereafter. His brother, Héctor Trujillo, was President from 1947 until August 1960, when he was replaced by Dr Joaquín Balaguer Ricardo, hitherto Vice-President. After Rafael Trujillo's death, President Balaguer remained in office, but in December 1961 he permitted moderate opposition groups to participate in a Council of State, which exercised legislative and executive powers. Balaguer resigned in January 1962, when the Council of State became the Provisional Government. A presidential election in December 1962, the country's first free election for 38 years, was won by Dr Juan Bosch Gaviño, the founder and leader of the Partido Revolucionario Dominicano (PRD), who had been in exile since 1930. President Bosch, a left-of-centre democrat, took office in February 1963 but was overthrown in the following September by a military coup. The leaders of the armed forces transferred power to a civilian triumvirate, led by Emilio de los Santos. In April 1965 a revolt by supporters of ex-President Bosch overthrew the triumvirate. Civil war broke out between pro-Bosch forces and military units headed by Gen. Elías Wessin y Wessin, who had played a leading role in the 1963 coup. The violence was eventually suppressed by the intervention of some 23,000 US troops, who were formally incorporated into an Inter-American peace force by the Organization of American States (OAS). The peace force withdrew in September 1965.

Following a period of provisional government under Héctor García Godoy, a presidential election in June 1966 was won by Balaguer, the candidate of the Partido Reformista Social Cristiano (PRSC). The PRSC, founded in 1964, also won a majority of seats in both houses of the new National Congress. A new Constitution was promulgated in November. Despite his association with the Trujillo dictatorship, Balaguer initially proved to be a popular leader, and in May 1970 he was re-elected for a further four years. In February 1973 a state of emergency was declared when guerrilla forces landed on the coast. Captain Francisco Caamaño Deño, the leader of the 1965 revolt, and his followers were killed. Bosch and other opposition figures went into hiding. Bosch later resigned as leader of the PRD (founding the Partido de la Liberación Dominicana—PLD), undermining hopes of a united opposition in the May 1974 elections, when Balaguer was re-elected with a large majority.

In the May 1978 presidential election, Balaguer was defeated by the PRD candidate, Silvestre Antonio Guzmán Fernández. This was the first occasion in the country's history when an elected President yielded power to an elected successor. An attempted military coup in favour of Balaguer was prevented by pressure from the US Government. On assuming office in August, President Guzmán undertook to professionalize the armed forces by removing politically ambitious high-ranking officers. In June 1981 he declared his support for Jacobo Majluta Azar, his Vice-President, as his successor, but in November the PRD rejected Majluta's candidacy in favour of Dr Salvador Jorge Blanco, a left-wing senator, who was elected President in May 1982. In the congressional elections, held at the same time, the PRD gained a majority in both the Senate and the Chamber of Deputies. Guzmán committed suicide in July after allegations of fraud were made against his Government and members of his family. Vice-President Majluta was immediately sworn in as interim President until Blanco assumed office in August. Although a member of the Socialist International, Blanco maintained good relations with the USA (on which the country is economically dependent) and declared that he would not resume relations with Cuba.

In April 1984 a series of public protests against substantial increases in the cost of essential items erupted into violent confrontations between the security forces and demonstrators in Santo Domingo and four other cities, which lasted for three days. In the course of the protests, more than 50 people were killed. In May the Government responded to the prospect of further demonstrations by ordering the arrest of more than 100 trade union and left-wing leaders. In August, in anticipation of civil unrest at the announcement of new price increases, more arrests were made among trade union and opposition leaders. Further demonstrations, including one attended by 40,000 people in Santo Domingo, were held in protest at the continuing economic decline.

In February 1985 a further series of substantial price increases led to violent clashes between demonstrators and the security forces, during which four people died. Public unrest was exacerbated by the Government's decision, in April, to accept the International Monetary Fund's (IMF) terms for further financial aid. In June a 24-hour general strike was organized by trade unions, in protest at the Government's economic policy and its refusal to increase the minimum wage. In July, however, the threat of a 48-hour general strike prompted the Government to order an immediate increase in the minimum wage.

Further violence preceded the presidential and legislative elections of May 1986. The three principal candidates in the presidential election were all former Presidents: Balaguer of the PRSC; Majluta, who, having registered La Estructura, his right-wing faction of the PRD, as a separate political party in July 1985, nevertheless secured the candidacy of the ruling PRD; and Bosch of the PLD. The counting of votes was suspended twice, following allegations by Majluta of fraud by the PRSC and by the Junta Central Electoral (JCE—Central Electoral Board). Balaguer was finally declared the winner by a narrow margin of votes over Majluta, his closest rival. In the simultaneous legislative elections, the PRSC won 21 of the 30 seats in the Senate and 56 of the 120 seats in the Chamber of Deputies.

Upon taking office as President (for the fifth time) in August 1986, Balaguer initiated an investigation into alleged corrupt practices by members of the outgoing administration. Blanco, the outgoing President, was charged with embezzlement and the illegal purchase of military vehicles. (In August 1991 he was finally convicted of 'abuse of power' and misappropriation of public funds, and sentenced to 20 years' imprisonment. However, in September 1994 legislation granting him amnesty was approved by the Chamber of Deputies.) The financial accounts of the armed forces were examined, and the former Secretary of State for the Armed Forces was subsequently imprisoned. In September 1987 the Cabinet resigned, at the request of the President, to enable him to restructure the Government. Some 35,000 government posts were abolished, in an attempt to reduce public spending, and expenditure was to be redirected to a programme of public works projects, which were expected to create almost 100,000 new jobs. Nevertheless, strike action continued. The situation deteriorated in February 1988, when demonstrations took place throughout the country, to protest against the high cost of living, following an increase in the price of staple foods. Six people were killed as the security forces intervened to quell the protests. Subsequently, the Roman Catholic Church mediated between the opposing sides, and Balaguer agreed to stabilize prices of staple foods and to increase the minimum wage by 33%. However, prices continued to rise, provoking a new wave of strikes in June.

In 1989 opposition to the Government's economic policies intensified. Popular discontent was aggravated by the deterioration of public utilities, particularly water and electricity. In June a national strike committee called a 48-hour general strike. More than 300 organizations supported the action, which reportedly paralysed the country for two days. The major demands included the doubling of the minimum wage, a reduction in the prices of staple commodities, and the ending of interruptions in the supplies of water and electricity. Four people were killed and an estimated 3,000 were arrested during the protests. Despite mediation efforts by the Roman Catholic Church, the Government made no concessions to union demands. In October, following a 66% rise in fuel prices, there were further violent demonstrations.

With presidential and legislative elections due to take place in May 1990, Balaguer's prospects for re-election were impeded considerably by the continuing deterioration of the economy (particularly rapid inflation), the worsening energy crisis, and criticism of government spending on expansive public works programmes, which had resulted in a severe depletion of the country's reserves of foreign exchange. The principal contender for the presidency was the PLD candidate, Bosch, who concentrated his election campaign on seeking support from the private sector, promising privatization of state-owned companies. When the initial results indicated a narrow victory for Balaguer, Bosch accused the ruling PRSC and the JCE of fraud, necessitating a re-count, supervised by monitors from the OAS. Almost two months after the election, Balaguer was declared the official winner. The PRSC secured a narrow majority in the Senate, with 16 of the 30 seats; the PLD won 12 and the PRD two. At elections to the Chamber of Deputies the PLD obtained 44 of the 120 seats, while the PRSC won 42, the PRD 32 and the Partido Revolucionario Independiente (PRI) two. However, the lack of an outright majority in the Chamber of Deputies did not threaten seriously to impede government policies, in view of Balaguer's extensive powers to govern by decree.

In August 1990, in an attempt to reduce inflation by cutting government subsidies, the Government announced a programme of austerity measures, including substantial increases in the cost of fuel and food. Petrol and essential foodstuffs were almost doubled in price. The trade unions reacted angrily to the austerity measures, calling a 48-hour general strike. This action was violently suppressed by the security forces, and the ensuing conflict resulted in as many as 14 deaths. The price increases were partially offset by an increase of 30% in the salaries of army personnel and civilian employees in the public sector. The trade unions, however, rejected an identical offer by the private sector and threatened further strike action if their demands for basic food subsidies and considerable wage increases were not satisfied. In September a three-day general strike, organized by the Organizaciones Colectivas Populares (OCP), led to further arrests, injuries and at least one death. In the following month another general strike was called by the OCP and the Central General de Trabajadores (CGT), with the stated aim of ousting Balaguer from power. Violent clashes with the security forces in Santo Domingo resulted in a further four deaths.

In July 1991 a government announcement that a stand-by agreement had been concluded with the IMF prompted a series of general strikes in opposition to the accord and its concomitant economic guidelines. The strikes, called by the Confederación de Trabajadores Unitaria (CTU), also supported demands for a 100% rise in the minimum wage for state employees. Despite the adverse public response, the IMF agreement was formally signed in August.

In April 1992 evidence emerged of a serious rift within the PLD. Following the expulsion from the party, by the PLD's predominantly right-wing political committee, of a deputy and trade unionist who had criticized the party's position on a new labour code under discussion in Congress, 47 high-ranking, and mainly left-wing, members announced their resignation from the PLD. In June more than 400 former PLD members held a 'national assembly' to form a new political movement, the Alianza por la Democracia (APD), which was officially established in August.

In late September 1992 a Dominican human rights leader, Rafael Efraín Ortiz, was shot dead by police during a demonstration in Santo Domingo, protesting at government plans to celebrate the 500th anniversary of the arrival in the Caribbean of Christopher Columbus. The demonstrations were the result of increasing public anger at the inordinate expense of the construction of the commemorative Columbus Lighthouse (estimated to have cost in excess of US $25m.). Protesters also denounced the celebration of the Spanish conquest, which had led to the enslavement and destruction of the indigenous Taino Indian population. In response to the death of Efraín, general strikes were called in several cities, and violent protests broke out, resulting in a further death as rioters clashed with the security forces.

In April 1993 the APD split into two factions. In January 1994 the PLD announced that it had formed an alliance with the right-wing Fuerza Nacional Progresista (FNP) in order to contest the forthcoming general election. In the same month Balaguer officially announced his intention to contest the forthcoming presidential election, and his nomination received the support of the majority of the PRSC. However, his decision prompted 20 members of the PRSC executive to withdraw from the party in order to support the presidential candidate of the Unidad Democrática (UD), Fernando Alvarez Bogaert, himself a defecting member of the PRSC. The UD subsequently signed an electoral pact with the PRD.

The official results of the presidential and legislative elections of 16 May 1994 were delayed, amid accusations of widespread voting irregularities. Interim results, announced on 24 May, indicated a narrow victory for Balaguer in the presidential election. However, the PRD claimed that polling stations had been issued with abbreviated electoral rolls and that the PRSC, which had effective control of the JCE, had removed the names of some 200,000 PRD supporters from the lists. A full recount began on 25 May. In June the JCE rejected a request, made by the US Department of State, that fresh elections be conducted wherever voting irregularities had been detected. In the same month Bosch resigned as leader of the PLD. In July an investigative commission confirmed that, as a result of serious irregularities, some 73,000 of the registered electorate had been denied a vote. Despite an atmosphere of growing political instability, Balaguer rejected opposition demands for the formation of a provisional government. Strike action in protest at the electoral irregularities was reported to have seriously affected several regions, including the capital, during that month. On 2 August the JCE announced the final election results, having apparently overlooked the findings of the electoral investigative commission. Balaguer was proclaimed the winner of the presidential election by a margin of less than 1% of the votes cast, with 43.6%. In the Senate the alliance of the PRD and the UD secured 15 seats, while the PRSC won 14 and the PLD one seat. In the Chamber of Deputies the PRD/UD alliance obtained 57 seats, while the PRSC gained 50 and the PLD 13 seats.

Talks aimed at ending the political crisis caused by the election were held in early August 1994, with the mediation of the OAS and the Roman Catholic Church, and resulted in the signing of the Pact for Democracy. Under the terms of the accord (agreed by all the major parties), a fresh presidential election was to be held in November 1995 and a series of constitutional reforms would be adopted, providing for the prohibition of the re-election of a president to a consecutive term, the replacement of the JCE, and the reorganization of the judiciary. As a result of the accord, José Francisco Peña Gómez, the PRD leader, cancelled a series of planned strikes and demonstrations organized by his party. However, at a session of the National Congress, held on 14 August, the deputies of the PRSC, with the support of those of the PLD, voted to extend Balaguer's mandate from 18 months to two years. The PRD withdrew from the legislature in protest, and Peña Gómez announced that his party would boycott Congress and resume strike action. The OAS also criticized Congress for violating the terms of the Pact for Democracy. The constitutional amendments that the Pact envisaged were, however, approved by Congress. On 16 August Balaguer was inaugurated as President for a seventh term, and a new Cabinet was appointed over the following days.

The year 1995 was marked by a series of protests and disturbances, largely provoked by the deteriorating standards of public services. In March a protest at increases in public transport fares resulted in four deaths (there were further protests in August after the Government increased fares by a further 25%). In April, following the most severe electricity shortages since 1990, the administrator of the state electricity company, the Corporación Dominicana de Electricidad (CDE), was dismissed.

In May a 24-hour general strike in protest at increases in food prices and at the deterioration of electricity and transport services took place, and in the following month there were renewed disturbances in Santo Domingo and other towns to the north of the capital. Violent confrontations occurred between security forces and workers in September at a sugar plantation in San Luis, where workers had been protesting the decision of the state sugar council, the Consejo Estatal de Azúcar, to dismiss some 12,700 of its work-force.

In April 1996 the energy shortfall again reached crisis proportions, with power cuts averaging between 14 and 20 hours per day, following the decision by a major private power station, owned by the US consortium Smith-Enron, to withdraw from the national grid pending the settlement of a debt of US $4.5m. owed to it by the CDE. Although the dispute was resolved later that month, the crisis prompted renewed demands for Congress to expedite legislation enabling the privatization of CDE, which, owing largely to inefficiency and corruption, operated at a considerable loss.

The presidential election of 16 May 1996, the first for some 30 years in which Balaguer was not a candidate, was conducted according to a new system, introduced since 1994, whereby a second round of voting would be conducted between the two leading candidates should no candidate secure an absolute majority in the initial ballot. In the first round Peña Gómez won 45.9% of the votes, while the candidate of the PLD, Leonel Fernández Reyna, obtained 38.9%. The candidate of the PRSC, Jacinto Peynado (who had received only nominal support from Balaguer), obtained just 15.0% of the votes. At the second round of the presidential election, conducted on 30 June, Fernández secured a narrow victory, winning 51.25% of the votes, while Peña Gómez obtained 48.75%. The establishment, earlier in the month, of an electoral alliance between the PLD and PRSC, entitled the Frente Nacional Patriótico, had ensured Fernández the support of the PRSC voters. While the PRSC failed to retain the presidency, Balaguer appeared to have succeeded in retaining considerable influence in the new administration, since the PLD had only minority representation in Congress and would be dependent on the support of the PRSC to implement planned institutional reforms. However, in early August relations between Fernández and Balaguer appeared to have deteriorated when the PRSC signed an unexpected agreement with the PRD, which guaranteed the PRSC the presidency of the Senate while the PRD obtained that of the Chamber of Deputies. On 16 August Fernández was inaugurated, and the Cabinet, consisting almost exclusively of PLD members, was sworn in.

In 1997, as part of a campaign to eliminate deep-seated corruption in the country's institutions (which was estimated to cost the State some 30,000m. pesos per year), Fernández restructured both the police and the judiciary. In August Fernández, in his role as Chairman of the Consejo Nacional de la Magistratura (National Judiciary Council), oversaw a restructuring of the Supreme Court, including the appointment of 15 new judges. Responsibility for appointing judges at all other levels of the judicial system was transferred from the Senate to the Supreme Court, principally to avoid appointments being influenced by political considerations.

Growing dissatisfaction with the continuing deterioration of public services and Fernández's failure to honour promises made during his election campaign provoked widespread disturbances and strike action throughout the country in 1997. Between July and September numerous violent confrontations between demonstrators and the security forces resulted in several deaths. In October, in an effort to defuse the volatile social and political climate, Fernández introduced a recovery plan aimed at overcoming electricity and food shortages. However, in the following month a two-day general strike was organized by an 'umbrella' protest group, the Coordinadora de Organizaciones Populares, in support of demands for pay increases, reductions in the price of fuel and basic foodstuffs and improved public services. In February 1998 the continuing deterioration of public utilities and popular discontent regarding unfulfilled government promises provoked renewed violent protest in Santo Domingo and in the north of the country.

At legislative elections held on 16 May 1998 the PRD won 83 seats in the 149-seat Chamber of Deputies (enlarged from 120 seats), while the PLD obtained 49 seats and the PRSC secured the remaining 17 seats. In the Senate the PRD gained 24 seats, while the PLD won four and the PRSC two seats. The number of registered voters who abstained from participating in the poll

was, at some 48%, the highest on record. As a result of the success of the opposition PRD, and the considerable losses incurred by the PRSC (on whom the PLD Government had hitherto depended for support in the legislature), it was considered likely that Fernández would encounter considerable difficulty in implementing his legislative programme for the remainder of his term of office, due to end in 2000. In July 1998 the outgoing Congress approved controversial legislation granting an amnesty to all public officials accused of corruption since 1978. The new legislature was inaugurated in August 1998. However, the PRD failed to secure the presidency of the Chamber of Deputies when a dissident group of PRD deputies joined forces with the PLD and the PRSC to re-elect the outgoing President of the Chamber, Héctor Rafael Peguero Méndez, to the post. Peguero had been expelled from the PRD in July, after refusing to accept the party's choice of candidate for the position.

In January 1999 conflict within the legislature threatened to jeopardize the disbursement of some US $216m. in reconstruction loans from the World Bank and the Inter-American Development Bank, which had been made available following the destruction caused by 'Hurricane Georges' in September 1998. The dispute concerned the election for the post of Secretary-General of the Liga Municipal Dominicana (LMD), an association of local government bodies with significant financial powers, which directed local government expenditure amounting to some 4% of the national budget. In the event, two separate elections were held independently of one another: the PRD, which controlled the legislature, elected its own candidate. However, the governing PLD and its ally, the PRSC, elected and swore in the candidate of the PRSC. In February the PRD initiated legal proceedings to contest the Government's claim to control the LMD, while also signalling its intention to use its legislative majority to prevent the ratification of the reconstruction loans until agreement had been reached on the dispute. An accord was finally achieved in April, when it was agreed to appoint an impartial commission to manage the LMD pending a judicial ruling on the election.

Violent protest against electricity and water shortages and declining living standards continued in 1998 and throughout 1999. In May 1999 the privatization of the CDE began. In October a general strike was organized in protest against the introduction of fuel price increases of up to 34% and a concomitant rise in transport fares. The protest effectively paralysed the public transport sector before being abandoned on its second day. In February 2001 the Senate finally passed legislation on the reform of the electricity sector. However, the bill was still to be approved by the Chamber of Deputies.

In the first round of the presidential election, held on 16 May 2000, Rafael Hipólito Mejía Domínguez, the PRD candidate, received 49.9% of the votes cast, while the PRD candidate, Danilo Medina Sánchez, won 24.9%. Former President Joaquín Balaguer, standing as the PRSC's candidate for a potential eighth presidential term, won 24.6% of the ballot. Despite Mejía's failure to secure the constitutionally required 50%, a second ballot was not held and the JCE allowed Mejía to declare himself the winner. He was inaugurated as President on 16 August and a new Cabinet was officially appointed. In February 2001 President Mejía initiated a poverty mitigation programme, including education, health and housing reforms.

The continuing illegal import of plantation labour into the Dominican Republic from Haiti was a major issue for successive Governments. In June 1991, in reaction to increasing criticism of the Dominican Republic's human rights record (and, in particular, the Government's apparent acquiescence in the exploitation of Haitian child labourers), President Balaguer ordered the repatriation of all Haitian residents aged under 16 or over 60 years. Protests made by the Haitian Government that such a unilateral measure contravened normal diplomatic procedure were rejected by Balaguer. Following the army coup of September 1991 in Haiti, tens of thousands of Haitians were estimated to have fled to the Dominican Republic. However, few were granted refugee status, according to the United Nations High Commissioner for Refugees. In mid-1994 reports of smuggling on a large scale from the Dominican Republic to Haiti, in defiance of UN sanctions against the Haitian military dictatorship, prompted the UN to seek assurances of co-operation from Balaguer. An agreement was reached, providing for a UN monitoring mission to observe the enforcement of the embargo until the lifting of UN sanctions (in October 1994). In 1997 relations with Haiti became strained following the expulsion from the Dominican Republic over a three-month period of some 20,000

Haitians who had been residing illegally in the country. In late February Fernández and his Haitian counterpart met in Antigua, and agreement was reached to put an immediate end to large-scale repatriations. Accord was also achieved providing for the repatriation process to be monitored by an international body to ensure the observance of human rights. In June 1998 Fernández became the first Dominican Head of State to visit Haiti since 1936. Fernández and the Haitian President met in Port-au-Prince, where they reached agreement on the establishment of joint border patrols to combat the traffic of drugs, arms and other contraband across the countries' joint border. In late 1999, following the summary deportation of some 8,000 Haitians, the two Governments signed a protocol limiting the repatriations.

In late 2000 the Dominican Republic was to testify before the Inter-American Court of Human Rights (part of the OAS) regarding the mistreatment of Haitians. The new President, Rafael Hipólito Mejía, stated that one of his new Government's priorities was bilateral relations with Haiti. In early 2001, following an increase in tensions in Haiti, a plan to protect Dominican territory was implemented; military forces deployed on the Dominican–Haitian border also were reinforced in an attempt to prevent both illegal immigration and drugs-trafficking.

Government

The Dominican Republic comprises 30 provinces, each administered by an appointed governor, and a Distrito Nacional (DN) containing the capital. Under the 1966 Constitution (as amended in 1994), legislative power is exercised by the bicameral National Congress, with a Senate of 30 members and a Chamber of Deputies (149 members). Members of both houses are elected for four years by universal adult suffrage. Executive power lies with the President, who is also elected by direct popular vote for four years. He is assisted by a Vice-President and a Cabinet comprising Secretaries of State.

Defence

Military service is voluntary and lasts for four years. In August 2000 the armed forces totalled 24,500 men: army 15,000, air force 5,500 and navy 4,000. Paramilitary forces numbered 15,000. The defence budget for 2000 was an estimated RD $2,400m.

Economic Affairs

In 1998, according to estimates by the World Bank, the Dominican Republic's gross national product (GNP), measured at average 1996–98 prices, was US $14,629m., equivalent to $1,770 per head (or $4,337 per head on an international purchasing-power parity basis). During 1990–98, it was estimated, GNP per head increased, in real terms, at an average rate of 3.4% annually. Over the same period, the population increased by an average of 2.1% per year. In 1999 GNP was estimated at $16,000m. The Dominican Republic's gross domestic product (GDP) increased, in real terms, by an average of 5.7% per year in 1990–99. Real GDP increased by 8.3% in 1999.

Agriculture, including forestry and fishing, contributed an estimated 11.3% of GDP, at constant 1970 prices, in 1999, and employed an estimated 18.1% of the labour force in 1998. The principal cash crops are sugar cane (sugar and sugar derivatives accounted for an estimated 12.0% of total export earnings in 1999), coffee and cocoa beans and tobacco. Agricultural GDP increased, in real terms, by an average of 3.8% per year during 1990–99, and by 6.8% in 1999. In 2001 the Government intended to implement a US $400m. development plan for fruit cultivation.

Industry (including mining, manufacturing, construction and power) employed 25.1% of the economically active population in 1997, and contributed an estimated 34.3% of GDP, at constant prices, in 1999. Industrial GDP increased, in real terms, by an average of 6.8% per year during 1990–99, and by 10.6% in 1999.

Mining contributed an estimated 1.8% of GDP, at constant prices, in 1999, but employed only 0.3% of the economically active population in 1997. The major mineral export is ferronickel (providing 30.0% of total export earnings in 1995). Gold and silver are also exploited, and there are workable deposits of gypsum, limestone and mercury. The GDP of the mining sector decreased, in real terms, by an average of 1.3% per year during 1990–99, and by an estimated 1.5% in 1999. In 2001 the Government was negotiating the privatization and reopening of the Rosario gold, silver and zinc mine at Cotuí and there were plans to develop other mines throughout the country.

Manufacturing contributed an estimated 17.0% of GDP, at constant prices, in 1999, and employed 18.2% of the economically active population in 1997. Important branches of manufacturing in 1997 included refined sugar, beer, cigarettes and petroleum. The most dynamic sector in 1999 was construction, in particular cement production. The GDP of the manufacturing sector increased, in real terms, at an average rate of 7.5% per year during 1990–99, and by 6.7% in 1999.

Energy is derived principally from petroleum; however, there is no domestic petroleum production. Imports of mineral fuels accounted for an estimated 13.2% of the total cost of imports in 1996. In 2000 construction began on a 300 MW oil-fired power-station and a 300 MW gas-fired power-station; both were to be completed by 2002. There were also plans to build a 500 MW gas-fired power-station.

The services sector contributed an estimated 54.3% of GDP in 1999, and employed 54.9% of the economically active population in 1997. The GDP of the services sector expanded at an average annual rate of 5.7% during 1990–99, and by 7.2% in 1999. Tourism accounted for approximately 13.3% of GDP in 1995.

In 1999 the Dominican Republic recorded a visible trade deficit of US $2,904.4m., and there was a deficit of $429.2m. on the current account of the balance of payments. In 1997 the principal source of imports was the USA (63.9%); other major suppliers were Japan, Panama and Mexico. In the same year the USA was the principal market for exports (50.5% of the total, excluding exports from free-trade zones); other significant purchasers were Puerto Rico and Belgium. The principal exports in 1999 were iron and steel and sugar and sugar derivatives. In 1999 exports from the free-trade zones amounted to an estimated US $3,200.4m. The principal imports in 1999 were petroleum and petroleum products, and food products.

In 1998 there was an estimated budgetary surplus of RD $2,109.8m. (equivalent to 0.9% of GDP). The Dominican Republic's total external debt at the end of 1998 was US $4,451m., of which $3,530m. was long term public debt In that year the cost of debt-servicing was equivalent to 4.2% of total revenue from exports of goods and services. In 1990–98 the average annual rate of inflation was 11.2%. Consumer prices increased by an average of 6.5% in 1999. An estimated 14.3% of the economically active population were unemployed in 1998.

In July 1984 the Dominican Republic was granted observer status in CARICOM (see p. 142). In December 1989 the country was accepted as a member of the ACP nations covered by the Lomé Convention (which expired in February 2000 and was replaced by the Cotonou Agreement in June—see p. 208). In 1990 the Dominican Republic's application for full membership of CARICOM was threatened when ACP nations accused the Dominican Republic of breaking an agreement made under the Lomé Convention concerning the export of bananas to countries of the European Community (now the European Union).

In the 1990s the economy of the Dominican Republic was severely affected by the unstable nature of the country's electricity supply. The situation reached crisis proportions in 1990 and again in 1995–98, when interruptions in the supply of electricity lasted up to 20 hours per day. A plan for the restructuring of the state electricity company (Corporación Dominicana de Electricidad—CDE) was agreed in principle in 1993. However, implementation of the plan was repeatedly delayed, while the CDE continued to operate at a significant loss. In May 1999 the generating and distribution operations of the CDE were partially privatized, with the divestment of 50%-shares producing revenue of US $644m. and saving the Government some $147m. per year in subsidies. Legislation on the reform of the electricity sector was finally given approval by the Senate in early 2001; however, the bill was still to be discussed in the Chamber of Deputies. In 1996 an emergency plan was introduced to revive the ailing sugar company, the Consejo Estatal de Azúcar (CEA). By 1999 the CEA had accumulated debts totalling more than $250m. In September four private consortiums were granted 30-year contracts to manage the CEA's operations, providing the Government with a further $11m. per year in revenue. Despite the structural difficulties in the state power and sugar sectors, the economy continued to record significant growth in the late 1990s, based on expansion in tourism and the free-trade zones. Damages resulting from the impact of 'Hurricane Georges' in September 1998 were estimated by the Government at $2,000m.; the most adversely affected sectors were agriculture, manufacturing and tourism. In October the Government announced a 3,500m. pesos-emergency programme for reconstruction, which was to be partly financed by foreign grants. The Government also sought a rescheduling of debt-servicing obligations with the 'Paris Club' of creditors. In June 1999 the Government and the opposition agreed to sign a pact committing them to expedite delayed economic and financial legislation, including measures to reform the system of tariffs and taxation. GDP growth of 7.8% was estimated in 2000, and at 6.5% in 2001, while inflation in 2000 was 9.0%. An estimated 7.0% increase in consumer prices was envisaged for 2001. The budget for 2001 was some 65,000m. pesos. In late 2000 the new President, Rafael Hipólito Mejía, announced a programme of fiscal measures, including an increase in consumer taxes, a rise in tariffs on imported luxury goods, and a tax increase on cars, insurance, advertising, flights, security, commercial rents, gambling, cigarettes and beer. In March 2001 the International Monetary Fund (IMF) praised the country's economic progress and President Mejía's fiscal adjustment programme. However, it maintained that further progress in the privatization process, particularly in the electricity sector, was necessary, as was a review of the public finances.

Social Welfare

A voluntary national contributory scheme, introduced in 1947, provides insurance cover for sickness, unemployment, accidental injury, maternity, old age and death. Only 42% of the population are thought to benefit from the system. In 1998 there were 861 hospitals and clinics, 8,134 physicians and 10,010 hospital beds under the auspices of the public health and welfare department and the Institute of Social Security. In 1997 there were an estimated 215.6 physicians per 100,000 inhabitants and 29.9 nurses per 100,000 inhabitants. The central Government's 1997 budget allocated 4,027.7m. pesos (11.2% of total expenditure) to the health sector.

Education

Education is, where possible, compulsory for children between the ages of six and 14 years. Primary education begins at the age of six and lasts for eight years. Secondary education, starting at 14 years of age, lasts for four years. In 1997 the total enrolment at primary and secondary schools was equivalent to 84.9% of the school-age population (males 82%; females 87.9%). In that year primary enrolment included an estimated 91.3% of children in the relevant age-group (males 89.0%; females 93.6%), while secondary enrolment included an estimated 78.5% of children in the relevant age-group (males 74.9%; females 82.1%). In 1994/95 there were 4,001 primary schools, and in 1996/97 there were an estimated 1,737 secondary schools. There are eight universities. Budgetary expenditure on education by the Secretariat of State for Education and Culture in 1997 was 5,114.7m. pesos, representing 14.3% of total government spending. In 1998, according to UNDP estimates, the average rate of adult illiteracy was 17.2% (males 17.1%; females 17.2%).

Public Holidays

2001: 1 January (New Year's Day), 6 January (Epiphany), 21 January (Our Lady of Altagracia), 26 January (Duarte), 27 February (Independence), 13 April (Good Friday), 14 April (Pan-American Day), 1 May (Labour Day), 16 July (Foundation of Sociedad la Trinitaria), 16 August (Restoration Day), 24 September (Our Lady of Mercedes), 12 October (Columbus Day), 24 October (United Nations Day), 1 November (All Saints' Day), 6 November (Constitution Day), 25 December (Christmas Day).

2002: 1 January (New Year's Day), 6 January (Epiphany), 21 January (Our Lady of Altagracia), 26 January (Duarte), 27 February (Independence), 29 March (Good Friday), 14 April (Pan-American Day), 1 May (Labour Day), 16 July (Foundation of Sociedad la Trinitaria), 16 August (Restoration Day), 24 September (Our Lady of Mercedes), 12 October (Columbus Day), 24 October (United Nations Day), 1 November (All Saints' Day), 6 November (Constitution Day), 25 December (Christmas Day).

Weights and Measures

The metric system is officially in force but the imperial system is often used.

Statistical Survey

Sources (unless otherwise stated): Oficina Nacional de Estadística, Edif. de Oficinas Gubernamentales, Avda México, esq. Leopoldo Navarro, Santo Domingo; tel. 682-7777; fax 685-4424; e-mail direccion@one.gov.do; internet www.one.gov.do; Banco Central de la República Dominicana, Calle Pedro Henríquez Ureña, esq. Leopoldo Navarro, Apdo 1347, Santo Domingo; tel. 221-9111; fax 686-7488; e-mail info@bancentral.gov.do; internet www.bancentral.gov.do.

Area and Population

AREA, POPULATION AND DENSITY

Area (sq km)	
Land	48,072
Inland water	350
Total	48,422*
Population (census results)†	
12 December 1981	5,647,977
24 September 1993	
Males	3,550,797
Females	3,742,593
Total	7,293,390
Population (official estimates at mid-year)‡	
1999	8,324,945
2000	8,518,483
Density (per sq km) at mid-2000	175.9

* 18,696 sq miles.
† Excluding adjustment for underenumeration.
‡ Not adjusted to take account of the results of the 1993 census.

PROVINCES (estimated population, 2000)

Distrito Nacional .	2,677,056	Maria Trinidad Sánchez	142,030
Santiago . .	836,614	La Altagracia . .	128,627
San Cristóbal .	519,906	Bahoruco . .	124,592
La Vega . .	390,314	Peravía . .	113,273
Duarte . .	318,151	San José de Ocoa .	110,000
Puerto Plata .	302,799	Salcedo . .	106,450
San Juan . .	265,562	El Seybo . .	105,447
San Pedro de Macorís	260,629	Monte Cristi . .	103,711
Azua . . .	243,157	Hato Mayor . .	87,595
Espaillat . .	228,173	Samaná . .	82,135
La Romana . .	213,628	Dajabón . .	78,045
Valverde . .	198,979	Elias Piña . .	66,267
Sánchez Ramírez .	194,282	Santiago Rodríguez. .	65,853
Barahona . .	179,945	Independencia . .	41,778
Monseñor Nouel .	174,923	Pedernales. . .	19,698
Monte Plata .	174,126		

PRINCIPAL TOWNS (population at 1993 census)

Santo Domingo, DN (capital) . .	1,609,699	San Francisco de Macorís . .	108,485
Santiago de los Caballeros . .	365,463	San Felipe de Puerto Plata . .	89,423
La Romana . .	140,204	Beneménta de San	
San Pedro de Macorís . .	124,735	Cristóbal . .	88,605
		La Vega . .	87,162

Births and deaths (1997): Registered live births 164,556 (birth rate 25.2 per 1,000); Registered deaths 26,301 (death rate 5.8 per 1,000).

Expectation of life (UNDP estimates, years at birth, 1995–2000): 70.6 (Source: UNDP, *Human Development Report*).

ECONOMICALLY ACTIVE POPULATION

(ISIC Major Divisions, '000 persons aged 10 years and over, official estimates, 1997)

	Males	Females	Total
Agriculture, hunting and forestry ⎫			
Fishing . . . . ⎬	512.5	16.5	529.0
Mining and quarrying	7.5	0.9	8.4
Manufacturing	332.7	150.7	483.3
Electricity, gas and water supply .	13.7	6.6	20.3
Construction	150.4	3.1	153.6
Wholesale and retail trade . .	356.1	176.1	532.3
Hotels and restaurants . .	59.5	55.8	115.3
Transport, storage and communications	190.0	12.9	202.7
Financial intermediation . . ⎫			
Real estate, renting and business activities . . . . . ⎬	17.3	16.8	34.0
Public administration and defence	99.5	25.9	125.4
Education . . . . . ⎫			
Health and social work . . . ⎬	152.2	295.3	447.5
Other community, social and personal service activities . ⎭			
Total employed	**1,891.4**	**760.6**	**2,652.0**
Unemployed	199.0	304.7	503.7
Total labour force	**2,090.4**	**1,065.3**	**3,155.7**

Source: ILO, *Yearbook of Labour Statistics*.

Mid-1998 (estimates in '000): Agriculture, etc. 644. Total labour force 3,553 (Source: FAO, *Production Yearbook*).

Agriculture

PRINCIPAL CROPS ('000 metric tons)

	1997	1998	1999
Rice (paddy)	508.5	474.6	562.8
Maize	33.9	34.2	30.3
Sorghum	21.8	21.7*	7.8
Potatoes	22.3	18.8	29.3
Sweet potatoes . . .	28.9	44.2	53.0
Cassava (Manioc) . . .	97.0	126.5	126.5
Yams	10.6	13.0	11.0
Other roots and tubers . .	200.2	244.0	261.4
Dry beans	24.4	24.3	25.8
Groundnuts (in shell) . .	1.8	1.8*	1.8*
Coconuts	154.6	160.2	184.4
Tomatoes	253.7	277.6	280.7
Sugar cane	6,294.4	5,028.1	4,452.7
Oranges.	106.8	135.6	89.4
Lemons and limes . . .	8.1*	8.5	8.5*
Avocados	155.0*	155.0*	89.4
Mangoes	185.0*	185.0	180.0*
Pineapples	112.0	107.8	72.5
Bananas	389.3	359.0	432.0
Plantains	327.0	341.4	229.3
Coffee (green)	41.7	56.9	34.6
Cocoa beans	58.3	67.7	25.9
Tobacco (leaves)	36.5	43.3	16.0

* FAO estimate(s).

Source: FAO.

LIVESTOCK ('000 head, year ending September)

	1997	1998	1999
Horses	329.0	329.0	329.0
Mules	135.0	135.0	135.0
Asses	144.5	144.5	144.5
Cattle	2,481.4	2,528.3	1,904.4
Pigs*	960.0	960.0	539.6
Sheep	135.0	135.0	105.5
Goats	570.0	570.0*	163.5

Chickens (million): 43.0 in 1997; 37.7 in 1998; 42.0* in 1999.

* FAO estimate(s).

Source: FAO.

LIVESTOCK PRODUCTS ('000 metric tons)

	1997	1998	1999
Beef and veal	79.2	76.8	65.5
Poultry meat	156.3	157.7	182.7
Cows' milk	390.2	358.4	411.1
Butter	1.5*	1.5†	1.5†
Cheese	2.5	2.5†	2.5†
Hen eggs	48.0	48.9	53.6
Cattle hides (fresh)	9.2	9.3	8.3

* Unofficial figure.　† FAO estimate(s).

Source: FAO.

Forestry

ROUNDWOOD REMOVALS ('000 cubic metres, excl. bark)

	1996	1997	1998
Sawlogs, veneer logs and logs for sleepers	4	4	4
Other industrial wood	3	3	3
Fuel wood	556	556	556
Total	562	562	562

Source: FAO, *Yearbook of Forest Products*.

Fishing

('000 metric tons, live weight)

	1996	1997	1998
Capture	13.8	14.5	10.2
Mozambique tilapia	—	0.3	0.4
Other tilapia	1.0	0.3	0.1
Groupers, seabasses	0.5	0.3	0.4
Southern red snapper	0.3	0.5	0.2
Yellowtail snapper	0.8	0.5	0.2
Other snappers and jobfishes	0.1	0.2	0.9
Porgies	0.4	1.1	—
Wrasses, hogfishes, etc.	0.5	1.5	0.1
Atlantic Spanish mackerel	1.6	0.6	0.3
Northern bluefin tuna	0.1	0.6	0.2
Blackfish tuna	0.5	0.3	0.1
Caribbean spiny lobster	0.4	1.1	0.9
Aquaculture	0.8	0.7	0.8
Total catch	14.6	15.2	11.0

Source: FAO, *Yearbook of Fishery Statistics*.

Mining

	1996	1997	1998
Ferro-nickel ('000 metric tons)*	78	n.a.	n.a.
Gold (metric tons)	3.3	3.5	3.5
Silver (million troy ounces)	0.5	0.4	0.2

* Source: US Bureau of Mines (Washington, DC).

Industry

SELECTED PRODUCTS
('000 metric tons, unless otherwise indicated)

	1995	1996	1997
Wheat flour	249	203	203
Refined sugar	98	112	114
Cement	1,450	1,642	1,835
Beer ('000 hectolitres)	2,082	2,199	2,593
Cigarettes (million)	4,070	4,068	3,972
Motor spirit (gasoline)	356	363	370
Electricity (million kWh)	6,506	6,847	7,335

Source: UN, *Industrial Commodity Statistics Yearbook*.

Finance

CURRENCY AND EXCHANGE RATES

Monetary Units
100 centavos = 1 Dominican Republic peso (RD $ or peso oro)

Sterling, Dollar and Euro Equivalents (29 December 2000)
£1 sterling = 24.88 pesos;
US $1 = 16.67 pesos;
€1 = 15.52 pesos;
1,000 Dominican Republic pesos = £40.19 = US $59.97 = €64.45.

Average Exchange Rate (RD $ per US $)
1998　15.267
1999　16.033
2000　16.415

BUDGET (RD $ million)

Revenue*	1995	1996	1997
Tax revenue	23,624.5	25,474.8	33,418.8
Taxes on income and profits	4,074.9	4,566.7	6,017.7
Taxes on goods and services	8,823.4	9,345.8	12,522.9
Taxes on international trade and transactions	9,521.9	10,183.2	13,126.6
Other current revenue	2,395.0	2,171.2	2,989.3
Property income	1,119.8	944.9	1,445.0
Fees and charges	1,082.5	1,032.9	1,189.6
Capital revenue	77.1	299.0	268.7
Total	26,096.6	27,945.0	36,676.8

Expenditure†	1995	1996	1997
General public services . . .	1,654.9	1,739.6	4,193.3
Defence	940.3	1,149.0	1,682.1
Public order and safety . . .	692.6	815.4	1,401.7
Education	3,150.0	3,610.3	5,114.7
Health	2,701.6	3,197.4	4,027.7
Social security and welfare . .	937.2	1,313.0	2,019.3
Housing and community amenities	3,619.8	3,783.3	4,730.0
Recreational, cultural and			
religious affairs and services	222.2	327.2	421.9
Economic affairs and services . .	8,629.7	10,482.3	10,821.4
Fuel and energy . . .	1,216.2	1,343.0	2,354.8
Agriculture, forestry and fishing	1,956.2	2,555.9	3,266.9
Mining and mineral resources,			
manufacturing and			
construction	2,221.3	2,206.1	1,730.8
Transport and communications	3,043.2	3,871.0	2,627.9
Other purposes	1,511.6	1,054.1	1,113.3
Sub-total	24,059.9	27,471.6	35,525.4
Adjustment	924.2	1,181.5	338.9
Total	24,984.1	28,653.1	35,864.3
Current‡	14,090.4	16,446.2	24,907.8
Capital	10,510.9	11,613.6	9,203.2
Adjustment	382.8	593.3	1,753.3

* Excluding grants received (RD $ million): 152.5 in 1995; 213.7 in 1996; 125.6 in 1997.
† Excluding lending minus repayments (RD $ million): 18.5 in 1995; 23.8 in 1996; 93.3 in 1997.
‡ Including interest payments (RD $ million): 1,511.6 in 1995; 1,054.1 in 1996; 1,113.3 in 1997.

Source: IMF, *Government Finance Statistics Yearbook*.

INTERNATIONAL RESERVES (US $ million at 31 December)

	1998	1999	2000
Gold*	5.3	5.2	5.0
IMF special drawing rights . .	0.3	0.3	0.4
Foreign exchange . . .	501.6	689.1	625.1
Total	507.2	694.6	630.5

* Valued at market-related prices.
Source: IMF, *International Financial Statistics*.

MONEY SUPPLY (RD $ million at 31 December)

	1998	1999	2000
Currency outside banks . .	12,568	16,889	15,076
Demand deposits at commercial			
banks	16,782	18,884	20,290
Total money (incl. others) . .	29,416	35,840	35,445

Source: IMF, *International Financial Statistics*.

COST OF LIVING
(Consumer Price Index; base: 1990 = 100)

	1995	1996	1997
Food	188.2	196.7	211.7
Clothing	181.3	186.0	189.3
Rent	222.0	237.4	255.5
All items (incl. others) . .	196.6	207.2	224.4

Source: ILO, *Yearbook of Labour Statistics*.

All items (base: 1995 = 100): 119.3 in 1998; 127.0 in 1999 (Source: IMF, *International Financial Statistics*).

NATIONAL ACCOUNTS
National Income and Product (RD $ million at current prices)

	1997	1998	1999
GDP in purchasers' values .	215,064	241,910	278,939
Net factor income from abroad .	−11,342	−13,565	−15,265
Gross national product (GNP) .	203,722	228,345	263,674
Less Consumption of fixed capital .	12,904	14,515	16,737
National income in market prices	190,818	213,830	246,937

Source: IMF, *International Financial Statistics*.

Expenditure on the Gross Domestic Product
(RD $ million at current prices)

	1997	1998	1999
Government final consumption expenditure . . .	16,403	19,449	22,797
Private final consumption expenditure	166,323	187,528	209,556
Increase in stocks . . .	620	698	804
Gross fixed capital formation .	41,945	56,026	69,201
Total domestic expenditure .	183,346	207,675	233,157
Exports of goods and services .	100,513	113,752	130,085
Less Imports of goods and services	110,739	135,542	153,504
GDP in purchasers' values .	215,064	241,910	278,939
GDP at constant 1970 prices .	5,324	5,714	6,188

Source: IMF, *International Financial Statistics*.

Gross Domestic Product by Economic Activity
(RD $ million at constant 1970 prices)

	1997	1998*	1999*
Agriculture, hunting, forestry and fishing	650.4	657.4	702.3
Mining and quarrying . . .	132.6	111.5	109.8
Manufacturing	929.9	987.5	1,053.6
Electricity, gas and water† . .	106.0	120.6	130.2
Construction	587.2	702.1	830.9
Wholesale and retail trade, restaurants and hotels . . .	1,005.5	1,093.1	1,195.7
Transport, storage and communications . . .	588.6	664.9	740.5
Finance, insurance and real estate	485.5	500.2	516.4
Community, social, personal and business services‡	838.0	876.4	908.7
Total	5,323.8	5,713.8	6,188.2

* Preliminary figures.
† Refers to electricity and water only.
‡ Including gas.

BALANCE OF PAYMENTS (US $ million)

	1997	1998	1999
Exports of goods f.o.b.	4,613.7	4,980.5	5,136.7
Imports of goods f.o.b.	−6,608.7	−7,597.3	−8.041.1
Trade balance	−1,995.0	−2,616.8	−2,904.4
Exports of services	2,446.6	2,501.5	2,850.3
Imports of services	−1,171.3	−1,319.5	−1,248.0
Balance on goods and services	−719.7	−1,434.8	−1,302.1
Other income received	140.4	168.2	218.3
Other income paid	−935.8	−1,058.3	−1,193.2
Balance on goods, services and income	−1,515.1	−2,324.9	−2,277.0
Current transfers received	1,373.1	2,016.9	1,997.1
Current transfers paid	−21.0	−30.4	−149.3
Current balance	−163.0	−338.4	−429.2
Direct investment from abroad	420.6	699.8	1,337.8
Portfolio investment assets	−5.6	−17.5	−433.0
Portfolio investment liabilities	−1.9	−3.8	−3.8
Other investment assets	−220.1	−66.4	−53.4
Other investment liabilities	254.6	76.0	213.4
Net errors and omissions	−193.7	−338.6	−480.4
Overall balance	90.9	11.1	151.4

Source: IMF, *International Financial Statistics*.

External Trade

PRINCIPAL COMMODITIES

Imports f.o.b. (US $ '000)*	1984	1985	1986
Cars and other vehicles (incl. spares)	65,300	84,633	161,619
Chemical and pharmaceutical products	59,649	64,436	106,229
Cotton and manufactures	9,660	15,212	7,045
Foodstuffs	112,295	171,793	115,248
Petroleum and petroleum products	504,842	426,782	253,849
Iron and steel manufactures (excl. building materials)	56,874	43,500	56,357
Machinery (incl. spares)	83,360	119,311	218,185
Total (incl. others)	1,257,134	1,285,910	1,351,732

* Provisional figures.

Total imports f.o.b. (US $ million): 1,792.8 in 1990; 1,728.8 in 1991; 2,174.6 in 1992; 2,118.4 in 1993; 2,283.8 in 1994; 2,588.0 in 1995; 3,205.1 in 1996; 4,192.0 in 1997; 4,896.6 in 1998; 5,206.8 in 1999 (Source: IMF, *International Financial Statistics*). Note: Figures exclude imports into free-trade zones.

Exports f.o.b. (US $ million)*	1998	1999†
Vegetable products	140.3	104.2
Edible vegetables	21	21.3
Edible fruits and nuts, peel of citrus and melons	39.3	46.1
Coffee, tea, maté and spices	68.1	24.0
Prepared food; beverages, spirits and tobacco	331.9	220.5
Sugars and sugar confectionery	127.4	76.5
Cocoa and cocoa preparations	85.6	24.8
Preparations of vegetables, fruits and nuts, etc.	18.3	17.6
Beverages, spirits and vinegar	20.2	22.5
Tobacco and manufactured tobacco substitutes	66.3	54.6
Products of chemical or allied industries	33.9	31.9
Organic chemicals	14.8	14.5
Plastics and articles thereof	13.5	15.6
Textiles and textile articles	19.2	15.7
Pearls, stones, precious metals, imitation jewellery, coins	16.2	6.5
Base metals and articles of base metal	145.9	161.2
Iron and steel	127.6	140.8
Re-exported products	13.5	19.3
Total (incl. others)	780.0	638.2

* Excluding exports from free-trade zones: (US $ million): 3,019.2 in 1998; 3,200.4 in 1999.
† Provisional figures.
Source: Centro Dominicano de Promoción de Exportaciones.

PRINCIPAL TRADING PARTNERS (US $ '000)

Imports c.i.f.	1997
Argentina	40,172.1
Japan	132,247.7
Mexico	88,409.6
Panama	89,141.3
Puerto Rico	68,673.6
USA	2,357,757.5
Venezuela	46,299.9
Total (incl. others)	3,689,269.1

Exports f.o.b.*	1996	1997†
Belgium–Luxembourg	40,860.6	102,032.5
Canada	19,163.5	21,673.5
Germany	8,531.7	6,152.2
Haiti	24,440.9	26,451.1
Honduras	5,490.0	9,973.7
Italy	12,970.7	16,840.2
Japan	16,489.4	24,693.6
Korea, Republic	46,948.2	43,603.9
Netherlands	87,166.2	18,492.9
Panama	13,227.6	7,380.5
Puerto Rico	60,682.3	121,412.1
Spain	12,584.0	10,422.6
USA	429,741.2	484,207.4
Total (incl. others)	835,712.9	958,229.3

* Excluding exports from free-trade zones.
† Provisional figures.

Transport

ROAD TRAFFIC (motor vehicles in use at 31 December, estimates)

	1997	1998
Passenger cars	305,477	353,177
Buses and coaches	27,380	32,619
Lorries and vans	147,523	167,728

SHIPPING

Merchant Fleet (registered at 31 December)

	1996	1997	1998
Number of vessels	27	25	20
Total displacement ('000 grt) . .	12.0	11.3	9.0

Source: Lloyd's Register of Shipping, *World Fleet Statistics*.

International Sea-borne Freight Traffic ('000 metric tons)

	1996	1997	1998
Goods loaded	112	152	139

Source: UN, *Monthly Bulletin of Statistics*.

CIVIL AVIATION (traffic on scheduled services)

	1995	1996	1997
Kilometres flown (million) . .	1	1	1
Passengers carried ('000) . . .	67	30	34
Passengers-km (million) . .	28	14	16
Total ton-km (million) . . .	3	1	1

Source: UN, *Statistical Yearbook*.

Tourism

ARRIVALS BY NATIONALITY

	1996	1997	1998
Canada	127,683	152,777	170,027
USA	412,016	402,039	437,803
Argentina	62,996	64,404	78,764
United Kingdom	121,778	216,790	188,184
Italy	104,218	118,551	110,332
Spain	91,367	106,398	110,782
Austria	40,262	36,753	30,017
Belgium	35,309	46,590	40,145
France	32,479	57,507	95,771
Germany	327,772	328,860	366,599
Total (incl. others) . . .	1,948,464	2,184,688	2,334,493

Source: WTO, *Yearbook of Tourism Statistics*.

Receipts from Tourism (US $ million): 2,099.4 in 1997; 2,153.1 in 1998; 2,524.0 (preliminary) in 1999.

Arrivals ('000, 1999): Total 2,930 (by air 2,649; by sea 281).

Communications Media

	1995	1996	1997
Radio receivers ('000 in use) . .	1,380	1,410	1,440
Television receivers ('000 in use) .	728	750	770
Telephones ('000 main lines in use)	581	622	709
Telefax stations (number in use) .	n.a.	2,300	n.a.
Mobile cellular telephones (subscribers)	53,973	77,795	130,149

Daily newspapers: 12 in 1996 (estimated average circulation 416,000 copies).

Sources: UNESCO, *Statistical Yearbook*; UN, *Statistical Yearbook*.

Education

(1996/97)

	Institu-tions	Teachers	Students Males	Students Females	Students Total
Pre-primary*	n.a.	8,571	96,252	94,289	190,541
Primary . .	4,001†	39,860	691,675	668,369	1,360,044
Secondary:					
General . .	1,737	11,033	145,560*	184,384*	329,944*
Teacher-training†	n.a.	86	549	743	1,292
Vocational†	n.a.	1,211	9,147	12,356	21,503
Higher . .	n.a.	9,041	75,223	101,772	176,995

* 1997/98 figure(s).   † 1994/95 figure(s).

Source: UNESCO, *Statistical Yearbook*.

Directory

The Constitution

The Constitution of the Dominican Republic was promulgated on 28 November 1966. Its main provisions are summarized below:

The Dominican Republic is a sovereign, free, independent state; no organizations set up by the State can bring about any act which might cause direct or indirect intervention in the internal or foreign affairs of the State or which might threaten the integrity of the State. The Dominican Republic recognizes and applies the norms of general and American international law and is in favour of and will support any initiative towards economic integration for the countries of America. The civil, republican, democratic, representative Government is divided into three independent powers: legislative, executive and judicial.

The territory of the Dominican Republic is as laid down in the Frontier Treaty of 1929 and its Protocol of Revision of 1936.

The life and property of the individual citizen are inviolable; there can be no sentence of death, torture nor any sentence which might cause physical harm to the individual. There is freedom of thought, of conscience, of religion, freedom to publish, freedom of unarmed association, provided that there is no subversion against public order, national security or decency. There is freedom of labour and trade unions; freedom to strike, except in the case of public services, according to the dispositions of the law.

The State will undertake agrarian reform, dedicating the land to useful interests and gradually eliminating the latifundios (large estates). The State will do all in its power to support all aspects of family life. Primary education is compulsory and all education is free. Social security services will be developed. Every Dominican has the duty to give what civil and military service the State may require. Every legally entitled citizen must exercise the right to vote, i.e. all persons over 18 years of age and all who are or have been married even if they are not yet 18.

GOVERNMENT

Legislative power is exercised by Congress which is made up of the Senate and Chamber of Deputies, elected by direct vote. Senators, one for each of the 30 Provinces and one for the Distrito Nacional, are elected for four years; they must be Dominicans in full exercise of their citizen's rights, and at least 25 years of age. Their duties are to elect judges, the President and other members of the Electoral and Accounts Councils, and to approve the nomination of diplomats. Deputies, one for every 50,000 inhabitants or fraction over 25,000 in each Province and the Distrito Nacional, are elected for four years and must fulfil the same conditions for election as Senators.

Decisions of Congress are taken by absolute majority of at least half the members of each house; urgent matters require a two-thirds' majority. Both houses normally meet on 27 February and 16 August each year for sessions of 90 days, which can be extended for a further 60 days.

Executive power is exercised by the President of the Republic, who is elected by direct vote for a four-year term. The President must be a Dominican citizen by birth or origin, over 30 years of age and in full exercise of citizen's rights. The President must not have engaged in any active military or police service for at least a year prior to election. The President takes office on 16 August following the election. The President of the Republic is Head of the Public Administration and Supreme Chief of the armed forces and police forces. The President's duties include nominating Secretaries and Assistant Secretaries of State and other public officials, promulgating and publishing laws and resolutions of Congress and seeing to their faithful execution, watching over the collection and just investment of national income, nominating, with the approval of the Senate, members of the Diplomatic Corps, receiving foreign Heads of State, presiding at national functions, decreeing a State of Siege or Emergency or any other measures necessary during a public crisis. The President may not leave the country for more than 15 days without authorization from Congress. In the absence of the President, the Vice-President will assume power, or failing him, the President of the Supreme Court of Justice.

LOCAL GOVERNMENT

Government in the Distrito Nacional and the Municipalities is in the hands of local councils, with members elected proportionally to the number of inhabitants, but numbering at least five. Each Province has a civil Governor, designated by the Executive.

JUDICIARY

Judicial power is exercised by the Supreme Court of Justice and the other Tribunals; no judicial official may hold another public office or employment, other than honorary or teaching. The Supreme Court is made up of at least nine judges, who must be Dominican citizens by birth or origin, at least 35 years old, in full exercise of their citizen's rights, graduates in law and have practised professionally for at least 12 years. There are also five Courts of Appeal, a Lands Tribunal and a Court of the First Instance in each judicial district; in each Municipality and in the Distrito Nacional there are also Justices of the Peace.

Elections are directed by the Central Electoral Board. The armed forces are essentially obedient and apolitical, created for the defence of national independence and the maintenance of public order and the Constitution and Laws.

The artistic and historical riches of the country, whoever owns them, are part of the cultural heritage of the country and are under the safe-keeping of the State. Mineral deposits belong to the State. There is freedom to form political parties, provided they conform to the principles laid down in the Constitution. Justice is administered without charge throughout the Republic.

This Constitution can be reformed if the proposal for reform is supported in Congress by one-third of the members of either house or by the Executive. A special session of Congress must be called and any resolutions must have a two-thirds' majority. There can be no reform of the method of government, which must always be civil, republican, democratic and representative.

Note: In August 1994 Congress resolved that the current President's term of office should be restricted to two years. Presidential elections were, therefore, scheduled for 1996. Other constitutional amendments included provisions for the prohibition of the re-election of the President to a consecutive term in office, the adoption of a two-round voting system for presidential elections, the reorganization of the judicial system and the replacement of the Central Electoral Board.

The Government

HEAD OF STATE

President: RAFAEL HIPÓLITO MEJÍA DOMÍNGUEZ (took office 16 August 2000).

Vice-President: Dra MILAGROS ORTIZ BOSCH.

CABINET
(April 2001)

Secretary of State to the Presidency: SERGIO GRULLÓN.

Secretary of State for External Relations: Dr HUGO TOLENTINO DIPP.

Secretary of State for the Interior and Police: Dr RAFAEL SUBERVÍ BONILLA.

Secretary of State for the Armed Forces: Maj.-Gen. JOSÉ MIGUEL SOTO JIMÉNEZ.

Secretary of State for Finance: FERNANDO ALVAREZ BOGAERT.

Secretary of State for Education: Dra MILAGROS ORTIZ BOSCH.

Secretary of State for Agriculture: ELIGIO JAQUEZ CRUZ.

Secretary of State for Public Works and Communications: MIGUEL VARGAS MALDONADO.

Secretary of State for Public Health and Social Welfare: Dr JOSÉ RODRÍGUEZ SOLDEVILLA.

Secretary of State for Industry and Commerce: ANGEL LOCKWARD.

Secretary of State for Labour: Dr MILTON RAY GUEVARA.

Secretary of State for Tourism: RAMÓN ALFREDO BORDAS.

Secretary of State for Sport, Physical Education and Recreation: CÉSAR CEDEÑO.

Secretary of State for Art and Culture: TONY RAFUL TEJADA.

Secretary of State for Women: Dra YADIRA HENRÍQUEZ.

Secretary of State for Youth: FRANCISCO ANTONIO PEÑA GUABA.

Secretary of State for the Environment and Natural Resources: FRANK MOYA PONS.

Secretaries of State without Portfolio: ANGEL MIOLAN, RAMÓN EMILIO JIMÉNEZ, ANTONIO TORRES, ELIAS WESSIN Y WESSIN.

Administrative Secretary to the Presidency: Dr PEDRO FRANCO BADÍA.

Technical Secretary to the Presidency: RAFAEL CALDERÓN.

Legal Counsel to the Presidency: GUIDO GÓMEZ MAZARA.

Attorney-General: VIRGILIO BELLO ROSA.

Governor of the Central Bank: Francisco Manuel Guerrero Prats.

Director of the Corporation of State Enterprises: Félix Calvo.

SECRETARIATS OF STATE

Administrative Secretariat of the Presidency: Palacio Nacional, Avda México, esq. Dr Delgado, Santo Domingo, DN; tel. 686-4771; fax 688-2100; internet www.presidencia.gov.do.

Technical Secretariat of the Presidency: Avda México, esq. Dr Delgado, Santo Domingo, DN; tel. 221-5140; fax 221-8627.

Secretariat of State for Agriculture: Autopista Duarte, Km 6.5, Los Jardines del Norte, Santo Domingo, DN; tel. 547-3888; fax 227-1268; internet www.agricultura.gov.do.

Secretariat of State for Defence: Plaza de la Independencia, Avda 27 de Febrero, esq. Luperón, Santo Domingo, DN; tel. 530-5149; fax 531-1309.

Secretariat of State for Education, Art and Culture: Avda Máximo Gómez 10, esq. Santiago, Santo Domingo, DN; tel. 688-9700; fax 689-8907.

Secretariat of State for External Relations: Avda Independencia 752, Santo Domingo, DN; tel. 535-6280; fax 533-5772; internet www.serex.gov.do.

Secretariat of State for the Environment: Santo Domingo, DN.

Secretariat of State for Finance: Avda México 45, Santo Domingo, DN; tel. 687-5131; fax 688-6561.

Secretariat of State for Industry and Commerce: Edif. de Oficinas Gubernamentales, 7°, Avda Francia, esq. Leopoldo Navarro, Santo Domingo, DN; tel. 685-5171; fax 686-4741; e-mail ind .comercio@codetel.net.do; internet www.seic.gov.do.

Secretariat of State for the Interior and Police: Edif. de Oficinas Gubernamentales, 3°, Avda Francia, esq. Leopoldo Navarro, Santo Domingo, DN; tel. 686-6251; fax 221-8234.

Secretariat of State for Labour: Centro de los Héroes, Calle Jiménez Moya 9, Santo Domingo, DN; tel. 535-4404; fax 535-4590; internet www.set.gov.do.

Secretariat of State for Public Health and Social Welfare: Avda Tiradentes, esq. San Cristóbal, Ensanche La Fe, Santo Domingo, DN; tel. 541-3121; fax 540-6445.

Secretariat of State for Public Works and Communications: Avda San Cristóbal, esq. Tiradentes, Ensanche La Fe, Santo Domingo, DN; tel. 565-2811; fax 562-3382.

Secretariat of State for Sport, Physical Education and Recreation: Avda Ortega y Gasset, Centro Olímpico, Santo Domingo, DN; tel. 540-4010; fax 563-6586.

Secretariat of State for Tourism: Bloque D, Edif. de Oficinas Gubernamentales, Avda México, esq. 30 de Marzo, Apdo 497, Santo Domingo, DN; tel. 221-4660; fax 682-3806; internet www .dominicana.com.do.

Secretariat of State for Women: Bloque D, Edif. de Oficinas Gubernamentales, Avda México, esq. 30 de Marzo, Santo Domingo, DN; tel. 685-3755; fax 686-0911.

Secretariat of State for Youth: Santo Domingo, DN.

President and Legislature

PRESIDENT

Election, 16 May 2000

Candidate	% of votes cast
Rafael Hipólito Mejía Domínguez (PRD)	49.87
Danilo Medina Sánchez (PLD)	24.94
Dr Joaquín Balaguer Ricardo (PRSC)	24.60
Total (incl. others)	100.0

CONGRESO NACIONAL

The National Congress comprises a Senate and a Chamber of Deputies.

President of the Senate: Rafael Albuquerque Ramírez (PRD).

President of the Chamber of Deputies: Dra Rafaela Alburquerque de González.

General Election, 16 May 1998

	Seats	
	Senate	Chamber of Deputies
Partido Revolucionario Dominicano (PRD)	24	83
Partido de la Liberación Dominicana (PLD)	4	49
Partido Reformista Social Cristiano (PRSC)	2	17
Total	30	149

Political Organizations

Alianza por la Democracia (APD): Santo Domingo, DN; f. 1992 by breakaway group of the PLD; split into two factions (led, respectively, by Max Puig and Nélsida Marmolejos) in 1993; Sec.-Gen. Vicente Bengoa.

Fuerza Nacional Progresista (FNP): Santo Domingo, DN; rightwing; Leader Mario Vinicio Castillo.

Fuerza de la Revolución: Avda Independencia 258, Apdo 2651, Santo Domingo, DN; e-mail fr@nodo50.ix.apc.org; internet www .nodo50.org/fr; f. 2000 by merger of the Partido Communista Dominicano, Movimiento Liberador 12 de Enero, Fuerza de Resistencia y Liberación Popular, Fuerza Revolucionaria 21 de Julio and other revolutionary groups; Marxist-Leninist.

Movimiento de Conciliación Nacional (MCN): Calle Pina 207, Santo Domingo, DN; f. 1969; centre party; 659,277 mems; Pres. Dr Jaime M. Fernández; Sec. Víctor Mena.

Movimiento de Integración Democrática (MIDA): Las Mercedes 607, Santo Domingo, DN; tel. 687-8895; centre-right; Leader Dr Francisco Augusto Lora.

Movimiento Popular Dominicano: Santo Domingo, DN; leftwing; Leader Julio de Peña Valdés.

Participación Ciudadana: Desiderio Arias 25, La Julia, Santo Domingo, DN; tel. 535-6200; fax 535-6631; e-mail p.ciudadana@ codetel.net.do; internet www.pciudadana.com; f. 1993; Leaders Javier Cabreja Polanco, Melba Barnett, Juan Bolívar Díaz.

Partido Demócrata Popular: Arz. Meriño 259, Santo Domingo, DN; tel. 685-2920; Leader Luis Homero Lájara Burgos.

Partido de la Liberación Dominicana (PLD): Avda Independencia 401, Santo Domingo, DN; tel. 685-3540; f. 1973 by breakaway group of PRD; left-wing; Leader Leonel Fernández Reyna; Sec.-Gen. José Tomás Pérez.

Partido Quisqueyano Demócrata (PQD): Bolívar 51, esq. Uruguay, Santo Domingo, DN; tel. 565-0244; internet www.geocities .com/CapitolHill/Senate/7090/; f. 1968; right-wing; 600,000 mems; Pres. Lic. Pedro Bergés; Sec.-Gen. Dr Elías Wessin Chávez.

Partido Reformista Social Cristiano (PRSC): Avda San Cristóbal, Ensanche La Fe, Apdo 1332, Santo Domingo, DN; tel. 566-7089; f. 1964; centre-right party; Leader Dr Joaquín Balaguer Ricardo; Pres. Donald Reid Cabral.

Partido Revolucionario Dominicano (PRD): Espaillat 118, Santo Domingo, DN; tel. 687-2193; internet www.prd.partidos.com; f. 1939; democratic socialist; mem. of Socialist International; 400,000 mems; Pres. Rafael Hipólito Mejía Domínguez; Sec.-Gen. Hatuey Decamps.

Partido Revolucionario Independiente (PRI): Santo Domingo; f. 1985 after split by the PRD's right-wing faction; Pres. José Rafael Molina Ureña; Sec.-Gen. Stormi Reynoso.

Partido Revolucionario Social Cristiano: Las Mercedes 141, Santo Domingo, DN; tel. 688-3511; f. 1961; left-wing; Pres. Dr Claudio Isidoro Acosta; Sec.-Gen. Dr Alfonso Lockward.

Partido de los Trabajadores Dominicanos: Avda Duarte 69 (Altos), Santo Domingo, DN; tel. 685-7705; f. 1979; workers' party; Sec.-Gen. José González Espinoza.

Unidad Democrática (UD): Santo Domingo; Leader Fernando Alvarez Bogaert.

Other parties include Unión Cívica Nacional (UCN), Partido Alianza Social Demócrata (ASD—Leader Dr José Rafael Abinader), Movimiento Nacional de Salvación (MNS—Leader Luis Julián Pérez), Partido Comunista del Trabajo de la República Dominicana (Sec.-Gen. Rafael Chaljub Mejía), Partido de Veteranos Civiles (PVC), Partido Acción Constitucional (PAC), Partido Unión Patriótica (PUP—Leader Roberto Santana), Partido de Acción Nacional (right-wing) and Movimiento de Acción Social Cristiana (ASC).

Diplomatic Representation

EMBASSIES IN THE DOMINICAN REPUBLIC

Argentina: Avda Máximo Gómez 10, Santo Domingo, DN; tel. 682-2977; fax 221-2206; Ambassador: ADRIÁN GUILLERMO MIRSON.

Brazil: Avda Winston Churchill 32, Edif. Franco-Acra y Asociados, 2°, Apdo 1655, Santo Domingo, DN; tel. 532-0868; Ambassador: P. G. VILAS-BÔAS CASTRO.

Chile: Avda Anacaona 11, Mirador del Sur, Santo Domingo, DN; tel. 532-7800; fax 530-8310; Ambassador: PATRICIO POZO RUIZ.

China (Taiwan): Edif. Palic, 1°, Avda Abraham Lincoln, esq. José Amado Soler, Apdo 4797, Santo Domingo, DN; tel. 562-5555; fax 563-4139; Ambassador: KUO KANG.

Colombia: Avda Abraham Lincoln 502, 2°, Santo Domingo, DN; tel. 567-6836; Ambassador: JOSÉ JOAQUÍN GORI CABRERA.

Costa Rica: Calle Malaquías Gil 11 Altos, Santo Domingo, DN; tel. 683-7209; fax 565-6467; e-mail emb.costarica@codetel.net.do; Ambassador: MARIO GARNIER BORELLA.

Ecuador: Calle Rafael Augusto Sánchez 17, Ensanche Naco, Apdo 808, Santo Domingo, DN; tel. 563-8363; fax 563-8153; e-mail mecuador@codetel.net.do; Ambassador: LUIS NARVÁEZ RIVADENEIRA.

El Salvador: Calle José A. Brea Peña 12, Ensanche Evaristo Morales, Santo Domingo, DN; tel. 565-4311; fax 541-7503; Ambassador: Dr BYRON F. LARIOS L.

France: Calle Las Damas 42, Zona Colonial, Santo Domingo, DN; tel. 689-2161; fax 221-8408; Ambassador: FRANÇOIS-XAVIER DENIAU.

Germany: Calle Rafael Augusto Sánchez 33, esq. Avda Lope de Vega, Ensanche Naco, Santo Domingo, DN; tel. 565-8811; fax 567-5014; Ambassador: IMMO VON KESSEL.

Guatemala: Z No 8, Ensanche Naco, Santo Domingo, DN; tel. 567-0110; fax 567-0115; Ambassador: Gen. ROBERTO MATA.

Haiti: 33 Juan Sánchez Ramírez, Santo Domingo, DN; tel. 686-5778; fax 686-6096; Chargé d'affaires: GUY G. LAMOTHE.

Holy See: Avda Máximo Gómez 27, Apdo 312, Santo Domingo, DN (Apostolic Nunciature); tel. 682-3773; fax 687-0287; Apostolic Nuncio: Most Rev. FRANÇOIS BACQUÉ, Titular Archbishop of Gradisca.

Honduras: Condominio Anacaona II, Edif. I, Apt 202, Avda Anacaona, Apdo 1486, Santo Domingo, DN; tel. 482-7992; fax 482-7505; Ambassador: ANDRÉS VÍCTOR ARTILES.

Israel: Pedro Henríquez Ureña 80, Santo Domingo, DN; tel. 541-8974; fax 562-3555; e-mail emb.israel@codetel.net.do; Ambassador: ELIAHU LÓPEZ.

Italy: Rodríguez Objío 4, Santo Domingo, DN; tel. 689-3684; fax 682-8296; e-mail ambital@codetel.net.do; Ambassador: STEFANO ALBERTO CANAVESIO.

Japan: Torre BHD, 8°, Avda Winston Churchill, esq. Luis F. Thomén, Santo Domingo, DN; tel. 567-3365; fax 566-8013; Ambassador: TSUNODA KATSUHIKO.

Korea, Republic: Avda Sarasota 98, Santo Domingo, DN; tel. 532-4314; fax 532-3807; Ambassador: YUN PARK.

Mexico: Rafael Hernández 11, Ensanche Naco, Santo Domingo, DN; tel. 565-2744; Ambassador: HUMBERTO LIRA MORA.

Nicaragua: Angel Cevero Cabral 32, Sánchez Juliete, Santo Domingo, DN; tel. 563-2311; fax 565-7961; Ambassador: ELSA ITALIA MEJÍA DE BERMUDEZ.

Panama: Hotel Embajador, Apdo 25338, Santo Domingo, DN; tel. 685-6950; Chargé d'affaires a.i.: Lic. ANTONIO PUELLO.

Peru: Cancillería, Avda Winston Churchill, Santo Domingo, DN; tel. 565-5851; Ambassador: RAÚL GUTIÉRREZ.

Russia: Santo Domingo, DN; Ambassador: VLADIMIR GONCHARENKO.

Spain: Independencia 1205, Santo Domingo, DN; tel. 535-1615; fax 535-1595; Ambassador: RICARDO DÍEZ HOCHLEITNER.

United Kingdom: Edif. Corominas Pepin, 7°, Avda 27 de Febrero 233, Santo Domingo; tel. 472-7111; fax 472-7574; Ambassador: DAVID WARD.

USA: César Nicolás Pensón, esq. Leopoldo Navarro, Santo Domingo, DN; tel. 541-2171; Ambassador: JANICE JACOBS (acting).

Uruguay: Avda México 169, Santo Domingo, DN; tel. 565-2669; Ambassador: JAIME WOLFSON KOT.

Venezuela: Cancillería, Avda Anaconda 7, Mirador Sur, Santo Domingo, DN; tel. 537-8578; fax 537-8780; Ambassador: Lic. MARÍA CLEMENCIA LÓPEZ-JIMÉNEZ.

Judicial System

The Judicial Power resides in the Supreme Court of Justice, the Courts of Appeal, the Tribunals of the First Instance, the municipal courts and the other judicial authorities provided by law. The Supreme Court is composed of at least nine judges (15 in December 1997) and the Attorney-General, and exercises disciplinary authority over all the members of the judiciary. The Attorney-General of the Republic is the Chief of Judicial Police and of the Public Ministry which he represents before the Supreme Court of Justice. The Consejo Nacional de la Magistratura (National Judiciary Council) appoints the members of the Supreme Court, which in turn appoints judges at all other levels of the judicial system.

Corte Suprema: Centro de los Héroes de Constanza, Santo Domingo, DN; tel. 533-3522; internet www.suprema.gov.do.

President: Dr JORGE SUBERO ISA.

Attorney-General: VIRGILIO BELLO ROSA.

Religion

The majority of the inhabitants belong to the Roman Catholic Church, but freedom of worship exists for all denominations. The Baptist, Evangelist and Seventh-day Adventist churches and the Jewish faith are also represented.

CHRISTIANITY

The Roman Catholic Church

The Dominican Republic comprises two archdioceses and nine dioceses. At 31 December 1998 adherents represented about 90.8% of the population.

Bishops' Conference: Conferencia del Episcopado Dominicano, Apdo 186, Santo Domingo, DN; tel. 685-3141; fax 689-9454; f. 1985; Pres. Cardinal NICOLÁS DE JESÚS LÓPEZ RODRÍGUEZ, Archbishop of Santo Domingo.

Archbishop of Santiago de los Caballeros: Most Rev. JUAN ANTONIO FLORES SANTANA, Arzobispado, Calle Duvergé 14, Apdo 679, Santiago de los Caballeros; tel. 582-2094; fax 581-3580.

Archbishop of Santo Domingo: Cardinal NICOLÁS DE JESÚS LÓPEZ RODRÍGUEZ, Arzobispado, Isabel la Católica 55, Apdo 186, Santo Domingo, DN; tel. 685-3141; fax 688-7270; e-mail f.j.arnaiz@codetel .net.do.

The Anglican Communion

Anglicans in the Dominican Republic are under the jurisdiction of the Episcopal Church in the USA. The country is classified as a missionary diocese, in Province IX.

Bishop of the Dominican Republic: Rt Rev. JULIO CÉSAR HOLGUÍN KHOURY, Calle Santiago 114, Apdo 764, Santo Domingo, DN; tel. 688-6016; fax 686-6364; e-mail h.khoury@codetel.net.do.

BAHÁ'Í FAITH

National Spiritual Assembly of the Bahá'ís of the Dominican Republic: Cambronal 152, esq. Beller, Santo Domingo, DN; f. 1961; tel. 687-1726; fax 687-7606; e-mail bahai.rd.aen@codetel.net.do; 402 localities.

The Press

Dirección General de Información, Publicidad y Prensa: Santo Domingo, DN; f. 1983; government supervisory body; Dir-Gen. LUIS GONZÁLEZ FABRA.

DAILIES

Santo Domingo, DN

El Caribe: Autopista Duarte, Km 7½, Apdo 416, Santo Domingo, DN; tel. 566-8161; fax 544-4003; f. 1948; morning; circ. 32,000; Editor ANTONIO EMILIO ORNÉS.

Diario Las Américas: Avda Tiradentes, Santo Domingo, DN; tel. 566-4577.

Hoy: Avda San Martín 236, Santo Domingo, DN; tel. 565-5581; fax 567-2424; f. 1981; morning; Dir MARIO ALVAREZ DUGAN; circ. 40,000.

Listín Diario: Paseo de los Periodistas 52, Ensanche Miraflores, Santo Domingo, DN; tel. 686-6688; fax 686-6595; e-mail listin .diario@codetel.net.do; internet www.codetel.net.do/listin-diario; f. 1889; morning; Dir RAFAEL MOLINA MORILLO; circ. 88,050.

El Nacional: San Martín 236, Apdo 1402, Santo Domingo, DN; tel. 565-5581; fax 565-4190; f. 1966; evening and Sunday; Dir MARIO ALVAREZ DUGAN; circ. 45,000.

La Noticia: Julio Verne 14, Santo Domingo, DN; tel. 535-0815; f. 1973; evening; Pres. JOSÉ A. BREA PEÑA; Dir BOLÍVAR BELLO.

El Nuevo Diario: Ensanche Gazcue, Santo Domingo, DN; tel. 687-6205; fax 688-0763; morning; Dir PERSIO MALDONADO.

El Siglo: Calle San Antonio 2, Zona Industrial de Herrera, Santo Domingo, DN; tel. 530-1000; fax 530-8412; e-mail editorial.golfo@ codetel.net.do; morning; Dir FEDERICO HENRÍQUEZ GRATEREAUX.

El Sol: Santo Domingo, DN; tel. 532-9511; morning; Pres. QUITERIO CEDEÑO; Dir-Gen. MIGUEL ANGEL CEDEÑO.

Ultima Hora: Paseo de los Periodistas 52, Ensanche Miraflores, Santo Domingo, DN; tel. 688-3361; fax 688-3019; e-mail ultimahora@codetel.net.do; internet www.codetel.net.do/ultimahora; f. 1970; evening; Dir RUDDY L. GONZÁLEZ C.; circ. 40,000.

Puerto Plata

El Porvenir: Calle Imbert 5, Apdo 614, Puerto Plata; f. 1872; Dir CARLOS ACEVEDO.

Santiago de los Caballeros, SD

La Información: Carretera Licey, Km 3, Santiago de los Caballeros, SD; tel. 581-1915; fax 581-7770; f. 1915; morning; Editor FERNANDO A. PÉREZ MEMÉN; circ. 15,000.

PERIODICALS AND REVIEWS

Agricultura: Santo Domingo, DN; organ of the State Secretariat of Agriculture; f. 1905; monthly; Dir MIGUEL RODRÍGUEZ, Jr.

Agroconocimiento: Apdo 345-2, Santo Domingo, DN; monthly; agricultural news and technical information; Dir DOMINGO MARTE; circ. 10,000.

¡Ahora!: San Martín 236, Apdo 1402, Santo Domingo, DN; tel. 565-5581; f. 1962; weekly; Dir MARIO ALVAREZ DUGAN.

La Campiña: San Martín 236, Apdo 1402, Santo Domingo, DN; f. 1967; Dir Ing. JUAN ULISES GARCÍA B.

Carta Dominicana: Avda Tiradentes 56, Santo Domingo, DN; tel. 566-0119; f. 1974; monthly; economics; Dir JUAN RAMÓN QUIÑONES M.

Deportes: San Martín 236, Apdo 1402, Santo Domingo, DN; f. 1967; sports; fortnightly; Dir L. R. CORDERO; circ. 5,000.

Eva: San Martín 236, Apdo 1402, Santo Domingo, DN; f. 1967; fortnightly; Dir MAGDA FLORENCIO.

Horizontes de América: Santo Domingo, DN; tel. 565-9717; f. 1967; monthly; Dir ARMANDO LEMUS CASTILLO.

Letra Grande, Arte y Literatura: Leonardo da Vinci 13, Mirador del Sur, Avda 27 de Febrero, Santo Domingo, DN; tel. 531-2225; f. 1980; monthly; art and literature; Dir JUAN RAMÓN QUIÑONES M.

Renovación: Calle José Reyes, esq. El Conde, Santo Domingo, DN; fortnightly; Dir OLGA QUISQUEYA VIUDA MARTÍNEZ.

FOREIGN PRESS BUREAUX

Agencia EFE (Spain): Galerías Comerciales, 5°, Of. 507, Avda 27 de Febrero, Santo Domingo, DN; tel. 567-7617; Bureau Chief ANTONIO CASTILLO URBERUAGA.

Agenzia Nazionale Stampa Associata (ANSA) (Italy): Calle Leopoldo Navarro 79, 3°, Sala 17, Apdo 20324, Huanca, Santo Domingo, DN; tel. 685-8765; fax 685-8765; Bureau Chief HUMBER ANDRÉS SUAZO.

Inter Press Service (IPS) (Italy): Calle Cambronal, No. 4-1, Ciudad Nueva, Santo Domingo, DN; tel. 593-5153; Correspondent VIANCO MARTÍNEZ.

United Press International (UPI) (USA): Carrera A. Manoguaybo 16, Manoguaybo, DN; tel. 689-7171; Chief Correspondent SANTIAGO ESTRELLA VELOZ.

Publishers

Santo Domingo, DN

Arte y Cine, C por A: Isabel la Católica 42, Santo Domingo, DN.

Editora Alfa y Omega: José Contreras 69, Santo Domingo, DN; tel. 532-5577.

Editora de las Antillas: Calle Pedro Henríquez Ureña, Santo Domingo, DN; tel. 685-2197.

Editora Dominicana, SA: 23 Oeste, No 3 Lup., Santo Domingo, DN; tel. 688-0846.

Editora El Caribe, C por A: Autopista Duarte, Km 7½, Apdo 416, Santo Domingo, DN; tel. 566-8161; fax 544-4003; f. 1948; Man. Dir RAFAEL DUARTE.

Editora Hoy, C por A: San Martín, 236, Santo Domingo, DN; tel. 566-1147.

Editora Listín Diario, C por A: Paseo de los Periodistas 52, Ensanche Miraflores, Apdo 1455, Santo Domingo, DN; tel. 686-6688; fax 686-6595; f. 1889; Pres. Dr ROGELIO A. PELLERANO.

Editorama, SA: Calle Justiniano Bobea, esq. Eugenio Contreras, Apdo 2074, Santo Domingo, DN; tel. 596-6669; fax 594-1421.

Editorial Padilla: San F. de Macorís 14, Santo Domingo, DN; tel. 682-3101.

Editorial Santo Domingo: Santo Domingo, DN; tel. 532-9431.

Editorial Stella: 19 de Marzo, Santo Domingo, DN; tel. 682-2281.

Julio D. Postigo e Hijos: Santo Domingo, DN; f. 1949; fiction; Man. J. D. POSTIGO.

Publicaciones Ahora, C por A: Avda San Martín 236, Apdo 1402, Santo Domingo; tel. 565-5580; fax 565-4190; Pres. JULIO CASTAÑO.

Publicaciones América: Santo Domingo, DN; Dir PEDRO BISONÓ.

Santiago de los Caballeros, SD

Editora el País, SA: Carrera Sánchez, Km 6½, Santiago de los Caballeros, SD; tel. 532-9511.

Broadcasting and Communications

Dirección General de Telecomunicaciones: Isabel la Católica 73, Santo Domingo, DN; tel. 682-2244; fax 682-3493; government supervisory body; Dir-Gen. RUBÉN MONTAS; Dir-Gen. of Television NELSON ARTURO MARTE.

Instituto Dominicano de Telecomunicaciones (INDOTEL): Santo Domingo, DN; Pres. ORLANDO JORGE MERA.

TELECOMMUNICATIONS

Compañía Dominicana de Teléfonos (Codetel): Avda Lincoln 1101, Apdo 1377, Santo Domingo, DN; tel. 220-2000; fax 543-1301; e-mail e.burri@codetel.net.do; internet www.codetel.net.do; f. 1930; Pres. JORGE IVAN RAMÍREZ; Gen. Man. GUILLERMO AMORE.

Tricom Telecomunicaciones de Voz, Data y Video: Avda Lope de Vega 95, Santo Domingo, DN; tel. 542-7556; fax 567-4412; internet www.tricom.net; Pres. ARTURO PELLERANO; Chief of Int. Relations CÉSAR A. FRANCO.

BROADCASTING

Radio

There were some 130 commercial stations in 2000. The government-owned broadcasting network, Radio Televisión Dominicana, operates nine radio stations.

Asociación Dominicana de Radiodifusoras (ADORA): Calle Paul Harris 3, Centro de los Héroes, Santo Domingo; tel. 535-4057; Pres. IVELISE DE TORRES.

Television

Corporación Dominicana de Radio y Televisión, Canal 9: Calle Emilio A. Morel, esq. Luis E. Pérez, Ensanche La Fe, Apdo 30043, Santo Domingo, DN; tel. 566-5876; fax 544-3607; commercial station; Channel 9; Dir-Gen. MANUEL QUIROZ GARCÍA.

Radio Televisión Dominicana: Dr Tejada Florentino 8, Apdo 869, Santo Domingo, DN; tel. 689-2120; government station; three channels, two relay stations; Dir-Gen. NELSON ARTURO MARTE; Gen. Man. AGUSTÍN MERCADO.

Rahintel Televisión: Centro de los Héroes de Constanza, Avda Independencia, Apdo 1220, Santo Domingo, DN; tel. 532-2531; fax 535-4575; commercial station; two channels; Pres. LEONEL ALMONTE V.

Teleantillas, Canal 2: Autopista Duarte, Km 7½, Los Prados, Apdo 30404, Santo Domingo, DN; tel. 567-7751; fax 540-4912; Gen. Man. JOSÉ A. MORENO.

Telecentro, SA: Avda Pasteur 204, Santo Domingo, DN; tel. 687-9161; fax 542-7582; Channel 13 for Santo Domingo and east region; Pres. JASINTO PEYNADO.

Tele-Inde Canal 13: Avda Pasteur 101, Santo Domingo, DN; tel. 687-9161; commercial station; Dir JULIO HAZIM.

Telesistema, Canal 11: Avda 27 de Febrero 52, Sector Bergel, Santo Domingo, DN; tel. 563-6661; fax 472-1754; Pres. JOSÉ L. CORREPIO.

Finance

(cap. = capital; dep. = deposits; m = million; p.u. = paid up; res = reserves; amounts in pesos)

BANKING

Supervisory Body

Superintendencia de Bancos: Avda México, esq. Leopoldo Navarro, Apdo 1326, Santo Domingo, DN; tel. 685-8141; fax 685-0859; f. 1947; Superintendent Lic. ALBERTO ELÍS ATALA LAJAN.

Central Bank

Banco Central de la República Dominicana: Calle Pedro Henríquez Ureña, esq. Leopoldo Navarro, Apdo 1347, Santo Domingo, DN; tel. 689-7121; fax 687-7488; e-mail info@bancentral.gov.do; internet www.bancentral.gov.do; f. 1947; cap. 0.7m., res 92.3m., dep. 6,321.7m. (Dec. 1996); Gov. FRANCISCO MANUEL GUERRERO PRATS; Man. NIEVES MÁRMOL DE PERICHE.

Commercial Banks

Banco BHD, SA: Avda 27 de Febrero, esq. Winston Churchill, Apdo 266-2, Santo Domingo, DN; tel. 243-3232; fax 562-4396; e-mail bhd@codetel.net.do; internet www.codetel.net.do.bhd; f. 1972; total assets 11,902m. (1999); Pres. José Antonio Caro; Gen. Man. Luis Molina A.; 35 brs.

Banco Dominicano del Progreso, SA: Avda John F. Kennedy 3, Apdo 1329, Santo Domingo, DN; tel. 563-3233; fax 563-2455; f. 1974; total assets 9,947m. (1999); Chair. Tomás A. Pastoriza; Exec. Vice-Pres. Pedro E. Castillo L.; 17 brs.

Banco Fiduciario, SA: Avda 27 de Febrero 50, Santo Domingo, DN; tel. 473-9400; fax 472-1466; total assets 7,876m. (1999); f. 1983; Exec. Vice-Pres. George Manuel Hazoury Peña.

Banco Global, SA: Avda R. Batancourt 1, esq. Avda A. Lincoln, Santo Domingo, DN; tel. 532-3000; fax 535-7070; total assets 11,486m. (1999).

Banco Intercontinental, SA: Avda Abraham Lincoln Casias, esq. José Contreras, Santo Domingo, DN; tel. 535-5500; fax 532-2474; total assets 10,129m. (1999).

Banco Mercantil: Avda Pastoriza 303, Santo Domingo; tel. 567-4444; fax 549-6509; internet www.mercantil.com.do; total assets 9,579m. (1999); Pres. Andrés Aybar Báez; Exec. Vice-Pres. Juan R. Oller; 11 brs.

Banco Metropolitano: Avda Lope de Vega, esq. Gustavo Mejía Ricart, Apdo 1872, Santo Domingo, DN; tel. 562-2442; fax 540-1566; f. 1974; total assets 12,055m. (1999); Pres. Agustín Verdeja; Gen. Dir Adalberto Pérez Perdomo; 7 brs.

Banco Nacional de Crédito, SA: Avda John F. Kennedy, esq. Tiradentes, Apdo 1408, Santo Domingo, DN; tel. 540-4441; fax 567-4854; e-mail info@bancredito.com; internet www.bancredito.com; f. 1981; total assets 10,365m. (1999); Pres. Máximo Pellerano; Vice-Pres. Marina de Garrigó.

Banco Popular Dominicano: Avda John F. Kennedy 20, Torre Popular, Apdo 1441, Santo Domingo, DN; tel. 544-8000; fax 544-5899; internet www.bpd.com.do; f. 1963; total assets 9,905m. (1999); Pres. Manuel Alejandro Grullón; 45 brs.

Banco de Reservas de la República Dominicana: Isabel la Católica 201, Apdo 1353, Santo Domingo, DN; tel. 687-5366; fax 685-0602; f. 1941; cap. 250.0m., res 681.8m., dep. 14,996.9m. (Dec. 1999); Chair. Daniel Toribio M.; Gen. Administrator Manuel Antonio Lara Hernández; 23 brs.

Development Banks

Banco Agrícola de la República Dominicana: Avda G. Washington 601, Apdo 1057, Santo Domingo, DN; tel. 533-1171; fax 535-8088; e-mail bagricola.refor@codetel.net.do; f. 1945; government agricultural development bank; Pres. Lic. Rafael Angeles Suárez; Gen. Administrator Radhamés Rodríguez Valerio.

Banco Hipotecario Bancomercio, SA: Avda Máximo Gómez, Santo Domingo, DN; tel. 541-6231.

Banco Hipotecario de la Construcción, SA (BANHICO): Avda Tiradentes (Altos Plaza Naco), Santo Domingo, DN; tel. 562-1281; f. 1977; Man. Dr Jaime Alvarez Dugan.

Banco Hipotecario Popular, SA: Avda 27 de Febrero 261, Santo Domingo, DN; tel. 544-6700; f. 1978; Pres. Manuel E. Jiménez F.

Banco Nacional de la Construcción: Avda Alma Mater, esq. Pedro Henríquez Ureña, Santo Domingo, DN; tel. 685-9776; f. 1977; Gen. Man. Luis Manuel Pellerano.

Foreign Banks

Bank of Nova Scotia (Canada): Avda John F. Kennedy, esq. Lope de Vega, Apdo 1494, Santo Domingo, DN; tel. 544-1700; fax 567-5732; f. 1920; Vice-Pres. and Gen. Man. Ariel D. Pérez; 13 brs.

Citibank NA (USA): Avda John F. Kennedy 1, Apdo 1492, Santo Domingo, DN; tel. 566-5611; fax 683-0906; f. 1962; Vice-Pres. and Gen. Man. Henry Comber; 7 brs.

STOCK EXCHANGE

Santo Domingo Securities Exchange Inc: Edif. Disesa, Suite 302, Avda Abraham Lincoln, Santo Domingo; tel. 567-6694; fax 567-6697; Pres. Felipe Auffant.

INSURANCE

Supervisory Body

Superintendencia de Seguros: Secretaría de Estado de Finanzas, Avda México, esq. Leopoldo Navarro, Santo Domingo, DN; tel. 688-1245; internet www.superseguro.gov.do; f. 1969; Superintendent Dr Domingo Batista.

Insurance Companies

American Life and General Insurance Co, C por A: Edif. ALICO, 5°, Avda Abraham Lincoln, Santo Domingo, DN; tel. 533-7131; fax 533-5969; general; Gen. Man. Frank Cabreja.

La Americana, SA: Edif. La Cumbre, Avda Tiradentes, Apdo 25241, Santo Domingo, DN; tel. 567-1211; f. 1975; life; Pres. Marino Ginebra H.

Atlantica Insurance, SA: Avda 27 de Febrero 265A. 2°, Apdo 826, Santo Domingo, DN; tel. 565-5591; fax 565-4343; Pres. Lic. Rhina Ramírez.

Bankers Security Life Insurance Society: Gustavo Mejia Ricart 61, Apdo 1123, Santo Domingo, DN; tel. 544-2626; fax 567-9389; Pres. Viriato Fiallo.

Bonanza Compañía de Seguros, SA: Edif. Santanita I, Of. 201, Avda San Martín 253, Santo Domingo, DN; tel. 565-5525; fax 565-5630; e-mail bonanza.seg@codetel.net.do; internet www.bonanza.dominicana.com.do; Pres. Lic. Dario Lama.

Britanica de Seguros, SA: Max Henríquez Ureña 35, Apdo 3637, Santo Domingo, DN; tel. 542-6863; fax 544-4542; e-mail wharper@codetel.net.do; Pres. John Harper Saleta.

Centro de Seguros La Popular, C por A: Gustavo Mejía Ricart 61, Apdo 1123, Santo Domingo, DN; tel. 566-1988; fax 567-9389; f. 1965; general except life; Pres. Lic. Rosa Fiallo.

La Colonial, SA: Edif. Haché, 2°, Avda John F. Kennedy, Santo Domingo, DN; tel. 565-9926; f. 1971; general; Pres. Dr Miguel Feris Iglesias.

Compañía Nacional de Seguros, C por A: Avda Máximo Gómez 31, Apdo 916, Santo Domingo, DN; tel. 687-5390; fax 682-3269; e-mail infocns@bancredito.com; internet www.cns.com.do; f. 1964; general; Chair. Dr Máximo A. Pellerano.

Compañía de Seguros Palic, SA: Avda Abraham Lincoln, esq. José Amado Soler, Apdo 1132, Santo Domingo, DN; tel. 562-1271; fax 562-1825; e-mail cia.seg.palic2@codetel.net.do; Pres. Lic. Eduardo Tolentino.

Confederación del Canada Dominicana: Salvador Sturla 17, Santo Domingo, DN; tel. 544-4144; fax 540-4740; Pres. Lic. Moises A. Franco Llenas.

Federal Insurance Company: Edif. La Cumbre, 4°, Avda Tiradentes, esq. Presidente González, Santo Domingo, DN; tel. 567-0181; fax 567-8909; Pres. Diego Ramón Sosa.

General de Seguros, SA: Avda Sarasota 55, Bella Vista, Santo Domingo, DN; tel. 535-8888; fax 532-4451; f. 1981; general; Pres. Dr Fernando A. Ballista Díaz.

La Intercontinental de Seguros, SA: Plaza Naco, 2°, Avda Tiradentes, Apdo 825, Santo Domingo, DN; tel. 562-1211; general; Pres. Lic. Ramón Báez Romano.

Magna Compañía de Seguros, SA: Edif. Magna Motors, Avda Abraham Lincoln, esq. John F. Kennedy, Santo Domingo, DN; tel. 544-1400; fax 562-5723; f. 1974; general and life; Pres. E. Antonio Lama S.; Man. Milagros de los Santos.

La Mundial de Seguros, SA: Avda Máximo Gómez, No 31, Santo Domingo, DN; tel. 685-2121; fax 682-3269; general except life and financial; Pres. Pedro D'acunha.

La Peninsular de Seguros, SA: Edif. Corp. Corominas Pepín, 3°, Avda 27 de Febrero 233, Santo Domingo, DN; tel. 472-1166; fax 563-2349; general; Pres. Lic. Ernesto Romero Landrón.

Reaseguradora Hispaniola, SA: Avda 27 de Febrero 205, Of. 202, Santo Domingo, DN; tel. 683-6150; fax 540-5288; Pres. Manuel de Jesús Colón.

Seguros La Antillana, SA: Avda Abraham Lincoln 708, Apdo 146 y 27, Santo Domingo, DN; tel. 567-4481; fax 541-2927; f. 1947; general and life; Pres. Lic. Oscar Lama.

Seguros La Isleña, C por A: Edif. Centro Coordinador Empresarial, Avda Nuñez de Caceres, esq. Guarocuya, Santo Domingo, DN; tel. 567-7211; fax 565-1448; Pres. María del Pilar Rodríguez.

Seguros Pepín, SA: Edif. Corp. Corominas Pepín, Avda 27 de Febrero 233, Santo Domingo, DN; tel. 472-1006; general; Pres. Dr Bienvenido Corominas.

Seguros San Rafael, C por A: Leopoldo Navarro 61, esq. San Francisco de Macorís, Santo Domingo, DN; tel. 688-2231; general; Admin. Victor Rodríguez.

El Sol de Seguros, SA: Torre Hipotecaria, 2°, Avda Tiradentes 25, Santo Domingo, DN; tel. 542-6063; general; Pres. Guillermo Armenteros.

Sudamericana de Seguros, SA: El Conde 105, frente al Parque Colón, Santo Domingo, DN; tel. 685-0141; fax 688-8074; Pres. Vincenzo Mastrolilli.

Transglobal de Seguros, SA: Avda Lope de Vega 16, esq. Porfirio Herreral, Apdo 1869, Santo Domingo, DN; tel. 683-4877; fax 567-9398; e-mail transglobal@codetel.net.do; Dirs José Manuel Vargas, Oscar Lama.

Universal América, C por A: Santo Domingo, DN; tel. 544-7200; fax 544-7999; internet www.universal.com.do; f. 1964 as La Universal de Seguros; merged with Grupo Asegurador América in 2000; general; Pres. Ing. Ernesto Izquierdo.

Insurance Association

Cámara Dominicana de Aseguradores y Reaseguradores, Inc:
Edif. Torre BHD, 5°, Calle Luis F. Thomen, esq. Winston Churchill,
Santo Domingo, DN; tel. 566-0019; fax 566-2600; e-mail cadoar@
codetel.net.do; internet www.cadoar.org.do; f. 1972; Pres. Lic.
NELSON HEDI HERNÁNDEZ.

Trade and Industry

GOVERNMENT AGENCIES

Comisión para la Reforma de la Empresa Pública: Santo
Domingo, DN; commission charged with divestment and restructuring of state enterprises; Pres. JOSÉ DEL CARMEN MARCANO.

Consejo Estatal del Azúcar (CEA) (State Sugar Council): Centro
de los Héroes, Apdo 1256/1258, Santo Domingo, DN; tel. 533-1161;
fax 533-7393; f. 1966; management of operations contracted to private consortiums in 1999; Dir-Gen. VÍCTOR MANUEL BÁEZ.

Corporación Dominicana de Empresas Estatales (CORDE)
(Dominican State Corporation): Avda General Antonio Duvergé,
Apdo 1378, Santo Domingo, DN; tel. 533-5171; f. 1966 to administer,
direct and develop state enterprises; Dir-Gen. FÉLIX CALVO.

Instituto de Estabilización de Precios (INESPRE): Avda Luperón, Santo Domingo, DN; tel. 530-0020; fax 530-0343; f. 1969; price
commission; Dir PABLO MERCEDES.

Instituto Nacional de la Vivienda: Antiguo Edif. del Banco
Central, Avda Pedro Henríquez Ureña, esq. Leopoldo Navarro, Apdo
1506, Santo Domingo, DN; tel. 685-4181; f. 1962; low-cost housing
institute; Dir-Gen. Ing. JUAN ANTONIO VARGAS.

DEVELOPMENT ORGANIZATIONS

**Departamento de Desarrollo y Financiamento de
Proyectos—DEFINPRO:** c/o Banco Central de la República Dominicana, Calle Pedro Henríquez Ureña, esq. Leopoldo Navarro, Apdo
1347, Santo Domingo, DN; tel. 221-9111; fax 687-7488; f. 1993;
associated with AID, IDB, WB, KFW; encourages economic development in productive sectors of economy, excluding sugar; authorizes
complementary financing to private sector for establishing and
developing industrial and agricultural enterprises and free-zone
industrial parks; Dir ANGEL NERY CASTILLO PIMENTEL.

Fundación Dominicana de Desarrollo (Dominican Development
Foundation): Calle Mercedes No 4, Apdo 857, Santo Domingo, DN;
f. 1962 to mobilize private resources for collaboration in financing
small-scale development programmes; 384 mems; Dir Lic. ADA WIS-
COVICTH.

Instituto de Desarrollo y Crédito Cooperativo (IDECOOP):
Centro de los Héroes, Apdo 1371, Santo Domingo, DN; tel. 533-
8131; fax 535-5148; f. 1963 to encourage the development of co-
operatives; Dir JAVIER PEÑA NUÑEZ.

CHAMBERS OF COMMERCE

Cámara de Comercio y Producción de Santo Domingo: Arz.
Nouel 206, Zona Colonial, Apdo 815, Santo Domingo, DN; tel. 682-
7206; fax 685-2228; e-mail cámara.sto.dgo.@codetel.net.do; f. 1910;
1,500 active mems; Pres. JOSÉ MANUEL ARMENTEROS; Exec. Dir MIL-
AGROS J. PUELLO.

**Cámara Americana de Comercio de la República Domin-
icana:** Torre BHD, 4°, Avda Winston Churchill, Santo Domingo,
DN; tel. 544-2222; fax 544-0502; e-mail amcham@codetel.net.do;
internet www.amcham.org.do; Pres. ANDRÉS AYBAR BÁEZ.

There are official Chambers of Commerce in the larger towns.

INDUSTRIAL AND TRADE ASSOCIATIONS

Asociación Dominicana de Hacendados y Agricultores Inc:
Avda Sarasota 20, Santo Domingo, DN; tel. 565-0542; farming and
agricultural org.; Pres. Lic. CESARIO CONTRERAS.

Asociación de Industrias de la República Dominicana Inc:
Avda Sarasota 20, Apdo 850, Santo Domingo, DN; tel. 535-9111; fax
533-7520; f. 1962; industrial org.; Pres. NASSIM ALEMANY.

**Centro Dominicano de Promoción de Exportaciones
(CEDOPEX):** Plaza de la Bandera, Apdo 199-2, Santo Domingo,
DN; tel. 530-5505; fax 530-8208; e-mail cedopex@codetel.net.do;
internet www.cedopex.gov.do; organization for the promotion of
exports; Dir ROLANDO GALVÁN.

Consejo Nacional de la Empresa Privada (CONEP): Santo
Domingo, DN; Pres. Lic. MARINO GINEBRA.

Consejo Promotor de Inversiones (Investment Promotion
Council): Avda Abraham Lincoln, 2°, Santo Domingo; tel. 532-3281;
fax 533-7029; Exec. Dir and CEO FREDERIC EMAM ZADÉ.

Corporación de Fomento Industrial (CFI): Avda 27 de Febrero,
Plaza Independencia, Apdo 1452, Santo Domingo, DN; tel. 530-

0010; fax 530-1303; f. 1962 to promote agro-industrial development;
Dir-Gen. JOSÉ OVALLE.

Dirección General de Minería e Hidrocarburos: Edif. de Oficinas Gubernamentales, 10°, Avda México, esq. Leopoldo Navarro,
Santo Domingo, DN; tel. 687-7557; fax 686-8327; f. 1947; government
mining and hydrocarbon org.; Dir-Gen. PEDRO VÁSQUEZ.

Instituto Agrario Dominicano (IAD): Avda 27 de Febrero, Santo
Domingo, DN; tel. 530-8272; Dir-Gen. TOMÁS HERNÁNDEZ ALBERTO.

Instituto Dominicano de Tecnología Industrial (INDOTEC):
Avda Nuñez de Caceres, esq. Olof Palme, Santo Domingo, DN;
tel. 566-8121; fax 227-8808; e-mail indotec@codetel.net.do; internet
www.indotec.gov.do; Dir ANTONIO ALMONTE REYNOSO.

Instituto Nacional del Azúcar (INAZUCAR): Avda Jiménez
Moya, Apdo 667, Santo Domingo, DN; tel. 532-5571; internet
www.inazucar.gov.do; sugar institute; f. 1965; Dir-Gen. RAFAEL MON-
TILLA.

EMPLOYERS' ORGANIZATIONS

Confederación Patronal de la República Dominicana: Edif.
Mella, Cambronal/G. Washington, Santo Domingo, DN; tel. 688-
3017; Pres. Ing. HERIBERTO DE CASTRO.

Consejo Nacional de Hombres de Empresa Inc: Edif. Motor-
ámbar, 7°, Avda Abraham Lincoln 1056, Santo Domingo, DN; tel.
562-1666; Pres. JOSÉ MANUEL PALIZA.

Federación Dominicana de Comerciantes: Carretera Sánchez
Km 10, Santo Domingo, DN; tel. 533-2666; Pres. IVAN GARCÍA.

UTILITIES

Electricity

Corporación Dominicana de Electricidad (CDE): Centro de los
Héroes, Apdo 1428, Santo Domingo, DN; tel. 535-1100; fax 535-
7472; f. 1955; state electricity company; partially privatized in 1999;
Dir-Gen. MARCELO JORGE PÉREZ; Admin. CÉSAR DOMINGO SÁNCHEZ
TORRES.

Superintendencia de Electricidad: Santo Domingo, DN; Superintendent JOSÉ D. OVALLE TEJADA.

Water

Instituto Nacional de Aguas Potables (INAPA): Santo Domingo,
DN; Exec. Dir JUAN ROBERTO RODRÍGUEZ HERNÁNDEZ.

Instituto Nacional de Recursos Hidráulicos: Centro de los
Héroes, Santo Domingo, DN; tel. 532-3271; f. 1965; Dir FRANK RODRÍ-
GUEZ.

TRADE UNIONS

Central General de Trabajadores (CGT): Calle 26, esq. Duarte,
Santo Domingo, DN; tel. 688-3932; f. 1972; 13 sections; Sec.-Gen.
FRANCISCO ANTONIO SANTOS; 65,000 mems.

Central de Trabajadores Independientes (CTI): Calle Juan
Erazo 133, Santo Domingo, DN; tel. 688-3932; f. 1978; left-wing;
Sec.-Gen. RAFAEL SANTOS.

Central de Trabajadores Mayoritarias (CTM): Tunti Cáceres
222, Santo Domingo, DN; tel. 562-3392; Sec.-Gen. NÉLSIDA MARMO-
LEJOS.

Confederación Autónoma de Sindicatos Clasistas (CASC)
(Autonomous Confederation of Trade Unions): J. Erazo 39, Santo
Domingo, DN; tel. 687-8533; f. 1962; supports PRSC; Sec.-Gen.
GABRIEL DEL RÍO.

**Confederación Nacional de Trabajadores Dominicanos
(CNTD)** (National Confederation of Dominican Workers): Santo
Domingo, DN; f. 1988 by merger; 11 provincial federations totalling
150 unions are affiliated; Sec.-Gen. JULIO DE PEÑA VÁLDEZ; 188,000
mems (est.).

Confederación de Trabajadores Unitaria (CTU) (United Workers' Confederation): Santo Domingo, DN; f. 1991.

Transport

RAILWAYS

In 2001 a proposal for the construction of a US $200m. passenger
and freight railway between Santo Domingo and Santiago, with the
possibility of extension to other areas, was under discussion.

Dirección General de Tránsito Terrestre: Avda San Cristóbal,
Santo Domingo, DN; tel. 565-2811; f. 1966; operated by Secretary
of State for Public Works and Communications; Dir-Gen. Ing. LUIS
EMILIO PINA.

Ferrocarriles Unidos Dominicanos: Santo Domingo; government-owned; 142 km of track from La Vega to Sánchez and from
Guayubín to Pepillo principally used for the transport of exports.

There are also a number of semi-autonomous and private railway companies for the transport of sugar cane, including:

Ferrocarril de Central Romana: La Romana; 375 km open; Pres. C. MORALES.

Ferrocarril Central Río Haina: Apdo 1258, Haina; 113 km open.

ROADS

In 1996 there were an estimated 12,600 km of roads, of which about 6,225 were paved. There is a direct route from Santo Domingo to Port-au-Prince in Haiti. In 2001 plans were proceeding for the construction of a toll road between Boca and San Pedro de Macorís at a cost of US $65m.

Dirección General de Mantenimiento de Carreteras y Caminos Vecinales: Santo Domingo, DN; f. 1987; government supervisory body; Dir-Gen. JESÚS MARIA MARTÍNEZ.

SHIPPING

The Dominican Republic has 14 ports, of which Santo Domingo is by far the largest, handling about 80% of imports.

A number of foreign shipping companies operate services to the island.

Agencias Navieras B&R, SA: Avda Abraham Lincoln 504, Apdo 1221, Santo Domingo; tel. 544-2200; fax 562-3383; e-mail jperiche@navierasbr.com; internet www.navierasbr.com; f. 1919; shipping agents and export services; Man. JUAN PERICHE PIDAL.

Armadora Naval Dominicana, SA: Isabel la Católica 165, Apdo 2677, Santo Domingo, DN; tel. 689-6191; Man. Dir Capt. EINAR WETTRE.

Autoridad Portuaria Dominicana: Avda Máximo Gómez, Santo Domingo, DN; tel. 535-8462; Exec. Dir Prof. ANÍBAL GARCÍA DUVERGÉ.

Líneas Marítimas de Santo Domingo, SA: José Gabriel García 8, Apdo 1148, Santo Domingo, DN; tel. 689-9146; fax 685-4654; Pres.C. LLUBERES; Vice-Pres. JUAN T. TAVARES.

CIVIL AVIATION

There are international airports at Santo Domingo (Aeropuerto Internacional de las Américas José Francisco Peña Gómez), Puerto Plata and Barahona (Aeropuerto Internacional María Móntez). A further international airport, at Samaná, was under construction. In December 2000 a new 421m.-peso international airport opened in La Romana. The international airports were undergoing privatization in 1999–2000. Most main cities have domestic airports.

Dirección General de Aeronáutica Civil: Santo Domingo, DN; f. 1955; government supervisory body; Dir-Gen. Dr ANÍBAL AMPARO GARCÍA DÍAZ.

Aerochago: Aeropuerto Internacional de las Américas, Santo Domingo; tel. 549-0709; fax 549-0708; f. 1973; operates cargo and charter service in Central America and the Caribbean; Gen. Man. PEDRO RODRÍGUEZ.

Aerolíneas Argo: Avda 27 de Febrero 409, Santo Domingo, DN; tel. 566-1844; f. 1971; cargo and mail services to the USA, Puerto Rico and the US Virgin Islands.

Aerolíneas Dominicanas (Dominair): Calle el Sol 62, Apdo 202, Santiago; tel. 581-8882; fax 582-5074; f. 1974; scheduled and charter passenger services; Pres. JOSÉ ARMANDO BERMÚDEZ; Gen. Man. MARÍA TERESA VELÁSQUEZ.

Aerolíneas Santo Domingo: Edif. J.P., Avda 27 de Febrero 272, esq. Calle Seminario, Santo Domingo; e-mail asd@codetel.net.do; internet www.airsantodomingo.com; f. 1996; operates scheduled and charter internal, regional and international flights; Pres. HENRY W. AZAR.

Aeromar Airlines: Aeropuerto Internacional de las Américas, Santo Domingo; tel. 549-0281; fax 542-0152; cargo services.

Compañía Dominicana de Aviación C por A: Avda Jiménez de Moya, esq. José Contreras, Apdo 1415, Santo Domingo, DN; tel. 532-8511; fax 535-1656; f. 1944; operates on international routes connecting Santo Domingo with the Netherlands Antilles, Aruba, the USA, Haiti and Venezuela; operations suspended 1995, privatization pending; Chair. Dr RODOLFO RINCÓN; CEO MARINA GINEBRA DE BONNELLY.

Tourism

Strenuous efforts were made in the 1980s and 1990s to improve the tourism infrastructure, with 200m. pesos spent on increasing the number of hotel rooms by 50%, road improvements and new developments. In 2001 the Government announced a tourist development in the south-western province of Pedernales, consisting of a preliminary 2,400 hotel rooms. The total number of visitors to the Dominican Republic in 1999 was 2,930,000, of whom 281,000 were cruiseship passengers. In that year receipts from tourism totalled US $2,524m. There were 52,000 hotel rooms in the Dominican Republic in 2000, with a further 7,000 rooms under construction.

Secretaría de Estado de Turismo: Bloque D, Edif. de Oficinas Gubernamentales, Avda México, esq. 30 de Marzo, Apdo 497, Santo Domingo, DN; tel. 221-4660; fax 682-3806; Sec. of State for Tourism RAMÓN ALFREDO BORDAS.

Asociación Dominicana de Agencias de Viajes: Carrera Sánchez 201, Santo Domingo, DN; tel. 687-8984; Pres. RAMÓN PRIETO.

Consejo de Promoción Turística: Avda México 66, Santo Domingo, DN; tel. 687-4676; fax 687-4727; e-mail cpt@codetel.net.do.

EAST TIMOR

Introductory Survey

Location, Climate, Language, Religion, Flag, Capital

East Timor, which is styled Timor Loro Sa'e (Timor of the rising sun) in the principal indigenous language, Tetum, occupies the eastern half of the island of Timor, which lies off the north coast of Western Australia. The western half of the island is Indonesian territory and constitutes part of the East Nusa Tenggara Province. In addition to the eastern half of Timor island, the territory also includes an enclave around Ocusse (Oekussi) Ambeno on the north-west coast of the island, and the islands of Ataúro (Pulo Cambing) and Jaco (Pulo Jako). Timor's climate is dominated by intense monsoon rain, succeeded by a pronounced dry season. The north coast of the island has a brief rainy season from December to February; the south coast a double rainy season from December to June, with a respite in March. The mountainous spine of the island has heavy rains that feed torrential floods. The National Council of Timorese Resistance (CNRT) has proposed the adoption of Tetum as a national language, and Portuguese as an official language. Hitherto, Bahasa Indonesia (a form of Malay) has been the principal medium of instruction in the public school system. More than 30 languages are in use in East Timor. The predominant religion is Christianity; 86% of the population were adherents of Roman Catholicism in 1997. Islam and animism are also practised. By early 2001 a national flag had not yet been officially adopted. The capital is Dili.

Recent History

The Portuguese began trading in Timor in about 1520, principally for sandalwood, and they later established settlements and several ports on the island. They were forced to move to the north and east of the island by the Dutch, who had arrived in the early part of the 18th century and had established themselves at Kupana in the south-west. The division of the island between Portugal and the Netherlands was formalized in a treaty of 1859, although the boundaries were modified slightly in 1904. Portuguese Timor and Macau were administered as a single entity until 1896, when Portuguese Timor became a separate province. The eastern half remained a Portuguese overseas province when the Dutch recognized the western area as part of Indonesia in 1949.

The military coup in Portugal in April 1974 was followed by increased political activity in Portuguese Timor. In August 1975 the União Democrática Timorense (UDT, Timorese Democratic Union) demanded independence for Timor. The UDT allied with two other parties, the Associação Popular Democrática de Timor (APODETI) and Kota, against the alleged threat of a Communist regime being established by the Frente Revolucionária do Timor Leste Independente (Fretilin, Revolutionary Front for an Independent East Timor), and fighting broke out. The UDT forces were supported by the Indonesians. Gains on both sides were uneven, with Fretilin in control of Dili in mid-September. In the same month the Portuguese administration abandoned the capital and moved to the offshore island of Ataúro. A Portuguese attempt to arrange peace talks was rejected in October. The Indonesians intervened directly and by the beginning of December Indonesian troops controlled the capital. Portuguese-Indonesian peace talks in Rome in November were unsuccessful, and diplomatic relations were suspended after Indonesian military involvement. Two meetings of the UN Security Council voted for immediate withdrawal of Indonesian troops. Fretilin's unilateral declaration of independence in November was recognized in December by the People's Republic of China. In December the enclave of Ocusse (Oekussi) Ambeno in West Timor was declared part of Indonesian territory. In May 1976 the People's Representative Council of East Timor voted for integration with Indonesia. The United Nations did not recognize the composition of the Council as being representative, however, and by mid-1976 the Portuguese had not formally ceded the right to govern, although they had no remaining presence in the territory.

In July 1976 East Timor was declared the 27th province of Indonesia. Human rights organizations claimed that as many as 200,000 people, from a total population of 650,000, might

have been killed by the Indonesian armed forces during the annexation. In February 1983 the UN Commission on Human Rights adopted a resolution affirming East Timor's right to independence and self-determination, and in early 1999 the UN continued to withhold recognition of Indonesia's absorption of the territory. In September 1983, following a five-month cease-fire (during which government representatives negotiated with Fretilin), the armed forces launched a major new offensive. During 1984 conditions in East Timor deteriorated, with widespread hunger, disease and repression among civilians, and continuing battles between rebels and Indonesian troops. The rebels suffered a serious set-back in August 1985, when the Australian Government recognized Indonesia's incorporation of East Timor. In November 1988 Gen. Suharto, the President of Indonesia, visited East Timor, prior to announcing that travel restrictions (in force since the annexation in 1976) were to be withdrawn. The territory was opened to visitors in late December. In October 1989 the Pope visited East Timor, as part of a tour of Indonesia, and made a plea to the Government to halt violations of human rights. Following a mass conducted by the Pope in the provincial capital, Dili, anti-Government protesters clashed with security guards. In January 1990 a visit to East Timor by the US ambassador to Indonesia prompted further demonstrations, which were violently suppressed by the armed forces. In October student protests led to the occupation of two schools by the armed forces and to the arrest, and alleged torture, of nearly 100 students. In November the Government rejected proposals by the military commander of Fretilin, José Alexandre (Xanana) Gusmão, for unconditional peace negotiations aimed at ending the armed struggle in East Timor.

In 1991 tension in East Timor increased prior to a proposed visit by a Portuguese parliamentary delegation. Some Timorese alleged that the armed forces had initiated a campaign of intimidation to discourage demonstrations during the Portuguese visit. The mission, which was to have taken place in November, was postponed, owing to Indonesia's objection to the inclusion of an Australian journalist who was a prominent critic of Indonesia's policies in East Timor. In November the armed forces fired on a peaceful demonstration (believed to have been originally organized to coincide with the Portuguese visit) at the funeral of a separatist sympathizer in Dili. The Indonesian Armed Forces (ABRI), which admitted killing 20 civilians, claimed that the attack had been provoked by armed Fretilin activists. Independent observers and human rights groups refuted this and estimated the number of deaths at between 100 and 180. There were also subsequent allegations of the summary execution of as many as 100 witnesses. Under intense international pressure, Suharto established a National Investigation Commission. The impartiality of the Commission was challenged, however, on the grounds that it excluded non-governmental organizations, and Fretilin announced that it would boycott the investigation. Despite this, the Commission's findings received cautious foreign approbation, as they were mildly critical of ABRI and stated that 50 people had died, and 90 disappeared, in the massacre. The senior military officers in East Timor were replaced, and 14 members of the armed forces were tried by a military tribunal. The most severe penalty received by any of the soldiers involved was 18 months' imprisonment; this contrasted starkly with the sentences of convicted demonstrators, which ranged from five years' to life imprisonment.

In July 1992 Indonesia and Portugal agreed to resume discussions on East Timor under the auspices of the UN Secretary-General (although without a representative from Fretilin, which had indicated in May that it was prepared to take part in the negotiations). In August the UN General Assembly adopted its first resolution condemning Indonesia's violations of fundamental human rights in East Timor. In September the appointment of Abílio Soares as Governor of East Timor provoked widespread criticism in the province; although Soares was a native of East Timor, he was a leading advocate of the Indonesian occupation. In October the US Congress suspended defence training aid to Indonesia, in protest at the killing of separatist demonstrators in November 1991. In October 1992, prior to the anniversary of the massacre, Amnesty International reported that hundreds of suspected supporters of independence had been arrested and tortured to prevent a commemorative demonstration.

In late November 1992 Xanana Gusmão was arrested. He was subsequently taken to Jakarta, where he was to be tried in February 1993 on charges of subversion and illegal possession of firearms. Xanana Gusmão's detention provoked international concern, and his replacement as leader of Fretilin, António Gomes da Costa (Mau Huno—who was himself arrested in April), claimed that his predecessor had been tortured. Two weeks after his capture, Xanana Gusmão publicly recanted his opposition to Indonesian rule in East Timor and advised Fretilin members to surrender. It transpired, however, that he was only co-operating with the authorities in order to gain the opportunity to speak publicly at a later date. During his trial, he was prevented from reading a prepared statement; the document was, however, illicitly conveyed to the press and was widely disseminated. In May Xanana Gusmão was found guilty of rebellion, conspiracy, attempting to establish a separate state and illegal possession of weapons, and was condemned to life imprisonment. The sentence was commuted to 20 years by Suharto in August. During the same month it was announced that all government combat forces were to be withdrawn from East Timor, leaving only troops involved in development projects. In September, however, the new acting leader of Fretilin, Konis Santana, declared that, contrary to announcements, the Indonesians were renewing their forces in East Timor and that killings and atrocities continued.

In December 1993 Xanana Gusmão managed to convey letters to the Portuguese Government and the International Commission of Jurists (see p. 322), demanding an annulment of his trial, owing to the lack of impartiality of his defence lawyer. The Government subsequently banned Xanana Gusmão from receiving visitors. Also in December the first reconciliation talks took place in the United Kingdom between an Indonesian government official and a former leader of Timorese exiles opposed to Indonesia's occupation of East Timor. In January 1994 Indonesia announced to the UN Secretary-General's envoy that it would facilitate access to East Timor by human rights and UN organizations. In late May, however, a privately-organized human rights conference being held in the Philippines, entitled the Asia-Pacific Conference on East Timor, provoked diplomatic tension with the Indonesian Government, which had attempted to force the abandonment of the conference. The outcome of the conference was the establishment of an Asia-Pacific coalition on East Timor, which consisted mainly of non-governmental organizations active in the region.

In July 1994 the Indonesian authorities suppressed a demonstration in Dili, following weeks of increasing tension in the capital; at least three people were reportedly killed and an estimated 20 injured during the protest. In August it was reported that the armed forces had held talks with Xanana Gusmão, included in which was the discussion of the possibility of holding a referendum under the auspices of the UN to determine the future status of the disputed territory. A second round of reconciliation talks between Indonesian officials and East Timorese exiles was held between late September and early October in the United Kingdom, and was attended by a UN envoy, although the main East Timorese opposition groups opposed the discussions, on the grounds that the participating East Timorese exiles were mostly in favour of Indonesian rule. The Indonesian Minister of Foreign Affairs, Ali Alatas, also held discussions in October in New York, in the USA, with José Ramos Horta, the Secretary for International Relations of Fretilin, the first such talks to be officially recognized. At the beginning of November President Suharto agreed to hold talks with exiled East Timorese dissidents. The Government's increasingly conciliatory position on East Timor was, however, reported largely to be a superficial attempt to improve the country's human rights image prior to the holding of the Asia-Pacific Economic Co-operation (APEC—see p. 128) summit meeting in Bogor, 60 km south of Jakarta, in mid-November. On 12 November, the third anniversary of the Dili massacre in 1991, 29 East Timorese protesters began an occupation of the US embassy in Jakarta, which coincided with the attendance of the US President, Bill Clinton, at the summit. The students demanded, unsuccessfully, a meeting with the visiting US Secretary of State and the release of Xanana Gusmão. They were eventually granted political asylum in Portugal and were shortly afterwards allowed by the Indonesian authorities to leave the embassy compound. Also in November riots involving more than 1,000 demonstrators broke out in Dili as delegates began arriving in Jakarta for the opening of the APEC summit meeting. Further disturbances later in the month were blamed by the authorities on incitement by the Western media.

In January 1995 Alatas, the Portuguese Minister of Foreign Affairs and the UN Secretary-General met in Geneva, Switzerland, for the fifth round of talks on East Timor. Agreement was reached to convene a meeting between separatist and pro-integrationist Timorese activists under the auspices of the UN, called the All-Inclusive Intra-East Timorese Dialogue (AETD). The AETD, which was held in June 1995, March 1996 and October 1997, failed to achieve any conclusive progress. The sixth and seventh rounds of talks between the Portuguese and Indonesian ministers responsible for foreign affairs took place in July 1995 and January 1996, again with little progress.

In September 1995 the worst rioting that year took place in protest against Indonesian Muslim immigrants, following an Indonesian prison official's alleged insult to Roman Catholicism. Mosques and Muslim businesses were burned, and some Muslims were forced to flee the island. Further riots erupted in October, in which rival groups of separatists and integrationists clashed on the streets. The Roman Catholic Apostolic Administrator in Dili, the Rt Rev. Carlos Filipe Ximenes Belo, persuaded the rioters to return home following an agreement with ABRI; however, the agreement was subsequently broken by the armed forces, who arrested more than 250 alleged rioters. In November the fourth anniversary of the Dili massacre passed without incident, owing to unprecedentedly high security.

From September 1995 East Timorese activists began forcing entry into foreign embassies in Jakarta and appealing for political asylum. They were granted asylum by the Portuguese, who were still officially recognized by the UN as the administrative power in East Timor. The Indonesian Government permitted the asylum-seekers to leave, but denied that there was any persecution in East Timor. The culmination of the successful campaign was the storming in December of the Dutch and Russian embassies by 58 and 47 activists respectively. The demonstrators, some of whom were non-Timorese and belonged to a radical group called the People's Democratic Union, demanded unsuccessfully a meeting with the UN High Commissioner for Human Rights, José Ayala Lasso, who was visiting Indonesia and who, following a brief visit to East Timor, confirmed the occurrence of severe violations of human rights in the province. In 1996 several further groups of East Timorese sought asylum in foreign embassies; the majority of these were successful.

In February 1996 President Suharto and the Portuguese Prime Minister met in Bangkok (the first meeting on East Timor by heads of government). During the negotiations Portugal offered to re-establish diplomatic links in return for the release of Xanana Gusmão and the guarantee of human rights in East Timor. International awareness of East Timor was heightened in October, when Belo and José Ramos Horta were jointly awarded the Nobel Prize for Peace. The Indonesian Government, displeased with the Nobel committee's choice, declared that there would be no change in its policy on East Timor. Four days after the announcement of the award, Suharto visited East Timor for the first time in eight years.

Following the announcement of the Nobel Peace Prize, Bishop Belo repeated demands that the Government conduct a referendum on the issue of autonomy for East Timor. In November 1996 he became involved in a controversy regarding an interview that he had given to a German periodical, *Der Spiegel*, which quoted several controversial remarks, allegedly made by Belo, about the treatment of the East Timorese people by the Indonesian Government and ABRI. Belo denied having made the remarks, but was requested to appear before a parliamentary commission in Jakarta to explain the matter. This controversy, and the temporary confiscation of Belo's passport by the Indonesian authorities (which threatened to prevent Belo's visit to Norway to receive the Nobel award), prompted five days of demonstrations in his support in Dili. The rallies were reportedly the largest since 1975, but were conducted peacefully.

The award of the Nobel Peace Prize to José Ramos Horta proved even more controversial. The Governor of East Timor accused Ramos Horta of ordering the torture and killing of East Timorese people. Ramos Horta himself declared that the award should have been made to Xanana Gusmão and invited the Indonesian Government to enter into serious negotiations on the future of East Timor. Ramos Horta was banned from visiting the Philippines for the duration of an APEC summit meeting which took place there in late 1996; this ban was subsequently extended.

In November 1996 the Indonesian Government withdrew permission for foreign journalists to visit East Timor, where they had planned to attend a press conference conducted by Belo. In December Ramos Horta and Belo attended the Nobel Prize ceremony in Oslo, Norway. On receiving the award, Belo emphasized his role as a spiritual, rather than a political, leader to the people of East Timor. Riots in Dili (following a gathering of Belo's supporters to welcome him upon his return) resulted in the death of a member of ABRI; it was reported later in the month that at least one East Timorese citizen had been killed by the Indonesian authorities in a raid to capture those believed to be responsible for the soldier's death. (It was, however, generally recognized by non-governmental organizations working in East Timor that the Indonesian authorities had become more lenient about allowing demonstrations in 1996.)

Following an increase in clashes between resistance forces and ABRI prior to the general election, in June 1997 a military commander of Fretilin, David Alex, was apprehended by the Indonesian armed forces. His subsequent death in custody was highly controversial; resistance groups rejected the official explanation that he had been fatally injured in a clash with security forces and claimed that he had been tortured to death. Guerrilla activity subsequently intensified and in September at least seven Indonesian soldiers were killed in a clash with resistance forces. Further fighting took place in November and December.

In July 1997 the President of South Africa, Nelson Mandela, met Xanana Gusmão, with the approval of Suharto. Mandela subsequently announced that he had written to Suharto to request the prisoner's release. In September Mandela continued his attempts to mediate in the Timorese conflict by holding talks with Bishop Belo; despite international optimism, however, Mandela's initiative ultimately proved fruitless.

In November 1997 the Australia-East Timor Association released a report cataloguing human rights abuses perpetrated by members of the Indonesian armed forces against Timorese women; abuses cited in the report included enforced prostitution, rape and compulsory sterilization programmes. Also in November shots were fired when Indonesian troops stormed the campus of the University of East Timor in Dili, following a vigil held by students to commemorate the massacre in Dili in 1991. According to reports, at least one student was killed in the incident, a number of others were injured and many were arrested. Belo accused the Indonesian security forces of having used 'excessive force', and this was confirmed by a report made by the Indonesian National Commission on Human Rights in early December. Also in December the Commission demanded the abolition of the country's anti-subversion legislation. In the same month two Timorese were sentenced to death under the legislation for their part in an ambush of election security officials earlier in the year, prompting threats of increased guerrilla activities by separatist forces, and a further four were sentenced to 12 years' imprisonment for taking part in armed resistance operations. Also in December 1997 Abílio Soares, who had been re-elected as Governor of East Timor in September, ordered the arrest of the leaders of the recently-formed Movement for the Reconciliation and Unity of the People of East Timor (MRUPT), which he declared to be a proscribed movement.

In January 1998 Ramos Horta attempted to exploit the Government's economic difficulties by urging Suharto to agree to a cease-fire and to co-operate with the UN in creating protection zones to ensure the safety of disarmed resistance fighters; the Government, however, failed to respond to his requests. In the same month it was announced that a Timorese resistance congress that was due to be held in Portugal in March was to be replaced by a national convention to ensure the participation of the UDT. The convention, held in late April, unanimously approved the 'Magna Carta' of East Timor, a charter intended to provide the basis for the constitution of future self-determination within the territory, and ratified plans for the establishment of the National Council of Timorese Resistance (CNRT), a body intended to give the Timorese resistance movement a single national structure and to bring together representatives of the defunct National Council of Maubere Resistance (CNRM), Fretilin and the UDT. Xanana Gusmão was appointed President of the new CNRT, and Ramos Horta was named as Vice-Presi-

dent. In March 1998, meanwhile, Konis Santana, the acting military leader of Fretilin, died following an accident; Taur Matan Ruak was appointed as his successor.

The accession of B. J. Habibie to the Indonesian presidency in May 1998 raised hopes that independence for East Timor might be granted in the near future. However, while President Habibie publicly suggested that the territory might be given a new 'special' status within Indonesia and that troops might be withdrawn, there was no initial indication that the Government was contemplating independence for the territory. While a number of prominent political prisoners were released soon after Habibie replaced Suharto as President, Xanana Gusmão's 20-year sentence was reduced by a mere four months. Following the killing of an East Timorese youth by Indonesian soldiers in June, the Government renewed efforts to demonstrate its conciliatory position and, in late July, effected a much-publicized withdrawal of a limited number of troops from the territory. However, opposition groups subsequently claimed that fresh troops were being sent by the Indonesian Government to replace those leaving (a claim denied by Indonesian military leaders).

In August 1998 it was announced that Indonesia and Portugal had agreed to hold discussions on the possibility of 'wide-ranging' autonomy for East Timor, and in early November the UN was reported to be opening discussions with the two countries regarding a UN plan for extensive autonomy for the territory. Following an outbreak of severe violence in the Alas region of East Timor later that month, in which 82 people were reported to have been killed, Portugal suspended its involvement in the talks; however, in January 1999 it was announced that the talks were to resume. During his visit to East Timor in mid-December 1998, UN special envoy Jamsheed Marker held talks with both Xanana Gusmão and Belo; in the same month, Xanana Gusmão reportedly advocated that the Timorese people should consider the UN's proposal for autonomy, but only as a transitional stage prior to the holding of a referendum (the possibility of which, in December, was still ruled out by the Indonesian Government).

In January 1999 the Australian Government announced a significant change in its policy on East Timor, stating that it intended actively to promote 'self-determination' in the territory (although the precise intended meaning of 'self-determination' remained unclear). Later the same month, total independence for East Timor in the near future emerged as an apparent possibility when, in its boldest move to date to appease the East Timorese and the international community, the Indonesian Government suggested that a vote might be held in the national legislature, the Majelis Permusyawaratan Rakyat (MPR, People's Consultative Assembly), following the election to the House of Representatives (part of the MPR) scheduled for June, on the issue of Indonesia's granting independence to the territory. As a result of a request from the UN Secretary-General, Kofi Annan, the Government also announced that it was to allow Xanana Gusmão to serve the remainder of his 20-year prison sentence under house arrest in Jakarta. Following the Government's announcement regarding the possibility of independence for East Timor, a number of outbreaks of violence, attributed to supporters of the territory's integration with Indonesia, were reported to have occurred.

On 27 January 1999 the Indonesian Government unexpectedly announced that, if the East Timorese voted to reject Indonesia's proposals for autonomy, it would consider granting independence to the province. Although the Indonesian Government was initially opposed to a referendum on the issue of independence for East Timor, it signed an agreement with Portugal on 5 May, giving its assent to a process of 'popular consultation' taking the form of a UN-supervised poll to determine the future status of East Timor. The United Nations Mission in East Timor (UNAMET) was established by the UN Security Council in June to organize the poll in which the East Timorese could opt for a form of political autonomy or for independence. The 'popular consultation' was initially scheduled to be held on 8 August, and all East Timorese, including those living in exile, were to be allowed to participate in the ballot.

Following the announcement of the scheduled referendum, violence in the territory escalated. Anti-independence militia groups based within East Timor initiated a campaign of violence and intimidation in advance of the poll, which included summary killings, kidnappings, harassment and the forced recruitment of young East Timorese. The Indonesian military itself was discovered to be not only supporting but also recruiting, training and organizing many of the militias. Violence continued to escalate throughout the territory during April and May 1999. In one incident in April anti-independence militia members massacred 57 people in a churchyard in the town of Liquiça (Likisia); further massacres were reported to have occurred in other areas, including Dili. Also in April Xanana Gusmão (who in February had been moved from Cipinang prison in Jakarta to serve the remainder of his 20-year sentence under effective house arrest in the capital) responded to the increasing violence from anti-independence militias by reversing his previous position and urging guerrillas in Fretilin's military wing, the Forças Armadas Libertação Nacional de Timor Leste (Falintil), to resume their struggle. Although rival pro-independence and integrationist factions signed a peace accord in June supporting a cease-fire and disarmament in advance of the scheduled referendum, the violence continued unabated.

The escalating violence in the territory, together with logistical difficulties, led the UN to postpone the referendum to 21 August 1999 and then to 30 August. Although intimidation and violence by the militias continued, the referendum proceeded on 30 August. About 98.5% of those eligible to vote participated in the poll, which resulted in an overwhelming rejection, by 78.5% of voters, of the Indonesian Government's proposals for autonomy and in the endorsement of independence for East Timor. The announcement of the result of the referendum, however, precipitated a rapid descent into anarchy. Pro-Jakarta militias embarked upon a campaign of murder and destruction in which hundreds of civilians were killed; as many as 500,000 (according to the UN) were forced to flee their homes, and many buildings were destroyed in arson attacks. While many of those who were displaced from their homes sought refuge in the hills, about one-half were estimated by the UN to have left the territory (a large number having entered West Timor), some involuntarily. In one incident during the campaign of extreme violence that followed the announcement of the result of the referendum, anti-independence militia members stormed the residence of Bishop Belo, evicting at gunpoint some 6,000 refugees who had sought shelter in the compound; the home of the bishop was burned down and dozens of East Timorese were reported to have been killed in the attack. Bishop Belo was evacuated to Australia, while Xanana Gusmão (who was released from house arrest in Jakarta by the Indonesian Government on 7 September) took refuge in the British embassy in Jakarta. Thousands of civilians besieged the UN compound in Dili, the premises of other international agencies, churches and police stations, seeking protection from the indiscriminate attacks of the militias. On 7 September martial law was declared in the territory, and a curfew was imposed. The violence continued unabated, however, and in mid-September, following international condemnation of the situation and intense diplomatic pressure, the Indonesian Government reversed its earlier opposition to a proposal by the Australian Government and agreed to permit the deployment of a multi-national peacekeeping force. As the massacre of civilians continued, thousands of refugees were airlifted to safety in northern Australia, along with the remaining employees of the UN (many local staff members of UNAMET were among the victims of the violence); shortly after the UN withdrew its staff, anti-independence militia members set fire to the UN compound in Dili. Meanwhile, aid agencies warned that as many as 300,000 East Timorese people would starve if humanitarian assistance were not urgently provided.

The first contingent of several thousand UN peace-keeping troops, forming the International Force for East Timor (Interfet), was deployed in the territory on 20 September 1999. Led by Australia, which committed 4,500 troops, the force gradually restored order. Other substantial contributions to the operation were made by the Philippines and Thailand, each of which provided 1,000 soldiers. A week later the Indonesian armed forces formally relinquished responsibility for security to the multi-national force. At the end of October, after 24 years as an occupying force, the last Indonesian soldiers left East Timor. In late September Indonesia and Portugal reiterated their agreement for the transfer of authority in East Timor to the UN. On 19 October the result of the referendum was ratified by the MPR, thus permitting East Timor's accession to independence to proceed. Shortly thereafter, on 25 October, the UN Security Council established the United Nations Transitional Administration in East Timor (UNTAET, see p. 64) as an integrated peacekeeping operation fully responsible for the administration of East Timor during its transition to independence. UNTAET, with an initial mandate until 31 January 2001, was to exercise all judicial and executive authority in East Timor, to undertake the establishment and training of a new police force, and to assume responsibility for the co-ordination and provision of humanitarian assistance and emergency rehabilitation; the transfer of command of military operations in the territory from Interfet to the UNTAET peace-keeping force was completed on 23 February 2000. Meanwhile, the UN also began a large-scale emergency humanitarian relief effort; however, many displaced and homeless East Timorese remained without access to adequate food supplies, shelter and basic health-care facilities.

Following reports that in mid-October 1999 Indonesian troops and militias had entered the isolated East Timorese enclave of Ocusse (situated within West Timor) and allegedly massacred around 50 people, Interfet troops were deployed in Ocusse; most of the enclave's population of 57,000 were believed to have been removed to refugee camps in West Timor, and by early November only 10,000 of its citizens had been accounted for. Following his popularly-acclaimed return to Dili in October, Xanana Gusmão met with the UNTAET Transitional Administrator, Sérgio Vieira de Mello, in November, and reportedly communicated the concerns of local East Timorese organizations that they were being marginalized by UNTAET officials. In late November he visited Jakarta in order to establish relations with the Indonesian Government, and in early December he visited Australia, where he met with representatives of the Australian Government to discuss the Timor Gap Treaty. (The Treaty, which had been concluded between Australia and Indonesia in 1991, provided a framework for petroleum and gas exploration in the maritime zone between Australia and East Timor and for the division of any resulting royalties between Australia and Indonesia. Indonesia ceased to be party to the original Treaty when it relinquished control of East Timor in October 1999, however, and the transitional administration in East Timor subsequently expressed a desire to renegotiate the terms of the Treaty, which the UN considered to have no legal standing, as Indonesian sovereignty over East Timor had never been recognized by the international body. In February 2000 a memorandum of understanding (MOU) relating to the Treaty was signed by the Australian Government and East Timor's UN administrators, temporarily maintaining the arrangement for the division of royalties (although between Australia and East Timor rather than Australia and Indonesia), and East Timor received its first payment of royalties from Australia under the MOU in October 2000. In the same month, however, the formal renegotiation of the Treaty began, with East Timor requesting the redrawing of the boundaries covered by the Treaty and a larger share of petroleum and gas royalties.)

On 1 December 1999 José Ramos Horta returned to East Timor after 24 years of exile. Ramos Horta, who commanded much popular support, urged the East Timorese people to show forgiveness towards their former oppressors and called for reconciliation between Indonesia and East Timor. On 11 December Vieira de Mello convened the first meeting of the National Consultative Council (NCC) in Dili; the 15-member Council, comprising members of the CNRT and other East Timorese political representatives as well as UNTAET officials, was established in late 1999 to advise UNTAET.

A number of mass graves containing the bodies of suspected victims of the violence perpetrated by the anti-independence militias both before and after the holding of the referendum in August 1999 were discovered in East Timor (including two in the Ocusse enclave) in late 1999 and early 2000. In December 1999 Sonia Picado Sotela, the Chair of the International Commission of Inquiry in East Timor, confirmed that the team of UN investigators had discovered evidence of 'systematic killing'. The UN announced in March 2000 that at least 627 East Timorese had been killed in the violence that followed the referendum, although this number was likely to increase as investigations continued.

In late January 2000 a panel appointed by the Indonesian Government to investigate human rights abuses in East Timor delivered its report to the Indonesian Attorney-General. The panel reportedly named 24 individuals whom it recommended should be prosecuted for their alleged involvement in violations of human rights in the territory. One of those named was the former Minister of Defence and Security and Commander-in-Chief of the Indonesian armed forces, Gen. Wiranto, who had since been appointed Co-ordinating Minister for Politics and Security in the Indonesian Government; also named were a number of senior military officers, as well as leaders of the pro-Jakarta militias responsible for the extreme violence perpetrated during the period following the referendum. However, pro-independence leaders in East Timor strongly criticized the report as inadequate. Also in late January the International Commission of Inquiry in East Timor recommended that the UN establish an independent international body to investigate allegations of human rights violations in East Timor, and an international tribunal to deal with the cases of those accused by the investigators. In February the recently-appointed President of Indonesia, Abdurrahman Wahid, visited East Timor and publicly apologized for the atrocities committed by the Indonesian armed forces during the Republic's occupation of the territory. During his visit Wahid laid wreaths at Dili's Santa Cruz cemetery—the site of the 1991 Dili massacre—and at a cemetery containing the graves of members of the Indonesian armed forces. Also in February 2000 Wahid reaffirmed the commitment of the Indonesian Government to the prosecution of any individuals implicated in the violation of human rights in East Timor. In the same month Wahid suspended Gen. Wiranto from the Indonesian Government. (Wiranto subsequently resigned in May.) The UN Secretary-General, Kofi Annan, made an official visit to East Timor in mid-February, during which he pledged that investigations into violations of human rights in the territory would be carried out. The President of Portugal, Dr Jorge Fernando Branco de Sampaio, also made a three-day official visit to East Timor in that month, during which he expressed the solidarity of the people of Portugal with the East Timorese.

In early April 2000 UNTAET signed an agreement with the Indonesian Government regarding the extradition to East Timor of Indonesian citizens facing charges relating to the violence of 1999, and in July 2000 a team from the Indonesian Attorney-General's Office visited East Timor to investigate a limited number of cases of human rights violations. However, relations between East Timor and Indonesia remained tense, and the introduction in August 2000 (in the closing stages of the annual session of the country's principal legislative body, the MPR) of an amendment to Indonesia's Constitution providing for the exclusion of military personnel from retroactive prosecution prompted fears among many international observers that the possibility of the prosecution of members of the Indonesian military believed responsible for recent human rights abuses in East Timor would be placed in serious jeopardy (despite the suggestions of senior Indonesian legislators that the amendment would probably not apply to crimes such as genocide, war crimes and terrorism). In early September the Indonesian Attorney General's Office named 19 people whom it suspected of involvement in the violence of 1999. Whilst human rights groups in both East Timor and Indonesia welcomed the publication of the list, which included the names of several former high-ranking members of the Indonesian armed forces, there was widespread disappointment that Gen. Wiranto was not among those named.

In June 2000 an agreement was reached between UNTAET and East Timorese leaders on the formation of a new transitional coalition Government, in which the two sides were to share political responsibility. The Cabinet of the new transitional Government, which was formally appointed on 15 July and met for the first time on 17 July, initially included four East Timorese cabinet ministers: João Carrascalão, President of the UDT and a Vice-President of the CNRT, who was allocated responsibility for infrastructure; Mari Alkatiri, Secretary-General of Fretilin, who was appointed Minister for Economic Affairs; Father Filomeno Jacob, who was appointed to oversee social affairs; and Ana Pessoa, who was placed in charge of internal administration. The new Cabinet also included four international representatives: Jean-Christian Cady, the UNTAET Deputy Special Representative of the Secretary-General for Governance and Public Administration, was allocated responsibility for the police and emergency services, while the three remaining non-East Timorese cabinet members were to be responsible for the judicial affairs, finance and political affairs portfolios. Mariano Lopes da Cruz, an East Timorese national, was appointed as Inspector-General. It was reported that Xanana Gusmão, whilst holding no formal position in the new Government, was to be consulted on an informal basis by Sérgio Vieira de Mello (who was to retain ultimate control over the approval of any draft legislation proposed to the Cabinet) with respect to all political decisions. In October the Cabinet was expanded to nine members, with the appointment of José Ramos Horta as Minister of Foreign Affairs.

In mid-July 2000 UNTAET approved the establishment of a 'National Council' to advise the new Cabinet. The East Timorese National Council, the membership of which was expanded from 33 to 36 in October, consisted of a selection of East Timorese representatives from the political, religious and private sectors. The new National Council was inaugurated on 23 October and replaced the 15-member NCC, which had held its last meeting a few days earlier. In the same month Xanana Gusmão was elected to lead the National Council, and by January 2001 34 of the National Council's 36 members had been appointed.

On 20 August 2000, meanwhile, Xanana Gusmão retired as the Military Commander of Falintil, in order to concentrate on his political role in the process of guiding East Timor towards full independence. Xanana Gusmão relinquished control of the guerrilla army to his deputy, Taur Matan Ruak. Initially, Falintil faced an uncertain future, and the refusal of the UN to allow the active involvement of the unit in attempts to combat incursions by Indonesian paramilitaries into East Timor led Xanana Gusmão to voice indirect criticism of the international organization in his resignation speech. In early February 2001, however, a new East Timorese Defence Force was established, consisting of an initial 650 recruits drawn exclusively from the ranks of Falintil, which was itself to be dissolved. The former Military Commander of the guerrilla army, Taur Matan Ruak, was promoted to the rank of Brigadier-General and appointed to command the new force. Meanwhile, a fund was established to finance the support and retraining of an estimated 1,000 Falintil veterans who were to be demobilized. Training of the new Defence Force was to be conducted by Portugal and Australia, and it was anticipated that the force, which was ultimately to include 1,500 regulars and 1,500 reservists, would be fully operational by late 2001. The role of the new force was described as that of 'policing', with the defence of the territory remaining the responsibility of UNTAET peace-keeping troops.

In August 2000 the first anniversary of the East Timorese people's vote for independence was marked by religious services at churches throughout East Timor. A mass held at Dili's cathedral on 30 August, conducted by Bishop Belo, was attended by more than 1,000 people. Also in August 2000 Xanana Gusmão, speaking at a multi-party congress organized by the CNRT, called for unity and urged the 450 East Timorese delegates in attendance to 'embrace democracy'.

Four of the five East Timorese members of the transitional Cabinet threatened to resign in December 2000, reportedly in protest at their treatment by the UN. The ministers, who allegedly claimed that they were merely 'puppet ministers' in the new coalition Government, demanded further clarification of the legal status of the Cabinet and of their authority as individual cabinet ministers, and called for the establishment of a more clearly defined relationship between UNTAET and the Cabinet. Further complaints about UNTAET's treatment of East Timorese officials were voiced at a donors' conference for East Timor held in the same month, and press reports suggested the existence of a level of public resentment of the UN's presence in East Timor. However, in January 2001 Ramos Horta warned that any attempt to scale down the UN's presence in East Timor would destabilize the territory's progression towards independence. In late January 2001 the UN Security Council extended UNTAET's mandate (which had initially been scheduled to expire on 31 January 2001) until 31 January 2002. It was acknowledged, however, that modifications of the mandate might be necessary to take into account developments in East Timor's progression towards full independence.

From August 2000, meanwhile, in a move that allowed for greater formal East Timorese influence in the governing of the territory during the period preceding the territory's accession to full independence, a process commenced whereby the transitional Government began to be redefined as the East Timorese Transitional Administration (ETTA). Consisting of both UNTAET and East Timorese staff, ETTA was composed of the transitional Cabinet, the National Council and the judiciary. Final authority over ETTA rested with the Special Representative of the UN Secretary-General and Transitional Administrator, Sérgio Vieira de Mello.

In February 2001 legislation providing for an election to an 88-seat Constituent Assembly, to be conducted on 30 August, was approved. The single chamber was to comprise 75 deputies elected on a national basis, using proportional representation, and one elected delegate from each of East Timor's 13 districts, chosen on a 'first-past-the-post' basis. The members of the Constituent Assembly were to be responsible for the preparation and adoption (within 90 days) of a constitution, which would require the endorsement of at least 60 members. Meanwhile, a

National Constitutional Commission, comprising representatives of various groups, was to be established in order to facilitate consultation with the people of East Timor. The new Constitution was to be duly proclaimed on 15 December 2001, whereupon the Constituent Assembly was to become the National Parliament.

In March 2001, following the arrest in Dili of three suspects in connection with a threat to assassinate Xanana Gusmão, rioters set fire to buildings in Baucau. Sérgio Vieira de Mello also received threats to his life. Security was intensified in Dili and also in Viqueque, where clashes between hundreds of youths belonging to rival gangs had reportedly resulted in two deaths and compelled dozens of aid workers to seek refuge in the UN compound.

In December 2000 UNTAET issued its first indictments for crimes committed against humanity in connection with the violence that had surrounded the referendum in 1999, charging 11 people (including an officer of the Indonesian special forces) with the murder of nine civilians in September 1999. In January 2001 an East Timor court sentenced a former pro-Jakarta militia member to 12 years' imprisonment for the murder of a village chief in September 1999, marking the first successful prosecution related to the violence of 1999.

In February 2000, meanwhile, the Australian Government announced that all 470 East Timorese refugees remaining in Australia were expected to be returned to East Timor by the end of the month. Also in February, however, the UN expressed its concern that very few of the estimated 90,000 East Timorese refugees remaining in camps across the border in West Timor were returning to East Timor; it had earlier been reported that pro-Jakarta militias had been intimidating the refugees in West Timor and preventing them from returning home. In September the UN temporarily suspended its relief work among East Timorese refugees in West Timor, following the murder by pro-Jakarta militias of three UN aid workers in the territory earlier in the month. The murders prompted international criticism of the Indonesian Government for its failure to control the militia groups operating in West Timor. In November Ramos Horta alleged that estimates of the number of East Timorese refugees residing in West Timor (reported by some sources to be as high as 130,000) were being deliberately exaggerated by the Indonesian Government, and estimated the actual number of refugees to be no higher than 60,000–70,000. In December 2000 and January 2001, in an attempt to dispel the fears of refugees remaining in West Timor about the security situation in East Timor, UNTAET arranged for a number of groups of refugees to visit their homeland. The visits resulted in a number of refugees opting to return permanently to East Timor.

Government

On 25 October 1999 the United Nations Security Council established the United Nations Transitional Administration in East Timor (UNTAET, see p. 64) as an integrated, multi-dimensional peace-keeping operation responsible for the administration of East Timor during its transition to independence. Under the terms of UN Security Council Resolution 1272 of 25 October 1999, UNTAET is empowered to exercise all legislative and executive authority in East Timor, including the administration of justice. In December 1999 a 15-member National Consultative Council (NCC), the role of which was to make policy recommendations to UNTAET, met for the first time. In October 2000, however, the NCC was replaced by the 36-member East Timorese National Council, which included political, religious and district representatives, as well as representatives of civic organizations. Following an agreement reached between UNTAET and East Timorese leaders in June on the formation of a new coalition Government, whereby the two sides were to share political responsibility, an eight-member transitional Cabinet was appointed in mid-July. In October the Cabinet was expanded to include nine members, five of whom were East Timorese and four of whom were international representatives. Meanwhile, from August 2000 the transitional Government of East Timor began a process of redefinition as the East Timorese Transitional Administration (ETTA). Comprising the transitional Cabinet, the National Council and also the judiciary, ETTA incorporates both UNTAET and East Timorese staff. An 88-member Constituent Assembly, which was to be responsible for drafting a new constitution for East Timor, was scheduled to be elected in August 2001. A total of 75 deputies were to be elected nationally by proportional representation, the remaining members being elected by each of East Timor's 13 districts.

Defence

Within the framework of its mandate, the United Nations Transitional Administration in East Timor (UNTAET, see p. 64) was required to provide security and to maintain law and order throughout East Timor. At 1 January 2001 there were 7,889 peace-keeping troops, 1,398 civilian police and 2,655 other UNTAET personnel in East Timor. (The authorized maximum strength of UNTAET was 8,950 troops, 200 military observers and 1,640 civilian police.) In early February 2001 a new East Timorese Defence Force was established; the force was to fulfil a 'policing' role, with the defence of the territory remaining the responsibility of UNTAET troops. The first 650 recruits for the new Defence Force, which was ultimately to consist of 1,500 regulars and 1,500 reservists, were drawn from the ranks of the former guerrilla army, Falintil. The new force was to be trained by Portugal and Australia, and was expected to be fully operational by late 2001.

Economic Affairs

In 1998 East Timor's gross domestic product (GDP), measured in current prices, was US \$375m., equivalent to US \$424 per head. In 1999 GDP was estimated to have declined to US \$228m., equivalent to US \$304 per head. Average annual GDP growth was estimated at more than 10%, in real terms, in 1994–96. GDP increased by 4.1% in 1997, but decreased by 2.1% in 1998 and by an estimated 38.5% in 1999.

The economy of East Timor is based principally on the agricultural sector, which normally employs more than 90% of the Timorese population. In 1999 the agricultural sector contributed an estimated 21.3% of GDP. The only significant export commodity is coffee. Subsistence crops include rice and maize. Livestock raised includes cattle and water buffalo. In addition to ocean fishing, there is also some small-scale aquaculture. Agricultural GDP increased at an average annual rate of 2.7%, in real terms, in 1994–96. Following annual increases of 7.1% and 0.2% in 1997 and 1998 respectively, the GDP of the sector decreased by an estimated 48.4% in 1999, as a consequence of the widespread destruction and violence that followed the referendum on independence held in that year.

There is a small industrial sector, which is mainly concerned with the production of textiles, the bottling of water and the processing of coffee. In 1999 the manufacturing sector provided an estimated 3.5% of GDP. The GDP of the manufacturing sector increased at an average annual rate of 15%, in real terms, in 1994–96. Following an annual increase of 11.7% in 1997, however, the GDP of the sector decreased by 4.2% in 1998 and by an estimated 37.4% in 1999.

The mining sector contributed an estimated 1.4% of GDP in 1999. The GDP of the mining sector increased at an average annual rate of 11%, in real terms, in 1994–96. However, following an increase of 22.2% in 1997, the GDP of the sector decreased by 8.6% in 1998 and by an estimated further 13.8% in 1999.

The construction sector contributed an estimated 23.2% of GDP in 1999. The GDP of the sector increased at an average annual rate of 12.1%, in real terms, in 1994–96. However, following an increase of 2.1% in 1997, the sector's GDP decreased by 9.1% in 1998 and by an estimated 9.0% in 1999.

The power sector (including electricity, gas and water) provided an estimated 0.7% of GDP in 1999. East Timor's generating capacity amounted to some 40 MW prior to the civil conflict in 1999, of which about 50% was contained in two power stations at Dili. However, the territory's power facilities suffered extensive damage in the civil conflict, and in 2001 supplies of electricity remained intermittent. The GDP of the power sector increased at an average annual rate of 19.1%, in real terms, in 1994–96. The sector's GDP increased by 4.8% in 1997 and by 4.2% in 1998, but decreased by an estimated 49.9% in 1999.

The services sector (including trade, transport and communications, finance, public administration and other services) contributed an estimated 49.8% of GDP in 1999. The GDP of all branches of the services sector recorded a sharp contraction in 1999.

In 1999 East Timor recorded a visible trade deficit of an estimated US \$36m. In early 2001 substantial official aid continued to dominate East Timor's trade flows. Although this aid contributed towards the rehabilitation and reconstruction of the economy, it also resulted in a marked deterioration in the territory's trade and current-account deficits. Exports declined following the violence of 1999, and export earnings in 2000, including those from coffee (East Timor's principal export commodity), were projected to be significantly below the pre-conflict average. At mid-2000 the IMF emphasized that the recovery of exports of coffee continued to be dependent upon the rehabilitation of the transport and processing infrastructure and on the re-establishment of distribution channels (particularly to Indonesia, traditionally the principal market for East Timor's coffee exports).

The preliminary budget for 2000, prepared by UNTAET, was presented to donors at a meeting in Tokyo in December 1999. The budget, which incorporated proposals for the introduction of a new taxation structure (including a 10% wage withholding tax, eventually introduced in January 2001), was consistent with the aim of providing sufficient revenue to finance one-half of the recurrent expenditures in the initial year and most of the recurrent budget at the end of a three-year period. Preliminary budgetary spending for 2000 totalled US $107m. (comprising US $30m. in recurrent and US $77m. in reconstruction and development expenditure), taking into account humanitarian assistance provided through the Consolidated Appeals Process. The draft budget for the financial year ending 30 June 2001 was approved by the National Consultative Council in early June 2000. Total spending for that financial year was projected at around US $172m., of which 25% represented current spending; expenditures were to be concentrated in infrastructure, health, education and agriculture. A fiscal deficit of about US $155m. was projected for the same financial year. Consumer prices increased by 10% in 1997, by 80% in 1998 and by an estimated 140% in 1999. In late 2000 the rate of unemployment in East Timor was estimated at around 80%. In January 2000 a regulation was passed by the UNTAET Transitional Administrator establishing the US dollar as the official currency of East Timor; however, as a result of the scarcity of low-denomination dollar notes, the absence of coins and a lack of familiarity with the new currency amongst the East Timorese, the use of the US dollar in 2000 was not as widespread as had been anticipated.

In December 1999 the Joint Assessment Mission of the World Bank reported that both the public and private sectors of the East Timorese economy had suffered almost total collapse as a consequence of the recent violence in the territory, with real GDP having declined by an estimated 38.5% in 1999. In early 2000, according to the Joint Assessment Mission, urgent priorities included restarting the flow of goods and services; the establishment of a payments system, currency arrangements and exchange houses; the re-establishment of branch units of Indonesian banks in order to permit the settlement of credits and depositor claims; and the introduction of fiscal measures with the aim of achieving sustainable government finances. At a meeting in Tokyo in December 1999 international donors pledged US $523m. to the humanitarian aid programme for East Timor, and in February 2000 the World Bank disbursed the first instalment of aid to the territory. Significant economic progress was made in 2000, with real GDP growing at an estimated average annual rate of 15% in the first six months of that year. In October 2000 East Timor received its first payment of royalties from Australia for petroleum and gas mined in the Timor Gap, under the Timor Gap Treaty originally concluded between Australia and Indonesia in 1991. (Since the signing of the original Treaty in 1991, sizeable natural gas fields had been discovered in and around the Timor Gap zone, and petroleum reserves in the region were estimated by some sources to total

a potential 500m. barrels, valued at more than US $17,000m. in early 2001. Although East Timor had agreed temporarily to maintain the arrangement covering the sharing of petroleum and gas royalties with Australia after Indonesia ceased to be party to the original Treaty in 1999, the transitional administration in East Timor ultimately considered the Treaty to be invalid and sought to secure a larger share of the royalties for East Timor. Formal renegotiation of the Treaty began in October 2000.) Real GDP was projected to increase by at least 15% in 2000 and 2001, growth being led by agriculture, commerce, basic services and reconstruction of public and residential buildings. According to the IMF, investment was also likely to increase as the process of economic recovery and reconstruction gained momentum. In early 2001, however, external aid continued to be of absolutely vital importance to the East Timorese economy, and the IMF cautioned that sound economic management would be critical to the preservation of macroeconomic stability, along with the provision of reasonable assurances to donors and other parties that the resources made available to East Timor were being used effectively and accounted for properly.

Social Welfare

Prior to the civil conflict in 1999, health indicators in East Timor were substantially inferior to those elsewhere in Indonesia. Infant mortality was high, at 124 deaths under one year of age per 1,000 live births. According to official figures, life expectancy at birth averaged 52 years, compared with an average for the whole of Indonesia of 61.5 years. As a result of the civil conflict almost all health services collapsed, with the loss of all fixed equipment and consumables. Some 130 of East Timor's 160 physicians were reported to have departed. Prior to the civil conflict, personnel engaged in the provision of health care numbered about 3,500. However, at mid-2000, according to the East Timorese Health Professionals Working Group, approximately 2,000 health workers were present in East Timor, and the number of East Timorese doctors remaining in the country was just 35. There are two hospitals operating in Dili (one of which, at mid-2000, was administered by the International Committee of the Red Cross), one in Baucau and one small hospital in Los Palos, in the east of the country. The draft budget for 2000/01 envisaged expenditure of US $13m. on health services.

Education

Prior to the civil conflict in 1999 there were 167,000 primary students, 32,000 junior secondary students and 19,000 senior secondary students. Primary school enrolment included 70% of those in the relevant age-group and secondary enrolment about 39%. Some 4,000 students were engaged in further education at the university and the polytechnic in Dili, while in addition several thousand East Timorese were following courses at Indonesian universities. It was estimated that, as a result of the civil conflict in 1999, 75%–80% of primary and secondary schools were either partially or completely destroyed. A total of 240,000 students registered for the 2000/01 academic year, however, a much higher number than anticipated. Literacy rates were reported to have reached only 41% by 1998, with lower rates recorded for women than for men. The draft budget for 2000/01 allocated US $12m. to the education sector.

Statistical Survey

Sources (unless otherwise stated): Indonesian Central Bureau of Statistics, Jalan Dr Sutomo 8, Jakarta 10710, Indonesia; tel. (21) 363360; fax (21) 3857046; IMF, *East Timor: Establishing the Foundations of Sound Macroeconomic Management.*

AREA AND POPULATION

Area: 14,609 sq km (5,641 sq miles).

Population: 555,350 at census of 31 October 1980; 747,750 (males 386,939, females 360,811) at census of 31 October 1990; 1998: 884,000; 1999 (estimate): 750,000.

Density (estimate, 1999): 51.3 per sq km.

Births and Deaths (UN estimates, annual averages): Birth rate per 1,000: 1980–85: 44.1; 1985–90: 43.3; 1990–95: 36.4; Death rate per 1,000: 1980–85: 23.0; 1985–90: 20.4; 1990–95: 17.4. Source: UN, *World Population Prospects: The 1998 Revision.*

Expectation of Life (UN estimates, years at birth, 1990–95): 45.0 (males 44.2; females 45.9). Source: UN, *World Population Prospects: The 1998 Revision.*

Economically Active Population (survey, persons aged 10 years and over, August 1993): Total employed 336,490; Unemployed 5,397; Total labour force 341,887.

AGRICULTURE, ETC.

Principal Crops ('000 metric tons, 1996): Rice (paddy) 46; Maize 101; Cassava (Manioc) 66; Sweet potatoes 16; Soybeans 1; Potatoes 6; Cabbages 3; Mustard greens 2; Avocados 1; Mangoes 5; Oranges 1; Papayas 1; Pineapples 2; Bananas 4.

Livestock ('000 head, 1996): Cattle 137; Sheep 32; Goats 187; Pigs 378; Horses 32; Buffaloes 69; Chickens 1,021; Ducks 28.

Fishing (metric tons): Total catch 2,459 in 1994; 2,462 in 1995.

FINANCE

Currency and Exchange Rate: United States currency is used: 100 cents = 1 US dollar ($). *Sterling and Euro Equivalents* (29 December 2000): £1 sterling = US $1.4922; €1 = 93.05 US cents; US $100 = £67.02 = €107.47.

Budget (million rupiah, year ending 31 March 1999): *Revenue:* Federal tax revenue 106,225 (Income tax 47,964, Value-added tax and sales tax 23,485, Revenue-sharing 34,108); Provincial tax revenue 7,637 (Vehicle taxes 5,105, Vehicle ownership fees 2,399); Other receipts 3,012; Total 116,874.

Expenditure: Current expenditure 207,132 (Salaries and wages 146,529, Goods 36,474); Capital expenditure 319,956; Total 527,088.

Money Supply (estimate, '000 million rupiah, 31 December 1998): Currency in circulation 58.

Cost of Living (Consumer Price Index for Dili; base: year ending March 1989 = 100): 146.4 in 1994; 158.6 in 1995; 169.3 in 1996.

Gross Domestic Product (million rupiah at current prices): 996,000 in 1997; 1,272,000 in 1998; 1,878,000* in 1999. * Preliminary figure.

Balance of Payments: (estimates, US $ million, 1999): Exports of goods 46; Imports of goods –82; *Trade balance* –36; Services and other income (net) –12; *Balance on goods, services and income* –48; Current transfers 49; *Current balance* 1; Capital transfers 3; Other capital flows (net) –3; Net errors and omissions –1; *Overall balance* 0.

EXTERNAL TRADE

Principal Commodities (US $ million, 1998): *Imports:* Rice 13; Other foodstuffs 22; Petroleum products 14; Construction materials 20; Total (incl. others) 135. *Exports:* Products of agriculture, forestry and fishing 51 (Food crops 8, Other crops 28, Livestock 12); Products of manufacturing 3; Total (incl. others) 55.

Principal Trading Partner (US $ million, 1998): *Imports:* Indonesia 135. *Exports:* Indonesia 53.

TOURISM

Tourist Arrivals ('000 foreign visitors, excl. Indonesians, at hotels): 0.8 in 1996; 1.0 in 1997; 0.3 in 1998. Figures exclude arrivals at non-classified hotels: 204 in 1996; 245 in 1997; 41 in 1998.

Directory

The Constitution

A new constitution was to be drawn up in the latter part of 2001, following the election of a Constituent Assembly, scheduled for August of that year. A National Constitutional Commission, which was to comprise members of the National Council's standing committee on political affairs, church representatives, women's and youth groups as well as representatives of all political parties, was to be established for the purposes of popular consultation. The new Constitution was to be proclaimed on 15 December 2001.

The Government

The United Nations Transitional Administration in East Timor (UNTAET, see International Organizations, p. 64), which in January 2001 had its mandate extended until 31 January 2002 by the United Nations Security Council, was initially empowered to exercise all legislative and executive authority in East Timor. UNTAET's mandate comprised the following elements: to provide security and maintain law and order throughout the territory of East Timor; to establish an effective administration; to assist in the development of civil and social services; to ensure the co-ordination and delivery of humanitarian assistance, rehabilitation and development assistance; to support capacity-building for self-government; to assist in the establishment of conditions for sustainable development. A 15-member National Consultative Council (NCC)—which included members of the National Council of Timorese Resistance (CNRT), representatives of political groups outside the CNRT which were in existence prior to the referendum on independence, a Roman Catholic priest, the UNTAET Transitional Administrator and three other UNTAET officials—was established in early December 1999 to advise UNTAET.

In June 2000 an agreement was reached between UNTAET and East Timorese leaders on the formation of a new transitional coalition Government, in which the two sides were to share political responsibility. An eight-member transitional Cabinet, composed of four East Timorese members and four international representatives, was subsequently appointed on 15 July (and, in October, was expanded to include nine members, five of whom were East Timorese). On 20 October the composition of a 36-member National Council, the East Timor National Council—which included political, religious and district representatives as well as representatives of civic organizations and which was comprised entirely of East Timorese members—was announced. The East Timor National Council was inaugurated on 23 October and replaced the 15-member NCC, which held its last meeting on 20 October. By January 2001, 34 of the intended 36 members had been appointed to the National Council.

In August 2000 a process commenced whereby the transitional Government of East Timor began to be redefined as the East Timorese Transitional Administration (ETTA). ETTA, which is formally comprised of three branches of government (the transitional Cabinet, the National Council and the judicial system), includes both UNTAET and East Timorese staff; final authority over ETTA rests with the United Nations' Special Representative of the Secretary-General and Transitional Administrator.

UNITED NATIONS TRANSITIONAL ADMINISTRATION IN EAST TIMOR

Special Representative of the Secretary-General and Transitional Administrator: Sérgio Vieira de Mello (Brazil).

Deputy Special Representative of the Secretary-General for Governance and Public Administration: Jean-Christian Cady (France).

Director of UNTAET/Jakarta: Lakhan Lal Mehrotra (India).

Force Commander: Lt-Gen. Boonsrang Niumpradit (Thailand).

Chief Military Liaison Officer: Brig.-Gen. Louis Gardiner (New Zealand).

Chief of Civilian Police: Police Commr José Luís da Costa e Sousa (Portugal).

NATIONAL COUNCIL

Speaker: Manuel Carrascalão.

TRANSITIONAL CABINET
(April 2001)

Minister for Police and Emergency Services: Jean-Christian Cady.

Minister for Internal Administration: Ana Pessoa.
Minister for Political Affairs: Peter W. Galbraith.
Minister for Foreign Affairs: José Ramos Horta.
Minister for Infrastructure: João Carrascalão.
Minister for Judicial Affairs: Gita Honwana-Welch.
Minister for Economic Affairs: Mari Alkatiri.
Minister for Finance: Michael Francino.
Minister for Social Affairs: Father Filomeno Jacob.
Inspector-General: Mariano Lopes da Cruz.

Legislature

A single-chamber Constituent Assembly was to be elected by popular vote on 30 August 2001. Its 88 members were to include 75 deputies elected under a national system of proportional representation and one representative from each of East Timor's 13 districts, elected under a 'first-past-the-post' system. Upon the proclamation of East Timor's Constitution, scheduled for 15 December 2001, the Constituent Assembly was to become the National Parliament.

Political Organizations

East Timor People's Front: fmrly supported integration with Indonesia; Leader Salvador Soares.

Frente Revolucionária do Timor Leste Independente (Fretilin) (Revolutionary Front for an Independent East Timor): f. 1974 to seek full independence for East Timor; entered into alliance with the UDT in 1986; Sec. for International Relations José Ramos Horta.

Movement for the Reconciliation and Unity of the People of East Timor (MRUPT): f. 1997; Chair. Manuel Viegas Carrascalão.

National Council of Timorese Resistance (CNRT): alliance of fmr East Timorese resistance movements (Fretilin, the UDT and the defunct National Council of Maubere Resistance); Pres. José Alexandre (Xanana) Gusmão; Vice-Pres. José Ramos Horta.

Partido Socialista de Timor (Socialist Party of Timor).

Timorese People's Party (PPT): f. 2000; supports candidacy of Xanana Gusmão for presidency of East Timor; Leader Hermínio da Silva da Costa.

União Democrática Timorense (UDT) (Timorese Democratic Union): based in Dili; e-mail fitini@yahoo.com; f. 1974; allied itself with Fretilin in 1986; Pres. João Carrascalão; Sec.-Gen. Domingos Oliveira.

Judicial System

All legislative and executive authority with respect to the administration of the judiciary in East Timor is vested in UNTAET and is exercised by the Transitional Administrator. An independent Transitional Judicial Service Commission was established in early December 1999. The Commission, which is composed of three members of East Timorese origin and two international experts and is chaired by an East Timorese citizen, is responsible for the recommendation of candidates for provisional judicial or prosecutorial office, the provision of advice on the removal of judges or prosecutors and the preparation of a Code of Ethics for judges and prosecutors. The first East Timorese judges and prosecutors were appointed in January 2000, and in March legislation was adopted that provided a legal framework for some aspects of the functioning of the courts and established a two-tier court structure consisting of District Courts and a Court of Appeal. By January 2001 four district courts had been established (one each in Dili, Baucau, Ocusse (Oekussi) and Suai); the Court of Appeal is situated in Dili.

Religion

In 1997 it was estimated that about 86% of the total population were Roman Catholic.

CHRISTIANITY
The Roman Catholic Church

East Timor comprises the dioceses of Dili and Baucau, directly responsible to the Holy See. In December 1998 the territory had an estimated 735,573 Roman Catholics.

Bishop of Baucau: (vacant); Apostolic Administrator: Rt Rev. Basílio do Nascimento Martins (Titular Bishop of Septimunicia), Largo da Catedral, Baucau 88810; tel. (399) 21209; fax (399) 21380.

Bishop of Dili: (vacant); Apostolic Administrator: Rt Rev. Carlos Filipe Ximenes Belo (Titular Bishop of Lorium), Jln. Gov. Alves Aldeia 25, POB 1038, Dili 88010; tel. (390) 321665.

Protestant Church

Igreja Protestante iha Timor Lorosa'e: Jl. Raya Comoro, POB 1186, Dili 88110; tel. and fax (390) 323128; f. 1988 as Gereja Kristen Timor Timur (GKTT); adopted present name 2000; Moderator Rev. Arlindo Marcal; Gen. Sec. Rev. Francisco de Vasconcelos; 30,000 mems.

The Press

The office and printing plant of the largest newspaper in East Timor under Indonesian rule, *Suara Timor Timur* (Voice of East Timor, circulation of 8,000), were destroyed prior to the referendum on independence in August 1999.

Lalenok (Mirror): Rua Gov. Celestino da Silva, Farol, Dili; tel. (390) 321607; e-mail lalenok@hotmail.com; f. 2000; publ. by Kamelin Media Group; Tetum; 3 a week; Dir Gen. and Chief Editor Virgílio da Silva Guterres; Editor José Maria Pompela; circ. 300.

The Official Gazette of East Timor: f. 1999; forum for publication of all UNTAET regulations and directives, acts of organs or institutions of East Timor and other acts of public interest requiring general notification; published by UNTAET in English, Portuguese and Tetum, with translations in Bahasa Indonesia available on request.

Tais Timor: Dili; f. 2000; published by the Office of Communication and Public Information (OCPI) of the United Nations; Tetum, English, Portuguese and Bahasa Indonesia; every fortnight; distributed free of charge; circ. 75,000.

Talit@kum: Dili; f. 2000; news magazine; publ. by Kdadlak Media Group; Bahasa Indonesia; monthly; Chief Editor Hugo Fernandez.

Timor Post: Rua D. Aleixo Corte Real No. 6, Dili; f. 2000; managed by editors and staff of the former *Suara Timor Timur*; Bahasa Indonesia, Tetum, Portuguese and English; daily.

PRESS ASSOCIATION

Timor Lorosae Journalists Association (TLJA): Dili; f. 1999; Co-ordinator Otelio Ote.

Broadcasting and Communications

TELECOMMUNICATIONS

Prior to the civil conflict in 1999, East Timor's telephone lines totalled about 12,000. Telecommunications transmission towers were reported to have suffered significant damage in the civil conflict. Indonesia withdrew its telecommunication services in September. A cellular telephone network service was subsequently provided by an Australian company.

RADIO

The UN launched a 24-hour radio station, Radio UNTAET, broadcasting news in English and Tetum. The Roman Catholic Church also operates a radio station, Radio Kamanak, while a third populist station, Voz Esperança, broadcasts in Dili. A fourth radio station, Radio Falintil FM, also operates in Dili. In late July 2000 the US radio station, Voice of America, began broadcasting to East Timor seven days a week in English, Portuguese and Bahasa Indonesia.

TELEVISION

Televizaun's Timor Lorosae (TV–TL): Dili; f. 2000 by UNTAET; broadcasts in Tetum and Portuguese.

Finance

In January 2000 a Central Fiscal Authority was established by the UNTAET Transitional Administrator. The Authority is responsible for the overall financial management of the consolidated budget of East Timor. On 24 January the National Consultative Council formally adopted the US dollar as East Timor's transitional currency; however, the Indonesian rupiah continues to be widely used as a means of payment throughout the territory.

BANKING

East Timor's banking system collapsed as a result of the violent unrest that afflicted the territory in 1999. In late 1999 Portugal's main overseas bank, Banco Nacional Ultramarino, opened a branch in Dili. In January 2001 the Australia and New Zealand Banking Group also opened a branch in the capital. In February the East Timor Central Payments Office was officially opened. In early 2001, however, the re-establishment of a banking system in East Timor remained an urgent priority.

Central Payments Office (CPO): Dili; inaugurated 2001; formulates and implements payment system policies; provides payment and storage services for foreign governments and foreign banks; conversion to Payments and Monetary Authority pending, as precursor to central bank; Gen. Man. Fernando de Peralta.

Foreign Banks

Australia and New Zealand Banking Group Ltd (ANZ) (Australia): POB 264, Dili; tel. (390) 324800; fax (390) 324822; e-mail etimor@anz.com; internet www.anz.com; retail and commercial banking services; Gen. Man. Chris Durman; Chief Operating Officer Richard Hare.

Banco Nacional Ultramarino (Portugal): Dili; internet www.bnu.pt.

Trade and Industry

UTILITIES

East Timor's total generating capacity amounted to some 40 MW. As a result of the civil conflict in 1999, some 13–23 power stations were reported to require repairs ranging from moderate maintenance to almost complete rehabilitation.

Transport

ROADS

The road network in East Timor is poorly designed and has suffered from long-term neglect. In December 1999 the World Bank reported that some 57% of East Timor's 1,414 km of paved roads were in poor or damaged condition. Many gravel roads are rough and potholed and are inaccessible to most vehicles.

SHIPPING

East Timor's maritime infrastructure includes ports at Dili, Carabela and Com, smaller wharves at Ocusse (Oekussi) and Liquiça (Likisia), and slip-landing structures in Ocusse, Batugade and Suai.

CIVIL AVIATION

East Timor has two international airports and eight grass runways. At mid-2000 operators of international flights to East Timor included Qantas Airways and Air North of Australia.

ECUADOR

Introductory Survey

Location, Climate, Language, Religion, Flag, Capital

The Republic of Ecuador lies on the west coast of South America. It is bordered by Colombia to the north, by Peru to the east and south, and by the Pacific Ocean to the west. The Galápagos Islands, about 960 km (600 miles) off shore, form part of Ecuador. The climate is affected by the Andes mountains, and the topography ranges from the tropical rain forest on the coast and in the eastern region to the tropical grasslands of the central valley and the permanent snowfields of the highlands. The official language is Spanish, but Quechua and other indigenous languages are very common. Almost all of the inhabitants profess Christianity, and more than 90% are Roman Catholics. The national flag (proportions 2 by 1) has three horizontal stripes, of yellow (one-half of the depth), blue and red. The state flag has, in addition, the national emblem (an oval cartouche, showing Mt Chimborazo and a steamer on a lake, surmounted by a condor) in the centre. The capital is Quito.

Recent History

Ecuador was ruled by Spain from the 16th century until 1822, when it achieved independence as part of Gran Colombia. In 1830 Ecuador seceded and became a separate republic. A long-standing division between Conservatives (Partido Conservador), whose support is generally strongest in the highlands, and Liberals (Partido Liberal, subsequently Partido Liberal Radical), based in the coastal region, began in the 19th century. Until 1948 Ecuador's political life was characterized by a rapid succession of presidents, dictators and juntas. Between 1830 and 1925 the country was governed by 40 different regimes. From 1925 to 1948 there was even greater instability, with a total of 22 heads of state.

Dr Galo Plaza Lasso, who was elected in 1948 and remained in power until 1952, was the first President since 1924 to complete his term of office. He created a climate of stability and economic progress. Dr José María Velasco Ibarra, who had previously been President in 1934–35 and 1944–47, was elected again in 1952 and held office until 1956. A 61-year-old tradition of Liberal Presidents was broken in 1956, when a Conservative candidate, Dr Camilo Ponce Enríquez, took office. He was succeeded in 1960 by Velasco, who campaigned as a non-party Liberal. In the following year, however, President Velasco was deposed by a coup, and was succeeded by his Vice-President, Dr Carlos Julio Arosemena Monroy. The latter was himself deposed in 1963 by a military junta, led by Capt. (later Rear-Adm.) Ramón Castro Jijón, the Commander-in-Chief of the Navy, who assumed the office of President. In 1966 the High Command of the Armed Forces dismissed the junta and installed Clemente Yerovi Indaburu, a wealthy business executive and a former Minister of Economics, as acting President. Yerovi was forced to resign when the Constituent Assembly, elected in October, proposed a new Constitution which prohibited the intervention of the armed forces in politics. In November he was replaced as provisional President by Dr Otto Arosemena Gómez, who held office until the elections of 1968, when Velasco returned from exile to win the presidency for the fifth time.

In 1970 Velasco, with the support of the army, suspended the Constitution, dissolved the National Congress and assumed dictatorial powers to confront a financial emergency. In 1972 he was overthrown for the fourth time by a military coup, led by Brig.-Gen. Guillermo Rodríguez Lara, the Commander-in-Chief of the Army, who proclaimed himself Head of State. In 1976 President Rodríguez resigned, and power was assumed by a three-man military junta, led by Vice-Adm. Alfredo Poveda Burbano, the Chief of Staff of the Navy. The new junta announced its intention to lead the country to a truly representative democracy. A national referendum approved a newly-drafted Constitution in January 1978 and presidential elections took place in July. No candidate achieved an overall majority, and a second round of voting was held in April 1979, when a new Congress was also elected. Jaime Roldós Aguilera of the Concentración de Fuerzas Populares (CFP) was elected President and he took office in August, when the Congress was inaugurated and the new Constitution came into force. Roldós

promised social justice and economic development, and guaranteed freedom for the press, but he encountered antagonism from both the conservative sections of the Congress and the trade unions. In 1981 Roldós died and was replaced by the Vice-President, Dr Osvaldo Hurtado Larrea. Hurtado encountered opposition from left-wing politicians and unions for his efforts to reduce government spending and from right-wing and commercial interests, which feared encroaching state intervention in the private economic sector. In January 1982 the heads of the armed forces resigned and the Minister of Defence was dismissed, when they opposed Hurtado's attempts to settle amicably the border dispute with Peru (see below).

In March 1983 the Government introduced a series of austerity measures, which encountered immediate opposition from the trade unions and private-sector employees. Discontent with the Government's performance was reflected in the results of the presidential and congressional elections of January 1984, when the ruling party, Democracia Popular–Unión Demócrata Cristiana (DP–UDC), lost support. At a second round of voting in May León Febres Cordero, leader of the Partido Social Cristiano (PSC) and presidential candidate of the conservative Frente de Reconstrucción Nacional, unexpectedly defeated Dr Rodrigo Borja Cevallos, representing the left-wing Izquierda Democrática (ID), with 52.2% of the votes cast.

The dismissal of the Chief of Staff of the Armed Forces, Lt-Gen. Frank Vargas Pazzos, brought about a military crisis in 1986. Vargas and his supporters barricaded themselves inside the Mantas military base until they had forced the resignation of both the Minister of Defence and the army commander, who had been accused by Vargas of embezzlement. Vargas then staged a second rebellion at the military base where he had been detained. Troops loyal to the President made an assault on the base, captured Vargas and arrested his supporters. In January 1987 President Febres Cordero was abducted and, after being held for 11 hours, was released in exchange for Vargas, who was granted an amnesty. In July 58 members of the air force were sentenced to up to 16 years' imprisonment for involvement in the abduction of the President.

In June 1986 President Febres Cordero lost the majority that his coalition of parties had held in the Congress. In May 1988 Dr Rodrigo Borja Cevallos (of the ID) won the presidential election, securing 46% of the votes cast in a second round of voting, defeating Abdalá Bucaram Ortiz of the Partido Roldosista Ecuatoriano (PRE), who won 41%. Borja took office as President in August, promising to act promptly to address Ecuador's increasing economic problems and to change the country's isolationist foreign policy. However, large demonstrations in protest against the rise in the price of fuel and against other anti-inflationary economic measures swiftly followed. In October the guerrilla organization, Montoneros Patria Libre (MPL), proposed the establishment of dialogue between the Government and the rebels. In the same month the President of the Supreme Court of Justice was murdered in Quito by unknown assassins.

In February 1989 the Government conducted a campaign to confiscate weapons belonging to paramilitary organizations. In March Alfaro Vive ¡Carajo! (AVC), a leading opposition (hitherto guerrilla) group, urged paramilitary groups across the political spectrum to surrender their weapons. The Government agreed to guarantee the civil rights of AVC members and promised to initiate a national dialogue in return for the group's demobilization. The MPL dissociated itself from the agreement between the Government and the AVC and pledged to continue violent opposition.

In October 1989 a plot to organize a coup to overthrow the President and replace him with the Vice-President was revealed. The alleged conspirators were based in the Guayaquil municipality, where the local business community resented the perceived growing centralization of power in Quito. Radical right-wing groups, headed by former President Febres Cordero, led the movement. In January 1990 Febres Cordero was detained and charged with embezzlement of public funds.

At mid-term legislative elections in June 1990, the ID lost 16 seats and conceded control of Congress to an informal alliance of the PSC and the PRE. In October a serious conflict arose between the Government and Congress when the newly-elected President of Congress, Dr Averroes Bucaram, attempted to stage a legislative coup against President Borja. Bucaram initially impeached several ministers, who were subsequently dismissed by Congress. Congress then dismissed the Supreme Court justices and other high-ranking members of the judiciary, and appointed new courts with shortened mandates. Both the Government and the judiciary refused to recognize these actions, on the grounds that Congress had exceeded its constitutional powers. Bucaram then announced that Congress would initiate impeachment proceedings against Borja himself. However, this move was averted when three opposition deputies transferred their allegiance, so restoring Borja's congressional majority. Bucaram was subsequently dismissed as President of Congress. None the less, impeachment proceedings against government ministers continued into 1991, and by August of that year a total of six ministers had been dismissed. The Government accused the opposition of using the proceedings as part of a deliberate campaign to undermine the prospects of the ID in the forthcoming elections.

In May 1990 about 1,000 indigenous Indians marched into Quito to demand official recognition of land rights for the indigenous population. In the following month the Confederación Nacional de Indígenas del Ecuador (CONAIE—National Confederation of the Indigenous Population of Ecuador) organized an uprising covering seven Andean provinces. Roads were blockaded, *haciendas* occupied, and supplies to the cities interrupted. Following the arrest of 30 Indians by the army, the rebels took military hostages. The Government offered to hold conciliatory negotiations with CONAIE, in return for the release of the hostages. Among the demands made by the Indians were the return of traditional community-held lands, recognition of Quechua as an official language and compensation from petroleum companies for environmental damage. Discussions between CONAIE and President Borja collapsed in August. In January 1991 the Frente Unitario de Trabajadores (FUT) announced a joint anti-Government campaign with CONAIE. The FUT was protesting against the Government's decision on the level of increase of the minimum monthly wage. In February discussions between CONAIE and the Government were resumed, following the seizure by Indian groups in the Oriente of eight oil wells. The protest was halted two weeks later, when the Government promised to consider the Indians' demands for stricter controls on the operations of the petroleum industry, and for financial compensation.

In September 1991 the British Embassy in Quito was occupied by eight members of a dissident faction of the AVC. The siege, which ended peacefully after two days, formed part of a campaign to win the release of the dissidents' leader from prison. In February 1991 the AVC had concluded the process of demobilization that it had begun in February 1989. In October 1991 the party was absorbed by the ID.

In April 1992 several thousand Amazon Indians marched from the Oriente to Quito to demand that their historical rights to their homelands be recognized. In mid-May President Borja agreed to grant legal title to more than 1m. ha of land in the province of Pastaza to the Indians.

At legislative elections in May 1992 the PSC gained the highest number of seats in the enlarged National Congress, winning 21 of the 77 seats, while the PRE secured 13. The Partido Unidad Republicano (PUR) was formed prior to the elections by the former PSC presidential candidate, Sexto Durán Ballén, in order to contest the presidential election (since the PSC had nominated the President of the party, Jaime Nebot Saadi, as its candidate). The PUR won 12 seats, the ID only seven and the Partido Conservador (PC) six seats. In the second round of the presidential election, Durán secured 58% of the votes cast, defeating Nebot, who won 38%. The PUR was to govern with its ally, the PC. However, as the two parties' seats did not constitute a majority in Congress, support from other centre-right parties, particularly the PSC, was sought.

In September 1992 the Government's announcement of a programme of economic austerity measures, including the restructuring of the public sector, prompted violent demonstrations and several bomb attacks in Quito and Guayaquil and a general strike in May 1993. The 'Modernization Law', a crucial part of the controversial austerity programme (which was to provide for the privatization of some 160 state-owned companies

and the reduction in the number of employees in the public sector by 100,000), was approved by Congress in August. In November striking teachers organized demonstrations throughout the country, demanding wage increases and reforms in the education system. During the protests two demonstrators were killed and many injured. Furthermore, the Government's decision in January 1994 to increase the price of fuel by more than 70% provoked violent demonstrations throughout the country and a general strike. In the following month the Tribunal of Constitutional Guarantees declared the rise to be unconstitutional, although Durán refused to recognize the ruling. The unpopularity of President Durán's PUR-PC governing alliance was demonstrated at mid-term congressional elections in May, when it won only nine of the 77 seats. The PSC secured 26 seats, while the PRE remained the second-largest party in Congress, winning 11 seats.

Environmental concerns regarding the exploitation of the Oriente by the petroleum industry continued to be expressed by national and international groups during 1993. In November five Amazon Indian tribes initiated legal proceedings against the international company Texaco to claim compensation totalling US $1,500m. for its part in polluting the rain forest. (It was estimated that some 17m. barrels of oil had been spilt during the company's 25 years of operations in the region.) Protests intensified in January 1994, when the Government initiated a round of bidding for petroleum-exploration licences for 10 hydrocarbon regions, including sites in the eastern Oriente, previously withheld because of opposition from environmentalists and indigenous communities. In mid-1997 a US court provoked outrage among indigenous organizations by rejecting their claim for compensation from Texaco. The organizations announced their intention to pursue the matter.

In June 1994 the increasingly vociferous indigenous movement organized large-scale demonstrations across the country, in protest at a recently-approved Land Development Law. The law, which allowed for the commercialization of Amerindian lands for farming and resource extraction, provoked serious unrest and a general strike, during which a state of emergency was declared and the army mobilized. Seven protesters were killed, and many injured, in clashes with the security forces. The law was subsequently judged to be unconstitutional by the Tribunal of Constitutional Guarantees, although Durán refused to accept the ruling. In early July, however, the law was modified to extend the rights of landowners and those employed to work on the land.

In August 1994 a national referendum on constitutional reform finally took place, at President Durán's instigation, following much disagreement between the Government and the judiciary and opposition parties. All but one of the eight proposed reforms (which included measures to alter the electoral system and the role of Congress and the establishment of a bicameral legislature) were approved; however, only some 50% of eligible voters participated, of whom some 20% returned void ballot papers.

Protests against the Government's economic programme of austerity measures and privatizations in January 1995 resulted in the deaths of two students in Quito during clashes with riot police. In March the Minister of Finance resigned (the third to do so since the Government came to power), apparently because of differences within the Cabinet concerning economic policy. During May and June the FUT launched a national strike against a new series of 'corrective' economic measures, introduced by the Government in an attempt to reduce the impact of the financial crisis caused by the border conflict with Peru (see below), and in July oil workers initiated a strike in protest at the impact of government policy on the petroleum industry. Later in that month, however, the country was plunged into a serious political crisis when Vice-President Alberto Dahik admitted giving funds from the state budget to opposition deputies (allegedly for use in local public-works projects) in return for their support for the Government's economic reform programme. Dahik refused to resign, despite the initiation of impeachment proceedings, and rejected the criminal charges against him. In a further development (believed by some observers to be an attempt to obstruct the case against Dahik) the President of the Supreme Court and two other justices were dismissed. Critics of the Government's action claimed that the dismissals themselves were unconstitutional, as they did not respect the separation of powers of the judiciary from the legislature and executive. In September impeachment proceedings began against the new Minister of Finance, Mauricio Pinto, for his role in various alleged financial irregularities. Meanwhile, the Superintendent of Banks resigned his post, following accusations that he had attempted to hinder the case against Dahik in the Supreme Court. Impeachment proceedings against Dahik began on 2 October, and on 11 October, following an appeal by Durán, the Vice-President resigned. A former Minister of Education, Dr Eduardo Peña Triviño, was subsequently elected as Vice-President by Congress. A further two cabinet ministers offered their resignations in support of Dahik, and on 13 October the entire Cabinet resigned in order that a reorganization of portfolios could take place.

In addition to the political crisis provoked by the scandal surrounding the Vice-President during mid-1995, the administration continued to be troubled by various industrial disputes and strikes. In September troops were dispatched to the Galápagos Islands, following disturbances among the islanders. The protesters were demanding the Government's acceptance of a special law granting increased political and financial autonomy to the islands, in addition to some US \$16m. in priority economic aid. Concerned about the potentially disastrous effect of the protests on the country's important tourist industry, the Government quickly withdrew its opposition to the proposed legislation and agreed to establish a specialist commission to draft a new law acceptable to all parties. Moreover, in October petroleum workers resumed strike action in protest at the Government's privatization plans, and in one incident occupied the PETROECUADOR building, taking two cabinet ministers hostage for several hours. The dispute ended following the resignation of the Minister of Energy and Mines at the end of the month. The strike, however, together with a severe drought, which halted production at the Paute hydroelectric plant (which, under normal circumstances, provided 60%–70% of the country's electricity), resulted in serious energy shortages in late 1995, further exacerbating the country's troubled political and economic situation.

A referendum on government proposals for constitutional reform was held in November 1995. All of the proposed changes were rejected in the plebiscite, which was widely regarded as a reflection of the Government's continued unpopularity. Despite its decisive defeat, the Government announced its intention to pursue its programme of reforms. Widespread strikes and demonstrations by teachers and students in the same month, in which one student was killed in clashes with police, led to the resignation of the Minister of Education. The initiation of impeachment proceedings against one cabinet minister, and the resignation of another, further weakened the President's position, and pressure for him to resign intensified. Industrial action among employees in the energy sector continued, and in January 1996 army units were deployed at prominent sites throughout the country in order to prevent further unrest. Furthermore, an industrial dispute by transport workers in March resulted in serious disruption in the capital and prompted a series of strikes in other sectors.

A presidential election, held in May 1996, failed to produce an outright winner, thus necessitating a second round of voting for the two leading contenders. The PSC candidate, Jaime Nebot Saadi, secured 27.1% of the votes in the first round, while Abdalá Bucaram Ortiz of the PRE won 25.6%. An increasingly vocal and politically-organized indigenous movement resulted in the strong performance of Freddy Ehlers, the candidate for the newly-formed Movimiento Nuevo País-Pachakutik (MNPP), a coalition organization composed of Amerindian and labour groups. Ehlers secured 21% of the votes. At legislative elections held concurrently the PSC won 27 of the 82 seats in the enlarged National Congress, while the PRE secured 19 and Democracia Popular (DP—formerly DP-UDC) won 12. The MNPP emerged as a significant new force in Congress, with a total of eight seats. At the second round of voting in the presidential election in July, Bucaram was the unexpected victor, receiving 54.5% of total votes. The success of Bucaram was widely interpreted as a rejection of the policies of the outgoing Government (which Nebot had promised to continue) and an expression of disenchantment with established party politics. Following his inauguration in August, Bucaram sought to allay the fears of the business community (prompted by his proposals for costly social reform, put forward during his electoral campaign) stating that existing economic arrangements would be maintained. Moreover, a team of prominent businessmen was assigned the role of advising the President on economic policy.

A scandal at the Ministry of Finance in September 1996, which resulted in the arrest of seven senior officials on charges

of embezzlement (estimated at more than US \$300m.) was claimed by Bucaram as a victory for his anti-corruption policies. However, concern at the President's idiosyncratic style of leadership and increasingly eccentric behaviour began to intensify in late 1996. Moreover, a perceived inconsistency in many of Bucaram's policies and the apparently arbitrary nature of his decisions, together with his use of undiplomatic language, contributed to a rapid decline in his popularity.

A 48-hour general strike began in early January 1997, prompted by increases of up to 600% in the price of certain commodities and a climate of considerable dissatisfaction with the President's leadership. Protests intensified in early February when several hundred thousand demonstrators marched through the streets of Quito demanding Bucaram's resignation. The President responded by declaring a national holiday and a one-week closure of schools across the country, and stated his support for the strike. Meanwhile, troops were deployed throughout the capital as violent clashes erupted between protesters and security personnel and Bucaram was barricaded inside the presidential palace. On 6 February, at an emergency session, Congress voted by 44 votes to 34 to dismiss the President on the grounds of mental incapacity; by questioning the President's sanity, Congress was able to evade the normal impeachment requirements of a two-thirds' majority. A state of emergency was declared, and the erstwhile Speaker, Fabián Alarcón Rivera, who had assumed the presidency in an acting capacity, urged demonstrators to storm the presidential palace. Bucaram, however, refused to leave office and claimed that he would retain power by force if necessary. The situation was further complicated by the claim of the Vice-President, Rosalia Arteaga, to be the legitimate constitutional successor to Bucaram. Political confusion over the correct procedure prompted fears of a military coup, despite a declaration of neutrality by the armed forces. Bucaram reportedly fled from the presidential palace on 9 February, and on the following day Arteaga was declared interim President after narrowly winning a congressional vote. However, by 11 February Arteaga had resigned, amid continued constitutional uncertainty, and Alarcón was reinstated as President. Alarcón, who stated that his priorities as President were political reform and the restoration of economic confidence, announced a reorganization of cabinet portfolios (which included no members of the two largest parties in Congress, the PSC and the PRE) and the creation of a commission to investigate allegations of corruption against Bucaram and his administration. In March Bucaram's extradition from Panama (where he had fled and successfully sought political asylum) was requested in order that he face charges of misappropriating some US \$90m. of government funds. Bucaram responded by stating that if he were fit to face criminal charges he could not be insane and should, therefore, be reinstated as President. He also reiterated his view that his removal from office constituted a *coup d'état*. In the following month the President of the Supreme Court announced that extradition would only be possible once a prison sentence had been issued. Furthermore, in May Bucaram declared his intention to stand as a presidential candidate at Ecuador's next elections. The announcement prompted Congress to vote almost unanimously in favour of a motion to impose an indefinite ban on Bucaram's candidacy in any future presidential election. The legislature similarly voted to curtail the term of office of the Vice-President, Rosalia Arteaga, such that it would terminate, along with that of the interim President, in August 1998, when elections would take place.

On 25 May 1997 a national referendum sought public opinion on a variety of matters, including electoral reform, the modernization of the judiciary and the authenticity of Alarcón's position. Although some 40.7% of the electorate did not participate, the vote revealed considerable support for the decision to remove Bucaram from office (75.7%) and for the appointment of Alarcón as interim President (68.3%). Some 64.5% of voters also favoured the creation of a national assembly to consider constitutional reform. Alarcón's apparent success in the referendum, however, was undermined in early June by the launch of an official congressional inquiry into allegations that leading drugs-traffickers in the country had contributed to political party funds, and, particularly, to Alarcón's Frente Radical Alfarista (FRA).

In July 1997 Congress dismissed all 31 judges of the Supreme Court, claiming that its action was in accordance with the views on the depoliticization of the judiciary (which is nominated by the legislature) expressed in the recent referendum. The President of the Supreme Court condemned the action as unconstitutional.

The announcement in August 1997 that a national assembly to review the Constitution (as proposed in the referendum of May 1997) would not be installed until August 1998 was widely opposed, and provoked a 48-hour strike in protest, which virtually paralyzed the country by means of numerous roadblocks. The strike was supported most strongly by Indian and peasant organizations, who insisted that an assembly should be convened as soon as possible in order to discuss indigenous rights and the proposed privatization of key areas of the economy. In response to the apparent strength of public opinion, it was announced in September that elections for the 70 representatives to the assembly would take place in late November. However, 11 indigenous organizations demonstrated their lack of confidence in the Government to address their concerns by convening a mass rally in Quito to establish guidelines for their own constitution.

The uneasy relationship between Alarcón and Arteaga became more apparent in August 1997, when the Vice-President publicly expressed support for the striking indigenous groups, and when Alarcón refused to transfer power to Arteaga while he left the country on a brief foreign tour. Alarcón's problems in office were further exacerbated by charges of embezzlement filed against him in the Supreme Court by a former FRA colleague. In January 1998 the Supreme Court issued a four-year prison sentence to Bucaram for libel. Numerous other legal suits against the ex-President remained pending.

In January 1998, following persistent pleas from international environmental and scientific organizations for greater protection of the Galápagos Islands, Congress approved a law which aimed to preserve the islands' unique environment more effectively. An element of the law, providing for an extension of the marine reserve around the islands from 15 to 40 nautical miles, attracted intense criticism from powerful fishing interests in the country and was, consequently, vetoed by Alarcón, prompting condemnation by environmentalists and small-scale fishing concerns, who claimed that the President had acceded to commercial pressures.

In February 1998 the recently-established National Constituent Assembly (convened to review the Constitution) announced a number of institutional reforms, including the enlargement of Congress from 82 to 121 seats, the extension of the presidential term (for Alarcón's successor) from four years to four years, five months and five days, the abolition of mid-term elections and the completion of a presidential term by the Vice-President in the case of the indefinite absence of the President. The new Constitution, which retained the majority of the provisions of the 1979 Constitution, officially came into force on 10 August.

At a presidential election on 31 May 1998 the DP candidate and mayor of Quito, Jamil Mahuad Witt, emerged as the strongest contender, securing 35.2% of total votes cast. Alvaro Noboa Pontón for the PRE, whose popularity was concentrated in Guayaquil and the coastal regions, received 26.5% of votes, while ex-President Borja and Freddy Ehlers won 15.6% and 14.3%, respectively. At concurrent elections to the newly-enlarged Congress the DP secured 32 of the 121 seats, the PSC won 27, the PRE 24 and the ID 18 seats. At the second round of voting in the presidential election on 12 July, Mahuad narrowly defeated Noboa with 51.2% of total votes. Noboa rejected the result, alleging widespread voting irregularities, none of which was upheld by the Supreme Electoral Tribunal or the international observers present in the country. Mahuad was consequently sworn in on 10 August and appointed a Cabinet consisting predominantly of independent members. The new President's stated objectives focused on the stimulation of economic recovery, following a series of serious reversals, including a decrease in world petroleum prices and the infrastructural and sociological damage caused by El Niño (a periodic warming of the tropical Pacific Ocean—see below). In addition, Mahuad proposed a number of social programmes (involving the creation of new jobs and the construction of low-cost homes), which prompted scepticism amongst observers, who doubted the feasibility of such plans.

A programme of severe adjustment measures, which included huge rises in the cost of domestic gas and electricity, as well as substantial increases in public transport fares and fuel prices, was introduced in September 1998, prompting a general strike, organized by FUT and CONAIE, in the following month. Subsequent rioting and violent confrontation between demonstrators and security personnel resulted in the deaths of four people. In February 1999 disagreement over economic policy led to the resignation of the Minister of Finance, Fidel Jaramillo Buendia, and severe disruption arising from extensive fuel shortages prompted the resignation of the Minister of Energy and Mines, Patricio Rivadeneira García. In the same month the leader of the left-wing Movimiento Popular Democrático and member of Congress, Jaime Hurtado González, was assassinated in Quito. The killing was linked to a right-wing Colombian paramilitary group. In March former interim President Alarcón was arrested on charges of illegally hiring personnel during his term in office as Speaker of Congress.

In early March 1999 a substantial decrease in the value of the sucre led President Mahuad to declare a week-long bank holiday in an attempt to prevent the withdrawal of deposits and reduce the pressure on the currency. A few days later a 60-day state of emergency was declared by the Government in response to a two-day strike, organized by leaders of the main trade unions and Indian groups. In addition, the Government announced an economic retrenchment programme in an attempt to restore investor confidence and prevent economic collapse. Measures included an increase in fuel prices of up to 160%, a number of tax reforms (notably an increase in value-added tax—VAT), the partial 'freezing' of bank accounts, and the planned privatization of certain state-owned companies. These prompted a further series of protests and the resignation of four of the five members of the board of the central bank (citing differences over government financial policies). The main opposition party, the PSC, similarly refused to endorse the austerity programme, thus compelling the President to compromise with the proposal of less severe economic measures, which were narrowly approved by Congress. These new measures included a partial reduction of fuel price increases, and the reinstatement of income tax; following their approval, Mahuad lifted the state of emergency. However, a further rise in prices and the collapse of a major bank (the Guayaquil-based Banco del Progreso) later in March led to renewed protests.

In April 1999 the Government announced an emergency plan entitled 'Ecuador 2000', which aimed to revive the economy and which included a number of requisite measures to gain the support of the International Monetary Fund (IMF). The plan incorporated numerous social and public works development schemes, tax reforms and moves towards less centralized government. The plan was approved by the IMF, and, following the appointment of four new board members of the central bank in June, hopes were renewed that the IMF would provide an estimated US $400m. in initial funding. However, in July taxi drivers and public transport workers took nation-wide industrial action in protest at increases in fuel prices and at the new economic retrenchment plan proposed by the IMF. In response to the ensuing massive disruption, the Government imposed a further state of emergency and called in the military. An agreement between transport officials and the Government was reached in mid-July, when Mahuad agreed to 'freeze' fuel prices and to allow co-operatives and transport companies access to 'frozen' bank deposits. The state of emergency was then lifted.

In late August 1999 the Government announced its intention to default on US $96m. in interest payments on $6,000m. in outstanding foreign debt repayments (on so-called Brady bonds—restructured commercial bank loans) for a period of 30 days, and to attempt to restructure its large external debts. The move, which was supported by the IMF, was implemented owing to the country's inability to honour repayments on its foreign debt (which, at a total of more than $13,000m., was equivalent to some 90% of GDP). In early September the Minister of Finance, Ana Lucia Armijos, resigned, prompted by the unpopularity of the recent economic measures (her successor, however, remained in the post only six weeks before himself resigning). Nevertheless, at the end of September, the IMF signed a preliminary agreement with Ecuador which was expected to provide up to $1,250m. in funding (comprising a $400m. stand-by loan from the IMF and $850m. in loans from other multilateral agencies).

In early January 2000 President Mahuad imposed a state of emergency in an attempt to curb increasing unrest, amid indications that the economic crisis was deteriorating. On 21 January President Mahuad was forced to flee from the presidential palace, following large-scale protests by thousands of Indian demonstrators, who were supported by sections of the armed forces, in Quito over the President's perceived mismanagement of the economic crisis (including his controversial decision to replace the sucre with the US dollar). A three-man council was established to oversee the country. However, Gen. Carlos

Mendoza, the Chief of Staff of the Armed Forces, disbanded the council within only 24 hours of its creation, and announced the appointment of former Vice-President Gustavo Noboa Bejerano as President. This move followed talks with US officials, who had warned that foreign aid to Ecuador would be curtailed if power were not restored to the elected Government. The coup was widely condemned by governments around the world and by international organizations. Noboa, whose appointment as Head of State was endorsed by a large majority in Congress, promised to restore economic stability to the country. However, Indian activists who had supported the short-lived three-member council (one of whose members had been the leader of CONAIE, Antonio Vargas) continued to demonstrate against the assumption of the presidency by Noboa, whom they viewed as ideologically similar to Mahuad. Noboa appointed Pedro Pinto Rubianes as the new Vice-President on 27 January and formed a new Cabinet, comprising members of the DP, the PSC and the PRE, in February. Heinz Moeller Freile was appointed Minister of Foreign Affairs and Francisco Huerta Montalvo was named Minister of the Interior.

In early February 2000 four members of the armed forces, who allegedly participated in the events leading up to Mahuad's removal from office, were apprehended on charges of insurrection. It was later announced that as many as 113 army officers were to be charged in connection with the previous month's events. In May the entire military high command was replaced, even though later that month Congress approved an amnesty for military officers and civilians arrested in connection with the coup.

In February 2000 Noboa secured congressional approval for a controversial economic reform programme, the Ley de Transformación Económica (Economic Transformation Law), which included the adoption of the US dollar as the official currency, as well as fiscal adjustments and an acceleration in the privatization process. CONAIE, which had returned to prominence following its role in the removal of President Mahuad, organized a series of demonstrations in protest at the dollarization policy and to demand a referendum on the dissolution of Congress and the Supreme Court. Palliative measures introduced by the Government, including an increase in the minimum wage, were rejected by trade unions and indigenous organizations. Nevertheless, the process of dollarization formally began in March and was completed in September, when the US dollar officially became Ecuador's sole currency. In late April the Minister of the Interior, Huerta Montalvo, resigned (to be replaced by his deputy, Antonio Andretta), after he failed to secure an agreement with CONAIE to end the protests. The announcement by the Government in May of an IMF-approved economic adjustment package, which included a sharp increase in the price of fuel, not only provoked further antagonism between the Government and trade unions and indigenous organizations, but also resulted in the resignation of the Minister of Finance and Public Credit, Jorge Guzmán Ortega. However, in September CONAIE entered into renewed negotiations with the Government after its calls for mass demonstrations in the previous month had met with only moderate support. In the same month the Supreme Electoral Tribunal disallowed a petition from CONAIE requesting that a referendum on various aspects of the Ley de Transformación Económica be held, owing to irregularities in the collection of signatures.

Both the DP and the PSC performed well in municipal and provincial elections held throughout the country in May 2000, suggesting significant popular acceptance of the structural reforms (although the ID candidate, Paco Moncayo, won the strategically important mayoral election in Quito). However, relations between the DP and the PSC came under increasing strain in August when the independent Susana González was controversially elected legislative President for the remaining two years of the current presidential term (until August 2002). The PSC claimed that, as the second largest party in Congress, its nominee should fill the position and a Constitutional Tribunal was organized to determine the legality of the result. In the same month the Government offered to resign in support to the President after the governing coalition lost its majority in Congress (divisions within the DP had resulted in several of its members aligning themselves with the centre-left opposition). The coalition's lack of a parliamentary majority endangered the proposed reform (also known as Trole 11) of the labour and petroleum sectors, as well as the privatization process. At the end of August, however, the impasse between the Government and Congress was resolved after the Constitutional Tribunal ruled that a new election to the congressional presidency must be held; Hugo Quevado of the PSC was subsequently elected to the post.

However, the relationship between the legislature and the executive was further strained in late August 2000 after Noboa resorted to presidential decree to pass the proposed Trole 11 legislation. CONAIE and trade union organizations appealed to the Constitutional Tribunal to rule on the legality of such a move. In January 2001 the Constitutional Tribunal upheld almost one-third of the objections against Trole 11, and, most notably, declared unconstitutional the clause concerning the proposed privatization of state-owned companies.

In December 2000 two attacks on the trans-Ecuadorean oil pipeline resulted in at least 16 fatalities and 41 injuries. President Noboa attributed blame for the attack to terrorists attempting to destabilize the country and prevent economic modernization. In the same month the Minister of Finance and Public Credit, Luis Yturralde, submitted his resignation, apparently a result of his opposition to economic reforms advocated by the IMF, which included an increase in VAT from 12% to 15%. Popular resentment against the Government erupted at the end of January 2001 after significant increases in fuel prices and transport costs were implemented. Thousands of Indian protesters occupied Quito and roadblocks were erected across the Andean highlands and the Amazon lowlands. In early February the Government imposed a national state of emergency, which was lifted only after the Government acceded to the demands for a reduction in fuel prices in return for an end to the protests, which were marred by violence. In late March transport workers staged a 24-hour strike in protest at the Government's proposed tax reforms as well as a planned reduction in transportation costs.

In late January 2001 an environmental catastrophe was feared when an oil tanker ran aground less than one kilometre from the Galapagos Islands. About 80% of the tanker's 240,000-gallon cargo leaked into the sea, thus posing a threat to the unique sanctuary of animals and plants that inhabit the islands. At least 76,000 gallons of petroleum were recovered and favourable winds and currents appeared to have limited the extent of the ecological damage. However, the long-term damage caused by the spill had yet to be assessed.

In April 1999 the World Trade Organization (WTO) upheld the complaint, put forward by the USA, Ecuador and four other Latin American countries, that the European Union (EU) unfairly favoured Caribbean banana producers, and authorized the USA to impose trade sanctions against EU goods. A two-tier tariff rate quota arrangement was subsequently agreed at a meeting between Ecuadorean government officials and leaders of Caribbean banana-producing countries in November 1999, easing restrictions on Latin American banana exporters and consequently assisting Ecuadorean producers.

The long-standing border dispute with Peru over the Cordillera del Cóndor erupted into war in January 1981. A cease-fire was declared a few days later under the auspices of the guarantors of the Rio Protocol of 1942 (Argentina, Brazil, Chile and the USA). The Protocol was not recognized by Ecuador as it awarded the area, which affords access to the Amazon river system, to Peru. Further clashes occurred along the border with Peru in December 1982 and January 1983. In January 1992 discussions on the border dispute were resumed. A number of minor incidents along the border were reported during 1994. However, in January 1995 serious fighting broke out between the two sides, following reports of Peruvian incursions into Ecuadorean territory. Both Governments denied responsibility for initiating hostilities and issued contradictory reports concerning subsequent clashes. Following offers from the Organization of American States (OAS) and the four guarantor nations of the Rio Protocol, representatives of the two Governments met for negotiations in Rio de Janeiro, Brazil, and a cease-fire agreement was eventually concluded in February. An observer mission, representing the four guarantor nations, was dispatched to the border, to oversee the separation of forces and demilitarization of the border area. Despite mutual accusations of the cease-fire having been broken, the separation of forces continued and both Governments ordered the release of a number of prisoners taken during the conflict. Following intensive negotiations, agreement on the delimitation of the demilitarized zone in the disputed area was reached in July and in October Ecuador finally repealed the state of emergency. A resumption of negotiations in September 1996 resulted in the signing of the Santiago Agreement by both sides in the following month, which was to provide a framework for a definitive solution on the border issue. In March 1997 Ecuador lodged an official complaint against the Peruvian army's use of land-mines along the border. Following further talks in Brasília, beginning in April, in August the two countries signed an agreement aimed at ensuring transparent mechanisms in arms procurement. The agreement, however, failed to prevent a series of rumours that Ecuador had secretly purchased considerable quantities of armaments from Israel. Furthermore, Ecuador's insistence on including the issue of a sovereign outlet to the Amazon river threatened the progress of the talks.

Following further negotiations in early 1998 a number of commissions were established to examine specific aspects of a potential agreement between Ecuador and Peru, including a trade and navigation treaty and the fixing of frontier markers on the ground in the Cordillera del Cóndor. Talks culminated in the signing of an accord in Brasília on 26 October by the Ministers of Foreign Affairs of Ecuador and Peru in the presence of the two countries' Presidents and of six other regional leaders. The accord confirmed Peru's claim regarding the delineation of the border, but granted Ecuador navigation and trading rights on the Amazon and its tributaries and the opportunity to establish two trading centres in Peru (although this was not to constitute sovereign access). Moreover, Ecuador was given 1 sq km of territory, as private property, at Tiwintza in Peru where many Ecuadorean soldiers, killed during the conflict in 1995, were buried. Both countries were committed to establish ecological parks along the border where military personnel would not be allowed access. Although considerable opposition to the accord was expressed in Peru, international reaction was very favourable and resulted in several offers of finance from multilateral agencies for cross-border development projects.

An official ceremony in May 1999 marked the transfer of Tiwintza from Peru to Ecuador, and both parties confirmed that two ecological parks were to be created along the common border. Presidents Mahuad and Alberto Fujimori reiterated their intention to seek US $3,000m. in funding, over a 10-year period, to finance a number of development projects (including the construction of new roads and health and education centres) and to organize the removal of land mines in the border area.

Following the suspected involvement of Colombian guerrillas in the murder of an Ecuadorean politician in Quito in March 1999 (see above) and reports (denied by the Ecuadorean Government) of the presence of Colombian paramilitary troops in the country, Ecuador's military presence was strengthened at its border with Colombia. In September 12 foreigners, several of whom were employees of a petroleum company operating in the region, were kidnapped by suspected Colombian guerrillas in the jungle near the Colombian border. In November an explosion which damaged an oil pipeline in the same area was linked to a Colombian rebel group, although any foreign involvement in the incident was denied by the Ecuadorean Government. However, as the internal conflict in Colombia escalated in 2000, Ecuador received an increasing number of refugees onto its territory as well as higher levels of violence on its border with Colombia. Between September 2000 and January 2001 about 2,100 Colombians sought refuge in the Ecuadorean border town of Lago Agrio. In February 2001 the Minister of Foreign Affairs, Heinz Moeller Freile, announced his intention to ask the US Government for financial aid to support the creation of an economic and military 'buffer' zone between Ecuador and Colombia. In March the Government assigned 10,000 troops to police the border with Colombia.

Government

Executive power is vested in the President, who is directly elected by universal adult suffrage for a four-year term (starting from 15 January of the year following his election). The President is not eligible for re-election. Legislative power is held by the 121-member unicameral Congress, which is also directly elected for a four-year term: 12 members are elected on a national basis and serve a four-year term, while 65 members are elected on a provincial basis. Ecuador comprises 21 provinces, composed of 193 cantons, 322 urban parishes and 757 rural parishes. Each province has a Governor, who is appointed by the President.

Defence

Military service, which lasts one year, is selective for men at the age of 20. In August 2000 there were 57,500 men in the armed forces: army 50,000, navy 4,500 (including 1,500 marines)

and air force 3,000. Defence expenditure in 1999 was estimated to be 4,000,000m. sucres.

Economic Affairs

In 1998, according to estimates by the World Bank, Ecuador's gross national product (GNP), measured at average 1996–98 prices, was US $18,450m., equivalent to $1,520 per head (or $3,003 per head on an international purchasing-power parity basis). During 1990–98, it was estimated, GNP per head increased, in real terms, at an average annual rate of 0.8%. Over the same period, the population increased at an average annual rate of 2.4%. In 1999, according to preliminary World Bank data, GNP was about $16,200m. ($1,310 per head). Ecuador's gross domestic product (GDP) increased, in real terms, at an average annual rate of 2.2% in 1990–99. Real GDP rose by 3.7% in 1997 and by 0.4% in 1998.

Agriculture (including hunting, forestry and fishing) contributed 13.0% of GDP in 1999. An estimated 27.2% of the economically active population were employed in the agricultural sector in 1998. The principal cash crops are bananas, coffee and cocoa. The seafood sector, particularly the shrimp industry, expanded rapidly in the 1980s, and in 1995 Ecuador was the second largest producer of shrimps in the world. Ecuador's extensive forests yield valuable hardwoods, and the country is a leading producer of balsawood. Exports of cut flowers increased from US $0.5m. in 1985 to $144.6m. in 1998. During 1990–99 agricultural GDP increased at an average annual rate of 2.0%. It rose by 4.1% in 1997, but declined by 1.4% in 1998 and by a further 1.3% in 1999.

Industry (including mining, manufacturing, construction and power) employed 18.1% of the labour force in 1990, and provided 40.0% of GDP in 1999. During 1990–99 industrial GDP increased at an average annual rate of 2.7%. It rose by 3.4% in 1997, but fell by 0.6% in 1998 and by 3.6% in 1999.

Mining contributed 12.2% of GDP in 1999, although the mining sector employed only 0.6% of the labour force in 1990. Petroleum and its derivatives remained the major exports in the late 1990s. In 1998 some 388,000 barrels of crude petroleum were produced per day, of which 40% was exported. Earnings from petroleum exports amounted to some US $1,400m. in 1997, but declined to $791m. in 1998. Natural gas is extracted, but only a small proportion is retained. Gold, silver, copper, antimony and zinc are also mined. In real terms, the GDP of the mining sector increased at an average rate of 4.6% per year during 1990–98. Mining GDP rose by 3.5% in 1997, but declined by 3.3% in 1998 and by 0.3% in 1999.

Manufacturing contributed 22.7% of GDP in 1999, and employed 11.2% of the labour force in 1990. Measured by the value of output, the most important branches of manufacturing in 1996 were food products (accounting for 33.1% of the total), petroleum refineries (16.5%), chemicals (7.3%) and pulp and paper products (6.0%). During 1990–98 manufacturing GDP increased at an average annual rate of 2.9%. It rose by 3.5% in 1997 and by 0.4% in 1998, but declined by 7.2% in 1999.

Energy is derived principally from thermoelectric and hydroelectric plants. Imports of mineral fuels and lubricants comprised 6.1% of the value of total imports in 1998.

The services sector contributed 47.0% of GDP in 1999. Around 46% of the active population were employed in services in 1990. The sector's GDP increased at an average annual rate of 1.9% during 1990–99. It rose by 2.6% in 1997 and by 0.8% in 1998, but declined by 9.9% in 1999.

In 1999 Ecuador recorded a visible trade surplus of US $1,665m., and a surplus of $955m. on the current account of the balance of payments. In 1998 the principal source of imports was the USA (accounting for 29.4% of the total), which was also the principal market for exports (38.9%). Other major trading partners were Colombia, Japan, Germany, Italy and the Republic of Korea. The principal exports in 1998 were seafood and seafood products (28.8%), bananas (25.8%) and petroleum and petroleum derivatives (22.3%). The principal imports in 1998 were machinery and transport equipment (35.2%), chemicals (16.0%) and basic manufactures (16.9%).

In 1999 there was a budgetary deficit of about 1,167,200m. sucres. In 1996 some 40% of government expenditure was financed by revenue from petroleum. Ecuador's total external debt was US $15,150m. at the end of 1998, of which $12,589m. was long-term public debt. In that year the cost of debt-servicing was equivalent to 28.8% of the total value of exports of goods and services. The average annual rate of inflation in 1990–99 was 37.4%; the rate averaged 51.7% in 1999 and 96.1% in 2000.

The rate of unemployment decreased from an average of 14.4% in 1999 to 9.0% in 2000.

Ecuador is a member of the Andean Community (see p. 122), the Organization of American States (OAS—see p. 261) and of the Asociación Latinoamericana de Integración (ALADI— p. 230). In 1992 Ecuador withdrew from the Organization of the Petroleum Exporting Countries (OPEC—p. 269) and announced its intention of seeking associate status. In 1995 Ecuador joined the World Trade Organization (WTO—p. 292).

In the mid-1990s Ecuador's proven petroleum reserves almost tripled, following discoveries in the Amazon region, and the Government signed contracts with numerous companies for further exploration and drilling. In late 1997 work to expand the capacity of the trans-Ecuadorean pipeline from 330,000 b/d to 410,000 b/d began. Construction of a new pipeline, financed by a consortium of private companies at a cost of US \$594m., was also expected to begin in 2001. Flooding of the coastal lowlands in mid-1997, caused by El Niño (a periodic warming of the tropical Pacific Ocean), adversely affected various cash crops (notably bananas) and fishing catches, and cost the country an estimated US \$250m. in lost agricultural income. In 1998 Ecuador's economy was adversely affected by a significant decrease in world petroleum prices, a decrease in foreign investment and the depreciation of the sucre by 35.1%. The implementation of a privatization programme, first proposed in 1992, was repeatedly impeded by political turmoil and trade union opposition (including several general strikes). In 1999 a further decline in revenue from petroleum exports, another substantial depreciation in the value of the sucre and the resultant rise in inflation, as well as the partial 'freezing' of bank accounts and a series of strikes and violent protests, contributed to a worsening of the economic crisis (with Ecuador unable to honour its massive external debt repayments) and had serious political repercussions (see Recent History). In April 2000 the IMF approved a 12-month stand-by credit for Ecuador worth SDR 226.7m. (about US \$304m.) to support the costly dollarization process, implemented in a bid to reduce inflation and to rebuild the country's fragile banking system. The loan was conditional on fiscal reforms, including the significant increase in fuel prices (in order to reduce costly subsidies), as well as structural reform in the labour and oil sectors and the privatization programme. However, opposition from Congress as well as from indigenous organizations and trade unions stalled the implementation of these policies and thus endangered further IMF support. In December Congress approved the 2001 budget with minor adjustments, including the transfer of \$72m. to social spending from debt repayments; however, there was concern that the budget was too dependent on high petroleum prices, which were predicted to fall in 2001. The economy grew by about 2% in 2000 and was forecast to increase by 3.5% in 2001.

Social Welfare

Social insurance is compulsory for all employees. Benefits are available for sickness, industrial accidents, disability, mat-

ernity, old age, widowhood and orphanhood. Hospitals and welfare institutions are administered by Central Public Assistance Boards. Budgetary expenditure on social welfare and labour was 134,697m. sucres (2.4% of total spending) in 1994. In 1993 there were 433 hospitals, and in 1997 there were 18,510 hospital beds and 15,866 physicians in the country. In the same year there were 70.1 nurses per 100,000 population. Budgetary expenditure on health and community development by the central Government was 319,470m. sucres (5.8% of total spending) in 1994.

Education

Education is compulsory for 10 years, to be undertaken between five and 15 years of age, and all state schools are free. Private schools continue to play a vital role in the educational system. Primary education begins at six years of age and lasts for six years. Secondary education, in general and specialized technical or humanities schools, begins at the age of 12 and lasts for up to six years, comprising two equal cycles of three years each. In 1997 the total enrolment at primary and secondary schools was equivalent to 89.5% of the school-age population (122% in primary schools and 57% in secondary schools). In 1993/94 there were 2,868 secondary schools and in 1996/97 there were 17,367 primary schools. University courses extend for up to six years, and include programmes for teacher training. A number of adult schools and literacy centres have been built, aimed at reducing the rate of adult illiteracy, which averaged an estimated 4.1% of the urban population (males 3.4%; females 4.8%) in 1997. Total expenditure on education by the central Government was estimated at 1,957,051m. sucres (equivalent to 3.5% of GNP) in 1996. In many rural areas, Quechua and other indigenous Indian languages are used in education.

Public Holidays

2001: 1 January (New Year's Day), 6 January (Epiphany), 26–27 February (Carnival), 12 April (Holy Thursday), 13 April (Good Friday), 14 April (Easter Saturday), 1 May (Labour Day), 24 May (Battle of Pichincha), 14 June (Corpus Christi), 24 July (Birth of Simón Bolívar), 10 August (Independence of Quito), 9 October (Independence of Guayaquil), 12 October (Discovery of America), 1 November (All Saints' Day), 2 November (All Souls' Day), 3 November (Independence of Cuenca), 6 December (Foundation of Quito), 25 December (Christmas Day).

2002: 1 January (New Year's Day), 6 January (Epiphany), 11–12 February (Carnival), 28 March (Holy Thursday), 29 March (Good Friday), 30 March (Easter Saturday), 1 May (Labour Day), 24 May (Battle of Pichincha), 30 May (Corpus Christi), 24 July (Birth of Simón Bolívar), 10 August (Independence of Quito), 9 October (Independence of Guayaquil), 12 October (Discovery of America), 1 November (All Saints' Day), 2 November (All Souls' Day), 3 November (Independence of Cuenca), 6 December (Foundation of Quito), 25 December (Christmas Day).

Weights and Measures

The metric system is in force.

Statistical Survey

Sources (unless otherwise stated): Banco Central del Ecuador, Quito; Ministerio de Industrias, Comercio, Integración y Pesquería, Quito; Instituto Nacional de Estadística y Censos, 10 de Agosto 229, Quito; tel. (2) 519-320; internet www.inec.gov.ec.

Area and Population

AREA, POPULATION AND DENSITY

Area (sq km)	272,045*
Population (census results)†	
28 November 1982	8,060,712
25 November 1990	
Males	4,796,412
Females	4,851,777
Total	9,648,189
Population (official estimates at mid-year)†	
1998	12,174,628
1999	12,411,232
2000	12,646,095
Density (per sq km) at mid-2000	46.5

* 105,037 sq miles.

† Figures exclude nomadic tribes of indigenous Indians. Census results also exclude any adjustment for underenumeration, estimated to have been 5.6% in 1982 and 6.3% in 1990.

PROVINCES (official estimates, mid-1999)*

	Population	Capital
Azuay	617,247	Cuenca
Bolívar	180,035	Guaranda
Cañar	214,820	Azogues
Carchi . . .	165,132	Tulcán
Cotopaxi . . .	302,177	Latacunga
Chimborazo . . .	422,676	Riobamba
El Oro . . .	548,121	Machala
Esmeraldas . . .	407,555	Esmeraldas
Guayas	3,346,804	Guayaquil
Imbabura . . .	325,475	Ibarra
Loja	425,490	Loja
Los Ríos . . .	652,078	Babahoyo
Manabí	1,249,073	Portoviejo
Morona Santiago . . .	139,531	Macas
Napo	155,375	Tena
Pastaza . . .	60,527	Puyo
Pichincha . . .	2,409,712	Quito
Sucumbíos . . .	139,371	Nueva Loja
Tungurahua . . .	440,771	Ambato
Zamora Chinchipe . . .	100,281	Zamora
Archipiélago de Colón (Galápagos) . . .	16,184	Puerto Baquerizo (Isla San Cristóbal)
Total	**12,318,435**	

* Figures exclude persons in unspecified areas, totalling 92,797.

PRINCIPAL TOWNS (estimated population at mid-1997)

Guayaquil . . .	1,973,880		Manta . . .	156,981
Quito (capital) . .	1,444,363*		Eloy Alfaro . .	127,832*
Cuenca . . .	255,028		Quevedo . .	120,640
Machala . . .	197,350		Milagro . .	119,371
Santo Domingo de			Esmeraldas . .	117,722
los Colorados	183,219		Loja . . .	117,365
Portoviejo . . .	167,956		Riobamba . .	114,322*
Ambato . . .	160,302		Ibarra . .	113,791*

* Population at mid-1996.

Source: UN, *Demographic Yearbook*.

BIRTHS, MARRIAGES AND DEATHS*
(excluding nomadic Indian tribes)

	Registered live births		Registered marriages		Registered deaths	
	Number	Rate (per 1,000)	Number	Rate (per 1,000)	Number	Rate (per 1,000)
1994 . .	350,838	31.3	71,289	6.4	51,165	4.6
1995 . .	408,983	35.7	70,480	6.2	50,867	4.4
1996 . .	302,217	25.8	72,094	6.2	52,300	4.5
1997 . .	288,803	24.2	66,967	5.6	52,089	4.4
1998 . .	199,079	16.4	n.a.	n.a.	54,357	4.5

* Registrations incomplete.

Sources: Instituto Nacional de Estadística y Censos; UN, *Demographic Yearbook*.

Expectation of life (UN estimates, years at birth, 1990-95): 68.5 (males 66.4, females 71.4) (Source: UN, *World Population Prospects: The 1998 Revision*).

ECONOMICALLY ACTIVE POPULATION*
(ISIC Major Divisions, 1990 census)

	Males	Females	Total
Agriculture, hunting, forestry and fishing . .	904,701	131,011	1,035,712
Mining and quarrying . . .	18,849	2,021	20,870
Manufacturing	248,157	122,181	370,338
Electricity, gas and water. . .	10,741	1,919	12,660
Construction. . . .	192,034	4,682	196,716
Trade, restaurants and hotels .	295,855	180,875	476,730
Transport, storage and communications . . .	123,807	7,277	131,084
Financing, insurance, real estate and business services . . .	54,043	27,314	81,357
Community, social and personal services . . .	483,821	354,308	838,129
Activities not adequately defined .	111,919	45,811	157,730
Total labour force	**2,443,927**	**877,399**	**3,321,326**

* Figures refer to persons aged 8 years and over, excluding those seeking work for the first time, totalling 38,441 (males 27,506; females 10,935).

1997: Total employed 3,062,185; Total unemployed 311,625; Total labour force 3,373,810.

Agriculture

PRINCIPAL CROPS ('000 metric tons)

	1997	1998	1999
Wheat	20	20	19
Rice (paddy)	1,072	1,043	1,290
Barley	35	36	34
Maize	688	382	568
Potatoes	602	534	563
Cassava (Manioc)	138	74	125
Dry beans	41	30	31
Soybeans (Soya beans)	9	10	77
Seed cotton	15	10	6
Coconuts	31	23	22
Palm kernels	41	45	28
Tomatoes	45	65	62
Pumpkins, squash and gourds*	40	40	41
Sugar cane*	5,000	7,000	7,864
Apples	25	25	12
Oranges	217	122	122
Other citrus fruits	106	39	52
Pineapples	30	80	124
Mangoes	3	69	21
Avocados	44	24	21
Bananas	7,494	4,563	6,392
Plantains	894	466	658
Papayas	69	68	112
Coffee (green)	87	48	133
Cocoa beans	83	35	95

* FAO estimate(s).

Source: FAO.

LIVESTOCK ('000 head)

	1997	1998	1999
Cattle	5,150	5,076	5,106
Sheep	1,802	2,081	2,180
Pigs	2,708	2,708	2,786
Horses*	520	520	521
Goats	309	280	284
Asses*	267	268	269
Mules*	156	157	157
Poultry	100,040	100,233	130,200

* FAO estimate(s).

Source: FAO.

LIVESTOCK PRODUCTS ('000 metric tons)

	1997	1998	1999
Beef and veal	156	158	164
Mutton and lamb	6	6	8
Pig meat	107	100	110
Goat meat	1	1	1
Poultry meat	177	108	146
Cows' milk	1,929	1,983	1,994
Sheep's milk	6	6	6
Goats' milk	2	2	2
Butter	5	5	5
Cheese*	7	7	7
Hen eggs	58	60	55
Wool:			
greasy	2	2*	2*
clean*	1	1	n.a.
Cattle hides (fresh)	31	32	33

* FAO estimate(s).

Source: FAO.

Forestry

ROUNDWOOD REMOVALS ('000 cubic metres, excluding bark)

	1996	1997	1998
Sawlogs, veneer logs and logs for sleepers	4,814	5,168	5,168
Pulpwood	635	682	682
Other industrial wood	65	70	70
Fuel wood	5,048	5,420	5,420
Total	10,562	11,340	11,340

Source: FAO, *Yearbook of Forest Products*.

SAWNWOOD PRODUCTION
('000 cubic metres, including railway sleepers)

	1996	1997	1998
Coniferous (softwood)	377	416	416
Broadleaved (hardwood)	1,509	1,663	1,663
Total	1,886	2,079	2,079

Source: FAO, *Yearbook of Forest Products*.

Fishing

('000 metric tons, live weight)

	1996	1997	1998
Capture	703.0	549.0	310.0
Chilean jack mackerel	56.8	30.3	25.9
South American pilchard	356.5	57.2	1.0
Red-eye round herring	34.3	1.1	8.9
Pacific thread herring	41.0	43.1	40.5
Pacific anchoveta	26.4	89.2	44.5
Skipjack tuna	37.5	67.4	67.5
Yellowfin tuna	19.3	19.6	31.1
Bigeye tuna	17.9	26.1	17.9
Chub mackerel	79.5	192.2	44.7
Aquaculture	108.7	135.3	146.6
Blue shrimp	10.0	13.3	14.4
Whiteleg shrimp	97.9	119.4	129.6
Total catch	811.7	684.3	456.6

Source: FAO, *Yearbook of Fishery Statistics*.

Mining

	1994	1995	1996
Crude petroleum ('000 metric tons)	17,391	20,100	19,243
Natural gas (petajoules)	15	15	26
Natural gasoline ('000 metric tons)	43	42*	42
Gold-bearing ores (kilograms)†	13,000	15,500	17,700

* Provisional or estimated figure.
† Estimated gold content (data from the US Bureau of Mines).

1997 (estimated figures): Natural gas (petajoules) 24; Gold-bearing ores (kilograms) 17,700.

Source: UN, *Industrial Commodity Statistics Yearbook*.

Industry

SELECTED PRODUCTS ('000 metric tons, unless otherwise indicated)

	1994	1995	1996
Jet fuels.	181	239	253
Kerosene	80	89	78
Motor spirit (gasoline)	1,302	1,567	1,937
Distillate fuel oils	1,533	1,562	1,812
Residual fuel oils	2,999	3,059	3,215
Liquefied petroleum gas	253	374	440
Crude steel	22	29	21
Cement .	2,085	2,459	2,930
Electric energy (million kWh)	8,163	8,349	9,260

Source: partly UN, *Industrial Commodity Statistics Yearbook*.

Finance

CURRENCY AND EXCHANGE RATES

Monetary Units

United States currency is used: 100 cents = 1 US dollar ($).

Sterling and Euro Equivalents (29 December 2000)
£1 sterling = US $1.4922;
€1 = 93.05 US cents;
US $100 = £67.02 = €107.47.

Note: Ecuador's national currency was formerly the sucre. From 13 March 2000 the sucre was replaced by the US dollar, at an exchange rate of $1 = 25,000 sucres. Both currencies were officially in use for a transitional period of 180 days, but from 9 September sucres were withdrawn from circulation and the dollar became the sole legal tender. Some figures in this Survey are still in terms of sucres. The average exchange rate of sucres per dollar was: 5,446.6 in 1998; 11,786.8 in 1999; 24,988.4 in 2000.

BUDGET (million sucres)

Revenue	1992	1993	1994
Petroleum revenue	1,537,698	2,069,852	2,345,187
Tax revenue	68,627	31,197	42,965
Non-tax revenue	1,469,071	2,038,655	2,302,222
Price increases on petroleum by-products for internal consumption	470,993	851,920	1,172,573
For export	998,078	1,186,735	1,129,649
Non-petroleum revenue	1,570,059	2,162,669	3,138,030
Tax revenue	1,368,994	2,034,925	2,808,630
External trade	274,413	392,470	606,631
Exports	—	—	—
Imports	274,413	392,470	606,631
Domestic taxes	1,094,581	1,642,455	2,201,999
Income tax	253,415	331,231	503,864
Taxes on financial transactions.	66,246	43,013	110,576
Taxes on production and consumption	744,757	1,152,491	1,495,902
Other taxes	30,163	115,720	91,657
Non-tax revenue	201,065	127,744	329,400
Transfers	22,034	82,051	164,426
Total	3,129,791	4,314,572	5,647,643

Expenditure	1992	1993	1994
General services .	736,416	1,144,175	1,679,092
Education and culture	605,075	746,993	1,066,535
Social welfare and labour.	43,092	99,421	134,697
Health and community development	200,421	202,593	319,470
Farming and livestock development	88,631	146,023	230,227
Natural and energy resources	14,121	31,323	47,144
Industry and trade	43,041	25,507	33,674
Transport and communications	126,629	327,585	446,366
Public debt interest	473,826	500,841	898,153
Other purposes	216,730	539,389	677,075
Total	2,547,982	3,763,850	5,532,433

Source: Banco Central del Ecuador.

1995 ('000 million sucres): Total revenue 8,030.4; Total expenditure 8,450.6.
1996 ('000 million sucres): Total revenue 10,633.9; Total expenditure 10,916.7.

1997 ('000 million sucres): Total revenue 13,515.3; Total expenditure 14,680.5.
1998 ('000 million sucres): Total revenue 17,866.6; Total expenditure 17,492.3.
1999 ('000 million sucres): Total revenue 31,884.4; Total expenditure 33,051.5.

Source (for 1995–99): IMF, *International Financial Statistics*.

INTERNATIONAL RESERVES (US $ million at 31 December)

	1998	1999	2000
Gold*	166.7	166.4	114.1
IMF special drawing rights	0.3	2.3	0.3
Reserve position in IMF	24.2	23.5	22.3
Foreign exchange	1,595.3	1,616.5	924.3
Total	1,786.5	1,808.7	1,061.0

* National valuation (US $403 per troy ounce at 31 December 1998; $402 per ounce at 31 December 1999; $275 per ounce at 31 December 2000).

Source: IMF, *International Financial Statistics*.

MONEY SUPPLY ('000 million sucres at 31 December)

	1997	1998	1999
Currency outside banks	2,384.6	2,911.7	9,287.7
Demand deposits at deposit money banks.	3,911.2	4,975.4	7,134.1
Total money*	6,955.9	9,081.9	19,129.2

* Includes private-sector deposits at the Central Bank.

Source: IMF, *International Financial Statistics*.

COST OF LIVING
(Consumer Price Index; annual averages for middle- and low-income families in urban area; base: 1990 = 100)

	1996	1997	1998
Food (excl. beverages)	597.8	813.8	1,146.4
Fuel and light	313.2	502.8	961.8
Clothing (incl. footwear)	523.1	642.7	788.5
Rent	903.5	1,118.1	1,331.6
All items (incl. others)	648.8	847.4	1,153.1

1999: Food (excl. beverages) 1,574.1; All items 1,749.1.

Source: ILO, *Yearbook of Labour Statistics*.

NATIONAL ACCOUNTS

Expenditure on the Gross Domestic Product
('000 million sucres at current prices)

	1996	1997	1998
Government final consumption expenditure	7,146	9,147	12,524
Private final consumption expenditure	38,791	53,153	75,610
Increase in stocks	−300	902	3,938
Gross fixed capital formation	10,798	15,053	22,550
Statistical discrepancy	−1	—	—
Total domestic expenditure	56,436	78,255	114,622
Exports of goods and services	18,514	23,711	27,170
Less Imports of goods and services	14,223	22,926	34,371
GDP in purchasers' values .	60,727	79,040	107,421
GDP at constant 1975 prices	219	227	228

Source: IMF, *International Financial Statistics*.

Gross Domestic Product by Economic Activity

('000 million sucres at current prices)

	1997	1998	1999
Agriculture, hunting, forestry and fishing	9,556.5	12,941.5	19,606.6
Petroleum and other mining	6,968.8	6,064.7	18,451.7
Manufacturing	16,878.4	23,501.0	34,290.8
Electricity, gas and water	215.4	302.5	441.3
Construction	3,667.5	5,289.7	7,295.8
Trade	15,655.5	21,691.4	29,632.2
Transport	7,359.8	10,259.9	15,109.3
Financial services	4,330.3	6,042.1	8,954.2
Government services	9,862.0	13,612.4	17,387.3
Sub-total	**74,494.2**	**99,705.2**	**151,169.0**
Adjustments	4,545.8	7,715.8	10,181.4
GDP in purchasers' values	**79,040.0**	**107,421.0**	**161,350.3**

BALANCE OF PAYMENTS (US $ million)

	1997	1998	1999
Exports of goods f.o.b.	5,264	4,203	4,451
Imports of goods f.o.b.	−4,666	−5,198	−2,786
Trade balance	**598**	**−995**	**1,665**
Exports of services	826	808	812
Imports of services	−1,459	−1,531	−1,304
Balance on goods and services	**−35**	**−1,718**	**1,173**
Other income received	102	82	49
Other income paid	−1,172	−1,309	−1,368
Balance on goods, services and income	**−1,105**	**−2,945**	**−146**
Current transfers received	438	840	1,151
Current transfers paid	−47	−64	−50
Current balance	**−714**	**−2,169**	**955**
Direct investment from abroad	625	814	690
Other investment liabilities	829	1,300	53
Net errors and omissions	−477	−352	−2,024
Overall balance	**263**	**−407**	**−326**

Source: IMF, *International Financial Statistics*.

External Trade

PRINCIPAL COMMODITIES (distribution by SITC, US $ million)

Imports c.i.f.	1996	1997	1998
Food and live animals	308.7	359.2	582.2
Cereals and cereal preparations	134.4	139.7	221.5
Wheat and meslin (unmilled)	86.0	88.3	88.4
Crude materials (inedible) except fuels	128.0	143.4	154.8
Mineral fuels, lubricants, etc.	165.6	385.2	335.4
Petroleum, petroleum products, etc.	53.1	299.0	247.4
Refined petroleum products	47.8	257.8	183.0
Kerosene and other medium oils	15.1	206.4	139.3
Gas (natural and manufactured)	112.3	86.1	87.6
Liquefied petroleum gases, etc.	111.6	86.1	87.5
Chemicals and related products	700.0	820.1	880.2
Organic chemicals	94.0	106.0	93.9
Medicinal and pharmaceutical products	173.3	206.9	235.8
Medicaments (incl. veterinary)	138.0	166.8	196.2
Artificial resins, plastic materials, etc.	120.6	144.7	141.2
Products of polymerization, etc.	93.8	113.2	108.1
Disinfectants, insecticides, fungicides, etc.	81.5	104.6	112.6
Basic manufactures	738.5	778.5	930.4
Paper, paperboard and manufactures	124.1	108.7	132.4
Paper and paperboard (not cut to size or shape)	100.6	82.0	103.5
Textile yarn, fabrics, etc.	65.4	86.4	110.1
Non-metallic mineral manufactures	82.4	83.0	107.8
Iron and steel	262.3	237.2	297.5
Ingots and other primary forms	84.8	65.4	79.2
Machinery and transport equipment	1,323.3	1,624.9	1,934.3
Power-generating machinery and equipment	133.5	167.1	179.3
Machinery specialized for particular industries	167.6	179.2	260.4
General industrial machinery, equipment and parts	231.0	282.3	318.0
Telecommunications and sound equipment	89.6	235.9	216.3
Other electrical machinery, apparatus, etc.	160.0	183.0	284.5
Road vehicles and parts*	440.6	454.1	494.2
Passenger motor cars (excl. buses)	218.1	222.4	186.2
Motor vehicles for goods transport and special purposes	121.0	147.1	170.7
Goods vehicles (lorries and trucks)	114.4	139.3	149.6
Miscellaneous manufactured articles	301.0	338.9	416.2
Total (incl. others)	**3,733.0**	**4,510.7**	**5,502.8**

* Data on parts exclude tyres, engines and electrical parts.

Exports f.o.b.	1996	1997	1998
Food and live animals	2,415.1	2,953.0	2,586.1
Fish, crustaceans and molluscs	871.0	1,155.1	1,190.7
Fresh, chilled or frozen fish	87.4	102.5	85.7
Fresh, chilled, frozen, salted or dried crustaceans and molluscs	631.4	874.5	853.9
Prepared or preserved fish, crustaceans and molluscs	151.0	176.5	250.3
Prepared or preserved fish	150.3	175.0	243.7
Vegetables and fruit	1,054.4	1,420.0	1,169.5
Fresh or dried fruit and nuts (excl. oil nuts)	985.1	1,331.8	1,080.4
Bananas and plantains	973.0	1,327.0	1,070.2
Coffee, tea, cocoa and spices	324.3	246.8	152.4
Coffee and coffee substitutes	159.1	114.1	104.4
Coffee (incl. husks and skins) and substitutes containing coffee	129.1	86.3	71.3
Unroasted coffee, husks and skins	129.0	86.3	71.2
Cocoa	157.5	126.3	42.9
Crude materials (inedible) except fuels	160.8	194.4	197.1
Cut flowers and foliage	99.1	119.1	144.6
Mineral fuels, lubricants, etc.	1,776.1	1,550.0	925.2
Petroleum, petroleum products, etc.	1,776.1	1,550.0	925.2
Crude petroleum oils, etc.	1,520.8	1,404.3	791.3
Refined petroleum products	216.5	118.0	107.7
Gas oils (distillate fuels)	185.6	117.4	106.7
Basic manufactures	187.9	190.5	154.8
Machinery and transport equipment	87.5	106.0	97.1
Non-monetary gold (excl. ores and concentrates)	127.4	65.2	15.0
Total (incl. others)	4,889.8	5,214.2	4,141.1

Source: UN, *International Trade Statistics Yearbook*.

PRINCIPAL TRADING PARTNERS (US $ million)

Imports c.i.f.	1996	1997	1998
Argentina	81.2	90.4	135.7
Aruba	4.4	80.9	33.2
Belgium-Luxembourg	64.5	46.4	62.4
Brazil	142.6	134.0	196.5
Canada	49.5	52.3	102.7
Chile	135.2	152.1	200.8
China, People's Republic	0.8	45.3	65.3
Colombia	378.5	478.9	591.5
France (incl. Monaco)	34.6	81.1	47.7
Germany	155.5	188.2	228.2
Italy	98.1	124.5	157.2
Japan	209.8	263.0	493.7
Korea, Republic	60.2	61.5	101.7
Mexico	197.7	149.9	155.7
Netherlands	49.8	49.2	57.7
Panama	97.1	112.3	179.9
Peru	40.4	59.7	98.3
Russian Federation	19.6	35.6	67.2
Spain	170.1	161.1	112.2
Switzerland-Liechtenstein	40.0	37.5	36.6
United Kingdom	45.7	54.3	63.9
USA	1,174.1	1,376.3	1,617.5
Venezuela	172.6	301.9	259.3
Total (incl. others)	3,733.0	4,510.6	5,502.8

Exports f.o.b.	1996	1997	1998
Argentina	84.1	76.0	76.3
Belgium-Luxembourg	108.2	98.9	88.8
Chile	220.5	237.9	137.7
China, People's Republic	67.1	157.3	51.9
Colombia	300.5	352.1	274.3
El Salvador	53.5	76.1	39.3
France (incl. Monaco)	82.9	87.6	93.6
Germany	176.0	204.0	128.4
Italy	195.4	271.4	254.6
Japan	138.7	155.7	122.8
Korea, Republic	314.4	171.4	95.2
Mexico	57.7	41.8	46.4
Netherlands	77.4	86.7	80.7
Panama	211.7	175.0	128.0
Peru	53.3	222.8	201.4
Russia	82.5	141.2	112.5
Spain	133.2	127.5	136.2
United Kingdom	125.1	94.3	60.5
USA	1,851.5	1,992.0	1,609.4
Venezuela	72.4	49.8	57.7
Total (incl. others)	4,889.8	5,214.1	4,141.0

Source: mainly UN, *International Trade Statistics Yearbook*.

1999 (US $ million): Total imports c.i.f. 3,017.3; Total exports f.o.b. 4,451.0. (Source: IMF, *International Financial Statistics*.)

Transport

RAILWAYS (traffic)

	1994	1995	1996
Passenger-kilometres (million)	20	14	11
Net ton-kilometres (million)	9	3	1

Source: UN, *Statistical Yearbook*.

ROAD TRAFFIC (motor vehicles in use at 31 December)

	1995	1996	1997
Passenger cars	446,192	464,902	483,897
Buses and coaches	8,753	8,688	8,504
Lorries and vans	43,340	43,942	41,327
Road tractors	2,813	2,959	2,930

Source: IRF, *World Road Statistics*.

SHIPPING
Merchant Fleet (registered at 31 December)

	1996	1997	1998
Number of vessels	145	154	167
Total displacement ('000 grt)	178.2	145.1	171.3

Source: Lloyd's Register of Shipping, *World Fleet Statistics*.

International Sea-borne Freight Traffic ('000 metric tons)

	1988*	1989*	1990
Goods loaded	8,402	10,020	11,783
Goods unloaded	2,518	2,573	1,958

* Source: UN, *Monthly Bulletin of Statistics*.

CIVIL AVIATION (traffic on scheduled services)

	1995	1996	1997
Kilometres flown (million)	15	15	23
Passengers carried ('000)	1,671	1,925	1,791
Passenger-km (million)	1,591	1,663	2,035
Total ton-km (million)	174	181	235

Source: UN, *Statistical Yearbook*.

Tourism

FOREIGN VISITOR ARRIVALS*

Country of residence	1996	1997	1998
Chile	13,417	15,740	14,349
Colombia	159,091	164,859	165,596
France	16,389	16,494	16,034
Germany	21,421	20,363	21,701
Peru	34,795	33,543	29,821
Spain	11,755	12,545	12,306
United Kingdom	12,152	12,321	12,051
USA	104,978	124,924	113,155
Venezuela	12,056	12,148	12,255
Total (incl. others) . . .	493,727	529,492	510,627

* Figures refer to total arrivals (including same-day visitors), except those of Ecuadorean nationals residing abroad.

Tourism receipts (US $ million): 252 in 1994; 255 in 1995; 281 in 1996.

Source: World Tourism Organization, *Yearbook of Tourism Statistics*.

Communications Media

	1995	1996	1997
Radio receivers ('000 in use) . .	3,800	4,000	4,150
Television receivers ('000 in use)	1,100	1,500	1,550
Mobile cellular telephones .	49,776	59,852	160,061
Daily newspapers	24	29	n.a.
Telephones ('000 main lines in use)	748	857	899

Source: mainly UNESCO, *Statistical Yearbook*.

Telefax stations: 30,000 in use in 1996 (Source: UN, *Statistical Yearbook*).

Education

(1996/97)

	Teachers	Pupils/ Students
Pre-primary	9,980	156,772
Primary	74,601	1,888,172
Secondary:		
General	62,630*	765,073†
Teacher-training	258‡	802*
Vocational	13,949§	279,189*
Higher‖	12,856	206,541

* 1992/93 figure.   † 1994/95 figure.
‡ 1980/81 figure.   § 1985/86 figure.
‖ 1990/91 figures.

1997/98: Pre-primary teachers 10,992; Pre-primary pupils 167,582; Pre-primary schools 4,009.

In 1996/97 there were 17,367 primary schools.

Source: UNESCO, *Statistical Yearbook*.

Directory

The Constitution

The 1945 Constitution was suspended in June 1970. In January 1978 a referendum was held to choose between two draft Constitutions, prepared by various special constitutional committees. In a 90% poll, 43% voted for a proposed new Constitution and 32.1% voted for a revised version of the 1945 Constitution. The new Constitution came into force on 10 August 1979. In November 1997 a National Constituent Assembly was elected for the purpose of reviewing the Constitution, and a new Constitution, which retained many of the provisions of the 1979 Constitution, came into force on 10 August 1998. The main provisions of the Constitution are summarized below:

CHAMBER OF REPRESENTATIVES

The Constitution of 1998 states that legislative power is exercised by the Chamber of Representatives which sits for a period of 60 days from 10 August. The Chamber is required to set up four full-time Legislative Commissions to consider draft laws when the House is in recess. Special sessions of the Chamber of Representatives may be called.

Representatives are elected for four years from lists of candidates drawn up by legally recognized parties. Twelve are elected nationally; two from each Province with over 100,000 inhabitants, one from each Province with fewer than 100,000; and one for every 200,000 citizens or fractions of over 150,000. Representatives are eligible for re-election.

In addition to its law-making duties, the Chamber ratifies treaties, elects members of the Supreme and Superior Courts, and (from panels presented by the President) the Comptroller-General, the Attorney-General and the Superintendent of Banks. It is also able to overrule the President's amendment of a bill which it has submitted for Presidential approval. It may reconsider a rejected bill after a year or request a referendum, and may revoke the President's declaration of a state of emergency. The budget is considered in the first instance by the appropriate Legislative Commission and disagreements are resolved in the Chamber.

PRESIDENT

The presidential term is four years (starting from 15 January of the year following his election), and there is no re-election. The President appoints the Cabinet, the Governors of Provinces, diplomatic representatives and certain administrative employees, and is responsible for the direction of international relations. In the event of foreign invasion or internal disturbance, the President may declare a state of emergency and must notify the Chamber, or the Tribunal for Constitutional Guarantees if the Chamber is not in session.

As in other post-war Latin-American Constitutions, particular emphasis is laid on the functions and duties of the State, which is given wide responsibilities with regard to the protection of labour; assisting in the expansion of production; protecting the Indian and peasant communities; and organizing the distribution and development of uncultivated lands, by expropriation where necessary.

Voting is compulsory for every Ecuadorean citizen who is literate and over 18 years of age. An optional vote has been extended to illiterates (under 15% of the population by 1981). The Constitution guarantees liberty of conscience in all its manifestations, and states that the law shall not make any discrimination for religious reasons.

The Government

HEAD OF STATE

President: GUSTAVO NOBOA BEJERANO (assumed office on 26 January 2000).
Vice-President: PEDRO PINTO RUBIANES.

CABINET
(April 2001)

Minister of National Defence: Adm. HUGO UNDA AGUIRRE.
Minister of the Interior: JUAN MANRIQUE MARTINEZ.
Minister of Foreign Affairs: Dr HEINZ MOELLER FREILE.
Minister of Finance and Public Credit: JORGE GALLARDO.
Minister of Foreign Trade, Industrialization and Fishing: ROBERTO PEÑA DURINI.
Minister of Labour and Social Action: MARTÍN INSUA-CHANG.

Minister of Energy and Mines: PABLO TERÁN RIBADENEIRA.
Minister of Agriculture: GALO PLAZA PALLARES.
Minister of Urban Development and Housing: NELSON MURGUEYTIO PEÑAHERRERA.
Minister of Education and Culture: ROBERTO HANSSE SALEM.
Minister of Public Health: FERNANDO BUSTAMENTE.
Minister of the Environment: RODOLFO RENDON.
Minister of Tourism: ROCÍO VÁSQUEZ.
Minister of Public Works and Communications: JOSÉ MACHIAVELLO.
Minister of Social Welfare: RAÚL PATIÑO ARCOA.

The following are, *ex officio*, members of the Cabinet: the National Secretary of Administrative Development, the Co-ordinator of the Social Expenditure Fund (FISE), the State Comptroller-General, the State Procurator-General, the Chairman of the National Monetary Board, the General Manager of the State Bank, the General Manager of the Central Bank, the Secretary-General of the National Planning Council (CONADE), the President of the National Financial Corporation, the President of the National Modernization Council (CONAM), the Presidential Private Secretary, the Subsecretary-General of Public Administration and the Presidential Press Secretary.

MINISTRIES

Office of the President: Palacio Nacional, García Moreno 1043, Quito; tel. (2) 216-300.

Office of the Vice-President: Manuel Larrea y Arenas, Edif. Consejo Provincial de Pichincha, 21°, Quito; tel. (2) 504-953; fax (2) 503-379.

Ministry of Agriculture: Avda Eloy Alfaro y Amazonas, Quito; tel. (2) 504-433; fax (2) 564-531.

Ministry of Education and Culture: Mejía 322, Quito; tel. (2) 216-224; fax (2) 580-116.

Ministry of Energy and Mines: Juan León Mera y Orellana, 5°, Quito; tel. (2) 550-041; fax (2) 550-018; e-mail menergia2@andinanet.net.

Ministry of the Environment: Avda Eloy Alfaro y Amazonas, edificio M.A.G., Quito; tel. (2) 563-487; fax (2) 563-487; e-mail mma@ambiente.gov.ec.

Ministry of Finance and Public Credit: Avda 10 de Agosto 1661 y Jorge Washington, Quito; tel. (2) 544-500; fax (2) 530-703.

Ministry of Foreign Affairs: Avda 10 de Agosto y Carrión, Quito; tel. (2) 230-100; fax (2) 564-873; e-mail webmast@mmrree.gov.ec; internet www.mmrree.gov.ec.

Ministry of Foreign Trade, Industrialization and Fishing: Avda Eloy Alfaro y Amazonas, Quito; tel. (2) 527-988; fax (2) 503-549.

Ministry of the Interior: Espejo y Benalcázar, Quito; tel. (2) 580-970; fax (2) 442-771.

Ministry of Labour and Social Action: Clemente Ponce 255 y Piedrahita, Quito; tel. (2) 566-148; fax (2) 503-122; e-mail mintrab@accessinter.net.

Ministry of National Defence: Exposición 208, Quito; tel. (2) 216-150; fax (2) 569-386.

Ministry of Public Health: Juan Larrea 444, Quito; tel. (2) 529-163; fax 569-786; e-mail msp@accessinter.net; internet www.msp.gpv.ec.

Ministry of Public Works: Avda Juan León Mera y Orellana, Quito; tel. (2) 222-749; fax (2) 223-077.

Ministry of Urban Development and Housing: Avda 10 de Agosto 2270 y Corotero, Quito; tel. (2) 238-060; fax (2) 566-785.

Ministry of Tourism: Quito; tel. (2) 540-920; fax (2) 255-172.

Office for Public Administration: Palacio Nacional, García Morena 1043, Quito; tel. (2) 515-990.

President and Legislature

PRESIDENT*

Elections of 31 May and 12 July 1998

Candidate	% of votes cast in first ballot	% of votes cast in second ballot
JAMIL MAHUAD WITT (DP)	35.2	51.2
ALVARO NOBOA PONTÓN (PRE) . . .	26.5	48.8
RODRIGO BORJA CEVALLOS (ID) . . .	15.6	—
FREDDY EHLERS ZURITA (MNPP) . .	14.3	—
ROSHAUA ARTEAGA SERRANO (MIRA) . .	5.1	—
Total (incl. others).	100.0	100.0

* President Mahuad was deposed in a coup on 21 January 2000; the erstwhile Vice-President, GUSTAVO NOBOA BEJERANO, was sworn in as Ecuador's new President on 26 January.

CONGRESO NACIONAL

Cámara Nacional de Representantes

President: HUGO QUEVADO.

Election, 31 May 1998

Political parties	Seats
Democracia Popular (DP)	32
Partido Social Cristiano (PSC) . . .	27
Partido Roldosista Ecuatoriano (PRE) . .	24
Izquierda Democrática (ID)	18
Movimiento Nuevo País-Pachakutik (MNPP).	9
Frente Radical Alfarista (FRA) . . .	5
Partido Conservador (PC)	3
Movimiento Popular Democrático (MPD) .	2
Concentración de Fuerzas Populares (CFP) .	1
Total	121

Political Organizations

Acción Popular Revolucionaria Ecuatoriana (APRE): centrist; Leader Lt-Gen. FRANK VARGAS PAZZOS.

Coalición Nacional Republicana (CNR): Quito; f. 1986; fmrly Coalición Institucionalista Demócrata (CID).

Concentración de Fuerzas Populares (CFP): Quito; f. 1946; Leader GALO VAYAS; Dir Dr AVERROES BUCARAM SAXIDA.

Democracia Popular (DP): Calle Luis Saá 153 y Hnos Pazmiño, Casilla 17-01-2300, Quito; tel. (2) 547-654; fax (2) 502-995; f. 1978 as Democracia Popular-Unión Demócrata Cristiana; Christian democrat; Leader Lic. ABSALÓN ROCHA.

Frente Radical Alfarista (FRA): Quito; f. 1972; liberal; Leader IVÁN CASTRO PATIÑO.

Izquierda Democrática (ID): Polonia 161, entre Vancouver y Eloy Alfaro, Quito; tel. (2) 564-436; fax (2) 569-295; f. 1977; absorbed Fuerzas Armadas Populares Eloy Alfaro—Alfaro Vive ¡Carajo! (AVC) (Eloy Alfaro Popular Armed Forces—Alfaro Lives, Damn It!) in 1991; Leader RODRIGO BORJA CEVALLOS; National Dir ANDRÉS VALLEJO.

Movimiento Independiente para una República Auténtica (MIRA): Quito; f. 1996; Leader Dra ROSALIA ARTEAGA SERRANO.

Movimiento Nuevo País-Pachakutik (MNPP): Quito; represents indigenous, environmental and social groups; Leader FREDDY EHLERS ZURITA.

Movimiento Popular Democrático (MPD): Maoist; Leader (vacant).

Partido Comunista Marxista-Leninista de Ecuador: Sec.-Gen. CAMILO ALMEYDA.

Partido Conservador (PC): Wilsón 578, Quito; tel.(2) 505-061; f. 1855; incorporated Partido Unidad Republicano in 1995; centre-right; Leader SEXTO DURÁN BALLÉN.

Partido Demócrata (PD): Quito; Leader Dr FRANCISCO HUERTA MONTALVO.

Partido Liberal Radical (PLR): Quito; f. 1895; held office from 1895 to 1944 as the Liberal Party, which subsequently divided into various factions; perpetuates the traditions of the Liberal Party; Leader CARLOS JULIO PLAZA A.

Partido Republicano (PR): Quito; Leader GUILLERMO SOTOMAYOR.

Partido Roldosista Ecuatoriano (PRE): Quito; f. 1982; populist; Dir ABDALÁ BUCARAM ORTIZ.

Partido Social Cristiano (PSC): Carrión 548 y Reina Victoria, Casilla 9454, Quito; tel. (2) 544-536; fax (2) 568-562; f. 1951; centre-right party; Pres. JAIME NEBOT SAADI; Leaders LEÓN FEBRES CORDERO RIVADENEIRA, Lic. CAMILO PONCE GANGOTENA, Dr HEINZ MOELLER FREILE, Lic. PASCUAL DEL CIOPPO ARAGUNDI.

Partido Socialista-Frente Amplia (PS-FA): Avda Gran Colombia y Yaguachi, Quito; tel. (2) 221-764; fax (2) 222-184; f. 1926; Pres. Dr MANUEL SALGADO TAMAYO.

Unión Alfarista-FRA: Quito; f. 1998; centrist; Leader CÉSAR VERDUGA VÉLEZ.

The following guerrilla groups are active:

Grupo de Combatientes Populares (GCP): claims to defend human rights and to fight poverty.

Montoneros Patria Libre (MPL): f. 1986; advocates an end to authoritarianism.

Partido Maoísta-Comunista 'Puka Inti': Sec.-Gen. RAMIRO CELI.

Diplomatic Representation

EMBASSIES IN ECUADOR

Argentina: Avda Amazonas 22-147 y Roca, 8°, Quito; tel. (2) 562-292; fax (2) 568-177; e-mail embarge2@andinanet.net; Ambassador: HERNÁN HIPÓLITO CORNEJO.

Belgium: Juan León Mera 23-103 y Wilson, Apdo. 17-21-532, Quito; tel. (2) 545-340; e-mail quito@diplobel.org; Ambassador: ROBERT VANREUSEL.

Bolivia: Avda Eloy Alfaro 2432 y Fernando Ayarza, Casilla 17-210003, Quito; tel: (2) 446-652; fax (2) 244-033; e-mail embolivia-quito@rree.gov.bo; Chargé d'affaires a.i.: CARLOS ANTONIO BARRIENTOS TERÁN.

Brazil: Avda Amazonas 1429 y Colón, Apdo 231, Quito; tel. (2) 563-846; fax (2) 509-468; e-mail ebrasil@uio.satnet.net; Ambassador: VERA PEDROSA MARTINS DE ALMEIDA.

Canada: Edif. Josueth Gonzales, Avda 6 de Diciembre 28-16 y Paul Rivet, 4°, Apdo 17-11-65-12, Quito; tel. (2) 506-162; e-mail quito@dfait-maeci.gc.ca; Ambassador: JOHN G. KNEALE.

Chile: Edif. Xerox, 4°, Juan Pablo Sanz y Amazonas, Quito; tel. (2) 249-403; e-mail embchile@waccom.nt.com; Ambassador: RODRIGO ASENJO ZEGERS.

China, People's Republic: Avda Atahualpa y Amazonas, Quito; tel. (2) 458-927; fax (2) 444-364; e-mail embchina@uio.telconet.net; Ambassador: LIU JUNXIU.

Colombia: Edif. Arista, Avda Colón 1133 y Amazonas, 7°, Apdo 17-07-9164, Quito; tel. (2) 228-926; Ambassador: ELISEO RESTREPO LONDOÑO.

Costa Rica: Rumipamba 692 y República, 2°, Apdo 17-03-301, Quito; tel. (2) 254-945; e-mail embajcr@uio.satnet; Ambassador: LUZ ARGENTINA CALDERÓN DE AGUILAR.

Cuba: Mercurio 365, entre La Razón y El Vengador, Quito; tel. (2) 456-936; fax (2) 430-594; Chargé d'affaires a.i.: FÉLIX RAÚL ROJAS CRUZ.

Dominican Republic: Edif. Albatros, Avda de los Shyris 1240 y Portugal, 2°, Apdo 17-01-387-A, Quito; Ambassador: RAFAEL JULIAN CEDANO.

Egypt: Edif. Araucaria, 9°, Baquedano 222 y Reina Victoria, Apdo 9355, Sucursal 7, Quito; tel. (2) 235-046; Ambassador: NAPOLEON THABET ABDUL-RAHIM.

El Salvador: Avda Republica de El Salvador 733 y Portugal, 201°, Quito; tel. (2) 433-670; Ambassador: RAFAEL A. ALFARO.

France: Plaza 107 y Avda Patria, Apdo 536, Quito; tel. (2) 560-789; fax (2) 566-424; e-mail francie@uio.satnet.net; Ambassador: SERGE PINOT.

Germany: Edif. Citiplaza, 14°, Avda Naciones Unidas y República de El Salvador, Casilla 17-17-536, Quito; tel. (2) 970-820; fax (2) 970-815; e-mail alemania@interactive.net.ec; Ambassador: WALTER NOCKER.

Guatemala: Edif. Gabriela III, Avda República de El Salvador 733 y Portugal, Apdo 17-03-294, Quito; tel. (2) 459-700; Ambassador: LUIS PEDRO QUEZADA.

Holy See: (Apostolic Nunciature), Avda Orellana 692, Apdo 17-07-8980, Quito; tel. (2) 505-200; fax (2) 564-810; e-mail nunapec@impsat.net.ec; Apostolic Nuncio: Most Rev. ALAIN PAUL LEBEAUPIN, Titular Archbishop of Vico Equense.

Honduras: Avda 12 de Octubre 1942 y Cordero, Apdo 17-03-4753, Quito; tel. (2) 223-985; Chargé d'affaires a.i.: HUMBERTO LÓPEZ VILLAMIL.

Israel: Edif. Plaza 2000, Avda 12 de Octubre y Fco. Salazar, Apdo 17-21-08, Quito; tel. (2) 237-474; e-mail isremuio@uio.telconet.net; Ambassador: YOSHEP HASEEN.

Italy: Calle La Isla 111 y Humberto Alborñoz, Casilla 17-03-72, Quito; tel. (2) 561-077; fax (2) 502-818; e-mail ambital@ambitalquito.org; Ambassador: PAOLO LEGNAIOLI.

Japan: Juan León Mera 130 y Avda Patria, 7°, Quito; tel. (2) 561-899; fax (2) 503-670; e-mail japembec@uio.satnet.net; Ambassador: MASANORI TODA.

Korea, Republic: Edif. Citiplaza, 8°, Avda Naciones Unidas y Avda de El Salvador, Quito; tel. (2) 970-625; fax (2) 970-630; e-mail ecemco@interactive.net.ec; Ambassador: PIL-JOO SUNG.

Mexico: Avda 6 de Diciembre 4843 y Naciones Unidas, Casilla 17-11-6371, Quito; tel. (2) 457-820; fax (2) 448-245; e-mail embmxec@uio.satnet.net; Ambassador: MANUEL MARTINEZ DEL SOBRAL.

Netherlands: Edif. WTC, 1°, Avda 12 de Octubre 1942 y Cordero, Quito; tel. (2) 229-230; fax (2) 567-917; e-mail holgui@ibm.net; internet www.embajadadeholanda.com/embassy.html; Ambassador: MAARTEN M. VAN DER GAAG.

Panama: Edif. Posada de las Artes, 3°, Diego de Almagro 1550 y Pradera, Apdo 17-07-9017, Quito; tel. (2) 565-234; fax (2) 566-449; e-mail pmaemecu@interactive.net.ec; Ambassador: ARMANDO TERÁN MORALES.

Paraguay: Avda Gaspar de Villarroel 2013 y Amazonas, Casilla 139A, Quito; tel. (2) 245-871; fax (2) 251-446; e-mail embapar@uio-telconet.net; Ambassador: Dr CARLOS VILLAGRA MARSAL.

Peru: Avda República de El Salvador 495 e Irlanda, Quito; tel. (2) 468-410; fax (2) 252-560; e-mail embpeecu@uio.satnet.net; Ambassador: OSCAR MAURTUA DE ROMAÑA.

Russia: Reina Victoria 462 y Roca, Quito; tel. (2) 561-361; e-mail embrusia@accessinter.net; Ambassador: GIORGII P. KOROLIOV.

Slovakia: Gen. Francisco Salazar 459 y Coruña, Quito.

Spain: La Pinta 455 y Amazonas, Casilla 9322, Quito; tel. (2) 237-132; e-mail embespec@uio.satnet.net: EDUARDO CERRO GODINHO.

Switzerland: Edif. Xerox, 2°, Juan Pablo Sanz 120 y Amazonas, Casilla 17-11-4815, Quito; tel. (2) 434-948; fax (2) 449-314; Ambassador: PETER VON GRAFFENRIED.

United Kingdom: Edif. Citiplaza, 14°, Avda Naciones Unidas y República de El Salvador, Casilla 17-01-314, Quito; tel. (2) 970-800; fax (2) 970-809; e-mail britembq@impsat.net.ec; internet www.britembquito.org.ec; Ambassador: IAN GERKEN.

USA: Avda 12 de Octubre y Patria 120, Quito; tel. (2) 562-890; fax (2) 502-052; internet www.usis.org.ec; Ambassador: GWEN C. CLARE.

Uruguay: Edif. Josueth González, 9°, Avda 6 de Diciembre 2816 y James Orton, Casilla 17-12-282, Quito; tel. (2) 563-762; fax (2) 563-763; e-mail emburugl@emburuguay.int.ec; Ambassador: DUNCAN B. CROCI DE MULA.

Venezuela: Avda Los Cabildos 115, Apdo 17-01-688, Quito; tel. (2) 268-636; fax (2) 502-630; e-mail embavenecua@interactive.net.ec; Ambassador: CARLOS RODOLFO SANTIAGO MARTÍNEZ.

Yugoslavia: Gen. Francisco Salazar 958 y 12 de Octubre, Quito; tel. (2) 526-218; Ambassador: SAMUILO PROTIĆ.

Judicial System

Attorney-General: ROBERTO GÓMEZ MERA.

Supreme Court of Justice: Palacio de Justicia, Avda 6 de Diciembre y Piedrahita 332, Quito; tel. (2) 900-424; fax (2) 900-425; e-mail dni-cnj@access.net.ec; internet www.justiciaecuador.gov.ec; f. 1830; Pres. GALO PICO MANTILLA.

Higher or Divisional Courts: Ambato, Azogues, Babahoyo, Cuenca, Esmeraldas, Guaranda, Guayaquil, Ibarra, Latacunga, Loja, Machala, Portoviejo, Quito, Riobamba and Tulcán; 90 judges.

Provincial Courts: there are 40 Provincial Courts in 15 districts; other courts include 94 Criminal; 219 Civil; 29 dealing with labour disputes; 17 Rent Tribunals.

Special Courts: National Court for Juveniles.

Religion

There is no state religion but more than 90% of the population are Roman Catholics. There are representatives of various Protestant Churches and of the Jewish faith in Quito and Guayaquil.

CHRISTIANITY

The Roman Catholic Church

Ecuador comprises four archdioceses, 11 dioceses, seven Apostolic Vicariates and one Apostolic Prefecture. At 31 December 1998 there were an estimated 11,880,390 adherents in the country, equivalent to some 92.5% of the population.

Bishops' Conference: Conferencia Episcopal Ecuatoriana, Avda América 1805 y La Gasca, Apdo 17-01-1081, Quito; tel. (2) 524-568; fax (2) 501-429; f. 1939 (statutes approved 1999); Pres. JOSÉ MARIO RUIZ NAVAS, Archbishop of Portoviejo.

Archbishop of Cuenca: LUIS ALBERTO LUNA TOBAR, Arzobispado, Calle Bolívar 7-64, Apdo 01-01-0046, Cuenca; tel. (7) 831-651; fax (7) 844-436.

Archbishop of Guayaquil: JUAN IGNACIO LARREA HOLGUÍN, Arzobispado, Calle Clemente Ballén 501 y Chimborazo, Apdo 09-01-0254, Guayaquil; tel. (4) 322-778; fax (4) 329-695.

Archbishop of Portoviejo: JOSÉ MARIO RUIZ NAVAS, Arzobispado, Avda Universitaria, Apdo 24, Portoviejo; tel. (5) 630-404; fax (5) 634-428; e-mail arzobis@ecua.net.ec.

Archbishop of Quito: Cardinal ANTONIO JOSÉ GONZÁLEZ ZUMÁRRAGA, Arzobispado, Calle Chile 1140 y Venezuela, Apdo 17-01-00106, Quito; tel. (2) 284-429; fax (2) 580-973.

The Anglican Communion

Anglicans in Ecuador are under the jurisdiction of Province IX of the Episcopal Church in the USA. The country is divided into two dioceses, one of which, Central Ecuador, is a missionary diocese.

Bishop of Littoral Ecuador: Rt Rev. ALFREDO MORANTE, Calle Bogotá 1010, Barrio Centenario, Apdo 5250, Guayaquil.

Bishop of Central Ecuador: Rt Rev. JOSÉ NEPTALÍ LARREA MORENO, Apdo 17-11-6165, Quito; e-mail ecuacen@uio.satnet.net.

The Baptist Church

Baptist Convention of Ecuador: Casilla 3236, Guayaquil; tel. (4) 384-865; Pres. Rev. HAROLT SANTE MATA; Sec. JORGE MORENO CHAVARRÍA.

The Methodist Church

Methodist Church: Evangelical United Church, Rumipamba 915, Casilla 17-03-236, Quito; tel. (2) 456-714; fax (2) 529-933; 800 mems, 2,000 adherents.

BAHÁ'Í FAITH

National Spiritual Assembly of the Bahá'ís: Apdo 869A, Quito; tel. (2) 563-484; e-mail ecua9nsa@uio.satnet.net; mems resident in 1,121 localities.

The Press

PRINCIPAL DAILIES
Quito

El Comercio: Avda Pedro Vicente Maldonado 11515 y el Tablón, Casilla 17-01-57, Quito; tel. (2) 670-999; fax (2) 670-466; e-mail elcomercio@elcomercio.com; internet www.elcomercio.com; f. 1906; morning; independent; Proprs Compañía Anónima El Comercio; Pres. GUADALUPE MANTILLA DE ACQUAVIVA; circ. 160,000.

Hoy: Avda Occidental N71-345, Casilla 17-07-09069, Quito; tel. (2) 490-888; fax (2) 491-881; e-mail hoy@edimpres.com.ec; internet www.hoy.com.ec; f. 1982; morning; independent; Dir BENJAMÍN ORTIZ BRENNAN; Man. JAIME MANTILLA ANDERSON; circ. 72,000.

El Tiempo: Avda América y Villalengua, Apdo 3117, Quito; f. 1965; morning; independent; Proprs Editorial La Unión, CA; Pres. ANTONIO GRANDA CENTENO; Editor EDUARDO GRANDA GARCÉS; circ. 35,000.

Ultimas Noticias: Avda Pedro Vicente Maldonado 11515 y el Tablón, Casilla 17-01-57, Quito; tel. (2) 670-999; fax (2) 674-923; f. 1938; evening; independent; commercial; Proprs Compañía Anónima El Comercio; Dir DAVID MANTILLA CASHMORE; circ. 60,000.

Guayaquil

Expreso: Avda Carlos Julio Arosemena, Casilla 5890, Guayaquil; tel. (4) 201-100; fax (4) 200-291; f. 1973; morning; independent; Dir GALO MARTÍNEZ MERCHÁN; circ. 60,000.

El Extra: Avda Carlos Julio Arosemena, Casilla 5890, Guayaquil; tel. (4) 201-100; fax (4) 200-291; f. 1975; morning; Pres. ERROL CARTWRIGHT BETANCOURT; Gen. Man. GALO MARTÍNEZ MERCHÁN; circ. 200,000.

La Razón: Avda Constitución y las Americas, Casilla 5832, Guayaquil; tel. (4) 280-100; fax (4) 285-110; f. 1965; morning; independent; Propr ROBERTO ISAÍAS DASSUM; Dir JORGE E. PÉREZ PESANTES; circ. 35,000.

La Segunda: Calle Colón 526 y Boyacá, Casilla 6366, Guayaquil; tel. (4) 320-635; fax (4) 320-539; f. 1983; morning; Propr CARLOS MANSUR; Dir VICENTE ADUM ANTÓN; circ. 60,000.

El Telégrafo: Avda 10 de Agosto 601 y Boyacá, Casilla 415, Guayaquil; tel. (4) 326-500; fax (4) 323-265; e-mail cartas@telegrafo.com.ec; internet www.telegrafo.com.ec; f. 1884; morning;

independent; commercial; Proprs El Telégrafo CA; Dir Dr ROBERTO HANZE SALEM; circ. 45,000 (weekdays), 55,000 (Sundays).

El Universo: Avda Domingo Comín y Alban, Casilla 09-01-531, Guayaquil; tel. (4) 490-000; fax (4) 491-034; e-mail editores@telconet.net; internet www.eluniverso.com; f. 1921; morning; independent; Pres. FRANCISCO PÉREZ FEBRES CORDERO; Dir CARLOS PÉREZ PERASSO; circ. 174,000 (weekdays), 290,000 (Sundays).

There are local daily newspapers of low circulation in other towns.

PERIODICALS
Quito

La Calle: Casilla 2010, Quito; f. 1956; weekly; politics; Dir CARLOS ENRIQUE CARRIÓN; circ. 20,000.

Cámara de Comercio de Quito: Avda Amazona y República, Casilla 202, Quito; tel. (2) 443-787; fax (2) 435-862; f. 1906; monthly; commerce; Pres. ANDRÉS PÉREZ ESPINOSA; Exec. Dir ARMANDO TOMASELLI; circ. 10,000.

Carta Económica del Ecuador: Toledo 1448 y Coruña, Apdo 3358, Quito; f. 1969; weekly; economic, financial and business information; Pres. Dr LINCOLN LARREA B.; circ. 8,000.

El Colegial: Calle Carlos Ibarra 206, Quito; tel. (2) 216-541; f. 1974; weekly; publ. of Student Press Association; Dir WILSON ALMEIDA MUÑOZ; circ. 20,000.

Ecuador Guía Turística: Mejía 438, Of. 43, Quito; f. 1969; fortnightly; tourist information in Spanish and English; Propr Prensa Informativa Turística; Dir JORGE VACA O.; circ. 30,000.

Integración: Solano 836, Quito; quarterly; economics of the Andean countries.

Letras del Ecuador: Casa de la Cultura Ecuatoriana, Avda 6 de Diciembre, Casilla 67, Quito; f. 1944; monthly; literature and art; non-political; Dir Dr TEODORO VANEGAS ANDRADE.

El Libertador: Olmedo 931 y García Moreno, Quito; f. 1926; monthly; Pres. Dr BENJAMÍN TERÁN VAREA.

Mensajero: Benalcázar 478, Apdo 17-01-4100, Quito; tel. (2) 219-555; f. 1884; monthly; religion, culture, economics and politics; Man. OSWALDO CARRERA LANDÁZURI; circ. 5,000.

Nueva: Apdo 3224, Quito; tel. (2) 542-244; f. 1971; monthly; left-wing; Dir MAGDALENA JARAMILLO DE ADOUM.

Quince Dias: Sociedad Periodistica Ecuatoriana, Los Pinos 315, Panamericana Norte km 51/2, Quito; tel. (2) 474-122; fax (2) 566-741; fortnightly; news and regional political analysis.

Solidaridad: Calle Oriente 725, Quito; tel. (2) 216-541; f. 1982; monthly; publ. of Confederation of Catholic Office Staff and Students of Ecuador; Dir WILSON ALMEIDA MUÑOZ; Man. JOHNY MERIZALDE; circ. 15,000.

Guayaquil

Análisis Semanal: Elizalde 119, 10°, Apdo 4925, Guayaquil; tel. (4) 326-590; fax (4) 326-842; e-mail wspurrie@gye.satnet.net; internet www.ecuadoranalysis.com; weekly; economic and political affairs; Editor WALTER SPURRIER BAQUERIZO.

Ecuador Ilustrado: Guayaquil; f. 1924; monthly; literary; illustrated.

El Financiero: Casilla 6666, Guayaquil; tel. (4) 304-050; weekly; business and economic news.

Revista Estadio: Aguirre 730 y Boyacá, Apdo 1239, Guayaquil; tel. (4) 327-200; fax (4) 320-499; e-mail estadio@vistazo.com; f. 1962; fortnightly; sport; Editor LUIS SÁNCHEZ; circ. 70,000.

Hogar: Aguirre 724 y Boyacá, Apdo 1239, Guayaquil; tel. (4) 327-200; f. 1964; monthly; Man. Editor ROSA AMELIA ALVARADO; circ. 35,000.

Vistazo: Aguirre 724 y Boyacá, Apdo 1239, Guayaquil; tel. (4) 327-200; fax (4) 320-499; e-mail vistazo@vistazo.com; f. 1957; fortnightly; general; Pres. XAVIER ALVARADO ROCA; circ. 85,000.

NEWS AGENCIES
Foreign Bureaux

Agencia EFE (Spain): Palacio Arzobispal, Chile 1178, Apdo 4043, Quito; tel. (2) 512-427; Bureau Chief EMILIO CRESPO.

Agenzia Nazionale Stampa Associata (ANSA) (Italy): Calle Venezuela 1013 y esq. Mejía, Of. 26, Quito; tel. (2) 580-794; fax (2) 580-782; Correspondent FERNANDO LARENAS.

Associated Press (AP) (USA): Edif. Sudamérica, 4°, Of. 44, Calle Venezuela 1018 y Mejía, Quito; tel. (2) 570-235; Correspondent CARLOS CISTERNAS.

Deutsche Presse-Agentur (dpa) (Germany): Edif. Atrium, Of. 5-7, González Suárez 894 y Gonnessiat, Quito; tel. (2) 568-986; Correspondent JORGE ORTIZ.

Informatsionnoye Telegrafnoye Agentstvo Rossii—Telegrafnoye Agentstvo Suverennykh Stran (ITAR—TASS) (Russia):

Calle Roca 328 y 6 de Diciembre, 2°, Dep. 6, Quito; tel. (2) 511-631; Correspondent VLADIMIR GOSTEV.

Inter Press Service (IPS) (Italy): Urbanización Los Arrayanes Manzanas 20, Casa 15, Calle León Pontón y Pasaje E, Casilla 17-01-1284, Quito; tel. (2) 662-362; fax (2) 661-977; e-mail jfrias@uio .telconet.net; Correspondent KINTTO LUCAS.

Prensa Latina (Cuba): Edif. Sudamérica, 2°, Of. 24, Calle Venezuela 1018 y Mejía, Quito; tel. (2) 519-333; Bureau Chief ENRIQUE GARCÍA MEDINA.

Reuters (United Kingdom): Avda Amazonas 3655, 2°, Casilla 17-01-4112, Quito; tel. (2) 431-753; fax (2) 432-949; Correspondent JORGE AGUIRRE CHARVET.

United Press International (UPI) (USA): Quito; Correspondent RICARDO POLIT.

Xinhua (New China) News Agency (People's Republic of China): Edif. Portugal, Avda Portugal y Avda de la República del Salvador 730, 10°, Quito; Bureau Chief LIN MINZHONG.

Publishers

Artes Gráficas Ltda: Avda 12 de Octubre 1637, Apdo 533, Casilla 456A, Quito; Man. MANUEL DEL CASTILLO.

Centro de Educación Popular: Avda America 3584, Apdo 17-08-8604, Quito; tel. (2) 525-521; fax (2) 542-369; e-mail centro@cedep.ec; f. 1978; communications, economics; Dir DIEGO LANDÁZURI.

CEPLAES: Avda 6 de Diciembre 2912 y Alpallana, Apdo 17-11/6127, Quito; tel. (2) 548-547; fax (2) 566-207; f. 1978; agriculture, anthropology, education, health, social sciences, women's studies; Exec. Dir ALEXANDRA AYALA.

CIDAP: Hno Miguel 3-23, Casilla 01011943, Cuenca; tel. (7) 829-451; fax (7) 831-450; e-mail cidapl@cidap.org.ec; art, crafts, games, hobbies; Dir CLAUDIO MALO GONZALES.

CIESPAL (Centro Internacional de Estudios Superiores de Comunicación para America Latina): Avda Almagro y Andrade Marin, Apdo 17-01-548, Quito; tel. (2) 234-031; fax (2) 548-011; f. 1959; communications, technology; Dir Dr LUIS E. PROANO.

Corporación de Estudios y Publicaciónes: Acuna 168 y J. Agama, Casilla 17-21-0086, Quito; tel. (2) 221-711; fax (2) 226-256; e-mail cep@accessinter.net; f. 1963; law, public administration.

Corporación Editora Nacional: Apdo 17-12-886, Quito; tel. (2) 554-358; fax (2) 566-340; f. 1978; archaeology, economics, education, geography, political science, history, law, literature, philosophy, social sciences.

Cromograf, SA: Coronel 2207, Casilla 4285, Guayaquil; tel. (4) 346-400; children's books, paperbacks, art productions.

Ediciones Abya-Yala: Avda 12 de Octubre 1430, Quito; tel. (2) 562-633; fax (2) 506-255; e-mail admin-info@abyayala.org; internet www.abyayala.org; f. 1975; anthropology, environmental studies, languages, theology; Dir Fr JUAN BOTTASSO.

Editorial de la Casa de la Cultura Ecuatoriana 'Benjamín Carrión': Avda 6 de Diciembre 679 y Patria, Apdo 67, Quito; tel. (2) 235-611; f. 1944; general fiction and non-fiction, general science; Pres. MILTON BARRAGÁN DUMET.

Editorial y Librería Selecciones: Avda 9 de Octubre 724 y Boyacá, Guayaquil; tel. (4) 305-807; history, geography and sociology.

Eguez-Pérez en Nombre Colectivo/Abrapalabra Editores: America 5378, Casilla 464A, Quito; tel. and fax (2) 544-178; f. 1990; drama, education, fiction, literature, science fiction, social sciences; Man. IVAN EGUEZ.

Libresa S A: Murgeon 364 y Ulloa, Quito; tel. (2) 230-925; fax (2) 502-992; e-mail libresa@interactive.net.ec; f. 1979; education, literature, philosophy; Pres. FAUSTO COBA ESTRELLA.

Libros Técnicos Litesa Cía Ltda: Avda América 542, Apdo 456A, Quito; tel. (2) 528-537; Man. MANUEL DEL CASTILLO.

Pontificia Universidad Católica del Ecuador, Centro de Publicaciones: Avda 12 de Octubre 1076 y Carrión, Apdo 17-01-2184, Quito; tel. (2) 529-250; fax (2) 567-117; e-mail puce@edu.ec; internet www.puce.edu.ec; f. 1946; literature, natural science, law, anthropology, sociology, politics, economics, theology, philosophy, history, archaeology, linguistics, languages and business; Rector Dr JOSÉ RIBADENEIRA ESPINOSA; Dir JESÚS AGUINAGA ZUMÁRRAGA.

Universidad Central del Ecuador: Departamento de Publicaciones, Servicio de Almacén Universitario, Ciudad Universitaria, Avda America y A. Perez Guerrero, POB 3291, Quito; tel. (2) 226-080; fax (2) 501-207.

Universidad de Guayaquil: Departamento de Publicaciones, Biblioteca General 'Luis de Tola y Avilés', Apdo 09-01-3834, Guayaquil; tel. (4) 516-296; f. 1930; general literature, history, philosophy, fiction; Man. Dir LEONOR VILLAO DE SANTANDER.

Broadcasting and Communications

TELECOMMUNICATIONS

Andinatel: Edif. Zeta, Avda Amazonas y Veitimilla, Quito; tel. (2) 561-004; fax (2) 562-240; e-mail wmaster@andinatel.com; internet www.andinatel.com; Exec. Pres. Ing. ALBERTO SANDOVAL.

Asociación Ecuatoriana de Radiodifusión (AER): Edif. Gran Pasaje, Avda 9 de Octubre 424, 9°, Oficina 915, Guayaquil; tel. and fax (4) 562-448; independent association; Pres. Abog. MARIO CANESSA ONETO.

Consejo Nacional de Telecomunicaciones (CONATEL): Avda Diego de Almagro 31-95 y Alpallana, Casilla 17-07-9777, Quito; tel. (2) 225-614; fax (2) 225-030; e-mail jpileggi@conatel.gov.ec; internet www.conatel.gov.ec; Pres. Dr JOSÉ PILEGGI VÉLIZ.

Pacifitel: Calle Panamá y Roca, Guayaquil; tel. (4) 308-724; Exec. Pres. Ing. WILSON CORREA.

Secretaría Nacional de Telecomunicaciones: Avda Diego de Almagro 31-95 y Alpallana, Casilla 17-07-9777, Quito; tel. (2) 502-197; fax (2) 901-010; Secretario Nacional de Telecomunicaciones Ing. CARLOS DEL POZO CAZAR.

Superintendencia de Telecomunicaciones: Edif. Olimpo, Avda 9 de Octubre 1645 y Berlín, Casilla 17-21-1797, Quito; tel. (2) 222-449; fax (2) 566-688; Superintendente de Telecomunicaciones Ing. HUGO RUIZ CORAL.

BROADCASTING

Regulatory Authority

Consejo Nacional de Radiodifusión y Televisión (CONARTEL): Calle La Pinta 225 y Rábida, Quito; tel. (2) 233-492; fax (2) 523-188; Pres. Ing. ALOO OTTATI PINO.

Radio

There are nearly 300 commercial stations, 10 cultural stations and 10 religious stations. The following are among the most important stations:

CRE (Cadena Radial Ecuatoriana): Edif. El Torreón, 9°, Avda Boyacá 642 y Padre Solano, Apdo 4144, Guayaquil; tel. (4) 564-290; fax (4) 560-386; e-mail aguerrero@cre.com.ec; Dir RAFAEL GUERRERO VALENZUELA.

Emisoras Gran Colombia: Calle Galápagos 112 y Guayaquil, Quito; tel. (2) 442-951; fax (2) 443-147; f. 1943; Pres. MARIO JOSÉ CANESSA ONETO.

Radio Católica Nacional: Avda América 1830 y Mercadillo, Casilla 17-03-540, Quito; tel. (2) 541-557; fax (2) 567-309; f. 1985; Pres. ANTONIO GONZÁLEZ.

Radio Centro: Avda República de El Salvador 836 y Portugal, Quito; tel. (2) 448-900; fax (2) 504-575; f. 1977; Pres. EDGAR YÁNEZ VILLALOBOS.

Radio Colón: Edif. Granda Centeno, Avda América OE4-22 y Villalengua, Casilla 17-08-8167, Quito; tel. (2) 247-467; fax (2) 241-994; f. 1934; Pres. JOSÉ ENRÍQUEZ ONTANEDA; Dir MARGARITA MOLINA GRANDA.

Radio Nacional del Ecuador: Mariano Echeverría 537 y Brasil, Casilla 17-01-82, Quito; tel. (2) 459-555; fax (2) 455-266; f. 1961; state-owned; Dir ANA MALDONADO ROBLES.

Radio Quito: Avda 10 de Agosto 2441 y Colón, Casilla 17-21-1971, Quito; tel. (2) 508-301; fax (2) 503-311; f. 1940; Pres. GUADALUPE MANTILLA MOSQUERA.

Radio Sonorama (HCAEL): Eloy Alfaro 5400 y Los Granados, Casilla 130B, Quito; tel. (2) 448-403; fax (2) 445-858; f. 1975; Pres. SANTIAGO PROAÑO.

Radio Sucre: JUAN Tanca Marengo, Casilla 117114, Guayaquil; tel. (4) 680-586; fax (4) 680-592; e-mail rsucre@gye.satnet.net; internet www.radiosucre.com.ec; f. 1983; Pres. VICENTE ARROBA DITTO.

Radio Zacaray: Avda Quito 1424 y Pasaje Aguavil, Santo Domingo de los Colorados; tel. (2) 750-140; fax (2) 449-207; f. 1959; Pres. HÓLGER VELASTEGUÍ DOMÍNGUEZ.

La Voz de los Andes (HCJB): Villalengua 884 y Avda 10 de Agosto, Casilla 17-17-691, Quito; tel. (2) 264-768; fax (2) 447-263; e-mail helpdesk@hcjb.org.ec; f. 1931; operated by World Radio Missionary Fellowship; programmes in 44 languages and dialects, including Spanish, English and Quechua; private, non-commercial, cultural, religious; Programme Dir GUILLERMO BOSSANO; Man. Dir GLEN VOLKHARDT.

Television

Corporación Ecuatoriana de Televisión—Ecuavisa Canal 2: Cerro El Carmen, Casilla 1239, Guayaquil; tel. (4) 300-150; fax (4) 303-677; f. 1967; Pres. XAVIER ALVARADO ROCA; Gen. Man. FRANCISCO AROSEMENA ROBLES.

Cadena Ecuatoriana de Televisión—TCTelevisión Canal 10: Avda de las Américas, frente al Aeropuerto, Casilla 09-01-673, Guayaquil; tel. (4) 397-664; fax (4) 287-544; e-mail tctvl@tctv.com.ec; f. 1969; commercial; Pres. ROBERTO ISAÍAS; Gen. Man. JORGE KRONFLE.

Televisora Nacional—Ecuavisa Canal 8: Bosmediano 447 y José Carbo, Bellavista, Quito; tel. (2) 446-472; fax (2) 445-488; commercial; f. 1970; Pres. PATRICIO JARAMILLO.

Televisión del Pacífico, SA—Gamavisión: Eloy Alfaro 5400 y Rio Coca, Quito; tel. (2) 262-222; fax (2) 440-259; e-mail gamavision@telconet.net; internet www.gamavision.com; Pres. MARCEL RIVAS SÁENZ.

Teleamazonas Cratel, CA: Granda Centeno y Brasil, Casilla 17-11-04844, Quito; tel. (2) 430-350; fax (2) 451-387; f. 1974; commercial; Pres. EDUARDO GRANDA GARCÉS.

Teleandina Canal 23: Avda de la Prensa 3920 y Fernández Salvador, Quito; tel. (2) 599-403; fax (2) 592-600; f. 1991; Pres. HUMBERTO ORTIZ FLORES; Dir PATRICIO AVILES.

Finance

(cap. = capital; p.u. = paid up; res = reserves; dep. = deposits; m. = million; amounts in sucres)

Junta Monetaria Nacional (National Monetary Board): Quito; tel. (2) 514-833; fax (2) 570-258; f. 1927; Pres. FRANCISCO SWETT.

Supervisory Authority

Superintendencia de Bancos y Seguros: Avda 12 de Octubre 561 y Madrid, Quito; tel. (2) 541-326; fax (2) 506-812; e-mail alejo@e-mail.superban.gov.ec; internet www.superban.gov.ec; f. 1927; supervises national banking system, including state and private banks and other financial institutions; Superintendent JUAN FALCONI PUIG.

BANKING

Central Bank

Banco Central del Ecuador: Avda 10 de Agosto y Briceño, Plaza Bolívar, Casilla 339, Quito; tel. (2) 582-577; fax (2) 955-458; internet www.bce.fin.ec; f. 1927; cap. 1,482m., res 2,533m., dep. 666,608m. (Dec. 1987); Pres. JOSÉ LUIS YCAZA PAZMIÑO; Gen. Man. LEOPOLDO R. BÁEZ CARRERA; 19 brs.

Other State Banks

Banco del Pacífico: Francisco de P. Ycaza 200, Guayaquil; tel. (4) 566-010; fax (4) 564-636; internet www.bp.fin.ec; f. 1999 by merger of Banco del Pacífico and Banco Continental; Exec. Pres. MARCEL J. LANIADO.

Banco Ecuatoriano de la Vivienda: Avda l0 de Agosto 2270 y Cordero, Casilla 3244, Quito; tel. (2) 521-311; f. 1962; cap. 5,006m., res 952m., dep. 7,389m. (Dec. 1986); Pres. Abog. JUAN PABLO MONCAGATTA; Gen. Man. Dr PATRICIO CEVALLOS MORÁN.

Banco del Estado (BDE): Avda Atahualpa 628 y 10 de Agosto, Casilla 17-01-00373, Quito; tel. (2) 250-800; fax (2) 250-320; f. 1979; cap. 115,587.5m., res 8,481.5m. (Aug. 1991); Pres. Econ. CÉSAR ROBALINO; Gen. Man. Econ. MARTÍN COSTA MARCH.

Banco Nacional de Fomento: Ante 107 y 10 de Agosto, Casilla 685, Quito; tel. (2) 572-248; fax (2) 580-910; e-mail bnf1@bnfomento.fin.ec; f. 1928; cap. 3,000m., res 14,914m., dep. 117,067m. (Dec. 1987); Pres. Dr IGNACIO HIDALGO VILLAVICENCIO; Gen. Man. MARCELO PEÑA DURINI; 70 brs.

Corporación Financiera Nacional (CFN): Avda Juan León Mera 130 y Patria, Casilla 163, Quito; tel. (2) 564-900; fax (2) 562-519; e-mail pnoboa@cfn.fin.ec; f. 1964; cap. 2,000m., res 8,417m. (July 1987); Pres. MILTON SALGADO; Gen. Man. Ing. RAFAEL CUESTA ALVAREZ.

Filanbanco: Avda 9 de Octubre 203 y Pichincha, Casilla 149, Guayaquil; tel. (4) 322-780; fax (4) 326-916; internet www.filanbanco.com; f. 1908; acquired by the State in 1999.

Commercial Banks

Quito

Banco Amazonas, SA: Avda Amazonas 4430 y Villalengua, Casilla 121, Quito; tel. (2) 260-400; fax (2) 255-123; e-mail basacomp@porta.net; f. 1976; affiliated to Banque Paribas; cap. 21,400m., res 8,970m., dep. 145,740m. (Dec. 1994); Pres. RAFAEL FERRETTI BENÍTEZ; Vice-Pres. ROBERTO SEMINARIO.

Banco Caja de Crédito Agrícola Ganadero, SA: Avda 6 de Diciembre 225 y Piedrahita, Quito; tel. (2) 528-521; f. 1949; cap 132m., res 41m., dep. 592m. (Aug. 1984); Man. HUGO GRIJALVA GARZÓN; Pres. NICOLÁS GUILLÉN.

Banco Consolidado del Ecuador: Avda Patria 740 y 9 de Octubre, Casilla 9150, Suc. 7, Quito; tel. (2) 560-369; fax (2) 560-719; e-mail jcalarco@gnb.fin.ec; f. 1981; cap. 2,874m., res 4,338m., dep. 5,545m. (Oct. 1998); Chair. JAIME GILINSKI; Gen. Man. ANTONIO COY; 2 brs.

Banco General Rumiñahui: Avda Orellana y Amazonas, Casilla 2952, Quito; tel. (2) 505-446; fax (2) 505-366; Gen. Man. Gen. GUSTAVO HERRERA.

Banco Internacional, SA: Avda Patria E-421 y 9 de Octubre, Casilla 17-01-2114, Quito; tel. (2) 565-547; fax (2) 565-758; e-mail cromero@bancointernacional.com.ec; internet www .bancointernacional.com.ec; f. 1973; cap. US $8,600m. (Dec. 2000); Pres. DAMIÁN VALLEJO; Gen. Man. Econ. RAÚL GUERRERO ANDRADE; 58 brs.

Banco Pacífico Popular (BPP): Avda Amazonas 353 y Juan Pablo Sanz, Casilla 696, Quito; tel. (2) 444-700; fax (2) 444-794; f. 1998 by merger of Banco Popular del Ecuador, Banco del Pacífico and Banco COFIEC; cap. US $251m., dep. US $1,598m., total assets US $2,859m. (Nov. 1998); Chair. ARTURO QUIROS; Exec. Pres. NICOLÁS LANDÉS; Pres. FRANCISCO ROSALES.

Banco del Pichincha, CA: Avda Amazonas 4560 y Pereira, Casilla 261, Quito; tel. (2) 980-980; fax (2) 981-187; internet www.pichincha .com; f. 1906; cap. 153,000m., dep. 6,773,832m. (Dec. 1998); Exec. Pres. and Chair. Dr FIDEL EGAS GRIJALVA; Gen. Man. ANTONIO ACOSTA ESPINOSA; 127 brs.

Produbanco: Avda Amazonas 3775 y Japón, Casilla 17-03-38-A, Quito; tel. (2) 260-150; fax (2) 447-319; internet www.produbanco .com; f. 1978 as Banco de la Producción; name changed as above in 1996; cap. 112,000m., res 64,840m., dep. 906,613.2 (Dec. 1997); Exec. Pres. and Gen. Man. Econ. ABELARDO PACHANO BERTERO; Exec. Vice-Pres. FERNANDO VIVERO LOZA.

UniBanco: Avda 10 de Agosto 937 y Buenos Aires, Casilla 2244, Quito; tel. (2) 544-188; fax (2) 227-898; f. 1964 as Banco de Cooperativas del Ecuador, name changed as above in 1995; Pres. Dr JACINTO MONTERO ZAMORA; Vice-Pres. Dr HUGO ENRÍQUEZ; 4 brs.

Ambato

Banco de Tungurahua: Montalvo 630, Casilla 173, Ambato; tel. (2) 821-122; fax (2) 840-426; f. 1979; cap. 50m., res 2m., dep. 329m. (June 1984); Pres. GEORG SONNENHOLZNER; Gen. Man. Econ. CAMILO AMPUERO SÁNCHEZ.

Cuenca

Banco del Austro: Sucre y Borrero (esq.), Casilla 01-01-0167, Cuenca; tel. (7) 831-646; fax (7) 832-633; f. 1977; cap. 34,000m., dep. 141,000m. (July 1994); Pres. JUAN ELJURI ANTÓN; Gen. Man. PATRICIO ROBAYO IDROVO; 19 brs.

Guayaquil

Banco Bolivariano, CA: Junín 200 y Panamá, Casilla 09-01-10184, Guayaquil; tel. (4) 560-799; fax (4) 566-707; e-mail crivera@ bolivariano.fin.ec; internet www.bolivariano.com; f. 1978; cap. 90,000m., res 23,470.9m., dep. 579,890.1m. (Dec. 1998); Chair. JOSÉ SALAZAR BARRAGÁN; Exec. Pres. MIGUEL BABRA LYON; 22 brs.

Banco Industrial y Comercial—Baninco: Pichincha 335 e Illingworth, Casilla 5817, Guayaquil; tel. (4) 323-488; f. 1965; cap. and res 2m., dep. 10m. (June 1988); Pres. Ing. CARLOS MANZUR PERES; Gen. Man. GABRIEL MARTÍNEZ INTRIAGO; 2 brs.

Banco Territorial, SA: Panamá 814 y V. M. Rendón, Casilla 09-01-227, Guayaquil; tel. (4) 566-695; fax (4) 566-695; f. 1886; cap. 3,800m., res 3,769m. (June 1993); dep. 516m. (Sept. 1991); Pres. ROBERTO GOLDBAUM; Gen. Man. Ing. GUSTAVO HEINERT.

Loja

Banco de Loja: esq. Bolívar y Rocafuerte, Casilla 11-01-300, Loja; tel. (4) 571-682; fax (4) 573-019; f. 1968; cap. 10,000m., res 4,207m., dep. 70,900m. (Dec. 1996); Pres. Lic. AUGUSTO EGUIGUREN EGUIGUREN; Man. Lic. FERNANDO BURBANO TORAL.

Machala

Banco de Machala, SA: Avda 9 de Mayo y Rocafuerte, Casilla 711, Machala; tel. (4) 930-100; fax (4) 922-744; f. 1972; Pres. Dr RODOLFO VINTIMILLA FLORES; Exec. Pres. and Gen. Man. ESTEBAN QUIROLA FIGUEROA; 2 brs.

Portoviejo

Banco Comercial de Manabí, SA: Avda 10 de Agosto 600 y 18 Octubre, Portoviejo; tel. (4) 653-888; fax (4) 635-527; f. 1980; cap. 117m., res 21m., dep. 720m. (June 1985); Pres. Dr RUBÉN DARÍO MORALES; Gen. Man. ARISTO ANDRADE DÍAZ.

Foreign Banks

ABN AMBO Bank NV (Netherlands): Avda Amazonas 4272, Casilla 17-17-1534, Quito; tel. (2) 266-666; fax (2) 443-151; internet www.abnamro.com.ec. f. 1960; cap. 23m.; Gen. Man. SJEF MARTINOT; 6 brs.

Citibank, NA (USA): Juan León Mera 130 y Patria, Casilla 17-01-1393, Quito; tel. (2) 563-300; fax (2) 566-895; f. 1959; cap. 7,000m., res 1,000m., dep. 62,000m. (Dec. 1996); Gen. Man. BENJAMÍN FRANCO; 3 brs.

ING Bank NV (Netherlands): Edificio Centro Financiero, Avda Amazonas 4545 y Pereira, Quito; tel. (2) 981-650; fax (2) 981-665.

Lloyds TSB (BLSA) Ltd (United Kingdom): Avda Amazonas 580, esq. Jerónimo Carrión, Casilla 17-03-556, Quito; tel. (2) 564-177; fax (2) 568-997; e-mail lloydsec@interactive.net.ec; f. 1988 (in succession to the Bank of London and South America, f. 1936); cap. US $1,500m., res US $8,300m., dep. US $80,000m. (Dec. 2000); Man. G. BELTRÁN M.

'Multibanco'

Banco de Guayaquil, SA: Plaza Ycaza 105 y Pichincha, Casilla 09-01-1300, Guayaquil; tel. (4) 517-100; fax (4) 514-406; e-mail servicios@bankguay.com; internet www.bankguay.com; f. 1923; absorbed the finance corpn, FINANSUR, in 1990 to become Ecuador's first 'multibanco', carrying out commercial and financial activities; cap. 145,000m., dep. 3,198,862m. (Dec. 1998); Exec. Pres. Dr GUILLERMO LASSO MENDOZA; Vice-Pres ANGELO CAPUTI, CARMEN SORIANO; 50 brs.

Finance Corporations

Financiera Guayaquil, SA: Carchi 702 y 9 de Octubre, 6°, Casilla 2167, Guayaquil; f. 1976; cap. 900m., res 142m. (June 1987); Gen. Man. Dr MIGUEL BABRA LYON.

FINANSA—Financiera Nacional, SA: Avda 6 de Diciembre 2417, entre Orellana y la Niña, Casilla 6420-CCI, Quito; tel. (2) 546-200; f. 1976; cap. 694m., res 103.6m. (June 1986); Gen. Man. RICHARD A. PEARSE; Dir LEONARDO STAGG.

Associations

Asociación de Bancos Privados del Ecuador: Edif. Delta, 7°, Avda República de El Salvador 890 y Suecia, Casilla 17-11-6708, Quito; tel. (2) 466-670; fax (2) 466-701; e-mail echiribo@ asobancos.org.ec; f. 1965; 36 mems; Pres. ANTONIO ACOSTA ESPINOSA; Exec. Pres. ERNESTO CHIRIBOGA BLONDET (acting).

Asociación de Compañías Financieras del Ecuador—AFIN: Robles 653 y Amazonas, 13°, Of. 1310-1311, Casilla 17-07-9156, Quito; tel. (2) 550-623; fax (2) 567-912; Pres. Ing. FRANCISCO ORTEGA.

STOCK EXCHANGES

Bolsa de Valores de Guayaquil: 9 de Octubre 110 y Pichincha, Guayaquil; tel. (4) 564-30; fax (4) 561-871; internet www4.bvg.fin.ec/ eng; CEO ENRIQUE AROSEMENA; Dir of Operations ERNESTO MURILLO.

Bolsa de Valores de Quito: Avda Amazonas 540 y J. Carrión, Quito; tel. (2) 526-805; fax (2) 526-048; e-mail pazosc@ccbvq.com; internet www.ccbvq.com; f. 1969; volume of operations US $1,700m. (1995); Pres GONZALO CHIRIBOGA CHÁVEZ; Exec. Pres. ARTURO QUIROZ RIUMALLÓ.

INSURANCE

Instituto Ecuatoriano de Seguridad Social: Avda 10 de Agosto y Bogotá, Apdo 2640, Quito; tel. (2) 547-400; fax (2) 504-572; f. 1928; various forms of state insurance provided; directs the Ecuadorean social insurance system; provides social benefits and medical service; Dir-Gen. Dr RAÚL ZAPATER HIDALGO.

National Companies

In 1992 there were some 35 insurance companies operating in Ecuador. The following is a list of the eight principal companies, selected by virtue of capital.

Amazonas Cía Anónima de Seguros: V. M. Rendón 401 y Córdova, Apdo 3285, Guayaquil; tel. (4) 566-300; fax (4) 563-192; e-mail contacto@segurosamazonas.com.ec; internet www.segurosama zonas.com.ec; f. 1966; Gen. Man. ANTONIO AROSEMENA.

Cía Reaseguradora del Ecuador, SA: Junín 105 y Malecón Simón Bolívar, Casilla 09-01-6776, Guayaquil; tel. (4) 566-326; fax (4) 564-454; e-mail oespinoz@ecuare.fin.ec; f. 1977; Man. Dir Ing. OMAR ESPINOSA ROMERO.

Cía de Seguros Condor, SA: Plaza Ycaza 302, Apdo 09-01-5007, Guayaquil; tel. (4) 565-888; fax (4) 560-144; f. 1966; Gen. Man. JAIME GUZMÁN ITURRALDE.

Cía de Seguros Ecuatoriano-Suiza, SA: Avda 9 de Octubre 2101 y Tulcán, Apdo 09-01-0937, Guayaquil; tel. (4) 372-222; fax (4) 500-209; f. 1954; Gen. Man. Econ. ENRIQUE SALAS CASTILLO.

La Nacional Cía de Seguros Generales, SA: Edif. World Trade Centre, Avda.fra de Arellana, 5°, Guayaquil; tel. (4) 630-170; fax (4) 630-175; f. 1940; Gen. Man. Dr MIGUEL BABRA LEÓN.

Panamericana del Ecuador, SA: Calle Portugal 305 y Eloy Alfaro, Quito; tel. (2) 469-460; fax (2) 469-650; f. 1973; Gen. Man. GERMAN DAVILA.

Seguros Rocafuerte, SA: Plaza Carbo 505 y 9 de Octubre, Apdo 6491, Guayaquil; f. 1967; Gen. Man. Ing. DANIEL CAÑIZARES AGUILAR.

Directory

La Unión Cía Nacional de Seguros: Km. 5½, Vía a la Costa, Apdo 09-01-1294, Guayaquil; tel. (4) 851-500; fax (4) 851-700; e-mail launion2@porta.net; f. 1943; Man. DAVID ALBERTO GOLDBAUM MORALES.

Trade and Industry

GOVERNMENT AGENCIES

Consejo Nacional de Modernización del Estado (CONAM): Edif. CFN, 9°, Avda Juan León Mera 130 y Patria, Quito; tel. (2) 509-432; fax (2) 228-450; e-mail cdelgado@uio.conam-pertal.gov.ec; f. 1994; Pres. Ing. RICARDO NOBOA; Exec. Dir Ing. ANTONIO PERÉ YCAZA.

Empresa de Comercio Exterior (ECE): Quito; f. 1980 to promote non-traditional exports; State owns 33% share in company; share capital 25m. sucres.

Fondo de Promoción de Exportaciones (FOPEX): Juan León Mera 130 y Patria, Casilla 163, Quito; tel. (2) 564-900; fax (2) 562-519; f. 1972; export promotion; Dir ELIANA SANTAMARÍA M.

Instituto Ecuatoriano de Reforma Agraria y Colonización (IERAC): f. 1973 to supervise the Agrarian Reform Law under the auspices and co-ordination of the Ministry of Agriculture; Dir LUIS LUNA GAYBOR.

Superintendencia de Compañías del Ecuador: Roca 660 y Amazonas, Casilla 17-21-0687, Quito; tel. (2) 541-606; fax (2) 566-685; e-mail estudi@q.supercias.gov.ec; f. 1964; responsible for the legal and accounting control of commercial enterprises; Supt Dr XAVIER MUÑOZ CHÁVEZ.

DEVELOPMENT ORGANIZATIONS

Centro Nacional de Promoción de la Pequeña Industria y Artesanía (CENAPIA): Quito; agency to develop small-scale industry and handicrafts; Dir Econ. EDGAR GUEVARA (acting).

Centro de Reconversión Económica del Azuay, Cañar y Morona Santiago (CREA): Avda México entre Unidad Nacional y las Américas, Casilla 01-01-1953, Cuenca; tel. (7) 817-500; fax (7) 817-134; f. 1959; development organization; Dir Dr JUAN TAMA.

Consejo Nacional de Desarrollo (CONADE): Juan Larrea y Arenas, Quito; formerly Junta Nacional de Planificación y Coordinación Económica; aims to formulate a general plan of economic and social development and supervise its execution; also to integrate local plans into the national; Chair. GALO ABRIL OJEDA; Sec. PABLO LUCIO PAREDES.

Fondo de Desarrollo del Sector Rural Marginal (FODERUMA): f. 1978 to allot funds to rural development programmes in poor areas.

Fondo Nacional de Desarrollo (FONADE): f. 1973; national development fund to finance projects as laid down in the five-year plan.

Instituto de Colonización de la Región Amazónica (INCREA): f. 1978 to encourage settlement in and economic development of the Amazon region; Dir Dr DIMAS GUZMÁN.

Instituto Ecuatoriano de Recursos Hidráulicos (INERHI): undertakes irrigation and hydroelectric projects; Man. Ing. EDUARDO GARCÍA GARCÍA.

Organización Comercial Ecuatoriana de Productos Artesanales (OCEPA): Carrión 1236 y Versalles, Casilla 17-01-2948, Quito; tel. (2) 541-992; fax (2) 565-961; f. 1964; to develop and promote handicrafts; Gen. Man. MARCELO RODRÍGUEZ.

Programa Nacional del Banano y Frutas Tropicales: Guayaquil; to promote the development of banana and tropical-fruit cultivation; Dir Ing. JORGE GIL CHANG.

Programa Regional de Desarrollo del Sur del Ecuador (PREDESUR): Pasaje María Eufrasia 100 y Mosquera Narváez, Quito; tel. (2) 544-415; f. 1972 to promote the development of the southern area of the country; Dir Ing. LUIS HERNÁN EGUIGUREN CARRIÓN.

CHAMBERS OF COMMERCE AND INDUSTRY

Federación Nacional de Cámaras de Comercio del Ecuador: Avda Olmedo 414 y Boyacá, Guayaquil; tel. (4) 323-130; fax (4) 323-478; Pres. Ing. LUIS TRUJILLO BUSTAMANTE; Exec. Vice-Pres. Dr ROBERTO ILLINGWORTH.

Cámara de Comercio de Cuenca: Avda Federico Malo 1-90, Casilla 4929, Cuenca; tel. (7) 827-531; fax (7) 833-891; f. 1919; 5,329 mems; Pres. ENRIQUE MORA VÁZQUEZ.

Cámara de Comercio de Quito: Edif. Las Cámaras, 6°, Avda República y Amazonas, Casilla 17-01-202, Quito; tel. (2) 443-787; fax (2) 435-862; e-mail ccq@uio.satnet.net; f. 1906; 8,000 mems; Chair. JAVIER ESPINOSA; Pres. DOMINGO CÓRDOVEZ PÉREZ.

Cámara de Comercio de Guayaquil: Avda Olmedo 414 y Boyacá, Guayaquil; tel. (4) 323-130; fax (4) 323-478; e-mail camcomg@g

.camcom.org.ec; f. 1889; 16,500 mems; Pres. Ing. LUIS TRUJILLO BUSTAMENTE; Exec. Sec. Dr ROBERTO ILLINGWORTH CABANILLA.

Federación Nacional de Cámaras de Industrias: Avda República y Amazonas, Casilla 2438, Quito; tel. (2) 452-994; fax (2) 448-118; f. 1974; Pres. Ing. PEDRO KOHN.

Cámara de Industrias de Cuenca: Edif. Las Cámaras, Avda Federico Malo 1-90, Casilla 01-01-326, Cuenca; tel. (7) 830-845; fax (7) 830-945; f. 1936; Pres. Ing. FRANK TOSI IÑIGUEZ.

Cámara de Industrias de Guayaquil: Avda 9 de Octubre 910 y Rumichaca, Casilla 09-01-4007, Guayaquil; tel. (4) 561-556; fax (4) 320-924; f. 1936; Pres. Ing. ERNESTO NOBOA BEJARANO.

INDUSTRIAL AND TRADE ASSOCIATIONS

Centro de Desarrollo Industrial del Ecuador (CENDES): Avda Orellana 1715 y 9 de Octubre, Casilla 2321, Quito; tel. (2) 527-100; f. 1962; carries out industrial feasibility studies, supplies technical and administrative assistance to industry, promotes new industries, supervises investment programmes; Gen. Man. CLAUDIO CREAMER GUILLÉN.

Corporación de Desarrollo e Investigación Geológico-Minero-Metalúrgica (CODIGEM): Avda 10 de Agosto 5844 y Pereira, Casilla 17-03-23, Quito; tel. (2) 254-673; fax (2) 254-674; e-mail prodemi2@prodeminca.org.ec; f. 1991 to direct mining exploration and exploitation; Exec. Pres. Ing. JORGE BARRAGÁN G.

Fondo Nacional de Preinversión (FONAPRE): Jorge Washington 624 y Amazonas, Casilla 17-01-3302, Quito; tel. (2) 563-261; f. 1973 to undertake feasibility projects before investment; Pres. LUIS PARODÍ VALVERDE; Gen. Man. Ing. EDUARDO MOLINA GRAZZIANI.

Petróleos del Ecuador (PETROECUADOR): Avda 6 de Diciembre, Casilla 5007-8, Quito; tel. (2) 229-043; state petroleum co; operations in at least seven oilfields were expected to be transferred to the private sector; Pres. RODOLFO BARNIOL.

EMPLOYERS' ORGANIZATIONS

Asociación de Cafecultores del Cantón Piñas: García Moreno y Abdón Calderón, Quito; coffee growers' association.

Asociación de Comerciantes e Industriales: Avda Boyacá 1416, Guayaquil; traders' and industrialists' association.

Asociación de Industriales Textiles del Ecuador (AITE): Edif. Las Cámaras, 8°, Avda República y Amazonas, Casilla 2893, Quito; f. 1938; textile manufacturers' association; 40 mems; Pres. Ing. RAMIRO LEÓN PAEZ; Exec. Pres. Dr ANTONIO JOSÉ COBO.

Asociación de Productores Bananeros del Ecuador (APROBANA): Malecón 2002, Guayaquil; banana growers' association; Pres. NICOLÁS CASTRO.

Asociación Nacional de Empresarios (ANDE): Edif. España, 6°, Of. 67, Avda Amazonas 1429 y Colón, Casilla 17-01-3489, Quito; tel. (2) 238-507; fax (2) 509-806; e-mail ande@vio.satnet.net; internet www.ande.net; national employers' association.

Asociación Nacional de Exportadores de Cacao y Café: Casilla 4774, Manta; cocoa and coffee exporters' association.

Asociación Nacional de Exportadores de Camarones: Pres. LUIS VILLACÍS.

Cámara de Agricultura: Casilla 17-21-322, Quito; tel. (2) 230-195; Pres. ALBERTO ENRÍQUEZ PORTILLA.

Consorcio Ecuatoriano de Exportadores de Cacao y Café: cocoa and coffee exporters' consortium.

Corporación Nacional de Exportadores de Cacao y Café: Guayaquil; cocoa and coffee exporters' corporation.

Federación Nacional de Cooperativas Cafetaleras: Quito; coffee co-operatives federation.

Unión Nacional de Periodistas: Joaquín Auxe Iñaquito, Quito; national press association.

There are several other coffee and cocoa organizations.

UTILITIES

Regulatory Authorities

Ministry of Energy and Mines: see section on The Government (Ministries).

Comisión Ecuatoriana de Energía Atómica: Juan Larrea 534 y Riofrío, Casilla 17-01-2517, Quito; tel. (2) 545-861; fax (2) 563-336; e-mail comecenl@comecenat.gov.ec; atomic energy commission; Exec. Dir CELIANO ALMEIDA.

Consejo Nacional de Electricidad (CONELEC): Avda Amazonas 33-299 e Inglaterra, Quito; tel. (2) 268-746; fax (2) 268-737; e-mail conelec@conelec.gov.ec; internet www.conelec.gov.ec; f. 1999; supervises electricity industry following transfer of assets of the former Instituto Ecuatoriano de Electrificación (INECEL) to the Fondo de Solidaridad; pending privatization as six generating companies, one transmission company and 19 distribution companies in late 2000 ; Pres. DIEGO PÉREZ PALLARES.

Directorate of Alternative Energy (Ministry of Energy and Mines): Edif. Interandina, Ulpiano Paéz 24-06 y Mercadillo, POB 17-15-007C, Quito; tel. (2) 565-980; fax (2) 565-474; e-mail mbalseca@uio.satnet.net; f. 1995; research and development of new and renewable energy sources; Dir Ing. MILTON BALSECA G.

Directorate-General of Hydrocarbons: Avda 10 de Agosto 321, Quito; supervision of the enforcement of laws regarding the exploration and development of petroleum.

Electricity

Empresa de Electricidad del Ecuador (EMELEC): La Garzota, Sector 3, Manzana 47; tel. (4) 248-057; fax (4) 246-952; major producer and distributor of electricity, mostly using oil-fired or diesel generating capacity.

Empresa Eléctrica Quito, SA: Avda 10 de Agosto y Las Casas, Quito; tel (2) 543-833; fax (2) 503-817; internet www.eeq.com.ec; f. 1894; produces electricity for the region around Quito, mostly from hydroelectric plants; Gen. Man. HERNÁN ANDINO ROMERO.

Water

Instituto Ecuatoriano de Obras Sanitarias: Toledo 684 y Lérida, Troncal, Quito; tel. (2) 522-738.

TRADE UNIONS

Frente Unitario de Trabajadores (FUT): f. 1971; left-wing; 300,000 mems; Pres. EDGAR PONCE; comprises:

Confederación Ecuatoriana de Organizaciones Clasistas (CEDOC): Calle Río de Janeiro 407 y Juan Larrea, Casilla 3207, Quito; tel. (2) 548-086; f. 1938; affiliated to CMT and CLAT; humanist; Pres. RAMIRO ROSALES NARVÁEZ; Sec.-Gen. JORGE MUÑOZ; 150,000 mems (est.) organized in 20 provinces.

Confederación Ecuatoriana de Organizaciones Sindicales Libres (CEOSL): Casilla 17-01-1373, Quito; tel. (2) 522-511; fax (2) 500-836; e-mail ceosl@hoy.net.; f. 1962; affiliated to ICFTU and ORIT; Pres. JOSÉ CHÁVEZ CHÁVEZ; Sec.-Gen. WILSON BECERRA ROSERO.

Confederación de Trabajadores del Ecuador (CTE) (Confederation of Ecuadorean Workers): Olmedo y Benalcázar, 3°, Casilla 4166, Quito; fax (2) 580-747; f. 1944; admitted to WFTU and CPUSTAL; Leaders EDGAR PONCE; 1,200 affiliated unions, 70 national federations.

Central Católica de Obreros: Avda 24 de Mayo 344, Quito; tel. (2) 213-704; f. 1906; craft and manual workers and intellectuals; Pres. CARLOS E. DÁVILA ZURITA.

A number of trade unions are not affiliated to the above groups. These include the Federación Nacional de Trabajadores Marítimos y Portuarios del Ecuador (FNTMPE) (National Federation of Maritime and Port Workers of Ecuador) and both railway trade unions.

Transport

RAILWAYS

All railways are government-controlled. In 1997 the total length of track was 956 km.

Empresa Nacional de Ferrocarriles del Estado: Calle Bolívar 443, Casilla 159, Quito; tel. (2) 216-180; Gen. Man. M. ARIAS SALAZAR.

There are divisional state railway managements for the following lines: Guayaquil–Quito, Sibambe–Cuenca and Quito–San Lorenzo.

ROADS

There were 43,198 km of roads in 1998, of which 16.8% were paved. The Pan-American Highway runs north from Ambato to Quito and to the Colombian border at Tulcán and south to Cuenca and Loja. Major rebuilding projects were undertaken in late 1998 with finance from several development organizations to restore roads damaged by the effects of El Niño (a periodic warming of the tropical Pacific Ocean).

SHIPPING

The following are Ecuador's principal ports: Guayaquil, Esmeraldas, Manta and Puerto Bolívar.

Acotramar, CA: General Gómez 522 y Coronel Guayaquil, Casilla 4044, Guayaquil; tel. (4) 401-004; fax (4) 444-852.

Ecuanave, CA: Junin 415 y Córdova, 4°, Casilla 09-01-30H, Guayaquil; tel. (4) 293-808; fax (4) 289-257; e-mail ecuanav@ecua.net.ec.; Chair. Ing. P. ERNESTO ESCOBAR; Man. Dir A. GUILLERMO SERRANO.

Flota Bananera Ecuatoriana, SA: Edif. Gran Pasaje, 9°, Plaza Ycaza 437, Casilla 6883, Guayaquil; tel. (4) 309-333; f. 1967; owned by Govt and private stockholders; Pres. DIEGO SÁNCHEZ; Gen. Man. JORGE BARRIGA.

Flota Mercante Grancolombiana, SA: Calle 2 Aguirre 104 y Malecón Simón Bolívar, Guayaquil; tel. (4) 512-791; f. 1946 with Colombia and Venezuela; on Venezuela's withdrawal, in 1953, Ecuador's 10% interest was increased to 20%; operates services from Colombia and Ecuador to European ports, US Gulf ports and New York, Mexican Atlantic ports and East Canada; offices in Quito, Cuenca, Bahía, Manta and Esmeraldas; Man. Naval Capt. J. ALBERTO SÁNCHEZ.

Flota Petrolera Ecuatoriana—FLOPEC: Edif. FLOPEC, Avda Amazonas 1188 y Cordero, Casilla 535-A, Quito; tel. (2) 564-058; fax (2) 569-794; f. 1972; e-mail g.general@flopec.com.ec; internet www.flopec.com.ec; Gen. Man. Vice-Adm. JORGE DONOSO MORAN.

Logística Marítima, CA (LOGMAR): Avda Córdova 812 y V. M. Rendón, 1°, Casilla 9622, Guayaquil; tel. (4) 307-041; Pres. J. COELLOG; Man. IGNACIO RODRÍGUEZ BAQUERIZO.

Naviera del Pacífico, CA (NAPACA): El Oro 101 y La Ría, Casilla 09-01-529, Guayaquil; tel. (4) 342-055; Pres. LUIS ADOLFO NOBOA NARANJO.

Servicios Oceánicos Internacionales, SA: Avda Domingo Comin y Calle 11, Casilla 79, Guayaquil; Pres. CARLOS VALDANO RAFFO; Man. FERNANDO VALDANO TRUJILLO.

Transfuel, CA: Junin 415 y Cordova, 4°, Casilla 09-01-30H, Guayaquil; tel. (4) 304-142; Chair. Ing. ERNESTO ESCOBAR PALLARES; Man. Dir CARLOS MANRIQUE A.

Transportes Navieros Ecuatorianos—Transnave: Edif. Citibank, 4°–7°, Avda 9 de Octubre 416 y Chile, Casilla 4706, Guayaquil; tel. (4) 561-455; fax (4) 566-273; transports general cargo within the European South Pacific Magellan Conference, Japan West Coast South America Conference and Atlantic and Gulf West Coast South America Conference; Pres. Vice-Adm. YÉZID JARAMILLO SANTOS; Gen. Man. RUBÉN LANDÁZURI ZAMBRANO.

CIVIL AVIATION

There are two international airports: Mariscal Sucre, near Quito, and Simón Bolívar, near Guayaquil.

Ecuatoriana: Edif. Torres de Almagro, Avda Reina Victoria y Colón, Torres de Almagro, Casilla 17-07-8475, Quito; tel. (2) 563-003; fax (2) 563-920; e-mail eu@impsat.comec; f. 1974 as Empresa Ecuatoriana de Aviación; nationalized 1974; ceased operations in 1993, aircraft subsequently sold or repossessed, and routes to the USA assigned to SAETA; airline subsequently reactivated; scheduled domestic and international services to Latin America and the USA; Dir. RICARDO VIO GUERRERO.

SAETA Air Ecuador (Sociedad Anónima Ecuatoriana de Transportes Aereos): Avda. Carlos Julio Arosemena Km. 2½, Guayaquil; tel. (4) 201-152; fax (4) 201-153; e-mail ehbuzon@saeta .com.ec; internet www.saeta.com.ec; f. 1967; domestic and regional scheduled flights; charter cargo services; Chair. ROBERTO DUNN BARREIRO; Exec. Dir ROBERTO D. SUÁREZ.

Servicios Aereos Nacionales (SAN): Km. 2½, Avda Carlos Julio Arrosemena, Apdo 7138, Guayaquil; tel. (4) 202-832; fax (4) 201-152; f. 1964; scheduled passenger and cargo services linking Guayaquil with Quito and the Galápagos Islands and Quito with Cuenca; Dir of Operations Capt. LUGIEBRE JEPEZ.

Transportes Aéreos Militares Ecuatorianos (TAME): Avda Amazonas 1354 y Colón, 6°, Casilla 17-07-8736, Sucursal Almagro, Quito; tel. (2) 547-000; fax (2) 500-736; e-mail tame1@tame.com.ec; internet wwwpub4.ecua.net.ec/tame/; f. 1962; domestic scheduled and charter services for passengers and freight; Pres. WILLIAM BIRKETT.

The following airlines also offer national and regional services:

Aerotaxis Ecuatorianos, SA (ATESA); Cía Ecuatoriana de Transportes Aéreos (CEDTA); Ecuastol Servicios Aéreos, SA; Ecuavia Cía Ltda; Aeroturismo Cía Ltda (SAVAC).

Tourism

Tourism has become an increasingly important industry in Ecuador, with 510,627 foreign arrivals (including same-day visitors) in 1998. Of total visitors in that year, some 32% came from Colombia, 6% were from Peru, 10% from other Latin American countries, 22% from the USA and 21% from Europe. Receipts from the tourism industry amounted to US $281m. in 1996.

Asociación Ecuatoriana de Agencias de Viajes y Turismo—ASECUT: Edif. Banco del Pacífico, 5°, Avda Amazonas 720 y Veintimilla, Casilla 9421, Quito; tel. (2) 503-669; fax (2) 285-872; f. 1953; Pres. KATBE I. TOUMA ABUHAYAR.

Corporación Ecuatoriana de Turismo—CETUR: Avda Eloy Alfaro y Carlos Tobar, Quito; tel. (2) 507-555; fax (2) 507-564; f. 1964; govt-owned; Exec. Dir KATBE I. TOUMA ABUHAYAR.

EGYPT

Introductory Survey

Location, Climate, Language, Religion, Flag, Capital

The Arab Republic of Egypt occupies the north-eastern corner of Africa, with an extension across the Gulf of Suez into the Sinai Peninsula, sometimes regarded as lying within Asia. Egypt is bounded to the north by the Mediterranean Sea, to the north-east by Israel, to the east by the Red Sea, to the south by Sudan, and to the west by Libya. The climate is arid, with a maximum annual rainfall of only 200 mm (8 ins) around Alexandria. More than 90% of the country is desert, and some 99% of the population live in the valley and delta of the River Nile. Summer temperatures reach a maximum of 43°C (110°F) and winters are mild, with an average day temperature of about 18°C (65°F). Arabic is the official language. Many educated Egyptians also speak English or French. More than 80% of the population are Muslims, mainly of the Sunni sect. The remainder are mostly Christians, principally Copts. The national flag (proportions 3 by 2) has three equal horizontal stripes, of red, white, and black; the white stripe has, in the centre, the national emblem (a striped shield superimposed on an eagle, with a cartouche beneath bearing the inscription, in Kufic script, 'Arab Republic of Egypt') in gold. The capital is Cairo (Al-Qahirah).

Recent History

Egypt, a province of Turkey's Ottoman Empire from the 16th century, was occupied by British forces in 1882. The administration was controlled by British officials, although Egypt remained nominally an Ottoman province until 1914, when a British protectorate was declared. Egypt was granted titular independence on 28 February 1922. Fuad I, the reigning Sultan, became King of Egypt. He was succeeded in 1936 by his son, King Faruq (Farouk). The Anglo-Egyptian Treaty of 1936 recognized full Egyptian sovereignty and provided for the gradual withdrawal of British troops, while giving the United Kingdom the right to maintain a garrison on the Suez Canal, and to use Alexandria and Port Said as naval bases. After the Second World War British forces withdrew from Egypt, except for a military presence in the Suez Canal Zone. When the British mandate in Palestine was ended in 1948, Arab armies intervened to oppose the newly-proclaimed State of Israel. A cease-fire was agreed in 1949, leaving Egyptian forces occupying the Gaza Strip.

On 23 July 1952 King Farouk's unpopular regime was overthrown in a bloodless coup. Power was seized by a group of young army officers led by Lt-Col (later Col) Gamal Abd an-Nasir (Nasser). Farouk abdicated in favour of his infant son, Ahmad Fuad II, and went into exile. Gen. Muhammad Nagib (Neguib) was appointed Commander-in-Chief of the army and Chairman of the Revolution Command Council (RCC). In September Neguib was appointed Prime Minister and Military Governor, with Nasser as Deputy Prime Minister. In December the 1923 Constitution was abolished, and all political parties were dissolved in January 1953. The monarchy was abolished on 18 June 1953, and Egypt was proclaimed a republic, with Neguib as President and Prime Minister. In April 1954 Neguib was succeeded as Prime Minister by Nasser. In October Egypt and the United Kingdom signed an agreement providing for the withdrawal of all British forces from the Suez Canal by June 1956. In November 1954 President Neguib was relieved of all his remaining posts, and Nasser became acting Head of State.

The establishment of military rule was accompanied by wide-ranging reforms, including the redistribution of land, the promotion of industrial development and the expansion of social welfare services. In foreign affairs, the new regime was strongly committed to Arab unity, and Egypt played a prominent part in the Non-aligned Movement (see p. 318). In 1955, having failed to secure Western armaments on satisfactory terms, Egypt accepted military assistance from the USSR.

On 23 June 1956 a new Constitution was approved by a national referendum and Nasser was elected President unopposed, whereupon the RCC was dissolved. In July, following the departure of British forces, the US and British Governments withdrew their offers of financial assistance for Egypt's construction of the Aswan High Dam. In response, Nasser announced the nationalization of the Suez Canal Company, so that revenue from Canal tolls could be used to finance the dam's construction. The take-over of the Canal was a cause of great concern to Israel, Britain and France, and Israel invaded the Sinai Peninsula on 29 October. Britain and France launched military operations against Egypt two days later. Strong pressure from the UN and the US Government resulted in a cease-fire on 6 November, and supervision by the UN of the invaders' withdrawal.

Egypt and Syria merged in February 1958 to form the United Arab Republic (UAR), with Nasser as President. The new nation strengthened earlier ties with the USSR and other countries of the communist bloc. In September 1961 Syria seceded from the UAR, but Egypt retained this title until September 1971. In 1958 the UAR and Yemen formed a federation styled the United Arab States, but this was dissolved in 1961.

President Nasser enjoyed immense prestige nationally, where he was regarded as the founder of modern Egypt, throughout the Arab world and beyond. In December 1962 he established the Arab Socialist Union (ASU) as the country's only recognized political organization. In May 1967 he secured the withdrawal of the UN Emergency Force from Egyptian territory. Egypt subsequently reoccupied Sharm esh-Sheikh, on the Sinai Peninsula, and closed the Straits of Tiran to Israeli shipping. This precipitated the 'Six-Day War' of June 1967, when Israel quickly defeated neighbouring Arab states, including Egypt. The war left Israel in control of the Gaza Strip and a large area of Egyptian territory, including the whole of the Sinai Peninsula. The Suez Canal was blocked, and remained closed until June 1975.

Nasser died suddenly in September 1970, and was succeeded by his Vice-President, Col Anwar Sadat. In September 1971 the UAR was renamed the Arab Republic of Egypt, and a new Constitution took effect. Egypt, Libya and Syria formed a Federation of Arab Republics in 1972, but this proved to be ineffective. In 1976 Egypt terminated its Treaty of Friendship with the USSR. Relations with the USA developed meanwhile, as President Sadat came to rely increasingly on US aid.

An uneasy cease-fire with Israel lasted until October 1973, when Egyptian troops crossed the Suez Canal to recover territory lost in 1967. After 18 days of fighting, a cease-fire was achieved. In 1974–75 the US Secretary of State, Dr Henry Kissinger, negotiated disengagement agreements whereby Israel evacuated territory in Sinai and Israeli and Egyptian forces were separated by a buffer zone under the control of UN forces. In a dramatic peace-making initiative, opposed by many Arab countries, Sadat visited Israel in 1977 and addressed the Knesset (parliament). The leaders of Syria, Libya, Algeria, Iraq, the People's Democratic Republic of Yemen (PDRY) and the Palestine Liberation Organization (PLO) condemned Egypt, which responded by severing diplomatic relations with the five dissenting countries. In September 1978, following talks held at the US presidential retreat at Camp David, Maryland, Sadat and the Israeli Prime Minister, Menachem Begin, signed two agreements: the first provided for a five-year transitional period during which the inhabitants of the Israeli-occupied West Bank of Jordan and the Gaza Strip would obtain full autonomy and self-government; the second provided for a peace treaty between Egypt and Israel. The latter was signed in March 1979, whereafter Israel made phased withdrawals from the Sinai Peninsula, the last taking place in April 1982. Syria, Algeria, Libya and the PLO had condemned the Camp David agreements, and in March 1979 the League of Arab States (the Arab League, see p. 232) expelled Egypt and imposed political and economic sanctions. Egypt continued to forge relations with Israel, and in February 1980 the two countries exchanged ambassadors for the first time.

In 1974 Sadat began to introduce a more liberal political and economic regime. Political parties (banned since 1953) were allowed to participate in the 1976 elections for the People's Assembly, and in July 1978 Sadat formed the National Democratic Party (NDP), with himself as leader. In 1979 the special constitutional status of the ASU was ended. In October 1981 Sadat was assassinated by members of Islamic Jihad, a group of militant fundamentalist Islamists. Sadat was succeeded by

Lt-Gen. Hosni Mubarak, his Vice-President and a former Commander-in-Chief of the air force. A new electoral law required parties to receive a minimum of 8% of the total vote in order to secure representation in the People's Assembly. This prompted opposition parties to boycott elections to local councils and to the Shura (Advisory) Council. At legislative elections in May 1984 the ruling NDP won 72.9% of the total vote. Of the four other participating parties, only the New Wafd Party, with 15.1%, achieved representation. The campaign by Islamist fundamentalists for the Egyptian legal system fully to adopt the principles of the *Shari'a* (Islamic holy law) intensified in 1985. The People's Assembly rejected proposals for immediate changes and advocated a thorough study of the small proportion of Egyptian law that did not conform to Islamic precepts.

Meanwhile, a division in the Arab world between a 'moderate' grouping (including Jordan, Iraq and the Gulf states), which viewed the participation of Egypt as indispensable to any diplomatic moves towards solving the problems of the region, and a 'radical' grouping, led by Syria, became increasingly evident. The PLO leader, Yasser Arafat, visited President Mubarak for discussions in December 1983, signifying the end of estrangement between Egypt and the PLO. In 1984 Jordan resumed diplomatic relations with Egypt. These two developments led to the profound involvement of Egypt under Mubarak in the pursuit of a negotiated settlement of the Palestinian question. Egypt proposed two formulas for a peaceful settlement of the Iran–Iraq War, but neither was adopted by Iran or Iraq. President Mubarak, accompanied by King Hussein of Jordan, made an unexpected visit to Baghdad in March 1985, to demonstrate his support for the Iraqi President, Saddam Hussain, although there had been no formal diplomatic relations between Egypt and Iraq since 1979. Relations with Libya remained poor. In November 1987, at a summit conference in Jordan attended by the majority of Arab leaders, President Hafiz Assad of Syria obstructed proposals to readmit Egypt to the Arab League. However, recognizing Egypt's support for Iraq in the Iran–Iraq War and acknowledging the influence that Egypt could exercise on the problems of the region, the conference approved a resolution placing the establishment of diplomatic links with Egypt at the discretion of member states.

In November 1986 President Mubarak accepted the resignation of Dr Ali Lutfi, the Prime Minister since September 1985. A new Council of Ministers was appointed under the premiership of Dr Atif Sidqi, hitherto head of the Central Auditing Agency. A general election was held in April 1987, following a campaign marred by clashes between Christians and Muslims and by accusations of government corruption. The election resulted in a large majority for the ruling NDP. Of the 448 elective seats in the People's Assembly, the NDP won 346, the opposition parties together won 95, and independents seven. An electoral alliance of the Socialist Labour Party (SLP), the Liberal Socialist Party (LSP) and the Muslim Brotherhood won a combined total of 60 seats, of which the Brotherhood took 37 to become the largest single opposition group in the legislature. At a referendum held in October Mubarak was confirmed as President for a second six-year term of office by 97% of voters.

In March 1988 the national state of emergency first declared after the assassination of President Sadat was renewed for a further three years. In April and May 1989, in response to increasing popular discontent over price increases and food shortages, the Government acted to pre-empt disturbances during the month of Ramadan by detaining more than 2,000 Islamist fundamentalists. In June elections to the Shura Council were contested by opposition parties for the first time since the Council's establishment in 1980; opponents of the Government subsequently alleged that the NDP had achieved its victory by fraudulent means.

A visit by King Fahd of Saudi Arabia to Cairo in March 1989 was a further indication of Egypt's improved status in the Arab world, and in May Egypt was readmitted to the Arab League. President Mubarak represented Egypt at an emergency summit conference of the League, convened to rally support for the diplomatic initiatives of Yasser Arafat, following the Palestinian declaration of independence. Col Muammar al-Qaddafi of Libya attended the meeting and had separate discussions with President Mubarak. The border between the two countries was reopened in June, and in October Qaddafi visited Egypt for further discussions.

Following Iraq's invasion and annexation of Kuwait in August 1990, Egypt convened an emergency summit meeting of Arab leaders. Egypt demanded the withdrawal of Iraqi forces from Kuwait, and 12 of the 20 Arab League states voted to send an Arab force to the Persian (Arabian) Gulf region, in response to Saudi Arabia's request for international assistance to deter potential aggression by Iraq. The Egtian contingent within the multinational force eventually amounted to 35,000 troops. Egypt emerged from the Gulf conflict with its international reputation enhanced, largely as a result of what was regarded as Mubarak's firm leadership of 'moderate' Arab opinion.

Legislative elections in November and December 1990 were conducted amid comprehensive security operations, in view of the Gulf crisis and following the assassination, in October, of the Speaker of the outgoing People's Assembly. Under new electoral laws, the requirement for a party to win a minimum of 8% of the total vote in order to gain representation in the People's Assembly was abolished and restrictions on independent candidates were removed. The elections were, none the less, boycotted by the principal opposition parties, in protest at the Government's refusal to concede to demands that the elections be removed from the supervision of the Ministry of the Interior and that the state of emergency be repealed. The credibility of the polls was further undermined by the low rate of participation by voters, estimated at 20%–30% of the registered electorate. Of the 444 elective seats in the new Assembly, the NDP won 348, the National Progressive Unionist Party six, and independent candidates (the majority of whom were affiliated to the NDP) 83. Voting in the remaining seven seats was suspended. Following a reorganization of the Council of Ministers in May 1991, President Mubarak stated that domestic political reform, in particular the extension of the democratic franchise, was to be one of the administration's principal aims. The national state of emergency was renewed for a further three-year period in June, in view of what the Government stated was the continued threat of internal and external subversion.

President Mubarak was formally proposed for a third term of office in July 1993, and in October his nomination was approved by some 94.9% of the valid votes cast at a national referendum. The official figure of an electoral turn-out of 84% was regarded with scepticism by many observers. The opposition parties, none of which had endorsed Mubarak's candidature demanded reforms including amendment of the Constitution to allow direct presidential elections, the unrestricted formation of political parties, and the introduction of a two-term limit to the presidency. Later in October Sidqi formed a new Council of Ministers, including 10 new ministers, although the allocation of most principal portfolios remained unchanged.

In May 1994 representatives of all Egypt's legal political parties and of its professional associations were chosen to form preparatory committees for a National Dialogue Congress. The Muslim Brotherhood, which was barred from forming its own political party, was excluded from the Congress, although it was believed that some of its supporters might attend as trade union representatives. The credibility of the Congress was undermined in advance by the withdrawal of the New Wafd Party and the Nasserist Party from preparatory committees, with the New Wafd Party accusing the Government of seeking to manipulate the agenda of the dialogue. The National Dialogue Congress held its first procedural session in late June and ended less than two weeks later. Three committees (charged, respectively, with consideration of political, economic and social affairs) were reported to have forwarded to the President only general, non-binding recommendations. With regard to political reform, the Congress was said to have suggested, *inter alia*, that elections should be supervised by the judiciary and that voting should be reorganized on the basis of party lists.

These recommendations were not implemented at legislative elections held in November–December 1995, at which candidates of the NDP won 316 seats, thus retaining a decisive (albeit reduced) majority in the People's Assembly.. The New Wafd Party took six seats, the National Progressive Unionist Party (NPUP) five and the LSP and the Nasserist Party one seat each. Of the 115 independent candidates elected, 99 were reported to have immediately joined or rejoined the NDP. Allegations of the intimidation of opposition supporters and of other electoral malpractices on the part of agents acting for the NDP were widespread. A new Council of Ministers was appointed in January 1996, with Kamal Ahmad al-Ganzouri (hitherto Minister of Planning) replacing Sidqi as Prime Minister. The Government was reorganized in July 1997, when Mubarak also appointed new governors to 10 of the country's governorates; the former head of state security, Gen. Mustafa Abd al-Qader, notably became governor of Menia, where there had been persistent Islamist attacks and, recently, violent protests against a new legislation removing rent controls on agricultural land.

During 1998 domestic criticism of the Government resulted in the imposition of severe restrictions on the freedom of the press (in place of more liberal legislation adopted in 1996). Dissenting editors of a number of newspapers were replaced with Government supporters, while six journalists were imprisoned on charges of libel between January and October. Moreover, a new law was introduced whereby individuals were prohibited from owning publishing companies, and in June stringent printing restrictions were imposed on two leading independent English-language newspapers. At mid-term elections to the Shura Council in June 1998 the NDP retained 85 of the 88 contested seats. Most opposition parties boycotted the poll.

In June 1999 Mubarak was formally nominated for a fourth presidential term; his nomination was approved by 93.8% of the valid votes cast in a national referendum held on 26 September. Voter turn-out was reported to be 79.2%. Of the four main legal opposition parties, only the Nasserist Party had refused to endorse Mubarak's candidature. In October Mubarak appointed Dr Atif Muhammad Obeid, previously Minister of the Public Enterprise Sector and responsible for the Government's privatization programme, to succeed al-Ganzouri as Prime Minister. Obeid's appointment was widely interpreted as an indication that economic reforms would be accelerated in Egypt. None the less, although his Council of Ministers included 13 new ministers (among them Dr Midhat Hasanayn as Minister of Finance), most strategic portfolios did not change hands. Meanwhile, in September an assailant was killed by presidential escorts following an alleged attack in Port Said on President Mubarak, who sustained a slight injury in the incident. The authorities claimed that the attack was not politically motivated.

Legislation concerning the activities of non-governmental organizations (NGOs), approved by the People's Assembly in May 1999, attracted strong criticism from human rights groups, which claimed that the new law would compromise the independence of the organizations through stringent state regulation of their activities. In early June 2000, in response to a judicial challenge by a local NGO, the Supreme Constitutional Court annulled the implementation of the law, ruling it to be unconstitutional on the grounds that it interfered with the fundamental right of freedom of association.

In early February 2000 President Mubarak's son, Gamal, was appointed to the 24-member general secretariat of the NDP. None the less, Gamal Mubarak strenuously denied rumours that he was preparing to stand as an NDP candidate in the forthcoming general election. Also in February the People's Assembly approved a presidential decree extending the state of emergency for a further three years. In the following month the Political Parties Committee approved the formation of a new political party, Hizb al-Wifaq al-Qawmi (or the National Accord Party), bringing the number of officially recognized parties to 15.

Some 2,000 students were involved in clashes with the security forces outside the Al-Azhar University in Cairo in May 2000. The students were protesting against a decision taken by the Ministry of Culture in November 1999 to reprint a book by a well-known Syrian author, Haidar Haidar, which they claimed was insulting to Islam. (The book, first published in 1983, had been banned in most other Arab countries). Police used rubber bullets and tear gas to quell the disturbance, and it was reported that six policemen and more than 40 students were injured during the skirmishes. Although several students were arrested, charges issued against them for crimes such as vandalism and rioting were abandoned in mid-July 2000. Following the riots the Government ordered that the book be removed from sale. The protest was the culmination of a campaign by the SLP's newspaper *Ash-Shaa'b* against the book, and in late May the Political Parties Committee suspended both the SLP and *Ash-Shaa'b* on the grounds that the party had exceeded its political mandate. In mid-July charges were filed against leaders of the SLP (among them the editor of *Ash-Shaa'b*, Magdi Hussein), including 'offering a platform to incite to harm general order' and having links with the prohibited Muslim Brotherhood. Later that month, however, an administrative court in Cairo ruled that the suspension of the SLP and its newspaper was unconstitutional. None the less, the SLP's activities remained officially in abeyance, but in early September the Judicial Administrative Court overturned the decision to suspend *Ash-Shaa'b* on the grounds that the ban on publication contravened constitutional

guarantees regarding freedom of expression; however, it also ruled that it did not have the jurisdiction to decide on the legality of the suspension of the SLP, and referred the matter to a higher court. Meanwhile, in June the Government ordered the closure of the Ibn Khaldoun Centre for Social and Development Studies, and the centre's director, Prof. Sa'adeddin Ibrahim (a prominent academic and pro-democracy activist), was arrested on suspicion of collecting funds without prior authority and defaming Egypt through his work. It was alleged that Ibrahim had accepted more than US $220,000 from the European Commission to produce a video documentary on the electoral process in Egypt. The decision provoked forceful criticism from the USA and other Western governments as well as from national and international human rights organizations. Ibrahim was released on bail in early August, but it was announced in September that he was to be tried on charges of receiving funds from abroad without official permission. Furthermore, in November military prosecutors announced that they were to investigate charges of espionage against Ibrahim.

Meanwhile, in June 2000 the State Security Court in Cairo sentenced three NDP parliamentary deputies (including a former Minister of Tourism) to 10 years' imprisonment, with hard labour, for their role in the embezzlement of an estimated £E1,600m. from five banks during the early 1990s. A further NDP deputy received a one-year prison sentence, and 28 businessmen and bank officials also implicated in the scandal received custodial terms ranging from one to 15 years, many with hard labour.

The Supreme Constitutional Court issued a judgment in mid-July 2000 that the People's Assembly elected in 1995 was illegitimate (as was the Assembly elected in 1990), and that the existing electoral system was invalid since the constitutional requirement that the judiciary have sole responsibility for the supervision of elections had not been adhered to. Later that month President Mubarak called an extraordinary session of the Assembly, at which two amendments to the existing electoral legislation were unanimously approved: these provided for judges to monitor voting in the impending general election, which was to be held over three stages in October–November 2000. Fourad Serag ed-Din, the leader of the New Wafd Party died in August; the party elected Nu'man Jum'ah as his successor in the following month.

Almost 4,000 candidates contested the 444 elective seats in the People's Assembly at polls conducted in three rounds, each of two stages, beginning on 18 October, 29 October and 8 November 2000. According to figures published by the Ministry of the Interior in mid-November, the NDP increased its majority, with candidates of the ruling party taking 353 seats. Independent candidates secured 72 seats, but it was reported that 35 of these had either joined or rejoined the NDP shortly after the elections. The New Wafd Party won seven seats, the NPUP six, the Nasserist Party three and the LSP one seat. The rate of participation by voters at the various stages was officially stated to be between 15% and 40%. There were reports of outbreaks of violence in many parts of the country, primarily involving the security forces and members of the outlawed Muslim Brotherhood, and voting for the two seats in one constituency in Alexandria was postponed following the arrest of some 20 Muslim Brotherhood activists. At least 14 people were killed, and hundreds of others injured, during the voting period, while large numbers of Islamists were arrested for public order offences. At its inaugural session in mid-December the new Assembly re-elected as its Speaker Ahmad Fathi Surur, who had held the post since 1990.

The summit meeting of the Arab League held in Jordan in late March 2001 appointed Amr Moussa, Egypt's Minister of Foreign Affairs since 1991, as the organization's Secretary-General. Ahmad Maher was appointed to replace Moussa in his government post in mid-May 2001.

Since 1992 the Government's attempts to suppress Islamist fundamentalism has dominated the domestic political agenda. During the early 1990s militant violence increasingly targeted foreign tourists visiting Egypt, as well as foreign investors, and there were frequent confrontations between Islamist militants and the security forces. In May 1993 a report published by a prominent human rights organization, Amnesty International, alleged that the Egyptian Government was systematically maltreating political detainees, and in November the organization accused the Government of breaching the UN Convention against Torture and Other Cruel, Inhuman or Degrading Treatment or Punishment.

In January 1994 the security forces were reported to have detained some 1,000 suspected fundamentalist activists in response to attacks on their members during that month. In March nine members of the Vanguard of Conquest (a faction of Islamic Jihad) were sentenced to death after having been convicted of conspiring to assassinate the Prime Minister in November 1993. In April 1994 the chief of the anti-terrorist branch of the State Security Investigation Section was assassinated by members of Jama'ah al-Islamiyah (one of Egypt's principal militant Islamist groups), prompting retaliatory security operations. Following the assassination emergency laws giving the security forces wide powers to arrest and detain suspects were renewed for a further three years. (The state of emergency was renewed in 1997 and again in 2000—see above.) In July 1994 a further five members of the Vanguard of Conquest were sentenced to death for the attempted assassination of the Minister of the Interior in August 1993.

In early 1995 the Government began to take steps to isolate the more moderate Muslim Brotherhood and to weaken its political influence in the approach to that year's legislative elections. Several leading members of the Brotherhood were arrested, and both President Mubarak and the Minister of the Interior claimed that there was evidence of links between the movement and Islamist extremists. The Government also acted to curb Islamist influence within professional organizations; in February the judiciary was accorded wide powers to intervene in union elections and to prevent Muslim Brotherhood members from standing. In January, meanwhile, clashes between extremists and security forces in Upper Egypt resulted in 87 deaths. In June Mubarak escaped an assassination attempt in Ethiopia while he was travelling to a summit meeting of the Organization of African Unity (OAU) in Addis Ababa; it was widely believed that the assailants were members of either Islamic Jihad or Jama'ah al-Islamiyah. Egypt's claim that the gunmen had been aided by Sudanese agents was denied by the Sudanese Government. (In September 1996 three Egyptians, reported to be members of unspecified Islamist groups, were sentenced to death by the Ethiopian Supreme Court for their involvement in the attempted assassination.)

In April 1996 12 prominent members of the Muslim Brotherhood were arrested and charged with attempting to revive the movement's activities and restore its links with extremist groups. For the first time the detainees included a member of the Brotherhood's Supreme Guidance Council. Three of those arrested were founder members of a new political organization, the Al-Wasat (Centre) Party, which the authorities claimed was serving as a 'front' for Brotherhood activities. The party's founders—who included Muslims, Christians, leftists and Nasserist activists—insisted, however, that they were seeking to create a political group that occupied the middle ground between the State and its fundamentalist Islamist opponents. (Twice in 1998 and again in June 1999 Al-Wasat was denied legal status by the authorities.) Also in April 1996 18 Greek tourists were killed in an attack on an hotel in Cairo. Jama'ah al-Islamiyah admitted responsibility for the deaths, but claimed that its intended targets had been Israeli tourists in order to avenge the victims of Israeli military operations in Lebanon. In the following month the Egyptian Government was reported to have rejected an offer by Islamist fundamentalists halt to their campaign of violence against security forces and tourists, on the grounds that it would not negotiate with 'militant groups'.

In September 1997 a military court in Haekstep, north of the capital, conducted a military trial on an unprecedented scale of suspected Islamist militants; of 98 defendants convicted, four were sentenced to death and eight to life imprisonment. A few days later nine German tourists were killed, and 11 others injured, as a result of an attack on a tourist bus in Cairo. Although the perpetrators of the assault were widely believed to be members of Jama'ah al-Islamiyah, the Egyptian Government claimed, in an apparent attempt to protect the country's vital tourism industry, that the attack was an isolated incident unconnected with terrorism. (In May 1998 two men were hanged, having been convicted in October 1997 of the attack.) In November 1997 the massacre near Luxor of 70 people, including 58 foreign tourists, by members of Jama'ah al-Islamiyah severely undermined both the crucial tourism sector and the claims of the Government to have suppressed Islamist violence. Mubarak was critical of the security forces for failing to protect tourists, and publicly discredited the Minister of the Interior, Hussein Muhammad al-Alfi, who had formulated the Government's uncompromising policies aimed at eradicating

Islamist militancy; al-Alfi was replaced by Habib Ibrahim el-Adli, hitherto the head of the state security services. Mubarak ordered a heightened security presence at all tourist sites and placed the Prime Minister at the head of a special committee charged with devising a plan to safeguard the tourism sector. (In June 1998 two senior police-officers—the first to stand trial for 18 years—who had been responsible for security at Luxor's tourist sites at the time of the massacre were dismissed and fined, after a police disciplinary hearing found them guilty of gross negligence.) In December 1997 a number of Jama'ah al-Islamiyah's exiled leaders claimed that the Luxor massacre had been perpetrated by a 'rogue' element acting without the authorization of the group's central leadership; furthermore, the leaders in exile announced that Jama'ah al-Islamiyah (at least, those members under their specific authority) would no longer target tourists in their conflict with the Government. (In May 1999 security officials in Switzerland alleged that the Saudi Arabian-born militant Islamist, Osama bin Laden, had been responsible for the Luxor killings.)

New state security measures adopted by the Ministry of the Interior during 1998 included a relaxation of the criteria whereby affiliation to Islamist groups was assumed, and the release of some Islamist prisoners who had renounced connections with illegal organizations. By June 106 death sentences had been imposed upon Islamist fundamentalists since 1992, of which 72 had been exacted. Internal dissent within Jama'ah al-Islamiyah remained evident: in October one of the group's imprisoned leaders urged all Islamist groups to form a 'world Islamic front' that would employ exclusively peaceful means; however, reports that the group had changed its political strategy were later denied by another senior member. In early 1999 one of Jama'ah al-Islamiyah's founders denied reports that the organization was planning to establish a political party, although speculation surrounding the issue continued. In March Jama'ah al-Islamiyah declared a unilateral cease-fire and announced a new strategy of exerting maximum political pressure on the Government without the use of violence. However, it remained unclear as to whether the group's military wing would end its violent campaign. Although the Government gave no formal acknowledgement of the cease-fire, an acceleration in the release of imprisoned Islamist militants was subsequently evident. In April the Ministry of the Interior released some 1,200 Jama'ah al-Islamiyah detainees (reportedly among them two of the group's leaders who were involved in the assassination of President Sadat in 1981), and a further 1,200 were released in December. Nevertheless, government officials strongly denied that any deal had been concluded with the proscribed organization, and arrests and trials of suspected Islamist militants continued throughout 1999. In February it was reported that three men suspected of involvement in the 1997 Luxor attack had been arrested on the Uruguayan–Brazilian border and were expected to stand trial in Cairo. In the same month proceedings began against 107 alleged members of Islamic Jihad who were charged with conspiring to overthrow the Government, in the largest security trial in Egypt since 1992. In April 1999 nine of the defendants were sentenced to death, 78 received sentences ranging from one year to life imprisonment, all with hard labour, while 20 were acquitted. In May the security services detained 23 suspects on the grounds that they were seeking to revive the activities in Egypt of the Vanguard of Conquest. In the following month 20 members of Jama'ah al-Islamiyah were given custodial sentences, having been convicted by a military court of planning a bomb attack on President Mubarak's Alexandria residence in 1996; that death sentences were not imposed was interpreted by the organization's lawyers as a positive response to the recent cease-fire declaration.

The unofficial truce between the Government and Jama'ah al-Islamiyah was apparently jeopardized in September 1999, when security forces in Giza shot dead four alleged members of the organization, including the commander of its military wing, Farid Salem al-Kedwani, in their first security action against the group since the implementation of the cease-fire in March. In November charges against 20 alleged members of the Muslim Brotherhood, who had been arrested in the previous month on charges of plotting to overthrow the Government and of infiltrating professional syndicates in order to undermine national security, were modified by the military court where they were standing trial from 'belonging' to the Muslim Brotherhood to 'participating in the founding and management' of the organization; any conviction under these charges was likely to result in much harsher sentences. The trial was initially postponed for procedural reasons but resumed in January 2000 (see below). Meanwhile, in October 1999 the Egyptian Organization for Human Rights (EOHR) drew attention to the campaign of arrests against moderate Islamists, asserting that 200 members of the Muslim Brotherhood had been arrested since the beginning of the year, of whom 100 remained in detention.

In early January 2000 three days of violent clashes between Muslims and Copts in the southern village of el-Kosheh, reported to be the worst incidence of sectarian violence in Egypt for decades, resulted in the deaths of 20 Christians and 1 Muslim. Although the EOHR claimed that during 1991–98 about 99 Copts had been killed by militant Islamists, the conclusions of the organization's inquiry into the violence of January 2000, the findings of which were published the following month, inferred that the primary cause of the violence was the 'economic inequalities' between the relatively prosperous Coptic majority and the poorer Muslim minority. There was a further outbreak of violence in el-Kosheh in late February. (In February 2001 four Muslims were sentenced to custodial terms of up to 10 years for their part in the violence of early 2000; a further 92 defendants were acquitted.)

Meanwhile, in late October 1999 there were newspaper reports that a new military leadership of Jama'ah al-Islamiyah had been established under Ala Abd ar-Raziq. It was rumoured later in the year that a power struggle was taking place within the group, and that the new Chairman of its Shura Council was Moustafa Hamzah, the chief suspect in the 1995 assassination attempt on President Mubarak. In early February 2000 senior members of the leadership of Islamic Jihad publicly urged the cessation of the organization's armed activities, appealing to militants to concentrate their activities on the liberation of the al-Aqsa Mosque in Jerusalem; this, noted as the first time that the group's leaders had called for a cease-fire, followed recent reports that a 'coup' within Islamic Jihad had resulted in the removal from the high command of Dr Ayman az-Zawahri. Later in February eight prominent Islamists were arrested on charges of seeking to revive the Muslim Brotherhood, shortly after the proscribed organization had issued a statement denouncing the Government's decision to extend the state of emergency for a further three years. In March, none the less, between 500 and 1,000 Islamists, mostly members of Jama'ah al-Islamiyah or Islamic Jihad, were reportedly released from prison; a further 500 Islamists were freed in July. Despite regular releases of large numbers of militants since 1998, human rights organizations maintained that more than 15,000 remained in detention, many of whom were being held without charge under the country's emergency laws. Furthermore, during the approach to the legislative elections the authorities arrested increasing numbers of Muslim Brotherhood members, in what was widely acknowledged as an effort to prevent their standing as candidates for the People's Assembly. In mid-November 2000 the Higher Military Court in Cairo pronounced guilty verdicts on 15 of those arrested in late 1999 on charges of reviving the Brotherhood, sentencing them to between three and five years' imprisonment; the five other defendants were acquitted.

Egyptian mediation was prominent in the Middle East peace process throughout the 1990s. The country played an important role in the efforts leading to the convening of the Middle East peace conference in Madrid, Spain, in October 1991, and an Egyptian delegation attended the first, symbolic session of the conference. Egyptian mediators were influential in the secret negotiations between Israel and the PLO that led to the signing of the Declaration of Principles on Palestinian Self-Rule in September 1993, and PLO and Israeli delegations subsequently began to meet regularly in Cairo or at the Red Sea port of Taba to discuss the detailed implementation of the Declaration of Principles. In November King Hussein of Jordan visited Cairo for talks on the Middle East peace process—his first visit since the Gulf crisis of 1990–91, which had damaged relations between the two countries. In May 1994 an agreement on Palestinian self-rule in the Gaza Strip and the Jericho area (for full details, see the chapter on Israel) was signed in Cairo by the Israeli Prime Minister, Itzhak Rabin, and the PLO Chairman, Yasser Arafat, at a ceremony presided over by Mubarak. Two months later the Egyptian President travelled to the Syrian capital, Damascus, in an effort to break the deadlock in the peace negotiations between Syria and Israel. However, despite an official visit to Egypt by President Ezer Weizman in December (the first such visit by an Israeli Head of State), relations between Egypt and Israel began to deteriorate. Egypt was concerned that the Middle East peace process might collapse

unless Israel showed more flexibility and the Palestinians secured tangible benefits from the peace agreement as quickly as possible. Egypt hosted summit meetings of Arab leaders in December 1994 and February 1995, prompting further censure from the Israeli Government. Further tension arose when Mubarak reiterated his warning that Egypt would not sign the Treaty on the Non-Proliferation of Nuclear Weapons (or Non-Proliferation Treaty—NPT, see p. 77), which was due for renewal in April 1995, unless Israel also agreed to sign it; he urged other states to do likewise. In March 1995 Israel offered to sign the NPT once it had concluded peace treaties with all of the Arab states and with Iran, and to allow Egypt to inspect its research nuclear reactor at Nahal Shorek (but not the nuclear facility at Dimona). Egypt rejected both offers, but adopted a more conciliatory line on the issue. Meanwhile, Egypt's stance with regard to the NPT antagonized the USA, which insisted that the continuation of US aid to Egypt depended on Egypt's signing the Treaty.

President Mubarak made his first visit to Jordan since the Gulf crisis in January 1995, when he met King Hussein at Aqaba. The visit was regarded as a sign of an improvement in relations between the two countries, following Jordan's signing of a peace treaty with Israel in July 1994.

Although relations between Egypt and Israel deteriorated in August 1995, after it was revealed that Israeli soldiers had killed a large number of Egyptian prisoners of war during the Suez crisis in 1956 and the Six-Day War in 1967, Egypt continued its mediatory role in the complex negotiations that eventually led to the signing, in Washington, DC, of the Israeli-Palestinian Interim Agreement on the West Bank and the Gaza Strip in September 1995. In November Mubarak made his first visit to Israel as President of Egypt, to attend the funeral of the assassinated Israeli Prime Minister, Itzhak Rabin. Egypt also participated in meetings leading to the resumption of peace negotiations between Israel and Syria at the end of 1995. In March 1996, following a series of Palestinian suicide bomb attacks in Israel, Egypt and the USA co-hosted a one-day 'Summit of Peacemakers' at the Red Sea resort of Sharm esh-Sheikh. Egypt's relations with Israel deteriorated again in April, as a consequence of Israeli military operations in Lebanon (q.v.). In June, in response to the apparently rejectionist stance of the new Israeli administration of Binyamin Netanyahu with regard to the exchange of land for peace, Mubarak convened an emergency summit meeting of the Arab League in Cairo—the first such meeting for six years. The summit's final communiqué reaffirmed the Arab states' commitment to peace, but warned that peace and any further *rapprochement* between them and Israel depended on Israel's returning all the Arab land that it occupied in 1967. In July Netanyahu visited Egypt for talks with Mubarak; this was the Israeli Prime Minister's first official visit to an Arab country since his election to the premiership. The Arab League again met in emergency session in Cairo in September, in response to a serious escalation in Palestinian–Israeli hostilities. In March 1997 Egypt, in common with the other Arab League members, condemned the Israeli Government for ordering the start of construction work on the new Israeli settlement of Har Homa in East Jerusalem; this controversial decision by Israel effectively brought about the suspension of the peace process for the remainder of that year. In April 1998 Mubarak and Netanyahu met (in Cairo) for the first time in 11 months to discuss a US initiative, supported by Egypt, to revive the peace process. However, Netanyahu rejected the proposal, and the renewed strain in Israeli–Egyptian relations became increasingly apparent. In June, after talks were held with Yasser Arafat to discuss an Israeli proposal for a new Madrid peace conference, Mubarak accused Netahyahu of 'destroying the peace process' by seeking to annul the first Madrid agreement, and bilateral relations were subsequently reported to have deteriorated to their worst level since 1979.

President Mubarak cautiously welcomed the Wye River Memorandum signed by Netanyahu and Arafat in October 1998 (see the chapter on Israel). However, in January 1999 Egypt suspended all contacts with the Israeli Government over its decision to suspend the implementation of the agreement. In March Egypt and Jordan made a joint declaration in support of the Palestinians' right to declare an independent state after the scheduled expiry of the Oslo accords in May. Subsequently, however, owing to an increasingly volatile security situation in the Israeli-Occupied Territories and in view of the forthcoming Israeli general election, Egypt and Jordan joined other countries in urging Yasser Arafat to postpone his planned declaration of statehood. The election, in May, of the leader of the One Israel alliance, Ehud Barak, to the Israeli premiership was generally welcomed in Egypt, but in July the Egyptian Minister of Foreign Affairs emphasized that there could be no normalization of Egyptian–Israeli relations prior to the resumption of comprehensive peace talks. In that month Mubarak became the first Arab leader to meet the new Israeli Prime Minister, expressing optimism that Barak could revitalize the stalled peace process. Egyptian mediation was subsequently influential in discussions between Israeli and Palestinian negotiators that led to the signing of the Sharm esh-Sheikh Memorandum by Barak and Arafat in early September 1999 (see the chapter on Israel).

In mid-February 2000 President Mubarak made his first ever visit to Lebanon. The main purpose of the visit was to demonstrate Egypt's solidarity with Lebanon following Israeli air attacks, condemned by Mubarak as 'criminal acts', on targets in Lebanon earlier in the month. None the less, Egypt continued to play an important role in the peace process during 2000. In early March Arafat and Barak attended a summit meeting in Sharm esh-Sheikh, at which the two leaders agreed a formula for the resumption of peace talks. Mubarak stressed that Egypt would recognize the unilateral declaration of Palestinian statehood in September, which Arafat intended to announce if no final settlement had been negotiated by then. Barak and Arafat both made brief visits to Cairo prior to the US-hosted summit at Camp David in July. Following the apparent failure of the summit, Mubarak emphasized that he would not pressure Arafat to make concessions regarding the central issue of the status of Jerusalem, and urged all Arab states to unite in support of the Palestinians until they regained all their legitimate rights in accordance with the pertinent UN resolutions.

Following the outbreak in Jerusalem in late September 2000 of violent clashes between Palestinians and Israeli security forces, which swiftly spread throughout the West Bank and Gaza, Mubarak assumed an important role in attempting to prevent the violence from escalating into a major regional crisis. In early October Mubarak hosted a continuation of talks between Yasser Arafat and the US Secretary of State, Madeleine Albright, that had begun in Paris, France; Barak refused to attend the session in Egypt. In mid-October, following mediation by the UN Secretary-General, Kofi Annan, Barak and Arafat agreed to lead delegations to a summit meeting at Sharm esh-Sheikh, brokered by US President Bill Clinton. An agreement concluded after two days of intensive negotiations proved unviable, and violence persisted. Later that month an emergency meeting of Heads of State of Arab League countries was convened in Cairo, at which Arab leaders held Israel solely to blame for the violence. In late November Egypt recalled its ambassador to Tel–Aviv, denouncing Israel's 'escalation of aggression and deliberate use of force against the Palestinian people'. Relations between the two countries deteriorated further at the end of that month when an Egyptian engineer was charged with having gathered information regarding Egyptian economic and military projects for the Israeli overseas intelligence service.

During a visit to Cairo in April 1996 the US Secretary of Defense, William Perry, announced that the USA would supply advanced military equipment to Egypt, including 21 F-16 fighter aircraft, in acknowledgement of the country's key role in the Middle East peace process. However, there have remained frequent tensions in relations between Egypt and the USA. In August 1998 Egypt was highly critical of US military air-strikes against targets in Afghanistan and Sudan held by the US administration to be associated with the militant Islamist Osama bin Laden (who was believed to be based in Afghanistan). Tensions were further exacerbated by the air-strikes undertaken against Iraq (q.v.) by US and British forces in December 1998, since Mubarak had consistently urged a diplomatic solution to the issue of weapons inspections. Differences persisted as US Secretary of Defense William Cohen visited Cairo and other regional capitals in March 1999 to seek support for a renewed air campaign against Iraq. While in Egypt Cohen agreed to supply Egypt with US $3,200m. of US defence equipment, including a further 24 F-16 fighter aircraft. Following a further visit by Cohen, it was announced in April 2000 that the USA would supply short-range missiles in order to modernize Egypt's air-defence system. Meanwhile, Mubarak visited Washington in June 1999 and the two countries made significant progress on proposals for the resumption of Middle East peace talks, culminating in the signing of the Sharm esh-Sheikh Memorandum in September. In late 2000 the Mubarak and

Clinton administrations co-operated closely in their efforts to mediate in the Middle East crisis (see above).

Egypt's relations with Libya improved steadily during the 1990s, and Egypt joined the Community of the Sahel-Saharan States, which was established in Tripoli in 1997. Meanwhile, bilateral links were dominated by the repercussions of the Lockerbie bombing (see the chapter on Libya). Egypt was active in seeking to avert a confrontation between Libya and the USA and its Western allies, which could threaten not only the livelihood of some 1m. expatriate Egyptian workers in Libya but also a steadily growing market for its exports. Following the suspension of UN sanctions against Libya in April 1999, the national carrier, EgyptAir, resumed regular flights to Tripoli in July 2000; Libyan air services to Egypt resumed later that month.

Egypt has a long-standing border dispute with Sudan concerning the so-called Halaib triangle. Relations deteriorated sharply in mid-1995, after Egypt accused Sudan of complicity in the attempted assassination of President Mubarak in Addis Ababa (see above). Egypt strengthened its control of the Halaib triangle, and subsequently (in contravention of a bilateral agreement concluded in 1978) imposed visa and permit requirements on Sudanese nationals visiting or resident in Egypt. In September 1995 the OAU accused Sudan of direct involvement in the assassination attempt, and in December the organization demanded that Sudan extradite immediately three individuals sought in connection with the attack. (It was reported in mid-1999 that one of the suspects had been extradited to Cairo.) In February 1996 the Sudanese authorities introduced permit requirements for Egyptian nationals resident in Sudan. President Mubarak met with his Sudanese counterpart, Omar al-Bashir, at the Arab League summit meeting in Cairo in May. In July, however, Egypt accused Sudan of harbouring Egyptian terrorists, contrary to an agreement concluded at the summit meeting. None the less, Egypt opposed the imposition by the UN of more stringent economic sanctions against Sudan (q.v.), on the grounds that they would harm the Sudanese people more than the regime.

In June 1997 the al-Bashir regime accused Egypt of providing Sudanese opposition forces with military training, and in October there were Sudanese press reports that Egypt was obstructing the import of medical supplies to Halaib. Despite such accusations, and claims made by members of the Sudanese opposition in January 1998 that the al-Bashir administration was supporting Egypt's armed Islamist groups, there was evidence of attempts to normalize relations. Bilateral security talks recommenced in August 1997 after a year-long suspension. In February 1998 river transport resumed between the Egyptian port of Aswan and Wadi Halfa in Sudan, and in April the two countries agreed to establish a joint ministerial committee (involving the Ministers of Higher Education, Defence and Irrigation). Although Sudan considered the presence of Sudanese opposition leaders in Egypt an obstacle to the normalization process, a meeting in Cairo, in May 1999, between representatives of the Sudanese Government and Sudan's former President Gaafar Mohammed Nimeri, to discuss arrangements for his return from exile, represented significant progress on this issue. In December Egypt and Sudan agreed to a full normalization of relations, and resolved to co-operate in addressing their border dispute. Taking up his post in Khartoum in March 2000, the new Egyptain ambassador to Sudan expressed optimism regarding the future of diplomatic relations between the two countries. In September the two countries signed a number of bilateral co-operation accords.

In February 2000 Pope John Paul II became the first Roman Catholic Pontiff to visit Egypt, where he held talks with President Mubarak, with the Grand Sheikh of the Al-Azhar University, Muhammad Said, and with the Patriarch of the Orthodox Coptic church, Shenoudah III.

Government

Legislative power is held by the unicameral Majlis ash-Sha'ab (People's Assembly), which has 454 members: 10 nominated by the President and 444 directly elected for five years from 222 constituencies. The Assembly nominates the President, who is elected by popular referendum for six years (renewable). The President, who is Head of State, has executive powers and appoints one or more Vice-Presidents, a Prime Minister and a Council of Ministers. There is also a 210-member advisory body, the Shura Council. The country is divided into 27 governorates.

Defence

In August 2000 Egypt had total armed forces of 448,500 (army 320,000, air defence command 80,000, navy an estimated 18,500, air force 30,000), with 254,000 reserves. There is a selective three-year period of national service. The state public budget for the year ending 30 June 1999 allocated £E8,290m (equivalent to 11.0% of total spending) to defence.

Economic Affairs

In 1998, according to estimates by the World Bank, Egypt's gross national product (GNP), measured at average 1996–98 prices, was US $79,185m., equivalent to $1,290 per head (or $3,146 per head on an international purchasing-power parity basis). During 1990–98, it was estimated, GNP per head increased, in real terms, by an average of 2.7% per year. Over the same period, the population increased by an average of 2.3% per year. Total GNP for 1999 was estimated at $87,500m., equivalent to $1,400 per head. Gross domestic product (GDP) increased at an average annual rate of 4.4% in 1990–99. At factor cost, real GDP increased by 6.0% in the year ending 30 June 1999.

Measured at constant 1996/97 prices, agriculture (including forestry and fishing) contributed 17.0% of GDP in 1998/99, and employed an estimated 34.0% of the economically active population in 1999. The principal crops include cotton, rice, wheat, sugar cane, maize and tomatoes. Exports of food and live animals accounted for 6.9% of total exports in 1997. During 1990–99 agricultural GDP increased at an average annual rate of 3.1%. Agricultural GDP grew by 3.7% in 1998/99.

Industry (including mining, manufacturing, construction and power) engaged 23.4% of the employed labour force at the time of the 1996 census, and provided 32.7% of GDP (at 1996/97 prices) in 1998/99. During 1990–99 industrial GDP expanded at an average annual rate of 4.7%. Industrial GDP increased by 6.7% in 1998/99.

Mining and manufacturing together contributed 25.1% of GDP (at 1996/97 prices) in 1998/99. Egypt's mineral resources include petroleum, natural gas, phosphates, manganese, uranium, coal, iron ore and gold. Although the mining sector employed only 0.4% of the working population in 1996, the petroleum industry contributed 6.0% of GDP in 1998/99, and petroleum and petroleum products accounted for 44.3% of total export earnings in 1997. Petroleum production averaged an estimated 700,000 barrels per day in 2000, and in that year Egypt's oil reserves were estimated to total about 8,200m. barrels (sufficient to sustain production at 2000 levels for almost 12 years), compared with oil industry figures of proven reserves of 2,900m. (sustainable for 10 years) at the end of 1999. At the end of 1999 Egypt's proven natural gas reserves totalled 1,000,000m. cu m. In 2000 all the natural gas produced (about 65m. cu m per day) was consumed domestically, but the Government planned to begin exporting in 2001.

Manufacturing engaged 13.8% of the employed labour force in 1996. Based on the value of output, the main branches of manufacturing in 1995 were food products (accounting for 18.8% of the total), petroleum refineries (15.6%) and textiles (10.4%). During 1990–98 the real GDP of the manufacturing sector increased by an average of 5.3% per year. The combined GDP of the mining and manufacturing sectors expanded by 5.8% in 1998/99.

Energy is derived principally from hydroelectric power and coal. In 1998 fuel imports accounted for about 5% of the value of merchandise imports.

Services contributed 50.3% of GDP (at 1996/97 prices) in 1998/99, and employed 45.7% of the working population in 1996. By the late 1980s tourism had become one of the most dynamic sectors of the Egyptian economy. For much of the 1990s, however, the sector was severely undermined by the campaign of violence aimed by fundamentalist Islamists at tourist targets, and visitor numbers and tourism revenues declined significantly. By 1999, however, there were signs of a recovery in the sector. In 1990–99 the real GDP of the services sector increased by an average of 4.3% per year. Services GDP increased by 6.4% in 1998/99.

In 1999 Egypt recorded a visible trade deficit of US $9,928m., while there was a deficit of $1,635m. on the current account of the balance of payments. In 1997 the principal source of imports (13.1%) was the USA; other major suppliers were Germany, Italy and France. The USA was also the principal market for exports (11.4%), followed by Italy (11.2%), Israel, Germany and the Netherlands. Egypt's principal exports in 1997 were petroleum and petroleum products, textiles, food, clothing and chemicals. The principal imports were machinery and transport equipment, basic manufactures, chemicals and cereals.

For the financial year ending 30 June 1998 there was a consolidated budget deficit of £E2,591m., equivalent to 0.9% of GDP. For 2000/01 there was a projected deficit of £E14,000m. in the state public budget. Egypt's external debt totalled US $31,964m. at the end of 1998, of which $27,670m. was long-term public debt. In that year the cost of servicing the foreign debt was equivalent to 9.5% of the value of exports of goods and services. The annual rate of inflation averaged 9.7% in 1990–99. Consumer prices increased by an average of 3.0% in 1999. Some 8.5% of the total labour force were unemployed at the time of the 1996 census.

Egypt is a member of the Common Market for Eastern and Southern Africa (COMESA, see p. 148), the Organization of Arab Petroleum Exporting Countries (OAPEC, see p. 264), the African Petroleum Producers' Association (see p. 303), and the Arab Co-operation Council (see p. 306).

The continued strategy under the Government of Dr Atif Obeid of maintaining sizeable foreign-exchange reserves as well as a high exchange rate against the US dollar has rendered the task of undertaking wide-ranging reforms without exacerbating an already high level of poverty and risking social unrest extremely complex. Since the introduction of the Government's economic reform programme in 1991, under which a major privatization scheme was launched, 135 companies have been transferred to private control. However, progress slowed during 2000, with protracted delays in the privatization of Telecom Egypt and the four major state-owned banks. A liquidity crisis during 1999 and early 2000–the major causes of which were the government arrears to the private sector, increased expenditure by the al-Ganzouri administration on major infrastructure projects, and a depletion in the main sources of hard currency (principally petroleum sales, tourism, and Suez Canal revenues)–eventually prompted intervention by the Government and the Central Bank in mid-2000; this resulted in the informal abandonment of the Egyptian pound's fixed exchange rate against the US dollar, and Government officials estimated that the Egyptian economy would require a year to recover from this reverse. Nevertheless, the revival of the tourism industry and the revival of earnings from exports of petroleum (reflecting the sustained recovery in international oil prices), in conjunction with a continued decrease in both the rate of inflation and the number of unemployed, offered cause for optimism, and GDP growth of some 6% was forecast for the 2000/01 fiscal year. Furthermore, the imminent signing of a partnership agreement with the European Union was expected to result in a marked increase in the volume of Egyptian exports to Europe, and thus in revenue from this lucrative market.

Social Welfare

Substantial progress has been made in social welfare services in recent years. There are comprehensive state schemes for sickness benefits, pensions, health insurance and training. In 1982 Egypt had 1,521 hospital establishments, with a total of 87,685 beds. (The number of hospital beds had increased to an estimated 132,182 by mid-1999, while in the same year there were an estimated 7,863 medical treatment units, including 321 general and district hospitals.) According to WHO data, there were 202 physicians per 100,000 inhabitants and 233 nursing personnel per 100,000 population working in the country in 1996. Government expenditure on health in 1998/99 was projected at some £E4,600m. (an estimated 5.0% of total spending).

Education

Education at all levels is available free of charge, and is officially compulsory for eight years between six and 14 years of age. Primary education, beginning at six years of age, lasts for five years. Secondary education, from 11 years of age, lasts for a further six years, comprising two cycles (the first being preparatory) of three years each. In 1997 total enrolment at primary and secondary schools was equivalent to 89% of the school-age population (males 94%; females 83%). In 1996 primary enrolment included 93% of children in the relevant age-group (males 98%; females 88%), while the comparable ratio for secondary enrolment was 67% (males 71%; females 64%). There are 14 universities. The Al-Azhar University and its various preparatory and associated institutes provide instruction and training in various disciplines, with emphasis on adherence to Islamic principles and teachings. Budget forecasts for 2000/01 allocated £E18,100m. (some 16.2% of total expenditure) to education. The 1996 census recorded the rate of adult illiteracy as 38.6%, compared with 49.6% in the 1986 census; this was interpreted as a direct result of a government initiative to expand education.

Public Holidays

2001: 1 January (New Year), 6 March* (Id al-Adha, Feast of the Sacrifice), 26 March* (Muharram, Islamic New Year), 16 April (Sham an-Nessim, Coptic Easter Monday), 25 April (Sinai Day), 4 June* (Mouloud/Yum an-Nabi, Birth of Muhammad), 23 July (Revolution Day), 6 October (Armed Forces Day), 15 October (Leilat al-Meiraj, Ascension of Muhammad), 24 October (Popular Resistance Day), 17 December* (Id al-Fitr, end of Ramadan), 23 December (Victory Day).

2002: 1 January (New Year), 23 February* (Id al-Adha, Feast of the Sacrifice), 15 March* (Muharram, Islamic New Year), 25 April (Sinai Day), 6 May (Sham an-Nessim, Coptic Easter Monday), 24 May* (Mouloud/Yum an-Nabi, Birth of Muhammad), 23 July (Revolution Day), 4 October Leilat al-Meiraj, Ascension of Muhammad), 6 October (Armed Forces Day), 24 October (Popular Resistance Day), 6* December (Id al-Fitr, end of Ramadan), 23 December (Victory Day).

* These holidays are dependent on the Islamic lunar calendar and may vary by one or two days from the dates given.

Coptic Christian holidays include: Christmas (7 January), Palm Sunday and Easter Sunday.

Weights and Measures

The metric system is in force, but some Egyptian measurements are still in use.

Statistical Survey

Sources (unless otherwise stated): Central Agency for Public Mobilization and Statistics, POB 2086, Cairo (Nasr City); tel. (2) 4024632; fax (2) 4024099; internet www.capmas.gov.eg; Research Department, National Bank of Egypt, Cairo.

Area and Population

AREA, POPULATION AND DENSITY

Area (sq km)	1,002,000*
Population (census results)†	
17–18 November 1986	48,254,238
31 December 1996	
Males	30,351,390
Females	28,961,524
Total	59,312,914
Density (per sq km) at 31 December 1996	59.2

* 386,874 sq miles. Inhabited and cultivated territory accounts for 55,039 sq km (21,251 sq miles).

† Excluding Egyptian nationals abroad, totalling an estimated 2,250,000 in 1986 and an estimated 2,180,000 in 1996.

Population (official estimates at December, excluding Egyptian nationals abroad): 60,706,000 in 1997; 61,994,000 in 1998; 63,234,000 in 1999.

GOVERNORATES (population at 1996 census*)

Governorate	Area (sq km)†	Population ('000)	Capital
Cairo	214.20	6,801.0	Cairo
Alexandria . . .	2,679.36	3,339.1	Alexandria
Port Said . . .	72.07	472.3	Port Said
Ismailia . . .	1,441.59	714.8	Ismailia
Suez	17,840.42	417.5	Suez
Damietta . . .	589.17	913.6	Damietta
Dakahlia . . .	3,470.90	4,223.9	El-Mansoura
Sharkia . . .	4,179.55	4,281.1	Zagazig
Kalyoubia . . .	1,001.09	3,301.2	Banha
Kafr esh-Sheikh . .	3,437.12	2,223.7	Kafr esh-Sheikh
Gharbia . . .	1,942.21	3,406.0	Tanta
Menoufia . . .	1,532.13	2,760.4	Shebien el-Kom
Behera . . .	10,129.48	3,994.3	Damanhour
Giza . . .	85,153.56	4,784.1	Giza
Beni-Suef . . .	1,321.50	1,859.2	Beni-Suef
Fayoum . . .	1,827.10	1,989.8	El-Fayoum
Menia . . .	2,261.70	3,310.1	El-Menia
Asyout . . .	1,553.00	2,802.3	Asyout
Suhag . . .	1,547.20	3,123.1	Suhag
Qena . . .	1,850.60	2,442.0	Qena
Aswan . . .	678.45	974.1	Aswan
Red Sea . . .	203,685.00	157.3	Hurghada
El-Wadi el-Gidid .	376,505.00	141.8	El-Kharga
Matruh . . .	212,112.00	212.0	Matruh
North Sinai . .	} 60,714.00 {	252.2	El-Areesh
South Sinai . .		54.8	Et-Tour

* Figures exclude data for the recently-created governorate of Luxor City, with an area of 55 sq km and a population (in '000) of 361.1.

† The sum of these figures is 997,738.40 sq km, compared with the official national total of 1,002,000 sq km.

PRINCIPAL TOWNS (estimated population at 1 July 1992)

Cairo (Al-Qahirah, the capital)* . .	6,800,992	Asyout (Asyut) . . .	321,000
		Zagazig (Az-Zaqaziq) .	287,000
Alexandria		Ismailia (Al-Ismailiyah)	255,000
(Al-Iskandariyah)* .	3,339,076	El-Fayum (Al-Fayyum) .	250,000
Giza (Al-Jizah)* . .	4,784,099	Kafr ed-Dawar	
Shoubra el-Kheima		(Kafr ad-Dawwar) .	226,000
(Shubra al-Khaymah)	834,000	Damanhour (Damanhur) .	222,000
Port Said (Bur Sa'id)*	472,335	Aswan	220,000
Suez (As-Suways)* .	417,527	El-Menia (Al-Minya) .	208,000
El-Mahalla el-Koubra		Beni-Suef (Bani-Suwayf) .	179,000
(Al-Mahallah al-Kubra)	408,000	Shebien el-Kom	
Tanta	380,000	(Shibin al-Kawn) . .	158,000
El-Mansoura		Suhag (Sawhaj) . .	156,000
(Al-Mansurah) . .	371,000		

* At census of December 1996.

Source: mainly UN, *Demographic Yearbook*.

BIRTHS, MARRIAGES AND DEATHS

	Registered live births		Registered marriages		Registered deaths	
	Number	Rate (per 1,000)	Number	Rate (per 1,000)	Number	Rate (per 1,000)
1992 .	1,521,000	28.1	397,000	7.3	385,000	7.1
1993 .	1,622,000	29.4	432,000	7.8	382,000	6.9
1994 .	1,636,000	29.0	452,000	8.0	388,000	6.9
1995 .	1,605,000	27.9	471,000	8.2	385,000	6.7
1996 .	1,662,000	28.3	489,000	8.3	380,000	6.5
1997 .	1,655,000	27.5	493,000	8.2	389,000	6.5
1998 .	1,687,000	27.5	504,000	8.2	399,000	6.5
1999* .	1,693,000	27.0	520,000	8.3	401,000	6.4

* Provisional figures.

Expectation of life (years at birth, 1996): males 65.1; females 69.0.

ECONOMICALLY ACTIVE POPULATION

('000 persons aged 15 years and over, 1996 census)

	Males	Females	Total
Agriculture, hunting, forestry and fishing	4,640.7	240.2	4,880.9
Mining and quarrying . . .	60.9	2.8	63.7
Manufacturing	1,967.8	209.6	2,177.4
Electricity, gas and water supply	145.1	14.3	159.4
Construction	1,261.9	20.9	1,282.8
Wholesale and retail trade; repair of motor vehicles, motorcycles and personal and household goods . . .	1,313.2	120.0	1,433.2
Hotels and restaurants . .	195.3	10.5	205.9
Transport, storage and communications . . .	871.6	44.9	916.5
Financial intermediation . . .			
Real estate, renting and business activities	} 483.6	225.1	708.7
Public administration and defence; compulsory social security	1,196.4	336.5	1,533.0
Education	888.0	623.0	1,511.0
Health and social work . .	190.8	182.7	373.5
Other community, social and personal service activities . .	304.8	43.9	348.7
Activities not adequately defined	146.9	26.9	173.8
Total employed . . .	13,666.9	2,101.3	15,768.2
Unemployed	932.0	530.4	1,462.4
Total labour force . . .	14,598.9	2,631.7	17,230.6

Agriculture

PRINCIPAL CROPS ('000 metric tons)

	1997	1998	1999
Wheat	5,849	6,093	6,347
Rice (paddy)	5,480	4,450	5,816
Barley	126	148	114
Maize	5,806	6,337	5,437*
Sorghum	787	887	937†
Potatoes	1,803	1,984	1,900*
Sweet potatoes	190	226	199*
Taro (Coco yam)	93	77	69*
Dry broad beans	476	523	307
Other pulses	59	64	64
Soybeans (Soya beans)	35	48	19
Groundnuts (in shell)	126	132	181†
Sunflower seed	26	34	43*
Cotton (lint)	342	230	243*
Olives*	180	200	205
Cabbages	490	526	332†
Tomatoes	5,873	5,753	5,900*
Cauliflowers	93	115	1,100*
Pumpkins, squash and gourds	568	616	620*
Cucumbers and gherkins*	255	258	260
Aubergines*	555*	560*	565
Green chillies and peppers	363	385	635
Onions (dry)	396	652	1,017
Garlic	159	174	224
Green beans	220	179	160
Green peas	154	159	187*
Carrots	138	129	135*
Other vegetables	1,117	1,078	79
Watermelons	1,735	1,409	1,500*
Melons	547	467	500*
Grapes	868	958	970*
Dates	741	840	850*
Sugar cane	13,726	14,353	15,325*
Sugar beets	1,143	1,951	2,560
Apples	403	388	400*
Pears	57	41	41*
Peaches and nectarines	377	430	420*
Plums	35	22	22*
Oranges	1,522	1,442	1,525*
Tangerines, mandarins, clementines and satsumas	435	422	425*
Lemons and limes	264	253	259*
Apricots	41	45	45*
Mangoes	231	223	231*
Bananas	635	656	600*
Other fruits and berries*	615	627	629

* FAO estimate(s).

Source: FAO.

LIVESTOCK ('000 head, year ending September)

	1997	1998	1999*
Cattle	3,117	3,217	3,150
Buffaloes	3,096	3,149	3,180
Sheep	4,260	4,352	4,400
Goats	3,187	3,217	3,150
Pigs*	28	29	29
Horses	43*	45*	46
Asses*	2,990	2,995	3,000
Camels*	128	113	116

Chickens (FAO estimates, million): 90* in 1997; 86 in 1998; 87* in 1999.
Ducks (FAO estimates, million): 9 in 1997; 9 in 1998; 9 in 1999.

* FAO estimate(s).

Source: FAO.

LIVESTOCK PRODUCTS ('000 metric tons)

	1997	1998	1999
Beef and veal	311	252	265*
Buffalo meat*	225	231	262
Mutton and lamb*	64	65	66
Goat meat*	56	56	57
Pig meat*	3	3	3
Poultry meat	541	535	541
Other meat	102	102	105
Cows' milk	1,324	1,352	1,352*
Buffaloes' milk	1,890	2,022	2,050
Sheep's milk*	91	93	93
Goats' milk*	14	15	15
Butter and ghee	91	91	91*
Cheese	400	427	430
Hen eggs	168	168	169*
Honey	9	8	9*
Wool: greasy	7	7	7*
Cattle and buffalo hides*	49	44	49
Sheepskins	8	8	8
Goatskins	7	7	7

* FAO estimate(s).

Source: FAO.

Forestry

ROUNDWOOD REMOVALS
('000 cubic metres, excluding bark)

	1996	1997	1998
Industrial wood	126	129	131
Fuel wood	2,597	2,647	2,698
Total	2,723	2,776	2,829

Source: FAO, *Yearbook of Forest Products*.

Fishing

('000 metric tons, live weight)

	1996	1997	1998
Capture	320.3	345.2	365.6
Grass carp	15.3	12.3	4.2
Nile tilapia	125.3	131.0	128.4
Mudfish	20.4	22.4	21.6
Other mullets	14.8	16.6	18.0
Sardinellas	15.1	16.3	28.9
Aquaculture	75.8	73.5	139.4
Common carp	23.4	22.3	50.8
Nile tilapia	27.9	30.4	52.8
Flathead grey mullet	20.1	16.0	28.4
Total catch	396.1	418.7	505.0

Source: FAO, *Yearbook of Fishery Statistics*.

Mining

('000 metric tons, year ending 30 June)

	1996/97	1997/98	1998/99*
Crude petroleum	42,000	40,000	4,000
Iron ore†	2,744	3,001	3,002
Salt (unrefined)	2,024	2,488	2,588
Phosphate rock	1,428	1,059	1,165
Gypsum (crude)	1,839	2,423	2,666
Kaolin	259	286	314

* Figures are provisional.
† Figures refer to gross weight. The estimated iron content is 50%.

Natural gas (estimates, petajoules): 530 in 1995; 563 in 1996; 581 in 1997 (Source: UN, *Industrial Commodity Statistics Yearbook*).

Industry

SELECTED PRODUCTS ('000 metric tons, unless otherwise indicated)

	1995	1996	1997
Wheat flour	3,767	4,657	4,739
Raw sugar*	1,132	1,222	1,230
Cottonseed oil (refined)	305	288	n.a.
Beer ('000 hectolitres)	360	380	n.a.
Cigarettes (million)	42,469	49,959	51,789
Cotton yarn (pure)†	250.3	211.6	n.a.
Jute yarn	19.8	15.3	14.9
Jute fabrics	19.3	n.a.	12.9
Wool yarn	14.1	14.1	7.3
Paper and paperboard*	221	221	282
Rubber tyres and tubes ('000)‡	3,690	3,046	3,501
Sulphuric acid (100%)	133	299	84
Caustic soda (Sodium hydroxide)	48	38	43
Nitrogenous fertilizers†§	6,136	3,337	2,813
Phosphate fertilizers‖	913	418	322
Jet fuels	860	850	n.a.
Motor spirit (petrol)	4,520	4,789	5,070
Kerosene	1,169	1,328	n.a.
Distillate fuel oils	5,792	5,652	5,870
Residual fuel oil (Mazout)	12,044	12,745	12,928
Petroleum bitumen (asphalt)	740	696	n.a.
Cement	14,237	15,569	15,480
Pig-iron	69	15	15
Radio receivers ('000)	n.a.	n.a.	n.a.
Television receivers ('000)	243	336	114
Passenger motor cars—assembly (number)	9,000	13,000	13,000
Electric energy (million kWh)†	49,500	50,258	n.a.

* Data from the FAO.
† Figures refer to the year ending 30 June.
‡ Tyres and inner tubes for road motor vehicles (including motorcycles) and bicycles.
§ Production in terms of nitrogen.
‖ Production in terms of phosphoric acid.

Source: mainly UN, *Industrial Commodity Statistics Yearbook*.

Finance

CURRENCY AND EXCHANGE RATES

Monetary Units

1,000 millièmes = 100 piastres = 5 tallaris = 1 Egyptian pound (£E).

Sterling, Dollar and Euro Equivalents (29 December)

£1 sterling = £E5.506;
US $1 = £E3.690;
€1 = £E3.434;
£E100 = £18.16 sterling = $27.10 = €29.12.

Note: From February 1991 foreign exchange transactions were conducted through only two markets, the primary market and the free market. With effect from 8 October 1991, the primary market was eliminated, and all foreign exchange transactions are effected through the free market. For external trade purposes, the average value of the Egyptian pound was 29.509 US cents in 1997, 29.516 US cents in 1998 and 29.452 US cents in 1999.

STATE PUBLIC BUDGET (£E million, year ending 30 June)

Revenue	1996/97	1997/98	1998/99
Current revenue	60,753	63,889	66,626
Central Government	57,179	60,035	62,449
Tax revenue	40,518	43,962	47,149
Taxes on income and profits	14,589	15,306	15,641
Domestic taxes on goods and services	11,325	12,925	14,313
Customs duties	8,125	8,886	10,108
Stamp duties	3,168	3,215	3,342
Other current revenue	16,661	16,073	15,300
Profit transfers	11,423	10,780	9,802
Petroleum Authority	4,778	3,870	2,227
Suez Canal Authority	2,828	2,940	2,914
Central Bank of Egypt	2,587	2,617	3,222
Local government	2,354	2,426	2,601
Service authorities	1,220	1,428	1,576
Capital revenue	3,745	4,047	4,669
Total	64,498	67,963	71,295

Expenditure	1996/97	1997/98	1998/99
Current expenditure	53,430	55,690	59,570
Wages	15,368	17,025	18,833
Pensions	4,300	4,647	5,009
Goods and services	3,520	3,734	3,888
Defence	7,373	7,772	8,290
Public debt interest	15,451	14,943	15,676
Local	12,337	12,219	13,251
Foreign	3,114	2,724	2,425
Subsidies	4,134	4,161	4,498
Capital expenditure (net)	13,396	15,093	15,715
Total	66,826	70,783	75,285

1999/2000 (projections, £E million, year ending 30 June): Revenue 90,593 (current 79,108, capital 11,485); Expenditure 99,453 (current 77,110, capital 22,343).
2000/01 (projections, £E million, year ending 30 June): Revenue 97,700; Expenditure 111,700.

INTERNATIONAL RESERVES (US $ million at 31 December)

	1997	1998	1999
Gold*	609	541	475
IMF special drawing rights	113	160	41
Reserve position in IMF	73	76	165
Foreign exchange	18,479	17,888	14,278
Total	19,274	18,665	14,959

* Valued at market-related prices.

Source: IMF, *International Financial Statistics*.

MONEY SUPPLY (£E million at 31 December)

	1997	1998	1999
Currency outside banks	28,215	31,502	35,310
Demand deposits at deposit money banks	18,920	19,335	20,506
Total money (incl. others)	48,708	58,577	59,066

Source: IMF, *International Financial Statistics*.

COST OF LIVING (Consumer Price Index; base: 1990 = 100)

	1996	1997	1998
Food, beverages and tobacco	176.5	183.8	190.9
Fuel and light	310.9	324.1	324.1
Clothing and footwear	203.8	215.4	220.8
Rent	152.2	153.9	154.8
All items (incl. others)	191.6	200.4	207.5

Source: ILO, *Yearbook of Labour Statistics*.

NATIONAL ACCOUNTS
(£E million, year ending 30 June)

Expenditure on the Gross Domestic Product (at current prices)

	1996/97	1997/98	1998/99
Government final consumption expenditure	26,050	28,250	30,420
Private final consumption expenditure	192,700	207,740	224,250
Increase in stocks	200	2,730	8,460
Gross fixed capital formation	49,400	59,600	64,430
Total domestic expenditure	268,350	298,320	327,560
Exports of goods and services	51,700	47,200	48,440
Less Imports of goods and services	63,800	65,300	73,700
GDP in purchasers' values	256,250	280,220	302,300

Source: IMF, *International Financial Statistics*.

Gross Domestic Product by Economic Activity
(at constant 1996/97 factor cost)

	1996/97	1997/98	1998/99
Agriculture, hunting, forestry and fishing	42,325	43,905	45,530
Mining and quarrying }	59,237	63,734	67,401
Manufacturing			
Electricity	4,220	4,470	4,824
Construction	12,750	14,100	15,580
Transport and communications	22,695	23,802	24,874
Trade, restaurants and hotels	45,275	46,898	50,379
Finance, insurance and real estate	13,957	15,187	16,736
Government services and social insurance	19,980	21,023	22,164
Other services	19,061	19,971	20,910
Total	239,500	253,090	268,398

BALANCE OF PAYMENTS (US $ million)

	1997	1998	1999
Exports of goods f.o.b.	5,525	4,403	5,237
Imports of goods f.o.b.	−14,157	−14,617	−15,165
Trade balance	−8,632	−10,214	−9,928
Exports of services	9,380	8,141	9,494
Imports of services	−6,770	−6,492	−6,452
Balance on goods and services	−6,021	−8,565	−6,886
Other income received	2,122	2,030	1,788
Other income paid	−1,185	−1,075	−1,045
Balance on goods, services and income	−5,085	−7,610	−6,143
Current transfers received	4,738	5,166	4,564
Current transfers paid	−363	−122	−55
Current balance	−711	−2,566	−1,635
Direct investment abroad	−129	−45	−38
Direct investment from abroad	891	1,076	1,065
Portfolio investment assets	n.a.	−63	−22
Portfolio investment liabilities	816	−537	617
Other investment assets	−170	39	−1,805
Other investment liabilities	551	1,431	−1,240
Net errors and omissions	−1,882	−722	−1,558
Overall balance	−635	−1,387	−4,614

Source: IMF, *International Financial Statistics*.

External Trade

Note: Figures exclude trade in military goods.

PRINCIPAL COMMODITIES (distribution by SITC, US $ million)

Imports c.i.f.	1995	1996	1997
Food and live animals	2,611.8	3,058.1	2,698.6
Cereals and cereal preparations	1,309.8	1,720.2	1,257.6
Wheat and meslin (unmilled)	875.7	1,232.1	821.1
Maize (unmilled)	349.3	435.5	385.4
Sugar and honey preparations	219.2	260.6	358.3
Crude materials (inedible) except fuels	1,059.1	1,142.1	1,119.8
Cork and wood	551.0	502.2	538.1
Simply worked wood and railway sleepers	522.3	452.5	502.3
Simply worked coniferous wood	445.7	346.7	410.3
Sawn coniferous wood	445.6	346.7	410.2
Animal and vegetable oils, fats and waxes	510.1	512.9	484.3
Fixed vegetable oils and fats	466.7	482.0	444.7
Chemicals and related products	1,526.4	1,596.2	1,727.3
Organic chemicals	289.2	277.4	285.9
Medicinal and pharmaceutical products	227.6	238.5	315.2
Artificial resins, plastic materials, etc.	498.5	549.4	584.2
Products of polymerization, etc.	381.9	427.8	469.5
Basic manufactures	2,375.5	2,602.8	2,574.7
Paper, paperboard and manufactures	534.8	413.7	388.7
Paper and paperboard (not cut to size or shape)	499.6	365.5	355.5
Textile yarn, fabrics, etc.	279.7	289.7	300.3
Iron and steel	782.8	1,012.3	919.8
Other metal manufactures	236.8	249.6	276.6
Machinery and transport equipment	2,957.7	3,302.8	3,547.0
Machinery specialized for particular industries	475.9	608.7	768.0
General industrial machinery, equipment and parts	786.0	845.4	791.2
Heating and cooling equipment	238.3	154.1	138.0
Telecommunications and sound equipment	212.1	238.0	278.9
Other electrical machinery, apparatus, etc.	463.4	532.5	517.4
Road vehicles and parts*	624.7	601.2	596.1
Miscellaneous manufactured articles	409.1	439.2	533.8
Total (incl. others)	11,739.0	13,019.6	13,168.5

* Excluding tyres, engines and electrical parts.

Exports f.o.b.	1995	1996	1997
Food and live animals	321.0	355.0	269.6
Cereals and cereal preparations	63.2	124.1	77.2
Rice	56.8	117.8	71.4
Vegetables and fruit	206.9	170.1	140.5
Fresh or simply preserved vegetables	152.9	121.0	89.6
Fresh potatoes (excl. sweet)	102.2	80.0	41.3
Crude materials (inedible) except fuels	241.0	180.1	203.0
Textile fibres (excl. wool tops) and waste	169.1	102.5	117.5
Cotton	157.9	92.6	111.2
Raw cotton (excl. linters)	152.3	91.9	110.3
Mineral fuels, lubricants, etc.	1,283.0	1,682.2	1,772.4
Petroleum, petroleum products, etc.	1,231.8	1,634.8	1,731.9
Crude petroleum oils, etc.	719.2	816.6	668.2
Refined petroleum products	496.4	810.2	968.4
Residual fuel oils	461.6	809.3	886.3
Chemicals and related products	200.9	176.6	197.8

Exports f.o.b. — *continued*	1995	1996	1997
Basic manufactures . . .	1,035.7	788.7	1,004.0
Textile yarn, fabrics, etc. . . .	571.3	426.5	533.5
Textile yarn	322.6	204.2	285.0
Cotton yarn	305.8	193.5	280.7
Woven cotton fabrics (excl. narrow or special fabrics) . .	109.3	88.8	104.9
Unbleached fabrics (not mercerized)	105.9	83.9	97.7
Other textile goods . . .	91.9	89.8	95.3
Linens etc.	83.8	78.8	77.8
Other non-metal mineral manufactures	27.5	28.0	121.2
Iron and steel	160.0	69.1	108.6
Non-ferrous metals	199.8	186.9	151.1
Aluminium and aluminium alloys	197.6	185.1	148.8
Unwrought aluminium and alloys	149.8	164.8	125.5
Worked aluminium and alloys	47.9	20.4	23.3
Miscellaneous manufactured articles	330.0	323.5	395.3
Clothing and accessories (excl. footwear)	252.6	239.4	259.0
Knitted or crocheted undergarments (incl. foundation garments of non-knitted fabrics) . . .	75.1	73.8	94.9
Cotton undergarments, non-elastic	75.0	73.8	94.9
Other miscellaneous manufactured articles	34.9	37.6	79.8
Total (incl. others) . . .	3,444.2	3,534.5	3,908.0

Source: UN, *International Trade Statistics Yearbook*.

PRINCIPAL TRADING PARTNERS
(countries of consignment, US $ million)

Imports c.i.f.	1995	1996	1997
Argentina	115.1	237.7	339.4
Australia	123.8	386.2	480.3
Belgium-Luxembourg . . .	236.8	211.9	206.4
Brazil	189.9	265.6	257.3
China, People's Repub. . .	295.9	283.6	295.6
Finland	183.0	166.4	177.4
France (incl. Monaco) . . .	685.2	577.1	805.4
Germany	1,044.6	1,089.2	1,141.8
India	160.7	184.4	223.1
Ireland	217.9	131.7	140.2
Italy	731.1	870.9	929.9
Japan	314.0	344.9	446.5
Korea, Republic . . .	227.1	192.9	233.1
Malaysia	220.4	241.0	232.5
Netherlands	381.4	363.5	379.2
Romania	160.4	197.0	218.5
Russia	405.3	370.8	379.2
Saudi Arabia	248.9	290.5	440.3
Spain	184.5	210.8	221.4
Sweden	259.6	306.6	299.8
Switzerland-Liechtenstein . .	311.9	334.1	340.8
Turkey	179.6	252.9	174.1
Ukraine	102.9	112.0	230.9
United Kingdom	379.8	441.1	427.0
USA	2,211.0	2,608.8	1,719.8
Total (incl. others) . . .	11,739.0	13,019.6	13,168.5

Exports f.o.b.	1995	1996	1997
Belgium-Luxembourg . . .	110.5	50.5	62.8
France (incl. Monaco) . . .	144.3	144.7	150.2
Germany	207.1	162.9	265.6
Greece	137.3	142.4	175.0
India	53.0	14.1	44.0
Israel	176.3	351.8	327.9
Italy	458.8	438.4	438.0
Japan	43.7	41.4	90.8
Jordan	30.9	44.6	26.1
Korea, Republic . . .	51.6	35.6	60.4
Lebanon	43.5	33.0	32.3
Libya	52.9	51.7	69.6
Netherlands	166.7	364.8	264.4
Portugal	21.5	24.0	40.4
Romania	41.3	36.9	64.3
Russia	31.9	37.7	24.4
SACU*	4.6	35.0	40.3
Saudi Arabia	113.1	122.7	138.5
Singapore	92.8	90.1	152.7
Spain	157.3	98.2	111.9
Syria	56.1	55.0	34.6
Thailand	4.7	1.0	44.2
Turkey	82.7	115.3	96.6
United Arab Emirates . .	41.0	44.4	34.2
United Kingdom	142.4	165.7	90.2
USA	522.1	459.9	447.2
Yemen	12.5	36.5	32.5
Total (incl. others) . . .	3,444.1	3,534.5	3,908.0

* Southern African Customs Union, comprising Botswana, Lesotho, Namibia, South Africa and Swaziland.

Source: partly UN, *International Trade Statistics Yearbook*.

Transport

RAILWAYS (traffic, year ending 30 June)

	1995/96	1996/97	1997/98*
Passengers (million) . .	1,089	1,218	1,314
Passenger-km (million) . .	50,665	52,929	56,667

* Estimate.

1995/96: Freight ton-km (million): 4,117 (Source: UN, *Statistical Yearbook*).

ROAD TRAFFIC (licensed motor vehicles in use at 31 December)

	1995*	1996	1997
Passenger cars . . .	1,280,000	1,099,583	1,154,753
Buses and coaches . . .	36,630	39,781	43,740
Lorries and vans . . .	387,000	489,542	510,766
Motorcycles and mopeds . .	397,000	427,864	439,756

* Estimates from IRF, *World Road Statistics*.

SHIPPING
Merchant Fleet (registered at 31 December)

	1996	1997	1998
Number of vessels . . .	375	378	379
Displacement ('000 grt) . .	1,230	1,288	1,368

Source: Lloyd's Register of Shipping, *World Fleet Statistics*.

International sea-borne freight traffic ('000 metric tons, incl. ships' stores, 1998): Goods loaded 23,868; Goods unloaded 31,152 (Source: UN, *Monthly Bulletin of Statistics*).

Suez Canal Traffic

	1997	1998	1999
Transits (number) . . .	14,430	13,471	13,490
Displacement ('000 net tons) . .	368,720	386,069	384,994
Northbound goods traffic ('000 metric tons)	144,448	160,346	153,582
Southbound goods traffic ('000 metric tons)	151,456	118,107	153,088
Net tonnage of tankers ('000) . .	78,012	89,976	67,872

Source: Suez Canal Authority, *Yearly Report*.

CIVIL AVIATION (traffic on scheduled services)

	1995	1996	1997
Kilometres flown (million) . .	55	62	65
Passengers carried ('000) . .	3,897	4,282	4,416
Passenger-km (million) . .	7,678	8,742	9,018
Total ton-km (million) . .	864	993	1,029

Source: UN, *Statistical Yearbook*.

Tourism

ARRIVALS BY NATIONALITY ('000)*

	1996	1997	1998
Belgium, Luxembourg and Netherlands	133.1	141.8	115.9
France	242.2	259.0	175.3
Germany	436.8	438.4	273.8
Israel	321.1	292.5	372.1
Italy	366.3	389.1	373.1
Japan	89.8	91.4	22.8
Kuwait	76.2	67.6	69.8
Libya	150.9	175.3	186.0
Palestine	143.0	181.1	195.9
Saudi Arabia	216.2	207.7	233.6
Switzerland	98.3	113.2	31.0
Syria	68.5	68.1	74.2
USSR (former)	124.9	120.7	133.8
United Kingdom	328.2	334.0	239.0
USA	174.7	176.3	153.6
Total (incl. others) . . .	3,895.9	3,961.4	3,453.9

* Figures refer to arrivals at frontiers of visitors from abroad. Excluding same-day visitors (excursionists), the total number of tourist arrivals (in '000) was: 3,528 in 1996 and 3,657 in 1997.

Source: World Tourism Organization, *Yearbook of Tourism Statistics*.

Tourism receipts (£E million): 5,043.4 in 1996; 5,837.8 in 1997; 4,062.9 in 1998.

Communications Media

	1995	1996	1997
Radio receivers ('000 in use) . .	19,400	20,000	20,500
Television receivers ('000 in use) .	6,850	7,500	7,700
Telephones ('000 main lines in use)*	2,716	3,025	3,453
Telefax stations (number in use)* .	27,332	31,394	n.a.
Mobile cellular telephones (subscribers)*	7,368	7,369	7,224
Daily newspapers:			
Number	15	17	n.a.
Average circulation ('000 copies)	2,373	2,400†	n.a.

* Year ending 30 June.
† Estimate.

Book production (1995): 2,215 titles; 92,353,000 copies.

Sources: UNESCO, *Statistical Yearbook*; UN, *Statistical Yearbook*.

Education

(1998/99, unless otherwise indicated)

	Schools	Teachers	Students
Pre-primary	3,172	14,894	289,995*
Primary	15,566	314,528	7,351,118
Prepatory	7,325	193,469	4,152,624
Secondary			
General	1,562	79,218	968,708
Technical	1,767	145,050	1,852,332
Higher	356†	n.a.	1,316,491*

* 1996/97 figure. Source: partly UNESCO, *Statistical Yearbook*.

† Official estimate.

Source: Ministry of Education.

Al-Azhar (1998/99): *Primary:* 2,655 schools; 730,170 students. *Preparatory:* 1,715 schools; 314,574 students. *Secondary:* 964 schools; 223,258 students.

Directory

The Constitution

A new Constitution for the Arab Republic of Egypt was approved by referendum on 11 September 1971.

THE STATE

Egypt is an Arab Republic with a democratic, socialist system based on the alliance of the working people and derived from the country's historical heritage and the spirit of Islam.

The Egyptian people are part of the Arab nation, who work towards total Arab unity.

Islam is the religion of the State; Arabic is its official language and the Islamic code is a principal source of legislation. The State safeguards the freedom of worship and of performing rites for all religions.

Sovereignty is of the people alone which is the source of all powers.

The protection, consolidation and preservation of the socialist gains is a national duty: the sovereignty of law is the basis of the country's rule, and the independence of immunity of the judiciary are basic guarantees for the protection of rights and liberties.

THE FUNDAMENTAL ELEMENTS OF SOCIETY

Social solidarity is the basis of Egyptian society, and the family is its nucleus.

The State ensures the equality of men and women in both political and social rights in line with the provisions of Muslim legislation.

Work is a right, an honour and a duty which the State guarantees together with the services of social and health insurance, pensions for incapacity and unemployment.

The economic basis of the Republic is a socialist democratic system based on sufficiency and justice in a manner preventing exploitation.

Ownership is of three kinds: public, co-operative and private. The public sector assumes the main responsibility for the regulation and growth of the national economy under the development plan.

Property is subject to the people's control.

Private ownership is safeguarded and may not be sequestrated except in cases specified in law nor expropriated except for the general good against fair legal compensation. The right of inheritance is guaranteed in it.

Nationalization shall only be allowed for considerations of public interest in accordance with the law and against compensation.

Agricultural holding may be limited by law.

The State follows a comprehensive central planning and compulsory planning approach based on quinquennial socio-economic and cultural development plans whereby the society's resources are mobilized and put to the best use.

The public sector assumes the leading role in the development of the national economy. The State provides absolute protection of this sector as well as the property of co-operative societies and trade unions against all attempts to tamper with them.

PUBLIC LIBERTIES, RIGHTS AND DUTIES

All citizens are equal before the law. Personal liberty is a natural right and no one may be arrested, searched, imprisoned or restricted in any way without a court order.

Houses have sanctity, and shall not be placed under surveillance or searched without a court order with reasons given for such action.

The law safeguards the sanctities of the private lives of all citizens; so have all postal, telegraphic, telephonic and other means of communication which may not therefore be confiscated, or perused except by a court order giving the reasons, and only for a specified period.

Public rights and freedoms are also inviolate and all calls for atheism and anything that reflects adversely on divine religions are prohibited.

The freedom of opinion, the Press, printing and publications and all information media are safeguarded.

Press censorship is forbidden, so are warnings, suspensions or cancellations through administrative channels. Under exceptional circumstances, as in cases of emergency or in wartime, censorship may be imposed on information media for a definite period.

Egyptians have the right to permanent or provisional emigration and no Egyptian may be deported or prevented from returning to the country.

Citizens have the right to private meetings in peace provided they bear no arms. Egyptians also have the right to form societies which have no secret activities. Public meetings are also allowed within the limits of the law.

SOVEREIGNTY OF THE LAW

All acts of crime should be specified together with the penalties for the acts.

Recourse to justice is a right of all citizens. Those who are financially unable will be assured of means to defend their rights.

Except in cases of *flagrante delicto,* no person may be arrested or their freedom restricted unless an order authorizing arrest has been given by the competent judge or the public prosecution in accordance with the provisions of law.

SYSTEM OF GOVERNMENT

The President, who must be of Egyptian parentage and at least 40 years old, is nominated by at least one-third of the members of the People's Assembly, approved by at least two-thirds, and elected by popular referendum. His term is for six years and he 'may be re-elected for another subsequent term'. He may take emergency measures in the interests of the State but these measures must be approved by referendum within 60 days.

The People's Assembly, elected for five years, is the legislative body and approves general policy, the budget and the development plan. It shall have 'not less than 350' elected members, at least half of whom shall be workers or farmers, and the President may appoint up to 10 additional members. In exceptional circumstances the Assembly, by a two-thirds vote, may authorize the President to rule by decree for a specified period but these decrees must be approved by the Assembly at its next meeting. The law governing the composition of the People's Assembly was amended in May 1979 (see People's Assembly, below).

The Assembly may pass a vote of no confidence in a Deputy Prime Minister, a Minister or a Deputy Minister, provided three days' notice of the vote is given, and the Minister must then resign. In the case of the Prime Minister, the Assembly may 'prescribe' his responsibility and submit a report to the President: if the President disagrees with the report but the Assembly persists, then the matter is put to a referendum: if the people support the President the Assembly is dissolved; if they support the Assembly the President must accept the resignation of the Government. The President may dissolve the Assembly prematurely, but his action must be approved by a referendum and elections must be held within 60 days.

Executive Authority is vested in the President, who may appoint one or more Vice-Presidents and appoints all Ministers. He may also dismiss the Vice-Presidents and Ministers. The President has 'the right to refer to the people in connection with important matters related to the country's higher interests.' The Government is described as 'the supreme executive and administrative organ of the state'. Its members, whether full Ministers or Deputy Ministers, must be at least 35 years old. Further sections define the roles of Local Government, Specialized National Councils, the Judiciary, the Higher Constitutional Court, the Socialist Prosecutor-General, the Armed Forces and National Defence Council and the Police.

POLITICAL PARTIES

In June 1977 the People's Assembly adopted a new law on political parties, which, subject to certain conditions, permitted the formation of political parties for the first time since 1953. The law was passed in accordance with Article Five of the Constitution which describes the political system as 'a multi-party one' with four main parties: 'the ruling National Democratic Party, the Socialist Workers (the official opposition), the Liberal Socialists and the Unionist Progressive'. (The legality of the re-formed New Wafd Party was established by the courts in January 1984.)

1980 AMENDMENTS

On 30 April 1980 the People's Assembly passed a number of amendments, which were subsequently massively approved at a referendum the following month. A summary of the amendments follows:

(i) the regime in Egypt is socialist-democratic, based on the alliance of working people's forces.

(ii) the political system depends on multiple political parties; the Arab Socialist Union is therefore abolished.

(iii) the President is elected for a six-year term and can be elected for 'other terms'.

(iv) the President shall appoint a Consultative Council to preserve the principles of the revolutions of 23 July 1952 and 15 May 1971.

(v) a Supreme Press Council shall safeguard the freedom of the press, check government censorship and look after the interests of journalists.

(vi) Egypt's adherence to Islamic jurisprudence is affirmed. Christians and Jews are subject to their own jurisdiction in personal status affairs.

(vii) there will be no distinction of race or religion.

The Government

THE PRESIDENCY

President: MUHAMMAD HOSNI MUBARAK (confirmed as President by referendum, 13 October 1981, after assassination of President Sadat; re-elected and confirmed by referendum, 5 October 1987, 4 October 1993 and 26 September 1999).

COUNCIL OF MINISTERS
(May 2001)

Prime Minister: Dr ATIF MUHAMMAD OBEID.

Deputy Prime Minister and Minister of Agriculture and Land Reclamation: Dr YOUSUF AMIN WALI.

Minister of Defence and of Military Production: Field Marshal MUHAMMAD HUSSAIN TANTAWI.

Minister of Information: MUHAMMAD SAFWAT MUHAMMAD YOUSUF ASH-SHARIF.

Minister of Foreign Affairs: AHMAD MAHER.

Minister of Justice: FAROUK MAHMOUD SAYF AN-NASR.

Minister of Culture: FAROUK ABD AL-AZIZ HOSNI.

Minister of Education: Dr HUSSAIN KAMAL BAHA ED-DIN.

Minister of Economy and Foreign Trade: Dr YOUSUF BOUTROS-GHALI.

Minister of Tourism: Dr MUHAMMAD MAMDOUH AHMAD EL-BELTAGI.

Minister of Construction, Housing and New Urban Communities: Dr Eng. MUHAMMAD IBRAHIM SULAYMAN.

Minister of Labour and Migration: AHMAD AHMAD EL-AMAWI.

Minister of Awqaf (Islamic Endowments): Dr MAHMOUD HAMDI ZAKZOUK.

Minister of Health and Population: Dr ISMAIL AWADALLAH SALAM.

Minister of Higher Education and Scientific Research: Dr MUFID MAHMOUD SHEHAB.

Minister of Public Works and Water Resources: Dr MAHMOUD ABD AL-HALIM ABU ZEID.

Minister of the Interior: Maj.-Gen. HABIB IBRAHIM EL-ADLI.

Minister of Insurance and Social Affairs: Dr AMINAH HAMZEH MAHMOUD AL-JUNDI.

Minister of Industry and Technological Development: Dr MOUSTAFA MUHAMMAD OSMAN AR-RIFA'I.

Minister of Electricity and Energy: Dr ALI FAHMI IBRAHIM AS-SA'IDI.

Minister of Transport: Dr IBRAHIM MUHAMMAD MUTAWALLI AD-DUMEIRI.

Minister of Youth: Dr ALI AD-DIN HELAL AD-DASUQI.

Minister of Supply and Internal Trade: Dr HASSAN ALI KHIDR.

Minister of Planning and Minister of State for International Co-operation: Dr AHMAD MAHRUS AD-DARSH.

Minister of the Public Enterprise Sector: Dr MUKHTAR ABD AL-MUN'IM KHATTAB.

Minister of Finance: Dr MUHAMMAD MIDHAT ABD AL-ATTI HASANAYN.

Minister of Communications and Information Technology: Dr AHMAD MAHMOUD MUHAMMAD NAZIF.

Minister of Petroleum: Dr AMIN SAMIH SAMIR FAHMI.

Minister of State for Parliamentary Affairs: KAMAL MUHAMMAD ASH-SHAZLI.

Minister of State for Administrative Development: Dr MUHAMMAD ZAKI ABU AMER.

Minister of State for Environmental Affairs: Dr NADIA RIAD MAKRAM OBEID.

Minister of State for Local Development: MOUSTAFA MUHAMMAD ABD AL-QADIR.

Minister of State for Military Production: Dr SAID ABDUH MOUSTAFA MASH'AL.

Cabinet Secretary: AHMAD HASSAN ABU TALEB.

MINISTRIES

Office of the Prime Minister: Sharia Majlis ash-Sha'ab, Cairo; tel. (2) 7958014; fax (2) 7958016; e-mail primemin@idsc.gov.eg.

Ministry of Administrative Development: Sharia Salah Salem, Cairo (Nasr City); tel. (2) 4022910; fax (2) 2614126.

Ministry of Agriculture and Land Reclamation: Sharia Nadi es-Sayed, Dokki, Giza; tel. (2) 3772566; fax (2) 3498128; e-mail sea@idsc.gov.eg; internet www.agri.gov.eg.

Ministry of Awqaf (Islamic Endowments): Sharia Sabri Abu Alam, Bab el-Louk, Cairo; tel. (2) 3929403; fax 3900362; e-mail mawkaf@idsc1.gov.eg.

Ministry of Communications and Information Technology: Ramses Sq., Cairo; tel. (2) 5770000; fax (2) 5744215.

Ministry of Construction, Housing and New Urban Communities: 1 Ismail Abaza, Sharia Qasr el-Eini, Cairo; tel. (2) 3553468; fax (2) 3557836; e-mail mhuuc@idsc1.gov.eg.

Ministry of Culture: 2 Sharia Shagaret ed-Dor, Cairo (Zamalek); tel. (2) 7380761; fax (2) 7356449; e-mail mculture@idsc.gov.eg.

Ministry of Defence: Sharia 23 July, Kobri el-Kobra, Cairo; tel. (2) 2602566; fax (2) 2916227; e-mail mod@idsc.gov.eg.

Ministry of Economy and Foreign Trade: 8 Sharia Adly, Cairo; tel. (2) 3919661; fax (2) 3903029; e-mail minecon@idsc1.gov.eg; internet www.economy.gov.eg.

Ministry of Education: 4 Sharia Ibrahim Nagiv, Cairo (Garden City); tel. (2) 5787643; fax (2) 7962952; e-mail moe@idsc.gov.eg; internet home.moe.edu.

Ministry of Electricity and Energy: Sharia Ramses, Abbassia, Cairo (Nasr City); tel. (2) 2616317; fax (2) 2616302; e-mail mee@idsc.gov.eg.

Ministry of the Environment: 30 Sharia Helwan, Cairo; tel. (2) 5256463; fax (2) 5256461.

Ministry of Finance: Justice and Finance Bldg, Sharia Majlis ash-Sha'ab, Lazoughli Sq., Cairo; tel. (2) 3541055; fax (2) 3551537; e-mail mofinance@idsc1.gov.eg.

Ministry of Foreign Affairs: Corniche en-Nil, Cairo (Maspiro); tel. (2) 5749820; fax (2) 5749533; e-mail minexter@idsc1.gov.eg; internet www.mfa.gov.eg.

Ministry of Health and Population: Sharia Majlis ash-Sha'ab, Lazoughli Sq., Cairo; tel. (2) 7941507; fax (2) 7953966; e-mail moh@idsc.gov.eg.

Ministry of Higher Education and Scientific Research: 101 Sharia Qasr el-Eini, Cairo; tel. (2) 7956962; fax (2) 7941005; e-mail mheducat@idsc.gov.eg; internet www.egy-mhe.gov.eg.

Ministry of Industry and Technological Development: 2 Sharia Latin America, Cairo (Garden City); tel. (2) 3557034; fax (2) 3555025; e-mail moimw@idsc1.gov.eg.

Ministry of Information: Radio and TV Bldg, Corniche en-Nil, Cairo (Maspiro); tel. (2) 5748984; fax (2) 5748981; e-mail rtu@idsc.gov.eg.

Ministry of Insurance and Social Affairs: Sharia Sheikh Rihan, Bab el-Louk, Cairo; tel. (2) 3370039; fax (2) 3375390; e-mail msi@idsc.gov.eg.

Ministry of the Interior: Sharia Sheikh Rihan, Bab el-Louk, Cairo; tel. (2) 3557500; fax (2) 5792031; e-mail moi2@idsc.gov.eg.

Ministry of Justice: Justice and Finance Bldg, Sharia Majlis ash-Sha'ab, Lazoughli Sq., Cairo; tel. (2) 7951176; fax (2) 7955700; e-mail mojeb@idsc1.gov.eg.

Ministry of Labour and Migration: 3 Sharia Yousuf Abbas, Abbassia, Cairo (Nasr City); tel. (2) 4042910; fax (2) 2609891; e-mail mwlabor@idsc1.gov.eg; internet www.emigration.gov.eg.

Ministry of Local Development: Sharia Nadi es-Seid, Cairo (Dokki); tel. (2) 3497470; fax (2) 3497788.

Ministry of Military Production: 5 Sharia Ismail Abaza, Qasr el-Eini, Cairo; tel. (2) 3552428; fax (2) 3548739.

Ministry of Parliamentary Affairs: Sharia Majlis ash-Sha'ab, Lazoughli Sq., Cairo; tel. (2) 3557750; fax (2) 3557681.

Ministry of Petroleum: Sharia el-Mokhayem ed-Dayem, Cairo (Nasr City); tel. (2) 2626060; fax (2) 2636060; e-mail mop@egyptonline.com.

Ministry of Planning: Sharia Salah Salem, Cairo (Nasr City); tel. (2) 4014615; fax (2) 4014733.

Ministry of the Public Enterprise Sector: Sharia Majlis ash-Sha'ab, Lazoughli Sq., Cairo; tel. (2) 3558026; fax (2) 3555882; e-mail mops@idsc.gov.eg.

Ministry of Public Works and Water Resources: Sharia Corniche en-Nil, Imbaba, Cairo; tel. (2) 3123304; fax (2) 3123357; e-mail mpwwr@idsc.gov.eg; internet www.starnet.com.eg/mpwwr.

Ministry of Supply and Internal Trade: 99 Sharia Qasr el-Eini, Cairo; tel. (2) 3557598; fax (2) 3544973; e-mail msit@idsc.gov.eg.

Ministry of Tourism: Misr Travel Tower, Abbassia Sq., Cairo; tel. (2) 2828439; fax (2) 2859551; e-mail mol@idsc.gov.eg; internet www.touregypt.net.

Ministry of Transport: 105 Sharia Qasr el-Eini, Cairo; tel. (2) 3555566; fax (2) 3555564; e-mail garb@idsc.gov.eg.

Legislature
MAJLIS ASH-SHA'AB
(People's Assembly)

There are 222 constituencies, which each elect two deputies to the Assembly. Ten deputies are appointed by the President, giving a total of 454 seats.

Speaker: Dr AHMAD FATHI SURUR.

Deputy Speakers: Dr ABD AL-AHAD GAMAL AD-DIN, AHMAD ABU ZEID, Dr AMAL UTHMAN.

Elections, 18 and 29 October and 8 November 2000

	Seats
National Democratic Party*	353
New Wafd Party	7
National Progressive Unionist Party	6
Nasserist Party	3
Liberal Socialist Party	1
Independents	72
Total†	442‡

* Official candidates of the National Democratic Party (NDP) gained 353 seats in the three rounds of voting. However, after the elections it was reported that 35 of the 72 candidates who had successfully contested the elections as independents had either joined or rejoined the NDP.
† There are, in addition, 10 deputies appointed by the President.
‡ The results for the two seats in one constituency in Alexandria were annulled by a court ruling. (Elections were scheduled to be reheld there in early 2001).

MAJLIS ASH-SHURA
(Advisory Council)

In September 1980 elections were held for a 210-member **Shura (Advisory) Council**, which replaced the former Central Committee of the Arab Socialist Union. Of the total number of members, 140 are elected and the remaining 70 are appointed by the President. The opposition parties boycotted elections to the Council in October 1983, and again in October 1986, in protest against the 8% electoral threshold. In June 1989 elections to 153 of the Council's 210 seats were contested by opposition parties (the 'Islamic Alliance', consisting of the Muslim Brotherhood, the LSP and the SLP). However, all of the seats in which voting produced a result (143) were won by the NDP. NDP candidates won 88 of the 90 seats on the Council to which mid-term elections were held in June 1995. The remaining two elective seats were gained by independent candidates. On 21 June new appointments were made to 47 vacant, non-elective seats. Mid-term elections to the Council were held again in June 1998. The NDP won 85 of the 88 contested seats, while independent candidates won the remaining three seats. Most opposition parties chose not to contest the elections.

Speaker: Dr MUSTAFA KAMAL HELMI.

Deputy Speakers: THARWAT ABAZAH, AHMAD AL-IMADI.

Political Organizations

Democratic People's Party: f. 1992; Chair. ANWAR AFIFI.

Democratic Unionist Party: f. 1990; Pres. IBRAHIM ABD AL-MONEIM TURK.

Et-Takaful (Solidarity): f. 1995; advocates imposition of 'solidarity' tax on the rich in order to provide needs of the poor; Chair. Dr USAMA MUHAMMAD SHALTOUT.

Green Party: f. 1990; Chair. Dr ABD AL-MONEIM EL-AASAR.

Hizb al-Wifaq al-Qawmi (National Accord Party): f. 2000.

Ikhwan (Brotherhood): f. 1928; officially illegal, the (Muslim) Brotherhood advocates the adoption of the *Shari'a*, or Islamic law, as the sole basis of the Egyptian legal system; Sec.-Gen. MAAMOUN AL-HODAIBY.

Liberal Socialist Party (LSP): Cairo; f. 1976; advocates expansion of 'open door' economic policy and greater freedom for private enterprise and the press; Leader (vacant).

Misr el-Fatah (Young Egypt Party): f. 1990; Chair. GAMAL RABIE.

Nasserist Party: Cairo; f. 1991; Chair. DIAA ED-DIN DAOUD.

National Democratic Party (NDP): Cairo; f. 1978; government party established by Anwar Sadat; has absorbed Arab Socialist Party; Leader MUHAMMAD HOSNI MUBARAK; Sec.-Gen. Dr YOUSUF AMIN WALI; Political Bureau: Chair. MUHAMMAD HOSNI MUBARAK.

National Progressive Unionist Party (Tagammu): 1 Sharia Karim ed-Dawlah, Cairo; f. 1976; left-wing; Leader KHALED MOHI ED-DIN; Sec. Dr RIFA'AT ES-SAID; 160,000 mems.

New Wafd Party (The Delegation): Cairo; original Wafd Party f. 1919; banned 1952; re-formed as New Wafd Party Feb. 1978; disbanded June 1978; re-formed 1983; Leader NU'MAN JUM'AH; Sec.-Gen. IBRAHIM FARAG.

Social Justice Party: f. 1993; Chair. MUHAMMAD ABD AL-AAL.

Socialist Labour Party (SLP): 12 Sharia Awali el-Ahd, Cairo; f. 1978; official opposition party; pro-Islamist; Leader IBRAHIM SHUKRI; Dep. Chair. ADEL HUSSEIN.

The following organizations are proscribed by the Government:

Islamic Jihad (Holy Struggle): militant Islamist grouping established following the imposition of a ban on the Muslim Brotherhood.

Jama'ah al-Islamiyah (Islamic Group): militant Islamist group founded following the imposition of a ban on the Muslim Brotherhood; declared a cease-fire in March 1999; Spiritual Leader Sheikh OMAR ABD AR-RAHMAN; Chair. of the Shura Council MOUSTAFA HAMZAH; Mil. Cmmdr ALA ABD AR-RAQIL.

Muslim Brotherhood (Ikhwan al-Muslimun): internet www.ummah.org.uk/ikhwan; f. 1928 with the aim of establishing an Islamic society; banned in 1954; moderate; Dep. Supreme Guide MA'MUN AL-HUDA BI.

Vanguards of Conquest: militant Islamist grouping; breakaway group from Islamic Jihad; Leader YASIR AS-SIRRI.

Diplomatic Representation

EMBASSIES IN EGYPT

Afghanistan: 59 Sharia el-Orouba, Cairo (Heliopolis); tel. (2) 666653; fax (2) 662262; Ambassador: SAYED FAZLULLAH FAZIL.

Albania: 29 Sharia Ismail Muhammad, Cairo (Zamalek); tel. (2) 3415651; fax (2) 3413732; Ambassador: ARBEN PANDI CICI.

Algeria: 14 Sharia Bresil, Cairo (Zamalek); tel. (2) 3418527; fax (2) 3414158; Ambassador: MOUSTAFA CHERIF.

Angola: 12 Midan Fouad Mohi ed-Din, Mohandessin, Cairo; tel. (2) 3498259; fax (2) 3378683; Ambassador: HERMINO JOAQUIM ESCORCIO.

Argentina: 8 Sharia es-Saleh Ayoub, Cairo (Zamalek); tel. (2) 6401501; fax (2) 3414355; e-mail argemb@idsc.gov.eg; Ambassador: DOMINGO CULLEN.

Armenia: 20 Sharia Muhammad Mazhar, Cairo (Zamalek); tel. (2) 3424157; fax (2) 3424158; e-mail armenemb@idsc.gov.eg; Ambassador: Dr EDWARD NALBANDIAN.

Australia: 11th Floor, World Trade Centre, Corniche en-Nil, Cairo 11111 (Boulac); tel. (2) 5750444; fax (2) 5781638; e-mail cairo.austremb@dfat.gov.au; Ambassador: VICTORIA OWEN.

Austria: 5th Floor, Riyadh Tower, 5 Sharia Wissa Wassef, cnr of Sharia en-Nil, Cairo 11111 (Giza); tel. (2) 5702975; fax (2) 5702979; e-mail aec@gega.net; Ambassador: FERDINAND TRAUTTMANSDORFF.

Bahrain: 15 Sharia Bresil, Cairo (Zamalek); tel. (2) 3407996; fax (2) 3416609; Ambassador: EBRAHIM AL-MAJED.

Bangladesh: 47 Sharia Ahmad Heshmat, Cairo (Zamalek); tel. (2) 3412645; fax (2) 3402401; e-mail bdoot@wnet1.worldnet.com.eg; Ambassador: RUHUL AMIN.

Belarus: 12–49 Misakha Sq., Cairo (Dokki); tel. and fax (2) 3493743; Chargé d'affaires: IGOR LESCHENYA.

Belgium: POB 37, 20 Sharia Kamal esh-Shennawi, Cairo 11511 (Garden City); tel. (2) 7947494; fax (2) 7943147; e-mail cairo@diplobel.org; Ambassador: PAUL PONJAERT.

Bolivia: 2 Sharia Hod el-Labban, Cairo (Garden City); tel. (2) 3546390; fax (2) 3550917; Ambassador: HERNANDO VELASCO.

Bosnia and Herzegovina: 26 July Square, Cairo (Agouza); tel. (2) 3474514; fax (2) 3456029; e-mail ebihebosnia@isdc.gov.eg; Chargé d'affaires a.i.: AVDIJA HADROVIĆ.

Brazil: 1125 Corniche en-Nil, Cairo 11561 (Maspiro); tel. (2) 5756938; fax (2) 761040; e-mail brazemb@idsc.gov.eg; Ambassador: CELSO MARCOS VIEIRA DE SOUZA.

Brunei: 24 Sharia Hassan Assem, Cairo (Zamalek); tel. (2) 7360097; fax (2) 7386375; e-mail ebdic@mail.link.net; Ambassador: Dato' Paduka Haji ALI BIN HAJI HASSAN.

Bulgaria: 6 Sharia el-Malek el-Ajdal, Cairo (Dokki); tel. (2) 3413025; fax (2) 3413826; Ambassador: PETKO DIMITROV.

Burkina Faso: POB 306, Ramses Centre, 9 Sharia el-Fawakeh, Mohandessin, Cairo; tel. (2) 3758956; fax (2) 3756974; Ambassador: MAHAMOUDOU OUÉDRAOGO.

Burundi: 22 Sharia en-Nakhil, Madinet ed-Dobbat, Cairo (Dokki); tel. (2) 3373078; fax (2) 3378431; Ambassador: GERVAIS NDIKUMAGNEGE.

Cambodia: 2 Sharia Tahawia, Cairo (Giza); tel. (2) 3489966; Ambassador: IN SOPHEAP.

Cameroon: POB 2061, 15 Sharia Muhammad Sedki Soliman, Mohandessin, Cairo; tel. (2) 3441101; fax (2) 3459208; Ambassador: MOUCHILI NJI MFOUAYO ISMAILA.

Canada: POB 1667, 5 Midan es-Saraya el-Kobra, Cairo (Garden City); tel. (2) 7943110; fax (2) 7963548; e-mail cairo@dtait-maeci.gc.ca; Ambassador: MARIE-ANDRÉE BEAUCHEMIN.

Central African Republic: 41 Sharia Mahmoud Azmy, Mohandessin, Cairo (Dokki); tel. (2) 3446873; Ambassador: HENRY KOBA.

Chad: POB 1869, 12 Midan ar-Refaï, Cairo 11511 (Dokki); tel. (2) 3373379; fax (2) 3373232; Ambassador: AMIN ABBA SIDICK.

Chile: 5 Sharia Shagaret ed-Dor, Cairo (Zamalek); tel. (2) 3408711; fax (2) 3403716; e-mail chilemb@idsc.gov.eg; Ambassador: NELSON HADAD HERESI.

China, People's Republic: 14 Sharia Bahgat Aly, Cairo (Zamalek); tel. (2) 3411219; fax (2) 3409459; e-mail chinaemb@idsc.gov.eg; Ambassador: AN HUIHOU.

Colombia: 6 Sharia Gueriza, Cairo (Zamalek); tel. (2) 3414203; fax (2) 3407429; e-mail colombemb@idsc.gov.eg; Ambassador: JAIME GIRÓN DUARTE.

Congo, Democratic Republic: 5 Sharia Mansour Muhammad, Cairo (Zamalek); tel. (2) 3403662; fax (2) 3404342; Ambassador: KAMIMBAYA WA DJONDO.

Côte d'Ivoire: 39 Sharia el-Kods esh-Sherif, Madinet el-Mohandessin, Cairo (Dokki); tel. and fax (2) 3460109; Ambassador: Gen. FÉLIX ORY.

Croatia: 3 Abou el-Feda St, Cairo (Zamalek); tel. (2) 7353155; fax (2) 7355812; e-mail croem@soficom.com.eg; Ambassador: (vacant).

Cuba: Apartment 4, 14 Sharia Madinah Munawarah, Cairo (Dokki); tel. (2) 3371649; fax (2) 3350390; e-mail cubaemb@idsc.gov.eg; Ambassador: LUIS E. MARISY FIGUEREDO.

Cyprus: 23A Sharia Ismail Muhammad, 1st Floor, Cairo (Zamalek); tel. (2) 3411288; fax (2) 3415299; Ambassador: CHARALAMBOS KAPSOS.

Czech Republic: 1st Floor, 4 Sharia Dokki, Cairo 12511 (Giza); tel. (2) 3485531; fax (2) 3485892; e-mail caiembcz@intouch.com; Ambassador: DANA HUŇÁTOVÁ.

Denmark: 12 Sharia Hassan Sabri, Cairo 11211 (Zamalek); tel. (2) 7357411; fax (2) 7361780; e-mail rdemb@commnet.com.eg; internet www.danemb.org.eg/cairo-dk.html; Ambassador: CHRISTIAN OLDENBURG.

Djibouti: 11 Sharia el-Gazaer, Aswan Sq., Cairo (Agouza); tel. (2) 3456546; fax (2) 3456549; Ambassador: Sheikh ADEN HASSEN.

Ecuador: Suez Canal Bldg, 4 Sharia Ibn Kasir, Cairo (Giza); tel. (2) 3496782; fax (2) 3609327; e-mail ecuademb@idsc.gov.eg; Ambassador: FRANKLIN BAHAMONDE.

Ethiopia: 6 Sharia Abd ar-Rahman Hussein, Midan Gomhuria, Cairo (Dokki); tel. (2) 3353696; fax (2) 3353699; Ambassador: KONGIT SINEGIORGIS.

Finland: 3 Sharia Abou el-Feda, Cairo (Zamalek); tel. (2) 3411487; fax (2) 3405170; Ambassador: AAPO POLHO.

France: POB 1777, 29 Sharia Giza, Cairo (Giza); tel. (2) 5703916; fax (2) 5710276; Ambassador: FRANÇOIS DOPFFER.

Gabon: 17 Sharia Mecca el-Moukarama, Cairo (Dokki); tel. (2) 3379699; Ambassador: MAMBO JACQUES.

Germany: 8B Sharia Hassan Sabri, Cairo (Zamalek); tel. (2) 7399600; fax (2) 7360530; e-mail germemb@gega.net; internet www.germ-embassy.org.eg; Ambassador: PAUL VON MALTZAHN.

Ghana: 1 Sharia 26 July, Cairo (Zamalek); tel. (2) 3444455; fax (2) 3032292; Ambassador: BON OHANE KWAPONG.

Greece: 18 Sharia Aicha at-Taimouria, Cairo (Garden City); tel. (2) 3551074; fax (2) 3563903; Ambassador: GEORGE ASIMAKOPOULOS.

Guatemala: POB 346, 11 Sharia 10, Maadi, Cairo; tel. (2) 3802914; fax (2) 3802915; e-mail guatemb@infinity.com.eg; Ambassador: JUAN ALFREDO RENDÓN.

Guinea: 46 Sharia Muhammad Mazhar, Cairo (Zamalek); tel. (2) 3408109; fax (2) 3411446; Ambassador: MOHAMED TSSIOGA KOUROUMA.

Guinea-Bissau: 37 Sharia Lebanon, Madinet el-Mohandessin, Cairo (Dokki).

Holy See: Apostolic Nunciature, Safarat al-Vatican, 5 Sharia Muhammad Mazhar, Cairo (Zamalek); tel. (2) 7352250; fax (2) 7356152; e-mail nunteg@rite.com; Apostolic Nuncio: Most Rev. PAOLO GIGLIO, Titular Archbishop of Tindari.

Honduras: 21 Sharia Aicha at-Taimouria, Cairo (Garden City); tel. (2) 3409510; fax (2) 3413835.

Hungary: 29 Sharia Muhammad Mazhar, Cairo (Zamalek); tel. (2) 7350659; fax (2) 7358648; e-mail huembcai@soficom.com.eg; Ambassador: LÁSZLÓ KÁDÁR.

India: 5 Sharia Aziz Abaza, Cairo (Zamalek); tel. (2) 3413051; fax (2) 3414038; e-mail indiaemb@idsc.gov.eg; Ambassador: KENWAL GIBAL; also looks after Iraqi interests at 5 Aziz Abaza St, Cairo (Zamalek) (tel. (2) 3409815).

Indonesia: POB 1661, 13 Sharia Aicha at-Taimouria, Cairo (Garden City); tel. (2) 3547200; fax (2) 3562495; Ambassador: Dr BOER MAUNA.

Iraq: *Interests served by India.*

Ireland: POB 2681, 3 Sharia Abou el-Feda, Cairo (Zamalek); tel. (2) 7358264; fax (2) 7362863; e-mail irishemb@rite.com; Ambassador: PETER GUNNING.

Israel: 6 Sharia Ibn el-Malek, Cairo (Giza); tel. (2) 3610545; fax (2) 3610414; Ambassador: ZVI MAZEL.

Italy: 15 Sharia Abd ar-Rahman Fahmi, Cairo (Garden City); tel. (2) 7943194; fax (2) 7940657; e-mail ambcairo@brainy1.ie-eg.com; internet www.italemb.org.eg; Ambassador: FRANCESCO ALOISI DE LARDEREL.

Japan: Cairo Centre Bldg, 2nd and 3rd Floors, 2 Sharia Abd al-Kader Hamza or 106 Sharia Qasr el-Eini, Cairo (Garden City); tel. (2) 3553962; fax (2) 3563540; e-mail center@embjapan.org.eg; internet www.mofa.go.jp/embjapan/egypt; Ambassador: TAKESHI OHARA.

Jordan: 6 Sharia Juhaini, Cairo; tel. (2) 3485566; fax (2) 3601027; Ambassador: NABIH AN-NIMR.

Kazakhstan: 4 Sharia Abay Kunanbayuli, New Maadi, Cairo; tel. and fax (2) 5194522; e-mail kazaemb@ids.gov.eg; Ambassador: BOLATKHAN K. TAIZHANOV.

Kenya: POB 362, 7 Sharia el-Mohandes Galal, Cairo (Dokki); tel. (2) 3453628; fax (2) 3443400; Ambassador: MUHAMMAD M. MAALIM.

Korea, Democratic People's Republic: 6 Sharia as-Saleh Ayoub, Cairo (Zamalek); tel. (2) 3408219; fax (2) 3414615; Ambassador: JANG MYONG-SON.

Korea, Republic: 3 Sharia Boulos Hanna, Cairo (Dokki); tel. (2) 3611234; fax (2) 3611238; Ambassador SHIM KYOUNG-BO.

Kuwait: 12 Sharia Nabil el-Wakkad, Cairo (Dokki); tel. (2) 3602661; fax (2) 3602657; ABD AR-RAZAK ABD AL-KADER AL-KANDRI.

Lebanon: 22 Sharia Mansour Muhammad, Cairo (Zamalek); tel. (2) 7382823; fax (2) 7382818; Ambassador: SAMI KRONFOL.

Liberia: 11 Sharia Bresil, Cairo (Zamalek); tel. (2) 3419864; fax (2) 3473074; Ambassador: Dr BRAHIMA D. KABA.

Libya: 7 Sharia as-Saleh Ayoub, Cairo (Zamalek); tel. (2) 3401864; Ambassador: JUM'AH AL-MAHDI AL-FAZZANI.

Malaysia: 29 Sharia Taha Hussein, Cairo (Zamalek); tel. (2) 3410863; fax (2) 3411049; Ambassador: Dato RAJA MANSUR RAZMAN.

Mali: 3 Sharia al-Kawsar, Cairo (Dokki); tel. (2) 3371641; fax (2) 3371841; Ambassador: ALLAYE ALPHADY CISSÉ.

Malta: 25 Sharia 12, Maadi, Cairo; tel. (2) 3804451; fax (2) 3804452; e-mail maltaemb@link.net; Ambassador: GAETAN NAUDI ACIS.

Mauritania: 114 Mohi ed-Din, Abou-el Ezz, Mohandessin, Cairo; tel. (2) 3490671; fax (2) 3489060; MUHAMMAD LEMINE OULD.

Mauritius: 156 Sharia es-Sudan, Mohandessin, Cairo; tel. (2) 3618102; fax (2) 3618101; e-mail embamaurathe@wayout.net; Ambassador: (vacant).

Mexico: 5th Floor, 17 Sharia Port Said, 11431 Cairo (Maadi); tel. (2) 3500258; fax (2) 3511887; e-mail mexemb@idsc.gov.eg; Ambassador: HÉCTOR CÁRDENAS.

Mongolia: 3 Midan en-Nasr, Cairo (Dokki); tel. (2) 3460670; Ambassador: SONOMDORJIN DAMBADARJAA.

Morocco: 10 Sharia Salah ed-Din, Cairo (Zamalek); tel. (2) 3409849; fax (2) 3411937; e-mail morocemb@idsc.gov.eg; Ambassador: ABD AL-LATIF MOULINE.

Myanmar: 24 Sharia Muhammad Mazhar, Cairo (Zamalek); tel. (2) 3404176; fax (2) 3416793; Ambassador: U AUNG GYI.

Nepal: 9 Sharia Tiba, Madinet el-Kobah, Cairo (Dokki); tel. (2) 3603426; fax (2) 704447; Ambassador: JITENDRA RAJ SHARMA.

Netherlands: 36 Sharia Muhammad Mazhar, Cairo (Zamalek); tel. (2) 3406434; fax (2) 3415249; e-mail nlgovkai@access.com.eg; internet www.hollandemb.org.eg; Ambassador: SJOERD LEENSTRA.

Niger: 101 Sharia Pyramids, Cairo (Giza); tel. (2) 3865607; Ambassador: MAMANE OUMAROU.

Nigeria: 13 Sharia Gabalaya, Cairo (Zamalek); tel. (2) 3406042; fax (2) 3403907; Chargé d'affaires a.i.: P. S. O. EROMOBOR.

Norway: 8 Sharia el-Gezirah, Cairo (Zamalek); tel. (2) 3403340; fax (2) 3420709; e-mail emb.cairo@mfa.no; Ambassador: BJØRN FRODE ØSTERN.

Oman: 52 Sharia el-Higaz, Mohandessin, Cairo; tel. (2) 3036011; fax (2) 3036464; Ambassador: ABDULLAH BIN HAMED AL-BUSAIDI.

Pakistan: 8 Sharia es-Salouli, Cairo (Dokki); tel. (2) 3487806; fax (2) 3400784; Ambassador: GUL HANEEF.

Panama: POB 62, 4A Sharia Ibn Zanki, 11211 Cairo (Zamalek); tel. (2) 3400784; fax (2) 3411092; Chargé d'affaires a.i.: ROY FRANCISCO LUNA GONZÁLEZ.

Peru: 8 Sharia Kamel esh-Shenawi, Cairo (Garden City); tel. (2) 3562973; fax (2) 3557985; Ambassador: MANUEL VERAMENDI I. SERRA.

Philippines: 5 Sharia Ibn el-Walid, Cairo (Dokki); tel. (2) 3480396; fax (2) 3480393; Ambassador: MENANDRO P. GALENZOGA.

Poland: 5 Sharia el-Aziz Osman, Cairo (Zamalek); tel. (2) 3409583; fax (2) 3405427; Ambassador: ROMAN CZYZYCKI.

Portugal: 57 Sharia el-Giza, Cairo (Giza); tel. (2) 3363950; fax (2) 3363952; Ambassador: MANUEL TAVARES DE SOUSA.

Qatar: 10 Sharia ath-Thamar, Midan an-Nasr, Madinet al-Mohandessin, Cairo; tel. (2) 3604693; fax (2) 3603618; Ambassador: BADIR AD-DAFA.

Romania: 6 el-khamel Muhammad, Cairo (Zamalek); tel. (2) 7360107; fax (2) 7360851; e-mail roembegy@access.com.eg; Ambassador: DORU COSTEA.

Russia: 95 Sharia Giza, Cairo (Giza); tel. (2) 3489353; fax (2) 3609074; Ambassador: VLADIMIR GOUDEV.

Rwanda: 23 Sharia Babel, Mohandessin, Cairo (Dokki); tel. (2) 3350532; fax (2) 3351479; Ambassador: CÉLESTIN KABANDA.

San Marino: 5 Sharia Ramez, Mohandessin, Cairo; tel. (2) 3602718.

Saudi Arabia: 2 Sharia Ahmad Nessim, Cairo (Giza); tel. (2) 3490775; Ambassador: ASSAD ABD AL-KAREM ABOU AN-NASR.

Senegal: 46 Sharia Abd al-Moneim Riad, Mohandessin, Cairo (Dokki); tel. (2) 3460946; fax 3461039; Ambassador: MAMADOU SOW.

Sierra Leone: *Interests served by Saudi Arabia.*

Singapore: 40 Sharia Babel, Cairo (Dokki); tel. (2) 3490468; fax (2) 3481682; e-mail singemb@link.com.eg; Ambassador: V. K. RAJAN.

Slovakia: 3 Sharia Adel Hussein Rostom, Cairo (Giza); tel. (2) 3358240; fax (2) 3355810; e-mail zukahira@gega.net; Chargé d'affaires a.i.: ZIGMUND BERTEK.

Slovenia: 5 es-Saraya el-Kobra Sq., Cairo (Garden City); tel. (2) 3555798; Ambassador: ANDREJ ŽLEBNIK.

Somalia: 27 Sharia es-Somal, Cairo (Dokki), Giza; tel. (2) 3374577; Ambassador: ABDALLA HASSAN MAHMOUD.

South Africa: 18th Floor, Nile Tower Bldg, 21–23 Sharia Giza, Cairo; tel. (2) 5717238; fax (2) 5717241; Ambassador: JUSTUS DE GOEDE.

Spain: 41 Sharia Ismail Muhammad, Cairo (Zamalek); tel. (2) 3406397; fax (2) 3405829; e-mail spainemb@idsc.gov.eg; Ambassador: JUAN ALFONSO ORTIZ.

Sri Lanka: POB 1157, 8 Sharia Sri Lanka, Cairo (Zamalek); tel. (2) 7350047; fax (2) 7367138; e-mail slembarc@menanet.net; Ambassador: D. SERASINGHE.

Sudan: 4 Sharia el-Ibrahimi, Cairo (Garden City); tel. (2) 3545043; fax (2) 3542693; Ambassador: AHMAD ABD AL-HALIM.

Sweden: POB 131, 13 Sharia Muhammad Mazhar, Cairo (Zamalek); tel. (2) 3414132; fax 3404357; e-mail sveamcai@link.com.eg; Ambassador: CHRISTER SYLVÉN.

Switzerland: POB 633, 10 Sharia Abd al-Khalek Sarwat, Cairo; tel. (2) 5758284; fax (2) 5745236; e-mail vertretung@cai.rep.admin.ch; Ambassador: BLAISE GODET.

Syria: 18 Sharia Abd ar-Rehim Sabry, POB 435, Cairo (Dokki); tel. (2) 3358806; fax (2) 3377020; Ambassador: YUSUF AL-AHMAD.

Tanzania: 9 Sharia Abd al-Hamid Lotfi, Cairo (Dokki); tel. (2) 704155; Ambassador: MUHAMMAD A. FOUM.

Thailand: 2 Sharia al-Malek el-Afdal, Cairo (Zamalek); tel. (2) 3410094; fax (2) 3400340; e-mail thaiemb@idsc.gov.eg; Ambassador: BUNTHAM BAIRAJ-VINICHAI.

Tunisia: 26 Sharia el-Jazirah, Cairo (Zamalek); tel. (2) 3418962; Ambassador: ABD AL-HAMID AMMAR.

Turkey: 25 Sharia Felaki, Cairo (Bab el-Louk); tel. (2) 3563318; fax (2) 3558110; Ambassador: YAŞAR YAKIŞ.

Uganda: 9 Midan el-Messaha, Cairo (Dokki); tel. (2) 3486070; fax (2) 3485980; Ambassador: IBRAHIM MUKIIBI.

Ukraine: 9 Sharia el-Saraya, Appt 31-32, Cairo (Dokki); tel. (2) 3491030; fax (2) 3360159.

United Arab Emirates: 4 Sharia Ibn Sina, Cairo (Giza); tel. (2) 3609721; e-mail uaeembassyca@online.com.eg; Ambassador: AHMAD AL-MAHMOUD MUHAMMAD.

United Kingdom: 17 Sharia Ahmad Ragheb, Cairo (Garden City); tel. (2) 7940852; fax (2) 7940859; e-mail info@britishembassy.org.eg; internet www.britishembassy.org.eg; Ambassador: GRAHAM BOYCE.

USA: 8 Sharia Kamal ed-Din, Cairo (Garden City); tel. (2) 3557371; fax (2) 3573000; Ambassador: DANIEL KURTZER.

Uruguay: 6 Sharia Lotfallah, Cairo (Zamalek); tel. (2) 3415137; fax (2) 3418123; Ambassador: JULIO CÉSAR FRANZINI.

Venezuela: 15A Sharia Mansour Muhammad, Cairo (Zamalek); tel. (2) 3413517; fax (2) 3417373; e-mail eov@idsc.gov.eg; Ambassador: DARIO BAUDER.

Viet Nam: 39 Sharia Kambiz, Cairo (Dokki); tel. (2) 3371494; fax (2) 3496597; Ambassador: NGUYEN LE BACH.

Yemen: 28 Sharia Amean ar-Rafai, Cairo (Dokki); tel. (2) 3614224; fax (2) 3604815; Ambassador: ABD AL-GHALIL GHILAN AHMAD.

Yugoslavia: 33 Sharia Mansour Muhammad, Cairo (Zamalek); tel. (2) 3404061; fax (2) 3403913; Ambassador: Dr IVAN IVEKOVIĆ.

Zambia: 6 Abd ar-Rahman Hussein, Mohandessin, Cairo (Dokki); tel. (2) 3610282; fax (2) 3610833; Ambassador: Dr ANGEL ALFRED MWENDA.

Zimbabwe: 40 Sharia Ghaza, Mohandessin, Cairo; tel. (2) 3030404; fax (2) 3059741; Ambassador: Dr HENRY V. MOYANA.

Judicial System

The Courts of Law in Egypt are principally divided into two juridical court systems: Courts of General Jurisdiction and Administrative Courts. Since 1969 the Supreme Constitutional Court has been at the top of the Egyptian judicial structure.

THE SUPREME CONSTITUTIONAL COURT

The Supreme Constitutional Court is the highest court in Egypt. It has specific jurisdiction over: (i) judicial review of the constitutionality of laws and regulations; (ii) resolution of positive and negative jurisdictional conflicts and determination of the competent court between the different juridical court systems, e.g. Courts of General Jurisdiction and Administrative Courts, as well as other bodies exercising judicial competence; (iii) determination of disputes over the enforcement of two final but contradictory judgments rendered by two courts each belonging to a different juridical court system; (iv) rendering binding interpretation of laws or decree laws in the event of a dispute in the application of said laws or decree laws, always provided that such a dispute is of a gravity requiring conformity of interpretation under the Constitution.

COURTS OF GENERAL JURISDICTION

The Courts of General Jurisdiction in Egypt are basically divided into four categories, as follows: (i) The Court of Cassation; (ii) The Courts of Appeal; (iii) The Tribunals of First Instance; (iv) The District Tribunals; each of the above courts is divided into Civil and Criminal Chambers.

(i) Court of Cassation: Is the highest court of general jurisdiction in Egypt. Its sessions are held in Cairo. Final judgments rendered by Courts of Appeal in criminal and civil litigation may be petitioned to the Court of Cassation by the Defendant or the Public Prosecutor in criminal litigation and by any of the parties in interest in civil litigation on grounds of defective application or interpretation of the law as stated in the challenged judgment, on grounds of irregularity of form or procedure, or violation of due process, and on grounds of defective reasoning of judgment rendered. The Court of Cassation is composed of the President, 41 Vice-Presidents and 92 Justices.

President: Hon. ABD AL-BORHAN NOOR.

(ii) The Courts of Appeal: Each has geographical jurisdiction over one or more of the governorates of Egypt. Each Court of Appeal is divided into Criminal and Civil Chambers. The Criminal Chambers try felonies, and the Civil Chambers hear appeals filed against such judgment rendered by the Tribunals of First Instance where the law so stipulates. Each Chamber is composed of three Superior Judges. Each Court of Appeal is composed of President, and sufficient numbers of Vice-Presidents and Superior Judges.

(iii) The Tribunals of First Instance: In each governorate there are one or more Tribunals of First Instance, each of which is divided into several Chambers for criminal and civil litigations. Each Chamber is composed of: (a) a presiding judge, and (b) two sitting judges. A Tribunal of First Instance hears, as an Appellate Court, certain litigations as provided under the law.

(iv) District Tribunals: Each is a one-judge ancillary Chamber of a Tribunal of First Instance, having jurisdiction over minor civil and criminal litigations in smaller districts within the jurisdiction of such Tribunal of First Instance.

PUBLIC PROSECUTION

Public prosecution is headed by the Attorney-General, assisted by a number of Senior Deputy and Deputy Attorneys-General, and a sufficient number of chief prosecutors, prosecutors and assistant prosecutors. Public prosecution is represented at all levels of the Courts of General Jurisdiction in all criminal litigations and also in certain civil litigations as required by the law. Public prosecution controls and supervises enforcement of criminal law judgments.

Attorney-General: MAHIR ABD AL-WAHID.

Prosecutor-General: MUHAMMAD ABD AL-AZIZ EL-GINDI.

ADMINISTRATIVE COURTS SYSTEM (CONSEIL D'ETAT)

The Administrative Courts have jurisdiction over litigations involving the state or any of its governmental agencies. The Administrative Courts system is divided into two courts: the Administrative Courts and the Judicial Administrative Courts, at the top of which is the High Administrative Court. The Administrative Prosecutor investigates administrative crimes committed by government officials and civil servants.

President of Conseil d'Etat: Hon. MUHAMMAD HILAL QASIM.

Administrative Prosecutor: Hon. RIFA'AT KHAFAGI.

THE STATE COUNCIL

The State Council is an independent judicial body which has the authority to make decisions in administrative disputes and disciplinary cases within the judicial system.

THE SUPREME JUDICIAL COUNCIL

The Supreme Judicial Council was reinstituted in 1984, having been abolished in 1969. It exists to guarantee the independence of the judicial system from outside interference and is consulted with regard to draft laws organizing the affairs of the judicial bodies.

Religion

According to the 1986 census, some 94% of Egyptians are Muslims (and almost all of these follow Sunni tenets). According to government figures published in the same year, there are about 2m. Copts (a figure contested by Coptic sources, whose estimates range between 6m. and 7m.), forming the largest religious minority, and about 1m. members of other Christian groups. There is also a small Jewish minority.

ISLAM

There is a Higher Council for the Isamic Call, on which sit: the Grand Sheikh of al-Azhar (Chair); the Minister of Awqaf (Islamic Endowments); the President and Vice-President of Al-Azhar University; the Grand Mufti of Egypt; and the Secretary-General of the Higher Council for Islamic Affairs.

Grand Sheikh of al-Azhar: Sheikh MUHAMMAD SAYED ATTIYAH TANTAWI.

Grand Mufti of Egypt: NASR WASSEL.

CHRISTIANITY

Orthodox Churches

Armenian Apostolic Orthodox Church: 179 Sharia Ramses, Cairo, POB 48-Faggalah; tel. (2) 5901385; fax (2) 906671; Archbishop ZAVEN CHINCHINIAN; 7,000 mems.

Coptic Orthodox Church: St Mark Cathedral, POB 9035, Anba Ruess, 222 Sharia Ramses, Abbassia, Cairo; tel. (2) 2857889; fax (2) 2825683; e-mail coptpope@tecmina.com; internet www.copticpope .org; f. AD 61; Patriarch Pope SHENOUDA III; c. 13m. followers in Egypt, Sudan, other African countries, the USA, Canada, Australia, Europe and the Middle East.

Greek Orthodox Patriarchate: POB 2006, Alexandria; tel. (3) 4868595; fax (3) 4875684; e-mail goptalex@tecmina.com; internet www.greece.org/goptalex; f. AD 64; Pope and Patriarch of Alexandria and All Africa His Beatitude PETROS VII; 3m. mems.

The Roman Catholic Church

Armenian Rite

The Armenian Catholic diocese of Alexandria, with an estimated 1,287 adherents at 31 December 1998, is suffragan to the Patriarchate of Cilicia. The Patriarch is resident in Beirut, Lebanon.

Bishop of Alexandria: (vacant), Patriarcat Arménien Catholique, 36 Sharia Muhammad Sabri Abou Alam, 11111 Cairo; tel. (2) 3938429; fax (2) 3932025; e-mail pacal@gega.net.

Chaldean Rite

The Chaldean Catholic diocese of Cairo had an estimated 500 adherents at 31 December 1998.

Bishop of Cairo: YOUSSEF IBRAHIM SARRAF, Evêché Chaldéen, Basilique-Sanctuaire Notre Dame de Fatima, 141 Sharia Nouzha, 11361 Cairo (Heliopolis); tel. and fax (2) 6355718.

Coptic Rite

Egypt comprises the Coptic Catholic Patriarchate of Alexandria and five dioceses. At 31 December 1998 there were an estimated 88,000 adherents in the country.

Patriarch of Alexandria: His Beatitude STEPHANOS II (ANDREAS GHATTAS), Patriarcat Copte Catholique, POB 69, 34 Sharia Ibn Sandar, Koubbeh Bridge, 11712 Cairo; tel. (2) 2571740; fax (2) 4545766.

Latin Rite

Egypt comprises the Apostolic Vicariate of Alexandria (incorporating Heliopolis and Port Said), containing an estimated 9,570 adherents at 31 December 1998.

Vicar Apostolic: (Titular Bishop of Ida in Mauretania), 10 Sharia Sidi el-Metwalli, Alexandria; tel. (3) 4876065; fax (3) 4878169.

Maronite Rite

The Maronite diocese of Cairo had an estimated 5,000 adherents at 31 December 1998.

Bishop of Cairo: JOSEPH DERGHAM, Evêché Maronite, 15 Sharia Hamdi, Daher, 11271 Cairo; tel. (2) 5939610.

Melkite Rite

His Beatitude MAXIMOS V HAKIM (resident in Damascus, Syria) is the Greek-Melkite Patriarch of Antioch, of Alexandria and of Jerusalem.

Patriarchal Exarchate of Egypt and Sudan: Patriarcat Grec-Melkite Catholique, 16 Sharia Daher, 11271 Cairo; tel. (2) 5905790; 6,500 adherents (31 December 1998); Exarch Patriarchal Mgr PAUL ANTAKI, Titular Archbishop of Nubia.

Syrian Rite

The Syrian Catholic diocese of Cairo had an estimated 1,763 adherents at 31 December 1998.

Bishop of Cairo: JOSEPH HANNOUCHE, Evêché Syrien Catholique, 46 Sharia Daher, 11271 Cairo; tel. (2) 5901234.

The Anglican Communion

The Anglican diocese of Egypt, suspended in 1958, was revived in 1974 and became part of the Episcopal Church in Jerusalem and the Middle East, formally inaugurated in January 1976. The Province has four dioceses: Jerusalem, Egypt, Cyprus and the Gulf, and Iran, and its President is the Bishop in Egypt. The Bishop in Egypt has jurisdiction also over the Anglican chaplaincies in Algeria, Djibouti, Eritrea, Ethiopia, Libya, Somalia and Tunisia.

Bishop in Egypt: Most Rev. GHAIS ABD AL-MALIK, Diocesan Office, POB 87, 5 Sharia Michel Lutfalla, Cairo (Zamalek); tel. (2) 3320313; fax (2) 3408941; e-mail diocese@intouch.com.

Other Christian Churches

Coptic Evangelical Organization for Social Services: POB 162-11811, Panorama, Cairo; tel. (2) 2975901; fax (2) 2975878; e-mail gm@ceoss.org.eg.

Other denominations active in Egypt include the Coptic Evangelical Church (Synod of the Nile) and the Union of the Armenian Evangelical Churches in the Near East.

JUDAISM

The 1986 census recorded 794 Jews in Egypt.

Jewish Community: Office of the Community, President ESTHER WEINSTEIN, 13 Sharia Sebil el-Khazindar, Abbassia, Cairo; tel. (2) 4824613; internet www.geocities.com/rain/forest/vines/5855.

The Press

Despite a fairly high illiteracy rate in Egypt, the country's press is well developed. Cairo is one of the region's largest publishing centres.

All newspapers and magazines are supervised, according to law, by the Supreme Press Council. The four major publishing houses of al-Ahram, Dar al-Hilal, Dar Akhbar al-Yawm and Dar at-Tahrir operate as separate entities and compete with each other commercially.

The most authoritative daily newspaper is the very long-established *Al-Ahram*.

DAILIES

Alexandria

Bareed ach-Charikat (Companies' Post): POB 813, Alexandria; f. 1952; Arabic; evening; commerce, finance, insurance and marine affairs; Editor S. BENEDUCCI; circ. 15,000.

Al-Ittihad al-Misri (Egyptian Unity): 13 Sharia Sidi Abd ar-Razzak, Alexandria; f. 1871; Arabic; evening; Propr ANWAR MAHER FARAG; Dir HASSAN MAHER FARAG.

Le Journal d'Alexandrie: 1 Sharia Rolo, Alexandria; French; evening; Editor CHARLES ARCACHE.

La Réforme: 8 Passage Sherif, Alexandria; French.

As-Safeer (The Ambassador): 4 Sharia as-Sahafa, Alexandria; f. 1924; Arabic; evening; Editor MUSTAFA SHARAF.

Tachydromos-Egyptos: 4 Sharia Zangarol, Alexandria; tel. (3) 35650; f. 1879; Greek; morning; liberal; Publr PENNY KOUTSOUMIS; Editor DINOS KOUTSOUMIS; circ. 2,000.

Cairo

Al-Ahram (The Pyramids): Sharia al-Galaa, Cairo 11511; tel. (2) 5801600; fax (2) 5786023; e-mail ahramdaily@ahram.org.eg; f. 1875; Arabic; morning, incl. Sundays (international edition published in London, England; North American edition published in New York, USA); Chair. and Chief Editor IBRAHIM NAFEH; circ. 900,000 (weekdays), 1.1m. (Friday).

Al-Ahram al-Misaa' (The Evening *Al-Ahram*): Sharia al-Galaa, Cairo 11511; f. 1990; Arabic; evening; Editor-in-Chief MORSI ATALLAH.

Al-Ahrar: 58 Manshyet as-Sadr, Kobry al-Kobba, Cairo; tel. (2) 4823046; fax (2) 4823027; f. 1977; organ of Liberal Socialist Party; Editor-in-Chief SALAH QABADAYA.

Al-Akhbar (The News): Dar Akhbar al-Yawm, 6 Sharia as-Sahafa, Cairo; tel. (2) 5782600; fax (2) 5782520; f. 1952; Arabic; Chair. IBRAHIM ABU SADAH; Man. Editor GALAL DEWIDAR; circ. 780,000.

Arev: 3 Sharia Sulayman Halabi, Cairo; tel. (2) 754703; f. 1915; Armenian; evening; official organ of the Armenian Liberal Democratic Party; Editor AVEDIS YAPOUDJIAN.

The Egyptian Gazette: 24–26 Sharia Zakaria Ahmad, Cairo; tel. (2) 5783333; fax (2) 5781110; e-mail 100236.3241@compuserve.com; f. 1880; English; morning; Chair. SAMIR RAGAB; Editor-in-Chief MUHAMMAD ALI IBRAHIM; circ. 90,000.

Al-Gomhouriya (The Republic): 24 Sharia Zakaria Ahmad, Cairo; tel. (2) 5783333; fax (2) 5781717; f. 1953; Arabic; morning; mainly economic affairs; Chair. and Editor-in-Chief SAMIR RAGAB; circ. 900,000.

Al-Misaa' (The Evening): 24 Sharia Zakaria Ahmad, Cairo; tel. (2) 5781010; fax (2) 5784747; f. 1956; Arabic; evening; political, social and sport; Editor-in-Chief MUHAMMAD FOUDAH; Man. Dir ABD AL-HAMROSE; circ. 450,000.

Phos: 14 Sharia Zakaria Ahmad, Cairo; f. 1896; Greek; morning; Editor S. PATERAS; Man. BASILE A. PATERAS; circ. 20,000.

Le Progrès Egyptien: 24 Sharia Zakaria Ahmad, Cairo; tel. (2) 5783333; fax (2) 5781110; f. 1890; French; morning including Sundays; Chair. SAMIR RAGAB; Editor-in-Chief KHALED ANWAR BAKIR; circ. 60,000.

Al-Wafd: 1 Sharia Boulos Hanna, Cairo (Dokki); tel. (2) 3482079; fax (2) 3602007; f. 1984; organ of the New Wafd Party; Editor-in-Chief GAMAL BADAWI; circ. 360,000.

PERIODICALS

Alexandria

Al-Ahad al-Gedid (New Sunday): 88 Sharia Said M. Koraim, Alexandria; tel. (3) 807874; f. 1936; Editor-in-Chief and Publr GALAL M. KORAITEM; circ. 60,000.

Alexandria Medical Journal: 4 G. Carducci, Alexandria; tel. (3) 4829001; fax (3) 4833076; internet www.who.sci.eg; f. 1922; English, French and Arabic; quarterly; publ. by Alexandria Medical Asscn; Editor Prof. TOUSSOUN ABOUL AZM.

Amitié Internationale: 59 ave el-Hourriya, Alexandria; tel. (3) 23639; f. 1957; publ. by Asscn Egyptienne d'Amitié Internationale; Arabic and French; quarterly; Editor Dr ZAKI BADAOUI.

L'Annuaire des Sociétés Egyptiennes par Actions: 23 Midan Tahrir, Alexandria; f. 1930; annually in Dec.; French; Propr ELIE I. POLITI; Editor OMAR ES-SAYED MOURSI.

L'Echo Sportif: 7 Sharia de l'Archevêché, Alexandria; French; weekly; Propr MICHEL BITTAR.

Egyptian Cotton Gazette: POB 1772, 12 Sharia Muhammad Tala'at Nooman, Alexandria 21111; tel. (3) 4806971; fax (3) 4833002; e-mail alcotexa@idsc.gov.eg; internet www.welcome.to/alcotexa; f. 1947; organ of the Alexandria Cotton Exporters' Association; English; 2 a year; Chief Editor GALA EL REFAI.

Informateur des Assurances: 1 Sharia Sinan, Alexandria; f. 1936; French; monthly; Propr ELIE I. POLITI; Editor SIMON A. BARANIS.

La Réforme Illustré: 8 Passage Sherif, Alexandria; French; weekly; general.

Sina 'at en-Nassig (L'Industrie Textile): 5 rue de l'Archevêché, Alexandria; Arabic and French; monthly; Editor PHILIPPE COLAS.

Voce d'Italia: 90 Sharia Farahde, Alexandria; Italian; fortnightly; Editor R. AVELLINO.

Cairo

Al-Ahali (The People): Sharia Kareem ad-Dawli, Tala'at Harb Sq., Cairo; tel. (2) 7786583; fax (2) 3900412; f. 1978; weekly; publ. by the National Progressive Unionist Party; Chair. LOTFI WAKID; Editor-in-Chief ABD AL-BAKOURY.

Al-Ahram al-Arabi: Sharia al-Galaa, Cairo 11511; f. 1997; Arabic; weekly; political, social and economic affairs; Chair. IBRAHIM NAFIE; Editor-in-Chief OSAMA SARAYA.

Al-Ahram Hebdo: POB 1057, Sharia al-Galaa, Cairo 11511; tel. (2) 5783104; fax (2) 5782631; e-mail hebdo@ahram.org.eg; internet www.ahram.org.eg/hebdo; f. 1993; French; weekly; Editor-in-Chief MUHAMMAD SALMAWI.

Al-Ahram al-Iqtisadi (The Economic *Al-Ahram*): Sharia al-Galaa, Cairo 11511; tel. (2) 5786100; fax (2) 5786833; Arabic; weekly (Monday); economic and political affairs; owned by Al-Ahram publrs; Chief Editor ISSAM RIFA'AT; circ. 83,280.

Al-Ahram Weekly (The Pyramids): Al-Ahram Bldg, Sharia al-Galaa, Cairo 11511; tel. (2) 5786100; fax (2) 5786833; e-mail weeklyweb@ahram.org.eg; internet www.ahram.org.eg/weekly; f. 1989; English; weekly; publ. by Al-Ahram publications; Editor-in-Chief HOSNI GUINDY; circ. 150,000.

Akhbar al-Adab: 6 Sharia as-Sahafa, Cairo; tel. (2) 5782500; fax (2) 5782510; f. 1993; literature and arts for young people; Editor-in-Chief GAMAL AL-GHITANI.

Akhbar al-Hawadith: 6 Sharia as-Sahafa, Cairo; tel. (2) 5782600; fax (2) 5782510; f. 1993; weekly; crime reports; Editor-in-Chief MUHAMMAD BARAKAT.

Akhbar al-Nogoome: 6 Sharia as-Sahafa, Cairo; tel. (2) 5782600; fax (2) 5782510; f. 1991; weekly; theatre and film news; Editor-in-Chief AMAL OSMAN.

Akhbar ar-Riadah: 6 Sharia as-Sahafa, Cairo; tel. (2) 5782600; fax (2) 5782510; f. 1990; weekly; sport; Editor-in-Chief IBRAHIM HEGAZY.

Akhbar al-Yaum (Daily News): 6 Sharia as-Sahafa, Cairo; tel. (2) 5782600; fax (2) 5782520; f. 1944; Arabic; weekly (Saturday); Chair. and Editor-in-Chief IBRAHIM ABU SEDAH; circ. 1,184,611.

Akher Sa'a (Last Hour): Dar Akhbar al-Yawm, Sharia as-Sahafa, Cairo; tel. (2) 5782600; fax (2) 5782530; f. 1934; Arabic; weekly (Sunday); independent; consumer and news magazine; Editor-in-Chief MAHMOUD SALAH; circ. 150,000.

Aqidaty (My Faith): 24–26 Sharia Zakaria Ahmad, Cairo; tel. (2) 5783333; fax (2) 5781110; weekly; Muslim religious newspaper; Editor-in-Chief ABD AR-RAOUF ES-SAYED; circ. 300,000.

Al-Arabi an-Nassiri: Cairo; f. 1993; publ. by the Nasserist Party; Editor-in-Chief MAHMOUD EL-MARAGHI.

Al-Azhar: Idarat al-Azhar, Sharia al-Azhar, Cairo; f. 1931; Arabic; Islamic monthly; supervised by the Egyptian Council for Islamic Research of Al-Azhar University; Dir MUHAMMAD FARID WAGDI.

Al-Bitrul (Petroleum): Cairo; monthly; publ. by the Egyptian General Petroleum Corporation.

Cairo Today: POB 2098, 1079 Corniche en-Nil, Cairo (Garden City); monthly.

Computerworld Middle East: World Publishing Ltd (Egypt), 41A Masaken al-Fursan Bldg, Sharia Kamal Hassan Ali, Cairo 11361; tel. (2) 3460601; fax (2) 3470118; English; monthly; specialist computer information.

Contemporary Thought: University of Cairo, Cairo; quarterly; Editor Dr Z. N. MAHMOUD.

Ad-Da'wa (The Call): Cairo; Arabic; monthly; organ of the Muslim Brotherhood.

Ad-Doctor: 8 Sharia Hoda Sharawi, Cairo; f. 1947; Arabic; monthly; Editor Dr AHMAD M. KAMAL; circ. 30,000.

Droit al-Haqq: Itihad al-Mohameen al-Arab, 13 Sharia Itihad, Cairo; publ. by the Arab Lawyers' Union; 3 a year.

Echos: 1–5 Sharia Mahmoud Bassiouni, Cairo; f. 1947; French; weekly; Dir and Propr GEORGES QRFALI.

The Egyptian Mail: 24–26 Sharia Zakaria Ahmad, Cairo; weekly; Sat. edn of *The Egyptian Gazette*; English; circ. 40,000.

El-Elm Magazine (Sciences): 24 Sharia Zakaria Ahmad, Cairo; tel. (2) 5781010; fax (2) 5784747; f. 1976; Arabic; monthly; publ. with the Academy of Scientific Research in Egypt; circ. 70,000.

Al-Fusoul (The Seasons): 17 Sharia Sherif Pasha, Cairo; Arabic; monthly; Propr and Chief Editor SAMIR MUHAMMAD ZAKI ABD AL-KADER.

Al-Garidat at-Tigariyat al-Misriya (The Egyptian Business Paper): 25 Sharia Nubar Pasha, Cairo; f. 1921; Arabic; weekly; circ. 7,000.

Hawa'a (Eve): Dar al-Hilal, 16 Sharia Muhammad Ezz el-Arab, Cairo 11511; tel. (2) 3625450; fax (2) 3625469; f. 1892; women's magazine; Arabic; weekly (Sat.); Chief Editor EKBAL BARAKA; circ. 210,502.

Al-Hilal Magazine: Dar al-Hilal, 16 Sharia Muhammad Ezz el-Arab, Cairo 11511; tel. (2) 3625450; fax (2) 3625469; f. 1895; Arabic; literary monthly; Editor MOUSTAFA NABIL.

Horreyati: 24 Sharia Zakaria Ahmad, Cairo; tel. (2) 5781010; fax (2) 5784747; f. 1990; weekly; social, cultural and sport; Editor-in-Chief MUHAMMAD NOUR ED-DIN; circ. 250,000.

Huwa wa Hiya (He and She): Middle East Foundation, POB 525, Cairo 11511; tel. (2) 5167400; fax (2) 5167325; f. 1977; monthly; news, leisure, sport, health, religion, women's issues; Dir GEORGE TAWFIK.

Industrial Egypt: POB 251, 26A Sharia Sherif Pasha, Cairo; tel. (2) 3928317; fax (2) 3928075; f. 1924; quarterly bulletin and year book of the Federation of Egyptian Industries in English and Arabic; Editor ALI FAHMY.

Informateur Financier et Commercial: 24 Sharia Sulayman Pasha, Cairo; f. 1929; weekly; Dir HENRI POLITI; circ. 15,000.

Al-Iza'a wat-Television (Radio and Television): 16 Sharia Muhammad Ezz el-Arab, Cairo 11511; tel. (2) 3643314; fax (2) 3543030; f. 1935; Arabic; weekly; Man. Editor MAHMOUD ALI; circ. 80,000.

Al-Kerazeh (The Sermon): Cairo; Arabic; weekly newspaper of the Coptic Orthodox Church.

Al-Kawakeb (The Stars): Dar al-Hilal, 16 Sharia Muhammad Ezz el-Arab, Cairo 11511; tel. (2) 3625450; fax (2) 3625469; f. 1952; Arabic; weekly; film magazine; Editor-in-Chief RAGAA AN-NAKKASH; circ. 86,381.

Kitab al-Hilal: Dar al-Hilal, 16 Sharia Muhammad Ezz el-Arab, Cairo 11511; tel. (2) 3625450; fax (2) 3625469; monthly; Founders EMILE and SHOUKRI ZEIDAN; Editor MOUSTAFA NABIL.

Al-Kora wal-Malaeb (Football and Playgrounds): 24 Sharia Zakaria Ahmad, Cairo; tel. (2) 5783333; fax (2) 5784747; f. 1976; Arabic; weekly; sport; circ. 150,000.

Al-Liwa' al-Islami (Islamic Standard): 11 Sharia Sherif Pasha, Cairo; f. 1982; Arabic; weekly; govt paper to promote official view of Islamic revivalism; Propr AHMAD HAMZA; Editor MUHAMMAD ALI SHETA; circ. 30,000.

Lotus Magazine: 104 Sharia Qasr el-Eini, Cairo; f. 1992; English, French and Arabic; quarterly; computer software magazine; Editor BEREND HARMENS.

Magallat al-Mohandessin (The Engineer's Magazine): 28 Sharia Ramses, Cairo; f. 1945; publ. by The Engineers' Syndicate; Arabic and English; 10 a year; Editor and Sec. MAHMOUD SAMI ABD AL-KAWI.

Al-Magallat az-Zira'ia (The Agricultural Magazine): Cairo; monthly; agriculture; circ. 30,000.

Mayo (May): Sharia al-Galaa, Cairo; f. 1981; weekly; organ of National Democratic Party; Chair. ABDULLAH ABD AL-BARY; Chief Editor SAMIR RAGAB; circ. 500,000.

Medical Journal of Cairo University: Qasr el-Eini Hospital, Sharia Qasr el-Eini, Cairo; tel. (2) 3655768; f. 1933; Qasr el-Eini Clinical Society; English; quarterly; Editor M. MOATZ ESH-SHERBINI.

MEN Economic Weekly: Middle East News Agency, 4 Sharia Hoda Sharawi, Cairo; tel. (2) 3933000; fax 3935055.

The Middle East Observer: 41 Sharia Sherif, Cairo; tel. (2) 3926919; fax (2) 3939732; e-mail fouda@soficom.com.eg; f. 1954; English; weekly; specializing in economics of Middle East and African markets; also publishes supplements on law, foreign trade and tenders; agent for IMF, UN and IDRC publications, distributor of World Bank publications; Man. Owner AHMAD FODA; Chief Editor MUHAMMAD ABDULLAH HESHAM A. RAOUF; circ. 20,000.

Middle East Times Egypt: 2 Sharia el-Malek el-Afdal, Cairo (Zamalek); tel. (2) 3419930; fax (2) 3413725; e-mail met@ritsec1.com.eg; f. 1983; English; weekly; Man. Editor ROD CRAIG; circ. 6,000.

Al-Musawar: Dar al-Hilal, 16 Sharia Muhammad Ezz el-Arab, Cairo 11511; tel. (2) 3625450; fax (2) 3625469; f. 1924; Arabic; weekly; news; Chair. and Editor-in-Chief MAKRAM MUHAMMAD AHMAD; circ. 130,423.

Nesf ad-Donia: Sharia al-Galaa, Cairo 11511; tel. (2) 5786100; f. 1990; weekly; women's magazine; publ. by Al-Ahram Publications; Editor-in-Chief SANAA AL-BESI.

October: Dar al-Maaref, 1119 Sharia Corniche en-Nil, Cairo; tel. (2) 5777077; fax (2) 5744999; f. 1976; weekly; Chair. and Editor-in-Chief RAGAB AL-BANA; circ. 140,500.

Al-Omal (The Workers): 90 Sharia al-Galaa, Cairo; publ. by the Egyptian Trade Union Federation: Arabic; weekly; Chief Editor AHMAD HARAK.

PC World Middle East: World Publishing Ltd (Egypt), 41A Masaken al-Fursan Bldg, Sharia Kamal Hassan Ali, Cairo 11361; tel. (2) 34606; fax (2) 3470118; monthly; computers.

Le Progrès Dimanche: 24 Sharia al-Galaa, Cairo; tel. (2) 5781010; fax (2) 5784747; French; weekly; Sunday edition of *Le Progrès Egyptien*; Editor-in-Chief KHALED ANWAR BAKIR; circ. 35,000.

Rose al-Yousuf: 89A Sharia Qasr el-Eini, Cairo; tel. (2) 3540888; fax (2) 3556413; f. 1925; Arabic; weekly; political; circulates throughout all Arab countries; Chair. of Board and Editor-in-Chief MUHAMMAD ABD AL-MONEIM; circ. 35,000.

As-Sabah (The Morning): 4 Sharia Muhammad Said Pasha, Cairo; f. 1922; Arabic; weekly (Thurs.); Editor RAOUF TAWFIK.

Sabah al-Kheir (Good Morning): 89A Sharia Qasr el-Eini, Cairo; tel. (2) 3540888; fax (2) 3556413; f. 1956; Arabic; weekly (Thurs.); light entertainment; Chief Editor RAOUF TAWFIK; circ. 70,000.

Ash-Shaab (The People): 313 Sharia Port Said, Sayeda Zeinab, Cairo; tel. (2) 3909716; fax (2) 3900283; e-mail elshaab@idsc.gov.eg; f. 1979; organ of Socialist Labour Party; bi-weekly (Tues. and Fri.); Editor-in-Chief MAGDI AHMAD HUSSEIN; circ. 130,000.

Shashati (My Screen): 24 Sharia Zakaria Ahmad, Cairo; tel. (2) 5781010; fax (2) 5784747; weekly; art, culture, fashion and television news.

As-Siyassa ad-Dawliya: Al-Ahram Bldg, 12th Floor, Sharia al-Galaa, Cairo 11511; tel. (2) 5786022; fax (2) 5786833; e-mail siyassa@ahram.org.eg; quarterly; politics and foreign affairs; Editor-in-Chief Dr OSAMA AL-GHAZALI.

Tabibak al-Khass (Family Doctor): Dar al-Hilal, 16 Sharia Muhammad Ezz el-Arab, Cairo; tel. (2) 3625473; fax (2) 3625442; monthly.

At-Tahrir (Liberation): 5 Sharia Naguib, Rihani, Cairo; Arabic; weekly; Editor ABD AL-AZIZ SADEK.

At-Taqaddum (Progress): c/o 1 Sharia Jarim ed-Dawlah, Cairo; f. 1978; weekly; organ of National Progressive Unionist Party.

Tchehreh Nema: 14 Sharia Hassan el-Akbar (Abdine), Cairo; f. 1904; Iranian; monthly; political, literary and general; Editor MANUCHEHR TCHEHREH NEMA MOADEB ZADEH.

Up-to-Date International Industry: 10 Sharia al-Galaa, Cairo; Arabic and English; monthly; foreign trade journal.

Watani (My Country): 27 Sharia Abd al-Khalek Sarwat, Cairo; tel. (2) 3927201; fax (2) 3935946; f. 1958; Arabic; independent Sun. newspaper addressing Egyptians in general and the Christian Copts in particular; Editor-in-Chief Dr SAMI AZIZ; Publr ANTOINE SIDHOM; circ. 50,000.

Yulio (July): July Press and Publishing House, Cairo; f. 1986; weekly; Nasserist; Editor ABDULLAH IMAM; and a monthly cultural magazine, Editor MAHMOUD AL-MARAGHI.

NEWS AGENCIES

Middle East News Agency (MENA): 17 Sharia Hoda Sharawi, Cairo; tel. (2) 3933000; fax (2) 3935055; e-mail newsroom@mena.org.eg; f. 1955; regular service in Arabic, English and French; Chair. and Editor-in-Chief MOUSTAFA NAGUIB.

Foreign Bureaux

Agence France-Presse (AFP): POB 1437-15511, 2nd Floor, 10 Misaha Sq, Cairo; tel. (2) 3481236; fax (2) 3603282; Chief SAMMY KETZ.

Agencia EFE (Spain): 35A Sharia Abou el-Feda, 4th Floor, Apt 14, Cairo (Zamalek); Correspondent DOMINGO DEL PIÑO.

Agenzia Nazionale Stampa Associata (ANSA) (Italy): 19 Sharia Abd al-Khalek Sarwat, Cairo; tel. (2) 3929821; fax (2) 3938642; Chief ANTONELLA TARQUINI.

Allgemeiner Deutscher Nachrichtendienst (ADN) (Germany): 17 Sharia el-Brazil, Apt 59, Cairo (Zamalek); tel. (2) 3404006; Correspondent RALF SCHULTZE.

Associated Press (AP) (USA): POB 1077, 1117 Sharia Corniche en-Nil, (Maspiro), Cairo 11221; tel. (2) 5784091; fax (2) 5784094; internet www.ap.org; Chief of Middle East Services EARLEEN FISHER.

Deutsche Presse-Agentur (dpa) (Germany): 14th Floor, 1125 Corniche en-Nil, Cairo; tel. (2) 5780351; fax (2) 5780354; e-mail 101234,46@compuserve.com; Chief HANS DAHNE.

Informatsionnoye Telegrafnoye Agentstvo Rossii—Telegrafnoye Agentstvo Suverennykh Stran (ITAR—TASS) (Russia): 30 Sharia Muhammad Mazhar, Cairo (Zamalek); tel. 3419784; fax (2) 3417268; Dir MIKHAIL I. KROUTIKHIN.

Jiji Press (Japan): 9 Sharia el-Kamal Muhammad, Cairo (Zamalek); tel. (2) 7356237; fax (2) 7355244; e-mail jijipresscairo@yahoo.com; Chief TETSUYA KATAYAMA.

Kyodo News (Japan): Flat 301, 15 Sharia Hassan Sabri, Cairo 11211 (Zamalek); tel. (2) 7361756; fax (2) 7356105; e-mail kyodocr@intouch.com; Chief SUSUMU SAKATA.

Reuters (United Kingdom): POB 2040, 21st Floor, Bank Misr Tower, 153 Sharia Muhammad Farid, Cairo; tel. (2) 5777150; fax (2) 5771133; e-mail cairo.newsroom@reuters.com; internet www.reuters.com; Chief ALISTAIR LYON.

United Press International (UPI) (USA): POB 872, 4 Sharia Eloui, Cairo; tel. (2) 3928106.

Xinhua (New China) News Agency (People's Republic of China): 2 Moussa Galal Sq., Mohandessin, Cairo; tel. (2) 3448950.

The Iraqi News Agency (INA) reopened its office in Cairo in 1985. The Saudi Press Agency (SPA) is also represented in Cairo.

PRESS ASSOCIATIONS

Egyptian Press Syndicate: Cairo; Chair. IBRAHIM NAFEH.

Foreign Press Association: Room 2037, Mariot Hotel, Cairo; tel. (2) 3419957.

Publishers

General Egyptian Book Organization: POB 1660, 117 Sharia Corniche en-Nil, Boulac, Cairo; tel. (2) 5775371; fax (2) 5754213; e-mail ssarhan@idsc.gov.eg; f. 1961; editing, publishing and distribution; organizer of Cairo International Book Fair; affiliated to the Ministry of Culture; Chair. Dr SAMIR SARHAN; Commercial Dir SAMIR SAAD KHALIL.

Alexandria

Alexandria University Press: Shatby, Alexandria.

Dar al-Matbo al-Gadidah: 5 Sharia St Mark, Alexandria; tel. (3) 4825508; fax (3) 4833819; agriculture, information sciences; social sciences.

Egyptian Printing and Publishing House: Ahmad es-Sayed Marouf, 59 Safia Zaghoul, Alexandria; f. 1947.

Maison Egyptienne d'Editions: Ahmad es-Sayed Marouf, Sharia Adib, Alexandria; f. 1950.

Maktab al-Misri al-Hadith li-t-Tiba wan-Nashr: 7 Sharia Noubar, Alexandria; also at 2 Sharia Sherif, Cairo; Man. AHMAD YEHIA.

Cairo

Al-Ahram Establishment: Al-Ahram Bldg, 6 Sharia al-Galaa, Cairo 11511; tel. (2) 5786100; fax (2) 5786023; e-mail ahram@ahram.org.eg; internet www.ahram.org.eg; f. 1875; publ. newspapers, magazines and books, incl. *Al-Ahram*; Chair. and Chief Editor IBRAHIM NAFEI; Dep. Chair. and Gen. Man. ALI GHONEIM.

Akhbar al-Yawm Publishing Group: 6 Sharia as-Sahafa, Cairo; tel. (2) 5748100; fax (2) 5748895; f. 1944; publ. *Al-Akhbar* (daily), *Akhbar al-Yawm* (weekly), and colour magazine *Akher Sa'a* (weekly); Pres. IBRAHIM SAAD.

Boustany's Publishing House: 29 Sharia Faggalah, Cairo 11271; tel. (2) 5915315; fax (2) 4177915; e-mail bph@ritsec3.com.eg; internet www.boustanys.com; f. 1900; fiction, poetry, history, biography, philosophy, language, literature, politics, religion, archaeology, Egyptology; Chief Exec. Mrs FADWA BOUSTANY.

Cairo University Press: Al-Giza, Cairo; tel. (2) 846144.

Dar al-Gomhouriya: 24 Sharia Zakaria Ahmad, Cairo; tel. (2) 5781010; fax (2) 5784747; affiliate of At-Tahrir Printing and Publishing House; publications include the dailies, *Al-Gomhouriya*, *Al-Misaa'*, *Egyptian Gazette* and *Le Progrès Egyptien*; Pres. SAMIR RAGAB.

Dar al-Hilal Publishing Institution: 16 Sharia Muhammad Ezz el-Arab, Cairo 11511; tel. (2) 3625450; fax (2) 3625469; f. 1892; publ. *Al-Hilal, Riwayat al-Hilal, Kitab al-Hilal, Tabibak al-Khass* (monthlies); *Al-Mussawar, Al-Kawakeb, Hawaa, Samir, Mickey* (weeklies); Chief Exec. MAKRAN MUHAMMAD AHMAD.

Dar al-Kitab al-Masri: POB 156, 33 Sharia Qasr en-Nil, Cairo 11511; tel. (2) 3922168; fax (2) 3924657; e-mail hlelzein@datum .com.eg; f. 1929; publishing, printing and distribution; publishers of books on Islam and history, as well as dictionaries, encyclopaedias, textbooks, children's books and books of general interest; Pres. and Man. Dir HASSAN EZ-ZEIN.

Dar al-Maaref: 1119 Sharia Corniche en-Nil, Cairo; tel. (2) 5777077; fax (2) 5744999; e-mail maaref@idselgov.eg; f. 1890; publishing, printing and distribution of wide variety of books in Arabic and other languages; publishers of *October* magazine; Chair. and Man. Dir RAGAB AL-BANA.

Dar an-Nahda al-Arabia: 32 Sharia Abd al-Khalek Sarwat, Cairo; tel. (2) 3926931; f. 1960; literature, law.

Dar an-Nashr (formerly Les Editions Universitaires d'Egypte): POB 1347, 41 Sharia Sherif, Cairo 11511; tel. (2) 3934606; fax (2) 3921997; f. 1947; university textbooks, academic works, encyclopaedia.

Dar ash-Shorouk Publishing House: 8 Sharia Sebaweh el-Masri, Nasr City, Cairo 11371; tel. (2) 4023399; fax (2) 4037567; e-mail imoallem@shorouk.com; f. 1968; publishing, printing and distribution; publishers of books on politics, history, Islamic studies, economics, literature, art and children's books; Chair. IBRAHIM EL-MOALLEM.

Dar ath-Thakafah al-Gadidah: 32 Sharia Sabry Abou Alam, Cairo; tel. (2) 42718; f. 1968; Pres. MUHAMMAD YOUSUF ELGUINDI.

Editions le Progrès: 6 Sharia Sherif Pasha, Cairo; Propr WADI SHOUKRI.

Egyptian Co for Printing and Publishing: 40 Sharia Noubar, Cairo; tel. (2) 21310; Chair. MUHAMMAD MAHMOUD HAMED.

Elias Modern Publishing House: 1 Sharia Kenisset ar-Rum el-Kathulik, Daher, Cairo; tel. (2) 5903756; fax (2) 5880091; e-mail eliasmph@gega.net; internet www.eliaspublishing.com; f. 1913; publishing, printing and distribution; publs dictionaries, children's books and books on linguistics, poetry and arts; Man. Dir LAURA KFOURY; Gen. Man. NADIM ELIAS.

Al-Khira Press: 8 Sharia Soliman el-Halabi, Cairo; tel. and fax (2) 5744809; Owner ABD AL-MEGUID MUHAMMAD.

Lagnat at-Taalif wat-Targama wan-Nashr (Committee for Writing, Translating and Publishing Books): 9 Sharia el-Kerdassi (Abdine), Cairo.

Librairie La Renaissance d'Egypte (Hassan Muhammad & Sons): POB 2172, 9 Sharia Adly, Cairo; f. 1930; religion, history, geography, medicine, architecture, economics, politics, law, philosophy, psychology, children's books, atlases, dictionaries; Man. HASSAN MUHAMMAD.

Maktabet Misr: POB 16, 3 Sharia Kamal Sidki, Cairo; tel. (2) 5898553; fax (2) 5907593; f. 1932; publs wide variety of fiction, biographies and textbooks for schools and universities; Man. AMIR SAID GOUDA ES-SAHHAR.

Middle East Book Centre: 45 Sharia Qasr en-Nil, Cairo; tel. (2) 910980; f. 1954; biography, fiction, history, language, literature, religion, philosophy, sciences; Man. Dir Dr A. M. MOSHARRAFA.

National Centre for Educational Research and Development: 12 Sharia Waked, el-Borg el-Faddy, POB 836, Cairo; tel. (2) 3930981; f. 1956; formerly Documentation and Research Centre for Education (Ministry of Education); bibliographies, directories, information and education bulletins; Dir Prof. ABD EL-FATTAH GALAL.

National Library Press (Dar al-Kutub): Midan Ahmad Maher, Cairo; bibliographic works.

Senouhy Publishers: 54 Sharia Abd al-Khalek Sarwat, Cairo; f. 1956; history, poetry, regional interests, religion, non-fiction; Man. Dir LEILA A. FADEL.

At-Tahrir Printing and Publishing House: 24 Sharia Zakaria Ahmad, Cairo; tel. (2) 5781222; fax (2) 2784747; e-mail eltahrir@eltahrir.net; internet www.eltahrir.net; f. 1953; affil. to Shura (Advisory) Council; Pres. and Chair. of Bd SAMIR RAGAB.

Watani: Sharia Tala'at Harb, Cairo; tel. (2) 3927201; fax (2) 3935946; Editor-in-Chief Dr SAMI AZIZ.

Broadcasting and Communications

TELECOMMUNICATIONS

Telecom Egypt: POB 2271, Sharia Ramses, Cairo 11511; tel. (2) 5793444; fax (2) 5744244; f. 1957; partial privatization scheduled for 2001; Chair. AKIL HAMED BESHIR.

Egyptian Company for Mobile Services (MobiNil): Cairo; e-mail customercare@mobinil.com; internet www.mobinil.com; began operation of the existing state-controlled mobile telecommunications network in early 1998; CEO OSMAN SULTAN.

MisrFone (Click GSM): Cairo; f. 1998; mobile telephone service provider; majority-owned by Vodafone Air Touch (UK/US); Chair. MUHAMMAD NOSSAIR; CEO and Gen. Man. MUHAMMAD EL-HAMASY.

BROADCASTING

Radio

Egyptian Radio and Television Union (ERTU): POB 11511, Cairo 1186; tel. (2) 5787120; fax (2) 746989; internet www.sis.gov.eg/vidaudio/html/audiofm.htm; f. 1928; 450 hours daily. Home Service radio programmes in Arabic, English and French; foreign services in Arabic, English, French, Swahili, Hausa, Bengali, Urdu, German, Spanish, Armenian, Greek, Hebrew, Indonesian, Malay, Thai, Hindi, Pushtu, Persian, Turkish, Somali, Portuguese, Fulani, Italian, Zulu, Shona, Sindebele, Lingala, Afar, Amharic, Yoruba, Wolof, Bambara; Pres. AMIN BASSIOUNI.

Middle East Radio: Société Egyptienne de Publicité, 24-26 Sharia Zakaria Ahmad, Cairo; tel. (2) 5781010; fax (2) 5784747; internet www.tahriv.net.

Television

Egyptian Radio and Television Union (ERTU): (see Radio).

Finance

(cap. = capital; dep. = deposits;
res = reserves; m. = million; brs = branches;
amounts in Egyptian pounds unless otherwise stated)

BANKING

Central Bank

Central Bank of Egypt: 31 Sharia Qasr en-Nil, Cairo; tel. (2) 3931514; fax (2) 3926361; e-mail research@cbe.org.eg; internet www.cbe.org.eg; f. 1961; privatization scheduled for 2001; dep. 95,411m., total assets 136,650m. (June 1999); Gov. and Chair. ISMAIL HASSAN MUHAMMAD; Dep. Gov. MAHMOUD IBRAHIM ABOUL-EIOUN; 3 brs.

Commercial and Specialized Banks

Alexandria Commercial and Maritime Bank, SAE: POB 2376, 85 ave el-Hourriya, Alexandria 21519; tel. (3) 4921556; fax (3) 4913706; f. 1981; cap. 74.9m., res 133.1m., dep. 1,372.1m., total assets 1,665.6m. (Dec. 1999); Chair. MUHAMMAD ADEL EL-BARKOUKI; Gen. Man. SALAH ED-DIN M.H. OMAR; 6 brs.

Arab Land Bank: POB 26, 78 Sharia Gamaat ad-Duwal Alarabiya, Cairo; tel. (2) 3383691; fax (2) 3383561; f. 1947; state-owned; cap. 95m., res 62.5m., dep. 4,572m., total assets 5,028.7m. (June 1998); Chair. ALAA ALOUSSIYA; Gen. Man. AHMAD EL-AROUSSI.

Bank of Alexandria: 6 Sharia Salah Salem, Alexandria; and 49 Sharia Qasr en-Nil, Cairo; tel. (3) 4830159 (Alexandria), (2) 3913822 (Cairo); fax (3) 4839968 (Alexandria), (2) 3919805 (Cairo); e-mail foreign@alexbank.com; internet www.alexbank.com; f. 1957; privatization scheduled for 2001; cap. 700m., res 421.2m., dep. 17,994m., total assets 20,527.9m. (June 1999); Chair. MAHMOUD ABD AS-SALAM OMAR; 184 brs.

Bank of Commerce and Development (At-Tegaryoon): POB 1373, 13 Sharia 26 July, Mohandessin, Cairo (Agouza); tel. (2) 3472063; fax (2) 3023963; f. 1980; cap. 205.9m., dep. 701.9m., total assets 903.4m. (Dec. 1998); Chair. and Man. Dir SAMIR MUHAMMAD FOUAD EL-QASRI; 6 brs.

Banque du Caire, SAE: POB 1495, 30 Sharia Rushdi, Cairo (Abdeen); tel. (2) 3904554; fax (2) 3908992; internet www.bdc.com.eg; f. 1952; state-owned; cap. 750.0m., res 543.8m., dep. 29,777.5m., total assets 32,829.9m. (June 1998); Chair. AHMAD-MONIR EL-BARDAI; Vice Chair. BADAWY HASSAN HASSANEIN; 257 brs in Egypt, 5 abroad.

Banque Misr: 151 Sharia Muhammad Farid, Cairo; tel. (2) 3912711; fax (2) 3919779; internet www.banquemisr.com; f. 1920; privatization scheduled for 2001; cap. 1,000m., res 807.9m., dep. 47,403.5m., total assets 51,854.0m. (June 1999); Chair. Dr BAHAA ED-DIN HELMY; 496 brs.

Commercial International Bank (Egypt), SAE: POB 2430, Nile Tower Bldg, 21-23 Sharia Giza, Cairo (Giza); tel. (2) 5701949; fax (2) 5703172; e-mail info@cibeg.com; internet www.cibeg.com; f. 1975 as Chase National Bank (Egypt) SAE; adopted present name 1987; National Bank of Egypt has 19.5% interest, International Finance Corpn 5%; cap. 650m., dep. 11,056.7m., total assets 15,015.7m. (Dec. 1999); Exec. Chair. and Man. Dir MAHMOUD ABD AL-AZIZ; Vice Chair. MAHMOUD HELAL; 27 brs.

Egyptian British Bank, SAE: POB 126, Abou el-Feda Bldg, 3 Sharia Abou el-Feda, Cairo (Zamalek); tel. (2) 3409186; fax (2) 3414010; f. 1982; the Hongkong and Shanghai Banking Corporation has a 40% shareholding, Egyptian interests 51%, other Arab interests 9%; cap. 161.2m., res 80.2m., dep. 2,632.8m., total assets 3,140.1m. (Dec. 1998); Chair. Dr IBRAHIM ABOU EL-EYOUN A. KAMAL; Man. Dir ABD AS-SALAM EL-ANWAR; 7 brs.

Export Development Bank of Egypt (EDBE): 108 Mohyee el-Din Aboul Ezz, Doki 12311; f. 1983 to replace National Import-Export Bank; tel. (2) 3385383; fax (2) 3385940; cap. 250m., res 237.6m., dep. 3,933.4m., total assets 5,106.0m. (June 1999); Chair. MAHMOUD MUHAMMAD MAHMOUD; Vice-Chair. SALAH ED-DIN FAHMY; 13 brs.

National Bank for Development (NBD): POB 647, 5 Sharia el-Borsa el-Gedida, Cairo 11511; tel. (2) 3928849; fax (2) 3905681; e-mail nbd@internetegypt.com; internet www.nbdegypt.com; f. 1980; cap. 200.0m., res 154.2m., dep. 5,489m., total assets 6,250m. (Dec. 1999); Chair. MUHAMMAD ZAKI EL-ORABI; 67 brs; there are affiliated National Banks for Development in 16 governorates.

National Bank of Egypt: POB 11611, National Bank of Egypt Tower, 1187 Corniche en-Nil, Cairo; tel. (2) 5749101; fax (2) 5762672; e-mail nbe@nbe.com.eg; internet www.nbe.com.eg; f. 1898; privatization scheduled for 2001; handles all commercial banking operations; cap. 1,000m., res 2,464m., dep. 54,715m., total assets 65,297m. (June 1999); Chair. AHMAD DIAA ED-DIN FAHMY; Dep. Chair. HUSSEIN ABD AL-AZIZ HUSSEIN; 343 brs.

Principal Bank for Development and Agricultural Credit: POB 11669, 110 Sharia Qasr el-Eini, Cairo; tel. (2) 3551204; fax (2)

3548337; f. 1976 to succeed former credit organizations; state-owned; cap. 1,105m., res 245m., dep. 5,244m., total assets 10,257m. (June 1997); Chair. HASSAN KHIDR; 8 brs.

Société Arabe Internationale de Banque (SAIB): POB 54, 56 Sharia Gamet ed-Dowal al-Arabia, Mohandessin, Cairo (Giza); tel. (2) 3499463; fax (2) 3603497; f. 1976; the Arab International Bank has a 39.3% share, other interests 60.7%; cap. US $42m., res US $33.0m., dep. US $328.8m., total assets US $434.7m. (Dec. 1999); Chair. Dr HASSAN ABBAS ZAKI; Man. Dir MUHAMMAD NOUR; 4 brs.

United Bank of Egypt (UBE): Cairo Center, 106 Sharia Kasr el-Eini, Cairo; tel. (2) 7920146; fax (2) 7920153; e-mail info@ube.net; internet www.ube.net; f. 1981 as Dakahlia National Bank for Development; current name adopted in 1997; cap. 200m., total assets 3,104m. (Dec. 2000); Chair. and Man. Dir SEIF COUTRY; 9 brs.

Social Bank

Nasser Social Bank: POB 2552, 35 Sharia Qasr en-Nil, Cairo; tel. (2) 3924484; fax (2) 3921930; f. 1971; state-owned; interest-free savings and investment bank for social and economic activities, participating in social insurance, specializing in financing co-operatives, craftsmen and social institutions; cap. 20m.; Chair. NASSIF TAHOON.

Multinational Banks

Arab African International Bank: 5 Midan Al-Saray el-Koubra, POB 60, Majlis el-Sha'ab, Cairo 11516; tel. (2) 7945094; fax (2) 7958493; internet www.aaibank.com; f. 1964 as Arab African Bank, renamed 1978; cap. US $100.0m., res US $20.4m., dep. US $662.0m., total assets US $957.0m. (Dec. 1999); commercial investment bank; shareholders are Govts of Kuwait, Egypt, Algeria, Jordan and Qatar, Bank Al-Jazira (Saudi Arabia), Rafidain Bank (Iraq), individuals and Arab institutions; Chair. and Man. Dir Dr FAHED MOHAMMED AL-RASHED; Gen. Man. HASSAN ABDALLA; 6 brs in Egypt, 4 abroad.

Arab International Bank: POB 1563, 35 Sharia Abd al-Khalek Sarwat, Cairo; tel. (2) 3918794; fax (2) 3916233; internet www.aib_egypt.com; f. 1971 as Egyptian International Bank for Foreign Trade and Investment, renamed 1974; cap. US $240m., res US $101.5m., dep. US $1,982.7m., total assets US $2,370.3m. (June 1999); offshore bank; aims to promote trade and investment in shareholders' countries and other Arab countries; owned by Egypt, Libya, UAE, Oman, Qatar and private Arab shareholders; Chair. Dr MUSTAFA KHALIL; Man. Dir ALY DABBOUS; 6 brs in Egypt, 1 in Bahrain.

Commercial Foreign Venture Banks

Alwatany Bank of Egypt: POB 63, 13 Sharia Semar, Dr Fouad Mohi ed-Din Sq., Gamet ed-Dewal al-Arabia, Mohandessin, Cairo 12655; tel. (2) 3388816; fax (2) 3379302; e-mail watany@alwatany .com.eg; internet www.alwatany.com.eg; f. 1980; cap. 105.0m., res 206.1m., dep. 2,733.4m., total assets 3,257.7m. (Dec. 1998); Chair. ADEL HUSSEIN EZZI; Man. Dir FATMA I. LOTFY; 13 brs.

Banque du Caire et de Paris: POB 2441, 3 Sharia Latin America, Cairo (Garden City); tel. (2) 7948323; fax (2) 7940619; e-mail bcpegypt@bcpegypt.com; f. 1977; BNP Group Paribas has 76% interest and Banque du Caire 22%; cap. 50.5m., res 30.6m., dep. 878.6m., total assets 1,135.2m. (Dec. 1998); Chair. JEAN THOMAGEAU; Man. Dir NOUR NAHAURI; 6 brs.

Cairo Barclays Bank, SAE: POB 110, 12 Midan esh-Sheikh Yousuf, Cairo (Garden City); tel. (2) 3662600; fax (2) 3662810; f. 1975 as Cairo Barclays Int. Bank; name changed to Banque du Caire Barclays International in 1983; renamed in 1999; Barclays Bank has 60%, Banque du Caire 40%; cap. 50m., res 116.0m., dep. 2,472m., total assets 2,890m. (Dec. 1999); Chair. ANDREW BUXTON; Man. Dir WAGDI RABBAT; 4 brs.

Cairo Far East Bank, SAE: POB 757, 104 Corniche en-Nil, Cairo (Dokki); tel. (2) 3362516; fax (2) 3483818; f. 1978; cap. 62.5m., res 12.9m., dep. 279.8m., total assets 369.1m. (Dec. 1998); Chair. Dr HASSAN FAG EN-NOUR; Man. Dir FAWZIA YOUSUF; 3 brs.

Crédit International d'Egypte: 46 Sharia el-Batal Ahmad Abd al-Aziz, Mohandessin, Cairo; tel. (2) 3361897; fax (2) 3608673; e-mail cie@soficom.com.eg; f. 1977; Crédit Commercial de France has 93.3% interest, others 6.7%; cap. 60.2m., res 32.4m., total assets 909.0m. (Dec. 1999); Chief Gen. Man. GEORGES CHOUEIRI; 3 brs.

Delta International Bank: POB 1159, 1113 Corniche en-Nil, Cairo; tel. (2) 5753492; fax (2) 5743403; e-mail dibbank@ mst1.mist.com.eg; f. 1978; cap. 300m., res 100.1m., dep. 1,258m., total assets 1,774m. (Dec. 1998); Chair. and Man. Dir ALI MUHAMMAD NEGM; 16 brs.

Egyptian American Bank: POB 1825, 4 & 6 Sharia Hassan Sabri, Cairo (Zamalek); tel. (2) 3391575; fax (2) 3420265; e-mail kafali@ eab-online.com; internet www.eab-online.com; f. 1976; Amex Holdings Inc. has 40.8% interest, Bank of Alexandria 35.8% and Public 23.4%; cap. 144m., res 359m., dep. 4,709m., total assets 5,764m. (Dec. 1999); Chair. MAHMOUD ABD AS-SALAM OMAR; Man. Dir JAMES D. VAUGHN; 30 brs.

Egyptian Commercial Bank: POB 92, 4th Floor, Evergreen Bldg, 10 Sharia Talaat Harb, Majlis ash-Sha'ab, Cairo; tel. (2) 5779766; fax (2) 5799862; f. 1978 as Alexandria-Kuwait International Bank, name changed as above in 1997; cap. 150m., res 14.1m., dep. 1,715.5m., total assets 1,945.2m. (Dec. 1999); Chair. MUHAMMAD ABD AL-WAHAD; Gen. Man. AHMAD NABIL EL-MINOUFI; 6 brs.

Egyptian Gulf Bank: POB 56, El-Orman Plaza Bldg, 8–10 Sharia Ahmad Nessim, Cairo (Giza); tel. (2) 3606640; fax (2) 3606512; e-mail h.r.egb@mst1.mist.com.eg; f. 1981; Misr Insurance Co has 20.2% interest, cap. 217.7m., res 22.0m., dep. 1,951.7m., total assets 2,332.1m. (Dec. 1998); Chair. JAWAD BU KHAMSEEN; Man. Dir MUHAMMAD BARAKAT; 5 brs.

Egyptian-Saudi Finance Bank: POB 188, Es-Sabbah Tower, 8 Sharia Ibrahim Naguib, Cairo (Garden City); tel. (2) 7946208; fax (2) 7942911; internet www.esfbank.com; f. 1980 as Pyramids Bank; cap. 103.5m., res 23.1m., dep. 1,627.1m., total assets 1,813.0m. (Dec. 1999); Chair. Sheikh SALEH ABDULLAH KAMAL; Man. Dir SOBHY BADAWY YAHIA; 7 brs.

Faisal Islamic Bank of Egypt: POB 2446, 1113 Corniche en-Nil, Cairo 11511; tel. (2) 5753109; fax (2) 777301; f. 1979; all banking operations conducted according to Islamic principles; cap. 263.7m., res 35.8m., dep. 6,080.5m., total assets 6,843.6m. (June 1998); Chair. Prince MUHAMMAD AL-FAISAL AS-SA'UD; 14 brs.

Misr Exterior Bank, SAE: Cairo Plaza Bldg, Corniche en-Nil, Boulaque, Cairo; tel. (2) 778701; fax (2) 762806; e-mail meb2@rite.com; internet www.misrext.com; f. 1981; Misr International Bank has 30.1% interest, Banque Misr 19.5%; cap. 51.1m., res 214.7m., dep. 5,048.4m., total assets 5,488.7m. (Dec. 1998); Chair. and Man. Dir ABDULLAH TAYEL; 9 brs.

Misr International Bank, SAE: POB 218, 54 Sharia el-Batal Ahmad Abd al-Aziz, Mohandessin, Cairo 12411; tel. (2) 3497091; fax (2) 3498072; f. 1975; the Banque Misr has 26.0% interest, Banco di Roma 10%, UBAF London 8.5%, Europartners 7.9%; cap. 112.5m., res 552.8m., dep. 7,657.1m., total assets 9,140.9m. (Dec. 1998); Chair. ESSAM ED-DIN MUHAMMAD EL-AHMADY; 14 brs.

Misr-America International Bank: POB 1003, 12 Sharia Nadi es-Seid, Cairo 11511 (Dokki); tel. (2) 7616623; fax (2) 7616610; e-mail maib@instinct.net; f. 1977; Banque du Caire has 33% interest, Misr Insurance Co 33%, Industrial Development Bank of Egypt 17%, S.A. for Investments, Luxembourg 17%; cap. 75m., res 28.5m., dep. 871.1m., total assets 1,024.5m. (Dec. 1998); Chair. and Man. Dir Dr YOUSRY ALI MOUSTAFA; 8 brs.

Misr-Romanian Bank, SAE: 54 Sharia Lebanon, Mohandessin, Cairo; tel. (2) 3039825; fax (2) 3039804; e-mail mrbeg@ie-eg.com; internet www.mrb.com.eg; f. 1977; Banque Misr has 33% interest, Romanian Commercial Bank (Bucharest) 19%, Bank of Agriculture (Bucharest) 15%, and Romanian Bank for Development (Bucharest) 15%; cap. 75.1m., res 199.0m., dep. 1,494.8m, total assets 1,963.6m. (Dec. 1999); Chair. Dr AHMAD METWALLY HUSSAIN; 5 brs in Egypt, 2 in Romania.

Mohandes Bank: POB 170, 3–5 Sharia Mossadek, Cairo (Dokki); tel. (2) 3373110; fax (2) 3362741; internet www.mohandesbank.com; f. 1979; cap. 161m., res 5.9m., dep. 4,163.0m., total assets 4,444.3m. (Dec. 1997); Chair. and Man. Dir MUHAMMAD ADEL HASHISH; 10 brs.

Nile Bank, SAE: POB 2741, 35 Sharia Ramses, Abd al-Moneim Riad Sq., Cairo; tel. (2) 5741417; fax (2) 5756296; e-mail nilebank@egyptonline.com; f. 1978; cap. 32.2m., res 86.8m., dep. 1,289.5m., total assets 1,594.1m. (Dec. 1999); Chair. ISSA EL-AYOUTY; Man. Dir MUHAMMAD ES-SABAGH; 18 brs.

Suez Canal Bank, SAE: POB 2620, 11 Sharia Muhammad Sabry Abou Alam, Cairo; tel. (2) 3931033; fax (2) 3913522; e-mail seif@scbank.com.eg; internet www.scbank.com.eg; f. 1978; cap. 100m., res 390.5m., dep. 7,341.1m., total assets 8,270.2m. (Dec. 1998); Chair. and Man. Dir MOUSTAFA FAYEZ HABLAS; 16 brs.

Non-Commercial Banks

Arab Banking Corporation—Egypt, SAE: POB 61, Majlis ash-Sha'ab, 5 Midan es-Saray, al-Koubra, Cairo 11511 (Garden City); tel. (2) 7952608; fax (2) 7925994; e-mail abcegypt@arabbanking.com.eg; internet www.arabbanking.com.eg; f. 1982 as Egypt Arab African Bank; acquired by Arab Banking Corporation (Bahrain) in 1999; Arab Banking Corporation has 93% interest, other interests 7%; cap. 75m., res 67m., dep. 793m., total assets 1,138m. (Dec. 1998); merchant and investment bank services; Chair. ESSA MUHAMMAD GHANEM ELSWEDY; Vice Chair. ASHRAF ABOU ALAM; 6 brs.

Arab Investment Bank: POB 826, Cairo Sky Center Bldg, 8 Sharia Abd al-Khalek Sarwat, Cairo; tel. (2) 768097; fax (2) 770329; e-mail arinbank@mst1.mist.com.eg; f. 1978 as Union Arab Bank for Development and Investment; Egyptian/Syrian/Libyan joint venture; cap. 85.8m., res 2.5m., dep. 1,316m., total assets 1,457.6m. (Dec. 1998); Chair. Prof. Dr MUHAMMAD AHMAD AR-RAZAZ; 13 brs.

Housing and Development Bank, SAE: POB 234, 12 Sharia Syria, Mohandessin, Cairo; tel. (2) 3492013; fax (2) 3600712; e-mail

hdbank@internetegypt.com; f. 1979; cap. 54m., res 175.3m., dep. 1,505.4m., total assets 5,450.3m. (Dec. 1998); Chair. and Man. Dir MUHAMMAD TALA'AT ABOU SEDA; 24 brs.

Islamic International Bank for Investment and Development: POB 180, 4 Sharia Ali Ismail, Mesaha Sq., Cairo (Dokki); tel. (2) 3489983; fax (2) 3600771; e-mail ibid@infinitycom.eg; internet www.iibid.com; f. 1980; cap. 133.8m., res −25.7m., dep. 2,517.2m., total assets 2,693.0m. (Dec. 1998); Chair. FATH ALLAH AMIN ZAYED; Gen. Man. SAYED MUHAMMAD EL-MENSHAWY; 8 brs.

Misr Iran Development Bank: POB 219, Nile Tower Bldg, 21–23 Charles de Gaulle Ave, Sharia Giza, Cairo (Giza); tel. (2) 5727311; fax (2) 5701185; e-mail midb@mst1.mist.com.eg; f. 1975; the Bank of Alexandria has 39.73% interest, Misr Insurance Co 39.73%, Iran Foreign Investment Co 20.54%; cap. 211.4m., res 115.5m., dep. 825.4m., total assets 1,244.8m. (Dec. 1998); Chair. Dr MAHMOUD SALAH ED-DIN HAMED; Man. Dir Dr AL-MOTAZ MANSOUR; 7 brs.

National Société Générale Bank, SAE: POB 2664, Evergreen Bldg, 10 Sharia Tala'at Harb, Cairo; tel. (2) 5749376; fax (2) 5776249; e-mail runsgbcr@rusys.eg.net; f. 1978; the National Bank of Egypt has 18% interest, Société Générale de Paris 51%, other interests 31%; cap. 180m., res 197.6m., dep. 3,803.5m., total assets 4,534.7m. (Dec. 1999); Chair. MUHAMMAD MADBOULY; CEO JEROME GUIRAUD; 9 brs.

STOCK EXCHANGES

Capital Market Authority: 20 Sharia Emad ed-Din, Cairo; tel. (2) 5741000; fax (2) 5755339; e-mail cmauth@idsc.gov.eg; f. 1979; Chair. ABDELHAMID IBRAHIM; Dep. Chair. ASHRAF SHAMS ED-DIN.

Cairo Stock Exchange: 4 Sharia esh-Sherifein, Cairo; tel. (2) 3921447; fax (2) 3928526; internet www.egyptse.com; f. 1904; Chair. Dr SAMEH AT-TORGOMAN.

Alexandria Stock Exchange: 11 Sharia Talaat Harb, Menshia, Alexandria; tel. (3) 4835432; fax (3) 4823039; internet www.egyptse.com; f. 1861; Chair. Dr SAMEH AT-TORGOMAN.

INSURANCE

Al-Ahly Insurance: Cairo; state-owned; scheduled for privatization.

Arab International Insurance Co: POB 2704, 28 Sharia Talaat Harb, Cairo; tel. (2) 5746322; fax (2) 760053; f. 1976; a joint-stock free zone company established by Egyptian and foreign insurance companies; Chair. and Man. Dir HASSAN MUHAMMAD HAFEZ.

Ach-Chark Insurance Co: 15 Sharia Qasr en-Nil, Cairo; tel. (2) 5740455; fax (2) 5753316; e-mail ins_chark@frcu.eun.eg; f. 1931; due to be privatized in 2000; general and life; Chair. ANWAR ZEKRY.

Egyptian Reinsurance Co, SAE: POB 950, 7 Sharia Abd al-Latif Boltia, Cairo (Garden City); tel. (2) 3543354; fax (2) 3557483; e-mail egyptre@intouch.com; internet www.egyptre.com.eg; f. 1957; due to be privatized in 2000; Chair. ABD AL-MONEM M. EMAM.

L'Epargne, SAE: POB 548, Immeuble Chemla, Sharia 26 July, Cairo; all types of insurance.

Al-Iktisad esh-Shabee, SAE: 11 Sharia Emad ed-Din, Cairo; f. 1948; Man. Dir and Gen. Man. W. KHAYAT.

Misr Insurance Co: POB 261, 44A Sharia Dokki, Cairo (Dokki); tel. (2) 3355350; fax (2) 3370428; e-mail micfin@frcu.eun.eg; internet www.frcu.eun.eg; f. 1934; all classes of insurance and reinsurance; due to be privatized in 2000; Chair. MUHAMMAD ET-TEIR.

Mohandes Insurance Co: POB 62, 3 El-Mesaha Sq., Cairo (Dokki); tel. (2) 3352162; fax (2) 3352697; e-mail mohandes@mist1.mist.com.eg; f. 1980; privately-owned; insurance and reinsurance; Chair. and Man. Dir SAMIR MOUSTAFA METWALLI.

Al-Mottahida: POB 804, 9 Sharia Sulayman Pasha, Cairo; f. 1957.

National Insurance Co of Egypt, SAE: POB 592, 41 Sharia Qasr en-Nil, Cairo; tel. (2) 3910731; fax (2) 3909133; f. 1900; cap. 100m.; due to be privatized in 2000; Chair. MUHAMMAD ABUL-YAZEED.

Provident Association of Egypt, SAE: POB 390, 9 Sharia Sherif Pasha, Alexandria; f. 1936; Man. Dir G. C. VORLOOU.

Trade and Industry

GOVERNMENT AGENCY

Egyptian Geological Survey and Mining Authority (EGSMA): 3 Salah Salem Rd, Abbassia, Cairo; tel. (2) 6828013; fax (2) 4820128; f. 1896; state supervisory authority concerned with geological mapping, mineral exploration and other mining activities; Chair. Dr A. SUEDAN.

DEVELOPMENT ORGANIZATION

General Authority for Investment (GAFI): POB 1007, 8 Sharia Adly, Cairo; tel. (2) 3906163; fax (2) 3907315; Chair. Dr Eng. MUHAMMAD EL-GHAMRAWI DAWOUD.

CHAMBERS OF COMMERCE

Federation of Chambers of Commerce: 4 el-Falaki Sq., Cairo; tel. (2) 3551164; fax (2) 3557940; Pres. MAHMOUD EL-ARABY.

Alexandria

Alexandria Chamber of Commerce: 31 Sharia el-Ghorfa Altogariya, Alexandria; tel. (3) 809339; fax (2) 808993; Pres. MOUSTAFA EN-NAGGAR.

Cairo

American Chamber of Commerce in Egypt: Cairo; e-mail web@amcham.org.eg; internet www.amcham.org.eg.

Cairo Chamber of Commerce: 4 el-Falaki Sq., Cairo; tel. (2) 3558261; fax (2) 3563603; f. 1913; Pres. MAHMOUD EL-ARABY; Sec.-Gen. MOSTAFA ZAKI TAHA.

In addition, there are 20 local chambers of commerce.

EMPLOYERS' ORGANIZATION

Federation of Egyptian Industries: POB 251, 26A Sharia Sherif Pasha, Cairo, and 65 Gamal Abd an-Nasser Ave, Alexandria; tel. (2) 3928317 (Cairo), (3) 4928622 (Alexandria); fax (2) 3928075; f. 1922; Pres. MUHAMMAD FARID KHAMIS; represents the industrial community in Egypt.

PETROLEUM AND GAS

Arab Petroleum Pipelines Co (SUMED): POB 158, Es-Saray, 431 El-Geish Ave, Louran, Alexandria; tel. (3) 5864138; fax (3) 5871295; f. 1974; Suez–Mediterranean crude oil transportation pipeline (capacity: 117m. tons per year) and petroleum terminal operators; Chair. and Man. Dir Eng. HAZEM AMIN HAMMAD.

Belayim Petroleum Co (PETROBEL): POB 7074, Sharia Gharb el-Estad, Cairo (Nasr City); tel. (2) 2621738; fax (2) 2609792; f. 1978; capital equally shared between EGPC and International Egyptian Oil Co, which is a subsidiary of ENI of Italy; petroleum and gas exploration, drilling and production; Chair. and Man. Dir FAROUK KENAWY.

Egyptian General Petroleum Corporation (EGPC): POB 2130, 4th Sector, Sharia Palestine, New Maadi, Cairo; tel. (2) 3531452; fax (2) 3531457; state supervisory authority generally concerned with the planning of policies relating to petroleum activities in Egypt with the object of securing the development of the petroleum industry and ensuring its effective administration; Chair. MUHAMMAD TAWILA; Dep. Chair. HASAB EN-NABI ASAL.

General Petroleum Co (GPC): POB 743, 8 Sharia Dr Moustafa Abou Zahra, Cairo (Nasr City); tel. (2) 4030975; fax (2) 4037602; f. 1957; wholly-owned subsidiary of EGPC; operates mainly in Eastern Desert; Chair. HUSSEIN KAMAL.

GASCO: Sheraton Heliopolis, 6A Sharia Moustafa Rifaat, Cairo (Heliopolis); tel. (2) 2666458; fax (2) 2666469; e-mail gasco@gasco.com.eg; internet www.gasco.com.eg; f. 1997; Gen. Man. Eng. MUHAMMAD IBRAHIM.

Gulf of Suez Petroleum Co (GUPCO): POB 2400, 4th Sector, Sharia Palestine, New Maadi, Cairo; tel. (2) 3520985; fax (2) 3531286; f. 1965; partnership between EGPC and Amoco-Egypt Oil Co, which is a subsidiary of BP (UK/US); developed the el-Morgan oilfield in the Gulf of Suez, also holds other exploration concessions in the Gulf of Suez and the Western Desert; Chair. and Man. Dir IBRAHIM SALAH MAHMOUD; Gen. Man. L. D. McVAY.

Western Desert Petroleum Co (WEPCO): POB 412, Alexandria; tel. (3) 4928710; f. 1967 as partnership between EGPC (50% interest) and Phillips Petroleum (35%) and later Hispanoil (15%); developed Alamein, Yidma and Umbarka fields in the Western Desert and later Abu Qir offshore gas field in 1978 followed by NAF gas field in 1987; Chair. Eng. MUHAMMAD MOHI ED-DIN BAHGAT.

Numerous foreign petroleum companies are prospecting for petroleum in Egypt under agreements with EGPC.

UTILITIES

Electricity

In 1998 seven new electricity generation and distribution companies were created, under the direct ownership of the Egyptian Electricity Authority. The Government is planning the privatization of all seven companies, beginning with the Cairo Electricity Company in 2001.

Egyptian Electricity Authority (EEA): Sharia Ramses, Cairo (Nasr City); tel. (2) 2616301; fax (2) 2616512; Chair. MOUSTAFA SUWAYDAN.

Alexandria Electricity Distribution: 9 Sharia Sidi el-Liban, Alexandria; tel. (3) 4935726; fax (3) 4933223.

Cairo Electricity Co: 53 Sharia 26 July, Cairo; tel. (2) 766612.

Cairo Electricity Distribution: 53 Sharia 26 July, Cairo; tel. (2) 766400; fax (2) 760383; Gen. Man. LOFTY EL-MOSHTLY.

Water

National Association for Potable Water and Sanitary Drainage (NOPWASD): 6th Floor, Mogamma Bldg, et-Tahrir Sq., Cairo; tel. (2) 3557664; fax (2) 3562869; f. 1981; water and sewerage authority; Chair. MUHAMMAD KHALED MOUSTafa.

TRADE UNIONS

Egyptian Trade Union Federation (ETUF): 90 Sharia al-Galaa, Cairo; tel. (2) 5740362; fax (2) 5753427; f. 1957; 23 affiliated unions; 5m. mems; affiliated to the International Confederation of Arab Trade Unions and to the Organization of African Trade Union Unity; Pres. MUHAMMAD ES-SAYED RASHID; Gen. Sec. MUHAMMAD ES-SAYED MORSI.

General Trade Union of Air Transport: 5 Sharia Ahmad Sannan, St Fatima, Cairo (Heliopolis); 11,000 mems; Pres. ABD AL-MONEM FARAG EISA; Gen. Sec. SHEKATA ABD AL-HAMID.

General Trade Union of Banks and Insurance: 2 Sharia el-Kady el-Fadel, Cairo; 56,000 mems; Pres. MAHMOUD MUHAMMAD DABBOUR; Gen. Sec. ABDOU HASSAN MUHAMMAD ALI.

General Trade Union of Building and Wood Workers: 9 Sharia Emad ed-Din, Cairo; tel. (2) 5913486; fax (2) 5915849; 500,000 mems; Pres. TAHA HASSAN SAGED; Gen. Sec. YEHIA EMAM ABDEL GAWAD.

General Trade Union of Chemical Workers: 90 Sharia al-Galaa, Cairo; fax (2) 5750490; 120,000 mems; Pres. IBRAHIM EL-AZHARY; Gen. Sec. GAAFER ABD EL-MONEM.

General Trade Union of Commerce: 54D Sharia el-Gomhouriya, Alfy Borg, Cairo; tel. (2) 5903159; fax (2) 5914144; f. 1903; 120,000 mems; Pres. FOUAD TOMA; Gen. Sec. SAMIR A. SHAFI.

General Trade Union of Food Industries: 3 Sharia Housni, Hadaek el-Koba, Cairo; 111,000 mems; Pres. SAAD M. AHMAD; Gen. Sec. ADLY TANOUS IBRAHIM.

General Trade Union of Health Services: 22 Sharia esh-Sheikh Qamar, es-Sakakiny, Cairo; 56,000 mems; Pres. IBRAHIM ABOU EL-MUTI IBRAHIM; Gen. Sec. AHMAD ABD AL-LATIF SALEM.

General Trade Union of Hotels and Tourism Workers: POB 606, 90 Sharia al-Galaa, Cairo; tel. and fax (2) 773901; 70,000 mems; Pres. MUHAMMAD HILAL ESH-SHARKAWI.

General Trade Union of Maritime Transport: 36 Sharia Sharif, Cairo; 46,000 mems; Pres. THABET MUHAMMAD ES-SEFARI; Gen. Sec. MUHAMMAD RAMADAN ABOU TOR.

General Trade Union of Military Production: 90 Sharia al-Galaa, Cairo; 64,000 mems; Pres. MOUSTAFA MUHAMMAD MOUNGI; Gen. Sec. FEKRY IMAM.

General Trade Union of Mine Workers: 5 Sharia Ali Sharawi, Hadaek el-Koba, Cairo; 14,000 mems; Pres. ABBAS MAHMOUD IBRAHIM; Gen. Sec. AMIN HASSAN AMER.

General Trade Union of Petroleum Workers: 5 Sharia Ali Sharawi, Hadaek el-Koba, Cairo; tel. (2) 4820091; fax (2) 4834551; 60,000 mems; Pres. FAUZI ABD AL-BARI; Gen. Sec. AMIR ABD ES-SALAM.

General Trade Union of Postal Workers: 90 Sharia al-Galaa, Cairo; 80,000 mems; Pres. HASSAN MUHAMMAD EID; Gen. Sec. SALEM MAHMOUD SALEM.

General Trade Union of Press, Printing and Information: 90 Sharia al-Galaa, Cairo; tel. (2) 740324; 55,000 mems; Pres. MUHAMMAD ALI EL-FIKKI; Gen. Sec. AHMAD ED-DESSOUKI.

General Trade Union of Public and Administrative Workers: 2 Sharia Muhammad Haggag, Midan et-Tahrir, Cairo; tel. (2) 5742134; fax (2) 5752044; 250,000 mems; Pres. Dr AHMAD ABDELZAHER; Gen. Sec. MUKHTAR HAMOUDA.

General Trade Union of Public Utilities Workers: 30 Sharia Sharif, Cairo; tel. and fax (2) 3938293; 290,000 mems; Pres. MUHAMMAD ES-SAYED MORSI; Gen. Sec. MUHAMMAD TALA'AT HASSAN.

General Trade Union of Railway Workers: POB 84 (el-Faggalah), 15 Sharia Emad ed-Din, Cairo; tel. (2) 5930305; fax (2) 5917776; 90,000 mems; Pres. SABER AHMAD HUSSAIN; Gen. Sec. YASIN SOLUMAN.

General Trade Union of Road Transport: 90 Sharia al-Galaa, Cairo; tel. (2) 5740413; fax (2) 5752955; 245,000 mems; Pres. MOUNIR BADR CHETA; Gen. Sec. SALINI GUNIDI.

General Trade Union of Telecommunications Workers: POB 651, Cairo; 60,000 mems; Pres. KHAIRI HACHEM; Sec.-Gen. IBRAHIM SALEH.

General Trade Union of Textile Workers: 327 Sharia Shoubra, Cairo; 244,000 mems; Pres. ALI MUHAMMAD DOUFDAA; Gen. Sec. HASSAN TOULBA MARZOUK.

General Trade Union of Workers in Agriculture and Irrigation: 31 Sharia Mansour, Cairo (Bab el-Louk); tel. (2) 3541419;

150,000 mems; Pres. Mukhtar Abd al-Hamid; Gen. Sec. Fathi A. Kurtam.

General Trade Union of Workers in Engineering, Metal and Electrical Industries: 90 Sharia al-Galaa, Cairo; tel. (2) 742519; 160,000 mems; Pres. Said Gomaa; Gen. Sec. Muhammad Fares.

Transport

RAILWAYS

The area of the Nile Delta is well served by railways. Lines also run from Cairo southward along the Nile to Aswan, and westward along the coast to Salloum.

Egyptian National Railways: Station Bldg, Midan Ramses, Cairo 11794; tel. (2) 5751000; fax (2) 5740000; f. 1852; length 8,600 km; 42 km electrified; a 346-km line to carry phosphate and iron ore from the Bahariya mines, in the Western Desert, to the Helwan iron and steel works in south Cairo, was opened in 1973, and the Qena–Safaga line (length 223 km) came into operation in 1989; Chair. (vacant).

Alexandria Passenger Transport Authority: POB 466, Aflaton, esh-Shatby, Alexandria 21111; tel. (3) 5975223; fax (3) 5971187; e-mail chrmapta@cns-egypt.com; f. 1860; controls City Tramways (28 km), Ramleh Electric Railway (16 km), suburban buses and minibuses (1,688 km); 121 tram cars, 42 light railway three-car sets; Chair. and Tech. Dir Eng. Medhat Hafez.

Cairo Metro: National Authority for Tunnels, POB 466, Ramses Bldg, Midan Ramses, Cairo 11794; tel. (2) 5742968; fax (2) 5742950; construction of the first underground transport system in Africa and the Middle East began in Cairo in 1982; connects electrified Helwan line of Egyptian railways with the diesel el-Marg line, via a 4.2-km tunnel with five stations beneath central Cairo, making a 44-km regional line with a total of 34 stations; gauge 1,435 mm, electrified; work on the first stage of the system was completed in July 1987, and it was opened in September; the second stage was completed in 1989; work on a second line linking Shoubra el-Kheima with central Cairo and Giza commenced in 1992. This new line will have a total length of 18.3 km. (13 km in tunnel) and 18 stations, two of which will interconnect with the first line. The first stage started operating between Shoubra el-Kheima and Ramses Square in 1996, the service extending to Tahrir Square in 1997. By mid-1999 15.8 km of the line was operational; the rest of the line, extending to Cairo University, is under construction and is due to be completed at the end of 2000; work on a third line connecting Imbaba with Cairo International Airport was due to commence in 2001; Chair. Dr Eng. Mokbel M. esh-Shafie.

Cairo Transport Authority: POB 254, Madinet Nasr, Cairo; tel. (2) 830533; length 78 km (electrified); gauge 1,000 mm; operates 16 tram routes and 24 km of light railway; 720 cars; Chair. M. E. Abd es-Salam.

Lower Egypt Railway: El-Mansoura; f. 1898; length 160 km; gauge 1,000 mm; 20 diesel railcars.

ROADS

There are good metalled main roads as follows: Cairo–Alexandria (desert road); Cairo–Banha–Tanta–Damanhour–Alexandria; Cairo–Suez (desert road); Cairo–Ismailia–Port Said or Suez; Cairo–Fayoum (desert road); in 1997 there were some 41,300 km of roads, including 22,000 km of highways. The total length of road network at the end of 1999 was 44,000 km. The Ahmad Hamdi road tunnel (1.64 km) beneath the Suez Canal was opened in 1980. A 320-km macadamized road linking Mersa Matruh, on the Mediterranean coast, with the oasis town of Siwa was completed in 1986.

General Authority for Roads, Bridges and Land Transport—Ministry of Transport: 105 Sharia Qasr el-Eini, Cairo; tel. (2) 3557429; fax (2) 3550591; e-mail garb@idsc.gov.eg; Chair. Muhammad Nabil el-Koussy.

SHIPPING

Egypt's principal ports are Alexandria, Port Said and Suez. A port constructed at a cost of £E315m., and designed to handle up to 16m. metric tons of grain, fruit and other merchandise per year (22% of the country's projected imports by 2000) in its first stage of development, was opened at Damietta in 1986. The second stage will increase handling capacity to 25m. tons per year. A ferry link between Nuweibeh and the Jordanian port of Aqaba was opened in 1985.

Alexandria Port Authority: 106 ave Gamal Abd an-Nasser, Alexandria; Head Office: 106 Sharia el-Hourriya, Alexandria; tel. (3) 4831640; fax (3) 4829714; e-mail apa@alexcomm.net; internet www.alexport.com; f. 1966; Chair. Adm. Hassan Hosni Amin; Vice-Chair. Adm. Kamal A. en-Nahta.

Major Shipping Companies

Alexandria Shipping and Navigation Co: POB 812, 557 ave el-Hourriya, Alexandria; tel. (3) 62923; services between Egypt, N. and W. Europe, USA, Red Sea and Mediterranean; 5 vessels; Chair. Eng. Mahmoud Ismail; Man. Dir Abd al-Aziz Qadri.

Arab Maritime Petroleum Transport Co (AMPTC): POB 143, 9th Floor, Nile Tower Bldg, 21 Sharia Giza, Cairo 12211 (Giza); tel. (2) 5701311; fax (2) 3378080; e-mail amptc09@rite.com; 11 vessels; Chair. Dr Ramadan es-Sanoussi Belhag; Gen. Man. Sulayman al-Bassam.

Egyptian Navigation Co: POB 82, 2 Sharia en-Nasr, Alexandria 21511; tel. (3) 4803608; fax (3) 4831345; e-mail enc@idsc.gov.eg; internet www.enc.com.eg; f. 1930; owners and operators of Egypt's mercantile marine; services Alexandria/Europe, USA, Black Sea, Adriatic Sea, Mediterranean Sea, Indian Ocean and Red Sea; 24 vessels; Chair. Abdullah Ali Fahim; Man. Dir Abd al-Wahab Yacout.

Memnon Tours Co: POB 2533, 18 Sharia Hoda Sharawi, Cairo; tel. (2) 3930195; fax (2) 3917410; 7 vessels.

Misr Petroleum Co: POB 228, Misr Petroleum House, 6 Sharia Orabi, Cairo; tel. (2) 5755000; fax (2) 5745436; 8 vessels; Chair. Eng. Salah ed-Din Hassan.

Misr Shipping Co: POB 157, 29 Sharia Masgid en-Nasr, Soumoha, Sidi Gaber, Alexandria; tel. (3) 4206769; fax (3) 4218425; 8 vessels; Chair. Adm. Redda Rashed; Man. Dir Adm. Yousri Hanafy.

National Navigation Co: 4 Sharia Ehegaz, Cairo (Heliopolis); tel. (2) 4525575; fax (2) 4526171; 11 vessels; Chair. and Man. Dir Muhammad Shawki Younis.

Pan-Arab Shipping Co: POB 39, 404 ave el-Hourriya, Rushdi, Alexandria; tel. (3) 5468835; fax (3) 5469533; f. 1974; Arab League Co; 5 vessels; Chair. Adm. Muhammad Sherif es-Sadek; Gen. Man. Capt. Mamdouh el-Guindy.

As-Salam Shipping & Trading Establishment: Apartment 203, 24 Sharia Ahmad Talceer, Cairo (Heliopolis); tel. (2) 908535; fax (2) 4175390; 6 vessels.

Samatour Shipping Co: As-Salam Bldg, 4 Sharia Naguib er-Rihani, Rami Station, Alexandria; tel. (3) 4822028; fax (3) 4832003; 5 vessels; Chair. Salem A. Salem.

Sayed Nasr Navigation Lines: 5 Sharia Dr Ahmad Amin, Cairo (Heliopolis); tel. (2) 2457643; fax (2) 2457736; 6 vessels.

Société Cooperative des Pétroles: Cooperative Bldg, 94 Sharia Qasr el-Eini, Cairo; tel. (2) 7360623; fax (2) 7956404; Chair. Dr Tamer Abu Bakr; Gen. Dir Osama Ibrahim.

THE SUEZ CANAL

In 1999 a total of 13,490 vessels, with a net displacement of 385m. tons, used the Suez Canal, linking the Mediterranean and Red Seas.

Length of canal 190 km; maximum permissible draught: 17.68 m (58 ft); breadth of canal at water level and breadth between buoys defining the navigable channel at −11 m: 365 m and 225 m, respectively, in the northern section and 305 m and 205 m in the southern section.

Suez Canal Authority (Hay'at Canal as-Suways): Irshad Bldg, Ismailia; tel. (64) 330000; fax (64) 320784; Cairo Office: 6 Sharia Lazoughli, Cairo (Garden City); f. 1956; Chair. Adm. Ahmad Ali Fadel.

CIVIL AVIATION

The main international airports are at Heliopolis (23 km from the centre of Cairo) and Alexandria (7 km from the city centre). An international airport was opened at Nuzhah in 1983.

In the 12-month period ending 30 June 1997 an estimated 14m. passengers and 109,000 metric tons of cargo passed through Egypt's airports.

EgyptAir: Administration Complex, Cairo International Airport, Cairo (Heliopolis); tel. (2) 2674700; fax (2) 2663773; internet www.egyptair.com.eg; f. 1932 as Misr Airwork; known as United Arab Airlines 1960–1971; operates internal services in Egypt and external services throughout the Middle East, Far East, Africa, Europe and the USA; cap. US $3,100m.; Chair. Eng. Muhammad Fahim Rayan.

Egyptian Civil Aviation Authority (ECAA): ECAA Complex, Sharia Airport, Cairo 11776; tel. (2) 2677610; fax (2) 2470351; e-mail egoca@idsc.gov.eg; Chair. Abd al-Fattah Kattu.

Tourism

Tourism is currently Egypt's second-largest source of revenue, generating £E4,063m. in 1998. Traditionally the industry has attracted tourists to its pyramids and monuments. Recently the industry has diversified; the Red Sea coastline has 1,000 km of beaches along which developments, including two international airports at Taba and Suba Bay, are under construction. The tourism industry was adversely affected in the mid-1990s by the campaign of violence by Islamist fundamentalists, although some recovery in tourist numbers was recorded by the end of the decade.

Ministry of Tourism: Misr Travel Tower, Abbassia Sq., Cairo; tel. (2) 2828439; fax (2) 2859551; e-mail mol@idsc.gov.eg; internet www.touregypt.net; f. 1965; brs at Alexandria, Port Said, Suez, Luxor and Aswan; Minister of Tourism Dr MAMDOUH EL-BELTAGI.

Egyptian General Authority for the Promotion of Tourism: Misr Travel Tower, Abbassia Sq., Cairo; tel. (2) 2853576; fax (2) 2854363; Chair. ADEL ABD AL-AZIZ.

Egyptian General Co for Tourism and Hotels: 4 Sharia Latin America, Cairo (Garden City); tel. (2) 3542914; fax (2) 3564830; f. 1961; affiliated to the holding co for Housing, Tourism and Cinema; Chair. Dr ALI ISMAIL EL-EMBABY.

EL SALVADOR

Introductory Survey

Location, Climate, Language, Religion, Flag, Capital

The Republic of El Salvador lies on the Pacific coast of Central America. It is bounded by Guatemala to the west and by Honduras to the north and east. The climate varies from tropical on the coastal plain to temperate in the uplands. The language is Spanish. About 85% of the population are Roman Catholics, and other Christian churches are represented. The civil flag (proportions 3 by 2) consists of three equal horizontal stripes, of blue, over white, over blue. The state flag differs by the addition, in the centre of the white stripe, of the national coat of arms. The capital is San Salvador.

Recent History

El Salvador was ruled by Spain until 1821, and became independent in 1839. Since then the country's history has been one of frequent coups and outbursts of political violence. General Maximiliano Hernández Martínez became President in 1931, and ruthlessly suppressed a peasant uprising, with an alleged 30,000 killings (including that of Farabundo Martí, the leader of the rebel peasants), in 1932. President Hernández was deposed in 1944, and the next elected President, Gen. Salvador Castañeda Castro, was overthrown in 1948. His successor as President, Lt-Col Oscar Osorio (1950–56), relinquished power to Lt-Col José María Lemus, who was deposed by a bloodless coup in 1960. He was replaced by a military junta, which was itself supplanted by another junta in January 1961. Under this Junta, the conservative Partido de Conciliación Nacional (PCN) was established and won all 54 seats in elections to the Asamblea Legislativa (Legislative Assembly) in December. A member of the Junta, Lt-Col Julio Adalberto Rivera, was elected unopposed to the presidency in 1962. He was succeeded by the PCN candidate, Gen. Fidel Sánchez Hernández, in 1967.

In the 1972 presidential election Col Arturo Armando Molina Barraza, candidate of the ruling PCN, was elected. His rival, José Napoleón Duarte, the leader of the left-wing coalition party, Unión Nacional de Oposición, staged an abortive coup in March, and Col Molina took office in July, despite allegations of massive electoral fraud. Similar allegations were made during the 1977 presidential election, after which the PCN candidate, Gen. Carlos Humberto Romero Mena, took office.

Reports of violations of human rights by the Government were widespread in 1979. The polarization of left and right after 1972 was characterized by an increase in guerrilla activity. In October 1979 President Romero was overthrown and replaced by a Junta of civilians and army officers. The Junta, which promised to install a democratic system and to organize elections, declared a political amnesty and invited participation from the guerrilla groups, but violence continued between government troops and guerrilla forces, and elections were postponed. In January 1980 an ultimatum from progressive members of the Government resulted in the formation of a new Government, a coalition of military officers and the Partido Demócrata Cristiano (PDC). In March the country moved closer to full-scale civil war following the assassination of the Roman Catholic Archbishop of San Salvador, Oscar Romero y Galdames, an outspoken supporter of human rights.

In December 1980 José Napoleón Duarte, the 1972 presidential candidate and a member of the Junta, was sworn in as President. In January 1981 the guerrillas launched their 'final offensive' and, after initial gains, the opposition front, Frente Democrático Revolucionario—FDR (allied with the guerrilla front, the Frente Farabundo Martí para la Liberación Nacional—FMLN), proposed negotiations with the USA. The US authorities referred them to the Salvadorean Government, which refused to recognize the FDR while it was linked with the guerrillas. The USA affirmed its support for the Duarte Government and provided civilian and military aid. During 1981 the guerrilla forces unified and strengthened their control over the north and east of the country. Attacks on economic targets continued, while the army retaliated by acting indiscriminately against the local population in guerrilla-controlled areas. By December there were an estimated 300,000 Salvadorean refugees, many of whom had fled to neighbouring countries.

At elections to a National Constituent Assembly, conducted in March 1982, the PDC failed to win an absolute majority against the five right-wing parties, which, together having obtained 60% of the total votes, formed a Government of National Unity. Major Roberto D'Aubuisson Arrieta, leader of the extreme right-wing Alianza Republicana Nacionalista (ARENA), emerged as the most powerful personality within the coalition and became President of the National Constituent Assembly. In April a politically independent banker, Dr Alvaro Magaña Borja, was elected interim President of El Salvador, after pressure from the armed forces. However, the Assembly voted to award itself considerable power over the President. Military leaders then demanded that five ministerial posts be given to members of the PDC, fearing that, otherwise, US military aid would be withdrawn. A presidential election was scheduled for 1983, and a new constitution was to be drafted.

During 1982 about 1,600 Salvadorean troops were trained in the USA, and US military advisers were reported to be actively participating in the conflict. In November a military coup was forestalled by Gen. José Guillermo García, the Minister of Defence, who removed several right-wingers from important military posts. President Magaña's position was strengthened in December, when a division within the PCN resulted in the moderates achieving a majority in the Assembly.

The presidential election was postponed until March 1984, as a result of disagreement in the National Constituent Assembly over the new Constitution, which finally became effective in December 1983. The issue of agrarian reform caused a serious dispute between Maj. D'Aubuisson's ARENA party and the PDC, and provoked a campaign by right-wing 'death squads' against trade unionists and peasant leaders. (In 1980 the governing Junta had nationalized some 60% of the country's prime arable land as part of a three-phase agrarian reform initiative, which envisaged the eventual redesignation of 90% of El Salvador's farmland. However, subsequent phases of the expropriation and reallocation programme had been suspended in March 1981 and May 1982, prompting US Government threats to withdraw financial and military assistance.) In December 1983 ARENA secured the support of the Assembly for the reactivation of a severely compromised reform programme, which provided for a maximum permissible landholding of 245 ha (rather than 100 ha as originally envisaged). This represented an important victory for the ARENA party, which had been isolated in the Assembly following the collapse of its alliance with the PCN in February.

Following a period of intense activity by 'death squads' in September and October 1983, when the weekly total of murders exceeded 200, the US Government urged the removal of several high-level officials, military officers and political figures who were linked to the murders. The failure of the US-trained 'rapid reaction' battalions and frequent reports of army atrocities undermined both public confidence in the Government and US President Ronald Reagan's efforts to secure further US aid for El Salvador. In February 1984, following a number of strategic territorial advances, the FDR-FMLN proposed the formation of a broadly-based provisional government, as part of a peace plan without preconditions. The plan was rejected by the Government. The guerrillas refused to participate in the presidential election, conducted in March 1984, and attempted to prevent voting in various provinces. As no candidate emerged with a clear majority, a second round of voting was held in May, when José Napoleón Duarte, the candidate of the PDC, obtained 54% of the votes cast to defeat Maj. D'Aubuisson, the ARENA candidate.

Following his inauguration in June 1984, President Duarte instituted a purge of the armed forces and the reorganization of the police force, including the disbanding of the notorious Treasury Police. Both the FDR-FMLN and the President expressed their willingness to commence peace negotiations. Following pressure from the Roman Catholic Church and trade unions, the Government opened discussions with guerrilla leaders in Chalatenango in October. A second round of negotiations, held in November, ended amid accusations of intransigence from both sides.

At legislative and municipal elections in March 1985 the PDC won a convincing victory over the ARENA-PCN electoral alliance, thereby securing a clear majority in the new Asamblea Nacional (National Assembly). The PDC's victory, coupled with internal divisions within the right-wing grouping, precipitated a decline in the popularity and influence of the alliance, which culminated in the resignation of ARENA's leader, Roberto D'Aubuisson, in September.

Despite a perceived decline in political violence and abuses of human rights in 1985–86, the failure of the Government and the rebels to agree an agenda for renewed negotiations during this period prompted speculation that a military solution would be sought to end the civil war. Such speculation was supported by reports of the armed forces' growing domination of the conflict and by the success of the army's 'Unidos para reconstruir' campaign, a social and economic programme, launched in July 1986, to recover areas that had been devastated by the protracted fighting.

In February 1987 the Government suffered a humiliating defeat when its attempt to introduce a 'war tax' was ruled unconstitutional by the Supreme Court. Furthermore, in March guerrillas carried out a successful attack on the army garrison at El Paraíso, which enabled them to take the military initiative in the civil war. Later in 1987, however, the Salvadorean Government's participation in a peace plan for Central America, which was signed on 7 August in Guatemala City, encouraged hopes that a peaceful solution could be found to the conflict. Discussions between the Government and the FDR-FMLN were eventually held in October, when agreement was reached on the formation of two committees to study the possibility of a cease-fire and an amnesty.

Despite the inauguration, in September 1987, of a National Reconciliation Commission, appointed by the President in August, and the Government's proclamation, in November, of a unilateral cease-fire, no long-term cessation of hostilities was maintained by either side. In late 1987 the political situation deteriorated further, following President Duarte's public denunciation of Roberto D'Aubuisson's complicity in the murder of Archbishop Romero y Galdames in March 1980.

In early 1988 there were increasing reports of the resurgence of 'death squads', and it was suggested that abuses of human rights were rapidly returning to the level reached at the beginning of the internal conflict. In February the FMLN launched a campaign of bombings and transport disruptions, in order to undermine preparations for the forthcoming legislative and municipal elections. At the elections, in March, ARENA secured control of more than 200 municipalities, including San Salvador, hitherto held for more than 20 years by the PDC. However, a dispute developed over the distribution of seats in the legislature, with both ARENA and the PDC claiming the same seat in one region. Following protracted arguments, ARENA was able to resume an overall majority in the Asamblea, when a deputy of the PCN transferred allegiance to ARENA, thereby giving the party 31 seats, compared with the PDC's 23 seats. In May the PDC suffered another reverse when it was revealed that President Duarte was suffering from a terminal illness (he died in February 1990).

In mid-1988 the Convergencia Democrática (CD), a left-wing alliance comprising two of the leading groups within the FDR-FMLN and the Partido Social Demócrata, announced that Dr Guillermo Ungo would be its candidate at the forthcoming presidential election. In September, however, the guerrillas launched a major new offensive, and in November took advantage of a transitional period following the installation of a new military high command to attack the headquarters of the National Guard in San Salvador.

By the end of 1988, it was estimated that as many as 70,000 Salvadoreans had died in the course of the civil war, while the US administration had provided some US $3,000m. in aid to the Government. Moreover, by early 1989 many areas appeared to be without government, following the resignations of some 75 mayors and nine judges, purportedly because of death threats by the FMLN. In late January, however, radical new peace proposals were announced by the FMLN, which, for the first time, expressed its willingness to participate in the electoral process. The FMLN proposed that the presidential election be postponed from March to September, and offered a 60-day cease-fire (30 days on each side of a September election date). However, negotiations about this proposal failed to produce agreement.

When Duarte announced that the election would proceed on the scheduled date of 19 March, the FMLN advocated a boycott of the election and intensified its campaign of violence, resulting in the deaths of more than 40 people on election day alone. The election resulted in victory for the ARENA candidate, Alfredo Cristiani Burkard. The level of abstention was estimated at almost 50%. Cristiani took office on 1 June 1989.

In August 1989 the Heads of State of five Central American countries signed an agreement in Tela, Honduras. The accord included an appeal to the FMLN to abandon its military campaign and to 'initiate dialogue' with the Salvadorean Government. In the spirit engendered by the Tela agreement, representatives of the Government and the FMLN began negotiations in Mexico City in September. A second round of discussions took place in San José, Costa Rica, in October and a third round was planned for Caracas, Venezuela, in November. However, it was abandoned following a bomb attack in late October, allegedly perpetrated by the Salvadorean army, on the headquarters of the Salvadorean Workers' National Union Federation (FENASTRAS), in which 10 people were killed. On 7 November, in accordance with the Tela agreement, the UN Security Council authorized the creation of the UN Observer Group for Central America (ONUCA), a multinational military force, to monitor developments in the region.

On 11 November 1989 the FMLN launched a military offensive, and throughout the month the fiercest fighting for nine years took place. The Government declared a state of siege, and stability was further undermined when, on 16 November, gunmen murdered the head of a San Salvador Jesuit university and five other Jesuit priests. On 12 January 1990, however, the FMLN announced that it would accept an offer made by the Salvadorean Government whereby the UN Secretary-General, Javier Pérez de Cuéllar, was to arrange the reopening of peace talks. In March President Cristiani announced that he was willing to offer a comprehensive amnesty, territorial concessions and the opportunity to participate fully in political processes to members of the FMLN, as part of a broad-based peace proposal. Later in 1990, however, hopes for the successful negotiation of a peaceful settlement were frustrated by the failure of the two sides to reach a consensus, at a series of UN-sponsored discussions, on the crucial issue of the future role, structure and accountability of the armed forces.

In May 1990 guerrilla forces had launched their first major offensive since November 1989, coinciding with demonstrations in San Salvador by some 40,000 trade unionists and opposition supporters in protest at economic austerity measures and the breakdown of peace negotiations. By the end of September all hopes for a cease-fire had been abandoned. A renewed FMLN offensive was undertaken by the newly-proclaimed National Army for Democracy (the establishment of which marked the reorganization of the FMLN's previous divisions into a more conventional army structure) in several departments in November. The conflict was considered to have entered into a new phase when, in the same month, a government aircraft was shot down by guerrilla forces armed with surface-to-air missiles (supplied by Nicaraguan military personnel). In January 1991 a US military helicopter, en route to operations in Honduras, was shot down by rebel forces in El Salvador. Public and political outrage in the USA increased when it became known that two of the three US servicemen who died in the incident had been executed, following the crash, by members of the FMLN.

Negotiations between the Government and the FMLN continued throughout 1991, interspersed by violent exchanges between the guerrillas and the security forces. On 10 March elections to the Asamblea (enlarged from 60 to 84 seats) and to 262 municipalities were conducted. While guerrilla forces refrained from disrupting the proceedings (the FMLN announced a three-day cease-fire), it was reported that many voters were intimidated by an escalation in military operations, and more than 50% of the electorate failed to cast a vote. A long delay in announcing the final results prompted left-wing groups to level accusations of electoral fraud against the Central Electoral Commission, which was under right-wing control. The final results revealed that ARENA had lost its majority in the Asamblea, but continued to command considerable support, with 44.3% of the votes and 39 seats. The party also retained significant support in the local elections, with victories in 175 of the 262 municipalities.

In late March 1991 a new initiative for the negotiation of a peace settlement was presented by the FMLN in Managua, Nicaragua, following a meeting between foreign affairs ministers from Central America and the European Community (EC, now European Union–EU). This new proposal dispensed with previous stipulations put forward by the guerrillas that military and constitutional reforms should be effected prior to any cease-fire, and suggested that concessions on both sides could be adopted simultaneously. The constitutional requirement that amendments to the Constitution be ratified by two successive legislative assemblies lent impetus to negotiations in April, the current Asamblea being scheduled to dissolve at the end of the month. Despite the attempts of uncompromising right-wing members of the Asamblea to sabotage the proceedings, a last-minute agreement on human rights (including the creation of a three-member 'truth commission', to be appointed by the UN Secretary-General) and on judicial and electoral reform was reached by the Government and the FMLN, and was swiftly approved by the Asamblea, prior to its dissolution. The working structure of a cease-fire and the detailed reform and purge of the armed forces were set aside for negotiation at a later date.

In May 1991 the UN Security Council voted to create an observer mission to El Salvador (ONUSAL), to be charged with the verification of accords reached between the Government and the FMLN. Initially the mission was to be resident in six regional centres for a 12-month period, and was expected to participate in any future cease-fire and peaceful reintegration programme. The creation of ONUSAL was denounced by right-wing groups within El Salvador as unwarranted interference and as an insult to national sovereignty.

In August 1991, following a personal invitation from the UN Secretary-General, Javier Pérez de Cuéllar, both sides attended a round of discussions in New York, where a new framework for peace was agreed. A National Commission for the Consolidation of Peace (COPAZ) was to be created (comprising representatives of both sides, as well as of all major political parties), which would supervise the enforcement of guarantees for the political integration of the guerrillas. The FMLN also secured guaranteed territorial rights for peasants settled in guerrilla-controlled areas, and the participation of former FMLN members in a National Civilian Police, which was to be under the control of a new Ministry of the Interior and Public Security. At the same time, the Asamblea approved constitutional reforms, whereby the Central Electoral Commission would be replaced by a Supreme Electoral Tribunal, composed of five magistrates (one from each of the five most successful parties at the previous presidential election), to be elected by the Asamblea.

In December 1991, following renewed discussions between the Government and the guerrilla leaders in New York, a new peace initiative was announced. Under the terms of the agreement, a formal cease-fire was to be implemented on 1 February 1992, under the supervision of some 1,000 UN personnel. The FMLN was to begin a process of disarmament, to be implemented in five stages (simultaneous with the dissolution of the notorious, military-controlled, 17,000-strong rapid deployment battalions), leading to full disarmament by 31 October. The success of the cease-fire agreement was expected to be dependent upon the adequate implementation, by the Government, of previously agreed reforms to the judiciary, the electoral system, guarantees of territorial rights, human rights, and guerrilla participation in civil defence, and of newly agreed reforms whereby the armed forces would be purged of those most responsible for abuses of human rights during the previous 12 years, and would be reduced in size by almost one-half, over a 22-month period.

In mid-January 1992 the UN Security Council approved the dispatch of some 1,000 police and military personnel to El Salvador to supervise the implementation of the first stage of the cease-fire. On 16 January, at Chapultepec Castle in Mexico City, the formal peace accord was ratified and was witnessed by the new UN Secretary-General, Boutros Boutros-Ghali, the US Secretary of State, James Baker, Heads of State from Central America, South America and Europe, representatives of El Salvador's military high command and all 84 members of the Asamblea. On 1 February some 30,000 Salvadoreans gathered in San Salvador to celebrate the first day of the cease-fire and to attend the formal installation of COPAZ.

Although mutual allegations of failure to comply with the terms of the peace accord persisted during 1992, prompting the temporary withdrawal, in May, of the FMLN from COPAZ, and resulting in further UN mediation and the negotiation of a revised timetable for disarmament, the cease-fire was carefully observed by both sides. In San Salvador on 15 December (declared National Reconciliation Day), at a ceremony attended by President Cristiani, FMLN leaders, the UN Secretary-General and Central American Heads of State and government representatives, the conflict was formally concluded, the terms of the December 1991 agreement having been fulfilled to the satisfaction of both sides. On the same day the FMLN was officially registered and recognized as a legitimate political party.

In November 1992, in accordance with the terms of the December 1991 peace accord, the Comisión de la Verdad (Truth Commission) announced the names of more than 200 military personnel alleged to have participated in abuses of human rights during the civil war. By early 1993, however, despite the urgences of the UN Secretary-General, the reluctance of the Government to comply with the conditions of the peace accord, relating to the removal from the armed forces of those personnel (particularly officers) identified by the Commission, threatened the further successful implementation of the process of pacification, and prompted the FMLN to delay the demobilization of its forces and the destruction of its remaining arsenals. The situation was exacerbated in March by the publication of the report of the Commission, which attributed responsibility for the vast majority of the war's 75,000 fatalities to the counter-insurgency measures of the armed forces, including the systematic eradication, by the security forces, of civilians thought to harbour left-wing sympathies. Some 400 murders were attributed to the FMLN. Forty military personnel, identified by name as those responsible for various human rights atrocities, included the ARENA founder Roberto D'Aubuisson Arrieta (who died in 1992), who was identified as the authority behind the organization of 'death squads' in the early 1980s, and the murder, in 1980, of the Archbishop of San Salvador, Oscar Romero y Galdames; also identified was the Minister of Defence and Public Security, Gen. René Emilio Ponce, his deputy, Gen. Orlando Zepeda, and the former air force chief, Gen. Juan Rafael Bustillo, who were believed to have ordered the murder of six prominent Jesuits in 1989. (In September 1991 Col Guillermo Benavides and an army lieutenant were found guilty of murder and sentenced to a maximum of 30 years' imprisonment; the seven other men charged were acquitted, on the grounds that they were simply following orders.) The report recommended that the judiciary should be reorganized, having failed to protect human rights during the war, and that all individuals identified by the report should be permanently excluded from all institutions of national defence and public security, and should be barred from holding public office for a period of 10 years.

While the conclusions of the report were welcomed by the FMLN, representatives of the Government and the armed forces challenged the legal validity of the document, despite the insistence of UN officials that the recommendations of the report were mandatory under the terms of the peace accord. However, later in March 1993, the strength of ARENA's representation in the Asamblea overcame opposition from the PDC, the CD and the Movimiento Nacional Revolucionario (MNR), and secured the approval of an amnesty law to extend to all political crimes committed before 1992, prompting widespread public outrage, which was compounded, in April 1993, by the release of the two prisoners sentenced in January 1992 for the murder of six prominent Jesuits, as the first beneficiaries of the amnesty. In late June 1993 the Government compromised, to some extent, by announcing the compulsory retirement of several veteran military officers, including Gen. Ponce, although their immunity from prosecution was guaranteed.

The findings of the Truth Commission, together with the disclosure of information following the declassification by the US administration, in November 1993, of hitherto confidential documents relating to the administrations of former US Presidents Ronald Reagan and George Bush, suggested that detailed knowledge of abuses of human rights was suppressed by US officials in order to continue to secure congressional funding for the Government in El Salvador in the 1980s. Evidence also emerged that US military training had been provided, in at least one instance, for a civilian group in El Salvador operating as a 'death squad'. In June 1998 three members of the National Guard, convicted in 1984 of the murder, in 1980, of three US nuns and a US lay worker, were granted a conditional release from prison on the grounds that they were simply following orders. In May 1999 legal proceedings were initiated in a US court against Gen. (retd) Carlos Eugenio Vides Casanova and Gen. (retd) José Guillermo García for their alleged involvement in the killings; however, in November 2000 they were acquitted of all charges.

Meanwhile, in June 1993 the FMLN had agreed to comply with an ultimatum issued by the UN, that the location and destruction of all remaining arms caches in El Salvador and neighbouring countries should be swiftly implemented. At the first national convention of the FMLN as a political organ, convened in September, the party confirmed its political alliance with the CD, selecting Francisco Lima as vice-presidential co-candidate with Rubén Zamora Rivas, the presidential candidate of the CD. In December this alliance was expanded to incorporate the MNR.

Voting to elect a new president, vice-president, legislature, 262 mayors and 20 members of the Central American parliament took place on 20 March 1994. Early indications were of a high level of support for ARENA's presidential candidate, Armando Calderón Sol, the mayor of San Salvador whose name had been linked to a 1981 plot to kidnap left-wing sympathisers by documents declassified by the US administration in November 1993. However, Calderón Sol failed to secure the clear majority needed for outright victory in the first poll, and was forced to contest a second round of voting against the second-placed candidate, Zamora Rivas, on 24 April 1994, which the ARENA candidate won with 68.2% of the votes. ARENA candidates also achieved considerable success in the legislative elections (retaining 39 seats in the Asamblea) and in the municipal poll (securing an estimated 200 municipalities). FMLN candidates were also considered to have performed well in the party's first electoral contest, winning 21 seats in the Asamblea and a number of rural municipalities. Calderón Sol was inaugurated on 1 June and a new Cabinet was installed simultaneously. In late June, in response to a recent intensification of political violence and organized crime, President Calderón Sol announced a new initiative for national security, which attracted opposition for its virtual exclusion of the transitional National Civilian Police.

Meanwhile, serious divisions emerged within the FMLN during 1994, and members of two constituent parties, the Resistencia Nacional (RN) and the Expresión Renovadora del Pueblo (ERP—formerly the Fuerzas Armadas de la Resistencia Nacional and the Ejército Revolucionario Popular guerrilla groups, respectively) became increasingly alienated following a decision, taken by the FMLN national council in May, to suspend several prominent members of the two parties from their positions within the FMLN executive for failing to comply with a party directive to boycott elections to the new directorate of the Asamblea. In December the RN and the ERP announced their withdrawal from the FMLN, owing to a divergence of political interests. In March 1995 the Secretary-General of the ERP, Joaquín Villalobos (who had been highly critical of the predominance of political extremism), announced the formation of a new centre-left political force, the Partido Demócrata (PD), comprising the ERP, the RN, the MNR and a dissident faction of the PDC. The new party demonstrated an immediate willingness to co-operate with the country's most prominent political forces.

Political manoeuvring in preparation for congressional and municipal elections scheduled for March 1997, began in mid-1996 with the PD's announcement of its withdrawal from the legislative pact forged with ARENA in May 1995, owing to the Government's failure to honour pledges to increase spending on health and education and to safeguard the jobs of employees at state concerns scheduled for privatization. (The Government's divestment and rationalization programme had provoked industrial action in the public sector early in the year) The PD subsequently announced that it would contest the March 1997 elections in an electoral alliance of the 'democratic centre', with the PDC. In early January 1997 ARENA's congressional strength was further undermined by the defection, to the PCN, of three prominent ARENA deputies, who complained of constrictive practices within the party.

The results of municipal and legislative elections, conducted on 16 March 1997, demonstrated a significant increase in support for the FMLN, particularly in the capital, where the party won seven of the 16 contested seats. Héctor Silva, the FMLN-led coalition candidate, was elected Mayor of San Salvador, defeating the incumbent ARENA candidate, Mario Valiente. The results of the legislative poll revealed a considerable erosion of ARENA's predominance in the Asamblea, with the party securing 29 seats, just one more than the FMLN. Widespread concern was expressed at the high level of voter abstention, estimated to be some 60%.

In May 1997 the FMLN secured sufficient support in the legislature to repeal a law providing for the privatization of the state telecommunications concern ANTEL. However, a revised privatization bill prepared by an *ad hoc* joint commission, involving all parties with representation in the Asamblea Nacional, was approved by the legislature in July, despite the continued opposition of the FMLN. ANTEL was to be divided into two separate companies, Compañía de Telecomunicaciones de El Salvador (CTE), which would control the terrestrial network, and Internacional de Telecomunicaciones (Intel), which would manage the sale of telecommunications frequencies. In June a new Ministry of the Environment and Natural Resources was created to address the country's serious environmental problems.

The presidential election of 7 March 1999 was won by Francisco Flores Pérez, the candidate of ARENA, who obtained 51.96% of the votes, thereby obviating the need for a second round of voting. Despite contesting the election in alliance with the Unión Social Cristiana, the candidate of the FMLN, Facundo Guardado, received only 29.05% of the votes, prompting him to resign as Co-ordinator of the party. He was succeeded in July by Fabio Castillo. Voter participation was the lowest recorded in the country's history, with more than 60% of the 3.2m. registered voters choosing to abstain. President Flores was inaugurated on 1 June, when a new Council of Ministers was installed. Flores stated that his Government's priority was to address the problem of violent crime, and an initiative was unveiled that included provision for the restructuring of the National Civilian Police force and a revision of the penal code. However, economic measures announced later that month, which included the rationalization of public bodies, prompted a succession of strikes by public-sector workers demanding salary increases and job security. In August two demonstrators were killed during a confrontation between the security forces and former paramilitaries who were protesting at not having received credits and pensions promised to them in return for their demobilization at the conclusion of the civil war. Furthermore, the Government was embarrassed by allegations that foreign funds, donated for disaster relief following the impact of 'Hurricane Mitch' in November 1998, had been diverted by ARENA to former paramilitaries in an attempt to buy votes for Flores in the presidential election. The issue was being investigated by the Comptroller-General's office.

Dissatisfaction with the ARENA Government was demonstrated in the results of the legislative elections of 12 March 2000, in which the FMLN became the largest single party in the Asamblea Nacional, winning 31 of the 84 seats. ARENA secured 29 seats, followed by the PCN (14 seats), the PDC (five seats), the Centro Democrático Unido (CDU—an electoral alliance comprising the CD and the Partido Social Demócrata, three seats) and the Partido Acción Nacional (PAN, two seats). Voter turn-out was only 33%. In concurrently-held municipal elections the FMLN also performed well, gaining control of 78 of the 262 municipalities, while ARENA won 127. On 21 March the FMLN proposed a governability pact with ARENA. However, relations between the two parties immediately became strained, and on 1 May ARENA formed an alliance with the PCN and the PDC in order to prevent the FMLN claiming the presidency of the Asamblea. Although the party gaining the most seats was, traditionally, given the presidency, in order to prevent a political impasse it was decided that the post was to be rotated annually among the three largest parties, the PCN, ARENA and the FMLN.

On 22 November 2000 President Flores unexpectedly announced that, from 1 January 2001, the US dollar would be introduced as an official currency alongside the colón, anchored to the colón at a fixed rate of exchange. The 'dollarization' was an attempt to stabilize the economy, lower interest rates, and stimulate domestic and foreign investment. Despite opposition to the move from the FMLN, the so-called Law of Monetary Integration was approved by the Asamblea Nacional in December.

On 13 January 2001 an earthquake, measuring 7.6 on the Richter scale, hit El Salvador, causing landslides in many areas, including in the Las Colinas suburb of Santa Tecla. Some 726 people were killed, with many more unaccounted for, an estimated 4,000 people were injured, and a further 50,000 people were left homeless. President Flores immediately declared a state of emergency and 87 medical and evacuee centres were established. Besides numerous aftershocks, a second earthquake, measuring 6.6 on the Richter scale, struck on 12

February, causing further damage and loss of life. Total damages and losses were estimated at US $1,600m., representing around 10% of gross domestic product (GDP) in 2000. Particularly badly affected were the housing, health and education services, and communications sectors. Agriculture, industry and trade all suffered losses, with the private sector particularly badly affected. In March 2001 the Inter-American Development Bank pledged some US $1,278.5m. in aid, mainly for economic, social and environmental development projects.

A severe increase in violent criminal activity from late 1995 caused widespread concern and prompted the Government to introduce a number of uncompromising emergency laws, in March 1996, which sought to address the problem. However, human rights organizations expressed concern that the new laws represented a serious infringement of civil liberties. These concerns were reiterated in October, following the Asamblea's approval of a constitutional amendment whereby the death penalty for civilians (abolished in 1971) was to be reinstated for a number of offences including rape, kidnapping and aggravated murder.

In December 1993, bowing to pressure from the UN, President Cristiani inaugurated a four-member commission of investigation (the Joint Group for the Investigation of Illegal Armed Groups), comprising representatives of the Government, the Office of the Ombudsman for Human Rights, and of ONUSAL, to examine allegations of political motivation behind an escalation in violent attacks against members of the FMLN in late 1993. The conclusions of the commission claimed that officials from numerous government departments, together with current and former members of the security forces, were continuing to participate in organized crime and in politically motivated acts of violence, prompting President Calderón Sol to declare his full commitment to all efforts to bring to justice anyone engaged in criminal activity.

In September 1994 and January 1995, in protest at the Government's failure to honour the terms of the 1992 peace accord with regard to financial compensation and other benefits for demobilized military personnel, retired soldiers occupied the Asamblea and took a number of deputies hostage. On both occasions the occupation was ended swiftly and peacefully following the Government's agreement to enter into direct negotiations with the former soldiers. The Association of the Demobilized Armed Forces had earlier threatened to sabotage the economy by disrupting transport communications and foreign businesses throughout the country if the Government failed to meet its obligations, and had organized a series of co-ordinated protests throughout the country in January 1995. Further demonstrations by army veterans during March and November were forcibly curtailed by the security forces, prompting concern that such incidents might provoke a renewed escalation of armed conflict.

In May 1994 the UN Security Council voted to extend the ONUSAL mandate for a further six months in order to supervise the full implementation of the outstanding provisions of the peace agreement. Of particular concern were delays in the reform of the judiciary, the initiation of the land reform programme and the full integration and activation of the National Civilian Police. In September the UN Secretary-General appealed to the Government and to the international community for increased financial commitment to the peace process. In the same month, in the context of increasing levels of crime and social unrest, the ONUSAL mandate was further extended, pending the effective habilitation of the National Civilian Police; a further extension, until the end of April 1995, was approved by the UN Security Council in November. A small contingent of UN observers, MINUSAL, was mandated to remain in El Salvador until April 1996 (the revised deadline for the fulfilment of the outstanding terms of the peace accord). By this date, however, full implementation of those terms of the accord relating to land allocation for refugees and former combatants, and to the reform of the judiciary and the electoral code, had yet to be achieved. A reduced MINUSAL contingent was further mandated to oversee Government efforts to fulfil the outstanding terms of the agreement, and the mission was formally terminated on 31 December 1996.

In an attempt to resolve a territorial dispute between El Salvador and Honduras over three islands in the Gulf of Fonseca and a small area of land on the joint border, President Duarte and President Azcona of Honduras submitted the dispute to the International Court of Justice (ICJ) for arbitration in December 1986. In September 1992 both countries accepted the ruling of the ICJ, which awarded one-third of the disputed mainland and two of the three disputed islands to El Salvador. Following the ruling, negotiations began towards a protocol defining the nationality and property rights of the inhabitants of the redesignated land. Although the ICJ recommended that all those involved should be granted dual nationality, a provision of the Honduran Constitution precluded this possibility. A resolution of the issue, which had led to numerous disputes between the two countries, was finally achieved in January 1998, when the parties signed a convention specifying the rights and obligations of those affected, including the right to choose between Honduran and Salvadorean citizenship.

Government

Executive power is held by the President, assisted by the Vice-President and the Council of Ministers. The President is elected for a five-year term by universal adult suffrage. Legislative power is vested in the Asamblea Nacional—National Assembly, with 84 members elected by universal adult suffrage for a three-year term.

Defence

Military service is by compulsory selective conscription of men between 18 and 30 years of age for one year. In August 2000 the armed forces totalled 16,800 men, comprising the army 15,000, the navy 700 and the air force 1,100. The National Civilian Police force, created in 1991, numbered around 12,000 personnel by 2000 and there were plans for it to total some 16,000. The defence budget for 2000 totalled 980m. colones.

Economic Affairs

In 1998, according to estimates by the World Bank, El Salvador's gross national product (GNP), measured at average 1996–98 prices, was US $11,207m., equivalent to $1,850 per head (or $4,008 per head on an international purchasing-power parity basis). During 1990–98, it was estimated, GNP per head increased, in real terms, by an average of 3.2% per year. Over the same period, the population increased at an average annual rate of 2.4%. El Salvador's gross domestic product (GDP) increased, in real terms, at an average annual rate of 4.9% in 1990–99. GDP grew by 3.4% in 1999 and by a preliminary 2.5% in 2000.

Agriculture (including hunting, forestry and fishing) contributed an estimated 10.4% of GDP in 1999 and employed some 25.1% of the employed labour force in 1998. The principal cash crops are coffee (which accounted for 25.8% of export earnings in 1998) and sugar cane. Maize, beans, rice and millet are the major subsistence crops. Shrimps and honey are increasingly significant export commodities. During 1990–99 agricultural GDP increased at an average annual rate of 0.9%. The sector's GDP increased by an estimated 6.6% in 1999 and decreased by a preliminary 0.8% in 2000. The agricultural sector was badly affected by the earthquakes that struck the country in early 2001. In March the Inter-American Development Bank (IDB) pledged some US $1,278.5m. in emergency assistance, of which US $132.6m. was intended for rehabilitation and development of agriculture; a further US $101.0m. was made available for redevelopment of the coffee industry, which had been particularly badly affected.

Industry (including mining, manufacturing, construction and power) contributed an estimated 29.6% of GDP in 1999, and engaged 24.6% of those employed in 1998. During 1990–99 industrial GDP increased at an average annual rate of 5.6%. The sector's GDP increased by an estimated 3.5% in 1999.

El Salvador has no significant mineral resources, and the mining sector employed less than 0.1% of the economically active population in 1998, and contributed only an estimated 0.4% of GDP in that year. Small quantities of gold, silver, sea-salt and limestone are mined or quarried.

Manufacturing contributed an estimated 22.6% of GDP in 1999, and employed 18.7% of the active labour force in 1998. Measured by the gross value of output, the most important branches of manufacturing (excluding the in-bond industry) in 1996 were food products (about 23.5% of the total), chemical products (16.1%), petroleum products, textiles, apparel (excl. footwear) and beverages. During 1990–99 manufacturing GDP increased at an average annual rate of 5.6%. The sector's GDP increased by an estimated 3.7%, in real terms, in 1999 and by a preliminary 4.5% in 2000. There is a thriving offshore (*maquila*) manufacturing sector. By the late 1990s manufacturing had become the highest earning export sector, generating the equivalent of 53% of total exports in 1999. Following the earthquakes in early 2001, the IDB pledged some US $62.2m. to the industry and commerce sector and a further $574.7m. to the housing sector to fund a renovation and reconstruction programme.

Energy is derived principally from imported fuel, which accounted for an estimated 10.4% of the cost of merchandise imports in 1998. An estimated 41.6% of total electricity production in 1998 was contributed by hydroelectric installations. In 2001 construction was to begin on an electricity interconnection between El Salvador and Honduras, part of a planned Central American regional power network.

The services sector contributed an estimated 60.0% of GDP in 1999 and employed 50.4% of the economically active population in 1998. The GDP of the services sector increased by an average of 5.6% per year in 1990–99. Growth in the sector was estimated at 1.4% in 1999. The promising tourism sector was severely damaged by the civil war, but recovered in the late 1990s. In 1998 receipts from tourism totalled US $125m., compared with $67m. in the previous year.

In 1999 El Salvador recorded a visible trade deficit of US $1,358.9m., while there was a deficit of $241.9m. on the current account of the balance of payments. Workers' remittances from abroad were equivalent to some 10% of annual GDP during 1990–98, and totalled about $1,370m. in 1999. In 1998 the principal source of imports (38.5%) was the USA; other major suppliers were Guatemala, Mexico, Japan, Costa Rica and Panama. The principal market for exports was Guatemala (taking 22.5% of exports in that year); other significant purchasers were the USA, Honduras, Germany and Costa Rica. In 1998 the main exports were coffee and coffee substitutes, textile yarn and fabrics, sugar, paper and paperboard manufactures, and chemicals and related products. In the same year the principal imports were machinery and transport equipment, basic manufactures and chemical products.

In 1998 there was an estimated budgetary deficit of 3,812m. colones, equivalent to some 3.6% of GDP. El Salvador's external debt totalled US $3,705m. at the end of 1999. In that year the cost of debt-servicing was $345m. The average annual rate of inflation was 9.0% in 1990–99; consumer prices increased by an average of 0.3% in 1999 and by 2.3% in 2000. Some 7.3% of the labour force were unemployed in 1998.

El Salvador is a member of the Central American Common Market (CACM, see p. 147), which aims to increase trade within the region and to encourage monetary and industrial co-operation.

The administration of Calderón Sol (1994–99) achieved considerable progress in reducing financial imbalances and in addressing the problem of widespread poverty. However, following strong growth in 1995, the economy slowed in 1996, reflecting declining coffee prices and the effect of increased competition from Mexico on receipts from non-traditional and *maquila* exports. There was strong recovery in 1997 as exports increased, and restructuring continued in 1998 with the divestment of state assets in the sectors of electricity distribution and telecommunications. A private pensions system also began operating in that year and was to replace gradually the existing state system. The Flores administration, inaugurated in June 1999, announced a plan for economic reactivation designed to galvanize agricultural and industrial production. In particular, the introduction of value-added tax on imported consumer goods and the prospect of more easily available credit were expected to improve the competitiveness of the agricultural sector. A revision of the tax system was expected to produce a significant increase in revenue. Following economic expansion of 3.4% in

1999, economic growth slowed in 2000, to 2.5%. Growth of between 3.5% and 4.0% was envisaged for 2001, with an inflation rate of around 3.5%.

Social Welfare

In 1952 the Instituto Salvadoreño del Seguro Social (ISSS) was established. This institute provides hospital facilities, medicines and benefits for industrial injury, sickness, accident, disability, maternity, old age and death. Health and welfare insurance is financed by contributions from workers, employers and the State. In 1997 there were an estimated 107.1 physicians per 100,000 inhabitants and 34.9 nurses per 100,000 inhabitants. In 1996 there were an estimated 4,904 hospital beds. The Ministry of Public Health and Social Welfare administers 250 medical units, including 14 hospitals. Following the earthquakes in early 2001, the IDB pledged some US $234.2m. to strengthen the institutional capacity of the Red Cross and other organizations, to recover the Ministry of Health vaccine bank, and to improve epidemiological vigilance. In 1997 budgetary expenditure by the central Government (excluding the ISSS) included 1,235.4m. colones (10.3% of total expenditure) on health and a further 654.8m. colones (5.4%) on social security and welfare.

Education

There are two national universities and more than 30 private universities. Education is provided free of charge in state schools, and there are also numerous private schools. Primary education, beginning at seven years of age and lasting for nine years, is officially compulsory. In 1997 enrolment at primary schools was equivalent to 89.1% of children in the relevant age-group (males 89.1%; females 89.1%). Secondary education begins at the age of 16 and lasts for three years. In 1997 enrolment at secondary schools was equivalent to just 36.4% of students in the relevant age-group (males 36.1%; females 36.7%). In 1998, according to estimates by the United Nations Development Programme, the illiteracy rate among people aged 15 years and over was 22.2% (males 19.2%; females 25.0%). Following the earthquakes in early 2001, the IDB pledged some US $43.6m. for infrastructure reconstruction and child protection. Budgetary expenditure on education by the central Government in 1997 was 2,361.9m. colones, equivalent to 19.6% of total expenditure.

Public Holidays

2001: 1 January (New Year's Day), 11–15 April (Easter), 1 May (Labour Day), 14 June (Corpus Christi), 4–6 August* (El Salvador del Mundo Festival), 15 September (Independence Day), 12 October (Discovery of America), 2 November (All Souls' Day), 5 November (First Call of Independence), 24–25 December (Christmas), 31 December (New Year's Eve).

2002: 1 January (New Year's Day), 27–31 March (Easter), 1 May (Labour Day), 30 May (Corpus Christi), 4–6 August* (El Salvador del Mundo Festival), 15 September (Independence Day), 12 October (Discovery of America), 2 November (All Souls' Day), 5 November (First Call of Independence), 24–25 December (Christmas), 31 December (New Year's Eve).

* 5–6 August outside the capital.

Weights and Measures

The metric system is officially in force. Some old Spanish measures are also used, including:

    25 libras = 1 arroba;
    4 arrobas = 1 quintal (46 kg);
    1 manzana = 0.699 ha.

Statistical Survey

Sources (unless otherwise stated): Banco Central de Reserva de El Salvador, Alameda Juan Pablo II y 17 Avda Norte, Apdo 01-106, San Salvador; tel. 271-0011; fax 271-4575; Dirección General de Estadística y Censos, Edif. Centro de Gobierno, Alameda Juan Pablo II y Calle Guadalupe, San Salvador; tel. 286-4260; fax 286-2505; internet www.minec.gob.sv/estadis.htm.

Area and Population

AREA, POPULATION AND DENSITY

Area (sq km)	
Land	20,721
Inland water	320
Total	21,041*
Population (census results)†	
28 June 1971	3,554,648
27 September 1992	
Males	2,485,613
Females	2,632,986
Total	5,118,599
Population (official estimates at mid-year)	
1998	6,031,000
1999	6,154,000
2000	6,276,000
Density (per sq km) at mid-2000	298.3

* 8,124 sq miles.
† Excluding adjustments for underenumeration.

PRINCIPAL TOWNS* (population at 1992 census)

San Salvador (capital)	415,346	San Miguel	127,696
Soyapango	261,122	Nueva San Salvador	116,575
Santa Ana	139,389	Ciudad Delgado	104,790
Mejicanos	131,972	Apopa	100,763

* Figures refer to *municipios*, which may each contain rural areas as well as an urban centre.

Source: UN, *Demographic Yearbook*.

BIRTHS, MARRIAGES AND DEATHS

	Registered live births		Registered marriages		Registered deaths	
	Number	Rate (per 1,000)	Number	Rate (per 1,000)	Number	Rate (per 1,000)
1991	151,210	28.3	22,658	4.2	27,066	5.1
1992	154,014	28.1	23,050	4.2	27,869	5.1
1993*	n.a.	29.9	n.a.	n.a.	n.a.	6.3
1994*	160,772	28.5	27,761	4.9	29,407	5.2
1995	n.a.	28.1	n.a.	n.a.	n.a.	n.a.
1996	163,007	28.2	n.a.	n.a.	28,904	5.0
1997	n.a.	27.8	n.a.	n.a.	n.a.	n.a.
1998	158,350	26.3	25,937	4.3	29,919	5.0

* Rates based on UN population estimate.

Note: Registration is incomplete. According to UN estimates, the average annual rates in 1990–95 were: births 29.6 per 1,000; deaths 6.7 per 1,000.

Expectation of life (UN estimates, years at birth, 1998): 69.7 (males 66.7; females 72.7) (Source: UNDP, *Human Development Report*).

ECONOMICALLY ACTIVE POPULATION
(ISIC Major Divisions, '000 persons aged 10 years and over, 1998)

	Males	Females	Total
Agriculture, hunting, forestry and fishing	502.2	55.9	558.0
Mining and quarrying	1.7	0.2	1.9
Manufacturing	199.7	215.9	415.6
Electricity, gas and water	7.7	0.9	8.7
Construction	117.9	3.3	121.2
Trade, restaurants and hotels	228.4	327.5	555.9
Transport, storage and communication	84.8	5.2	90.0
Financing, insurance, real estate and business services	49.7	32.9	82.6
Community, social and personal services	153.7	239.9	393.6
Total employed	**1,345.8**	**881.7**	**2,227.5**
Unemployed	119.9	55.8	175.7
Total labour force	**1,465.7**	**937.5**	**2,403.2**

Source: ILO, *Yearbook of Labour Statistics*.

Agriculture

PRINCIPAL CROPS ('000 metric tons)

	1997	1998	1999
Rice (paddy)	65.3	71.8	60.4
Maize	501.6	551.8	683.5
Sorghum	197.3	217.0	181.5
Dry beans	66.7	46.1	71.7
Sugar cane	4,642.9	5,650.9	5,500.0
Coffee (green)	124.5	117.2	143.8

Source: FAO.

LIVESTOCK ('000 head, year ending September)

	1997	1998	1999
Horses*	95.8	95.8	95.8
Mules*	23.8	23.8	23.8
Cattle	1,162.1	1,037.7	1,141.5
Pigs	294.0	312.0	335.1
Sheep*	5.2	5.2	5.2
Goats*	15.3	15.3	15.3

Chickens* (million): 8 in 1997; 9 in 1998; 9 in 1999.

* FAO estimates.

Source: FAO.

LIVESTOCK PRODUCTS ('000 metric tons)

	1997	1998	1999
Beef and veal	34.7	33.9	34.4
Pig meat	10.7	11.4	11.4
Poultry meat	43.5	47.9	46.2
Cows' milk	367.7	404.5	410.0
Cheese	2.6	2.6	2.6
Hen eggs*	45.0	45.7	45.0

* FAO estimates.

Source: FAO.

Forestry

ROUNDWOOD REMOVALS
('000 cubic metres, excl. bark)

	1996	1997	1998
Sawlogs, veneer logs and logs for sleepers	155	466	427
Other industrial wood . .	56	200	183
Fuel wood	4,119	4,519	4,519
Total	4,330	5,185	5,129

Source: FAO, *Yearbook of Forest Products.*

SAWNWOOD PRODUCTION
(FAO estimates, '000 cubic metres, incl. railway sleepers)

	1996	1997	1998
Coniferous (softwood) . .	57	57	57
Broadleaved (hardwood) . .	14	14	14
Total	70	70	70

Source: FAO, *Yearbook of Forest Products.*

Fishing

('000 metric tons, live weight)

	1996	1997	1998
Capture	12.8	10.6	15.0
Nile tilapia	1.1	1.3	1.5
Jaguar guapote . . .	0.6	0.4	0.4
Other freshwater fishes .	1.1	1.1	1.2
Croakers and drums . .	0.3	0.3	0.3
Sharks, rays, skates, etc. .	0.3	1.2	1.1
Whiteleg shrimp . . .	0.5	n.a.	1.1
Penaeus shrimps . . .	1.4	1.2	1.7
Pacific seabobs . .	4.8	2.1	6.1
Aquaculture	0.4	0.4	0.4
Total catch	13.2	11.0	15.4

Source: FAO, *Yearbook of Fishery Statistics.*

Industry

SELECTED PRODUCTS ('000 metric tons, unless otherwise indicated)

	1994	1995	1996
Raw sugar	323	302	310
Motor spirit (petrol) . . .	185	178	202
Distillate fuel oils . . .	264	218	107
Residual fuel oils . . .	262	217	309
Cement	915	914	938
Electric energy (million kWh) .	3,203	3,398	3,452

Source: UN, *Industrial Commodity Statistics Yearbook.*

Finance

CURRENCY AND EXCHANGE RATES

Monetary Units
100 centavos = 1 Salvadorean colón.

Sterling, Dollar and Euro Equivalents (29 December 2000)
£1 sterling = 13.064 colones;
US $1 = 8.755 colones;
€1 = 8.147 colones;
1,000 Salvadorean colones = £76.54 = $114.22 = €122.75.

Note: The foregoing information refers to the principal exchange rate, applicable to official receipts and payments, imports of petroleum and exports of coffee. In addition, there is a market exchange rate, applicable to other transactions. The principal rate has been maintained at 8.755 colones per US dollar since May 1995.

BUDGET (million colones)

Revenue*	1996	1997	1998
Current revenue†	10,321.7	11,195.1	11,296.6
Taxation	10,599.1	10,290.8	10,784.0
Taxes on income, profits and capital gains . . .	3,054.0	2,911.7	2,999.1
Taxes on property . . .	86.1	119.5	126.1
Domestic taxes on goods and services	6,014.1	5,909.2	6,355.6
Sales or turnover taxes .	5,306.4	5,195.1	5,698.9
Excises	630.8	632.0	571.1
Taxes on international trade and transactions . .	1,424.6	1,307.5	1,268.8
Customs duties . . .	1,411.3	1,305.2	1,268.1
Other current revenue . . .	396.7	823.8	523.4
Entrepreneurial and property income	280.3	624.4	346.9
Administrative fees, non-industrial and incidental sales	89.3	92.6	90.4
Capital revenue	206.2	32.9	30.2
Capital transfers from non-governmental sources . .	194.8	—	—
Total	10,527.9	11,228.0	11,326.8

Expenditure‡	1995	1996	1997
General public services . .	1,779.3	1,674.0	1,639.0
Defence	848.9	843.2	853.2
Public order and safety . .	1,438.2	1,908.2	1,964.2
Education	1,655.8	2,006.4	2,361.9
Health	1,044.2	1,217.7	1,235.4
Social security and welfare .	1,078.7	596.3	654.8
Housing and community amenities	148.5	670.5	219.5
Recreational, cultural and religious affairs and services .	125.0	206.1	202.8
Economic services . . .	1,541.7	1,831.9	2,053.8
Agriculture, forestry and fishing	192.1	355.3	263.1
Transport and communications	1,079.8	1,199.8	1,487.4
Other expenditure . . .	1,188.5	1,346.1	1,431.1
Total expenditure . . .	11,376.3	12,305.6	12,027.3
Current§	9,486.1	10,298.9	10,367.6
Capital‖	1,362.7	2,001.5	2,248.1

* Excluding grants received (million colones): 105.2 in 1996; 42.3 in 1997; 18.3 in 1998.

† Including adjustment (million colones): −674.1 in 1996; 80.5 in 1997; −10.8 in 1998.

‡ Excluding lending minus repayments (million colones): −747.2 in 1995; −1,209.6 in 1996; −176.3 in 1997.

§ Including interest payments (million colones): 1,188.5 in 1995; 1,346.1 in 1996; 1,431.1 in 1997.

‖ Excluding adjustment to cash basis and expenditure under previous budgets (million colones): 527.5 in 1995; 5.2 in 1996; −588.4 in 1997.

Source: IMF, *Government Finance Statistics Yearbook.*

1998 (million colones, provisional figures): Expenditure 15,261.3 (excl. lending minus repayments −103.9).

CENTRAL BANK RESERVES (US $ million at 31 December)

	1998	1999	2000
Gold*	19.8	19.8	19.8
IMF special drawing rights	25.0	25.0	25.0
Foreign exchange	1,577.9	1,969.5	1,889.8
Total	1,622.7	2,014.3	1,934.6

* Valued at US $42.22 per troy ounce.

Source: IMF, *International Financial Statistics*.

MONEY SUPPLY (million colones at 31 December)

	1997	1998	1999
Currency outside banks	3,250	3,531	4,716
Demand deposits at deposit money banks	4,921	5,268	5,416
Total money (incl. others)	9,693	10,064	10,880

Source: IMF, *International Financial Statistics*.

COST OF LIVING
(Consumer Price Index; base: 1990 = 100)

	1997	1998	1999
Food	243.6	248.3	246.2
Rent	163.2	171.9	176.7
Fuel and light	155.2	176.1	176.2
Clothing	153.9	153.0	151.4
All items (incl. others)	210.5	216.1	216.7

Source: ILO, *Yearbook of Labour Statistics*.

NATIONAL ACCOUNTS (million colones at current prices)
National Income and Product

	1991	1992	1993
Domestic factor incomes*	39,747	46,232	55,844
Consumption of fixed capital	—	—	—
Gross domestic product at factor cost	42,594	49,841	60,522
Indirect taxes, *less* subsidies	2,847	3,609	4,678
GDP in purchasers' values	45,441	53,450	65,200
Net factor income from abroad	—	—	—
Gross national product	41,386	48,226	59,803
Less Consumption of fixed capital	—	—	—
National income in market prices	41,386	48,226	59,803

* Compensation of employees and the operating surplus of enterprises. The amount is obtained as a residual.

Source: UN, *National Accounts Statistics*.

Expenditure on the Gross Domestic Product

	1998	1999	2000
Government final consumption expenditure	10,178	10,981	11,993
Private final consumption expenditure	88,831	93,624	99,612
Increase in stocks	990	123	90
Gross fixed capital formation	17,365	17,619	18,737
Total domestic expenditure	117,364	122,347	130,432
Exports of goods and services	26,407	27,432	30,949
Less Imports of goods and services	38,863	40,694	45,665
GDP in purchasers' values	104,907	109,086	115,716
GDP at constant 1990 prices	54,028	55,883	57,293

Source: IMF, *International Financial Statistics*.

Gross Domestic Product by Economic Activity

	1996	1997	1998*
Agriculture, hunting, forestry and fishing	11,746.4	12,744.3	12,388.0
Mining and quarrying	406.5	438.4	411.8
Manufacturing	18,762.3	20,349.6	22,166.6
Construction	3,877.4	4,219.6	4,510.9
Electricity, gas and water	1,369.2	1,599.4	1,739.7
Transport, storage and communications	6,822.5	7,756.7	8,446.1
Wholesale and retail trade	18,758.3	19,159.5	20,068.0
Finance, insurance, etc.	3,026.1	3,601.2	3,894.2
Owner-occupied dwellings	6,938.1	7,785.6	8,378.1
Public administration	5,982.3	6,533.7	7,026.1
Other	9,570.1	10,455.2	11,260.5
Sub-total	87,259.2	94,643.2	100,290.0
Import duties / Value-added tax	6,717.7	7,128.0	7,677.9
Less Imputed bank service charge	2,928.7	3,843.0	4,155.7
Total	91,048.2	97,928.2	103,812.2

* Preliminary figures.

BALANCE OF PAYMENTS (US $ million)

	1997	1998	1999
Exports of goods f.o.b.	2,429.2	2,459.7	2,500.4
Imports of goods f.o.b.	−3,532.5	−3,762.7	−3,859.3
Trade balance	−1,103.3	−1,303.0	−1,358.9
Exports of services	370.4	558.2	634.8
Imports of services	−548.7	−678.8	−791.5
Balance on goods and services	−1,281.6	−1,423.6	−1,515.5
Other income received	75.1	111.4	112.9
Other income paid	−221.7	−266.8	−395.9
Balance on goods, services and income	−1,428.2	−1,579.0	−1,798.5
Current transfers received	1,363.6	1,507.6	1,565.6
Current transfers paid	—	−7.3	−9.0
Current balance	−64.6	−78.7	−241.9
Capital account (net)	—	4.6	31.6
Direct investment abroad	—	—	−2.9
Direct investment from abroad	59.0	1,103.7	231.3
Portfolio investment assets	—	—	−2.1
Portfolio investment liabilities	111.0	−221.5	75.4
Other investment assets	2.0	−8.0	−148.8
Other investment liabilities	457.6	136.2	461.5
Net errors and omissions	−202.4	−633.1	−199.9
Overall balance	362.6	303.2	204.2

Source: IMF, *International Financial Statistics*.

External Trade

PRINCIPAL COMMODITIES (distribution by SITC, US $ million).

Imports c.i.f.	1996	1997	1998
Food and live animals . . .	358.6	403.0	405.5
Dairy products and birds' eggs .	52.0	61.4	60.8
Cereals and cereal preparations .	128.7	140.1	127.3
Crude materials (inedible) except fuels	95.2	100.3	117.9
Textile fibres and their wastes .	55.2	61.6	69.1
Mineral fuels, lubricants, etc. .	325.4	336.7	322.0
Petroleum, petroleum products, etc.	299.7	311.5	296.2
Crude petroleum . . .	121.6	119.6	86.7
Refined petroleum products .	175.2	188.5	206.4
Residual fuel oils . . .	114.0	125.2	120.4
Animal and vegetable oils, fats and waxes	76.2	76.9	82.4
Chemicals and related products	455.4	503.4	472.4
Medicinal and pharmaceutical products	109.7	115.2	94.3
Medicaments	89.9	90.8	75.4
Perfumes and cleansing preparations, etc. . .	70.6	80.3	76.2
Plastic materials, etc. . . .	85.2	95.3	106.4
Products of polymerization, etc.	71.8	80.2	87.1
Basic manufactures . . .	435.4	499.5	572.4
Paper, paperboard and manufactures . . .	90.3	94.1	112.5
Paper and paperboard . .	68.4	68.2	87.9
Textile yarn, fabrics, etc. . .	45.9	64.3	73.4
Iron and steel	99.0	111.6	134.8
Machinery and transport equipment	700.1	783.8	853.9
Power-generating machinery and equipment . . .	58.1	44.0	65.2
Machinery specialized for particular industries . .	87.2	136.0	127.1
General industrial machinery, equipment and parts . .	85.2	114.7	131.4
Office machines and automatic data-processing equipment . .	57.7	76.5	62.1
Telecommunications and sound equipment . . .	68.5	67.2	84.2
Other electrical machinery, apparatus, etc. . . .	94.1	97.4	95.1
Road vehicles	237.2	234.6	260.8
Passenger motor cars (except buses)	79.0	78.5	91.9
Lorries and special purpose motor vehicles . . .	96.4	90.0	102.1
Lorries and trucks . . .	89.0	86.0	95.3
Miscellaneous manufactured articles	204.8	237.0	260.1
Total (incl. others) . . .	2,670.1	2,961.5	3,108.1

Source: UN, *International Trade Statistics Yearbook.*

Exports f.o.b.	1996	1997	1998
Food and live animals . . .	509.1	715.5	557.1
Fish, crustaceans and molluscs .	43.7	34.2	38.6
Fresh, chilled, frozen, salted or dried crustaceans and molluscs	40.9	31.6	33.9
Cereals and cereal preparations	19.6	23.8	30.3
Cereal preparations, etc. . .	17.6	21.9	25.6
Sugar, sugar preparations and honey	53.1	74.8	85.3
Sugar and honey . . .	45.7	68.0	77.7
Sugars, beet and cane (raw, solid)	31.6	52.9	63.7
Coffee, tea, cocoa, etc. . .	341.9	519.8	328.1
Coffee and coffee substitutes .	340.0	517.5	324.6
Coffee (incl. husks and skins) and substitutes containing coffee	339.1	515.9	322.0
Mineral fuels, lubricants, etc.	33.2	44.5	47.6
Petroleum, petroleum products, etc.	33.2	44.4	47.6
Refined petroleum products . .	33.1	44.3	47.2
Chemicals and related products	141.2	166.5	178.0
Medicinal and pharmaceutical products	49.7	53.2	58.8
Medicaments	45.7	48.0	53.6
Perfumes and cleansing preparations, etc. . . .	48.4	63.7	68.7
Soap, etc.	33.8	42.9	46.1
Basic manufactures . . .	188.6	232.6	252.7
Paper, paperboard and manufactures	57.0	64.4	64.6
Shaped or cut articles of paper and paperboard . . .	40.6	45.8	45.7
Textile yarn, fabrics, etc. . . .	67.3	84.2	90.8
Iron and steel	21.6	26.9	34.8
Non-ferrous metals . . .	21.0	23.0	27.1
Aluminium	20.7	22.1	26.1
Machinery and transport equipment	35.3	50.2	50.0
Miscellaneous manufactured articles	77.3	98.5	130.9
Clothing and accessories . .	27.5	39.4	54.9
Total (incl. others) . . .	1,024.3	1,354.0	1,257.1

Source: UN, *International Trade Statistics Yearbook.*

PRINCIPAL TRADING PARTNERS
(US $ million)

Imports c.i.f.	1996	1997	1998
Brazil	29.4	23.6	26.0
China, People's Republic . . .	7.9	14.0	53.4
Colombia	19.0	42.2	32.8
Costa Rica	101.7	116.3	115.1
Ecuador	29.2	79.3	85.5
Germany	97.2	93.6	89.7
Guatemala	279.8	323.7	346.8
Honduras	70.3	85.1	87.8
Italy	31.2	31.2	31.6
Japan	114.1	91.2	145.1
Mexico	172.3	235.3	238.4
Netherlands	30.4	18.2	27.2
Netherlands Antilles . . .	30.3	20.7	37.0
Nicaragua	54.1	51.1	49.4
Panama	175.9	65.5	106.1
Spain	24.2	39.5	49.0
USA	1,067.6	1,224.6	1,197.6
Venezuela	59.6	63.6	41.8
Total (incl. others) . . .	2,670.1	2,961.5	3,108.0

Exports f.o.b.				1996	1997	1998
Belgium .	.	.	.	60.6	60.9	24.7
Costa Rica	.	.	.	93.3	111.4	110.3
Dominican Republic	.	.	.	8.1	11.4	13.4
France	.	.	.	4.7	16.8	13.2
Germany	.	.	.	159.0	237.5	139.9
Guatemala	.	.	.	210.7	264.1	282.5
Honduras	.	.	.	97.5	136.0	148.8
Japan	.	.	.	10.3	14.1	12.5
Mexico .	.	.	.	12.6	17.8	17.3
Netherlands .	.	.	.	31.3	29.1	21.9
Nicaragua	.	.	.	53.7	64.6	75.0
Panama	.	.	.	24.5	24.5	24.3
Russia .	.	.	.	0.0	0.0	22.2
United Kingdom .	.	.	.	9.9	29.9	19.4
USA	.	.	.	197.4	260.1	270.1
Total (incl. others)	.	.	.	1,024.3	1,353.9	1,257.1

Source: UN, *International Trade Statistics Yearbook*.

Transport

RAILWAYS (traffic)

				1997	1998
Number of passengers ('000)	.	.	.	460.4	355.3
Passenger-kilometres (million)	.	.	.	7.1	5.5
Freight ('000 metric tons).	.	.	.	161.1	239.8
Freight ton-kilometres (million)	.	.	.	17.4	24.8

Source: UN, *Statistical Yearbook*.

ROAD TRAFFIC (motor vehicles in use at 31 December)

				1995	1996	1997
Passenger cars	.	.	.	151,081	168,234	177,488
Buses and coaches	.	.	.	29,293	32,238	33,087
Lorries and vans	.	.	.	125,101	142,916	151,772
Motorcycles and mopeds	.	.	.	28,888	38,330	27,476

Source: IRF, *World Road Statistics*.

SHIPPING
Merchant Fleet (registered at 31 December)

			1996	1997	1998
Number of vessels	.	.	12	12	12
Total displacement ('000 grt)	.	.	1.5	1.5	1.5

Source: Lloyd's Register of Shipping, *World Fleet Statistics*.

CIVIL AVIATION (traffic on scheduled services)

			1995	1996	1997
Kilometres flown (million)	.	.	21	22	20
Passengers carried ('000) .	.	.	1,698	1,800	1,701
Passenger–km (million)	.	.	2,077	2,181	2,080
Total ton-km (million)	.	.	227	212	204

Source: UN, *Statistical Yearbook*.

Tourism

TOURIST ARRIVALS BY COUNTRY OF ORIGIN
(excluding Salvadorean nationals residing abroad)

					1996	1997	1998
Canada .	.	.	.	.	8,855	9,052	9,282
Costa Rica	.	.	.	.	19,497	19,919	28,804
Guatemala	.	.	.	.	54,210	83,685	163,485
Honduras	.	.	.	.	20,644	36,515	84,299
Mexico .	.	.	.	.	11,276	19,737	19,912
Nicaragua	.	.	.	.	14,104	24,546	60,735
Panama .	.	.	.	.	9,050	6,883	10,498
Spain .	.	.	.	.	8,242	8,779	7,631
USA	.	.	.	.	88,905	123,355	97,838
Total (incl. others)	.	.	.		282,835	387,052	541,863

Receipts from tourism (US $ million): 44 in 1996; 67 in 1997; 125 in 1998.

Source: World Tourism Organization, *Yearbook of Tourism Statistics*, World Bank, *World Development Indicators*.

Communications Media

	1995	1996	1997
Radio receivers ('000 in use) . .	2,600	2,670	2,750
Television receivers ('000 in use) .	3,900	3,910	4,000
Telephones ('000 main lines in use)	285	325	n.a.
Mobile cellular telephones (subscribers)	13,475	23,270	40,163
Daily newspapers:			
Number	6	5	n.a.
Total circulation ('000) . . .	280	278	n.a.
Non-daily newspapers:			
Number	6	6	n.a.
Total circulation ('000) . . .	48	52	n.a.

Source: mainly UNESCO, *Statistical Yearbook*.

Education

(1997)

		Insti-tutions	Teachers	Students		
				Males	Females	Total
Pre-primary	. .	3,679*	6,009*	88,447	90,599	179,046
Primary	. .	5,025*	34,496*	610,528	580,524	1,191,052
Secondary	. .	n.a.	9,255*	73,295	79,179	152,474
Tertiary:						
University level .	.	32	5,610*	53,183*	54,292*	107,475*
Other higher	.	n.a.	309*	2,747*	2,044*	4,791*

* 1996 figure.

Source: UNESCO, *Statistical Yearbook*.

Directory

The Constitution

The Constitution of the Republic of El Salvador came into effect on 20 December 1983.

The Constitution provides for a republican, democratic and representative form of government, composed of three Powers—Legislative, Executive, and Judicial—which are to operate independently. Voting is a right and duty of all citizens over 18 years of age. Presidential and congressional elections may not be held simultaneously.

The Constitution binds the country, as part of the Central American Nation, to favour the total or partial reconstruction of the Republic of Central America. Integration in a unitary, federal or confederal form, provided that democratic and republican principles are respected and that basic rights of individuals are fully guaranteed, is subject to popular approval.

LEGISLATIVE ASSEMBLY

Legislative power is vested in a single chamber, the Asamblea Nacional, whose members are elected every three years and are eligible for re-election. The Asamblea's term of office begins on 1 May. The Asamblea's duties include the choosing of the President and Vice-President of the Republic from the two citizens who shall have gained the largest number of votes for each of these offices, if no candidate obtains an absolute majority in the election. It also selects the members of the Supreme and subsidiary courts; of the Elections Council; and the Accounts Court of the Republic. It determines taxes; ratifies treaties concluded by the Executive with other States and international organizations; sanctions the Budget; regulates the monetary system of the country; determines the conditions under which foreign currencies may circulate; and suspends and reimposes constitutional guarantees. The right to initiate legislation may be exercised by the Asamblea (as well as by the President, through the Council of Ministers, and by the Supreme Court). The Asamblea may override, with a two-thirds majority, the President's objections to a Bill which it has sent for presidential approval.

PRESIDENT

The President is elected for five years, the term beginning and expiring on 1 June. The principle of alternation in the presidential office is established in the Constitution, which states the action to be taken should this principle be violated. The Executive is responsible for the preparation of the Budget and its presentation to the Asamblea; the direction of foreign affairs; the organization of the armed and security forces; and the convening of extraordinary sessions of the Asamblea. In the event of the President's death, resignation, removal or other cause, the Vice-President takes office for the rest of the presidential term; and, in case of necessity, the Vice-President may be replaced by one of the two Designates elected by the Asamblea.

JUDICIARY

Judicial power is exercised by the Supreme Court and by other competent tribunals. The Magistrates of the Supreme Court are elected by the Legislature, their number to be determined by law. The Supreme Court alone is competent to decide whether laws, decrees and regulations are constitutional or not.

The Government

HEAD OF STATE

President: Francisco Flores Pérez (assumed office 1 June 1999).
Vice-President: Carlos Quintanilla Schmidt.

COUNCIL OF MINISTERS
(April 2001)

Minister of Foreign Affairs: María Eugenia Brizuela de Avila.
Minister of the Interior: Mario Ernesto Acosta Oertel.
Minister of Public Security and Justice: Francisco Bertrand Galindo.
Minister of the Economy: Miguel Ernesto Lacayo Argüello.
Minister of Education: Ana Evelyn Jacir de Lovo.
Minister of National Defence: Maj. Gen. Juan Antonio Martínez Varela.
Minister of Labour and Social Security: Jorge Isidoro Nieto Menéndez.

Minister of Public Health and Social Welfare: José López Beltrán.
Minister of the Treasury: José Luis Trigueros.
Minister of Agriculture and Livestock: Salvador Urrutia Loucel.
Minister of Public Works: José Angel Quiros.
Minister of the Environment and Natural Resources: Ana María Majano Guerrero.

MINISTRIES

Ministry for the Presidency: Avda Cuba, Calle Darió González 806, Barrio San Jacinto, San Salvador; tel. 221-8483; fax 771-0950; internet www.casapres.gob.sv.

Ministry of Agriculture and Livestock: Alameda Roosevelt, San Salvador; tel. 779-1579; fax 779-1941; internet www.mag.gob.sv.

Ministry of the Economy: Centro de Gobierno, Alameda Juan Pablo II y Calle Guadalupe, San Salvador; tel. 281-1122; fax 221-5446; internet www.minec.gob.sv.

Ministry of Education: Dirección de Publicaciones, 17 Avda Sur 430, San Salvador; tel. 222-0665; fax 271-1071; internet www.mined.gob.sv.

Ministry of the Environment and Natural Resources: Edif. Torre El Salvador, 3°, Alameda Roosevelt y 55 Avda Norte, San Salvador; tel. 260-8900; fax 260-3117; e-mail medioambiente@marn.gob.sv; internet www.marn.gob.sv.

Ministry of Foreign Affairs: 5500 Alameda Dr Manuel Enrique Araújo, Km 6, Carretera a Santa Tecla, San Salvador; tel. 243-3712; fax 243-3714; internet www.rree.gob.sv.

Ministry of the Interior: Centro de Gobierno, Alameda Juan Pablo II y Calle Guadalupe, San Salvador; tel. 222-5000; e-mail informacion@minter.gob.sv; internet www.minter.gob.sv.

Ministry of Labour and Social Security: Avda La Capilla 223, Col. San Benito, San Salvador; tel. 779-0388; fax 779-0877.

Ministry of National Defence: Alameda Dr Manuel Enrique Araújo, Km 5, Carretera a Santa Tecla, San Salvador; tel. 223-0233; fax 998-2005.

Ministry of Public Health and Social Welfare: Calle Arce 827, San Salvador; tel. 771-0008; internet www.mspas.gob.sv.

Ministry of Public Security and Justice: Centro de Gobierno, Edif. B-1, Alameda Juan Pablo II y Avda Norte 17, San Salvador; tel. 221-3688; fax 221-3956; e-mail mjministro@telemovil.com.

Ministry of Public Works: 1a Avda Sur 603, San Salvador; tel. 222-1505; fax 771-2881.

Ministry of the Treasury: Edif. Ministerio de Hacienda, Blvd Los Héroes 1231, San Salvador; tel. 225-5500; fax 225-7491; internet www.mh.gob.sv.

President and Legislature

PRESIDENT

Election, 7 March 1999

Candidates	% of votes cast
Francisco Flores Pérez (ARENA)	51.96
Facundo Guardado (FMLN/USC)	29.05
Rubén Ignacio Zamora (CD)	7.50
Rodolfo Parker (PDC)	5.68
Rafael Hernán Contreras (PCN)	3.82
Salvador Nelson García (LIDER)	1.63
Francisco Ayala de Paz (PUNTO)	0.36
Total	100.0

ASAMBLEA NACIONAL

President: Ciro Cruz Zapeda.

General Election, 12 March 2000

Party	Seats
Frente Farabundo Martí para la Liberación Nacional (FMLN)	31
Alianza Republicana Nacionalista (ARENA)	29
Partido de Conciliación Nacional (PCN)	14
Partido Demócrata Cristiano (PDC)	5
Centro Democrático Unido (CDU)*	3
Partido Acción Nacional (PAN)	2
Total	**84**

* Electoral alliance comprising the Convergencia Democrática (CD) and the Partido Social Demócrata (PSD).

Political Organizations

Alianza Republicana Nacionalista (ARENA): Prolongación Calle Arce 2423 y Avda Norte, San Salvador; tel. 260-4400; f. 1981; right-wing; Leader (vacant).

Convergencia Democrática (CD): Blvd Tutunichapa y Calle Roberto Masferrer 1313, Urb. La Esperanza, San Salvador; tel. 226-1928; f. 1993; left-wing alliance; contested 2000 elections as part of the Centro Democrático Unido electoral alliance; Leader Vinicio Peñate; Sec.-Gen. Ruben Zamora; the alliance comprised three groups:

Movimiento Nacional Revolucionario (MNR): Blvd María Cristina 128, Urbanización La Esperanza, San Salvador; tel. 226-4194; fax 225-3166; f. 1967; also mem. of FMLN; Sec.-Gen. Dr Víctor Manuel Valle.

Movimiento Popular Social Cristiano (MPSC): formed by dissident members of PDC; also mem. of FMLN; Leader Rubén Zamora Rivas.

Partido Social Demócrata (PSD): f. 1987; left-wing; contested 2000 elections as part of the Centro Democrático Unido electoral alliance; Sec.-Gen. Mario Reni Roldán.

Frente Farabundo Martí para la Liberación Nacional (FMLN): 27 Calle Poniente 1316 y 9a Avda Norte 229, San Salvador; tel. 225-2961; internet www.fmln.org.sv; f. 1980 as the FDR (Frente Democrático Revolucionario-FMLN as a left-wing opposition front to the PDC-military coalition Government; the FDR was the political wing and the FMLN was the guerrilla front; military operations were co-ordinated by the Dirección Revolucionaria Unida (DRU); achieved legal recognition 1992; Co-ordinator Fabio Castillo; the front comprised c. 20 groups, of which the principal were:

Bloque Popular Revolucionario (BPR): guerrilla arm: Fuerzas Populares de Liberación (FPL; Leader 'Commander Gerónimo'); based in Chalatenango; First Sec. Leonel González; Second Sec. Dimas Rodríguez.

Frente de Acción Popular Unificado (FAPU): guerrilla arm: Fuerzas Armadas de la Resistencia Nacional (FARN); Leaders Fermán Cienfuegos, Saúl Villalta.

Frente Pedro Pablo Castillo: f. 1985.

Ligas Populares del 28 de Febrero (LP-28): guerrilla arm: Ejército Revolucionario Popular (ERP); Leaders Joaquín Villalobos, Ana Guadalupe Martínez.

Movimiento Nacional Revolucionario (MNR): (see above).

Movimiento Obrero Revolucionario Salvado Cayetano Carpio (MOR).

Movimiento Popular Social Cristiano (MPSC): (see above).

Unión Democrática Nacionalista (UDN): f. 1969; Communist; Sec.-Gen. Mario Aguinada Carranza.

Liga Democrática Republicana (LIDER): San Salvador; republican.

Movimiento Auténtico Cristiano (MAC): San Salvador; f. 1988; Leader Julio Adolfo Rey Prendes.

Movimiento Estable Republicano Centrista (MERECEN): San Salvador; f. 1982; centre party; Sec.-Gen. Juan Ramón Rosales y Rosales.

Partido Acción Democrática (AD): San Salvador; f. 1981; centre-right; observer mem. of Liberal International; Leader Ricardo González Camacho.

Partido Acción Nacional (PAN): San Salvador.

Partido Acción Renovadora (PAR): San Salvador; f. 1944; advocates a more just society; Leader Ernesto Oyarbide.

Partido Auténtico Institucional Salvadoreño (PAISA): San Salvador; f. 1982; formerly right-wing majority of the PCN; Sec.-Gen. Dr Roberto Escobar García.

Partido de Conciliación Nacional (PCN): Calle Arce 1128, San Salvador; tel. 221-3752; f. 1961; right-wing; Leader Francisco José Guerrero; Sec.-Gen. Ciro Cruz Zepeda.

Partido Demócrata (PD): Blvd Héctor Silva 128, Urb. Médica, San Salvador; tel. 225-3166; f. 1995 by Movimiento Nacional Revolucionario and a dissident faction of the PDC, together with Expresión Renovadora del Pueblo (f. 1994, fmrly the ERP, see above) and Resistencia Nacional (f. 1994, fmrly the FARN, see above), following their withdrawal from the FMLN; centre-left; Leaders Jorge Meléndez, Juan Medrano.

Partido Demócrata Cristiano (PDC): 3a Calle Poniente 836, San Salvador; tel. 222-1815; fax 998-1526; f. 1960; 150,000 mems; anti-imperialist, advocates self-determination and Latin American integration; Sec.-Gen. Rene Aguiluz.

Partido de Orientación Popular (POP): San Salvador; f. 1981; extreme right-wing.

Partido Liberal Democrático (PLD): Calle El Progreso y Col. El Rosal 11, San Salvador; tel. 224-2143; f. 1994; right-wing; Leader Kirio Waldo Salgado.

Partido Popular Laborista (PPL): Calle Poniente 23 y Col. Layco 1518, San Salvador; tel. 235-6260; f. 1997; Sec.-Gen. Ernesto Vilanova.

Partido Popular Salvadoreño (PPS): San Salvador; f. 1966; right-wing; represents business interests; Sec.-Gen. Francisco Quiñónez Avila.

Partido Unionista Centroamericana (PUCA): San Salvador; advocates reunification of Central America; Pres. Dr Gabriel Piloña Araújo.

Pueblo Unido Nuevo Trato (PUNTO): San Salvador.

Unión Social Cristiana (USC): Calle Poniente 12 y Avda Sur 31, Col. Flor Blanca, San Salvador; tel. 222-0571; f. 1997 by merger of Movimiento de Unidad, Partido de Renovación Social Cristiano and Movimiento de Solidaridad Nacional; Leader Abraham Rodríguez.

Other parties include Partido Centrista Salvadoreño (f. 1985; Leader Tomás Chafoya Martínez); Partido de Empresarios, Campesinos y Obreros (ECO, Leader Dr Luis Rolando López); Partido Independiente Democrático (PID, f. 1985; Leader Eduardo García Tobar); Partido de la Revolución Salvadoreña (Sec.-Gen. Joaquín Villalobos); Patria Libre (f. 1985; right-wing; Leader Hugo Barrera).

OTHER GROUPS

The following groups were active during the internal disturbances of the 1980s and early 1990s:

Partido de Liberación Nacional (PLN): political-military organization of the extreme right; the military wing was the Ejército Secreto Anti-comunista (ESA); Sec.-Gen. and C-in-C Aquiles Baires.

The following guerrilla groups were dissident factions of the Fuerzas Populares de Liberación (FPL):

Frente Clara Elizabeth Ramírez: f. 1983; Marxist-Leninist group.

Movimiento Laborista Cayetano Carpio: f. 1983.

There were also several right-wing guerrilla groups and 'death squads', including the Fuerza Nacionalista Roberto D'Aubuisson (FURODA), not officially linked to any of the right-wing parties.

Diplomatic Representation

EMBASSIES IN EL SALVADOR

Argentina: 79 Avda Norte 704, Col. Escalón, Apdo 384, San Salvador; tel. 263-3638; fax 263-3687; Ambassador: Jorge Telesforo Pereira.

Belize: Calle el Bosque Norte, Col. La Lima, San Salvador; tel. 248-1423; fax 248-1423; e-mail embassyofbelizeinelsalvar@yahoo.com; Ambassador: Darwin Gabourel.

Brazil: Blvd de Hipódromo 305, Col. San Benito, San Salvador; tel. 298-2751; fax 279-3934; e-mail brasembes@netcomsa.com; Ambassador: Luis Enrique Pereira da Fonseca.

Canada: Centro Financiero Gigante, 63 Avda Sur y Alameda Roosevelt, San Salvador; tel. 279-4655; fax 279-0765; Ambassador: Allan Culham.

Chile: Pasaje Belle Vista 121, Entre 9a C.P. y 9a C.P. bis, Col. Escalón, San Salvador; tel. 263-4285; fax 263-4308; Ambassador: Hector Horacio Wood Armas.

China (Taiwan): Condominio Penthouse, 7°, Paseo General Escalón 5333, Col. Escalón, Apdo 956, San Salvador; tel. 263-1275; fax 263-1329; Ambassador: Gen. Bing F. Yen.

Colombia: Calle El Mirador 5120, Col. Escalón, San Salvador; tel. 263-1936; fax 263-1942; Ambassador: Guillermo Orjuela.

Costa Rica: 85 Avda Sur y Calle Cuscatlán 4415, Colonia Escalón, San Salvador; tel. 264-3863; fax 264-3866; e-mail embaricasal@ sicanet.org.sv; Ambassador: CARMEN MARÍA MADRIZ CONTRERAS.

Dominican Republic: Avda República Federal de Alemania 163, Col. Escalón, San Salvador; tel. 263-1816; fax 263-1816; Ambassador: JORGE ADALBERTO SANTIAGO PÉREZ.

Ecuador: 77 Avda Norte 208, Col. Escalón, San Salvador; tel. 263-5323; fax 263-5258; Ambassador: ENRIQUE GARCÉS FÉLIX.

Egypt: 9a Calle Poniente y 93 Avda Norte 12-97, Col. Escalón; tel. 263-2426; fax 263-2411; Chargé d'affaires a.i.: FAWZI MOHAMED ALSAID GOHAR.

France: 1 Calle Poniente 3718, Col. Escalón, Apdo 474, San Salvador; tel. 279-4016; fax 298-1536; e-mail ambafrance@es.com.sv; Ambassador: LYDIE GAZARIAN.

Germany: 7a Calle Poniente 3972 esq. 77a Avda Norte, Col. Escalón, Apdo 693, San Salvador; tel. 263-2088; fax 263-2091; Ambassador: SEPP WOELKER.

Guatemala: 15 Avda Norte 135, San Salvador; tel. 271-2225; fax 221-3019; Ambassador: OSCAR AUGUSTO ZELAYA CORONADO.

Holy See: 87a Avda Norte y 7a Calle Poniente, Col. Escalón, Apdo 01-95, San Salvador (Apostolic Nunciature); tel. 263-2931; fax 263-3010; e-mail nunapes@es.com.sv; Apostolic Nuncio: Most Rev. GIACINTO BERLOCO, Titular Archbishop of Fidene.

Honduras: 7a Calle Poniente 3697, Col. Escalón, San Salvador; tel. 264-7814; fax 223-2221; Ambassador: ROBERTO ARITA QUIÑONEZ.

Israel: Centro Financiero Gigante, Torre B, 11°, Alameda Roosevelt y Avda Sur 63, San Salvador; tel. 211-3434; fax 211-3443; Ambassador: ARYEH ZUR.

Italy: Calle la Reforma 158, Col. San Benito, Apdo 0199, San Salvador; tel. 223-4806; fax 298-3050; e-mail italemb@embitaliaes .org; internet www.embitaliaes.org; Ambassador: ROBERTO FALASCHI.

Japan: Calle Loma Linda 258, Col. San Benito, San Salvador; tel. 224-4740; fax 298-6685; Ambassador: SABURO YAZAWA.

Malta: Calle Juan José Cañas 251, entre 79 y 81 Avda Sur, Col. Escalón; tel. 216-0222; fax 216-0727; Ambassador: LOUIS CHIURATO.

Mexico: Calle Circunvalación y Pasaje 12, Col. San Benito, Apdo 432, San Salvador; tel. 243-3190; fax 243-0437; Ambassador: ANGONIO GUILLERMO VILLEGAS.

Nicaragua: 71a Avda Norte y 1a Calle Poniente 164, Col. Escalón, San Salvador; tel. 223-7729; fax 223-7201; Ambassador: JULIO ALEJANDRO ESPINAL.

Panama: Alameda Roosevelt 2838 y Avda Norte 55, Apdo 104, San Salvador; tel. 260-5452; fax 260-5453; Ambassador: RAFAEL ANTONIO MORENO.

Peru: 7a Calle Poniente 4111, Col. Escalón, San Salvador; tel. 263-3326; fax 263-3310; e-mail embperu@telesal.net; Ambassador: ANTONIO GRUTER VÁSQUEZ.

Spain: Calle La Reforma 167, Col. San Benito, San Salvador; tel. 298-1188; fax 298-0402; Ambassador: RICARDO PEIDRÓ CONDE.

United Kingdom: Edif. Inter Inversión, Paseo General Escalón 4828, Apdo 1591, San Salvador; tel. 263-6527; fax 263-6516; Ambassador: PATRICK MORGAN.

USA: Blvd Santa Elena Sur, Antiguo Cuscatlán, San Salvador; tel. 278-4444; fax 278-6011; internet www.usinfo.org.sv; Ambassador: ROSE M. LIKINS.

Uruguay: Edif. Gran Plaza, 4°, Blvd del Hipódromo, Col. San Benito, San Salvador; tel. 279-1627; fax 279-1626; Ambassador: Dr ENRIQUE DELGADO GENTA.

Venezuela: 7a Calle Poniente, entre 75 y 77 Avda Norte, Col. Escalón, San Salvador; tel. 263-3977; fax 263-3979; Ambassador: JUAN JOSÉ MONSANT.

Judicial System

Supreme Court of Justice: Centro de Gobierno José Simeón Cañas, San Salvador; tel. 771-3511; fax 771-3379; f. 1824; composed of 14 Magistrates, one of whom is its President. The Court is divided into four chambers: Constitutional Law, Civil Law, Penal Law and Litigation.

President: JOSÉ DOMINGO MÉNDEZ.

Chambers of 2nd Instance: 14 chambers composed of two Magistrates.

Courts of 1st Instance: 12 courts in all chief towns and districts.

Courts of Peace: 99 courts throughout the country.

Attorney-General: BELISARIO ARTIGA.

Secretary-General: ERNESTO VIDAL RIVERA GUZMÁN.

Attorney-General of the Poor: Dr VICENTE MACHADO SALGADO.

Religion

Roman Catholicism is the dominant religion, but other denominations are also permitted. In 1982 there were about 200,000 Protestants. Seventh-day Adventists, Jehovah's Witnesses, the Baptist Church and the Church of Jesus Christ of Latter-day Saints (Mormons) are represented.

CHRISTIANITY

The Roman Catholic Church

El Salvador comprises one archdiocese and seven dioceses. At 31 December 1998 Roman Catholics represented some 79.8% of the total population.

Bishops' Conference: Conferencia Episcopal de El Salvador, 15 Avda Norte 1420, Col. Layco, Apdo 1310, San Salvador; tel. 225-8997; fax 226-5330; f. 1974; Pres. Most Rev. FERNANDO SÁENZ LACALLE, Archbishop of San Salvador.

Archbishop of San Salvador: Most Rev. FERNANDO SÁENZ LACALLE, Arzobispado, Avda Dr Emilio Alvarez y Avda Dr Max Bloch, Col. Médica, Apdo 2253, San Salvador; tel. 226-0501; fax 226-4979; e-mail arzfsl@ejje.com.

The Anglican Communion

El Salvador comprises one of the five dioceses of the Iglesia Anglicana de la Región Central de América.

Bishop of El Salvador: Rt Rev. MARTÍN DE JESÚS BARAHONA PASCACIO, 47 Avda Sur, 723 Col. Flor Blanca, Apdo 01-274, San Salvador; tel. 223-2252; fax 223-7952; e-mail martinba@gbm.net.

The Baptist Church

Baptist Association of El Salvador: Avda Sierra Nevada 922, Col. Miramonte, Apdo 347, San Salvador; tel. 226-6287; f. 1933; Exec. Sec. Rev. CARLOS ISIDRO SÁNCHEZ.

The Press

DAILY NEWSPAPERS

San Miguel

Diario de Oriente: Avda Gerardo Barrios 406, San Miguel.

San Salvador

Co Latino: 23a Avda Sur 225, Apdo 96, San Salvador; tel. 271-0671; fax 271-0971; e-mail colatino@es.com.sv; f. 1890; evening; Editor FRANCISCO ELÍAS VALENCIA; circ. 15,000.

El Diario de Hoy: 11 Calle Oriente 271, Apdo 495, San Salvador; tel. 271-0100; fax 271-2040; e-mail comedh@es.com.sv; internet www.elsalvador.com; f. 1936; morning; independent; Dir ENRIQUE ALTAMIRANO MADRIZ; circ. 115,000.

Diario Oficial: 4a Calle Poniente 829, San Salvador; tel. 221-9101; f. 1875; Dir LUD DREIKORN LÓPEZ; circ. 2,100.

El Mundo: 2a Avda Norte 211, Apdo 368, San Salvador; tel. 771-4400; fax 771-4342; internet www.sadecu.com/el-mundo; f. 1967; evening; Dir CRISTÓBAL IGLESIAS; circ. 58,032 (weekdays), 61,822 (Sundays).

La Noticia: Edif. España, Avda España 321, San Salvador; tel. 222-7906; fax 771-1650; f. 1986; evening; general information; independent; Dir CARLOS SAMAYOA MARTÍNEZ; circ. 30,000 (weekdays and Saturdays).

La Prensa Gráfica: 3a Calle Poniente 130, San Salvador; tel. 271-1010; fax 271-4242; e-mail lpg@gbm.net; internet www.laprensa .com.sv; f. 1915; general information; conservative, independent; Editor RODOLFO DUTRIZ; circ. 97,312 (weekdays), 115,564 (Sundays).

Santa Ana

Diario de Occidente: 1a Avda Sur 3, Santa Ana; tel. 441-2931; f. 1910; Editor ALEX E. MONTENEGRO; circ. 6,000.

PERIODICALS

Anaqueles: 8a Avda Norte y Calle Delgado, San Salvador; review of the National Library.

Cultura: Concultura, Ministerio de Educación, 17 Avda Sur 430, San Salvador; tel. 222-0665; fax 271-1071; quarterly; educational; Dir Dr RICARDO ROQUE BALDOVINOS.

El Salvador Filatélico: San Salvador; f. 1940; publ. quarterly by the Philatelic Society of El Salvador.

Orientación: 1a Calle Poniente 3412, San Salvador; tel. 998-6838; fax 224-5099; f. 1952; Catholic weekly; Dir P. FABIAN AMAYA TORRES; circ. 8,000.

Proceso: Universidad Centroamericana, Apdo 01-575, San Salvador; tel. 224-0011; fax 273-3556; f. 1980; weekly newsletter, published by the Documentation and Information Centre of the

Universidad Centroamericana José Simeón Cañas; Dir LUIS ARMANDO GONZÁLEZ.

Revista del Ateneo de El Salvador: 13a Calle Poniente, Centro de Gobierno, San Salvador; tel. 222-9686; f. 1912; 3 a year; official organ of Salvadorean Athenaeum; Pres. Lic JOSÉ OSCAR RAMÍREZ PÉREZ; Sec.-Gen. Lic. RUBÉN REGALADO SERMEÑO.

Revista Judicial: Centro de Gobierno, San Salvador; tel. 222-4522; organ of the Supreme Court; Dir Dr MANUEL ARRIETA GALLEGOS.

PRESS ASSOCIATIONS

Asociación de Corresponsales Extranjeros en El Salvador: San Salvador; Dir CRISTINA HASBÚN.

Asociación de Periodistas de El Salvador (Press Association of El Salvador): Edif. Casa del Periodista, Paseo General Escalón 4130, San Salvador; tel. 223-8943; Pres. JORGE ARMANDO CONTRERAS.

FOREIGN NEWS AGENCIES

Agencia EFE (Spain): San Salvador; Bureau Chief CRISTINA HASBÚN DE MERINO.

Agenzia Nazionale Stampa Associata (ANSA) (Italy): Edif. 'Comercial 29', 29 Calle Poniente y 11 Avda Norte, San Salvador; tel. 226-8008; fax 774-5512; Bureau Chief RENÉ ALBERTO CONTRERAS.

Associated Press (AP) (USA): San Salvador; Correspondent ANA LEONOR CABRERA.

Deutsche Presse-Agentur (dpa) (Germany): San Salvador; Correspondent JORGE ARMANDO CONTRERAS.

Inter Press Service (IPS) (Italy): Apdo 05152, San Salvador; tel. 998-0760; Correspondent PABLO IACUB.

Reuters (United Kingdom): 5 Calle La Mascota, Carretera a Santa Tecla, San Salvador; tel. 223-4736; Bureau Chief ALBERTO BARRERA.

United Press International (UPI) (USA): Calle y Pasaje Palneral, Col. Toluca, Apdo 05-185, San Salvador; tel. 225-4033; Correspondent (vacant).

Publishers

CENITEC (Centro de Investigaciones Tecnológicas y Científicas): 85 Avda Norte 905 y 15c Pte, Col. Escalón, San Salvador; tel. 223-7928; f. 1985; politics, economics, social sciences; Dir IVO PRÍAMO ALVARENGA.

Clásicos Roxsil, SA de CV: 4a Avda Sur 2–3, Nueva San Salvador; tel. 229-6742; fax 228-1212; e-mail silviaa@navegante.com.sv; f. 1976; textbooks, literature; Dir ROSA VICTORIA SERRANO DE LÓPEZ.

Editorial Delgado: Universidad 'Dr José Matías Delgado', Km 8.5, Carretera a Santa Tecla, Ciudad Merliot; tel. 278-1011; f. 1984; Dir LUCÍA SÁNCHEZ.

Editorial Universitaria: Ciudad Universitaria de El Salvador, Apdo 1703, San Salvador; tel. 226-0017; f. 1963; Dir TÍRSO CANALES.

D'TEXE (Distribuidora de Textos Escolares): Edif. C, Col., Paseo y Condominio Miralvalle, San Salvador; tel. 274-2031; f. 1985; educational; Dir JORGE A. LÓPEZ HIDALGO.

Dirección de Publicaciones e Impresos: Ministerio de Educación, 17a Avda Sur 430, San Salvador; tel. 222-0665; fax 271-1071; e-mail dpi@netcomsa.com; f. 1953; educational and general; Dir MIGUEL HUEZO MIXCO.

UCA Editores: Apdo 01-575, San Salvador; tel. 273-4400; fax 273-3556; f. 1975; social science, religion, economy, literature and textbooks; Dir RODOLFO CARDENAL.

PUBLISHERS' ASSOCIATIONS

Asociación Salvadoreña de Agencias de Publicidad: Centro Profesional Presidente Loc. 33a, Col. San Benito, San Salvador; tel. 243-3535; f. 1962; Dir ANA ALICIA DE GONZÁLEZ.

Cámara Salvadoreña del Libro: 4a Avda Sur 2–3, Apdo 2296, Nueva San Salvador; tel. 228-1832; fax 228-1212; f. 1974; Pres. ADELA CELARIÉ.

Broadcasting and Communications

TELECOMMUNICATIONS

Telecom de El Salvador: 63 Avda Sur y Alameda Roosevelt, Centro Financiero Gigante, San Salvador; tel 271-7200; fax 221-4849; e-mail servicioalcliente@cte.com.sv; internet www.telecom .com.sv; terrestrial telecommunications network, frmly part of Administración Nacional de Telecomunicaciones (Antel) which was divested in 1998, changed its name from CTE Antel Telecom in 1999; 51% owned by France Télécom; Pres. DOMINIQUE ST JEAN.

Telefónica El Salvador: San Salvador; internet www.telefonica .com.sv; manages sale of telecommunications frequencies, frmly Internacional de Telecomunicaciones (Intel) which was divested in 1998; controlling interest owned by Telefónica de España; allied with Amzak International in March 2000 to form Telefónica Multiservicios, offering cable-based television, telephone and internet access; Dir-Gen. LUIS ANTÓN.

Superintendencia General de Electricidad y Telecomunicaciones (SIGET): Sexta Décima Calle Poniente y 37 Avda Sur 2001, Col. Flor Blanca; tel. 257-4438; internet www.siget.gob.sv/ index.htm; f. 1996; Supt Lic. ERNESTO LIMA MENA.

RADIO

Asociación Salvadoreña de Radiodifusores (ASDER): Avda Izalco, Bloco 6 No 33, Residencial San Luis, San Salvador; tel. 222-0872; fax 274-6870; f. 1965; Pres. MANUEL A. FLORES B.

YSS Radio Nacional de El Salvador: Dirección General de Medios, Calle Monserrat, Plantel Ex-IVU, San Salvador; tel. 773-4170; non-commercial cultural station; Dir-Gen. ALFONSO PÉREZ GARCÍA.

There are 64 commercial radio stations. Radio Venceremos and Radio Farabundo Martí, operated by the former guerrilla group FMLN, were legalized in April 1992. A new station, Radio Mayavisión (operated by FMLN supporters), began broadcasting in November 1993.

TELEVISION

Canal 2, SA: Carretera a Nueva San Salvador, Apdo 720, San Salvador; tel. 223-6744; fax 998-6565; commercial; Pres. BORIS ESERSKI; Gen. Man. SALVADOR I. GADALA MARÍA.

Canal 4, SA: Carretera a Nueva San Salvador, Apdo 720, San Salvador; tel. 224-4555; commercial; Pres. BORIS ESERSKI; Man. RONALD CALVO.

Canal 6, SA: Km 6, Carretera Panamericana a Santa Tecla, San Salvador; tel. 243-3966; fax 243-3818; e-mail tv6@gbm.net; internet www.elnoticiero.com.sv; f. 1972; commercial; Exec. Dir JUAN CARLOS ESERSKI; Man. Dr PEDRO LEONEL MORENO MONGE.

Canal 8 and 10 (Televisión Cultural Educativa): Avda Robert Baden Powell, Apdo 104, Nueva San Salvador; tel. 228-0499; fax 228-0973; f. 1964; government station; Dir TOMÁS PANAMEÑO.

Canal 12: Urb. Santa Elena 12, Antiguo Cuscatlán, San Salvador; tel. 278-0622; fax 278-0722; f. 1984; Pres. RICARDO SALINAS PLIEGO.

Canal 15: 4a Avda Sur y 5a Calle Oriente 301, San Miguel; tel 661-3298; fax 661-3298; f. 1994; Gen. Man. JOAQUÍN APARICIO.

Canal 19 Sistemas de Video y Audio INDESI: Final Calle Los Abetos 1, Col. San Francisco, San Salvador; Gen. Man. MARIO CAÑAS.

Canal 21 (Megavisión): Final Calle Los Abetos 1, Col San Francisco, Apdo 2789, San Salvador; tel. 298-5311; fax 298-6492; f. 1993; Pres. OSCAR ANTONIO SAFIE; Dir HUGO ESCOBAR.

Canal 25 (Auvisa de El Salvador): Final Calle Libertad 100, Nueva San Salvador; commercial; Gen. Man. MANUEL BONILLA.

Canal 33 (Teleprensa): Istmania 262, Col Escalón, San Salvador; tel. 224-6040; fax 224-3193; f. 1957; Dir and Gen. Man. GUILLERMO DE LEÓN.

Finance

(cap. = capital; p.u. = paid up; res = reserves; dep. = deposits; m. = million; brs = branches; amounts in colones unless otherwise stated)

BANKING

The banking system was nationalized in March 1980. In June 1991 the Government initiated the transfer to private ownership of six banks and seven savings and loans institutions, as part of a programme of economic reform, which was completed in 1994.

Supervisory Body

Superintendencia del Sistema Financiero: 7a Avda Norte 240, Apdo 2942, San Salvador; tel. 281-2444; fax 281-1621; internet www.ssf.gob.sv/princip.htm; Supt Lic. GUILLERMO ARGUMEDO.

Superintendencia de Valores: Antiguo Edif. BCR, 1a Calle Poniente y 7a Avda Norte, San Salvador; tel. 281-8900; fax 281-8912; Supt Lic. JOSÉ ENRIQUE SORTO CAMPBELL.

Central Bank

Banco Central de Reserva de El Salvador: Alameda Juan Pablo II y 17 Avda Norte, Apdo 01-106, San Salvador; tel. 281-8000; fax 281-8011; e-mail comunicaciones@bcr.gob.sv; internet www .bcr.gob.sv; f. 1934; nationalized Dec. 1961; sole right of note issue; entered monetary integration process 1 Jan. 2001; cap. 1,000m., res

2,000m., dep. 6,500m. (Sept. 2000); Pres. Rafael Barraza; First Vice-Pres. Carmen Elena de Alemán.

Commercial and Mortgage Banks

Ahorromet Scotiabank: Edif. Torre Ahorromet, Avda Olímpica y 53 Avda Sur, San Salvador; tel. 245-1455; fax 224-2815; f. 1972; Pres. Lic. Juan Federico Salaverría.

Banco Agrícola: Paseo General Escalón y 69 Avda Sur 3635, Col. Escalón, San Salvador; tel. 267-5000; fax 267-5775; internet www.bancoagricola.com; f. 1955; privately owned; cap. 324.0m., res 703.6m., dep. 11,947.9m. (Dec. 1998); merged with Banco Desarrollo in July 2000; Pres. Archi Baldochi Dueñas; 150 brs world-wide.

Banco Capital: 1a Calle Poniente 3649, Col. Escalón, San Salvador; tel. 298-5776; fax 298-0772; privately owned; Gen. Man. Lic. Arturo Núñez.

Banco de Comercio de El Salvador: Edif. Ex Americana, 25 Avda Norte y 21 Calle Poniente, San Salvador; tel. 226-4577; fax 226-9466; f. 1949; privately owned; total assets 9,074m. (1999); Pres. José Gustavo Belismelis Vides; 23 brs.

Banco Credomatic: Edif. Credomatic, Avda Olímpica y 55 Avda Sur, San Salvador; tel. 279-4344; fax 224-4138; Pres. Raúl Ernesto Cardenal.

Banco Cuscatlán: Edif. Pirámide Cuscatlán, Km 10, Carretera a Santa Tecla, Apdo 626, San Salvador; tel. 212-3333; fax 228-5700; e-mail cuscatlan@bancocuscatlan.com; internet www .bancocuscatlan.com; f. 1972; privately owned; cap. 80m., res 68.9m., dep. 1,312.0m. (Dec. 2000); Pres. Mauricio Samayoa Rivas; Vice-Pres. Roberto Ortiz; 31 brs.

Banco Hipotecario de El Salvador: Pasaje Senda Florida Sur, Col. Escalón, Apdo 999, San Salvador; tel. 298-2072; fax 298-0447; f. 1935; state-owned mortgage and commercial bank; cap. 104.0m., dep. 1,852m. (Dec. 1998); Pres. Lic. Gino Bettaglio; 13 brs.

Banco Promérica: 71 Avda Sur y Paseo General Escalón 3669, Col. Escalón, San Salvador; tel. 211-5501; fax 211-4257; privately owned; Pres. Lic. Eduardo Ernesto Vilanova.

Banco Salvadoreño, SA (BANCOSAL): Edif. Centro Financiero, Avda Olímpica 3550, Apdo 06-73, San Salvador; tel. 298-4444; fax 298-0102; internet www.gbm.net/bancosal; f. 1885; privately-owned commercial bank; cap. 12,000m., dep. 8,900m. (Aug. 2000); merged with Banco de Construcción y Ahorro, SA (BANCASA) in July 2000; Pres. Lic. Félix Simán Jacir; Vice-Pres. Ing. Moisés Castro Maceda; 53 brs.

Banco UNO: Paseo General Escalón y 69 Avda Sur 3563, Col. Escalón, San Salvador; tel. 245-0055; fax 245-0080; Pres. Ing. Albino Román.

Citibank, NA: Edif. Century Plaza, Alameda Dr Manuel Enrique Araujo, San Salvador; tel. 224-3011; fax 245-1842; Pres. Steven J. Puig.

Financiera Calpiá: 37 Avda Sur 2, Col. Flor Blanca, San Salvador; tel. 260-6859; fax 260-6922; Pres. Pedro Dalmau Gorrita.

First Commercial Bank: Centro Comercial Gigante, Torre Telefónica, 3°, 63 Avda Sur y Alameda Roosevelt, San Salvador; tel. 211-2121; fax 211-3130; Vice-Pres. Peter Ming-Fung Lan.

UNIBANCO: Alameda Roosevelt, entre 47 y 49, Avda Sur 2511, San Salvador; tel. 245-0651; fax 245-0655; privately owned; Pres. Ing. José Roberto Navarro.

Public Institutions

Banco de Fomento Agropecuario: Km 10.5, Carretera al Puerto de la Libertad, Nueva San Salvador; tel. 228-5199; fax 229-2930; e-mail rgprieto@gbm.net; f. 1973; state-owned; cap. 605.0m., dep. 872.0m. (Oct. 1997); Pres. José Guillermo Funes Araujo; Gen. Man. Juan A. Martínez; 27 brs.

Banco Multisectoral de Inversiones: Alameda Manuel E. Araujo, Century Plaza, San Salvador; tel. 267-0000; fax 267-0038; f. 1994; Pres. Dr Nicola Angelucci.

Federación de Cajas de Crédito: 25 Avda Norte y 23 Calle Poniente, San Salvador; tel. 225-5922; fax 226-7059; f. 1943; Pres. Lic. Marco Tulio Rodríguez Mena.

Fondo Social Para la Vivienda: Calle Rubén Darío y 17 Avda Sur, San Salvador; tel. 271-2774; Pres. Lic. Edgar Ramiro Mendoza.

Banking Association

Asociación Bancaria Salvadoreña—ABANSA: Pasaje Senda Florida Norte 140, Col. Escalón, San Salvador; tel. 298-6938; fax 223-1079; Pres. Ing. Mauricio Samayoa; Exec. Dir Dr Claudio de Rosa.

STOCK EXCHANGE

Mercado de Valores de El Salvador, SA de CV (Bolsa de Valores): Edif. La Centroamericana, 6°, Alameda Roosevelt 3107, San Salvador; tel. 298-4244; fax 223-2898; internet www .bolsavalores.com.sv; Pres. Rolando Duarte Schlageter.

INSURANCE

AIG Unión y Desarrollo, SA: Calle Loma Linda 265, Col. San Benito, Apdo 92, San Salvador; tel. 298-5455; fax 298-5084; e-mail jorge.guirola@uni-desa.com; f. 1998 following merger of Unión y Desarrollo, SA and AIG; Pres. Francisco R. de Sola.

American Life Insurance Co.: Edif. Omnimotores, 2°, Km 4½, Carretera a Santa Tecla, Apdo 169, San Salvador; tel. 223-4925; f. 1963; Man. Carlos F. Pereira.

Aseguradora Agrícola Comercial, SA: Alameda Roosevelt 3104, Apdo 1855, San Salvador; tel. 260-3344; fax 260-5592; f. 1973; Pres. Luis Alfredo Escalante; Gen. Man. Federico Peraza F.

Aseguradora Popular, SA: Paseo General Escalón 5338, Col. Escalón, San Salvador; tel. 998-0700; fax 224-6866; f. 1975; Exec. Pres. Dr Carlos Armando Lahúd.

Aseguradora Suiza Salvadoreña, SA: Calle la Reforma, Col. San Benito, Apdo 1490, San Salvador; tel. 298-5222; fax 298-5060; f. 1969; Pres. Mauricio M. Cohen; Gen. Man. Rodolfo Schildknecht.

Internacional de Seguros, SA: Centro financiero Banco Salvadoreño, 5°, Avda Olímpica 3550, Col. Escalón, San Salvador; tel. 298-0202; fax 224-6935; f. 1958; Pres. Félix José Simán Jacir; Gen. Man. Alejandro Cabrera Rivas.

La Centro Americana, SA, Cía Salvadoreña de Seguros: Alameda Roosevelt 3107, Apdo 527, San Salvador; tel. 223-6666; fax 223-2687; f. 1915; Pres. Rufino Garay.

Compañía Anglo Salvadoreña de Seguros, SA: Paseo General Escalón 3848, San Salvador; tel. 224-2399; fax 224-4394; f. 1976; Pres. José Arturo Gómez; Vice-Pres. Julio E. Payes.

Compañía General de Seguros, SA: Calle Loma Linda 223, Col. San Benito, Apdo 1004, San Salvador; tel. 779-2777; fax 998-2870; f. 1955; Pres. José Gustavo Belismelis Vides; Gen. Man. Lic. Heriberto Pérez Aguirre.

Seguros e Inversiones, SA (SISA): Alameda Dr Manuel Enrique Araújo 3530, Apdo 1350, San Salvador; tel. 998-1199; fax 998-2882; f. 1962; Pres. Alfredo Félix Cristiani Burkard.

Seguros Universales, SA: Paseo Escalón y 81 Avda Norte 205, Col. Escalón, San Salvador; tel. 779-3533; fax 779-1830; Pres. Dr Enrique García Prieto.

Trade and Industry

GOVERNMENT AGENCIES AND DEVELOPMENT ORGANIZATIONS

Consejo Nacional de Ciencia y Tecnología (CONACYT): Col. Médica, Avda Dr Emilio Alvarez, Pasaje Dr Guillermo Rodríguez Pacas 51, San Salvador; tel. 226-2800; fax 225-6255; internet www.conacyt.gob.sv; f. 1992; formulation and guidance of national policy on science and technology; Exec. Dir Carlos Federico Paredes Castillo.

Corporación de Exportadores de El Salvador (COEXPORT): Condomínios del Mediterráneo, Edif. 'A', No 23, Col. Jardines de Guadalupe, San Salvador; tel. 243-1328; fax 243-3159; e-mail info@coexport.com; internet www.coexport.com; f. 1973 to promote Salvadorean exports; Exec. Dir Lic. Silvia M. Cuéllar.

Corporación Salvadoreña de Inversiones (CORSAIN): 1a Calle Poniente, entre 43 y 45 Avda Norte, San Salvador; tel. 224-4242; fax 224-6877; Pres. Lic. Mario Emilio Redaelli.

Fondo de Financiamiento y Garantía para la Pequeña Empresa (FIGAPE): 9a Avda Norte 225, Apdo 1990, San Salvador; tel. 771-1994; f. 1994; government body to assist small-sized industries; Pres. Lic. Marco Tulio Guardado.

Fondo Social para la Vivienda (FSV): Calle Rubén Darío y 17 Avda Sur 455, San Salvador; tel. 271-1662; fax 271-2910; internet www.fsv.gob.sv; f. 1973; Pres. Edgar Ramiro Mendoza Jerez; Gen. Man. Francisco Antonio Guevara.

Instituto Salvadoreño de Transformación Agraria (ISTA): Km 5½, Carretera a Santa Tecla, San Salvador; tel. 224-6000; fax 224-0259; f. 1976 to promote rural development; empowered to buy inefficiently cultivated land; Pres. José Roberto Molina Morales.

Instituto de Vivienda Urbana (IVU): San Salvador; f. 1950; government housing agency, transferred to private ownership in 1991; Pres. Lic. Pedro Alberto Hernández P.

CHAMBER OF COMMERCE

Cámara de Comercio e Industria de El Salvador: 9a Avda Norte y 5a Calle Poniente, Apdo 1640, San Salvador; tel. 771-2055; fax 771-4461; internet www.camarasal.com; f. 1915; 1,800 mems; Pres. Ricardo Simán; Exec. Dir Ing. Francisco Castro Funes; Gen. Man. Albero Padilla; branch offices in San Miguel, Santa Ana and Sonsonate.

INDUSTRIAL AND TRADE ASSOCIATIONS

Asociación Cafetalera de El Salvador (ACES): 67 Avda Norte 116, Col. Escalón, San Salvador; tel. 223-3024; fax 223-7471; f. 1930; coffee growers' asscn; Pres. Ing. EDUARDO E. BARRIENTOS.

Asociación de Ganaderos de El Salvador: 1a Avda Norte 1332, San Salvador; tel. 225-7208; f. 1932; livestock breeders' asscn; Pres. Lic. CARLOS ARTURO MUYSHONDT.

Asociación Salvadoreña de Beneficiadores y Exportadores de Café (ABECAFE): 87a Avda Norte 720, Col. Escalón, Apdo A, San Salvador; tel. 223-3292; fax 223-3292; coffee producers' and exporters' asscn; Pres. VICTORIA DALTÓN DE DÍAZ.

Asociación Salvadoreña de Industriales: Calles Roma y Liverpool, Col. Roma, Apdo 48, San Salvador; tel. 279-2488; fax 279-2070; e-mail asi@asi.com.sv; internet www.asi.com.sv; f. 1958; 400 mems; manufacturers' asscn; Pres. LEONEL MEJÍA; Exec. Dir Lic. JORGE ARRIAZA.

Cooperativa Algodonera Salvadoreña, Ltda: San Salvador; f. 1940; 185 mems; cotton growers' asscn; Pres. ULISES FERNANDO GONZÁLEZ; Gen. Man. Lic. MANUEL RAFAEL ARCE.

Instituto Nacional del Azúcar: Paseo General Escalón y 87a Avda Norte, San Salvador; tel. 224-6044; fax 224-5132; national sugar institute, scheduled for privatization; Pres. Lic. JAIME ÁLVAREZ GOTÁN.

Instituto Nacional del Café (INCAFE): San Salvador; f. 1942; national coffee institute, scheduled for privatization; Pres. ROBERT SUÁREZ SUAY; Gen. Man. MIGUEL ANGEL AGUILAR.

UCAFES: San Salvador; union of coffee-growing co-operatives; Pres. FRANCISCO ALFARO CASTILLO.

EMPLOYERS' ORGANIZATIONS

There are several business associations, the most important of which is the **Asociación Nacional de Empresa Privada (ANEP—National Private Enterprise Association):** 1a Calle Pte. y 71a Avda Norte 204, Col. Escalón, Apdo1204, San Salvador; tel. 224-1236; fax 223-8932; e-mail anep@telesal.net; internet www.anep .org.sv; national private enterprise association; Pres. RICARDO FÉLIX SIMÁN; Exec. Dir Lic. LUIS MARIO RODRÍGUEZ .

UTILITIES

Electricity

Comisión Ejecutiva Hidroeléctrica del Río Lempa (CEL): 9a Calle Poniente 950, San Salvador; tel. 271-0855; fax 228-1911; state energy agency dealing with electricity generation and transmission, and non-conventional energy sources; scheduled for privatization; Pres. GUILLERMO A. SOL BANG.

Superintendencia General de Electricidad y Telecomunicaciones (SIGET): Sexta Décima Calle Poniente y 37 Avda Sur 2001, Col. Flor Blanca; tel. 257-4438; internet www.siget.gob.sv/ index.htm; f. 1996; Supt Lic. ERNESTO LIMA MENA.

Water

Administración Nacional de Acueductos y Alcantarillados (ANDA): Edif. ANDA, Final Avda Don Bosco, Col Libertad, San Salvador; tel. 225-3534; fax 225-3152; f. 1961; maintenance of water supply and sewerage systems; Pres. CARLOS AUGUSTO PERLA.

TRADE UNIONS

Asociación de Sindicatos Independientes—ASIES (Association of Independent Trade Unions): San Salvador.

Central de Trabajadores Democráticos—CTD (Democratic Workers' Confederation): San Salvador; Pres. SALVADOR CARAZO.

Central de Trabajadores Salvadoreños—CTS (Salvadorean Workers' Confederation): Calle Darío González 616, Barrio San Jacinto, San Salvador; f. 1966; Christian Democratic; 35,000 mems; Sec.-Gen. MIGUEL ANGEL VÁSQUEZ.

Confederación General de Sindicatos—CGS (General Confederation of Unions): 3a Calle Oriente 226, San Salvador; f. 1958; admitted to ICFTU/ORIT; 27,000 mems.

Confederación General del Trabajo—CGT (General Confederation of Workers): 2a Avda Norte 619, San Salvador; tel. 222-5980; f. 1983; 20 affiliated unions; Sec.-Gen. JOSÉ LUIS GRANDE PREZA; 85,000 mems.

Coordinadora de Solidaridad de los Trabajadores—CST (Workers' Solidarity Co-ordination): San Salvador; f. 1985; conglomerate of independent left-wing trade unions.

Federación Campesina Cristiana de El Salvador-Unión de Trabajadores del Campo—FECCAS-UTC (Christian Peasant Federation of El Salvador—Union of Countryside Workers): Universidad Nacional, Apdo 4000, San Salvador; allied illegal Christian peasants' organizations.

Federación Nacional de Sindicatos de Trabajadores de El Salvador (FENASTRAS) (Salvadorean Workers' National Union Federation): San Salvador; f. 1975; left-wing; 35,000 mems in 16 affiliates.

Federación Revolucionaria de Sindicatos (Revolutionary Federation of Unions): San Salvador; Sec.-Gen. SALVADOR CHÁVEZ ESCAL-ANTE.

Federación Unitaria Sindical Salvadoreña—FUSS (United Salvadorean Union Federation): Centro de Gobierno, Apdo 2226, San Salvador; tel. and fax 225-3756; f. 1965; left-wing; Sec.-Gen. JUAN EDITO GENOVEZ.

MUSYGES (United Union and Guild Movement): San Salvador; labour federation previously linked to FDR; 50,000 mems (est.).

Unión Comunal Salvadoreña—UCS (Salvadorean Communal Union): San Salvador; peasants' association; 100,000 mems; Gen. Sec. GUILLERMO BLANCO.

Unidad Nacional de Trabajadores Salvadoreños—UNTS (National Unity of Salvadorean Workers): San Salvador; f. 1986; largest trade union conglomerate; Leader MARCO TULIO LIMA; affiliated unions include:

> **Unidad Popular Democrática—UPD** (Popular Democratic Unity): San Salvador; f. 1980; led by a committee of 10; 500,000 mems.

Unión Nacional Obrera-Campesina—UNOC (Worker-Peasant National Union): San Salvador; f. 1986; centre-left labour organization; 500,000 mems.

Some unions, such as those of the taxi drivers and bus owners, are affiliated to the Federación Nacional de Empresas Pequeñas Salvadoreñas—Fenapes, the association of small businesses.

Transport

Comisión Ejecutiva Portuaria Autónoma (CEPA): Edif. Torre Roble, Blvd de Los Héroes, Apdo 2667, San Salvador; tel. 224-1133; fax 224-0907; f. 1952; operates and administers the ports of Acajutla (on Pacific coast) and Cutuco (on Gulf of Fonseca) and the El Salvador International Airport, as well as Ferrocarriles Nacionales de El Salvador; Pres. RUY CÉSAR MIRANDA; Gen. Man. Lic. ARTURO GERMÁN MARTÍNEZ.

RAILWAYS

In 1998 there were 547 km of railway track in the country. The main track links San Salvador with the ports of Acajutla and Cutuco and with San Jerónimo on the border with Guatemala. The 429 km Salvadorean section of the International Railways of Central America runs from Anguiatú on the El Salvador–Guatemala border to the Pacific ports of Acajutla and Cutuco and connect San Salvador with Guatemala City and the Guatemalan Atlantic ports of Puerto Barrios and Santo Tomás de Castilla.

A project to connect the Salvadorean and Guatemalan railway systems between Santa Ana and Santa Lucia (in Guatemala) is under consideration.

Ferrocarriles Nacionales de El Salvador (FENADESAL): Avda Peralta 903, Apdo 2292, San Salvador; tel. 271-5632; fax 271-5650; 562 km open; in 1975 Ferrocarril de El Salvador and the Salvadorean section of International Railways of Central America (429 km open) were merged and are administered by the Railroad Division of CEPA (see above); Gen. Man. TULIO O. VERGARA.

ROADS

The country's highway system is well integrated with its railway services. There were some 9,977 km of roads in 1996, including: the Pan-American Highway: 306 km; paved highways: 1,985 km. A coastal highway, with interconnecting roads, was under construction in the early 1990s. Following the earthquakes of early 2001, the Inter-American Development Bank (IDB) pledged some US $106.0m. to the transport sector for the restoration and reconstruction of roads and bridges.

SHIPPING

The port of Acajutla is administered by CEPA (see above). Services are also provided by foreign lines. The port of Cutuco has been inactive since 1996; however, in 2000 it was being considered for privatization.

CIVIL AVIATION

The El Salvador International Airport is located 40 km (25 miles) from San Salvador in Comalapa. An expansion of the airport was completed in 1998, with a second expansion phase of hotel and commercial space to be completed early in the 21st century. The former international airport at Ilopango is used for military and private civilian aircraft; there are an additional 88 private airports, four with permanent-surface runways.

AESA Aerolíneas de El Salvador, SA de CV: San Salvador; cargo and mail service between San Salvador and Miami; Pres. E. CORNEJO LÓPEZ; Gen. Man. JOSÉ ROBERTO SANTANA.

TACA International Airlines: Edif. Caribe, 2°, Col. Escalón, San Salvador; tel. 339-9155; fax 223-3757; f. 1939; passenger and cargo services to Central America and the USA; Pres. FEDERICO BLOCH; Gen. Man. BEN BALDANZA.

Tourism

El Salvador was one of the centres of the ancient Mayan civilization, and the ruined temples and cities are of great interest. The volcanoes and lakes of the uplands provide magnificent scenery, while there are fine beaches along the Pacific coast. The civil war, from 1979 to 1992, severely affected the tourism industry. However, in the late 1990s the number of tourist arrivals increased from 282,835 in 1996 to 541,863 in 1998. Tourism receipts in 1998 were US \$125m. Following the earthquakes of early 2001, the Inter-American Development Bank (IDB) pledged some US \$3.6m. to the tourism and historical and cultural heritage sectors, for the reconstruction and renovation of recreational centres, the promotion of tourism, and the development of culture and heritage.

Buró de Convenciones y Visitantes de la Ciudad de San Salvador: Edif. Olimpic Plaza, 73 Avda Sur 28, 2°, San Salvador; tel. 224-0819; fax 223-4912; f. 1973; assists in organization of national and international events; Pres. (vacant); Exec. Dir ROSY MEJÍA DE MARCHESINI.

Cámara Salvadoreña de Turismo: San Salvador; tel. 223-9992; Pres. ARNOLDO JIMÉNEZ; co-ordinates:

    Comité Nacional de Turismo (CONATUR): San Salvador; comprises hotels, restaurants, tour operators, airlines and Instituto Salvadoreño de Turismo; Sec. MERCEDES MELÉNDEZ.

    Corporación de Turismo (CORSATUR): 508 Blvd del Hipódromo, Col. San Benito, San Salvador; tel. 243-7835: fax 243-0427: internet www.elsalvadorturismo.gob.sv.

    Feria Internacional de El Salvador (FIES): Avda La Revolución 222, Col. San Benito, Apdo 493, San Salvador; tel. 243-0244; fax 243-3161; e-mail fies@es.com.sv; internet www.fies.gob.sv; Pres. JOSÉ CARLOS LIÉVANO.

Instituto Salvadoreño de Turismo (ISTU) (National Tourism Institute): Calle Rubén Darío 619, San Salvador; tel. 222-0960; fax 222-1208; f. 1950; Pres. CARLOS HIRLEMANN; Dir EDUARDO LÓPEZ RIVERA.

EQUATORIAL GUINEA

Introductory Survey

Location, Climate, Language, Religion, Flag, Capital

The Republic of Equatorial Guinea consists of the islands of Bioko (formerly Fernando Póo and subsequently renamed Macías Nguema Biyogo under the regime of President Macías), Corisco, Great Elobey, Little Elobey and Annobón (previously known also as Pagalu), and the mainland region of Río Muni (previously known also as Mbini) on the west coast of Africa. Cameroon lies to the north and Gabon to the east and south of Río Muni, while Bioko lies off shore from Cameroon and Nigeria. The small island of Annobón lies far to the south, beyond the islands of São Tomé and Príncipe. The climate is hot and humid, with average temperatures higher than 26°C (80°F). The official languages are Spanish and French. In Río Muni the Fang language is spoken, as well as those of coastal tribes such as the Combe, Balemke and Bujeba. Bubi is the indigenous language on Bioko, although Fang is also widely used, and Ibo is spoken by the resident Nigerian population. An estimated 90% of the population are adherents of the Roman Catholic Church, although traditional forms of worship are also followed. The national flag (proportions 3 by 2) has three equal horizontal stripes, of green, white and red, with a blue triangle at the hoist and the national coat of arms (a silver shield, containing a tree, with six yellow stars above and a scroll beneath) in the centre of the white stripe. The capital is Malabo (formerly Santa Isabel).

Recent History

Portugal ceded the territory to Spain in 1778. The mainland region and the islands were periodically united for administrative purposes. In July 1959 Spanish Guinea, as the combined territory was known, was divided into two provinces: Río Muni, on the African mainland, and Fernando Póo (now Bioko), with other nearby islands. From 1960 the two provinces were represented in the Spanish legislature. In December 1963 they were merged again, to form Equatorial Guinea, with a limited measure of self-government.

After 190 years of Spanish rule, independence was declared on 12 October 1968. Francisco Macías Nguema, Equatorial Guinea's first President, formed a coalition Government from all the parties represented in the new National Assembly. In March 1969 the Minister for Foreign Affairs, Atanasio Ndongo Miyone, was killed by security forces during a failed coup attempt.

In February 1970 the President outlawed all existing political parties and formed the Partido Unico Nacional (PUN), which later became the Partido Unico Nacional de los Trabajadores (PUNT). Macías appointed himself Life President in July 1972. A new Constitution, giving absolute powers to the President was adopted in July 1973. Macías controlled both radio and press and all citizens were forbidden to leave the country, although many fled during his rule. During 1975–77 there were many arrests and executions. Nigerian workers were repatriated in 1976, following reports of maltreatment and forced labour. The Macías regime maintained close relations with the Soviet bloc.

In August 1979 President Macías was overthrown in a coup led by his nephew, Lt-Col (later Brig.-Gen.) Teodoro Obiang Nguema Mbasogo, hitherto the Deputy Minister of Defence. (Obiang Nguema subsequently ceased to use his forename.) Macías was found guilty of treason, genocide, embezzlement and violation of human rights, and was executed in September. The Spanish Government, which admitted prior knowledge of the coup, was the first to recognize the new regime, and remained a major supplier of financial and technical aid. Obiang Nguema appointed civilians to the Government for the first time in December 1981. In August 1982 he was reappointed President for a further seven years, and later that month a new Constitution, which provided for an eventual return to civilian government, was approved by 95% of voters in a referendum. At legislative elections held in August 1983 some 41 candidates, who had been nominated by the President, were elected (unopposed) to a new House of Representatives.

The imposition, from 1979 to 1991, of a ban on organized political activity within Equatorial Guinea, and persistent allegations against the Obiang Nguema regime of human rights abuses and corruption, resulted in the development of a substantial opposition in exile. Opposition coalitions were formed in Spain and France during the 1980s. In 1991 the Coordinación Democrática de los Partidos de Oposición de Guinea Ecuatorial was established in Libreville, Gabon, and in 1999 unregistered opposition parties exiled in Spain formed the Coordinadora de la Oposición Conjunta (see below).

During the 1980s Obiang Nguema's rule was threatened on a number of occasions. Attempted coups were reported in April 1981, May 1983 and November 1983. In January 1986 the President reinforced his control by assuming the post of Minister of Defence. An attempt in July by senior civilian and military officials to occupy the presidential palace in Malabo was quelled by loyalist forces. In the following month the alleged leader of the coup attempt, Eugenio Abeso Mondu (a former diplomat and a member of the House of Representatives), was sentenced to death and executed, while prison sentences were imposed on 12 others who had been convicted of complicity in the plot. In August 1987 Obiang Nguema announced the establishment of a 'governmental party', the Partido Democrático de Guinea Ecuatorial (PDGE), while continuing to reject demands for the legalization of opposition parties. At legislative elections held in July 1988, 99.2% of voters endorsed a single list of candidates who had been nominated by the President. In September severe sentences of imprisonment were imposed on nine civilians and military officers who had been convicted of plotting to overthrow Obiang Nguema; these included the Secretary-General of the Partido del Progreso de Guinea Ecuatorial, José Luis Jones. Jones was, however, released in January 1989, prior to an official visit to Spain by Obiang Nguema.

In June 1989, at the first presidential election to be held since independence, Obiang Nguema, the sole candidate, reportedly received the support of more than 99% of the electorate. Opposition groupings criticized the conduct of the election and declared the result invalid. Following his success, the President appealed to dissidents to return to Equatorial Guinea and declared an amnesty for political prisoners. However, Obiang Nguema reiterated his opposition to the establishment of a multi-party system, and in December 1990 it was reported that about 30 advocates of the introduction of a plural political system had been imprisoned. The human rights organization, Amnesty International, has frequently reiterated accusations against the Equato-Guinean authorities of detaining and torturing political opponents.

In April 1991 opposition groups in exile in Gabon formed a coalition, the Coordinación Democrática de los Partidos de Oposición de Guinea Ecuatorial. In early August the ruling PDGE held its first national extraordinary congress, at which delegates demanded the introduction of a new democratic constitution, the legalization of other political parties and the removal of restrictions on the media. Nevertheless, in mid-August a prominent opposition leader in exile was refused a passport to travel to Equatorial Guinea in order to campaign for democracy, and shortly afterwards it was reported that the Equato-Guinean Ambassador to Spain had been arrested during a return visit to Equatorial Guinea, for allegedly liaising with opposition movements. In the following month Amnesty International claimed that torture was 'accepted practice' in Equatorial Guinea, and reported the deaths in custody of at least six Equato-Guineans since 1988. Later in September the Government announced the formation of a human rights commission.

A new Constitution, containing provisions for a multi-party political system, was approved by an overwhelming majority of voters at a national referendum in November 1991. However, opposition movements rejected the Constitution, owing to the inclusion of clauses exempting the President from any judicial procedures arising from his tenure of office and prohibiting citizens who had not been continuously resident in Equatorial Guinea for 10 years from standing as election candidates, while requiring all political parties to submit an excessively large deposit (which could not be provided by funds from abroad) as a condition of registration. In addition, there was inadequate provision for the upholding of human rights. In January 1992 a transitional Government was formed (comprising only members of the PDGE), and, during that month, a general amnesty was extended to all political exiles. The UN published a report in January that adversely criticized the human rights record of the Equato-Guinean authorities and some of the provisions incorporated in the new Constitution. Throughout 1992 the security forces continued to arrest members of opposition parties. During November a new alliance of opposition organizations, the Plataforma de la Oposición Conjunta (POC), was created.

In January 1993 an electoral law was promulgated. In February the UN released another report in which it alleged a serious disregard for human rights by the Obiang Nguema regime. During February and March the Government and several opposition organizations negotiated a national pact which established conditions for the conduct of legislative elections that were due to take place in 1993, including the freedom to organize political activity and the provision of equal access to the media for all political parties. However, the Government was soon accused of violating the pact, and further arrests and mistreatment of its political opponents were reported. During August violent clashes occurred on the island of Annobón between anti-Government demonstrators and the security forces. Accusations by the Equato-Guinean authorities that Spain had incited the unrest were strongly denied by the Spanish Government.

Multi-party legislative elections took place in November 1993. The elections were, however, boycotted by most of the parties in the POC, in protest at Obiang Nguema's refusal to review contentious clauses of the electoral law or to permit impartial international observers to inspect the electoral register. The UN declined a request by the Equato-Guinean authorities to monitor the elections, contending that correct electoral procedures were evidently being infringed. Representatives of the OAU were present and estimated that 50% of the electorate participated. The PDGE won 68 of the 80 seats in the House of Representatives, while, of the six opposition parties that presented candidates, the Convención Socialdemocrática Popular obtained six seats, the Unión Democrática y Social de Guinea Ecuatorial won five seats and the Convención Liberal Democrática secured one. Widespread electoral irregularities were alleged to have occurred and, prior to the elections, opposition politicians were reportedly subjected to intimidation by the security forces. In early December the Government announced that all party political gatherings would henceforth be subject to prior official authorization. In mid-December Silvestre Siale Bileka, hitherto Prime Minister of the interim Government, was appointed Prime Minister of the new administration. Shortly afterwards Bileka nominated a Council of Ministers, which included no opposition representatives.

In April 1994 Severo Moto Nsa, the founding leader of one of the most influential exiled opposition parties, the Partido del Progreso de Guinea Equatorial (PPGE), based in Spain, returned to Equatorial Guinea. In June, in response to pressure from international aid donors, the Government agreed to amend the controversial electoral law and to conduct a preliminary electoral census prior to the holding of local elections. In September, however, the authorities began to compile a full population census, instead of preparing for the local elections, which had been scheduled for November. The census was boycotted by opposition parties, and many people were arrested in ensuing clashes with the security forces. The local elections were postponed. In October the Speaker and Deputy Speaker of the National Assembly resigned, accusing the Obiang Nguema administration of incompetence and disregard for human rights. In November Moto Nsa alleged that the Government had sanctioned the assassination of Vicente Moto, who was his brother and a senior figure in the POC.

In early 1995 the Constitution and electoral law were amended to reduce from 10 to five the minimum number of years required for candidates to have been resident in Equatorial Guinea. In February several leading members of the PPGE, including Moto Nsa, were arrested for allegedly plotting to overthrow Obiang Nguema; in April they were found guilty by a military court and sentenced to terms of imprisonment. (Moto Nsa received a sentence of 28 years.) The convictions and sentences were widely condemned by foreign Governments and in August, following representations by President Chirac of France, Obiang Nguema unexpectedly pardoned all the convicted PPGE members.

Local elections (which had been postponed in 1994—see above) were staged, on a multi-party basis, in September 1995. According to the official results, the ruling PDGE won an overall victory, securing a majority of the votes cast in two-thirds of local administrations. Allegations by the opposition (which claimed to have obtained 62% of the votes) that serious electoral malpractice had occurred were supported by the Spanish Ambassador to Equatorial Guinea. A monitoring team of international observers agreed that some electoral irregularities had taken place.

At a presidential election held in February 1996 Obiang Nguema was returned to office, reportedly securing more than 90% of the votes cast. However, influential opposition leaders boycotted the contest, in protest at alleged electoral irregularities and official intimidation. In late March Obiang Nguema appointed a new Prime Minister, Angel Serafin Seriche Dougan (hitherto a Deputy Minister); an enlarged Council of Ministers was announced in early April. Representatives of opposition parties had declined a presidential invitation to participate in the new administration. During March the POC was dissolved.

In August 1996 Obiang Nguema awarded himself the military rank of General. In November a military court found 11 army officers guilty of conspiring to overthrow the Government; all were sentenced to terms of imprisonment.

In April 1997 representatives of the Government and of 13 opposition parties concluded a new national pact. During the following month Moto Nsa was arrested by the Angolan authorities with a consignment of arms, which were reportedly intended for use in a planned coup in Equatorial Guinea. Following his release in June, Moto Nsa was granted refuge in Spain. Meanwhile, the PPGE was banned; the party subsequently divided into two factions, of which one was led by Moto Nsa. In August Moto Nsa and 11 others were convicted *in absentia* of treason; Moto Nsa was sentenced to 101 years' imprisonment. In September the Government protested strongly to Spain over its offer of political asylum to Moto Nsa. Shortly afterwards French was declared the second official national language. In January 1998 the Government resigned. Shortly afterwards Seriche Dougan was re-appointed as Prime Minister, and a new, enlarged Council of Ministers was formed. In the following month a new electoral law was approved by the House of Representatives; this banned political coalitions, and was expected to disadvantage the opposition at the next legislative elections.

In late January 1998 armed protesters launched three successive attacks against military targets on Bioko, killing four soldiers and three civilians. The terrorist action was alleged to have been perpetrated by members of the secessionist Movimiento para la Autodeterminación de la Isla de Bioko (MAIB), which was founded in 1993 by ethnic Bubis (the original inhabitants of the island, who, following independence, had become outnumbered by the mainland Fang). Subsequently hundreds of Bubis and resident Nigerians were arrested; many were reportedly also severely tortured. In late May 1998 some 116 detainees were tried by a military court in connection with the January attacks, on charges including terrorism and treason. Fifteen of the defendants were found guilty of the most serious charges and sentenced to death; in response to international pressure, however, the death sentences were commuted to sentences of life imprisonment in September. In July Martin Puye, a prominent MAIB leader who had been sentenced to 27 years in prison following the May trial, died in detention, arousing widespread international condemnation of the conditions of imprisonment in Equatorial Guinea.

During early 1999 six unregistered opposition parties exiled in Spain, including the MAIB and Moto Nsa's faction of the PPGE, formed a new alliance, the Coordinadora de la Oposición Conjunta. Equatorial Guinea's second multi-party legislative elections took place in early March amid allegations of electoral malpractice and of the systematic intimidation of opposition candidates by the security forces. The elections were contested by 13 parties (excluding the divided PPGE, which had been banned in 1997—see above), and some 99% of the electorate was estimated to have voted. According to the official results, the ruling PDGE obtained more than 90% of the votes, increasing its representation from 68 to 75 of the 80 seats in the House of Representatives. Two opposition parties, the Unión Popular (UP) and the Convergencia para la Democracia Social (CPDS), secured four seats and one seat respectively. Both parties, however, refused to participate in the new administration, in protest at alleged violations of the electoral law. (This policy subsequently led to an internal crisis within the UP and a change of leadership was instigated in August 2000.) The UP, the CPDS and five other opposition organizations campaigned, without success, to have the election results annulled. Following the election, Seriche Dougan was reappointed to the premiership, and in late July a new Council of Ministers was announced. It was reported during late 1999 that Obiang Nguema was seriously ill.

The new administration dismissed hundreds of civil servants, including a number of high-ranking officials, during its first three months in office, as part of efforts to eradicate corruption. Furthermore, in January 2000 a number of judicial officials, including the President of the Supreme Court and the President of the Constitutional Court, were dismissed. Former Prime Minister, Silvestre Siale Bileka, was appointed to the presidency of the Supreme Court. Nevertheless, in March 2000, the new Special Representative for Equatorial Guinea at the UN Human Rights Commission condemned the Equatorial Guinean authorities for systematic and serious human rights violations. The Special Representative further stated that, despite some minor advances, real democracy did not exist in the country and accused the Government of refusing to authorize the formation of human rights non-governmental organizations.

Municipal elections were held on 28 May, but were boycotted by the CPDS, the UP and the Alianza Democrática Progresista (ADP). Consequently, the PDGE obtained 95.7% of the votes cast and secured control of all 30 municipal councils. The opposition dismissed the elections as invalid. In October Obiang Nguema reportedly urged Seriche Dougan to resign after the House of Representatives severely criticized the Prime Minister for failing to address adequately the problem of corruption in government. In November six opposition parties, including the CPDS, the UP and the ADP, formed the Frente de la Oposición Democrática in order to create a common front to promote democracy.

In late February 2001 Seriche Dougan announced the resignation of his Government, in response to further pressure from the President and the legislature. Cándido Muatetema Rivas, formerly Deputy Secretary-General of the PDGE, was subsequently appointed as Prime Minister and formed a new Council of Ministers. Five members of the opposition were appointed to the new Government, including Jeremias Ondo Ngomo, the President of the UP, as Minister-delegate for Communications and Transport.

Equatorial Guinea enjoyed exceptionally high revenues from petroleum exports during the late 1990s; allegations emerged, however, that members of the Obiang Nguema regime were accruing private profits from national petroleum exports.

While Spain (the former colonial power) has traditionally been a major trading partner and aid donor, Equatorial Guinea's entry in 1983 into the Customs and Economic Union of Central Africa (replaced in 1999 by the Communauté économique et monétaire de l'Afrique centrale—see p. 211) represented a significant move towards a greater integration with neighbouring francophone countries. In 1985 Equatorial Guinea joined the Franc Zone (see p. 210), with financial assistance from France. Obiang Nguema has regularly attended Franco-African summit meetings. In late 1988 Obiang Nguema postponed a visit to Spain, following allegations, in the Spanish legislature, of the misappropriation of Spanish development aid to the former colony; the visit was, however, eventually undertaken in January 1989, when the continuation of bilateral links between the two countries was confirmed and the Spanish Government agreed to cancel one-third of Equatorial Guinea's public debt to Spain. In 1991 Spain cancelled a further one-third of the bilateral debt, and in November of that year the Prime Minister of Spain made an official visit to Equatorial Guinea. From mid-1993, however, Equato-Guinean-Spanish relations deteriorated, and in January 1994 the Spanish Government withdrew one-half of its aid to Equatorial Guinea in retaliation for the expulsion in December 1993 of a Spanish diplomat whom the Equato-Guinean authorities had accused of interfering in the country's internal affairs. In November 1994 the Equato-Guinean Government accused Spain of sponsoring the passage of a resolution adopted by the European Parliament condemning violations of human rights in Equatorial Guinea. In September 1997 the Obiang Nguema administration protested strongly to the Spanish Government over Spain's offer of political asylum to the opposition leader Severo Moto Nsa (see above). On several occasions in 1998 the Equato-Guinean Government accused Spain of attempting to destabilize Equatorial Guinea by prov-

iding funds to opposition organizations. In October 1999 the Spanish Government agreed to resume full assistance to its former colony. However, in the same month the medical aid agency, Médecins sans frontières, withdrew its mission from Equatorial Guinea in protest against the alleged manipulation of humanitarian aid by the Government. During the 1990s the European Union withdrew financial aid to Equatorial Guinea, and the United Nations Development Programme suspended some projects.

Despite Equatorial Guinea's close military links with Nigeria, relations between the two countries became strained in 1988, when evidence emerged that Equatorial Guinea, keen to attract foreign investment, had formed links with South Africa. However, reciprocal official visits in 1990 by the Equato-Guinean and Nigerian Heads of State heralded an improvement in relations between the two countries. In November 1999 Equatorial Guinea, Angola, Cameroon, the Republic of the Congo, Gabon, Nigeria and São Tomé and Príncipe established an international committee to demarcate maritime borders in the Gulf of Guinea. The development of petroleum reserves in the region during the 1990s had revived long-standing frontier disputes. In September 2000 Equatorial Guinea and Nigeria formally resolved their maritime border dispute, reaching an agreement on the demarcation of the border, which was expected to encourage further petroleum exploration and development in that area. In February 2001 Equatorial Guinea and Libya resolved to strengthen bilateral relations and agreed to establish embassies in their respective capitals.

Government

In November 1991 a new Constitution was approved in a referendum, providing for the introduction of multi-party democracy. Executive power is vested in the President, whose seven-year term of office is renewable indefinitely. The President is immune from prosecution for offences committed before, during or after his tenure of the post. Legislative power is held by an 80-member House of Representatives, which serves for a term of five years. Both the President and the House of Representatives are directly elected by universal adult suffrage. The President appoints a Council of Ministers, headed by a Prime Minister, from among the members of the House of Representatives.

Defence

In August 2000 there were 1,100 men in the army, 120 in the navy and 100 in the air force. There was also a paramilitary force, trained by French military personnel. Military service is voluntary. The estimated defence budget for 2000 was 8,000m. francs CFA. Spain has provided military advisers and training since 1979, and military aid has also been received from the USA.

Economic Affairs

In 1998, according to estimates by the World Bank, Equatorial Guinea's gross national product (GNP), measured at average 1996–98 prices, was US $478m., equivalent to $1,110 per head. During 1990–98, it was estimated, GNP per head increased, in real terms, at an average annual rate of 13.1%. Over the same period, the population increased by an average of 2.9% per year. GNP totalled an estimated $516m. in 1999, equivalent to $1,170 per head. Equatorial Guinea's gross domestic product (GDP) increased, in real terms, by an average of 22.9% annually during 1992–98. Real GDP grew by 29.1% in 1996, by 71.2% in 1997 and by an estimated 22.0% in 1998.

Agriculture (including hunting, forestry and fishing) contributed an estimated 21.8% of GDP in 1998 (compared with 51.6% of GDP in 1995). The sector employed an estimated 71.2% of the labour force in 1999. The principal cash crop is cocoa, which contributed an estimated 1.5% of export earnings in 1998. Coffee is also a traditional export. The Government is encouraging the production of bananas, spices (vanilla, black pepper and coriander) and medicinal plants for export. The main subsistence crops are cassava and sweet potatoes. Exploitation of the country's vast forest resources (principally of okoumé and akoga timber) provided an estimated 9.2% of export revenue in 1998. Almost all industrial fishing activity is practised by foreign fleets, notably by those of countries of the EU.

Industry (including mining, manufacturing, construction and power) contributed an estimated 66.4% of GDP in 1998 (compared with 27.3% of GDP in 1995).

Extractive activities were minimal during the 1980s, and the mining sector employed less than 0.2% of the working population in 1983. However, the development of onshore and offshore reserves of petroleum and of offshore deposits of natural gas led to unprecedented economic growth during the 1990s. Exports of petroleum commenced in 1992 and provided an estimated 87% of total export earnings by 1998. In that year exports of natural gas (which commenced in 1997) accounted for an estimated 1.6% of export earnings. The petroleum sector contributed an estimated 61.8% of GDP in 1998 (compared with 18.2% of GDP in 1995). The existence of deposits of gold, uranium, iron ore, tantalum and manganese has also been confirmed.

The manufacturing sector contributed only an estimated 0.4% of GDP in 1998. Wood-processing constitutes the main commercial manufacturing activity.

A total of 20m. kWh of electric energy was generated in 1995. Bioko is supplied by a 3.6-MW hydroelectric installation, constructed on the Riaba river. There is a further 3.6-MW installation on the mainland. Imports of fuel products comprised 7.7% of the value of total imports in 1990.

The services sector contributed an estimated 11.8% of GDP in 1998. The dominant services are trade, restaurants and hotels, and government services.

In 1996 there was a visible trade deficit of US $116.73m., while the deficit on the current account of the balance of payments was $344.04m. In 1998 the USA was both the principal source of imports (35.4%) and the main market for exports (62.0%). Other major trading partners were Spain, France, Cameroon and the People's Republic of China. In 1998 crude petroleum (87%), wood and cocoa constituted the principal sources of export revenue, while in 1990 the principal imports were ships and boats, petroleum and related products and food and live animals.

In 1998 the budgetary deficit was estimated at 3,754m. francs CFA. Equatorial Guinea's external debt was US $306.1m. at the end of 1998, of which $216.5m. was long-term public debt. In that year the cost of debt-servicing was equivalent to 1.4% of the value of exports of goods and services. The rate of inflation averaged 7.5% per year in 1990–98. Following the devaluation of the currency (see below), consumer prices rose by an estimated annual average of 38.9% in 1994; in 1998, however, prices increased by an estimated annual average of 7.8%. The annual average rate of inflation was only 0.6% in 1999 and 4.5% in 2000.

Equatorial Guinea is a member of the central African organs of the Franc Zone (see p. 210), including the Communauté économique et monétaire de l'Afrique centrale (CEMAC, see p. 211).

Equatorial Guinea suffered a severe economic decline under the Macías regime. The Obiang Nguema administration has achieved some success in rehabilitating and diversifying the primary sector, and exceptional economic growth was recorded from the late 1990s, stimulated by the commencement in 1992 of petroleum exports. GNP per head nearly trebled in 1996–98. The devaluation of the CFA franc by 50% against the French franc in January 1994 significantly enhanced export competitiveness, particularly in the timber sector. An immediate sharp rise in the prices of consumer goods, however, increased hardship for vulnerable sections of the population. An economic development programme for 1994–96, supported by the IMF, was largely unsuccessful in its aim to restructure the public and financial sectors. Revenue from the profitable petroleum and timber sectors has been undermined by the country's inefficient taxation system and by poor budgetary discipline. In addition, it has been widely alleged that members of the Equato-Guinean regime have profited personally from national petroleum exports. The IMF has urged the Equato-Guinean Government to improve its financial management and to invest petroleum revenues in initiatives to foster economic diversification, improve the inadequate transport infrastructure and develop social welfare and educational resources. Equatorial Guinea remains burdened by a large external debt. Spain and France have traditionally been important bilateral donors. However, economic relations with the USA have strengthened in recent years as a result of major investments in the development of Equato-Guinean oilfields by US energy companies and the approval by the US Overseas Private Investment Corporation, in June 2000, of financing, worth US $373m., for the construction and operation of a methanol plant on Bioko.

Social Welfare

Health services are extremely limited, and diseases such as malaria, infectious hepatitis, whooping cough and dysentery are endemic. In 1996, according to estimates by the World Health Organization, there were 24.6 physicians and 39.5 nurses for every 100,000 inhabitants.

Education

Education is officially compulsory and free for five years between the ages of six and 11 years. Primary education starts at six years of age and normally lasts for five years. Secondary education, beginning at the age of 12, spans a seven-year period, comprising a first cycle of four years and a second cycle of three years. In 1982 the total enrolment at primary and secondary schools was equivalent to 81% of the school-age population. In 1993/94 primary education was provided for 75,751 pupils in 781 schools with 1,381 teachers. More advanced education for 16,616 pupils was provided in that year, with 588 teachers. In 1990 there were 578 pupils in higher education. Since 1979, assistance in the development of the educational system has been provided by Spain. Two higher education centres, at Bata and Malabo, are administered by the Spanish Universidad Nacional de Educación a Distancia. The French Government also provides considerable financial assistance. In 1995, according to UNESCO estimates, the average rate of adult illiteracy was 22.2% (males 10.7%; females 32.8%). In 1993 budgetary expenditure on education by the central Government amounted to 734m. francs CFA (1.8% of total expenditure).

Public Holidays

2001: 1 January (New Year's Day), 5 March (Independence Day), 13–16 April (Easter), 1 May (Labour Day), 25 May (OAU Day), 10 December (Human Rights Day), 25 December (Christmas).

2002: 1 January (New Year's Day), 5 March (Independence Day), 29 March–1 April (Easter), 1 May (Labour Day), 25 May (OAU Day), 10 December (Human Rights Day), 25 December (Christmas).

Weights and Measures

The metric system is in force.

Statistical Survey

Source (unless otherwise stated): Dirección Técnica de Estadística, Secretaría de Estado para el
Plan de Desarrollo Económico, Malabo.

AREA AND POPULATION

Area: 28,051 sq km (10,831 sq miles): Río Muni 26,017 sq km, Bioko 2,017 sq km, Annobón 17 sq km.

Population: 246,941 (Río Muni 200,106, Bioko 44,820, Annobón 2,015) at December 1965 census; 300,000 (Río Muni 240,804, Bioko 57,190, Annobón 2,006), comprising 144,268 males and 155,732 females, at census of 4–17 July 1983. (Source: Ministerio de Asuntos Exteriores, Madrid); 442,000 (UN estimate) at mid-1999.

Provinces (population, census of July 1983): Kié-Ntem 70,202, Litoral 66,370, Centro-Sur 52,393, Wele-Nzas 51,839, Bioko Norte 46,221, Bioko Sur 10,969, Annobón 2,006.

Principal Towns (population at 1983 census): Malabo (capital) 15,253, Bata 24,100.

Births and Deaths (UN estimates, annual averages): Birth rate 43.5 per 1,000 in 1990–95; Death rate 18.0 per 1,000 in 1990–95. Source: UN, *World Population Prospects: The 1998 Revision.*

Expectation of Life (UN estimates, years at birth, 1990–95): 48.0 (males 46.4; females 49.6) (Source: UN, *Demographic Yearbook.*)

Economically Active Population (persons aged 6 years and over, 1983 census): Agriculture, hunting, forestry and fishing 59,390; Mining and quarrying 126; Manufacturing 1,490; Electricity, gas and water 224; Construction 1,929; Trade, restaurants and hotels 3,059; Transport, storage and communications 1,752; Financing, insurance, real estate and business services 409; Community, social and personal services 8,377; Activities not adequately defined 984; Total employed 77,740 (males 47,893, females 29,847); Unemployed 24,825 (males 18,040, females 6,785); Total labour force 102,565 (males 65,933, females 36,632). Note: Figures are based on unadjusted census data, indicating a total population of 261,779. The adjusted total is 300,000. Source: International Labour Office, *Yearbook of Labour Statistics.*

AGRICULTURE, ETC.

Principal Crops ('000 metric tons, 1999): Sweet potatoes 36; Cassava 42; Coconuts 6; Palm kernels 3; Bananas and plantains 20; Cocoa beans 6; Green coffee 4. Source: FAO.

Livestock (FAO estimates, '000 head, year ending September 1999): Cattle 5; Pigs 5; Sheep 36; Goats 8. Source: FAO.

Forestry (1998): Roundwood removals ('000 cu m): Fuel wood 447 (assumed to be unchanged since 1983); Sawlogs, veneer logs and logs for sleepers 364; Total 811. Source: FAO, *Yearbook of Forest Products.*

Fishing (metric tons, live weight, 1998): Freshwater fishes 970, Flatfishes 325, Gadiformes 603, Demersal percomorphs 225, Clupeoids 850, Tuna-like fishes 392, Chub mackerel 400, Sharks, rays, skates, etc. 779, Marine crustaceans 430; Total catch (incl. others) 6,005. Source: FAO, *Yearbook of Fishery Statistics.*

MINING

Crude Petroleum ('000 metric tons): 821.7 in 1996; 2,754.6 in 1997; 4,036.7 (provisional) in 1998. Source: IMF, *Equatorial Guinea: Recent Economic Developments* (October 1999).

INDUSTRY

Palm Oil ('000 metric tons): 4.4 in 1997 (FAO estimate); 4.3 in 1998 (FAO estimate); 4.5 in 1999. Source: FAO.

Veneer Sheets ('000 cubic metres): 9 in 1996; 9 in 1997; 9 in 1998. Source: FAO, *Yearbook of Forest Products.*

Electric Energy (million kWh): 19 in 1994; 20 in 1995; 20 in 1996. Source: UN, *Industrial Commodity Statistics Yearbook.*

FINANCE

Currency and Exchange Rates: 100 centimes = 1 franc de la Coopération financière en Afrique centrale (CFA). *Sterling, Dollar and Euro Equivalents* (29 December 2000): £1 sterling = 1,051.93 francs CFA; US $1 = 704.95 francs CFA; €1 = 655.96 francs CFA; 10,000 francs CFA = £9.506 = $14.185 = €15.245. *Average Exchange Rate* (francs CFA per US dollar): 589.95 in 1998; 615.70 in 1999; 711.98 in 2000. *Note:* An exchange rate of 1 French franc = 50 francs CFA, established in 1948, remained in force until January 1994, when the CFA franc was devalued by 50%, with the exchange rate adjusted to 1 French franc = 100 francs CFA. This relationship to French currency remained in effect with the introduction of the euro

on 1 January 1999. From that date, accordingly, a fixed exchange rate of €1 = 655.957 francs CFA has been in operation.

Budget (estimates, million francs CFA, 1998): *Revenue:* Petroleum sector 53,489; Taxation 14,608 (Taxes on income and profits 2,253; Taxes on domestic goods and services 6,501; Taxes on international trade 5,064; Other taxes 786); Other revenue 7,080; Total revenue 75,177, excl. grants from abroad (1,797). *Expenditure:* Current expenditure 33,788 (Wages and salaries 9,129; Other goods and services 12,917; Subsidies and transfers 7,284; Interest payments 4,458); Capital expenditure 29,410; Unclassified expenditure 17,530; Total expenditure 80,728. Source: IMF, *Equatorial Guinea: Recent Economic Developments* (October 1999).

International Reserves (US $ million at 31 December 1999): Foreign exchange 3.35. Source: IMF, *International Financial Statistics.*

Money Supply ('000 million francs CFA at 31 December 1999): Currency outside deposit money banks 12.06; Demand deposits at deposit money banks 16.39; Total money 28.45. Source: IMF, *International Financial Statistics.*

Cost of Living (Consumer price index; base: January 1990 = 100): 161.1 in 1996; 166.0 in 1997; 179.0 (estimate) in 1998. Source: IMF, *Equatorial Guinea: Recent Economic Developments* (October 1999).

Expenditure on the Gross Domestic Product ('000 million francs CFA at current prices, 1997): Government final consumption expenditure 32.0; Private final consumption expenditure 133.2; Gross capital formation 190.8; *Total domestic expenditure* 356.0; Exports of goods and services 292.9; *Less* Imports of goods and services 358.4; *GDP in purchasers' values* 290.5. Source: IMF, *Equatorial Guinea: Recent Economic Developments* (October 1999).

Gross Domestic Product by Economic Activity (million francs CFA at current prices, 1997): Agriculture, hunting, forestry and fishing 67,268; Petroleum sector 187,429; Manufacturing 962; Electricity, gas and water 3,121; Construction 5,768; Trade, restaurants and hotels 8,819; Transport and communications 1,920; Finance, insurance, real estate and business services 1,967; Government services 8,235; Other services 2,823; *Sub-total* 288,312; Import duties 2,205; *GDP in purchasers' values* 290,517. Source: IMF, *Equatorial Guinea: Recent Economic Developments* (October 1999).

Balance of Payments (US $ million, 1996): Exports of goods f.o.b. 175.31; Imports of goods f.o.b. –292.04; *Trade balance* –116.73; Exports of services 4.88; Imports of services –184.58; *Balance on goods and services* –296.43; Other income received 0.16; Other income paid –45.18; *Balance on goods, services and income* –341.44; Current transfers received 4.03; Current transfers paid –6.62; *Current balance* –344.04; Direct investment from abroad 376.18; Other investment liabilities –62.43; Net errors and omissions 24.82; *Overall balance* –5.46. Source: IMF, *International Financial Statistics.*

EXTERNAL TRADE

Principal Commodities (distribution by SITC, US $ '000, 1990): *Imports c.i.f.:* Food and live animals 4,340; Beverages and tobacco 3,198, (Alcoholic beverages 2,393); Crude materials (inedible) except fuels 2,589 (Crude fertilizers and crude minerals 2,102); Petroleum and petroleum products 4,738; Chemicals and related products 2,378; Basic manufactures 3,931; Machinery and transport equipment 35,880 (Road vehicles and parts 3,764, Ships, boats and floating structures 24,715); Miscellaneous manufactured articles 2,725; Total (incl. others) 61,601. *Exports f.o.b.:* Food and live animals 6,742 (Cocoa 6,372); Beverages and tobacco 3,217 (Tobacco and tobacco manufactures 2,321); Crude materials (inedible) except fuels 20,017 (Sawlogs and veneer logs 12,839, Textile fibres and waste 7,078); Machinery and transport equipment 24,574 (Ships, boats and floating structures 23,852); Total (incl. others) 61,705. Source: UN, *International Trade Statistics Yearbook.*

1997 (US $ '000): Imports c.i.f. 352,800; Exports f.o.b. 498,444. Source: IMF, *Equatorial Guinea: Recent Economic Developments* (October 1999).

Principal Trading Partners (US $ '000, 1991): *Imports c.i.f.:* Cameroon 29,141; France 5,915; Italy 3,001; Liberia 22,032; Spain 11,640; USA 33,366; Total (incl. others) 113,545. *Exports f.o.b.:* Cameroon 47,212; Gabon 2,389; Netherlands 2,103; Nigeria 8,955; São Tomé and Príncipe 1,952; Spain 11,645; Total (incl. others) 86,151. Source: UN, *International Trade Statistics Yearbook.*

TRANSPORT

Road Traffic (estimates, motor vehicles in use at 31 December 1996): Passenger cars 1,520; Lorries and vans 540. Source: IRF, *World Road Statistics*.

Shipping: *Merchant Fleet* (at 31 December 1998): Vessels 87; Total displacement 58,506 grt. Source: Lloyd's Register of Shipping, *World Fleet Statistics*. International Sea-borne Freight Traffic ('000 metric tons, 1990): Goods loaded 110; Goods unloaded 64. Source: UN, *Monthly Bulletin of Statistics*.

Civil Aviation (traffic on scheduled services, 1997): Passengers carried ('000) 21; Passenger-km (million) 4. Source: UN, *Statistical Yearbook*.

COMMUNICATIONS MEDIA

1996: 175,000 radio receivers in use; 4,000 television receivers in use; 4,000 main telephone lines in use; 100 telefax stations in use; 61 mobile cellular telephone subscribers; 1 daily newspaper (estimated circulation 2,000); Book production 17 titles (1988).

1997: 180,000 radio receivers in use; 4,000 television receivers in use.

Sources: UNESCO, *Statistical Yearbook*; UN, *Statistical Yearbook*.

EDUCATION

Primary (1993/94): Schools 781; Teachers 1,381; Pupils 75,751.
Secondary and Further (1993/94): Teachers 588; Pupils 16,616.
Higher (1990/91): Teachers 58; Pupils 578.
Source: UNESCO, *Statistical Yearbook*.

Directory

The Constitution

The present Constitution was approved by a national referendum on 16 November 1991 and amended in January 1995. It provided for the introduction of a plural political system and for the establishment of an 80-member legislative House of Representatives. The term of office of the President is seven years, renewable on an indefinite number of occasions. The President is immune from prosecution for offences committed before, during or after his tenure of the post. The House of Representatives serves for a term of five years. Both the President and the House of Representatives are directly elected by universal adult suffrage. The President appoints a Council of Ministers, headed by a Prime Minister, from among the members of the House of Representatives.

The Government

HEAD OF STATE

President and Supreme Commander of the Armed Forces: Gen. (TEODORO) OBIANG NGUEMA MBASOGO (assumed office 25 August 1979; elected President 25 June 1989; re-elected 25 February 1996).

COUNCIL OF MINISTERS
(April 2001)

Prime Minister and Head of Government: CÁNDIDO MUATETEMA RIVAS.

Deputy Prime Minister and Minister of the Civil Service and Administrative Co-ordination: IGNACIO MILAM TANG.

Minister of State for Presidential Missions: ALEJANDRO EVUNA OWONO ASANGONO.

Secretary-General of the Government: FRANCISCO PASCUAL OBAMA EYEGUE.

Minister of State for Parliamentary Relations and Judicial Affairs: (vacant).

Minister of State for Communications and Transport: MARCELINO OYONO NTUTUMU.

Minister of State for Education and Science, Government Spokesman: ANTONIO FERNANDO NVE NGU.

Minister of State for Health and Social Welfare: MARCELINO NGUEMA ONGUENE.

Minister of State for Labour and Social Security: RICARDO MANGUE OBAMA NFUBE.

Minister of State for Agriculture, Livestock and Rural Development: GREGORIO BOHO CAMO.

Minister of State for Forestry, Fisheries and the Environment: TEODORO NGUEMA OBIANG MANGUE.

Minister of State for Information, Tourism and Culture: LUCAS NGUEMA ESONO.

Minister of Foreign Affairs, International Co-operation and Francophone Affairs: SANTIAGO NSOBEYA EFUMAN.

Minister of Justice and Worship: RUBÉN MAYE NSUE.

Minister of the Interior and Local Corporations: CLEMENTE ENGONGA NGUEMA ONGUENE.

Minister of the Economy and Finance: BALTASAR ENGONGA EDJO.

Minister of Industry, Commerce and Small- and Medium-sized Enterprises: CONSTANTINO EKONG NSUE.

Minister of Mines and Energy: CRISTÓBAL MEÑANA ELA.

Minister of Social Affairs and Women's Development: TERESA EFUA ASANGONO.

Minister of Public Works, Housing and Urban Affairs: FLORENTINO NKOGO NDONG.

Minister of Planning and Economic Development: FORTUNATO OFA MBO.

Minister of Youth and Sports: JUAN ANTONIO BIBANG NTUTUMU.

In addition, there are eight Ministers-delegate, eight Deputy Ministers and five Secretaries of State.

MINISTRIES

All ministries are in Malabo.

Ministry of Agriculture, Livestock and Rural Development: Apdo 504, Malabo.

Ministry of the Economy and Finance: Malabo; tel. (9) 31-05; fax (9) 32-05.

Ministry of Foreign Affairs, International Co-operation and Francophone Affairs: Malabo; tel. (9) 32-20.

Ministry of Mines and Energy: Calle 12 de Octobre s/n, Malabo; tel. (9) 35-67; fax (9) 33-53.

Legislature

CÁMARA DE REPRESENTANTES DEL PUEBLO
(House of Representatives)

Speaker: SALOMON NGUEMA OWONO.

General Election, 7 March 1999

Party		Seats
Partido Democrático de Guinea Ecuatorial (PDGE) .		75
Unión Popular (UP)		4
Convergencia para la Democracia Social (CPDS) . .		1
Total		80

Political Organizations

Acción Popular (AP): Pres. MIGUEL ESONO.

Alianza Democrática Progresista (ADP): Pres. VICTORINO BOLEKIA.

Alianza Nacional para la Restauración Democrática de Guinea Ecuatorial (ANRD): 95 Ruperto Chapi, 28100 Madrid, Spain; tel. (1) 623-88-64; f. 1974; Sec.-Gen. LUIS ONDO AYANG.

Convención Liberal Democrática (CLD): Pres. ALFONSO NSUE MIFUMU.

Convención Socialdemocrática Popular (CSDP): Leader SECUNDINO OYONO.

Convergencia para la Democracia Social (CPDS): Pres. SANTIAGO OBAMA; Sec.-Gen. PLÁCIDO MICÓ ABOGO.

Coordinación Democrática de los Partidos de Oposición de Guinea Ecuatorial: based in Libreville, Gabon; f. 1991; coalition of the following groups:

Frente Democrático para la Reforma: Sec.-Gen. BIYONGO BI-TUNG.

Movimiento Nacional para la Nueva Liberación de Guinea Ecuatorial.

Partido Republicano.

Partido de Reunificación (PR).

Unión para la Democracia y el Desarrollo Social (UDDS): f. 1990; Sec.-Gen. ANTONIO SIBACHA BUEICHEKU.

Coordinadora de la Oposición Conjunta (CODE): based in Spain; f. 1999; alliance of seven opposition parties; Leader JOAQUÍN ELEMA BORENGUE.

Foro-Democracia Guinea Ecuatorial (FDGE).

Frente de la Oposición Democrátia (FOD): f. 2000; alliance of six opposition groups, incl. the ADP, the CPDS and the UP.

Fuerza Demócrata Republicana (FDR): f. 1995; Chair. FELIPE ONDO OBIANG.

Movimiento para la Autodeterminación de la Isla de Bioko (MAIB): f. 1993 by Bubi interests seeking independence of Bioko; Spokesman JOAQUÍN MAHO.

Partido de la Convergencia Social Demócrata (PCSD): Pres. BUENAVENTURA MOSUY.

Partido Democrático de Guinea Ecuatorial (PDGE): Malabo; f. 1987; sole legal party 1987–92; Chair. Gen. (TEODORO) OBIANG NGUEMA MBASOGO.

Partido del Progreso de Guinea Ecuatorial (PPGE): f. 1983; Christian Democrat; faction led by SEVERO MOTO NSA.

Partido Social Demócrata (PSD): Pres. BENJAMÍN BALINGA.

Partido Socialista (PS): Sec.-Gen. TOMÁS MACHEBA.

Unión Democrática Independiente (UDI): Leader DANIEL OYONO.

Unión Democrática Nacional (UDEMA): Pres. JOSÉ MECHEBA.

Unión Democrática y Social de Guinea Ecuatorial (UDS): Pres. CARMELO MODÚ AKUNE.

Unión Popular (UP): f. 1992; socialist; Pres. JEREMIAS ONDO NGOMO.

Unión para la Reconciliación y el Progreso (URP).

Diplomatic Representation

EMBASSIES IN EQUATORIAL GUINEA

Cameroon: 37 Calle Rey Boncoro, Apdo 292, Malabo; tel. and fax (9) 22-63; Ambassador: JOHN NCHOTU AKUM.

China, People's Republic: Carretera del Aeropuerto, Apdo 44, Malabo; tel. (9) 35-05; fax (9) 23-81; Ambassador: HUAILONG CHEN.

France: Carretera del Aeropuerto, Apdo 326, Malabo; tel. (9) 20-05; Ambassador: GÉRARD BRUNET DE COURSSOU.

Gabon: Apdo 648, Douala, Malabo; tel. (9) 420; Ambassador: JEAN-BAPTISTE MBATCHI.

Korea, Democratic People's Republic: Malabo; Ambassador: PAK MYONG HAK.

Nigeria: 4 Paseo de los Cocoteros, Apdo 78, Malabo; tel. (9) 23-86; Chargé d'affaires: EDWARD NWADA.

Russia: Malabo; Ambassador: LEV ALEKSANDROVICH VAKHRAMEYEV.

Spain: Parque de las Avenidas de Africa, Malabo; tel. (9) 20-20; fax (9) 26-11; Ambassador: JACOBO GONZÁLEZ-ARNAO.

Judicial System

The structure of Judicial Administration was established in 1981. The Supreme Tribunal in Malabo, consisting of a President of the Supreme Tribunal, the Presidents of the three chambers (civil, criminal and administrative), and two magistrates from each chamber, is the highest court of appeal. There are Territorial High Courts in Malabo and Bata, which also sit as courts of appeal. Courts of first instance sit in Malabo and Bata, and may be convened in the other provincial capitals. Local courts may be convened when necessary.

President of the Supreme Tribunal: SILVESTRE SIALE BILEKA.

Religion

An estimated 90% of the population are adherents of the Roman Catholic Church. Traditional forms of worship are also followed.

CHRISTIANITY

The Roman Catholic Church

Equatorial Guinea comprises one archdiocese and two dioceses. There were an estimated 370,304 adherents in the country at 31 December 1998.

Bishops' Conference: Arzobispado, Apdo 106, Malabo; tel. (9) 29-09; fax 21-76; e-mail arzobispadomalabo@hotmail.com; f. 1984; Pres. Rt Rev. ILDEFONSO OBAMA OBONO, Archbishop of Malabo.

Archbishop of Malabo: Most Rev. ILDEFONSO OBAMA OBONO, Arzobispado, Apdo 106, Malabo; tel. (9) 29-09; fax (9) 21-76.

Protestant Church

Iglesia Reformada Evangélica de Guinea Ecuatorial (Evangelical Reformed Church of Equatorial Guinea): Apdo 195, Malabo; f. 1960; c. 8,000 mems; Sec.-Gen. Rev. JAIME SIPOTO.

The Press

El Patio: Apdo 180, Malabo; tel. (9) 27-20; fax (9) 27-22; Spanish; cultural review; 6 a year; publ. by Centro Cultural Hispano-Guineano; Editor GABRIELA GÓMEZ-PIMPOLLO.

El Sol: 24 Calle Camerún, Apdo 944, Malabo; f. 1994; Spanish; weekly; Chief Editor FERMÍN-NVO MBOMIO AVOMO; circ. 3,500.

Hoja Parroquial: Malabo; weekly.

La Gaceta: Malabo; f. 1996; bi-weekly.

La Verdad: Malabo; opposition monthly; publ. by the Convergencia para la Democracia Social; Editor PLÁCIDO MIKÓ ABOGO.

Voz del Pueblo: Malabo; publ. by the Partido Democrático de Guinea Ecuatorial.

FOREIGN NEWS BUREAU

Agencia EFE (Spain): 50 Calle del Presidente Nasser, Malabo; tel. (9) 31-65; Bureau Chief DONATO NDONGO-BIDYOGO.

Publisher

Centro Cultural Hispano-Guineano: Apdo 180, Malabo; tel. (9) 27-20; fax (9) 27-22.

Broadcasting and Communications

RADIO

Radio Africa and Radio East Africa: Apdo 851, Malabo; e-mail pabcomain@aol.com; commercial station; owned by Pan American Broadcasting; music and religious programmes in English.

Radio Malabo: Malabo; Spanish and French programmes.

Radio Nacional de Guinea Ecuatorial: Apdo 749, Barrio Comandachina, Bata; tel. (8) 25-92; fax (8) 20-93; and Apdo 195, 90 ave 30 de Agostó, Malabo; tel. (9) 22-60; fax (9) 20-97; govt-controlled; commercial station; programmes in Spanish, French and vernacular languages; Dir (Bata) SEBASTIÁN ELÓ ASEKO; Dir (Malabo) JUAN EYENE OPKUA NGUEMA.

TELEVISION

Televisión Nacional: Malabo; broadcasts in Spanish and French; Dir ANTONIO NKULU OYE.

Finance

(cap. = capital; p.u. = paid up; res = reserves; m. = million; br. = branch; amounts in francs CFA)

BANKING

Central Bank

Banque des Etats de l'Afrique Centrale (BEAC): Apdo 510, Malabo; tel. (9) 20–10; fax (9) 20–06; HQ in Yaoundé, Cameroon; f. 1973; bank of issue for mem. states of the Communauté économique et monétaire de l'Afrique centrale (CEMAC, fmrly Union douanière et économique de l'Afrique centrale), comprising Cameroon, the Central African Repub., Chad, the Repub. of the Congo, Equatorial Guinea and Gabon; cap. 45,000m., res 172,198m., total assets 1,407,908m. (Dec. 1999); Gov. JEAN-FÉLIX MAMALEPOT; Dir in Equatorial Guinea FRANCISCO GARCIA BERNIKON.

Commercial Banks

Caisse Commune d'Epargne et d'Investissement Guinea Ecuatorial (CCEI-GE): Pres. Nasser St, POB 428, Malabo; tel. (9) 31-21; fax (9) 33-11; f. 1995; dep. 4,725m. (Dec. 1998); Man. Dir JOSEPH TINDJOU.

Société Générale des Banques GE (SGBGE): 6 Calle de Argelia, Apdo 686, Malabo; tel. (9) 93-37; fax (9) 33-66; f. 1986, present name adopted 1998; 60% owned by Société Générale SA (France), 33% state-owned; dep. 10,330m. (Dec. 1998); Pres. CASTRO NVONO AKELE; Gen. Man. CHARLES SANLAVILLE; brs in Bata and Malabo.

Development Banks

Banco de Fomento y Desarrollo (BFD): Malabo; f. 1998; 30% state-owned; cap. 50m.

Banque de Développement des Etats de l'Afrique Centrale (see Franc Zone, p. 127).

Financial Institution

Caja Autónoma de Amortización de la Deuda Pública: Ministry of the Economy and Finance, Malabo; tel. (9) 31-05; fax (9) 32-05; management of state funds; Dir-Gen. BALTASAR ESONO-EWORO NFONO.

Trade and Industry

GOVERNMENT AGENCIES

Cámaras Oficiales Agrícolas de Guinea: Bioko and Bata; purchase of cocoa and coffee from indigenous planters, who are partially grouped in co-operatives.

Empresa General de Industria y Comercio (EGISCA): Malabo; f. 1986; parastatal body jtly operated with the French Société pour l'Organisation, l'Aménagement et le Développement des Industries Alimentaires et Agricoles (SOMDIA); import-export agency.

Oficina para la Cooperación con Guinea Ecuatorial (OCGE): Malabo; f. 1981; administers bilateral aid from Spain.

DEVELOPMENT ORGANIZATION

Sociedad Anónima de Desarrollo del Comercio (SOADECO–Guinée): Malabo; f. 1986; parastatal body jtly operated with the French Société pour l'Organisation, l'Aménagement et le Développement des Industries Alimentaires et Agricoles (SOMDIA); development of commerce.

CHAMBER OF COMMERCE

Cámara de Comercio, Agrícola y Forestal de Malabo: Apdo 51, Malabo; tel. (9) 151.

INDUSTRIAL AND TRADE ASSOCIATIONS

INPROCAO: Malabo; production, marketing and distribution of cocoa.

Total Ecuatoguineana de Gestion (GE–Total): Malabo; f. 1984; 50% state-owned, 50% by CFP-Total (France); petroleum marketing and distribution; Chair. of Bd of Dirs Minister of Public Works, Housing and Urban Affairs.

Unión General de Empresas Privadas de la República de Guinea Ecuatorial (UGEPRIGE): Apdo 138, Malabo.

UTILITIES
Electricity
ENERGE: Malabo; state-owned electricity board.

TRADE UNIONS

A law permitting the establishment of trade unions was introduced in 1992.

Transport

RAILWAYS

There are no railways in Equatorial Guinea.

ROADS

In 1996 there were an estimated 2,880 km of roads and tracks.

Bioko: a semi-circular tarred road serves the northern part of the island from Malabo down to Batete in the west and from Malabo to Bacake Grande in the east, with a feeder road from Luba to Moka and Bahía de la Concepción.

Río Muni: a tarred road links Bata with the town of Mbini (Río Benito) in the west; another road, partly tarred, links Bata with the frontier post of Ebebiyín in the east and then continues into Gabon; other earth roads join Acurenam, Mongomo and Anisok.

SHIPPING

The main ports are Bata (general cargo and most of the country's export timber), Malabo (general), Luba (bananas, timber), Mbini and Cogo (timber).

CIVIL AVIATION

There are two international airports, at Malabo (Santa Isabel Airport) and Bata (the latter was completed with Italian aid in 1995). The national carrier, EGA–Ecuato Guineana de Aviación (which has been in liquidation since 1990), continues to provide limited regional and domestic services, as well as a weekly service to Madrid. Scheduled services between Malabo and Madrid are operated by IBERIA, Líneas Aéreas de España, and Swissair is also developing an international service from Malabo. Cameroon Airlines (CAM-AIR) carries passengers between Malabo and Douala (Cameroon). Air Afrique operates a cargo service linking Equatorial Guinea with West African destinations.

EGA–Ecuato Guineana de Aviación: Apdo 665, Malabo; tel. (9) 23-25; fax (9) 33-13; regional and domestic passenger and cargo services.

Tourism

Tourism remains undeveloped. Future interest in this sector would be likely to focus on the unspoilt beaches of Río Muni and Bioko's scenic mountain terrain.

ERITREA

Introductory Survey

Location, Climate, Language, Religion, Flag, Capital

The State of Eritrea, which has a coastline on the Red Sea extending for almost 1,000 km, is bounded to the north-west by Sudan, to the south and west by Ethiopia, and to the south-east by Djibouti. Its territory includes the Dahlak islands, a low-lying coralline archipelago off shore from Massawa. Rainfall is less than 500 mm per year in lowland areas, increasing to 1,000 mm in the highlands. The temperature gradient is similarly steep: average annual temperatures range from 17°C (63°F) in the highlands to 30°C (86°F) in Massawa. The Danakil depression in the south-east, which is more than 130 m below sea-level in places, experiences some of the highest temperatures recorded, frequently exceeding 50°C (122°F). The major language groups in Eritrea are Afar, Bilien, Hedareb, Kunama, Nara, Rashaida, Saho, Tigre and Tigrinya. English is rapidly becoming the language of business and is the medium of instruction at secondary schools and at university. Arabic is also widely spoken. The population is fairly evenly divided between Tigrinya-speaking Christians (mainly Orthodox), the traditional inhabitants of the highlands, and the Muslim communities of the western lowlands, northern highlands and east coast; there are also systems of traditional belief adhered to by a small number of the population. The national flag (proportions 2 by 1) consists of a red triangle with its base corresponding to the hoist and its apex at the centre of the fly, in which is situated, towards the hoist, an upright gold olive branch with six clusters of three leaves each, framed by a wreath of two gold olive branches; the remainder of the field is green at the top and light blue at the base. The capital is Asmara.

Recent History

Eritrea, as a political entity, first emerged following Italian occupation of the Red Sea port of Massawa and other coastal enclaves in the 1880s. In 1889 Italy signed the Treaty of Ucciali with the Ethiopian Emperor, Menelik, and in 1890 named its new possession 'Eritrea'. The treaty gave the Italian Government control over the colony, and the borders agreed upon therein are now the borders of the State of Eritrea. Italian farmers were encouraged to settle on areas declared Italian Crown Land by the colonial government, covering, in particular, the fertile highland area. Italian exploitation of the colony continued until the defeat of the Axis powers by the Allied powers in East Africa during the Second World War. During 1941–52 Eritrea was under British administration. The Eritrean national identity, which was established during the Italian colonial period, was further subjugated under British rule, which led to the neglect and decline of Eritrean industry and permitted the continued exploitation of Eritrea's agricultural resources by Italian settler farmers. As the Allied powers and the UN discussed the future of the former Italian colony, Ethiopian territorial claims helped to foment a more militant nationalism among the Eritrean population. In 1952 a compromise agreement was reached, whereby a federation was formed between Eritrea and Ethiopia. However, the absence of adequate provisions for the creation of federal structures allowed Ethiopia to reduce Eritrea's status to that of an Ethiopian province by 1962.

Resistance to the Ethiopian annexation was first organized in the late 1950s around emerging opposition groups, in particular the Eritrean Liberation Movement, founded in 1958, which was succeeded shortly afterwards by the Eritrean Liberation Front (ELF). The ELF launched an armed struggle in 1961. However, not until the mid-1970s, when a reformist group broke away from the ELF and formed the Popular Liberation Forces (renamed the Eritrean People's Liberation Front, EPLF, in 1977), did the military confrontation with the Ethiopian Government begin in earnest. A major consequence of the split between the two groups was the civil war of 1972–74. After two phases of desertion from the ELF to the EPLF, firstly in 1977–78 and secondly in 1985 (following a second civil war), the ELF was left without a coherent military apparatus. However, a number of disaffected factions remained loyal to the ELF, particularly

those associated with Ahmed Nasser, the leader of the ELF—Revolutionary Council (ELF—RC).

Following the 1974 revolution in Ethiopia and the assumption of power by Mengistu Haile Mariam in 1977, thousands of new recruits joined the EPLF and the armed struggle eventually transformed into full-scale warfare. The numerically and materially superior Ethiopian forces (armed mainly by the USSR) initially achieved significant victories over the EPLF. Following defeat in the highlands, the EPLF was forced to retreat to its stronghold in the north of Eritrea. During Ethiopia's 'red star' offensive in 1982, the EPLF captured sufficient quantities of heavy artillery and tanks to transform it from a guerrilla force into a regular army. From its secure base, the EPLF launched counter-attacks throughout the late 1980s and slowly drove back the Ethiopian forces on all fronts. By 1989 the EPLF had gained control of the north and the west of the country and in late 1989 the EPLF captured Massawa port, thereby severing a major supply-route to the Ethiopian forces, who were by now besieged in Asmara. In May 1991 units of the EPLF entered Asmara, after the Ethiopian troops had fled, and immediately established an interim EPLF administration.

Following the liberation of Asmara by the EPLF, and of Addis Ababa by the Ethiopian People's Revolutionary Democratic Front (EPRDF), a conference was convened in London, United Kingdom, in August 1991, under the chairmanship of the US Assistant Secretary of State for Africa. Representatives of the EPLF attended in a delegation separate from the EPRDF, now in control of Ethiopia and sympathetic to Eritrean national aspirations. Both the USA and the Ethiopian delegation accepted the EPLF administration as the legitimate provisional Government of Eritrea, and the EPLF agreed to hold a referendum on independence in 1993. The provisional Government, which was to administer Eritrea during the two years prior to the referendum, drew most of its members from the EPLF. The Government struggled to rehabilitate and develop Eritrea's war-torn economy and infrastructure, and to feed a population of whom 80% remained dependent on food aid. The agricultural sector had been severely disrupted by the war, and urban economic activity was almost non-existent. The Government was confronted by the additional problem of how to reintegrate some 750,000 refugees, of whom approximately 500,000 lived in Sudan, mostly at subsistence level.

The UN-supervised referendum on independence was held in April 1993; of the 1,102,410 Eritreans who voted, 99.8% endorsed national independence. The anniversary of the liberation of Asmara, 24 May, was proclaimed Independence Day, and on 28 May Eritrea formally attained international recognition. In June Eritrea was admitted to the Organization of African Unity (OAU). Following Eritrea's accession to independence, a four-year transitional period was declared, during which preparations were to proceed for establishing a constitutional and pluralist political system. At the apex of the transitional Government were three state institutions: the Consultative Council (the executive authority formed from the ministers, provincial administrators and heads of government authorities and commissions); the National Assembly (the legislative authority formed from the Central Committee of the EPLF together with 30 members from the Provincial Assemblies and 30 individuals selected by the Central Committee); and the judiciary. One of the National Assembly's first acts was the election as Head of State of Issaias Afewerki, the Secretary-General of the EPLF, by a margin of 99 votes to five.

At its third congress, held in Asmara in February 1994, the EPLF transformed itself into a political party, called the People's Front for Democracy and Justice (PFDJ). An 18-member Executive Committee and a 75-member Central Committee were elected; President Afewerki was elected Chairman of the latter. In March the National Assembly adopted a series of resolutions whereby the former executive body, the Consultative Council, was formally superseded by a State Council. Other measures adopted by resolutions of the Assembly included the creation of a 50-member Constitutional Commission, and the establishment of a committee charged with the reorganization of the country's administrative divisions. It was decided that the National Assembly would henceforth comprise the 75 members of the PFDJ Central Committee and 75 directly elected members. However, no mechanism was announced for their election. All but eight of the 50-member Constitutional Commission were government appointees, and there was no provision for any opposition participation in the interim system.

A draft constitution was discussed at international conventions, held by the Constitutional Commission, in July 1994 and January 1995, and more than 1,000 popular meetings took place in the first six months of 1995 to allow wider discussion of the proposed constitution. A third stage of consultation began in October, when former soldiers of the EPLF armed forces were invited to discuss the draft law. Meanwhile, in May the National Assembly approved proposals to create six administrative regions to replace the 10 regional divisions that had been in place since colonial rule. In November the Assembly approved new names for the regions and finalized details of their exact boundaries and sub-divisions.

Since the establishment of the EPLF Government, an effective ban on other political groups had been in effect and many political activists were allegedly detained in prison. In April 1994 26 members of the ELF—RC faction were detained in Ethiopia; other ELF—RC members were reported to have been forcibly repatriated to Eritrea.

In early 1997 the Government established a Constituent Assembly, comprising 527 members (150 from the National Assembly; the remainder selected from representatives of Eritreans residing abroad or elected by regional assemblies), to discuss and ratify the draft constitution. On 23 May the Constituent Assembly adopted the Constitution, authorizing 'conditional' political pluralism and instituting a presidential regime, with a President elected for a maximum of two five-year terms. The President, as Head of State, would appoint a Prime Minister and judges of the Supreme Court; his mandate could be revoked should two-thirds of the members of the National Assembly so demand. The Constituent Assembly was disbanded and a Transitional National Assembly (consisting of the 75 members of the PFDJ Central Committee, 60 members of the Constituent Assembly and 15 representatives of Eritreans residing abroad) was empowered to act as the legislature until the holding of elections to a new National Assembly. Meanwhile, in February 1997 President Afewerki carried out a wide-ranging reorganization of the State Council; notably, no public announcement was made of the changes. In October 2000 Afewerki effected a minor cabinet reshuffle. Meanwhile, it was announced that Eritrea's first post-independence elections, which were scheduled to have been held in 1998 but were postponed indefinitely following the outbreak of hostilities with Ethiopia (see below), would take place in December 2001.

External relations have proved problematic. The transitional Government has attempted to consolidate good relations with Eritrea's neighbours and to develop stronger links with the USA, China and other major powers. However, the complexity of regional relations, and of Eritrea's position therein, became evident in July 1993, when President Afewerki had to counter allegations, made during a visit to Saudi Arabia, that Israel was establishing a military presence in Eritrea. Prior to the referendum, harsh reactions had been provoked in the Arab press after Afewerki visited Israel for medical treatment. The Eritrean Government is keen to maintain good relations with its Arab neighbours (one of which, namely Saudi Arabia, had previously provided support to the ELF) but not to the detriment of what it regards as important ties with Israel.

Relations between the transitional Government and Sudan, which had supported the EPLF during the war, deteriorated in December 1993, following an incursion by members of an Islamist group, the Eritrean Islamic Jihad (EIJ), into Eritrea from Sudan. In a clash with Eritrean forces, all the members of the group, and an Eritrean commander, were killed. In response to the incident, President Afewerki stressed the links between the EIJ and the Sudanese National Islamic Front, led by Dr Hassan at-Turabi, implying that the latter had prior knowledge of the incursion. However, following a swift denial by the Sudanese Government that it would interfere in the affairs of neighbouring states, Afewerki reaffirmed his support for the Sudanese authorities and his commitment to improving bilateral relations. In August 1993 it was reported that the EIJ had split between its political faction, led by Sheikh Mohamed Arafa, and a military wing.

In August 1994 Eritrea and Sudan signed an agreement concerning borders, security and the repatriation of refugees, and in November the office of the UN High Commissioner for Refugees (UNHCR) initiated a repatriation programme for Eritrean refugees currently in Sudan. Some 500,000 Eritreans had taken refuge in Sudan in the early 1990s as a result of separatist conflicts, although by 1995 an estimated 125,000 had returned spontaneously, particularly following Eritrea's accession to independence. Owing to delays in the implementation of the UNHCR programme, an estimated 342,100 Eritrean refugees remained in Sudan in late 1999.

Relations between Eritrea and Sudan deteriorated in November 1994, when the Eritrean authorities accused Sudan of training 400 terrorists since August. Sudan accused Eritrea of training some 3,000 Sudanese rebels in camps within Eritrea. In December Eritrea severed diplomatic relations with Sudan. Further destabilization was provoked in early 1995 by attacks and infiltration in Barka Province by commandos of the military wing of the EIJ. The Eritrean authorities subsequently claimed to have identified six training camps on the Sudanese side of the border, and also alleged that large numbers of Eritrean refugees in Sudan had been arrested by Sudanese security forces. Sudan responded by proposing Eritrea's suspension from the Intergovernmental Authority on Drought and Development (IGADD, now the Intergovernmental Authority on Development—IGAD, see p. 214), which had been attempting to mediate in Sudan's civil war. The Sudanese Government protested strongly against Eritrea's growing support for the Sudanese opposition grouping, the National Democratic Alliance (NDA), which held conferences in Asmara in December 1994, June 1995 and January 1996. In February 1996 Eritrea granted Sudanese opposition leaders permission to use Sudan's embassy in Asmara as their headquarters; limited radio transmissions to Sudan were also allowed. In January 1997 Sudan accused Eritrean troops of launching an attack on Sudanese forces in the frontier region, resulting in numerous casualties. In May Sudan temporarily closed its border with Eritrea, apparently fearing an imminent Eritrean attack. Meanwhile, Eritrean security forces announced that they had foiled a plot by the Sudanese Government to assassinate President Afewerki in that month. Eritrea subsequently protested against alleged repeated violations of its airspace by Sudanese aircraft. In February 1998 Sudan closed the border with Eritrea in an attempt to prevent incursions into Sudan. Further attacks on Sudanese forces by Eritrean troops were reported during 1998, including an alleged offensive in eastern Sudan in October. In November the Ministers of Foreign Affairs of the two countries attended a mediation meeting in Qatar, at the conclusion of which they signed a memorandum of understanding to normalize relations. Tensions remained, however, and mutual recriminations regarding border incidents continued.

In early 1999 Sudan took steps to resolve its differences with Ethiopia, thus increasing the tension between Eritrea and Sudan. In March the Alliance of Eritrean National Forces (AENF) was launched in Khartoum by 10 Eritrean opposition organizations with Ethiopia's support. Shortly afterwards the AENF announced its intention to establish an Eritrean government-in-exile. In the following month, however, Sudan indicated its willingness also to improve relations with Eritrea, and in May President Afewerki and his Sudanese counterpart signed a reconciliatory agreement in Qatar, which, *inter alia*, restored diplomatic relations between the two countries. In June Sudan accused Eritrea of violating the agreement by allowing a Sudanese opposition group to hold a rally in Asmara. However, relations improved further after President Afewerki ordered Sudanese anti-Government activists occupying the Sudanese embassy building to cease political activities and to vacate the premises. In January 2000 President al-Bashir of Sudan visited Afewerki in Asmara, where they pledged further to improve bilateral relations between the two countries. Following the renewed outbreak of hostilities between Eritrea and Ethiopia in May (see below), some 94,000 Eritreans fleeing the Ethiopian advances crossed the border into Sudan. After the cessation of fighting in June, many Eritrean refugees were repatriated with the assistance of the UNHCR, however, a large number of refugees remained in Sudan in early 2001. During 2000 the Eritrean Government assumed a mediatory role in the conflict between the Sudanese Government and opposition groups based in Eritrea. In August 2000 the two countries exchanged ambassadors, and in September al-Bashir travelled to Asmara where he met with the leader of the opposition NDA for the first time since 1989.

In November 1995 there were reports that Eritrean troops had attempted to land on the Red Sea island of Greater Hanish, one of three islands (the others being Lesser Hanish and Zuqar) claimed by both Eritrea and Yemen. The incursion had reportedly been provoked by Yemen's announced intention to develop Greater Hanish as a tourist resort, and its subsequent refusal to comply with an Eritrean demand that the island be evacuated. The disputed islands had been used by Eritrea (with apparent Yemeni approval) during its struggle for independence from Ethiopia. Yemen had subsequently resumed its claims to the islands, because of both their strategic importance (located close to a principal shipping lane) and the possible existence of exploitable petroleum reserves in their surrounding waters. Negotiations in Eritrea and Yemen failed to defuse the crisis, and in mid-December fighting erupted between the two sides, resulting in the deaths of six Eritrean and three Yemeni soldiers. Two days later Eritrea and Yemen agreed to a cease-fire, but fighting resumed on the following day, and Eritrean forces succeeded in occupying Greater Hanish. The cease-fire was adhered to thenceforth, and some 180 captured Yemeni soldiers were released at the end of the month. The Ethiopian and Egyptian Governments attempted, unsuccessfully, to promote an agreement, and in January 1996 France assumed the mediatory role. In May representatives of Eritrea and Yemen signed an arbitration accord in Paris, France, whereby the two sides agreed to submit the dispute to an international tribunal. France subsequently undertook to observe and supervise military movements in the area around the disputed islands. In August, despite the accord, Eritrean troops occupied Lesser Hanish; however, later in the month Eritrea withdrew its soldiers after mediation by France and a UN Security Council instruction to evacuate the island forthwith. In October Eritrea and Yemen confirmed that they would submit the dispute to an international tribunal. In October 1998 the tribunal ruled that Yemen had sovereignty over Greater and Lesser Hanish, and all islands to their north-west, while Eritrea had sovereignty over the Mohabaka islands. The court recommended that the fishing traditions around the islands be maintained, thereby granting access to the Hanish islands to Eritrean and Yemeni fishermen. Both countries accepted the ruling, and shortly afterwards agreed to establish a joint committee to strengthen bilateral co-operation.

In November 1995 Eritrea and Djibouti pledged to enhance bilateral co-operation, following a meeting between Eritrea's Minister of Foreign Affairs, Petros Solomon, and Djibouti's President Gouled. However, relations between the two countries were strained in April 1996 when Gouled reportedly rejected a map (produced by Italy in 1935) submitted by Solomon, which apparently indicated that a 20-km strip of land currently claimed by Djibouti was, in fact, Eritrean territory. Meanwhile, Eritrea denied reports of an attempted occupation of a border post in Djibouti (within the disputed territory) by Eritrean troops. Relations between the two countries subsequently improved; however, in November 1998 Djibouti suspended diplomatic relations with Eritrea, following allegations by the Eritrean authorities that it was supporting Ethiopia in the Eritrea–Ethiopia border conflict (see below). The two countries re-established diplomatic relations in March 2000, following Libyan mediation.

In September 1993 the first meeting of the Ethiopian-Eritrean joint ministerial commission was held in Asmara, during which agreement was reached on measures to allow the free movement of nationals between each country, and on co-operation regarding foreign affairs and economic policy. Meetings held between President Afewerki and the Ethiopian President, Meles Zenawi, in December underlined the good relations prevailing between the two Governments and their efforts to co-ordinate policy with regard to Somalia. In June the OAU had appointed Afewerki to work on behalf of Africa towards solving the Somalia problem, an appointment supported by the UN Security Council and other member states of the UN.

Relations with Ethiopia deteriorated in late 1997, following Eritrea's adoption of a new currency (the nakfa) to replace the Ethiopian birr and the subsequent disruption of cross-border trade. In early May 1998 fighting erupted between Eritrean and Ethiopian troops in the border region after both countries accused the other of having invaded their territory. As many as 100 people were killed in clashes around the towns of Badme and Sheraro. Hostilities escalated in June around Badme, Zal-

ambessa and Assab, resulting in numerous casualties for both sides. A peace plan devised by the USA and Rwanda in early June met with little success, as one of its preconditions for negotiations was the withdrawal of Eritrean troops to the positions occupied before the eruption of hostilities—a proviso vehemently rejected by Eritrea, which demanded the bilateral demilitarization of the area. The US-Rwandan plan had also envisaged the demilitarization of the border region and the dispatch of an observer mission to Badme. In mid-June Eritrea and Ethiopia agreed to an aerial cease-fire, following mediation by the USA and Italy, but a UN Security Council resolution passed later that month, demanding the immediate cessation of hostilities, was not adhered to. The OAU, meanwhile, established a mediation committee in an attempt to resolve the crisis, and in July an OAU delegation visited the two countries. In August the committee presented its report to the Ministers of Foreign Affairs of Eritrea and Ethiopia at an OAU meeting in Ouagadougou, Burkina Faso. The OAU proposals, which endorsed the US-Rwandan peace plan, were rejected by Eritrea, which maintained that it would not withdraw its troops from the disputed territory prior to negotiations. Meanwhile, it was alleged that thousands of Eritreans were being deported from Ethiopia, while Ethiopia claimed that its citizens were being harassed in Eritrea and prevented from leaving the country. In November President Afewerki and Prime Minister Meles of Ethiopia were present at different sessions of a special meeting of the OAU mediation committee in Ouagadougou, which was also attended by the Heads of State of Burkina Faso, Zimbabwe and Djibouti. The committee's peace proposals, which again stressed the need to demilitarize and demarcate the disputed territory, were accepted by Ethiopia, but rejected by Eritrea. Eritrea, moreover, demanded that Djibouti withdraw from the committee, accusing it of providing assistance to Ethiopia in the conflict. Djibouti suspended diplomatic relations with Eritrea, in protest at the allegations. Other international mediation attempts in late 1998 (including that of Anthony Lake, a former US national security adviser) failed to resolve the dispute, and in February 1999 the aerial cease-fire was broken and intense fighting resumed in the border region. In April both sides claimed that they were now prepared to accept and implement the OAU peace proposals, but accused each other of violating its conditions. Following further unsuccessful OAU attempts in May, both sides confirmed their commitment to the OAU's Framework Agreement at the OAU summit held in Algiers, Algeria in July. President Afewerki announced that Eritrean troops would be withdrawn from all territory captured from Ethiopia since 6 May 1998. Under the agreement, Ethiopia was also required to withdraw from all Eritrean territory captured since 6 February 1999, which, in effect, would see both sides return to their positions before the war. The UN subsequently announced it would demarcate the border using maps drawn up by Italy in around 1900. After requesting clarification of technical arrangements to end the war, Ethiopia informed the OAU in September that it had rejected the peace agreement, owing to inconsistencies contained therein. Eritrea accused Ethiopia of attempting to buy time while secretly preparing for a fresh offensive.

Throughout late 1999 and early 2000 there were reports of numerous clashes between Eritrean and Ethiopian troops and both countries continued to promote and assist opposition groups hostile to their foe. In late February 2000 Prime Minister Ahmed Ouyahia of Algeria, the OAU's special envoy, visited Asmara and Addis Ababa with Lake in an attempt to persuade Eritrea and Ethiopia to accept the OAU's peace proposals; however, no agreement was reached. In March, with severe drought once again threatening widespread famine in the Horn of Africa, the Eritrean authorities agreed to allow large quantities of food aid destined for Ethiopia to be transported through the port of Assab. It was reported in the Ethiopian press, however, that this offer had been rejected by the Ethiopian Government. In late April delegations from both countries agreed to attend OAU-sponsored talks in Algiers, although they refused to meet directly, forcing Algerian diplomats to act as mediators. After six days of negotiations the talks collapsed with representatives from both sides blaming the other for the breakdown. In mid-May hostilities between the two countries broke out again; Ethiopia launched a major offensive near the disputed towns of Badme and Zalambessa and succeeded in repulsing the Eritrean forces. The UN Security Council immediately adopted a resolution providing for the imposition of sanctions and an embargo on the sale of all military supplies to the two warring countries, if fighting was not halted within three days. Nevertheless, hostilities continued, despite fears of a grave humanitarian crisis in the region, and the UN Security Council unanimously approved the imposition of a 12-month arms embargo on Eritrea and Ethiopia. Ethiopian forces continued to drive deeper into Eritrean territory, capturing the strategically important town of Barentu and taking control of the western front. By late May Ethiopian forces had seized Zalambessa and the Eritrean authorities had announced that they would withdraw troops from the disputed areas, although Afewerki maintained that this was merely a 'gesture of goodwill' designed to revive the peace talks, which resumed in Algiers on 29 May. Two days later the Ethiopian Prime Minister, Meles Zenawi, stated that the war was over and that his troops had withdrawn from most of the territory it had captured from Eritrea. However, despite the ongoing discussions in Algiers, fighting continued, with each side accusing the other of resuming hostilities: the Eritrean Government claimed that Ethiopian troops had launched an attack on Assab, but this claim was refuted by the Ethiopian authorities. Following extensive negotiations in early June, both sides expressed their readiness, in principle, to accept the OAU's cease-fire agreement, and on 18 June the Ethiopian and Eritrean Ministers of Foreign Affairs signed an agreement, which provided for an immediate cease-fire and the deployment of a UN peace-keeping force in a 25-km 'temporary security zone' inside Eritrea until the issue of the demarcation of the border had been settled. It was estimated that about 100,000 people had been killed and up to 1.5m. Eritreans displaced since the conflict had begun in 1998. Indirect negotiations to discuss the technical issues of the peace accord, involving representatives from both countries, took place in Washington, DC, USA in early July and continued in Algiers in October. Meanwhile, in September the UN Security Council approved the deployment of the UN Mission in Ethiopia and Eritrea, a 4,200-strong peace-keeping force, which was expected to be fully in place by late January 2001. On 12 December 2000 Eritrea and Ethiopia signed an agreement in Algiers, which formally ended the conflict between the two countries. The agreement provided for a permanent cessation of all hostilities, the immediate return of all prisoners of war, the demarcation of the common border by an independent commission and the establishment of a Claims Commission to assess the issues of compensation and reparations. Furthermore, both countries pledged to co-operate with an independent investigation, which aimed to determine the origins of the conflict.

Government

In May 1991 the Eritrean People's Liberation Front (EPLF, restyled as the People's Front for Democracy and Justice—PFDJ—in February 1994) established a provisional Government to administer Eritrea, pending the holding of a national referendum on the issue of independence. The EPLF did not invite other organizations to participate, although it promised that free elections would be held following the referendum. The referendum was held in April 1993, and Eritrea was proclaimed an independent state in the following month. A transitional Government was established, at the apex of which were three state institutions: the Consultative Council (the executive authority formed from the ministers, provincial administrators and heads of government authorities and commissions); the National Assembly (the legislative authority comprising the Central Committee of the EPLF, 30 additional members from the Provincial Assemblies and 30 individuals selected by the Central Committee); and the judiciary. In March 1994 the Consultative Council was superseded by a State Council. At independence a four-year transitional period was declared, during which preparations were to proceed for the establishment of a constitutional and pluralist political system. Meanwhile, in March 1994 the National Assembly voted to alter its composition: it would thenceforth comprise the 75 members of the PFDJ Central Committee and 75 directly elected members. In May 1997, following the adoption of the Constitution, the Constituent Assembly empowered a Transitional National Assembly (comprising the 75 members of the PFDJ Central Committee, 60 members of the former Constituent Assembly and 15 representatives of Eritreans residing abroad) to act as the legislature until elections were held for a new National Assembly.

Defence

In August 2000 Eritrea's armed forces were estimated to number 9,600, including an army of about 8,000, a navy of 200 and an air force of about 200. National service is compulsory for all Eritrean citizens between 18 and 40 years of age (with certain exceptions), for an 18-month period, including six months of military training. The defence budget for 2000 was estimated at US $263m.

Economic Affairs

In 1998, according to estimates by the World Bank, Eritrea's gross national product (GNP), measured at average 1996–1998 prices, was US $781m., equivalent to $200 per head (or $984 per head on an international purchasing-power parity basis). In 1999 GNP was estimated at $800m., equivalent to $200 per head. During 1990–1998 the population increased by an average of 3.0% per year. In 1999 GDP was estimated to be 5,828.3m. nakfa, with a real growth rate of 3.0%.

By far the most important sector of the economy is agriculture, which, despite a reduction in food production of roughly 40% between 1980 and 1990, still sustains 90% of the population. In 1999 agricultural production (including forestry and fishing) accounted for an estimated 16.0% of GDP. In that year the sector employed an estimated 77.8% of the economically active population. Most sedentary agriculture is practised in the highlands, where rainfall is sufficient to cultivate the main crops: teff (an indigenous grain), sorghum, millet, barley and wheat. The 1994 harvest was considerably higher than in the previous few years, owing to high levels of rainfall and an extensive government programme of rehabilitation of communications and irrigation systems. Crop production declined in 1995 (despite good rainfall), owing to a severe locust infestation, but increased slightly in the following year. The effects of successive crop failures in 1999 and 2000 were exacerbated by the outbreak of hostilities between Eritrea and Ethiopia, and in mid-2000 it was estimated that more than 50% of the population was critically dependent on food aid. Although fishing activity is on a very small scale, the total catch increased considerably in the first half of the 1990s, reaching 3,212 metric tons in 1996. The total catch declined to 978 tons in 1997, but rose to 1,576 tons in 1998. According to the UN, sustainable yields of as much as 70,000 tons per year may be possible.

As a result of serious environmental degradation (caused directly and indirectly by the war of independence), water scarcity and unreliable rainfall, projects have been undertaken to build water reservoirs and small dams, while badly eroded hillsides have been terraced and new trees planted in order to prevent soil erosion. Since 1994 several international organizations have granted loans for the development of the agricultural sector.

Eritrea's industrial base traditionally centred on the production of glass, cement, footwear and canned goods, but most industrial enterprises were badly damaged during the war of independence. In 1999 industrial production (comprising mining, manufacturing, construction and utilities) accounted for an estimated 27.3% of GDP. Although some of the 42 public-sector factories—producing textiles, footwear, beverages and other light industrial goods—were operating in 1991, they were doing so at only one-third of capacity. By 1995 production had increased considerably, mostly as a result of substantial government aid. The Government has calculated that the cost of industrial recovery would be US $20m. for the private sector and $66m. for the state sector.

The manufacturing sector provided an estimated 13.9% of GDP in 1999. Until mid-1997 imported petroleum was processed at the Assab refinery, whose entire output of petroleum products was delivered to Ethiopia. The authorities announced that they would import refined petroleum for the immediate future. Eritrea purchases its own petroleum requirements from Ethiopia under a quota arrangement; however, trade between the two countries was disrupted by the outbreak of hostilities in May 1998.

Eritrea's mineral resources are believed to be of significant potential value, although in 1999 mining and quarrying accounted for only 0.1% of GDP. Of particular importance, in view of Eritrea's acute energy shortage, is the possibility of large reserves of petroleum and natural gas beneath the Red Sea. Production-sharing agreements for the exploration of petroleum and gas were signed with the Anadarko Petroleum Corpn of the USA in 1995 and 1997. However, Anadarko's first three deep drills were dry, and in May 1999 the company began reducing operations by removing most of its operational staff. Other mineral resources include potash, zinc, magnesium, copper, iron ore, marble and gold. New legislation on mining, adopted in 1995, declared all mineral resources to be state assets, but recognized an extensive role for private investors in their exploitation.

Most electric energy is provided by four thermal power stations, largely dependent on fuel imported from Ethiopia. However, electricity is provided to only some 10% of the population, the remainder relying on fuelwood and animal products. In 1994 the Kuwait Fund for Arab Economic Development allocated US $158m. for improvements in electricity production and distribution. In mid-1999 the discovery of geothermal potential at the Alid volcanic centre raised hopes that Eritrea's energy problems could soon be alleviated.

The services sector contributed an estimated 56.6% of GDP in 1999. The dominant services are trade, public administration and transport.

In 1999, according to estimates by the IMF, Eritrea recorded a trade deficit of US $480.7m., and there was a deficit of $166.8m. on the current account of the balance of payments. In 1998 the principal sources of non-petroleum imports were Italy (accounting for 17.4% of the total), the United Arab Emirates (16.2%) and Germany (5.7%). Exports in that year were mostly to Sudan (27.2%) and Ethiopia (26.5%). The principal exports to these countries were crude materials (45.5% of the total), food and live animals, and basic manufactures. The main non-petroleum imports were machinery and transport equipment (38.3% of the total), basic manufactures, and food and live animals.

In 1999 it was estimated that Eritrea's budget deficit reached 2,551.9m. nakfa, equivalent to 43.8% of GDP. Eritrea's external debt at the end of 1998 totalled US $149.3m., of which $144.1m. was long-term public debt. The cost of debt-servicing represented 1.5% of the value of exports of goods and services in that year. There are no overall price indices for Eritrea, but statistics for Asmara showed that prices rose by 10.5% in the year to December 1997, compared with 3.4% in the previous 12 months. Unemployment and underemployment are estimated to affect as many as 50% of the labour force.

In 1993 Eritrea was admitted to the group of African, Caribbean and Pacific (ACP) countries party to the Lomé Convention (see p. 206). Eritrea became a member of the IMF in 1994.

Since Eritrea achieved independence, the establishment of a strong market-based economy has been a government priority. In 1993 the authorities adopted a two-year Recovery and Rehabilitation Programme (funded by a series of loans on concessionary terms) to address the extensive economic problems generated by years of war and infrastructural neglect. Emphasis was placed on improving agricultural productivity, promoting export-orientated industries, developing financial and tourism services, and restructuring the public administration. Although significant progress was made in attracting domestic and foreign investment, increasing receipts from exports, reforming taxation policy and improving revenue administration, during 1995 and 1996 the budget deficit rose sharply, primarily as a result of extraordinary capital expenditure. An increase in revenue and external grants, together with a decline in total expenditure, reduced the deficit significantly in 1997. The Government's programme of privatization, initiated in 1993, gathered momentum in late 1997 with the announcement that all 39 state-owned manufacturing enterprises would be divested. By mid-1998 11 of these had been privatized, although foreign investment in the sector remained limited. In November 1997 the Government introduced the nakfa as the national currency (Eritrea had retained the Ethiopian birr as its monetary unit since independence), initially at par with the birr. The adoption of the new currency led to tensions with Ethiopia, adversely affecting cross-border trade, and, following the outbreak of hostilities with that country in May 1998, Ethiopia re-routed its maritime commerce via Djibouti. The conflict had a devastating effect on the Eritrean economy. Trade with Ethiopia, which previously accounted for two-thirds of Eritrean exports, virtually ceased, and Eritrea was estimated to have spent at least US $1m. per day on the war. This expenditure, coupled with the failure of successive harvests, has increased Eritrea's already considerable reliance on donations from aid organizations, and the need to feed, clothe and shelter the vast numbers of people displaced during the war is expected further to increase the strain on government finances during 2001.

Social Welfare

In the period 1990–95 the infant mortality rate was estimated to be 101 per 1,000 live births, and average life expectancy at birth was 49.6 years; in 1996 there were an estimated three physicians per 100,000 people. By mid-1994 there were 17 hospitals, 32 health centres and 120 health stations under the administration of the Government (compared with eight, four and 45, respectively, in 1991). An estimated 60,000 children were left crippled by the war, and another 45,000 orphaned. The war has also created some 600,000 refugees. Government expenditure on health in 1997 was 172.2m. nakfa (4.5% of total spending).

Education

Education is provided free of charge in government schools and at the University of Asmara. There are also some fee-paying private schools. Education is officially compulsory for children between seven and 13 years of age. Primary education begins at the age of seven and lasts for five years. Secondary education, beginning at 12 years of age, lasts for as much as six years, comprising a first cycle of two years and a second of four years. In 1996 the total enrolment at primary and secondary schools was equivalent to 37% of the school-age population (41% of boys; 33% of girls). In that year primary enrolment included 31% of children in the relevant age-group (males 32%; females 29%), while the comparable ratio for secondary enrolment was only 16% (males 17%; females 15%). Government expenditure on education and training in 1998 was 253.4m. nakfa (6.6% of total spending). By mid-1994 Eritrea had about 600 schools, almost three times as many as in 1991. In 1997 there were 3,096 students enrolled at the University of Asmara or at equivalent level institutions. The overall rate of adult illiteracy in Eritrea in the mid-1990s was estimated to be 80% (among demobilized women fighters the rate was believed to be as high as 95%).

Public Holidays

2001: 1 January (New Year's Day), 6 January (Epiphany), 6 March* (Id al-Adha/Arafat), 24 May (Independence Day), 20 June (Martyrs' Day), 1 September (anniversary of the start of the armed struggle), 17 December* (Id al-Fitr, end of Ramadan), 25 December (Christmas).

2002: 1 January (New Year's Day), 6 January (Epiphany), 23 February* (Id al-Adha/Arafat), 24 May (Independence Day), 20 June (Martyrs' Day), 1 September (anniversary of the start of the armed struggle), 6 December* (Id al-Fitr, end of Ramadan), 25 December (Christmas).

* These holidays are dependent on the Islamic lunar calendar and may vary by one or two days from the dates given.

Weights and Measures

The metric system is in force.

Statistical Survey

Source (unless otherwise stated): Ministry of Trade and Industry, POB 1844, Asmara; tel. (1) 118386; fax (1) 120586.

Area and Population

AREA, POPULATION AND DENSITY*

Area (sq km)	121,144†
Population (census results)	
9 May 1984	
Males	1,374,452
Females	1,373,852
Total	2,748,304
Population (UN estimates at mid-year)‡	
1997	3,433,000
1998	3,577,000
1999	3,719,000
Density (per sq km) at mid-1999	30.7

* Including the Assab district.
† 46,774 sq miles.
‡ Source: UN, *World Population Prospects: The 1998 Revision.*

PRINCIPAL TOWN (estimated population at mid-1990)

Asmara (capital)	358,100

Source: UN, *Demographic Yearbook.*

BIRTHS AND DEATHS (UN estimates, averages per year)

	1980–85	1985–90	1990–95
Birth rate (per 1,000) . . .	45.2	44.7	43.1
Death rate (per 1,000) . . .	20.0	17.0	15.5

Expectation of life (UN estimates, years at birth, 1990–95): 49.6 (males 48.0; females 51.4).

Source: UN, *World Population Prospects: The 1998 Revision.*

Agriculture

PRINCIPAL CROPS ('000 metric tons)

	1997	1998	1999*
Wheat	6	23†	15
Barley	12	57†	40
Maize	6	29†	15
Millet	11	52†	30
Sorghum	59	268†	150
Potatoes.	42	45*	38
Other roots and tubers . .	85	85*	87
Pulses	49	55*	44
Groundnuts (in shell). . .	2	2†	2
Sesame seed	4	5†	4
Linseed	1	1*	1
Vegetables	30	32*	28
Fruits and berries . . .	5	6*	4

* FAO estimate(s).   † Unofficial figure.
Source: FAO.

LIVESTOCK ('000 head, year ending September)

	1997	1998	1999*
Cattle	1,450*	1,500†	1,550*
Sheep*	1,550	1,560	1,570
Goats*	1,600	1,650	1,700
Camels*	73	74	75
Poultry*	4,500	4,550	4,600

* FAO estimate(s).
† Unofficial figure.
Source: FAO.

LIVESTOCK PRODUCTS (FAO estimates, '000 metric tons)

	1997	1998	1999
Beef and veal*	11	12	13
Mutton and lamb* . . .	5	5	6
Goat meat*	5	5	6
Poultry meat	6	6	6
Cows' milk*	34	36	37
Goats' milk	8	8	9
Sheep's milk	4	4	4
Hen eggs	6	6	6
Wool: greasy*	1	1	1
Cattle hides	2	2	3
Sheepskins	1	1	1
Goatskins	1	1	1

* FAO estimates.
Source: FAO.

Fishing

(metric tons, live weight)

	1996	1997	1998
Sea catfishes	9	—	149
Groupers	141	95	117
Snappers	281	219	294
Grunts and sweetlips . . .	367	13	47
Emperors (Scavengers) . .	767	90	104
Barracudas	185	21	57
Carangids	815	13	184
Narrow-barred Spanish mackerel .	181	174	182
Tuna-like fishes	4	29	110
Total catch (incl. others) . .	3,212	978	1,576

Source: FAO, *Yearbook of Fishery Statistics.*

Finance

CURRENCY AND EXCHANGE RATES

Monetary Units
100 cents = 1 nakfa.

Sterling, Dollar and Euro Equivalents (30 November 2000)
£1 sterling = 13.50 nakfa;
US $1 = 9.50 nakfa;
€1 = 8.25 nakfa;
1,000 nakfa = £74.08 = $105.26 = €121.22.

Note: Following its secession from Ethiopia in May 1993, Eritrea retained the Ethiopian currency, the birr. An exchange rate of US $1 = 5.000 birr was introduced in October 1992 and remained in force until April 1994, when it was adjusted to $1 = 5.130 birr. Further adjustments were made subsequently. In addition to the official exchange rate, the Bank of Eritrea applied a marginal auction rate (determined at fortnightly auctions of foreign exchange, conducted by the National Bank of Ethiopia) to aid-funded imports and to most transactions in services. A more depreciated preferential rate applied to remittances of foreign exchange by Eritreans abroad, to proceeds from exports and to most payments for imports. On 1 April 1997 Eritrea unified the official and preferential exchange rates at $1 = 7.20 birr (which had been the preferential rate since January 1996). In November 1997 the Government introduced a separate national currency, the nakfa, replacing (and initially at par with) the Ethiopian birr. The exchange rate in relation to the US dollar was initially set at the prevailing unified rate, but from 1 May 1998 a mechanism to provide a market-related exchange rate was established.

BUDGET (million birr/nakfa)

Revenue*	1997	1998	1999†
Tax revenue	959.4	976.9	982.5
Direct taxes	447.9	512.3	474.9
Taxes on personal income .	117.2	128.0	132.5
Taxes on business profits . .	292.9	334.1	291.4
Rehabilitation tax . .	18.1	17.5	12.6
Domestic sales tax (incl. stamp duties)	212.8	198.5	243.3
Import duties and taxes . .	298.7	266.1	264.3
Port fees and charges . . .	444.3	99.7	104.7
Other current revenue . . .	619.1	499.5	361.8
Extraordinary revenue . . .	—	175.3	251.1
Capital revenue	20.0	149.1	122.7
Total	2,042.8	1,900.5	1,822.9

Expenditure	1996	1997	1998
Current expenditure	1,883.3	1,445.5	2,336.7
General services	1,233.1	886.0	1,776.3
Internal affairs . . .	74.7	56.6	21.1
Regional administration . .	40.6	55.5	161.8
Foreign affairs	77.1	84.5	88.4
Defence‡	968.1	634.2	1,458.8
Economic services	186.4	140.8	66.3
Agriculture and natural resources	15.4	32.8	36.0
Mining and energy . . .	5.5	4.0	3.3
Construction and urban development	61.8	9.7	3.0
Transport and communications	85.4	85.0	12.8
Social services	188.0	279.5	323.0
Education and training . .	70.7	139.3	159.2
Health	56.0	81.1	99.4
Demobilization of ex-combatants	14.0	—	—
Capital expenditure . . .	838.2	1,143.3	1,495.5
General services . . .	163.9	99.6	188.3
Economic development . .	471.4	709.7	1,056.5
Agriculture and natural resources	256.1	180.6	410.6
Trade, industry and tourism .	35.0	83.1	76.7
Construction, transport and communications	73.6	242.1	370.8
Social development . . .	202.9	334.0	250.7
Education	49.3	99.3	94.2
Health	87.7	55.0	72.8
Total	2,721.5	2,588.8	3,832.2

* Excluding grants received (million birr/nakfa): 290.5 in 1997 (current 32.7, capital 257.8); 458.4 in 1998 (current 32.4, capital 426.0); 376.7 (preliminary) in 1999 (current 125.5, capital 251.2).
† Provisional figures.
‡ Including some demobilization costs.

1999: Total expenditure (million birr/nakfa, provisional): 4,628.7 (current 2,644.3, capital 1,984.4).
Source: IMF, *Eritrea: Statistical Appendix* (April 2000).

MONEY SUPPLY (million birr/nakfa at 31 December)

	1996	1997	1998
Demand deposits at banks . .	1,670.9	1,597.9	1,808.7

Source: IMF, *Eritrea: Statistical Appendix* (April 2000).

COST OF LIVING*
(price index for Asmara at December; base: January 1992 = 100)

	1995	1996	1997
All items	141.3	146.1	161.5

* The index has been constructed using estimated weights for various categories of commodity prices, compiled by the Ministry of Trade and Industry.
Source: IMF, *Eritrea: Selected Issues* (September 1998).

NATIONAL ACCOUNTS (million birr/nakfa at current prices)
Gross Domestic Product by Economic Activity

	1997	1998	1999*
Agriculture, forestry and fishing .	390.3	734.9	853.6
Mining and quarrying . . .	4.5	3.8	4.7
Manufacturing†	656.0	644.7	741.2
Electricity and water	65.1	71.7	84.0
Construction	515.4	530.5	624.9
Wholesale and retail trade . .	1,134.1	991.2	1,139.4
Transport and communications .	488.9	472.1	542.7
Financial services	85.7	97.6	114.4
Dwellings and domestic services .	103.7	115.8	135.1
Public administration and services	706.8	844.2	1,014.4
Other services	50.8	56.8	66.5
GDP at factor cost . . .	4,201.4	4,563.4	5,320.7
Indirect taxes, *less* subsidies .	511.5	464.6	507.6
GDP in purchasers' values . .	4,712.9	5,028.0	5,828.3

* Preliminary figures.
† Including handicrafts and small-scale industry.

Source: IMF, *Eritrea: Statistical Appendix* (April 2000).

BALANCE OF PAYMENTS (US $ million)

	1997	1998	1999*
Exports of goods f.o.b. . . .	53.5	27.9	26.3
Imports of goods c.i.f. . . .	−494.6	−526.8	−506.9
Trade balance	−441.1	−498.9	−480.7
Exports of services	149.8	80.8	73.6
Imports of services	−94.4	−70.0	−55.2
Balance on goods and services	−385.7	−488.1	−462.3
Other income (net)	−3.4	4.4	3.4
Balance on goods, services and income	−389.1	−483.7	−458.9
Private unrequited transfers (net) .	352.1	245.4	240.2
Official unrequited transfers (net) .	51.4	62.9	51.9
Current balance	14.4	−175.4	−166.8
Direct investment (net) . . .	38.7	31.7	36.0
Official long-term capital (net) .	28.9	65.5	83.3
Portfolio investment (net) . . .	—	3.1	16.4
Short-term capital (net) . . . } Net errors and omissions . . . }	−142.7	−89.7	−39.1
Overall balance	−60.7	−164.8	8.0

* Preliminary figures.
Source: IMF, *Eritrea: Statistical Appendix* (April 2000).

External Trade

PRINCIPAL COMMODITIES (million birr/nakfa)

Imports c.i.f. (excl. petroleum)	1996	1997	1998
Food and live animals . . .	542.9	599.9	460.1
Crude materials (inedible) except fuels	116.5	67.7	43.7
Animal and vegetable oils, fats and waxes	55.0	57.6	71.3
Chemicals and related products .	209.7	182.8	152.2
Basic manufactures	733.8	678.5	642.4
Machinery and transport equipment	1,091.1	1,158.2	1,030.1
Miscellaneous manufactured articles	250.8	242.7	231.4
Total (incl. others)	3,062.8	3,062.0	2,693.0

Exports f.o.b.	1996	1997	1998
Food and live animals . . .	92.4	81.3	58.3
Beverages and tobacco . .	26.2	8.9	0.2
Crude materials (inedible) except fuels	123.0	129.5	89.6
Chemicals and related products .	13.4	8.2	4.1
Basic manufactures . . .	88.3	64.3	26.1
Machinery and transport equipment . . .	27.7	10.8	4.7
Miscellaneous manufactured articles	146.6	70.9	13.8
Total (incl. others) . . .	520.4	375.3	196.9

Source: IMF, *Eritrea: Statistical Appendix* (April 2000).

PRINCIPAL TRADING PARTNERS (million birr/nakfa)

Imports c.i.f. (excl. petroleum)	1996	1997	1998
Belgium.	84.1	26.8	47.3
Djibouti	78.6	79.0	57.3
Ethiopia.	261.8	274.6	25.0
Germany	217.0	168.4	152.7
Italy	429.1	420.1	469.8
Japan	111.2	125.5	107.1
Korea, Repub. . . .	126.0	—	118.4
Netherlands	49.4	51.2	60.1
Saudi Arabia . . .	465.6	480.2	15.4
Sudan	97.9	20.3	22.0
United Arab Emirates . .	365.9	402.0	436.8
United Kingdom . . .	68.5	142.1	120.5
USA	83.1	96.4	113.9
Total (incl. others) . . .	3,062.9	3,062.2	2,693.1

Exports f.o.b.	1996	1997	1998
Ethiopia.	342.4	238.1	52.2
Italy	22.3	18.3	10.4
Japan	—	—	26.0
Saudi Arabia . . .	20.0	7.3	2.3
Sudan	51.5	62.3	53.5
USA	39.9	3.2	4.0
Total (incl. others) . . .	520.4	375.3	196.9

Source: IMF, *Eritrea: Statistical Appendix* (April 2000).

Transport

ROAD TRAFFIC (motor vehicles in use)

	1996	1997	1998
Number of registered vehicles. .	27,013	31,276	35,942

SHIPPING
Merchant Fleet (registered at 31 December)

	1996	1997	1998
Number of vessels . . .	4	6	7
Displacement (grt) . . .	830	6,777	7,335

Source: Lloyd's Register of Shipping, *World Fleet Statistics*.

CIVIL AVIATION

	1996	1997	1998
Passengers ('000)	168.1	173.8	105.2

Tourism

ARRIVALS BY NATIONALITY

	1996	1997	1998
Ethiopia.	248,814	275,534	117,087
Total (incl. others) . . .	416,596	409,544	187,647

Tourism receipts (US $ million): 69 in 1996.
Source: World Tourism Organization, *Yearbook of Tourism Statistics*.

Communications Media

	1995	1996	1997
Radio receivers ('000 in use) . .	310	330	345
Television receivers ('000 in use) .	1	1	1
Telephones ('000 main lines in use)	17	19	21
Telefax stations (number in use) .	777	1,101	1,388

Book production (1993): 106 titles (including 23 pamphlets) and 420,000 copies (including 60,000 pamphlets). Figures for books, excluding pamphlets, refer only to school textbooks (64 titles; 323,000 copies) and government publications (19 titles; 37,000 copies).
Telephones ('000 main lines in use): 24 in 1998.
Sources: mainly UNESCO, *Statistical Yearbook*; UN, *Statistical Yearbook*.

Education

(1996/97)

	Institutions	Teachers	Pupils
Pre-primary	61	207	7,443
Primary	549	5,476	240,737
Secondary:			
General	n.a.	1,959	88,054
Teacher-training . . .	n.a.	33	359
Vocational	n.a.	79	674
University and equivalent level* .	n.a.	198	3,096

* Figures refer to 1997/98.
Source: UNESCO, *Statistical Yearbook*.

Directory

The Constitution

On 23 May 1997 the Constituent Assembly unanimously adopted the Eritrean Constitution. A presidential regime was instituted, with the President to be elected for a maximum of two five-year terms. The President, as Head of State, has extensive powers and appoints, with the approval of the National Assembly (the Legislature), the ministers, the commissioners, the Auditor-General, the president of the central bank and the judges of the Supreme Court. The President's mandate can be revoked if two-thirds of the members of the National Assembly so demand. 'Conditional' political pluralism is authorized. Pending the election of a new National Assembly, legislative power was to be held by a Transitional National Assembly, comprising the 75 members of the PFDJ Central Committee, 60 members of the former Constituent Assembly and 15 representatives of Eritreans residing abroad.

The Government

HEAD OF STATE

President: ISSAIAS AFEWERKI (assumed power May 1991; elected President by National Assembly 8 June 1993).

CABINET
(April 2001)

President: ISSAIAS AFEWERKI.
Minister of Defence: Gen. SEBHAT EPHREM.
Minister of Justice: FAWZIA HASHIM.
Minister of Foreign Affairs: ALI SAYYID ABDULLAH.
Minister of Information: BARAKI GEBRESELASSIE.
Minister of Finance: GEBRESELASSIE YOSIEF.
Minister of Trade and Industry: HAILE WOLDETENSAE.
Minister of Agriculture: AREFAINE BERHE.
Minister of Local Government: MAHMOUD AHMED SHERIFO.
Minister of Labour and Human Welfare: ASKALU MENKERIOS.
Minister of Fisheries: PETROS SOLOMON.
Minister of Construction: ABRAHA ASFAHA.
Minister of Energy and Mines: TESFAI GEBRESELASSIE.
Minister of Education: OSMAN SALIH MUHAMMAD.
Minister of Health: Dr SALIH MEKKI.
Minister of Transport and Communications: SALEH KEKIA.
Minister of Tourism: AHMED HAJI ALI.
Minister of Land, Water and the Environment: TESFAI GHIRMAZION.

MINISTRIES AND COMMISSIONS

Office of the President: POB 257, Asmara; tel. (1) 119701; fax (1) 125123.
Ministry of Agriculture: POB 1048, Asmara; tel. (1) 181499; fax (1) 181415.
Ministry of Construction: POB 841, Asmara; tel. (1) 119077; fax (1) 120661.
Ministry of Defence: POB 629, Asmara; tel. (1) 115493; fax (1) 124920.
Ministry of Education: POB 5610, Asmara; tel. (1) 113044; fax (1) 113866.
Ministry of Energy and Mines: POB 5285, Asmara; tel. (1) 116872; fax (1) 127652.
Ministry of Finance: POB 896, Asmara; tel. (1) 118131; fax (1) 127947.
Ministry of Fisheries: POB 923, Asmara; tel. (1) 114271; fax (1) 112185.
Ministry of Foreign Affairs: POB 190, Asmara; tel. (1) 127838; fax (1) 123788; e-mail tesfai@wg.eol.
Ministry of Health: POB 212, Asmara; tel. (1) 117549; fax (1) 112899.
Ministry of Information: POB 242, Asmara; tel. (1) 117111; fax (1) 124647.
Ministry of Justice: POB 241, Asmara; tel. (1) 127739; fax (1) 126422.
Ministry of Labour and Human Welfare: POB 5252, Asmara; tel. (1) 181846; fax (1) 181649; e-mail mlhw@eol.com.er.

Ministry of Land, Water and the Environment: POB 976, Asmara; tel (1) 118021; fax (1) 123285.
Ministry of Local Government: POB 225, Asmara; tel. (1) 127734.
Ministry of Tourism: POB 1010, Asmara; tel. (1) 126997; fax (1) 126949; e-mail ona@eol.com.er.
Ministry of Trade and Industry: POB 1844, Asmara; tel. (1) 118386; fax (1) 110586.
Ministry of Transport and Communications: POB 6465, Asmara; tel. (1) 114307; fax (1) 127048; e-mail motc_rez@eol.com.er.
Eritrean Relief and Refugee Commission: POB 1098, Asmara; tel. (1) 182222; fax (1) 182970; e-mail john@errec.er.punchdown.org.
Land and Housing Commission: POB 348, Asmara; tel. (1) 117400.

Provincial Administrators

There are six administrative regions in Eritrea, each with regional, sub-regional and village administrations.

Anseba Province: ALAMIN SHEIKH SALIH.
Debub Province: MESFIN HAGOS.
Debubawi Keyih Bahri Province: ABDELLA ADEM.
Gash-Barka Province: MUSTAFA NUR HUSSEIN.
Maakel Province: WELDENKIEL ABRAHA.
Semenawi Keyih Bahri Province: IBRAHIM IDRIS TOTIL.

Legislature

NATIONAL ASSEMBLY

In accordance with transitional arrangements formulated in Decree No. 37 of May 1993, the National Assembly consists of the Central Committee of the People's Front for Democracy and Justice (PFDJ) and 60 other members: 30 from the Provincial Assemblies and an additional 30 members, including a minimum of 10 women, to be nominated by the PFDJ Central Committee. The legislative body 'outlines the internal and external policies of the government, regulates their implementation, approves the budget and elects a president for the country'. The National Assembly is to hold regular sessions every six months under the chairmanship of the President. In his role as Head of the Government and Commander-in-Chief of the Army, the President nominates individuals to head the various government departments. These nominations are ratified by the legislative body. In March 1994 the National Assembly voted to alter its composition: it would henceforth comprise the 75 members of the Central Committee of the PFDJ and 75 directly elected members. In May 1997, following the adoption of the Constitution, the Constituent Assembly empowered a Transitional National Assembly (comprising the 75 members of the PFDJ, 60 members of the former Constituent Assembly and 15 representatives of Eritreans residing abroad) to act as the legislature until elections were held for a new National Assembly.

Chairman of the Transitional National Assembly: ISSAIAS AFEWERKI.

Political Organizations

At independence in May 1993, many of the rival political organizations to the Eritrean People's Liberation Front (now the People's Front for Democracy and Justice) declared their support for the transitional Government.

Democratic Movement for the Liberation of Eritrea: opposition group; Leader HAMID TURKY.
Eritrean Islamic Jihad (EIJ): radical opposition group; in Aug. 1993 split into a mil. wing and a political wing, led by Sheikh MOHAMED ARAFA.
Eritrean Liberation Front (ELF): f. 1958; commenced armed struggle against Ethiopia in 1961; subsequently split into numerous factions (see below); mainly Muslim support; opposes the PFDJ; principal factions:

Eritrean Liberation Front–Central Command (ELF–CC): f. 1982; Chair. ABDALLAH IDRISS.
Eritrean Liberation Front–National Council (ELF–NC): Leader HASSAN ALI ASSAD.
Eritrean Liberation Front–Revolutionary Council (ELF–RC): Leader IBRAHIM MOHAMED ALI.

People's Front for Democracy and Justice (PFDJ): POB 1081, Asmara; tel. (1) 121399; fax (1) 120848; f. 1970 as the Eritrean Popular Liberation Forces, following a split in the Eritrean Liberation Front; renamed the Eritrean People's Liberation Front in 1977; adopted present name in Feb. 1994; Christian and Muslim support; in May 1991 took control of Eritrea and formed provisional Govt; formed transitional Govt in May 1993; Chair. ISSAIAS AFEWERKI; Sec.-Gen. ALAMIN MOHAMED SAID.

Red Sea Afar Democratic Organization: Afar opposition group; Sec.-Gen. AMIN AHMMAD.

Diplomatic Representation

EMBASSIES IN ERITREA

China, People's Republic: 16 Ogaden St, POB 204, Asmara; tel. (1) 185271; fax (1) 185275; Ambassador: SHI YONGJIU.

Denmark: Ras Dashan St 11, POB 6300, Asmara; tel. (1) 124346; fax (1) 124343; e-mail dkemb@eol.com.er; Chargé d'affaires a.i.: PETER TRUELSEN.

Djibouti: POB 5589, Asmara; tel. (1) 354961; fax (1) 351831; Ambassador: AHMAD ISSA.

Egypt: POB 5577, Asmara; tel. (1) 123603; fax (1) 123294; Ambassador: Dr RIFAT AL-ANSARI.

Ethiopia: Franklin D. Roosevelt St, POB 5688, Asmara; tel. (1) 116365; fax (1) 116144; Ambassador: AWALOM WOLDU (recalled May 1998).

France: POB 209, Asmara; tel. (1) 126599; fax (1) 121036; e-mail af@gemel.com.er; Ambassador: LOUIS LE VERT.

Germany: 24 Ogaden Ave, POB 5589, Asmara; tel. (1) 182670; fax (1) 182900; Ambassador: ELMAR TIMPE.

Israel: POB 5600, Asmara; tel. (1) 185626; fax (1) 185550; e-mail isremb@eol.com.er; Ambassador: URI SAVIR.

Italy: POB 220, Asmara; tel. (1) 120160; fax (1) 121115; e-mail iea@eol.com.er; Ambassador: ANTONIO BANDINI.

Libya: Asmara.

Russia: POB 5667, Asmara; tel. (1) 127172; fax (1) 182033; Ambassador: ALEKSANDR OBLOV.

Saudi Arabia: POB 5599, Asmara; tel. (1) 120171; fax (1) 121027; Ambassador: ABDUL R. IBRAHIM AT-TOELMI.

Sudan: Asmara.

USA: Franklin D. Roosevelt St, POB 211, Asmara; tel. (1) 120004; fax (1) 127584; Ambassador: WILLIAM D. CLARKE.

Yemen: POB 5566, Asmara; tel. (1) 114434; fax (1) 117921; Ambassador: Dr AKRAM ABD AL-MARIK AL-QABRI.

Judicial System

The judicial system operates on the basis of transitional laws which incorporate pre-independence laws of the Eritrean People's Liberation Front, revised Ethiopian laws, customary laws and post-independence enacted laws. The independence of the judiciary in the discharge of its functions is unequivocally stated in Decree No. 37, which defines the powers and duties of the Government. It is subject only to the law and to no other authority. At present, the court structure is composed of first instance sub-zonal courts, appellate and first instance zonal courts, appellate and first instance high courts and a panel of high court judges, presided over by the president of the high court, as a court of last resort. With the implementation of the 1997 ratified Constitution, a supreme court will be established, whose judges will be appointed by the President of the State, subject to confirmation by the National Assembly.

High Court: POB 241, Asmara; tel. (1) 115210.

Religion

Eritrea is almost equally divided between Muslims and Christians. Most Christians are adherents of the Orthodox Church, although there are Protestant and Roman Catholic communities. A small number of the population follow traditional beliefs.

CHRISTIANITY

The Eritrean Orthodox Church

In September 1993 the separation of the Eritrean Orthodox Church from the Ethiopian Orthodox Church was agreed by the respective church leaderships. The Eritrean Orthodox Church announced that it was to create a diocese of each of the country's then 10 provinces. The first five bishops of the Eritrean Orthodox Church were consecrated in Cairo in September 1994. In May 1998 Eritrea's first Patriarch (Abune) was consecrated in Asmara.

Patriarch (Abune): Archbishop PHILIPPOS.

The Roman Catholic Church

At 31 December 1998 there were an estimated 133,192 adherents in the country.

Bishop of Asmara: Rt Rev. ZEKARIAS YOHANNES, 19 Gonder St, POB 244, Asmara; tel. (1) 120206; fax (1) 126519.

Bishop of Barentu: Rt Rev. LUCA MILESI, POB 9, Barentu; tel. (1) 120631; fax (1) 122322.

Bishop of Keren: Rt Rev. TESFAMARIAM BEDHO, POB 460, Keren; tel. (1) 401907; fax (1) 401604; e-mail cek@gemel.com.er.

The Anglican Communion

Within the Episcopal Church in Jerusalem and the Middle East, Eritrea lies within the jurisdiction of the Bishop in Egypt.

Leader: ASFAHA MAHARY.

ISLAM

Eritrea's main Muslim communities are concentrated in the western lowlands, the northern highlands and the eastern coastal region.

Leader: Sheikh AL-AMIN OSMAN AL-AMIN.

The Press

Chamber News: POB 856, Asmara; tel. (1) 120045; fax (1) 120138; monthly; Tigrinya, Arabic and English; publ. by Asmara Chamber of Commerce.

Eritrea Profile: POB 247, Asmara; f. 1994; weekly; English; publ. by the Ministry of Information and Culture.

Hadas Eritra (New Eritrea): Asmara; f. 1991; three times a week; in English, Tigrinya and Arabic; govt publ.; Editor YITBAREK ZEROM; circ. 25,000.

Newsletter: POB 856, Asmara; tel. (1) 120045; fax (1) 120138; e-mail encc@aol.com.er; monthly; Tigrinya, Arabic and English; publ. by Eritrean National Chamber of Commerce; Editor MUHAMMED-SFAF HAMMED.

Trade and Development Bulletin: POB 856, Asmara; tel. (1) 121388; fax (1) 120138; monthly; Tigrinya, Arabic and English; publ. by Asmara Chamber of Commerce; Editor TAAME FOTO.

Broadcasting and Communications

Ministry of Transport and Communications (Communications Department): POB 4918, Asmara; tel. (1) 115847; fax (1) 126966; e-mail motc_rez@eol.com.er; Dir-Gen. ESTIFANOS AFEWERKI.

TELECOMMUNICATIONS

Telecommunications Services of Eritrea: 11 Semaetat St, POB 234, Asmara; tel. (1) 117547; fax (1) 120938; f. 1991; Gen. Man. GOITOM OGBAZGHI.

BROADCASTING

Radio

Voice of the Broad Masses of Eritrea (Dimseehafash): POB 242, Asmara; tel. (1) 117111; fax (1) 124847; govt-controlled; programmes in Arabic, Tigrinya, Tigre, Saho, Oromifa, Amharic, Afar and Kunama; Dir-Gen. MAHMUD CHIRUM.

Television

ERI-TV: Asmara; f. 1992; govt station providing educational, tech. and information service; broadcasting began in 1993 in Arabic, Tigre and Tigrinya; transmissions limited to Asmara and surrounding areas.

Finance

(cap. = capital; dep. = deposits; m. = million; brs = branches; amounts in Ethiopian birr)

In November 1997 Eritrea adopted the nakfa as its unit of currency, replacing the Ethiopian birr, which had been Eritrea's monetary unit since independence.

BANKING

Central Bank

Bank of Eritrea: POB 849, 21 Victory Ave, Asmara; tel. (1) 123036; fax (1) 123162; e-mail tekieb@boe.gov.er; f. 1993; bank of issue; Gov. TEKIE BEYENE.

Other Banks

Commercial Bank of Eritrea: POB 219, Asmara; tel. (1) 121844; fax (1) 124887; f. 1991; dep. 5,100m. (Dec. 1996); Gen. Man. YAMANE TESFAI; 15 brs.

Eritrean Development and Investment Bank: POB 1266, Asmara; tel. (1) 123787; f. 1996; cap. 45m.; provides medium- to long-term credit; 13 brs.

Housing and Commerce Bank of Eritrea: POB 235, Asmara; tel. (1) 120350; fax (1) 120401; e-mail hcb@gemel.com.er; f. 1994; cap. 33m., total assets 1,008m. (Dec. 1998); finances residential and commercial construction projects and commercial loans; CEO Dr ARAIA TSEGGAI; 7 brs.

INSURANCE

National Insurance Corporation of Eritrea (NICE): NICE Bldg, POB 881, Asmara; tel. (1) 123000; fax (1) 123240; e-mail nice@eol.com.er; Gen. Man. ZERU WOLDEMICHAEL.

Trade and Industry

CHAMBER OF COMMERCE

Eritrean National Chamber of Commerce: POB 856, Asmara; tel. (1) 121388; fax (1) 120138; e-mail encc@aol.com.er.

TRADE ASSOCIATION

Red Sea Trading Corporation: 29/31 Ras Alula St, POB 332, Asmara; tel. (1) 127846; fax (1) 124353; f. 1983; import and export services; operated by the PFDJ; Gen. Man. KUBROM DAFLA.

UTILITIES
Electricity

Eritrean Electricity Authority (EEA): POB 911, Asmara; fax (1) 121468; e-mail eeahrg@eol.com.er.

Water

Dept of Water Resources: Asmara; tel. (1) 119636; fax (1) 124625.

Transport

Eritrea's transport infrastructure was severely damaged during the three decades of war prior to independence. International creditors have since provided loans for the repair and reconstruction of the road network and for the improvement of port facilities.

RAILWAYS

The 306-km railway connection between Agordat, Asmara and the port of Massawa was severely damaged during the war of independence and ceased operation in 1975. In 1999 an 81-km section of the Asmara–Massawa line (between Massawa and Embatkala) became operational; the 36-km railway connection between Embatkala and Asmara was under rehabilitation.

Eritrean Railway: POB 6081, Asmara; tel. (1) 123365; fax (1) 201785; Co-ordinator, Railways Rehabilitation Project AMANUEL GEBRESELLASIE.

ROADS

In 1997 there were approximately 3,900 km of roads in Eritrea, of which some 900 km were paved. Roads that are paved require considerable repair, as do many of the bridges across seasonal water courses destroyed in the war. Road construction between Asmara and the port of Massawa was given particular priority in the Recovery and Rehabilitation Programme.

SHIPPING

Eritrea has two major seaports: Massawa, which sustained heavy war damage in 1990, and Assab, which has principally served Addis Ababa, in Ethiopia. Under an accord signed between the Ethiopian and Eritrean Governments in 1993, the two countries agreed to share the facilities of both ports. Since independence, activity in Massawa has increased substantially; however, activity at Assab declined following the outbreak of hostilities with Ethiopia in May 1998. In 1998 a total of 463 vessels docked at Massawa, handling 1.2m. metric tons of goods; 322 vessels docked at Assab, which handled 1.0m. tons of goods.

Dept of Maritime Transport: POB 679, Asmara; tel. (1) 121317; fax (1) 121316; e-mail motc_rez@eol.com.er; Dir-Gen. IBRAHIM SAÏD IDRIS.

Port and Maritime Transport Authority: POB 851, Asmara; tel. (1) 111399; fax (1) 113647; Dir WELDE MIKAEL ABRAHAM.

Eritrean Shipping Lines: 80 Semaetat Ave, POB 1110, Asmara; tel. (1) 120359; fax (1) 120331; f. 1992; provides shipping services in Red Sea and Persian (Arabian) Gulf areas and owns and operates four cargo ships; Gen. Man. TEWELDE KELATI.

CIVIL AVIATION

The international airport is at Asmara.

Civil Aviation Department: POB 252, Asmara; tel. (1) 124335; fax (1) 124334; e-mail motc_rez@eol.com.er; handles freight and passenger traffic for eight scheduled carriers which use Asmara airport; Dir-Gen. PAULOS KAHSAY.

Eritrean Airlines: POB 222, Asmara; tel. (1) 181822; fax (1) 181255; Man. Dir ABRAHA GHIRMAZION.

Tourism

The Ministry of Tourism is overseeing the development of this sector, although its advance since independence has been inhibited by the country's war-damaged transport infrastructure, and by subsequent conflicts with Ethiopia and other regional tensions. Eritrea possesses many areas of scenic and scientific interest, including the Dahlak Islands (a coralline archipelago rich in marine life), off shore from Massawa, and the massive escarpment rising up from the coastal plain and supporting a unique ecosystem. In 1998 tourist arrivals in Eritrea totalled 187,647, compared with 409,544 in 1997; in 1996 tourism receipts amounted to US $69m.

Eritrean Tourism Service Corporation: Asmara; operates govt-owned hotels.

ESTONIA

Introductory Survey

Location, Climate, Language, Religion, Flag, Capital

The Republic of Estonia (formerly the Estonian Soviet Socialist Republic) is situated in north-eastern Europe. The country is bordered to the south by Latvia, and to the east by the Russian Federation. Estonia's northern coastline is on the Gulf of Finland and its territory includes more than 1,520 islands, mainly off its western coastline in the Gulf of Rīga and the Baltic Sea. The largest of the islands are Saaremaa and Hiiumaa, in the Gulf of Rīga. The climate is influenced by Estonia's position between the Eurasian land mass and the Baltic Sea and the North Atlantic Ocean. The mean January temperature in Tallinn is –0.6°C (30.9°F); in July the mean temperature is 17.1°C (62.8°F). Average annual precipitation is 568 mm. The official language is Estonian, which is a member of the Baltic-Finnic group of the Finno-Ugric languages; it is written in the Latin script and is closely related to Finnish. Many of the Russian residents, who comprise nearly 30% of the total population, do not speak Estonian. Most of the population profess Christianity and, by tradition, Estonians belong to the Evangelical Lutheran Church. Smaller Protestant sects and the Eastern Orthodox Church are also represented. The national flag (proportions 11 by seven) consists of three equal horizontal stripes, of blue, black and white. The capital is Tallinn.

Recent History

The Russian annexation of Estonia, formerly under Swedish rule, was formalized in 1721. During the latter half of the 19th century, as the powers of the dominant Baltic German nobility declined, Estonians experienced a national cultural revival, which culminated in political demands for autonomy during the 1905 Russian Revolution, and for full independence after the beginning of the First World War. On 30 March 1917 the Provisional Government in Petrograd (St Petersburg), which had taken power after the abdication of Tsar Nicholas II in February, approved autonomy for Estonia. A Land Council was elected as the country's representative body. However, in October the Bolsheviks staged a coup in Tallinn, and declared the Estonian Soviet Executive Committee as the sole government of Estonia. As German forces advanced towards Estonia, in early 1918, the Bolshevik troops were forced to leave. The major Estonian political parties united to form the Estonian Salvation Committee, and on 24 February an independent Republic of Estonia was proclaimed. A Provisional Government, headed by Konstantin Päts, was formed, but Germany refused to recognize Estonia's independence and the country was occupied by German troops until the end of the First World War. Following the capitulation of Germany in November, the Provisional Government assumed power. After a period of armed conflict between Soviet and Estonian troops, the Republic of Estonia and Soviet Russia signed the Treaty of Tartu on 2 February 1920, under the terms of which the Soviet Government recognized Estonia's independence and renounced any rights to its territory. Estonian independence was recognized by the major Western powers in January 1921, and Estonia was admitted to the League of Nations.

This period of independence lasted until 1940. During most of this time the country had a liberal-democratic political system, in which the Riigikogu (State Assembly) was the dominant political force. Significant social, cultural and economic advances were made in the 1920s, including radical land reform. However, the decline in trade with Russia and the economic depression of the 1930s, combined with the political problems of a divided parliament, caused public dissatisfaction. In March 1934 Prime Minister Päts seized power in a bloodless coup and introduced a period of authoritarian rule. The Riigikogu and political parties were disbanded, but in 1938 a new Constitution was adopted, which provided for a presidential system of government, with a bicameral legislature. In April 1938 Päts was elected President.

In August 1939 the USSR and Germany signed a non-aggression treaty (the Nazi-Soviet or Molotov-Ribbentrop Pact). The 'Secret Protocols' to the treaty provided for the occupation of Estonia by the USSR. In September Estonia was forced to sign an agreement that permitted the USSR to base Soviet troops in Estonia. In June 1940 the Government, in accordance with a Soviet ultimatum, resigned, and a new administration was appointed by the Soviet authorities, with Johannes Vares-Barbarus as Prime Minister. In July elections were held, in which only candidates approved by the Soviet authorities were permitted to participate. On 21 July the Estonian Soviet Socialist Republic was proclaimed by the new legislature, and on 6 August the republic was formally incorporated into the USSR.

Soviet rule in Estonia lasted less than one year, before German forces occupied the country. In that short period, Soviet policy resulted in mass deportations of Estonians to Siberia, the expropriation of property, severe restrictions on cultural life and the introduction of Soviet-style government in the republic.

German forces entered Estonia in July 1941 and remained in occupation until September 1944. After a short-lived attempt to reinstate Estonian independence, Soviet troops occupied the whole of the country, and the process of 'sovietization' was continued. By the end of 1949 most Estonian farmers had been forced to join collective farms. Heavy industry was expanded, with investment concentrated on electricity generation and the chemical sector. Structural change in the economy was accompanied by increased political repression, with deportations of Estonians continuing until the death of Stalin (Iosif V. Dzhugashvili), in 1953. The most overt form of opposition to Soviet rule was provided by the 'forest brethren' (metsavennad), a guerrilla movement, which continued to conduct armed operations against Soviet personnel and institutions until the mid-1950s. In the late 1960s, as in other Soviet republics, more traditional forms of dissent appeared, concentrating on cultural issues, provoked by the increasing domination of the republic by immigrant Russians and other Slavs.

During the late 1970s and the 1980s the issues of 'russification' and environmental degradation became subjects of intense debate in Estonia. The policy of glasnost, introduced by the Soviet leader, Mikhail Gorbachev, in 1986, allowed such discussion to spread beyond dissident groups. The first major demonstrations of the 1980s were organized in protest against plans to increase open-cast phosphorite mining in north-eastern Estonia. Public opposition to the plans caused the Soviet Government to reconsider its proposals, and this success prompted further protests. In August 1987 a demonstration, attended by some 2,000 people, commemorated the anniversary of the signing of the Nazi-Soviet Pact. Following the demonstration, an Estonian Group for the Publication of the Molotov-Ribbentrop Pact (MRP-AEG) was formed. During 1988 the Nazi-Soviet Pact was duly published, and the MRP-AEG re-formed as the Estonian National Independence Party (ENIP), proclaiming the restoration of Estonian independence as its political objective. Another opposition group, the Estonian Popular Front (EPF), which had been established in April, was formally constituted at its first congress, in October, and included many members of the ruling Communist Party of Estonia (CPE). The EPF was more cautious than the ENIP in its approach, advocating the transformation of the USSR into a confederal system; the CPE was forced to adapt its policies to retain a measure of public support. On 16 November the Estonian Supreme Soviet (legislature) adopted a declaration of sovereignty, which included the right to annul all-Union (USSR) legislation. The Presidium of the USSR Supreme Soviet declared the sovereignty legislation unconstitutional, but the Estonian Supreme Soviet affirmed its decision in December.

The adoption of Estonian as the state language was accepted by the Supreme Soviet in January 1989, and the tricolor of independent Estonia was reinstated as the official flag. Despite the successes of the opposition, differing political tactics were employed by the radical ENIP and the EPF. The ENIP refused to nominate candidates for elections to the all-Union Congress of People's Deputies in March. Instead, the ENIP leadership announced plans for the registration by citizens' committees of all citizens of the pre-1940 Republic of Estonia and their descendants. Voters on an electoral register, thus compiled, would elect a Congress of Estonia as the legal successor to the pre-1940 Estonian legislature. The EPF, however, participated in the elections to the Congress of People's Deputies and won 27 of the 36 contested seats. Five seats were won by the International Movement, a political group composed predominantly of Russian immigrants, which was established in July 1988 to oppose the growing influence of the Estonian opposition movements in the republic.

In October 1989 delegates at the second congress of the EPF, influenced by the growing popularity of the ENIP and the citizens' committees, voted to adopt the restoration of Estonian independence as official policy. In November the Estonian Supreme Soviet voted to annul the 1940 decision of its predecessor to enter the USSR, declaring that the decision had been reached under coercion from Soviet armed forces.

On 2 February 1990 a mass rally was held to commemorate the anniversary of the 1920 Treaty of Tartu. Deputies attending the rally later met to approve a declaration urging the USSR Supreme Soviet to begin negotiations on restoring Estonia's independence. On 22 February the Estonian Supreme Soviet approved the declaration, and on the following day it voted to abolish the constitutional guarantee of power enjoyed by the CPE. This formal decision permitted largely free elections to take place to the Estonian Soviet in March. The EPF won 43 of the 105 seats, and 35 were won by the Association for a Free Estonia and other pro-independence groups. The remainder were won by members of the International Movement. Candidates belonging to the CPE, which was represented in all these groups, won 55 seats.

At the first session of the new legislature, Arnold Rüütel, previously Chairman of the Presidium of the Supreme Soviet, was elected to the new post of Chairman of the Supreme Soviet, in which was vested those state powers that had been the preserve of the First Secretary of the CPE. On 30 March 1990 the Supreme Soviet adopted a declaration that proclaimed the beginning of a transitional period towards independence and denied the validity of Soviet power in the republic.

In late February and early March 1990 some 580,000 people took part in elections to the rival parliament to the Supreme Soviet, the Congress of Estonia. The Congress convened on 11–12 March and declared itself the constitutional representative of the Estonian people. The participants adopted resolutions demanding the restoration of Estonian independence and the withdrawal of Soviet troops from Estonia.

In early April 1990 the Supreme Soviet elected Edgar Savisaar, a leader of the EPF, as Prime Minister and on 8 May it voted to restore the first five articles of the 1938 Constitution, which described Estonia's independent status. The formal name of pre-1940 Estonia, the Republic of Estonia, was also restored, as were the state emblems, flag and anthem. On 16 May a transitional system of government was approved.

Although formal economic sanctions were not imposed on Estonia (as was the case with Lithuania), relations with the Soviet authorities were severely strained. In mid-May 1990 President Gorbachev annulled the republic's declaration of independence, declaring that it violated the USSR Constitution. The Estonian leadership's request for negotiations on the status of the republic was refused by Gorbachev, who insisted that the independence declaration be rescinded before negotiations could begin. There was also opposition within the republic, mostly from ethnic Russians affiliated to the International Movement.

When troops of the USSR's Ministry of Internal Affairs attempted military intervention in Latvia and Lithuania in January 1991, the Estonian leadership anticipated similar confrontation. Barricades and makeshift defences were erected, but no military action was taken. However, events in the other Baltic republics intensified popular distrust of Estonian involvement in a new union, which was being negotiated by other Soviet republics. Consequently, Estonia refused to participate in a referendum on the future of the USSR, which took place in nine of the republics in March 1991. The Estonian authorities had conducted a poll on the issue of independence earlier in the same month. According to the official results, 82.9% of the registered electorate took part, of which 77.8% voted in favour of Estonian independence.

When the State Committee for the State of Emergency announced that it had seized power in the USSR on 19 August 1991, Estonia, together with the other Baltic republics, expected military intervention to overthrow the pro-independence governments. Gen. Fyodor Kuzmin, the Soviet commander of the Baltic military district, informed Arnold Rüütel, the Chairman of the Supreme Council (as the legislature was now known), that he was taking full control of People's. Military vehicles

entered Tallinn on 20 August, and troops occupied the city's television station. However, the military command did not prevent a session of the Estonian Supreme Council from convening on the same day. Deputies adopted a resolution declaring the full and immediate independence of Estonia, thus ending the transitional period that had begun in March 1990. Plans were also announced for the formation of a government-in-exile, should the Government and the Supreme Council be disbanded by Soviet troops.

After it became evident, on 22 August 1991, that the Soviet coup had collapsed, the Government began to take measures against persons who had allegedly supported the coup. The anti-Government movements, the International Movement and the United Council of Work Collectives were banned, as was the Communist Party of the Soviet Union. Several directors of Soviet enterprises were dismissed, and the Committee of State Security (KGB) was ordered to terminate its activities in Estonia.

As the Estonian Government moved to assert its authority over former Soviet institutions, other countries quickly began to recognize its independence. On 6 September the USSR State Council finally recognized the re-establishment of Estonian independence. Later in the month Estonia, together with the other Baltic states, was admitted to the UN as well as to the Conference on Security and Co-operation in Europe (CSCE, renamed the Organization for Security and Co-operation in Europe—OSCE—in December 1994). During the remainder of 1991 Estonia re-established diplomatic relations with most major states and was offered membership of leading international organizations. In internal politics there was hope for a cessation of conflict between the radical Congress of Estonia and the Supreme Council, with the establishment of a Constitutional Assembly, composed of equal numbers of delegates from each body, which was to draft a new constitution.

In January 1992, following a series of disputes with the Supreme Council concerning economic management, the issue of citizenship and the Government's failure to persuade the legislature to impose an economic state of emergency, Savisaar resigned as Prime Minister and was replaced by the erstwhile Minister of Transport, Tiit Vähi. A new Council of Ministers, which included seven ministers from the previous Government, was approved by the Supreme Council at the end of the month.

The draft Constitution that had been prepared by the Constitutional Assembly was approved by an overwhelming majority of the electorate (some 91%) in a referendum held in late June 1992. Under the recently adopted Citizenship Law, only citizens of pre-1940 Estonia and their descendants, or those who had successfully applied for citizenship, were entitled to vote. This ruling drew strong criticism from Russian leaders, concerned that the rights of the large Russian minority in Estonia, most of whom had not been granted citizenship and who were thus disenfranchised, were being violated. The new Constitution, which entered into force in early July 1992, provided for a parliamentary system of government, with a strong presidency. A new legislature, the Riigikogu, was to replace the Supreme Council (and the Congress of Estonia), and an election to the new body were to be held in September. A direct presidential election was to take place simultaneously (although subsequent presidents would be elected by the Riigikogu).

Legislative and presidential elections were duly held on 20 September 1992, with the participation of some 67% of the electorate. The country's Russian and other ethnic minorities, who now represented 42% of the total population, were again barred from voting (with the exception of those whose applications for citizenship had been granted). The election to the 101-seat Riigikogu was contested by a total of 633 candidates, representing some 40 parties and movements, largely grouped into eight coalitions. The nationalist alliance Isamaa (Pro Patria, or Fatherland) emerged with the largest number of seats (29). The centrist Popular Front alliance (led by the EPF) won an unexpectedly low total of 15 seats. The Secure Home alliance, which comprised some former Communists, obtained 17 seats. The Moderates electoral alliance obtained 12 seats and the ENIP, which was not part of a coalition, won 10 seats. None of the four candidates in the presidential election won an overall majority of the votes. It thus fell to the Riigikogu to choose from the two most successful candidates, Arnold Rüütel, now a leading member of the Secure Home alliance, and Lennart Meri, a former Minister of Foreign Affairs, who was supported by Isamaa. In early October the Isamaa-dominated Riigikogu elected Meri to be Estonia's President, by 59 votes to 31.

A new coalition Government, with a large representation of Isamaa members, as well as members of the Moderates and the ENIP, was announced in mid-October 1992. Earlier in the month Mart Laar, a 32-year-old historian and the leader of Isamaa, had been chosen as Prime Minister. Laar indicated that the principal objectives of his administration would be to negotiate the withdrawal of all Russian troops remaining in Estonia, as well as to accelerate the country's privatization programme. In late November four of the five constituent parties of the Isamaa alliance united to form the National Fatherland Party (NFP), with Laar as its Chairman. In the same month the CPE was renamed the Estonian Democratic Labour Party.

The NFP suffered a considerable loss of support at local elections held in October 1993. In Tallinn the Party secured only five of the 64 seats on the city council. In the following month Laar survived a vote of 'no confidence', proposed to the Riigikogu by opposition deputies, who accused the Prime Minister of incompetence and 'strategic errors in foreign affairs'. In January 1994 Laar reshuffled four key portfolios in the Council of Ministers (finance, economy, defence and foreign affairs), overcoming initial opposition by President Meri to two of the nominees. Meanwhile, in November 1993, the EPF was disbanded; it was stated that the party had largely fulfilled its aims.

The NFP continued to lose popular support in early 1994. At the same time the governing coalition, led by the NFP, was increasingly afflicted by internal divisions, largely prompted by what was perceived as Laar's authoritarian style of leadership. In May–June four members of the Council of Ministers resigned from their posts. Defections from the Isamaa faction within the Riigikogu resulted in Laar's supporters retaining control of only 19 seats in the legislature by early September. Following the revelation, in that month, that Laar had secretly contravened an agreement with the International Monetary Fund (IMF), a vote of 'no confidence' in the Prime Minister was endorsed by 60 members of the Riigikogu (with 27 votes against). In late October Andres Tarand, hitherto Minister of the Environment, was appointed to replace Laar. A new Council of Ministers, which included representatives of Isamaa and the Moderates, the ENIP and liberal and right-wing parties, was announced in the following month.

In early January 1995 seven electoral alliances and eight parties were registered to participate in the general election scheduled for 5 March. The result of the election reflected widespread popular dissatisfaction with the parties of the governing coalition. The largest number of seats in the Riigikogu (41 of the total of 101) was won by an alliance of the centrist Estonian Coalition Party (ECP, led by the former Prime Minister, Tiit Vähi) and the Rural Union (comprising various agrarian parties, most prominently Rüütel's Estonian Country People's Party). A coalition of the newly established Estonian Reform Party (ERP, led by Siim Kallas, the President of the Bank of Estonia) and liberal groups obtained 19 seats, followed by Edgar Savisaar's Estonian Centre Party (16). The NFP (in coalition with the ENIP) won only eight seats, while the Moderates alliance (which included Andres Tarand) gained six seats. The 'Estonia is Our Home' pact (which united three new parties representing the Russian-speaking minority) also won six seats; this development was broadly welcomed as a potentially stabilizing factor in both the domestic and foreign affairs of the country. The remaining five seats were taken by a coalition of right-wing parties. The participation rate was almost 70%.

In late March 1995 Tiit Vähi was nominated by President Meri to form a new Council of Ministers. Vähi was confirmed as Prime Minister by the legislature in early April, and the new Government—a coalition of the ECP/Rural Union and the Estonian Centre Party—was appointed later in the month. The Government survived only until early October, when it was revealed that Edgar Savisaar, the Minister of the Interior, had made clandestine recordings of conversations that he had held with other politicians, following the general election in March, concerning the formation of a new coalition government. Although Savisaar was dismissed by Vähi, the Estonian Centre Party (of which Savisaar was the leader) refused to accept his dismissal. As a result of the effective collapse of the coalition, Vähi and the remaining members of the Council of Ministers tendered their resignations. In mid-October President Meri reappointed Vähi as Prime Minister and charged him with the formation of a new Government. This emerged in late October, and represented a coalition of the ECP/Rural Union and the ERP. Meanwhile, Savisaar resigned as Chairman of the

Estonian Centre Party. In December the NFP and the ENIP, which had campaigned jointly in the legislative election in March, merged to form the Pro Patria (Fatherland) Union. In March 1996 tension within the Estonian Centre Party, following the scandal surrounding Savisaar, resulted in the emergence of two factions: Andra Veidemann, the Chairman of the Party, and six deputies from the Riigikogu established the New Democratic Association, subsequently to become the liberal-centrist Development Party, while Savisaar was re-elected as Chairman of the Estonian Centre Party.

A presidential election was held in the Riigikogu on 26 August 1996, and was contested by the incumbent, Lennart Meri, and Arnold Rüütel of the Estonian Country People's Party. A further two rounds of voting took place on the following day, since neither candidate had secured the requisite 68 votes; however, these were also inconclusive. A larger electoral college, comprising the 101 deputies of the legislature and 273 representatives of local government, was therefore convened on 20 September. Five candidates contested the first round, but, as none of the contenders secured an overall majority of the votes, a second round of voting was held to choose between the leading candidates, Meri and Rüütel. The election was won by Meri, with some 52% of the votes cast, and in October he was duly sworn in as President for a second term.

In October 1996 local government elections were held, in which the ERP gained control of Tallinn city council. In November 1996 the ECP concluded a co-operation agreement with the Estonian Centre Party (excluded from the Government since October 1995), which pledged to seek to involve the centrists in the governing coalition. Disagreements among the coalition partners led to the collapse of the Tallinn council leadership, and Savisaar was appointed as the new Chairman of the council, replacing the newly elected ERP candidate. The ERP threatened to leave the Government unless the co-operation agreement with the Estonian Centre Party was cancelled, and on 22 November 1996 six ministers, including the Chairman of the ERP and the Minister for Foreign Affairs, Siim Kallas, resigned, thus causing the collapse of the ruling coalition. Following the failure of negotiations between the ECP, the Estonian Centre Party and the Development Party a minority Government, comprising the ECP, the Rural Union and independent members, was appointed, with the support of 41 deputies, in early December. In early 1997 a series of allegations of abuse of office were made against Tiit Vähi. A legislative motion of 'no confidence', presented by the leaders of four opposition parties (the Pro Patria—Fatherland—Union, the Reform Party, the Moderates' Party and the Republican Party) in early February, was defeated by a narrow margin, but Vähi, nevertheless, tendered his resignation at the end of that month, while denying the allegations made against him. Mart Siimann, the leader of the ECP parliamentary faction, was appointed Prime Minister, having received the support of the majority of deputies, and was asked to form a new Government (the resignation of the Prime Minister automatically entailed that of the Government). In mid-March a new minority Government, which comprised a coalition of the ECP, the Rural Union and independent members, was appointed. In September former Prime Minister Vähi announced his resignation from the ECP and his retirement from political life. His position as Chairman of the ECP was assumed by Prime Minister Siimann.

During 1998 there was considerable political consolidation and realignment in preparation for the legislative election expected in the following year. In January the Rural Union entered into a co-operation agreement with the opposition Estonian Centre Party, and in April the smaller Estonian Farmers' Party (to which the formerly independent Minister of Foreign Affairs, Toomas Hendrik Ilves, pledged his political allegiance in December 1997) and People's Party of Republicans and Conservatives merged to form the People's Party, with Ilves as leader. The new party immediately concluded a co-operation agreement with the ECP, although it did not enter the governing coalition. In May, in an attempt to broaden the appeal of both political platforms, the Estonian Green Party was absorbed by the Estonian Centre Party. Meanwhile, the six members of the Riigikogu representing the three major Russian-speaking minority parties announced that they were setting aside former differences in order to present a united front in the legislature, in support of their common interests. In late September, following repeated criticism of his leadership of a party not represented in the governing coalition or the legislature, Ilves resigned the foreign affairs portfolio. As a result, the co-operation agreement concluded between the People's Party and the ECP in April was abandoned. In October an independent former diplomat, Raul Malk, was appointed as Ilves's successor. In November, in an attempt to rationalize and simplify the forthcoming election campaign, the Riigikogu voted to proscribe the formation of formal political alliances. It was expected that the legislation would make the efforts of smaller parties to gain legislative representation increasingly difficult; many members of the parties participating in the incumbent coalition Government abstained from or opposed the vote. In early December President Meri announced that the election to the Riigikogu would be conducted on 7 March 1999.

At the general election held on 7 March 1999 the Estonian Centre Party won 28 of the 101 seats in the legislature; the ERP and the Pro Patria (Fatherland) Union each secured 18 seats, the Moderates (in alliance with the People's Party) claimed 17 seats, the Estonian Country People's Party received seven seats and the United People's Party of Estonia won six seats. According to official sources, the level of participation was just 57.4% of the electorate. Although the Estonian Centre Party obtained the largest number of seats, it was unable to form a majority coalition. A centre-right coalition Government was thus formed by the ERP, the Pro Patria Union and the Moderates, with each party receiving five ministerial posts; Mart Laar, leader of the Pro Patria Union, was appointed Prime Minister (a post that he had held in 1992–94). The new Government pledged to continue the policy of free-market reforms and confirmed its objective to obtain membership of the European Union (EU) by 2003. In May 1999 it was announced that non-native Estonians (numbering an estimated 300,000) were to be allowed to participate in local elections to be held in October. Later in May large demonstrations took place in the mainly Russian-speaking border town of Narva, in protest at rising unemployment in the region.

At the local elections held in October 1999 the governing ERP/Pro Patria (Fatherland) Union/Moderates alliance gained control in 13 of Estonia's 15 counties. Following prolonged negotiations, the alliance joined with four members of the People's Trust Party and one member of the People's Choice bloc, which both represented the Russian-speaking population, to take control of Tallinn city council. Rein Voog of the ERP was elected Chairman of the council and Jüri Mõis was appointed Mayor of Tallinn, after resigning as Minister of Internal Affairs; he was replaced by Tarmo Loodus. Later in October draft legislation proposed by the Estonian Centre Party to institute direct presidential elections was defeated in the Riigikogu. In November the Moderates' Party and the People's Party merged to form the People's Party Moderates.

During 2000 repeated unsuccessful votes of 'no confidence' were brought against both cabinet members and local government officials. In April the Minister of Finance, Siim Kallas, survived a confidence motion relating to an ongoing corruption scandal that dated back to his time as President of the Bank of Estonia. Early the following month a motion of 'no confidence' against the Minister of Internal Affairs, Tarmo Loodus, accused of failing to prevent the spread of crime and corruption, was defeated. Meanwhile, in mid-June a new party, the Estonian People's Union, was formed by the merger of the Estonian Rural People's Party, the Rural Union and the Pensioners' and Families' Party. In November Jüri Mõis, the Mayor of Tallinn, won a vote of 'no confidence' brought by the Estonian Centre Party. Confidence votes were, similarly, brought against Rein Voog, the Chairman of the city council of Tallinn, and the Chairmen of three other towns. It was alleged that the opposition was seeking to undermine the composition of local government, in anticipation of the presidential election due to be held in the legislature in 2001, when, should initial rounds of voting prove inconclusive, representatives of local government would form part of an extended electoral college. Mõis was subjected to another unsuccessful vote of 'no confidence' in February 2001. Meanwhile, in January the Minister of Transport and Communications, Toivo Jürgensen, held responsible by the opposition for difficulties connected with the privatization of the rail industry, also survived a confidence vote. In the following month Prime Minister Laar was implicated in a scandal concerning an incident in 1999, when he and other officials were alleged to have carried out informal shooting practice aimed at a picture of the controversial Estonian Centre Party leader, Edgar Savisaar; a vote of 'no confidence' in the Prime Minister was suspended, pending the completion of an enquiry.

Since the restoration of Estonian independence in 1991, the republic's relations with its eastern neighbour, the Russian Federation, have been strained by a number of issues, most notably the presence of former Soviet troops (under Russian jurisdiction) and the rights of the large Russian minority in Estonia. Under the Citizenship Law of 1992 (a modified version of that adopted in 1938), non-ethnic Estonians who settled in the republic after its annexation by the USSR in 1940 were obliged to apply for naturalization (as were their descendants). Many of the requirements for naturalization—including two years' residency in Estonia as well as an examination in the Estonian language—were criticized by the Russian Government as being excessively stringent, and discriminatory against the Russian-speaking minority. A new citizenship law, adopted in January 1995, extended the residency requirement to five years. Non-citizens were given until 12 July 1995 to apply for residence and work permits, by which time almost 330,000 people (more than 80% of the total) had submitted applications. The deadline was extended until 30 November 1996, following which non-citizens were required to hold either an alien's passport (which served as an international travel document) or a residence permit. (Former Soviet passports were valid for identification purposes within Estonia until the relevant documents had been issued.) By October 1996 some 110,000 people had taken Russian citizenship, while continuing to live in Estonia. In May 1997 the Ministry of Internal Affairs announced that Soviet passports were no longer valid in Estonia. An amendment to the Language Law, adopted by the Riigikogu in November 1997, provoked outrage among the Russian-speaking minority. Under the terms of the amended law, parliamentary deputies and local government officials who had not received elementary education at an Estonian language school were to be required to demonstrate their knowledge of the language. The amendment was denounced by ethnic Russian members of the legislature (who had opposed the legislation) as unconstitutional, and the amendment was vetoed by President Meri in December 1997 and in January 1998. Meri's objections to the legislation were upheld by a ruling of the Supreme Court in early February. However, revised legislation requiring elected officials to demonstrate sufficient command of Estonian to participate in the basic bureaucratic procedures of office was approved by the Riigikogu in mid-December, despite opposition from the OSCE, which had urged President Meri to veto the law. The legislation became effective in May 1999. On 1 July a further amendment to the Language Law came into force, which stipulated that all people employed in the services sector be able to communicate with clients in Estonian. In early August the leader of the Tallinn Union of Russian Citizens in Estonia, Oleg Morozov, was arrested and charged with violating Estonian residency laws. He was subsequently sentenced to 20 days' imprisonment, whereupon he commenced a hunger strike and demanded recognition as a political prisoner. Morozov had refused to obtain a residency permit, owing to the fact that he had been born in Estonia and had been permanently resident there. In protest at the sentence, another member of the Union, Eduard Shaumyan, began a hunger strike in front of the Russian embassy in Tallinn; a member of the Russian legislature, Sergei Glotov, appealed to the Parliamentary Assembly of the Council of Europe to take measures to prevent further alleged violations of the Russian-speaking minority's civil rights. Officials of the Russian Ministry of Foreign Affairs, however, urged Morozov to end his protest. Following his release, Morozov was informed that he would be placed under administrative supervision and be obliged to legalize his stay by 30 January 2000 or leave the country. In late December 1999 Petr Rozhok, another prominent member of the Union, was arrested and notified that, if acquitted of extortion charges, he would also be required to obtain a residency permit or leave Estonia. Meanwhile, in September it was announced that only 34 parents had applied for Estonian citizenship on behalf of their children, following the introduction of legislation in mid-July that entitled non-citizens' children under the age of 15, who were born in Estonia, to full Estonian citizenship. Estimates had indicated that some 6,000 children would be eligible to apply.

With the dissolution of the USSR in 1991, several thousand former Soviet troops remained stationed (under Russian command) on Estonian territory. Their withdrawal was commenced in 1992, but the Russian leadership increasingly linked the progress of the troop withdrawals with the question of the citizenship, and other rights, of the Russian-speaking minority in Estonia. Withdrawals of the troops were suspended temporarily on several occasions in response to allegations of violations of the Russian minority's rights. In November 1993 a resolution by the UN General Assembly demanded a complete withdrawal of the ex-Soviet troops, and the Russian Government proposed 31 August 1994 as the final deadline for the withdrawals. Negotiations continued in 1994 on the terms for the withdrawal of the troops, but were complicated by Russian demands that the 12,000 retired Russian military servicemen (and their dependants) living in Estonia be granted unqualified citizenship rights and social guarantees. In July talks were held in the Russian capital, Moscow, between President Meri and President Yeltsin of the Russian Federation, at which Meri pledged that civil and social rights would be guaranteed to all Russian military pensioners in Estonia, while Yeltsin confirmed that Russia would remove its military presence by the end of August. The withdrawal of former Soviet troops from Estonia was finally completed on 29 August 1994. The agreements on the withdrawal of troops and on Russian military pensioners were ratified by the Russian and Estonian legislatures in 1995, despite opposition from many Estonian politicians who argued that, as Russia had been an occupying force, its servicemen should not be allowed to retire in Estonia. By December 1996 the Estonian Government had granted residence permits to over 20,000 retired servicemen and their dependants.

A further cause of tension in Estonian-Russian relations concerned Estonia's demand for the return of some 2,000 sq km (770 sq miles) of territory that had been ceded to Russia in 1944. This matter remained unresolved at inter-governmental talks held in 1992–93, with Estonia insisting that the Russian-Estonian state border be determined by the terms of the Treaty of Tartu of 1920, in which Russia recognized Estonia's independence. In June 1994 President Yeltsin ordered the unilateral demarcation of Russia's border with Estonia according to the Soviet boundary, although no agreement with Estonia had been concluded. During 1995 Estonia abandoned its demand for the return of the disputed territories. Instead, during Russian-Estonian border negotiations, the Estonian Government appealed only for minor amendments to be made to the existing line of demarcation, in order to improve border security; more importantly, it insisted that Russia recognize the Treaty of Tartu as the basis of future relations between the two countries. However, the Russian Government maintained that the Treaty had lost its legal force, having been superseded by the declaration on bilateral relations signed by Russia and Estonia in 1991.

Relations between Russia and Estonia deteriorated in 1996. The re-establishment of the Estonian Apostolic Orthodox Church (see section on Religion) was perceived by Russia as a threat to the rights of the Russian-speaking minority in Estonia, and the assertion of jurisdiction in Estonia by the Ecumenical Patriarch of Constantinople in February led to the temporary cessation of relations with the Moscow Patriarchate. Relations were restored in May, when it was agreed that congregations should be permitted to decide which Patriarchate they wished to support. Tensions increased later that month, when Russia expelled an Estonian diplomat, allegedly for espionage; Estonia retaliated by expelling a Russian diplomat. Negotiations concerning the adoption of the border agreement were held throughout 1996, but Russia continued to reject the inclusion in the agreement of the Treaty of Tartu, fearing that it would legitimize Estonia's claims on Russian territory (despite the fact that Estonia had abandoned such claims). In November it was announced that Estonia was prepared to omit the Treaty of Tartu from the border agreement. The Estonian Government approved the draft agreement in late November, and declared that it would be signed by Estonia and Russia at the Lisbon summit of the OSCE in December. However, the Russian Government refused to sign the agreement until other issues had been addressed, in particular the rights of the Russian-speaking minority in Estonia. Further talks on the delimitation of the border were conducted in Moscow in August 1998, but no agreement was signed. By 2000 relations between the two countries remained strained, and in March of that year Russia arrested a suspected British spy, who, it was alleged, had received assistance from the Estonian security service. In a further incident, in September, Estonia expelled two Russian diplomats on suspicion of espionage; Russia retaliated by expelling two Estonian diplomats. In the same month Estonia decreed that from 2001 a full visa regime would come into effect between the two countries, despite Russia's disapproval. Moreover, in February 2001 a visiting Russian official declared that Estonia's admission to NATO would lead to a complete breakdown in

relations between the two countries. However, the terms for both Estonia's accession to the EU and Russia's membership of the World Trade Organization demanded improved relations.

Estonia actively pursues close relations with its Baltic neighbours, Latvia and Lithuania. In late 1991 the three states established a consultative interparliamentary body, the Baltic Assembly, with the aim of developing political and economic co-operation. In early 1992 it was agreed to abolish almost all trade restrictions between the three countries and to introduce a common visa policy, and a tripartite agreement on free trade and regional security was signed in late 1993. A customs agreement came into force in June 1996, which constituted the first stage of the establishment of a unified customs system. At two separate meetings during November 1997 the three countries agreed to reject Russian overtures to provide unilateral security guarantees, and to remove all non-tariff customs barriers between them. In January 1998 the Presidents of the three states met President Clinton of the USA in Washington, DC, and all parties signed a Charter of Partnership. Estonia is a member of the Council of Baltic Sea States (established in March 1992). In July 1996 the member states signed a programme of co-operation aimed at encouraging economic development and integration between the countries of the Council. In July 1999 the Estonian, Latvian and Lithuanian Prime Ministers met in Palanga, Lithuania, where they agreed to develop the Baltic Common Economic Area and to remove obstacles to the further implementation of trilateral agreements on free trade.

An important focus of Estonia's foreign policy is the attainment of full membership of the EU. In July 1995 Estonia became an associate member, and in December it officially applied for full membership. At a meeting of the European Council of Ministers convened in Luxembourg in December 1997, the EU confirmed that Estonia was among six states with which it wished to begin bilateral talks; formal accession negotiations began on 31 March 1998. A number of political and economic agreements concluded between the EU and the Baltic states in 1995, with the aim of facilitating their membership of the EU, came into effect on 1 February 1998. In March, in accordance with the European Convention on Human Rights and Fundamental Freedoms, the Riigikogu voted to abolish the death penalty. Among the EU states, Estonia enjoys particularly cordial relations with Finland (its largest trading partner), with which it shares close cultural and linguistic ties. Estonia is also a member of the Council of Europe (see p. 165), of which it held the Presidency for six months from May 1996. In addition, Estonia pursues the goal of membership of NATO (Estonia joined NATO's 'Partnership for Peace' programme of military co-operation in 1994). Despite Russian opposition to the expansion of NATO into Eastern Europe and, particularly, into the former USSR, Estonia hoped to obtain full NATO membership by 2002.

Government

Legislative authority resides with the Riigikogu (State Assembly), which has 101 members, elected by universal adult suffrage for a four-year term. The Riigikogu elects the President (Head of State) for a term of five years. The President is also Supreme Commander of Estonia's armed forces. Executive power is held by the Council of Ministers, which is headed by the Prime Minister, who is nominated by the President. For administrative purposes, Estonia is divided into 15 counties (*maakonds*), 47 towns and 207 rural municipalities.

Defence

Before regaining independence in 1991, Estonia had no armed forces separate from those of the USSR. Following the establishment of its own Ministry of Defence in April 1992, Estonia began to form an independent army. By August 2000 total armed forces numbered 4,710 (army 4,320, navy 250, air force 140). There was also a reserve militia of some 14,000. There is a paramilitary border guard numbering 2,800 troops, under the command of the Ministry of the Interior. In July 2000 the standard duration of military service was reduced from 12 to eight months. Also in 2000 a plan for the reform of the armed forces was approved. In February 1994 Estonia joined NATO's 'Partnership for Peace' programme of military co-operation (see p. 243). In 1998 the Baltic states agreed to establish a joint airspace observation system (BALTNET), a defence college and a peace-keeping battalion (BALTBAT); from 2001 this was to be divided into three national battalions and Estbat was to recruit an extra three battalions. A Baltic naval unit (BALTRON) was established in mid-1998. Full NATO membership was scheduled to be achieved by 2002 and Estonia is implementing measures to increase its defence expenditure, in line with NATO requirements that countries aspiring to membership should assign at least 2.0% of annual GDP for defence. Central government expenditure on defence in 1998 totalled 969.4m. kroons, which represented 4.0% of total central government spending and was equivalent to 1.5% of GDP in that year. Projected budgetary expenditure on defence for 2001 was 1,460m. kroons.

Economic Affairs

In 1998, according to the World Bank, Estonia's gross national product (GNP), measured at average 1996–98 prices, was US $4,878m., equivalent to $3,360 per head (or $7,563 per head on an international purchasing-power parity basis). During 1990–98, it was estimated, GNP per head declined, in real terms, at an average annual rate of 1.4%. Over the same period the population was estimated to have declined by an annual average of 1.1%. Estonia's gross domestic product (GDP) was estimated to have increased, in real terms, by an average of 2.2% per year during 1980–90, but to have decreased by an annual average of 1.3% during 1990–99. According to the IMF, real GDP decreased by 2.0% in 1994, but increased by 4.3% in 1995, by 4.0% in 1996, by 10.6% in 1997 and by 4.7% in 1998, before decreasing by 1.1% in 1999.

Agriculture (including forestry and fishing) contributed 5.7% of GDP in 1999. In that year the sector provided some 8.3% of employment. Animal husbandry is the main activity in the agricultural sector. Some 27.4% of Estonia's land is cultivable. The principal crops are grains, potatoes and fruits and berries. Forestry products are also important. During 1990–99, according to the World Bank, agricultural GDP declined at an average annual rate of 3.4%. The value of gross agricultural output increased, in real terms, by 2.9% in 1995, but decreased by 6.3% in 1996, by 1.5% in 1997, by 5.0% in 1998 and by 8.2% in 1999.

Industry (including mining and quarrying, manufacturing, construction and power) contributed 25.3% of GDP in 1999. In that year the sector provided 32.3% of employment. The sector is dominated by machine-building, electronics and electrical engineering. During 1990–99, according to the World Bank, industrial GDP declined at an average annual rate of 4.5%. However, following declines of 18.6% in 1993 and 3.1% in 1994, industrial production (excluding construction) increased by 1.9% in 1995, by 2.9% in 1996, by 14.7% in 1997 and by 1.8% in 1998, before decreasing by 7.6% in 1999.

Mining and quarrying contributed 1.2% of GDP in 1999, when it provided 1.4% of employment. Estonia's principal mineral resource is oil-shale, and there are also deposits of peat and phosphorite ore. There are total estimated reserves of oil-shale of some 4,000 metric tons. Annual extraction of oil-shale reached some 31m. metric tons in 1980, but had decreased to 9.6m. tons in 1999. Phosphorite ore is processed to produce phosphates for use in agriculture, but development of the industry has been accompanied by increasing environmental problems. The value of mining GDP decreased, in real terms, by 6.0% in 1994 and by 6.8% in 1995, but increased by 7.4% in 1996 and by 13.4% in 1997. However, it decreased by 11.8% in 1998 and by 6.5% in 1999.

In 1999 the manufacturing sector accounted for 15.2% of GDP and engaged an estimated 21.2% of the employed labour force. The sector is based on products of food- and beverage-processing (especially dairy products), textiles and clothing, fertilizers and other chemical products, and wood and timber products (particularly furniture). The value of manufacturing GDP decreased, in real terms, by 3.4% in 1994, but increased by 10.0% in 1995, by 2.7% in 1996, by 18.1% in 1997 and by 2.8% in 1998, before decreasing by 2.7% in 1999.

The country relies on oil-shale for about 65% of its energy requirements. Some 50% of electricity produced in this way is exported. In 1999 imports of fuel and energy products accounted for an estimated 6% of total imports. In 1999 Estonia imported some 700m. cu m of natural gas from Russia.

Estonia's services sector was the most developed in the former USSR. The sector accounted for 62.8% of GDP in 1999, and engaged 61.2% of the employed population. During 1990–99, according to the World Bank, the GDP of the services sector increased by an annual average of 1.4%. Although the GDP of the sector declined by an annual average of 27.1% per year in 1990–94, it subsequently expanded substantially, and increased by an estimated 5.0%, in real terms, in 1996, by 8.0% in 1997, by 5.4% in 1998 and by 2.6% in 1999.

In 1999 Estonia recorded a visible trade deficit of US $877.5m., while there was a deficit of $294.7m. on the current account of the balance of payments. Of all the former republics of the USSR, Estonia experienced the most rapid reorientation of its trade after 1991: trade with Western countries, particularly Scandinavia, increased considerably, while trade with former Soviet republics declined from about 90% of the pre-1991 total to some 30% in 1995. In 1999 Finland was Estonia's principal trading partner, accounting for 22.8% of imports and 19.4% of exports; other important trading partners were Russia, Sweden, Germany and Latvia. In 1999 the principal exports were machinery and electrical goods (20.9% of total export revenue), timber products (14.5%), textiles (11.8%), base metals (9.9%), chemical products (9.3%), miscellaneous manufactured articles (6.4%) and prepared foodstuffs (5.6%). The principal imports were machinery and electrical goods (27.4%), base metals (9.7%), chemical products (9.3%), textiles (7.8%), mineral products (7.4%), prepared foodstuffs (7.1%) and transport equipment (7.0%).

In 1998, according to official sources, there was a general consolidated budgetary deficit of 67.5m. kroons. Estonia's external debt totalled US $781.7m. at the end of 1998, of which $231.3m. was long-term public debt. In 1998 the cost of debt-servicing was equivalent to 2.1% of the value of exports of goods and services. The annual rate of inflation averaged 3.3% in 1980–89, rising to 17% in 1990, to 202% in 1991 and to as high as 1,069% in 1992. However, in 1993, following a programme of radical monetary reform, the average annual rate of inflation was reduced to 89%. During 1992–99 the annual rate of inflation averaged 28.5%. Consumer prices increased by an average of 19.3% in 1996, by 10.6% in 1997, by 8.2% in 1998, by 3.3% in 1999 and by 4.0% in 2000. Some 46,318 people (approximately 5.3% of the labour force) were officially registered as unemployed in 2000.

In 1992 Estonia became a member of the IMF and the World Bank. It also joined the European Bank for Reconstruction and Development (see p. 176). In 1994 Estonia signed a free-trade agreement with the EU; in June 1995 Estonia became an associate member of the EU, and in December it applied for full membership. In November 1999 Estonia became a member of the World Trade Organization (WTO, see p. 292).

Even before it regained independence in mid-1991, Estonia had begun a transition to a market economy, which included the nationalization of formerly Soviet-controlled enterprises and the establishment of a central bank, as well as a private banking system. Further far-reaching economic reforms were continued in the early 1990s. Despite Estonia's relative prosperity during the Soviet period, the collapse of the USSR and its internal economic system resulted in serious economic difficulties. An annual decline in output was recorded in all sectors in 1991 and 1992. However, from 1993 a rapid increase in the volume of exports and growing foreign investment helped to reverse this trend. In June 1992 Estonia introduced a new currency, the kroon, which remained pegged at a rate of 8:1 against the Deutsche Mark, thus further enhancing international financial confidence in Estonia. By October 1997 it was estimated that total investment from abroad since independence amounted to some US $700m., and inflation has decreased considerably since 1993. In 1999, however, Estonia suffered a number of economic reverses, largely related to the Russian financial crisis of the previous year. Negative growth was recorded, compared with growth of 4.0% in 1998, and unemployment increased dramatically. In March 2000 the IMF approved an 18-month credit arrangement to support Estonia's economic programme for 2001–01, although the Government stated that it regarded the measure as precautionary, and did not intend to draw upon it. In July the IMF emphasized the need to reduce the high level of unemployment, to balance the budget and to increase the age of retirement. In 2000 the economy was aided by the export trade to EU member countries, a recovery in industrial production (which had declined significantly in the previous year) and comparatively healthy domestic demand. Budgetary proposals for 2001, approved by the Riigikogu in December 2000, envisaged an average rate of inflation of 4.1% and GDP growth of 5.5%; the Riigikogu also approved a balanced budget. The Government's spending priorities for 2001 were identified as education and social welfare, improvements to the country's infrastructure, in particular the road network, and defence. Although Estonia had hoped to adopt the common European currency, the euro, by 2002, in advance of its accession to the EU, the proposal was rejected by the EU, as being in contravention of fundamental EU accords.

Social Welfare

In pre-1940 Estonia, health care was provided by both state and private facilities. A comprehensive state-funded health system was introduced under Soviet rule. This system was restructured in the early 1990s. Social security is administered by the state and provided through specialized agencies, while social assistance and social services are the responsibility of local municipalities. The system of social security comprises pensions insurance (introduced in 1993), health insurance (1991), family benefits (1994), unemployment benefits (1995) and funeral grants (1993). Under the social assistance programme, subsistence cash benefits are paid according to means-testing. In early 1998 an estimated 366,876 Estonians were receiving state pensions totalling a monthly average of 1,096m. kroons. There is a relatively high number of physicians, equivalent to 31 per 10,000 inhabitants in 1999, but a shortage of auxiliary staff. There were 78 hospitals and 72 hospital beds per 10,000 inhabitants in 1999. The official retirement age was 62 years for men and 57 years for women. However, the male retirement age was to increase to 63 years from 2001. In 1998 central government expenditure on health amounted to 3,948.6m. kroons, equivalent to 16.4% of central government spending. In the same year local government expenditure on health totalled 108.7m. kroons, which represented 1.7% of total local government spending. Central government expenditure on social security and welfare totalled 7,384.9m. kroons in that year, equivalent to 30.6% of total central government spending. Local government expenditure on social security and welfare was 738.6m. kroons in 1998, which represented 11.5% of total local government spending.

Education

The Estonian education system consists of pre-school, primary, secondary, vocational, university/higher, and adult education. Compulsory education begins at the age of seven and lasts for nine years: primary school (Grades 1–6) and lower secondary (Grades 7–9). Students may then attend either general secondary school (Grades 10–12) or vocational school. In 1999/2000 there were 34 higher-education institutions in Estonia, including Tartu University (founded in 1632) and the Tallinn Technical University, with a total of 49,574 students enrolled. The language of instruction at all levels is either Estonian or Russian. In 1998 29% of students at general day schools took classes with Russian as the language of instruction. In 1992/93 the proportion of students instructed in Estonian was: primary and lower secondary 64%, upper secondary 76%, vocational and technical 65% and higher 81%. In 1999 the enrolment at primary schools was equivalent to 96.6% of the corresponding age group. At secondary school level enrolment was equivalent to 77.2% of the school-age population and in tertiary education it was equivalent to 53.7%. In 1989, according to census results, only 0.3% of the adult population were illiterate and official figures for 1999 recorded a rate of illiteracy of just 0.2%. Central government expenditure on education totalled 2,875.5m. kroons in 1999; local government expenditure amounted to 2,791.2m. kroons. Total public-sector expenditure on education in that year was equivalent to an estimated 7% of GDP.

Public Holidays

2001: 1 January (New Year's Day), 24 February (Independence Day), 13 April (Good Friday), 1 May (Spring Day), 23 June (Victory Day, anniversary of the Battle of Võnnu in 1919), 24 June (Midsummer Day, Jaanipäev), 20 August (Restoration of Independence Day), 25–26 December (Christmas).

2002: 1 January (New Year's Day), 24 February (Independence Day), 29 March (Good Friday), 1 May (Spring Day), 23 June (Victory Day, anniversary of the Battle of Võnnu in 1919), 24 June (Midsummer Day, Jaanipäev), 20 August (Restoration of Independence Day), 25–26 December (Christmas).

Weights and Measures

The metric system is in force.

Statistical Survey

Source (unless otherwise stated): Statistical Office of Estonia, Endla 15, Tallinn 0100; tel. 625-9202; fax 625-9370; e-mail stat@stat.ee; internet www.stat.ee.

Area and Population

AREA, POPULATION AND DENSITY

Area (sq km)	45,227*
Population (census results)†	
12 January 1989	
Males	731,392
Females	834,270
Total	1,565,662
31 March 2000‡	
Males	631,900
Females	738,600
Total	1,370,500
Population (official estimates at 1 January)†	
1998	1,453,844
1999	1,445,580
2000	1,439,197
Density (per sq km) at 1 January 2000	31.8

* 17,462 sq miles.
† Figures refer to permanent inhabitants. The *de facto* total at the 1989 census was 1,572,916.
‡ Provisional results.

POPULATION BY NATIONALITY
(estimated permanent inhabitants at 1 January 2000)

	Number	%
Estonian	939,310	65.3
Russian	403,925	28.1
Ukrainian	36,467	2.5
Belarusian	21,125	1.5
Finnish	12,762	0.9
Tatar	3,232	0.2
Latvian	2,638	0.2
Jewish	2,275	0.2
Polish	2,290	0.2
Lithuanian	2,188	0.2
German	1,228	0.1
Others	11,757	0.8
Total	1,439,197	100.0

POPULATION BY ADMINISTRATIVE COUNTY
(estimated permanent inhabitants at 1 January 2000)

Harjumaa	532,883	Raplamaa	40,086
Hiiumaa	11,723	Saaremaa	39,971
Ida-Virumaa	193,610	Tartumaa	151,912
Jõgevamaa. . . .	40,992	Valgamaa	38,370
Järvamaa	42,970	Viljandimaa	61,933
Läänemaa	31,822	Võrumaa	42,579
Lääne-Virumaa . . .	75,421	**Total**	1,439,197
Põlvamaa	35,272		
Pärnumaa	99,653		

PRINCIPAL TOWNS
(estimated population, excluding suburbs, at 1 January 2000)

Tallinn (capital) . .	408,329	Kohtla-Järve . . .	51,170
Tartu	101,744	Pärnu	50,966
Narva	73,295		

BIRTHS, MARRIAGES AND DEATHS

	Registered live births		Registered marriages		Registered deaths	
	Number	Rate (per 1,000)	Number	Rate (per 1,000)	Number	Rate (per 1,000)
1992 . .	18,006	11.7	8,878	5.7	20,115	13.0
1993 . .	15,170	10.0	7,745	5.1	21,267	14.0
1994 . .	14,178	9.5	7,378	4.9	22,150	14.8
1995 . .	13,560	9.1	7,006	4.7	20,872	14.1
1996 . .	13,291	9.1	5,517	3.8	19,019	13.0
1997 . .	12,626	8.7	5,589	3.8	18,566	12.7
1998 . .	12,269	8.5	5,430	3.7	19,446	13.4
1999 . .	12,545	8.7	5,590	3.9	18,455	12.8

Expectation of life (years at birth, 1998): males 65.4; females 76.1.

EMPLOYMENT
(labour force sample surveys, annual averages, '000 persons aged 15 years and over, excl. armed forces)

	1997	1998	1999
Agriculture, hunting and forestry	53.6	52.9	47.8
Fishing	7.2	5.2	3.4
Mining and quarrying . . .	7.6	8.2	8.6
Manufacturing	144.1	139.5	130.2
Electricity, gas and water supply	17.6	18.2	17.5
Construction	47.4	46.9	41.8
Wholesale and retail trade . .	90.6	90.6	86.9
Hotels and restaurants . .	14.6	14.4	13.8
Transport, storage and communications	59.4	58.3	62.7
Financial intermediation . . .	7.5	8.6	9.1
Real estate, renting and business activities	35.1	38.9	39.1
Public administration and defence	34.3	36.7	36.9
Education	58.9	56.5	52.6
Health and social work . . .	36.9	35.1	32.6
Activities not adequately defined	33.8	30.2	31.1
Total employed . . .	648.4	640.2	614.0
Unemployed	69.4	70.2	86.2
Total labour force . . .	717.8	710.4	700.2
Males	376.7	370.7	365.6
Females	341.0	339.7	334.7

1989 census ('000 persons aged 15 years and over): Total labour force 856 (males 428; females 428).

Agriculture

PRINCIPAL CROPS ('000 metric tons)

	1997	1998	1999
Wheat	111	118	88
Barley	312	273	186
Rye	72	55	39
Oats	115	99	71
Other cereals	41	31	17
Potatoes	437	317	404
Cabbages	20	18	19
Tomatoes	3	3	3
Cucumbers and gherkins . .	7	6	6
Carrots	9	13	7
Other vegetables	15	13	14
Fruits and berries . . .	29	18	22

Source: FAO.

LIVESTOCK ('000 head, year ending September)

	1997	1998	1999
Cattle	343.0	325.6	307.5
Pigs	298.4	306.3	326.4
Sheep	39.2	35.6	30.8
Chickens	2,295*	2,574*	2,636
Ducks	20*	20*	20†
Geese	10*	8*	8†

* Unofficial figure.   † FAO estimate.

Source: FAO.

LIVESTOCK PRODUCTS

('000 metric tons, unless otherwise indicated)

	1997	1998	1999
Beef and veal	19	19	22
Pig meat	30	32	31
Poultry meat	4	8	8
Cows' milk	717	729	626
Butter	17	15*	16†
Cheese	18	16	16
Poultry eggs	18	19	17
Honey (metric tons)	303	115	336

* Unofficial figure.   † FAO estimate.

Source: FAO.

Forestry

ROUNDWOOD REMOVALS ('000 cu m, excl. bark)

	1996	1997	1998
Sawlogs, veneer logs and logs for sleepers	1,490	1,548	1,698
Pulpwood	1,611	2,200	2,545
Other industrial wood	196	275	303
Fuel wood	573	1,370	1,515
Total	3,901	5,393	6,061

Source: FAO, *Yearbook of Forest Products.*

SAWNWOOD PRODUCTION ('000 cu m, incl. railway sleepers)

	1996	1997	1998
Coniferous (softwood)	360	684	547
Broadleaved (hardwood)	40	45	36
Total	400	729	583

* FAO estimate.

Source: FAO, *Yearbook of Forest Products.*

Fishing

('000 metric tons, live weight)

	1996	1997	1998
Capture	108.4	123.6	118.7
Blue whiting	11.0	5.7	6.3
Atlantic redfishes	7.1	3.7	4.0
Atlantic herring	45.3	52.4	42.7
European sprat	22.5	39.7	32.2
Chub mackerel	4.5	2.0	7.2
Atlantic mackerel	3.7	6.3	7.4
Northern prawn	3.2	5.0	7.2
Aquaculture	0.3	0.3	0.3
Total catch	108.7	123.9	119.0

Source: FAO, *Yearbook of Fishery Statistics.*

Mining

('000 metric tons)

	1997	1998	1999
Oil-shale	12,860	10,913	9,602
Peat	1,074	334	1,266

Industry

SELECTED PRODUCTS ('000 metric tons, unless otherwise indicated)

	1995	1996	1997
Wine and spirits ('000 hectolitres)	173	84*	n.a.
Beer ('000 hectolitres)	492	459	543
Soft drinks ('000 hectolitres)	435	544	638
Textile fabrics (million sq metres)	94	124*	n.a.
Footwear ('000 pairs)	682	711	793
Plywood ('000 cubic metres)	11.2	18	20
Paper	5.9	19.5*	n.a.
Paperboard	0.4	0.9*	n.a.
Building bricks (million)	31	26	23
Cement	418	388	422
Electric energy (million kWh)	8,693	9,103	n.a.

* Provisional.

Source: partly UN, *Industrial Commodity Statistics Yearbook.*

Finance

CURRENCY AND EXCHANGE RATES

Monetary Units

100 cents = 1 kroon.

Sterling, Dollar and Euro Equivalents (29 December 2000)

£1 sterling = 25.10 kroons;

US $1 = 16.82 kroons;

€1 = 15.65 kroons;

1,000 kroons = £39.84 = $59.45 = €63.89.

Average Exchange Rate (kroons per US $)

1998   14.075

1999   14.678

2000   16.969

Note: In June 1992 Estonia reintroduced its national currency, the kroon, replacing the rouble of the former USSR, initially at a rate of one kroon per 10 roubles.

BUDGET (million kroons)*

Revenue†	1997	1998	1999
Tax revenue	19,592.0	21,913.4	21,505.2
Taxes on income, profits and capital gains	3,544.1	4,675.7	4,508.9
Individual	2,315.7	2,761.6	2,870.1
Corporate	1,228.4	1,914.1	1,638.8
Social security contributions	6,867.4	7,937.5	7,793.8
Domestic taxes on goods and services	9,179.6	9,300.1	9,202.5
General sales, turnover or value-added taxes	6,686.2	6,413.4	6,418.9
Excises	2,400.9	2,789.2	2,686.5
Other current revenue	2,190.6	1,344.1	1,155.3
Entrepreneurial and property income	682.0	457.2	269.0
Administrative fees and charges, non-industrial and incidental sales	741.9	696.8	764.6
Capital revenue	577.9	749.0	209.0
Sales of land and intangible assets	468.7	676.8	141.1
Total	22,360.5	24,006.5	22,869.5

Expenditure‡	1996	1997	1998
General public services . . .	1,141.2	1,183.2	1,191.6
Defence	845.5	944.5	969.4
Public order and safety . . .	1,503.2	1,811.1	1,769.3
Education	1,808.5	2,087.1	2,066.5
Health	2,944.2	3,232.0	3,948.6
Social security and welfare . .	5,743.4	6,581.5	7,384.9
Housing and community amenities	50.8	82.9	10.0
Recreational, cultural and			
religious affairs and services	841.2	899.8	1,061.0
Economic affairs and services .	2,153.7	2,300.9	3,069.0
Agriculture, forestry, fishing and			
hunting	859.4	885.9	1,442.5
Transport and communications	1,106.3	1,173.1	1,444.2
Other purposes	682.0	1,428.8	2,633.0
Total	17,713.7	20,551.8	24,103.3
Current§	16,114.6	18,695.8	22,020.3
Capital	1,599.1	1,856.0	2,083.0

* Figures represent a consolidation of the operations of the central Government, comprising the Republican Budget, the Medical Insurance Fund, the Social Security Fund and various extrabudgetary funds.
† Excluding grants received (million kroons): 25.0 in 1997; 124.0 in 1998; 29.5 in 1999.
‡ Excluding lending minus repayments (million kroons): 205.5 in 1996; 281.4 in 1997; 94.7 in 1998.
§ Including interest payments (million kroons): 208.1 in 1996; 211.6 in 1997; 225.5 in 1998.

INTERNATIONAL RESERVES
(US $ million at 31 December)

	1997	1998	1999
Gold*	2.39	2.37	2.38
IMF special drawing rights . .	0.01	0.07	1.36
Reserve position in IMF . .	0.01	0.01	0.01
Foreign exchange	757.70	810.53	851.69
Total	760.11	812.98	855.44

* National valuation.

Source: IMF, *International Financial Statistics*.

MONEY SUPPLY (million kroons at 31 December)

	1997	1998	1999
Currency outside banks . .	4,588.5	4,538.6	5,741.3
Demand deposits at banks . .	8,582.5	8,207.7	11,174.7
Total money (incl. others) . .	13.223.3	12,750.0	16,918.7

Source: IMF, *International Financial Statistics*.

COST OF LIVING (Consumer price index; base: 1997 = 100)

	1998	1999
Food (incl. beverages)	104.9	100.9
Fuel and light	111.3	122.2
Clothing (incl. footwear)	112.0	119.8
Rent	111.2	120.5
All items (incl. others)	108.2	111.8

Source: ILO, *Yearbook of Labour Statistics*.

NATIONAL ACCOUNTS (million kroons at current prices)
Expenditure on the Gross Domestic Product

	1997	1998	1999
Government final consumption			
expenditure	14,219.2	15,996.6	17,827.8
Non-profit institutions . . .	404.4	469.1	511.1
Private final consumption			
expenditure	37,586.0	43,174.0	43,603.1
Increase in stocks	1,882.4	−189.0	−408.3
Gross fixed capital formation .	17,962.4	21,761.0	18,893.9
Total domestic expenditure . .	72,054.4	81,211.7	80,427.6
Exports of goods and services f.o.b.	50,238.1	58,590.4	57,987.9
Less Imports of goods and services			
f.o.b.	57,661.1	66,259.6	62,470.6
Statistical discrepancy . . .	−307.7	−217.2	−584.7
GDP in purchasers' values . .	64,323.7	73,325.3	75,360.2
GDP at constant 1995 prices .	46,789.0	48,995.7	48,468.5

Gross Domestic Product by Economic Activity

	1997	1998	1999
Agriculture and forestry . . .	3,621	3,872	3,670
Fishing	278	283	199
Mining and quarrying . . .	830	796	801
Manufacturing	9,386	10,789	10,359
Electricity, gas and water supply .	1,984	2,411	2,422
Construction	3,314	4,234	3,681
Trade	9,737	10,890	10,907
Hotels and restaurants . . .	676	779	906
Transport and communications .	6,928	9,123	9,916
Finance and insurance . . .	2,798	2,563	2,842
Real estate, renting and business			
activities	5,560	7,307	8,325
Public administration . . .	2,597	2,900	3,384
Education	3,082	3,584	4,014
Health and social care . . .	2,187	2,368	2,602
Other services	3,879	4,018	4,279
Sub-total	56,858	65,918	68,308
Less Imputed bank service charge	1,171	999	1,169
GDP at factor cost . . .	45,828	64,919	67,139
Net indirect taxes	8,407	8,222	8,222
GDP in purchasers' values . .	64,324	73,325	75,360

Source: Bank of Estonia.

BALANCE OF PAYMENTS (US $ million)

	1997	1998	1999
Exports of goods f.o.b. . . .	2,291.3	2,690.1	2,453.0
Imports of goods f.o.b. . . .	−3,415.6	−3,804.9	−3,330.6
Trade balance	−1,124.3	−1,114.8	−877.5
Exports of services . . .	1,318.0	1,479.6	1,486.7
Imports of services . . .	−726.6	−910.1	−901.9
Balance on goods and services .	−532.9	−545.3	−292.7
Other income received . . .	115.1	133.5	134.2
Other income paid . . .	−260.8	−214.5	−254.3
Balance on goods, services and			
income	−678.6	−626.3	−412.8
Current transfers received . .	135.3	172.9	139.4
Current transfers paid . . .	−18.6	−24.5	−41.4
Current balance	−561.9	−477.9	−314.7
Capital account (net) . . .	−0.2	1.8	1.1
Direct investment abroad . .	−136.6	−6.3	−74.2
Direct investment from abroad .	266.2	580.5	306.5
Portfolio investment assets .	−165.0	−10.9	−134.6
Portfolio investment liabilities .	427.5	1.1	157.0
Other investment assets . .	−334.2	−168.5	−104.7
Other investment liabilities .	744.8	112.1	290.8
Net errors and omissions . .	−24.9	5.3	−8.0
Overall balance	215.9	37.3	119.3

Source: IMF, *International Financial Statistics*.

External Trade

PRINCIPAL COMMODITIES
(million kroons)

Imports c.i.f.	1997	1998	1999
Live animals and animal products	2,572.4	3,369.1	1,731.8
Vegetable products	1,486.7	1,773.1	1,605.8
Prepared foodstuffs, beverages, spirits, vinegar and tobacco	5,656.7	5,881.6	4,313.3
Mineral products	5,458.1	4,216.7	4,488.9
Products of the chemical or allied industries	5,051.0	5,462.9	5,648.1
Plastics, rubber and articles thereof	2,520.8	2,834.9	2,676.4
Wood pulp, paper and paperboard	2,379.1	2,153.3	1,885.7
Textiles and textile articles	4,609.9	5,022.3	4,744.6
Base metals and articles of base metal	4,817.6	6,293.5	5,851.6
Machinery (incl. electrical) and parts	13,582.0	17,147.9	16,589.9
Transport equipment	7,435.0	6,296.1	4,213.8
Optical, photographic, measuring, precision and medical apparatus; clocks and watches; musical instruments	1,210.5	1,240.2	1,423.4
Miscellaneous manufactured articles	1,392.4	1,553.3	1,383.6
Total (incl. others)	61,610.1	67,363.8	60,475.2

Exports f.o.b.	1997	1998	1999
Live animals and animal products	2,581.1	2,838.4	1,923.4
Prepared foodstuffs, beverages, spirits, vinegar and tobacco	3,533.7	3,726.9	2,423.4
Mineral products	2,982.2	2,002.3	2,218.3
Products of the chemical or allied industries	3,161.4	3,278.6	2,820.2
Plastics, rubber and articles thereof	822.7	1,031.3	994.5
Wood and cork products, etc.	4,681.6	5,772.1	6,247.7
Wood pulp, paper and paperboard	942.5	1,097.9	899.8
Textiles and textile articles	4,649.4	5,248.4	5,083.1
Base metals and articles of base metal	2,686.1	3,862.5	4,292.4
Machinery (incl. electrical) and parts	6,903.8	8,966.0	9,009.2
Vehicles, aircraft, vessels and associated transport equipment	3,150.1	2,180.4	1,628.1
Miscellaneous manufactured articles	1,939.8	2,421.5	2,773.8
Total (incl. others)	40,662.3	45,551.4	43,164.5

PRINCIPAL TRADING PARTNERS (million kroons)

Imports c.i.f.	1997	1998	1999
Belgium	814.9	934.2	935.3
China, People's Repub.	332.7	510.3	706.3
Côte d'Ivoire	1,135.6	1,222.6	905.3
Denmark	1,592.8	1,859.1	1,505.8
Finland	14,421.2	15,226.2	13,769.9
France	1,384.8	1,675.5	1,276.3
Germany	6,191.9	7,303.1	5,621.9
Italy	1,838.4	2,198.9	1,915.9
Japan	2,075.1	3,314.4	2,855.3
Korea, Repub.	1,044.8	537.4	311.7
Latvia	1,081.3	1,365.8	1,313.2
Lithuania	933.6	1,101.8	994.2
Netherlands	1,583.3	1,732.4	1,486.1
Norway	656.8	804.8	663.2
Poland	694.1	908.2	1,170.5
Russia	8,889.1	7,481.1	8,171.2
Sweden	5,608.1	6,096.9	5,603.8
Switzerland	646.8	640.6	601.4
Ukraine	631.7	704.6	588.5
United Kingdom	1,894.2	2,001.6	1,437.5
USA	2,293.0	3,095.9	2,680.7
Total (incl. others)	61,661.1	67,377.9	60,475.2

Exports f.o.b.	1997	1998	1999
Belarus	559.4	418.7	268.5
Belgium	466.8	547.2	557.2
Denmark	1,302.7	1,657.1	1,696.6
Finland	6,386.5	8,542.0	8,378.5
France	285.4	412.7	517.4
Germany	2,277.8	2,512.6	3,237.2
Italy	307.7	331.9	468.5
Latvia	3,516.7	4,298.6	3,766.3
Lithuania	2,479.1	2,128.0	1,675.2
Netherlands	1,374.2	1,002.7	1,441.5
Norway	659.9	940.9	1,056.0
Russia	7,679.5	6,080.7	3,969.8
Sweden	5,498.0	7,609.7	8,103.6
Switzerland	785.2	709.7	196.6
Ukraine	2,036.3	2,268.9	1,234.4
United Kingdom	1,492.9	1,941.9	1,930.9
USA	764.7	874.9	1,056.6
Total (incl. others)	40,785.4	45,575.2	43,157.0

Transport

DOMESTIC PASSENGER TRAFFIC (million passenger-kilometres)

	1997	1998	1999
Railway traffic	262	236	238
Road traffic (bus traffic)	2,238	2,265	2,222
Sea traffic	302	372	433
Air traffic	209	227	298
Total public transport	3,011	3,100	3,191

DOMESTIC FREIGHT TRAFFIC (million ton-kilometres)

	1997	1998	1999
Railway traffic	5,102	6,079	7,295
Road traffic	2,773	3,791	3,975
Sea traffic	26,524	24,764	19,221
Air traffic	5	3	4
Total public transport	34,404	34,637	30,495

ROAD TRAFFIC ('000 motor vehicles in use at 31 December)

	1997	1998	1999
Passenger cars	427.7	451.0	458.7
Buses and coaches	6.5	6.3	6.2
Lorries and vans	76.6	80.6	81.0
Motor cycles	5.3	6.1	6.7

SHIPPING
Merchant Fleet (registered at 31 December)

	1996	1997	1998
Number of vessels	220	229	239
Total displacement ('000 grt)	545	602	522

Source: Lloyd's Register of Shipping.

International Sea-borne Freight Traffic ('000 metric tons)

	1997	1998	1999
Goods loaded	18,763	22,725	28,588
Goods unloaded	4,476	4,632	5,767

CIVIL AVIATION (traffic on scheduled services)

	1995	1996	1997
Kilometres flown (million) . .	4	4	5
Passengers carried ('000) . .	169	149	231
Passenger-km (million) . .	107	114	147
Total ton-km (million) . . .	10	11	14

Source: UN, *Statistical Yearbook*.

1998: Passengers carried 324,200; Freight carried (incl. mail) 4,700 metric tons; Passenger-km 227.3m.
1999: Passengers carried 336,200; Freight carried (incl. mail) 5,500 metric tons; Passenger-km 297.6m.

Tourism

FOREIGN TOURIST ARRIVALS BY COUNTRY OF ORIGIN

	1997	1998	1999
Finland	1,000,112	1,331,993	1,199,584
Sweden	19,607	26,696	33,148
USA and Canada . . .	19,074	34,589	32,065
Total (incl. others) . . .	1,099,448	1,467,411	1,350,366

Receipts from tourism (US $ million): 465 in 1997, 534 in 1998. (Sources: World Tourism Organization, *Yearbook of Tourism Statistics* and World Bank, *World Development Indicators*.)

Communications Media

(At 1 January)

	1997	1998	1999
Telephones ('000 main lines in use)	469	499	515
Mobile cellular telephones ('000 subscribers)	151	249	388
Books published (titles)* . . .	3,317	3,090	3,265
Daily newspapers (number) . .	15	16	17
Non-daily newspapers (number) . .	87	93	88
Periodicals (number)	572	578	930

* Including pamphlets.

Radio receivers in use: 221,000 in 1996.
Television receivers in use: 455,000 in 1996.
Telefax stations: 13,000 in 1995. (Source: UN, *Statistical Yearbook*.)

Education

(1999/2000)

	Institutions	Teachers	Students
Pre-primary	663	8,070*	51,100
Primary	425 ⎫		184,700 ⎫
General secondary . . .	236 ⎬ 18,045		37,500 ⎬
Special	45 ⎭		5,700
Vocational and professional . .	86	1,345†	31,147‡
Universities, etc.	33	3,052§	46,409‡

* Figure refers to 1997/98. Including staff in child care and pre-school institutions (Source: UNESCO, *Statistical Yearbook*).
† Full-time teachers only.
‡ Including students enrolled in evening and correspondence courses.
§ Figure refers to 1996/97.

Directory

The Constitution

A new Constitution, based on that of 1938, was adopted by a referendum held on 28 June 1992. It took effect on 3 July. The following is a summary of its main provisions:

FUNDAMENTAL RIGHTS, LIBERTIES AND DUTIES

Every child with one parent who is an Estonian citizen has the right, by birth, to Estonian citizenship. Anyone who, as a minor, lost his or her Estonian citizenship has the right to have his or her citizenship restored. The rights, liberties and duties of all persons, as listed in the Constitution, are equal for Estonian citizens as well as for citizens of foreign states and stateless persons who are present in Estonia.

All persons are equal before the law. No one may be discriminated against on the basis of nationality, race, colour, sex, language, origin, creed, political or other persuasions. Everyone has the right to the protection of the state and the law. Guaranteeing rights and liberties is the responsibility of the legislative, executive and judicial powers, as well as of local government. Everyone has the right to appeal to a court of law if his or her rights or liberties have been violated.

The state organizes vocational education and assists in finding work for persons seeking employment. Working conditions are under state supervision. Employers and employees may freely join unions and associations. Estonian citizens have the right to engage in commercial activities and to form profit-making associations. The property rights of everyone are inviolable. All persons legally present in Estonia have the right to freedom of movement and choice of abode. Everyone has the right to leave Estonia.

Everyone has the right to health care and to education. Education is compulsory for school-age children. Everyone has the right to instruction in Estonian.

The official language of state and local government authorities is Estonian. In localities where the language of the majority of the population is other than Estonian, local government authorities may use the language of the majority of the permanent residents of that locality for internal communication.

THE PEOPLE

The people exercise their supreme power through citizens who have the right to vote by: i) electing the Riigikogu (legislature); ii) participating in referendums. The right to vote belongs to every Estonian citizen who has attained the age of 18 years.

THE RIIGIKOGU

Legislative power rests with the Riigikogu (State Assembly). It comprises 101 members, elected every four years in free elections on the principle of proportionality. Every citizen entitled to vote who has attained 21 years of age may stand as a candidate for the Riigikogu.

The Riigikogu adopts laws and resolutions; decides on the holding of referendums; elects the President of the Republic; ratifies or rejects foreign treaties; authorizes the candidate for Prime Minister to form the Council of Ministers; adopts the national budget and approves the report on its execution; may declare a state of emergency, or, on the proposal of the President, declare a state of war, order mobilization and demobilization.

The Riigikogu elects from among its members a Chairman (Speaker) and two Deputy Chairmen to direct the work of the Riigikogu.

THE PRESIDENT

The President of the Republic is the Head of State of Estonia. The President represents Estonia in international relations; appoints and recalls, on the proposal of the Government, diplomatic representatives of Estonia and accepts letters of credence of diplomatic representatives accredited to Estonia; declares regular (and early) elections to the Riigikogu; initiates amendments to the Constitution; nominates the candidate for the post of Prime Minister; and is the Supreme Commander of Estonia's armed forces.

The President is elected by secret ballot of the Riigikogu for a term of five years. No person may be elected to the office for more than two consecutive terms. Any Estonian citizen by birth, who is at least 40 years of age, may stand as a candidate for President.

Should the President not be elected after three rounds of voting, the Speaker of the Riigikogu convenes, within one month, an Electoral Body to elect the President.

THE GOVERNMENT

Executive power is held by the Government of the Republic (Council of Ministers). The Government implements national, domestic and foreign policies; directs and co-ordinates the work of government institutions; organizes the implementation of legislation, the resolutions of the Riigikogu, and the edicts of the President; submits draft legislation to the Riigikogu, as well as foreign treaties; prepares a draft of the national budget and presents it to the Riigikogu; administers the implementation of the national budget; and organizes relations with foreign states.

The Government comprises the Prime Minister and Ministers. The President of the Republic nominates a candidate for Prime Minister, who is charged with forming a new government.

JUDICIAL SYSTEM

Justice is administered solely by the courts. They are independent in their work and administer justice in accordance with the Constitution and laws. The court system is comprised of rural and city, as well as administrative, courts (first level); district courts (second level); and the Supreme Court of the Republic of Estonia (the highest court in the land).

The Government

HEAD OF STATE

President: Lennart Meri (elected 5 October 1992, re-elected 20 September 1996).

COUNCIL OF MINISTERS
(March 2001)

A coalition of the Estonian Reform Party (ERP), the Pro Patria (Fatherland) Union and the People's Party Moderates.

Prime Minister: Mart Laar (Pro Patria—Fatherland—Union).

Minister of Internal Affairs: Tarmo Loodus (Pro Patria—Fatherland—Union).

Minister of Foreign Affairs: Toomas Hendrik Ilves (Moderates).

Minister of Justice: Märt Rask (ERP).

Minister of Economic Affairs: Mikhel Pärnoja (Moderates).

Minister of Finance: Siim Kallas (ERP).

Minister of Transport and Communications: Toivo Jürgenson (Pro Patria—Fatherland—Union).

Minister of the Environment: Heiki Kranich (ERP).

Minister of Culture: Signe Kivi (ERP).

Minister of Education: Tõnis Lukas (Pro Patria—Fatherland—Union).

Minister of Agriculture: Ivari Padar (Moderates).

Minister of Social Affairs: Eiki Nestor (Moderates).

Minister of Defence: Jüri Luik (Pro Patria—Fatherland—Union).

Minister without Portfolio (responsible for Ethnic Issues): Katrin Saks (Moderates).

Minister without Portfolio (responsible for Regional Affairs): Toivo Asmer (ERP).

Secretary of State of the State Chancellery: Aino Lepik von Wirén.

MINISTRIES

Office of the Prime Minister: Rahukohtu 3, Tallinn 15161; tel. 631-6701; fax 631-6704; e-mail peaminister@rk.ee; internet www.riik.ee/primeminister/.

State Chancellery: Rahukohtu 3, Tallinn 15161; tel. 693-5860; fax 693-5914; e-mail riigikantselei@rk.ee; internet www.riik.ee/chancellery/.

Ministry of Agriculture: Lai 39/41, Tallinn 15056; tel. 625-6101; fax 625-6200; e-mail pm@agri.ee; internet www.agri.ee.

Ministry of Culture: Suur Karja 23, Tallinn 15076; tel. 628-2222; fax 628-2200; e-mail info@kul.ee; internet www.kul.ee.

Ministry of Defence: Sakala 1, Tallinn 10141; tel. 640-6012; fax 640-6001; e-mail info@kmin.ee; internet www.mod.gov.ee.

Ministry of Economic Affairs: Harju 11, Tallinn 15072; tel. 625-6342; fax 631-3660; e-mail info@mineco.ee; internet www.mineco.ee.

Ministry of Education: Tõnismägi 9/11, Tallinn 15192; tel. 628-1333; fax 631-1213; e-mail hm@hm.ee; internet www.hm.ee.

Ministry of the Environment: Toompuiestee 24, Tallinn 15172; tel. 626-2800; fax 626-2801; e-mail min@ekm.envir.ee; internet www.envir.ee.

Ministry of Finance: Suur-Ameerika 1, Tallinn 15006; tel. 611-3558; fax 696-6810; e-mail info@fin.ee; internet www.fin.ee.

Ministry of Foreign Affairs: Islandi Väljak 1, Tallinn 15049; tel. 631-7000; fax 631-7099; e-mail vminfo@vm.ee; internet www.vm.ee.

Ministry of Internal Affairs: Pikk 61, Tallinn 15065; tel. 612-5001; fax 612-5087; e-mail sisemin@sisemin.gov.ee; internet www.sisemin.gov.ee.

Ministry of Justice: Tõnismägi 5A, Tallinn 15191; tel. 620-8100; fax 620-8109; e-mail sekretar@just.ee; internet www.just.ee.

Ministry of Social Affairs: Gonsiori 29, Tallinn 15191; tel. 626-9700; fax 626-9802; e-mail smin@sm.ee; internet www.sm.ee.

Ministry of Transport and Communications: Viru 9, Tallinn 15081; tel. 639-7659; fax 639-7606; e-mail info@tsm.ee; internet www.tsm.ee/tsm.

President and Legislature

PRESIDENT

The presidential election was held on 26–27 August 1996 in the Riigikogu. LENNART MERI and ARNOLD RÜÜTEL were the contenders. A two-thirds' majority (68 votes) was needed, but, in three rounds of voting, neither contender achieved this. A larger electoral college, comprising the 101 parliamentary deputies and 273 representatives from local government, was convened on 20 September. Five candidates contested the first round of the election and, as no candidate achieved the necessary 188 votes, the leading two candidates, LENNART MERI and ARNOLD RÜÜTEL, proceeded to the second round of voting. The election was won by LENNART MERI, with 196 votes.

Election, 20 September 1996

| | Votes | |
Candidate	First Round	Second Round*
LENNART MERI	139	196
ARNOLD RÜÜTEL	85	126
TUNNE KELAM	76	—
ENN TOUGU	47	—
SIIRI OVIIR	25	—

* There were 44 abstentions and six invalid votes, with two electors absent.

RIIGIKOGU
(State Assembly)

Riigikogu: Lossi plats 1A, Tallinn 0100; tel. 631-6331; fax 631-6334; e-mail margit.liivoja@riigikogu.mailnet.fi.

Speaker: TOOMAS SAVI.

Deputy Speakers: TUNNE KELAM, SIIRI OVIIR.

General Election, 7 March 1999

Parties	% of votes	Seats
Estonian Centre Party	23.41	28
Pro Patria (Fatherland) Union	16.09	18
Estonian Reform Party	15.92	18
Moderates*†	15.21	17
Estonian Coalition Party*‡	7.58	7
Estonian Country People's Party	7.27	7
United People's Party of Estonia*§	6.13	6
Others	8.39	0
Total	**100.00**	**101**

* As political parties require a minimum of 5% of the votes cast to obtain representation in the Riigikogu, several smaller parties formed informal alliances (formal alliances were proscribed in November 1998) and campaigned on the same electoral list under one party's name.

† Nine seats were won by the People's Party and eight by the Moderates. The two parties subsequently merged to form the People's Party Moderates in November 1999.

‡ Three seats were won by the Estonian Coalition Party, two by the Estonian Rural Union and two by the Estonian Pensioners' and Families' Party.

§ Two seats were won by the Estonian Social-Democratic Labour Party and the remaining four seats were taken by the United People's Party of Estonia and the Russian Unity Party.

Political Organizations

Estonian Blue Party (Eesti Sinine Erakond): Ahtri 6/112, Tallinn 10151; tel. 625-9895; fax 625-9810; e-mail sinine.erakond@mail.ee; internet www.gaia.gi.ee/ese/ese2.html; Sec.-Gen. ANNELI MILISTVER.

Estonian Centre Party (Eesti Keskerakond): Toom-Rüütli 3/5, Tallinn 10130; POB 3737, Tallinn 0090; tel. 627-3460; fax 627-3461; e-mail keskerakond@keskerakond.ee; internet www.keskerakond.ee; absorbed the Estonian Green Party in mid-1998; f. 1991; Chair. EDGAR SAVISAAR.

Estonian Christian People's Party (Eesti Kristlik Rahvapartei): Narva mnt. 51, Tallinn 10152; tel. 627-5730; fax 527-5708; e-mail ekrpkesk@uninet.ee; internet www.ekrpi.ee/sisu.htm.

Estonian Coalition Party (ECP) (Eesti Koonderakond): Tulika 19, Tallinn 10613; tel. 650-5113; fax 650-5114; e-mail koondera@online.ee; internet www.koonderakond.ee; f. 1991; Chair. MÄRT KUBO; Sec.-Gen. JUHAN HINDOV.

Estonian Democratic Party: Tallinn; f. 2000 by merger of the Development Party and members of the Estonian Blue Party.

Estonian National Progressive Party: Tallinn; f. 1993; Chair. ANTS ERM.

Estonian People's Union (Eestimaa Rahvaliit): Marja 4D, Tallinn 10617; tel. 611-2909; fax 611-2908; e-mail erl@erl.ee; internet www.erl.ee; f. 2000 by merger of the Estonian Pensioners' and Families' Party and the Estonian Rural People's Union; Chair. ARNOLD RÜÜTEL; Deputy Chair. MAI TREIAL.

Estonian Reform Party (ERP) (Eesti Reformierakond): Tõnismagi 3A–15, Tallinn 0001; tel. 640-8740; fax 640-8741; e-mail info@reform.ee; internet www.reform.ee; f. 1994; Gen. Sec. HEIKI KRANICH; Chair. SIIM KALLAS.

Estonian Royalist Party (Eesti Rojalistlik Partei): POB 300, Tartu 2400; tel. (7) 432-986; fax (7) 431-466; f. 1989; advocates the establishment of a Kingdom of Estonia; Chair. KALLE KULBOK.

Estonian Russian-Baltic Party: Uus 32, Tallinn 10111; tel. 699-7046; fax 699-7047; e-mail partei@vbee.ee; internet www.vbee.ee; f. 2000; Russian-speaking party; upholds the rights of minority nationalities; Chair. SERGEY IVANOV.

Estonian Social-Democratic Labour Party (Eesti Sotsiaaldemokraatlik Tööpartei): Central Post Office, POB 4102, Tallinn 10111; tel. (2) 493-965; fax (2) 472-147; f. 1920 as the Communist Party of Estonia; renamed Estonian Democratic Labour Party in 1992 and as above in 1998; Chair. TIIT TOOMSALU; Dep. Chair. ENDEL PAAP; 1,041 mems (1998).

Estonian United People's Party (Eestimaa Ühendatud Rahvapartei): Estonia pst. 3/5, Tallinn 10141; tel. 645-5335; fax 645-5336; e-mail yhendatudfr@riigikogu.ee; internet www.stv.ee/~eurp/; f. 1994; represents the Russian-speaking minority in Estonia; Chair. VIKTOR ANDREYEV.

Farmers' Union (Põllumeeste Kogu): POB 543, Tallinn 0010; tel. (2) 437-733; f. 1992; Chair. ELDUR PARDER.

Moderates' Women's Assembly (Moodukad Naiskogu): Tallinn; e-mail moodukad@dafanet.ee; f. 1996 to encourage women to take part in politics; Pres. HELSO PIKHOF.

People's Party Moderates (Moodukad): Valli 4, Tallinn 10148; POB 3437, Tallinn 19090; tel. (6) 620-7980; fax 620-7988; e-mail kirjod@moodukad.ee; internet www.moodukad.ee; f. 1999 by merger of the People's Party and the Moderates' Party; Chair. ANDRES TARAND; Sec.-Gen. TONU KOIV.

Progressive Party (Arengupartei): Tallinn; e-mail arengupartei@online.ee; f. 1996 following a split in the Estonian Centre Party; Chair. ANDRA VEIDEMANN; Sec.-Gen. TOIVO KEVA; 1,300 mems.

Pro Patria (Fatherland) Union (Isamaaliit): Wismari 11, Tallinn 10136; tel. (6) 263-325; fax (6) 263-324; e-mail info@isamaaliit.ee; internet www.isamaaliit.ee; f. 1995 by merger of the National Fatherland Party (Isamaa, f. 1992) and the Estonian National Independence Party (f. 1988); Chair. MART LAAR; 2,800 mems.

Republican Party (Vabariiklik): Kuperjanovi 5b-5, Tartu; tel. 521-4512; e-mail leping.vp@mail.ee; internet www.hot.ee/vabpar; f. 1999; Chair. KRISTJAN OLARI LEPING.

Russian Christian Union: Tallinn; f. 1996; represents Russians in Estonia; Founder BORIS PILAR.

Russian Democratic Movement: Tallinn; tel. (2) 440-421; fax (2) 441-237; f. 1991 to promote domestic peace and mutual understanding between Estonians and Russians living in Estonia.

Russian Party of Estonia: c/o Riigikogu, Lossi plats 1A, Tallinn 0100; f. 1994; merged with the Russian People's Party of Estonia in early 1996; part of the Our Home is Estonia alliance; represents the Russian-speaking minority in Estonia; Chair. NIKOLAI MASPANOV; 1,250 mems.

Russian Unity Party (RUP): Tallinn; f. 1997 by former members of the Russian Party of Estonia; Leader GENNADI KULKOV.

Social Democratic Labour Party: Tallinn.

Diplomatic Representation

EMBASSIES IN ESTONIA

Belarus: Tallinn; Ambassador: MIKHAIL MARYNICH.

Canada: Tallinn; Ambassador: PETER MCKELLAR.

China, People's Republic: Narva mnt. 98, Tallinn 15009; tel. 601-5830; fax 601-5833; Ambassador: ZOU MINGONG.

Czech Republic: Roosikrantsi 11, Tallinn 10119; tel. 627-4400; fax 631-4716; Ambassador: VLADISLAV LABUDEK.

Denmark: Wismari 5, Tallinn 15047; tel. 630-6400; fax 630-6421; e-mail tllamb@tllamb.um.dk; internet www.denmark.ee; Ambassador: JØRGEN MUNK RASMUSSEN.

Finland: Kohtu 4, Tallinn 15180; tel. 610-3200; fax 610-3281; internet www.finemb.ee; Ambassador: PEKKA OINONEN.

France: Toom-Kuninga 20, Tallinn 0100; tel. 631-1492; fax 631-1385; internet www.viabalt.ee/estfra/; Ambassador: JEAN-JACQUES SUBRENAT.

Germany: Toom-Kuninga 11, Tallinn 15048; tel. 627-5300; fax 627-5304; e-mail saksasaa@online.ee; Ambassador: Dr GERHARD ENVER SCHRÖMBGENS.

Italy: Vene 4, Tallinn 10140; tel. 625-6444; fax 631-1370; e-mail italemb1@online.ee; internet www.online.ee/italemb; Ambassador: LUCHINO CORTESE.

Japan: Harju 6, Tallinn 15069; tel. 631-0531; fax 631-0533; e-mail jaapansk@online.ee; Chargé d'affaires a.i.: RYUTARO FUJII.

Latvia: Tõnismägi 10, Tallinn 0100; tel. 646-1313; fax 631-1366; Ambassador: ANDRIS PIEBALGS.

Lithuania: Uustn 15, Tallinn 0001; tel. 631-4030; fax 641-2013; Ambassador: RIMANTAS TOMKUNAS.

Moldova: Tallinn; Ambassador: NICOLAE DUDAU.

Norway: Harju 6, Tallinn 15054; tel. 627-1000; fax 627-1001; e-mail emb.tallinn@mfa.no; Ambassador: PER KR. PEDERSEN.

Poland: Pärnu mnt. 8, Tallinn 10503; tel. 627-8206; fax 644-5221; e-mail ambrptal@netexpress.ee; internet www.online.ee/~poolabrh; Ambassador: JAKUB WOLASIEWICZ.

Portugal: Tallinn; Ambassador: MANUEL DOS MOREIRA DE ANDRADE.

Russia: Pikk 19, Tallinn 10133; tel. 646-4175; fax 646-4178; e-mail vensaat@online.ee; Ambassador: KONSTANTIN PROVALOV.

Slovakia: Tallinn; Ambassador: JOZEF DRAVECKY.

Sweden: Pikk 28, Tallinn 15055; tel. 640-5600; fax 640-5695; Ambassador: ELISABET BORSIIN BONNIER.

Switzerland: Tallinn; Ambassador: HANSRUDOLF HOFFMANN.

Turkey: Tallinn; Ambassador: ALI NAZIM BELGER.

Ukraine: Lahe 6, Tallinn; tel. 601-5815; fax 631-1556; e-mail embukr@eol.ee; internet www.uninet.ee/~embukra; Ambassador: MYKOLA MAKAREVYCH.

United Kingdom: Wismari 6, Tallinn 10136; tel. 667-4700; fax 667-4724; e-mail information@britishembassy.ee; Ambassador: SARAH SQUIRE.

USA: Kentmanni 20, Tallinn 15099; tel. 668-8100; fax 668-8134; Ambassador: MELISSA WELLS.

Judicial System

Supreme Court of the Republic of Estonia: Lossi 17, Tartu 50093; tel. (7) 309-002; fax (7) 309-003; e-mail nc@nc.ee; internet www.nc.ee.

   Chief Justice: UNO LÕHMUS.

   Chairman of the Constitutional Review Chamber: UNO LÕHMUS.

   Chairman of the Civil Chamber: JAANO ODAR.

   Chairman of the Criminal Chamber: JÜRI ILVEST.

   Chairman of the Administrative Law Chamber: TÕNU ANTON.

Legal Chancellor's Office: Tõnismägi 16, Tallinn 15193; tel. 693-8400; fax 693-8401; e-mail info@lc.gov.ee; internet www.gov.ee/estno/oiguskantsler.html; f. 1993; reviews general application of legislative and executive powers and of local governments for conformity with the constitution, supervises activities of state agencies in guaranteeing constitutional rights and freedoms; Legal Chancellor ALLAR JOKS.

Public Prosecutor's Office: Wismari 7, Tallinn 15188; tel. 631-3002; fax 645-1475; e-mail riigiprok@rprok.just.ee; internet www.prokuratuur.ee; State Prosecutor-Gen. RAIVO SEPP.

Religion

CHRISTIANITY

Protestant Churches

Consistory of the Estonian Evangelical Lutheran Church of Estonia: Kiriku plats 3, Tallinn 10130; tel. 627-7350; fax 627-7352; e-mail eelk@eelk.ee; internet www.zzz.ee/eelk; Archbishop JAAN KIIVIT.

Estonian Conference of Seventh-day Adventists: Lille 18, Tartu 51010; tel. (7) 343-211; fax (7) 343-389; f. 1917; e-mail advent@uninet.ee; Chair. TÕNU JUGAR.

Union of Evangelical Christian and Baptist Churches of Estonia: Pargi 9, Tallinn 11620; tel. 670-0698; fax 650-6008; e-mail eekbl@ekklesia.ee; internet www.ekklesia.ee; Pres. HELARI PUU.

United Methodist Church in Estonia: Apteegi 3, Tallinn 10146; tel. (2) 445-447; fax 631-3482; e-mail keskus@emk.edu.ee; f. 1907; Superintendent OLAV PÄRNAMETS.

The Eastern Orthodox Church

Between 1923 and 1940 the Estonian Apostolic Orthodox Church (EAOC) was subordinate to the Constantinople Ecumenical Patriarchate (based in Istanbul, Turkey). Following the Soviet occupation of Estonia in 1940, the EAOC was banned and its churches and communities were placed under the jurisdiction of the Moscow Patriarchate. The leaders of the EAOC went into exile in Stockholm (Sweden). After the restoration of Estonian independence in 1991, negotiations were held between the Constantinople and Moscow Patriarchates over the status of the more than 50 of Estonia's 84 Orthodox congregations that wished to return to Constantinople's jurisdiction. As no agreement was reached, in February 1996 the Constantinople Patriarchate decided unilaterally to restore the EAOC to its jurisdiction. In response, the Russian Orthodox Church suspended relations with Constantinople. The Estonian Government stated that freedom of worship would be guaranteed to the (predominantly Russian-speaking) congregations that wished to remain under the jurisdiction of the Moscow Patriarchate. Relations with Constantinople were restored in May 1996, when the holy synods of the two churches agreed that congregations should be permitted to decide under which jurisdiction they wished to remain.

Estonian Apostolic Orthodox Church: Tallinn; Chair. of Synod NIKOLAI SUURESOOT.

Estonian Orthodox Church of Moscow Patriarchy: Pikk 64/4, Tallinn 10133; tel. 641-1301; fax 641-1302; Archbishop KORNELIUS.

The Roman Catholic Church

At 1 January 2000 there were an estimated 3,500 Roman Catholic adherents in Estonia.

Office of the Apostolic Administrator: Jaan Poska 47, Tallinn 0001; tel. (2) 423-147; fax (2) 426-440; Apostolic Administrator Most Rev. ERWIN JOSEF ENDER (Titular Archbishop of Germania in Numidia), Apostolic Nuncio to Lithuania, Estonia and Latvia (resident in Vilnius, Lithuania).

Roman Catholic Parish of St Peter and St Paul in Tallinn: Vene 18, Tallinn 0001; tel. 644-6367; fax 644-4678; Parish Priest Fr ZBIGNIEW PIŁAT.

Tallinn Parish of the Ukrainian Catholic (Uniate) Church: Võrgu 13–6, Tallinn; tel. 632-4306; Chair. of Bd ANATOLII LYUTYUK.

ISLAM

Estonian Islamic Congregation: Sütiste 52–76, Tallinn 0034; tel. (2) 522-403; f. 1928; Chair. of Bd TIMUR SEIFULLEN.

JUDAISM

Hineirry Jewish Progressive Community of Narva: Narva Partisani 2, Narva 2000; tel. (35) 409-97; Chair. of Bd YEVGENII BORINSKII.

Jewish Community of Estonia: Karu 16, Tallinn; POB 3576, Tallinn 10507; tel. and fax 662-3034; e-mail ciljal@icom.ee; Chair. CILJA LAUD.

Jewish Progressive Community in Tallinn: POB 200, Tallinn; Chair. of Bd DAVID SLOMKA.

The Press

In 1999 there were 105 officially registered newspapers published in Estonia, including 73 in Estonian, and 930 periodicals, including 725 in Estonian. There were 17 daily newspapers in 1999, including 13 in Estonian.

PRINCIPAL NEWSPAPERS

In Estonian except where otherwise stated.

Äripäev (Business Daily): Pärnu mnt. 105, Tallinn 19094; tel. 667-0222; fax 667-0165; e-mail mbp@mbp.ee; internet www.mbp.ee; f. 1989; five days a week; business and finance; Editor-in-Chief IGOR RÕTOV; circ. 17,200.

Den za Dujan (Day After Day): Pärnu mnt. 130, Tallinn 11313; tel. 678-8288; fax 678-8290; e-mail ambre@dd.ee; f. 1991; weekly; in Russian; Editor-in-Chief JANA LITVINOVA; circ. 20,000.

Eesti Ekspress (Estonian Express): Narva mnt. 11E, Tallinn 10151; tel. 669-8080; fax 669-8154; e-mail ekspress@ekspress.ee; f. 1989; weekly; Editor-in-Chief AAVO KOKK; circ. 49,300.

Eesti Kirik (Estonian Church): Ülikooli, Tartu 51003; tel. (7) 431-437; fax (7) 433-243; f. 1923; weekly; Editor-in-Chief SIRJE SEMM; circ. 2,100.

Eesti Päevaleht (Estonian Daily): Pärnu mnt. 67A, POB 433, Tallinn 10151; tel. 614-4498; fax 614-4334; e-mail mail@epl.ee; f. 1905; daily; Editor-in-Chief PRIIT HÕBEMÄGI; circ. 37,000.

Estonija: Madala 16, Tallinn 10315; tel. 665-1100; fax 665-1111; e-mail vestimg@teleport.ee; internet www.vesti.ee; f. 1940; five days a week in Russian (with Estonian edn Mon.); Editor-in-Chief VITALIY KHAITOV; circ. 7,700.

Maaleht (Country News): Toompuiestee 16, Tallinn 10137; tel. 661-3718; fax (2) 662-292; e-mail ml@maaleht.ee; internet www .maaleht.ee; f. 1987; weekly; problems and aspects of politics, culture, agriculture and country life; Editor-in-Chief SULEV VALNER; circ. 46,000.

ME: POB 120, Kentmanni 18, Tallinn 10502; tel. 628-6123; fax 646-1623; e-mail moles@infonet.ee; three days a week; in Russian; Editor-in-Chief ARKADII PRISJAZHNÕI; circ. 5,100.

Meie Meel (Our Mind): POB 104, Tallinn 0090; tel. (2) 681-253; fax 646-1625; e-mail meiemeel@zzz.ee; f. 1991; weekly; youth paper; Editor-in-Chief MARE VETEMAA; circ. 20,700.

Postimees (Postman): Maakri 23A, Tallinn 10145; tel. 666-2302; fax 666-2301; e-mail erik.roose@postimees.ee; f. 1857; daily; Editor-in-Chief URMAS KLAAS; circ. 60,200.

Sirp: POB 388, Tallinn 10503; tel. 644-8868; fax 644-9247; f. 1940; weekly; Editor-in-Chief MIHKEL MUTT; circ. 3,500.

SL Õhtuleht (Evening Gazette): Narva mnt. 13, POB 106, Tallinn 10501; tel. 614-4805; fax 614-4001; e-mail priit@sloleht.ee; internet www.sloleht.ee; f. 2000 by merger of Õhtuleht and Sõnumileht newspapers; daily; in Estonian; Editor-in-Chief VÄINO KOORBERG; circ. 67,200.

PRINCIPAL PERIODICALS

Akadeemia: Ülikooli 21, Tartu 51007; tel. (7) 431-117; fax (7) 431-373; e-mail akadeemia@akad.ee; f. 1989; monthly; journal of the Union of Writers; Editor-in-Chief AIN KAALEP; circ. 2,200.

Eesti Arst (Estonian Physician): Pepleri 32, Tartu 51010; tel. and fax (7) 427-825; f. 1922; monthly; Editor-in-Chief VÄINO SINISALU; circ. 1,400.

Eesti Loodus (Estonian Nature): Veski 4, POB 100, Tartu 50002; tel. (7) 421-186; fax (7) 427-432; e-mail toimetus@el.loodus.ee; internet www.loodus.ee/el; f. 1933; monthly; popular science; illustrated; Editor-in-Chief UNO SIITAN; circ. 5,200.

Eesti Naine (Estonian Woman): Maakri 23A, Tallinn 10145; tel. 666-2627; fax 666-2557; e-mail katrin.streimann@kirjastus.ee; internet www.kirjastus.ee/eestinaine; f. 1924; monthly; Editor-in-Chief KATRIN STREIMANN; circ. 24,000.

Hea Laps (Good Kid): Harju 1, Tallinn 10146; tel. 631-4428; monthly; for children; Editor-in-Chief LEELO TUNGAL.

Horisont (Horizon): Narva mnt. 5, Tallinn 0117; tel. 661-6163; fax 641-8033; e-mail horisont@horisont.ee; f. 1967; 6 a year; popular scientific; Editor-in-Chief INDREK ROHTMETS; circ. 3,000.

Keel ja Kirjandus (Language and Literature): Roosikrantsi 6, Tallinn 10119; tel. 644-9228; fax 644-1800; e-mail kk@eki.ee; f. 1958; monthly; joint edition of the Academy of Sciences and the Union of Writers; Editor-in-Chief MART MERI; circ. 1,500.

Kodukiri (Your Home): Maakri 23A, Tallinn 10145; tel. 666-2550; fax 666-2558; e-mail velve.saar@kirjastus.ee; f. 1992; monthly; Editor-in-Chief KATRIN KUUSEMÄE; circ. 50,000.

Linguistica Uralica: Roosikrantsi 6, Tallinn 10119; tel. 644-0745; e-mail lu@eki.ee; internet www.gaid.gi.ee/eap/l.-u.htm; f. 1965; Editor-in-Chief VÄINO KLAUS; circ. 400.

Looming (Creation): Harju 1, Tallinn 10146; tel. (2) 627-6420; e-mail looming@hot.ee; f. 1923; journal of the Union of Writers; fiction, poetry, literary criticism; Editor-in-Chief UDO UIBO; circ. 2,000.

Loomingu Raamatukogu (Library of Creativity): Harju 1, Tallinn 10146; tel. 627-6425; f. 1957; journal of the Union of Writers; poetry, fiction and non-fiction by Estonian and foreign authors; Editor-in-Chief TOOMAS HAUG; circ. 1,800.

Maakodu (Country Home): Toompuiestee 16, Tallinn 10137; tel. 660-5306; fax 662-2292; e-mail meelim@maaleht.ee; f. 1989; monthly; Editor-in-Chief MEELI MÜÜRIPEAL; circ. 12,000.

Maamajandus (Country Economy): Toompuiestee 16, Tallinn 10137; tel. 660-5305; fax 662-2292; e-mail ylo@maaleht.ee; montly; Editor-in-Chief ÜLO KALM; circ. 2,000.

Oil Shale: Estonia pst. 7, Tallinn 10143; tel. 646-7512; fax 646-6026; e-mail aili@argus.chemnet.ee; internet gaia.gi.ee/oilshale; f. 1984; quarterly; geology, chemistry, mining, oil-shale industry; Editor-in-Chief JÜRI KANN; circ. 350.

Põllumajandus (Agriculture): Lai 39, Tallinn 0001; tel. 641-1161; f. 1932; monthly; Editor-in-Chief ARVO SIRENDI; circ. 1,000.

Täheke (Little Star): Pärnu mnt. 67A, Tallinn 10134; tel. 646-3697; e-mail tell@tallpost.ee; f. 1960; monthly; illustrated; for 6–10-year-olds; Editor-in-Chief ELJU SILD; circ. 3,500.

Teater, Muusika, Kino (Theatre, Music, Cinema): POB 3200, Narva mnt. 5, Tallinn 10117; tel. 660-1828; fax (2) 660-1887; e-

mail tmk@estpak.ee; f. 1982; monthly; Editor-in-Chief JÜRI AARMA; circ. 1,500.

Vikerkaar (Rainbow): Voorimehe 9, Tallinn 10146; tel. 646-4059; fax (2) 442-484; e-mail vikerkaar@teleport.ee; f. 1986; monthly; fiction, poetry, critical works; in Estonian and Russian; Editor-in-Chief MÄRT VÄLJATAGA; circ. 1,500.

NEWS AGENCIES

BNS (Baltic News Service): Pärnu mnt. 105, Tallinn 15043; tel. 610-8800; fax 610-8811; e-mail bns@bns.ee; internet www.bns.ee; f. 1990; Dir OLEG HARLAMOV.

ETA Interactive: Pärnu mnt. 142, Tallinn 10134; tel. 630-0800; fax 630-0816; e-mail eta@eta.ee; internet www.eta.ee/telefon.html; f. 1918; Dir TIIT LÕHMUS.

PRESS ORGANIZATIONS

Estonian Journalists' Union: Niguliste 4, Tallinn 10134; tel. 646-3699; fax 646-3672; e-mail eal@eal.ee; internet www.eal.ee; f. 1919; Chair. ALLAN ALAKÜLA.

Estonian Newspaper Association: Pärnu mnt. 67A, Tallinn 10134; tel. 646-1005; fax 631-1210; e-mail eall@eall.ee; internet www.eall.ee; f. 1990; 47 mem. newspapers; Man. Dir TARMU TAMMERK.

Estonian Press Council: Pärnu mnt. 67A, Tallinn 10134; tel. 646-1005; fax 631-1210; e-mail eall@eall.ee; Chair. URMAS LOIT.

Publishers

Eesti Raamat (Estonian Book): Laki 26, Tallinn 12915; tel. and fax 658-7889; f. 1940; fiction; Dir ANNE-ASTRI KASK.

Estonian Encyclopaedia Publishers Ltd: Mustamäe 5, Tallinn 10616; tel. 625-9415; fax 656-6542; e-mail encyclo@online.ee; internet www.ene.ee; f. 1991; Man. Dir TÕNU KOGER.

Huma: Vene 14, Tallinn 10123; tel. and fax 644-0955; e-mail huma@online.ee; fiction, non-fiction, children's books, art, calendars; Dir LIIVI KESKPAIK.

Ilmamaa: Vanemuise 19, Tartu 51014; tel. (7) 427-290; fax (2) 427-320; e-mail ilmamaa@ilmamaa.ee; internet www.ilmamaa.ee; general fiction, philosophy, cultural history, electronic publishing; Dir MART JAGOMÄGI.

Koolibri: Pärnu mnt. 10, Tallinn 10148; tel. 644-5223; fax 644-6813; e-mail koolibri@koolibri.ee; internet www.koolibri.ee; f. 1991; textbooks, dictionaries, children's books; Dir ANTS LANG.

Kunst (Fine Art): Lai 34, Tallinn 10133; POB 105, Tallinn 10502; tel. 641-1764; fax 641-1762; e-mail kunst.lai@mail.ee; f. 1957; fine arts, fiction, tourism, history, biographies; Dir SIRJE HELME.

Kupar: Pärnu mnt. 67A, Tallinn 10134; tel. 628-6174; fax 646-2076; e-mail kupar@netexpress.ee; f. 1987; contemporary fiction; Dir IVO SANDRE.

Logos: Toompuiestee 23, Tallinn 10149; tel. and fax 631-1501; f. 1991; religious publications; Chair. INGMAR KURG.

Monokkel: POB 311, Tallinn 10503; tel. 501-6307; fax 656-9176; f. 1988; history, fiction; Dir ANTS ÖÖBIK.

Olion: Laki 26, Tallinn 12915; tel. 655-0175; fax 655-0173; e-mail olion@hot.ee; f. 1989; politics, reference, history, biographies, children's books; Dir ÜLLE UNT.

Õllu: Harju 1, Tallinn 10146; tel. 652-2038; fiction; Chair. of Bd HEINO KIIK.

Olympia: Pikk 2, Tallinn 10123; tel. 644-2549; fax 661-2853; e-mail olympia@online.ee; sports; Editor-in-Chief PAAVO KIVINE.

Perioodika (Periodicals): Voorimehe 9, Tallinn 10146; POB 3648, Tallinn 10507; tel. 644-1252; fax 644-2484; f. 1964; newspapers, guidebooks, periodicals, fiction, children's books in foreign languages; Dir UNO SILLAJÕE.

Publishing House ILO: Modara 14, Tallinn 10612; tel. 661-0553; fax 661-0347; e-mail ilo@ilo.ee; internet www.ilo.ee; dictionaries, encyclopaedias, business, management and law; Dir SILVI-AIRE VILLO.

Tartu University Press: Tiigi 78, Tartu 50410; tel. (7) 375-961; fax (7) 375-944; e-mail tyk@psych.ut.ee; internet www.psych.ut.ee/tup; f. 1958; science, textbooks, etc; Chair. VAIKO TIGANE.

Tiritamm: Laki 15, Tallinn 12915; tel. and fax 656-3616; e-mail tiritamm@hot.ee; f. 1991; children's books; Dir SIRJE SAIMRE.

Valgus Publishers: Tulika 19, Tallinn 10613; tel. 650-5025; fax 650-5104; e-mail info@kirjastusvalgus.ee; internet www .kirjastusvalgus.ee; f. 1965; scientific literature, resource materials and textbooks; Man. Dir MARIKA TAMM.

PUBLISHERS' ASSOCIATION

Estonian Publishers' Association: Laki 17, Tallinn 0006; POB 3366, Tallinn 0090; tel. 650-5592; fax 650-5590; f. 1991; unites 31 publishing houses; Chair. of Bd TÕNU KOGER.

Broadcasting and Communications

TELECOMMUNICATIONS

Regulatory Authorities

Broadcasting Council: Gonsiori 21, Tallinn 15020; tel. 611-4305; fax 611-4457; e-mail rhn@er.ee.

National Communications Board: Ädala 4D, Tallinn 10614; tel. 693-1154; fax 693-1155; e-mail postbox@sa.ee; internet www.sa.ee; Dir JÜRI JÕEMA.

Major Provider

Eesti Telekom AS (Estonian Telecom Ltd): Roosikrantsi 2, Tallinn 10119; tel. 631-1212; fax 631-1224; e-mail mailbox@telekom.ee; internet www.telekom.ee; f. 1992 as Eesti Telefon; privatized in 1999; operates national telecommunications system; Dir-Gen. TOOMAS SOMERA; Chief Exec. JAAN MÄNNIK.

BROADCASTING

Radio

In 2000 there were 30 radio broadcasters operating in Estonia, one on the basis of an international licence, 14 on the basis of a regional licence and 15 on the basis of a local broadcasting licence.

Eesti Raadio (Estonian Radio): Gonsiori 21, Tallinn 15020; tel. 611-4115; fax 611-4457; e-mail raadio@er.ee; internet www.er.ee; f. 1926; five 24-hour channels (three in Estonian, one in Russian and one in English, French and German); external service in English; Chair. and Dir-Gen. AIN SAARNA.

Kristlik Pereraadio (Christian Family Radio): Annemõisa 8, Tartu 50708; tel. and fax (78) 488-458; owned by Tartu Pereraadio Ühing (Family Radio Union of Tartu); Exec. Dir PAAVO PIHLAK.

Raadio Elmaar: Õpetaja 9A, Tartu 51003; tel. (7) 427-927; fax (7) 742-044; owned by AS Radio Elmaar; Dir JAAN HABICHT.

Raadio Kuku: Narva mnt. 63, Tallinn 20606; tel. 630-7660; fax 601-5759; owned by AS Trio LSL; Chair. of Council REIN LANG.

Raadio Sky Pluss: Pärnu mnt. 139C, Tallinn 11317; tel. 654-3210; fax 654-3110; owned by Taevaraadio AS; Chair. HARALD TEHVER.

Raadio Uuno: Narva mnt. 63, Tallinn 20606; tel. 630-7660; fax 601-5759; owned by AS Trio LSL; Chair. of Council REIN LANG.

Raadio V6: Koidula 17, Tallinn 51003; tel. (7) 427-927; fax (7) 420-444; owned by AS Wodlinger International Tallinn; Chair. SIGNE HARMA.

Star Fm: Peterburi tee 81, Tallinn 11415; tel. 622-0288; fax 622-0294; owned by AS Mediainvest Holding; Chair. SVEN NUTMANN.

Television

There are four commercial television stations in Estonia, three of which operate on regional licences, and one of which operates on a local licence. In addition, five cable television licences have been issued. The principal commercial stations are:

Eesti Televisioon (Estonian Television): Faehlmanni 12, Tallinn 15029; tel. 628-4113; fax 628-4155; e-mail etv@etv.ee; internet www.etv.ee; f. 1955; one channel; programmes in Estonian and Russian; Chair. AARE URM.

EVTV: Peterburi 81, Tallinn 0014; tel. 632-8228; fax 632-3650; commercial station; Chair. AARE URM.

Kanal 2 (Channel 2): Maakri 23A, Tallinn 10145; tel. 666-2450; fax 666-2451; e-mail info@kanal2.ee; internet www.kanal2.ee; f. 1993; commercial station; owned by AS Kanal 2; Chair. HANS ERIK MATRE.

TV1: Pirita tee 12, Tallinn 10127; tel. 627-7700; fax 627-7709; owned by Eesti Sóltumatu Televisiooni AS; Chair. RAIT KILLANDI.

TV3: Peterburgi tee 81, Tallinn 11415; tel. 622-0200; fax 622-0201; owned by AS TV3, Exec. Dir MART LUIK.

Finance

(cap. = capital; res = reserves; dep. = deposits; m. = million; brs = branches; amounts in kroons, unless otherwise stated)

BANKING

The bank of Estonia was re-established in 1990, as was a private banking system. During a crisis in the financial sector in 1992 a number of weaker banks collapsed and others merged. New legislation was subsequently enacted to strengthen the sector, with increased supervision. A currency board became responsible for monetary supervision in 1992.

Central Bank

Bank of Estonia (Eesti Pank): Estonia pst. 13, Tallinn 15095; tel. 668-0719; fax 668-0836; e-mail info@epbe.ee; internet www.ee/epbe; f. 1918, re-established 1990; central bank of Estonia; bank of issue; cap. and res 2,220.7m., dep. 4,911.2m. (Dec. 1999); Pres. VAHUR KRAFT.

Commercial Banks

Estonian Credit Bank (Eesti Krediidipank): Narva mnt. 4, Tallinn 15014; tel. 640-5000; fax 661-6037; e-mail krediidipank@ekp.ee; f. 1992; cap. 71.5m., res 24.6m., dep. 474.8m. (Dec. 1999); Pres. REIN OTSASON; Vice-Pres. ANDRUS KLUGE; 12 brs.

Esttexbank: Sakala 1, Tallinn 0100; tel. (2) 666-657; fax (2) 444-102; f. 1989; Chair. MART SILD; 30 employees.

EVEA Bank: Pronski 19, Tallinn 10124; tel. 667-1300; fax 667-1033; e-mail info@evb.ee; internet www.evb.ee; f. 1989; cap. 61.0m., res 14.7m., dep. 653.1m. (Dec. 1997); Pres. and Chief Exec. BORIS SHPUNGIN; 12 brs.

Hansabank: Liivalaia 8, Tallinn 15040; tel. 613-1310; fax 613-1410; e-mail webmaster@hansa.ee; internet www.hansa.ee; f. 1991; cap. 787.6m., res 3,177.3m., dep. 19,458.8m. (Dec. 1999); merger with Estonian Savings Bank (Eesti Hoiupank) approved in July 1998; Chair. of Bd INDREK NEIVELT; 127 brs.

Land Bank of Estonia (Eesti Maapank): Narva mnt 11A, Tallinn 0001; tel. 640-8300; fax 640-8301; f. 1989 as Virumaa Kommertspank, current name adopted in 1996; cap. 72.0m., res 7.1m., dep. 932.8m. (Dec. 1996); Chair. MALLE EENMAA.

Sampo Bank: Narva mnt. 11, Tallinn 15015; tel. 630-2100; fax 630-2200; e-mail bank@optiva.ee; internet www.optiva.ee; f. 1998 as Optiva Bank, by merger of Estonian Forexbank and Estonian Investment Bank; name changed as above in January 2001 following the purchase in 2000 of a 93% stake by the Sampo—Leonia group; cap. 473.2m., res 49.5m., dep. 3,076.2m. (Dec. 1999); Chair. HARMO VÄRK; 7 brs.

Tallinn Business Bank Ltd (Tallinna Äripanga AS): Estonia pst. 3–5, Tallinn 15097; tel. 668-8000; fax 668-8001; e-mail info@tbb.ee; internet www.tbb.ee; f. 1991; cap. 63.4m., dep. 172.2m. (Dec. 1998); Pres. NEEME ROOSIMÄGI.

Union Bank of Estonia (Eesti Ühispank): Tornimäe 2, Tallinn 15010; tel. 665-5100; fax 665-5102; e-mail postkast@eyp.ee; internet www.eyp.ee; f. 1992; cap. 665.6m., res 1,645.1m., dep. 9,183.9m. (Dec. 1999); merged with North Estonia Bank in Jan. 1997 and with Tallinna Pank in July 1998; Pres. AIN HANSCHMIDT; 90 brs.

Foreign Bank

Merita Bank Ltd (Finland): Hobujaama 4, Tallinn 10051; tel. 628-3200; fax 628-3201; e-mail merita@estpak.ee; f. 1995; Gen. Man. HEIKKI VIITANEN.

Banking Association

Estonian Banking Association (Eesti Pangaliit): Ahtri 12, Tallinn 10151; tel. 611-6567; fax 611-6568; e-mail post@pangaliit.ee; internet www.pangaliit.ee; f. 1992; Chair. HARMO VÄRK; Man. Dir VIKTOR HÜTT.

STOCK EXCHANGE

Tallinn Stock Exchange: Pärnu mnt. 12, Tallinn 10148; tel. 640-8840; fax 640-8801; e-mail tse@tse.ee; internet www.tse.ee; f. 1995; Chair. GERT TIIVAS.

INSURANCE

Insurance Supervisory Authority of Estonia: Lauteri 5, Tallinn 10114; tel. 610-6700; fax 610-6701; e-mail secretary@eisa.ee; internet www.eisa.ee; f. 1993; Dir-Gen. KAIDO TROPP.

Principal non-life companies include Balti Kindlustus (BICO) Ltd, Eesti Varakindlustus Ltd, ETAS Kindlustus Ltd, Hansa Kindlustus Ltd, Inges Kindlustus Ltd, Kalju Ltd, Leks Kindlustus Ltd, Nordika Kindlustus Ltd, Polaris-Vara Ltd, Salva Kindlustus Ltd, Sampo Kindlustus Ltd, Seesam Rahvusvaheline Kindlustus Ltd and Ühiskindlustus.

Principal life companies include AB Elukindlustus Ltd, Bico Elukindlustus Ltd, Eesti Elukindlustus Ltd, Hansapanga Kindlustus Ltd, Leks Elukindlustus Ltd, Nordika Elukindlustus Ltd, Polaris-Elu Ltd and Seesam Elukindlustus Ltd.

Trade and Industry

GOVERNMENT AGENCIES

Consumer Protection Board: Kiriku 4, Tallinn 15071; tel. 620-1700; fax 620-1701; e-mail info@consumer.ee; Dir-Gen. HELLE ARUNIIT.

Estonian Export Agency: Rävala pst 6–602B, Tallinn 0001; tel. 631-3851; fax 641-0312; Dir KRISTJAN KIVIPALU.

Estonian Grain Board: Hobujaama 1, Tallinn 0001; tel. (2) 432-815; fax 641-9075; Dir-Gen. AGO SOOTS.

Estonian Investment Agency: Roosikrantsi 11, Tallinn 10119; tel. 627-9420; fax 627-9427; e-mail info@eia.ee; internet www.investinestonia.com; Dir MAIT MARRAN.

Estonian Privatization Agency (Eesti Erastamisagentuur): Rävala 6, Tallinn 0105; tel. 630-5600; fax 630-5699; e-mail eea@eea.ee; internet www.eea.ee/; Dir-Gen. VÄINO SARNET.

Estonian Trade Council: Kiriku 2, Tallinn 0100; tel. (2) 444-703; fax 631-4117; f. 1991; Dir AARE PUUR.

National Standards Board of Estonia: Aru 10, Tallinn 10317; tel. 651-9200; fax 651-9220; e-mail info@evs.ee; Dir-Gen. ARNO UNIVER.

Enterprise Estonia: Roosikrantsi 11, Tallinn 10119; tel. 627-9279; fax 627-9427; e-mail info@eia.ee; internet www.eia.ee; Chair. URMAS VAHUR.

CHAMBER OF COMMERCE

Estonian Chamber of Commerce and Industry (ECCI): Toom-Kooli 17, Tallinn 10130; tel. 646-0244; fax 646-0245; e-mail koda@koda.ee; internet www.koda.ee; f. 1925; Pres. TOOMAS LUMAN; Gen. Dir MART RELVE.

INDUSTRIAL AND TRADE ASSOCIATIONS

Association of Construction Material Producers of Estonia (Eesti Ehitusmaterjalide Tootjate Liit): Kiriku 6, Tallinn 10130; tel. 629-1018; fax 648-9062; e-mail eetl@hot.ee; internet www.hot.ee/eetl; Pres. VAMBOLA JUURMANN.

Association of Estonian Electrotechnical and Electronic Industry: Pirita 20, Tallinn 0001; tel. (2) 238-981; fax (2) 237-827; Pres. GUNNAR TOOMSOO.

Association of Estonian Food Industry: Gonsiori 29, Tallinn 10147; tel. (2) 422-246; fax 631-2718; e-mail ettl@online.ee; internet www.online.ee/~ettl; f. 1993; Man. Dir HELVE REMMEL.

Association of Estonian International Road Carriers (Eesti Rahvusvaheliste Autovedajate Assotsiatsioon): Narva mnt. 91, Tallinn 10127; tel. 627-3740; fax 627-3741; e-mail info@eraa.ee; internet www.eraa.ee; Sec.-Gen. TOLVO KULDKEPP.

Association of Estonian Local Industry: Gonsiori 29, Tallinn 0100; tel (2) 422-367; fax (2) 424-962; Chair. HEINO VASAR.

Estimpex Foreign Trade Association: Uus 32/34, Tallinn 0101; tel. (2) 601-462; fax (2) 602-184; import and export of household fixtures, foodstuffs, souvenirs and oil-based products; Gen. Dir OSVALD KALDRE.

Estonian Agricultural Producers Central Union (Eestimaa Pollumajandustootjate Keskliit): Lai 39/41, Tallinn 0100; tel. (2) 602-045; fax (2) 440-601; Chair. of Bd HEINO PRIIMÄGI.

Estonian Asphalt Pavement Association (Eesti Asfaldiliit): Parnu 24, Tallinn 10141; tel. 611-9365; fax 611-9360; f. 1991; co-ordinates Estonian asphalt paving and mixing companies; Chair. of Bd ALEKSANDER KALDAS.

Estonian Association of Construction Entrepreneurs (Eesti Ehitusettevõtjate Liit): Kiriku 6, Tallinn 10130; tel. and fax 641-0071; e-mail eeel@eeel.ee; internet www.hot.ee/eeel; Man. Dir ILMAR LINK.

Estonian Association of Small and Medium-sized Enterprises (EVEA): Pronksi 3, Tallinn 10124; tel. 640-3935; fax 631-2451; e-mail sme@evea.ee; internet www.evea.ee; f. 1988; Pres. RIIVO SINIJÄRV; Man. Dir MARGIT KALLASTE.

Estonian Clothing and Textile Association (Eesti Rõivaja Tekstiililiit): Tartu mnt. 63, Tallinn 10115; tel. 611-5567; fax 611-5568; e-mail ertl@online.ee; internet www.online.ee/~ertl; Chair. MADIS VÕÕRAS.

Estonian Dairy Association (Eesti Piimaliit): Vilmsi 53, Tallinn 10147; tel. (2) 430-715; fax (2) 643-0418 Chair. ENN SOKK.

Estonian Fisheries Association: Liivalaia 14, Tallinn 0100; tel. (2) 683-442; fax (2) 682-283; Chair. HEINO PALU.

Estonian Forest Federation (Eesti Metsaliit): Gonsiori 29, Tallinn 0001; tel. (2) 421-559; fax (2) 423-739; Pres. MART ERIK.

Estonian Gas Association (Eesti Gaasiliit): Liivalaia 9, Tallinn 0001; tel. 646-1571; fax 631-4340; Chair. of Bd ANDRES SAAR.

Estonian Hotel and Restaurant Association (Easti Hotellide ja Restoranide Liit): Kiriku 6, Tallinn 10130; tel. 641-1428; fax 641-1425; e-mail info@ehrl.ee; Chair. of Bd TARMO SUMBERG.

Estonian Meat Association (Eesti Lihaliit): Lai 39/41, Tallinn 10133; tel. and fax 641-1035; f. 1989; 29 mem. companies (1999); Chair. of Bd PEETER MASPANOV.

ETK Managers' Club: Narva mnt. 7, Tallinn 10117; tel. 630-2324; fax 630-2333; f. 1991; Pres. GEORG ILVEST.

Federation of Estonian Chemical Industries: Kiriku 6, Tallinn 10130; tel. and fax 648-9004; e-mail info@keemia.ee; internet www.keemia.ee; f. 1991; 32 mem. enterprises; Chair. ILMAR VESIALIIK.

Federation of Estonian Engineering Industry: Mustamäe 4, Tallinn 10621; tel. 611-5893; fax 656-6640; e-mail eml@ltnet.ee; f. 1991; 80 mem. enterprises; Chair. of Bd MIHKEL PIKNER.

Union of Estonian Automobile Enterprises (Eesti Autoettevõtete Liit): Magasini 31, Tallinn 10138; tel. 643-9476; fax 644-3345; e-mail al@autoettevoteliit.ee; Pres. MATI MÄGI.

Union of Estonian Breweries (Eesti Õlletootjate Liit): Tähtvere 58/62, Tartu 2400; tel. (7) 434-330; fax (7) 431-193; Chair. of Bd MADIS PADDAR.

Union of Estonian Paper Manufacturers (Eesti Paberitööstuse Liit): Tööstuse 19, Kohila 3420; tel. (48) 33-564; fax (48) 32-132; e-mail kohila pv@netexpress.ee; Chair. of Bd HENNO PAVELSON.

Union of Estonian Wine Producers (Eesti Veinitootjate Liit): Karksi, Karksi vald, Vilijandi mk. 69104; tel. and fax (43) 54-022; e-mail veinilitt@hot.ee; Chair. of Bd JÜRI KERT.

EMPLOYERS' ORGANIZATION

Confederation of Estonian Industry and Employers: Gonsiori 29, Tallinn 0100; tel. (2) 422-235; fax (2) 424-962; f. 1991 as Confederation of Estonian Industry, name changed as above 1995; Man. Dir VILJAR VESKIVÄLI.

UTILITIES

Electricity

Eesti Energia AS (Estonian Energy Ltd): Estonia pst 1, Tallinn 10143; tel. 625-2222; fax 625-2200; e-mail kaja.malts@energia.ee; internet www.energia.ee; f. 1939; producer of thermal and electric energy; manufacture of electric motors; electrical engineering; scheduled for privatization in 2000; Chair. GUNNAR OKK; 8,000 employees.

Gas

Eesti Gaasiliit (Estonian Gas Association): Liivalaia 9, Tallinn 10118; tel. 646-1571; fax 631-4340; e-mail egl@online.ee; internet www.gaas.ee; f. 1993; purchases and transports natural gas, constructs pipelines, calibrates gas meters; Chair. ALLAN SEPP; 405 employees.

Water

Tallinn Water Ltd (AS Tallinna Vesi): Adala 10, POB 174, Tallinn 10502; tel. 626-2200; fax 626-2300; e-mail tvesi@tvesi.ee; internet www.tallvesi.ee; f. 1997; supply and treatment of water; collection and treatment of waste water; 50.4% owned by British International Water UU; Chair. BRIAN HILL.

TRADE UNIONS

Association of Estonian Chemical Industry Workers' Trade Unions: Järveküla 40, Kohtla-Järve 30328; tel. (33) 478-28; fax (33) 457-98; f. 1990; Chair. MIHKEL ISKÜL.

Association of Estonian Radio and Electronics Industry Workers' Trade Unions: Rävala 4, Tallinn 0100; tel. (2) 432-318; Chair. LYUBOV SEROVA.

Confederation of Estonian Food and Landworkers' Unions: 32 Raua Str, Tallinn 10152; tel. and fax 641-0249; e-mail aare.etmk@mail.ee; f. 1989; Chair. AARE-LEMBIT NEEVE.

Confederation of Estonian Trade Unions: Rävala 4, Tallinn 10143; tel. 661-2383; fax 661-2542; e-mail eakl@eakl.ee; f. 1990; Chair. KADI PARNITS.

Estonian Light Industry Workers' Trade Union: Rävala 4, Tallinn 0100; tel. and fax (2) 431-640; Chair. EVI JAAGURA.

Society of Estonian Economy Workers' Trade Unions: Rävala 4, Tallinn 10143; tel. and fax 661-2414; e-mail emal@online.ee.

Trade Union of Oil-Shale Industry Workers: Jaama 10, Jõhvi 41502; tel. (33) 70575; e-mail ental@en.ee; Chair. ENDEL PAAP.

Transport

RAILWAYS

In 1998 there were 1,018 km of railway track in use, of which 132 km were electrified. Main lines link Tallinn with Narva and St Petersburg (Russia), Tartu and Pskov (Russia), Tartu and Valga (Latvia), and Pärnu and Rīga (Latvia).

Estonian Railways Ltd (AS Eesti Raudtee): Pikk 36, Tallinn 15073; tel. 615-8610; fax 615-8710; e-mail raudtee@evr.ee; internet www.evr.ee; f. 1918; scheduled for privatization in 2001; freight carriers; Chair. ARDO OJASSIN; 5,000 employees.

ROADS

In 1998 Estonia had a total road network of 49,480 km of which 3,823 km were main roads, 12,532 km were secondary roads and 33,050 km were local roads. The motorway network totalled 75 km. In 2000 there were plans to construct an international motorway, to be known as the Via Baltica, between Tallinn and Warsaw (Poland). The project was to be partly funded by the EU. In 1997 about 51% of the total road network was asphalted.

Estonian Road Administration: Pärnu Road 24, Tallinn 10141; tel. 611-9300; fax 611-9360; e-mail estroad@mnt.ee; internet www.mnt.ee; Gen. Dir RIHO SÕRMUS.

SHIPPING

Tallinn is the main port for freight transportation. There are regular passenger services between Tallinn and Helsinki (Finland). A service between Tallinn and Stockholm (Sweden) was inaugurated in 1991.

Estonian National Maritime Board: Sadama 29, Terminal B, Tallinn 10111; tel. 620-5500; fax 620-5506; e-mail eva@enmb.ee; internet www.enmb.ee; f. 1990; administers and implements state maritime safety policies, ship-control, pilot, lighthouse and hydrography services; Gen. Dir Capt. KALLE PEDAK; 500 employees.

Shipowning Company

Estonian Shipping Company Ltd (AS Eesti Merelaevardus): Estonia Blvd 3/5, Tallinn 15096; tel. 640-9500; fax 640-9595; f. 1991; transferred to private ownership in mid-1997; liner services, ship chartering and cargo shipping; Chair. ENN PANT; Dir-Gen. TOIVO NINNAS; 2,380 employees.

Shipowners' Association

Estonian Shipowners' Association (Eesti Laevaomanike Liit): Luise 1A, Tallinn 10142; tel. and fax 646-0109; e-mail reeder@teleport.ee; Pres. REIN MERISALU.

Port Authority

Port of Tallinn: Sadama 25, Tallinn 15051; tel. 631-8002; fax 631-8166; e-mail portoftallinn@portoftallinn.com; internet www.portoftallinn.com; Chair. RIHO RASMANN; Harbour Master E. HUNT.

CIVIL AVIATION

Estonia has air links with several major cities in the former USSR, including Moscow and St Petersburg (Russia), Kiev (Ukraine), Minsk (Belarus), Riga (Latvia) and Vilnius (Lithuania), and with several western European destinations.

Estonian Civil Aviation Administration: Pärnu mnt. 6, Tallinn 10148; tel. 631-3620; fax 631-2681; e-mail ecaa@trenet.ee; f. 1990; Dir Gen. EDUARD TÜÜR.

Elk Airways (Estonian Aviation Company Ltd): Eesti Vabariik, Majaka 26, Tallinn 11416; tel. 638-0972; fax 638-0975; e-mail elk@infonet.ee; internet www.elk.ee; f. 1992; international and domestic passenger and cargo flights to Europe and the CIS; Man. Dir VLADIMIR SLONTCHEVSH.

Estonian Air: Lennujaama 2, Tallinn 0011; tel. 640-1101; fax 631-2740; internet www.estonian-air.ee; f. 1991; passenger and cargo flights to Europe and the CIS; Chair. MADIS ÜÜRIKE.

Tourism

Estonia has a wide range of attractions for tourists, including the historic towns of Tallinn and Tartu, extensive nature reserves and coastal resorts. In 1990 the National Tourism Board was established to develop facilities for tourism in Estonia. In 1999 there were an estimated 1.4m. visitors to Estonia, with Finland the main source of tourists.

Estonian Association of Travel Agents (Eesti Turismifirmade Liit): Kiriku 6, Tallinn 10130; tel. 631-3013; fax 631-3622; e-mail info@etfl.ee; internet www.etfl.ee; f. 1990; Pres. DAISY JÄRVA.

Estonian Marine Tourism Association: Regati pst. 1, 6K, Tallinn 11911; tel. 639-8933; fax 639-8899; e-mail helle.hallika@mail.ee; f. 1990; Man. Dir HELLE HALLIKA.

Estonian Tourist Board: Mundi tn. 2, Tallinn 10146; tel. 699-0420; fax 699-0432; e-mail info@tourism.ee; internet www.visitestonia.com; f. 1990; Dir RIINA LOHMUS.

ETHIOPIA

Introductory Survey

Location, Climate, Language, Religion, Flag, Capital

The Federal Democratic Republic of Ethiopia is a land-locked country in eastern Africa; it has a long frontier with Somalia near the Horn of Africa. Sudan lies to the west, Eritrea to the north, Djibouti to the north-east and Kenya to the south. The climate is mainly temperate because of the high plateau terrain, with an average annual temperature of 13°C (55°F), abundant rainfall in some years and low humidity. The lower country and valley gorges are very hot and subject to recurrent drought. The official language is Amharic, but many other local languages are also spoken. English is widely used in official and commercial circles. The Ethiopian Orthodox (Tewahido) Church, an ancient Christian sect, has a wide following in the north and on the southern plateau. In much of the south and east the inhabitants include Muslims and followers of animist beliefs. The national flag (proportions 3 by 2) has three equal horizontal stripes, of green, yellow and red. The capital is Addis Ababa.

Recent History

Ethiopia was dominated for more than 50 years by Haile Selassie, who became Regent in 1916, King in 1928 and Emperor in 1930. He continued his autocratic style of rule (except during the Italian occupation of 1936–41) until September 1974, when he was deposed by the armed forces. Haile Selassie died, a captive of the military regime, in August 1975.

The 1974 revolution was organized by an Armed Forces Co-ordinating Committee, known popularly as the Dergue (Shadow), which established a Provisional Military Administrative Council (PMAC), led by Brig.-Gen. Teferi Benti. In December Ethiopia was declared a socialist state, and in 1975 land, financial institutions and large industrial companies were nationalized. A radical programme of social and economic reforms led to widespread unrest, and in February 1977 Lt-Col Mengistu Haile Mariam executed Teferi and his closest associates, and replaced him as Chairman of the PMAC and as Head of State.

During 1977–78, in an attempt to end opposition to the regime, the Government imprisoned or killed thousands of its opponents. Political power was consolidated in a Commission for Organizing the Party of the Working People of Ethiopia (COPWE), largely dominated by military personnel. In September 1984, at the COPWE's third congress, the Workers' Party of Ethiopia (WPE) was formally inaugurated. Lt-Col Mengistu was unanimously elected Secretary-General of the party, which modelled itself on the Communist Party of the Soviet Union. In mid-1986, in preparation for the eventual transfer of power from the PMAC to a civilian government, a draft Constitution was published. In February 1987 it was endorsed by a referendum, obtaining the support of some 81% of the votes cast. In June national elections were held to an 835-seat legislature, the National Shengo (Assembly). In September, at the inaugural meeting of the new legislature, the PMAC was abolished, and the People's Democratic Republic of Ethiopia was declared. The National Shengo unanimously elected Lt-Col Mengistu as President of the Republic, and a 24-member Council of State was also elected, to act as the Shengo's permanent organ.

Numerous groups, encouraged by the confusion resulting from the 1974 revolution, launched a number of armed insurgencies against the Government. Of these, the most effective were based in the Ogaden, Eritrea and Tigrai regions. Somalia laid claim to the Ogaden, which is populated mainly by ethnic Somalis. Somali troops supported incursions by forces of the Western Somali Liberation Front, and in 1977 the Somalis made major advances in the Ogaden. In 1978, however, they were forced to retreat, and by the end of 1980 Ethiopian forces had gained control of virtually the whole of the Ogaden region, although armed clashes continued.

The former Italian colony of Eritrea was merged with Ethiopia, in a federal arrangement, in September 1952, and annexed to Ethiopia as a province in November 1962. A secessionist movement, the Eritrean Liberation Front (ELF), was founded in Egypt in 1958. In the late 1960s and early 1970s the ELF enjoyed considerable success against government troops, but eventually split into several rival factions, the largest of which was the Eritrean People's Liberation Front (EPLF). In 1978 government troops re-established control in much of Eritrea, and the EPLF was forced to retreat to the remote northern town of Nakfa. In 1982 a military offensive by government troops failed to capture Nakfa, and in 1984 the EPLF made several successful counter-attacks. In mid-1985 the Government launched a large-scale offensive in Eritrea and made significant gains. The EPLF, however, continued to attack strategic targets, and in mid-1986 government forces abandoned the north-east coast to the rebels.

An insurgent movement also emerged in Tigrai province in the late 1970s. The Tigrai People's Liberation Front (TPLF) was armed and trained by the EPLF, but relations between the two groups deteriorated sharply in the mid-1980s. The TPLF was weakened by conflict with other anti-Government groups, and in 1985 and 1986 government forces had considerable success against the TPLF.

The conflict in the north of the country during 1984–85 compounded difficulties being experienced in areas of Ethiopia already severely affected by famine. In 1984 the rains failed for the third consecutive crop season, and in May it was estimated that 7m. people could suffer starvation. Emergency food aid was received from many Western nations, but distribution was hampered, both by the continuing conflict and by the inadequacy of Ethiopia's infrastructure. Some rainfall in 1985 eased the drought in the northern provinces, but there were further fears of famine in 1987, when the crops failed again.

In September 1987 the newly-elected National Shengo announced that five areas, including Eritrea and Tigrai, were to become 'autonomous regions' under the new Constitution. Eritrea was granted a considerable degree of self-government, but both the EPLF and the TPLF rejected the proposals. In March 1988 EPLF forces captured the town of Afabet, and claimed to have killed one-third of all Ethiopian troops in Eritrea. Following the town's capture, the TPLF took advantage of the movement of government forces from Tigrai to Eritrea and overran all the garrisons in north-western and north-eastern Tigrai. In May the Government declared a state of emergency in Eritrea and Tigrai, and in June government troops regained control of some of the captured garrison towns in Tigrai, suffering heavy losses in the process. However, in early 1989, following major defeats in north-west Tigrai, government forces abandoned virtually the whole region to the TPLF.

US-sponsored negotiations held in late 1989 between representatives of the Ethiopian Government and the EPLF proved inconclusive. Negotiations between the TPLF and the Ethiopian Government, in late 1989 and early 1990, were also unsuccessful. A third round of negotiations, held in Rome, Italy, in March 1990, collapsed over the TPLF's insistence that substantive negotiations should involve a joint delegation of the TPLF and their allies, the Ethiopian People's Democratic Movement (EPDM).

Severe drought in 1989 threatened widespread famine, and the UN estimated that some 4m. people in northern areas would require food aid in 1990. Substantial aid was supplied by Western governments and non-governmental organizations, but its distribution to the most needy areas remained difficult, owing to the disruption of supply convoys by both rebel and government forces. The recurrent food crises prompted further criticism of the Mengistu Government's commitment to collectivist agricultural policies and its 'villagization' programme (combining several villages in single administrative units, mainly for security reasons).

Following the capture of Massawa port by the EPLF in February 1990 (presenting a direct threat to the continued survival of the Ethiopian army in Eritrea), President Mengistu was obliged to make further concessions. In March Ethiopian socialism was virtually abandoned, when the ruling WPE was renamed the Ethiopian Democratic Unity Party, and membership was opened to non-Marxists. Mengistu began introducing elements of a market economy and dismantling many of the economic structures that had been established after the 1974 revolution. However, heavy defeats of government forces continued during 1990 and early 1991. Peace negotiations held in the USA in February 1991 between representatives of the EPLF and the Ethiopian Government failed to end the military conflict.

By late April 1991, troops of the Ethiopian People's Revolutionary Democratic Front (EPRDF—an alliance of the TPLF and the EPDM, formed in September 1989) had captured Ambo, a town 130 km west of Addis Ababa, while EPLF forces were 50 km north of Assab, Ethiopia's principal port. On 21 May, faced with the prospect of the imminent defeat of his army, Mengistu fled the country. Lt-Gen. Tesfaye, the Vice-President, assumed control. On 28 May, following the failure of negotiations in the United Kingdom, and with the public support of the USA, units of the EPRDF entered Addis Ababa. They encountered little resistance, and the EPRDF established an interim Government, pending the convening, in July, of a multi-party conference, which was to elect a transitional government. Meanwhile, the EPLF had gained control of the Eritrean capital, Asmara, and announced the establishment of a provisional Government to administer Eritrea until the holding of a referendum, within two years, on the issue of independence.

In July 1991 a national conference adopted amendments to a national charter, presented by the EPRDF, and elected an 87-member Council of Representatives, which was to govern for a transitional period of two years, after which free national elections were to be held. The national charter provided guarantees for freedom of association and expression, and for self-determination for Ethiopia's various ethnic groups. The EPLF was not officially represented at the conference, but came to an agreement with the EPRDF, whereby the EPRDF accepted the formation of the EPLF's provisional Government of Eritrea and the determination by referendum of the future of the region. In late July the Council of Representatives established a commission to draft a new constitution and elected Meles Zenawi, the leader of the EPRDF (and of the TPLF), as Chairman of the Council, a position that made him President of the transitional Government and Head of State, and in August it appointed a Council of Ministers. However, violent conflict continued in many parts of the country in the latter half of the year.

In November 1991, in accordance with the national charter's promise of self-determination for Ethiopia's peoples, the transitional Government announced the division of the country into 14 regional administrations, which would have autonomy in matters of regional law and internal affairs. A transitional economic policy, designed to accelerate economic reform, was also approved.

In early 1992 skirmishes continued between forces of the EPRDF and the Oromo Liberation Front (OLF) in the south and east of the country, severely hampering the distribution of food aid to some 6.5m. people affected by drought and to a further 1.4m. people displaced during the continuing conflict. In April a cease-fire between the two sides was agreed upon, under the auspices of the USA and the EPLF. Local elections were held in many parts of the country in April and May, and regional elections in June. These latter elections were boycotted by the OLF and other political groups, amid widespread allegations of intimidation of opposition candidates by the EPRDF. (There was also evidence, however, that the OLF had harassed civilians and election officials.) An international observer group, including representatives of the UN, the Organization of African Unity (OAU) and the European Community (EC, now the European Union—EU), indicated that claims of electoral malpractice by the EPRDF in many areas were, at least in part, justified. Shortly after the elections, in which the EPRDF and associated parties obtained 90% of the votes cast, the OLF withdrew its support from the transitional Government. In July 10 political organizations that were signatories to the national charter of July 1991 demanded the annulment of the results of the regional elections. The transitional Government established a board 'to correct election errors' at the end of the month, but by late August the regional councils were functioning in all parts of the country except the Afar and Somali areas, where the elections had been postponed. Hopes that the transitional Government had truly democratic intentions were also undermined by reports from the Ethiopian Human Rights Council, which by mid-1992 had documented more than 2,000 cases of people who had been detained without being charged, of whom the majority were political opponents of the EPRDF.

In June 1992 OLF troops reportedly captured the town of Asbe Teferi, about 150 km from Addis Ababa; the EPRDF's numerically greatly superior forces, however, ensured that the transitional Government's control of the capital was secure. In October talks between the EPRDF and the OLF ended in failure, with the OLF continuing to demand that the results of the June elections be annulled, while the EPRDF urged the OLF to rejoin the transitional Government. Hostilities between the two sides continued in various parts of the country, with the EPRDF taking prisoners in massive numbers.

Throughout 1992 people in many parts of the country continued to suffer acute food shortages, caused by drought and ineffective distribution of aid: in August it was estimated that 13.5m. people were affected. In the following year inadequate rainfall resulted in widespread crop failure in southern, northern and eastern Ethiopia.

Meanwhile the provisional Government of Eritrea announced in November 1992 that a UN-supervised referendum on the area's status would be held in April 1993. The Sudanese Government expressed its readiness to assist the Eritrean Referendum Commission in conducting a plebiscite among some 250,000 Eritrean refugees still residing in Sudan. The referendum revealed overwhelming support for Eritrean independence, which was duly proclaimed on 24 May 1993.

In July 1993 the EPRDF experienced serious internal unrest when its executive committee issued a statement denouncing an undisclosed number of party members. It was believed that a purge was under way of middle-ranking TPLF members who had criticized the Government's policy of ethnic regionalization and the slow pace of economic liberalization. Delays in the dispatch of humanitarian aid in early 1994 resulted in the deaths (from hunger and disease) of some 5,000 people in southern Ethiopia. By August relief food was reaching those in need, and by October the threat of famine had been brought under control with help from international donors.

Elections to a Constituent Assembly were conducted in June 1994, in which the EPRDF won 484 of the 547 seats. The elections were boycotted by the All-Amhara People's Organization, the recently-formed Council of Alternative Forces for Peace and Democracy in Ethiopia (CAFPDE—incorporating 30 opposition groups) and the OLF, whose leaders alleged that the Meles administration had intimidated their supporters and refused opposition parties permission to open offices. The Constituent Assembly was inaugurated in October to debate a draft Constitution, which it ratified in December. The new Constitution provided for the establishment of a federal government and the division of the country (renamed the Federal Democratic Republic of Ethiopia) into nine states and two chartered cities. It provided for regional autonomy, including the right of secession. A new legislature, the Federal Parliamentary Assembly, was to be established, comprising two chambers: the House of People's Representatives (consisting of no more than 550 directly-elected members) and the House of the Federation (composed of 117 deputies, elected by the new state assemblies).

The EPRDF and its allies won an overwhelming victory in elections to the House of People's Representatives and state assemblies in May 1995. In Tigrai region the TPLF won all the seats in both the federal and state assemblies; EPRDF parties were equally successful in Amhara and Oromia regions. The EPRDF itself won all 92 local assembly seats in Addis Ababa. The largest opposition party to participate in the elections, the Ethiopian National Democratic Movement, contested 80 seats, but none of its candidates was elected. Elections in Afar and Somali regions, where opposition to the EPRDF was strong, were postponed until June, when pro-EPRDF parties won narrow victories. Most opposition parties boycotted the poll. International observers at the elections accepted that the polls were conducted in a largely free and fair manner. In July EU ambassadors to Ethiopia expressed concern that the overwhelming victory of the EPRDF would impede the further development of political pluralism in the country.

On 21 August 1995 legislative power was transferred from the transitional Council of Representatives to the Federal Parliamentary Assembly. On 22 August the transitional administration was terminated, and the country's new Constitution and designation as the Federal Democratic Republic of Ethiopia were formally instituted. Later that day Dr Negasso Gidada (formerly the Minister of Information), a member of the Oromo People's Democratic Organization (OPDO, which is in alliance with the EPRDF) and the nominee of the EPRDF, was elected President of the Federal Republic. A new Prime Minister, ex-President Meles Zenawi, was elected from among the members of the House of People's Representatives; Meles nominated a

17-member Council of Ministers, which was duly approved by the Federal Parliamentary Assembly.

During late 1995 and early 1996 the Meles administration was criticized for its harsh treatment of opposition activists. In June 1996 Dr Taye Wolde Semayat, the Secretary-General of the Ethiopian Teachers' Association, was arrested with several associates and accused of leading a clandestine political organization (the Ethiopian National Patriotic Front — ENPF), which, allegedly, had been responsible for several terrorist acts. The arrests were strongly criticized by human rights groups, which claimed that the detainees were guilty only of expressing discontent at certain government policies. Meanwhile, the Somali-based al-Ittihad al-Islam (Islamic Union Party—which has sought independence for Ethiopia's Ogaden province) claimed responsibility for bomb explosions at hotels in Addis Ababa and Dire Dawa in early 1996, and for the attempted assassination in July of Dr Abdul-Mejid Hussen, the Minister of Transport and Communications. Government forces launched reprisal attacks on al-Ittihad bases in Somalia on numerous occasions during 1996–98, resulting in the deaths of several hundred al-Ittihad members.

In September 1996 the authorities announced a campaign to address the problem of corruption, which reportedly had become endemic in the country. In the following month Tamirat Layne was accused of 'indiscipline' (he was later implicated in corrupt activities) and removed from the post of Deputy Prime Minister and Minister of Defence; he was also dismissed as Secretary-General of the Amhara National Democratic Movement (ANDM, as the EPDM had been renamed in 1994), and ejected from its central committee. (In February 2000 Layne was found guilty of abuse of power, embezzlement and corruption, and was subsequently sentenced to 18 years' imprisonment. Meanwhile, hundreds of officials from regional administrations were arrested or dismissed during 1996–97 following EPRDF-organized peace, democracy and development conferences.

In late 1996 the Government announced plans to establish a 25,000-strong Afar military force (under the command of the Afar People's Democratic Organization) to counter an increase in armed attacks on government troops by militant members of the Afar Revolutionary Democratic Unity Front (ARDUF). The authorities subsequently withdrew government forces from sensitive Afar regions and granted concessions regarding political prisoners in an attempt to persuade the ARDUF to cease its military activities. In August 1997 the ARDUF reportedly agreed to renounce the use of violence in its campaigning.

In February 1997 two people were killed and nine were injured in a grenade attack on a hotel in Harar. Similar attacks in Addis Ababa in April and September resulted in as many as 100 casualties, including three fatalities. The authorities attributed the incidents to the OLF, and in December 31 OLF members stood trial for crimes including terrorism and illegally amassing weapons. Six of the accused were allegedly implicated in the grenade attacks. In mid-1998, moreover, the authorities accused the OLF of conspiring with al-Ittihad and the Eritrean leadership to undermine the Ethiopian regime.

Attempts by the authorities to stifle the opposition continued during 1997–98, with the arrest of numerous journalists and the closure of several independent periodicals. In September, meanwhile, some 30 delegates attended a meeting in Paris, France, of Ethiopian opposition movements, during which eight groups agreed to establish a new bloc, the Coalition of Ethiopian Opposition Political Organizations (CEOPO). At the conclusion of the meeting, the delegates (who included representatives of the CAFPDE, the Southern Ethiopian People's Democratic Coalition (SEPDC), the ARDUF and Ethiopians in exile) urged the Ethiopian authorities to facilitate national dialogue. A CEOPO-organized demonstration held in Addis Ababa in late January 1999 was attended by some 5,000 people.

In June 1999 Dr Taye Wolde Semayat, head of the banned ENPF, was sentenced to 15 years' imprisonment for destabilizing public order after allegedly raiding state economic, military and security institutions. In July severe drought once again threatened to cause wide-scale famine, and the UN appealed for US $50m. to help to alleviate the most severe case of starvation since 1984.

In August 1999 it was announced that elections for the House of the Federation and the House of People's Representatives were to be held in May 2000, and registration for political parties began. Following this, there were several attempts by coalition groups to form a united opposition to the ruling EPRDF alliance; however, meetings in Frankfurt am Main, Germany, and Washington, DC, in September 1999, organized by the CEOPO and the ENC respectively, merely led to greater divisions. In October the SEPDC withdrew from the CEOPO, and in November the CAFPDE split into two rival factions.

The trial of 69 former government officials, including Mengistu, opened in Addis Ababa in December 1994, although proceedings were adjourned on numerous occasions. The defendants, 23 of whom were being tried *in absentia* (including Mengistu, who was in exile in Zimbabwe) and five of whom had died while awaiting trial, were accused of crimes against humanity and of genocide, perpetrated during 1974–91. In February 1997 the office of the Special Prosecutor announced that an additional 5,198 people would be indicted for war crimes and genocide, of whom nearly 3,000 would be tried *in absentia*. In November 1999 South Africa refused a request from the Ethiopian Government to extradite ex-President Mengistu, after it emerged that he was receiving medical treatment in that country.

In December 1999 the Ethiopian authorities prohibited the publication of 12 weekly newspapers on financial grounds. The following month the Deputy Editor of *Maebel* newspaper, who had been arrested on several occasions for allegedly violating press legislation, committed suicide. The incident was preceded by the imprisonment of two other journalists on similar charges and prompted the International Federation of Journalists to express its concern at the treatment of journalists in Ethiopia. In March 2000 the Ethiopian Government finally granted the Ethiopian Free Press Journalists' Association official recognition.

Elections to the House of People's Representatives and the House of the Federation were held concurrently on 14 May 2000, except in the Somali regional state, where voting was postponed until 31 August, owing to severe drought. Voting was also repeated in several constituencies after accusations of irregularities were upheld by the National Electoral Board (NEB). According to results published by the NEB in September, following the completion of all voting, the OPDO won the largest number of seats in the House of Representatives, taking 178 of the 546 available. The OPDO's major partners in the EPRDF coalition, the ANDM and the TPLF, gained 134 and 38 seats, respectively, while a number of smaller groups in the EPRDF won a further 19 seats. The EPRDF thus comfortably retained its large majority in the lower chamber, although notably the Deputy Prime Minister and Minister of Justice, Tefera Walwa, lost his parliamentary seat. He was subsequently replaced by Addiso Leggese, the former President of Amhara state. In mid-October the new legislature was sworn in and re-elected Meles as Prime Minister.

In September 2000 more than 50 privately-owned Ethiopian newspapers suspended publication for one week in protest at a recent steep increase in printing costs, which had been introduced by state-owned printing houses. The rise was officially attributed to a world-wide increase in the cost of pulp paper; however, many independent journalists maintained that the Government had levied increased charges in an attempt to suppress the independent media. In November, more than 25 years after his death, Haile Selassie was accorded a state funeral. The Government had previously refused to allow a state burial as it claimed that the former Emperor had imposed a regime of oppression, terror and brutality upon the people of Ethiopia.

Ethiopia's foreign affairs after Mengistu's coup in 1977 were dominated by relations with the USSR, which replaced the USA as the principal supplier of armaments to Ethiopia and provided military advisers and economic aid. In the late 1980s, however, changes in Soviet foreign policy weakened the relationship, and the Soviet Government began to urge a political, rather than military, solution to Ethiopia's regional conflicts.

In April 1989 Ethiopia sought to upgrade its diplomatic relations with the USA, receiving a cautious initial response. The USA subsequently encouraged the EPRDF's seizure of power in May 1991 and expressed its approval of proposals for a transition to a multi-party democratic system. In late 1993 representatives of Ethiopia and the USA signed an agreement on economic and technical co-operation, the first such agreement for 17 years.

Relations with Somalia have been problematic since the Ogaden War of 1977–78. However, in April 1988 Ethiopia and Somalia agreed to re-establish diplomatic relations, to withdraw troops from their common border and to exchange prisoners of war. During 1988–91 an estimated 600,000 Somali refugees entered Ethiopia from northern Somalia, of whom more than 150,000 arrived in the first half of 1991. The transitional Government of Ethiopia declared a policy of non-interference in the affairs of neighbouring states and adopted a neutral stance in Somalia's civil conflict. During 1993–98 Ethiopia hosted reconciliation conferences between Somalia's warring factions. In August 1998 Ethiopia's Minister of Foreign Affairs held discussions with Hussein Aidid, the leader of the Somali National Alliance (SNA), on resolving Somalia's conflict. Aidid was also requested to cease providing support to al-Ittihad and Oromo organizations opposed to the Ethiopian administration. In February 1999 tensions escalated when Aidid accused the Ethiopian Government of interfering in Somali affairs and supplying arms to three anti-SNA factions. In April heavily-armed Ethiopian forces, which claimed to be pursuing OLF insurgents, entered Somalia. Aidid appealed to the UN and the OAU to take action against Ethiopia. Meanwhile, more than 20,000 Somali refugees were reported to have fled to Ethiopia during the previous two months. In early June the Somali-based Rahawin Resistance Army (RRA), assisted by some 3,000 Ethiopian troops, captured the town of Baidoa, which had been controlled by Aidid, after heavy fighting. Aidid's continuing support of the Eritrean Government and Ethiopian insurgent groups led many observers to believe that the conflict between Eritrea and Ethiopia was in danger of spreading elsewhere in the Horn of Africa. The Ethiopian Government claimed, however, that its actions were merely attempts to protect the border from attacks initiated by Somali-based rebel opposition groups. Following mediation attempts involving the two sides in October, Ethiopia withdrew its forces from Somalia, although the Ethiopian Government reiterated its demand that the SNA sever its connections with Eritrea and the Oromo rebels. In November 2000 the President of Somalia, Abdulkassim Salad Hasan, visited Ethiopia for the first time since his election in August. This followed a visit to Ethiopia by the President of the self-proclaimed 'Republic of Somaliland' earlier that month. During his visit Hasan held talks with senior Ethiopian officials but, although relations between the two countries were reported to have improved as a result of the discussions, the Ethiopian authorities continued to refuse to recognize officially the Hasan administration and urged it to reach agreements with its opponents. In January 2001 relations between the countries deteriorated once again after the Somali Prime Minister accused Ethiopia of continuing to assist the RRA, which had taken control of a number of towns in south-west Somalia, and maintained that Ethiopia was behind an assassination attempt on the Speaker of Somalia's transitional legislature. The accusations were strenuously denied by the Ethiopian authorities, which stated that no Ethiopian troops were in Somali territory.

Following the military coup in Sudan in April 1985 (which deposed President Nimeri), full diplomatic relations were restored between Ethiopia and Sudan. Relations between the two countries were strained, however, by the influx into Ethiopia, in the late 1980s, of thousands of Sudanese refugees, fleeing from famine and civil war in southern Sudan. The vast majority of an estimated 380,000 refugees were reported to have returned to Sudan by early 1991, as a result of the civil war in Ethiopia. The change of government in Ethiopia in May 1991 led to a considerable improvement in relations between Ethiopia and Sudan. In October President Meles and Sudan's leader, Lt-Gen. al-Bashir, signed an agreement on friendship and co-operation. Bilateral relations deteriorated again in January 1994, when the Ethiopian Minister of Foreign Affairs accused the Sudanese National Islamic Front of supporting Islamic extremists in Ethiopia. In September 1995 the Ethiopian administration adopted a number of sanctions against Sudan, including the suspension of air flights between the two countries and a reduction in Sudanese diplomatic representation in Ethiopia, after the Sudanese authorities refused to extradite to Ethiopia three men allegedly involved in an assassination attempt on President Mubarak of Egypt in Addis Ababa in June. In December there were reports of military clashes between Ethiopian and Sudanese forces in the border region. Accusations of border incursions intensified during 1996–97. Although attacks against Sudanese positions were known to have been launched by the Sudan People's Liberation Army (SPLA), operating from Ethiopia, the Ethiopian authorities denied any knowledge of their activities. Relations between the two countries subsequently improved, and in late October 1998 Ethiopia reportedly resumed air flights to Sudan. The Ethiopian authorities were also reported to have closed the SPLA offices in western Ethiopia, while Sudan closed the OLF base in Khartoum. In November 1999 Prime Minister Meles received Lt-Gen. al-Bashir in Addis

Ababa, where they discussed the possible reactivation of the Ethio-Sudan Joint Ministerial Commission and announced their intent to form closer economic ties between the two countries.

In November 1991 the leaders of Ethiopia and Kenya signed a co-operation agreement, although in October 1992 it was reported that the Kenyan Government was secretly giving asylum to Ethiopian dissidents. In April 1997 the two countries agreed to strengthen border controls following an attack by Ethiopian tribesmen in Kenya's frontier region; 41 civilians and 16 security personnel were killed during the incident. Additional security measures were agreed in late 1998, following an incursion by Ethiopian tribesmen into Kenya, which resulted in some 140 fatalities. In March 1999 Kenyan security forces exchanged fire with Ethiopian troops pursuing OLF rebels across the border. Kenya accused Ethiopia of violating international law, and relations between the two countries became further strained after Ethiopian soldiers attacked villages along the border. Bilateral relations deteriorated yet further during late 2000 and early 2001 after it was reported that some 50 Kenyans had been killed by Ethiopian militia forces. In January 2001 representatives from both countries met in Nairobi, Kenya, and agreed to take steps aimed at ending disputes along the common border.

Relations with many Arab states improved substantially following the collapse of the Mengistu regime in 1991. In November 1993 Ethiopia removed all remaining sanctions against South Africa and announced that normal financial, trade and investment relations between the two countries would now be possible.

In 1984 some 13,000 Falashas, a Jewish group in Ethiopia, reached Sudan, from where they were flown to Israel in a secret airlift. Following the renewal of formal diplomatic relations (severed in 1973) between Ethiopia and Israel in 1989, the Ethiopian Government removed restrictions on 'Falashas' leaving the country, and Israel began to provide Ethiopia with more armaments and anti-guerrilla training. In May 1991 Israel evacuated a further 14,000 Falashas from Addis Ababa; some 10,000 Falashmura (Ethiopian Christians whose forefathers had converted from Judaism) were subsequently granted Israeli citizenship on humanitarian grounds. In mid-1998 the Israeli authorities closed an aid camp in Addis Ababa for Ethiopians claiming Jewish descent, and officially ended the airlifts from Ethiopia. In March 1999 the Israeli Prime Minister, Binyamin Netanyahu, pledged to examine the possibility of bringing the estimated 19,000 Jews remaining in Ethiopia to Israel. In June, following negotiations between the Israeli Minister of Foreign Affairs and the Ethiopian ambassador to Israel, a first group of around 70 Jews, of a total of 4,000 stranded in refugee camps in the Quara region of Ethiopia, was airlifted to Israel. In April 2000 the Israeli Minister of the Interior visited Ethiopia to investigate the claims of some 26,000 Ethiopians who asserted that they belonged to the Falashmura community and were thus eligible to settle in Israel under Israeli law. Officials from the Jewish Agency for Israel, however, estimated the number of Falashmura eligible at just 5,000.

After May 1991 the EPLF governed Eritrea as a *de facto* independent state and conducted its affairs with foreign countries accordingly. Ethiopia and the newly-independent Eritrea signed a treaty of co-operation during a visit by the Eritrean President, Issaias Afewerki, to Addis Ababa in July 1993. The agreement included provisions on the joint utilization of resources and co-operation in the energy, transport, defence and education sectors. A further agreement, signed in late 1994, provided for the free movement of goods between the two countries without payment of customs dues.

In late 1997 relations with Eritrea deteriorated, following that country's adoption of a new currency (to replace the Ethiopian birr) and the subsequent disruption of cross-border trade. Fighting between Ethiopian and Eritrean troops erupted in the border region in early May 1998, with both countries accusing the other of having invaded their territory. Eritrea rejected a peace plan drafted by the USA and Rwanda in early June, as it refused to comply with a precondition to withdraw its troops from the disputed region. The US-Rwandan plan had also envisaged the demilitarization of the border region and the dispatch of an observer mission to Badme. In mid-June the USA and Italy successfully mediated an aerial cease-fire, but a resolution passed by the UN Security Council later that month, demanding that Ethiopia and Eritrea cease hostilities forthwith, was ignored. The OAU established a mediation committee in June in an attempt to end the dispute, and in July an OAU delegation visited the two countries. The committee presented its report to the Ethiopian and Eritrean Ministers of Foreign Affairs at a meeting in Ouagadougou, Burkina Faso, in August; however, its proposals were rejected by Eritrea, necessitating the convening of a special meeting of the mediation committee in Ouagadougou in November. Prime Minister Meles and President Afewerki attended different sessions of the meeting, at which the Heads of State of Burkina Faso, Djibouti and Zimbabwe were also present. Ethiopia welcomed the committee's proposals, which stressed the need to demilitarize and demarcate the disputed region, but Eritrea rejected the plans and accused Djibouti of favouring Ethiopia in the conflict. Other international mediation attempts continued in late 1998 (including that of Anthony Lake, a former US national security adviser), but failed to resolve the dispute.

In early February 1999 hundreds of people were killed during armed clashes in the disputed territory. Each side accused the other of having broken the aerial cease-fire and of escalating the conflict. After two weeks of intense fighting, Ethiopia recaptured the disputed town of Badme and the Eritrean Government announced that it had accepted the OAU peace plan that it had previously rejected in late 1998. However, Ethiopia appeared eager to maximize this opportunity to secure access to the coast, and ignored appeals by the UN Security Council for an immediate cease-fire. Fighting erupted again in March 1999, as the two sides continued to blame each other for obstructing the OAU's peace efforts. Ethiopia insisted on Eritrea's unilateral withdrawal from its territory; however, Eritrea repeatedly rejected this demand and insisted that it did not form part of the OAU peace agreement. Mutual distrust persisted on both sides, and Ethiopia claimed that Eritrea had accepted the OAU agreement (which Ethiopia had accepted in November 1998) only in order to regroup its forces, and was actually continuing to attack Ethiopian troops stationed on the border. The deadlock continued into May as Eritrea steadfastly refused to withdraw from the territory that it occupied, and, despite the UN Security Council's repeated insistence on an immediate cessation of fighting, Ethiopian military aircraft bombed the Eritrean port of Massawa.

In mid-July 1999 the Algerian President, Abdelaziz Bouteflika, attempted to mediate between Ethiopia and Eritrea at the OAU summit meeting in Algiers. The deadlock appeared to have been broken when the two warring countries confirmed their commitment to the OAU peace proposals, under which both sides would withdraw from all territory captured since the outbreak of the conflict, thus effectively returning both sides to their pre-war frontiers. However, the situation was complicated by Eritrean demands for war reparations and Ethiopian requests for clarification of the technical arrangements regarding the withdrawal of troops from the disputed territory. In August Eritrea formally accepted the latest OAU peace plan; however, in the following month Ethiopia announced that it had rejected the proposals because, in its opinion, the technical arrangements were inconsistent with the other elements (the framework agreement and the modalities) of the peace propositions and did not guarantee a return to the *status quo ante*. Both sides were reported to be re-arming on a large scale. In October Eritrea claimed Zalambessa as its sovereign territory, and, while both sides publicly insisted that they were intent on finding a peaceful solution to the conflict, their mutual reluctance to make concessions meant that the situation remained unresolved. In late February 2000 Lake and Prime Minister Ahmed Ouyahia of Algeria, the OAU's special envoy, visited Addis Ababa and Asmara with the aim of persuading the two warring parties to accept the OAU's peace proposals. However, despite strenuous efforts, no agreement was reached. By March it was evident that the Horn of Africa was on the verge of widespread famine and the Eritrean authorities offered to allow large quantities of food aid destined for Ethiopia to be transported through the port of Assab. This offer was, however, rejected by the Ethiopian Government, which claimed that about 100,000 tons of food aid destined for Ethiopia in May 1998 had been looted by Eritreans at Assab. In April 2000 it was announced that some 8m. people in Ethiopia were in danger of starvation and both the Ethiopian and Eritrean Governments were strongly criticized by aid agencies for continuing to spend vast amounts on funding their war efforts, while millions of their citizens endured severe food shortages. In late April delegations from both countries agreed to attend OAU-sponsored talks in Algiers, although neither side would agree to a direct meeting. After six days of negotiations the talks collapsed, with both parties blaming each other for the breakdown.

In mid-May 2000 Ethiopian troops launched a major offensive near the disputed towns of Badme and Zalambessa, repelling the Eritrean forces. An announcement by the UN Security Council that it would impose sanctions and an embargo on the sale of all military supplies to the two countries, if fighting did not cease within three days, provoked violent protests outside the British and US embassies in Addis Ababa. However, hostilities continued and on 18 May the UN Security Council unanimously approved the imposition of a 12-month arms embargo on Ethiopia and Eritrea. Shortly afterwards Ethiopian forces captured the strategically vital town of Barentu, thus taking control of the western front. Zalambessa subsequently fell to the Ethiopian forces and on 25 May the Eritrean Government announced the withdrawal of its troops from all disputed areas. Despite the resumption of peace talks in Algiers on 29 May, Ethiopian forces continued to capture Eritrean towns and on 30 May Ethiopian aircraft bombed the military airfield in Asmara. The following day Prime Minister Meles stated that Ethiopia had no territorial claims over Eritrea and that the war between the two countries was over. Nevertheless, sporadic fighting continued to take place. Following extensive indirect negotiations in Algiers during early June, both sides expressed their willingness, in principle, to accept the OAU's peace proposals. On 18 June the Ethiopian and Eritrean Ministers of Foreign Affairs signed an agreement, which provided for an immediate cease-fire and the establishment of a 25-km 'temporary security zone' on the Eritrean side of the common border until the issue of the final demarcation of the border had been settled. It was estimated that as many as 120,000 people had been killed since the beginning of the conflict in 1998, and that more than 350,000 Ethiopians had been internally displaced. Indirect negotiations involving representatives from both countries, at which the technical issues of the peace agreement were to be discussed, commenced in Washington, DC, USA, in early July and continued in Algiers in October. Meanwhile, in mid-September the UN Security Council approved the deployment of the 4,200-strong UN Mission in Ethiopia and Eritrea (UNMEE), which was expected to be in place by late January 2001.

On 12 December 2000 Ethiopia and Eritrea signed an agreement in Algiers, which formally brought an end to the conflict. The agreement provided for a permanent cessation of all hostilities, the return of all prisoners of war, the demarcation of the common border by an independent commission, and the establishment of a Claims Commission to assess the issues of compensation and reparations. Furthermore, both countries pledged to co-operate with an independent investigation into the origins of the conflict. Later that month the first exchange of prisoners of war between the two countries took place and thousands more were due to be exchanged in early 2001. By mid-February 2001 the majority of the UNMEE force had arrived in the region and Ethiopian troops had begun to withdraw from the territory they had captured from Eritrea. In mid-March the UN Security Council extended UNMEE's mandate (which was about to expire) until 15 September.

Government

In August 1995 the Council of Representatives, a body established in 1991 to govern the country during the transitional period after the overthrow of the Mengistu regime, formally transferred power to a newly-elected legislature, the Federal Parliamentary Assembly. Under the provisions of a new Constitution, adopted in December 1994, the country became a federation, consisting of nine states and two chartered cities, the capital, Addis Ababa, and Dire Dawa. The states have their own parliamentary assemblies, which also elect representatives to the House of the Federation, the upper chamber of the Federal Parliamentary Assembly. The lower chamber, the House of People's Representatives, consists of no more than 550 directly elected deputies. The Federal Parliamentary Assembly elects a President as Head of State. However, the President fulfils mainly ceremonial functions, executive power being the preserve of the Prime Minister. The Prime Minister, who is elected by the House of People's Representatives, appoints the Council of Ministers (subject to approval by the legislature), and acts as Commander-in-Chief of the armed forces.

Defence

In December 1991 Ethiopia's transitional Government announced that a 'national defence army', based on already active EPRDF troops, would constitute Ethiopia's armed forces during the transitional period. In October 1993 the Minister of Defence announced that preparations were under way to create a 'multi-ethnic defence force', comprising members of all the different ethnic groups in Ethiopia. Extensive demobilization of former members of the TPLF has since taken place. In September 1996 the Government sold its naval assets. Owing to the war with Eritrea, there was a large increase in the size of the armed forces and in defence expenditure. In August 2000 Ethiopia's active armed forces numbered an estimated 352,500, including an air force of some 2,500. The defence budget for 2000 was estimated at 3,700m. birr.

Economic Affairs

In 1998, according to estimates by the World Bank, the gross national product (GNP) of Ethiopia, measured at average 1996–98 prices, was US $6,169m., equivalent to $100 per head (or $566 per head on an international purchasing-power parity basis): one of the lowest recorded levels of GNP per caput for any country in the world. During 1990–98, it was estimated, GNP per head increased, in real terms, at an average annual rate of 2.6%. Over the same period, the population also increased by an average of 2.6% per year. In 1999 GNP was estimated at $6,600m. ($100 per head). Ethiopia's gross domestic product (GDP) increased, in real terms, by an average of 4.8% per year during 1990–99. Measured at factor cost, real GDP rose by 5.2% in 1996/97, but declined by 0.5% in 1997/98.

Agriculture (including forestry and fishing) contributed 45.7% of GDP (at constant 1980/81 prices) in 1997/98, and employed an estimated 82.8% of the economically active population in 1999. The principal cash crop is coffee (which accounted for 70.7% of export earnings in 1997/98). The principal subsistence crops are cereals (barley, maize, sorghum and teff) and sugar cane. During 1990–99 agricultural GDP increased by an average of 2.5% per year. It rose by 3.4% in 1996/97, but declined by 10.3% in 1997/98. In 1995 the Government initiated a five-year programme (supported by the World Bank), which aimed to make Ethiopia self-sufficient in food production. In 1998 agricultural production declined by 8.3%, compared with the previous year, while the cereal harvest declined by 26.3% as a result of drought and severe flooding.

Industry (including mining, manufacturing, construction and power) employed 2.0% of the labour force in 1995, and provided 11.6% of GDP (at constant prices) in 1997/98. During 1990–99 industrial GDP increased by an average of 6.3% per year. It rose by 6.8% in 1996/97 and by 6.3% in 1997/98.

Mining contributed only 0.5% of GDP in 1997/98, and employed less than 0.1% of the labour force in 1995. During 1989/90–94/95 mining GDP increased by an average of 16.8% per year. It rose by 13.0% in 1996/97 and by 10.1% in 1997/98. Ethiopia has reserves of petroleum, although these have not been exploited, and there are also deposits of copper and potash. Gold, tantalite, soda ash, kaolin, dimension stones, precious metals and gemstones, salt, and industrial and construction materials are mined. In April 2000 a US company discovered large petroleum deposits in the west of the country.

Manufacturing employed only 1.6% of the labour force in 1995 and contributed 6.7% of GDP in 1997/98. During 1990–1998 manufacturing GDP increased by an average of 6.6% per year. It rose by 5.9% in 1996/97 and by 5.8% in 1997/98. Measured by the value of output, the principal branches of manufacturing in 1996/97 were beverages and food products (accounting for 37.2% of the total), textiles (11.%), non-metallic mineral manufactures (8.7%), leather tanning, dressing and processing (8.1%) and cement, lime and plaster (6.0%).

Services, which consisted mainly of wholesale and retail trade, public administration and defence, and transport and communications, employed 9.5% of the labour force in 1995, and contributed 42.7% of GDP (at constant prices) in 1997/98. The combined GDP of the service sectors increased, in real terms, at an average rate of 6.7% per year during 1990–99. It rose by 7.1% in 1996/97, and by 10.4% in 1997/98.

In years of normal rainfall, energy is derived principally from Ethiopia's massive hydroelectric power resources. Imports of mineral fuels accounted for an estimated 16.2% of the cost of total imports in 1997/98. In 1993 agreement was reached with the World Bank on the financing of a project to construct a liquefied gas unit to exploit gas reserves in the Ogaden. In late 1995 the Government announced plans to develop geothermal energy sources at 15 sites in various regions of the country. Ethiopia's electricity generating capacity is expected to be doubled (to 713 MW) by 2005.

In 1999 Ethiopia recorded a visible trade deficit of US $797.1m., and there was a deficit of $316.2m. on the current account of the balance of payments. In 1997 the principal source of imports (10.5%) was Japan, and in 1998 the principal market for exports (24.8%) was Germany. Other major trading partners were Saudi Arabia, Italy, the USA, Djibouti, the United Kingdom and India. The principal exports in 1997/98 were coffee, leather and leather products, and oilseeds. The principal imports in that year were machinery and transport equipment, basic manufactures, and mineral fuels and related products.

In the fiscal year 1997/98 it was estimated that Ethiopia's budgetary deficit reached 1,787m. birr (equivalent to 4.0% of GDP). Ethiopia is the principal African recipient of concessionary funding, and the largest recipient of EU aid (US $387m. for the first five years of the period covered by the Lomé IV Convention). At the end of 1998 Ethiopia's total external debt was $10,352m., of which $9,618m. was long-term public debt. In that year the cost of debt-servicing was equivalent to an estimated 11.3% of total earnings from the export of goods and services. In late 1992 debts repayable to various countries and international organizations amounting to $595m., including interest, were cancelled. Commercial debts worth $250m. were cancelled in early 1996. The annual rate of inflation averaged 7.7% in 1990–97. Although the rate rose considerably in 1991 (to 35.7%), in the following years it remained constant at about 10%, and in 1996 and 1997 consumer prices declined by 5.1% and 3.7%, respectively. However, consumer prices rose by 0.9% in 1998 and by 3.8% in 1999. There were 28,350 persons registered as applicants for work in the 12 months to June 1996.

Ethiopia is a member of the African Development Bank (see p. 120) and the Common Market for Eastern and Southern Africa (see p. 148), and adheres to the Lomé Convention of the EU (see p. 206).

Ethiopia remains one of the poorest countries in the world and the country's economy continues to suffer from the effects of recurrent, catastrophic drought, which severely disrupts agricultural production (the country's economic base). During 1991–95 the transitional Government adopted many elements of a market economy, resulting in a greater readiness on the part of developed countries to provide economic assistance to Ethiopia, and the resumption of relations with the World Bank and the IMF. The Ethiopian economy is heavily dependent on assistance and grants from abroad, particularly in times of drought. However, many donors suspended aid for the duration of the war with Eritrea, resulting in the loss of an estimated US $1,000m. worth of assistance. Ethiopia's economic difficulties were further exacerbated by its vast military expenditure on the conflict and the renewed failure of crop harvests in 1999 and 2000. Following the cessation of fighting between Ethiopia and Eritrea in mid-2000 (see above), the World Bank agreed to resume development assistance to Ethiopia and, in December, approved a credit of $400.6m. in support of the Ethiopian Government's planned recovery and rehabilitation projects as well as the demobilization of its armed forces. The divestiture of some 120 state-owned enterprises and the construction of road and rail links to connect land-locked Ethiopia with ports in Djibouti, Kenya and Sudan were among the Government's main priorities. The budget for 2000/2001 envisaged much reduced defence expenditure, a significant increase in spending on social services and agricultural development and GDP growth of 10%.

Social Welfare

The scope of modern health services has been greatly extended since 1960, but they still reach only a small section of the population. In 1977 free medical care for the needy was introduced. In 1980 Ethiopia had 86 hospital establishments. During 1974–87 26 new hospitals were built. By 1987 there were a total of 11,400 hospital beds, while 1,204 physicians and 3,105 nurses were working in the health service. Relative to the size of the population, the provision of hospital beds and physicians was the lowest among African countries. By 1987 there were also 2,095 clinics and 159 health centres. It was estimated that in the early 1990s there were four doctors and eight nurses per 100,000 people. With foreign assistance, health centres and clinics are steadily expanding into the rural areas. In times of famine, however, Ethiopian health services are totally inadequate. In late 1998 the World Bank announced that it would lend Ethiopia US $100m. to finance the first five-year phase of an ambitious government programme to improve health services. It was envisaged that more than 400 health centres and hospitals would be built or restored during the 20-year project. The 1997/98 budget allocated an estimated 6.0% (677.3m. birr) of total expenditure to public health.

Education

Education in Ethiopia is available free of charge up to grade 10, and, after a rapid growth in numbers of schools, it became compulsory between the ages of seven and 13 years. Since 1976 most primary and secondary schools have been controlled by local peasant associations and urban dwellers' associations. In 1994 Ethiopia adopted a new Education and Training Policy and Strategy (ETPS), which restructured the education system and aimed to improve the quality of education. Primary education begins at seven years of age and lasts for eight years. Secondary education, beginning at 15 years of age, lasts for a further four years, comprising two cycles of two years each, the second of which provides preparatory education for entry to the tertiary level. A system of vocational and technical education also exists parallel to the preparatory programme. In 2000 total enrolment at primary schools was equivalent to 51.0% of children in the appropriate age-group (60.9% of boys; 40.7% of girls); enrolment at secondary schools was equivalent to 10.3% of children in the relevant age-group (12.0% of boys; 8.5% of girls). The 1999/2000 budget allocated an estimated 11.3% (2,304m. birr) of total expenditure to education. In 1995, according to UNESCO estimates, the rate of adult illiteracy stood at 66.8% (males 60.1%; females 73.5%). There are 17 institutions of higher education in Ethiopia, including six universities (in Addis Ababa, Bahir Dar, Alemanya, Jimma, Awassa and Makele).

Public Holidays

2001: 7 January* (Christmas), 19 January* (Epiphany), 2 March (Battle of Adowa), 6 March† (Id al-Adha/Arafat), 13 April* (Good Friday), 16 April* (Easter Monday), 1 May (May Day), 5 May (Patriots' Victory Day), 28 May (Downfall of the Dergue), 4 June† (Mouloud, Birth of the Prophet), 11 September (New Year's Day), 27 September* (Feast of the True Cross), 17 December† (Id al-Fitr, end of Ramadan).

2002: 7 January* (Christmas), 19 January* (Epiphany), 23 February† (Id al-Adha/Arafat), 2 March (Battle of Adowa), 29 March* (Good Friday), 1 April* (Easter Monday), 1 May (May Day), 5 May (Patriots' Victory Day), 24 May† (Mouloud, Birth of the Prophet), 28 May (Downfall of the Dergue), 11 September (New Year's Day), 27 September* (Feast of the True Cross), 6 December† (Id al-Fitr, end of Ramadan).

* Coptic holidays.

† These holidays are dependent on the Islamic lunar calendar and may vary by one or two days from the dates given.

Note: Ethiopia uses its own solar calendar; the Ethiopian year 1993 began on 11 September 2000.

Weights and Measures

The metric system is officially in use. There are also many local weights and measures.

Statistical Survey

Source (unless otherwise stated): Central Statistical Authority, POB 1143, Addis Ababa; tel. (1) 553010; fax (1) 550334.

Note: Unless otherwise indicated, figures in this Survey refer to the territory of Ethiopia after the secession of Eritrea in May 1993.

Area and Population

AREA, POPULATION AND DENSITY

Area (sq km)	1,133,380*
Population (census results)	
9 May 1984†	39,868,501
11 October 1994	
Males	26,910,698
Females	26,566,567
Total	53,477,265
Population (official estimates at mid-year)	
1997	58,117,000
1998	59,880,000
1999	61,672,000
Density (per sq km) at mid-1999	54.4

* 437,600 sq miles.

† Including an estimate for areas not covered by the census.

ADMINISTRATIVE DIVISIONS (estimated population at mid-1999)

	Population ('000)		
	Males	Females	Total
Regional States			
1 Tigrai	1,767	1,826	3,593
2 Afar	667	521	1,188
3 Amhara	7,938	7,912	15,850
4 Oromia	10,833	10,861	21,694
5 Somali	1,952	1,650	3,602
6 Benishangul/Gumuz . .	264	259	523
7 Southern Nations, Nationalities and Peoples	6,029	6,103	12,132
8 Gambela	105	101	206
9 Harari	78	76	154
Chartered Cities			
1 Dire Dawa	154	152	306
2 Addis Ababa	1,169	1,255	2,424
Total	**30,956**	**30,716**	**61,672**

PRINCIPAL TOWNS (census results of October 1994)

Addis Ababa (capital)	2,084,588
Dire Dawa	164,851
Nazret	127,842
Harar	122,932
Mekele	119,779
Jimma	119,717
Dessie	117,268
Bahir Dar	115,531
Debrezit	105,963

Source: UN, *Demographic Yearbook*.

BIRTHS AND DEATHS (UN estimates, annual averages)

	1980–85	1985–90	1990–95
Birth rate (per 1,000) . . .	48.0	49.0	46.5
Death rate (per 1,000) . . .	22.1	20.0	19.2

Expectation of life (UN estimates, years at birth, 1990–95): 45.2 (males 43.9; females 46.7).

Source: UN, *World Population Prospects: The 1998 Revision*.

ECONOMICALLY ACTIVE POPULATION (official estimates, ISIC Major Divisions, persons aged 10 years and over, mid-1995)*

	Males	Females	Total
Agriculture, hunting, forestry and fishing	12,681,037	8,924,280	21,605,317
Mining and quarrying . . .	12,114	4,426	16,540
Manufacturing	224,106	160,889	384,995
Electricity, gas and water . .	14,799	2,267	17,066
Construction	55,906	5,326	61,232
Trade, restaurants and hotels . .	335,353	600,584	935,937
Transport, storage and communications	87,975	15,179	103,154
Financing, insurance, real estate and business services . .	14,513	4,938	19,451
Community, social and personal services	777,907	474,317	1,252,224
Total labour force . . .	**14,203,710**	**10,192,206**	**24,395,916**

* The figures exclude persons seeking work for the first time, totalling 210,184 (males 100,790; females 109,394), but include other unemployed persons.

Source: ILO, *Yearbook of Labour Statistics*.

Mid-1999 (estimates in '000): Agriculture, etc. 22,170; Total labour force 26,764 (Source: FAO).

Agriculture

PRINCIPAL CROPS ('000 metric tons)

	1997	1998	1999
Wheat	1,093	1,143	1,150†
Barley	953	983	970†
Maize	2,987	2,344	2,840†
Oats	67	56	55†
Millet (Dagusa) . . .	296	260	381
Sorghum	2,040	1,083	1,340†
Other cereals	2,037	1,328	1,670
Potatoes*	360	365	370
Sweet potatoes* . . .	159	160	165
Yams*	265	266	267
Other roots and tubers . .	3,394	3,400*	3,450*
Dry beans	97	78	102
Dry peas	142	97	98
Dry broad beans . . .	361	339	285
Chick-peas	118	137	139
Lentils	33	36	28
Other pulses	152	135	132
Sugar cane	1,490	1,650*	2,200*
Soybeans*	23	24	25
Groundnuts (in shell)* .	56	57	58
Castor beans* . . .	15	15	16
Rapeseed*	82	83	84
Sesame seed*	42	55	50
Linseed	32*	33*	35
Safflower seed* . . .	35	36	37
Cotton (lint)† . . .	15	15	15*
Vegetables and melons* . .	589	596	599
Bananas*	80	81	81
Other fruit (excl. melons)*	149	150	150
Tree nuts*	68	69	68
Coffee (green)† . . .	228	230	232
Tobacco (leaves) . . .	4†	4*	3*
Fibre crops (excl. cotton) .	19	19	19*

* FAO estimate(s). † Unofficial figure(s).

Source: FAO.

LIVESTOCK ('000 head, year ending September)

	1997	1998	1999
Cattle	32,612	35,372	35,095
Sheep*	21,850	21,900	22,000
Goats*	16,850	16,900	16,950
Asses*	5,200	5,200	5,200
Horses*	2,750	2,750	2,750
Mules*	630	630	630
Camels*	1,030	1,040	1,050
Pigs*	23	24	25
Poultry*	55,000	55,200	55,400

* FAO estimates.

Source: FAO.

LIVESTOCK PRODUCTS ('000 metric tons)

	1997	1998	1999
Beef and veal	270	274	290
Mutton and lamb*	81	81	81
Goat meat*	63	63	63
Pig meat*	1	1	1
Poultry meat*	73	73	74
Other meat	134	135	135
Cows' milk	938	949	961
Goats' milk	93	93	94
Sheep's milk	55	55	55
Butter	11	12	12
Cheese	4	4	4
Hen eggs*	75	75	76
Honey	28	28	29
Wool:			
greasy*	12	12	12
Cattle hides	51	54	56
Sheepskins	15	15	15
Goatskins	13	13	13

* FAO estimates.

Source: FAO.

Forestry

ROUNDWOOD REMOVALS ('000 cubic metres, excl. bark)

	1996	1997	1998
Sawlogs, veneer logs and logs for sleepers	92	60	60
Pulpwood	7	7	7
Other industrial wood	2,340	2,416	2,416
Fuel wood	45,379	46,521	47,665
Total	47,818	49,004	50,148

Source: FAO, *Yearbook of Forest Products*.

SAWNWOOD PRODUCTION
('000 cubic metres, incl. railway sleepers)

	1996	1997	1998
Total	33	33	33

Source: FAO, *Yearbook of Forest Products*.

Fishing

(metric tons, live weight)

	1996	1997	1998
Capture	8,770	10,370	14,000
Rhinofishes	1,994	2,007	3,168
Other cyprinids	542	857	918
Tilapias	5,066	6,076	7,952
North African catfish	812	1,200	1,677
Nile perch	270	230	191
Aquaculture*	38	44	44
Total catch	8,808	10,414	14,044

* FAO estimates.

Source: FAO, *Yearbook of Fishery Statistics*.

Mining

('000 metric tons, unless otherwise indicated)

	1993	1994	1995
Gold (kilograms)	3,404	2,370*†	4,500*†
Salt (unrefined)†	53	5	5
Limestone ('000 cu metres)†	100	261	n.a.
Gypsum†	3	31	54
Marble ('000 sq metres)†	n.a.	n.a.	184

Gold (kilograms): 5,000*† in 1996.

Salt (unrefined, '000 metric tons): 5† in 1996; 1† in 1997.

* Provisional figure.

† Data from US Bureau of Mines.

Source: UN, *Industrial Commodity Statistics Yearbook*.

Industry

SELECTED PRODUCTS
('000 metric tons, unless otherwise indicated; year ending 7 July)

	1992/93*	1993/94	1994/95
Edible oils	4.0	4.2	5.6
Wheat flour	62.3	74.7	116.0
Flour of other cereals	0.3	2.3	1.6
Macaroni and pasta	5.7	11.2	19.1
Raw sugar	136.7	123.3	129.3
Wine ('000 hectolitres)	68.9	57.3	70.9
Beer ('000 hectolitres)	522.3	634.4	723.5
Mineral waters ('000 hectolitres)	159.3	199.3	298.4
Soft drinks ('000 hectolitres)	553.8	546.2	710.5
Cigarettes (million)	1,932.0	1,468.4	1,582.8
Cotton yarn (metric tons)	3,448	5,669	4,934
Woven cotton fabrics ('000 sq metres)	36,423	60,591	50,016
Nylon fabrics ('000 sq metres)	3,840	3,752	4,910
Leather footwear ('000 pairs)	928.8	1,999.2	1,159.4
Canvas and rubber footwear ('000 pairs)	2,030.9	1,609.4	2,196.3
Plastic footwear ('000 pairs)	123.5	62.3	395.7
Paper	—	—	7.1
Soap	17.3	15.0	15.2
Tyres ('000)	99.8	171.3	167.5
Clay building bricks ('000)	19.8	19.5	19.3
Quicklime	3.7	2.7	4.9
Cement	377.1	464.4	609.3

* Including Eritrea.

Electricity (estimates, million k Wh): 1,399 in 1993; 1,302 in 1994; 1,328 in 1995; 1,316 in 1996 (Source: UN, *Industrial Commodity Statistics Yearbook*).

1996 ('000 metric tons; data from FAO): Wheat flour 185; Raw sugar 182 (Source: UN, *Industrial Commodity Statistics Yearbook*).

Finance

CURRENCY AND EXCHANGE RATES

Monetary Units
100 cents = 1 birr.

Sterling, Dollar and Euro Equivalents (29 December 2000)
£1 sterling = 12.406 birr;
US $1 = 8.314 birr;
€1 = 7.736 birr;
1,000 birr = £80.61 = $120.28 = €129.26.

Average Exchange Rate (birr per US $)
1998   7.1159
1999   7.9423
2000   8.2173

GENERAL BUDGET (million birr, year ending 7 July)

Revenue*	1995/96	1996/97†	1997/98†
Taxation	4,723.3	5,358.2	5,261.1
Taxes on income and profits	1,848.8	1,745.3	1,849.5
Personal income	337.4	366.3	429.3
Business profits	1,222.3	1,264.7	1,088.6
Domestic indirect taxes	1,155.6	1,289.9	1,180.6
Sales/excise taxes	955.3	1,067.9	942.2
Alcohol and tobacco	359.2	397.9	356.1
Import duties	1,694.4	2,025.1	2,037.2
Customs duties	889.1	1,066.9	1,012.4
Excise taxes	805.3	958.2	1,024.8
Export duties	119.5	138.5	181.2
Other revenue	2,242.9	2,519.3	3,139.1
Government investment income	822.4	1,118.5	1,400.4
Reimbursements and property sales	177.4	116.4	92.2
Proceeds from privatization	—	347.0	312.5
Total	**6,966.2**	**7,877.5**	**8,400.2**

* Excluding grants received from abroad (million birr): 1,096.8 in 1995/96; 1,504.0† in 1996/97; 1,273.3† in 1997/98.
† Estimate(s).

Expenditure	1995/96	1996/97*	1997/98*
Current expenditure	5,582.2	5,717.4	7,094.9
General services	1,949.5	1,860.2	287.5
Organs of state	343.1	239.2	287.5
Judiciary	66.6	220.2	258.9
Defence	771.9	334.7	2,083.5
Public order and security	347.4	185.2	216.4
Economic services	620.5	661.0	659.9
Agriculture and natural resources	378.6	408.0	486.5
Social services	1,422.0	1,488.4	1,723.1
Education	941.0	1,025.7	1,126.8
Health	328.1	331.5	400.4
Pension payments	290.6	303.4	308.7
Interest and charges	922.5	918.7	835.6
External assistance (grants)†	142.7	256.5	160.0
Capital expenditure	3,562.6	4,299.8	4,265.1
Economic development	2,618.8	3,000.4	2,451.1
Agriculture and settlement	357.7	277.2	370.2
Water and natural resources	422.2	513.2	464.0
Mining and energy	384.4	796.0	429.0
Industry	358.3	288.1	93.2
Road construction	670.6	742.1	898.5
Transport and communications	218.0	385.5	194.7
Financial agencies	207.1	n.a.	n.a.
Social development	712.0	843.5	1,013.4
Education	441.9	421.9	436.8
Public health	153.9	251.8	276.9
Urban development and housing	116.2	169.8	299.7
General services and compensation	231.8	355.9	305.6
External assistance (grants)†	n.a.	100.0	495.0
Equity contribution	1,049.2	—	100.0
Total	**10,194.0**	**10,017.2**	**11,460.1**

* Estimates.
† Imputed value of goods and services provided mainly in kind.

Source: National Bank of Ethiopia.

NATIONAL BANK RESERVES (US $ million, at 31 December)

	1997	1998	1999
Gold*	0.4	0.4	0.3
IMF special drawing rights	0.1	0.1	0.1
Reserve position in IMF	9.5	10.0	9.7
Foreign exchange	491.4	501.0	448.7
Total	**501.5**	**511.5**	**458.8**

* National valuation.
Source: IMF, *International Financial Statistics*.

MONEY SUPPLY (million birr, at 31 December)

	1997	1998	1999
Currency outside banks	4,964	3,978	4,507
Demand deposits at commercial banks	5,123	5,326	6,018
Total money	**10,087**	**9,304**	**10,524**

Source: IMF, *International Financial Statistics*.

COST OF LIVING (General Index of Retail Prices for Addis Ababa; base: 1997 = 100)

	1998	1999
Food	101.8	111.2
Clothing (incl. footwear)	92.9	89.2
All items (incl. others)	**100.9**	**104.7**

Source: ILO, *Yearbook of Labour Statistics*.

NATIONAL ACCOUNTS
(million birr at current prices; year ending 7 July)

Expenditure on the Gross Domestic Product

	1995/96	1996/97	1997/98
Government final consumption expenditure	4,158	4,526	6,251
Private final consumption expenditure	31,291	32,831	35,472
Gross capital formation	7,246	7,049	7,927
Total domestic expenditure	**42,695**	**44,406**	**49,650**
Exports of goods and services	4,962	6,731	7,251
Less Imports of goods and services	9,719	9,672	11,866
GDP in purchasers' values	**37,938**	**41,465**	**45,035**

Source: IMF, *International Financial Statistics*.

Gross Domestic Product by Economic Activity
(at constant 1980/81 factor cost)

	1995/96	1996/97	1997/98
Agriculture, hunting, forestry and fishing	7,206.2	7,453.9	6,687.0
Mining and quarrying	55.4	62.6	68.9
Manufacturing	881.0	932.8	986.9
Electricity, gas and water	203.2	215.1	223.1
Construction	349.3	379.6	412.1
Trade, hotels and restaurants	1,115.5	1,208.9	1,263.3
Transport, storage and communications	799.2	853.2	907.8
Finance, insurance and real estate	879.7	954.5	999.2
Public administration and defence	1,391.5	1,483.4	1,848.3
Education	298.0	311.1	327.0
Health	154.0	160.1	175.9
Domestic and other services	654.1	694.7	731.5
Total	**13,987.1**	**14,709.9**	**14,631.0**

Source: IMF, *Ethiopia: Recent Economic Developments* (September 1999).

BALANCE OF PAYMENTS (US $ million)

	1997	1998	1999
Exports of goods f.o.b.	588.3	560.3	447.7
Imports of goods f.o.b.	−1,001.6	−1,309.8	−1,244.9
Trade balance	−413.4	−749.4	−797.1
Exports of services	390.8	428.8	476.6
Imports of services	−394.2	−482.3	−447.7
Balance on goods and services	−416.8	−802.9	−768.2
Other income received	24.2	21.0	16.6
Other income paid	−65.5	−58.0	−44.1
Balance on goods, services and income	−458.1	−839.9	−795.7
Current transfers received	425.5	589.8	499.7
Current transfers paid	−7.6	−15.7	−20.2
Current balance	−40.2	−265.8	−316.2
Capital account (net)	−0.8	—	—
Investment assets	318.5	45.1	−182.9
Investment liabilities	−77.3	−68.6	−72.3
Net errors and omissions	−627.9	−75.6	−384.5
Overall balance	−427.7	−364.9	−186.9

Source: IMF, *International Financial Statistics*.

External Trade

PRINCIPAL COMMODITIES (distribution by SITC, US $ '000)

Imports c.i.f.	1994	1995	1996
Food and live animals	150,811	123,677	26,783
Cereals and cereal preparations	121,279	84,432	19,287
Mineral fuels, lubricants, etc.	n.a.	124,378	119,455
Crude petroleum oils, etc.	80,274	67,197	47,285
Refined petroleum products	65,795	57,000	71,822
Chemicals and related products	n.a.	n.a.	n.a.
Medicinal and pharmaceutical products	32,622	29,561	26,634
Medicaments	n.a.	27,499	22,282
Manufactured fertilizers	8,821	60,967	66,171
Basic manufactures	n.a.	n.a.	n.a.
Rubber manufactures	33,962	36,033	51,258
Textile yarn, fabrics, etc.	31,688	47,121	52,761
Iron and steel	n.a.	58,530	80,544
Universals, plates and sheets	n.a.	45,714	55,910
Machinery and transport equipment	n.a.	n.a.	n.a.
Electrical machinery, apparatus, etc.*	n.a.	53,255	69,459
Road vehicles and parts†	146,467	198,335	194,946
Passenger motor cars (excl. buses)	n.a.	43,304	57,066
Motor vehicles for goods transport, etc.	n.a.	102,023	94,397
Parts and accessories for cars, buses, lorries, etc.†	n.a.	23,373	22,097
Total (incl. others)	918,589	1,121,297	1,117,884

* Excluding telecommunications and sound equipment.

† Excluding tyres, engines and electrical parts.

Exports f.o.b.	1994	1995	1996
Food and live animals	n.a.	n.a.	n.a.
Vegetables and fruit	2,561	16,111	3,495
Coffee, tea, cocoa and spices	n.a.	270,829	278,485
Coffee and coffee substitutes	218,430	270,707	278,485
Crude materials (inedible) except fuels	n.a.	n.a.	n.a.
Raw hides, skins and furskins	48,315	56,450	71,078
Raw hides and skins (excl. furs)	48,315	56,450	71,078
Cattle hides	n.a.	8,809	4,559
Sheep skins	n.a.	24,301	50,114
Mineral fuels, lubricants, etc.	17,409	11,842	13,701
Petroleum, petroleum products, etc.	17,409	11,842	13,701
Total (incl. others)	334,894	414,483	417,411

Exports f.o.b. (US $ '000, 1997): Vegetables and fruit 23,576; Coffee, tea, cocoa and spices 382,703 (Coffee and coffee substitutes 382,314); Raw hides, skins and furskins 60,590 (Raw hides and skins, excl. furs 60,590); Total (incl. others) 557,376.

Exports f.o.b. (US $ '000, 1998): Vegetables and fruit 39,958; Coffee, tea, cocoa and spices 420,313 (Coffee and coffee substitutes 419,763); Raw hides, skins and furskins 49,572 (Raw hides and skins, excl. furs 49,572); Total (incl. others) 593,393.

Source: National Bank of Ethiopia.

PRINCIPAL TRADING PARTNERS (million birr)

Imports c.i.f.	1995	1996	1997*
Belgium-Luxembourg	217.4	160.2	114.4
China, People's Repub.	163.4	207.5	366.1
Denmark	66.3	83.4	n.a.
Djibouti	174.3	186.5	40.0
France	183.7	130.2	149.5
Germany	539.6	504.9	749.5
India	177.2	243.8	430.6
Italy	863.8	863.9	726.7
Japan	588.5	565.9	796.8
Kenya	214.9	211.3	154.9
Korea, Repub.	155.6	200.6	358.5
Netherlands	194.1	342.2	344.9
Saudi Arabia	828.4	724.7	735.2
Sweden	198.7	188.6	n.a.
Turkey	36.6	83.7	121.3
United Kingdom	417.5	321.6	454.7
USA	910.4	374.5	358.5
Total (incl. others)	7,041.7	7,103.1	7,615.1

* Preliminary estimates.

Exports f.o.b.	1996	1997	1998*
Belgium-Luxembourg	54.7	142.5	176.2
Djibouti	230.9	298.9	147.0
France	94.2	127.5	144.0
Germany	827.1	811.9	984.4
Israel	8.8	18.9	56.1
Italy	206.7	307.8	270.3
Japan	333.6	441.0	479.5
Netherlands	35.9	57.5	73.8
Saudi Arabia	296.3	337.1	392.5
Switzerland	21.9	62.6	22.8
United Kingdom	86.6	115.0	98.1
USA	169.9	448.0	271.2
Total (incl. others)	2,783.1	3,941.3	3,966.0

* Preliminary estimates.

Source: IMF, *Ethiopia: Recent Economic Developments* (September 1999).

Transport

RAILWAYS (traffic, year ending 7 July)*

	1996/97	1997/98	1998/99
Addis Ababa–Djibouti:			
Passenger-km (million) . .	157	167	150
Freight (million net ton-km)	106	90	116

* Including traffic on the section of the Djibouti–Addis Ababa line which runs through the Republic of Djibouti. Data pertaining to freight include service traffic.

Source: Ministry of Transport and Communications, Addis Ababa.

ROAD TRAFFIC (motor vehicles in use, year ending 7 July)

	1996/97	1997/98	1998/99
Cars	42,318	48,307	48,534
Buses and coaches . . .	22,460	21,959	24,199
Lorries and vans	24,367	26,000	26,007
Motorcycles and mopeds . . .	1,151	1,172	1,353
Road tractors . . .	5,888	5,445	5,367
Total	96,184	102,883	105,460

Source: Ministry of Transport and Communications, Addis Ababa.

SHIPPING
Merchant Fleet (registered at 7 July)

	1997	1998	1999
Number of vessels . . .	11	11	12
Displacement (grt) . . .	86,592	81,508	82,503

Source: Ethiopian Shipping Lines Corporation.

International Sea-borne Shipping (freight traffic, '000 metric tons, year ending 7 July)

	1996/97	1997/98	1998/99
Goods loaded	242	201	313
Goods unloaded	777	1,155	947

Source: Ministry of Transport and Communications, Addis Ababa.

CIVIL AVIATION (traffic on scheduled services, year ending 7 July)

	1996/97	1997/98	1998/99
Kilometres flown (million) . .	28	n.a.	n.a.
Passengers carried ('000) . .	808	807	779
Passenger-km (million) . .	1,915	1,944	1,999
Total ton-km (million) . .	129	149	115

Source: Ministry of Transport and Communications, Addis Ababa.

Tourism

TOURIST ARRIVALS BY COUNTRY OF ORIGIN

	1996	1997	1998
Canada	3,811	4,703	3,421
Djibouti	4,247	6,197	4,698
France	4,029	4,818	3,837
Germany	5,554	6,081	5,151
India	2,069	2,066	2,067
Italy	7,621	7,458	6,922
Japan	2,830	2,868	2,383
Kenya	5,336	6,769	4,821
Netherlands	2,504	2,983	2,455
Russia	3,702	2,869	3,460
Saudi Arabia . . .	4,246	5,277	3,620
Sudan	3,485	2,408	3,516
Switzerland . . .	3,159	3,443	2,950
United Kingdom . . .	6,424	6,769	5,949
USA	8,819	9,762	8,002
Yemen	3,920	4,475	3,148
Total (incl. others)*	108,885	114,732	116,686

* Including Ethiopian nationals residing abroad.

Source: World Tourism Organization, *Yearbook of Tourism Statistics*.

1999: Tourist arrivals 91,859.

Receipts from tourism (million birr): 230 in 1997; 129 in 1998; 130 in 1999.

Source: Ethiopian Tourism Commission.

Communications Media

	1995	1996	1997
Radio receivers ('000 in use) . .	10,900	11,300	11,750
Television receivers ('000 in use) .	250	300	320
Telephones ('000 main lines in use)*	142	149	157
Telefax stations (number in use)* .	1,445	1,624	2,038
Daily newspapers:			
Number	4	4	n.a.
Average circulation ('000 copies)	92†	86	n.a.

* Year ending 30 June.
† Estimate.

Book production: 240 titles (including 93 pamphlets) in 1991.

Non-daily newspapers: 17 in 1995 (average combined circulation 159,000).

Source: mainly UNESCO, *Statistical Yearbook*.

Education

(1999/2000)

	Institutions	Teachers	Students
Pre-primary	834	2,877	99,710
Primary	11,490	115,777	6,462,503
Secondary:			
General	410	13,154	571,719
Teacher-training . . .	12	294	4,813
Skill development centres .	25	367	2,474
Technical and vocational:			
Government	16	523	3,427
Non-Government . .	9	125	1,837
University level . . .	6	1,779	40,894
Other higher:			
Government . . .	11	578	18,412
Non-Government . . .	4	140	8,376

Source: Ministry of Education, Addis Ababa.

Directory

The Constitution

The Constitution of the Federal Democratic Republic of Ethiopia was adopted by the transitonal Government on 8 December 1994. The following is a summary of the main provisions of the Constitution, which came into force on 22 August 1995.

GENERAL PROVISIONS

The Constitution establishes a federal and democratic state structure and all sovereign power resides in the nations, nationalities and peoples of Ethiopia. The Constitution is the supreme law of the land. Human rights and freedoms, emanating from the nature of mankind, are inviolable and inalienable. State and religion are separate and there shall be no state religion. The State shall not interfere in religious matters and vice versa. All Ethiopian languages shall enjoy equal state recognition; Amharic shall be the working language of the Federal Government.

FUNDAMENTAL RIGHTS AND FREEDOMS

All persons are equal before the law and are guaranteed equal and effective protection, without discrimination on grounds of race, nation, nationality, or other social origin, colour, sex, language, religion, political or other opinion, property, birth or other status. Everyone has the right to freedom of thought, conscience and religion and the freedom, either individually or in community with others, and in public or private, to manifest his religion or belief in worship, observance, practice and teaching. Every person has the inviolable and inalienable right to life, privacy, and the security of person and liberty.

DEMOCRATIC RIGHTS

Every Ethiopian national, without discrimination based on colour, race, nation, nationality, sex, language, religion, political or other opinion, or other status, has the following rights: on the attainment of 18 years of age, to vote in accordance with the law; to be elected to any office at any level of government; to freely express oneself without interference; to hold opinions without interference; to engage in economic activity and to pursue a livelihood anywhere within the national territory; to choose his or her means of livelihood, occupation and profession; and to own private property.

Every nation, nationality and people in Ethiopia has the following rights: an unconditional right to self-determination, including the right to secession; the right to speak, to write and to develop its own language; the right to express, to develop and to promote its culture, and to preserve its history; the right to a full measure of self-government which includes the right to establish institutions of government in the territory that it inhabits. Women shall, in the enjoyment of rights and protections provided for by this Constitution, have equal right with men.

STATE STRUCTURE

The Federal Democratic Republic of Ethiopia shall have a parliamentarian form of government. The Federal Democratic Republic shall comprise nine States. Addis Ababa shall be the capital city of the Federal State.

STRUCTURE AND DIVISION OF POWERS

The Federal Democratic Republic of Ethiopia comprises the Federal Government and the member States. The Federal Government and the States shall have legislative, executive and judicial powers. The House of People's Representatives is the highest authority of the Federal Government. The House is responsible to the people. The State Council is the highest organ of state authority. It is responsible to the people of the State. State government shall be established at state and other administrative levels deemed necessary. Adequate power shall be granted to the lowest units of government to enable the people to participate directly in the administration of such units. The State Council has legislative power on matters falling under state jurisdiction. Consistent with the provisions of this Constitution, the Council has the power to draft, adopt and amend the state constitution. The state administration constitutes the highest organ of executive power. State judicial power is vested in its courts. The States shall respect the powers of the Federal Government. The Federal Government shall likewise respect the powers of the States. The Federal Government may, when necessary, delegate to the States powers and functions granted to it by the Constitution.

THE FEDERAL HOUSES

There shall be two Federal Houses: The House of People's Representatives and the House of the Federation.

Members of the House of People's Representatives shall be elected by the people for a term of five years on the basis of universal suffrage and by direct, free and fair elections held by secret ballot. Members of the House, on the basis of population and special representation of minority nationalities and peoples, shall not exceed 550; of these, minority nationalities and peoples shall have at least 20 seats. The House of People's Representatives shall have legislative power in all matters assigned by this Constitution to federal jurisdiction. The political party or coalition of political parties, that has the greatest number of seats in the House of People's Representatives shall form and lead the Executive. Elections for a new House shall be concluded one month prior to the expiry of the House's term.

The House of the Federation is composed of representatives of nations, nationalities and peoples. Each nation, nationality and people shall be represented in the House of the Federation by at least one member. Each nation or nationality shall be represented by one additional representative for each one million of its population. Members of the House of the Federation shall be elected by the State Councils. The State Councils may themselves elect representatives to the House of the Federation, or they may hold elections to have the representatives elected by the people directly. The House of the Federation shall hold at least two sessions annually. The term of mandate of the House of the Federation shall be five years. No one may be a member of the House of People's Representatives and of the House of the Federation simultaneously.

PRESIDENT OF THE REPUBLIC

The President of the Federal Democratic Republic of Ethiopia is the Head of State. The House of People's Representatives shall nominate the candidate for President. The nominee shall be elected President if a joint session of the House of People's Representatives and the House of the Federation approves his candidacy by a two-thirds majority vote. The term of office of the President shall be six years. No person shall be elected President for more than two terms. The President's duties include the opening of the Federal Houses; appointing ambassadors and other envoys to represent the country abroad; granting, upon recommendation by the Prime Minister and in accordance with law, high military titles; and granting pardons.

THE EXECUTIVE

The highest executive powers of the Federal Government are vested in the Prime Minister and in the Council of Ministers. The Prime Minister and the Council of Ministers are responsible to the House of People's Representatives. In the exercise of state functions, members of the Council of Ministers are collectively responsible for all decisions they make as a body. Unless otherwise provided in this Constitution, the term of office of the Prime Minister is the duration of the mandate of the House of People's Representatives. The Prime Minister is the Chief Executive, the Chairman of the Council of Ministers, and the Commander-in-Chief of the national armed forces. The Prime Minister shall submit for approval to the House of People's Representatives nominees for ministerial posts from among members of the two Houses or from among persons who are not members of either House and possess the required qualifications. The Council of Ministers is responsible to the Prime Minister and, in all its decisions, is responsible to the House of People's Representatives. The Council of Ministers ensures the implementation of laws and decisions adopted by the House of People's Representatives.

STRUCTURE AND POWERS OF THE COURTS

Supreme Federal judicial authority is vested in the Federal Supreme Court. The House of People's Representatives may, by two-thirds majority vote, establish nation-wide, or in some parts of the country only, the Federal High Court and First-Instance Courts it deems necessary. Unless decided in this manner, the jurisdictions of the Federal High Court and of the First-Instance Courts are hereby delegated to the state courts. States shall establish State Supreme, High and First-Instance Courts. Judicial powers, both at federal and state levels, are vested in the courts. Courts of any level shall be free from any interference of influence of any governmental body, government official or from any other source. Judges shall exercise their functions in full independence and shall be directed solely by the law. The Federal Supreme Court shall have the highest and final judicial power over Federal matters. State Supreme Courts shall have the highest and final judicial power over state matters. They shall also exercise the jurisdiction of the Federal High Court.

MISCELLANEOUS PROVISIONS

The Council of Ministers of the Federal Government shall have the power to decree a state of emergency in the event of an external invasion, a breakdown of law and order that endangers the constitutional order and cannot be controlled by the regular law enforcement agencies and personnel, a natural disaster or an epidemic. State executives can decree a state-wide state of emergency should a natural disaster or an epidemic occur.

A National Election Board independent of any influence shall be established, to conduct free and fair elections in federal and state constituencies in an impartial manner.

The Government

HEAD OF STATE

President: Dr NEGASSO GIDADA (took office 22 August 1995).

COUNCIL OF MINISTERS
(April 2001)

Prime Minister: MELES ZENAWI.

Deputy Prime Minister and Head of Economic Affairs: Dr KASSA YLALA.

Deputy Prime Minister and Minister of Defence: ADDISO LEGGESE.

Minister of Foreign Affairs: SEYOUM MESFIN.

Minister of Health: Dr LAMIESO HAISSO (acting).

Minister of Energy and Mines: EZEDIN ALI.

Minister of Economic Development and Co-operation: GIRMA BIRU.

Minister of Information and Culture: WOLDE MIKAEL CHAMO.

Minister of Education: GENET ZEWDE.

Minister of Agriculture: Dr MENGISTU HULUKA.

Minister of Commerce and Industry: KASAHUN AYELE.

Minister of Finance: SUFYAN AHMED.

Minister of Justice: WEREDE WOLDU WOLDE.

Minister of Works and Urban Development: HAILE SELASSIE ASEGIDE.

Minister of Labour: HASAN ABDELA.

Minister of Water Resources: SHIFERAW JARSO.

Minister and Head of the Revenue Collectors Board: DESTA AMARE.

Minister of Transport and Communications: MOHAMOUD DIRIR GHEDDI.

MINISTRIES AND COMMISSIONS

Office of the Prime Minister: POB 1013, Addis Ababa; tel. (1) 552044.

Ministry of Agriculture: POB 62347, Addis Ababa; tel. (1) 152816; fax (1) 512984.

Ministry of Commerce and Industry: POB 704, Addis Ababa; tel. (1) 518025; fax (1) 515411.

Ministry of Defence: POB 125, Addis Ababa; tel. (1) 445555.

Ministry of Economic Development and Co-operation: POB 2559, Addis Ababa; tel. (1) 552800.

Ministry of Education: POB 1367, Addis Ababa; tel. (1) 553133.

Ministry of Energy and Mines: POB 486, Addis Ababa; tel. (1) 518250; fax (1) 517874.

Ministry of Finance: POB 1905, Addis Ababa; tel. (1) 552400; fax (1) 551355.

Ministry of Foreign Affairs: POB 393, Addis Ababa; tel. (1) 447345; fax (1) 514300.

Ministry of Health: POB 1234, Addis Ababa; tel. (1) 518031; fax 519366.

Ministry of Information and Culture: POB 1020, Addis Ababa; tel. (1) 517020.

Ministry of Justice: POB 1370, Addis Ababa; tel. (1) 517390.

Ministry of Labour: POB 2056, Addis Ababa; tel. (1) 517080.

Ministry of Transport and Communications: POB 1238, Addis Ababa; tel. (1) 516166; fax (1) 515665.

Ministry of Water Resources: POB 5744, Addis Ababa, tel. (1) 611111; fax (1) 610885.

Ministry of Works and Urban Development: POB 3386, Addis Ababa; tel. (1) 150000.

Regional Governments

Ethiopia comprises nine regional governments, one chartered city (Addis Ababa) and one Administrative Council (Dire Dawa), which are vested with authority for self-administration. The executive bodies are respectively headed by Presidents (regional states) and Chairmen (Addis Ababa and Dire Dawa).

PRESIDENTS

Tigrai: TSEGAYE BERHE (acting).
Afar: ESMAEL ALISERO.
Amhara: YOSEF RETA.
Oromia: KUMA DEMEKSA.
Somali: IBRAHIM DULENI.
Benishangul/Gumuz: YAREGAL AYSHESHIM.
Southern Nations, Nationalities and Peoples: ABATE KISHO.
Gambela: OKALO GNIGELO.
Harari: FUAD IBRAHIM.

CHAIRMEN

Dire Dawa: SOLOMON HAILU.
Addis Ababa: ALI ABDO.

Legislature

FEDERAL PARLIAMENTARY ASSEMBLY

The legislature comprises an upper house, the House of the Federation (Yefedereshn Mekir Bet), with 108 seats (members are selected by state assemblies and are drawn one each from 22 minority nationalities and one from each professional sector of the remaining nationalities, and serve for a period of five years), and a lower house of no more than 550 directly-elected members, the House of People's Representatives (Yehizbtewekayoch Mekir Bet), who are also elected for a five-year term.

Speaker of the House of the Federation: ALMAZ MEKO.

Yehizbtewekayoch Mekir Bet
(House of People's Representatives)

Speaker: DAWIT YOHANES.

General Election, 14 May and 31 August* 2000

Party	Seats
Oromo People's Democratic Organization (OPDO)	178
Amhara National Democratic Movement (ANDM)	134
Tigrai People's Liberation Front (TPLF)	38
Walayta, Gamo, Gofa, Dawro, and Konta People's Democratic Organization (WGGPDO)	30
Ethiopian People's Revolutionary Democratic Front (EPRDF)	19
Somali People's Democratic Party (SPDP)	19
Sidama People's Democratic Organization (SPDO)	18
Gurage Nationalities' Democratic Movement (GNDM)	15
Kafa Shaka People's Democratic Organization (KSPDO)	10
Afar National Democratic Party (ANDP)	8
Gedeyo People's Revolutionary Democratic Front (GPRDF)	7
South Omo People's Democratic Movement (SOPDM)	7
Benishangul Gumuz People's Democratic Unity Front (BGPDUF)	6
Kembata, Alabaa and Tembaro (KAT)	6
Bench Madji People's Democratic Organization (BMPDO)	5
Hadiya Nation Democratic Organization (HNDO)	5
Gambela People's Democratic Front (GPDF)	3
South Ethiopia People's Democratic Front (SEPDF)	3
Council of Alternative Forces for Peace and Democracy in Ethiopia (CAFPDE)	2
Derashe People's Democratic Organization (DPDO)	2
Ethiopian Democratic Party (EDP)	2
Hadiya People's Democratic Organization (HPDO)	2
Southern Ethiopian People's Democratic Union (SEPDU)	2
All Amhara People's Organization (AAPO)	1
Argoba People's Democratic Movement (APDM)	1
Burgi People's Democratic Union (BPDU)	1
Gambella People's Democratic Congress (GPDC)	1
Konso People's Democratic Organization (KPDO)	1
Kore Nationality Democratic Organization (KNDO)	1
Oromo Liberation Unity Front (OLUF)	1
Oromo National Congress (ONC)	1
Oyda Nationality Democratic Organization (ONDO)	1
Sidama Hadicho People's Democratic Organization (SHPDO)	1
Silte People's Democratic Unity Party (SPDUP)	1
Yem People's Democratic Unity Party (YPDUP)	1
Independents	13
Total*	546

* Owing to irregularities and violence at some polling stations, voting was reheld in 16 constituencies. Furthermore, voting in the

Somali regional state was postponed until 31 August because of severe drought affecting the area.

Political Organizations

Afar People's Democratic Organization (APDO): fmrly Afar Liberation Front (ALF); based in fmr Hararge and Wollo Admin. Regions; Leader ISMAIL ALI SIRRO.

Council of Alternative Forces for Peace and Democracy in Ethiopia (CAFPDE): f. 1993 as a broadly-based coalition of groups opposing the EPRDF; split into two factions in Dec. 1999, led by former Vice-Chairman KIFLE TIGNEH ABATE and by Dr BEYENE PETROS.

Coalition of Ethiopian Democratic Forces (COEDF): f. 1991 in the USA by the Ethiopian People's Revolutionary Party–EPRP (the dominant member), together with a faction of the Ethiopian Democratic Union (EDU) and the Ethiopian Socialist Movement (MEISON); opposes the EPRDF; Chair. MERSHA YOSEPH.

Coalition of Ethiopian Opposition Political Organizations (CEOPO): f. 1998 in France as a coalition of groups opposing the EPRDF; Chair. NEGEDE GOBEZIE; Chair. (Ethiopia) KIFLEH TIGNEH ABATE.

Ethiopian Democratic Unity Party (EDUP): Addis Ababa; f. 1984 as Workers' Party of Ethiopia; adopted present name in 1990, when its Marxist-Leninist ideology was relaxed and membership opened to non-Marxist and opposition groups; sole legal political party until May 1991; Leader RAS MENGESHA; Sec.-Gen. Lt-Gen. TESFAYE GEBRE KIDAN.

Ethiopian National Congress (ENC): USA-based organization aims to form a unified opposition among anti-Govt parties; Chair. GEBEYEHU IJUGU.

Ethiopian National Democratic Party (ENDP): f. 1994 by merger of five pro-Govt orgs with mems in the Council of Representatives; comprises: the Ethiopian Democratic Organization, the Ethiopian Democratic Organization Coalition (EDC), the Gurage People's Democratic Front (GPDF), the Kembata People's Congress (KPC), and the Wolaita People's Democratic Front (WPDF); Chair. FEKADU GEDAMU.

Ethiopian People's Revolutionary Democratic Front (EPRDF): Addis Ababa; f. 1989 by the TPLF as an alliance of insurgent groups seeking regional autonomy and engaged in armed struggle against the EDUP Govt; Leader MELES ZENAWI; in May 1991, with other orgs, formed transitional Govt; alliance comprises:

> **Amhara National Democratic Movement (ANDM):** based in Tigrai; represents interests of the Amhara people; fmrly the Ethiopian People's Democratic Movement (EPDM); adopted present name in 1994; Sec.-Gen. TEFERA WALWA.

> **Oromo People's Democratic Organization (OPDO):** f. 1990 by the TPLF to promote its cause in Oromo areas; based among the Oromo people in the Shoa region; Dep. Sec.-Gen. KUMA DEMEKSA.

> **Tigrai People's Liberation Front (TPLF):** f. 1975; the dominant org. within the EPRDF; Leader MELES ZENAWI.

Gambela People's Democratic Front (GPDF): pro-Govt group based in the Gambela region; Chair. AKILO NIGILIO.

Oromo Liberation Front (OLF): seeks self-determination for the Oromo people; participated in the Ethiopian transitional Govt until June 1992; Chair. KATABE MAYU (acting); Vice-Chair. ABDULFATTAH A. MOUSSA BIYYO.

Somali Abo Liberation Front (SALF): operates in fmr Bale Admin. Region; has received Somali military assistance; Sec.-Gen. MASURAD SHU'ABI IBRAHIM.

Somali People's Democratic Party: f. 1998 by merger of Ogaden National Liberation Front (ONLF) and the Ethiopian Somali Democratic League (ESDL—an alliance comprising the Somali Democratic Union Party, the Issa and Gurgura Liberation Front, the Gurgura Independence Front, the Eastern Gabooye Democratic Organization, the Eastern Ethiopian Somali League, the Horyal Democratic Front, the Social Alliance Democratic Organization, the Somali Abo Democratic Union, the Shekhash People's Democratic Movement, the Ethiopian Somalis' Democratic Movement and the Per Barreh Party); Chair. MOHAMOUD DIRIR GHEDDI; Sec.-Gen. SULTAN IBRAHIM.

Southern Ethiopian People's Democratic Coalition (SEPDC): opposition alliance; Chair. Dr BEYENE PETROS.

Southern Ethiopian People's Democratic Union (SEPDU): f. 1992 as an alliance of 10 ethnically-based political groups from the south of the country; was represented in the transitional Council of Representatives, although five of the participating groups were expelled from the Council in April 1993.

United Liberation Forces of Oromia (ULFO): f. 2000 in Asmara, Eritrea, as a common Oromo Front seeking to overthrow the Ethiopian Government; alliance comprises:

> **Islamic Front for the Liberation of Oromia:** Leader ABDELKARIM IBRAHIM HAMID.

Oromo Liberation Congress (OLC).

Oromo Liberation Front (OLF): see above.

Oromo People's Liberation Front (OPLF).

Oromo People's Liberation Organization (OPLO).

United Oromo People's Liberation Front (UDPLF): Chair. WAQO CUTU.

Western Somali Liberation Front (WSLF): POB 978, Mogadishu, Somalia; f. 1975; aims to unite the Ogaden region with Somalia; maintains guerrilla forces of c. 3,000 men; has received support from regular Somali forces; Sec.-Gen. ISSA SHAYKH ABDI NASIR ADAN.

The following parties all have parliamentary representation: **Afar National Democratic Party (ANDP); All Amhara People's Organization (AAPO):** Pres. HAILU SHAWEL; **Argoba People's Democratic Movement (APDM); Bench Madji People's Democratic Organization (BMPD); Benishangul Gumuz People's Democratic Unity Front (BGPDUF); Burgi People's Democratic Union (BPDU); Derashe People's Democratic Organization (DPDO); Ethiopian Democratic Party (EDP):** Pres. ADMASSU GEBEYEHU; Sec.-Gen. LIDETU AYALEW; **Gambella People's Democratic Congress (GPDC); Gedeyo People's Revolutionary Democratic Front (GPRDF); Gurage Nationalities' Democratic Movement (GNDM), Hadiya Nation Democratic Organization (HNDO); Hadiya People's Democratic Organization (HPDO); Kafa Shaka People's Democratic Organization (KSPDO); Kembata, Alabaa and Tembaro (KAT); Konso People's Democratic Organization (KPDO); Kore Nationality Democratic Organization (KNDO); Oromo Liberation Unity Front (OLUF); Oromo National Congress (ONC):** Leader MERERA GUDINA; **Oyda Nationality Democratic Organization (ONDO); Sidama Hadicho People's Democratic Organization (SHPDO); Sidama People's Democratic Organization (SPDO); Silte People's Democratic Unity Party (SPDUP); South Ethiopia People's Democratic Front (SEPDF); South Omo People's Democratic Movement (SOPDM); Southern Ethiopian People's Democratic Union (SEPDU); Walayta, Gamo, Gofa, Dawro, and Konta People's Democratic Organization (WGGPDO); Yem People's Democratic Organization Unity Party (YPDUP).**

Diplomatic Representation

EMBASSIES IN ETHIOPIA

Algeria: POB 5740, Addis Ababa; tel. (1) 652300; fax (1) 650187; e-mail algemb@telecom.net.et; Ambassador: SMAIL CHERGUI.

Angola: POB 2962, Addis Ababa; tel. (1) 510085; fax (1) 514922; e-mail angola.embassy@telecom.net.et; Ambassador: MIGUEL NETO.

Austria: POB 1219, Addis Ababa; tel. (1) 712144; fax (1) 712140; Ambassador: THOMAS MICHAEL BAIER.

Belgium: POB 1239, Addis Ababa; tel. (1) 611813; fax (1) 613646; e-mail embel.et@telecom.net.et; Ambassador: LEOPOLD CARREWYN.

Bulgaria: POB 987, Addis Ababa; tel. (1) 610032; fax (1) 613373; Chargé d'affaires a.i.: MIROSLAV KOMAROV.

Burkina Faso: POB 19685, Addis Ababa; tel. (1) 615863; fax (1) 612094; e-mail ambfet@telecom.net.et; Ambassador: ZEONDRE B. BASSOLE.

Burundi: POB 3641, Addis Ababa; tel. (1) 651300; e-mail burundi.emb@telecom.net.et; Ambassador: MELCHIOR BWAKIRA.

Cameroon: Bole Rd, POB 1026, Addis Ababa; tel. and fax (1) 504488; Ambassador: JEAN-HILAIRE MBÉA MBÉA.

Canada: Old Airport Area, Higher 23, Kebele 12, House No. 122, POB 1130, Addis Ababa; tel. (1) 713022; fax (1) 713033; Ambassador: JOHN R. SCHRAM.

Chad: POB 5119 Addis Ababa; tel. (1) 613819; fax (1) 612050; Ambassador: MAHAMAT ABDELKERIM.

China, People's Republic: POB 5643, Addis Ababa tel. (1) 711960; fax (1) 712457; e-mail chinesembassy@telecom.net.et; Ambassador: JIANG ZHENGYUN.

Congo, Democratic Republic: Makanisa Rd, POB 2723, Addis Ababa; tel. (1) 710111; fax (1) 713466; e-mail rdca@telecom.net.et; Chargé d'affaires a.i.: MARGRET RASHID KABAMBA.

Congo, Republic: POB 5639, Addis Ababa; tel. (1) 514188; Chargé d'affaires a.i.: CASIMIR MPIERA.

Côte d'Ivoire: POB 3668, Addis Ababa; tel. (1) 712178; e-mail coted.aa@telecom.net.et; Ambassador: PIERRE YÉRÉ.

Cuba: Jimma Road Ave, POB 5623, Addis Ababa; tel. (1) 620459; fax (1) 620460; Ambassador: ANGEL ARZUAGA REYES.

Czech Republic: POB 3108, Addis Ababa; tel. (1) 516132; fax (1) 513471; Ambassador: ZDENÉK POLÁČEK.

Djibouti: POB 1022, Addis Ababa; tel. (1) 613200; fax (1) 612786; Ambassador: (vacant).

Egypt: POB 1611, Addis Ababa; tel. (1) 553077; fax (1) 552722; Ambassador: MARWAN BADR.

Equatorial Guinea: POB 246, Addis Ababa; tel. (1) 615973; Ambassador: APLINAR MOIHE ECHEK.

Eritrea: POB 2571, Addis Ababa; tel. (1) 512844; fax (1) 514911; Chargé d'affaires a.i.: SAHIH OMER.

Finland: Higher 17, Kebele 19, House No. 163, POB 1017, Addis Ababa; tel. (1) 611575; fax (1) 615964; e-mail finland.embassy@ telecom.net.et; Chargé d'affaires a.i.: HELI SIRVE.

France: Kabana, POB 1464, Addis Ababa; tel. (1) 550066; fax (1) 551441; e-mail ambfrance@telecom.net.et; Ambassador: JACQUES DEWATRE.

Gabon: POB 1256, Addis Ababa; tel. (1) 611090; fax (1) 613760; Ambassador: EMMANUEL MENDOUME-NZE.

Germany: Kabana, POB 660, Addis Ababa; tel. (1) 550433; fax (1) 551311; Ambassador: HERBERT HONSOWITZ.

Ghana: POB 3173, Addis Ababa; tel. (1) 711402; fax (1) 712511; e-mail ghmfa24@telecom.net.et; Ambassador: FRITZ KWABENA POKU.

Greece: off Debre Zeit Rd, POB 1168, Addis Ababa; tel. (1) 654911; fax (1) 654883; e-mail greekembassy@telecom.net.et; internet www.telecom.net.et/~greekemb; Ambassador: SPYROS ALIAGAS.

Guinea: POB 1190, Addis Ababa; tel. (1) 651308; fax (1) 651250; Ambassador: MAMADI DIAWARA.

Holy See: POB 588, Addis Ababa (Apostolic Nunciature); tel. (1) 712100; fax (1) 711499; e-mail vatican.embassy@telecom.net.et; Apostolic Nuncio: Most Rev. SILVANO M. TOMASI, Titular Archbishop of Asolo.

Hungary: Abattoirs Rd, POB 1213, Addis Ababa; tel. (1) 651850; Ambassador: Dr SÁNDOR ROBEL.

India: Kabena, POB 528, Addis Ababa; tel. (1) 552394; fax (1) 552521; e-mail indembassy@podis.gn.apc.org; Ambassador: KADAKATH PATHROSE ERNEST.

Indonesia: Mekanisa Rd, POB 1004, Addis Ababa; tel. (1) 710122; fax (1) 710873; e-mail kbriadis@telecom.net.et; Ambassador: HADITMO HARSOJO.

Iran: POB 70488, Addis Ababa; tel. (1) 200794; fax (1) 711915; email csiri@telecom.net.et; internet www.telecom.net.et/~iranet/; Ambassador: SEYED HOSSEIN RAJABI.

Ireland: POB 9585, Addis Ababa; tel. (1) 710835; fax (1) 710988; e-mail ireland.emb@telecom.net.et; Chargé d'affaires a.i.: PAULINE CONWAY.

Israel: POB 1266, Addis Ababa; tel (1) 610998; fax (1) 612456; e-mail israel.embassy@telecom.net.et; Ambassador: ARIEL KEREM.

Italy: Villa Italia, POB 1105, Addis Ababa; tel. (1) 553042; fax (1) 550218; e-mail italembadd@telecom.net.et; Ambassador: MARCELLO RICOVERI.

Jamaica: National House, Africa Ave, POB 5633, Addis Ababa; tel. (1) 613656; Ambassador: OWEN A. SINGH.

Japan: Sunshine Bldg, Bole Rd, POB 5650, Addis Ababa; tel. (1) 511088; fax (1) 511350; e-mail japanembassy@telecom.net.et; Ambassador: TAKEHISA NOGAMI.

Kenya: Fikre Mariam Rd, POB 3301, Addis Ababa; tel. (1) 610033; fax (1) 611433; e-mail kenya.embassy@telecom.net.et; Ambassador: GEORGE AGOI.

Korea, Democratic People's Republic: POB 2378, Addis Ababa; tel. (1) 182828; fax (1) 625417; Ambassador: O. NAM JUNG.

Korea, Republic: Jimma Rd, Old Airport Area, POB 2047, Addis Ababa; tel. (1) 655230; Ambassador: JA CHOL-HAHN.

Kuwait: Higher 20, Kebele 17, House No. 128, Bole Rd, Addis Ababa; tel. (1) 615411; fax (1) 612621; Ambassador: MUHAMMAD AL-AWADHI.

Lesotho: POB 7483, Addis Ababa; tel. (1) 614368; fax (1) 612837; Ambassador: MASHULA H. LETEKA.

Liberia: POB 3116, Addis Ababa; tel. (1) 513655; Ambassador: MARCUS M. KOFA.

Libya: POB 5728, Addis Ababa; tel. (1) 511077; fax (1) 511383; Ambassador: ALI ABDALLA AWIDA.

Madagascar: POB 60004, Addis Ababa; tel. (1) 612555; fax (1) 610127; e-mail amba.mad.addis@telecom.net.et; Ambassador: CHRISTIAN RÉMI RICHARD.

Malawi: POB 2316, Addis Ababa; tel. (1) 615866; fax (1) 615436; e-mail malemb@telecom.net.et; Ambassador: WILLIE CHAKANI.

Mali: POB 4561, Addis Ababa; tel. (1) 201528; fax (1) 712601; Ambassador: AL MAAMOUN KEITA.

Mexico: Tsige Mariam Bldg 292/21, 4th Floor, Churchill Rd, POB 2962, Addis Ababa; tel. (1) 443456; Ambassador: CARLOS FERRER.

Morocco: 210 Bole Rd, POB 60033, Addis Ababa; tel. (1) 531700; fax (1) 511828; e-mail morocco.emb@telecom.net.et; Ambassador: SIDI MUHAMMAD RAHHALI.

Mozambique: POB 5671, Addis Ababa; tel. (1) 710020; fax (1) 613824; e-mail embamoc-add@telecom.net.et; Ambassador: ALEXANDRE ZANDAMELA.

Namibia: Higher 17, Kebele 19, House No. 002, POB 1443, Addis Ababa; tel. (1) 611966; fax (1) 612677; e-mail embassy@telecom .net.et; Ambassador: GEORGE OBANGA.

Netherlands: POB 1241, Addis Ababa; tel. (1) 711100; fax (1) 711577; e-mail netherlands.emb@telecom.net.et; internet www .telecom.net.et/~nethemb/body.htm; Ambassador: PIETER J. T. MARRES.

Niger: Debrezenit Rd, Higher 18, Kebele 41, House No. 057, POB 5791, Addis Ababa; tel. (1) 651305; Ambassador: ASSANE IGODOE.

Nigeria: POB 1019, Addis Ababa; tel. (1) 552307; Ambassador: J. K. SHINKAYE.

Norway: POB 8383, Addis Ababa; tel. (1) 710799; fax (1) 711255; e-mail ambassade-addis@telecom.net.et; Ambassador: S. OSKARSSON.

Poland: Bole Rd, POB 1123, Addis Ababa; tel. (1) 610197; Ambassador: TADEUSZ WUJEK.

Romania: 17 Woreda, Kebele 19, 10 Bole Rd, POB 2478, Addis Ababa; tel. (1) 610156; fax (1) 611191; Chargé d'affaires a.i.: VASILE BONDARET.

Russia: POB 1500, Addis Ababa; tel. (1) 612060; fax (1) 613795; e-mail russemb@telecom.net.et; Ambassador: VALERY N. LIPNYAKOV.

Rwanda: Africa House, Higher 17, Kebele 20, POB 5618, Addis Ababa; tel. (1) 610300; fax (1) 610411; e-mail rwanda.emb@telecom .net.et; Ambassador: Dr NGOGA PASCAL.

Saudi Arabia: Old Airport Area, POB 1104, Addis Ababa; tel. (1) 712952; fax (1) 711799; Ambassador: SAOUD A. M. AL-YAHAYA.

Senegal: Africa Ave, POB 2581, Addis Ababa; tel. (1) 611376; fax (1) 610020; Ambassador: PAPA LOUIS FALL.

Sierra Leone: POB 5619, Addis Ababa; tel. (1) 710033; fax (1) 711911; Ambassador: FODE M. DABOR.

Somalia: Addis Ababa; Ambassador: ABRAHIM HAJI NUR.

South Africa: POB 1091, Addis Ababa; tel. (1) 713034; fax (1) 711330; e-mail sa.embassy.addis@telecom.net.et; Ambassador: JEREMIAH N. MAMABOLO.

Spain: Entoto St, POB 2312, Addis Ababa; tel. (1) 550222; fax (1) 551131; e-mail embespet@mail.mae.es; Ambassador: PABLO ZALDIVAR MIQUELARENA.

Sudan: Kirkos, Kebele, POB 1110, Addis Ababa; tel (1) 516477; fax (1) 518141; e-mail sudan.embassy@telecom.net.et; Ambassador: OSMAN AS-SAYED.

Swaziland: Addis Ababa; Ambassador: SOLOMON DLAMINI.

Sweden: Ras Ababa Aregaye Ave, POB 1142, Addis Ababa; tel. (1) 511255; fax (1) 515830; e-mail sweden.embassy@telecom.net.et; Ambassador: JOHAN HOLMBERG.

Switzerland: Jimma Rd, Old Airport Area, POB 1106, Addis Ababa; tel. (1) 711107; fax (1) 712177; e-mail swissemadd@telecom.net.et; Ambassador: PAOLO BROGINI.

Tanzania: POB 1077, Addis Ababa; tel. (1) 511063; fax (1) 517358; Ambassador: CHARLES S. KILEO.

Togo: Addis Ababa; Ambassador: KATI OHARA KORGA.

Tunisia: Wereda 17, Kebele 19, Bole Rd, POB 100069, Addis Ababa; tel. (1) 612063; fax (1) 614568; e-mail embassy.tunisia@telecom .net.et; Ambassador: ZOUHEIR ALLAGUI.

Turkey: POB 1506, Addis Ababa; tel. (1) 613161; fax (1) 611688; e-mail turk.emb@telecom.net.et; Ambassador: MURAT BILHAN.

Uganda: Addis Ababa; tel. (1) 513088; fax (1) 514355; Ambassador: Dr ALEX KAMUGISHA.

United Kingdom: POB 858, Addis Ababa; tel. (1) 612354; fax (1) 610588; e-mail b.emb4@telecom.net.et; Ambassador: MYLES WICKSTEAD.

USA: Entoto St, POB 1014, Addis Ababa; tel. (1) 550666; fax (1) 551328; e-mail usembassy@telecom.net.et; internet www.telecom .net.et/~usemb-et/; Ambassador: TIBOR P. NAGY, Jr.

Venezuela: Debre Zeit Rd, POB 5584, Addis Ababa; tel. (1) 654790; Chargé d'affaires a.i.: ALFREDO HERNÁNDEZ-ROVATI.

Viet Nam: POB 1288, Addis Ababa; Ambassador: NGUYEN DUY KINH.

Yemen: POB 664, Addis Ababa; Ambassador: MANSUR ABD AL-JALIL ABD AL-RAB.

Yugoslavia: POB 1341, Addis Ababa; tel. (1) 517804; fax (1) 514192; e-mail yugoslav.embassy@telecom.net.et; Ambassador: VOJISLAV VUCIEVIC.

Zambia: POB 1909, Addis Ababa; tel. (1) 711302; fax (1) 711566; Ambassador: SIMATAA AKAPELWA.

Zimbabwe: POB 5624, Addis Ababa; tel. (1) 613877; fax (1) 613476; e-mail zimbabwe.embassy@telecom.net.et; Ambassador: NVILLE NDONDO.

Judicial System

The 1994 Constitution stipulates the establishment of an independent judiciary in Ethiopia. Judicial powers are vested in the courts, both at federal and state level. The supreme federal judicial authority is the Federal Supreme Court. This court has the highest and final power of jurisdiction over federal matters. The federal states of the Federal Democratic Republic of Ethiopia can establish Supreme, High and First-Instance Courts. The Supreme Courts of the federal States have the highest and the final power of jurisdiction over state matters. They also exercise the jurisdiction of the Federal High Court. According to the Constitution, courts of any level are free from any interference or influence from government bodies, government officials or any other source. In addition, judges exercise their duties independently and are directed solely by the law.

Federal Supreme Court: Addis Ababa; tel. (1) 448425; comprises civil, criminal and military sections; its jurisdiction extends to the supervision of all judicial proceedings throughout the country; the Supreme Court is also empowered to review cases upon which final rulings have been made by the courts (including the Supreme Court) where judicial errors have occurred; Pres. ASEFA LIBEN.

Federal High Court: Addis Ababa; hears appeals from the state courts; has original jurisdiction; Pres. WUBISHET KIBRU.

Awraja Courts: Regional courts composed of three judges, criminal and civil.

Warada Courts: Sub-regional; one judge sits alone with very limited jurisdiction, criminal only.

Religion

About 45% of the population are Muslims and about 40% belong to the Ethiopian Orthodox (Tewahido) Church. There are also significant Evangelical Protestant and Roman Catholic communities. The Pentecostal Church and the Society of International Missionaries carry out mission work in Ethiopia. There are also Hindu and Sikh religious institutions. Virtually all of Ethiopia's small Jewish population had been evacuated by the Israeli Government by mid-1999. It has been estimated that 5%–15% of the population follow animist rites and beliefs.

CHRISTIANITY

Ethiopian Orthodox (Tewahido) Church

The Ethiopian Orthodox (Tewahido) Church is one of the five oriental orthodox churches. It was founded in AD 328, and in 1989 had more than 22m. members, 20,000 parishes and 290,000 clergy. The Supreme Body is the Holy Synod and the National Council, under the chairmanship of the Patriarch (Abune). The Church comprises 25 archdioceses and dioceses (including those in Jerusalem, Sudan, Djibouti and the Western Hemisphere). There are 32 Archbishops and Bishops. The Church administers 1,139 schools and 12 relief and rehabilitation centres throughout Ethiopia.

Patriarchate Head Office: POB 1283, Addis Ababa; tel. (1) 116507; Patriarch (Abune) Archbishop PAULOS; Gen. Sec. L. M. DEMTSE GEBRE MEDHIN.

The Roman Catholic Church

At 31 December 1998 Ethiopia contained an estimated 68,357 adherents of the Alexandrian-Ethiopian Rite and 378,113 adherents of the Latin Rite.

Bishops' Conference: Ethiopian and Eritrean Episcopal Conference, POB 21322, Addis Ababa; tel. (1) 550300; fax (1) 553113; f. 1966; Pres. Most Rev. BERHANE-YESUS DEMEREW SOURAPHIEL, Archbishop of Addis Ababa.

Alexandrian-Ethiopian Rite

Adherents are served by one archdiocese (Addis Ababa) and one diocese (Adigrat).

Archbishop of Addis Ababa: Most Rev. BERHANE-YESUS DEMEREW SOURAPHIEL, Catholic Archbishop's House, POB 21903, Addis Ababa; tel. (1) 111667; fax (1) 553113.

Latin Rite

Aherents are served by the five Apostolic Vicariates of Awasa, Harar, Meki, Nekemte and Soddo-Hosanna, and by the Apostolic Prefecture of Jimma-Bonga.

Other Christian Churches

The Anglican Communion: Within the Episcopal Church in Jerusalem and the Middle East, the Bishop in Egypt has jurisdiction over seven African countries, including Ethiopia.

Armenian Orthodox Church: Deacon VARTKES NALBANDIAN, St George's Armenian Church, POB 116, Addis Ababa; f. 1923.

Ethiopian Evangelical Church (Mekane Yesus): Pres. Rev.YADESA DABA, POB 2087, Addis Ababa; tel. (1) 531919; fax (1) 534148; e-mail eecmy.co@telecom.net.et; f. 1959; affiliated to Lutheran World Fed., All Africa Conf. of Churches and World Council of Churches; c. 3.2m. mems (1999).

Greek Orthodox Church: Metropolitan of Axum Most Rev. PETROS GIAKOUMELOS, POB 571, Addis Ababa.

Seventh-day Adventist Church: Pres. TINSAE TOLESSA, POB 145, Addis Ababa; tel. (1) 511319; e-mail sdaeum@telecom.net.et; f. 1907; 130,000 mems.

ISLAM

Leader: Haji MOHAMMED AHMAD.

JUDAISM

A phased emigration to Israel of about 27,000 Falashas (Ethiopian Jews) took place during 1984–91. An estimated further 4,000 Falashas were assisted to emigrate to Israel in mid-1999, leaving only a small number remaining in the country.

The Press

DAILIES

Addis Zemen: POB 30145, Addis Ababa; f. 1941; Amharic; publ. by the Ministry of Information and Culture; Editor-in-Chief (vacant); circ. 40,000.

The Daily Monitor: POB 22588, Addis Ababa; tel (1) 611880; fax (1) 518409; f. 1993; English; Editor-in-Chief LULLIT MICKAEL; circ. 6,000.

Eletawi Addis (Addis Daily): Addis Ababa; f. 2000; Amharic; Editors-in-Chief SOLOMON ABATE, DEREJE DESTA.

Ethiopian Herald: POB 30701, Addis Ababa; tel. (1) 119050; f. 1943; English; publ. by the Ministry of Information and Culture; Editor-in-Chief KIFLOM HADGOI; circ. 37,000.

PERIODICALS

Abyotawit Ethiopia: POB 2549, Addis Ababa; fortnightly; Amharic.

Addis Tribune: Tambek International, POB 2395, Addis Ababa; tel. (1) 615228; fax (1) 615227; e-mail tambek@telecom.net.et; internet www.addistribune.ethiopiaonline.com; f. 1993; weekly; English; Editor-in-Chief (vacant); circ. 6,000.

Addis Zimit: POB 2395, Addis Ababa; tel. (1) 118613; fax (1) 552110; f. 1993; weekly; Amharic; Editor-in-Chief (vacant); circ. 8,000.

Al-Alem: POB 30232, Addis Ababa; tel. (1) 158046; fax (1) 516819; f. 1941; weekly; Arabic; publ. by the Ministry of Information; Editor-in-Chief TELSOM AHMED; circ. 2,500.

Berisa: POB 30232, Addis Ababa; f. 1976; weekly; Oromogna; publ. by the Ministry of Information; Editor BULO SIBA; circ. 3,500.

Beza: Addis Ababa; weekly; Editor-in-Chief YARED KEMFE.

Birhan Family Magazine: Addis Ababa; monthly; women's magazine.

Birritu: National Bank of Ethiopia, POB 5550, Addis Ababa; tel. (1) 517430; fax (1) 514588; e-mail nbe.excd@telecom.net.et; f. 1968; quarterly; Amharic and English; banking, insurance and macroeconomic news; circ. 2,000; Editor-in-Chief SEMENEH ADGE.

Ethiopis Review: Editor-in-Chief TESFERA ASMARE.

Mabruk: Addis Ababa; weekly; Editor-in-Chief TESAHALENNE MENGESHA.

Maebel: Addis Ababa; weekly; Amharic; Editor-in-Chief ABERA WOGI.

Meskerem: Addis Ababa; quarterly; theoretical politics; circ. 100,000.

Negarit Gazzetta: POB 1031, Addis Ababa; irregularly; Amharic and English; official gazette.

Nigdina Limat: POB 2458, Addis Ababa; tel. (1) 513882; fax (1) 511479; monthly; Amharic; publ. by the Ethiopian Chamber of Commerce; circ. 6,000.

Press Digest: POB 12719, Addis Ababa; tel. (1) 504200; fax (1) 513523; e-mail phoenix.universal@telecom.net.et; internet pressdigest.phoenixuniversal.com; f. 1993; weekly.

Tequami: Addis Ababa; weekly; Editor-in-Chief SAMSON SEYUM.

Tinsae (Resurrection): Addis Ababa; tel. (1) 116507; Amharic and English; publ. by the Ethiopian Orthodox Church.

Tobia Magazine: POB 22373, Addis Ababa; tel. (1) 556177; fax (1) 552654; e-mail akpac@telecom.net.et; monthly; Amharic; Man. Goshu Moges; circ. 30,000.

Tobia Newspaper: POB 22373, Addis Ababa; tel. (1) 556177; fax (1) 552654; e-mail akpac@telecom.net.et; weekly; Amharic; Man. Goshu Moges; circ. 25,000.

Wetaderna Alamaw: POB 1901, Addis Ababa; fortnightly; Amharic.

Yezareitu Ethiopia (Ethiopia Today): POB 30232, Addis Ababa; weekly; Amharic and English; publ. by the Ministry of Information and Culture; Editor-in-Chief Imiru Worku; circ. 30,000.

NEWS AGENCIES

Ethiopian News Agency (ENA): Patriot St, POB 530, Addis Ababa; tel. (1) 550011; fax (1) 551609; e-mail ena@telecom.net.et; internet www.telecom.net.et/~ena; Chief Amare Aregawi.

Foreign Bureaux

Agence France-Presse (AFP): POB 3537, Addis Ababa; tel. (1) 511006; Chief Saba Seyoum.

Agenzia Nazionale Stampa Associata (ANSA) (Italy): POB 1001, Addis Ababa; tel. (1) 111007; Chief Brahame Ghebrezghi-Abiher.

Associated Press (AP): Addis Ababa; tel. (1) 161726; Correspondent Abebe Andualam.

Deutsche Presse-Agentur (dpa) (Germany): Addis Ababa; tel. (1) 510687; Correspondent Ghion Hagos.

Informatsionnoye Telegrafnoye Agentstvo Rossii—Telegraf-noye Agentstvo Suverennykh Stran (ITAR—TASS) (Russia): Addis Ababa; tel. (1) 181255; Bureau Chief Gennadii G. Gabrielyan.

Prensa Latina (Cuba): Gen. Makonnen Bldg, 5th Floor, nr Ghion Hotel, opp. National Stadium, Addis Ababa; tel. (1) 519899; Chief Hugo Rius Blein.

Reuters (UK): Addis Ababa; tel. (1) 156505; Correspondent Tsegaye Tadesse.

Rossiiskoye Informatsionnoye Agentstvo—Novosti (RIA—Novosti) (Russia): POB 239, Addis Ababa; Chief Vitalii Polikarpov.

Xinhua (New China) News Agency (People's Republic of China): POB 2497, Addis Ababa; tel. (1) 515676; fax (1) 514742; Correspondent Chen Cailin.

PRESS ASSOCIATION

Ethiopian Free Press Journalists' Association (EFJA): POB 31317; Addis Ababa; tel. (1) 555021; fax (1) 922939; e-mail efja@telecom.net.et; internet www.ifex.org/members/efja; f. 1993; granted legal recognition in 2000; Pres. Kifle Mulat.

Ethiopian Journalists' Association: POB 30288, Addis Ababa; tel. (1) 117852; fax (1) 513365; Pres. Kefale Mammo.

Publishers

Addis Ababa University Press: POB 1176, Addis Ababa; tel. (1) 119148; fax (1) 550655; f. 1968; educational and reference works in English; Editor Messelech Habte.

Ethiopia Book Centre: POB 1024, Addis Ababa; tel. (1) 116844; f. 1977; privately-owned; publr, importer, wholesaler and retailer of educational books.

Kuraz Publishing Agency: POB 30933, Addis Ababa; tel. (1) 551688; state-owned.

Government Publishing House

Government Printing Press: POB 1241, Addis Ababa.

Broadcasting and Communications

TELECOMMUNICATIONS

Ethiopian Telecommunications Corpn (ETC): POB 1047, Addis Ababa; tel. (1) 510500; fax (1) 515777; etc-hq@telecom.net.et; internet www.telecom.net.et; Man. Dir Asmare Abate.

BROADCASTING

Radio

Radio Ethiopia: POB 1020, Addis Ababa; tel. (1) 121011; f. 1941; Amharic, English, French, Arabic, Afar, Oromifa, Tigre, Tigrinya and Somali; Gen. Man. Kasa Miloko.

Radio Torch: Addis Ababa; f. 1994; Amharic; autonomous station; Gen. Man. Seifu Ture Getachew.

Radio Voice of One Free Ethiopia: Amharic; broadcasts twice a week; opposes current Govts of Ethiopia and Eritrea.

Voice of the Revolution of Tigrai: POB 450, Mekele; tel. (4) 400600; fax (4) 405485; f. 1985; Tigrinya and Afargna; broadcasts 57 hours per week; supports Tigrai People's Liberation Front.

Television

Ethiopian Television: POB 5544, Addis Ababa; tel. (1) 516977; fax (1) 512685; f. 1964; semi-autonomous station; accepts commercial advertising; programmes transmitted from Addis Ababa to 26 regional stations; Dir-Gen. Wole Gurmu.

Finance

(cap. = capital; p.u. = paid up; res = reserves; dep. = deposits; m. = million; brs = branches; amounts in birr)

BANKING
Central Bank

National Bank of Ethiopia: POB 5550, Addis Ababa; tel. (1) 517430; fax (1) 514588; e-mail nbe@telecom.net.et; f. 1964; bank of issue; cap. and res 1,117.5m., dep. 6,022.8m. (May 1999); Gov. Teklewold Atnafu; Vice-Gov. Legesse Motta; 4 brs.

Other Banks

Awash International Bank: POB 12638, Addis Ababa; tel. (1) 612919; fax (1) 614477; e-mail awash.bank@telecom.net.et; f. 1994; cap. and res 66.6m., dep. 455.4m. (December 1999); Gen. Man. Leikun Berhanu; 18 brs.

Bank of Abyssinia: POB 12947, Addis Ababa; tel. (1) 514130; fax (1) 511575; e-mail abyssinia@telecom.net.et; f. 1905 (closed 1935 and reopened 1996); commercial banking services; cap. and res 28.0m., dep. 255.4m. (March 1999); CEO Tekalign Gedamu; 7 brs.

Commercial Bank of Ethiopia: Unity Sq., POB 255, Addis Ababa; tel. (1) 511271; fax (1) 514522; e-mail cbe/ibd@telecom.net.et; internet www.combanketh.com; f. 1943, reorg. 1996; state-owned; cap. and res 995.7m., dep. 14,931.0m. (June 1999); Pres. Tilahun Abbay; 168 brs.

Construction and Business Bank: Higher 21, Kebele 04, POB 3480, Addis Ababa; tel. (1) 512300; fax (1) 515103; e-mail cbb@telecom.net.et; f. 1975 as Housing and Savings Bank; provides credit for construction projects and a range of commercial banking services; state-owned; cap. p.u. 68.7m., total assets 1,045.3m. (March 1999); Gen. Man. Admassu Techane; 20 brs.

Dashen Bank: POB 12752, Addis Ababa; tel. (1) 650286; fax (1) 653037; e-mail dashenbank@telecom.net.et; cap. and res 48.9m., dep. 489.4m. (June 1999); CEO Lulseged Teferi; 16 brs.

Development Bank of Ethiopia: POB 1900, Addis Ababa; tel. (1) 511188; fax (1) 511606; provides devt finance for industry and agriculture, technical advice and assistance in project evaluation; state-owned; cap. and res 385.2m., dep. 727.7m. (March 1999); Gen. Man. Moges Chemere; 32 brs.

United Bank: POB 19963, Addis Ababa; tel. (1) 655222; fax (1) 655243; f. 1998; commercial banking services; cap. and res 41.6m., dep. 70.6m. (June 2000); Gen. Man. Kebede Temesgen; 7 brs.

Wegagen Bank: POB 1018, Addis Ababa; tel. (1) 655015; fax (1) 653330; e-mail wegagen@telecom.net.et; f. 1997; commercial banking services; cap. and res 43.0m.; dep. 218.4m. (March 1999); CEO Brutayit Dawit Abdi; 13 brs.

INSURANCE

Africa Insurance Co: POB 12941, Addis Ababa; tel. (1) 517861; fax (1) 510376; Gen. Man. Alem Tesfatsion.

Awash Insurance Co: POB 12637, Addis Ababa; tel. (1) 614420; fax (1) 614419; Gen. Man. Tsegaye Kemas.

Ethiopian Insurance Corpn: POB 2545, Addis Ababa; tel. (1) 512400; fax (1) 517499; e-mail eic.md@telecom.net.et; internet www.telecom.net.et/~eic; f. 1976; Man. Dir Habtamu Haile Mariam.

Global Insurance SC: POB 180112, Addis Abba; tel. (1) 560483; fax (1) 533308; f. 1997; Gen. Man. Masresha G. Meskel.

Lion Insurance SC: POB 661, Addis Ababa; tel. (1) 513305; fax (1) 710091; f. 1998; Gen. Man. Tesfaye Natnael.

National Insurance Co of Ethiopia: POB 12645, Addis Ababa; tel. (1) 661129; fax (1) 650660; e-mail nice@telecom.net.et; Gen. Man. Abate Fantaye.

Nile Insurance Co: POB 12836, Addis Ababa; tel. (1) 150580; fax (1) 514592; f. 1995; Gen. Man. Mahtsentu Feleke.

Nyala Insurance SC: POB 12753, Addis Ababa; tel. (1) 626707; fax (1) 626706; e-mail nisco@telecom.net.et; Man. Dir Nahu-Senaye Araya.

United Insurance Co: POB 1156, Addis Ababa; tel. (1) 515656; fax (1) 513258; e-mail united.insurance@telecom.net.et; Man. Dir. Iyesuswork Zafu.

Trade and Industry

CHAMBERS OF COMMERCE

Ethiopian Chamber of Commerce: Mexico Sq., POB 517, Addis Ababa; tel. (1) 518240; fax (1) 517699; f. 1947; city chambers in Addis Ababa, Asella, Awasa, Bahir Dar, Dire Dawa, Nazret, Jimma, Gondar, Dessie, Mekele and Shashemene; Pres. ASCHALEW HAILE; Sec.-Gen. ADANE GUDINA.

Addis Ababa Chamber of Commerce: POB 2458, Addis Ababa; tel. (1) 513882; fax (1) 511479; e-mail AAchamber1@telecom.net.et; internet www.addischamber.com; Chair. BERHANE MEWA; Vice-Chair. IYESUSWORK ZAFU.

INDUSTRIAL AND TRADE ASSOCIATIONS

Ethiopian Beverages Corporation: POB 1285, Addis Ababa; tel. (1) 186185; Gen. Man. MENNA TEWAHEDE.

Ethiopian Cement Corporation: POB 5782, Addis Ababa; tel. (1) 552222; fax (1) 551572; Gen. Man. REDI GEMAL.

Ethiopian Chemical Corporation: POB 5747, Addis Ababa; tel. (1) 184305; Gen. Man. ASNAKE SAHLU.

Ethiopian Coffee Export Enterprise: POB 2591, Addis Ababa; tel. (1) 515330; fax (1) 510762; f. 1977; Gen. Man. DERGA GURMESSA.

Ethiopian Food Corporation: POB 2345, Addis Ababa; tel. (1) 518522; fax (1) 513173; f. 1975; produces and distributes food items including edible oil, ghee substitute, pasta, bread, maize, wheat flour etc.; Gen. Man. BEKELE HAILE.

Ethiopian Fruit and Vegetable Marketing Enterprise: POB 2374, Addis Ababa; tel. (1) 519192; fax (1) 516483; f. 1980; sole wholesale domestic distributor and exporter of fresh and processed fruit and vegetables, and floricultural products; Gen. Man. KAKNU PEWONDE.

Ethiopian Grain Trade Enterprise: POB 3321, Addis Ababa; tel. (1) 653166; fax (1) 652792; e-mail egte@telecom.net.et; Gen. Man. GIRMA BEKELE.

Ethiopian Handicrafts and Small-Scale Industries Development Agency: Addis Ababa; tel. (1) 157366; f. 1977.

Ethiopian Import and Export Corporation (ETIMEX): Addis Ababa; tel. (1) 511112; fax (1) 515411; f. 1975; state trading corpn under the supervision of the Ministry of Commerce and Industry; import of building materials, foodstuffs, stationery and office equipment, textiles, clothing, chemicals, general merchandise, capital goods; Gen. Man. ASCHENAKI G. HIWOT.

Ethiopian National Metal Works Corporation: Addis Ababa; fax (1) 510714; Gen. Man. ALULA BERHANE.

Ethiopian Oil Seeds and Pulses Export Corporation: POB 5719, Addis Ababa; tel. (1) 550597; fax (1) 553299; f. 1975; Gen. Man. ABDOURUHMAN MOHAMMED.

Ethiopia Peasants' Association (EPA): f. 1978 to promote improved agricultural techniques, home industries, education, public health and self-reliance; comprises 30,000 peasant asscns with c. 7m. mems; Chair. (vacant).

Ethiopian Petroleum Enterprise: POB 3375, Addis Ababa; fax (1) 512938; e-mail ethpetroleum@telecom.net.et; f. 1976; Gen. Man. YIGZAW MEKONNEN.

Ethiopian Pharmaceuticals and Medical Supplies Corporation (EPHARMECOR): POB 21904, Addis Ababa; tel. (1) 134577; fax (1) 752555; f. 1976; manufacture, import, export and distribution of pharmaceuticals, chemicals, dressings, surgical and dental instruments, hospital and laboratory supplies; Gen. Man. GIRMA BEPASSO.

Ethiopian Sugar Corporation: POB 133, Addis Ababa; tel. (1) 519700; fax (1) 513488; Gen. Man. ABATE LEMENGH.

Green Star Food Corporation: POB 5579, Addis Ababa; tel. (1) 500969; fax (1) 507848; f. 1984; fmrly the Ethiopian Livestock and Meat Corpn; production and marketing of canned and frozen foods; Gen. Man. DAWIT BEKELE.

National Leather and Shoe Corporation: POB 2516, Addis Ababa; tel. (1) 514075; fax (1) 513525; f. 1975; produces and sells semi-processed hides and skins, finished leather, leather goods and footwear; Gen. Man. GIRMA W. AREGAI.

National Textiles Corporation: POB 2446, Addis Ababa; tel. (1) 157316; fax (1) 511955; f. 1975; production of yarn, fabrics, knitwear, blankets, bags, etc.; Gen. Man. FIKRE HUGIANE.

Natural Gums Processing and Marketing Enterprise: POB 62322, Addis Ababa; tel. (1) 159930; fax (1) 518110; f. 1976; Gen. Man. AREGA HABTEWOLD.

UTILITIES

Electricity

Ethiopian Electric Power Corporation (EEPCO): De Gaulle Sq., POB 1233, Addis Ababa; tel. (1) 111443; fax (1) 551324; Chair. HAILE SELASSIE ASEGIDE; Gen. Man. MIHRET DEBEBE (acting).

Water

Addis Ababa Water Sewerage Authority: Addis Ababa.

Water Resources Development Authority: POB 1045, Addis Ababa; tel. (1) 612999; fax (1) 611245; Gen. Man. GETACHEW GIZAW.

TRADE UNIONS

Ethiopian Trade Union (ETU): POB 3653, Addis Ababa; tel. (1) 514366; f. 1975; comprises nine industrial unions and 22 regional unions with a total membership of 320,000 (1987); Chair. (vacant).

Transport

RAILWAYS

Djibouti-Ethiopian Railway (Chemin de Fer Djibouti-Ethiopien–CDE): POB 1051, Addis Ababa; tel. (1) 517250; fax (1) 513533; f. 1909, adopted present name in 1981; jtly-owned by Govts of Ethiopia and Djibouti; 781 km of track (681 km in Ethiopia), linking Addis Ababa with Djibouti; Pres. SALEH OMAR HILDID; Dir-Gen. ALI ABDALLAH GADID.

ROADS

In 1998 the total road network comprised an estimated 26,053 km of primary, secondary and feeder roads, of which 3,656 km were paved, the remainder being gravel roads. In addition, there are some 30,000 km of unclassified tracks and trails. A highway links Addis Ababa with Nairobi in Kenya, forming part of the Trans-East Africa Highway. In early 1998 the World Bank granted Ethiopia a loan of US $309.2m. to help finance the first five-year phase of an ambitious 10-year government programme to rebuild and upgrade rural and urban roads.

Comet Transport Enterprise: POB 2402, Addis Ababa; tel. (1) 151864; fax (1) 514254; f. 1994; Gen. Man. FELEKE YIMER.

Ethiopian Freight Transport Corporation: Addis Ababa; restructured into five autonomous enterprises in 1994.

Ethiopian Road Transport Authority: POB 2504, Addis Ababa; tel. (1) 510244; fax (1) 510715; enforcement of road transport regulations, registering of vehicles and issuing of driving licences; Gen. Man. KASAHUN H. MARIAM.

Ethiopian Roads Authority: POB 1770, Addis Ababa; tel. (1) 517170; fax (1) 514866; f. 1951; construction and maintenance of roads, bridges and airports; Gen. Man. TESFA MICHAEL NAHUSENAI.

Public Transport Corporation: POB 5780, Addis Ababa; tel. (1) 153117; fax (1) 510720; f. 1977; urban bus services in Addis Ababa and Jimma, and services between towns; restructured into three autonomous enterprises in 1994 and scheduled for privatization; Man. Dir AHMED NURU.

SHIPPING

The formerly Ethiopian-controlled ports of Massawa and Assab now lie within the boundaries of the State of Eritrea (q.v.). Although an agreement exists between the two Governments allowing Ethiopian access to the two ports, which can handle more than 1m. metric tons of merchandise annually, in mid-1998 Ethiopia ceased using the ports, owing to the outbreak of hostilities. Ethiopia's maritime trade currently passes through Djibouti (in the Republic of Djibouti), and also through the Kenyan port of Mombasa. At 7 July 1999 Ethiopia's registered merchant fleet numbered 12 vessels, with a total displacement of 82,503 grt.

Ethiopian Shipping Lines Corporation: POB 2572, Addis Ababa; tel. (1) 518280; fax (1) 519525; e-mail esl@telecom.net.et; f. 1964; serves Red Sea, Europe, Mediterranean, Gulf and Far East with its own fleet and chartered vessels; Chair. G. TSADKAN GEBRE TENSAY; Gen. Man. AMBACHEW ABRAHA.

Marine Transport Authority: Maritime Dept, POB 1861, Addis Ababa; tel. (1) 158227; fax (1) 515665; f. 1993; regulates maritime transport services; Chair. TESHOME WOLDEGIORGIS.

Maritime and Transit Services Enterprise: POB 1186, Addis Ababa; tel. (1) 518197; fax (1) 514097; e-mail mtse@telecom.net.et; internet www.telecom.net/~mtse; f. 1979; services include stevedoring, bagging, forwarding and transporting; Chair. DESTA AMARE; Gen. Man. AHMED YASSIN.

CIVIL AVIATION

Ethiopia has two international airports (at Addis Ababa and Dire Dawa) and around 40 airfields. Bole International Airport in the capital handles 95% of international air traffic and 85% of domestic flights. A programme to modernize the airport, at an estimated cost of 819m. birr (US $130m.), was to be undertaken during 1997–2001. Construction of airports at Aksum, Lalibela and Gonda was completed in April 2000, while renovation work continued at a further eight domestic airports during 2001.

Civil Aviation Authority: POB 978, Addis Ababa; tel. (1) 610277; fax (1) 612533; e-mail civilaviation@telecom.net.et; constructs and maintains airports; provides air navigational facilities; Dir-Gen. MESHESHA BELAYNEH.

Ethiopian Airlines: Bole International Airport, POB 1755, Addis Ababa; tel. (1) 612222; fax (1) 611474; e-mail eal@telecom.net.et; internet www.flyethiopian.com; f. 1945; operates regular domestic services and flights to 47 international destinations in Africa, Europe, Middle East, Asia and the USA; CEO BISRAT NIGATU.

Tourism

Ethiopia's tourist attractions include the early Christian monuments and churches, the ancient capitals of Gondar and Axum, the Blue Nile Falls and the National Parks of the Semien and Bale Mountains. Tourist arrivals in 1996 totalled 108,885 and provided US $28m. in foreign exchange. In 1998 116,686 tourists visited Ethiopia.

Ethiopian Tourism Commission: POB 2183, Addis Ababa; tel. (1) 517470; fax (1) 513899; e-mail tour-com@telecom.net.et; f. 1964; formulates national tourism policy, publicizes tourist attractions and regulates standards of tourist facilities; Commr YOUSUF ABDULLAHI SUKKAR.

FIJI

Introductory Survey

Location, Climate, Language, Religion, Flag, Capital

The Republic of Fiji comprises more than 300 islands, of which 100 are inhabited, situated about 1,930 km (1,200 miles) south of the equator in the Pacific Ocean. The four main islands are Viti Levu (on which almost 70% of the country's population lives), Vanua Levu, Taveuni and Kadavu. The climate is tropical, with temperatures ranging from 16°C to 32°C (60°F–90°F). Rainfall is heavy on the windward side. Fijian and Hindi are the principal languages but English is also widely spoken. In 1986 about 53% of the population were Christians (mainly Methodists), 38% Hindus and 8% Muslims. The national flag (proportions 2 by 1) is light blue, with the United Kingdom flag as a canton in the upper hoist. In the fly is the main part of Fiji's national coat of arms: a white field quartered by a red upright cross, the quarters containing sugar canes, a coconut palm, a stem of bananas and a dove bearing an olive branch; in chief is a red panel with a yellow crowned lion holding a white cocoa pod. The capital is Suva, on Viti Levu.

Recent History

The first Europeans to settle on the islands were sandalwood traders, missionaries and shipwrecked sailors, and in October 1874 Fiji was proclaimed a British possession. In September 1966 the British Government introduced a new Constitution for Fiji. It provided for a ministerial form of government, an almost wholly elected Legislative Council and the introduction of universal adult suffrage. Rather than using a common roll of voters, however, the Constitution introduced an electoral system that combined communal (Fijian and Indian) rolls with cross-voting. In September 1967 the Executive Council became the Council of Ministers, with Ratu Kamisese Mara, leader of the multiracial (but predominantly Fijian) Alliance Party (AP), as Fiji's first Chief Minister. Following a constitutional conference in April–May 1970, Fiji achieved independence, within the Commonwealth, on 10 October 1970. The Legislative Council was renamed the House of Representatives, and a second parliamentary chamber, the nominated Senate, was established. The British-appointed Governor became Fiji's first Governor-General, while Ratu Sir Kamisese Mara (as he had become in 1969) took office as Prime Minister.

Fiji was, however, troubled by racial tensions. Although the descendants of indentured Indian workers who were brought to Fiji in the late 19th century had grown to outnumber the native inhabitants, they were discriminated against in political representation and land ownership rights. A new electoral system was adopted in 1970 to ensure a racial balance in the legislature.

At the general election held in March and April 1977 the National Federation Party (NFP), traditionally supported by the Indian population, won 26 of the 52 seats in the House of Representatives, but was unable to form a government and subsequently split into two factions. The AP governed in a caretaker capacity until the holding of a further general election in September, when it was returned with its largest-ever majority. While the two main parties professed multiracial ideas, the Fijian Nationalist Party campaigned in support of its 'Fiji for the Fijians' programme in order to foster nationalist sentiment.

In 1980 Ratu Sir Kamisese Mara's suggestion that a Government of National Unity be formed was overshadowed by renewed political disagreement between the AP and the NFP (whose two factions had drawn closer together again) over land ownership. Fijians owned 83% of the land and were strongly defending their traditional rights, while the Indian population was pressing for greater security of land tenure. The general election held in July 1982 was also dominated by racial issues. The AP retained power after winning 28 seats, but its majority had been reduced from 20 to four. The NFP won 22 seats and the Western United Front (WUF), which professed a multiracial outlook, took the remaining two seats.

A meeting of union leaders in May 1985 represented the beginning of discussions that culminated in the founding of the Fiji Labour Party (FLP), officially inaugurated in Suva in July.

Sponsored by the Fiji Trades Union Congress (FTUC), and under the presidency of Dr Timoci Bavadra, the new party was formed with the aim of presenting a more effective parliamentary opposition, and declared the provision of free education and a national medical scheme to be among its priorities. The FLP hoped to work through farmers' organizations to win votes among rural electorates, which traditionally supported the NFP. During 1985–86 disagreements between the Government and the FTUC over economic policies became increasingly acrimonious, leading to an outbreak of labour unrest and the withdrawal, in June 1986, of government recognition of the FTUC as the unions' representative organization.

At a general election in April 1987 a coalition of the FLP and NFP won 28 seats (19 of which were secured by ethnic Indian candidates) in the House of Representatives, thus defeating the ruling AP, which won only 24 seats. The new Government, led by Bavadra, was therefore the first in Fijian history to contain a majority of ministers of Indian, rather than Melanesian, origin. Bavadra, himself, was of Melanesian descent. On 14 May, however, the Government was overthrown by a military coup, led by Lt-Col (later Maj.-Gen.) Sitiveni Rabuka. The Governor-General, Ratu Sir Penaia Ganilau, responded by declaring a state of emergency and appointed a 19-member advisory council, including Bavadra and Rabuka. However, Bavadra refused to participate in the council, denouncing it as unconstitutional and biased in its composition.

Widespread racial violence followed the coup, and there were several public demands for Bavadra's reinstatement as Prime Minister. In July 1987 the Great Council of Fijian Chiefs, comprising the country's 70 hereditary Melanesian leaders, approved plans for constitutional reform. In September negotiations began, on the initiative of Ganilau, between delegations led by the two former Prime Ministers, Bavadra and Mara, to resolve the political crisis. On 22 September it was announced that the two factions had agreed to form an interim bipartisan Government.

On 25 September 1987, however, before the new plan could be implemented, Rabuka staged a second coup and announced his intention to declare Fiji a republic. Despite Ganilau's refusal to recognize the seizure of power, Rabuka revoked the Constitution on 1 October and proclaimed himself Head of State, thus deposing the Queen. Ganilau conceded defeat and resigned as Governor-General. At a meeting in Canada, Commonwealth Heads of Government formally declared that Fiji's membership of the Commonwealth had lapsed. An interim Cabinet, comprising mainly ethnic Fijians, was installed by Rabuka. In late October Rabuka announced that he would resign as Head of State as soon as he had appointed a new President of the Republic. Several cases of violations of human rights by the Fijian army were reported, as the regime assumed powers of detention without trial and suspended all political activity.

On 6 December 1987 Rabuka resigned as Head of State. Although he had previously refused to accept the post, Ganilau, the former Governor-General, became the first President of the Fijian Republic. Mara was reappointed Prime Minister, and Rabuka became Minister of Home Affairs. A new interim Cabinet was announced on 9 December, containing 11 members of Rabuka's administration, but no member of Bavadra's deposed Government.

In February 1988 Rotuma (the only Polynesian island in the country), which lies to the north-west of Vanua Levu, declared itself politically independent of Fiji, whose newly-acquired republican status it refused to recognize. Fijian troops were dispatched to the island, however, and soon quelled the dissent.

A new draft Constitution was approved by the interim Government in September 1988. The proposed Constitution was rejected, however, by a multiracial constitutional committee, which considered unnecessary the specific reservation of the principal offices of state for ethnic Fijians. In September 1989 the committee published a revised draft, which was still, however, condemned by Bavadra and the FLP-NFP coalition. In November Bavadra died and was replaced as leader of the FLP-NFP coalition by his widow, Adi Kuini Bavadra.

In January 1990 Rabuka resigned from the Cabinet and returned to his military duties. Mara agreed to remain as Prime Minister until the restoration of constitutional government. In June the Great Council of Chiefs approved the draft Constitution. At the same time, the Great Council of Chiefs stated its intention to form a new party, the Soqosoqo ni Vakavulewa ni Taukei (SVT) or Fijian Political Party, to advocate the cause of ethnic Fijians. The new Constitution was finally promulgated on 25 July by President Ganilau, and was immediately condemned by the FLP-NFP coalition, which announced that it would boycott any elections held in accordance with the Constitution's provisions. Angered by the fact that a legislative majority was guaranteed to ethnic Fijians (who were reserved 37 of the 70 elective seats, compared with 27 Indian seats), and that the Great Council of Chiefs was to nominate ethnic Fijians to 24 of the 34 seats in the Senate and to appoint the President of the Republic, the opposition organized anti-Constitution demonstrations. The new Constitution was similarly condemned for its racial bias by India, New Zealand and Australia at the UN General Assembly, meeting in New York in October. In May 1991 the Commonwealth stated that Fiji would not be re-admitted to the organization until it changed its Constitution.

In July 1991 Rabuka resigned as Commander of the Armed Forces in order to rejoin the Cabinet as Deputy Prime Minister and Minister of Home Affairs, although towards the end of 1991, he relinquished the post in order to assume the leadership of the SVT.

Disagreements between the Government and the FTUC re-emerged at the beginning of 1991. In February a strike by more than 900 members of the Fijian Miners' Union over union recognition, pay and poor working conditions led to the dismissal of some 400 of the workers. In May the Government announced a series of reforms to the labour laws, including the abolition of the minimum wage, restrictions on strike action and derecognition of unions that did not represent at least two-thirds of the work-force. A significant political development announced by the Government in late 1992 was the official recognition of the FTUC (withheld since 1986) as the sole representative of workers in Fiji.

At legislative elections in May 1992 the SVT secured 30 of the 37 seats reserved for ethnic Fijians, while the NFP won 14 and the FLP 13 of the seats reserved for Indian representatives. Following the election, the FLP agreed to participate in Parliament and to support Rabuka in his campaign for the premiership, in return for a guarantee from the SVT of a full review of the Constitution and of trade union and land laws. Rabuka was, therefore, appointed Prime Minister and formed a coalition Government (consisting of 14 members of the SVT and five others).

Remarks made by the Prime Minister in an Australian television interview in October 1992, expressing his implicit support for the repatriation of Fijian Indians, attracted controversy and prompted renewed fears that any reform of the Constitution would be merely superficial. Nevertheless, in December Rabuka formally invited the opposition leaders, Jai Ram Reddy of the NFP and Mahendra Chaudhry of the FLP (formerly the National Secretary of the FTUC), to form a Government of National Unity. The move was largely welcomed, but Indian politicians expressed reluctance to take part in a government whose political control remained fundamentally vested with ethnic Fijians. Rabuka was criticized equally by nationalist extremists of the Taukei Solidarity Movement, who accused him of conceding too much political power to Fijian Indians. Following the appointment of a new Cabinet in June, all 13 of the FLP legislative members began an indefinite boycott of Parliament, in protest at Rabuka's failure to implement the reforms, which he had agreed to carry out in return for their support for his election to the premiership in June 1992.

In December 1993 President Ganilau died, following a long illness, and was replaced by Ratu Sir Kamisese Mara, who took office on 18 January 1994 (re-elected on 18 January 1999).

At legislative elections held in February 1994 the SVT increased the number of its seats in the House of Representatives to 31, while the Fijian Association Party (FAP, established in January by former members of the SVT) secured only five seats, of a total of 37 reserved for ethnic Fijians. Of the 27 seats reserved for ethnic Indian representatives, 20 were secured by the NFP. The SVT subsequently formed a governing coalition with the General Voters' Party (GVP, which represented the interests of the General Electors—i.e. the minority Chinese and European communities and people from other Pacific Islands

resident in Fiji) and an independent member, under the premiership of Rabuka, who announced the formation of a new Cabinet composed entirely of ethnic Fijians. In response to international concern regarding the continued existence of Fiji's racially-biased Constitution, Rabuka announced in June that a Constitutional Review Commission had been established, which, it was hoped, would have completed a review of the Constitution by 1997.

In January 1995 the Government announced that it was to recommend that Parliament vote to repeal the Sunday observance law (imposed after the coups of 1987), which prohibited work, organized entertainment and sport on that day. It was believed that the law had become increasingly unpopular, particularly among the Indian community. However, the announcement aroused intense opposition from nationalist politicians and Methodist church leaders, who organized demonstrations in three cities, attended by more than 12,000 people. In February, however, the House of Representatives voted in favour of removing the regulations. The Senate narrowly rejected the proposal, thus effectively delaying the implementation of any changes. The Sunday observance law was finally repealed in November.

The issue of independence for the island of Rotuma was revived in September 1995 with the return of the King of Rotuma from exile in New Zealand. King Gagaj Sa Lagfatmaro, who had fled to New Zealand following death threats made against him during the military coups of 1987, appeared before the Constitutional Review Commission to petition for the island's independence within the Commonwealth, reiterating his view that Rotuma remained a British colony rather than a part of Fiji.

In September 1995 the Government decided to transfer all state land (comprising some 10% of Fiji's total land area), hitherto administered by the Government Lands Department, to the Native Land Trust Board. The decision was to allow the allocation of land to indigenous Fijians on the basis of native custom. However, concern among the Fijian Indian population increased following reports in early 1996 that many would not be able to renew their land leases (most of which were due to expire between 1997 and 2024) under the Agricultural Landlords and Tenants Act (ALTA). The reports were strongly denied by the Government, despite statements by several Fijian land-owning clans that Indians' leases would not be renewed. Moreover, a recently-formed sugar cane growers' association solely for ethnic Fijians, the Taukei Cane Growers' Association, announced its intention to campaign for ethnic Fijian control of the sugar industry, largely by refusing to renew land leases to ethnic Indians (who held some 85% of sugar farm leases). In mid-1999 a government survey indicated that at least 70% of leases were likely to be renewed under ALTA, although there were continuing reports that ethnic Fijian landowners were unwilling to sign new contracts under the act. Concern was expressed that mounting tensions between landowners and tenants could lead to violence, and that the situation was affecting investor confidence. The Government, which claimed that certain political groups were using the lease issue to achieve their aim of destabilizing the country, responded by reaffirming its commitment to finding a solution acceptable to both parties and to retaining the viability and stability of the sugar industry. By the end of 2000 almost 2,000 land leases had expired, leaving many tenant farmers and their families homeless. Some 70 farmers, who had expressed a wish not to be resettled, received rehabilitation grants of $F28,000 in December 2000, although the authorities were criticized for their apparent slowness in processing the applications. In January 2001 the administration of native land leases was transferred from ALTA to the Native Lands Trust Act (NLTA), prompting fears of increased bias in favour of ethnic Fijian landowners and further instability in the sugar industry. A further 1,500 leases were due to expire during 2001.

Meanwhile, racial tension intensified in October 1995, following the publication of the SVT's submission to the Constitutional Review Commission. In its report the party detailed plans to abandon the present multiracial form of government, recommending instead the adoption of an electoral system based on racial representation, in which each ethnic group would select its own representatives. The expression of numerous extreme anti-Indian sentiments in the document was widely condemned (by both ethnic Fijians and ethnic Indians) as offensive.

A rift within the GVP in early 1996, which resulted in two of the four GVP members of the House of Representatives withdrawing their support for the Government, prompted Rabuka to seek alternative coalition partners from among the opposition, in an attempt to establish a more secure majority. However, the Prime Minister was unsuccessful in persuading parliamentary members of the FAP (which had strongly criticized the SVT's submission to the Constitutional Review Commission the previous year) to join the Government. The administration's troubles during 1996 contributed to the defeat of the SVT in virtually every municipality at local elections, which took place in September.

Existing divisions within the Government were further exacerbated by the presentation to the House of Representatives, in September 1996, of the Constitutional Review Commission's report. The report included recommendations to enlarge the House of Representatives to 75 seats, with 25 seats reserved on a racial basis (12 for ethnic Fijians, 10 for Fijian Indians, two for General Electors and one for Rotuma Islanders), and also proposed that the size of the Senate should be reduced from 34 to 32 members (and the number of nominated ethnic Fijian senators be reduced from 24 to 15), and that the Prime Minister should be a Fijian of any race, while the President should continue to be an indigenous Fijian. Rabuka and Mara both endorsed the findings of the report, while several nationalist parties, including the Vanua Independent Party, the Fijian Nationalist United Front Party (FNUFP) and the Taukei Solidarity Movement, expressed extreme opposition to the proposals, and formed a coalition in an attempt to further their influence within Parliament. In addition, a number of SVT members of the House of Representatives aligned themselves with the nationalists, and in early 1997 were reported to be responsible for a series of political manoeuvres within the Cabinet, aimed at undermining Rabuka's position. The parliamentary committee reviewing the report agreed on a majority of the 700 recommendations, but proposed that the House of Representatives be enlarged to only 71 seats, with 46 seats reserved on a racial basis (23 for ethnic Fijians, 19 for Indians, three for General Electors and one for Rotuma Islanders) and 25 seats open to all races. The committee's modified proposals were presented in May to the Great Council of Chiefs, which officially endorsed the recommendations in early June. The Constitution Amendment Bill was approved unanimously by the House of Representatives and the Senate in the following month. Rabuka was anxious to reassure extremist nationalist Fijians, who had vociferously opposed the reforms throughout the debate, that their interests would be protected under the amended Constitution (which was not due to take effect until July 1998) and that indigenous Fijians would continue to play a pre-eminent role in the government of the country.

Despite opposition from both the FLP and the nationalist parties, Fiji was readmitted to the Commonwealth at a meeting of member states in October 1997. In the same month Rabuka was granted an audience with Queen Elizabeth II in London, at which he formally apologized for the military coups of 1987. Events in early 1998 were dominated by political reaction to the imminent promulgation of the new Constitution. An extremist nationalist group of former SVT supporters, including senior church, military and police officials, were rumoured to be planning to overthrow Rabuka's Government. Meanwhile, it was reported that opponents of the Constitution were discussing the establishment of several new political parties. The new Constitution, none the less, came into effect on 27 July 1998.

Following a period of severe drought, nation-wide water restrictions were introduced in early 1998. The sugar industry was drastically affected by the drought, resulting in an annual crop some 60% lower than predicted, with exporters unable to meet commitments to foreign buyers. By September of that year more than one-quarter of the population were dependent on emergency food and water rations, and the Government announced its intention to reduce public expenditure in order to provide greater relief for those worst affected by the drought.

A dispute between tribal landowners and the Government over compensation payments for land flooded by the Monosavu hydroelectric power station erupted into violence in July 1998. Landowners, who had been demanding compensation worth some $A30m. since the plant was constructed in 1983, seized control of the station (which supplies 90% of Fiji's electricity) and carried out a series of arson attacks on Fiji Electricity Authority property. In October the Government agreed to pay the landowners compensation totalling some $A12m., although many involved in the dispute rejected the offer and announced their intention of pursuing a legal claim against the Government.

The prospect of legislative elections, to be held in early May 1999, prompted reports of political manoeuvring as parties sought to increase their influence by forming alliances. In addition, a number of changes in the country's political organizations occurred in late 1998. Following the death of Josefata Kamikamica, Adi Kuini Vuikaba Speed (widow of ex-President Bavadra) was elected leader of the FAP. Meanwhile, the GVP and the General Electors' Party merged to form the United General Party (UGP) under the leadership of the Minister for Tourism, Transport and Civil Aviation, David Pickering, and Rabuka was re-elected leader of the SVT (despite the party being required to amend its constitution in order for this to be possible). The formation of a new party, the Veitokani ni Lewenivanua Vakarisito (VLV, Christian Democratic Alliance), by several senior church and military leaders and former members of the nationalist Taukei Solidarity Movement, was widely criticized for its extremist stance and refusal to accept the newly-formed, multiracial Constitution.

At legislative elections held on 8–15 May 1999, the first to be held under the new Constitution, Rabuka's coalition Government was defeated by Mahendra Chaudhry, leader of the Indian-dominated FLP, who thus became Fiji's first ethnic Indian Prime Minister. Chaudhry's broad-based Government (a coalition of the FLP, FAP, VLV and the Party of National Unity—PANU) initially seemed threatened by the reluctance of FAP members to serve under an Indian Prime Minister. The leaders were persuaded to remain in the coalition in the interests of national unity, after the intervention of President Mara. However, in June there were renewed demands for the FAP to withdraw from the coalition because of the alleged discontent of party members at the lack of representation afforded to the party in the senate nominations presented by Chaudhry. Political stability after the elections was marred by demands for Chaudhry's resignation by the Fijian Nationalist Vanua Takolavo Party (NVTLP), and by a number of arson attacks, allegedly linked to the outgoing SVT (although these allegations were denied by Rabuka). Following the SVT's decisive defeat in the elections, Rabuka resigned as party leader; he was replaced by Ratu Inoke Kubuabola, the former Minister for Communications, Works and Energy. Rabuka was later appointed the first independent Chairman of the newly-autonomous Great Council of Chiefs. The NVTLP was widely suspected to have been responsible for three bomb explosions in Suva in August 1999. In the same month a parliamentary vote of 'no confidence' against Prime Minister Chaudhry was overwhelmingly defeated. In the latter half of 1999 there were persistent demands by various nationalist groups (including the SVT) that Chaudhry be replaced by a leader of indigenous Fijian descent, and a number of demonstrations were organized, expressing disillusionment with the Government. In October the opposition coalition was successful in gaining control of a majority of councils in local elections, while the FLP won control of four municipal councils (having previously been in charge of none).

The Government's decision to disband the Fiji Intelligence Service from December 1999 was criticized by the opposition as 'foolish' and racially motivated. An announcement by the Chief Justice in December of a project to amend a number of laws that did not comply with the terms of the new Constitution, together with reports that the Government was planning to withdraw state funds previously provided to assist indigenous Fijian business interests, prompted further accusations of racism by the Government against ethnic Fijians. Consequently, the SVT and the VLV held talks to discuss ways of consolidating the ethnic Fijian political base. Proposed legislation, which would alter the distribution of power between the President and the Prime Minister, attracted further criticism from the opposition, and in February 2000 a faction of the FAP announced its withdrawal from the governing coalition, citing dissatisfaction with Chaudhry's leadership. Of greater significance, however, was the announcement in April that the extremist nationalist Taukei Movement (which had been inactive for several years) had been revived with the sole intention of removing the Prime Minister from office. The group subsequently publicized a campaign of demonstrations and civil disobedience, prompting the army to issue a statement distancing itself from any anti-Government agitation and pledging loyalty to Chaudhry. The campaign attracted considerable public support, however, and culminated in a march through Suva by some 5,000 people in early May.

On 19 May 2000 a group of armed men, led by businessman George Speight, invaded the parliament building and ousted the Government, taking hostage Chaudhry and 30 other members of the governing coalition. President Mara condemned the coup and declared a state of emergency as Speight's supporters rampaged through the streets of Suva, looting and setting fire to Indian businesses. Speight declared that he had reclaimed Fiji for indigenous Fijians and had dissolved the Constitution. Moreover, he threatened to kill the hostages if the military intervened. On 22 May Mara formally invited Rabuka, in his role as chairman of the Great Council of Chiefs, to seek a resolution of the crisis. In the following days the Great Council of Chiefs convened to discuss the situation and proposed the replacement of Chaudhry's Government with an interim administration, an amnesty for Speight and the rebels, and the amendment of the Constitution. Speight rejected the proposals, demanding that Mara also be removed from office. Meanwhile, violent clashes erupted at the headquarters of Fiji Television when the rebels stormed the building following the broadcast of an interview with an opponent of the coup. A police-officer was shot dead, television equipment was destroyed and the station's employees were taken hostage. On 29 May Mara resigned and the Commander of the Armed Forces, Frank Bainimarama, announced the imposition of martial law and a curfew, in an attempt to restore calm and stability to the country. In an expression of his apparent reluctance to assume the role, Bainimarama gave Mara a whale's tooth, a traditional Fijian symbol of regret.

Negotiations between the newly-installed Military Executive Council and the Great Council of Chiefs continued throughout June 2000. Failure to reach a conclusive outcome seemed to be the result of inconsistencies in Speight's demands and an ambivalent attitude on the part of the military towards the coup. Regular patrols by the security forces curbed rioting in Suva, although outbreaks of violence in rural areas (mostly in the form of attacks on Indian Fijians, the looting and burning of Indian-owned farms and the occupation of several tourist resorts) were reported. On 25 June the four female hostages were released from the parliament building. The Military Executive Council announced its intention to appoint an interim government without consulting Speight and demanded that the rebel leader release the remaining hostages. Speight reiterated his threat to kill all those held if any rescue attempts were made.

An interim administration of 19 indigenous Fijians led by Laisenia Qarase (the former managing director of the Merchant Bank of Fiji) was sworn in on 4 July 2000. Minutes after the ceremony a gun battle erupted outside the parliament building in which four civilians and one rebel were injured; the rebel subsequently died. Speight announced that he not recognize the interim authority, and most of Fiji's mainstream political parties similarly denounced it, although the Methodist Church declared its support for the body. On 12 July a further nine hostages were released and on the following day the remaining 18, including Chaudhry, were liberated. In accordance with Speight's wishes, Ratu Josefa Iloilo, hitherto the First Vice-President, was then installed as President.

Incidents of civil unrest (including the occupation of the hydroelectric dam at Monasavu and of the army barracks on Vanua Levu) continued throughout July 2000 as Speight sought to manipulate existing grievances, particularly disputes over land ownership, in order to mobilize additional support. On 29 July, however, Speight was finally arrested, along with dozens of his supporters, for breaking the terms of his amnesty by refusing to relinquish weapons. Armed rebels responded violently to the arrest, and in Labasa Indian Fijians were rounded up and detained in army barracks by supporters of Speight. In early August more than 300 rebels appeared in court on a variety of firearms and public order offences. Speight was similarly charged with several minor offences. On 11 August Speight and 14 of his supporters were formally charged with treason. During September Speight made several applications for bail, all of which were refused. Meanwhile, the suspended police commissioner, Isikia Savua, revealed that police were conducting an investigation into a commercial deal involving the Fijian mahogany trade, which, it was believed, might have precipitated the coup; Speight had been chairman of both Fiji Pine Corporation and Fiji Hardwood Corporation before being dismissed in 1999. This view was reiterated by the deposed Prime Minister on an overseas tour during October, when

Chaudhry expressed his commitment to the restoration of democracy and constitutional rule and stated his belief that the coup had been motivated by commercial vested interests rather than by concern over indigenous rights.

In early November 2000 about 40 soldiers staged a mutiny at army headquarters in Suva. Troops loyal to Bainimarama, who narrowly escaped capture, retook the barracks following an eight-hour assault in which five rebels and four loyal soldiers were killed. It was later revealed that a number of the rebel soldiers had been involved in the coup in May and speculation spread that the mutiny had been another attempted coup. The chairman of the Great Council of Chiefs, Sitiveni Rabuka, denied allegations by New Zealand's Minister of Foreign Affairs and Trade, Phil Goff, that he had been involved in the mutiny.

On 15 November 2000 the High Court ruled that the existing Constitution remained valid and that the elected Parliament, ousted in the coup, remained Fiji's legitimate governing authority. Laisenia Qarase responded by lodging an appeal against the ruling and by declaring that the interim authority, of which he was leader, would continue as the country's national government until new elections could be organized and a new constitution drafted within 18 months.

In mid-December 2000 Chaudhry's campaign to re-establish his Government suffered a significant reversal when the ministers of foreign affairs of Australia and New Zealand announced that they were abandoning their appeal for its reinstatement, although they would continue to support a return to the 1997 Constitution. However, within Fiji supporters of a return to democracy formed the Fiji First Movement, which aimed to consolidate opposition to the post-coup regime. The group organized a series of protests across the country in late 2000 and early 2001.

In February 2001 an international panel of judges at the Court of Appeal began the hearing against the November 2000 ruling, which found the abrogation of the 1997 Constitution to be illegal. In its final judgment the court ruled that the 1997 Constitution remained the supreme law of Fiji, that the interim civilian government could not prove that it had the support of a majority of Fijian people and was therefore illegal and that, following Mara's resignation, the office of President remained vacant. The ruling was welcomed by many countries in the region, including Australia and New Zealand, and appeared to be accepted by the interim authority, which announced that it would organize elections as soon as possible. However, on 14 March Iloilo informed Chaudhry in a letter that he had been dismissed as Prime Minister, claiming that by advising Iloilo to dissolve the authority in preparation for elections he had accepted that he no longer had the mandate of Parliament. Chaudhry rejected the decision as unconstitutional and unlawful. Ratu Tevita Momoedonu was appointed Prime Minister on the same day. On the following day, however, Iloilo dismissed Momoedonu, on the advice of the Great Council of Chiefs, and reinstated Laisenia Qarase as head of the interim authority. It was announced that a general election would be held between 25 August and 1 September 2001.

In November 1989 the Fijian Government expelled the Indian ambassador to Fiji for allegedly interfering in Fiji's internal affairs, and the status of the Indian embassy was downgraded to that of a consulate. Relations between Fiji and India deteriorated following the coup of May 1987, when many ethnic Indians emigrated. In January 1989 statistical information, released by the interim Government, indicated that the islands' ethnic Fijians were in a majority for the first time since 1946. Following the adoption of significant constitutional reforms in 1997 diplomatic relations improved considerably, and in October the Indian Government invited Fiji to open a High Commission in New Delhi. In February 1999 India lifted its trade embargo against Fiji (which had been in force for 10 years), and in May India reopened its High Commission in Suva. However, Fiji's relations with the international community suffered a major reversal following the coup of May 2000, which was condemned by the UN, the Commonwealth, the United Kingdom, Australia, New Zealand and several other nations in the region. In June Fiji was partially suspended from the Commonwealth (having been readmitted in October 1997 following its expulsion after the coups of 1987) and a delegation of ministers of foreign affairs from the organization visited the islands to demand the reinstatement of the 1997 Constitution.

Government

The 1998 Constitution provided for a parliamentary form of government with a bicameral legislature, comprising the elected

71-seat House of Representatives and the appointed Senate, with 32 members. The Constitution states that 46 seats in the House are reserved on a racial basis (23 for ethnic Fijians, 19 for Indians, three for other races—General Electors—and one for Rotuma Islanders) and 25 seats are open to all races. The Senate was to be appointed by the President of the Republic, 14 members on the advice of the Great Council of Chiefs (a 70-member traditional body comprising every hereditary chief (Ratu) of a Fijian clan), nine on the advice of the Prime Minister, eight on the advice of the Leader of the Opposition and one on the advice of the Rotuma Island Council.

Defence

The Fiji Military Forces consist of men in the regular army, the Naval Squadron, the conservation corps and the territorials. The conservation corps was created in 1975 to make use of unemployed labour in construction work. In August 2000 the total armed forces numbered 3,500 men: 3,200 in the army and 300 in the navy. Budgetary expenditure on defence in 2000 was projected at $F58m.

Economic Affairs

In 1998, according to estimates by the World Bank, Fiji's gross national product (GNP), measured at average 1996–98 prices, was $1,748m, equivalent to $2,210 per head (or $4,094 on an international purchasing-power parity basis). In the following year GNP was estimated at US $1,771m., again equivalent to $2,210 per head. During 1990–98, it was estimated, GNP per head increased, in real terms, at an average annual rate of 0.5%. Over the same period, the population increased at an average annual rate of 1.0%. According to the Asian Development Bank (ADB), Fiji's gross domestic product (GDP) increased at an estimated average annual rate of 2.4% between 1990 and 1999. Real GDP expanded by an estimated 1.5% in 1998 and by 6.6% in 1999.

In 1999, according to the ADB, agriculture (including forestry and fishing) contributed an estimated 16.0% of GDP (at constant 1989 prices). In 1998 the sector engaged 41.0% of the economically active population. The principal cash crop is sugar cane, which normally accounts for about 80% of total agricultural production. Sugar and its derivatives provided 27.0% of Fiji's total export earnings in 1998. Output in the industry decreased significantly in 1998, when a prolonged drought resulted in the country's failure to meet its export commitments. However, sugar cane production increased by 81% in 1999, as a consequence of the successful implementation of a crop rehabilitation programme, although the industry subsequently experienced a sharp decline in output owing to problems arising from the coup in May 2000 and from the issue of expiring land leases (see above). Other important export crops are coconuts and ginger, while the most important subsistence crop is paddy rice. Fishing became an increasingly important activity in the mid-1990s, earning some $F49.5m. in 1998 in exports (equivalent to 5.5% of domestic export revenue). During 1990–99, according to ADB estimates, agricultural GDP rose by an average annual rate of 0.5%. Having declined by an estimated 7.2% in 1998, the sector's GDP was estimated to have increased by 15.8% in 1999.

Industry (including mining, manufacturing, construction and power) engaged 31.4% of the employed labour force in 1996, and provided an estimated 27.0% of GDP in 1999. The GDP of the industrial sector increased at an average rate of 4.6% per year during 1990–99. The industrial sector's GDP was estimated by the ADB to have increased by some 3.1% in 1998 and by 12.9% in 1999.

Mining contributed an estimated 2.8% of GDP in 1999, and employed 2.1% of the labour force in 1996. Gold and silver are the major mineral exports. Production of gold totalled 3,885 kg in 1998, when exports earned $F70.5m, equivalent to 7.8% of total export earnings Gold exploration activity increased dramatically in the mid-1990s (with the number of prospecting licences totalling 49 in late 1998), and it was forecast that annual exports of gold would total some 11,500 kg and earn an estimated $F200m. by 2003. A copper-mining project in Namosi, central Viti Levu, began operations in 1997.

Manufacturing contributed an estimated 15.4% of GDP in 1999, and engaged 22.4% of the employed labour force in 1996. The sector's GDP increased at an average rate of 4.8% per year during 1990–99. Compared with the previous year, manufacturing GDP rose by 5.6% in 1999. The most important branch of the sector is food-processing, in particular sugar, molasses and copra. The ready-made garment industry is also important and has particularly benefited from the tax-exemption scheme

implemented by the Government in 1987. In 1997 there were 156 tax-exempt factories operating in the country, of which 96 were dedicated to garment manufacture. The ready-made garment industry accounted for 33.4% of domestic export earnings in 1998, and engaged 85.8% of the 13,400 people employed in the tax-free sector in 1994. In late 1998 the Government sought to increase its trade quota with the USA, with the aim of exporting more garments to that country. Output from the garment industry increased by some 10% in 1999 owing to the introduction of preferential trade arrangements with Australia and New Zealand, but declined considerably in the following year as a result of sanctions imposed by those countries in protest at the coup of May 2000.

Energy is derived principally from hydroelectric power, which provided some 90% of Fiji's electricity in the late 1990s. The electricity, gas and water sector accounted for 3.9% of GDP in 1999. Imports of mineral fuels represented 11.1% of the total cost of imports in 1998.

The services sector contributed an estimated 57.0% of GDP in 1999. During 1990–99 the sector's GDP rose by an average annual rate of 2.1%. According to the ADB, the GDP of the services sector increased by some 3.4% in 1998 and by an estimated 1.1% in 1999. Tourism is Fiji's largest source of foreign exchange, earning some $F541.2m. in 1999, when visitor arrivals totalled 409,955. In the following year, however, arrivals fell to 282,677 and earnings to $F344m., as a result of the events surrounding the coup of May 2000.

In 1999 Fiji recorded a visible trade deficit of US $115.6m., but a surplus of US $12.7m. on the current account of the balance of payments. In 1998 the principal sources of imports were Australia (40.1%), the USA (14.9%), New Zealand (14.1%) and Japan (5.3%). The principal markets for exports were Australia (37.4%), the United Kingdom (23.2%) and the USA (14.1%). The principal imports in that year were machinery and transport equipment, basic manufactured goods, mineral fuels and food. The principal exports were sugar, gold, re-exported petroleum products and ready-made garments.

In 1997 there was a budgetary deficit of $F196.0m. and a projected budgetary deficit for 1998 of $F106.1m. The latter was forecast at the equivalent of 3.4% of GDP (compared with an estimated 6.5% for 1997). A deficit equivalent to 1.2% of GDP was projected for 1999. Fiji's total external debt was US $192.8m. at the end of 1998, of which US $172.2m. was long-term public debt. In that year the cost of debt-servicing was equivalent to 3.6% of revenue from exports of goods and services. The annual rate of inflation averaged 3.7% in 1990–99. The rate decreased to 1.7% in 1999 and stood at 1.8% for the year ending October 2000. In 1998 an estimated 5.4% of the labour force were unemployed, while there were 112,500 people in paid employment. Since 1987 Fiji's economy has suffered considerably from large-scale emigration. Between 1987 and 1995 some 72,688 citizens emigrated from Fiji, of whom some 90% were Fijian Indians, with an estimated 30% described as professional or semi-professional workers.

Fiji is a member of the UN Economic and Social Commission for Asia and the Pacific (see p. 28), the Pacific Islands Forum (formerly the South Pacific Forum—see p. 276), the Pacific Community (formerly the South Pacific Commission—see p. 275) and the International Sugar Organization (see p. 305). Fiji is also a signatory of the South Pacific Regional Trade and Economic Co-operation Agreement—SPARTECA (see p. 278) and the Lomé Convention with the European Union (EU—see p. 206). In 1996 Fiji was admitted to the Melanesian Spearhead Group.

Fiji's economic performance in the 1980s was adversely affected by the world recession and by political instability resulting from the two coups of 1987. The subsequent recovery of the economy was aided by strong sugar prices on the international market, an increase in tourist arrivals, the introduction of tax-free zones, and growth in foreign investment (notably from Japan). Fiji's GDP declined by 3.9% in 1998, mainly owing to a decrease in sugar production as a result of drought, as well as a decline in gold prices. Nevertheless, the continuing expansion of the tourism and garment industries, and the devaluation of the Fiji dollar helped to offset a serious financial crisis. Strong economic growth in 1999 was attributed to a recovery in the sugar sector, a buoyant tourist industry and an increase in garment production, although the sugar industry continued to experience problems relating to the land tenure issue, poor industrial relations and the prospect of losing preferential access to European markets. The overthrow of the Government during a coup in May 2000 and the subsequent installation of an unelected authority, however, had a severe impact on Fiji's economy. A significant amount of that year's sugar crop was not harvested, and a large proportion of tourist bookings were cancelled. In addition, the islands lost a considerable sum of revenue owing to the withdrawal of foreign aid and faced further hardship through the imposition of economic sanctions and trade union boycotts from abroad (which particularly affected the mining sector and garment manufacture). It was estimated that the economy contracted by some 8% during 2000 and that 6,700 people lost their jobs in the second half of the year, the overwhelming majority of these having been engaged either in tourist-related activities or in manufacturing.

Social Welfare

The Fiji National Provident Fund, established in 1966, contains provision for retirement pensions, widows' pensions, an insurance scheme and housing loans. Employers and employees contribute equally. In 1995 Parliament approved legislation providing for the establishment of a national non-contributory pension scheme. Medical and dental treatment is provided for all at a nominal charge. In 1997 Fiji had 25 hospitals (with a total of 1,805 beds) and 409 physicians. The budget proposals for 2000 allocated $F108m. for health services and $F11m. for social welfare and included provisions for the construction of several new hospitals.

Education

Education in Fiji is not compulsory, but in 1992 about 95% of school-age children were enrolled at the country's schools, and the Government provided free education for the first eight years of schooling. Primary education begins at six years of age and lasts for six years. Secondary education, beginning at the age of 12, lasts for a further six years. State subsidies are available for secondary and tertiary education in cases of hardship. In

1995 there were 709 primary schools (with a total enrolment of 142,781 pupils in 1997), 146 secondary schools (with an enrolment of 70,098 pupils in 1997), and in 1994 there were 31 vocational and technical institutions (with 1,876 students in 1997). In 1994 Fiji had four teacher-training colleges (with 903 students in 1997), and in 1989 there were two schools of medicine (with 493 students). In 1996 a total of about 4,000 students were enrolled on campus at the University of the South Pacific and there were a further 6,000 extension students. Budgetary expenditure on education by the central Government in 1998 was $F121.4m., representing 23.4% of total spending. The budget proposals for 2000 allocated $F198m. for education. The adult illiteracy rate in 2000 averaged an estimated 7.1% (males 5.0%; females 9.1%).

Public Holidays

2001: 1 January (New Year's Day), 16 February (National Youth Day), 13–16 April (Easter), 28 May (Ratu Sir Lala Sukuna Day), 4 June* (Birth of the Prophet Muhammad), 18 June (Queen's Official Birthday), 23 July (Constitution Day), 8 October (Fiji Day), 14 November (Diwali), 25–26 December (Christmas).

2002: 1 January (New Year's Day), 15 February (National Youth Day), 29 March–1 April (Easter), 27 May (Ratu Sir Lala Sukuna Day), 24 May* (Birth of the Prophet Muhammad), June† (Queen's Official Birthday), 22 July (Constitution Day), 7 October (Fiji Day), October/November (Diwali), 25–26 December (Christmas).

* This Islamic holiday is dependent on the lunar calendar and may vary by one or two days from the dates given.

† Date to be announced in 2001.

Weights and Measures

The metric system is in force.

Statistical Survey

Sources (unless otherwise stated): Bureau of Statistics, POB 2221, Government Bldgs, Suva; tel. 315144; fax 303656; Reserve Bank of Fiji, POB 1220, Suva; tel. 313611; fax 301688; e-mail rbf@reservebank.gov.fj; internet www.reservebank.gov.fj.

AREA AND POPULATION

Area (incl. the Rotuma group): 18,376 sq km (7,095 sq miles). Land area of 18,333 sq km (7,078 sq miles) consists mainly of the islands of Viti Levu (10,429 sq km—4,027 sq miles) and Vanua Levu (5,556 sq km—2,145 sq miles).

Population: 715,375 (males 362,568, females 352,807) at census of 31 August 1986; 775,077 (males 393,931, females 381,146) at census of 25 August 1996.

Density (August 1996): 42.2 per sq km.

Principal Towns (population at 1996 census): Suva (capital) 77,366; Lautoka 36,083; Nadi 9,170; Labasa 6,491; Ba 6,314.

Ethnic Groups (1996 census): Fijians 393,575; Indians 338,818; Part-European 11,685; European 3,103; Rotuman 9,727; Chinese 4,939; Other Pacific Islanders 10,463; Others 2,767; Total 775,077.

Births, Marriages and Deaths (registrations, 1995): Live births 19,577 (birth rate 24.6 per 1,000); Marriages 7,903 (marriage rate 9.9 per 1,000); Deaths 4,993 (death rate 6.3 per 1,000).

Expectation of Life (years at birth, 1996 census): 66.6 (males 64.5; females 68.7).

Economically Active Population (persons aged 15 years and over, census of 31 August 1986): Agriculture, hunting, forestry and fishing 106,305; Mining and quarrying 1,345; Manufacturing 18,106; Electricity, gas and water 2,154; Construction 11,786; Trade, restaurants and hotels 26,010; Transport, storage and communications 13,151; Financing, insurance, real estate and business services 6,016; Community, social and personal services 36,619; Activities not adequately defined 1,479; Total employed 222,971 (males 179,595, females 43,376); Unemployed 18,189 (males 10,334, females 7,855); Total labour force 241,160 (males 189,929, females 51,231). *1996* (total labour force at 31 December): 297,800.

AGRICULTURE, ETC.

Principal Crops (mostly FAO estimates, '000 metric tons, 1999): Sugar cane 2,098; Coconuts 209; Copra 14 (1998); Cassava 27; Rice (paddy) 17; Sweet potatoes 7; Bananas 6; Yams 3; Taro 26. Source: FAO.

Livestock (FAO estimates, '000 head, year ending September 1999): Cattle 345; Pigs 112; Goats 235; Horses 44; Chickens 3,900. Source: FAO.

Livestock Products (mostly FAO estimates, metric tons, 1999): Poultry meat 8,170; Beef and veal 9,310; Goat meat 930; Pig meat 3,460; Hen eggs 3,300; Cows' milk 54,000; Butter and ghee 1,800; Honey 62. Source: FAO.

Forestry ('000 cubic metres, 1998): *Roundwood removals* (excl. bark): Sawlogs and veneer logs 557; Fuel wood 37; Total 594. *Sawnwood production* (incl. sleepers): 131. Source: FAO, *Yearbook of Forest Products*.

Fishing ('000 metric tons, live weight, 1998): Capture 28.2 (Groupers 1.2, Snappers 1.2, Emperors 1.7, Barracudas 1.6, Mullets 1.2, Narrow-barred Spanish mackerel 1.5, Albacore 2.1, Yellowfin tuna 0.9, Crustaceans 1.1, Freshwater molluscs 4.5, Anadara clams 2.8, Other marine molluscs 3.3); Aquaculture 0.3; Total catch 28.5. Figures exclude aquatic plants ('000 metric tons): 10.1 (Capture 0.1, Aquaculture 10.0). Also excluded are trochus shells (115 metric tons), pearl oyster shells (10 tons) and corals (1,280 tons). Source: FAO, *Yearbook of Fishery Statistics*.

MINING

Production (1997): Gold 4,671 kg; Silver 2,594 kg; Crushed metal 133,891 cu m (1984).

INDUSTRY

Production (metric tons, 1997): Sugar 351,000; Molasses 142,000; Coconut oil 6,664; Soap 8,318; Cement 95,800; Paint 2,578 ('000 litres); Beer 17,000 ('000 litres); Soft drinks 10,059 ('000 litres); Cigarettes 511; Matches 159 ('000 gross boxes); Electric energy 610 (million kWh); Ice cream 2,489 ('000 litres); Toilet paper 12,905 ('000 rolls).

FINANCE

Currency and Exchange Rates: 100 cents = 1 Fiji dollar ($F). *Sterling, US Dollar and Euro Equivalents* (29 December 2000): £1 sterling = $F3.262; US $1 = $F2.186; €1 = $F2.034; $F100 = £30.66

= US $45.75 = €49.17. *Average Exchange Rate* ($F per US $): 1.9868 in 1998; 1.9696 in 1999; 2.1286 in 2000.

General Budget ($F million, 1996): *Revenue:* Taxation 633.52 (Taxes on income, profits and capital gains 236.29, Domestic taxes on goods and services 238.25, Taxes on international trade and transactions 157.29); Other current revenue 96.37 (Entrepreneurial and property income 71.01, Administrative fees and charges, non-industrial and incidental sales 10.76); Capital revenue 6.29; Total 736.18, excl. grants received from abroad (7.34). *Expenditure:* General public services 229.46; Defence 51.17; Public order and safety 43.80; Education 160.34; Health 76.43; Social security and welfare 36.42; Housing and community amenities 25.35; Recreational, cultural and religious affairs and services 7.66; Economic affairs and services 166.74 (Agriculture, forestry, fishing and hunting 31.67, Transport and communications 70.33); Interest payments 84.07; Total 881.44 (Current 677.68, Capital 203.76), excl. lending minus repayments (9.12). Figures exclude the accounts of central government units with individual budgets. Source: IMF, *Government Finance Statistics Yearbook*.

1997 ($F million): *Revenue:* Taxation 664.8; Other current revenue 129.3; Capital revenue 10.0; Total 804.1, incl. grants (8.2). *Expenditure:* Total 1,000.1 (Current 739.8; Capital 260.3), incl. net lending. Source: IMF, *Fiji: Statistical Appendix* (November 1998).

1998 ($F million): *Revenue:* Taxation 731.7; Other current revenue 99.6; Capital revenue 296.3; Total 1,127.6; *Expenditure:* Total 963.9 (Current 821.2; Capital 142.7). Source: ADB, *Key Indicators of Developing Asian and Pacific Countries*.

International Reserves (US $ million at 31 December 1999): Gold (valued at market-related prices) 0.24; IMF special drawing rights 5.63; Reserve position in IMF 20.50; Foreign exchange 402.55; Total 428.69. Source: IMF, *International Financial Statistics*.

Money Supply ($F million at 31 December 1999): Currency outside banks 189.9; Demand deposits at commercial banks 497.6; Total money (incl. others) 694.5. Source: IMF, *International Financial Statistics*.

Cost of Living (Consumer Price Index; base: 1995 = 100): 106.5 in 1997; 112.6 in 1998; 114.8 in 1999. Source: IMF, *International Financial Statistics*.

Expenditure on the Gross Domestic Product ($F million at current prices, 1998): Government final consumption expenditure 565.0; Private final consumption expenditure 2,261.0; Increase in stocks 40.0; Gross fixed capital formation 377.6; *Total domestic expenditure* 3,243.6; *Less* Exports of goods and services 2,094.0; *Less* Imports of goods and services 2,163.4; *GDP in purchasers' values* 3,134.2. Source: IMF, *International Financial Statistics*.

Gross Domestic Product by Economic Activity ($F million at constant 1989 prices, 1998): Agriculture, forestry and fishing 299.2; Mining and quarrying 49.7; Manufacturing 262.5; Electricity, gas and water 81.4; Building and construction 80.7; Wholesale and retail trade 228.8; Hotels and restaurants 57.2; Transport and communications 252.1; Finance, real estate, etc. 248.9; Community, social and personal services 363.5; Other services 14.4; Sub-total 1,938.4; *Less* Imputed bank service charges 130.0; GDP at factor cost 1,808.4. Source: Fiji Islands Trade and Investment Bureau.

Balance of Payments (US $ million, 1999): Exports of goods f.o.b. 537.7; Imports of goods f.o.b. –653.3; *Trade balance* –115.6; Exports of services 525.1; Imports of services –389.8; *Balance on goods and services* 19.7; Other income received 47.3; Other income paid –82.8; *Balance on goods, services and income* –15.8; Current transfers received 42.7; Current transfers paid –14.2; *Current balance* 12.7; Capital account (net) 14.0; Direct investment abroad –53.0; Direct investment from abroad –33.2; Other investment assets –62.2; Other investment liabilities 44.4; Net errors and omissions 32.5; *Overall balance* –44.9. Source: IMF, *International Financial Statistics*.

EXTERNAL TRADE

Principal Commodities ($F million, 1998): *Imports c.i.f.* (distribution by SITC): Food and live animals 205.9; Mineral fuels, lubricants, etc. 159.2; Chemicals and related products 89.9; Basic manufactures 391.9; Machinery and transport equipment 376.6; Miscellaneous manufactured articles 167.7; Total (incl. others) 1,434.2. *Exports f.o.b.:* Fresh fish 27.3; Canned fish 22.2; Sugar 244.2; Forestry products 62.4; Gold 70.5; Clothing 302.8; Total (incl. others) 905.6 (excl. re-exports 110.7).

Principal Trading Partners ($F million, 1998): *Imports c.i.f.:* Australia 575.0; China, People's Republic 28.2; Hong Kong 27.4;

India 19.6; Japan 76.3; Korea, Republic 23.0; New Zealand 202.2; Singapore 72.8; United Kingdom 13.3; USA 213.2; Total (incl. others) 1,434.2. *Exports:* American Samoa 18.4; Australia 339.0; France 19.1; Japan 41.5; New Zealand 39.1; United Kingdom 210.1; USA 128.1; Total (incl. others) 905.6 (excl. re-exports 110.7).

TRANSPORT

Road Traffic (motor vehicles registered at 31 December 1998): Passenger cars 47,053; Goods vehicles 34,182; Buses 1,801; Taxis 2,956; Rental vehicles 4,714; Motorcycles 4,409; Tractors 5,404; Total (incl. others) 104,760.

Shipping: *Merchant Fleet* (registered at 31 December 1998): Vessels 53; Total displacement ('000 grt) 29.3. Source: Lloyd's Register of Shipping, *World Fleet Statistics. International Freight Traffic* ('000 metric tons, 1990): Goods loaded 568; Goods unloaded 625. Source: UN, *Monthly Bulletin of Statistics.*

Civil Aviation (traffic on scheduled services, 1997): Passengers carried 517,000; Passenger-kilometres 2,000 million; Total ton-kilometres 200 million. Source: UN, *Statistical Yearbook.*

TOURISM

Foreign Visitors by Country of Residence (excluding cruise-ship passengers, 1999): Australia 118,272, Canada 13,552, Japan 37,930, New Zealand 72,156, United Kingdom 40,316, USA 62,131; **Total** (incl. others) 409,955. Note: Figures exclude Fijian nationals residing abroad.

Tourism Receipts ($F million): 481.9 in 1998; 541.2 in 1999.

COMMUNICATIONS MEDIA

Radio Receivers (1997): 500,000 in use*.
Television Receivers (1997): 21,000 in use*.
Telephones (1997): 71,403 main lines in use.
Telefax Stations (1997): 3,800 in use†.
Mobile Cellular Telephones (1997): 5,200 subscribers†.
Book Production (1980): 110 titles (84 books, 26 pamphlets); 273,000 copies (229,000 books, 44,000 pamphlets).
Daily Newspaper (1996): 1 (estimated circulation 40,000)*.
Non-daily Newspapers (provisional, 1988): 7 (combined circulation 99,000)*.

* Source: UNESCO, *Statistical Yearbook.*
† Source: UN, *Statistical Yearbook.*

EDUCATION

Pre-primary (1992): 366 schools (1994); 422 teachers; 8,209 pupils.
Primary (1997): 709 schools (1995); 5,011 teachers; 142,781 pupils.
General Secondary (1997): 146 schools (1995); 3,519 teachers; 70,098 pupils.
Vocational and Technical: 31 institutions (1994); 71 teachers (1995); 1,876 students (1997).
Teacher Training (1997): 4 institutions (1994); 92 teachers; 903 students.
Medical (1989): 2 institutions; 493 students.
University (1991): 1 institution; 277 teachers; 7,908 students.
Source: mainly UNESCO, *Statistical Yearbook*, and UN, *Statistical Yearbook for Asia and the Pacific.*

Directory

The Constitution

On 27 July 1998 President Mara promulgated a new Constitution, after the Great Council of Chiefs (Bose Levu Vakaturaga—a traditional body, with some 70 members, consisting of every hereditary chief or Ratu of each Fijian clan) had approved the draft. The following is a summary of the main provisions:

The Constitution, which declares Fiji to be a sovereign, democratic republic, guarantees fundamental human rights, a universal, secret and equal suffrage and equality before the law for all Fijian citizens. Citizenship may be acquired by birth, descent, registration or naturalization and is assured for all those who were Fijian citizens before 6 October 1987. Parliament may make provision for the deprivation or renunciation of a person's citizenship. Ethnic Fijians, and the Polynesian inhabitants of Rotuma, receive special constitutional consideration. The Judicial and Legal Services Commission, the Public Service Commission and the Police Service Commission are established as supervisory bodies.

THE GREAT COUNCIL OF CHIEFS

The Great Council of Chiefs (Bose Levu Vakaturaga) derives its authority from the status of its members and their chiefly lineage. The Great Council appoints the President of the Republic and selects the 14 nominees for appointment to the Senate, the upper chamber of the Parliament.

The Great Council became fully independent of the Government in mid-1999.

THE EXECUTIVE

Executive authority is vested in the President of the Republic, who is appointed by the Great Council of Chiefs, for a five-year term, to be constitutional Head of State and Commander-in-Chief of the armed forces. The Presidential Council advises the President on matters of national importance. The President, and Parliament, can be empowered to introduce any necessary measures in an emergency or in response to acts of subversion which threaten Fiji.

In most cases the President is guided by the Cabinet, which conducts the government of the Republic. The Cabinet is led by the Prime Minister, who is a Fijian of any ethnic origin and is appointed by the President from among the members of Parliament, on the basis of support in the legislature. The Prime Minister selects the other members of the Cabinet (the Attorney-General, the minister responsible for defence and security and any other ministers) from either the House of Representatives or the Senate on a multi-party and multiracial basis. The Cabinet is responsible to Parliament.

THE LEGISLATURE

Legislative power is vested in the Parliament, which comprises the President, the appointed upper house or Senate and an elected House of Representatives. The maximum duration of a parliament is five years.

The Senate has 32 members, appointed by the President of the Republic for the term of the Parliament. A total of 14 senators are nominated by the Great Council of Chiefs, nine are appointed on the advice of the Prime Minister, eight on the advice of the Leader of the Opposition and one on the advice of the Rotuma Island Council. The Senate is a house of review, with some powers to initiate legislation, but with limited influence on financial measures. The Senate is important in the protection of ethnic Fijian interests, and its consent is essential to any attempt to amend, alter or repeal any provisions affecting ethnic Fijians, their customs, land or tradition.

The House of Representatives has 71 elected members, who themselves elect their presiding officials and the Speaker from outside the membership of the House, and Deputy Speaker from among their number (excluding ministers). Voting is communal, with universal suffrage for all citizens of the Republic aged over 21 years. For general elections to the House 46 seats are reserved on a racial basis (23 for ethnic Fijians, 19 for Indians, three for other races—General Electors—and one for Rotuma Islanders) and 25 seats are open to all races. Elections must be held at least every five years and are to be administered by an independent Supervisor of Elections. An independent Boundaries Commission determines constituency boundaries.

THE JUDICIARY

The judiciary is independent and comprises the High Court, the Fiji Court of Appeal and the Supreme Court. The High Court and the Supreme Court are the final arbiters of the Constitution. The establishment of Fijian courts is provided for, and decisions of the Native Lands Commission (relating to ethnic Fijian customs, traditions and usage, and on disputes over the headship of any part of the Fijian people, with the customary right to occupy and use any native lands) are declared to be final and without appeal.

Note: Following the coup of May 2000, the Constitution was declared to have been abrogated.

The Government

HEAD OF STATE

President: Ratu JOSEFA ILOILO (appointed 12 July 2000 by an interim authority established following the coup of 19 May 2000).

Vice-President: Ratu JOPE SENILOLI.

THE CABINET
(March 2001)

An interim civilian government appointed following the coup of 19 May 2000.

Prime Minister and Minister for National Reconciliation: LAISENIA QARASE.

Deputy Prime Minister and Minister for Fijian Affairs: Ratu EPELI NAILATIKAU.

Minister for Foreign Affairs, External Trade and Sugar: KALIOPATE TAVOLA.

Minister for Finance, National Planning and Public Enterprise: Ratu JONE KUBUABOLA.

Attorney-General and Minister for Justice: ALIPATE QETAKI.

Minister for Lands and Mineral Resources: MITIELI BULANAUGA.

Minister for Information and Communications: Ratu INOKE KUBUABOLA.

Minister for Works and Energy: JOKETANI COKANASIGA

Minister for Education: NELSON DELAILOMALOMA.

Minister for Tourism and Transport: KONISI YABAKI.

Minister for Labour and Industrial Relations: Ratu TEVITA MOMOEDONU.

Minister for Commerce, Business Development and Investment: TOMASI VUETILOVONI.

Minister for Public Enterprise and Public Sector Reform: HECTOR HATCH.

Minister for Local Government, Housing and Environment: Ratu COKANAUTO TU'UAKITAU.

Minister of Health: PITA NACUVA.

Minister for Agriculture, Fisheries, Forests and Agricultural Landlords and Tenants Act (ALTA): APISAI TORA.

Minister for Regional Development and Multi-Ethnic Affairs: ILAITIA TUISESE.

Minister for Women, Culture and Social Welfare: RO TEMUMU KEPA.

Minister for Youth, Employment Opportunities and Sports: KENI DAKUIDREKETI.

Minister for Home Affairs and Immigration: Ratu TALEMO RATAKELE.

MINISTRIES

Office of the President: Government Bldgs, POB 2513, Suva; tel. 314244; fax 301645.

Office of the Prime Minister: Government Bldgs, POB 2353, Suva; tel. 211201; fax 306034; e-mail pmsoffice@is.com.fj; internet www.fiji.gov.fj.

Office of the Attorney-General: Government Bldgs, Victoria Parade, POB 2213, Suva; tel. 309866; fax 305421.

Ministry of Agriculture, Fisheries, Forestry and Agricultural Landlords and Tenants Act (ALTA): PMB, Raiwaqa; tel. 384233; fax 385048; e-mail maffinfo@is.com.fj.

Ministry of Commerce, Business Development and Investment: Government Bldgs, POB 2118, Suva; tel. 305411; fax 302617.

Ministry of Education: Marela House, Thurston St, PMB, Suva; tel. 314477; fax 315245.

Ministry of Fijian Affairs: Government Bldgs, POB 2100, Suva; tel. 304200; fax 302585.

Ministry of Finance and National Planning: Government Bldgs, POB 2212, Suva; tel. 307011; fax 300834.

Ministry of Foreign Affairs, External Trade and Sugar: Government Bldgs, POB 2220, Suva; tel. 211458; fax 301741; e-mail foreignaffairs@govnet.gov.fj.

Ministry of Health: Government Bldgs, POB 2223, Suva; tel. 306177; fax 306163; e-mail irokvada@health.gov.fj.

Ministry of Home Affairs and Immigration: Government Bldgs, POB 2349, Suva; tel. 211401; fax 300346.

Ministry of Information and Communications: Government Bldgs, POB 2225, Suva; tel. 211250; fax 303146; e-mail info@fiji.gov.fj.

Ministry of Justice: POB 11869, Suva; tel. 308600; fax 303676.

Ministry of Labour and Industrial Relations: Government Bldgs, POB 2216, Suva, tel. and fax 304701; e-mail minlabour@is.com.fj.

Ministry of Lands and Mineral Resources: Government Bldgs, POB 2222, Suva; tel. 211556; fax 302730; e-mail brao@mrd.gov.fj.

Ministry of Local Government, Housing and Environment: *National Planning:* Government Bldgs, POB 2351, Suva; tel. 313411; fax 304809; *Local Government:* Government Bldgs, POB 2131; tel. 211310; fax 303515; *Environment:* Government Bldgs, POB 2131; tel. 311069; fax 312879; e-mail msovaki@ govnet.gov.fj.

Ministry of Public Enterprise and Public Sector Reform: Government Bldgs, POB 2278, Suva; tel. 315577; fax 315035.

Ministry of Regional Development and Multi-ethnic Affairs: Government Bldgs, POB 2219, Suva; tel. 313400; fax 313035.

Ministry of Tourism and Transport: Third Floor, Civic Tower, POB 1260, Suva; tel. 312788; fax 302060; e-mail infodesk@fijivb.gov.fj; internet www.bulafiji.com.

Ministry of Women, Culture and Social Welfare: POB 14068, Suva; tel. 312199; fax 303829; e-mail slomaloma@govnet.gov.fj.

Ministry of Works and Energy: Nasilivata House, Kings Rd, PMB, Samabula; tel. 384111; fax 383198.

Ministry of Youth, Employment Opportunities and Sports: Government Bldgs, POB 2448, Suva; tel. 315960; fax 305348.

Legislature

PARLIAMENT

Senate

Under the Constitution promulgated in July 1998, the upper chamber comprised 32 appointed members (see The Constitution).

House of Representatives

The lower chamber comprised 71 elected members: 23 representing ethnic Fijians, 19 representing ethnic Indians, three representing other races (General Electors), one delegate from Rotuma Island and 25 seats open to all races.

Speaker: Dr APENISA KURISAQILA.

General Election, 8–15 May 1999

	Communal Seats			Open Seats	Total Seats
	Fijian	Indian	Other*		
Fiji Labour Party (FLP) . . .	—	19	—	18	37
Fijian Association Party (FAP)	9	—	—	1	10
Soqosoqo ni Vakavulewa ni Taukei (SVT)	5	—	—	3	8
Party of National Unity (PANU)	4	—	—	—	4
Veitokani ni Lewenivanua Vakarisito (VLV) . . .	3	—	—	—	3
United General Party (UGP)	—	—	1	1	2
Nationalist Vanua Takolavo Party (NVTLP)	1	—	—	1	2
Independents	1	—	3	1	5
Total	**23**	**19**	**4**	**25**	**71**

* One Rotuman and three General Electors' seats.

Note: All parliamentary activity was suspended as a result of the coup of May 2000. In March 2001 it was announced that a general election would take place between 25 August and 1 September 2001.

Political Organizations

Fiji Indian Congress: POB 3661, Samabula, Suva; tel. 391211; fax 340117; f. 1991; Gen. Sec. VIJAY RAGHWAN.

Fiji Indian Liberal Party: Rakiraki; f. 1991; represents the interests of the Indian community, particularly sugar-cane farmers and students; Sec. SWANI KUMAR.

Fiji Labour Party (FLP): POB 2162, Suva; tel. 308602; fax 307829; f. 1985; Pres. JOKAPECI KOROI; Sec.-Gen. MAHENDRA CHAUDHRY.

Fijian Association Party (FAP): Suva; f. 1995 by merger of Fijian Association (a breakaway faction of the SVT) and the multiracial All Nationals Congress; Leader Ratu TU'UAKITAU COKANAUTO (acting); Pres. Ratu VILIAME DREUNIMISIMISI.

Fijian Conservative Party: Suva; f. 1989 by former mems of the Fiji Nationalist Party and the Alliance Party; Leader ISIRELI VUIBAU.

Fijian Nationalist United Front Party (FNUFP): POB 1336, Suva; tel. 362317; f. 1992 to replace Fijian Nationalist Party; seeks additional parliamentary representation for persons of Fijian ethnic origin, the introduction of other pro-Fijian reforms and the repatriation of ethnic Indians; Leader SAKEASI BAKEWA BUTADROKA.

Janata Party: Suva; f. 1995 by former mems of NFP and FLP.

National Federation Party (NFP): POB 13534, Suva; tel. 305811; fax 305317; f. 1960 by merger of the Federation Party, which was multiracial but mainly Indian, and the National Democratic Party; Leader JAI RAM REDDY; Pres. SHIU CHARAN; Gen. Sec. ATTAR SINGH.

Nationalist Vanua Takolavo Party (NVTLP): c/o House of Representatives, Suva; Leader SAULA TELAWA.

New Labour Movement: Suva; Gen. Sec. MICHAEL COLUMBUS.

Party of National Unity (PANU): Ba; f. 1998 to lobby for increased representation for the province of Ba; Leader MELI BOGILEKA.

Soqosoqo ni Vakavulewa ni Taukei (SVT) (Fijian Political Party): Suva; f. 1990 by Great Council of Chiefs; supports constitutional dominance of ethnic Fijians but accepts multiracialism; Pres. Ratu INOKE KUBUABOLA; Sec.-Gen. JONE BANUVE.

Taukei Movement: Lautoka; f. 1988, following merger of Taukei Liberation Front and Domo Ni Taukei; extreme right-wing indigenous Fijian nationalist group; Pres. Ratu TEVITA BOLOBOLO; Vice-Pres. MELI VESIKULA.

United General Party (UGP): Suva; f. 1998 by the merger of the General Electors' Party and the General Voters' Party (fmrly the General Electors' Association, one of the three wings of the Alliance Party—AP, the ruling party 1970–87); represents the interests of the minority Chinese and European communities and people from other Pacific Islands resident in Fiji, all of whom are classed as General Electors under the 1998 Constitution; Pres. DAVID PICKERING.

Vanua Independent Party: Leader ILIESA TUVALOVO; Sec. URAIA TUISOVISOVI.

Veitokani ni Lewenivanua Vakarisito (VLV) (Christian Democratic Alliance): c/o House of Representatives, Suva; f. 1998 in opposition to constitutional reforms and to defend Christian and Melanesian interests; Leader POESCI WAQALEVU BUNE; Sec. TANIELA TABU.

Other minor parties that contested the 8–15 May 1999 general election included the Coalition of Independent Nationals Party, the Farmers and General Workers Coalition Party, the National Democratic Party, the Natural law Party, the Lio'on Famor Rotuma Party, the Party of the Truth, the United National Labour Party and the Viti Levu Dynamic Multiracial Democratic Party.

Supporters of secession are concentrated in Rotuma.

Diplomatic Representation

EMBASSIES AND HIGH COMMISSIONS IN FIJI

Australia: 37 Princes Rd, POB 214, Suva; tel. 382211; fax 382065; e-mail austembassy@is.com.fj; High Commissioner: SUSAN BOYD.

China, People's Republic: 147 Queen Elizabeth Drive, PMB, Nasese, Suva; tel. 300215; fax 300950; e-mail chinaemb@is.com.fj; Ambassador: CHEN JINGHUA.

France: Dominion House, 7th Floor, Thomson St, Suva; tel. 312233; fax 301894; e-mail vidon@ambafrance.org.fj; Ambassador: JEAN-PIERRE VIDON.

India: POB 471, Suva; tel. 301125; fax 301032; e-mail hicomindsuva @is.com.fj; High Commissioner: ISHWAR SINGH CHAUHAN.

Japan: Dominion House, 2nd Floor, POB 13045, Suva; tel. 304633; fax 302984; e-mail eojfiji@is.com.fj; Ambassador: HISATO MURAYAMA.

Korea, Republic: Vanua House, 8th Floor, PMB, Suva; tel. 300977; fax 303410; Ambassador: LIM DAE-TAEK.

Malaysia: Pacific House, 5th Floor, POB 356, Suva; tel. 312166; fax 303350; e-mail mwsuva@is.com.fj; High Commissioner: MOHAMMED TAKWIR DIN.

Marshall Islands: 41 Borron Rd, Government Bldgs, POB 2038, Suva; tel. 387899; fax 387115; Ambassador: MACK KAMINAGA.

Micronesia, Federated States: 37 Loftus St, POB 15493, Suva; tel. 304566; fax 300842; e-mail fsmsuva@sopacsun.sopac.org.fj; Ambassador: KODARO MARTIN GALLEN.

Nauru: Ratu Sukuna House, 7th Floor, Government Bldgs, POB 2420, Suva; tel. 313566; fax 302861; High Commissioner: CAMILLA SOLOMON.

New Zealand: Reserve Bank of Fiji Bldg, 10th Floor, Pratt St, POB 1378, Suva; tel. 311422; fax 300842; e-mail nzhc@is.com.fj; High Commissioner: TIA BARRETT.

Papua New Guinea: Credit Corporation House, 3rd Floor, Government Bldgs, POB 2447, Suva; tel. 304244; fax 300178; e-mail kundufj@is.com.fj; High Commissioner: BABANI MARAGA.

Tuvalu: 16 Gorrie St, POB 14449, Suva; tel. 300697; fax 301023; High Commissioner: ENELE SOSENE SOPOAGA.

United Kingdom: Victoria House, 47 Gladstone Rd, POB 1355, Suva; tel. 311033; fax 301406; e-mail ukinfo@bhc.org.fj; internet www.ukinthepacific.bhc.org.fj; High Commissioner: MICHAEL PRICE.

USA: 31 Loftus Rd, POB 218, Suva; tel. 314466; fax 300081; e-mail usembsuva@is.com.fj; internet www.amembassy-fiji.gov; Chargé d'affaires: OSMAN SIDDIQUE.

Judicial System

Justice is administered by the Supreme Court, the Fiji Court of Appeal, the High Court and the Magistrates' Courts. The Supreme Court of Fiji is the superior court of record presided over by the Chief Justice. The 1990 Constitution provided for the establishment of Fijian customary courts and declared as final decisions of the Native Lands Commission in cases involving Fijian custom, etc.

Supreme Court: Suva; tel. 211524; fax 300674.

Chief Justice: Sir TIMOCI TUIVAGA.

President of the Fiji Court of Appeal: (vacant).

Director of Public Prosecutions: KENNETH WILKINSON (acting).

Solicitor-General: NAINENDRA NAND.

Religion

CHRISTIANITY

Most ethnic Fijians are Christians. Methodists are the largest Christian group, followed by Roman Catholics. In the census of 1986 about 53% of the population were Christian (mainly Methodists).

Fiji Council of Churches: POB 2300, Government Bldgs, Suva; tel. (1) 313798; f. 1964; seven mem. churches; Pres. Most Rev. PETERO MATACA (Roman Catholic Archbishop of Suva); Gen. Sec. EMI FRANCES.

The Anglican Communion

In April 1990 Polynesia, formerly a missionary diocese of the Church of the Province of New Zealand, became a full and integral diocese. The diocese of Polynesia is based in Fiji but also includes Wallis and Futuna, Tuvalu, Kiribati, French Polynesia, Cook Islands, Tonga, Samoa and Tokelau.

Bishop of Polynesia: Rt Rev. JABEZ LESLIE BRYCE, Bishop's House, 7 Disraeli Rd, POB 35, Suva; tel. 302553; fax 302687.

The Roman Catholic Church

Fiji comprises a single archdiocese. At 31 December 1998 there were an estimated 84,236 adherents in the country.

Bishops' Conference: Episcopal Conference of the Pacific Secretariat (CEPAC), 14 Williamson Rd, POB 289, Suva; tel. 300340; fax 303143; e-mail cepac@is.com.fj; f. 1968; 17 mems; Pres. Most Rev. MICHEL MARIE CALVET, Archbishop of Nouméa, New Caledonia; Gen. Sec. Rev. ARTHUR TIERNEY.

Regional Appeal Tribunal for CEPAC: 14 Williamson Rd, POB 289, Suva; tel. 300340; fax 303143; e-mail cepac@is.com.fj; f. 1980; 17 mems; Judicial Vicar Rev. THEO KOSTER.

Archbishop of Suva: Most Rev. PETERO MATACA, Archdiocesan Office, Nicolas House, Pratt St, POB 109, Suva; tel. 301955; fax 301565.

Other Christian Churches

Methodist Church in Fiji (Lotu Wesele e Viti): Epworth Arcade, Nina St, POB 357, Suva; tel. 311477; fax 303771; f. 1835; autonomous since 1964; 215,416 mems (1999); Pres. Rev. TOMASI KANAILAGI; Gen. Sec. Rev. LAISIASA RATABACACA.

Other denominations active in the country include the Assembly of God (with c. 7,000 mems), the Baptist Mission, the Congregational Christian Church and the Presbyterian Church.

HINDUISM

Most of the Indian community are Hindus. According to the census of 1986, 38% of the population were Hindus.

ISLAM

In 1993 some 8% of the population were Muslim. There are several Islamic organizations:

Fiji Muslim League: POB 3990, Samabula, Suva; tel. 384566; fax 370204; f. 1926; Pres. Haji FAZAL KHAN; Gen. Sec. MASUM ALI BUKSH; 26 brs and 3 subsidiary orgs.

SIKHISM

Sikh Association of Fiji: Suva; Pres. HARKEWAL SINGH.

BAHÁ'Í FAITH

National Spiritual Assembly: National Office, POB 639, Suva; tel. 387574; fax 387772; e-mail nsafijiskm@suva.is.com.fj; mems resident in 490 localities; national headquarters for consultancy and co-ordination.

The Press

NEWSPAPERS AND PERIODICALS

Coconut Telegraph: POB 249, Savusavu, Vanua Levu; f. 1975; monthly; serves widely-scattered rural communities; Editor LEMA LOW.

Fiji Calling: POB 12095, Suva; tel. 305916; fax 301930; publ. by Associated Media Ltd; every 6 months; English; Publr YASHWANT GAUNDER.

Fiji Cane Grower: POB 12095, Suva; tel. 305916; fax 305256.

Fiji Daily Post: 10–16 Toorak Rd, POB 2071, Govt Bldgs, Suva; f. 1987 as *Fiji Post*, daily from 1989; English; 45% govt-owned; Gen. Man. ANURA BANDARA (acting); Editor JALE MOALA.

Fiji Islands Business: 46 Gordon St, POB 12718; Suva; tel. 303108; fax 301423; e-mail editor@ibi.com.fj; monthly; English; Editor-in-Chief PETER LOMAS.

Fiji Magic: POB 12095, Suva; tel. 305916; fax 301930; e-mail review@is.com.fj; publ. by The Review Ltd; monthly; English; Publr YASHWANT GAUNDER.

Fiji Republic Gazette: Printing Dept, POB 98, Suva; tel. 385999; fax 370203; f. 1874; weekly; English.

Fiji Sun: Suva; re-established 1999; daily; Editor MARK GARRET.

Fiji Times: 20 Gordon St, POB 1167, Suva; tel. 304111; fax 301521; f. 1869; publ. by Fiji Times Ltd; daily; English; Man. Dir ALAN ROBINSON; Editor SAMISONI KAKAIUALU; circ. 34,000.

Fiji Trade Review: The Rubine Group, POB 12511, Suva; tel. 313944; monthly; English; Publr GEORGE RUBINE; Editor MABEL HOWARD.

Islands Business: 46 Gordon St, POB 12718, Suva; tel. 303108; fax 301423; e-mail editor@ibi.com.fj; f. 1980; regional monthly news and business magazine; English; Publr ROBERT KEITH-REID; Editor-in-Chief PETER LOMAS; circ. 11,950; to merge with *Pacific* magazine (Honolulu).

Na Tui: 422 Fletcher Rd, POB 2071, Govt Bldgs, Suva; f. 1988; weekly; Fijian; Publr TANIELA BOLEA; Editor SAMISONI BOLATAGICI; circ. 7,000.

Nai Lalakai: 20 Gordon St, POB 1167, Suva; tel. 304111; fax 301521; e-mail fijitimes@is.com.fj; f. 1962; publ. by Fiji Times Ltd; weekly; Fijian; Editor SAMISONI KAKAIVALU; circ. 18,000.

Pacific Business: POB 12095, Suva; tel. 305916; fax 301930; publ. by Associated Media Ltd; monthly; English; Publr YASHWANT GAUNDER.

Pacific Telecom: POB 12095, Suva; tel. 300591; fax 302852; e-mail review@is.com.fj; publ. by Associated Media Ltd; monthly; English; Publr YASHWANT GAUNDER.

Pactrainer: PMB, Suva; tel. 303623; fax 303943; e-mail pina@is.com.fj; monthly; newsletter of Pacific Journalism Development Centre; Editor PETER LOMAS.

PINA Nius: Pacific Islands News Association, 46 Gordon St, PMB, Suva; tel. 303623; fax 303943; e-mail pina@is.com.fj; internet www.pressasia.org/pfa/; monthly newsletter of Pacific Islands News Association; Editor NINA RATULELE.

The Review: POB 12095, Suva; tel. 305916; fax 301930; e-mail review@is.com.fj; publ. by Associated Media Ltd; monthly; English; Publr YASHWANT GAUNDER.

Sartaj: John Beater Enterprises Ltd, Raiwaqa, POB 5141, Suva; f. 1988; weekly; Hindi; Editor S. DASO; circ. 15,000.

Shanti Dut: 20 Gordon St, POB 1167, Suva; f. 1935; publ. by Fiji Times Ltd; weekly; Hindi; Editor M. C. VINOD; circ. 8,000.

Top Shot: Suva; f. 1995; golf magazine; monthly.

Volasiga: 10–16 Toorak Rd, POB 2071, Suva; f. 1988; weekly; Fijian; Gen. Man. ANURA BANDARA (acting); Editor SAMISONI BOLATAGICI.

The Weekender: 2 Dension Rd, POB 15652, Suva; tel. 315477; fax 305346; publ. by Media Resources Ltd; weekly; English; Publr JOSEFATA NATA.

PRESS ASSOCIATIONS

Fiji Islands Media Association: c/o Vasiti Ivaqa, POB 12718, Suva; tel. 303108; fax 301423; national press asscn; operates Fiji Press Club and Fiji Journalism Training Institute; Sec. NINA RATULELE.

Pacific Islands News Association: 46 Gordon St, PMB, Suva; tel. 303623; fax 303943; e-mail pina@is.com.fj; internet www .pressasia.org/pfa/; regional press asscn; defends freedom of information and expression, promotes professional co-operation, provides training and education; Administrator NINA RATULELE; Pres. WILLIAM PARKINSON.

Publishers

Fiji Times Ltd: POB 1167, Suva; tel. 304111; fax 302011; f. 1869; Propr News Corpn Ltd; largest newspaper publr; also publrs of books and magazines; Man. Dir ALAN ROBINSON.

Lotu Pasifika Productions: POB 2401, Suva; tel. 301314; fax 301183; f. 1973; cookery, education, poetry, religion; Gen. Man. SERU L. VEREBALAVU.

University of the South Pacific: University Media Centre, POB 1168, Suva; tel. 313900; fax 301305; e-mail farkas_g@nsp.ac.fj; f. 1986; education, natural history, regional interests.

Government Publishing House

Printing and Stationery Department: POB 98, Suva; tel. 385999; fax 370203.

Broadcasting and Communications

TELECOMMUNICATIONS

Fiji International Telecommunicatons Ltd (FINTEL): 158 Victoria Parade, POB 59, Suva; tel. 312933; fax 300750; e-mail philip .richards@cwhkt.cwplc.com; 51% govt-owned; 49% C&Wplc; Gen. Man. PHILIP RICHARDS.

Telcom Fiji Ltd: Private Mail Bag, Suva; tel. 304019; fax 301765; internet www.tfl.com.fj/; Chair. LIONEL YEE; CEO WINSTON THOMPSON.

Vodafone Fiji Ltd: Private Mail Bag, Suva; tel. 312000; fax 312007; 51% owned by Telecom Fiji, 41% by Vodafone Holdings Australia; Man. Dir ASLAM KHAN.

BROADCASTING

Radio

Fiji Broadcasting Commission—FBC (Radio Fiji): Broadcasting House, POB 334, Suva; tel. 314333; fax 301643; f. 1954; statutory body; jointly funded by govt grant and advertising revenue; Chair. DANIEL WHIPPY; CEO SIRELI KINI.

Radio Fiji 1 broadcasts nationally on AM in English and Fijian.

Radio Fiji 2 broadcasts nationally on AM in English and Hindi.

Radio Fiji Gold broadcasts nationally on AM and FM in English.

104 FM and Radio Rajdhani 98 FM, mainly with musical programmes, broadcast in English and Hindi respectively, but are received only on Viti Levu.

Bula FM, musical programmes, broadcasts in Fijian, received only on Viti Levu.

Communications Fiji Ltd: 231 Waimanu Rd, PMB, Suva; tel. 314766; fax 303748; e-mail cfl@fm96.com.fj; f. 1985; operates three commercial stations; Man. Dir WILLIAM PARKINSON; Gen. Man. IAN JACKSON.

FM 96, f. 1985, broadcasts 24 hours per day, on FM, in English.

Navtarang, f. 1989, broadcasts 24 hours per day, on FM, in Hindi.

Viti FM, f. 1996, broadcasts 24 hours per day, on FM, in Fijian.

Radio Light: Shop 11B, Pacific Harbour Culture Centre, POB 319, Pacific Harbour; tel. and fax 450007; e-mail radiolight@is.com.fj; f. 1990; non-profit religious organization; broadcasts on FM 106 and FM 93.6; Station Man. and Programmes Dir DOUGLAS ROSE.

Radio Pasifik: POB 1168, University of the South Pacific, Suva; tel. 313900; fax 312591; e-mail schuster_a@usp.ac.fj; Gen. Man. ALFRED SCHUSTER.

Television

Film and Television Unit (FTU): c/o Ministry of Information and Communications, Govt Bldgs, POB 2225, Suva; tel. 314688; fax 300196; video library; production unit established by Govt and Hanns Seidel Foundation (Germany); a weekly news magazine and local documentary programmes.

Fiji Television Ltd: 20 Gorrie St, POB 2442, Suva; tel. 305100; fax 305077; e-mail fijitv@is.com.fj; internet www.fijitv.com; f. 1994; operates two services, Fiji 1, a free channel, and Sky Fiji, a three-channel subscription service; Chair. ISOA KALOUMAIRA; CEO KEN CLARK; Head of Programmes CAROLYN JALAL.

Fiji Vision Ltd: Suva; f. 1997; subscription television; jointly-owned by Yasana Holdings Ltd and a Hawaiian consortium.

In 1990 two television stations were constructed at Suva and Monsavu, with aid from the People's Republic of China. A permanent television station became operational in July 1994.

Finance

In 1996 the Ministry of Finance announced that it had secured financial assistance for the undertaking of a study to investigate the possibility of developing an 'offshore' financial centre in Fiji.

BANKING

(cap. = capital; res = reserves; dep. = deposits; m. = million; brs = branches; amounts in Fiji dollars)

Central Bank

Reserve Bank of Fiji: Pratt St, PMB, Suva; tel. 313611; fax 301688; e-mail rbf@reservebank.gov.fj; internet www.reservebank.gov.fj; f. 1984 to replace Central Monetary Authority of Fiji; bank of issue; administers Insurance Act; cap. and res 32.1m., dep. 143.1m. (Dec. 2000); Chair. and Gov. SAVENACA NARUBE.

Commercial Bank

National Bank of Fiji Ltd: 3 Central St, POB 1166, Suva; tel. 314400; fax 302190; f. 1974; 51% acquired from Fiji Govt by Colonial Ltd in 1999; cap. 11.5m., dep. 145.1m. (June 1998); Chair. LIONEL YEE; Man. Dir KENNETH R. MCARTHUR; 13 brs; 66 agencies.

Development Bank

Fiji Development Bank: 360 Victoria Parade, POB 104, Suva; tel. 314866; fax 314886; f. 1967; finances the development of natural resources, agriculture, transportation and other industries and enterprises; statutory body; cap. 50.8m., res 14.0m., dep. 182.6m. (June 1993); Chair. CHARLES WALKER; 9 brs.

Merchant Banks

Merchant Bank of Fiji Ltd: 231 Waimanu Rd, POB 14213, Suva; tel. 314955; fax 300026; e-mail merchantbk@is.com.fj; f. 1986; owned by the Fijian Holdings Ltd; Man. Dir (vacant); 4 brs.

National MBf Finance (Fiji) Ltd: Burns Philp Bldg, 2nd Floor, POB 13525, Suva; tel. 302232; fax 305915; e-mail mbf@is.com.fj; f. 1991; 51% owned by the National Bank of Fiji, 49% by MBf Asia Capital Corpn Holding Ltd (Hong Kong); Chief Operating Officer SIEK KART; 4 brs.

Foreign Banks

Agence Française de Développement (ADF) (France): Suva; licensed to operate in Fiji in 1997.

Australia and New Zealand (ANZ) Banking Group Ltd: ANZ House, 25 Victoria Parade, POB 179, Suva; tel. 213000; fax 312527; bought Bank of New Zealand in Fiji (8 brs) in 1990; Gen. Man. (Fiji) DAVID BELL; 17 brs; 9 agencies.

Bank of Baroda (India): Bank of Baroda Bldg, Marks St, POB 57, Suva; tel. 311400; fax 302510; f. 1908; CEO S. K. BAGCHI; 7 brs; 2 agencies.

Bank of Hawaii (USA): 67–69 Victoria Parade, POB 273, Suva; tel. 312144; fax 312464; f. 1993; Gen. Man. BRIAN BLISS; 3 brs.

Habib Bank (Pakistan): Narsey's Bldg, Renwick Rd, POB 108, Suva; tel. 304011; fax 304835; Chief Man. (Fiji) ABDUL MATIN; licensed to operate in Fiji 1990; 3 brs.

Westpac Banking Corporation (Australia): 1 Thomson St, Suva; tel. 300666; fax 301813; Chief Man. (Pacific Islands region) TREVOR WISEMANTEL; 12 brs; 9 agencies.

STOCK EXCHANGE

South Pacific Stock Exchange: Level 2, Plaza One, Provident Plaza, 33 Ellery St, POB 11689, Suva; tel. 304130; fax 304145; e-mail suvastockex@is.com.fj; internet www.suvastockex.com; formerly Suva Stock Exchange; name changed as above in 2000; Chair. FOANA T. NEMANI; Man. MESAKE NAWARI.

INSURANCE

Blue Shield (Pacific) Ltd: Parade Bldg, POB 15137, Suva; tel. 311733; fax 300318; Fijian co; subsidiary of Colonial Mutual Life Assurance Society Ltd; medical and life insurance; Chief Exec. SIALENI VUETAKI.

Colonial Mutual Life Assurance Society Ltd: Colonial Bldg, PMB, Suva; tel. 314400; fax 303448; f. 1876; inc in Australia; life; Gen.Man. SIMON SWANSON.

Dominion Insurance Ltd: Civic House, POB 14468, Suva; tel. 311055; fax 303475; partly owned by Flour Mills of Fiji Ltd; general insurance; Man. Dir GARY S. CALLAGHAN.

FAI Insurance (Fiji) Ltd: Suva.

Fiji Reinsurance Corpn Ltd: RBF Bldg, POB 12704, Suva; tel. 313471; fax 305679; 20% govt-owned; reinsurance; Chair. Ratu JONE Y. KUBUABOLA; Man. PETER MARIO.

Fijicare Mutual Assurance: 41 Loftus St, POB 15808, Suva; tel. 302717; fax 302119; f. 1992; CEO JEFF PRICE.

Insurance Trust of Fiji: Loftus St, POB 114; Suva; tel. 311242; fax 302541; Man. SAMUEL KRISHNA.

National Insurance Co of Fiji Ltd: McGowan Bldg, Suva; tel. 315955; fax 301376; owned by New Zealand interests; Gen. Man. GEOFF THOMPSON.

New India Assurance Co Ltd: Harifam Centre, POB 71, Suva; tel. 313488; fax 302679; Man. MILIND A. KHARAT.

Queensland Insurance (Fiji) Ltd: Queensland Insurance Center, Victoria Parade, POB 101, Suva; tel. 315455; fax 300285; owned by Australian interests; Gen. Man. PETER J. NICHOLLS.

There are also two Indian insurance companies operating in Fiji.

Trade and Industry

GOVERNMENT AGENCIES

Fiji National Training Council (FNTC): Beaumont Rd, POB 6890, Nasinu; tel. 392000; fax 340184; e-mail gen-enq@fntc.ac.fj; internet www.fntc.ac.fj; Dir-Gen. NELSON DELAILOMALOMA.

Fiji Trade and Investment Board: Civic House, 6th Floor, Victoria Parade, Suva; tel. 315988; fax 301783; e-mail ftibinfo@ftib.org.fj; internet www.ftib.org.fj; f. 1980, restyled 1988, to promote and stimulate foreign and local economic development investment; Chair. JAMES DATTA; CEO JESONI VITUSAGAVULU.

Mineral Resources Department: Private Mail Bag; Suva; tel. 381611; fax 370039; internet www.mrd.gov.fj/index.html.

DEVELOPMENT ORGANIZATIONS

Fiji Development Company Ltd: POB 161, FNPF Place, 350 Victoria Parade, Suva; tel. 304611; fax 304171; e-mail hfc@is.com.fj; f. 1960; subsidiary of the Commonwealth Development Corpn; Man. F. KHAN.

Fiji-United States Business Council: CI-FTIB; POB 2303; Suva; f. 1998 to develop and expand trade links between the two countries; Pres. RAMENDRA NARAYAN.

Fijian Development Fund Board: POB 122, Suva; tel. 312601; fax 302585; f. 1951; funds derived from payments of $F20 a metric ton from the sales of copra by indigenous Fijians; deposits receive interest at 2.5%; funds used only for Fijian development schemes; Chair. Minister for Fijian Affairs; CEO VINCENT TOVATA.

Land Development Authority: c/o Ministry for Agriculture, Fishery and Forestry, POB 358, Suva; tel. 311233; fax 302478; f. 1961 to co-ordinate development plans for land and marine resources; Chair. Ratu Sir JOSAIA TARAIQIA.

CHAMBERS OF COMMERCE

Ba Chamber of Commerce: POB 99, Ba; tel. 670134; fax 670132; Pres. DIJENDRA SINGH.

Labasa Chamber of Commerce: POB 121, Labasa; tel. 811262; fax 813009; Pres. SHIVLAL NAGINDAS.

Lautoka Chamber of Commerce: POB 366, Lautoka; tel. 661834; fax 662379; Pres. NATWARLAL VAGH.

Levuka Chamber of Commerce: POB 85, Levuka; tel. 440248; fax 440252; Pres. ISHRAR ALI.

Nadi Chamber of Commerce: POB 2735, Nadi; tel. 701704; fax 702314; e-mail arunkumar@is.com.fj; Pres. VENKAT RAMANI AIYER.

Nausori Chamber of Commerce: POB 228, Nausori; tel. 478235; fax 400134; Pres. ROBERT RAJ KUMAR.

Sigatoka Chamber of Commerce: POB 882, Sigatoka; tel. 500064; fax 520006; Pres. NATWAR SINGH.

Suva Chamber of Commerce: 29 Ackland St, Vatuwara, POB 337, Suva; tel. 303854; fax 300475; f. 1902; Pres. NAVIN CHANDRA; 150 mems.

Tavua-Vatukoula Chamber of Commerce: POB 698, Tavua; tel. 680390; fax 680390; Pres. SOHAN SINGH.

INDUSTRIAL AND TRADE ASSOCIATIONS

Fiji Forest Industries (FFI): Suva; Deputy Chair. Ratu SOSO KATONIVERE.

Fiji National Petroleum Co Ltd: Suva; f. 1991; govt-owned, distributor of petroleum products.

Fiji Sugar Corporation Ltd: 2nd and 3rd Floors, Western House, Cnr of Bila and Vidilo St, PMB, Lautoka; tel. 662655; fax 664685; nationalized 1974; buyer of sugar-cane and raw sugar mfrs; Chair. HAFIZUD D. KHAN; Man. Dir JONETANI K. GALUINADI.

Fiji Sugar Marketing Co Ltd: Dominion House, 5th Floor, Thomson St, POB 1402, Suva; tel. 311588; fax 300607; Man. Dir JONETANI GALUINADI.

Mining and Quarrying Council: 42 Gorrie St, Suva; tel. 302188; fax 302183; e-mail employer@is.com.fj.

National Trading Corporation Ltd: POB 13673, Suva; tel. 315211; fax 315584; f. 1992; a govt-owned body set up to develop markets for agricultural and marine produce locally and overseas; processes and markets fresh fruit, vegetables and ginger products; CEO APIAMA CEGUMALINA.

Native Lands Trust Board: Suva; manages holdings of ethnic Fijian landowners; Gen. Man. MAIKA QARIKAU.

Pacific Fishing Co: Suva; fish-canning; govt-owned.

Sugar Cane Growers' Council: Canegrowers' Bldg, 3rd Floor, 75 Drasa Ave, Lautoka; tel. 650466; fax 650624; e-mail canegrower@is.com.fj; f. 1985; aims to develop the sugar industry and protect the interests of registered growers; CEO JAGANNATH SAMI; Chair. RUSIATE MUSUDROKA.

Sugar Commission of Fiji: POB 5993, Lautoka; tel. 664866; fax 664051; e-mail scof@is.com.fj; Chair. GERALD BARRACK.

EMPLOYERS' ORGANIZATIONS

Fiji Employers' Federation: 42 Gorrie St, POB 575, Suva; tel. 313188; fax 302183; e-mail employer@fef.com.fj; represents 206 major employers; Pres. K. J. CLEMENS; CEO KENNETH A. J. ROBERTS.

Fiji Manufacturers' Association: POB 1308, Suva; tel. 212223; fax 302567; e-mail volau-m@usp.ac.fj; internet www.fijibusiness.com; f. 1902; Pres. DESMOND WHITESIDE; 55 mems.

Local Inter-Island Shipowners' Association: POB 152, Suva; fax 303389; Pres. VITI G. WHIPPY.

Textile, Clothing and Footwear Council: POB 10015, Nabua; tel. 384777; fax 370446; Sec. R. DUNSTAN.

UTILITIES
Electricity

Fiji Electricity Authority (FEA): PMB, Suva; tel. 311133; fax 311882; f. 1966; govt-owned; responsible for the generation, transmission and distribution of electricity throughout Fiji; CEO NIZAM UD-DEAN.

Water

Water and Sewerage Section: Public Works Department, Ministry of Works and Energy, Nasilivata House, Kings Rd, PMB, Samabula; tel. 211250; fax 303146; e-mail fkau@info.gov.fj; Dir RAM SUMER SHANDIL.

TRADE UNIONS

Fiji Trades Union Congress (FTUC): 32 Des Voeux Rd, POB 1418, Suva; tel. 315377; fax 300306; e-mail ftucl@is.com.fj; f. 1951; affiliated to ICFTU and ICFTU—APRO; 35 affiliated unions; more than 42,000 mems; Pres. DANIEL URAI; Gen. Sec. FELIX ANTHONY. Principal affiliated unions:

   Association of USP Staff: POB 1168, Suva; tel. 313900; fax 301305; f. 1977; Pres. GANESH CHAND; Sec. D. R. RAO.

   Federated Airline Staff Association: Nadi Airport, POB 9259, Nadi; tel. 722877; fax 790068; Sec. RAM RAJEN.

   Fiji Aviation Workers' Association: FTUC Complex, 32 Des Voeux Rd, POB 5351, Raiwaqa; tel. 303184; fax 311805; Pres. VALENTINE SIMPSON; Gen. Sec. ATTAR SINGH.

   Fiji Bank and Finance Sector Employees' Union: 101 Gordon St, POB 853, Suva; tel. 301827; fax 301956; e-mail fbeu@is.com.fj; Nat. Sec. DIWAN C. SHANKAR.

   Fiji Electricity and Allied Workers Union: POB 1390, Lautoka; tel. 666353; e-mail feawu@is.com.fj; Pres. LEONE SAKETA; Sec. J. A. PAUL.

   Fiji Garment, Textile and Allied Workers' Union: c/o FTUC, Raiwaqa; f. 1992.

   Fiji Nurses' Association: POB 1364, Suva; tel. 312841; Gen. Sec. KITI VATANIMOTO.

   Fiji Public Service Association: 298 Waimanu Rd, POB 1405, Suva; tel. 311922; fax 301099; e-mail fpsa@is.com.fj; f. 1943; 3,434 mems; Pres. AISEA BATISARESARE; Gen. Sec. RAJESHWAR.SINGH.

   Fiji Sugar and General Workers' Union: 84 Naviti St, POB 330, Lautoka; tel. 660746; fax 664888; 25,000 mems; Pres. SHIU LINGAM; Gen. Sec. FELIX ANTHONY.

   Fiji Teachers' Union: 1–3 Berry Rd, Govt Bldgs, POB 2203, Suva; tel. 314099; fax 305962; e-mail ftu@is.com.fj; f. 1930; 3,200 mems; Pres. BALRAM; Gen. Sec. AGNI DEO SINGH.

Fijian Teachers' Association: POB 14464, Suva; tel. 315099; fax 304978; e-mail fta@.com.fj; Pres. TARITA KOREI; Gen. Sec. MAIKA NAMUDU.

Insurance Officers' Association: POB 71, Suva; tel. 313488; Pres. JAGDISH KHATRI; Sec. DAVID LEE.

Mineworkers' Union of Fiji: POB 876, Tavua; f. 1986; Pres. HENNESY PETERS; Sec. KAVEKINI NAVUSO.

National Farmers' Union: POB 522, Labasa; tel. 811838; 10,000 mems (sugar-cane farmers); Pres. DEWAN CHAND; Gen. Sec. M. P. CHAUDHRY; CEO MOHAMMED LATIF SUBEDAR.

National Union of Factory and Commercial Workers: POB 989, Suva; tel. 311155; 3,800 mems; Pres. CAMA TUILEVEUKA; Gen. Sec. JAMES R. RAMAN.

National Union of Hotel and Catering Employees: Nadi Airport, POB 9426, Nadi; tel. 70906; fax 700181; Pres. EMOSI DAWAI; Sec. TIMOA NAIVAHIWAQA.

Public Employees' Union: POB 781, Suva; tel. 304501; 6,752 mems; Pres. SEMI TIKOICINA; Gen. Sec. FILIMONE BANUVE.

Transport and Oil Workers' Union: POB 903, Suva; tel. 302534; f. 1988; following merger of Oil and Allied Workers' Union and Transport Workers' Union; Pres. J. BOLA; Sec. MICHAEL COLUMBUS.

There are several independent trade unions, including Fiji Registered Ports Workers' Union (f. 1947; Pres. JIOJI TAHOLOSALE).

Transport

RAILWAYS

Fiji Sugar Corporation Railway: Rarawai Mill, POB 155, Ba; tel. 674044; fax 670505; for use in cane-harvesting season, May–Dec.; 595 km of permanent track and 225 km of temporary track (gauge of 600 mm), serving cane-growing areas at Ba, Lautoka and Penang on Viti Levu and Labasa on Vanua Levu; Gen. Man. ADURU KUVA.

ROADS

At the end of 1996 there were some 3,440 km of roads in Fiji, of which 49.2% were paved. A 500-km highway circles the main island of Viti Levu.

SHIPPING

There are ports of call at Suva, Lautoka, Levuka and Savusavu. The main port, Suva, handles more than 800 ships a year, including large passenger liners. Lautoka handles more than 300 vessels and liners and Levuka, the former capital of Fiji, mainly handles commercial fishing vessels. In 1996 a feasibility study into the possible establishment of a free port at Suva was commissioned. In May 1997 the Government approved 14 new ports of entry in the northern, western and central eastern districts of Fiji.

Maritime and Ports Authority of Fiji (MPAF): Administration Bldg, Princes Wharf, POB 780, Suva; tel. 312700; fax 300064; corporatized in 1998; Chair. DANIEL ELISHA; Port Master Capt. GEORGE MACOMBER.

Ports Terminals Ltd: POB S13, Suva; tel. 304725; fax 304769; f. 1998, following corporatization of Ports Authority of Fiji (now MPAF, see above).

Burns Philp Shipping (Fiji) Ltd: Rodwell Rd, POB 15832, Suva; tel. 315444; fax 302754; e-mail burshipfiji@is.com.fj; shipping agents, customs agents and international forwarding agents; Gen. Man. DANNY REES.

Consort Shipping Line Ltd: Muaiwalu Complex, Rona St, Walubay, POB 152, Suva; tel. 313344; fax 303389; CEO HECTOR SMITH; Man. Dir JUSTIN SMIT.

Fiji Maritime Services Ltd: c/o Fiji Ports Workers and Seafarers Union, 36 Edinburgh Drive, Suva; f. 1989 by PAF and the Ports Workers' Union; services between Lautoka and Vanua Levu ports.

Inter-Ports Shipping Corpn Ltd: 25 Eliza St, Walu Bay; POB 152, Suva; tel. 313638; f. 1984; Man. Dir JUSTIN SMITH.

Transcargo Express Fiji Ltd: POB 936, Suva; f. 1974; Man. Dir LEO B. SMITH.

Wong's Shipping Co Ltd: Suite 647, Epworth House, Nina St, POB 1269, Suva; tel. 311867.

CIVIL AVIATION

There is an international airport at Nadi (about 210 km from Suva), a smaller international airport at Nausori (Suva) and 15 other airfields. Nadi is an important transit airport in the Pacific and in 1990 direct flights to Japan also began.

Airports Fiji Ltd: Nadi International Airport, Nadi; Chair. DINESH SHANKAR; CEO JONE KOROITAMANA.

Air Fiji Ltd: 219 Victoria Parade, POB 1259, Suva; tel. 314666; fax 300771; internet www.airfiji.net; operates 65 scheduled services daily to 15 domestic destinations; daily service to Tonga and Tuvalu and direct flights to Auckland and Sydney commenced in 1999; charter operations, aerial photography and surveillance also conducted; partly owned by the Fijian Govt, which was expected to sell a majority of its shares in 2001; Chair. DOUG HAZARD; CEO KEN MACDONALD.

Air Pacific Ltd: Air Pacific Centre, POB 9266, Nadi International Airport, Nadi; tel. 720777; fax 720512; internet www.airpacific.com; f. 1951 as Fiji Airways, name changed in 1971; domestic and international services from Nausori Airport (serving Suva) to Nadi and international services to Tonga, Solomon Islands, Cook Islands, Vanuatu, Samoa, Japan, Australia, New Zealand and the USA; 51% govt-owned, 46.05% owned by Qantas (Australia); Chair. GERALD BARRACK; Man. Dir and CEO MICHAEL McQUAY.

Fijian Airways International: POB 10138, Nadi International Airport, Nadi; tel. 724702; fax 724654; f. 1997; service to London via Singapore and Mumbai (India) planned; Chair. NEIL UNDERHILL; CEO ALAN LINDREA.

Hibiscus Air Ltd: Nadi International Airport, Nadi; domestic airline operating charter and non-scheduled flights around Fiji.

Sunflower Airlines Ltd: POB 9452, Nadi International Airport, Nadi; tel. 723555; fax 720085; e-mail sun@is.com.fj; internet www.fiji.to; f. 1980; scheduled flights to domestic destinations, also charter services; Man. Dir DON IAN COLLINGWOOD.

Vanua Air Charters: Labasa; f. 1993; provides domestic charter and freight services; Proprs Ratu Sir KAMISESE MARA, CHARAN SINGH.

Tourism

Scenery, climate, fishing and diving attract visitors to Fiji, where tourism is an important industry. The number of foreign tourist arrivals increased by 10.4% (compared with the previous year) in 1999, when 409,955 people visited the country (excluding cruise-ship passengers who numbered 14,030 in that year). Receipts from tourism increased by 12.3% to $F541.2m. in 1999. In that year some 28.8% of visitors came from Australia, 17.6% from New Zealand, 15.2% from the USA, 9.8% from the United Kingdom and 9.2% from Japan. A total of 5,777 rooms in 186 hotels were available in 1999. The South Pacific Tourism Organization (formerly the Tourism Council of The South Pacific) is based in Suva. In 1998 the Government announced its intention further to develop the tourist industry in Fiji through the establishment of the Fiji Tourism Development Plan: 1998–2005. In April 1999 construction began on a new luxury resort at Korotoga, situated half-way between Suva and Nadi. The industry was severely affected by the coup of May 2000.

Fiji Hotel Association (FHA): 42 Gorrie St, POB 13560, Suva; tel. 302980; fax 300331; e-mail fha@is.com.fj; represents 72 hotels; Pres. ROBERT WADE; Chief Exec. OLIVIA PARETI.

Fiji Visitors' Bureau: POB 92, Suva; tel. 302433; fax 300970; e-mail infodesk@fijifvb.gov.fj; internet www.bulafiji.com; f. 1923; Chair. SITIVENI WELEILAKEBA; Chief Exec. SITIVENI YAQONA; Dir of Tourism ERONI LUVENIYALI.

FINLAND

Introductory Survey

Location, Climate, Language, Religion, Flag, Capital

The Republic of Finland lies in northern Europe, bordered to the far north by Norway and to the north-west by Sweden. Russia adjoins the whole of the eastern frontier. Finland's western and southern shores are washed by the Baltic Sea. The climate varies sharply, with warm summers and cold winters. The mean annual temperature is 5°C (41°F) in Helsinki and –0.4°C (31°F) in the far north. There are two official languages: more than 93% of the population speak Finnish and 6% speak Swedish. There is a small Lapp population in the north. Almost all of the inhabitants profess Christianity, and about 85% belong to the Evangelical Lutheran Church. The national flag (proportions 18 by 11) displays an azure blue cross (the upright to the left of centre) on a white background. The state flag has, at the centre of the cross, the national coat of arms (a yellow-edged red shield containing a golden lion and nine white roses). The capital is Helsinki.

Recent History

Finland formed part of the Kingdom of Sweden until 1809, when it became an autonomous Grand Duchy under the Russian Empire. During the Russian revolution of 1917 the territory proclaimed its independence. Following a brief civil war, a democratic Constitution was adopted in 1919. The Soviet regime that came to power in Russia attempted to regain control of Finland but acknowledged the country's independence in 1920.

Demands by the USSR for military bases in Finland and for the cession of part of the Karelian isthmus, in south-eastern Finland, were rejected by the Finnish Government in November 1939. As a result, the USSR attacked Finland, and the two countries fought the 'Winter War', a fiercely contested conflict lasting 15 weeks, before Finnish forces were defeated. Following its surrender, Finland ceded an area of 41,880 sq km (16,170 sq miles) to the USSR in March 1940. In the hope of recovering the lost territory, Finland joined Nazi Germany in attacking the USSR in 1941. However, a separate armistice between Finland and the USSR was concluded in 1944.

In accordance with a peace treaty signed in February 1947, Finland agreed to the transfer of about 12% of its pre-war territory (including the Karelian isthmus and the Petsamo area on the Arctic coast) to the USSR, and to the payment of reparations, which totalled about US $570m. when completed in 1952. Meanwhile, in April 1948 Finland and the USSR signed the Finno-Soviet Treaty of Friendship, Co-operation and Mutual Assistance (the YYA treaty), which was extended for periods of 20 years in 1955, 1970 and again in 1983. A major requirement of the treaty was that Finland repel any attack made on the USSR by Germany, or its allies, through Finnish territory. (The treaty was replaced by a non-military agreement in 1992, see below.)

Since independence in 1917, the politics of Finland have been characterized by coalition governments (including numerous minority coalitions) and the development of consensus between parties. The Finnish Social Democratic Party (Suomen Sosialidemokraattinen Puolue, SDP) and the Finnish Centre Party (Suomen Keskusta—Kesk) have usually been the dominant participants in government. The conservative opposition gained significant support at a general election in March 1979, following several years of economic crises. A new centre-left coalition Government was formed in May, however, by Dr Mauno Koivisto, a Social Democratic economist and former Prime Minister. This four-party Government, comprising Kesk, the SDP, the Swedish People's Party (Svenska folkpartiet, SFP) and the Finnish People's Democratic League (Suomen Kansan Demokraattinen Liitto, SKDL—an electoral alliance, which included the communists), continued to pursue deflationary economic policies, although there were disagreements within the Council of State (Cabinet) in 1981, over social welfare policy and budgetary matters.

Dr Urho Kekkonen, President since 1956, resigned in October 1981. Dr Koivisto was elected President in January 1982. He was succeeded as head of the coalition by a former Prime Minister, Kalevi Sorsa, a Social Democrat. Towards the end of 1982 the SKDL refused to support austerity measures or an increase in defence spending. This led to the re-formation of the coalition in December, without the SKDL, until the general election of March 1983.

At this election the SDP won 57 of the 200 seats in the Eduskunta (Parliament), compared with 52 in the 1979 election; while the conservative opposition National Coalition Party (Kansallinen Kokoomus—Kok) lost three seats. In May Sorsa formed another centre-left coalition, comprising the SDP, the SFP, Kesk and the Finnish Rural Party (Suomen Maaseudun Puolue, SMP): the coalition parties held a total of 122 parliamentary seats.

At a general election held in March 1987, the combined non-socialist parties gained a majority in the Eduskunta for the first time since the election of 1945. Although the SDP remained the largest single party, losing one seat and retaining 56, the system of modified proportional representation enabled Kok to gain an additional nine seats, winning a total of 53, while increasing its share of the votes cast by only 1%. President Koivisto eventually invited Harri Holkeri, a former Chairman of Kok, to form a coalition Government comprising Kok, the SDP, the SFP and the SMP, thus avoiding a polarization of the political parties within the Eduskunta. The four parties controlled 131 of the 200 seats. Holkeri became the first conservative Prime Minister since 1946, and Kesk joined the opposition for the first appreciable length of time since independence.

In February 1988 Koivisto retained office after the first presidential election by direct popular vote (in accordance with constitutional changes adopted in the previous year), following his campaign for a reduction in presidential power. He did not win the required absolute majority, however, and an electoral college was convened. Koivisto was re-elected after an endorsement by the Prime Minister, Holkeri, who had also contested the presidency and who had received the third highest number of direct votes (behind Paavo Väyrynen, the leader of Kesk).

At a general election held in March 1991, Kesk obtained 55 of the 200 seats in the Eduskunta, the SDP gained 48 seats, and Kok 40 seats. In April a coalition Government, comprising Kesk, Kok, the SFP and the Finnish Christian Union (Suomen Kristillinen Liitto, SKL), took office. The new coalition constituted the country's first wholly non-socialist Government for 25 years. The Chairman of Kesk, Esko Aho, became Prime Minister. In March 1993 President Koivisto announced that he would not present himself as a candidate for a third term in the forthcoming presidential election. In the first stage of the election, which took place in January 1994, the two most successful candidates were Martti Ahtisaari (the SDP candidate and a senior United Nations official), with 25.9% of the votes cast, and Elisabeth Rehn (the SFP candidate and Minister of Defence), with 22%. The Kesk candidate (Paavo Väyrynen) obtained 19.5% of the votes cast, and the Kok candidate 15.2%. Both of the leading candidates were firm supporters of Finland's application for membership of the European Union (EU, see p. 181), as the European Community (EC) had been restyled in late 1993. In accordance with constitutional changes adopted since the previous election (stipulating that, if no candidate gained more than 50% of the votes cast, the electorate should choose between the two candidates with the most votes), a second stage of the election took place on 6 February 1994. It was won by Ahtisaari (with 53.9% of the votes cast), who took office on 1 March.

At a general election held on 19 March 1995, the SDP obtained 63 of the 200 seats in the Eduskunta, Kesk secured 44 seats, Kok 39 seats, and the Left Alliance (Vasemmistoliitto Vänsterförbundet, formed in 1990 by a merger of the communist parties and the SKDL) 22 seats. A new coalition Government was formed in April, comprising the SDP, Kok, the SFP, the Left Alliance and the Green League (Vihreä Liitto). Paavo Lipponen, the leader of the SDP, replaced Aho as Prime Minister, and Sauli Niinistö, the Chairman of Kok, was appointed Deputy Prime Minister. The first election of Finnish representatives to the European Parliament was held in October 1996. The SDP performed relatively poorly, securing 21.5% of the votes cast, compared with 28.3% at the 1995 election to the Finnish Parliament, while Kesk achieved 24.6% (19.9% in 1995) and Kok 20.2% (17.9% in 1995). The disappointing result for the SDP was attributed, in part, to the Government's decision, a week earlier, to commit Finland to entering the exchange rate mechanism (ERM) of the EU's European Monetary System.

Following a general election held on 21 March 1999, the SDP remained the largest party in the Eduskunta, gaining 51 of the 200 seats. Kesk won 48 seats and Kok 46 in an election that was characterized by the second lowest rate of voter participation—68%—since 1945. In April the five parties of the outgoing Government—the SDP, Kok, the SFP, the Left Alliance and the Green League—agreed to form a new coalition. The terms of the new coalition agreement stipulated that the SDP leader, Paavo Lipponen, should remain in office as Prime Minister, while the leader of Kok, Sauli Niinistö, was reappointed as Minister of Finance. The remaining portfolios of the Council of State were redistributed among the coalition partners. Another element of the coalition agreement was that there should be no increase (in real terms) in public expenditure during the term in office of the new legislature.

Presidential elections were held in January and February 2000, at which Ahtisaari did not seek re-election, following his failure to secure the nomination of the SDP. In mid-January seven candidates contested the first round of the ballot, which was won by Tarja Halonen (the SDP candidate and Minister of Foreign Affairs), who received 40% of votes cast; the second largest share of the vote (34.4%) was obtained by Esko Aho (the Kesk candidate). As Halonen had failed to win 50% of the vote, a second round of voting was held on 6 February, contested by Halonen and Aho. This second stage of the election was won by Halonen (with 51.6% of the votes cast), who took office as the first female President on 1 March. Following the conclusion of the elections, a minor reorganization of the Council of State was effected, in which Halonen was replaced as Minister of Foreign Affairs by Erkki Tuomioja, the former Minister of Trade and Industry.

A new Constitution entered into force on 1 March 2000, under the provisions of which the executive power of the President was significantly reduced while the real authority of the Parliament was increased, with the power of decision-making being divided more equally between the Parliament, the Council of State and the President. According to the 1919 Constitution, the President appointed the Prime Minister and the other ministers; however, under the new Constitution, the Parliament elects the Prime Minister (who is then officially appointed by the President) and the other government ministers are appointed by the President on the basis of nominations by the Prime Minister. In addition, according to new constitutional provisions, the President was to co-operate more closely with the Council of State with regard to issues of foreign policy.

Following his defeat in the presidential election, the Chairman of the opposition Kesk, Aho, took leave from domestic politics for one year from August 2000 to lecture at Harvard University in the USA. His decision was believed to be a reflection of the stability of the government coalition, which, despite its disparate composition, seemed likely to last until 2003. Anneli Jäättenmäki, a former Minister of Justice, was elected to replace Aho during his sabbatical. At the municipal elections, which took place on 22 October 2000, however, the two principal parties in the coalition suffered losses whilst Kesk, under the leadership of Jäätteenmäki, secured the largest gains, winning 23.8% of the votes cast to become the largest municipal party. Voter participation for the local elections was only 55.8% of the electorate (compared with 61.3% in 1996).

In November 2000, the stability of the coalition Government was threatened by a controversial proposal by a Finnish electricity company to build a fifth nuclear reactor in Finland, the first such proposal in western Europe since the mid-1980s. The Government was believed to be divided over the issue, with the SDP Minister of Trade and Industry, Sinikka Mönkäre, in favour of the proposal while the Green League was strongly opposed to nuclear expansion and threatened to leave the coalition should the proposal be accepted.

In foreign affairs, Finland has traditionally maintained a neutral stance, although the pursuance of friendly relations with the USSR, and latterly Russia, has generally been regarded as a priority. In October 1989 Mikhail Gorbachev became the first Soviet Head of State to visit Finland since 1975, and recognized Finland's neutral status. The 1948 Finno-Soviet Treaty of Friendship, Co-operation and Mutual Assistance, which bound Finland to a military defence alliance with the USSR and prevented the country from joining any international organization (including the EC) whose members posed a military threat to the USSR, was replaced in January 1992 by a 10-year agreement, signed by Finland and Russia, which involved no military commitment. The agreement was to be automatically renewed for five-year periods unless annulled by either signatory. The new treaty also included undertakings by the two countries not to use force against each other and to respect the inviolability of their common border and each other's territorial integrity. In 1998 a Russian diplomat to Finland, reportedly involved in an incident of espionage, left the country at the request of the Finnish authorities; a second Russian diplomat, also allegedly involved in the incident, left the country voluntarily, while an official from the Finnish Ministry of Foreign Affairs was suspended. In June 2000 he was found guilty of espionage and passing secret EU documents to the Russian diplomats; the details of the case were declared secret for 30 years. In the same month the Finnish President, Halonen, paid an official visit to Russia and held a cordial meeting with the Russian President, Vladimir Putin. During 1992 Finland established diplomatic relations with the former Soviet republics.

In July 2000 Finland recalled its ambassador to Namibia at the express request of the Namibian Government. He had not been accused of any impropriety, and the Namibian Government refused to either confirm or deny the dismissal, however it was believed that he had been asked to leave after openly criticizing the Namibian Government.

Finland joined the United Nations and the Nordic Council (see p. 237) in 1955 but became a full member of the European Free Trade Association (EFTA, see p. 178) only in 1986. In 1989 Finland joined the Council of Europe (see p. 165). A free-trade agreement between Finland and the EC took effect in 1974. In March 1992 the Finnish Government formally applied to join the EC, despite opposition from farmers, who feared the impact of membership on Finland's strongly-protected agricultural sector. In a referendum on the question of Finland's accession to membership of the EU, which was held on 16 October 1994, 56.9% of the votes cast were in favour of membership, and in November the treaty of accession was ratified after protracted debate in the Eduskunta. Opponents of EU membership highlighted the benefits of Finland's traditional policy of neutrality, particularly with regard to Russian national security considerations, and warned that the country would now be increasingly forced to identify with Western security policy. The Government declared, however, that Finland's neutral stance would not be compromised either by joining the EU or by its stated intention to participate in NATO's 'partnership for peace' programme, and announced that it would not seek full membership of NATO (see p. 241) or Western European Union (WEU, see p. 286). The decision not to apply for membership of NATO was reiterated in May 1995 by the new Prime Minister, Paavo Lipponen. Finland left EFTA and joined the EU, as scheduled, on 1 January 1995.

Finland has proved its commitment to European integration. For instance, the so-called 'rainbow coalition', formed in 1995 and renewed in 1999, ensured the country's adherence to the economic 'convergence' criteria for Stage III of economic and monetary union (EMU), which commenced on 1 January 1999. In July Finland assumed the presidency of the EU for the first time. During its six-month incumbency the Government had intended to promote economic and cultural links in the so-called 'Northern Dimension'—the Nordic countries, the Baltic states and Russia. In the event, this agenda was superseded by the conflict over the Serbian region of Kosovo and Metohija in Yugoslavia, which led to Western military intervention from March. Finland was deemed to have distinguished itself through its diplomacy, in particular the role of the Finnish President, which was important in securing an end to the hostilities in Yugoslavia.

Government

Finland has a republican Constitution, under the provisions of which executive power is divided between the Parliament (Eduskunta), the Council of State (Cabinet) and the President. The unicameral Parliament has 200 members, elected by universal adult suffrage for four years on the basis of proportional representation. The President is elected for six years by direct popular vote. Legislative power is exercised by Parliament. The Parliament elects the Prime Minister, who is then appointed by the President. The other government ministers are appointed by the President on the basis of nominations by the Prime Minister. Finland is divided into 452 municipalities, which are guaranteed self-government and are entitled to levy taxes. The province of Ahvenanmaa (the Åland Islands) has rights of legislation in internal affairs (see separate section at end of chapter).

Defence

In August 2000 the armed forces of Finland numbered 31,700 (of whom 23,100 were conscripts serving up to 12 months), comprising an army of 24,000 (19,000 conscripts), an air force of 2,700 (1,500 conscripts) and a navy of 5,000 (2,600 conscripts). There were also some 485,000 reserves and 3,400 frontier guards. The proposed defence budget for 2001 was 9,544m. markkaa (equivalent to 4.6% of total proposed budgetary expenditure).

Economic Affairs

In 1998, according to estimates by the World Bank, Finland's gross national product (GNP), measured at average 1996–98 prices, was US $125,091m., equivalent to $24,280 per head (or $20,641 per head on an international purchasing-power parity basis). During 1990–98 it was estimated that GNP per head increased in real terms at an average annual rate of 1.8%. Over the same period, the population increased by an average of 0.5% per year. In 1999, according to preliminary World Bank data, Finland's GNP was about $122,900m. ($23,780 per head). The country's gross domestic product (GDP) increased, in real terms, by an average of 5.1% per year in 1995–99. Real GDP increased by 5.3% in 1998 and by 4.4% in 1999.

Agriculture (including hunting, forestry and fishing) contributed an estimated 3.6% of GDP in 1999 and employed 6.3% of the working population in that year. Forestry is the most important branch of the sector, with products of the wood and paper industries providing about 28.5% of export earnings in 1999. Animal husbandry is the predominant form of farming. The major crops are barley, sugar beet and oats. During 1995–99 agricultural GDP increased, in real terms, by an average of 0.5% per year; agricultural GDP declined by 3.7% in 1998 and by 2.2% in 1999.

Industry (including mining, manufacturing, construction and power), provided 32.2% of GDP in 1999 and employed 27.8% of the working population in the same year. Industrial GDP increased, in real terms, by an average of 7.0% per year during 1995–99; industrial GDP grew by 8.2% in 1998 and by 6.2% in 1999.

Mining and quarrying contributed 0.3% of GDP in 1999 and employed 0.2% of the working population in the same year. The GDP of the mining sector increased, in real terms, at an average rate of 3.4% per year during 1995–99; mining GDP declined by 17.8% in 1998 but increased by 18.0% in 1999. Gold is the major mineral export, and zinc ore, copper ore and lead ore are also mined in small quantities.

Manufacturing provided 24.4% of GDP in 1999 and in the same year employed 20.1% of the working population. The most important branches of manufacturing are the electronics industry, particularly mobile telephones, transport equipment, metal products and food and beverages. The GDP of the manufacturing sector increased, in real terms, at an average rate of 7.3% per year during 1995–99; the sector's GDP increased by 9.5% in 1998 and by 7.1% in 1999.

Of total energy generated in 2000, 41% was derived from petroleum, natural gas and other bio-combustibles, 28% from nuclear power and 16% from hydro-electric power. At the end of 2000 there were four nuclear reactors in operation, and plans for a fifth reactor, which would increase nuclear power's share of electricity generation to 35%, had been submitted to Parliament for approval. Imports of mineral fuels comprised 8.5% of the total cost of imports in 1999.

Services engaged 65.9% of the employed labour force in 1999 and provided 64.2% of GDP in that year. In real terms, the combined GDP of the service sectors increased at an average rate of 4.3% per year during 1995–99; growth in the sector's GDP was recorded at 4.4% in 1998 and by 3.8% in 1999.

In 1999 Finland recorded a visible trade surplus of US $11,655m., and there was a surplus of $7,141m. on the current account of the balance of payments. In 1999 the principal source of imports was Germany (15.3%); other major sources were Sweden (11.2%), the USA (7.9%), Russia (7.2%) and the United Kingdom (6.6%). Germany was also the principal market for exports in the same year (13.0%); other major purchasers were Sweden (10.0%), the United Kingdom (9.1%), the USA (7.9%) and France (5.3%). The EU accounted for some 53.8% of exports and 52.8% of imports in 1999. The principal exports in 1999 were machinery and transport equipment (mainly electronic products, notably mobile telephones), basic manufactures (mainly paper, paperboard and manufactures) and crude materials (mainly wood and pulp). The principal imports were machinery and transport equipment, basic manufactures, chemicals and related products and miscellaneous manufactured articles.

Finland's overall budget surplus for 1999 was 1,411m. markkaa (equivalent to 0.2% of GDP). At the end of September 1999 Finland's gross public debt amounted to some €49,340m.. The average annual rate of inflation was 1.8% during 1990–99. Consumer prices increased by an average of 1.4% in 1998, by 1.2% in 1999 and by 3.4% in 2000. The rate of unemployment declined from 15.4% in 1995 to 10.4% in 1999.

Finland is a member of the Nordic Council (see p. 237) and the Organisation for Economic Co-operation and Development (p. 247). In January 1995 it left the European Free Trade Association and joined the European Union (EU, see p. 181).

In the early 1990s the Finnish economy was characterized by recession and crisis in the financial sector, precipitated by the break-up of the USSR on which much of Finland's economy had depended. In the mid-1990s, however, recovery commenced as industrial production and exports improved and Finland's membership of the EU helped stimulate investment in the economy. Finland's improved economic performance facilitated its participation in the final stage of European economic and monetary union (EMU), the introduction of the European single currency, the euro, which came into effect (in 11 countries) on 1 January 1999. Between 1995 and 2000 the Finnish economy expanded consistently faster than the European average. The loss of control over monetary policy under EMU became an increasing problem for Finland as its economic cycle demanded higher interest rates than those set by the European Central Bank, to prevent the risk of rising inflation. However, strict fiscal policy proved effective and although inflation in 2000 was higher than in most European countries, it remained moderate. The strength of the Finnish economy was largely the result of a surge in exports, which benefited both from the weakness of the euro and from improved economic growth inside the euro zone increasing the demand for goods. Much of Finland's success was due to the mobile telephone manufacturer, Nokia, which alone accounted for more than 20% of exports in 1999, representing a divergence away from the traditional industries of pulp and paper production and metal engineering. However, economic development was uneven with the principal cities and areas dominated by the information technology industry (which had grown up around Nokia) flourishing, while many northern and eastern parts of the country were depressed with unemployment far above the national average. Even the national average for unemployment, although significantly reduced, remained high at an estimated 9.6% in 2000, with the unemployed lacking the skills to fill the jobs available in the high-technology sector. Presenting the 2001 budget in August 2000, the Finnish Government announced tax cuts valued at 6,400 markkaa, reducing the larger than average tax burden in the country. In response to fears of the risk of increasing inflation, the Government argued that although the tax reductions might add to consumer demand they would also help to minimize pay settlements at the end of 2000. It was hoped that the reduction in tax levels on low-paid jobs would encourage those dependent on state benefits to enter the labour force, thus reducing unemployment.

Social Welfare

Benefits are paid to compensate for loss of income owing to sickness, unemployment, maternity, old age, disability and death of a family's principal source of income. Child allowances and living allowances are also paid. Pension coverage consists of a basic pension scheme, covering all persons who are permanently resident in Finland, and earnings-related pension schemes. Some 90% of employees are members of unemployment insurance funds. All children under seven years of age are entitled to day care provided by local authorities. (In 1995 about one-half of children of that age were exercising their entitlement.) The public health services (including both primary and specialized health care) cover the whole population, and are financed mainly by the state and local authorities. The National Health Act of 1972 provided for the establishment of health centres in every municipality. In 1994 Finland had 46,400 hospital beds and there were 14,500 physicians working in the country. Of total budgetary expenditure by the central

Government in 2001, 44,694m. markkaa (21.4%) was allocated to the Ministry of Social Welfare and Health.

Education

Compulsory education was introduced in 1921. By the 1977/78 school year, the whole country had transferred to a new comprehensive education system. Tuition is free and the core curriculum is the same for all students. The right to pre-school education, and the corresponding obligation for local authorities to provide it, was due to come into force in August 2001. Compulsory attendance lasts for nine years, and is divided into a six-year lower stage, beginning at the age of seven, and a three-year upper stage (or lower secondary stage), beginning at the age of 13. After comprehensive school, the pupil may continue his or her studies, either at a general upper secondary school, or a vocational upper secondary school. The upper secondary school curriculum is designed for three years but may be completed in two or four years. Courses leading to basic vocational qualifications take three years to complete. The matriculation examination taken at the end of three years of general upper secondary school gives eligibility for higher education as do three-year vocational diplomas. Higher education is provided by 20 universities and 29 polytechnics. Of total budgetary expenditure by the central Government in 2001, 30,200m. markkaa (14.4%) was allocated to the Ministry of Education.

Public Holidays

2001: 1 January (New Year's Day), 6 January (Epiphany), 13 April (Good Friday), 16 April (Easter Monday), 30 April–1 May (May Day), 24 May (Ascension Day), 4 June (Whitsun), 25–26 June (Midsummer Day), 1 November (All Saints' Day), 6 December (Independence Day), 24–26 December (Christmas).

2002: 1 January (New Year's Day), 6 January (Epiphany), 29 March (Good Friday), 1 April (Easter Monday), 30 April–1 May (May Day), 9 May (Ascension Day), 20 May (Whitsun), 21–22 June (Midsummer Day), 1 November (All Saints' Day), 6 December (Independence Day), 24–26 December (Christmas).

Weights and Measures

The metric system is in force.

Statistical Survey

Source (unless otherwise specified): Statistics Finland, 00022 Helsinki; tel. (9) 17342220; fax (9) 17342279.
Note: Figures in this Survey include data for the autonomous Åland Islands.

Area and Population

AREA, POPULATION AND DENSITY

Area (sq km)	
Land	304,529
Inland water	33,615
Total	338,145*
Population (census results)	
31 December 1990	4,998,478
31 December 1995	
Males	2,491,701
Females	2,625,125
Total	5,116,826
Population (official estimates at 31 December)	
1997	5,147,349
1998	5,159,646
1999	5,171,302
Density (per sq km) at 31 December 1999†	17.0

* 130,559 sq miles.
† Excluding inland waters.

REGIONS (estimated population at 31 December 1999)

	Land Area (sq km)*	Population	Density (per sq km)
Uusimaa (Nyland)	6,366	1,290,619	202.7
Itä-Uusimaa (Östra Nyland) . .	2,747	89,094	32.4
Varsinais-Suomi (Egentliga Finland)	10,623	445,542	41.9
Satakunta	8,290	239,950	28.9
Kanta-Häme (Egentliga Tavastland)	5,204	165,190	31.7
Pirkanmaa (Birkaland) . .	12,605	447,023	35.5
Päijät-Häme (Päijänne-Tavastland)	5,133	197,347	38.4
Kymenlaakso (Kymmenedalen) .	5,106	188,633	36.9
Etelä-Karjala (Södra Karelen) .	5,674	137,377	24.2
Etelä-Savo (Södra Savolax) . .	14,436	168,770	11.7
Pohjois-Savo (Norra Savolax) . .	16,510	253,792	15.4
Pohjois-Karjala (Norra Karelen) .	17,782	172,551	9.7
Keski-Suomi (Mellersta Finland) .	16,248	260,513	16.0
Etelä-Pohjanmaa (Södra Österbotten)	13,458	196,795	14.6
Pohjanmaa (Österbotten) . . .	7,675	173,533	22.6
Keski-Pohjanmaa (Mellersta Österbotten)	5,286	71,646	13.6
Pohjois-Pohjanmaa (Norra Österbotten)	35,291	362,388	10.3
Kainuu (Kajanaland) . . .	21,567	91,081	4.2
Lappi (Lappland)	93,003	194,352	2.1
Ahvenanmaa (Åland) . . .	1,527	25,706	16.8
Total	304,529	5,171,302	17.0

* Excluding inland waters, totalling 33,615 sq km.

PRINCIPAL TOWNS (estimated population at 31 December 1999)

Helsinki (Helsingfors) (capital)	551,123
Espoo (Esbo)	209,667
Tampere (Tammerfors)	193,174
Vantaa (Vanda)	176,386
Turku (Åbo)	172,107
Oulu (Uleåborg)	117,670
Lahti	95,666
Kuopio	86,575
Jyväskylä	77,879
Pori (Björneborg)	76,220
Lappeenranta (Villmanstrand)	57,583
Vaasa (Vasa)	56,658
Kotka	55,238
Joensuu	51,514
Hämeenlinna (Tavastehus)	45,980

BIRTHS, MARRIAGES AND DEATHS

	Registered live births*		Registered marriages†		Registered deaths*	
	Number	Rate (per 1,000)	Number	Rate (per 1,000)	Number	Rate (per 1,000)
1991 . .	65,395	13.0	24,732	5.0	49,294	9.8
1992 . .	66,877	13.2	23,093	4.6	49,523	9.8
1993 . .	64,826	12.8	24,660	4.9	50,488	10.1
1994 . .	65,231	12.8	24,898	4.9	48,000	9.4
1995 . .	63,067	12.3	23,737	4.6	49,280	9.6
1996 . .	60,723	11.8	24,464	4.8	49,167	9.6
1997 . .	59,329	11.5	23,444	4.6	49,108	9.6
1998 . .	57,108	11.1	24,023	4.7	49,262	9.6
1999 . .	57,574	11.1	24,271	4.7	49,345	9.6

* Including Finnish nationals temporarily outside the country.
† Data relate only to marriages in which the bride was domiciled in Finland.

Expectation of life (years at birth, 1996): males 73.0; females 80.5.

ECONOMICALLY ACTIVE POPULATION*
(annual averages, '000 persons aged 15 to 74 years)

	1997	1998	1999
Agriculture, forestry and fishing . . .	153	144	144
Mining and quarrying	6	6	5
Manufacturing	436	447	460
Electricity, gas and water	22	22	22
Construction	130	139	149
Trade, restaurants and hotels . . .	329	339	355
Transport, storage and communications . .	164	170	168
Finance, insurance, real estate and business services	240	249	267
Community, social and personal services .	684	700	719
Activities not adequately defined . . .	7	8	6
Total employed	2,169	2,222	2,296
Unemployed	314	285	261
Total labour force	2,484	2,507	2,557

* Excluding persons on compulsory military service (25,000 in 1997, 25,000 in 1998, 21,000 in 1999).

Agriculture

PRINCIPAL CROPS
('000 metric tons; farms with arable land of 1 hectare or more)

	1997	1998	1999
Wheat	464	397	254
Barley	2,004	1,316	1,568
Rye	47	49	24
Oats	1,243	975	990
Mixed grain	49	35	44
Potatoes	754	591	791
Rapeseed	93	64	88
Sugar beet	1,360	892	1,172

LIVESTOCK

('000 head at 1 May; farms with arable land of 1 hectare or more)

	1997	1998	1999
Horses*	53.1	55.2	54.5
Cattle	1,142.4	1,117.1	1,086.8
Sheep	150.1	128.3	106.6
Reindeer	203.0	196.0	195.0
Pigs†	1,467.0	1,401.0	1,351.3
Poultry	5,439.3	4,986.5	4,386.6
Beehives‡	40.0	42.0	39.0

* Including horses not on farms.
† Including piggeries of dairies.   ‡ '000 hives.

LIVESTOCK PRODUCTS ('000 metric tons)

	1997	1998	1999
Beef	99.2	93.5	90.2
Veal	0.4	0.3	0.2
Pig meat	179.7	184.5	181.9
Poultry meat	52.7	61.1	66.1
Cows' milk*	2,301.0	2,293.7	2,324.6
Butter†	56.5	57.3	59.7
Cheese‡	82.9	87.7	87.6
Hen eggs	66.7	63.9	58.9

* Million litres.
† Including amount of butter in vegetable oil mixture.
‡ Excluding curd.

Forestry

ROUNDWOOD REMOVALS ('000 cu m, excl. bark)

	1996	1997	1998
Sawlogs, veneer logs and logs for sleepers	21,210	24,976	25,585
Pulpwood	20,968	22,312	24,053
Other industrial wood	325	325	n.a.
Fuel wood	4,094	4,041	4,032
Total	46,597	51,329	53,670

Source: FAO, *Yearbook of Forest Products.*

SAWNWOOD PRODUCTION ('000 cu m, incl. railway sleepers)

	1996	1997	1998
Coniferous (softwood)	9,300	10,600	11,300
Broadleaved (hardwood)	70	60	60
Total	9,370	10,660	11,360

Source: FAO, *Yearbook of Forest Products.*

Fishing

('000 metric tons, live weight)

	1996	1997	1998
Capture	179.0	180.1	181.3
Roaches	8.9	9.0	9.0
Northern pike	12.3	12.4	12.4
European perch	17.6	17.9	17.9
Vendace	6.0	6.0	6.0
Atlantic herring	94.5	91.5	86.8
European sprat	14.4	19.9	27.0
Aquaculture	17.7	16.4	16.0
Rainbow trout	17.5	16.3	15.9
Total catch	196.7	196.5	197.3

Source: FAO, *Yearbook of Fishery Statistics.*

Mining

('000 metric tons, unless otherwise indicated)

	1996	1997	1998
Copper ore*	9.2	8.5	9.5
Lead ore	1.2	2.2	1.8
Zinc ore*	26.3	31.2	30.7
Gold (kilograms)	1,670	1,900	2,370

* Figures refer to metal content.

Industry

SELECTED PRODUCTS ('000 metric tons, unless otherwise indicated)

	1997	1998*	1999*
Cellulose	5,534	6,724	6,977
Newsprint	1,557	1,483	1,490
Other paper, boards and cardboards	10,635	11,221	11,433
Plywoods and veneers ('000 cubic metres)	965	1,014	1,103
Cement	1,152	1,100	1,162
Pig iron and ferro-alloys	2,786	2,920	2,954
Electricity (net, million kWh)	65,950	67,094	66,629
Sugar	161	149	n.a.
Rolled steel products (metric tons)	3,351	3,715	3,783
Copper cathodes (metric tons)	116,328	122,894	115,080
Cigarettes (million)	6,473	5,510	n.a.

* Preliminary data.

Finance

CURRENCY AND EXCHANGE RATES

Monetary Units
100 penniä (singular: penni) = 1 markka (Finnmark).

Sterling, Dollar and Euro Equivalents (29 December 2000)
£1 sterling = 9.5349 markkaa;
US $1 = 6.3898 markkaa;
€1 = 5.9457 markkaa;
100 markkaa = £10.49 = $15.65 = €16.82.

Average Exchange Rate (markkaa per US $)
1998   5.3441
1999   5.5808
2000   6.4535

Note: Since the introduction of the euro, with Finnish participation, on 1 January 1999, a fixed exchange rate of €1 = 5.94573 markkaa has been in operation.

BUDGET (million markkaa)*

Revenue	1999	2000†	2001‡
Taxes and other levies	157,933	199,579	209,172
on income and property	63,718	70,001	74,695
on turnover	53,654	57,665	62,120
Excise duties	26,962	27,614	27,630
Miscellaneous revenues	50,621	26,853	26,645
Sub-total	208,554	226,432	235,817
Interest on investments and profits received	3,886	4,255	4,634
Loans receivable	683	606	925
Total	213,124	199,579	209,172

Expenditure			1999	2000†	2001‡
President of the Republic	.	.	45	40	37
Parliament	.	.	364	395	496
Council of State	.	.	211	209	222
Ministry of Foreign Affairs		.	3,652	3,635	3,866
Ministry of Justice	.	.	3,121	3,137	3,117
Ministry of the Interior	.	.	6,576	7,069	7,524
Ministry of Defence	.	.	9,230	9,828	9,544
Ministry of Finance	.	.	28,859	29,636	31,221
Ministry of Education	.	.	26,645	27,924	30,200
Ministry of Agriculture and Forestry	.	.	12,374	13,234	13,997
Ministry of Transport and Communications	.	.	7,485	7,363	7,061
Ministry of Trade and Commerce	.		4,818	4,809	5,184
Ministry of Social Welfare and Health	.	.	41,930	43,491	44,694
Ministry of Labour	.	.	12,105	11,316	11,361
Ministry of the Environment	.	.	3,959	3,755	3,639
Public debt	.	.	49,340	33,735	27,008
Total	.	.	211,713	199,575	209,172

* Figures refer to the General Budget only, excluding the operations of the Social Insurance Institution and of other social security funds with their own budgets.

† Projections.

‡ Proposals.

INTERNATIONAL RESERVES (US $ million at 31 December)

			1997	1998	1999
Gold*	.	.	321.4	427.8	459.0
IMF special drawing rights	.	.	326.1	348.5	290.1
Reserve position in IMF	.	.	558.8	837.8	637.3
Foreign exchange	.	.	7,531.7	8,508.2	6,747.0
Total	.	.	8,738.0	10,122.3	8,133.4

* Valued at market-related prices.

Source: IMF, *International Financial Statistics.*

MONEY SUPPLY (million markkaa at 31 December)

			1997	1998	1999*
Currency in circulation	.	.	17,817	17,689	3,350
Demand deposits at banking institutions	.	.	201,557	211,632	38,277

* Figures for 1999 are in million euros.

Source: IMF, *International Financial Statistics.*

COST OF LIVING (Consumer Price Index; base: 1995 = 100)

			1997	1998	1999
Food	.	.	99.6	101.3	101.0
Beverages and tobacco	.	.	104.6	106.0	107.8
Clothing and footwear	.	.	99.9	98.5	99.5
Rent, heating and lighting	.	.	102.5	104.8	106.1
Furniture, household equipment	.		101.0	101.2	102.4
All items	.	.	101.8	103.2	104.4

NATIONAL ACCOUNTS (million markkaa at current prices)
National Income and Product

			1997	1998	1999*
Compensation of employees	.	.	308,407	330,984	346,758
Operating surplus	.	.	141,993	161,991	168,314
Domestic factor incomes	.	.	450,400	492,975	516,072
Consumption of fixed capital	.		106,286	111,656	116,562
Gross domestic product at factor cost	.	.	556,686	604,631	632,634
Indirect taxes	.	.	94,669	100,838	105,319
Less Subsidies	.	.	15,823	15,946	15,995
GDP in purchasers' values	.	.	635,532	689,523	721,958
Factor income received from abroad ⎱ *Less* Factor income paid abroad ⎰			−12,700	−16,829	−13,785
Gross national product	.	.	622,832	672,694	708,173
Less Consumption of fixed capital			106,286	111,656	116,562
National income in market prices	.	.	516,546	561,038	591,611

* Provisional figures.

Expenditure on the Gross Domestic Product

	1997	1998	1999*
Government final consumption expenditure	142,641	149,428	155,376
Private final consumption expenditure	323,563	346,021	363,529
Increase in stocks . . .	2,781	6,816	3,522
Gross fixed capital formation . .	114,300	128,913	135,956
Statistical discrepancy . . .	398	−2,472	4,163
Total domestic expenditure	583,684	628,706	662,546
Exports of goods and services	248,306	267,467	270,756
Less Imports of goods and services	196,458	206,650	211,344
GDP in purchasers' values . .	635,532	689,523	721,958

* Provisional figures.

Gross Domestic Product by Economic Activity

	1997	1998	1999*
Agriculture, hunting, forestry and fishing . . .	23,480	22,986	23,107
Mining and quarrying . .	1,717	1,643	1,675
Manufacturing . . .	136,736	153,040	155,376
Electricity, gas and water . .	13,291	14,131	13,159
Construction	25,723	30,298	35,314
Trade, restaurants and hotels .	68,157	73,274	76,999
Transport, storage and communication	55,311	60,890	64,366
Finance, insurance and business services	51,092	56,120	61,451
Owner-occupied dwellings . .	51,353	54,326	57,397
Public administration and welfare	103,296	107,975	111,784
Other community, social and personal services . . .	32,566	35,031	38,121
Sub-total	562,722	609,714	638,749
Less Imputed bank service charge	14,858	14,439	15,526
GDP in basic values . .	547,864	595,275	623,223
Commodity taxes . . .	93,359	99,354	103,722
Less Commodity subsidies . .	5,691	5,106	4,987
GDP in purchasers' values . .	635,532	689,523	721,958

* Provisional figures.

BALANCE OF PAYMENTS (US $ million)

	1997	1998	1999
Exports of goods f.o.b.	41,148	43,393	41,983
Imports of goods f.o.b.	−29,604	−30,903	−30,328
Trade balance	11,544	12,490	11,655
Exports of services	6,640	6,703	6,524
Imports of services	−8,235	−7,767	−7,522
Balance on goods and services	9,949	11,427	10,656
Other income received	4,136	4,237	5,208
Other income paid	−6,600	−7,320	−7,690
Balance on goods, services and income	7,485	8,143	8,174
Current transfers received	1,210	1,523	1,606
Current transfers paid	−2,062	−2,521	−2,639
Current balance	6,633	7,345	7,141
Capital account (net)	247	91	115
Direct investment abroad	−5,260	−18,698	−5,954
Direct investment from abroad	2,129	12,029	4,754
Portfolio investment assets	−4,600	−3,906	−14,317
Portfolio investment liabilities	3,843	3,866	13,127
Financial derivatives assets	−72	89	—
Financial derivatives liabilities	114	−725	−419
Other investment assets	−2,201	331	−4,967
Other investment liabilities	3,072	5,292	2,921
Net errors and omissions	−1,600	−5,418	−2,499
Overall balance	2,304	296	−97

Source: IMF, *International Financial Statistics*.

External Trade

PRINCIPAL COMMODITIES (distribution by SITC, million markkaa)

Imports c.i.f.	1997	1998	1999
Food and live animals	9,027.3	9,268.5	9,019.4
Crude materials (inedible) except fuels	10,999.4	11,202.7	11,451.7
Metalliferous ores and metal scrap	5,000.2	4,665.0	5,002.5
Mineral fuels, lubricants, etc.	15,499.2	12,735.3	14,901.3
Petroleum, petroleum products, etc.	10,357.6	7,964.6	11,102.4
Crude petroleum oils, etc.	7,303.9	5,803.6	8,181.2
Refined petroleum products	2,909.7	2,046.0	2,796.9
Chemicals and related products	18,732.0	19,276.7	19,508.0
Chemical elements and compounds	3,210.0	2,789.3	2,972.4
Plastic materials, etc.	3,265.5	3,442.8	3,223.0
Basic manufactures	21,568.4	22,484.4	20,875.7
Textile yarn, fabrics, etc.	3,034.2	3,221.0	3,103.5
Iron and steel	5,551.9	5,610.5	4,876.9
Machinery and transport equipment	63,350.0	75,234.5	75,927.2
Non-electric machinery	25,789.6	29,832.5	20,875.7
Electrical machinery, apparatus, etc.	22,780.9	26,830.0	29,038.4
Transport equipment	14,769.6	18,571.9	19,071.1
Road vehicles and parts*	11,511.2	13,992.8	14,236.9
Passenger motor cars (excl. buses)	5,510.7	7,185.8	7,484.8
Miscellaneous manufactured articles	17,705.6	18,179.9	18,793.8
Scientific instruments, watches, etc.	2,920.3	3,082.6	3,264.7
Total (incl. others)	160,994.7	172,819.2	175,842.7

* Excluding tyres, engines and electrical parts.

Exports f.o.b.	1997	1998	1999
Food and live animals	5,211.0	4,462.0	3,655.2
Crude materials (inedible) except fuels	17,111.7	16,046.0	16,307.5
Wood, lumber and cork	9,130.1	8,983.6	9,141.2
Shaped or simply worked wood	7,531.4	8,522.1	8,365.8
Sawn coniferous lumber	8,203.8	7,433.4	8,254.5
Pulp and waste paper	4,204.3	3,822.9	4,587.5
Chemical wood pulp	3,972.6	3,580.5	4,291.9
Mineral fuels, lubricants, etc.	4,935.0	4,292.3	5,631.8
Petroleum, petroleum products, etc.	4,618.5	4,136.6	5,536.2
Refined petroleum products	4,533.8	4,096.4	5,490.6
Chemicals and related products	13,707.0	14,287.7	14,551.7
Basic manufactures	73,892.6	78,710.6	77,250.7
Wood and cork manufactures (excl. furniture)	4,702.0	4,855.1	4,767.0
Paper, paperboard and manufactures	43,689.0	48,317.5	47,810.9
Paper and paperboard	39,239.4	44,027.5	43,949.7
Newsprint paper	3,271.4	3,404.5	3,423.7
Other printing and writing paper in bulk	23,336.4	27,847.0	27,626.6
Kraft paper and paperboard	2,694.6	2,585.3	2,598.3
Iron and steel	9,807.5	10,402.4	9,571.6
Non-ferrous metals	6,092.2	5,294.8	5,766.6
Machinery and transport equipment	82,678.5	96,271.2	99,139.4
Non-electric machinery	34,773.7	35,672.3	32,271.7
Electrical machinery, apparatus, etc.	35,969.9	47,217.4	53,224.6
Transport equipment	11,934.9	13,381.4	13,643.1
Ships and boats	4,735.7	5,578.8	5,962.3
Miscellaneous manufactured articles	13,041.6	13,715.6	13,376.4
Total (incl. others)	212,840.4	230,568.7	232,601.4

PRINCIPAL TRADING PARTNERS (million markkaa)*

Imports c.i.f.	1997	1998	1999
Belgium/Luxembourg	4,056.1	4,550.3	4,213.3†
China, People's Republic	2,876.8	3,171.7	4,102.0
Denmark	5,469.1	6,175.1	6,442.2
Estonia	2,189.0	3,045.4	3,208.9
France	7,748.7	8,433.2	7,550.3
Germany	23,339.8	26,191.7	26,891.2
Italy	6,471.1	7,137.4	6,564.6
Japan	8,596.1	9,768.2	10,991.7
Netherlands	6,477.8	7,302.6	7,112.4
Norway	5,905.2	6,016.1	6,325.9
Russia	12,532.2	11,360.3	12,702.6
Spain	2,272.9	2,922.3	2,809.4
Sweden	19,469.8	20,243.4	19,740.1
United Kingdom	12,589.0	12,552.1	11,580.0
USA	11,807.2	14,148.1	13,847.3
Total (incl. others)	160,994.7	172,819.2	175,842.7

Exports f.o.b.	1997	1998	1999
Belgium/Luxembourg	4,919.8	5,759.8	6,032.9†
China, People's Republic	3,806.7	6,766.0	5,743.9
Denmark	6,543.5	6,464.2	6,579.6
Estonia	6,758.6	7,597.2	7,021.4
France	9,019.6	11,732.1	12,258.7
Germany	23,450.5	27,277.0	30,353.9
Italy	6,333.8	8,863.2	8,796.6
Netherlands	8,769.2	10,441.3	10,123.8
Norway	6,229.6	7,552.5	6,507.1
Russia	15,258.9	13,804.4	9,485.4
Spain	4,626.4	5,805.7	6,273.3
Sweden	20,925.8	21,770.8	23,383.0
United Kingdom	21,312.8	21,255.5	21,264.5
USA	14,783.1	16,845.3	18,384.5
Total (incl. others)	212,840.4	230,568.7	232,601.4

* Imports by country of production; exports by country of consumption.
† Excluding trade with Luxembourg.

Transport

RAILWAYS (traffic)

	1997	1998	1999
Passenger-km (million)	3,376	3,377	3,415
Freight ton-km (million)	9,856	9,885	9,753

ROAD TRAFFIC (registered motor vehicles at 31 December)

	1997	1998	1999
Passenger cars	1,948,126	2,021,116	2,082,580
Buses and coaches	8,450	9,040	9,487
Lorries and vans	266,944	280,610	293,707

SHIPPING

Merchant Fleet (registered at 31 December)

	1996	1997	1998
Number of vessels	274	277	284
Total displacement ('000 grt)	1,511	1,559	1,629

Source: Lloyd's Register of Shipping, *World Fleet Statistics*.

1999: Number of vessels 620; Total displacement ('000 grt) 1,715.

International Sea-borne Freight Traffic

	1997	1998	1999
Number of vessels entered	25,203	26,255	27,705
Goods ('000 metric tons):			
Loaded	36,164	37,524	39,307
Unloaded	39,018	39,070	38,196

CANAL TRAFFIC

	1997	1998	1999
Vessels in transit	74,963	49,319	50,819*
Timber rafts in transit	2,422	1,181	n.a.
Goods carried ('000 metric tons)	5,471	4,493	4,230
Passengers carried ('000)	356	n.a.	n.a.†

* Excludes vessels on self-service lock canals.

† In 2000 some lock canals were converted into self-service lock canals, for which only the total number of lock uses can be included. These figures are therefore no longer available.

CIVIL AVIATION (traffic on scheduled services, '000)

	1997	1998	1999
Kilometres flown	105,000	108,000	108,000
Passenger-kilometres	11,924,000	13,096,000	12,916,000
Cargo ton-kilometres	312,596	295,654	336,375

Tourism

NUMBER OF NIGHTS AT ACCOMMODATION FACILITIES

Country of Domicile	1997	1998	1999
France	118,523	122,914	140,498
Germany	453,953	458,235	483,507
Italy	103,971	119,736	140,764
Japan	132,385	120,541	129,002
Netherlands	122,308	142,637	149,449
Norway	164,280	168,803	195,169
Russia	549,104	540,337	388,556
Sweden	626,451	570,640	581,447
United Kingdom	248,470	290,572	319,925
USA	198,754	201,037	222,854
Total (incl. others)	3,645,854	3,700,396	3,773,959

Communications Media

	1997	1998	1999
Telephone lines ('000)	2,861	2,855	2,850
Mobile cellular telephones ('000 subscribers)	2,163	2,947	3,364
Television receivers ('000)*	1,947	1,972	1,994
Book production: titles	12,717	12,887	13,173
Newspapers and periodicals	5,238	5,298	5,349

* Number of licences (note: one licence can cover several receivers in the same household).

1997: Radio receivers in use ('000) 7,700 (Source: UNESCO, *Statistical Yearbook*).

Education

(1998)

	Institutions	Teachers	Students
Comprehensive schools*	4,228	41,631	595,300
Senior secondary schools	458	6,693	137,400
Vocational and professional institutions	406	14,869	242,500
Polytechnics	21	3,133	72,300
Universities	20	7,252	141,300

* Comprising six-year primary stage and three-year lower secondary stage.

Directory

The Constitution

The Constitution of Finland entered into force on 1 March 2000, amending the Constitution of July 1919. Its main provisions are summarized below:

FUNDAMENTAL PROVISIONS

Finland is a sovereign republic. The powers of the State are vested in the people, who are represented by the Parliament. Legislative power is exercised by the Parliament, which also decides on state finances, governmental power is held by the President of the Republic and the Council of State, and judicial power is exercised by independent courts of law. The basic rights and liberties of the individual are guaranteed in the Constitution.

PARLIAMENT

The unicameral Parliament comprises 200 representatives, who are elected for a term of four years by a direct, proportional and secret vote. For the parliamentary elections the country is divided, on the basis of the number of Finnish citizens, into at least 12 and at most 18 constituencies. In addition, the Åland Islands form their own constituency for the election of one representative. Registered political parties, and groups of persons who have the right to vote, are entitled to nominate candidates in parliamentary elections. The President of the Republic, in response to a proposal by the Prime Minister, may order that extraordinary parliamentary elections be held. The Parliament elects from among its members a Speaker and two Deputy Speakers for each parliamentary session. The proposal for the enactment of legislation is initiated in the Parliament either by the Government or through a motion submitted by a representative.

PRESIDENT

The President of the Republic is elected by a direct vote for a term of six years (with the same person restricted to a maximum of two consecutive terms in office). The President will be a native-born Finnish citizen. The candidate who receives more than one-half of the votes cast in the election will be elected President. If none of the candidates receives a majority of the votes cast, a further election will be held between the two candidates who have received the most votes. The right to nominate a candidate in the presidential election is held by any registered political party from which at least one representative was elected to the Parliament in the most recent elections, as well as by any group of 20,000 persons who have the right to vote. The President of the Republic makes decisions on the basis of proposals submitted by the Council of State. The foreign policy of Finland is directed by the President of the Republic in co-operation with the Council of State.

COUNCIL OF STATE

The Council of State comprises the Prime Minister and the necessary number of ministers. The Parliament elects the Prime Minister, who is thereafter appointed to the office by the President of the Republic. The President appoints the other ministers on the basis of nominations made by the Prime Minister.

JUDICIARY

The Supreme Court, the Courts of Appeal and the District Courts are the general courts of law. The Supreme Administrative Court and the regional Administrative Courts are the general courts of administrative law. Justice in civil, commercial and criminal matters in the final instance is administered by the Supreme Court, while justice in administrative matters in the final instance is administered by the Supreme Administrative Court. The High Court of Impeachment deals with charges brought against a member of the Government, the Chancellor of Justice, the Parliamentary Ombudsman or a member of the supreme courts for unlawful conduct in office. Tenured judges are appointed by the President of the Republic.

ADMINISTRATION AND SELF-GOVERNMENT

In addition to the Government, the civil administration of the State may consist of agencies, institutions and other bodies. The Åland Islands are guaranteed self-government. Finland is divided into municipalities, which are guaranteed self-government, and are entitled to levy tax. In their native region the Sami have linguistic and cultural autonomy.

The Government

HEAD OF STATE

President: Tarja Halonen (elected 6 February 2000 and took office on 1 March 2000).

COUNCIL OF STATE
(Valtioneuvosto)

(April 2001)

A coalition of the Social Democratic Party (SDP), National Coalition Party (Kok), Swedish People's Party (SFP), Left Alliance (V) and Green League (VL), with one independent (Ind.).

Prime Minister: Paavo Lipponen (SDP).

Deputy Prime Minister and Minister of Finance: Sauli Niinistö (Kok).

Minister of Foreign Affairs: Erkki Tuomioja (SDP).

Minister of the Interior: Ville Itälä (Kok).

Minister of Regional and Municipal Affairs: Matti Korhonen (V).

Minister of Defence: Jan-Erik Enestam (SFP).

Minister at the Ministry of Finance: Suvi-Anne Siimes (V).

Minister of Education: Maija Rask (SDP).

Minister of Culture: Suvi Linden (Kok).

Minister of Agriculture and Forestry: Kalevi Hemilä (Ind.).

Minister of Transport and Communications: Olli-Pekka Heinonen (Kok).

Minister of Trade and Industry: Sinikka Mönkäre (SDP).

Minister of Social Affairs and Health: Maija Perho (Kok).

Minister of Health and Social Services: Osmo Soininvaara (VL).

Minister for Foreign Trade: Kimmo Sasi (Kok).

Minister of Justice: Johannes Koskinen (SDP).

Minister of Labour: Tarja Filatov (SDP).

Minister of the Environment: Satu Hassi (VL).

MINISTRIES

Prime Minister's Office: Snellmaninkatu 1A, POB 23, 00170 Helsinki; tel. (9) 1601; fax (9) 478711; e-mail kirjaamo@vnk.vn.fi; internet www.vn.fi/vnk.

Ministry of Agriculture and Forestry: Hallituskatu 3A, 00170 Helsinki; tel. (9) 1601; fax (9) 1602190.

Ministry of Defence: Fabianinkatu 2, POB 31, 00130 Helsinki; tel. (9) 1601; fax (9) 653254.

Ministry of Education: Meritullinkatu 10, 00171 Helsinki; POB 29, 00023 Government; tel. (9) 134171; fax (9) 1359335; e-mail pia.ekqvist@minedu.fi; internet www.minedu.fi.

Ministry of the Environment: Kasarmikatu 25, POB 380, 00131 Helsinki; tel. (9) 19911; fax (9) 19919545.

Ministry of Finance: Snellmaninkatu 1A, 00170 Helsinki; tel. (9) 1601; fax (9) 1603090; internet www.vn.fi/vm/index.html.

Ministry of Foreign Affairs: Merikasarmi, POB 176, 00161 Helsinki; tel. (9) 134151; fax (9) 629840; internet formin.finland.fi.

Ministry of the Interior: Kirkkokatu 12, 00170 Helsinki; tel. (9) 1601; fax (9) 1602927.

Ministry of Justice: Eteläesplanadi 10, POB 1, 00131 Helsinki; tel. (9) 18251; fax (9) 18257730.

Ministry of Labour: Eteläesplanadi 4, POB 524, 00101 Helsinki; tel. (9) 18561; fax (9) 1857950.

Ministry of Social Affairs and Health: Meritullinkatu 8, POB 33, 00170 Helsinki; tel. (9) 1601; fax (9) 1604716; e-mail kirjaamo.stm@stm.vn.fi; internet www.stm.fi.

Ministry of Trade and Industry: Aleksanterinkatu 4, POB 230, 00171 Helsinki; POB 32, 00023 Government; tel. (9) 1601; fax (9) 1603666; internet www.vn.fi/ktm.

Ministry of Transport and Communications: Eteläesplanadi 16–18, POB 235, 00131 Helsinki; tel. (9) 1601; fax (9) 1602596; e-mail info@mintc.fi; internet www.mintc.fi.

President and Legislature

PRESIDENT

Elections of 16 January and 6 February 2000

	Popular vote (%)	
	First Round	Second Round
Tarja Halonen (SDP)	40.0	51.6
Esko Aho (Kesk)	34.4	48.4
Riitta Uosukainen (Kok)	12.8	—
Märta Elisabeth Rehn (SFP) . .	7.9	—
Heidi Hautala (VL)	3.3	—
Ilkka Hakalehto (PS)	1.0	—
Risto Kuisma (REM)	0.6	—
Total	100.0	100.0

EDUSKUNTA
(Parliament)

Speaker: Riitta Uosukainen (Kok).
Secretary-General: Seppo Tiitinen.

General Election, 21 March 1999

	% of votes	Seats
Finnish Social Democratic Party . . .	22.9	51
Finnish Centre Party	22.4	48
National Coalition Party	21.0	46
Left Alliance	10.9	20
Green League	7.5	11
Swedish People's Party	5.1	11
Finnish Christian Union	4.2	10
True Finns	1.0	1
Independents	1.1	1
Others	4.2	1
Total	100.0	200

Political Organizations

Eco-Diverse Party: Mannerheimintie 40A, 00100 Helsinki; tel. (9) 4323566; fax (9) 4322717; Chair. Pertti Virtanen; Sec. Jukka Wallenius.

Kansallinen Kokoomus (Kok) (National Coalition Party): Pohjoinen Rautatiekatu 21B, 00100 Helsinki; tel. (9) 1603004; fax (9) 1603004; e-mail firstname.lastname@kokoomus.fi; internet www.kokoomus.fi; f. 1918; moderate conservative political ideology; Chair. Sauli Niinistö; Sec.-Gen. Matti Kankare; Chair. Parliamentary Group Ben Zyskowicz; 50,000 mems.

Liberaalinen Kansanpuolue (LKP) (Finnish Liberal Party): POB 266, 00121 Helsinki; tel. (9) 644323; fax (9) 61248100; e-mail liberal@liberaalit.fi; internet www.liberaalit.fi; f. 1965 as a coalition of the Finnish People's Party and the Liberal Union; Chair. Altti Majava; Sec.-Gen. Marjut Palomäki; 4,000 mems.

Perussuomalaiset-Sannfinländarna rp (True Finns): Mannerheimintie 40 13 56, 00100 Helsinki; tel. (9) 4540411; fax (9) 4540466; e-mail peruss@persussuomalaiset.fi; internet www.perussuomalaiset.fi; Chair. Timo Soini; Sec. Hannu Purmo.

Reform Group: Mannerheimintie 40A, 00100 Helsinki; tel. (9) 4143352; fax (9) 645379; Chair. Risto Kuisma; Sec. Seija Lahti.

Suomen Keskusta (Kesk) (Finnish Centre Party): Apollonkatu 11A, 00100 Helsinki; tel. (9) 75144200; fax (9) 75144240; internet www.keskusta.fi; f. 1906; a radical centre party founded to promote the interests of the rural population, now a reformist 'green' movement favouring individual enterprise, equality and decentralization; Chair. Esko Aho; Acting Chair. (Aug. 2000–Aug. 2001) Anneli Jäätteenmäki; Sec.-Gen. Eero Lankia; Chair. Parliamentary Group Mauri Pekkarinen; 270,000 mems.

Suomen Kristillinen Liitto (SKL) (Finnish Christian Union): Karjalankatu 2c, 7., 00520 Helsinki; tel. (9) 34882200; fax (9) 34882228; e-mail merja.erapolku@eduskunta.fi; internet www.skl.fi; f. 1958; Chair. Bjarne Kallis; Sec. Milla Kalliomaa; Chair. Parliamentary Group Jouko Jääskeläinen; 16,500 mems.

Suomen Maaseudun Puolue (SMP) (Finnish Rural Party): Hämeentie 157, 00560 Helsinki; tel. (9) 790299; fax (9) 790299; f. 1959; non-socialist programme; represents lower-middle-class elements, small farmers, small enterprises etc.; Chair. Raimo Vistbacka; Sec. Timo Soini; Chair. Parliamentary Group Lea Mäkipää.

Suomen Sosialidemokraattinen Puolue (SDP) (Finnish Social Democratic Party): Saariniemenkatu 6, 00530 Helsinki; tel. (9) 478988; fax (9) 712752; e-mail palaute@sdp.fi; internet www.sdp.fi; f. 1899; constitutional socialist programme; mainly supported by the urban working and middle classes; Chair. Paavo Lipponen; Gen. Sec. Kari Laitinen; Chair. Parliamentary Group Antti Kalliomäki; 62,000 mems.

Svenska folkpartiet (SFP) (Swedish People's Party): Simonsgatan 8A, 00100 Helsinki; tel. (9) 693070; fax (9) 6931968; internet www.sfp.fi; f. 1906; a liberal party representing the interests of the Swedish-speaking minority; Chair. Jan-Erik Enestam; Sec. Peter Heinström; Chair. Parliamentary Group Ulla-Maj Wideroos; 42,000 mems.

Vasemmistoliitto Vänsterförbundet (Left Alliance): Viherniemenkatu 5A, 2., 00530 Helsinki; tel. (9) 774741; fax (9) 77474200; e-mail vas@vasemmistoliitto.fi; internet www.vasemmistoliitto.fi; f. 1990 as a merger of the Finnish People's Democratic League (f. 1944), the Communist Party of Finland (f. 1918), the Democratic League of Finnish Women, and left-wing groups; Chair. Suvi-Anne Siimes; Sec.-Gen. Ralf Sund; Chair. Parliamentary Group Martti Korhonen; 14,000 mems.

Vihreä Liitto (VL) (Green League): Runeberginkatu 5B, 00100 Helsinki; tel. (9) 58604160; fax (9) 58604161; e-mail vihreat@vihrealiitto.fi; internet www.vihrealiitto.fi; f. 1988; Chair. Satu Hassi; Sec. Ari Heikkinen.

Young Finns: Lönnrotinkatu 23A, 00180 Helsinki; tel. (9) 6856211; fax (9) 6856233; Chair. Risto E. J. Penttilä; Sec. Marita Vuorinen.

Diplomatic Representation

EMBASSIES IN FINLAND

Argentina: Bulevardi 5A 11, 00120 Helsinki; tel. (9) 607630; fax (9) 646788; Ambassador: Silvio H. Newman.

Austria: Keskuskatu 1A, 00100 Helsinki; tel. (9) 171322; fax (9) 665084; e-mail austrian.embassy@kolumbus.fi; Ambassador: Dr Christoph Quernter.

Belgium: Kalliolinnantie 5, 00140 Helsinki; tel. (9) 170412; fax (9) 628842; e-mail aubel.helsinki@kolumbus.fi; Ambassador: Louis Mouraux.

Brazil: Itäinen puistotie 4B 1, 00140 Helsinki; tel. (9) 177922; fax (9) 650084; e-mail brasemb.helsinki@kolumbus.fi; Ambassador: Luiz Henrique Pereira da Fonseca.

Bulgaria: Kuusisaarentie 2B, 00340 Helsinki; tel. (9) 4584055; fax (9) 4584550; e-mail bulembfi@icon.fi; Ambassador: Dr Elena Kirtcheva.

Canada: Pohjoisesplanadi 25B, 00100 Helsinki; tel. (9) 171141; fax (9) 601060; internet www.canada.fi; Ambassador: Craig MacDonald.

Chile: Erottajankatu 11, 00130 Helsinki; tel. (9) 6126780; fax (9) 61267825; e-mail echilefi@kolumbus.fi; Ambassador: Montserrat Palou.

China, People's Republic: Vanha Kelkkamäki 9–11, 00570 Helsinki; tel. (9) 22890110; fax (9) 22890168; Ambassador: Lü Xinhua.

Colombia: Ratakatu 1B A1, 00120 Helsinki; tel. (9) 6802799; fax (9) 6802180; e-mail emcolhel.emba@kolumbus.fi; Chargé d'affaires a.i.: Carmen Lucia Tristancho.

Croatia: Eteläesplanadi 12, 1., 00130 Helsinki; tel. (9) 6222232; fax (9) 6222221; Ambassador: Zeljko Bošnjak.

Cuba: Uudenmankatu 26A, 3, 00120 Helsinki; tel. (9) 6802022; fax (9) 643163; e-mail manual.vinas@embacuba.inet.fi; Ambassador: Marianela Ferriol Echevarria.

Cyprus: Bulevardi 5A, 23, 00120 Helsinki; tel. (9) 6962820; fax (9) 69628230; e-mail cyemb.hel@kolumbus.fi.

Czech Republic: Armfeltintie 14, 00150 Helsinki; tel. (9) 171169; fax (9) 630655; e-mail helsinki@embassy.mzv.cz; Ambassador: Radek Pech.

Denmark: Keskuskatu 1A, POB 1042, 00101 Helsinki; tel. (9) 6841050; fax (9) 68410540; e-mail danmark@kolumbus.fi; internet www.kolumbus.fi/danmark; Ambassador: Niels Helskov.

Egypt: Munkkiniemen puistotie 25, 00330 Helsinki; tel. (9) 4777470; fax (9) 47774721; Ambassador: Zeinab Soheim.

Estonia: Itäinen puistotie 10, 00140 Helsinki; tel. (9) 6220260; fax (9) 62202610; e-mail sekretar@estemb.fi; Ambassador: Mati Vaarmann.

France: Itäinen puistotie 13, 00140 Helsinki; tel. (9) 618780; fax (9) 61878323; e-mail ambassade.france@kolumbus.fi; Ambassador: Gilles d'Humières.

Germany: POB 5, 00331 Helsinki; tel. (9) 458580, fax (9) 45858258; e-mail saksa@germanembassy.fi; internet www.germanembassy.fi; Ambassador: Henning von Wistinghausen.

Greece: Maaneesikatu 2A 4, 00170 Helsinki; tel. (9) 2781100; fax (9) 2781200; e-mail grpress@dlc.fi; Ambassador: Basil Ch. Patsikakis.

Hungary: Kuusisaarenkuja 6, 00340 Helsinki; tel. (9) 484144; fax (9) 480497; Ambassador: JÓZSEF VIG.

Iceland: Pohjoisesplanadi 27C, 00100 Helsinki; tel. (9) 6122460; fax (9) 61224620; e-mail icemb.helsinki@utn.stjr.is; interest www .islanti.fi; Ambassador: KORNELIUS SIGMUNDSSON.

India: Satamakatu 2A 8, 00160 Helsinki; tel. (9) 608927; fax (9) 6221208; e-mail indemb.fin@iehlk.pp.fi; Ambassador: C. R. BALA-CHANDRA.

Indonesia: Kuusisaarentie 3, 00340 Helsinki; tel. (9) 4470370; fax (9) 4582882; Ambassador: AHMAD FAUZIE GANI.

Iran: Kolosaarentie 9, 00570 Helsinki; tel. (9) 6869240; fax (9) 68692410; e-mail iri.embassy@kolumbus.fi; Ambassador: SEYED ABBAS ARAGHCHI.

Iraq: Lars Sonckin tie 2, 00570 Helsinki; tel. (9) 6849177; fax (9) 6848977; Chargé d'affaires a.i.: MOHAMMED R. A. JASSIM.

Ireland: Erottajankatu 7A, 00130 Helsinki; tel. (9) 646006; fax (9) 646022; e-mail ireland@ireland.pp.fi; Ambassador: GEARÓID Ó BROIN.

Israel: Vironkatu 5A, 00170 Helsinki; tel. (9) 1356177; fax (9) 1356959; e-mail postmaster@ilemb.pp.fi; internet www.mfa.gov.il; Ambassador: MIRYAM SHOMRAT.

Italy: Itäinen puistotie 4, 00140 Helsinki; tel. (9) 6811280; fax (9) 175976; e-mail info@italia.fi; internet www.italia.fi; Ambassador: PIETRO LONARDO.

Japan: Eteläranta 8, 00130 Helsinki; tel. (9) 6860200; fax (9) 633012; e-mail emb2@japan.inet.fi; internet www.personal.inet.fi/koti/jpnembassy; Ambassador: NORIMASA HASEGAWA.

Korea, Republic: Annankatu 32A, 00100 Helsinki; tel. (9) 6866230; fax (9) 68662355; e-mail koreanembassy@kolumbus.fi; Ambassador: YANG DONG-CHIL.

Latvia: Armfeltintie 10, 00150 Helsinki; tel. (9) 47647244; fax (9) 47647233; e-mail latemb.fin@latemb.inet.fi; Ambassador: VALDIS KRASTINS.

Lithuania: Rauhankatu 13A, 00170 Helsinki; tel. (9) 608210; fax (9) 608220; e-mail embassy@liettua.pp.fi; Ambassador: NERIS GERMANAS.

Mexico: Simonkatu 12A, 00100 Helsinki; tel. (9) 5860430; fax (9) 6949411; e-mail mexican.embassy@co.inet.fi; Ambassador: CRISTINA DE LA GARZA.

Morocco: Mikonkatu 8A, 00100 Helsinki; tel. (9) 635740; fax (9) 635160; e-mail embassyofmorocco@co.inet.fi; Chargé d'affaires a.i.: AZIZ OUARRAK.

Netherlands: Eteläesplanadi 24A, 00130 Helsinki; tel. (9) 661737; fax (9) 654734; e-mail nlgovhel@kolumbus.fi; Ambassador: J. VAN DER VELDEN.

Norway: Rehbinderintie 17, 00150 Helsinki; tel. (9) 6860180; fax (9) 657807; e-mail emb.helsinki@mfa.no; Ambassador: REGINALD NORBY.

Peru: Annankatu 31–33C 44, 00100 Helsinki; tel. (9) 6933681; fax (9) 6933682; Ambassador: MARTHA CHAVARRI DUPUY.

Poland: Armas Lindgrenin tie 21, 00570 Helsinki; tel. (9) 6848077; fax (9) 6847477; e-mail emb.poland@helsinki.inet.fi; internet www.embassyofpoland.fi; Ambassador: STANISŁAW STEBELSKI.

Portugal: Itäinen puistotie 11B, 00140 Helsinki; tel. (9) 68243715; fax (9) 663550; Ambassador: MANUEL MOREIRA DE ANDRADE.

Romania: Stenbäckinkatu 24, 00250 Helsinki; tel. (9) 2413624; fax (9) 2413272; e-mail romamb@clinet.fi; Ambassador: SMARANDA ENACHE.

Russia: Tehtaankatu 1B, 00140 Helsinki; tel. (9) 661876; fax (9) 661006; Ambassador: ALEXANDER K. PATSEV.

Slovakia: Annankatu 25, 00100 Helsinki; tel. (9) 70018460; fax (9) 640105; e-mail skemb.hels@sci.fi; Chargé d'affaires a.i.: Dr EMIL KUCHÁR.

South Africa: Rahapajankatu 1A 5, 00160 Helsinki; tel. (9) 68603100; fax (9) 68603160; e-mail saemb@icon.fi; Ambassador: FRANKI VERWEY.

Spain: Kalliolinnantie 6, 00140 Helsinki; tel. (9) 6877080; fax (9) 170923; e-mail embassy.spain@kolumbus.fi; Ambassador: FERNANDO CARDERERA.

Sweden: Pohjoisesplanadi 7B, 00170 Helsinki; tel. (9) 7877660; fax (9) 655285; e-mail ambassaden.helsingfoss@foreign.ministry.se; internet www.sverige.se; Ambassador: KERSTIN ASP-JOHNSSON.

Switzerland: Uudenmaankatu 16A, 00120 Helsinki; tel. (9) 649422; fax (9) 649040; e-mail vertretung@hel.rep.admin.ch; Ambassador: HANSRUDOLF HOFFMANN.

Turkey: Puistokatu 1B A 3, 00140 Helsinki; tel. (9) 68110312; fax (9) 655011; e-mail turkish.embassay@pp.htv.fi; Ambassador: ONUR GÖKÇE.

Ukraine: Vähäniityntie 9, 00570 Helsinki; tel. (9) 2289000; fax (9) 2289001; e-mail ukrainian.embassy@kolumbus.fi; Ambassador: IHOR PODOLIEV.

United Kingdom: Itäinen puistotie 17, 00140 Helsinki; tel. (9) 22865100; fax (9) 22865262; e-mail info@ukembassy.fi; internet www.ukembassy.fi; Ambassador: ALYSON BAILES.

USA: Itäinen puistotie 14A, 00140 Helsinki; tel. (9) 171931; fax (9) 174681; internet www.usembassy.fi; Ambassador: ERIC S. EDELMAN.

Venezuela: Bulevardi 1A, POB 285, 00101 Helsinki; tel. (9) 641522; fax (9) 640971; e-mail embavene.finland@dlc.fi; Ambassador: JOSÉ E. LÓPEZ CONTRERAS.

Yugoslavia: Kulosaarentie 36, 00570 Helsinki; tel. (9) 6848522; fax (9) 6848783; Ambassador: DUŠAN CRNOGORČEVIĆ.

Judicial System

The administration of justice is independent of the Government and judges can be removed only by judicial sentence.

SUPREME COURT

Korkein oikeus/Högsta domstolen: Pohjoisesplanadi 3, POB 301, 00171 Helsinki; tel. (9) 12381; fax (9) 1238354; consists of a President and 20 Justices appointed by the President of the Republic. Final court appeal in civil and criminal cases, supervises judges and executive authorities.

President: OLAVI HEINONEN.

SUPREME ADMINISTRATIVE COURT

Korkein hallinto-oikeus/Högsta förvaltningsdomstolen: Unioninkatu 16, POB 180, 00131 Helsinki; tel. (9) 18531; fax (9) 1853382; consists of a President and 20 Justices appointed by the President of the Republic. Highest tribunal for appeals in administrative cases.

President: PEKKA HALLBERG.

COURTS OF APPEAL

There are Courts of Appeal at Turku, Vaasa, Kuopio, Helsinki, Kouvola, and Rovaniemi, consisting of a President and an appropriate number of members.

DISTRICT COURTS

Courts of first instance for almost all suits. Appeals lie to the Court of Appeal, and then to the Supreme Court. The composition of the District Court is determined by the type of case to be heard. Civil cases and 'ordinary' criminal cases can be considered by one judge. Other criminal cases and family law cases are heard by a judge and a panel of three lay judges (jurors). Other civil cases are heard by three legally-qualified judges.

CHANCELLOR OF JUSTICE

The Oikeuskansleri is responsible for seeing that authorities and officials comply with the law. He is the chief public prosecutor, and acts as counsel for the Government.

Chancellor of Justice: PAAVO NIKULA.

PARLIAMENTARY SOLICITOR-GENERAL

The Eduskunnan Oikeusasiamies is the Finnish Ombudsman appointed by Parliament to supervise the observance of the law.

Parliamentary Solicitor-General: LAURI LEHTIMAJA.

Religion

CHRISTIANITY

Suomen ekumeeninen neuvosto/Ekumeniska rådet i Finland (Finnish Ecumenical Council): Katajanokankatu 7, POB 185, 00161 Helsinki; tel. (9) 18021; fax (9) 174313; e-mail sen@kolumbus.fi; f. 1917; 12 mem. churches; Pres. Archbishop JUKKA PAARMA (Archbishop of Karelia and All Finland, Evangelical Lutheran Church of Finland); Gen. Sec. Rev. JAN EDSTRÖM.

National Churches

Suomen Evankelis-luterilainen Kirkko (Evangelical Lutheran Church of Finland): Dept for International Relations, Satamakatu 11, POB 185, 00161 Helsinki; tel. (9) 18021; fax (9) 1802230; about 85.2% of the population are adherents; Archbishop Dr JUKKA PAARMA.

Suomen Ortodoksinen Kirkko (Orthodox Church of Finland): Karjalankatu 1, 70110 Kuopio; tel. (17) 2872230; fax (17) 2872231; e-mail archbishop@ort.fi; internet www.ort.fi; 58,000 mems; Leader JOHANNES, Archbishop of Karelia and all Finland.

Other Churches

Anglican Church in Finland: Mannerheimintie 19A 7, 00250 Helsinki; tel. (9) 490424; fax (9) 447987; chaplaincy founded 1921; part of diocese of Gibraltar in Europe; 122 mems.

Finlands svenska baptistmission (Finland Swedish Baptist Union): POB 54, 65101 Vasa; tel. (6) 3178559; fax (6) 3178550; e-mail fsb@pp.qnet.fi; 1,450 mems.

Jehovan Todistajat (Jehovah's Witnesses): Puutarhatie 60, 01300 Vantaa; tel. (9) 825885; fax (9) 82588285; 19,631 mems.

Katolinen kirkko Suomessa (Roman Catholic Church in Finland): Rehbinderintie 21, 00150 Helsinki; tel. (9) 637907; fax (9) 639820; e-mail kat.hiippak@kanslia.pp.fi; Finland comprises the single diocese of Helsinki, directly responsible to the Holy See; 7,312 mems (Jan. 1999); Apostolic Administrator JOHANNES AARTS.

Myöhempien Aikojen Pyhien Jeesuksen Kristuksen Kirkko (Church of Jesus Christ of Latter-day Saints—Mormon): Neits-ytpolku 3A, 00140 Helsinki; tel. (9) 177311; 3,101 mems.

Suomen Adventtikirkko (Seventh-day Adventist Church in Finland): POB 94, 33101 Tampere; tel. (3) 3611111; fax (3) 3600454; e-mail advent@sdafin.org; internet www.sdafin.org; f. 1894; 5,745 mems; Pres. PEKKA POHJOLA; Sec. JOEL NIININEN.

Suomen Baptistiyhdyskunta (Baptists, Finnish-speaking): Kissanmaankatu 19, 33530 Tampere; tel. (3) 2530901; fax (3) 2530913; e-mail kharis@sci.fi; 1,821 mems; Pres. Rev. JORMA LEMPINEN.

Suomen Vapaakirkko (Evangelical Free Church of Finland): POB 198, 13101 Hämeenlinna; tel. (3) 6445150; fax (3) 6122153; e-mail svk@svk.fi; internet www.svk.fi; f. 1923; 14,054 mems; Pres. Rev. JORMA KUUSINEN.

Svenska Kyrkan i Finland (Church of Sweden in Finland): Minervagatan 6, 00100 Helsinki; tel. (9) 443831; fax (9) 4546059; e-mail christina.myman@olausjetri.inet.fi; f. 1919; 1,500 mems; Rector Dr JARL JERGMAR.

United Methodist Church in Northern Europe: Vänrikki Stoolinkatu 6, 00100 Helsinki; tel. (9) 4542620; fax (9) 45426226; e-mail umc.vaxby@kolumbus.fi; Bishop HANS VÄXBY.

Finlands svenska metodistkyrka (United Methodist Church in Finland—Swedish-speaking): Apollonkatu 5, 00100 Helsinki; tel. (9) 449874; fax (9) 406098; 1,000 mems; District Superintendents Rev. FREDRIK WEGELIUS, Rev. GÖSTA SÖDERSTRÖM.

Suomen Metodistikirkko (United Methodist Church—Finnish-speaking): Punavuorenkatu 2, 00120 Helsinki; tel. (9) 628135; 767 mems; District Superintendent Rev. TXAPANI RAJAMAA.

The Salvation Army is also active in the country.

BAHÁ'Í FAITH

Suomen Bahá'í-yhteisö (Bahá'í Community of Finland): POB 423, 00600 Helsinki; tel. (9) 790875; fax (9) 790058; e-mail secretariat@bahai.fi; f. 1953; 600 mems.

JUDAISM

Helsingin Juutalainen Seurakunta (Jewish Community of Helsinki): Synagogue and Community Centre, Malminkatu 26, 00100 Helsinki; tel. (9) 5860310; fax (9) 6948916; e-mail helsinki.jc@hjc.pp.fi; 1,200 mems; Pres. GIDEON BOLOTOWSKY; Exec. Dir DAN KANTOR.

ISLAM

Suomen Islamilainen Yhdyskunta (Islamic Community of Finland): POB 87, 00101 Helsinki; tel. (9) 3512190; fax (9) 6121156; 936 mems; Imam ENVER YILDIRIM.

The Press

In 2000 there were 205 daily newspapers in Finland (including 27 printed seven days a week), with a total circulation of some 3.3m. A number of dailies are printed in Swedish. The most popular daily papers are *Helsingin Sanomat, Aamulehti, Turun Sanomat* and *Ilta-Sanomat*. Most respected for its standard of news coverage and commentary is *Helsingin Sanomat*, an independent paper.

In 2000 there were about 2,800 periodicals. The principal 'consumer' periodicals, in terms of circulation, are the weekly family magazines *Apu* and *Seura*, the children's weekly *Aku Ankka* (Donald Duck), and the monthlies *Kotivinkki* (for women), *ET-lehti* (for the elderly) and *Valitut Palat* (Reader's Digest). A larger circulation is enjoyed by 'customer' magazines, such as *Pirkka* (K-retail group) and *Matkaviesti* (Sonera). Prominent business and management magazines include *Taloustaito* (economics and taxation) and *Kunta ja me*.

PRINCIPAL DAILIES

Espoo

Hevosurheilu: Tulkinkuja 3, 02600 Espoo; tel. (9) 51100300; fax (9) 51100390; e-mail hevosurheila@hevosurheilulehti.fi; internet www.hippos.fi; independent; Man. Dir ILMARI HALINEN; Editor-in-Chief JORMA KEMILÄINEN; circ. 27,691.

Helsinki

Demari: Paasivuorenkatu 3, POB 338, 00531 Helsinki; tel. (9) 701041; fax (9) 7010570; e-mail toimitus@demari.fi; internet www.demari.fi; f. 1918; chief organ of the Social Democratic Party; Man. Dir and Editor-in-Chief KARI AROLA; circ. 25,669.

Helsingin Sanomat: Töölönlahdenkatu 2, POB 77, 00089 Sanomat; tel. (9) 1221; fax (9) 605709; e-mail janne.virkkunen@sanoma.fi; internet www.helsinginsanomat.fi; f. 1889; independent; Publr SEPPO KIEVARI; Senior Editor-in-Chief JANNE VIRKKUNEN; circ. 446,972 weekdays, 529,007 Sunday.

Hufvudstadsbladet: Mannerheimvägen 18, POB 217, 00101 Helsinki; tel. (9) 12531; fax (9) 642930; e-mail centralred@mail.hbl.fi; internet www.hbl.fi; f. 1864; Swedish language; independent; Editor ERIK WAHLSTRÖM; circ. 55,084 weekdays, 57,845 Sunday.

Iltalehti: Aleksanterinkatu 9, 4., 00100 Helsinki; tel. (9) 507721; fax (9) 177313; internet ww.iltalehti.fi; f. 1981; afternoon; independent; Man. Dir. VELI-MATTI ASIKAINEN; Editor-in-Chief PEKKA KARHUVAARA; circ. 101,980 weekdays, 129,443 Saturday.

Ilta-Sanomat: POB 45, 00089 Sanomat; tel. (9) 1221; fax (9) 1223419; e-mail iltasanomat@sanoma.fi; internet www.iltsanomat.fi; f. 1932; afternoon; independent; Man. Dir SEPPO KIEVARI; Editor-in-Chief VESA-PEKKA KOLJONEN; circ. 218,010 weekdays, 250,098 weekend.

Kansan Uutiset: POB 43, 00501 Helsinki; tel. (9) 75881; f. 1957; organ of the Left Alliance; Editor YRJÖ RAUTIO; circ. 42,415.

Kauppalehti (The Commercial Daily): POB 189, 00101 Helsinki; tel. (9) 50781; fax (9) 5078419; internet www.kauppalehti.fi; f. 1898; morning; Man. Dir HEIKKI SARASTE; Editor-in-Chief LAURI HELVE; circ. 81,764.

Maaseudun Tulevaisuus: Simonkatu 6, POB 440, 00100 Helsinki; tel. (9) 131151; fax (9) 6944766; internet www.maaseuduntulevaisuus.fi; f. 1916; independent; Man. Dir KIMMO VARJOUA-ARA; Editor-in-Chief LAURI KONTRO; circ. 91,804.

Hämeenlinna

Hämeen Sanomat: Vanajantie 7, POB 530, 13111 Hämeenlinna; tel. (3) 61511; fax (3) 6151492; internet www.hameensanomat.fi; f. 1879; independent; Man. Dir ARTO KAJANTO; Editor-in-Chief TERTTU HÄKKINEN; circ. 30,510.

Joensuu

Karjalainen: Kosti Aaltosentie 9, POB 99, 80141 Joensuu; tel. (13) 2551; fax (13) 2552363; e-mail toimitus@karjalainen.fi; internet www.karjalainen.fi; f. 1874; independent; Man. Dir LEO KARVONEN; Editor PEKKA SITARI; circ. 48,209.

Jyväskylä

Keskisuomalainen: Aholaidantie 3, POB 159, 40101 Jyväskylä; tel. (14) 622000; fax (14) 622272; e-mail tiepal@keskisuomalainen.fi; internet www.keskisuomalainen.fi; f. 1871; Man. Dir ERKKI PORANEN; Editor ERKKI LAATIKAINEN; circ. 76,315.

Kajaani

Kainuun Sanomat: Viestitie 2, POB 150, 87101 Kajaani; tel. (8) 61661; fax (8) 6166307; e-mail toimitus@kainuunsanomat.fi; internet www.kainuunsanomat.fi; f. 1918; independent; Editor-in-Cheif HEIKKI LÄÄKKÖLÄ; circ. 23,628.

Kemi

Pohjolan Sanomat: Sairaalakatu 2,94100 Kemi; tel. (16) 2911; fax (16) 291300; e-mail ps.toimitus@pohjolansanomat.fi; internet www.pohjolansanomat.fi; f. 1915; organ of the Finnish Centre Party; Man. Dir MATTI NIKKANEN; Editor-in-Chief HEIKKI LÄÄKKÖLÄ; circ. 24,024.

Kokkola

Keskipohjanmaa: Kosila, POB 45, 67101 Kokkola; tel. (6) 8272000; fax (6) 8220208; internet www.kpk.fi/keskipohjanmaa; f. 1917; independent; Man. Dir EINO LAUKKA; Editor LASSI JAAKKOLA; circ. 29,182.

Kotka

Kymen Sanomat: POB 27, 48101 Kotka; tel. (5) 2100111; fax (5) 216377; e-mail kysatoimitus@kylmedia.fi; internet www.kymensanomat.fi; f. 1902; independent; Man. Dir ANTTI MÄKELÄ; Editor MARKKU ESPO; circ. 27,879.

Kouvola

Kouvolan Sanomat: POB 40, 45101 Kouvola; tel. (5) 828911; fax (5) 3115335; e-mail ks.toimitus@kouvolansanomat.fi; internet www.kouvolansanomat.fi; f. 1909; independent; Man. Dir ANTTI MÄKELA; Editor-in-Chief VILLE POHJONEN; circ. 30,322.

Kuopio

Savon Sanomat: POB 68, 70101 Kuopio; tel. (17) 303111; fax (17) 303347; e-mail lukijansanomat@iwn.fi; internet www.savonsanomat

.fi; f. 1907; independent; Man. Dir HEIKKI AURASMAA; Editor-in-Chief TAPANI LEPOLA; circ. 72,757.

Lahti

Etelä-Suomen Sanomat: Ilmarisentie 7, POB 80, 15101 Lahti; tel. (3) 7575; fax (3) 7575466; internet www.ess.fi; f. 1900; independent; Man. Dir JUKKA OTTELA; Editor-in-Chief HEIKKI HAKALA; circ. 62,328.

Lappeenranta

Etelä-Saimaa: POB 3, 53501 Lappeenranta; tel. (5) 677111; fax (5) 4516936; internet www.esaimaa.fi; f. 1885; independent; Man. Dir. ANTERO JUNTTILA; Editor JORMA HERNESMAA; circ. 35,191.

Mikkeli

Länsi-Savo: POB 6, 50101 Mikkeli; tel. (15) 3501; fax (15) 350280; e-mail toimitus@lansi-savo.fi; internet www.lansi-savo.fi; independent; Man. Dir JUKKA TIKKA; Editor-in-Chief KARI JUUTILAINEN; circ. 26,496.

Oulu

Kaleva: POB 170, 90401 Oulu; tel. (8) 5377111; fax (8) 5377195; e-mail kaleva@kaleva.fi; internet www.kaleva.fi; f. 1899; independent; Man. Dir TAISTO RISKI; Editor-in-Chief TEUVO MÄLLINEN; circ. 84,292.

Pori

Satakunnan Kansa: POB 58, 28101 ·Pori; tel. (2) 6228111; fax (2) 6228392; e-mail sk.toimitus@satakunnankansa.fi; internet www .satakannankanska.fi; f. 1873; independent; Man. Dir TUOMO SAARINEN; Editor-in-Chief ERKKI TEIKARI; circ. 57,060.

Rauma

Länsi-Suomi: Susivuorentie 2, 26100 Rauma; tel. (2) 83361; fax (2) 8336299; f. 1905; independent; circ. 18,067.

Rovaniemi

Lapin Kansa: Veitikantie 2–8, 96100 Rovaniemi; tel. (16) 320011; fax (16) 32003045; e-mail lktoimitus@lapinkansa.fi; internet www.lapinkansa.fi; f. 1928; independent; Man. Dir HEIKKI OLLILA; Editor-in-Chief HEIKKI TUOMI-NIKULA; circ. 36,259.

Salo

Salon Seudun Sanomat: Örninkatu 14, POB 117, 24101 Salo; tel. (2) 770211; fax (2) 7702300; internet www.sss.fi; independent; Man. Dir KIRSTI KIRJONEN; Editor-in-Chief JARMO VÄHÄSILTA; circ. 21,684.

Savonlinna

Itä-Savo: POB 35, 57231 Savonlinna; tel. (15) 29171; organ of the Finnish Centre Party; Editor ESKO SUIKKANEN; circ. 23,502.

Seinäjoki

Ilkka: POB 60, Kouluk, 60101 Seinäjoki; tel. (6) 4186555; fax (6) 4186500; e-mail ilkaa.toimitus@ilkka.fi; internet www.ilkka.fi; f. 1906; independent; Man. Dir MATTI KORKIATUPA; Editor-in-Chief KARI HOKKANEN; circ. 55,034.

Tampere

Aamulehti: POB 327, 33101 Tampere; tel. (3) 2666111; fax (3) 2666259; internet www.aamulehti.fi; f. 1881; Editors MATTI APUNEN; circ. 134,779 weekdays, 143,043 Sunday.

Turku

Turun Sanomat: POB 95,20101 Turku; tel. (2) 2693311; fax (2) 2693274; e-mail ts.toimitus@ts-group.fi; internet www .turunsanomat.fi; f. 1904; independent; Man. Dir KEIJO KETONEN; Editors-in-Chief ARI VALJAKKA, RAIMO VAHTERA, AIMO MASSINEN; circ. 113,411 weekdays, 125,318 Sunday.

Tuusula

Keski-Uusimaa: POB 52, 04301 Tuusula; tel. (9) 273000; fax (9) 27300205; e-mail toimitus@keskiuusimaa.fi; internet www .kcskiuusimaa.fi; independent; Man. Dir JUKKA VIRTA; Editor-in-Chief REIJO HIRVONEN; circ. 21,986.

Vaasa

Pohjalainen: Pitkäkatu 37, POB 37, 65101 Vaasa; tel. (6) 3249111; fax (6) 3249352; e-mail kari.manty@pohjalainen.fi; internet www.pohjalainen.fi; f. 1903; independent; Editor KARI MANTY; circ. 34,500.

Vasabladet: Sandögatan 6, POB 52, 65101 Vaasa; tel. (6) 3260211; fax (6) 3129003; e-mail tips@vasabladet.fi; internet www .vasabladet.fi; f. 1856; Swedish language; Liberal independent; Editor MAJ-BRITT HÖGLUND; circ. 26,700.

PRINCIPAL PERIODICALS

7 päivää: POB 124, 00151 Helsinki; tel. (9) 177777; fax (9) 177477; weekly; television and radio; circ. 127,810.

Ahjo: POB 107, 00531 Helsinki; tel. (9) 77071; fax (9) 7707400; e-mail ahjo@metalliliitto.fi; fortnightly; for metal industry employees; Editor-in-Chief HEIKKI PISKONEN; circ. 164,000.

Aku Ankka (Donald Duck): POB 40, 00040 Helsinki; tel. (9) 1201; fax (9) 1205569; f. 1951; weekly; children's; Editor-in-Chief MARKKU KIVEKÄS; circ. 283,334.

Apu: Hitsaajankatu 10, 00081 Helsinki; tel. (9) 75961; fax (9) 781911; e-mail matti.saari@apu.fi; internet www.apu.fi; f. 1933; weekly; family journal; Editor-in-Chief MATTI SAARI; circ. 251,853.

Avotakka: Hitsaajankatu 7/6, 00081 A-lehdet, Helsinki; tel. (9) 75961; fax (9) 7591268; e-mail avotakka@a-lehdet.fi; internet www.a-lehdet.fi/avotakka; f. 1967; monthly; interior decorating; Editor-in-Chief TARJA HURME; circ. 102,162.

Birka: Kanavakatu 3B, 00160 Helsinki; tel. (9) 1053010; fax (9) 105336235; quarterly; trade; in Swedish; circ. 76,322.

Diabetes: Kirjoniementie 15, 33680 Tampere; tel. (3) 2860111; fax (3) 3600462; e-mail lehdet@diabetes.fi; internet www.diabetes .fi; f. 1949; monthly; health; circ. 53,590.

Eeva: Hitsaajankatu 7/7, 00081 A-lehdet, Helsinki; tel. (9) 75961; fax (9) 786858; e-mail eeva@a-lehdet.fi; internet www.a-lehdet.fi/ eeva; f. 1933; monthly; women's; Editor-in-Chief LIISA JÄPPINEN; circ. 99,678.

Elbladet: POB 184, 00131 Helsinki; tel. (9) 6861676; fax (9) 68616786; e-mail ari.vesa@energia.fi; f. 1939; quarterly; Editor-in-Chief ARI J. VESA; circ. 101,575.

Erä: Esterinportti 1, 00015 Kuvalehdet, Helsinki; tel. (9) 15661; fax (9) 15666210; e-mail era@kuvalehdet.fi; internet www.kuvalehdet.fi; monthly; sport fishing and outdoor leisure; Editor SEPPO SUURONEN; circ. 51,370.

ET-lehti: POB 100, 00040 Helsinki; tel. (9) 1201; fax (9) 1205428; e-mail kaisa.larmela@helsinkimedia.fi; monthly; over 50s magazine; Editor-in-Chief KAISA LARMELA; circ. 250,000.

Gloria: POB 100, 00040 Helsinki; tel. (9) 1201; fax (9) 1205427; e-mail gloria@helsinkimedia.fi; monthly; women's; Editor-in-Chief RIITTA LINDEGREN; circ. 64,000.

Hippo: POB 308, 00101 Helsinki; tel. (9) 4041; fax (9) 4042165; 4 a year; Editor-in-Chief STINA SUOMINEN; circ. 188,141.

Hymy: Maistraatinportti 1, 00240 Helsinki; tel. (9) 15661; fax (9) 15666206; monthly; family journal; Editor ESKO TULUSTO; circ. 94,527.

Hyvä Terveys: POB 100, 00040 Helsinki; tel. (9) 1201; fax (9) 1205456; e-mail hyva.terveys@helsinkimedia.fi; 11 a year; health; Editor-in-Chief JXALI RUUSKANEN; circ. 82,000.

IT-Invalidityö: Kumpulantie 1A, 00520 Helsinki; tel. (9) 613191; fax (9) 1461443; e-mail it-lehti@invalidiliitto.fi; internet www .it-lehti.fi; 12 a year; for handicapped people; Editor-in-Chief VOITTO KORHONEN; circ. 51,611.

Kaks' Plus: Maistraatinportti 1, 00015 Kuvalehdet; tel. (9) 1566591; fax (9) 1566550; e-mail kaksplus@kuvalehdet.fi; internet www .kaksplus.fi; f. 1969; monthly; for families with young children; Editor-in-Chief MARI IKONEN; circ. 43,972.

Katso: Hitsaajankatu 7/5, 00081 A-lehdet, Helsinki; tel. (9) 75961; fax (9) 7596342; e-mail katso@a-lehdet.fi; internet www.a-lehdet.fi/ katso; f. 1960; weekly; TV, radio, film and video; Editor-in-Chief MARKKU VEIJALAINEN; circ. 70,388.

Kauneus ja terveys: Hitsaajankatu 10, 00081 Helsinki; tel. (9) 75961; fax (9) 786858; monthly; health and beauty; circ. 61,647.

Kirkko ja kaupunki: POB 137, 00201 Helsinki; tel. (9) 613021; fax (9) 61302342; weekly; church and community; Editor-in-Chief SEPPO SIMOLA; circ. 199,793.

Kodin Kuvalehti: POB 100, 00040 Helsinki; tel. (9) 1201; fax (9) 1205468; e-mail kodin.kuvalehti@helsinkimedia.fi; fortnightly; family magazine; Editor LEENA KARO; circ. 180,068.

Kotilääkäri: Maistraatinportti 1, 00240 Helsinki; tel. (9) 15661; fax (9) 1566507; e-mail kotilaakari@kuvalehdet.fi; f. 1889; monthly; health and beauty; Editor-in-Chief TARJA HURME; circ. 64,769.

Kotiliesi: Maistraatinportti 1, 00240 Helsinki; tel. (9) 15661; fax (9) 147724; f. 1922; fortnightly; women's; Editor-in-Chief ELINA SIMONEN-HYVÄRINEN; circ. 200,474.

Kotivinkki: Kalevankatu 56, 00180 Helsinki; tel. (9) 773951; fax (9) 77395399; monthly; women's; Editor-in-Chief ANNELI MYLLER; circ. 207,550.

Me Naiset: POB 100, 00040 Helsinki; tel. (9) 1201; fax (9) 1205414; internet www.menaiset.fi; f. 1952; weekly; women's; Editor ULLA-MAIJA PAAVILAINEN; circ. 115,000.

Metsälehti: Soidinkj 4, 00700 Helsinki; tel. (9) 1562333; fax (9) 1562335; e-mail paavo.seppanen@metsalehti.mailnet.fi; internet www.metsalehti.fi; f. 1933; fortnightly; forestry; Editor PAAVO SEPPÄNEN; circ. 33,375.

MikroPC: POB 920, 00101 Helsinki; tel. (9) 148801; fax (9) 6856631; 20 a year; computers; circ. 39,000.

Nykyposti: Maistraatinportti 1, 00240 Helsinki; tel. (9) 15661; fax (9) 144595; f. 1977; monthly; family journal; Editor JAANA LAUKKANEN; circ. 107,375.

Partio: Kylänvanhimmantie 29, 00640 Helsinki; tel. (9) 25331133; fax (9) 25331160; e-mail hanne.partanen@sp.partio.fi; 6 a year; the Scout movement; circ. 57,188.

Pellervo: POB 77, 00101 Helsinki; tel. (9) 4767501; fax (9) 6948945; e-mail toimisto@pellervo.fi; internet www.pellervo.fi; f. 1899; monthly; agricultural and co-operative journal; organ of the central organization of co-operatives; Editor-in-Chief KAISU RÄSÄNEN; circ. 35,188.

Pirkka: Kanavakatu 3B, 00160 Helsinki; tel. (9) 1053010; fax (9) 105336235; 10 a year; Swedish; trade; Editor-in-Chief KAISA PEUTERE; circ. 2,278,939.

Reserviläinen: Döbelninkatu 2, 00260 Helsinki; tel. (9) 40562018; fax (9) 499875; monthly; military; circ. 64,593.

Sähköviesti: POB 184, 00131 Helsinki; tel. (9) 68616716; fax (9) 68616786; e-mail ari.vesa@energia.fi; f. 1939; quarterly; publ. by Ascn of Finnish Electric Utilities; Editor-in-Chief ARI J. VESA; circ. 1,400,000.

Sampovisio: POB 2, 00040 Helsinki; tel. (9) 1205964; fax (9) 1205999; 6 a year; business, finance; circ. 65,000.

Seura: Maistraatinportti 1, 00240 Helsinki; tel. (9) 15661; fax (9) 1496472; f. 1934; weekly; family journal; Editor-in-Chief JOUNI FLINKKILÄ; circ. 268,553.

STTK—lehti: POB 248, 00171 Helsinki; tel. (9) 131521; fax (9) 652367; e-mail forename.surname@sttk.fi; 8 a year; organ of Finnish Confederation of Salaried Employees; Editor-in-Chief MATTI HYNYNEN; circ. 40,000.

Suomen Kuvalehti: Maistraatinportti 1, 00015 Yhtyneet Kuvalehdet; tel. (9) 15661; fax (9) 144076; e-mail suomen.kuvalehti@kuvalehdet.fi; internet saunalahti.fi/suomenkuvalehti; f. 1916; weekly; illustrated news; Editor-in-Chief TAPANI RUOKANEN; circ. 96,902.

Suosikki: Maistraatinportti 1, 00015 Yhtyneet Kuvalehdet; tel. (9) 1566553; fax (9) 1445595; e-mail suosikki@kuvalehdet.fi; internet www.magnet.fi; monthly; pop music; Editor-in-Chief JYRKI HÄMÄLÄINEN; circ. 77,445.

Suuri Käsityölehti: POB 100, 00040 Helsinki; tel. (9) 1201; fax (9) 1205428; f. 1974; monthly; needlework, knitting and dress-making magazine; Editor KRISTINA TÖTTERMAN; circ. 126,858.

Talouselämä: Malminkatu 30, POB 920, 00101 Helsinki; tel. (9) 148801; fax (9) 6856650; e-mail te@talentum.fi; internet www .talouselama.fi; f. 1938; 43 a year; economy, administration; Man. Dir JIKKA SEPPÄLÄ; Editor-in-Chief PEKKA SEPPÄNEN; circ. 70,029.

Tekniikan Maailma: Esterinportti 1, 00240 Helsinki; tel. (9) 15661; fax (9) 15666313; e-mail tekniikan.maailma@kuvalehdet.fi; internet www.tekniikanmaailma.fi; f. 1953; 20 a year; technical review; Editor-in-Chief MARTTI J. MERILINNA; circ. 129,343.

Trendi: Kalevankatu 56A, 00180 A-lehdet, Helsinki; tel. (9) 773951; fax (9) 77395399; 10 a year; women's lifestyle; circ. 62,063.

Tuulilasi: Hitsaajankatu 7/6, 00081 Helsinki; tel. (9) 75961; fax (9) 787311; e-mail tuulilasi@a-lehdet.fi; internet www.a-lehdet.fi/tuulilasi; f. 1963; monthly; motoring; Editor-in-Chief LAURI LARMELA; circ. 87,484.

Työ Terveys Turvallisuus: Topeliuksenkatu 41A, 00250 Helsinki; tel. (9) 47471; fax (9) 47472478; f. 1971; 12 a year; occupational safety and health; Editor-in-Chief MATTI TAPIAINEN; circ. 69,923.

Valitut Palat: POB 46, 00441 Helsinki; tel. (9) 503441; fax (9) 5034499; monthly; Finnish Reader's Digest; Editor-in-Chief TOM LUNDBERG; circ. 354,103.

Voi Hyvin: Hitsaajankatu 7, 00081 Helsinki; tel. (9) 75961; fax (9) 786858; e-mail voihyvin@a-lehdet.fi; 6 a year; health; circ. 75,000.

Yhteishyvä: POB 171, 00511 Helsinki; tel. (9) 1881; fax (9) 1882626; f. 1905; monthly; free to members of co-operative group; Editor-in-Chief PENTTI TÖRMÄLÄ; circ. 695,000.

NEWS AGENCIES

Oy Suomen Tietotoimisto-Finska Notisbyrån Ab (STT-FNB): Albertinkatu 33, POB 550, 00101 Helsinki; tel. (9) 695811; fax (9) 69581335; e-mail toimitus@stt.fi; internet www.stt.fi; f. 1887; nine provincial branches; independent national agency distributing domestic and international news in Finnish and Swedish; Chair. SEPPO KIEVARI; Gen. Man. and Editor-in-Chief MIKAEL PENTIKÄINEN.

Foreign Bureaux

Agence France-Presse (AFP) (France): Hämeentie 101B, 38, 00500 Helsinki; tel. (9) 737693; fax (9) 27095339; Correspondent PASCAL ZERLING.

Agenzia Nazionale Stampa Associata (ANSA) (Italy): Albertinkatu 33, 00180 Helsinki; tel. (9) 695811; fax (9) 69581335; Correspondent ANNA TORVALDS.

Associated Press (AP) (USA): Erottasankatu 9A, 00130 Helsinki; tel. (9) 6802394; fax (9) 6802310; Correspondent MATTI HUUHTANEN.

Informatsionnoye Telegrafnoye Agentstvo Rossii—Telegrafnoye Agentstvo Suverennykh Stran (ITAR—TASS) (Russia): Ratakatu 1A B 10, 00120 Helsinki; tel. (9) 601877; fax (9) 601151; e-mail ryhels@hotmail.com; internet www.itar-tass.com; Dir YURI ROMANTSOV.

Inter Press Service (IPS) (Italy): Suomen IPS, Käenkuja 3–5E, 00500 Helsinki; tel. (9) 7536954; fax (9) 7536964; e-mail ips@kaapeli .fi; Editor MILLA SUNDSTRÖM.

Reuters (UK): Yrjönkatu 23B 7, POB 550, 00100 Helsinki; tel. (9) 68050247; fax (9) 6802284; Correspondent ADAM JASSER.

Rossiyskoye Informatsionnoye Agentstvo—Novosti (RIA—Novosti) (Russia): Lönnrotinkatu 25A, 00180 Helsinki; tel. (9) 6820580; fax (9) 6942357; Dir LEONID LAAKSO; Correspondent RUDOLF HILTUNEN.

Xinhua (New China) News Agency (People's Republic of China): Hopeasalmentie 14, 00570 Helsinki; tel. (9) 6847587; fax (9) 6848629; Correspondents ZHENG HUANGING, QIE SHUANGTAO.

PRESS ASSOCIATIONS

Aikakauslehtien Liitto (Periodical Publishers' Association): Lönnrotinkatu 11, 00120 Helsinki; tel. (9) 22877280; fax (9) 603478; internet www.aikakaus.fi; f. 1946; aims to further the interests of publishers of magazines and periodicals, to encourage co-operation between publishers, and to improve standards; Man. Dir MATTI AHTOMIES.

Suomen Journalistiliitto—Finlands Journalistförbund r.y. (Union of Journalists): Hietalahdenkatu 2B 22, 00180 Helsinki; tel. (9) 6122330; fax (9) 644120; f. 1921; 11,759 mems; Pres. PEKKA LAINE; Sec.-Gen. EILA HYPPÖNEN.

Sanomalehtien Liitto—Tidningarnas Förbund (Finnish Newspapers Association): Lönnrotinkatu 11, 00120 Helsinki; tel. (9) 22877300; fax (9) 607989; e-mail info@sanomalehdet.fi; f. 1908; negotiates newsprint prices, postal rates; represents the press in relations with Government and advertisers; undertakes technical research; promotes newspaper advertising; 210 mems; Man. Dir VEIKKO LÖYTTYNIEMI.

Publishers

Art House Oy: Bulevardi 19C, 00120 Helsinki; tel. (9) 6932727; fax (9) 6949028; f. 1975; Finnish and foreign fiction, non-fiction, popular science, horror, fantasy, science fiction, detective fiction; Publr PAAVO HAAVIKKO.

Gummerus Kustannus Oy: Arkadiankatu 23B, POB 749, 00101 Helsinki; tel. (9) 584301; fax (9) 58430200; e-mail publisher@gummerus.fi; internet www.gummerus.fi/kustannus; f. 1872; fiction, non-fiction, encyclopaedias, dictionaries, textbooks and reference books; Man. Dir AHTI SIRKIÄ.

Helsinki Media Oy: POB 100, 00040 Helsinki; tel. (9) 1201; fax (9) 1205171; internet www.helsinkimedia.fi; f. 1993; magazines, directories, children's books, comics, non-fiction; Pres. EIJA AILASMAA.

Karisto Oy: Paroistentie 2, POB 102, 13101 Hämeenlinna; tel. (3) 6161551; fax (3) 6161555; f. 1900; non-fiction and fiction, the printing industry; Man. Dir SIMO MOISIO.

Kirjapaja: POB 137, 00101 Helsinki; tel. (9) 613021; fax (9) 61302341; f. 1942; Christian literature, general fiction, non-fiction, reference, juvenile; Man. Dir KALEVI VIRTANEN.

Kustannus-Mäkelä Oy: POB 14, 03601 Karkkila; tel. (9) 2257995; fax (9) 2257660; f. 1971; juvenile, fiction; Man. Dir ORVO MÄKELÄ.

Oy Like Kustannus Ltd: Meritullinkatu 21, 00170 Helsinki; tel. (9) 1351385; fax (9) 1351372; e-mail likekustannus@dlc.fi; f. 1987; film literature, fiction, non-fiction, comics; Man. Dir HANNU PALOVIITA.

Otava Publishers: Uudenmaankatu 10, 00120 Helsinki; tel. (9) 19961; fax (9) 643136; e-mail otava@otava.fi; internet www.otava.fi; f. 1890; non-fiction, fiction, the printing industry, science, juvenile, and textbooks; Man. Dir ANTTI REENPÄÄ.

Schildts Förlags Ab: Rusthållargatan 1, 02270 Espoo; tel. (9) 8870400; fax (9) 8043257; e-mail schildts@schildts.fi; f. 1913; subjects mainly in Swedish; Man. Dir JOHAN JOHNSON.

Söderström & Co Förlags Ab: Wavulinsvägen 4, 00210 Helsinki; tel. (9) 68418620; fax (9) 68418621; e-mail soderstr@soderstrom.fi; f. 1891; all subjects in Swedish only; Man. Dir MARIANNE BARGUM.

Suomalaisen Kirjallisuuden Seura, SKS (Finnish Literature Society): POB 259, 00171 Helsinki; tel. (9) 131231; fax (9) 13123220; f. 1831; Finnish and other Finno-Ugric languages, Finnish literature, literary scholarship, folklore, comparative ethnology and history; Publishing Dir MATTI SUURPÄÄ.

Tammi Publishers: Urho Kekkosen katu 4–6E, 00100 Helsinki; tel. (9) 6937621; fax (9) 69376266; e-mail tammi@tammi.net; internet www.tammi.net; f. 1943; fiction, non-fiction, juvenile; Man. Dir PENTTI MOLANDER.

Weilin & Göös Oy: Kappelitie 8, 02200 Espoo; tel. (9) 43771; fax (9) 4377270; e-mail weegee@wg.fi; internet www.wg.fi; f. 1872; non-fiction, encyclopaedias; Man. Dir JUHANI MIKOLA.

Werner Söderström Corporation (WSOY): Bulevardi 12, 00120 Helsinki; tel. (9) 61681; fax (9) 61683560; internet www.wsoy.fi; f. 1878; fiction and non-fiction, science, juvenile, textbooks, reference, comics, the printing industry; Pres. ANTERO SILJOLA.

PUBLISHERS' ASSOCIATION

Suomen Kustannusyhdistys (Finnish Book Publishers' Association): POB 177, 00121 Helsinki; tel. (9) 22877258; fax (9) 6121226; e-mail finnpubl@skyry.pp.fi; internet www.sky.cultnet.fi; f. 1858; Chair. OLLI ARRAKOSKI; Man. Dir VEIKKO SONNINEN; 88 mems.

Broadcasting and Communications

TELECOMMUNICATIONS

Telecommunications Administration Centre: Itämerinkatu 3A, POB 313, 00181 Helsinki; tel. (9) 69661; fax (9) 6966410; e-mail info@thk.fi; internet www.thk.fi; affiliated to Ministry of Transport and Communications; CEO RAUNI HAGMAN.

Elisa Communications: Korkeavuorenkatu 35–37, POB 148, 00131 Helsinki; tel. (0) 1026000; fax (9) 664480; internet www.elisa .com; Pres. and CEO MATTI MATTHEISZEN.

Finnet International Ltd: POB 94, 00131 Helsinki; tel. (9) 69550212; fax (9) 69550301.

Nokia Telecommunications: POB 226, 00045 Nodia Group; tel. (9) 18071; fax (9) 656338; internet www.nokia.com; Pres. and Chief Exec. JORMA OLLILA.

Sonera Ltd: Teollisuuskatu 15, POB 106, 00051 Helsinki; tel. (9) 20401; fax (9) 20403647; internet www.sonera.net; fmrly Telecom Finland Ltd; 80%-owned by the state-owned Sonera Group PLC; partially privatized in 1998; government holding of 53.3% to be sold during 2001; Pres. and CEO AULIS SALIN.

Telecon Ltd: POB 110, Teollisuuskatu 15, 00511 Helsinki; tel. (0) 20405390; fax (0) 20405389; e-mail telecon@telecon.fi; Man. Dir YRJÖ SIRKEINEN.

RADIO

Yleisradio Oy (YLE) (Finnish Broadcasting Company): POB 96, 00024 Yleisradio; tel. (9) 14801; fax (9) 14803390; e-mail fbc@yle.fi; internet www.yle.fi/fbc; f. 1926; 99.9% state-owned, with management appointed by the Administrative Council; YLE owns all the national terrestrial radio and television distribution networks in Finland; Dir-Gen. ARNE WESSBERG; Dir of Radio and Deputy Dir-Gen. TAPIO SIIKALA; Dir of Television HEIKKI LEHMUSTO; Dir of Swedish-language Radio and Television Programmes ANN SANDELIN.

Digita Oy: f. 1999; 100%-owned by Yleisradio Oy (YLE); provides transmission services to YLE, MTV3, Channel Four Finland and Radio Nova.

YLE R1 (Radio Ylen Ykkönen): 24-hour arts and culture in Finnish; Dir OLLI ALHO.

YLE R2 (Radiomafia): 24-hour popular culture for young people in Finnish; Dir JUKKA HAARMA.

YLE R3 (Radio Suomi): 24-hour news, current affairs, sport, regional programmes in Finnish; Dir RAIMO VANNINEN.

YLE R4 (Radio Extrem): Swedish-language channel for young people; Dir RICHARD NORDGREN.

YLE R5 (Radio Vega): news, current affairs, art, culture and regional programmes in Swedish; Dir PEIK HENRICHSON.

Capital FM: 24-hour local service in the Helsinki area combining broadcasts by YLE and several foreign radio stations.

Radio Peili: Finland's first digital radio service, began operations in 1998.

Sámi Radio: Sámi-language network covering northern Lapland.

Radio Finland: Broadcasts in Finnish, Swedish, English, German, French, Russian and Classical Latin.

Experimental Finnish local radio began operations in 1984, and in 1995 there were 61 local radio stations, of which two were broadcasting on a semi-national basis.

TELEVISION

Oy Yleisradio Ab (YLE) (see above) operates two national networks, TV 1 and TV 2, and leases the third network to the commercial company MTV Finland (see below).

YLE/TV 1: POB 97, 00024 Helsinki; tel. (9) 14801; fax (9) 14803424; e-mail astrid.gartz@yle.fi; f. 1957; programmes in Finnish; Dir ASTRID GARTZ.

YLE/TV 2: POB 196, 33101 Tampere; tel. (3) 3456111; fax (3) 3456892; f. 1964; programmes in Finnish and Swedish; Dir JYRKI PAKARINEN.

YLE/TV 4: relays programmes from Sweden for coastal areas in southern Finland.

MTV Finland: 00033 MTV3, 00240 Helsinki; tel. (9) 15001; fax (9) 1500707; f. 1957; independent nationwide commercial television company producing programmes on the third national network (MTV3), leased from YLE, the state broadcasting company (see above); about 120 hours per week; Pres. and CEO (vacant).

Oy Kolmostelevisio Ab (MTV3 Finland): 00033 MTV3, 00240 Helsinki; tel. (9) 15001; fax (9) 1500673; subsidiary of MTV Finland; sport and other subcontracted programming on MTV 3; Man. Dir HEIKKI VAHALA.

Finance

The Bank of Finland is the country's central bank and the centre of Finland's monetary and banking system. It functions 'under guarantee and supervision of Parliament and the Bank supervisors delegated by Parliament'.

In late 1998 Finland's three groups of deposit banks (commercial banks, co-operative banks and savings banks) had a total of 1,655 branches. There were three large commercial banks and six smaller ones, and 293 co-operative banks, with their own extensive branch networks. In December 1998 (following a number of mergers in the early 1990s) there were 40 savings banks. There were also three mortgage banks and six specialized credit institutions. Insurance companies (numbering about 60) also grant credit. Foreign banks were permitted to open branches in Finland from the beginning of 1991.

BANKING

(cap. = capital; dep. = deposits; m. = million; res = reserves; brs = branches; amounts in markkaa (FIM) or euros (€), unless otherwise indicated)

Supervisory Authority

Financial Supervision Authority: Kluuvikatu 5, POB 159, 00101 Helsinki; tel. (9) 18351; fax (9) 1835328; f. 1995; maintains confidence in the financial markets by supervising the markets and the bodies working within them. It functions administratively in connection with the Bank of Finland, but operates as an independent decision-making body; Dir-Gen. KAARLO JÄNNÄRI.

Central Bank

Suomen Pankki/Finlands Bank (The Bank of Finland): Snellmaninaukio, POB 160, 00101 Helsinki; tel. (9) 1831; fax (9) 174872; e-mail info@bof.fi; internet www.bof.fi; f. 1811; Bank of Issue under the guarantee and supervision of Parliament; cap. FIM 5,000m., res FIM 764m. (Dec. 1998); Gov. MATTI VANHALA; 4 brs.

Commercial and Mortgage Banks

Sampo-Leonea PLC: Eteläesplanadi 8, Helsinki, 00075 Sampo; tel. (10) 51510; fax (10) 5132608; internet www.sampo-leonia.fi; f. 1886 as Postipankki Ltd; changed name Leonia Bank PLC in 1998; formed by merger with Sampo PLC; cap. FIM 630m., res FIM 2,907.0m., dep. FIM 96,950.0m. (Dec. 1998); CEO EINO KEINANEN; 63 brs.

Mandatum Bank PLC: Bulevardi 10, POB 152, 00121 Helsinki; tel. (9) 166721; fax (9) 632705; internet www.mandatum.fi; f. 1988 as Interbank Ltd; changed name as above in 1998; cap. FIM 80.1m., res FIM 225.5m., dep. FIM 2,801.5m. (Dec. 1998); Chair. KURT LUNDMARK.

Merita Nordbanken: Aleksanterinkatu 30, 00010 Helsinki; tel. (9) 1651; fax (9) 16542838; internet www.merita.fi/s/; f. 1998 by merger of Merita Pankki Oy (Merita Bank Ltd, f. 1995) and a Swedish bank; cap. FIM 6,024m., res. FIM 6,697m., dep. FIM 248,931m. (Dec. 1997); Chair. and CEO HANS DALBORG; Pres. PXERTTI VOUTILAINEN; 479 brs.

OKO—Investointiluottopankki Oyj (OKO Mortgage Bank PLC): Teollisuuskatu 1B, POB 930, 00101 Helsinki; tel. (9) 4041; fax (9) 4044209; f. 1916; cap. and res €58.6m. (Dec. 1999); Chair. TIMO RITAKALLIO; Man. Dir JOUKO IMMONEN.

Okobank (Osuuspankkien Keskuspankki Oyj) (Co-operative Banks of Finland Ltd): Teollisuuskatu 1B, POB 308, 00101 Helsinki; tel. (9) 4041; fax (9) 4042002; internet www.okobank.fi; f. 1902; cap. FIM 2,314m., dep. FIM 18,312m., total assets FIM 27,000m. (Dec. 1998); Chair. and CEO ANTTI TANSKANEN; Man. Dir MIKAEL SILVENNOINEN.

OP-Kotipankki Oy: Lummetie 2, 01300 Vantaa; tel. (9) 4041; fax (9) 4044042; cap. and res FIM 96m., dep. FIM 588m. (Dec. 1994); Man. Dir MATTI KORKEELA.

Suomen Hypoteekkiyhdistys (Mortgage Society of Finland): Yrjönkatu 9, POB 509, 00101 Helsinki; tel. (9) 228361; fax (9) 647443; f. 1860; cap. and res FIM 220m. (Dec. 1996); Pres. Risto Piepponen.

Savings Bank

Aktia Säästöpankki Oyj (Aktia Savings Bank PLC): Mannerheimintie 14, 00100 Helsinki; tel. (10) 2475000; fax (10) 2476356; e-mail kommunikation@aktia.fi; internet www.aktia.fi; current name adopted in September 1997; cap FIM 423.1m., dep. FIM 12,758.7m. (Dec. 1998); Man. Dir Erik Anderson; 65 brs.

Investment Bank

Nordiska Investeringsbanken (Nordic Investment Bank): Fabianinkatu 34, POB 249, 00171 Helsinki; tel. (9) 18001; fax (9) 1800210; e-mail info@nib.fi; internet www.nibank.org; f. 1976; owned by govts of Denmark, Finland, Iceland, Norway and Sweden; cap. €384m., total assets €11,200m. (Nov. 1999); Pres. and CEO Jon Sigurdsson.

Banking Associations

Säästöpankkiliitto (Finnish Savings Banks Association): Mannerheimintie 14A, 00100 Helsinki; tel. (9) 618440; fax (20) 6029108; internet www.savings-banks.fi; f. 1906; 40 mems; 256 brs; Chair. Eino Linnakangas; Man. Dir Markku Ruutu.

Suomen Pankkiyhdistys r.y. (The Finnish Bankers' Association): Museokatu 8A, POB 1009, 00101 Helsinki; tel. (9) 4056120; fax (9) 40561291; e-mail info@pankkiyhdistys.fi; internet www.pankkiyhdistys.fi; f. 1914; Chair. Pertti Voutilainen; Man. Dir Matti Sipilä.

STOCK EXCHANGE

Helsinki Exchanges (HEX Ltd, Helsinki Securities and Derivatives Exchange, Clearing House): Fabianinkatu 14, POB 361, 00131 Helsinki; tel. (9) 616671; fax (9) 61667366; e-mail juhani.erma@hex.fi; internet www.hex.fi; f. 1912; current name adopted following merger between Helsinki Stock Exchange Ltd and SOM Ltd in December 1997; from 1999 Finnish derivatives were to be traded within the Swiss–German exchange, the Eurex, and from 2000 the cash market was to use the German Xetra trading system; 132 listed companies at end of December 1998; Chair. of Bd of Dirs Jussi Laitinen; CEO Juhani Erma.

INSURANCE

A list is given below of some of the more important insurance companies:

A-Vakuutus keskinäinen yhtiö (A-Vakuutus Mutual Insurance Co): Hietalahdenranta 3, POB 165, 00151 Helsinki; tel. (10) 5040; fax (10) 5045200; non-life; Man. Dir Esko Rinkinen.

Aurum Life Insurance Co. Ltd: POB 308, 00101 Helsinki; tel. (9) 4042528; fax (9) 4043501; Man. Dir Jukka Ruuskanen.

Eurooppalainen Insurance Co Ltd: Lapinmäentie 1, 00013 Pohjola; tel. (10) 55911; fax (10) 5592205; non-life; Man. Dir Jouni Aaltonen.

Garantia Insurance Co Ltd: Salomonkatu 17A, POB 600, 00101 Helsinki; tel. (9) 685811; fax (9) 68581301; internet www.garantia.fi; non-life; Man. Dir Mikael Englund.

Henkivakuutusosakeyhtiö Pohjola (Pohjola Life Assurance Co Ltd): POB 1068, 00101 Helsinki; tel. (10) 55911; fax (10) 5596799; internet www.pohjola.fi; Man. Dir Jarmo Kuisma.

Henkivakuutusosakeyhtiö Verdandi (Verdandi Life Insurance Co Ltd): Olavintie 2, POB 133, 20101 Turku; tel. (10) 55010; fax (10) 5501690; Man. Dir Folke Lindström.

Keskinäinen Eläkevakuutusyhtiö Ilmarinen (Ilmarinen Mutual Pension Insurance Co): Eerikinkatu 41, 00018 Jimarinen; tel. (9) 1841; fax (9) 1843445; e-mail info@ilmarinen.fi; internet www.ilmarinen.fi; f. 1961; statutory employment pensions; Man. Dir Kari Puro.

Keskinäinen Eläkevakuutusyhtiö Tapiola (Tapiola Mutual Pension Insurance Co): 02010 Tapiola; tel. (9) 4531; fax (9) 4532146; internet www.tapiola.fi; Pres. Asmo Kalpala; Man. Dir Tom Liljeström.

Keskinäinen Eläkevakuutusyhtio Varma-Sampo (Varma-Sampo Mutual Pension Insurance Company): POB 1, 00098 Varma-Sampo; tel. (10) 51513; fax (10) 5154752; e-mail asiakaspalvelu@varma-sampo.fi; internet www.varma-sampo.fi; Man. Dir Paavo Pitkänen.

Keskinäinen Henkivakuutusosakeyhtiö Suomi (Suomi Mutual Life Assurance Co): Lönnrotinkatu 5, 00120 Helsinki; tel. (10) 55911; fax (10) 5596799; Man. Dir Jukka Rantala.

Keskinäinen Henkivakuutusyhtiö Tapiola (Tapiola Mutual Life Assurance Co): 02010 Tapiola; tel. (9) 4531; fax (9) 4532146; internet www.tapiola.fi; Pres. Jari Saine.

Keskinäinen Vakuutusyhtiö Kaleva (Kaleva Mutual Insurance Co): Bulevardi 56, 00025 Sampo; tel. (10) 515225; fax (10) 5147449; Man. Dir Matti Rantanen.

Keskinäinen Vakuutusyhtiö Tapiola (Tapiola General Mutual Insurance Co): 02010 Tapiola; tel. (9) 4531; fax (9) 4532146; internet www.tapiola.fi; non-life; Pres. Asmo Kalpala; Man. Dir Pertti Heikkala.

Keskinäinen Yhtiö Yrittäjäinvakuutus—Fennia (Enterprise Fennia Mutual Insurance Co): Asemamiehenkatu 3, 00520 Helsinki; tel. (10) 5031; fax (10) 5035300; non-life; Man. Dir Kari Elo.

Lähivakuutus Keskinäinen Yhtiö (Local Insurance Mutual Co): Lintuvaarantie 2, POB 50, 02601 Espoo; tel. (9) 511011; fax (9) 51101335; internet www.lahivakuutus.fi; non-life; Man. Dir Harri Kainulainen.

Leonia Henkivokuutus Oy (Leonia Life Insurance Co Ltd): Fabianinkatu 7 00007 Helsinki; tel. (20) 4256099; fax (20) 4256299; Man. Dir Arto Jurttila.

Merita Henkivakaatus Oy (Merita Life Assurance Ltd): Asemakuja 2, 00020 Merita; tel. (9) 16527601; fax (9) 8594622; internet www.merita.fi/selekta; Man. Dir Seppo Ilvessalo.

Palonvara Mutual Insurance Co: Saimaankatu 20, 15140 Lahti; tel. (3) 873300; fax (3) 8733050; e-mail palvelu@palonvara.fi; internet www.palonvara.fi; f. 1912; non-life; Man. Dir Jukka Hertti.

Pankavara Insurance Co Ltd: Kanavaranta 1, POB 309, 00101 Helsinki; tel. (20) 46111; fax (20) 4621447; non-life; Man. Dir Jukka Kähönen.

Pohjanti Keskäinen Vakuutusyhtiö (Pohjantähti Mutual Insurance Co): Raatihuoneenkatu 19, POB 164, 13101 Hämeenlinna; tel. (3) 62671; fax (3) 6169303; e-mail polvelu@pohjantahti.fi; internet www.pohjantahti.fi; f. 1895; non-life; Man. Dir Eero Ylä-Soininmäki.

Säästöpankkien Keskinäinen Vakuutusyhtiö (Mutual Insurance Co of the Savings Banks): Mannerheimintie 7, 00100 Helsinki; tel. (20) 4401; fax (20) 4407320; non-life; Man. Dir Hannu Loponen.

Sampo-Leonia Insurance Company PLC: Eteläesplanadi 8, Helsinki; 00075 Sampo; tel. (10) 51510; fax (10) 5132608; internet www.sampo.fi; life and non-life; Man. Dir Jouko K. Leskinen.

Spruce Insurance Ltd: POB 330, 00101 Helsinki; tel. (10) 8611; fax (10) 8621107; e-mail leena.laakso@kemira.com; non-life; Man. Dir Leena Laakso.

Teollisuusvakuutus Oy (Industrial Insurance Co Ltd): Vattuniemenkuja 8A, 00035 Helsinki; tel. (10) 51512; fax (10) 5145232; internet www.sampo.fi; non-life; Man. Dir Juha Toivola.

Vakuutusosakeyhtiö Pohjola (Pohjola Insurance Co Ltd): Lapinmäentie 1, 00013 Pohjola; tel. (10) 55911; fax (10) 5592205; non-life; Man. Dir Joukko Bergius.

Insurance Associations

Federation of Accident Insurance Institutions: Bulevardi 28, POB 275, 00121 Helsinki; tel. (9) 680401; fax (9) 68040389; e-mail forename.surname@vakes.fi; f. 1920; Man. Dir Tapani Miettinen.

Federation of Finnish Insurance Companies: Bulevardi 28, 00120 Helsinki; tel. (9) 680401; fax (9) 68040216; e-mail asmo.kalpala@vakcs.fi; internet www.vakcs.fi/svk; f. 1942; Chair. Iiro Viinanen; Man. Dir Asmo Kalpala; 50 mems.

Finnish Atomic Insurance Pool, Finnish Pool of Aviation Insurers, Finnish General Reinsurance Pool: Ratakatu 9, 00120 Helsinki; tel. (9) 680149; Man. Dir K.-M. Strömmer.

Finnish Motor Insurers' Centre: Bulevardi 28, 00120 Helsinki; tel. (9) 680401; fax (9) 68040391; f. 1938; Man. Dir Pentti Ajo.

Finnish Pension Alliance RLA: Lastenkodinkuja 1, 00180 Helsinki; tel. (9) 695560; fax (9) 69556200; f. 1964; Man. Dir Esa Swanlvung.

Trade and Industry

GOVERNMENT AGENCIES

Finnish Foreign Trade Association: Arkadiankatu 2, POB 908, 00101 Helsinki; tel. (20) 46951; fax (20) 4695535; e-mail info@exports.finland.fi; internet www.exports.finland.fi; f. 1919; Chair. Jorma Ollila; Chair. of Board Johannes Koroma; CEO Seppo Härkönen.

Invest in Finland Bureau: Aleksanterinkatu 17, POB 800, 00101 Helsinki; tel. (9) 6969125; fax (9) 69692530: e-mail investinfinland-cawtc.fi; internet www.investinfinland.fi.

DEVELOPMENT ORGANIZATION

Altia Group: Salmisaarenranta 7, POB 350, 00101 Helsinki; tel. (9) 13311; fax (9) 1333361; internet www.altiagroup.fi; f. 1932;

development, manufacture, import, export, wholesale and marketing of alcoholic beverages; 100% state-owned; Pres. and CEO Veikko Kasurinen.

CHAMBERS OF COMMERCE

Helsinki Chamber of Commerce: Kalevankatu 12, 00100 Helsinki; tel. (9) 228601; f. 1917; Pres. Kurt Nordman; Man. Dir Heikki Heliö; 4,100 mems.

Keskuskauppakamari (Central Chamber of Commerce): Aleksanterinkatu 17, POB 1000, 00101 Helsinki; tel. (9) 696969; fax (9) 650303; internet www.keskuskauppakamari.fi; f. 1918; Pres. Vesa Vainio; Gen. Man. Kari Jalas; represents 21 regional chambers of commerce.

INDUSTRIAL AND TRADE ASSOCIATIONS

Kalatalouden Keskusliitto (Federation of Finnish Fisheries Associations): Köydenpunojankatu 7B 23, 00180 Helsinki; tel. (9) 6844590; fax (9) 68445959; e-mail kalastus@ahven.net; internet www.ahven.net; f. 1891; Sec. M. Myllylä; 616,000 mems.

Kaukomarkkinat Oy: Kutojantie 4, 02630 Espoo; tel. (9) 5211; fax (9) 5216641; internet www.kaukomarkkinat.fi; f. 1947; export, import and international trade; Pres. Kari Ansio.

Kaupan Keskusliitto (Federation of Finnish Commerce and Trade): Mannerheimintie 76A, 00250 Helsinki; tel. (9) 43156122; fax (9) 43156302; e-mail@kaupankl.fi; internet www.kaupankl.fi; f. 1992; Man. Dir Guy Wires; 40 mem. asscns with over 14,000 firms.

Kesko Oyj (Retailers' Wholesale Co): Satamakatu 3, 00160 Helsinki; tel. (9) 5311; fax (9) 174398; f. 1941; retailer-owned wholesale corporation, trading in foodstuffs, textiles, shoes, consumer goods, agricultural and builders' supplies, and machinery; Pres. Matti Honkala.

Oy Labor Ab (Agricultural Machinery): Mikkolantie 1, 00640 Helsinki; tel. (9) 7291; f. 1898; Gen. Man. Kimmo Varjovaara.

Maa- ja metsätaloustuottajain Keskusliitto MTK r.y. (Central Union of Agricultural Producers and Forest Owners): Simonkatu 6, 00100 Helsinki; tel. (9) 131151; fax (9) 13115425; e-mail paavo-makinen@mtk.fi; internet www.mtk.fi; f. 1917; Chair. of Board of Dirs Esa Härmälä; Sec.-Gen. Paavo Mäkinen; 179,000 mems.

Metsäteollisuus r.y. (Finnish Forest Industries Federation): Snellmaninkatu 13, POB 336, 00171 Helsinki; tel. (9) 13261; fax (9) 1324445; e-mail timo-poranen@forestindustries.fi; internet www.forestindustries.fi; f. 1918; Man. Dir Timo Poranen; mems: 120 companies in the forestry industry and the following sales or trade associations:

> **Finncell** (Finnish Pulp Exporters' Association): Eteläesplanadi 2, POB 60, 00101 Helsinki; tel. (9) 132480; fax (9) 1324892; f. 1918; Man. Dir T. Nykopp; 4 mems.

> **Suomen Lastulevy-yhdistys** (Finnish Particle Board Association): Rikhardinkatu 1B 19, 00130 Helsinki; tel. (9) 657122; fax (9) 657145; Man. Dir Pentti Saarro; 2 mems.

> **Suomen Vaneriyhdistys** (Association of Finnish Plywood Industry): Rikhardinkatu 1B 19, 00130 Helsinki; tel. (9) 657122; fax (9) 657145; f. 1939; Man. Dir Pentti Saarro; 4 mems.

Suomalaisen Työn Liitto (Association for Finnish Work): Mannerheimintie 8, POB 429, 00101 Helsinki; tel. (9) 6962430; fax (9) 69624333; e-mail stl@avainlippu.fi; internet www.avainlippu.fi; f. 1978; public relations for Finnish products and for Finnish work; Chair. of Council Kimmo Sasi; Chair. of Board of Dirs Hannu Jaakkola; Man. Dir Lars Collin; about 1,200 mems.

Suomen Betoniteollisuuden Keskusjärjestö r.y. (Association of the Concrete Industry of Finland): Helsinki; tel. (9) 648212; fax (9) 642597; f. 1929; Chair. Erkki Inkinen; Man. Dir Erkki Tikkanen; 78 mems.

Suomen Osuuskauppojen Keskusliitto (SOKL) r.y. (Finnish Co-operative Union): POB 171, 00511 Helsinki; tel. (9) 1882222; fax (9) 1882580; f. 1908; Chair. Matti Vanto; Man. Dir Tapio Peltola; 44 mems.

Svenska Lantbruksproducenternas centralförbund (Central Union of Swedish-speaking Agricultural Producers): Fredriksgatan 61A, 00100 Helsinki; tel. (9) 5860460; fax (9) 6941358; internet www.slc.fi; f. 1945; Swedish-speaking producers; Chair. O. Rosendahl; 18,000 mems.

Teknisen Kaupan Liitto (Association of Finnish Technical Traders): Sarkiniementie 3, 00210 Helsinki; tel. (9) 6824130; fax (9) 68241310; e-mail tekninen.kauppa@tkl.fi; internet www.tkl.fi; f. 1918; organization of the main importers dealing in steel and metals, machines and equipment, heavy chemicals and raw materials; Chair. Heimo Aho; Man. Dir Klaus Katara; 225 mems.

EMPLOYERS' ORGANIZATIONS

Autoliikenteen Työnantajaliitto r.y. (Employers' Federation of Road Transport): Nuijamiestentie 7A, 00400 Helsinki; tel. (9) 47899480; fax (9) 5883995; internet www.altnet.fi; Chair. Pertti Korhonen; Man. Dir Hannu Parvela; 995 mems.

Autonrengasliitto r.y. (Tyre Specialists of Finland): Eteläranta 10, 00130 Helsinki; tel. (9) 172841; fax (9) 179588; e-mail osten.brannas@toimialaliitot.ttliitot.fi; f. 1944; Chair. Tuomo Räsänen; Exec. Dir Östen Brännäs; 77 mems.

Kultaseppien Työnantajaliitto r.y. (Employers' Association of Goldsmiths): Eteläranta 10, 00130 Helsinki; tel. (9) 172841; fax (9) 179588; e-mail sari.vannela@ryhma.ttliitot.fi; Chair. Ilkka Ruohola; Exec. Dir Sari Vannela.

Liiketyönantajain Keskusliitto (LTK) r.y. (Employers' Confederation of Service Industries): Eteläranta 10, 00130 Helsinki; tel. (9) 172831; fax (9) 655588; f. 1945; seven mem. asscns consisting of about 5,800 enterprises with 234,000 employees; Man. Dir Jarmo Pellikka.

Suomen Tiiliteollisuusliitto r.y. (Finnish Brick Industry Association): POB 11, 00131 Helsinki; tel. (9) 17284431; fax (9) 17284444; e-mail jyrki.malmio@rtt.ttliitot.fi; Chair. Leo Seppälä.

Teollisuuden ja Työnantajain Keskusliitto (TT) (Confederation of Finnish Industry and Employers): Eteläranta 10, POB 30, 00131 Helsinki; tel. (9) 68681; fax (9) 68682812; internet www.tt.fi; f. 1907 (renamed 1992); aims to promote co-operation between companies and member organizations and to protect the interests of mems in employment issues; 30 asscns consisting of about 5,600 enterprises with 500,000 employees; Chair. Jurki Juusela; Dir-Gen. Johannes Koroma.

> **Elintarviketeollisuusliitto r.y.** (Finnish Food and Drinks Industries' Federation): Pasilankatu 2, 00240 Helsinki; tel. (9) 148871; fax (9) 14887201; e-mail food.industry@etl.fi; internet www.etl.fi; Chair. Bertel Paulig; Dir Gen. Pekka Hämäläinen.

> **Energia-alan Keskusliitto r.y. Finergy** (Finnish Energy Industries Federation): Eteläranta 10, 00130 Helsinki; tel. (9) 686161; fax (9) 6861630; e-mail info@finergy.fi; internet www.energia.fi; Chair Timo Rajala.

> **Kemianteollisuus (KT) r.y.** (Chemical Industry Federation): Eteläranta 10, POB 4, 00131 Helsinki; tel. (9) 172841; fax (9) 630225; internet www.chemind.fi; Chair. Tauno Pihlava; Man. Dir Hannu Vornamo.

> **Kenkä- ja Nahkateollisuus r.y.** (Association of Finnish Shoe and Leather Industries): Eteläranta 10, 00130 Helsinki; tel. (9) 172841; fax (9) 179588; e-mail sari.vannela@ryhma.ttliitot.fi; Chair. Olavi Viljanmaa; Exec. Dir Sari Vannela.

> **Kulutustavara- ja Erikoistuoteteollisuus Ket** (Association of Consumer Goods and Special Products Industries): Eteläranta 10, 00130 Helsinki; tel. (9) 686121; fax (9) 653305; Chair. Tapani Jarva; Man. Dir Matti Järventie.

> **Kumiteollisuusyhdistys r.y.** (Rubber Manufacturers' Association): Eteläranta 10, 00130 Helsinki; tel. (9) 6220410; fax (9) 176135; e-mail tuula.rantalaiho@kumittliitot.fi; internet www.kumiteollisuus.fi; Chair. Kim Gran; Man. Dir Tuula Rantalaiho.

> **Lääketeollisuus r.y.** (Pharma Industry Finland—PIF): Sörnäisten rantatie 23, POB 108, 00501 Helsinki; tel. (9) 5842400; fax (9) 58424728; e-mail pif@pif.fi; internet www.pif.fi; Chair. Pekka Kalvola; Man. Dir Jarmo Lehtonen.

> **Metalliteollisuuden Keskusliitto r.y.** (Federation of Finnish Metal, Engineering and Electrotechnical Industries): Eteläranta 10, POB 10, 00131 Helsinki; tel. (9) 19231; fax (9) 624462; internet www.met.fi; f. 1903; Chair. Stig Gustavsson; Man. Dir Marti Mäenpää.

> **Metsäteollisuus r.y.** (Finnish Forest Industries): Snellmaninkatu 13, 00170 Helsinki; tel. (9) 13261; fax (9) 1324445; Chair. Juha Niemelä; Man. Dir Timo Poranen.

> **Palvelualojen Toimialaliitto r.y.** (Association of Support Service Industries): Eteläranta 10, 00130 Helsinki; tel. (9) 172841; fax (9) 176877; Chair. Arne Wessberg; Man. Dir Peter Forsström.

> **PT:n Työnantajaliitto r.y.** (PT Employers' Federation): Mannerheiminaukio 1A, 00100 Helsinki; tel. (9) 613151; fax (9) 61315082; Chair. Pekka Vennamo; Man. Dir Juha Kivinen.

> **Puusepänteollisuuden Liitto r.y.** (Association of the Finnish Furniture and Joinery Industries): Snellmaninkatu 13, POB 336, 00171 Helsinki; tel. (9) 13261; fax (9) 1324447; f. 1917; Chair. Hannu Roine; Man. Dir Jukka Nevala; 90 mems.

> **Rakennusteollisuuden Keskusliitto r.y.** (Confederation of the Finnish Construction Industries): Unioninkatu 14 VI, 00130 Helsinki; tel. (9) 12991; fax (9) 1299252; internet www.rtk.fi; f. 1920; Chair. Mikko Pekkala; Man. Dir Terho Salo; 1,630 mems.

> **Rakennustuoteteollisuus RTT r.y.** (Finnish Association of Construction Product Industries): Eteläranta 10, 00130 Helsinki; tel. (9) 172841; fax (9) 17284444; e-mail rtt@rtt.ttliitot.fi; internet www.rttry.fi; f. 1992; Chair. Lauri Ratia; Man. Dir Raimo Taivalkoski.

Rannikko- ja Sisävesiliikenteen Työnantajaliitto (RASILA) r.y. (Coastal and Inland Waterway Employers' Association): Satamakatu 4A, 00160 Helsinki; tel. (9) 62267312; fax (9) 669251; Chair. STEFAN HÅKANS; Man. Dir HENRIK LÖNNQVIST.

Sähkö- ja telealan työnantajaliitto r.y. (Finnish Association of Electrical and Telecommunications Employers): Yrjönkatu 13, 00120 Helsinki; tel. (9) 695900; fax (9) 69590111; Chair. ANTTI RANTANEN; Man. Dir MATTI HÖYSTI; 110 mems.

Suomen Kiinteistöliitto r.y. (Finnish Real-Estate Association): Annankatu 24, 00100 Helsinki; tel. (9) 166761; fax (9) 16676400; f. 1907; Chair. ARTO PALSALA; Man. Dir UKKO LAURILA.

Suomen Lastauttajain Liitto (SLL) r.y. (Federation of Finnish Master Stevedores): Köydenpunojankatu 8, 00180 Helsinki; tel. (9) 6949800; fax (9) 6944585; f. 1906; Chair. HANS MARTIN; Man. Dir HARRI TUULENSU.

Suomen Muoviteollisuusliitto r.y. (Finnish Plastics Industries' Federation): Eteläranta 10, 00130 Helsinki; tel. (9) 172841; fax (9) 171164; Chair. JYRKI ANT-WUORINEN; Man. Dir KARI TEPPOLA.

Suomen Varustamoyhdistys r.y. (Finnish Shipowners' Association): see under Shipping.

Suunnittelu- ja konsulttitoimistojen liitto (SKOL) r.y. (Finnish Association of Consulting Firms—SKOL): Pohjantie 12A, 02100 Espoo; tel. (9) 4160122; fax (9) 467642; e-mail skolry@skolry.fi; internet www.skolry.fi; Chair. KARI LAUTSO; Man. Dir TIMO MYLLYS; 252 mems.

Teknokemian Yhdistys r.y. (Finnish Cosmetic, Toiletry and Detergent Association): Eteläranta 10, 00130 Helsinki; tel. (9) 172841; fax (9) 666561; e-mail stig.granqvist@ty.ttliitot.fi; internet www.teknokem.fi; Chair. JARL STORGÅRDS; Man. Dir STIG GRANQVIST.

Tekstiili- ja vaatetusteollisuus r.y. (Federation of Finnish Textile and Clothing Industries): Aleksis Kivenkatu 10, POB 50, 33211 Tampere; tel. (3) 3889111; fax (3) 3889120; internet www.finatex.fi; f. 1905; Chair. HANNU JAAKKOLA; Man. Dir MATTI JÄRVENTIE.

Toimistoteknisen Kaupan Yhdistys (TTK) r.y. (Finnish Association of Office Technology Traders): Mannerheimintie 76A, 00250 Helsinki; tel. (9) 441651; fax (9) 496142; Chair. KARI SOLALA; Man. Dir EERO PERITALO.

Tupakkateollisuusliitto r.y. (Finnish Tobacco Industries' Federation): POB 115, 00241 Helsinki; tel. (9) 644373; fax (9) 14887201; e-mail asta.morsky@etl.fi; Chair. MATTI RIHKO.

Työnantajain Yleinen Ryhmä r.y. (Finnish Employers' General Group): Eteläranta 10, 00130 Helsinki; tel. (9) 172841; fax (9) 179588; e-mail sari.vannela@ryhma.ttliitot.fi; Chair. MARKKU JOKINEN; Exec. Dir SARI VANNELA.

Viestintätyönantajat VTA (Media Employers' Association): Lönnrotinkatu 11A, 00120 Helsinki; tel. (9) 22877200; fax (9) 603527; Chair. MATTI PACKALÉN; Man. Dir MATTI SUTINEN.

Yleinen Teollisuusliitto r.y. (General Industry Association): Eteläranta 10, 00130 Helsinki; tel. (9) 6220410; fax (9) 176135; Chair. MARKKU TALONEN; Man. Dir MARKKU KÄPPI.

UTILITIES

Finnish Energy Industries Federation: Etelarento 10, POB 21, 00131 Helsinki; tel. (9) 686161; fax (9) 6861630; e-mail info@finergy.fi; internet www.energia.fi/finergy.

Fortum: Helsinki; internet www.fortum.com; f. 1998 following merger of the Imatran Voima Group and the Neste Group; international energy co with core businesses in oil, gas, power and heat; listed on the Helsinki exchanges in December 1998; Chair. MATTI VUORIA; Pres. and CEO HEIKKI MARTTINEN.

Helsingin Kaupungin Energialaitos (Helsinki Energy Board): POB 469, 00101 Helsinki; tel. (9) 6171; fax (9) 6172360; f. 1909; municipal undertaking; generates and distributes electrical power and district heating; distributes natural gas.

Electricity

Kemijoki Oy: Valtakatu 9 11, POB 8131, 96101 Rovaniemi; tel. (16) 7401; fax (16) 7402325; e-mail info@kemijoki.fi; f. 1954; electric power; 70.03% state-owned; Chair. of Supervisory Board KALEVI NUMMINEN; Chair. of Board of Management MARKKU AUTTI; 412 employees.

Suomen Sähkölaitosyhdistys r.y. (Association of Finnish Electric Utilities): Mannerheimintie 76A, 00250 Helsinki; POB 100, 00101 Helsinki; tel. (9) 408188; fax (9) 442994; f. 1926; 122 mems; development of technical, economic and administrative functions of utilities; consultant services in electricity supply; educational activities; research and advice on electrical applications; collection and publication of electricity statistics; publishes consumer magazine *Sähköviesti/Elbladet*; domestic and international co-operation; safety at work and environmental conservation.

Water

Helsinki Water: Iimalankuja 2A, 00240 Helsinki; POB 1100, 00099 Helsinki; tel. (9) 47371; fax (9) 47342010; responsible for water supply and sewerage of the greater Helsinki area.

CO-OPERATIVES

Pellervo (Confederation of Finnish Co-operatives): Simonkatu 6, POB 77, 00100 Helsinki; tel. (9) 4767501; fax (9) 6948845; e-mail toimisto@pellervo.fi; f. 1899; central organization of co-operatives; CEO SAMULI SKURNIK; 400 mem. societies (incl. 7 central co-operative societies).

Munakunta (Co-operative Egg Producers' Association): POB 6, 20761 Piispanristi; tel. 2214420; fax 22144222; f. 1921; Man. Dir JAN LÄHDE; 9,991 mems.

Valio Ltd (Finnish Co-operative Dairies' Association): POB 10, 00039 Valio; tel. (10) 381121; fax (10) 3812059; f. 1905; production and marketing of dairy products; Pres. and CEO OLAVI KUUSELA.

TRADE UNIONS

AKAVA (Confederation of Unions for Academic Professionals): Rautatieläisenkatu 6, 00520 Helsinki; tel. (9) 141822; fax (9) 142595; internet www.akava.fi; f. 1950; 32 affiliates, incl. asscns of doctors, engineers, social workers and teachers; total membership 360,000; Pres. RISTO PIEKKA.

Suomen Ammattiliittojen Keskusjärjestö (SAK) r.y. (Central Organization of Finnish Trade Unions): Siltasaarenkatu 3A, POB 157, 00531 Helsinki; tel. (9) 77211; fax (9) 7721447; internet www.sak.fi; f. 1907; 25 affiliated unions; 1,110,000 mems (1996); Pres. LAURI IHALAINEN; Dirs TUULIKKI KANNISTO, PEKKA AHMAVAARA.

Principal affiliated unions:

Auto- ja Kuljetusalan Työntekijäliitto (AKT) r.y. (Transport Workers): John Stenbergin ranta 6, POB 313, 00531 Helsinki; tel. (9) 613110; fax (9) 739287; e-mail juhani.koivunen@akt.fi; internet www.akt.fi; f. 1948; Pres. KAUKO LEHIKOINEN; Secs MATTI VEHKAOJA, JUHANI KOIVUNEN; 50,721 mems.

Hotelli- ja Ravintolahenkilökunnan Liitto (HRHL) r.y. (Hotel and Restaurant Workers): Toinen linja 3, POB 327, 00531 Helsinki; tel. (9) 77561; fax (9) 7756223; e-mail hrhl@hrhl.fi; f. 1933; Pres. JORMA KALLIO; Sec. LEENA RAUTAVUORI; 50,919 mems.

Kemianliitto-Kemifacket r.y. (Chemical Workers): Haapaniemenkatu 7–9B, POB 324, 00531 Helsinki; tel. (9) 773971; fax (9) 7538040; internet www.kemianliitto.fi; f. 1993; Pres. TIMO VALLITTU; Sec. SULO KORHONEN; 35,000 mems.

Kiinteistötyöntekijäin Liitto r.y. (Caretakers): Viherniemenkatu 5A, 00530 Helsinki; tel. (9) 750075; fax (9) 761427; f. 1948; Pres. RISTO SORSA; Sec. TAUNO ROSTEN; 12,645 mems.

Kunta-alan Ammattiliitto (KTV) r.y. (Municipal Sector): Kolmas linja 4, POB 101, 00531 Helsinki; tel. (9) 77031; fax (9) 7703397; internet www.ktv.fi; f. 1931; Pres. JOUNI RISKILÄ; 211,031 mems.

Metallityöväen Liitto r.y. (Metalworkers): Siltasaarenkatu 3–5A, POB 107, 00531 Helsinki; tel. (9) 77071; fax (9) 7707277; internet www.metalliliitto.fi; f. 1899; Pres. PER-ERIK LUNDH; Sec. ERIK LINDFORS; 164,000 mems.

Palvelualojen ammattiliitto PAM r.y. (Service Union United): Paasivuorenkatu 4–6, POB 54, 00531 Helsinki; tel. (9) 77571; fax (9) 7011119; f. 1987 as Liikealan ammattiliitto r.y.; present name adopted 2000; Pres. MAJ-LEN REMAHL; Vice-Pres JORMA KALLRO KAARLO JULKUNEN; 210,000 mems.

Paperiliitto r.y. (Paperworkers): Paasivuorenkatu 4–6A, POB 326, 00531 Helsinki; tel. (9) 70891; fax (9) 7012279; f. 1906; Pres. JARMO LÄHTEENMÄKI; Gen. Sec. ARTTURI PENNANEN; 48,569 mems.

Puu- ja erityisalojen Liitto r.y. (Wood and Allied Workers): Haapaniemenkatu 7–9B, POB 318, 00531 Helsinki; tel. (9) 615161; fax (9) 761160; e-mail puuliitto@puuliitto.fi; internet www.puuliitto.fi; f. 1993 by merger of two unions; Pres. KALEVI VÄISÄNEN; 55,000 mems.

Rakennusliitto r.y. (Construction Workers): Siltasaarenkatu 4, POB 307, 00531 Helsinki; tel. (9) 77021; fax (9) 7702241; e-mail info@rakennusliitto.fi; internet www.rakennusliitto.fi; f. 1930; Pres. PEKKA HYNÖNEN; 89,000 mems.

Sähköalojen ammattiliitto r.y. (Electrical Workers): Aleksanterinkatu 15, POB 747, 33101 Tampere; tel. (3) 2520111; fax (3) 2520210; e-mail lauri.lyly@sahkoliitto.fi; internet www.sahkoliitto.fi; f. 1955; Pres. LAURI LYLY; Sec. HEIMO RINNE; 30,000 mems.

Suomen Elintarviketyöläisten Liitto (SEL) r.y. (Food Workers): Siltasaarenkatu 6, POB 213, 00531 Helsinki; tel. (9) 393881; fax (9) 712059; f. 1905; Pres. RITVA SAVTSCHENKO; 42,000 mems.

Suomen Merimies-Unioni r.y. (Seamen): Uudenmaankatu 16B, POB 249, 00121 Helsinki; tel. (9) 6152020; fax (9) 61520227;

e-mail forename.surname@smury.fi; internet www.smury.fi; f. 1916; Pres. SIMO ZITTING; Sec. ERKKI UKKONEN; 10,099 mems.

Tekstiili- ja vaatetustyöväen liitto Teva r.y. (Textile and Garment Workers): Salhojankatu 27, POB 87, 33101 Tampere; tel. (3) 2593111; fax (3) 2593343; e-mail tevaliitto@tevaliitto.fi; internet www.tevaliitto.fi; f. 1970; Pres. AULI KORHONEN; 19,000 mems.

Valtion yhteisjärjestö (VTY) r.y. (Joint Organization of State Employees): Haapaniemenkatu 7–9B, POB 317, 00531 Helsinki; tel. (9) 584211; fax (9) 739513; f. 1946; Pres. RAIMO RANNISTO; Sec.-Gen. JAAN VINGISAAR; 37,000 mems.

Viestintäalan ammattiliitto r.y. (Media Union): Sutasarrntatu 4, 00530 Helsinki; tel. (9) 616581; fax (9) 61658333; f. 1894; Pres. PENTTI LEIVO; Sec. PEKKA LAMTINEN; 32,000 mems.

STTK (Finnish Confederation of Salaried Employees): Pohjoisranta 4A, POB 248, 00171 Helsinki; tel. (9) 131521; fax (9) 652367; internet www.sttk.fi.

The principal independent trade unions (formerly affiliated to the now-dissolved Confederation of Salaried Employees—TVK, f. 1922) include the following:

Erityisalojen Toimihenkilöliitto ERTO r.y. (Special Service and Clerical Employees): Asemamiehenkatu 2, 00520 Helsinki; tel. (9) 613231; fax (9) 61323390; e-mail info.erto@erto.fi; internet www.erto.fi; f. 1968; Chair. MATTI HELLSTEN; 20,000 mems.

Hallintovirkailijoiden Keskusliitto (HVK) (Civil Servants): Ratamestarinkatu 11, 00520 Helsinki; tel. (9) 1551; f. 1992; Chair. HEIKKI KUJANPÄÄ; 12,500 mems.

Kunnallisvirkamiesliitto r.y. (KVL) (Municipal Officers): Asemamiehenkatu 4, 00520 Helsinki; tel. (9) 1551; fax (9) 1552333; f. 1918; Chair. KATRIINA PERKKA-JORTIKKA; 74,000 mems.

Maanpuolustuksen ja Turvallisuuden Ammattijärjestöt (MTAJ) r.y. (Defence and Security Employees): Ratamestarinkatu 11, 00520 Helsinki; tel. (9) 1551; f. 1992; Chair. PIRKKO MATTILA; 7,800 mems.

Suomen Perushoitajaliitto (Enrolled Nurses): Asemamiehenkatu 2, 00520 Helsinki; tel. (9) 141833; f. 1948; Chair. KAARINA MUHLI; 36,000 mems.

Suomen Poliisijärjestöjen Liitto (Police): Asemamiehenkatu 2, 00520 Helsinki; tel. (9) 1551; f. 1990; Chair. MATTI KRATS; 13,600 mems.

Suomen Rahoitus- ja Erityisalojen ammattiliitto r.y. (Financial Sector Union): Ratamestarinkatu 12, 00520 Helsinki; tel. (9) 229141; fax (9) 22914300; f. 1931; Pres. CHRISTINA HOLMLUND; Sec.-Gen. SIMO LEIVO; 40,000 mems.

Suomen Teollisuustoimihenkilöiden Liitto (Salaried Employees in Industry): Asemamiehenkatu 4, 00520 Helsinki; tel. (9) 1551; fax (9) 1481930; internet www.stl.fi; f. 1917; Pres. HELENA RISSANEN; Admin. Dir MARJATTA VÄISÄNEN; 46,000 mems.

Tehy (The Union of Health and Social Care Services): POB 10, 00060 Helsinki; tel. (9) 1551; fax (9) 1483038; f. 1982; Chair. JAANA LAITINEN-PESOLA; 110,000 mems.

Vakuutusväen Liitto r.y. (Insurance Employees): Asemamiehenkatu 2, 00520 Helsinki; tel. (9) 85672400; fax (9) 85672401; e-mail sirpa.spoljari@jttpalvelut.fi; internet www.vvl.fi; f. 1945; Chair. SIRPA KOMONEN; Gen. Sec. SIRPA SPOLJARI; 11,000 mems.

Valtion Laitosten ja Yhtiöiden Toimihenkilöliitto (Employees in State-owned Institutions and Companies): Topparikuja 7, 00520 Helsinki; tel. (9) 348050; fax (9) 145135; e-mail joan.vingisar@vty.fi; f. 1945; Gen. Sec. PEKKA ELORANTA; 10,000 mems.

Transport

RAILWAYS

Finland has 5,836 km of railways, providing internal services and connections with Sweden and Russia. An underground railway service has been provided by Helsinki City Transport since 1982.

Ratahallintokeskus (RHK) (Finnish Rail Administration): POB 185, 00101 Helsinki; tel. (9) 58405111; fax (9) 58405100; e-mail info@rhk.fi; internet www.rhk.fi; f. 1995; civil service department under the Ministry of Transport and Communications; owns the rail network, together with its equipment, structures and land holdings; responsible for management, maintenance and development of railways; Chief Dir O. NIEMIMUUKKO.

Karhula Railway: Ratakatu 8, 48600 Karhula; tel. (5) 298221; fax (5) 298225; f. 1937; goods transport; operates 10 km of railway (1,524 mm gauge); Man. PERTTI HONKALA.

VR Group: Vilhonkatu 13, POB 488, 00101 Helsinki; tel. (9) 7071; fax (9) 7073700; internet www.vr.fi; began operating 1862; joint-stock co since 1995; operates 5,836 km of railways; wide gauge

(1,524 mm); 2,234 km of route are electrified; Pres. and CEO HENRI KUITUNEN; Exec. Vice-Pres. JUHANI KOPPERI.

ROADS

At 31 December 1998 there were 77,895 km of public roads, of which 473 km were motorways, 12,798 km other main roads, 28,657 km secondary or regional roads and 35,967 other roads.

In the beginning of 2001 Tielaitos (National Road Administration) was divided into the following organizations:

Tiehallinto (Finnish Road Administration): POB 33, 00521 Helsinki; tel. (204) 22150; fax (204) 222202; e-mail uusimaa.liikennekeskus@tiehallinto.fi; internet www.tiehallinto.fi; f. 1799; government agency; supervises nine road districts; manages the public road network including bridges and ferries; organizes bids for road construction and maintenance; Dir-Gen. EERO KARJALUOTO.

Tieliikelaitos (Finnish Road Enterprises): POB 33, 00521 Helsinki; tel. (204) 4411; e-mail etunimi.sukunimi@tieliikelaitos.fi; internet www.tieliikelaitos.fi; unincorporated state enterprise; provides transport infrastructure and transport environment services; Man. Dir HEIKKI KOIVISTO.

INLAND WATERWAYS

Lakes cover 31,500 sq km. The inland waterway system comprises 7,842 km of buoyed-out channels, 40 open canals and 30 lock canals. The total length of canals is 116 km. In 1999 the cargo vessel traffic on inland waterways amounted to 2.0m. metric tons, and the passenger traffic to 504,000 passengers.

In 1968 the southern part of the Saimaa Canal, which was leased to Finland by the USSR, was opened for vessels. In 1999 a total of 1.6m. metric tons of goods were transported along the canal.

SHIPPING

The chief port of export is Kotka. Reclamation of land is currently under way to build a second container port in Kotka. It is scheduled to open in 2001 and will have the capacity to handle 500,000 20-ft equivalent units (TEUs) of cargo per year. The main port of import is Helsinki, which has three specialized harbours. The West Harbour handles most of the container traffic, the North Harbour cargo ferry (ro-ro) traffic and the South Harbour passenger traffic. Other important international ports are Turku (Abo), Rauma and Hamina. The ports handled 90m. metric tons of cargo in 1999.

Port Authority Association

Suomen Satamaliitto (Finnish Port Association): Toinen Linja 14, 00530 Helsinki; tel. (9) 7711; fax (9) 7530474; e-mail alpo.naski@satamaliitto.fi; internet www.finnports.com; Gen. Dir MATTI AURA.

Port Authorities

Hamina: POB 14, 49401 Hamina; tel. (5) 7495400; fax (5) 7495419; e-mail office@portofhamina.fi; internet www.hamina.fi/satama; Port Man. SEPPO HERRALA; Harbour Master MARKKU KOSKINEN.

Helsinki: Helsinki Port Authority, Olympiaranta 3, 00140 Helsinki; tel. (9) 173331; fax (9) 17333232; e-mail port.helsinki@hel.fi; internet www.hel.fi/port; Harbour Master K. WALLIN.

Kotka: Port of Kotka Ltd, Laivurinkatu 7, 48100 Kotka; tel. (5) 2344280; fax (5) 2181375; e-mail port@kotka.fi; internet www.port.kotka.fi; Marketing Dir DIRK BECQUART.

Rauma: Port Authority of Rauma, Hakunintie 19, 26100 Rauma; tel. (2) 8344712; fax (2) 8226369; e-mail harbour.office@portofrauma.com; internet www.portofrauma.com; Dir HANNU ASUM-ALAHTI.

Turku: Turku Port Authority, Linnankatu 80, 20100 Turku; tel. (2) 2674111; fax (2) 2674125; Harbour Master TOM JOUTSIA.

Shipowners' Association

Suomen Varustamoyhdistys r.y. (Finnish Shipowners' Association): Satamakatu 4, POB 155, 00161 Helsinki; tel. (9) 6226730; fax (9) 669251; f. 1932; Chair. ANTTI LAGERROOS; Man. Dir KAJ ERIKSSON; 10 mems.

Principal Companies

Bore: Veistämönaukio 1 3, POB 144, 20101 Turku; tel. (2) 2813600; fax (2) 2534036; e-mail info@boret.com; f. 1897; Man. Dir KAJ ERIKSSON; 6 cargo ferries; 43,085 dwt.

ESL Shipping Oy: Suolakivenkatu 10, 00810 Helsinki; tel. (9) 7595777; fax (9) 787315; world-wide tramp services; Man. Dir H. HÖCKERT.

FG Shipping Oy Ab: Lönnrotinkatu 21, POB 406, 00121 Helsinki; tel. (10) 21640; fax (9) 2164243; e-mail fgs@fg-shipping.fi; f. 1947 (until 1989 Oy Finnlines Ltd); ship management, marine consulting; Pres. ESKO MUSTAMÄKI.

Finncarriers Oy Ab: Porkkalankatu 7, POB 197, 00180 Helsinki; tel. (9) 1034350; fax (9) 103435200; e-mail info@finncarriers.fi;

internet www.finncarriers.fi; f. 1975; liner and contract services between Finland and other European countries; overland and inland services combined with direct sea links; contract services in the North Atlantic and bulk traffic in the Baltic; Man. Dir ASSER AHLE-SKOG; 3 cargo ferries; 28,335 dwt.

Finnish Maritime Agencies (Fimag) Oy: POB 124, 00241 Helsinki; tel. (9) 1483070; fax (9) 145737; Man. Dir JOUNI AHRELA; 1 oil tanker; 11,474 dwt.

Finnlines Oyj: Lönnrotinkatu 21, POB 182, 00121 Helsinki; tel. (10) 55440; fax (10) 5544425; e-mail info@finnlines.fi; Pres. and CEO ANTTI LAGERROOS.

Fortum Oil and Gas Oy: POB 100, 00048 Fortum Keilaniemi, 02150 Spoo; tel. (10) 4511; fax (10) 4524777; internet www.fortum.com; Senior Vice-Pres. JUKKA LAAKSOVIRJA.

Alfons Håkans OYAB: Linnankatu 36C, 20100 Turku; tel. (2) 515500; fax (2) 2515873; e-mail office.turku@alfonshakans.fi; 30 tugs.

Rederi Ab Engship: Linnankatu 33B, 20100 Turku; tel. (2) 5125500; fax (2) 2502087; e-mail engship@engship.fi; Man. Dir KAJ ENGBLOM; 14 dry cargo vessels; 96,000 dwt.

Silja Line Oy: POB 880, 00101 Helsinki; tel. (9) 18041; fax (9) 1804484; internet www.silja.com; f. 1883; cruise and ferry services in the Baltic; Man. Dir NILS-GUSTAF PALMGREN; 7 passenger vessels.

CIVIL AVIATION

An international airport is situated at Helsinki-Vantaa, 19 km from Helsinki. International and domestic services also operate to and from airports at Ivalo, Joensuu, Jyväskylä, Kajaani, Kemi-Tornio, Kruunupyy, Kuopio, Lappeenranta, Mariehamn, Oulu, Pori, Rovaniemi, Savonlinna, Tampere-Pirkkala, Turku, Vaasa and Varkaus.

Domestic services are available at airports at Enontekiö, Kittilä, Kuusamo and Mikkeli.

In 1999 13.1m. passengers passed through Finnish airports.

Ilmailulaitos (Civil Aviation Administration): POB 50, 01531 Vantaa; tel. (9) 82771; fax (9) 82772099; e-mail ilmailulaitos@fcaa.fi; internet www.ilmailulaitos.com.

Principal Airlines

Air Botnia: POB 168, 01531 Vantaa; tel. (9) 61512900; fax (9) 61512919; e-mail airbotnia@sas.se; internet www.airbotnia.fi; f. 1994; intra-nordic services; acquired by Scandinavian Airlines System in early 1998; Pres. and CEO KJELL FREDHEIM.

Finnair Oyj: Tietotie 11A, POB 15, 01053 Vantaa; tel. (9) 81881; fax (9) 8184401; internet www.finnair.fi; f. 1923; 58.4% state-owned; 21 domestic services and 50 international services (to Europe, North America, the Middle East and the Far East); Pres. and CEO KEIJO SUILA.

Tourism

Europe's largest inland water system, vast forests, magnificent scenery and the possibility of holiday seclusion are Finland's main attractions. Most visitors come from other Nordic countries, Germany, Russia, the United Kingdom and the USA. Registered accommodation establishments recorded 3,773,959 overnight stays by foreigners in 1999.

Matkailun edistämiskeskus (Finnish Tourist Board): Töölönkatu 11, POB 625, 00101 Helsinki; tel. (9) 4176911; fax (9) 41679333; e-mail mek@mek.fi; internet www.mek.fi; f. 1973; Chair. BO GÖRAN ERIKSSON; Dir JAAKKO LEHTONEN.

FINNISH EXTERNAL TERRITORY

THE ÅLAND ISLANDS

Introductory Survey

Location, Language, Religion, Flag, Capital

The Åland Islands are a group of 6,554 islands (of which some 60 are inhabited) in the Gulf of Bothnia, between Finland and Sweden. About 94% of the inhabitants are Swedish-speaking, and Swedish is the official language. The majority profess Christianity and belong to the Evangelical Lutheran Church of Finland. The flag displays a red cross, bordered with yellow, on a blue background, the upright of the cross being to the left of centre. The capital is Mariehamn, which is situated on Åland, the largest island in the group.

History and Government

For geographical and economic reasons, the Åland Islands were traditionally associated closely with Sweden. In 1809, when Sweden was forced to cede Finland to Russia, the islands were incorporated into the Finnish Grand Duchy. However, following Finland's declaration of independence from the Russian Empire, in 1917, the Ålanders demanded the right to self-determination and sought to be reunited with Sweden. Their demands were supported by the Swedish Government and people. In 1920 Finland granted the islands autonomy but refused to acknowledge their secession, and in 1921 the Åland question was referred to the League of Nations. In June the League granted Finland sovereignty over the islands, while directing that certain conditions pertaining to national identity be included in the autonomy legislation offered by Finland and that the islands should be a neutral and non-fortified region. Elections were held in accordance with the new legislation, and the new provincial parliament (Landsting) held its first plenary session on 9 June 1922. The revised Autonomy Act of 1951 provided for independent rights of legislation in internal affairs and for autonomous control over the islands' economy. This Act could not be amended or repealed by the Finnish Eduskunta without the consent of the Åland Landsting.

In 1988 constitutional reform introduced the principle of a majority parliamentary government, to be formed by the Lantrådskandidat, the member of the Landsting nominated to conduct negotiations between the parties. These negotiations may yield two alternative outcomes: either the nominee will submit a proposal to create a new government or the nominee will fail to reach agreement on a new government (in which case renewed negotiations will ensue). The first formal parliamentary government and opposition were duly established. The governing coalition consisted of the three largest parties that had been elected to the Landsting in October 1987 (the Centre Party, the Liberals and the Moderates), which together held 22 seats in the 30-member legislature.

At a general election held on 20 October 1991 the Centre Party increased its share of the seats in the Landsting to 10, while the Liberal Party secured seven seats and the Moderates and Social Democrats won six and four seats respectively. The parties forming the new coalition Government included the Centre and Moderate Parties, as before, while the Liberal Party was replaced by the Social Democratic Party.

A revised Autonomy Act, providing Åland with a greater degree of autonomous control, was adopted in 1991 and took effect on 1 January 1993. The rules regarding legislative authority were modernized, and the right of the Åland legislature (henceforth known as the Lagting) to enact laws was extended. Åland was given greater discretion with respect to its budget, and the revised Act also introduced changes in matters such as right of domicile, land ownership regulations and administrative authority. The Autonomy Act contains a provision that, in any treaty which Finland may conclude with a foreign state and to which Åland is a party, the Lagting must consent to the statute implementing the treaty in order for the provision to enter into force in Åland. This procedure gave Åland the opportunity not to consent to membership of the European Union (EU, see p. 181). A referendum on the issue of Åland's proposed accession to membership of the EU in 1995 was held in Nov-ember 1994, immediately after similar referendums in Finland and Sweden had shown a majority in favour of membership. (A small majority of Åland citizens had supported Finland's membership.) Despite low participation in the referendum, 73.7% of the votes cast supported membership and Åland duly joined the EU, together with Finland and Sweden, on 1 January 1995. Under the terms of the treaty of accession, Åland was accorded special exemption from tax union with the EU in order to stimulate the ferry and tourist industries. (In 1998 two of Europe's largest ferry operators, Silja and Viking—both Finnish—re-routed their major services via Åland in order to continue to conduct duty-free sales, which were later abolished within the rest of the EU.)

A general election was held on 15 October 1995. The Centre Party secured nine seats and the Liberal Party won eight seats, while the Moderates and Social Democrats maintained the representation that they had achieved in the previous parliament. The new coalition Government was composed of members of the Centre and Moderate Parties and one independent.

At a general election held on 17 October 1999 the Centre Party and the Liberal Party each won nine seats. The Moderate Party, meanwhile, gained only four seats, compared with six at the previous election, while the Social Democrats maintained its level of representation with three seats. Independents grouped together in the Obunden samling won four seats. A coalition Government was formed comprising the Centre Party, the Moderate Party and the Independents. In March 2001, following a 'no-confidence' motion in the Lagting, the Chairman (Lantråd) of the Government, Roger Nordlund of the Centre Party, dissolved the coalition and formed a new administration comprising members of the Centre Party and the Liberal Party.

Economic Affairs

In 1996 the gross domestic product (GDP) of the Åland Islands, measured at current prices, was 4,052m. markkaa. In 1997 7.9% of the working population were employed in the agriculture sector Forests cover 40% of the islands, and only 9% of the total land area is arable. The principal crops are cereals, sugar-beet, potatoes and fruit. Dairy-farming and sheep-rearing are also important.

Since 1960 the economy of the islands has expanded and diversified. Fishing has declined as a source of income, and shipping (particularly the operation of ferry services between Finland and Sweden), trade and tourism have become the dominant economic sectors. In 1997 services engaged 77.2% of the employed labour force. The transport sector, including shipping, employed 19.4%. The political autonomy of the islands and their strategic location between Sweden and Finland have contributed to expanding banking and trade sectors; financial services engaged 7.4% of the employed labour force in 1997, while trade and hotels employed 12.6%. Consumer prices increased at an average annual rate of 1.3% in 1996–99; prices rose by only 0.9% in 1999. Unemployment stood at 2.5% in 1999, compared with 5.2% in 1996.

Education and Social Welfare

The education system is similar to that of Finland, except that Swedish is the language of instruction and Finnish an optional subject. In 1998 government medical services included two hospitals, with a total of 148 beds. There were 51 physicians working in the Åland Islands in 1997.

Statistical Survey

Source: Government of Åland, Department of Statistics and Economic Research, POB 60, 22101 Mariehamn; tel. (18) 25000; fax (18) 19495; internet www.asub.aland.fi.

AREA, POPULATION AND DENSITY

Area: 6,784 sq km (2,619 sq miles), of which 1,527 sq km (589 sq miles) is land and 5,258 sq km (2,030 sq miles) is water.

Population (31 December 1999): 25,706.

Density per sq km: 16.8.

Principal Town: Mariehamn (capital), population 10,492 at 31 December 1999.

Vital Statistics (1998): Registered live births 311 (birth rate 12.2 per 1,000); Deaths 237 (death rate 9.3 per 1,000); Marriages 93 (marriage rate 3.6 per 1,000).

Expectation of Life (years at birth, 1998): Males 77.4; Females 84.8.

Employed Labour Force (1997): Agriculture 947; Manufacturing 1,160; Construction 630; Trade 1,519; Transport 2,339; Financial services 892; Public services 4,070; Other services 477; Total employed 12,034.

AGRICULTURE AND FISHING

Agricultural Production (metric tons, 1999): Milk 14,232; Beef 576; Pork 147; Poultry 1,020; Wheat 5,357; Barley, oats 3,844; Sugar beets 41,801; Potatoes 12,330; Onions 5,975; Chinese cabbage, head lettuce 2,411; Apples 1,450.

Forestry Production (cu m, roundwood, 1997): Logs 35,270; Pulp 114,910.

Fishing (metric tons, live weight, 1999): Capture 7,606 (Baltic herring 7,061, Whitefish 157, Perch 178, Pike-perch 49, Pike 51, Other fish 110); Aquaculture 5,100; total catch 12,706.

FINANCE

Currency: Finnish currency: 100 penniä (singular: penni) = 1 markka.

Government Accounts ('000 markkaa, 1998): Revenue 1,319,909; Expenditure 1,123,954.

Cost of Living (consumer price index; base: 1995 = 100): 101.1 in 1997; 102.9 in 1998; 103.9 in 1999.

Gross Domestic Product (million markkaa at current prices): 3,799 in 1994; 3,842 in 1995; 4,052 in 1996.

EXTERNAL TRADE

1996 (million markkaa): Imports 3,473; Exports 4,250.

TRANSPORT AND TOURISM

Road Traffic (registered motor vehicles, 1999): Private motor cars 13,525; Goods vehicles 914; Buses 38; Motor cycles 577; Tractors 3,245.

Shipping (1999): Merchant fleet 40 vessels (car and passenger ferries 11, archipelago ferries 8); total displacement 873,194 grt (car and passenger ferries 269,078 grt, archipelago ferries 6,641). Note: Figures include 9 vessels registered under flags other than Åland or Finland, total displacement 454,000 grt.

Tourist Arrivals (1999): 1,734,578.

EDUCATION

Primary and Secondary Schools (1999): Institutions 28 (Comprehensive schools 24, Upper stage schools 9); Pupils 2,933 (Comprehensive schools 2,039, Upper stage schools 894). Note: Five schools offer both comprehensive and upper stage education.

Pupils Enrolled in Education After Comprehensive Schools (1999): Preparatory study programme 518 (males 227, females 291); Vocational programme 641 (males 388, females 253); Advanced vocational programme 237 (males 137, females 100); Other 57 (males 25, females 32).

Directory

Government and Legislature

The Governor of Åland represents the Government of Finland and is appointed by the Finnish President (with the agreement of the Speaker of the Åland legislature). The legislative body is the Lagting, comprising 30 members, elected every four years on a basis of proportional representation. All Ålanders over the age of 18 years, possessing Åland regional citizenship, have the right to vote and to seek election. An executive council (Landskapsstyrelse), consisting of five to seven members, is elected by the Lagting, and its Chairman (Lantråd) is the highest-ranking politician in Åland after the Speaker (Talman) of the Lagting. The President has the right to veto Lagting decisions only when the Lagting exceeds its legislative competence, or when there is a threat to the security of the country.

Governor: HENRIK GUSTAFSSON.

LANDSKAPSSTYRELSE
(March 2001)

The governing coalition comprises members of the Centre Party and the Liberal Party.

Chairman (Lantråd): ROGER NORDLUND (Centre Party).

Deputy Chairman: OLOF ERLAND (Liberal Party).

Members: SUNE ERIKSSON (Liberal Party), RUNAR KARLSSON (Centre Party), RITVA SARIN-GRUFBERG (Liberal Party), GUN CARLSSON (Centre Party).

LAGTING

Speaker (Talman): SUNE ERIKSSON (Liberal Party).

Election, 17 October 1999

	% of votes cast	Seats
Liberalerna på Åland (Liberal Party) . .	28.7	9
Åländsk Center (Centre Party) . .	27.3	9
Frisinnad samverkan (Moderate Party) .	14.5	4
Obunden samling (Independents) . . .	12.8	4
Ålands socialdemokrater (Social Democratic Party) .	11.8	3
Ålands Framstegsgrupp (Progress Group) .	4.8	1
Total	**100.0**	**30**

Political Organizations

Unless otherwise indicated, the address of each of the following organizations is: Ålands Lagting, POB 69, 22101 Mariehamn; tel. (18) 25000; fax (18) 13302; internet www.lagtinget.aland.fi.

Åländsk Center (Centre Party): e-mail centern@lagtinget.aland.fi.; Chair. ROGER NORDLUND; Leader JAN-ERIK MATTSSON; Sec. ROBERT BRANÉR.

Ålands Framstegsgrupp (Progress Group).

Ålands socialdemokrater (Social Democratic Party): e-mail socialdemokraterna@laetinget.aland.fi; internet www.social demokraterna.aland.fi; Chair. BARBRO SUNDBACK.

Frisinnad samverkan (Moderate Party): Chair. HARRIET LINDEMAN; Leader MAX SIRÉN; Sec.-Gen. NINA DANIELSSON.

Liberalerna på Åland (Liberal Party): tel. (18) 25362; fax (18) 16075; e-mail liberalerna@lagtinget.aland.fi; Chair. OLOF ERLAND; Leader LISBETH ERIKSSON; Gen. Sec. BIRGITTA GUSTAVSSON.

Obunden samling (Independents): Chair. BERIT HAMPF; Leader ERIK TUDEER.

Religion

CHRISTIANITY

In 1998 93.3% of the population were adherents of the Lutheran National Church.

The Press

Åland: POB 50, 22101 Mariehamn; tel. (18) 26026; fax (18) 15505; 5 a week; circ. 10,705.

Nya Åland: POB 21, 22101 Mariehamn; tel. (18) 23444; fax (18) 23449; 4 a week; circ. 7,768.

Broadcasting and Communications

RADIO

Ålands Radio och TV: POB 140, 22101 Mariehamn; tel. (18) 26060; fax (18) 26520; e-mail redaktion@radiotv.aland.fi; internet www.radiotv.aland.fi; f. 1996; broadcasts radio programmes in Swedish, 115.5 hours a week; Man. Dir PIA ROTHBERG-OLOFSSON; Editor-in-Chief ASTRID OLHAGEN.

Finance

BANKS

(cap. = capital; res = reserves; dep. = deposits; m. = million; amounts in markkaa unless otherwise stated; brs = branches)

Ålandsbanken Abp (Bank of Åland Ltd): Nygatan 2, POB 3, 22101 Mariehamn; tel. (18) 29011; fax (18) 29228; e-mail info@ alandsbanken.fi; internet www.alandsbanken.fi; f. 1919 as Ålands Aktiebank; name changed as above in 1980; merged with Ålands Hypoteksbank Ab in November 1995; cap. €20m., res €21m., dep. €1,059m. (Dec. 2000); Man. Dir FOLKE HUSELL; 25 brs.

Andelsbanken för Åland: POB 34, 22101 Mariehamn; tel. (18) 26000; Dirs HÅKAN CLEMES, ROLAND KARLSSON.

Lappo Andelsbank: 22840 Lappo; tel. (18) 56621; fax (18) 56699; Dir TORSTEN NORDBERG.

Merita Bank: Torggatan 10, 22100 Mariehamn; tel. (18) 5330; fax (18) 12499; Dirs ERLING GUSTAFSSON, JAN-ERIK RASK.

Postbanken: Leonia, Torggatan 4, 22100 Mariehamn; tel. (18) 6360; fax (18) 636608.

INSURANCE

Alandia Group: Ålandsvägen 31, POB 121, 22101 Mariehamn; tel. (18) 29000; fax (18) 12290; e-mail mhamn@alandiabolagen.com; internet www.alandiabolagen.com; f. 1938; life, non-life and marine; comprises three subsidiaries; Gen. Man. JOHAN DAHLMAN.

Ålands Ömsesidiga Försäkringsbolag (Åland Mutual Insurance Co): Köpmansgatan 6, POB 64, 22101 Mariehamn; tel. (18) 27600; fax (18) 27610; f. 1866; property; Man. Dir BJARNE OLOFSSON.

Cabanco Insurance Co Ltd: Köpmansgatan 6, POB 64, 22101 Mariehamn; tel. (18) 27690; fax (18) 27699; Man. Dir BO-STURE SJÖLUND.

Hamnia Reinsurance Co Ltd: Köpmansgatan 6, POB 64, 22101 Mariehamn; tel. (18) 27690; fax (18) 27699; Man. Dir BO-STURE SJÖLUND.

Trade and Industry

CHAMBER OF COMMERCE

Ålands Handelskammare: Nygatan 9, 22100 Mariehamn; tel. (18) 29029; fax (18) 21129; e-mail info@hk.aland.fi; internet www.hk .aland.fi; f. 1945; Chair. ANDERS NORDLUND; Man. Dir AGNETA ERLANDSSON-BJÖRKLUND.

TRADE ASSOCIATION

Ålands Företagareförening (Åland Business Asscn): Nygatan 9, 22100 Mariehamn; tel. (18) 29033; fax (18) 21129; f. 1957; Chair. SIGVARD PERSSON; Sec. BO HELENIUS.

EMPLOYERS' ORGANIZATIONS

Ålands Arbetsgivareförening (Åland Employers' Asscn): Nygatan 9, 22100 Mariehamn; tel. (18) 291474; fax (18) 21129; f. 1969; Chair. ERIK SUNDBLOM; Man. Dir ANDERS KULVES.

Ålands Fiskodlarförening (Åland Fish Farmers' Asscn): Storagatan 14, 22100 Mariehamn; tel. (18) 17834; fax (18) 17833; e-mail al.fishfarm@pb.alcom.aland.fi; Chair. MARCUS ERIKSSON; Sec. OLOF KARLSSON.

Ålands köpmannaförening (Åland Businessmen's Asscn): Ålandsvägen 34, 22100 Mariehamn; tel. (18) 13650; f. 1927; Chair. TOM FORSBOM; Sec. STEFAN BLOMQVIST.

Ålands producentförbund (Åland Agricultural Producers' Asscn): Ålands Landsbygdscentrum, 22150 Jomala; tel. (18) 329640; fax (18) 329639; e-mail henry.lindstrom@landsbygd.aland.fi; f. 1946; Chair. LOUISE KARLSSON; Man. Dir HENRY LINDSTROM.

Frakfartygsföreningen r.f. (Cargo Ship's Asscn): Norragatan 7A, 22100 Mariehamn; tel. (18) 23662; fax (18) 23644; e-mail small.ton@ aland.net; f. as Ultrikesfartens Småtonnagförening; present name adopted 2000; Chair. OLOF WIDÉN.

TRADE UNIONS

AKAVA-Åland (Professional Asscn): Storagatan 14, 22100 Mariehamn; tel. (18) 16348; fax (18) 12125; e-mail akava-a@aland.net; Chair. PEKKA ERÄMETSÄ; Gen. Sec. MARIA HAGMAN.

FFC/SAK; s Lokalorganisation på Åland (SAK Regional Trade Union in Åland): POB 108, 22101 Mariehamn; tel. (18) 16207; fax (18) 17207; e-mail kurt.gustafsson@sak.fi; internet www.facket .aland.fi; Chair. HELGE FREDRIKSSON; Gen. Sec. KURT GUSTAFSSON.

Fackorgan för offentliga arbetsomraden på Åland (FOA-Å) (Joint Organization of Civil Servants and Workers (VTY) in Åland): Ålandsvägen 55, 22100 Mariehamn; tel. (18) 16976; Chair. ULLA ANDERSSON; Gen. Sec. ULLA BRITT DAHL.

Tjänstemannaorganisationerna på Åland, TCÅ r.f. (Union of Salaried Employees in Åland): Strandgatan 23, 22100 Mariehamn; tel. (18) 16210; e-mail tca@aland.net; Chair. ANNE SJÖLUND; Dir. TUULA MATTSSON.

Transport

The islands are linked to the Swedish and Finnish mainlands by ferry services and by air services from Mariehamn airport.

ROADS

In 1999 there was a road network of 912.7 km, of which 646.8 km was paved.

SHIPPING

Ålands Redarförening r.f. (Åland Shipowners' Association): Hamngatan 8, 22100 Mariehamn; tel. (18) 13430; fax (18) 22520; e-mail info@alship.aland.fi; f. 1934; Chair. WIKING JOHANSSON; Man. Dir HANS AHLSTRÖM.

Principal Companies

Birka Line Abp: POB 175, 22101 Mariehamn; tel. (18) 27027; fax (18) 27343; e-mail info@birkaline.com; internet www.birkaline.com; f. 1971; shipping service; Chair. K.J. HAGMAN; Man. Dir WIKING JOHANSSON.

Lundqvist Rederierna: Norra Esplanadgatan 9B, 22100 Mariehamn; tel. (18) 26050; fax (18) 26428; e-mail info@lundqvist.aland.fi; f. 1927; tanker and ro-ro services; Pres. BEN LUNDQVIST; total tonnage 1.0m. dwt.

Rederi Ab Lillgaard: Nygatan 5, POB 136, 22101 Mariehamn; tel. (18) 13120; fax (18) 17220.

Rederiaktiebolaget Gustaf Erikson: POB 49, 22101 Mariehamn; tel. (18) 27070; fax (18) 12670; e-mail gustaf.erikson@geson.aland.fi; f. 1913; Man. Dir GUN ERIKSON-HJERLING; manages dry cargo and refrigerated vessels.

United Shipping Ltd Ab: Storagatan 11, POB 175, 22101 Mariehamn; tel. (18) 27320; fax (18) 23223; e-mail info@unitedshipping.fi; internet www.unitedshipping.fi.

Viking Line Abp: Norragatan 4, 22100 Mariehamn; tel. (18) 27000; fax (18) 12099; internet www.vikingline.fi; f. 1963; Chair. BEN LUNDQVIST; Man. Dir NILS-ERIK EKLUND; 7 car/passenger vessels; total tonnage 205,860 grt.

Viking Line Marketing Ab Oy: Storagatan 2, POB 35, 22101 Mariehamn; tel. (18) 26011; fax (18) 15811; internet www .vikingline.fi; Man. Dir BORIS EKMAN.

Tourism

Ålands TuristFörbund (Åland Tourist Asscn): Storagatan 8, 22100 Mariehamn; tel. (18) 24000; fax (18) 24265; internet www .goaland.net; f. 1989; Chair. MAGNUS LUNDBERG; Man. Dir GUNILLA G. NORDLUND.

FRANCE

Introductory Survey

Location, Climate, Language, Religion, Flag, Capital

The French Republic is situated in western Europe. It is bounded to the north by the English Channel (la Manche), to the east by Belgium, Luxembourg, Germany, Switzerland and Italy, to the south by the Mediterranean Sea and Spain, and to the west by the Atlantic Ocean. The island of Corsica is part of metropolitan France, while four overseas departments, two overseas 'collectivités territoriales' and four overseas territories also form an integral part of the Republic. The climate is temperate throughout most of the country, but in the south it is of the Mediterranean type, with warm summers and mild winters. The principal language is French, which has numerous regional dialects, and small minorities speak Breton and Basque. Almost all French citizens profess Christianity, and about 78% are adherents of the Roman Catholic Church. Other Christian denominations are represented, and there are also Muslim and Jewish communities. The national flag (proportions three by two) has three equal vertical stripes, of blue, white and red. The capital is Paris.

Recent History

In September 1939, following Nazi Germany's invasion of Poland, France and the United Kingdom declared war on Germany, thus entering the Second World War. In June 1940 France was forced to sign an armistice, following a swift invasion and occupation of French territory by German forces. After the liberation of France from German occupation in 1944, a provisional Government took office under Gen. Charles de Gaulle, leader of the 'Free French' forces during the wartime resistance. The war in Europe ended in May 1945, when German forces surrendered at Reims. In 1946, following a referendum, the Fourth Republic was established and Gen. de Gaulle announced his intention to retire from public life.

France had 26 different Governments from 1946 until the Fourth Republic came to an end in 1958 with an insurrection in Algeria (then an overseas department) and the threat of civil war. In May 1958 the President, René Coty, invited Gen. de Gaulle to form a government. In June the National Assembly invested him as Prime Minister, with the power to rule by decree for six months. A new Constitution was approved by referendum in September and promulgated in October; thus the Fifth Republic came into being, with Gen. de Gaulle taking office as President in January 1959. The new system provided a strong presidency, the authority of which would be strengthened by national referendums and a stable executive.

France was a founder member of the European Community (EC, now European Union, EU—see p. 181) and of the North Atlantic Treaty Organization (NATO, see p. 241). In 1966 it withdrew from the integrated military structure of NATO, desiring a more self-determined defence policy, but remained a member of the alliance (see below).

The early years of the Fifth Republic were overshadowed by the Algerian crisis. De Gaulle granted Algeria independence in 1962, withdrew troops and repatriated French settlers. In May 1968 students and workers joined in a revolt against the Government's authoritarian education and information policies, low wage rates and lack of social reform. For a time the republic appeared threatened, but the student movement collapsed and the general strike was settled by large wage rises. In April 1969 President de Gaulle resigned following his defeat in a referendum on regional reform.

Georges Pompidou, de Gaulle's Prime Minister between April 1962 and July 1968, was elected President in June 1969. The Gaullist hold on power was, however, undermined by the agreement of a common programme for contesting legislative elections by the Parti Socialiste (PS) and the Parti Communiste Français (PCF). At a general election for the National Assembly in March 1973, the government coalition was returned with a reduced majority. Pompidou died in April 1974. In the presidential election held in May, Valéry Giscard d'Estaing, formerly leader of the Républicains Indépendants (RI) narrowly defeated François Mitterrand, the First Secretary of the PS. A coalition Government was formed from members of the RI, the Union des Démocrates pour la Republique (UDR) and the centre parties. In August 1976 Jacques Chirac resigned as Prime Minister and subsequently undertook to transform the UDR into a new Gaullist party, the Rassemblement pour la République (RPR). In February 1978 the governing non-Gaullist parties formed the Union pour la Démocratie Française (UDF) to compete against RPR candidates in the National Assembly elections held in March, when the governing coalition retained a working majority.

In the April/May 1981 presidential elections Mitterrand, with the support of communist voters, defeated Giscard d'Estaing. At elections for a new Assembly, held in June, the PS and associated groups, principally the Mouvement des Radicaux de Gauche (MRG), won an overall majority of seats, following which four members of the PCF were appointed to the Council of Ministers. The new Government introduced a programme of social and labour reforms; several major industrial enterprises and financial institutions were brought under state control; and administrative and financial power was transferred from government-appointed Préfets to locally-elected departmental assemblies.

A legislative election took place in March 1986, using a party-list based system of proportional representation for the first time. Although the PS remained the largest single party in the new National Assembly, the centre-right RPR-UDF alliance, with the support of other right-wing parties, commanded a majority of seats. The PCF suffered a severe decline in support, while the far-right Front National (FN) won seats in the Assembly for the first time. A period of political 'cohabitation' ensued as Mitterrand invited the RPR leader, Chirac, to form a new Council of Ministers.

In April 1986 Chirac introduced legislation that allowed his Government to legislate by decree on economic and social issues and on the proposed reversion to a voting system comprising single-member constituencies for legislative elections. However, Mitterrand insisted on exercising the presidential right to withhold approval of decrees that reversed the previous Government's social reforms. In July Chirac thus resorted to the 'guillotine' procedure (setting a time-limit for consideration of legislative proposals) to gain parliamentary consent for legislation providing for the transfer to the private sector of 65 state-owned companies, which, since it had been approved by the predominantly right-wing Senate and the Constitutional Council, the President was legally bound to approve.

Mitterrand was returned for a further term as President in May 1988, gaining 54% of the votes cast at the second round of voting to defeat Chirac. The PS-dominated Government under the premiership of Michel Rocard failed to command a reliable majority in the 577-seat National Assembly. A general election took place in June, with voting based on the reintroduced single-seat majority system. An alliance of the PS and the MRG secured a total of 276 seats, whilst an alliance of the RPR, the UDF and other right-wing candidates, styled the Union du Rassemblement et du Centre, won 272. The PCF won 27 seats, and the FN one. Rocard, reappointed as Prime Minister, formed an administration in which members of the previous Government retained the principal portfolios, although six UDF members and a number of independents were also included.

Rocard resigned in May 1991, weakened by disunity within the PS and by his failure to negotiate the passage of three government bills. Edith Cresson, France's first female Prime Minister, succeeded him. Cresson, who had resigned eight months previously from her post as Minister of European Affairs, in protest at Rocard's economic policies and the pace of their implementation, undertook to increase government control over economic and industrial planning.

In April 1992, in response to poor results recorded by the PS at recent regional and cantonal elections, Mitterrand replaced Edith Cresson as Prime Minister, appointing Pierre Bérégovoy, hitherto the Minister of State for the Economy, Finance and the Budget, as her successor. In June the National Assembly approved constitutional changes allowing the ratification of the EC's Treaty on European Union (the 'Maastricht Treaty'), subject to approval in a national referendum. In the referendum, held in September, 69.7% of the electorate voted, of whom 51.1% were in favour of the ratification of the Treaty.

In October 1992 two senior health service officials received prison sentences, following the discovery that unscreened blood infected with the human immunodeficiency virus (HIV) had been used in transfusions. It was subsequently estimated that some 4,300 people had been infected with HIV, of whom more than 1,000 had died by 1999. Public pressure mounted to have three former government members—including the PS leader, Laurent Fabius, who had been Prime Minister in 1984–86—indicted for their alleged part in the scandal. In December 1992 the Senate voted by an overwhelming majority to endorse the decision of the National Assembly that the three should be brought to trial before the Conseil d'Etat. In 1999 Fabius and the former Minister of Social Affairs and National Solidarity, Georgina Dufoix, were acquitted of charges of manslaughter and criminal negligence, while the former Secretary of State for Health, Edmond Hervé, was convicted on two counts but released without sentence.

Elections to the National Assembly in March 1993 resulted in a clear defeat for the PS; this was mainly attributable to the high level of unemployment and a succession of scandals in which members of the ruling party had been implicated. Several government ministers failed to retain their seats. In the first round of voting the RPR and the UDF (which had presented joint candidates, as the Union pour la France, in some 500 constituencies) together received 39.5% of total votes cast, while the PS obtained 17.6%. Following the second round of voting, the RPR won 247 of the 577 seats in the Assembly, the UDF 213 and the PS 54. Despite polling well at the first round of voting, neither the FN nor the alliance of the two main environmental parties, Les Verts and Génération Ecologie, won any seats. Chirac, as the leader of the largest party in the new legislature, had made it known that he intended to concentrate on his candidacy in the 1995 presidential election, and consequently was not available for the post of Prime Minister. Mitterrand therefore asked another RPR member, Edouard Balladur, a former Minister of Finance, to form a government. Balladur's centre-right coalition enacted stricter laws on immigration and the conferral of French citizenship during 1993–94, together with controversial legislation giving the police wider powers to make random security checks.

In the first round of voting in the presidential election, on 23 April 1995, Lionel Jospin, the candidate of the PS, won 23% of the votes, while Chirac and Balladur, both representing the RPR, took 21% and 19% respectively. Jean-Marie Le Pen, the leader of the FN, won 15%. In the second round, on 7 May, Chirac (with 53% of the votes) defeated Jospin. Balladur resigned as Prime Minister, and Chirac appointed Alain Juppé (Minister of Foreign Affairs in the previous Government) as his successor. Juppé formed an administration in which the principal portfolios were evenly shared between the RPR and the UDF. In October Juppé was elected President of the RPR, while Jospin was elected First Secretary of the PS.

Following widespread strikes and demonstrations by public-sector workers in late 1995, proposed reforms to public-sector pension arrangements were abandoned. In May 1996 the Government approved proposals submitted by President Chirac to restructure the armed forces. A 30% reduction in military personnel, the elimination of compulsory military service, a restriction on the defence budget and the privatization of state-owned companies in the defence industry were envisaged to be implemented by 2002, with further restructuring to be completed by 2015. In February 1997 immigration legislation approved in the National Assembly provoked a demonstration by some 100,000 people in Paris. The protests were widely believed to have resulted in the Government's decision to exclude a controversial clause in the bill, requiring French citizens to register the arrival and departure of any foreign guests with the local authorities. Renewed controversy surrounding the conduct of French institutions during the Second World War arose in early 1997, following reports that French banks had failed to transfer the deposits of Jews killed in the Holocaust to the State, as required by law. Similar revelations that museums in France, including the Louvre, continued to hold some 2,000 valuable works of art seized from Jews under the Vichy regime (1940–44) prompted the Government to announce the creation of a commission to trace and catalogue the misappropriated property.

In April 1997 Chirac announced that legislative elections would take place in May–June, some 10 months earlier than required, a decision that was widely viewed as an attempt to secure a mandate for a number of policies relating to economic and monetary union (EMU – see p. 199) within the EU. In the first round of voting, held on 25 May, the PS secured 23.5% of total votes cast, the RPR 15.7%, the FN 14.9% and the UDF 14.2%. Following the second round of voting, held on 1 June, the PS secured 241 seats, the RPR 134, the UDF 108 and the PCF 38. Despite its strong performance in the first round, the FN won only one seat.

The unexpected victory of the PS, which began a further period of 'cohabitation', was widely attributed to dissatisfaction with Juppé's administration and the imposition of economic austerity measures necessitated under the terms of EMU. Jospin, leader of the PS, became Prime Minister, and formed a coalition with several left-wing and ecologist parties. The new Government's stated objectives included the reduction of youth unemployment by the creation of some 700,000 new jobs and the reform of immigration law.

In December 1997 a series of demonstrations began in Marseille, in protest at the Government's perceived failure to address adequately the problem of unemployment. The demonstrations soon spread to other parts of the country, and in many towns erupted into violence as unemployed youths attacked public-service workers (leading to strikes by public transport operators), clashed with police and set fire to buildings and vehicles. Meanwhile, protesters began an occupation of welfare offices across the country (which lasted several weeks), demanding a review of the benefits system. Measures announced by the Government in January 1998, which aimed to placate the demonstrators, were rejected by groups representing the unemployed. Furthermore, the support of communist and ecologist members of the Government for the protests highlighted divisions within the governing coalition on the matter. In February legislation shortening the maximum working week from 39 to 35 hours, regarded as central to the Government's job creation policy, was approved by the National Assembly.

At regional council elections held in March 1998, the governing socialist coalition won 39.4% of the total vote, the centre-right opposition secured 35.6%, and the FN 15.5%. A subsequent offer by the FN to form alliances with the RPR and the UDF in order to secure control of a number of councils caused much controversy. Both parties instructed their members to ignore the proposal; however, five members of the UDF defied their leadership and consequently obtained council presidencies. Two later resigned, while the remaining three were expelled from the party; one of these, Charles Millon, subsequently formed a new political organization called La Droite (subsequently renamed La Droite Libérale Chrétienne). A further two senior UDF members left the party in protest at the expulsions, amid serious criticism of party President, François Léotard's, management of the crisis. In April the mayor of Paris, Jean Tiberi, dismissed 12 members of the RPR who had joined a new right-wing grouping on the Paris city council. In an attempt to counteract the increasing fragmentation of the country's political centre right, the RPR and the UDF announced the formation in May of a loose umbrella organization called Alliance pour La France (APF), although this grouping collapsed in February 1999, following the decision of the UDF to present a separate list of candidates at forthcoming elections to the European Parliament. In late June the National Assembly voted to reform the system of regional elections, largely as a result of the problems experienced following the elections in March. The changes, which aimed to ensure coherent majorities in the regional councils, included the replacement of the previous one-round system with a two-round poll in which a party with an outright majority in the first round of voting would automatically receive 25% of the seats available.

From the late 1990s the influence of the FN began to wane. At a by-election in May 1998 the party narrowly lost its only seat in the National Assembly to the PS. In April a court banned Le Pen from holding or seeking public office for two years (reduced to one year on appeal) and gave him a three-month suspended prison sentence after finding him guilty of physical assault on a socialist candidate in the 1997 general elections. The selection of a potential replacement for Le Pen, necessitated by the ban, to lead the FN list of candidates in the following year's elections to the European Parliament (of which the FN leader was a member), resulted in a major dispute within the party and the creation of two rival factions. Le Pen's decision to nominate his wife, Jany Le Pen, as his replacement infuriated supporters of Bruno Mégret, the party's second-in-command. Deepening divisions between supporters of the rivals led, in December, to Mégret's suspension, and later expulsion, from the party, together with six other senior party officials. In January 1999 Mégret launched his own party, the Front National—Mouvement National, which was subsequently renamed the Mouvement National Républicain (MNR). A significant proportion of Mégret supporters within the FN subsequently transferred their allegiance or membership to the MNR, although the electoral performance of the party was in general somewhat poorer than that of the weakened FN. In October 2000 Le Pen was finally expelled from his seat in the European Parliament, following the rejection of his final appeal against his 1998 conviction in the European Court of Human Rights. However, in January 2001 the European Court of Justice ruled that the President of the European Parliament had illegally excluded Le Pen from the legislature as the expulsion had been predicated on French national law.

In 1999, following the dissolution of the APF, the RPR suffered further reverses; in April Philippe Séguin resigned as party President, citing his dissatisfaction with what he termed Chirac's political manoeuvrings. His interim replacement, Nicolas Sarkozy, in turn resigned, following poor results for the party in elections to the European Parliament held in June. The RPR, in alliance with Alain Madeline's Démocratie Libérale (DL), gained 12.8% of the votes cast, less than both the PS, which won 22.0% of votes cast, and a breakaway Gaullist group, opposed to the terms of the Maastricht Treaty, the Rassemblement pour la France (RPF), led by Charles Pasqua, which gained 13.1% of the votes cast. Les Verts took 9.7%, the UDF 9.3%, and the PCF 6.8%. A populist organization, which sought to defend participants in country sports from legislative changes demanded by the EU, Chasse Pêche Nature Traditions (CPNT) secured 6.8% of the vote nationwide, yet was the second most popular party in some regions, while the FN, apparently weakened by the recent divisions, gained 5.7% of the vote. Following the electoral success of the RPF, Pasqua announced that the movement would be reformulated as an active political party, although a subsequent split ensued when a faction led by Philippe de Villiers defected in order to re-establish the Mouvement pour la France, which, like the RPF, had originally been formed in the mid-1990s, thereby further fragmenting the far-right and nationalist vote. In December 1999 Michèle Alliot-Marie was elected President of the RPR.

In late 1999 there were protests in Paris by employers critical of the Government's 35-hour working week policy, due to enter effect fully by 2002. Employers claimed that the scheme, aimed at lowering unemployment levels, would harm smaller businesses unable to cope with the reduction in working hours. Although, in response to criticism from employers and trade unions alike, the Government abandoned plans to draw on social security surpluses to fund the scheme, the implementation of the first stage of the policy, in February 2000, was greeted by widespread protests, including the blockade of border posts by road hauliers (who were also protesting about a proposed increased in diesel prices) and strike action by public-sector workers. Concessions by the Government, notably to the hauliers, soon relieved tensions, although trade unions remained dissatisfied. The principal employers' group, Mouvement des Entreprises de France (MEDEF), threatened to withdraw from the social security fund if the latter were used to finance the shortfall in employers' contributions caused by the implementation of the 35-hour week. Public- and private-sector employees staged a one-day national strike in January 2001 in protest at MEDEF's proposal to extend the minimum age of retirement with full benefits from 60 to 65 in order to finance future pensions in the light of demographic changes. The Government rejected MEDEF's recommendations, which clashed with the administration's goal of reducing unemployment. In November 1999 Dominique Strauss-Kahn was obliged to step down as Minister of Finance, Economy and Industry, following allegations of fraudulent behaviour (see below). He was replaced by Christian Sautter. In March 2000 Jospin carried out the first major reorganization of the Council of Ministers since taking office. Fabius, who had recently been cleared of any involvement in the HIV-infected blood case (see above), returned to office as Minister of Finance, in which role he was regarded as a supporter of reform and greater economic liberalization. The hitherto First Vice-President of the National Assembly, Raymond Forni, replaced him as its President. The reshuffle was widely regarded as seeking to ensure that all factions in the PS were represented in the Government, in advance of the presidential election scheduled for 2002, which Jospin was expected to contest, and also was believed to reflect the failure of the outgoing ministers to resolve ongoing disputes with trade unions over reforms proposed in the taxation and education sectors. Jack Lang, a former Minister of Culture under President Mitterrand, returned to senior office as Minister of Education. Two new ministers-delegate from Les Verts and the PCF were appointed, while the Parti Radical de Gauche (as the MRG had been restyled) received their first ministerial appointment.

In August 2000, the Minister of the Interior, Jean-Pierre Chevènement, the leader and sole minister of the Mouvement des Citoyens, resigned in protest at government policy towards Corsica (see below), although he emphasized that his party would continue to support the Government on every other policy. Daniel Vaillant of the PS was appointed in his place. In a further reshuffle in October, Marylise Lebranchu replaced Elisabeth Guigou as Minister of Justice, while Guigou became Minister of Employment in place of Martine Aubry, who resigned to focus on her campaign to become mayor of Lille.

Throughout 2000 the tensions caused by a prolonged period of 'cohabitation' promoted moves towards constitutional change. In May Valéry Giscard d'Estaing submitted proposals to reduce the parliamentary term from seven to five years, in order to bring it into line with the life of a parliament. Although Chirac had rejected similar proposals as recently as July 1999, it appeared that both the President and Prime Minister were now supportive of reform. In June 2000 the National Assembly voted in favour of the proposed constitutional amendment, presented in the chamber by Elisabeth Guigou, by a margin of 466 in favour to 28 opposed, with 73 abstentions. Amid concerns that the more conservative Senate might not support the bill by the two-thirds majority required for a constitutional change to be approved, Chirac called for a referendum, to be held on 24 September. The referendum took place amid increasing accusations of widespread corruption among both the RPR and PS (see below), and attracted only a 30.6% participation rate, by far the lowest in any constitutional referendum held in France. Of those who voted, 73.2% were in favour of the change, which thereby was enacted, to take effect from the 2002 presidential elections.

Following this constitutional change, a proposal previously raised by the UDF President, François Bayrou, to the effect that presidential elections in 2002 be held in March, prior to the parliamentary elections due in May, gained in popularity, particularly among deputies of the UDF and PS, who were concerned to prevent a further period of 'cohabitation', which they felt might be more likely to result were the government to be elected prior to a President, as provided for under the existing electoral calendar. The RPR opposed the proposal as a partisan move intended to strengthen Jospin's position as a presidential candidate in 2002, and that of the PS in the proposed subsequent parliamentary elections. Although Chirac's popularity as President appeared to decline during 2000, the RPR and other Gaullists had expected to win a majority in the parliamentary elections of 2002, in part as a consequence of the splintering and decline of the far-right vote. The PCF and Les Verts rejected the proposed change as granting an unacceptable increase in power to the President. None the less, on 20 December the National Assembly voted in favour of the proposal.

In late August 2000 fishermen blocked major ports on the English Channel and the Mediterranean Sea in order to protest against the high price of marine fuel. Although the dispute ended within a week, following the announcement of tax cuts, in early September an alliance of road hauliers, farmers, taxi and coach drivers and ambulance operators began a blockade of oil refineries across France, in order to protest at the high level of taxation on fuel. The blockade, which subsequently included the obstruction of railways and motorways, continued for seven days and received widespread public support despite causing significant disruption. The dispute ended suddenly, following the Government's decision to backdate the tax cut on fuel already promised to farmers to the beginning of the year, and to grant further concessions to taxi and coach drivers. The protests in France received widespread international publicity and were regarded as an inspiration for similar disputes that erupted in the United Kingdom, Germany and in other European countries in late 2000.

From the late 1990s a number of serious scandals affected almost every major political party in France. In early 1998 the home and offices of Roland Dumas, the President of the Constitutional Council and a former Minister of Foreign Affairs, were raided by police as part of an ongoing investigation into the alleged fraudulent handling of commission payments, estimated at US $500m., on the sale of six frigates to Taiwan in 1991. Dumas resisted pressure to resign as President of the Constitutional Council but took leave of absence from the post in March 1999, following the reopening that month of a magistrate's inquiry into his involvement in the corruption scandals at the formerly state-owned petroleum company, Elf Aquitaine. He did, however, resign in March 2000 when it was announced that he would stand trial for his participation in corrupt practices at Elf; the decision followed allegations by Dumas's former mistress, Christine Deviers-Joncour, that he had knowingly accepted inducements from the petroleum company during his tenure as Minister of Foreign Affairs, and that he had arranged for her employment in a spurious but well-paid position. His trial was postponed until January 2001, and was further delayed, in February, following the extradition to France, in relation to further charges of corruption within Elf Aquitaine, of former company executive, Alfred Sirven. Meanwhile, in early 2000, allegations that Elf had been involved in providing illicit funding to the political party of the former German Chancellor, Helmut Kohl, gained publicity; among those implicated were former Prime Minister, Edith Cresson, who was also under investigation for reputed fraud in the European Commission in Brussels. The wrongdoing in Germany was linked primarily to the acquisition of the former East German petroleum company, Leuna, and reportedly had taken place with the knowledge of the late President Mitterrand. Sirven had been placed on trial in his absence, and was believed to have played a key role in the misallocation of state funds in the company between 1989 and 1993, before it was privatized. He was arrested in the Philippines, following investigations by the magazine *Paris Match*, and was extradited to Germany before in turn being delivered to the French authorities. Sirven refused to co-operate with the trial when brought to court in March 2001. In that month it was announced that a judgment in the trial regarding the abuse of public money by former employees of Elf Aquitaine would be made in late May.

During 1999–2000, the former Minister of the Economy, Finance and Industry, Dominique Strauss-Kahn, was implicated in a number of cases of alleged corruption. He had been forced to resign in November 1999 in response to allegations that he had received 603,000 francs in payments from a students' mutual fund in respect of a fictitious job, although these charges were subsequently reduced to the falsification of documents related to this employment. However, in January 2000 Strauss-Kahn was placed under formal investigation on charges of complicity in the misuse of public funds that he had allegedly received, by means of his secretary, from Elf Aquitaine. Strauss-Kahn was also under investigation in relation to the concealment of evidence of fraud in the corruption scandal involving Paris city council (see below), and was also implicated in allegations of corruption in the PS-controlled Ile-de-France regional council.

In mid-1998 allegations of corruption emerged involving the inclusion of at least 300 fictitious employees on the payroll of the Paris city council, under Chirac's tenure as mayor. It was claimed that the payroll included friends and relatives of council members, RPR supporters and unsuccessful RPR candidates. In March 1999, despite the disclosure of documentation purporting to show that he had been aware of the bogus employees' scheme, Chirac's immunity from prosecution, which had been assured for the duration of his presidential term by a Constitutional Council ruling in January, was upheld by a Paris public prosecutor. (This was confirmed by an appeal court ruling in January 2000.) In June 1999 Tiberi, who had been responsible for the payroll in the period in question, and who was Chirac's successor as mayor, was placed under formal investigation. By early 2000 the RPR came under increasing pressure to distance itself from Tiberi before he sought re-election in March 2001. As allegations surfaced that around 1,500 fictitious persons had also been listed on the RPR membership roll in Paris during Tiberi's period as mayor, and that membership of the party could result in the provision of employment or accommodation by the city council, the RPR President, Michèle Alliot-Marie, removed Tiberi from his position in the party, and supported Philippe Séguin's candidacy for mayor. Tiberi was suspended from the party in October, following his announcement that he would contest the post none the less. In July 2000 Tiberi's

wife, Xavière Tiberi, became the subject of scrutiny, following allegations that she had added over 6,000 fictitious names to the electoral roll in her husband's constituency. She stood trial in November on a charge that in 1994 she had accepted payment for a fictitious job in a council outside of Paris. As Chirac increasingly distanced himself from Tiberi, Tiberi threatened to disclose evidence that he alleged would implicate Chirac in the party funding scandal.

Evidence of corruption deepened in September 2000, when a transcript of a video cassette made by Jean-Claude Méry, a former RPR official who had been imprisoned on charges of embezzlement in the mid-1990s, was published posthumously in *Le Monde*. In the recording Méry stated that Chirac had personally ordered Méry to arrange for city funds to be illicitly used to support political parties. Strauss-Kahn admitted that he had received the original copy of the cassette in 1999, when Méry's lawyer, had presented it to him as Minister of Finance in exchange for Strauss-Kahn's agreement to illegally reduce a tax penalty owed by a high-profile client, the couturier, Karl Lagerfeld. Strauss-Kahn's involvement in the affair effectively implicated the PS and other political parties in the allegations of corruption and illicit funding in Paris that previously had been restricted to the RPR. Moreover, in December 2000 Chirac gave a televised interview in which he denied involvement in corrupt party funding in Paris during his tenure as mayor. This followed the arrest earlier that month of Michel Roussin, who had been Chirac's principal private secretary from 1989 to 1993 and the questioning of Louise Casetta, who had worked as the unofficial treasurer for the RPR under Chirac's leadership. Their testimony, which was leaked to the press, included details of the systematic levying of an illegal 2% commission on public works contracts awarded by the Paris administration. Although the RPR was allegedly the major recipient of this funding, the PS and the PCF were also implicated in the scheme. In October 2000, the leader of the PCF, Robert Hué, stood trial for allegedly receiving illegal funding from Compagnie Générale des Eaux (now Vivendi) in exchange for the granting of contracts to the company in PCF-run municipalities. The trial was, however, suspended in late October, following defence allegations concerning the impartiality of the judge.

Municipal and cantonal elections, held in two rounds in March 2001, which had been widely regarded as a significant measure of the standing of the political parties prior to the presidential and legislative elections to be held in early 2002, provided largely inconclusive results. Although the PS won some high profile victories, overall the party's performance was widely regarded as disappointing, and that of the right-of-centre parties as better than had been anticipated. (In villages and towns with more than 3,000 inhabitants the mainstream right gained 49.8% of the votes while the mainstream left secured 46.3%.) Although the PS candidate, Bertrand Delanoë, was successful, with support from Les Verts, in becoming the first socialist mayor of Paris since the introduction of the elected office in 1977, and the left was successful in gaining control of Lyon, several members of the Government, including Jack Lang, Elisabeth Guigou and Dominique Voynet, failed to gain election as mayors. The share of the vote awarded to the PCF also fell notably, whilst the MNR and FN retained control of three of the four municipalities in the South of France the FN had gained in 1995, but lost control of Toulon to Démocratie Libérale, largely because of a three-way split in the far-right vote and because of a court judgment against the incumbent mayor, Jean-Marie Le Chevallier, formerly a member of the FN, charging him with benefiting fraudulently from fictive employment. In the cantonal elections, although the PS gained control of five departments, it lost two others, and had the number of its councillors reduced by some 50 nation-wide, largely to the benefit of other small left-wing parties or independent candidates. The UDF and RDR also lost around 100 councillors, with the beneficiaries again smaller parties or independent candidates.

As a result of decentralization legislation of 1982, the status of Corsica was elevated to that of a 'collectivité territoriale', with its own directly-elected 61-seat Assembly, and an administration with augmented economic and social executive powers. None the less, terrorist campaigns by several groups that called for the independence or greater autonomy of the island continued throughout the 1980s. In November 1990, in proposals known as the Joxe Plan (after the Minister of the Interior, Pierre Joxe) the French Government proposed the granting of greater autonomy to Corsica, incorporating the formation of a seven-member executive council, to be chosen from a 51-member

Corsican assembly, which would be elected in 1992. The legislation, which was opposed both by Corsican separatists and Gaullist members of the National Assembly, was adopted in April 1991. Throughout the 1990s, none the less, an unprecedented series of armed robberies, bombings and deliberately raised forest fires threatened to undermine the economically significant Corsican tourist industry. In February 1997 a series of explosions on the island followed the arrest of several high-profile separatists. In one of the most serious incidents of violence on Corsica in its recent history, the Préfet, Claude Erignac, was assassinated in early February 1998. The killing was condemned by the pro-independence Front de Libération Nationale de la Corse (FLNC), leading observers to speculate that the assassination had been carried out by a splinter group (Sampieru), which had previously admitted responsibility for the kidnapping of a police-officer in September 1997. In May 1998 the FLNC claimed responsibility for a bomb attack, which caused serious damage to the regional council building in Marseille.

In January 1999 the FLNC declared a cease-fire, on Corsican territory only, in an apparent attempt to prevent further attacks from damaging the separatist cause in regional assembly elections scheduled to take place in March. The elections strengthened the position of the Corsican nationalist parties, with Corsica Nazione winning almost 17% of votes cast. An arson attack on a bar in the island's capital, Ajaccio, in April led to the arrest and dismissal of the island's Préfet, Bernard Bonnet, and the disbandment of the anti-terrorist unit, the Groupe de pelotons de sécurité (GPS), that had been established after the murder of Erignac. Bonnet's arrest was made in response to allegations that the head of the GPS, Henri Mazères, had ordered the attack on the bar. In May, following the arrest of four Corsican nationalists in connection with the murder of Erignac, the Jospin Government narrowly avoided a motion of censure, proposed by the opposition parties in protest at the Government's handling of the situation on the island. In late 1999, following a visit to Corsica by Jospin, two explosions in public buildings in Ajaccio injured six people. The Prime Minister had reiterated that an end to the violence was a necessary precondition for the development of negotiations on increased autonomy.

Talks involving the Government and representatives of the island, including two Corsican nationalists, commenced in Paris in December 1999. Four groups of Corsican militants called an unconditional and unlimited cease-fire as the negotiations began, and pledged to disarm should their aims, including the recognition of the Corsican people as a nation, and the granting of official status to the Corsican language on the island, be achieved. The peace process resulted in agreement on a number of proposals known as the Matignon Accords. On 28 July 2000 the proposals were approved in the Corsican Assembly by an overwhelming majority. Under the proposals, subject to the maintenance of peace on Corsica, and the approval of the French National Assembly, revisions would be made to the French Constitution by 2004 to introduce a single political and administrative body for the island with formal, but limited legislative powers, to be elected by a form of proportional representation, replacing the two existing administrative departments. The proposals also provided for instruction in the Corsican language to take place in all primary schools. In August the Government rejected nationalist demands for an amnesty for all those held on crimes related to the struggle for autonomy on the island. The Minister of the Interior, Jean-Pierre Chevènement, resigned in protest over the proposals, claiming that they represented a surrender to the demands of terrorist groups, as well as a weakening of the republican structure of government. President Chirac and other leading figures in the RPR also expressed their opposition to this proposed act of decentralization, although Jospin emphasized that granting devolution was not an immediate priority for his Government.

Although most dissident groups maintained a cease-fire following the signature of the Matignon Accords, a series of bombings against state buildings occurred on the island in the second half of 2000, and two prominent nationalists, who were sympathetic to the government proposals, were assassinated in August. Corsican nationalists had been implicated in the planting of a bomb, which failed to detonate, in Paris late in June. These attacks were, in an unprecedented manner, denounced by the majority of nationalist and separatist groups, including those who had until recently justified the use of violence in their campaign. The attacks continued following a

visit to Corsica by the new Minister of the Interior, Daniel Vaillant, in November, during which he presented a draft document outlining the additional powers to be devolved to the Corsican Assembly from January 2002. In January 2001 Armata Corse, an organization founded in June 1999 by dissenting members of a faction of the FLNC, FLNC-Canal Historique, and which had until August 2000 been supportive of the peace process, claimed responsibility for two 'executions' and eight bombings on Corsica, in addition to planting a 'car bomb', which failed to detonate, in Marseille. President Chirac maintained his opposition to granting greater autonomy to Corsica, as allegations of widespread organized crime and corruption on the island surfaced, and following the announcement in October 2000 that groups in support of greater autonomy or independence for other regions of the French Republic, including Brittany, the Basque country, and certain Overseas Departments and Territories, had formed an alliance in response to what they regarded as a positive resolution of Corsica's status. In April 2000 Breton separatist terrorists, who had been waging a low-level bombing campaign intermittently since the late 1960s, but without causing any deaths, and who were reportedly linked with Basque groups, were reputedly responsible for an explosion at a fast-food restaurant in Dinan, in which one person was killed. However, allegations subsequently emerged that state intelligence services were implicated in the attack. A further attack in November, in which a civil servant was killed in southern Brittany, was also attributed to the Breton separatist movement.

In June 1995 Chirac announced that France was to end a moratorium on nuclear testing imposed by Mitterrand in 1992. Eight tests were to be conducted on Mururoa and Fangataufa atolls in French Polynesia, in the Pacific Ocean, between September 1995 and May 1996 (although this was later reduced to six). The announcement caused almost universal outrage in the international community, and was condemned for its apparent disregard for South Pacific regional opinion, as well as for undermining the considerable progress made by Western nations towards a world-wide ban on nuclear-weapons tests.

In November 1998, following an enduring campaign for the independence of the Pacific overseas territory of New Caledonia by indigenous Melanesian (Kanak) separatists, in conflict with the wishes of settlers of European origin (see French Overseas Possessions, p. 1651), a referendum on self-determination was held. At the referendum a gradual transfer of powers to local institutions over a period of between 15 and 20 years was approved, and the Republican Constitution amended accordingly. In October 1999 the Senate approved legislation granting French Polynesia the new status of 'pays d'outre-mer' (overseas country). By March 2001, however, the constitutional amendment was still awaiting final ratification

France granted independence to most of its former colonies after the Second World War. In Indo-China, after prolonged fighting, Laos, Cambodia and Viet Nam became fully independent in 1954. In Africa most of the French colonies in the West and Equatorial regions attained independence in 1960, but retained their close economic and political ties with France (particularly within the framework of the Franc Zone: see p. 210). From the second half of the 1990s, France was active in promoting the establishment of regional peace-keeping forces for Africa, and the reorganization of the French armed forces notably entailed a reduction in military commitments in its former African colonies.

In the early 1990s a contingent of French troops was dispatched to Rwanda to train forces of the Rwandan Government and to supply military equipment, following the outbreak of armed conflict between the Government and the opposition Rwandan Patriotic Front (FPR). In April 1994 French troops re-entered Rwanda to establish a 'safe humanitarian zone' for refugees fleeing the civil war. Although France declared its presence to be restricted to a transitional period prior to the arrival of UN peace-keeping forces, the FPR accused France of using the operation secretly to transport alleged war criminals out of the country. In January 1998 new evidence emerged in support of allegations that France had sold arms to Rwanda during the massacres in 1994, after the imposition of a UN embargo on the delivery of military equipment to any party in the conflict, although the Government denied the accusations. A commission of inquiry, established to investigate the affair, effectively exonerated France but implicated the international community (and particularly the USA) for failing to provide adequate support for UN forces in the country, although the Rwandan Government rejected these findings.

In September 1994, following the killing by Islamist terrorists of five French officials at the French embassy in Algiers, the French Government initiated an extensive security operation, the results of which included the detention and subsequent expulsion from France of a number of alleged Islamist fundamentalist activists. In December members of the French security forces killed four Islamist terrorists on board an Air France aircraft, which had been hijacked in Algiers and flown to Marseille. The following day four Catholic priests, three of them French citizens, were killed in Algeria, in an apparent reprisal attack. Eight people were killed in the second half of 1995 in a series of bombings in Paris and Lyon, for which the Armed Islamic Group (GIA), an extremist Algerian terrorist organization, was widely believed to be responsible. Terrorist activity resumed in December 1996 when four people were killed and many injured in an explosion on a crowded commuter train in Paris. Although no organization claimed responsibility for the attack it was speculated that the bombing might be in protest against the imminent trial in Paris of 30 young men of north African extraction who were accused of involvement in terrorist activities in Morocco in 1994. In December 1996 the GIA warned that it would continue its terrorist campaign in France, unless the French Government undertook to sever ties with the Algerian Government. France has been accused by Islamist groups in Algeria of providing covert military assistance to the Algerian Government following the suspension of the 1992 general election in Algeria (q.v.). In February 1998 36 Islamist militants were sentenced to up to 10 years' imprisonment for providing logistical support to the GIA during its bombing campaign in 1995. In late 1999 24 Islamist militants, reputedly linked to the GIA, were found guilty of a series of bombings, perpetrated in 1995, in which 10 people died. Diplomatic contacts between the Algerian President, Abdelaziz Bouteflika, and the French Minister of Foreign Affairs resulted in the reopening of a number of French consulates in Algeria, and in the state visit of Bouteflika to Paris in May 2000.

Relations with the People's Republic of China (PRC) were severely prejudiced in 1993 by France's decision to sell armaments to China (Taiwan) (see above). In January 1994 France suspended further sales of military equipment to Taiwan and announced the renewal of normal working relations with the PRC.

In October 1999 France refused to revoke its ban on imports of British beef, despite the formal ending in July of the ban imposed in 1996 by the EU, following the outbreak in the United Kingdom of Bovine Spongiform Encephalopathy (BSE—'Mad Cow Disease') and its human variant, Creutzfeldt-Jakob Disease, v-CJD). The French Government disregarded warnings that it would be in breach of EU policy were it to continue to block imports of British beef. The situation was further complicated when a report published by the European Commission in late October revealed the presence of human waste and sewage in French animal feed. In response to action by British farmers trying to prevent imports of French products, French farmers blockaded British trucks in Calais. In January 2000 the European Commission instituted legal proceedings against France in response to its refusal to lift the ban on the import of British beef; a judgment was, however, not expected for about 18 months. Meanwhile, by the end of 2000 162 cases of BSE-infected cattle had been found in France, while by the end of the year two humans had died from v-CJD as a result of eating infected beef. As BSE spread in France, a number of the country's major export markets for beef placed restrictions on the import of meat from France. In November 2000, in an attempt to alleviate concern both among the wider public and those directly economically affected by the crisis, Jospin imposed restrictions on the sale of certain cuts of beef and announced an emergency programme of aid worth 3,200,000m. francs to farmers and the meat industry. Allegations surfaced in early 2001 that high-level government officials had knowingly allowed consumers to risk infection by v-CJD. With the Government threatened by a loss of public confidence similar to that experienced after the case of HIV-infected blood knowingly given in transfusions in the mid 1980s (see above), over 30,000 cattle suspected of being liable to BSE infection were destroyed in January 2001.

Following legal pressure from the European Commission, France ended the monopoly of Electricité de France in its electricity markets in February 2000, almost one year later than had been required by EU legislation on competition. None the less, in June, the European Commission commenced legal proceedings against France for failing to ensure that the resulting competition would be fair. Although the establishment of separate departments in Gaz de France, announced in mid-2000, to deal with the transmission and trading of gas, was in compliance with the demands of EU competition law, it appeared that France would also fail to comply with its obligations to create competition in this sector.

In May 1992 France and Germany announced that they would establish a joint defence force of 50,000 troops, the 'Eurocorps', which was intended to provide a basis for a European army under the aegis of Western European Union (WEU, see p. 286) and which became operational on 30 November 1995. Belgium, Spain and Luxembourg also agreed to participate in the force. In January 1993 an agreement was signed between NATO and the French and German Governments, establishing formal links between the corps and NATO's military structure. In December 1995 it was announced that France would rejoin the military structure of NATO, although it would not initially become a full member of NATO's integrated military command and would retain control of its independent nuclear forces. France's proposed re-entry into the integrated military command has been delayed as a result of an ongoing dispute with the USA over command of the alliance troops in southern Europe, which France insists must be under the command of a European officer. In late 2000 it was announced that France would contribute 12,000 troops, of a total of 66,000 that would form a European rapid reaction force, to participate in peace-keeping missions from 2003. Relations between France and the command structure of NATO were further strained following the insistence of France, and particularly of President Chirac, that the operation and planning to be undertaken by the future European rapid reaction force be independent of NATO.

Government

Under the 1958 Constitution, legislative power is held by the bicameral Parliament, comprising a Senate and a National Assembly. The Senate has 321 members (296 for metropolitan France, 13 for the overseas departments, 'collectivités territoriales' and territories, and 12 for French nationals abroad). Senators are elected for a nine-year term by an electoral college composed of the members of the National Assembly, delegates from the Councils of the Departments and delegates from the Municipal Councils. One-third of the Senate is renewable every three years. The National Assembly has 577 members, with 555 for metropolitan France and 22 for overseas departments, 'collectivités territoriales' and territories. Members of the Assembly are elected by universal adult suffrage, under a single-member constituency system of direct election, using a second ballot if the first ballot failed to produce an absolute majority for any one candidate. The Assembly's term is five years, subject to dissolution. Executive power is held by the President. Since 1962 the President had been directly elected by popular vote (using two ballots if necessary) for seven years, although a constitutional amendment passed on 2 October 2000 shortened the term of office to five years. The President appoints a Council of Ministers, headed by the Prime Minister, which administers the country and is responsible to Parliament. Under constitutional amendments and legislation instituted in 1998-2000, political parties are penalized financially if they do not ensure parity of men and women in candidatures for elections.

Metropolitan France comprises 21 administrative regions containing 96 departments. Under the decentralization law of March 1982, administrative and financial power in metropolitan France was transferred from the Préfets, who became Commissaires de la République, to locally-elected departmental assemblies (Conseils généraux) and regional assemblies (Conseils régionaux). The special status of a 'collectivité territoriale' was granted to Corsica, which has its own directly-elected Legislative Assembly. There are four overseas departments (French Guiana, Guadeloupe, Martinique and Réunion), two overseas 'collectivités territoriales' (Mayotte and St Pierre and Miquelon), three overseas territories (French Polynesia, the French Southern and Antarctic Territories and the Wallis and Futuna Islands) and one 'pays d'outre-mer' (New Caledonia), all of which are integral parts of the French Republic (see p. 1605). Each overseas department is administered by an elected Conseil général and Conseil régional, each 'collectivité territoriale' by an appointed government commissioner, each overseas territory by an appointed high commissioner, and New Caledonia by its Government. In 1998 a referendum granted a transfer of powers to local institutions in New Caledonia over a period of 15–20 years. In 2000 plans to grant greater autonomy to Corsica, and to merge its two departments into one, by 2004, subject to several conditions, were announced, while in early 2001 plans to create a second department in Réunion were under discussion.

Defence

French military policy is decided by the Supreme Defence Council. Military service is currently compulsory and lasts for 10 months, although proposals to create fully professional armed forces, which were submitted to the National Assembly in 1996, meant that the practice of conscription was expected to cease in 2002. The cessation of conscription and decreased defence expenditure were expected to result in a reduction in the number of military personnel of some 25% by 2002. In August 2000 the total active armed forces numbered 294,430 (including 58,710 conscripts), including an army of 169,300, a navy of 49,400, an air force of 60,500, central service staff numbering 5,200, a medical corps of 8,600 and a directorate of fuel of 1,340. In addition, there was a paramilitary gendarmerie of 94,500 (including 15,600 conscripts). Total reserves stood at 419,000 (army 242,500; navy 97,000; air force 79,500) in August 1999, prior to further reorganization. Government expenditure on defence in 1999 amounted to 239,000m. francs. Defence expenditure was estimated at 187,900m. francs for 2000, with similar annual expenditure projected for 2001 and 2002. Although a member of NATO, France withdrew from its integrated military organization in 1966, and possesses its own nuclear weapons. In 1995, however, it was announced that France was to rejoin NATO's defence committee, and in 1996 President Chirac declared France's intention to rejoin NATO's integrated military command, although by early 2001 there had been no firm indication as to when or if this latter move was likely to occur. In mid-2000, France announced that it would be the third-largest contributor of troops, behind Germany and the United Kingdom, to the European rapid reaction force, that would enter service, primarily on peace-keeping missions, in 2003.

Economic Affairs

In 1998, according to estimates by the World Bank, France's gross national product (GNP), measured at average 1996-98 prices, was US $1,465,399m., equivalent to $24,210 per head (or $21,214 on an international purchasing-power parity basis). During 1990–98, it was estimated, GNP per head expanded, in real terms, at an average annual rate of 1.2%. Over the same period, the population increased by an average of 0.5% per year. In 1999 France's GNP (including the overseas departments, French Guiana, Guadeloupe, Martinique and Réunion) was US $1,427,200m, equivalent to US $23,480 per head. France's gross domestic product (GDP) increased, in real terms, by an average of 1.6% per year in 1990–99. Real GDP grew by 3.0% in 1998, by 2.8% in 1999.

Agriculture (including forestry and fishing) contributed 3.3% of GDP in constant 1995 prices in 1999, and engaged 3.7% of the economically active population in 1998. The principal crops are wheat, sugar beet, maize and barley. Livestock, dairy products and wine are also important. Agricultural GDP increased, in real terms, by an average of 1.7% per year in 1990–99; it increased by 2.6% in 1998 and by 1.5% in 1999.

Industry (including mining, manufacturing, construction and power) provided 25.1% of GDP in constant 1995 prices in 1999, and employed 26.6% of the working population in 1994. Industrial GDP increased, in real terms, by an average of 0.8% per year during 1990–99; it increased by 1.0% in 1998 and by 2.6% in 1999.

Mining and quarrying contributed 0.4% of GDP in 1995 and employed 0.3% of the working population in 1994. Coal is the principal mineral produced, while petroleum and natural gas are also extracted. In addition, metallic minerals, including iron ore, copper and zinc, are mined. In real terms, the GDP of the mining sector increased by 9.5% in 1993, but declined by 8.4% in 1994.

Manufacturing provided 20.1% of GDP in 1995 and employed 18.8% of the working population in 1994. Measured by the value of output, the most important branches of manufacturing in 1995 were machinery and transport equipment (accounting for 31% of the total), food, beverages and tobacco (17%), chemicals (10%) and fabricated metal products (6%). According to the World Bank, manufacturing GDP increased, in real terms, at an annual average rate of 1.0% in 1989–99.

In 1997 nuclear power provided 78.2% of total electricity production, hydroelectric power 13.9% and thermal power 7.9%.

Imports of mineral fuels comprised 5.9% of the value of total imports in 1998. The GDP of the energy sector increased, in real terms, at an annual average rate of 1.5% in 1990–99.

Services accounted for 71.5% of GDP in constant 1995 prices in 1999 and employed 68.7% of the working population in 1994. The combined GDP of all service sectors increased, in real terms, at an average rate of 1.6% per year in 1990–99; it increased by 3.4% in 1998 and by 2.8% in 1999.

In 1999 France recorded a trade surplus of US $19,390m., and there was a surplus of $36,580m. on the current account of the balance of payments. In 1998 the principal source of imports (17.3%) was Germany; other major sources were Italy (9.9%), the USA (8.9%), the United Kingdom (8.4%) Belgium and Luxembourg (7.7%), Spain (7.1%) and the Netherlands (5.1%). Germany was also the principal market for exports (16.0%); other major trading partners were the United Kingdom (10.0%), Italy (9.2%), Spain (8.7%), Belgium and Luxembourg (7.7%) and the USA (7.4%). The EU as a whole provided 62.4% of imports in 1998 and took 63.1% of exports. The principal exports in 1998 were machinery and transport equipment, basic manufactures, chemicals and food and live animals. The principal imports were machinery and transport equipment, basic manufactures and miscellaneous manufactured articles.

The budget deficit for 1997 amounted to 284,400m. francs, equivalent to 3.6% of GDP. The deficit was equivalent to 3.0% of GDP in 1998 and 2.5% in 1999. In 1999 gross state debt was equivalent to 58.9% of annual GDP. The average annual rate of inflation in 1990–99 was 1.7%. In 1999 consumer prices increased by only 0.5%, the lowest annual average for more than 40 years; in 2000, however, the rate of inflation had increased to 1.7%. The rate of unemployment was 8.8% in February 2001.

France is a member of the European Union (EU, see p. 181) and of the Organisation for Economic Co-operation and Development (see p. 247), and presides over the Franc Zone (see p. 210).

As one of the initial 11 member countries of the EU that had chosen to participate in a single currency under economic and monetary union (EMU, see p. 199), France adopted the euro on 1 January 1999 as a single currency unit for transactions throughout the euro zone and as an internationally traded currency. The euro was expected to become legal tender in France in February 2002. The economy exhibited vigorous growth in the late 1990s, which was principally due to high levels of private consumption and investment, supported by strong consumer and business confidence. Growth was also fuelled by the depreciation of the euro which promoted external demand. The rapid growth of the economy has facilitated the attainment of one of the stated economic priorities of the Jospin administration, the reduction of the country's persistently high rate of unemployment. The implementation in February 2000 of legislation reducing the duration of the working week from 39 to 35 hours for public-sector workers and employees of companies with more than 20 employees (to be extended to cover small firms from February 2002), also contributed to the reductions in unemployment. A number of major state-owned corporations have been wholly or partially privatized since 1993. In February 2001 the acquisition of Banque Hervet, the final bank in which the state had a significant (97.5%) share, by Crédit Commercial de France, was announced. At the end of August 2000 the Government announced tax reductions equivalent to 1.3% of GDP, which were to be implemented during 2001–03: the measures included reductions in all income tax brackets, rebates at the lower level on social security contributions and cuts in corporate income tax. The announcement in January 2001, of a tax credit for the low-paid, in preference to an increase in the minimum wage, was regarded as marking a significant shift in fiscal policy by the Socialist Government. The budget for 2001 aimed at further reducing the budget deficit to 1.0%, whilst increasing real expenditure by 1.3%. Despite the rise in international petroleum prices, which had a slight adverse effect on demand, analysts forecast a continuation of strong growth in output and employment with low and stable inflation. In the longer term, public finances needed to be further improved in order to cope with the problem of an ageing population, the pressures of which would begin to take effect in 2005. This demographic change also necessitated further reform of the pension system including the development of a complementary private pension sector.

Social Welfare

France has evolved a comprehensive system of social security, which is compulsory for all wage-earners and self-employed people. A national minimum hourly wage is in force, and is periodically adjusted in accordance with fluctuations in the cost of living. State insurance of wage-earners requires contributions from both employers and employees, and provides for sickness, unemployment, maternity, disability through industrial accident and substantial allowances for large families. War veterans receive pensions and certain privileges, and widows the equivalent of three months' salary and pension. About 95% of all medical practitioners adhere to the state scheme. The patient pays directly for medical treatment and prescribed medicines, and then obtains reimbursement for all or part of the cost. Sickness benefits and pensions are related to the insured person's income, age and the length of time for which he or she has been insured. Proposed budgetary expenditure by the central Government in 1998 included 73,163m. francs for social services and health (4.6% of total budgetary spending). Of total government expenditure (including disbursements by government-controlled social security funds) in 1992, about 487,700m. francs (15.5%) was for health, and a further 1,419,900m. francs (45.1%) for social security and welfare. The Caisse d'Amortissement de la Dette Sociale (CADES), a financial institution created in 1996, is responsible for eliminating the deficit in the social services sector (estimated at 120,000m. francs in 1994–95 and projected at 17,000m. francs for 1996). CADES is funded by a special income tax, levied since 1996. In 1997 France had 4,186 hospital establishments (of which 1,063 were public), with a total of 659,539 beds (459,792 of which were in public establishments). In 1998 there were an estimated 175,000 physicians registered in France In 1998 spending on national health care was equivalent to 9.4% of GDP.

Education

France is divided into 27 educational districts, called Académies, each responsible for the administration of education, from primary to higher levels, in its area. Education is compulsory and free for children aged six to 16 years. Primary education begins at six years of age and lasts for five years. At the age of 11 all pupils enter the first cycle of the Enseignement secondaire, with a four-year general course. At the age of 15 they may then proceed to the second cycle, choosing a course leading to the baccalauréat examination after three years or a course leading to vocational qualifications after two or three years, with commercial, administrative or industrial options. From 1963 junior classes in the Lycées were gradually abolished in favour of new junior comprehensives, called Collèges. Alongside the collèges

and lycées, technical education is provided in the Lycées professionnels and the Lycées techniques. About 17% of children attend France's 10,000 private schools, most of which are administered by the Roman Catholic Church.

Educational reforms, introduced in 1980, aimed to decentralize the state school system: the school calendar now varies according to three zones, and the previously rigid syllabus has been replaced by more flexibility and choice of curricula. Further decentralization measures included, from 1986, the transfer of financial responsibility for education to the local authorities.

The minimum qualification for entry to university faculties is the baccalauréat. There are three stages of university education. The first level, the Diplôme d'études universitaires générales (DEUG), is reached after two years of study, and the first degree, the Licence, is obtained after three years. The master's degree (Maîtrise) is obtained after four years of study, while the doctorate requires six or seven years' study and the submission of a thesis. The prestigious Grandes Ecoles complement the universities; entry to them is by competitive examination, and they have traditionally supplied France's administrative élite. The 1968 reforms in higher education aimed to increase university autonomy and to render teaching methods less formal. Enrolment at schools in 1996 included 100% of children in the relevant age-group for primary education and 95% (males 94%; females 95%) for secondary education. Expenditure on education by all levels of government in 1999 totalled an estimated 92,600m. euros (7.2% of GDP). Proposed budgetary expenditure on education by the central Government amounted to 334,378m. francs in 1998 (21.1% of total budgetary expenditure).

Public Holidays

2001: 1 January (New Year's Day), 16 April (Easter Monday), 1 May (Labour Day), 8 May (Liberation Day), 24 May (Ascension Day), 4 June (Whit Monday), 14 July (National Day, Fall of the Bastille), 15 August (Assumption), 1 November (All Saints' Day), 11 November (Armistice Day), 25 December (Christmas Day).

2002: 1 January (New Year's Day), 1 April (Easter Monday), 1 May (Labour Day), 8 May (Liberation Day), 9 May (Ascension Day), 20 May (Whit Monday), 14 July (National Day, Fall of the Bastille), 15 August (Assumption), 1 November (All Saints' Day), 11 November (Armistice Day), 25 December (Christmas Day)

Weights and Measures

The metric system is in force.

Statistical Survey

Unless otherwise indicated, figures in this survey refer to metropolitan France, excluding Overseas Departments and Territories.
Source (unless otherwise stated): Institut national de la statistique et des études économiques, 18 boulevard Adolphe Pinard, 75675 Paris Cédex 14; tel. 1-45-17-50-50; internet www.insee.fr.

Area and Population

AREA, POPULATION AND DENSITY

Area (sq km)	543,965*
Population (census results, *de jure*)†	
5 March 1990	56,615,155
8 March 1999	
Males	28,419,419
Females	30,101,269
Total	58,520,688
Population (official estimates at mid-year)	
1998	58,397,800
1999‡	58,620,400
2000‡	58,891,900
Density (per sq km) at mid-2000	108.3

* 210,026 sq miles.
† Excluding professional soldiers and military personnel outside the country with no personal residence in France.
‡ Provisional.

NATIONALITY OF THE POPULATION
(numbers resident in France at 1990 census*)

Country of citizenship	Population	%
France	53,026,709	93.63
Algeria	619,923	1.09
Belgium	59,705	0.11
Germany	51,483	0.09
Italy	253,679	0.45
Morocco	584,708	1.03
Poland	46,283	0.08
Portugal	645,578	1.14
Spain	216,015	0.38
Tunisia	207,496	0.37
Turkey	201,480	0.36
Yugoslavia	51,697	0.09
Others	669,543	1.18
Total	**56,634,299**	**100.00**

* Figures include double counting. The revised total is 56,615,155.

REGIONS (population at 1999 census, revised figures)

	Area (sq km)	Population	Density (per sq km)
Alsace	8,280.2	1,733,732	209.4
Aquitaine	41,308.4	2,908,953	70.4
Auvergne	26,012.9	1,308,656	50.3
Basse-Normandie . . .	17,589.3	1,422,436	80.9
Bourgogne (Burgundy) . .	31,582.0	1,610,407	51.0
Bretagne (Brittany) . .	27,207.9	2,907,178	106.9
Centre	39,150.9	2,439,962	62.3
Champagne–Ardenne . .	25,605.8	1,342,202	52.4
Corse (Corsica) . . .	8,679.8	260,149	30.0
Franche-Comté . . .	16,202.3	1,117,257	69.0
Haute-Normandie . . .	12,317.4	1,780,439	144.5
Île-de-France	12,012.3	10,951,136	911.7
Languedoc–Roussillon . .	27,375.8	2,296,357	83.9
Limousin	16,942.3	710,792	42.0
Lorraine	23,547.4	2,310,023	98.1
Midi–Pyrénées	45,347.9	2,552,696	56.3
Nord–Pas-de-Calais . .	12,414.1	3,995,871	321.9
Pays de la Loire . . .	32,081.8	3,222,784	100.5
Picardie (Picardy) . .	19,399.5	1,857,105	95.7
Poitou–Charentes . . .	25,809.5	1,640,453	63.6
Provence–Alpes–Côte d'Azur .	31,399.6	4,506,253	143.5
Rhône–Alpes	43,698.2	5,645,847	129.2
Total	**543,965.3**	**58,520,688**	**107.6**

PRINCIPAL TOWNS* (population at 1999 census, revised figures)

Paris (capital) . .	2,125,246	Brest	149,634
Marseille		Le Mans . . .	146,105
(Marseilles) . .	798,430	Clermont-Ferrand .	137,140
Lyon (Lyons) . .	445,452	Amiens . . .	135,501
Toulouse . .	390,350	Aix-en-Provence .	134,222
Nice . . .	342,738	Limoges . . .	133,968
Nantes . .	270,251	Nîmes . . .	133,424
Strasbourg . .	264,115	Tours . . .	132,820
Montpellier .	225,392	Villeurbanne . .	124,215
Bordeaux . .	215,363	Metz . . .	123,776
Rennes . .	206,229	Besançon . .	117,733
Le Havre . .	190,905	Caen . . .	113,987
Reims (Rheims) .	187,206	Orléans . .	113,126
Lille . . .	184,493	Mulhouse . .	110,359
Saint-Étienne . .	180,210	Rouen . . .	106,592
Toulon . .	160,639	Boulogne-	
Grenoble . .	153,317	Billancourt . .	106,367
Angers . .	151,279	Perpignan . .	105,115
Dijon . . .	149,867	Nancy . . .	103,605

* Figures refer to the population of communes (municipalities).

BIRTHS, MARRIAGES AND DEATHS*

	Registered live births		Registered marriages		Registered deaths	
	Number	Rate (per 1,000)	Number	Rate (per 1,000)	Number	Rate (per 1,000)
1990 . .	762,407	13.4	287,099	5.1	526,201	9.3
1991 . .	759,056	13.3	280,175	4.9	524,685	9.2
1992 . .	743,658	13.0	271,427	4.7	521,530	9.1
1993 . .	711,610	12.3	255,190	4.4	532,263	9.2
1994 . .	710,993	12.3	253,746	4.4	519,965	9.0
1995 . .	729,609	12.6	254,651	4.4	531,618	9.2
1996 . .	734,338	12.7	280,072	4.8	535,775	9.2
1997 . .	726,768	12.5	283,984	4.9	530,319	9.1

* Including data for national armed forces outside the country.
1998 (provisional figures): 738,100 registered live births (birth rate 12.6 per 1,000); 271,400 registered marriages (marriage rate 4.6 per 1,000); 534,000 registered deaths (death rate 9.1 per 1,000).
1999 (provisional figures): 744,100 registered live births (birth rate 12.7 per 1,000); 541,600 registered deaths (death rate 9.2 per 1,000).

Expectation of life (years at birth, 1999, provisional figures): Males 74.9; Females 82.4.

ECONOMICALLY ACTIVE POPULATION*
(annual averages, '000 persons aged 15 years and over)

	1992	1993	1994
Agriculture, hunting, forestry and fishing	1,150.3	1,100.8	1,048.4
Mining and quarrying	72.0	69.9	65.9
Manufacturing	4,479.0	4,269.3	4,162.2
Electricity, gas and water.	204.0	204.9	203.7
Construction.	1,568.3	1,487.8	1,443.1
Trade, restaurants and hotels	3,715.2	3,680.5	3,715.7
Transport, storage and communications	1,418.4	1,403.1	1,397.0
Financing, insurance, real estate and business services	2,295.2	2,265.1	2,340.4
Community, social and personal services†	7,405.4	7,596.2	7,733.8
Total employed	22,307.6	22,078.2	22,110.0
Persons on compulsory military service	221.1	219.9	212.4
Unemployed .	2,590.7	2,929.0	3,163.8
Total labour force	25,119.4	25,227.1	25,486.2

* Figures are provisional. The revised totals (in '000) are: Employed 22,306.0 in 1992, 22,052.7 in 1993, 22,043.8 in 1994; Persons on compulsory military service 225.0 in 1992; Unemployed 2,590.0 in 1992, 2,929.4 in 1993, 3,117.0 in 1994; Labour force 25,121.0 in 1992, 25,202.0 in 1993, 25,373.2 in 1994.
† Figures include regular members of the armed forces, officially estimated at 304,200 (males 286,000; females 18,200) in 1986.
Source: mainly ILO, *Yearbook of Labour Statistics.*

1996 (annual averages, '000 persons aged 15 years and over): Total employed 22,246.7; Persons on compulsory military service 199.9; Unemployed 3,137.2; Total labour force 25,583.8 (males 14,176.7, females 11,407.1).

1997 (annual averages, '000 persons aged 15 years and over, provisional): Total employed 22,327.2; Persons on compulsory military service 169.4; Unemployed 3,192.0; Total labour force 25,688.6 (males 14,236.6, females 11,452.0).

1999 (annual averages, '000 persons aged 15 years and over): Total employed 23,055.0; Persons on compulsory military service 85.0; Unemployed 3,402.0; Total labour force 26,542.0.

Agriculture

PRINCIPAL CROPS ('000 metric tons)

	1997	1998	1999
Wheat	33,847	39,809	37,050
Rye .	197	216	186
Barley	10,124	10,591	9,548
Oats	568	888	551
Maize*	16,832	15,206	15,656
Sorghum	459	361	328
Rice (paddy) .	121	107	103
Sugar beet	34,372	31,156	32,919
Potatoes.	6,690	6,053	6,644
Pulses	3,121	3,310	2,715
Soybeans	269	284	272
Sunflower seed	1,995	1,713	1,868
Rapeseed	3,495	3,734	4,469
Tobacco (leaves) .	25	26	26
Artichokes	76	85	75
Cabbages	237	232	239
Carrots .	652	662	672
Cauliflowers.	509	439	425
Cucumbers and gherkins .	140	143	147
Melons	278	325	322
Onions (dry) .	328	330	349
Garlic	45	45	41
Beans (green)	115	127	125
Peas (green) .	515	550	557
Tomatoes	805	884	921
Apples	2,473	2,210	2,643
Apricots .	158	80	181
Grapes	7,191	7,013	8,137
Peaches and nectarines	464	341	478
Pears	268	260	300
Plums	196	206	185

* Figures refer to main, associated and catch crops.
Source: FAO.

LIVESTOCK ('000 head, year ending 30 September)

	1997	1998	1999
Cattle	20,664	20,371	20,214
Pigs.	14,976	14,501	14,682
Sheep	10,463	10,316	10,240
Goats	1,202	1,200	1,199
Horses	340	347	348
Asses*	25	25	25
Mules	14	14	14
Chickens (million)	231	238	240
Ducks (million) .	23	22	24
Turkeys (million)	42	43	44

* FAO estimates.
Source: FAO.

LIVESTOCK PRODUCTS ('000 metric tons)

	1997	1998	1999
Beef and veal	1,718	1,630	1,604
Mutton and lamb	141	134	131
Goat meat	8	10	10
Pig meat	2,220	2,127	2,154
Horse meat	11	10	9
Poultry meat	2,125	2,169	2,092
Other meat	285	285	285
Cows' milk	24,916	24,741	24,609
Sheep's milk .	243	243	244
Goats' milk	489	492	496
Butter	466	463	464†
Cheese .	1,622	1,653	1,661
Honey .	16	17	18*
Hen eggs	1,009	1,009	1,051
Wool:			
greasy.	22†	22†	22*
clean .	12*	12†	n.a.
Cattle hides*	163	154	151
Sheepskins* .	17	16	16

* FAO estimate(s).   † Unofficial figure.
Source: FAO.

Forestry

ROUNDWOOD REMOVALS ('000 cubic metres, excluding bark)

	1997	1998	1999
Sawlogs, veneer logs and logs for sleepers	21,134	21,967	22,550
Pulpwood	9,698	10,273	10,500
Other industrial wood	484	478	480
Fuel wood	9,800*	2,809	2,850
Total	41,116	35,527	36,380

* FAO estimate.
Source: FAO, *Yearbook of Forest Products.*

SAWNWOOD PRODUCTION
('000 cubic metres, including railway sleepers)

	1997	1998	1999
Coniferous (softwood).	6,800	7,197	7,450
Broadleaved (hardwood) .	2,807	3,023	3,050
Total	9,607	10,220	10,500

Source: FAO, *Yearbook of Forest Products.*

Fishing*

('000 metric tons, live weight)

	1996	1997	1998
Capture	560.2	567.5	536.3
European anchovy . . .	19.5	16.2	25.4
Skipjack tuna	63.1	48.4	48.3
Yellowfin tuna	70.2	61.8	52.4
Crustaceans	20.6	21.0	17.4
Molluscs	49.4	61.9	55.0
Aquaculture	285.6	287.5	273.6
Rainbow trout . . .	50.6	50.5	44.7
Pacific cupped oyster . .	149.6	147.2	143.0
Blue mussel	50.0	52.4	50.0
Total catch	845.8	855.0	809.9

* Figures exclude aquatic plants ('000 metric tons): 146.4 (capture 84.4, aquaculture 62.0) in 1996, 137.5 (capture 75.5, aquaculture 62.0) in 1997, 129.9 (capture 67.0, aquaculture 62.0) in 1998; coral (metric tons): 2 in 1996, 3 in 1997, 5 in 1998; and sponges (metric tons, FAO estimates): 7 in 1996, 5 in 1997, 5 in 1998. Also excluded are aquatic mammals, recorded by number rather than by weight. The number of toothed whales caught was: 29 in 1996, 321 in 1997, 48 in 1998.

Source: FAO, *Yearbook of Fishery Statistics*.

Mining

('000 metric tons, unless otherwise indicated)

	1997	1998	1999*
Hard coal	5,779	5,300	n.a.
Brown coal (incl. lignite) . .	690	800	n.a.
Iron ore:			
gross weight	523	250	250
metal content	150*	75	35
Crude petroleum	1,780	n.a.	n.a.
Potash salts†	725	656	300
Salt (unrefined)	7,085	7,000*	7,000
Natural gas (million cubic metres)	2,600	2,600*	n.a.

* Estimate(s).

† Figures refer to recovered quantities of K_2O.

Source: mainly US Geological Survey.

Industry

SELECTED PRODUCTS
('000 metric tons, unless otherwise indicated)

	1994	1995	1996
Margarine and other prepared fats	134.8	131.2	138.3
Wheat flour*	5,186	5,282	5,400
Raw sugar†	4,014	4,198	4,179
Wine ('000 hectolitres) . .	54,850	n.a.	n.a.
Beer ('000 hectolitres) . .	17,688	18,311	17,140
Cigarettes (million) . .	48,188	46,361	46,931
Cotton yarn—pure (metric tons)[1]	110,400	n.a.	n.a.
Woven cotton fabrics—pure and mixed (metric tons) . .	87,000	n.a.	n.a.
Wool yarn—pure and mixed (metric tons)	15,800	n.a.	n.a.
Woven woollen fabrics—pure and mixed (metric tons) . .	25,850	n.a.	n.a.
Non-cellulosic continuous filaments (metric tons) . .	63,100	n.a.	n.a.
Non-cellulosic discontinuous fibres (metric tons) . .	61,600	n.a.	n.a.
Woven fabrics of non-cellulosic (synthetic) fibres (metric tons) .	14,028	n.a.	n.a.
Mechanical wood pulp . .	886	934	757
Chemical wood pulp‡ . .	1,901	1,884	1,758
Newsprint	844	890	783
Other printing and writing paper .	3,268	3,096	3,141
Other paper and paperboard .	4,589	4,633	4,632
Synthetic rubber . . .	518.4	619.4	n.a.
Rubber tyres ('000)[2] . .	66,744	n.a.	n.a.

— continued	1994	1995	1996
Sulphuric acid	2,227	2,382	n.a.
Caustic soda (Sodium hydroxide) .	1,561	1,501	n.a.
Nitrogenous fertilizers (a)[3,4] . .	1,720	n.a.	n.a.
Phosphate fertilizers (b)[3] . .	936	n.a.	n.a.
Potash fertilizers (c)[3,4] . .	870	n.a.	n.a.
Liquefied petroleum gas[5] . .	2,488	2,459	2,802
Motor spirit (petrol) . . .	17,696	17,946	18,094
Jet fuels	5,297	5,649	6,397
Kerosene	51	45	54
Distillate fuel oils . . .	30,501	30,877	32,568
Residual fuel oils . . .	10,668	9,427	10,536
Petroleum bitumen (asphalt) . .	3,348	3,132	n.a.
Coke-oven coke . . .	5,880	5,566	5,580
Cement	20,184	19,896	n.a.
Pig-iron	12,444	12,876	12,132
Crude steel	18,242	18,101	17,633
Aluminium (unwrought):			
primary	481.5	364.5	380.1
secondary (incl. alloys) . .	227.4	253.6	236.8
Refined copper—unwrought (metric tons) . . .	51,600	54,000	62,000
Lead (unwrought):			
primary	105.3	128.7	139.1
secondary	75.4	168.0	162.0
Zinc (unwrought):			
primary	293.0	300.0	324.3
Secondary	29.3		
Radio receivers ('000) . .	2,804	n.a.	n.a.
Television receivers ('000) . .	2,796	n.a.	n.a.
Merchant ships launched ('000 gross reg. tons) . . .	172	70	124
Passenger motor cars ('000) . .	3,176	n.a.	n.a.
Lorries and vans ('000) . .	453.3	n.a.	n.a.
Electric energy (million kWh) .	476,209	493,785	508,224

1997 ('000 metric tons, unless otherwise indicated): Newsprint 783; Other printing and writing paper 3,141; Liquefied petroleum gas 2,758; Motor spirit (petrol) 18,734; Jet fuels 6,598; Kerosene 78; Distillate fuel oils 35,112; Residual fuel oils 11,052; Coke-oven coke 5,441; Pig-iron 13,428; Crude steel 19,767; Aluminium (unwrought): primary 399.4; Aluminium (unwrought): secondary 232.8; Refined copper-unwrought (metric tons) 59,100; Lead (unwrought): primary 114.0; Lead (unwrought): secondary 168.0; Zinc (unwrought) 317.2; Electric energy (million kWh) 509,878.

* Deliveries.

† Estimated production during crop year ending 30 September.

‡ Including semi-chemical pulp, but excluding dissolving grades.

[1] Including tyre-cord yarn.

[2] Tyres for road motor vehicles other than bicycles and motor cycles.

[3] Production of fertilizers is in terms of plant nutrients: (a) nitrogen; (b) phosphoric acid; or (c) potassium oxide.

[4] Figures refer to output during the 12 months ending 30 June of year stated.

[5] Excluding production in natural gas processing plants ('000 metric tons): 228 in 1994; 203 in 1995; n.a. in 1996.

Source: mainly UN, *Industrial Commodity Statistics Yearbook*.

Finance

CURRENCY AND EXCHANGE RATES

Monetary Units:
100 centimes = 1 French franc.

Sterling, Dollar and Euro Equivalents (29 December 2000)
£1 sterling = 10.5193 francs;
US $1 = 7.0495 francs;
€1 = 6.5596 francs;
1,000 French francs = £95.06 = $141.85 = €152.45.

Average Exchange Rate (francs per US $)

1998	5.8995
1999	6.1570
2000	7.1198

Note: Since the introduction of the euro, with French participation, on 1 January 1999, a fixed exchange rate of €1 = 6.55957 French francs has been in operation.

GENERAL BUDGET (estimates, million francs)

Revenue	1996	1997	1998*
Tax revenue .	1,620,124	1,671,051	1,725,035
Income tax	314,136	290,000	296,550
Corporation tax	171,700	203,100	220,200
Value-added tax	728,244	753,000	776,770
Stamp duty, etc.†	85,443	91,850	91,750
Other taxes	320,601	333,101	339,765
Non-tax revenue .	138,989	137,449	140,857
Sub-total	1,759,113	1,808,500	1,865,892
Tax relief and reimbursements	−260,788	−267,400	−278,330
Other deductions, e.g. EU	−243,016	−252,970	−255,724
Total	1,255,309	1,288,130	1,331,838

* Projected figures.
† Including registration duties and tax on stock exchange transactions.

Expenditure	1997	1998*
General non-salary disbursements (net)	336,323	339,587
Education	324,218	334,378
Culture and communications .	15,126	15,109
Social services and health	70,930	73,163
Employment .	150,381	155,812
Agriculture and fisheries .	35,244	35,172
Housing .	40,348	39,834
Transport, tourism and public works	83,663	85,194
Financial services	45,844	46,547
Industry .	25,158	16,367
Home affairs .	76,195	77,829
Foreign affairs	14,462	14,387
Defence†	243,344	238,265
Judiciary	23,903	24,867
Research and development	28,909	39,611
Other purposes	49,969	49,185
Total	1,564,017	1,585,307

* Projected figures.
† Including expenditure allocated for retired personnel.

Source: Ministère du Budget.

INTERNATIONAL RESERVES (US $ million at 31 December)*

	1997	1998	1999
Gold†	30,927	44,312	39,701
IMF special drawing rights	971	1,107	347
Reserve position in IMF	2,859	4,452	5,421
Foreign exchange	27,097	38,753	33,933
Total	61,854	88,624	79,402

* Excluding deposits made with the European Monetary Institute (now the European Central Bank).
† Valued at market-related prices.

Source: IMF, *International Financial Statistics.*

MONEY SUPPLY ('000 million francs for 1997 and 1998, million euros for 1999, at 31 December)

	1997	1998	1999
Currency outside banks .	283	287	49,282
Demand deposits at banking institutions	1,674	n.a.	243,949

Source: IMF, *International Financial Statistics.*

COST OF LIVING (Consumer Price Index for Urban Households, average of monthly figures; base: 1990 = 100)

	1997	1998	1999
Food (incl. beverages)	109.0	110.7	111.4
Fuel and light	107.3	104.3	104.7
Clothing and household linen .	108.8	108.6	110.4
Rent	125.8	128.3	130.6
All items (incl. others)	115.2	116.0	116.6

Source: ILO, *Yearbook of Labour Statistics.*

NATIONAL ACCOUNTS

National Income and Product (million francs at current prices)

	1993	1994	1995
Compensation of employees	3,737,354	3,827,608	3,981,150
Operating surplus	1,548,596	1,677,023	1,734,558
Domestic factor incomes	5,285,950	5,504,631	5,715,708
Consumption of fixed capital .	925,815	954,624	985,611
Gross domestic product (GDP) at factor cost .	6,211,765	6,459,255	6,701,319
Indirect taxes	1,035,458	1,102,813	1,159,926
Less Subsidies .	170,136	172,413	186,434
GDP in purchasers' values .	7,077,087	7,389,654	7,674,811
Factor income received from abroad	395,607	359,227	375,752
Less Factor income paid abroad	451,799	412,193	407,714
Gross national product (GNP) .	7,020,895	7,336,688	7,642,849
Less Consumption of fixed capital	925,815	954,624	985,611
National income in market prices .	6,095,080	6,382,064	6,657,238
Other current transfers from abroad .	186,232	179,259	183,478
Less Other current transfers paid abroad .	210,192	214,974	212,840
National disposable income	6,071,120	6,346,349	6,627,876

Source: UN, *National Accounts Statistics.*

Expenditure on the Gross Domestic Product
('000 million francs at current prices)

	1997	1998	1999
Government final consumption expenditure .	1,986.2	2,009.6	2,088.1
Private final consumption expenditure .	4,509.1	4,696.5	4,837.6
Increase in stocks*	−7.7	40.5	2.5
Gross fixed capital formation*	1,473.0	1,564.9	1,675.5
Total domestic expenditure	7,960.6	8,311.5	8,603.8
Exports of goods and services	2,093.5	2,228.9	2,299.6
Less Imports of goods and services	−1,849.2	−2,006.1	−2,087.9
GDP in purchasers' values .	8,204.6	8,534.3	8,815.5
GDP at constant 1995 prices	7,987.4	8,246.3	8,488.1

* Construction of non-residential buildings is included in 'Increase in stocks'.

Source: mainly Institut national de la statistique et des études économiques.

Gross Domestic Product by Economic Activity
(provisional, million francs at current prices)

	1993	1994	1995
Agriculture, hunting, forestry and fishing	165,859	177,863	183,444
Mining and quarrying	31,662	31,943	31,938
Manufacturing	1,380,297	1,423,067	1,478,011
Electricity, gas and water .	171,619	173,396	178,069
Construction .	357,982	342,298	342,836
Trade, restaurants and hotels	1,080,595	1,107,301	1,154,202
Transport, storage and communications	414,197	427,443	433,518
Finance, insurance, real estate and business services*	1,570,139	1,697,018	1,745,956
Government services†	1,211,348	1,261,469	1,323,570
Other community, social and personal services	443,280	458,920	479,774
Sub-total	6,826,978	7,100,718	7,351,318
Value-added tax and import duties	525,336	552,068	586,403
Less Imputed bank service charges	275,227	263,132	262,910
Total	7,077,087	7,389,654	7,674,811

* Including imputed rents of owner-occupied dwellings.
† Including private non-profit services to households.

Source: UN, *National Accounts Statistics.*

BALANCE OF PAYMENTS (US $ '000 million)*

	1997	1998	1999
Exports of goods f.o.b.	286.07	303.02	298.22
Imports of goods f.o.b.	−259.17	−278.08	−278.83
Trade balance	26.90	24.94	19.39
Exports of services	80.79	84.96	83.79
Imports of services	−64.16	−67.73	−64.67
Balance on goods and services	43.52	42.17	38.51
Other income received	57.13	66.67	67.87
Other income paid	−50.04	−58.00	−56.82
Balance on goods, services and income	50.62	50.83	49.55
Current transfers received	19.61	19.65	18.80
Current transfers paid	−32.43	−32.79	−31.78
Current balance	37.80	37.70	36.58
Capital account (net)	1.48	1.47	1.47
Direct investment abroad	−35.49	−45.70	−106.84
Direct investment from abroad	23.05	29.52	38.83
Portfolio investment assets	−60.79	−105.22	−129.84
Portfolio investment liabilities	35.32	59.75	115.43
Financial derivatives liabilities	4.10	−0.44	−2.23
Other investment assets	−53.64	26.11	−31.86
Other investment liabilities	49.85	6.70	75.34
Net errors and omissions	4.26	9.94	1.67
Overall balance	5.94	19.82	−1.45

* Figures refer to transactions of metropolitan France, Monaco and the French Overseas Departments and Territories with the rest of the world.

Source: IMF, *International Financial Statistics*.

External Trade

Note: Figures refer to the trade of metropolitan France, French Overseas Departments (French Guiana, Guadeloupe, Martinique and Réunion) and Monaco with the rest of the world, excluding trade in war materials, goods exported under the off-shore procurement programme, war reparations and restitutions and the export of sea products direct from the high seas. The figures include trade in second-hand ships and aircraft, and the supply of stores and bunkers for foreign ships and aircraft.

PRINCIPAL COMMODITIES (distribution by SITC, US $ million)

Imports c.i.f.	1996	1997	1998
Food and live animals	23,611.2	22,026.5	22,687.9
Vegetables and fruit	6,063.0	5,549.8	5,827.3
Crude materials (inedible) except fuels	8,697.3	8,525.7	8,484.3
Mineral fuels, lubricants, etc. (incl. electric current)	22,857.6	21,891.9	16,813.3
Petroleum, petroleum products, etc.	17,691.3	16,651.2	11,997.8
Crude petroleum oils, etc.	12,746.4	12,379.1	8,694.6
Chemicals and related products	32,862.7	32,322.4	34,980.3
Organic chemicals	7,431.9	7,495.3	8,096.1
Medicinal and pharmaceutical products	5,723.0	5,875.4	7,166.0
Artificial resins, plastic materials, etc.	6,938.6	6,692.2	6,954.4
Basic manufactures	42,980.7	42,267.0	45,531.3
Paper, paperboard and manufactures	6,790.0	6,454.7	7,095.3
Textile yarn, fabrics, etc.	7,083.5	6,989.6	7,511.9
Iron and steel	8,010.4	7,872.9	8,982.1
Non-ferrous metals	5,766.7	6,084.6	5,770.3
Other metal manufactures	6,395.7	6,135.0	6,695.9
Machinery and transport equipment	99,648.4	96,774.9	111,869.1
Power-generating machinery and equipment	6,713.4	7,666.2	9,724.1
Machinery specialized for particular industries	7,501.3	6,834.8	7,726.3

Imports c.i.f. — *continued*	1996	1997	1998
General industrial machinery, equipment and parts	11,801.2	11,259.2	12,663.8
Office machines and automatic data-processing equipment	13,342.5	13,681.2	15,597.2
Automatic data-processing machines and units	7,936.1	8,212.4	9,579.2
Telecommunications and sound equipment	6,686.6	7,418.8	8,549.0
Other electrical machinery, apparatus, etc.	17,339.2	18,001.9	20,109.4
Thermionic valves, tubes, etc.	5,292.2	5,682.1	6,809.0
Road vehicles and parts*	28,485.8	23,474.4	28,121.5
Passenger motor cars (excl. buses)	16,043.8	12,103.7	14,835.1
Parts and accessories for cars, buses, lorries, etc.*	5,618.0	5,576.8	6,597.1
Other transport equipment and parts*	5,853.0	6,639.6	7,295.7
Aircraft, associated equipment and parts*	5,021.8	5,732.7	6,684.7
Miscellaneous manufactured articles	38,828.3	37,995.6	40,571.2
Clothing and accessories (excl. footwear)	10,897.9	10,759.9	11,658.6
Total (incl. others)	274,913.8	266,575.4	286,035.9

* Data on parts exclude tyres, engines and electrical parts.

Exports f.o.b.	1996	1997	1998
Food and live animals	29,974.8	27,870.4	26,866.5
Cereals and cereal preparations	7,600.2	6,630.1	6,231.3
Beverages and tobacco	8,378.7	8,608.6	9,206.0
Beverages	8,087.0	8,277.3	8,833.6
Alcoholic beverages	7,328.5	7,492.9	8,011.2
Crude materials (inedible) except fuels	6,081.9	5,702.0	5,603.4
Mineral fuels, lubricants, etc. (incl. electric current)	7,429.4	7,234.1	6,527.8
Chemicals and related products	40,217.5	36,319.7	38,312.7
Organic chemicals	8,732.2	5,835.7	5,936.2
Medicinal and pharmaceutical products	7,244.8	7,900.9	9,314.6
Medicaments (incl. veterinary medicaments)	5,324.9	5,936.4	7,248.0
Essential oils, perfume materials and cleansing preparations	7,636.8	7,630.6	7,817.7
Perfumery, cosmetics and toilet preparations (excl. soaps)	5,877.3	5,762.9	5,848.0
Artificial resins, plastic materials, etc.	6,883.1	5,765.0	5,734.4
Products of polymerization, etc.	6,208.6	5,056.2	4,937.3
Basic manufactures	45,742.1	43,998.6	45,374.4
Paper, paperboard and manufactures	5,924.7	5,637.3	5,834.5
Textile yarn, fabrics, etc.	7,644.7	7,545.3	7,850.3
Iron and steel	10,343.4	9,775.3	10,015.5
Machinery and transport equipment	115,326.9	117,947.7	131,663.9
Power-generating machinery and equipment	9,098.1	9,084.3	11,102.7
Machinery specialized for particular industries	7,497.5	7,367.4	7,990.2
General industrial machinery, equipment and parts	13,292.8	13,150.4	14,564.9
Office machines and automatic data-processing equipment	9,815.4	10,279.8	10,831.0
Automatic data-processing machines and units	6,496.9	6,925.1	7,476.2
Telecommunications and sound equipment	6,797.3	8,075.5	10,364.9
Other electrical machinery, apparatus, etc.	20,307.4	20,870.5	22,213.2
Thermionic valves, tubes, etc.	6,113.9	6,729.7	7,593.4

Exports f.o.b. — *continued*	1996	1997	1998
Road vehicles and parts*	31,618.6	32,235.3	36,144.1
Passenger motor cars (excl. buses)	15,803.8	17,345.3	19,414.5
Parts and accessories for cars, buses, lorries, etc.*	10,346.6	9,942.2	10,894.6
Other transport equipment and parts*	15,577.3	15,458.9	17,074.6
Aircraft, associated equipment and parts*	13,223.9	13,613.9	15,054.0
Miscellaneous manufactured articles	28,201.2	27,507.8	28,885.2
Total (incl. others)	283,901.4	283,345.8	300,571.2

* Data on parts exclude tyres, engines and electrical parts.

Source: UN, *International Trade Statistics Yearbook*.

PRINCIPAL TRADING PARTNERS (US $ million)

Imports c.i.f.	1996	1997	1998
Belgium-Luxembourg	23,345	21,414	22,115
China, People's Republic	6,028	6,637	7,219
Germany	48,266	44,115	49,343
Ireland	3,811	4,078	5,204
Italy	28,125	26,071	28,406
Japan	8,967	8,928	9,517
Netherlands	14,419	13,366	14,490
Norway	4,622	4,864	3,992
Portugal	3,197	3,035	3,150
Russia	3,976	3,485	2,787
Saudi Arabia	2,908	2,642	1,788
Spain	19,177	17,727	20,336
Sweden	3,929	3,843	4,088
Switzerland-Liechtenstein	6,872	6,363	7,104
United Kingdom	23,129	22,229	23,996
USA	22,421	23,358	23,549
Total (incl. others)	274,914	266,575	286,036

Exports f.o.b.	1996	1997	1998
Austria	3,143	2,970	3,294
Belgium-Luxembourg	24,147	22,760	23,280
China, People's Republic	2,423	3,421	3,308
Germany	49,120	44,979	48,001
Hong Kong	3,516	2,944	3,106
Italy	26,421	26,310	27,506
Japan	5,354	4,876	4,666
Netherlands	13,029	13,263	13,849
Portugal	3,898	3,992	4,471
Spain	22,712	22,763	26,217
Sweden	4,050	4,144	4,395
Switzerland-Liechtenstein	11,084	9,971	10,347
Turkey	2,554	2,861	2,850
United Kingdom	26,853	28,641	30,108
USA	17,312	18,446	22,274
Total (incl. others)	283,901	283,346	300,571

Source: UN, *International Trade Statistics Yearbook*.

Transport

RAILWAYS (traffic)

	1997	1998	1999
Paying passengers ('000 journeys)	n.a.	823,000	861,000
Freight carried ('000 metric tons)	n.a.	136,100	134,000
Passenger-km (million)	61,830	64,500	66,590
Freight ton-km (million)*	54,820	53,800	52,110

* Including passengers' baggage.

Sources: UN, *Statistical Yearbook*, Société Nationale des Chemins de fer Français, Paris.

ROAD TRAFFIC ('000 motor vehicles in use at 31 December)

	1996	1997	1998
Passenger cars	25,500	25,930	26,800
Lorries and vans	4,976	5,057	5,418
Buses	82	82	82

Source: mainly International Road Federation, *World Road Statistics*.

INLAND WATERWAYS

	1997	1998	1999
Freight carried ('000 metric tons)	48,493	50,793	54,991
Freight ton-km (million)	5,682	6,207	6,829

Source: Voies navigables de France.

SHIPPING

Merchant Fleet (vessels registered at 30 June)

	Displacement ('000 gross reg. tons)		
	1995	1996	1997
Oil tankers	2,370	2,440	2,560
Total (incl. others)	4,080	4,163	4,119

Source: Direction de la Flotte de Commerce (Ministère de l'Equipement, du Logement, des Transports et du Tourisme).

Sea-borne Freight Traffic ('000 metric tons)

	1995	1996	1997
Goods loaded (excl. stores)	81,250	82,409	94,987
International	73,382	74,449	87,022
Coastwise	7,868	7,960	7,965
Goods unloaded (excl. fish)	215,433	215,916	229,016
International	204,261	204,236	217,751
Coastwise	11,172	11,679	11,265

Source: Ministère de l'Equipement, du Logement, des Transports et du Tourisme, Direction des Ports et de la Navigation Maritimes.

CIVIL AVIATION (revenue traffic on scheduled services)*

	1995	1996	1997
Kilometres flown (million)	528	609	669
Passengers carried ('000)	36,020	41,253	42,344
Passenger-km (million)	68,192	81,594	84,037
Total ton-km (million)	11,570	13,151	13,750

* Including data for airlines based in French Overseas Departments and Territories.

Source: UN, *Statistical Yearbook*.

Tourism

FOREIGN TOURIST ARRIVALS BY COUNTRY OF ORIGIN ('000)

	1996	1997	1998
Belgium and Luxembourg	7,375	8,395	8,364
Germany	13,378	14,593	14,770
Italy	5,299	5,533	5,836
Netherlands	8,115	9,008	10,203
Spain	2,759	2,935	2,875
Switzerland	3,737	3,715	3,682
United Kingdom and Ireland	9,926	10,496	11,359
USA	2,603	2,746	2,911
Total (incl. others)	62,406	67,310	70,040

Source: World Tourism Organization, *Yearbook of Tourism Statistics*.

Net earnings from tourism (million francs): 54,287 (receipts 145,076, expenditure 90,789) in 1996; 66,732 (receipts 163,488, expenditure 96,756) in 1997; 71,615 (receipts 176,562, expenditure 104,947) in 1998.

Communications Media

	1993	1994	1995
Radio receivers ('000 in use) . .	51,200	51,450	52,000
Television receivers ('000 in use) .	n.a.	34,100	34,250
Book production (titles)* . . .	41,234	45,311	34,766
Telephones ('000 main lines in use)	30,900	31,600	32,400
Mobile cellular telephones ('000 subscribers)	572	883	1,302
Telefax stations ('000 in use) .	1,221	1,600	1,900

* Including pamphlets (about 32% of all titles produced in 1984).

Sources: UN, *Statistical Yearbook*; UNESCO, *Statistical Yearbook*.

Telephones ('000 main lines in use): 32,900 in 1996; 33,700 in 1997.

Mobile cellular telephones ('000 subscribers): 2,463 in 1996; 5,817 in 1997; 11,200 in 1998; 20,600 in 1999.

Telefax stations ('000 in use): 2,400 in 1996; 2,800 in 1997.

Daily newspapers (estimates, 1996): 117 titles (combined circulation 12,700,000 copies per issue).

Non-daily newspapers (1995): 278 titles (circulation 1,714,000 copies in 1995).

Other periodicals (1993): 2,683 titles (circulation 120,018,000 copies in 1991).

Education

(1996/97, unless otherwise indicated)

	Institutions	Teachers	Students
Pre-primary	18,884*	106,581	2,451,210
Primary	41,000*	211,192	4,004,704
Secondary†	11,212‡	483,493	5,979,690
Higher‡:			
Universities . . .	n.a.	46,196	1,395,103
Other	n.a.	6,467	688,129

* Figures are for 1995/96.

† Including vocational education (1,646,377 students).

‡ Figures are for 1993/94.

1998/99: Students: Pre-primary and primary 6,337,300; Secondary 5,472,900; Higher 2,089,000.

Source: partly UNESCO, *Statistical Yearbook*.

Directory

The Constitution

The Constitution of the Fifth Republic was adopted by referendum on 28 September 1958 and promulgated on 6 October 1958.

PREAMBLE

The French people hereby solemnly proclaims its attachment to the Rights of Man and to the principles of national sovereignty as defined by the Declaration of 1789, confirmed and complemented by the Preamble of the Constitution of 1946.

By virtue of these principles and that of the free determination of peoples, the Republic hereby offers to the Overseas Territories that express the desire to adhere to them, new institutions based on the common ideal of liberty, equality and fraternity and conceived with a view to their democratic evolution.

Article 1. (As amended by legislation of 4 August 1995.) France shall be a Republic, indivisible, secular, democratic and social. It shall ensure the equality of all citizens before the law, without distinction of origin, race or religion. It shall respect all beliefs.

I. ON SOVEREIGNTY

Article 2. (As amended by legislation of 25 June 1992.) The language of the Republic shall be French.

The national emblem shall be the tricolour flag, blue, white and red.

The national anthem shall be the 'Marseillaise'.

The motto of the Republic shall be 'Liberty, Equality, Fraternity'.

Its principle shall be government of the people, by the people, and for the people.

Article 3. (As amended by legislation of 8 July 1999.) National sovereignty belongs to the people, who shall exercise this sovereignty through their representatives and through the referendum.

No section of the people, nor any individual, may arrogate to themselves or himself the exercise thereof.

Suffrage may be direct or indirect under the conditions stipulated by the Constitution. It shall always be universal, equal and secret.

All French citizens of both sexes who have reached their majority and who enjoy civil and political rights may vote under the conditions to be determined by law.

The law shall promote equal access by women and men to elective offices and positions.

Article 4. (As amended by legislation of 8 July 1999.) Political parties and groups are instrumental in the exercise of suffrage. They may form and carry on their activities freely. They must respect the principles of national sovereignty and of democracy. They shall contribute to the implementation of the principle set out in the last paragraph of article 3 as provided by the law.

II. THE PRESIDENT OF THE REPUBLIC

Article 5. (As amended by legislation of 4 August 1995.) The President of the Republic shall see that the Constitution is respected. He shall ensure, by his arbitration, the regular functioning of the governmental authorities, as well as the continuity of the State.

He shall be the guarantor of national independence, of the integrity of the territory, and of respect for treaties.

Article 6. (As amended by legislation of 6 November 1962 and 2 October 2000.) The President of the Republic shall be elected for five years by direct universal suffrage. The method of implementation of the present article shall be determined by an organic law.

Article 7. (As amended by legislation of 6 November 1962 and 18 June 1976.) The President of the Republic shall be elected by an absolute majority of the votes cast. If such a majority is not obtained at the first ballot, a second ballot shall take place on the second following Sunday. Those who may stand for the second ballot shall be only the two candidates who, after the possible withdrawal of candidates with more votes, have gained the largest number of votes on the first ballot.

Voting shall begin at the summons of the Government. The election of the new President of the Republic shall take place not less than 20 days and not more than 35 days before the expiry of the powers of the President in office. In the event that the Presidency of the Republic has been vacated for any reason whatsoever, or impeded in its functioning as officially declared by the Constitutional Council, after the matter has been referred to it by the Government and which shall give its ruling by an absolute majority of its members, the functions of the President of the Republic, with the exception of those covered by Articles 11 and 12 hereunder, shall be temporarily exercised by the President of the Senate or, if the latter is in his turn unable to exercise his functions, by the Government.

In the case of vacancy or when the impediment is declared to be permanent by the Constitutional Council, the voting for the election of the new President shall take place, except in case of force majeure officially noted by the Constitutional Council, not less than 20 days and not more than 35 days after the beginning of the vacancy or of the declaration of the final nature of the impediment.

If, in the seven days preceding the latest date for the lodging of candidatures, one of the persons who, at least 30 days prior to that date, publicly announced his decision to be a candidate dies or is impeded, the Constitutional Council may decide to postpone the election.

If, before the first ballot, one of the candidates dies or is impeded, the Constitutional Council orders the postponement of the election.

In the event of the death or impediment, before any candidates have withdrawn, of one of the two candidates who received the greatest number of votes in the first ballot, the Constitutional Council shall declare that the electoral procedure must be repeated in full; the same shall apply in the event of the death or impediment of one of the two candidates standing for the second ballot.

All cases shall be referred to the Constitutional Council under the conditions laid down in paragraph 2 of article 61 below, or under those determined for the presentation of candidates by the organic law provided for in Article 6 above.

The Constitutional Council may extend the periods stipulated in paragraphs 3 and 5 above provided that polling shall not take place more than 35 days after the date of the decision of the Constitutional Council. If the implementation of the provisions of this paragraph results in the postponement of the election beyond the expiry of the powers of the President in office, the latter shall remain in office until his successor is proclaimed.

Articles 49 and 50 and Article 89 of the Constitution may not be put into application during the vacancy of the Presidency of the Republic or during the period between the declaration of the final nature of the impediment of the President of the Republic and the election of his successor.

Article 8. The President of the Republic shall appoint the Prime Minister. He shall terminate the functions of the Prime Minister when the latter presents the resignation of the Government.

At the suggestion of the Prime Minister, he shall appoint the other members of the Government and shall terminate their functions.

Article 9. The President of the Republic shall preside over the Council of Ministers.

Article 10. The President of the Republic shall promulgate laws within 15 days following the transmission to the Government of the finally adopted law.

He may, before the expiry of this time limit, ask Parliament for a reconsideration of the law or of certain of its articles. This reconsideration may not be refused.

Article 11. (As amended by legislation of 4 August 1995.) The President of the Republic, on the proposal of the government during [Parliamentary] sessions, or on joint motion of the two Assemblies published in the *Journal Officiel*, may submit to a referendum any bill dealing with the organization of the governmental authorities, with reforms related to the economic or social policy of the nation and to the public services contributing thereto or providing for authorization to ratify a treaty that, without being contrary to the Constitution, might affect the functioning of the institutions.

Where the referendum is held in response to a proposal by the Government, the latter shall make a statement before each Assembly, which shall be followed by a debate.

Where the referendum decides in favour of the government bill, the President of the Republic shall promulgate the law within 15 days following the proclamation of the results of the vote.

Article 12. (As amended by legislation of 4 August 1995.) The President of the Republic may, after consultation with the Prime Minister and the Presidents of the Assemblies, declare the dissolution of the National Assembly.

A general election shall take place 20 days at the least and 40 days at the most after the dissolution.

The National Assembly shall convene by right on the second Thursday following its election. If this meeting takes place between the period provided for the ordinary session, a session shall, by right, be opened for a 15-day period.

There may be no further dissolution within a year following this election.

Article 13. The President of the Republic shall sign the ordinances and decrees decided upon in the Council of Ministers.

Directory

He shall make appointments to the civil and military posts of the State.

Councillors of State, the Grand Chancellor of the Legion of Honour, Ambassadors and Envoys Extraordinary, Master Councillors of the Audit Court, prefects, representatives of the Government in the Overseas Territories, general officers, rectors of academies [regional divisions of the public educational system] and directors of central administrations shall be appointed in meetings of the Council of Ministers.

An organic law shall determine the other posts to be filled by decision of the Council of Ministers, as well as the conditions under which the power of the President of the Republic to make appointments to office may be delegated by him to be exercised in his name.

Article 14. The President of the Republic shall accredit Ambassadors and Envoys Extraordinary to foreign powers; foreign Ambassadors and Envoys Extraordinary shall be accredited to him.

Article 15. The President of the Republic shall be commander of the armed forces. He shall preside over the higher councils and committees of national defence.

Article 16. When the institutions of the Republic, the independence of the nation, the integrity of its territory or the fulfilment of its international commitments are threatened in a grave and immediate manner and the regular functioning of the constitutional governmental authorities is interrupted, the President of the Republic shall take the measures required by these circumstances, after official consultation with the Prime Minister and the Presidents of the Assemblies, and the Constitutional Council.

He shall inform the nation of these measures in a message.

These measures must be prompted by the desire to ensure to the constitutional governmental authorities, in the shortest possible time, the means of accomplishing their mission. The Constitutional Council shall be consulted with regard to such measures.

Parliament shall meet by right.

The National Assembly may not be dissolved during the exercise of exceptional powers.

Article 17. The President of the Republic shall have the right of pardon.

Article 18. The President of the Republic shall communicate with the two Assemblies of Parliament by means of messages, which he shall cause to be read, and which shall not be the occasion for any debate.

Between sessions, the Parliament shall be convened especially to this end.

Article 19. Official decisions of the President of the Republic, other than those provided for under Articles 8 (first paragraph), 11, 12, 16, 18, 54, 56 and 61, shall be counter-signed by the Prime Minister and, where applicable, by the appropriate ministers.

III. THE GOVERNMENT

Article 20. The Government shall determine and conduct the policy of the nation.

It shall have at its disposal the administration and the armed forces.

It shall be responsible to the Parliament under the conditions and according to the procedures stipulated in Articles 49 and 50.

Article 21. The Prime Minister shall direct the operation of the Government. He shall be responsible for national defence. He shall ensure the execution of the laws. Subject to the provisions of Article 13, he shall have regulatory powers and shall make appointments to civil and military posts.

He may delegate certain of his powers to the ministers.

He shall replace, should the occasion arise, the President of the Republic as the Chairman of the councils and committees provided for under Article 15.

He may, in exceptional instances, replace him as the chairman of a meeting of the Council of Ministers by virtue of an explicit delegation and for a specific agenda.

Article 22. The official decisions of the Prime Minister shall be counter-signed, when circumstances so require, by the ministers responsible for their execution.

Article 23. The functions of Members of the Government shall be incompatible with the exercise of any parliamentary mandate, with the holding of any office, at the national level, in business, professional or labour organizations, and with any public employment or professional activity.

An organic law shall determine the conditions under which the holders of such mandates, functions or employments shall be replaced.

The replacement of the members of Parliament shall take place in accordance with the provisions of Article 25.

IV. THE PARLIAMENT

Article 24. The Parliament shall comprise the National Assembly and the Senate.

The deputies to the National Assembly shall be elected by direct suffrage.

The Senate shall be elected by indirect suffrage. It shall ensure the representation of the territorial units of the Republic. French nationals living outside France shall be represented in the Senate.

Article 25. An organic law shall determine the term for which each Assembly is elected, the number of its members, their emoluments, the conditions of eligibility, and the offices incompatible with membership of the Assemblies.

It shall likewise determine the conditions under which, in the case of a vacancy in either Assembly, persons shall be elected to replace the deputy or senator whose seat has been vacated until the holding of new complete or partial elections to the Assembly concerned.

Article 26. (As amended by legislation of 4 August 1995.) No Member of Parliament may be prosecuted, subjected to inquiry, arrested, detained or tried as a result of the opinions expressed or votes cast by him in the exercise of his functions.

No Member of Parliament shall be subjected, in regard to any criminal or correctional matter, to arrest or any other custodial or semi-custodial measures other than with the authorization of the Assembly of which he is a member. Such authorization shall not be required in the case of a serious crime or other major offence committed *in flagrante delicto* or a final conviction.

The detention, subjection to custodial or semi-custodial measures, or prosecution of a Member of Parliament shall be suspended for the duration of the session if the Assembly of which he is a member so requires.

The Assembly concerned shall convene as of right for additional sittings in order to permit the preceding paragraph to be applied should circumstances so require.

Article 27. Any compulsory vote shall be null and void.

The right to vote of the members of Parliament shall be personal.

An organic law may, under exceptional circumstances, authorize the delegation of a vote. In this case, no member may be delegated more than one vote.

Article 28. (As amended by legislation of 4 August 1995.) Parliament shall convene by right in one ordinary session a year, which shall start on the first working day of October and shall end on the last working day of June.

The number of days for which each Assembly may sit during the ordinary session shall not exceed one hundred and twenty. The sitting weeks shall be determined by each Assembly.

The Prime Minister, after consulting the President of the Assembly concerned, or the majority of the members of each Assembly, may decide to meet for additional sitting days.

The days and hours of sittings shall be determined by the rules of procedure of each Assembly.

Article 29. Parliament shall convene in extraordinary session at the request of the Prime Minister or of the majority of the members comprising the National Assembly, to consider a specific agenda.

When an extraordinary session is held at the request of the members of the National Assembly, the closure decree shall take effect as soon as the Parliament has exhausted the agenda for which it was called, and at the latest 12 days from the date of its meeting.

Only the Prime Minister may ask for a new session before the end of the month following the closure decree.

Article 30. Apart from cases in which Parliament meets by right, extraordinary sessions shall be opened and closed by decree of the President of the Republic.

Article 31. The members of the Government shall have access to the two Assemblies. They shall be heard when they so request.

They may call for the assistance of Commissioners of the Government.

Article 32. The President of the National Assembly shall be elected for the duration of the legislature. The President of the Senate shall be elected after each partial re-election [of the Senate].

Article 33. The meetings of the two Assemblies shall be public. An *in extenso* report of the debates shall be published in the *Journal Officiel*.

Each Assembly may sit in secret committee at the request of the Premier or of one-tenth of its members.

V. ON RELATIONS BETWEEN PARLIAMENT AND THE GOVERNMENT

Article 34. (As amended by legislation of 22 February 1996.) Laws shall be voted by Parliament.

Legislation shall establish the regulations concerning:

Civil rights and the fundamental guarantees granted to the citizens for the exercise of their public liberties; the obligations imposed by the national defence upon the person and property of citizens;

Nationality, status and legal capacity of persons; marriage contracts, inheritance and gifts;

Determination of crimes and misdemeanours as well as the penalties imposed therefor; criminal procedure; amnesty; the creation of new juridical systems and the status of magistrates;

The basis, the rate and the methods of collecting taxes of all types; the issue of currency.

Legislation likewise shall determine the regulations concerning:

The electoral system of the Parliamentary Assemblies and the local assemblies;

The establishment of categories of public institutions;

The fundamental guarantees granted to civil and military personnel employed by the State;

The nationalization of enterprises and the transfers of the property of enterprises from the public to the private sector.

Legislation shall determine the fundamental principles of:

The general organization of national defence;

The free administration of local communities, of their competencies and their resources;

Education;

Property rights, civil and commercial obligations;

Legislation pertaining to employment unions and social security.

The financial laws shall determine the financial resources and obligations of the State under the conditions and with the reservations to be provided for by an organic law.

Social security finance bills shall determine the general conditions for the financial balance of social security and, taking account of their revenue forecasts, shall determine expenditure targets in the manner and under the reserves provided for by an organic law.

Laws pertaining to national planning shall determine the objectives of the economic and social action of the State.

The provisions of the present article may be detailed and supplemented by an organic law.

Article 35. Parliament shall authorize the declaration of war.

Article 36. Martial law shall be decreed in a meeting of the Council of Ministers.

Its extension beyond 12 days may be authorized only by Parliament.

Article 37. Matters other than those that fall within the domain of law shall be of a regulatory character.

Legislative texts concerning these matters may be modified by decrees issued after consultation with the Council of State. Those legislative texts which shall be passed after the entry into force of the present Constitution shall be modified by decree only if the Constitutional Council has stated that they have a regulatory character as defined in the preceding paragraph.

Article 38. The Government may, in order to carry out its programme, ask Parliament for authorization to take through ordinances, during a limited period, measures that are normally within the domain of law.

The ordinances shall be enacted in meetings of Ministers after consultation with the Council of State. They shall come into force upon their publication but shall become null and void if the bill for their ratification is not submitted to Parliament before the date set by the enabling act.

At the expiry of the time limit referred to in the first paragraph of the present article, the ordinances may be modified only by the law in respect of those matters which are within the legislative domain.

Article 39. (As amended by legislation of 22 February 1996.) The Prime Minister and the Members of Parliament alike shall have the right to initiate legislation.

Government bills shall be discussed in the Council of Ministers after consultation with the Council of State and shall be filed with the secretariat of one of the two Assemblies. Finance bills shall be submitted first to the National Assembly. Finance bills and social security finance bills shall be submitted first to the National Assembly.

Article 40. Private members' bills and amendments shall be inadmissible when their adoption would have as a consequence either a diminution of public financial resources or an increase in public expenditure.

Article 41. If it shall appear in the course of the legislative procedure that a Parliamentary bill or an amendment is not within the domain of law or is contrary to a delegation granted by virtue of Article 38, the Government may declare its inadmissibility.

In case of disagreement between the Government and the President of the Assembly concerned, the Constitutional Council, upon the request of one or the other, shall rule within a time limit of eight days.

Article 42. The discussion of bills shall pertain, in the first Assembly to which they have been referred, to the text presented by the Government.

An Assembly given a text passed by the other Assembly shall deliberate on the text that is transmitted to it.

Article 43. Government and private members' bills shall, at the request of the Government or of the Assembly concerned, be sent for study to committees especially designated for this purpose.

Government and private members' bills for which such a request has not been made shall be sent to one of the permanent committees, the number of which is limited to six in each Assembly.

Article 44. Members of Parliament and of the Government have the right of amendment.

After the opening of the debate, the Government may oppose the examination of any amendment which has not previously been submitted to committee.

If the Government so requests, the Assembly concerned shall decide, by a single vote, on all or part of the text under discussion, retaining only the amendments proposed or accepted by the Government.

Article 45. Every government or private member's bill shall be considered successively in the two Assemblies of Parliament with a view to the adoption of an identical text.

When, as a result of disagreement between the two Assemblies, it has been impossible to adopt a Government or private member's bill after two readings by each Assembly, or, if the Government has declared the matter urgent, after a single reading by each of them, the Prime Minister shall have the right to bring about a meeting of a joint committee composed of an equal number from both Assemblies charged with the task of proposing a text on the matters still under discussion.

The text elaborated by the joint committee may be submitted by the Government for approval of the two Assemblies. No amendment shall be admissible except by agreement with the Government.

If the joint committee does not succeed in adopting a common text, or if this text is not adopted under the conditions set forth in the preceding paragraph, the Government may, after a new reading by the National Assembly and by the Senate, ask the National Assembly to rule definitively. In this case, the National Assembly may reconsider either the text elaborated by the joint committee, or the last text voted by it, modified when circumstances so require by one or several of the amendments adopted by the Senate.

Article 46. The laws that the Constitution characterizes as organic shall be passed and amended under the following conditions:

A Government or private member's bill shall be submitted to the deliberation and to the vote of the first Assembly notified only at the expiration of a period of 15 days following its introduction;

The procedure of Article 45 shall be applicable. Nevertheless, lacking an agreement between the two Assemblies, the text may be adopted by the National Assembly on final reading only by an absolute majority of its members;

The organic laws relative to the Senate must be passed in the same manner by the two Assemblies;

The organic laws may be promulgated only after a declaration by the Constitutional Council on their constitutionality.

Article 47. The Parliament shall pass finance bills under the conditions to be stipulated by an organic law.

Should the National Assembly fail to reach a decision on first reading within a time limit of 40 days after a bill has been filed, the Government shall refer it to the Senate, which must rule within a time limit of 15 days. The procedure set forth in Article 45 shall then be followed.

Should Parliament fail to reach a decision within a time limit of 70 days, the provisions of the bill may be enforced by ordinance.

Should the finance bill establishing the resources and expenditures of a fiscal year not be filed in time for it to be promulgated before the beginning of that fiscal year, the Government shall urgently request Parliament for authorization to collect taxes and shall make available by decree the funds needed to meet the Government commitments already voted.

The time limits stipulated in the present article shall be suspended when the Parliament is not in session.

The Audit Court shall assist Parliament and the Government in supervising the implementation of the finance laws.

Article 47–1. (Appended by legislation of 22 February 1996.) Parliament shall pass social security finance bills in the manner provided for by an organic law.

Should the National Assembly fail to reach a decision on first reading within twenty days following the introduction of a bill, the Government shall refer the bill to the Senate, which must rule within fifteen days. The procedure set out in article 45 shall then apply.

Should Parliament fail to reach a decision within fifty days, the provisions of the bill may be implemented by ordinance.

The time limits set by this article shall be suspended when Parliament is not in session and, as regards each assembly, during the weeks when it has decided not to sit in accordance with the second paragraph of article 28.

The Audit Court shall assist Parliament and the Government in monitoring the implementation of social security finance Acts.

Article 48. (As amended by legislation of 4 August 1995.) Without prejudice to the application of the last three paragraphs of article 28, the discussion of the bills tabled or agreed upon by the Government shall have priority on the agenda of the Assemblies in the order determined by the Government.

At least one meeting a week shall be reserved, by priority, for questions asked by Members of Parliament and for answers by the Government.

One meeting a month shall be reserved, by priority, for the agenda determined by each Assembly.

Article 49. (As amended by legislation of 4 August 1995.) The Prime Minister, after deliberation by the Council of Ministers, shall make the Government responsible, before the National Assembly, for its programme or, should the occasion arise, for a declaration of general policy.

The National Assembly may challenge the responsibility of the Government by a motion of censure. Such a motion is admissible only if it is signed by at least one-tenth of the members of the National Assembly. The vote may not take place before 48 hours after the motion has been filed. Only the votes that are favourable to a motion of censure shall be counted; the motion of censure may be adopted only by a majority of the members comprising the Assembly. Except as provided for in the following paragraph, a Deputy shall not sign more than three motions of censure during a single ordinary session and more than one during a single extraordinary session.

The Prime Minister may, after deliberation by the Council of Ministers, make the Government responsible before the National Assembly for the adoption of a bill. In this case, the text shall be considered as adopted unless a motion of censure, filed during the twenty-four hours that follow, is carried under the conditions provided for in the preceding paragraph.

The Prime Minister shall have the right to request the Senate for approval of a declaration of general policy.

Article 50. When the National Assembly adopts a motion of censure, or when it disapproves the programme or a declaration of general policy of the Government, the Prime Minister must hand the resignation of the Government to the President of the Republic.

Article 51. (As amended by legislation of 4 August 1995.) The closure of the ordinary or of extraordinary sessions shall by right be delayed, should the occasion arise, in order to permit the application of Article 49. Additional sittings shall by right be held for the same purpose.

VI. ON TREATIES AND INTERNATIONAL AGREEMENTS

Article 52. (As amended by legislation of 4 August 1995.) The President of the Republic shall negotiate and ratify treaties.

He shall be informed of all negotiations leading to the conclusion of an international agreement not subject to ratification.

Article 53. Peace treaties, commercial treaties, treaties or agreements relative to international organization, those that commit the finances of the State, those that modify provisions of a legislative nature, those relative to the status of persons, those that call for the cession, exchange or addition of territory may be ratified or approved only by a law.

They shall go into effect only after having been ratified or approved.

No cession, no exchange, or addition of territory shall be valid without the consent of the populations concerned.

Article 53–1. (Appended by legislation of 25 November 1993.) The Republic may conclude, with European states that are bound by commitments identical with its own in the matter of asylum and the protection of human rights and fundamental liberties, agreements determining their respective competence in regard to the consideration of requests for asylum submitted to them.

However, even if the request does not fall within their competence under the terms of these agreements, the authorities of the Republic shall remain empowered to grant asylum to any foreigner who is persecuted for his action in pursuit of liberty or who seeks the protection of France for some other reason.

Article 53–2. (Appended by legislation of 8 July 1999.) The Republic may recognize the jurisdiction of the International Criminal Court as provided for by the treaty signed on 18 July 1998.

Article 54. (As amended by legislation of 25 June 1992.) If the Constitutional Council, the matter having been referred to it by the President of the Republic, by the Prime Minister, by the President of one or the other Assembly, or by any 60 Deputies or 60 Senators, shall declare that an international commitment contains a clause contrary to the Constitution, the authorization to ratify or approve the commitment in question may be given only after amendment of the Constitution.

Article 55. Treaties or agreements duly ratified or approved shall, upon their publication, have an authority superior to that of laws, subject, for each agreement or treaty, to its application by the other party.

VII. THE CONSTITUTIONAL COUNCIL

Article 56. The Constitutional Council shall consist of nine members, whose mandates shall last nine years and shall not be renewable. One-third of the membership of the Constitutional Council shall be renewed every three years. Three of its members shall be appointed by the President of the Republic, three by the President of the National Assembly, three by the President of the Senate.

In addition to the nine members provided for above, former Presidents of the Republic shall be members *ex officio* for life of the Constitutional Council.

The President shall be appointed by the President of the Republic. He shall have the deciding vote in case of a tie.

Article 57. The office of member of the Constitutional Council shall be incompatible with that of minister or Member of Parliament. Other incompatibilities shall be determined by an organic law.

Article 58. The Constitutional Council shall ensure the regularity of the election of the President of the Republic.

It shall examine complaints and shall announce the results of the vote.

Article 59. The Constitutional Council shall rule, in the case of disagreement, on the regularity of the election of deputies and senators.

Article 60. The Constitutional Council shall ensure the regularity of the referendum procedure and shall announce the results thereof.

Article 61. (As amended by legislation of 29 October 1974.) Organic laws, before their promulgation, and regulations of the parliamentary Assemblies, before they come into application, must be submitted to the Constitutional Council, which shall rule on their constitutionality.

To the same end, laws may be submitted to the Constitutional Council, before their promulgation, by the President of the Republic, the Prime Minister, the President of the National Assembly, the President of the Senate, or any 60 deputies or 60 senators.

In the cases provided for by the two preceding paragraphs, the Constitutional Council must make its ruling within a time limit of one month. Nevertheless, at the request of the Government, in case of urgency, this period shall be reduced to eight days.

In these same cases, referral to the Constitutional Council shall suspend the time limit for promulgation.

Article 62. A provision declared unconstitutional may not be promulgated or implemented.

The decisions of the Constitutional Council may not be appealed to any jurisdiction whatsoever. They shall be binding on the governmental authorities and on all administrative and juridical authorities.

Article 63. An organic law shall determine the rules of organization and functioning of the Constitutional Council, the procedure to be followed before it, and in particular of the periods of time allowed for laying disputes before it.

VIII. ON JUDICIAL AUTHORITY

Article 64. The President of the Republic shall be the guarantor of the independence of the judicial authority.

He shall be assisted by the High Council of the Judiciary.

An organic law shall determine the status of the judiciary.

Judges may not be removed from office.

Article 65. (As amended by legislation of 27 July 1993.) The High Council of the Judiciary shall be presided over by the President of the Republic. The Minister of Justice shall be its Vice-President *ex officio*. He may preside in place of the President of the Republic.

The High Council of the Judiciary shall consist of two sections, one with competence for judges, the other for public prosecutors.

The section with competence for judges shall include, in addition to the President of the Republic and the Minister of Justice, five judges and one public prosecutor, one senior member of the Council of State appointed by the Council of State, and three prominent citizens who are neither members of Parliament nor the judiciary, appointed respectively by the President of the Republic, the President of the National Assembly and the President of the Senate.

The section with jurisdiction for public prosecutors shall include, in addition to the President of the Republic and the Minister of Justice, five public prosecutors and one judge, the senior member of the Council of State and the three prominent citizens referred to in the preceding paragraph.

The section of the High Council of the Judiciary with jurisdiction for judges shall make nominations for the appointment of judges in the Court of Cassation, for the First Presidents of the courts of appeal and the presidents of the tribunaux de grande instance. Other judges shall be appointed with its assent.

It shall serve as the disciplinary council for judges. When acting in that capacity, it shall be presided over by the First President of the Court of Cassation.

The section of the High Council of the Judiciary with jurisdiction for public prosecutors shall give its opinion on the appointment of public prosecutors, with the exception of posts to be filled in the Council of Ministers. It shall give its opinion on disciplinary penalties with regard to public prosecutors. When acting in that capacity, it shall be presided over by the Chief Public Prosecutor at the Court of Cassation.

An organic law shall determine the manner in which this article is to be implemented.

Article 66. No one may be arbitrarily detained.

The judicial authority, guardian of individual liberty, shall ensure the respect of this principle under the conditions stipulated by law.

IX. THE HIGH COURT OF JUSTICE

Article 67. A High Court of Justice shall be instituted.

It shall be composed, in equal number, of members elected, from among their membership, by the National Assembly and by the Senate after each general or partial election to these Assemblies. It shall elect its President from among its members.

An organic law shall determine the composition of the High Court, its rules, as well as the procedure to be applied before it.

Article 68. (As amended by legislation of 27 July 1993.) The President of the Republic shall not be held accountable for actions performed in the exercise of his office except in the case of high treason. He may be indicted only by the two Assemblies ruling by identical vote in open balloting and by an absolute majority of the members of said Assemblies. He shall be tried by the High Court of Justice.

X. ON THE CRIMINAL LIABILITY OF MEMBERS OF GOVERNMENT

(title and section appended by legislation of 27 July 1993)

Article 68–1. The members of the Government shall be criminally liable for actions performed in the exercise of their office and rated as crimes or misdemeanours at the time they were committed.

They shall be tried by the Court of Justice of the Republic.

The Court of Justice of the Republic shall be bound by such definition of serious crimes and other major offences and such determination of penalties as are laid down by the law.

Article 68–2. The Court of Justice of the Republic shall consist of fifteen members: twelve Members of Parliament, elected in equal number from among their ranks by the National Assembly and the Senate after each general or partial election to these Assemblies, and three judges of the Court of Cassation, one of whom shall preside over the Court of Justice of the Republic.

Any person claiming to be a victim of a crime or misdemeanour committed by a member of the Government in the exercise of his duties may lodge a complaint with a commission of requests.

This committee shall order either the closure of the case or that it be forwarded to the chief public prosecutor at the Court of Cassation for referral to the Court of Justice of the Republic.

The Chief Public Prosecutor at the Court of Cassation may also make a reference *ex officio* to the Court of Justice of the Republic with the assent of the commission of requests.

An organic law shall determine the manner in which this article is to be implemented.

Article 68–3. (Appended by legislation of 4 August 1995.) The provisions of this title shall apply to acts committed before its entry into force *(on 27 July 1993.)*

XI. THE ECONOMIC AND SOCIAL COUNCIL

Article 69. The Economic and Social Council, at the referral of the Government, shall give its opinion on the Government bills, draft ordinances and decrees, as well as on the private members' bills submitted to it.

A member of the Economic and Social Council may be designated by the Council to present, before the Parliamentary Assemblies, the opinion of the Council on the Government or private members' bills that have been submitted to it.

Article 70. (As amended by legislation of 4 August 1995.) The Economic and Social Council may likewise be consulted by the Government on any problem of an economic or social character. Any plan, or any bill dealing with a plan, of an economic or social character shall be submitted to it for advice.

Article 71. The composition of the Economic and Social Council and its rules of procedure shall be determined by an organic law.

XII. ON TERRITORIAL UNITS

Article 72. The territorial units of the Republic shall be the communes, the Departments, and the Overseas Territories. Any other territorial unit shall be created by law.

These units shall be free to govern themselves through elected councils and under the conditions stipulated by law.

In the Departments and the Territories, the Delegate of the Government shall be responsible for the national interests, for administrative supervision, and for seeing that the laws are respected.

Article 73. Measures of adjustment required by the particular situation of the Overseas Departments may be taken with regard to the legislative system and administrative organization of those Departments.

Article 74. (As amended by legislation of 25 June 1992.) The Overseas Territories of the Republic shall have a particular organization, taking account of their own interests within the general interests of the Republic. The statutes governing the Overseas Territories shall be established by organic laws that define, *inter alia,* the competencies of their own institutions; they shall be amended in accordance with the same procedure after consultation with the territorial assembly concerned.

Other provisions concerning their particular form of organization shall be defined and amended by law after consultation with the territorial assembly concerned.

Article 75. Citizens of the Republic who do not have ordinary civil status, the only status referred to in Article 34, may keep their personal status as long as they have not renounced it.

XIII. TRANSITIONAL PROVISIONS RELATING TO NEW CALEDONIA

(Section appended by legislation of 20 July 1998)

Article 76. The population of New Caledonia is called upon to vote by 31 December 1998 on the provisions of the agreement signed at Nouméa on 5 May 1998, and published in the *Journal officiel* of the French Republic on 27 May 1998.

Persons satisfying the requirements laid down in article 2 of Act No. 88-1028 of 9 November 1988 shall be eligible to take part in the vote.

The measures required to organize the ballot shall be taken by decree adopted after consultation with the *Conseil d'Etat* and discussion in the Council of Ministers.

Article 77. After approval of the agreement by the vote provided for in article 76, the organic law passed after consultation with the deliberative assembly of New Calendonia shall determine, in order to ensure the development of New Caledonia in accordance with the guidelines set out in that agreement and as required for its implementation:

the competencies of the State which are to be transferred definitively to the institutions of New Caledonia, at what time and in what manner such transfers are to be made, and how the costs incurred thereby are to be apportioned

the rules for the organization and operation of the institutions of New Caledonia, incuding the circumstances in which certain categories of instrument passed by the deliberative assembly may be referred to the Constitutional Council for review before publication

the rules concerning citizenship, the electoral system, employment, and ordinary civil status

the circumstances and the time limits within which the population concerned in New Caledonia is to vote on the attainment of full sovereignty.

Any other measures required to give effect to the agreement referred to in article 76 shall be determined by law.

[A former Article 76, permitting Overseas Territories to retain their former status within the republic and a section 'On the Community' (Articles 77–87), providing for a community of autonomous states of common citizenship, were repealed by legislation of 4 August 1995.]

XIV. ON AGREEMENTS OF ASSOCIATION

Article 88. The Republic may make agreements with States that wish to associate themselves with it in order to develop their own civilizations.

XV. ON THE EUROPEAN COMMUNITIES AND THE EUROPEAN UNION

(Section appended by legislation of 25 June 1992)

Article 88–1. The Republic shall participate in the European Communities and in the European Union constituted by States that have freely chosen, by virtue of the treaties that established them, to exercise some of their powers in common.

Article 88–2 (Amended by legislation of 25 January 1999.) Subject to reciprocity and in accordance with the terms of the Treaty on European Union signed on 7 February 1992, France agrees to the transfer of competencies necessary for the establishment of European economic and monetary union.

Subject to the same reservation and in accordance with the terms of the Treaty establishing the European Community, as amended by the treaty signed on 2 October 1997, the transfer of competencies necessary for the determination of rules concerning freedom of movement for persons and related areas may be agreed.

Article 88–3. Subject to reciprocity and in accordance with the terms of the Treaty on European Union signed on 7 February 1992, the right to vote and stand as a candidate in municipal elections shall be granted only to citizens of the Union residing in France. Such citizens shall neither exercise the office of mayor or deputy mayor nor participate in the designation of senate electors or in the election of Senators. An organic law passed in identical terms by the two Assemblies shall determine the manner of implementation of this article.

Article 88–4. (Amended by legislation of 25 January 1999.) The Government shall present to the National Assembly and the Senate any proposals for or drafts of acts of the European Communities or the European Union containing provisions of a legislative nature as soon as they have been transmitted to the Council of the European Union. It may also present to them other proposals or drafts of acts or any document emanating from a European Union institution.

In the manner laid down by the rules of procedure of each Assembly, resolutions may be passed, even if Parliament is not in session, on the drafts, proposals or documents referred to in the preceding paragraph.

XVI. ON AMENDMENT

Article 89. The initiative for amending the Constitution shall belong both to the President of the Republic on the proposal of the Prime Minister and to the Members of Parliament.

The Government or private member's bill for amendment must be passed by the two Assemblies in identical terms. The amendment shall become definitive after approval by a referendum.

Nevertheless, the proposed amendment shall not be submitted to a referendum when the President of the Republic decides to submit it to Parliament convened in Congress; in this case, the proposed amendment shall be approved only if it is accepted by a three-fifths majority of the votes cast. The Secretariat of the Congress shall be that of the National Assembly.

No amendment procedure may be undertaken or followed if it is prejudicial to the integrity of the territory.

The republican form of government shall not be the object of an amendment.

ELECTORAL LAW, JULY 1986

The 577 Deputies of the National Assembly are to be directly elected under the former single-member constituency system (in force before the implementation of a system of proportional representation imposed by the electoral law of 1985). Participating parties can nominate only one candidate and designate a reserve candidate, who can serve as a replacement if the elected Deputy is appointed a Minister or a member of the Constitutional Council, or is sent on a government assignment scheduled to last more than six months, or dies. A candidate must receive an absolute majority and at least one-quarter of registered votes in order to be elected to the National Assembly. If these conditions are not fulfilled, a second ballot will be held a week later, for voters to choose between all candidates receiving 12.5% of the total votes on the first ballot. The candidate who receives a simple majority of votes on the second ballot will then be elected. Candidates polling less than 5% of the votes will lose their deposit.

The Government

HEAD OF STATE

President: JACQUES CHIRAC (took office 17 May 1995).

COUNCIL OF MINISTERS
(March 2001)

A coalition of the Parti Socialiste (PS), the Parti Communiste Français (PCF), the Parti Radical de Gauche (PRG) and Les Verts (Green).

Prime Minister: LIONEL JOSPIN (PS).

Minister of the Economy, Finance and Industry: LAURENT FABIUS (PS).

Minister of Employment and Solidarity: ELISABETH GUIGOU (PS).

Minister of Justice, Keeper of the Seals: MARYLISE LEBRANCHU (PS).

Minister of the Interior: DANIEL VAILLANT (PS).

Minister of National Education: JACK LANG (PS).

Minister of Foreign Affairs: HUBERT VÉDRINE (PS).

Minister of Defence: ALAIN RICHARD (PS).

Minister of Capital Works, Transport and Housing: JEAN-CLAUDE GAYSSOT (PCF).

Minister of Culture and Communication: CATHERINE TASCA (PS).

Minister of Agriculture and Fisheries: JEAN GLAVANY (PS).

Minister of Town and Country Planning and the Environment: DOMINIQUE VOYNET (Green).

Minister of Relations with Parliament: JEAN-JACK QUEYRANNE (PS).

Minister of the Civil Service and the Reform of the State: MICHEL SAPIN (PS).

Minister of Youth and Sport: MARIE-GEORGE BUFFET (PCF).

Minister of Research: ROGER-GÉRARD SCHWARTZENBERG (PRG).

There are also five Ministers-Delegate and 12 Secretaries of State.

MINISTRIES

Office of the President: Palais de l'Elysée, 55–57 rue du Faubourg Saint Honoré, 75008 Paris; tel. 1-42-92-81-00; fax 1-47-42-24-65; internet www.elysee.fr.

Office of the Prime Minister: Hôtel Matignon, 57 rue de Varenne, 75007 Paris; tel. 1-42-75-80-00; fax 1-42-75-75-04; e-mail premier -ministre@premier-ministre.gouv.fr; internet www.premier -ministre-gouv.fr.

Ministry of Agriculture and Fisheries: 78 rue de Varenne, 75349 Paris 07; tel. 1-49-55-49-55; fax 1-49-55-40-39; internet www .agriculture.gouv.fr.

Ministry of Capital Works, Transport and Housing: 246 blvd Saint-Germain, 75007 Paris; tel. 1-40-81-21-22; internet www .equipement.gouv.fr.

Ministry of the Civil Service: 72 rue de Varenne, 75007 Paris; tel. 1-42-75-80-00; fax 1-47-05-93-32; internet www.fonction-publique .gouv.fr.

Ministry of Culture: 3 rue de Valois, 75001 Paris; tel. 1-40-15-80-00; fax 1-42-61-35-77; internet www.culture.gouv.fr.

Ministry of Defence: 14 rue Saint Dominique, 75007 Paris; tel. 1-42-19-30-11; fax 1-47-05-40-91; internet www.defense.gouv.fr.

Ministry of the Economy, Finance and Industry: 139 rue de Bercy, 75572 Paris Cédex 12; tel. 1-40-04-04-04; fax 1-43-43-75-97; internet www.finances.gouv.fr.

Ministry of Employment and Solidarity: 127 rue de Grenelle, 75007 Paris; tel. 1-44-38-38-38; fax 1-44-38-20-10; internet www .travail.gouv.fr.

Ministry of Foreign Affairs: 37 quai d'Orsay, 75007 Paris Cédex 07; tel. 1-43-17-53-53; fax 1-43-17-52-03; internet www.diplomatie .gouv.fr.

Ministry of the Interior: place Beauvau, 75008 Paris; tel. 1-49-27-49-27; fax 1-43-59-89-50; e-mail sirp@cybercable.fr; internet www.interieur.gouv.fr.

Ministry of Justice: 13 place Vendôme, 75042 Paris Cédex 01; tel. 1-42-75-80-00; fax 1-44-77-70-20; internet www.justice.gouv.fr.

Ministry of National Education: 110 rue de Grenelle, 75357 Paris 07; tel. 1-55-55-10-10; fax 1-45-51-53-63; internet www .education.gouv.fr.

Ministry of Relations with Parliament: 69 rue de Varenne, 75007 Paris; tel. 1-42-75-80-00; fax 1-42-75-87-93.

Ministry of Research: 1 rue Descartes, 75005 Paris; tel. 1-49-55-10-10; internet www.recherche.gouv.fr.

Ministry of Town and Country Planning and the Environment: 20 ave de Ségur, 75302 Paris Cédex 07; tel. 1-42-19-20-21; internet www.environment.gouv.fr.

Ministry of Youth and Sport: 78 rue Olivier de Serres, 75015 Paris; tel. 1-40-45-90-00; fax 1-42-50-42-49; internet www .jeunesse-sports.gouv.fr.

President and Legislature

PRESIDENT
Elections of 23 April and 7 May 1995

	First ballot	Second ballot
EDOUARD BALLADUR (Rassemblement pour la République)	5,658,796	—
JACQUES CHEMINADE (Fédération pour une nouvelle solidarité)	84,959	—
JACQUES CHIRAC (Rassemblement pour la République)	6,348,375	15,763,027
ROBERT HUE (Parti Communiste Français)	2,632,460	—
LIONEL JOSPIN (Parti Socialiste) . . .	7,097,786	14,180,644
ARLETTE LAGUILLER (Lutte Ouvrière) . .	1,615,552	—
JEAN-MARIE LE PEN (Front National) . .	4,570,838	—
PHILIPPE DE VILLIERS (Mouvement pour la France)	1,443,186	—
DOMINIQUE VOYNET (Les Verts) . . .	1,010,681	—

PARLEMENT
(Parliament)

Assemblée Nationale
(National Assembly)

President: RAYMOND FORNI.

General Election, 25 May and 1 June 1997

Party	% of votes cast in first ballot	% of votes cast in second ballot*	Seats
Parti Socialiste (PS) . . .	23.53	38.05	241
Rassemblement pour la République (RPR) . .	15.70	22.82	134
Union pour la Démocratie Française (UDF) . . .	14.22	20.77	108
Parti Communiste Français (PCF) . . .	9.94	3.84	38
Parti Radical Socialiste (PRS) .	1.45	2.19	12
Front National (FN) . . .	14.94	5.60	1
Various ecologist candidates	6.81	1.62	7
Various right-wing candidates	6.70	2.45	14
Various left-wing candidates	5.32	2.55	21
Others	1.39	0.11	1
Total.	100.00	100.00	577

* Held where no candidate had won the requisite overall majority in the first ballot, between candidates who had received at least 12.5% of the votes in that round.

Sénat
(Senate)

President: CHRISTIAN PONCELET.

Members of the Senate are indirectly elected for a term of nine years, with one-third of the seats renewable every three years.

After the most recent election, held on 27 September 1998, the Senate had 321 seats: 296 for metropolitan France; 13 for the overseas departments and territories; and 12 for French nationals abroad. The strength of the parties was as follows:

	Seats
Groupe du Rassemblement pour la République . . .	99
Groupe socialiste	78
Groupe de l'Union centriste des Démocrates de Progrès	52
Groupe de l'Union des Républicains et des Indépendants .	47
Groupe du Rassemblement démocratique et européen .	22
Groupe communiste, républicain et citoyen	16
Non-attached	7
Total	321

Political Organizations

Les Alternatifs: 40 rue de Malte, 75011 Paris; tel. 1-43-57-44-80; fax 1-43-57-64-50; e-mail alternatifs@wanadoo.fr; internet www.alternatifs.org; f. 1998 to replace Alternative Rouge et Verte (f. 1993); left-wing ecologist party; Leaders JEAN-JACQUES BUISLAR-OUSSIE, MATHIEU COLLOGHAN, MARIE-FRANÇOISE PIROT, ROGER WINTER-HALTER.

Centre National des Indépendants et Paysans (CNI): 6 rue Quentin Bauchart, 75008 Paris; tel. 1-47-23-47-00; fax 1-47-23-47-03; f. 1949; right-wing; Pres. ANNICK DU ROSCOAT; Sec.-Gen. BRUNO COTTARD.

Chasse Pêche Nature Traditions (CPNT): Centre d'Affaires Praxis, 245 blvd de la Paix, 64000 Pau; tel. 5-59-14-71-71; fax 5-59-14-71-72; e-mail cpnt@cpnt.asso.fr; internet www.cpnt.asso.fr; f. 1989 as Chasse-Pêche-Traditions; emphasizes defence of rural traditions, field sports, populist; Pres. JEAN SAINT-JOSSE; Sec.-Gen. MICHEL RAYMOND.

Démocratie Libérale (DL): 113 rue de l'Université, 75007 Paris; tel. 1-40-62-30-30; fax 1-40-62-30-40; internet demlib.com; formed May 1977 as Parti Républicain, a grouping of the Fédération Nationale des Républicains Indépendants (FNRI) and three smaller 'Giscardian' parties, name changed as above in 1997; Leader ALAIN MADELIN.

Droite Libérale Chrétienne (DLC): Paris, f. 1998 as La Droite by breakaway faction of UDF; Leader CHARLES MILLON.

Front National (FN): BP 290, 4 rue Vauguyon, 92210 Saint-Cloud; tel. 1-41-12-10-00; fax 1-41-12-10-86; e-mail webmastre@ front-nat.fr; internet www.front-nat.fr; f. 1972; extreme right-wing nationalist; Pres. JEAN-MARIE LE PEN; Sec.-Gen. CARL LANG.

Génération Ecologie: 7 villa Virginie, 75014 Paris; tel. 1-56-53-53-73; fax 1-56-53-53-70; e-mail generation-ecologie@wanadoo.fr; internet www.generation-ecologie.com; f. 1990; emphasis on environmental matters; Leader BRICE LALONDE.

Ligue Communiste Révolutionnaire (LCR): c/o Rouge, 2 rue Richard Lenoir, 93108 Montreuil; tel. 1-48-70-42-30; fax 1-48-59-23-28; e-mail lcr@lcr-rouge.org; internet www.lcr-rouge.org; f. 1974; Trotskyist; 1,500 mems (1996); Leader ALAIN KRIVINE.

Lutte Ouvrière (LO): BP 233, 75865 Paris Cédex 18; f. 1968; Trotskyist; Leaders ARLETTE LAGUILLER, F. DUBURG, J. MORAND.

Mouvement des Citoyens: 9 rue du Faubourg Poissonnière, 75009 Paris; internet www.mdc-france.org; f. 1992; socialist; sceptical of increased European integration or devolution of powers from the nation-state; Leader JEAN-PIERRE CHEVÈNEMENT; Sec.-Gen. PAUL LORIDANT.

Mouvement Ecologiste Indépendant: 34 chemin du pont d'Y, 44600 Saint-Nazaire; tel. and fax 2-40-91-91-92; e-mail contact@ mei-fr.org; internet www.mei-fr.org; f. 1994; emphasis on environmental matters; 3,000 mems; Pres. ANTOINE WAECHTER; Nat. Sec. JEAN-ROLLAND LASSALLE.

Mouvement National Républicain (MNR): 15 rue de Cronstadt, 75015 Paris; tel. 1-56-56-64-34; fax 1-56-56-52-47; e-mail m-n-r@ m-n-r.com; internet m-n-r.com; f. 1999 as FN-MN by breakaway faction of FN; Leader BRUNO MÉGRET .

Mouvement des Réformateurs (MR): 7 rue de Villersexel, 75007 Paris; tel. 1-45-44-61-50; fax 1-45-44-91-90; f. 1992; centrist; formed by merger of Association des Démocrates, France Unie and Performance et Partage; Sec.-Gen. JEAN-PIERRE SOISSON.

Mouvement pour la France (MPF): 35 ave de la Motte-Piquet, 75007 Paris; tel. 1-44-42-02-42; fax 1-44-42-02-43; e-mail mpf-villiers .org; internet www.mpf-villiers.org; f. 1995; right-wing; opposes terms of the Maastricht Treaty; Pres. PHILIPPE DE VILLIERS.

Nouvelle Union pour la Démocratie Française (UDF): 133 rue de l'Université, 75007 Paris; tel. 1-53-59-20-00; fax 1-53-59-20-59; internet www.udf.org; f. 1978 to unite for electoral purposes non-Gaullist 'majority' candidates; has frequently formed electoral alliances with RPR (q.v.); Pres. FRANÇOIS BAYROU; Sec.-Gen. PIERRE-ANDRÉ WILTZER.

Affiliated parties:

Parti Populaire pour la Démocratie Française (PPDF): 250 blvd Saint Germain, 75007 Paris; tel. 1-42-22-69-51; fax 1-42-22-59-49; f. 1965, present name since 1995; Leader HERVÉ DE CHARETTE.

Parti Radical: 1 place de Valois, 75001 Paris; tel. 1-42-61-56-32; fax 1-42-61-49-65; e-mail radical@partiradical.net; internet www .partiradical.net; f. 1901; Pres. FRANÇOIS LOOS; Sec.-Gen. ARLETTE FRUCTUS.

Parti social-démocrate (PSD): Paris; tel. 1-47-53-84-41; fax 1-47-05-73-53; f. 1973 as Mouvement des démocrates socialistes de France, name changed 1982; Pres. MAX LEJEUNE; Sec.-Gen. ANDRÉ SANTINI.

Parti Communiste Français (PCF): 2 place du Colonel Fabien, 75940 Paris Cédex 19; tel. 1-40-40-12-12; fax 1-40-40-13-56; e-mail pcf@pcf.fr; internet www.pcf.fr; subscribed to the common programme of the United Left (with the Parti Socialiste) until 1977; advocates an independent foreign policy; Nat. Sec. ROBERT HUE.

Parti Radical de Gauche (PRG): 13 rue Duroc, 75007 Paris; tel. 1-45-66-67-68; fax 1-45-66-47-93; e-mail prg-nat@club-internet.fr; internet www.radical-gauche.org; f. 1972 as the Mouvement des Radicaux de Gauche; left-wing; Pres. JEAN-MICHEL BAYLET.

Parti Socialiste (PS): 10 rue de Solférino, 75333 Paris Cédex 07; tel. 1-45-56-77-00; fax 1-47-05-15-78; e-mail infops@parti -socialiste.fr; internet www.parti-socialiste.fr; f. 1971; subscribed to the common programme of the United Left (with the Parti Communiste) until 1977; advocates full employment and a mixed economy; 109,000 mems (1996); First Sec. FRANÇOIS HOLLANDE.

Rassemblement pour la France (RPF): 159 ave Charles de Gaulle, 92521 Neuilly-sur-Seine Cédex; tel. 1-55-62-24-24; e-mail rpf@rpf-ie.org; internet www.rpf-ie.org; f. 1994; opposes terms of the Maastricht Treaty; Pres. CHARLES PASQUA; Gen-Sec. JEAN JACQUES GUILLET.

Rassemblement pour la République (RPR): 123 rue de Lille, 75007 Paris; tel. 1-49-55-63-00; fax 1-45-51-44-79; internet www.rpr.org; f. 1976 from the Gaullist party Union des Démocrates pour la République; has frequently formed electoral alliances with UDF (q.v.); 150,000 mems ; Pres. MICHÈLE ALLIOT-MARIE; Sec.-Gen. SERGE LEPELTIER.

Les Verts: 107 ave Parmentier, 75011 Paris; tel. 1-43-55-10-01; fax 1-43-55-16-15; e-mail secretar@verts.imaginet.fr; internet www .verts.imaginet.fr; f. 1984; ecologist party; Spokespersons MARTINE

BILLARD, DENIS BAUPIN, STÉPHANE POCRAIN, MARYSE ARDITI; National Sec. JEAN-LUC BENNAHMIAS.

Diplomatic Representation

EMBASSIES IN FRANCE

Afghanistan: 32 ave Raphaël, 75016 Paris; tel. and fax 1-45-25-05-29; e-mail ambassade.afg@worldonline.fr; internet www .ambafghane.com; Chargé d'affaires: MEHRABODIN MASSTAN.

Albania: 57 ave Marceau, 75116 Paris; tel. 1-47-24-31-00; fax 1-47-23-59-85; e-mail ambalbpa@aol.com; Ambassador: LUAN RAMA.

Algeria: 50 rue de Lisbonne, 75008 Paris; tel. 1-53-93-20-20; fax 1-42-25-10-25; Ambassador: HOCINE DJOUDI.

Andorra: 30 rue d'Astorg, 75008 Paris; tel. 1-40-06-03-30; fax 1-40-06-03-64; e-mail ambaixada@andorra.ad; internet www .amb-andorre.fr; Ambassador: IMMA TOR FAUS.

Angola: 19 ave Foch, 75116 Paris; tel. 1-45-01-58-20; fax 1-45-00-33-71; e-mail anginfos@club-internet.fr; Ambassador: ASSUNÇÃO DOS ANJOS.

Antigua and Barbuda: 43 ave de Friedland, 75008 Paris; tel. 1-53-96-93-96; fax 1-53-96-93-97; Ambassador: RONALD MICHAEL SANDERS.

Argentina: 6 rue Cimarosa, 75116 Paris; tel. 1-44-34-22-00; fax 1-44-34-22-09; Ambassador: JUAN ARCHIBALDO LANUS.

Armenia: 9 rue Viète, 75017 Paris; tel. 1-42-12-98-01; fax 1-42-12-98-03; Ambassador: VAHAN PAPAZIAN.

Australia: 4 rue Jean Rey, 75724 Paris Cédex 15; tel. 1-40-59-33-00; fax 1-40-59-33-10; e-mail information.paris@dfat.gov.au; internet www.austgov.fr; Ambassador: WILLIAM NORMAN FISHER.

Austria: 6 rue Fabert, 75007 Paris; tel. 1-40-63-30-63; fax 1-45-55-63-65; e-mail ambaut@worldnet.fr; internet www.bmaa.gv.at/embassy/fr/index.html.fr; Ambassador: FRANZ CESKA.

Azerbaijan: 209 rue de l'Université, 75007 Paris; tel. 1-44-18-60-20; fax 1-44-18-60-25; e-mail ambazer@compuserve.com; Ambassador: ELÉONORA HUSSEÏNOVA.

Bahrain: 3 bis place des Etats-Unis, 75116 Paris; tel. 1-47-23-48-68; fax 1-47-20-55-75; Ambassador: Sheikha HAYA RASHED AL-KHALIFA.

Bangladesh: 39 rue Erlanger, 75116 Paris; tel. 1-46-51-90-33; fax 1-46-51-90-35; e-mail bdootpar@club-internet.fr; Ambassador: SYED MUAZZEM ALI.

Belarus: 38 blvd Suchet, 75016 Paris; tel. 1-44-14-69-79; fax 1-44-14-69-70; Ambassador: VLADIMIR SENKO.

Belgium: 9 rue de Tilsitt, 75017 Paris; tel. 1-44-09-39-39; fax 1-47-54-07-64; e-mail ambabelge@noos.fr; Ambassador: ALAIN RENS.

Benin: 87 ave Victor Hugo, 75116 Paris; tel. 1-45-00-98-82; fax 1-45-01-82-02; Ambassador: ANDRÉ-GUY OLOGOUDOU.

Bolivia: 12 ave Président Kennedy, 75016 Paris; tel. 1-42-24-93-44; fax 1-45-25-86-23; Ambassador: GONZALO CAMPERO PAZ.

Bosnia and Herzegovina: 174 rue de Courcelles, 75017 Paris; tel. 1-42-67-34-22; fax 1-40-53-85-22; Ambassador: NIKOLA KOVAČ.

Brazil: 34 cours Albert 1er, 75008 Paris; tel. 1-45-61-63-00; fax 1-42-89-03-45; e-mail ambassade@bresil.org; internet www.bresil.org; Ambassador: MARCOS CASTRISTO DE AZAMBUJA.

Brunei: 7 rue de Presbourg, 75116 Paris; tel. 1-53-64-67-60; fax 1-53-64-67-83; Ambassador: Pengiran Hajah MASRAINAH BINTI Pengiran Haji AHMAD.

Bulgaria: 1 ave Rapp, 75007 Paris; tel. 1-45-51-85-90; fax 1-45-51-18-68; internet www.amb-bulgarie.fr; Ambassador: STÉPHANE TAFROV.

Burkina Faso: 159 blvd Haussmann, 75008 Paris; tel. 1-43-59-90-63; fax 1-42-56-50-07; Ambassador: FILIPPE SAWADOGO.

Burundi: 24 rue Raynouard, 75016 Paris; tel. 1-45-20-60-61; fax 1-41-12-99-42; Ambassador: JEAN-BAPTISTE MBONYINGINGO.

Cambodia: 4 rue Adolphe Yvon, 75116 Paris; tel. 1-45-03-47-20; fax 1-45-03-47-40; Ambassador: PRAK SOKHONN.

Cameroon: 73 rue d'Auteuil, 75116 Paris; tel. 1-47-43-98-33; fax 1-46-51-24-52; Ambassador: PASCAL BILOA TANG.

Canada: 35 ave Montaigne, 75008 Paris; tel. 1-44-43-29-00; fax 1-44-43-29-99; internet www.amb-canada.fr; Ambassador: RAYMOND CHRÉTIEN.

Cape Verde: 80 rue Jouffroy d'Abbans, 75017 Paris; tel. 1-42-12-73-50; fax 1-40-53-04-36; Ambassador: RUI ALBERTO DE FIGUEIREDO SOARES.

Central African Republic: 30 rue des Perchamps, 75116 Paris; tel. 1-42-24-42-56; fax 1-46-51-00-21; Ambassador: JEAN POLOKO.

Chad: 65 rue des Belles Feuilles, 75116 Paris; tel. 1-45-53-36-75; fax 1-45-53-16-09; inAmbassador: MAHAMAT AHMAD ALHABO.

Chile: 2 ave de la Motte Picquet, 75007 Paris; tel. 1-44-18-59-60; fax 1-44-18-59-61; e-mail echilefr@iway.fr; Ambassador: FABIO VIO UGARTE.

China, People's Republic: 11 ave George V, 75008 Paris; tel. 1-47-23-34-45; fax 1-47-20-24-22; internet www.amb-chine.fr; Ambassador: WU JIANMIN.

Colombia: 22 rue de l'Elysée, 75008 Paris; tel. 1-42-65-46-08; fax 1-42-66-18-60; e-mail embcolombia@wanadoo.fr; Ambassador: ADOLFO CARVAJAL.

Comoros: 20 rue Marbeau, 75116 Paris; tel. 1-40-67-90-54; fax 1-48-59-87-26; Ambassador: SAID HASSAN SAID HACHIM.

Congo, Democratic Republic: 32 cours Albert 1er, 75008 Paris; tel. 1-42-25-57-50; fax 1-64-61-02-76; Ambassador: (vacant).

Congo, Republic : 37 bis rue Paul Valéry, 75116 Paris; tel. 1-45-00-60-57; fax 1-45-00-34-26; Ambassador: HENRI LOPES.

Costa Rica: 78 ave Emile Zola, 75015 Paris; tel. 1-45-78-96-96; fax 1-45-78-99-66; Ambassador: EDGAR MOHS.

Côte d'Ivoire: 102 ave Raymond Poincaré, 75116 Paris; tel. 1-53-64-62-62; fax 1-45-00-47-97; e-mail bureco-fr@cotedivoire.com; internet www.cotedivoire.com/indexfr.htm; Ambassador: ALASSANE SALIF N'DIAYE.

Croatia: 39 ave Georges Mandel, 75116 Paris; tel. 1-53-70-02-80; fax 1-53-70-02-90; e-mail secretariat@ambcroatie.fr; internet www.amb-croatie.fr; Ambassador: MARKO ŽAJA.

Cuba: 16 rue de Presles, 75015 Paris; tel. 1-45-67-55-35; fax 1-45-66-80-92; e-mail embacu@club-internet.fr; Ambassador: EUMELIO CABALLERO RODRÍGUEZ.

Cyprus: 23 rue Galilée, 75116 Paris; tel. 1-47-20-86-28; fax 1-40-70-13-44; e-mail embrecyp@worldnet.fr; internet home.worldnet.fr/~embrecyp; Ambassador: ANDRÉAS D. MAVROYIANNIS.

Czech Republic: 15 ave Charles Floquet, 75007 Paris; tel. 1-40-65-13-00; fax 1-47-83-50-78; Ambassador: PETR JANYŠKA.

Denmark: 77 ave Marceau, 75116 Paris; tel. 1-44-31-21-21; fax 1-44-31-21-88; e-mail ambadk@parfr.um.dk; internet www .amb-danemark.fr; Ambassador: HANS HENRIK BRUUN.

Djibouti: 26 rue Emile Ménier, 75116 Paris; tel. 1-47-27-49-22; fax 1-45-53-50-53; e-mail webmaster@amb-djibouti.org; internet www .amb-djibouti.org; Ambassador: DJAMA OMAR IDLEH.

Dominican Republic: 45 rue de Courcelles, 75008 Paris; tel. 1-53-53-95-95; fax 1-45-63-35-63; e-mail embajadom@wanadoo.fr; internet www.amba-dominicaine-paris.com; Ambassador: NORMAN G. DE CASTRO-CAMPBELL.

Ecuador: 34 ave de Messine, 75008 Paris; tel. 1-45-61-10-21; fax 1-42-56-06-64; e-mail ambecuad@infonie.fr; Ambassador: JUAN CUEVA JARAMILLO.

Egypt: 56 ave d'Iéna , 75116 Paris; tel. 1-53-67-88-30; fax 1-47-23-06-43; Ambassador: ALY MAHER EL-SAYED.

El Salvador: 12 rue Galilée, 75116 Paris; tel. 1-47-20-42-02; fax 1-40-70-01-95; Ambassador: RAMIRO ZEPEDA ROLDAN.

Equatorial Guinea: 6 rue Alfred de Vigny, 75008 Paris; tel. 1-47-66-44-33; fax 1-47-09-26-38; Ambassador: LINO SIMO EKUA AVOMO.

Estonia: 46 rue Pierre Charron, 75008 Paris; tel. 1-56-62-22-00; fax 1-49-52-05-65; Ambassador: RUTH LAUSMA LUIK.

Ethiopia: 35 ave Charles Floquet, 75007 Paris; tel. 1-47-83-83-95; fax 1-43-06-52-14; e-mail embethe@starnet.fr; Ambassador: MULUG-ETTA ETAFFA.

Finland: 1 place de Finlande, 75007 Paris; tel. 1-44-18-19-20; e-mail pia.setala@formin.fi; internet www.info.finlande.fr; Ambassador: ANTTI HYNNINEN.

Gabon: 26 bis ave Raphaël, 75116 Paris; tel. 1-44-30-22-30; fax 1-42-24-62-42; Ambassador: HONORINE DOSSOU-NAKI.

The Gambia: 117 rue St Lazare, 75008 Paris; tel. 1-42-94-09-30; fax 1-42-94-11-91; Ambassador: JOHN P. BOJANG.

Georgia: 104 ave Raymond Poincaré, 75116 Paris; tel. 1-45-02-16-01; fax 1-45-02-16-01; Ambassador: GOTCHA TCHOGOVADZE.

Germany: 13–15 ave Franklin D. Roosevelt, 75008 Paris; tel. 1-53-83-45-00; fax 1-43-59-74-18; e-mail ambassade@amb-allemagne.fr; internet www.amb-allemagne.fr; Ambassador: Dr PETER HARTMANN.

Ghana: 8 Villa Saïd, 75116 Paris; tel. 1-45-00-09-50; fax 1-45-00-81-95; Ambassador: HARRY OSEI BLAVO.

Greece: 17 rue Auguste Vacquerie, 75116 Paris; tel. 1-47-23-72-28; fax 1-47-23-73-85; internet www.amb-grece.fr/presse; Ambassador: ELIAS CLIS.

Guatemala: 73 rue de Courcelles, 75008 Paris; tel. 1-42-27-78-63; fax 1-47-54-02-06; e-mail embguatefrancia@wanadoo.fr; Ambassador: ANTONIO PALLARÉS BUONAFINA.

Guinea: 51 rue de la Faisanderie, 75116 Paris; tel. 1-47-04-81-48; fax 1-47-04-57-65; e-mail isylla@club-internet.fr; Ambassador: IBRAHIMA SYLLA.

Guinea-Bissau: 94 rue Saint Lazare, 75009 Paris; Ambassador: Fali Embalo.

Haiti: 10 rue Théodule Ribot, 75017 Paris; tel. 1-47-63-47-78; fax 1-42-27-02-05; e-mail haiti01@francophonie.org; Ambassador: Marc A. Trouillot.

Holy See: 10 ave du Président Wilson, 75116 Paris (Apostolic Nunciature); tel. 1-53-23-01-50; fax 1-47-23-65-44; e-mail noncapfr@worldnet.fr; Apostolic Nuncio: Most Rev. Fortunato Baldelli, Titular Archbishop of Bevagna.

Honduras: 8 rue Crevaux, 75116 Paris; tel. 1-47-55-86-45; fax 1-47-55-86-48; e-mail ambassade.honduras@wanadoo.fr; Ambassador: Enrique Ortez Colindres.

Hungary: 7 sq. Vergennes, 75015 Paris; tel. 1-56-36-07-54; fax 1-56-36-02-68; e-mail ambassade-de-hongrie@wanadoo.fr; internet www.hongrie.org; Ambassador: Dezső Kékessy.

Iceland: 8 ave Kléber, 75116 Paris; tel. 1-44-17-32-85; fax 1-40-67-99-96; e-mail icemb.paris@utn.stjr.is; Ambassador: Sigridur A. Snaevarr.

India: 15 rue Alfred Dehodencq, 75016 Paris; tel. 1-40-50-70-70; fax 1-40-50-09-96; e-mail administra@amb-inde.fr; internet www.amb-inde.fr; Ambassador: Kanwal Sibal.

Indonesia: 47–49 rue Cortambert, 75116 Paris; tel. 1-45-03-07-60; fax 1-45-04-50-32; internet www.amb-indonesie.fr; Ambassador: Dadang Sukandar.

Iran: 4 ave d'Iéna, 75116 Paris; tel. 1-40-69-79-00; fax 1-40-70-01-57; Ambassador: (vacant).

Iraq (Interests Section): 53 rue de la Faisandrie, 75016 Paris; tel. 1-45-53-33-70; fax 1-45-53-33-80; e-mail paris@embassyiraq.com; internet www.embassyiraq.com; Head of Mission: Dr Ghazzi Faisel Hussain.

Ireland: 4 rue Rude, 75116 Paris; tel. 1-44-17-67-00; fax 1-44-17-67-60; e-mail irembparis@wanadoo.fr; Ambassador: Patrick O'Connor.

Israel: 3 rue Rabelais, 75008 Paris; tel. 1-40-76-55-00; fax 1-40-76-55-55; e-mail info@amb-israel.fr; internet www.amb-israel.fr; Ambassador: Eytan Bentsur.

Italy: 51 rue de Varenne, 75007 Paris; tel. 1-49-54-03-00; fax 1-45-49-35-81; Ambassador: Sergio Vento.

Japan: 7 ave Hoche, 75008 Paris; tel. 1-48-88-62-00; fax 1-42-27-50-81; e-mail i-richard@amb-japon.fr; internet www.amb-japon.fr; Ambassador: Kazuo Ogoura.

Jordan: 11 rue Alfred Dehodencq, 75016 Paris; tel. 1-55-74-73-73; fax 1-55-74-73-74; Ambassador: Adnan Talhouni.

Kazakhstan: 59 rue Pierre Charron, 75008 Paris; tel. 1-45-61-52-00; fax 1-45-61-52-01; Ambassador: Akmaral Arystanbekova.

Kenya: 3 rue Freycinet, 75116 Paris; tel. 1-56-62-25-25; fax 1-47-20-44-41; Ambassador: Steven A. Loyatum.

Korea, Republic: 125 rue de Grenelle, 75007 Paris; tel. 1-47-53-01-01; fax 1-47-53-00-41; e-mail koremb-fr@mofat.go.kr; internet www.amb-coreesud.fr; Ambassador: Kwon In-Hyuk.

Kuwait: 2 rue de Lübeck, 75116 Paris; tel. 1-47-23-54-25; fax 1-47-20-33-59; Ambassador: Ahmad al-Ebrahim.

Laos: 74 ave Raymond Poincaré, 75116 Paris; tel. 1-45-53-02-98; fax 1-47-57-27-89; Ambassador: Khamphan Simmalavong.

Latvia: 6, villa Saïd, 75016 Paris; tel. 1-53-64-58-10; fax 1-53-64-58-19; e-mail ambleton@wanadoo.fr; Ambassador: Sandra Kalniete.

Lebanon: 3 villa Copernic, 75116 Paris; tel. 1-40-67-75-75; fax 1-40-67-16-42; e-mail ambliban@club-internet.fr; Ambassador: Raymond Baaklini.

Liberia: 12 place du Général Catroux, 75017 Paris; tel. 1-47-63-58-55; fax 1-42-12-76-14; e-mail libem.paris@wanadoo.fr; Ambassador: Christopher Minikon (delegate).

Libya: 2 rue Charles Lamoureux, 75116 Paris; tel. 1-47-04-71-60; fax 1-47-55-96-25; Ambassador: Abn al-Salam al-Mazughi.

Lithuania: 14 blvd Montmartre, 75009 Paris; tel. 1-48-01-00-33; fax 1-48-01-03-31; e-mail amb.lituanie@magic.fr; internet www.amb-lituanie-paris.fr; Ambassador: Skaisgirytė Liauškienė.

Luxembourg: 33 ave Rapp, 75007 Paris; tel. 1-45-55-13-37; fax 1-45-51-72-29; Ambassador: Jean-Marc Hoscheit.

Macedonia, former Yugoslav republic: 21 rue Sébastian Mercier, 75015 Paris; tel. 1-45-77-10-50; fax 1-45-77-14-84; Ambassador: Luan Starova.

Madagascar: 4 ave Raphaël, 75016 Paris; tel. 1-45-04-62-11; fax 1-45-03-58-70; Ambassador: Malala-Zo Raolison.

Malawi: 20 rue Euler, 75008 Paris; tel. 1-47-20-20-27; fax 1-47-23-62-48; Ambassador: Augustine W. Mnthambala.

Malaysia: 2 bis rue Bénouville, 75116 Paris; tel. 1-45-53-11-85; fax 1-47-27-34-60; Ambassador: Dr Rajmah Hussain.

Mali: BP 175, 89 rue du Cherche-Midi, 75263 Paris; tel. 1-45-48-58-43; fax 1-45-48-55-34; Ambassador: Madina Ly-Tall.

Malta: 92 ave des Champs Elysées, 75008 Paris; tel. 1-56-59-75-90; fax 1-45-62-00-36; Ambassador: Prof. Salvino Buscuttil.

Mauritania: 5 rue de Montévidéo, 75116 Paris; tel. 1-45-04-88-54; fax 1-40-72-82-96; Ambassador: Mohamed Ben Mbirek.

Mauritius: 127 rue de Tocqueville, 75017 Paris; tel. 1-42-27-66-70; fax 1-40-53-02-91; e-mail amb-maurice-paris@goformet.com; Ambassador: Marie-France Roussety.

Mexico: 9 rue de Longchamp, 75116 Paris; tel. 1-53-70-27-70; fax 1-47-55-65-29; e-mail embamex_francia@wanadoo.fr; internet www.sre.gob.mx/francia; Ambassador: Claude Heller.

Moldova: 1 rue de Sfax, 75116 Paris; tel. 1-40-67-11-20; fax 1-40-67-11-23; e-mail ambassade.moldavie@free.fr; Ambassador: Mihai Popov.

Monaco: 22 blvd Suchet, 75116 Paris; tel. 1-45-04-74-54; fax 1-45-04-45-16; Ambassador: Christian Orsetti.

Mongolia: 5 ave Robert Schuman, 92100 Boulogne-Billancourt; tel. 1-46-05-28-12; fax 1-46-05-30-16; e-mail 106513.2672@compuserve.com; Ambassador: Gotoudorjiin Lousan.

Morocco: 3–5 rue Le Tasse, 75116 Paris; tel. 1-45-20-69-35; fax 1-45-20-22-58; Ambassador: Mohamed Berrada.

Mozambique: 82 rue Laugier, 75017 Paris; tel. 1-47-64-91-32; fax 1-44-15-90-13; e-mail embamocparis@compuserve.com; Ambassador: José Rui Mota do Amaral.

Myanmar: 60 rue de Courcelles, 75008 Paris; tel. 1-42-25-56-95; fax 1-42-56-49-41; Ambassador: U Nyunt Tin.

Namibia: 80 ave Foch, 75016 Paris; tel. 1-44-17-32-65; fax 1-44-17-32-73; e-mail namparis@club-internet.fr; Ambassador: Leonard Iipumbu.

Nepal: 45 bis rue des Acacias, 75017 Paris; tel. 1-46-22-48-67; fax 1-42-27-08-65; e-mail nepal@worldnet.fr; Ambassador: Indra Bahadur Singh.

Netherlands: 7–9 rue Eblé, 75007 Paris; tel. 1-40-62-33-00; fax 1-40-62-34-56; e-mail ambassade@amb-pays-bas.fr; internet www.amb-pays-bas.fr; Ambassador: Ronald van Beuge.

New Zealand: 7 ter rue Léonard de Vinci, 75116 Paris; tel. 1-45-01-43-43; fax 1-45-01-43-44; e-mail nzembassy-paris@wanadoo.fr; Ambassador: Dr Richard Grant.

Nicaragua: 34 ave Bugeaud, 75116 Paris; tel. and fax 1-44-05-90-42; e-mail embanifr@cybercable.fr; internet www.blue-brain.com/embassy/nicaragua; Ambassador: Joaquín Gómez.

Niger: 154 rue de Longchamp, 75116 Paris; tel. 1-45-04-80-60; fax 1-45-04-62-26; Ambassador: Mariama Hima.

Nigeria: 173 ave Victor Hugo, 75116 Paris; tel. 1-47-04-68-65; fax 1-47-04-47-54; e-mail embassy@nigeriaparis.com; internet www.nigeriaparis.com; Ambassador: E. A. Aina.

Norway: 28 rue Bayard, 75008 Paris; tel. 1-53-67-04-00; fax 1-53-67-04-40; e-mail emb.paris@mfa.no; internet www.amb-norvege.fr; Ambassador: Rolf Trolle Andersen.

Oman: 50 ave d'Iéna, 75116 Paris; tel. 1-47-23-01-63; fax 1-47-23-02-25; Ambassador: Jaifer Salim al-Said.

Pakistan: 18 rue Lord Byron, 75008 Paris; tel. 1-45-62-23-32; fax 1-45-62-89-15; e-mail pakemb_paris@yahoo.com; Ambassador: Shaharyar M. Khan.

Panama: 145 ave de Suffren, 75015 Paris; tel. 1-47-83-23-32; fax 1-45-67-99-43; e-mail panaemba@worldnet.fr; internet services.worldnet.net/panaemba; Ambassador: Arístides Royo.

Papua New Guinea: 1 rue Miollis, B-347, 75015 Paris; tel. 1-45-68-31-21; fax 1-47-34-15-51; e-mail dl.papua-new-guinea@unesco.org; Chargé d'affaires: Kappa Yamka.

Paraguay: 1 rue St Dominique, 75007 Paris; tel. 1-42-22-85-05; fax 1-42-22-83-57; Ambassador: Rubén Bareiro Saguier.

Peru: 50 ave Kléber, 75116 Paris; tel. 1-53-70-42-00; fax 1-47-55-98-30; e-mail perou@noos.net; internet www-amb-perou.fr; Chargé d'affaires a.i.: Augusto Thornberry.

Philippines: 4 hameau de Boulainvilliers, 75016 Paris; tel. 1-44-14-57-00; fax 1-46-47-56-00; e-mail ambaphil-paris@compuserve.com; Ambassador: Hector K. Villaroel.

Poland: 1–3 rue de Talleyrand, 75343 Paris Cédex 07; tel. 1-43-17-34-05; fax 1-43-17-35-07; e-mail info@ambassade.pologne.net; Ambassador: Stefan Meller.

Portugal: 3 rue de Noisiel, 75116 Paris; tel. 1-47-27-35-29; fax 1-47-55-00-40; internet www.embaixada-portugal-fr.org; Ambassador: Leonardo Mathias.

Qatar: 57 quai d'Orsay, 75007 Paris; tel. 1-45-51-90-71; fax 1-45-51-77-07; Ambassador: Saad Mohamed al-Kobaisi (designate).

Romania: 5 rue de l'Exposition, 75007 Paris; tel. 1-40-62-22-02; fax 1-45-56-97-47; e-mail amb.paris.ro@francophonie.org; Ambassador: Dumitru Ciausu.

Russia: 40-50 blvd Lannes, 75116 Paris; tel. 1-45-04-05-50; fax 1-45-04-17-65; e-mail rusembfr@club-internet.fr; Ambassador: NIKOLAI AFANASSIEVSKII.

Rwanda: 12 rue Jadin, 75017 Paris; tel. 1-42-27-36-31; fax 1-42-27-74-69; Chargé d'affaires a.i.: MODESTE RUTABAYIRU.

San Marino: 21 rue Auguste Vacquerie, 75116 Paris; tel. 1-47-23-77-32; fax 1-47-23-78-05; Ambassador: Countess ISA CORINALDI DE BENEDETTI.

Saudi Arabia: 5 ave Hoche, 75008 Paris; tel. 1-56-79-40-00; fax 1-56-79-40-01; e-mail ambsaudi@club-internet.fr; Ambassador: FAISAL ABDULAZIZ ALHEGELAN.

Senegal: 14 ave Robert Schuman, 75007 Paris; tel. 1-47-05-39-45; fax 1-45-56-04-30; internet www.amb-senegal.fr; Ambassador: KÉBA BIRANE CISSÉ.

Seychelles: 51 ave Mozart, 75016 Paris; tel. 1-42-30-57-47; fax 1-42-30-57-40; e-mail ambsey@aol.com;Ambassador: CALLIXTE D'OFFAY.

Singapore: 12 Square de l'ave Foch, 75116 Paris; tel. 1-45-00-33-61; fax 1-45-00-61-79; e-mail ambsing@club-internet.fr; Ambassador: THAMBYNATHAN JASUDASEN.

Slovakia: 125 rue du Ranelagh, 75016 Paris; tel. 1-44-14-56-00; fax 1-42-88-76-53; e-mail zuparis@wanadoo.fr; Ambassador: VLADIMIR VALACH.

Slovenia: 21 rue Bouquet de Longchamp, 75116 Paris; tel. 1-47-55-65-90; fax 1-47-55-60-05; Ambassador: JOŽEF KUNIČ.

Somalia: 26 rue Dumont d'Urville, 75116 Paris; tel. 1-45-00-76-51; Ambassador: Said Hagi MUHAMMAD FARAH.

South Africa: 59 quai d'Orsay, 75343 Paris Cédex 07; tel. 1-53-59-23-23; fax 1-53-59-23-68; e-mail info@afriquesud.net; Ambassador: THUTHUKILE SKWEYIYA.

Spain: 22 ave Marceau, 75008 Paris; tel. 1-44-43-18-00; fax 1-47-23-59-55; e-mail ambespfr@mail.mae.es; internet www.amb-espagne.fr; Ambassador: FRANCISCO JAVIER ELORZA.

Sri Lanka: 15 rue d'Astorg, 75008 Paris; tel. 1-42-66-35-01; fax 1-40-07-00-11; internet sl.france@wanadoo.fr; Ambassador: CASIE CHETTY.

Sudan: 56 ave Montaigne, 75008 Paris; tel. 1-42-25-55-71; fax 1-54-63-66-73; Ambassador: EL TIGANI SALIH FIDAIL.

Sweden: 17 rue Barbet de Jouy, 75007 Paris; tel. 1-44-18-88-00; fax 1-44-18-88-40; e-mail presseinfo@amb-suede.fr; internet www.amb-suede.fr; Ambassador: ÖRJAN BERNER.

Switzerland: 142 rue de Grenelle, 75007 Paris; tel. 1-49-55-67-00; fax 1-45-55-67-67; e-mail vertretung@par.rep.admin.ch; Ambassador: BENEDIKT VON TSCHARNER.

Syria: 20 rue Vaneau, 75007 Paris; tel. 1-40-62-61-00; fax 1-47-05-92-73; Ambassador: ELIAS NAJMÉH.

Tanzania: 13 ave Raymond Poincaré, 75116 Paris; tel. 1-53-70-63-66; fax 1-47-55-05-46; e-mail tanzanie@infonie.fr; Ambassador: KASSIM M. J. MWAWADO.

Thailand: 8 rue Greuze, 75016 Paris; tel. 1-56-26-50-50; fax 1-56-26-04-46; e-mail thaipar@wanadoo.fr; Ambassador: SAROJ CHAVANAVIRAJ.

Togo: 8 rue Alfred Roll, 75017 Paris; tel. 1-43-80-12-13; fax 1-43-80-90-71; Ambassador: KONDI CHARLES MADJOME AGBA.

Tunisia: 25 rue Barbet de Jouy, 75007 Paris; tel. 1-45-55-95-98; fax 1-45-56-02-64; Ambassador: MONGI BOUSNINA.

Turkey: 16 ave de Lamballe, 75016 Paris; tel. 1-53-92-72-11; fax 1-45-20-41-91; e-mail ambtrparis@cie.fr; Ambassador: SÖNMEZ KÖKSAL.

Turkmenistan: 13 rue Picot, 75116 Paris; tel. 1-47-55-05-36; fax 1-47-55-05-68; e-mail turkmenamb@aol.com; Ambassador: TCHARY G. NIIAZOV.

Uganda: 13 ave Raymond Poincaré, 75116 Paris; tel. 1-53-70-62-70; fax 1-53-70-85-15; Ambassador: DAVID KAZUNGU.

Ukraine: 21 ave de Saxe, 75007 Paris; tel. 1-43-06-07-37; fax 1-43-06-02-94; Ambassador: YURI KOCHUBEY.

United Arab Emirates: 3 rue de Lota, 75116 Paris; tel. 1-44-34-02-00; fax 1-47-55-61-04; Ambassador: ABDUL AZIZ N. R. AL-SHAMSI.

United Kingdom: 35 rue du Faubourg Saint Honoré, 75383 Paris Cédex 08; tel. 1-44-51-31-00; fax 1-44-51-41-27; internet www.amb-grandebretagne.fr; Ambassador: Sir MICHAEL JAY.

USA: 2 ave Gabriel, 75382 Paris Cédex 08; tel. 1-43-12-22-22; fax 1-42-66-97-83; internet www.amb-usa.fr/pagefr.htm; Chargé d'affaires a.i: DOUGLAS L. McELHANEY.

Uruguay: 15 rue Le Sueur, 75016 Paris; tel. 1-45-00-81-37; fax 1-45-01-25-17; e-mail urugali@fr.inter.net; internet www.amb-uruguay-france.org; Ambassador: MICHEL ANGEL SEMINO.

Uzbekistan: 22 rue d'Aguesseau, 75008 Paris; tel. 1-53-30-03-53; fax 1-53-30-03-54; e-mail ambsssade.ouzbekistan@freesbee.fr; internet www.oaric.com/ouzbekistan.html; Ambassador: TOKHIRJON MAMAJANOV.

Venezuela: 11 rue Copernic, 75116 Paris; tel. 1-45-53-29-98; fax 1-47-55-64-56; e-mail embavzla@club-internet.fr; internet www.embavenez-paris.com; Ambassador: HIRAM GAVIRIA.

Viet Nam: 62 rue Boileau, 75016 Paris; tel. 1-44-14-64-00; fax 1-45-24-39-48; Ambassador: NGUYÊN CHIÊN THANG.

Yemen: 25 rue Georges Bizet, 75116 Paris; tel. 1-47-23-61-76; fax 1-47-23-69-41; Ambassador: ABDULLAH AL-ERYANI.

Yugoslavia: 54 rue de la Faisanderie, 75116 Paris; tel. 1-40-72-24-24; fax 1-40-72-24-11; Ambassador: BOGDAN TRIFUNOVIĆ.

Zimbabwe: 12 rue Lord Byron, 75008 Paris; tel. 1-56-88-16-00; fax 1-56-88-16-09; Ambassador: JOEY MAZORODZE BIMHA.

Judicial System

The Judiciary is independent of the Government. Judges of the Court of Cassation and the First President of the Court of Appeal are appointed by the executive from nominations of the High Council of the Judiciary.

Subordinate cases are heard by Tribunaux d'instance, of which there are 471, and more serious cases by Tribunaux de grande instance, of which there are 181. Parallel to these Tribunals are the Tribunaux de commerce, for commercial cases, composed of judges elected by traders and manufacturers among themselves. These do not exist in every district. Where there is no Tribunal de commerce, commercial disputes are judged by Tribunaux de grande instance.

The Conseils de Prud'hommes (Boards of Arbitration) consist of an equal number of workers or employees and employers ruling on the differences which arise over Contracts of Work.

The Tribunaux correctionnnels (Correctional Courts) for criminal cases correspond to the Tribunaux de grande instance for civil cases. They pronounce on all graver offences (délits), including those involving imprisonment. Offences committed by juveniles of under 18 years go before specialized tribunals for children.

From all these Tribunals appeal lies to the Cours d'appel (Courts of Appeal).

The Cours d'assises (Courts of Assize) have no regular sittings, but are called when necessary to try every important case, for example, murder. They are presided over by judges who are members of the Cours d'appel, and are composed of elected judges (jury). Their decision is final, except where shown to be wrong in law, and then recourse is had to the Cour de cassation (Court of Cassation). The Cour de cassation is not a supreme court of appeal but a higher authority for the proper application of the law. Its duty is to see that judgments are not contrary either to the letter or the spirit of the law; any judgment annulled by the Court involves the trying of the case anew by a court of the same category as that which made the original decision.

A programme of extensive reforms in the judicial system, which aimed to reduce political control of the Judiciary and to increase citizens' rights, was introduced in stages between 1997 and 2000.

COUR DE CASSATION

Palais de Justice, 5 quai de l'Horloge, 75001 Paris; tel. 1-44-32-50-50; fax 1-44-32-78-28; internet www.courdecassation.fr.

First President: GUY CANIVET.

Presidents of Chambers: JEAN-PIERRE DUMAS (Chambre commerciale), JACQUES LEMONTEY (1ère Chambre civile), JEAN BUFFET (2ème Chambre civile), ROGER BEAUVOIS (3ème Chambre civile), GERARD GELINEAU-LARRIVET (Chambre sociale), BRUNO COTTE (Chambre criminelle).

Solicitor-General: JEAN-FRANÇOIS BURGELIN.

There are 85 Counsellors, one First Attorney-General and 22 Attorneys-General.

Chief Clerk of the Court: MARLÈNE TARDI.

Council of Advocates at Court of Cassation: Pres. JEAN BARTHÉLEMY.

COUR D'APPEL DE PARIS

Palais de Justice, blvd du Palais, 75001 Paris; tel. 1-44-32-52-52.

First President: JEAN-MARIE COULON.

There are also 69 Presidents of Chambers.

Solicitor-General: JEAN-LOUIS NADAL.

There are also 121 Counsellors, 24 Attorneys-General and 38 Deputies.

TRIBUNAL DE GRANDE INSTANCE DE PARIS

4 blvd du Palais, 75055 Paris RP; tel. 1-44-32-51-51; fax 1-43-29-12-55.

President: JEAN-CLAUDE MAGENDIE.

Solicitor of Republic: GABRIEL BESTARD.

TRIBUNAL DE COMMERCE DE PARIS

1 quai de Corse, 75181 Paris Cédex 04.

President: JEAN-PIERRE MATTEÏ.

TRIBUNAUX ADMINISTRATIFS

Certain cases arising between civil servants (when on duty) and the Government, or between any citizen and the Government are judged by special administrative courts.

The Tribunaux administratifs, of which there are 22, are situated in the capital of each area; the Conseil d'Etat (see below) has its seat in Paris.

TRIBUNAL DES CONFLITS

Decides whether cases shall be submitted to the ordinary or administrative courts.

President: The Minister of Justice.

Vice-President: PIERRE NICOLAI.

There are also four Counsellors of the Cour de cassation and three Counsellors of State.

COUR DES COMPTES

13 rue Cambon, 75100 Paris RP; tel. 1-42-98-95-00; fax 1-42-60-01-59; internet www.ccomptes.fr.

An administrative tribunal (Audit Court) competent to judge the correctness of public accounts. It is the arbiter of common law of all public accounts laid before it. The judgments of the Court may be annulled by the Conseil d'Etat.

First President: FRANÇOIS LOGEROT.

Presidents: FRANÇOIS LOGEROT, GUY BERGER, JEAN-FRANÇOIS COLLINET, ANTOINE BRUNET, JEAN MARMOT, GABRIEL MIGNOT, BERNARD MENASSEYRE.

Solicitor-General: HÉLÈNE GISSEROT.

CHAMBRES RÉGIONALES DES COMPTES

In 1983 jurisdiction over the accounts of local administrations (Régions, Départements and Communes) and public institutions (hospitals, council housing, etc.) was transferred from the Cour des comptes to local Chambres régionales. The 25 courts are autonomous but under the jurisdiction of the State. Appeals may be brought before the Cour des comptes.

CONSEIL D'ETAT

Palais-Royal, 75100 Paris; tel. 1-40-20-80-00; fax 1-40-20-83-72; internet www.conseil-etat.fr.

The Council of State is a council of the central power and an administrative tribunal, with 201 members in active service. As the consultative organ of the Government, it gives opinions in the legislative and administrative domain (interior, finance, public works and social sections). In administrative jurisdiction it has three functions: to judge in the first and last resort such cases as appeals against excess of power laid against official decrees or individuals; to judge appeals against judgments made by Tribunaux administratifs and resolutions of courts of litigation; and to annul decisions made by various specialized administrative authorities which adjudicate without appeal, such as the Cour des comptes.

President: The Prime Minister.

Vice-President: RENAUD DENOIX DE SAINT-MARC.

Presidents of Sections: JEAN MASSOT, JEAN-FRANÇOIS THERY, MICHEL ROUX, JEAN-PIERRE LECLERC, DANIEL LABETOULLE, MICHEL FRANC.

General Secretary: MARTINE DE BOISDEFFRE.

Religion

CHRISTIANITY

Conseil d'Eglises Chrétiennes en France: 80 rue de l'Abbé-Carton, 75014 Paris; tel. 1-53-90-25-50; fax 1-45-42-03-07; e-mail unite.chretiens.revue@wanadoo.fr; f. 1987; ecumenical organization comprising representatives from all Christian denominations to express opinions on social issues; 21 mems; Pres Most Rev. LOUIS-MARIE BILLÉ, Pastor JEAN-ARNOLD DE CLERMONT, Most Rev. JÉRÉMIE CALIGIORGIS; Secs Pastor GILL DAUDÉ; Fr CHRISTIAN FORSTER, Fr MICHEL EVDOKIMOV.

The Roman Catholic Church

For ecclesiastical purposes, France comprises nine Apostolic Regions, together forming 19 archdioceses (of which two, Marseille and Strasbourg, are directly responsible to the Holy See), 95 dioceses (including one, Metz, directly responsible to the Holy See) and one Territorial Prelature. The Archbishop of Paris is also the Ordinary for Catholics of Oriental Rites. At the end of 1997 there were an estimated 45.9m. adherents of the Roman Catholic Church in France, equivalent to some 78.3% of the population.

Bishops' Conference: Conférence des Evêques de France, 106 rue du Bac, 75341 Paris Cédex 07; tel. 1-45-49-69-90; fax 1-45-49-69-95; e-mail cef@cef.fr; internet www.cef.fr; Pres. Cardinal LOUIS-MARIE BILLÉ, Archbishop of Lyon.

Latin Rite

Archbishop of Lyon and Primate of Gaul: Cardinal LOUIS-MARIE BILLÉ, Archevêché, 1 place de Fourvière, 69321 Lyon Cédex 05; tel. 4-72-38-80-90; fax 4-78-36-06-00; e-mail dioceselyon@wanadoo.fr; internet catholique-lyon.cef.fr.

Archbishop of Aix: Most Rev. CLAUDE FEIDT.

Archbishop of Albi: Most Rev. PIERRE-MARIE CARRÉ.

Archbishop of Auch: Most Rev. MAURICE FRÉCHARD.

Archbishop of Avignon: Most Rev. RAYMOND BOUCHEX.

Archbishop of Besançon: Most Rev. LUCIEN DALOZ.

Archbishop of Bordeaux: Cardinal PIERRE EYT.

Archbishop of Bourges: Most Rev. HUBERT BARBIER.

Archbishop of Cambrai: Most Rev. FRANÇOIS GARNIER.

Archbishop of Chambéry: Most Rev. LAURENT ULRICH.

Archbishop of Marseille: Most Rev. BERNARD PANAFIEU.

Archbishop of Paris: Cardinal JEAN-MARIE LUSTIGER.

Archbishop of Reims: Most Rev. THIERRY JORDAN.

Archbishop of Rennes: Most Rev. FRANÇOIS SAINT-MACARY.

Archbishop of Rouen: Most Rev. JOSEPH DUVAL.

Archbishop of Sens: Most Rev. GEORGES GILSON.

Archbishop of Strasbourg: Most Rev. JOSEPH DORÉ.

Archbishop of Toulouse: Most Rev. EMILE MARCUS.

Archbishop of Tours: Most Rev. ANDRÉ VINGT-TROIS.

Armenian Rite

Bishop of Sainte-Croix-de-Paris: KRIKOR GHABROYAN, 10 bis rue Thouin, 75005 Paris; tel. 1-40-51-11-90; fax 1-40-51-11-99; e-mail epaparis@francenet.fr; 30,000 adherents (1986).

Ukrainian Rite

Apostolic Exarch in France: MICHEL HRYNCHYSHYN (Titular Bishop of Zygris), 186 blvd Saint-Germain, 75006 Paris; tel. 1-45-48-48-65; 16,000 adherents (1989).

Protestant Churches

There are some 950,000 Protestants in France.

Eglise Méthodiste: 3 rue Paul Verlaine, 30100 Alès; tel. 4-66-86-20-72; the total Methodist community was estimated at 2,900 mems in 1982.

Fédération Protestante de France: 47 rue de Clichy, 75311 Paris Cédex 09; tel. 1-44-53-47-00; fax 1-48-74-66-31; e-mail fpf@protestants.org; internet perso.wanadoo.fr/fpf; f. 1905; Pres. Pastor JEAN-ARNOLD DE CLERMONT; Gen. Sec. Pastor CHRISTIAN SEYTRE.

The Federation includes:

Armée du Salut: 60 rue des Frères Flavien, 75976 Paris; tel. 1-43-62-25-00; fax 1-43-62-25-56; e-mail salut@teaser.fr; internet www.teaser.fr/salut; f. 1881; Pres. Col GLEN SHEPHERD.

Communauté protestant évangélique de Vannes: 18 blvd Edouard Herriot, 56000 Vannes; tel. 2-97-47-16-75; fax 2-97-42-44-93; Pres. Pastor JEAN-MARC THOBOIS.

Eglise apostolique (EA): 5 rue de l'Est, 94600 Choisy-le-Roi; tel. 2-35-31-47-45; 1,000 mems; Pres. JACQUES VAVASSEUR.

Eglise de la Confession d'Augsbourg d'Alsace et de Lorraine: 1b quai Saint Thomas, 67081 Strasbourg Cédex; tel. 3-88-25-90-05; fax 3-88-25-90-99; e-mail epal-directoire@protestants.org; internet www.protestants.org/epal; 218,000 mems; Pres. Prof. MARC LIENHARD.

Eglise évangélique de Rochefort: 30 Quéreux de la Laiterie, 17300 Rochefort; tel. 5-46-99-63-79; Pres. Pastor PIERRE ROCHAT.

Eglise évangélique luthérienne de France: 13 rue Godefroy, 75013 Paris; tel. 1-45-82-19-99; fax 1-44-24-36-18; 40,000 mems; f. 1872; Pres. JEAN-MICHEL STURM; Sec. FREDERIC KALTERMARK.

Eglise réformée d'Alsace et de Lorraine: 1 quai St Thomas, 67081 Strasbourg Cédex; tel. 3-88-25-90-10; fax 3-88-25-90-80; e-mail epal@protestants.org; internet www.protestants.org/epal; 33,000 mems; Pres. Pastor JEAN-PAUL HUMBERT.

Eglise réformée de France: 47 rue de Clichy, 75311 Paris Cédex 09; tel. 1-48-74-90-92; fax 1-42-81-52-40; internet www.eglise-reformee-fr.org; 350,000 mems; Pres. National Council Pastor MICHEL BERTRAND; Gen. Sec. Pastor MARC RICHALOT.

Fédération des Eglises évangéliques baptistes de France: 48 rue de Lille, 75007 Paris; tel. 1-42-61-13-96; fax 1-40-20-05-26; e-mail feebf@aol.com; internet www.feebf.com; 6,000 mems; f. 1910; Pres. MICHEL CHARLES; Gen. Sec. Pastor ETIENNE LHERMENAULT.

Mission évangélique tzigane de France: 'Les Petites Brosses', 45500 Neuvoy; tel. 2-38-67-38-00; 70,000 mems; f. 1946; Pres. Pastor GEORGES MEYER.

Mission populaire évangélique de France: 47 rue de Clichy, 75311 Paris Cédex 09; tel. 1-48-74-98-58; fax 1-48-78-52-37; e-mail mpef@free.fr; 4,000 mems; f. 1871; Pres. JEAN-JACQUES DEMOUVEAUX; Gen. Sec. Pastor JEAN-FRANÇOIS FABA.

Union des Eglises évangeliques libres de France: 12 rue Claude-Perrault, 31500 Toulouse; tel. 5-61-26-06-18; fax 5-61-92-92-82; internet services.worldnet.net/ueel; 2,500 mems; Pres. Pastor ANDRÉ COURTIAC; Sec. CLIVE CHARLTON.

Union Nationale des Eglises réformées évangéliques indépendantes de France: 30900 Nîmes; tel. 4-66-62-93-96; 13,000 mems; Pres. PAUL AIMÉ LANDES; Gen. Sec. GÉRARD FINES.

The Orthodox Churches

There are about 200,000 Orthodox believers in France, of whom 100,000 are Russian Orthodox and 50,000 Greek Orthodox. There are 85 parishes and eight monasteries.

Administration of Russian Orthodox Churches in Europe (Jurisdiction of the Ecumenical Patriarchate): 12 rue Daru, 75008 Paris; tel. 1-46-22-38-91; Pres. Most Rev. SERGE (KONOVALOV), Archbishop of Russian Orthodox Churches in Europe.

Greek Orthodox Church: Cathedral of St Stéphane, 7 rue Georges Bizet, 75116 Paris; tel. 1-47-20-82-35; fax 1-47-20-83-15; Exarch Most Rev. JÉRÉMIE (KALIGIORGIS), Greek Archbishop of France, Spain and Portugal.

The Anglican Communion

Within the Church of England, France forms part of the diocese of Gibraltar in Europe. The Bishop is resident in London (United Kingdom).

Archdeacon of France: Ven. MARTIN DRAPER, St. George's Church, 7 rue Auguste Vacquerie, 75116 Paris; tel. 1-47-20-22-51.

Other Christian Churches

Société Religieuse des Amis (Quakers) et Centre Quaker International: 114 rue de Vaugirard, 75006 Paris; tel. 1-45-48-74-23.

ISLAM

In numerical terms, Islam is the second most important religion in France; in 1997 there were about 3.2m. adherents, of whom more than 750,000 resided in the Marseille area. A High Council of Islam in France was founded in Paris in 1995.

Conseil Représentatif des Musulmans de France: c/o Paris Mosque, 2 place du Puits de l'Ermite, 75005 Paris; f. 1994; Pres. HAMLAOUI MÉKÉCHÉRA; Sec.-Gen. DJELLOUL SEDDIKI.

Fédération Nationale des Musulmans de France (FNMF): c/o Paris Mosque, 2 place du Puits de l'Ermite, 75005 Paris; f. 1985; 20 asscns; Pres. DANIEL YOUSSOF LECLERQ.

Institut Musulman de la Grande Mosquée de Paris: 2 bis place du Puits de l'Ermite, 75005 Paris; tel. 1-45-35-97-33; fax 1-45-35-16-23; e-mail boubakeur@mosquee-de-paris.com; internet www .mosquee-de-paris.com; f. 1923; cultural, diplomatic, social, judicial and religious sections; research and information and commercial annexes; Dir Dr DALIL BOUBAKEUR.

JUDAISM

There are about 700,000 Jews in France.

Consistoire Central—Union des Communautés Juives de France: 19 rue Saint Georges, 75009 Paris; tel. 1-49-70-88-00; fax 1-42-81-03-66; e-mail consis@club-internet.fr; f. 1808; 230 asscns; Chief Rabbi of France JOSEPH SITRUK; Pres. JEAN KAHN; Dir.-Gen. FRÉDÉRIC ATTALI.

Consistoire Israélite de Paris: 17 rue Saint Georges, 75009 Paris; tel. 1-40-82-76-76; internet www.consistoire.org; f. 1808; 40,000 mems; Pres. MOÏSE COHEN; Chief Rabbi of Paris DAVID MESSAS; Chief Rabbi of the Consistoire Israélite de Paris ALAIN GOLDMANN; Sec.-Gen. MOCHÉ COHEN.

BUDDHISM

Dojo Zen de Paris: 175 rue Tolbiac, 75013 Paris; tel. 1-53-80-19-19; fax 1-53-80-14-33; e-mail courrier@dojozendeparis.com; internet www.dojozendeparis.com; f. 1970; Pres. KATIA ROBEL.

World Federation of Buddhists, French Regional Centre: 98 chemin de la Calade, 06250 Mougins; Sec. Mme TEISAN PERUSAT STORK.

The Press

Most major daily newspapers are owned by individual publishers or by the powerful groups which have developed round either a company or a single personality. The major groups are as follows:

Amaury Group: 25 ave Michelet, 93408 Saint Ouen Cédex; tel. 1-40-10-30-30; fax 1-40-11-15-26; owns *Le Parisien, Aujourd'hui en France,*

the sports daily *L'Equipe,* the weeklies *L'Equipe Magazine* and *France-Football,* and the monthly *Vélo;* Man. Dir PHILIPPE AMAURY.

Bayard Presse: 3 rue Bayard, 75008 Paris; tel. 1-44-35-60-60; fax 1-44-35-61-61; e-mail communication@bayard-presse.com; internet www.bayardpresse.fr; Catholic press group; owns 102 publs worldwide (49 within France), incl. the national *La Croix, Pèlerin Magazine, Panorama, Notre Temps,* magazines for young people and the over 50s, and several specialized religious publications; Pres. ALAIN CORDIER.

Emap France: 43 rue du Colonel Pierre Avia, 75754 Paris Cédex 15; tel. 1-41-33-50-00; fax 1-41-33-57-19; internet www.emapfrance .com; frmly Editions Mondiales; owns several popular magazines, incl. *Nous Deux, Studio, Télé-Star, Top Santé, Les Veillées des Chaumières, Télé-Poche, Auto Plus,* and also specialized magazines; Man. Dir ARNAUD DE PUYFONTAINE.

Expansion Group: 14 blvd Poissonnière, 75308 Paris Cédex 9; tel. 1-53-24-40-40; fax 1-53-24-41-05; e-mail webmaster@groupe -expansion.com; internet www.groupe-expansion.com; f. 1967; owns a number of magazines, incl. *L'Expansion, L'Entreprise, Business Solo, Courrier International, Voyages, La Vie Financière;* Chair. and Man. Dir JEAN-LOUIS SERVAN-SCHREIBER.

Hachette Filipacchi Médias Group: 149 rue Anatole-France, 92534 Levallois-Peret Cédex; tel. 1-41-34-60-00; internet www .hachette-filipacchi.com; f. 1999 by merger of Filipacchi Group and Hachette Groupe Presse; controls a number of large-circulation magazines incl. *Paris-Match, Echo des Savanes, Pariscope, Jeune et Jolie, Photo France-Dimanche, Elle, Maximum, Télé 7 Jours, Parents, Var Matin;* Pres. GÉRALD DE ROQUEMAUREL.

Socpresse: one of the largest of the provincial daily press groups; frmly Hersant Group; owns 20 dailies, numerous weeklies, fortnightlies and periodicals; dailies incl. *Le Progrès, Le Figaro, France-Soir, Le Dauphiné Libéré, Nord-Matin* and *Nord-Eclair;* Chair. and Man. Dir YVES DE CHAISEMARTIN.

DAILY PAPERS (PARIS)

La Croix: 3-5 rue Bayard, 75393 Paris Cédex 08; tel. 1-44-35-60-60; fax 1-44-35-60-01; f. 1883; Catholic; Dir BRUNO FRAPPAT; Editor-in-Chief DOMINIQUE QUINIO; circ. 98,233.

Les Echos: 46 rue la Boétie, 75381 Paris Cédex 08; tel. 1-49-53-65-65; fax 1-45-61-48-92; internet www.lesechos.fr; f. 1908; economic and financial; Chair. DANIEL GUNAUEL; Editor NICOLAS BEYTOUT; circ. 135,000.

L'Equipe: 4 rue Rouget-de-l'Isle, 92130 Issy-les-Moulineaux Cédex; tel. 1-40-93-20-20; fax 1-40-93-20-08; e-mail emortureux@lequipe.fr; internet www.lequipe.fr; f. 1946; sport; Chair. LOUIS GILLET; circ. 390,788 (1999).

Le Figaro: 37 rue du Louvre, 75002 Paris; tel. 1-42-21-62-00; fax 1-42-21-64-05; e-mail hchateauneuf@lefigaro.fr; internet www .lefigaro.fr; f. 1828; morning; news and literary; magazine on Saturdays; three weekly supplements; Editor-in-Chief DOMINIQUE BAUDIS; circ. 375,000.

France-Soir: 37 rue du Louvre, 75002 Paris; tel. 1-44-82-87-00; f. 1941 as *Défense de la France,* present title 1944; Editor-in-Chief YVES THREARD; circ. 184,000.

L'Humanité: 32 rue Jean Jaurès, 93528 Saint-Denis Cédex; tel. 1-49-22-72-72; fax 1-49-22-73-00; f. 1904 by Jean Jaurès; communist; morning; Dir PIERRE ZARKA; Editor-in-Chief CLAUDE CABANES; circ. 117,005.

International Herald Tribune: 6 bis rue des Graviers, 92521 Neuilly-sur-Seine Cédex; tel. 1-41-43-93-00; fax 1-41-43-93-93; e-mail iht@iht.com; internet www.iht.com; f. 1887; English language; Co-Chairs KATHARINE GRAHAM, ARTHUR O. SULZBERGER; CEO PETER GOLDMARK; Exec. Editor MICHAEL GETLER; circ. 210,000.

Le Journal Officiel de la République Française: 26 rue Desaix, 75727 Paris Cédex 15; tel. 1-40-58-75-00; fax 1-45-79-17-84; f. 1870; official journal of the Government; publishes laws, decrees, parliamentary proceedings, and economic bulletins; Dir JEAN-PAUL BOLUFER.

Libération: 11 rue Béranger, 75154 Paris Cédex 03; tel. 1-42-76-17-89; fax 1-42-72-94-93; e-mail webmaster@liberation.fr; internet www.liberation.com; f. 1973; 65%-owned by the Chargeurs group from 1996; independent; Publr SERGE JULY; Dir-Gen. EVENCE-CHARLES COPPÉE; Editor-in-Chief JACQUES AMALRIC; circ. 169,427 (1999).

Le Monde: 21 bis rue Claude-Bernard, 75242 Paris Cédex 05; tel. 1-42-17-20-00; fax 1-42-17-21-21; e-mail lemonde@lemonde.fr; internet www.lemonde.fr; f. 1944; left-wing liberal; independent; Pres. JEAN-MARIE COLOMBANI; Dir-Gen. DOMINIQUE ALDUY; Editor-in-Chief EDWY PLENEL; circ. 402,443 (2000).

Le Parisien: 25 ave Michelet, 93408 Saint-Ouen Cédex; tel. 1-40-10-30-30; fax 1-40-10-35-16; e-mail infoat@leparisien.fr; internet www.leparisien.fr; f. 1944; morning; sold in Paris area and surrounding départements; Man. Dir JACQUES GUERIN; Editorial Dir CHRISTIAN DE VILLENEUVE; circ. 478,152 (1999).

Aujourd'hui en France: f. 1994; national version of *Le Parisien*.

Le Quotidien du Médecin: 140 rue Jules Guesde, 92300 Levallois-Perret; tel. 1-41-40-75-00; fax 1-41-40-75-75; e-mail quotidien@wanadoo.fr; internet www.quotimed.com; medical journal; Dir Dr MARIE-CLAUDE TESSON-MILLET; Editor-in-Chief RICHARD LISCIA; Editors RENÉE CARTON, BRUNO KELLER, EMMANUEL DE VIEL; circ. 82,000.

La Tribune: 42–46 rue Notre Dame des Victoires, 75002 Paris; tel. 1-40-13-13-13; fax 1-44-82-17-92; internet www.latribune.fr; economic and financial; Chair. FABRICE LARUE; Man. Dir ELISABETH DESCOMBES; circ. 80,000.

SUNDAY PAPERS (PARIS)

Le Journal du Dimanche: 149 rue Anatole France, 92534 Levallois-Perret Cédex; tel. 1-41-34-60-00; fax 1-41-34-70-76; Dir JEAN-CLAUDE MAURICE; Editor-in-Chief CHRISTIAN SAUVAGE; circ. 298,000 (1998).

Le Parisien Dimanche: 25 ave Michelet, 93408 Saint Ouen Cédex; tel. 1-40-10-30-30; fax 1-40-10-35-16.

PRINCIPAL PROVINCIAL DAILY PAPERS

Amiens

Le Courrier Picard: 29 rue de la République, BP 1021, 80010 Amiens Cédex 01; tel. 3-22-82-60-00; fax 3-22-82-60-12; e-mail jquemere@courier-picard.fr; internet www.courier-picard.fr; f. 1944; Chair., Man. DOMINIQUE FONTAINE; Dir JEAN QUÉMÉRÉ; Editor-in-Chief FRANÇOIS PERRIER; circ. 82,739.

Angers

Le Courrier de l'Ouest: 4 blvd Albert Blanchoin, BP 728, 49007 Angers Cédex 01; tel. 2-41-68-86-88; fax 2-41-68-13-27; f. 1944; Chair., Man. Dir CHRISTIAN COUSTAL; Editor-in-Chief JACQUES BOSSEAU; circ. 108,802.

Angoulême

Charente Libre: BP 1025, 16001 Angoulême Cédex; tel. 5-45-94-16-00; fax 5-45-94-16-19; e-mail charente@charente.com; internet www.charente.com; Man. Dir MICHEL LÉPINAY; Editors-in-Chief JEAN-LOUIS HERVEIS, JACQUES GUYON; circ. 40,496.

Auxerre

L'Yonne Républicaine: 8-12 ave Jean Moulin, 89025 Auxerre Cédex; tel. 3-86-49-52-00; fax 3-86-46-99-90; f. 1944; Dir-Gen. JOËL LOUBERT; Editor-in-Chief GILLES DAUXERRE: circ. 40,400.

Bordeaux

Sud-Ouest: Place Jacques Lemoine, 33094 Bordeaux Cédex; tel. 5-56-00-33-33; fax 5-56-00-32-17; e-mail a.igorra@sudouest.com; internet www.sudouest.com; f. 1944; independent; Chair., Man. Dir PIERRE JEANTET; Editor-in-Chief PATRICK VENRIES; circ. 359,204.

Chalon-sur-Saône

Le Journal de Saône-et-Loire: 9 rue des Tonneliers, BP 134, 71100 Chalon-sur-Saône; tel. 3-85-44-68-68; fax 3-85-93-02-96; e-mail jslmediatheque@le-journal-de-saone-et-loire.fr; internet jsl.sdv.fr; f. 1826; Dir FRANÇOIS PRETET; circ. 83,000.

Chartres

L'Echo Républicain: 37 rue de Châteaudun, BP 189, 28000 Chartres; f. 1929; Chair., Man. Dir JACQUES CAMUS; Sec.-Gen. J. P. COUSIN; circ. 35,000.

Clermont-Ferrand

La Montagne: 28 rue Morel Ladeuil, BP 83, 63000 Clermont-Ferrand Cédex 1; tel. 4-73-17-17-17; fax 4-73-17-18-19; e-mail lamontagne@centrefrance.com; f. 1919; independent; Man. Dir JEAN-PIERRE CAILLARD; Editor-in-Chief JEAN-LOUP MANOUSSI; circ. 250,100.

Dijon

Le Bien Public: 7 blvd du Chanoine Kir, BP 550, 21015 Dijon Cédex; tel. 3-80-42-42-42; fax 3-80-42-42-73; e-mail y.mezou@pbnetb.fr; internet www.bienpublic.com; f. 1850; Dir-Gen. FRANÇOIS PRETET; Editors-in-Chief YVON MEZOU, MICHEL BEY; circ. 61,492.

Les Dépêches: 5 rue Pierre Palliot, BP 570, 21015 Dijon; tel. 3-80-42-16-16; f. 1936; Chair. XAVIER ELLIE; Man. Dir PIERRE VILLEZ; circ. 42,000.

Epinal

Liberté de l'Est: 40 quai des Bons Enfants, BP 273, 88007 Epinal Cédex; tel. 3-29-82-98-00; fax 3-29-82-99-29; e-mail contact@lalibertedelest.fr; internet www.lalibertedelest.fr; f. 1945; Chair., Man. Dir THIERRY BECUWE; Editor-in-Chief JEAN-MARIE RIAT; circ. 30,630 (1998).

Grenoble

Le Dauphiné Libéré: Les Iles-Cordées, 38913 Veurey-Voroize Cédex; tel. 4-76-88-71-00; fax 4-76-88-70-96; e-mail redaction@ledauphinlibere.com; internet www.ledauphinlibere.com; f. 1945; Chair., Man. Dir DENIS HUERTAS; Editor-in-Chief HUBERT PERRIN; circ. weekdays 281,416, Sunday 397,282.

Lille

La Voix du Nord: 8 place du Général de Gaulle, BP 549, 59023 Lille Cédex; tel. 3-20-78-40-40; fax 3-20-78-42-44; e-mail webvdn@lavoixdunord.fr; internet www.lavoixdunord.fr; f. 1944; Chair., Man. Dir JEAN-LOUIS PRÉVOST; Editor-in-Chief PHILIPPE CARON; circ. 410,000.

Limoges

L'Echo du Centre: 29 rue C. H. Gorceix, 87022 Limoges Cédex 9; tel. 5-55-04-49-99; fax 5-55-04-49-78; f. 1943; five editions; Communist; Man. Dir CHRISTIAN AUDOUIN; Editor-in-Chief BERNARD CUNY; circ. 69,200.

Le Populaire du Centre: rue du Général Catroux, 87011 Limoges Cédex; tel. 5-55-58-59-60; fax 5-55-58-69-79; f. 1905; Chair. Man. Dir MARCEL TOURLONIAS; Editor-in-Chief SERGE JOFFRE; circ. 58,773 (1997).

Lyon

Le Progrès: 93 ave du Progrès, 69680 Chassieu; tel. 4-72-22-23-23; fax 4-78-90-52-40; internet www.leprogres.fr; f. 1859; Chair., Man. Dir XAVIER ELLIE; Editor-in-Chief JEAN PAUL LARDY; circ. 299,047.

Le Mans

Le Maine Libre: 28–30 place de l'Eperon, BP 299, 72007 Le Mans Cédex; tel. 2-43-83-72-50; fax 2-43-83-72-59; Chair., Man. Dir GÉRARD CHOL; Editor-in-Chief RAYMOND MAUDET; circ. 54,891.

Marseille

La Marseillaise: 19 cours Honoré d'Estienne d'Orves, BP 1862, 13001 Marseille; tel. 4-91-57-75-00; fax 4-91-57-75-25; f. 1944; Communist; Man. Dir PAUL BIAGGINI; Editor-in-Chief CHRISTIAN DIGNE; circ. 78,900.

La Provence: 248 ave Roger-Salengro, 13015 Marseille; tel. 4-91-84-45-45; fax 4-91-84-49-95; e-mail redaction@laprovence-presse.fr; internet www.laprovence-presse.fr; f. 1996 following merger of *Le Provençal* with *Le Méridional*; Chair., Man. Dir GHISLAIN LELEU; Editor-in-Chief LAURENT GILARDINO.

Metz

Le Républicain Lorrain: 3 rue Saint-Eloy, 57140 Woippy; tel. 3-87-34-17-89; fax 3-87-33-28-18; e-mail pm.pernet@republicain-lorrain.fr; internet www.republicain-lorrain.fr; f. 1919; independent; Chair. CLAUDE PUHL; Man. Dir MATHIEU PUHL; Editor-in-Chief JEAN CHARLES BOURDIER; circ. 184,861.

Montpellier

Midi-Libre: 34923 Montpellier Cédex; tel. 4-67-07-67-07; fax 4-67-07-68-13; internet www.midilibre.fr; f. 1944; Chair., Man. Dir NOËL-JEAN BERGEROUX; Editor-in-Chief ALAIN PLOMBAT; circ. 175,420.

Morlaix

Le Télégramme de Brest et de l'Ouest: 7 voie d'Accès au Port, BP 243, 29205 Morlaix Cédex; tel. 2-98-62-11-33; fax 2-98-88-76-65; e-mail telegramme@bretagne-online.com; internet www.bretagne-online.com; f. 1944; Chair., Man. Dir EDOUARD COUDURIER; Editor-in-Chief JEAN CLAUDE CASSENAC; circ. 199,710.

Mulhouse

L'Alsace: 18 rue de Thann, BP 1160, 68053 Mulhouse; tel. 3-89-32-70-00; fax 3-89-32-11-26; e-mail redaction@alsapresse.com; internet www.alsapresse.com; f. 1944; Chair. JEAN-DOMINIQUE PRETET; Editor-in-Chief JEAN-MARIE HAEFFELLE; circ. 124,997.

Nancy

L'Est Républicain: rue Théophraste-Renaudot, Nancy Houdemont, 54185 Heillecourt Cédex; tel. 3-83-59-80-54; fax 3-83-59-80-13; e-mail er-secretariat-general@wanadoo.fr; internet www.estrepublican.fr; f. 1889; Chair., Man. Dir GÉRARD LIGNAC; Editor-in-Chief PIERRE TARIBO; circ. 230,922.

Nantes

Presse Océan: 5 rue Santeuil, BP 22418, 44024 Nantes Cédex 1; tel. 2-40-44-24-00; fax 2-40-44-24-59; f. 1944; Chair. CHRISTIAN COUSTAL; Editor-in-Chief ETIENNE CHARBONNEAU; circ. 77,931.

Nevers

Le Journal du Centre: 3 rue du Chemin de Fer, BP 106, 58001 Nevers; tel. 3-86-71-45-00; fax 3-86-71-45-20; e-mail lejournalducentre@wanadoo.fr; f. 1943; Man. Dir LOUIS COTTIER; Editor-in-Chief FRANÇOISE GILARDI; circ. 37,348.

Nice

Nice-Matin: 214 route de Grenoble, BP 4, 06290 Nice Cédex 3; tel. 4-93-18-28-38; fax 4-93-83-93-97; internet www.nicematin.fr; f. 1945; Chair., Man. Dir MICHEL COMBOUL; Editor-in-Chief HUBERT PERRIN; circ. 169,800; also Corsican edition *Corse-Matin*.

Orléans

La République du Centre: rue de la Halte, 45770 Saran; tel. 2-38-78-79-80; fax 2-38-78-79-79; f. 1944; Chair., Man. Dir JACQUES CAMUS; Editor-in-Chief DENIS LEGER; circ. 61,044.

Perpignan

L'Indépendant: Le Mas de la Garrigue, 2 ave Alfred Sauvy, 66605 Rivesaltes Cédex; tel. 4-68-64-88-88; fax 4-68-64-88-38; f. 1846; also **Indépendant-Dimanche** (Sunday); Dir-Gen. ROGER BÈNE; circ. 82,595.

Reims

L'Union: 87 place Drouet d'Erlon, 51083 Reims Cédex; tel. 3-26-50-50-50; fax 3-26-50-51-69; f. 1944; Chair. MICHEL NOZIÈRE; Man. Dir DANIEL HUTIER; Editor-in-Chief MICHEL GRENOUILLOUX; circ. 137,518.

Rennes

Ouest-France: 10 rue du Breil, 35051 Rennes Cédex 09; tel. 2-99-32-60-00; fax 2-99-32-60-25; internet www.ouest-france.fr; f. 1944; Chair., Man. Dir FRANÇOIS RÉGIS HUTIN; Editor-in-Chief DIDIER PILLET; circ. 786,205.

Roubaix

Nord-Eclair: 15–21 rue du Caire, BP 58, 59052 Roubaix Cédex 1; tel. 3-20-75-92-56; fax 3-20-82-83-63; f. 1944; Chair., Man. Dir MICHEL PROUVOT; Editor-in-Chief ANDRÉ FARINE; circ. 96,661.

Rouen

Paris-Normandie: 19 place du Général de Gaulle, 76000 Rouen; tel. 2-35-14-56-56; fax 2-35-14-56-15; internet www.paris-normandie.com; f. 1944; Chair., Man. Dir PHILIPPE HERSANT; Editor-in-Chief GILLES DAUXERRE; circ. 104,327.

Strasbourg

Les Dernières Nouvelles d'Alsace: 17–21 rue de la Nuée Bleue, BP 406/R1, 67077 Strasbourg Cédex; tel. 3-88-21-55-00; fax 3-88-21-56-41; e-mail dnasug@sdv.fr; internet www.dna.fr; f. 1877; non-party; Chair., Man. Dir GÉRARD LIGNAC; Editor-in-Chief ALAIN HOWILLER; circ. 215,460.

Toulon

Var Matin: Toulon; tel. 4-94-06-91-91; fax 4-94-63-49-98; internet www.varmatin.com; f. 1975; Dir MICHEL COMBOUL; Editorial Dir HUBERT PERRIN; circ. 93,000.

Toulouse

La Dépêche du Midi: ave Jean Baylet, 31095 Toulouse Cédex; tel. 5- 62-11-33-00; fax 5-61-44-74-74; internet www.ladepeche.com; f. 1870; radical; Chair., Man. Dir JEAN MICHEL BAYLET; Editors-in-Chief GUY-MICHEL EMPOCIELLO, HENRI AMAR; circ. 218,214.

Tours

La Nouvelle République du Centre-Ouest: 232 ave de Grammont, 37048 Tours Cédex; tel. 2-47-31-70-00; fax 2-47-31-70-70; e-mail admin@nrco.com; internet www.nrco.com; f. 1944; non-party; Co-Chairs DAVID BOHBOT, JACQUES SAINT-CRICQ, CHRISTIAN ALLORY; Editor-in-Chief HERVÉ GUÉNERON; circ. 285,825.

Troyes

L'Est-Eclair: 71 ave du Maréchal Leclerc, 10120 St André les Vergers; tel. 3-25-79-90-10; fax 3-25-79-58-54; f. 1945; Dir FRANÇOIS LE SACHÉ; circ. 33,000.

SELECTED PERIODICALS
General, Current Affairs and Politics

Annales—Histoire, Sciences sociales: 54 blvd Raspail, 75006 Paris; tel. 1-49-54-23-77; fax 1-49-54-26-88; e-mail annales@ehess.fr; f. 1929; every 2 months.

Armées d'Aujourd'hui: Délégation à l'Information et à la Communication de la Défense, BP 33, 14 rue St Dominique, 75997 Paris; 10 a year; military and technical; produced by the Service d'information et de relations publiques des armées (SIRPA); circ. 130,000.

Le Canard Enchaîné: 173 rue Saint Honoré, 75051 Paris Cédex 01; tel. 1-42-60-31-36; fax 1-42-27-97-87; f. 1915; weekly; political satire; Dir MICHEL GAILLARD; circ. 520,000.

Courrier International: 14 blvd Poissonière, 75308 Paris; tel. 1-53-24-44-24; fax 1-53-24-41-67; e-mail jean-christophe.rampal@groupe-expansion.com; internet www.courrierint.com; f. 1990;

weekly; current affairs and political; Dir HERVÉ LAVERGNE; Editor-in-Chief JEAN-MICHEL BOISSIER; circ. 87,000.

Le Crapouillot: Paris; tel. 1-47-42-21-72; fax 1-42-66-93-96; f. 1915; satire and humorous; Man. N. DUPATY; Publr, Editor ROLAND GAUCHER.

Croissance: Le monde en développement: 163 blvd Malesherbes, 75017 Paris; tel. 1-48-88-46-00; fax 1-42-27-29-03; f. 1961 as *Croissance des Jeunes Nations*; monthly on developing nations; circ. 25,000.

Europe Outremer: Paris; tel. 1-46-47-78-44; f. 1923; monthly; Dir R. TATON; circ. 17,800.

L'Evénement: 32 rue René Boulanger, 75467 Paris Cédex 10; tel. 1-53-72-00-00; f. 1984 as *L'Evénement du jeudi*; weekly; current affairs; Dir JEAN-FRANÇOIS KAHN; Editor-in-Chief BERNARD POULET; circ. 169,820 (1998).

L'Express: 17 rue de l'Arrivée, 75733 Paris Cédex 15; tel. 1-53-91-11-11; fax 1-53-91-12-05; internet www.lexpress.fr; f. 1953; weekly; Dir DENIS JEAMBAR; circ. 428,125.

Globe Hebdo: 73–77 rue Pascal, 75013 Paris; tel. 1-44-08-02-02; fax 1-44-08-02-49; weekly; current affairs; Dir GEORGES-MARC BENAMOU; Editors STÉPHANE BENAMOU, ROBERT MELCHER.

L'Humanité Hebdo: 32 rue Jean Jaurès, 93528 Saint-Denis Cedex; tel. 1-49-22-72-72; fax 1-49-22-73-00; current affairs; Editor MARTINE BULARD.

Ici-Paris: 10 rue Thierry le Luron, 92592 Levallois-Perret Cédex; tel. 1-49-53-49-53; fax 1-42-89-31-78; f. 1941; weekly; Dir GHISLAIN LE LEU; Editor ROBERT MADJAR; circ. 372,386.

Lutte Ouvrière: BP 233, 75865 Paris Cédex 18; f. 1968; weekly; left-wing; Editor MICHEL RODINSON.

Marianne: 32 rue René Boulanger, 75467 Paris Cédex 10; tel. 1-55-72-09-00; fax 1-53-72-09-10; e-mail journal@marianne-en-ligne.fr; internet www.marianne-en-ligne.fr; f. 1997; weekly; current affairs; Dir JEAN-FRANÇOIS KAHN.

Le Monde des Débats—Le Nouvel Observateur: 10-12 place de la Bourse, 75081 Paris Cédex 02; tel. 1-44-88-34-34; internet www.nouvelobs.com; f. 1964 as *Le Nouvel Observateur*, merged with *Le Monde des Débats* in 2001; weekly; left-wing political and literary; Chair. CLAUDE PERDRIEL; Dir JEAN DANIEL; circ. 432,433.

Le Monde Diplomatique: 21 bis rue Claude Bernard, 75005 Paris; tel. 1-42-17-29-16; fax 1-42-17-21-00; internet www.monde-diplomatique.fr; international affairs; circ. 193,804 (2000).

Paris-Match: 151 rue Anatole-France, 92598 Levallois-Perret Cédex; tel.1-41-34-62-43; fax 1-41-34-75-29; e-mail lesommire@parismatch.com; internet www.parismatch.com. f. 1949; weekly; magazine of French and world affairs; Gen. Man. ALAIN GENESTAR; circ. 776,700.

Passages: 17 rue Simone Weil, 75013 Paris; tel. 1-45-86-30-02; fax 1-44-23-98-24; e-mail passages@club-internet.fr; internet perso-club-internet.fr/passages; f. 1987; monthly; Jewish current affairs, humour and literary review; Dir EMILE MALET; circ. 75,000.

Le Peuple: 263 rue de Paris, Case 432, 93514 Montreuil Cédex; tel. 1-48-18-83-06; fax 1-48-59-28-31; e-mail lepeuple@cgt.fr; f. 1921; fortnightly; official organ of the Confédération Générale du Travail (trade union confederation); Dir DANIEL PRADA; Editor-in-Chief FRANÇOISE DUCHESNE.

Le Point: 74 ave du Maine, 75014 Paris; tel. 1-44-10-10-10; fax 1-43-21-43-24; e-mail courier@lepoint.tm.fr; internet www.lepoint.fr; f. 1972; weekly; politics and current affairs; Man. Dir BERNARD WOUTS; Editor-in-Chief FRANZ-OLIVIER GIESBERT; circ. 318,000.

Point de Vue: 142 rue du Bac, 75007 Paris; tel. 1-44-39-11-11; fax 1-42-84-17-34; e-mail contact@pointdevue.fr; internet www.pointdevue.fr; weekly; general illustrated; Dir and Editor LAURE BOULAY DE LA MEURTHE; circ. 370,311.

Politique Internationale: 11 rue du Bois de Boulogne, 75116 Paris; tel. 1-45-00-15-26; fax 1-45-00-38-79; f. 1978; quarterly; Dir and Editor-in-Chief PATRICK WAJSMAN.

Regards: 15 rue Montmartre, 75001 Paris; tel. 1-40-13-79-00; fax 1-40-13-79-29; e-mail regards@regards.fr; internet www.regards.fr; monthly; communist, politics, current affairs, culture; Editor-in-Chief JACKIE VIRUEGA.

Révolution: 15 rue Montmartre, 75001 Paris; tel. 1-42-33-61-26; fax 1-42-33-58-92; f. 1980; weekly; political and cultural; Dir GUY HERMIER; Editor-in-Chief JEAN-PAUL JOUARY.

Revue 'Défense Nationale': Ecole Militaire, 1 place Joffre, 75007 Paris; tel. 1-44-42-31-90; fax 1-44-42-31-89; e-mail redac@revuedefensenationale.comworldnet.fr; internet www.revuedefensenationale.com; f. 1939; monthly; publ. by Committee for Study of National Defence; military, economic, political and scientific problems; Chair. Gen. QUESNOT; Editor Adm. GIRARD.

Revue des Deux Mondes: 10 place du Général Catroux, 75017 Paris; tel. 1-40-54-11-00; fax 1-40-54-11-32; f. 1829; monthly; current affairs; Dir MARC LADREIT DE LACHARRIÈRE.

Rivarol: 1 rue St Hauteville, 75010 Paris; tel. 1-53-34-97-97; fax 1-53-34-97-98; e-mail galic@rivarol.com; internet www.rivarol.com; f. 1951; weekly; political, literary and satirical; Dir and Editor-in-Chief CAMILLE-MARIE GALIC; circ. 45,000.

La Vie: 163 blvd Malesherbes, 75017 Paris; tel. 1-48-88-46-00; fax 1-48-88-46-01; f. 1945; weekly; Catholic, general; Dir JEAN-CLAUDE PETIT; circ. 241,000.

VSD (Vendredi-Samedi-Dimanche): 15 rue Galvani, 75809 Paris Cédex 17; tel. 1-56-99-47-00; fax 1-56-99-51-28; e-mail lecteurs @vsd.fr; internet www.vsd.fr; f. 1977; weekly; current affairs, leisure; Editor-in-Chief THIERRY BRÉTAGNE; circ. 225,238 (1999).

The Arts

L'Architecture d'Aujourd'hui: 6 rue Lhomond, 75005 Paris; tel. 1-47-63-12-11; internet www.architecture-aujourdhui.presse.fr; f. 1930; publ. by Groupe Expansion; Editor-in-Chief FRANÇOIS CHASLIN; circ. 25,791.

Art et Décoration: 16–18 rue de l'Amiral Mouchez, 75686 Paris Cédex 14; tel. 1-45-65-48-48; f. 1897; 8 a year; Dir JEAN MASSIN; Editor-in-Chief DANIEL SOUBEYRAND; circ. 451,443.

Critique: 7 rue Bernard Palissy, 75006 Paris; tel. 1-45-44-23-16; fax 1-45-44-82-36; f. 1946; monthly; general review of French and foreign literature, philosophy, social sciences and history; Dir PHILIPPE ROGER; Editor ISABELLE CHAVE.

Diapason: 9–13 rue du Colonel Pierre Avia, 75754 Paris Cédex 15; tel. 1-46-62-20-00; fax 1-46-62-25-33; f. 1956; monthly; classical music; Pres. and Dir-Gen. CLAUDE POMMEREAU; Editor-in-Chief YVES PETIT DE VOIZE; circ. 70,000.

Ecrivain: Paris; f.1995; 6 a year; literature, history, philosophy, science; Dirs PIERRE BONCENNE, GÉRARD LARPENT.

Gazette des Beaux-Arts: 140 rue du Faubourg Saint Honoré, 75008 Paris; tel. 1-45-61-61-70; fax 1-45-61-61-71; f. 1859; monthly; the oldest review of the history of art; Dir DANIEL WILDENSTEIN.

Les Inrockuptibles: 144 rue du Rivoli, 75001 Paris; tel. 1-42-44-16-16; fax 1-42-44-16-00; e-mail mediator@inrocks.com; internet www1.lesinrocks.com; weekly; music, cinema, literature; Editor CHRISTIAN FEVRET.

Les Lettres Françaises: Ivry sur Seine; tel. 1-46-71-35-95; monthly arts magazines; Dir JEAN RISTAT.

Lire: 17 rue de l'Arrivée,75733 Paris Cédex 15; tel. 1-53-91-11-11; fax 1-53-91-11-04; internet www.lire.fr; monthly; literary review; Editor PIERRE ASSOULINE; circ. 110,000.

Livres-Hebdo: 35 rue Grégoire de Tours, 75006 Paris; tel. 1-44-41-28-00; fax 1-43-29-77-85; e-mail livreshebdo@electra.com; f. 1979; 46 a year; Dir JEAN-MARIE DOUBLET.

Livres de France: 35 rue Grégoire de Tours, 75006 Paris; tel. 1-44-41-28-00; fax 1-43-29-77-85; f. 1979; 11 a year; Dir JEAN-MARIE DOUBLET.

L'Oeil: Paris; tel. 1-45-25-85-60; fax 1-42-88-65-87; f. 1955; monthly; Editor-in-Chief SOLANGE THIERRY.

Magazine littéraire: 40 rue des Saints-Pères, 75007 Paris; tel. 1-45-44-14-51; fax 1-45-48-86-36; e-mail magazine@magazine -litteraire.com; internet www.magazine-litteraire.com; f. 1966; monthly; literature; Dir NICKY FASQUELLE; Editor JEAN-LOUIS HUE; circ. 100,000.

Le Matricule des Anges: BP 225, 34004 Montpellier Cédex; tel. and fax 4-67-92-29-33; e-mail lmda@lmda.net; internet www.lmda.net; f. 1992; literary criticism; Editor THIERRY GUICHARD.

Poétique: Editions du Seuil, 27 rue Jacob, 75261 Paris Cédex 06; tel. 1-40-46-50-50; fax 1-40-46-51-43; f. 1970; quarterly; literary review.

La Quinzaine Littéraire: 135 rue Saint-Martin, 75194, Paris Cédex 04; tel. 1-48-87-48-58; fax 1-48-87-13-01; e-mail selis@ wanadoo.fr; internet www.quinzaine-litteraire.presse.fr; f. 1966; fortnightly; Dir MAURICE NADEAU; circ. 20,000.

Les Temps Modernes: 4 rue Férou, 75006 Paris; tel. 1-43-29-08-47; fax 1-40-51-83-38; f. 1945 by J.-P. Sartre; four a year; literary review; publ. by Gallimard; Dir CLAUDE LANZMANN.

Economic and Financial

L'Expansion: 14 blvd Poissonnière, 75208 Paris Cédex 09; tel. 1-53-24-40-40; internet www.expansion.com; f. 1967; fortnightly; economics and business; Dir JEAN BOISSONNAT; Editor JACQUES BARRAUX; circ. 147,602 (2000).

Marchés Tropicaux et Méditerranéens: 190 blvd Haussmann, 75008 Paris; tel. 1-44-95-99-50; fax 1-44-95-99-79; e-mail webmaster-mtm@moreux.fr; internet www.marches-tropicaux.com; f. 1945; weekly; analysis and information on Africa and the Indian Ocean and on tropical products; Pres. SERGE MARPAUD; Editor F. GAULME.

Mieux Vivre Votre Argent: 32 rue Notre-Dame-des-Victoires, 75002 Paris; tel. 1-53-00-20-00; fax 1-42-33-44-98; e-mail jpviallon@ mieuxvivre.fr; internet www.mieuxvivre.fr; f. 1968; investment,

economics; Editorial Dir JEAN-ANTOINE BOUCHEZ; Editor-in-Chief FRANÇOIS DE WITT; circ. 248,387 (1999).

Le Nouvel Economiste: 10 rue du Faubourg Montmartre, 75009 Paris; tel. 1-55-33-30-00; fax 1-41-09-31-00; e-mail marcel.jalvy@ nouveleco.com; internet www.nouveleco.com; f. 1975 by merger; weekly; Chair. CLAUDE POSTERNAK; Editor-in-Chief YANNICK LE BOURDONNEC; circ. 117,090.

L'Usine Nouvelle: 12-14 rue Médéric 75815 Paris Cédex 17; tel.1-56-79-41-00; fax 1-56-79-42-34; internet www.usinenouvelle.com; f. 1945; weekly with monthly supplements; technical and industrial journal; Dir JEAN-LÉON VANDOOME; Editor-in-Chief JEAN-PIERRE GAUDARD; circ. 60,000.

Valeurs Actuelles: 10 place du Général Catroux, 75858 Paris Cédex 17; tel. 1-40-54-11-00; fax 1-40-54-12-85; internet www .valeursactuelles.com; f. 1966; weekly; politics, economics, international affairs; Editor FRANÇOIS D'ORCIVAL; circ. 100,000.

La Vie Financière: 14 blvd Poissonnière, 75308 Paris Cédex 09; tel. 1-53-24-40-40; fax 1-53-24-41-10; e-mail weblav@ groupe-expansion.com; f. 1945; weekly; economics and finance; Publishing Dir DAMIEN DUFOUR; Editorial Dir GEORGES VALANCE; circ. 102,605 (1999).

History and Geography

Acta geographica: 184 blvd Saint Germain, 75006 Paris; tel. 1-45-48-54-62; fax 1-42-22-40-93; e-mail socgeosg@societe-de-geographie .asso.fr; internet www.societe-de-geographie.asso.fr; f. 1821; quarterly of the Geographical Society of Paris; Chair. JEAN BASTIÉ.

Annales de géographie: 21 rue de Montparnasse, 75298 Paris; tel. 1-40-46-61-54; fax 1-40-46-62-21; f. 1891; every 2 months.

Cahiers de civilisation médiévale: 24 rue de la Chaine, 86022 Poitiers; tel. 5-49-45-45-63; fax 5-49-45-45-73; e-mail Marie-Helene .Debies@mshs-univ-poitiers.fr; f. 1958; quarterly; Dir MARTIN AURELL.

Historia: Paris; tel. 1-44-51-01-01; fax 1-44-51-01-00; internet www.historia.presse.fr; f. 1946; monthly; Dirs FRANÇOIS DE L'ESPEE, CHRISTIAN MELCHIOR-BONNET; circ. 104,097.

Revue d'histoire diplomatique: 13 rue Soufflot, 75005 Paris; tel. 1-43-54-05-97; fax 1-46-34-07-60; f. 1887; quarterly; Dirs MAURICE VAISSE, GEORGES-HENRI SOUTOU.

Revue Historique: Archives Nationales, 60 rue des Francs Bourgeois, 75003 Paris; f. 1876; quarterly; Dirs CLAUDE GAUVARD, JEAN-FRANÇOIS SIRINELLI.

Revue de synthèse: Centre International de Synthèse, 12 rue Colbert, 75002 Paris; tel. 1-42-97-50-68; fax 1-42-97-46-46; e-mail synthese@pour-la-science.org; internet synthese.pour-la-science .org; f. 1900; quarterly; Dir ERIC BRIAN.

Vingtième Siècle: Paris; f. 1984; 20th century history; Editor-in-Chief JEAN-PIERRE RIOUX.

Leisure Interests and Sport

Les Cahiers du Cinéma: 9 passage de la Boule Blanche, 75012 Paris; tel. 1-53-44-75-75; fax 1-43-43-95-04; e-mail courrier@ cahiersducinema.com; internet www.cahiersducinema.com; f. 1951; monthly; film reviews; Dir SERGE TOUBIANA; circ. 45,000.

Le Chasseur Français: 19 rue d'Orléans, 92200 Neuilly-sur-Seine; tel. 1-41-43-42-00; fax 1-41-43-42-90; f. 1885; monthly; hunting and shooting; Dir DANIEL DIGNE; Editor PIERRE LANCRENON; circ. 552,461 (2000).

France-Football: 4 rue Rouget de Lisle, 92793 Issy-les-Moulineaux Cédex 9; tel. 1-40-93-20-20; fax 1-40-93-20-08; f. 1946; twice-weekly; owned by Amaury Group; Editor GÉRARD ERNAULT; circ. 230,000 (Tues.), 100,000 (Fri.).

Pariscope: 149 rue Anatole France, 92534 Levallois-Perret Cédex; tel. 1-41-34-73-23; fax 1-41-34-78-30; internet www.pariscope.fr; f. 1965; listings and reviews of events in Paris and surrounding region; weekly; Editor-in-Chief PASCALE DACBERT-LEMAIRE; circ. 125,300.

Photo: 149 rue Anatole France, 92534 Levallois-Perret; tel. 1-41-34-73-27; fax 1-41-34-71-52; e-mail photo@hfp.fr; internet www .photo.fr; f. 1967; monthly; specialist photography magazine; circ. 87,400; Dir XAVIER GOUPY; Editor-in-Chief ERIC COLMET DAAGE.

Télé-Magazine: 28 rue Jean Jaurès, 92800 Puteaux; tel. 1-47-62-60-00; fax 1-47-76-07-29; f. 1955; weekly; Dir FRANCIS MOREL; Editor-in-Chief MONIQUE GAUTHIER; circ. 418,967.

Télé-Poche: 150 rue Galliéni, 92644 Boulogne-Billancourt; tel. 1-41-33-50-02; fax 1-41-33-57-48; f. 1966; weekly; television magazine; Pres., Dir-Gen. KEVIN HAND; Editor F. J. F. MORUZZI; circ. 1,800,000.

Télérama: 36 rue de Naples, 75008 129 blvd Malesherbes, 75017 Paris; tel. 1-48-88-48-88; fax 1-47-64-02-04; internet www.telerama.fr; f. 1972; weekly; radio, TV, film, literature and music; Dir PIERRE BÉRARD; circ. 599,912; also *Télérama Câble* (Dir CLAUDE SALES).

Télé 7 Jours: 149 rue Anatole-France, 92300 Levallois-Perret Cédex; tel. 1-40-88-60-00; fax 1-40-88-61-44; f. 1960; weekly; television; Dir FRANÇOIS DIWO; Editor-in-Chief ALAIN LAVILLE; circ. 2,800,000.

Vélo Magazine: 4 rue Rouget de Lisle, 92137 Issy-les-Moulineaux; tel. 1-40-93-23-45; fax 1-40-93-23-99; monthly; cycling.

Maritime

Le Droit Maritime Français: 190 blvd Haussmann, 75008 Paris; tel. 1-44-95-99-50; fax 1-42-89-08-72; f. 1949; monthly; maritime law; Editor STÉPHANE MIRIBEL.

Le Journal de la Marine Marchande et du Transport Multimodal: 190 blvd Haussmann, 75008 Paris; tel. 1-44-95-99-50; fax 1-42-89-08-72; e-mail moreux@club-internet.fr; internet www.moreux.fr/jmm/jourmm.htm; f. 1919; weekly shipping publication; Pres. SERGE MARPAUD; Editor-in-Chief JEAN-CLAUDE LUCAS.

Nouveautés Techniques Maritimes: 190 blvd Haussmann, 75008 Paris; tel. 1-44-95-99-50; fax 1-44-95-99-50; fax 1-44-95-99-50; fax 1-49-53-90-16; f. 1950; monthly; international shipbuilding and harbours; Editor ALAIN GIRARD.

La Pêche Maritime: 190 blvd Haussmann, 75008 Paris; tel. 1-44-95-99-50; fax 1-42-89-08-72; f. 1919; every 2 months; fishing industry; Pres. SERGE MARPAUD; Editor-in-Chief BERNARD LAVAGNE.

Religion and Philosophy

Actualité des Religions: 163 blvd Malesherbes, 75017 Paris; tel. 1-48-88-46-00; fax 1-42-27-04-19; internet actualite.religions@wanadoo.fr; f. 1999; Editor JEAN-PAUL GUETNY; circ. 40,000.

Études: 14 rue d'Assas, 75006 Paris; tel. 1-44-39-48-48; fax 1-44-39-48-17; e-mail assas@jesuites.com; internet perso.wanadoo.fr/assas-editions; f. 1856; monthly; general interest; Editor HENRI MADELIN.

France Catholique: 60 rue de Fontenay, 92350 Le Plessis Robinson; tel. 1-46-30-79-01; fax 1-46-30-04-64; e-mail francecath@aol.com; internet www.france-catholique.com; weekly; Dir ANNIE CHABADEL; circ. 20,000.

Pèlerin Magazine: 3 rue Bayard, 75008 Paris; tel. 1-44-35-60-60; fax 1-44-35-60-21; f. 1873; weekly; Dir BERNARD PORTE; Editor-in-Chief RENÉ POUJOL; circ. 344,974.

Prier: 163 blvd Malesherbes, 75017 Paris; tel. 1-48-88-46-00; fax 1-42-27-29-03; e-mail lecteurs@prier.org; internet www.prier.org; f. 1978; monthly; review of modern prayer and contemplation; circ. 62,611.

Revue des sciences philosophiques et théologiques: Librairie J. Vrin, 6 place de la Sorbonne, 75005 Paris; tel. 1-43-54-03-47; fax 1-43-54-48-18; e-mail contact@vrin.fr; internet www.vrin.fr; f. 1907; quarterly.

Témoignage Chrétien: 49 rue du Faubourg Poissonnière, 75009 Paris; tel. 1-44-83-82-82; fax 1-44-83-82-88; e-mail redac@tc-hebdo.com; f. 1941; weekly; Dirs PIERRE-LUC SEGUILLON, BERNARD GINISTY; circ. 30,000.

Tribune Juive: Paris; tel. 1-45-23-19-20; fax 1-45-23-13-04; internet www.col.fr/tj; fortnightly; Jewish affairs; Dir JEAN-PIERRE ALLALI.

La Voix Protestante: 14 rue de Trévise, 75009 Paris; tel. 1-47-70-23-53; fax 1-48-01-09-13; e-mail la.voix.protestante@wanadoo.fr; monthly review of Protestant churches; Editor DIDIER WEIL.

Science and Technology

Action Auto-Moto: 1 rue du Colonel Pierre Avia, 75015 Paris; tel. 1-46-48-48-48; fax 1-46-48-49-90; e-mail automoto@francenet.fr; internet www.auto-moto.com; monthly; cars; Dir PAUL DUPUY; Editor-in-Chief JEAN SAVARY.

Annales de Chimie—Science des Matériaux: Editions Scientifiques et Médicales Elsevier, 23 rue Linois, 75747 Paris Cédex 15; tel. 1-45-58-90-67; fax 1-45-58-94-24; e-mail jftimmel@elsevier.fr; f. 1789; 8 a year; chemistry and material science.

L'Argus de l'Automobile: 1 place Boieldieu, 75082 Paris Cédex 02; tel. 1-53-29-11-00; fax 1-49-27-09-50; internet www.argusauto.com; f. 1927; motoring weekly.

Astérisque: Montrouge; tel. 1-40-84-80-55; fax 1-40-84-80-52; f. 1973; monthly; mathematics; Dir L. SZPIRO; Sec. C. HÉTIER.

L'Astronomie: 3 rue Beethoven, 75016 Paris; tel. 1-42-24-13-74; fax 1-42-30-75-47; e-mail saf@calva.net; internet www.iap.fr/saf; f. 1887; monthly; publ. by Société Astronomique de France; Chair. ROGER FERLET.

L'Auto Journal: 43 rue du Colonel Pierre Avia, 75754 Paris; tel. 1-41-33-50-00; fax 1-41-33-57-04; fortnightly; cars; Editor-in-Chief MARC SCHLICKLIN.

Aviation Magazine International: Paris; tel. 1-42-02-40-41; f. 1950; fortnightly; circ. 30,000.

Biochimie: Centre universitaire des Saints Pères, 45 rue des Saints Pères, 75270 Paris Cédex 06; tel. 1-40-20-04-12; fax 1-40-20-04-22; e-mail redaction.biochimie@ibpc.fr; f. 1914; monthly; biochemistry; Editor-in-Chief M. GRUNBERG-MANAGO.

Electronique pratique: 2–12 rue de Bellevue, 75940 Paris Cédex 19; tel. 1-44-84-84-84; fax 1-42-41-89-40; e-mail redac@eprat.com; internet www.eprat.com; monthly; electronics; Editor BERNARD FIGHIERA.

Industries et techniques: 26 rue d'Oradour-sur-Glane, 75504 Paris Cédex 15; tel. 1-44-25-30-01; fax 1-45-58-15-19; e-mail webmaster-it@industries-techniques.com; internet www.industries-techniques.com; monthly; Dir PAUL WAGNER.

Ingénieurs de l'Automobile: 15 rue du 19 Janvier, 92380 Garches; tel. 1-47-01-30-08; fax 1-47-01-48-25; e-mail lcda@lcda.fr; internet www.lcda.fr; f. 1927; 8 a year; technical automobile review; Editor-in-Chief JEAN PIERRE GOSSELIN.

Matériaux et Techniques: 76 rue de Rivoli, 75004 Paris; tel. 1-42-78-52-20; fax 1-42-74-40-48; e-mail sirpe@cybercable.fr; f. 1913; monthly; review of engineering research and progress on industrial materials; Editor-in-Chief R. DROUHIN.

Le Monde Informatique: Immeuble Lafayette, 2 place des Vosges, 92051 Paris La Défense Cédex 65; tel. 1-49-04-79-00; fax 1-49-04-79-04; e-mail pahus@idg.fr; internet www.weblmi.fr; weekly; information science; Publshr MICHEL CRESTIN; Editor-in-Chief FRANÇOIS JEANNE.

Le Moniteur des Travaux Publics et du Bâtiment: 17 rue d'Uzès, 75002 Paris; tel. 1-40-13-30-30; fax 1-40-41-94-95; e-mail redac@groupemoniteur.fr; f. 1903; weekly; construction; Chair. MARC-NOËL VIGIER; Editor-in-Chief BERTRAND FABRÉ; circ. 67,000.

Psychologie française: 2 rue de la Liberté, 93526 Saint Denis, Paris Cédex 02; tel. 1-49-40-67-94; fax 1-49-40-64-73; f. 1956; quarterly; review of the Société Française de Psychologie; Editor NICOLE DUBOIS.

La Recherche: 57 rue de Seine, 75280 Paris Cédex 6; tel. 1-53-73-79-79; fax 1-46-34-75-08; e-mail courrier@larecherche.fr; internet www.larecherche.fr; monthly; review of the Société d'éditions scientifiques; Dir. STÉPHANE KHÉMIS; Editor-in-Chief GÉRARD CHEVALIER.

Science et vie: 1 rue du Colonel Pierre Avia, 75015 Paris; tel. 1-46-48-48-48; fax 1-46-48-48-67; internet www.science-et-vie.com; f. 1913; monthly; Pres. PAUL DUPUY; circ. 350,000.

Women's, Home and Fashion

Cosmopolitan: 10 blvd des Frères Voisin, 92792 Issy-les-Moulineaux Cédex 9; tel. 1-41-46-88-88; fax 1-41-48-84-93; Dir EVELYNE PROUVOST-BERRY; Editor JULIETTE BOISRIVEAUD.

Côté Femme: 3-5 rue Bayard, 75008 Paris; tel. 1-44-35-59-61; fax 1-44-35-60-37; f. 1922; weekly; Editor-in-Chief CLAUDINE LITAUD; circ. 234,637.

Elle: 149 rue Anatole-France, 92534 Levallois-Perret Cédex; tel. 1-41-34-60-11; fax 1-41-34-74-94; e-mail presse@elle.fr; internet www.elle.fr; f. 1945; weekly; Dir ANNE-MARIE PÉRIER-SARDOU; Editor-in-Chief VALÉRIE TORANIAN; circ. 358,400.

Femme Actuelle: 73–75 rue La Condamine, 75854 Paris Cédex 17; tel. 1-44-90-67-00; fax 1-44-90-67-14; e-mail femactu@prismapresse.com; f. 1984; weekly; Editor MARYSE BONNET; circ. 2,100,000.

Femme Pratique: Immeuble Nice, 455 promenade des Anglais, 06200 Nice; tel. 4-92-00-48-86; fax 1-64-25-21-01; f. 1958; monthly; Dir MAX BENSOUSSON; circ. 180,000 (1996).

Le Journal de la Maison: 20 rue de Billancourt, BP 406, 92103 Boulogne-Billancourt Cédex; tel. 1-41-10-13-00; fax 1-41-10-13-71; e-mail jean_francois.remy@bonnier.fr; monthly; home; Editor JEAN-FRANÇOIS REMY.

Marie-Claire: 10 blvd des Frères Voisin, 92792 Issy-les-Moulineaux Cédex 9; tel. 1-41-46-88-88; fax 1-41-46-86-86; internet www.marieclaire.presse.fr; f. 1954; monthly; Chair. EVELYNE PROUVOST-BERRY; Editor MONIQUE MAJEROWICZ; circ. 599,362.

Marie-Claire Maison: 10 blvd des Frères Voisin, 92792 Issy-les-Moulineaux; tel. 1-41-46-88-88; fax 1-41-46-86-86; f. 1967; monthly; home interest; Editor CAROLINE TINÉ; circ. 165,710.

Marie-France: 10 blvd des Frères Voisin, 92792 Issy-les-Moulineaux; tel. 1-41-46-88-88; fax 1-41-48-86-86; f. 1944; monthly; Editor CHARLOTTE SEELING; circ. 280,000.

Modes et travaux: 43 rue du Colonel Pierre Avià, 75015 Paris; tel. 1-42-99-40-40; fax 1-42-99-40-33; f. 1919; monthly; Editor CATHERINE GOURLAT; circ. 710,389.

Notre Temps: 3–5 rue Bayard, 75393 Paris Cédex 08; tel. 1-44-35-60-60; fax 1-44-35-60-31; e-mail notre.temps@wanadoo.fr; internet www.notretemps-mag.com; monthly; for retired people; Dir PATRICK DARDE; Editor REMY MICHEL.

Nous Deux: 152 rue Galliéni, 92644 Boulogne-Billancourt Cédex; tel. 1-41-86-86-86; fax 1-41-86-84-02; e-mail nous-deux@emapfrance.com; internet www.nousdeux.com; f. 1947; weekly; Editor ANNE-MARIE LESAGE; circ. 823,397.

Parents: 10 rue Thierry-le-Luron, 92592 Levallois-Perret Cédex; tel. 1-41-34-61-88; fax 1-41-34-70-79; magazine for parents; Dir XAVIER GOUPY; Editor-in-Chief CATHERINE LILIÈVRE; circ. 378,100.

Pleine Vie: 152 rue Galliéni, 92644 Boulogne-Billancourt Cédex; tel. 1-41-86-84-15; fax 1-41-86-85-63; f. 1997; monthly; Dir. ANNICK ALOMBERT; circ. 1,105,000.

Questions de femmes: 117 rue de la Tour, 75116 Paris; tel. 1-45-03-80-00; fax 1-45-03-80-20; f. 1996; monthly; Editor-in-Chief NATHALIE COTTIN.

Santé Magazine: 110 rue Marius Aufan, BP 318, 92304 Levallois-Perret Cédex; tel. 1-41-49-41-49; fax 1-40-89-04-30; e-mail direction @santemagazine.fr; internet www.sante.mag.com; f. 1976; monthly; health; Editor ANDRÉ GIOVANNI.

Vogue: 56A rue du Faubourg Saint Honoré, 75008 Paris; tel. 1-41-49-41-49; fax 1-40-89-04-30; e-mail magazine@vogueparis.com; internet www.vogueparis.com; monthly; Publr GARDNER BELLANGER; Editor-in-Chief JOAN JULIET BUCK.

NEWS AGENCIES

In 1995 there were some 216 news agencies in France.

Agence France-Presse: 11–15 place de la Bourse, BP 20, 75061 Paris Cédex 02; tel. 1-40-41-46-46; fax 1-40-41-46-32; internet www.afp.com; f. 1944; 24-hour service of world political, financial, sporting news, and photographs; 165 agencies and 2,000 correspondents all over the world; Pres. BERTRAND EVENO; Editor-in-Chief ERIC WISHART.

Agence Parisienne de Presse: 18 rue Saint Fiacre, 75002 Paris; tel. 1-42-36-95-59; fax 1-42-33-83-24; f. 1949; Man. Dir MICHEL BURTON.

Infomedia M.C.: 8 rue de la Michodière, 75002 Paris; tel. 1-47-42-14-33; fax 1-47-42-14-39; f. 1988; economic and financial news; Dir FRANÇOIS COUDURIER.

Foreign Bureaux

Agence Maghreb Arabe Presse (MAP) (Morocco): 1 blvd de la Madeleine, 75001 Paris; tel. 1-42-65-40-45; fax 1-42-66-26-43; e-mail map@francophonie.org; f. 1959; Correspondent MOHAMED RED-DADI.

Agencia EFE (Spain): 10 rue Saint-Marc, 75002 Paris; tel. 1-44-82-65-40; fax 1-40-39-91-78; e-mail agencia.efe.paris@wanadoo.fr; f. 1939; Bureau Chief ANNE LEROUX.

Agenzia Nazionale Stampa Associata (ANSA) (Italy): 29 rue Tronchet, 75008 Paris; tel. 1-42-65-55-16; fax 1-42-65-12-11; e-mail ansa.paris@wanadoo.fr; Bureau Chief GIAMPIERO GRAMAGLIA.

Associated Press (AP) (USA): 162 rue du Faubourg Saint Honoré, 75008 Paris; tel. 1-43-59-86-76; fax 1-40-74-00-45; e-mail apmail@ associatedpress.fr; internet www.associatedpress.fr; Bureau Chief ABNER KATZMAN.

Deutsche Presse-Agentur (dpa) (Germany): 30 rue Saint Augustin, 75002 Paris; tel. 1-47-42-95-02; fax 1-47-42-51-75; Bureau Chief HANNS-JOCHEN KAFFSACK.

Informatsionnoye Telegrafnoye Agentstvo Rossii—Telegrafnoye Agentstvo Suverennykh Stran (ITAR-TASS) (Russia): 27 ave Bosquet, 75007 Paris; tel. 1-44-11-31-80; fax 1-47-05-33-98; Correspondent ALEKSANDR KONDRASHOV.

IPS—Inter Press Service (Italy): 11 rue de Saint Simon, 75007 Paris; tel. 1-45-49-81-62; e-mail godoy@aol.com; Correspondent JULIO GODOY.

Jiji Tsushin-sha (Japan): 27 blvd des Italiens, 75002 Paris; tel. 1-42-66-96-57; fax 1-42-66-96-61; Bureau Chief YUKIO YOSHINAGA.

Magyar Távirati Iroda (MTI) (Hungary): 365 rue de Vaugirard, 75015 Paris; tel. 1-45-33-22-59; fax 1-45-33-22-06; e-mail grakos@ yahoo.fr; Correspondent GYÖRGY RAKOS.

Middle East News Agency (Egypt): 6 rue de la Michodière, 75002 Paris; tel. 1-47-42-16-03; fax 1-47-42-44-52; f. 1956; Dir MOHAMED EL-SHAMY.

Prensa Latina (Cuba): Paris; tel. 1-42-60-22-18; Bureau Chief RAMÓN MARTÍNEZ CRUZ.

Reuters (UK): 101 rue Réaumur, 75080 Paris Cédex 02; tel. 1-42-21-50-00; fax 1-40-26-69-70; internet www.reuters.fr; Dir DANIEL FOGEL; Editor-in-Chief F. DURIAUD.

Rossiyskoye Informatsionnoye Agentstvo—Novosti (RIA—Novosti) (Russia): 14 place du Général Catroux, 75017 Paris; tel. 1-42-27-79-21; fax 1-43-80-96-83; Bureau Chief N. VIKHLAEV.

United Press International (UPI) (USA): Paris; tel. 1-42-60-23-68; fax 1-42-60-30-98; Bureau Chief EDUARDO CUE.

Xinhua (New China) News Agency (People's Republic of China): 27–31 rue Médéric, 92110 Clichy-la-Garenne; tel. 1-41-06-97-30; fax 1-42-70-61-28; Bureau Chief QI YANG.

PRESS ASSOCIATIONS

Comité de Liaison de la Presse: tel. 1-42-46-67-82; liaison organization for press, radio and cinema.

Fédération Française des Agences de Presse (FFAP): Paris; tel. 1-42-93-42-57; fax 1-42-93-15-32; e-mail info@agencesdepresse .fr; internet www.agencesdepresse.fr; comprises five syndicates (news, photographs, television, general information and multimedia) with a total membership of 109 agencies; Dir JACQUES MORANDAT.

Fédération Nationale de la Presse Française (FNPF): 13 rue La Fayette, 75009 Paris; tel. 1-53-20-90-50; fax 1-53-20-90-51; f. 1944; mems. Syndicat de la Presse Parisienne, Syndicat Professionnel de la Presse, Magazine et d'Opinion, Syndicat de la Presse Quotidienne Régionale, Syndicat des Quotidiens Départementaux, Fédération de la Presse Périodique Régionale, Fédération Nationale de la Presse d'Information Spécialisée; Pres. ALAIN BOULONNE; Vice-Pres. LIONEL GUERIN.

Fédération Nationale de la Presse d'Information Spécialisée: 37 rue de Rome, 75008 Paris; tel. 1-44-90-43-60; fax 1-44-90-43-72; e-mail contact@fnps.fr; internet www.fnps.fr. CEO JEAN-MICHEL HUAN.

Fédération de la Presse Périodique Régionale: 72 rue d'Hauteville, 75010 Paris; tel. 1-45-23-98-00; fax 1-45-23-98-01; f. 1978; mems Syndicat de la Presse Hebdomadaire Régionale, Syndicat National des Publications Régionales, Syndicat de la Presse Judiciaire de Province; Chair. BERNARD BIENVENU.

Syndicat de la Presse Quotidienne Régionale: 17 place des Etats Unis, 75116 Paris; tel. 1-40-73-80-20; fax 1-47-20-48-94; f. 1986; regional dailies; Pres. JEAN-LOUIS PRÉVOST; Dir-Gen. BRUNO HOCQUART DE TURTOT.

PRESS INSTITUTE

Institut Français de Presse et des Sciences de l'Information: 92 rue d'Assas, 75006 Paris; tel. 1-44-41-57-93; fax 1-44-41-59-49; e-mail ifp@u-paris2.fr; f. 1951; studies and teaches all aspects of communication and the media; maintains research and documentation centre; open to research workers, students, journalists; Dir NADINE TOUSSAINT-DESMOULINS.

Publishers

Editions Albin Michel: 22 rue Huyghens, 75680 Paris Cédex 14; tel. 1-42-79-10-00; fax 1-43-27-21-58; internet www.albin-michel.fr; f. 1901; general, fiction, history, classics; Pres FRANCIS ESMÉNARD; Man. Dir RICHARD DUCOUSSET.

Editions Arthaud: 20 rue Monsieur le Prince, 75006 Paris; tel. 1-40-51-31-00; fax 1-43-29-21-48; f. 1873; arts, history, travel books, reference; Chair. CHARLES-HENRI FLAMMARION; Man. Dirs ALAIN FLAMMARION, JEAN-PIERRE ARBON.

Editions de l'Atelier/Editions Ouvrières: 12 ave Soeur Rosalie, 75013 Paris; tel. 1-44-08-95-15; fax 1-44-08-95-00; e-mail editions .atelier@wanadoo.fr; internet www.maitron.org/maitron/Dico/ atelier1.htm; f. 1929; religious, educational, political and social, including labour movement; Man. Dir FRANÇOIS DE PALMAERT.

Editions Aubier—Montaigne: 13 quai de Conti, 75006 Paris; tel. 1-40-51-31-00; fax 1-43-29-71-04; f. 1924; psychoanalysis, literature, philosophy, history and sociology; Man. Dir M. AUBIER-GABAIL.

J. B. Baillière: Paris; tel. 1-49-53-69-00; fax 1-49-53-01-65; f. 1818; science, medicine and technical books; Man. Dir PHILIPPE LEDUC.

Editions Balland: 33 rue Saint André des Arts, 75006 Paris; tel. 1-43-25-74-40; fax 1-46-33-56-21; f. 1967; literature; Chair., Man. Dir JEAN-JACQUES AUGIER.

Bayard Editions—Centurion: 3 rue Bayard, 75393 Paris Cédex 08; tel. 1-44-35-60-60; fax 1-44-35-61-61; e-mail communication@ bayard-presse.com; internet www.bayardpresse.fr; f. 1870; children's books, religion, human sciences; Man. Dir JEAN-CLAUDE DUBOST.

Beauchesne Editeur: 7 cité du Cardinal Lemoine, 75005 Paris; tel. 1-53-10-08-18; fax 1-53-10-85-19; f. 1900; scripture, religion and theology, philosophy, religious history, politics, encyclopaedias, periodicals; Man. Dir JEAN-PIERRE DRUAUD.

Editions Belfond: 12 ave d'Italie, 75627 Paris; tel. 1-44-16-05-00; fax 1-44-16-05-06; f. 1963; fiction, poetry, documents, history, arts; Chair. JÉRÔME TALAMON; Man. Dir FABIENNE DELMOTE.

Berger-Levrault: 17 rue Rémy Dumoncel, 75014 Paris; tel. 1-40-64-42-32; fax 1-40-64-42-30; e-mail blc@berger-levrault.fr; internet www.berger-levrault.fr; f. 1976; fine arts, health, social and economic sciences, law; Chair. MARC FRIEDEL; Man. Dir BERNARD AJAC.

De Boccard, Edition-Diffusion: 11 rue de Médicis, 75006 Paris; tel. 1-43-26-00-37; fax 1-43-54-85-83; f. 1866; history, archaeology, religion, orientalism, medievalism; Man. Dir DOMINIQUE CHAULET.

Bordas: Paris; tel. 1-42-79-62-00; fax 1-43-22-85-18; f. 1946; encyclopaedias, dictionaries, history, geography, arts, children's and educational; Chair. and CEO PATRICE MAUBOURGUET.

Editions Bornemann: 62 rue Blanche, 75009 Paris; tel. 1-42-82-08-16; fax 1-48-74-14-88; f. 1829; art, fiction, sports, nature, easy readers; Chair. and Man. Dir PIERRE C. LAHAYE.

Bottin, SA: Créteil; tel. 1-49-81-56-56; fax 1-49-77-85-28; business, finance, medicine, sports; Pres. JEAN PAUL DEVAI.

Buchet-Chastel: 18 rue de Condé, 75006 Paris; tel. 1-44-32-05-60; fax 1-44-32-05-61; e-mail buchet_chastel@wanadoo.fr; f. 1929; literature, music, crafts, religion, practical guides; Chair. SARA MICHALSKI; Gen. Man. HENRY MARCELLIN.

Calmann-Lévy, SA: 3 rue Auber, 75009 Paris; tel. 1-47-42-38-33; fax 1-47-42-77-81; f. 1836; French and foreign literature, history, social sciences, economics, sport, leisure; Chair. JEAN-ETIENNE COHEN-SEAT.

Editions Casterman: 36 rue du Chemin Vert, 75011 Paris; tel. 1-55-28-12-00; fax 1-55-28-12-60; e-mail info@casterman.com; internet www.casterman.com; f. 1857; juvenile, comics, fiction, education, leisure, art; Chair. DIDIER PLATTEAU; Man. Dir SIMON CASTERMAN.

Les Editions du Cerf: 29 blvd de Latour Maubourg, 75340 Paris Cédex 07; tel. 1-44-18-12-12; fax 1-45-56-04-27; internet www.editionsducerf.fr; f. 1929; juvenile, religion, social science; Chair. MICHEL BON; Man. Dir NICOLAS SED.

Chiron (Editions): 10 rue Léon-Foucault, 78184 Saint-Quentin-en-Yveline; tel. 1-30-14-19-30; fax 1-30-14-19-46; f. 1907; technical, sport, education, fitness, health, dance, games; Chair. and Man. Dir DENYS FERRANDO-DURFORT.

Armand Colin Editeur: 21 rue du Montparnasse, 75283 Paris Cédex 06; tel. 1-44-39-54-47; fax 1-44-39-43-43; e-mail infos@armand-colin.com; internet www.armand-colin.com; f. 1870; literature, fine arts, history, science, school and university textbooks; Man. Dir JEAN-MAX LECLERC.

Editions Complexe: Paris; tel. 1-46-34-00-76; fax 1-43-26-73-81; f. 1971; literature, history, politics.

Editions Dalloz: 31-35 rue Froidevaux, 75685 Paris Cédex 14; tel. 1-40-64-54-54; fax 1-40-64-54-60; e-mail ventes@dalloz.fr; internet www.dalloz.fr; f. 1824; law, philosophy, political science, business and economics; subsidiary of Vivendi Universal Publishing; Pres. CHARLES VALLÉE; Dir-Gen. PHILIPPE CHAGNON.

Dargaud: 15-27 rue Moussorgski, 75895 Paris Cédex 18; tel. 1-53-26-32-32; fax 1-53-26-32-00; e-mail info@dargaud.fr; internet www.dargaud.fr; f. 1943; juvenile, cartoons, comics, video, graphic novels; Chair. and Man. Dir CLAUDE DE SAINT-VINCENT.

La Découverte: 9 bis rue Abel Hovelacque, 75013 Paris; tel. 1-44-08-84-00; fax 1-44-08-84-39; e-mail decouverte@dial.oleane.com; f. 1959; economic, social and political science, literature, history; Man. Dir FRANÇOIS GÈZE.

Denoël Editeur: 9 rue du Cherche-Midi, 75006 Paris; tel. 1-44-39-73-73; fax 1-44-39-73-79; f. 1929; general literature, science fiction, crime, history; imprint of Editions Gallimard; Man. Dir OLIVIER RUBINSTEIN.

Editions Des Femmes Antoinette Fouque: 6 rue de Mézières, 75006 Paris; tel. 1-42-22-60-74; fax 1-42-22-62-73; f. 1973; mainly women authors; fiction, essays, art, history, politics, psychoanalysis, talking books; Dirs ANTOINETTE FOUQUE, MARIE-CLAUDE GRUMBACH.

Desclée De Brouwer: 76 bis rue des Saints Pères, 75007 Paris; tel. 1-45-49-61-92; fax 1-42-22-61-41; e-mail info@descleedebrouwer.com; internet www.descleedebrouwer.com; f. 1877; religion, philosophy, arts, human sciences; Dir MARC LEBOUCHER.

Diderot Editeur: 20 rue Notre Dame de Nazareth, 75003 Paris; tel. 1-48-04-91-45; f. 1995; science, fine arts, history of art and culture.

La Documentation Française: 29 quai Voltaire, 75344 Paris Cédex 07; tel. 1-40-15-70-00; fax 1-40-15-72-30; e-mail postmaster@ladocfrancaise.gouv.fr; internet www.ladocfrancaise.gouv.fr; f. 1945; government publs; politics, law, economics, culture, science; Man. Dir SOPHIE MOATI.

Dunod Editeur: 5 rue Laromiguière, 75005 Paris Cédex; tel. 1-40-46-35-00; e-mail infos@dunod.com; internet www.dunod.com; f. 1800; science, computer science, electronics, economics, accountancy, management, psychology and humanities; subsidiary of Vivendi Universal Publishing; Chair. CHARLES VALLÉE; Dir-Gen. PHILIPPE CHAGNON.

Edisud: La Calade RN 7, 13090 Aix-en-Provence; tel. 4-42-21-61-44; fax 4-42-21-56-20; e-mail info@edisud.com; internet www.edisud.com; f. 1971; Dir CHARLY-YVES CHAUDOREILLE.

ESF Editeur: 17 rue Viète, 75017 Paris; tel. 1-44-15-62-00; fax 1-46-22-67-45; f. 1928; business, humanities, social sciences, law, communications, new technology; Chair. GÉRARD DIDIER; Man. Dir FRANÇOISE DAUZAT.

Eyrolles: 61 blvd Saint Germain, 75240 Paris Cédex 05; tel. 1-44-41-11-11; fax 1-44-41-11-44; f. 1918; science, technology, electronics, management, law; Man. Dirs JEAN-PIERRE TISSIER.

Fayard: 75 rue des Saints Pères, 75278 Paris Cédex 06; tel. 1-45-49-82-00; fax 1-42-22-40-17; internet www.editions-fayard.fr; f. 1857;

literature, biography, history, religion, essays, music; Chair. CLAUDE DURAND; Man. Editor JEAN-MARC ROBERTS.

Librairie Ernest Flammarion: 26 rue Racine, 75006 Paris; tel. 1-40-51-31-00; fax 1-43-29-76-44; f. 1875; general literature, art, human sciences, sport, children's books, medicine; Chair. CHARLES-HENRI FLAMMARION; Man. Dir DANIELLE NEES.

Fleuve Noir: 12 ave d'Italie, 75627 Paris Cédex 13; tel. 1-44-16-05-07; e-mail beatrice.duval@havaspoche.com; fax 1-44-16-05-11; subsidiary of Vivendi Universal Publishing; crime and science fiction; Chair. JEAN-CLAUDE DUBOST; Man. Dir BEATRICE DUVAL.

Les Editions Foucher: 31 rue du Fleurus, 75278 Paris Cédex 06; tel. 1-49-54-35-35; fax 1-49-54-35-00; e-mail cfages@editions-foucher.fr; internet www.editions-foucher.fr; f. 1936; science, economics, law, medicine text-books; Chair. and Man. Dir BERNARD FOULON.

Editions Gallimard: 5 rue Sébastien-Bottin, 75328 Paris Cédex 7; tel. 1-49-54-42-00; fax 1-45-44-94-03; e-mail pub@gallimard.fr; internet www.gallimard.fr; f. 1921; general fiction, literature, history, poetry, children's, philosophy; Man. Dir PIERRE MARCHAND.

Editions Grasset et Fasquelle: 61 rue des Saints-Pères, 75006 Paris; tel. 1-44-39-22-00; fax 1-42-22-64-18; e-mail afarges@edition-grasset.fr; internet www.edition-grasset.fr; f. 1907; contemporary literature, criticism, general fiction and children's books; Pres. OLIVIER NORA.

Groupe Fleurus-Mame: 15-27 rue Moussorgski, 75895 Paris Cédex 18; tel. 1-53-26-33-35; fax 1-53-26-33-36; arts, education, leisure; Chair. VINCENT MONTAGNE; Man. Dir PIERRE-MARIE DUMONT; also Fleurus Idées, Fleurus Enfants, Fleurus Jeunesse, Fleurus Tardy, Critérion, Desclée, Droguet-Ardant.

Librairie Gründ: 60 rue Mazarine, 75006 Paris; tel. 1-43-29-87-40; fax 1-43-29-49-86; internet www.grund.fr; f. 1880; art, natural history, children's books, guides; Chair. ALAIN GRÜND.

Hachette Livre: 43 quai de Grenelle, 75905 Paris Cédex 15; tel. 1-43-92-30-00; fax 1-43-92-30-30; internet www.hachette-livre.fr; f. 1826; group includes Hachette Education, Hachette Jeunesse, Hachette Littératures, Hachette Référence; Chair., Man. Dir JEAN-LOUIS LISIMACHIO.

L'Harmattan Edition: 7 rue de l'Ecole Polytechnique, 75005 Paris; tel. 1-43-54-79-10; fax 1-43-25-82-03; e-mail harmat@worldnet.fr; internet www.editions-harmattan.fr; f. 1975; politics, human sciences, developing countries; Dir DENIS PRYEN.

Editions Hatier: 8 rue d'Assas, 75278 Paris Cédex 06; tel. 1-49-54-49-54; fax 1-40-49-00-45; e-mail mnmalapert@editions-hatier.fr; internet www.editions-hatier.fr; f. 1880; children's books, fiction, history, science, nature guides; Chair. BERNARD FOULON.

Hermann: 293 rue Lecourbe, 75015 Paris; tel. 1-45-57-45-40; fax 1-40-60-12-93; f. 1870; sciences and art, humanities; Chair. PIERRE BERÈS.

I.D. Music, SA: 29 rue de Bitche, 92400 Courbevoie; tel. 1-41-88-98-98; fax 1-47-68-74-28; e-mail idmusic@easynet.fr; f. 1988; music; Dir PHILIPPE AGEON.

Editions Ibolya Virag: 11 rue du Grand-Prieuré, 75011 Paris; tel. and fax 1-43-07-70-16; e-mail virag@optyma.fr; f. 1996; fiction, history, Central and Eastern Europe, Russia and Central Asia; Dir IBOLYA VIRAG.

J'ai Lu: 84 rue de Grenelle, 75007 Paris; tel. 1-44-39-34-70; fax 1-45-44-65-52; e-mail ajasmin@jailu.com; internet www.jailu.com; f. 1958; fiction, paperbacks; subsidiary of Flammarion; Chair. CHARLES-HENRI FLAMMARION; Man. Dir FRÉDÉRIC MOREL.

Julliard: 24 ave Marceau, 75008 Paris; tel. 1-53-67-14-00; fax 1-53-67-14-14; internet www.lafont.fr/julliard/index.htm; f. 1931; general literature, biography, essays; imprint of Editions Robert Laffont; subsidiary of Vivendi Universal Publishing.

Karthala Éditions—diffusion: 22–24 blvd Arago, 75013 Paris; tel. 1-43-31-15-59; fax 1-45-35-27-05; e-mail www.karthala.com; e-mail karthala@wanadoo.fr; politics, history, developing countries.

Jeanne Laffitte: 25 Cours d'Estienne d'Orves, BP 1903, 13225 Marseille Cédex 01; tel. 4-91-59-80-49; fax 4-91-54-76-33; e-mail lafitte-jeanne@pacwan.fr; f. 1972; art, geography, culture, medicine, history; Chair. and Man. Dir JEANNE LAFFITTE.

Editions Robert Laffont: 24 ave Marceau, 75381 Paris Cédex 08; tel. 1-53-67-14-00; fax 1-53-67-14-14; e-mail bvernet@robert.laffont.fr; internet www.laffont.fr; f. 1941; literature, history, translations; subsidiary of Vivendi Universal Publishing; Chair. LEONELLO BRANDOLINI.

Librairie Larousse, SA: 21 rue du Montparnasse, 75298 Paris Cédex 06; tel. 1-44-39-44-00; fax 1-44-39-43-43; internet www.larousse.net; f. 1852; general, specializing in dictionaries, illustrated books on scientific subjects, encyclopaedias, classics, textbooks and periodicals; subsidiary of Vivendi Universal Publishing; Chair. and Man. Dir CHRISTIAN BREGOU.

Editions Jean-Claude Lattès: 17 rue Jacob, 75006 Paris; tel. 1-44-41-74-00; fax 1-43-25-30-47; e-mail mpageix@editions-jclattes.fr;

f. 1968; general fiction and non-fiction, biography; Man. Dir ISABELLE LAFFONT.

Letouzey et Ané: 87 blvd Raspail, 75006 Paris; tel. 1-45-48-80-14; fax 1-45-49-03-43; e-mail letouzey@free.fr; f. 1885; theology, religion, archaeology, history, ecclesiastical encyclopaedias and dictionaries, biography; Man. Dir FLORENCE LETOUZEY.

LGDJ—Montchrestien: Paris; tel. 1-43-35-01-67; fax 1-43-20-07-42; f. 1836; law and economy; Chair. LIONEL GUÉRIN; Man. Dir NATHALIE JOUVEN.

LITEC: 27 place Dauphine, 75001 Paris; tel. 1-43-26-26-86; fax 1-43-54-52-09; f. 1927; law, economics, taxation; Dirs ANJER HOLL, MARIELLE BERNARD.

Le Livre de Poche: 43 quai de Grenelle, 75905 Paris Cédex 15; tel. 1-43-92-30-00; fax 1-43-92-35-90; *Le Livre de Poche* paperback series, general literature, dictionaries, encyclopaedias; f. 1953; Chair. DOMINIQUE GOUST.

Editions Magnard: 20 rue Berbier-du-Mets, 75647 Paris Cédex 13; tel. 1-44-08-85-85; fax 1-44-08-49-79; e-mail l.breton@magnard.fr; internet www.magnard.fr; f. 1933; children's and educational books; subsidiary of Editions Albin Michel; Man. Dir LOUIS MAGNARD.

Masson Editeur: 120 blvd Saint Germain, 75006 Paris; tel. 1-40-46-60-00; fax 1-40-46-60-01; e-mail infos@masson.fr; internet www.masson.fr; f. 1804; medicine and science, books and periodicals; publrs for various academies and societies; subsidiary of Vivendi Universal Publishing; Pres. PIERRE DUTILLEUL.

Mercure de France, SA: 26 rue de Condé, 75006 Paris; tel. 1-43-29-21-13; fax 1-43-54-49-91; f. 1894; general fiction, history, biography, sociology; Chair. and Man. Dir ANTOINE GALLIMARD; Editor NICOLAS BREHAL.

Les Editions de Minuit: 7 rue Bernard Palissy, 75006 Paris; tel. 1-44-39-39-20; fax 1-45-44-82-36; e-mail presse@leseditionsdeminuit.fr; internet www.leseditionsdeminuit.fr; f. 1945; general literature; Chair. JÉRÔME LINDON; Man. Dir IRÈNE LINDON.

Nathan Education: 9 rue Méchain, 75014 Paris; tel. 1-45-87-50-00; fax 1-47-07-57-57; internet www.nathan.fr; f. 1881; educational books for all levels; Chair. BERTRAND EVENO; Man. Dir JEAN-PAUL BAUDOIN.

Editions Ouest-France: 13 rue du Breil, BP 6339, 35063 Rennes Cédex; tel. 2-99-32-58-27; fax 2-99-32-58-30; history, guides; Chair. FRANCOIS-XAVIER HUTIN; Man. Dir SERVANE BIGUAIS.

Editions Payot: 106 blvd Saint Germain, 75006 Paris; tel. 1-44-41-39-90; fax 1-44-41-39-69; e-mail payotrivages@wanadoo.com; f. 1917; literature, human sciences, philosophy; Chair. and Dir JEAN-FRANÇOIS LAMUNIÈRE.

Perrin: 76 rue Bonaparte, 75284 Paris Cédex 06; tel. 1-44-41-35-00; fax 1-44-41-05-02; f. 1884; history, biography; Chair. OLIVIER ORBAN; Man. Dir XAVIER DE BARTILLAT.

A. et J. Picard: 82 rue Bonaparte, 75006 Paris; tel. 1-43-26-96-73; fax 1-43-26-42-64; e-mail livres@librairie-picard.com; internet www.abebooks.com/home/libpicard; f. 1869; archaeology, architecture, history of art, history, pre-history, auxiliary sciences, linguistics, musicological works, antiquarian books; Chair. and Man. Dir CHANTAL PASINI-PICARD.

Plon: 76 rue Bonaparte, 75284 Paris Cédex 06; tel. 1-44-41-35-00; fax 1-44-41-35-01; f. 1844; fiction, travel, history, anthropology, human sciences, biography; Chair. OLIVIER ORBAN.

Presses de Sciences Po: 44 rue du Four, 75006 Paris; tel. 1-44-39-39-60; fax 1-45-48-04-41; e-mail info@presses.sciences-po.fr; internet www.sciences-po.fr; f. 1975; history, politics, linguistics, economics, sociology; Dir BERTRAND BADIE.

Presses Universitaires de France: 6 ave Reille, 75014 Paris; tel. and fax 1-58-10-31-00; e-mail info@puf.com; internet www.puf.com; f. 1921; philosophy, psychology, psychoanalysis, psychiatry, education, sociology, theology, history, geography, economics, law, linguistics, literature, science; Chair. MICHEL PRIGENT.

Presses Universitaires de Grenoble: 1041 rue des Résidences, BP 47, 38040 Grenoble Cédex 09; tel. 4-76-82-56-51; fax 4-76-82-78-35; e-mail pug@pug.fr; internet www.pug.fr; f. 1972; psychology, law, economics, management, history, statistics, literature, medicine, science, politics; Man. Dir BERNARD WIRBEL.

Presses Universitaires de Nancy: 42–44 ave de la Libération, BP 3347, 54014 Nancy Cédex; tel. 3-83-96-84-30; fax 3-83-96-84-39; e-mail pun@clsh.univ-nancy2.fr; internet www.univ-nancy2.fr/pun/presentation.html; f. 1976; literature, history, law, social sciences, politics; Chair., Man. Dir ALAIN TROGNON.

Privat, SA: 14 rue des Arts, BP 828, 31080 Toulouse Cédex 06; tel. 5-61-11-03-20; fax 5-61-13-74-41; e-mail privat@starway.tm.fr; f. 1839; regional, national and international heritage, history, health; Dir DOMINIQUE PORTÉ.

Quillet Diffusion: 58 rue Jean Bleuzen, 92170 Vanves; tel. 1-40-95-21-93; fax 1-40-95-22-35; f. 1902; specializes in dictionaries and encyclopaedias; Chair. ETIENNE VENDROUX; Man. Dir JACQUES SOYER.

Editions du Seuil: 27 rue Jacob, 75261 Paris Cédex 06; tel. 1-40-46-50-50; fax 1-43-29-08-29; internet www.seuil.com; f. 1936; modern literature, fiction, illustrated books, non-fiction; Chair. and Man. Dir CLAUDE CHERKI.

Editions Signe: Eckbolsheim, Strasbourg; f. 1987; religion; Chair. and Man. Dir CHRISTIAN RIEHL.

Editions Stock: 23 rue Cassette, 75006 Paris; tel. 1-42-84-87-00; fax 1-42-84-87-09; internet www.editions-stock.fr; f. 1710; literature, translations, biography, human sciences, guides; Chair., Man. Dir JEAN-MARC ROBERTS.

Succès du Livre: 60 rue St. André des Arts, 75006 Paris; tel. 1-43-29-82-82; fax 1-43-29-60-75; f. 1987; fiction, biography; Chair. JACQUES DOMAS.

Editions de la Table Ronde: 7 rue Corneille, 75006 Paris; tel. 1-43-26-03-95; fax 1-44-07-09-30; f. 1944; fiction, essays, religion, travel, theatre, youth; Man. Dir DENIS TILLINAC.

Editions Tallandier: 74 ave du Maire, 75014 Paris; tel. 1-44-10-12-90; fax 1-44-10-12-94; internet www.historia.presse.fr/service/tallandier.html; f. 1909; history, reference; Man-Dir ANNE-MARIE FINKELSTEIN.

Editions Vigot Frères: 23 rue de l'Ecole de Médecine, 75006 Paris; tel. 1-43-29-54-50; fax 1-46-34-05-89; f. 1890; medicine, pharmacology, nature, veterinary science, sport; Chair. CHRISTIAN VIGOT; Man. Dir DANIEL VIGOT.

Vivendi Universal Publishing (VUP): 31 rue du Colisée, 75383 Paris Cédex 08; tel. 1-53-53-30-00; fax 1-53-53-37-37; e-mail nicolas.watrin@havas.fr; internet www.havas.fr/fr; frmly Havas (f. 1832), renamed in 2000; education, literature, reference; imprints include Bordas, Dunod, Fleuve Noir, Harrap, Laffont, Larousse, Masson, Robert; 100% owned by Vivendi, sale expected in 2001; Pres. ERIC LICOYS; Vice-Pres. and Dir-Gen. AGNÈS TOURAINE.

Librairie Philosophique J. Vrin: 6 place de la Sorbonne, 75005 Paris; tel. 1-43-54-03-47; fax 1-43-54-48-18; e-mail contact@vrin.fr; internet www.vrin.fr; f. 1911; university textbooks, philosophy, education, science, law, religion; Chair. and Man. Dir A. PAULHAC-VRIN.

Librairie Vuibert: 20 rue Berbier-du-Mets, 75647 Paris Cédex 13; tel. 1-44-08-49-00; fax 1-44-08-49-39; e-mail laurence.brunel@vuibert.fr; internet www.vuibert.com; f. 1877; school and university textbooks, psychology, law; subsidiary of Editions Albin Michel.

PUBLISHERS' AND BOOKSELLERS' ASSOCIATIONS

Cercle de la Librairie (Syndicat des Industries et Commerces du Livre): 35 rue Grégoire de Tours, 75006 Paris Cédex; tel. 1-44-41-28-00; fax 1-44-41-28-40; f. 1847; a syndicate of the book trade, grouping the principal asscns of publishers, booksellers and printers; Chair. CHARLES-HENRI FLAMMARION; Man. Dir JEAN-MARIE DOUBLET.

Chambre Syndicale des Editeurs de Musique de France: 215 rue du Faubourg Saint Honoré, 75008 Paris; tel. 1-53-83-84-50; fax 1-45-63-62-91; f. 1873; music publishers' asscn; Chair. JEAN-MANUEL MOBILLION DE SCARAND; Sec. TRISTAN DE CELEYRAN.

Chambre Syndicale de l'Edition Musicale (CSDEM): 62 rue Blanche, 75009 Paris; tel. 1-48-74-09-29; fax 1-42-81-19-87; e-mail csdem@club-internet.fr; internet www.csdem.org; f. 1978 by merger; music publishers.

Fédération Française Syndicale de la Librairie: 49 rue de Châteaudun, 75009 Paris; tel. 1-42-82-00-03; fax 1-42-82-10-51; f. 1892; booksellers' asscn; 2,000 mems; Chair. JEAN LEGUÉ; Gen. Man. JEAN-BAPTISTE DAELMAN.

Syndicat National de l'Edition: 115 blvd Saint-Germain, 75006 Paris; tel. 1-44-41-40-50; fax 1-44-41-40-77; e-mail sbaroghel@snedition.fr; internet www.snedition.fr; f. 1892; publishers' asscn; 550 mems; Chair. SERGE EYROLLES; Man. Dir JEAN SARZANA.

Syndicat National de la Librairie: 40 rue Grégoire de Tours, 75006 Paris; tel. 1-46-34-74-20; fax 1-44-07-14-73; booksellers' asscn; Pres. ALAIN DIART.

Broadcasting and Communications

TELECOMMUNICATIONS
Regulatory Authorities

Agence Nationale des Fréquences (ANFR): 78 ave du Général de Gaulle, BP 400, 94704 Maisons-Alfort Cédex; tel. 1-45-18-72-72; fax 1-45-18-72-00; e-mail parmentier@anfr.fr; internet www.anfr.fr; Pres. JEAN-CLAUDE GUIGUET; Gen. Man. JEAN-MARC CHADUC.

Autorité de Régulation des Télécommunications (ART): 7 sq. Max Hymans, 75730 Paris Cédex 15; tel. 1-40-47-70-00; fax 1-40-47-71-98; internet www.art-telecom.fr; Pres. JEAN-MICHEL HUBERT; Gen. Man. PIERRE-ALAIN JEANNENEY.

Direction des Postes et Télécommunications (DPT): 20 ave de Ségur, 75354 Paris 07; tel. 1-43-19-19-39; fax 1-43-19-63-00; e-mail emmanuel.gabla@industrie.gouv.fr; Dir PATRICK DE GUERRE.

Major Service Providers

Cegetel: 1 place Carpeaux, Tour de l'Esplanade, 92915 Paris Cédex; tel. 1-41-97-70-35; fax 1-41-97-72-55; internet www.cegetel-entreprises.fr; f. 1996; 44% owned by Vivendi, 26% by British Telecommunications plc; affiliated cos include SFR, le 7, AOL France; turnover 19,000m. frs (1998); Dir OLIVIER HUART.

France Télécom: 6 place d'Alleray, 75505 Paris Cédex 15; tel. 1-44-44-89-34; fax 1-44-44-03-59; internet www.francetelecom.fr; 54% state-owned; acquired Orange (UK) in 2000; turnover 182,200m. francs (1999); Chair. MICHEL BON.

BROADCASTING

Conseil Supérieur de l'Audiovisuel (CSA): Tour Mirabeau, 39–43 quai André Citroën, 75739 Paris Cédex 15; tel. 1-40-58-38-00; fax 1-45-79-00-06; internet www.csa.fr; f. 1989 as replacement for the Commission Nationale de la Communication et des Libertés (CNCL); supervises all French broadcasting; awards licences to private radio and television stations, allocates cable networks and frequencies, appoints heads of state-owned radio and television companies, monitors programme standards; consists of nine members, appointed for six years: three nominated by the Pres. of the Republic; three by the Pres. of the National Assembly; and three by the Pres. of the Senate; Pres. DOMINIQUE BAUDIS; Gen. Man. LAURENT TOUVET.

Institut National de l'Audiovisuel: 4 ave de l'Europe, 94366 Bry-sur-Marne Cédex; tel. 1-49-83-20-00; internet www.ina.fr; f. 1975; research and professional training in the field of broadcasting; radio and TV archives; Pres. FRANCIS BECK.

Télédiffusion de France (TDF), SA: 10 rue d'Oradour-sur-Glane, 75732 Paris Cédex 15; e-mail e-tdf@tdf.fr; internet www.tdf.fr; f. 1975, partly privatized in 1987; subsidiary of Groupe France Télécom, responsible for broadcasting programmes produced by the production companies, for the organization and maintenance of the networks, for study and research into radio and television equipment; operates a cable television network; administrative council comprising 16 members, of which six are representatives of the State; Chair. BRUNO CHETAILLE.

Radio
State-controlled Radio

Public radio services are provided by three entities: Radio France for the domestic audience; Radio-Télévision Française d'Outre-Mer for the French overseas departments and territories; and Radio France International for foreign countries (and those of foreign origin in France). Radio France began the digital broadcasting of certain of its channels in early 2000.

Société Nationale de Radiodiffusion (Radio France): 116 ave du Président Kennedy, 75786 Paris Cédex 16; tel. 1-42-30-22-22; fax 1-42-30-14-88; internet www.radio-france.fr; f. 1975; planning and production of radio programmes; provides five national services, 49 local stations and two European services (see below); Chair. and Man. Dir JEAN-MARIE CAVADA; Man. Dir CLAUDE NOREK.

Radio France provides the following domestic radio services for a nationwide audience:

France Inter (general programmes, for entertainment and information); Dir JEAN-LUC HEES.
France Culture; Dir LAURE ADLER.
France Info (continuous news and information); Dir PASCAL DELANNOY.
France Musiques; Dir PIERRE BOUTEILLER.
Le Mouv' (music and general interest for young people).
Radio Bleu (for older people).

Radio France's local services comprise:

France Inter (38 decentralized local radio stations); Dir PATRICK PÉPIN.
Réseau FIP (nine local stations, continuous music); Dir DOMINIQUE PENSEC.

Radio France's European services (broadcast by TDF1/TDF2 satellite) comprise:

Hector (mainly classical music);
France Culture Europe (cultural and information).

Radio France Internationale (RFI): 116 ave du Président Kennedy, BP 9516, 75786 Paris Cédex 16; tel. 1-42-30-12-12; fax 1-42-30-47-59; internet www.rfi.fr; broadcasts on medium wave and FM transmitters, mainly to Africa, Eastern Europe, North America, the Caribbean, South-East Asia and the Middle East, in French and 18 other languages; Pres. JEAN-PAUL CLUZEL; Dir-Gen. CHRISTIAN CHARPY; Dir MICHEL MEYER.

Réseau France Outre-mer (RFO): 35-37 rue Danton, 92240 Malakoff; tel. 1-55-22-71-00; fax 1-55-22-74-76; e-mail rfo@rfo.fr; internet www.rfo.fr; controls broadcasting in the French overseas territories; ten local stations providing two radio networks, two television channels, the latter broadcasting material from various state and private channels as well as local programmes, and one satellite television channel; Pres. ANDRÉ-MICHEL BESSE.

Independent Radio

BFM: 43 rue Marius Jacotôt, 92800 Puteaux; tel. 8-36-68-96-40; e-mail dgarnier@radiobfm.com; internet www.radiobfm.com; f. 1992; broadcasts on cable and 14 FM frequencies; politics, economics; Chair. PATRICK FILLIOUD.

Europe 1: 26 bis rue François 1er, 75008 Paris; tel. 1-42-32-90-00; fax 1-47-23-19-00; internet www3.europeinfos.com; owned by Groupe Lagardère, which also owns Europe 2 and RFM; broadcasting on long wave and 99 FM frequencies; Chair. ARNAUD LAGARDERE; Man. Dir JÉRÔME BELLAY.

Radio Monte-Carlo (RMC): 12 rue Magellan, 75008 Paris; tel. 1-40-69-88-00; fax 1-40-69-88-55; broadcasting on long wave and 102 FM frequencies; Man. Dir JEAN-NOEL TASSEZ.

RTL: 22 rue Bayard, 75008 Paris; tel. 1-40-70-40-70; fax 1-40-70-42-72; internet www.rtl.fr; broadcasting on long wave and 150 FM frequencies; Chair., Man. Dir RÉMY SAUTTER.

Television
State-controlled Television

La Cinquième: 10–14 rue Horace Vernet, 92136 Issy-les-Moulineaux Cédex; tel. 1-41-46-55-55; internet www.lacinquieme.fr; f. 1994; educational programmes; Pres. MARC TESSIER.

France Télévision: 1 place Henri de France, 75015 Paris; tel. 1-44-31-60-00; fax 1-47-20-24-54; f. 1992 as supervisory authority for the two national public television networks (France 2 and France 3: see below); Pres. MARC TESSIER; Sec.-Gen. FRANÇOIS GUILBEAU.

Société Nationale de Télévision—France 2 (F2): 7 Esplanade Henri de France, 75907 Paris Cédex 15; tel. 1-56-22-42-42; e-mail contact@france2.fr; internet www.france2.fr; f. 1975 as Antenne 2 (A2); general programmes for a nationwide audience; Dir-Gen. MICHÈLE PAPPALARDO.

Société Nationale de Programmes—France 3 (F3): 7 Esplanade Henri de France, 75907 Paris Cédex 15; tel. 1-56-22-30-30; internet www.france3.fr; f. 1975 as France Régions 3 (FR3); general programmes for a nationwide audience (with a larger proportion of cultural and educational programmes than F2), and regional programmes transmitted from 13 regional stations; Dir-Gen. RÉMY PFLIMLIN.

Arte France: 8 rue Marceau, 92785 Issy-les-Moulineaux Cédex 9; tel. 1-55-00-77-77; internet www.arte.tv.com; f. 1986 as La Sept; arts, cultural programmes; Pres. JEROME CLÉMENT.

Television programmes for France's overseas departments and territories are provided by Réseau France Outre-mer (see under Radio).

Independent Television

Canal Plus: 85–89 quai André Citroën, 75711 Paris Cédex 15; tel. 1-44-25-10-00; fax 1-44-25-12-34; internet www.cplus.fr; f. 1984; 34% owned by Vivendi, 15% by Richemont, and the remainder by other companies; coded programmes financed by audience subscription; uncoded programmes financed by advertising sold by Canal Plus; specializes in drama (including cinema films) and sport; launched a 'pay-per-view' service for sports events in 1996; produces 21 theme channels in six countries; Pres. PIERRE LESCURE.

Demain!: 1 rue Patry, 92220 Bagneux; fax 1-44-25-72-00; internet www.demain.fr; f. 1997; owned by Canal Plus; information about employment for job-seekers; Dir-Gen.: MARTINE MAULÉON.

LCI (La Chaîne Info): 78 rue Olivier de Serres, 75015 Paris; tel. 1-40-45-23-45; internet www.lci.fr; f. 1994; news, information; Pres. ÉTIENNE MOUGEOTTE; Dir-Gen. JEAN-CLAUDE DASSIER.

M6: 89 ave Charles de Gaulle, 92573 Neuilly-sur-Seine Cédex; tel. 1-41-92-66-66; fax 1-41-92-66-10; f. 1986 as TV6, re-formed as M6 in 1987; 34% owned by Lyonnaise des Eaux, 40% by CLT, and smaller percentages by other shareholders; specializes in drama, music and magazines; Pres. JEAN DRUCKER; Dir-Gen. NICOLAS DE TAVERNOST.

Télévision Française 1 (TF1): 1 quai du Point du Jour, 92656 Boulogne-Billancourt Cédex; tel. 1-41-41-12-34; fax 1-41-41-28-40; internet www.tf1.fr; f. 1975 as a state-owned channel, privatized 1987; 40.1% owned by Bouygues SA, 3.0% by Société Générale, and smaller percentages by other shareholders, including 2.4% by TF1 employees; general programmes; Pres. PATRICK LE LAY.

Satellite Television

In 1984 TV5 began broadcasting programmes relayed from French, Belgian and Swiss television stations by satellite. In the same year, the French Government reached an agreement with Luxembourg to finance jointly a communal direct-broadcasting satellite television system (TDF1). TDF1 was inaugurated in 1988, and another satellite television system, TDF2 (financed by private investors), was launched in 1989. In 1993 the TDF1/TDF2 satellites were transmitting television programmes for Arte, Canal Plus and the MCM-Euromusique music channel, and radio programmes for Radio France (Hector and Elisa). Two telecommunications satellites, Télécom 2A and Télécom 2B, were also transmitting programmes for the principal television channels. In 1995 the Astra, Eutelsat and Télécom satellites were transmitting to the majority of the 1.0m. households that were able to receive satellite television. In 1996, with the advent of digital television programming, three new satellites, Canal Satellite, Télévision par satellite and AB Sat, were launched.

Cable Television

In 1999 a total of 116 television channels were available in France, including terrestrial, cable and pay-to-view channels. This compared with a total of 68 channels available in 1995, or 26 in 1990. The channels available to subscribers of cable television included the specialized national channels: Canal J for children, Ciné-Cinémas, providing cinema films, Planète, specializing in documentaries, and Eurosport France, local channels and foreign channels. The following are the principal operators of cable television:

Est Vidéocommunication: 26, blvd du Président Wilson, 67954 Strasbourg Cédex 9; tel. 3-88-76-44-60; fax 3-88-76-44-69; e-mail estvideo@evc.net; internet www.evc.net; f. 1988; 93,816 subscribers (1998); affiliated to Electricité de Strasbourg; Dir-Gen. FRANÇOIS HOLVECK.

France Télécom Cable: 3 rue Danton, 92240 Malakoff; tel. 1-55-58-34-00; fax 1-55-58-34-06; e-mail ftc.communication@wanadoo.fr; internet www.francetelecomcable.fr; f. 1993; 753,900 subscribers (1998); turnover 784m. francs (1999); Chair. PATRICK PINOCHET.

NC Numéricâble: 12–16 rue Guynemer, 92445 Issy-les-Moulineaux; tel. 1-55-92-46-00; fax 1-55-92-46-90; e-mail communication@ncnumericable.com; internet www.ncnumericable .com; f. 1997; affiliated to Canal Plus; 602,937 subscribers (1998); Pres. BERNARD COTTIN; Dir-Gen. CHRISTIAN KOZAR.

Noos: 20 place des vins de France, 75614 Paris Cédex 12; tel. 1-53-44-86-52; fax 1-53-44-86-55; e-mail admin@cybercable.fr; internet www.noos.com; f. 1986 as Lyonnaise Communications, affiliated to Groupe Suez Lyonnaise des Eaux; 633,405 subscribers (1998); Chair GILLES PELISSON; Dir-Gen. FRANÇOIS GUICHARD.

Réseaux Câblés de France: 92130 Issy-les-Moulineaux; tel. 1-46-48-77-77; fax 1-46-48-79-05; 66,951 subscribers (1998); Chair., Man. Dir MICHEL GILLARD.

Finance

(cap. = capital; p.u. = paid up; dep. = deposits; res = reserves; m. = million; brs = branches; amounts in French francs, unless otherwise stated)

BANKING

Central Bank

Banque de France: 39 rue Croix des Petits Champs, BP 140-01, 75049 Paris; tel. 1-42-92-42-92; fax 1-42-92-45-00; internet www.banque-france.fr; f. 1800; nationalized in 1946; became independent in 1994; acts as banker to the Treasury, issues bank notes, controls credit and money supply and administers France's gold and currency assets; in 1993 the National Assembly approved legislation to make the Banque de France an independent central bank, with a General Council to supervise activities and appoint the principal officials, and a nine-member monetary policy committee, independent of government control, to be in charge of French monetary policy; cap. and res €24,260.7m., dep. €35,679.1m., total assets €140,967.1m. (Dec. 1999). Gov. JEAN-CLAUDE TRICHET; Dep. Govs HERVÉ HANNOUN, JEAN-PAUL REDOUIN; 214 brs.

State Savings Bank

Caisse des depôts et consignations: 56 rue de Lille, 75356 Paris; tel. 1-40-49-56-78; fax 1-40-49-88-99; internet www.caissedesdepots .fr; f. 1816; manages state savings system, holds widespread investments in industrial cos; res €9,812.0m, dep. €135,858.0m., total assets €177,103.0m. (Dec. 1999); Pres. and CEO DANIEL LEBÈGUE; 1 br.

Commercial Banks

American Express Bank (France) SA: 11 rue Scribe, 75009 Paris Cédex 09; tel. 1-47-14-50-00; fax 1-42-68-17-17; f. 1957; cap. 310m., res 36.7m., dep. 1,660.9m. (Dec. 1997); Pres. GIAMPIERO PIERO GRANDI; Country Man. PIERO GRANDI; 4 brs.

Banque AGF: 14 rue Halévy, 75009 Paris; tel. 1-53-24-47-70; fax 1-53-24-45-54; internet www.banqueagf.fr; f. 1991 by merger as Banque du Phénix; owned by ABN AMRO France; cap. 38.7m., res 0.8m., dep. 20,479.7m. (Dec. 1995); Pres. PHILIPPE TOUSSAINT.

Banque Arabe et Internationale d'Investissement (BAII): 12 place Vendôme, 75001 Paris; tel. 1-47-03-23-45; fax 1-47-03-28-00; f. 1973; investment bank; cap. 650.8m., total assets 19,468.3m. (Dec. 1990); subsidiary of BAII Holdings, Luxembourg; Chair. ROBERT K. SURSOCK; Dir-Gen. PHILIPPE GASTON.

Banque CGM—Caisse de Gestion Mobilière: 6 rue des Petit Pères, 75002 Paris Cédex 02; tel. 1-40-20-20-00; fax 1-42-86-90-05; f. 1929; subsidiary of Compagnie Parisienne de Réescompte; cap. 84.1m., res 123.7m.(Dec. 1993), dep. 15,903.0m. (Dec. 1992); Chair., Dir-Gen. PHILIPPE DELIENNE.

Banque de Bretagne: 18 quai Duguay-Trouin, 35084 Rennes Cédex; tel. 2-99-01-77-77; fax 2-99-01-75-00; f. 1909; 100% owned by BNP Paribas; cap. 325.7m., res 109.8m., dep. 6,918.3m. (Dec. 1998); Pres. PATRICK DE VILLEPIN; 70 brs.

Banque Commerciale pour l'Europe du Nord (EUROBANK), SA: 79–81 blvd Haussmann, 75382 Paris Cédex 08; tel. 1-40-06-43-21; fax 1-40-06-48-48; f. 1921; cap. 1,215.8m., res 370.9m., dep. 4,637.9m. (Dec. 1999); Pres. ANDREÏ MOVTCHAN; Chair. IOURI PONOMAREV.

Banque de l'Economie du Commerce et de la Monétique: 34 rue du Wacken, 67913 Strasbourg Cédex 9; tel. 3-88-14-74-74; fax 3-88-14-75-10; e-mail becm@becm.creditmutuel.fr; internet www.becm.fr; f. 1992 as Banque de l'Economie—Crédit Mutuel; cap. 400m; CEO RODOLPHE STADDLER; Chair. of Supervisory Bd ETIENNE PFLIMLIN.

Banque Fédérative du Crédit Mutuel, SA: 34 rue du Wacken, BP 412, 67000 Strasbourg Cédex; tel. 3-88-14-88-14; fax 3-88-14-67-00; internet www.creditmutuel.fr; f. 1933; cap. 620.1m., res 4,675.8m., dep. 204,370.5m. (Dec. 1997); Chair. ETIENNE PFLIMLIN; CEO MICHEL LUCAS.

Banque Française de Crédit Coopératif (BFCC): 33 rue des Trois Fontanot, BP 211, 92002 Nanterre Cédex; tel. 1-47-24-85-00; fax 1-47-24-89-25; e-mail doc@coopanet.com; internet www.bfcc.fr; f. 1969; cap. 521.3m., res 177.6m., dep. 27,107.0m. (Dec. 1999); Pres. JEAN-CLAUDE DETILLEUX; Gen. Man. ROBERT DURAND; 54 brs.

Banque Française de l'Orient: 30 ave George V, 75008 Paris; tel. 1-49-52-17-00; fax 1-49-52-18-00; f. 1989 by merger; cap. 500.0m., res 391.7m., dep. 21,866.4m. (Dec. 1998); Pres. BERNARD UNGER; Chair. JEAN CHEVAL.

Banque La Henin: 73 rue d'Anjou, 75381 Paris Cédex 08; tel. 1-44-51-20-20; fax 1-44-51-25-25; f. 1949; 99.9% owned by Crédisuez, Paris; cap. 650.0m., res 468.3m., dep. 25,441.5m. (Dec. 1998); Chair. JACQUES LEBHAR; Man. Dir MARIE DENISE PONCHET; 34 brs.

Banque Hervet, SA: 127 ave Charles de Gaulle, 92200 Neuilly; tel. 1-46-40-92-87; fax 1-46-40-96-51; f. 1830; 97.5% state-owned; privatization and acquisition by Crédit Commercial de France (CCF) impending in 2001; cap. 110.2m., res 1,051.7m., dep. 25,063.4m. (Dec. 1998); Chair., Man. Dir PATRICK CAREIL; Gen. Man. ALAIN CADIOU; 78 brs.

Banque Intercontinentale Arabe: 67 ave Franklin D. Roosevelt, 75008 Paris; tel. 1-53-76-62-62; fax 1-42-89-09-59; f. 1975; cap. €90.0m., res €3.2m., dep. €388.7m. (Dec. 1999); Pres. MOHAMED BENHALIMA; Gen. Man. FARAG MOHAMED SHALLOUF.

Banque Internationale de Placement: 108 blvd Haussman, 75008 Paris; tel. 1-44-70-80-80; fax 1-42-93-03-30; f. 1979; cap. 193m., res 1,196.1m. (Dec. 1996); Chair. JEAN-LOUIS LAURENS; Gen. Mans JEAN-MICHEL MEPUIS, DOMINIQUE OULD FERHAT, PATRICK HÉNAFF.

Banque Nationale de Paris Intercontinentale, SA: 20 blvd des Italiens, 75009 Paris; tel. 1-40-14-22-11; fax 1-40-14-69-34; internet www.bnpgroup.com; f. 1940; 100% owned by BNP Paribas; cap. €30.5m., res. €418.1m., dep. €3,128.2m. (Dec. 1999); Chair. PIERRE MARIANI; CEO VINCENT DE ROUX.

Banque de Neuflize, Schlumberger, Mallet, Demachy: 3 ave Hoche, 75410 Paris Cédex 08; tel. 1-56-21-70-00; fax 1-56-21-84-60; internet www.banque-nsmd.f; f. 1966; subsidiary of ABN AMRO Bank NV; cap. €197.2m., res €92.9m., dep. €6,455.2m. (Dec. 1999); Chair. Supervisory Bd ROGER PAPAZ; Chair. Man. Bd HENRI MOULARD; 18 brs.

Banque OBC—Odier Bungener Courvoisier, SA: 57 ave d'Iéna, BP 195, 75783 Paris Cédex 16; tel. 1-45-02-40-00; fax 1-45-00-77-79; internet www.banque-obc.fr; f. 1960; cap. €220.7m., res €77.3m., dep. €7,018.3m. (Dec. 1999); Chair. and CEO MAGGIEL SCALONGNE.

Banque Régionale de l'Ouest, SA: 7 rue Gallois, BP 49, 41003 Blois Cédex; tel. 2-54-56-54-56; fax 2-54-56-54-00; e-mail brocommunication@bro.cic.fr; internet www.bro.fr; f. 1913; mem. of Crédit Industriel et Commercial Group; cap. 217.2m., res 154.3m., dep. 13,642.0m. (Dec. 1998); Chair. and CEO MICHEL MICHENKO; Gen. Man. JEAN-PIERRE BICHON; 95 brs.

Banque Sanpaolo, SA: 52 ave Hoche, 75382 Paris Cédex 08; tel. 1-47-54-40-40; fax 1-47-54-46-57; cap. 2,100.0m., res 397.8m., dep. 30,632.5m. (Dec. 1999); Chair. LANFRANCO VIVARELLI; 52 brs.

Banque Scalbert-Dupont: 33 ave le Corbusier, BP 567, 59023 Lille Cédex; tel. 3-20-12-64-64; fax 3-20-12-64-05; e-mail international@bsd.tm.fr; f. 1977 by merger; cap. 300.0m., res 742.9m., dep. 31,055.9m. (Dec. 1999); Chair. CLAUDE LAMOTTE; Gen. Man. JÉRÔME GUILLEMARD; 150 agencies.

Banque Sudameris: 4 rue Meyerbeer, 75009 Paris; tel. 1-48-01-77-77; fax 1-42-46-32-13; e-mail webmaster@sudameris.fr; internet www.sudameris.com; f. 1910; cap. €185.0m., res €701.5m., dep. €14,346.1m. (Dec. 1999); active principally in South America; Chair. and Pres. E. MEUCCI.

Banque Worms, SA: Le Voltaire, 1 place des Degrés, Puteaux, 92800 Paris La Défense; tel. 1-49-07-50-50; fax 1-49-07-59-11; internet www. banque-worms.fr; f. 1928; 100% subsidiary of AXA; cap. 2,100.0m., res −423.9m., dep. 30,460.8m. (Dec. 1998); Chair. and CEO JÉRÔME MEYSONNIER; 18 brs.

Barclays Bank PLC: 21 rue Lafitte, 75002 Paris; tel. 1-44-79-79-79; fax 1-44-79-72-52; f. 1968; cap. 850m., res 278.2m., dep. 41,794.4m. (Dec. 1990); Gen. Man. CHRISTIAN MENARD; 71 brs and sub-brs.

BNP Finance: Paris; tel. 1-40-14-16-01; fax 1-40-14-16-80; f. 1980 as Banque Natiotrésorie; 100% owned by BNP Paribas; cap. 750.0m., res 96.5m., dep. 457,423.8m. (Dec. 1998); Chair JEAN-BERNARD LAFONTA; CEO FABRICE DE MEGLIO.

BNP Paribas: 16 blvd des Italiens, 75009 Paris; tel. 1-40-14-45-46; fax 1-40-14-69-40; internet www.bnpparibas.com; f. 1966 as Banque Nationale de Paris by merger, under state control, privatized 1993, acquired Paribas and renamed in 2000; cap. €1,799.0m., res €19,359.0m., dep. €457,175.0 (Dec. 1999); Chair. MICHEL PÉBEREAU.

BRED Banque Populaire: 18 quai de la Rapée, 75604 Paris Cédex 12; tel. 1-48-98-60-00; fax 1-40-04-71-57; internet www.bred.fr; f. 1919; fmrly Banque Régionale d'Escompte et de Dépôts; present name since 1994; cap. 1,250m., res 2,369.3m., dep. 46,304.3m. (Dec. 1999); Chair. STEVE GENTILI; Gen. Man. FRANÇOIS-XAVIER DE FOURNAS; 193 brs.

Caisse d'Epargne Ile de France Paris: 19 rue du Louvre, BP 9401, 75021 Paris Cédex 1; tel. 1-40-41-30-31; fax 1-42-33-45-18; f. 1818; savings bank; cap. €266.6m., res €303.1m., dep. €20,204.7m. (Dec. 1999); Pres. NICOLE MOREAU; Chair. BERNARD COMOLET; 301 brs.

Caisse Nationale de Crédit Agricole (CNCA), SA: 91–93 blvd Pasteur, 75015 Paris; tel. 1-43-23-52-02; fax 1-43-23-20-28; internet www.credit-agricole.fr; f. 1920; central institution for co-operative banking group comprising 53 Caisses Regionales; emphasis on agri-business; cap. 25,499.0m., res 114,640.0m., dep. 2,381,441.0m. (Dec. 1999); Chair. MARC BUÉ; CEO JEAN LAURENT; 7,958 brs.

Compagnie Financière du Crédit Mutuel de Bretagne: 29808 Brest Cédex 09; tel. 2-98-00-22-22; fax 2-98-60-27-24; internet www.cmb.fr; f. 1960; cap. 1,548.1m., res 2,779.0m., dep. 118,691.4m. (Dec. 1999); Chair. YVES LE BAQUER; Man. Dir CLAUDE FOUYET; 256 brs.

CPR: 30 rue Saint Georges, 75312 Paris Cédex 09; tel. 1-45-96-20-00; fax 1-45-96-25-55; e-mail dircom@cpr.fr; internet www.cpr.fr; f. 1928 as Compagnie Parisienne de Réescompte; present name adopted 1997; discount bank; cap. 88.6m., res 446.8m., dep. 13,957.7m. (Dec. 1998); Chair. ROBERT RAYMOND; Gen. Man. ALEC DE LEZARDIÈRE; 2 brs.

Crédit Agricole Indosuez: 9 rue Louis Murat, 75371 Paris Cédex 08; tel. 1-44-20-20-20; fax 1-44-20-29-56; internet www.ca-indosuez .com; f. 1975 as Banque Indosuez; owned by Caisse Nationale de Crédit Agricole (q.v.) since 1996; cap. 3,684.9m., res 10,543.4m., dep. 325,445m. (Dec. 1995).

Crédit Commercial de France (CCF), SA: 103 ave des Champs Elysées, 75008 Paris; tel. 1-40-70-70-40; fax 1-40-70-70-09; internet www.ccf.com; f. 1894; cap. €1,461.9m., res €809.4m., dep. €48,656.4m. (Dec. 1999); Chair. and CEO CHARLES DE CROISSET; 184 brs.

Crédit Foncier de France, SA: 19 rue des Capucines, BP 65, 75050 Paris Cédex 01; tel. 1-42-44-80-00; fax 1-42-44-99-96; e-mail communication@creditfoncier.fr; internet www.creditfoncier.fr; f. 1852; 90.6% owned by Caisse Nationale d'Epargne et de Prévoyance; mortgage banking; cap. 3,771.0m., res −2,541.7m., dep. 239,204.4m. (Dec. 1998); Chair. FRANÇOIS LEMASSON; Dir.Gen. ALAIN LEMAIRE.

Crédit Industriel d'Alsace et de Lorraine (CIC Banque CIAL): 31 rue Jean Wenger-Valentin, 67000 Strasbourg; tel. 3-88-37-61-23; fax 3-88-37-71-81; e-mail documentation@banquecial.fr; internet www.banquecial.fr; f. 1919; 99.99% owned by Crédit Industriel et Commercial; cap. 160.5m., res 3,819.2m. dep. 133,874.8m. (Dec. 1999); Chair. PHILIPPE VIDAL; Gen. Man. PIERRE JACHEZ; 147 brs and sub-brs.

Crédit Industriel et Commercial (CIC): 6 ave de Provence, 75452 Paris Cédex 09; tel. 1-45-96-96-96; fax 1-45-96-96-66; f. 1859; 68.9% owned by Banque Fédérative du Crédit Mutuel; cap. 3,501.0m., res 15,822.0m., dep. 601,301.0m. (Dec. 1999); Chair. MICHEL LUCAS.

Crédit Industriel de Normandie, SA (Banque CIN): 15 place de la Pucelle d'Orléans, BP 3026, 76041 Rouen Cédex; tel. 2-35-08-64-00; fax 2-35-08-64-38; f. 1932; 100% owned by Crédit Industriel et Commercial; cap. 400.0m., res 108.3m., dep. 14,202.4m. (Dec. 1999); Chair. GÉRARD ROMEDENNE; Gen. Man. JÉROME GUILLEMARD; 7 brs and 71 sub-brs.

Crédit Industriel de l'Ouest, SA (Banque CIO): 2 ave Jean-Claude Bonduelle, 44040 Nantes; tel. 2-40-12-91-91; fax 2-40-12-92-07; internet www.cic-banques.fr/cio; f. 1957; cap. 241.4m., res 805.9m., dep. 35,423.4m. (Dec. 1999); Chair. BENOÎT DE LA SEIGLIÈRE; Man. Dir GÉRARD GOULET; 13 brs and 181 sub-brs.

Crédit Lyonnais, SA: 19 blvd des Italiens, 75002 Paris; tel. 1-42-95-70-00; fax 1-53-02-73-83; internet www.creditlyonnais.com; f. 1863; privatized in July 1999; cap. 1,693.0m., res 5,100.0m., dep. 158,929.0m. (Dec. 1999); Chair. JEAN PEYRELEVADE; Gen. Man. DOMINIQUE FERRARO; 2,100 brs.

Crédit du Nord, SA: 59 blvd Haussmann, 75008 Paris; tel. 1-40-22-40-22; fax 1-47-70-71-70; f. 1848; 80% owned by Société Générale; cap. €740.5m., res €91.1m., dep. €13,835.6m. (Dec. 1999); Pres. of Management Bd BRUNO FLICHY; 640 brs.

Fortis Banque France, SA: 56 rue de Châteaudun, 75009 Paris; tel. 1-42-80-68-68; fax 1-42-81-53-35; e-mail courrier@fortisbanque .fr; internet www.fortisbanque.fr; f. 1920; frmly Banque Parisienne de Crédit; cap. 230.6m., res 828.6m., dep. 14,936.4m. (Dec. 1999); Chair. MICHEL CLERCKX; 69 brs.

HSBC Bank France, SA: 20 bis ave Rapp, 75332 Paris Cédex 07; tel. 1-44-42-70-00; fax 1-44-42-77-77; f. 1966; cap. 456.3m., res 2,597.4m., dep. 2,382.3m. (Dec. 1997); Chair. J. DAVIES.

ING Bank (France), SA: 89-91 rue du Faubourg Saint-Honoré, 75008 Paris; tel. 1-55-27-70-00; fax 1-55-27-77-77; f. 1953, name changed from Banque Bruxelles Lambert France in 2000; cap. 2,000m., res 620.1m., dep. 19,955.1m. (Dec. 1998); Chair. MICHEL TILMANT; Dir-Gen. GUY BENIADA; 1 br.

Lyonnaise de Banque, SA: 8 rue de la République, 69001 Lyon; tel. 4-78-92-02-12; fax 4-78-92-03-00; e-mail ddi@lb.cicomore.fr; internet www.l-b.fr; f. 1865; cap. 1,313.4m., res 1,429.5m., dep. 65,768.9m. (Dec. 1999); Chair. DENIS SAMUEL LAJEUNESSE; Man. Dir RÉMY WEBER; 300 brs.

Natexis Banques Populaires: 45 rue Saint-Dominique, 75007 Paris; tel. 1-48-00-48-00; fax 1-48-00-41-51; f. 1999 by merger of Natexis Banque (f. 1997) and Caisse Centrale des Banques Populaires, cap €531.0m., res €2,320.0m., dep. €81,069.0m.); Chair. PHILIPPE DUPONT; Gen. Man. PAUL LORIOT.

SBT-BATIF: 34/36 ave de Friedland, 75008 Paris; tel. 1-47-54-80-00; fax 1-47-54-82-91; f. 1991 by merger; cap. 2,518m., res 11,885m., dep. 53,447m. (Dec. 1993); Chair. CLAUDE-ERIC PAQUIN; Man. Dir CLAUDE HAUVILLE.

Société de Banque Occidentale (SDBO): 8 rue de la Rochefoucauld, BP 302, 75425 Paris Cédex 09; tel. 1-49-95-70-00; fax 1-49-95-72-00; f. 1907; wholly-owned subsidiary of Crédit Lyonnais; cap. 515m., res 263.1m., dep. 19,688.5m. (Dec. 1993); Chair., Man. Dir PIERRE DOREL; 6 brs.

Société Bordelaise de Crédit Industriel et Commercial, SA: 42 cours du Chapeau Rouge, 33000 Bordeaux; tel. 5-57-85-55-00; fax 5-57-85-57-50; f. 1880; 100% owned by Crédit Industrial et Commercial; cap. 290.7m., res 68.5m., dep. 9,979.3m. (Dec. 1999); Chair. JEAN-PAUL ESCANDE; Man. Dir JEAN-PHILIPPE BRINET; 93 brs.

Société Générale, SA: Tour Société Générale, 92972 Paris La Défense; tel. 1-42-14-20-00; fax 1-40-98-20-99; internet www.socgen .com; f. 1864; cap. €3,785.0m., res €5,797.0m., dep. €290,294.0m. (Dec. 1999); Chair. and CEO DANIEL BOUTON; 2,000 brs.

Société Générale Alsacienne de Banque (SOGENAL): 8 rue du Dôme, 67003 Strasbourg Cédex; tel. 3-88-77-66-55; fax 3-88-77-60-09; internet www.sogenal.com; f. 1881; cap. 376.2m., res 3,174.5m., dep. 72,935.3m. (Dec. 1998); Chair., Man. Dir HENRI LASSALLE; 101 brs.

Société Marseillaise de Crédit, SA: 75 rue Paradis, 13006 Marseille; tel. 4-91-13-33-33; fax 4-91-13-55-15; e-mail infos@smc.fr; f. 1865; 100% owned by Crédit Industriel et Commercial; cap. 100.0m., res 401.0m., dep. 19,448.1m. (Dec. 1998); Chair. and CEO JOSEPH PEREZ; Gen Mans MAURICE DADONNE, EMMANUEL BARTHELEMY; 162 brs.

Société Nancéienne Varin-Bernier (CIC Banque SNVB): 4 place André Maginot, 54074 Nancy Cédex; tel. 3-83-34-50-00; fax 3-83-34-50-99; e-mail snvinter@snvb.cic.fr; internet www.snvb.fr; f. 1881; 100% owned by Crédit Industriel et Commercial; cap. 388.2m., res 1,002.1m., dep. 35,100.2m. (Dec. 1998); Chair. PHILIPPE VIDAL; Gen. Man. LUC DYMARSKI; 148 brs.

Union de Banques à Paris, SA: 17–19 place Etienne Pernet, 75738 Paris Cédex 15; tel. 1-45-30-44-44; fax 1-45-30-44-57; f. 1935; 100% owned by Crédit Industriel et Commercial; cap. 331.3m., res −102.7m., dep. 9,307.8m. (Dec. 1998); Chair. RAYMOND BERT; CEO JEAN-FRANÇOIS LE TREIS; 53 brs.

Union de Banques Arabes et Françaises (UBAF): 190 ave Charles de Gaulle, 92523 Neuilly Cédex; tel. 1-46-40-61-01; fax 1-

47-38-13-88; internet www.ubafrance.com; f. 1970; cap. 1,492.0m., res 467.6m., dep. 14,518.1m. (Dec. 1999); Chair. Supervisory Bd MOHAMED SEQAT; Chair. Management Bd HUBERT DÉPINAY.

Union Française de Banques (UFB Locabail): 14 rue Louis Blériot, BP 229, 92858 Rueil–Malmaison Paris Cédex; tel. 1-41-42-60-60; fax 1-41-42-77-21; f. 1950; 97.2% owned by BNP Paribas; cap. and res 3,130.0m., dep. 26,540.0m. (Dec. 1998); Chair. FRANÇOIS DAMBRINE; Man. Dir JACQUES MALLET; 60 brs.

Via Banque: 10 rue Volney, BP 27, 75002 Paris; tel. 1-49-26-26-26; fax 1-49-26-29-99; e-mail via.banque@wanadoo.fr; internet www.viabanque.fr; f. 1974; cap. 534.0m., res 1,040.4m., dep. 9,196.6m. (Dec. 1999); Chair. JEAN-CHRISTIAN P. MENARD; Gen. Man. PIERRE LAFFINEUR.

Supervisory Body

Association Française des Etablissements de Crédit (AFEC): 36 rue Taitbout, 75009 Paris; tel. 1-48-24-34-34; fax 1-48-24-13-31; f. 1983; advises Government on monetary and credit policy and supervises the banking system; Pres. MICHEL FREYCHE; Gen. Man. ROBERT PELLETIER.

Banking Association

Association Française des Banques: 18 rue La Fayette, 75440 Paris Cédex 09; tel. 1-48-00-52-52; fax 1-42-46-76-40; e-mail afb@afb.fr; internet www.afb.fr; f. 1941; 430 mems; Pres. JEAN LAURENT; CEO BERNARD MAUREL.

STOCK EXCHANGES

The Paris Stock Exchange (Bourse) was established in 1725. There are provincial exchanges at Bordeaux, Lille, Lyon, Marseille, Nancy and Nantes. During the 1980s the Paris Bourse underwent extensive changes and deregulation and a fully computerized clearing and settlement system, called Relit, was installed. The reforms allowed member firms to open their capital to banks, insurance companies and other financial institutions.

In September 2000 Euronext, the largest stock exchange in the euro zone, was formed by the merger of the stock exchanges of Paris (Paris Bourse), Brussels, Belgium (Brussels Exchanges) and Amsterdam, The Netherlands (Amsterdam Exchanges).

Euronext Paris: 39 rue Cambon, 75001 Paris; tel. 1-49-27-10-00; fax 1-49-27-14-33; e-mail d.lande@euronext.fr; internet www.euronext.fr; Chair. JEAN-FRANÇOIS THÉODORE.

Marché à Terme International de France (MATIF): 115 rue Réaumur, 75002 Paris; tel. 1-40-28-82-82; fax 1-40-28-80-01; e-mail s.larrede@euronext.fr; internet www.matif.fr; f. 1986; financial and commodities futures exchange.

Marché des Options Négociables de Paris (MONEP): c/o Euronext Paris; internet www.monep.fr; f. 1987.

Stock Exchange Associations

Commission des Opérations de Bourse (COB): 17 place de la Bourse, 75002 Paris; tel. 1-53-45-60-25; fax 1-53-45-61-00; e-mail rel-pub@cob.fr; internet www.cob.fr; f. 1967; 240 mems; Chair. MICHEL PRADA.

Fédération Française des Clubs d'Investissement (FFCI): 39 rue Cambon, 75001 Paris; tel. 1-42-60-12-47; fax 1-42-60-10-14; e-mail fnaci@club-internet.fr; internet www.ffci.org; f. 1968; fmrly Fédération Nationale des Associations de Clubs d'Investissement (FNACI); represents investment clubs in matters concerning public and political institutions; Pres. CLAUDE VALLON.

INSURANCE

Abeille Vie: 57 rue Taitbout, 75442 Paris Cédex 09; tel. 1-55-50-55-50; fax 1-55-50-48-72; turnover 11,200m. frs (1999); Pres. BERNARD POTTIER; Dir BRUNO ROSTAIN.

Assurances du Crédit Mutuel IARD, SA: BP 373 R 10, 34 rue du Wacken, 67010 Strasbourg Cédex; tel. 3-88-14-90-90; fax 3-88-14-90-01; internet www.creditmutuel.fr; Pres. MICHEL LUCAS; Dir ALAIN SCHMITTER.

Assurances Générales de France (AGF): 87 rue de Richelieu, 75113 Paris Cédex 02; tel. 1-44-86-20-00; fax 1-49-27-99-57; internet www.agf.fr; f. 1968 by merger; affiliated to Groupe Allianz (Germany); insurance and reinsurance; cap. 407m.; Pres. ANTOINE JEANCOURT-GALIGNANI; Gen. Mans JEAN-FRANÇOIS DEBROIS, YVES MANSION.

AXA Assurances IARD: 21 rue de Châteaudun, 75441 Paris Cédex 09; tel. 1-53-21-16-00; fax 1-53-21-17-96; internet www.axa.com; Pres. CLAUDE TENDIL; Dir JEAN-LUC BERTOZZI.

Caisse Centrale des Assurances Mutuelles Agricoles: 8 rue d'Astorg, 75413 Paris Cédex 08; tel. 1-44-56-77-77; fax 1-44-56-72-74; affiliated to Groupama; Pres. JEAN BALIGNARD; Dir BERNARD DELAS.

Caisse Nationale de Prévoyance-Assurances (CNP): 4 place Raoul Dautry, 75716 Paris Cédex 15; tel. 1-42-18-88-88; fax 1-42-34-70-14; general insurance; Pres GILLES BENOIST, EDMOND ALPHANDERY.

Cardif Société Vie: 5 ave Kleber, 75798 Paris Cédex 16; tel. 1-41-42-83-00; fax 1-41-42-84-17; internet www.cardif.fr; general insurance; Pres. PIERRE DE VILLENEUVE; Dir-Gen. RENAUD DUMORA.

Ecureuil Vie: 5 rue Masseran, 75007 Paris; tel. 1-44-49-64-00; fax 1-45-66-93-04; life insurance; Pres. JEAN-JACQUES DELAPORTE; Dir JEAN BABY.

ERISA: Immeuble Ile de France, 4 pl. de la Pyramide, 92800 Paris La Défense; tel. 1-41-02-40-40; fax 1-41-02-49-84; life insurance; affiliated to HSBC France; Pres. PATRICK POLLET; Dir JOËLLE DURIEUX.

La Fédération Continentale: 11 blvd Haussman, 75009 Paris; tel. 1-55-32-74-00; fax 1-55-32-74-01; e-mail webmastre@federation-continentale.fr; internet www.federation-continentale.fr; f. 1961; life insurance; Pres. JEAN-PHILLIPE THIERRY; Dir DANIEL COLLIGNON.

Garantie Mutuelle des Fonctionnaires: 76 rue de Prony, 75857 Paris Cédex 17; tel. 1-47-54-10-10; fax 1-47-54-18-97; internet www.gmf.fr; f. 1934; turnover 11,302,000 Frs (1999); Pres. YVES CAZAUX; Dir CHRISTIAN SASTRE.

Generali France Assurances: 5 rue de Londres, 75456, Paris Cédex 09; tel. 1-55-32-40-00; fax 1-55-32-40-05; e-mail mberger@gfa.generali.fr; internet www.gfa.generali.fr; turnover 16,100m. Frs (1999); Pres. HENRI MOULARD; Dir ERIC LE GENTIL.

GPA Assurances—Groupe Generali: 18 place des Cinq Martyrs du Lycée Buffon, 75695 Paris Cédex 14; tel. 1-40-47-15-15; fax 1-42-18-06-20; Pres. HENRI MOULARD; Dirs HERVÉ DE SAINT-GERMAIN, JEAN-YVES HERMENIER.

Groupama Vie: 5 rue du Centre, 93199 Noisy Le Grand Cédex; tel. 1-49-31-31-31; fax 1-49-31-31-98; e-mail webmaster@groupama.fr; internet www.groupama.fr; life insurance; Pres. JEAN BALIGAND.

Groupe des Assurances Nationales (GAN): 8–10 rue d'Astorg, Paris 75008; tel. 1-42-47-50-00; fax 1-42-47-67-66; e-mail gan.rimbault.philippe@wanadoo.fr; internet www.gan.fr; f. 1820 (fire), 1830 (life), 1865 (accident), affiliated to Groupama; Pres. JEAN-FRANÇOIS LEMOUX; Dir HENRI GUS.

La Mondiale: 32 ave Émile Zola, Mons en Baroeul, 59896 Lille Cédex 9; tel. 3-20-67-37-00; fax 3-20-47-70-90; internet www.lamondiale.fr; f. 1905; life insurance; turnover 17.4m Frs (1999); Pres. PATRICK PEUGEOT.

La Mutuelle d'Assurances du Commerce et de l'Industrie (MACI): BP 609, 8 rue de Dammartin, 59671 Roubaix Cédex 1; tel. 3-20-45-72-00; fax 3-20-45-72-36; Pres. GILBERT TOULEMONDE; Dir LUCIEN CATRY.

La Mutuelle du Mans Assurances IARD: 19 rue Chanzy, 72030 le Mans Cédex 09; tel. 2-43-41-72-72; fax 2-43-42-60-85; internet www.mma.fr; life and general insurance; f. 1828; Pres. JEAN-CLAUDE SEYS; Dir JACQUES LENORMAND.

Predica: 50 rue de la Procession, 75724 Paris Cédex 15; tel. 1-43-23-58-00; fax 1-43-23-03-47; internet www.predica.com; affiliated to Caisse Nationale du Crédit Agricole; general insurance; Pres. MAURICE GRANGEY; Dir MICHEL VILLATTE.

Préservatrice Foncière Assurances Vie (PFA Vie): Immeuble Athena, Cédex 43, 92076 Paris La Défense; tel. 1-42-91-10-10; fax 1-42-91-19-19; general insurance; Pres. ANTOINE JEANCOURT-GALIGNANI; Dir YVES MANSION.

Previposte: BP 7162, 4 Place Raoul Dautry, 75716 Paris Cédex 15; tel. 1-42-18-91-80; fax 1-42-18-94-94; life insurance; Pres. JACQUES OUVAROFF; Dir PHILIPPE DELVAL.

Socapi: 42 rue des Mathurins, 75008 Paris; tel. 1-44-71-52-00; fax 1-40-17-02-33; internet www.socapi.fr; f. 1985; 55% owned by Groupe Crédit Industriel et Commercial, 45% by Groupe des Assurances Nationales; life insurance; turnover 10,069m. Frs (1999); Pres. JEAN-PAUL GUILLOU; Gen. Man. JEAN VECCHIERINI.

Suravenir: BP 103, 232 rue Général Paulet, 29802 Brest Cédex 09; tel. 2-98-34-65-00; fax 2-98-34-65-11; internet www.suravenir.fr; f. 1984; general insurance; turnover 6,200m. Frs (1999); Pres. DENIS GUYARD; Dir HUMBERT DE FRESNOYE.

Union des Assurances Fédérales (UAF): 27 ave Claude Vellefaux, 75499 Paris Cédex 10; tel. 1-40-03-10-61; fax 1-40-18-36-93; internet www.uafdirect.fr; life insurance; affiliated to Crédit Lyonnais; turnover 15,000m. Frs (1999); Pres. JEAN-PIERRE WIEDMER; Dir BRICE LEIBUNDGUT.

Insurance Associations

Fédération Française des Courtiers d'Assurances et de Réassurances (FCA): 91 rue Saint Lazare, 75009 Paris; tel. 1-48-74-19-12; fax 1-42-82-91-10; e-mail ffca@wanadoo.fr; internet www.ffca.fr; f. 1991; Chair. FRANÇOIS LE CORNEC; c. 750 mems.

Fédération Française des Sociétés d'Assurances (FFSA): 26 blvd Haussmann, 75009 Paris; tel. 1-42-47-90-00; fax 1-42-47-93-11; internet www.ffsa.fr; f. 1937; Chair. DENIS KESSLER; Gen. Man. JEAN-PIERRE MOREAU; Sec.-Gen. GILLES WOLKOWITSCH.

Fédération Nationale des Syndicats d'Agents Généraux d'Assurances de France: 104 rue Jouffroy d'Abbans, 75847 Paris

Cédex 17; tel. 1-44-01-18-00; fax 1-46-22-76-29; Chair. JEAN-CLAUDE LECHANOINE.

Syndicat Français des Assureurs-Conseils: 14 rue de la Grange Batelière, 75009 Paris; tel. 1-55-33-51-51; fax 1-48-00-93-01; internet www.sfac-assurance.fr; Chair. HERVÉ DE WAZIÈRES.

Trade and Industry

GOVERNMENT AGENCIES

Centre Français du Commerce Extérieur: 10 ave d'Iéna, 75783 Paris Cédex 16; tel. 1-40-73-38-88; fax 1-40-73-39-79; e-mail orientation@cfce.fr; internet www.cfce.fr; Pres. ARIANE OBOLENSKY; CEO JEAN-DANIEL GARDÈRE.

Conseil National du Commerce: 8 pl. d'Iéna, 75783 Paris Cédex 16; tel. 1-44-34-68-34; fax 1-47-55-18-54; Chair. JACQUES DERMAGNE.

DEVELOPMENT ORGANIZATIONS

Agence Pour la Création d'Entreprises (APCE): 14 rue Delambre, 75682 Paris Cédex 14; tel. 1-42-18-58-58; fax 1-42-18-58-00; e-mail info@apce.com; internet www.apce.com; Pres. MICHEL HERVÉ.

Groupe IDI: 18 ave Matignon, 75008 Paris; tel. 1-55-27-80-00; fax 1-40-17-04-44; f. 1970 as Institut de Développement Industriel; provides venture capital, takes equity shares in small and medium-sized businesses; Chair. CHRISTIAN LANGLOIS MEURINNE; CEO F. MARMISSOLLE.

CHAMBERS OF COMMERCE

There are Chambers of Commerce in all the larger towns for all the more important commodities produced or manufactured.

Assemblée des Chambres Françaises de Commerce et d'Industrie: 45 ave d'Iéna, 75116 Paris; tel. 1-40-69-37-00; e-mail contactdie@acfci.cci.fr; internet www.acfci.cci.fr; f. 1964; Pres. JEAN-PAUL NOURY.

Chambre de Commerce et d'Industrie de Paris: 27 ave de Friedland, 75382 Paris Cédex 08; tel. 1-42-89-70-00; fax 1-42-89-72-86; internet www.ccip.fr; f. 1803; 273,000 mems in Paris and surrounding regions; Chair. MICHEL FRANCK; Man. Dir JEAN-DANIEL MARZOLF.

INDUSTRIAL AND TRADE ASSOCIATIONS

Assemblée Permanente des Chambres d'Agriculture (APCA): 9 ave George V, 75008 Paris; tel. 1-53-57-10-10; fax 1-53-57-10-05; e-mail accueil@apca.chambagri.fr; internet paris.apca.chambagri.fr; f. 1929; Chair. JEAN FRANÇOIS HERVIEU; Dir-Gen. ALAIN MOULINIER.

Association Nationale des Industries Alimentaires (ANIA): 155 blvd Haussmann, 75008 Paris; tel. 1-53-83-86-00; fax 1-45-61-96-64; e-mail infos@ania.net; internet www.ania.net; f. 1971; food and agricultural produce; Chair. VICTOR SCHERRER.

Centre des Jeunes Dirigeants d'Entreprise (CJD): 19 ave Georges V, 75008 Paris; tel. 1-53-23-92-50; fax 1-40-70-15-66; e-mail cjd@cjd.net; internet www.cjd.net; f. 1938; asscn for young entrepreneurs (under 45 years of age); Pres. LOUISE GUERRE.

Chambre Syndicale de l'Ameublement, Négoce de Paris et de l'Île de France: 15 rue de la Cerisaie, 75004 Paris; tel. 1-42-72-13-79; fax 1-42-72-02-36; e-mail info@meubleparis.com.fr; internet www.meubleparis.com.fr; f. 1860; furnishing; Chair. NICOLE PHILIBERT; 350 mems.

Chambre Syndicale des Céramistes et Ateliers d'Art de France: 4 passage Roux, 75017 Paris; tel. 1-44-01-08-30; fax 1-44-01-08-35; e-mail ateliers.art.de.france@wanadoo.fr; internet www.ateliersdart.com; f. 1886; ceramics and arts; Chair. VICTOR DESCHANG.

Chambre Syndicale des Constructeurs de Navires: 47 rue de Monceau, 75008 Paris; tel. 1-53-89-52-01; fax 1-53-89-52-15; shipbuilding; Chair. ALAIN GRILL; Gen. Man. FABRICE THEOBALD.

Comité Central de la Laine et des Fibres Associées (CCLFA): BP 121, 37–39 rue de Neuilly, 92113 Clichy Cédex; tel. 1-47-56-31-41; fax 1-47-37-06-20; e-mail cclfahdp@aol.com; internet www.textile.fr:81/laine.htm; f. 1922; manufacture of wool and associated textiles; Chair. CAMILLE AMALRIC; Vice-Chairs OLIVIER TOULEMONDE, CHRISTIAN DEWAVRIN; 240 mems.

Comité Central des Armateurs de France: 47 rue de Monceau, 5008 Paris; tel. 1-53-89-52-52; fax 1-53-89-52-53; e-mail caf@ccaf.asso.fr; internet www.ccaf.asso.fr; f. 1903; shipping; Pres. ALAIN WILS; Delegate-Gen. EDOUARD BERLET; 110 mems.

Comité des Constructeurs Français d'Automobiles: 2 rue de Presbourg, 75008 Paris; tel. 1-49-52-51-00; fax 1-49-52-51-88; e-mail cmory@ccfa.fr; internet www.ccfa.fr; f. 1909; motor manufacturing; Chair. YVES DE BELABRE; 9 mems.

Comité National des Pêches Maritimes et des Elevages Marins (CNPMEM): 51 rue Salvador Allende, 92027 Nanterre Cédex; tel. 1-47-5-01-01; fax 1-49-00-06-02; e-mail cnpmem@comite-peches.fr; internet www.comite-peches.fr; marine fisheries.

Comité Professionnel du Pétrole: Tour Corosa, 3 rue Eugène et rmand Peugeot, BP 282, 92505 Rueil-Malmaison Cédex; tel. 1-47-6-94-60; fax 1-47-08-10-57; e-mail cpdp@cpdp.org; internet www.cpdp.org; f. 1950; petroleum industry; 80 mems.

Commissariat à l'Energie Atomique (CEA) (Atomic Energy Commission): 31-33 rue de la Fédération, 75752 Paris Cedex 15; tel. 1-40-56-10-00; fax 1-40-56-29-70; e-mail dcom@aramis.cea.fr; internet www.cea.fr; f. 1945; promotes the uses of nuclear energy in science, industry and national defence; involved in production of nuclear materials; reactor development; fundamental research; innovation and transfer of technologies; military applications; biotechnologies; robotics; electronics; new materials; radiological protection and nuclear safety; Gen. Administrator YANNICK D'ESCATHA; High Commissioner RENÉ PELLAT.

Confédération des Industries Céramiques de France: 15 ave ictor Hugo, 75116 Paris; tel. 1-45-00-18-56; fax 1-45-00-47-56; e-ail ceramique@wanadoo.fr; f. 1937; ceramic industry; Chair. JACQUES RUSSEIL; Man. Dir FRANÇOIS DE LA TOUR; 111 mems, 7 affiliates.

Confédération Générale des Petites et Moyennes Entreprises et du Patronat Réel (CGPME): 10 Terrasse Bellini, 92806 Puteaux Cédex; tel. 1-47-62-73-73; fax 1-47-73-08-86; internet www.cgpme.org; f. 1945; small and medium-sized enterprises; Chair. JACQUES FREIDEL; 3,500 affiliated asscns.

Fédération des Chambres Syndicales de l'Industrie du Verre: 3 rue la Boétie, 75008 Paris; tel. 1-42-65-60-02; e-mail le_verre@compuserve.com; internet www.verre-avenir.org; f. 1874; glass industry; Chair. JACQUES DEMARTY.

Fédération des Chambres Syndicales des Minerais, Minéraux Industriels et Métaux non-Ferreux: 30 ave de Messine, 75008 Paris; tel. 1-45-63-02-66; fax 1-45-63-61-54; e-mail fmmnfx@aol.com; f. 1945; minerals and non-ferrous metals; Chair. JEAU CHOUVEL; Delegate-Gen. G. JOURDAN; 16 affiliated syndicates.

Fédération des Exportateurs des Vins et Spiritueux de France: 95 rue de Monceau, 75008 Paris; tel. 1-45-22-75-73; fax 1-45-22-94-16; e-mail contact@feus.com; f. 1921; exporters of wines and spirits; Pres. BERTRAND DEVILLARD; Delegate-Gen. LOUIS RÉGIS AFFRE; 450 mems.

Fédération Française de l'Acier: Immeuble Pacific, 11-13 Cours Valmy, 92070 Paris La Défense Cédex; tel. 1-41-25-58-00; fax 1-41-25-59-81; e-mail ffa@ffa.fr; internet www.ffa.fr; f. 1945; steelmaking; Chair. FRANCIS MER; Delegate-Gen. J.-C. GEORGES FRANÇOIS.

Fédération Française du Bâtiment: 33 ave Kléber, 75784 Paris Cédex 16; tel. 1-40-69-51-00; fax 1-45-53-58-77; e-mail ffbbox@ffb.fr; internet www.ffbatiment.fr; f. 1906; building trade; Chair. ALAIN SIONNEAU; Dir-Gen. BERTRAND SABLIER; 50,000 mems.

Fédération Française de l'Industrie Cotonnière: BP 121, 37–39 rue de Neuilly, 92113 Clichy Cédex; tel. 1-47-56-30-40; fax 1-47-56-30-49; e-mail ffic@fedcoton-laine.com; internet www.textile.fr:81/coton/coton.htm; f. 1902; cotton manufacturing; Chair. DOMINIQUE MEILLASSOUX; Vice-Chair. DENIS CHAIGNE; mems 71 (spinning), 153 (weaving).

Fédération Française du Négoce de Bois d'Oeuvre et Produits Dérivés: 251 blvd Pereire, 75852 Paris Cédex 17; tel. 1-45-72-55-50; fax 1-45-72-55-56; e-mail bois@nat.fr; timber trade; Pres. ANDRÉ TALON; Dir-Gen. LIONEL THOMAS D'ANNEBAULT.

Fédération Française de la Tannerie-Mégisserie: 122 rue de Provence, 75008 Paris; tel. 1-45-22-96-45; fax 1-42-93-37-44; e-mail fftm@leatherfrance.com; f. 1885; leather industry; 100 mems.

Fédération de l'Imprimerie et de la Communication Graphique: 68 blvd Saint Marcel, 75005 Paris; tel. 1-44-08-64-46; fax 1-43-36-09-51; e-mail contact@ficg.fr; internet www.ficg.fr; printing; Pres. FRANÇOIS GUTLÉ.

Fédération des Industries de la Parfumerie (France): 33 Champs Elysées, 75008 Paris; tel. 1-56-69-67-89; fax 1-56-69-67-90; makers of perfume, cosmetics and toiletries; Pres. ALAIN GRANGÉ CABANE.

Fédération des Industries Electriques et Electroniques (FIEE): Paris; tel. 1-45-05-70-70; fax 1-45-53-03-93; e-mail comm@fieec.fr; internet www.fieec.fr; f. 1925; electrical and electronics industries; Chair. HENRI STARCK; Delegate-Gen. JEAN-CLAUDE KARPELÈS; c. 1,000 mems.

Fédération des Industries Mécaniques: 39–41 rue Louis Blanc, 92400 Courbevoie; tel. 1-47-17-60-00; fax 1-47-17-64-99; e-mail fim@club.internet.fr; internet www.fim.net; f. 1840; mechanical and metal-working; Chair. MARTINE CLÉMENT; Man. Dir MARC BAŸ.

Fédération des Industries Nautiques: Port de Javel Haut, 75015 Paris; tel. 1-44-37-04-00; fax 1-45-77-21-88; e-mail fin@france-nautic.com; internet www.france-nautic.com; f. 1965; pleasure-boating; Pres. ANNETTE ROUX; Man. Dir TIBOR SILLINGER; 500 mems.

Fédération Nationale du Bois: 6 rue François 1er, 75008 Paris; tel. 1-56-69-52-00; fax 1-56-69-52-09; e-mail infos@fnbois.com; internet www.fnbois.com; f. 1884; timber and wood products; Chair. DOMINIQUE JUILLOT; 1,850 mems.

Fédération Nationale des Chambres Syndicales des Horlogers, Bijoutiers, Joailliers et Orfèvres (HBJO): 249 rue Saint Martin, 75003 Paris; tel. 1-44-54-34-00; fax 1-44-54-34-07; e-mail fedhbjo@wanadoo.fr; internet www.fedehbjo.com; jewellery, watch-and clock-making; Pres. GÉRARD ATLAN; 1,200 mems.

Fédération Nationale de l'Industrie Hôtelière (FNIH): 22 rue d'Anjou, 75008 Paris; tel. 1-44-94-19-94; fax 1-42-65-16-21; e-mail fnih@imagenet.fr; Chair. ANDRÉ DAGUIN.

Fédération Nationale de l'Industrie Laitière: Paris; tel. 1-45-62-96-60; dairy products; Pres. XAVIER PAUL-RENARD.

Fédération Nationale des Industries Électrométallurgiques, Électrochimiques et Connexes: 30 ave de Messine, 75008 Paris; tel. 1-45-61-06-63; fax 1-45-63-61-54; Chair. JACQUES GANI.

Fédération Nationale de la Musique: 62 rue Blanche, 75009 Paris; tel. 1-48-74-09-29; fax 1-42-81-19-87; f. 1964; includes Chambre Syndicale de la Facture Instrumentale, Syndicat National de l'Edition Phonographique and other groups; musical instruments, publications and recordings; Chair. PIERRE HENRY; Sec.-Gen. FRANÇOIS WELLEBROUCK.

Les Fondeurs de France: 45 rue Louis Blanc, 92038 Paris La Défense Cédex; tel. 1-43-34-76-30; fax 1-43-34-76-31; e-mail contact@fondeursdefrance.org; internet www.fondeursdefrance .org; f. 1897; metal casting; Chair. FRANÇOIS DELACHAUX; Man. Dir OLIVIER DUCRU; 300 mems.

Groupe Intersyndical de l'Industrie Nucléaire (GIIN): Paris; tel. 1-42-67-30-68; f. 1958; aims to promote the interests of the French nuclear industry; 200 member firms.

Groupement des Industries Françaises Aéronautiques et Spatiales (GIFAS): 4 rue Galilée, 75782 Paris Cédex 16; tel. 1-44-43-17-00; fax 1-40-70-91-41; e-mail infogifas@gifas.asso.fr; internet www.gifas.asso.fr; aerospace industry; Pres. JEAN-PAUL BÉCHAT.

Syndicat Général des Cuirs et Peaux Bruts: Bourse de Commerce, 2 rue de Viarmes, 75040 Paris Cédex 01; tel. 1-45-08-08-54; fax 1-40-39-97-31; f. 1977; untreated leather and hides; Chair. PIERRE DUBOIS; 60 mems.

Syndicat Général des Fabricants d'Huile et de Tourteaux de France: 118 ave Achille Peretti, 92200 Neuilly-sur-Seine; tel. 1-46-37-22-06; fax 1-46-37-15-60; f. 1928; edible oils; Pres. HENRI RIEUX; Sec.-Gen. JEAN-CLAUDE BARSACQ.

Syndicat de l'Imprimerie et de la Communication Graphique de l'Ile-de-France (SICOGIF): 8 rue de Berri, 75008 Paris; tel. 1-42-25-04-35; fax 1-42-25-04-32; f. 1991; printers' asscn; 700 mems; Chair. JOËL CARDINAL; Sec.-Gen. PHILIPPE QUEINEC.

Syndicat National de l'Industrie Pharmaceutique (SNIP): 88 rue de la Faisanderie, 75782 Paris Cédex 16; tel. 1-45-03-88-88; fax 1-45-04-47-71; e-mail dcre@snip.fr; internet www.snip.fr; pharmaceuticals; Chair. JEAN-JACQUES BERTRAND.

Union des Armateurs à la Pêche de France: 59 rue des Mathurins, 75008 Paris; tel. 1-42-66-32-60; fax 1-47-42-91-12; e-mail uapf75@wanadoo.fr; f. 1945; fishing-vessels; Chair. PATRICK SOISSON; Delegate-Gen. MICHEL DION.

Union des Fabricants de Porcelaine de Limoges: 7 bis rue du Général Cérez, 87000 Limoges; tel. 5-55-77-29-18; fax 5-55-77-36-81; porcelain manufacturing; Chair. MICHEL BERNARDAUD; Sec.-Gen. MARIE-THÉRÈSE PASQUET.

Union des Industries Chimiques: Paris La Défense; tel. 1-47-78-50-00; e-mail uicgeneral@uic.fr; internet www.uic.fr; f. 1860; chemical industry; Chair. J.-C. ACHILLE; Dir-Gen. C. MARTIN; 58 affiliated unions.

Union des Industries Métallurgiques et Minières (UIMM): 56 ave de Wagram, 75017 Paris; tel. 1-40-54-20-20; fax 1-47-66-22-74; e-mail uimm@uimm.fr; internet www.uimm.fr; metallurgy and mining; Chair. DANIEL DEWAVRIN; 223 mems.

Union des Industries Papetières pour les Affaires Sociales (UNIPAS): 154 blvd Haussmann, 75008 Paris; tel. 1-53-89-25-25; fax 1-53-89-25-26; e-mail unipas@aol.com; f. 1864; paper, cardboard and cellulose; Chair. MICHEL SORIANO; Gen. Man. DANIEL PLOIX; 500 firms affiliated.

Union des Industries Textiles (Production): BP 121, 37–39 rue de Neuilly, 92113 Clichy Cédex; tel. 1-47-56-31-00; fax 1-47-30-25-28; e-mail marc_journoud.uit@textile.fr; internet www.textile.fr/UIT/indexO_i.htm; f. 1901; Chair. GUILLAUME SARKOZY; 2,500 mems.

EMPLOYERS' ORGANIZATIONS

Association des Grandes Entreprises Françaises (AGREF): 63 rue la Boétie, 75008 Paris; tel. 1-43-59-65-35; fax 1-43-59-81-17.

Centre des Jeunes Dirigeants d'Entreprise (CJD): 19 ave Georges V, 75008 Paris; tel. 1-53-23-92-50; fax 1-40-70-15-66; e-mail cjd@cjd.net; internet www.cjd.net; f. 1938; Pres. LOUISE GUERRE.

Confédération Générale des Petites et Moyennes Entreprises et du Patronat Réel (CGPME): 10 terrasse Bellini, 92806 Puteaux Cédex; tel. 1-47-62-73-73; fax 1-47-73-08-86; internet www.cgpme .org; small and medium-sized cos; Chair. JACQUES FREIDEL.

Les Entrepreneurs et Dirigeants Chrétiens (Les EDC): 24 rue Hamelin, 75016 Paris; tel. 1-45-53-09-01; fax 1-47-27-43-32; e-mail lesedc@lesedc.org; internet www.lesedc.org; frmly Centre Français du Patronat Chrétien; asscn of Christian employers; Pres. JEAN BRUNET LECOMTE.

Mouvement des Entreprises de France (MEDEF): 31 ave Pierre Ier de Serbie, 75784 Paris Cédex 16; tel. 1-40-69-44-44; fax 1-47-23-47-32; f. 1946 as Conseil National du Patronat Français, name changed as above in 1998; an employers' organization grouping 1.5m. companies from all sectors of activity; Chair. ERNEST-ANTOINE SEILLIÈRE DE LABORDE; Exec. Vice-Chair. DENIS KESSLER.

UTILITIES

Electricity

Alcatel: 54 rue la Boétie, 75382 Paris Cedex 08; tel. 1-40-76-10-10; fax 1-40-76-14-00; internet www.alcatel.com; f. 1898; energy, nuclear energy and electrical contracting (also involved in industrial process control, telecommunications and business systems, cables and batteries, transportation); 125,000 employees; Chair. and CEO SERGE TCHURUT; Pres. JEAN-PIERRE HALBRON.

Charbonnages de France (CdF): Tour Albert 1er, 65 ave de Colmar, 92507 Rueil-Malmaison Cédex; tel. 1-47-52-35-00; fax 1-47-51-30-75; e-mail cdf.com@wanadoo.fr; internet www.groupe charbonnages.fr; established under the Nationalization Act of 1946; responsible for coal mining, sales and research in metropolitan France; there are also engineering and electricity divisions; 8,000 employees; Chair. and Dir-Gen. PHILIPPE DE LADOUCETTE.

Electricité de France: 2 rue Louis Murat, 75834 Paris Cédex 8; tel. 1-40-42-53-33; e-mail masteredf@edfgdf.fr; internet www.edf.fr; established under the Electricity and Gas Industry Nationalization Act of 1946; responsible for generating and supplying electricity for distribution to consumers in metropolitan France; 120,000 employees; Chair. FRANÇOIS ROUSSELY.

Gas

Gaz de France: 23 rue Philibert Delorme, 75840 Paris Cédex 17; tel. 1-47-54-20-20; fax 1-47-54-21-87; internet www.gazdefrance.com; established under the Electricity and Gas Industry Nationalization Act of 1946; responsible for distribution of gas in metropolitan France; about 10% of gas was produced in France (Aquitaine) in 1993 and the rest imported from Algeria, the Netherlands, Norway and the territories constituting the former USSR; Chair. PIERRE GADONNEIX.

Water

Suez: 1 rue d'Astorg, 75008 Paris; f. 1858; internet www.suez.com; frmly Suez-Lyonnaise des Eaux; present name adopted 2001; Pres. and CEO GÉRARD MESTRALLET.

Vivendi: ave Friedland, Paris; fmrly Compagnie Générale des Eaux; provides water and other environmental services, as well as telecommunications and construction; Chair. JEAN-MARIE MESSIER.

TRADE UNIONS

In late 1995 it was estimated that some 8% of the French labour force belonged to trade unions (compared with 18% in 1980).

There are three major trade union organizations:

Confédération Générale du Travail (CGT): Complexe Immobilier Intersyndical CGT, 263 rue de Paris, 93516 Montreuil Cédex; tel. 1-48-18-80-00; fax 1-49-88-18-57; e-mail info@cgt.fr; internet www.cgt.fr; f. 1895; National Congress is held every three years; Sec.-Gen. BERNARD THIBAULT; 650,000 mems.

Affiliated unions:

Agro-Alimentaire et Forestière (FNAF): 263 rue de Paris, Case 428, 93514 Montreuil Cédex; tel. 1-48-18-83-27; fax 1-48-51-57-49; Sec.-Gen. FREDDY HUCK.

Bois Ameublement (Woodworkers): 263 rue de Paris, Case 414, 93514 Montreuil Cédex; tel. 1-48-18-81-61; fax 1-48-51-59-91; Sec.-Gen. HENRI SANCHEZ.

Cheminots CGT (Railway Workers): 263 rue de Paris, Case 546, 93515 Montreuil Cédex; tel. 1-49-88-61-00; fax 1-48-57-95-65; e-mail cgtchem_coord@post.club-internet.fr; Sec.-Gen. DIDIER LERESTE.

Construction (Building): 263 rue de Paris, Case 413, 93514 Montreuil Cédex; tel. 1-48-18-81-60; fax 1-48-59-10-37; e-mail fdconstruction@wanadoo.fr; Sec.-Gen. MARCEL LE GUEN.

Equipement et l'Environnement: 263 rue de Paris, Case 543, 93515 Montreuil Cédex; tel. 1-48-18-82-81; fax 1-48-51-62-50; e-mail equipement.cgt@wanadoo.fr; Sec.-Gen. DANIEL SALANDRE.

Fédération Education Recherche Culture (FERC): 263 rue de Paris, Case 544, 93515 Montreuil Cédex; tel. 1-48-18-82-44; fax 1-49-88-07-43; e-mail ferc@cgt.fr; internet www.ferc.cgt.fr; Sec.-Gen. CHRISTIAN DUBOT.

Fédération Nationale des Mines et de l'Energie: 263 rue de Paris, Case 535, 93515 Montreuil Cédex; tel. 1-48-18-82-25; fax 1-48-51-60-36; e-mail international@fnme-cgt.fr; internet www.fnme.cgt.fr; Sec.-Gen. DENIS COHEN.

Finances: 263 rue de Paris, Case 540, 93515 Montreuil Cédex; tel. 1-48-18-82-21; fax 1-48-18-82-52; e-mail finances@cgt.fr; internet www.finances.cgt.fr; Sec.-Gen. PIERRETTE CROSEMARIE.

Fonctionnaires (UGFF) (Civil Servants): 263 rue de Paris, Case 542, 93515 Montreuil Cédex; tel. 1-48-18-82-31; fax 1-48-18-82-11; e-mail ugff.cgt@wanadoo.fr; groups National Education, Finance, Technical and Administrative, Civil Servants, Police, etc.; mems about 70 national unions covered by six federations; Sec.-Gen. BERNARD LHUBERT.

Industries Chimiques (Chemical Industries): 263 rue de Paris, Case 429, 93514 Montreuil Cédex; tel. 1-48-18-80-36; fax 1-48-18-80-35; e-mail fnic@cgt.fr; internet www.fnic.cgt.fr; Sec.-Gen. GEORGES HERVO.

Industries du Livre du Papier et de la Communication (FILPAC) (Printing and Paper Products): 263 rue de Paris, Case 426, 93514 Montreuil Cédex; tel. 1-48-18-80-24; fax 1-48-51-99-07; e-mail filpac@cgt.fr; internet www.filpac.cgt.fr; Sec.-Gen. MICHEL MULLER.

Ingénieurs, Cadres et Techniciens (Engineers, Managerial Staff and Technicians): 263 rue de Paris, Case 408, 93514 Montreuil Cédex; tel. 1-48-18-81-25; fax 1-48-51-64-57; e-mail g.delahaye@ugict.cgt.fr; internet www.ugict.cgt.fr; f. 1963; Sec.-Gen. GÉRARD DELAHAYE.

Intérimaires (Temporary workers): 263 rue de Paris, Case 460, 93514 Montreuil Cédex; tel. 1-48-18-84-16; fax 1-48-18-82-59; Pres. SAMUEL GAULTIER.

Journalistes: 263 rue de Paris, Case 570, 93514 Montreuil Cédex; tel. 1-48-18-81-78; fax 1-48-51-58-08; Sec.-Gen. MICHEL DIARD.

Officiers de la Marine Marchande (Merchant Marine): Cercle Franklin, 119 Cours de la République, 76600 Le Havre; tel. 2-35-25-04-81; fax 2-35-24-23-77; Sec.-Gen. CHARLES NARELLI.

Fédération des Travailleurs de la Métallurgie (FTM) (Metalworkers): 263 rue de Paris, 93514 Montreuil Cédex; tel. 1-48-18-21-21; fax 1-48-59-80-66; e-mail ftm@ftm-cgt.fr; internet www.ftm-cgt.fr; f. 1891; Sec.-Gen. DANIEL SANCHEZ.

Organismes Sociaux: 263 rue de Paris, Case 536, 93515 Montreuil Cédex; tel. 1-48-18-83-56; fax 1-48-59-24-75; e-mail fede@orgasociauxcgt.fr; internet www.orgasociauxcgt.fr; Sec.-Gen. PHILIPPE HOURCADE.

Personnels du Commerce, de la Distribution et des Services: 263 rue de Paris, Case 425, 93514 Montreuil Cédex; tel. 1-48-18-83-11; fax 1-48-18-83-19; e-mail federation-cgt-commerce@wanadoo.fr; Sec.-Gen. JACQUELINE GARCIA.

Police: 263 rue de Paris, Case 550, 93514 Montreuil Cédex; tel. 1-48-18-81-85; fax 1-48-51-14-43; e-mail cgt-police@wanadoo.fr; internet perso.wanadoo.fr/cgt-police; f. 1906; Sec.-Gen. PASCAL MARTINI.

Ports et Docks: 263 rue de Paris, Case 424, 93514 Montreuil Cédex; tel. 1-48-18-82-96; fax 1-48-18-82-94; Sec.-Gen. DANIEL LEFÈVRE.

Postes et Télécommunications: 263 rue de Paris, Case 545, 93515 Montreuil Cédex; tel. 1-48-18-54-00; fax 1-48-59-25-22; e-mail fede@cgt-ptt.fr; internet www.cgt-ptt.fr; Sec.-Gen. MARYSE DUMAS.

Santé, Action Sociale, CGT (Health and Social Services): 263 rue de Montreuil, Case 538, 93514 Montreuil Cédex; tel. 1-48-18-20-99; fax 1-48-18-29-80; e-mail santeas@cgt.fr; internet www.cgt.fr/santeas; f. 1907; Sec.-Gen. NADINE PRIGENT.

Secteurs Financiers: 263 rue de Paris, Case 537, 93514 Montreuil Cédex; tel. 1-48-18-83-40; fax 1-49-88-16-36; e-mail fnpsf@cgt.fr; Sec.-Gen. PHILIPPE BOURGALE.

Services Publics (Community Services): 263 rue de Paris, Case 547, 93514 Montreuil Cédex; tel. 1-48-18-83-74; fax 1-48-51-98-20; e-mail fdsp@cgt.fr; internet www.spterritoriaux.cgt.fr; Sec.-Gen. VINCENT DEBEIR.

Sociétés d'études (Higher Education workers): 263 rue de Paris, Case 421, 93514 Montreuil Cédex; tel. 1-48-18-84-34; fax 1-48-18-84-86; e-mail fsetud@cgt.fr; Pres. NOËL LECHAT.

Sous-sol (Miners): 263 rue de Paris, Case 535, 93514 Montreuil Cédex; tel. 1-48-18-82-25; fax 1-48-51-60-36; Sec.-Gen. JACKY BERNARD.

Spectacle, Audio-Visuel et Action Culturelle (Theatre, Media and Culture): 14-16 rue des Lilas, 75019 Paris; tel. 1-48-03-87-60;

fax 1-42-40-90-20; e-mail fnsac@cgt.fr; internet www.fnsac.cgt.fr; Sec.-Gen. JEAN VOIRIN.

Syndicats Maritimes (Seamen): 263 rue de Paris, Case 420, 93514 Montreuil Cédex; tel. 1-48-18-84-21; fax 1-48-51-59-21; Sec.-Gen. ALAIN MERLET.

Tabac et Allumettes (Tobacco and Matches): 263 rue de Paris, Case 422, 93514 Montreuil Cédex; tel. 1-48-18-84-19; fax 1-48-51-54-53; e-mail cgt.tabacs.allumettes@wanadoo.fr; Sec.-Gen. BERTRAND PAGE.

Textiles, Habillement, Cuir—THC (Textiles): 263 rue de Paris, Case 415, 93514 Montreuil Cédex; tel. 1-48-18-82-98; fax 1-48-18-83-01; Sec.-Gen. CHRISTIAN LAROSE.

Transports: 263 rue de Paris, Case 423, 93514 Montreuil Cédex; tel. 1-48-18-80-82; fax 1-48-18-82-54; Sec.-Gen. ALAIN RENAULT.

Travailleurs de l'Etat (State Employees): 263 rue de Paris, Case 541, 93514 Montreuil Cédex; tel. 1-48-18-86-86; fax 1-48-18-86-87; e-mail cgt.fnte1@libertysurf.fr; Sec.-Gen. JEAN LOUIS NAUDET.

Verre et Céramique (Glassworkers and Ceramics): 263 rue de Paris, Case 417, 93514 Montreuil Cédex; tel. 1-48-18-80-13; fax 1-48-18-80-11; e-mail cgtverre_ceramique@libertysurf.fr; Sec.-Gen. JACQUES BEAUVOIR.

Voyageurs-Représentants, Cadres et Techniciens de la Vente (Commercial Travellers): Bourse du Travail, 3 rue du Château d'eau, 75010 Paris; tel. 1-42-39-02-99; fax 1-42-39-09-11; Sec.-Gen. ALAIN SERRE.

Force Ouvrière: 141 ave du Maine, 75680 Paris Cédex 14; tel. 1-40-52-82-00; fax 1-40-52-82-02; f. 1947 by breakaway from the more left-wing CGT (above); Force Ouvrière is a member of ICFTU and of the European Trade Union Confederation; Sec.-Gen. MARC BLONDEL; c. 1m. mems.

Affiliated federations:

Action Sociale: 7 passage Tenaille, 75680 Paris Cédex 14; tel. 1-40-52-85-80; fax 1-40-52-85-79; Sec. MICHEL PINAUD.

Administration Générale de l'État: 46 rue des Petites Ecuries, 75010 Paris; tel. 1-42-46-40-19; fax 1-42-46-19-57; e-mail flamarque@force-ouvriere.fr; f. 1948; Sec.-Gen. FRANCIS LAMARQUE; 20,000 mems.

Agriculture, Alimentation et Tabacs (Agriculture, Food and Tobacco): 7 passage Tenaille, 75680 Paris Cédex 14; tel. 1-40-52-85-10; fax 1-40-52-85-12; Sec.-Gen. RAFAËL NEDZYNSKI.

Bâtiment, Travaux Publics, Bois, Céramique, Papier Carton et Matériaux de Construction (Building, Public Works, Wood, Ceramics, Paper, Cardboard and Building Materials): 170 ave Parmentier, 75010 Paris; tel. 1-42-01-30-00; fax 1-42-39-50-44; Sec.-Gen. MICHEL DAUDIGNY.

Union des Cadres et Ingénieurs (UCI) (Engineers): 2 rue de la Michodière, 75002 Paris; tel. 1-47-42-39-69; fax 1-47-42-03-53; Sec.-Gen. HUBERT BOUCHET.

Fédération Syndicaliste Force Ouvrière des Cheminots (Railway Workers): 61 rue de la Chapelle, 75018 Paris; tel. 1-55-26-94-00; fax 1-55-26-94-01; e-mail force.ouvriere.fdcheminots@wanadoo.fr; f. 1948; Sec.-Gen. ERIC FALEMPIN; 10,000 mems.

Coiffeurs, Esthétique et Parfumerie (Hairdressers, Beauticians and Perfumery): 3 rue de la Croix Blanche, 18350 Nerondes; tel. 1-48-74-89-32; fax 1-48-74-81-26; Sec.-Gen. MICHEL BOURLON.

Cuirs, Textiles, Habillement (Leather, Textiles and Clothing): 7 passage Tenaille, 75680 Paris Cédex 14; tel. 1-40-52-83-00; fax 1-40-52-82-99; Sec.-Gen. JEAN-CLAUDE HUMEZ.

Défense, Industries de l'Armement et Secteurs Assimilés (Defence, Arms Manufacture and Related Industries): 46 rue des Petites Ecuries, 75010 Paris; tel. 1-42-46-00-05; fax 1-45-23-12-89; e-mail asparfel@force-ouvriere.fr; Sec.-Gen. ALAIN SPARFEL.

Employés et Cadres (Managerial Staff): 28 rue des Petits Hôtels, 75010 Paris; tel. 1-48-01-91-91; fax 1-48-01-91-92; e-mail rboutaric@fec-fo.com; Sec.-Gen. ROSE BOUTARIC.

Enseignement, Culture et Formation Professionnelle (Teaching, Culture and Professional Training): 7 passage Tenaille, 75680 Paris Cédex 14; tel. 1-40-52-85-30; fax 1-40-52-85-35; Sec.-Gen. FRANÇOIS CHAINTRON; 50,000 mems.

Equipement, Transports et Services (Transport and Public Works): 46 rue des Petites Ecuries, 75010 Paris; tel. 1-42-46-36-63; fax 1-48-24-38-32; f. 1932; Sec.-Gen. YVES VEYRIER; 50,000 mems.

Fédération Nationale de l'Energie et des Mines: 60 rue Vergniaud, 75640 Paris Cédex 13; tel. 1-44-16-86-20; fax 1-44-16-86-32; f. 1947; Sec.-Gen. GABRIEL GAUDY; 22,000 mems.

Fédération des Syndicats Généraux de la Police: 146-8 rue de Piapus, 75012 Paris; tel. 1-53-46-11-00; fax 1-44-68-07-41; Sec.-Gen. XAVIER BEUGNET.

Finances: 46 rue des Petites Ecuries, 75010 Paris; tel. 1-42-46-75-20; fax 1-47-70-23-92; e-mail finances@wanadoo.fr; internet pro.wanadoo.fr/fo.finances; Sec. JACKY LESUEUR.

Fonctionnaires (Civil Servants): 46 rue des Petites Ecuries, 75010 Paris; tel. 1-44-83-65-55; fax 1-42-46-97-80; internet www.fo-fonctionnaires.fr; Sec. ROLAND GAILLARD.

Industries Chimiques (Chemical Industries): 60 rue Vergniaud, 75640 Paris Cédex 13; tel. 1-45-80-14-90; fax 1-45-80-08-03; e-mail fedechimie_cgtfo@wanadoo.fr; f. 1948; Sec.-Gen. MICHEL DECAYEUX.

Livre (Printing Trades): 7 passage Tenaille, 75680 Paris Cédex 14; tel. 1-40-52-85-00; fax 1-40-52-85-01; e-mail livre.fo@wanadoo.fr; Sec.-Gen. MAURICE ROSSAT.

Métaux (Metals): 9 rue Baudouin, 75013 Paris; tel. 1-53-94-54-00; fax 1-45-83-78-87; internet www.fo-metaux.org; Sec.-Gen. MICHEL HUC.

Mineurs, Miniers et Similaires (Mine Workers): 7 passage Tenaille, 75014 Paris; tel. 1-40-52-85-50; fax 1-40-52-85-48; e-mail fo.mineurs@wanadoo.fr; Sec.-Gen. BERNARD FRAYSSE.

Personnels des Services des Départements et Régions (Local Public Services): 46 rue des Petites Ecuries, 75010 Paris; tel. 1-42-46-50-52; fax 1-47-70-26-06; e-mail fpspr.cgtfo@wanadoo.fr; Sec.-Gen. MICHÈLE SIMONNIN.

Pharmacie (Pharmacists): 7 passage Tenaille, 75680 Paris Cédex 14; tel. 1-40-52-85-60; fax 1-40-52-85-61; Sec.-Gen. GILBERT LEBRUMENT.

Police: 6 rue Albert Bayet, 75013 Paris; tel. 1-45-82-28-08; fax 1-45-82-64-24; f. 1948; Sec. JEAN JACQUES PENIN; 11,000 mems.

Postes et Télécommunications: 60 rue Vergniaud, 75640 Paris Cédex 13; tel. 1-40-78-31-50; fax 1-40-78-30-58; e-mail federation@fo-ptt.com; internet www.fo-ptt.com; f. 1947; Sec.-Gen. JACQUES LEMERCIER.

Services Publics et de Santé (Health and Public Services): 153–155 rue de Rome, 75017 Paris; tel. 1-44-01-06-00; fax 1-42-27-21-40; e-mail fedespsfo@wanadoo.fr; internet www.fo-sante.com; f. 1947; Sec.-Gen. CAMILLE ORDRONNEAU; 130,000 mems.

Syndicats des Arts des Spectacles de l'Audiovisuel et de la Presse et de la Communication F.O. (FASAPFO) (Theatre and Cinema Performers, Press and Broadcasting): 2 rue de la Michodière, 75002 Paris; tel. 1-47-42-35-86; fax 1-47-42-39-45; Sec.-Gen. BERTRAND BLANC.

Transports: 7 passage Tenaille, 75680 Paris Cédex 14; tel. 1-40-52-85-45; fax 1-40-52-85-09; Gen. Sec. ROGER POLETTI.

Voyageurs-Représentants-Placiers (Commercial Travellers): 6 rue Albert Bayet, 75013 Paris; tel. 1-45-82-28-28; fax 1-45-70-93-69; f. 1930; Sec. MICHEL BOUTELEUX.

Confédération Française Démocratique du Travail (CFDT): 4 blvd de la Villette, 75955 Paris Cédex 19; tel. 1-42-03-80-00; fax 1-42-03-81-44; e-mail confederation@cfdt.fr; internet www.cfdt.fr; constituted in 1919 as Confédération Française des Travailleurs Chrétiens—CFTC, present title and constitution adopted in 1964; moderate; co-ordinates 1,500 trade unions, 95 departmental and overseas unions, 3 confederal unions and 18 affiliated professional federations, all of which are autonomous. There are also 22 regional orgs; 808,581 mems (1999); affiliated to European Trade Union Confederation and to ICFTU; Sec.-Gen. NICOLE NOTAT; Nat. Secs JEAN-FRANÇOIS TROGRLIC, ANNIE THOMAS, MICHEL JALMAIN, MICHEL CARON, JEAN-MARIE TOULISSE, RÉMI JOUAN.

Affiliated federations:

Agroalimentaire (FGA): 47-49 ave Simon Bolivar, 75950 Paris Cédex 19; tel. 1-53-38-12-12; fax 1-53-38-12-00; e-mail fga@cfdt.fr; f. 1980; Sec.-Gen. ODILE BELLOUIN.

Banques (Fédération des Syndicats CFDT de Banques et Sociétés Financières) (Banking): 47-49 ave Simon Bolivar, 75950 Paris Cédex 19; tel. 1-44-52-71-20; fax 1-44-52-71-21; e-mail banques@cfdt.fr; internet www.cfdt-banques.fr; Sec.-Gen. BERNARD DUFIL.

Chimie-Energie (FCE-CFDT): 47-49 ave Simon Bolivar, 75950 Paris Cédex 19; tel. 1-44-84-86-00; fax 1-44-84-86-05; e-mail fce@cfdt.fr; internet www.fce.cfdt.fr; f. 1946; Sec.-Gen. JACQUES KHELIFF; 57,000 mems (1996).

Communication et Culture (FTILAC): 47-49 ave Simon Bolivar, 75950 Paris Cédex 19; tel. 1-44-52-52-70; fax 1-42-02-59-74; e-mail ftilac@cfdt.fr; Sec.-Gen. DANIÈLE RIVED.

Construction-Bois (FNCB) (Builders, wood-workers, architects, town-planners): 47-49 ave Simon Bolivar, 75950 Paris Cédex 19; tel. 1-53-72-87-20; fax 1-53-72-87-21; e-mail fncb@cfdt.fr; internet www.cfdt-construction-bois.fr; f. 1934; Sec.-Gen. JOSEPH MURGIA.

Education Nationale (SGEN-CFDT) (National Education): 47-49 ave Simon Bolivar, 75950 Paris Cédex 19; tel. 1-40-03-37-00; fax 1-42-02-50-97; e-mail sgen@cfdt.fr; internet www.sgen-cfdt.org; f. 1937; Sec.-Gen. JEAN-LUC VILLENEUVE.

Etablissements et Arsenaux de l'Etat: 47-49 ave Simon Bolivar, 75950 Paris Cédex 19; tel. 1-42-52-55-33; fax 1-44-52-55-44; e-mail feae@cfdt.fr; Sec.-Gen. JEAN-PIERRE LE VELLY.

Fédération Unifiée des Postes et des Télécoms CFDT (FUPT-CFDT) (Post and Telecommunications Workers): 47-49 ave Simon Bolivar, 75950 Paris Cédex 19; tel. 1-44-84-30-30; fax 1-42-02-42-10; e-mail fupt@cfdt.fr; Sec.-Gen. MARIE-PIERRE LIBOUTET.

Finances et Affaires Economiques (Finance): 47-49 ave Simon Bolivar, 75950 Paris Cédex 19; tel. 1-53-72-73-00; fax 1-42-02-49-91; e-mail finances@cfdt.fr; internet www.cfdt-finances.fr; f. 1936; civil servants and workers within government financial departments; Sec.-Gen. PHILIPPE LECLEZIO.

Fonctionnaires et Assimilés (UFFA-CFDT) (Civil Servants): 47-49 ave Simon Bolivar, 75950 Paris Cédex 19; tel. 1-42-02-44-70; fax 1-42-02-38-77; e-mail uffa@cfdt.fr; f. 1932; Sec.-Gen. MICHEL PÉRIER.

Formation et Enseignement Privés (Non-State education): 47-49 ave Simon Bolivar, 75950 Paris Cédex 19; tel. 1-40-18-53-53; fax 1-40-40-99-14; e-mail fep@cfdt.fr; internet fep-cfdt.fr; Sec.-Gen. PHILIPPE LEPEU.

Habillement, Cuir et Textile (HACUITEX-CFDT) (Clothing Industry): 47-49 ave Simon Bolivar, 75950 Paris Cédex 19; tel. 1-44-52-71-10; fax 1-42-01-02-98; e-mail hacuitex@cfdt.fr; f. 1963; Sec.-Gen. MARTIAL VIDET.

Mines et Métallurgie (Miners and Metal Workers): 47-49 ave Simon Bolivar, 75950 Paris Cédex 19; tel. 1-44-52-20-20; fax 1-44-52-20-52; e-mail fgmm@cfdt.fr; internet www.fgmm.cfdt.fr; Sec.-Gen. ROBERT BONNAND.

Personnel du Ministère de l'Intérieur et des Collectivités Locales (INTERCO-CFDT): 47–49 ave Simon Bolivar, 75950 Paris Cédex 19; tel. 1-40-40-85-50; fax 1-42-06-86-86; e-mail interco@cfdt.fr; internet www.interco-cfdt.fr; Sec.-Gen. ALEXIS GUÉNÉGO.

Protection Sociale, Travail, Emploi (Social Security): 47-49 ave Simon Bolivar, 75950 Paris Cédex 19; tel. 1-40-18-77-72; fax 1-40-18-77-79; e-mail pste@cfdt.fr; internet www.pstecfdt.com; Sec.-Gen. JEAN-LOUIS TARDIVAUN.

Santé et Services Sociaux (Health and Social Workers): 47-49 ave Simon Bolivar, 75950 Paris Cédex 19; tel. 1-40-40-85-00; fax 1-42-02-48-08; e-mail santesociaux@efdt.fr; internet www.fed-cfdt-sante-sociaux.org; Sec.-Gen. FRANÇOIS CHEREQUE.

Services: Tour Essor, 14 rue Scandicci, 93508 Pantin Cédex; tel. 1-48-10-65-90; fax 1-48-10-65-95; e-mail services@cfdt.fr; Sec.-Gen. RÉMY JOUAN.

Transports et Equipement: 47-49 ave Simon Bolivar, 75950 Paris Cédex 19; tel. 1-44-84-29-50; fax 1-42-02-49-96; e-mail fgte_cfdt@wanadoo.fr; f. 1977; Sec.-Gen. BRUNO DALBERTO.

Union Confédérale des Cadres (UCC-CFDT) (Managers, professionals, engineers): 47–49 ave Simon Bolivar, 75950 Paris Cédex 19; tel. 1-42-02-44-43; fax 1-42-02-48-58; e-mail ucc-cfdt@ucc-cfdt.fr; internet www.ucc-cfdt.fr; Sec.-Gen. MARIE ODILE PAULET.

Union Confédérale des Retraités (UCR): 47-49 ave Simon Bolivar, 75950 Paris Cédex 19; tel. 1-44-52-12-90; fax 1-42-02-34-51; e-mail union-retraites@cfdt.fr; Sec.-Gen. JACQUES SENSE.

Confédération Française de l'Encadrement (CFE—CGC): 59–63 rue du Rocher, 75008 Paris; tel. 1-55-30-12-12; fax 1-55-30-13-13; e-mail presse@cfecgc.fr; internet www.cgc.fr; f. 1944; organizes managerial staff, professional staff and technicians; co-ordinates unions in every industry and sector; Chair. JEAN-LUC CAZETTES; Vice Chair. CLAUDE CAMBUS; 192,842 mems.

Confédération Française des Travailleurs Chrétiens (CFTC): 13 rue des Ecluses Saint Martin, 75483 Paris Cédex 10; tel. 1-44-52-49-00; fax 1-44-52-49-18; e-mail communication@cftc.fr; internet www.cftc.fr; f. 1919; present form in 1964 after majority CFTC became CFDT (see above); mem. European Trade Union Confederation; Chair. ALAIN DELEU; Gen. Sec. JACKY DINTINGER; 250,000 mems.

Confédération des Syndicats Libres (CSL): 37 rue Lucien Sampaix, 75010 Paris; tel. 1-55-26-12-12; fax 1-55-26-12-00; e-mail csl@ifrance.com; internet www.ifrance.com/csl; f. 1947; right-wing; frmly Confédération française du Travail; Sec.-Gen. GÉRARD FOURMAL; 250,000 mems.

Fédération de l'Education Nationale (FEN): 48 rue La Bruyère, 75440 Paris Cédex 09; tel. 1-42-85-71-01; fax 1-40-16-05-92; f. 1948; e-mail presse@fen.fr; internet www.fen.fr; federation of teachers' unions; Sec.-Gen. HERVÉ BARO.

Fédération Nationale des Syndicats Autonomes: 19 blvd Sébastopol, 75001 Paris; f. 1952; groups unions in the private sector; Sec.-Gen. MICHEL-ANDRÉ TILLIÈRES.

Fédération Nationale des Syndicats d'Exploitants Agricoles (FNSEA) (National Federation of Farmers' Unions): 11 rue de la Baume, 75008 Paris; tel. 1-53-83-47-47; fax 1-53-83-48-48; e-mail fnsea@fnsea.fr; internet www.fnsea.fr; f. 1946; divided into 92 departmental federations and 32,000 local unions; Chair. Luc Guyau; Dir-Gen. Yves Salmon; 600,000 mems.

Fédération Syndicale Unitaire (FSU): 3–5 rue de Metz, 75010 Paris; tel. 1-44-79-90-30; fax 1-48-01-02-52; e-mail webmaster@ fsu.fr; internet www.fsu.fr; f. 1993, following split in FEN; federation of 19 teachers' unions; Sec.-Gen. Monique Vuaillat; 150,000 mems.

Syndicat National Unitaire des Instituteurs (SNUIPP): 128 blvd Blanqui, 75013 Paris; tel. 1-44-08-69-30; fax 1-44-08-69-40; e-mail snuipp@snuipp.fr; internet www.snuipp.fr; f. 1993; primary-school teachers; Secs-Gen. Daniel Le Bret, Laurent Zappi, Nicole Geneix.

Transport

RAILWAYS

Most of the French railways are controlled by the Société Nationale des Chemins de fer Français (SNCF) which took over the activities of the five largest railway companies in 1937. In 1997 the Réseau Ferré de France was created to manage track and infrastructure. The SNCF is divided into 23 régions (areas), all under the direction of a general headquarters in Paris. In 1993 the SNCF operated 32,579 km of track, of which 13,572 km were electrified. By 1999 total track length had been reduced to 31,735 km. High-speed services (trains à grande vitesse—TGV) operate between Paris and Lyon (TGV Sud-Est), Paris and Bordeaux (TGV Atlantique) and Paris and Calais (TGV Nord). The TGV network covered 1,281 km of track in 1999. The Parisian transport system is controlled by a separate authority, the Régie Autonome des Transports Parisiens (RATP, see below). A number of small railways in the provinces are run by independent organizations. In 1994 a rail link between France and the United Kingdom was opened, including a tunnel under the English Channel (la Manche), from Calais to Folkestone. In 1996 it was announced that the TGV network was to be extended to link Strasbourg with Paris. TGV Méditerranée, which will link Valence, Marseille and Nîmes, was expected to become operational in June 2001.

Réseau Ferré de France (RFF): Tour Pascal A, 92045 Paris La Défense Cédex; tel. 1-46-96-90-00; fax 1-46-96-90-73; f. 1977 to assume ownership and financial control of national rail infrastructure, previously the responsibility of SNCF; state-owned; Pres. Claude Martinand; Gen. Man. Jean-François Bénard.

Société Nationale des Chemins de fer Français (SNCF): 34 rue du Commandant Mouchotte, 75699 Paris Cédex 14; tel. 1-53-25-60-00; fax 1-53-25-61-08; e-mail webcom@sncf.fr; internet www.sncf.fr; f. 1937; 178,893 employees; Chair. Louis Gallois; Sec.-Gen. Paul Mingasson; Gen. Man. Guillaume Pepy.

Metropolitan Railways

Régie Autonome des Transports Parisiens (RATP): 54 quai de la Rapée, 75599 Paris Cédex 12; tel. 1-44-68-20-20; fax 1-44-68-31-60; internet www.ratp.fr; f. 1949; state-owned; operates the Paris underground, suburban railways (totalling 327 km in 2001), 3 suburban tram lines, and buses; Chair. and Dir-Gen. Jean-Paul Bailly.

Three provincial cities also have underground railway systems: Marseille, Lyon and Lille. The construction of an underground railway system in Rennes began in 1997, and was scheduled to enter service in 2001.

ROADS

At 31 December 1998 there were 10,300 km of motorways (auto-routes). There were also 28,000 km of national roads (routes nationales), 355,000 km of secondary roads and 500,000 km of major local roads.

Fédération Nationale des Transports Routiers (FNTR): 6 rue Ampère, 75017 Paris; tel. 1-44-29-04-29; fax 1-44-29-04-01; e-mail fntr@fntr.fr; internet www.fntr.fr; road transport; Chair. René Petit.

INLAND WATERWAYS

At 31 December 2000 there were 8,500 km of navigable waterways, of which 1,686 km were accessible to craft of 3,000 tons.

Voies navigables de France: 175 rue Ludovic Boutleux, BP 820, 62408 Béthune Cédex; tel. 3-21-63-24-42; e-mail direction-generale@ vnf.fr; internet www.vnf.fr; f. 1991; management and development of France's inland waterways; Pres. F. Bordry; Gen. Man. A. Borowski.

SHIPPING

In 1998 the principal ports, in terms of quantity of cargo, were Marseille, Le Havre and Dunkerque, and the principal passenger port was Calais. The six major seaports (Marseille, Le Havre, Dunkerque, Rouen, Nantes–Saint-Nazaire and Bordeaux) are oper-

ated by autonomous authorities, although the State retains supervisory powers.

Conseil National des Communautés Portuaires: 3 Square Desaise, 75007 Paris; tel. 1-40-81-86-11; f. 1987; central independent consultative and co-ordinating body for ports and port authorities; over 50 mems including 10 trade union mems; Pres. Jacques Dupuy-Dauby; Sec.-Gen. M. de Rocquigny du Fayel.

Principal Shipping Companies

Note: Not all the vessels belonging to the companies listed below are registered under the French flag.

Brittany Ferries: Port du Bloscon, BP 72, 29688 Roscoff Cédex; tel. 2-98-29-28-00; fax 2-98-29-27-00; e-mail agnes.suils@brittany -ferries.fr; internet www.brittany-ferries.fr; f. 1972 as Bretagne-Angleterre-Irlande (BAI); transport between France, Ireland, Spain and the United Kingdom; Chair. Alexis Gourvennec; Man. Dir Jean-Michel Masson; displacement 122,068 grt.

Bromstrom Tankers: 5 ave Percier, 75008 Paris; tel. 1-42-99-66-66; fax 1-42-99-66-20; e-mail brotank.paris@brostrom.fr; frmly Van Ommeren Tankers; oil product and chemical coastal tankers and tramping.

CETRAMAR, Consortium Européen de Transports Maritimes: 87 ave de la Grande Armée, 75782 Paris Cédex 16; tel. 1-40-66-11-11; fax 1-45-00-77-35; Chair. Philippe Poirier d'Angé d'Orsay; Man. Dir André Maire; displacement 564,291 grt.

Compagnie Nationale de Navigation: 128 blvd Haussmann, 75008 Paris; tel. 1-53-04-20-00; fax 1-53-04-20-14; f. 1930 as Compagnie Navale Worms; merged with Compagnie Nationale de Navigation and Société Française de Transports Maritimes, and changed name to Compagnie Nationale de Navigation in 1986; shipowning co with subsidiaries: Morbihannaise et Nantaise de Navigation (75%), MN-Langevin (100%), Héli-Union (100%), Compagnie Industrielle Maritime SNC (32%); turnover; €117.2m. (1999); Chair. Patrick Molis; Deputy Man. Dir Marie-Laure Breard; displacement 2,221,546 grt.

Esso SAF: 2 rue des Martinets, 92569 Rueil-Malmaison Cédex; tel. 1-47-10-60-00; fax 1-47-10-60-44; turnover 36,900m. Frs (1999); Chair., Man. Dir Jean Verré; Marine Man. Pierre Lange; 5 petroleum tankers, displacement 428,431 grt.

Groupe CMA—CGM: 4 quai d'Arenc, BP 2409, 13215 Marseille Cédex 02; tel. 4-91-39-30-00; fax 4-91-39-30-95; e-mail webmaster@ cma-cgm.com; internet www.cma-cgm.com; f. 1996 by merger of Compagnie Générale Maritime and Compagnie Maritime d'Affrètement; freight services to USA, Canada, the Caribbean, Central and South America, the Mediterranean, the Middle East, the Far East, India, Australia, New Zealand, Indonesia, East Africa and other Pacific and Indian Ocean areas; 18 ships owned; turnover 9,547m. Frs (1999); Chair. Jacques R. Saadé; Man. Dir Tristan Vielieux; displacement 1,300,000 grt (1999).

Louis-Dreyfus Armateurs (SNC): 87 ave de la Grande Armée, 75782 Paris Cédex 16; tel. 1-40-66-11-11; fax 1-45-00-23-97; internet www.lda.fr; gas and bulk carriers; CEO J. Veyrat; Chair. Philippe Louis-Dreyfus.

MARFRET (Compagnie Maritime Marfret): 13 quai de la Joliette, 13002 Marseille; tel. 4-91-56-91-00; fax 4-91-56-91-01; e-mail mfmedsea@marfret.fr; internet www.marfret.fr; freight services to the Mediterranean, South America, the Caribbean, Canada and northern Europe; Chair. Raymond Vidil; displacement 8,711 grt.

Mobil Oil Française: Tour Septentrion, 92081 Paris La Défense Cédex; tel. 1-41-45-42-41; fax 1-41-45-42-93; bulk petroleum transport; refining and marketing of petroleum products; Chair. G. Dupasquier; displacement 281,489 grt.

Navale Française SA: 8 blvd Victor Hugo, 34000 Montpellier; tel. 4-67-58-82-12; fax 4-67-92-98-34; Chair. Marc Chevallier.

Sea France: 3 rue Ambroise-Paré, 75010 Paris; tel. 1-49-95-58-92; fax 1-48-74-62-37; e-mail presse@seafrance.net; internet www .seafrance.fr; frmly Société Nouvelle d'Armement Transmanche; vehicle and passenger services between France and the United Kingdom, Ireland and the Channel Islands; turnover 1,324m. Frs (1999); Man. Dir Eudes Riblier.

Société d'Armement et de Transport (SOCATRA): 9 Allées de Tourny, 33000 Bordeaux; tel. 5-56-00-00-47; fax 5-56-48-51-23; e-mail direction@socatra.com; internet www.socatra.com; Chair. F. Bozzoni; Man. Dir. M. Dubourg.

Société Européenne de Transport Maritime: 9 allées de Tourny, 33000 Bordeaux; tel. 5-56-00-00-56; fax 5-56-48-51-23; Man. Dirs Gilles Bouthillier, Fernand Bozzoni; displacement 53,261 grt.

Société Nationale Maritime Corse-Méditerranée: 61 blvd des Dames, BP 1963, 13226 Marseille Cédex 02; tel. 4-91-56-32-00; fax 4-91-56-34-94; internet www.sncm.fr; passenger and roll on/roll off ferry services between France and Corsica, Sardinia, North Africa; Chair. Pierre Vieu; displacement 141,454 grt.

Société Navale Caennaise: Caen; tel. 2-31-72-54-00; fax 2-31-78-04-94; f. 1901; cargo services to Europe and West Africa; Chair., Man. Dir A. LABAT; displacement 59,680 grt.

Société Services et Transports: route du Hoc Gonfreville-L'Orcher, 76700 Harfleur; tel. 2-35-24-72-00; fax 2-35-53-36-25; petroleum and gas transport, passenger transport; Chair. YVES ROUSIER; Man. Dir JACQUES CHARVET; displacement 118,274 grt.

TotalFinaElf: 2 place de la Coupole, La Défense 6, 92400 Courbevoie; tel. 1-47-44-45-46; fax 1-47-44-78-78; f. 1999 by merger of Total, PetroFina and Elf Aquitaine; petroleum tankers; Chair. THIERRY DESMAREST.

CIVIL AVIATION

There are international airports at Orly, Roissy-Charles de Gaulle and Le Bourget (Paris), Bordeaux, Lille, Lyon, Marseille, Nice, Strasbourg and Toulouse.

Aéroports de Paris: 291 blvd de Raspail, 75675 Paris Cédex 14; tel. 1-43-35-70-00; fax 1-43-35-72-19; e-mail webmaster@adp.fr; internet www.adp.fr; state authority in charge of Paris airports; Chair. YVES COUSQUER; Man. Dir EMMANUEL DURET.

Airlines

Air France: 45 rue de Paris, 95747 Roissy Cédex; tel. 1-41-56-78-00; fax 1-41-56-70-29; internet www.airfrance.net; f. 1933; 56% state-owned; internal, international, European and inter-continental services; flights to Africa, the Americas, Middle and Far East and West Indies; turnover €10,300m. in 1999/2000; 39.8m. passengers carried in 1999/2000; Chair. JEAN-CYRIL SPINETTA; Pres. P. H. GOURGEUN.

Air Liberté: bâtiment 363, BP 854, 94551 Orly Aérogare Cédex; tel. 1-49-79-10-52; fax 1-49-79-13-97; internet www.air-liberte.fr; f. 1987; in 2000 merged with Air Littoral and AOM Compagnie Aérienne Française; operates international, regional and domestic passenger and cargo services; jointly owned by Marine Wendel Group Alpha and SAirLines (Swiss Air); CEO MARC ROCHET; Chair. RENÉ LAPAUTRE.

Brit Air: Aérodrome de Ploujean, BP 156, 29204 Morlaix; tel. 2-98-62-10-22; fax 2-98-62-77-66; f. 1973; operates some 200 daily European flights on more than 30 routes; 2.3m. passengers carried in 1999; turnover €257m. (1999); 99% owned by Air France from November 2000; Chair. XAVIER LECLERCQ; Dir JACQUES PELLERIN.

Euralair International: Aéroport du Bourget, 93350 Paris; tel. 1-49-34-62-00; fax 1-49-34-63-00; e-mail aviation_d_affaires@euralair.com; internet www.euralair.com; f. 1964; international services to Europe and the Mediterranean region; Pres. ANTOINE DE SIZEMONT.

Hex Air: Aéroport Le Puy, 43320 Loudes; tel. 4-71-08-62-28; fax 4-71-08-04-10; f. 1991; operates domestic scheduled and charter services; Pres. BERNARD GUICHON.

Regional Airlines: Aéroport Nantes Atlantique, 44345 Bougenais Cédex; tel. 2-40-13-53-00; fax 2-40-13-53-08; e-mail news@ regionalairlines.com; internet www.regionalairlines.com; f. 1992; operates European and domestic flights; 99% owned by Air France Finance from 2000; 0.9m. passengers carried in 1999; turnover 1,200m. Frs (1999); Pres. JEAN-PAUL DUBREUIL; Man. Dir GUY LE SANN.

TAT European Airlines: 47 rue Christiaan-Huygens, BP 7237, 37072 Tours Cédex 02; tel. 2-47-42-30-00; fax 2-47-54-29-50; f. 1968; fmrly Transport Aérien Transrégional; took over Air Alpes 1981; took over Air Alsace routes following its demise in 1982; wholly-owned by British Airways since 1996; regional charter services; Pres. RODOLPHE MARCHAIS; Chair. MARC ROCHET.

Airlines Associations

Chambre Syndicale du Transport Aérien (CSTA): 28 rue de Chateaudun, 75009 Paris; tel. 1-45-26-23-24; fax 1-45-26-23-95; e-mail info@fnam.fr; internet www.fnam.fr; f. 1946 to represent French airlines at national level; Chair. CÉDRIC PASTOUR; Delegate-Gen. JEAN-PIERRE LE GOFF; 10 mems.

Fédération Nationale de l'Aviation Marchande (FNAM): 28 rue de Chateaudun, 75009 Paris; tel. 1-45-26-23-24; fax 1-45-26-23-95; e-mail info@fnam.fr; internet www.fnam.fr; f. 1991; Chair. CÉDRIC PASTOUR; Delegate-Gen. JEAN-PIERRE LE GOFF.

Tourism

France attracts tourists from all over the world. Paris is famous for its boulevards, historic buildings, theatres, art treasures, fashion houses, restaurants and night clubs. The Mediterranean and Atlantic coasts and the French Alps are the most popular tourist resorts. Among other attractions are the many ancient towns, the châteaux of the Loire, the fishing villages of Brittany and Normandy, and spas and places of pilgrimage, such as Vichy and Lourdes. The theme park, Euro Disney, also attracts large numbers of tourists. There were 70,040,000 tourist arrivals in 1998; estimated tourist receipts in 1997 totalled US $66,732m. Most visitors are from the United Kingdom, Germany, Belgium, the Netherlands and Italy.

Direction du Tourisme: 2 rue Linois, 75740 Paris Cédex 15; tel. 1-44-37-36-00; fax 1-44-37-36-36; Dir PHILIPPE BOISADAM.

Maison de la France: 20 ave de l'Opéra, 75041 Paris Cédex 01; tel. 1-42-96-70-00; fax 1-42-96-70-11; internet www.maison-de-la-france.com; f. 1987; Pres. GÉRARD BRÉNOND.

Observatoire National du Tourisme: 8 ave de l'Opéra, 75001 Paris; tel. 1-44-77-95-40; fax 1-44-77-95-50; internet www.ont .asso.fr; f. 1991; conducts studies and publishes information on all aspects of tourism in France; Pres. MAURICE BERNADET; Dir ALAIN MONFERRAND.

There are Regional Tourism Committees in the 23 regions and 4 overseas départements. There are more than 3,200 Offices de Tourisme and Syndicats d'Initiative (tourist offices operated by the local authorities) throughout France.

FRENCH OVERSEAS POSSESSIONS

Ministry of Overseas Departments and Territories: 27 rue Oudinot, 75358 Paris 07 SP, France; tel. 1-53-69-20-00; fax 1-43-06-60-30.
Secretary of State for Overseas Departments and Territories: CHRISTIAN PAUL.
The national flag of France, proportions three by two, with three equal vertical stripes, of blue, white and red, is used in the Overseas Possessions.

French Overseas Departments

The four Overseas Departments (départements d'outre-mer) are French Guiana, Guadeloupe, Martinique and Réunion. They are integral parts of the French Republic. Each Overseas Department is administered by a Prefect, appointed by the French Government, and the administrative structure is similar to that of the Departments of metropolitan France. Overseas Departments, however, have their own Courts of Appeal. In 1974 each of the Overseas Departments was granted the additional status of a Region (a unit devised for the purpose of economic and social planning, presided over by a Regional Council). Under the decentralization law of March 1982, the executive power of the Prefect in each Overseas Department was transferred to the locally-elected General Council. As a compromise between autonomy and complete assimilation into France, the Regional Councils' responsibility for economic, social and cultural affairs was increased in 1983. In February of that year the first direct elections for the Regional Councils were held. Government proposals regarding the institutional future and socio-economic development of the Departments were provi-

sionally accepted by the National Assembly in May 2000 and, following a number of alterations, were subsequently adopted by the Senate. Changes proposed by the French Government included the creation on Réunion of a second department; the establishment on French Guiana, Guadeloupe and Martinique of congresses of the Regional and General Councils, which would discuss issues of common interest and formulate proposals concerning institutional reform and economic and social development; the transfer to the Regions of responsibilities in areas such as roads, territorial development, water resources and housing; and measures to increase the Departments' autonomy in conducting relations with neighbouring countries and territories. The amended proposals were definitively approved by the National Assembly in November (although the creation of a second department on Réunion was rejected) and by the Constitutional Council in December. The Overseas Departments continue to send elected representatives to the French National Assembly and to the Senate in Paris, and also to the European Parliament in Strasbourg.

FRENCH GUIANA

Introductory Survey

Location, Climate, Language, Religion, Capital

French Guiana (Guyane) lies on the north coast of South America, with Suriname to the west and Brazil to the south and east. The climate is humid, with a season of heavy rains from April to July and another short rainy season in December and January. Average temperature at sea-level is 27°C (85°F), with little seasonal variation. French is the official language, but a creole patois is also spoken. The majority of the population belong to the Roman Catholic Church, although other Christian churches are represented. The capital is Cayenne.

Recent History

French occupation commenced in the early 17th century. After brief periods of Dutch, English and Portuguese rule, the territory was finally confirmed as French in 1817. The colony steadily declined, after a short period of prosperity in the 1850s as a result of the discovery of gold in the basin of the Approuague river. French Guiana, including the notorious Devil's Island, was used as a penal colony and as a place of exile for convicts and political prisoners before the practice was halted in 1937. The colony became a Department of France in 1946.

French Guiana's reputation as an area of political and economic stagnation was dispelled by the growth of pro-independence sentiments, and the use of violence by a small minority, compounded by tensions between the Guyanais and large numbers of immigrant workers. In 1974 French Guiana was granted regional status, as part of France's governmental reorganization, thus acquiring greater economic autonomy. In that year, none the less, demonstrations against unemployment, the worsening economic situation and French government policy with regard to the Department led to the detention of leading trade unionists and pro-independence politicians. In 1975 the French Government announced plans to increase investment in French Guiana, but these were largely unsuccessful, owing partly to the problems of developing the interior (about 90% of the territory is covered by forest). Further industrial and political unrest in the late 1970s prompted the Parti Socialiste Guyanais (PSG), then the strongest political organization, to demand greater

autonomy for the Department. In 1980 there were several bomb attacks against 'colonialist' targets by an extremist group, Fo nou Libéré la Guyane. Reforms introduced by the French Socialist Government in 1982–83 devolved some power over local affairs to the new Regional Council. In the February 1983 elections to the Regional Council the left-wing parties gained a majority of votes, but not of seats, and the balance of power was held by the separatist Union des Travailleurs Guyanais (UTG), the political wing of which became the Parti National Populaire Guyanais (PNPG) in November 1985. At elections to the General Council held in March 1985, the PSG and left-wing independents secured 13 seats out of a total of 19.

For the general election to the French National Assembly in March 1986, French Guiana's representation was increased from one to two deputies. The incumbent PSG deputy was re-elected, the other seat being won by the Gaullist Rassemblement pour la République (RPR). At simultaneous elections to the Regional Council, the PSG increased its strength on the Council from 14 to 15 members, and Georges Othily of the PSG was re-elected President of the Council. The RPR won nine seats, and the centre-right Union pour la Démocratie Française (UDF) three, while the remaining four seats were secured by Action Démocratique Guyanaise.

Of the votes cast in the Department at the 1988 French presidential election, the incumbent François Mitterrand of the Parti Socialiste (PS) defeated Jacques Chirac of the RPR. In the legislative elections held in June, the RPR none the less retained a seat in the National Assembly. In September–October the left-wing parties won 14 of the 19 seats at elections to the General Council. In September 1989 Othily, the President of the Regional Council, was elected to take French Guiana's seat in the French Senate. Othily had recently been expelled from the PSG for having worked too closely with the opposition parties. However, he attracted support from those who regarded the party's domination of French Guiana as corrupt, and his victory over the incumbent senator, a PSG member, was believed to reflect the level of dissatisfaction within the party.

In March 1992 elections were held to both the General and Regional Councils. In the former, the PSG retained 10 seats, while other left-wing candidates took five seats. The PSG leader, Elie Castor, retained the presidency of the General Council.

The party also won 16 seats in the Regional Council, and the PSG Secretary-General, Antoine Karam, was subsequently elected as the body's President. In a referendum in September, 67.3% of voters in French Guiana approved ratification of the Treaty on European Union (see p. 181), although an abstention rate of 81.4% was recorded.

At the March 1993 elections to the French National Assembly Léon Bertrand of the RPR was re-elected in the Kourou, Saint-Laurent-du-Maroni constituency. Christiane Taubira-Delannon the founder of the independent left-wing Walwari movement and an outspoken critic of existing policies for the management of French Guiana's natural resources, was elected in the Cayenne–Macouria constituency (traditionally a PSG stronghold); she subsequently joined the République et liberté grouping in the National Assembly.

The PSG's representation in the General Council declined to eight seats following the March 1994 cantonal elections; none the less, one of its members, Stéphan Phinéra-Horth, was subsequently elected President of the Council (Elie Castor having left the party). Taubira-Delannon, defeated by Karam, failed to secure election, although another member of the Walwari movement did enter the Council. Taubira-Delannon was elected to the European Parliament in June, as a representative of the Energie radicale grouping—which secured the greatest percentage of the votes (36.3%) in the Department, ahead of the government list and a combined list of the parties of the left of the four Overseas Departments. An abstention rate of 80.4% was recorded.

At the first round of voting in the 1995 presidential elections, on 23 April, there was a considerable increase in support in French Guiana for Chirac, who took 39.8% of the votes cast, at the expense of the candidate of the PS, Lionel Jospin, who received the support of 24.2% of voters. The level of support for Jean-Marie Le Pen, of the extreme right-wing Front National, almost doubled (to 8.1%), compared with that at the 1988 election. At the second round, on 7 May 1995, Chirac won 57.4% of the valid votes cast. The rate of participation by voters at this round was 48.0%. At municipal elections in June the PSG retained control of the Cayenne council, although with reduced support.

Beginning in late October 1996 a boycott of classes by secondary-school pupils, who were demanding improved conditions of study, escalated in the following month into a crisis that was regarded as exemplifying wider social tensions between the Department and metropolitan France. The refusal of the Prefect, Pierre Dartout, to receive schools' representatives prompted protests in Cayenne, which swiftly degenerated into rioting and looting, apparently as the protesters were joined by disaffected youths from deprived areas. Considerable material damage was caused to government and commercial property during two nights of violence. The central Government dispatched anti-riot police to assist the local security forces (reinforcements numbered about 200 by mid-November), and it was announced that Jean-Jacques de Peretti and the Minister of National Education, François Bayrou, would visit French Guiana. However, the conviction, shortly afterwards, of several people implicated in the rioting provoked further protests and clashes with security forces, and a one-day general strike in Cayenne, organized by the UTG, resulted in the closure of most businesses and government departments. The extent of the security forces' actions in suppressing the demonstrations was criticized both by those involved in the schools' protest and by local politicians, while the competence of the Department's administrators in their approach to the crisis was the focus of considerable scrutiny. Local officials, meanwhile, denounced the role in the violence not only of unemployed youths but also of separatist groups, alleging that the latter were seeking to exploit the crisis for their own ends. Differences also emerged between the Department's education inspector, Jean-Marcel Coteret, and the Rector of the Antilles-Guyane Academy, Michèle Rudler, as Coteret openly criticized Rudler for remaining in Martinique (the seat of the Academy) throughout the crisis. Bayrou and de Peretti subsequently arrived in Cayenne to meet those involved in the crisis. Local administrators and schools' representatives had already reached agreement on the students' material demands, but, to considerable local acclaim, the ministers announced the establishment, effective from the beginning of 1997, of separate Academies for French Guiana, Guadeloupe and Martinique. The creation was also announced of additional primary educational facilities for some 3,000 children, and a programme was declared to improve academic standards in secondary schools. In all, the measures were to cost the French Government more than 500m. francs. The removal from his post of Coteret, in December 1996, and the appointment of a new Prefect in January 1997 were perceived as indicative of the central Government's desire to assuage tensions in French Guiana.

Elie Castor died in France in June 1996; prior to his death he had been under investigation in connection with allegations including fraud and abuse of influence during his time in public office. In May 1997 further details of irregularities in the General Council's administration of French Guiana during Elie Castor's presidency were revealed in a letter from the Antilles–Guyane Chambre régionale des comptes (responsible for monitoring public finances in the region) to Phinéra-Horth, Castor's successor as President of the Council.

In April 1997 violent incidents followed the arrest of five pro-independence activists suspected of setting fire to the home of the public prosecutor during the disturbances of November 1996. Five others, including leading members of the UTG and the PNPG, were subsequently detained in connection with the arson incident. The transfer of all 10 detainees to Martinique (termed a deportation by separatist organizations) prompted further violent protests in Cayenne. Police reinforcements were dispatched by the central Government to help suppress the violence, as nine gendarmes reportedly received gunshot wounds during two nights of rioting. In July one of the detainees, Jean-Victor Castor, a prominent member of the UTG and the pro-independence Mouvement pour la Décolonisation et l'Emancipation Sociale (MDES), who had been released the previous month, was rearrested and accused of assaulting a policeman during the April riots. Following the announcement, in August, that Castor was to remain in custody, some 200 demonstrators clashed with riot police in Cayenne. Castor was released shortly afterwards, and in September a further four separatists, who had been held on remand since April, were also freed.

In late May and early June 1997 Léon Bertrand, securing 63.3% of votes cast, and Christiane Taubira-Delannon, winning 64.8% of votes, were both re-elected to the French National Assembly in elections that were marked by a high rate of abstention. Candidates from pro-independence parties notably gained increased support, winning slightly more than 10% of the votes cast in both constituencies.

Elections to the Regional and General Councils were held in March 1998. The PSG's representation in the Regional Council declined to 11 seats, with other left-wing candidates securing a further 11 seats (including two won by Walwari). Antoine Karam was re-elected to the presidency of the Council. The PSG also lost seats in the General Council, retaining only five of the 19 seats, while other left-wing candidates took a further five, and independent candidates won seven seats. André Lecante, an independent left-wing councillor, was elected as the body's President, defeating the incumbent, Phinéra-Horth. In late September 1998 Othily was re-elected to the French Senate.

In January 1999 representatives of 10 separatist organizations from French Guiana, Guadeloupe and Martinique, including the MDES and the PNPG, signed a joint declaration denouncing 'French colonialism', in which they stated their intention to campaign for the reinstatement of the three Caribbean Overseas Departments on a UN list of territories to be decolonized. The political future of the Overseas Departments provoked much debate during 1999. In February members of the Regional and General Councils held a congress to discuss the political, economic and social future of French Guiana; the participants proposed the replacement of the two Councils with a single body, to which responsibility in several areas, such as economic development, health and education, would be transferred. Several RPR councillors boycotted the meeting. In October, however, during a visit to Guadeloupe and Martinique, Lionel Jospin, the Prime Minister, precluded from future legislation any merger of the Regional and General Councils. Following a series of meetings held in late 1999, in December the Presidents of the Regional Councils of French Guiana, Guadeloupe and Martinique signed a joint declaration in Basse-Terre, Guadeloupe, affirming their intention to propose, to the President and the Government, a legislative amendment, possibly constitutional, aimed at creating a new status of overseas region. The declaration, however, was dismissed by the Secretary of State for Overseas Departments and Territories, Jean-Jack Queyranne, in February 2000 as unconstitutional and exceeding the mandate of politicians responsible. In March, during a visit to the Department by Queyranne, rioting broke out following Queyranne's refusal to meet a delegation of separatist organizations. Later that month the Regional Council rejected, by 23 votes to seven, reforms proposed by Queyranne in February, which included the creation of a Congress in French Guiana, as well as the extension of the Departments' powers in areas such as regional co-operation. Nevertheless, the proposals were provisionally accepted by the French National Assembly in May, and were subsequently adopted, by a narrow margin, by the French Senate, following a number of modifications. In November the National Assembly approved the reforms, and in December they were ratified by the Constitutional Council. At a referendum held in September, French Guiana voted in favour (80%) of reducing the presidential mandate from seven years to five.

In late November 2000 several people were injured following riots in Cayenne. The demonstrations followed a march, organized by the UTG, demanding greater autonomy for French Guiana, as well as immediate negotiations with the new Secretary of State for Overseas Departments and Territories, Christian Paul. Protesters claimed they had been excluded from talks on French Guiana's status (Paul had invited leaders of various political parties in French Guiana to attend a meeting to be held in France in December, but the offer was rejected by MDES activists, who demanded the meeting be held in Cayenne). Nevertheless, discussions were held in mid-December in Paris at which Paul, various senior politicians from French Guiana and representatives from the PSG, the RPR, Walwari, and the Forces Démocratiques Guyanaises (FDG) were present. It was agreed that further talks were to be held between the Regional and General Councils of French Guiana before the end of 2001, eventually to be followed by a referendum in the Department; however, no constitutional changes were to be effected before the 2002 presidential and parliamentary elections. In early January 2001, following further consultations, it was agreed that a document detailing proposals for increased autonomy for French Guiana was to be drawn up by local officials and was to be presented to the French Government for approval.

At municipal elections held in March 2001, the PSG candidate for the mayorship of Cayenne, Jean-Claude Lafontaine, defeated the Walwari candidate, Christiane Taubira-Delannon. At concurrently-held elections to the presidency of the General Council the left-wing independent candidate Joseph Ho-Ten-You defeated André Lecante.

In 1986–87 French Guiana's relations with neighbouring Suriname deteriorated as increasing numbers of Surinamese refugees fled across the border to escape rebel uprisings in their own country. In late 1986 additional French troops were brought in to patrol the border, as a result of which the Surinamese Government accused the French Government of preparing an invasion of Suriname via French Guiana. It was also reported that Surinamese rebels were using French Guiana as a conduit for weapons and supplies. In 1989 there was an escalation in violent crime, which was generally attributed to the immigrant and refugee population. In August a 24-hour strike, in protest against the high rate of crime, was widely supported. In response to demands for more effective policing, the French Government dispatched 100 riot police from France as reinforcements for the Department's regular police. In 1992 the French Government implemented a programme under which all of the refugees from Suriname were to be repatriated by the end of September.

Government

France is represented in French Guiana by an appointed Prefect. There are two Councils with local powers: the General Council, with 19 members, and the Regional Council, with 31 members. Both are elected by universal adult suffrage for a period of six years. French Guiana elects two representatives to the French National Assembly in Paris, and sends one elected representative to the French Senate. French Guiana is also represented at the European Parliament.

Defence

At 1 August 2000 France maintained military forces of 3,250 in French Guiana, as well as a gendarmerie of 600.

Economic Affairs

In 1996 French Guiana's gross domestic product (GDP), measured at current prices, was 10,772m. French francs, equivalent to 76,671 francs per head. Between 1990 and 1996, it was estimated, GDP increased, in real terms, at an average rate of 4.3% per year. Between the censuses of 1990 and 1999, according to provisional figures, the population increased at an average annual rate of 3.6%.

Agriculture engaged about 11.4% of the employed labour force at the time of the 1990 census. However, according to official sources, by 1997 agriculture engaged an estimated 3.0% of the total employed. The dominant activities are fisheries and forestry, although the contribution of the latter to export earnings has declined in recent years. In 1997 exports of shellfish (particularly shrimps) provided some 19.4% of total export earnings. The principal crops for local consumption are cassava, vegetables and rice, and sugar cane is grown for making rum. Rice, pineapples and citrus fruit are cultivated for export. In 1995 agriculture (including hunting, forestry and fishing) contributed 5.5% of GDP.

Industry, including mining, manufacturing, construction and power, engaged about 20.7% of the employed labour force in 1990. According to official sources, by 1997 this figure had decreased to an estimated 16.8%. The mining sector is dominated by the extraction of gold, which involves small-scale alluvial operations as well as larger local and multinational mining concerns. Exploration activity intensified in the mid-1990s, and the proposed construction of a major new road into the interior of the Department was expected to encourage further development. Officially-recorded gold exports contributed some 27.4% of total export earnings in 1997: actual production levels and sales are believed to be higher than published levels. In 1998 2.8 metric tons (90,020 troy oz) of gold were mined. Crushed rock for the construction industry is the only other mineral extracted in significant quantities, although exploratory drilling of known diamond deposits began in 1995. Deposits of bauxite, columbo-tantalite and kaolin are also present. There is little manufacturing activity, except for the processing of fisheries products (mainly shrimp-freezing) and the distillation of rum. In 1995 industry contributed 19.0% of GDP.

French Guiana was heavily dependent on imported fuels for the generation of energy prior to the flooding of the Petit-Saut hydroelectric dam on the River Sinnamary, in 1994. Together with existing generating plants, the 116-MW dam was expected to satisfy the territory's electrical energy requirements for about 30 years. Imports of mineral fuels accounted for 5.3% of total imports in 1995.

The services sector engaged 67.9% of the employed labour force in 1990. By 1997, according to official estimates, this figure had increased to 72.7%. The European Space Agency's satellite-launching centre at Kourou (established in 1964 and expanded during the 1990s) has provided a considerable stimulus to the economy, most notably the construction sector (which engaged 7.4% of the employed labour force in 1997). Some 1,100 people were employed at the centre in 1991. In 1996 15 satellites were launched from 10 *Ariane-4* rockets, although the explosion of the new *Ariane-5* rocket, in July of that year, delayed the centre's programme. In October 1997 the *Ariane-5* rocket was successfully launched, and its first commercial mission was accomplished in December 1999. The tourist sector expanded during the 1980s and 1990s, although its potential is limited by the lack of infrastructure away from the coast. In 1999 68,211 visitor arrivals were recorded.

In 1998 French Guiana recorded a trade deficit of 2,852.2m. French francs. In 1997 the principal source of imports was metropolitan France (which supplied 51.9% of total imports in that year); the Department's other major suppliers were the USA and Trinidad and Tobago. Metropolitan France was also the principal market for exports in that year (62.0%); other important purchasers were Switzerland, Spain, Guadeloupe and Brazil. The principal imports in 1995 were machinery and transport equipment, food and live animals, manufactured articles, chemicals, mineral fuels and lubricants, and beverages and tobacco. The principal exports in 1997 were gold, parts for air and space vehicles, shellfish and rice.

In 1992 there was a combined deficit on the budgets of French Guiana's government authorities (state, regional, departmental and communal) of 974m. French francs. Under the 1997 regional budget it was envisaged that expenditure would total 447m. French francs. By September 1988 French Guiana's external debt had reached US $1,200m. The annual rate of inflation averaged 1.6% in 1990–98; consumer prices increased by an average of 0.5% in 1998 and by 0.2% in 1999. Unemployment in March 1998 was estimated at 26.5% of the total labour force. However, there is a shortage of skilled labour, offset partly by immigration.

As an integral part of France, French Guiana is a member of the European Union (EU—see p. 181). The French Overseas

Departments were to receive a total of ECU 1,500m. from EU regional funds during 1994–2000.

Economic development in French Guiana has been hindered by the Department's location, poor infrastructure away from the coast and lack of a skilled indigenous labour force, although there is considerable potential for further growth in the fishing, forestry and tourism (notably 'eco-tourism') sectors. A particular concern throughout the 1990s was the rapid rise in the rate of unemployment; youth unemployment and related social problems were widely interpreted as having contributed to the violence in Cayenne in late 1996 (see Recent History). French Guiana's geographical characteristics—large parts of the territory are accessible only by river—have resulted in difficulties in regulating key areas of the economy, such as gold-mining and forestry. Considerable concern has been expressed regarding the ecological consequences of such a lack of controls; moreover, the flooding of a large area of forest (some 340 sq km), as part of the Petit-Saut barrage project, has prompted disquiet among environmental groups, as has uncertainty regarding the ecological implications of the satellite-launching programme at Kourou. Proposals for the creation of a national park, covering 2.5m. ha of the south of French Guiana, with the aim of protecting an expanse of equatorial forest, were hindered in 2001 by the need to reconcile ecological concerns with economic priorities and the needs of the resident communities, notably the demands of gold prospectors. The budget deficit represents a significant obstacle to growth, while high demand for imported consumer goods (much of which is generated by relatively well-remunerated civil servants, who constitute about two-thirds of the working population) undermines progress in reducing the trade deficit.

Social Welfare

In 1997 there were two hospital complexes, a medical centre and three private clinics. In addition, each of the 22 communes has a health centre. There were 223 doctors, 41 dental surgeons and 48 pharmacists in 1998. The Institut Pasteur, in Cayenne, undertakes research into malaria and other tropical diseases. Welfare payments and the statutory minimum wage in the Overseas Departments are aligned with those of metropolitan France.

Education

Education is modelled on the system in metropolitan France, and is compulsory for 10 years between the ages of six and 16 years. Primary education begins at six years of age and lasts for five years. Secondary education, beginning at 11 years of age, lasts for up to seven years, comprising a first cycle of four years and a second of three years. Education at state schools (which accounted for more than 90% of total enrolment in 1992/93) is provided free of charge. Between 1980 and 1993 the number of children attending primary schools increased by more than 70%, and the number of pupils at secondary schools by 87%, although such expansion has placed considerable strain on existing facilities. Higher education in law, administration and French language and literature is provided by a branch of the Université Antilles-Guyane in Cayenne (the university as a whole had 10,919 enrolled students in the 1998/99 academic year, of which 666 were studying in Cayenne), and one department of a technical institute opened at Kourou in 1988. There is also a teacher-training college and an agricultural college. Total government expenditure on education amounted to 851m. French francs in 1993. An Academy for French Guiana was established in January 1997. In 1992 the average rate of adult illiteracy was 18.0% (males 17%; females 19%).

Public Holidays

2001: 1 January (New Year's Day), 26–27 February (Lenten Carnival), 28 February (Ash Wednesday), 13–16 April (Easter), 1 May (Labour Day), 24 May (Ascension Day), 4 June (Whit Monday), 10 June (Slavery Day), 14 July (National Day), 11 November (Armistice Day), 25 December (Christmas Day).

2002: 1 January (New Year's Day), 11–12 February (Lenten Carnival), 13 February (Ash Wednesday), 29 March–1 April (Easter), 1 May (Labour Day), 9 May (Ascension Day), 20 May (Whit Monday), 10 June (Slavery Day), 14 July (National Day), 11 November (Armistice Day), 25 December (Christmas Day).

Weights and Measures

The metric system is in use.

Statistical Survey

Sources (unless otherwise stated): Institut national de la statistique et des études économiques (INSEE), Service Régional de Guyane, ave Pasteur, BP 6017, 97306 Cayenne Cédex; tel. 29-73-00; fax 29-73-01; internet www.insee.fr; Ministère des départements et territoires d'outre-mer, 27 rue Oudinot, 75358 Paris 07 SP; tel. 1-53-69-20-00; fax 1-43-06-60-30; internet www.outre-mer.gouv.fr.

AREA AND POPULATION

Area: 83,534 sq km (32,253 sq miles).

Population: 73,012 at census of 9 March 1982; 114,808 (males 59,799, females 55,009) at census of 15 March 1990; 157,213 at census of 8 March 1999.

Density (at 1999 census): 1.9 per sq km.

Principal Towns (population at 1999 census, provisional): Cayenne (capital) 50, 594; Saint-Laurent-du-Maroni 19,211; Kourou 19,107; Matoury 18,032; Remire-Montjoly 15,555; Maripasoula 12,010; Mana 5,445; Macouria 5,050 .

Births, Marriages and Deaths (1997): Registered live births 4,453 (birth rate 29.8 per 1,000); Registered marriages 671 (marriage rate 4.5 per 1,000); Registered deaths 562 (death rate 3.8 per 1,000).

Expectation of Life (years at birth, 1997): 75.6 (males 72.4; females 78.7).

Economically Active Population (persons aged 15 years and over, 1990 census): Agriculture, hunting, forestry and fishing 4,177; Industry and energy 3,130; Construction 4,440; Trade 3,152; Transport and telecommunications 1,857; Financial services 408; Other marketable services 7,352; Non-marketable services 12,068; Total civilians employed 36,584; Military personnel 417; Unemployed 11,722. Total labour force 48,723 (males 30,110, females 18,613).

AGRICULTURE, ETC.

Principal Crops (FAO estimates, '000 metric tons, 1999): Sugar cane 5; Cassava 10; Other roots and tubers 4; Rice (paddy) 31. Source: FAO.

Livestock (FAO estimates, '000 head, year ending September 1999): Cattle 9; Pigs 11; Sheep 3; Goats 1. Source: FAO.

Livestock Products (metric tons, unless otherwise indicated, 1999): Beef and veal 400*; Pig meat 1,180*; Poultry meat 560; Cows' milk 250*; Hen eggs 450*.
* FAO estimate(s). Source: FAO.

Forestry ('000 cu m, 1998): *Roundwood removals* (excl. bark): Sawlogs, veneer logs and logs for sleepers 51; Other industrial wood 9; Fuel wood 60; Total 120. *Sawnwood production* (incl. railway sleepers): Total 15. Source: FAO, *Yearbook of Forest Products*.

Fishing (metric tons, live weight, 1998): Capture 7,709 (Marine fishes 3,500, Shrimps 4,209); Aquaculture 18; Total catch 7,727. Source: FAO, *Yearbook of Fishery Statistics*.

MINING

Production: Gold (metal content of ore, metric tons) 2.8 in 1998 (Source: Gold Fields Mineral Services Ltd, *Gold Survey 1999*); Sand and gravel ('000 metric tons) 3,000 in 1994 (Source: UN, *Industrial Commodity Statistics Yearbook*).

INDUSTRY

Production: Rum 2,600 hl in 1996; Electric energy 450 million kWh in 1996 (Source: UN, *Industrial Commodity Statistics Yearbook*).

FINANCE

Currency and Exchange Rates: 100 centimes = 1 French franc. *Sterling, Dollar and Euro Equivalents* (29 December 2000): £1 sterling = 10.5193 francs; US $1 = 7.0495 francs; €1 = 6.5596 francs; 1,000 French francs = £95.06 = $141.85 = €152.45. *Average Exchange Rate* (French francs per US dollar): 5.8995 in 1998; 6.1570 in 1999; 7.1198 in 2000.

Budget (million French francs, 1992): *French Government:* Revenue 706; Expenditure 1,505. *Regional Government:* Revenue 558; Expenditure 666. *Departmental Government:* Revenue 998; Expenditure 803. *Communes:* Revenue 998; Expenditure 982. **1997** (million French francs): *Regional Budget:* Expenditure 447.

Money Supply (million French francs at 31 December 1996): Currency outside banks 3,000; Demand deposits at banks 1,621; Total money 4,621.

Cost of Living (Consumer Price Index for Cayenne; base: 1990 = 100): 112.9 in 1997; 113.5 in 1998; 113.7 in 1999. Source: UN, *Monthly Bulletin of Statistics*.

Expenditure on the Gross Domestic Product (million French francs at current prices, 1995): Government final consumption expenditure 4,042; Private final consumption expenditure 5,898; Increase in stocks 121; Gross fixed capital formation 2,542; *Total domestic expenditure* 12,603; Exports of goods and services 7,746; *Less* Imports of goods and services 9,577; *GDP in purchasers' values* 10,772.

Gross Domestic Product by Economic Activity (million French francs at current prices, 1995): Agriculture, hunting, forestry and fishing 572; Mining, quarrying and manufacturing 988; Electricity, gas and water 139; Construction 858; Trade, restaurants and hotels 1,895; Transport, storage and communications 1,241; Finance, insurance, real estate and business services 815; Public administration 1,492; Other services 2,451; *Sub-total* 10,449; *Less* Imputed bank service charge 310; *GDP at basic prices* 10,139; Taxes, less subsidies, on products 633; *GDP in purchasers' values* 10,772.

EXTERNAL TRADE

Principal Commodities: *Imports c.i.f.* (US $ million, 1995): Food and live animals 104.3 (Meat and meat preparations 29.6, Dairy products and birds' eggs 15.6); Beverages and tobacco 39.0 (Beverages 34.3); Mineral fuels, lubricants, etc. 41.9 (Petroleum and petroleum products 40.5); Chemicals and related products 58.0 (Medicinal and pharmaceutical products 17.2); Basic manufactures 92.5; Machinery and transport equipment 330.0 (Power-generating machinery and equipment 27.0, General industrial machinery, equipment and parts 28.0, Office machines and automatic data-processing machines 22.2, Telecommunications and sound equipment 27.6, Road vehicles and parts 88.6, Other transport equipment 88.6); Miscellaneous manufactured articles 97.0 (Professional, scientific and controlling instruments, etc. 15.6); Total (incl. others) 783.3. Source: UN, *International Trade Statistics Yearbook*. *Exports f.o.b.*: (million French francs, 1997): Crustaceans 177.4; Rice 51.8; Parts for air and space vehicles 220.5; Gold 250.9; Total (incl. others) 915.7.

1998 (million French francs): *Imports:* 3,449.44; *Exports* 597.22.

Principal Trading Partners (million French francs, 1997): *Imports c.i.f.:* Belgium-Luxembourg 42.2; France (metropolitan) 1,889.9; Germany 58.3; Italy 72.2; Japan 59.0; Netherlands 66.5; Trinidad and Tobago 218.9; USA 519.9; Total (incl. others) 3,640.4. *Exports f.o.b.:* Brazil 47.6; France (metropolitan) 567.3; Guadeloupe 49.6; Martinique 44.5; Spain 54.8; Switzerland 66.5; USA 21.4; Total (incl. others) 915.7.

TRANSPORT

Road Traffic ('000 motor vehicles in use, 1995): Passenger cars 26.5; Commercial vehicles 8.1. Source: UN, *Statistical Yearbook*.

International Sea-borne Shipping (traffic, 1998): Vessels entered 318; Goods loaded 75,000 metric tons; Goods unloaded 501,400 metric tons; Passengers carried 275,300.

Civil Aviation (1998): Freight carried 6,600 metric tons; Passengers carried 422,100.

TOURISM

Tourist Arrivals (1999): 68,211. Source: Comité du Tourisme de la Guyane.

COMMUNICATIONS MEDIA

Radio Receivers ('000 in use) 104 in 1997; **Television Receivers** ('000 in use) 30 in 1997; **Telephones** ('000 main lines in use) 47 in 1997; **Telefax Stations** (number in use) 185 in 1990; **Daily Newspaper** 1 in 1996 (average circulation 2,000 copies). Sources: UNESCO, *Statistical Yearbook*; UN, *Statistical Yearbook*.

EDUCATION

Pre-primary (1998/99): 42 institutions (1993/94); 10,431 students (9,584 state, 847 private).

Primary* (1998/99): 125 institutions (118 state, 7 private); 1,349 teachers; 18,802 students (17,339 state, 1,463 private).

Secondary (1998/99): 33 institutions (28 state, 5 public); 1,198 teachers; 19,132 students (17,572 state, 3,870 private).

Higher (1998/99): 666 students.

* Figures for institutions and teachers in Primary education include Pre-primary education.

Directory

The Government

(April 2001)

Prefect: HENRI MASSE, Préfecture, rue Fiedmont, BP 7008, 97307 Cayenne Cédex; tel. 39-45-00; fax 30-02-77.

President of the General Council: JOSEPH HO-TEN-YOU (Independent left), Hôtel du Département, place Léopold Heder, BP 5021, 97307 Cayenne Cédex; tel. 29-55-00; fax 29-55-25.

Deputies to the French National Assembly: CHRISTIANE TAUBIRA-DELANNON (Independent left), LÉON BERTRAND (RPR).

Representative to the French Senate: GEORGES OTHILY (FDG).

REGIONAL COUNCIL

Conseil Regional, 66 ave du Général de Gaulle, BP 7025, 97307 Cayenne Cédex; tel. 29-20-35; fax 31-95-22; e-mail caberg@nplus.gf.

President: ANTOINE KARAM (PSG).

Election, 15 March 1998

	Seats†
Parti Socialiste Guyanais (PSG)	11
Rassemblement pour la République (RPR)	6
Walwari	2
Others	12*
Total	31

* Three independents and nine left-wing candidates.

† In 2000 one PSG and one RPR candidate defected from their respective parties; thus the new distribution of seats changed to PSG 10, RPR five, Walwari two and Others 14.

Political Organizations

Action Démocratique Guyanaise (ADG): Cayenne; Leader ANDRÉ LECANTE.

Forces Démocratiques Guyanaises (FDG): Cayenne; f. 1989 by a split in the PSG; Leader GEORGES OTHILY.

Mouvement pour la Décolonisation et l'Emancipation Sociale (MDES): Cayenne; pro-independence party; Sec.-Gen. MAURICE PINDARD.

Parti National Populaire Guyanais (PNPG): Cayenne; f. 1985; pro-independence party; Leader JEAN-CLAUDE RINGUET.

Parti Socialiste: Cayenne; tel. 37-81-33; local branch of the national party; Leader PIERRE RIBARDIÈRE.

Parti Socialiste Guyanais (PSG): 1 Cité Césaire, Cayenne; f. 1956; Sec.-Gen. MARIE-CLAUDE VERDANT.

Rassemblement pour la République (RPR): Cayenne; tel. 31-66-60; f. 1946; local branch of the national party; Gaullist; Leader PAULIN BRUNE.

Union pour la Démocratie Française (UDF): Cayenne; tel. 31-17-10; f. 1979; local branch of the national party; centre-right; Leader R. CHOW-CHINE.

Union Socialiste Démocratique (USD): Cayenne; Leader THÉODORE ROUMILLAC.

Walwari: Cayenne; left-wing; Leader CHRISTIANE TAUBIRA-DELANNON.

Judicial System

Courts of Appeal: see Judicial System, Martinique.

Tribunal de Grande Instance: Palais de Justice, 9 ave du Général de Gaulle, 97300 Cayenne; Pres. J. FAHET; Procurator-Gen. ANNE KAYANAKIS.

Religion

CHRISTIANITY

The Roman Catholic Church

French Guiana comprises the single diocese of Cayenne, suffragan to the archdiocese of Fort-de-France, Martinique. At 31 December 1998 there were an estimated 150,000 adherents in French Guiana, representing some 75% of the total population. French Guiana participates in the Antilles Episcopal Conference, currently based in Port of Spain, Trinidad and Tobago.

Bishop of Cayenne: Rt Rev. LOUIS SANKALÉ, Evêché, 24 rue Madame Payé, BP 378, 97328 Cayenne Cédex; tel. 31-01-18; fax 30-20-33; e-mail louisankale@wanadoo.fr.

The Anglican Communion

Within the Church in the Province of the West Indies, French Guiana forms part of the diocese of Guyana. The Bishop is resident in Georgetown, Guyana.

Other Churches

Assembly of God: 1051 route de Raban, 97300 Cayenne; tel. 25-62-22; fax 35-23-05; Pres. JACQUES RHINO.

Church of Jesus Christ of Latter-day Saints (Mormons): chemin Constant Chlore, 97354 Rémire-Montjoly; tel. 30-55-92; Br. Pres. FRANÇOIS PRATIQUE, allée des Cigales, route de Montabo, 97300 Cayenne; tel. 31-21-86.

Quadrangular Gospel Church: 97300 Cayenne; tel. 37-84-81.

Seventh-day Adventist Church: Mission Adventiste de la Guyane, 39 rue Schoëlcher, BP 169, 97324 Cayenne Cédex; tel. 25-64-26; fax 37-93-02; e-mail mission.adventiste@wanadoo.fr.

The Jehovah's Witnesses are also represented.

The Press

France-Guyane: 88 bis ave du Général de Gaulle, 97300 Cayenne; tel. 29-85-86; fax 31-11-57; daily; Dir PHILIPPE HERSANT; circ. 5,500.

La Presse de Guyane: 26 rue du Lieutenant Brassé, BP 6012, 97300 Cayenne; tel. 29-59-90; fax 30-20-25; 4 a week; circ. 1,000.

Broadcasting and Communications

TELECOMMUNICATIONS

France Telecom: 76 ave Voltaire, 97300 Cayenne; tel. 39-91-14; fax 39-93-02; local branch of national telecommunications co.

BROADCASTING

Réseau France Outre-mer (RFO): 43 rue du Dr Devèze, BP 7013, 97305 Cayenne; tel. 29-99-00; fax 30-26-49; e-mail rfosaf@nplus.gf; internet www.rfo.fr; fmrly Société Nationale de Radio-Télévision Française d'Outre-mer, renamed as above 1998; Radio-Guyane Inter: broadcasts 18 hours daily; Téléguyane: 2 channels, 32 hours weekly; Pres. ANDRÉ-MICHEL BESSE; Regional Dir ANASTASIE BOURQUIN.

Radio

Six private FM radio stations are in operation.

Cayenne FM: 88 ave Général de Gaulle, BP 428, 97300 Cayenne; tel. 31-37-38; private radio station broadcasting 126 hours weekly.

Radio Nou Men: private station; broadcasts in Creole and Boni.

Radio Tout Moune: rue des Mandarines, 97300 Cayenne; tel. 31-80-74; fax 30-91-19; f. 1982; private station; broadcasts 24 hours a day; Pres. R. BATHILDE; Dir GUY SAINT-AIME.

Television

Antenne Créole: 31 ave Louis Pasteur, 97300 Cayenne; tel. 31-20-20; private television station.

Canal Plus Guyane: Cayenne; private 'coded' television station.

Finance

(cap. = capital; res = reserves; dep. = deposits; m. = million; brs = branches; amounts in French francs)

BANKING

Central Bank

Institut d'Emission des Départements d'Outre-mer (IEDOM): 8 rue Christophe Colomb, BP 6016, 97306 Cayenne Cédex; tel. 29-36-50; fax 30-02-76.

Commercial Banks

Banque Française Commerciale Antilles–Guyane (BFC Antilles Guyane): 8 pl. des Palmistes, BP 111, 97345 Cayenne; tel. 29-11-11; fax 30-13-12 (see chapter on Guadeloupe).

BNP Paribas Guyane SA: 2 pl. Victor Schoëlcher, BP 35, 97300 Cayenne; tel. 39-63-00; fax 30-23-08; e-mail bnpg@mail.change-espace.gf; f. 1855; fmrly BNP Guyane; name changed July 2000; cap. 71.7m., res 100.0m., dep. 2,007m. (Dec. 1994); Man. Dir JEAN-CLAUDE HERIDE; 5 brs.

Caisse Centrale de Coopération Économique: route Baduel Heliconias, Cayenne; tel. 31-41-33; fax 30-63-32.

Crédit Populaire Guyanais: Caisse de Crédit Mutuel, 93 rue Lallouette, BP 818, 97338 Cayenne; tel. 30-15-32; fax 30-17-65.

Development Bank

Société financière pour le développement économique de la Guyane (SOFIDEG): PK 3, route de Baduel, BP 860, 97339 Cayenne Cédex; tel. 29-94-29; fax 30-60-44; f. 1982; Dir FRANÇOIS CHEVILLOTTE.

Trade and Industry

GOVERNMENT AGENCY

Direction Régionale de l'Industrie, de la Recherche et de l'Environnement (DRIRE): impasse Buzaré, BP 7001, 97307 Cayenne; tel. 29-75-00; fax 29-07-34; e-mail drire.antilles.guyane@wanadoo.fr; mining authority; responsible for assessing applications for and awarding exploration and exploitation rights; Regional Dir JEAN-CLAUDE BARA.

DEVELOPMENT ORGANIZATION

Agence Française de Développement (AFD): Cayenne; tel. 31-41-33; fmrly Caisse Française de Développement; Dir CLAUDE ALBINA.

CHAMBERS OF COMMERCE

Chambre de Commerce et d'Industrie: Hôtel Consulaire, pl. de l'Esplanade, BP 49, 97321 Cayenne Cédex; tel. 29-96-00; fax 29-96-34; internet www.guyane.cci.fr; Pres. JEAN-PAUL LEPELLETIER.

Chambre de Métiers de Guyane: Jardin Botanique, blvd de la République, BP 176, 97324 Cayenne Cédex; tel. 30-21-80; Pres. RICHARD HO-A-SIM.

Jeune Chambre Economique de Cayenne: Cité A. Horth, route de Montabo, BP 683, Cayenne; tel. 31-62-99; fax 31-76-13; f. 1960; Pres. FRANCK VERSET.

EMPLOYERS' ORGANIZATIONS

Organisation des Producteurs Guyanais de Crevettes (OPG): Kourou; tel. 32-27-26; fax 32-19-18; shrimp producers' asscn and export business; Man. ROBERT COTONNEC.

Syndicat des Exploitants Forestiers et Scieurs de la Guyane (SEFSEG): Macouria; tel. 31-72-50; fax 30-08-27; f. 1987; asscn of 14 forestry developers (450 employees); timber processers; Man. M. POMIES.

Syndicat des Exportateurs de la Guyane: Z. I. de Dégrad-des-Cannes, 97354 Rémire-Montjoly; tel. 35-40-78; Pres. JEAN PATOZ.

Union Patronale de la Guyane (UPDG): c/o SOFIDEG, km 3 route de Baduel, BP 820, 97338 Cayenne Cédex; tel. 31-17-71; fax 30-32-13; e-mail updg@nplus.gf; Pres. ALAIN CHAUMET.

UTILITIES

Electricity

Électricité de France Guyane (EDF): blvd Jubelin, BP 6002, 97300 Cayenne; tel. 39-64-00; fax 30-10-81; state-owned; Gen. Man. GUY EHRMANN.

Water

SGDE: PK 3 route de Montabo, 97305 Cayenne; tel. 30-32-32; fax 30-59-60; Gen. Man. MARC THEPOT.

TRADE UNIONS

Centrale Démocratique des Travailleurs de la Guyane (CDTG): 99-100 Cité Césaire, BP 383, 97300 Cayenne; tel. 31-50-72; fax 31-81-05; Sec.-Gen. GÉRARD FAUBERT.

Force Ouvrière (FO): 107 rue Barthélemy, Cayenne; Sec.-Gen. M. XAVERO.

SE/FEN (Syndicat des enseignants): 52 rue F. Arago, Cayenne; Sec.-Gen. GEORGINA JUDICK-PIED.

Union des Travailleurs Guyanais (UTG): 7 ave Ronjon, Cayenne; tel. 31-26-42; Sec.-Gen. CHRISTIAN RAVIN.

Transport

RAILWAYS

There are no railways in French Guiana.

ROADS

In 1988 there were 1,137 km (707 miles) of roads in French Guiana, of which 371 km were main roads. Much of the network is concentrated along the coast, although proposals for a major new road into the interior of the Department were under consideration in late 1997.

SHIPPING

Dégrad-des-Cannes, on the estuary of the river Mahury, is the principal port, handling 80% of maritime traffic in 1989. There are other ports at Le Larivot, Saint-Laurent-du-Maroni and Kourou. Saint-Laurent is used primarily for the export of timber, and Larivot for fishing vessels. There are river ports on the Oyapock and on the Approuague. There is a ferry service across the Maroni river between Saint-Laurent and Albina, Suriname. The rivers provide the best means of access to the interior, although numerous rapids prevent navigation by large vessels.

Direction Départementale des Affaires Maritimes: 2 bis rue Mentel, BP 307, 97305 Cayenne Cédex; tel. 31-00-08; Dir PIERRE-YVES ANDRIEUX.

Société de Transport Maritime Guyanes: 13 ave Pt Gaston Monnerville, Cayenne.

Somarig: Z. I. de Dégrad-des-Cannes, Remire, BP 81, 97322 Cayenne Cédex; tel. 35-42-00; fax 35-53-44; joint venture between the Compagnie Générale Maritime and Delmas; Dir DANIEL DOURET.

CIVIL AVIATION

Rochambeau International Airport, situated 17.5 km (11 miles) from Cayenne, is equipped to handle the largest jet aircraft. Access to remote inland areas is frequently by helicopter.

Air Guyane: Aéroport de Rochambeau, 97300 Matoury; tel. 35-65-55; operates internal services.

Guyane Aéro Services: Aéroport de Rochambeau, 97307 Matoury; tel. 35-65-55; f. 1980; fmrly Guyane Air Transport; Pres. PIERRE PRÉVÔT; Dir PATRICK LENCLOE.

Tourism

The main attractions are the natural beauty of the tropical scenery and the Amerindian villages of the interior. In 1999 there were 30 hotels with 1,200 rooms, and 68,211 tourist arrivals were recorded.

Comité du Tourisme de la Guyane: Pavillon du Tourisme, Jardin Botanique, 12 rue Lallouette, BP 801, 97338 Cayenne Cédex; tel. 29-65-00; fax 29-65-01; internet www.tourisme-guyane.gf.

Délégation Régionale au Tourisme, au Commerce et à l'Artisanat pour la Guyane: BP 7008, 97307 Cayenne; tel. 31-01-04; fax 31-84-91; e-mail drtguyan@nplus.gf; Delegate PATRICE MALLET.

Fédération des Offices de Tourisme et Syndicats de l'Initiative de la Guyane (FOTSIG): 12 rue Lallouette, 97300 Cayenne; tel. 30-96-29; fax 31-23-43; e-mail fotsig@nplus.gf; internet www.guyane.net.

GUADELOUPE

Introductory Survey

Location, Climate, Language, Religion, Capital

Guadeloupe is the most northerly of the Windward Islands group in the West Indies. Dominica lies to the south, and Antigua and Montserrat to the north-west. Guadeloupe is formed by two large islands, Grande-Terre and Basse-Terre, separated by a narrow sea channel (but linked by a bridge), with a smaller island, Marie-Galante, to the south-east, and another, La Désirade, to the east. There are also a number of small dependencies, mainly Saint-Barthélemy and the northern half of Saint-Martin (the remainder being part of the Netherlands Antilles), among the Leeward Islands. The climate is tropical, with an average temperature of 26°C (79°F), and a more humid and wet season between June and November. French is the official language, but a creole patois is widely spoken. The majority of the population profess Christianity, and belong to the Roman Catholic Church. The capital is the town of Basse-Terre; the other main town and the principal commercial centre is Pointe-à-Pitre, on Grande-Terre.

Recent History

Guadeloupe was first occupied by the French in 1635, and has remained French territory, apart from a number of brief occupations by the British in the 18th and early 19th centuries. It gained departmental status in 1946.

The deterioration of the economy and an increase in unemployment provoked industrial and political unrest during the 1960s and 1970s, including outbreaks of serious rioting in 1967. Pro-independence parties (which had rarely won more than 5% of the total vote at elections in Guadeloupe) resorted, in some cases, to violence as a means of expressing their opposition to the economic and political dominance of white, pro-French landowners and government officials. In 1980 and 1981 there was a series of bomb attacks on hotels, government offices and other targets by a group called the Groupe Libération Armée, and in 1983 and 1984 there were further bombings by a group styling itself the Alliance Révolutionnaire Caraïbe (ARC), which was also responsible for bomb attacks in French Guiana and Martinique at this time. The Government responded by outlawing the ARC and reinforcing the military and police presence throughout Guadeloupe. (The ARC merged with the Mouvement Populaire pour une Guadeloupe Indépendante—MPGI—in 1984). Further sporadic acts of violence continued into 1985, but in October of that year the ARC suspended its bombing campaign prior to the holding of legislative elections. A further series of bomb attacks began in November 1986, and in January 1988 responsibility for bomb explosions in various parts of the territory was claimed by a previously unknown pro-independence group, the Organisation Révolutionnaire Armée.

In 1974 Guadeloupe was granted the status of a Region, and an indirectly-elected Regional Council was formed. In direct elections to a new Regional Council in February 1983, held as a result of the recent decentralization reforms, the centre-right coalition succeeded in gaining a majority of the seats and control of the administration. In January 1984 Lucette Michaux-Chevry, the President of the General Council, formed a new conservative centre party, Le Parti de la Guadeloupe, which remained in alliance with the right-wing Rassemblement pour la République (RPR). However, at the elections for the General Council held in March 1985, the left-wing combination of the Parti Socialiste (PS) and the Parti Communiste Guadeloupéen (PCG) gained a majority of seats on the enlarged (42-member) Council, and the PS leader, Dominique Larifla, was elected its President. In July demonstrations and a general strike, organized by pro-separatist activists in order to obtain the release of a leading member of the MPGI, quickly intensified into civil disorder and rioting in the main commercial centre, Pointe-à-Pitre.

For the March 1986 general election to the French National Assembly, Guadeloupe's representation was increased from three to four deputies. The local branches of the RPR and the centre-right Union pour la Démocratie Française (UDF), which had campaigned jointly at the 1981 general election and the 1983 regional elections, presented separate candidates. Ernest

Moutoussamy and Frédéric Jalton, respectively the incumbent PCG and PS members of the Assembly, were re-elected, but the UDF deputy was not; the two remaining seats were won by RPR candidates (Michaux-Chevry and Henri Beaujean). In the concurrent elections for the 41 seats on the Regional Council, the two left-wing parties together won a majority of seats (PS 12, PCG 10). As a result, José Moustache of the RPR was replaced as President of the Council by Félix Proto of the PS. At the 1988 French presidential elections the incumbent President François Mitterrand of the PS defeated Jacques Chirac of the RPR. At elections to the French National Assembly in June, Larifla (for the PS) defeated Beaujean, while the three other deputies to the National Assembly retained their seats. In September–October the left-wing parties won 26 of the 42 seats at elections to the General Council, and Larifla was re-elected President of the Council.

In April 1989 the separatist Union Populaire pour la Libération de la Guadeloupe (UPLG) organized protests in Port Louis to demand the release of 'political prisoners', which led to violent clashes with the police. A number of activists of the now disbanded ARC (including its leader, Luc Reinette) staged a hunger strike while awaiting trial in Paris, accused in connection with politically-motivated offences in the Overseas Departments. In the following month the Comité Guadeloupéen de Soutien aux Prisonniers Politiques united 11 organizations in demonstrations against the Government. Demands included the release of the prisoners held in France, a rejection of the Single European Act and the granting of a series of social demands. In June the French National Assembly approved legislation granting an amnesty for crimes that had taken place before July 1988, and that were intended to undermine the authority of the French Republic in the Overseas Departments. The agreement of those seeking greater independence in Guadeloupe to work within the democratic framework had gained parliamentary support for the amnesty. However, when the freed activists returned to Guadeloupe in July 1989, they urged increased confrontation with the authorities in order to achieve autonomous rule. In March 1990 the UPLG declared that it would henceforth participate in elections, and would seek associated status (rather than full independence) for Guadeloupe.

In March 1992 concurrent elections were held to the General and Regional Councils. Larifla was re-elected as President of the General Council, despite his refusal to contest as part of the local official PS list of candidates and his leadership of a group of 'dissident' PS members. (The division was not recognized at national level.) In the elections to the Regional Council the official PS list (headed by Jalton) secured nine seats and the dissident PS members seven. Former members of the PCG, who had formed a new organization, the Parti Progressiste Démocratique Guadeloupéen (PPDG) in September 1991, won five seats, compared with only three for the PCG. The RPR, the UDF and other right-wing candidates formed an electoral alliance, Objectif Guadeloupe, to contest the elections, together securing 15 of the 41 seats in the Regional Council. Jalton's refusal to reach an agreement with the 'dissident' PS members prompted Larifla's list to support the presidential candidacy of Michaux-Chevry. Thus, despite an overall left-wing majority in the Regional Council, the right-wing Michaux-Chevry was elected as President with 21 votes. In December 1992, however, the French Conseil d'Etat declared the election to the Regional Council invalid, owing to the failure of Larifla's list to pay a deposit on each seat prior to the registration of its candidates. Seven other heads of lists, including Moutoussamy of the PPDG, were subsequently found to have submitted incomplete documents to the election commission, and (although malpractice was discounted) the electoral code necessitated that they be declared ineligible for election to the Regional Council for one year. Fresh elections took place in January 1994, at which Objectif Guadeloupe took 22 seats, while the PS and 'dissident' PS retained a total of only 10 seats.

In a referendum on 20 September 1992 67.5% of voters in Guadeloupe endorsed ratification of the Treaty on European Union (see p. 181), although an abstention rate of 83.4% was recorded. In November banana growers in Guadeloupe and Martinique suspended economic activity in their respective Departments by obstructing access to ports and airports and blocking roads, in protest at the threatened loss of special advantages under the Single European Act. Order was restored, however, following assurances that subsidies would be maintained and that products such as bananas (Guadeloupe's main export) would be protected under new proposals.

The persistence of divisions between the socialists was evident at the March 1993 elections to the French National Assembly. Michaux-Chevry of the RPR was re-elected, as were Moutoussamy (for the PPDG) and Jalton (representing the anti-Larifla faction of the PS). Larifla, meanwhile, was defeated by Edouard Chammougon, a candidate of the independent right, who was elected (despite his implication in several corruption scandals—see below) with the assistance of votes in the second round of those socialists who resented Larifla's support for Michaux-Chevry in 1992. Michaux-Chevry was appointed to the position of Minister-Delegate, with responsibility for human rights and humanitarian action, in Edouard Balladur's centre-right coalition Government.

The left retained control of the General Council following cantonal elections in March 1994. Larifla was subsequently re-elected President of the Council. At elections to the European Parliament in June, a combined list of parties of the left of the French Overseas Departments, including the PPDG (the list was headed by Moutoussamy), won the greatest share of the votes cast (37.2%) in Guadeloupe; an abstention rate of 85.4% was recorded.

Meanwhile, local political affairs were dominated by scandals involving prominent public figures. Twice during 1993 the Antilles-Guyane Chambre régionale des comptes—the body responsible for overseeing public finances in the region—rejected budget figures submitted by Guadeloupe's Regional Council, deeming that the Council's deficit projections were severely underestimated. In January 1994 an administrative tribunal in Basse-Terre ruled that Michaux-Chevry had been unjustified in dismissing (following the first rejection of the budget) the Regional Council's director of finances, who had submitted departmental accounts, as required by law, to the Chambre régional des comptes; this judgment was upheld at an appeal in Paris in April 1995. In January 1993 Chammougon, the Mayor of Baie-Mahault, was sentenced to three years' imprisonment, fined and deprived of his civic and civil rights for 10 years, following his conviction on corruption charges dating as far back as 1980. He remained at liberty pending an appeal and also, after March 1993, benefited from parliamentary immunity; the prison sentence was suspended and the fine lowered in November 1993, and in October 1994 a higher appeal reduced the deprivation of rights to five years. In September 1993 an investigation of alleged corruption among several of Chammougon's close associates resulted in the deputy's implication in further charges of 'passive corruption' and the abuse and misappropriation of public funds. In November 1994 the French Constitutional Council revoked Chammougon's membership of the National Assembly. In January 1995 Chammougon's wife (elected in the previous month to replace him as Mayor of Baie-Mahault) was elected to succeed him in the General Council, although Léo Andy, the candidate of the 'dissident' PS, was elected to the vacant seat in the National Assembly, defeating the candidate supported by both Chammougon and Michaux-Chevry.

The rate of abstention in Guadeloupe (64.5%) at the first round of the 1995 presidential election, held on 23 April, was the highest recorded at a presidential contest since 1965. Chirac emerged as the leading candidate, with 38.2% of the valid votes cast, ahead of the PS candidate, Lionel Jospin, who took 35.1%. At the second round, on 7 May 1995, Jospin secured 55.1% of the votes, having benefited from the expressed support of all the parties of the left. The level of abstention at this round was 55.2%. At municipal elections in June, Michaux-Chevry became mayor of Basse-Terre, defeating the incumbent PPDG candidate. Jalton, who was supplanted as mayor of Les Abymes by a candidate of the 'dissident' PS, died in November. Michaux-Chevry and Larifla were elected to the Senate in September; the defeat of one of the incumbents, Henri Bangou of the PPDG, was attributed to the continuing divisions within the left. Philippe Chaulet of the RPR was subsequently elected to take Michaux-Chevry's seat in the National Assembly.

At elections to the French National Assembly in late May and early June 1997, Moutoussamy, Andy and Chaulet all retained their seats, while Daniel Marsin, a candidate of the independent left, was elected in the constituency of Les Abymes, Pointe-à-Pitre. An abstention rate of 52.5% was recorded. The RPR

performed strongly in elections to the Regional Council in March 1998, securing 25 of the 41 seats, while the PS won 12; Michaux-Chevry was re-elected as President of the Council. The composition of the General Council remained largely unchanged following concurrent cantonal elections, with the left retaining a majority of 28 seats, although the RPR doubled its representation to eight seats; Marcellin Lubeth, of the PPDG, was elected to the presidency, defeating Larifla.

In January 1999 representatives of 10 separatist organizations from French Guiana, Guadeloupe and Martinique, including the UPLG, signed a joint declaration denouncing 'French colonialism', in which they stated their intention to campaign for the reinstatement of the three Caribbean Overseas Departments on a UN list of territories to be decolonized.

Social and industrial unrest intensified in Guadeloupe in late October 1999, prior to a two-day visit by Lionel Jospin, the Prime Minister. Demonstrations escalated into rioting in Pointe-à-Pitre, following the sentencing of Armand Toto, a leading member of the Union Générale des Travailleurs de la Guadeloupe (UGTG), to four months' imprisonment for assaulting two policemen and threatening to kill another while occupying the premises of a motor vehicle company in support of a dismissed worker. Further protests ensued a few days later when an appeal against Toto's sentence failed. Moreover, banana producers demonstrated around the port of Basse-Terre, demanding the disbursement of 100m. French francs, and additional assistance for the restructuring of their businesses, as compensation for a significant decline in banana prices on the European market. Meanwhile, an indefinite strike by hospital workers, organized by the UGTG, affected Guadeloupe's 16 private clinics. However, calls issued by several trade union and political organizations for a 48-hour general strike during Jospin's visit were largely ignored, and the Prime Minister announced an emergency plan for the banana sector.

Also in October 1999, 61 Chinese emigrants were rescued by French naval forces when the shrimp boat in which they were apparently attempting to reach the USA encountered difficulties off the coast of Guadeloupe. In December the French authorities refused to consider asylum claims made by 53 of the emigrants, despite a petition, signed by nearly 7,000 people, including Marcellin Lubeth and the Department's four deputies, urging the Government to give residence and work permits to the refugees.

The institutional future of the Overseas Departments provoked much discussion in 1999 and 2000. Following a series of meetings, in December 1999 the Presidents of the Regional Councils of French Guiana, Guadeloupe and Martinique signed a joint declaration in Basse-Terre, affirming their intention to propose, to the President and the Government, a legislative amendment, possibly constitutional, aimed at creating a new status of overseas region The declaration, however, was dismissed by the Secretary of State for Overseas Departments and Territories, Jean-Jack Queyranne, in February 2000 as unconstitutional and exceeding the mandate of politicians responsible. Proposals regarding the institutional evolution of Guadeloupe were provisionally accepted by the French National Assembly in May, and were subsequently adopted, by a narrow margin, by the French Senate, following a number of modifications. In November the National Assembly approved the amended proposals, and in December they were ratified by the Constitutional Council. At a referendum held in September, Guadeloupe voted overwhelmingly in favour (89%) of reducing the presidential mandate from seven years to five.

In municipal elections held in March 2001 Michaux-Chevry was re-elected mayor of Basse-Terre, despite corruption charges against her. Henri Bangou of the PPDG was also re-elected to the mayoralty of Pointe-à-Pitre. In the concurrently-held election to the presidency of the General Council Jacques Gillot of Guadeloupe Unie, Socialisme et Réalité (GUSR) defeated Marcellin Lubeth of the PPDG.

Government

France is represented in Guadeloupe by an appointed prefect. There are two councils with local powers: the 42-member General Council and the 41-member Regional Council. Both are elected by universal adult suffrage for a period of up to six years. Guadeloupe elects four deputies to the French National Assembly in Paris, and sends two indirectly-elected representatives to the Senate. The Department is also represented at the European Parliament.

Defence

At 1 August 2000 France maintained a military force of 3,800 and a gendarmerie of 860 in the Antilles, with headquarters in Fort-de-France (Martinique).

Economic Affairs

In 1996 Guadeloupe's gross domestic product (GDP), measured at current prices, was US $3,153m., equivalent to $7,316 per head. During 1990–95 GDP declined, in real terms, at an average annual rate of 0.1%; GDP increased by 1.9% in 1994, but declined by 2.9% in 1995. Between the censuses of 1990 and 1999, according to provisional figures, the population increased at an average annual rate of 1.0%.

Agriculture, hunting, forestry and fishing contributed 4.0% of GDP in 1995, and engaged an estimated 6.5% of the employed labour force in 1998. The principal cash crops are bananas and sugar cane; exports of the former provided 21.9% of total export earnings in 1997, while exports of raw sugar accounted for 23.7% of the total in that year. Yams, sweet potatoes and plantains are the chief subsistence crops. Fishing, mostly at an artisanal level, fulfilled about two-thirds of domestic requirements in the 1990s; shrimp-farming was developed during the 1980s. Agricultural GDP increased at an average annual rate of 4.9% in 1980–85, and by an average of 3.9% per year in 1985–89. Agricultural production increased at an average rate of 2.6% per year during 1990–98. It rose by 25.8% in 1997, but declined by 5.0% in 1998.

The industrial sector (including mining, manufacturing, construction and power) contributed 15.1% of GDP in 1995, and engaged 16.5% of the employed labour force in 1998. Manufacturing, mining and power provided 6.4% of GDP in 1995. The main manufacturing activity is food processing, particularly sugar production, rum distillation, and flour-milling. The sugar industry was in decline in the 1990s, owing to deteriorating equipment and a reduction in the area planted with sugar cane (from 20,000 ha in 1980 to 16,000 ha in 1990 and to only 9,600 ha in 1999). Industrial GDP increased at an average annual rate of 2.7% in 1980–85, and by an average of 1.8% per year in 1985–89.

Of some 700,000 tons of petroleum imported annually, about one-third is used for the production of electricity. Efforts are currently being concentrated on the use of renewable energy resources—notably solar, geothermal and wind power—for energy production; there is also thought to be considerable potential for the use of sugar cane as a means of generating energy in Guadeloupe. Imports of mineral fuels accounted for 5.8% of total expenditure on imports in 1995.

The services sector engaged 76.2% of the employed labour force in 1998 and provided 80.9% of GDP in 1995. Tourism superseded sugar production in 1988 as the Department's principal source of income, and there is significant potential for the further development of the sector, particularly 'eco-tourism'. In 1998 tourist arrivals totalled 693,000, and receipts from tourism amounted to US $499m. in 1997. In 1998 83.3% of arrivals came from metropolitan France or dependent territories.

In 1998 Guadeloupe recorded a trade deficit of 9,999.7m. French francs. In 1997 the principal source of imports (62.9%) was metropolitan France, which was also the principal market for exports (60.7%). Martinique, the USA and Germany are also important trading partners. The principal exports in 1997 were sugar, bananas, boats and rum. The principal imports in 1995 were machinery and transport equipment (mainly road vehicles), food and live animals, miscellaneous manufactured articles, basic manufactures and chemicals.

Guadeloupe's budget deficit was estimated by the metropolitan authorities to amount to some 800m. French francs (including arrears) in 1993. Under the 1997 regional budget it was envisaged that expenditure would total 1,700m. French francs. The annual rate of inflation averaged 2.1% in 1990–97; consumer prices increased by an average of 1.1% in 1997. Some 30.7% of the labour force were unemployed in 1998.

As an integral part of France, Guadeloupe belongs to the European Union (EU—see p. 181). Guadeloupe and the other French Overseas Departments were to receive a total of ECU 1,500m. from EU regional funds in 1994–2000.

Economic growth in Guadeloupe has been restricted by certain inherent problems: its location; the fact that the domestic market is too narrow to stimulate the expansion of the manufacturing base; the lack of primary materials; and the inflated labour and service costs compared with those of neighbouring countries. Economic activity was severely disrupted in September 1989, when 'Hurricane Hugo' struck the islands, causing widespread devastation. The French Government undertook to provide more than 2,000m. French francs for reconstruction, and additional aid for the modernization of the sugar industry. The banana-growing sector and the tourist industry, both of which were particularly adversely affected, had recovered well by the early 1990s. However, Hurricanes Luis and Marilyn, which struck in September 1995, caused severe infrastructural damage and destroyed banana plantations, hotels and public buildings. In the late 1990s Guadeloupe's banana sector was adversely affected by declining prices on the European market, while an ongoing dispute between the USA and four major Latin American producers and the EU over the latter's banana import regime also threatened the sector.

Social Welfare

In 1997 there were seven hospital complexes (including one for psychiatric care), two local hospitals, a physiotherapy clinic and 16 private clinics. In addition, each of the 34 communes has a clinic. In 1998 there were 760 doctors, 230 pharmacists and 135 dental surgeons in Guadeloupe. The social security legislation of metropolitan France is applicable in Guadeloupe. With effect from 1 January 1996 welfare payments and the statutory minimum wage in the Overseas Departments were aligned with those of metropolitan France.

Education

The education system is similar to that of metropolitan France (see chapter on French Guiana). In 1996 secondary education was provided at 40 junior comprehensives, or collèges, 10 vocational lycées, 10 general and technological lycées and one agricultural lycée. A branch of the Université Antilles-Guyane, at Pointe-à-Pitre, has faculties of law, economics, sciences, medicine and Caribbean studies. The university in Guadeloupe had 5,800 enrolled students in 1997. There is also a teacher training college. An Academy for Guadeloupe was established in January 1997. Total government expenditure on education amounted to 2,776m. French francs in 1993. In 1992 the average rate of adult illiteracy was 9.9% (males 10.3%; females 9.5%).

Public Holidays

2001: 1 January (New Year's Day), 26–27 February (Lenten Carnival), 13–16 April (Easter), 1 May (Labour Day), 8 May (Victory Day), 24 May (Ascension Day), 4 June (Whit Monday), 14 July (National Day), 21 July (Victor Schoëlcher Day), 15 August (Assumption), 1 November (All Saints' Day), 11 November (Armistice Day), 25 December (Christmas Day).

2002: 1 January (New Year's Day), 11–12 February (Lenten Carnival), 29 March–1 April (Easter), 1 May (Labour Day), 8 May (Victory Day), 9 May (Ascension Day), 20 May (Whit Monday), 14 July (National Day), 21 July (Victor Schoëlcher Day), 15 August (Assumption), 1 November (All Saints' Day), 11 November (Armistice Day), 25 December (Christmas Day).

Weights and Measures

The metric system is in use.

Statistical Survey

Sources (unless otherwise stated): Institut national de la statistique et des études économiques (INSEE), ave Paul Lacavé, BP 96, 97102 Basse-Terre; tel. 81-17-86; fax 81-07-15; Ministère des départements et territoires d'outre-mer, 27 rue Oudinot, 75700 Paris 07 SP; tel. 1-53-69-20-00; fax 1-43-06-60-30; internet www.outre-mer.gouv.fr.

AREA AND POPULATION

Area: 1,705 sq km (658.3 sq miles), incl. dependencies (La Désirade, Les Saintes, Marie-Galante, Saint-Barthélemy, Saint-Martin).

Population: 327,002 (males 160,112, females 166,890) at census of 9 March 1982; 387,034 (males 189,187, females 197,847) at census of 15 March 1990; 422,496 at census of 8 March 1999.

Density (at 1999 census): 247.8 per sq km.

Principal Towns (population at 1999 census): Basse-Terre (capital) 12,410; Les Abymes 63,054; Saint-Martin 29,078; Le Gosier 25,360; Baie-Mahault 23,389; Pointe-à-Pitre 20,948; Le Moule 20,827; Petit Bourg 20,528; Sainte Anne 20,410.

Births, Marriages and Deaths (1997, provisional figures): Registered live births 7,554 (birth rate 17.4 per 1,000); Registered marriages 1,936 (marriage rate 4.7 per 1,000); Registered deaths 2,441 (death rate 5.6 per 1,000).

Expectation of Life (UN estimates, years at birth, 1990–95): 75.9 (males 72.4, females 80.1). Source: UN, *World Population Prospects: The 1998 Revision.*

Economically Active Population (persons aged 15 years and over, 1990 census): Agriculture, hunting, forestry and fishing 8,391; Industry and energy 9,630; Construction and public works 13,967; Trade 15,020; Transport and telecommunications 6,950; Financial services 2,802; Other marketable services 26,533; Non-marketable services 34,223; Total employed 117,516 (males 68,258, females 49,258); Unemployed 54,926 (males 25,691, females 29,235); Total labour force 172,442 (males 93,949, females 78,493).

1998: Agriculture 8,200; Industry 7,900; Construction 13,000; Services 96,200; Not available 1,000; Total employed 126,300; Unemployed 55,900; Total labour force 182,200.

AGRICULTURE, ETC.

Principal Crops (FAO estimates, '000 metric tons, 1999): Sweet potatoes 3; Yams 9; Cassava 1; Other roots and tubers 3; Vegetables and melons 23; Watermelons 1; Pineapples 7; Bananas 141; Plantains 6; Sugar cane 500. Source: FAO.

Livestock (FAO estimates, '000 head, year ending September 1999): Cattle 80; Goats 63; Pigs 15; Sheep 4. Source: FAO.

Livestock Products (FAO estimates, '000 metric tons, 1999): Beef and veal 3; Pig meat 1; Poultry meat 1; Hen eggs 2. Source: FAO.

Forestry: Roundwood removals ('000 cu m, excl. bark, 1998): Total (fuel wood) 15. Source: FAO, *Yearbook of Forest Products.*

Fishing (metric tons, live weight, 1998): Capture 9,084 (Common dolphinfish 680, Blackfin tuna 470, Other mackerel-like fishes 1,450, Marine fishes 5,800, Stromboid conchs 550); Aquaculture 14; Total catch 9,098. Source: FAO, *Yearbook of Fishery Statistics.*

MINING

Production ('000 metric tons, 1995): Pozzolan 210.0. Source: UN, *Industrial Commodity Statistics Yearbook.*

INDUSTRY

Production: Raw sugar 38,400 metric tons in 1998; Rum 62,679 hl in 1998; Cement 283,000 metric tons in 1996; Electric energy (million kWh) 1,211 in 1997 (Source: UN, *Industrial Commodity Statistics Yearbook*).

FINANCE

Currency and Exchange Rates: French currency is used (see French Guiana).

Budget (million French francs): *State budget* (1990): Revenue 2,494; Expenditure 4,776. *Regional budget* (1997): Expenditure 1,700. *Departmental budget* (1989): Revenue 1,617; Expenditure 1,748.

Money Supply (million French francs at 31 December 1996): Currency outside banks 1,148; Demand deposits at banks 6,187; Total money 7,335.

Cost of Living (Consumer Price Index for urban areas; base: 1990 = 100): 112.4 in 1995; 114.0 in 1996; 115.3 in 1997. Source: ILO, *Yearbook of Labour Statistics.*

Expenditure on the Gross Domestic Product (million French francs at current prices, 1994): Government final consumption expenditure 5,721; Private final consumption expenditure 16,779; Increase in stocks 161; Gross fixed capital formation 5,218; *Total domestic expenditure* 27,879; Exports of goods and services 912; *Less* Imports of goods and services 9,040; *GDP in purchasers' values* 19,751.

Gross Domestic Product by Economic Activity (million French francs at current prices, 1992): Agriculture, hunting, forestry and fishing 1,206.9; Mining, quarrying and manufacturing 1,237.5; Electricity, gas and water 307.5; Construction 1,164.4; Trade, restaurants and hotels 2,907.9; Transport, storage and communications 1,415.4; Finance, insurance, real estate and business services 2,023.0; Government services 4,769.7; Other community, social and personal services 2,587.7; Other services 348.0; *Sub-total* 17,968.0; Import duties 699.4; Value-added tax 615.7; *Less* Imputed bank service charge 1,311.2; *GDP in purchasers' values* 17,972.0. Source: UN, *National Accounts Statistics.*

EXTERNAL TRADE

Principal Commodities: *Imports c.i.f.* (US $ million, 1995): Food and live animals 302.8 (Meat and meat preparations 74.7, Dairy products and birds eggs 51.9, Cereals and cereal preparations 55.6, Vegetables and fruit 51.4); Beverages and tobacco 88.1 (Beverages 78.8); Mineral fuels, lubricants, etc. 110.7 (Petroleum, petroleum

products, etc. 52.5, Gas, natural and manufactured 58.0); Chemicals and related products 172.8 (Medicinal and pharmaceutical products 78.1); Basic manufactures 259.5 (Paper, paperboard and manufactures 39.3); Machinery and transport equipment 607.0 (Office machines and automatic data-processing equipment 40.7, Telecommunications and sound equipment 43.0, Road vehicles and parts 217.7, Other transport equipment 100.0); Miscellaneous manufactured articles 282.6 (Furniture and parts 47.2, Clothing and accessories, excl. footwear, 52.6, Printed matter 39.5); Total (incl. others) 1,901.3. Source: UN, *International Trade Statistics Yearbook. Exports f.o.b.* (million French francs, 1997): Bananas 179.7; Melons and fresh papayas 33.8; Sugar 193.9; Rum 40.2; Wheaten or rye flour 35.3; Yachts and sports boats 50.7; Total (incl. others) 819.4.

1998 (million French francs): *Imports:* 10,703.9; *Exports:* 704.2.

Principal Trading Partners (million French francs, 1997): *Imports c.i.f.:* Belgium-Luxembourg 161.8; Curaçao (Netherlands Antilles) 212.6; France (metropolitan) 6,435.7; Germany 445.5; Italy 395.0; Japan 247.6; Martinique 114.0; Spain 190.2; Trinidad and Tobago 189.3; United Kingdom 151.7; USA 315.4; Total (incl. others) 10,236.6. *Exports f.o.b.:* Belgium-Luxembourg 23.0; France (metropolitan) 497.2; French Guiana 20.6; Italy 21.7; Martinique 152.2; United Kingdom 18.7; USA 36.6; Total (incl. others) 819.4.

TRANSPORT

Road Traffic ('000 motor vehicles in use, 1995): Passenger cars 97.0; Commercial vehicles 28.9. Source: UN, *Statistical Yearbook.*

Shipping *Merchant Fleet* (vessels registered, '000 grt at 31 December 1992): Total displacement 6. Source: Lloyd's Register of Shipping. *International sea-borne traffic,* (1998): Vessels entered 3,319 (1996); Goods loaded 324,500 metric tons; Goods unloaded 2,518,200 metric tons; Passengers carried 1,308,800.

Civil Aviation (1998): Passengers carried 1,978,000; Freight carried 16,500 metric tons.

TOURISM

Tourist Arrivals ('000): 693 in 1998.

Receipts from Tourism (US $ million): 458 in 1995; 496 in 1996; 499 in 1997. Source: World Tourism Organization, *Yearbook of Tourism Statistics.*

COMMUNICATIONS MEDIA

Radio Receivers ('000 in use) 113 in 1997; **Television Receivers** ('000 in use) 118 in 1997; **Telephones** ('000 main lines in use) 171 in 1996; **Telefax Stations** (number in use) 3,400 in 1996; **Mobile Cellular Telephones** (subscribers) 814 in 1990; **Daily Newspaper** 1 (estimate) in 1996 (estimated average circulation 35,000 copies). Sources: UNESCO, *Statistical Yearbook*; UN, *Statistical Yearbook.*

EDUCATION

Pre-primary (1993/94): 121 institutions; 760 teachers; 22,678 students (1994/95).

Primary (1992/93): 219 institutions; 1,920 teachers; 38,332 students (1994/95).

Secondary (1994/95): 3,467 teachers (1992/93); 41,656 general students 9,243 vocational students.

Source: UNESCO, *Statistical Yearbook.*

Higher (1997): 5,800 students (Université Antilles-Guyane).

Directory

The Government

(April 2001)

Prefect: JEAN-FRANÇOIS CARENCO, Préfecture, Palais d'Orléans, rue Lardenoy, 97109 Basse-Terre Cédex; tel. 99-39-00; fax 81-58-32.

President of the General Council: JACQUES GILLOT (GUSR), Hôtel du Département, blvd Félix Eboué, 97109 Basse-Terre; tel. 99-77-77; fax 99-76-00; e-mail info@cg971.com; internet www.cg971.com.

President of the Economic and Social Committee: GUY FRÉDÉRIC.

Deputies to the French National Assembly: ERNEST MOUTOUSSAMY (PPDG), LÉO ANDY ('dissident' PS), PHILIPPE CHAULET (RPR), DANIEL MARSIN (Independent left).

Representatives to the French Senate: LUCETTE MICHAUX-CHEVRY (RPR), DOMINIQUE LARIFLA ('dissident' PS).

REGIONAL COUNCIL

ave Paul Lacavé, Petit-Paris, 97109 Basse-Terre; tel. 80-40-40; fax 81-34-19; internet www.cr-guadeloupe.fr.

President: LUCETTE MICHAUX-CHEVRY (RPR).

Election, 15 March 1998

	Seats
Rassemblement pour la République (RPR)	25
Parti Socialiste (PS)	12
Parti Communiste Guadeloupéen (PCG)	2
Others*	2
Total	**41**

* Other right-wing candidates.

Political Organizations

Fédération de la Guadeloupe du Rassemblement pour la République (RPR): Lotissement SIG, Sainte-Anne; Gaullist; Departmental Sec. ALDO BLAISE.

Fédération Guadeloupéenne du Parti Socialiste (PS): 801 Residence Collinette, Grand Camp, 97139 Les Abymes; tel. and fax 82-19-32; divided into two factions to contest the March 1992 and March 1993 elections; First Sec. GEORGES LOUISOR. A 'dissident' faction of the party is led by DOMINIQUE LARIFLA.

Fédération Guadeloupéenne de l'Union pour la Démocratie Française (UDF): Pointe-à-Pitre; centrist.

Guadeloupe Unie, Socialisme et Réalité (GUSR): Pointe-à-Pitre.

Konvwa pou Liberayson Nasyon Gwadloup (KLNG): Pointe-à-Pitre; pro-independence; Leader LUC REINETTE.

Parti Communiste Guadeloupéen (PCG): 119 rue Vatable, 97110 Pointe-à-Pitre; tel. 82-19-45; fax 83-69-90; f. 1944; Sec.-Gen. CHRISTIAN CÉLESTE.

Parti Progressiste Démocratique Guadeloupéen (PPDG): Pointe-à-Pitre; f. 1991; includes a breakaway group of PCG militants; Leaders HENRI BANGOU; DANIEL GENIES.

Union Populaire pour la Libération de la Guadeloupe (UPLG): Basse-Terre; f. 1978; favours increased autonomy for Guadeloupe; Sec.-Gen. ROLAND THESAUROS.

Judicial System

Cour d'Appel: Palais de Justice, 4 blvd Félix Eboué, 97100 Basse-Terre; tel. 80-63-36; fax 80-63-39; First Pres. B. BACOU; Procurator-Gen. M. ZIRNHELT; two Tribunaux de Grande Instance, four Tribunaux d'Instance.

Religion

The majority of the population belong to the Roman Catholic Church.

CHRISTIANITY

The Roman Catholic Church

Guadeloupe comprises the single diocese of Basse-Terre, suffragan to the archdiocese of Fort-de-France, Martinique. At 31 December 1998 there were an estimated 340,000 adherents, representing some 79.4% of the total population. The Bishop participates in the Antilles Episcopal Conference, currently based in Port of Spain, Trinidad and Tobago.

Bishop of Basse-Terre: Rt Rev. ERNEST MESMIN LUCIEN CABO, Evêché, pl. Saint-François, BP 369, 97106 Basse-Terre Cédex; tel. 81-36-69; fax 81-98-23.

Other Denominations

Apostles of Infinite Love: Plaines, 97116 Pointe-Noire; tel. 98-01-19.

Mission Baptiste: 101 Belcourt, 97122 Baie-Mahault; tel. and fax 26-15-71; e-mail al.gary@wanadoo.fr.

The Press

L'Etincelle: 119 rue Vatable, 97110 Pointe-à-Pitre; tel. 91-12-77; fax 83-69-90; f. 1944; weekly; organ of the PCG; Dir RAYMOND BARON; circ. 5,000.

France-Antilles: 1 rue Hincelin, BP 658, 97159 Pointe-à-Pitre; tel. 90-25-25; fax 91-78-31; daily; Dir FRANÇOIS MERCADER; circ. 25,000.

Guadeloupe 2000: Résidence Massabielle, 97110 Pointe-à-Pitre; tel. 82-36-42; fax 91-52-57; fortnightly; right-wing extremist; Dir EDOUARD BOULOGNE; circ. 3,500.

Jakata: Pointe-à-Pitre; f. 1977; fortnightly; Dir FRANTZ SUCCAB; circ. 6,000.

Match: 33 rue Peyrier, 97110 Pointe-à-Pitre; tel. and fax 82-01-87; fortnightly; Dir MARIE ANTONIA JABBOUR; circ. 6,000.

Newsmagazine Guadeloupéen: Résidence Vatable, Bâtiment B, BP 1286, 97178 Pointe-à-Pitre; tel. 91-16-94; fax 82-22-38; f. 1994; fmrly *Magwa*; fortnightly; independent; Editor DANNICK ZANDRONIS; circ. 4,000.

Le Progrès social: rue Toussaint L'Ouverture, 97100 Basse-Terre; tel. 81-10-41; weekly; Dir JEAN-CLAUDE RODES; circ. 5,000.

7 Mag: Immeuble SOCOGAR, 97122 Baie-Mahault; Dir JACQUES CANNEVAL.

TV Magazine Guadeloupe: 1 rue Paul Lacavé, BP 658, 97169 Pointe-à-Pitre; tel. 90-25-25; weekly.

NEWS AGENCIES

Agence Centrale Parisienne de Presse (ACP): Pointe-à-Pitre; tel. 82-14-76; fax 83-78-73; Rep. RENÉ CAZIMIR-JEANON.

Foreign Bureaux

Agencia EFE (Spain): Pointe-à-Pitre; Correspondent DANNICK ZANDRONIS.

United Press International (UPI) (USA): BP 658, 97159 Pointe-à-Pitre; Rep. STÉPHANE DELANNOY.

Broadcasting and Communications

BROADCASTING

Réseau France Outre-mer (RFO): BP 402, 97163 Pointe-à-Pitre Cédex; tel. 93-96-96; fax 93-96-82; internet www.rfo.fr; fmrly Société Nationale de Radio-Télévision Française d'Outre-mer, renamed as above 1998; 24 hours radio and 24 hours television broadcast daily; Pres. ANDRÉ-MICHEL BESSE; Regional Dir MICHEL MEYER.

Radio

More than 30 private FM radio stations are in operation.

Radio Actif: Jarry, 97122 Baie-Mahault; commercial; satellite link to Radio Monte-Carlo (Monaco and France).

Radio Caraïbes International (RCI): BP 1309, 97187 Point-à-Pitre Cédex; tel. 83-96-96; fax 83-96-97; two commercial stations broadcasting 24 hours daily; Dir JEAN-FRANÇOIS FERANDIER-SICARD.

Radio Saint-Martin: Port de Marigot, 97150 Saint-Martin; commercial station broadcasting 94 hours weekly; Man. H. COOKS.

Radio Voix Chrétiennes de Saint-Martin: BP 103, Marigot, 97150 Saint-Martin; tel. 87-13-59; religious; Man. Fr CORNELIUS CHARLES.

Television

Archipel 4: Résidence Les Palmiers, Gabarre 2, 97110 Pointe-à-Pitre; tel. 83-63-50; commercial station.

Canal Antilles: 2 Lotissement Les Jardins de Houelbourg, 97122 Baie-Mahault; tel. 26-81-79; private 'coded' station.

TCI Guadeloupe: Montauban, 97190 Grosier; commercial station.

Finance

(cap. = capital; res = reserves; dep. = deposits; m. = million; brs = branches; amounts in French francs)

BANKING

Central Bank

Institut d'Emission des Départments d'Outre-mer: Pointe-à-Pitre.

Commercial Banks

Banque des Antilles Françaises: pl. de la Victoire, BP 696, 97171 Pointe-à-Pitre Cédex; tel. 93-16-00; fax 93-16-10; rue de Cours Nolivos, 97100 Basse-Terre; f. 1853; cap. 36.9m., res 44.2m., dep. 2,441.8m. (Dec. 1998); Chair. JACQUES GIRAULT; Gen. Man. JEAN TAUZIES.

Banque Française Commerciale Antilles-Guyane (BFC Antilles-Guyane): BP 13, 97151 Pointe-à-Pitre Cédex; tel. 89-64-00; fax 83-60-63; internet www.cosmobay.com/demo/bfcag; f. 1976 as branch of Banque Française Commerciale SA, separated 1984; total assets 3,609.1m (1998); Chair. YVES GUERIN; CEO and Gen. Man.FRANCIS LAMARQUE.

BNP Paribas, SA: pl. de la Rénovation, 97110 Pointe-à-Pitre; tel. 90-58-58; fax 90-04-07; Dir HENRI BETBEDER; 6 further brs in Guadeloupe.

Crédit Martiniquais: blvd Marquisat de Houelbourg, Zone Industrielle de Jarry, 97122 Baie-Mahault; tel. 25-45-00; fax 25-45-02; f. 1987; cap. 185.4m (1998)—see chapter on Martinique.

Société Générale de Banque aux Antilles (SGBA): 30 rue Frébault, BP 55, 97152 Pointe-à-Pitre; tel. 25-49-77; fax 25-49-78; e-mail sgba@wanadoo.fr; f. 1979; Chair. JEAN-LOUIS MATTEI; Gen. Man. BERNARD GILBERT; 8 brs in French West Indies.

INSURANCE

Mutuelle Antillaise d'Assurances, Société d'Assurances à forme mutuelle: 12 rue Gambetta, BP 409, 97110 Pointe-à-Pitre; tel. 83-23-32; fax 83-34-99; f. 1937; Dir-Gen. FÉLIX CHERDIEU D'ALEXIS; Man. A. ZOGG.

Foreign Companies

Some 30 of the principal European insurance companies are represented in Pointe-à-Pitre, and another six companies have offices in Basse-Terre.

Trade and Industry

DEVELOPMENT ORGANIZATIONS

Agence Française de Développement (AFD): Faubourg Frébault, BP 160, 97154 Pointe-à-Pitre; tel. 83-32-72; fmrly Caisse Française de Développement.

Agence pour la Promotion des Investissements en Guadeloupe (APRIGA): BP 514, 97165 Pointe-à-Pitre; tel. 83-48-97; fax 82-07-09; e-mail apriga@apriga.com; f. 1979 as Agence pour la Promotion de l'Industrie de la Guadeloupe; Pres. PATRICK DOQUIN; Dir CHARLY BLONDEAU.

Centre Technique Interprofessionnel de la Canne et du Sucre: Morne Epingle, Les Abymes, BP 397, 97162 Pointe-à-Pitre Cédex; tel. 82-94-70; fax 20-97-84; Pres. MICHEL MONTEIRO; Dir MICHEL MARCHAT.

CHAMBERS OF COMMERCE

Chambre de Commerce et d'Industrie de Pointe-à-Pitre: Hôtel Consulaire, rue Félix Eboué, 97159 Pointe-à-Pitre Cédex; tel. 93-76-00; fax 90-21-87; e-mail contacts@cci-pap.org; Pres. FÉLIX CLAIREVILLE; Dir-Gen. JACQUES GARRETA.

Chambre de Commerce et d'Industrie de Basse-Terre: 6 rue Victor Hugues, 97100 Basse-Terre; tel. 99-44-44; fax 81-21-17; internet www.basse-terre.cci.fr; f. 1832; 24 mems; Pres. JEAN-JACQUES FAYEL; Sec.-Gen. JEAN-CLAUDE BAPTISTIDE.

Chambre Départementale d'Agriculture de la Guadeloupe: 23 rue Lardenoy, 97100 Basse-Terre; tel. 81-34-61; Pres. MAURICE RAMASSAMY; Dir FRANCK LOMBION.

Chambre de Métiers de la Guadeloupe: route Choisy, BP 61, 97120 Saint-Claude; tel. 80-23-33; fax 80-08-93; Dir MAURICE SONGEONS.

EMPLOYERS' ORGANIZATIONS

Union Patronale de la Guadeloupe: Pointe-à-Pitre; Pres. MICHEL POMAREDE.

Société d'Intérêt Collectif Agricole (Sica-Assobag): Desmarais, 97100 Basse-Terre; tel. 81-05-52; f. 1967; banana producers; Pres. FRANÇOIS LE METAYER; Dir JEAN-CLAUDE PETRELLUZZI.

Syndicat des Producteurs-Exportateurs de Sucre et de Rhum de la Guadeloupe et Dépendances: Zone Industrielle de la Pointe Jarry, 97122 Baie-Mahault, BP 2015, 97191 Pointe-à-Pitre; tel. 26-62-12; fax 26-86-76; f. 1937; 4 mems; Pres. AMÉDÉE HUYGHUES-DESPOINTES.

TRADE UNIONS

Centrale des Travailleurs Unis (CTU): Logement Test 14, BP 676, Bergevin, 97169 Pointe-à-Pitre; tel. 83-16-50; fax 91-78-02;

affiliated to the Confédération Française Démocratique du Travail; Sec.-Gen. HENRI BERTHELOT.

Confédération Générale du Travail de la Guadeloupe (CGTG): 4 cité Artisanale de Bergevin, BP 779, 97173 Pointe-à-Pitre Cédex; tel. 82-34-61; fax 91-04-00; f. 1961; Sec.-Gen. CLAUDE MORVAN; 5,000 mems.

Union Départementale de la Confédération Française des Travailleurs Chrétiens: BP 245, 97159 Pointe-à-Pitre; tel. 82-04-01; f. 1937; Sec.-Gen. ALBERT SARKIS; 3,500 mems.

Union Départementale des Syndicats CGT-FO: 59 rue Lamartine, 97110 Pointe-à-Pitre; Gen. Sec. FERDINAND QUILLIN; 1,500 mems.

Union Générale des Travailleurs de la Guadeloupe: rue Paul Lacavé, 97110 Pointe-à-Pitre; tel. 83-10-07; confederation of pro-independence trade unions; Sec.-Gen. GABY CLAVIER; 4,000 mems.

Transport

RAILWAYS

There are no railways in Guadeloupe.

ROADS

In 1990 there were 2,069 km (1,286 miles) of roads in Guadeloupe, of which 323 km were Routes Nationales.

SHIPPING

The major port is at Pointe-à-Pitre, and a new port for the export of bananas has been built at Basse-Terre.

Compagnie Générale Maritime Antilles-Guyane: Z.I. de la Pointe Jarry, BP 92, 97100 Baie-Mahault; tel. 26-72-39; fax 26-74-62.

Direction Départementale des Affaires Maritimes de la Guadeloupe: 1 Quai Layrle, BP 473, 97164 Pointe-à-Pitre Cédex; tel. 82-03-13; fax 90-07-33; Dir RENÉ GOALLO.

Port Autonome de la Guadeloupe: Gare Maritime, BP 485, 97165 Pointe-à-Pitre Cédex; tel. 21-39-00; fax 21-39-69; e-mail webmaster@port-guadeloupe.com; internet www.port-guadeloupe.com; port authority; Gen. Man. PATRICK LAMBERT.

Société Guadeloupéenne de Consignation et Manutention (SGCM): 8 rue de la Chapelle, BP 2360, 97001 Jarry Cédex; tel. 38-05-55; fax 26-95-39; e-mail sgcma@outremer.com; f. 1994; shipping agents, stevedoring; Chair. LUC EMY; Gen. Man. MARTIN BUTRUILLE.

Société de Transport Maritimes Brudy Frères: 78 Centre St John Perse, 97110 Pointe-à-Pitre; tel. 82-52-25; fax 93-00-79.

CIVIL AVIATION

Raizet International Airport is situated 3 km (2 miles) from Pointe-à-Pitre and is equipped to handle jet-engined aircraft. There are smaller airports on the islands of Marie-Galante, La Désirade and Saint-Barthélémy.

Air Guadeloupe: Aéroport du Raizet, Immeuble Le Caducet, 97139 Abymes; tel. 82-47-34; fax 82-47-48; f. 1970; operates inter-island and regional services, flights to Miami (USA); Pres. and Dir-Gen. ERIC KOURY.

Tourism

Guadeloupe is a popular tourist destination, especially for visitors from metropolitan France (who account for some 82% of tourists) and the USA. The main attractions are the beaches, the mountainous scenery and the unspoilt beauty of the island dependencies. In 1998 693,000 tourists visited Guadeloupe, and receipts from tourism totalled US \$499m. in 1997. In 1998 there were 168 hotels, with 8,371 rooms.

Délégation Régionale au Tourisme: 5 rue Victor Hugues, 97100 Basse-Terre; tel. 81-15-60; fax 81-94-82; Dir HUGUES JONNIAUX.

Office du Tourisme: 5 square de la Banque, BP 1099, 97110 Pointe-à-Pitre Cédex; tel. 89-46-90; fax 83-89-22; Pres. PHILIPPE CHAULET.

Syndicat d'Initiative de la Guadeloupe: Pointe-à-Pitre; Pres. Dr EDOUARD CHARTOL.

MARTINIQUE

Introductory Survey

Location, Climate, Language, Religion, Capital

Martinique is one of the Windward Islands in the West Indies, with Dominica to the north and Saint Lucia to the south. The island is dominated by the volcanic peak of Mont Pelée. The climate is tropical, but tempered by easterly and north-easterly breezes. The more humid and wet season runs from July to November, and the average temperature is 26°C (79°F). French is the official language, but a creole patois is widely spoken. The majority of the population profess Christianity and belong to the Roman Catholic Church. The capital is Fort-de-France.

Recent History

Martinique has been a French possession since 1635. The prosperity of the island was based on the sugar industry, which was devastated by the volcanic eruption of Mont Pelée in 1902. Martinique became a Department of France in 1946, when the Governor was replaced by a Prefect, and an elected General Council was created.

During the 1950s there was a growth of nationalist feeling, as expressed by Aimé Césaire's Parti Progressiste Martiniquais (PPM) and the Parti Communiste Martiniquais (PCM). However, economic power remained concentrated in the hands of the *békés* (descendants of white colonial settlers), who owned most of the agricultural land and controlled the lucrative import-export market. This provided little incentive for innovation or self-sufficiency, and fostered resentment against lingering colonial attitudes.

In 1974 Martinique, together with Guadeloupe and French Guiana, was given regional status as part of France's governmental reorganization. An indirectly-elected Regional Council was created, with some control over the local economy. In 1982 and 1983 the socialist Government of President François Mitterrand, which had pledged itself to decentralizing power in favour of the Overseas Departments, made further concessions towards autonomy by giving the local councils greater control over taxation, local police and the economy. At the first direct elections to the new Regional Council, held in February 1983, left-wing parties (the PPM, the PCM and the Fédération Socialiste de la Martinique—FSM) won 21 of the 41 seats. This success, and the election of Aimé Césaire as the Council's President, strengthened his influence against the pro-independence elements in his own party. (Full independence for Martinique attracted support from only a small minority of the population; the majority sought reforms that would bring greater autonomy, while retaining French control.) The Mouvement Indépendantiste Martiniquais (MIM), the most vocal of the separatist parties, fared badly in the elections, obtaining less than 3% of the total vote. At elections to the enlarged General Council, held in March 1985, the left-wing parties increased their representation, but the centre-right coalition of the Union pour la Démocratie Française (UDF) and the Rassemblement pour la République (RPR) maintained their control of the administration.

For the general election to the French National Assembly in March 1986, Martinique's representation was increased from three to four deputies. Aimé Césaire and a member of the FSM were elected from a unified list of left-wing candidates, while the RPR and the UDF (which had also presented a joint list) each won one seat. For the concurrent elections to the Regional Council the left-wing parties (including the PPM, the FSM and the PCM) won 21 of the 41 seats, and the RPR and the UDF together won the remaining seats. Aimé Césaire retained the presidency of the Council until 1988, when he relinquished the post to Camille Darsières (the Secretary-General of the PPM). In September 1986 indirect elections were held for Martinique's two seats in the French Senate. As in the March elections, the left-wing parties united, and, as a consequence, Martinique acquired a left-wing senator for the first time since 1958, a PPM member, while the other successful candidate belonged to the UDF.

Following the recent trend in Martinique, the incumbent, François Mitterrand of the Parti Socialiste (PS), won a decisive majority of the island's votes at the 1988 French presidential election. Left-wing candidates secured all four seats at elections to the French National Assembly in June. Furthermore, in September–October, for the first time in 40 years, the parties of the left achieved a majority at elections to the General Council. Emile Maurice of the RPR was, none the less, elected President of the General Council for a seventh term.

In June 1990 the results of the 1986 election to the Regional Council were annulled because of a technicality, and another election was therefore held in October. Pro-independence candidates won nearly 22% of the votes, and secured nine seats (of which seven were won by the MIM). The PPM, the FSM and the PCM again formed a joint electoral list, but won only 14 seats, and consequently lost their absolute majority on the Council; Camille Darsières was, however, re-elected to the presidency of the Council. The success of the pro-independence candidates was attributed to local apprehension concerning the implications of plans within the European Community (EC, known as the European Union, EU—see p. 181—from November 1993) for a single market, which would, it was feared, expose Martinique's economy to excessive competition.

At elections to the General Council in March 1992, left-wing parties secured 26 seats and right-wing organizations 19. Claude Lise, a PPM deputy to the French National Assembly, was elected President of the General Council. In concurrent elections to the Regional Council the RPR and the UDF, contesting the election as the Union pour la France (UPF), won 16 seats, the MIM (which contested the election under the title Patriotes Martiniquais) and the PPM secured nine seats each, and the PCM (under the title Pour une Martinique au Travail) and the FSM (as the Nouvelle Génération Socialiste) won four and three seats, respectively. Following three rounds of voting, Emile Capgras of the PCM was finally elected President of the Regional Council.

In September 1992 72.3% of voters in Martinique approved ratification of the Treaty on European Union (see p. 181), although the abstention rate was 75.6%. In November of that year banana-growers in Guadeloupe and Martinique suspended economic activity in their respective Departments by obstructing access to ports and airports and blocking roads, in protest at the threatened loss of special advantages under the Single European Act. Order was restored after four days, however, following assurances that subsidies would be maintained and that certain products, such as bananas (one of Martinique's principal exports), would be protected under EC proposals.

At the March 1993 elections to the French National Assembly there was a marked swing in favour of the parties of the right: André Lesueur and Pierre Petit were elected to represent the RPR, while a third right-wing candidate, Anicet Turinay, campaigned successfully on behalf of the UPF. Aimé Césaire did not seek re-election, and was replaced at the National Assembly by Camille Darsières.

The composition of the General Council remained largely unchanged following cantonal elections in March 1994, at which the PPM retained 10 seats, the RPR seven and the UDF three; Claude Lise was subsequently re-elected President of the Council. At elections to the European Parliament in June, the government list secured the greatest proportion (36.6%) of the votes cast. A combined list of parties of the left of the four Overseas Departments (which included the PPM and the Parti Martiniquais Socialiste) took 20.2% of the votes.

At the first round of voting in the 1995 presidential election, on 23 April, Martinique was the only French overseas possession in which the candidate of the PS, Lionel Jospin, received the greatest proportion of the valid votes cast (34.4%). Jospin, supported by all the parties of the left, took 58.9% of the votes cast at the second round on 7 May. At municipal elections in June the PPM retained control of Martinique's principal towns. In September Claude Lise was elected to the Senate, while the incumbent PPM representative, Rodolphe Désiré, was returned to office.

At elections to the French National Assembly in May and June 1997, Anciet Turinay and Pierre Petit, representing the RPR, were re-elected, together with Camille Darsières of the PPM. Alfred Marie-Jeanne, the First Secretary and a founding member of the MIM, was elected in the constituency of Le François–Le Robert (hitherto held by the RPR). At elections to the Regional Council in March 1998, the left retained its majority. The pro-independence MIM performed well, increasing its representation by four seats, to 13, while the PPM secured seven seats, the RPR six and the UDF five. Marie-Jeanne was elected President of the Regional Council. In concurrent elections to the General Council the left again increased its majority, from 26 to 29 seats, with right-wing candidates winning 14 seats and independents two. Claude Lise was re-elected to the presidency of the Council.

In January 1999 representatives of 10 separatist organizations from French Guiana, Guadeloupe and Martinique, including the MIM, signed a joint declaration denouncing 'French colonialism', in which they stated their intention to campaign for the reinstatement of the three Caribbean Overseas Departments on a UN list of territories to be decolonized.

A two-month strike by workers in the banana sector, which had severely disrupted economic activity around the port of Fort-de-France, was ended in January 1999, when a pay agreement was reached. The social climate deteriorated further in May, as two companies were affected by strike action. Workers at the Toyota motor company were demanding substantial pay increases and a reduction in working hours, while employees of the Roger Albert distribution group were protesting against the dismissal of two colleagues. In early October tension escalated as trade unions took sympathetic action, blocking access to the main industrial and commercial zones around the capital for two days. Subsequent negotiations between the local authorities and a trade union delegation resulted in the removal of the blockades and an agreement to hold talks on the resolution of the two conflicts. The dispute at Roger Albert was concluded shortly afterwards, following the intervention of Alfred Marie-Jeanne, but, despite mediation efforts, industrial action at Toyota continued. In mid-October trade unions organized a week-long blockade of the port of Fort-de-France in protest against proposed redundancies at Toyota. Later that month, prior to a two-day visit to Martinique by Lionel Jospin, the Prime Minister, banana producers occupied the headquarters of the French naval forces for several days, demanding the disbursement of exceptional aid to compensate for the adverse effect on their industry of a dramatic decline in prices on the European market. Marie-Jeanne, who was opposed to the limited nature of the Government's plans for institutional reform, refused to participate in the events organized for Jospin's stay. The Prime Minister announced an emergency plan for the banana sector and, while attending a conference on regional co-operation, agreed, in principle, to a proposal for greater autonomy for the local authorities in conducting relations with neighbouring countries and territories. In November, following two weeks of direct negotiations between trade union representatives and the management of Toyota, a protocol was signed, marking the end of the five-month dispute; a pay increase was awarded and dismissal proceedings against 12 employees were annulled.

Following a series of meetings, in December 1999 the Presidents of the Regional Councils of French Guiana, Guadeloupe and Martinique signed a joint declaration in Basse-Terre, Guadeloupe, affirming their intention to propose, to the President and the Government, a legislative amendment, possibly constitutional, aimed at creating a new status of overseas region, despite an earlier statement by Jospin indicating that the Government did not envisage a change in status for the Departments. Further meetings of the three regional Presidents were held in January and February 2000. Proposals regarding the institutional future and socio-economic development of the Departments (see p. 1605) were provisionally accepted by the French National Assembly in May 2000, and a modified version of the proposals was subsequently adopted, by a narrow margin, by the French Senate. In November the National Assembly approved the proposals and in December they were ratified by the Constitutional Council.

At a referendum held in September 2000, Martinique voted overwhelmingly in favour (91%) of reducing the presidential mandate from seven years to five. In municipal elections held in March 2001 the PPM retained control of the majority of municipalities (including Fort-de-France, where Aimé Césaire, retiring as mayor after 55 years, was succeeded by a fellow PPM member, Sérge Letchimy, who defeated Alfred Marie-Jeanne, President of the Regional Council). In the concurrently-held election to the General Council Claude Lise was re-elected President.

Government

France is represented in Martinique by an appointed prefect. There are two councils with local powers: the 45-member General Council and the 41-member Regional Council. Both are elected by universal adult suffrage for a period of up to six years. Martinique elects four deputies to the French National Assembly in Paris, and sends two indirectly-elected representatives to the Senate. The Department is also represented at the European Parliament.

Defence

At 1 August 2000 France maintained a military force of 3,800 and a gendarmerie of 860 in the Antilles, with headquarters in Fort-de-France.

Economic Affairs

In 1996 Martinique's gross domestic product (GDP), measured at current prices, was estimated at US $3,876m., equivalent to about $10,095 per head. During 1990–95, it was estimated, GDP declined, in real terms, at an average rate of 0.1% per year; GDP increased by 1.9% in 1994, but declined by 2.9% in 1995. Between the censuses of 1990 and 1999, according to provisional figures, the population increased at an average annual rate of 0.7%.

Agriculture, hunting, forestry and fishing contributed 4.1% of GDP in 1995, and engaged an estimated 4.7% of the labour force in 1998. The principal cash crops are bananas (which accounted for some 36.6% of export earnings in 1997), sugar cane (primarily for the production of rum), limes, melons and pineapples. Severe damage to banana plantations was caused by 'Cyclone Debbie' in September 1994. The cultivation of cut flowers is also of some significance. Roots and tubers and vegetables are grown for local consumption. Agricultural production increased at an average rate of 1.3% per year during 1990–98. It increased by 6.7% in 1997, but declined by 0.2% in 1999.

The industrial sector (including mining, manufacturing, construction and power) contributed 16.1% of GDP in 1995, and engaged 17.3% of the employed labour force at the 1996 census. Mining, manufacturing and power provided 8.7% of GDP in 1995. The most important manufacturing activities are petroleum refining (exports of refined petroleum products accounted for some 16.0% of the value of total exports in 1997) and the processing of agricultural products—the production of rum being of particular significance. Exports of rum provided some 10.0% of export earnings in 1997. Martiniquais rum was accorded the designation of Appellation d'origine contrôlée (AOC) in 1996 (the first AOC to be designated outside metropolitan France). Other areas of activity include metals, cement, chemicals, plastics, wood, printing and textiles. Energy is derived principally from mineral fuels. Imports of mineral fuels (including crude petroleum destined for the island's refinery) accounted for 7.5% of the value of total imports in 1995.

The services sector engaged 75.1% of the employed labour force in 1996 and provided 79.8% of GDP in 1995. Tourism is a major activity on the island and one of the most important sources of foreign exchange. In 1999 946,389 tourists visited the island. In 1997 earnings from the tourism industry totalled US $400m.

In 1999 Martinique recorded a trade deficit of 8,890.5m. French francs. In 1997 the principal source of imports (62.1%) was metropolitan France, which was also the principal market for exports (45.1%). Guadeloupe, the United Kingdom, Venezuela and Belgium-Luxembourg were also significant trading partners. The principal exports in 1997 were bananas, refined petroleum products, rum, flavoured or sweetened water and boats. The principal imports in 1995 were machinery and transport equipment (especially road vehicles), food and live animals, miscellaneous manufactured articles, basic manufactures, chemicals and mineral fuels.

In 1999 the budget was expected to balance at 1,298m. French francs. The annual rate of inflation averaged 2.3% in 1990–98; consumer prices increased by an average of 1.3% in 1998 and by 0.4% in 1999. Some 28.1% of the labour force were unemployed in 1999. In 1990 the level of emigration from the island was estimated at about 15,000 per year; most of the emigrants were under 25 years of age.

As an integral part of France, Martinique belongs to the European Union (EU—see p. 181). Martinique and the other French Overseas Departments were to receive a total of ECU 1,500m. from EU regional funds during 1994–2000.

Martinique's economic development has created a society that combines a relatively high standard of living with a weak

Martinique

economic base in agricultural and industrial production, as well as a chronic trade deficit. Levels of unemployment and emigration are high (in 1990 some 30% of Martiniquais nationals were resident in France), although the rate of growth of both these factors has slowed since the mid-1980s. The linking of wage levels to those of metropolitan France, despite the island's lower level of productivity, has increased labour costs and restricted development. In the late 1990s the value of banana exports declined owing to a significant fall in prices on the European market, while an ongoing dispute between the USA and four Latin American countries and the EU over the latter's banana import regime also threatened Martinique's banana-growing sector. Moreover, a succession of industrial disputes severely disrupted economic activity in 1999.

Social Welfare

Martinique has a system of social welfare similar to that of metropolitan France. With effect from 1 January 1996 welfare payments and the statutory minimum wage in the Overseas Departments were aligned with those of metropolitan France. In 1997 Martinique had a regional and university hospital complex, 13 general hospitals, five maternity hospitals and a hospital complex specializing in physiotherapy. In 1998 there were 780 physicians, 130 dental surgeons and 240 pharmacists.

Education

The educational system is similar to that of metropolitan France (see chapter on French Guiana). Higher education in law, French language and literature, human sciences, economics, medicine and Creole studies is provided in Martinique by a branch of the Université Antilles-Guyane. The university as a whole had 11,199 enrolled students in the 1999/2000 academic year. There are also two teacher-training institutes, and colleges of agriculture, fisheries, hotel management, nursing, midwifery and child care. Separate Academies for Martinique, French Guiana and Guadeloupe were established in January 1997, replacing the single Academy for the Antilles-Guyane (which was based in Fort-de-France). Total government expenditure on education amounted to 2,842m. French francs in 1993.

Public Holidays

2001: 1 January (New Year's Day), 26–27 February (Carnival), 28 February (Ash Wednesday), 13–16 April (Easter), 1 May (Labour Day), 8 May (Victory Day), 24 May (Ascension Day), 4 June (Whit Monday), 14 July (National Day), 15 August (Assumption), 1 November (All Saints' Day), 11 November (Armistice Day), 25 December (Christmas Day).

2002: 1 January (New Year's Day), 11–12 February (Carnival), 13 February (Ash Wednesday), 29 March–1 April (Easter), 1 May (Labour Day), 8 May (Victory Day), 9 May (Ascension Day), 20 May (Whit Monday), 14 July (National Day), 15 August (Assumption), 1 November (All Saints' Day), 11 November (Armistice Day), 25 December (Christmas Day).

Weights and Measures

The metric system is in use.

Statistical Survey

Sources (unless otherwise stated): Institut national de la statistique et des études économiques (INSEE), Pointe de Jaham Schoëlcher, BP 605, 97261 Fort-de-France; tel. 5-96-60-73-73; fax 5-96-60-73-50; Ministère des départements et territoires d'outre-mer, 27 rue Oudinot, 75700 Paris 07 SP; tel. 1-53-69-20-00; fax 1-43-06-60-30; internet www.outre-mer.gouv.fr.

AREA AND POPULATION

Area: 1,100 sq km (424.7 sq miles).

Population: 326,717 (males 158,415, females 168,302) at census of 9 March 1982; 359,579 (males 173,878, females 185,701) at census of 15 March 1990; 381,427 at census of 8 March 1999.

Density (at 1999 census): 346.8 per sq km.

Principal Towns (at 1999 census): Fort-de-France (capital) 94,049; Le Lamentin 35,460; Le Robert 21,240; Schoelcher 20,845; Sainte-Marie 20,098; Le François 18,559; Saint-Joseph 15,785; Ducos 15,240.

Births, Marriages and Deaths (1997, provisional figures): Registered live births 5,735 (birth rate 15.2 per 1,000); Registered marriages 1,548 (marriage rate 4.1 per 1,000); Registered deaths 2,403 (death rate 6.4 per 1,000).

Expectation of Life (UN estimates, years at birth, 1990–95): 77.6 (males 74.7, females 81.5). Source: UN, *World Population Prospects: The 1998 Revision*.

Economically Active Population (persons aged 15 years and over, 1996 census): Agriculture, hunting, forestry and fishing 8,445; Industry and energy 9,706; Construction and public works 9,298; Trade 13,965; Transport and telecommunications 6,673; Financial services 2,952; Other marketable services 23,537; Non-marketable services 35,541; Total employed 110,117 (males 60,137, females 49,980); Unemployed 54,760 (males 26,416, females 28,344); Total labour force 164,877 (males 86,553, females 78,324).

1999: Total employed 119,900; Unemployed 46,900; Total labour force 166,800.

AGRICULTURE, ETC.

Principal Crops (FAO estimates, '000 metric tons, 1999): Yams 5; Sweet potatoes 1; Other roots and tubers 12; Sugar cane 189; Bananas 321; Plantains 13; Pineapples 20; Oranges 1; Source: FAO.

Livestock (FAO estimates, '000 head, year ending September 1999): Cattle 30; Sheep 42; Pigs 33; Goats 22. Source: FAO.

Livestock Products (FAO estimates, '000 metric tons, 1999): Beef and veal 3; Pig meat 2; Poultry meat 1; Cows' milk 2; Hen eggs 2. Source: FAO.

Forestry: Roundwood removals ('000 cu m, excluding bark, 1998): Sawlogs, veneer logs and logs for sleepers 2; Fuel wood 10; Total 12. Source: FAO, *Yearbook of Forest Products*.

Fishing (metric tons, live weight, 1998, estimates): Capture 5,500 (Common dolphinfish 420, Atlantic bonito 1,030, Cero 420, Blackfin tuna 910, Marine fishes 2,397); Aquaculture 55; Total catch 5,555. Source: FAO, *Yearbook of Fishery Statistics*.

MINING

Production (1995, '000 metric tons): Pumice 130.0. Source: UN, *Industrial Commodity Statistics Yearbook*.

INDUSTRY

Production (1996, '000 metric tons, unless otherwise indicated): Pineapple juice 3.2 (1994); Canned or bottled pineapples 18.4 (1994); Raw sugar 7 (1997); Rum ('000 hl) 78 (1994); Motor spirit (petrol) 151 (estimate); Kerosene 132; Gas-diesel (distillate fuel) oils 158; Residual fuel oils 275; Liquefied petroleum gas 21; Cement 225 (estimate); Electric energy (million kWh) 1,078 (1997). Source: UN, *Industrial Commodity Statistics Yearbook*.

1996: Rum 64,985 hl.
1997: Rum 70,040 hl.
1998: Raw sugar 6,543 metric tons; Rum 68,716 hl.

FINANCE

Currency and Exchange Rates: French currency is used (see French Guiana).

Budget (estimates, 1999): Revenue and expenditure to balance at 1,298 million French francs.

Expenditure by Metropolitan France (1988): 4,486 million French francs.

Money Supply (million French francs at 31 December 1996): Currency outside banks 1,252; Demand deposits at banks 5,275; Total money 6,527.

Cost of Living (Consumer Price Index; base: 1990 = 100): 118.5 in 1997; 120.0 in 1998; 120.5 in 1999. Source: UN, *Monthly Bulletin of Statistics*.

Expenditure on the Gross Domestic Product (million French francs at current prices, 1994): Government final consumption expenditure 6,962; Private final consumption expenditure 20,133; Increase in stocks 20; Gross fixed capital formation 5,102; *Total domestic expenditure* 32,217; Exports of goods and services 1,439; *Less* Imports of goods and services 9,150; *GDP in purchasers' values* 24,506.

Gross Domestic Product by Economic Activity (million French francs at current prices, 1992): Agriculture, hunting, forestry and fishing 1,106.3; Mining, quarrying and manufacturing 1,770.6; Electricity, gas and water 483.6; Construction 1,145.3; Trade, restaurants and hotels 4,022.1; Transport, storage and communications 1,427.6; Finance, insurance, real estate and business services 2,590.1; Government services 5,416.0; Other community, social and personal services 3,576.4; Other services 330.5; *Sub-total* 21,868.5; Import duties 791.0; Value-added tax 640.9; *Less* Imputed bank service charge 1,207.1; *GDP in purchasers' values* 22,093.4. Source UN, *National Accounts Statistics*.

EXTERNAL TRADE

Principal Commodities: *Imports c.i.f.* (US $ million, 1995): Food and live animals 319.6 (Meat and meat preparations 82.8, Dairy products and birds' eggs 53.6, Fish and fish preparations 38.6, Cereals and cereal preparations 45.6, Vegetables and fruit 49.1); Beverages and tobacco 52.0 (Beverages 45.0); Mineral fuels, lubricants, etc. 148.0 (Petroleum and petroleum products 146.2); Chemicals and related products 189.5 (Medicinal and pharmaceutical products 83.9); Basic manufactures 260.1 (Paper, paperboard and manufactures 45.1); Machinery and transport equipment 637.6 (Power-generating machinery and equipment 62.8, General industrial machinery, equipment and parts 83.2, Telecommunications and sound equipment 41.1, Road vehicles and parts 240.7, Ships and boats 50.3); Miscellaneous manufactured articles 288.5 (Furniture and parts 46.2, Clothing and accessories, excl. footwear 62.6); Total (incl. others) 1,969.8. Source: UN, *International Trade Statistics Yearbook*. *Exports f.o.b.* (million French francs, 1997): Bananas 462.2; Rum 126.7; Flavoured or sweetened water 78.8; Refined petroleum products 201.9; Yachts and sports boats 74.4; Total (incl. others) 1,263.3.

1997 (million French francs): *Imports:* 9,947.0; *Exports:* 1,239.0. *1998* (million French francs): *Imports:* 10,046.8; *Exports:* 1,701.4. *1999* (million French francs): *Imports:* 10,605.6; *Exports:* 1,715.1. Source: Direction Générale des Douanes.

Principal Trading Partners (million French francs, 1997): *Imports c.i.f.:* France (metropolitan) 6,178.9; Germany 352.0; Italy 350.1; Japan 180.3; Trinidad and Tobago 159.6; United Kingdom 108.3; USA 263.6; Venezuela 607.8; Total (incl. others) 9,957.5; *Exports f.o.b.:* Belgium-Luxembourg 76.4; France (metropolitan) 569.7; French Guiana 54.8; Guadeloupe 357.2; United Kingdom 110.5; Total (incl. others) 1,263.3.

TRANSPORT

Road Traffic ('000 motor vehicles in use, 1995): Passenger cars 95.0; Commercial vehicles 21.5. Source: UN, *Statistical Yearbook*.

Shipping *Merchant Fleet* (vessels registered '000 grt at 31 December, 1992): 1. Source: Lloyd's Register of Shipping. *International Sea-borne Traffic* (1999, provisional): Goods loaded 809,000 metric tons; Goods unloaded 1,927,000 metric tons. Source: Direction Départementale de l'Équipement.

Civil Aviation (1998): Passengers carried 1,821,063; Freight carried 16,166 metric tons. Source: Chambre de Commerce et d'Industrie de la Martinique.

TOURISM

Tourist Arrivals 942,432 in 1997; 1,007,451 in 1998; 946,389 in 1999.

Receipts from Tourism (US $ million): 384 in 1995; 382 in 1996; 400 in 1997. Source: World Tourism Organization, *Yearbook of Tourism Statistics*.

COMMUNICATIONS MEDIA

Radio Receivers ('000 in use) 82 in 1997; **Television Receivers** ('000 in use) 66 in 1997; **Telephones** ('000 main lines in use) 170 in 1997; **Telefax Stations** (number in use) 5,200 in 1997; **Mobile Cellular Telephones** (subscribers) 15,000 in 1997; **Daily Newspaper** 1 (estimate) in 1996 (estimated average circulation 32,000 copies). Sources: UNESCO, *Statistical Yearbook;* UN, *Statistical Yearbook*.

EDUCATION

Pre-primary (1995/96): 86 institutions; 660 teachers; 21,232 students.

Primary (1999/2000): 273 institutions; 3,266 teachers (3,026 state, 240 private); 54,327 students.

Secondary (1999/2000): 76 institutions; 4,227 teachers (3,897 state, 330 private); 48,893 students.

Higher (1999/2000): 11,199 students (Université Antilles-Guyane).

Source: UNESCO, *Statistical Yearbook*, and Académie de la Martinique.

Directory

The Government

(April 2001)

Prefect: MICHEL CADOT, Préfecture, 82 rue Victor Sévère, BP 647, 97200 Fort-de-France Cédex; tel. 39-36-00; fax 71-40-29.

President of the General Council: CLAUDE LISE (PPM), Conseil Général de la Martinique, 20 ave des Caraïbes, BP 679, 97264 Fort-de-France Cédex; tel. 55-26-00; fax 73-59-32; internet www.cg972.fr.

Deputies to the French National Assembly: ANICET TURINAY (RPR), PIERRE PETIT (RPR), CAMILLE DARSIÈRES (PPM), ALFRED MARIE-JEANNE (MIM).

Representatives to the French Senate: CLAUDE LISE (PPM), RODOLPHE DÉSIRÉ (PPM).

REGIONAL COUNCIL

Hôtel de Région, rue Gaston Deferre, BP 601, 97200 Fort-de-France Cédex; tel. 59-63-00; fax 72-68-10; e-mail Crg72 .com-ext@wanadoo.fr; internet www.cr-martinique.fr.

President: ALFRED MARIE-JEANNE (MIM).

Election, 15 March 1998

	Seats
Mouvement Indépendantiste Martiniquais (MIM) . .	13
Parti Progressiste Martiniquais (PPM)	7
Rassemblement pour la République (RPR) . . .	6
Union pour la Démocratie Française (UDF)* . . .	5
Parti Martiniquais Socialiste (PMS)	3
Others†	7
Total	**41**

* Re-established as the Forces Martiniquaises de Progrès in October 1998.

† Three of those elected were candidates of the right.

Political Organizations

Fédération Socialiste de la Martinique (FSM): Cité la Meynard, 97200 Fort-de-France; tel. 75-53-28; local branch of the **Parti Socialiste (PS)**; Sec.-Gen. JEAN CRUSOL.

Forces Martiniquaises de Progrès: f. 1998 to replace the local branch of the Union pour la Démocratie Française.

Groupe Révolution Socialiste (GRS): 97200 Fort-de-France; tel. 70-36-49; f. 1973; Trotskyist; Leader GILBERT PAGO.

Mouvement Indépendantiste Martiniquais (MIM): Fort-de-France; f. 1978; pro-independence party; First Sec. ALFRED MARIE-JEANNE.

Parti Communiste Martiniquais (PCM): Fort-de-France; f. 1920; affiliated to French Communist Party until 1957; Leader GEORGES ERICHOT.

Parti Martiniquais Socialiste (PMS): Fort-de-France; Pres. LOUIS JOSEPH DOGUÉ; Sec. ERNEST WAN AJOUHU.

Parti Progressiste Martiniquais (PPM): Fort-de-France; tel. 71-86-83; f. 1957; left-wing; Pres. AIMÉ CÉSAIRE; Sec.-Gen. CAMILLE DARSIÈRES.

Rassemblement pour la République (RPR): 97205 Fort-de-France; Gaullist.

Judicial System

Cour d'Appel de Fort-de-France: Fort-de-France; tel. 70-62-62; fax 63-52-13; e-mail ca-fort-de-france@justice.fr; highest court of appeal for Martinique and French Guiana; First Pres. CHRISTIAN AUDOUARD; Procurator-Gen. ROBERT FINIELZ.

There are two Tribunaux de Grande Instance, at Fort-de-France and Cayenne (French Guiana), and three Tribunaux d'Instance (two in Fort-de-France and one in Cayenne).

Religion

The majority of the population belong to the Roman Catholic Church.

CHRISTIANITY

The Roman Catholic Church

Martinique comprises the single archdiocese of Fort-de-France, with an estimated 280,000 adherents (some 77.8% of the total population) at 31 December 1998. The Archbishop participates in the Antilles Episcopal Conference, currently based in Port of Spain, Trinidad and Tobago.

Archbishop of Fort-de-France: Most Rev. MAURICE MARIE-SAINTE, Archevêché, 5–7 rue du Révérend Père Pinchon, BP 586, 97207 Fort-de-France Cédex; tel. 63-70-70; fax 63-75-21.

Other Churches

Among the denominations active in Martinique are the Assembly of God, the Evangelical Church of the Nazarene and the Seventh-day Adventist Church.

The Press

Antilla: BP 46, Lamentin; tel. 75-48-68; fax 75-58-46; e-mail antilla .hebdo@wanadoo.fr; weekly; Dir ALFRED FORTUNE.

Aujourd'hui Dimanche: Presbytère de Bellevue, Fort-de-France; tel. 71-48-97; weekly; Dir Père GAUTHIER; circ. 12,000.

Carib Hebdo: 97200 Fort-de-France; f. 1989; Dir GISÈLE DE LA FARGUE.

Combat Ouvrier: Fort-de-France; weekly; Dir M. G. BEAUJOUR.

France-Antilles: pl. Stalingrad, 97200 Fort-de-France; tel. 59-08-83; fax 60-29-96; f. 1964; daily; Dir HENRI MERLE; circ. 30,000 (Martinique edition).

Justice: rue Andrè Aliker, 97200 Fort-de-France; tel. 71-86-83; weekly; organ of the PPM; Dir G. THIMOTÉE; circ. 8,000.

Le Naif: Fort-de-France; weekly; Dir R. LAOUCHEZ.

Le Progressiste: Fort-de-France; weekly; organ of the PPM; Dir PAUL GABOURG; circ. 13,000.

Révolution Socialiste: BP 1031, 97200 Fort-de-France; tel. 70-36-49; f. 1973; weekly; organ of the GRS; Dir PHILIPPE PIERRE CHARLES; circ. 2,500.

Télé Sept Jours: rond-point du Vietnam Héroïque, 97200 Fort-de-France; tel. 63-75-49; weekly.

Broadcasting and Communications

BROADCASTING

Réseau France Outre-mer (RFO): La Clairère, BP 662, 97263 Fort-de-France; tel. 59-52-00; fax 63-29-88; internet www.rfo.fr; fmrly Société Nationale de Radio-Télévision Française d'Outre-mer, renamed as above 1998; broadcasts 24 hours of radio programmes daily and 37 hours of television programmes weekly; Pres. ANDRÉ-MICHEL BESSE; Regional Dir MARIJOSÉ ALIE; Editor-in-Chief GÉRARD LE MOAL.

Radio

There are some 40 licensed private FM radio stations.

Radio Caraïbe International (RCI): 2 blvd de la Marne, 97200 Fort-de-France Cédex; tel. 63-98-70; fax 63-26-59; internet www .fwinet.com/rci.htm; commercial station broadcasting 24 hours daily; Dir YANN DUVAL.

Television

ATV Antilles Télévision: 28 rue Arawaks, 97200 Fort de France; tel. 75-44-44; fax 75-55-65; commercial station.

Canal Antilles: Centre Commerciale la Galléria, 97232 Le Lamentin; tel. 50-57-87; private commercial station.

TCI Martinique: Immeuble RCI/TCI, Zone Industrielle, 92232 Le Lamentin; tel. 51-06-06; fax 51-85-62; private commercial station.

Finance

(cap. = capital; res = reserves; dep. = deposits; m. = million; brs = branches; amounts in French francs)

BANKING

Central Bank

Institut d'Emission des Départements d'Outre-mer: blvd du Général de Gaulle, BP 512, 97206 Fort-de-France Cédex; tel. 59-44-00; fax 59-44-04.

Major Commercial Banks

Banque des Antilles Françaises: 28–34 rue Lamartine, BP 582, 97207 Fort-de-France Cédex; tel. 73-93-44; fax 63-58-94; f. 1853; cap. 32.6m., res 42.9m., dep. 2,243.6m. (Dec. 1996); Chair. JACQUES GIRAULT.

Banque Française Commerciale: BP 986, 97425 Fort-de-France; tel. 63-82-57; fax 70-51-15; Man. JACQUES FACHON.

BNP Paribas, SA: 72 ave des Caraïbes, 97200 Fort-de-France; tel. 59-46-00; fax 63-71-42; Dir JEAN PASCAL DUMANS; 12 further brs in Martinique.

BRED Banque Populaire: 5 Place Monseigneur Romero, 97200 Fort-de-France; tel. 63-77-63; internet www.bred.fr; Chair. STEVE GENTILI.

Crédit Agricole: rue Case Nègre—Place d'Armes, 97232 Le Lamentin Cédex 2; tel. 66-59-39; fax 66-59-67; internet www.credit -agricole.fr; Chair MARC BUÉ.

Crédit Martiniquais: 17 rue de la Liberté, Fort-de-France; tel. 71-12-40; f. 1922; associated since 1987 with Chase Manhattan Bank (USA) and, since 1990, with Mutuelles du Mans Vie (France); cap. 185.4m. (1998); Administrator ALAIN DENNHARDT; 10 brs.

Société Générale de Banque aux Antilles: 19 rue de la Liberté, BP 408, 97200 Fort-de-France; tel. 71-69-83; f. 1979; cap. 15m.; Dir MICHEL SAMOUR.

INSURANCE

Cie Antillaise d'Assurances: 19 rue de la Liberté, 97205 Fort-de-France; tel. 73-04-50.

Caraïbe Assurances: 11 rue Victor Hugo, BP 210, 97202 Fort-de-France; tel. 63-92-29; fax 63-19-79.

Groupement Français d'Assurances Caraïbes (GFA Caraïbes): 46–48 rue Ernest Desproges, 97205 Fort-de-France; tel. 59-04-04; fax 73-19-72.

La Nationale (GAN): 30 blvd Général de Gaulle, BP 185, Fort-de-France; tel. 71-30-07; Reps MARCEL BOULLANGER, ROGER BOULLANGER.

Le Secours: 74 ave Duparquet, 97200 Fort-de-France; tel. 70-03-79; Dir Y. ANGANI.

Trade and Industry

DEVELOPMENT ORGANIZATIONS

Agence pour le Développement Economique de la Martinique: Fort-de-France; tel. 73-45-81; fax 72-41-38; f. 1979; promotion of industry.

Agence Française de Développement (AFD): 12 blvd du Général de Gaulle, BP 804, 97244 Fort-de-France Cédex; tel. 59-44-73; fax 59-44-88; fmrly Caisse Française de Développement; Dir JACQUES ALBUGUES; Regional Man. XAVIER BLANCHARD.

Bureau du Développement Economique: Préfecture, 97262 Fort-de-France; tel. 39-36-00; fax 71-40-29; research, documentation and technical and administrative advice on investment in industry and commerce; Chief VICTOR VÉLAIDOMESTRY.

Société de Crédit pour le Développement de la Martinique (SODEMA): 12 blvd du Général de Gaulle, BP 575, 97242 Fort-de-France Cédex; tel. 72-87-72; fax 72-87-70; e-mail sodema@ compuserve.com; f. 1970; cap. 25m. frs; medium- and long-term finance; Dir-Gen. JACKIE BATHANY.

Société de Développement Régional Antilles-Guyane (SODERAG): 111–113 rue Ernest Desproges, BP 450, 97205 Fort-de-France Cédex; tel. 59-71-00; fax 63-38-88; Dir-Gen. FULVIO MAZZEO; Sec.-Gen. OLYMPE FRANCIL.

CHAMBERS OF COMMERCE

Chambre d'Agriculture: pl. d'Armes, BP 312, 97286 Le Lamentin; tel. 51-75-75; fax 51-93-42; Pres. GUY OVIDE-ETIENNE.

Chambre de Commerce et d'Industrie de la Martinique: 50–54 rue Ernest Desproges, BP 478, 97241 Fort-de-France; tel. 55-28-00; fax 60-66-68; e-mail ccim.doi@martinique.cci.fr; internet www .martinique.cci.fr; f. 1907; Pres. JEAN-CLAUDE LUBIN; Dir-Gen. FERNAND LERYCHARD.

Chambre des Métiers de la Martinique: 2 rue du Temple, Morne Tartenson, BP 1194, 97200 Fort-de-France; tel. 71-32-22; fax 70-47-30; f. 1970; Pres. CHRISTIAN CAYOL; 8,000 mems.

EMPLOYERS' ORGANIZATIONS

Groupement de Producteurs d'Ananas de la Martinique: Fort-de-France; f. 1967; Pres. C. DE GRYSE.

Ordre des Médecins de la Martinique: 80 rue de la République, 97200 Fort-de-France; tel. 63-27-01; Pres. Dr RENÉ LEGENDRI.

Ordre des Pharmaciens de la Martinique: BP 587, 97207 Fort-de-France Cédex; tel. 52-23-67; fax 52-20-92.

Société Coopérative d'Intérêt Collectif Agricole Bananière de la Martinique (SICABAM): Domaine de Montgéralde, La Dillon, 97200 Fort-de-France; f. 1961; Pres. ALEX ASSIER DE POMPIGNAN; Dir GÉRARD BALLY; 1,000 mems.

Syndicat des Distilleries Agricoles: Fort-de-France; tel. 71-25-46.

Syndicat des Producteurs de Rhum Agricole: La Dillon, 97200 Fort-de-France.

Union Départementale des Coopératives Agricoles de la Martinique: Fort-de-France; Pres. M. URSULET.

TRADE UNIONS

Centrale Démocratique Martiniquaise des Travailleurs: BP 21, 97201 Fort-de-France; tel. 70-19-86; fax 71-32-25; Sec.-Gen. CATHERINE FELIX.

Confédération Générale des Travailleurs de la Martinique (1936): Maison des Syndicats, porte no 14, Jardin Desclieux, 97200 Fort-de-France; tel. 60-45-21; f. 1936; affiliated to World Federation of Trade Unions; Sec.-Gen. LUC BERNABÉ; c. 12,000 mems.

Syndicat des Enseignants de la Martinique: 31 rue Perrinon, 97200 Fort-de-France; tel. 70-24-52; fax 63-74-36; e-mail se-gen -972@cgit.com.

Union Départementale des Syndicats—FO: BP 1114, 97248 Fort-de-France Cédex; affiliated to International Confederation of Free Trade Unions; Sec.-Gen. ALBERT SABEL; c. 2,000 mems.

Transport

RAILWAYS

There are no railways in Martinique.

ROADS

There are 267 km of motorways and first-class roads, and 615 km of secondary roads.

SHIPPING

Direction des Concessions Services Portuaires: Quai de l'Hydro Base, BP 782, 97244 Fort-de-France Cédex; tel. 59-00-00; fax 71-35-73; port services management; Dir FRANTZ THODIARD; Operations Man. VICTOR ELISTACHE.

Direction Départementale des Affaires Maritimes: blvd Chevalier de Sainte-Marthe, BP 620, 97261 Fort-de-France Cédex; tel. 71-90-05; fax 63-67-30; Dir FRANÇOIS NIHOUL.

Alcoa Steamship Co, Alpine Line, Agdwa Line, Delta Line, Raymond Witcomb Co, Moore MacCormack, Eastern Steamship Co: c/o Etablissements Ren, Cottrell, Fort-de-France.

American President Lines: c/o Compagnie d'Agence Multiples Antillaise (CAMA), 44 rue Garnier Pages, 97205 Fort-de-France Cédex; tel. 71-31-00; fax 63-54-40.

CMA-CGM CGM Antilles-Guyane: 8 ave Maurice Bishop, BP 574, 97242 Fort-de-France Cédex; tel. 55-32-05; fax 60-47-84; e-mail fdf.jdurand@cma-cgm.com; internet www.cma-cgm.com; also represents other passenger and freight lines; Dir. JEAN-LUC DURAND.

Compagnie de Navigation Mixte: Immeuble Rocade, La Dillon, BP 1023, 97209 Fort-de-France; Rep. R. M. MICHAUX.

CIVIL AVIATION

Martinique's international airport is at Le Lamentin, 6 km from Fort-de-France. A new terminal was inaugurated in July 1995.

Air Martinique: Aéroport du Lamentin, 97232 Fort-de-France; tel. 51-08-09; fax 51-59-27; f. 1981 as Compagnie Antillaise d'Affrètements Aériens; operates regional services; Pres. MICHEL ZIEGLER; Man. Dir MICHEL GOUZE.

Tourism

Martinique's tourist attractions are its beaches and coastal scenery, its mountainous interior, and the historic towns of Fort-de-France and Saint Pierre. In 1999 tourist arrivals totalled 946,389. Tourism receipts in 1997 totalled US $400m. In 1999 there were 122 hotels, with some 6,051 rooms.

Agence Régionale pour le Développement du Tourisme en Martinique: Anse Gouraud, 97233 Schoelcher; tel. 61-61-77; fax 61-22-72.

Chambre Syndicale des Hôtels de Tourisme de la Martinique: Entrée Montgéralde, Route de Chateauboeuf, Fort-de-France; tel. 70-27-80.

Délégation Régionale au Tourisme: 41 rue Gabriel Périé 97200 Fort-de-France; tel. 63-18-61; Dir GILBERT LECURIEUK.

Fédération Martiniquaise des Offices de Tourisme et Syndicats d'Initiative (FMOTSI): Maison du Tourisme Vert, 9 blvd du Général de Gaulle, BP 491, 97207 Fort-de-France Cédex; tel. 63-18-54; fax 70-17-61; f. 1984; Pres. VICTOR GRANDIN.

Office Départemental du Tourisme de la Martinique: 2 rue Ernest Desproges, BP 520, 97206 Fort-de-France; tel. 63-79-60; fax 73-66-93.

RÉUNION

Introductory Survey

Location, Climate, Language, Religion, Capital

Réunion is an island in the Indian Ocean, lying about 800 km (500 miles) east of Madagascar. The climate varies greatly according to altitude: at sea-level it is tropical, with average temperatures between 20°C (68°F) and 28°C (82°F), but in the uplands it is much cooler, with average temperatures between 8°C (46°F) and 19°C (66°F). Rainfall is abundant, averaging 4,714 mm annually in the uplands, and 686 mm at sea-level. The population is of mixed origin, including people of European, African, Indian and Chinese descent. The official language is French. A large majority of the population are Christians belonging to the Roman Catholic Church. The capital is Saint-Denis.

Recent History

Réunion was first occupied by France in 1642, and was ruled as a colony until 1946, when it received full departmental status. In 1974 it became an Overseas Department with the status of a region.

In 1978 the Organization of African Unity (OAU, see p. 256) adopted a report recommending measures to hasten the independence of the island, and condemned its occupation by a 'colonial power'. However, this view seemed to have little popular support in Réunion. Although the left-wing political parties on the island advocated increased autonomy (amounting to virtual self-government), few people were in favour of complete independence.

In 1982 the French Government proposed a decentralization scheme, envisaging the dissolution of the General and Regional Councils in the Overseas Departments and the creation in each department of a single assembly, to be elected on the basis of proportional representation. As a result of considerable opposition in Réunion and the other Overseas Departments, the Government was eventually forced to abandon the project. Revised legislation on decentralization in the Overseas Departments, however, was approved by the French National Assembly in December 1982. Elections to the Regional Council took place in Réunion in February 1983, when left-wing candidates won 50.8% of the votes cast.

In elections to the French National Assembly in March 1986, Réunion's representation was increased from three to five deputies. The Parti Communiste Réunionnais (PCR) won two seats, while the Union pour la Démocratie Française (UDF), the Rassemblement pour la République (RPR) and a newly-formed right-wing party, France-Réunion-Avenir (FRA), each secured one seat. In the concurrent elections to the Regional Council, an alliance between the RPR and the UDF obtained 18 of the 45 seats, while the PCR secured 13 and the FRA eight. The leader of the FRA, Pierre Lagourgue, was elected as President of the Regional Council.

In the second round of the French presidential election in May 1988, François Mitterrand, the incumbent President and a candidate of the Parti Socialiste (PS), received 60.3% of the votes cast in Réunion, while Jacques Chirac, the RPR Prime Minister, obtained 39.7%. Mitterrand won an absolute majority of votes in all five electoral districts in Réunion, including the RPR stronghold of Saint-Denis. At elections to the French National Assembly in June, the PCR won two of the seats allocated to Réunion, while the UDF and the RPR (which contested the elections jointly as the Union du Rassemblement du Centre—URC), and the FRA each won one seat. (The RPR and FRA deputies later became independents, although they maintained strong links with the island's right-wing groups.) Relations between the PCR and the PS subsequently deteriorated, following mutual recriminations concerning their failure to co-operate in the general election.

In the elections for the newly-enlarged 44-member General Council in September and October 1988, the PCR and the PS won nine and four seats respectively, while left-wing independent candidates obtained two seats. The UDF secured six seats and right-wing independent candidates 19, but the RPR, which had previously held 11 seats, won only four. Later in October, Eric Boyer, a right-wing independent candidate, was elected as President of the General Council. The results of the municipal elections in March 1989 represented a slight decline in support for the left-wing parties; for the first time since the 1940s, however, a PS candidate, Gilbert Annette, became mayor of Saint-Denis.

In September 1990, following the restructuring of the RPR under the new local leadership of Alain Defaud, several right-wing and centrist movements, including the UDF and the RPR, established an informal alliance, known as the Union pour la France (UPF), to contest the regional elections in 1992. During a visit to Réunion in November 1990 the French Minister for Overseas Departments and Territories, Louis Le Pensec, announced a series of proposed economic and social measures, in accordance with the pledges made by Mitterrand in 1988 regarding the promotion of economic development and social equality between the Overseas Departments and metropolitan France. However, the proposals were criticized as insufficient by right-wing groups and by the PCR. Following a meeting in Paris between Le Pensec and a delegation from Réunion, the adoption of a programme of social and economic measures was announced in April 1991.

In March 1990 violent protests took place in support of an unauthorized television service, Télé Free-DOM, following a decision by the French national broadcasting commission, the Conseil Supérieur de l'Audiovisuel (CSA), to award a broadcasting permit to a rival company. In February 1991 the seizure by the CSA of Télé Free-DOM's broadcasting transmitters prompted renewed demonstrations in Saint-Denis. Some 11 people were killed in ensuing riots, and the French Government dispatched police reinforcements to restore order. Le Pensec, who subsequently visited Réunion, ascribed the violence to widespread discontent with the island's social and economic conditions. A visit to Réunion in March by the French Prime Minister, Michel Rocard, precipitated further rioting. In the same month a commission of enquiry attributed the riots in February to the inflammatory nature of television programmes that had been broadcast by Télé Free-DOM in the weeks preceding the disturbances, and cited the station's director, Dr Camille Sudre, as responsible. However, the commission refuted allegations by right-wing and centrist politicians that the PCR had orchestrated the violence.

In March 1992 Annette expelled Sudre, who was one of the deputy mayors of Saint-Denis, from the majority coalition in the municipal council, after Sudre presented a list of independent candidates to contest the forthcoming regional elections. In the elections to the Regional Council, which took place on 22 March, Sudre's list of candidates (known as Free-DOM) secured 17 seats, while the UPF obtained 14 seats, the PCR nine seats and the PS five seats. In concurrent elections to the General Council (newly enlarged to 47 seats), right-wing independent candidates won 20 seats, although the number of PCR deputies increased to 12, and the number of PS deputies to six; Boyer retained the presidency of the Council. Following the elections, the Free-DOM list of candidates formed an alliance with the PCR, thereby obtaining a narrow majority of 26 of the 45 seats in the Regional Council. Under the terms of the agreement, Sudre was to assume the presidency of the Regional Council, and Paul Vergès, of the PCR, the vice-presidency. Later in March Sudre was accordingly elected as President of the Regional Council by a majority of 27 votes, with the support of members of the PCR. The PS subsequently appealed against the results of the regional elections on the grounds of media bias; Sudre's privately-owned radio station, Radio Free-DOM, had campaigned on his behalf prior to the elections. Following his election to the presidency of the Regional Council, Sudre announced that Télé Free-DOM was shortly to resume broadcasting. The CSA indicated, however, that it would continue to regard transmissions by Télé Free-DOM as illegal, and liable to judicial proceedings. Jean-Paul Virapoullé, a deputy to the French National Assembly, subsequently proposed the adoption of legislation that would legalize Télé Free-DOM and would provide for the establishment of an independent media sector on Réunion. In April Télé Free-DOM's transmitters were returned, and at the end of May a full broadcasting service was resumed (without the permission of the CSA).

In June 1992 a delegation from the Regional Council met President Mitterrand to submit proposals for economic reforms, in accordance with the aim of establishing parity between Réunion and metropolitan France. In early July, however, the French Government announced increases in social security benefits that were substantially less than had been expected, resulting in widespread discontent on the island. In September the PCR demanded that the electorate refuse to participate in the forthcoming French referendum on ratification of the Treaty on European Union (see p. 181), in protest at the alleged failure of the French Government to recognize the requirements of the Overseas Departments. At the referendum, which took place later that month, the ratification of the Treaty was approved by the voters of Réunion, although only 26.3% of the registered electorate voted.

At the end of September 1992 Boyer and the former President of the Regional Council, Pierre Lagourgue, were elected as representatives to the French Senate. (The RPR candidate, Paul Moreau, retained his seat.) In October the investigation of allegations that members of the General Council had misappropriated funds and obtained contracts by fraudulent means commenced. In December increasing discontent with deteriorating economic conditions on Réunion prompted violent rioting in Saint-Denis and in the town of Le Port.

In March 1993 Sudre announced that he was to contest Virapoullé's seat on behalf of the Free-DOM–PCR alliance in the forthcoming elections to the French National Assembly. However, at the elections, which took place later that month, Sudre was defeated by Virapoullé in the second round of voting, while another incumbent right-wing deputy, André Thien Ah Koon (who contested the elections on behalf of the UPF), also retained his seat. The PCR, the PS and the RPR each secured one of the remaining seats.

In May 1993 the French Conseil d'Etat declared the results of the regional elections in March 1992 to be invalid, and prohibited Sudre from engaging in political activity for a year, on the grounds that programmes broadcast by Radio Free-DOM prior to the elections constituted political propaganda. Sudre subsequently nominated his wife, Margie, to assume his candidacy in further elections to the Regional Council. In the elections, which took place in June 1993, the Free-DOM list of candidates, headed by Margie Sudre, secured 12 seats, while the UDF obtained 10 seats, the RPR eight seats, the PCR nine seats and the PS six seats. Margie Sudre was subsequently elected as President of the Regional Council, with the support of the nine PCR deputies and three dissident members of the PS, obtaining a total of 24 votes.

In April 1993 a number of prominent business executives were arrested in connection with the acquisition of contracts by fraudulent means; several senior politicians, including Boyer and Pierre Vergès (the mayor of Le Port and son of Paul Vergès), were also implicated in malpractice, following the investigation into their activities. Both Boyer and Pierre Vergès subsequently fled in order to evade arrest. In August Boyer, who had surrendered to the security forces, was formally charged with corruption and placed in detention. (Joseph Sinimalé, a member of the RPR, temporarily assumed the office of President of the General Council.) In the same month the Vice-President of the General Council, Cassam Moussa, was also arrested and charged with corruption.

In January 1994 Jules Raux, a deputy mayor of Saint-Denis who was also the local treasurer of the PS, was arrested on charges of corruption: it was alleged that both local and French enterprises had obtained contracts from the Saint-Denis municipality in exchange for a share in profits (which was apparently used, in part, to finance PS activities on the island). In February two municipal councillors from Saint-Denis were arrested on suspicion of involvement in the affair. In the same month a French citizen (who was believed to have connections with members of the Djibouti Government) was arrested on Réunion on charges of having transferred the funds that had been illegally obtained by the Saint-Denis municipality to enterprises in Djibouti. In March Annette, who was implicated in the affair, resigned as mayor of Saint-Denis, and was subsequently charged with corruption. Later that month Boyer and Moussa were convicted and sentenced to terms of imprisonment.

At elections to the General Council, which took place in March 1994, the PCR retained 12 seats, while the number of PS deputies increased to 12 (despite adverse publicity attached to the PS as a result of the alleged corruption within the Saint-Denis municipality). The number of seats held by the RPR and

UDF declined to five and 11 respectively (compared with six and 14 in the previous Council). The RPR and UDF subsequently attempted to negotiate an alliance with the PCR; however, the PCR and PS established a coalition (despite the long-standing differences between the two parties), thereby securing the support of 24 of the 47 seats in the General Council. In April a member of the PS, Christophe Payet, was elected President of the General Council (obtaining 26 votes), defeating Sinimalé; the right-wing parties (which had held the presidency of the General Council for more than 40 years) boycotted the poll. The PS and PCR signed an agreement whereby the two parties were to control the administration of the General Council jointly, and indicated that centrist deputies might be allowed to join the alliance. In July, following a judicial appeal, Boyer's custodial sentence was reduced to a term of one year.

In November 1994 an official visit to Réunion by the French Prime Minister, Edouard Balladur (who intended to contest the French presidential election in early 1995), prompted strike action in protest at his opposition to the establishment of social equality between the Overseas Departments and metropolitan France. Jacques Chirac, who was the official presidential candidate of the RPR, visited the island in December; the organ of the PCR, *Témoignages* (which had criticized Balladur), declared its approval of Chirac's stated commitment to the issue of social equality. In the second round of the presidential election, which took place in May 1995, the socialist candidate, Lionel Jospin, secured 56% of votes cast on Réunion, while Chirac won 44% of the votes (although Chirac obtained the highest number of votes overall); the PCR and Free-DOM had urged their supporters not to vote for Balladur in the first round, owing to his opposition to the principle of social equality between the Overseas Departments and metropolitan France. Following Chirac's election to the French presidency, Margie Sudre was nominated Minister of State with responsibility for Francophone Affairs, prompting concern among right-wing organizations on Réunion.

In August 1995 Pierre Vergès was sentenced *in absentia* to a custodial term of 18 months; an appeal was rejected in July 1996. In September the mayor of Salazie, who was a member of the RPR, was also charged with corruption. In November 1995 Boyer lost an appeal against his 1994 conviction and was expelled from the French Senate.

With effect from the beginning of 1996 the social security systems of the Overseas Departments were aligned with those of metropolitan France. In February Alain Juppé, the French Prime Minister, invited more than 300 representatives from the Overseas Departments to Paris to participate in discussions on social equality and development; participants came from political parties, trade unions and other associations. The main issue uniting the political representatives from Réunion was the need to align the salaries of civil servants on the island with those in metropolitan France. Several trade unionists declared themselves willing to enter into negotiations, on the condition that only new recruits would be affected. The French Government remained undecided. President Chirac's visit to Réunion in March coincided with the 50th anniversary of France's establishment of Overseas Departments. The main issues that the President addressed during his visit were unemployment, the reinforcement of social policy, and equality with metropolitan France. Paul Vergès, joint candidate of the PCR and the PS, was elected to the French Senate in April, securing 51.9% of the votes cast. Fred K/Bidy won 40.0% of the votes, failing to retain Eric Boyer's seat for the RPR. In the by-election to replace Paul Vergès, which took place in September, Claude Hoarau, the PCR candidate, was elected as a deputy to the French National Assembly with 56.0% of the votes cast, while Margie Sudre obtained 44.0%. A new majority alliance between Free-DOM, the RPR and the UDF was subsequently formed in the Regional Council, with the re-election of its 19-member permanent commission in October.

In October 1996 the trial of a number of politicians and business executives, who had been arrested in 1993–94 on charges of corruption, took place, after three years of investigations. Gilbert Annette and Jules Raux were convicted and, in December 1996, received custodial sentences, although Annette's sentence was reduced on appeal in December 1997. Jacques de Châteauvieux, the Chairman of Groupe Sucreries de Bourbon (principally concerned with the production and exportation of sugar), was found guilty of bribery, and was also imprisoned. Two senior executives from the French enterprise, Compagnie Générale des Eaux, were given suspended sentences, although the public prosecutor subsequently appealed for part of the sentences to be made custodial. Some 20 others were also found guilty of corruption. Pierre Vergès surrendered to the authorities in December and appeared before a magistrate in Saint-Pierre, where he was subsequently detained; in February 1997 he was released by the Court of Appeal. Also in December 1996 voting on the regional budget for 1997 was postponed three times, as a result of the abstention of eight Free-DOM councillors, led by the first Vice-President of the Regional Council, Jasmin Moutoussamy, who demanded the dismissal of Gilbert Payet, a Sub-Prefect and special adviser to Sudre, and greater delegation of power to the Vice-Presidents. They also objected to Sudre's alliance with the RPR-UDF majority. In late March 1997 the regional budget was eventually adopted, although Sudre and many right-wing councillors abstained from voting because of the opposition's insistence on a number of amendments, most significantly to the composition of the Council's permanent commission, in which it had no representation. Following the vote, Sudre suspended the session to allow for discussion between the political organizations.

Meanwhile, civil servants and students protested violently against a French government proposal, made earlier in March 1997, to undertake reform of the civil service, including a reduction in the incomes of new recruits to bring them closer to those in metropolitan France. Senator Pierre Lagourgue was designated to mediate between the French Government and the civil servants' trade unions, but strike action and demonstrations continued into April, leading to violent clashes with the security forces.

Four left-wing candidates were successful in elections to the French National Assembly held in May and June 1997. Claude Hoarau (PCR) retained his seat and was joined by Huguette Bello and Elie Hoarau, also both from the PCR, and Michel Tamaya (PS), while André Thien Ah Koon, representing the RPR-UDF coalition, was re-elected.

In February 1998 the PCR (led by Paul Vergès), the PS and several right-wing mayors presented a joint list of candidates, known as the Rassemblement, to contest forthcoming elections. In the elections to the Regional Council, which took place on 15 March, the Rassemblement secured 19 seats, while the UDF obtained nine seats and the RPR eight, with various left-wing candidates representing Free-DOM winning five. Vergès was elected President of the Regional Council on 23 March, with the support of the deputies belonging to the Rassemblement and Free-DOM groups. In concurrent elections to an expanded 49-member General Council, right-wing candidates (including those on the Rassemblement's list) secured 27 seats, while left-wing candidates obtained 22 seats, with the PCR and the PS each winning 10 seats. At the end of the month Jean-Luc Poudroux, of the UDF, was elected President of the General Council, owing to the support of two left-wing deputies.

In October 1998 Réunion's three PCR deputies to the French National Assembly proposed legislation providing for the division of the island into two departments, with Saint-Pierre to join Saint-Denis as a departmental town. In December 1999, whilst attending the heads of state summit of the Indian Ocean Commission (IOC, see p. 308) on the island, President Chirac announced that he supported the creation of a second department on Réunion, as part of a number of proposed changes to the institutional future and socio-economic development of the French Overseas Departments (see p. 1605). In March 2000 the French Secretary of State for Overseas Departments, Jean-Jack Queyranne, declared that Réunion was to be divided into two departments, Réunion South and Réunion North, as of 1 January 2001. However, both the proposed date and the geographical division of the island were rejected by the PS, although it stated that it remained in favour of the creation of a second department. The leader of the UDF, Jean-Paul Virapoullé, expressed his opposition to the proposals. Demonstrations both for and against the division of the island took place in March 2000. It was subsequently agreed that the proposals would not be effected until 1 January 2002, and changes were made to the initial plans regarding the division of the island. However, on 15 June 2000 the creation of a second department was rejected by the French Senate by 203 votes to 111. In November the National Assembly definitively rejected the creation of a second department, but approved the changes to the institutional future of the Overseas Departments, which were finally ratified by the Constitutional Council in December. Also in that month Paul Vergès was arrested on charges of forgery and fraud in connection with his election to the Senate in 1996.

At municipal elections, held in March 2001, the left-wing parties experienced significant losses. Notably, the PS mayor of Saint-Denis, Michel Tamaya, was defeated by the RPR candidate, René-Paul Victoria. The losses were widely interpreted as a general rejection of Jospin's proposals to create a second department on the island. At elections to the General Council, held concurrently, the right-wing parties also made substantial gains, obtaining 38 of the 49 seats; the UDF retained its majority and Jean-Luc Poudroux was re-elected as President.

In January 1986 France was admitted to the IOC, owing to its sovereignty over Réunion. Réunion was given the right to host ministerial meetings of the IOC, but would not be allowed to occupy the presidency, owing to its status as a non-sovereign state.

Government

France is represented in Réunion by an appointed Prefect. There are two councils with local powers: the 49-member General Council and the 45-member Regional Council. Both are elected for up to six years by direct universal suffrage. Réunion sends five directly-elected deputies to the National Assembly in Paris and three indirectly-elected representatives to the Senate. The Department is also represented at the European Parliament.

Defence

Réunion is the headquarters of French military forces in the Indian Ocean. At 1 August 2000 there were 4,200 French troops stationed on Réunion and Mayotte, as well as a gendarmerie of 850.

Economic Affairs

Réunion's gross national product (GNP) in 1995 was estimated at 29,200m. French francs, equivalent to about 44,300 francs per head. During 1990–97, according to World Bank estimates, Réunion's population increased at an average annual rate of 1.7%. In 1995 Réunion's gross domestic product (GDP) was 42,577m. French francs, equivalent to 64,303 francs per head. GDP increased, in real terms, at an average annual rate of 3.4% in 1988–94. GDP grew by 1.5% in 1994 and by 6.3% in 1995.

Agriculture (including hunting, forestry and fishing) contributed 3.4% of GDP in 1995. An estimated 3.5% of the economically active population were employed in the sector in 1999. The principal cash crops are sugar cane (sugar accounted for 58.9% of export earnings in 1998), maize, tobacco, vanilla, and geraniums and vetiver root, which are cultivated for the production of essential oils. Fishing and livestock production are also important to the economy. According to the FAO, agricultural production increased at an average rate of 1.3% per year during 1990–98. It grew by 4.6% in 1997, but decreased by 5.1% in 1998.

Industry (including mining, manufacturing, construction and power) contributed 12.0% of GDP in 1995, and employed an estimated 13.7% of the working population in 1993. The principal branch of manufacturing is food-processing, particularly the production of sugar and rum. Other significant sectors include the fabrication of construction materials, mechanics, printing, metalwork, textiles and garments, and electronics.

There are no mineral resources on the island. Energy is derived principally from thermal and hydroelectric power. Imports of petroleum products comprised 5.4% of the value of total imports in 1998.

Services (including transport, communications, trade and finance) contributed 84.6% of GDP in 1995, and employed 71.7% of the working population in 1993. The public sector accounts for about one-half of employment in the services sector. Tourism is also significant; in 1999 394,000 tourists visited Réunion (a decrease of 1.5% compared with 1998), and tourism revenue totalled 1,850m. French francs.

In 1999 Réunion recorded a trade deficit of 14,282m. French francs. The principal source of imports (63.5%) in 1997 was metropolitan France; other major suppliers were Italy and Bahrain. Metropolitan France is also the principal market for exports (taking 72.1% of the total in 1997); other significant purchasers are Japan and Belgium-Luxembourg. The principal exports in 1998 were sugar and capital equipment. The principal imports in that year were road and rail vehicles, pharmaceutical products, and solid mineral fuels and petroleum products.

In 1998 there was an estimated state budgetary deficit of 8,048.9m. French francs. The annual rate of inflation averaged 2.2% in 1990–99; consumer prices increased by 0.9% in 1999. An estimated 36.5% of the labour force were unemployed in March 2000.

Réunion is represented by France in the Indian Ocean Commission (IOC, see p. 308). As an integral part of France, Réunion belongs to the European Union (EU—see p. 181).

Réunion has a relatively developed economy, but is dependent on financial aid from France. The economy has traditionally been based on agriculture, and is therefore vulnerable to poor climatic conditions. During the 1990s the production of sugar cane (which dominates this sector) was adversely affected by increasing urbanization, which resulted in a decline in agricultural land. In 1994 the Government indicated that it intended to give priority to the reduction of unemployment and announced a programme of economic and social development, which comprised measures to stimulate employment and to assist economic sectors that had been adversely affected by international competition. However, Réunion's rate of unemployment remained the highest of all the French Departments in 1997, with youth unemployment of particular concern. In November of that year the French Government and the authorities on Réunion signed an agreement that was designed to create nearly 3,500 jobs for young people over a period of three years. Although favourable economic progress was reported in 1998, sustained largely by tourism, economists have identified Réunion's need to expand external trade, particularly with fellow IOC members, if the island's economy is to continue to prosper. In May 2000 the French Government announced that it had agreed to equalize the minimum taxable wage in the Overseas Departments with that of metropolitan France within a period of three years; the current minimum taxable wage in Réunion was 20% lower than that of metropolitan France. This measure was approved by the French Senate in June.

Social Welfare

At 1 January 1999 there were 1,346 physicians, 2,906 nurses and 337 dentists working on Réunion. In 1999 there were four general hospitals, two local hospitals, a hospital complex specialized in psychiatric care and nine private surgical clinics. The island had a total of 2,734 hospital beds at 1 January 1998. There is a system of social welfare similar to that of metropolitan France. With effect from 1 January 1996 welfare payments and the statutory minimum wage in the Overseas Departments were aligned with those of metropolitan France. Expenditure on public health and welfare in the departmental budget for 2001 was forecast at 1,133.2m. French francs (equivalent to 27.2% of total expenditure).

Education

Education is modelled on the French system, and is compulsory for 10 years between the ages of six and 16 years. Primary education begins at six years of age and lasts for five years. Secondary education, which begins at 11 years of age, lasts for up to seven years, comprising a first cycle of four years and a second of three years. For the academic year 1998/99 there were 43,137 pupils enrolled at 176 pre-primary schools, 77,976 at 353 primary schools, and 95,132 at 111 secondary schools (comprising 71 junior comprehensives, or collèges, and 40 lycées). There is a university, with several faculties, providing higher education in law, economics, politics, and French language and literature, and a teacher-training college. In 1982 the illiteracy rate among the population over 15 years of age averaged 21.4% (males 23.5%; females 19.5%).

Public Holidays

2001: 1 January (New Year's Day), 16 April (Easter Monday), 1 May (Labour Day), 8 May (Liberation Day), 24 May (Ascension Day), 4 June (Whit Monday), 14 July (National Day, Fall of the Bastille), 15 August (Assumption), 1 November (All Saints' Day), 11 November (Armistice Day), 20 December (Abolition of Slavery Day), 25 December (Christmas Day).

2002: 1 January (New Year's Day), 1 April (Easter Monday), 1 May (Labour Day), 8 May (Liberation Day), 9 May (Ascension Day), 20 May (Whit Monday), 14 July (National Day, Fall of the Bastille), 15 August (Assumption), 1 November (All Saints' Day), 11 November (Armistice Day), 20 December (Abolition of Slavery Day), 25 December (Christmas Day).

Weights and Measures

The metric system is in use.

Statistical Survey

Source: Institut National de la Statistique et des Etudes Economiques, Service Régional de la Réunion, 15 rue de l'Ecole, 97490 Sainte-Clotilde; 48-81-00; fax 41-09-81.

AREA AND POPULATION

Area: 2,507 sq km (968 sq miles).

Population: 515,798 (males 252,997, females 262,801) at census of 9 March 1982; 597,828 (males 294,256, females 303,572) at census of 15 March 1990; 706,300 at census of 8 March 1999.

Density (8 March 1999): 281.7 per sq km.

Principal Towns (population at census of March 1999): Saint-Denis (capital) 131,557; Saint-Paul 87,712; Saint-Pierre 68,915; Le Tampon 60,323; Saint-Louis 43,519; Saint-André 43,174.

Births and Deaths (provisional figures, 1998): Registered live births 13,550 (birth rate 19.3 per 1,000); Registered deaths 3,805 (death rate 5.4 per 1,000).

Economically Active Population (persons aged 15 years and over, 1990 census): Agriculture, hunting, forestry and fishing 11,141; Mining, manufacturing, electricity, gas and water 11,295; Construction 16,563; Wholesale and retail trade 17,902; Transport, storage and communications 7,250; Financing, insurance, real estate and business services 3,005; Other services (incl. activities not adequately defined) 79,097; Total employed 146,253 (males 90,526, females 55,727); Unemployed 86,108 (males 45,889, females 40,219); Total labour force 232,361 (males 136,415, females 95,946). Figures exclude persons on compulsory military service. Source: International Labour Office, *Yearbook of Labour Statistics*.

Mid-1999 (estimates in '000): Agriculture, etc. 10; Total labour force 285. Source: FAO.

AGRICULTURE, ETC.

Principal Crops (FAO estimates, '000 metric tons, 1999): Sugar cane 1,938 (unofficial figure); Raw sugar 234 (unofficial figure); Maize 17; Vegetables and melons 67; Fruit (excl. melons) 49. Source: FAO.

Livestock (FAO estimates, '000 head, year ending September 1999): Cattle 27; Pigs 89; Sheep 2; Goats 38; Chickens 11,000. Source: FAO.

Livestock Products (FAO estimates, '000 metric tons, 1999): Beef and veal 1; Pig meat 13; Poultry meat 17; Cow's milk 14; Eggs 5. Source: FAO.

Forestry ('000 cubic metres): Roundwood removals: 36 in 1996; 36 in 1997; 36 in 1998. Source: FAO, *Yearbook of Forest Products*.

Fishing (metric tons, live weight, 1998): Capture 6,453 (Gadiformes 3,230, Porgies and seabreams 750, Swordfish 640, Other tuna-like fishes 750, Marine fishes 761, Tropical spiny lobsters 308); Aquaculture 63; Total catch 6,516. Source: FAO, *Yearbook of Fishery Statistics*.

INDUSTRY

Production (metric tons, 1998): Oil of geranium 6.25; Oil of vetiver root 0.24; Tobacco 22.0 (1992); Vanilla 116.5 (1992); Ginger 95.0 (1992); Pimento 405.6 (1992); Rum (hl) 68,169; Electric energy (million kWh) 1,566.

FINANCE

Currency and Exchange Rates: French currency is used (see French Guiana).

Budget (million francs, 1998): *State Budget:* Revenue 7,432.1, Expenditure 15,481.0; *Regional Budget:* Revenue 2,118, Expenditure 2,090; *Departmental Budget:* Revenue 4,624, Expenditure 4,300.

2001 (forecasts, million francs): Departmental Budget: *Revenue* 4,159.8 (State revenue 2,248.6, Direct and indirect taxation 1,107.8, Loans received 350.0, Investment funds and other interests 409.5, Other revenue 43.8); *Expenditure* 4,159.8 (Public health and welfare 1,133.2, Construction 655.7, Economic affairs and employment 495.6, Local development 167.1, Education, transport, sport and culture 308.1, Public debt 551.4, Other expenditure 848.8).

Money Supply (million francs at 31 December 1996): Currency outside banks 4,050; Demand deposits at banks 7,469; Total money 11,519.

Cost of Living (Consumer Price Index for urban areas, average of monthly figures; base: 1990 = 100): 119.3 in 1997; 120.8 in 1998; 121.9 in 1999. Source: UN, *Monthly Bulletin of Statistics*.

Expenditure on the Gross Domestic Product (million francs at current prices, 1995): Government final consumption expenditure 19,010; Private final consumption expenditure 27,209; Increase in stocks −262; Gross fixed capital formation 7,467; *Total domestic expenditure* 53,424; Exports of goods and services 3,167; *Less* Imports of goods and services 14,014; *GDP in purchasers' values* 42,577.

Gross Domestic Product by Economic Activity (million francs at current prices, 1995): Agriculture, forestry and fishing 1,392; Mining, manufacturing, electricity, gas and water 3,101; Construction 1,761; Wholesale and retail trade 6,140; Transport and communications 1,753; Finance and insurance 1,926; Real estate 2,669; Owner-occupied dwellings 2,767; Public administration 3,322; Other marketable services 5,228; Other non-market services 10,435; *Subtotal* 40,494; *Less* Imputed bank service charge 1,760; *GDP at basic prices* 38,734; Taxes on products, *less* subsidies on products 3,843; *GDP in purchasers' values* 42,577.

EXTERNAL TRADE

Principal Commodities (million francs, 1998): *Imports c.i.f.:* Agricultural products 437; Solid mineral fuels and petroleum products 824; Ceramic materials 403; Parachemical products 595; Pharmaceutical products 835; Metal manufactures 556; Industrial equipment 511; Electrical equipment 370; Electronic equipment 510; Road and rail vehicles 2,248; Meat and meat preparations 509; Milk and milk products 347; Preserves 309; Cereal preparations 446; Threads and hosiery products 350; Clothing 434; Manufactured wood products 320; Furnishings 324; Paper and cardboard 440; Printed matter 358; Plastic products 330; Total (incl. others) 15,310. *Exports f.o.b.:* Sugar 715.5; Capital equipment 212.3; Intermediate goods 43.7; Rum 30.5; Consumer goods 29.2; Total (incl. others) 1,214.9.

1999 (million francs): Imports c.i.f. 15,552; Exports f.o.b. 1,270.

Principal Trading Partners (million francs, 1996): *Imports c.i.f.:* Bahrain 519.4; Belgium-Luxembourg 302.0; France (metropolitan) 9,348.2; Germany 466.0; Italy 515.6; Japan 299.0; South Africa 291.5; Total (incl. others) 14,251.5. *Exports f.o.b.:* Belgium-Luxembourg 56.8; France (metropolitan) 759.3; Japan 56.1; Madagascar 34.1; Mauritius 36.2; Mayotte 48.7; United Kingdom 26.6; Total (incl. others) 1,071.2.

TRANSPORT

Road Traffic (1 Jan. 1999): Motor vehicles in use 234,578.

Shipping: *Merchant Fleet* (total displacement at 31 December 1992): 21,000 grt (Source: UN, *Statistical Yearbook*); *Traffic* (1998): Vessels entered 885; Freight unloaded 2,597,300 metric tons; Freight loaded 467,900 metric tons; Passenger arrivals 20,147; Passenger departures 22,189.

Civil Aviation (1998): Passenger arrivals 677,487; Passenger departures 674,651; Freight unloaded 15,060 metric tons; Freight loaded 7,270 metric tons.

TOURISM

Tourist Arrivals (by country of residence, 1998): France (metropolitan) 318,600, Mauritius 39,800, Madagascar 10,200, EU countries (excl. France) 8,600; Total (incl. others) 400,000.
1999: 394,000.

Tourism Receipts (million francs): 1,455 in 1997; 1,563 in 1998; 1,850 in 1999.

COMMUNICATIONS MEDIA

Radio Receivers (1997): 173,000 in use. Source: UNESCO, *Statistical Yearbook*.

Television Receivers (1997): 127,000 in use. Source: UNESCO, *Statistical Yearbook*.

Telephones (main lines at 31 Dec. 1997): 250,000.

Telefax Stations (1996): 9,164 in use. Source: UN, *Statistical Yearbook*.

Mobile Cellular Telephones (Sept. 1999): 85,000 subscribers.

Book Production (1992): 69 titles (50 books; 19 pamphlets). Source: UNESCO, *Statistical Yearbook*.

Daily Newspapers (1996): 3 (estimated average circulation 55,000 copies). Source: UNESCO, *Statistical Yearbook*.

Non-daily Newspapers (1988, estimates): 4 (average circulation 20,000 copies). Source: UNESCO, *Statistical Yearbook*.

EDUCATION

Pre-primary (1998/99): Schools 176; teachers 1,336 (1986); pupils 43,137.

Primary (1998/99): Schools 353; teachers 3,917 (1986); pupils 77,976.

Secondary (1998/99): Schools 111; teachers 6,479; pupils 98,897 (1999/2000).

University: (1998/99): Teaching staff 283; students 8,882.

Directory

The Government
(April 2001)

Prefect: JEAN D'AUBIGNY, Préfecture, Place du Barachois, 97405 Saint-Denis Cédex; tel. 40-74-03; fax 40-74-51; e-mail prefet974@guetali.fr.

President of the General Council: JEAN-LUC POUDROUX (UDF), Hôtel du Département, 2 rue de la Source, 97400 Saint-Denis; tel. 90-30-30; fax 90-39-99.

Deputies to the French National Assembly: HUGUETTE BELLO (PCR), CLAUDE HOARAU (PCR), ELIE HOARAU (PCR), MICHEL TAMAYA (PS), ANDRÉ THIEN AH KOON (RPR-UDF).

Representatives to the French Senate: EDMOND LAURET (RPR), LILIAN PAYET (MDLFT), PAUL VERGÈS (PCR).

GOVERNMENT OFFICES

Direction de l'Agriculture et de la Forêt: blvd de la Providence, 97400 Saint-Denis Cédex; tel. 48-61-00; fax 48-61-99.

Direction du Développement Économique et de l'Économie Solidaire: ave de la Victoire, 97488 Saint-Denis Cédex; tel. 90-31-90; fax 90-39-89.

Direction du Développement Local: ave de la Victoire, 97488 Saint-Denis Cédex; tel. 90-36-36; fax 90-39-94.

Direction de l'Environnement: 60 rue Fénélon, 97488 Saint-Denis Cédex; tel. 90-24-00; fax 90-39-48.

Direction des Finances: ave de la Victoire, 97488 Saint-Denis Cédex; tel. 90-39-39; fax 90-39-92.

Direction de l'Informatique: 19 route de la Digue, 97488 Saint-Denis Cédex; tel. 90-32-00; fax 90-32-99; e-mail fneyra@cg974.fr.

Direction des Infrastructures Départementales: 1 rue Charles Gounaud, 97488 Saint-Denis Cédex; tel. 41-56-52; fax 90-39-94.

Direction de la Logistique: 2 rue de la Source, 97488 Saint-Denis Cédex; tel. 90-31-38; fax 90-39-91.

Direction du Patrimoine: 6b rue Rontaunay, 97488 Saint-Denis Cédex; tel. 90-86-86; fax 90-86-90.

Direction de la Presse et de la Communication: 42 rue du Général de Gaulle, 97488 Saint-Denis Cédex; tel. 21-86-30; fax 21-39-45.

Direction de la Promotion Culturelle et Sportive: 18 rue de Paris, 97488 Saint-Denis Cédex; tel. 90-35-35; fax 20-26-03.

Direction de la Promotion de l'Enfance, de la Famille et de la Santé: 2 rue de la Source, 97488 Saint-Denis Cédex; tel. 90-33-33; fax 90-39-96.

Direction des Resources Humaines: 2 rue de la Source, 97488 Saint-Denis Cédex; tel. 90-37-37; fax 90-34-90.

Direction des Transports: 34 rue Notre Dame de la Source, 97488 Saint-Denis Cédex; tel. 20-38-08; fax 41-72-88.

Direction de la Vie Éducative: ave de la Victoire, 97488 Saint-Denis Cédex; tel. 90-31-31; fax 90-39-98.

REGIONAL COUNCIL

Hôtel de la Région Pierre Lagourgue, ave René Cassin, Moufia BP 402, 97494 Sainte-Clotilde Cédex; tel. 48-70-00; fax 48-70-71; e-mail region.reunion@cr-reunion.fr.

President: PAUL VERGÈS (PCR).

Election, 15 March 1998

Party	Seats
Le Rassemblement*	19
UDF	9
RPR	8
Free-DOM	5
Réunion France Europe	4
Total	45

* An alliance comprising the PCR, the PS and the MDLFT (a right-wing group).

Political Organizations

Front National (FN): Saint-Denis; f. 1972; extreme right-wing; Leader ALIX MOREL.

Mouvement des Radicaux de Gauche (MRG): Saint-Denis; f. 1977; advocates full independence and an economy separate from, but assisted by, France; Pres. JEAN-MARIE FINCK.

Mouvement pour l'Egalité, la Démocratie, le Développement et la Nature: affiliated to the PCR; advocates political unity; Leader RENÉ PAYET.

Mouvement pour l'Indépendance de la Réunion (MIR): f. 1981 to succeed the fmr Mouvement pour la Libération de la Réunion; grouping of parties favouring autonomy.

***Parti Communiste Réunnais (PCR):** 21 bis rue d l'Est, 97400 Saint-Denis; f. 1959; Pres. PAUL VERGÈS; Sec.-Gen. ELIE HOARAU.

***Parti Socialiste (PS)–Fédération de la Réunion:** 18 ave Stanislas Gimart, 97490 Saint-Denis; tel. 29-04-19; left-wing; Sec.-Gen. JEAN-CLAUDE FRUTEAU.

Rassemblement des Démocrates pour l'Avenir de la Réunion (RADAR): Saint-Denis; f. 1981; centrist.

Rassemblement des Socialistes et des Démocrates (RSD): Saint-Denis; Sec.-Gen. DANIEL CADET.

Rassemblement pour la République (RPR): 6 bis blvd Vauban, BP 11, 97400 Saint-Denis; tel. 20-21-18; Gaullist; Pres. EDMOND LAURET; Sec.-Gen. TONY MANGLOU.

Réunion France Europe: Saint-Denis.

Union pour la Démocratie Française (UDF): Saint-Denis; f. 1978; centrist; Pres. JEAN-PAUL VIRAPOULLÉ.

Les Verts Réunion: 13 allée des Terrasses, 97400 Saint-Denis; tel. and fax 30-18-28; e-mail verts.reunion@voila.fr; internet www.chez.com/rayonvert; regional branch of the French ecologist party Les Verts.

* In the March 1998 regional elections the PCR, the PS and the MDLFT (a right-wing group) presented a joint list of candidates, known as the Rassemblement.

Judicial System

Cour d'Appel: Palais de Justice, 166 rue Juliette Dodu, 97488 Saint-Denis; tel. 40-58-58; fax 21-95-32; Pres. JEAN CLAUDE CARRIÉ.

There are two **Tribunaux de Grande Instance**, one **Cour d'Assises**, four **Tribunaux d'Instance**, two **Tribunaux pour Enfants** and two **Conseils de Prud'hommes**.

Religion

A substantial majority of the population are adherents of the Roman Catholic Church. There is a small Muslim community.

CHRISTIANITY
The Roman Catholic Church

Réunion comprises a single diocese, directly responsible to the Holy See. At 31 December 1998 there were an estimated 590,000 adherents, equivalent to some 92.2% of the population.

Bishop of Saint-Denis de la Réunion: Mgr GILBERT AUBRY, Evêché, 36 rue de Paris, BP 55, 97461 Saint-Denis; tel. 94-85-70; fax 94-85-73.

The Press

DAILIES

Journal de l'Ile de la Réunion: 357 rue du Maréchal Leclerc, BP 166, 97463 Saint-Denis Cédex; tel. 90-46-76; fax 90-46-04; internet www.clicanso.com; f. 1956; Dir JACQUES TILLIER; circ. 35,000.

Quotidien de la Réunion: BP 303, 97712 Saint-Denis Cédex 9; tel. 92-15-15; fax 28-43-60; f. 1976; Dir MAXIMIN CHANE KI CHUNE; circ. 30,000.

PERIODICALS

Al-Islam: Centre Islamique de la Réunion, BP 437, 97459 Saint-Pierre Cédex; tel. 25-45-43; fax 35-58-23; f. 1975; 4 a year; Dir SAÏD INGAR.

Cahiers de la Réunion et de l'Océan Indien: 24 blvd des Cocotiers, 97434 Saint-Gilles-les-Bains; monthly; Man. Dir CLAUDETTE SAINT-MARC.

L'Economie de la Réunion: c/o INSEE, 15 rue de l'Ecole, BP 13 Le Chaudron, 97408 Saint-Denis; tel. 48-89-00; fax 48-89-89; 6 a year; Dir RENÉ JEAN; Editor-in-Chief COLETTE PAVAGEAU.

L'Eglise à la Réunion: 18 rue Montreuil, 97469 Saint-Denis; tel. 41-56-90; Dir P. FRANÇOIS GLÉNAC.

L'Enjeu: Saint-Denis; tel. 21-75-76; fax 41-60-62; Dir BLANDINE ETRAYEN; Editor-in-Chief JEAN-CLAUDE VALLÉE; circ. 4,000.

Le Journal de la Nature: 97489 Saint-Denis; tel. 29-45-45; fax 29-00-90; Dir J. Y. CONAN.

Le Memento Industriel et Commercial Réunionnais: 80 rue Pasteur, 97400 Saint-Denis; tel. 21-94-12; fax 41-10-85; e-mail memento@oceanes.fr; f. 1970; monthly; Dir CATHERINE LOUAPRE POTTIER; Editor GEORGES-GUILLAUME LOUAPRE POTTIER; circ. 10,000.

974 Ouest: Montgaillard, 97400 Saint-Denis; monthly; Dir DENISE ELMA.

La Réunion Agricole: Chambre d'Agriculture, 24 rue de la Source, BP 134, 97463 Saint-Denis Cédex; tel. 21-25-88; fax 21-06-17; e-mail chambagri.cda-97@wanadoo.fr; f. 1967; monthly; Dir JEAN-YVES MINATCHI; Chief Editor BÉATRICE TEVANÉE; circ. 8,000.

Télé 7 Jours Réunion: 6 rue Montyon, BP 405, 93200 Saint-Denis; weekly; Dir MICHEL MEKDOUD; circ. 25,000.

Témoignage Chrétien de la Réunion: 21 bis rue de l'Est, BP 192, 97465 Saint-Denis; weekly; Dir RENÉ PAYET; circ. 2,000.

Témoignages: 21 bis rue de l'Est, BP 192, 97465 Saint-Denis; tel. 21-13-07; f. 1944; publ. of the PCR; weekly; Dir ELIE HOARAU; circ. 6,000.

Visu: 97712 Saint-Denis Cédex 9; tel. 90-20-60; fax 90-20-61; weekly; Editor-in-Chief GUY LEBLOND; circ. 53,000.

Broadcasting and Communications

TELECOMMUNICATIONS

Cegetel: Saint-Denis; sole cellular telephone operator on Réunion; 93,000 subscribers.

BROADCASTING

Société Nationale de Radio-Télévision Française d'Outremer (RFO): 1 rue Jean Chatel, 97716 Saint-Denis Cédex; tel. 40-67-67; fax 21-64-84; internet www.rfo.fr; home radio and television relay services in French; operates two television channels; Chair. ANDRÉ-MICHEL BESSE; Dir ALBERT-MAX BRIAND.

Radio

Radio Free-DOM: BP 666, 97473 Saint-Denis Cédex; tel. 41-51-51; fax 21-68-64; e-mail freedom@guetali.fr; internet www.freedom.fr; f. 1981; privately-owned radio station; Dir Dr CAMILLE SUDRE.

In February 1998 there were a total of 44 authorized radio stations broadcasting in Réunion.

Television

Antenne Réunion: 33 chemin Vavangues, 97490 Sainte-Clotilde; tel. 48-28-28; fax 48-28-29; f. 1991; broadcasts 10 hours daily; Dir THIERRY MICHAUT.

Canal Réunion: 35 chemin Vavangues, 97490 Sainte-Clotilde; tel. 29-02-02; fax 29-17-09; subscription television channel; broadcasts a minimum of 19 hours daily; Chair. DOMINIQUE FAGOT; Dir JEAN-BERNARD MOURIER.

TV-4: 8 chemin Fontbrune, 97400 Saint-Denis; tel. 52-73-73; broadcasts 19 hours daily.

TV Sud: 10 rue Aristide Briand, 97430 Le Tampon; tel. 57-42-42; commenced broadcasting in 1993; broadcasts 4 hours daily.

Other privately-owned television services include TVB, TVE, RTV, Télé-Réunion and TV-Run.

Finance

(cap. = capital; res = reserves; dep. = deposits; m. = million;
brs = branches; amounts in French francs)

BANKING

Central Bank

Institut d'Emission des Départements d'Outre-mer: 4 rue de
la Compagnie, 97400 Saint-Denis Cédex; tel. 90-71-00; fax 21-41-
32; Dir Guy Debuys.

Commercial Banks

Banque Française Commerciale Océan Indien (BFCOI): 60
rue Alexis de Villeneuve, BP 323, 97468 Saint-Denis Cédex; tel.
40-55-55; fax 20-09-07; Chair. Philippe Brault; Dir Philippe Lavit
d'Hautefort; 8 brs.

Banque Nationale de Paris Intercontinentale: 67 rue Juliette
Dodu, BP 113, 97463 Saint-Denis; tel. 40-30-30; fax 41-39-09; e-mail
bnpipmv@guetali.fr; internet www.bnpgroup.com; f. 1927; Chair.
Michel Pebereau; Man. Dir Jean Tabaries; 11 brs.

Banque de la Réunion, SA: 27 rue Jean Chatel, 97711 Saint-
Denis Cédex; tel. 40-01-23; fax 40-00-61; internet www
.banquedelareunion.fr; f. 1849; cap. 121.0m., res 401.6m., dep.
6,155.8m. (Dec. 1999); Pres. Serge Robert; Gen. Man. Christian
Godefroy; 12 brs.

Crédit Agricole: Les Camélias, Cité des Lauriers, BP 84, 97462
Saint-Denis Cédex; tel. 40-81-81; fax 40-81-40; internet www.credit
-agricole.fr; f. 1949; affiliate of Caisse Nationale de Crédit Agricole;
Chair. Christian de la Giroday; Dir Eric Pradel.

Development Bank

Banque Populaire Fédérale de Développement: 33 rue Victor
MacAuliffe, 97400 Saint-Denis; tel. 21-18-11; Dir Olivier Devisme;
3 brs.

INSURANCE

More than 20 major European insurance companies are represented
in Saint-Denis.

Trade and Industry

DEVELOPMENT ORGANIZATIONS

Association pour le Développement Industriel de la Réunion:
8 rue Philibert, BP 327, 97466 Saint-Denis Cédex; tel. 94-43-00; fax
94-43-09; e-mail adir@guetali.fr; f. 1975; 190 mems; Pres. Maurice
Cerisola.

Chambre d'Agriculture de la Réunion: 24 rue de la Source, BP
134, 97463 Saint-Denis Cédex; tel. 21-25-88; fax 21-06-17; e-mail
chambagri.cda-97@wanadoo.fr; Pres. Jean-Yves Minatchy; Dir-Gen.
Fatma Badat.

Direction de l'Action Economique: Secrétariat Général pour les
Affaires Economiques, ave de la Victoire, 97405 Saint-Denis; tel.
40-77-10; fax 40-77-01.

Jeune Chambre Economique de Saint-Denis de la Réunion:
25 rue de Paris, BP 1151, 97483 Saint-Denis; f. 1963; 30 mems;
Chair. Jean-Christophe Duval.

**Société de Développement Economique de la Réunion—
SODERE:** 26 rue Labourdonnais, 97469 Saint-Denis; tel. 20-01-68;
fax 20-05-07; f. 1964; Chair. Raymond Vivet; Man. Dir Albert Tri-
maille.

CHAMBERS OF COMMERCE

Chambre de Commerce et d'Industrie de la Réunion: 5 bis
rue de Paris, 97400 Saint-Denis Cédex; tel. 94-20-00; fax 94-22-90;
internet www.reunion.cci.fr; f. 1830; Pres. Roger Roland.

Chambre de Métiers: 42 rue Jean Cocteau, 97490 Sainte-Clotilde;
tel. 21-04-35; fax 21-68-33; internet www.cm-reunion.fr.

INDUSTRIAL AND TRADE ASSOCIATIONS

**Fedération Réunionnaise du Bâtiment et des Travaux Pub-
lics:** BP 108, 97462 Saint-Denis Cédex; tel. 41-70-87; fax 21-55-07;
Pres. J. M. le Bourvellec.

**Syndicat des Exportateurs d'Huiles Essentielles, Plantes Aro-
matiques et Medicinales de Bourbon:** Saint-Denis; tel. 20-10-23;
exports oil of geranium, vetiver and vanilla; Pres. Rico Ploenières.

Syndicat des Fabricants de Sucre de la Réunion: BP 284,
97466 Saint-Denis Cédex; tel. 90-45-00; fax 41-24-13; e-mail
prestsuc@groupemace.com; Chair. Xavier Thieblin.

Syndicat des Producteurs de Rhum de la Réunion: BP 284,
97466 Saint-Denis; tel. 90-45-00; fax 41-24-13; e-mail prestsuc@
groupemace.com; Chair. Xavier Thieblin.

TRADE UNIONS

Confédération Générale du Travail de la Réunion (CGTR):
144 rue du Général de Gaulle, BP 1132, 97482 Saint-Denis Cédex;
Sec.-Gen. Georges Marie Lepinay.

Réunion also has its own sections of the major French trade union
confederations, **Confédération Française Démocratique du
Travail (CFDT), Force Ouvrière (FO), Confédération Française de l'Encadrement** and **Confédération Française des
Travailleurs Chrétiens (CFTC)**.

Transport

ROADS

A route nationale circles the island, generally following the coast
and linking the main towns. Another route nationale crosses the
island from south-west to north-east linking Saint-Pierre and Saint-
Benoît. In 1994 there were 370 km of routes nationales, 754 km of
departmental roads and 1,630 km of other roads; 1,300 km of the
roads were bituminized.

SHIPPING

In 1986 work was completed on the expansion of the Port de la
Pointe des Galets, which was divided into the former port in the
west and a new port in the east (the port Ouest and the port Est).
In 1998 some 3.1m. tons of freight were loaded and discharged at
the two ports.

Compagnie Générale Maritime (CGM): 1 rue Jesse Owens, BP
2007, 97822 Le Port Cédex; tel. 55-10-10; fax 43-23-04; e-mail
gmc-cgm@stor.fr; shipping agents; Dir Henri Felce.

Réunion Maritime: f. 1991; consortium of 15 import cos; freight
only.

Shipping Mediterranean Co: Le Port.

**Société de Manutention et de Consignation Maritime (SOM-
ACOM):** BP 7, Le Port; shipping agents.

Société Réunionnaise de Services Maritimes: Zac 2000, BP
2006, 97822 Le Port Cédex; tel. 55-17-55; fax 55-17-58; freight only;
Man. Jean Jacques René.

CIVIL AVIATION

Réunion's international airport, Roland Garros-Gillot, is situated
14 km from Saint-Denis. A programme to develop the airport was
completed in 1994, and in 1997 work commenced on the extension of
its terminal, at a cost of some 175m. French francs. The Pierrefonds
airfield, near Saint-Pierre, commenced operating as an international
airport in December 1998, serving daily flights to Mauritius, following its development at an estimated cost of nearly 50m. French
francs. An extension to the runway was planned for 2000 to enable
flights to Madagascar.

Air Austral: Zone Aéroportuaire, Aéroport de la Réunion Roland
Garros, 97438 Sainte-Marie, BP 611, 97473 Saint-Denis; tel. 93-10-
10; fax 29-28-95; internet www.air-austral.com; f. 1975; subsidiary
of Air France; scheduled regional services; Dir-Gen. Gérard Etheve.

Air Outre-Mer: Saint-Denis; f. 1990; scheduled services to Paris;
Chair. René Micaud.

Tourism

Tourism is being extensively promoted. Réunion's attractions
include spectacular scenery and a pleasant climate. In 1997 the
island had 49 hotels with a total of 1,810 rooms. In 1999 394,000
tourists visited Réunion, and revenue from tourism totalled 1,850m.
French francs, an 18.4% increase compared with 1998.

Comité du Tourisme de la Réunion (CTR): BP 615, 97472 Saint-
Denis Cédex; tel. 21-00-41; fax 21-00-21; e-mail ctr@la-reunion-
tourisme.com; internet www.la-reunion-tourisme.com; Pres. Margie
Sudre.

**Délégation Régionale au Commerce, à l'Artisanat et au Tour-
isme:** Préfecture de la Réunion, 97400 Saint-Denis; tel. 40-77-58;
fax 50-77-15; Dir Renaud Ferrand.

Office du Tourisme Intercommunal du Nord: 53 rue Pasteur,
97400 Saint-Denis; tel. 41-83-00; fax 21-37-76; e-mail otinord@
wanadoo.fr; Pres. Jean-Marie Dupuis.

French Overseas Collectivités Territoriales

The two overseas Collectivités Territoriales are Mayotte and St Pierre and Miquelon. Their status is between that of an Overseas Department and that of an Overseas Territory. They are integral parts of the French Republic and are each administered by a Prefect, who is appointed by the French Government. The Prefect is assisted by an elected General Council. In a

referendum held on 2 July 2000 on Mayotte, the population overwhelmingly approved the proposed transformation of the island into a Collectivité Départementale. The Collectivités Territoriales are represented in the French National Assembly and in the Senate in Paris, and also in the European Parliament in Strasbourg.

MAYOTTE

Introductory Survey

Location, Climate, Language, Religion, Capital

Mayotte forms part of the Comoros archipelago, which lies between the island of Madagascar and the east coast of the African mainland. The territory comprises a main island, Mayotte (Mahoré), and a number of smaller islands. The climate is tropical, with temperatures averaging between 24°C and 27°C (75°F to 81°F) throughout the year. The official language is French, and Islam is the main religion. The capital is Dzaoudzi, which is connected to the island of Pamandzi by a causeway.

Recent History

Since the Comoros unilaterally declared independence in July 1975, Mayotte has been administered separately by France. The independent Comoran state claims sovereignty of Mayotte, and officially represents it in international organizations, including the UN. In December 1976 France introduced the special status of Collectivité Territoriale for the island. Following a coup in the Comoros in May 1978 (see p. 1151), Mayotte rejected the new Government's proposal that it should rejoin the other islands under a federal system, and reaffirmed its intention of remaining linked to France. In December 1979 the French National Assembly approved legislation that extended Mayotte's special status for another five years, during which the islanders were to be consulted. In October 1984, however, the National Assembly further prolonged Mayotte's status, and the referendum on the island's future was postponed indefinitely. The UN General Assembly has adopted a number of resolutions in support of the sovereignty of the Comoros over the island. Until 1999 the main political party on Mayotte, the Mouvement Populaire Mahorais (MPM), demanded full departmental status for the island (as held by Réunion), but France was reluctant to grant this in view of Mayotte's lack of development.

At the general election to the French National Assembly in March 1986, Henry Jean-Baptiste, a member of the Centre des Démocrates Sociaux (CDS), which was affiliated to the Union pour la Démocratie Française (UDF), was elected as deputy for Mayotte. During a visit (the first by a French Prime Minister) to Mayotte in October, Jacques Chirac assured the islanders that they would remain French citizens for as long as they wished. Relations between the MPM and the French Government rapidly deteriorated after the Franco-African summit in November 1987, when Chirac expressed reservations concerning the elevation of Mayotte to the status of an Overseas Department (despite his announcement, in early 1986, that he shared the MPM's aim to upgrade Mayotte's status).

In the second round of the French presidential election, which took place in May 1988, François Mitterrand, the incumbent President and the candidate of the Parti Socialiste (PS), received 50.3% of the votes cast on Mayotte, defeating Chirac, the candidate of the Rassemblement pour la République (RPR). At elections to the French National Assembly, which took place in June, Jean-Baptiste retained his seat. (Later that month, he joined the newly-formed centrist group in the French National Assembly, the Union du Centre—UDC.) In elections to the General Council in September and October, the MPM retained the majority of seats. In November the General Council demanded that the French Government introduce measures to restrict immigration to Mayotte from neighbouring islands, particularly from the Comoros.

Following the assassination of the Comoran President, Ahmed Abdallah, in November 1989, Mayotte was used as a strategic military base, where additional French troops were stationed in December, in preparation for possible military intervention.

In 1989–1990 concern about the number of Comoran immigrants seeking employment on the island resulted in an increase in racial tension. In 1989 more than 150 Comoran refugees were prevented from landing on Mayotte by security forces. In January 1990 demonstrators in the town of Mamoudzou protested against illegal immigration to the island. A paramilitary organization, known as Caiman, was subsequently formed in support of the expulsion of illegal immigrants, but was refused legal recognition by the authorities.

At elections to the General Council, which took place in March 1991, the MPM secured an additional three seats, although Younoussa Bamana, the President of the General Council and leader of the MPM, was defeated in his canton, Keni-Keli, by the RPR candidate. In April, however, Bamana secured the majority of votes cast in a partial election, which took place in the canton of Chicani, and was subsequently re-elected to the presidency of the General Council.

In June 1991 a demonstration was held on the island of Pamandzi in protest at the relocation of a number of people as a result of the expansion of the airfield. Unrest among young people on Pamandzi culminated in violence in July, when demonstrators attempted to set fire to the town hall. Clashes between demonstrators and security forces ensued, and the Prefect, Jean-Paul Costes, requested that police reinforcements be dispatched from Réunion to restore order. An organization of young islanders, the Association des Jeunes pour le Développement de Pamandzi (AJDP), accused the mayor of mismanagement and demanded his resignation. The demonstrations, which threatened to destabilize the MPM, were believed to reflect general dissatisfaction among young people on Mayotte (who comprised about 60% of the population) with the authorities. Later in July five members of the AJDP, who had taken part in the demonstration at the airfield in June, received custodial sentences.

In June 1992 increasing resentment resulted in further attacks against Comoran immigrants resident in Mayotte. In early September representatives of the MPM met the French Prime Minister, Pierre Bérégovoy, to request the reintroduction of entry visas to restrict immigration from the Comoros. Later that month the MPM organized a boycott (which was widely observed) of Mayotte's participation in the French referendum on the Treaty on European Union (see p. 181), in support of the provision of entry visas. In December Costes and a number of other prominent officials were charged in connection with the deaths of six people in domestic fires, which had been caused by dangerous fuel imported from Bahrain. In February 1993 a general strike, which was staged in support of claims for wage increases, culminated in protracted violent rioting. Security forces were subsequently dispatched from Réunion to restore order, while trade unions agreed to end the strike. Later that month Costes was replaced as Prefect.

At elections to the French National Assembly, which took place in March 1993, Jean-Baptiste was returned, securing 53.4% of votes cast, while the Secretary-General of the RPR, Mansour Kamardine, received 44.3% of the votes. Kamardine (who contested the elections as an independent candidate) subsequently accused Jean-Baptiste of illegally claiming the support of an electoral alliance of the RPR and the UDF, known as the Union pour la France, by forging the signatures of party officials on a document. Jean-Baptiste, however, denied the allegations, and began legal proceedings against Kamardine for calumny.

Elections to the General Council (which was enlarged from 17 to 19 members) took place in March 1994: the MPM retained 12 seats, while the RPR secured four seats, and independent candidates three seats. During an official visit to Mayotte in November, the French Prime Minister, Edouard Balladur, announced the reintroduction of entry visas as a requirement for Comoran nationals, and the adoption of a number of security measures, in an effort to reduce illegal immigration to the island. In January 1995 the reimposition of visa requirements prompted widespread protests on the Comoros; the Comoran Government suspended transport links between Mayotte and the Comoros in response to the measure. In the first round of the French presidential election in April, Balladur received the highest number of votes on Mayotte (although Chirac subsequently won the election).

Following a further coup attempt by mercenaries in the Comoros, which took place in September 1995 (see p. 1153), the French Government dispatched additional troops to Mayotte, prior to staging a military intervention. In elections to the Senate in September, the incumbent MPM representative, Marcel Henry, was returned by a large majority. During a visit to Mayotte in October, the French Secretary of State for Overseas Departments and Territories pledged that a referendum on the future status of the island would be conducted by 1999. In October 1996 he confirmed that two commissions, based in Paris and Mayotte, were preparing a consultation document, which would be presented in late 1997, and announced that the resulting referendum would take place before the end of the decade.

Partial elections to fill nine seats in the General Council were held in March 1997; the MPM secured three seats (losing two that it had previously held), the RPR won three seats, the local PS one seat, and independent right-wing candidates two seats. In elections to the French National Assembly Jean-Baptiste, representing the alliance of the UDF and the Force Démocrate (FD, formerly the CDS), defeated Kamardine, securing 51.7% of votes cast in the second round of voting, which took place in June.

In July 1997 the relative prosperity of Mayotte was believed to have prompted separatist movements on the Comoran islands of Nzwani and Mwali to demand the restoration of French rule, and subsequently to declare their independence in August (see p. 1155). In September, following an unsuccessful military intervention, mounted by the Comoran Government in an attempt to quell the insurrection, many of those injured in the fighting were taken to Mayotte for medical treatment. Illegal immigration from the Comoros continued to prove a major concern for the authorities on Mayotte; during January–February 1997 some 6,000 Comorans were expelled from the island, with many more agreeing to leave voluntarily.

Meanwhile, uncertainty remained over the future status of Mayotte. In April 1998 one of the commissions charged with examining the issue submitted its report, which concluded that the present status of Collectivité Territoriale was no longer appropriate, but did not advocate an alternative. In May the MPM declared its support for an adapted form of departmental administration, and urged the French authorities to decide on a date for a referendum. In July Pierre Bayle succeeded Philippe Boisadam as Prefect. In December two rounds of preparatory talks on the island's future constitutional status took place between local political organizations and senior French government officials. However, further negotiations, which were planned to be held in February 1999, were suspended, owing to France's concerns over the political instability in the Comoros. In May Bamana made an appeal that the inhabitants of Mayotte be allowed to organize their own vote on their future, and later that month Jean-Baptiste introduced a draft piece of legislation to the French National Assembly, which proposed the holding of a referendum regarding the island's future before the end of 1999. In August, following negotiations between the French Secretary of State for Overseas Departments and Territories, Jean-Jack Queyranne, and island representatives, Mayotte members of the RPR and the PS and Bamana (the leader of the MPM) signed a draft document providing for the transformation of Mayotte into a Collectivité Départementale, if approved at a referendum. However, both Henry and Jean-Baptiste rejected the document. The two politicians subsequently announced their departure from the MPM and formed a new political party entitled the Mouvement Départementaliste Mahorais (MDM), whilst reiterating their demands that Mayotte be granted full overseas departmental status.

Following the approval of Mayotte's proposed new status by the General Council (by 14 votes to five) and the municipal councils, an accord to this effect was signed by Queyranne and political representatives of Mayotte on 27 January 2000. On 2 July a referendum was held, in which the population of Mayotte voted overwhelmingly in favour of the January accord, granting Mayotte the status of Collectivité Départementale for a period of 10 years. In November the commission established to define the terms of Mayotte's new status published a report, which envisaged the transfer of executive power from the Prefect to the General Council by 2004, the dissolution of the position of Prefect by 2007 and the concession of greater powers to the local Government, notably in the area of regional co-operation. Draft legislation confirming Mayotte's status was expected to be presented to the General Council in 2001.

At elections to the General Council, held in March 2001, no party established a majority. The MPM experienced significant losses, with only four of its candidates being elected, while the RPR won five seats, the Mouvement des Citoyens two, the MDM one, the PS one, and various right-wing independent candidates six seats. Yanoussa Bamana was re-elected as President of the Council.

(For further details of the recent history of the island, see the chapter on the Comoros, p. 1151.)

Government

The French Government is represented in Mayotte by an appointed Prefect. There is a General Council, with 19 members, elected by universal adult suffrage. Mayotte elects one deputy to the French National Assembly, and one representative to the Senate. Mayotte is also represented at the European Parliament. Under the terms of a proposed new status for Mayotte, executive power would be transferred from the Prefect to the General Council by 2004, and the position of Prefect would be dissolved by 2007.

Defence

At 1 August 2000 there were 4,200 French troops stationed in Mayotte and Réunion.

Economic Affairs

Mayotte's gross domestic product (GDP) per head in 1991 was estimated at 4,050 French francs. Between the censuses of 1991 and 1997 the population of Mayotte increased at an average annual rate of 5.7%.

The economy is based mainly on agriculture. In 1997 18.6% of the employed labour force were engaged in this sector. The principal export crops are ylang-ylang and vanilla. Rice, cassava and maize are cultivated for domestic consumption. Livestock-rearing and fishing are also important activities. However, Mayotte imports large quantities of foodstuffs, which comprised 22.8% of the value of total imports in 1997.

Industry (which is dominated by the construction sector) engaged 21.5% of the employed population in 1997. There are no mineral resources on the island. Imports of mineral products comprised 5.0%, and metals 10.3%, of the value of total imports in 1997.

Services engaged 59.8% of the employed population in 1997. The annual total of tourist arrivals (excluding cruise-ship passengers) increased from 6,700 in 1995 to 21,000 in 1999. Receipts from tourism in 1999 totalled 50m. French francs.

In 1998 Mayotte recorded a trade deficit of 896m. French francs. The principal source of imports in 1997 was France (60%); the other major supplier was South Africa. France was also the principal market for exports (taking 68% of exports in that year); the other significant purchaser was Réunion. The principal exports in 1997 were oil of ylang-ylang, transport equipment and foodstuffs. In that year falling prices and increased competition led to a significant decline in exports of vanilla (usually one of Mayotte's principal exports). The principal imports in 1997 were foodstuffs, electrical machinery, apparatus and appliances, transport equipment and metals.

In 1997 Mayotte's total budgetary revenue was estimated at 1,022.4m. French francs, while total expenditure was estimated at 964.2m. French francs. Official debt was 435.7m. French francs at 31 December 1995. The rate of inflation in the year to December 1997 was 2.1%. Some 41.2% of the labour force were unemployed in 1997.

Mayotte suffers from a persistently high trade deficit, owing to its reliance on imports, and is largely dependent on French aid. From the late 1980s the French Government granted substantial aid to finance a number of construction projects, in an attempt to encourage the development of tourism on the island. Mayotte's remote location, however, continued to prove an impediment to the development of the tourist sector. A five-year Development Plan (1986–91) included measures to improve infrastructure and to increase investment in public works; the Plan was subsequently extended to the end of 1993. In 1995 Mayotte received credit from France to finance further investment in infrastructure, particularly in the road network. As Mayotte's labour force has continued to increase (mostly owing to a high birth rate and continued illegal immigration), youth unemployment has caused particular concern. In 1997 37.8% of the unemployed population were under 25 years of age. In September 2000 an economic and social development agreement was signed with the French Government for the period 2000–04; Mayotte was to receive 4,386m. French francs to assist in its development.

Social Welfare

Medical services on Mayotte are available free of charge. The island is divided into six sectors, each of which is allocated a doctor or medical worker. In 1997 Mayotte had two hospitals, situated at Mamoudzou and at Dzaoudzi, which provided a total of 186 beds. In that year there were 57 physicians, four dentists and 131 qualified nurses working in Mayotte.

Education

Education is compulsory for children aged six to 15 years, and comprises five years' primary and five years' secondary schooling. In 1997 there were 99 primary schools on the island. In 1997 there were 14 secondary schools, comprising 12 collèges (junior comprehensives) and two lycées. There were also two vocational and technical institutions. In the same year 5,663 pre-primary school pupils, 24,681 primary school pupils and 10,616 secondary school pupils were enrolled. A further 1,449 students were enrolled at the vocational and technical institutions. In December 1996 the Caisse Française de Développement (now Agence Française de Développement) provided 21.6m. French francs for the construction of pre-primary and primary schools on Mayotte.

Public Holidays

The principal holidays of metropolitan France are observed.

Statistical Survey

Source (unless otherwise indicated): Institut National de la Statistique et des Etudes Economiques; 51 hauts des Jardins du Collège, BP 1369, 97600 Mamoudzou; tel. 61-36-65; fax 61-39-56.

AREA AND POPULATION

Area: 374 sq km (144 sq miles).
Population: 67,167 (census of August 1985); 94,410 (census of August 1991); 131,368 (males 66,600; females 64,768) at census of 5 August 1997; 142,000 (official estimate) at 1 January 1998. *Principal towns* (population of communes at 1997 census): Dzaoudzi (capital) 10,792, Mamoudzou 32,733, Koungou 10,165.
Density (1 January 1998): 379.7 per sq km.
Births and Deaths (1997): Registered live births 5,326 (birth rate 40.6 per 1,000); Death rate 5.6 per 1,000.
Economically Active Population (persons aged betweeen 15 and 64 years, census of August 1997): Agriculture and fishing 4,672; Electricity, gas and water 399; Industry 1,164; Construction and engineering 3,843; Wholesale and retail trade 2,717; Transport and telecommunications 1,563; Other marketable services 1,530; Finance and insurance 97; Other non-marketable services 9,108; Total employed 25,093 (males 18,200, females 6,893); Persons on compulsory military service 143 (males 139, females 4); Unemployed 17,660 (males 8,982, females 8,678); Total labour force 42,896 (males 27,321, females 15,575).

AGRICULTURE, ETC.

Livestock (1995): Cattle 15,000; Sheep 2,700; Goats 23,000.
Fishing (metric tons, live weight, 1998): Capture (Marine fishes 1,570; Aquaculture (FAO estimate) 2; Total catch 1,572. Source: FAO, *Yearbook of Fishery Statistics*.

FINANCE

Currency and Exchange Rates: French currency is used (see French Guiana).
Budget (million French francs, 1997): Total revenue 1,022.4 (current 783.7, capital 238.7); Total expenditure 964.2 (current 725.4, capital 238.7).
Money Supply (million French francs at 31 December 1997): Currency outside banks 789; Demand deposits 266; Total money 1,055.
Cost of Living (Consumer Price Index; base: December 1996 = 100). 102.1 in December 1997.

EXTERNAL TRADE

Total Trade (million French francs): *Imports:* 915 in 1998. *Exports:* 19 in 1998.
Principal Commodities (million French francs, 1997): *Imports:* Foodstuffs 188.1 (Beef and veal 19.2, Poultry and rabbit meat 26.4, Rice 33.6); Mineral products 41.0 (Hydraulic cements 31.4); Chemicals and related products 63.1 (Medicinal and pharmaceutical products 21.6); Plastic materials, ethers and resins 29.1; Wood, charcoal and wickerwork 25.5 (Sawnwood 16.2); Paper-making material, paper and paper products 20.8; Textiles 22.9; Base metals and metal products 84.6; Electrical machinery, apparatus and appliances 168.5; Transport equipment 101.1 (Passenger motor cars 44.3, Road motor vehicles for goods transport 25.2); Optical and photographic apparatus 21.4; Miscellaneous goods 20.1; Total (incl. others) 823.4. *Exports:* Foodstuffs 2.4 (Vanilla 0.8); Chemicals and related products 5.8 (Ylang-ylang 5.6); Paper-making materials, paper and paper products 1.5; Base metals and metal products 1.9; Electrical machinery, apparatus and appliances 2.2; Transport equipment 4.6 (Passenger motor cars 1.0, Road motor vehicles for goods transport 1.9); Total (incl. others) 20.2.
Principal Trading Partners (percentage of trade, 1997): *Imports:* France 60; South Africa 8. *Exports:* France 68; Réunion 7.

TRANSPORT

Road Traffic (1998): Motor vehicles in use 8,213.
Shipping: *Traffic* (metric tons, 1998): Goods unloaded 21,102; Goods loaded 8,165.
Civil Aviation (1998): *Passenger arrivals:* 42,260; *Passenger departures:* 45,774; *Freight carried:* 1,012 metric tons.

TOURISM

Visitor Arrivals (excluding cruise-ship passengers): 9,500 in 1997; 11,400 in 1998; 21,000 in 1999.
Tourism Receipts (million French francs): 50 in 1999.

COMMUNICATIONS MEDIA

Telephones (1997): 9,314 subscribers.

EDUCATION

Pre-primary (1997): 42 schools; 5,663 pupils.
Primary (1997): 99 schools; 24,681 pupils.
General Secondary (1997): 14 schools; 10,616 pupils.
Vocational and Technical (1997): 2 institutions; 1,449 students.

Directory

The Constitution

Under the status of *Collectivité Territoriale*, which was adopted in December 1976, Mayotte has an elected General Council, comprising 19 members, which assists the Prefect in the administration of the island. On 2 July 2000 a referendum was held on Mayotte, in which the population overwhelmingly approved the proposed transformation of the island into a *Collectivité Départementale*. In November a commisson established to define the terms of Mayotte's new status proposed the transfer of executive power from the Prefect to the General Council by 2004 and the suppression by 2007 of the position of Prefect.

The Government

Représentation du Gouvernement, BP 20, 97610 Dzaoudzi; tel. 60-10-54; fax 60-18-89.

(April 2001)

Prefect: PIERRE BAYLE.
Secretary-General: ANDRÉ DORSO.
Deputy to the French National Assembly: HENRY JEAN-BAPTISTE (MDM).

Representative to the French Senate: MARCEL HENRY (MDM).

Economic and Social Adviser: IBRAHIM ABUBACAR (PS).

GOVERNMENT DEPARTMENTS

Department of Agriculture and Forestry: 15 rue Mariage, BP 103, 97600 Mamoudzou; tel. 61-12-13; fax 61-10-31; e-mail daf .mayotte@wanadoo.fr.

Department of Education: rue du collège, 97600 Mamoudzou; tel. 61-10-24; fax 61-09-87.

Department of Health and Social Security: rue de l'Hôpital, 97600 Mamoudzou; tel. 61-12-25; fax 60-19-56.

Department of Work, Employment and Training: 4 place du Mariage, 97600 Mamoudzou; tel. 61-16-57; fax 61-03-37.

Department of Youth and Sports: rue Mariazé, BP 248, 97600 Mamoudzou; tel. 61-16-60; fax 61-01-26.

CONSEIL GÉNÉRAL

Conseil Général, BP 101, 8 rue de l'Hôpital, 97600 Mamoudzou; tel. 61-12-33; fax 61-10-18.

The General Council comprises 19 members. At elections in March 2001, the Fédération de Mayotte du Rassemblement pour la République secured five seats, the Mouvement Populaire Mahorais (MPM) four, the Mouvement des Citoyens (MDC) two, the Mouvement Départementaliste Mahorais (MDM) one, the Parti Socialiste one, and independent right-wing candidates six seats.

President of the General Council: YOUNOUSSA BAMANA.

Political Organizations

Fédération de Mayotte du Rassemblement pour la République: 97610 Dzaoudzi; local branch of the French (Gaullist) Rassemblement pour la République (RPR); Sec.-Gen. MANSOUR KAMARDINE.

Mouvement des Citoyens (MDC): Collège Tsim Koura, BP 04, 97620 Chirongui; Leader JEAN-CLAUDE MAHINC.

Mouvement Départementaliste Mahorais (MDM): 97610 Dzaoudzi; f. 1999 by former members of the MPM; seeks full overseas departmental status for Mayotte; Leader HENRY JEAN-BAPTISTE.

Mouvement Populaire Mahorais (MPM): 97610 Dzaoudzi; seeks departmental status for Mayotte; Leader YOUNOUSSA BAMANA.

Parti Socialiste: Dzaoudzi; local branch of the French party of the same name; Leader IBRAHIM ABUBACAR.

Judicial System

Tribunal Supérieur d'Appel: 16 rue de l'Hôpital, BP 106, 97600 Mamoudzou, tel. 61-11-15; fax 61-19-63; Pres. JEAN-BAPTISTE FLORI; Prosecutor JEAN-LOUIS BEC.

Procureur de la République: PATRICK BROSSIER.

Tribunal de Première Instance: Pres. ARLETTE MEALLONNIER-DUGUE.

Religion

Muslims comprise about 98% of the population. Most of the remainder are Christians, mainly Roman Catholics.

CHRISTIANITY

The Roman Catholic Church

Mayotte is within the jurisdiction of the Apostolic Administrator of the Comoros.

Office of the Apostolic Administrator: BP 1012, 97600 Mamoudzou; tel. and fax 61-11-53.

The Press

L'Insulaire: Immeuble Villa Bourhani, rue du Collège, BP 88, 97600 Mamoudzou; tel. 61-37-85; fax 61-37-86; weekly.

Le Kwezi: BP 5, 97600 Mamoudzou; tel. 61-30-00; fax 61-19-91; e-mail kwezi@wanadoo.fr; f. 1996; biweekly; Dir ZAÏDOU BAMANA; Editor-in-Chief LAURENT CANAVATE.

Broadcasting and Communications

TELECOMMUNICATIONS

France Télécom Mayotte: BP 105, 97610 Dzaoudzi; tel. 60-10-50; fax 60-19-09.

RADIO AND TELEVISION

Société Nationale de Radio-Télévision Française d'Outremer (RFO): BP 103, 97610 Dzaoudzi; tel. 60-10-17; fax 60-18-52;

e-mail jrv@wanadoo.fr; internet www.rfo.fr; f. 1977; govt-owned; radio broadcasts in French and Mahorian; television transmissions began in 1986; plans for a satellite service were announced in 1998; Pres. ANDRÉ-MICHEL BESSE; Dir-Gen. GEROGES CHOW-TOUN.

Finance

BANKS

Issuing Authority

Institut d'Emission d'Outre-mer: Route de la Préfecture, BP 500, 97600 Mamoudzou; tel. 61-05-05; fax 61-05-02.

Commercial Bank

Banque Française Commerciale Océan Indien: BP 322, 97600 Mamoudzou; tel. 61-10-91; fax 61-17-40; br. at Dzaoudzi.

Trade and Industry

DEVELOPMENT ORGANIZATION

Agence Française de Développement (AFD): Route de la Préfecture, BP 500, 97600 Mamoudzou; tel. 61-05-05; fax 61-05-02.

UTILITIES

Electricity

Electricité de Mayotte (EDM): Fongoujou, BP 37, 97615 Pamandzi; tel. 60-31-38; fax 60-31-39.

Water

Syndicat des Eaux: BP 289, 97600 Mamoudzou; tel. 62-11-11; fax 62-10-31.

TRADE UNION

Confédération Inter-Syndicale de Mayotte (CISMA): 18 rue Mahabou, BP 1038, 97600 Mamoudzou; tel. 61-12-38; fax 61-36-16; Gen. Sec. SAID BOINALI.

Transport

ROADS

In 1984 the main road network totalled approximately 93 km, of which 72 km were bituminized. There were 137 km of local roads, of which 40 km were tarred, and 54 km of minor tracks (unusable during the rainy season).

SHIPPING

Coastal shipping is provided by locally-owned small craft. There is a deep-water port at Longoni.

Affaires Maritimes: Zone Industrielle de Kaweni, BP 333, 97600 Mamoudzou; tel. 61-44-44; fax 60-10-92.

Service des Transports Maritimes (STM): BP 186, 97610 Dzaoudzi; tel. 60-10-69; fax 60-17-30.

CIVIL AVIATION

There is an airfield at Dzaoudzi, serving four-times weekly commercial flights to Réunion, twice-weekly services to Madagascar, Njazidja, Nzwani and Mwali, and a weekly service to Kenya. A direct service to Paris, expected to commence in 1999, was postponed, owning to the inadequacy of facilities at the island's airfield.

Tourism

Tropical scenery provides the main tourist attraction. In 1999 the island had six hotels, providing 118 rooms, five guest houses and eight apartments and lodges. Excluding cruise-ship passengers, Mayotte received 21,000 visitors in 1999, and tourism receipts totalled 50m. French francs in that year.

Comité du Tourisme de Mayotte: rue de la Pompe, BP 1169, 97600 Mamoudzou; tel. 61-09-09; fax 61-03-46; e-mail comite-du-tourisme-mayotte@wanadoo.fr; internet www.mayotte-island.com.

ST PIERRE AND MIQUELON

Introductory Survey

Location, Climate, Language, Religion, Capital

The territory of St Pierre and Miquelon (Iles Saint-Pierre-et-Miquelon) consists of a number of small islands which lie about 25 km (16 miles) from the southern coast of Newfoundland, Canada, in the North Atlantic Ocean. The principal islands are St Pierre, Miquelon (Grande Miquelon) and Langlade (Petite Miquelon)—the last two being linked by an isthmus of sand. Winters are cold, with temperatures falling to –20°C (–4°F), and summers are mild, with temperatures averaging between 10° and 20°C (50° and 68°F). The islands are particularly affected by fog in June and July. The language is French, and the majority of the population profess Christianity and belong to the Roman Catholic Church. The capital is Saint-Pierre, on the island of St Pierre.

Recent History

The islands of St Pierre and Miquelon are the remnants of the once extensive French possessions in North America. They were confirmed as French territory in 1816, and gained departmental status in July 1976. The departmentalization proved unpopular with many of the islanders, since it incorporated the territory's economy into that of the European Community (EC, now European Union, see p. 181), and was regarded as failing to take into account the islands' isolation and dependence on Canada for supplies and transport links. In March 1982 socialist and other left-wing candidates, campaigning for a change in the islands' status, were elected unopposed to all seats in the General Council. St Pierre and Miquelon was excluded from the Mitterrand administration's decentralization reforms, undertaken in 1982.

In 1976 Canada imposed an economic interest zone extending to 200 nautical miles (370 km) around its shores. Fearing the loss of traditional fishing areas and thus the loss of the livelihood of the fishermen of St Pierre, the French Government claimed a similar zone around the islands. Hopes of discovering valuable reserves of petroleum and natural gas in the area heightened the tension between France and Canada.

In December 1984 legislation was approved giving the islands the status of a Collectivité Territoriale with effect from 11 June 1985. This was intended to allow St Pierre and Miquelon to receive the investment and development aid suitable for its position, while allaying Canadian fears of EC exploitation of its offshore waters. Local representatives, however, remained apprehensive about the outcome of negotiations between the French and Canadian Governments to settle the dispute over coastal limits. (France continued to claim a 200-mile fishing and economic zone around St Pierre and Miquelon, while Canada wanted the islands to have only a 12-mile zone.) The dispute was submitted to international arbitration. Discussions began in March 1987, and negotiations to determine quotas for France's catch of Atlantic cod over the period 1988–91 were to take place simultaneously. In the mean time, Canada and France agreed on an interim fishing accord, which would allow France to increase its cod quota. The discussions collapsed in October, however, and French trawlers were prohibited from fishing in Canadian waters. In February 1988 Albert Pen and Gérard Grignon, St Pierre's elected representatives to the French legislature, together with two members of the St Pierre administration and 17 sailors, were arrested for fishing in Canadian waters. This episode, and the arrest of a Canadian trawler captain in May for fishing in St Pierre's waters, led to an unsuccessful resumption of negotiations in September. In November the President of the Inter-American Development Bank was appointed as mediator in the dispute, and agreement was reached on fishing rights in March 1989, whereby France's annual quotas for Atlantic cod and other species were determined for the period until the end of 1991. (Further quotas were subsequently stipulated for the first nine months of 1992.) At the same time the Governments agreed upon the composition of an international arbitration tribunal which would delineate the disputed maritime boundaries and exclusive economic zones. Meanwhile, in January 1989 two factory fishing ships from metropolitan France sailed to the area to catch the fish under agreed quotas, but there were protests by the islanders, who feared that damage might be caused to fishing stocks by the factory ships. After discussions with the French Prime Minister, it was agreed that one of the factory ships would return to France. In October 1990 the islanders protested to the Government concerning illegal fishing in their waters by a metropolitan-based company.

In July 1991 the international arbitration tribunal began its deliberations in New York, USA. The tribunal's ruling, issued in June 1992, was generally deemed to be favourable to Canada. France was allocated an exclusive economic zone around the territory totalling 2,537 square nautical miles (8,700 sq km), compared with its demand for more than 13,000 square nautical miles. The French authorities claimed that the sea area granted would be insufficient to sustain the islands' fishing community. Talks on new fishing quotas for the area off Newfoundland failed, and, in the absence of a new agreement, industrial fishing in the area was effectively halted until November 1994, when the Governments of the two countries signed an accord specifying new quotas for a period of 10 years. In the following month deputies in the French National Assembly expressed concern that the terms of the agreement would be detrimental to St Pierre and Miquelon's interests, although the Government asserted that the accord recognized the islanders' historic fishing rights in Canadian waters. Meanwhile, in January of that year St Pierre and Miquelon protested at what it alleged was an unauthorized entry into the islands' waters by Canadian coastguards (who had been attempting to intercept goods being smuggled from Saint-Pierre to Newfoundland).

At the March 1986 election to the French National Assembly the islands' incumbent deputy, Albert Pen of the Parti Socialiste (PS), was re-elected. Pen was also the sole candidate at the indirect election to choose the islands' representative in the French Senate in September. A fresh election for a deputy to the National Assembly was held in November, when Gérard Grignon, representing the centre-right Union pour la Démocratie Française (UDF), was elected. At the 1988 French presidential election Jacques Chirac of the right-wing Rassemblement pour la République (RPR) received 56% of the votes cast by the islanders in the second round, in May, against the successful PS incumbent, François Mitterrand. In June Grignon was re-elected to the National Assembly, taking 90.3% of the valid votes. In September–October, however, the parties of the left won a majority at elections to the General Council, securing 13 of the 19 seats.

In September 1992 64.2% of voters approved ratification of the Treaty on European Union (see p. 181), although only a small percentage of the electorate participated in the referendum. Grignon was re-elected to the National Assembly in March 1993; some 83% of the electorate participated in the poll. At the 1995 presidential election Chirac was the winning candidate at the second round on 7 May, taking 66.86% of the votes cast. The rate of abstention at the second round was 33.2%. At elections to the Senate in September, Pen was narrowly defeated at a second round of voting by Victor Reux of the RPR, since 1994 the Secretary of the islands' Economic and Social Council. Grignon was re-elected to the National Assembly at a second round of voting on 1 June 1997, with 52.34% of the votes cast.

A number of government proposals regarding the socio-economic and institutional development of the Overseas Departments, certain provisions of which were also to be applied to St Pierre and Miquelon, were provisionally accepted by the National Assembly in May 2000, and subsequently adopted by the Senate (following a number of modifications). The proposals were definitively approved by the National Assembly in November and were ratified by the Constitutional Council in December. Measures included provisions for improving and supporting the economic development of the islands, as well the introduction of proportional representation in elections to the General Council.

Government

The French Government is represented in St Pierre by an appointed Prefect. There is a General Council, with 19 members (15 for St Pierre and four for Miquelon), elected by adult universal suffrage for a period of six years. St Pierre and Miquelon elects one deputy to the French National Assembly and one representative to the Senate in Paris.

Defence
France is responsible for the islands' defence.

Economic Affairs
The soil and climatic conditions of St Pierre and Miquelon do not favour agricultural production, which is mainly confined to smallholdings, except for market-gardening and the production of eggs and chickens.

The principal economic activity of the islands is traditionally fishing and related industries, which employed some 18.5% of the working population in 1996. However, the sector has been severely affected by disputes with Canada regarding territorial waters and fishing quotas; the absence of quotas in 1992–94 effectively halted industrial fishing. New arrangements have been to the detriment of St Pierre and Miquelon, although there is some optimism regarding potential for the exploitation of shellfish, notably mussels and scallops, in the islands' waters. However, the total fish catch increased from 747 metric tons in 1996 to 3,571 tons in 1997, and to 6,108 tons in 1998.

Processing of fish provides the basis for industrial activity, which engages about 41% of the labour force. It is dominated by one major company, which produces frozen and salted fish, and fish meal for fodder. Following a sharp decrease in production in the late 1980s, much of the fish processed is now imported. Electricity is generated by two thermal power-stations, with a combined capacity of 23 MW. In 2000 plans were well advanced for the construction of a wind power-station, which, it was hoped, would generate some 40% of the islands' electricity requirements.

The replenishment of ships' (mainly trawlers') supplies was formerly an important economic activity, but has now also been adversely affected by the downturn in the industrial fishing sector. During the late 1980s efforts were made to promote tourism, and the opening of the St Pierre–Montréal air route in 1987 led to an increase in air traffic. Tourist arrivals in 1998 were estimated at 11,994. In 1999 the completion of a new airport capable of accommodating larger aircraft further improved transport links.

In 1997 St Pierre and Miquelon recorded a trade deficit of 356m. French francs; total exports were 29m. francs. Most trade is with Canada and France and other countries of the European Union. The only significant exports are fish and fish meal. The principal imports in 1994 were fuel, building supplies and food from Canada. Items such as clothing and other consumer goods are generally imported from France.

The annual rate of inflation averaged 6.3% in 1981–91, and consumer prices increased by an average of 2.1% per year between December 1991 and December 1996. Some 9.5% of the labour force were unemployed in the late 1990s.

Given the decline of the fishing sector, the development of the port of Saint-Pierre and the expansion of tourism (particularly from Canada and the USA) are regarded by St Pierre and Miquelon as the principal means of maintaining economic progress. The islands will, none the less, remain highly dependent on budgetary assistance from the French central Government.

Social Welfare
In 1997 there was one hospital complex, which included a retirement home and a centre for the handicapped. Citizens of St Pierre and Miquelon benefit from similar social security provisions to those of metropolitan France.

Education
The education system is modelled on the French system, and education is compulsory for children between the ages of six and 16 years. In 1997 there were nine primary schools, three secondary schools (one of which is private and has a technical school annex) and one technical school.

Public Holidays
2001: 1 January (New Year's Day), 13–16 April (Easter), 1 May (Labour Day), 24 May (Ascension Day), 4 June (Whit Monday), 14 July (National Day), 11 November (Armistice Day), 25 December (Christmas Day).

2002: 1 January (New Year's Day), 29 March–1 April (Easter), 1 May (Labour Day), 9 May (Ascension Day), 20 May (Whit Monday), 14 July (National Day), 11 November (Armistice Day), 25 December (Christmas Day).

Weights and Measures
The metric system is in use.

Statistical Survey

Source: Préfecture, Place du Lieutenant-Colonel Pigeaud, BP 4200, 97500 Saint-Pierre; tel. 41-10-10; fax 41-47-38.

AREA AND POPULATION
Area: 242 sq km (93.4 sq miles): St Pierre 26 sq km; Miquelon-Langlade 216 sq km.

Population: 6,392 at census of 15 March 1990: Saint-Pierre 5,683, Miquelon-Langlade 709; 6,316 at census of 8 March 1999.

Density (1997): 27.7 per sq km.

Births, Marriages and Deaths (1997): Live births 92; Marriages 36; Deaths 51.

Economically Active Population (1992): Fish and fish-processing 540; Construction 333; Transport 192; Dockers 44; Trade 409; Restaurants and hotels 154; Business services 417; Government employees 727; Activities not adequately defined 106; Total labour force 2,922.

FISHING
Total Catch (metric tons, live weight, 1998): Capture 6,108 (Greenland halibut 1,431, Witch flounder 57, Yellowtail flounder 59, Atlantic cod 3,123, Atlantic redfishes 654, Lumpfish 249, Queen crab 354).

FINANCE
Currency and Exchange Rates: French currency is used (see French Guiana).

Expenditure by Metropolitan France (1997): 280 million francs.

Budget (estimates, million francs, 1997): Expenditure 244 (current 128; capital 116).

Money Supply (million francs at 31 December 1997): Currency outside banks 281; Demand deposits at banks 897; Total money 1,178.

Cost of Living (Consumer price index; base: 1981 = 100): 183.0 in 1989; 189.6 in 1990; 196.5 in 1991.

EXTERNAL TRADE
Total (million francs, 1997): *Imports:* 385; *Exports:* 29. Most trade is with Canada, France (imports), other countries of the European Union (exports) and the USA.

TRANSPORT
Road Traffic (1997): 3,876 motor vehicles in use.

Shipping (1995): Ships entered 884; Freight entered 20,400 metric tons. *1997:* Ships entered 918.

Civil Aviation (1997): Passengers carried 30,341, Freight carried 105 metric tons.

TOURISM
Tourist Arrivals (estimate, 1998): 11,994. Source: Agence Régionale du Tourisme.

COMMUNICATIONS MEDIA
Radio Receivers (estimate, '000 in use): 5.0 in 1997.

Television Receivers (estimate, '000 in use): 3.5 in 1997.

EDUCATION
Primary (1997): 9 institutions; 50 teachers (1987); 877 students.
Secondary (1997): 3 institutions; 55 teachers (1987); 562 students.
Technical (1997): 1 institution; 194 students.

Directory
The Government
(April 2001)

Prefect: JEAN-FRANÇOIS TALLEC.
Deputy to the French National Assembly: GÉRARD GRIGNON (UDF-CDS).

Representative to the French Senate: VICTOR REUX (RPR).

GENERAL COUNCIL

Place de l'Eglise, 97500 Saint-Pierre; tel. 41-46-22; fax 41-22-97. The General Council has 19 members (St Pierre 15, Miquelon four).
President of the General Council: BERNARD LESOAVEC.

Political Organizations

Centre des Démocrates Sociaux (CDS): 97500 Saint-Pierre.

Parti Socialiste (PS): BP 984, 97500 Saint-Pierre; tel. 41-35-74; fax 41-78-90; e-mail psspm@altavista.net; f. 1996.

Rassemblement pour la République (RPR): BP 113, 97500 Saint-Pierre; tel. 41-35-73; fax 41-29-97; Gaullist.

Union pour la Démocratie Française (UDF): 97500 Saint-Pierre; centrist.

Judicial System

Tribunal Supérieur d'Appel: 97500 Saint-Pierre; tel. 41-47-26; fax 41-49-45; e-mail tsaspm@cancom.net; Pres. FRANÇOIS BILLON.

Tribunal de Première Instance: 14 rue Emile Sasco, BP 4215, 97500 Saint-Pierre; tel. 41-47-26; fax 41-49-45; e-mail tsaspm@cancom.net; Presiding Magistrate PASCAL MATHIS.

Religion

Almost all of the inhabitants are adherents of the Roman Catholic Church.

CHRISTIANITY

The Roman Catholic Church

The islands form the Apostolic Vicariate of the Iles Saint-Pierre et Miquelon. At 31 December 1997 there were an estimated 6,215 adherents.

Vicar Apostolic: LUCIEN FISCHER (Titular Bishop of Avioccala), Vicariat Apostolique, BP 4245, 97500 Saint-Pierre; tel. 41-20-35; fax 41-47-09.

The Press

L'Echo des Caps Hebdo: rue Georges Daguerre, BP 4213, 97500 Saint-Pierre; tel. 41-41-01; fax 41-49-33; e-mail echohebd@cancom.net; f. 1982; weekly; circ. 2,500.

Recueil des Actes Administratifs: 4 rue du Général Leclerc, BP 4233, 97500 Saint-Pierre; tel. 41-24-50; fax 41-20-85; f. 1866; monthly; Dir E. DEROUET.

Trait d'Union: BP 113, 97500 Saint-Pierre; tel. 41-35-73; fax 41-29-97; six a year; organ of the local branch of the RPR.

Le Vent de la Liberté: 1 rue Amiral Muselier, BP 1179, 97500 Saint-Pierre; tel. 41-42-19; fax 41-48-06; e-mail archipel@cancom.net; weekly; circ. 350; Dir GÉRARD GRIGNON.

Broadcasting and Communications

RADIO AND TELEVISION

Réseau France Outre-mer (RFO): BP 4227, 97500 Saint-Pierre; tel. 41-11-11; fax 41-22-19; internet www.rfo.fr; fmrly Société Nationale de Radio-Télévision Française d'Outre-mer, renamed as above 1998; broadcasts 24 hours of radio programmes daily and 195 hours of television programmes weekly on two channels; Pres. ANDRÉ-MICHEL BESSE; Dir JEAN-MICHEL CAMBIANICA.

Radio Atlantique: BP 1282, 97500 Saint-Pierre; tel. 41-24-93; fax 41-56-33; e-mail adlian@cancom.net; internet www.radioatlantique.com; private; broadcasts 24 hours of radio programmes daily; Pres. and Dir ROGER GUICHOT.

Finance

(cap. = capital, res = reserves, dep. = deposits; m. = million; amounts in French francs)

MAJOR BANKS

Banque des Iles Saint-Pierre-et-Miquelon: 2 rue Jacques Cartier, BP 4223, 97500 Saint-Pierre; tel. 41-25-43; fax 41-25-31; f. 1889; cap. 25m., res 10.0m., dep. 296.8m. (Dec. 1998); Pres. and Gen. Man. GUILLAUME DE CHALUS; Man. BERNARD DURDILLY.

Crédit Saint Pierrais: 20 place du Général de Gaulle, BP 4218, 97500 Saint-Pierre; tel. 41-22-49; fax 41-25-96; f. 1962; cap. 36.5m., res 3m., dep. 286m. (Dec. 1998); Pres. GUY SIMON; Man. PIERRE SPIETH.

PRINCIPAL INSURANCE COMPANIES

Mutuelle des Iles: 5 rue Maréchal Foch, BP 1112, 97500 Saint-Pierre; tel. 41-28-69; fax 41-51-13.

Paturel Assurances SARL, Agence PFA Athéna: 31 rue Maréchal Foch, BP 4288, 97500 Saint-Pierre; tel. 41-32-98; fax 41-51-65; Gen. Agent GUY PATUREL; Man. NATHALIE PATUREL.

Trade and Industry

GOVERNMENT AGENCY

Comité Economique et Social: 4 rue Borda, 97500 Saint-Pierre; tel. 41-45-50; fax 41-42-45.

DEVELOPMENT ORGANIZATION

SODEPAR: Palais Royal, rue Borda, BP 4365, 97500 Saint-Pierre; tel. 41-15-15; fax 41-15-16; e-mail sodepar@cancom.net; internet www.cancom.net/~sodepar; f. 1989; economic development agency; Chair. BERNARD LESOAVEC; Dir GÉRARD MERCHER.

CHAMBER OF COMMERCE

Chambre de Commerce, d'Industrie et de Métiers: 4 blvd Constant-Colmay, BP 4207, 97500 Saint-Pierre; tel. 41-45-12; fax 41-32-09; e-mail ccim975@cancom.net; Pres. JEAN LEBAILLY.

TRADE UNIONS

Union Interprofessionnelle CFDT–SPM: BP 4352, 97500 Saint-Pierre; tel. 41-23-20; fax 41-27-99; affiliated to the Confédération Française Démocratique du Travail; Sec.-Gen. PHILIPPE GUILLAUME.

Union Interprofessionnelle CFTC: BP 1117, 97500 Saint-Pierre; tel. 41-37-19; affiliated to the Confédération Française des Travailleurs Chrétiens.

Union Intersyndicale CGT de Saint-Pierre et Miquelon: 97500 Saint-Pierre; tel. 41-41-86; affiliated to the Confédération Générale du Travail; Sec.-Gen. RONALD MANET.

Union des Syndicats CGT-FO de Saint-Pierre et Miquelon; 15 rue Dr Dunan, BP 4241, 97500 Saint-Pierre; tel. 41-25-22; fax 41-46-55; affiliated to the Confédération Générale du Travail-Force Ouvrière; Sec.-Gen. MAX OLAISOLA.

Transport

SHIPPING

Packet boats and container services operate between Saint-Pierre, Halifax, Nova Scotia, and Boston, MA. The seaport at Saint-Pierre has three jetties and 1,200 metres of quays.

SPM Express: Agence Hôtel Robert, 10 rue du 11 novembre, 97500 Saint-Pierre; tel. 41-24-26; daily service between St-Pierre and Newfoundland.

CIVIL AVIATION

There is an airport on St Pierre, served by airlines linking the territory with France and Canada. Construction of a new airport, able to accommodate larger aircraft and thus improve air links, was completed in 1999.

Air Saint-Pierre: 18 rue Albert Briand, Saint-Pierre, BP 4225, 97500 Saint-Pierre; tel. 41-00-00; fax 41-00-02; e-mail asp@cancom.net; internet http://209.205.50.254/aspweb; f. 1964; connects the territory directly with Newfoundland, Nova Scotia and Québec; Pres. RÉMY L. BRIAND; Man. THIERRY BRIAND.

Tourism

There were an estimated 11,994 tourist arrivals in 1998.

Agence Régionale du Tourisme: 18 place du Général de Gaulle, BP 4274, 97500 Saint-Pierre; tel. 41-22-22; fax 41-33-55; e-mail tourispm@cancom.net; internet www.iquebec.com/A-R-T-spm; f. 1989; Pres. BERNARD LESOAVEC; Dir JEAN-HIGUES DETCHEVERRY.

French Overseas Territories

The three Overseas Territories (territoires d'outre-mer) are French Polynesia, the French Southern and Antarctic Territories, and the Wallis and Futuna Islands. They are integral parts of the French Republic. Each is administered by a High Commissioner or Chief Administrator, who is appointed by the French Government. Each permanently inhabited Territory also has a Territorial Assembly or Congress, elected by universal adult suffrage. Certain members of the Territorial Assembly or Congress sit in the French National Assembly and the Senate of the Republic in Paris. The Territories have varying degrees of internal autonomy.

FRENCH POLYNESIA

Introductory Survey

Location, Climate, Language, Religion, Flag, Capital

French Polynesia comprises several scattered groups of islands in the South Pacific Ocean, lying about two-thirds of the way between the Panama Canal and New Zealand. Its nearest neighbours are the Cook Islands, to the west, and the Line Islands (part of Kiribati), to the north-west. French Polynesia consists of the following island groups: the Windward Islands (Iles du Vent—including the islands of Tahiti and Moorea) and the Leeward Islands (Iles Sous le Vent—located about 160 km north-west of Tahiti) which, together, constitute the Society Archipelago; the Tuamotu Archipelago, which comprises some 80 atolls scattered east of the Society Archipelago in a line stretching north-west to south-east for about 1,500 km; the Gambier Islands, located 1,600 km south-east of Tahiti; the Austral Islands, lying 640 km south of Tahiti; and the Marquesas Archipelago, which lies 1,450 km north-east of Tahiti. There are 35 islands and 83 atolls in all. The average monthly temperature throughout the year varies between 20°C (68°F) and 29°C (84°F), and most rainfall occurs between November and April, the average annual precipitation being 1,625 mm (64 ins). The official languages are French and Tahitian. Polynesian languages are spoken by the indigenous population. The principal religion is Christianity; about 55% of the population are Protestant and some 34% Roman Catholic. The official flag is the French tricolour. Subordinate to this, there is a territorial flag (proportions 3 by 2), comprising three horizontal stripes, of red, white (half the depth) and red, with, in the centre, the arms of French Polynesia, consisting of a representation in red of a native canoe, bearing a platform supporting five stylized persons, on a circular background (five wavy horizontal dark blue bands, surmounted by 10 golden sunrays). The capital is Papeete, on the island of Tahiti.

Recent History

Tahiti, the largest of the Society Islands, was declared a French protectorate in 1842, and became a colony in 1880. The other island groups were annexed during the last 20 years of the 19th century. The islands were governed from France under a decree of 1885 until 1957, when French Polynesia became an Overseas Territory, administered by a Governor in Papeete. A Territorial Assembly and a Council of Government were elected to advise the Governor.

Between May 1975 and May 1982 a majority in the Territorial Assembly sought independence for French Polynesia. Following pressure by Francis Sanford, leader of the largest autonomist party in the Assembly, a new Constitution for the Territory was negotiated with the French Government and approved by a newly-elected Assembly in 1977. Under the provisions of the new statute, France retained responsibility for foreign affairs, defence, monetary matters and justice, but the powers of the territorial Council of Government were increased, especially in the field of commerce. The French Governor was replaced by a High Commissioner, who was to preside over the Council of Government and was head of the administration, but had no vote. The Council's elected Vice-President, responsible for domestic affairs, was granted greater powers. An Economic, Social and Cultural Council, responsible for all development matters, was also created, and French Polynesia's economic zone was extended to 200 nautical miles (370 km) from the islands' coastline.

Following elections to the Territorial Assembly in May 1982, the Gaullist Tahoeraa Huiraatira, led by Gaston Flosse, which secured 13 of the 30 seats, formed successive ruling coalitions, first with the Ai'a Api party and in September with the Pupu Here Ai'a Te Nunaa Ia Ora party. Seeking self-government, especially in economic matters, elected representatives of the Assembly held discussions with the French Government in Paris in 1983, and in September 1984 a new statute was approved by the French National Assembly. This allowed the territorial Government greater powers, mainly in the sphere of commerce and development; the Council of Government was replaced by a Council of Ministers, whose President was to be elected from among the members of the Territorial Assembly. Flosse became the first President of the Council of Ministers.

At elections held in March 1986 the Tahoeraa Huiraatira gained the first outright majority to be achieved in the Territory, winning 24 of the 41 seats in the Territorial Assembly. Leaders of opposition parties subsequently expressed dissatisfaction with the election result, claiming that the Tahoeraa Huiraatira victory had been secured only as a result of the allocation of a disproportionately large number of seats in the Territorial Assembly to one of the five constituencies. The constituency at the centre of the dispute was that comprising the Mangareva and Tuamotu islands, where the two French army bases at Hao and Mururoa constituted a powerful body of support for Flosse and the Tahoeraa Huiraatira, which, in spite of winning a majority of seats, had obtained a minority of individual votes in the election. At the concurrent elections for French Polynesia's two seats in the National Assembly in Paris, Flosse and Alexandre Léontieff, the candidates of the Rassemblement pour la République (RPR—to which Tahoeraa Huiraatira is affiliated), were elected, Flosse subsequently ceding his seat to Edouard Fritch. Later in March the French Prime Minister, Jacques Chirac, appointed Flosse to a post in the French Council of Ministers, assigning him the portfolio of Secretary of State for South Pacific Affairs.

In April 1986 Flosse was re-elected President of the Council of Ministers. However, he faced severe criticism from leaders of the opposition for his allegedly inefficient and extravagant use of public funds, and was accused, in particular, of corrupt electoral practice. Flosse resigned as President of the Territory's Council of Ministers in February 1987, and was replaced by Jacques Teuira.

In December 1987, amid growing discontent over his policies, Teuira and the entire Council of Ministers resigned and were replaced by a coalition of opposition parties and the Te Tiaraama party (a breakaway faction of the Tahoeraa Huiraatira) under the presidency of Alexandre Léontieff. The Léontieff Government survived several challenges in the Territorial Assembly to its continuation in office during 1988–89. Amendments to the Polynesian Constitution, which were approved by the French Parliament and enacted by July 1990, augmented the powers of the President of the Territorial Council of Ministers and increased the competence of the Territorial Assembly. The major purpose of these amendments was to clarify the areas of responsibility of the State, the Territory and the judiciary, which was considered particularly necessary following various disputes about the impending single market of the European Community (EC—now European Union, EU, see p. 181). In June 1989, in protest, 90% of the electorate had refused to vote in the elections to the European Parliament.

At territorial elections in March 1991 the Tahoeraa Huiraa-tira won 18 of the 41 seats. Flosse then formed a coalition with the Ai'a Api, thereby securing a majority of 23 seats in the Territorial Assembly. Emile Vernaudon, leader of the Ai'a Api, was elected President of the Assembly and Flosse was elected President of the Council of Ministers. In September Flosse announced the end of the coalition between his party and the Ai'a Api, accusing Vernaudon of disloyalty, and signed a new alliance with the Pupu Here Ai'a Te Nunaa Ia Ora led by Jean Juventin.

In April 1992 Flosse was found guilty of fraud (relating to an illegal sale of government land to a member of his family) and there were widespread demands for his resignation. In November Juventin and Léontieff were charged with 'passive' corruption, relating to the construction of a golf course by a Japanese company. In the following month the French Court of Appeal upheld the judgment against Flosse, who received a six-month, suspended prison sentence. The case provoked a demonstration by more than 3,000 people in January 1993, demanding the resignation of Flosse and Juventin. In September 1994 Flosse succeeded in having the conviction overturned, on a procedural issue, in a second court of appeal. In October 1997, however, Léontieff was found guilty of accepting substantial bribes in order to facilitate a business venture and was sentenced to three years in prison (half of which was to be suspended). In May 1998 Léontieff was sentenced to a further three years' imprisonment (two of which were to be suspended) for corruption.

French presidential elections took place in April/May 1995. During the second round of voting in the Territory, the socialist candidate, Lionel Jospin, received 39% of the total votes, while the RPR candidate, Jacques Chirac, won 61%. (Chirac was elected to the presidency with 52.6% of votes cast throughout the republic.)

In November 1995 the Territorial Assembly adopted a draft statute of autonomy, which proposed the extension of the Terri-tory's powers to areas such as fishing, mining and shipping rights, international transport and communications, broad-casting and the offshore economic zone. France, however, would retain full responsibility for defence, justice and security in the islands. Advocates of independence for French Polynesia criticized the statute for promising only relatively cosmetic changes, while failing to increase the democratic rights of the islanders. The statute was approved by the French National Assembly in December and came into force in April 1996.

At territorial elections held on 13 May 1996 the Gaullist Tahoeraa Huiraatira achieved an outright majority, although the principal pro-independence party, Tavini Huiraatira/Front de Libération de la Polynésie (FLP), made considerable gains throughout the Territory (largely owing to increased popular hostility towards France since the resumption of nuclear-wea-pons tests at Mururoa Atoll—see below). Tahoeraa Huiraatira secured 22 of the 41 seats in the Territorial Assembly, with 38.7% of total votes cast, while Tavini Huiraatira won 10 seats, with 24.8% of votes. Other anti-independence parties won a total of eight seats and an additional pro-independence grouping secured one seat. Flosse defeated the independence leader, Oscar Temaru, by 28 votes to 11 to remain as President of the Council of Ministers later in the month, and Justin Arapari was elected President of the Territorial Assembly. Allegations of voting irregularities led to legal challenges, which overturned the results in 11 constituencies. Following by-elections in May 1998 for the 11 seats, Tahoeraa Huiraatira increased its repre-sentation by one seat. Tavini Huiraatira again claimed that the elections had not been fairly conducted.

At elections for French Polynesia's two seats in the French National Assembly in May 1997 Michel Buillard and Emile Vernaudon, both supporters of the RPR, were elected with 52% and 59% of total votes cast, respectively. However, the pro-independence leader, Oscar Temaru, was a strong contender for the western constituency seat, securing 42% of the votes. Flosse was re-elected as the Territory's representative to the French Senate in September 1998.

In March 1999 proposals for an increase in French Polynesia's autonomy, as part of constitutional reforms, were announced in Paris. These proposals followed an initial agreement between the Territory and the French Government in late 1998, on the future of French Polynesia. In October 1999 the French Senate adopted a constitutional amendment granting French Polynesia a greater degree of autonomy. According to the bill (which had also been approved by the National Assembly in June), the status of the islands was to be changed from that of overseas territory to overseas country, and a new Polynesian citizenship was to be created. Although France was to retain control over areas such as foreign affairs, defence, justice and electoral laws, French Polynesia would have the power to negotiate with other Pacific countries and sign its own international treaties. The constitutional amendment was presented to a joint session of the French Senate and National Assembly for final ratification in late January 2000. However, no decision was taken on the matter and the issue was unlikely to be addressed again before May 2001.

In November 1999 Flosse was found guilty of corruption, on charges of accepting more than 2.7m. French francs in bribes from the owner of an illegal casino, allegedly to help fund his party. Flosse was sentenced to a two-year suspended prison term, a large fine, and a one-year ban on seeking office. Demon-strations, organized by the pro-independence FLP, took place in Tahiti, in protest at Flosse's refusal to resign from his post as President of the Territorial Council of Ministers. Flosse appealed against the ruling in October 2000; however, the case was adjourned until May 2001.

In December 2000 some 2,000 workers went on strike in Papeete, protesting against low wages, and demanding that their pay be raised to a level commensurate with the prosperous state of the Territory's economy. In early 2001 it was announced that elections to the newly-enlarged Territorial Assembly were scheduled to be held in May; in December 2000 provision was made for the number of seats in the Territorial Assembly to be increased from 41 to 49, in an attempt better to reflect demographic changes in the territory. At the elections, held on 6 May 2001, Tahoeraa Huiraatira secured 28 seats (see p. 1643). Gaston Flosse was subsequently re-elected President of the Territorial Assembly, and a government reorganization ensued.

The testing of nuclear devices by the French Government began in 1966 at Mururoa Atoll, in the Tuamotu Archipelago. In July 1985 the *Rainbow Warrior*, the flagship of the anti-nuclear environmentalist group, Greenpeace, which was to have led a protest flotilla to Mururoa, was sunk in Auckland Harbour, New Zealand, in an explosion that killed one crew member. Two agents of the French secret service, the Direction générale de sécurité extérieure (DGSE), were subsequently convicted of manslaughter and imprisoned in New Zealand, and relations between France and New Zealand were seriously affected by the resultant dispute, especially regarding the treatment of the two agents (see chapter on New Zealand for further details). In May 1991, during a visit to New Zealand, the French Prime Minister, Michel Rocard, formally apologized for the bombing of the *Rainbow Warrior*; however, in July tension between France and the region was exacerbated by the French Gov-ernment's decision to award a medal for 'distinguished service' to one of the agents convicted for his role in the bombing. Between 1975 and 1992 France performed 135 underground and 52 atmospheric nuclear tests in the Territory.

In April 1992 the French Government announced that nuclear tests would be suspended until the end of the year. Although the decision was welcomed throughout the South Pacific, con-cern was expressed in French Polynesia over the economic implications of the move, because of the Territory's dependence on income received from hosting the nuclear-test programme. Similarly, it was feared that unemployment resulting from the ban would have a serious impact on the economy. A delegation of political leaders subsequently travelled to Paris to express its concerns, and in January 1993 accepted assistance worth 7,000m. francs CFP in compensation for lost revenue and in aid for development projects.

Shortly after his election in May 1995, President Jacques Chirac announced that France would resume nuclear testing, with a programme of eight tests between September 1995 and May 1996. The decision provoked almost universal outrage in the international community, and was condemned for its apparent disregard for regional opinion, as well as for under-mining the considerable progress made by Western nations towards a worldwide ban on nuclear testing. Scientists also expressed concern at the announcement; some believed that further explosions at Mururoa could lead to the collapse of the atoll, which had been weakened considerably. Large-scale demonstrations and protest marches throughout the region were accompanied by boycotts of French products and the suspension of several trade and defence co-operation agreements. Opposi-tion to the French Government intensified in July 1995, when French commandos violently seized *Rainbow Warrior II*, the flagship of Greenpeace, and its crew, which had been protesting peacefully near the test site. Chirac continued to defy mounting pressure to reverse the decision from within the EU, from Japan and Russia, as well as from Australia, New Zealand and the South Pacific region. French Polynesia became the focus of world attention when the first test took place in September. The action attracted further statements of condemnation from Governments around the world, and provoked major demonstrations in many countries. In Tahiti hitherto peaceful protests soon developed into full-scale riots, as several thousand demonstrators rampaged through the capital, demanding an end to French rule. Meanwhile, violent clashes with police, and the burning of dozens of buildings in Papeete during the riots, left much of the capital in ruins. In defiance of world opinion, a further five tests were carried out, the sixth and final one being conducted in January 1996. In early 1996 the French Government confirmed reports by a team of independent scientists that radioactive isotopes had leaked into the waters surrounding the atoll, but denied that they represented a threat to the environment. However, following the election of a new socialist administration in France (in mid-1997), the French Minister of the Environment demanded in August 1998 that the matter be investigated further, stating that she had not been reassured by the initial reports. The Minister's demands were reiterated by church leaders in the Territory, who asked the Government to establish radiological surveillance systems at the former test sites, to conduct thorough medical studies on people exposed to radiation from the tests and to make military records accessible to the public, claiming that previous investigations had failed to address the concerns of the islanders. Work to dismantle facilities at the test site began in 1997 and was completed in July 1998.

In September 1998 the trial of more than 60 people charged with offences relating to the riots and protests of September 1995 began in Papeete. Hiro Tefaare, a pro-independence member of the Territorial Assembly and former police officer, was found guilty of instigating the riots and was sentenced to three years' imprisonment (of which 18 months were to be suspended). Furthermore, in September 1999 the French Government was ordered by the Administrative Tribunal to pay 204m. francs CFP in compensation for failing to maintain law and order.

In early 1999 a study by the French Independent Research and Information Commission reported that there was serious radio-active leakage into underground water, lagoons and the ocean at Mururoa and Fangataufa atolls. These claims were dismissed by a New Zealand scientist who had taken part in an earlier study by the International Atomic Energy Agency, which had claimed that radiation levels were nearly undetectable. In May a French government official admitted that fractures had been found in the coral cone at the Mururoa and Fangataufa nuclear testing sites. The reports, by Greenpeace, that the atoll was in danger of collapsing had always been previously denied by France. However, France's claim that no serious long-term damage had been done was contested by Greenpeace, which also suggested the need for an urgent independent study of the test sites. In January 2000, in what was considered to be a significant development, the commander of the French armed forces in French Polynesia admitted that there were significant cracks in the coral reef surrounding Mururoa, and that these could lead to the occurrence of a tsunami.

Government

The French Government is represented in French Polynesia by its High Commissioner to the Territory, and controls various important spheres of government, including defence, foreign diplomacy and justice. A local Territorial Assembly, with (from 2001) 49 members, is elected for a five-year term by universal adult suffrage. The Assembly may elect a President of an executive body, the Territorial Council of Ministers, who, in turn, submits a list of between six and 12 members of the Assembly to serve as ministers, for approval by the Assembly.

In addition, French Polynesia elects two deputies to the French National Assembly in Paris and one representative to the French Senate, all chosen on the basis of universal adult suffrage. French Polynesia is also represented at the European Parliament.

Defence

France tested nuclear weapons at Mururoa Atoll, in the Tuamotu Archipelago, between 1966 and 1996. In August 2000 France maintained a force of 3,100 military personnel in the Territory, as well as a gendarmerie of 600.

Economic Affairs

In 1998, according to official estimates, French Polynesia's gross domestic product (GDP), measured at current prices, was 404,886m. francs CFP, equivalent to 1,777,000 francs CFP per head. During 1988–98 the population increased at an average annual rate of 2.0%.

Agriculture, forestry and fishing contributed only 4.1% of GDP in 1997, but provided most of French Polynesia's exports. The sector engaged 14.6% of the employed labour force in 1996. Coconuts are the principal cash crop, and in 1998 the estimated harvest was 63,000 metric tons. Vegetables, fruit (especially pineapples and citrus fruit), vanilla and coffee are also cultivated. Most commercial fishing, principally for tuna, is conducted, under licence, by Japanese and Korean fleets. Another important activity is the production of cultured black pearls, of which the quantity exported increased from 112 kg in 1984 to 4,989 kg in 1997. In 1998 the Territory exported some 6,050 kg of black pearls, earning some 16,429m. francs CFP (compared with 14,453m. francs CFP and 14,658m. francs CFP in 1996 and 1997 respectively), and during the mid-1990s was estimated to have produced more than 95% of the world's cultured black pearls. In 1999 exports of black pearls increased to 8,182 kg, earning some 19,100m. francs CFP. Japan is the biggest importer of black pearls from the Territory, and in 1998 purchased an estimated 65% of black pearls produced in that year.

Industry (comprising manufacturing, construction and utilities) engaged 16.6% of the working population in 1998, and provided 15.5% of GDP in 1997. There is a small manufacturing sector, which is heavily dependent on agriculture. Coconut oil and copra are produced, as are beer, dairy products and vanilla essence. Important deposits of phosphates and cobalt were discovered during the 1980s. The manufacturing sector engaged 8.2% of the employed labour force in 1998, and provided 7.0% of GDP in 1997. Construction is an important industrial activity, contributing 5.3% of GDP in 1997, and engaging 8.4% of the employed labour force in 1998.

Hydrocarbon fuels are the main source of energy in the Territory, with the Papeete thermal power station providing about three-quarters of the electricity produced. Hydroelectric and solar energy also make a significant contribution to French Polynesia's domestic requirements. Hydroelectric power dams, with the capacity to generate the electricity requirements of 36% of Tahiti's population, have been constructed.

Tourism is the Territory's major industry. In 1990 the trade, restaurants and hotels sector contributed 22.7% of GDP. In 1999 some 210,800 tourists visited French Polynesia, and receipts from tourism totalled an estimated 47,300m. francs CFP. French Polynesia's hotel capacity amounted to 3,407 rooms in 1999. The services sector engaged 69.8% of the employed labour force in 1996, and provided 80.4% of GDP in 1997.

In 2000 French Polynesia recorded a trade deficit of 97,578m. francs CFP. In that year the principal sources of imports were France (which provided 36.0% of total imports), the USA (13.9%), Australia (9.3%) and New Zealand (7.4%). The principal markets for exports in that year were Hong Kong (accounting for 20.8% of the total), France (13.8%) and the USA (13.1%). The principal imports in 1997 included machinery and mechanical appliances (9.7% of the total) and electrical goods (6.6%). The principal commodity exports were cultured black pearls (providing 61.6% of total export revenue).

In 1999 there was an estimated territorial budgetary deficit of 28,990m. francs CFP. In 1999 expenditure by the French State in the Territory totalled 120,631m. francs CFP, 28.5% of which was on the military budget. The total external debt was estimated at US $390m. in 1992. The annual rate of inflation averaged 1.2% in 1990–99, standing at 0.7% in 1999. A high unemployment rate (recorded at 13.2% of the labour force in 1996) is exacerbated by the predominance of young people in the population (in 1996 some 43% of the population were under the age of 20 years).

French Polynesia forms part of the Franc Zone (see p. 210), and is a member of the Pacific Community (formerly the South Pacific Commission—see p. 275), which provides technical advice, training and assistance in economic, cultural and social development to countries in the region.

French Polynesia's traditional agriculture-based economy was distorted by the presence of large numbers of French military personnel (in connection with the nuclear-testing programme which began in 1966), stimulating employment in the construction industry and services at the expense of agriculture, and encouraging migration from the outer islands to Tahiti, where 75% of the population currently reside. These dramatic changes effectively transformed French Polynesia from a state of self-sufficiency to one of import dependency in less than a generation. The development of tourism had a similar effect. The Contract for Development, an agreement for metropolitan France to provide the Territory with 28,300m. francs CFP annually between 1996 and 2006, was concluded in 1995 and took effect upon completion of the last series of nuclear tests in early 1996. It was hoped that the arrangement would enable French Polynesia to establish an economy that was more reliant upon local resources and would consequently create greater employment, thereby enhancing the Territory's potential for durable independence. In an attempt to increase revenue, the Territorial Government announced the introduction of a value-added tax from October 1997. French Polynesia's steady economic growth has partly been as a result of the development of the services sector, notably in hotel construction and other tourism-related services, which has led to significant employment creation. Other sectors of the economy, such as pearl farming, however, have not expanded as rapidly, principally because of regional economic conditions (notably the recession in Japan, one of the largest importers of black pearls). GDP continued to grow throughout the late 1990s, increasing, according to the Bank of Hawaii, by some 6.2% in 1998, 4.0% in 1999 and by a projected 4.0% in 2000. This was principally due to the financial support provided by France, but also to a significant rise in the number of tourists visiting the territory (a 16.8% increase between 1997 and 1999), a trend that was expected to continue in the immediate future; it was hoped that revenue from tourism would eventually replace the grants provided by the French State.

Social Welfare

In 1991 there were 34 hospitals in French Polynesia. In 1996 there was a total of 981 hospital beds, and in that year there were 369 physicians working in the Territory. All medical services are provided free of charge for the inhabitants of French Polynesia. An estimated 32,892m. francs CFP was spent on health services in the Territory in 1995.

Education

Education is compulsory for eight years between six and 14 years of age. It is free of charge for day pupils in government schools. Primary education, lasting six years, is financed by the territorial budget, while secondary and technical education are supported by state funds. In 1996/97 there were 59 kindergartens, with 16,049 children enrolled, and 170 primary schools, with 29,415 pupils. Secondary education is provided by both church and government schools. In 1996/97 there were 28,438 pupils at general secondary schools, and 3,730 secondary pupils were enrolled at vocational institutions in 1992/93. The French University of the Pacific was established in French Polynesia in 1987. In 1999 it was divided into two separate branches, of which the University of French Polynesia is now based in Papeete. In 1995 the Papeete branch had 50 teachers and, in 1998/99, some 1,685 students. Total government expenditure on education in the Territory was 40,300m. francs CFP in 1999.

Public Holidays

2001: 1 January (New Year's Day), 16 April (Easter Monday), 1 May (Labour Day), 4 May (Liberation Day), 24 May (Ascension Day), 4 June (Whit Monday), 14 July (Fall of the Bastille), 11 November (Armistice Day), 25 December (Christmas Day).

2002: 1 January (New Year's Day), 1 April (Easter Monday), 1 May (Labour Day), 3 May (Liberation Day), 9 May (Ascension Day), 20 May (Whit Monday), 14 July (Fall of the Bastille), 11 November (Armistice Day), 25 December (Christmas Day).

Weights and Measures

The metric system is in force.

Statistical Survey

Source (unless otherwise indicated): Institut Statistique de la Polynésie Française, Immeuble Donald (2ᵉ étage), Angle rue Jeanne d'Arc et blvd Pomare, BP 395, 98713 Papeete; tel. 543232; fax 427252; e-mail ispf@ispf.pf; internet www.ispf.pf.

AREA AND POPULATION

Area: Total 4,167 sq km (1,609 sq miles); Land area 3,521 sq km (1,359 sq miles).

Population: 188,814 (98,345 males, 90,469 females) at census of 6 September 1988; 219,521 (males 113,934, females 105,587) at census of 3 September 1996; 231,500 (provisional estimate) at 1 January 2000.

Population by island group (1996 census): Society Archipelago 189,524 (Windward Islands 162,686, Leeward Islands 276,838); Marquesas Archipelago 8,064; Austral Islands 6,563; Tuamotu-Gambier Islands 15,370.

Density (January 2000): 55.6 per sq km.

Ethnic Groups (census of 15 October 1983): Polynesian 114,280; 'Demis' 23,625 (Polynesian-European 15,851, Polynesian-Chinese 6,356, Polynesian-Other races 1,418); European 19,320; Chinese 7,424; European-Chinese 494; Others 1,610; Total 166,753. *1988 census* ('000 persons): Polynesians and 'Demis' 156.3; Others 32.5.

Principal Towns (population at 1996 census): Papeete (capital) 25,553; Faaa 25,888; Punaauía 19,524; Pirae 13,974; Moorea-Maiao 11,965; Mahina 11,640; Paea 10,281.

Births, Marriages and Deaths (1999, provisional): Registered live births 4,580 (birth rate 19.9 per 1,000); Marriage rate 5.2 per 1,000 (1997); Registered deaths 1,003 (death rate 4.4 per 1,000).

Expectation of Life (years at birth, 1997): 72.5 (males 70.0; females 75.0). Source: UN, *Statistical Yearbook for Asia and the Pacific.*

Economically Active Population (persons aged 14 years and over, 1996 census): Agriculture, hunting, forestry and fishing 10,888; Mining and manufacturing 6,424; Electricity, gas and water 459; Construction 4,777; Trade, restaurants and hotels 9,357; Transport, storage and communications 3,788; Financial services 1,482; Real estate 383; Business services 3,710; Private services 9,033; Education, health and social welfare 10,771; Public administration 13,475; Total employed 74,547 (males 46,141, females 28,406); Persons on compulsory military service 1,049 (all males); Unemployed 11,525 (males 6,255, females 5,270); Total labour force 87,121 (males 53,445, females 33,676).

AGRICULTURE, ETC.

Principal Crops (metric tons, 1999): Roots and tubers 11,349*; Vegetables and melons 5,870*; Pineapples 3,026*; Other fruit 3,460*; Coconuts 63,000*; Copra 7,464*; Vanilla 16; Coffee (green) 16. Source: FAO and Service du Développement Rural.

* FAO estimate.

Livestock (FAO estimates, year ending September 1999): Cattle 9,200; Horses 2,200; Pigs 35,000; Goats 16,000; Sheep 420. Source: FAO.

Livestock Products (FAO estimates, metric tons, 1999): Cows' milk 894; Pig meat 1,123; Other meat 825; Hen eggs 1,576. Source: FAO.

Fishing ('000 metric tons, live weight, 1998): Capture 11.4 (Common dolphinfish 0.4, Skipjack tuna 0.8; Albacore 3.2, Yellowfin tuna 0.6, Bigeye tuna 0.4, Marlins and sailfishes 0.5; Marine fishes 4.7); Aquaculture 0.1; Total catch 11.5. Source: FAO, *Yearbook of Fishery Statistics.*

INDUSTRY

Production: Coconut oil 5,366 metric tons (1994); Oilcake 4,477 metric tons (1987); Beer 129,000 hectolitres (1992); Printed cloth 200,000 m (1979); Japanese sandals 600,000 pairs (1979); Electric energy 364.6m. kWh (1999).

FINANCE

Currency and Exchange Rates: 100 centimes = 1 franc de la Communauté française du Pacifique (franc CFP or Pacific franc). *Sterling, Dollar and Euro Equivalents* (29 December 2000): £1 sterling = 191.37 francs CFP; US $1 = 128.24 francs CFP; €1 = 119.33 francs CFP; 1,000 francs CFP = £5.226 = $7.798 = €8.380. *Average Exchange Rate* (francs CFP per US $): 107.26 in 1998; 112.01 in 1999; 129.52 in 2000. Note: Until 31 December 1998 the value of the franc CFP was fixed at 5.5 French centimes (1 French franc = 18.1818 francs CFP). Since the introduction of the euro, on 1 January 1999, an official exchange rate of 1,000 francs CFP = €8.38 (€1 = 119.332 francs CFP) has been in operation. Accordingly, the value of the franc CFP has been adjusted to 5.4969 French centimes (1 French franc = 18.1920 francs CFP), representing a 'devaluation' of 0.056%.

Territorial Budget (estimates, million francs CFP, 1999): *Revenue:* Current 96,136 (Indirect taxation 52,650). *Expenditure:* Current 88,136, Capital 36,990; Total 125,126.

French State Expenditure (million francs CFP, 1996): Civil budget 61,706 (Current 56,564, Capital 5,142); Military budget

46,119 (Current 37,160, Capital 8,959); Pensions 10,458; Total (incl. others) 123,774 (Current 109,060, Capital 14,714).

1997 (million francs CFP): 122,596 (incl. military budget 43,081).

1998 (million francs CFP): 121,788 (incl. military budget 37,982).

1999 (million francs CFP): 120,631 (incl. military budget 34,343).

Money Supply (million francs CFP at 31 December 1997): Currency in circulation 6,846; Demand deposits 81,141; Total money 87,987. Source: Institut National de la Statistique et des Etudes Economiques.

Cost of Living (Consumer Price Index; base: 1990 = 100): 108.0 in 1996; 109.4 in 1997; 110.9 in 1998. Source: Institut National de la Statistique et des Etudes Economiques.

Gross Domestic Product (million francs CFP at current prices): 372,168 in 1996; 378,501 in 1997; 404,886 in 1998 (provisional).

Expenditure on the Gross Domestic Product (million francs CFP at current prices, 1993): Government final consumption expenditure 126,127; Private final consumption expenditure 202,563; Increase in stocks −536; Gross fixed capital formation 53,494; *Total domestic expenditure* 381,648; Exports of goods and services 34,523; *Less* Imports of goods and services 86,905; *GDP in purchasers' values* 329,266. Source: UN, *National Accounts Statistics*.

Gross Domestic Product by Economic Activity (million francs CFP at current prices, 1997): Agriculture, forestry and fishing 15,534; Manufacturing 26,360*; Electricity, gas and water 12,221*; Construction 20,104; Trade 81,854; Transport and telecommunications 27,832. Other private services 96,714; Government services 97,238; Domestic services 646; *GDP in purchasers' values* 378,503. *Manufacturing of energy-generating products is included in electricity, gas and water. Source: UN, *National Accounts Statistics*.

EXTERNAL TRADE

Principal Commodities (million francs CFP, 1997): *Imports c.i.f.:* Meat and edible offal 4,886; Beverages, spirits and vinegar 1,903; Tobacco and manufactured tobacco substitutes 394; Pharmaceutical products 3,077; Articles of iron or steel 2,594; Machinery and mechanical appliances 9,591; Electrical machinery, sound and image recorders 6,605; Total (incl. others) 99,339. *Exports f.o.b.:* Vanilla 111.1; Mother of pearl 323.9; Coconut oil 391.9; Cultured pearls 14,658.0; Total (incl. others) 23,804. Source: UN, *Statistical Yearbook for Asia and the Pacific*.
1998: Imports c.i.f.: 116,355. *Exports f.o.b.:* Vanilla 89.3; Mother of pearl 151.0; Coconut oil 153.5; Cultured pearls 14,587.0; Total (incl. others) 26,462.
1999: Imports c.i.f.: 102,972 (Civilian 98,682; Military 4,290); *Exports c.i.f.:* Cultured pearls 17,328; Total (incl. others) 27,182.
2000: Imports c.i.f.: 126,407; *Exports c.i.f.* 28,829.
Source: ISPF—Service des Douanes.

Principal Trading Partners (million francs CFP, 2000): *Imports:* Australia 11,763; Belgium 6,004; China, People's Republic 3,566; France 45,531; Germany 1,775; Italy 3,828; Japan 5,116; Korea, Republic 1,544; New Zealand 9,338; Singapore 2,445; Spain 1,707; Taiwan 1,634; United Kingdom 2,447; USA 17,594; Total (incl. others) 126,407. *Exports:* France 3,989; Germany 499; Hong Kong 6,010; Japan 349; New Caledonia 1,440; New Zealand 297; USA 3,768; Total (incl. others) 28,829. Source: ISPF—Service des Douanes.

TRANSPORT

Road Traffic (1987): Total vehicles registered 54,979; (1996 census): Private cars 47,300.

Shipping (1990): *International traffic:* Passengers carried 47,616; Freight handled 642,314 metric tons. *Domestic traffic:* Passengers carried 596,185; Freight handled 261,593 metric tons. (1999): Goods unloaded 824,958 metric tons; Goods loaded 32,699 metric tons.

Civil Aviation (1999): *International traffic:* Passengers carried (incl. those in transit) 604,328; Freight handled 7,974 metric tons. *Domestic traffic:* Passengers carried 1,389,475; Freight handled 10,111 metric tons.

TOURISM

Visitors (excluding cruise passengers and excursionists): 180,440 in 1997; 188,933 in 1998; 210,800 in 1999.

Tourist Arrivals by Country of Residence (1999): Australia 8,264; France 58,705; Germany 6,381; Italy 10,969; Japan 14,256; New Zealand 8,805; United Kingdom 4,770; USA 66,169; Total (incl. others) 210,800.

Tourism Receipts (US $m.) 326 in 1995; 322 in 1996; 359 in 1997. Source: partly, World Tourism Organization, *Yearbook of Tourism Statistics*.
1998: 39,200m. francs CFP.
1999: 47,300m. francs CFP.
Source: Ministère du Tourisme.

COMMUNICATIONS MEDIA

Radio Receivers (1997): 128,000 in use*.
Television Receivers (1997): 40,000 in use*.
Telephones (1997): 52,000 main lines in use.
Telefax Stations (1997): 2,974 in use†.
Mobile Cellular Telephones (subscribers, 1997): 5,427†.
Daily Newspapers (2000): 2.
* Source: UNESCO, *Statistical Yearbook*.
† Source: UN, *Statistical Yearbook*.

EDUCATION

Pre-primary (1996/97): 59 schools; 408 teachers; 16,049 pupils.
Primary (1996/97): 170 schools; 2,811 teachers; 29,415 pupils.
General Secondary (1996/97): 1,897 teachers; 28,438 pupils.
Vocational (1992): 316 teachers; 3,730 students.
Tertiary (1993): 34 teachers; 892 students.
Source: partly UNESCO, *Statistical Yearbook*.

Directory

The Constitution

The constitutional system in French Polynesia is established under the aegis of the Constitution of the Fifth French Republic and specific laws of 1977, 1984 and 1990. The French Polynesia Statute 1984, the so-called 'internal autonomy statute', underwent amendment in a law of July 1990. A further extension of the Territory's powers under the statute was approved by the French National Assembly in December 1995. A constitutional amendment granting French Polynesia a greater degree of autonomy was presented to a joint session of the French Senate and National Assembly for final ratification in January 2000 (see History). By early 2001, however, no decision had been taken on the matter.

French Polynesia is declared to be an autonomous Territory of the French Republic, of which it remains an integral part. The High Commissioner, appointed by the French Government, exercises the prerogatives of the State in matters relating to defence, foreign relations, the maintenance of law and order, communications and citizenship. The head of the local executive and the person who represents the Territory is the President of the Territorial Government, who is elected by the Territorial Assembly from among its own number. The Territorial President appoints and dismisses the Council of Ministers and has competence in international relations as they affect French Polynesia and its exclusive economic zone, and is in control of foreign investments and immigration. The Territorial Assembly, which has financial autonomy in budgetary affairs and legislative authority within the Territory, is elected for a term of up to five years on the basis of universal adult suffrage. There are 49 members: 32 elected by the people of the Windward Islands (Iles du Vent—Society Islands), seven by the Leeward Islands (Iles Sous le Vent—Society Islands), four by the Tuamotu Archipelago and the Gambier Islands and three each by the Austral Islands and by the Marquesas Archipelago. The Assembly elects a Permanent Commission of between seven and nine of its members, and itself meets for two ordinary sessions each year and upon the demand of the majority party, the Territorial President or the High Commissioner. Local government is conducted by the municipalities. There is an Economic, Social and Cultural Council (composed of representatives of professional groups, trade unions and other organizations and agencies which participate in the economic, social and cultural activities of the Territory), a Territorial Audit Office and a judicial system which includes a Court of the First Instance, a Court of Appeal and an Administrative Court. The Territory, as a part of the French Republic, also elects two deputies to the National Assembly and one member of the Senate, and may be represented in the European Parliament.

The Government

(May 2001)

High Commissioner: JEAN ARIBAUD (appointed November 1997).
Secretary-General: CHRISTIAN MASSIMON.

COUNCIL OF MINISTERS

President and Minister for Foreign Affairs, the Pearl Culture Industry and Urban Development: GASTON FLOSSE.

Vice-President and Minister for Employment and Training, Outer Island Development, New Technologies and Post: EDOUARD FRITCH.

Minister for Economy and Finance: GEORGES PUCHON.

Minister for Housing, Land Use, Urban Affairs, Town Humanization and Government Spokesman: JEAN-CHRISTOPHE BOUISSOU.

Minister for Lands, Land Redistribution and Valuation: GASTON TONG SANG.

Minister for Education and Technical Training: NICOLAS SANQUER.

Minister for Ports and Utilities: JONAS TAHUAITU.

Minister for Transport and Energy: BRUNO SANDRAS.

Minister for Tourism, the Environment and Women's Affairs: NICOLE BOUTEAU.

Minister for Fisheries, Industry and Small and Medium Businesses: NINA VERNAUDON.

Minister for Agriculture and Livestock: FRÉDÉRIC RIVETA.

Minister for Health and Research: PATRICK TAHIATA HOWELL.

Minister for Solidarity and Family: PIA FAATOMO.

Minister for Youth and Sports, Youth Opportunities and Associative Affairs, responsible for Relations with the Territorial Assembly and the Economic, Social and Cultural Council: REYNALD TEMARII.

Minister for Labour, Social Dialogue, Public Service and Administrative Decentralization: ARMELLE MERCERON.

Minister for Culture and Higher Education, responsible for the Promotion of Polynesian Languages: LOUISE PELTZER.

Minister for Arts and Crafts: PASCALE HAITI.

GOVERNMENT OFFICES

Office of the High Commissioner of the Republic: Bureau du Haut Commissaire, ave Bruat, BP 115, 98713, Papeete; tel. 468686; fax 468689; e-mail courrier@haut-commissariat.pf.

Office of the President of the Territorial Government: BP 2551, 98713 Papeete; tel. 472000; fax 419781; e-mail presid@mail.pf; internet www.presidence.pf.

Territorial Government of French Polynesia: BP 2551, Papeete; tel. 543450; fax 419781; e-mail presid@mail.pf; all ministries; Delegation in Paris: 28 blvd Saint-Germain, 75005 Paris, France; tel. 1-55-42-65-10; fax 1-55-42-64-09.

Economic, Social and Cultural Council: Av. Bruat, BP 1657, 98716 Papeete; tel. 416500; fax 419242; e-mail cesc@cesc.gov.pf; Pres. BRUNO SANDRAS.

Legislature

ASSEMBLÉE TERRITORIALE

President: LUCETTE TAERO.

Territorial Assembly: Assemblée Territoriale, BP 28, Papeete; tel. 416100; fax 416160.

Election, 6 May 2001

Party	Seats
Tahoeraa Huiraatira/RPR	28
Tavini Huiraatira	13
Fe'tia Api	7
Tapura Amui No Tuhaa Pae	1
Total	**49**

PARLEMENT

Deputies to the French National Assembly: EMILE VERNAUDON (Ai'a Api/RPR), MICHEL BUILLARD (Tahoeraa Huiraatira/RPR).

Representative to the French Senate: GASTON FLOSSE (Tahoeraa Huiraatira/RPR).

Political Organizations

Ai'a Api (New Land): BP 11055, Mahina, Tahiti; tel. 481135; f. 1982 after split in Te E'a Api; Leader EMILE VERNAUDON.

Alliance 2000: c/o Assemblée Territoriale, BP 28, Papeete; pro-independence grouping.

Fe'tia Api (New Star): c/o Assemblée Territoriale, BP 28, Papeete; Leader BORIS LÉONTIEFF.

Haere i Mua: Leader ALEXANDRE LÉONTIEFF.

Heiura-Les Verts: BP 44, Borabora; tel. and fax 677174; e-mail heiura@mail.pf.

Ia Mana Te Nunaa: rue du Commandant Destrémau, BP 1223, Papeete; tel. 426699; f. 1976; advocates 'socialist independence'; Sec.-Gen. JACQUES DROLLET.

Polynesian Union Party: Papeete; Leader JEAN JUVENTIN.

Pupu Here Ai'a Te Nunaa Ia Ora: BP 3195, Papeete; tel. 420766; f. 1965; advocates autonomy; 8,000 mems.

Te Tiaraama: Papeete; f. 1987 by split from the RPR; Leader ALEXANDRE LÉONTIEFF.

Pupu Taina/Rassemblement des Libéraux: rue Cook, BP 169, Papeete; tel. 429880; f. 1976; seeks to retain close links with France; associated with the French Union pour la Démocratie Française (UDF); Leader MICHEL LAW.

Taatiraa Polynesia: BP 2916, Papeete; tel. 437494; fax 422546; f. 1977; Federal Pres. ARTHUR CHUNG; Exec. Pres. ROBERT TANSEAU.

Tahoeraa Huiraatira/Rassemblement pour la République—RPR: rue du Commandant Destrémeau, BP 471, Papeete; tel. 429898; fax 437758; f. 1958; supports links with France, with internal autonomy; Pres. GASTON FLOSSE; Hon. Pres. JACQUES TEUIRA.

Tapura Amui No Tuhaa Pae: c/o Assemblée Territoriale, BP 28, Papeete; represents the Austral Islands; Leader CHANTAL FLORES.

Tavini Huiraatira/Front de Libération de la Polynésie (FLP): independence movement; anti-nuclear; Leader OSCAR TEMARU.

Te Avei'a Mau (True Path): c/o Assemblée Territoriale, BP 28, Papeete; Leader TINOMANA EBB.

Te e'a No Maohi Nui: Leader JEAN-MARIUS RAAPOTO.

Te Henua Enata Kotoa: c/o Assemblée Territoriale, BP 28, Papeete; Leader LUCIEN KIMITETE.

Judicial System

Court of Appeal: Cour d'Appel de Papeete, BP 101, 98713 Papeete; tel. 415546; fax 415581; Pres. PATRICK MICHAUX; Attorney-General JACK GAUTHIER.

Court of the First Instance: Tribunal de Première Instance de Papeete, BP 101, Papeete; tel. 415500; fax 454012; Pres. JEAN-LOUIS THIOLET; Procurator MICHEL MAROTTE; Clerk of the Court MADELEINE VANQUIN.

Court of Administrative Law: Tribunal Administratif, BP 4522, Papeete; tel. 509025; fax 451724; e-mail tapapeete@mail.pf; Pres. ALFRED POUPET; Cllrs RAOUL AUREILLE, PATRICK DEMARQUET, MARIE-CHRISTINE LUBRANO.

Religion

About 54% of the population are Protestants and 30% are Roman Catholics.

CHRISTIANITY
Protestant Church

L'Eglise évangélique de Polynésie française (Etaretia Evaneria no Porinetia Farani): BP 113, Papeete; tel. 460600; fax 419357; e-mail eepf@mail.pf; f. 1884; autonomous since 1963; c. 95,000 mems; Pres. of Council Rev. JACQUES TERAI IHORAI; Sec.-Gen. (vacant).

The Roman Catholic Church

French Polynesia comprises the archdiocese of Papeete and the suffragan diocese of Taiohae o Tefenuaenata (based in Nuku Hiva, Marquesas Is). At 31 December 1998 there were an estimated 81,600 adherents in the Territory, representing about 37% of the total population. The Archbishop and the Bishop participate in the Episcopal Conference of the Pacific, based in Fiji.

Archbishop of Papeete: Most Rev. HUBERT COPPENRATH, Archevêché, BP 94, Vallée de la Mission, 98713 Papeete; tel. 420251; fax 424032; e-mail catholic@mail.pf.

Other Churches

There are small Sanito, Church of Jesus Christ of Latter-day Saints (Mormon), and Seventh-day Adventist missions.

The Press

La Dépêche de Tahiti: Société Océanienne de Communication, BP 50, Papeete; tel. 464343; fax 464350; e-mail journalistes@france-antilles.pf; internet www.ladepechedetahiti.com; f. 1964; daily; French; Editor-in-Chief DANIEL PARDON; Dir-Gen. PASCAL HEEMS; circ. 15,000.

Les Nouvelles de Tahiti: place de la Cathédrale, BP 629, Papeete; tel. 508100; fax 508109; e-mail nouvelles@mail.pf; f. 1956; daily; French; Editor MURIEL PONTAROLLO; Dir-Gen. PASCAL HEEMS; Publr PHILIPPE HERSANT; circ. 6,500.

Le Semeur Tahitien: BP 94, 98713 Papeete; tel. 420251; e-mail catholic@mail.pf; f. 1909; monthly; French; publ. by the Roman Catholic Church.

Tahiti Beach Press: BP 887, Papeete; tel. 426850; f. 1980; weekly; English; Publr G. WARTI; circ. 3,000.

Tahiti Pacifique Magazine: BP 368, Maharepa, Moorea; tel. 562894; fax 563007; e-mail tahitipm@mail.pf; internet www.tahiti-pacifique.com; monthly; French; Editor ALEX DU PREL; circ. 5,000.

Tahiti Rama: Papeete; weekly.

Tahiti Today: BP 887, 98713 Papeete; tel. 426850; fax 423356; f. 1996; quarterly; Publr G. WARTI; circ. 3,000.

La Tribune Polynésienne: place du Marché, BP 392, Papeete; tel. 481048; fax 481220; weekly; Dir LOUIS BRESSON.

Ve'a Katorika: BP 94, 98713 Papeete; f. 1909; monthly; publ. by the Roman Catholic Church.

Ve'a Porotetani: BP 113, Papeete; tel. 460623; fax 419357; e-mail eepf@mail.pf; f. 1921; monthly; French and Tahitian; publ. by the Evangelical Church; Editor RALF TEANORE; Dir IHORAI JACQUES; circ. 6,000.

NEWS AGENCIES

Tahitian Press Agency (ATP): Papeete; f. 2001; bilingual French and English news service providing pictures and radio reports.

Foreign Bureaux

Agence France-Presse (AFP): BP 629, Papeete; tel. 508100; fax 508109; e-mail international@france-antilles.pf; Correspondent CHRISTIAN BRETAULT.

Associated Press (AP) (USA): BP 912, Papeete; tel. 437562; Correspondent AL PRINCE.

Reuters (UK): BP 50, Papeete; tel. 464340; fax 464350; e-mail danielpardon@mail.pf; Correspondent DANIEL PARDON.

Publishers

Haere Po No Tahiti: BP 1958, Papeete; fax 582333; f. 1981; travel, history, botany, linguistics and local interest.

Scoop/Au Vent des Îles: BP 5670, 98716 Pirae; tel. 435456; fax 426174; e-mail scooptah@mail.pf; f. 1992; Gen. Man. ROBERT CHRISTIAN.

Government Printer

Imprimerie Officielle: 43 rue des Poilus-Tahitiens, BP 117, 98713 Papeete; tel. 425067; fax 425261; f. 1843; printers, publrs; Dir CLAUDINO LAURENT.

Broadcasting and Communications

TELECOMMUNICATIONS

Office des Postes et Télécommunications: 8 rue de la Reine Pomare IV, Papeete; tel. 414242; fax 436767; Dir-Gen. GEFFRY SALMON.

France Cables et Radio (FCR): Télécommunications extérieures de la Polynésie française, BP 99, Papeete; tel. 415400; fax 437553; e-mail fcr@mail.pf.

BROADCASTING

Radio

Radio-Télé-Tahiti: 410 rue Dumont d'Urville, BP 125, Papeete; tel. 861640; fax 861641; e-mail dirbi@rfo.pf; internet www .tahiti-explorer.com/rfo.html; f. 1951 as Radio-Tahiti; television service began 1965; operated by Société Nationale de Radio-Télévision Française d'Outre-Mer (RFO), Paris; daily programmes in French and Tahitian; Dir CLAUDE RUBEN; Dir (Programmes) JEAN-RAYMOND BODIN.

Private Stations

NRJ Radio: Papeete; tel. and fax 464346; e-mail nrj@mail.pf; French.

Radio Bleue: Papeete; tel. 483436; fax 480825; e-mail redaction@ radiobleue.pf; affiliated to the political party Ai'a Api; French.

Radio Maohi: Maison des Jeunes, Pirae; tel. 819797; fax 825493; e-mail tereo@mail.pf; owned by the political party Tahoeraa Huiraa-tira; French and Tahitian.

Radio One: Fare Ute, BP 3601, Papeete; tel. 434100; fax 423406; e-mail infos@radio1.pf.

Radio Tefana: Papeete; tel. 819797; fax 825493; e-mail tereo@ mail.pf; affiliated to the political party Tavini Huiraatira; French and Tahitian.

Radio Tiare: Fare Ute, Papeete; tel. 434100; fax 423406; e-mail contact@tiarefm.pf.

Television

Radio-Télé-Tahiti: (see Radio).

Canal Plus Polynésie: Immeuble Pomare, blvd Paofai, BP 20051, 98713 Papeete; tel. 540754; fax 540755; e-mail classagne@cplus.pf; privately-owned; Dir CHRISTOPHE LASSAGNE.

Telefenua: Papeete; tel. 461125; fax 431213; paying cable channel broadcasting in French, Tahitian and English.

TNTV (Tahiti Nui Television): Papeete; tel. 473600; e-mail emoniot@tntv.pf; local govt station broadcasting in French and Tahitian.

TNS (Tahiti Nui Satellite): (see TNTV); French.

Finance

(cap. = capital; res = reserves; dep. = deposits; m. = million; brs = branches; amounts in CFP francs)

BANKING
Commercial Banks

Banque de Polynésie SA: 355 blvd Pomare, BP 530, 9713 Papeete; tel. 466666; fax 466664; e-mail sec.gen@sg-bdp.pf; internet www .sg-bdp.pf; f. 1973; 80% owned by Société Générale (France); cap. and res 5,210.5m., dep. 65,456.4m. (Dec. 1999); Pres. JEAN-LOUIS MATTEI; Dir-Gen. ROGER MUNOZ; 19 brs.

Banque de Tahiti SA: rue François Cardella, BP 1602, Papeete; tel. 425389; fax 423376; e-mail dir.gene@bank-tahiti.pf; internet www.bank-tahiti.pf; f. 1969; owned by Bank of Hawaii (USA—94%) and Crédit Lyonnais (France—3%); merged with Banque Paribas de Polynésie, Aug. 1998; cap. 1,336m., res 3,739.4m., dep. 76,014.1m. (Dec. 1998); Pres. J. C. IRRMANN; Exec. Vice-Pres. MICHEL DUPIEUX; 16 brs.

Banque SOCREDO—Société pour le Crédit et le Développe-ment en Océanie: 115 rue Dumont d'Urville, BP 130, 98713 Papeete; tel. 415123; fax 433661; f. 1959; public body; affiliated to Banque Nationale de Paris (France); cap. 7,000m. (Dec. 1993), dep. 76,610m. (Dec. 1995); Pres. JEAN VERNAUDON; Dir ERIC POMMIER; 24 brs.

Trade and Industry

DEVELOPMENT ORGANIZATIONS

Agence pour l'Emploi et la Formation Professionnelle: BP 540, Papeete; tel. 426375; fax 426281.

Agence Française de Développement (ACFD): BP 578, Papeete; tel. 544600; fax 544601; public body; development finance institute.

Conseil Economique, Social et Culturel: ave Bruat, BP 1657, 98716 Papeete; tel. 416500; fax 419242; e-mail cesc@cesc.gov.pf; Dir BRUNO SANDRAS.

Service de l'Artisanat Traditionnel: BP 4451, 98713 Papeete; tel. 423225; fax 436478; e-mail teura.iriti@artisanat.gov.pf; Dir TEURA IRITI.

Service du Développement de l'Industrie et des Métiers: BP 20728, 98713 Papeete; tel. 533096; fax 412645; e-mail sdim2@ economie.gov.pf; industry and small business development admin-istration.

Société pour le Développement de l'Agriculture et de la Pêche: BP 1247, Papeete; tel. 836798; fax 856886; agriculture and marine industries.

SODEP—Société pour le Développement et l'Expansion du Pacifique: BP 4441, Papeete; tel. 429449; f. 1961 by consortium of banks and private interests; regional development and finance co.

CHAMBERS OF COMMERCE

Chambre de Commerce, d'Industrie, des Services et des Mé-tiers de Polynésie Française: 41 rue du Docteur Cassiau, BP 118, Papeete; tel. 472700; fax 540701; e-mail info@cci.pf; internet www.ccism.pf; f. 1880; 36 mems; Pres. NINA VERNAUDON.

Chambre d'Agriculture et de la Pêche Lagonaire: route de l'Hippodrome, BP 5383, Papeete; tel. 425393; fax 438754; f. 1886; 10 mems; Pres. SYLVAIN MILLAUD.

Jeune Chambre Economique de Tahiti: BP 2576, Papeete; tel. 454542; fax 466070; internet www.jce.pf; Pres. CATHY GOURBAULT.

EMPLOYERS' ORGANIZATIONS

Chambre Syndicale des Entrepreneurs du Bâtiment et des Travaux Publics: BP 2218, Papeete; tel. 438898; fax 423237; Pres. GEORGES TRAMINI.

Conseil des Employeurs: Immeuble FARNHAM, rue E. Ahnne, BP 972, Papeete; tel. 438898; fax 423237; f. 1983; Pres. GILLES YAU; Sec.-Gen. ASTRID PASQUIER.

Fédération Générale de Commerce (FGC): rue Albert Leboucher, BP 1607, 98713 Papeete; tel. 429908; fax 422359; Pres. GILLES YAU.

Fédération Polynésienne de l'Agriculture et de l'Elevage: Papara, Tahiti; Pres. MICHEL LEHARTEL.

Syndicat des Importateurs et des Négociants: BP 1607, Papeete.

Union Interprofessionnelle du Tourisme de la Polynésie Française: BP 4560, Papeete; tel. 439114; f. 1973; 1,200 mems; Pres. PAUL MAETZ; Sec.-Gen. JEAN CORTEEL.

Union Patronale: BP 317, Papeete; tel. 438898; fax 423237; f. 1948; 63 mems; Pres. DIDIER CHOMER.

UTILITES

Electricity

Electricité de Tahiti: route de Puurai, BP 8021, Faaa-Puurai; tel. 867777.

Water

Société Polynésienne des Eaux et Assainissements: Papeete, Tahiti.

Syndicat Central de l'Hydraulique: Tahiti.

TRADE UNIONS

Confédération Syndicale A Tia I Mua: Immeuble la Ora, BP 4523, Papeete; tel. 436038; fax 450245; e-mail atiaimua@ifrance .com; affiliated to CFDT (France); Gen. Sec. BRUNO SANDRAS.

Fédération des Syndicats de la Polynésie Française: BP 1136, Papeete; Pres. MARCEL AHINI.

Syndicat Territorial des Instituteurs et Institutrices de Polynésie: BP 3007, Papeete; Sec.-Gen. WILLY URIMA.

Union des Syndicats Affiliés des Travailleurs de Polynésie/Force Ouvrière-USATP/FO : BP 1201, Papeete; tel. 426049; fax 450635; Pres. COCO TERAIEFA CHANG; Sec.-Gen. PIERRE FRÉBAULT.

Union des Syndicats de l'Aéronautique: Papeete; Pres. JOSEPH CONROY.

Union des Travailleurs de Tahiti et des Iles: rue Albert Leboucher, Papeete; tel. 437369; Pres. JOHN TEFATUA-VAIHO.

Transport

ROADS

French Polynesia has 792 km of roads, of which about one-third are bitumen-surfaced and two-thirds stone-surfaced.

SHIPPING

The principal port is Papeete, on Tahiti.

Port Authority: Port Autonome de Papeete, Motu Uta, BP 9164, 98715 Papeete; tel. 505454; fax 421950; e-mail portppt@mail.pf; internet www.portoftahiti.com; Harbour Master Commdt CLAUDE VIGOR; Port Man. BÉATRICE CHANSIN.

Agence Maritime Internationale de Tahiti: BP 274, Papeete; tel. 428972; fax 432184; e-mail amitahiti@mail.pf; services to New Zealand, USA, Australia, American Samoa, Fiji, Europe and Asia.

CGM Tour du Monde SA: 80 rue du Général de Gaulle, BP 96, Papeete; tel. 420890; fax 436806; shipowners and agents; freight

services between Europe and many international ports; Dir HENRI C. FERRAND.

Compagnie de Développement Maritime des Tuamotu (CODEMAT): POB 1291, Papeete.

Compagnie Française Maritime de Tahiti: 2 rue de Commerce, POB 368, Papeete; tel. 426393; fax 420617; Man. M. GARBUTT.

Compagnie Maritime des Iles Sous le Vent: BP 9012, Papeete.

Compagnie Polynésienne de Transport Maritime: BP 220, Papeete; tel. 426240; fax 434889; e-mail aranui@mail.pf; internet www.aranui.com; Dir JEAN WONG.

Leprado Valere SARL: POB 3917, Papeete; tel. 450030; fax 421049.

Richmond Frères SARL: POB 1816, Papeete.

Société de Navigation des Australes: BP 1890; Papeete; tel. 509609; fax 420609.

Société de Transport Insulaire Maritime (STIM): BP 635, Papeete; tel. 452324.

Société de Transport Maritime de Tuamotu: BP 11366, Mahina; tel. 422358; fax 430373.

CIVIL AVIATION

There is one international airport, Faaa airport, 6 km from Papeete, on Tahiti, and there are about 40 smaller airstrips. International services are operated by Air France, Air New Zealand, LAN-Chile, Air Outre Mer, Air Calédonie International, Corsair and Hawaiian Airlines (USA).

Service d'État de l'Aviation Civile: Papeete; internet www .seac.pf; Dir GUY YEUNG.

Air Moorea: BP 6019, Faaa; tel. 864100; fax 864269; f. 1968; operates internal services between Tahiti and Moorea Island and charter flights throughout the Territory; Pres. MARCEL GALENON; Dir-Gen. FREDDY CHANSEAU.

Air Tahiti: blvd Pomare, BP 314, 98713 Papeete; tel. 864000; fax 864009; e-mail direction.generale@airtahiti.pf; f. 1953, Air Polynésie 1970–87; operates domestic services to 39 islands; Chair. CHRISTIAN VERNAUDON; Gen. Man. MARCEL GALENON.

Air Tahiti Nui: BP 1673, Papeete; tel. 160202; fax 460290; e-mail fly@airtahitinui.pf; internet www.airtahitinui-usa.com; f. 1996; commenced operations 1998; scheduled services to Osaka (Japan) and Auckland (New Zealand); Chair. and CEO NELSON LEVY.

Tourism

Tourism is an important and developed industry in French Polynesia, particularly on Tahiti, and 210,800 people visited the Territory in 1999. In that year some 27.8% of arrivals were from France, 31.3% from the USA and 6.8% from Japan. There were a total of 3,650 hotel rooms in Tahiti in 2000. In 1999 the tourism industry earned an estimated 47,300m. francs CFP.

GIE Tahiti Tourisme: Immeuble Paofai, bâtiment D, blvd Pomare, BP 65, 98713 Papeete; tel. 505700; fax 436619; e-mail tahiti-tourisme @mail.pf; internet www.tahiti-tourisme.com; f. 1966 as autonomous public body, transformed into private corpn in 1993; tourist promotion; CEO BRIGITTE VANIZETTE.

Service du Tourisme: Fare Manihini, blvd Pomare, BP 4527, Papeete; tel. 505700; fax 481275; govt dept; manages Special Fund for Tourist Development; Dir GÉRARD VANIZETTE.

Syndicat d'Initiative de la Polynésie Française: BP 326, Papeete; Pres. PIU BAMBRIDGE.

FRENCH SOUTHERN AND ANTARCTIC TERRITORIES

The French Southern and Antarctic Territories (Terres australes et antarctiques françaises) form an Overseas Territory but are administered under a special statute. The territory comprises Adélie Land, a narrow segment of the mainland of Antarctica together with a number of offshore islets, and three groups of sub-Antarctic islands (the Kerguelen and Crozet Archipelagos and St Paul and Amsterdam Islands) in the southern Indian Ocean.

Under the terms of legislation approved by the French Government on 6 August 1955, the French Southern and Antarctic Territories were placed under the authority of a chief administrator, who was responsible to the Secretary of State for Overseas Departments and Territories. The Chief Administrator is assisted by a Consultative Council, which meets at least twice annually. The Council is composed of seven members who are appointed for five years by the Minister of Defence and the Secretary of State responsible for Overseas Departments and Territories (from among members of the Office of Scientific Research and from those who have participated in scientific missions in the sub-Antarctic islands and Adélie Land) and by other designated ministers.

From 1987 certain categories of vessels were allowed to register under the flag of the Kerguelen Archipelago, provided that 25% of their crew (including the captain and at least two officers) were French. These specifications were amended to 35% of the crew and at least four officers in April 1990. At 1 January 2000 there were 166 registered vessels.

In 1992 the French Government created a 'public interest group', the Institut Français pour la Recherche et la Technologie Polaires (IFRTP), to assume responsibility for the organization of scientific and research programmes in the French Southern and Antarctic Territories.

France is a signatory to the Antarctic Treaty (see p. 456).

Statistical Survey

Area (sq km): Kerguelen Archipelago 7,215, Crozet Archipelago 515, Amsterdam Island 58, St Paul Island 8, Adélie Land (Antarctica) 432,000.

Population (the population, comprising members of scientific missions, fluctuates according to season, being higher in the summer; the figures given are approximate): Kerguelen Archipelago, Port-aux-Français 56; Amsterdam Island at Martin de Viviès 20; Adélie Land at Base Dumont-d'Urville 27; the Crozet Archipelago at Alfred Faure (on Ile de la Possession) 17; St Paul Island is uninhabited. Total population (January 1999): 120.

Fishing (catch quotas in metric tons): Crayfish (spiny lobsters) in Amsterdam and St Paul: 340 (1999/2000); fishing by French and foreign fleets in the Kerguelen Archipelago: 6,500 (1999/2000).

Currency: French currency is used (see French Guiana).

Budget: Projected at 125.0m. francs in 1999, of which official subventions comprised 47.5m. francs.

External Trade: Exports consist mainly of crayfish and other fish to France and Réunion. The Territories also derive revenue from the sale of postage stamps and other philatelic items.

Directory

Government: Chief Administrator Mme BRIGITTE GIRARDIN; there is a central administration in Paris (34 rue des Renaudes, 75017 Paris, France; tel. 1-40-53-46-53; fax 1-47-66-91-23); e-mail taaf .com@wanado.fr.

Consultative Council: Pres. JEAN-PIERRE CHARPENTIER.

Transport: An oceanographic and supply vessel, the *Marion Dufresne II*, operated by the French Government, provides regular links between Réunion and the sub-Antarctic islands. Another specialized vessel, the *Astrolabe*, owned by the Groupe Bourbon and operating from Hobart, Tasmania, calls five times a year at the Antarctic mainland.

Research Stations: There are meteorological stations and geophysical research stations on Kerguelen, Amsterdam, Adélie Land and Crozet. Research in marine microbiology is conducted from the Crozet and Kerguelen Archipelagos, and studies of atmospheric pollution are carried out on Amsterdam Island. The French atomic energy authority, the Commissariat à l'énergie atomique, also maintains a presence on Crozet, Kerguelen and Adélie Land.

WALLIS AND FUTUNA ISLANDS

Introductory Survey

Location, Climate, Language, Religion, Capital

The Territory of Wallis and Futuna comprises two groups of islands: the Wallis Islands, including Wallis Island (also known as Uvea) and 19 islets *(motu)* on the surrounding reef, and, to the south-west, Futuna (or Hooru), comprising the two small islands of Futuna and Alofi. The islands are located north-east of Fiji and west of Samoa. Temperatures are generally between about 23°C (73°F) and 30°C (86°F), and there is a cyclone season between December and March. French and Wallisian (Uvean), the indigenous Polynesian language, are spoken in the Territory, and nearly all of the population is nominally Roman Catholic. The capital is Mata'Utu, on Wallis Island.

Recent History

The Wallis and Futuna Islands were settled first by Polynesian peoples, Wallis from Tonga and Futuna from Samoa. Futuna was subsequently discovered by the Dutch navigators, Schouten and Le Maire, in 1616, and Uvea was discovered by Samuel Wallis in 1767. Three kingdoms later emerged, and in 1837 the first Marist missionaries arrived. By 1842 the majority of the population had been converted to Christianity. In April 1842 the authorities requested French protection, coinciding with a similar proclamation in Tahiti (now French Polynesia). In 1851 a *fakauvea* war between the Catholic majority and the Methodist minority assisted by Tonga (which had commenced in 1843) came to an end when 500 Wallisians left for Tonga. Protectorate status was formalized in 1887 for Wallis and in 1888 for the two kingdoms of Futuna, but domestic law remained in force. The islands were never formally annexed, and nor were French law or representative institutions introduced, although Wallis and Futuna were treated as a dependency of New Caledonia. During the Second World War, Wallis was used as an airforce base by the USA. In 1959 the traditional Kings and chiefs requested integration into the French Republic. The islands formally became an Overseas Territory in July 1961, following a referendum in December 1959, in which 94.4% of the electorate requested this status (almost all the opposition was in Futuna, which itself recorded dissent from only 22.2% of the voters; Wallis was unanimous in its acceptance).

Although there is no movement in Wallis and Futuna seeking secession of the Territory from France (in contrast with the situation in the other French Pacific Territories, French Polynesia and New Caledonia), the two Kings whose kingdoms share the island of Futuna requested in November 1983, through the Territorial Assembly, that the island groups of Wallis and Futuna become separate Overseas Territories of France, arguing that the administration and affairs of the Territory had become excessively concentrated on Uvea (Wallis Island).

At elections to the 20-member Territorial Assembly in March 1982, the Rassemblement pour la République (RPR) and its allies won 11 seats, while the remaining nine were secured by candidates belonging to, or associated with, the Union pour la Démocratie Française (UDF). Later that year one member of the Lua Kae Tahi, a group affiliated to the metropolitan UDF, defected to the RPR group. In November 1983, however, three of the 12 RPR members joined the Lua Kae Tahi, forming a new majority. In the subsequent election for President of the Territorial Assembly, this 11-strong bloc of UDF-associated members supported the ultimately successful candidate, Falakiko Gata, even though he had been elected to the Territorial Assembly in 1982 as a member of the RPR.

In April 1985 Falakiko Gata formed a new political party, the Union Populaire Locale (UPL), which was committed to giving priority to local, rather than metropolitan, issues.

In 1987 a dispute broke out between two families both laying claim to the throne of Sigave, the northern kingdom on the island of Futuna. The conflict arose following the deposition of the former King, Sagato Keletaona, and his succession by Sosefo Vanaï. The intervention of the island's administrative authorities, who attempted to ratify Vanaï's accession to the throne, was condemned by the Keletaona family as an interference in the normal course of local custom, according to which such disputes are traditionally settled by a fight between the protagonists.

At elections to the Territorial Assembly held in March 1987, the UDF (together with affiliated parties) and the RPR each won seven seats. However, by forming an alliance with the UPL, the RPR maintained its majority, and Falakiko Gata was subsequently re-elected President. At elections for the French National Assembly in June 1988, Benjamin Brial was re-elected Deputy. However, when the result was contested by an unsuccessful candidate, Kamilo Gata, the election was investigated by the French Constitutional Council and the result declared invalid, owing to electoral irregularities. When the election was held again in January 1989, Kamilo Gata was elected Deputy, obtaining 57.4% of total votes.

Statistical information, gathered in 1990, showed that the emigration rate of Wallis and Futuna islanders had risen to over 50%. In October of that year 13,705 people (of whom 97% were Wallisians and Futunians) lived in the Territory, while 14,186 were resident in New Caledonia. At the 1996 census the number of Wallisians and Futunians resident in New Caledonia had increased to 17,563. According to the results, a proportion of the islanders had chosen to emigrate to other French Overseas Possessions or to metropolitan France. The principal reason for the increase was thought to be the lack of employment opportunities in the islands.

At elections to the Territorial Assembly in March 1992 the newly-founded Taumu'a Lelei secured 11 seats, while the RPR won nine. The new Assembly was remarkable for being the first since 1964 in which the RPR did not hold a majority. At elections to the French National Assembly in March 1993, Kamilo Gata was re-elected Deputy, obtaining 52.4% of total votes cast to defeat Clovis Logologofolau. In June 1994 the Union Locale Force Ouvrière organized a general strike in protest at the increasing cost of living in the Territory and the allegedly inadequate education system. It was reported that demonstrations continued for several days, during which the Territorial Assembly building was damaged in an arson attack.

In October 1994 it was reported that the King of Sigave, Lafaele Malau, had been deposed by a unanimous decision of the kingdom's chiefs. The action followed the appointment of two customary leaders to represent the Futunian community in New Caledonia, which had led to unrest among the inhabitants of Sigave. He was succeeded by Esipio Takasi.

At elections to the Territorial Assembly in December 1994 the RPR secured 10 seats, while a coalition group, Union Populaire pour Wallis et Futuna (UPWF), won seven, and independent candidates three. Mikaele Tauhavili was subsequently elected President of the Assembly.

The refusal by 10 of the 20 members of the Territorial Assembly to adopt budgetary proposals in January 1996, led to appeals for the dissolution of the Government by France and the organization of new elections. The budget (which, at US $20m., was some US $4.5m. smaller than the previous year) aroused opposition for its apparent lack of provision for development funds, particularly for the islands' nascent tourist industry.

Elections to the Territorial Assembly took place on 16 March 1997. A participation rate of 87.2% was recorded at the poll, in which RPR candidates secured 14 seats and left-wing candidates (including independents and members of various political groupings) won six seats. Victor Brial, a representative of the RPR, was elected President of the Territorial Assembly. At the second round of elections to the French National Assembly, on 1 June, Brial defeated Kamilo Gata, obtaining 3,241 votes (51.3% of the total).

Allegations that electoral irregularities had occurred in the elections to the Territorial Assembly of March 1997 were investigated and upheld for 11 of the seats. As a result, new elections were organized for the 11 seats on 6 September 1998, at which the RPR's representation in the Assembly was reduced to 11 seats overall, while left-wing and independent members increased their share of seats to nine. Also in September 1998, in a second round of voting, Fr Robert Laufoaulu was elected to the French Senate, defeating Kamilo Gata in a vote by the Territorial Assembly. Laufoaulu, a priest and director of Catholic education in the islands, stood as a left-wing candidate, nominated by RPR candidates, but was elected with the support of right-wing politicians.

In late March 1999 festivities were held to commemorate the 40th anniversary of the accession of the King of Wallis Island, Lavelua Tomasi Kulimoetoke. An estimated 10,000 people paid homage to the King, who was crowned in 1959. In late 1999 Kamilo Gata was appointed Social and Economic Adviser by the French Government. In March 2000 a delegation from Wallis and Futuna visited New Caledonia to discuss mutual arrangements concerning free trade and employment rights between the two Territories.

Government

The Territory of Wallis and Futuna is administered by a representative of the French Government, the Chief Administrator, who is assisted by the Territorial Assembly. The Assembly has 20 members and is elected for a five-year term. The three traditional kingdoms, from which the Territory was formed, one on Wallis and two sharing Futuna, have equal rights, although the kings' powers are limited. In addition, the Territory elects one Deputy to the French National Assembly in Paris and one representative to the French Senate. The islands may also be represented at the European Parliament.

Economic Affairs

In 1995 it was estimated that Wallis and Futuna's gross domestic product (GDP) was US $28.7m., equivalent to some $2,000 per head. Most monetary income in the islands is derived from government employment and remittances sent home by islanders employed in New Caledonia. Traditional food products, mother of pearl (from the Trochus shell) and handicrafts are the only significant export commodities, earning an estimated 14.3m. francs CFP in 1998. Exports of copra from Wallis ceased in 1950, and from Futuna in the early 1990s. Tobacco is cultivated for local consumption. Yams, taro, bananas, cassava and other food crops are also cultivated. Imports, which are provided mainly by metropolitan France and New Caledonia, cost an estimated 2,961m. francs CFP in 1998 and, in 1995, consisted principally of raw materials, manufactured goods and petroleum products. Wallis imports an estimated 5 metric tons of kava per year from Fiji and Vanuatu. In 1998/99 imports from New Zealand totalled $NZ5m. and those from Australia cost $A7m. An estimated 1,000 pigs a year are reared on the islands, and two units rear 800 and 450 hens a year respectively, which are used principally for eggs, and meet an estimated 80% of the territory's commercial needs. Fishing activity in the Territory's exclusive economic zone increased during the 1990s; the total catch was estimated at 206 metric tons in 1998, compared with 70 tons in 1991. Mineral fuels are the main source of electrical energy, although it is hoped that hydroelectric power can be developed, especially on Futuna. There is a 4,000 KW thermal power station on Wallis, and a 2,600 KW thermal power station was expected to be completed on Futuna in 2000.

There were 366 businesses in the Territory in 1999, of which 28 were in the industrial and artisanal sector, 101 in construction and 237 in the service and commercial sectors; 72 of those businesses were located on Futuna.

In 1998 almost all the cultivated vegetation on the island of Wallis, notably the banana plantations, was destroyed by a cyclone. In response to the cyclone damage, the French Government provided exceptional aid of 80m. francs CFP to alleviate the situation. In August 1989 a new earth station for satellite communications was inaugurated. The islands also benefited from an increase in building activity and public works in the early 1990s. Plans, under consideration in the mid-1990s, to develop a small tourism industry on the islands were prompted in part by the expectation that France was to reduce its financial assistance to the Territory.

Social Welfare

In 1999 there was one hospital on Wallis Island (with a total of 60 beds in 1990), and in 1993 the construction of a 21-bed hospital in Futuna was completed. There was one private doctor on the island in 1999.

Education

In 2000/01 there were 19 state-financed primary schools (including three pre-primary, 14 primary and two homecraft centres), and seven secondary schools (including two vocational schools) in Wallis and Futuna, with a total of 5,214 pupils. In 1999/2000, 361 students attended various universities overseas.

Public Holidays

2001: 1 January (New Year's Day), 16 April (Easter Monday), 1 May (Labour Day), 8 May (Liberation Day), 24 May (Ascension Day), 4 June (Whit Monday), 14 July (Fall of the Bastille), 11 November (Armistice Day), 25 December (Christmas Day).

2002: 1 January (New Year's Day), 1 April (Easter Monday), 1 May (Labour Day), 8 May (Liberation Day), 9 May (Ascension Day), 20 May (Whit Monday), 14 July (Fall of the Bastille), 11 November (Armistice Day), 25 December (Christmas Day).

Weights and Measures

The metric system is in force.

Statistical Survey

AREA AND POPULATION

Area (sq km): 160.5. *By island:* Uvea (Wallis Island) 77.5, Other Wallis Islands 18.5; Futuna Island 45, Alofi Island 19.5.

Population (census of 15 February 1983): 12,408: Wallis Islands 8,084, Futuna Island 4,324, Alofi Island uninhabited; (October 1990 census): 13,705 (males 6,829, females 6,876): Wallis Islands 8,973, Futuna Island 4,732 (Alo 2,860, Sigave 1,872); 14,186 Wallisians and Futunians resided in New Caledonia. Total population 14,166 (males 6,984, females 7,182) at census of 1996. Total population 14,375 (estimate) at mid-1999.

Density (estimate, mid-1999): 89.6 per sq km.

Principal Town: Mata'Utu (capital), population 1,137 at 1996 census.

Births and Deaths (estimates, 1998): Birth rate 23.0 per 1,000; Death rate 4.8 per 1,000.

Expectation of Life (estimates, years at birth, 1998): 73.8 (males 73.2; females 74.4).

AGRICULTURE, ETC.

Principal Crops (FAO estimates, '000 metric tons, 1999): Cassava 2; Yams 1; Taro 2; Other roots and tubers 1; Coconuts 2; Bananas 4; Other fruit 5; Vegetables and melons 1. Source: FAO.

Livestock (FAO estimates, '000 head, year ending September 1999): Pigs 25; Goats 7. Source: FAO.

Livestock Products (FAO estimates, metric tons, 1999): Hen eggs 33; Honey 11. Source: FAO.

Fishing (metric tons, live weight, 1998): Capture 206 (Marine fishes 200). Source: FAO, *Yearbook of Fishery Statistics*.

FINANCE

Currency and Exchange Rates: see French Polynesia.

Budget: US $24.5m. in 1995; US $20m. in 1996; US $22m. in 1997.

Aid from France (million francs CFP, 1999): 7,048.

Money Supply: (million francs CFP, 1999): Currency in circulation 497; Demand deposits 1,779; Total money 2,277. Source: Institut National de la Statistique et des Etudes Economiques.

EXTERNAL TRADE

1998 (million francs CFP): *Imports:* 2,961. *Exports:* 14.3.

TRANSPORT

Shipping: *Merchant Fleet* (vessels registered, '000 grt, at 31 December 1998): 111.4. Source: Lloyd's Register of Shipping.

Civil Aviation (Uvea, 1999): aircraft arrivals and departures 853; freight handled 28.7 metric tons; passenger arrivals and departures 9,473; mail loaded and unloaded 14.1 metric tons.

TOURISM

Visitors: 400 in 1985.

Hotels (1999): Number 6; Rooms 39.

COMMUNICATIONS MEDIA

Telephones (1997): 1,000 main lines in use.

Telefax Stations (1993): 90 in use.

Source: UN, *Statistical Yearbook*.

EDUCATION

Pre-primary (2000/01): 3 institutions.

Primary (2000/01): 14 institutions.

Secondary (2000/01): 7 institutions (2 vocational); 2,119 students.

Directory
The Constitution

The Territory of the Wallis and Futuna Islands is administered according to a statute of 1961, and subsidiary legislation, under the Constitution of the Fifth Republic. The Statute declares the Wallis and Futuna Islands to be an Overseas Territory of the French Republic, of which it remains an integral part. The Statute established an administration, a Council of the Territory, a Territorial Assembly and national representation. The administrative, political and social evolution envisaged by, and enacted under, the Statute is intended to effect a smooth integration of the three customary kingdoms with the new institutions of the Territory. The Kings are assisted by ministers and the traditional chiefs. The Chief Administrator, appointed by the French Government, is the representative of the State in the Territory and is responsible for external affairs, defence, law and order, financial and educational affairs. The Chief Administrator is required to consult with the Council of the Territory, which has six members: three by right (the Kings of Wallis, Sigave and Alo) and three appointed by the Chief Administrator upon the advice of the Territorial Assembly. This Assembly assists in the administration of the Territory; there are 20 members elected on a common roll, on the basis of universal adult suffrage, for a term of up to five years. The Territorial Assembly elects, from among its own membership, a President to lead it. The Territory elects national representatives (one Deputy to the National Assembly, one Senator and one Economic and Social Councillor) and votes for representatives to the European Parliament in Strasbourg.

The Government
(March 2001)

Chief Administrator (Administrateur Supérieur): ALAIN WAQUET (appointed 2000).

CONSEIL DU TERRITOIRE

Chair: Chief Administrator.

Members by Right: King of Wallis, King of Sigave, King of Alo.

Appointed Members: MIKAELE HALAGAHU (Faipule), ATOLOTO UHILA (Kulitea), KELETO LAKALAKA (Sous réserves).

GOVERNMENT OFFICE

Government Headquarters: Bureau de l'Administrateur Supérieur, Havelu, BP 16, Mata'Utu, 98600 Uvea, Wallis Islands, Wallis and Futuna, via Nouméa, New Caledonia; tel. 722727; fax 722324; all departments.

Legislature
ASSEMBLÉE TERRITORIALE

The Territorial Assembly has 20 members and is elected for a five-year term. The most recent general election took place on 16 March 1997, at which RPR candidates secured a total of 14 seats and various left-wing candidates (including independents) won six seats. However, a reorganization of the election for 11 of the seats was held on 6 September 1998, following the investigation of widespread voting irregularities in the previous year's poll. These elections resulted in a reduction in the RPR's representation to 11 seats and an increase in that of left-wing members to nine seats.

President: SOANE MUNI UHILA (RPR).

Territorial Assembly: Assemblée Territoriale, Havelu, BP 31, Mata'Utu, 98600 Uvea, Wallis Islands, Wallis and Futuna, via Nouméa, New Caledonia; tel. 722504; fax 722054.

PARLEMENT

Deputy to the French National Assembly: VICTOR BRIAL (RPR).
Representative to the French Senate: Fr ROBERT LAUFOAULU.
Social and Economic Adviser: KAMILO GATA (UPWF).

The Kingdoms
WALLIS
(Capital: Mata'Utu on Uvea)

Lavelua, King of Wallis: TOMASI KULIMOETOKE.
Council of Ministers: Prime Minister (Kivalu) and five other ministers. Kivalu: TISIMASI HEAFALA.

The Kingdom of Wallis is divided into three districts (Hihifo, Hahake, Mua), and its traditional hierarchy includes three district chiefs (Faipule) and 20 village chiefs (Pule).

SIGAVE
(Capital: Leava on Futuna)

Keletaona, King of Sigave: PASILIO KELETAONA.
Council of Ministers: six ministers, chaired by the King.

The Kingdom of Sigave is located in the north of the island of Futuna; there are five village chiefs.

ALO
(Capital: Ono on Futuna)

Tuigaifo, King of Alo: SAGATO ALOFI.
Council of Ministers: five ministers, chaired by the King.

The Kingdom of Alo comprises the southern part of the island of Futuna and the entire island of Alofi. There are nine village chiefs.

Political Organizations

Rassemblement pour la République (RPR): c/o Assemblée Territoriale; Gaullist; Territorial Leader CLOVIS LOGOLOGOFOLAU.
Taumu'a Lelei (Bright Future): c/o Assemblée Territoriale; f. 1992; Leader SOANE MUNI UHILA.
Union pour la Démocratie Française (UDF): c/o Assemblée Territoriale; centrist; based on Uvean (Wallis) support.
Union Populaire pour Wallis et Futuna (UPWF): c/o Assemblée Territoriale; affiliated to the Parti Socialiste of France in 1998; f. 1994; Leader KAMILO GATA.

Religion

Almost all of the inhabitants profess Christianity and are adherents of the Roman Catholic Church.

CHRISTIANITY
The Roman Catholic Church

The Territory comprises a single diocese, suffragan to the archdiocese of Nouméa (New Caledonia). The diocese estimated that there were 14,316 adherents (99.0% of the population) at 31 December 1998. The Bishop participates in the Catholic Bishops' Conference of the Pacific, currently based in Fiji.

Bishop of Wallis and Futuna: Mgr LOLESIO FUAHEA, Evêché, Laro, BP G6, 98600 Mata'Utu, Uvea, Wallis Islands, Wallis and Futuna, via Nouméa, New Caledonia; tel. 722932; fax 722783; e-mail eveche.wallis@wallis.co.nc.

The Press

Te-Fenua Fo'ou: BP 435, 98600 Mata'Utu, Uvea, Wallis Islands, Wallis and Futuna, via Nouméa, New Caledonia; e-mail tff@wallis.co.nc; f. 1995; weekly; French, Wallisian and Futurian.

Broadcasting and Communications
TELECOMMUNICATIONS

France Telecom—FCR: Télécommunications extérieures de Wallis et Futuna, BP 54, 98600 Mata'Utu, Uvea, Wallis Islands, Wallis and Futuna, via Nouméa, New Caledonia; tel. 722436; fax 722255; e-mail admin@wallis.co.nc.
Service des Postes et Télécommunications: Administration Supérieure des Iles Wallis et Futuna, BP 00, 98600 Mata'Utu, Uvea, Wallis Islands, Wallis and Futuna, via Nouméa, New Caledonia; tel. 722121; fax 722500; e-mail adminspt.get@wallis.co.nc.

BROADCASTING
Radio and Television

Radio Wallis et Futuna: BP 102, 97911 Mata'Utu, Uvea, Wallis Islands, Wallis and Futuna, via Nouméa, New Caledonia; tel. 722020; fax 722346; internet www.rfo.fr; fmrly Radiodiffusion Française d'Outre-mer (RFO); transmitters at Mata'Utu (Uvea) and Alo (Futuna); programmes broadcast 24 hours daily in Uvean (Wallisian), Futunian and French; a television service on Uvea, transmitting for 12 hours daily in French, began operation in 1986; a television service on Futuna was inaugurated in December 1994; satellite television began operation in March 2000; Man. JOSEPH BLASCO; Head of Information BERNARD JOYEUX.

Finance
BANKING
Bank of Issue

Institut d'Emission d'Outre-Mer: 98600 Mata'Utu, Uvea, Wallis Islands, Wallis and Futuna, via Nouméa, New Caledonia; tel. 722505; f. 1998.

Other Banks

Agence Française de Développement: 98600 Mata'Utu, Uvea, Wallis Islands, Wallis and Futuna, via Nouméa, New Caledonia; tel. 722505; fmrly Caisse Française de Développement; development bank.

Banque de Wallis et Futuna: BP 59, 98600 Mata'Utu, Uvea, Wallis Islands, Wallis and Futuna, via Nouméa, New Caledonia; tel. 722124; fax 722156; f. 1991; 51% owned by BNP Paribas (New Caledonia).

Paierie de Wallis et Futuna: 98600 Mata'Utu, Uvea, Wallis Islands, Wallis and Futuna, via Nouméa, New Caledonia.

Trade and Industry

GOVERNMENT AGENCY

Economie Rurale et Pêche: BP 05, 98600 Mata'Utu, Uvea, Wallis Islands, Wallis and Futuna, via Nouméa, New Caledonia; tel. 720400; fax 720404; e-mail ecoru@wallis.co.nc; Antenne de Futuna, BP 05, 98620 Sigave, Futuna, Wallis and Futuna, via Nouméa, New Caledonia; tel. 723214; fax 723402.

UTILITIES

Electricité et Eau de Wallis et Futuna: 98600 Mata'Utu, Uvea, Wallis Islands, Wallis and Futuna, via Nouméa, New Caledonia; 32.3% owned by the territory and 66.64% owned by EEC of New Caledonia.

TRADE UNIONS

Union Interprofessionnelle CFDT Wallis et Futuna (UI CFDT): BP 178, 98600 Mata'Utu, Uvea, Wallis Islands, Wallis and Futuna, via Nouméa, New Caledonia; tel. 721880; Sec. Gen. KALOLO HANISI.

Union Locale Force Ouvrière: BP 325, Mata-Utu, Uvea, Wallis Islands, Wallis and Futuna, via Nouméa, New Caledonia; tel. 721732; fax 720132; Sec.-Gen. ANTONIO KULIFATA.

Transport

ROADS

Uvea has a few kilometres of road, one route circling the island, and there is also a partially-surfaced road circling the island of Futuna; the only fully-surfaced roads are in Mata'Utu.

SHIPPING

Mata'Utu serves as the seaport of Uvea and the Wallis Islands, while Sigave is the only port on Futuna. A total of 45 general freight ships and 17 gas and petroleum tankers docked in Wallis in 1999.

Services des Douanes et Affaires Maritimes: Aka'aka, 98600 Mata'Utu, Uvea, Wallis Islands, Wallis and Futuna, via Nouméa, New Caledonia; tel. 722571; fax 722986.

AMACAL (General Agent): POB 1080, Nouméa, New Caledonia; tel. 283384; fax 287388; e-mail amb.noumea@offratel.nc.

CIVIL AVIATION

There is an international airport in Hihifo district on Uvea, about 5 km from Mata'Utu. Air Calédonie International (New Caledonia) operates five flights a week from Wallis to Futuna, one flight a week from Wallis to Tahiti (French Polynesia) and two flights a week from Wallis to Nouméa (New Caledonia). The airport on Futuna is at Vele, in the south-east, in the Kingdom of Alo.

Tourism

Tourism remains undeveloped. There are four small hotels and a guest-house on Uvea, Wallis Islands. In 1985 there were some 400 tourist visitors, in total, to the islands. There are two small guest-houses for visitors on Futuna.

French Overseas Country

New Caledonia was formerly an Overseas Territory (see p. 1638) of France. The Nouméa Accord, concluded in 1998, provides for a gradual transfer of powers to New Caledonia. The Territory became an Overseas Country of France in 1999.

NEW CALEDONIA

Introductory Survey

Location, Climate, Language, Religion, Capital

New Caledonia comprises one large island and several smaller ones, lying in the South Pacific Ocean, about 1,500 km (930 miles) east of Queensland, Australia. The main island, New Caledonia (la Grande-Terre), is long and narrow, and has a total area of 16,372 sq km. Rugged mountains divide the west of the island from the east, and there is little flat land. The nearby Loyalty Islands, which are administratively part of New Caledonia, are 1,981 sq km in area, and a third group of islands, the uninhabited Chesterfield Islands, lies about 400 km northwest of the main island. The climate is generally mild, with an average temperature of about 24°C (75°F) and a rainy season between December and March. The average rainfall in the east of the main island is about 2,000 mm (80 ins) per year, and in the west about 1,000 mm (40 ins). French is the official language and the mother tongue of the Caldoches (French settlers); the indigenous Kanaks (Melanesians) also speak Melanesian languages. Other immigrants speak Polynesian and Asian languages. New Caledonians almost all profess Christianity; about 59% are Roman Catholics, and there is a substantial Protestant minority. The capital is Nouméa, on the main island.

Recent History

New Caledonia became a French possession in 1853, when the island was annexed as a dependency of Tahiti. In 1860 a separate administration was established, and in 1946 it became an Overseas Territory of the French Republic. Early European settlers on New Caledonia, supported by legislation, quickly assumed possession of Melanesian land, which provoked a number of rebellions by the indigenous Kanak (Melanesian) population.

In 1956 the first Territorial Assembly, with 30 members, was elected by universal adult suffrage, although the French Governor effectively retained control of the functions of government. New Caledonian demands for a measure of self-government were answered in 1976 by a new statute, which gave the Council of Government, elected from the Territorial Assembly, responsibility for certain internal affairs. The post of Governor was replaced by that of French High Commissioner to the Territory. In 1978 the Kanak-supported, pro-independence parties obtained a majority of the posts in the Council of Government. In early 1979, however, the French Government dismissed the Council, following its failure to support a proposal for a 10-year 'contract' between France and New Caledonia, because the plan did not acknowledge the possibility of New Caledonian independence. The Territory was then placed under the direct authority of the High Commissioner. A general election was held in July, but a new electoral law, which affected mainly the pro-independence parties, ensured that minor parties were not represented in the Assembly. Two parties loyal to France (Rassemblement pour la Calédonie dans la République—RPCR, and Fédération pour une Nouvelle Société Calédonienne—FNSC) together won 22 of the 36 seats.

Following the election of François Mitterrand as President of France, tension increased in September 1981 after the assassination of Pierre Declercq, the Secretary-General of the pro-independence party, Union Calédonienne (UC). In December of that year the French Government made proposals for change that included equal access for all New Caledonians to positions of authority, land reforms and the fostering of Kanak cultural institutions. To assist in effecting these reforms, the French Government simultaneously announced that it would rule by decree for a period of at least one year. In 1982 the FNSC joined with the opposition grouping, Front Indépendantiste (FI), to form a government that was more favourable to the proposed reforms.

In November 1983 the French Government proposed a five-year period of increased autonomy from July 1984 and a referendum in 1989 to determine New Caledonia's future. The statute was opposed in New Caledonia, both by parties in favour of earlier independence and by those against, and it was rejected by the Territorial Assembly in April 1984. However, the proposals were approved by the French National Assembly in September 1984. Under the provisions of the statute, the Territorial Council of Ministers was given responsibility for many internal matters of government, its President henceforth being an elected member instead of the French High Commissioner; a second legislative chamber, with the right to be consulted on development planning and budgetary issues, was created at the same time. All of the main parties seeking independence (except the Libération Kanak Socialiste (LKS) party, which left the FI) boycotted elections for the new Territorial Assembly in November 1984 and, following the dissolution of the FI, formed a new movement called the Front de Libération Nationale Kanak Socialiste (FLNKS). On 1 December, the FLNKS Congress established a 'provisional government', headed by Jean-Marie Tjibaou. The elections to the Territorial Assembly attracted only 50.1% of the electorate, and the anti-independence party Rassemblement pour la Calédonie dans la République (RPCR) won 34 of the 42 seats. An escalation of violence began in November, and in the following month three settlers were murdered by pro-independence activists and 10 Kanaks were killed by *métis* settlers.

In January 1985 Edgard Pisani, the new High Commissioner, announced a plan by which the Territory might become independent 'in association with' France on 1 January 1986, subject to the result of a referendum in July 1985. Kanak groups opposed the plan, insisting that the indigenous population be allowed to determine its own fate. At the same time, the majority of the population, which supported the RPCR, demonstrated against the plan and in favour of remaining within the French Republic. A resurgence of violence followed the announcement of Pisani's plan, and a state of emergency was declared after two incidents in which a leading member of the FLNKS was killed by security forces and the son of a French settler was killed by Kanak activists.

In April 1985 the French Prime Minister, Laurent Fabius, put forward new proposals for the future of New Caledonia, whereby the referendum on independence was deferred until an unspecified date not later than the end of 1987. Meanwhile, the Territory was to be divided into four regions, each to be governed by its own elected autonomous council, which would have extensive powers in the spheres of planning and development, education, health and social services, land rights, transport and housing. The elected members of all four councils together would serve as regional representatives in a Territorial Congress (to replace the Territorial Assembly).

The 'Fabius plan' was well received by the FLNKS, although the organization reaffirmed the ultimate goal of independence. It was also decided to maintain the 'provisional Government' under Tjibaou at least until the end of 1985. The RPCR, however, condemned the plan, and the proposals were rejected by the predominantly anti-independence Territorial Assembly in May. However, the necessary legislation was approved by the French National Assembly in July, and the Fabius plan came into force. Elections were held in September, and, as expected, only in the region around Nouméa, where the bulk of the population is non-Kanak, was an anti-independence majority recorded. However, the pro-independence Melanesians, in spite of their majorities in the three non-urban regions, would be in a minority in the Territorial Congress.

The FLNKS boycotted the general election to the French National Assembly in March 1986, in which only about 50% of the eligible voters in New Caledonia participated. In May the French Council of Ministers approved a draft law providing for a referendum to be held in New Caledonia within 12 months, whereby voters would choose between independence and a further extension of regional autonomy. In December, in spite of strong French diplomatic opposition, the UN General Assembly voted to reinscribe New Caledonia on the UN list of non-self-governing territories, thereby affirming the population's right to self-determination.

The FLNKS decided to boycott the referendum on 13 September 1987, at which 98.3% votes were cast in favour of New Caledonia's continuation as part of the French Republic and only 1.7% were cast in favour of independence. Of the registered electorate, almost 59% voted, a higher level of participation than was expected, although 90% of the electorate abstained in constituencies inhabited by a majority of Kanaks.

In October 1987 seven pro-French loyalists were acquitted on a charge of murdering 10 Kanak separatists in 1984. Tjibaou, who reacted to the ruling by declaring that his followers would have to abandon their stance of pacifism, and his deputy, Yeiwéné Yeiwéné, were indicted for 'incitement to violence'. In April 1988 four gendarmes were killed, and 27 held hostage in a cave on the island of Ouvéa, by supporters of the FLNKS. Two days later, Kanak separatists prevented about one-quarter of the Territory's polling stations from opening when local elections were held. The FLNKS boycotted the elections. Although 12 of the gendarmes taken hostage were subsequently released, six members of a French anti-terrorist squad were captured. French security forces immediately laid siege to the cave and, in the following month, made an assault upon it, leaving 19 Kanaks and two gendarmes dead. Following the siege, allegations that three Kanaks had been executed or left to die, after being arrested, led to an announcement by the new French Socialist Government that a judicial inquiry into the incident was to be opened.

At the elections to the French National Assembly in June 1988, both New Caledonian seats were retained by the RPCR. Michel Rocard, the new French Prime Minister, chaired negotiations in Paris, between Jacques Lafleur (leader of the RPCR) and Tjibaou, who agreed to transfer the administration of the Territory to Paris for 12 months. Under the provisions of the agreement (known as the Matignon Accord), the Territory was to be divided into three administrative Provinces prior to a territorial plebiscite on independence to be held in 1998. Only people resident in the Territory in 1988, and their direct descendants, would be allowed to vote in the plebiscite. The agreement also provided for a programme of economic development, training in public administration for Kanaks, and institutional reforms. The Matignon Accord was presented to the French electorate in a referendum, held on 6 November 1988, and approved by 80% of those voting (although an abstention rate of 63% of the electorate was recorded). The programme was approved by a 57% majority in New Caledonia, where the rate of abstention was 37%. In November, under the terms of the agreement, 51 separatists were released from prison, including 26 Kanaks implicated in the incident on Ouvéa.

In May 1989 the leaders of the FLNKS, Tjibaou and Yeiwéné, were murdered by separatist extremists, alleged to be associated with the Front Uni de Libération Kanak (FULK), a grouping which had until then formed part of the FLNKS, but which opposed the Matignon Accord on the grounds that it conceded too much to the European settlers. The assassinations were regarded as an attempt to disrupt the implementation of the Accord. Elections to the three Provincial Assemblies were nevertheless held, as scheduled, in June: the FLNKS won a majority of seats in the Province of the North and the Province of the Loyalty Islands, while the RPCR obtained a majority in the Province of the South, and also emerged as the dominant party in the Territorial Congress, with 27 of the 54 seats; the FLNKS secured 19 seats.

The year of direct rule by France ended, as agreed, on 14 July 1989, when the Territorial Congress and Provincial Assemblies assumed the administrative functions allocated to them in the Matignon Accord (see below under Government). In November the French National Assembly approved an amnesty (as stipulated in the Matignon Accord) for all who had been involved in politically-motivated violence in New Caledonia before August 1988, despite strong opposition from the right-wing French parties.

In April 1991 the LKS announced its intention to withdraw from the Matignon Accord, accusing the French Government, as well as several Kanak political leaders, of seeking to undermine Kanak culture and tradition. The RPCR's policy of encouraging the immigration of skilled workers from mainland France and other European countries continued to be a source of conflict between the conservative coalition and the FLNKS.

At elections for the Representative to the French Senate in September 1992, the RPCR's candidate, Simon Loueckhote, narrowly defeated Rock Wamytan, the Vice-President of the FLNKS.

Debate concerning the political future of the Territory continued in 1994. In October the RPCR leader, Jacques Lafleur, proposed that New Caledonia abandon the planned 1998 referendum on self-determination, in favour of a 30-year agreement with France, similar to the Matignon Accord, but with provision for greater autonomy in judicial matters. The UC, however, rejected the proposal and reiterated its demand for a gradual transfer of power from France to New Caledonia, culminating in a return to sovereignty in 1998.

French presidential elections took place in April/May 1995. During the second round of voting in the Territory, the socialist candidate, Lionel Jospin, received 25.9% of the total votes, while the candidate of the Gaullist Rassemblement pour la République (RPR), Jacques Chirac, won 74.1%. (Chirac was elected to the presidency with 52.6% of votes cast throughout the republic.)

At provincial elections in July 1995 the RPCR remained the most successful party, although its dominance was reduced considerably. The FLNKS remained in control of the Provinces of the North and the Loyalty Islands, while the RPCR retained a large majority in the Province of the South. The RPCR retained an overall majority in the Territorial Congress, while the FLNKS remained the second largest party. Considerable gains were made by a newly-formed party led by a Nouméa businessman, Une Nouvelle-Calédonie pour Tous (UNCT), which secured seven seats in the Territorial Congress and seven seats in the Provincial Government of the South. An estimated 67% of the electorate participated in the elections. However, a political crisis subsequently arose as a result of the UNCT's decision to align itself with the FLNKS, leaving the RPCR with a minority of official positions in the congressional committees. Lafleur would not accept a situation in which the UNCT appeared to be the dominant party in Congress, and Pierre Frogier, the RPCR's President of Congress, refused to convene a congressional sitting under such circumstances. The deadlock was broken only when the FLNKS released a statement in October, reiterating the importance of the relationship between the FLNKS and the RPCR as signatories of the Matignon Accord, and proposing the allocation of congressional positions on a proportional basis.

Negotiations between the French Government and delegations from the FLNKS and the RPCR were held in Paris in late 1995. It was agreed that further discussions would take place in early 1996, involving representatives from numerous interest groups in the Territory, to examine the possibility of achieving a consensus solution on the future of the islands. Thus, the major political groups in New Caledonia sought to achieve a consensus solution on the Territory's future, which could be presented to the electorate for approval in the 1998 referendum. It was widely believed that this was preferable to a simple 'for' or 'against' vote on independence, which would necessarily polarize the electorate and create a confrontational political climate.

Elections to the French National Assembly in May–June 1997 were boycotted by the pro-independence FLNKS and LKS, resulting in a relatively low participation rate among the electorate. Jacques Lafleur and Pierre Frogier, both candidates of the RPCR, were elected to represent New Caledonia. Intensive negotiations involving the RPCR, the FLNKS and the French Government took place throughout early 1996. The process, however, was disrupted by a dispute over the disclosure of confidential information regarding the talks to the French press (responsibility for which was later admitted by Jacques Lafleur) and the belief by pro-independence leaders that France had apparently reneged on its promise to consider all available options for the Territory's political future by discounting the possibility of outright independence. France's refusal to grant final approval for a large-scale nickel smelter project in the North Province (see Economic Affairs) until the achievement of consensus in the discussions on autonomy prompted accusations of blackmail from several sources within the Territory and fuelled suspicions that metropolitan France would seek to retain control of the islands' valuable mineral resources in any settlement on New Caledonia's future status. The issue proved to be a serious obstacle in the negotiations and resulted in the virtual cessation of discussions between the two sides during the remainder of 1996. The FLNKS argued that the smelter project should be administered by local interests, consistent with the process of reallocating responsibility for the economy from metropolitan France to the Territory as advocated in the Matignon Accord. Their demands were supported by widespread industrial action in the mining sector during late 1996.

In February 1997 the French Minister for Overseas Territories travelled to the Territory in an attempt to achieve an exchange agreement on nickel between the Société Minière du Sud-Pacifique (SMSP), controlled by the North Province, and the French-owned company, with numerous interests in the islands, Société Le Nickel (SLN). The minister failed to resolve the dispute during his visit; however, at the end of the month, in a complete reversal of its previous position, the French Government announced its decision not to compensate SLN for any losses incurred. The decision provoked strong criticism from SLN and Eramet, the French mining conglomerate, of which SLN is a subsidiary, and attracted protests from shareholders and employees of the company. During March large-scale demonstrations were held by the UC and the pro-independence trade union, USTKE, in support of the SMSP's acquisition of the smelter. Meanwhile, another trade union, USOENC (which represents a high proportion of SLN employees), organized a protest rally against the unequal exchange of mining sites. In mid-1997 the newly-elected French Government announced the appointment of Philippe Essig (a former head of the French national railway company) in the role of adviser and mediator in the dispute. The search for an agreement between SLN and the SMSP had become centred on the issue of access to nickel resources. Essig compiled a report on the matter, published in November 1997, which proposed the creation of an independent body to supervise the management of deposits, gradually ceding control to the operators once an agreement had been reached. Frustrated at SLN's seemingly intransigent position in the negotiations, the FLNKS organized protests and blockades at all the company's major mining installations. Supporters of the pro-independence organization also restricted shipments of ore around the Territory. Consequently, four mines were forced to close, while a 25% reduction in working hours was imposed on 1,500 mine workers, prompting protests by SLN employees and demands from USOENC that the blockades be removed. In January 1998 Roch Wamytan urged the French Prime Minister, Lionel Jospin, to settle the dispute by the end of the month in order that official negotiations on the political future of the Territory, in preparation for the referendum, might begin. The position of the FLNKS had been somewhat undermined by the decision, in the previous month, of a breakaway group of pro-independence politicians (including prominent members of the UC, Palika, the UMP and the LKS) to begin negotiations on that subject with the RPCR. A draft agreement on the exchange of deposits was signed by SLN and the SMSP on 1 February, and in April a deal between the SMSP and a Canadian company for the establishment of the nickel smelter was concluded. If construction of the smelter had not begun by the end of 2005, control of the nickel deposits transferred to the SMSP was to revert to SLN. Meanwhile, the French Government agreed to pay compensation of some 1,000m. French francs to Eramet for the reduction in the company's reserves.

Following the signing of the nickel agreement (see above), tripartite talks on the constitutional future of New Caledonia resumed in Paris in late February 1998. Discussions between representatives of the French Government, the FLNKS and the RPCR continued in March, despite a temporary boycott of the talks by the RPCR delegation, who requested the inclusion of various other minor political groups at the negotiations. On 21 April, following a final round of talks in Nouméa, an agreement was concluded by the three sides. The agreement, which became known as the Nouméa Accord, postponed the referendum on independence for a period of between 15 and 20 years but provided for a gradual transfer of powers to local institutions. The document also acknowledged the negative impact of many aspects of French colonization on the Territory and emphasized the need for greater recognition of the importance of the Kanak

cultural identity in the political development of the islands. The Nouméa Accord was signed on 5 May.

On 6 July 1998 the French Parliament (the National Assembly and the Senate) voted in favour of adopting the proposed changes regarding the administration of New Caledonia, which were to be incorporated in an annex to the French Constitution. In the following month the French Minister for Overseas Territories returned to New Caledonia for discussion on draft legislation for the devolution process. In September a new political group, called the Comité Provisoire pour la Défense des Principes Républicains de la Nouvelle-Calédonie Française, was formed in opposition to the Nouméa Accord, with support from members of the Front National and other right-wing parties. The UNCT, which was dissatisfied with several aspects of the accord, also urged its supporters to vote against the agreement.

The Nouméa Accord was presented to the electorate in New Caledonia in a referendum on 8 November 1998, when it was decisively approved, with 71.9% of votes cast in favour of the agreement. The Province of the North registered the strongest vote in favour of the accord (95.5%), while the Province of the South recorded the most moderate level of approval (62.9%). In late December the French National Assembly unanimously approved draft legislation regarding the definitive adoption of the accord. The Senate similarly approved the legislation in February 1999. In March of that year, however, the French Constitutional Council declared its intention to allow any French person who had resided in New Caledonia for 10 years or more to vote in provincial elections. This decision was criticized by Roch Wamytan, leader of the FLNKS, as well as by politicians in the French National Assembly and Senate, who claimed that this was in breach of the Nouméa Accord, whereby only those residing in New Caledonia in 1998 would be permitted to vote in provincial elections. Pro-independence groups threatened to boycott the elections (to be held in May). In response to this, the French Government announced that the Accord would be honoured, claiming that the Constitutional Council had breached the Nouméa Accord, and stating that this contravention would be rectified. In June the French Council of Ministers and the Legal Committee of the French National Assembly adopted draft legislation restricting eligibility for voting in provincial elections and in any future referendums on sovereignty, to those who had been eligible to vote in the November 1998 referendum on the Nouméa Accord, and to their children upon reaching the age of majority. This decision was condemned by the right-wing Front National, and by the leader of the RPCR.

At a general election held on 9 May 1999, no party gained an absolute majority. However, Lafleur's anti-independence RPCR won 24 of the 54 seats in the Territorial Congress, and formed a coalition with the newly-established Fédération des Comités de Coordination des Indépendantistes (FCCI) and, on an informal level, with the Front National, thus creating an anti-independence block of 31 seats in the chamber. The pro-independence FLNKS won 18 seats. Simon Loueckhote was re-elected as President of the Territorial Congress in late May. Results of the elections in the Loyalty Island Province were officially challenged by the moderate independence LKS and FCCI parties, as well as by the RPCR, following the issue by the electoral commissioner for the Province of a report claiming that a large number of irregularities had occurred. A new election was held in June 2000, at which a coalition of the RPCR, FCCI, LKS and FULK obtained 44.8% of votes and six seats. The FLNKS obtained 37.3% of votes and six seats, and Palika 17.8% of votes and two seats. The composition of the Territorial Congress therefore remained unchanged. Robert Xowie was re-elected as President of the Province.

On 28 May 1999 the Territorial Congress elected Jean Lèques as the first President of the Government of New Caledonia, under the increased autonomy terms of the Nouméa Accord. The new Government was elected on the basis of proportional representation and replaced the French High Commissioner as New Caledonia's executive authority. The election of Léopold Jorédié, leader of the FCCI, as Vice-President was denounced by the FLNKS, which argued that, as the second largest party in Congress and as joint negotiators in the Nouméa Accord, the post should have gone to its leader, Roch Wamytan. In the formation of the Government the RPCR was awarded seven positions and the FLNKS four.

In October 1999 Wamytan threatened to withdraw from the Government, in protest at the lack of co-operation among parties. He claimed that sections of the Nouméa Accord requiring power to be distributed among the various political parties had not been observed (see above). In December Vice-President Léopold Jorédié received a one-year suspended prison sentence following accusations of misuse of public funds. Jorédié was charged with illegally obtaining grants totalling an estimated 5.5m. francs CFP, for the benefit of his son.

In July 2000 concern was expressed by the French Government over the implementation of the 'collegiality' clause in the Nouméa Accord, which provides for greater political co-operation among parties. Repeated threats by the FLNKS to withdraw from the Government because of its discontent with the RPCR's lack of power-sharing led to the establishment of an agreement between New Caledonia and the French State detailing the role of the two Governments in areas such as education and foreign policy; the role of the traditional chiefs in legal matters was also specified. In August Lafleur resigned from his seat in the French National Assembly, following the upholding of a ruling convicting him of slander against Bruno Van Peteghem, an activist opposing construction plans for a complex near Nouméa. However, in early September Lafleur reversed his decision following pleas by RPCR members.

At the FLNK's annual conference, held in November 2000, Wamytan was re-elected President of the party (Wamytan was also narrowly re-elected leader of the UC); at the same time a new pro-independence party, the Groupe UC du Congrès, formed by a breakaway faction of the UC, was officially recognized by both the UC and the FLNKS.

In April 2001 Pierre Frogier of the RPCR was elected President, after Jean Lèques decided to relinquish the post. The new coalition Government comprised members of the RPCR, FCCI, FLNKS and UC.

Government

The French Government is represented in New Caledonia by its High Commissioner, and controls a number of important spheres of government, including external relations, defence, justice, finance, external trade and secondary education. In July 1989 administrative reforms were introduced, as stipulated in the Matignon Accord (which had been approved by national referendum in November 1988). New Caledonia was divided into three Provinces (North, South and Loyalty Islands), each governed by an assembly, which is elected on a proportional basis. The members of the three Provincial Assemblies together form the Territorial Congress. Members are subject to re-election every five years. The responsibilities of the Territorial Congress include New Caledonia's budget and fiscal affairs, infrastructure and primary education, while the responsibilities of the Provincial Assemblies include local economic development, land reform and cultural affairs. The Government of New Caledonia is elected by the Territorial Congress, and comprises between seven and 11 members. Under the terms of the Nouméa Accord (which was approved by a referendum in November 1998), it replaces the French High Commissioner as New Caledonia's executive authority. A gradual transfer of power from metropolitan France to local institutions was to be effected over a period of between 15 and 20 years under the terms of the Nouméa Accord.

In addition, New Caledonia elects two deputies to the French National Assembly in Paris and one representative to the French Senate on the basis of universal adult suffrage; one Economic and Social Councillor is also nominated. New Caledonia may also be represented at the European Parliament.

Defence

In August 2000 France was maintaining a force of 3,100 military personnel in New Caledonia, including a gendarmerie of 1,050.

Economic Affairs

In 2000, according to estimates by the Bank of Hawaii (BOH), New Caledonia's gross domestic product (GDP), measured at current prices, totalled US $3,058m., equivalent to US $14,616 per head. During 1990–2000, it was estimated, New Caledonia's GDP increased, in real terms, at an average annual rate of 1.6%. Over the same period, real GDP per head decreased at an average rate of 0.5% per year. GDP declined by 3.2% in 1998, but increased by 0.9% in 1999 and by 2.1% in 2000. New Caledonia's population increased at an average annual rate of 2.2% in 1990–99.

Agriculture and fishing contributed only 1.9% of GDP in 1999, and 7.2% of the employed labour force were engaged in the sector in 1996. In 1997 only some 0.7% of total land area was used for arable purposes or permanent crops. Maize, yams, sweet potatoes and coconuts have traditionally been the prin-

cipal crops. However, pumpkins (squash) became an important export crop for the Japanese market during the 1990s, with 3,000 metric tons produced in 1998 (compared with 500 tons in 1993). Livestock consists mainly of cattle and pigs. New Caledonia also began to export deer, principally to Thailand, in 1994. In 1998 an Australian company announced major investment in a chicken-farming project in the North Province, increasing the number of chickens from 1,000 in 1995 to 330,000 in 1998. The main fisheries products are tuna and shrimps (most of which are exported to Japan). A total of 1,906 metric tons of shrimps were produced in 1999 (compared with 632 tons in 1993), and a giant clam project was undertaken in 1996.

Industry (comprising mining, manufacturing, construction and utilities) provided 19.6% of GDP in 1997, and employed 27.4% of the working population in 1995. Although mining employed only 3.2% of New Caledonia's working population in 1995, it constitutes the most important industrial sector. In 1999 mining and quarrying contributed an estimated 10% of GDP. New Caledonia possesses the world's largest known nickel deposits, accounting for about 30% of the world's known reserves, and is the world's largest producer of ferro-nickel. Sales of nickel accounted for 89.3% of export revenues in 1999 (of which 56.2% was ferro-nickel). In 1999 a Canadian company opened a pilot smelter at Goro, in the South Province, at a cost of US $50m. It was hoped that the plant would produce up to 27,000 tons of nickel per year by 2003. The project, which was to cost an estimated US $1,060m., envisaged the construction of a deep-water port, international airport, power station and associated infrastructure, and was expected to provide 2,000 jobs. In 1998, however, the nickel industry was adversely affected by the Asian financial crisis, which resulted in a dramatic decline in demand, a period of unrest among workers at the most severely affected mines and the consequent loss of some 300 jobs.

The manufacturing sector, which provided 6.6% of GDP in 1992 and (together with electricity, gas and water) engaged 10.9% of the employed labour force in 1995, consists mainly of small and medium-sized enterprises, most of which are situated around the capital, Nouméa, producing building materials, furniture, salted fish, fruit juices and perishable foods.

Electrical energy is provided by thermal power stations (71.0% in 1999) and by hydroelectric plants. Mineral products accounted for 9.4% of total imports in 1998. In 1996 construction began on a plant producing wind-generated electricity near Nouméa, at a cost of US $7m., which provides some 4.5m. kWh of energy per year.

Service industries together contributed 73.7% of GDP in 1999 and engaged 69.4% of the employed labour force in 1996. The tourism sector in New Caledonia, however, has failed to witness similar expansion to that experienced in many other Pacific islands. Tourist arrivals were seriously affected by political unrest and outbreaks of violence in mid-1988 between the Caldoches and Kanaks. However, by 1997 annual arrivals of foreign visitors had increased to 105,137. Arrivals however, decreased slightly to 103,835 in 1998, and to 99,735 in 1999. Receipts from tourism declined from US $140m. in 1997 to $112m. in 1998.

In 1999 there was a trade deficit of some 60,420m. francs CFP. The principal imports in that year were mineral fuels, foodstuffs and machinery and transport equipment. France is the main trading partner, providing 39.7% of imports in that year and purchasing 27.7% of exports in 1996; other major trading partners in 1999 were other European Union (EU) countries (14.6% of exports), Australia, New Zealand and the USA.

The territorial budget for 1999 envisaged a surplus of 3,529m. francs CFP. In 1996 the islands received official development assistance totalling US $396.1m., 99.0% of which was from France. In 1999 aid from France totalled US $336.0m. The annual rate of inflation in Nouméa averaged 2.0% in 1990–99. Consumer prices increased by an average of 0.2% in 1999. Some 11.2% of the labour force were unemployed in 1999.

New Caledonia forms part of the Franc Zone (see p. 210), is an associate member of the UN's Economic and Social Commission for Asia and the Pacific (ESCAP—see p. 28) and is a member, in its own right, of the Pacific Community (formerly the South Pacific Commission—see p. 275). Following the adoption of the Nouméa Accord in 1998 (see Recent History), New

Caledonia obtained observer status at the Pacific Islands Forum (formerly the South Pacific Forum) in 1999.

New Caledonia's economy is vulnerable to factors affecting the islands' important nickel industry, which included political unrest during the 1980s and fluctuations in international prices for the commodity in the 1990s. The industry was adversely affected by the Asian financial crisis in 1998. The Nouméa Accord, approved by referendum in November 1998 (see Recent History), aimed to improve the economic conditions of the Kanak population and to increase their participation in the market economy and in public administration. Despite previous attempts to redress the balance of New Caledonian society (most importantly in the Matignon Accord of 1988), the indigenous population remained largely excluded from New Caledonia's economic and political administration, and a considerable proportion continued to experience economic hardship in the late 1990s. In mid-1999 the RPCR leader, Jacques Lafleur, revealed proposals for the creation of an inter-provincial committee for economic development, which would allow the comparatively wealthy South Province to assist the economic development of the other Provinces. Moreover, it was hoped that the development of those sectors generally considered not to have reached their full potential (notably tourism, aquaculture, fishing and farm agriculture) would alleviate the economic uncertainty created by the need to reduce dependency on France. In late 1999 a joint French and Australian research mission discovered what was believed to be the world's largest gas deposit, measuring an estimated 18,000 sq km. It was hoped that this indicated the presence of considerable petroleum reserves. Construction of facilities at two nickel mines was expected to commence in 2002–04, and it was thought that this would significantly increase nickel production.

Social Welfare

In 1994 there were 1,226 hospital beds in New Caledonia. A total of 358 physicians and 669 nurses were working in New Caledonia.

Education

Education is compulsory for 10 years between six and 16 years of age. Schools are operated by both the State and churches, under the supervision of three Departments of Education: the Provincial department responsible for primary level education, the New Caledonian department responsible for primary level inspection, and the State department responsible for secondary level education. The French Government finances the state secondary system. Primary education begins at six years of age, and lasts for five years; secondary education, beginning at 11 years of age, comprises a first cycle of four years and a second, three-year cycle. In 1999 there were 73 pre-primary schools, 282 primary schools (of which 95 were private schools), and 56 secondary schools (of which 25 were private). Also in that year there were 19 technical and higher institutions (of which 11 were private). Some 400 students attend universities in France. In 1987 the French University of the Pacific (based in French Polynesia) was established, with a centre in Nouméa, and in 1999 it was divided into two universities. In 2000 the University of New Caledonia had 60 teachers and 1,600 students. Several other vocational tertiary education centres exist in New Caledonia. In 1989 the rate of adult illiteracy averaged 6.9% (males 6.0%, females 7.9%). According to UNESCO, total public expenditure on education in 1993 was 1,652m. French francs.

Public Holidays

2001: 1 January (New Year's Day), 16 April (Easter Monday), 1 May (Labour Day), 8 May (Liberation Day), 24 May (Ascension Day), 4 June (Whit Monday), 14 July (Fall of the Bastille), 24 September (anniversary of possession by France), 11 November (Armistice Day), 25 December (Christmas Day).

2002: 1 January (New Year's Day), 1 April (Easter Monday), 1 May (Labour Day), 8 May (Liberation Day), 9 May (Ascension Day), 20 May (Whit Monday), 14 July (Fall of the Bastille), 24 September (anniversary of possession by France), 11 November (Armistice Day), 25 December (Christmas Day).

Weights and Measures

The metric system is in force.

Statistical Survey

Source (unless otherwise stated): Institut Territorial de la Statistique et des Etudes Economiques, BP 823, 98845 Nouméa; tel. 275481; fax 288148; internet www.itsee.nc.

AREA AND POPULATION

Area (sq km): New Caledonia island (Grande-Terre) 16,372; Loyalty Islands 1,981 (Lifou 1,207, Maré 642, Ouvéa 132); Isle of Pines 152; Belep Archipelago 70; Total 18,575 (7,172 sq miles).

Population: 164,173 (males 83,862, females 80,311) at census of 4 April 1989; 196,836 (males 100,762, females 96,074) at census of 16 April 1996; *Population by province* (1996 census): Loyalty Islands 20,877, North Province 41,413, South Province 134,546; 209,222 (official estimate) at 1 January 2000.

Density (1 January 2000): 11.3 per sq km.

Ethnic Groups (census of 1996): Melanesians 86,788; French and other Europeans 67,151; Wallisians and Futunians (Polynesian) 17,763; Indonesians 5,003; Tahitians (Polynesian) 5,171; Others 14,960.

Principal Town (1996): Nouméa (capital), population 76,293.

Births, Marriages and Deaths (1999): Registered live births 4,316 (birth rate 20.8 per 1,000); Registered marriages 943 (marriage rate 4.5 per 1,000); Registered deaths 1,095 (death rate 5.3 per 1,000).

Expectation of Life (years at birth, 1999): Males 69.8; Females 75.8.

Employment (persons aged 14 years and over, 1995, provisional): Agriculture, hunting, forestry and fishing 2,489; Mining and quarrying 1,651; Manufacturing and Electricity, gas and water 5,583; Construction 6,824; Trade, restaurants and hotels 8,477; Transport, storage and communications 2,754; Financing, insurance, real estate and business services 5,676; Community, social and personal services 9,710; Activities not adequately defined 7,920; Total employed 51,260; Unemployed 7,410; Total labour force 58,670. Source: UN, *Statistical Yearbook for Asia and the Pacific*.

1996 (census results, excluding military conscripts): Agriculture 4,663; Industry 8,177; Construction 6,890; Services 44,647; Total employed 64,377; Unemployed 15,048.

1999: Total employed 58,698; Unemployed 7,390; Total labour force 66,088. Source: Institut d'Emission d'Outre-Mer, *Annual Report*.

AGRICULTURE, ETC.

Principal Crops (FAO estimates, '000 metric tons, 1999): Maize 2; Taro 2; Potatoes 2; Sweet potatoes 3; Yams 11; Cassava 3; Coconuts 15; Vegetables and melons 4; Fruit 4. Source: FAO.

Livestock (FAO estimates, '000 head, year ending September 1999): Horses 12; Cattle 120; Pigs 40; Sheep 4; Goats 17; Chickens ('000) 330 (Source: FAO); Rabbits ('000, 1984) 5.3.

Livestock Products ('000 metric tons, 1999): Beef and veal 4; Pig meat 1; Poultry meat 1; Cows' milk 4; Hen eggs 2. Source: FAO.

Forestry: Roundwood removals ('000 cubic metres): 5 in 1996; 5 in 1997; 5 in 1998. Source: FAO, *Yearbook of Forest Products*.

Fishing (metric tons, live weight, 1998): Capture 2,880 (Albacore 860, Yellowfin tuna 185, Bigeye tuna 498, Other tuna-like fishes 150, Marine fishes 442, Sea cucumbers 390); Aquaculture 1,614 (Crustaceans 1,569); Total catch 4,494. Source: FAO, *Yearbook of Fishery Statistics*.

MINING

Production ('000 metric tons): Nickel ore (metal content) 136.5 in 1997; 125.3 in 1998; 111.6 in 1999.

INDUSTRY

Production: Ferro-nickel and nickel matte 56,424 metric tons (metal content, 1999); Electric energy 1,620m. kWh (1999).

Cement: 89,000 metric tons in 1996 (Source: UN, *Statistical Yearbook for Asia and the Pacific*).

FINANCE

Currency and Exchange Rates: see French Polynesia.

Territorial Budget (million francs CFP, 1999): *Revenue:* 77,747; *Expenditure:* 74,218. French government transfers 88,758. Source: Bank of Hawaii, *An Update on New Caledonia*.

Aid from France (US $ million): 442.2 in 1995; 392.0 in 1996; 336.0 in 1997. Source: UN, *Statistical Yearbook for Asia and the Pacific*.

Money Supply (million francs CFP at 31 December 1997): Currency in circulation 9,414; Demand deposits 65,444; Total money 74,858. Source: Institut National de la Statistique et des Etudes Economiques.

Cost of Living (Consumer Price Index for Nouméa; base: December 1992 = 100): 109.9 in 1997; 111.2 in 1998; 111.4 in 1999.

Gross Domestic Product (million francs CFP at current prices): 337,000 in 1998.

Expenditure on the Gross Domestic Product (million francs CFP at current prices, 1992): Government final consumption expenditure 94,770; Private final consumption expenditure 159,514; Increase in stocks 416; Gross fixed capital formation 66,818; *Total domestic expenditure* 321,518; Exports of goods and services 47,246; *Less* Imports of goods and services 88,403; *Sub-total* 280,361; Statistical discrepancy 1,066; *GDP in purchasers' values* 281,427. Source: UN, *National Accounts Statistics*.

Gross Domestic Product by Economic Activity (million francs CFP at current prices, 1997): Agriculture and food processing 12,835; Energy, mining and metallurgy 37,232; Other manufactures 13,815; Construction and public works 17,447; Transport and communication 23,415; Services and commerce 152,659; Salaries 91,857; Total 349,260. Source: Bank of Hawaii, *An Update on New Caledonia*.

EXTERNAL TRADE

Principal Commodities (million francs CFP, 1999): *Imports:* Prepared foodstuffs, beverages, spirits and vinegar, tobacco and manufactured substitutes 18,233; Mineral products 10,579; Products of chemical or allied industries 8,860; Plastics, rubber and articles thereof 4,526; Paper-making material, paper and paperboard and articles thereof 3,115; Textiles and textile articles 3,967; Base metals and articles thereof 8,048; Machinery and mechanical appliances, electrical equipment, sound and television apparatus 22,617; Vehicles, aircraft, vessels and associated transport equipment 17,613; Total (incl. others) 112,808. *Exports:* Ferro-nickel 29,445; Nickel matte 8,764; Nickel ore 8,583; Prawns 1,868; Total (incl. others) 52,388.

Principal Trading Partners (% of total; 1999): *Imports:* Australia 13.4; France (metropolitan) 39.7; New Zealand 5.0; USA 6.1; European Union (excluding France) 14.6. *Exports:* (US $ '000, 1996) Australia 3,754; France (metropolitan) 13,921; Germany 1,031; Japan 12,848; USA 4,885; Total (incl. others) 50,225.

Source: Institut National de la Statistique et des Etudes Economiques.

TRANSPORT

Road Traffic (1993): Passenger cars in use 58,500; Commerical vehicles in use 22,600; (1999): Vehicles in use 80,339. Source: partly UN, *Statistical Yearbook*.

Shipping (1999): Vessels entered 510; Goods unloaded 1,254,662 metric tons, Goods loaded 3,790,064 metric tons. *Merchant Fleet* (vessels registered, '000 grt, at 31 December 1992): 14.

Civil Aviation (La Tontouta airport, Nouméa, 1999): Passengers arriving 171,887, Passengers departing 170,815; Freight unloaded 3,914 metric tons, Freight loaded 1,163 metric tons.

TOURISM

Visitors (arrivals by air): 105,137 in 1997; 103,835 in 1998; 99,735 in 1999.

Tourist Arrivals by Country of Residence (1999): Australia 14,567, France 29,500, Japan 31,017, New Zealand 7,090; Total (incl. others) 99,735.

Receipts (US $ million): 140.0 in 1997; 111.8 in 1998.

Source: partly World Tourism Organization, *Yearbook of Tourism Statistics*.

COMMUNICATIONS MEDIA

Radio Receivers (1997): 107,000 in use*.

Television Receivers (1997): 52,000 in use*.

Telephones (1999): 50,652 main lines in use.

Telefax Stations (1996): 2,200 in use†.

Mobile Cellular Telephones (1997): 5,427 subscribers†.

Daily Newspapers (1999): 1.

* Source: UNESCO, *Statistical Yearbook*.
† Source: UN, *Statistical Yearbook*.

EDUCATION

Pre-primary (1999): 73 schools; 461 teachers (1995); 14,000 pupils.

Primary (1999): 284 schools; 1,628 teachers; 36,667 pupils.

Secondary (1999): 85 schools; 2,212 teachers; 27,877 pupils.

Higher (1999): 6 institutions; 899 teachers (1996); 1,866 students.

Source: Partly UNESCO, *Statistical Yearbook*, and Ministère de l'Education Nationale, de la Recherche et de la Technologie, France.

Directory

The Constitution

The constitutional system in New Caledonia is established under the Constitution of the Fifth French Republic and specific laws, the most recent of which were enacted in July 1989 in accordance with the terms agreed by the Matignon Accord. A referendum on the future of New Caledonia (expected to be conducted in 1998) was postponed for a period of between 15 and 20 years while a gradual transfer of power from metropolitan France to local institutions is effected under the terms of the Nouméa Accord, concluded in 1998. Under the terms of the Nouméa Accord, the islands are declared to be an Overseas Country of the French Republic, of which they remain an integral part. The High Commissioner is the representative of the State in the Territory and is appointed by the French Government. The High Commissioner is responsible for external relations, defence, law and order, finance and secondary education. New Caledonia is divided into three Provinces, of the South, the North and the Loyalty Islands. Each is governed by a Provincial Assembly, which is elected on a proportional basis and is responsible for local economic development, land reform and cultural affairs. Members of the Assemblies (40 for the South, 22 for the North and 14 for the Loyalty Islands) are subject to re-election every five years. A proportion of the members of the three Provincial Assemblies together form the Congress of New Caledonia (32 for the South, 15 for the North, and seven for the Loyalty Islands), which is responsible for the territorial budget and fiscal affairs, infrastructure and primary education. The Assemblies and the Congress each elect a President to lead them. The Government of New Caledonia is elected by the Congress, and comprises between seven and 11 members. Under the terms of the Nouméa Accord, it replaces the French High Commissioner as the Territory's executive authority. Provision is also made for the maintenance of Kanak tradition: there are eight custom regions, each with a Regional Consultative Custom Council. These eight Councils, with other appropriate authorities, are represented on the Customary Senate, which is composed of 16 members (two elected from each regional council for a six-year period); the Senate is consulted by the Congress and the Government. Local government is conducted by 33 communes. New Caledonia also elects two deputies to the National Assembly in Paris and one Senator, on the basis of universal adult suffrage. One Economic and Social Councillor is also nominated. New Caledonia may be represented in the European Parliament.

The Government

(April 2001)

STATE GOVERNMENT

High Commissioner: THIERRY LATASTE (took office July 1999).

Secretary-General: JÉRÔME GUTTON.

Deputy Secretary-General: ALAIN MARC.

LOCAL GOVERNMENT

Secretary-General: BERNARD DELADRIÈRE.

Deputy Secretary-General: PATRICK JAMIN.

COUNCIL OF MINISTERS

President: PIERRE FROGIER (RPCR).

Vice-President and Minister for Culture, Youth and Sports: DÉWÉ GORODEY (FLNKS).

Minister for Agriculture and Fishing: MAURICE PONGA (RPCR).

Minister for Education: LÉOPOLD JORÉDIÉ (FCCI).

Minister for Employment, Public Service and Professional Training: FRANÇOISE HORHANT (RPCR).

Minister for Transport and Communications and relations with Congress, responsible for Audiovisual Affairs: PIERRE MARESCA (RPCR).

Minister for Economic Affairs and relations with the Economic and Social Council: ALAIN LAZARE (RPCR).

Minister for Finance and the Budget, responsible for the development of New Caledonia: HERVÉ CHATELAIN (RPCR).

Minister for Customary Affairs and relations with the Senate and the Custom Consultative Council: ROCH WAMYTAN (FLNKS).

Minister for Social Security and Health: AUKUSITINO MANUO-HALALO (FLNKS).

Minister for Infrastructure: Gérald Cortot (UC).

GOVERNMENT OFFICES

Office of the High Commissioner: Haut-commissariat de la République en Nouvelle-Calédonie, 1 ave Maréchal Foch, BP C5, 98848 Nouméa Cédex; tel. 266300; fax 272828; internet www.etat.nc.

New Caledonian Government: *Présidence du Gouvernement:* 19 ave Maréchal Foch, BP M2, 98849 Nouméa Cédex; tel. 246565; fax 246550; *Congrès de la Nouvelle-Calédonie:* 1 blvd Vauban, BP 31, 98845 Nouméa Cédex; tel. 273129; fax 276219.

Office of the Secretary-General of New Caledonia: Immeuble administratif Jacques Iekawe, 18 ave Paul Doumer, BP C5, 98844 Nouméa Cédex; tel. 256000; fax 286848; internet www.gouv.nc.

Government of the Province of the Loyalty Islands: Gouvernement Provincial des Iles Loyauté, BP 50, 98820 Wé, Lifou, Loyalty Islands; tel. 454400; fax 451440; e-mail loyalty@loyalty.nc; internet www.loyalty.nc.

Government of the Province of the North: Gouvernement Provincial du Nord, BP 41, 98860 Koné, Grande-Terre; tel. 477100; fax 355475.

Government of the Province of the South: Hôtel de la Province Sud, 9 Route des Artifices Artilleries, Port Moselle, BP 4142, 98846 Nouméa Cédex; tel. 258000; fax 274900; internet www.province-sud.nc.

GOVERNMENT DEPARTMENTS

Department of Administrative Services and Computer Technology: 3 rue Gustave Flaubert, Baie de l'Orphelinat, BP 8231, 98807 Nouméa Cédex; tel. 275858; fax 281919; e-mail smai@territoire.nc; internet www.gouv.nc/smai.

Department of Agriculture, Forestry and the Environment: 209 rue Anatole Bénébig, BP 180, 98845 Nouméa Cedex; tel. 255100; fax 255129; e-mail dafe@offratel.nc; internet sfdnouvelle-caledonie@educagri.fr.

Department of Civil Aviation: 179 rue Gervolino, BP H1, 98845 Nouméa Cédex; tel. 265200; fax 265202; e-mail bpasqualini@canl.nc; internet www.dgac.fr.

Department of Culture: 75 rue Sébastopol, BP C5, Nouméa; tel. 241281; fax 242180.

Department of Education: Vice-Réctorat, 22 rue J. B. Dézarnaulds, BP G4, 98848 Nouméa Cédex; tel. 266100; fax 273048; internet www.ac-nouméa.nc.

Department of Employment: 12 rue de Verdun, BP 141, 98845 Nouméa Cédex; tel. 275572; fax 270494; e-mail dt@gouv.nc; internet www.gouv.nc/dtnc.

Department of Finance: 4 rue Monchovet, BP E4, 98848 Nouméa Cédex; tel. 279200; fax 272675; e-mail tg162.contact@cpfinances.gouv.fr; internet www.finances.gouv.fr.

Department of Human Resources and Civil Service: Nouméa.

Department of Infrastructure, Topography and Transport: 1 bis rue Edouard Unger, 1ère Vallée du Tir, BP A2, 98848 Nouméa Cédex; tel. 280300; fax 281760; e-mail dittt@territoire.nc; internet www.gouv.nc/ditt.

Department of Justice: 2 blvd Extérieur, BP F4, Nouméa; tel. 279350; fax 272756.

Department of Maritime Affairs: 2 bis rue Russeil, BP 36, Nouméa Cédex; tel. 272600; fax 287286; e-mail affmar@gouv.nc; internet www.mer.gouv.fr.

Department of Mines and Energy: 1 ter, rue Edouard Unger, 1ère Vallée du Tir, BP 465, 98845 Nouméa Cédex; tel. 273944; fax 272345; e-mail mines@gouv.nc; internet www.gouv.nc/sme.

Department of Social Security and Health: 5 rue Général Galliéni, BP 3278, 98846 Nouméa Cédex; tel. 243700; fax 277346; e-mail dtass@territoire.nc; internet www.gouv.nc/dtass.

Department of Youth and Sports: 23 ave Jean Jaurès, BP810, 98845 Nouméa Cedex; tel. 252384; fax 254585; e-mail dtjs@gouv.nc.

Legislature

ASSEMBLÉES PROVINCIALES

Members of the Provincial Assemblies are elected on a proportional basis for a five-year term. Each Provincial Assembly elects its President. A number of the members of the Provincial Assemblies sit together to make up the Territorial Congress. The Assembly of the Northern Province has 22 members (including 15 sitting for the Territorial Congress), the Loyalty Islands 14 members (including seven for the Congress) and the Southern Province has 40 members (including 32 for the Congress).

Election, 9 May 1999 (results by province)

Party	North	South	Loyalty Islands
Rassemblement pour la Calédonie dans la République (RPCR)	4	25	2
Front de Libération Nationale Kanak Socialiste (FLNKS)	6	6	6
Union Nationale pour l'Indépendance (UNI—PALIKA)	8	—	—
Fédération des Comités de Coordination des Indépendantistes (FCCI)	4	—	2
Front National (FN)	—	5	—
Alliance pour la Calédonie (APLC)	—	4	—
Libération Kanak Socialiste (LKS)	—	—	2
Parti de Libération Kanak (PALIKA)	—	—	2
Total	22	40	14

Province of the North: President Paul Néaoutyine (UNI—PALIKA).
Province of the South: President Jacques Lafleur (RPCR).
Province of the Loyalty Islands: President Robert Xowie (FLNKS).

Note: following allegations of irregularities in the Loyalty Islands poll, a second election in that province was held on 25 June 2000, following which the distribution of seats remained unchanged.

CONGRÈS

A proportion of the members of the three Provincial Assemblies sit together, in Nouméa, as the Congress of New Caledonia. There are 54 members (out of a total of 76 sitting in the Provincial Assemblies).
President: Simon Loueckhote (RPCR).

Election, 9 May 1999 (results for the Territory as a whole)

Party	Votes	%	Seats
RPCR	30,774	38.80	24
FLNKS	13,824	17.43	12
UNI	4,831	6.09	5
FCCI	7,515	9.48	4
FN	5,374	6.78	4
APLC	4,830	6.09	3
LKS	2,046	2.58	1
PALIKA	1,335	1.68	1
Others	8,789	11.08	1
Total	79,321	100.00	54

PARLEMENT

Deputies to the French National Assembly: Jacques Lafleur (RPCR).

Representative to the French Senate: Simon Loueckhote (RPCR).

Political Organizations

Alliance pour la Calédonie (APLC): c/o Congrès de la Nouvelle-Calédonie; Leader Didier Leroux.

Fédération des Comités de Coordination des Indépendantistes (FCCI): f. 1998 by breakaway group from FLNKS; Leaders Léopold Jorédié, Raphaël Mapou, François Burck.

Front Calédonien (FC): extreme right-wing; Leader M. Sarran.

Front de Libération Nationale Kanak Socialiste (FLNKS): Nouméa; tel. 272599; f. 1984 (following dissolution of Front Indépendantiste); pro-independence; Pres. Roch Wamytan; a grouping of the following parties:

Groupe UC du Congrès: Nouméa; f. 2000 by breakaway faction of the UC; Leader Pascal Naouna.

Parti de Libération Kanak (PALIKA): f. 1975; 5,000 mems; Leader Paul Néaoutyine.

Rassemblement Démocratique Océanien (RDO): Nouméa; f. 1994 by breakaway faction of UO; supports Kanak sovereignty; Pres. Aloisio Sako.

Union Calédonienne (UC): f. 1952; 11,000 mems; Pres. Roch Wamytan; Sec.-Gen. Daniel Yeiwéné.

Union Nationale pour l'Indépendance (UNI): c/o Congrès de la Nouvelle-Calédonie; Leader PAUL NÉAOUTYINE.

Union Progressiste Mélanésienne (UPM): f. 1974 as the Union Progressiste Multiraciale; 2,300 mems; Pres. VICTOR TUTUGORO; Sec.-Gen. RENÉ POROU.

Front National (FN): Nouméa; extreme right-wing; Leader GUY GEORGE.

Génération Calédonienne: f. 1995; youth-based; aims to combat corruption in public life; Pres. JEAN RAYMOND POSTIC.

Libération Kanak Socialiste (LKS): Maré, Loyalty Islands; moderate, pro-independence; Leader NIDOÏSH NAISSELINE.

Rassemblement pour la Calédonie dans la République (RPCR): 19 ave du Maréchal Foch, BP 306, 98845 Nouméa; tel. 282620; fax 284033; f. 1977; affiliated to the metropolitan Rassemblement pour la République (RPR); in favour of retaining the status quo in New Caledonia; Leader JACQUES LAFLEUR; a coalition of the following parties:

Centre des Démocrates Sociaux (CDS): f. 1971; Leader JEAN LÈQUES.

Parti Républicain (PR): Leader PIERRE MARESCA.

Union Océanienne (UO): Nouméa; f. 1989 by breakaway faction of RPCR; represents people whose origin is in the French Overseas Territory of Wallis and Futuna; conservative; Leader MICHEL HEMA.

Other political organizations participating in the elections of May 1999 included: **Développer Ensemble pour Construire l'Avenir, (DECA), Renouveau, Citoyens Ensemble, La Calédonie Autrement, Front Uni de Libération Kanak (FULK), Groupe Alliance Multiraciale (GAM)** and **Indépendance et Progrès.**

Judicial System

Court of Appeal: Palais de Justice, BP F4, 98848 Nouméa; tel. 279350; fax 269185; e-mail pg.ca-noumea@canl.nc; First Pres. GERARD FEY; Procurator-Gen. GÉRARD NÉDELLEC.

Court of the First Instance: 2 blvd Extérieur, BP F4, 98848 Nouméa; Pres. JEAN PRADAL; Procurator of the Republic ROBERT BLASER. There are two subsidiary courts, with resident magistrates, at Koné (Province of the North) and Wé (Province of the Loyalty Islands).

Custom Consultative Council: Conseil Consultatif Coutumier; 68 ave J. Cook, Nouville; tel. 242000; fax 249320; f. 1990; consulted by Govt on all matters affecting land and Kanak tradition; mems: 40 authorities from eight custom areas; Pres. BERGE KAWA; Vice-Pres. JOSEPH PIDJOT.

Religion

The majority of the population is Christian, with Roman Catholics comprising about 55% of the total in 1998. About 3% of the inhabitants, mainly Indonesians, are Muslims.

CHRISTIANITY

The Roman Catholic Church

The Territory comprises a single archdiocese, with an estimated 110,000 adherents in 1998. The Archbishop participates in the Catholic Bishops' Conference of the Pacific, based in Fiji.

Archbishop of Nouméa: Most Rev. MICHEL-MARIE-BERNARD CALVET, Archevêché, BP 3, 4 rue Mgr-Fraysse, 98845 Nouméa; tel. 265353; fax 265352; e-mail archeveche@ddec.nc.

The Anglican Communion

Within the Church of the Province of Melanesia, New Caledonia forms part of the diocese of Vanuatu (q.v.). The Archbishop of the Province is the Bishop of Central Melanesia (resident in Honiara, Solomon Islands).

Protestant Churches

Eglise évangélique en Nouvelle-Calédonie et aux Iles Loyauté: BP 277, Nouméa; f. 1960; Pres. Rev. SAILALI PASSA; Gen. Sec. Rev. TELL KASARHEROU.

Other churches active in the Territory include the Assembly of God, the Free Evangelical Church, the Presbyterian Church, the New Apostolic Church, the Pentecostal Evangelical Church and the Tahitian Evangelical Church.

The Press

L'Avenir Calédonien: 10 rue Gambetta, Nouméa; organ of the Union Calédonienne; Dir PAÏTA GABRIEL.

La Calédonie Agricole: BP 111, 98845 Nouméa Cédex; tel. 243160; fax 284587; every 2 months; official publ. of the Chambre d'Agriculture; Pres. ANDRÉ MAZURIER; Man. GEORGES ROUCOU; circ. 3,000.

Eglise de Nouvelle-Calédonie: BP 3, 98845 Nouméa; fax 265352; f. 1976; monthly; official publ. of the Roman Catholic Church; circ. 450.

Les Nouvelles Calédoniennes: 41–43 rue de Sébastopol, BP 179, Nouméa; tel. 272584; fax 279443; internet www.nouvelles-caledoniennes.nc; f. 1971; daily; Publr PHILIPPE HERSANT; Dir BRUNO FRANCESCHI; Editor MARC SPISSER; circ. 18,500.

Télé 7 Jours: route de Vélodome, BP 2080, 98846 Nouméa Cédex; tel. 284598; weekly.

NEWS AGENCY

Agence France-Presse (AFP): 15 rue Docteur Guégan, 98800 Nouméa; tel. 263033; fax 278699; Correspondent FRANCK MADOEUF.

Publishers

Editions d'Art Calédoniennes: 3 rue Guynemer, BP 1626, Nouméa; tel. 277633; fax 281526; art, reprints, travel.

Editions du Santal: 5 bis rue Emile-Trianon, 98846 Nouméa; tel. and fax 262533; e-mail santal@offratel.nc; history, art, travel; Dir PAUL-JEAN STAHL.

Grain de Sable: BP 577, Nouméa; tel. 273057; fax 285707; literature, travel.

Île de Lumière: BP 8401, Nouméa Sud; tel. 289858; history, politics.

Savannah Editions SARL: 49 rue de la Boudeuse magenta Que mo, 98846 Nouméa; tel. 252919; fax 282470; f. 1994; sports, travel, leisure.

Société d'Etudes Historiques de Nouvelle-Calédonie: BP 63, Nouméa; tel. 263662.

Broadcasting and Communications

TELECOMMUNICATIONS

France Cables et Radio (FCR): Télécommunications extérieures de la Nouvelle-Calédonie, BP A1, 98848 Nouméa Cédex; tel. 266600; fax 266666; Dir PHILIPPE DUPUIS.

Offices des Postes et Télécommunications: Le Waruna, 2 rue Monchovet, Port Plaisance, 98841 Nouméa Cédex; tel. 268210; fax 262927; e-mail direction@opt.nc; Dir JEAN-YVES OLLIVAUD.

BROADCASTING

Radio

NRJ Nouvelle-Calédonie: 41–43 rue Sebastopol, BP 3260, Nouméa; tel. 279446; fax 279447.

Radio Djiido: 29 rue du Maréchal Juin, BP 1671, 98803 Nouméa Cédex; tel. 253515; fax 272187; f. 1985; community station; broadcasts in French; pro-independence.

Radio Nouvelle Calédonie: Mont Coffin, BP 93, Nouméa Cédex; tel. 274327; fax 281252; f. 1942; fmrly Radiodiffusion Française d'Outre-mer (RFO); 24 hours of daily programmes in French; Dir ALAIN LE GARREC; Editor-in-Chief FRANCIS ORNY.

Radio Rythme Bleu: BP 578, Nouméa; tel. 254646; fax 284928; Dir ALAIN PROST.

Television

RFO-Télé Nouvelle-Calédonie: Radio Télévision Française d'Outre Mer (RFO), Mont Coffin, BP 93, Nouméa; tel. 274327; fax 281252; f. 1965; transmits 10 hours daily; Dir ALAIN LE GARREC.

Canal Calédonie: 8 rue de Verneilh, Nouméa; subscription service.

Canal Outre-mer (canal+): Nouméa; f. 1995; cable service.

Finance

(cap. = capital; res = reserves; dep. = deposits; m. = million; brs = branches; amounts in CFP francs unless otherwise stated)

BANKING

Agence Française de Développement: 5 Rue Barleux, BP JI, 98849 Nouméa Cédex; tel. 282088; fax 282413.

Bank of Hawaii—Nouvelle-Calédonie: 25 ave de la Victoire, BP L3, 98849 Nouméa Cédex; tel. 257400; fax 274147 and 275619; internet www.boh.nc; f. 1974; owned by Bank of Hawaii (USA—94.5%) and Crédit Lyonnais (France—3%); cap. 3,617.7m., res 940.2m. dep. 46,462.2m. (Dec. 1998); Pres. WILLIAM MICHAEL ORD; Gen. Man. CHARLES GIORDAN; 9 brs.

Banque Calédonienne d'Investissement (BCI): BP K5, 50 ave de la Victoire, 98849 Nouméa; tel. 256565; fax 274035.

Banque Nationale de Paris Nouvelle-Calédonie (France): 37 ave Henri Lafleur, BP K3, 98800 Nouméa Cédex; tel. 258400; fax

258459; e-mail bnp.nc@bnpparibas.com; f. 1969 as Banque Nationale de Paris; present name adopted in 1978; cap. 30.0m. French francs, res 159.0m. French francs, dep. 1,927.0m. French francs (Dec. 1994); Gen. Man. GÉRARD D'HERE; Gen. Man. JEAN CLAUDE DANG; 10 brs.

Société Générale Calédonienne de Banque: 56 ave de la Victoire, BP G2, 98848 Nouméa Cédex; tel. 272264; fax 276245; f. 1981; cap. 825.0m., res 2,000.8m., dep. 36,326.0m. (Dec. 1997); Pres. JEAN-LOUIS MATTEI; Gen. Man. JOËL BREDELET; 12 brs.

Trade and Industry

DEVELOPMENT ORGANIZATIONS

New Caledonia Economic Development Agency (ADECAL): 15 rue Guynemer, BP 2384, 98846 Nouméa Cédex; tel. 249077; fax 249087; e-mail adecal@offratel.nc; internet www.adecal.nc/; f. 1995; promotes investment within New Caledonia; Dir JEAN-MICHEL ARLIE.

Agence de Développement de la Culture Canaque: Centre Culturel Jean-Marie Tjibaou, rue des Accords de Matignon BP 378, 98845 Nouméa Cédex; tel. 414545; fax 414546; e-mail adck.nc; internet www.adck.nc. Pres. MARIE-CLAUDE TJIBAOU; Dir-Gen. OCTAVE TOGNA.

Agence de Développement Rural et d'Aménagement Foncier (ADRAF): 1 rue de la Somme, BP 4228, 98847 Nouméa Cédex; tel. 258600; fax 258604; e-mail dgadraf@offratel.nc; f. 1986, reorganized 1989; acquisition and redistribution of land; Chair. THIERRY LATASTE; Dir-Gen. LOUIS MAPOU.

Agence pour l'Emploi de Nouvelle Calédonie: 3 rue de la Somme, BP 497, 98845 Nouméa Cédex; tel. 281082; fax 272079; internet www.apenc.nc.

Comité Economique et Social: 19 ave Maréchal Foch, BP 4766, 98847 Nouméa Cédex; tel. 278517; fax 278509; e-mail ces@gouv.nc; represents trade unions and other organizations that are involved in the economic, social and cultural life of the Territory; Pres. BERNARD PAUL; Gen. Sec. YOLAINE ELMOUR.

Institut Calédonien de Participation: Nouméa; f. 1989 to finance development projects and encourage the Kanak population to participate in the market economy.

CHAMBERS OF COMMERCE

Chambre d'Agriculture: 3 rue A. Desmazures, BP 111, 98845 Nouméa Cédex; tel. 243160; fax 284587; e-mail canc-gr@canl.nc; f. 1909; 33 mems; Pres. ANDRÉ MAZURIER.

Chambre de Commerce et d'Industrie: 15 rue de Verdun, BP M3, 98849 Nouméa Cédex; tel. 243100; fax 243131; e-mail cci@cci.nc; internet www.cci.nc; f. 1879; 29 mems; Pres. MICHEL QUINTARD; Gen. Sec. MICHEL MERZEAU.

Chambre des Métiers: 10 ave James Cook, BP 4186, 98846 Nouméa Cédex; tel. 282337; fax 282729.

STATE-OWNED INDUSTRIES

Société Minière du Sud-Pacifique (SMSP): Nouméa; 87% owned by SOFINOR, 5% owned by SODIL; nickel-mining co; subsidiaries: Compagnie Maritime Calédonienne (stevedoring), Nouméa Nickel, Nord Industrie Services, Nickel Mining Corporation (NMC); Man. Dir ANDRÉ DANG VAN NHA.

Société Le Nickel (SLN): Doniambo; 60% owned by the French state-owned mining conglomerate Eramet; nickel mining, processing and sales co; CEO YVES RAMBAUD.

EMPLOYERS' ORGANIZATION

Fédération Patronale de Nouvelle-Calédonie: Immeuble Jules Ferry, 1 rue de la Somme, BP 466, 98845 Nouméa Cédex; tel. 273525; fax 274037; e-mail fedepat@canl.nc; f. 1936; represents the leading companies of New Caledonia in the defence of professional interests, co-ordination, documentation and research in socio-economic fields; Pres. JEAN-MARC MOULEDOUS; Sec.-Gen. FRANÇOIS PERONNET.

TRADE UNIONS

Confédération des Travailleurs Calédoniens: Nouméa; Sec.-Gen. R. JOYEUX; grouped with:

Fédération des Fonctionnaires: Nouméa; Sec.-Gen. GILBERT NOUVEAU.

Syndicat Général des Collaborateurs des Industries de Nouvelle Calédonie: Sec.-Gen. H. CHAMPIN.

Union Syndicale des Travailleurs Kanak et des Exploités (USTKE): BP 4372, Nouméa; tel. 277210; fax 277687; Leader LOUIS KOTRA UREGEÏ.

Union des Syndicats des Ouvriers et Employés de Nouvelle-Calédonie (USOENC): BP 2534, Vallée du Tir, Nouméa; tel. and fax 259640; e-mailc1vr@canl.nc; Sec.-Gen. DIDIER GUENANT-JEANSON.

Union Territoriale Force Ouvrière: 13 rue Jules Ferry, BP 4773, 98847 Nouméa; tel. 274950; fax 278202; e-mail utfonc98@ifrance.com; internet fo98000.ifrance.com; f. 1982; Sec.-Gen. ROBERT FORT.

Transport

ROADS

In 1983 there was a total of 5,980 km of roads on New Caledonia island; 766 km were bitumen-surfaced, 589 km unsealed, 1,618 km stone-surfaced and 2,523 km tracks in 1980. The outer islands had a total of 470 km of roads and tracks in 1980.

SHIPPING

Most traffic is through the port of Nouméa. Passenger and cargo services, linking Nouméa to other towns and islands, are regular and frequent. There are plans to develop Nepoui, in the Province of the North, as a deep-water port and industrial centre.

Port Autonome de la Nouvelle-Calédonie: BP 14, 98845 Nouméa Cédex; tel. 255000; fax 275490; e-mail noumeaportnc@canl.nc; Port Man. and Harbour Master PHILIPPE LAFLEUR.

Compagnie Wallisienne de Navigation: BP 1080, Nouméa; tel. 283384; fax 287388; Chair. ARMAND BALLANDE; Man. Dir JEAN-YVES BOILEAU.

Somacal: BP 2099, 98846 Nouméa; tel. 273898; fax 259315.

CIVIL AVIATION

There is an international airport, Tontouta, 47 km from Nouméa, and an internal network, centred on Magenta airport, which provides air services linking Nouméa to other towns and islands. Air France operates a service four times a week between Nouméa and Paris via Tokyo, Air Calédonie International operates two flights weekly from Nouméa to Osaka, two weekly flights to Sydney and Brisbane, and one weekly flight to Auckland and Papeete (French Polynesia) and AOM two flights weekly, from Paris to Nouméa via Sydney. Other airlines providing services to the island include Air New Zealand, Air Vanuatu and Qantas.

Air Calédonie: BP 212, Nouméa; tel. 250300; fax 254869; e-mail commercial@air-caledonie.nc; internet www.air-caledonie.nc; f. 1954; services throughout New Caledonia; 283,593 passengers carried in 1999–2000; Pres. and CEO OLIVIER RAZAVET.

Air Calédonie International (Aircalin): 8 rue Frédéric Surleau, BP 3736, 98846 Nouméa Cédex; tel. 265546; fax 272772; e-mail dg.aci@canl.nc; internet www.aircalin.nc/aci.htm; f. 1983; 62% owned by Territorial Govt; services to Sydney and Brisbane (Australia), Auckland (New Zealand), Nadi (Fiji), Papeete (French Polynesia), Wallis and Futuna Islands, Port Vila (Vanuatu) and Osaka and Tokyo (Japan); Chair. CHARLES LAVOIX; CEO JEAN-MICHEL MASSON.

Tourism

An investment programme was begun in 1985 with the aim of developing and promoting tourism. A total of 2,388 hotel rooms were available in 1999. In that year there were 99,735 visitors to New Caledonia, of whom 31.1% came from Japan, 29.6% from France, 14.6% from Australia and 7.1% from New Zealand. The industry earned US $111.8m. in 1998.

New Caledonia Tourism: Immeuble Nouméa-Centre, 20 rue Anatole France; BP 688, 98845 Nouméa Cédex; tel. 242080; fax 242070; e-mail tourisme@offratel.nc; internet www.new-caledonia-tourism.nc; f. 1990; international promotion of tourism in New Caledonia; Chair. GABY BRIAULT; Dir JEAN-MICHEL FOUTREIN.

GABON

Introductory Survey

Location, Climate, Language, Religion, Flag, Capital

The Gabonese Republic is an equatorial country on the west coast of Africa, with Equatorial Guinea and Cameroon to the north and the Congo to the south and east. The climate is tropical, with an average annual temperature of 26°C (79°F) and an average annual rainfall of 2,490 mm (98 ins). The official language is French, but Fang (in the north) and Bantu dialects (in the south) are also widely spoken. About 60% of the population are Christians, mainly Roman Catholics. Most of the remainder follow animist beliefs. The national flag (proportions 4 by 3) has three equal horizontal stripes, of green, yellow and blue. The capital is Libreville.

Recent History

Formerly a province of French Equatorial Africa, Gabon was granted internal autonomy in November 1958, and proceeded to full independence on 17 August 1960. Léon M'Ba, the new Republic's President, established Gabon as a one-party state. Following his death in November 1967, M'Ba was succeeded by the Vice-President, Albert-Bernard Bongo, who organized a new ruling party, the Parti démocratique gabonais (PDG). Gabon enjoyed political stability and rapid economic growth in the 1970s, underpinned by substantial foreign investment in the development and exploitation of its petroleum reserves. However, the social and economic problems that accompanied the subsequent decline in world petroleum prices led to the emergence in 1981 of a moderate opposition group, the Mouvement de redressement national (MORENA), which demanded the restoration of a multi-party system. Bongo maintained his commitment to a single-party framework, in which he undertook to allow democratic debate. MORENA responded by forming a government-in-exile in Paris, from which it unsuccessfully sought to put forward a candidate to challenge Bongo in the presidential election held in November 1986.

Following a period of preoccupation with internal divisions, MORENA resumed its campaign against the Government in early 1989. In May the Chairman of MORENA, Fr Paul M'Ba Abessole, visited Gabon, and, after a meeting with Bongo, announced that he and many of his supporters would return to Gabon. In January 1990 representatives of MORENA announced that M'Ba Abessole had been dismissed from the leadership of the movement, following his declaration of support for the Government. M'Ba Abessole subsequently formed a breakaway faction, known as MORENA des bûcherons (renamed Rassemblement national des bûcherons in 1991 to avoid confusion with the rival MORENA—originels.).

A number of arrests took place in October 1989, following an alleged conspiracy to overthrow the Government. It was claimed that the plot had been instigated by Pierre Mamboundou, the leader of the Union du peuple gabonais (UPG, an opposition movement based in Paris). Further arrests took place in November, after the alleged discovery of a second plot to overthrow the Government.

In early 1990 a series of strikes and demonstrations reflected increasing public discontent with economic austerity measures. In February a 'special commission for democracy' (which had been established by the PDG) submitted a report condemning Gabon's single-party political system. Bongo subsequently announced that extensive political reforms were to be introduced and that the ruling party was to be replaced by a new organization, the Rassemblement social-démocrate gabonais (RSDG). However, strike action continued in a number of sectors, resulting in severe disruption.

In March 1990 the PDG announced that a multi-party system was to be introduced, under the supervision of the RSDG, at the end of a five-year transitional period. A national conference was convened in late March to determine the programme for the reforms. The conference (which was attended by representatives of more than 70 political organizations, as well as professional bodies and other special interest groups) rejected Bongo's proposals for a transitional period of political reform under the aegis of the RSDG, and demanded the immediate establishment of a multi-party system and the formation of a new government,

which would hold office only until legislative elections could take place. Bongo acceded to the decisions of the conference, and in late April Casimir Oye Mba, the Governor of the Banque des états de l'Afrique centrale, was appointed Prime Minister of a transitional administration, which included several opposition members.

In May 1990 the Central Committee of the PDG and the National Assembly approved constitutional changes that would facilitate the transition to a multi-party political system. The existing presidential mandate (effective until January 1994) was to be respected; thereafter, elections to the presidency would be contested by more than one candidate, and the tenure of office would be reduced to five years, renewable only once. At the same time, Bongo resigned as Secretary-General of the PDG, claiming that this role was now incompatible with his position as Head of State. In the same month, however, the death, in suspicious circumstances, of Joseph Rendjambe, the Secretary-General of the opposition Parti gabonais du progrès (PGP), provoked violent demonstrations in protest at Bongo's alleged complicity in the death. A national curfew was imposed in response to the increasing unrest, while French troops were briefly deployed in Gabon, to protect the interests of the 20,000 resident French nationals, and several hundred Europeans were evacuated. It was announced in early June that the French military reinforcements were to be withdrawn, and the national curfew was lifted in the following month. Port-Gentil, however, remained under a state of emergency until mid-August.

Legislative elections were scheduled for 16 and 23 September 1990: however, only political parties that had registered during the national conference in March were allowed to offer candidates. The first round of the elections was disrupted by violent protests by voters who claimed that the PDG was engaging in electoral fraud. Following further allegations of widespread electoral malpractices, results in 32 constituencies were declared invalid, although the election of 58 candidates (of whom 36 were members of the PDG) was confirmed. The interim Government subsequently conceded that electoral irregularities had taken place, and further voting was postponed until 21 and 28 October. A commission, representing both the PDG and opposition parties, was established to supervise polling. At the elections the PDG won an overall majority in the 120-member National Assembly, with 62 seats, while opposition candidates secured 55 seats.

On 27 November 1990 a government of national unity, under Casimir Oye Mba, was formed. Sixteen posts were allocated to members of the PDG, while the remaining eight portfolios were distributed among members of five opposition parties. A new draft Constitution, which was promulgated on 22 December, endorsed reforms that had been included in the transitional Constitution, introduced in May. Further measures included the proposed establishment of an upper house, to be known as the Senate, which was to control the balance and regulation of power. A Constitutional Council was to replace the administrative chamber of the Supreme Court, and a National Communications Council was to be formed to ensure the impartial treatment of information by the state media.

The final composition of the National Assembly was determined in March 1991, when elections took place in five constituencies, where the results had been annulled, owing to alleged malpractice. Following the completion of the elections, the PDG held a total of 66 seats in the National Assembly, while various opposition groups held 54 seats. The two most prominent opposition movements, the PGP and the Rassemblement national des bûcherons (RNB), held 19 and 17 seats respectively.

In May 1991 six opposition parties formed an alliance, known as the Co-ordination de l'opposition démocratique (COD), in protest at the delay in the implementation of the new Constitution. The COD also demanded the appointment of a new Prime Minister, the abolition of certain institutions under the terms of the Constitution, and the liberalization of the state-controlled media. Following a general strike, organized by the COD, Bongo announced the resignation of the Council of Ministers, and declared that he was prepared to implement fully the new

Constitution. He also claimed that, in accordance with the Constitution, several institutions, including the High Court of Justice, had been dissolved, and that a Constitutional Court and a National Communications Council had been established. However, opposition parties within the COD refused to be represented in a new government of national unity, of which Oye Mba was appointed as Prime Minister. Later that month opposition deputies who had taken part in the boycott of the National Assembly resumed parliamentary duties. On 22 June Oye Mba appointed a new coalition Government, in which 14 members of the previous Council of Ministers retained their portfolios. Members of MORENA–originels, the Union socialiste gabonaise (USG) and the Association pour le socialisme au Gabon (APSG) were also represented in the Government.

In February 1992 MORENA–originels, the USG and the Parti socialiste gabonais formed an alliance within the COD, known as the Forum africain pour la reconstruction (FAR). In the same month a general strike, which was organized by the RNB (without the support of other opposition groups), in an attempt to oblige the Government to comply with the demands presented by the COD, was only partially observed. Later in February the Government announced that a multi-party presidential election, would take place in December 1993; a population census was to be conducted prior to the election.

In mid-February 1992 a meeting of supporters of the RNB was violently suppressed by security forces. In the same month the university in Libreville was closed, and a ban on political gatherings and demonstrations was imposed, following protests by students against inadequate financing. Later in February the COD organized a one-day general strike in Port-Gentil (which was only partially observed), followed by a one-day campaign of civil disobedience, which suspended economic activity in Port-Gentil and Libreville. At the end of February the Government reopened the university, and ended the ban on political gatherings and demonstrations. In March, however, the COD instigated a further one-day campaign of civil disobedience in Libreville, following the violent suppression of a demonstration by teachers who were demanding improvements in salaries and working conditions. In early April the PDG organized a pro-Government demonstration, in an attempt to gain public support.

In early July 1992 the National Assembly adopted a new electoral code (which had been submitted by the Government), despite protests by the FAR that the Government had failed to comply with the demands presented by the COD in October 1991. Later in July a motion of censure against the Government, proposed by opposition deputies in the National Assembly in response to the postponement of local government elections, was defeated. The Council of Ministers was reshuffled in August, and in December three members of the PDG, including a former minister, were expelled from the party, after establishing a faction, known as the Cercle des libéraux réformateurs (CLR).

Social unrest continued during the first half of 1993. In April security forces were dispatched to restore order, after protesters blockaded roads in central and southern Gabon, in support of demands for improved social infrastructure. In the same month Jules Bourdès-Ogouliguendé (who had resigned from the PDG in January) relinquished his post as President of the National Assembly, prior to standing as a candidate in the forthcoming presidential election. In July Bongo reorganized the Council of Ministers, following the resignation of the Minister of Labour, Employment, Professional Training and Human Resources, Simon Oyono Aba'a, who had been nominated as the presidential candidate of MORENA–originels. In November 1993 five political associations, the PDG, the USG, the APSG, the CLR and the Parti de l'unité du peuple gabonais, agreed to support Bongo's candidacy in the presidential election, while eight opposition candidates established an informal alliance, known as the Convention des forces du changement. Later in the same month a number of demonstrations were staged by members of the opposition, in support of demands for the revision of the electoral register. Clashes between opposition and government supporters ensued, following opposition allegations that irregularities in the electoral register indicated deliberate malpractice on the part of the Government. In early December the Government agreed to revise the register in part, but rejected opposition demands that the election be postponed.

At the presidential election, which took place on 5 December 1993, Bongo was re-elected, winning 51.18% of votes cast, while M'Ba Abessole (the leader of the RNB) secured 26.51% of the votes. The official announcement of the results prompted rioting by opposition supporters, in which several foreign nationals were attacked (apparently as a result of dissatisfaction with international observers, who declared that no electoral irregularities had taken place). Five deaths were reported after security forces suppressed the unrest, and a national curfew and state of alert were subsequently imposed. M'Ba Abessole, however, claimed that he had won the election, and formed a High Council of the Republic, later redesignated as the High Council of Resistance (HCR), which included the majority of opposition presidential candidates, and a parallel government. Despite the reports by international observers that the elections had been conducted fairly, the opposition appealed to the Constitutional Court to annul the results, on the grounds that the Government had perpetrated electoral malpractice. In mid-December Bongo condemned M'Ba Abessole's formation of a parallel administration, and invited the other candidates who had contested the election to participate in a government of national consensus. As a result of the administrative confusion, local government elections, which were due to take place in late December, were postponed until March 1994. (In February 1994 they were further postponed, to August.)

In early January 1994 the USA criticized Bongo's administration for alleged infringement of human rights, after three opposition leaders, including two presidential candidates, were prevented from leaving the country. Later that month the Constitutional Court ruled against the appeal by the opposition and endorsed the election results. On 22 January Bongo was officially inaugurated as President. In mid-February the national curfew and the state of alert, which had been in force since December 1993, were repealed, but later that month were reimposed, after a general strike, in support of demands for an increase in salaries to compensate for a devaluation of the CFA franc in January (see Economic Affairs), degenerated into violence. Security forces destroyed the transmitters of a radio station owned by the RNB (which had supported the strike), and attacked M'Ba Abessole's private residence, resulting in clashes with protesters. Strike action was suspended after four days, following negotiations between the Government and trade unions; nine people had been killed during that period, according to official figures (although the opposition claimed that a total of 38 had died). At the end of February 1994 the Minister of State Control in charge of Parastatal Affairs resigned from the Government and from the PDG, owing to disagreement with the increasingly authoritarian stance adopted by Bongo.

In March 1994 Oye Mba resigned and dissolved the Council of Ministers. Later that month he was reappointed as Prime Minister, and, following the opposition's refusal to participate in a government of national unity, formed a 38-member administration, solely comprising representatives of the presidential majority (apart from one member of the PGP, who was expected to be expelled from that party). The size of the new Government, in view of the deterioration of the economy, prompted widespread criticism, and two of the newly-appointed ministers subsequently refused to assume their allocated posts, apparently owing to disagreement regarding the composition of the portfolios. In the same month the National Assembly approved a constitutional amendment that provided for the establishment of a Senate (which the opposition had resisted) and repealed legislation prohibiting unsuccessful presidential candidates from participating in the Government within a period of 18 months. In June opposition parties agreed to a further postponement of the local government elections, to early 1995. In August opposition parties announced that they were prepared to participate in a coalition government, on condition that it was installed as a transitional organ pending legislative elections. In September negotiations between the Government and opposition took place in Paris, under the auspices of the Organization of African Unity (OAU, see p. 256), in order to resolve remaining differences concerning the results of the presidential election and the proposed formation of a government of national unity. In mid-September the RNB, which was attending the discussions, indicated that it would refuse to join a coalition government.

At the end of September 1994 an agreement was reached, as a result of the Paris meetings, whereby a transitional coalition government was to be installed, with local government elections scheduled to take place after a period of one year, followed by legislative elections six months later; the electoral code was to be revised and an independent electoral commission established, in an effort to ensure that the elections be conducted fairly. In early October Oye Mba resigned from office and dissolved the Council of Ministers. Shortly afterwards Bongo appointed Dr

Paulin Obame-Nguema, a member of the PDG who had served in former administrations, as Prime Minister. Obame-Nguema subsequently formed a 27-member Council of Ministers, which included six opposition members. The composition of the new Government was, however, immediately criticized by the opposition, on the grounds that it was entitled to one-third of ministerial portfolios in proportion to the number of opposition deputies in the National Assembly; the HCR announced that the opposition would boycott the new administration, which, it claimed, was in violation of the Paris accord. Four opposition members consequently refused to accept the portfolios allocated to them, although two of these finally agreed to join the Government. (The portfolios that remained vacant were later assigned to a further two opposition members.) Following the inauguration of the Council of Ministers in early November, a motion expressing confidence in the new Prime Minister was adopted by 99 of 118 votes cast in the National Assembly. In the same month associates of Bongo established an informal grouping, known as the Mouvement des amis de Bongo.

In January 1995 controversy emerged over the extent of the authority vested in the National Assembly, after members of the HCR refused to participate in the drafting of the new electoral code until the Paris agreement was ratified. The Constitutional Court subsequently ruled that the National Assembly was not empowered, under the terms of the Constitution, to ratify the agreement. In early February, however, opposition deputies ended a boycott of the National Assembly, following a further ruling by the Constitutional Court that the National Assembly was entitled to act as a parliamentary body, pending the installation of a Senate after the legislative elections in 1996, but that the constitutional provisions adopted under the terms of the Paris accord would require endorsement by referendum. Following a declaration by the authorities that all illegal immigrants remaining in Gabon by mid-February would be arrested, some 55,000 foreign nationals left the country by the stipulated date. In April Bongo announced that a referendum to endorse the constitutional amendments would take place in June. In the same month, in accordance with the Paris accord, the Cabinet approved legislation providing for the release of prisoners detained on charges involving state security. Later in April Gabon withdrew its ambassador in Paris, in protest at reports by the French media regarding Bongo's alleged involvement with prostitutes; a number of demonstrations in support of Bongo took place in Libreville. Government efforts to prohibit two pro-opposition newspapers, which had published French press reports considered to be critical of Bongo, were rejected by the National Communications Council. At the national referendum (which had been postponed until 24 July), the constitutional amendments were approved by 96.5% of votes cast, with 63% of the electorate participating. In September 1995, following dissent within the UPG, Sébastien Mamboundou Mouyama, the Minister of Social Affairs and National Solidarity, was elected party Chairman, replacing Pierre Mamboundou. However, the latter subsequently regained the leadership of the UPG. (Mamboundou Mouyama formed a new political party, the Mouvement alternatif, in August 1996.)

During early 1996 opposition parties criticized the Government for delaying the implementation of the electoral timetable contained in the Paris accord. At the beginning of May, following a meeting attended by all the officially recognized political parties, Bongo agreed to establish a National Electoral Commission to formulate a timetable for local, legislative and senatorial elections, in consultation with all the official parties. It was also decided that access to state-controlled media and election funding should be equitably divided. On 20 May 1996 the National Assembly's mandate expired, and Obame-Nguema's Government resigned at the beginning of June, in accordance with the Paris accord. Bongo, however, rejected the resignation on the grounds that the Government should, before leaving office, organize the elections and finalize pending agreements with the IMF and the World Bank. At the beginning of October the National Electoral Commission adopted a timetable for legislative elections: the first round was to take place on 17 November, with a second round scheduled for 1 December. HCR representatives denounced the timetable, withdrew their participation from the commission and demanded the postponement of the local and legislative elections. In mid-October Pierre-Claver Maganga Moussavou, the leader of the PSD, was forced to resign from the Government, following his condemnation of the electoral timetable. The Chairman of the HCR claimed that

the 'dismissal' was a violation of the Paris accord. Later that month a minor reshuffle of the Council of Ministers was effected.

Organizational problems disrupted the local elections, which were held on 20 October 1996, having been postponed twice previously; according to reports, only 15% of the electorate participated. The PDG gained control of the majority of the municipalities, although the PGP secured victory in Port-Gentil, while the RNB was successful in the north of the country. Elections in Fougamou (where voting had not taken place) and Libreville (where the results had been invalidated) were eventually rescheduled for 24 November, although the RNB demanded the validation of the original results. On 24 November the RNB secured 62 of the 98 seats available in Libreville; M'Ba Abessole was subsequently elected mayor.

Legislative elections were rescheduled on several occasions, owing to the delay in the release of the local election results and the failure to revise electoral registers in time. The first round of the elections took place on 15 December 1996, without major incidents. Later that month it was reported that the PDG had obtained 47 of the 55 seats that were decided in the first round of voting. The opposition disputed the results, and there were demands for protest marches and a boycott of the second round of voting. The PDG secured a substantial majority of the seats decided in the second round, which was held on 29 December, winning 84 seats, while the RNB obtained seven, the PGP six and independent candidates four, with the remaining 14 seats shared by the CLR, the UPG, the USG and others. Polling was unable to proceed for the five remaining seats, and results in a number of other constituencies were later annulled, owing to irregularities. (Following by-elections held in August 1997, during which five people were reportedly killed in violent incidents in north-east Gabon, the PDG held 88 seats, the PGP nine and the RNB five.) Guy Ndzouba Ndama was elected President of the new National Assembly. Obame-Nguema was reappointed Prime Minister on 27 January, and a new Council of Ministers, dominated by members of the PDG, was announced on the following day. The PGP, the main opposition party represented in the National Assembly, had refused to participate in the new Government.

Elections to the new Senate took place on 26 January and 9 February 1997, with senators to be elected by members of municipal councils and departmental assemblies. The PDG won 53 of the Senate's 91 seats, while the RNB secured 20 seats, the PGP four, the Alliance démocratique et républicaine (ADERE) three, the CLR one, and the RDP one, with independent candidates obtaining nine seats. The results for a number of seats were annulled, however, and in subsequent by-elections, held later that year, the PDG increased its representation to 58 seats, while the RNB held 20 seats and the PGP four.

On 18 April 1997, at a congress of deputies and senators, constitutional amendments which extended the presidential term to seven years, provided for the creation of the post of Vice-President and formally designated the Senate as an upper chamber of a bicameral legislature were adopted, despite the protests of opposition leaders who objected to the creation of a vice-presidency and demanded that a referendum be held. The Vice-President was to deputize for the President as required, but was not to have any power of succession. In late May Didjob Divungui-di-N'Dingue, a senior member of the ADERE and a candidate in the 1993 presidential election, was appointed to the new post. Although officially part of the HCR, the ADERE had signed a number of local electoral agreements with other parties, including the PDG, prior to the legislative elections.

In April 1998 the Government established a National Democracy Council, a consultative body whose members were to include the Prime Minister, the Presidents of the Senate and the National Assembly, and the leaders of all political parties with parliamentary representation. Divisions within the leadership of the RNB led to a split in the party in July, following the expulsion of its Secretary-General, Pierre-André Kombila, who was subsequently elected to chair a dissident group within the party.

In September 1998 opposition parties withdrew their members from the National Electoral Commission in protest at alleged irregularities in the voter registration process for the forthcoming presidential election. In mid-October President Bongo confirmed that he was to seek re-election; his candidature was formally accepted later that month, together with those of Kombila, M'Ba Abessole and Alain Egouang Nze for the RNB, Pierre Mamboundou for the HCR, Maganga Moussavou for the PSD, and two independents.

At the presidential election, which was held on 6 December 1998, Bongo was re-elected by 66.55% of votes cast, while Mamboundou received 16.54% of the votes and M'Ba Abessole secured 13.41%. The reported rate of participation was 53.8%. Opposition parties rejected the results, again alleging electoral malpractice, and called for fresh elections to be held. None the less, Bongo was inaugurated as President on 21 January 1999, and a new 42-member Council of Ministers, headed by Jean-François Ntoutoume Emane, was subsequently appointed. A minor reshuffle took place in February. In early 1999 student demonstrations and strike action by civil servants severely disrupted health and education services, with some schools closed for up to three months. In December it was announced that Bongo had reduced the Council of Ministers in size from 42 to 31 members.

In August 2000 four opposition parties, including the RNB (which subsequently changed its name to the Rassemblement pour le Gabon—RPG), formed a coalition, the Front des parties du changement, in preparation for legislative and local elections scheduled to be held in 2001. In January 2001 a minor cabinet reshuffle was effected after the Minister for Equipment and Construction, Zacharie Myboto, resigned, on the grounds that his position had become untenable, owing to an alleged campaign to discredit him because of his objections to democratic reforms. Later that month post and telecommunications workers began a nation-wide strike in support of their demands for improved working conditions. The industrial action ended in early February when the Government agreed to the financial demands of the workers.

President Bongo has pursued a policy of close co-operation with France in the fields of economic and foreign affairs. Relations became strained in March 1997, however, when allegations that Bongo had been a beneficiary in an international fraud emerged, during a French judicial investigation into the affairs of the petroleum company Elf-Aquitaine. The Chairman of Elf-Gabon, André Tarallo, was temporarily detained, and overseas bank accounts, said to contain Gabonese government funds, were blocked. In response, Bongo cancelled a visit to France and reportedly threatened to impose economic sanctions on French oil interests in Gabon. He insisted that the Elf enquiry was a matter for the French judiciary and was not the concern of Gabon. Tarallo, who had been replaced as chairman of Elf-Gabon, came under further investigation in November 1997.

In October 1999 a further judicial investigation into the affairs of Elf-Aquitaine, carried out by Swiss authorities, revealed that Tarallo had used bank accounts in that country secretly to transfer large sums of money to several African heads of state, among them Bongo. Bongo denied personally receiving direct payments from Elf and maintained that such 'bonus' payments were made only to the Gabonese Government. However, a report released in November, following a separate investigation by the US Congress into money 'laundering' and corruption among political figures, alleged that the US banking group Citibank had assisted Bongo in transferring 'political gifts', including some US $50m. contributed to his 1993 election campaign fund, which had been paid into 'offshore' accounts by Elf.

Bongo has often acted as an intermediary in regional disputes, chairing the OAU *ad hoc* committee seeking to resolve the border dispute between Chad and Libya, and encouraging dialogue between Angola and the USA. In 1997 he mediated in civil conflicts in Zaire (now the Democratic Republic of the Congo), the Central African Republic and the Republic of the Congo. In July of that year the Government expressed concern at the large numbers of refugees arriving in Gabon and subsequently announced plans for repatriation. Throughout late 1998 Bongo participated in discussions with other central African leaders in an attempt to find a solution to the political and military crisis in the Democratic Republic of the Congo (DRC), which had been invaded by Rwandan and Ugandan troops in August of that year. At a summit meeting held in Libreville in September, it was decided that Bongo would chair a monitoring and consultations committee on the conflict.

In July 1999 a summit meeting of Central African heads of government took place in Libreville to discuss the problem of displaced people in the region. Bongo appealed for regional solidarity in addressing this issue, and proposed the formation of a new organization to assist the region's refugees. Later that month the Gabonese Government appealed for international assistance following a further influx of refugees from renewed fighting in the DRC. At the Gulf of Guinea summit held in Libreville in November the seven countries represented agreed

to form the Commission du Golfe de Guinée, a consultation framework designed to promote co-operation and development among the member countries as well as to take measures towards the prevention and resolution of conflicts affecting those countries. In the same month Gabon established diplomatic relations with Libya.

In January 2000 African leaders and representatives of the IMF met in Libreville to discuss the alleviation of poverty in Africa. Later that month, under the framework of the Renforcement des capacités africaines de maintien de la paix (a French initiative designed to enhance the abilities of African countries to intervene in conflicts on their own continent), a military exercise involving personnel from eight countries from the Central African region took place in Lambaréné, Gabon. Known as 'Gabon 2000', the exercise was orientated towards conflict resolution and was supported, with technical assistance, by eight industrialized nations, including France, Belgium, the United Kingdom and the USA.

In February 1996 the northern part of Gabon was quarantined in response to an outbreak of Ebola haemorrhagic fever, in which at least 13 people died, according to the World Health Organization (WHO). In April it was reported that the World Bank and the World Wide Fund for Nature were seeking to identify areas of equatorial forest for conservation, amid fears that increasing exploitation by logging companies would imperil the survival of indigenous plant and animal species. It was also feared that opening up the forest could lead to another outbreak of the Ebola virus, of which forest-dwelling fauna are believed to be carriers. In October a second outbreak claimed 14 lives in the north-east of the country, and by January 1997 a further 40 deaths had been reported.

Government

The Constitution of March 1991 provides for a multi-party system, and vests executive power in the President, who is directly elected by universal suffrage for a period of seven years. The President appoints the Prime Minister, who is Head of Government and who (in consultation with the President) appoints the Council of Ministers. The legislative organ is the National Assembly, comprising 120 members, who are elected by direct universal suffrage for a term of five years. Provision is made for the formation of an upper house. Elections to a 91-member Senate took place in January and February 1997. The independence of the judiciary is guaranteed by the Constitution. Gabon is divided into nine provinces, each under an appointed governor, and 37 prefectures.

Defence

At 1 August 2000 the army consisted of 3,200 men, the air force of 1,000 men, and the navy of an estimated 500 men. Paramilitary forces numbered 2,000. Military service is voluntary. France maintains a military detachment of 680 in Gabon. The defence budget for 2000 was estimated at 89,000m. francs CFA.

Economic Affairs

In 1998, according to estimates by the World Bank, Gabon's gross national product (GNP), measured at average 1996–98 prices, was US $4,922m., equivalent to $4,170 per head (or $5,615 per head on an international purchasing-power parity basis). During 1990–98, it was estimated, GNP per head increased, in real terms, by 0.3% per year, while the population increased at an average annual rate of 3.0%. GNP was estimated at $4,043m. in 1999, equivalent to $3,350 per head. Gabon's gross domestic product (GDP) increased, in real terms, at an average annual rate of 3.3% in 1990–98. The IMF estimated that real GDP growth declined by 9.6% in 1999.

Agriculture (including forestry and fishing) contributed an estimated 7.9% of GDP in 1999. About 39.2% of the labour force were employed in the agricultural sector in 1999. Cocoa, coffee, oil palm and rubber are cultivated for export. Gabon has yet to achieve self-sufficiency in staple crops: imports of foods accounted for 33.8% of the value of total imports in 1996. The principal subsistence crops are plantains, cassava and maize. The exploitation of Gabon's forests (which cover about 75% of the land area) is a principal economic activity. The forestry sector accounted for an estimated 2.7% of GDP in 1999, and engaged an estimated 15% of the working population in 1991. In 1999 okoumé timber accounted for an estimated 68% of all timber production. Although Gabon's territorial waters contain important fishing resources, their commercial exploitation is minimal. Agricultural GDP declined at an average annual rate of 2.3% in 1990–98. The IMF estimated an increase of 5.4% in agricultural GDP in 1999.

Industry (including mining, manufacturing, construction and power) contributed an estimated 52.7% of GDP in 1999. About 14.1% of the working population were employed in the sector in 1991. Industrial GDP increased at an average annual rate of 2.7% in 1990–98. The IMF estimated a decline of 12.4% in industrial GDP in 1999.

Mining accounted for an estimated 41.6% of GDP in 1999 (of which 39.5% was contributed by the petroleum sector). In 1999 sales of petroleum and petroleum products provided an estimated 74.4% of export revenue. Gabon is among the world's foremost producers and exporters of manganese (which contributed an estimated 5.7% of export earnings in 1999). Significant deposits of uranium have been exploited since the late 1950s at Mounana; however, with all reserves having been exhausted, operations ceased in early 1999. Major reserves of iron ore remain undeveloped, owing to the lack of appropriate transport facilities. Small amounts of gold are extracted, and the existence of many mineral deposits, including talc, barytes, phosphates, rare earths, titanium and cadmium, has also been confirmed. In 1999 it was expected that mining of substantial niobium (columbium) reserves at Mabounie would commence in the near future. The IMF estimated a decline of 11.5% in mining GDP in 1999.

The manufacturing sector contributed an estimated 6.1% of GDP in 1999. The principal activities are the refining of petroleum and the processing of other minerals, the preparation of timber and other agro-industrial processes. The chemicals industry is also significant. Manufacturing GDP increased at an average annual rate of 0.9% in 1990–98. The IMF estimated a decline in manufacturing GDP of 1.5% in 1999.

Electrical energy is derived principally from hydroelectric installations. Imports of fuel and energy comprised an estimated 21.3% of the total value of imports in 1995.

Services engaged 18.8% of the economically active population in 1991 and provided an estimated 39.4% of GDP in 1999. The GDP of the services sector increased at an average annual rate of 4.8% in 1990–98. Services GDP declined by an estimated 6.6% in 1999.

In 1995 Gabon recorded a visible trade surplus of US $1,744.4m., and there was a surplus of $99.8m. on the current account of the balance of payments. In 1999 the principal source of imports (50.2%) was France; other major sources were the USA and Italy. The principal market for exports in that year was the USA (50.6%); France was also an important purchaser. The principal exports in 1999 were petroleum and petroleum products, timber and manganese. The principal imports in 1996 were machinery and transport equipment, basic manufactures, food products and chemicals and related products.

In 1999 there was an estimated budgetary surplus of 38,500m. francs CFA (equivalent to 1.4% of GDP). Gabon's external debt totalled US $4,425m. at the end of 1998, of which $3,833m. was long-term public debt. In that year the cost of debt-servicing was equivalent to 12.0% of the value of exports of goods and services. In 1990–97 the average annual rate of inflation was 3.3%. The annual rate of inflation increased to 36.1% in 1994, following the 50% devaluation of the CFA franc in January of that year, but had declined to 4.0% by 1997. The IMF estimated that consumer prices declined by 0.7% in 1999. The Government estimated about 20% of the labour force to be unemployed in 1996.

Gabon is a member of the Central African organs of the Franc Zone (see p. 210), and of the Communauté économique des états de l'Afrique centrale (CEEAC, see p. 307). In 1996 Gabon, which had been a member of OPEC (see p. 269) since 1973, withdrew from the organization.

Gabon's potential for economic growth is based upon its considerable mineral and forestry resources. In the mid-1980s, however, the country's vulnerability to fluctuations in international prices and demand for its principal commodities precipitated a decline in export and budget revenue. By the early 1990s the country's economic and financial situation had deteriorated, owing to a decline in the international price for petroleum and

the accumulation of debt arrears. Following the devaluation of the CFA franc by 50% in relation to the French franc in January 1994, a programme for economic recovery was agreed with the IMF. In 1995 the IMF approved a three-year credit under an extended facility, in support of the Government's programme for 1995–98, which aimed to stimulate employment through economic diversification, to liberalize the regulatory framework and further to develop the non-petroleum sector. In 1997 the divestiture of Gabon's electricity and water services was the first major privatization project to be implemented. Gabon's economic situation deteriorated substantially in 1998–99. Falling petroleum prices and the negative impact of the Asian economic crisis on timber exports forced the Government to revise budget estimates downwards in 1999. Further strain was placed on the heavily-indebted economy by the suspension of loans from the Agence française de développement, and from March 1999 Gabon had no IMF programme. The economy began to recover in 2000 as a result of higher petroleum prices and improved timber export revenues. In October the IMF approved an 18-month stand-by credit, worth some US $119m., in support of the Government's economic programme for 2000-01, and in December the 'Paris Club' of international creditors agreed to reschedule about $532m. of Gabon's debt. Priorities for 2001 included the successful implementation of Gabon's privatization programme (including the sale of Air Gabon), as well as increased investment in non-petroleum sectors, such as tourism and agriculture.

Social Welfare

There is a national Fund for State Insurance, and a guaranteed minimum wage. In January 1985 Gabon had 28 hospitals, 87 medical centres and 312 dispensaries, with a total of 5,156 hospital beds. In the early 1990s there were 19 physicians per 100,000 people and 56 nurses per 100,000 people working in the country. Maternal and infant health is a major priority. The 1988 budget allocated 18,000m. francs CFA (10% of total administrative spending) to health expenditure.

Education

Education is officially compulsory for 10 years between six and 16 years of age: in 1993 89% of children in the relevant age-group attended primary and secondary schools (90% of boys; 88% of girls). Primary and secondary education is provided by state and mission schools. Primary education begins at the age of six and lasts for six years. Secondary education, beginning at 12 years of age, lasts for up to seven years, comprising a first cycle of four years and a second of three years. The Université Omar Bongo, at Libreville, had 2,741 students in 1986. The Université des Sciences et des Techniques de Masuku was opened in 1986, with an enrolment of 550 students. In 1995, according to estimates by UNESCO, adult illiteracy averaged 36.7% (males 26.3%; females 46.6%). The 1994 budget allocated 78,850m. francs CFA (19% of total administrative spending) to expenditure on education.

Public Holidays

2001: 1 January (New Year's Day), 6 March* (Id al-Adha, feast of the Sacrifice), 12 March (Anniversary of Renovation, foundation of the Parti démocratique gabonais), 16 April (Easter Monday), 1 May (Labour Day), 4 June (Whit Monday and Mouloud, birth of Muhammad), 17 August (Anniversary of Independence), 1 November (All Saints' Day), 17 December* (Id al-Fitr, end of Ramadan), 25 December (Christmas).

2002: 1 January (New Year's Day), 23 February* (Id al-Adha, feast of the Sacrifice), 12 March (Anniversary of Renovation, foundation of the Parti démocratique gabonais), 1 April (Easter Monday), 1 May (Labour Day), 20 May (Whit Monday), 24 May* (Mouloud, birth of Muhammad), 17 August (Anniversary of Independence), 1 November (All Saints' Day), 6 December* (Id al-Fitr, end of Ramadan), 25 December (Christmas).

* These holidays are dependent on the Islamic lunar calendar and may vary by one or two days from the dates given.

Weights and Measures

The metric system is in official use.

Statistical Survey

Source (unless otherwise stated): Direction Générale de l'Economie, Ministère de la Planification, de l'Economie et de l'Administration Territoriale, Libreville.

Area and Population

AREA, POPULATION AND DENSITY

Area (sq km)	267,667*
Population (census results)	
8 October 1960–May 1961	448,564
31 July 1993	
Males	501,784
Females	513,192
Total	1,014,976
Population (official estimate at mid-year)†	
1999	1,385,000
Density (per sq km) at mid-1999	5.2

* 103,347 sq miles.
† Source: UN, *Population and Vital Statistics Report.*

REGIONS (1993 census, provisional)

Region	Area (sq km)	Population*	Density (per sq km)	Chief town
Estuaire . . .	20,740	462,086	22.3	Libreville
Haut-Ogooué . .	36,547	102,387	2.8	Franceville
Moyen-Ogooué .	18,535	41,827	2.3	Lambaréné
N'Gounié . .	37,750	77,871	2.1	Mouila
Nyanga . . .	21,285	39,826	1.9	Tchibanga
Ogooué-Ivindo .	46,075	48,847	1.1	Makokou
Ogooué-Lolo .	25,380	42,783	2.1	Koula-Moutou
Ogooué-Maritime .	22,890	98,299	4.3	Port-Gentil
Woleu-N'Tem .	38,465	97,739	2.5	Oyem
Total . . .	**267,667**	**1,011,665**	**3.8**	

* Excluding 45 persons in unspecified regions.
Source: UN, *Demographic Yearbook.*

PRINCIPAL TOWNS (population in 1988)

Libreville (capital) .	352,000	Franceville . . .	75,000
Port-Gentil . . .	164,000		

BIRTHS AND DEATHS (UN estimates, annual averages)

	1980–85	1985–90	1990–95
Birth rate (per 1,000) . . .	33.1	35.7	36.6
Death rate (per 1,000) . . .	18.1	17.0	16.1

Expectation of life (UN estimates, years at birth, 1990–95): 52.3 (males 50.8; females 54.0).
Source: UN, *World Population Prospects: The 1998 Revision.*

ECONOMICALLY ACTIVE POPULATION
(estimates, '000 persons, 1991)

	Males	Females	Total
Agriculture, etc.	187	151	338
Industry	62	9	71
Services	69	26	95
Total labour force . . .	**318**	**186**	**504**

Source: UN Economic Commission for Africa, *African Statistical Yearbook.*
Mid-1999 (estimates, '000 persons): Agriculture, etc. 213; Total 544.
Source: FAO.

Agriculture

PRINCIPAL CROPS ('000 metric tons)

	1997	1998	1999
Maize*	31	31	31
Cassava (Manioc)* . . .	218	220	225
Yams*	140	145	150
Taro (Coco yam)* . . .	58	58	59
Vegetables*	34	34	35
Bananas*	11	11	12
Plantains*	270	275	280
Cocoa beans . . .	1	1†	1†
Groundnuts (in shell)* . .	17	17	17
Sugar cane*	175	173	175

* FAO estimates. † Unofficial figures.
Source: FAO.

LIVESTOCK ('000 head, year ending September)

	1997	1998	1999
Cattle	33	34*	35*
Pigs*	210	211	212
Sheep*	187	191	195
Goats*	88	89	90
Chickens*	2,900	3,000	3,100

* FAO estimate(s).
Source: FAO.

LIVESTOCK PRODUCTS
1999 ('000 metric tons): Meat 32; Hen eggs 2 (FAO estimate).
Source: FAO.

Forestry

ROUNDWOOD REMOVALS ('000 cubic metres)

	1996	1997	1998
Sawlogs, veneer logs and logs for sleepers	2,409	2,775	2,775
Fuel wood	2,425	2,491	2,557
Total	**4,834**	**5,266**	**5,332**

Source: FAO, *Yearbook of Forest Products.*

SAWNWOOD PRODUCTION
('000 cubic metres, incl. railway sleepers)

	1996	1997	1998
Total	50	30	30

Source: FAO, *Yearbook of Forest Products.*

Fishing

('000 metric tons, live weight)

	1996	1997	1998
Capture	45.3	44.7	53.6
Tilapias	3.6	4.2	3.5
Torpedo-shaped catfishes . .	2.1	2.1	2.0
Other freshwater fishes . .	4.3	3.6	3.5
Sea catfishes . . .	2.8	2.7	1.3
Grunts, sweetlips, etc. . .	0.8	0.9	1.7
West African croakers . .	5.0	3.8	6.2
Lesser African threadfin . .	3.8	3.2	3.5
Bonga shad . . .	13.0	14.7	19.3
Sharks, rays, skates, etc. . .	0.6	0.8	2.0
Southern pink shrimp . .	1.0	0.8	2.3
Aquaculture	0.1	0.1	0.1*
Total catch	45.4	44.8	53.7

* FAO estimate.

Source: FAO, *Yearbook of Fishery Statistics*.

Mining

('000 metric tons, unless otherwise indicated)

	1995	1996	1997
Crude petroleum	18,246	18,277	18,462
Natural gas (petajoules) . .	32	25	26
Uranium ore (metric tons)† . .	653*	568	516
Manganese ore*†‡ . . .	891	915	878
Gold (kilograms)*†‡ . . .	70	70	70

* Provisional or estimated figure(s).

† Figures refer to the metal content of ores.

‡ Data from the US Bureau of Mines.

Source: UN, *Industrial Commodity Statistics Yearbook*.

Industry

PETROLEUM PRODUCTS ('000 metric tons)

	1995	1996*	1997
Liquefied petroleum gas . . .	11*	11	10
Motor spirit (petrol) . . .	78	76	71
Kerosene	55*	68	81
Jet fuel	17*	28	23
Distillate fuel oils . . .	169	165	230
Residual fuel oils . . .	315*	308	285
Bitumen (asphalt) . . .	10	14	10

* Provisional or estimated figure(s).

Source: UN, *Industrial Commodity Statistics Yearbook*.

SELECTED OTHER PRODUCTS

('000 metric tons, unless otherwise indicated)

	1995	1996	1997
Palm oil (crude)*	7	7	7
Flour*	27	26	n.a.
Cement†	130	n.a.	n.a.
Electric energy (million kWh)‡ .	1,135	1,213	1,257

* Data from the FAO.

† Data from the US Bureau of Mines.

‡ Estimated production.

Beer ('000 hectolitres): 905 in 1993; 801 in 1994; 816 in 1995.

Soft drinks ('000 hectolitres): 390 in 1993; 351 in 1994; 416 in 1995.

Source: UN, *Industrial Commodity Statistics Yearbook*.

Plywood ('000 cu metres): 25 in 1996; 25 in 1997; 53 in 1998 (Source: FAO, *Yearbook of Forest Products*).

Veneer sheets (FAO estimates, '000 cu metres): 2 in 1995; 5 in 1996; 10 in 1997 (Source: FAO, *Yearbook of Forest Products*).

Finance

CURRENCY AND EXCHANGE RATES

Monetary Units

100 centimes = 1 franc de la Coopération financière en Afrique centrale (CFA).

Sterling, Dollar and Euro Equivalents (29 December 2000)

£1 sterling = 1,051.93 francs CFA;

US $1 = 704.95 francs CFA;

€1 = 655.96 francs CFA;

10,000 francs CFA = £9.506 = $14.185 = €15.245.

Average Exchange Rate (francs CFA per US $)

1998	589.95
1999	615.70
2000	711.98

Note: An exchange rate of 1 French franc = 50 francs CFA, established in 1948, remained in force until January 1994, when the CFA franc was devalued by 50%, with the exchange rate adjusted to 1 French franc = 100 francs CFA. This relationship to French currency remained in effect with the introduction of the euro on 1 January 1999. From that date, accordingly, a fixed exchange rate of €1 = 655.957 francs CFA has been in operation.

BUDGET ('000 million francs CFA)

Revenue	1997	1998*	1999†
Petroleum revenue . . .	643.9	498.3	368.7
Profits tax	337.8	272.6	172.3
Royalties	198.6	129.5	165.8
Production-sharing and assets .	6.0	4.4	7.7
Dividends	60.5	48.8	22.8
Other	41.0	43.0	n.a.
Non-petroleum revenue . .	386.0	413.8	445.0
Tax revenue . . .	377.1	405.8	420.9
Direct taxes . . .	100.3	107.6	91.6
Company taxes . .	61.2	69.2	53.7
Individual taxes . .	39.0	38.4	37.9
Indirect taxes . . .	72.5	72.8	58.2
Turnover taxes . .	64.5	59.0	44.4
Taxes on goods and services .	8.0	13.8	13.8
Taxes on refined petroleum products .	2.5	2.5	2.0
Taxes on international trade and transactions . .	190.9	214.5	164.6
Import duties . .	168.3	200.8	146.7
Export duties . .	22.6	13.7	17.9
Other revenue . . .	22.3	18.8	130.6
Total	1,029.8	912.1	813.7

Expenditure	1997	1998*	1999†
Current expenditure . . .	630.6	918.8	660.6
Wages and salaries . . .	195.7	204.9	214.0
Other goods and services .	140.1	204.2	124.2
Transfers and subsidies . .	102.8	308.1	126.5
Interest payments . .	192.0	201.6	195.9
Capital expenditure . . .	349.6	362.8	118.9
Sub-total	980.2	1,281.6	779.5
Adjustment for payment arrears	54.0	−80.9	−4.3
Total (cash basis) . . .	1,034.2	1,200.7	775.2

* Preliminary figures.

† Estimates.

Source: IMF, *Gabon: Statistical Annex* (November 2000).

INTERNATIONAL RESERVES (US $ million at 31 December)

	1997	1998	1999
Gold*	3.74	3.69	2.43
IMF special drawing rights .	—	0.01	0.01
Reserve position in IMF . .	0.09	0.09	0.15
Foreign exchange . . .	282.51	15.30	17.79
Total	286.34	19.09	20.38

* Valued at market-related prices.

Source: IMF, *International Financial Statistics*.

MONEY SUPPLY ('000 million francs CFA at 31 December)

	1997	1998	1999
Currency outside banks . .	121.03	124.72	105.26
Demand deposits at commercial and development banks .	174.41	156.99	161.85
Total money (incl. others) . .	298.25	283.12	268.61

Source: IMF, *International Financial Statistics*.

COST OF LIVING
(Retail Price Index for African families in Libreville; base: 1995 = 100)

	1996	1997
All items	100.7	104.7

Source: IMF, *International Financial Statistics*.

NATIONAL ACCOUNTS ('000 million francs CFA at current prices)
Expenditure on the Gross Domestic Product

	1997*	1998*	1999†
Government final consumption expenditure	335.8	409.1	338.2
Private final consumption expenditure	1,028.4	1,218.5	1,206.7
Increase in stocks . . .	19.0	30.3	—
Gross fixed capital formation . .	959.5	1,003.6	681.7
Total domestic expenditure	2,342.7	2,661.5	2,226.6
Exports of goods and services . .	2,011.8	1,232.5	1,655.8
Less Imports of goods and services	1,245.4	1,249.0	1,051.7
GDP in purchasers' values . .	3,109.1	2,645.0	2,830.7

* Preliminary figures.
† Estimates.
Source: IMF, *Gabon: Statistical Annex* (November 2000).

Gross Domestic Product by Economic Activity

	1997*	1998*	1999†
Agriculture, livestock, hunting and fishing	132.0	134.0	137.4
Forestry.	92.4	51.7	72.4
Petroleum exploitation and research	1,281.8	726.1	1,049.8
Other mining	52.7	62.3	56.9
Manufacturing	145.3	164.6	161.5
Electricity and water. . . .	35.9	29.3	33.7
Construction and public works .	152.4	158.8	99.3
Trade	232.0	250.8	244.6
Transport	164.4	172.1	148.2
Financial services . . .	23.6	19.1	18.6
Government services . . .	259.1	278.1	294.9
Other services	322.3	362.3	340.3
GDP at factor cost . .	2,893.9	2,409.2	2,657.6
Import duties	215.2	235.8	173.1
GDP in purchasers' values .	3,109.1	2,645.0	2,830.7

* Preliminary figures.
† Estimates.
Source: IMF, *Gabon: Statistical Annex* (November 2000).

BALANCE OF PAYMENTS (US $ million)

	1993	1994	1995
Exports of goods f.o.b. . . .	2,326.2	2,365.3	2,642.9
Imports of goods f.o.b. . . .	−845.1	−776.7	−898.5
Trade balance	1,481.1	1,588.6	1,744.4
Exports of services . . .	311.1	219.6	272.9
Imports of services	−1,022.7	−826.7	−949.4
Balance on goods and services	769.5	981.4	1,067.8
Other income received . .	32.1	11.9	13.4
Other income paid	−658.3	−509.9	−783.5
Balance on goods, services and income	143.4	483.4	297.7
Current transfers received . .	48.0	18.7	4.4
Current transfers paid . . .	−240.5	−184.8	−202.3
Current balance	−49.1	317.4	99.8
Direct investment abroad. . .	−2.5	—	n.a.
Direct investment from abroad .	−113.7	−99.6	−113.4
Other investment assets . .	−7.8	−258.6	−5.4
Other investment liabilities . .	−265.2	−386.7	−293.9
Net errors and omissions . .	−13.6	254.6	−108.2
Overall balance	−451.9	−173.0	−421.2

Source: IMF, *International Financial Statistics*.

External Trade

PRINCIPAL COMMODITIES

Imports c.i.f. (US $ million)*	1993	1994	1996
Food and live animals . .	131.5	105.8	145.7
Meat and meat preparations . .	34.8	32.0	37.8
Fresh, chilled or frozen meat	31.5	28.9	32.8
Fresh or frozen bovine meat	16.7	13.1	10.1
Dairy products and birds' eggs .	16.1	10.7	15.5
Fish and fish preparations .	15.4	8.7	13.6
Cereals and cereal preparations .	35.5	32.3	48.4
Beverages and tobacco . .	17.7	15.5	23.1
Mineral fuels, lubricants, etc. .	14.5	17.1	31.6
Petroleum, petroleum products, etc.	14.3	16.9	28.3
Refined petroleum products .	14.2	16.8	27.4
Chemicals and related products	83.6	70.1	93.0
Medicinal and pharmaceutical products	30.7	18.4	33.4
Medicaments (incl. veterinary)	28.3	16.7	30.7
Basic manufactures . . .	123.8	112.1	150.2
Paper, paperboard and manufactures . . .	19.4	14.1	16.8
Iron and steel	30.9	27.3	37.3
Tubes, pipes and fittings . .	23.7	19.7	24.3
Machinery and transport equipment	316.4	314.3	351.9
Power-generating machinery and equipment	26.9	25.9	26.3
Machinery specialized for particular industries . .	21.0	46.4	36.9
Civil engineering and contractors' plant and equipment	12.1	30.9	23.2
General industrial machinery, equipment and parts . .	67.0	82.2	105.9
Pumps for liquids, etc. . .	10.7	14.1	10.0
Other pumps, centrifuges, etc.	14.6	18.5	35.8
Office machines and automatic data-processing equipment . .	15.2	12.3	19.7
Telecommunications and sound equipment	19.0	16.6	22.8
Other electrical machinery, apparatus, etc. . . .	40.0	29.8	42.8
Switchgear, resistors, printed circuits, switchboards, etc.	15.3	9.1	11.9

Imports c.i.f. (US $ million)* — continued	1993	1994	1996
Road vehicles and parts . . .	68.7	57.6	84.2
Passenger motor cars (excl. buses) . . .	30.8	18.6	29.4
Motor vehicles for goods transport, etc. . . .	18.8	14.1	23.3
Goods vehicles (lorries and trucks) . . .	17.7	13.2	19.8
Other transport equipment . .	57.8	42.8	12.3
Ships, boats and floating structures . . .	50.8	37.9	4.1
Miscellaneous manufactured articles	77.9	62.3	89.1
Professional, scientific and controlling instruments, etc.	21.3	16.9	29.8
Measuring and controlling instruments . . .	15.3	14.3	24.2
Total (incl. others) . . .	774.9	707.5	898.1

* Figures for 1995 are not available.

Source: UN, *International Trade Statistics Yearbook*.

Exports ('000 million francs CFA)	1997	1998*	1999†
Petroleum and petroleum products	1,401.9	833.4	1,153.8
Manganese	84.8	87.0	88.3
Timber	230.5	130.9	246.7
Total (incl. others) . . .	1,790.5	1,124.8	1,550.6

* Preliminary figures.
† Estimates.

Source: IMF, *Gabon: Statistical Annex* (November 2000).

PRINCIPAL TRADING PARTNERS (US $ million)

Imports c.i.f.*	1993	1994	1996
Belgium-Luxembourg . . .	22.5	24.5	37.1
Cameroon	6.3	12.0	12.1
Côte d'Ivoire	6.3	7.6	13.7
France (incl. Monaco) . . .	370.4	281.4	384.8
Germany	27.8	39.7	41.1
Italy	24.3	29.6	31.3
Japan	n.a.	n.a.	53.8
Morocco	10.1	4.5	6.6
Netherlands	36.0	35.1	40.8
Panama	—	11.3	—
SACU†	3.5	4.5	9.3
Spain	11.2	11.4	21.0
Thailand	4.3	3.3	15.3
United Kingdom	29.4	45.1	42.8
USA	71.0	83.5	93.4
Total (incl. others) . . .	774.9	707.5	898.1

Exports f.o.b.*	1993	1994	1996
Canada	52.3	—	—
Chile	81.6	22.6	17.5
China, People's Repub. . .	29.4	54.5	136.2
France (incl. Monaco) . .	505.6	361.6	239.8
Gibraltar	17.2	42.0	n.a.
Israel	9.9	19.8	34.5
Japan	n.a.	n.a.	66.1
Korea, Repub. . . .	16.1	35.4	24.2
Morocco	14.5	76.2	16.8
Netherlands	2.9	89.0	30.7
Netherlands Antilles . . .	n.a.	n.a.	121.4
Portugal	1.9	91.2	6.3
Singapore	17.1	40.6	2.0
Spain	32.9	92.5	36.8
Switzerland-Liechtenstein .	10.8	9.8	34.7
United Kingdom . . .	93.1	61.8	7.3
USA	1,388.2	1,192.9	2,015.3
Total (incl. others) . . .	2,637.0	2,391.0	3,145.6

* Figures for 1995 are not available.
† Southern African Customs Union, comprising Botswana, Lesotho, Namibia, South Africa and Swaziland.

Source: UN, *International Trade Statistics Yearbook*.

Transport

RAILWAYS (traffic)

	1997*	1998*	1999†
Passengers carried ('000) . . .	195	195	215
Freight carried ('000 metric tons)	2,944	3,291	2,893

* Preliminary figures.
† Estimates.

Source: IMF, *Gabon: Statistical Annex* (November 2000).

ROAD TRAFFIC (estimates, motor vehicles in use)

	1994	1995	1996
Passenger cars	22,310	24,000	24,750
Lorries and vans	14,850	15,840	16,490

Source: IRF, *World Road Statistics*.

INTERNATIONAL SEA-BORNE SHIPPING
(freight traffic, '000 metric tons)

	1988	1989	1990
Goods loaded	8,890	10,739	12,828
Goods unloaded	610	213	212

Source: UN, *Monthly Bulletin of Statistics*.

CIVIL AVIATION (traffic on scheduled services)

	1995	1996	1997
Kilometres flown (million) . .	7	7	8
Passengers carried ('000) . .	508	431	469
Passenger-kilometres (million) .	623	728	826
Total ton-kilometres (million) . .	89	100	112

Source: UN, *Statistical Yearbook*.

Tourism

	1995	1996	1997
Tourist arrivals	127,332	141,170	167,197
Tourism receipts (US $ million)	7	7	7

Sources: Centre Gabonais de Promotion Touristique (GABONTOUR) and World Tourism Organization, *Yearbook of Tourism Statistics.*

Communications Media

	1995	1996	1997
Radio receivers ('000 in use) . .	195	201	208
Television receivers ('000 in use) .	51	60	63
Telephones ('000 main lines in use)	32	35	37
Telefax stations (number in use) .	360	503	501
Mobile cellular telephones			
(subscribers)	4,000	6,800	9,500
Daily newspapers:			
Number	2	2	n.a.
Average circulation			
('000 copies)	30	33	n.a.

Sources: UNESCO, *Statistical Yearbook*; UN, *Statistical Yearbook.*

Education

(1996)

	Institu-tions	Teachers	Pupils		
			Males	Females	Total
Pre-primary* . .	9	37	465	485	950
Primary . . .	1,147	4,944	126,208	124,398	250,606
Secondary:					
General . .	88	1,107	31,318	28,863	60,181
Technical . .	5	181	5,521	1,033	6,554
Vocational . .	6	52	291	189	480
University level* .	2	299	2,148	852	3,000
Other higher .	n.a.	257†	1,033‡	315‡	1,348‡

* 1991/92 figures.   † 1983/84 figure.   ‡ 1986/87 figure.

Sources: Ministère de l'Education Nationale; UNESCO, *Statistical Yearbook.*

Directory

The Constitution

The Constitution of the Gabonese Republic was adopted on 14 March 1991. The main provisions are summarized below:

PREAMBLE

Upholds the rights of the individual, liberty of conscience and of the person, religious freedom and freedom of education. Sovereignty is vested in the people, who exercise it through their representatives or by means of referenda. There is direct, universal and secret suffrage.

HEAD OF STATE*

The President is elected by direct universal suffrage for a five-year term, renewable only once. The President is Head of State and of the Armed Forces. The President may, after consultation with his ministers and leaders of the National Assembly, order a referendum to be held. The President appoints the Prime Minister, who is Head of Government and who is accountable to the President. The President is the guarantor of national independence and territorial sovereignty.

EXECUTIVE POWER

Executive power is vested in the President and the Council of Ministers, who are appointed by the Prime Minister, in consultation with the President.

LEGISLATIVE POWER

The National Assembly is elected by direct universal suffrage for a five-year term. It may be dissolved or prorogued for up to 18 months by the President, after consultation with the Council of Ministers and President of the Assembly. The President may return a bill to the Assembly for a second reading, when it must be passed by a majority of two-thirds of the members. If the President dissolves the Assembly, elections must take place within 40 days.

The Constitution also provides for the establishment of an upper chamber (the Senate), to control the balance and regulation of power.

POLITICAL ORGANIZATIONS

Article 2 of the Constitution states that 'Political parties and associations contribute to the expression of universal suffrage. They are formed and exercise their activities freely, within the limits delineated by the laws and regulations. They must respect the principles of democracy, national sovereignty, public order and national unity'.

JUDICIAL POWER

The President guarantees the independence of the Judiciary and presides over the Conseil Supérieur de la Magistrature. Supreme judicial power is vested in the Supreme Court.

* A constitutional amendment, adopted by the legislature on 18 April 1997, extended the presidential term to seven years and provided for the creation of the post of Vice-President.

The Government

HEAD OF STATE

President: El Hadj OMAR (ALBERT-BERNARD) BONGO (took office 2 December 1967, elected 25 February 1973, re-elected December 1979, November 1986, December 1993 and December 1998).
Vice-President: DIDJOB DIVUNGUI-DI-N'DINGUE.

COUNCIL OF MINISTERS
(May 2001)

Prime Minister and Head of Government: JEAN-FRANÇOIS NTOU-TOUME EMANE.
Vice-Prime Minister, Minister of National Solidarity and Social Welfare: EMMANUEL ONDO-METHOGO.
Minister of State for Equipment and Construction: EGIDE BOUNDONO-SIMANGOYE.
Minister of State for Planning, Development and Territorial Administration: CASIMIR OYÉ MBA.
Minister of State for Foreign Affairs, Co-operation and Francophone Affairs: JEAN PING.
Minister of State for Communications, Posts and Information Technology: JEAN-RÉMY PENDY-BOUYIKI.

Minister of State for Labour, Employment and Professional Training: PAULETTE MISSAMBO.
Minister of State for the Interior, Security and Decentralization: ANTOINE MBOUMBOU MIYAKOU.
Minister of State for Housing, Urbanization and Cadastral Services: JACQUES ADIAHÉNOT.
Minister of Mining, Energy and Water Resources: PAUL TOUNGUI.
Minister of Justice, Guardian of the Seals: PASCAL DÉSIRÉ MISSONGO.
Minister of Water, Forestry, Fishing, Reafforestation and the Environment: RICHARD ONOUVIET.
Minister of Transport and Merchant Navy: Gen. IDRISS NGARI.
Minister of Trade and Industrial Development: ALFRED MABICKA.
Minister of National Education and Government Spokesperson: ANDRÉ MBA OBAME.
Minister of National Defence: ALI BONGO.
Minister of Economic Affairs, Finance, the Budget and Privatization: ÉMILE DOUMBA.
Minister of Higher Education, Research and Technology: ANDRÉ-DIEUDONNÉ BERRE.
Minister of Public Health and Population: FAUSTIN BOUKOUBI.
Minister of Agriculture, Livestock and Rural Development: FABIEN OWONO ESSONO.
Minister of Culture, the Arts, Popular Education, Youth and Sports: DANIEL ONA-ONDO.
Minister of Small- and Medium-sized Enterprises: PAUL BIYOGHÉ-MBA.
Minister of Family Affairs and Women: ANGELIQUE NGOMA.
Ministry of Tourism and Crafts: JEAN MASSIMA.

There were also eight Ministers-delegate.

MINISTRIES

Office of the Prime Minister: BP 546, Libreville; tel. 77-89-81.
Ministry of Agriculture, Livestock and Rural Development: BP 551, Libreville; tel. 72-09-60.
Ministry of the Civil Service, Administrative Reform and Modernization of the State: BP 496, Libreville; tel. 76-38-86.
Ministry of Communications, Posts and Information Technology: Libreville.
Ministry of Culture, the Arts and Popular Education: BP 2280, Libreville; tel. 76-61-83.
Ministry of Economic Affairs, Finance, the Budget and Privatization: BP 165, Libreville; tel. 76-12-10; fax 76-59-74.
Ministry of Equipment and Construction: BP 49, Libreville; tel. 76-38-56; fax 74-80-92.
Ministry of Family Affairs and Women: BP 5684, Libreville; tel. 77-50-32.
Ministry of Foreign Affairs, Co-operation and Francophone Affairs: BP 2245, Libreville; tel. 73-94-65.
Ministry of Higher Education and Research Technology: BP 2217, Libreville; tel. 72-41-08.
Ministry of Housing, Urbanization and Cadastral Services: BP 512, Libreville; tel. 77-31-02.
Ministry of Human Rights and Relations with Constitutional Institutions: Libreville.
Ministry of the Interior, Security and Decentralization: BP 2110, Libreville; tel. 72-00-75.
Ministry of Justice: BP 547, Libreville; tel. 74-66-28; fax 72-33-84.
Ministry of Labour, Employment and Professional Training: BP 4577, Libreville; tel. 74-32-18.
Ministry of Mining and Energy: BP 576, Libreville; tel. 77-22-39.
Ministry of National Defence: BP 13493, Libreville; tel. 77-86-94.
Ministry of National Education: BP 6, Libreville; tel. 76-13-01; fax 74-14-48.
Ministry of National Solidarity and Social Welfare: Libreville.
Ministry of Planning, Development and Territorial Administration: Libreville.
Ministry of Public Health and Population: BP 50, Libreville; tel. 76-36-11.

Ministry of Small- and Medium-sized Enterprises: BP 3096, Libreville; tel. 74-59-21.

Ministry of Social Welfare: Libreville.

Ministry of Tourism and Crafts: BP 178, Libreville; tel. 76-34-62.

Ministry of Trade and Industrial Development: Libreville.

Ministry of Transport and Marine Resources: BP 803, Libreville; tel. 74-71-96; fax 77-33-31.

Ministry of Water, Forestry, Fishing and Reafforestation: BP 3974, Libreville; tel. 76-01-09; fax 76-61-83.

Ministry of Youth and Sports: BP 2150, Libreville; tel. 74-00-19; fax 74-65-89.

President and Legislature

PRESIDENT

Presidential Election, 6 December 1998

Candidate	% of votes
El Hadj OMAR (ALBERT-BERNARD) BONGO	66.55
PIERRE MAMBOUNDOU	16.54
Fr PAUL M'BA ABESSOLE	13.41
PIERRE-ANDRÉ KOMBILA	1.54
PIERRE-CLAVER MAGANGA MOUSSAVOU	0.99
Others	0.97
Total	**100.00**

ASSEMBLÉE NATIONALE

President: GUY NDZOUBA NDAMA.

Secretary-General: PIERRE NGUEMA-MVE.

General Election, 15 and 29 December 1996

Party	Seats
Parti démocratique gabonais (PDG)	84
Rassemblement national des bûcherons (RNB)*	7
Parti gabonais du progrès (PGP)	6
Independents	4
Cercle des libéraux réformateurs (CLR)	3
Union du peuple gabonais (UPG)	2
Union socialiste gabonais (USG)	2
Others	7
Total	**115†**

* Renamed Rassemblement pour le Gabon (RPG) in October 2000.

† Voting was unable to proceed normally in five constituencies, and results in a number of other constituencies were later annulled. Following subsequent by-elections, the PDG held 89 seats, the PGP nine and the RNB six.

SÉNAT

President: GEORGES RAWIRI.

Secretary-General: FÉLIX OWANSANGO DEACKEU.

Election, 26 January and 9 February 1997*

Party	Seats
Parti démocratique gabonais (PDG)	53
Rassemblement national des bûcherons (RNB)†	20
Independents	9
Parti gabonais du progrès (PGP)	4
Alliance démocratique et républicaine (ADERE)	3
Cercle des libéraux réformateurs (CLR)	1
Rassemblement pour la démocratie et le progrès (RDP)	1
Total	**91**

* Following the annulment of a number of results, the PDG gained a further five seats at by-elections held later in 1997.

† Renamed Rassemblement pour le Gabon (RPG) in October 2000.

Political Organizations

Alliance démocratique et républicaine (ADERE): Pres. MBOUMBOU NGOMA; Sec.-Gen. DIDJOB DIVUNGUI-DI-N'DINGUE.

Alliance des républicains pour le développement (ARD): f. 2001; Pres. MARIE-AUGUSTINE HOUANGNI AMBOUROUE.

Association pour le socialisme au Gabon (APSG): Pres. V. MAPANGOU MOUCANI MOUETSA.

Cercle des libéraux réformateurs (CLR): f. 1993 by breakaway faction of the PDG; Leader JEAN-BONIFACE ASSELE.

Cercle pour le renouveau et le progrès (CRP).

Congrès pour la démocratie et la justice (CDJ): Pres. JULES BOURDES OGOULIGUENDE.

Convention des forces du changement: f. 1993 as an informal alliance of eight opposition presidential candidates.

Coordination de l'opposition démocratique (COD): f. 1991 as an alliance of eight principal opposition parties; Chair. SÉBASTIEN MAMBOUNDOU MOUYAMA.

Forum africain pour la reconstruction (FAR): f. 1992; a factional alliance within the COD; Leader Prof. LÉON MBOU-YEMBI; comprises three political parties:

> **Mouvement de redressement national (MORENA-originels):** f. 1981 in Paris, France; Leader (vacant).

> **Parti socialiste gabonais (PSG):** f. 1991; Leader Prof. LÉON MBOYEBI.

> **Union socialiste gabonais (USG):** Leader Dr SERGE MBA BEKALE.

Forum centriste de socialisme africain: f. 2000; Leader ANDRÉ EYEGHE.

Front national (FN): f. 1991; Leader MARTIN EFAYONG.

Front des parties du changement (FPC): f. 2000 as an alliance of four opposition parties to contest the 2001 legislative elections.

Gabon Avenir: f. 1999; Leader SYLVESTRE OYOUOMI.

Mouvement alternatif: f. 1996; Leader SÉBASTIEN MAMBOUNDOU MOUYAMA.

Mouvement pour la démocratie, le développement et la reconciliation nationale (Modern): Libreville; f. 1996; Leader GASTON MOZOGO OVONO.

Parti démocratique gabonais (PDG): BP 268, Libreville; tel. 70-31-21; fax 70-31-46; f. 1968; sole legal party 1968–90; Leader OMAR BONGO; Sec.-Gen. SIMPLICE GUEDET MANZELA.

Parti gabonais du centre indépendant (PGCI): Leader JEAN-PIERRE LEMBOUMBA LEPANDOU.

Parti gabonais du progrès (PGP): f. 1990; Pres. PIERRE-LOUIS AGONDJO-OKAWÉ; Sec.-Gen. ANSELME NZOGHE.

Parti des libéraux démocrates (PLD): Leader MARC SATURNIN NAN NGUEMA.

Parti social-démocrate (PSD): f. 1991; Leader PIERRE-CLAVER MAGANGA MOUSSAVOU.

Parti de l'unité du peuple gabonais (PUP): Libreville; f. 1991; Leader LOUIS GASTON MAYILA.

Rassemblement des démocrates (RD): f. 1993.

Rassemblement pour la démocratie et le progrès (RDP): Pres. PIERRE EMBONI.

Rassemblement pour le Gabon (RPG): f. 1990 as MORENA des bûcherons, renamed Rassemblement national des bûcherons in 1991, name changed as above in 2000; Leader Fr PAUL M'BA ABESSOLE; Sec.-Gen. Prof. VINCENT MOULENGUI BOUKOSSO.

Rassemblement des Gaullois: Libreville; f. 1994, registered 1998; 5,000 mems; Pres. MAX ANICET KOUMBA-MBADINGA.

Union pour la démocratie et le développement Mayumba (UDD).

Union démocratique et sociale (UDS): f. 1996; Leader HERVÉ ASSAMANET.

Union nationale pour la démocratie et le développement (UNDD): f. 1993; supports President Bongo.

Union du peuple gabonais (UPG): f. 1989 in Paris, France; Leader PIERRE MAMBOUNDOU.

Diplomatic Representation

EMBASSIES IN GABON

Algeria: BP 4008, Libreville; tel. 73-23-18; fax 73-14-03; e-mail ambalgabon@tiggabon.com; Ambassador: ABDELHAMID CHEBCHOUB.

Angola: BP 4884, Libreville; tel. 73-04-26; fax 73-76-24; Ambassador: BERNARDO DOMBELE M'BALA.

Argentina: BP 4065, Libreville; tel. 74-05-49; Ambassador: HUGO HURTUBEI.

Belgium: BP 4079, Libreville; tel. 73-29-92; Ambassador: VICTOR WEI.

Bénin: BP 3851, Akebe, Libreville; tel. 73-76-82; fax 73-77-75; Ambassador: TIMOTHÉE ADANLIN.

Brazil: BP 3899, Libreville; tel. 76-05-35; fax 74-03-43; e-mail emblibreville@inet.ga; Ambassador: SERGIO SEABRA DE NORONAHA.

Cameroon: BP 14001, Libreville; tel. 73-28-00; Ambassador: JEAN KOE NTONGA.

Canada: BP 4037, Libreville; tel. 74-34-64; fax 74-34-66; e-mail lbrve@dfait-maeci.gc.ca; Ambassador: ROBERT NOBLE.

Central African Republic: Libreville; tel. 72-12-28; Ambassador: FRANÇOIS DIALLO.

China, People's Republic: BP 3914, Libreville; tel. 74-32-07; Ambassador: GUO TIANMIN.

Congo, Democratic Republic: BP 2257, Libreville; tel. 74-32-53; Ambassador: KABANGI KAUMBU BULA.

Congo, Republic: BP 269, Libreville; tel. 73-29-06; Ambassador: PIERRE OBOU.

Côte d'Ivoire: BP 3861, Libreville; tel. 73-82-68; Ambassador: GÉORGES GOHO BAH.

Egypt: BP 4240, Libreville; tel. 73-25-38; fax 73-25-19; Ambassador: SIHAM SALEM RAHMY MOKHTAR.

Equatorial Guinea: BP 1462, Libreville; tel. 75-10-56; Ambassador: CRISANTOS NDONGO ABA MESSIAN.

France: blvd de l'Indépendance, BP 2125, Libreville; tel. 76-10-56; fax 74-48-78; e-mail ambafran@inet.ga; internet www.chez.com/ambafrangabon; Ambassador: PHILIPPE SELZ.

Germany: blvd de l'Indépendance, BP 299, Libreville; tel. 76-01-88; fax 72-40-12; e-mail amb-allegmagne@inet.ga; Ambassador: ADALBERT RITTMÜLLER.

Guinea: BP 4046, Libreville; tel. 73-85-09; Ambassador: MOHAMED SAMPIL.

Holy See: blvd Monseigneur Bessieux, BP 1322, Libreville (Apostolic Nunciature); tel. 74-45-41; Apostolic Nuncio: Most Rev. MARIO ROBERTO CASSARI, Titular Archbishop of Tronto.

Iran: BP 2158, Libreville; tel. 73-05-33; Ambassador: AHMAD SOBHAM.

Italy: Immeuble Personnaz et Gardin, rue de la Mairie, BP 2251, Libreville; tel. 74-28-92; fax 74-80-35; e-mail ambiasciata-italia@internetgabon.com; Ambassador: LUDOVICO TASSONI ESTENSE DE CASTELVECCHIO.

Japan: BP 3341, Libreville; tel. 73-22-97; fax 73-60-60; Ambassador: ASAHI HIDEKI.

Korea, Republic: BP 2620, Libreville; tel. 73-40-00; fax 73-00-79; Ambassador: OH SANG-SHIK.

Lebanon: BP 3341, Libreville; tel. 73-96-45; Ambassador: CHARAMY HABIB AYOUB.

Mauritania: BP 3917, Libreville; tel. 74-31-65; Ambassador: El Hadj THIAM.

Morocco: BP 3983, Libreville; tel. 77-41-51; fax 77-41-50; Ambassador: MOHAMED GHALI TAZI.

Nigeria: BP 1191, Libreville; tel. 73-22-03; Ambassador: IGNATIUS HEKAIRE AJURU.

Philippines: BP 1198, Libreville; tel. 72-34-80; Chargé d'affaires a.i.: ARCADIO HERRERA.

Russia: BP 3963, Libreville; tel. 72-48-68; fax 72-48-70; Ambassador: USEVOLD SOUKHOV.

São Tomé and Príncipe: BP 489, Libreville; tel. 72-09-94; Ambassador: URBINO JOSÉ GONHALVES BOTELÇO.

Senegal: BP 3856, Libreville; tel. 77-42-67; Ambassador: OUMAR WELE.

South Africa: Immeuble les Arcades, 142 rue des Chavannes, BP 4063, Libreville; tel. 77-45-30; fax 77-45-36; Ambassador: MONGEHI SAMUEL MONAISA.

Spain: Immeuble Diamant, blvd de l'Indépendance, BP 2105, Libreville; tel. 72-12-64; fax 74-88-73; Ambassador: DOMINGO DE SILOS MANSO GARCÍA.

Togo: BP 14160, Libreville; tel. 73-29-04; Ambassador: AHLONKO KOFFI AQUEREBURU.

Tunisia: BP 3844, Libreville; tel. 73-28-41; Ambassador: EZZEDINE KERKENI.

USA: blvd de la Mer, BP 4000, Libreville; tel. 76-20-03; fax 74-55-07; internet usembassy.state.gov/posts/gb1/wwwhmain.html; Ambassador: JAMES V. LEDESMA.

Venezuela: BP 3859, Libreville; tel. 73-31-18; fax 73-30-67; Ambassador: VÍCTOR CROQUER-VEGA.

Yugoslavia: Libreville; tel. 73-30-05; Ambassador: ČEDOMIR STRBAC.

Judicial System

Supreme Court: BP 1043, Libreville; tel. 72-17-00; three chambers: judicial, administrative and accounts; Pres. BENJAMIN PAMBOU-KOMBILA.

Constitutional Court: Libreville; tel. 72-57-17; fax 72-55-96; Pres. MARIE MADELEINE MBORANTSUO.

Courts of Appeal: Libreville and Franceville.

Court of State Security: Libreville; 13 mems; Pres. FLORENTIN ANGO.

Conseil Supérieur de la Magistrature: Libreville; Pres. El Hadj OMAR BONGO; Vice-Pres. Pres. of the Supreme Court (ex officio).

There are also Tribunaux de Première Instance (County Courts) at Libreville, Franceville, Port-Gentil, Lambaréné, Mouila, Oyem, Koula-Moutou, Makokou and Tchibanga.

Religion

About 60% of Gabon's population are Christians, mainly adherents of the Roman Catholic Church. About 40% are animists, and fewer than 1% are Muslims.

CHRISTIANITY
The Roman Catholic Church

Gabon comprises one archdiocese and three dioceses. At 31 December 1998 the estimated number of adherents in the country was equivalent to 50.4% of the total population.

Bishops' Conference: Conférence Episcopale du Gabon, BP 2146, Libreville; tel. 72-20-73; f. 1989; Pres. Most Rev. BASILE MVÉ ENGONE, Archbishop of Libreville.

Archbishop of Libreville: Most Rev. BASILE MVÉ ENGONE, Archevêché, Sainte-Marie, BP 2146, Libreville; tel. 72-20-73.

Protestant Churches

Christian and Missionary Alliance: active in the south of the country; 16,000 mems.

Eglise Evangélique du Gabon: BP 10080, Libreville; tel. 72-41-92; f. 1842; independent since 1961; 120,000 mems; Pres. Pastor SAMUEL NANG ESSONO; Sec. Rev. EMILE NTETOME.

The Evangelical Church of South Gabon and the Evangelical Pentecostal Church are also active in Gabon.

The Press

Afric'Sports: BP 3950, Libreville; tel. 76-24-74; monthly; sport; CEO SERGE ALFRED MPOUHO; Man. YVON PATRICE AUBIAN; circ. 5,000.

Le Bûcheron: BP 6424, Libreville; tel. 72-50-20; f. 1990; weekly; official publ. of the Rassemblement national des bûcherons; Editor DÉSIRÉ ENAME.

Bulletin Evangélique d'Information et de Presse: BP 80, Libreville; monthly; religious.

Bulletin Mensuel de Statistique de la République Gabonaise: BP 179, Libreville; monthly; publ. by Direction Générale de l'Economie.

La Cigale Enchantée: Libreville; bi-monthly; satirical.

L'Economiste Gabonais: BP 3906, Libreville; quarterly; publ. by the Centre gabonais du commerce extérieur.

Gabon d'Aujourd'hui: BP 750, Libreville; weekly; publ. of the Ministry of Culture, the Arts and Popular Education.

Gabon Libre: BP 6439, Libreville; tel. 72-42-22; weekly; Dir DZIME EKANG; Editor RENÉ NZOVI.

Gabon-Matin: BP 168, Libreville; daily; publ. by Agence Gabonaise de Presse; Man. HILARION VENDANY; circ. 18,000.

La Griffe: BP 4928, Libreville; tel. 74-73-45; f. 1990; weekly; independent; satirical; Editor-in-Chief RAPHAEL NTOUTOUME NKOGHE; Editor NDJOUMBA MOUSSOCK.

Journal Officiel de la République Gabonaise: BP 563, Libreville; f. 1959; fortnightly; Man. EMMANUEL OBAMÉ.

Ngondo: BP 168, Libreville; monthly; publ. by Agence Gabonaise de Presse.

Le Progressiste: blvd Léon-M'Ba, BP 7000, Libreville; tel. 74-54-01; f. 1990; Dir BENOÎT MOUITY NZAMBA; Editor JACQUES MOURENDE-TSIOBA.

La Relance: Libreville; tel. 70-31-66; weekly; publ. of the Parti démocratique gabonais; Pres. JACQUES ADIAHÉNOT; Dir RENÉ NDE-MEZO'O OBIANG.

Le Reveil: BP 20386, Libreville; tel. and fax 73-17-21; weekly; Man. ALBERT YANGARI; Editor RENÉ NZOVI; circ. 8,000.

La Tribune des Affaires: BP 2234, Libreville; tel. 72-20-64; fax 74-12-20; monthly; publ. of the Chambre de Commerce, d'Agriculture, d'Industrie et des Mines du Gabon.

La Voix du Peuple: BP 4049, Libreville; tel. 76-20-45; f. 1991; Publisher Parti de l'unité du peuple gabonais; weekly; Editor-in-Chief JEAN KOUMBA; Editor MAURIC-BLAISE NDZADIENGA MAYILA; circ. 4,000.

Sept Jours: BP 213, Libreville; weekly.

L'Union: Sonapresse, BP 3849, Libreville; tel. 73-58-61; fax 73-58-62; f. 1974; 75% state-owned; daily; official govt publ.; Man. Dir ALBERT YANGARI; Editor NGOYO MOUSSAVOU; circ. 20,000.

NEWS AGENCIES

Agence Gabonaise de Presse (AGP): BP 168, Libreville.

Association Professionnelle de la Presse Ecrite Gabonais (APPEG): BP 3849, Libreville; e-mail wmestre@gabon-presse.org.

BERP International: BP 8483, Libreville; tel. 33-80-16; fax 77-58-81; e-mail BERP8483@hotmail.com; f. 1995; Dir ANTOINE LAWSON.

Foreign Bureau

Agence France-Presse (AFP): Immeuble Sogapal, Les Filaos, BP 788, Libreville; tel. 76-14-36; fax 72-45-31; e-mail afp-libreville@tiggabon.com; Dir JEAN-PIERRE REJETE.

Publishers

Gabonaise d'Imprimerie (GABIMP): BP 154, Libreville; tel. 70-22-55; fax 70-31-85; f. 1973; Dir BÉATRICE CAILLOT.

Multipress Gabon: blvd Léon-M'Ba, BP 3875, Libreville; tel. 73-22-33; f. 1973; Chair. PAUL BORY.

Société Imprimerie de l'Ogooué (SIMO): BP 342, Port-Gentil; f. 1977; Man. Dir URBAIN NICOUE.

Société Nationale de Presse et d'Edition (SONAPRESSE): BP 3849, Libreville; tel. 73-21-84; f. 1975; Pres. and Man. Dir JOSEPH RENDJAMBE.

Broadcasting and Communications

TELECOMMUNICATIONS

Office des Postes et des Télécommunications (OPT): BP 2000, Libreville; tel. 78-70-05; fax 78-67-70; scheduled for privatization during 2001; Dir-Gen. THOMAS SOUAH.

Société des Télécommunications Internationales Gabonaises (TIG): BP 2261, Libreville; tel. 78-77-56; fax 74-19-09; f. 1971; cap. 3,000m. francs CFA; 61% state-owned; planning and devt of international telecommunications systems; Man. Dir A. N'GOUMA MWYUMALA.

Celtel Gabon, Libertis and Telecel Gabon operate mobile telecommunication services in Gabon.

BROADCASTING
Radio

The national network, 'La Voix de la Rénovation', and a provincial network broadcast for 24 hours each day in French and local languages.

Africa No. 1: BP 1, Libreville; tel. 76-00-01; fax 74-21-33; e-mail africa1@inet.ga; internet www.africa1.com; f. 1980; 35% state-controlled; international commercial radio station; daily programmes in French and English; Pres. LOUIS BARTHÉLEMY MAPANGOU; Sec.-Gen. MICHEL KOUMBANGOYE.

Radiodiffusion-Télévision Gabonaise (RTG): BP 150, Libreville; tel. 73-20-25; f. 1959; state-controlled; Dir-Gen. JOHN JOSEPH MBOUROU; Dir of Radio GILLES TERENCE NZOGHE.

Radio Fréquence 3: f. 1996.

Radio Génération Nouvelle: f. 1996; Dir JEAN-BONIFACE ASSELE.

Radio Mandarine: f. 1995.

Radio Soleil: f. 1995; affiliated to Rassemblement national des bûcherons.

Radio Unité: f. 1996.

Television

Radiodiffusion-Télévision Gabonaise (RTG): BP 150, Libreville; tel. 73-21-52; fax 73-21-53; f. 1959; state-controlled; Dir-Gen. JOHN JOSEPH MBOUROU; Dir of Television JULES CÉSAR LEKOGHO.

Télé-Africa: Libreville; tel. 76-20-33; private channel; daily broadcasts in French.

Télédiffusion du Gabon: f. 1995.

Finance

(cap. = capital; res = reserves; dep. = deposits; m. = million; brs = branches; amounts in francs CFA)

BANKING
Central Bank

Banque des Etats de l'Afrique Centrale (BEAC): BP 112, Libreville; tel. 76-13-52; fax 74-45-63; HQ in Yaoundé, Cameroon; f. 1973; bank of issue for mem. states of the Communauté économique et monétaire de l'Afrique centrale (CEMAC, fmrly Union douanière et économique de l'Afrique centrale), comprising Cameroon, the Central African Repub., Chad, the Repub. of the Congo, Equatorial Guinea and Gabon; cap. 45,000m., res 172,198m., total assets 1,407,908m. (Dec. 1999); Gov. JEAN-FÉLIX MAMALEPOT; Dir in Gabon PHILIBERT ANDZEMBE; 3 brs in Gabon.

Commercial Banks

Banque Internationale pour le Commerce et l'Industrie du Gabon, SA (BICIG): ave du Colonel Parant, BP 2241, Libreville; tel. 76-26-13; fax 74-64-10; e-mail bicigdoi@inet.ga; f. 1973; 27.7% state-owned; cap. 12,000m., res 32,614m., dep. 205,508m. (Dec. 1999); Pres. ETIENNE GUY MOUVAGHA TCHIOBA; 9 brs.

Banque Internationale pour le Gabon: Immeuble Concorde, blvd de l'Indépendance, BP 106, Libreville; tel. 76-26-26; fax 76-20-53.

BGFIBANK: BP 2253, Libreville; tel. 76-23-26; fax 74-08-94; e-mail bgfi@internetgabon.com; internet www.bgfi.com; f. 1972 as Banque Gabonaise et Française Internationale (BGFI); name changed as above in March 2000; 33.4% state-owned; cap. and res 23,706.5m., dep. 65,499.7m. (Dec. 1999); Chair. PATRICE OTHA; Dir-Gen. HENRI-CLAUDE OYIMA; 3 brs.

Crédit Foncier du Gabon: blvd de l'Indépendance, BP 3905, Libreville; tel. 72-47-45; fax 76-08-70; 90% state-owned; under enforced administration since June 1996; Interim Admin. FABIEN OVONO-NGOUA.

Union Gabonaise de Banque, SA (UGB): ave du Colonel Parant, BP 315, Libreville; tel. 77-70-00; fax 76-46-16; f. 1962; 25% state-owned; cap. 5,000m., res 9,359m., dep. 85,192m. (Dec. 1999); Chair. MARCEL DOUPAMBY-MATOKA; Pres. PIERRE-PARFAIT GONDJOUT; Man. Dir JEAN-CLAUDE DUBOIS; 6 brs.

Development Banks

Banque Gabonaise de Développement (BGD): rue Alfred Marche, BP 5, Libreville; tel. 76-24-29; fax 74-26-99; e-mail bdg@internetgabon.com; f. 1960; 69% state-owned; cap. 21,000.0m., res 5,859.3m., dep. 14,738.4m. (Dec. 1998); Pres. MICHEL ANCHOUEY; Chair. VICTOR AFENE; Dir-Gen. RICHARD ONOUVIET.

Banque Gabonaise et Française Internationale Participations: blvd de l'Indépendance, BP 2253, Libreville; tel. 76-23-26; fax 74-08-94; e-mail bgfi@internetgabon.com; internet www.bgfi.com; f. 1997; cap. 1,500m. (Dec. 1999); Dir-Gen. HENRI-CLAUDE OYIMA.

Banque Nationale de Crédit Rural (BNCR): ave Bouet, BP 1120, Libreville; tel. 72-47-42; fax 74-05-07; f. 1986; 74% state-owned; cap. 1,350m., total assets 6,885m. (Dec. 1998); Pres. GÉRARD MEYO M'EMANE; Man. Dir GEORGES ISSEMBE.

Société Nationale d'Investissement du Gabon (SONADIG): BP 479, Libreville; tel. 72-09-22; fax 74-81-70; f. 1968; state-owned; cap. 500m.; Pres. ANTOINE OYIEYE; Dir-Gen. MASSALA TSAMBA.

Financial Institution

Caisse Autonome d'Amortissement du Gabon: BP 912, Libreville; tel. 74-41-43; management of state funds; Dir-Gen. MAURICE EYAMBA TSIMAT.

INSURANCE

Agence Gabonaise d'Assurance et de Réassurance (AGAR): BP 1699, Libreville; tel. 74-02-22; fax 76-59-25; f. 1987; Man. Dir LOUIS GASTON MAYILA.

Assurances Générales Gabonaises (AGG): ave du Colonel Parant, BP 2148, Libreville; tel. 76-09-73; fax 76-57-41; f. 1974; Dir-Gen. ALAIN WELLER.

Assureurs Conseils Franco-Africains du Gabon (ACFRA-GABON): BP 1116, Libreville; tel. 72-32-83; Chair. FRÉDÉRIC MARRON; Dir M. GARNIER.

Assureurs Conseils Gabonais-Faugère et Jutheau & Cie: Immeuble Shell-Gabon, rue de la Mairie, BP 2138, Libreville; tel. 72-04-36; fax 76-04-39; represents foreign insurance cos; Dir GÉRARD MILAN.

Groupement Gabonais d'Assurances et de Réassurances (GGAR): Immeuble les Horizons, blvd Triomphal Omar Bongo, BP 3949, Libreville; tel. 74-28-72; f. 1985; Chair. RASSAGUIZA AKEREY; Dir-Gen. DENISE OMBAGHO.

Mutuelle Gabonaise d'Assurances: ave du Colonel Parant, BP 2225, Libreville; tel. 72-13-91; fax 76-47-49; Sec.-Gen. M. YENO-OLINGOT.

Omnium Gabonais d'Assurances et de Réassurances (OGAR): 546 blvd Triomphal Omar Bongo, BP 201, Libreville; tel. 76-15-96; fax 76-58-16; f. 1976; 10% state-owned; general; Pres. MARCEL DOUPAMBY-MATOKA; Man. Dir EDOUARD VALENTIN.

Société Nationale Gabonaise d'Assurances et de Réassurances (SONAGAR): ave du Colonel Parant, BP 3082, Libreville;

tel. 76-28-97; f. 1974; owned by l'Union des Assurances de Paris (France); Dir-Gen. JEAN-LOUIS MESSAN.

SOGERCO-Gabon: BP 2102, Libreville; tel. 76-09-34; f. 1975; general; Dir M. RABEAU.

L'Union des Assurances du Gabon (UAG): ave du Colonel Parant, BP 2141, Libreville; tel. 74-34-34; fax 74-14-53; f. 1976; Chair. ALBERT ALEWINA CHAVIOT; Dir EKOMIE AFENE.

Trade and Industry

GOVERNMENT AGENCY

Conseil Economique et Social de la République Gabonaise: BP 1075, Libreville; tel. 73-19-46; fax 73-19-44; comprises representatives from salaried workers, employers and Govt; commissions on economic, financial and social affairs and forestry and agriculture; Pres. LOUIS GASTON MAYILA.

DEVELOPMENT ORGANIZATIONS

Agence Française de Développement: BP 64, Libreville; tel. 74-33-74; fax 74-51-25; fmrly Caisse Française de Développement; Dir ANTOINE BAUX.

Agence Nationale de Promotion de la Petite et Moyenne Entreprise (PROMO-GABON): BP 3939, Libreville; tel. 74-31-16; f. 1964; state-controlled; promotes and assists small and medium-sized industries; Pres. SIMON BOULAMATARI; Man. Dir JEAN-FIDÈLE OTANDO.

Centre Gabonais de Commerce Extérieur (CGCE): BP 3906, Libreville; tel. 76-11-67; promotes foreign trade and investment in Gabon; Man. Dir MICHEL LESLIE TEALE.

Commerce et Développement (CODEV): BP 2142, Libreville; tel. 76-06-73; f. 1976; 95% state-owned, proposed transfer to private ownership announced 1986; import and distribution of capital goods and food products; Chair. and Man. Dir JÉRÔME NGOUA-BEKALE.

Mission Française de Coopération: BP 2105, Libreville; tel. 76-10-56; fax 74-55-33; administers bilateral aid from France; Dir JEAN-CLAUDE QUIRIN.

Office Gabonais d'Amélioration et de Production de Viande (OGAPROV): BP 245, Moanda; tel. 66-12-67; f. 1971; development of private cattle farming; manages ranch at Lekedi-Sud; Pres. PAUL KOUNDA KIKI; Dir-Gen. VINCENT EYI-NGUI.

Palmiers et Hévéas du Gabon (PALMEVEAS): BP 75, Libreville; f. 1956; state-owned; palm-oil development.

Société de Développement de l'Agriculture au Gabon (AGRO-GABON): BP 2248, Libreville; tel. 76-40-82; fax 76-44-72; f. 1976; 92% state-owned; Man. Dir ANDRÉ PAUL-APANDINA.

Société de Développement de l'Hévéaculture (HEVEGAB): BP 316, Libreville; tel. 72-08-29; fax 72-08-30; f. 1981; 99.9% state-owned; development of rubber plantations in the Mitzic, Bitam and Kango regions; Chair. FRANÇOIS OWONO-NGUEMA; Man. Dir RAYMOND NDONG-SIMA.

Société Gabonaise de Recherches et d'Exploitations Minières (SOGAREM): blvd de Nice, Libreville; state-owned; research and development of gold mining; Chair. ARSÈNE BOUNGUENZA; Man. Dir SERGE GASSITA.

Société Gabonaise de Recherches Pétrolières (GABOREP): BP 564, Libreville; tel. 75-06-40; fax 75-06-47; exploration and exploitation of hydrocarbons; Chair. HUBERT PERRODO; Man. Dir P. F. LECA.

Société Nationale de Développement des Cultures Industrielles (SONADECI): Libreville; tel. 76-33-97; f. 1978; state-owned; agricultural development; Chair. PAUL KOUNDA KIKI; Man. Dir GEORGES BEKALÉ.

CHAMBER OF COMMERCE

Chambre de Commerce, d'Agriculture, d'Industrie et des Mines du Gabon: BP 2234, Libreville; tel. 72-20-64; fax 74-12-20; f. 1935; regional offices at Port-Gentil and Franceville; Pres. JOACHIM BOUSSAMBA-MAPAGA; Sec.-Gen. DOMINIQUE MANDZA.

EMPLOYERS' ORGANIZATIONS

Confédération Patronale Gabonaise: BP 410, Libreville; tel. 76-02-43; fax 74-86-52; f. 1959; represents industrial, mining, petroleum, public works, forestry, banking, insurance, commercial and shipping interests; Pres. J. C. BALOCHE; Sec.-Gen. ERIC MESSERSCHMITT.

Conseil National du Patronat Gabonais (CNPG): Libreville; Pres. RAHANDI CHAMBRIER; Sec.-Gen. THOMAS FRANCK EYA'A.

Syndicat des Entreprises Minières du Gabon (SYNDIMINES): BP 260, Libreville; Pres. ANDRÉ BERRE; Sec.-Gen. SERGE GREGOIRE.

Syndicat des Importateurs Exportateurs du Gabon (SIMPEX): Libreville; Pres. ALBERT JEAN; Sec.-Gen. R. TYBERGHEIN.

Syndicat des Producteurs et Industriels du Bois du Gabon: BP 84, Libreville; tel. 72-26-11; fax 77-44-43; e-mail synfoga@inet.ga; Pres. HEIRIC CHENEAU.

Syndicat Professionnel des Usines de Sciages et Placages du Gabon: Port-Gentil; f. 1956; Pres. PIERRE BERRY.

Union des Représentations Automobiles et Industrielles (URAI): BP 1743, Libreville; Pres. M. MARTINENT; Sec. R. TYBERGHEIN.

Union Nationale du Patronat Syndical des Transports Urbains, Routiers et Fluviaux du Gabon (UNAPASYFTU-ROGA): BP 1025, Libreville; f. 1977; Pres. LAURENT BELLAL BIBANG-BI-EDZO; Sec.-Gen. MARTIN KOMBILA-MOMBO.

UTILITIES

Société d'Energie et d'Eau du Gabon (SEEG): BP 2082, Libreville; tel. 72-19-11; fax 76-11-34; f. 1950; 51% owned by Cie Générale des Eaux (France) and Electricity Supply Board International (Ireland); controls 35 electricity generation and distribution centres and 32 water production and distribution centres; Chair. of Bd FRANÇOIS OMBANDA.

TRADE UNIONS

Confédération Gabonaise des Syndicats Libres (CGSL): BP 8067, Libreville; tel. 77-37-82; fax 74-45-25; f. 1991; Sec.-Gen. FRANCIS MAYOMBO; 16,000 mems.

Confédération Syndicale Gabonaise (COSYGA): BP 14017, Libreville; f. 1969 by the Govt, as a specialized organ of the PDG, to organize and educate workers, to contribute to social peace and economic development, and to protect the rights of trade unions; Gen. Sec. MARTIN ALLINI.

Transport

RAILWAYS

The construction of the Transgabonais railway, which comprises a section running from Owendo (the port of Libreville) to Booué (340 km) and a second section from Booué to Franceville (357 km), was completed in 1986. By 1989 regular services were operating between Libreville and Franceville. Some 2m. metric tons of freight and 200,000 passengers were carried on the network in 1996. In 1998 the railways were transferred to private management.

Office du Chemin de Fer Transgabonais (OCTRA): BP 2198, Libreville; tel. 70-24-78; fax 70-20-38; f. 1972; management transferred to the private sector in late 1998; Dir-Gen. CÉLESTIN NDOLIA-NHAUD.

ROADS

In 1996 there were an estimated 7,670 km of roads, including 30 km of motorways, 3,780 km of main roads and 2,420 km of secondary roads; about 8.2% of the road network was paved.

INLAND WATERWAYS

The principal river is the Ogooué, navigable from Port-Gentil to Ndjolé (310 km) and serving the towns of Lambaréné, Ndjolé and Sindara.

Compagnie de Navigation Intérieure (CNI): BP 3982, Libreville; tel. 72-39-28; fax 74-04-11; f. 1978; state-owned; responsible for inland waterway transport; agencies at Port-Gentil, Mayumba and Lambaréné; Chair. JEAN-PIERRE MENGWANG ME NGYEMA; Dir-Gen. JEAN LOUIS POUNAH-NDJIMBI.

SHIPPING

The principal deep-water ports are Port-Gentil, which handles mainly petroleum exports, and Owendo, 15 km from Libreville, which services mainly barge traffic. The main ports for timber are at Owendo, Mayumba and Nyanga, and there is a fishing port at Libreville. The construction of a deep-water port at Mayumba is planned. A new terminal for the export of minerals, at Owendo, was opened in 1988. In 1998 the merchant shipping fleet had a total displacement of 26,532 grt. In 1997 the Islamic Development Bank granted a loan of 11,000m. francs CFA for the rehabilitation of Gabon's ports.

Compagnie de Manutention et de Chalandage d'Owendo (COMACO): BP 2131, Libreville; tel. 70-26-35; f. 1974; Pres. GEORGES RAWIRI; Dir in Libreville M. RAYMOND.

Office des Ports et Rades du Gabon (OPRAG): BP 1051, Libreville; tel. 70-00-48; fax 70-37-35; f. 1974; state-owned; national port authority; Pres. ALI BONGO; Dir-Gen. MARTIN LOURY.

SAGA Gabon: BP 518, Port-Gentil; tel. 55-54-00; fax 55-21-71; Chair. G. COGNON; Man. Dir J. C. SIMON.

Société Nationale d'Acconage et de Transit (SNAT): BP 3897, Libreville; tel. 70-04-04; fax 70-13-11; f. 1976; 51% state-owned; freight transport; Dir-Gen. GUSTAVE BONGO.

Société Nationale de Transports Maritimes (SONATRAM): BP 3841, Libreville; tel. 74-06-32; fax 74-59-67; f. 1976; relaunched 1995; 51% state-owned; river and ocean cargo transport; Man. Dir RAPHAEL MOARA WALLA.

Société du Port Minéralier d'Owendo: f. 1987; majority holding by Cie Minière de l'Ogooué; management of a terminal for minerals at Owendo.

SOCOPAO–Gabon: BP 4, Libreville; tel. 70-21-40; fax 70-02-76; f. 1983; freight transport and storage; Dir DANIEL BECQUERELLE.

CIVIL AVIATION

There are international airports at Libreville, Port-Gentil and Franceville, 65 other public and 50 private airfields linked mostly with the forestry and petroleum industries.

Air Affaires Gabon: BP 3962, Libreville; tel. 73-25-13; fax 73-49-98; f. 1975; domestic passenger chartered and scheduled flights; Chair. RAYMOND BELLANGER; Dir-Gen. DIEUDONNÉ MFOUBOU MOUD-HOUMA.

Air Service Gabon (ASG): BP 2232, Libreville; tel. 73-24-08; fax 73-60-69; f. 1965; charter flights; Chair. JEAN-LUC CHEVRIER; Gen. Man. FRANÇOIS LASCOMBES.

Compagnie Nationale Air Gabon: BP 2206, Libreville; tel. 73-00-27; fax 73-01-11; f. 1951 as Cie Aérienne Gabonaise; began operating international services in 1977, following Gabon's withdrawal from Air Afrique (see under Côte d'Ivoire); 80% state-owned; internal and international cargo and passenger services; Chair. MARTIN BONGO; Dir-Gen. RENÉ MORVAN.

Société de Gestion de l'Aéroport de Libreville (ADL): BP 363, Libreville; tel. 73-62-44; fax 73-61-28; e-mail adl@inet.ga; f. 1988; 26.5% state-owned; management of airport at Libreville; Pres. CHANTAL LIDJI BADINGA; Dir-Gen. PIERRE ANDRÉ COLLET.

Tourism

Tourist arrivals were estimated at 167,197 in 1997, and receipts from tourism totalled US $7m. in 1996. The tourism sector is being extensively developed, with new hotels and associated projects and the promotion of national parks. In 1996 there were 74 hotels, with a total of 4,000 rooms.

Centre Gabonais de Promotion Touristique (GABONTOUR): BP 2085, Libreville; tel. 72-85-04; fax 72-85-03; e-mail gabontour@ internetgabon.com; internet www.internetgabon.com; f. 1988; Dir-Gen. JOSEPH ADJEMBIMANDE.

Office National Gabonais du Tourisme: BP 161, Libreville; tel. 72-21-82.

THE GAMBIA

Introductory Survey

Location, Climate, Language, Religion, Flag, Capital

The Republic of The Gambia is a narrow territory around the River Gambia on the west coast of Africa. Apart from a short coastline on the Atlantic Ocean, the country is a semi-enclave in Senegal. The climate is tropical, with a rainy season from July to September. Away from the river swamps most of the terrain is covered by savannah bush. Average temperatures in Banjul range from 23°C (73°F) in January to 27°C (81°F) in July, while temperatures inland can exceed 40°C (104°F). English is the official language, while the principal vernacular languages are Mandinka, Fula and Wolof. About 85% of the inhabitants are Muslims; most of the remainder are Christians, and there are a small number of animists. The national flag (proportions 3 by 2) has red, blue and green horizontal stripes, with two narrow white stripes bordering the central blue band. The capital is Banjul.

Recent History

Formerly administered with Sierra Leone, The Gambia became a separate British colony in 1888. Party politics rapidly gained momentum following the establishment of a universal adult franchise in 1960. Following legislative elections in May 1962, the leader of the People's Progressive Party (PPP), Dr (later Sir) Dawda Kairaba Jawara, became Premier. Full internal self-government followed in October 1963. On 18 February 1965 The Gambia became an independent country within the Commonwealth, with Jawara as Prime Minister. The country became a republic on 24 April 1970, whereupon Jawara took office as President. He was re-elected in 1972 and again in 1977, as a result of overwhelming PPP victories in legislative elections.

In July 1981 a coup was attempted while Jawara was visiting the United Kingdom. Left-wing rebels formed a National Revolutionary Council, and proclaimed their civilian leader, Kukoi Samba Sanyang, as Head of State. Under the terms of a mutual defence pact, Senegalese troops assisted in suppressing the rebellion. About 1,000 people were arrested and more than 60 people were subsequently sentenced to death, although no executions took place. A state of emergency remained in force until February 1985. All those convicted of involvement in the insurrection were released by early 1991.

The first presidential election by direct popular vote was held in May 1982. Jawara was re-elected, with 72% of the votes cast; he was opposed by the leader of the National Convention Party (NCP), Sherif Mustapha Dibba (who was in detention for his alleged involvement in the abortive coup). In the concurrent legislative elections the PPP won 27 of the 35 elective seats in the House of Representatives. At legislative elections in March 1987 the PPP took 31 of the 36 directly-elected seats in the House of Representatives: the NCP won the remaining five elective seats. In the presidential election Jawara was re-elected with 59% of the votes cast; Dibba (who had been acquitted and released from detention in June 1982) received 27% of the votes, and Assan Musa Camara, a former Vice-President who had recently formed the Gambian People's Party (GPP), won 14%. Rumours of financial impropriety, corruption and the abuse of power at ministerial level persisted throughout the decade, and apparently prompted the dismissal of at least four government members between 1984 and 1990.

Plans were announced in August 1981 for a confederation of The Gambia and Senegal, to be called Senegambia. The confederal agreement came into effect on 1 February 1982; a Confederal Council of Ministers, headed by President Abdou Diouf of Senegal (with President Jawara as his deputy), held its inaugural meeting in January 1983, as did a 60-member Confederal Assembly. Agreements followed on co-ordination of foreign policy, communications, defence and security, but Senegal was critical of Jawara's reluctance to proceed towards full economic and political integration. In August 1989 Diouf announced that Senegalese troops were to leave The Gambia, apparently in protest at a request by Jawara that The Gambia be accorded more power within the confederal structures. The confederation was dissolved in the following month, and a period of tension between the two countries followed: The Gambia alleged that the Senegalese authorities had introduced trade and travel restrictions, while Senegal accused The Gambia of harbouring rebels of the Mouvement des forces démocratiques de la Casamance (MFDC), an organization seeking independence for the Casamance region—which is virtually separated from the northern segment of Senegal by the enclave of The Gambia. In January 1991 the two countries signed an agreement of friendship and co-operation. However, relations were again strained in September 1993, when Senegal unilaterally closed the border, apparently in connection with anti-smuggling operations.

The Commander of the National Gendarmerie and Army resigned in June 1991, following a brief rebellion in Banjul by soldiers who were demanding the payment of overdue allowances. A Nigerian national was subsequently appointed Commander of the Gambian armed forces, and a defence co-operation agreement was signed by the two countries in early 1992. In March 1992 seven people were arrested following a government announcement that a Libyan-backed rebel force, led by Kukoi Samba Sanyang, was preparing to invade The Gambia.

Despite an earlier announcement that he would not be seeking a sixth presidential mandate, Jawara was re-elected in April 1992, receiving 58% of the votes cast. Dibba took 22% of the votes cast. In elections to the House of Representatives the PPP lost six seats but retained a clear majority, with 25 elected members. The NCP secured six seats, the GPP two and independent candidates the remaining three. In April 1993 the House of Representatives approved the abolition of the death penalty: although a total of 87 death sentences had been imposed (mostly in cases of high treason) since independence, only one execution had taken place.

On 22 July 1994 Jawara was deposed by a self-styled Armed Forces Provisional Ruling Council (AFPRC), a group of young army officers led by Lt (later Col) Yahya Jammeh, in an abrupt but bloodless coup. Jawara and members of his entourage, including several government ministers, left The Gambia aboard a US navy vessel. Jawara later took up permanent residence in the United Kingdom.

The five-member AFPRC suspended the Constitution and banned all political activity. The new regime undertook to eliminate the institutionalized corruption that it claimed had been fostered under Jawara, pledging a return to civilian rule once this had been accomplished, and also promised to recover state funds allegedly misappropriated by former public officials. Jammeh officially pronounced himself Head of State, and appointed a mixed civilian and military Government. Members of Jawara's Government who had been arrested following the coup were released shortly afterwards. Purges of the armed forces and public institutions were implemented, and in November 1994 it was announced that 10 of Jawara's former ministers would be tried on charges of corruption.

The AFPRC's timetable for a transition to civilian rule, published in October 1994, envisaged a programme of reform culminating in the inauguration of new elected institutions, of what was to be designated the Second Republic, in December 1998. The length of the transition period prompted criticism both internationally and domestically. In November it was revealed that a coup attempt, involving military officers who were said by the AFPRC to wish to install an entirely military regime, had been foiled. Some 50 soldiers, including the coup leaders, were reported to have been killed during the attempt and its suppression, and several arrests were made. Later in the month some of the police and army officers who had been detained since July were released.

At the end of November 1994 Jammeh commissioned a National Consultative Committee (NCC) to make recommendations regarding a possible shortening of the period of transition to civilian rule. In January 1995 two members of the AFPRC (the Vice-President, Sana Sabally, and Sadibou Hydara, the Minister of the Interior), both of whom were said to be opposed to the NCC's recommendations for a curtailment of the transition period (the Committee proposed a return to civilian government in July 1996), were arrested, following an alleged attempt to seize power. In December Sabally was sentenced by court martial to nine years' imprisonment for plotting to overthrow Jammeh; Hydara was reported to have died of natural causes while in detention. Meanwhile, Fafa Idriss M'bai, a principal instigator of the NCC, was dismissed from the Government in March 1995, and was subsequently arrested and charged with corruption.

The death penalty was restored by government decree in August 1995, reportedly in response to a recent increase in the murder rate. In October Capt. Ebou Jallow, since January the official spokesman of the AFPRC, sought asylum in Senegal, accusing Jammeh's regime of complicity in murder and arbitrary arrests. For its part, the AFPRC asserted that Jallow had embezzled government funds prior to his departure and that he was conspiring with Jawara. In January 1998 a Swiss court ordered the return of US $3m. that Jallow had transferred from the Central Bank of The Gambia to a personal bank account in Geneva.

In November 1995 a government decree was issued conferring wide powers of arrest and detention on the Minister of the Interior: under its terms, the police were authorized to detain without trial for a period of up to three months any person considered to be a threat to state security. In January 1996 Jawara was charged *in absentia* with embezzlement, following investigations into the alleged diversion of proceeds from the sale of petroleum donated by Nigeria. In subsequent months the confiscation was ordered of the assets in The Gambia of Jawara and 11 former government members. In July the Minister of Health and Social Welfare was arrested and charged with the misappropriation of state funds.

Although the AFPRC stated its commitment to freedom of expression, a ban on the publication of journals by political organizations was introduced shortly after the July 1994 coup. The alleged harassment of journalists in The Gambia provoked considerable international concern, as there were periodic incidents of the arrest of, or fines against, journalists, while several non-Gambian journalists were deported.

A Constitutional Review Commission was inaugurated in April 1995, and submitted its recommendations to Jammeh in November; the draft was published in March 1996. Despite demands by the European Union (EU) and the Commonwealth, as well as by individual countries that had previously been major donors to The Gambia (most notably the United Kingdom and the USA), for an early return to civilian rule, the AFPRC continued to assert that it would adhere to its revised timetable. In April it was announced that it would be impossible to complete the return to elected civilian government by July, and in May new dates were set for the presidential and legislative elections, which would now take place in September and December, respectively. The draft Constitution was to be submitted to a national referendum in August. Opponents of the AFPRC criticized provisions of the Constitution that, they alleged, had been formulated with the specific intention of facilitating Jammeh's election to the presidency (although the Head of State had frequently asserted that he would not seek election) and of giving political advantage to his supporters.

The constitutional referendum took place on 8 August 1996. The rate of participation was high (85.9%), and 70.4% of voters endorsed the new document. A presidential decree was issued in the following week reauthorizing party political activity. Shortly afterwards, however, a further decree (Decree 89) was promulgated, according to which all holders of executive office in the 30 years prior to July 1994 were to be prohibited from seeking public office, with the PPP, the NCP and the GPP barred from contesting the forthcoming presidential and parliamentary elections. Thus, the only parties from the Jawara era authorized to contest the elections were the People's Democratic Organization for Independence and Socialism (PDOIS) and the People's Democratic Party (PDP). The effective ban on the participation of all those associated with political life prior to the military takeover in the restoration of elected institutions was strongly criticized by the Commonwealth and its Ministerial Action Group on the Harare Declaration (CMAG, see p. 151), which had hitherto made a significant contribution to the transition process. At the same time the AFPRC announced that, following consultations between the military authorities and the Provisional Independent Electoral Commission (PIEC), which had expressed concern that newly-authorized political organizations would have insufficient time to campaign for the elections, the presidential poll was to be postponed by two weeks, to 26 September 1996.

Jammeh formally announced his intention to contest the presidency in mid-August 1996. At the end of the month the establishment of a political party supporting Jammeh, the Alliance for Patriotic Reorientation and Construction (APRC), was reported. In early September Jammeh resigned from the army, in order to contest the presidency as a civilian, as required by the Constitution. The presidential election proceeded, as scheduled, on 26 September. Three people were reportedly killed, and more than 30 injured, in violence shortly before the poll. According to official results, issued by the PIEC, Jammeh secured the presidency, with 55.77% of the total votes cast, ahead of Ousainou Darboe, the leader of the United Democratic Party (UDP), who received 35.84% of votes cast. Darboe sought refuge for several days in the residence of the Senegalese ambassador. The rate of participation by voters was again high, especially in rural areas. However, observers, including CMAG, expressed doubts as to the credibility of the election results. The dissolution of the AFPRC was announced the same day. Jammeh was inaugurated as President on 18 October. In November an unconditional amnesty was extended to more than 40 political detainees, among them former government ministers detained since July 1994.

In November 1996 an attack on an army camp at Farafenni, 100 km east of Banjul, resulted in the deaths of six people. Shortly afterwards the legislative elections, due to take place on 11 December, were postponed until 2 January 1997. All the registered parties presented candidates for the 45 elective seats in the new National Assembly. Voting took place as scheduled, and the Gambian authorities, opposition groups and most international observers expressed broad satisfaction at the conduct of the poll. (The Commonwealth did not send observers, owing to the continued ban on former members of Jawara's administration from seeking public office.) As expected, the APRC won an overwhelming majority of seats. The final results, as issued by the PIEC, allocated 28 seats to Jammeh's party (additionally, the APRC had been unopposed in five constituencies), seven to the UDP, two to the National Reconciliation Party and one to the PDOIS; independent candidates took the two remaining seats. The overall rate of participation by voters (again higher in rural areas) was 73.2%. As Head of State, Jammeh was empowered by the Constitution to nominate four additional members of parliament, from whom the Speaker (and Deputy Speaker) would be chosen. The opening session of the National Assembly, on 16 January, accordingly elected Mustapha Wadda, previously Secretary-General of the APRC and Secretary at the Presidency, as Speaker. This session denoted the full entry into force of the Constitution and thus the inauguration of the Second Republic.

Under the new Constitution government ministers of cabinet rank were designated Secretaries of State, and the Government was reorganized to this effect in March 1997. Isatou Njie-Saidy, Secretary of State for Health, Social Welfare and Women's Affairs, was appointed Vice-President. However, most of the responsibilities hitherto associated with this post were transferred to the Secretary of State for the Office of the President, a position now held by Edward Singhateh: although Singhateh had succeeded Sabally as AFPRC Vice-President in early 1995, he was, under the terms of the new Constitution, too young (at 27 years of age) to assume the office of Vice-President. In April 1997 civilian appointees, including Jawara's former head of police, replaced the remaining four military regional governors.

Supporters of the new regime attributed the electoral success of Jammeh and the APRC to the popularity within The Gambia of the ambitious infrastructural projects undertaken since July 1994, citing in particular the construction of more new schools and hospitals than had been built in 30 years by the Jawara administration, as well as a new airport terminal and modernized port facilities, a television station, and plans for a national university. However, Jammeh's critics condemned what they regarded as excessive expenditure on 'prestige' projects.

In February 1997 CMAG reiterated its earlier concerns regarding the implications of Decree 89, and in July again urged the immediate removal of the ban on political activities by those connected with the Jawara administration. Additionally, CMAG appealed to the Government to investigate allegations of the harassment of opposition activists. In September, none the less, CMAG reported signs of progress in the democratization process.

In April 1997 the trial began (in camera) of five alleged mercenaries suspected of involvement in the November 1996 attack on the Farafenni barracks. The accused apparently confirmed reports that they had formed part of a 40-strong commando group, trained in Libya and led by Kukoi Samba Sanyang, which had fought for Charles Taylor's National Patriotic Front of Liberia during the early 1990s. Four of the accused (three Gambians and one Senegalese national) were subsequently sentenced to death on charges of treason; the fifth defendant had died in detention in May 1997. In October, however, the Supreme Court ruled that the convictions, were unsustainable, and ordered that the four be retried on conspiracy charges. Meanwhile, the arrest of a further mercenary had been reported in April; some 13 other suspects remained at large.

In September 1997 members of the Pakistani Ahmadi Islamic sect left The Gambia (where they had been working for more than 20 years), accusing the Secretary of State for the Interior and Religious Affairs, Momodou Bojang, of fomenting religious intolerance by describing the sect as 'infidels' and by allowing Gambian Islamic leaders to deliver sermons hostile to the Ahmadi. Responsibility for religious affairs was transferred to the Secretary of State for Youth and Sports in the following month.

In February 1998 the director and a journalist of a private radio station, Citizen FM, were detained, and the Government ordered the closure of the station and an associated newspaper, *New Citizen*, citing the station's failure to comply with new tax requirements for independent broadcasters (taxes had been doubled). However, opponents of the closure noted that the station had recently broadcast information concerning the National Intelligence Agency. The director of Citizen FM, Baboucar Gaye, subsequently launched a legal appeal against the closure of the station, and, following several adjournments, accused the Government of employing delaying tactics. Further concern about press freedom arose in May 1999, when the *Daily Observer*, the only remaining newspaper that openly criticized the Government, was purchased by Amadou Samba, a businessman closely associated with Jammeh. Despite Samba's assurances that he would not interfere in editorial matters, staff who had criticized the Government were subsequently removed from their posts. In July *The Independent*, a privately-owned newspaper, which had recently been launched, was ordered to suspend publication because of alleged irregularities in its registration. It was, however, claimed that the Government had ordered the suspension following the publication of an article which repeated accusations, made by the UDP, of widespread corruption in the Jammeh regime.

Opposition activists continued to allege harassment by the Government throughout 1998 and early 1999. In May 1998 nine people were arrested in a raid on the mosque at Brikama; among those detained was Lamine Wa Juwara, a prominent critic of Jammeh. A member of the UDP, Juwara was involved in a lawsuit seeking compensation for alleged wrongful imprisonment for 20 months without charge following the 1994 coup. The UDP leader, Ousainou Darboe, was also briefly imprisoned. In July Juwara was forcibly removed from a seminar on government structures, conducted under the auspices of the Department of State for Local Government and Lands, by APRC militants. The Government accused Juwara of fomenting unrest; meanwhile, critics claimed that the activities of APRC's so-called 'Action Group' were officially condoned. At the end of July Juwara's claim for damages was rejected by the Supreme Court on the grounds that a clause in the Constitution granted immunity to the former AFPRC in connection with the transition period. In May 1999 the leader of the youth wing of the UDP, Momodou Shyngle Nyassi, was reportedly abducted by the security forces and subjected to ill-treatment. He was released without charge after nearly a month, following the intervention of the Gambian High Court and diplomatic pressure from the EU.

In January 1999 four cabinet members were dismissed, as was the Managing Director of the National Water and Electricity Company, amid allegations that financial mismanagement had occurred in certain government departments.

In early January 2000 allegations of government corruption emerged after the disclosure in legal proceedings in the United Kingdom that significant sums of money generated by the sale of crude petroleum had been paid into an anonymous Swiss bank account. The crude petroleum had been granted to The Gambia for trading purposes by the Nigerian Government between August 1996 and June 1998, reportedly in recognition of Jammeh's opposition in 1995 to the imposition of sanctions by the Commonwealth against Nigeria. Jammeh vigorously

denied any involvement in the matter. In mid-January Jammeh effected a minor cabinet reshuffle, appointing Hassan Sallah as Secretary of State for Agriculture to replace Abdoulie Sallah, who was assigned the health and social welfare portfolios, which had previously been the responsibility of the Vice-President.

On 15 January 2000 the security forces announced that they had forestalled an attempted military coup. It was reported that during efforts to arrest the conspirators a lieutenant in the State Guard had been killed and the Commander of the State Guard, Lt Landing Sanneh, the officer in charge of security at the presidential palace, had been wounded. Another member of the State Guard was killed on the following day while attempting to evade arrest. The Secretary of State for the Interior, Ousman Badjie, strenuously denied rumours that the authorities had invented the conspiracy as a pretext to purge the State Guard and as a means of diverting press attention from the petroleum scandal, and opposition demands that the Government produce evidence of the existence of the plot were rejected. (In February 2001 Sanneh was acquitted of charges of treason, but was immediately rearrested and was expected to be tried by a court martial.)

In March 2000 it was announced that municipal and rural elections were to be held in November, while presidential elections were to be held in October 2001. In late March Col (retd) Sam Sillah, who henceforth was expected to contest the presidential elections of 2001, was appointed President of the UDP.

In April 2000 student demonstrations in Banjul, Brikama and Serrekunda degenerated into serious disturbances, during which police and fire stations were burned down. The protests occurred in response to the death of a student, who had been found, apparently after having been tortured, in firemen's barracks, and to the alleged rape of a schoolgirl by an officer of the security forces. Following the intervention of the security forces, 14 people were killed and 30 were injured. The authorities initially denied that the security forces had fired on the crowd, suggesting that the demonstrators had included foreigners and armed bandits. However, it later became apparent that the security forces had in fact used live ammunition against the demonstrators. In May Jammeh assured the UN Secretary-General, Kofi Annan, who was visiting The Gambia, that those responsible for the deaths would be brought to justice, and called for co-operation with a commission of inquiry that had been established to investigate the disturbances.

Also in May 2000, amid allegations that he had accepted bribes, Capt. (retd) Lamin Bajo was dismissed as Secretary of State for Local Government, Lands and Religious Affairs. In June it was announced that the UDP leader, Darboe, had been arrested and accused, along with 80 of his supporters, of murdering an APRC activist.

In July 2000 the Supreme Court finally upheld Baboucar Gaye's appeal against the closure of Citizen FM in February 1998 and ordered that Gaye's confiscated broadcasting equipment be returned to him; the radio station was re-opened later in the year. However, an arson attack in the following month on the premises of another independent radio station, Radio 1 FM, was widely believed to be linked to a critical interview, recently broadcast on the station, with the President's Director of Press and Public Relations.

In August 2000 the APRC suggested that it would not be possible to hold local government elections in November as scheduled, as the National Assembly had yet to approve the local government act, which was intended to regulate voter registration and electoral boundaries. A major cabinet reshuffle also took place in August. Changes included the appointment as Secretary of State for Fisheries and Natural Resources of Susan Waafa-Ogoo, who was replaced as Secretary of State for Tourism and Culture by Yankuba Touray, hitherto Secretary of State for Youth and Sports. Edward Singhateh remained in his position as Secretary of State for Presidential Affairs, and also took on responsibility for works, communications and information.

In December 2000, with a revised schedule for the postponed municipal elections yet to be announced, Jammeh dismissed Anglican Bishop Solomon Tilewa Johnson from his position as Chairman of the Independent Electoral Commission (IEC), stating his incompetence for the post. Johnson's predecessor, Gabriel Roberts, was reappointed, despite allegations that he had been involved in fraudulent behaviour to benefit the APRC at the parliamentary and presidential elections of 1996. The dismissal of Johnson, which the opposition described as unconstitutional, followed his instigation of a court case in response to the Government's failure to enact the local government act, as a result of which the municipal elections had been postponed.

In January 2001 the commission of inquiry into the student unrest of the April 2000 published its report. The Government rejected the commission's recommendation that the Secretary of State for the Interior, Badjie, and senior police officials should accept responsibility for the disturbances. Shortly afterwards Pap Cheyassin Secka was dismissed as Secretary of State for Justice and Attorney-General and replaced by Joseph Henry Joof. Secka's dismissal was widely welcomed by opposition members, who claimed that he had increased political interference in the judiciary, particularly regarding the findings of the commission of inquiry, and also emphasized his role in justifying Johnson's removal from the IEC.

In February 2001 the IEC proposed a new code of practice for election campaigns, including the regulation of the amount of broadcast time allocated to parties and the prohibition of campaigning for more than one party to occur in any one location simultaneously. The code of practice, which was not to be legally enforceable, was condemned by representatives of the media and opposition groups.

In February 2001 Jammeh assured the Secretary-General of the Commonwealth, Don McKinnon, that Decree 89 would be repealed in the near future, although domestic political discourse appeared to indicate that this was not regarded as a priority by the Government. Omar Jallow, a government minister under Jawara, announced that he had filed a lawsuit at the Court of Appeal challenging the validity of Decree 89, after the High Court had declared in 2000 that it lacked the authority to hear the case. In March 2001 it was reported that the Government intended to propose a constitutional amendment extending the presidential term from five to seven years.

In the months that followed the 1994 coup The Gambia's traditional aid donors and trading partners suspended much co-operation (although vital aid projects generally continued). The Jammeh administration therefore sought new links: diplomatic relations with Libya, severed in 1980, were restored in November 1994 and numerous co-operation agreements ensued. Links with Taiwan, ended in 1974, were also re-established in July 1995, whereupon Taiwan became one of the Gambia's major sources of funding. In November 1999 Jammeh visited Teheran in order to establish closer bilateral relations between The Gambia and Iran.

Despite the presence in Senegal of prominent opponents of his Government, Jammeh also sought to improve relations with that country, and in January 1996 the two countries signed an agreement aimed at increasing bilateral trade and at minimizing cross-border smuggling. A further agreement, concluded in April 1997, was designed to facilitate the trans-border movement of goods destined for re-export. In June the two countries agreed to take joint measures to combat insecurity, illegal immigration, arms-trafficking and drugs-smuggling. In January 1998 the Government of Senegal welcomed an offer by Jammeh to mediate in the conflict in the southern province of Casamance: the separatist MFDC is chiefly composed of the Diola ethnic group, of which Jammeh is a member. In June 2000 the Gambian Government refuted opposition allegations that it was involved in arms-trafficking to the separatists, and in December sent a delegation to participate in talks between the MFDC and the Senegalese Government. In June 1998 Jammeh offered to mediate in the conflict between the Government and rebel forces in Guinea-Bissau (q.v.); the rebel leader, Brig. Ansumane Manè, was a Diola of Gambian extraction. In January 1999 The Gambia agreed to provide troops for an ECOMOG (see Economic Community of West African States, p. 172) peace-keeping mission in Guinea-Bissau. After the defeat of government forces in Guinea-Bissau in May 1999, the Gambian authorities secured in June the safe passage of former President Vieira to The Gambia on medical grounds, from where he departed for Portugal. In late June the interim President of Guinea-Bissau, Malam Bacai Sanha, visited Jammeh to thank him for his intervention; both Presidents expressed their desire to co-operate to attain a lasting peace in the region, and a joint communiqué to that effect was signed in April 2000. The killing of Manè in December 2000 was widely regarded as a serious setback for Gambian foreign policy. In January 2001 the Gambian Government denied that it was implicated, as stated in a UN report, in the illicit trafficking of diamonds to benefit dissident groups in Angola and Sierra Leone.

Government

The Constitution of the Second Republic of The Gambia, which was approved in a national referendum on 8 August 1996, entered into full effect on 16 January 1997. Under its terms, the Head of State is the President of the Republic, who is directly elected by universal adult suffrage (the minimum age for voters is 18 years). No restriction is placed on the number of times a President may seek re-election. Legislative authority is vested in the National Assembly, comprising 45 members elected by direct suffrage and four members nominated by the President of the Republic. The President appoints government members, who are responsible both to the Head of State and to the National Assembly.

Defence

In August 2000 the Gambian National Army comprised 800 men (including a marine unit of about 70 and a presidential guard) in active service. Military service has been mainly voluntary; however, the Constitution of the Second Republic, which entered into full effect in January 1997, makes provision for compulsory service. The defence budget for 2000 was estimated at D190m.

Economic Affairs

In 1998, according to estimates by the World Bank, The Gambia's gross national product (GNP), measured at average 1996–98 prices, was US $408m., equivalent to $340 per head (or $1,428 on an international purchasing-power parity basis). During 1990–98, it was estimated, GNP per head declined, in real terms, at an average annual rate of 0.5%. During the same period the population increased at an average annual rate of 4.0%. GNP in 1999 was estimated at $430m. ($340 per head). During 1990/91–1999 (financial years, until 1997, ending 30 June), according to data published by the IMF, The Gambia's gross domestic product (GDP) increased, in real terms, at an average annual rate of an estimated 3.1%. Real GDP increased by an estimated 4.9% in 1998, and by an estimated 5.6% in 1999.

Agriculture (including forestry and fishing) contributed an estimated 33.3% of GDP in 1999. About 79.2% of the labour force were employed in the sector in that year. The dominant agricultural activity is the cultivation of groundnuts. Exports of groundnuts and related products accounted for an estimated 68.2% of domestic export earnings in 1999; however, a significant proportion of the crop is frequently smuggled for sale in Senegal. Cotton, citrus fruits, mangoes, avocados and sesame seed are also cultivated for export. The principal staple crops are rice, millet, sorghum and maize, although The Gambia remains heavily dependent on imports of rice and other basic foodstuffs. Fishing makes an important contribution both to the domestic food supply and to export earnings: exports of fish and fish products contributed an estimated 13.6% of the value of domestic exports in 1998. Agricultural GDP increased at an estimated average annual rate of 4.0% in 1990/91–1999; the sector's GDP increased by an estimated 8.0% in 1998, and by an estimated 17.5% in 1999, largely reflecting a sharp increase in the groundnut crop.

Industry (including manufacturing, construction, mining and power) contributed an estimated 12.6% of GDP in 1999. About 9.7% of the labour force were employed in the sector at the time of the 1993 census. Industrial GDP increased at an average annual rate of 1.1% in 1990/91–1999, with growth of an estimated 3.6% in 1999.

The Gambia has no economically viable mineral resources, although seismic surveys have indicated the existence of deposits of petroleum. Deposits of kaolin and salt are currently unexploited. Manufacturing contributed an estimated 5.3% of GDP in 1999, and employed about 6.3% of the labour force in 1993. The sector is dominated by agro-industrial activities, most importantly the processing of groundnuts and fish. Beverages and construction materials are also produced for the domestic market. Manufacturing GDP increased at an average annual rate of 1.1% in 1990/91–1999; the sector's GDP increased by an estimated 2.9% in 1999.

The Gambia is highly reliant on imported energy. According to figures published by the IMF, imports of petroleum products accounted for an estimated 8.5% of the value of imports for domestic use in 1998.

The services sector contributed an estimated 54.1% of GDP in 1999. The tourist industry is of particular significance as a generator of foreign exchange. Tourism contributed about 10% of annual GDP in the early 1990s, and employed about one-third of workers in the formal sector at that time. The international response to the 1994 coup and its aftermath had a severe impact on tourism to The Gambia, although the industry recovered strongly from 1996 onwards. The Jammeh administration has expressed its intention further to exploit the country's potential as a transit point for regional trade and also as a centre for regional finance and telecommunications. The GDP of the services sector increased at an average annual rate of 3.5% in 1990/91–1999; growth in 1999 was estimated at 4.3%.

In 1997 The Gambia recorded a visible trade deficit of US $87.48m., while there was a deficit of $23.56m. on the current account of the balance of payments. In 1999 the principal source of imports was Germany, which supplied an estimated 13.8% of total imports; other major sources were the United Kingdom, France, the People's Republic of China and Belgium. The two largest market for exports in that year were Belgium (an estimated 7.7% of total exports) and the United Kingdom. The Gambia's principal domestic exports in 1999 were groundnuts and related products, fish and fish products, and fruit and vegetables. The principal imports in that year were food and live animals, machinery and transport equipment, basic manufactures and mineral fuels and lubricants.

In 1999 there was an estimated overall budget deficit of D208.2m. (equivalent to 4.2% of that year's GDP). The Gambia's total external debt was US $477.0m. at the end of 1998, of which $451.3m. was long-term public debt. In that year the cost of debt-servicing was equivalent to 9.7% of the value of exports of goods and services. The average annual rate of inflation was 4.2% in 1991–98; consumer prices increased by an average of 1.1% in 1998 and by 3.8% in 1999. The rate of unemployment was estimated at some 26% of the labour force in mid-1994.

The Gambia is a member of the Economic Community of West African States (ECOWAS, see p. 170), of The Gambia River Basin Development Organization (OMVG, see p. 308), of the African Groundnut Council (see p. 303), of the West Africa Rice Development Association (WARDA, see p. 306), and of the Permanent Inter-State Committee on Drought Control in the Sahel (CILSS, see p. 309).

The military coup of July 1994 caused considerable economic disruption to The Gambia: the country's principal donors suspended much financial co-operation, while there was also a dramatic decline in both entrepôt trade and tourism. None the less, the Jammeh Government undertook numerous infrastructural projects, with the aim of strengthening and expanding the economy. A return to growth from 1995 was, in large part, underpinned by the recovery in the tourism sector. The installation of elected civilian institutions in early 1997 prompted a return to full support by the international economic community. The World Bank resumed co-operation in late 1997, and in mid-1998 the IMF approved a three-year Enhanced Structural Adjustment Facility (subsequently renamed the Poverty Reduction and Growth Facility, PRGF) to support the Government's economic programme for 1998–2000. The programme aimed to reduce the overall fiscal deficit from 4.5% in 1998 to 2.5% in 2000 (although this figure was subsequently revised to 3.5%), and to restrict average inflation to 2.5% per year. A further loan, worth US $13m., was approved in principle by the IMF, under the terms of the PRGF, in December 2000. In the same month it was announced that The Gambia was receive $91m. in debt-service relief over 15 years under the Heavily Indebted Poor Countries (HIPC) initiative. Investor confidence in The Gambia was weakened by the nationalization in early 1999 of the Gambia Groundnut Corporation. Proposed legislation submitted to the National Assembly in October 2000 envisaged the establishment of an agency to oversee the privatization programme. The Gambia's overriding dependence on the groundnut sector remains an obstacle to sustained growth. The sector lags behind others in terms of modernization and productivity, although the gradual introduction of reforms,

which sought to improve relations between public- and private-sector interests in the sector, commenced in 2000. Concern has also been expressed at the level of borrowing incurred by the Jammeh Government to finance its infrastructural programme; the level of The Gambia's international indebtedness has risen sharply since 1995.

Social Welfare

There were 128 government physicians working in The Gambia in 1997 (compared with 43 in 1980). In 1998 there were three referral hospitals, with the construction of a fourth planned, seven major and 12 minor health centres, and 17 dispensaries. In addition, there was a network of 177 maternity and child welfare clinics and 396 village health posts throughout the country in 1997. A major programme to improve health and social welfare facilities has been undertaken since 1994. In 1999 current expenditure by the central Government on health was estimated at D88.7m, equivalent to 13.9% of non-interest current spending. Estimated current spending by the central Government on social welfare in 1996/97 was D600,000, equivalent to less than 0.1% of current spending allocations.

Education

Primary education, beginning at seven years of age, is free but not compulsory and lasts for six years. Secondary education, from 13 years of age, comprises two cycles, each lasting three years. A revised education policy, to be implemented in 1998–2003, envisaged the merging of the first three-year cycle of secondary education with primary education to provide nine years of consolidated elementary education. In 1997 total enrolment at primary schools was equivalent to 73% of children in the relevant age-group (61% of girls), while the comparable ratio for secondary enrolment was only 19% (13% of girls). According to UNESCO estimates, adult illiteracy in 1995 averaged 69.1% (males 62.2%; females 75.6%). The Jammeh administration has, since 1994, embarked on an ambitious project to improve educational facilities and levels of attendance and attainment. A particular aim has been to ameliorate access to schools for pupils in rural areas. Post-secondary education is available in teacher training, agriculture, health and technical subjects. Some 1,591 students were enrolled at tertiary establishments in 1994/95. The University of The Gambia, at Banjul, was officially opened in 2000. In 1977 The Gambia introduced Koranic studies at all stages of education, and many children attend Koranic schools (daara). In 1999 current expenditure by the central Government on education was an estimated D146.0m., equivalent to 22.9% of non-interest current spending.

Public Holidays

2001: 1 January (New Year's Day), 18 February (Independence Day), 6 March* (Eid al-Kebir, Feast of the Sacrifice), 13 April (Good Friday), 1 May (Workers' Day), 4 June* (Eid al-Moulid, Birth of the Prophet), 22 July (Anniversary of the Second Republic), 15 August (Assumption/St Mary's Day), 17 December* (Eid al-Fitr, end of Ramadan), 25 December (Christmas).

2002: 1 January (New Year's Day), 18 February (Independence Day), 23 February* (Eid al-Kebir, Feast of the Sacrifice), 29 March (Good Friday), 1 May (Workers' Day), 24 May* (Eid al-Moulid, Birth of the Prophet), 22 July (Anniversary of the Second Republic), 15 August (Assumption/St Mary's Day), 6 December* (Eid al-Fitr, end of Ramadan), 25 December (Christmas).

* These holidays are dependent on the Islamic lunar calendar and may vary by one or two days from the dates given.

Weights and Measures

Imperial weights and measures are used. Importers and traders also use the metric system.

Statistical Survey

Source (unless otherwise stated): Department of Information, 14 Daniel Goddard St, Banjul; tel. 225060; fax 227230.

Area and Population

AREA, POPULATION AND DENSITY

Area (sq km)	11,295*
Population (census results)	
15 April 1983	
Total	687,817
15 April 1993	
Males	514,530
Females	511,337
Total	1,025,867
Population (UN estimates at mid-year)†	
1997	1,189,000
1998	1,229,000
1999	1,268,000
Density (per sq km) at mid-1999	112.3

* 4,361 sq miles.
† Source: UN, *World Population Prospects: The 1998 Revision.*

ETHNIC GROUPS

1993 census (percentages): Mandinka 39.60; Fula 18.83; Wollof 14.61; Jola 10.66; Serahule 8.92; Serere 2.77; Manjago 1.85; Bambara 0.84; Creole/Aku 0.69; Others 1.23.

PRINCIPAL TOWNS (population at 1993 census)

Banjul (capital)	.	42,326	Lamin	10,668
Brikama	. .	41,761	Gunjur . . .	9,983
Bakau	. . .	28,882	Basse	9,265
Farafenni	. .	20,956	Soma	7,988
Serrekunda	. .	18,901	Bansang . . .	5,743
Sukuta	. . .	16,667		

BIRTHS AND DEATHS (UN estimates, annual averages)

	1980–85	1985–90	1990–95
Birth rate (per 1,000) . . .	48.2	46.3	43.3
Death rate (per 1,000) . .	23.1	21.2	19.2

Expectation of life (UN estimates, years at birth, 1990–95): 45.0 (males 43.4; females 46.6).

Source: UN, *World Population Prospects: The 1998 Revision.*

ECONOMICALLY ACTIVE POPULATION*
(persons aged 10 years and over, 1993 census)

	Males	Females	Total
Agriculture, hunting and forestry	82,886	92,806	175,692
Fishing	5,610	450	6,060
Mining and quarrying . .	354	44	398
Manufacturing . . .	18,729	2,953	21,682
Electricity, gas and water supply	1,774	84	1,858
Construction	9,530	149	9,679
Wholesale and retail trade; repair of motor vehicles, motorcycles and personal and household goods	33,281	15,460	48,741
Hotels and restaurants . .	3,814	2,173	5,987
Transport, storage and communications . . .	13,421	782	14,203
Financial intermediation . .	1,843	572	2,415
Other community, social and personal service activities .	25,647	15,607	41,254
Activities not adequately defined	10,421	6,991	17,412
Total	207,310	138,071	345,381

* Figures exclude persons seeking work for the first time.

Mid-1999 (estimates in '000): Agriculture, etc. 514; Total 649 (Source: FAO).

Agriculture

PRINCIPAL CROPS ('000 metric tons)

	1997	1998	1999
Millet	66	65	80
Sorghum	13	10	18
Rice (paddy)	17	27	29
Maize	8	8	6
Cassava (Manioc)* . . .	6*	6	6
Pulses*	4*	4	4
Palm kernels*	2*	2	2
Groundnuts (in shell) . .	78	73	126
Vegetables*	8*	8	8
Fruits*	4*	4	4

* FAO estimate(s).

Source: FAO.

LIVESTOCK ('000 head, year ending September)

	1997	1998*	1999*
Cattle	346	360	360
Goats	250	265	265
Sheep	182	190	190
Pigs*	14	14	14
Asses	33	34	34
Horses	16	17	17
Poultry	639	680	680

* FAO estimates.

Source: FAO.

LIVESTOCK PRODUCTS ('000 metric tons)

	1997	1998	1999
Beef and veal	3	3	3
Goat meat	1	1	1
Mutton and lamb . . .	1	1	1
Poultry meat	2	2	2*
Other meat	1	1	1*
Cows' milk	7	7	7
Poultry eggs	1	1	1*

* FAO estimate.

Source: FAO.

Forestry

ROUNDWOOD REMOVALS
('000 cubic metres, excluding bark)

	1996	1997	1998
Sawlogs, veneer logs and logs for sleepers	106	106	106
Other industrial wood . .	7	7	7
Fuel wood	700	700	700
Total	813	813	813

Source: FAO, *Yearbook of Forest Products.*

Fishing

('000 metric tons, live weight)

	1996	1997	1998
Capture	31.6	32.3	29.0
Tilapias	1.2	1.1	1.1
Sea catfishes	0.2	1.2	0.5
Bonga shad	22.6	21.5	22.0
Croakers and drums	1.3	1.0	0.9
Sharks, rays, skates	0.4	3.2	0.6
Aquaculture	0.0	0.0*	0.0*
Total catch	31.6	32.3	29.0

* FAO estimate.

Source: FAO, *Yearbook of Fishery Statistics*.

Industry

SELECTED PRODUCTS

	1993	1994	1995
Salted, dried or smoked fish ('000 metric tons)*	0.9	1.1	0.9
Palm oil—unrefined ('000 metric tons)*	3	3	3
Electric energy (million kWh)†	73	73	74

* Data from the FAO.   † Provisional or estimated figures.

Source: UN, *Industrial Commodity Statistics Yearbook*.

Palm oil—unrefined (FAO estimates, '000 metric tons): 3 in 1997; 3 in 1998, 3 in 1999. Source: FAO.

Finance

CURRENCY AND EXCHANGE RATES

Monetary Units
100 butut = 1 dalasi (D).

Sterling, Dollar and Euro Equivalents (31 October 2000)
£1 sterling = 20.37 dalasi;
US $1 = 14.06 dalasi;
€1 = 11.83 dalasi;
1,000 dalasi = £49.10 = $71.13 = €84.51.

Average Exchange Rate (dalasi per US $)
1997   10.200
1998   10.643
1999   11.395

BUDGET (million dalasi)

Revenue*	1997	1998†	1999‡
Tax revenue	714.7	751.1	773.7
Direct taxes	168.5	185.1	201.8
Taxes on personal incomes	72.3	76.4	81.3
Taxes on corporate profits	81.8	93.7	81.3
Indirect taxes	546.2	566.0	571.8
Domestic taxes on goods and services	71.5	65.3	77.3
Domestic sales tax	57.1	63.0	64.7
Taxes on international trade	474.7	500.7	494.5
Customs duties	119.7	145.1	183.0
Sales tax on imports	146.4	149.9	158.6
Petroleum taxes	208.5	205.8	152.9
Duty	178.6	177.3	132.3
Sales tax	29.9	28.5	20.6
Other current revenue	84.8	80.4	105.0
Government services and charges	40.1	35.1	75.1
Interest, dividends and property	23.0	38.6	22.0
Central Bank profit	17.4	4.0	4.6
Total	799.5	831.5	878.7

Expenditure§	1997	1998†	1999‡
Current expenditure	794.6	799.8	887.0
Expenditure on goods and services	470.9	447.5	490.8
Wages and salaries	269.3	282.9	301.7
Other goods and services	201.6	164.5	189.1
Interest payments	214.7	236.9	248.3
Internal	155.2	180.4	187.5
External	59.5	56.4	60.9
Subsidies and transfers	109.0	115.4	129.8
Emergency relief	—	—	18.0
Capital expenditure¶	349.9	259.9	261.0
Total	1,144.5	1,059.7	1,148.0

* Excluding grants received (million dalasi): 53.0 in 1997; 88.5 in 1998; 65.8 in 1999.
† Estimates.
‡ Preliminary figures.
§Excluding lending minus repayments (million dalasi): −20.9 in 1997; −31.2 in 1998; −29.8 in 1999.
¶ Including foreign-financed extrabudgetary expenditure (million dalasi): 60.6 in 1997; 0.0 in 1998; 0.0 in 1999.

Source: IMF, *The Gambia: Selected Issues* (August 2000).

INTERNATIONAL RESERVES (US $ million at 31 December)

	1997	1998	1999
IMF special drawing rights	0.11	0.42	0.67
Reserve position in IMF	2.00	2.09	2.04
Foreign exchange	93.92	103.85	108.54
Total	96.04	106.36	111.25

Source: IMF, *International Financial Statistics*.

MONEY SUPPLY (million dalasi at 31 December)

	1997	1998	1999
Currency outside banks	360.51	347.55	379.72
Demand deposits at commercial banks	268.90	279.02	336.32
Total money	629.41	626.57	716.04

Source: IMF, *International Financial Statistics*.

COST OF LIVING

(Consumer Price Index for Banjul and Kombo St Mary's; base: 1974 = 100)

	1997	1998†	1999‡
Food	1,511.8	1,565.8	1,628.8
Fuel and light	2,145.8	1,854.9	2,076.0
Clothing*	937.5	981.8	999.9
Rent	1,409.6	1,431.3	1,428.6
All items (incl. others)	1,441.5	1,457.3	1,512.9

* Including household linen.

NATIONAL ACCOUNTS

(million dalasi at current prices)

Expenditure on the Gross Domestic Product

	1997*	1998*	1999†
Government final consumption expenditure	735.1	743.3	753.6
Private final consumption expenditure	3,146.2	3,399.4	3,758.9
Increase in stocks	717.7	819.8	880.5
Gross fixed capital formation			
Total domestic expenditure	4,599.0	4,962.5	5,393.0
Exports of goods and services	1,884.8	2,263.1	2,353.0
Less Imports of goods and services	2,303.7	2,746.5	2,790.4
GDP in purchasers' values	4,180.1	4,479.1	4,955.6
GDP at constant 1976/77 prices	641.0	672.5	710.1

Gross Domestic Product by Economic Activity

	1997*	1998*	1999†
Agriculture, hunting, forestry and fishing	1,074.8	1,228.1	1,466.5
Manufacturing	218.8	219.0	234.6
Electricity and water	59.8	70.0	82.0
Construction	205.3	218.2	236.2
Trade, restaurants and hotels	587.3	647.4	735.0
Transport and communications	636.7	656.8	717.6
Real estate and business services	280.6	282.1	299.8
Government services	375.9	394.1	421.6
Other services‡	194.6	197.5	204.4
GDP at factor cost	3,633.9	3,913.1	4,397.6
Indirect taxes, *Less* Subsidies	546.2	566.0	558.0
GDP in purchasers' values	4,180.1	4,479.1	4,955.6

* Estimates.
† Preliminary figures.
‡ Including banking and insurance, net of imputed bank service charges.
Source: IMF, *The Gambia: Selected Issues* (August 2000).

BALANCE OF PAYMENTS (US $ million, year ending 30 June).

	1995	1996	1997
Exports of goods f.o.b.	122.96	118.75	119.61
Imports of goods f.o.b.	−162.53	−217.10	−207.09
Trade balance	−39.57	−98.35	−87.48
Exports of services	53.71	101.21	109.35
Imports of services	−69.25	−77.03	−74.67
Balance on goods and services	−55.11	−74.17	−52.81
Other income received	4.37	6.01	3.73
Other income paid	−9.58	−9.28	−11.30
Balance on goods, services and income	−60.32	−77.44	−60.38
Current transfers received	55.81	35.10	45.04
Current transfers paid	−3.68	−5.35	−8.22
Current balance	−8.19	−47.70	−23.56
Capital account (net)	—	8.52	5.74
Direct investment from abroad	7.78	10.80	11.98
Other investment assets	−3.66	5.62	10.28
Investment liabilities	20.65	42.18	17.19
Net errors and omissions	−15.63	−4.94	−14.22
Overall balance	0.95	14.47	7.40

Source: IMF, *International Financial Statistics*.

External Trade

PRINCIPAL COMMODITIES (million dalasi)

Imports c.i.f.	1997	1998	1999
Food and live animals	570.9	956.6	726.3
Beverages and tobacco	48.9	74.4	83.1
Raw materials	28.9	26.6	36.5
Mineral fuels, lubricants, etc.	124.4	142.8	121.3
Animal and vegetable oils	62.8	98.7	66.8
Chemicals	170.0	131.2	116.1
Manufactured goods classified by material	160.0	241.1	253.9
Machinery and transport equipment	373.7	502.7	456.4
Miscellaneous manufactured articles	201.7	207.5	273.1
Total (incl. others)	1,773.8	2,426.4	2,206.9

Exports f.o.b.*	1997	1998	1999
Groundnuts and groundnut products	49.2	139.9	197.6
Fish and fish products	44.2	33.6	36.6
Fruit and vegetables	11.5	25.9	19.2
Cotton products	9.6	6.7	2.4
Total (incl. others)	139.4	229.4	289.8

* Excluding re-exports (million dalasi) 11.0 in 1997; 50.2 in 1998; 23.2 in 1999.

PRINCIPAL TRADING PARTNERS (million dalasi)

Imports c.i.f.	1997	1998	1999
Belgium	86.8	163.1	126.8
China, People's Repub.	68.9	140.5	140.8
Côte d'Ivoire	104.3	145.2	89.8
France (incl. Monaco)	167.3	220.6	148.3
Germany	148.0	179.6	305.3
Hong Kong	50.5	82.8	96.7
Italy	47.9	30.6	31.8
Japan	55.3	77.2	71.5
Netherlands	84.5	163.8	105.3
Senegal	42.8	38.1	50.0
Spain	67.8	87.1	38.1
Thailand	6.2	125.6	27.3
United Kingdom	261.2	338.5	235.1
USA	171.2	168.9	109.2
Total (incl. others)	1,773.8	2,426.4	2,206.9

Exports f.o.b.	1997	1998	1999
Belgium	7.3	16.8	24.2
China, People's Repub.	2.6	6.9	1.4
France (incl. Monaco)	27.5	153.9	2.3
Germany	3.5	20.6	10.1
Hong Kong	2.6	1.4	0.8
Japan	3.2	5.3	2.1
Netherlands	7.4	9.0	3.3
Senegal	5.3	7.3	5.9
Spain	29.2	8.9	7.7
United Kingdom	22.0	34.8	15.7
USA	6.5	1.4	3.0
Total (incl. others)	150.4	279.6	313.0

Transport

ROAD TRAFFIC (estimates, motor vehicles in use)

	1995	1996	1997
Passenger cars	6,972	6,925	7,267
Lorries and vans	3,778	4,045	4,147

SHIPPING
Merchant Fleet (registered at 31 December)

	1996	1997	1998
Number of vessels	6	7	8
Total displacement (grt)	1,490	1,600	1,884

Source: Lloyd's Register of Shipping, *World Fleet Statistics*.

International Sea-borne Freight Traffic ('000 metric tons)

	1996	1997	1998
Goods loaded	55.9	38.1	47.0
Goods unloaded	482.7	503.7	493.2

CIVIL AVIATION (traffic on scheduled services)

	1992	1993	1994
Kilometres flown (million) . .	1	1	1
Passengers carried ('000) . . .	19	19	19
Passenger-km (million) . . .	50	50	50
Total ton-km (million) . . .	5	5	5

Source: UN, *Statistical Yearbook*.

Tourism

FOREIGN VISITORS BY COUNTRY OF ORIGIN*

	1996	1997	1998
Belgium.	6,366	3,795	3,703
Denmark	2,445	2,237	2,836
Germany	4,692	18,460	22,189
Netherlands . . .	13,207	10,365	10,762
Sweden	6,317	5,478	5,574
United Kingdom . . .	37,295	38,378	37,437
Total (incl. others) . . .	76,814	84,758	91,106

* Air charter tourist arrivals.

Source: National Tourist Office, Banjul.

1999 (Air charter tourist arrivals): 121,797.

Receipts from tourism (million dalasi): 347.6 in 1996/97, 326.1 in 1997, 511.8 in 1998.

Source: IMF, *The Gambia: Selected Issues* (August 2000).

Communications Media

	1994	1995	1996
Radio receivers ('000 in use) . .	176	182	189
Television receivers ('000 in use) .	3	4	4
Daily newspapers			
Number	2	1	1
Average circulation ('000 copies)	2*	1	2
Books published†			
Titles	21	n.a.	14
Copies ('000)	20	n.a.	10

* Estimate.　† Including pamphlets: 5 titles, 9,000 copies in 1994.

1997 ('000 in use): Radio receivers 196; Television receivers 4.

Telephones: ('000 main lines in use, excluding public call offices, year ending 31 March): 19 in 1995/96; 21 in 1996/97; 25 in 1997/98.

Telefax stations (number in use, year ending 31 March): 1,030 in 1995/96; 1,096 in 1996/97; 1,149 in 1997/98.

Mobile cellular telephones (subscribers, year ending 31 March): 1,442 in 1995/96; 3,096 in 1996/97; 4,734 in 1997/98.

Non-daily newspapers (1996): 4; Average circulation (estimate) 6,000 copies.

Sources: UNESCO, *Statistical Yearbook*; UN, *Statistical Yearbook*.

Education

(1998/99, unless otherwise indicated)

	Teachers	Students		
		Males	Females	Total
Pre-primary . . .	408*	15,205	13,618	28,823
Primary . . .	4,578	81,360	69,043	150,403
Junior Secondary .	1,338	20,142	14,018	34,160
Senior Secondary .	598	8,102	4,507	12,609
Tertiary* . . .	155	1,018	573	1,591

* 1994/95 figure(s).

Source: Department of State for Education, Banjul.

Directory

The Constitution

Following the *coup d'état* of July 1994, the 1970 Constitution was suspended and the presidency and legislature, as defined therein, dissolved. A Constitutional Review Commission was inaugurated in April 1995; the amended document was approved in a national referendum on 8 August. The new Constitution of the Second Republic of The Gambia entered into full effect on 16 January 1997.

Decrees issued during the transition period (1994–96) are deemed to have been approved by the National Assembly and remain in force so long as they do not contravene the provisions of the Constitution of the Second Republic.

The Constitution provides for the separation of the powers of the executive, legislative and judicial organs of state. The Head of State is the President of the Republic, who is directly elected by universal adult suffrage. No restriction is placed on the number of times a President may seek re-election. Legislative authority is vested in the National Assembly, comprising 45 members elected by direct universal suffrage and four members nominated by the President of the Republic. The Speaker and Deputy Speaker of the Assembly are elected, by the members of the legislature, from among the President's nominees. The Constitution upholds the principle of executive accountability to parliament. Thus, the Head of State appoints government members, but these are responsible both to the President and to the National Assembly. Ministers of cabinet rank take the title of Secretary of State. Committees of the Assembly have powers to inquire into the activities of ministers and of government departments, and into all matters of public importance.

In judicial affairs, the final court of appeal is the Supreme Court. Provision is made for a special criminal court to hear and determine all cases relating to the theft and misappropriation of public funds.

The Constitution provides for an Independent Electoral Commission, an Independent National Audit Office, an Office of the Ombudsman, a Lands Commission and a Public Service Commission, all of which are intended to ensure transparency, accountability and probity in public affairs.

The Constitution guarantees the rights of women, of children and of the disabled. Tribalism and other forms of sectarianism in politics are forbidden. Political activity may be suspended in the event of a state of national insecurity.

The Government

HEAD OF STATE

President: Col (retd) Dr Alhaji YAHYA A. J. J. JAMMEH (proclaimed Head of State 26 July 1994; elected President 26 September 1996).

Vice-President: ISATOU NJIE-SAIDY.

THE CABINET
(April 2001)

President: Col (retd) Dr Alhaji YAHYA A. J. J. JAMMEH.

Vice-President and Secretary of State for Women's Affairs: ISATOU NJIE-SAIDY.

Secretary of State for Presidential Affairs, Works, Communication and Information, responsible for the National Assembly and the Civil Service: Capt. (retd) EDWARD DAVID SINGHATEH.

Secretary of State for Youth and Sports: SARJO JALLOW.

Secretary of State for the Interior and Religious Affairs: OUSMAN BADJIE.

Secretary of State for Trade, Industry and Employment: MUSA SILLAH.

Secretary of State for Foreign Affairs: MOMODOU LAMINE SEDAT JOBE.

Secretary of State for Education: ANN THERESE NDONG-JATTA.

Secretary of State for Tourism and Culture: Capt (retd) YANKUBA TOURAY.

Secretary of State for Agriculture: HASSAN SALLAH.

Secretary of State for Fisheries and Natural Resources: SUSAN WAFFA-OGOO.

Secretary of State for Finance and Economic Affairs: FAMARA JATTA.

Secretary of State for Local Government and Lands: MOMODOU NAI CEESAY.

Secretary of State for Justice, Attorney-General: JOSEPH HENRY JOOF.

Secretary of State for Health and Social Welfare: YANKUBA GASSAMA.

Secretary-General: JULIA JOINER.

MINISTRIES

Office of the President: State House, Banjul; tel. 227881; fax 227034.

Office of the Vice-President: State House, Banjul; tel. 227605; fax 224012.

Department of State for Agriculture: The Quadrangle, Banjul; tel. 228291; fax 223578.

Department of State for Education: Bedford Place Bldg, POB 989, Banjul; tel. 227236; fax 224180.

Department of State for Finance and Economic Affairs: The Quadrangle, Banjul; tel. 228291; fax 227954.

Department of State for Fisheries and Natural Resources: Banjul.

Department of State for Foreign Affairs: 4 Col Muammar Ghadaffi Ave, Banjul; tel. 225654; fax 223578.

Department of State for Health, Social Welfare and Women's Affairs: The Quadrangle, Banjul; tel. 227881; fax 228505.

Department of State for the Interior and Religious Affairs: Ecowas Ave, Banjul; tel. 228511; fax 223063.

Department of State for Justice: Col Muammar Ghadaffi Ave, Banjul; tel. 228181; fax 225352.

Department of State for Local Government and Lands: The Quadrangle, Banjul; tel. 228291.

Department of State for Tourism and Culture: New Administrative Bldg, The Quadrangle, Banjul; tel. 228496; fax 227753.

Department of State for Trade, Industry and Employment: Independence Drive, Banjul; tel. 228229.

Department of State for Works, Communication and Information: MID Rd, Kanifing, Banjul; tel. 227449; fax 226655.

Department of State for Youth and Sports: The Quadrangle, Banjul; tel. 227449; fax 225066.

President and Legislature

PRESIDENT
Presidential Election, 26 September 1996

Candidate	Votes	% of votes
YAHYA A. J. J. JAMMEH	220,011	55.77
OUSAINOU DARBOE	141,387	35.84
HAMAT N. K. BAH	21,759	5.52
SIDIA JATTA	11,337	2.87
Total	394,494	100.00

NATIONAL ASSEMBLY

Speaker: MUSTAPHA WADDA.

General Election, 2 January 1997

Party	Seats
Alliance for Patriotic Reorientation and Construction	33*
United Democratic Party	7
National Reconciliation Party	2
People's Democratic Organization for Independence and Socialism	1
Independents	2
Total	45†

* Including five seats taken in constituencies in which the party was unopposed.

† The President of the Republic is empowered by the Constitution to nominate four additional members of parliament.

Political Organizations

Alliance for Patriotic Reorientation and Construction (APRC): GAMSTAR Bldg, Banjul; f. 1996; Chair. President YAHYA A. J. J. JAMMEH.

National Reconciliation Party (NRP): Banjul; f. 1996; Leader HAMAT N. K. BAH.

People's Democratic Organization for Independence and Socialism (PDOIS): 1 Sambou St, Churchill, Srerekunda; tel. 393177; fax 466180; f. 1986; radical socialist; Leaders HALIFA SALLAH, SAM SARR, SIDIA JATTA.

United Democratic Party (UDP): 16 Ecowas Ave, Banjul; tel. 227442; fax 223894; internet www.udpgambia.org; f. 1996; Pres. Col (retd) SAM SILLAH; Leader OUSAINOU DARBOE.

Note: The **Gambia People's Party**, of ASSAN MUSA CAMARA, the **National Convention Party**, of SHERIF MUSTAPHA DIBBA, and the **People's Progressive Party**, of fmr Pres. Sir DAWDA KAIRABA JAWARA, were banned from contesting the 1996 presidential election and the 1997 legislative elections.

Diplomatic Representation

EMBASSIES AND HIGH COMMISSIONS IN THE GAMBIA

China (Taiwan): 26 Radio Gambia St, Kanifing South, POB 916, Banjul; tel. 374046; fax 374055; Ambassador: CHEN-HSIUNG LEE.

Guinea-Bissau: 16 Wellington St, Banjul; tel. and fax 228134; Ambassador: ABEL COELHO DE MENDONÇA.

Liberia: Garba-Jahumpa Rd, Bakau Newtown, POB 2982, Banjul; tel. 496775; fax 396629; Chargé d'affaires a.i.: ERIC R. TOGBA.

Libya: 73 Gloucester St, Banjul; tel. 223213; fax 223214; Chargé d'affaires a.i.: ABDUSSALAM ABUZAID.

Nigeria: Garba Jahumpa Rd, Bakau Newtown, POB 630, Banjul; tel. 495803; fax 496456; High Commissioner: AYUBA JACOB NGBAKO.

Senegal: Kairaba Ave, POB 385, Banjul; tel. 373752; fax 373750; Ambassador: Gen. MOMODOU DIOP.

Sierra Leone: 67 Daniel Goddard St, POB 448, Banjul; tel. 228206; fax 229814; High Commissioner: IBRAHIM MORIKEH FOFANA.

United Kingdom: 48 Atlantic Rd, Fajara, POB 507, Banjul; tel. 495133; fax 495134; e-mail bhcbanjul@gamtel.gm; High Commissioner: JOHN PERROTT.

USA: The White House, Kairaba Ave, Fajara, PMB 19, Banjul; tel. 392856; fax 392475; Ambassador: GEORGE WILLIFORD BOYCE HALEY.

Judicial System

The judicial system of The Gambia is based on English Common Law and legislative enactments of the Republic's Parliament which include an Islamic Law Recognition Ordinance whereby an Islamic Court exercises jurisdiction in certain cases between, or exclusively affecting, Muslims.

The Constitution of the Second Republic guarantees the independence of the judiciary. The Supreme Court is defined as the final court of appeal. Provision is made for a special criminal court to hear and determine all cases relating to theft and misappropriation of public funds.

Supreme Court of The Gambia: Law Courts, Independence Drive, Banjul; tel. 227383; fax 228380; consists of the Chief Justice and four other judges.

Chief Justice: FELIX LARTEY.

The Banjul Magistrates Court (f. 1997), the **Kanifing Magistrates Court** and the **Divisional Courts** are courts of summary jurisdiction presided over by a magistrate or in his absence by two or more lay justices of the peace. There are resident magistrates in all divisions. The magistrates have limited civil and criminal jurisdiction, and appeal from these courts lies with the Supreme Court.

Islamic Courts have jurisdiction in matters between, or exclusively affecting, Muslim Gambians and relating to civil status, marriage, succession, donations, testaments and guardianship. The Courts administer Islamic (Shari'a) Law. A cadi, or a cadi and two assessors, preside over and constitute an Islamic Court. Assessors of the Islamic Courts are Justices of the Peace of Islamic faith.

District Tribunals have appellate jurisdiction in cases involving customs and traditions. Each court consists of three district tribunal members, one of whom is selected as president, and other court members from the area over which it has jurisdiction.

Attorney-General: JOSEPH HENRY JOOF.

Solicitor-General: RAYMOND SOCK.

Religion

About 85% of the population are Muslims. The remainder are mainly Christians, and there are a few animists, mostly of the Jola and Karoninka ethnic groups.

ISLAM

Banjul Central Mosque: Box Bar Road, Banjul; tel. 228094; Imam Ratib Alhaji ABDOULIE M. JOBE; Dep. Imam Ratib Alhaji TAFSIR GAYE.

Imam Ratib of Banjul: Alhaji ABDOULIE M. JOBE, King Fahd Bun Abdul Aziz Mosque, 39 Lancaster St, POB 562, Banjul; tel. 228094.

Supreme Islamic Council: Banjul; Chair. Alhaji BANDING DRAMMEH; Vice-Chair. Alhaji OUSMAN JAH.

CHRISTIANITY

The Gambia Christian Council: POB 27, Banjul; tel. and fax 392092. 1966; seven mems (churches and other Christian bodies); Chair. Rev. TITUS K. A. PRATT (Gen. Supt of the Methodist Church of The Gambia); Sec.-Gen. HANNAH ACY PETERS.

The Anglican Communion

The diocese of The Gambia, which includes Senegal and Cape Verde, forms part of the Church of the Province of West Africa. The Archbishop of the Province is the Bishop of Koforidua, Ghana. There are about 1,500 adherents in The Gambia.

Bishop of The Gambia: Rt Rev. SOLOMON TILEWA JOHNSON, Bishopscourt, POB 51, Banjul; tel. 227405; fax 373803; e-mail 106617.1404@compuserve.com.

The Roman Catholic Church

The Gambia comprises a single diocese (Banjul), directly responsible to the Holy See. At 31 December 1998 there were an estimated 33,000 adherents of the Roman Catholic Church in the country. The diocese administers a development organization (Caritas, The Gambia), and runs 63 schools and training centres. The Bishop of Banjul is a member of the Inter-territorial Catholic Bishops' Conference of The Gambia and Sierra Leone (based in Freetown, Sierra Leone).

Bishop of Banjul: Rt Rev. MICHAEL J. CLEARY, Bishop's House, POB 165, Banjul; tel. 393437; fax 390998; e-mail mcleary@gamtel.gm.

Protestant Churches

Abiding Word Ministries: POB 207, Serrekunda; tel. and fax 394035; e-mail ncwc.awm@commit.gm; f. 1988; Senior Pastor Rev. FRANCIS FORBES.

Methodist Church: POB 288, Banjul; f. 1821; tel. 227425; Chair. and Gen. Supt Rev. TITUS K. A. PRATT.

The Press

All independent publications are required to register annually with the Government and to pay a registration fee.

The Daily Observer: POB 131, Banjul; tel. 496608; fax 496878; e-mail observer@qanet.gm; internet www.qanet.gm/observer/observer.html; f. 1992; daily; independent; Man. Dir BUBACARR BALOEH; Editor-in-Chief PASCHAL EZE (acting).

Foroyaa (Freedom): Bundunka Kunda, POB 2306, Serrekunda; tel. 393177; fax 393177; e-mail foroyaa@qanet.gm; internet www.gambian.com/foroyaa/foroyaa.htm; weekly; publ. by the PDOIS; Editors HALIFA SALLAH, SAM SARR, SIDIA JATTA.

The Gambia Daily: Dept of Information, 14 Daniel Goddard St, Banjul; tel. 225060; fax 227230; e-mail gamna@gamtel.gm; internet www.gambianews.com; f. 1994; govt organ; Dir of Information EBRUMA COLE; circ. 500.

The Gambia Onward: Banjul; 3 a week; Editor RUDOLPH ALLEN.

The Gambian: Banjul; 3 a week; Editor NGAING THOMAS.

The Gambian Times: 21 OAU Blvd, POB 698, Banjul; tel. 445; f. 1981; fortnightly; publ. by the PPP; Editor MOMODOU GAYE.

The Independent: next to A-Z Supermarket, Kairaba Ave, Banjul; f. 1999; e-mail independent@qanet.gm; internet www.qanet.gm/independent/independent.html; 2 a week; independent; Editor-in-Chief DEMBA JAWO (acting); Man. Editor YORRO JALLOW.

The Nation: People's Press, 3 Boxbar Rd, POB 334, Banjul; fortnightly; Editor FABAKARY TAAL; circ. 1,000.

The Point: 2 Garba Jahumpa Rd, Fajara, Banjul; tel. 497441; fax 497442; e-mail point@qanet.gm; internet www.qanet.gm/point/point.html; f. 1991; 2 a week; Man. Editor DEYDA HYDARA; circ. 4,000.

The Spectator: Banjul; tel. 226072; e-mail thespectatormagazine@yahoo.com; f. 1999; independent; weekly magazine.

The Toiler: 31 OAU Blvd, POB 698, Banjul; Editor PA MODOU FALL.

The Worker: 6 Albion Place, POB 508, Banjul; publ. by the Gambia Labour Union; Editor M. M. CEESAY.

NEWS AGENCIES

Gambia News Agency (GAMNA): Dept of Information, 14 Daniel Goddard St, Banjul; tel. 225060; fax 227230; e-mail gamna@gamtel.ga; Dir EBRIMA COLE.

Spice News Services: Banjul; e-mail ahes_ttsmart_spi@hotmail.com.

PRESS ASSOCIATION

Gambia Press Union: 10 Atlantic Rd, Fajara, POB 1440, Banjul; tel. 497945; fax 497946; e-mail gpu@qanet.gm; affiliated to West African Journalists' Association; Pres. DEMBA ALI JAWO.

Publisher

Government Printer: MacCarthy Sq., Banjul; tel. 227399.

Broadcasting and Communications

TELECOMMUNICATIONS

Gambia Telecommunications Co Ltd (GAMTEL): Gamtel House, 3 Nelson Mandela St, POB 387, Banjul; tel. 229999; fax 227214; e-mail gen-info@gamtel.gm; internet www.gamtel.gm; f. 1984; state-owned; Man. Dir BAKARY K. NJIE.

BROADCASTING
Radio

Citizen FM: Banjul; independent commercial broadcaster; Propr BABOUCAR GAYE; News Editor EBRIMA SILLAH.

Farafenni Community Radio: Farafenni; tel. 735527.

FM B Community Radio Station: Brikama; tel. 483000; FM broadcaster.

Gambia Radio and Television Services: Serrekunda Exchange Complex, Kairaba Ave, Serrekunda; tel. 374223; fax 374242; e-mail tombongs@hotmail.com; internet www.qanet.com; f. 1962; state-funded, non-commercial broadcaster; radio broadcasts in English, Mandinka, Wolof, Fula, Jola, Serer and Serahuli; Dir TOMBONG SAIDY.

Radio 1 FM: 44 Kairaba Ave, POB 2700, Serrekunda, Fajara; tel. 394900; fax 396071; e-mail george.radio1@qanet.gm; f. 1990; private station broadcasting FM music programmes to the Greater Banjul area; Dir GEORGE CHRISTENSEN.

Radio Gambia: Mile 7, Banjul; tel. 495101; fax 495932.

Radio Syd: POB 279, Banjul; tel. and fax 226490; f. 1970; medium-wave commercial station broadcasting mainly music; programmes in English, French, Wolof, Mandinka and Fula; also tourist information in Swedish; Dir CONSTANCE WADNER ENHÖRNING; Man. BENNY HOLGERSON.

Sud FM: ECOWAS Ave, POB 94, Banjul; tel. 222359; fax 222394.

West Coast Radio: Manjai Kunda, POB 2687, Serrekunda; tel. 460911; fax 461193; e-mail wcr@delphi.com; FM broadcaster.

The Gambia also receives broadcasts from Radio Democracy for Africa (f. 1998); a division of the Voice of America.

Television

Gambia Radio and Television Services: (see Radio); television broadcasts commenced 1996.

Finance

(cap. = capital; res = reserves; dep. = deposits; m. = million; brs = branches; amounts in dalasi)

BANKING
Central Bank

Central Bank of The Gambia: 1–2 Ecowas Ave, Banjul; tel. 228103; fax 226969; e-mail centralbank.gambia@qanet.gm; f. 1971; bank of issue; monetary authority; cap. 1.0m., res 3.0m., dep. 993.6m. (Dec. 1998); Gov. MOMODOU CLARKE BAJO; Gen. Man. VALDEMAR R. JENSEN.

Other Banks

Arab-Gambian Islamic Bank: 7 Ecowas Ave, POB 1415, Banjul; tel. 223773; fax 223770; e-mail agib@qanet.gm; f. 1996, operations commenced 1997; 30.1% owned by Islamic Development Bank; cap. 5.8m., total assets 58.8m. (Dec. 1999); Chair. Dr OMAR ZUHAIR HAFIZ; Man. Dir MAMOUR MALICK JAGNE; 1 br.

Continent Bank Ltd: 61 Ecowas Ave, POB 142, Banjul; tel. 222000; fax 229711; e-mail continent.bank@gamtel.gm; internet www.gambianews.com/continentbank; f. 1990; cap. 3.6m., dep. 66.6m. (Dec. 1999); Chair. KARIM BAYZID; Gen. Man. MURAD BAYZID; 2 brs.

First International Bank Ltd: 6 OAU Blvd, POB 1997, Banjul; tel. 202003; fax 202000; e-mail fib@gamtel.gm; f. 1999; 52.5% owned by Slok Nigeria Ltd; cap. 10.0m., res. 1.3m., dep. 4.4m. (Dec. 1999); Chair. Dr BABACAR NDIAYE; Man. Dir ONWUCHEKWA ONWUCHEKWA (acting).

International Bank for Commerce and Industry (Gambia) Ltd: 11A Liberation Ave, POB 211, Banjul; tel. 218144; fax 229312; f. 1968; owned by Banque Mauritanienne pour le Commerce et l'Industrie; cap. and res 16.5m., dep. 179.1m. (Dec. 1999); Chair. SIDI MOHAMED ABBASS; Man. Dir BABA OULDAH; 3 brs.

Standard Chartered Bank Gambia Ltd: 8 Ecowas Ave, POB 259, Banjul; tel. 228681; fax 227714; f. 1978; 75% owned by Standard Chartered Holdings BV, Amsterdam; cap. and res 65.9m., dep. 542.4m. (Dec. 1999); Chair. Dr PETER JOHN N'DOW; Chief Exec. S. TSIKIRAYI; 5 brs.

Trust Bank Ltd (TBL): 3–4 Ecowas Ave, POB 1018, Banjul; tel. 225778; fax 225781; e-mail trust@gamtel.gm; f. 1992; fmrly Meridien BIAO Bank Gambia Ltd, name changed 1997; 30% owned by Data Bank, 25% by Social Security and Housing Finance Corpn, 10% by Boule & Co Ltd; cap. and res 16.5m., total assets 179.1m. (Dec. 1999); Chair. KEN OFORI ATTA; Man. Dir PA MACOUMBA NJIE; 5 brs.

INSURANCE

There were seven insurance companies and four insurance brokers operating in The Gambia at the end of 1998.

Capital Insurance Co Ltd: 22 Anglesea St, POB 268, Banjul; tel. 227480; fax 229219; e-mail capinsur@gamtel.gm; f. 1986; CEO DOUDOU TAAL; Man. Dir JOSEPH C. FYE.

The Gambia National Insurance Co Ltd: 19 Kairaba Ave, Fajara, POB 750, Banjul; tel. 395726; fax 395716; e-mail info@gnic.gm; internet www.gnic.gm; f. 1974; privately-owned; Chair. BAI MATARR DRAMMEH; 3 brs.

GAMSTAR Insurance Co Ltd: 79 Daniel Goddard St, POB 1276, Banjul; tel. 226021; fax 229755; f. 1991; Man. Dir BAI NDONGO FAAL.

Great Alliance Insurance Co: 10 Nelson Mandela St, POB 1160, Banjul; tel. 227839; fax 229444; e-mail info@gaic.gm; internet www.gaic.gm; f. 1989; Man. Dir YABOR FORSTER.

Prime Insurance Co Ltd: 10c Nelson Mandela St, POB 277, Banjul; tel. 222476; e-mail prime@qanet.gm; f. 1997; Man. Dir PA ALASSAN JAGNE.

Insurance Association

Insurance Association of The Gambia (IAG): Banjul.

Trade and Industry

GOVERNMENT AGENCIES

Indigenous Business Advisory Services: Serrekunda; tel. 496098.

National Environmental Agency (NEA): 5 Fitzgerald St, Banjul; tel. 228056; fax 229701.

National Investment Promotion Authority (NIPA): Independence Drive, Banjul; tel. 228332; fax 229220; f. 1994 to replace the National Investment Bd; CEO S. M. MBOGE.

National Trading Corpn of The Gambia Ltd (NTC): 1–3 Liberation Avenue, POB 61, Banjul; tel. 228323; fax 227790; f. 1973; transfer pending to private-sector ownership; Man. Dir. CHARBEL N. ELHAJJ; 15 brs.

CHAMBER OF COMMERCE

Gambia Chamber of Commerce and Industry (GCCI): NTC Complex, Ecowas Ave, POB 333, Banjul; tel. 227042; fax 229671; e-mail gcci@qanet.gm; internet www.gambiachamber.gm; f. 1967 by merger; Man. Dir. BAI NDONGO FALL; Chief Exec. KEBBA T. N'JAI.

UTILITIES

National Water and Electricity Company (NAWEC): 10th St East, POB 609, Fajara; tel. 496430; fax 496971; f. 1996, in 1999 control was transferred to the Bassau Development Corporation, Côte d'Ivoire, under a 15-year contract; Man. Dir. MUSTAPHA CORR.

CO-OPERATIVES

Federation of Agricultural Co-operatives: Banjul.

The Gambia Co-operative Union (GCU): POB 505, Banjul; tel. 374788; fax 392582; f. 1959; co-operative for groundnut producers; Gen. Man. LAMIN WILLY JAMMEH; 110,000 mems.

TRADE UNIONS

Association of Gambia Sailors: c/o 31 OAU Blvd, POB 698, Banjul; tel. 223080; fax 227214.

Dock Workers' Union: Albert Market, POB 852, Banjul; tel. 229448; fax 225049.

Gambia Labour Union: 6 Albion Place, POB 508, Banjul; tel. 641; f. 1935; Pres. B. B. KEBBEH; Gen. Sec. MOHAMED CEESAY; 25,000 mems.

Gambia Workers' Confederation: 12 Clarkson St, POB 979, Banjul; f. 1958 as The Gambia Workers' Union, present name adopted in 1985; Sec.-Gen. PA MODOU FALL.

The Gambia National Trades Union Congress (GNTUC): Trade Union House, 31 OAU Blvd, POB 698, Banjul; Sec.-Gen. EBRIMA GARBA CHAM.

Transport

Gambia Public Transport Corporation: Factory St, Kanifing Industrial Estate, POB 801, Kanifing; tel. 392230; fax 392454; f. 1975; operates road transport and ferry services; Chair. SALIFU KUJABI.

RAILWAYS

There are no railways in The Gambia.

ROADS

In 1996 there were an estimated 2,700 km of roads in The Gambia, of which 850 km were main roads, and 520 km were secondary roads. In that year only about 35% of the road network was paved. Some roads are impassable in the rainy season. The expansion and upgrading of the road network is planned, as part of the Jammeh administration's programme to improve The Gambia's transport infrastructure. Among intended schemes is the construction of a motorway along the coast, with the aid of a loan of US $8.5m. from Kuwait. In early 1999 Taiwan agreed to provide $6m. for road construction programmes, and in early 2000 work began on the construction of a dual carriageway between Serrekunda-Mandina-Ba, supported by funds from the Islamic Development Fund.

Gambia Public Transport Corpn (GPTC): Banjul; tel. 392230; fax 392454; provides bus services; state-owned.

SHIPPING

The River Gambia is well suited to navigation. A weekly river service is maintained between Banjul and Basse, 390 km above Banjul, and a ferry connects Banjul with Barra. Small ocean-going vessels can reach Kaur, 190 km above Banjul, throughout the year. Facilities at the port of Banjul were modernized and expanded during the mid-1990s, with the aim of enhancing The Gambia's potential as a transit point for regional trade. In 1999 three advanced storage warehouses were commissioned with total storage space of 8,550 sq m.

Gambia Ports Authority: 34 Liberation Ave, POB 617, Banjul; tel. 229940; fax 227268; e-mail gamport@gamtel.gm; internet www.gamport.gm; Man. Dir IBRAHIMA JANGANA.

The Gambia River Transport Co Ltd: Banjul; tel. 227664; river transport of groundnuts and general cargo; Man. Dir. LAMIN JUWARA; 200 employees.

The Gambia Shipping Agencies Ltd: Liberation Ave, Banjul; tel. 227518; fax 227929; shipping agents and forwarders; Man. NILS LANGGAARD SORENSEN; 30 employees.

Interstate Shipping Co (Gambia) Ltd: POB 437, Banjul; tel. 227644; fax 229347; transport and storage.

CIVIL AVIATION

Banjul International Airport, at Yundum, 27 km from the capital, handled some 275,000 passengers and 3,000 metric tons of cargo in 1992. Construction of a new terminal, at a cost of some US $10m., was completed in late 1996. Facilities at Yundum have been upgraded by the US National Aeronautics and Space Administration (NASA), to enable the airport to serve as an emergency landing site for space shuttle vehicles.

Gambia Civil Aviation Authority: Banjul National Airport, Yundum; tel. 472831; fax 472190.

Gambia International Airlines: 8 Hagan St, Banjul; tel. 223702; fax 472750; e-mail info@gia.gm; internet www.gia.gm; f. 1996; state-owned; sole handling agent at Banjul, sales agent; Man. Dir VICTOR J. CARVALHO.

Tourism

Tourists are attracted by The Gambia's beaches and also by its abundant birdlife. A major expansion of tourism facilities was carried out in the early 1990s. Although there was a dramatic decline in tourist arrivals in the mid-1990s (owing to the political instability), the tourism sector recovered well; an estimated 121,797 tourists visited The Gambia in 1999. In 1998 estimated earnings from tourism were D511.8m. An annual 'Roots Festival' was inaugurated in 1996, with the aim of attracting African-American visitors to The Gambia.

National Tourist Office: Dept of State for Tourism and Culture, New Administrative Bldg, The Quadrangle, Banjul; tel. 229563; fax 224019; Dir of Tourism M. B. O. CHAM.

The Gambia Hotels' Association: c/o The Bungalow Beach Hotel, POB 2637, Serrekunda; tel. 465288; fax 466180; Chair. ARDE SARGE.

GEORGIA

Introductory Survey

Location, Climate, Language, Religion, Flag, Capital

Georgia is situated in west and central Transcaucasia, on the southern foothills of the Greater Caucasus mountain range. There is a frontier with Turkey to the south-west and a western coastline on the Black Sea. The northern frontier with the Russian Federation follows the axis of the Greater Caucasus, and includes borders with the Russian republics of Dagestan, Chechnya, Ingushetiya, North Ossetia (Osetiya), Kabardino-Balkariya and Karachai-Cherkessiya. To the south lies Armenia, and to the south-east is Azerbaijan. Georgia includes two autonomous republics (Abkhazia and Ajaria) and the autonomous region of South Ossetia. (In the late 1990s the status of these three territories was in dispute.) The Black Sea coast and the Rion plains have a warm, humid, subtropical climate, with annual rainfall of more than 2,000 mm and average temperatures of 6°C (42°F) in January and 23°C (73°F) in July. Eastern Georgia has a more continental climate, with cold winters and hot, dry summers. The official language is Georgian (a member of the Caucasian language group), which is written in the Georgian script. Most of the population are adherents of Christianity; the principal denomination is the Georgian Orthodox Church. Islam is professed by Ajarians, Azerbaijanis, Kurds and some others. Most Ossetians in Georgia are Eastern Orthodox Christians, although their co-nationals in North Ossetia are mainly Sunni Muslims. There are also other Christian groups, and a small number of adherents of the Jewish faith (both European and Georgian Jews). The national flag (proportions 5 by 3) consists of a field of cornelian red, with a canton, divided into two equal horizontal stripes of black over white, in the upper hoist. The capital is Tbilisi.

Recent History

A powerful kingdom in medieval times, Georgia subsequently came under periods of foreign domination, becoming annexed by the Russian Empire during the 19th century. After the collapse of the Russian Empire in 1917, an independent Georgian state was established on 26 May 1918; ruled by a Menshevik Socialist Government, it received recognition from the Bolshevik Government of Soviet Russia by treaty in May 1920. However, Georgia was invaded by Bolshevik troops in early 1921, and a Georgian Soviet Socialist Republic (SSR) was proclaimed on 25 February. In December 1922 it was absorbed into the Transcaucasian Soviet Federative Socialist Republic (TSFSR), which, on 22 December, became a founder member of the USSR. The Georgian SSR became a full union republic in 1936, when the TSFSR was disbanded.

During the 1930s Georgians suffered persecution under the Soviet leader, Stalin (Iosif V. Dzugashvili), himself an ethnic Georgian. The first victims had been opponents of Stalin during his time as a revolutionary leader in Georgia, but later the persecution became more indiscriminate. Most members of the Georgian leadership were dismissed after Stalin's death in 1953. There was a further purge in 1972, when Eduard Shevardnadze became First Secretary of the Communist Party of Georgia (CPG) and attempted to remove officials who had been accused of corruption. Despite Soviet policy, Georgians retained a strong national identity. Opposition to a perceived policy of 'russification' was demonstrated in 1956, when anti-Russian riots were suppressed by security forces, and in 1978, when there were mass protests against the weakened status of the Georgian language in the new Constitution. Shevardnadze remained leader of the CPG until July 1985, when he became Minister of Foreign Affairs in the Government of the USSR.

The increased freedom of expression that followed the election of Mikhail Gorbachev as the Soviet leader in 1985 allowed the formation of unofficial groups, which campaigned on linguistic, environmental and ethnic issues. Such groups were prominent in organizing demonstrations in November 1988 against russification in Georgia. In February 1989 Abkhazians renewed a campaign, begun in the 1970s, for secession of their autonomous republic (in north-western Georgia) from the Georgian SSR (see below). Counter-demonstrations were staged in the capital, Tbilisi, by Georgians demanding that Georgia's territorial integrity be preserved. On the night of 8–9 April 1989 Soviet security forces attacked demonstrators in Tbilisi, who were demanding that Abkhazia remain within the republic and advocating the restoration of Georgian independence, killing 16 people and injuring many more. Despite the subsequent resignation of state and party officials (including the First Secretary of the CPG, Jumber Patiashvili) and the announcement of an official investigation into the deaths, anti-Soviet sentiment and inter-ethnic conflict increased sharply in the republic. Public outrage over the killings and the increasing influence of unofficial groups forced the CPG to adapt its policies to retain some measure of popular support. In November the Georgian Supreme Soviet (legislature), which was dominated by CPG members, declared the supremacy of Georgian laws over all-Union (USSR) laws. In February 1990 the same body declared Georgia 'an annexed and occupied country', and in the following month Article Six of the Georgian Constitution, which ensured that the CPG retained a monopoly on power, was abolished. Pressure from the newly established opposition parties forced the elections to the Georgian Supreme Soviet, which were scheduled for 25 March, to be postponed to allow time for a more liberal election law to be drafted. Legislation permitting full multiparty elections was finally adopted in August.

Despite their success in influencing the position of the CPG, there were considerable differences between the many opposition parties. Attempts to create a united front for the independence movement were unsuccessful. In early 1990, however, many of the principal political parties united in the Round Table–Free Georgia coalition. This and other leading parties aimed to achieve independence by parliamentary means and were willing, in the mean time, to participate in elections to Soviet institutions such as the Georgian Supreme Soviet. Many of the more radical parties, however, united in the National Forum, headed by Giorgi Chanturia, which announced its intention to boycott the elections to the Supreme Soviet and, instead, to elect a rival parliament, the National Congress. The announcement of elections to the Congress, to be held on 30 September (thus pre-empting the elections to the Supreme Soviet, scheduled for late October), caused increased tension and acts of violence between parties of the two tendencies. The elections to the National Congress took place as scheduled, but only 51% of the electorate participated. Many parties did not present candidates, preferring to contest the elections to the Supreme Soviet.

In the elections to the Supreme Soviet, held on 28 October and 11 November 1990, the Round Table–Free Georgia coalition, led by Zviad Gamsakhurdia, won 155 seats in the 250-seat chamber, with 64% of the votes cast. All 14 of the political parties and coalitions involved in the election campaign, including the CPG, were united in seeking Georgia's independence. The CPG won only 64 seats, while the remainder were won by the Georgian Popular Front (GPF), smaller coalitions and independents. The elections were boycotted by many non-ethnic Georgians, since parties limited to one area of the country were prevented from participating.

The new Supreme Soviet convened for the first time on 14 November 1990 and elected Gamsakhurdia as its Chairman. Two symbolic gestures of independence were adopted: the territory was, henceforth, to be called the Republic of Georgia and the white, black and cornelian-coloured flag of independent Georgia was officially adopted. Tengiz Sigua, also a member of the Round Table–Free Georgia coalition, was appointed Chairman of the Council of Ministers. The new Supreme Soviet adopted several controversial laws at its first session, declaring illegal the conscription of Georgians into the Soviet armed forces. Many young men were reported to have joined nationalist paramilitary groups or were ready to join the National Guard (a de facto republican army), which the Supreme Soviet established in January 1991.

The Georgian authorities officially boycotted the all-Union referendum on the future of the USSR, held in nine other Soviet republics, in March 1991, but polling stations were opened in the autonomous territories of South Ossetia and Abkhazia, and in local military barracks. In South Ossetia 43,950 people took part in the referendum; of these, only nine voted against the preservation of the USSR. In Abkhazia almost the entire non-Georgian population voted to preserve the Union. The Georgian leadership refused to participate in the negotiations on a new union treaty. Instead, on 31 March the Government conducted a referendum asking whether 'independence should be restored on the basis of the act of independence of 26 May 1918'. Of those eligible to vote, 95% participated in the referendum, 93% of whom voted for independence. On 9 April 1991 the Georgian Supreme Soviet approved a decree formally restoring Georgia's independence. Georgia thus became the first republic to secede from the USSR. Direct elections to the newly established post of executive President, held in May, were won by Gamsakhurdia, who received 86.5% of the votes cast. Voting did not take place in South Ossetia or Abkhazia.

Despite the high level of popular support that Gamsakhurdia received from the electorate, there was considerable opposition from other politicians to what was perceived as an authoritarian style of rule. His actions during the failed Soviet coup attempt of August 1991 were also strongly criticized, and he initially refrained from publicly condemning the coup leaders. After the coup had collapsed, Gamsakhurdia's position became tenuous. Tengiz Kitovani, the leader of the National Guard (who had been officially dismissed by Gamsakhurdia on 19 August, when the Soviet coup attempt began), announced that 15,000 of his men had remained loyal to him and were no longer subordinate to the President. Kitovani was joined in opposition to Gamsakhurdia by Tengiz Sigua, who had resigned as Chairman of the Council of Ministers in mid-August. In September 30 opposition parties united to demand the resignation of Gamsakhurdia and organized a series of anti-Government demonstrations. When opposition supporters occupied the television station in Tbilisi, several people were killed in clashes between Kitovani's troops and those forces still loyal to Gamsakhurdia.

Throughout October 1991 demonstrations by both supporters and opponents of Gamsakhurdia continued, but the strength of Gamsakhurdia's support among the rural and working-class population, his arrests of prominent opposition leaders and imposition of a state of emergency in Tbilisi, and his effective monopoly of the republican media all weakened the position of the opposition. In December armed conflict broke out, as the opposition resorted to force to oust the President. Kitovani and Jaba Ioseliani, the leader of the paramilitary *Mkhedrioni* (Horsemen) group were joined by other opposition figures and increasing numbers of former Gamsakhurdia supporters. The fighting was mostly confined to central Tbilisi, around the parliament buildings, where Gamsakhurdia was besieged. More than 100 people were believed to have been killed. Gamsakhurdia and some of his supporters fled Georgia on 6 January 1992 (eventually taking refuge in southern Russia). A few days previously the opposition had declared Gamsakhurdia deposed and formed a Military Council, led by Kitovani and Ioseliani, which appointed Tengiz Sigua as acting Chairman of the Council of Ministers. The office of President was abolished, and the functions of Head of State were to be exercised by the Chairman of the Supreme Soviet.

In mid-January 1992 Sigua began the formation of a new Government, and also announced plans for significant economic reforms. An Interim Consultative Council, comprising representatives of all the major political groups, was established, in an attempt to create stability. (The Council did not include the CPG, which had been disbanded in August 1991.) In early March 1992 Eduard Shevardnadze returned to Georgia, and a State Council was created to replace the Military Council in legislative and executive matters. The State Council, of which Shevardnadze was designated Chairman, comprised 50 members, drawn from all the major political organizations, and included Sigua, Ioseliani and Kitovani. Shevardnadze succeeded in reconciling the various factions of the State Council, as well as the leaders of the two principal military bodies, the National Guard and the *Mkhedrioni*. The loyalty of these forces was essential to Shevardnadze in suppressing repeated attempts by Gamsakhurdia and his supporters in early 1992 to re-establish control. Further civil unrest ensued, especially in the western strongholds (including Abkhazia) of Gamsakhurdia's supporters (or 'Zviadists'), and curfews were imposed in Tbilisi and other towns. By April it was reported that government troops had re-established control in the rebellious areas. In July, however, one of Georgia's deputy premiers was taken hostage by 'Zviadists' in western Georgia. This was followed by the kidnapping of Roman

Gventsadze, the Georgian Minister of Internal Affairs, and several other officials. In response, the State Council dispatched more than 3,000 National Guardsmen to Abkhazia, where the hostages were believed to be held, prompting armed resistance by Abkhazian militia. In mid-August three of the hostages, including Gventsadze, were released.

An election to the Supreme Council (as the Supreme Soviet was now known) was held on 11 October 1992, against a background of intensified hostilities in Abkhazia and the threat of disruptive actions by the 'Zviadists'. In the event, however, the election was conducted peacefully, although it was boycotted in South Ossetia, Mengrelia and parts of Abkhazia. An estimated 75% of the total electorate participated. Of the more than 30 parties and alliances contesting the election, none succeeded in gaining a significant representation in the 235-seat legislature. The largest number of seats (just 29) was won by the centrist Peace bloc, which mainly comprised former Communists as well as intellectuals. Of greater consequence, however, was the direct election of the legislature's Chairman—effectively a presidential role—which was held simultaneously. Shevardnadze was the sole candidate for the post, winning more than 95% of the total votes cast, thus obtaining the legitimate popular mandate that he had hitherto lacked.

The Supreme Council convened for the first time in early November 1992 and adopted a decree on state power, whereby supreme executive authority was vested in Shevardnadze as the Council's Chairman (or Head of State), in conjunction with the Council of Ministers, while the Supreme Council remained the highest legislative body. Shevardnadze was also elected Commander-in-Chief of the Georgian armed forces and Tengiz Sigua was re-elected Chairman of the Council of Ministers. One of the principal aims of the new Government was to create a unified army; an 11-member National Security and Defence Council was established for this purpose in early 1993. A comprehensive programme of economic reform was also initiated.

Almost directly after his election, Shevardnadze was confronted by opposition from within his own administration. In response to rumours that Kitovani was plotting to overthrow him, Shevardnadze suspended the National Security and Defence Council in May 1993, also dismissing Kitovani from his post as Minister of Defence. In August the entire Council of Ministers tendered its resignation, following the legislature's rejection of the proposed budget. In the following month Shevardnadze appointed a new Council of Ministers, which was headed by Otar Patsatsia, a former CPG official. Shevardnadze himself tendered his resignation as Head of State in mid-September, in response to accusations of dictatorial methods. However, crowds blockaded the parliament building, demanding his reinstatement, and the Supreme Council voted overwhelmingly to reject Shevardnadze's resignation.

By late September 1993 Georgia appeared ungovernable: confronted by growing political and economic crisis and military defeat in Abkhazia (see below), Shevardnadze's position was made more precarious by the reappearance of Gamsakhurdia and the 'Zviadists' in western Georgia. In early October the former President's forces captured the Black Sea port of Poti as well as the strategic town of Samtredia, blocking all rail traffic to Tbilisi. As the rebel forces advanced further eastwards, Shevardnadze persuaded the Supreme Council to agree to Georgia's immediate membership of the Commonwealth of Independent States (CIS, see p. 157), established in December 1991 by 11 former Soviet republics. In late October 1993 Russian troops were dispatched to Georgia, and by early November the 'Zviadists' had been entirely routed from the republic. In early January 1994 it was reported that Gamsakhurdia had committed suicide, after having been surrounded by government troops in western Georgia.

Georgia's formal admittance to the CIS was delayed until early December 1993, when all of the member states finally granted their approval. Despite the restoration of some measure of stability in the republic, in November Shevardnadze extended the state of emergency (which had been declared in September) until early 1994. Shevardnadze also created his own party, the Citizens' Union of Georgia (CUG), formed from several existing parties. In February 1994 the *Mkhedrioni* group was transformed into a 'Rescue Corps', as part of the continuing process of creating a unified army.

Throughout 1994 Shevardnadze sought to curb the increasing level of organized crime in the republic; however, the incidence of assassinations and other acts of political violence remained high, as rival paramilitary groups—often based on regional affiliations or loyalty to certain powerful figures—competed for influence. Shevardnadze's own administration was undermined by clan-based rivalries. Popular opposition to the regime escalated, and regular demonstrations against Shevardnadze were held. New opposition parties emerged: a National Liberation Front (NLF) was established by Sigua and Kitovani with the declared aim to restore Georgia's territorial integrity (i.e. regain Abkhazia); in June several small parties claiming to be successors to the CPG merged as the United Communist Party of Georgia (UCPG). Nevertheless, in May more than 30 political and public organizations, including leading opposition parties (such as the GPF and Giorgi Chanturia's National Democratic Party of Georgia—NDPG) signed a declaration 'of national unity and accord' in an attempt to bring stability to Georgian politics. In December, however, the wave of political violence culminated in the assassination of Chanturia. (A former member of the *Mkhedrioni* confessed to his murder in April 1997.) In January 1995 Kitovani led an armed convoy of some 350 NLF supporters towards Abkhazia in an apparent attempt to 'liberate' the region. The convoy was halted and disarmed by government security forces; Kitovani was arrested and the NLF was banned. Attempts to curtail the criminal activities of the numerous politico-military groups operating in Georgia culminated in May, when the leading such group, Ioseliani's Rescue Corps, was ordered to surrender its arms; in July Ioseliani was reported to have established a political organization from elements of the *Mkhedrioni*.

In August 1995 the Supreme Council adopted Georgia's new Constitution, which had been prepared by a special constitutional commission. The document provided for a strong executive presidency and a 235-member unicameral Georgian Parliament. The Government was to be directly subordinate to the President, to whom it would act as an advisory body. The post of Prime Minister was abolished; the most senior position in the Government was henceforth to be that of the Minister of State, who was to co-ordinate the ministers' work and liaise with the President. The country (the official title of which was changed from the Republic of Georgia to Georgia) was described as 'united and undivided'; however, the territorial status of Abkhazia and South Ossetia was not defined. It was stated that, following the eventual conclusion of political settlements in those regions, the Georgian Parliament would be transformed into a bicameral body (comprising a Council of the Republic and a Senate, the latter representing the various territorial units of Georgia).

The Constitution was due to be signed at an official ceremony on 29 August 1995. However, following an assassination attempt on Shevardnadze, the signing was postponed; it eventually took place on 17 October. Security forces began a large-scale search for the would-be assassins, and the Minister of State Security, Igor Giorgadze, was dismissed for having failed to prevent the attack. Giorgadze was subsequently named by state prosecutors as the chief instigator of the plot, along with his deputy and a leading member of the Rescue Corps. Warrants were issued for their arrest; however, the three men fled abroad. (In February 1998 Georgia requested their extradition.) Shevardnadze announced the complete disbandment of the Rescue Corps, and in November Ioseliani was arrested, charged with complicity in the assassination attempt.

A direct election to the restored post of President of Georgia was held on 5 November 1995. Shevardnadze won a convincing victory, receiving almost 75% of the total votes cast. His closest rival (with only 19%) was Jumber Patiashvili, the former First Secretary of the CPG. The election of the new Georgian Parliament was held simultaneously with the presidential election. A mixed system of voting was employed: 150 seats were to be filled by proportional representation of parties, while the remaining 85 deputies were to be elected by majority vote in single-member constituencies. The election was boycotted in Abkhazia and in parts of South Ossetia. Only three parties contesting the 150 proportional seats succeeded in gaining the 5% of the votes necessary for representation in the Parliament. Of these, Shevardnadze's CUG won the largest number of seats (90), followed by the NDPG (31) and the All-Georgian Union of Revival, chaired by Aslan Abashidze, the regional leader of Ajaria (25 seats). Only about one-half of the single-mandate seats were filled; however, following a further two rounds of voting, all 85 deputies were elected. These included 17 members of the CUG and 29 independent candidates, as well as 12 deputies from Abkhazia (elected in 1992), whose mandates were renewed. This produced a total of 231 parliamentarians (representing 11 parties); the CUG emerged with a total of 107

seats, but it was supported by many of the other parties that gained representation. Four seats remained vacant. Approximately 64% of the registered electorate was believed to have participated in the legislative election.

The Georgian Parliament convened for the first time in late November 1995 and elected as its Chairman (Speaker) Zurab Zhvania, General Secretary of the CUG and a close associate of Shevardnadze. In early December Shevardnadze appointed Nikoloz Lekishvili, formerly Mayor of Tbilisi, as Minister of State. The remaining members of the Government were appointed later in the month. In January 1996, in accordance with the Constitution, a National Security Council was established as a consultative body dealing with issues relating to defence and security and the elimination of terrorism and corruption.

Meanwhile, in late 1995 criminal proceedings commenced in Tbilisi against Kitovani, in connection with the NLF's attempted raid on Abkhazia in early 1995 (see above). In May 1996 Ioseliani, the former leader of the *Mkhedrioni*, was convicted of complicity in the assassination attempt against Shevardnadze in August 1995 (he was sentenced to 11 years' imprisonment in November 1998), and in June 1996 supporters of former President Gamsakhurdia received lengthy prison sentences for their role in the civil war of 1993. Kitovani was convicted on charges of establishing an illegal armed formation in September 1996 and was sentenced to eight years' imprisonment. (He was released by presidential decree in May 1999.) In March 1997 nine opposition parties, which supported Gamsakhurdia, formed the Front for the Reinstatement of Legitimate Power in Georgia.

Allegations that the Ministry of State Security had authorized the illegal monitoring of senior journalists' telephone calls were confirmed in a closed session of the Georgian Parliament by the Procurator-General. Although the Georgian legislature did not hold the Minister, Shota Kviraia, personally responsible, he nevertheless tendered his resignation in July 1997. A review of the state security system was announced following the discovery of documentary evidence of corruption within the Ministries of Defence and of the Interior. Judicial and administrative reforms were also implemented, with the establishment of the Justice Council, which was formed to co-ordinate the appointment of members of the judiciary. A Civil Code, second in importance only to the Constitution, was adopted in June, and capital punishment was formally abolished.

On 9 February 1998 President Shevardnadze survived a second attempt on his life, when unidentified gunmen attacked the presidential motorcade as it drove through Tbilisi, killing two bodyguards. The USA sent experts to investigate the attack, the perpetrators of which were suspected of having Russian connections. A blockade was consequently imposed on the Russian military bases in Georgia. In mid-February seven people were detained, one of whom confessed to having participated in the attack. Investigations into the assassination attempt, which reportedly involved 20 'Zviadists' (including six Chechens), were completed in December, although the results were not made public. In March Guram Absandze, the Minister of Finance under the Gamsakhurdia administration, was arrested in the Russian capital, Moscow, at the request of the Georgian Government, and sent back to Georgia to be tried for his alleged involvement in attacks on Shevardnadze in 1992 and 1998. The Minister of Internal Affairs, Kakha Targamadze, tendered his resignation in May, on the grounds of his failure to prevent the assassination attempt in February; Shevardnadze, however, refused to accept it. Three deputy ministers were, none the less, dismissed for failing to dispatch help promptly to the scene of the attack.

In March 1998 the question of banning all Communist parties in Georgia was raised in Parliament. However, in October the Supreme Court ruled that the UCPG was entitled to participate in local elections, which were due to be held the following month. In June members of the opposition staged a parliamentary 'walkout' in protest against a decision taken by the Central Election Committee to annul the results of two by-elections in eastern Georgia. In July most of the Government resigned, including the Minister of State, Nikoloz Lekishvili, to permit the President to carry out a major ministerial reorganization. In the following month Georgia's former ambassador to Russia, Vazha Lortkipanidze, was appointed the new Minister of State, having received virtually unanimous support in Parliament.

Meanwhile, on 19 February 1998 four observers from the UN Observer Mission in Georgia (UNOMIG, see below) were taken hostage in the western town of Zugdidi by Gamsakhurdia supporters, who demanded the withdrawal of Russian troops from

Georgia, the release of 'political' prisoners and a meeting between the current and the 'legitimate' (i.e. Gamsakhurdia's former administration) Georgian authorities. A few days later the hostages were released, after Shevardnadze agreed to hold talks with the political representatives of their captors in Tbilisi. The leader of the kidnappers, Gocha Esebua (who was also suspected of involvement in the assassination attempt earlier in February), was killed in a gun battle with Georgian police in Zugdidi in late March. There were violent scenes at his funeral procession, during which five people were reportedly killed. In October a two-day armed insurrection by rebel troops in western Georgia ended when the 'Zviadist' mutineers surrendered to government forces at Kutaisi. Following this incident and the subsequent escape of the rebel leaders, the Minister of State Security, Jemal Gakhokidze, resigned in late October. In early January 1999 the police prevented a rally being held in Tbilisi by Gamsakhurdia supporters. A number of arrests were made, including that of Gamsakhurdia's widow, who was released later that day. In January the Round Table—Free Georgia coalition announced its intention to participate in parliamentary elections later that year. In March the Round Table—Free Georgia leader, Soso Jajanidze, was arrested and charged with possessing illegal arms. He denied the charges, and staged a hunger strike in protest at his detention.

In May 1999 13 people, including Guram Absandze, were charged with state treason for the attempt to assassinate Shevardnadze in February 1998. Later in May 17 people were arrested following the discovery of a coup plot. Reportedly, all of those detained were connected to Igor Giorgadze, and the group included current and former state officials. In January 2000 one of the alleged coup plotters died in detention; although his relatives claimed that he had been killed, an official post-mortem examination stated that he had died from natural causes.

Meanwhile, in July 1999 Parliament approved a constitutional amendment, which increased the minimum requirement for parliamentary representation from 5% to 7% of the votes cast under the system of proportional representation, by which 150 of the 235 seats are allocated. A number of blocs and alliances were formed following the announcement in August of a legislative election, to be held on 31 October. The most significant of these, chaired by Aslan Abashidze, was the Union for the Revival of Georgia, comprising the All-Georgian Union of Revival, the Socialist Party, the Union of Traditionalists, the People's Party and the 21st Century bloc. The election was contested by 32 parties and blocs, with the participation of 68% of the electorate. A second round of voting, between the two leading candidates, where no majority had been achieved, was held on 14 November. Final results showed a resounding victory for the CUG, which obtained 130 seats (85 proportional and 45 constituency). The Union for the Revival of Georgia bloc and the Industry Will Save Georgia bloc secured 58 seats (51 proportional, 7 constituency) and 15 seats (14 proportional, 1 constituency), respectively. Of the remaining single-member constituency seats, 17 were won by independents and two were won by the Georgian Labour Party. One seat remained vacant. As in 1995, the mandate of the 12 Abkhazian deputies was extended. Despite opposition allegations of irregularities, observers from the Organization for Security and Co-operation in Europe (OSCE, see p. 252) declared the election lawful. The new Parliament re-elected Zurab Zhvania as Chairman. In late November Lortkipanidze was awarded presidential powers for the settlement of conflicts in Georgia. In the following month the responsibilities of the Minister of State were expanded further by the President, and Lortkipanidze was accorded powers similar to those of a prime minister, including the right to convene ministerial meetings.

In the presidential election of 9 April 2000, Shevardnadze demonstrated the strength of his position against the fragmented opposition, securing 79.8% of the votes cast, with only Jumber Patiashvili, the former Communist official, obtaining any other significant result, with 16.7% of the votes. Electoral violations were noted by the OSCE, but the Parliamentary Assembly of the Council of Europe (see p. 253) and the Central Election Committee reported no major infringements of voting procedure. The only opponent who had been considered likely to pose a threat to the incumbent President was the Ajarian leader, Aslan Abashidze, who withdrew his candidacy on 6 April. Following the presidential election, a government reshuffle took place, in accordance with the Constitution, and on 11 May the Georgian Parliament endorsed the appointment of Gia Arsen-

ishvili as the new Minister of State. The Parliament also approved a reduction in the number of ministries, from 21 to 18. The Ministries of the Economy and of Industry were merged, as were the Ministries of Communications and Post and of Transport, while the Ministry of Trade and Foreign Economic Relations was incorporated into the Ministry of Foreign Affairs. On 14 May the new cabinet was approved, with four new appointments: Zurab Noghaideli replaced Davit Onoprishvili as Minister of Finance, Ivane Chkhartishvili was appointed Minister of Economics and Industry, Sesili Gogoberidze became Minister of Culture and Malkhaz Kakabadze was appointed Minister without Portfolio (with responsibility for conflict resolution). However, the nomination of Bakur Gulua, the incumbent Minister of Agriculture, was rejected by Parliament, owing to his alleged involvement in an embezzlement scandal; he was replaced by Davit Kirvalidze. At the beginning of October 12 prisoners accused of complicity in the assassination attempt on the President in February 1998, including Guram Absandze, escaped from a maximum security prison in Tbilisi. Although the prisoners were subsequently recaptured, the Minister of Justice, Dzhoni Khetsuriani, resigned as a result of the incident; he was replaced by Mikheil Saakashvili. Khetsuriani was later appointed parliamentary secretary to Shevardnadze.

Following his return to Georgia in March 1992, Shevardnadze struggled to resolve the inter-ethnic tensions in Georgia's autonomous territories, which had intensified following the election of Gamsakhurdia's nationalist Government in 1990, and which led to serious armed conflict in South Ossetia and Abkhazia. Ossetia, the original inhabitants of which are an East Iranian people, was divided into two parts under Stalin, North Ossetia falling under Russian jurisdiction and South Ossetia becoming an autonomous region of Georgia. At the census of 1979 ethnic Ossetians comprised 66% of the region's population. The long-standing Georgian animosity towards the Ossetians stems not only from ethnic differences but also from the Ossetians' traditional pro-Russian stance. The current dispute began in 1989, when Ossetian demands for greater autonomy and eventual reunification with North Ossetia (which would entail secession from Georgia and integration into the Russian Federation) led to violent clashes between local Georgians and Ossetians. Troops of the Soviet Ministry of Internal Affairs were dispatched to South Ossetia in January 1990, but in September the South Ossetian Supreme Soviet (legislature) proclaimed South Ossetia's independence and state sovereignty within the USSR. This decision was declared unconstitutional by the Georgian Supreme Soviet, which in December formally abolished the region's autonomous status. Following renewed violence, the Georgian legislature declared a state of emergency in Tskhinvali, the South Ossetian capital.

In January 1991 Soviet President Gorbachev annulled both South Ossetia's declaration of independence and the Georgian Supreme Soviet's decision of December 1990. However, violence continued throughout 1991, with the resulting displacement of many thousands of refugees. There was a series of cease-fires, all of which were almost immediately violated. In December the South Ossetian Supreme Soviet declared both a state of emergency and a general mobilization, in response to the Georgian Government's dispatch of troops to the region. In the same month the South Ossetian legislature adopted a second declaration of the region's independence, as well as a resolution in favour of its integration into the Russian Federation. The resolutions were overwhelmingly endorsed by South Ossetians at a referendum held in January 1992. While denouncing these developments, the new administration in Tbilisi (the Military Council) none the less declared its willingness to discuss the issue. However, hostilities continued between the rival factions, compounded by the intervention of Georgian government troops (which, by April, were attacking Tskhinvali). The situation was further complicated by the arrival of volunteer fighters from North Ossetia, in support of their South Ossetian neighbours.

Negotiations between Shevardnadze and President Yeltsin of the Russian Federation in late June 1992, and their agreement to secure a lasting cease-fire, promised a peaceful solution to the conflict (in which more than 400 Georgians and 1,000 Ossetians had been killed since 1989). Peace-keeping monitors (comprising Georgians, Ossetians and Russians) were deployed in South Ossetia during July, with the simultaneous withdrawal of all armed forces from the region. The return of refugees to South Ossetia began in that month. However, although the cease-fire subsequently remained in force, no political settlement to the conflict was reached at talks held in 1993–94, and

South Ossetia remained effectively a seceded territory; on 23 December 1993 it introduced a new Constitution. The lack of a formal settlement delayed the repatriation of refugees: in early 1994 some 11,000 South Ossetians remained in North Ossetia, while some 7,000 ethnic Georgians had yet to return to their homes in South Ossetia. In July 1995 representatives from Georgia, Russia, North Ossetia and South Ossetia reopened talks on a political settlement, under the aegis of the OSCE; negotiations continued in 1996. The South Ossetian leadership demanded recognition of the region's independence, rejecting proposals to grant South Ossetia the status of an autonomous republic within Georgia. However, a significant breakthrough was achieved in April, when a memorandum 'on strengthening mutual trust and security measures' was initialled in Tskhinvali;. the memorandum was signed in Moscow in the following month. A series of meetings was subsequently held between President Shevardnadze and Ludvig Chibirov, the Chairman of the South Ossetian legislature, to negotiate South Ossetia's political status. In September, however, the legislature of the separatist region approved an amendment to its Constitution to allow the introduction of a presidential government. Despite the Georgian leadership's declaration that the results of any election would be considered illegitimate, an election to the post of President of South Ossetia was held on 10 November, and was won by Chibirov. Shevardnadze, while criticizing the election, insisted that the search for a political settlement would continue.

Quadripartite negotiations were held at intervals throughout 1997, at which it was agreed that the policing role of peace-keeping forces deployed in South Ossetia was to be transferred to regional law-enforcement bodies; the issue of the revival of the region's economy was also discussed. Talks held in Moscow in March confirmed the principle of Georgia's territorial integrity, while allowing a measure of self-determination for South Ossetia. In September, at a meeting between Shevardnadze and Chibirov, an agreement was signed on the return of refugees to South Ossetia, described as the main concern of the two sides. In June 1998 a joint statement was signed by Shevardnadze and Chibirov, deferring political discussions in favour of economic accord. At talks held in South Ossetia in January 1999, however, South Ossetia refused to allow the sharing of customs revenue with the Georgian authorities. The first round of legislative elections took place in South Ossetia in May; the Communist Party secured about 39% of the votes cast. They were not recognized by the OSCE or by the Georgian authorities, who refused to fill the four seats (of 33) reserved for ethnic Georgian deputies. In October of that year the region requested a new round of talks with Georgia. A referendum on proposed amendments to the 1993 Constitution was scheduled to be held in South Ossetia in April 2001.

The cease-fire that was declared in South Ossetia in mid-1992 coincided with a resurgence of violence in the Autonomous Republic of Abkhazia. As in South Ossetia, a movement for Abkhazian secession from Georgia had been revived in 1989. Abkhazians are a predominantly Muslim people and their region had enjoyed virtual sovereignty within Georgia during the 1920s. However, in 1930 Abkhazia was made an autonomous republic and, on Stalin's orders, large numbers of western Georgians were resettled in the region. As a result, by 1989 ethnic Abkhazians comprised only 18% of the area's population, while Georgians constituted the largest ethnic group (46%). The Georgian Government repeatedly rejected Abkhazian secessionist demands on these demographic grounds. The movement for Abkhazian independence was also fiercely resisted by the local Georgian population. In July 1989 there were violent clashes between ethnic Georgians and Abkhazians in Sukhumi, the republic's capital, resulting in 14 deaths. A state of emergency was imposed throughout Abkhazia, but troops did not succeed in preventing further inter-ethnic violence.

In August 1990 the Abkhazian Supreme Soviet voted to declare independence from Georgia. This declaration was pronounced invalid by the Georgian Supreme Soviet, and Georgians living in Abkhazia staged protests and began a rail blockade of Sukhumi. In late August Georgian deputies in the Abkhazian legislature succeeded in reversing the declaration of independence. Inter-ethnic unrest continued during late 1990 and in 1991. Following the overthrow of Zviad Gamsakhurdia, in January 1992, there was renewed unrest in Abkhazia, as large numbers of ethnic Georgians demonstrated in support of the former President. In July the Abkhazian legislature declared Abkhazia's sovereignty as the 'Republic of Abkhazia'.

A period of violent armed conflict began in August 1992, when the Georgian Government dispatched some 3,000 members of the National Guard to the secessionist republic. It was claimed that the troops had been sent to release senior officials who had been taken hostage by the 'Zviadists' and who were allegedly being held in Abkhazia (see above), but the covert reason for their deployment, it was believed, was to suppress the growing secessionist movement. Abkhazian militia launched a series of attacks against the Georgian troops, but failed to retain control of Sukhumi. The Chairman of the Abkhazian legislature and leader of the independence campaign, Vladislav Ardzinba, retreated north with his forces, establishing his base at Gudauta. The situation was complicated by the dispatch of Russian paratroopers to the region to protect Russian military bases.

Relations between Georgia and Russia became strained, following Georgian accusations that conservative elements within the Russian leadership and armed forces were supplying military equipment and personnel to the Abkhazians. In October 1992 the Abkhazians launched a successful counter-offensive, regaining control of all of northern Abkhazia, and reportedly killing hundreds of its ethnic Georgian inhabitants. Hostilities intensified in the first half of 1993. Peace talks were held at regular intervals, finally culminating in the signing of a provisional peace agreement, in July, by Georgian and Abkhazian leaders. The cease-fire held (albeit with minor violations) until mid-September, when the Abkhazians launched surprise attacks in parts of the region, capturing Sukhumi after 11 days of intense fighting. Shevardnadze, who had arrived in Sukhumi at the start of the offensive (vowing to remain until the town was securely under government control), was forced to flee by air, under heavy bombardment. By late September almost all Georgian forces had been expelled from Abkhazia, and the region was declared 'liberated'.

Several hundred people were believed to have been killed during the fighting, and more than 200,000 ethnic Georgians and others fled Abkhazia. Many thousands of the refugees were subsequently stranded, in freezing conditions, in the mountainous border region separating Abkhazia and Georgia, where large numbers perished. The situation in Abkhazia following the rout of the Georgian forces was reported to be close to anarchy, with atrocities allegedly being perpetrated against remaining ethnic Georgians and other nationalities by Abkhazians. Nevertheless, in early December 1993 Georgian and Abkhazian officials signed an eight-point 'memorandum of understanding' at UN-sponsored talks in Geneva, Switzerland. A small number of UN military personnel, part of UNOMIG (see p. 64) were subsequently dispatched to Sukhumi in a peace-keeping capacity.

Outbreaks of violence continued in Abkhazia throughout 1994, despite the holding of peace talks (under UN and other auspices) at regular intervals. The fundamental disagreement between the Georgian and Abkhazian delegations concerned the future status of Abkhazia: Ardzinba demanded full independence (or confederal ties at the least) for Abkhazia, while the Georgian Government insisted on the preservation of Georgia's territorial integrity. However, hope for a peaceful solution was raised in May, by the declaration of a full cease-fire (only statements or memorandums had been issued up to this point). Under the accord, a contingent of some 2,500 CIS (mainly Russian) peace-keepers were deployed in June, joining the (augmented) UN observer force in Abkhazia. Nevertheless, the peace-keeping presence was unable to prevent renewed hostilities.

In November 1994 the Abkhazian legislature adopted a new Constitution, which declared the 'Republic of Abkhazia' to be a sovereign state. Ardzinba was elected to the new post of 'President'. The declaration of sovereignty was condemned by the Georgian Government, and the peace negotiations were subsequently suspended. Protests were also voiced by the USA, Russia and the UN Security Council, all of which reaffirmed their recognition of Georgia's territorial integrity. Peace negotiations were resumed in 1995, despite periodic outbreaks of violence in Abkhazia. In January 1996, at a summit meeting of CIS leaders in Moscow, it was agreed to implement Shevardnadze's request for economic sanctions to be imposed against Abkhazia until it consented to rejoin Georgia. In July the UN Security Council extended the mandate of the UNOMIG observers until January 1997 (when it was extended for a further six months). The CIS peacekeepers' mandate was extended in August 1996 until January 1997, and allowed for the peace-keepers to adopt measures to protect returning refugees.

On 23 November 1996 an election to the secessionist Abkhazian legislature, the People's Assembly, was held. The UN and the OSCE severely criticized the holding of the election, while the Georgian authorities declared the election results to be invalid. President Shevardnadze organized a simultaneous plebiscite among refugees from Abkhazia; voters were asked whether they supported the holding of a parliamentary election in Abkhazia prior to the restoration of Georgia's territorial integrity and the repatriation of refugees, and it was reported that some 99% of refugees had taken part, of whom almost all had voted against the holding of the election.

The mandate of the CIS peace-keeping forces in Abkhazia was the focus of much controversy in 1997. Members of the Abkhazeti faction in the Georgian Parliament staged a hunger strike in March, demanding the withdrawal of the CIS peace-keepers. However, at the CIS summit meeting later in that month the peace-keepers' mandate was extended until the end of July, and expanded to include the whole district of Gali, in order to facilitate the repatriation of refugees. The Abkhazian legislature claimed that the decision could not be implemented, since it required the approval of all parties in the conflict. Regular demands for the resumption of peace negotiations met with little success, and the diversion of Abkhazian long-distance telephone connections via Tbilisi, in April, coupled with the Abkhazian leadership's failure to achieve the lifting of economic sanctions against the region, further hampered the renewal of talks.

Violent clashes took place in the Kodori Gorge region of Abkhazia in early July 1997, with 20 people reported killed. Peace talks sponsored by the UN were subsequently held in Geneva, but no formal conclusion was reached. The UN observers' mandate, which expired on 31 July, was renewed for a further six months (and was subsequently granted successive six-monthly extensions, the most recent of which was until 31 July 2001). The status of the CIS peace-keepers remained undecided, since, upon the expiry of their mandate at the end of July, the Georgian National Security Council approved a resolution neither to request their immediate withdrawal, nor to demand an extension of their mandate.

Russian proposals for a settlement of the conflict, which provided for substantial autonomy for Abkhazia, while retaining Georgia's territorial integrity, were welcomed by Shevardnadze, but rejected by Ardzinba, who continued to demand equal status for Abkhazia within a confederation. In August 1997, for the first time since 1992, Ardzinba visited Georgia, together with the Russian Minister of Foreign Affairs, Yevgenii Primakov. Talks were held with Shevardnadze and, although no political consensus was reached, a reaffirmation of both sides' commitment to a peaceful resolution of the conflict was made. At further talks in September 1997 progress was reportedly achieved on the conditions for the repatriation of refugees, although the political status of the region remained a subject of dispute.

At the CIS summit meeting held in October 1997, the mandate of the CIS peace-keepers was extended until 31 January 1998. Shevardnadze, while welcoming the decision, criticized the peace-keepers' failure to create the conditions necessary for the safe return of ethnic Georgian refugees. The refugees, and the Tbilisi-based official leadership of Abkhazia, continued to demand the withdrawal of the Russian forces, fearing an escalation of Russian military intervention in the republic. A partial lifting by Russia of the economic sanctions against Abkhazia was condemned by Shevardnadze. UN-sponsored talks were convened in mid-November 1997, when a measure of progress in the search for a peaceful resolution of the conflict was achieved. A joint co-ordinating council was to be established, with the task of incorporating working groups to resolve the three main issues: a cessation of armed hostilities, the repatriation of refugees and the settlement of economic and social issues. Representatives of the parties to the conflict, as well as Russian, UN and European Union (EU, see p. 181) delegates were to participate in the council. Shevardnadze's declaration that he would favour the use of force to establish peace in Abkhazia, should further peace talks fail, was criticized by Ardzinba, who warned that any deployment of international forces in Abkhazia would be viewed as an act of aggression.

In March 1998 the Georgian Parliament declared the forthcoming local elections (due to be held later that month) in Abkhazia invalid. In May tension escalated when there was a renewal of hostilities, following a move by Abkhazian troops to enter the neutral zone separating Abkhazia from Georgia, in order to force ethnic Georgians out of the district of Gali. The

Georgian forces were put on full combat alert, and tens of thousands of ethnic Georgian refugees fled into Georgia. Following emergency peace talks, a cease-fire was agreed and came into force on 26 May. UN observers reported the following day that hostilities had ceased and Ardzinba imposed a three-month state of emergency in the area (which was extended in August). Peace negotiations were resumed in June; Georgia's key demand was the prompt and unconditional repatriation to Gali of some 35,000 ethnic Georgians who had been forced to flee the city by Abkhazian troops.

In July 1998 the transfer of responsibility for patrolling Georgia's maritime borders from Russian to Georgian guards provoked tension. The Abkhazian authorities criticized the new arrangement and threatened to attack any Georgian patrol vessel entering its territorial waters and demanded control of its own section of the maritime border. A special joint group to settle inland border issues was established in August. In September four observers from UNOMIG were injured when their vehicle was attacked by gunmen in Sukhumi. Abkhazia and Georgia blamed each other for the attack, and Ardzinba imposed a curfew on the region. Ensuing peace talks proved unsuccessful and hostilities continued. In January 1999, however, Ardzinba agreed to permit ethnic Georgian refugees to return to Gali from 1 March. Their return was, however, hindered by a blockade of the road bridge connecting Georgia with Abkhazia, which had begun in mid-February, by refugees demanding, *inter alia*, that Georgia leave the CIS and that persecution of ethnic Georgian guerrillas be stopped. The Russian peace-keeping forces and UNOMIG were not permitted to pass, thus thwarting scheduled quadripartite talks on Abkhazia, due to be held in Gali. The protest ended in mid-March. In August the Georgian Security Council voted to extend the mandate of the CIS peace-keepers. Periodic violence continued throughout 1999.

On 3 October 1999 Ardzinba, the sole candidate, was re-elected President with 99% of the votes cast; the rate of participation was 87.7%. The election was declared illegal by international observers. In a referendum held simultaneously, 97% of the votes cast upheld the 1994 Constitution, proclaiming the region as an independent, democratic republic. Shortly afterwards the Abkhazian legislature unanimously passed the State Independence Act. None the less, Georgia remained determined to pursue peace talks. In July 2000 a UN-sponsored protocol on stabilization measures was signed by both Abkhazia and Georgia. Violent incidents continued in 2000. Most prominently, a number of UN military observers were kidnapped in both June and December, and in August the leader of the Abkhazian opposition and human-rights consultant to the UN, Zurab Achba, was assassinated.

In March 2001 Russia joined Georgia in refusing to recognize the legitimacy of local elections held in Abkhazia. The holding of the elections was also condemned by the UN and the OSCE. However, some progress was made in mid-March, at a summit meeting held in Yalta, Ukraine, under UN auspices, when Abkhazia and Georgia signed an accord renouncing the use of force; the two sides also agreed a programme of confidence-building measures.

The Autonomous Republic of Ajaria proved to be the least troubled of Georgia's three autonomous territories. Despite being of ethnic Georgian origin, the Ajars, whose autonomous status was the result of a Soviet–Turkish Treaty of Friendship (1921), retained a sense of separate identity, owing to their adherence to Islam. In recent years some Christian Georgians have considered the Muslim Ajars a threat to a unified Georgian nation. Tensions between Muslims and Christians increased in 1991, after the Georgian Supreme Soviet ruled as unconstitutional a law relating to elections to the Ajar Supreme Soviet, which restricted nominations for the forthcoming election to permanent residents of Ajaria. In April there were prolonged demonstrations in protest against proposals to abolish Ajar autonomy and against perceived 'christianization' of the Muslim population. Ajaria remained calm from the latter half of 1991, in an otherwise volatile region. In February 1993, however, there were reports of provocations against Russian troops in Ajaria by armed Ajar groups. Nevertheless, the situation remained stable during 1994. In February 1995 there was reported to have been an assassination attempt against Aslan Abashidze, the Chairman of the Ajar Supreme Council (regional leader), and against the commander of Russian military forces in Ajaria. Elections to the Supreme Council (legislature) of Ajaria were held in September 1996 and the majority of seats were won by the All-Georgian Union of Revival party. Abashidze was re-elected Chairman of the Council. In December the deployment of armoured vehicles, allegedly from Russian military units, on the streets of Batumi, the republic's capital, led to tension between the Georgian authorities and the leadership of Ajaria. Abashidze denied reports in the Georgian press that a state of emergency had been declared, and announced that the military units were carrying out deployment exercises. The Georgian leadership responded by issuing a statement declaring that it had full control of the situation, although it appeared unable to verify on whose orders the vehicles had been deployed.

In October 1999 relations between Ajaria and Georgia deteriorated when Abashidze called Shevardnadze the 'father of terrorists'. In the same month, Ajaria refused to release prisoners who had been pardoned by Shevardnadze under an amnesty; criminal proceedings were subsequently instigated against the region. Abashidze was highly vocal in his criticism of the Georgian elections held in October and November 1999, and in late November he relinquished his parliamentary mandate, citing his inability to attend sittings in Tbilisi, owing to his fear of assassination; his seat was allocated to a member of his party. Relations with Georgia were also adversely affected by Ajaria's strong objections to military manoeuvres, due to be held in the region in 2001 under NATO's 'Partnership for Peace' programme of military co-operation.

Georgia was one of only four republics of the USSR not to join the CIS at its formation in December 1991. However, as civil and separatist conflicts threatened to destroy the country altogether, Shevardnadze was forced to reverse official Georgian policy on the CIS, and in late 1993 the republic was admitted to that body, including its collective security system. In May 1999, however, Georgia failed to sign the Collective Security Treaty on its expiry, as it did not consider the system relevant to the problems affecting it. Georgia's relations with the Russian Federation were strained by developments in secessionist Abkhazia in 1992–93 and by Georgian accusations of Russian involvement. However, in February 1994 Georgia and Russia signed a 10-year treaty of friendship and co-operation. The treaty provided, *inter alia*, for the establishment of Russian military bases in Georgia to 'protect the security of the CIS'. Abkhazian and South Ossetian leaders opposed the treaty, claiming that Russian-Georgian military co-operation would lead to an escalation of tension in the region. Nationalist opposition forces in Georgia also opposed the strengthening of the republic's ties with Russia. In 1996 President Shevardnadze and the Georgian legislature threatened to close the Russian military bases, unless Russia adopted a firmer stance against the separatists in South Ossetia and Abkhazia. In 1997–98 Russia continued to participate in the search for a resolution of the Abkhaz conflict. Tension between Georgia and Russia increased, however, over the issue of the CIS peace-keepers and the partial lifting of economic sanctions against Abkhazia (see above). Furthermore, Georgia criticized its exclusion by Russia and Ukraine from decisions pertaining to the division of the former Black Sea Fleet. In July 1998 Georgia assumed control of its maritime borders, following the withdrawal of Russian maritime patrols. A 150-km section of the state land border with Turkey was transferred from Russian to Georgian control in December. In May 2000 representatives of Bulgaria, Georgia, Romania, Russia, Turkey and Ukraine agreed to establish an international naval unit, Blackseafor.

The lifting of restrictions on the Russian-Abkhazian border in September 1999 angered Georgia, and further tension occurred later in the year, owing to the Russian-Chechen conflict. Georgia denied allegations that it was harbouring Chechen soldiers and selling arms to the breakaway republic. Shevardnadze consistently reiterated his refusal to comply with Russian requests for Russian and Georgian troops to patrol jointly the Georgian border with Dagestan and confirmed his opposition to the use of existing Russian bases to initiate attacks on Chechnya. In August, following an accidental bomb attack by Russia on the border with Chechnya, it was agreed that all Russian border guards deployed in Abkhazia and Ajaria would be withdrawn by the beginning of November. Furthermore, in November it was agreed that two of the four Russian military bases on Georgian territory would be withdrawn by mid-2001. In 2000 there were violent disturbances in the Pankisi Gorge, close to the Chechen border, which was inhabited by both ethnic Chechens and Chechen refugees. There were repeated kidnappings; in August three International Committee of the Red Cross (ICRC, see p. 222) workers were taken hostage for a

period of nine days, and that organization had frequently to suspend its activities there. In December local people began to patrol the troubled zone themselves. Despite this, in the same month Shevardnadze reiterated Georgia's refusal to carry out joint operations in the area with Russian troops.

Russia's decision to implement a full visa regime for Georgian citizens entering its territory from December 2000 caused renewed antagonism between the two countries, particularly since citizens of both Abkhazia and South Ossetia were to be exempt from the requirement. Russia claimed that it had introduced the regime in order to prevent the unrestricted movement of Chechen insurgents, but Georgia interpreted it as an attempt to undermine its territorial integrity, in retaliation for Georgia's unwillingness to assist Russia in the Chechen conflict; Russia confirmed, however, that the visa regime was to be a temporary measure only.

Georgia sought to develop its international relations in the late 1990s. In April 1996, together with Armenia and Azerbaijan, it signed an agreement on partnership and co-operation with the EU, and in January 1999 it joined the Council of Europe (see p. 165). In October it was announced that Georgia planned to apply for membership of the North Atlantic Treaty Organization (NATO, see p. 241) by 2005, although in 2000 President Shevardnadze indicated that the country might eventually declare itself to have neutral status. Relations with Ukraine were strengthened in 2000, as the result of significant increases in trade and the signature of trade and co-operation agreements. Moreover, in March 2001, as President of the UN Security Council, Ukraine played an important role in the mediation between Georgia and Abkhazia.

Government

Under the Constitution of August 1995, the President of Georgia is Head of State and the head of the executive, and also Commander-in-Chief of the Armed Forces. The President is directly elected for a five-year term (and may not hold office for more than two consecutive terms). The Government (headed by the Minister of State), is accountable to the President, to whom it acts as an advisory body. The supreme legislative body is the unicameral 235-member Georgian Parliament, which is directly elected for four years. (The Constitution provides for a future bicameral Parliament, comprising a Council of the Republic and a Senate, following the eventual restoration of Georgia's territorial integrity.)

Defence

One of the principal objectives of the Government following independence in 1991 was to create a unified army from the various existing paramilitary and other groups. A National Security Council (headed by the President of Georgia) was established in early 1996 as a consultative body co-ordinating issues related to defence and security. Compulsory military service lasts for two years. In August 2000 total armed forces numbered some 26,900: 23,800 army, 800 navy, 1,870 air force, and 430 troops attached to the Ministry of Defence. There were also 5,000 Russian troops based in Georgia. However, a law was passed in June, which was to reduce the total number of troops to 20,000 by the end of the year. In late 1993 Georgia joined the CIS and its collective security system. However, Georgia failed to renew its participation in the system upon its expiry in May 1999. In March 1994 Georgia joined NATO's 'Partnership for Peace' programme of military co-operation (see p. 243). The 2000 budget allocated 43.7m. lari to defence.

Economic Affairs

In 1998, according to estimates by the World Bank, Georgia's gross national product (GNP), measured at average 1996–98 prices, was US $5,281m., equivalent to $970 per head (or $3,429 per head on an international purchasing-power parity basis). During 1990–98, it was estimated, GNP per head declined, in real terms, at an average annual rate of 11.3%. In the same period the population decreased by an average of 0.1% per year. Georgia's gross domestic product (GDP) decreased, in real terms, by an average of 10.3% annually during 1990–99. Real GDP declined by 11.4% in 1994, but increased by 2.6% in 1995. Real GDP rose by 11.2% in 1996, and by 10.8% in 1997. However, GDP growth of only 2.9% was recorded in 1998, and GDP increased by 3.1% in 1999.

Agriculture contributed an estimated 33.2% of GDP in 1999 and in 1995 the sector (including forestry) provided 29.8% of employment. According to the FAO, in 1999 20% of the economically active population were engaged in agriculture.

Georgia's exceedingly favourable climate allows the cultivation of subtropical crops, such as tea and citrus fruit. Non-citrus fruit (including wine grapes), flowers, tobacco and grain are also cultivated. The mountain pastures are used for sheep- and goat-farming. In 1996 private agricultural production provided more than 85% of total output. During 1990–95, according to the World Bank, agricultural GDP decreased, in real terms, by an average of 31.4% per year. In 1994 agricultural GDP declined by about 58%, compared with 1993, but in 1995 growth of 18% was recorded. Agricultural output increased, according to the FAO, by 10.9% in 1995, by 0.5% in 1996 and by 2.2% in 1997, but declined by 6.0% in 1998, before undergoing a reversal, and increasing by 6.0% in 1999. However, a serious drought in 2000 caused up to 70% of total grain, sunflowers and wine-grape production to be destroyed.

Industry (comprising mining, manufacturing and utilities) contributed an estimated 13.0% of GDP in 1999, and provided 20.5% of employment in 1995. The most significant parts of the sector are the agro-processing and energy industries. According to the World Bank, industrial GDP decreased, in real terms, by an average of 34.1% per year in 1990–95. In 1995 industrial GDP declined by 10%, but in 1996 the sector recorded growth of 7.7%.

The principal minerals extracted are coal, petroleum and manganese ore, but reserves of high-grade manganese ore are largely depleted. There are also deposits of coal, copper, gold and silver. Substantial natural gas deposits were discovered in 1994–96.

The manufacturing sector contributed an estimated 12.9% of GDP in 1995. The machinery and metal-working industries, traditionally the most important parts of the sector, were in decline in the late 1990s. According to the World Bank, manufacturing GDP increased, in real terms, by an average of 0.7% per year in 1990–99.

Georgia has traditionally been highly dependent on imports of fuel and energy, in particular the import of natural gas from Turkmenistan, and crude petroleum from Russia. However, since 1993, when the prices of imported energy were raised to international market prices, there has been a significant reduction in the amount of fuel imported, leading to widespread energy shortages. The import of natural gas from Turkmenistan ceased in 1994. In mid-1996 the Georgian Government was negotiating with international organizations to construct some 200 hydroelectric power stations over the next 10 years. Imports of fuel and energy comprised an estimated 24.3% of total imports in 1998. In April 1999 a pipeline to transport petroleum to Supsa, on Georgia's Black Sea coast, from Baku, Azerbaijan, officially entered into service. A natural-gas pipeline from Baku to Erzurum, Turkey, via Georgia, was scheduled for completion in 2002. In the mean time, Georgia obtained natural gas from Russia, via Armenia.

The services sector contributed an estimated 50.1% of GDP in 1999 and engaged 49.7% of the employed labour force in 1995. Trade and transport and communications are the most significant activities of the sector, and tourism is expected to expand. According to the World Bank, the GDP of the sector decreased, in real terms, by an average of 22.3% annually in 1990–95. However, in 1995 the sector was estimated to have grown by 5.3%. In 1996 trade increased by more than 8%, compared with 1995.

In 1999 Georgia recorded a visible trade deficit of US $533.9m., while there was a deficit of $198.4m. on the current account of the balance of payments. In 1997 Russia was the principal source of imports (13.4% of total imports); other major sources were Azerbaijan, Turkey and the USA. The principal market for exports in that year was also Russia (29.8% of total exports); other important purchasers were Turkey, Azerbaijan and Armenia. According to government sources, in January–November 2000 Georgia's main trading partners were Turkey (accounting for 16.7% of total trade turnover), Russia (15.7%), Germany (8.7%) and the USA (7.6%). The principal exports in 1998 were ferro-alloys, wine and related products, and copper ore. The principal imports in that year were petroleum products, cigars and cigarettes, and cars.

In 1998 there was a budgetary deficit of 309.9m. lari. At the end of 1998 Georgia's total external debt was US $1,674m., of which $1,311m. was long-term public debt. The cost of debt-servicing in that year was equivalent to 7.6% of the value of exports of goods and services. The annual rate of inflation averaged 1,816% during 1991–95. Consumer prices increased by an average annual rate of 15,606.5% in 1994 and by 162.7%

in 1995. In 1996 the rate of increase declined to 39.4%. In 1997 the rate of inflation was 7.1%, decreasing to 3.5% in 1998, before rising again, to 19.2% in 1999. According to government estimates, the rate of increase was 4.6% in 2000. In 1999 some 277,500 people were unemployed.

In 1992 Georgia became a member of the IMF and the World Bank, as well as joining the European Bank for Reconstruction and Development (EBRD, see p. 176). Georgia is also a member of the Organization for Black Sea Economic Co-operation (see p. 265). In June 2000 Georgia became a full member of the World Trade Organization (WTO, see p. 292).

The collapse of the USSR in 1991 and the outbreak of three armed conflicts in Georgia adversely affected the country's economy. Output declined sharply in all sectors, and Georgia became increasingly dependent on international financial and humanitarian aid; at the same time the instability in the republic discouraged investment by foreign companies. However, with the return of relative political stability in 1994, the Government embarked on a programme of comprehensive stabilization. By early 1998 the programme of structural reform had achieved considerable success and there was growth in all sectors. In mid-1998, however, adverse domestic developments and the Russian financial crisis severely disrupted the Georgian economy, causing an increase in inflation and a lower rate of growth. However, the currency had stabilized by mid-1999, following a crisis in December 1998, and the opening of the Baku–Supsa petroleum pipeline in April 1999 brought much-needed revenue. At the end of 1999 Georgia established a new Ministry of Tax and Revenue, demonstrating its commitment to increasing income from taxation. In October 2000, however, an IMF review observed that tax revenue remained too low, resulting in difficulties in settling wages' and pensions' arrears. Nevertheless, the Fund praised the budget for that year and the country's campaign against corruption. In order for the IMF to resume its lending activities in Georgia, suspended in July 1999, it had to obtain agreement from the country's creditors. In order to obtain such approval from Russia, Georgia agreed, in January 2001, to the so-called 'zero option' (already negotiated with many successor states), whereby Russia assumed responsibility for Georgia's share of the Soviet debt, in exchange for its renunciation of any claim to Soviet assets. The IMF duly resumed lending to Georgia, pledging US $141m. over a three-year period. Similarly, the World Bank was to allocate $215m. towards structural reform over the same period. Moreover, in March the 'Paris Club' of official creditors agreed to implement beneficial debt restructuring for Georgia. The budget for 2001, approved by the Georgian Parliament in December 2000, envisaged a budgetary deficit of some 277.6m. lari, equivalent to around 4% of GDP. The budget aimed, in particular, to bring about a reduction in the level of foreign debt.

Social Welfare

Georgia's social welfare system was enormously strained by the civil and separatist conflicts in the early 1990s, and radical reforms were subsequently implemented. Three extrabudgetary funds provide social welfare benefits: the Social Security Fund, established in 1991, which distributes old-age, invalidity and widows' pensions; the Employment Fund, also established in 1991, which provides unemployment, sickness and maternity benefits; and the Health Fund, established in 1995. The Government aimed to privatize most health care facilities by 1998 and was covering only 30% of direct costs (such as medical supplies) of health care provision in that year. However, free medical care was to continue to be provided to the neediest sections of the population. In March 1997 some 287,000 refugees received assistance from the Government.

In 1996 there were 1,000 people per 4.8 hospital beds. The 1996 budget allocated 10.7% of total expenditure (82.5m. lari) to social services, and a further 2.2% (16.9m. lari) to health care. Total public expenditure on health in 1998 was 42.2m. lari. In 1996 the retirement age was raised from 60 to 65 years for men and from 55 to 60 years for women; early retirement was eliminated in 1998. There were 890,000 registered pensioners by the end of 1998.

Education

Until the late 1980s the education system was an integrated part of the Soviet system. Considerable changes were made following the restoration of independence in 1991, including the ending of the teaching of ideologically orientated subjects, and greater emphasis on Georgian language and history. Education is officially compulsory for nine years, between the ages of six and 14. Primary education begins at six years of age and lasts for four years. Secondary education, beginning at 10, lasts for a maximum of seven years, comprising a first cycle of five years and a second cycle of two years. Free secondary education is available for the highest-achieving 30% of primary-school pupils. In 1997 34% of children of the relevant age-group attended pre-primary schools. Primary enrolment in that year was equivalent to 88% of the relevant age group (89% for males, 88% for females), while the comparable ratio for secondary enrolment was 77% (78% males, 76% females). In the 1994/95 academic year there were 3,139 secondary schools, with a total enrolment of 700,472 pupils; of these, 75.4% were taught in Georgian-language schools, while 3.9% were taught in Russian-language schools, 3.7% in Armenian-language schools, 6.1% in Azerbaijani-language schools and 9.6% in mixed Georgian- and Russian-language schools. In 1996/97 163,345 students were enrolled at institutions of higher education (including universities); enrolment was equivalent to 42% of the relevant age-group. In 1995 it was estimated that the illiteracy rate had decreased to 0.5% of the adult population. In 1998 113.2m. lari (equivalent to 2.4% of GDP) was allocated to education; however, the Government spent a total of 99.5m. lari in that year.

Public Holidays

2001: 1 January (New Year), 7 January (Christmas), 19 January (Epiphany), 3 March (Mother's Day), 13–16 April (Easter), 26 May (Independence Day), 28 August (St Mary's Day, Mariamoba), 14 October (Svetitskovloba), 23 November (St Georgi's Day, Giorgoba).

2002: 1 January (New Year), 7 January (Christmas), 19 January (Epiphany), 3 March (Mother's Day), 4–6 May (Easter), 26 May (Independence Day), 28 August (St Mary's Day, Mariamoba), 14 October (Svetitskovloba), 23 November (St Georgi's Day, Giorgoba).

Weights and Measures

The metric system is in force.

Statistical Survey

Principal sources: IMF, *Georgia — Economic Review* and *Georgia — Recent Economic Developments*; World Bank, *Statistical Handbook: States of the Former USSR*.

Area and Population

AREA, POPULATION AND DENSITY

Area (sq km)	69,700*
Population (census results)†	
17 January 1979	4,993,182
12 January 1989	
Males	2,562,040
Females	2,838,801
Total	5,400,841
Population (official estimates at mid-year)‡§	
1996	5,411,000
1997	5,434,000
1999	5,399,000
Density (per sq km) at mid-1999	77.5

* 26,911 sq miles.
† Population is *de jure*. The *de facto* total at the 1989 census was 5,443,359.
‡ Figures include persons registered in Georgia but residing abroad. As a result of large-scale emigration from Georgia in the early 1990s, the population was estimated to have declined to about 4,600,000 by late 1994.
§ Figures for 1998 are not available.

POPULATION BY NATIONALITY (1989 census result)

										%
Georgian	.	.	.	.	.	.	.	.	.	68.8
Armenian	.	.	.	.	.	.	.	.	.	9.0
Russian .	.	.	.	.	.	.	.	.	.	7.4
Azerbaijani	.	.	.	.	.	.	.	.	.	5.1
Ossetian.	.	.	.	.	.	.	.	.	.	3.2
Greek	.	.	.	.	.	.	.	.	.	1.9
Abkhazian	.	.	.	.	.	.	.	.	.	1.7
Others .	.	.	.	.	.	.	.	.	.	2.9
Total	.	.	.	.	.	.	.	.	.	**100.0**

PRINCIPAL TOWNS
(estimated population at 1 January 1990)

Tbilisi (capital).	.	1,268,000	Batumi	. . .	. 137,000
Kutaisi	. .	236,000	Sukhumi	. . .	. 122,000
Rustavi	. .	160,000			

Source: UN, *Demographic Yearbook*.

BIRTHS, MARRIAGES AND DEATHS

	Registered live births		Registered marriages		Registered deaths	
	Number	Rate (per 1,000)	Number	Rate (per 1,000)	Number	Rate (per 1,000)
1993 . .	61,594	11.3	24,105	4.4	48,938	9.0
1994 . .	57,311	10.6	21,908	4.0	41,596	7.7
1995 . .	56,341	10.4	21,481	4.0	37,874	7.0
1996 . .	53,669	9.9	19,253	3.6	34,414	6.4
1997 . .	52,000	10.7	17,100	3.5	37,700	7.7
1998 . .	46,800	9.1	15,300	3.0	39,400	7.6

Source: UN, *Demographic Yearbook*; Caucasus Health International Forum.

Expectation of life (years at birth, 1998): 73 (Source: World Bank, *World Development Indicators*).

EMPLOYMENT (annual averages, '000 persons)*

	1993	1994	1995
Material sphere	1,201.2	1,203	1,169
Industry†	303.4	277	264
Construction	125.3	64	90
Agriculture	553.4	539	510
Forestry	9.0	6	6
Transport and communications .	57.4	63	52
Trade and other services . .	152.7	254	257
Non-material sphere	590.6	547	561
Housing and municipal services.	66.3	53	52
Science, research and development	40.6	36	36
Education, culture and arts. .	222.5	216	228
Health, social security and sports	155.8	155	160
Banking and financial institutions	12.4	10	10
Government	49.0	35	35
Other non-material services .	44.3	42	40
Total	**1,791.8**	**1,750**	**1,730**

1996 (annual averages, '000 persons)*: 2,036.2.
1997 (annual averages, '000 persons)*: 2,233.2.

* Figures exclude employment in the informal sector, estimated to total about 750,000 persons at mid-1996.
† Comprising manufacturing (except printing and publishing), mining and quarrying, electricity, gas, water, logging and fishing.

Unemployment ('000 persons): 291.0 (males 159.7, females 131.3) in 1998, 277.5 (males 160.1, females 117.4) in 1999 (Source: ILO, *Yearbook of Labour Statistics*).

Agriculture

PRINCIPAL CROPS ('000 metric tons)

	1997	1998	1999
Wheat	292	145	226
Barley	45	20	51
Maize	546	420	490
Potatoes.	353	350	443
Sunflower seed	32	23	41
Cabbages	105*	80	110*
Tomatoes	277*	220	310*
Cucumbers and gherkins* . .	40	30	42
Onions (dry). . . .	35	36	45*
Carrots	11*	5	8*
Other vegetables. . . .	45	9	10*
Watermelons	11*	32	66*
Grapes	309	238	220
Apples	76*	93	110*
Pears	30*	37	41*
Peaches and nectarines . .	11*	15	18*
Plums	19*	21	25*
Citrus fruit	57	85	56
Apricots	3*	2	3*
Tea (made)	33	47	60
Tobacco (leaves)	0	3	2

* Unofficial figure(s).

Source: FAO.

LIVESTOCK ('000 head at 1 January)

	1997	1998	1999
Horses	26	28	30
Cattle	1,008	1,027	1,051
Buffaloes*	18	16	16
Pigs.	333	330	366
Sheep†	600	525	522
Goats†	45	41	37
Chickens (million) . .	15	16	8

* FAO estimates.   † Unofficial figures.

Source: FAO.

LIVESTOCK PRODUCTS ('000 metric tons)

	1997	1998	1999
Beef and veal	56	43	41
Mutton and lamb . . .	7	8	7
Pig meat	47	42	41
Poultry meat . . .	11	10	11
Cows' milk	593	635	660
Cheese	3	3	3
Hen eggs*	21	21	22

* Unofficial figures.

Source: FAO.

Fishing

(metric tons, live weight)

	1996	1997	1998
Capture	2,453	2,583	3,001
Whiting	223	58	53
European sprat . . .	185	85	24
European anchovy . . .	1,232	2,288	2,346
Sharks, rays and skates . .	71	1	550
Sea snails	711	118	—
Aquaculture	101	61	96
Common carp	84	49	42
Total catch (incl. others) . .	2,554	2,644	3,097

Source: FAO, *Yearbook of Fishery Statistics*.

Mining*

('000 metric tons, unless otherwise indicated)

	1996	1997	1998
Coal	22.5	4.6	14.7
Crude petroleum . . .	128.0	134.0	119.2
Natural gas (million cu m) . .	3.3	—	—
Manganese ore	101.9	14.2	16.0

* Data for South Ossetia and Abkhazia are not included.

Industry*

SELECTED PRODUCTS ('000 metric tons, unless otherwise indicated)

	1996	1997	1998
Refined sugar	25.8	19.7	—
Canned foodstuffs . . .	7.9	9.0	1.9
Wine ('000 hectolitres) . .	228	245	217
Beer ('000 hectolitres) . .	47	78	74
Soft drinks ('000 hectolitres) .	160	400	290
Mineral water ('000 hectolitres) .	180	332	281
Cigarettes (million) . . .	1,200	900	600
Wool yarn	0.2	0.1	0.0
Cotton yarn	0.4	0.1	0.1
Textile fabrics (million sq metres) .	1.3	0.5	0.2
Mineral fertilizers . . .	68.0	80.9	55.4
Synthetic ammonia . . .	93.2	102.1	77.5
Motor spirit (petrol) . . .	—	4.4	2.4
Distillate fuel oil (diesel fuel) . .	4.5	8.1	4.7
Building bricks (million) . .	9.4	11.7	13.1
Steel	82.7	103.0	56.4
Steel pipes	34.0	23.5	8.8
Electric energy (million kWh) . .	7,200	7,200	8,100

* Data for South Ossetia and Abkhazia are not included.

Finance

CURRENCY AND EXCHANGE RATES

Monetary Units
    100 tetri = 1 lari.

Sterling, Dollar and Euro Equivalents (29 December 2000)
    £1 sterling = 2.947 lari;
    US $1 = 1.975 lari;
    €1 = 1.838 lari;
    100 lari = £33.93 = $50.63 = €54.41.

Average Exchange Rate (lari per US $)
    1998   1.3898
    1999   2.0245
    2000   1.9762

Note: On 25 September 1995 Georgia introduced the lari, replacing interim currency coupons at the rate of 1 lari = 1,000,000 coupons. From April 1993 the National Bank of Georgia had issued coupons in various denominations, to circulate alongside (and initially at par with) the Russian (formerly Soviet) rouble. From August 1993 coupons became Georgia's sole legal tender, but their value rapidly depreciated. The transfer from coupons to the lari lasted one week, and from 2 October 1995 the lari became the only permitted currency in Georgia.

BUDGET (million lari)*

Revenue†	1996	1997	1998
Tax revenue	317.9	484.6	526.1
Taxes on income . . .	44.5	76.9	87.8
Taxes on profits . . .	37.9	38.8	50.5
Value-added tax . . .	133.8	205.5	219.7
Customs duties . . .	19.9	61.2	67.0
Other current revenue . . .	50.0	66.3	97.1
Extrabudgetary revenue‡ . . .	91.7	102.5	117.5
Total	459.6	653.5	740.8

Expenditure§	1996	1997	1998
Current expenditure . . .	736.7	890.5	997.3
Wages and salaries. . .	103.7	155.5	176.7
Other goods and services‖ . .	303.9	274.0	202.4
Subsidies and transfers. .	59.0	103.4	119.3
Interest payments . . .	57.6	85.1	114.8
Extrabudgetary expenditure¶ .	103.8	168.4	212.5
Local government expenditure .	108.7	104.2	171.7
Capital expenditure . . .	68.9	73.4	65.5
Total	**805.6**	**963.9**	**1,062.8**

* Figures represent a consolidation of the State Budget (covering the central Government and local administrations) and extrabudgetary funds.

† Excluding grants received (million lari): 71.1 in 1996; 15.5 in 1997; 45.7 in 1998.

‡ Comprising the revenues of the Social Security Fund, the Employment Fund, the Health Fund (until July 1997), the Privatization Fund and the Road Fund (established in October 1995).

§ Excluding net lending (million lari): 4.2 in 1996; 18.5 in 1997; 33.6 in 1998.

‖ Comprising other goods and services, other current expenditure and unclassified expenditure.

¶ Including the payment of pensions and unemployment benefit.

INTERNATIONAL RESERVES (US $ million at 31 December)

	1997	1998	1999
Gold	0.50	0.50	0.54
IMF special drawing rights . .	0.13	5.20	8.42
Reserve position in the IMF . .	0.01	0.01	0.01
Foreign exchange . . .	199.66	117.78	123.96
Total	**200.30**	**123.49**	**132.93**

Source: IMF, *International Financial Statistics*.

MONEY SUPPLY (million lari at 31 December)

	1997	1998	1999
Currency outside banks . .	239.87	212.19	244.00
Demand deposits. . . .	38.67	38.38	31.51
Total money	**278.54**	**250.58**	**275.50**

Source: IMF, *International Financial Statistics*.

COST OF LIVING (Consumer price index for five cities; base: 1995 = 100)

	1997	1998	1999
Food, beverages and tobacco . .	139.2	144.6	171.4
Fuel and light	159.8	196.8	305.6
Clothing (incl. footwear) . .	150.2	147.3	168.4
All items (incl. others) . .	**149.3**	**154.6**	**184.3**

Source: ILO, *Yearbook of Labour Statistics*.

NATIONAL ACCOUNTS

Gross Domestic Product (million lari at current prices)

	1995	1996	1997
GDP in purchasers' values . .	3,694	5,724	6,798

Gross Domestic Product by Economic Activity (% of total)

	1997	1998	1999
Agriculture	34.5	31.6	33.2
Industry*	13.6	13.0	13.0
Construction	3.6	4.4	3.8
Health and education . .	4.2	4.3	3.6
Housing	9.5	9.2	8.2
Transport and communications .	7.8	11.2	11.6
Trade	11.2	10.9	11.7
Other	15.8	15.4	15.0
Total	**100.0**	**100.0**	**100.0**

* Principally mining, manufacturing, electricity, gas and water.

BALANCE OF PAYMENTS (US $ million)

	1997	1998	1999
Exports of goods f.o.b. . .	376.5	299.9	329.5
Imports of goods f.o.b. . .	−1,162.9	−994.5	−863.4
Trade balance	**−786.4**	**−694.6**	**−533.9**
Exports of services . . .	198.0	365.3	216.9
Imports of services . . .	−249.7	−345.2	−224.0
Balance on goods and services.	**−838.1**	**−674.5**	**−541.0**
Other income received . .	186.6	243.4	211.4
Other income paid . . .	−59.2	−52.7	−64.5
Balance on goods, services and income	**−710.7**	**−483.8**	**−394.1**
Current transfers received . .	205.5	219.9	228.7
Current transfers paid . .	−9.0	−11.8	−33.0
Current balance . . .	**−514.2**	**−275.7**	**−198.4**
Capital account (net) . . .	−6.5	−6.1	−7.1
Direct investment abroad . .	—	—	−1.0
Direct investment from abroad	242.5	265.3	82.3
Portfolio investment liabilities .	2.4	—	6.2
Other investment assets . .	−24.8	−86.9	9.3
Other investment liabilities .	102.6	170.4	38.7
Net errors and omissions . .	136.0	−170.5	55.7
Overall balance	**−62.0**	**−103.5**	**−14.3**

Source: IMF, *International Financial Statistics*.

External Trade

PRINCIPAL COMMODITIES (US $ million)

Imports f.o.b.	1996	1997	1998
Crude petroleum and natural gas	87.9	75.8	58.5
Petroleum products . .	160.0	152.2	130.3
Sugar	33.2	39.1	16.2
Cigars and cigarettes . . .	30.8	107.8	120.0
Electricity	14.4	26.8	25.7
Wheat and flour . . .	49.6	37.1	26.5
Wheat and rye by-products .	63.7	57.2	31.8
Medicines	14.6	35.9	36.3
Coffee and coffee substitutes .	11.6	n.a.	n.a.
Radio receivers . . .	6.8	n.a.	n.a.
Automobiles	n.a.	45.3	65.2
Electronic devices . .	n.a.	17.6	20.2
Pipes and other related products	n.a.	n.a.	16.2
Total (incl. others) . .	**686.8**	**943.5**	**884.3**

Exports f.o.b.	1996	1997	1998
Ferro alloys	7.7	15.5	22.3
Non-ferrous metal pipes . .	15.7	17.5	6.4
Crude petroleum and natural gas	6.7	14.4	n.a.
Petroleum products . .	17.4	13.4	9.2
Tea	16.8	18.5	8.9
Fertilizers	11.9	13.8	10.6
Citrus fruits (incl. dry fruits) .	8.2	9.1	9.5
Copper ore	13.4	14.1	15.1
Alcoholic beverages (excl. wine)	6.3	5.2	5.5
Wine and related products .	12.5	12.5	15.4
Non-alloyed steel and cast iron	10.2	9.3	6.2
Mineral water . . .	17.5	18.5	7.2
Electricity	13.1	11.9	n.a.
Total (incl. others) . .	**198.9**	**239.8**	**192.3**

1999 (US $ million): Total imports 551.6; Total exports 233.8. Source: *Macro Micro Economics*.

PRINCIPAL TRADING PARTNERS (US $ million)

Imports f.o.b.	1994	1995	1996
Armenia	1.1	11.4	17.3
Austria	0.3	10.1	8.4
Azerbaijan	23.5	42.8	77.9
Bulgaria	2.1	26.6	43.3
China, People's Republic	0.1	0.1	1.4
Czech Republic	0.1	0.5	2.4
France	0.3	1.6	25.4
Germany	4.8	10.6	27.1
Netherlands	0.9	3.9	12.9
Romania	3.3	31.4	40.8
Russia	26.5	48.8	127.3
Turkey	38.6	84.6	80.3
Turkmenistan	215.8	41.2	4.7
Ukraine	4.2	7.7	38.5
United Kingdom	0.3	11.8	34.3
USA	5.1	14.5	48.3
Total (incl. others)	337.8	385.4	718.4

Exports f.o.b.	1994	1995	1996
Armenia	12.9	18.9	20.5
Azerbaijan	14.7	12.7	24.9
Belarus	3.3	2.1	1.4
Bulgaria	0.1	5.7	12.2
Czech Republic	0.2	0.0	0.0
Italy	0.1	2.8	1.7
Kazakhstan	9.0	1.8	2.4
Russia	52.3	47.0	56.8
Switzerland	2.1	6.1	7.5
Turkey	23.6	34.9	25.9
Turkmenistan	15.5	6.9	13.4
Ukraine	6.1	5.6	5.4
USA	3.7	0.6	1.3
Uzbekistan	2.7	0.6	2.9
Total (incl. others)	155.8	154.3	199.4

Transport

RAILWAYS (traffic)

	1991	1992	1993
Passenger-km (million)	2,135	1,210	1,003
Freight net ton-km (million)	9,916	3,677	1,750

Source: UN, *Statistical Yearbook*.

ROAD TRAFFIC ('000 motor vehicles in use)

	1994	1995	1996*
Passenger cars	468.8	441.8	427.0
Commercial vehicles	48.7	42.1	34.7

* Estimates.

Source: International Road Federation, *World Road Statistics*.

SHIPPING
Merchant Fleet (registered at 31 December)

	1996	1997	1998
Number of vessels	84	97	95
Total displacement ('000 grt)	206.0	128.1	117.8

Source: Lloyd's Register of Shipping, *World Fleet Statistics*.

CIVIL AVIATION (traffic on scheduled services)

	1995	1996	1997
Kilometres flown (million)	4	5	3
Passengers carried ('000)	177	152	110
Passenger-km (million)	308	288	206
Total ton-km (million)	30	28	20

Source: UN, *Statistical Yearbook*.

Passengers carried ('000): 230 in 1998; 171 in 1999 (Source: Georgian Investment Centre).

Tourism

FOREIGN TOURIST ARRIVALS BY COUNTRY OF ORIGIN

	1996	1997	1998
CIS countries*	46,843	185,884	177,162
Turkey	50,529	99,826	102,160
USA	2,746	3,691	4,633
Total (incl. others)	116,980	313,290	317,063

* Comprising Armenia, Azerbaijan, Belarus, Kazakhstan, Kyrgyzstan, Moldova, Russia, Tajikistan, Turkmenistan, Ukraine and Uzbekistan.

Tourism receipts (US $ million): 170 in 1996; 416 in 1997; 423 in 1998.

Source: World Tourism Organization, *Yearbook of Tourism Statistics* and World Bank, *World Development Indicators*.

Communications Media

	1995	1996	1997
Telephones ('000 main lines in use)	554	567	620
Telefax stations (number in use)	n.a.	500	n.a.
Mobile cellular telephones (subscribers)	150	2,300	30,000
Radio receivers ('000 in use)	3,005	3,010	2,570
Television receivers ('000 in use)	2,550	2,560	3,020
Book production*:			
Titles	1,104	581	n.a.
Copies ('000)	1,627	834	n.a.

* Including pamphlets.

Sources: UN, *Statistical Yearbook*; UNESCO, *Statistical Yearbook*.

Education

(1996/97, unless otherwise indicated)

	Institutions	Teachers	Students
Pre-primary schools	1,322*	9,368	71,407
Primary schools	3,201	16,542	293,325
Secondary schools	3,139†	57,963	444,058
State secondary specialized schools	76‡	n.a.	30,153‡
Private secondary specialized schools	98†	n.a.	14,200†
Vocational/technical schools	115†	2,146	19,593
Higher schools (incl. universities)	23‡	25,549	163,345

* 1995/96.   † 1994/95.   ‡ 1993/94.

Sources: UNESCO, *Statistical Yearbook* and Ministry of Education, Tbilisi.

Directory

The Constitution

A new Constitution was approved by the Georgian legislature on 24 August 1995; it entered into force on 17 October. The Constitution replaced the Decree on State Power of November 1992 (which had functioned as an interim basic law). The following is a summary of the Constitution's main provisions:

GENERAL PROVISIONS

Georgia is an independent, united and undivided state, as confirmed by the referendum conducted throughout the entire territory of the country (including Abkhazia and South Ossetia) on 31 March 1991, and in accordance with the Act on the Restoration of the State Independence of Georgia of 9 April 1991. The Georgian state is a democratic republic. Its territorial integrity and the inviolability of its state borders are confirmed by the republic's Constitution and laws.

All state power belongs to the people, who exercise this power through referendums, other forms of direct democracy, and through their elected representatives. The State recognizes and defends universally recognized human rights and freedoms. The official state language is Georgian; in Abkhazia both Georgian and Abkhazian are recognized as state languages. While the State recognizes the exceptional role played by the Georgian Orthodox Church in Georgian history, it declares the complete freedom of faith and religion as well as the independence of the Church from the State. The capital is Tbilisi.

FUNDAMENTAL HUMAN RIGHTS AND FREEDOMS

Georgian citizenship is acquired by birth and naturalization. A Georgian citizen may not concurrently be a citizen of another state. Every person is free by birth and equal before the law, irrespective of race, colour, language, sex, religion, political and other views, national, ethnic and social affiliation, origin and place of residence. Every person has the inviolable right to life, which is protected by law. No one may be subjected to torture or inhuman, cruel or humiliating treatment or punishment.

Freedom of speech, thought, conscience and faith are guaranteed. The mass media are free. Censorship is prohibited. The right to assemble publicly is guaranteed, as is the right to form public associations, including trade unions and political parties. Every citizen who has attained the age of 18 years has the right to participate in referendums and elections of state and local administrative bodies.

THE GEORGIAN PARLIAMENT

The Georgian Parliament is the supreme representative body, implementing legislation and determining the basis of the country's domestic and foreign policies. It controls the activities of the Government, within the limits prescribed by the Constitution, and has other powers of implementation.

Parliament is elected on the basis of universal, equal and direct suffrage by secret ballot, for a term of four years. It is composed of 235 members: 150 elected by proportional representation (with a minimum requirement of 7% of the votes cast to secure parliamentary representation) and 85 by majority vote in single-member constituencies. Any citizen who has attained the age of 25 years and has the right to vote may be elected a member of Parliament. The instigation of criminal proceedings against a member of Parliament, and his/her detention or arrest, are only permitted upon approval by Parliament. A member of Parliament may not hold any position in state service or engage in entrepreneurial activities.

Parliament elects a Chairman and Deputy Chairmen (including one Deputy Chairman each from deputies elected in Abkhazia and Ajaria), for the length of its term of office. Members of Parliament may unite to form parliamentary factions. A faction must have no fewer than 10 members.

(Following the creation of the appropriate conditions throughout the territory of Georgia and the formation of bodies of local self-government, the Georgian Parliament will be composed of two chambers: the Council of the Republic and the Senate. The Council of the Republic will be composed of deputies elected according to the proportional system. The Senate will be composed of deputies elected in Abkhazia, Ajaria and other territorial units of Georgia, and five members appointed by the President of Georgia.)

THE PRESIDENT OF GEORGIA AND THE GOVERNMENT

The President of Georgia is Head of State and the head of executive power. The President directs and implements domestic and foreign policy, ensures the unity and territorial integrity of the country, and supervises the activities of state bodies in accordance with the Constitution. The President is the supreme representative of Georgia in foreign relations. He/she is elected on the basis of universal, equal and direct suffrage by secret ballot, for a period of five years. The President may not be elected for more than two consecutive terms. Any citizen of Georgia who has the right to vote and who has attained the age of 35 years and lived in Georgia for no less than 15 years, is eligible to be elected President.

The President of Georgia concludes international treaties and agreements and conducts negotiations with foreign states; with the consent of Parliament, appoints and dismisses Georgian ambassadors and other diplomatic representatives; receives the credentials of ambassadors and other diplomatic representatives of foreign states and international organizations; with the consent of Parliament, appoints members of the Government and Ministers; is empowered to remove Ministers from their posts; submits to Parliament the draft state budget, after agreeing upon its basic content with parliamentary committees; in the event of an armed attack on Georgia, declares a state of war, and concludes peace; during war or mass disorders, when the country's territorial integrity is threatened, or in the event of a *coup d'état* or an armed uprising, an ecological catastrophe or epidemic, or in other instances when the bodies of state power cannot implement their constitutional powers normally, declares a state of emergency; with the consent of Parliament, has the right to halt the activities of representative bodies of self-government or territorial units (if their activities create a threat to the sovereignty and territorial integrity of the country) as well as to halt state bodies in the exercise of their constitutional powers; signs and promulgates laws; decides questions of citizenship and the granting of political asylum; grants pardons; schedules elections to Parliament and other representative bodies; has the right to revoke acts of subordinate executive bodies; is the Commander-in-Chief of the Armed Forces; and appoints members of the National Security Council, chairs its meetings, and appoints and dismisses military commanders.

The President enjoys immunity. During his/her period in office, he/she may not be arrested, and no criminal proceedings may be instigated against him/her. In the event that the President violates the Constitution, betrays the State or commits other crimes, Parliament may remove him/her from office (with the approval of the Constitutional Court or the Supreme Court).

Members of the Government are accountable to the President. They do not have the right to hold other posts (except party posts), to engage in entrepreneurial activities or to receive a wage or any other permanent remuneration for any other activities. Members of the Government may be removed from their posts by an edict of the President or by Parliament. Ministries perform state management in specific spheres of state and public life. Each Ministry is headed by a Minister, who independently adopts decisions on questions within his/her sphere of jurisdiction.

JUDICIAL POWER

Judicial power is independent and is implemented only by the courts. Judges are independent in their activities and are subordinate only to the Constitution and the law. Court proceedings are held in public (except for certain specified instances). The decision of the court is delivered in public. Judges enjoy immunity. It is prohibited to instigate criminal proceedings against a judge or to detain or arrest him/her, without the consent of the Chairman of the Supreme Court.

The Constitutional Court is the legal body of constitutional control. It is composed of nine judges, three of whom are appointed by the President, three elected by Parliament, and three appointed by the Supreme Court. The term of office of members of the Constitutional Court is 10 years.

The Supreme Court supervises legal proceedings in general courts according to the established judicial procedure and, as the court of first instance, examines cases determined by law. On the recommendation of the President of Georgia, the Chairman and judges of the Supreme Court are elected by Parliament for a period of at least 10 years.

The Procurator's Office is an institution of judicial power which carries out criminal prosecution, supervises the preliminary investigation and the execution of a punishment, and supports the state prosecution. On the recommendation of the President of Georgia, the Procurator-General is appointed by Parliament for a term of five years. Lower-ranking procurators are appointed by the Procurator-General.

DEFENCE OF THE STATE

Georgia has armed forces to protect the independence, sovereignty and territorial integrity of the country, and also to fulfil international obligations. The President of Georgia approves the structure of the armed forces and Parliament ratifies their numerical strength, on the recommendation of the National Security Council. The National Security Council, which is headed by the President of Georgia, carries out military organizational development and the defence of the country.

The Government

HEAD OF STATE

President of Georgia: EDUARD SHEVARDNADZE (elected by direct popular vote 5 November 1995; re-elected 9 April 2000).

GOVERNMENT
(May 2001)

Minister of State and Head of the State Chancellery: GIA ARSENISHVILI.

Minister of Agriculture and Produce: DAVIT KIRVALIDZE.

Minister of State Property Management: LEVAN DZNELADZE.

Minister of Culture: SESILI GOGOBERIDZE.

Minister of Defence: Gen. DAVIT TEVZADZE.

Minister of Economics and Industry: IVANE CHKHARTISHVILI.

Minister of Education: ALEKSANDZRE KARTOZIA.

Minister of Environmental Protection and Natural Resources: NINO CHKHOBADZE.

Minister of Finance: ZURAB NOGHAIDELI.

Minister of Foreign Affairs: IRAKLI MENAGHARISHVILI.

Minister of Fuel and Energy: DAVIT MIRTSKHULAVA.

Minister of Health Care and Social Security: AVTANDIL JORBENADZE.

Minister of Internal Affairs: KAKHA TARGAMADZE.

Minister of Justice: MIKHEIL SAAKASHVILI.

Minister of Refugees and Resettlement: VALERI VASHAKIDZE.

Minister of State Security: VAKHTANG KUTATELADZE.

Minister of Tax and Revenue: MIKHEIL MACHAVARIANI.

Minister of Transport and Communications: Dr MERAB ADEISHVILI.

Minister of Urban Affairs and Construction: MERAB CHKHENKELI.

Minister without Portfolio: MALKHAZ KAKABADZE.

MINISTRIES

Office of the President: 300002 Tbilisi, Rustaveli 29; tel. (32) 99-74-75; fax (32) 99-96-30; e-mail office@presidpress.gov.ge.

Office of the Government: 380018 Tbilisi, Ingorokva 7; tel. (32) 93-59-07; fax (32) 98-23-54.

Ministry of Agriculture and Produce: 380023 Tbilisi, Kostava 41; tel. (32) 99-02-72; fax (32) 99-94-44.

Ministry of Culture: 380008 Tbilisi, Rustaveli 37; tel. (32) 93-74-33; fax (32) 99-90-37; internet www.parliament.ge/culture.

Ministry of Defence: 380007 Tbilisi, Universitetis 2A; tel. (32) 98-39-30; fax (32) 98-39-29.

Ministry of Economics and Industry: 380008 Tbilisi, Chanturia 12; tel. (32) 93-33-61; fax (32) 93-15-35.

Ministry of Education: 380002 Tbilisi, Uznadze 52; tel. (32) 95-88-86; fax (32) 77-00-73; internet www.parliament.ge/education.

Ministry of Environmental Protection and Natural Resources: 380015 Tbilisi, Kostava 68A; tel. (32) 23-06-64; fax (32) 94-34-20; e-mail irisi@gmep.kneta.ge; internet www.parliament.ge/governance/gov/enviro/parliament/ministry.htm.

Ministry of Finance: 380062 Tbilisi, Abashidze 70; tel. (32) 22-68-05; fax (32) 29-23-68.

Ministry of Foreign Affairs: 380018 Tbilisi, 9 April 4; tel. (32) 98-93-77; fax (32) 99-72-48; internet www.mfa.gov.ge.

Ministry of Fuel and Energy: 380007 Tbilisi, Lermontov 10; tel. (32) 99-60-98; fax (32) 93-35-42.

Ministry of Health Care and Social Security: 380060 Tbilisi, K. Gamsakhurdia 30; tel. (32) 38-70-71; fax (32) 37-00-86.

Ministry of Internal Affairs: 380014 Tbilisi, Didikheivani 10; tel. (32) 99-62-96; fax (32) 98-65-32.

Ministry of Justice: 380008 Tbilisi, Griboedov 19; tel. (32) 93-27-21; fax (32) 93-02-25.

Ministry of Refugees and Resettlement: 380008 Tbilisi, Dadiani 30; tel. (32) 94-16-11; fax (32) 92-14-27.

Ministry of State Property Management: 380062 Tbilisi, Chavchavadze 64; tel. (32) 29-48-75; fax (32) 22-52-09.

Ministry of State Security: 380018 Tbilisi, 9 April 4; tel. (32) 92-23-15; fax (32) 93-27-91.

Ministry of Tax and Revenue: 380062 Tbilisi, Chavchavadze 55; tel. (32) 25-15-38; fax (32) 93-15-84.

Ministry of Transport and Communications: 380060 Tbilisi, Aleksandr Kazbegi 12; tel. (32) 93-28-46; fax (32) 93-91-45.

Ministry of Urban Affairs and Construction: 380060 Tbilisi, Vazha Pshavela 16; tel. (32) 37-42-76; fax (32) 22-05-41.

President and Legislature

PRESIDENT
Presidential Election, 9 April 2000

Candidates	Votes	%
EDUARD SHEVARDNADZE	1,870,311	79.82
JUMBER PATIASHVILI	390,486	16.66
KARTLOS GHARIBASHVILI	7,863	0.34
AVTANDIL JOGLIDZE	5,942	0.25
VAZHA ZHGHENTI	3,363	0.14
TENGIZ ASANIDZE	2,793	0.12
Total*	2,343,176	100.00

* Including 62,418 spoilt voting papers (2.66% of the total).

GEORGIAN PARLIAMENT

Sakartvelos Parlamenti: 380028 Tbilisi, Rustaveli 8; tel. (32) 93-61-70; fax (32) 99-93-86; internet www.parliament.ge.

Chairman: ZURAB ZHVANIA.

Deputy Chairmen: GIORGI TSERETELI, ELDAR SHENGELAIA, ROSTOM JAPARIDZE, VAKHTANG KOLBAIIA, VAKHTANG RCHEULISHVILI.

General Election, 31 October and 14 November 1999

Parties and blocs	Party lists		Single-member constituency seats	Total seats
	% of votes*	Seats		
Citizens' Union of Georgia	41.9	85	45	130
Union for the Revival of Georgia bloc	25.7	51	7	58
Industry Will Save Georgia bloc	7.8	14	1	15
Georgian Labour Party	6.7	0	2	2
Abkhazian deputies†	—	—	12	12
Independent candidates	—	—	17	17
Total (incl. others)	100.00	150	84	234‡

* In order to win seats, parties needed to obtain at least 7% of the total votes cast.

† Owing to the electoral boycott in the secessionist region of Abkhazia, the mandates of 12 deputies from Abkhazia (elected to the legislature in 1992) were renewed.

‡ One of the single-member constituency seats remained unfilled.

According to the Constitution of August 1995, the unicameral Georgian Parliament would be transformed into a bicameral body following the eventual restoration of Georgia's territorial integrity. The future Parliament would comprise a Council of the Republic and a Senate (the latter representing the various territorial units of the country).

Political Organizations

More than 40 parties and alliances contested the legislative election of 31 October 1999. The following are among the most prominent parties in Georgia:

Agrarian Party of Georgia: Tbilisi; f. 1994; Chair. ROIN LIPARTELIANI.

All Georgian Union of Revival: Batumi, Gogebashvili 7; tel. (200) 76-500; f. 1992; 200,000 mems; Chair. ASLAN ABASHIDZE.

Christian Democratic Union of Georgia: Tbilisi, Kostava 63; tel. (32) 36-38-28; fax (32) 33-58-40; f. 1990.

Citizens' Union of Georgia (CUG): Tbilisi, Marshal Gelovani 4; tel. (32) 95-98-25; fax (32) 95-83-25; e-mail cug@access.sanet.ge; f. 1993; 300,000 mems; Chair. EDUARD SHEVARDNADZE; Gen. Sec. EDUARD SURMANIDZE.

Communist Party of Georgia: Tbilisi, Montin 2; tel. (32) 53-25-17; f. 1992; Chair. IVANE TSIKLAURI.

Conservative Party of Georgia: Tbilisi, Sabaduri 32; tel. (32) 72-44-73; f. 1995; legal successor to the Liberal–Conservative Party; separated from the Monarchist Party; Chair. GEORGI KARTOZIA.

Georgian Labour Party: Tbilisi, Javakhishvili 88; tel. (32) 96-06-46; fax (32) 99-62-13; f. 1997; main aim is the social protection of the population; Chair. SHALVA NATELASHVICI; 64,000 mems.

Georgian People's Party: Tbilisi; f. 1996 by dissident members of the National Democratic Party of Georgia.

Georgian Social Democratic Party: 380018 Tbilisi, Tskhra Aprilis 2; tel. (32) 99-95-50; fax (32) 98-73-89; f. 1893; ruling party 1918–21; re-established 1990; Chair. Prof. JEMAL KAKHNIASHVILI.

Georgian Social-Realistic Party: f. 1999; centrist party aimed at building united democratic Georgian state; Chair. Dr GURAM BEROZASHVILI.

Georgian Union of Reformers and Agrarians: Tbilisi; f. 1999; merger of Reformers' Union of Georgia and the Agrarian Union.

Industry Will Save Georgia: Tbilisi, Barnovi 69; tel. (32) 23-53-35; f. 1999; opposition alliance; Chair. GIORGI TOPADZE.

Liberal Democratic Party: Tbilisi; Chair. MIKHEIL NANEISHVILI.

Mtsvanta Partia (Green Party of Georgia): c/o Sakartvelos Mtsvaneta Modzraoba, 380012 Tbilisi, Davit Aghmashenebeli 182; tel. (32) 95-20-33; fax (32) 35-16-74; e-mail party@greens.org.ge; f. 1990; Leader ZURAB ZHVANIA; Chair. GEORGI GACHECHILADZE.

National Democratic Party of Georgia: 380008 Tbilisi, Rustaveli 21; tel. (32) 98-35-36; fax (32) 93-19-78; e-mail ndpfc@parliament.ge; f. 1981; Leader IRINA SHARISHVILI-CHANTURIA.

National Independence Party: 380007 Tbilisi, Machabeli 8; tel. (32) 98-27-70; f. 1988; Chair. IRAKLI TSERETELI.

Nationalist Party: Tbilisi, Zaziashvili 1; tel. (32) 95-14-85; f. 1993; Chair. ZAZA VASHAKMADZE.

Party for Liberation of Abkhazia: Tbilisi; advocates the restoration of the jurisdiction of Georgia and constitutional order in Abkhazia; f. 1998; Chair. TAMAZ NADAREISHVILI.

People's Patriotic Union of Georgia: Tbilisi; left-wing alliance; Chair. YEVGENII DZHUGHASHVILI.

People's Party—Didgori: Tbilisi, Uznadze 56; tel. (32) 96-03-69; fax (32) 93-57-98; e-mail pppess@parliament.ge; f. 1996; Chair. MAMUKA GIORGIADZE.

Republican Party of Georgia: Tbilisi, Antoneli 31/2; tel. and fax (32) 93-25-36; e-mail cdc@access.sanet.ge; f. 1995; absorbed Georgian Popular Front (f. 1989); Chair. IVLIANE KHAINDRAVA.

Rightist Alternative Alliance: Tbilisi; alliance between the Union of Georgian Traditionalists and the Liberal Economic Party; f. 2000.

Round Table—Free Georgia: Tbilisi, Dgebuadze 4; tel. (32) 95-48-20; f. 1990; opposition party uniting supporters of former President Zviad Gamsakhurdia; Chair. SOSO JAJANIDZE.

Socialist Party of Georgia: Tbilisi, Leselidze 41; tel. (32) 98-33-67; fax (32) 93-27-09; f. 1995; Chair. VAKHTANG RCHEULISHVILI.

Union for the Revival of Georgia: Batumi, Ninoshvili 5; tel. (200) 76-500; fax (200) 76-505; principal opposition alliance including parties loyal to the former President, Zviad Gamsakhurdia (the All-Georgian Union of Revival, the Socialist Party of Georgia, the Union of Traditionalists, the People's Party and the 21st Century bloc); Chair. ASLAN ABASHIDZE.

Union of Georgian Realists: f. 1997; aims to achieve political and economic stability in a united Georgia.

Union of Georgian Traditionalists: Tbilisi, Arsena 10; f. 1990; Chair. AKAKI ASATIANI.

United Communist Party of Georgia: Tbilisi, Budapeshti 6; tel. (32) 38-41-65; f. 1994; 87,000 mems (2000); First Sec. PANTELEIMON GIORGADZE.

Diplomatic Representation

EMBASSIES IN GEORGIA

Armenia: 380002 Tbilisi, Tetelashvili 4; tel. (32) 95-94-43; fax (32) 99-01-26; Ambassador: GEORGE KHOSROEV.

Azerbaijan: 380079 Tbilisi, Mukhadze 4; tel. and fax (32) 23-40-37; Ambassador: HAJAN HAJIYEV.

China, People's Republic: 380007 Tbilisi, Barnov 52; tel. (32) 99-80-11; fax (32) 93-12-76; Ambassador: ZHANG YONGQUAN.

Czech Republic: 380054 Tbilisi, Tsereteli 57; tel. (32) 34-33-10; Ambassador: JIŘÍ NEKVASIL.

France: 380008 Tbilisi, Gogebashvili 15; tel. (32) 93-42-10; fax (32) 95-33-75; internet www.multimania.com/ambafce/index.htm; Ambassador: MIREILLE MUSSO.

Germany: 380012 Tbilisi, Davit Aghmashenebeli 166; tel. (32) 95-09-36; fax (32) 95-89-10; Ambassador: Dr WOLFDIETRICH VOGEL.

Greece: 380003 Tbilisi, Arakishvili 5; tel. and fax (32) 93-89-81; Ambassador: SPYRIDON GEORGILES.

Holy See: 380086 Tbilisi, Dzhgenti 40, Nutsubidze Plateau; tel. (32) 94-13-05; fax (32) 29-39-44; e-mail nuntius@access.sanet.ge; Apostolic Nuncio: Most Rev. PETER STEPHAN ZURBRIGGEN, Titular Archbishop of Glastonia (Glastonbury).

Iran: 380060 Tbilisi, Zovreti 16; tel. (32) 98-69-90; fax (32) 98-69-93; Ambassador: ABOLFAZL KHAZAEE TORSHIZI.

Israel: 380012 Tbilisi, Davit Aghmashenebeli 61; tel. (32) 96-02-13; fax (32) 95-17-09; Ambassador: EHUD EITAM.

Italy: 380003 Tbilisi, Telavi 20, Sheraton Metcochi Place; tel. (32) 94-64-44; fax (32) 95-73-76; e-mail ambita.tbilisi@access.sanet.ge; Ambassador: MICHELANGELO PIPANI.

Korea, Republic: Tbilisi; Ambassador: YI CHONG-PIN.

Poland: Tbilisi, Brothers Zubalashvili 19; tel. (32) 92-03-98; fax (32) 92-03-97; Chargé d'affaires: PIOTR BORAWSKI.

Romania: Tbilisi, Lvov 7; tel. (32) 25-00-98; fax (32) 25-00-97; Ambassador: KONSTANTIN GIRBEA.

Russia: 380002 Tbilisi, Tsinamdzgvrishvili 90; tel. (32) 95-59-11; fax (32) 95-52-33; Ambassador: VLADIMIR GUDEV.

Turkey: 380012 Tbilisi, Davit Aghmashenebeli 61; tel. (32) 95-20-14; fax (32) 95-18-10; e-mail turkem_tifl@yahoo.com; Ambassador: BURAK GURSEL.

Ukraine: 380060 Tbilisi, Davit Aghmashenebeli 61; tel. (32) 98-93-62; fax (32) 23-71-45; Ambassador: STEFAN VOLKOVETSKII.

United Kingdom: 380003 Tbilisi, Sheraton Palace Hotel; tel. and fax (32) 95-54-97; email british.embassy@caucasus.net; Ambassador: DEBORAH BARNES-JONES.

USA: 380026 Tbilisi, Atoneli 25; tel. (32) 98-99-67; fax (32) 93-37-59; internet www.georgia.net.ge/usis; Ambassador: KENNETH SPENCER YALOWITZ.

Judicial System

Constitutional Court: Tbilisi, Rustaveli 29; e-mail court@const.gov.ge; internet www.constcourt.gov.ge; Chair. AVTANDIL DEMETRASHVILI.

Supreme Court: 380010 Tbilisi, Zubalashvilebi 32; tel. (32) 99-65-46; fax (32) 93-52-94; Chair. LADO CHANTURIA.

Procurator-General: GIORGI MEPARISHVILI.

First Deputy Procurator-General: VENEDI BENIDZE.

Council of Justice: Tbilisi, Davit Aghmashenebeli 80; tel. and fax (32) 95-75-99; f. 1997; 12-member council that co-ordinates the appointment of judges and their activities; four mems nominated by the President, four by Parliament and four by the Supreme Court; Chair. MIKHEIL SAAKASHVILI; Sec. ASLAN PAGHAVA.

Religion

CHRISTIANITY

The Georgian Orthodox Church

The Georgian Orthodox Church is divided into 27 dioceses, and includes not only Georgian parishes, but also several Russian, Greek and Armenian Orthodox communities, which are under the jurisdiction of the Primate of the Georgian Orthodox Church. There are 40 monasteries and convents, two theological academies and four seminaries.

Patriarchate: 380005 Tbilisi, Erekle II Moedani 1; tel. (32) 99-03-78; fax (32) 98-71-14; e-mail ecclesi@access.sanet.ge; internet www.orthodox-patriarchate-of-georgia.org.ge; Catholicos-Patriarch of All Georgia ILIYA II.

The Roman Catholic Church

The Apostolic Administrator of the Caucasus is the Apostolic Nuncio to Georgia, Armenia and Azerbaijan, who is resident in Tbilisi (see Diplomatic Representation, above).

ISLAM

There are Islamic communities among the Ajarians, Abkhazians, Azerbaijanis, Kurds and some Ossetians. The country falls under the jurisdiction of the Muslim Board of Transcaucasia, based in Baku (Azerbaijan).

The Press

Department of the Press: 380008 Tbilisi, Jorjiashvili 12; tel. (32) 98-70-08; govt regulatory body; Dir V. RTSKHILADZE.

PRINCIPAL NEWSPAPERS

In Georgian, except where otherwise stated.

Akhalgazrda Iverieli (Young Iberian): Tbilisi, Kostava 14; tel. (32) 93-31-49; 3 a week; organ of the Georgian Parliament; Editor MERAB BALARJISHVILI.

Droni (Times): Tbilisi, Kostava 14; tel. (32) 99-56-54; internet www.opentext.org.ge/droni/; Editor-in-Chief SOSO SIMONISHVILI.

Eri (Nation): Tbilisi; weekly; organ of the Georgian Parliament; Editor A. SILAGADZE.

Ertoba: Tbilisi; f. 1918; weekly; organ of the Georgian Social Democratic Party.

Georgian Times: Tbilisi, Chavchavadze 55; tel. and fax (32) 22-76-21; e-mail times@gtze.com.ge; internet www.sanet.ge/gtze; f. 1993; daily; in English; Editor-in-Chief ZAZA GACHECHILADZE.

Iberia Spektri (Iberian Spectrum): Tbilisi, Machabeli 11; tel. (32) 98-73-87; fax (32) 98-73-88; internet www.opentext.org.ge/iberia-spektri/; Editor IRAKLI GOTSIRIDZE.

Literaturuli Sakartvelo (Literary Georgia): Tbilisi, Gudiashvili Sq. 2; tel. (32) 99-84-04; internet www.opentext.org.ge/literaturulisakartvelo/; weekly; organ of the Union of Writers of Georgia; Editor TAMAZ TSIVTSIVADZE.

Mamuli (Native Land): Tbilisi; fortnightly; organ of the Rustaveli Society; Editor T. CHANTURIA.

Respublika (Republic): 380096 Tbilisi, Kostava 14; tel. and fax (32) 93-43-91; f. 1990; weekly; independent; Editor J. NINUA; circ. 40,000.

Rezonansi: Tbilisi, Davit Aghmashenebeli 89–24; tel. (32) 95-69-38; fax (32) 96-92-60; e-mail n1001@geo.net.ge; f. 1992; daily; Editor-in-Chief MALKHAZ RAMISHVILI; circ. 10,000.

Sakartvelo (Georgia): 380096 Tbilisi, Kostava 14; tel. (32) 99-92-26; internet www.opentext.org.ge/sakartvelo/; 5 a week; organ of the Georgian Parliament; Editor (vacant).

Shvidi Dghe (Seven Days): Tbilisi, Krilov 5; tel. (32) 94-35-52; fax (32) 95-40-76; e-mail dge7@caucasus.net; internet www.opentext.org.ge_7dge; f. 1991; weekly; Dir GELA GURGENIDZE; Editor KOBA AKHALBEDASHVILI; circ. 3,000.

Svobodnaya Gruziya (Free Georgia): Tbilisi, Rustaveli 42; tel. (32) 93-13-54; fax (32) 93-17-06; e-mail new@caucasus.net; internet www.svobodnaya-gruzia.com; in Russian; Editor-in-Chief APOLON SILAGADZE.

Tavisupali Sakartvelo (Free Georgia): 380008 Tbilisi, POB W227; tel. (32) 95-48-20; weekly; organ of Round Table—Free Georgia party.

Tbilisi Times: Tbilisi; e-mail david@tbilisitimes.com; internet www.tbilisitimes.com; in English and Georgian; independent, non-profit; Dirs DAVID DZIDZIKASHVILI, SHAVLEG SHAVERDASHVILI.

Vestnik Gruzii (Georgian Herald): Tbilisi; 5 a week; organ of the Georgian Parliament; in Russian; Editor V. KESHELAVA.

Weekly Post: 380002 Tbilisi, POB 85; tel. and fax (32) 94-07-07; e-mail weekpost@iberiapac.ge; f. 1991; Editor BESIK KHARANAULI.

PRINCIPAL PERIODICALS

Alashara: 394981 Sukhumi, Govt House, kor. 1; tel. (300) 2-35-40; organ of the Abkhazian Writers' Organization of the Union of Writers of Georgia; in Abkhazian.

Dila (Morning): 380096 Tbilisi, Kostava 14; tel. (32) 99-41-30; f. 1904; monthly; illustrated; for 5–10 year-olds; Editor-in-Chief REVAZ INANISHVILI; circ. 168,000.

Drosha (Banner): Tbilisi; f. 1923; monthly; politics and fiction; Editor O. KINKLADZE.

Fidiyag: Tskhinvali, Kostava 3; tel. 2-22-65; organ of the South Ossetian Writers' Organization of the Union of Writers of Georgia; in Ossetian.

Khelovneba (Art): Tbilisi; f. 1953, fmrly *Sabchota Khelovneba* (Soviet Art); monthly; journal of the Ministry of Culture; Editor N. GURABANIDZE.

Kritika (Criticism): 380008 Tbilisi, Rustaveli 42; tel. (32) 93-22-85; f. 1972; every 2 months; publ. by Merani Publishing House; journal of the Union of Writers of Georgia; literature, miscellaneous; Editor V. KHARCHILAVA.

Literaturnaya Gruziya (Literary Georgia): 380008 Tbilisi, Kostava 5; tel. (32) 93-65-15; f. 1957; quarterly; journal of the Union of Writers of Georgia; politics, art and fiction; in Russian; Editor Z. ABZIANIDZE.

Metsniereba da Tekhnika (Science and Technology): 380060 Tbilisi; f. 1949; monthly; publ. by the Metsniereba Publishing House; journal of the Georgian Academy of Sciences; popular; Editor Z. TSILOSANI.

Mnatobi (Luminary): 380004 Tbilisi, Rustaveli 28; tel. (32) 99-51-56; f. 1924; monthly; journal of the Union of Writers of Georgia; fiction, poetry and arts; Editor T. CHILADZE.

Nakaduli (Stream): Tbilisi, Kostava 14; tel. (32) 93-31-81; f. 1926; fmrly *Pioneri*; monthly; journal of the Ministry of Education; illustrated; for 10–15-year-olds; Editor V. GINCHARADZE; circ. 5,000.

Niangi (Crocodile): 380096 Tbilisi, Kostava 14; f. 1923; fortnightly; satirical; Editor Z. BOLKVADZE.

Politika (Politics): Tbilisi; theoretical, political, social sciences; Editor M. GOGUADZE.

Sakartvelos Kali (Georgian Woman): 380096 Tbilisi, Kostava 14; tel. (32) 99-98-71; f. 1957; popular, socio-political and literary; Editor-in-Chief NARGIZA MGELADZE; circ. 25,000.

Sakartvelos Metsnierebata Akedemiis Matsne (Herald of the Georgian Academy of Sciences, Biological Series): Tbilisi; f. 1975; 6 a year; in Georgian, English and Russian; Editor-in-Chief VAZHA OKUJAVA.

Sakartvelos Metsnierebata Akedemiis Matsne (Herald of the Georgian Academy of Sciences, Chemical Series): Tbilisi; f. 1975; quarterly; in Georgian, English and Russian; Editor-in-Chief TEIMURAZ ANDRONIKASHVILI.

Sakartvelos Metsnierebata Akademiis Moambe (Bulletin of Georgian Academy of Sciences): 380008 Tbilisi, Rustaveli 52; tel. (32) 99-75-93; fax (32) 99-88-23; e-mail bulletin@presid.achet.ge; f. 1940; 6 a year; in Georgian and English; Editor-in-Chief ALBERT TAVKHELIDZE.

Saunje (Treasure): 380007 Tbilisi, Dadiani 2; tel. (32) 72-47-31; f. 1974; 6 a year; organ of the Union of Writers of Georgia; foreign literature in translation; Editor S. NISHNIANIDZE.

Tsiskari (Dawn): 380007 Tbilisi, Dadiani 2; tel. (32) 99-85-81; f. 1957; monthly; organ of the Union of Writers of Georgia; fiction; Editor I. KEMERTELIDZE.

NEWS AGENCIES

BS Press: Tbilisi, Rustaveli 42; tel. (32) 93-51-20; fax (32) 93-13-02; Dir DEVI IMEDASHVILI.

Iberia: Tbilisi, Marjanishvili 5; tel. (32) 93-64-22; Dir KAKHA GAGLOSHVILI.

Iprinda: Tbilisi, Rustaveli 19; tel. (32) 99-03-77; fax (32) 98-73-65; Dir KETEVAN BOKHUA.

Kontakt: Tbilisi, Kostava 68; tel. (32) 36-04-79; fax (32) 22-18-45; Dir DIMITRI KIKVADZE.

Prime News Agency: Tbilisi, Kutateladze 5; tel. (32) 92-32-12; fax (32) 92-32-02; e-mail pna@pna.com.ge; internet www.prime-news.com.ge; f. 1997 after dissolution of BGI news agency.

Sakinform: 380008 Tbilisi, Rustaveli 42; tel. (32) 93-19-20; fax (32) 99-92-00; e-mail gha@lberiapac.ge; f. 1921; state information agency; Dir KAKHA IMNADZE.

Sarke Information Agency: 380002 Tbilisi, Davit Aghmashenebeli 63; tel. (32) 95-06-59; fax (32) 95-08-37; e-mail info@sarke.com; internet www.sarke.com; f. 1992.

Publishers

Ganatleba (Education): 380025 Tbilisi, Orjonikidze 50; f. 1957; educational, literature; Dir L. KHUNDADZE.

Georgian National Universal Encyclopaedia: Tbilisi, Tsereteli 1; Editor-in-Chief A. SAKVARELIDZE.

Khelovneba (Art): 380002 Tbilisi, Davit Aghmashenebeli 179; f. 1947; Dir N. JASHI.

Merani (Writer): 380008 Tbilisi, Rustaveli 42; tel. (32) 99-64-92; fax (32) 93-29-96; e-mail merani@caucasus.net; f. 1921; fiction; Dir G. GVERDTSITELI.

Metsniereba (Science): 380060 Tbilisi, Kutuzov 19; f. 1941; publishing house of the Georgian Academy of Sciences; Editor S. SHENGELIA.

Nakaduli (Stream): 380060 Tbilisi, Gamsakhurdia 28; f. 1938; books for children and youth; Dir O. CHELIDZE.

Publishing House of Tbilisi State University: 380079 Tbilisi, Chavchavadze 14; f. 1933; scientific and educational literature; Editor V. GAMKRELIDZE.

Sakartvelo (Georgia): 380002 Tbilisi, Marjanishvili 16; tel. (32) 95-42-01; f. 1921; fmrly *Sabchota Sakartvelo* (Soviet Georgia); political, scientific and fiction; Dir D. A. TCHARKVIANI.

Broadcasting and Communications

TELECOMMUNICATIONS

National Regulatory Authority: Tbilisi; Chair. VAKHTANG ABASHIDZE.

Telecom Georgia: 380058 Tbilisi, Rustaveli 31; tel. (32) 99-91-97; fax (32) 00-11-11; provides telecommunications services.

BROADCASTING

State Department of Television and Radio: Tbilisi, Kostava 68; tel. (32) 36-81-66; e-mail gtvr@iberiapac.ge; Chair. (vacant).

Television

Channel 7: Tbilisi; tel. (32) 94-31-65; fax (32) 33-12-33; e-mail channel@macrocom.ge; internet www.macrocom.com.ge; f. 2000; cable television.

Georgian Television: 380015 Tbilisi, Kostava 68; tel. (32) 36-22-94; fax (32) 36-23-19; two stations; relays from Russian television.

Rustavi 2: 380077 Tbilisi, Vazha-Pshavela 45; tel. (32) 32-22-71; fax (32) 25-00-31; e-mail tv@rustavi2.com; internet www.rustavi2.com; f. 1994; independent; Exec. Dir EROSI KITSMARISHVILI.

Radio

Georgian Radio: 380015 Tbilisi, Kostava 68; tel.(32) 36-83-62; fax (32) 36-86-65; govt controlled; broadcasts in Georgian and Russian, with regional services for Abkhazia, Ajaria and South Ossetia; foreign service in English and German; Dir VAKHTANG NANITASHVILI.

Finance

(cap. = capital; res = reserves; dep. = deposits;
m. = million; brs = branches; amounts in lari, unless otherwise indicated)

BANKING

In August 1991 the Georgian Supreme Soviet adopted legislation which nationalized all branches of all-Union (USSR) banks in Georgia. Georgian branches of the USSR State Bank (Gosbank) were transferred to the National Bank of Georgia.

At the beginning of 1993 the Georgian banking system comprised the National Bank, five specialized state commercial banks (consisting of the domestic branches of the specialized banks of the former USSR) and 72 private commercial banks. However, of the last, only about one-half satisfied general legal provisions and only five properly complied with the paid-in capital requirement. As a result, in 1995 more than 50% of the commercial banks in Georgia (then numbering almost 230) were closed down. The remaining banks were to be audited by the National Bank to verify their commercial viability. In April 1995 three of the five specialized state commercial banks—Sakeksimbanki (Export-Import Bank), Industriabanki and Akhali Kartuli Banki (Savings Bank)—merged to form the United Georgian Bank. In 1996 the authorized capital requirement was raised to 5m. lari. By December 1999 there were 38 banks in Georgia.

Central Bank

National Bank of Georgia: 380005 Tbilisi, Leonidze 3–5; tel. (32) 99-65-05; fax (32) 99-98-85; e-mail nbg@access.sunet.ge; f. 1991; cap. 1.3m., res 9.3m., dep. 298.8m., total assets 1,190m. (Dec. 1998); Pres. and Chair. of Bd IRAKLI MANAGADZE.

Other Banks

Absolute Bank: 380008 Tbilisi, Ingorokva 8; tel. (32) 98-99-47; fax (32) 99-61-82; e-mail absolutebank@absolutebank.ge; cap. 4.5m., dep. 26.1m. (Apr. 1999); Chair. LOUIS LLOYD; Pres. DEREK FARMER; 3 brs.

Agrobank: 380005 Tbilisi, Trasury 3; tel. (32) 23-46-29; fax (32) 98-21-46; f. 1991 as specialized state commercial bank; 63 brs.

Bank of Georgia: 380005 Tbilisi, Pushkin 3; tel. (32) 99-77-26; fax (32) 98-32-58; e-mail info@bankofgeorgia.com.ge; internet www .bankofgeorgia.com.ge; f. 1991 as Zhilsotsbank—Social Development Bank, one of five specialized state commercial banks; renamed as above 1994; universal joint-stock commercial bank; cap. 6.9m., dep. 46m. (Dec. 1999); Pres. VLADIMER PATEISHVILI; 32 brs.

Cavcasioni: 380062 Tbilisi, Chubinishvili 41; tel. (32) 95-14-44; fax (32) 95-93-93; e-mail caucasioni@iberiapac.ge; f. 1992; cap. 3m., res 0.1m., dep. 0.4m. (Dec. 1999); Pres. BESO MAGRADZE; Chair. ZAZIA PANKVELASHVILI.

Georgian Maritime Bank: 384517 Batumi, Gogebashvili 60; tel. (222) 7-65-82; fax (222) 7-60-01; e-mail inter@gmb-batumi.com; f. 1993; cap. 3.6m., res 0.3m., dep. 13m. (Dec. 1998); Chair. NUGZAR MIKELADZE.

Intellectbank: 380064 Tbilisi, Davit Aghmashenebeli 127; tel. (32) 23-70-83; fax (32) 23-70-82; e-mail intellect@iberiapac.ge; f. 1993; cap. 4m., dep. 21.5m. (Dec. 1998); Pres. KAKHA GIUASHVILI; Gen. Dir VLADIMER CHANISHVILI; 13 brs.

JSC Cartu Bank: 380062 Tbilisi, Chavchavadze 39A; tel. (32) 23-00-21; fax (32) 23-03-83; e-mail zcc_cartu@global-erty.net; f. 1996, name changed as above Sept. 1998; cap. 12.5m., res 1.9m., dep. 3.7m. (Dec. 2000); Chair. G. CHRDILELI.

TBC-Bank: 380079 Tbilisi, Chavchavadze 11; tel. (32) 22-06-61; fax (32) 22-04-06; e-mail info@tbcbank.com.ge; internet www.tbcbank .com.ge; f. 1992; cap. 3.0m., res 7.6m., dep. 54.2m. (Dec. 1999); Pres. MAMUKA KAZARADZE; Gen. Dir VAKHTANG BUTSKHRIKIDZE; 3 brs.

TbilCreditBank: 380002 Tbilisi, Davit Aghmashenebeli 79; tel. (32) 95-12-92; fax (32) 98-27-83; e-mail tbilcred@caucasus.net; internet www.tbilcreditbank.com; cap. 5.5m., dep. 7m. (Dec. 1999); Chair. DAVIT BUADZE.

Tbiluniversalbank Ltd: 380071 Tbilisi, Kostava 70; tel. (32) 99-82-92; fax (32) 98-61-68; f. 1994 as Superbank; name changed as above 1995; cap. 2.8m., dep. 1.4m. (Dec. 1998); Chair. TARIEL GVALIA.

JSC United Georgian Bank: 380002 Tbilisi, Uznadze 37; tel. (32) 95-60-98; fax (32) 95-60-85; e-mail head@ugb.com.ge; internet www.ugb.com.ge; f. 1995 by merger of three specialized state commercial banks; cap. 23.8m., res 2.8m., dep. 31.8m. (Dec. 1999); Gen. Dir IRAKLI KOVZANADZE; Chair. TAMAZ MAGLAKEUDZE; 20 brs.

CURRENCY EXCHANGE

Tbilisi Interbank Currency Exchange (TICEX): 380005 Tbilisi, Galaktion Tabidze 4; tel. (32) 92-34-43; fax (32) 92-23-01; Gen. Dir DAVIT KLDIASHVILI.

Trade and Industry

GOVERNMENT AGENCIES

Georgian Investment Centre: 380077 Tbilisi, Kazbegi 42; e-mail gic@access.sanet.ge; internet www.georgiainvestment.com; f. 1996 to promote foreign and domestic investment; Dir. SABA SARISHVILI.

State Property Management Agency: Tbilisi; f. 1992; responsible for divestment of state-owned enterprises.

INSURANCE

Aldagi Insurance Co: 380062 Tbilisi, Chavchavadze 62; tel. (32) 29-49-05; fax (32) 29-49-06; e-mail aldagi@caucasus.net; f. 1990; Chair. DAVIT GAMKRELIDZE; Gen. Dir TENGIZ MEZURNISHVILI.

Anglo-Georgian Insurance Co: 380030 Tbilisi, Abashidze 29, kv. 14; tel. (32) 25-03-51; fax (32) 25-03-50; e-mail administrator@agic .com.ge; internet www.georgia.net.ge/agic; f. 1998 as a joint-stock company; Gen. Dir ROBERT MURPHY.

Central Insurance Co: 380019 Tbilisi, Tsereteli 126; tel. (32) 98-87-18; Gen. Dir NIKOLAI A. DVALADZE.

Georgian International Insurance Ltd: 380075 Tbilisi, Saakadze Sq. 1; tel. (32) 33-16-89; f. 1993; Dir IGOR KARPOVICH.

CHAMBER OF COMMERCE

Chamber of Commerce and Industry of Georgia: 380079 Tbilisi, Chavchavadze 11; tel. (32) 29-33-75; fax (32) 23-57-60; e-mail ktm@ean.kheta.ge; internet www.gcci.org.ge; brs in Sukhumi and Batumi; Chair. GURAM D. AKHVLEDIANI.

TRADE ASSOCIATION

Georgian Import Export (Geoimpex): 380008 Tbilisi, Giorgiashvili 12; tel. (32) 99-70-90; fax (32) 98-25-41; Gen. Dir T. A. GOGOBERIDZE.

UTILITIES

Electricity

Department of Power Supply: Tbilisi, V. Vekua 1; tel. (32) 98-05-65; attached to the Ministry of Fuel and Energy.

Sakenergo: 380005 Tbilisi, V. Vekua 1; tel. (32) 98-98-14; fax (32) 98-31-97; formerly state-owned energy supplier; in 1996 restructured into three cos (generation, transmission and distribution); transformation into joint-stock cos in progress in 1997; Gen. Dir VAZHA METREVELI.

Sakenergogeneratsia: 38005 Tbilisi, V. Vekua 1; tel. and fax (32) 98-98-13; state power-generating co; Gen. Dir G. BADURASHVILI.

Gas

International Gas Corpn of Georgia: joint-stock co; Chair. ALEKSANDR GOTSIRIDZE.

Sakgazi: 380007 Tbilisi, Lermontova 10; tel. (32) 99-18-30; fax (32) 99-60-93; gas production co; Chair. DAVIT ELIASHVILI.

Saktransgasmretsvi: 380077 Tbilisi, Delisi III 22; tel. (32) 53-61-96; fax (32) 53-61-93; state-owned gas distribution co; Gen. Dir IVAN ZAZASHVILI.

TRADE UNIONS

Confederation of Trade Unions of Georgia: 380122 Tbilisi, Shartava 7; tel. (32) 38-29-95; fax (32) 22-46-63; f. 1995; comprises branch unions with a total membership of approx. 1.4m.; Chair. IRAKLI TUGUSHI.

Free Trade Union of Journalists: Tbilisi, Vazha Pshavela pr. 43; f. 2000; over 100 mems; Chair. BEZHAN MESKHI.

Transport

RAILWAYS

In 1997 Georgia's rail network (including the sections within the secessionist republic of Abkhazia) totalled approximately 1,600 km. However, some 500 km of track was reported to be in a poor state of repair, as a result of which the capacity of some sections of the network had decreased by more than 75% since 1990. The main rail links are with the Russian Federation, along the Black Sea coast, with Azerbaijan, with Armenia and with Iran. The Georgian–Armenian railway continues into eastern Turkey. Various civil conflicts in the mid-1990s disrupted sections of the railway network. The separatist war in Abkhazia resulted in the severance of Georgia's rail connection with the Russian Federation. However, services to the Russian capital, Moscow, resumed in mid-1997, following a four-year interruption. In mid-1998 it was announced that the European Bank for Reconstruction and Development was to assist with the refurbishment of the railways.

The first section of the Tbilisi Metro was opened in 1966; by 1999 the system comprised two lines with 20 stations, totalling 23 km in length, and three extensions, totalling 15 km, were under construction.

Georgian Railways: 380012 Tbilisi, Tsaritsa Tamara 15; tel. (32) 99-40-12; fax (32) 95-02-25; f. 1992, following the dissolution of the former Soviet Railways; Chair. AKAKI CHKHAIDZE.

Tbilisi Metropolitena: 380012 Tbilisi, Pl. Vokzalnaya 2; Gen. Man. I. G. MELKADZE.

ROADS

In 1996 the total length of roads in use was an estimated 20,700 km (6,170 km of highways and 14,500 km of secondary roads), of which 93.5% were paved.

SHIPPING

There are international shipping services with Black Sea and Mediterranean ports. The main ports are at Batumi, Poti and Sukhumi.

Shipowning Company

Georgian Shipping Company: 384517 Batumi, Gogebashvili 60; tel. (222) 14-02-312; fax (222) 73-91-114; Pres. Capt. B. VARSHANIDZE.

CIVIL AVIATION

Air Georgia: 380062 Tbilisi, I. Chavchavadze 49A; tel. (32) 29-40-53; fax (32) 23-34-23; e-mail airgeo@caucasus.net; internet www.air-georgia.com; national and international transport of passengers and freight; Dir ELGOUDZHA DVALI.

Iveria: Tbilisi; f. 1998 as a joint-stock co following merger.

Orbi (Georgian Airlines): 380058 Tbilisi, Tbilisi Airport; tel. (32) 98-73-28; fax (32) 49-51-51; successor to the former Aeroflot division in Georgia; charter and scheduled services to destinations in the CIS and the Middle East; Chief Exec. VASILI S. JAMILBAZISHVILI.

Sukhumi United Aviation Detachment (Taifun—Adjal Avia): 384962 Sukhumi, Babushara Airport; tel. (122) 22021; domestic scheduled and chartered flights; Cmmdr ZAUR K. KHAINDRAVA.

Tourism

Prior to the disintegration of the USSR, Georgia attracted some 1.5m. tourists annually (mainly from other parts of the USSR), owing to its location on the Black Sea and its favourable climate. However, following the outbreak of civil conflict in the early 1990s in South Ossetia and Abkhazia, there was an almost complete cessation in tourism. It was hoped that with the signing of cease-fire agreements with the secessionist republics, tourist numbers would increase. Efforts to regenerate the sector were made in the late 1990s, with the historic buildings of Tbilisi and the surrounding area one of the primary attractions. The ski resort at Gudauri also remained very popular with foreign tourists in the winter months. In 1998 there was just one international hotel in the capital. According to the World Tourism Organization, in 1997 receipts from tourism totalled US $416m. and in 1998 there were 317,000 tourist arrivals.

Department of Tourism: 380074 Tbilisi, Chavchavadze 80; tel. (32) 22-61-25; fax (32) 29-40-52; Chair. KONSTANTINE SALIA.

GERMANY

Introductory Survey

Location, Climate, Language, Religion, Flag, Capital

The Federal Republic of Germany, which was formally established in October 1990 upon the unification of the Federal Republic of Germany (FRG, West Germany) and the German Democratic Republic (GDR, East Germany), lies in the heart of Europe. Its neighbours to the west are the Netherlands, Belgium, Luxembourg and France, to the south Switzerland and Austria, to the east the Czech Republic and Poland, and to the north Denmark. The climate is temperate, with an average annual temperature of 9°C (48°F), although there are considerable variations between the North German lowlands and the Bavarian Alps. The language is German. There is a small Sorbian-speaking minority (numbering about 100,000 people). About 33% of the population are Protestants and a further 33% are Roman Catholics. The national flag (proportions 5 by 3) consists of three equal horizontal stripes, of black, red and gold. The capital is Berlin.

Recent History

Following the defeat of the Nazi regime and the ending of the Second World War in 1945, Germany was divided, according to the Berlin Agreement, into US, Soviet, British and French occupation zones. Berlin was similarly divided. The former German territories east of the Oder and Neisse rivers, with the city of Danzig (now Gdańsk), became part of Poland, while the northern part of East Prussia, around Königsberg (now Kaliningrad), was transferred to the USSR. After the failure of negotiations to establish a unified German administration, the US, French and British zones were integrated economically in 1948. In May 1949 a provisional Constitution, the Grundgesetz (Basic Law), came into effect in the three zones (except in Saarland—see below), and federal elections were held in August. On 21 September 1949 a new German state, the Federal Republic of Germany (FRG), was established in the three Western zones. The FRG was governed from Bonn in Nordrhein-Westfalen. (Saarland was not incorporated into the FRG until 1957.) In October 1949 Soviet-occupied Eastern Germany declared itself the German Democratic Republic (GDR), with the Soviet zone of Berlin as its capital. This left the remainder of Berlin (West Berlin) as an enclave of the FRG within the territory of the GDR.

The FRG and GDR developed sharply divergent political and economic systems. The leaders of the GDR created a socialist state, based on the Soviet model. As early as 1945 large agricultural estates in eastern Germany were nationalized, followed in 1946 by major industrial concerns. Exclusive political control was exercised by the Sozialistische Einheitspartei Deutschlands (SED, Socialist Unity Party of Germany), which had been formed in April 1946 by the merger of the Communist Party of Germany and the branch of the Sozialdemokratische Partei Deutschlands (SPD, Social Democratic Party of Germany) in the Soviet zone. Other political parties in eastern Germany were under the strict control of the SED, and no political activity independent of the ruling party was permitted. In 1950 Walter Ulbricht was appointed Secretary-General (later restyled First Secretary) of the SED.

The transfer, as war reparations, of foodstuffs, livestock and industrial equipment to the USSR from eastern Germany had a devastating effect on the area's economy in the immediate post-war period. In June 1953 increasing political repression and severe food shortages led to uprisings and strikes, which were suppressed by Soviet troops. The continued failure of the GDR to match the remarkable economic recovery of the FRG prompted a growing number of refugees to cross from the GDR to the FRG (between 1949 and 1961 an estimated 2.5m. GDR citizens moved permanently to the FRG). Emigration was accelerated by the enforced collectivization of many farms in 1960, and in August 1961 the GDR authorities hastily constructed a guarded wall between East and West Berlin.

In May 1971 Ulbricht was succeeded as First Secretary of the SED by Erich Honecker. Ulbricht remained Chairman of the Council of State (Head of State), a post that he had held since 1960, until his death in August 1973. He was initially succeeded in this office by Willi Stoph, but in October 1976 Stoph returned to his previous post as Chairman of the Council of Ministers, and Honecker became Chairman of the Council of State. Under Honecker, despite some liberalization of relations with the FRG, there was little relaxation of repressive domestic policies. Honecker strongly opposed the political and economic reforms that began in the USSR and some other Eastern European countries in the mid-1980s.

The 1949 elections in the FRG resulted in victory for the conservative Christlich-Demokratische Union Deutschlands (CDU, Christian Democratic Union of Germany), together with its sister party in Bavaria, the Christlich-Soziale Union (CSU, Christian Social Union). The SPD was the largest opposition party. Dr Konrad Adenauer, the leader of the CDU, was elected Federal Chancellor by the Bundestag (Federal Assembly); Theodor Heuss became the first President of the Republic. Under Adenauer's chancellorship (which lasted until 1963) and the direction of Dr Ludwig Erhard, his Minister of Economics (and successor as Chancellor), the FRG rebuilt itself rapidly to become one of the most affluent and economically dynamic states in Europe, as well as an important strategic ally of other Western European states and the USA. The Paris Agreement of 1954 gave full sovereign status to the FRG from 5 May 1955, and also granted it membership of NATO (see p. 241).

The CDU/CSU ruled in coalition with the SPD from 1966 to 1969, under the chancellorship of Dr Kurt Kiesinger, but lost support at the 1969 general election, allowing the SPD to form a coalition Government with the Freie Demokratische Partei (FDP, Free Democratic Party), under the chancellorship of Willy Brandt, the SPD leader. Following elections in November 1972, the SPD became, for the first time, the largest party in the Bundestag. In May 1974, however, Brandt resigned as Chancellor, after the discovery that his personal assistant had been a clandestine agent of the GDR. He was succeeded by Helmut Schmidt of the SPD, hitherto the Minister of Finance. A deteriorating economic situation was accompanied by a decline in the popularity of the Government and increasing tension between the coalition partners. In the general election of October 1976 the SPD lost its position as largest party in the Bundestag, but the SPD-FDP coalition retained a slender majority.

At the general election of October 1980 the SPD-FDP coalition secured a 45-seat majority in the Bundestag. However, over the next two years the coalition became increasingly unstable, with the partners divided on issues of nuclear power, defence and economic policy. In September 1982 the coalition finally collapsed when the two parties failed to agree on budgetary measures. In October the FDP formed a Government with the CDU/CSU, under the chancellorship of Dr Helmut Kohl, the leader of the CDU. This new partnership was consolidated by the results of the general election of March 1983, when the CDU/CSU substantially increased its share of the votes cast, obtaining 48.8% of the total, compared with 38.8% for the SPD, now led by Hans-Jochen Vogel. An environmentalist party, Die Grünen (The Greens), gained representation in the Bundestag for the first time. In July 1984 Carstens was succeeded as Federal President by Dr Richard von Weizsäcker, also of the CDU. The CDU/CSU-FDP coalition retained power after the general election of January 1987, although with a reduced majority; Kohl was reappointed Chancellor by the Bundestag.

During the period 1949–69 the FRG, under the CDU/CSU, remained largely isolated from Eastern Europe, owing to the FRG Government's refusal to recognize the GDR as an independent state or to maintain diplomatic relations with any other states that recognized the GDR. When Willy Brandt of the SPD became Chancellor in 1969, he adopted a more conciliatory approach to relations with Eastern Europe and, in particular, towards the GDR, a policy which came to be known as Ostpolitik. In 1970 formal discussions were conducted between representatives of the GDR and the FRG for the first time, and there was a significant increase in diplomatic contacts between the FRG and the other countries of Eastern Europe. In 1970 treaties were signed with the USSR and Poland, in which the FRG formally renounced claims to the eastern territories of the

Third Reich and recognized the 'Oder–Neisse Line' as the border between Germany (actually the GDR) and Poland. Further negotiations between the GDR and the FRG, following a quadripartite agreement on West Berlin in September 1971, clarified access rights to West Berlin and also allowed West Berliners to visit the GDR. In December 1972 the two German states signed a 'Basic Treaty', agreeing to develop normal, neighbourly relations with each other, to settle all differences without resort to force, and to respect each other's independence. The Treaty permitted both the FRG and the GDR to join the UN in September 1973, and allowed many Western countries to establish diplomatic relations with the GDR, although both German states continued to deny formal diplomatic recognition to each other.

In December 1981 the first official meeting took place between the two countries' leaders for 11 years, when Chancellor Schmidt of the FRG travelled to the GDR for discussions with Honecker. Inter-German relations deteriorated following the deployment, in late 1983, of US nuclear missiles in the FRG, and the subsequent siting of additional Soviet missiles in the GDR. Nevertheless, official contacts were maintained, and Honecker made his first visit to the FRG in September 1987.

Relations between the two German states were dramatically affected by political upheavals that occurred in the GDR in late 1989 and 1990. In the latter half of 1989 many thousands of disaffected GDR citizens emigrated illegally to the FRG, via Czechoslovakia, Poland and Hungary. The exodus was accelerated by the Hungarian Government's decision, in September 1989, to permit citizens of the GDR to leave Hungary without exit visas. Meanwhile, there was a growth in popular dissent within the GDR, led by Neues Forum (New Forum), an independent citizens' action group that had been established to encourage discussion of democratic reforms, justice and environmental issues.

In early October 1989, following official celebrations to commemorate the 40th anniversary of the foundation of the GDR, anti-Government demonstrations erupted in East Berlin and other large towns. Eventually, as the demonstrations attracted increasing popular support, intervention by the police ceased. (It was later reported that the SED Politburo had voted narrowly against the use of the armed forces to suppress the civil unrest.) In mid-October, as the political situation became more unsettled, Honecker resigned as General Secretary of the SED, Chairman of the Council of State and Chairman of the National Defence Council, ostensibly for reasons of ill health. He was replaced in all these posts by Egon Krenz, a senior member of the SED Politburo. Krenz immediately offered concessions to the opposition, initiating a dialogue with the members of Neues Forum (which was legalized in early November) and with church leaders. There was also a noticeable liberalization of the media, and an amnesty was announced for all persons who had been detained during the recent demonstrations and for those imprisoned for attempting to leave the country illegally. However, large demonstrations, to demand further reforms, continued in many towns throughout the GDR.

On 7 November 1989, in a further attempt to placate the demonstrators, the entire membership of the GDR Council of Ministers (including the Chairman, Willi Stoph) resigned. On the following day the SED Politburo also resigned. On 9 November restrictions on foreign travel for GDR citizens were ended, and all border crossings to the FRG were opened. During the weekend of 10–11 November an estimated 2m. GDR citizens crossed into West Berlin, and the GDR authorities began to dismantle sections of the wall dividing the city. Dr Hans Modrow, a leading member of the SED who was regarded as an advocate of greater reforms, was appointed Chairman of a new Council of Ministers. The new Government pledged to introduce comprehensive political and economic reforms and to hold free elections in 1990.

In early December 1989 the Volkskammer (the GDR's legislature) voted to remove provisions in the Constitution that protected the SED's status as the single ruling party. However, the mass demonstrations continued, prompted by revelations of corruption and personal enrichment by the former leadership and of abuses of power by the state security service (Staatssicherheitsdienst, known colloquially as the Stasi, which was subsequently disbanded). A special commission was established to investigate such charges, and former senior officials, including Honecker and Stoph, were expelled from the SED and placed under house arrest, pending legal proceedings. As the political situation became increasingly unstable, the entire membership of the SED Politburo and Central Committee, including Krenz,

resigned, and both bodies, together with the post of General Secretary, were abolished. Shortly afterwards, Krenz also resigned as Chairman of the Council of State; he was replaced by Dr Manfred Gerlach, the Chairman of the Liberal-Demokratische Partei Deutschlands (LDPD, Liberal Democratic Party of Germany). Dr Gregor Gysi, a prominent defence lawyer who was sympathetic to the opposition, was elected to the new post of Chairman of the SED (restyled the Partei des Demokratischen Sozialismus—PDS, Party of Democratic Socialism, in February 1990).

In December 1989 and January 1990 all-party talks took place in the GDR, resulting in the formation, in early February, of a new administration, designated the Government of National Responsibility (still led by Modrow), to remain in office until elections were held. The GDR's first free legislative elections took place on 18 March 1990, with the participation of 93% of those eligible to vote. The East German CDU obtained 40.8% of the total votes cast, while the newly re-established East German SPD and the PDS secured 21.8% and 16.4% of the votes respectively. In April a coalition Government was formed, headed by Lothar de Maizière, leader of the Eastern CDU. Five parties were represented in the new Government: the CDU, the SPD, the Liga der Freien Demokraten (League of Free Democrats) and two smaller parties, the Deutsche Soziale Union (German Social Union), and Demokratische Aufschwung (Democratic Departure). The PDS was not invited to join the coalition.

As a result of the changes within the GDR and the subsequent free contact between Germans of east and west, the issue of possible unification of the two German states inevitably emerged. In November 1989 Chancellor Kohl proposed a plan for the eventual unification of the two countries by means of an interim confederal arrangement. In December Kohl made his first visit to the GDR, where he held discussions with the East German leadership. The two sides agreed to develop contacts at all levels and to establish joint economic, cultural and environmental commissions. However the GDR Government initially insisted that the GDR remain a sovereign, independent state. Nevertheless, in February 1990, in response to growing popular support among GDR citizens for unification, Modrow publicly advocated the establishment of a united Germany. Shortly afterwards, Kohl and Modrow met in Bonn, where they agreed to establish a joint commission to achieve full economic and monetary union between the GDR and the FRG. The new coalition Government of the GDR, formed in April 1990, pledged its determination to achieve German unification in the near future. In mid-May the legislatures of the GDR and the FRG approved the Treaty Between the FRG and the GDR Establishing a Monetary, Economic and Social Union; the Treaty came into effect on 1 July. Later in July the Volkskammer approved the re-establishment on GDR territory of the five Länder (states)—Brandenburg, Mecklenburg-Vorpommern (Mecklenburg-Western Pomerania), Sachsen (Saxony), Sachsen-Anhalt (Saxony-Anhalt) and Thüringen (Thuringia)—which had been abolished by the GDR Government in 1952 in favour of 14 Berzirke (districts). On 31 August the Treaty Between the FRG and the GDR on the Establishment of German Unity was signed in East Berlin by representatives of the two Governments. The treaty stipulated, *inter alia*, that the newly-restored Länder would accede to the FRG on 3 October 1990, and that the 23 boroughs of East and West Berlin would jointly form the Land (state) of Berlin.

Owing to the complex international status of the FRG and the GDR and the two countries' membership of opposing military alliances (respectively, NATO and the now-defunct Warsaw Pact), the process of German unification also included negotiations with other countries. In February 1990 representatives of 23 NATO and Warsaw Pact countries agreed to establish the so-called 'two-plus-four' talks (the FRG and the GDR, plus the four countries that had occupied Germany after the Second World War—France, the USSR, the United Kingdom and the USA) to discuss the external aspects of German unification. In June both German legislatures approved a resolution recognizing the inviolability of Poland's post-1945 borders, stressing that the eastern border of a future united Germany would remain along the Oder–Neisse line. In July, at bilateral talks in the USSR with Chancellor Kohl, the Soviet leader, Mikhail Gorbachev, agreed that a united Germany would be free to join whichever military alliance it wished, thus permitting Germany to remain a full member of NATO. The USSR also pledged to withdraw its armed forces (estimated at 370,000 in 1990) from GDR territory within four years, and it was agreed that a united

Germany would reduce the strength of its armed forces to 370,000 within the same period. This agreement ensured a successful result to the 'two-plus-four' talks, which were concluded in September in Moscow, where the Treaty on the Final Settlement with Respect to Germany was signed. In late September the GDR withdrew from the Warsaw Pact.

On 1 October 1990 representatives of the four countries that had occupied Germany after the Second World War met in New York to sign a document in which Germany's full sovereignty was recognized. Finally, on 3 October, the two German states were formally unified. On the following day, at a session of the Bundestag (which had been expanded to permit the representation of former deputies of the GDR Volkskammer), five prominent politicians from the former GDR were sworn in as Ministers without Portfolio in the Federal Government.

Prior to unification, the CDU, the SPD and the FDP of the GDR had merged with their respective counterparts in the FRG to form three single parties. At state elections in the newly-acceded Länder, held in mid-October 1990, the CDU obtained an average of 41% of the total votes and won control of four Land legislatures, while the SPD received an average of 27% of the total votes and gained a majority only in Brandenburg. This surge of support for Chancellor Kohl and the CDU was confirmed by the results of elections to the Bundestag in early December (the first all-German elections since 1933). The CDU (together with the CSU) won 43.8% of the total votes cast, and thus secured a total of 319 seats in the 662-member Bundestag. The SPD achieved its poorest result in a general election since 1957, receiving 33.5% of the votes cast and winning 239 seats in the legislature (a result attributed, in large part, to the party's cautious stance on unification). The FDP won 11% of the total votes cast, and consequently 79 seats in the Bundestag, its most successful result in legislative elections since 1961. Unexpectedly, the West German Grünen lost the 42 seats that they had previously held in the legislature, having failed to obtain the necessary 5% of the votes cast in the area formerly constituting the FRG. However, as a result of a special clause in the electoral law (adopted in October 1990, and valid only for the legislative elections of December 1990), which permitted representation in the Bundestag for parties of the former GDR that received at least 5% of the total votes cast in former GDR territory, the party's eastern German counterpart, in coalition with Bündnis 90 (Alliance 90), secured eight seats in the legislature. Under the same ruling, the PDS won 17 seats in the Bundestag (having received almost 10% of the total votes cast in the area formerly constituting the GDR).

Dr Kohl was formally re-elected to the post of Federal Chancellor in mid-January 1991, immediately after the formation of the new Federal Government. This comprised 20 members, but included only three politicians from the former GDR. The FDP's representation was increased from four to five ministers, reflecting the party's success in the recent legislative elections.

Investigations into the abuse of power by the administration of the former GDR, conducted during the early 1990s, prompted the dismissal or resignation from government posts of several former SED politicians. In January 1991 the German authorities temporarily suspended efforts to arrest Honecker on charges of manslaughter (for complicity in the deaths of people who had been killed while attempting to escape from the GDR), owing to the severe ill health of the former GDR leader. In March it was announced that Honecker had been transferred, without the permission of the German authorities, to the USSR, and in December he took refuge in the Chilean embassy in Moscow.

One of the most serious problems confronting the Government immediately following unification was that of escalating unemployment in eastern Germany, as a result of the introduction of market-orientated reforms that were intended to integrate the economic system of the former GDR with that of the rest of the country. A substantial increase in the crime rate in eastern Germany was also recorded. A further disturbing social issue, particularly in the eastern Länder, was the resurgence of extreme right-wing and neo-Nazi groups. Moreover, there were also fears of a resurgence of political violence, following a series of terrorist acts culminating in the assassination, in April 1991, of Detlev Rohwedder, the executive head of the Treuhandanstalt (the trustee agency that had been established in March 1990 to supervise the privatization of state-owned enterprises in the former GDR). Responsibility for this and other attacks was claimed by the Rote Armee Fraktion (RAF, Red Army Faction), a terrorist organization that had been active in the FRG during the 1970s. (The RAF eventually disbanded in 1998.)

Increasing popular discontent with the Government's post-unification policies was reflected in successive victories for the SPD in Land elections in the first half of 1991, causing the SPD to regain its majority in the Bundesrat, which it had lost to the CDU/CSU-FDP coalition in October 1990. In June 1991 the Bundestag voted in favour of Berlin as the future seat of the legislature and of government; it was envisaged that the transfer of organs of government from Bonn to Berlin would be completed by 2000.

At the beginning of January 1992 some 2m. Stasi files were opened to public scrutiny. In February Erich Mielke, the former head of the Stasi, was brought to trial on charges of murder, and in September Markus Wolf, the former head of East Germany's intelligence service, was charged with espionage, treason and corruption; both were subsequently found guilty and each was sentenced to six years' imprisonment. Meanwhile, Honecker returned to Germany from Russia in July 1992. He was brought to trial in November, together with five other defendants (among them Mielke and Stoph), on charges of manslaughter and embezzlement. In April 1993, however, the charges against Honecker were suspended. (The former East German leader, who was terminally ill, had been allowed to leave for Chile in January of that year; he died in May 1994.) Stoph was also released on grounds of ill health. In May 1993 Hans Modrow was found guilty of electoral fraud at communal elections that had taken place in the former GDR in 1989; Modrow was subsequently sentenced to nine months' imprisonment (suspended).

The issue of asylum-seekers dominated domestic politics during the early 1990s. At Land elections which took place in April 1992, both the CDU and the SPD lost considerable support to right-wing extremist parties. In June the Bundestag approved controversial legislation that aimed to accelerate the processing of applications by refugees and introduced stricter rules for the granting of asylum. A six-week limit was imposed on the time that could be devoted to the consideration of each case, during which period applicants would be required to stay in special camps. Extreme nationalistic sentiment in some quarters led to an escalation in brutal attacks against asylum seekers and foreign workers during the early 1990s. In August 1992 neo-Nazi youths attacked refugee centres in more than 15 towns and bombed a memorial to the Holocaust (the Nazis' extermination of an estimated 6m. Jews) in Berlin. Sporadic attacks continued throughout Germany (though mainly in the east) in September and October. Several neo-Nazi vandals were arrested, but there was criticism of the lenient sentences imposed on those convicted. The murder in November of three Turkish immigrants in an arson attack in Mölln, Schleswig-Holstein, prompted the Government to ban several right-wing groups that were believed to have been responsible for co-ordinating attacks on foreigners. In December the main political parties reached agreement on the terms of a constitutional amendment to the law of asylum, and the new provisions, empowering immigration officials to refuse entry to economic migrants while still facilitating the granting of asylum to persons who were deemed to be political refugees, were approved by the Bundestag and the Bundesrat in May 1993. The Ministry of the Interior estimated that a record total of 438,191 people had sought asylum in Germany during 1992. By 1998, however, mainly as a result of the 1993 legislation, the number of applications had fallen to 98,644. During May 1993 the deaths of five Turkish women in an arson attack near Köln precipitated protest demonstrations throughout Germany and widespread condemnation in the international media. In May 1994 the Bundesrat approved measures to impose stricter penalties on perpetrators of right-wing violence and on those who denied the existence of the Holocaust; further strong measures against nationalist extremists were adopted in September.

The CDU/CSU-FDP coalition was re-elected at a general election held in October 1994; its majority in the Bundestag (enlarged to 672 seats) was, however, sharply reduced, from 134 to 10 seats. The CDU (with the CSU) won 41.4% of the votes cast and 294 seats, the SPD 36.4% of the votes cast and 252 seats, Bündnis 90/Die Grünen 7.3% of the votes cast and 50 seats, the FDP (which had lost representation at several Land parliament elections during 1994) 6.9% of the votes cast and 47 seats, and the PDS 4.4% of the votes cast and 30 seats. (The PDS secured 17.7% of the votes cast in the eastern Länder.) The right-wing extremist organizations did not attract strong support. In early November the ruling coalition negotiated a new political programme, with the creation of jobs a priority.

Shortly afterwards Dr Kohl was formally re-elected as the Federal Chancellor, by a narrow margin of five votes.

In May 1995 the Federal Constitutional Court ruled that alleged former East German spies should not be prosecuted by Federal courts regarding crimes that were committed against the Federal Republic on behalf of the former GDR prior to unification; consequently in October the 1992 conviction of Markus Wolf on espionage charges was overturned. In November 1996 the Federal Constitutional Court ruled that the legal principles of the FRG regarding human rights could be retroactively applied to actions carried out within the former GDR. Thus, in January 1997 Wolf was charged with abduction, coercion and assault. In August Egon Krenz and two other former senior SED members, Günther Schabowski and Günther Kleiber, were found guilty of the manslaughter and attempted manslaughter of people who had sought to flee the former GDR; all three were sentenced to terms of imprisonment. The convictions were upheld in November 1999, following unsuccessful appeals. Krenz appeared before the European Court of Human Rights in November 2000 to appeal against his conviction; a judgment was expected in 2001. Schabowski and Kleiber were pardoned in September 2000 and were released on the eve of the 10th anniversary of German reunification in early October.

The activities of extreme right-wing organizations increased significantly in 1997, and during the latter half of the year a series of incidents were reported that suggested the infiltration of some sections of the armed forces by neo-Nazi interests. In late April 1998 the extreme right-wing and openly xenophobic Deutsche Volksunion (German People's Union, DVU) won unprecedented support at an election to the Land parliament for the economically depressed Sachsen-Anhalt region of eastern Germany, securing 12.9% of the votes cast.

Tensions within the CDU/CSU-FDP coalition became apparent in 1997, mainly concerning the desirability and means of meeting the so-called 'convergence criteria' for participation in European economic and monetary union (EMU) by 1999. Record levels of unemployment continued to cause concern, as well as an unexpectedly large deficit on the 1997 budget. In January 1998 three economists and a professor of law initiated a challenge at the Federal Constitutional Court to Germany's proposed participation in EMU, on the grounds that it would contravene the Government's constitutional duty to pursue sound monetary policy. However, in early April the Court ruled that the issue of a common European currency was outside its jurisdiction and was, rather, the responsibility of the Government. In late April, despite evidence of widespread opposition to the new currency, the Bundestag voted strongly in favour of Germany's participation in EMU.

At the general election held in late September 1998 the CDU/CSU-FDP coalition was decisively defeated by the SPD, which won 298 of the total seats in the Bundestag (reduced to 669). The CDU took 198 seats, both the CSU and Bündnis 90/Die Grünen secured 47, the FDP 43 and the PDS 36. The Republikaner and the DVU did not gain representation in the federal legislature. Following the election, Kohl resigned as Chairman of the CDU; he was replaced by the party's parliamentary leader, Dr Wolfgang Schäuble. Meanwhile, the SPD and Bündnis 90/Die Grünen swiftly negotiated a coalition pact, which envisaged the implementation of measures to create employment, to reform Germany's restrictive citizenship laws and to withdraw from dependence on nuclear power. The agreement was formally approved by both parties at conferences in late October. Shortly afterwards Gerhard Schröder of the SPD (formerly the Minister President of Niedersachsen) was elected Federal Chancellor by a large majority of Bundestag members; the following day a new Cabinet was announced, which included three ministers representing Bündnis 90/Die Grünen. The most prominent of these was the new Federal Vice-Chancellor and Minister of Foreign Affairs, Joseph (Joschka) Fischer, who was formerly the parliamentary leader of the ecological parties. Oskar Lafontaine, the Chairman of the SPD, was appointed Minister of Finance, charged with the responsibility for guiding Germany into EMU. The SPD–Bündnis 90/Die Grünen coalition had a 21-seat majority in the Bundestag.

In early November 1998 Schröder delivered his first major policy statement, placing high priority on reducing the rising level of unemployment; measures were also planned to expedite the economic reconstruction of the eastern Länder, to reform the pension system, to impose an 'ecological' tax on energy consumption and gradually to curtail the country's nuclear energy programme. It soon became apparent, however, that the two coalition partners envisaged very different timescales for the abandonment of atomic power. While the SPD favoured the phased closure of the 19 national nuclear power plants over a minimum period of 25 years, the ecological parties aimed to act far more swiftly. In mid-December Schröder overruled his Bündnis 90/Die Grünen Minister of the Environment, Nature Conservation and Nuclear Safety, Jürgen Trittin, when Trittin unilaterally attempted both to cancel contracts with British and French companies for the reprocessing of German nuclear waste and to dismiss the chiefs of the national atomic power safety commissions.

In early March 1999 Lafontaine resigned as Minister of Finance, apparently in protest at an evident lack of support for his economic policies and management from within both the business community and the Cabinet; he also vacated his seat in the Bundestag and the Chairmanship of the SPD. Hans Eichel of the SPD, hitherto the Minister-President of Hesse, was appointed as the new Minister of Finance. In the following month Schröder was elected to the post of SPD Chairman. In early May the Government approved legislation that enabled people born in Germany of resident foreign parents to hold both German citizenship (hitherto denied them) and the nationality of one parent until adulthood, whereupon they would be required to relinquish one. This represented a significant departure from previous ethnically-orientated citizenship legislation, and was intended to encourage the social assimilation of Germany's foreign population (numbering some 7m. in 1999). The opposition CDU had strongly opposed an initial proposal to grant a full right of dual nationality.

At the beginning of June 1999 Dr Roman Herzog of the CDU was replaced as Federal President by Prof. Dr Johannes Rau of the SPD, formerly Minister-President of Nordrhein-Westfalen. During mid-1999 most organs of government moved from Bonn to Berlin (the capital and henceforth permanent seat of government). Both the Bündnis 90/Die Grünen alliance (which was becoming increasingly polarized between idealist and more pragmatic elements) and the SPD (which was popularly regarded as having betrayed its avowed commitment to social justice following the announcement in June of a package of economic austerity measures designed to redress the decelerating economic growth rate and to appease the alienated business sector) performed poorly at several elections to Land legislatures during the second half of 1999; by late 1999 the ruling coalition had control of less than two-fifths of votes in the Bundesrat (Federal Council). Nevertheless, in early December Schröder was re-elected to the post of SPD Chairman, by a higher margin of support than that achieved at the April party election.

During November 1999 the opposition CDU became embroiled in a scandal concerning the discovery of a system of secret bank accounts, which had been used to deposit undisclosed donations to the party throughout the 1990s. (In accordance with the Grundgesetz—Basic Law—all substantial funding of political parties must be declared.) Allegations subsequently emerged that the CDU leadership had covertly (and possibly with the knowledge of former French President François Mitterrand) accepted a large bribe from the then state-owned French oil company, Elf Aquitaine, in connection with its purchase in 1992 of an eastern German oil refinery. It was also alleged that, in 1998, the CDU had granted an export licence to an arms exporting interest in return for an undeclared party donation. The former Chancellor, Kohl, admitted knowledge of some secret party funding, but repeatedly refused to name any sources; in late December 1999 he became the subject of a criminal investigation. Kohl resigned his honorary chairmanship of the CDU following an ultimatum from party members to clarify his role in the scandal or risk suspension from his honorary position. The current CDU leadership was also implicated in the scandal, including the party Chairman, Dr Schäuble, who had been a close ally of Kohl under the previous administration. Schäuble was, however, confirmed by the party as CDU Chairman in January 2001, despite his offer of resignation, following his belated confession earlier in the month that in 1994 he had accepted a donation of DM 100,000 in cash from an arms dealer, Karlheinz Schreiber, who was implicated in the funding scandal. (In August 2000 a court ruled that Schreiber should stand trial on charges of tax evasion, bribery and conspiracy to defraud in connection with the German Government's sale of 36 tanks to Saudi Arabia during the Gulf War.) Schäuble established a CDU independent inquiry into the funding scandal in January, which subsequently revealed that funding irregularities had persisted for decades in German politics. The inquiry established that during the 1970s between US $15m. and $20m. was paid in cash to the main political parties by the German intelligence agency to support developing democracies in Spain and Portugal. Throughout January 2000 further revelations emerged, including the secretion of more than DM 13m. in illegal foreign accounts by the Hesse regional branch of the CDU. The Minister-President of Hesse, Roland Koch, however, retained the support of both his party and its regional coalition partner, the FDP. In September Koch also won a vote of confidence in the state legislature following fresh media accusations that he had benefited from large corporate donations in the late 1990s. In February 2000 the CDU was fined DM 41m. for irregularities in the Hesse accounts for 1998. The following day Schäuble resigned as Chairman of the CDU, accepting responsibility for mishandling the funding scandal. In March a formal investigation was launched into suspected illegal party financing by the former head of the Chancellery under Schröder, Bodo Hombach; the SPD had not previously been implicated in the party funding scandals.

Following the withdrawal from contention in March 2000 of the former Minister of Defence, Volke Rühe (owing to the party's poor performance under his leadership in the state legislative election in Schleswig Holstein in late February), the CDU's Secretary General, Angela Merkel, was elected Chairman at the party congress in April. Merkel, who had secured significant support as a result of her determination to expose the CDU's financial irregularities, was considered more liberal than her predecessors. In March excerpts from transcripts of telephone conversations of the CDU treasurer under Kohl, Uwe Lüthje, and other CDU officials, which had been illegally recorded by the Stasi, appeared to indicate that Kohl was aware of the irregular party funding earlier than he had previously admitted. Following a campaign by Kohl, the leaders of the principal parties agreed in May to forbid the use of the transcripts by the parliamentary committee investigating financial irregularities in the CDU. However, in the same month the state prosecutor concluded that there were sufficient grounds for the criminal prosecution of Kohl on charges of fraud and bribery (although as an incumbent member of the legislature Kohl was immune from prosecution). In his testimony in June to the parliamentary committee Kohl continued to admit accepting illegal secret contributions to party funds but refuted allegations that such donations had influenced government policy decisions (including the sale of an East German oil refinery to Elf Aquitaine). Kohl's credibility was diminished still further that month when a report was published revealing that two-thirds of chancellery records relating to the period in question had been destroyed following Kohl's defeat in the 1998 general election. (This issue had first emerged during the parliamentary inquiry in February.) The files were however, discovered in July in the archives of the Konrad Adenauer Foundation, a right-wing policy unit.

In September 2000 Kohl resumed his seat in the legislature for the first time since December 1999. He declined an invitation to the 10th anniversary celebration of reunification in October on the grounds that, despite his central role in achieving reunification, he was not invited to speak. In December 2000 another fine, of DM 7.7m., was imposed on the CDU by the Speaker of the Bundestag, Wolfgang Thierce, as a consequence of illegal fund-raising. Kohl had transferred DM 8m. (largely raised through donations) to the CDU in June to contribute to the payment of fines. The CDU's appeal against the previous fine of DM 41m. was upheld by a court in January 2001 although Thierce announced his intention to appeal against the ruling. In February Kohl accepted the proposal of the state prosecutor that he should pay a fine of DM 300,000 in exchange for the abandonment of the criminal investigation into his acceptance of illegal contributions to the CDU in the 1990s; this arrangement subsequently gained judicial approval. The parliamentary inquiry would, however, continue.

In December 1999 the German Government agreed to pay a substantial sum in compensation to people who had worked as forced labourers for German companies or been deprived of their assets under the Nazi regime; it was hoped that this would forestall a growing number of lawsuits taken out against German industrial interests and banks by survivors of the Holocaust. Chancellor Schröder announced that the Government would raise DM 5,000m. towards the proposed DM 10,000m. fund; the other DM 5,000m. was to be raised by Germany's largest banks and companies. The Government's

share was to be financed by state privatizations and contributions from the Länder. The USA agreed to contribute US $10m. as a show of solidarity. In March 2000 Schröder announced an improved agreement, which resolved differences between categories of victims and added a further DM 200m. to the compensation fund. The extra money was to derive from interest income and from a separate settlement between Swiss banks and Holocaust victims. The Evangelical Bishop of Berlin, Bishop Wolfgang Huber, revealed that both the Protestant and the Catholic Churches had used forced labour during the Second World War; he said that his Evangelical Church would contribute DM 10m. to the Government's compensation fund. The Catholic Church in Germany provoked fierce criticism when it announced that it would pay only DM 5m. to compensate forced labourers, and that it would do so separately from the Government's fund; a further DM 5m. was allocated for 'reconciliation work' to be distributed among the Church's charities. The larger German insurers had hitherto declined to contribute to the DM 5,000m. fund being raised by industry because of potentially overlapping claims from separate negotiations involving many leading European insurers. The agreement was eventually signed in July 2000, however by the beginning of 2001 payments had yet to begin because 'legal peace' (the dismissal of all Holocaust-related lawsuits which have been brought against German companies in the USA—one of the conditions of the settlement) had yet to be achieved.

In June 2000, following months of negotiations between the Government and the nuclear industry, Schröder announced that an agreement had been concluded to decommission the country's 19 nuclear power plants (which accounted for almost one-third of power requirements) without compensation by 2021. Under the accord reprocessing of nuclear fuel would end by 2005 (although the transportation of spent fuel for reprocessing elsewhere could continue under certain conditions). Despite some reservations by members of the Bündnis 90/Die Grünen, who had favoured an immediate cessation of nuclear power generation, the agreement was endorsed at a party conference later that month.

In August 2000, in response to growing fears concerning the escalation of neo-Nazi violence against immigrants, the Government announced a series of measures to combat racist attacks, including the establishment of a panel to investigate a potential ban on the extremist right-wing party, the National-demokratische Partei Deutschlands (NPD, National Democratic Party). Despite some opposition to the plan, on the grounds that it was unconstitutional and would afford neo-Nazis an undesirably high level of publicity, in early October the Federal Minister of the Interior proposed the ban, which subsequently received the support of 14 of the 16 Länder. The application to the Constitutional Court to ban the NPD on the grounds that it was anti-Semitic, racist and supported violence was approved by the Bundesrat in November and by the Bundestag in December; the Court was expected to take two years to produce a definitive ruling. Schröder called for stricter application of existing legislation and tougher sentencing from the courts when dealing with right-wing extremists. In August 2000 the perpetrators of the racially-motivated murder in June of a black Mozambique-born German received lengthy sentences which were applauded by the Chancellor. In the same month the Government approved the expenditure of DM 75m. over three years to support local youth initiatives committed to fighting racism, anti-Semitism and xenophobia, and in January 2001 the Minister of Justice, Herta Däubler-Gmelin, announced that her Ministry would provide DM 10m. to compensate the victims of far-right violence, threats or insults. In September the Government banned the neo-Nazi music distributor, Blood and Honour, together with the associated White Youth group on the grounds that both had engaged in activities that breached the Constitution (i.e. spreading Nazi propaganda).

In November 2000 Reinhard Klimmt, the Minister of Transport, Building and Housing, resigned after he was charged with three counts of aiding and abetting fraud in Saarland and fined DM 27,000. In January 2001 a series of photographs emerged which appeared to show the Minister of Foreign Affairs assaulting a police officer during a demonstration in Frankfurt in 1973. Fischer had never hidden his leftist militant past, but claimed he was a firm advocate of peaceful protest. He admitted to having fought unarmed against the police, but only after intense provocation, and flatly denied ever having used weapons. Nevertheless he apologized 'for the wrongdoing to others', a statement which led to calls for his resignation. Schröder however offered his unequivocal support to Fischer. The photographs were supplied to the press by Bettina Röhl, the daughter of the terrorist leader Ulrika Meinhoff; Röhl claimed to possess further compromising material on Fischer, and accused Fischer of inciting demonstrators to throw Molotov cocktails, but later retracted the allegation. Fischer gave evidence later that month as a character witness in the trial of a former international terrorist, Hans Joachim Klein, when he again asserted that he had never favoured armed struggle. Although calls for his resignation continued from the conservative opposition, Fischer retained both popular and political support. However, a criminal investigation into allegations of perjury by Fischer in the Klein trial was opened in February following claims by Margrit Schiller, a former member of the terrorist RAF, that she had lived in Fischer's house during 1973; Fischer had testified that he had never knowingly had contact with members of the RAF.

In January 2001 Andrea Fischer, the Minister of Health, and Karl-Heinz Funke, the Minister of Food, Agriculture and Forestry, resigned amid growing national alarm at the spread of bovine spongiform encephalopathy (BSE) in cattle and accusations that they had ignored the risks posed by infected beef, which was linked to a new strain of Creutzfeldt-Jakob disease, a fatal degenerative illness affecting humans. Despite the crisis that had afflicted the United Kingdom Funke had insisted that special anti-BSE measures were inappropriate in Germany. Such measures were, however, introduced in November 2000 following the confirmation of the first two cases of BSE in German cattle. By the end of January 2001 confirmed cases of BSE in German cattle had increased to 20. In response to public fears about BSE, Schröder created a new Ministry of Consumer Protection, Food and Agriculture, to which he appointed Renate Künast, a leader of the Bündnis 90/Die Grünen. The health portfolio was allocated to Ulla Schmidt of the SPD, who became the subject of scandal, following reports that as a student she had worked as a waitress in a bar which offered prostitution services and that her finances had become entangled with those of a friend who was arrested for trying to exchange counterfeit money. However the Government announced that there were no doubts as to her integrity.

In May 2000 a radical transformation of the armed forces was announced to provide more rapidly deployable troops for the purposes of future peace-keeping missions. In January 2001 the Government announced the reduction of the armed forces from 310,000 to 280,000, with conscripts declining from 130,000 to 80,000 as a result of a decision in June 2000 to reduce the time served from 10 months to nine months; 59 of the 588 garrisons were to be closed and the level of civilian employment by the military was to decline from 140,000 to 100,000. The savings that would ensue would be invested in military technology. From January 2001 women would be able to enrol in military units with a combat role, following a ruling by the European Court of Justice in January 2000 that a prohibition on women serving in combat roles in the German armed forces constituted gender discrimination.

The orientation of Germany's foreign policy after unification broadly followed that of the pre-1990 FRG. The united Germany remained committed to a leading role in the European Community (EC—now European Union, EU), of which the FRG was a founding member, and NATO, while placing greater emphasis on defence co-operation with France. The country was also strongly committed to close relations with Eastern Europe, in particular with the USSR and, subsequently, its successor states. Relations between the FRG and the USSR had improved significantly during the 1980s, culminating in the signing, in September 1990, of a Treaty on Good-Neighbourliness, Partnership and Co-operation. In April 1992 Germany and Russia agreed to a mutual cancellation of debts, and in December of the same year the two countries concluded an agreement whereby the Russian Government would grant autonomy to the 2.5m. ethnic Germans in the Volga region of Russia. In September 1996 the Land interior ministers agreed that the Länder could begin deporting some of the 320,000 refugees from Bosnia and Herzegovina who had been given temporary refuge in Germany. In October the German Government signed an agreement with the Federal Republic of Yugoslavia (FRY), providing for the return of about 135,000 Yugoslav refugees to the FRY over a three-year period (from the beginning of December). In January 1997, following more than a year of complex diplomatic negotiations, Dr Kohl and the Prime Minister of the Czech Republic, Václav Klaus, signed a joint declaration regretting

past wrongs committed on both sides before, during and after the Second World War.

Following the Iraqi invasion and annexation of Kuwait in August 1990, the German Government expressed support for the deployment of US-led allied forces in the region of the Persian (Arabian) Gulf, and contributed substantial amounts of financial and technical aid to the effort to liberate Kuwait, although there were mass demonstrations against the allied action in many parts of Germany. Despite criticism from certain countries participating in the alliance, Germany did not contribute troops to the allied force, in accordance with a provision in the Grundgesetz that was widely interpreted as prohibiting intervention outside the area of NATO operations. In July 1992, however, the Government announced that it was to send a naval destroyer and reconnaissance aircraft to the Adriatic Sea to participate in the UN force monitoring the observance of UN sanctions on the FRY. This deployment was subsequently approved by the Bundestag. In April 1993 the Constitutional Court ruled that German forces could join the UN operation to enforce an air exclusion zone over Bosnia and Herzegovina. Germany dispatched troops to assist the UN relief effort in Somalia in mid-1993. In May 1994 the Constitutional Court declared the participation of German military units in collective international defence and security operations, with the approval of the Bundestag in each instance, to be compatible with the Grundgesetz. In March 1997, while supervising the evacuation from Albania of citizens of western European states, German troops opened fire on hostile forces for the first time since 1945. From March to early June 1999 Germany participated in the ongoing NATO military offensive against the FRY, despite misgivings from left-wing elements within the ruling SPD-Bündnis 90/Die Grünen coalition.

In May 1992 Germany and France reached agreement on the establishment of a combined defence corps, which, they envisaged, would provide the basis for a pan-European military force under the aegis of Western European Union (WEU, see p. 286). The so-called Eurocorps became operational in November 1995. In December 2000 the heads of government of the EU (except Denmark) endorsed the plan for a European Rapid Reaction Force (RRF), which had been adopted by EU ministers in November (although NATO was to remain central to European defence). The RRF's first commander was to be a German, Lt-Gen. Rainer Schuwirth; Germany had pledged the largest number of troops for a deployed RRF, 13,500.

In December 1992 the Bundestag ratified the Treaty on European Union, which had been approved by EC Heads of Government at Maastricht in December 1991. At the same time the lower house approved an amendment to the Grundgesetz (negotiated in May 1992 with the Länder), whereby the state assemblies would be accorded greater involvement in the determination of German policy within the EC. The Bundesrat ratified the Maastricht Treaty later in December 1992. In April 1998 the Bundestag approved Germany's participation in EMU, which took effect in January 1999. In conjunction with other EU member states Germany suspended normal diplomatic relations with neighbouring (and fellow EU member) Austria in early February 2000, following the formation in that country of a coalition Government that included the far right-wing Freiheitlichen (Freedom Party); sanctions were lifted in September.

Government

Germany is composed of 16 Länder (states), each Land having its own constitution, legislature and government.

The country has a parliamentary regime, with a bicameral legislature. The Upper House is the Bundesrat (Federal Council), with 69 seats. Each Land has between three and six seats, depending on the size of its population. The term of office of Bundesrat members varies in accordance with Land election dates. The Lower House, and the country's main legislative organ, is the Bundestag (Federal Assembly), with 669 deputies, who are elected for four years by universal adult suffrage (using a mixed system of proportional representation and direct voting).

Executive authority rests with the Federal Government, led by the Federal Chancellor, who is elected by an absolute majority of the Bundestag and appoints the other Ministers. The Federal President is elected by a Federal Convention (Bundesversammlung), which meets only for this purpose and consists of the Bundestag and an equal number of members elected by Land parliaments. The President is a constitutional Head of State with little influence on government.

Each Land has its own legislative assembly, with the right to enact laws except on matters which are the exclusive right of the Federal Government, such as defence, foreign affairs and finance. Education, police, culture and environmental protection are in the control of the Länder. Local responsibility for the execution of Federal and Land laws is undertaken by the Gemeinden (communities).

Defence

Germany is a member of the North Atlantic Treaty Organization (NATO—see p. 241). Military service is compulsory for a period of 10 months (see below). In August 2000 Germany's armed forces totalled 321,000, including 128,400 conscripts. The strength of the army stood at 221,100, including 102,100 conscripts. The navy numbered 26,000 (including 4,200 conscripts), and there were 73,300 in the air force (20,800 conscripts). The defence budget for 2001 was projected at DM 47,800m. In January 2001 the Government announced that the armed forces were to be reduced to 280,000, with conscripts reduced to 80,000 through the reduction of military service from 10 months to nine months.

At German unification, the National People's Army of the former GDR was dissolved, and 50,000 of its members were incorporated into the German Bundeswehr (armed forces). In accordance with a Soviet-German agreement, concluded in September 1990, the USSR withdrew its 370,000 troops from the territory of the former GDR during 1990–94, while Germany significantly reduced the total strength of its armed forces during the 1990s. In August 2000 the USA, the United Kingdom and France had approximately 80,880 troops stationed in Germany, while Belgium and the Netherlands maintained, respectively, forces of 2,000 and 3,000 men.

Economic Affairs

In 1998, according to estimates by the World Bank, Germany's gross national product (GNP), measured at average 1996–98 prices, was US $2,179,802m., equivalent to $26,570 per head (or $22,026 per head on an international purchasing-power parity basis). During 1991–99, according to official estimates, GNP per head, measured in real terms, expanded at an average annual rate of 0.8%. Over the same period, the population increased by an average of 0.3% per year. GNP was estimated at $2,079,200m. in 1999, equivalent to $25,350 per head. Germany's gross domestic product (GDP) increased by an average of 1.6% annually during 1992–99. GDP grew by 2.6% in 1998, by 1.8% in 1999 and by an estimated 3.0% in 2000.

Agriculture (including hunting, forestry and fishing) employed 2.8% of the total working population in 1999 and provided 1.2% of Germany's GDP in that year. The principal cash crops are potatoes, sugar beet, barley and wheat. Wine production is also important in western Germany. Agricultural GDP increased, in real terms, at an average annual rate of 1.8% in 1992–99; it expanded by 3.2% in 1998 and by 1.8% in 1999.

Industry (including mining, power, manufacturing and construction) engaged 33.4% of the employed labour force and contributed 30.4% of GDP in 1999. Industrial GDP increased, in real terms, by a negligible average annual rate in 1992–99; it increased by 2.2% in 1998 and by 0.6% in 1999.

The mining sector engaged 0.4% of the employed labour force in 1999 and contributed 0.3% of GDP in 1998. The principal mining activities are the extraction of lignite (low-grade brown coal), hard coal and salts.

The manufacturing sector engaged 23.4% of the employed labour force in 1999 and provided 22.9% of GDP in that year. Measured by value of output, the principal branches of manufacturing in 1998 were transport equipment (accounting for 17.3% of the total), non-electric machinery (12.3%), chemical products (10.1%) and food products (9.8%). Passenger motor cars remain an important export. During the 1990s companies specializing in microelectronics and biotechnology performed well in both eastern and western Germany. In 1997 Germany was the world's highest issuer of patents.

Of the total energy produced in 1999 coal amounted to 52.9% (27.7% was hard coal and 25.1% was lignite, or brown coal, which is primarily used in the eastern Länder), nuclear power accounted for 29.2%, natural gas 11.2%, hydroelectric power 3.8%, heating oil 1% and other sources for the remaining 1.1%. In 1999 imports of mineral fuels accounted for an estimated 5.9% of Germany's total imports. In June 2000 the Government announced plans to abandon the use of nuclear power by 2021 (see Recent History above).

Services engaged 63.7% of the employed labour force in 1999 and contributed 68.4% of GDP in 1998. The GDP of the services sector increased, in real terms, at an annual average rate of 2.3% in 1992–99: it grew by 2.8% in 1998 and by 2.3% in 1999.

In 1999 Germany recorded a visible trade surplus of US $72,000m., while there was a deficit of $19,310m. on the current account of the balance of payments. More than one-half of Germany's total trade in that year was conducted with other countries of the European Union (EU—see p. 181). France is the most significant individual trading partner, supplying an estimated 10.5% of imports and purchasing an estimated 11.5% of exports in 1999. The other principal sources of imports in that year were the USA (8.3%), the Netherlands (8.1%), Italy (7.4%) and the United Kingdom (7.0%); the other major purchasers of exports were the USA (10.2%), the United Kingdom (8.4%), Italy (7.4%), the Netherlands (6.6%) and Austria (5.4%). The principal imports in 1999 were road vehicles (9.9%), various categories of electrical machinery (7.2%), office machines and automatic data-processing equipment (5.7%) and clothing and accessories (4.5%). The principal exports were road vehicles (18.0%), non-electrical machinery, various categories of electrical machinery and metals and metal products (especially iron and steel).

The budgetary deficit for 1999 totalled DM 44,531m. (equivalent to 1.2% of GDP). The average annual rate of inflation was 1.0% during 1991–99. Consumer prices rose by 1.9% in 1997, by 0.9% in 1998 and by 0.6% in 1999. An estimated 10.1% of the labour force were unemployed in January 2000. In April 2000 the unemployment rate in the eastern Länder stood at 17.3%, compared with a rate of 7.8% in the territory constituting the former FRG.

Germany is a member of the EU, including the European Monetary System (EMS—see p. 198), and of the Organisation for Economic Co-operation and Development (OECD—see p. 247).

From the mid-1990s austerity measures were introduced in Germany to reduce the budgetary deficit (which had expanded rapidly, owing to the costs of unification) prior to the third stage of European economic and monetary union (EMU): the introduction in January 1999 of a single currency unit for transactions throughout the euro zone and as an internationally traded currency. The euro was expected to become legal tender in Germany in February 2002. Following slow real GDP growth in the late 1990s, largely owing to the crises in Asia and Russia as well as the continuing effects of reunification, economic performance improved during 2000 with an estimated annual growth rate of 3%. The recovery was led by the manufacturing sector, with a rapid increase in industrial output and exports, which benefited both from an increase in international demand and the advantageous effects of the low value of the euro. Private consumption remained subdued although was expected to increase following the introduction in mid-2000 of significant reductions in both corporate and personal income tax, which were expected to raise consumer and business confidence and increase investment, stimulating job creation, The rate of unemployment began to stabilize in late 1999, having reached a record post-war level during the year. However, improvements in the national figures disguised the disparity of employment levels in the former East Germany and the Federal Republic. Future economic growth was threatened both by the inefficient labour market, which urgently required structural reform, and by the growing cost of providing pensions for the ageing population. Proposals for the reform of the pension system included the reduction of state benefits to 64% of final pay from the current 70%, and the introduction of tax breaks and subsidies for new private and occupational pension schemes. However, far more radical reform of the sector needed to take place in the longer term. Wage settlements were moderate in 2000, contributing (with the continuing deregulation of the utilities sector) to a low underlying rate of inflation although the consumer price index had risen, largely as a result of the rapid increase in international petroleum prices. In mid-2000 auctions of third generation mobile telephone licences raised DM 98,800m., all of which was allocated to repaying public debt. At the same time the Minister of Finance announced plans to limit government expenditure during 2001, thereby reducing government borrowing; the measures were part of a long-term plan to balance the federal budget by 2006.

Social Welfare

Social legislation has established comprehensive insurance cover for sickness, accidents, retirement, disability, unemployment and long-term care. The insurance schemes for disability, retirement and unemployment are compulsory for all employees. Insurance is administered by autonomous federal, regional and local organizations. Pensions are based on contributions paid; the amount is related to national average earnings and regularly adjusted. Proposed reforms to the pensions system were due to be voted on in 2002 (see Economic Affairs above). Health insurance pays for all medical attention. During the first six weeks of illness the employer is legally committed to pay 100% of the normal wage. Subsequent to this period, sickness insurance provides a benefit of 70% of the normal gross wage. Of total expenditure on social benefits (DM 1,236,100m. by the Federal Government, the Länder Governments, the municipalities, the private sector and social insurance institutions) in 1999, DM 428,900m. (32.8%) was for health services, DM 485,000m. (37.1%) for old-age pensions, DM 182,600m. for family benefits (14.0%) and DM 162,100m. (12.4%) for employment initiatives and unemployment benefit.

In 1998 there were 2,263 hospitals in Germany, with a total of 571,629 beds. Provisional figures for 1999 show that there were 2,252 hospitals in Germany, with an approximate total of 565,000 beds.

Education

The Basic Law assigns the control of important sectors of the education system to the governments of the Länder. These do, however, co-operate quite closely to ensure a large degree of conformity in the system. Compulsory schooling begins at six years of age and continues for nine years (in some Länder for 10). Until the age of 18, all young people who do not continue to attend a full-time school must attend a part-time vocational school (Berufsschule). Primary education lasts four years (six years in some Länder) and is provided free of charge. Attendance at the Grundschule (elementary school) is obligatory for all

children, after which their education continues at one of four types of secondary school. Approximately one-third of this age-group attend the Hauptschule (general school) for five or six years, after which they may enter employment, but continue their education part-time for three years at a vocational school. Alternatively, pupils may attend the Realschule (intermediate school) for up to nine years, the Gymnasium (grammar school) for nine years (for eight years in some Länder), or the Gesamtschule (comprehensive school, not available in all parts of the country) for up to nine years. The Abitur (grammar school leaving certificate) is a necessary prerequisite for university education

In 1997 total expenditure on education by the Federal Government, the Länder Governments and the municipalities amounted to DM 172,600m. (9.2% of total public expenditure).

Public Holidays

2001: 1 January (New Year's Day), 6 January (Epiphany)*, 13 April (Good Friday), 16 April (Easter Monday), 1 May (Labour Day), 24 May (Ascension Day), 4 June (Whit Monday), 14 June (Corpus Christi)*, 15 August (Assumption)*, 3 October (Day of Unity), 1 November (All Saints' Day)*, 25–26 December (Christmas).

2002: 1 January (New Year's Day), 6 January (Epiphany)*, 29 March (Good Friday), 1 April (Easter Monday), 1 May (Labour Day), 9 May (Ascension Day), 20 May (Whit Monday), 30 May (Corpus Christi)*, 15 August (Assumption)*, 3 October (Day of Unity), 1 November (All Saints' Day)*, 25–26 December (Christmas).

* Religious holidays observed in certain Länder only.

Weights and Measures

The metric system is in force.

Statistical Survey

Source (unless otherwise indicated): Statistisches Bundesamt, 65180 Wiesbaden; tel. (611) 752405; fax (611) 753330; e-mail info@statistik-bund.de; internet www.statistik-bund.de.

Area and Population

AREA, POPULATION AND DENSITY

Area (sq km)*	357,022
Population (official estimates at 31 December)	
1997	82,057,379
1998	82,037,011
1999	82,163,475†
Density (per sq km) at 31 December 1999	230.1

* 137,846 sq miles.

† Of the total (rounded to the nearest 100), 42,072,700 were males and 40,090,800 females.

STATES

	Area (sq km)	Population ('000) at 31 Dec. 1999	Density (per sq km)	Capital
Baden-Württemberg	35,752	10,467	293	Stuttgart
Bayern (Bavaria)	70,548	12,155	172	München
Berlin	890	3,387	3,806	Berlin
Brandenburg	29,476	2,601	88	Potsdam
Bremen	404	663	1,641	Bremen
Hamburg	755	1,705	2,258	Hamburg
Hessen (Hesse)	21,115	6,052	287	Wiesbaden
Mecklenburg-Vorpommern (Mecklenburg-Western Pomerania) .	23,171	1,789	77	Schwerin
Niedersachsen (Lower Saxony)	47,614	7,899	166	Hannover
Nordrhein-Westfalen (North Rhine-Westphalia) . . .	34,080	18,000	528	Düsseldorf
Rheinland-Pfalz (Rhineland-Palatinate)	19,847	4,031	203	Mainz
Saarland	2,570	1,072	417	Saarbrücken
Sachsen (Saxony)	18,413	4,460	242	Dresden
Sachsen-Anhalt (Saxony-Anhalt)	20,447	2,649	130	Magdeburg
Schleswig-Holstein	15,769	2,777	176	Kiel
Thüringen (Thuringia)	16,172	2,449	151	Erfurt
Total	357,022	82,163	230	—

PRINCIPAL TOWNS (estimated population at 30 June 1998)

Berlin (capital) . .	3,417,200	Gelsenkirchen . .	285,300
Hamburg . . .	1,700,800	Karlsruhe . .	276,400
München (Munich) .	1,192,100	Wiesbaden . .	267,600
Köln (Cologne) . .	963,600	Mönchengladbach .	265,300
Frankfurt am		Halle an der Saale*	265,000
Main . . .	643,600	Münster . .	264,300
Essen . . .	606,200	Chemnitz† . .	255,800
Dortmund . .	593,600	Augsburg . .	255,500
Stuttgart . . .	584,600	Braunschweig	
Düsseldorf . .	570,100	(Brunswick) .	248,000
Bremen . . .	545,000	Aachen	
Duisburg . .	526,300	(Aix-la-Chapelle) .	244,900
Hannover		Krefeld . .	244,600
(Hanover) . .	518,200	Magdeburg . .	243,400
Nürnberg		Kiel . . .	238,800
(Nuremberg) . .	488,200	Oberhausen . .	223,100
Dresden . . .	456,300	Lübeck . .	214,800
Leipzig . . .	442,300	Rostock . .	210,600
Bochum . . .	394,500	Hagen . .	208,300
Wuppertal . .	374,500	Erfurt . . .	204,400
Bielefeld . .	322,500	Freiburg im Breisgau	200,300
Mannheim . .	309,700	Kassel . . .	199,300
Bonn . . .	304,500		

* Including Halle-Neustadt.

† Chemnitz was renamed Karl-Marx-Stadt in 1953, but its former name was restored in 1990.

BIRTHS, MARRIAGES AND DEATHS

	Registered live births		Registered marriages		Registered deaths	
	Number	Rate (per 1,000)	Number	Rate (per 1,000)	Number	Rate (per 1,000)
1992 . .	809,114	10.0	453,428	5.6	885,443	11.0
1993 . .	798,447	9.8	442,605	5.5	897,270	11.1
1994 . .	769,603	9.5	440,244	5.4	884,661	10.9
1995 . .	765,221	9.4	430,534	5.3	884,588	10.8
1996 . .	796,013	9.7	427,297	5.2	882,843	10.8
1997 . .	812,173	9.9	422,776	5.2	860,389	10.5
1998 . .	785,034	9.6	417,420	5.1	852,382	10.4
1999 . .	770,744	9.4	430,674	5.2	846,330	10.3

Expectation of life (years at birth, 1996–98): Males 74.0; Females 80.3.

IMMIGRATION AND EMIGRATION

	1996	1997	1998
Immigrant arrivals	959,691	840,633	802,456
Emigrant departures	677,494	746,969	755,358

ECONOMICALLY ACTIVE POPULATION
(sample surveys, '000 persons aged 15 years and over, at April)

	1997	1998	1999
Agriculture, hunting and forestry	1,043	1,016	1,020
Fishing	6	8	6
Mining and quarrying	202	182	161
Electricity, gas and water	8,475	8,461	8,532
Manufacturing	339	305	311
Construction	3,271	3,183	3,146
Wholesale and retail trade; repair of motor vehicles, motorcycles and personal and household goods	5,111	5,154	5,208
Hotels and restaurants	1,133	1,130	1,188
Transport, storage and communications	1,941	1,920	1,953
Financial intermediation	1,257	1,273	1,291
Real estate, renting and business activities	2,475	2,581	2,738
Public administration and defence; compulsory social security	3,295	3,174	3,178
Education	1,887	1,927	1,948
Health and social work	3,437	3,534	3,665
Other community, social and personal service activities	1,772	1,826	1,879
Private households with employed persons	133	150	141
Extra-territorial organizations and bodies	29	36	37
Total employed	35,805	35,860	36,402
Unemployed	3,890	3,849	3,503
Total labour force	39,694	39,709	39,905
Males	22,632	22,583	22,564
Females	17,062	17,126	17,341

Source: ILO, *Yearbook of Labour Statistics.*

Agriculture

PRINCIPAL CROPS ('000 metric tons)

	1997	1998	1999
Wheat	19,827	20,188	19,615
Barley	13,399	12,242	13,301
Maize	3,188	2,782	3,257
Rye	4,580	4,775	4,329
Oats	1,599	1,279	1,339
Mixed grain	2,893	3,039	2,611
Potatoes	11,659	11,338	11,569
Dry broad beans	92	94	96
Sunflower seed*	85	85	81
Rapeseed	2,867	3,388	4,285
Cabbages	736	686	786
Cauliflowers	156	157	157
Cucumbers and gherkins	177	182	194
Onions (dry)	227	260	262
Green beans	46	46	44
Carrots	313	372	380
Grapes*†	1,250	1,408	1,648
Sugar beets‡	25,769	26,787	27,569
Apples§	765	977	1,036
Pears§	37	55	54
Cherries§	34	55	75
Plums§	32	48	55
Strawberries§	79	82	109
Currants*	121	136	155

* Source: FAO.
† Unofficial figures.
‡ Deliveries to sugar factories.
§ Marketed production only.

LIVESTOCK ('000 head at December)

	1997	1998	1999
Horses	680.0*†	680.0*†	471.0
Cattle	15,227.2	14,942.0	14,657.2
Pigs	24,795.2	26,294.0‡	26,002.7
Sheep	2,301.9	2,302.0*	2,298.0†
Goats*	103.0	110.0	114.0
Chickens	103,000.0*†	103,000.0*†	107,175.8
Geese	n.a.	n.a.	400.0
Ducks	2,000.0*†	2,000.0*†	1,924.8
Turkeys	7,000.0*†	7,000.0*†	7,991.6

* Source: FAO; year ending September.
† FAO estimate.
‡ At November.

LIVESTOCK PRODUCTS ('000 metric tons)

	1997	1998	1999
Beef and veal	1,595	1,459	1,439
Mutton and lamb	44	44	44
Pig meat	3,564	3,746	3,980
Poultry meat	734	790	807
Cows' milk	28,702	28,329	28,334
Goats' milk	22	22	22
Butter	442	426	426*
Cheese	1,558	1,569	1,439
Hen eggs	850	854	866
Honey	15	16	20
Wool: greasy*	15	15	15
Cattle hides*	176	161	161

* FAO estimate(s).
Source: FAO.

Forestry

ROUNDWOOD REMOVALS
('000 cubic metres, excluding bark)

	1996	1997	1998
Sawlogs, veneer logs and logs for sleepers	23,175	25,387	24,633
Pulpwood	10,241	10,241	10,417
Other industrial wood	1,122	1,363	1,391
Fuel wood	2,476	2,719	2,611
Total	37,014	38,207	39,052

Source: FAO, *Yearbook of Forest Products.*

SAWNWOOD PRODUCTION
('000 cubic metres, including railway sleepers)

	1996	1997	1998
Coniferous (softwood)	13,123	13,682	13,807
Broadleaved (hardwood)	1,144	1,048	1,165
Total	14,267	14,730	14,972

Source: FAO, *Yearbook of Forest Products.*

Fishing

('000 metric tons, live weight)

	1996	1997	1998
Capture	236.4	259.4	266.6
Freshwater fishes	23.2	23.3	23.3
Atlantic cod	37.6	26.5	23.1
Saithe (Pollock)	15.2	16.0	13.6
Blue whiting (Poutassou)	6.9	4.7	18.0
Atlantic redfishes	22.5	21.1	20.3
Atlantic horse mackerel	22.0	38.1	34.4
Atlantic herring	42.1	42.7	47.0
Sardinellas	10.1	23.9	17.4
Atlantic mackerel	16.3	16.5	21.8
Common shrimp	16.0	19.9	14.8
Aquaculture	75.2	59.4	67.0
Common carp	12.0	12.0	10.7
Rainbow trout	25.0	25.0	25.0
Blue mussel	38.0	22.3	31.2
Total catch	311.6	318.8	333.6

Note: Figures exclude aquatic mammals, recorded by number rather than by weight. The number of long-finned pilot whales caught was: 8 in 1996. The number of harbour porpoises caught was: 6 in 1996; 4 in 1997; 5 in 1998.

Source: FAO, *Yearbook of Fishery Statistics.*

Mining

('000 metric tons, unless otherwise indicated)

	1997	1998	1999
Hard coal	46,792	41,642	39,523
Brown coal	177,099	165,977	161,228
Crude petroleum	2,821	2,895	2,739
Natural gas (petajoules)*	719.8	708.9	751.8
Salt (unrefined)	7,100	6,345	8,405

* Source: UN, *Monthly Bulletin of Statistics.*

Industry

SELECTED PRODUCTS

('000 metric tons, unless otherwise indicated)

	1997	1998	1999
Margarine	731	721	595
Flour	4,095	4,124	4,118
Refined sugar	4,285	3,939	4,345
Beer ('000 hl)	108,729	106,993	107,479
Cigarettes (million)	181,747	181,904	204,631
Cotton yarn (pure and mixed)	106	96	80
Woven cotton fabrics ('000 sq metres)	449,099	478,886	403,404
Carpets and rugs ('000 sq metres)	177,221	169,653	159,475
Plywood	396	371	n.a.
Newsprint	1,802	1,780	1,750
Brown-coal briquettes	3,546	2,345	2,072
Pig-iron*	30,939	30,162	27,931
Crude steel*	45,009	44,046	42,056
Motor spirit (petrol)	24,481	25,232	25,557
Diesel oil†	44,194	46,786	44,123
Cement	35,932	36,378	38,099
Sulphuric acid	1,514	n.a.	1,720
Nitrogenous fertilizers (N)	1,103	1,116	1,152
Artificial resins and plastics	11,225	11,611	12,655
Synthetic rubber	450	512	598
Soap	123	n.a.	n.a.
Aluminium (unwrought):			
Primary	361	381	412
Secondary	373	397	455
Refined lead (unwrought)	199	218	265
Refined zinc (unwrought)	336	357	347
Refined copper	544	548	550

— continued	1997	1998	1999
Passenger cars and minibuses ('000)	4,744	5,444	5,418
Bicycles ('000)	2,440	2,558	2,822
Clocks, watches and non-electronic time-measuring instruments ('000)	15,727	14,661	5,156
Footwear ('000 pairs)‡	30,669	33,146	31,480
Electricity (million kWh)	549,746	n.a.	n.a.

* Source: US Geological Survey.
† Including light heating oil.
‡ Excluding rubber and plastic footwear.

Finance

CURRENCY AND EXCHANGE RATES

Monetary Units
100 Pfennige = 1 Deutsche Mark (DM).

Sterling, Dollar and Euro Equivalents (29 December 2000)
£1 sterling = 3.1365 DM;
US $1 = 2.1019 DM;
€1 = 1.9558 DM;
100 DM = £31.88 = $47.58 = €51.13.

Average Exchange Rate (DM per US $)
1998   1.7597
1999   1.8358
2000   2.1229

Note: Since the introduction of the eruo, with German participation, on 1 January 1999, a fixed exchange rate of €1 = 1.95583 DM has been in operation.

BUDGET (million DM)*

Revenue	1997	1998	1999
Current receipts	1,713,328	1,702,238	1,742,783
Taxes and similar revenue	1,494,369	1,533,469	1,585,221
Income from economic activity	35,381	51,030	43,850
Interest	12,138	13,797	10,200
Allocations and grants for current purposes	428,814	448,585	434,759
Other receipts	143,071	76,554	75,817
Less Deductible payments on the same level	400,445	421,197	407,064
Capital receipts	74,392	83,947	72,067
Sale of property	41,982	52,811	40,417
Loans and grants for investment	63,122	54,769	51,632
Repayment of loans	22,631	22,145	24,052
Public sector borrowing	1,975	1,493	1,232
Less Deductible payments on the same level	55,318	47,271	45,266
Total	1,787,720	1,786,185	1,814,850

Expenditure	1997	1998	1999
Current expenditure . . .	1,703,051	1,657,621	1,686,068
Personnel expenses . . .	390,203	346,519	350,994
Goods and services . . .	418,381	395,552	409,300
Interest	133,095	134,704	137,602
Allocations and grants for current purposes	1,161,817	1,202,043	1,195,508
Less Deductible payments on the same level	400,445	421,197	407,064
Capital expenditure . . .	173,332	176,787	173,313
Construction	67,201	62,066	61,903
Purchase of property . . .	22,003	19,349	20,669
Allocations and grants for investment	101,907	106,898	103,921
Loans	30,024	26,996	24,655
Sale of shares	5,481	6,958	5,371
Repayment expenses in the public sector	2,035	1,792	2,059
Less Deductible payments on the same level	55,318	47,271	45,266
Total	1,876,383	1,834,408	1,859,381

* Figures represent a consolidation of the accounts of all public authorities, including the Federal Government and Land administrations.

INTERNATIONAL RESERVES (US $ million at 31 December)*

	1998	1999	2000
Gold†	10,227	32,436	30,606
IMF special drawing rights . .	1,868	1,959	1,763
Reserve position in IMF . . .	8,023	6,419	5,460
Foreign exchange . . .	64,133	52,661	49,677
Total	84,251	93,475	87,506

* Data on gold and foreign exchange holdings exclude deposits made with the European Monetary Institute (now the European Central Bank).
† National valuation.

Source: IMF, *International Financial Statistics*.

MONEY SUPPLY ('000 million euros at 31 December)

	1998*	1999	2000
Currency in circulation . . .	271.0	148.2	142.2
Demand deposits at banking institutions	n.a.	426.0	448.2

* Figures for 1998 are in '000 million Deutsche Marks.
Source: IMF, *International Financial Statistics*.

COST OF LIVING
(Consumer Price Index for All Private Households; base: 1995 = 100)

	1997	1998	1999
Food	102.0	103.0	101.7
Clothes and shoes . . .	101.1	101.5	101.8
Rent . . . . . }	105.1	106.0	107.4
Energy . . . . . }			
Furniture, domestic appliances and other household expenses .	101.1	101.8	102.1
Transport	104.3	104.7	107.6
Communications	97.9	97.3	88.2
Health	108.7	114.4	110.6
Entertainment and culture . .	102.5	103.1	103.4
All items	103.3	104.3	104.9

NATIONAL ACCOUNTS
(provisional, million DM at current prices)

National Income and Product

	1997	1998	1999
Compensation of employees . .	1,990,110	2,027,830	2,058,370
Operating surplus . . .	778,640	835,540	842,460
Domestic factor incomes . .	2,768,750	2,863,370	2,900,830
Consumption of fixed capital . .	3,066,670	3,153,030	574,710
Gross domestic product at factor cost	3,315,170	3,414,910	3,475,540
Indirect taxes	418,500	438,640	472,030
Less Subsidies	67,070	69,350	70,470
GDP in purchasers' values .	3,666,600	3,784,200	3,877,100
Factor income from abroad . .	153,630	150,840	163,600
Less Factor income paid abroad .	170,850	180,990	201,170
Gross national product . .	3,649,380	3,754,050	3,893,530
Less Consumption of fixed capital .	546,420	561,540	574,710
National income in market prices	3,102,960	3,192,510	3,264,820
Other current transfers from abroad	15,530	15,780	16,270
Less Other current transfers paid abroad	51,820	55,260	54,320
National disposable income .	3,066,670	3,153,030	3,226,770

Expenditure on the Gross Domestic Product

	1997	1998	1999
Government final consumption expenditure	714,200	719,420	736,210
Private final consumption expenditure	2,106,760	2,174,720	2,238,760
Increase in stocks . . .	7,110	29,640	47,110
Gross fixed capital formation . .	784,960	797,150	811,750
Total domestic expenditure .	3,613,030	3,720,930	3,833,830
Exports of goods and services . .	1,020,870	1,092,120	1,134,140
Less Imports of goods and services	967,300	1,028,850	1,088,870
GDP in purchasers' values .	3,666,600	3,784,200	3,877,100
GDP at constant 1995 prices .	3,601,100	3,678,600	3,732,300

Gross Domestic Product by Economic Activity

	1997	1998	1999
Agriculture, hunting and forestry .	43,930 ⎫	43,870	42,240
Fishing	400 ⎭		
Mining and quarrying . . .	10,430	9,190 ⎫	82,600
Electricity, gas and water supply	81,550	81,360 ⎭	
Manufacturing	769,640	812,800	826,960
Construction.	204,780	193,390	189,830
Wholesale and retail trade; repair of motor vehicles, motorcycles and personal and household goods .	364,740	375,970	381,110
Hotels and restaurants . .	42,880	42,530	42,620
Transport, storage and communications	195,240	203,700	204,630
Financial intermediation . .	178,240	181,080 ⎫	1,077,270
Real estate, renting and business activities*	816,550	853,890 ⎟	
Public administration and defence; compulsory social security	221,310	221,870 ⎟	
Education	145,980	148,120 ⎟	
Health and social work . .	208,970	214,710 ⎬	770,600
Other community, social and personal service activities .	160,760	166,530 ⎟	
Private households with employed persons	4,500	4,660 ⎭	
Sub-total	3,449,900	3,553,670	3,617,860
Less Imputed bank service charges	137,110	137,550	137,800
GDP at basic prices . .	3,312,790	3,416,120	3,480,060
Taxes on products . . .	373,340	387,600	417,290
Less subsidies on products .	19,530	19,520	20,250
GDP in purchasers' values .	3,666,600	3,784,200	3,877,100

* Including imputed rents of owner-occupied dwellings.

BALANCE OF PAYMENTS (US $ million)*

	1997	1998	1999
Exports of goods f.o.b. . .	510,710	542,800	542,960
Imports of goods f.o.b. . .	−439,900	−463,910	−470,960
Trade balance	70,810	78,890	72,000
Exports of services . . .	83,230	83,820	83,070
Imports of services . . .	−125,150	−130,270	−134,340
Balance on goods and services.	28,890	32,450	20,730
Other income received . .	80,330	84,020	85,900
Other income paid . . .	−81,760	−90,690	−98,610
Balance on goods, services and income .	27,460	25,780	8,020
Current transfers received .	16,460	16,460	17,010
Current transfers paid . .	−46,830	−46,800	−44,340
Current balance . . .	−2,900	−4,560	−19,310
Capital account (net). . .	−	720	−120
Direct investment abroad. .	−41,680	−92,400	−98,840
Direct investment from abroad	11,660	20,140	52,230
Portfolio investment assets .	−90,080	−141,100	−189,320
Portfolio investment liabilities	90,860	144,790	164,690
Financial derivatives liabilities	−8,820	−6,710	2,160
Other investment assets . .	−83,540	−85,110	−71,060
Other investment liabilities .	122,100	168,760	106,250
Net errors and omissions . .	−1,350	−5,200	39,210
Overall balance . . .	−3,760	4,010	−14,110

* Figures are rounded to the nearest $10 million.

Source: IMF, *International Financial Statistics*.

(public and private development aid to developing countries and multilateral agencies, million DM)

	1996	1997	1998
Public development co-operation .	11,437	10,156	9,819
Bilateral	6,824	6,310	6,141
Multilateral	4,613	3,847	3,678
Other public transactions. . .	292	−836	−565
Bilateral	792	−336	−65
Multilateral	−500	−500	−500
Private development aid . . .	1,571	1,546	1,710
Other private transactions . .	18,730	23,442	27,614
Bilateral	18,448	23,103	25,251
Multilateral	281	339	2,363
Total	32,030	34,309	38,577

External Trade

Note: Figures include trade in second-hand ships, and stores and bunkers for foreign ships and aircraft. Imports exclude military supplies under the off-shore procurement programme and exports exclude war reparations and restitutions, except exports resulting from the Israel Reparations Agreement.

PRINCIPAL COMMODITIES
(distribution by SITC, million DM)

Imports c.i.f.	1997	1998	1999
Food and live animals . .	58,532	59,725	52,436
Vegetables and fruit . . .	19,594	19,946	18,302
Crude materials (inedible) except fuels	31,177	32,080	28,164
Mineral fuels, lubricants, etc. .	57,970	46,303	48,523
Petroleum, petroleum products, etc.	40,104	30,100	34,419
Chemicals and related products	68,287	79,805	76,127
Organic chemicals . . .	16,405	21,083	20,436
Basic manufactures . .	114,621	125,727	113,621
Textile yarn, fabrics, etc. . .	18,663	20,491	18,166
Iron and steel	20,120	22,539	18,130
Non-ferrous metals . . .	17,429	17,857	16,016
Other metal manufactures . .	17,940	20,168	19,579
Machinery and transport equipment	266,564	310,196	323,700
Power-generating machinery and equipment	20,330	24,201	27,343
General industrial machinery, equipment and parts . . .	25,189	29,501	29,081
Office machines and automatic data-processing equipment .	37,455	46,016	49,022
Telecommunications and sound equipment	19,258	22,179	24,268
Other electrical machinery, apparatus and appliances . .	53,206	59,795	61,203
Road vehicles (incl. air-cushion vehicles) and parts[1] . .	75,692	81,935	84,555
Other transport equipment . .	17,964	25,954	27,768
Miscellaneous manufactured articles	111,528	118,390	114,439
Articles of apparel and clothing accessories (excl. footwear) . .	39,586	40,577	38,111
Total (incl. others)[2] . . .	772,149	828,200	853,077

[1] Excluding tyres, engines and electrical parts.
[2] Including monetary gold and government imports. Also included are returns and replacements, not allocated to their appropriate headings.

Exports f.o.b.	1997	1998	1999
Food and live animals . .	35,372	37,848	33,586
Chemicals and related products	118,553	124,726	128,049
Organic chemicals . . .	22,891	21,811	22,352
Medicinal and pharmaceutical products	20,209	24,973	27,170
Plastics in primary forms. . .	20,507	20,205	20,942
Basic manufactures . .	137,503	146,347	137,550
Paper, paperboard and manufactures	18,633	20,380	19,958
Textile yarn, fabrics, etc. . .	22,937	24,055	21,851
Iron and steel	26,808	27,835	23,070
Machinery and transport equipment . .	445,960	496,223	505,071
Power-generating machinery and equipment	27,548	31,376	32,862
Machinery specialized for particular industries . .	52,217	55,144	50,352
General industrial machinery and equipment	61,628	66,453	65,418
Office machines and automatic data-processing equipment .	21,700	25,102	25,559
Telecommunications and sound equipment	21,963	21,848	25,520
Other electrical machinery, apparatus and appliances .	71,368	76,569	77,408
Road vehicles (incl. air-cushion vehicles) and parts[1] . .	148,978	171,362	176,981
Other transport equipment .	21,746	28,321	33,644
Miscellaneous manufactured articles . .	87,378	95,319	96,552
Professional scientific and controlling instruments, etc. .	22,190	24,615	26,482
Total (incl. others)[2] . . .	888,616	955,170	984,065

[1] Excluding tyres, engines and electrical parts.
[2] Including monetary gold. Also included are returns and replacements, not allocated to their appropriate headings.

PRINCIPAL TRADING PARTNERS*
(million DM, including gold)

Imports c.i.f.	1997	1998	1999
Austria	29,082.0	33,077.6	34,549.9
Belgium/Luxembourg. . .	47,420.8	46,437.2	n.a.
China, People's Republic .	21,534.3	23,180.5	26,750.0
Czech Republic . . .	13,830.7	17,182.4	19,856.5
Denmark	14,653.9	13,879.5	13,379.5
France	81,090.1	88,914.4	89,689.4
Hungary	10,857.1	14,588.2	17,503.3
Ireland	8,861.0	14,171.6	15,939.9
Italy	61,074.1	64,512.7	63,341.7
Japan	37,477.6	41,047.2	41,984.8
Netherlands	67,536.7	69,424.7	68,908.1
Norway	15,538.0	13,182.4	13,507.6
Poland	14,356.9	16,443.9	18,009.5
Portugal.	8,884.6	9,093.5	9,324.3
Russia	17,164.6	15,061.5	16,342.4
Spain	25,940.9	27,801.1	27,782.9
Sweden	14,818.6	16,331.0	15,613.1
Switzerland	29,857.7	32,550.1	33,412.5
Taiwan	9,096.0	10,043.3	10,530.6
Turkey	9,925.2	10,736.5	11,043.9
United Kingdom . . .	54,341.5	56,693.7	59,430.8
USA	59,039.4	68,306.5	71,169.9
Total (incl. others) . . .	772,149.0	828,199.6	853,076.8

Exports f.o.b.	1997	1998	1999
Austria	46,679.5	51,760.1	52,693.2
Belgium/Luxembourg. . .	51,666.0	54,288.2	n.a.
China, People's Republic . .	10,628.6	11,900.4	13,591.4
Czech Republic . . .	16,499.2	18,743.4	19,635.8
Denmark	16,023.0	16,563.3	16,533.7
France	94,419.9	105,901.2	112,936.1
Hungary	11,665.4	15,268.7	16,596.8
Italy	65,052.6	70,532.6	73,340.6
Japan	20,475.7	18,310.4	20,457.3
Netherlands	63,054.1	66,910.2	64,464.3
Poland	20,666.2	24,135.9	24,156.5
Portugal.	9,459.0	10,572.3	11,191.5
Russia	16,433.5	14,512.1	9,893.8
Spain	33,070.9	38,454.0	43,359.3
Sweden	20,630.3	21,874.3	22,301.1
Switzerland	39,847.1	42,685.8	44,679.4
Turkey	13,769.2	13,629.0	11,533.0
United Kingdom . . .	74,961.5	81,355.7	83,275.0
USA	76,617.0	89,750.7	100,837.4
Total (incl. others) . . .	888,615.7	955,169.8	984,065.1

* Imports by country of production; exports by country of consumption. The distribution by countries excludes stores and bunkers for ships and aircraft (million DM): Imports 942.7 in 1997; 1,041.5 in 1998; 1,045.3 in 1999; Exports 2,492.0 in 1997; 2,306.6 in 1998; 2,275.8 in 1999.

Transport

FEDERAL RAILWAYS (traffic)

	1997	1998	1999
Passengers (million) . . .	1,980	1,919	1,943
Passenger-km (million) . .	73,917	72,389	73,587
Freight net ton-km (million) . .	72,703	73,560	71,356

ROAD TRAFFIC
('000 licensed vehicles)

	1998*	1999*	2000†
Passenger cars . . .	41,673.8	42,323.7	42,423.3
Lorries	2,370.6	2,465.5	2,491.1
Buses	83.3	84.7	84.9
Motor cycles	2,925.8	3,177.4	3,178.5
Trailers	4,521.4	4,655.8	4,749.7

* At 1 July.   † At 1 January.

SHIPPING
Inland Waterways

	1996	1997	1998
Freight ton-km (million) . . .	61,291.5	61,153.2	64,267.3

Merchant Fleet (registered at 31 December)

	1996	1997	1998
Number of vessels . . .	1,101	1,125	1,158
Displacement ('000 grt) . . .	5,842.1	6,949.6	8,083.6

Source: Lloyd's Register of Shipping, *World Fleet Statistics.*

Sea-borne Traffic

	1997	1998	1999
Vessels entered ('000 net registered tons)*			
Domestic (coastwise) . . .	19,785	43,667	21,213
International	260,553	263,470	269,637
Vessels cleared ('000 net registered tons)*			
Domestic	19,664	67,036	20,529
International	235,110	237,071	246,887
Freight unloaded ('000 metric tons)†			
International	136,249	140,846	137,759
Freight loaded ('000 metric tons)†			
International	69,058	69,098	73,858
Total domestic freight ('000 metric tons)	8,011	7,444	10,005

* Loaded vessels only.
† Including transhipments.

CIVIL AVIATION (traffic on scheduled services)

	1995	1996	1997
Kilometres flown (million) . .	622	653	704
Passengers carried ('000) . .	34,680	40,118	45,805
Passenger-km (million) . .	64,233	77,765	86,189

Source: UN, *Statistical Yearbook.*

Tourism

FOREIGN TOURIST ARRIVALS ('000)*

Country of Residence	1997	1998	1999
Austria	636.3	672.4	723.5
Belgium and Luxembourg . .	571.8	614.9†	723.4
Denmark	576.6	625.4	653.3
France	784.3	803.8	824.1
Italy	862.1	922.9	998.6
Japan	818.6	814.5	818.0
Netherlands	1,806.8	1,824.2	1,923.1
Poland	313.5	307.3	311.1
Spain	355.6	655.1	399.2
Sweden	618.6	893.7	684.3
Switzerland	843.8	380.2	954.9
United Kingdom	1,408.7	1,525.5	1,598.8
USA	1,750.8	1,954.8	2,016.5
Total (incl. others) . . .	14,891.2	15,593.8	16,137.1

* Figures refer to arrivals at registered accommodation establishments.
† Figure for 1998 excludes Luxembourg.

Communications Media

	1994	1995	1996
Radio receivers ('000 in use) . .	76,000	77,000	77,500
Television receivers ('000 in use) .	45,500	46,000	46,300
Telephones ('000 main lines in use)	38,800	40,400	n.a.
Telefax stations ('000 in use) . .	1,447	n.a.	n.a.
Mobile cellular telephones ('000 subscribers)	2,491	3,750	n.a.
Book production: titles* . . .	70,643	74,174	71,515
Daily newspapers:			
Number	411	389	375
Average circulation ('000 copies)	25,757	25,600	25,500
Non-daily newspapers:			
Number	n.a.	38†	36
Average circulation ('000 copies)	n.a.	6,900†	6,600

1997: Radio receivers ('000 in use) 77,800; Television receivers ('000 in use) 46,500.

* Including pamphlets.   † Estimate.

Sources: UNESCO, *Statistical Yearbook*; UN, *Statistical Yearbook.*

Education

(1997)

	Teachers	Students
Pre-primary	5,400	75,700
Primary	173,378	3,746,200
Secondary:		
First stage	314,010	5,177,100
Second stage	61,980	741,700
Special	56,506	406,100
Higher:		
Non-university institutions	16,730*	438,400
Universities and equivalent institutions . .	137,738*	1,394,400

* 1996 figures.

Source: Ministry of Education and Research, Berlin.

Directory

The Constitution

The Basic Law (Grundgesetz), which came into force in the British, French and US Zones of Occupation in Germany (excluding Saarland) on 23 May 1949, was intended as a provisional Constitution to serve until a permanent one for Germany as a whole could be adopted. (Saarland was incorporated into the Federal Republic of Germany in 1957.) The Parliamentary Council which framed the Basic Law intended to continue the tradition of the Constitution of 1848–49, and to preserve some continuity with subsequent German constitutions (with Bismarck's Constitution of 1871, and with the Weimar Constitution of 1919), while avoiding the mistakes of the past.

With the accession of the five newly re-established eastern Länder and East Berlin to the Federal Republic on 3 October 1990, the Basic Law became the Constitution of the entire German nation.

The Basic Law has 182 articles, divided into 14 sections, and is introduced by a short preamble.

I. BASIC RIGHTS

The opening articles of the Constitution guarantee the dignity of man, the free development of his personality, the equality of all persons before the law, and freedom of faith and conscience. Men and women shall have equal rights, and no one shall suffer discrimination because of sex, descent, race, language, homeland and origin, faith or religion or political opinion.

No one may be compelled against his conscience to perform war service as a combatant (Article 4). All Germans have the right to assemble peacefully and unarmed and to form associations and societies. Everyone has the right freely to express and to disseminate his opinion through speech, writing or pictures. Freedom of the press and freedom of reporting by radio and motion pictures are guaranteed (Article 5). Censorship is not permitted.

The State shall protect marriage and the family, property and the right of inheritance. The care and upbringing of children is the natural right of parents. Illegitimate children shall be given the same conditions for their development and their position in society as legitimate children. Schools are under the supervision of the State. Religion forms part of the curriculum in the State schools, but parents have the right to decide whether the child shall receive religious instruction (Article 7).

A citizen's dwelling is inviolable; house searches may be made only by Court Order. No German may be deprived of his citizenship if he would thereby become stateless. The politically persecuted enjoy the right of asylum (Article 16).

II. THE FEDERATION AND THE LÄNDER

Article 20 describes the Federal Republic (Bundesrepublik Deutschland) as a democratic and social federal state. The colours of the Federal Republic are black-red-gold, the same as those of the Weimar Republic. Each Land within the Federal Republic has its own Constitution, which must, however, conform to the principles laid down in the Basic Law. All Länder, districts and parishes must have a representative assembly resulting from universal, direct, free, equal and secret elections (Article 28). The exercise of governmental powers is the concern of the Länder, in so far as the Basic Law does not otherwise prescribe. Where there is incompatibility, Federal Law overrides Land Law (Article 31). Every German has in each Land the same civil rights and duties.

Political parties may be freely formed in all the states of the Federal Republic, but their internal organization must conform to democratic principles, and they must publicly account for the sources of their funds. Parties which seek to impair or abolish the free and democratic basic order or to jeopardize the existence of the Federal Republic of Germany are unconstitutional (Article 21). So are activities tending to disturb the peaceful relations between nations, and, especially, preparations for aggressive war, but the Federation may join a system of mutual collective security in order to preserve peace (Articles 26 and 24). The rules of International Law shall form part of Federal Law and take precedence over it and create rights and duties directly for the inhabitants of the Federal territory (Article 25).

The territorial organization of the Federation may be restructured by Federal Law, subject to regional plebiscites and with due regard to regional, historical and cultural ties, economic expediency and the requirements of regional policy and planning.

III. THE BUNDESTAG

The Federal Assembly (Bundestag) is the Lower House. Its members are elected by the people in universal, free, equal, direct and secret elections, for a term of four years.* Any person who has reached the age of 18 is eligible to vote and any person who has reached the age of 18 is eligible for election (Article 38). A deputy may be arrested for a punishable offence only with the permission of the Bundestag, unless he be apprehended in the act or during the following day.

The Bundestag elects its President and draws up its Standing Orders. Most decisions of the House require a majority vote. Its meetings are public, but the public may be excluded by the decision of a two-thirds majority. Upon the motion of one-quarter of its members the Bundestag is obliged to set up an investigation committee.

IV. THE BUNDESRAT

The Federal Council (Bundesrat) is the Upper House, through which the Länder participate in the legislation and the administration of the Federation, and in matters relating to the European Union (see p. 181). The Bundesrat consists of members of the Land governments, which appoint and recall them (Article 51). Each Land has at least three votes; Länder with more than two million inhabitants have four, and those with more than six million inhabitants have five. Länder with more than seven million inhabitants have six votes. The votes of each Land may only be given as a block vote. The Bundesrat elects its President for one year. Its decisions are taken by simple majority vote. Meetings are public, but the public may be excluded. The members of the Federal Government have the right, and, on demand, the obligation, to participate in the debates of the Bundesrat.

V. THE FEDERAL PRESIDENT

The Federal President (Bundespräsident) is elected by the Federal Convention (Bundesversammlung), consisting of the members of the Bundestag and an equal number of members elected by the Land Parliaments (Article 54). Every German eligible to vote in elections for the Bundestag and over 40 years of age is eligible for election. The candidate who obtains an absolute majority of votes is elected, but if such majority is not achieved by any candidate in two ballots, whoever receives most votes in a further ballot becomes President. The President's term of office is five years. Immediate re-election is permitted only once. The Federal President must not be a member of the Government or of any legislative body or hold any salaried office. Orders and instructions of the President require the counter-signature of the Federal Chancellor or competent Minister, except for the appointment or dismissal of the Chancellor or the dissolution of the Bundestag.

The President represents the Federation in its international relations and accredits and receives envoys. The Bundestag or the Bundesrat may impeach the President before the Federal Constitutional Court on account of wilful violation of the Basic Law or of any other Federal Law (Article 61).

VI. THE FEDERAL GOVERNMENT

The Federal Government (Bundesregierung) consists of the Federal Chancellor (Bundeskanzler) and the Federal Ministers (Bundesminister). The Chancellor is elected by an absolute majority of the Bundestag on the proposal of the Federal President (Article 63). Ministers are appointed and dismissed by the President upon the proposal of the Chancellor. Neither he nor his Ministers may hold any other salaried office. The Chancellor determines general policy and assumes responsibility for it, but within these limits each Minister directs his department individually and on his own responsibility. The Bundestag may express its lack of confidence in the Chancellor only by electing a successor with the majority of its members; the President must then appoint the person elected (Article 67). If a motion of the Chancellor for a vote of confidence does not obtain the support of the majority of the Bundestag, the President may, upon the proposal of the Chancellor, dissolve the House within 21 days, unless it elects another Chancellor within this time (Article 68).

VII. THE LEGISLATION OF THE FEDERATION

The right of legislation lies with the Länder in so far as the Basic Law does not specifically accord legislative powers to the Federation.

---

* The elections of 1949 were conducted on the basis of direct election, with some elements of proportional representation. In January 1953 the draft of a new electoral law was completed by the Federal Government and was approved shortly before the dissolution. The new law represents a compromise between direct election and proportional representation, and is designed to prevent the excessive proliferation of parties in the Bundestag.

Distinction is made between fields within the exclusive legislative powers of the Federation and fields within concurrent legislative powers. In the field of concurrent legislation the Länder may legislate so long and so far as the Federation makes no use of its legislative right. The Federation has this right only in matters relating to the creation of equal living conditions throughout the country and in cases where the preservation of legal and economic unity is perceived to be in the national interest. Exclusive legislation of the Federation is strictly limited to such matters as foreign affairs, Federal finance, citizenship, migration, currency, copyrights, customs, railways, waterways, shipping and post and telecommunications. In most other fields, as enumerated (Article 74), concurrent legislation exists.

The legislative organ of the Federation is the Bundestag, to which Bills are introduced by the Government, by members of the Bundestag or by the Bundesrat (Article 76). After their adoption they must be submitted to the Bundesrat, which may demand, within three weeks, that a committee of members of both houses be convened to consider the Bill (Article 77). In so far as its express approval is not needed, the Bundesrat may veto a law within two weeks. This veto can be overruled by the Bundestag, with the approval of a majority of its members. When the Bill requires the consent of the Bundesrat, such an overruling may not take place.

An amendment of the Basic Law requires a majority of two-thirds in both houses, but an amendment affecting the division of the Federation into Länder and the basic principles contained in Articles 1 and 20 is inadmissible (Article 79).

VIII. THE EXECUTION OF FEDERAL LAWS AND THE FEDERAL ADMINISTRATION

The Länder execute Federal Laws as matters of their own concern in so far as the Basic Law does not otherwise determine. In doing so, they regulate the establishment of the authorities and the administrative procedure, but the Federal Government exercises supervision in order to ensure that the Länder execute Federal Laws in an appropriate manner.

In order to avert imminent danger to the existence of the democratic order, a Land may call in the police forces of other Länder; and if the Land in which the danger is imminent is itself not willing or able to fight the danger, the Federal Government may place the police in the Land, or the police forces in other Länder, under its instructions (Article 91).

IX. THE ADMINISTRATION OF JUSTICE

Judicial authority is vested in independent judges, who are subject only to the law and who may not be dismissed or transferred against their will (Article 97).

Justice is exercised by the Federal Constitutional Court, by the Supreme Federal Courts and by the Courts of the Länder. The Federal Constitutional Court decides on the interpretation of the Basic Law in cases of doubt, on the compatibility of Federal Law or Land Law with the Basic Law, and on disputes between the Federation and the Länder or between different Länder. Supreme Federal Courts are responsible for the spheres of ordinary, administrative, fiscal, labour and social jurisdiction. If a Supreme Federal Court intends to judge a point of law in contradiction to a previous decision of another Supreme Federal Court, it must refer the matter to a special senate of the Supreme Courts. Extraordinary courts are inadmissible.

The freedom of the individual may be restricted only on the basis of a law. No one may be prevented from appearing before his lawful judge (Article 101). Detained persons may be subjected neither to physical nor to mental ill-treatment. The police may hold no one in custody longer than the end of the day following the arrest without the decision of a court. Any person temporarily detained must be brought before a judge who must either issue a warrant of arrest or set him free, at the latest on the following day. A person enjoying the confidence of the detainee must be notified forthwith of any continued duration of a deprivation of liberty. An act may be punished only if it was punishable by law before the act was committed, and no one may be punished more than once for the same criminal act. A criminal act may not be punished by sentence of death.

X. FINANCE

The Federation has the exclusive power to legislate only on customs and fiscal monopolies; on most other taxes, especially on income, property and inheritance, it has concurrent power to legislate with the Länder (see VII above).

Customs, fiscal monopolies, excise taxes (with exception of the beer tax) and levies within the framework of the European Union are administered by Federal finance authorities, and the revenues thereof accrue to the Federation. The remaining taxes are administered, as a rule, by the Länder and the Gemeinden (communities) to which they accrue. Income tax, corporation tax and value-added tax are shared taxes, accruing jointly to the Federation and the Länder (after deduction of a proportion of income tax for the municipalities; Article 106). The Federation and the Länder shall be self-supporting and independent of each other in their fiscal administration (Article 109). In order to ensure the working efficiency of the Länder with low revenues and to equalize their differing burdens of expenditure, there exists a system of revenue sharing among the Länder; in addition, the Federation may make grants, out of its own funds, to the poorer Länder. All revenues and expenditures of the Federation must be estimated for each fiscal year and included in the budget, which must be established by law before the beginning of the fiscal year. Decisions of the Bundestag or the Bundesrat which increase the budget expenditure proposed by the Federal Government require its approval (Article 113).

XI. TRANSITIONAL AND CONCLUDING PROVISIONS

Articles 116–146 regulate a number of unrelated matters of detail, such as the relationship between the old Reich and the Federation. Article 143 contains divergences from the Basic Law, with regard to the newly-acceded Länder, as stipulated in the Unification Treaty.

The Government

HEAD OF STATE

Federal President: Prof. Dr JOHANNES RAU (inaugurated 1 July 1999).

THE FEDERAL GOVERNMENT
(March 2001)

A coalition of the Sozialdemokratische Partei Deutschlands (Social Democratic Party–SPD) and Bündnis 90/Die Grünen (Alliance 90/ Greens).

Federal Chancellor: GERHARD SCHRÖDER (SPD).

Federal Vice-Chancellor and Minister of Foreign Affairs: JOSEPH (JOSCHKA) FISCHER (Bündnis 90/Die Grünen).

Head of the Federal Chancellery: BODO HOMBACH (SPD).

Minister of the Interior: OTTO SCHILY (SPD).

Minister of Justice: Prof. Dr HERTA DÄUBLER-GMELIN (SPD).

Minister of Finance: HANS EICHEL (SPD).

Minister of Economics and Technology: WERNER MÜLLER (Independent).

Minister of Consumer Protection, Food and Agriculture: RENATE KÜNAST (Bündnis 90/Die Grünen).

Minister of Labour and Social Affairs: WALTER RIESTER (SPD).

Minister of Defence: RUDOLF SCHARPING (SPD).

Minister of Family Affairs, Senior Citizens, Women and Youth: DR CHRISTINE BERGMANN (SPD).

Minister of Health: ULLA SCHMIDT (SPD).

Minister of Transport, Building and Housing: KURT BODEWIG (SPD).

Minister of the Environment, Nature Conservation and Nuclear Safety: JÜRGEN TRITTIN (Bündnis 90/Die Grünen).

Minister of Education and Research: EDELGARD BULMAHN (SPD).

Minister of Economic Co-operation and Development: HEIDEMARIE WIECZOREK-ZEUL (SPD).

Minister for Special Tasks at the Federal Chancellery: DR FRANK WALTER STEINMEIER (SPD).

MINISTRIES

Office of the Federal President: Schloss Bellevue, 11010 Berlin; tel. (30) 20000; internet www.bundespraesident.de.

Federal Chancellery: Schlossplatz 1, 10178 Berlin; tel. (30) 40000; fax (30) 40001818; e-mail bundeskanzler@bundeskanzler.de; internet www.bundeskanzler.de.*

Press and Information Office of the Federal Government: Neustädtische Kirchstrasse 15, 10117 Berlin; tel. (1888) 2720; fax (1888) 2722555; e-mail posteingang@bpa.bund.de; internet www .government.de.

Ministry of Defence: Stauffenbergstr. 18, 10785 Berlin; tel. (30) 200400; fax (30) 20048333; e-mail poststelle@bmug.bund400.de; internet www.bundeswehr.de.

* When the Government moved from Bonn to Berlin the Federal Chancellerey was temporarily located in the former GDR State Council Building. The new Chancellerey building was expected to be completed in the Spring of 20001. The new address will be: Willy-Brandt Str. 1, 10557 Berlin. There was to be no change in the telephone or fax numbers.

Ministry of Economic Co-operation and Development: Stresemannstr. 92, Europahaus, 10963 Berlin; tel. (30) 25030; fax (30) 25034847; e-mail poststelle@bm2.bund.de; internet www.bmz.de.

Ministry of Economics and Technology: Scharnhorststr. 34–37, 10115 Berlin; tel. (1888) 6159; fax (1888) 6157010; e-mail info@bmwi.bund.de; internet www.bmwi.de.

Ministry of Education and Research: Hannoversche Str. 30, 10115 Berlin; tel. (30) 285400; fax (30) 285405270; e-mail bmbf@bmbf.bund400.de; internet www.bmbf.de.

Ministry of the Environment, Nature Conservation and Nuclear Safety: Alexanderplatz 6, 10178 Berlin; tel. (1888) 3050; fax (1888) 3054375; e-mail service@bmu.de; internet www.bmu.de.

Ministry of Family Affairs, Senior Citizens, Women and Youth: Taubenstr. 42/43, 10117 Berlin; tel. (30) 206550; fax (30) 206551145; e-mail info@bmfsfj.bund.de; internet www.bmfsfj.de.

Ministry of Finance: Wilhelmstr. 97, 10117 Berlin; tel. (30) 22420; fax (30) 22423260; e-mail poststelle@bmf.bund.de; internet www.bundesfinanzministerium.de.

Ministry of Consumer Protection, Food and Agriculture: Postfach 42, 10177 Berlin; Wilhelmstr. 54, 10121 Berlin; tel. (30) 20060; fax (30) 20064262; e-mail internet@bml.bund.de; internet www.bml.de.

Ministry of Foreign Affairs: Werderscher Markt 1, 10117 Berlin; tel. (1888) 170; fax (1888) 173402; e-mail poststelle@auswaertiges-amt.de; internet www.auswaertiges-amt.de.

Ministry of Health: Postfach 080163, 10117 Berlin; Mohrenstr. 62, 10001 Berlin; tel. (30) 206400; fax (30) 206404974; e-mail info@bmg.bund.de; internet www.bmgesundheit.de.

Ministry of the Interior: Alt-Moabit 101, 10559 Berlin; tel. (1888) 6810; fax (1888) 6812926; e-mail poststelle@bmi.bund400.de; internet www.bmi.bund.de.

Ministry of Justice: Jerusalemer Str. 27, 10117 Berlin; tel. (30) 202570; fax (30) 20259525; e-mail poststelle@bmj.bund.de; internet www.bmj.bund.de.

Ministry of Labour and Social Affairs: Wilhelmstr. 49, 10117 Berlin; tel. (30) 20140; fax (30) 2014922; e-mail info@bma.bund.de; internet www.bma.bund.de.

Ministry of Transport, Building and Housing: Krausenstr. 17–20, 10117 Berlin; tel. (30) 20080; fax (30) 20081920; e-mail buergerinfo@bmvbw.bund.de; internet www.bmvbw.de.

Legislature

BUNDESTAG
(Federal Assembly)

President: WOLFGANG THIERSE (SPD).

Vice-Presidents: ANKE FUCHS (SPD), RUDOLF SEITERS (CSU), Dr ANTJE VOLLMER (Bündnis 90/Die Grünen), Dr HERMANN OTTO SOLMS (FDP), PETRA BLÄSS (PDS).

General Election, 27 September 1998

Parties and Groups	Votes*	%	Seats
Sozialdemokratische Partei Deutschlands (SPD)	20,178,838	40.93	298
Christlich-Demokratische Union Deutschlands (CDU)	14,004,907	28.41	198
Christlich-Soziale Union Deutschlands (CSU)	3,324,325	6.74	47
Bündnis 90/Die Grünen	3,300,133	6.69	47
Freie Demokratische Partei (FDP)	3,080,661	6.25	43
Partie des Demokratischen Sozialismus (PDS)	2,513,788	5.10	36
Die Republikaner	905,200	1.84	—
Deutsche Volksunion (DVU)	600,194	1.22	—
Others	1,392,409	2.82	—
Total	49,300,455	100.00	669

* Figures refer to valid second votes (i.e. for state party lists). Details of the numbers of valid first votes (for individual candidates) are not available.

BUNDESRAT
(Federal Council)

President: Prof. Dr KURT BIEDENKOPF (CDU).

The Bundesrat has 69 members. Each Land (state) has three, four, five or six votes, depending on the size of its population, and may send as many members to the sessions as it has votes. The head of government of each Land is automatically a member of the Bundesrat. Members of the Federal Government attend the sessions, which are held every two to three weeks.

Länder	Seats
Nordrhein-Westfalen (North Rhine-Westphalia)	6
Bayern (Bavaria)	6
Baden-Württemberg	6
Niedersachsen (Lower Saxony)	6
Hessen (Hesse)	4
Sachsen (Saxony)	5
Rheinland-Pfalz (Rhineland-Palatinate)	4
Berlin	4
Sachsen-Anhalt (Saxony-Anhalt)	4
Thüringen (Thuringia)	4
Brandenburg	4
Schleswig-Holstein	4
Mecklenburg-Vorpommern (Mecklenburg-Western Pomerania)	3
Hamburg	3
Saarland	3
Bremen	3

The Land Governments

The 16 Länder of Germany are autonomous but not sovereign states, enjoying a high degree of self-government and extensive legislative powers. Thirteen of the Länder have a Landesregierung (Government) and a Landtag (Assembly). The equivalent of the Landesregierung in Berlin, Bremen and Hamburg is the Senate. The equivalent of the Landtag is the House of Representatives in Berlin and the City Council in Bremen and Hamburg.

BADEN-WÜRTTEMBERG

The Constitution was adopted by the Assembly in Stuttgart on 11 November 1953 and came into force on 19 November. The Minister-President, who is elected by the Assembly, appoints and dismisses Ministers. The Government, which is responsible to the Assembly, is currently formed by a coalition of the CDU and the FDP/DVP.

Minister-President: ERWIN TEUFEL (CDU).

The composition of the Assembly, as the result of elections held on 25 March 2001, is as follows:

President of Assembly: PETER STRAUB (CDU).

Party	Seats
Christlich-Demokratische Union Deutschlands (CDU)	63
Sozialdemokratische Partei Deutschlands (SPD)	45
Bündnis 90/Die Grünen	10
Freie Demokratische Partei/Demokratische Volkspartei (FDP/DVP)	10

The Land is divided into four administrative districts: Stuttgart, Karlsruhe, Tübingen and Freiburg.

BAYERN (BAVARIA)

The Constitution of Bayern provides for a bicameral Assembly and a Constitutional Court. Provision is also made for referendums. The Minister-President, who is elected by the Assembly for four years, appoints the Ministers and Secretaries of State with the consent of the Assembly. The Government is currently formed from the majority party (CSU).

Minister-President: Dr EDMUND STOIBER (CSU).

The composition of the Assembly, as a result of elections held on 13 September 1998, is as follows:

President of Assembly: JOHANN BÖHM (CSU).

Party	Seats
Christlich-Soziale Union Deutschlands (CSU)	123
Sozialdemocratische Partei Deutschlands (SPD)	67
Bündnis 90/Die Grünen	13
Independent	1

The Senate, or second chamber, consists of 60 members, divided into 10 groups representing professional interests, e.g. agriculture, industry, trade, the professions and religious communities. Every two years one-third of the Senate is newly elected. In February 1998 a majority of voters who participated in a Land referendum on the future of the Senate favoured its abolition.

President of the Senate: HERIBERT THALLMAIR (CSU).

Bayern is divided into seven districts: Mittelfranken, Oberfranken, Unterfranken, Schwaben, Niederbayern, Oberpfalz and Oberbayern.

BERLIN

The House of Representatives (Abgeordnetenhaus) is the legislative body. The executive agency is the Senate, which is composed of the Governing Mayor (Regierender Bürgermeister) and up to 10 Senators, from among whom the deputy mayor is elected. The Governing Major and the senators are elected by a majority of the House of Representatives. The Senate is responsible to the House of Representatives and dependent on its confidence. The Senate is currently composed of a coalition of the CDU and the SPD.

Regierender Bürgermeister: EBERHARD DIEPGEN (CDU).

The composition of the House of Representatives, as the result of elections held on 10 October 1999, is as follows:

President of House of Representatives: REINHARD FÜHRER (CDU).

Party	Seats
Christlich-Demokratische Union Deutschlands (CDU)	75
Sozialdemocratische Partei Deutschlands (SPD) . .	42
Partie des Demokratischen Sozialismus (PDS) . .	33
Bündnis 90/Die Grünen	18

BRANDENBURG

The Government is currently formed from a coalition of the SPD and the CDU.

Minister-President: Dr MANFRED STOLPE (SPD).

The composition of the Assembly, as a result of elections held on 5 September 1999, is as follows:

President of Assembly: Dr HERBERT KNOBLICH (SPD).

Party	Seats
Sozialdemocratische Partei Deutschlands (SPD) . .	37
Christlich-Demokratische Union Deutschlands (CDU)	25
Partie des Demokratischen Sozialismus (PDS) . .	22

BREMEN

The Constitution of the Free Hanseatic City of Bremen was sanctioned by referendum of the people on 12 October 1947. The main constitutional organs are the City Council (legislature), the Senate (government) and the Constitutional Court. The Senate is the executive organ elected by the Council for the duration of its own tenure of office. The Senate elects from its own ranks two Mayors (Bürgermeister), one of whom becomes President of the Senate. Decisions of the Council are subject to the delaying veto of the Senate. The Senate is currently formed from a coalition of the SPD and the CDU.

First Bürgermeister and President of the Senate: Dr HENNING SCHERF (SPD).

The election of 6 June 1999 resulted in the following composition:

President of the City Council: CHRISTIAN WEBER (CDU).

Party	Seats
Sozialdemocratische Partei Deutschlands (SPD) . .	47
Christlich-Demokratische Union Deutschlands (CDU)	42
Bündnis 90/Die Grünen	10
Deutsche Volksunion (DVU)	1

HAMBURG

The Constitution of the Free and Hanseatic City of Hamburg was adopted in June 1952. The City Council (legislature) elects the members of the Senate (government), which in turn elects the President and the President's deputy from its own ranks. The President remains in office for one year, but may stand for re-election. The Senate is currently formed by a coalition of the SPD and Bündnis 90/Die Grünen.

President of Senate and First Bürgermeister: ORTWIN RUNDE (SPD).

The City Council was elected on 21 September 1997, and is composed as follows:

President: Dr DOROTHEE STAPELFELDT (SPD).

Party	Seats
Sozialdemocratische Partei Deutschlands (SPD) . .	54
Christlich-Demokratische Union Deutschlands (CDU)	46
Bündnis 90/Die Grünen	21

HESSEN (HESSE)

The Constitution of this Land dates from 1 December 1946. The Minister-President is elected by the Assembly, and appoints and dismisses Ministers with its consent. The Assembly can force the resignation of the Government by a vote of no confidence. The Government is currently formed from a coalition of the CDU and FDP.

Minister-President: ROLAND KOCH (CDU).

The Assembly, elected on 7 February 1999, is composed as follows:
President of Assembly: KLAUS PETER MÖLLER (CDU).

Party	Seats
Christlich-Demokratische Union Deutschlands (CDU)	50
Sozialdemokratische Partei Deutschlands (SPD) . .	46
Bündnis 90/Die Grünen	8
Freie Demokratische Partei (FDP)	6

Hessen is divided into three governmental districts: Kassel, Gießen and Darmstadt.

MECKLENBURG-VORPOMMERN (MECKLENBURG-WESTERN POMERANIA)

The Constitution was adopted by the Assembly on 14 May 1993. The Government is currently formed from a coalition of the SPD and the PDS.

Minister-President: HARALD RINGSTORFF (SPD).

The composition of the Assembly, as a result of elections held on 27 September 1998, is as follows:

President of Assembly: HINRICH KUESSNER (SPD).

Party	Seats
Sozialdemokratische Partei Deutschlands (SPD) . .	27
Christlich-Demokratische Union Deutschlands (CDU)	24
Partie des Demokratischen Sozialismus (PDS) . .	20

NIEDERSACHSEN (LOWER SAXONY)

The Constitution was adopted by the Assembly on 19 May 1993 and came into force on 1 June. The Government is currently formed from the majority party (SPD).

Minister-President: SIGMAR GABRIEL.

As a result of elections held on 1 March 1998, the Assembly is composed as follows:

President of Assembly: Prof. ROLF WERNSTEDT (SPD).

Party	Seats
Sozialdemokratische Partei Deutschlands (SPD) . .	83
Christlich-Demokratische Union Deutschlands (CDU)	62
Bündnis 90/Die Grünen	12

Niedersachsen is divided into four governmental districts: Braunschweig, Hannover, Lüneburg and Weser-Ems.

NORDRHEIN-WESTFALEN (NORTH RHINE-WESTPHALIA)

The present Constitution was adopted by the Assembly on 6 June 1950, and was endorsed by the electorate in the elections held on 18 June. The Government is presided over by the Minister-President, who appoints Ministers. It is currently formed from a coalition of the SPD and Bündnis 90/Die Grünen.

Minister-President: WOLFGANG CLEMENT (SPD).

The Assembly, elected on 14 May 2000, is composed as follows:
President of Assembly: ULRICH SCHMIDT (SPD).

Party	Seats
Sozialdemokratische Partei Deutschlands (SPD) . .	102
Christlich-Demokratische Union Deutschlands (CDU)	88
Freie Demokratische Partei (FDP)	24
Bündnis 90/Die Grünen	15

The Land is divided into five governmental districts: Düsseldorf, Münster, Arnsberg, Detmold and Köln.

RHEINLAND-PFALZ (RHINELAND-PALATINATE)

The three chief agencies of the Constitution of this Land are the Assembly, the Government and the Constitutional Court. The Minister-President is elected by the Assembly, with whose consent he/

she appoints and dismisses Ministers. The Government, which is dependent on the confidence of the Assembly, is currently composed of a coalition of the SPD and the FDP.

Minister-President: KURT BECK (SPD).

The members of the Assembly are elected according to a system of proportional representation. Its composition, as the result of elections held on 25 March 2001, is as follows:

President of Assembly: CHRISTOPH GRIMM (SPD).

Party	Seats
Sozialdemokratische Partei Deutschlands (SPD) . .	49
Christlich-Demokratische Union Deutschlands (CDU)	38
Freie Demokratische Partei (FDP)	8
Bündnis 90/Die Grünen	6

Rheinland-Pfalz is divided into three districts: Koblenz, Rheinhessen-Pfalz (Rheinhessen-Palatinate) and Trier.

SAARLAND

Under the Constitution which came into force on 1 January 1957, Saarland was politically integrated into the FRG as a Land. It was economically integrated into the FRG in July 1959. The Minister-President is elected by the Assembly. The Government is currently formed from a coalition of the CDU and the SPD.

Minister-President: PETER MÜLLER (CDU).

The composition of the Assembly, as a result of elections held on 5 September 1999, is as follows:

President of the Assembly: HANS LEY (CDU).

Party	Seats
Christlich-Demokratische Union Deutschlands (CDU)	26
Sozialdemokratische Partei Deutschlands (SPD) . .	25

SACHSEN (SAXONY)

The Government is formed by the majority party (CDU).

Minister-President: Prof. Dr KURT BIEDENKOPF (CDU).

The composition of the Assembly, as a result of elections held on 19 September 1999, is as below.

President of Assembly: ERICH ILTGEN (CDU).

Party	Seats
Christlich-Demokratische Union Deutschlands (CDU)	76
Partie des Demokratischen Sozialismus (PDS) . .	30
Sozialdemokratische Partei Deutschlands (SPD) . .	14

SACHSEN-ANHALT (SAXONY-ANHALT)

The Government is currently formed by the majority party (SPD).

Minister-President: Dr REINHARD HÖPPNER (SPD).

The composition of the Assembly, as a result of elections held on 26 April 1998, is as follows:

President of Assembly: WOLFGANG SCHAEFER (SPD).

Party	Seats
Sozialdemokratische Partei Deutschlands (SPD) . .	47
Christlich-Demokratische Union Deutschlands (CDU)	28
Partei des Demokratischen Sozialismus (PDS) . .	25
Deutsche Volksunion (DVU)	16

Sachsen-Anhalt is divided into three governmental districts: Magdeburg, Halle and Dessau.

SCHLESWIG-HOLSTEIN

The Provisional Constitution was adopted by the Assembly on 13 December 1949. The Government consists of the Minister-President and the Ministers appointed by the Minister-President. The Government is currently formed from a coalition of the SPD and Bündnis 90/Die Grünen.

Minister-President: HEIDE SIMONIS (SPD).

The composition of the Assembly, as the result of elections held on 27 February 2000, is as follows:

President of Assembly: HEINZ-WERNER ARENS (SPD).

Party	Seats
Sozialdemokratische Partei Deutschlands (SPD) . .	41
Christlich-Demokratische Union Deutschlands (CDU)	33
Freie Demokratische Partei (FDP)	7
Bündnis 90/Die Grünen	5
Südschleswigscher Wählerverband*	3

* Represents the Danish minority in Schleswig-Holstein.

THÜRINGEN (THURINGIA)

The Assembly Government is currently led by the CDU.

Minister-President: Dr BERNHARD VOGEL (CDU).

The composition of the Assembly, as a result of elections held on 12 September 1999, is as follows:

President of Assembly: CHRISTINE LIEBERKNECHT (CDU).

Party	Seats
Christlich-Demokratische Union Deutschlands (CDU)	49
Partei des Demokratischen Sozialismus (PDS) . .	21
Sozialdemokratische Partei Deutschlands (SPD) . .	18

Political Organizations

Bündnis 90/Die Grünen (Alliance 90/Greens): Platz vor dem Neuen Tor 1, 10115 Berlin; tel. (30) 284420; fax (30) 28442210; e-mail bgst@gruene.de; internet www.gruene.de; f. 1993 by merger of Bündnis 90 (f. 1990, as an electoral political asscn of citizens' movements of the former GDR) and Die Grünen (f. 1980, largely comprised of the membership of the Grüne Aktion Zukunft, the Grüne Liste, Umweltschutz and the Aktionsgemeinschaft Unabhängiger Deutscher, also including groups of widely varying political views); essentially left-wing party programme includes ecological issues, democratization of society at all levels, social justice, comprehensive disarmament; Speaker of Exec. AUDJE RADCKE; Parliamentary Leaders RENATE KÜNAST, FRITZ KUHN.

Christlich-Demokratische Union Deutschlands (in Bavaria: **Christlich-Soziale Union Deutschlands**) **(CDU/CSU)** (Christian Democratic and Christian Social Union):

CDU: Konrad-Adenauer-Haus, Klingelhöferstr. 8, 10785 Berlin; tel. (30) 220700; fax (30) 22070111; e-mail post@cdu.de; internet www.cdu.de; f. 1945, became a federal party in 1950; stands for the united action between Catholics and Protestants for rebuilding German life on a Christian-Democratic basis, while guaranteeing private property and the freedom of the individual, and for a 'free and equal Germany in a free, politically united and socially just Europe'; other objectives are to guarantee close ties with allies within NATO and the principle of self-determination; in Oct. 1990 incorporated the CDU of the former GDR; c. 630,173 mems (April 2000); Chair. Dr ANGELA MERKEL; Sec.-Gen. LAURENZ MEYER; Parliamentary Leader FRIEDRICH MERZ.

CSU: Nymphenburger Str. 64, 80335 München; tel. (89) 12430; fax (89) 1243220; f. 1946; Christian Social party, aiming for a free market economy 'in the service of man's economic and intellectual freedom'; also combines national consciousness with support for a united Europe; 181,000 mems; Chair. Dr EDMUND STOIBER; Sec.-Gen. Dr THOMAS GOPPEL.

Deutsche Kommunistische Partei (DKP) (German Communist Party): Hoffnungstr. 18, 45127 Essen; tel. (201) 225148. fax (201) 202467; e-mail dkp.pv@t-online-de; internet www.dkp.de; 7,000 mems (1998); Chair. HEINZ STEHR.

Deutsche Volksunion (DVU) (German People's Union): Postfach 600464, 81204 München; tel. (89) 896085; fax (89) 8341534; internet www.dvu.net; f. 1987; right-wing, xenophobic.

Freie Demokratische Partei (FDP) (Free Democratic Party): Reinhardtstr. 14, 10117 Berlin; tel. (30) 2849580; fax (30) 28495822; e-mail tdh@fdp.de; internet www.fdp.de; f. 1948; represents democratic and social liberalism and makes the individual the focal point of the state and its laws and economy; in Aug. 1990 incorporated the three liberal parties of the former GDR—the Association of Free Democrats, the German Forum Party and the FDP; approx. 70,000 mems (Nov. 1999); Chair. Dr GUIDO WESTERWELLE; Deputy Chair. CORNELIA PIEPER, RAINER BRÜDERLE, Dr WALTER DÖRING; Chair. in Bundestag Dr GUIDO WESTERWELLE; Sec.-Gen. (vacant).

Freie Demokratische Partei/Demokratische Volkspartei (FDP/DVP): Konrad Adenauer-Str. 12, 70173 Stuttgart; tel. (711) 2063625; fax (711) 2063610; e-mail post@fdp.landtag-bw.de; internet www.fdp-dvp-fraktion.de; f. 1948; Chair ERNST PFISTER.

Nationaldemokratische Partei Deutschlands (NPD) (National Democratic Party of Germany): Postfach 840157, 12531 Berlin;

internet www.npd.de; f. 1964; right-wing; 15,000 mems; youth organization Junge Nationaldemokraten (JN), 6,000 mems; Chair. UDO VOIGT.

Neues Forum (New Forum): Bergstr. 23, 99089 Erfurt; tel. (361) 2110114; fax (361) 2118123; e-mail bv@neuesforum.de; internet www.neuesforum.de; f. 1989 as a citizens' action group; played a prominent role in the democratic movement in the former GDR; Leaders KAROLIN SCHUBERT, MATTHIAS BÜCHNER, MICHAEL BONEHR.

Partei des Demokratischen Sozialismus (PDS) (Party of Democratic Socialism): Kleine Alexanderstr. 28, 10178 Berlin; tel. (30) 240090; fax (30) 24009425; e-mail pdspv@aol.com; internet www.pds-online.de; the dominant political force in the former GDR until late 1989; formed in 1946 as the Socialist Unity Party (SED), as a result of a unification of the Social Democratic Party and the Communist Party in Eastern Germany; in Dec. 1989 renamed the SED-PDS; adopted present name in Feb. 1990; has renounced Stalinism, opposes fascism, right-wing extremism and xenophobia, advocates international disarmament and a socially- and ecologically-orientated market economy with public ownership of the means of production; 105,000 mems (Dec, 1997); Chair. Prof. GABRIELLE ZIMMER; Chair. of Parliamentary Party Dr GREGOR GYSI; Hon. Chair. Dr HANS MODROW.

Die Republikaner (REP) (Republican Party): Postfach 870210, 13162 Berlin; tel. (30) 79098310; fax (30) 79098315; e-mail republikaner-bgs@t-online.de; internet www.rep.de; f. 1983; conservative right wing; approx. 15,000 mems; Chair. Dr ROLF SCHLIERER.

Sozialdemokratische Partei Deutschlands (SPD) (Social Democratic Party of Germany): Wilhelmstr. 141, 10963 Berlin; tel. (30) 259910; fax (30) 410; e-mail parteivorstand@spd.de; internet www.spd.de; f. 1863; maintains that a vital democracy can be built only on the basis of social justice; advocates for the economy as much competition as possible, as much planning as necessary to protect the individual from uncontrolled economic interests; favours a positive attitude to national defence, while supporting controlled disarmament; rejects any political ties with Communism; in September 1990 incorporated the SPD of the former GDR; approx. 755,244 mems (Oct. 1999); Chair. GERHARD SCHRÖDER; Gen. Sec. FRANZ MÜNTEFERING.

There are also numerous other small parties, none of them represented in the Bundestag, covering all shades of the political spectrum and various regional interests.

Diplomatic Representation

EMBASSIES IN GERMANY*

Afghanistan: Liebfrauenweg 1A, 53125 Bonn; tel. (228) 251927; fax (228) 255310; Chargé d'affaires: AMANULLAH JAYHOON.

Albania: Friedrichstr. 231, 10969 Berlin; tel. (30) 2593050; fax (30) 25930599; Ambassador: BASHKIM ZENELI.

Algeria: Görschstr. 45–46, 13187 Berlin; tel. (30) 4816170; fax (30) 4863137; MOHAMMED HANECHE.

Angola: Wallstr. 58, 10179 Berlin; e-mail botschaftangola@t-online .de; Ambassador: ALBERTO DO CARMO BENTO RIBIERO.

Argentina: Adenauerallee 50–52, 53113 Bonn; tel. (228) 228010; fax (228) 2280130; internet www.argentinischebotschaft.de; Ambassador: Dr ANDRÉS GUILLERMO PESCI-BOUREL.

Armenia: Hillmannstr. 5, 13467 Berlin; tel. (30) 4050910; fax (30) 40509125; e-mail armemb@t-online.de; Ambassador: Dr ASHOT VOSKANIAN.

Australia: Friedrichstr. 200, 10117 Berlin; tel. (30) 8800880; fax (30) 880088310; Ambassador: PAUL O'SULLIVAN.

Austria: Friedrichstr. 60, Quartier 203, 10117 Berlin; tel. (30) 202870; fax (30) 2290569; e-mail austria.berlin@t-online.de; internet www.oesterreichische-botschaft.de; Ambassador: Dr MARKUS LUTTEROTTI.

Azerbaijan: Schlossallee 12, 53179 Bonn; tel. (228) 943890; fax (228) 858644; Ambassador: HUSSEIN-AGA M. SSADIGOV.

Bahrain: Plittersdorferstr. 91, 53173 Bonn; tel. (228) 957610; fax (228) 9576199; Ambassador: Dr AHMED ABBAS AHMED.

Bangladesh: Dovestr. 1, 10587 Berlin; Ambassador: KAZI ANWARUL MASUD.

Belarus: Am Treptower Park, 12345 Berlin; tel. (30) 5363590; fax (30) 53635923; Ambassador: VLADIMIR SKWORZOW.

Belgium: Friedrichstr. 95, 10117 Berlin; tel. (30) 203520; fax (30) 20352200; Ambassador: DOMINICUS STRUYE DE SWIELANDE.

Benin: Postfach 200254, 53179 Bonn; Rüdigerstr. 10, 53132 Bonn; tel. (228) 943870; fax (228) 857192; Ambassador: CORNEILLE MEHISSOU.

Bolivia: Wichmannstr. 6, 10787 Berlin; tel. (30) 2639150; fax (30) 2639515; e-mail embolberlin@t-online.de; internet www.bolivia.de; Ambassador: Dr ERNESTO FERNANDO SCHILLING KRIETE.

Bosnia and Herzegovina: Bürgerstr. 12, 53173 Bonn; Ambassador: ANTON BALKOVIC.

Brazil: Wallstr. 57, 10179 Berlin; tel. (30) 726280; fax (30) 72628320; e-mail brazil@brasemberlin.de; Ambassador: ROBERTO PINTO FERREIRA MAMERI ABDENUR.

Brunei: Kronenstr. 55–58, 10117 Berlin; tel. (30) 2060760; Ambassador: MAHADI BIN Haji WASLI.

Bulgaria: Mauerstr. 11, 10117 Berlin; tel. (30) 2010922; fax (30) 2086838; e-mail bbotschaft@myokay.net; Ambassador: NIKOLAI APOSTOLOFF.

Burkina Faso: Wendelstadtallee 18, 53179 Bonn; tel. (228) 952970; fax (228) 9529720; e-mail embassy-burkina-faso@t-online.de; Ambassador: JEAN-BAPTISTE ILBOUDO.

Burundi: Mainzerstr. 174, 53179 Bonn; tel. (228) 345032; fax (228) 340148; Ambassador: ALOYS MBONAYO.

Cambodia: Benjamin-Vogelsdorf-Str., 13187 Berlin; Ambassador: KHEK LERANG.

Cameroon: Rheinallee 76, 53173 Bonn; tel. (228) 356038; fax (228) 359058; Ambassador: JEAN MELAGA.

Canada: Friedrichstr. 95, 10117 Berlin; tel. (30) 203120; fax (30) 20312590; internet www.kanada-info.de; Ambassador: MARK BERNARD-MEUNIER.

Cape Verde: Dorotheenstr. 43, 10117 Berlin; tel. (30) 20450955; fax (30) 20450966; Ambassador: VICTOR ALFONSO G. FIDALGO.

Central African Republic: Rheinaustr. 120, 53225 Bonn; tel. (228) 233564; Ambassador: MARTIN-GÉRARD TEBITO.

Chad: Basteistr. 80, 53173 Bonn; tel. (228) 356026; fax (228) 355887; Ambassador: BINTOU MALLOUM.

Chile: Kronprinzstr. 20, 53173 Bonn; tel. (228) 955840; fax (228) 9558440; e-mail echilede@t-online.de; Ambassador: RICARDO HORMAZÁBAL SÁNCHEZ.

China, People's Republic: Kurfürstenallee 12, 53177 Bonn; tel. (228) 955970; fax (228) 361635; Ambassador: LU QIUTAN.

Colombia: Kurfürstenstr. 84, 10797 Berlin; tel. (30) 2639610; fax (30) 26396125; e-mail cultura.emcol@t-online.de; Ambassador: HERNAN BELTZ-PERALTA.

Congo, Democratic Republic: Im Meisengarten 133; 53179 Bonn; tel. (228) 858160; fax (228) 340398; Ambassador: LHELO BOLOTO.

Congo, Republic: Rheinallee 45, 53173 Bonn; tel. (228) 358355; fax (228) 358355; Chargé d'affaires a.i.: SERGE MICHEL ODZOCKI.

Costa Rica: Langenbachstr. 19, 53113 Bonn; tel. (228) 540040; fax (228) 549053; e-mail 100730.1020@compuserve.com; Ambassador: Prof. Dr RAFAEL ANGEL HERRA.

Côte d'Ivoire: Königstr. 93, 53115 Bonn; tel. (228) 212098; fax (228) 217313; Ambassador: JEAN VINCENT ZINSOU.

Croatia: Kurfürstendamm 72, 10709 Berlin; tel. (30) 3237635; fax (30) 3237630; Ambassador: Prof. Dr ZORAN JASIC.

Cuba: Stavanger Str. 20, 10439 Berlin; tel. (30) 91611810; fax (30) 9164553; Ambassador: OSCAR ISRAEL MARTÍNEZ CORDOVÉS.

Cyprus: Wallstr. 27, 10179 Berlin; tel. (30) 3086830; fax (30) 27591454; e-mail cyprusembassy@t-online.de; Ambassador: Dr CHRISTOS N. PSILOGENIS.

Czech Republic: Wilhelmstr. 44, 10117 Berlin; tel. (30) 226380; fax (30) 2294033; e-mail berlin@embassy.mzv.cz; Ambassador: FRANTIŠEK CERNÝ.

Denmark: Postfach 301245, 10789 Berlin; Rauchstr. 1, 10722 Berlin; tel. (30) 50502009; fax (30) 50502050; e-mail beramb@beramb.um.dk; internet www.daenemark.org; Ambassador: BENT HAAKONSEN.

Dominican Republic: Burgstr. 87, 53177 Bonn; tel. (228) 364956; fax (228) 352576; Ambassador: Prof. Dr VINICIO ALFONSO TOBAL UREÑA.

Ecuador: Koblenzer Str. 37, 53173 Bonn; tel. (228) 352544; fax (228) 361765; Ambassador: Dr WERNER MOELLER FRIELE.

Egypt: Kronprinzenstr. 2, 53173 Bonn; tel. (228) 956830; fax (228) 364304; Ambassador: MAHMOUD AHMED FATHY MOUBARAK.

El Salvador: Joachim-Karnatz-Allee 47, 10557 Berlin; tel. (30) 2064660; fax (30) 22488244; e-mail embasalva.rfa@t-online.de; Ambassador: (vacant).

Eritrea: Marktstr. 8, 50968 Köln; tel. (221) 373016; fax (221) 3404128; Ambassador: PETROS TSEGGAI.

Estonia: Kurfürstendamm 56, 10707 Berlin; tel. (30) 32705355; fax (30) 32707263; e-mail saatkond-berlinis@berlin.estemb.de; Ambassador: MARGUS LAIDRE.

Ethiopia: Boothstr. 20A, 12207 Berlin; tel. (30) 772060; fax (30) 7720624; Ambassador: Dr BERHANE TENSAY WOLDESENBET.

Finland: Rauchstr. 1, 10787 Berlin; tel. (30) 505030; fax (30) 5050333; internet www.finlandemb.de; Ambassador: ARTO OLAVI MANSALA.

France: Kochstr. 6/7, 10969 Berlin; tel. (30) 2063900; fax (30) 20639010; Ambassador: CLAUDE MARTIN.

Gabon: Kronprinzenstr. 52, 53173 Bonn; tel. (228) 365844; fax (228) 359195; Ambassador: SYLVESTRE RATANGA.

Georgia: Am Kurpark 6, 53177 Bonn; tel. (228) 957510; fax (228) 9575120; Ambassador: Dr KONSTANTIN GABASCHWILI.

Ghana: Rheinallee 58, 53173 Bonn; tel. (228) 367960; fax (228) 363498; Ambassador: GEORGE ROBERT NIPAH.

Greece: Jägerstr. 54–55, 10117 Berlin; tel. (30) 206260; fax (30) 20626444; internet www.griechenland-botschaft.de; Ambassador: DIMITRIOS NEZERITIS.

Guatemala: Joachim-Karnatz-Allee 47, 10557 Berlin; tel. (30) 2064363; fax (30) 20643659; internet www.guatemala.travel.com.gt; Ambassador: FRANSISCO VILLAGRAN DE LEON.

Guinea: Rochusweg 50, 53129 Bonn; tel. (228) 231098; fax (228) 231097; Ambassador: NAMANKOUMBA KOUYATE.

Haiti: Schlossallee 10, 53179 Bonn; tel. (228) 340351; fax (228) 857700; e-mail haibot@aol.com; Ambassador: Dr ALRICH NICOLAS.

Holy See: Turmstr. 29 (Apostolic Nunciature), 53175 Bonn; tel. (228) 959010; fax (228) 379180; Apostolic Nuncio: Mgr GIOVANNI LAJOLO.

Honduras: Ubierstr. 1, 53173 Bonn; tel. (228) 356394; fax (228) 351981; e-mail embahonbn@t-online.de; Ambassador: MAX VELÁS-QUEZ DÍAZ.

Hungary: Markgrafenstr. 36, 10117 Berlin; tel. (30) 203100; fax (30) 2291314; e-mail huembber@attmail.com; Ambassador: GER-GELY PRÓHLE.

Iceland: Rauchstr. 1, 10787 Berlin; tel. (30) 50504000; fax (30) 50504300; e-mail icemb.berlin@utn.stjr.is; internet www.botschaft-island.de; Ambassador: INGIMUNDUR SIGFÚSSON.

India: Adenauerallee 262–264, 53113 Bonn; tel. (228) 54050; fax (228) 5405154; Ambassador: RANENDRA SEN.

Indonesia: Bernkasteler Str. 2, 53175 Bonn; tel. (228) 382990; fax (228) 311393; Ambassador: IZHAR IBRAHIM.

Iran: Podbielskiallee 67, 14195 Berlin; tel. (30) 8419180; fax (30) 8329874; Ambassador: AHMAD AZIZI.

Iraq: Annaberger Str. 289, 53175 Bonn; Chargé d'affaires: SHAMIL A. MOHAMMED.

Ireland: Friedrichstr. 200, 10117 Berlin; e-mail info@irish-embassy .de; Ambassador: NOEL FAHEY.

Israel: Schinkelstr. 10, 14193 Berlin; tel. (30) 89045500; fax (30) 89045222; e-mail botschaft@israel.de; Ambassador: (vacant).

Italy: Dessauerstr. 28–29, 10963 Berlin; tel. (30) 254400; fax (30) 25440116; e-mail ambitalia.segr@t-online.de; Ambassador: ENZO PERLOT.

Jamaica: Schmagendorfer Str. 32, 12159 Berlin; tel. and fax (30) 8599450; e-mail info@jamaican-embassy-berlin.de; Ambassador: PETER CARLYSLE BLACK.

Japan: Kleiststr. 23–26, 10787 Berlin; tel. (30) 210940; fax (30) 21094222; Ambassador: KUNISADA KUME.

Jordan: Beethovenallee 21, 53173 Bonn; tel. (228) 357046; fax (228) 353951; Ambassador: HUSSEIN AHMAD HAMMAMI.

Kazakhstan: Nordendstr. 14/15, 13156 Berlin; tel. (30) 470070; fax (30) 47007125; Ambassador: VYACHESLAV GIZZATOV.

Kenya: Villichgasse 17, 53177 Bonn; tel. (228) 935800; fax (228) 9358050; Ambassador: JOHN LEPI LANYASUNYA.

Korea, Republic: Schöneberger Ufer 89/91, 10785 Berlin; tel. (30) 260650; fax (30) 2606551; Ambassador: KICHOO LEE.

Kuwait: Griegstr. 5–7, 14193 Berlin; tel. (30) 8973000; fax (30) 89730070; Ambassador: FAISAL RASHED AL-GHAIS.

Kyrgyzstan: Otto-Suhr-Allee 146, 10585 Berlin; e-mail 101477.1160@compuserve.com; Ambassador: Dr APAS DSCHMAGULOV.

Laos: Am Lessing 6, 53639 Königswinter; tel. (223) 21501; fax (223) 3065; Ambassador: PHANTHONG PHOMMAHAXAY.

Latvia: Reinerzstr. 40–41, 14193 Berlin; tel. (30) 8260020; fax (30) 82600233; Ambassador: ANDRIS TEIKMANIS.

Lebanon: Berliner Str. 127, 13187 Berlin; tel. (30) 4749860; fax (30) 47497858; Ambassador: MOHAMAD ISSA.

Lesotho: Godesberger Allee 50, 53175 Bonn; tel. (228) 308430; fax (228) 3084322; e-mail lesoembger@aol.com; Ambassador: LEBOHANG NTSINYI.

Liberia: Mainzerstr. 259, 53179 Bonn; tel. (228) 340822; Ambas-sador: RUFUS WEBSTER SIMPSON.

Libya: Beethovenallee 12A, 53173 Bonn; tel. (228) 820090; fax (228) 364260; Secretary of the People's Committee: MOHAMMED ALBARANI.

Lithuania: Katharinenstr. 9, 10711 Berlin; tel. (30) 890681; fax (30) 890681; e-mail botschaftlitauen@t-online.de; Ambassador: Prof. Dr HABIL VAIDIEVUTIS GERALAVIČIUS.

Luxembourg: Klingelhöfer Str. 7, 10785 Berlin; tel. (30) 12639570; fax (30) 126395727; e-mail berlin.amb@mae.etat.lu; Ambassador: Dr JULIEN ALEX.

Macedonia, former Yugoslav republic: Königsallee 2, 14193 Berlin; tel. (30) 8906950; fax (30) 89541194; Ambassador: Dr SRGJAN KERIM.

Madagascar: Rolandstr. 48, 53179 Bonn; tel. (228) 953590; fax (228) 334628; e-mail madagaskar-botschaft@t-online.de; internet www.botschaft-madagaskar.de; Ambassador: ZAFERA A. RABESA.

Malawi: Mainzer Str. 124, 53179 Bonn; tel. (228) 943350; fax (228) 9433537; e-mail malawibonn@ool.com; Ambassador: Rev Dr S. S. NCOZANA.

Malaysia: Kurfürstendamm 50, 10707 Berlin; tel. (30) 8857490; fax (30) 88729028; Ambassador: Dato' ABDUL KADIR MOHAMED DEEN.

Mali: Basteistr. 86, 53173 Bonn; tel. (228) 357048; fax (228) 361922; Ambassador: OUSMANE DEMBÉLÉ.

Malta: Klingellnöferstr. 7, 10785 Berlin; tel. (30) 2639110; fax (30) 26391123; e-mail maltaembgrm@ndh.net; Ambassador: WILLIAM C. SPITERI.

Mauritania: Bonnerstr. 48, 53173 Bonn; tel. (228) 364024; fax (228) 361788; Ambassador: HAMOUD OULD ELY.

Mexico: Kurfürstendamm 72, 10709 Berlin; tel. (30) 3249047; fax (30) 32771121; e-mail rfaemb@edina.xnc.com; internet www .embamex.de; Ambassador: ROBERTO EMILIO FRIEDRICH HEINZE.

Moldova: Gotlandstr. 16, 10439 Berlin; tel. (30) 44652970; fax (30) 2835237; e-mail 113145.334@compuserve.com; Ambassador: Dr AURELIAN DÁNILÁ.

Monaco: Zitelmannstr. 16, 53113 Bonn; tel. (228) 232007; fax (228) 236282; Chargé d'affaires: EVA WITTENBERG.

Mongolia: Gotlandstr. 12, 10439 Berlin; tel. (30) 4469320; fax (30) 4469321; e-mail mongolbot@aol.com; Ambassador: BAZARRAGCHA BAYARSAIHAN.

Morocco: Niederwallstr. 39, 10117 Berlin; tel. (30) 2061240; fax (30) 20612420; Ambassador: Dr ABDELADIM LHAFI.

Mozambique: Adenauerallee 46A, 53113 Bonn; tel. (228) 263921; fax (228) 213920; e-mail emoza@ad.com; Ambassador: MANUEL TOMÁS LUBISSE.

Myanmar: Schumann Str. 112, 53113 Bonn; tel. (228) 210091; fax (228) 219316; e-mail k.oh@wunsch.com; Ambassador: U. SAN THIEN.

Namibia: Friedrichstr. 60, 10787 Berlin; Ambassador: HINYANGERWA PIUS ASHEEKE.

Nepal: Guerickestr. 27, 10587 Berlin; tel. (30) 3435992022; fax (30) 34359906; e-mail rneberlin@t-online.de; internet www .nepalembassy-germany.com; Ambassador: BALRAM SINGH MALLA.

Netherlands: Friedrichstr. 95, 10117 Berlin; tel. (30) 209560; fax (30) 20956441; e-mail nlgovbon@nlgovbon.bn.uunet.de; internet www.dutchembassy.de; Ambassador: Dr NIKOLAOS VAN DAM.

New Zealand: Friedrichstr. 60, 10117 Berlin; tel. (30) 206210; fax (30) 20621114; e-mail nzemb@t-online.de; Ambassador: W. A. COCHRANE.

Nicaragua: Konstantinstr. 41, 53179 Bonn; tel. (228) 362505; fax 354001; Ambassador: SUYAPA INDIANA PADILLA TERCERO.

Niger: Dürenstr. 9, 53173 Bonn; tel. (228) 3682061; fax (228) 3682062; Ambassador: ADAMOU OUMAROU.

Nigeria: Goldbergweg 13, 53177 Bonn; tel. (228) 322071; fax (228) 328088; Chargé d'affaires a.i.: BABA GANA WAKIL.

Norway: Rauchstr. 1, 10787 Berlin; tel. (30) 505050; fax (30) 505055; e-mail emb.berlin@mfa.no; internet www.norwegen.org; Ambassador: MORTEN WETLAND.

Oman: Lindenallee 11, 53173 Bonn; tel. (228) 357031; fax (228) 357045; Ambassador: AHMED M. AL-HINAI.

Pakistan: Schaper Str. 29, 10719 Berlin; Ambassador: Gen. ASAD DURRANI.

Panama: Lützowstr. 1, 53173 Bonn; tel. (228) 361036; fax (228) 363558; Ambassador: FLOR DE MARIA MONTEVERDE.

Papua New Guinea: Moltkestr. 44–46, 53173 Bonn; e-mail 106555.326@compuserve.com; Chargé d'affaires: PETER RAKA.

Paraguay: Uhlandstr. 32, 53173 Bonn; tel. (228) 356727; fax (228) 366663; Ambassador: Dr MARCOS MARTÍNEZ MENDIETA.

Peru: Godesberger Allee 125, 53175 Bonn; tel. (228) 3084570; fax (228) 379475; e-mail eprfa@aol.com; internet members.aol.com/ perusipan; Chargé d'affaires a.i.: ZOSIMO ROBERTO MORILLO HERRODA.

Philippines: Argelanderstr. 1, 53115 Bonn; tel. (228) 267990; fax (228) 221968; Ambassador: JOSÉ A. ZAIDE.

Poland: Lassenstr. 19–21, 14193 Berlin; tel. (30) 223130; fax (30) 2213155; e-mail post@botschaft-polen.de; internet www .botschaft-polen.de; Ambassador: Dr ANDRZEJ BYRT.

Portugal: Zimmerstr. 56, 10117 Berlin; tel. (30) 590063500; fax (30) 590063600; Ambassador: Dr JOÃO DIOGO CORREIA SARAIVA NUNES.

Qatar: Hagenstr. 56, 14193 Berlin; Ambassador: MOHAMED HASSAN AL-JABER.

Romania: Legionsweg 14, 53117 Bonn; tel. (228) 68380; fax (228) 680247; Ambassador: TUDOR GAVRIL DUNCA.

Russia: Unter den Linden 63–65, 10117 Berlin; tel. (30) 2291110; fax (30) 2299397; e-mail russembassyg@trionet.de; Ambassador: SERGEI BORISOVICH KRYLOV.

Rwanda: Beethovenallee 72, 53173 Bonn; tel. (228) 355228; fax (228) 351922; e-mail ambrwabonn@aol.com; Ambassador: (vacant).

Saudi Arabia: Kurfürstendamm 63, 10787 Berlin; Ambassador: ABBAS FAIG GHAZZAWI.

Senegal: Argelanderstr. 3, 53115 Bonn; tel. (228) 218008; fax (228) 217815; Ambassador: Gen. MOHAMADOU KEÏTA.

Sierra Leone: Rheinallee 20, 53173 Bonn; tel. (228) 352001; fax (228) 364269; e-mail uwurie@aol.com; Ambassador: UMARU BUNDU WURIE.

Singapore: Friedrichstr. 200, 10117 Berlin; tel. (30) 2263430; fax (30) 22634355; e-mail sing.emb.berlin@t-online.de; Ambassador: WALTER WOON.

Slovakia: Leipziger Str. 36, 10117 Berlin; tel. (30) 2044538; fax (30) 2082459; Ambassador: JÁN FOLTIN.

Slovenia: Hausvogteiplatz 3–4, 10117 Berlin; tel. (30) 2061450; fax (30) 20614570; Ambassador: ALFONZ NABERŽNIK.

South Africa: Friedrichstr. 60, 10117 Berlin; tel. (30) 220730; fax (30) 22073190; e-mail botschaft@suedafrika.org; internet www .suedafrika.org; Ambassador: Prof. Dr SIGUSISO M. B. BENGU.

Spain: Schöneberger Ufer 89–91, 10785 Berlin; tel. (30) 2540070; fax (30) 25799557; Ambassador: JOSÉ PEDRO SEBASTIÁN DE ERICE.

Sri Lanka: Niklasstr. 19, 14163 Berlin; tel. (30) 80909764; fax (30) 80909764; e-mail amb@slemb.bn.eunet.de; Ambassador: S. B. ATU-GODA.

Sudan: Kurfürstendamm 151, 10709 Berlin; tel. (30) 8906980; fax (30) 89409693; Ambassador: AHMED GAAFAN ABDELKARIM.

Sweden: Rauchstr. 1, 10787 Berlin; tel. (30) 505060; fax (30) 50506789; internet www.schweden.org; Ambassador: MATS HELLSTRÖM.

Switzerland: Haus am Wasser, Kirchstr. 13, 10557 Berlin; tel. (30) 3904000; fax (30) 3911030; Ambassador: THOMAS BORER-FIELDING.

Syria: Andreas-Hermes-Str. 5, 53175 Bonn; tel. (228) 819920; fax (228) 8199299; Ambassador: WALID HEZBOR.

Tajikistan: Otto-Suhr-Allee 84, 10585 Berlin; tel. (30) 3479300; fax (30) 34793029; Ambassador: AKBAR MIRZOYEV.

Tanzania: Theaterplatz 26, 53177 Bonn; tel. (228) 358051; fax (228) 358226; Ambassador: ANDREW M. DARAJA.

Thailand: Lepsiusstr. 64–66, 12163 Berlin; tel. (30) 794810; fax (30) 79481511; Ambassador: KASIT PIROMYA.

Togo: Beethovenallee 13, 53173 Bonn; tel. (228) 355091; fax (228) 351639; Ambassador: SOGOYOU K. KEGUEWE.

Tunisia: Godesberger Allee 103, 53175 Bonn; tel. (228) 376981; fax (228) 374223; Ambassador: SLAHEDDINE BEN M'BAREK.

Turkey: Rungestr. 9, 10179 Berlin; tel. (30) 275850; fax (30) 27585700; Ambassador: TUGAY ULUCEVIK.

Turkmenistan: Langobardenallee 14, 14052 Berlin; tel. (30) 30102452; fax (30) 30102453; e-mail botschaft-turkmenistan@ t-online.de; Chargé d'affaires a.i.: CHARY ISHANIYAZOV.

Ukraine: Albrechtstr. 26, 10117 Berlin; tel. (30) 288870; fax (30) 28887163; Ambassador: Dr ANATOLIY PONOMARENKO.

United Arab Emirates: Erste Fährgasse 6, 53113 Bonn; tel. (228) 267070; fax (228) 2670714; Ambassador: MOHAMMAD ALI AL-ZAROUNI.

United Kingdom: Wilhelmstr. 70, 10117 Berlin; tel. (30) 204570; fax (30) 20457574; e-mail presse@fco.mail.gov.uk; internet www .britischebotschaft.de; Ambassador: Sir PAUL LEVER.

USA: Neustädtische Kirche 4/5, 10117 Berlin; tel. (30) 83052805; fax (30) 20453644; internet www.usembassy.de; Ambassador: JOHN CHRISTIAN KORNBLUM.

Uruguay: Gotenstr. 1–3, 53175 Bonn; tel. (228) 356570; fax (228) 361410; Ambassador: JUAN JOSÉ REAL PERRERA.

Uzbekistan: Mauerstr. 83–84, 10117 Berlin; tel. (30) 22487457; fax (30) 22679963; Ambassador: Dr VLADIMIR IMAMOVICH NOROV.

Venezuela: Grosse Weinmeisterstr. 53, 14469 Potsdam; e-mail 100635.154@compuserve.com; Ambassador: ERIK BECKER BECKER.

Viet Nam: Konstantinstr. 37, 53179 Bonn; tel. (228) 957540; fax (228) 351866; Ambassador: LE KINH TAI.

Yemen: Adenauerallee 77, 53113 Bonn; tel. (228) 220273; fax (228) 229364; Ambassador: MOHY A. AL-DHABBI.

Zambia: Mittelstr. 39, 53175 Bonn; tel. (228) 376813; fax (228) 379536; Ambassador: ELIAS MARKO CHISHA CHIPIMO.

Zimbabwe: Villichgasse 7, 53177 Bonn; tel. (228) 356071; fax (228) 356309; Ambassador: GIFT PUNUNGWE.

* Owing to the transfer of several organs of state from Bonn to Berlin in 1999, many foreign embassies also relocated to the capital.

Judicial System

The Unification Treaty, signed by the FRG and the GDR in August 1990, provided for the extension of Federal Law to the territory formerly occupied by the GDR, and also stipulated certain exceptions where GDR Law was to remain valid.

Judges are not removable except by the decision of a court. Half of the judges of the Federal Constitutional Court are elected by the Bundestag and half by the Bundesrat. A committee for the selection of judges participates in the appointment of judges of the Superior Federal Courts.

FEDERAL CONSTITUTIONAL COURT

Bundesverfassungsgericht (Federal Constitutional Court): Postfach 1771, 76006 Karlsruhe; Schlossbezirk 3, 76131 Karlsruhe; tel. (721) 91010; fax (721) 9101382; e-mail bverfg@bundesverfas sungsgericht.de.

President: Prof. Dr JUTTA LIMBACH.

Vice-President: Prof. Dr HANS-JÜRGEN PAPIER.

Director: Dr ELKE LUISE BARNSTEDT.

Judges of the First Senate: Prof. Dr DIETER GRIMM, Dr JÜRGEN KÜHLING, RENATE JAEGER, Dr EVELYN HAAS, Dr DIETER HÖMIG, Prof. Dr UDO STEINER, Dr CHRISTINE HOHMANN-DENNHARDT.

Judges of the Second Senate: Prof. Dr PAUL KIRCHOF, KLAUS WINTER, BERTOLD SOMMER, Dr HANS-JOACHIM JENTSCH, Prof. Dr WIN-FRIED HASSEMER, Dr SIEGFRIED BROSS, Prof. Dr LERKE OSTERLOH.

SUPERIOR FEDERAL COURTS

Bundesgerichtshof (Federal Court of Justice): Herrenstr. 45A, 76133 Karlsruhe; tel. (721) 1590; fax (721) 159830; internet www .uni-karlsruhe.de.

President: KARLMANN GEISS.

Vice-President: Dr BURKHARD JÄHNKE.

Presidents of the Senate: Prof. Dr WILLI ERDMANN, Dr VOLKER RÖHRICHT, Dr EBERHARD RINNE, Dr KARL BERNARD SCHMITZ, WERNER GROSS, Dr KATHARINA DEPPERT, Dr BERND PAULUSCH, RÜDGER ROGGE, Dr FRIEDRICH BLUMENRÖHR, Dr GERHARD SCHÄFER, Dr BURKHARD JÄHNKE, KLAUS KUTZER, Dr LUTZ MEYER-GOSSNER, Prof. Dr EIKE ULLMANN, GERD NOBBE, MONIKA HARMS.

Federal Solicitor-General: KAY NEHM.

Federal Prosecutors: REINER SCHULTE, VOLKHARD WACHE, Dr HANS-JOACHIM KURTH.

Bundesverwaltungsgericht (Federal Administrative Court): Postfach 120341, 10593 Berlin; Hardenbergstr. 31, 10623 Berlin; tel. (30) 31971; fax (30) 3123021; internet www.bverwg.de.

President: Dr EVERHARDT FRANSSEN.

Vice-President: Dr INGEBORG FRANKE.

Presidents of the Senate: Dr ERICH BERMEL, WERNER MEYER, Dr NORBERT NIEHUES, FRIEDRICH SEEBASS, Dr GÜNTER GAENTZSCH, Dr HORST SÄCKER, Prof. Dr HANS-JOACHIM DRIEHAUS, Dr JOACHIM MAI-WALD, Dr NIKOLAUS VOGELGESANG, Dr OSWIN MÜLLER, ECKART HIEN.

Bundesfinanzhof (Federal Financial Court): Postfach 860240, 81629 München; Ismaningerstr. 109, 81675 München; tel. (89) 92310; fax (89) 9231201.

President: Dr IRIS EBLING.

Vice-President: (vacant).

Presidents of the Senate: Dr SIEGFRIED WIDMANN, Dr REINHARD SUNDER-PLASSMANN, Dr HANS JOACHIM HERRMANN, Dr GEORG GRUBE, Dr GERHARD MÖSSLANG, Dr WERNER HEIN, Prof. Dr WALTER DRENSECK, Prof. Dr FRANZ WASSERMEYER.

Religion

CHRISTIANITY

Arbeitsgemeinschaft Christlicher Kirchen in Deutschland (Council of Christian Churches in Germany): Postfach 900617, 60446 Frankfurt a.M.; Ludolfusstr. 2–4, 60487 Frankfurt a.M.; tel. (69) 2470270; fax (69) 24702730; e-mail ackoec@t-online.de; 21 affiliated Churches, including the Roman Catholic Church and the Greek Orthodox Metropoly.

The Roman Catholic Church

Germany comprises seven archdioceses and 20 dioceses. It is estimated that about 33% of the population are adherents of the Roman Catholic Church.

Bishops' Conference: Deutsche Bischofskonferenz, Postfach 2962, 53019 Bonn; Kaiserstr. 163, 53113 Bonn; tel. (228) 103290; fax (228) 103335; e-mail sekretariat@dbk.de; Pres. Cardinal Dr Dr KARL LEHMANN, Bishop of Mainz; Sec. Pater Dr HANS LANGENDÖRFER.

Archbishop of Bamberg: Dr KARL BRAUN, Postfach 120153, 96049 Bamberg; Domplatz 3, 96033 Bamberg; tel. (951) 5020; fax (951) 502212.

Archbishop of Berlin: Cardinal GEORG MAXIMILIAN STERZINSKY, Wundtstr. 48–50, 14057 Berlin; tel. (030) 326840; fax (030) 32684276.

Archbishop of Freiburg im Breisgau: Dr OSKAR SAIER, Herrenstr. 35, 79098 Freiburg i. Br.; tel. (761) 21881; fax (761) 2188599.

Archbishop of Hamburg: Dr LUDWIG AVERKAMP, Postfach 101925, 20013 Hamburg; Danzigerstr. 52A, 20099 Hamburg; tel. (40) 248770; fax (40) 24877233; e-mail egv@erzbistum-hamburg.de; internet www.erzbistum-hamburg.de.

Archbishop of Köln: Cardinal Dr JOACHIM MEISNER, Generalvikariat, Marzellenstr. 32, 50668 Köln; tel. (221) 16420; fax (221) 1642700.

Archbishop of München and Freising: Cardinal Dr FRIEDRICH WETTER, Postfach 330360, 80079 München; Rochhusstr. 5–7, 80063 München; tel. (89) 21370; fax (89) 21371585.

Archbishop of Paderborn: Cardinal Dr JOHANNES JOACHIM DEGENHARDT, Erzbischöfliches Generalvikariat, Domplatz 3, 33098 Paderborn; tel. (5251) 1250; fax (5251) 125470.

Commissariat of German Bishops—Catholic Office: Postfach 040660, 10115 Berlin; Hannoversche Str. 5, 10063 Berlin; tel. (30) 288780; fax (30) 28878108; e-mail post@kath-buero.de; represents the German Conference of Bishops before the Federal Govt on political issues; Leader Prälat Dr KARL JÜSTEN.

Central Committee of German Catholics: Hochkreuzallee 246, 53175 Bonn; tel. (228) 382970; fax (228) 3829744; e-mail info@zdk.de; internet www.zdk.de; f. 1868; summarizes the activities of Catholic laymen and lay-organizations in Germany; Pres. Prof. Dr HANS JOACHIM MEYER; Gen. Sec. Dr STEFAN VESPER.

Evangelical (Protestant) Churches

About 33% of the population are members of the Evangelical Churches.

Evangelische Kirche in Deutschland (EKD) (Evangelical Church in Germany): Herrenhäuser Str. 12, 30419 Hannover; tel. (511) 27960; fax (511) 2796707; e-mail presse@ekd.de; internet www.ekd.de. The governing bodies of the EKD are its Synod of 120 clergy and lay members which meets at regular intervals, the Conference of member churches, and the Council, composed of 15 elected members; the EKD has an ecclesiastical secretariat of its own (the Evangelical Church Office), including a special office for foreign relations; Chair. of the Council Präses MANFRED KOCK; Pres. of the Office VALENTIN SCHMIDT.

Synod of the EKD: Herrenhäuser Str. 12, 30419 Hannover; tel. (511) 2796114; fax (511) 2796707; e-mail synode@ekd.de; Pres. Dr JÜRGEN SCHMUDE.

Deutscher Evangelischer Kirchentag (German Evangelical Church Assembly): Postfach 480, 36004 Fulda; Magdeburgerstr. 59, 36037 Fulda; tel. (661) 969500; fax (661) 9695090; e-mail fulda@kirchentag.de; internet www.kirchentag.de; Pres. MARTIN DOLDE; Gen. Sec. FREDERIKE WOLDT.

Churches and Federations within the EKD:

Arnoldshainer Konferenz: Jebensstr. 3, 10623 Berlin; tel. (30) 310010; fax (30) 31001200; e-mail akf@eku-kirche.de; internet www.eku-kirche.de; f. 1967; a loose federation of the church governments of one Lutheran, two Reformed Territorial and all United Churches, aiming at greater co-operation between them; Chair. of Council Bischof Prof. Dr CHRISTIAN ZIPPERT.

Evangelische Kirche der Union (EKU) (Evangelical Church of the Union): Chancellery, Jebensstr. 3, 10623 Berlin; tel. (30) 310010; fax (30) 31001200; e-mail postfach@eku-online.de; internet www.eku-online.de; composed of Lutheran and Reformed elements; includes the Evangelical Churches of Anhalt, Berlin-Brandenburg, Silesian Oberlausitz, Pomerania, the Rhineland, Saxony and Westphalia; Chair. of Synod Vizepräses NIKOLAUS SCHNEIDER; Chair. of Council Präses MANFRED SORG; Pres. of Administration Dr WILHELM HÜFFMEIER.

Reformierter Bund (Reformed Alliance): Vogelsangstr. 20, 42109 Wuppertal; tel. (202) 755111; fax (202) 754202; f. 1884; unites the Reformed Territorial Churches and Congregations of Germany (with an estimated 2m. mems). The central body of the Reformed League is the 'Moderamen', the elected representation of the various Reformed Churches and Congregations; Moderator Rev. PETER BUKOWSKI; Gen. Sec. Rev. HERMANN SCHAEFER.

Vereinigte Evangelisch-Lutherische Kirche Deutschlands (VELKD) (The United Evangelical-Lutheran Church of Germany): Postfach 510409, 30634 Hannover; Richard-Wagner-Str. 26, 30177 Hannover; tel. (511) 62611; fax (511) 62611511; e-mail zentrale@nbvelkd.de; internet www.velkd.de; f. 1948; mems 11.2m.; a body uniting all but three of the Lutheran territorial Churches within the Evangelical Church in Germany; Presiding Bishop Bischof Dr HANS CHRISTIAN KNUTH (Schleswig).

Affiliated to the EKD:

Bund Evangelisch-Reformierter Kirchen (Association of Evangelical Reformed Churches): Ferdinandstr. 21, 20095 Hamburg; tel. (40) 3010040; Chair. Präses SABINE DRESSLER-KROMMINGA.

Herrnhuter Brüdergemeine or **Europäisch-Festländische Brüder-Unität** (Moravian Church): f. 1457; there are 25 congregations in Germany, Switzerland, Denmark, Sweden, Estonia and the Netherlands, with approximately 30,000 mems; Chair. Rev. HANS-BEAT MOTEL; Badwasen 6, 73087 Bad Boll; tel. (7164) 94210; fax (7164) 942199).

†**Evangelical Church in Baden:** Postfach 2269, 76010 Karlsruhe; Blumenstr. 1, 76133 Karlsruhe; tel. (721) 9175100; fax (721) 9175550; Landesbischof Prof. Dr ULRICH FISCHER.

***Evangelical-Lutheran Church in Bayern:** Meiserstr. 11–13, 80333 München; tel. (89) 55950; fax (89) 5595444; e-mail poep@elkb.de; internet www.bayern-evangelisch.de; Landesbischof Dr JOHANNES FRIEDRICH.

†**Evangelical Church in Berlin-Brandenburg:** Georgenkirchstr. 69/70, 10249 Berlin; tel. (30) 2434400; fax (30) 24344500; e-mail kirche@ekibb.com; internet www.ekibb.com; Bischof Prof. Dr WOLFGANG HUBER.

Evangelical-Lutheran Church in Braunschweig: Dietrich-Bonhoeffer-Str. 1, 38300 Wolfenbüttel; tel. (5331) 8020; fax (5331) 802707; e-mail info@luth-braunschweig.de; internet www.luth-braunschweig.de; Landesbischof Dr CHRISTIAN KRAUSE.

†**Bremen Evangelical Church:** Postfach 106929, Franziuseck 2–4, 28199 Bremen; tel. (421) 55970; Pres. HEINZ HERMANN BRAUER.

***Evangelical-Lutheran Church of Hannover:** Haarstr. 6, 30169 Hannover; tel. (511) 800188; fax (511) 880438; e-mail margot.kraesmann@evlka.de; internet www.evlka.de; Landesbischof Dr MARGOT KÄSSMANN.

†**Evangelical Church in Hessen and Nassau:** Paulusplatz 1, 64276 Darmstadt; tel. (6151) 405284; fax (6151) 405441; Pres. Prof. Dr PETER STEINACKER.

†**Evangelical Church of Kurhessen-Waldeck:** Postfach 410260, 34131 Kassel-Wilhelmshöhe; Wilhelmshöher Allee 330, 34114 Kassel; tel. (561) 937807; fax (561) 9378400; e-mail landeskirchenamt@ekkw.de; Bischof Prof. Dr CHRISTIAN ZIPPERT.

†**Church of Lippe:** Leopoldstr. 27, 32756 Detmold; tel. (5231) 97660; fax (5231) 976850; e-mail oeff@lippische-landeskirche.de; internet www.lippische-landeskirche.de; Landessuperintendent GERRIT NOLTENSMEIER.

Evangelical-Lutheran Church of Mecklenburg: Münzstr. 8, 19010 Schwerin; tel. (385) 51850; fax (385) 5185170; e-mail okt@ellmode; internet kirche-mv.de; Landes-bischof HERMANN BESTE.

***Evangelical-Lutheran Church of North Elbe:** Bischof Dr HANS CHRISTIAN KNUTH (Plessenstr. 5A, 24837 Schleswig; tel. (4621) 22056; fax (4621) 22194); Bischof KARL LUDWIG KOHLWAGE (23564 Lübeck, Bäckerstr. 3–5; tel. (451) 790201); Bishop MARIA JEPSEN (20457 Hamburg, Neue Burg 1; tel. (40) 373050); Pres. of North Elbian Church Administration Prof. Dr KLAUS BLASCHKE (24103 Kiel, Dänische Str. 21–23; tel. (431) 97975).

Evangelical-Reformed Church in North-West Germany: Saarstr. 6, 26789 Leer; tel. (491) 91980; fax (491) 9198251; e-mail info@reformiert.de; internet www.reformiert.de; Moderator GARRELT DUIN; Synod Clerks Rev. WALTER HERRENBRÜCK, ERNST-JOACHIM PAGENSTECHER.

Evangelical-Lutheran Church in Oldenburg: Philosophenweg 1, 26121 Oldenburg; tel. (441) 77010; fax (441) 7701299; e-mail ips@ev-kirche-oldenburg.de; internet www.ev-kirche-oldenburg.de; Bischof PETER KRUG.

†**Evangelical Church of the Palatinate:** Domplatz 5, 67346 Speyer; tel. (6232) 6670; fax (6232) 667228; e-mail evkpfalz@speyer.she.de; internet www.evpfalz.de; Pres. EBERHARD CHERDRON.

†**Evangelical Church in the Rhineland:** Postfach 300339, 40476 Düsseldorf; Hans-Böckler-Str. 7, 40403 Düsseldorf; tel. (211) 45620; fax (211) 4562490; e-mail pressestelle@ekir.de; internet www.ekir.de; Pres. MANFRED KOCK.

Evangelical-Lutheran Church of Saxony: Postfach 320101, 01033 Dresden; Lukasstr. 6, 01069 Dresden; tel. (351) 46920; fax (351) 4692144; e-mail kirche@evlks.de; internet www.evlks.de; Landesbischof VOLKER KRESS.

***Evangelical-Lutheran Church of Schaumburg-Lippe:** Herderstr. 27, 31675 Bückeburg; tel. (5722) 9600; e-mail lka-bueckeburg@t-online.de; Landesbischof HEINRICH HERRMANNS.

Evangelical-Lutheran Church in Thuringia: Dr-Moritz-Mitzenheim Str. 2A, 99817 Eisenach; tel. (3691) 67899; e-mail landes landeskirchenamt@elkth.de; internet www.ev-kirche-thueringen .de; Landesbischof ROLAND HOFFMANN.

†**Evangelical Church of Westfalen:** Altstädter Kirchplatz 5, 33602 Bielefeld; tel. (521) 5940; fax (521) 594129; e-mail landes kirchenamt@lka.ekvw.de; internet www.ekvw.de; Präses MANFRED SORG.

†**Evangelical-Lutheran Church of Württemberg:** Postfach 101342, Gänsheidestr. 4, 70184 Stuttgart; tel. (711) 21490; fax (711) 2149236; e-mail landesbischof@elk.wue.de; Landesbischof EBERHARDT RENZ.

(* Member of the VELKD; † member of the EKU)

Other Evangelical (Protestant) Churches

Arbeitsgemeinschaft Mennonitischer Gemeinden in Deutschland (Asscn of Mennonite Congregations in Germany): Ringstr. 3, 67677 Eukenbach-Alsenborn; tel. (6303) 3883; fax (6303) 983739; e-mail rwrc.funck@t-online.de; f. 1886, re-organized 1990; Chair. WERNER FUNCK.

Bund Evangelisch-Freikirchlicher Gemeinden (Union of Evangelical Free Church Congregations; Baptists): Friedberger Str. 101, 61350 Bad Homburg v. d. H.; tel. (6172) 80040; fax (6172) 800436; e-mail befg@baptisten.org; internet www.baptisten .org; f. 1849; Pres. Dr WOLFGANG LORENZ; Dirs HEINZ SAGER, Rev. HANS-DETLEF SASS, Rev. LUTZ REICHARDT.

Bund Freier evangelischer Gemeinden (Covenant of Free Evangelical Churches in Germany): Postfach 4005, 58426 Witten; Goltenkamp 4, 58452 Witten; tel. (2302) 9370; fax (2302) 93799; e-mail kandwischer@bund.feg.de; internet www.feg.de; f. 1854; Pres. PETER STRAUCH; Administrator KLAUS KANWISCHER; 31,500 mems.

Evangelisch-altreformierte Kirche von Niedersachsen (Evangelical Reformed Church of Lower Saxony): Ehm-Schipper-Weg 2, 26736 Krummhörn-Campen; tel. (4927) 329; fax (4927) 912969; Sec. Rev. G. SCHRADER.

Evangelisch-methodistische Kirche (United Methodist Church): Wilhelm-Leuschner-Str. 8, 60329 Frankfurt a.M.; tel. (69) 2425210; fax (69) 24252129; e-mail emk.kirchenkanzlei@t-online.de; f. 1968; Bishop Dr WALTER KLAIBER.

Gemeinschaft der Siebenten-Tags-Adventisten (Seventh-Day Adventist Church): Postfach 4260, 73745 Ostfildern; Senefelderstr. 15, 73760 Ostfildern; tel. (711) 448190; fax (711) 4481960; e-mail sdv.zentrale@adventisten.de.

Heilsarmee in Deutschland (Salvation Army in Germany): Salierring 23–27, 50677 Köln; tel. (221) 208190; fax (221) 208951; e-mail heils@rmee.de; internet www.heilsarmee.de; f. 1886; Leader Col SIEGFRIED OLAUSEN.

Mülheimer Verband Freikirchlich-Evangelischer Gemeinden (Pentecostal Church): Haubenhauser Dorfstr. 27, 28279 Bremen; tel. (421) 8399130; fax (421) 8399136; e-mail mv-bremen@ t-online.de; f. 1913.

Selbständige Evangelisch-Lutherische Kirche (Independent Evangelical-Lutheran Church): Schopenhauerstr. 7, 30625 Hannover; tel. (511) 557808; fax (511) 551588; e-mail selk@selk.de; f. 1972; Bishop Dr DIETHARDT ROTH; Exec. Sec. Rev. MICHAEL SCHÄTZEL.

Other Christian Churches

Alt-Katholische Kirche (Old Catholic Church): Gregor-Mendel-Str. 28, 53115 Bonn; tel. (228) 232285; fax (228) 238314; e-mail info@alt-katholisch.de; internet www.alt-katholisch.de; seceded from the Roman Catholic Church as a protest against the declaration of Papal infallibility in 1870; belongs to the Utrecht Union of Old Catholic Churches; in full communion with the Anglican Communion; Pres. Bischof JOACHIM VOBBE (Bonn); 28,000 mems.

Apostelamt Jesu Christi: Madlower Hauptstr. 38, 03050 Cottbus; tel. (355) 541227; Pres. WALDEMAR ROHDE.

Armenisch-Apostolische Orthodoxe Kirche in Deutschland: Allensteiner Str. 5, 50735 Köln; tel. (221) 7126223; fax (221) 7126267; Archbishop KAREKIN BEKDJIAN.

Griechisch-Orthodoxe Metropolie von Deutschland (Greek Orthodox Metropoly of Germany): Postfach 300555, 53185 Bonn; Dietrich-Bonhoeffer-Str. 2, 53227 Bonn; tel. (228) 462041; fax (228) 464989.

Religiöse Gesellschaft der Freunde (Quäker) (Society of Friends): Planckstr. 20, 10117 Berlin; tel. 2082284; f. 1925; 311 mems.

Russische Orthodoxe Kirche—Berliner Diözese (Russian Orthodox Church): Postfach 17, 10267 Berlin; Wildensteiner Str. 10, 10138 Berlin; tel. (30) 5099611; fax (30) 5098153; e-mail red .stimme@snafu.de; Archbishop FEOFAN.

ISLAM

There are an estimated 2.6m. Muslims in Germany.

JUDAISM

The membership of Jewish synagogues in Germany numbered some 74,289 in 1998.

Zentralrat der Juden in Deutschland (Central Council of Jews in Germany): Tucholskystr. 9, Leo-Baeck-Haus, 10117 Berlin; tel. (30) 2844560; fax (30) 28445613; e-mail info@zentralratjuden.de; internet www.zentralratjuden.de; Pres. Board of Dirs PAUL SPIEGEL; Exec. Dir STEPHAN J. KRAMER.

Jüdische Gemeinde zu Berlin (Jewish Community in Berlin): Fasanenstr. 79–80, 10623 Berlin; e-mail vorstand@jg-berlin.org; Pres. Dr ANDREAS NACHAMA.

The Press

The German Press Council was founded in 1956 as a self-regulatory body, and is composed of publishers and journalists. It formulates guide-lines and investigates complaints against the press.

In 1968 a government commission stipulated various limits on the proportions of circulation that any one publishing group should be allowed to control: (1) 40% of the total circulation of newspapers or 40% of the total circulation of magazines; (2) 20% of the total circulation of newspapers and magazines together; (3) 15% of the circulation in one field if the proportion owned in the other field is 40%.

Deutscher Presserat (German Press Council): Postfach 7160, 53071 Bonn; tel. (228) 985720; fax (228) 9857299; e-mail info@ presserat.de; internet www.presserat.de; Dir LUTZ TILLMANNS.

The principal newspaper publishing groups are:

Axel Springer Verlag AG: Axel-Springer-Str. 65, 10888 Berlin; tel. (30) 25910; fax (30) 251606; Axel-Springer-Platz 1, 20355 Hamburg; tel. (40) 34700; fax (40) 345811; internet www.asv.de; f. 1946; the largest newspaper publishing group in continental Europe; includes five major dailies (*Die Welt, Hamburger Abendblatt, Bild, Berliner Morgenpost, BZ*), three Sunday papers (*Welt am Sonntag, Bild am Sonntag, BZ am Sonntag*), and radio, television, women's and family magazines; Chair. AUGUST A. FISCHER.

Gruner + Jahr AG & Co Druck- und Verlagshaus: Am Vossbarg, 25524 Itzehoe; tel. (4821) 7771; fax (4821) 777449; and Am Baumwall 11, 20459 Hamburg; tel. (40) 37030; fax (40) 3703600; internet www.co.guj.de; owns, amongst others, *Stern, Brigitte, Capital, Eltern, Schöner Wohnen, Hamburger Morgenpost; Financial Times Deutschland*, a jt venture with *Financial Times* (UK), was launched in Feb. 2000.

Süddeutscher-Verlag GmbH: Sendlingerstr. 80, 80331 München; tel. (89) 21830; fax (89) 2183787; internet www.sueddeutsche.de; f. 1945; owns *Süddeutsche Zeitung*, special interest periodicals.

JahreszeitenVerlag GmbH: Possmoorweg 5, 22301 Hamburg; tel. (40) 27170; fax (40) 27172056; f. 1948; owns, amongst others, the periodicals *Für Sie* and *Petra*; Pres. THOMAS GANSKE.

Heinrich-Bauer-Verlag: Postfach 4660, 20077 Hamburg; Burchardstr. 11, 20095 Hamburg; tel. (40) 30190; fax (40) 30191043; and Charles-de-Gaulle-Str. 8, 81737 München; tel. (89) 678600; fax (89) 6702033; internet www.hbv.de; owns 29 popular illustrated magazines, including *Quick* (München), *Neue Revue* (Hamburg), *Praline, Neue Post, TV Horen + Sehen* and *Bravo*; Pres. HEINRICH BAUER.

Burda GmbH: Arabellastr. 23, 81925 München; tel. (89) 92502745; fax (89) 92502745; internet www.burda.de; f. 1908; publs incl. *Bunte, Burda Moden, Bild+Funk, Focus, Freundin, Meine Familie & ich* and *Schweriner Volkszeitung*; 10 Mans.

PRINCIPAL DAILIES

Aachen

Aachener Nachrichten: Postfach 110, 52002 Aaachen; Dresdner Str. 3, 52068 Aachen; tel. (241) 51010; fax (241) 5101399; internet www.an-online.de; f. 1872; circ. 67,000.

Aachener Zeitung: Postfach 500110, 52085 Aachen; Dresdner Str. 3, 52068 Aachen; tel. (241) 51010; fax (241) 5101399; internet www.aachener-zeitung.de; f. 1946; Editor-in-Chief BERND MATHIEU; circ. 106,000.

Ansbach

Fränkische Landeszeitung: Postfach 1362, 91504 Ansbach; Nürnberger Str. 9–17, 91522 Ansbach; tel. (981) 95000; fax (981) 13961; Editors-in-Chief GERHARD EGETEMAYER, PETER M. SZYMANOWSKI; circ. 50,000.

Aschaffenburg

Main-Echo: Postfach 548, 63736 Aschaffenburg; Weichertstr. 20, 63739 Aschaffenburg a.M.; tel. (6021) 3960; fax (6021) 396499; e-mail redaktionssekretariat@main-echo.de; internet www

.main-echo.de; Editors HELMUT WEISS, Dr HELMUT TEUFEL; circ. 93,000.

Augsburg

Augsburger Allgemeine: Curt-Frenzel-Str. 2, 86167 Augsburg; tel. (821) 7770; fax (821) 704471; e-mail chefredaktion@ augsburger-allgemeiner.de; internet www.augsburger-allgemeine .de; daily (Mon. to Sat.); Editors-in-Chief RAINER BONHORST, WALTER ROLLER, KLAUS-DIETER DÜSTER; circ. 370,000.

Baden-Baden

Badisches Tagblatt: Postfach 120, 76481 Baden-Baden; Stefanienstr. 1–3, 76530 Baden-Baden; tel (7221) 215241; fax (7221) 215240; Editors-in-Chief HARALD BESINGER, VOLKER-BODO ZANGER; circ. 41,000.

Bamberg

Fränkischer Tag: Gutenbergstr. 1, 96050 Bamberg; tel. (951) 1880; fax (951) 188118; internet www.fraenkischer-tag.de; Publr Dr HELMUTH JUNGBAUER; circ. 75,800.

Bautzen

Serbske Nowiny: Tuchmacher Str. 27, 02625 Bautzen; tel. (3591) 577232; e-mail serbske-nowiny@t-online.de; evening; Sorbian language paper; Editor BENEDIKT DYRLICH; circ. 1,500.

Berlin

Berliner Kurier: Karl-Liebknecht-Str. 29, 10178 Berlin; tel. (30) 2442403; fax (30) 2442274; evening; publ. by Gruner + Jahr AG; circ. 186,200.

Berliner Morgenpost: Axel-Springer-Str. 65, 10888 Berlin; tel. (30) 25910; fax (30) 2516071; e-mail redaktion@berliner-morgen post.de; internet www.berliner-morgenpost.de; f. 1898; publ. by Axel Springer Verlag AG; Editor-in-Chief HERBERT WESSELS; circ. 184,100.

Berliner Zeitung: Karl-Liebknecht-Str. 29, 10178 Berlin; tel. (2) 23279; fax (30) 23275533; internet www.berlinonline.de; f. 1945; morning; publ. by Gruner + Jahr AG; Editor DIETER SCHRÖDER; circ. 216,600.

BZ (Berliner Zeitung): Axel-Springer-Str. 65, 10888 Berlin; tel. (30) 25910; fax (30) 2510928; internet www.bz-berlin.de; f. 1877; publ. by Axel Springer Verlag AG; Editor WOLFGANG KRYSZOHN; circ. 313,500.

Junge Welt: Mauerstr. 39–40, 1080 Berlin; tel. (30) 22330; fax (30) 1302865; internet www.jungewelt.de; f. 1947; morning; Editor JENS KÖNIG; circ. 158,000.

Neues Deutschland: Alt-Stralau 1–2, 10245 Berlin; tel. (30) 293905; fax (30) 29390600; f. 1946; morning; independent; Editor WOLFGANG SPICKERMANN; circ. 72,400.

Der Tagesspiegel: Postfach 304330, 10723 Berlin; Potsdamer Str. 87, 10785 Berlin; tel. (30) 260090; fax (30) 26009332; f. 1945; circ. 130,200.

Die Welt: Axel-Springer-Str. 65, 10888 Berlin; tel. (30) 25910; fax (30) 251606; internet www.welt.de; f. 1946; publ. by Axel Springer Verlag AG; Editor Dr THOMAS LÖFFELHOLZ; circ. 216,800.

Bielefeld

Neue Westfälische: Postfach 100225, 33502 Bielefeld; Niedernstr. 21–27, 33602 Bielefeld; tel. (521) 5550; fax (521) 555520; internet www.nw-news.de; f. 1967; circ. 219,850.

Westfalen-Blatt: Postfach 8740, 33531 Bielefeld; Südbrackstr. 14–18, 33611 Bielefeld; tel. (521) 5850; fax (521) 585370; internet www.westfalen-blatt.de; f. 1946; Editor CARL-W. BUSSE; circ. 147,400.

Bonn

General-Anzeiger: Justus-von-Liebig-Str. 15, 53121 Bonn; tel. (228) 66880; fax (228) 6688170; internet www .general-anzeiger-bonn.de; f. 1725; independent; Publrs HERMANN NEUSSER, Hermann Neusser, Jr, MARTIN NEUSSER; Editor Dr HELMUT HERLES; circ. 90,000.

Braunschweig

Braunschweiger Zeitung: Postfach 3263, 38022 Braunschweig; Hamburger Str. 277, 38114 Braunschweig; tel. (531) 39000; fax (531) 3900610; internet www.newsclick.de; circ. 170,400.

Bremen

Bremer Nachrichten: Postfach 107801, 28078 Bremen; Martinistr. 43, 28195 Bremen; tel. (421) 36710; fax (421) 3379233; f. 1743; Publr HERBERT C. ORDEMANN; Editor DIETRICH IDE; circ. 44,000.

Weser-Kurier: Postfach 107801, 28078 Bremen; Martinistr. 43, 28195 Bremen; tel. (421) 36710; fax (421) 3379233; internet www.weser-kurier.de; f. 1945; Publr HERBERT C. ORDEMANN; Editor VOLKER WEISE; circ. 185,000.

Bremerhaven

Nordsee-Zeitung: Postfach 27512, 27512 Bremerhaven; Hafenstr. 140, 27576 Bremerhaven 1; tel. (471) 5970; fax (471) 597551; internet www.nordsee-zeitung.de; Chief Editor JÖRG JUNG; circ. 77,500.

Chemnitz

Freie Presse: Postfach 261, Brückenstr. 15, 09111 Chemnitz; tel. (371) 6560; fax (371) 643042; internet www.freiepresse.de; f. 1963; morning; Editor DIETER SOIKA; circ. 461,900.

Cottbus

Lausitzer Rundschau: Postfach 100279, 03002 Cottbus; Str. der Jugend 54, 03050 Cottbus; tel. (355) 4810; fax (355) 481245; internet www.lr-online.de; independent; morning; Chief Officers FRANK LÜDECKE, J. FRIEDRICH ORTHS; circ. 190,000.

Darmstadt

Darmstädter Echo: Postfach 100155, 64276 Darmstadt; Holzhofallee 25–31, 64295 Darmstadt; tel. (6151) 3871; fax (6151) 387448; internet www.echo-online.de; f. 1945; Publrs Dr HANS-PETER BACH, HORST BACH; Editor-in-Chief ROLAND HOF; circ. 87,300.

Dortmund

Ruhr-Nachrichten: Postfach 105051, Westenhellweg 86–88, 44047 Dortmund; internet www.westline.de; f. 1949; Editor FLORIAN LENSING-WOLFF; circ. 215,400.

Westfälische Rundschau: Postfach 105067, 44047 Dortmund; Brüderweg 9; Dortmund 44135; tel. (201) 8040; fax (201) 8042841; internet www.westfaelische-rundschau.de; Editor FRANK BÜNTE; circ. 250,000.

Dresden

Dresdner Morgenpost: Ostra-Allee, 01067 Dresden; tel. (51) 4864; fax (51) 4951116; circ. 126,700.

Dresdner Neueste Nachrichten/Union: Hauptstr. 21, 01097 Dresden; tel. (351) 8075210; fax (351) 8075212; morning; Editor-in-Chief DIRK BIRGEL; circ. 39,000.

Sächsische Zeitung: Haus der Presse, Ostra-Allee 20, 01067 Dresden; tel. (351) 48640; fax (351) 48642354; e-mail redaktion@ sz-online.de; internet www.sz-online.de; f. 1946; morning; publ. by Gruner + Jahr AG; Editor-in-Chief PETER CHRIST; circ. 397,700.

Düsseldorf

Düsseldorf Express: Postfach 1132, 40002 Düsseldorf; Königsallee 27, 40212 Düsseldorf; tel. (211) 13930; fax (211) 324835.

Handelsblatt: Postfach 102741, 40018 Düsseldorf; Kasernenstr. 67, 40213 Düsseldorf; tel. (211) 8870; fax (211) 329954; e-mail handelsblatt@rhb.de; internet www.handelsblatt.de; 5 a week; Publr DIETER VON HOLTZBRINCK; circ. 156,473.

Rheinische Post: Zülpicherstr. 10, 40549 Düsseldorf; tel. (211) 5050; fax (211) 5052575; internet www.rp-online.de; f. 1946; Editor ULRICH REITZ; circ. 349,200.

Westdeutsche Zeitung: Postfach 101132, 40002 Düsseldorf; Königsallee 27, 40212 Düsseldorf; tel. (211) 83820; fax (211) 822225; internet www.wz-newsline.de; Editor-in-Chief MICHAEL HARTMANN; Publr Dr M. GIRARDET; circ. 176,800.

Erfurt

Thüringer Allgemeine: Gottstedter Landstr. 6, 99092 Erfurt; tel. (361) 2274; fax (361) 2275144; f. 1946; morning; Editor-in-Chief SERGEJ LOCHTHOFEN; circ. 330,000.

Essen

Neue Ruhr Zeitung: Friedrichstr. 34–38, 45128 Essen; tel. (201) 8042605; fax (201) 8042121; Editor-in-Chief Dr RICHARD KIESSLER; circ. 215,000.

Westdeutsche Allgemeine Zeitung: Friedrichstr. 34–38, 45128 Essen; tel. (201) 8040; fax (201) 8042841; Editor RALF LEHMANN; circ. 650,000.

Flensburg

Flensburger Tageblatt: Postfach 1553, 25804 Flensburg; Nikolaistr. 7, 24937 Flensburg; tel. (461) 8080; fax (461) 8082121.

Frankfurt am Main

Frankfurter Allgemeine Zeitung: Hellerhofstr. 2–4, 60327 Frankfurt a.M.; tel. (69) 75910; fax (69) 75911743; internet www.faz.de; f. 1949; Editors JÜRGEN JESKE, BERTHOLD KOHLER, Dr HUGO MÜLLER-VOGG, Dr GÜNTHER NONNENMACHER, Dr FRANK SCHIRRM-ACHER; circ. 400,000.

Frankfurter Neue Presse: Postfach 100801, 60008 Frankfurt a.M.; Frankenallee 71–81, 60327 Frankfurt a.M.; tel. (69) 75010; fax (69) 75014330; internet www.fnp.de; independent; Editor GERHARD MUMME; circ. 110,440.

Frankfurter Rundschau: Grosse Eschenheimer Str. 16–18; 60313 Frankfurt a.M.; tel. (69) 21991; fax (69) 2199328; internet www.fr-aktuell.de; Editor RODERICH REIFENRATH; circ. 189,000.

Frankfurt an der Oder

Märkische Oderzeitung: Postfach 178, 15201 Frankfurt a.d. Oder; Kellenspring 6, 15230 Frankfurt a.d. Oder; tel. (335) 55300; fax (335) 23214; morning; Editor Dr FRANZ KADELL; circ. 150,633.

Freiburg im Breisgau

Badische Zeitung: Pressehaus, Basler Str. 88, 79115 Freiburg i. Br.; tel. (761) 4960; fax (761) 4965008; e-mail redaktion@badische-zeitung.de; internet www.badische-zeitung.de; f. 1946; Editor Dr JÜRGEN BUSCHE; circ. 171,005.

Gera

Ostthüringer Zeitung: De-Smit-Str. 18, 6500 Gera; tel. (70) 6120; fax (70) 51233; morning; Editor-in-Chief ULLRICH ERZIGKEIT; circ. 237,537.

Göttingen

Göttinger Tageblatt: Postfach 1953, 37009 Göttingen; Dransfelder Str. 1, 37079 Göttingen; tel. (551) 9011; fax (551) 901229; e-mail info@goettinger.tageblatt.de; internet www.goettinger-tageblatt.de; f. 1889; Man. Dirs HERBERT FLECKEN, GÜNTER GRIFFELS; Editor-in-Chief BERNO HILDER; circ. 50,200.

Hagen

Westfalenpost: Schürmannstr. 4, 58097 Hagen; tel. (2331) 9170; fax (2331) 9174263; e-mail westfalenpost@cityweb.de; f. 1946; Chief Editor BODO ZAPP; circ. 160,000.

Halle

Haller Kreisblatt: Postfach 1452, 33779 Halle; Gutenbergstr. 2, 33790 Halle.

Hamburg

Bild: Axel-Springer-Platz 1, 20355 Hamburg; tel. (40) 34700; fax (40) 345811; internet www.bild.de; f. 1952; publ. by Axel Springer Verlag AG; Chief Editor UDO RÖBEL; circ. 4,412,200.

Hamburger Abendblatt: Axel-Springer-Platz 1, 20355 Hamburg; tel. (40) 34700; fax (40) 345811; internet www.abendblatt.de; publ. by Axel Springer Verlag AG; Editor-in-Chief KLAUS KRUSE; circ. 315,600.

Hamburger Morgenpost: Griegstr. 75, 22763 Hamburg; tel. (40) 8830303; fax (40) 88303237; e-mail iamedien@www.mopo.de; internet www.mopo.de; publ. by Gruner + Jahr AG; circ. 140,700.

Hannover

Hannoversche Allgemeine Zeitung: Bemeroder Str. 58, 30148 Hannover, 30559 Hannover; tel. (511) 5180; fax (511) 527328; internet www.niedersachsen.com; circ. 269,600.

Neue Presse: Postfach 149, 30001 Hannover; Bemeroder Str. 58, 30559 Hannover; tel. (511) 51010; fax (511) 524554.

Heidelberg

Rhein-Neckar-Zeitung: Postfach 104560, 69035 Heidelberg; Hauptstr. 23, 69117 Heidelberg; tel. (6221) 5191; fax (6221) 519217; internet www.rnz-online.de; f. 1945; morning; Publrs Dr LUDWIG KNORR, WINFRIED KNORR, Dr DIETER SCHULZE; circ. 104,600.

Heilbronn

Heilbronner Stimme: Allee 2, 74072 Heilbronn; tel. (7131) 6150; fax (7131) 615200; e-mail gl@stimme.de; internet www.stimme.de; f. 1946; Editor-in-Chief Dr WOLFGANG BOK; circ. 102,500.

Hof-Saale

Frankenpost: Postfach 1320, 95012 Hof-Saale; Poststr. 9–11, 95028 Hof-Saale; tel. (9281) 8160; fax (9281) 816283; e-mail fp-redaktion@frankenpost.de; internet www.frankenpost.de; Publr Frankenpost Verlag GmbH; Editor-in-Chief MALTE BUSCHBECK; circ 100,000.

Ingolstadt

Donaukurier: Postfach 100259, 85002 Ingolstadt; Stauffenbergstr. 2A, 85051 Ingolstadt; tel. (841) 96660; fax (841) 9666255; e-mail redaktion@donaukurier.de; internet www.donaukurier.de; f. 1872; Publr ELIN REISSMÜLLER; circ. 84,700.

Kassel

Hessische/Niedersächsische Allgemeine: Postfach 101009, 34010 Kassel; Frankfurter Str. 168, 34121 Kassel; tel. (561) 20300; fax (561) 2032116; internet www.hna.de; f. 1959; independent; circ. 189,200.

Kempten

Allgäuer Zeitung: Postfach 3155, 87440 Kempten; Heisinger Str. 14, 87437 Kempten; tel. (831) 2060; fax (831) 206379; internet www.all-in.de; f. 1968; Publrs GEORG Fürst VON WALDBURG-ZEIL, GÜNTER HOLLAND; circ. 117,900.

Kiel

Kieler Nachrichten: Postfach 1111, 24100 Kiel; Fleethörn 1–7, 24103 Kiel; tel. (431) 9030; fax (431) 903935; internet www.kn-online.de; Publ. by Axel Springer Verlag; Chief Editor JÜRGEN HEINEMANN; circ. 113,400.

Koblenz

Rhein-Zeitung: Postfach 1540, August-Horch-Str. 28, 56070 Koblenz; tel. (261) 89200; fax (261) 892476; internet www.rhein-zeitung.de; Editor MARTIN LOHMANN; circ. 246,100.

Köln

Express: Postfach 100410, 50450 Köln; Breite Str. 70, 50667 Köln; tel. (221) 2240; fax (211) 2242524; internet www.express.de; f. 1964; Publr ALFRED NEVEN DUMONT; circ. 370,000.

Kölner Stadt-Anzeiger: Amsterdamer Str. 192, 50735 Köln; tel. (221) 2240; fax (221) 2242524; internet www.ksta.de; f. 1876; Publr ALFRED NEVEN DUMONT; Editor FRANZ SOMMERFELD; circ. 294,400.

Kölnische Rundschau: Postfach 102145, 50461 Köln; Stolkgasse 25–45, 50667 Köln; tel. (221) 16320; fax (221) 1632491; internet www.rundschau-online.de; f. 1946; Publr HELMUT HEINEN; Editor-in-Chief DIETER BREUERS; circ. 155,100.

Konstanz

Südkurier: Postfach 102001, Presse- und Druckzentrum, 78420 Konstanz; Max-Stromeyer-Str. 178, 78467 Konstanz; tel. (7531) 9990; fax (7531) 999485; e-mail redaktion@suedkurier.de; internet www.skol.de; f. 1945; circ. 148,990.

Leipzig

Leipziger Volkszeitung: Peterssteinweg 19, 04107 Leipzig; tel. (341) 21811; fax (341) 310992; internet www.lvz-online.de; f. 1894; morning; publ. by Axel Springer Verlag AG; circ. 264,000.

Leutkirch im Allgäu

Schwäbische Zeitung: Postfach 1145, 88291 Leutkirch im Allgäu; Rudolf-Roth-Str. 18, 88299 Leutkirch im Allgäu; tel. (7561) 800; fax (7561) 80134; e-mail redaktion@schwaebische-zeitung.de; internet www.schwaebische-zeitung.de; f. 1945; Editor JOACHIM UMBACH; circ. 196,000.

Lübeck

Lübecker Nachrichten: Herrenholz 10–12, 23556 Lübeck; tel. (451) 1440; fax (451) 1441022; internet www.ln-online.de; f. 1945; publ. by Axel Springer Verlag AG; Chief Editor THOMAS LUBOWSKI; circ. 115,900.

Ludwigshafen

Die Rheinpfalz: Postfach 211147, 67011 Ludwigshafen; Amtsstr. 5–11, 67059 Ludwigshafen; tel. (621) 590201; fax (621) 5902336; Dir Dr THOMAS SCHAUB; circ. 249,410.

Magdeburg

Magdeburger Volksstimme: Bahnhofstr. 17, 39104 Magdeburg; tel. (391) 59990; fax (391) 388400; f. 1890; morning; publ. by Magdeburger Verlags- und Druckhaus GmbH; Editor-in-Chief Dr HEINZGEORG OETTE; circ. 316,900.

Mainz

Allgemeine Zeitung: Postfach 3120, 55021 Mainz; Erich-Dombrowski-Str. 2, 55127 Mainz; tel. (6131) 1440; fax (6131) 144504; internet www.main-rheiner.de; publ. by Rhein-Main-Presse; circ. 134,000.

Mannheim

Mannheimer Morgen: Postfach 102164, 68021 Mannheim; Dudenstr. 12–26, 68167 Mannheim; tel. (621) 39201; fax (621) 3921376; e-mail redaktion@mamo.de; internet www.morgenweb.de; f. 1946; Publr R. VON SCHILLING; Chief Editor HORST ROTH; circ. 97,600.

München

Abendzeitung: Sendlingerstr. 10, 80331 München; tel. (89) 23770; fax (89) 2377478; f. 1948; publ. by Süddeutscher-Verlag GmbH; Dir CHRISTOPH MATTES; Editor-in-Chief KURT RÖLLGEN; circ. 184,697.

Münchner Merkur: Paul-Heyse-Str. 2–4, 80336 München; tel. (89) 53060; fax (89) 5306201; internet www.merkur-online.de; Publr Dr DIRK IPPEN; Editor PETER FISCHER; circ. 203,200.

Süddeutsche Zeitung: Sendlingerstr. 8, 80331 München; tel. (89) 21830; fax (89) 2183787; internet www.sueddeutsche.de; f. 1945;

publ. by Süddeutscher-Verlag GmbH; Editors-in-Chief HANS-WERNER KILZ, Dr GERNOT SITTNER; circ. 427,644.

TZ: Paul-Heyse-Str. 2–4, 80336 München; tel. (89) 53060; fax (89) 530552; e-mail kschermann@tz-online.de; f. 1968; Editor KARL SCHERMANN; circ. 154,600.

Münster

Münstersche Zeitung: Postfach 5560, 48030 Münster; Neubrückenstr. 8–11, 48143 Münster; tel. (251) 5920; fax (251) 592212; e-mail mz-redaktion@westline.de; internet www.westline.de; f. 1871; independent; Editor Dr GREGOR BOTHE; circ. 46,860.

Westfälische Nachrichten: Soester Str. 13, 48155 Münster; tel. (251) 6900; fax (251) 690105; internet www.wnonline.de; Chief Editor Dr NORBERT TIEMANN; circ. 125,900.

Neubrandenburg

Nordkurier: Flurstr. 2, 17034 Neubrandenburg; tel. (395) 45750; fax (395) 4575694; internet www.nordkurier.de; circ. 340,000.

Nürnberg

Nürnberger Nachrichten: Marienstr. 9–11, 90402 Nürnberg; tel. (911) 2160; fax (911) 2162326; internet www.nn-online.de; f. 1945; Editor FELIX HARTLIEB; circ. 344,000.

Oberndorf-Neckar

Schwarzwälder Bote: Postfach 1380, 78722 Oberndorf-Neckar; Kirchtorstr. 14, 78727 Oberndorf-Neckar; tel. (7423) 780; fax (7423) 7873; internet www.swol.de; circ. 104,300.

Oelde

Die Glocke: Engelbert-Holterdorf-Str. 4–6, 59302 Oelde; tel. (2522) 730; fax (2522) 73216; f. 1880; Editors FRIED GEHRING, ENGELBERT HOLTERDORF; circ. 65,500.

Offenbach

Offenbach Post: Postfach 100263, 63002 Offenbach; Waldstr. 226, 63071 Offenbach; tel. (69) 850080; fax (69) 85008198; internet www.op-online.de; f. 1947; Publr UDO BINTZ; circ. 53,200.

Oldenburg

Nordwest-Zeitung: Postfach 2527, 26015 Oldenburg; Peterstr. 28–34, 26121 Oldenburg; tel. (441) 998801; fax (441) 99882029; internet www.nwz-online.de; publ. by Nordwest-Zeitung Verlagsgesellschaft mbH & Co KG; Editor ROLF SEELHEIM; circ. 130,000.

Osnabrück

Neue Osnabrücker Zeitung: Postfach 4260, 49032 Osnabrück; Breiter Gang 10–14 and Grosse Str. 17–19, 49074 Osnabrück; tel. (541) 3250; fax (541) 325275; e-mail redoktion@neue-oz.de; internet www.neue-oz.de; f. 1967; Chief Editor F. SCHMEDT; circ. 179,700.

Passau

Passauer Neue Presse: Medienstr. 5, 94036 Passau; tel. (851) 8020; fax (851) 802256; internet www.pnp.de; f. 1946; circ. 162,900.

Potsdam

Märkische Allgemeine: Postfach 601153, 14411 Potsdam; Friedrich-Engels-Str. 24, 14473 Potsdam; tel. (331) 28400; fax (331) 2840301; f. 1990; morning; independent; Editor HANS-ULRICH KONRAD; circ. 220,400.

Regensburg

Mittelbayerische Zeitung: Margaretenstr. 4, 93047 Regensburg; tel. (941) 207270; fax (941) 207307; internet www.donau.et.net; f. 1945; Editor PETER ESSER; circ. 134,202.

Rostock

Ostsee-Zeitung: Richard-Wagner-Str. 1A, 18055 Rostock; tel. (81) 3650; fax (81) 365244; internet www.ostsee-zeitung.de; f. 1952; publ. by Axel Springer Verlag AG; Editor GERD SPILKER; circ. 214,300.

Saarbrücken

Saarbrücker Zeitung: Gutenbergstr. 11–23, 66117 Saarbrücken; tel. (681) 5020; fax (681) 5022500; internet www.sz-newsline.de; f. 1761; Editor RUDOLPH BERNHARD; circ. 183,500.

Schwerin

Schweriner Volkszeitung: Gutenbergstr. 1, 19061 Schwerin; tel. (385) 63780; fax (385) 3975140; internet www.svz.de; f. 1946; Editor CHRISTOPH HAMM; circ. 144,800.

Straubing

Straubinger Tagblatt: Ludwigsplatz 30, 94315 Straubing; tel. (9421) 940115; fax (9421) 940155; e-mail service@idowa.de; internet www.idowa.de; f. 1860; morning; Chief Editor Dr HERMANN BALLE; circ. 140,000.

Stuttgart

Stuttgarter Nachrichten: Postfach 104452, 70039 Stuttgart; Plieninger Str. 150, 70567 Stuttgart; tel. (711) 72050; fax (711) 7205300; internet www.stuttgarter-nachrichten.de; f. 1946; Editor-in-Chief JÜRGEN OFFENBACH; circ. 59,300.

Stuttgarter Zeitung: Postfach 106032, 70049 Stuttgart; Plieninger Str. 150, 70567 Stuttgart; tel. (711) 72050; fax (711) 7205300; internet www.stuttgarter-zeitung.de; f. 1945; Chief Editor Dr UWE VORKÖTTER; circ. 151,600.

Trier

Trierischer Volksfreund: Postfach 3770, 54227 Trier; Am Nikolaus-Koch-Platz 1–3, 54290 Trier; tel. (651) 71990; fax (651) 7199990; internet www.intrinet.de; Chief Editor WALTER W. WEBER; circ. 100,000.

Ulm

Südwest Presse: Frauenstr. 77, 89073 Ulm; tel. (731) 1560; fax (731) 156308; internet www.suedwest-presse.de; circ. 107,800.

Weiden

Der Neue Tag: Postfach 1340, 92603 Weiden; Weigelstr. 16, 92637 Weiden; tel. (961) 850; fax (961) 44499; Editor-in-Chief HANS KLEMM; circ. 87,400.

Weimar

Thüringische Landeszeitung: Marienstr. 14, 99423 Weimar; tel. (3643) 206411; fax (3643) 206413; f. 1945; morning; Editor HANS HOFFMEISTER; circ. 62,000.

Wetzlar

Wetzlarer Neue Zeitung: Elsa-Brandström-Str. 18, 35578 Wetzlar; tel. (6441) 9590; fax (6441) 71684; f. 1945; Editor WULF EIGENDORF; circ. 75,000.

Wiesbaden

Wiesbadener Kurier: Postfach 6029, 65050 Wiesbaden; Langgasse 21, 65183 Wiesbaden; tel. (611) 3550; fax (611) 355377; internet www.main-rheiner-de; Chief Editors MATTHIAS FRIEDRICH, FRIEDRICH ROEINGH; circ. 86,700.

Würzburg

Main-Post: Berner Str. 2, 97084 Würzburg; tel. (931) 60010; fax (931) 6001242; internet www.mainpost.de; f. 1883; independent; Publrs Dr HANS GASSER, MANFRED WINTERBACH; Editors-in-Chief DAVID BRANDSTÄTTER, ANTON SAHLENDER; circ. 153,300.

SUNDAY AND WEEKLY PAPERS

Bayernkurier: Nymphenburger Str. 64, 80636 München; tel. (89) 120041; weekly; organ of the CSU; Chief Editor W. SCHARNAGL; circ. 156,300.

Bild am Sonntag: Axel-Springer-Platz 1, 20350 Hamburg; tel. (40) 34700; fax (40) 345811; f. 1956; Sunday; publ. by Axel Springer Verlag AG; Chief Editor MICHAEL H. SPRENG; circ. 2,647,629.

BZ am Sonntag: Axel-Springer-Str. 65, 10888 Berlin; tel. (30) 25910; fax (30) 2510928; f. 1992; publ. by Axel Springer Verlag AG; circ. 157,714.

Frankfurter Allgemeine Sonntagszeitung: Hellerhofstr. 2–4, 60327 Frankfurt a.M.; tel. (69) 75910; fax (69) 75911773; internet www.faz.de; Sunday; Publr Dr HUGO MÜLLER-VOGG; Editor-in-Chief CORNELIA VON WRANGEL; circ. 95,000.

Rheinischer Merkur: Postfach 201164, 53141 Bonn; Godesberger Allee 91, 53175 Bonn; tel. (228) 8840; fax (228) 884299; internet www.merkur.de; f. 1946; weekly; circ. 110,100.

Sonntag aktuell: Plienigerstr. 150, 70567 Stuttgart; tel. (711) 72050; fax (711) 7205930; Sunday; circ. 869,500.

Welt am Sonntag: Axel-Springer-Platz 1, 20355 Hamburg; tel. (40) 34700; fax (40) 34724912; e-mail wams.leser@asv.de; internet www.welt.de; Sunday; publ. by Axel Springer Verlag AG; Editor Dr THOMAS GAMUS; circ. 442,005.

Die Zeit: Speersort 1, Pressehaus, 20095 Hamburg; tel. (40) 32800; fax (40) 327111; internet www.zeit.de; f. 1946; weekly; Editors-in-Chief Dr MICHAEL NAUMANN, Dr JOSEF JOFFE; circ. 455,000.

SELECTED PERIODICALS
Agriculture

Agrar Praxis: Ernst-Mey-Str. 8, 7022 Leinfelden-Echterdingen; tel. (711) 7594423; f. 1882; monthly; Editor-in-Chief KLAUS NIE-HÖRSTER; circ. 60,250.

Bauernzeitung: Postfach 310448, 10634 Berlin; Wilhelmsaue 36/37, 10713 Berlin; e-mail bauernzeitung@bauernverlag.de; f. 1960; agricultural weekly; Editor RALF STEPHAN; circ. 36,000.

Bayerisches Landwirtschaftliches Wochenblatt: Postfach 400320, 80703 München; Lothstr. 29, 80797 München; e-mail redbaywo@t.online.de; f. 1810; weekly; organ of the Bayerischer Bauernverband; Editor-in-Chief JOHANNES URBAN; circ. 115,800.

Eisenbahn-Landwirt: Postfach 110664, Am Ellenbogen 12, 4300 Essen 11; tel. (201) 670525; f. 1918; monthly; Dir HANS HÜSKEN; circ. 120,000.

Das Landvolk: Warmbüchenstr. 3, 30159 Hannover; fax (511) 3670468; fortnightly; issued by Landbuch-Verlag GmbH; Chief Editor GÜNTHER MARTIN BEINE; circ. 98,000.

Landpost: Wollgrasweg 31, 70599 Stuttgart; tel. (711) 451275; fax (711) 456603; e-mail vdaw-e.v.@t-online.de; internet www.vdaw.de; f. 1945; weekly; agriculture and gardening; Editor ERICH REICH; circ. 60,000.

Art, Drama, Architecture and Music

Art. Das Kunstmagazin: Am Baumwall 11, 20459 Hamburg; tel. (40) 37030; fax (40) 37036618; publ. by Gruner + Jahr AG.

Intelligente Architektur: Fasanenweg 18, 70771 Leinfelden-Echterdingen; tel. (711) 7591286; fax (711) 7591410; e-mail ait-red@ait-online.de; internet www.ait-online.de; f. 1890; monthly; Editors Dr D. DANNER, P. STEPHAN; circ. 16,000.

Theater der Zeit: Klosterstr. 68–70, 10179 Berlin; tel. (30) 2423626; fax (30) 24722415; f. 1946; monthly; theatre, drama, opera, musical, children's theatre, puppet theatre, ballet; Editor (vacant); circ. 8,000.

Theater heute: Reinhardtstr. 29, 10117 Berlin; tel. (30) 25449510; fax (30) 25449512; e-mail redaktion@theaterheute.de; internet www.theaterheute.de; f. 1960; monthly; Editors BARBARA BURCKHARDT, Dr MICHAEL MERSCHMEIER, Prof. Dr HENNING RISCHBIETER, Dr FRANZ WILLE.

Economics, Finance and Industry

absatzwirtschaft: Postfach 101102, 40002 Düsseldorf; Kasernenstr. 67, 40213 Düsseldorf; tel. (211) 8871422; fax (211) 8871420; e-mail absatzwirtschaft@vhb.de; internet www.absatzwirtschaft.de; f. 1958; monthly; journal for marketing; Dir UWE HOCH; Editor FRIEDHELM PÄLIKE; circ. 23,000.

atw—Internationale Zeitschrift für Kernenergie: Postfach 101102, 40002 Düsseldorf; tel. (211) 8871442; fax (211) 8871440; e-mail w.liebholz@vhb.de; f. 1956; monthly; technical, scientific and economic aspects of nuclear engineering and technology; Editors W.-M. LIEBHOLZ, Dr E. PASCHE; circ. 4,500.

Der Betrieb: Postfach 101102, 40002 Düsseldorf; Kasernenstr. 67, 40123 Düsseldorf; tel. (211) 8871451; fax (211) 8871450; e-mail der-betrieb@vhb.de; weekly; business administration, revenue law, labour and social legislation; circ. 36,000.

Capital: Gruner + Jahr AG, 20444 Hamburg; tel. (40) 37032480; fax (40) 37035607; f. 1962; monthly; business magazine; circ. 295,440.

Creditreform: Postfach 1102, Kasernenstr. 67, 40002 Düsseldorf; tel. (211) 8871461; fax (211) 8871463; f. 1879; Editor KLAUS-WERNER ERNST; circ. 124,870.

Finanzwirtschaft: Am Friedrichshain 22, 104010 Berlin; tel. (30) 42151237; fax (30) 42151332; 12 a year; finance and economics; circ. 4,818.

Getränketechnik, Zeitschrift für das technische Management: Breite Gasse 58–60, 8500 Nürnberg 1; tel. (911) 23830; fax (911) 204956; 6 a year; trade journal for the brewing and beverage industries; circ. 8,518.

HV-Journal Handelsvermittlung und Vertrieb: Postfach 101937, 60019 Frankfurt a.M.; Mainzer-Land-Str. 251, 60326 Frankfurt a.M.; Siegel-Verlag Otto Müller GmbH; tel. (69) 75890950; fax (69) 75890960; e-mail hv-journal@svffm.de; internet www.svffm.de; f. 1949; fortnightly; Editor Dr ANDREAS PAFFHAUSEN; circ. 19,000.

Industrie-Anzeiger: Postfach 100252, 70746 Leinfelden-Echterdingen; e-mail ia.redaktion@kanradin.de; internet www.industrienet.de; f. 1879; weekly; Editor-in-Chief Dr R. LANGBEIN; circ. 50,000.

Management International Review: Abraham-Lincoln-Str. 46, 65189 Wiesbaden; tel. (611) 7878230; fax (611) 7878411; quarterly; issued by Gabler Verlag; English; Editor Prof. Dr K. MACHARZINA (Stuttgart-Hohenheim).

VDI Nachrichten: Postfach 101054, Heinrichstr. 24, 40001 Düsseldorf; tel. (211) 61880; fax (211) 6188306; e-mail internet@vdi-nachrichten.com; internet www.vdi-nachrichten.com; f. 1946; weekly; circ. 155,000.

Versicherungswirtschaft: Klosestr. 22, 76137 Karlsruhe; tel. (721) 35090; fax (721) 31833; e-mail rehnert@vvw.de; internet www.vvw.de; f. 1946; fortnightly; Editors KARL-HEINZ REHNERT, HUBERT CLEMENS; circ. 12,000.

Wirtschaftswoche: Kasernenstr. 67, 40213 Düsseldorf; tel. (211) 8770; fax (211) 133374; internet wiwo.de; weekly; business; Publrs

Dr HEIK AFHELDT, Dr RENATE MERKLEIN; Editor STEFAN BARON; circ. 163,000.

Education and Youth

Bravo: Charles-de-Gaulle-Str. 8, 81737 München; tel. (89) 6786700; fax (89) 6702033; weekly; for young people; circ. 1,659,360.

Computer Bild: Axel-Springer-Platz 1, 20350 Hamburg; tel. (40) 34724300; fax (40) 34724683; e-mail redaktion@computerbild.de; internet www.computerbild.de; f. 1996; publ. by Axel Springer Verlag AG; circ. 923,432.

Deutsche Lehrerzeitung: Lindenstr. 54B, 10117 Berlin; tel. (2) 23809414; fax (2) 20183645; f. 1954; weekly for teachers; Editor RAINER WINKEL; circ. 22,000.

Erziehung und Wissenschaft: Goldammerweg 16, 45134 Essen; tel. (201) 843000; fax (201) 472590; e-mail info@stamm.de; internet www.gew.de; f. 1948; monthly; Editor-in-Chief STEFFEN WELZEL; circ. 270,000.

Geographische Rundschau: Georg-Westermann-Allee 66, 38104 Braunschweig; tel. (531) 708385; fax (531) 708329; e-mail gr@westermann.de; f. 1949; monthly; Man. Editor REINER JUENGST; circ. 12,000.

PÄDAGOGIK: Werderstr. 10, 69469 Weinheim; tel. (40) 454595; fax (40) 4108564; f. 1949; monthly; Editor Prof. Dr J. BASTIAN; circ. 13,000.

Praxis Deutsch: Postfach 100150, 30917 Seelze; tel. (511) 40004139; fax (511) 40004219; e-mail redaktion.pd@friedrich-verlag.de; 6 a year; German language and literature; circ. 25,000.

Law

Deutsche Richterzeitung: Seufertstr. 27, 53173 Bonn; fax (228) 334723; f. 1909; monthly; circ. 11,000.

Juristenzeitung: Postfach 2040, 72010 Tübingen; Wilhelmstr. 18, 72074 Tübingen; tel. (7071) 92352; fax (7071) 92367; e-mail jz@mohr.de; f. 1944; fortnightly; Editor HEIDE SCHAPKA; circ. 6,000.

Juristische Rundschau: Postfach 303421, 10728 Berlin; Genthiner Str. 13, 10785 Berlin; tel. (30) 2600123; fax (30) 26005329; e-mail wdg-info@degruyter.de; internet www.degruyter.de; f. 1922; monthly; Editors-in-Chief Prof. Dr DIRK OLZEN, Prof. Dr HERBERT TRÖNDLE.

Neue Juristische Wochenschrift: Palmengartenstr. 14, 60325 Frankfurt a.M.; Wilhelmstr. 5–9, 80703 München; tel. (69) 7560910; fax (69) 75609149; f. 1947; weekly; 5 Editors; circ. 55,000.

Rabels Zeitschrift für ausländisches und internationales Privatrecht: Mittelweg 187, 20148 Hamburg; tel. (40) 41900263; fax (40) 41900288; f. 1927; quarterly; Editors JÜGEN BASEDOW, KLAUS J. HOPT, HEIN KÖTZ.

Versicherungsrecht: Klosestr. 22, 76137 Karlsruhe; tel. (721) 35090; fax (721) 31833; e-mail rehnert@vvw.de; f. 1950; 3 a month; Editors Prof. Dr EGON LORENZ, KARL-HEINZ REHNERT; circ. 8,800.

Zeitschrift für die gesamte Strafrechtswissenschaft: Postfach 303421, 10728 Berlin, Genthiner Str. 13, 10785 Berlin; tel. (30) 26005123; fax (30) 26005329; e-mail wdg-info@degruyter.de; internet www.degruyter.de; f. 1881; quarterly; Editor-in-Chief Prof. Dr Dr HANS JOACHIM HIRSCH.

Politics, Literature, Current Affairs

Akzente: Kolbergerstr. 22, 81631 München; tel. (89) 998300; fax (89) 9827119; f. 1954; Editor MICHAEL KRÜGER.

Buch Aktuell: Postfach 101852/62, 44018 Dortmund; Königswall 21, 44137 Dortmund; tel. (231) 90560; fax (231) 9056110; e-mail post@harenberg.de; internet www.harenberg.de; 3 a year; Editor BODO HARENBERG; circ. 630,000.

Focus: Arabellastr. 23, 81925 München; tel. (89) 92500; fax (89) 92502026; e-mail anzeigen@focus.de; internet www.focus.de; f. 1993; weekly; political, general; publ. by Burda GmbH; circ. 764,000.

Gegenwartskunde: Postfach 300551, Leske Verlag + Budrich GmbH, 51334 Leverkusen (Opladen); tel. (2171) 49070; fax (2171) 490711; e-mail lesbudpubl@aol.com; internet www.leske-budrich.de; quarterly; economics, politics, education; Editors S. REINHARDT, H.-H. HARTWICH, B. SCHÄFERS, R. STURM.

Internationale Politik: Rauchstr. 18, 10787 Berlin; tel. (30) 25423146; fax (30) 25423167; e-mail ip@dgap.org; f. 1946; monthly; journal of the German Society for Foreign Affairs; publ. W. Bertelsmann Verlag GmbH & Co KG, Bielefeld; Editor Prof. Dr WERNER WEIDENFELD; Exec. Editor Dr ANGELIKA VOLLE; circ. 4,800.

Merian Jahreszeiten Verlag: Harvestehuder Weg 42, 20149 Hamburg; tel. (40) 44188240; fax (40) 44188310; e-mail redaktion@merian.de; internet www.merian.jalag.de; f. 1948; monthly; every issue deals with a country or a city; Chief Editor HOLGER SCHNITGERHAUS; circ. 150,000.

Merkur (Deutsche Zeitschrift für europäisches Denken): Pfisterstr. 10, 80331 München; tel. (89) 29163111; fax (89) 29163114;

internet www.merkur.de; f. 1947; monthly; literary, political; Editors KARL HEINZ BOHRER, KURT SCHEEL; circ. 6,000.

Neue Deutsche Literatur: Neue Promenade 6, 10178 Berlin; tel. (30) 28394238; fax (30) 28394100; e-mail ndl@aufbau-verlag.de; f. 1953; 6 a year; review of literature; Editor JÜRGEN ENGLER.

Neue Gesellschaft—Frankfurter Hefte: Hiroshimastr. 17, 10785 Berlin; tel. (30) 26935818; fax (30) 26935855; e-mail norbert.seitz@fes.de; f. 1946; monthly; cultural, political; Editors HOLGER BÖRNER, KLAUS HARPPRECHT, JOHANNES RAU, CAROLA STERN, HANS-JOCHEN VOGEL; circ. 11,000.

Neue Rundschau: Neue Gräustr. 17, 10179 Berlin; tel. (30) 30863912; fax (30) 30863910; f. 1890; quarterly; literature and essays; Editor MARTIN BAUER; circ. 6,000.

Sozialdemokrat Magazin: Am Michaelshof 8, 5300 Bonn 2; tel. (228) 361011; Publr Vorwärts Verlag GmbH; circ. 834,599.

Der Spiegel: Brandstwiete 19/Ost-West-Str. 23, 20457 Hamburg; tel. (40) 30070; fax (40) 30072247; e-mail spiegel@spiegel.de; internet www.spiegel.de; f. 1947; weekly; political, general; Publr RUDOLF AUGSTEIN; Editor-in-Chief STEFAN AUST; circ. 1,050,000.

Universitas: Postfach 101061, 70009 Stuttgart; Birkenwaldstr. 44, 70109 Stuttgart; tel. (711) 25820; fax (711) 2582290; f. 1946; monthly; scientific, literary and philosophical; Editor Dr CHRISTIAN ROTTA; circ. 6,500.

VdK-Zeitung: Wurzerstr. 4A, 53175 Bonn; tel. (228) 820930; fax (228) 8209343; e-mail info@vdk.de; internet www.vdk.de; f. 1950; monthly; Publr Sozialverband VdK Deutschland eV; Editors ULRICH LASCHET, SABINE KOHLS, KRISTINA JOCHUM, MICHAEL PAUSDER, THOMAS A. SEEHUBER; circ. 1,000,000.

VdK-Zeitung, Bayern: Schellingstr. 31, 80799 München; tel. (89) 21170; fax (89) 2117280; e-mail info@vdk.de; internet www.vdk.de; f. 1948; monthly; Publr Sozialverband VdK Deutschland e.V.; Editor ALBRECHT ENGER; circ. 1,100,000.

Welt des Buches: Axel-Springer-Str. 65, 10888 Berlin; tel. (30) 25912916; fax (30) 25912939; e-mail literatur@welt.de; f. 1971; weekly; literary supplement of *Die Welt*.

Popular

Anna: Arabellastr. 23, 81925 München; tel. (89) 92502772; fax (89) 92502745; f. 1974; publ. by Burda GmbH; knitting and needlecrafts; Editor AENNE BURDA.

Auto Bild: Axel-Springer-Platz 1, 20355 Hamburg, tel. (40) 34700; fax (40) 345660; e-mail autobild@asv.de; internet www.autobild.de; f. 1986; publ. by Axel Springer Verlag AG; circ. 837,013.

Das Beste Readers Digest: Postfach 106020, 70049 Stuttgart; Augustenstr. 1, 70178 Stuttgart; tel. (711) 66020; fax (711) 6602547; e-mail verlag@dasbeste.de; internet www.dasbeste.de; magazines, general, serialized and condensed books, music and video programmes; Man. Dir WERNER NEUNZIG; circ. 1,100,000.

Bild der Frau: Axel-Springer-Platz 1, 20355 Hamburg; tel. (40) 34700; f. 1983; publ. by Axel Springer Verlag AG; circ. 1,858,711.

Bild + Funk: Arabellastr. 23, 81925 München; tel. (89) 92502772; fax (89) 92502745; internet www.burda.de; publ. by Burda GmbH; radio and television weekly; Editor GÜNTER VAN WAASEN; circ. 1,040,829.

Brigitte: Gruner + Jahr AG, Am Baumwell 11, 20459 Hamburg; tel. (40) 37030; fax (40) 37035679; internet www.brigitte.de; fortnightly; women's magazine; circ. 1,300,000.

Bunte: Arabellastr. 23, 81925 München; tel. (89) 92500; fax (89) 92503427; internet www.bunte.de; f. 1948; weekly family illustrated; publ. by Burda GmbH; circ. 850,000.

Burda Moden: Arabellastr. 23, 81925 München; tel. (89) 92502772; fax (89) 92502745; e-mail vab@vabab.burda.com; internet www.burda.de; f. 1949; monthly; publ. by Burda GmbH; fashion, beauty, cookery; circ. 2,000,000.

Deutschland: Postfach 10081, 60008 Frankfurt a.M.; Frankenallee 71–81, 60327 Frankfurt a.M.; tel. (69) 75010; fax (69) 75094361; e-mail vertrieb.deutschland@thein-main.net; internet www.magazine-deutschland.de; 6 a year; editions in German, Chinese, English, French, Hebrew, Hungarian, Japanese, Polish, Portuguese, Russian, Spanish, Turkish, Ukrainian; circ. 450,000.

Elle: Arabellastr. 23, 81925 München; tel. (89) 92500; fax (89) 92503030; e-mail elle.mail@icpro.de; publ. by Burda GmbH.

Eltern: Am Baumwall 11, 20459 Hamburg; tel. (89) 41520; fax (89) 4152651; f. 1966; monthly; publ. by Gruner + Jahr AG; for parents; Editor NORBERT HINZE; circ. 645,000.

Eulenspiegel: Gubener Str. 47, 10243 Berlin; tel. (30) 29346311; fax (30) 29346322; e-mail eule@eulenspiegel.b.uunet.de; internet www.bmp.de/eulenspiegel; f. 1946; political satirical and humorous monthly; Editors JÜRGEN NOWAK, HARTMUT BERLIN; circ. 120,000.

Familie & Co: Axel-Springer-Platz 1, 20355 Hamburg; tel. (40) 34700; fax (40) 345811; internet www.familie.de; f. 1996; monthly; publ. by Axel Springer Verlag AG; circ. 243,710.

FF: Mauerstr. 86–88, 10117 Berlin; tel. (30) 231010; fax (30) 23101265; weekly; Editor ALFRED WAGNER; circ. 610,000.

Frau aktuell: Adlerstr. 22, Düsseldorf; tel. (211) 36660; fax (211) 3666231; f. 1965; Editor INGRID THEIS; circ. 450,000.

Frau im Spiegel: Griegstr. 75, 22763 Hamburg; tel. (40) 8830305; fax (40) 88303486; women's magazine; circ. 690,861.

Freundin: Arabellastr. 23, 81925 München; tel. (89) 92500; fax (89) 92503991; e-mail freundin@fmc.burda.com; internet www.freundin.com; f. 1948; fortnightly for young women; publ. by Burda GmbH; Chief Editor ULRIKE SCHLÜTER; circ. 660,070.

Funk Uhr: Axel-Springer-Platz 1, 20355 Hamburg; tel. (40) 34726315; fax (40) 726977; f. 1952; radio and television weekly; publ. by Axel Springer Verlag AG; Editor IMRE KUSZTRICH; circ. 1,305,749.

Für Dich: Karl-Liebknecht-Str. 29, 10178 Berlin; tel. (2) 2440; fax (2) 2443327; f. 1962; women's weekly; Editors HANS EGGERT, Dr PETER PANKAU; circ. 350,000.

Für Sie: Possmoorweg 5, 22301 Hamburg; tel. (40) 27172300; fax (40) 27172048; e-mail anzeigen@fuer-sie.de; internet www.jalag.de; fortnightly; women's magazine; circ. 572,159.

Gong: Innere Cramer-Klett-Str. 6, 90403 Nürnberg; fax (911) 5325197; internet www.gonginfo.de; f. 1948; radio and TV weekly; Editor RAINER STILLER.

Guter Rat!: Mollstr. 1, 10178 Berlin; tel. (30) 23876600; fax (30) 23876395; e-mail redaktion@guter-rat.de; f. 1945; monthly consumer magazine; Editor-in-Chief Dr RAINER BIELING; circ. 260,000.

Hörzu: Postfach 4110, Axel-Springer-Platz 1, 20355 Hamburg; tel. (40) 34700; fax (40) 34722628; f. 1946; radio and television; publ. by Axel Springer Verlag AG; Editor MICHAEL HOHMANN; circ. 2,300,000.

Journal für die Frau: Axel-Springer-Platz 1, 20355 Hamburg; tel. (40) 34700; fax (40) 34727023; e-mail chefredaktion-jfdf@asv.de; f. 1978; fortnightly women's magazine; publ. by Axel Springer Verlag AG; circ. 480,000.

Kicker-Sportmagazin: Badstr. 4–6, 90402 Nürnberg; tel. (911) 2160; e-mail info@kicker.de; internet www.kicker.de; f. 1946; sports weekly illustrated; publ. by Olympia Verlag; Man. Dir DIETRICH PUSCHMANN; circ. 265,978.

Marie Claire: Am Baumwall 11, 20459 Hamburg; tel. 3703226; publ. by Gruner + Jahr AG; circ. 163,388.

Meine Familie & ich: Arabellastr. 23, 81925 München; tel. (89) 92500; fax (89) 92503030; publ. by Burda GmbH; circ. 620,000.

Neue Post: Postfach 100444, Burchardstr. 11, 20095 Hamburg; weekly; circ. 1,728,750.

Neue Revue: Postfach 2411, Ost-West-Str. 20, 20077 Hamburg; tel. (40) 30190; fax (40) 30194401; e-mail neue-revue@hbv.de; f. 1946; illustrated weekly; Editor-in-Chief PETER BARTEL; circ. 1,121,184.

Petra: Jahreszeiten Verlag, Possmoorweg 1, 22301 Hamburg; tel. (40) 27173009; fax (40) 27173020; e-mail redaktion@petra.de; internet www.petra.de; monthly; circ. 390,681.

Praline: Hammerbrookstr. 5, 20097 Hamburg; fax (40) 24870190; weekly; women's magazine; circ. 569,300.

Schöner Wohnen: Am Baumwall 11, 20459 Hamburg; tel. (40) 37032226; monthly; publ. by Gruner + Jahr AG; homes and gardens; Editor ANGELIKA JAHR; circ. 365,000.

7 Tage: Postfach 100450, 76485 Baden-Baden; Stadelhofer Str. 14, 76530 Baden-Baden; tel. (7221) 3501391; fax (7221) 3501399; f. 1843; weekly; Chief Editor KARIN KARSTEN; circ. 480,000.

Sport Bild: Axel-Springer-Platz 1, 20355 Hamburg; tel. (40) 34700; fax (40) 345811; internet www.sportbild.de; f. 1988; weekly; publ. by Axel Springer Verlag AG; circ. 584,921.

Stern: 20444 Hamburg; tel. (40) 37030; fax (40) 37035631; e-mail info@stern.de; internet www.stern.de; illustrated weekly; publ. by Gruner + Jahr AG; Editor-in-Chief Dr MICHAEL MAIER; circ. 1,102,075.

TV Hören+Sehen: Burchardstr. 11, 20095 Hamburg; tel. (40) 30194001; fax (40) 30194081; f. 1962; weekly; Chief Editor MARION HORN; circ. 2,936,670.

TVneu: Axel-Springer-Platz 1, 20355 Hamburg; tel. (40) 34700; fax (40) 345811; publ. by Axel Springer Verlag AG; circ. 917,293.

Wochenend: Burchardstr. 11, 20095 Hamburg; tel. (40) 30190; fax (40) 30194081; f. 1948; weekly; Editor GERD ROHLOF; circ. 668,278.

Religion and Philosophy

Christ in der Gegenwart: Hermann-Herder-Str. 4, 79104 Freiburg i. Br.; tel. (761) 2717276; fax (761) 2717518; e-mail cig@herder.de; f. 1948; weekly; Editor JOHANNES RÖSER; circ. 36,000.

Die Christliche Familie: Ruhrtalstr. 52–60, 45239 Essen; tel. (201) 8492411; f. 1885; weekly; Publr Dr DIRK HERMANN VOSS; Editors ROBERT HIMMRICH, HELGA MECKNER, SABINE SANKE-WASSERMANN.

Der Dom: Karl-Schurz-Str. 26, 33100 Paderborn; tel. (5251) 1530; fax (5251) 153104; f. 1946; weekly; Catholic; Publr Bonifatius GmbH, Druck-Buch-Verlag; circ. 95,000.

Europa Magazin: Postfach 104864, Landhausstr. 82, 70190 Stuttgart; tel. (711) 285500; fax (711) 2855083; e-mail verlag@europa magazin.de; f. 1949; 6 a year; Publr Verlag Axel B. Trunkel.

Evangelischer Digest: Postfach 104864, Landhausstr. 82, 70190 Stuttgart; tel. (711) 285500; fax (711) 2855083; e-mail verlag@ trunkel.de; internet www.trunkel.de; f. 1958; monthly; Publr Verlag Axel B. Trunkel; circ. 9,300.

Katholischer Digest: Postfach 104864, Landhausstr. 82, 70190 Stuttgart; tel. (711) 285500; fax (711) 2855083; e-mail verlag@ trunkel.de; internet www.trunkel.de; f. 1949; monthly; Publr Verlag Axel B. Trunkel; circ. 28,900.

Katholisches Sonntagsblatt: Senefelderstr. 12, 73760 Ostfildern; tel. (711) 44060; fax (711) 4406101; e-mail ks@schwabenverlag.de; internet www.schwabenverlag.de; f. 1848; weekly; Publr Schwaben-verlag AG; circ. 71,500.

Die Kirche: Ziegelstr. 30, 10117 Berlin; tel. (30) 28303922; fax (30) 2829321; f. 1945; Protestant weekly; Editors-in-Chief GERHARD THOMAS, LUTZ BORGMANN; circ. 35,000.

Kirche und Leben: Postfach 4320, 48024 Münster, Antoniuskirch-platz 21, 48151 Münster; tel. (251) 48390; fax (251) 4839122; e-mail k-und-l@muenster.de; internet www.kirche-und-leben .muenster.de; f. 1945; weekly; Catholic; Chief Editor Dr HANS-JOSEF RIESENBECK; circ. 195,000.

Kirchenzeitung für das Erzbistum Köln: Postfach 102041, 50460 Köln; Ursulaplatz 1, 50668 Köln; tel. (221) 1619131; fax (221) 1619216; weekly; Chief Editor Mgr ERICH LÄUFER; circ. 120,000.

Philosophisches Jahrbuch: Ludwig-Maximilians-Universität, Geschwister-Scholl-Platz 1, 80539 München; f. 1893; 2 a year.

Der Sonntagsbrief: Postfach 104864, Landhausstr. 82, 70190 Stuttgart; tel. (711) 285500; fax (711) 2855083; e-mail verlag@ trunkel.de; internet www.trunkel.de; f. 1974; monthly; Publr Verlag Axel B. Trunkel; circ. 36,000.

Standpunkt: Fennstr. 16, 1190 Berlin; tel. (2) 6350915; f. 1973; Protestant monthly; circ. 3,000.

Der Weg: Postfach 102253, 40013 Düsseldorf; tel. (211) 915110; e-mail wegredaktion@ekir.de; weekly; Protestant; Editor ANDREAS KRZOK; circ. 50,000.

Weltbild: Steinerne Furt 67, 86131 Augsburg; tel. (821) 70048350; fax (821) 70048349; fortnightly; Catholic; Editor ALBERT HERCHEN-BACH; circ. 270,000.

Science and Medicine

Angewandte Chemie: Postfach 101161, 69451 Weinheim; tel. (6201) 606315; fax (6201) 602328; e-mail angewandte@wiley-vch.de; f. 1888; fortnightly; circ. 4,000; international edition in English, f. 1962; circ. 3,000.

Ärztliche Praxis: Hans-Cornelius-Str. 4, 82166 Gräfelfing; tel. (89) 898170; fax (89) 89817120; 2 a week; Editor WOLFRAM HAASE; circ. 60,000.

Berichte der Bunsen-Gesellschaft für physikalische Chemie: VCH Verlagsgesellschaft mbH, Postfach 101161, Pappelallee 3, 69451 Weinheim/Bergstr.; tel. (6201) 6060. 1894; monthly; Editors R. AHLRICHS, W. FREYLAND, M. KAPPES, P. C. SCHMIDT; circ. 2,300.

Chemie-Ingenieur-Technik: Postfach 101161, 69451 Weinheim, tel. (6201) 606519; fax (6201) 606500; f. 1928; monthly; Editor R. PFEFFERKORN; circ. 7,807.

Der Chirurg: Kirschnerstr. 1 (INF 110), 69120 Heidelberg; tel. (6221) 402813; fax (6221) 402014; f. 1928; monthly; Editor Prof. Dr Ch. HERFARTH; circ. 7,650.

Deutsche Apotheker Zeitung: Postfach 101061, 70009 Stuttgart; Birkenwaldstr. 44, 70191 Stuttgart; tel. (711) 2582238; fax (711) 2582291; e-mail daz@deutscher-apotheker-verlag.de; f. 1861; weekly; Editor PETER DITZEL; circ. 34,000.

Deutsche Medizinische Wochenschrift: Rüdigerstr. 14, 70469 Stuttgart; tel. (711) 8931232; fax (711) 8931235; e-mail dmw@ thieme.de; internet www.thieme.de/dmw; f. 1875; weekly; Editor-in-Chief M. MIDDEKE; circ. 30,000.

Deutsche Zahnärztliche Zeitschrift: Kolbergerstr. 22, 81679 München; tel. (89) 998300; fax (89) 984809; e-mail info@hanser.de; internet www.zahnheilkunde.de; f. 1945; monthly; dental medicine; Editors Prof. Dr GEURTSEN, Prof. Dr TH. KERSCHBAUM, Dr G. MASCH-INSKI; circ. 5,300.

Elektro-Anzeiger: Ernst-Mey-Str. 8, 70771 Leinfelden-Echterd-ingen; tel. (711) 7594279; fax (711) 7594221; f. 1948; monthly; Editor H. KLEWE; circ. 18,100.

Europa Chemie: Karlstr. 21, 60329 Frankfurt a.M.; tel. (69) 25561516; fax (69) 239564; e-mail europa-chemie@metronet.de; f. 1949; 3 a month; industrial chemistry, the environment and economics; Editor-in-Chief Dr G. SCHRIMPF; circ. 2,800.

Geologische Rundschau: Geologische Vereinigung e.V., Vulk-anstr. 23, 56743 Mendig; tel. (2652) 989360; fax (2652) 989361; e-mail geol.ver@t-online.de; internet www.g-v.de; f. 1910; quarterly; general, geological; Pres. Prof. Dr W. FRANKE; circ. 2,400.

Handchirurgie, Mikrochirurgie, Plastische Chirurgie: Postfach 300504, 70445 Stuttgart; Rüdigerstr. 14, 70469 Stuttgart; tel. (711) 89310; fax (711) 8931453; 6 a year; Editors Prof. Dr med. D. BUCK-GRAMCKO, Prof. Dr W. SCHNEIDER.

Journal of Neurology: Platz der Deutschen Einheit 25, 64293 Dasmstadt; tel. (6151) 828990; fax (6151) 8289940; e-mail tschech.stk@springer.de; f. 1891; official journal of the European Neurological Society; Editors-in-Chief T. BRANDT, D. H. MILLER.

Kerntechnik: Bundesamt für Strahlenschutz, Institut für Strah-lenhygiene, Ingolstaedter Landstr. 1, 85764 Oberschleissheim; tel. (89) 31603101; fax (89) 31603140; e-mail schmitt@bfs.de; f. 1958; publ. by Carl Hanser GmbH; 6 a year; independent journal on nuclear engineering, energy systems and radiation; Editor ANNE-MARIE SCHMITT-HANNIG; circ. 900.

Kosmos: Postfach 106012, Neckarstr. 121, 7000 Stuttgart 10; tel. (711) 26310; fax (711) 2631107; f. 1904; monthly; popular nature journal; Editor Dr RAINER KÖTHE; circ. 80,000.

Mund-, Kiefer- und Gesichtschirurgie: Glückstr. 11, 91054 Erlangen; tel. (9131) 8553601; fax (9131) 8536228; e-mail friedrich.neukam@mkg.imed.uni-erlangen.de; internet www.mkg .uni-erlangen.de; 7 a year; oral and maxillofacial surgery and oral pathology; Editor Prof. Dr Dr FRIEDRICH W. NEUKAM.

Medizinische Klinik: Lindwurmstr. 95, 80337 München; tel. (89) 532920; fax (89) 53292100; e-mail verlag@urban-vogel.de; internet www.urban-vogel.de; f. 1904; monthly; Editor Prof. Dr J. KÖBBER-LING; circ. 10,000.

Nachrichten aus der Chemie: Postfach 900440, 60444 Frankfurt a.M.; tel. (69) 7917462; fax (69) 7917463; e-mail nachrichten@ gdch.de; f. 1953; monthly; journal of the German Chemical Society; Editor-in-Chief Dr ERNST. GUGGOLZ; circ. 30,000.

Naturwissenschaftliche Rundschau: Postfach 101061, 70009 Stuttgart; Birkenwaldstr. 44, 70191 Stuttgart; tel. (711) 2582295; fax (711) 2582283; e-mail nr@wissenschaftliche-verlagsgesell schaft.de; f. 1948; monthly; scientific; Editor KLAUS REHFELD; circ. 7,600.

Planta Medica: Postfach 301120, 70451 Stuttgart, Georg Thieme Verlag, Rüdigerstr. 14, 70469 Stuttgart; tel. (711) 89310; fax (711) 8931298; e-mail leser.service@thieme.de; f. 1952; 8 a year; journal of the Society of Medicinal Plant Research; Editor Prof. Dr ADOLF NAHRSTEDT.

rfe: Am Friedrichshain 22, 10407 Berlin; tel. (30) 42151313; fax (30) 42151208; f. 1952; monthly; technology and marketing of con-sumer good electronics, multimedia, audio, video, broadcasting, TV; circ. 30,000.

Zahnärztliche Praxis: HansCornelius-Str. 4, 82166 München-Gräfelfing; tel. (89) 898170; fax (89) 853799; monthly; circ. 16,500.

Zeitschrift für Allgemeinmedizin: Postfach 300504, 70445 Stuttgart; Steiermärker Str. 3–5, 70469 Stuttgart; tel. (711) 89310; fax (711) 8931706; e-mail ruth.auschra@hippokrates.de; f. 1924; fortnightly; general and family medicine; publ. by Hippokrates Verlag GmbH; Editors Dr W. MAHRINGER, Dr U. MARSCH-ZIEGLER, Prof. Dr M. KOCHEN, Dr H.-H. ABHOLZ; Dr W. NIEBLING, circ. 4,000.

Zeitschrift für Klinische Psychologie u. Psychotherapie: Postfach 2540, Jühenplatz am Rathaus, 33055 Paderborn; f. 1952; quarterly; Editor Prof. Dr F. PETERMANN.

Zeitschrift für Metallkunde: Heisenbergstr. 5, 70569 Stuttgart; tel. (711) 6861200; fax (711) 6861255; f. 1911; monthly; metal research; Editors G. PETZOW, M. RÜHLE, P. P. SCHEPP.

Zeitschrift für Psychologie mit Zeitschrift für angewandte Psychologie: Postfach 100109, 04001 Leipzig; tel. (341) 9929200; fax (341) 9929209; internet www.psychologie.huberlin.de/ psyzeit.html; f. 1890; 4 a year; psychology and applied psychology; Editors Prof. Dr F. KLIX, Prof. Dr W. HACKER, Prof. Dr E. VAN DER MEER, Dr M. ZIESSLER, Dr H. HAGENDORF, R. GRUHN; circ. 600.

Zentralblatt für Neurochirurgie: Heinrich-Heine-Universität, Moorenstr. 5, 40225 Düsseldorf; tel. (211) 8117910; fax (211) 316512; f. 1936; 4 a year; neuro-surgery, spine surgery, traumatology; Editor Prof. Dr W. J. BOCK; circ. 1,000.

NEWS AGENCIES

Allgemeiner Deutscher Nachrichtendienst GmbH (ADN): Mollstr. 1, 10178 Berlin; tel. (30) 231220; fax (30) 23122118; e-mail redaktion@adn.de; internet www.adn.de; f. 1946; fmrly official news agency of the GDR; maintains 20 branch offices in Germany; prov-ides a daily news service and features in German; Man. Dirs LUTZ SCHUMACHER, Dr MARCUS ENGLERT.

Deutsche Presse-Agentur GmbH (dpa): Mittelweg 38, 20148 Hamburg; tel. (40) 41130; fax (40) 41132219; e-mail info@dpa.de;

f. 1949; supplies all the daily newspapers, broadcasting stations and more than 1,000 further subscribers throughout Germany with its national and regional text, photo, audio, graphics and online services. English, Spanish, Arabic and German language news is also transmitted via direct satellite and the internet to press agencies, newspapers, radio and television stations, online services and non-media clients in more than 100 countries; Dir Gen. Dr WALTER RICHTBERG; Editor-in-Chief Dr WILM HERLYN.

VWD: Niederurseler Allee 8–10, 65760 Eschborn; tel. (6196) 4050; fax (6196) 482007; e-mail hbutterweck@vwd.de; internet www.vwd.de; economic and financial news.

Foreign Bureaux

Agence France-Presse (AFP): Friedrichstr. 108–109, 10117 Berlin; tel. (30) 30876110; fax (30) 30876270; e-mail post@afp.de; internet www.afp.de; Mans N. C. WORTMANN, P. FEUILLY.

Agencia EFE (Spain): Heussallee 2–10, Pressehaus II/12–14, 53113 Bonn; tel. (228) 214058; fax (228) 224147; Bureau Chief GUILLERMO DÍAZ.

Agenzia Nazionale Stampa Associata (ANSA) (Italy): Savignyplatz 6, 10623 Berlin; tel. (30) 3127745; fax (30) 3127747; Bureau Chief FLAMINIA BUSSOTTI.

Associated Press GmbH (AP) (USA): Moselstr. 27, Frankfurt a.M; tel. (69) 272300; fax (69) 251289; also in Hamburg, Stuttgart, Berlin, Munich; Man. STEPHEN H. MILLER.

Česká tisková kancelář (ČTK) (Czech Republic): Heussallee 2–10, Pressehaus I/207, 53113 Bonn; tel. (228) 215811; fax 214189; f. 1918; Correspondent FRANTIŠEK VACLAVIK.

Informatsionnoye Telegrafnoye Agentstvo Rossii-Telegrafnoye Agentstvo Suverennykh Stran (ITAR-TASS) (Russia): Heussallee 2–10, Pressehaus I/133, 53113 Bonn; tel. (228) 215665; fax (228) 210627.

Inter Press Service (IPS) (Italy): Heussallee 2–10, Pressehaus II/205, 53113 Bonn; tel. (228) 9145710; fax (228) 261205; Bureau Chief RAMESH JAURA.

Jiji Tsushin-sha (Japan): Mittelweg 38, 20148 Hamburg; tel. (40) 445553; fax (40) 456849.

Kyodo Tsushin (Japan): Bonn-Center, Bundeskanzlerplatz 2–10, 53113 Bonn; tel. (228) 225543; fax (228) 222198; Chief Correspondent KAKUYA OGATA.

Magyar Távirati Iroda (MTI) (Hungary): Heussallee 2–10, Pressehaus I/202, 53113 Bonn; tel. (228) 210820; fax (228) 210821; Correspondent LÁSZLÓ DOROGMAN.

Reuters (UK): Friedrich-Ebert-Anlage 49, 60327 Frankfurt a.M.; tel. (69) 75651000; fax (69) 75651515; internet www.reuters.de.

United Press International (UPI) (USA): Heussallee 2–10, Pressehaus II/224, Bonn; tel. (228) 263787; Bureau Man. and Chief Correspondent PETER G. BILD.

Xinhua (New China) News Agency (People's Republic of China): Lyngsbergstr. 33, 5300 Bonn 2; tel. (228) 331845; fax (228) 331247; Chief Correspondent HU XUDONG.

RIA–Novosti (Russia) is also represented.

PRESS AND JOURNALISTS' ASSOCIATIONS

Bundesverband Deutscher Zeitungsverleger eV (German Newspaper Publishers' Association): Postfach 205002, 53170 Bonn; Riemenschneiderstr. 10, 53175 Bonn; tel. (228) 810040; fax (228) 8100415; e-mail bdzv@bdzv.de; internet www.bdzv.de; 11 affiliated Land Asscns; Pres. WILHELM SANDMANN; Chief Sec. Dr VOLKER SCHULZE.

Deutscher Journalisten-Verband (German Journalists' Association): Bennauerstr. 60, 53115 Bonn; tel. (228) 201720; fax (228) 2017233; e-mail djv@djv.de; internet www.djv.de; Chair. Dr HERMANN MEYN; Man. Dir HUBERT ENGEROFF; 16 Land Asscns.

Verband Deutscher Zeitschriftenverleger eV (Association of German Publishers of Periodicals): Markgrafenstr. 15, 10969 Berlin; tel. (30) 726298101; fax (30) 7262898103; e-mail info@vdz.de; internet www.vdz.de; seven affiliated Land Asscns; Pres. Dr HUBERT BURDA; Man. Dir WOLFGANG FÜRSTNER.

Verein der Ausländischen Presse (VAP) (Foreign Press Association): Heussallee 2–10, Pressehaus I/35, 53113 Bonn; tel. (228) 210810; fax (228) 219672; f. 1951; Chair. AHMET KÜLAHCI.

Publishers

The following is a selection of the most prominent German publishing firms:

ADAC Verlag GmbH: Am Westpark 8, 81373 München; tel. (89) 76760; fax (89) 76764621; e-mail clare.billig@zentrale.adac.de; internet www.adac.de; f. 1958; guidebooks, legal brochures, maps,

magazines ADAC-Motorwelt, Deutsches Autorecht; Man. Dir MANFRED M. ANGELE.

Ariston Verlag GmbH & Co KG: Boschetsrieder Str. 12, 81379 München; tel. (89) 7241034; fax (89) 7241718; f. 1964; medicine, psychology; Man. Dir FRANK AUERBACH.

Aufbau-Verlag GmbH: Neue Promenade 6, 10178 Berlin; tel. (30) 283940; fax (30) 28394100; e-mail info@aufbau-verlag.de; f. 1945; fiction, non-fiction, classical literature; Dir PETER DEMPEWOLF.

J.P. Bachem Verlag GmbH: Ursulaplatz 1, 50668 Köln; tel. (221) 16190; fax (221) 1619159; f. 1818; economics, social science, religion; Dirs Dr CLEMENS J. B. SANDMANN, LAMBERT BACHEM.

Bauverlag GmbH: Am Klingenweg 4A, 65396 Walluf; tel. (61213) 7000; fax (61213) 700122; f. 1929; civil engineering, architecture, environment, energy, etc.; Dirs OTTO GMEINER, REINER GROCHOWSKI.

Verlag C. H. Beck oHg: Postfach 400340, 80703 München, Wilhelmstr. 9, 80801 München; tel. (89) 381890; fax (89) 38189398; e-mail info@beck.de; internet www.beck.de; f. 1763; law, science, theology, archaeology, philosophy, philology, history, politics, art, literature; Dirs Dr HANS DIETER BECK, WOLFGANG BECK.

Bertelsmann Buch AG: Neumarkterstr. 18, 81673 München; tel. (89) 43720; fax (89) 43722938; f. 1994; general, reference; Chair. FRANK WÖSSNER.

Bibliographisches Institut und F. A. Brockhaus GmbH: Postfach 100311, 68167 Dudenstr. 6, 68003 Mannheim; tel. (621) 390101; fax (621) 3901391; f. 1805; encyclopaedias, dictionaries, travel, natural sciences, memoirs, archaeology; Dirs HUBERTUS BROCKHAUS, CLAUS GREUNER, Dr MICHAEL WEGNER.

BLV Verlagsgesellschaft mbH: Lothstr. 29, 80797 München; tel. (89) 127050; fax (89) 12705354; e-mail blv-verlag@t-online.de; internet www.blv.de; f. 1946; gardening, nature, sports, fitness, equestrian, hunting, fishing, travel, food and drink, agriculture; Man. Dirs HARTWIG SCHNEIDER (books), HANS-PETER KLIEMANN (magazines).

Breitkopf & Härtel: Postfach 1707, Walkmühlstr. 52, 65195 Wiesbaden; tel. (611) 450080; fax (611) 4500859; f. 1719; music and music books; Dirs LIESELOTTE SIEVERS, GOTTFRIED MÖCKEL.

Brönner Verlag GmbH: Stuttgarter Str. 18–24, 6000 Frankfurt a.M. 1; tel. (69) 26000; fax (69) 2600223; art; Dirs KLAUS BREIDENSTEIN, HANS-JÜRGEN BREIDENSTEIN.

Verlag Bruckmann München: Nymphenburgerstr. 86, 80636 München; tel. (89) 125701; fax (89) 1257269; f.1858; books, calendars, video cassettes, magazines, fine art prints, original prints; Man. Dir Dr JÖRG D. STIEBNER.

Bund-Verlag GmbH: Postfach 900168, 60441 Frankfurt; Theodor-Heuss-Allee 90–96, 60486 Frankfurt; tel. (69) 7950100; fax (69) 79501010; e-mail kontakt@bund-verlag.de; internet www.bund-verlag.de; f. 1947; legal studies and commentaries, economics, politics, etc.; Man. Dir CHRISTIAN POULSEN.

Verlag Georg D. W. Callwey GmbH & Co: Streitfeldstr. 35, 81673 München; tel. (89) 4360050; fax (89) 436005113; e-mail buch@callwey.de; internet www.callwey.de; f. 1884; architecture, painting, gardens, art restoration, crafts, do-it-yourself; Man. Dirs HELMUTH BAUR-CALLWEY, Dr VERONIKA BAUR-CALLWEY.

Carlsen Verlag GmbH: Postfach 500380, 22703 Hamburg; Völckersstr. 14–20, 22765 Hamburg; tel. (40) 3910090; fax (40) 39100962; e-mail kaempfe-burghard@carlsen.de; internet www.carlsen.de; f. 1953; children's and comic books; Dirs KLAUS HUMANN, KLAUS KÄMPFE-BURGHARDT.

Cornelsen Verlag GmbH & Co: Mecklenburgische Str. 53, 14197 Berlin; tel. (30) 897850; fax (30) 89786299; e-mail e-mail@cornelsen.de; internet www.cornelsen.de; f. 1946; school textbooks, educational software; Man. Dirs HANS-JÖRG DÜLLEMANN, ALFRED GRÜNER, JÜRGEN L. PETER, Dr HANS WEYMAR.

Delius Klasing Verlag: Siekerwall 21, 33602 Bielefeld; tel. (521) 5590; fax (521) 559113; e-mail info@delius-klasing.de; internet www.delius-klasing.de; f. 1911; yachting, motor boats, surfing, mountain biking, race biking, basketball, motor cars; Dir KONRAD DELIUS.

Deutsche Verlags-Anstalt GmbH: Postfach 106012, 70049 Stuttgart; Neckarstr. 121, 70190 Stuttgart; tel. (711) 26310; fax (711) 2631292; e-mail info@dva.de; f. 1831; general; CEO JÜRGEN HORBACH.

Deutscher Taschenbuch Verlag GmbH & Co KG (dtv): Postfach 400422, 80704 München; Friedrichstr. 1A, 80801 München; tel. (89) 381670; fax (89) 346428; e-mail verlag@dtv.de; internet www.dtv.de; f. 1961; general fiction, history, music, reference, children, natural and social science, medicine, textbooks; Man. Dirs WOLFGANG BALK, MARKUS ANGST.

Verlag Moritz Diesterweg: Hedderichstr. 108–110, 60596 Frankfurt a.M.; tel. (69) 420810; fax (69) 42081205; f. 1860; text books, languages, social sciences, sciences, pedagogics; Dirs RALF MEIER, KARL SLIPEK.

Droemersche Verlagsanstalt Th. Knaur Nachf GmbH & Co: Rauchstr. 9–11, 81679 München; tel. (89) 92710; fax (89) 9271168; f. 1901; general literature, non-fiction, art books, paperbacks; Man. Dirs Peter Schaper, Dr Günther Fetzer.

DuMont Buchverlag GmbH & Co KG: Amsterdamer Str. 192, 50735 Köln; tel. (221) 224190; fax (221) 2241812; internet www .dumontverlag.de; f. 1956; archaeology, art, design, garden, travel, guidebooks, cookery, calendars, etc.; Publr Dr Gottfried Honne-felder.

Econ Verlagsgruppe: Postfach 151329, Goethestr. 43, 80336 München; fax (89) 5148229; e-mail michael.then@verlag.goethestr .com; general fiction and non-fiction, business and computing books; Publr Christian Strasser; Editor-in-Chief Margit Ketterle.

Egmont Pestalozzi Verlag GmbH: Schleifsheimer Str. 267, 80809 München; tel. (89) 358116; fax (89) 35811869; internet www .pestalozzi-verlag.de; f. 1844; children's books; Man. Dirs Rehné Herzig, Frank Knau.

Egmont VGS Verlagsgesellschaft mbH: Gertrudenstr. 30–36, 50667 Köln; tel. (221) 208110; fax (221) 2081166; e-mail info@vgs.de; internet www.vgs.de; f. 1970; fiction, hobbies, natural sciences, culture, popular culture, TV, history, etc.; Dir Michael Schweins.

Eichborn Verlag: Kaiserstr. 66, 60329 Frankfurt a.M. 1; tel. (69) 2560030; fax (69) 25600330; f. 1980; literature non-fiction, historical science, humour, cartoons; Man. Dir Dr Matthias Kierzek.

Europaverlag: Mauerkirchestr. 8, 81679 München; tel. (89) 9827790; fax (89) 98277950; e-mail info@europaverlag.de; fiction, non-fiction, poetry, biography and current events; Dirs Gisela Anna Stümpel, Wolfgang Weidmann.

Falk-Verlag GmbH: Im Gleisdreieck 5, 21035 Hamburg; tel. (40) 725990; fax (40) 72599200; f. 1945; maps, guidebooks, phrasebooks; Man. Dir Dr Helge Lintzhöft.

Falken-Verlag GmbH: Schöne Aussicht 21, 65527 Niedernhausen; tel. (6127) 7020; fax (6127) 702133; internet www.falken.de; f. 1923; health, cooking, management, business; Man. Dir Dr Hans-Ulrich von Freyberg.

S. Fischer Verlag GmbH: Postfach 700355, 60553 Frankfurt a.M.; Hedderichstr. 114, 60596 Frankfurt a.M.; tel. (69) 60620; fax (69) 6062319; e-mail info@s-fischer.de; internet www.s-fischer.de; f. 1886; general, paperbacks; Publr Monika Schoeller; Man. Dirs Dr Hubertus Schenkel, Frank Trümper.

Franzis' Verlag GmbH: Gruber Str. 46, 85586 Poing; tel. (8121) 950; fax (8121) 951696; internet www.franzis.de; f. 1924; Gen. Man. Dr Rüdiger Henniss.

Gräfe und Unzer Verlag GmbH: Grillparzer Str. 12, 81675 München; tel. (89) 419810; fax (89) 41981113; internet www .graefe-und-unzer.de; f. 1722; cookery, health, nature, travel, business; Man. Dirs Frank H. Häger, Dr Stefan Hoyer, Claudia Reitter.

Walter de Gruyter GmbH & Co KG Verlag: Postfach 303421, 10728 Berlin; Genthiner Str. 13, 10785 Berlin; tel. (30) 260050; fax (30) 26005251; internet www.degruyter.de; f. 1919; humanities and theology, law, science, medicine, mathematics, economics, general; Man. Dirs Reinhold Tokar, Dr Hans-Robert Cram.

Hallwag Verlag GmbH: Postfach 4266, 73745 Ostfildern; Brunnwiesenstr. 23, 73760 Ostfildern; tel. (711) 449840; fax (711) 44984-60; maps, travel guides, wine, other reference.

Carl Hanser Verlag: Kolbergerstr. 22, 81679 München; tel. (89) 998300; fax (89) 984809; internet www.hanser.de; f. 1928; modern literature, plastics, technology, chemistry, science, dentistry; Man. Dirs Wolfgang Beisler, Stephan D. Joss, Michael Krüger.

Harenberg Kommunikation Verlags- und Mediengesellschaft mbH & Co KG: Postfach 101852, 44018 Dortmund; Königswall 21, 44137 Dortmund; tel. (231) 90560; fax (231) 9056110; e-mail post@ harenberg.de; internet www.harenberg.de; f. 1973; almanacs, encyclopaedias, calendars, periodicals; Man. Dir Bodo Harenberg.

Rudolf Haufe Verlag GmbH & Co KG: Hindenburgstr. 64, 79102 Freiburg i. Br.; tel. (761) 36830; fax (761) 3683195; e-mail online @haufe.de; internet haufe.de; f. 1934; business, law, finance, social science; Man. Dirs Uwe Renald Müller, Martin Laqua, Helmuth Hopfner.

Verlag Herder GmbH & Co KG: Hermann-Herder-Str. 4; 79104 Freiburg i. Br., tel. (761) 27170; fax (761) 2717520; e-mail vertrieb@ herder.de; f. 1801; religion, philosophy, psychology, history, education, art, encyclopaedias, children's books, gift books, periodicals; Proprs Dr Hermann Herder, Manuel Gregor Herder.

Wilhelm Heyne Verlag: Türkenstr. 5–7, 80333 München; tel. (89) 286350; fax (89) 2800943; e-mail verlag@heyne; internet www .heyne.de; f. 1934; fiction, biography, history, cinema, etc.; Publr Rolf Heyne.

Hoffmann und Campe Verlag: Postfach 1304445, 20139 Hamburg; Harvestehuderweg 42, 20149 Hamburg; tel. (40) 441880; fax (40) 44188202; e-mail cladia.fischer@hoca.de; internet

www.hoffmann-und-campe.de; f. 1781; biography, fiction, history, economics, science; Man. Dirs Dr Raimer Moritz, Uwe Matsen.

Dr Alfred Hüthig Verlag GmbH: Im Weiher 10, 6900 Heidelberg; tel. (6221) 4890; fax (6221) 489279; f. 1925; chemistry, chemical engineering, metallurgy, dentistry, etc.

Axel Juncker-Verlag: Postfach 401120, Neusser Str. 3, 80711 München; tel. (89) 360960; fax (89) 36096222; f. 1902; dictionaries, phrase-books; Man. Dirs Karl Ernst Tielebier-Langenscheidt, Andreas Langenscheidt.

S. Karger GmbH: Lörracherstr. 16A, 79115 Freiburg; tel. (761) 452070; fax (761) 4520714; f. 1890; medicine, psychology, natural science; Man. Dir S. Karger.

Gustav Kiepenheuer Verlag: Gerichtsweg 28, 04103 Leipzig; tel. (341) 9954600; fax (341) 9954620; f. 1909; fiction, non-fiction, cultural history; Chief Editor Birgit Peter.

Verlag Kiepenheuer & Witsch & Co: Rondorferstr. 5, 50968 Köln 51; tel. (221) 376850; fax (221) 388595; e-mail umolitor@ kiwi-koeln.de; internet www.kiwi-koeln.de; f. 1948; general fiction, biography, history, sociology, politics; Man. Dir Dr Reinhold Neven du Mont.

Ernst Klett Verlag: Postfach 106016, 70049 Stuttgart; tel. (711) 66720; fax (711) 6672800; f. 1844; secondary school and university textbooks (especially German as a foreign language), dictionaries, atlases, teaching aids; Dirs Michael Klett, Roland Klett, Dr Thomas Klett.

Verlag W. Kohlhammer GmbH: Hessbrühlstr. 69, 70565 Stuttgart; tel. (711) 78630; fax (711) 7863263; f. 1866; periodicals, general textbooks; Man. Dirs Dr Jürgen Gutbrod, Hans-Joachim Nagel.

Kösel-Verlag GmbH & Co: Flüggenstr. 2, 80639 München; tel. (89) 178010; fax (89) 1780111; f. 1593; philosophy, religion, psychology, esoteric, family and education; Dir Dr Christoph Wild.

Kreuz Verlag GmbH: Postfach 800669; Breitwiesenstr. 30, 70565 Stuttgart; tel. (711) 788030; fax (711) 7880310; f. 1983; theology, psychology, pedagogics; Man. Dir Dr Sabine Schubert.

Verlag der Kunst GmbH: Rosa-Menzer-Str. 12, 01309 Dresden; tel. (351) 3100052; fax (351) 3105245; e-mail verlag-der-kunst.dd@ t-online.de; www.txt.de/vdk; f. 1952; art books and reproductions; Dir Roger N. Greene.

Peter Lang GmbH: Postfach 940225, Eschborner Landstr. 42–50, 60489 Frankfurt a.M.; tel. (69) 7807050; fax (69) 78070550; e-mail 101622.27@compuserve.com; internet www.peterlang.de; sociology, politics, communications, linguistics, science of law, literature, theology, economics.

Langenscheidt-Verlag: Postfach 401120, 80807 München; Neusser Str. 3, Crellestr. 28–30, 10827 Berlin; tel. (89) 360960; fax (89) 36096222; internet www.langenscheidt.de; f. 1856; foreign languages, German for foreigners, dictionaries, textbooks, language guides, records, tapes, cassettes, video cassettes, software, electronic dictionaries; Man. Dirs Karl Ernst Tielebier-Langenscheidt, Andreas Langenscheidt.

Paul List Verlag KG: Goethestr. 43, 8000 München 2; tel. (89) 51480; fax (89) 5148185; f. 1894; general fiction, history, music, art, philosophy, religion, psychology, school books; Editorial Dir Gerald Trageiser.

Gustav Lübbe Verlag GmbH: Scheidtbachstr. 23–25, 51469 Bergisch Gladbach; tel. (2202) 1210; f. 1964; general fiction and non-fiction, biography, history, etc. Man. Dirs Peter Molden, Dr Peter Roggen.

Hermann Luchterhand Verlag GmbH: Postfach 2352, 56513 Neuwied; Heddesdorfer Str. 31, 56564 Neuwied; tel. (2631) 8010; fax (2631) 801210; e-mail into@luchterhand.de; internet www.luchter hand.de; f. 1924; insurance, law, taxation, labour; Man. Dir J. Luczak.

Mairs Geographischer Verlag: Postfach 3151, Marco-Polo-Zentrum, 7302 Ostfildern 4, tel. (711) 45020; fax (711) 4502310; f. 1848; road maps, atlases, tourist guides; Man. Dir Dr Volkmar Mair.

J. B. Metzler Verlag: Postfach 103241, Kernerstr. 43, 70028 Stuttgart; tel. (711) 229020; fax (711) 2290290; internet www .metzlerverlag.de; f. 1682; literature, music, pedagogics, linguistics, history, economics, commerce, textbooks; Dir Dr Bernd Lutz.

Verlag Moderne Industrie AG & Co KG: Justus-von-Liebig-Str. 1, 86895 Landsberg; tel. (8191) 1250; fax (8191) 125211; f. 1952; management, investment, technical; Man. Dir Dr Hans-Joachim Hartmann.

Morgenbuch Verlag GmbH: Seelenbinderstr. 152, 1170 Berlin; tel. (2) 6504151. 1958; belles-lettres, politics; Dir Dr Wolfgang Tenzler.

Verlagsgesellschaft Rudolf Müller GmbH & Co KG: Stolberger Str. 84, 50933 Köln; tel. (221) 54970; fax (221) 5497326; e-mail vbv@rudolf-mueller.de; internet www.rudolf-mueller.de; f. 1840;

architecture, construction, engineering, education; Publrs CHRISTOPH MÜLLER, RUDOLF M. BLESER, GÜNTER SANDSCHEPER.

Verlag Friedrich Oetinger: Poppenbütteler Chaussee 53, 22397 Hamburg; tel. (40) 60790902; fax (40) 6072326; e-mail oetlinger@vsg-hamburg.de; juvenile, illustrated books; Man. Dirs SILKE WEITENDORF, THOMAS HUGGLE.

R. Oldenbourg Verlag GmbH: Rosenheimerstr. 145, 81671 München; tel. (89) 4904110; fax (89) 490411207; internet www .oldenbourg.de; f. 1858; technology, science, history, textbooks, mathematics, economics, dictionaries, periodicals; Dirs Dr T. VON CORNIDES, Dr D. HOHM, WOLFGANG DICK, JOHANNES OLDENBOURG.

Omnis Verlag GmbH: Hohenzollerndamm 174, 10713 Berlin; tel. (30) 85962838; fax (30) 85962840; e-mail info@omnis-verlag.de; art, children's, belles-lettres, history.

Verlagsunion Erich Pabel–Arthur Moewig KG: Karlsruher Str. 31, 76437 Rastatt; tel. (7222) 130; fax (7222) 13301; Gen. Man. GERHARD STEDTFELD.

Verlag Paul Parey: Spitalerstr. 12, 20095 Hamburg; tel. (40) 339690; fax (40) 33969198; internet www.parey.de; f. 1848; biology, botany, zoology, ethology, veterinary science, laboratory animals science, food technology and control, agriculture, starch research and technology, brewing and distilling, forestry, horticulture, phytomedicine, plant and environment protection, water management, hunting, fishing, dogs, equitation; technical and scientific journals; Dirs Dr FRIEDRICH GEORGI, Dr RUDOLF GEORGI.

Manfred Pawlak Grossantiquariat und Verlagsgesellschaft mbH: Gachenau Str. 31, 8036 Herrsching; tel. (8152) 37070; fax (8152) 370748; f. 1949; history, art, general interest; Dir ULRIKE PAWLAK.

Piper Verlag GmbH: Postfach 430861, Georgenstr. 4, 80799 München; tel. (89) 3818010; fax (89) 338704; e-mail info@piper.de; f. 1904; literature, philosophy, theology, psychology, natural sciences, political and social sciences, history, biographies, music; Dir VIKTOR NIEMANN.

Quell Verlag: Postfach 897, Furtbachstr. 12A, 7000 Stuttgart 1; tel. (711) 601000; f. 1830; Protestant literature; Dirs Dr WOLFGANG REISTER, WALTER WALDBAUER.

Ravensburger Buchverlag Otto Maier GmbH: Postfach 1860, Marktstr. 22–26, 88188 Ravensburg, 88212 Ravensburg; tel. (751) 860; fax (751) 861289; e-mail info@ravensburger.de; internet www.ravensburger.de; f. 1883; Man. Dirs Dr DETLEV LUX, HANSJÖRG SCHIRMER.

Philipp Reclam jun. Verlag GmbH: Siemensstr. 32, 71254 Ditzingen bei Stuttgart; tel. (7156) 1630; fax (7156) 163197; e-mail werbung@reclam.de; internet www.reclam.de; f. 1828; literature, literary criticism, fiction, history of culture and literature, philosophy and religion, biography, fine arts, music; Partner FRANK RAINER MAX.

Rowohlt Taschenbuch Verlag GmbH: Hamburgerstr. 17, 21465 Reinbek bei Hamburg; tel. (40) 72721; fax (40) 7272319; internet www.rowohlt.de; f. 1908/1953; politics, science, fiction, translations of international literature; Dirs Dr HELMUT DÄHNE, NICOLAUS HANSEN.

K.G. Saur Verlag: Postfach 701649, 81316 München; Ortlerstr. 8, 81373 München; tel. (89) 769020; fax (89) 76902150; e-mail k.saur@saur.de; internet www.saur.de; f. 1949; library science, reference, dictionaries, microfiches; 2 brs in Leipzig and Zürich; subsidiary of the Gale Group, Div of Thomson Learning Int.

F.K. Schattauer Verlag GmbH: Postfach 104545, 70040 Stuttgart; Hoelderlinstr. 3, 70192 Stuttgart; tel. (711) 229870; fax (711) 2298750; e-mail info@schattauer.de; internet www.schattauer.de; f. 1949; medicine and related sciences; Publr DIETER BERGEMANN.

Scherz Verlag GmbH: Stievestr. 9, 8000 München 19; tel. (89) 172237; fax (89) 174030; f. 1957; general fiction, history, politics, etc.; Man. Dir RUDOLF STREIT-SCHERZ.

Verlag Dr Otto Schmidt KG: Unter den Ulmen 96–98, 50968 Köln; tel. (221) 9373801; fax (221) 93738943; f. 1905; university textbooks, jurisprudence, tax law; Man. Dir K. P. WINTERS.

Egmont Franz Schneider Verlag GmbH: Schleissheimer Str. 267, 80809 München; tel. (89) 358116; fax (89) 35811755; e-mail postmaster@schneiderbuch.de; f. 1913; children's books; Publr Dr WOLFGANG REINHARD.

Schroedel Schulbuchverlag GmbH: Hildesheimer Str. 202–206, 30519 Hannover; tel. (511) 83880; fax (511) 8388343; f. 1982; school textbooks and educational software; Man. Dirs THOMAS BAUMANN, Dr WERNER KUGEL.

Springer-Verlag GmbH & Co KG: Heidelberger Platz 3, 14197 Berlin; tel. (30) 827870; fax (30) 8214091; f. 1842; medicine, biology, mathematics, physics, chemistry, psychology, engineering, geosciences, philosophy, law, economics; Proprs Prof Dr DIETRICH GÖTZE, RÜDIGER GEBAUER, ARNOED KIEL, Dr HANS-DIETER HAENEL.

Stamm Verlag: Fuggerstr. 7, 51149 Köln; e-mail info@stam.de; internet www.stam.de; reference.

Stollfuss Verlag Bonn GmbH & Co KG: Dechenstr. 7, 53115 Bonn; tel. (228) 7240; fax (228) 659723; reference, fiscal law, economics, investment, etc.; Man. Dir WOLFGANG STOLLFUSS.

Suhrkamp Verlag GmbH & Co: Postfach 101945, 60019 Frankfurt a.M.; Suhrkamp Haus, Lindenstr. 29–35, 60325 Frankfurt a.M.; tel. (69) 756010; fax (69) 75601522; e-mail unseld@suhrkamp.de; internet www.suhrkamp.de; f. 1950; modern German and foreign literature, philosophy, poetry; Dir Dr SIEGFRIED UNSELD.

Sybex Verlag GmbH: Erkratherstr. 345–349, 40231 Düsseldorf; tel. (211) 97390; fax (211) 9739199; e-mail sybex@sybex.de; internet www.sybex.de; f. 1981; computer books and software; Man. Dirs HANS NOLDEN, RODNAY ZAKS.

Georg Thieme Verlag: Postfach 301120; 70451 Stuttgart; Rüdigerstr. 14, 70469 Stuttgart; tel. (711) 89310; fax (711) 8931298; e-mail info@thieme.com; internet www.thieme.com; f. 1886; medicine and natural science; Man. Dirs Dr GÜNTHER HAUFF, ALBRECHT HAUFF.

K. Thienemanns Verlag: Blumenstr. 36, 70182 Stuttgart; tel. (711) 210550; fax (711) 2105539; f. 1849; picture books, children's books, juveniles; Dirs HANSJÖRG WEITBRECHT, GUNTER EHNI.

transpress Verlagsgesellschaft mbH: Borkumstr. 2, 13181 Berlin; tel. (30) 47805151; fax (30) 47805160; f. 1990; specialized literature on transport and marketing; Man. Dr HARALD BÖTTCHER.

Verlag Eugen Ulmer GmbH & Co: Postfach 700561, 70574 Stuttgart; tel. (711) 45070; fax (711) 4507120; e-mail info@ulmer.de; f. 1868; agriculture, horticulture, science, periodicals; Dir ROLAND ULMER.

Verlag Ullstein GmbH: Charlottenstr. 13, 10969 Berlin; tel. (30) 25913570; fax (30) 25913523; f. 1894; literature, art, music, theatre, contemporary history, biography; Pres. Dr JÜRGEN RICHTER.

Urban & Fischer Verlag GmbH & Co KG: Postfach 100537, 07705 Jena; Löbdergraben 14A, 07745 Jena; tel. (3641) 6263; fax (3641) 626500; e-mail journals@urbanfischer.de; internet www .urbanfischer.de/journals; f. 1878; biological science, medical science; Dir BERND ROLLE.

Urban & Schwarzenberg GmbH: Landwehrstr. 61, 8000 München 2; tel. (89) 53830; fax (89) 5383221; f. 1866; medicine, natural sciences; Man. Dir MICHAEL URBAN.

Weltbild Verlag GmbH: Steinerne Furt 67–72, 86167 Augsburg; tel. (821) 70040; fax (821) 7004279; f. 1949; religion, philosophy, fashion, heraldry, nature and environment, culture, history, photography, literature, health, travel.

Georg Westermann Verlag GmbH: Postfach 3320, Georg-Westermann-Allee 66, 38023 Braunschweig; tel. (531) 7080; fax (531) 796569; f. 1838; non-fiction, paperbacks, periodicals; Dir Dr HANS-DIETER MÖLLER.

Wiley-VCH Verlag: Postfach 101161, Pappelallee 3, 69451 Weinheim; tel. (6201) 6060; fax (6201) 6063288; e-mail info@wiley-vch.de; internet www.wiley-vch.de; f. 1921; natural sciences, especially chemistry, chemical engineering, biotechnology, materials science, life sciences, information technology and physics, law, scientific software; Man. Dir Dr MANFRED ANTONI.

Verlag Klaus Wingefeld: Lindenstr. 12, 71686 Remseck; fax (7146) 871881; e-mail kinderbuchverlag@t-online.de.

PRINCIPAL ASSOCIATION OF BOOK PUBLISHERS AND BOOKSELLERS

Börsenverein des Deutschen Buchhandels eV (German Publishers and Booksellers Association): Postfach 100442, 60004 Frankfurt a.M.; Grosser Hirschgraben 17–21, 60311 Frankfurt a.M.; tel. (69) 13060; fax (69) 1306201; e-mail info@boev.de; internet www.boersenverein.de; f. 1825; Chair. ROLAND ULMER; Man. Dir Dr HARALD HEKER.

Broadcasting and Communications

TELECOMMUNICATIONS

debitel AG: 70545 Stuttgart; e-mail presse@de.debitel.com; internet www.debitel.com; owned by Swisscom AG.

Deutsche Telekom AG: Postfach 2000, 53105 Bonn; tel.(228) 1810; fax (228) 1818872; e-mail gd-bonn02@bonn02.telekom400.dbp.de; internet www.dtag.de; f. 1989; partially privatized 1996 with further privatization pending, 43% state-owned; fmr monopoly over national telecommunications network removed Jan. 1998; Chair. Supervisory Bd ROLF-DIETER LEISTER; CEO RON SOMMER.

e-plus Mobilfunk GmbH: Postfach 300307, 40403 Düsseldorf; E-Plus-Platz 1, 40468 Düsseldorf; tel. (211) 4480; fax (211) 4482222; internet www.eplus.de; f. 1995; Chair. Supervisory Bd ALAIN D. BANDLE.

Mannesmann Mobilfunk GmbH: Am Seestern 1, 40547 Düsseldorf; tel. (211) 5330; fax (211) 5332200; internet www .d2mannesmann.de; operates D2 mobile telephone network; subsidiary of Mannesmann AG, Telecommunications Division (takeover by Vodafone Airtouch Ltd, UK, pending); Chair. JÜRGEN VON KUCZKOWSKI.

Mannesmann o-tel-o GmbH: Deutz-Mulheimer-Str. 111, 51063 Köln; tel. (221) 8080; fax (221) 8087566; internet www.o-tel-o.com; operates fixed line telephone network; subsidiary of Mannesmann AG, Telecommunications Division (takeover by Vodafone Airtouch Ltd, UK, pending).

Mannesmann Arcor AG: Kölnerstr. 5, 65760 Eschborn; fax (69) 21694444; e-mail arcor@arcor.net; internet www.arcor.de; operates fixed line telephone network; subsidiary of Mannesmann AG, Telecommunications Division (takeover by Vodafone Airtouch Ltd, UK, pending).

MobilCom AG: Postfach 520, 24753 Rendsburg; Hollerstr. 126, 24782 Rendsburg; internet www.mobilcom.de; f. 1991; Chair. GERHARD SCHMID.

T-Mobil: internet www.t-mobil.de; f. 1992; subsidiary of Deutsche Telekom AG; f. 1992; operates T-D1 mobile telephone network.

Viag Interkom: internet www.viaginterkom.de; f. 1995; Chair. MAXIMILIAN ARDELT.

Associations

Deutscher Multimedia Verband (dmmv): Kaistr. 14, 40221 Düsseldorf; tel. (211) 6004560; fax (211) 60045633; e-mail info@dmmv.de; internet www.dmmv.de; 1,300 mems (Feb. 2001).

Verband Privater Rundfunk und Telekommunikation eV (VPRT) (Assocation of Commercial Broadcasting and Telecommunications Cos): 53177 Bonn; tel. (228) 934500; fax (228) 9345048; e-mail vprt@vprt.de; internet www.vprt.de; 160 mems (Feb. 2000).

Regulatory Authority

Regulierungsbehörde für Telekommunikation und Post (RegTP): Heussallee 2–10, Haus IV, 53113 Bonn; tel. (228) 140; fax (228) 148872; e-mail poststelle@regtp.de; internet www.regtp.de; f. 1997 as a regulatory body responsible for supervising the liberalization (commencing in January 1998) of the post and telecommunications sector; Pres. MATTHIAS KURTH.

BROADCASTING
Radio

Regional public radio stations are co-ordinated by the ARD (see below). There are also numerous regional commercial radio stations.

Public Stations

Arbeitsgemeinschaft der öffentlich-rechtlichen Rundfunkanstalten der Bundesrepublik Deutschland (ARD) (Association of Public Law Broadcasting Organizations): Bertramstr. 8, 60320 Frankfurt a.M.; tel. (69) 590607; fax (69) 1552075; e-mail info@ard.de; internet www.ard.de; f. 1950; Chair. Prof. Dr UDO REITER; the co-ordinating body of Germany's public service radio and television organizations; each of the following radio stations broadcasts 3–5 channels:

Bayerischer Rundfunk: Rundfunkplatz 1, 80300 München; tel. (89) 590001; fax (89) 59002375; internet www.bronline.de; Dir-Gen. Prof. ALBERT SCHARF; Chair. Broadcasting Council Prof. Dr WILHELM WIMMER; Chair. Admin. Bd JOHANN BÖHM.

Radio Bremen: Bürgermeister-Spitta-Allee 45, 28329 Bremen; tel. (421) 2460; fax (421) 2461010; internet www.radiobremen.de; f. 1945; radio and television; Dir-Gen. Dr HEINZ GLÄSSGEN.

Deutsche Welle: Raderberggürtel 50, 50968 Köln; tel. (221) 3892500; fax (221) 3892510; e-mail deutsche.welle@dw.gmd.de; internet www.dwelle.de; German short-wave radio and satellite television service; broadcasts daily in 35 languages for Europe and overseas; Dir-Gen. DIETER WEIRICH.

DeutschlandRadio: Hans Rosenthal Platz, 10825 Berlin; tel. (30) 85030; internet www.deutschlandradio.de; Dir-Gen. ERNST ELLITZ.

Hessischer Rundfunk: Bertramstr. 8, 60320 Frankfurt a.M.; tel. (69) 1551; fax (69) 1552900; internet www.hr-online.de; Dir-Gen. Prof. Dr KLAUS BERG.

Mitteldeutscher Rundfunk: Kanstr. 71–73, 04275 Leipzig; tel. (341) 3000; fax (341) 3005544; internet www.mdr.de; f. 1992; Dir-Gen. Prof. Dr UDO REITER.

Norddeutscher Rundfunk: Rothenbaumchaussee 132, 20149 Hamburg; tel. (40) 41560; fax (40) 447602; f. 1956; internet www.ndr.de; Dir-Gen. JOBST PLOG.

Ostdeutscher Rundfunk Brandenburg: August-Bebel-Str. 26–53, 14482 Potsdam; tel. (331) 7310; fax (331) 7213571; internet www.orb.de; Dir-Gen. Prof. HANSJÜRGEN ROSENBAUER.

Saarländischer Rundfunk: Funkhaus Halberg, 66100 Saarbrücken; tel. (681) 6020; fax (681) 6023874; internet www.sr-online.de; f. 1952; Dir-Gen. FRITZ RAFF.

Sender Freies Berlin: Masurenallee 8–14, 14057 Berlin; tel. (30) 30310; fax (30) 3015062; e-mail info@sfb.de; internet www.sfb.de; Dir-Gen. Dr HORST SCHÄTTLE; Chair. Broadcasting Council MARIANNE BRINCKMEIER; Dir of Radio JENS WENDLAND; Dir of TV BARBARA GROTH.

Süddeutscher Rundfunk: Postfach 106040, 70049 Stuttgart; Neckarstr. 230, 70190 Stuttgart; tel. (711) 9290; fax (711) 9292600; internet www.sdr.de; f. 1924; Dir-Gen. HERMANN FÜNFGELD.

Südwestrundfunk: Neckarstr. 230, 70150 Stuttgart; tel. (49) 9290; fax (49) 9292600; internet www.swr-online.de; Dir-Gen. PETER VOSS.

WDR (Westdeutscher Rundfunk): Appellhofplatz 1, 50667 Köln; tel. (221) 2200; fax (221) 2204800; internet www.wdr.de; Dir-Gen. FRITZ PLEITGEN.

Commercial Radio

Verband Privater Rundfunk und Telekommunikation eV (VPRT): (see under Telecommunications); represents privately-owned radio stations.

Television

There are three public service television channels. The autonomous regional broadcasting organizations combine to provide material for the First Programme which is produced by ARD. The Second Programme (Zweites Deutsches Fernsehen/ZDF) is completely separate and is controlled by a public corporation of all the Länder. It is partly financed by advertising. The Third Programme (also produced by ARD) provides a cultural and educational service in the evenings only with contributions from several of the regional bodies. Commercial television channels also operate.

Public Stations

ARD: Programmdirektion Deutsches Fernsehen: Arnulfstr. 42, 80335 München; tel. (89) 590001; fax (89) 59003249; Chair. INGO DAHRENDORF; co-ordinates the following regional public-service television organizations: Bayerischer Rundfunk Fernsehen, Hessischer Rundfunk Fernsehen, MDR Fernsehen, NDR Fernsehen, ORB Fernsehen, Radio Bremen Fernsehen, Saarländischer Rundfunk Fernsehen, SDR Fernsehen, SFB Fernsehen, SNF Fernsehen, WDR Fernsehen.

Zweites Deutsches Fernsehen (ZDF): Postfach 4040, 55100 Mainz, tel. (6131) 701; fax (6131) 702157; e-mail info@zdf.de; internet www.zdf.de; f. 1961 by the Länder Govts as a second television channel; 104 main transmitters; Dir-Gen. Prof. Dr DIETER STOLTE.

Commercial Television

Verband Privater Rundfunk und Telekommunikation eV (VPRT): (see under Telecommunications); represents privately-owned satellite, cable and digital television cos.

Finance

(cap. = capital; dep. = deposits; m. = million; res = reserves; brs = branches; amounts in Deutsche Marks (DM) or euros (€))

The Deutsche Bundesbank, the central bank of Germany, consists of the central administration in Frankfurt am Main (considered to be the financial capital of the country) and 9 main offices (Landeszentralbanken) with 140 branches. In carrying out its functions as determined by law the Bundesbank is independent of the Federal Government, but is required to support the Government's general economic policy. As a member of the European System of Central Banks, the Bundesbank implements the single monetary policy determined by the Governing Council of the European Central Bank.

All credit institutions other than the Bundesbank are subject to governmental supervision through the Federal Banking Supervisory Office (Bundesaufsichtsamt für das Kreditwesen) in Berlin. Banks outside the central banking system are divided into three groups: private commercial banks, credit institutions incorporated under public law and co-operative credit institutions. All these commercial banks are 'universal banks', conducting all kinds of customary banking business. There is no division of activities. As well as the commercial banks there are a number of specialist banks, such as private or public mortgage banks.

The group of private commercial banks includes all banks incorporated as a company limited by shares (Aktiengesellschaft—AG, Kommanditgesellschaft auf Aktien—KGaA) or as a private limited company (Gesellschaft mit beschränkter Haftung—GmbH) and those which are known as 'regional banks' because they do not usually function throughout Germany; and those banks which are established as sole proprietorships or partnerships and mostly have no branches outside their home town. The main business of all private commercial banks is short-term lending. The private bankers fulfil the most varied tasks within the banking system.

The public law credit institutions are the savings banks (Sparkassen) and the Landesbank-Girozentralen. The latter act as central banks and clearing houses on a national level for the savings banks. Laws governing the savings banks limit them to certain sectors—credits, investments and money transfers—and they concentrate on the areas of home financing, municipal investments and the trades. In December 1998 there were 594 savings banks and 13 Landesbank-Girozentralen in Germany.

The head institution of the co-operative system is the DG BANK Deutsche Genossenschaftsbank. In December 1998 there were three regional co-operative central banks and 2,256 local co-operative banks.

BANKS

The Central Banking System

Germany participates in the European System of Central Banks (ESCB), which consists of the European Central Bank (ECB) and the national central banks of all 15 EU member states. Stage III of European Monetary Union, the launch of the euro, commenced (with 11 initial participants) at the beginning of January 1999. Pending the initial issue of euro banknotes and coins, scheduled for the beginning of January 2002, the Deutsche Mark remains the sole legal tender in Germany.

Deutsche Bundesbank: Postfach 100602, 60006 Frankfurt a.M.; Wilhelm-Epstein-Str. 14, 60431 Frankfurt a.M.; tel. (69) 95661; fax (69) 5601071; e-mail presse-information@bundesbank.de; internet www.bundesbank.de; f. 1957; issues bank notes, regulates note and coin circulation and supply of credit; safeguards internal and external value of Deutsche Mark; aims, in conjunction with the other members of the ESCB, to safeguard the value of the euro. Credit institutions are required to maintain minimum reserves at the Bundesbank. The Bundesbank (which has nine regional offices—Landeszentralbanken) is the principal bank of the Federal Govt and Länder Govts, carrying accounts for public authorities, executing payments and assisting with borrowing on the capital market. The Bundesbank is the guardian of Germany's official monetary reserves, and invests them at interest. In addition there are gold holdings and reserve positions in, and claims on, the IMF and the ECB. The Central Bank Council determines the Bundesbank's business policy; members of the Federal Govt may take part in the deliberations of the Council but may not vote; Pres. ERNST WELTEKE; Vice-Pres. Dr JÜRGEN STARK.

Landeszentralbank in Baden-Württemberg: Marstallstr. 3, 70173 Stuttgart; tel. (711) 9440; fax (711) 9441903; e-mail landeszentralbank@lzb-bw.bundesbank.de; internet www.bundesbank.de/lzb-bw; total assets US $261,707.5m. (Dec. 1998); Pres. Bd of Management HELMUT SCHIEBER.

Landeszentralbank im Freistaat Bayern: Ludwigstr. 13, 80539 München; tel. (89) 28895; fax (89) 28893598; internet www.bundesbank.de/lzb-bayern; Pres. Bd of Management Dr FRANZ-CHRISTOPH ZEITLER.

Landeszentralbank in Berlin und Brandenburg: Postfach 110160, 10831 Berlin; tel. (30) 34750; fax (30) 34751990; e-mail volkswirtschaft@lzb-bbb.bundesbank.de; internet www.bundesbank.de/lzb-bbb; Pres. Bd of Management KLAUS-DIETER KUEHBACHER.

Landeszentralbank in der Freien Hansestadt Bremen, in Niedersachsen und Sachsen-Anhalt: 28203 Bremen, tel. (421) 32910; Pres. Bd of Management HANS-HELMUT KOTZ.

Landeszentralbank in der Freien und Hansestadt Hamburg, in Mecklenburg-Vorpommern und Schleswig-Holstein: Ost-West-Str. 73, 20459 Hamburg; tel. (40) 37070; fax (40) 37072205; e-mail lzb-hms-pressestelle@t-online.de; Pres. Bd of Management Prof. Dr HANS-JÜRGEN KRUPP.

Landeszentralbank in Hessen: Taunusanlage 5, 60329 Frankfurt a.M.; tel. (69) 23880; fax (69) 23882130; Pres. Dr HANS RECKERS.

Landeszentralbank in Nordrhein-Westfalen: Berliner Allee 14, 40212 Düsseldorf; tel. (211) 8740; e-mail lzb-nrw@t-online.de; internet www.bundesbank.de/lzb-nrw; Pres. EBERHARD HEINKE.

Landeszentralbank in Rheinland-Pfalz und im Saarland: Hegelstr. 65, 52122 Mainz; tel. (6131) 3770; fax (6131) 377750; e-mail vo.lzb_rs@t-online.de; internet www.bundesbank.de/lzb-rs; Pres. HANS-JÜRGEN KOEBNICK.

Landeszentralbank in den Freistaaten Sachsen und Thüringen: Postfach 901121, 04358 Leipzig; tel. (341) 8600; fax (341) 8602389; e-mail zentrale.mailstelle@lzb-sth.bundesbank.de; internet www.bundesbank.de/lzb-sth.

Private Commercial Banks

In December 1998 328 private commercial banks were operating in Germany. The most prominent of these are listed below:

Baden-Württembergische Bank AG: Postfach 106014, 70049 Stuttgart; Kleiner Schlossplatz 11, 70173 Stuttgart; tel. (711) 1800; fax (711) 1801712; e-mail info@bw-bank.de; f. 1977 by merger of Badische Bank, Handelsbank Heilbronn and Württembergische Bank; cap. €92m., res €536m., dep. €22,014m. (Dec. 1999); Chair. GERHARD STRATTHAUS; 53 brs.

Bankgesellschaft Berlin AG: Alexanderplatz 2, 10178 Berlin; tel. (30) 245500; fax (30) 24566333; e-mail ir@bankgesellschaft.de; internet www.bankgesellschaft.de; f. 1994; cap. €558m., res €3,658m., dep. €177,043m. (Dec. 1999); Chair. Supervisory Bd Prof. Dr DIETER FEDDERSEN.

Bayerische Hypo- und Vereinsbank AG (HypoVereinsbank): Postfach 80311, 80333 München; Am Tucherpark 16, 80538 München; tel. (89) 3780; fax (89) 378113422; e-mail info@hypovereinsbank.de; internet www.hypovereinsbank.de; f. 1998 by merger of Bayerische Hypotheken- und Wechsel Bank AG (f. 1835) and Bayerische Vereinsbank AG (f. 1869); cap. €1,265m., res €10,816m., dep. €442,429m. (Dec. 1999); Chair. Supervisory Bd Dr KURT VIERMETZ; Chair. Bd of Management Dr ALBRECHT SCHMIDT; 1,426 brs.

Berliner Volksbank eG: Volksbank-Center am Potsdamer Platz, Schellingstr. 1, 10785 Berlin; tel. (30) 30630; fax (30) 30631550; e-mail service@berliner-volksbank.de; internet www.berliner-volksbank.de; f. 1860; cap. DM 343m., res DM 345m., dep. DM 14,097m. (Dec. 1998); Chair. Prof. Dr DIETMAR WINJE.

BfG—Bank AG: Mainzer Landstr. 16, 60325 Frankfurt a.M.; tel. (69) 2580; fax (69) 2587578; info@bfg.de; internet www.bfg.de; f. 1958; cap. €775m., res 428m., dep. 25,895m. (Dec. 1999); Chair. KARL-HEINZ HÜLSMANN; 177 brs.

BHF-Bank AG: Bockenheimer Landstr. 10, 60323 Frankfurt a.M.; tel. (69) 7180; fax (69) 7182296; e-mail kontakt@bhfbank.com; internet www.bhf-bank.com; f. 1856; cap. €215m., res €1,515m., dep. €46,645m. (Dec. 1999); Man. Dir Dr PETER GLOYSTEIN.

Chase Manhattan Bank AG: Grüneburgweg 2, 60322 Frankfurt a.M.; tel. (69) 71581; fax (69) 71582209; f. 1947; cap. DM 220m., res DM 33m., dep. DM 5,046m. (Dec. 1996); Chair. RAINER GEBBE.

Citibank AG: Neue Mainzer Str. 75, 60311 Frankfurt a.M.; tel. (69) 13660; fax (69) 13661113; f. 1976; cap. DM 426m., res DM 74m., dep. DM 9,062m. (Dec. 1998); Chair. Supervisory Bd Prof. K. PETER MAILÄNDER; 3 brs.

Citibank Privatkunden AG: Kasernenstr. 10, 40213 Düsseldorf; tel. (211) 89840; fax (211) 8984222; internet www.citibank.de; f. 1926; cap. DM 156m., res. DM 778m., dep. DM 15,221m. (Dec. 1998).

Commerzbank AG: Kaiserplatz, 60311 Frankfurt a.M., tel. (69) 13620; fax (69) 285389; e-mail webmaster@commerzbank.de; internet www.commerzbank.de; f. 1870; cap. €1,335m., res €9,395m., dep. €320,670m. (Dec. 1999); Chair. Supervisory Bd DIETRICH-KURT FROWEIN; Chair. Bd of Management MARTIN KOHLHAUSSEN; 964 brs.

Deutsche Bank AG: Central Office: Taunusanlage 12, 60325 Frankfurt a.M.; tel. (69) 91000; fax (69) 91033422; e-mail db.presse@db.com; internet www.deutsche-bank.de; f. 1870; cap. €1,573m., res €20,868m., dep. €753,025m. (Dec. 1999); Chair. Supervisory Bd HILMAR KOPPER; 133 brs.

Dresdner Bank AG: Jürgen-Ponto-Platz 1, 60329 Frankfurt a.M., tel. (69) 2630; fax (69) 634004; e-mail investor.relations@dresdner-bank.com; internet www.dresdner-bank.de; f. 1872; cap. €1,354m., res €9,885m. (Dec. 2000); Chair. Supervisory Bd ALFONS TITZRATH; over 1,400 brs.

Dresdner Bank Lateinamerika AG: Postfach 301246, 20305 Hamburg; Neuer Jungfernstieg 16, 20354 Hamburg; tel. (40) 35950; fax (40) 35953314; e-mail public-relations@dbla.com; internet www.dbla.com; f. 1906; fmrly Deutsch-Südamerikanische Bank AG; cap. €100m., res €258m., dep. €9,917m. (Dec. 1999); Chair. Supervisory Bd Dr JOACHIM V. HARBOU; Chair. Bd of Management HELGER F. SOMMER.

DSL Bank Deutsche Siedlungs- und Landesrentenbank: Kennedyallee 62–70, 53175 Bonn; tel. (228) 8890; fax (228) 889624; internet www.dsl-bank.de; f. 1966; cap. DM 219m., res DM 746m., dep. DM 131,333m. (Dec. 1998); Spokesman Bd of Dirs STEFAN JÜTTE.

GZ-Bank AG: Bockenheimer Anlage 46, 60322 Frankfurt a.M.; tel. (69) 71390; fax (69) 71391309; e-mail info@gz-bank.de; internet www.gz-bank.de; f. 1883; cap. DM 400m., res DM 1,744m., dep. DM 63,055m. (Dec. 1998); Chair. Bd of Management Dr ULRICH BRIXNER.

HSBC Trinkaus & Burkhardt KGaA: Königsallee 21–23, 40212 Düsseldorf; tel. (211) 9100; fax (211) 910616; f. 1785; current name adopted 1999; cap. €67m., res €445m., dep. €7,914m. (Dec. 1999); 4 Partners; 6 brs.

Merck Finck & Co: Pacellistr. 16, 80333 München; tel. (89) 21040; fax (89) 299814; e-mail info@merckfinck.de; internet www.merckfinck.de; f. 1870; cap. €317m., dep. €2,560.4m. (Dec. 1999); Partners GERD SCHMITZ-MORKRAMER, UTZ-DIETER BOLSTORFF, ANDREW LAWSON.

Oldenburgische Landesbank AG: Stau 15–17, 26122 Oldenburg; tel. (441) 2210; fax (441) 210310; e-mail olb@olb.de; internet www.olb.de; f. 1868; cap. €57m., res €271m., dep. €7,200m. (Dec. 1999); Spokesman Bd of Management H.-D. GELLER.

Oppenheim (Sal) Jr & Cie KGaA: Unter Sachsenhausen 4; 50667 Köln; tel. (221) 14501; fax (221) 1451512; internet www .oppenheim.de; f. 1789; cap. DM 200m., res DM 944m., dep. DM 10,887m. (Dec. 1998); Chair. MATTHIAS GRAF VON KROCKOW.

Schmidt Bank KGaA: Ernst-Reuter-Str. 119, 95030 Hof; tel. (9281) 6010; fax (9281) 601427; e-mail kundenservice@schmidtbank.de; internet www.schmidtbank.de; f. 1828; cap. DM 417m., res DM 83,762m., dep. DM 83,762m. (Dec. 1999); Partners Dr KARL-GERHARD SCHMIDT, Dr HANS NUISSL; 125 brs.

Skandinaviska Enskilda Banken AG: Postfach 101957, 60019 Frankfurt a.M.; Rahmhofstr. 2–4, 60313 Frankfurt a.M.; tel. (69) 290210; fax (69) 284191; f. 1975; cap. DM 81m., res DM 64m., dep. DM 2,235m. (Dec. 1998); Chair. ZAID PEDERSEN; Man. Dirs WOLFGANG AZGELANDER, LARS TÖRNQUIST; 2 brs.

USB Warburg AG: Ulmenstr. 30, 60325 Frankfurt a.M.; tel. (69) 13690; fax (69) 13691366; internet www.wdr.com; f. 1998 as Warburg Dillon Read AG by merger of Schweizerischer Bankverein (Deutschland) and Union Bank of Switzerland (Deutschland) AG; present name a pted 2000; Man. Dirs PETER AARTS, DR RICHARD JAEKEL, STEFAN WINTER.

Vereins- und Westbank AG: 20457 Hamburg, Alter Wall 22; tel. (40) 369201; fax (40) 36922870; internet www.vuw.de; f. 1974 by merger; cap. €174m., res €598m., dep. €16,962m. (Dec. 1999); 190 brs.

Weberbank Berliner Industriebank KGaA: Hohenzollerndamm 134, 14199 Berlin; tel. (30) 897980; fax (30) 89798900; internet www.weberbank.de; f. 1949; cap. €52m., res €123m., dep. €6,244m. (Dec. 1999); 4 Partners; 4 brs.

Westfalenbank AG: Huestr. 21–25, 44787 Bochum; tel. (234) 6160; fax (234) 6164400; e-mail info@westfalenbank.de; internet www.westfalenbank.de; f. 1921; cap. DM 97m., res DM 217m., dep. €5,199m. (Dec. 1999); Chair. DIETMAR P. BINKOWSKA.

Public-Law Credit Institutions

Together with the private banks, the banks incorporated under public law (savings banks—Sparkassen—and their central clearing houses Landesbank-Girozentralen) play a major role within the German banking system. In 1998 there were 594 savings banks and 13 central clearing houses.

Bayerische Landesbank Girozentrale: Brienner Str. 20, 80333 München; tel. (89) 217101; fax (89) 21713579; e-mail kontakt@blb.de; internet www.bayernlb.de; f. 1972; cap. €3,339m., res €3,531m., dep. €253,921m. (Dec. 1999); Chair. Bd of Management ALFRED H. LEHNER.

Bremer Landesbank Kreditanstalt Oldenburg: Domshof 26, 28195 Bremen; tel. (421) 3320; fax (421) 3322625; e-mail kontakt@ bremerlandesbank.de; internet www.bremerlandesbank.de; f. 1983; cap. €498m., res €230m., dep. €30,746m. (Dec. 1999); Chair. Dr PETER HASSKAMP.

DGZ DekaBank: Postfach 110523, 60040 Frankfurt a.M.; Mainzer Landstr. 16, 60325 Frankfurt a.M.; tel. (69) 71470; fax (69) 71471376; internet www.dgz-dekabank.com; f. 1999 through merger of Deutsche Girozentrale-Deutsche Kommunalbank and Dekabank GmbH; issues Pfandbriefe (bonds); total assets €75,300m. (Dec. 2000); Chair. Bd of Management MANFRED ZASS.

Hamburgische Landesbank-Girozentrale: Gerhart-Hauptmann-Platz 50, 20095 Hamburg; tel. (40) 33330; fax (40) 33332707; e-mail info@hamburglb.de; internet www.hamburglb.de; f. 1938; cap. €1,884m., res €696m., dep. €67,340m. (Dec. 1999); Chair. ALEXANDER STUHLMANN; 4 brs.

Landesbank Baden-Württemberg: Am Hauptbahnhof 2, 70173 Stuttgart; tel. (711) 1270; fax (71) 1273278; e-mail kontakt@lbbw.de; internet www.lbbw.de; f. 1999 by merger of Landesgirokasse, L-Bank Landeskreditbank Baden-Württemberg and Südwestdeutsche Landesbank Girozentrale; cap. €2,202m., res €3,131m., dep. €241,223m. (Dec. 1999); Chair. WERNER SCHMIDT.

Landesbank Berlin Girozentrale: Bundesallee 171, 10889 Berlin-Wilmersdorf; tel. (30) 869801; fax (30) 86983074; e-mail information@lbb.de; internet www.lbb.de; f. 1818; cap. €844m., res €1,494m., dep. €86,355m. (Dec. 1999); Chair. Bd of Management ULF-WILHELM DECKEN; 173 brs.

Landesbank Hessen-Thüringen Girozentrale: Main Tower, Neue Mainzer Str. 52–58, 60297 Frankfurt a.M.; tel. (69) 913201; fax (69) 291517; internet www.helaba.de; cap. €60m., res €38m., dep. €4,444m. (Dec. 1999); Chair. WALTER SCHÄFER.

LRP Landesbank Rheinland-Pfalz Girozentrale: Grosse Bleiche 54–56, 55098 Mainz; tel. (6131) 1301; fax (6131) 132724; e-mail lrp@lrp.de; internet www.lrp.de; f. 1958; cap. €266m., res €506m., dep. €53,859m. (Dec. 1999); Chair. and CEO KLAUS G. ADAM.

Landesbank Saar Girozentrale: Ursulinenstr. 2, 66111 Saarbrücken; tel. (681) 38301; fax (681) 3831295; e-mail saarlb@aol.com.; internet www.saarlb.de; f. 1941; cap. €138m., res €101m., dep. €12,119m. (Dec. 1999); Chair. KARL HEINZ TRAUTMANN.

Landesbank Schleswig-Holstein Girozentrale: Martendsdamm 6, 24103 Kiel; tel. (431) 90001; fax (431) 9002446; e-mail info@ lb-kiel.de; internet www.lb-kiel.de; f. 1917; cap. €340m., res €2,508m., dep. €105,494m. (Dec. 1999); Chair. DR DIETRICH RÜMKER.

Norddeutsche Landesbank Girozentrale (NORD/LB): Georgsplatz 1, 30159 Hannover; tel. (511) 3610; fax (511) 3612502; internet www.nordlb.de; f. 1970 by merger of several north German banks; cap. €1,169m., res €2,234m., dep. €113,480m. (Dec. 1999); Chair. Dr MANFRED BODIN; 172 brs.

Westdeutsche Landesbank Girozentrale: Herzogstr. 15, 40217 Düsseldorf; tel. (211) 82601; fax (211) 8266119; e-mail presse@ westlb.de; internet www.westlb.de; f. 1969; cap. €1,182m., res €7,029m., dep. €358,344m. (Dec. 1999); Chair. Dr FRIEDEL NEUBER.

Central Bank of Co-operative Banking System

DG BANK Deutsche Genossenschaftsbank AG: Am Platz der Republik, 60265 Frankfurt a.M.; tel. (69) 744701; fax (69) 74471685; internet www.dgbank.de; f. 1949; cap. €1,469m., res €1,614m., dep. €224,694m. (Dec. 1999); Chair. Supervisory Bd WOLFGANG GRÜGER; Chair. Bd of Management Dr BERND THIEMANN; 46 brs.

DG BANK is a specialist wholesale bank and is the central institution in the German co-operative banking sector, which comprises 2,248 local co-operative banks, three regional central banks and a number of specialist financial institutions.

Specialist Banks

Although Germany is considered the model country for universal banking, banks which specialize in certain types of business are also extremely important. In December 1998 there were 51 specialist banks. A selection of the most prominent among these are given below:

Allgemeine Hypotheken Bank AG: Postfach 170162, 60075 Frankfurt a.M.; Bockenheimer Landstr. 25, 60325 Frankfurt a.M.; tel. (69) 71790; fax (69) 7179100; e-mail info@ahb-ag.com; internet www.ahb-ag.com; f. 1962; cap. €100m., res €804m., dep. €61,711m. (Dec. 2000); Chair. HORST ALEXANDER SPITZKOPF; 8 brs.

Bayerische Handelsbank AG: Von-der-Tann-Str. 2, 80539 München; tel. (89) 286270; fax (89) 28627304; internet www.bhb.de; f. 1869; cap. €46m., res €344m., dep. €26,096m. (Dec. 1999).

Berlin-Hannoversche Hypothekenbank AG: Budapester Str. 1, 10787 Berlin, tel. (30) 259990; fax (30) 25999131; e-mail kommunikation@berlinhyp.de; internet www.berlinhyp.de; f. 1996 by merger; cap. DM 144m., res DM 1,239m., dep. DM 77,761m. (Dec. 1998); Chair. Supervisory Bd Dr WOLFGANG RUPF.

Deutsche Hyp Deutsche Hypothekenbank Frankfurt-Hamburg AG: Postfach 160265, Taunusanlage 9, 60329 Frankfurt a.M.; tel. (69) 25480; fax (69) 2548113; e-mail info@deutschehyp.de; internet www.deutschehyp.de; f. 1998 by merger; cap. €196m., res €991m., dep. €89,186m. (Dec. 1999); Man. Dir WOLFGANG AHR.

Deutsche Hypothekenbank AG: Georgsplatz 8, 30159 Hannover; tel. (511) 30450; fax (511) 3045459; e-mail mail@deutsche-hypo.de; internet www.deutsche-hypo.de; f. 1872; total assets €21,990m. (Dec. 1999); Chair. Supervisory Bd LOUIS GRAF VON ZECH; 10 brs.

DePfa Deutsche Pfandbriefbank AG: Postfach 2169, 65011 Wiesbaden; Paulinenstr. 15, 65189 Wiesbaden; tel. (611) 3480; fax (611) 3482549; e-mail tsai-chin.kou@depfa.com; internet www .depfa.com; f. 1922; cap. €108m., res €1,785m., dep. €135,049m. (Dec. 1999); Chair. Supervisory Bd Dr JÜRGEN WESTPHAL.

Deutsche Postbank AG: Friedrich-Ebert-Allee 114–126, 53113 Bonn; tel. (228) 9200; fax (228) 9202818; internet www.postbank.de; f. 1990; cap. DM 800m., res DM 2,527m., dep. DM 109,086m. (Dec. 1999); state-owned; Chair. Prof. Dr WULF VON SCHIMMELMANN.

Eurohypo AG Europäische Hypothekenbank der Deutschen Bank: Junghofstr. 5–7, 60311 Frankfurt a.M.; tel. (69) 298980; fax (69) 288469; e-mail mailbox.eurohypo@db.com; internet www.eurohypo.de; f. 1998 by merger of Frankfurter Hypotheken-bank Centralboden AG (f. 1862) and Lübecker Hypothekenbank AG (f. 1927); cap. DM 242m., res DM 2,498m., dep. DM 113,918m. (Dec. 1998); Chair. Supervisory Bd CARL L. VON BOEHM-BEZING.

IKB Deutsche Industriebank AG: Postfach 101118, 40002 Düsseldorf; Willhelm-Bötzkes-Str.1, 40474 Düsseldorf; tel. (211) 82210; fax (211) 82212559; internet www.ikb.de; f. 1949; cap. €153m., res €46m., dep. €4,414m. (March 2000); Gen. Mans CLAUS MOMBURG, J. NEUPEL, S. ORTSEIFEN, G.-J. V. PUTTKAMER, Dr A. V. TIPPELSKIRCH.

Kreditanstalt für Wiederaufbau (KFW): Postfach 111141, 60046 Frankfurt a.M.; Palmengartenstr. 5–9, 60325 Frankfurt a.M.; tel. (69) 74310; fax (69) 74312944; e-mail kfw.vsb@kfw.de; internet www.kfw.de; f. 1948; cap. €511m., res €5,386m., dep. €176,779m. (Dec. 1999); Spokesman Bd of Management HANS W. REICH.

Münchener Hypothekenbank eG: Nussbaumstr. 12, 80036 München; tel. (89) 53870; fax (89) 5387333; e-mail mhbinfo@

t-online.de; internet www. muenchener-hyp.de; f. 1896; cap. DM 367m., res DM 358m., dep. DM 45,146m. (Dec. 1999); Chair. Prof. Dr WILLIBALD J. FOLZ.

RHEINHYP Rheinische Hypothekenbank AG: Taunustor 3, 60311 Frankfurt a.M.; tel. (69) 23820; fax (69) 23824202; e-mail info@rheinhyp-bank.de; internet www.rheinhyp-bank.de; f. 1871; cap. €74m., res €753m., dep. €61,493m. (Dec. 1999); Chair. Dr MARTIN KOHLHAUSSEN; 41 brs.

Süddeutsche Bodencreditbank AG: Ottostr. 21, 80333 München; tel. (89) 51120; fax (89) 5112406; internet www.suedboden.de; f. 1871; cap. €39m., res €305m., dep. €20,722m. (Dec. 1999); Chair. Dr ALBRECHT SCHMIDT; 9 brs.

Bankers' Organizations

Bundesverband deutscher Banken (Association of German Banks): Postfach 040307, 10062 Berlin; Burgstr. 28, 10178 Berlin; e-mail bdb@bdb.de; internet www.bdb.de; f. 1951; Pres. Dr FRANK HEINTZELER.

Bundesverband der Deutschen Volksbanken und Raiffeisenbanken eV (Association of German Industrial and Agricultural Credit Co-operatives): Schellingstr. 4, 10785 Berlin; e-mail poststelle@bur.de; internet www.vmet.de; f. 1971; Pres. Dr CHRISTOPHER PLEISTER; 1,800 mems.

Bundsverband Öffentlicher Banken Deutschlands eV (Association of German Public-Sector Banks): Godesberger Allee 88, 53175 Bonn; (228) 81920: e-mail postmaster@voeb.de; internet www .voeb.de.

Deutscher Sparkassen- und Giroverband eV (German Savings Banks Association). Postfach 1429, Simrockstr. 4, 53113 Bonn; tel. (228) 2040; fax (228) 204250; e-mail postmaster@dsgv.de; internet www.dsgv.de; Pres. Dr DIETRICH H. HOPPENSTEDT.

STOCK EXCHANGES

Frankfurt am Main: Deutsche Börse AG, Börsenplatz 4, 60313 Frankfurt a.M.; tel. (69) 21010; fax (69) 29977580; internet www .exchange.de; f. 1585 as Frankfurter Wertpapierbörse; also operates Neuer Markt (f. 1997) listing high growth cos; 269 mems; Chair. Supervisory Bd ROLF-ERNST BREUER; Chair. of Bd of Management Dr WERNER G. SEIFERT.

Berlin: Berliner Wertpapierbörse, Fasanenstr. 85, 10623 Berlin; tel. (30) 3110910; fax (30) 31109179; internet www .berlinerboerse.de; f. 1685; 82 mems; Pres. LEOPOLD TRÖBINGER.

Bremen: Bremer Wertpapierbörse, Postfach 100726, 28007 Bremen; Kohlhökerstr. 29, 28203 Bremen; tel. (421) 277440; fax (421) 2774490; e-mail info@boerse-bremer.de; internet www.boerser-bremer.de; 67 mems; Pres. HORST-GÜNTER LUCKE; Man. AXEL H. SCHUBERT.

Düsseldorf: Rheinisch-Westfälische Börse zu Düsseldorf, Postfach 104262, 40033 Düsseldorf; Ernst-Schneider-Platz 1, 40212 Düsseldorf; tel. (211) 13890; fax (211) 133287; f. 1935; 110 mem. firms; Pres. HERBERT H. JACOBI.

München: Bayerische Börse, Lenbachplatz 2A/1, 80333 München; tel. (89) 5490450; fax (89) 54904532; 125 mems; Chair. Council Dr NORBERT JUCHEM.

North Germany (Hamburg and Hannover): Börsen AG, Schauenburgerstr. 49, 20095 Hamburg, Rathenaustr. 2; 30159 Hannover; tel. (40) 3613020; fax (40) 36130223; tel. (511) 327661; fax (511) 324915; f. 1999 by merger of Hanseatische Wertpapierbörse Hamburg and Niedersächsische Börse zu Hannover; (109 and 81 mems, respectively); Pres. (Hamburg) UDO BANDOW; Chair. Pres. Rechtesanwalt (Hannover) FRIEDRICH KERSTING.

Stuttgart: Baden-Württembergische Wertpapierbörse, Königstr. 28, 70173 Stuttgart; tel. (711) 2229850; fax (711) 2268119; f. 1861; 141 mems; Pres. ROLF LIMBACH; Man. Dir Dr PETER LUDWIG.

INSURANCE

German law specifies that property and accident insurance may not be jointly underwritten with life, sickness, legal protection or credit insurance by the same company. Insurers are therefore obliged to establish separate companies to cover the different classes of insurance. In December 1997 there were 2,004 insurance companies (excluding reinsurance companies, of which there were 35 in 1997/98). A selection of the most prominent is given below.

Aachener und Münchener Lebensversicherung AG: Robert-Schuman-Str. 51, 52066 Aachen; tel. (241) 600101; fax (241) 60015138; f. 1868; Chair. Dr WOLFGANG KASKE; Gen. Man. Dr MICHAEL KALKA.

Albingia Versicherungs-AG: Ballindamm 39, 20095 Hamburg; tel. (40) 30220; fax (40) 30222585; e-mail infoa@albingia.de; internet www.albingia.de; f. 1901; Chair. Dr K. ASCHER; Gen. Man. V. BREMKAMP.

Allianz AG: Königinstr. 28, 80802 München; tel (89) 38000; fax (89) 349941; internet www.allianz.com; f. 1890; Chair. Supervisory Bd Dr KLAUS LIESEN; Chair. Bd of Mans Dr HENNING SCHULTE-NOELLE.

Allianz Lebensversicherungs-AG: Reinsburgstr. 19, 70178 Stuttgart; tel. (711) 6630; fax (711) 6632654; internet www .allianz-leben.de; f. 1922; Chair. Supervisory Bd Dr H. SCHULTE-NOELLE; Chair. Bd of Mans Dr G. RUPPRECHT.

Allianz Versicherungs AG: Elsa-Brandström-Str. 10–12, 80802 München; tel. (89) 38000; fax (89) 349941; e-mail medienzentrale@ allian.de; f. 1985; Chair. Dr H. SCHULTE-NOELLE; Gen. Man. Dr R. HAGEMANN.

AXA Colonia Krankenversicherung AG: 50592 Köln, tel. (221) 148125; fax (221) 14832602; f. 1962; Chair. CLAAS KLEYBOLDT. Gen. Man. Dr CARL HERMANN SCHLEIFFER.

AXA Colonia Lebensversicherung AG: Gereonstr. 71, 50670 Köln; tel. (1803) 556622; fax (221) 14822750; e-mail presse@ axa-colonia.de; internet www.axa-colonia.de; f. 1853; Chair Supervisory Bd CLAAS KLEYBOLDT; Chair. Bd of Management Dr CLAUS-MICHAEL DILL.

AXA Colonia Versicherung AG: Colonia-Allee 10–20, 50670 Köln; tel. (1803) 556622; fax (221) 14822740; e-mail service@axa-colonia .de; internet www.axa-colonia.de; f. 1839; Chair. Supervisory Bd CLAAS KLEYBOLDT; Chair. Bd of Management Dr CLAUS-MICHAEL DILL.

Continentale Krankenversicherung AG: Postfach 105032, 44047 Dortmund, tel. (231) 9190; fax (231) 9191799; f. 1926; Chair. F. LENSING-WOLFF; Gen. Man. Dr H. HOFFMANN.

DBV-Winterthur Lebensversicherung AG: Frankfurter Str. 50, 65178 Wiesbaden; tel. (611) 3630; fax (611) 3636565; e-mail info@dbv-winterthur.de; f. 1872; Chair. T. SCHULTE; Man. Dir H. FALK.

Debeka Krankenversicherungsverein AG: Ferdinand-Sauerbruch-Str. 18, 56058 Koblenz; tel. (261) 4980; fax (261) 41402; f. 1905; Chair. P. KUREPKAT; Gen. Man. P. GREISLER.

Deutsche Krankenversicherung AG: Postfach 100865, 50448 Köln; Aachener Str. 300, 50933 Köln; tel. (221) 5780; fax (221) 5783694; internet www.dkv.com; f. 1927; Chair. Dr HANS-JÜRGEN SCHINZLER; Gen. Man. Dr J. BOETIUS.

Deutscher Herold Lebensversicherungs-AG: Postfach 1448, 53004 Bonn, tel. (228) 26801; fax (228) 2683692; f. 1921; Chair. W. SOBOTA; Gen. Man. H. D. RITTERBEX.

Frankfurter Versicherungs-AG: 60257 Frankfurt a.M.; tel. (69) 71260; fax (69) 728750; f. 1929; Chair. Dr R. HAGEMANN; Gen. Man. Dr KARL LUDWIG Frhr VON FREYBERG.

Gerling-Konzern Allgemeine Versicherungs-AG: Postfach 100808, 50448 Köln; tel. (221) 1441; fax (221) 1443319; f. 1918; Chair. Supervisory Bd Dr J. ZECH; Chair. Bd of Management T. REINECKE.

Gothaer Versicherungsbank Versicherungsverein AG: Kaiser-Wilhelm-Ring 23–25, 50672 Köln; tel. (221) 574600; fax (221) 5746103; f. 1820; Chair. Supervisory Bd Prof. A. W. KLEIN; Chair. Bd Management Dr WOLFGANG PEINER.

Haftpflicht-Unterstützungs-Kasse kraftfahrender Beamter Deutschlands a.G. in Coburg (HUK-COBURG): Bahnhofsplatz, 96444 Coburg; tel. (9561) 960; fax (9561) 963636; e-mail huk-m@ huk.de; internet www.huk.de; f. 1933; CEO ROLF-PETER HOENEN.

HDI Haftpflichtverband der Deutschen Industrie Versicherungsverein a.G.: Postfach 510369, 30633 Hannover, tel. (511) 6450; fax (511) 6454545; internet www.hdi.de; f. 1903; Chair. Dr H.-J. FONK; Gen. Man. W.-D. BAUMGARTL.

Hamburg-Mannheimer Versicherungs-AG: Überseering 45, 22297 Hamburg; tel. (40) 63760; fax (40) 63762885; e-mail prr@ hamburg-mannheimer.de; internet www.hamburg-mannheimer.de; merger with Victoria Versicherung AG pending; f. 1899; Chair. Dr EDGAR JAMMOTT; Gen. Man. Dr GÖTZ WRICKE.

Iduna Vereinigte Lebensversicherung AG für Handwerk, Handel und Gewerbe: Postfach 302761, 20309 Hamburg, tel. (40) 41240; f. 1914; Chair. H. BECKER; Gen. Man. G. KUTZ.

LVM-Versicherungen: Kolde-Ring 21, 48126 Münster; tel. (251) 7020; fax (251) 7021099; e-mail info@lvm.de; internet www.lvm.de; f. 1896; Chair. H. OSTROP; Gen. Man. G. KETTLER.

R+V Versicherungsgruppe: Taunusstr. 1, 65193 Wiesbaden; tel. (611) 5330; fax (611) 5334500; f. 1922; group consists of 9 cos incl. R+V Allgemeine Versicherung AG, R+V Lebensversicherung AG and R+V Krankenversicherung AG; Chair. Dr J. BRIXNER; Gen. Man. Dr J. FÖRTERER.

SIGNAL Krankenversicherung AG: Joseph-Scherer-Str. 44139, 44139 Dortmund; tel. (231) 1350; fax (231) 1354638; f. 1907; Chair. PAUL SCHNITKER; Gen. Man. H. FROMMKNECHT.

Vereinte Krankenversicherung AG: Fritz-Schäffer-Str. 9, 81737 München; tel. (89) 67850; fax (89) 67856523; e-mail service-center@ vereinte.de; internet www.vereinte.de; f. 1925; Chair. Dr ULRICH RUMM.

Victoria Versicherung AG: Victoriaplatz 1–2, 40198 Düsseldorf; tel. (221) 4770; fax (211) 4772222; e-mail info@victoria.de; internet www.victoria.de; merger with Hamburg-Mannheimer Versicherungs-AG pending; f. 1904; Chair. Dr E. JANNOTT; Gen. Man. HORST DÖRING.

Victoria Lebensversicherung AG: Victoriaplatz 1–2, 40198 Düsseldorf; tel. (211) 4770; fax (211) 4772222; e-mail info@victoria.de; internet www.victoria.de; merger with Hamburg-Mannheimer Versicherungs-AG pending; f. 1929; Chair. Dr E. JANNOTT; Gen. Man. MICHAEL ROSENBERG.

Volksfürsorge Deutsche Lebensversicherung AG: Postfach 106420, 20043 Hamburg, tel. (40) 28650; fax (40) 28653369; f. 1913; Chair. Dr WOLFGANG KASKE; Gen. Man. Dr H. JÄGER.

Württembergische AG Versicherungs-Beteiligungsgesellschaft: Gutenbergstr. 30, 70176 Stuttgart; tel. (711) 6620; fax (711) 6622520; e-mail keu@wuerttembergische.de; internet www.wuerttembergische.de; f. 1828; Chair. Supervisory Bd Dr G. BÜCHNER; Chair. Bd of Management G. MEHL.

Reinsurance

Bayerische Rückversicherung AG: Sederanger 4–6, 80538 München; tel. (89) 38440; fax (89) 38442279; e-mail info@bayerischerueck.com; f. 1911; Chair. Dr G. BÜCHNER; Gen. Man. Dr S. LIPPE.

Deutsche Rückversicherung AG: Postfach 320269, 40417 Düsseldorf; Rossstr. 166, 40476 Düsseldorf; tel. (211) 455401; fax (211) 4554199; f. 1951; Chair. Dr G. SCHMIDT; Gen. Man. JÜRGEN REHMANN.

DARAG Deutsche Versicherungs- und Rückversicherungs-AG: Postfach 10, 13062 Berlin; Gustav-Adolf-Str. 130, 13086 Berlin; tel. (30) 477080; fax (30) 47708100; f. 1957, re-formed 1990; fire and non-life, technical, cargo transport, marine hull, liability, aviation insurance and reinsurance; Chair. KLAUS-DIETER LÄSSKER; Gen. Man. Dr INGO WELTHER.

ERC-Aachener Rückversicherungs-Gesellschaft AG: Postfach 25, 52001 Aachen, tel. (241) 93690; fax (241) 9369205; f. 1853; Chair. Supervisory Bd KAJ AHLMANN; Chair. Management Bd BERNHARD C. FINK.

ERC Frankona Rückversicherungs-AG: Postfach 860380, 81630 München; Maria-Theresia-Str. 35, 81675 München; tel. (89) 92280; fax (89) 9228395; f. 1886; Chair. DAVID L. CALHOUN; Gen. Man. BERNARD C. FINK.

Gerling-Konzern Globale Rückversicherungs-AG: Postfach 101544, 50597 Köln; tel. (221) 1441; fax (221) 1443718; internet www.ggre.com; f. 1954; Chair. A. KRACHT; Gen. Man. NORBERT STROHSCHEN.

Hamburger Internationale Rückversicherung AG: Postfach 1161, 25452 Rellingen; Halstenbekerweg 96A, 25462 Rellingen; tel. (4101) 4710; fax (4101) 471298; f. 1965; Chair. IVOR KIVERSTEIN; Gen. Man. R. SOLL.

Hannover Rückversicherungs-AG: Postfach 610369, 30603 Hannover; Karl-Wiechert-Allee 50, 30625 Hannover; tel. (511) 56040; fax (511) 56041188; e-mail info@hannover-re.com; internet www.hannover-re.com; f. 1966; Chair. Supervisory Bd W. BAUMGARTL; Chair. Management Bd W. ZELLER.

Kölnische Rückversicherungs-Gesellschaft AG: Postfach 102244, 50668 Köln; Theodor-Heuss-Ring 11, 50462 Köln; tel. (221) 97380; fax (221) 9738494; e-mail contact@gcre.com; internet www.gcre.com; f. 1846; Chair. PETER LÜTKE-BORNEFELD.

Münchener Rückversicherungs-Gesellschaft AG: Königinstr. 107, 80802 München; tel. (89) 38910; fax (89) 399056; e-mail info@munichre.com; internet www.munichre.com; f. 1880; all classes of reinsurance; Chair. ULRICH HARTMANN; Gen. Man. Dr HANS-JÜRGEN SCHINZLER.

R + V Versicherung-AG Reinsurance: Sonnenberger Str. 44, 65193 Wiesbaden; tel. (611) 533940; fax (611) 529610; f. 1935; all classes of reinsurance; Chair. W. GRÜGER; Gen. Man. Dr J. FÖRTERER.

Principal Insurance Association

Gesamtverband der Deutschen Versicherungswirtschaft eV: Friedrichstr. 191, 10117 Berlin; tel. (30) 20205000; fax (30) 20206000; f. 1948; affiliating one mem. asscn and 469 mem. cos; Pres. Dr BERND MICHAELS (Düsseldorf).

Trade and Industry

GOVERNMENT AGENCIES

Bundesstelle für Aussenhandelsinformation (Federal Foreign Trade Information Office): Postfach 100522, 50445 Köln; Agrippastr. 87–93, 50676 Köln; tel. (221) 20570; fax (221) 2057212; e-mail bfai@geod.geonet.de; internet www.bfa.de.

Bundesverband des Deutschen Gross- und Aussenhandels eV: Postfach 1349, 53003 Bonn; Bonner Talweg 57, 53113 Bonn; tel. (228)

260040; fax (228) 2600455; f. 1949; Dir-Gen. Dr PETER SPARY; 77 mem. asscns.

Hauptverband des Deutschen Einzelhandels eV: Postfach 250425, 50520 Köln; Gothaer Allee 2, 50969 Köln; tel. (221) 9365502; fax (221) 93655719; e-mail hde@einzelhandel.de; internet www.einzelhandel.de; f. 1947; Chair. HERMANN FRANZEN; Exec. Dir HOLGER WENZEL.

Industrial Investment Council (IIC): Charlottenstr. 57, 10104 Berlin; tel. (30) 20945660; fax (30) 20945666; internet www.iic.de; promotes investment in the eastern Länder; Chair. HANS CHRISTOPH VON ROHR.

Zentralverband Gewerblicher Verbundgruppen: Vorgebirgsstr. 43, 53119 Bonn; tel. (228) 985840; fax (228) 9858410; f. 1992; six dirs; c. 400 mems.

CHAMBERS OF COMMERCE

Deutscher Industrie- und Handelstag (Association of German Chambers of Industry and Commerce): Adenauerallee 148, 53113 Bonn; tel. (228) 1040; fax (228) 104158; Pres. Dipl. Ing. HANS PETER STIHL; Sec.-Gen. Dr FRANZ SCHOSER; affiliates 83 Chambers of Industry and Commerce.

There are Chambers of Industry and Commerce in all the principal towns and also fourteen regional associations including:

Arbeitsgemeinschaft Hessischer Industrie- und Handelskammern: Börsenplatz 4, 60313 Frankfurt a.M.; tel. (69) 21970; fax (69) 2197424; Chair. Dr FRANK NIETHAMMER; Sec.-Gen. Dr WOLFGANG LINDSTAEDT; 12 mems.

Arbeitsgemeinschaft der Industrie- und Handelskammern in Mecklenburg-Vorpommern: Schlossstr. 17, 19053 Schwerin; tel. (385) 51030; fax (385) 5103136; e-mail info@schwerin.ihk.de; Pres. HANSHEINRICH LIESBERG.

Arbeitsgemeinschaft der Industrie- und Handelskammern Rheinland-Pfalz: Herzogenbuscher Str. 12, 54292 Trier; tel. (651) 97770; fax (651) 9777105; e-mail huepel@trier.ihk.de; Sec. Dr WOLFGANG SCHNEIDER; four mems.

Arbeitsgemeinschaft der Industrie- und Handelskammern in Sachsen: Str. der Nationen 25, 0911 Chemnitz; tel. (371) 69000; fax (371) 643018.

Arbeitsgemeinschaft Norddeutscher Industrie- und Handelskammern: Adolphsplatz 1, 20457 Hamburg; tel. (40) 366382; Vice-Pres. Dr MARTIN WILLICH; Sec. Dr UWE CHRISTIANSEN.

Arbeitsgemeinschaft der Thuringer Industrie- und Handelskammern: Weimarische Str. 45, 99099 Erfurt; tel. (361) 34840; fax (361) 3485972; f. 1991; Pres. NIELS LUND CHRESTENSEN.

Baden-Württembergischer Industrie-und Handelskammertag: Jägerstr. 40, 70174 Stuttgart; tel. (711) 22550060; fax (711) 22550077; e-mail ihktag@baden-wuerttemberg.ihk.de; internet www.baden-wuerttemberg.ihk.de; Chair. TILL CASPER.

Bayerischer Industrie- und Handelskammertag: Max-Joseph-Str. 2, 80333 München, tel. (89) 51160; fax (89) 5116306; Pres. Dr CLAUS HIPP; Sec. Gen. Dr REINHARD DÖRFLER; 10 mems.

IHK-Vereinigung Schleswig-Holstein: Fackenburger Allee 2, 23554 Lübeck; tel. (451) 60060; fax (451) 6006999; e-mail ihk@luebeck.ihk.de; Chair. HANS GEORG RIECKMANN; Sec. Gen. WULF HERMANN (acting).

Industrie- und Handelskammer Magdeburg: Postfach 1840, Alter Markt 8, 39104 Magdeburg; tel. (391) 56930; fax (391) 5693193; f. 1825; Pres. Dr KLAUS HIECKMANN.

Industrie- und Handelskammern Potsdam: Grosse Weinmeisterstr. 59, 14469 Potsdam; tel. (331) 2786251; fax (331) 2786190; e-mail ullmann@potsdam.ihk.de; internet www.ihk.de/potsdam; f. 1990; Pres. Dr VICTOR STIMMING; CEO PETER EGENTER.

Vereinigung der Industrie- und Handelskammern in Nordrhein-Westfalen: Postfach 240120, 40090 Düsseldorf; tel. (211) 367020; fax (211) 3670221; CEO HANS GEORG CRONE-ERDMANN; Pres. Dr JÖRG MITTELSTEN SCHEID; 16 mems.

Vereinigung der Niedersächsischen Industrie- und Handelskammern: Postfach 3029, 30030 Hannover; Schiffgraben 49, 30175 Hannover; tel. (511) 3107289; fax (511) 3107383; f. 1899; Pres. DIETER SCHLECHT; Man. Dir Dr WILFRIED PREWO; seven mems.

INDUSTRIAL AND TRADE ASSOCIATIONS

Bundesverband der Deutschen Industrie eV (Federation of German Industry): Postfach 3029, 10178 Berlin, tel. (30) 20280; fax (30) 20282566; e-mail presse@bdi-online.de; Pres. HANS-OLAF HENKEL; Dir-Gen. Dr LUDOLF VON WARTENBERG; mems include some of the following asscns:

Arbeitsgemeinschaft Keramische Industrie eV (Ceramics): Postfach 1624, 95090 Selb; Schillerstr. 17, 95100 Selb; tel. (9287) 80844; fax (9287) 70492; Pres. WENDELIN VON BOCH; Man. PETER FRISCHHOLZ.

Bundesverband Baustoffe—Steine und Erden eV (Building): Postfach 150162, 60061 Frankfurt a.M.; Friedrich-Ebert-Anlage 38, 60325 Frankfurt a.M.; tel. (69) 7560820; fax (69) 75608212; e-mail bubaustoffe@aol.com; internet www.baustoffindustrie.de; f. 1948; Pres. Dr Jürgen Lose; Chief Dir Dr Wolfgang Mack.

Bundesverband Bekleidungsindustrie eV (Clothing): Postfach 100955, 50449 Köln; Mevissenstr. 15, 50668 Köln; tel. (221) 7744110; fax (221) 7744118; e-mail bbi@bbi-online.de; internet www .bbi-online. de; Pres. Dr Fritz Goost; Dirs-Gen. Bernd Kemper, Friedhelm N. Sartoris.

Bundesverband der Deutschen Entsorgungswirtschaft (BDE) (Waste Disposal and Recycling): Schönhauser Str. 3, 50968 Köln; tel. (221) 9347000; fax (221) 93470090; e-mail info@bde.org; internet www.bde.org; Pres. Bernard Kemper; Dir-Gen. Frank-Rainer Billigmann.

Bundesverband der Deutschen Luft- und Raumfahrtindustrie eV (BDLI) (German Aerospace Industries Asscn): Friedrichstr. 152, 10117 Berlin; tel. (30) 2061400; fax (30) 20614090; e-mail info@bdli.de; internet www.bdli.de; f. 1952; Pres. Dr Gustav Humbert; Man. Dir Dr Hans Eberhard Birke.

Bundesverband Druck eV (Printing): Postfach 1869, 65008 Wiesbaden; Biebricher Allee 79, 65187 Wiesbaden; tel. (611) 8030; fax (611) 803113; e-mail info@bvd-online.de; f. 1947; Pres. Alexander Schorsch; Man. Dirs Thomas Mayr, Peter Klemm; 12 mem. asscns.

Bundesverband Glasindustrie und Mineralfaserindustrie eV (Glass): Postfach 101753, 40008 Düsseldorf; Stresemannstr. 26, 40210 Düsseldorf; tel. (211) 168940; fax (211) 1689427; e-mail info@bvglas.de; Chair. Dr Leopold von Heimendahl; 6 mem. asscns.

Bundesverband Schmuck, Uhren, Silberwaren und Verwandte Industrien eV: Poststr. 1, 75172 Pforzheim; tel. (7231) 33041; fax (7231) 355887; Pres. Carl-Heinrich Lüth; Man. Dir Dr Alfred Schneider.

Bundesvereinigung der Deutschen Ernährungsindustrie eV (Food): Godesberger Allee 142–148, 53175 Bonn; tel. (228) 308290; fax (228) 3082999; e-mail bve@bve-online.de; internet www .bve-online.de; f. 1949; Chair. Dr Peter Traumann; Chief Gen. Man. Prof. Dr Matthias Horst.

Deutscher Giessereiverband (Foundries): Postfach 101961, 40100 Düsseldorf; Sohnstr. 70, 40237 Düsseldorf; tel. (211) 68710; fax (211) 6871333; e-mail info@dgv.de; internet www.dgv.de; Pres. Helmut Christmann; Man. Dir Dr Klaus Urbat.

Deutscher Hotel- und Gaststättenverband eV (DEHOGA): Am Weidendamm 1a, 10117 Berlin; tel. (30) 7262520; fax (30) 72625242; f. 1949; Pres. Dr Erich Kaub; Gen. Sec. Christian Ehlers; over 85,000 mems.

DVG Deutsche Verbundgesellschaft eV (Electricity): Ziegelhäuser Landstr. 5, 69120 Heidelberg; tel. (6221) 40370; fax (6221) 403771; e-mail info@dvg-heidelberg.de; internet www .dvg-heidelberg.de; Pres. Prof. Dr Rolf Winnmöller; Dir-Gen. Dr Jürgen Schwarz.

EBM Wirtschaftsverband (Metal Goods): Postfach 105121, 40858 Ratingen; An der Pont 48, 40885 Ratingen; tel. (2102) 1860; fax (2102) 186169; e-mail info@ebm.de; internet www.ebm.de; Pres. Günter Becker; Gen. Man. Ulrich Böshagen.

Gemeinschaftsausschuss der Deutschen gewerblichen Wirtschaft (Joint Committee for German Industry and Commerce): Gustav-Heinemann-Ufer 84–88, 5000 Köln 51; tel. (221) 370800; fax (221) 3708730; f. 1950; a discussion forum for the principal industrial and commercial orgs; Pres. Dr Tyll Necker; 16 mem. orgs, including:

Gesamtverband kunststoffverarbeitende Industrie eV (GKV) (Plastics): Am Hauptbahnhof 12, 60329 Frankfurt a.M.; tel. (69) 271050; fax (69) 232799; e-mail tenhagen-gkv@t-online.de; internet www.gkv.de; f. 1950; Chair. Günter Schwank; Sec.-Gen. Joachim ten Hagen; 750 mems.

Gesamtverband der Textilindustrie in der BRD (Gesamttextil) eV (Textiles): Postfach 5340, 65728 Eschborn; Frankfurter Str. 10–14, 65760 Eschborn; tel. (6196) 9660; fax (6196) 42170; f. 1948; internet www.textil-online.de; Dir-Gen. Dr Wolf R. Baumann.

Hauptverband der Deutschen Bauindustrie eV (Building): Wiesbaden; tel. (611) 7720; fax (611) 772240; f. 1948; Pres. Dr Othmar Franz; Dir-Gen. Michael Knipper; 23 mem. asscns.

Hauptverband der Deutschen Holz und Kunststoffe verarbeitenden Industrie und verwandter Industriezweige eV (HDH) (Woodwork): Flutgraben 2, 53604 Bad-Honnef; tel (2224) 93770; fax (2224) 937777; e-mail info@hdh-ev.de; internet www.hdh-ev.de; f. 1948; Pres. Helmut Lubke; Man. Dir Dirk-Uwe Klaas; 30 mem. asscns.

Hauptverband der Papier, Pappe und Kunststoffe verarbeitenden Industrie eV (HPV) (Paper, Board and Plastic): Strubbergstr. 70, 60489 Frankfurt a.M.; tel. (69) 9782810; fax (69)

97828130; e-mail info@hpv-ev.org; internet www.hpv-ev.org; f. 1948; 10 regional groups, 20 production groups; Pres. Lutz Boeder; Dir-Gen. Thomas Beck; 1,300 mems.

Mineralölwirtschaftsverband eV (Petroleum): Steindamm 55, 20099 Hamburg; tel. (40) 248490; fax (40) 24849-253; e-mail mwv@mwv.de; internet www.mwv.de; f. 1946; Chair. Pieter Berkhout; Man. Dir Dr Peter Schlüter.

Verband der Automobilindustrie eV (Motor Cars): Postfach 170563, 60079 Frankfurt a.M.; Westendstr. 61, 60325 Frankfurt a.M.; tel. (69) 975070; fax (69) 97507261; internet www.vda.de; Pres. Dr Bernd Gottschalk.

Verband der Chemischen Industrie eV (Chemical Industry): Karlstr. 21, 60329 Frankfurt a.M.; tel. (69) 25560; fax (69) 2556-1471; f. 1877; Pres. Dr Manfred Schneider; Dir-Gen. Dr Wilfried Sahm; 1,500 mems.

Verband der Cigarettenindustrie (Cigarettes): Königswinterer Str. 550, 53227 Bonn; tel. (228) 449060; fax (228) 442582; e-mail vdc@vdc.bonn.de; Chair. Karsten Schmidt; Dir-Gen. Dr Ernst Brückner.

Verband der Deutschen Feinmechanischen und Optischen Industrie eV (Optical and Precision Instruments): Kirchweg 2, 50858 Köln; tel. (221) 9486280; fax (221) 483428; e-mail info@ feinoptik.de; internet www.feinoptik.de; f. 1949; Chair. Randolf Rodenstock; Dir Harald Russegger.

Verband Deutscher Maschinen- und Anlagenbau eV (VDMA) (Machinery and Plant Manufacture): Postfach 710864, 60498 Frankfurt a.M.; Lyoner Str. 18, 60528 Frankfurt a.M.; tel. (69) 66030; fax (69) 66031511; e-mail pvoe@vdma.org; internet www.vdma.org; f. 1892; Pres. Eberhard Reuther; Gen. Man. Dr Martin Wansleben.

Verband Deutscher Papierfabriken eV (Paper): Adenauerallee 55, 53113 Bonn; tel. (228) 267050; fax (228) 2670562; Pres. Hans-Michael Gellenkamp; Dir-Gen. Klaus Windhagen.

Verband für Schiffbau und Meerestechnik eV (Shipbuilding): An der Alster 1, 20099 Hamburg; tel. (40) 2801520; fax (40) 28015230; e-mail vsm.e.v.@t-online.de; internet www.vsm.de; Gen. Dir Dr Werner Schöttelndreyer; Man. Dirs Volkhard Meier, Dr Mathias Münchau.

Verein der Zuckerindustrie (Sugar): Am Hofgarten 8, 53113 Bonn; tel. (228) 22850; fax (228) 2285100; e-mail wvz.wvz@t-online .de; internet www.zuckerwirtschaft.de; f. 1850; Chair. Dr Klaus Korn; Dir-Gen. Dr Dieter Langendorf.

Wirtschaftsverband der Deutschen Kautschukindustrie eV (W.d.K.) (Rubber): Zeppelinallee 69, 60487 Frankfurt a.M.; tel. (69) 79360; fax (69) 7936165 ; f. 1894; Pres. Robert Schaefer; Gen. Man. Klaus Mocker; 92 mems.

Wirtschaftsverband Erdöl- und Erdgasgewinnung eV (Association of Crude Oil and Gas Producers): Brühlstr. 9, 30169 Hannover; tel. (511) 121720; fax (511) 1217210; e-mail info@ erdoel-erdgas.de; f. 1945; Pres. Dr Karl Heinz Geisel; Gen. Man. Josef Schmid.

Wirtschaftsverband Stahlbau und Energietechnik (SET) (Steel and Energy): Postfach 320420, 40419 Düsseldorf; Sternstr. 36, 40479 Düsseldorf; tel. (211) 498700; fax (211) 4987036; e-mail setev@aol.com; internet www.set-online.de; Chair. S. Michelfelder; Dir-Gen. R. Maass.

Wirtschaftsverband Stahlumformung eV (Steelworks): Postfach 4009, 58040 Hagen; Goldene Pforte 1, 58093 Hagen; tel. (2331) 95880; fax (2331) 51046; Pres. Jürgen R. Thumann; Dir-Gen. Hans-Dieter Oelkers.

Centralvereinigung Deutscher Wirtschaftsverbände für Handelsvermittlung und Vertrieb: Am Weidendamm 1a, 10117 Berlin; tel. (30) 72625600; fax (30) 72625699; e-mail cdh .centralvereinigung@cdh.de; internet www.cdh.de; Pres. Horst Platz; Gen. Sec. Dr Andreas Paffhausen; 18,000 mems in all brs.

Wirtschaftsvereinigung Bergbau eV (Mining): Postfach 120753, 10597 Berlin; Am Schillertheater 4, 10625 Berlin; tel. (30) 3151820; e-mail wvb.berlin@t-online.de; internet www.wv-bergbau.de; Pres. Dr Volker Schäfer; Gen. Man. Karl-Ernst Kegel; 18 mem. asscns.

WirtschaftsVereinigung Metalle (Metal): Postfach 105463, 40045 Düsseldorf; Bonneshof 5, 40474 Düsseldorf; tel. (211) 47960; fax (211) 4796400; e-mail postmaster@ne-metalnet.de; internet www.ne-metalnet.de; Pres. Dr Werner Marnette; Dir-Gen. Martin Kneer.

Wirtschaftsvereinigung Stahl (Steel): Postfach 105464, 40045 Düsseldorf; Sohnstr. 65, 40237 Düsseldorf; tel. (211) 67070; fax (211) 6707310; e-mail wvstahl@wvstahl.de; internet www.stahl.online.de; Pres. Prof. Dr Dieter Ameling; Dir Albrecht Kormann.

Wirtschaftsvereinigung Ziehereien und Kaltwalzwerke eV (Metal): Drahthaus, Kaiserswerther Str. 137, 40474 Düsseldorf; tel. (211) 4564246; fax (211) 432154; Chair. Jürgen R. Thumann; Gen. Man. Günter Müller.

Zentralverband des Deutschen Handwerks: Johanniterstr. 1, Haus des Deutschen Handwerks, 53113 Bonn; tel. (228) 5450; fax

(228) 545205; f. 1949; Pres. HERIBERT SPÄTH; Gen. Sec. HANNS-EBERHARD SCHLEYER; 56 mem. chambers, 52 asscns.

Zentralverband Elektrotechnik- und Elektronikindustrie e V (ZVEI) (Electrical and Electronic Equipment): Postfach 701261, 60591 Frankfurt a.M.; Stresemannallee 19, 60596 Frankfurt a.M.; tel. (69) 63020; fax (69) 6302317; e-mail zvei@zvei.org; internet www.zvei.org; f. 1918; Chair. Dr DIETMAR HARTING; Dirs Dr FRANZ-JOSEF WISSING, NORBERT KNAUP, INGO RÜSCH, GOTTHARD GRAF; 1,300 mems.

EMPLOYERS' ORGANIZATIONS

Bundesvereinigung der Deutschen Arbeitgeberverbände (Confederation of German Employers' Associations): BDA im Haus des Deutschen Wirtschaft, 11054 Berlin; tel. (30) 20330; fax (30) 20331055; e-mail info@bda-online.de; internet www.bda-online.de; f. 1913; Pres. Dr DIETER HUNDT; Dirs Dr REINHARD GÖHNER, HEISE; represents the professional and regional interests of German employers in the social policy field, affiliates 14 regional asscns, and 54 branch asscns, of which some are listed under industrial asscns (see above).

Affiliated associations:

Arbeitgeberkreis Gesamttextil im Gesamtverband der Textilindustrie in der Bundesrepublik Deutschland eV (General Textile Employers' Organization): Frankfurter Str. 10–14, 65760 Eschborn; tel. (6196) 9660; fax (6196) 42170; internet www.textil-online.de; Chair. HARTMUT BIELEFELD; Dir Dr KLAUS SCHMIDT; 9 mem. asscns.

Arbeitgeberverband der Cigarettenindustrie (Employers' Association of Cigarette Manufacturers): Harvestehuder Weg 88, 20149 Hamburg; tel. (40) 445739; fax (40) 443039; f. 1949; Pres. Dr JÖRG SCHAPPEI; Dir LUTZ SANNIG.

Arbeitgeberverband der Deutschen Binnenschiffahrt eV (Employers' Association of German Inland Waterway Transport): Dammstr. 15–17, 47119 Duisburg; tel. (203) 8000631; fax (203) 8000628; e-mail vbw-eubinsch@t-online.de; Pres. Dr WOLFGANG HÖNEMANN; Dir G. DÜTEMEYER.

Arbeitgeberverband Deutscher Eisenbahnen eV (German Railway Employers' Association): Volksgartenstr. 54A, 50677 Köln; tel. (221) 9318450; fax (221) 93184588; Pres. KLAUS-DIETER BOLLHÖFER; Dir Dr HANS-PETER ACKMANN.

Arbeitgeberverband des Privaten Bankgewerbes eV (Private Banking Employers' Association): Burgstr. 28, 10178 Berlin; tel. (30) 590011270; f. 1954; 149 mems; Pres. Dr TESSEN VON HEYDERBRECK; Dir GERD BENRATH.

Arbeitgeberverband der Versicherungsunternehmen in Deutschland (Employers' Association of Insurance Companies): Arabellastr. 29, 81925 München; tel. (89) 9220010; fax (89) 92200150; Pres. HANS SCHREIBER; Dir-Gen. Dr JÖRG MULLER-STEIN.

Bundesarbeitsgeberverband Chemie eV (Federation of Employers' Associations in the Chemical Industry): Postfach 1280, Abraham-Lincoln-Str. 24, 65189 Wiesbaden; tel. (611) 778810; fax (611) 7788123; e-mail info.bavc@t-online.de; internet www.chemie-arbeitgeber.de; Pres. PAUL COENEN; Dir HANS PAUL FREY; 11 mem. asscns.

Bundesvereinigung der Arbeitgeber im Bundesverband Bekleidungsindustrie eV (Confederation of Employers of the Clothing Industry): Postfach 100955, 50449 Köln; Mevissenstr. 15, 50668 Köln; tel. (221) 7744110; fax (221) 7744118; e-mail bbi@bbi-online.de; internet www.bbi-online.de; Pres. WILFRIED BRANDES; Dir BERND KEMPER; 12 mem. asscns.

Gesamtverband der Deutschen Land- und Forstwirtschaftlichen Arbeitgeberverbände eV (Federation of Agricultural and Forestry Employers' Associations): Godesberger Allee 142–148, 53175 Bonn; tel. (228) 8198248; fax (228) 8198204; Pres. WOLF VON BUCHWALDT; Sec. MARTIN MALLACH.

Gesamtverband der metallindustriellen Arbeitgeberverbände eV (Federation of the Metal Trades Employers' Associations): Volksgartenstr. 54A, 50677 Köln; tel. (221) 33990; fax (221) 3399233; e-mail info@gesamtmetall.de; Pres. Dr WERNER STUMPFE; 15 mem. asscns.

Vereinigung der Arbeitgeberverbände der Deutschen Papierindustrie eV (Federation of Employers' Associations of the German Paper Industry): Adenauerallee 55, 53113 Bonn; tel. (228) 2672810; fax (228) 215270; Pres. HEINRICH AUGUST SCHOELLER; Dir PETER KARTHÄUSER; 8 mem. asscns.

Vereinigung der Arbeitgeberverbände energie- und versorgungswirtschaftlicher Unternehmungen (Employers' Federation of Energy and Power Supply Enterprises): Kurt Schumacher-Str. 24, 30159 Hannover; tel. (511) 911090; fax (511) 9110940; f. 1962; Pres. UDO CAHN VON SEELEN; Dir HERMANN D. STRÖHMBERG; 7 mem. asscns.

Regional employers' associations:

Landesvereinigung Baden-Württembergischer Arbeitgeberverbände eV: Postfach 700501, 70574 Stuttgart; Löffelstr. 22–24, 70597 Stuttgart; tel. (711) 76820; fax (711) 7651675; e-mail info@vmi.de; internet www.vmi.de; Pres. Dr DIETER HUNDT; Dir Dr ULRICH BROCKER; 47 mem. asscns.

Vereinigung der Bayerischen Wirtschaft (Federation of Employers' Associations in Bavaria): Max-Joseph-Str. 5, 80333 München; tel. (89) 55178200.

Vereinigung der Unternehmensverbände in Berlin und Brandenburg eV (Federation of Employers' Associations in Berlin and Brandenburg): Am Schillertheater 2, 10625 Berlin; tel. (30) 310050; fax (30) 31005120; internet www.uvb-bln-brbg.de; Pres. ERICH GERARD; Dir Dr HARTMANN KLEINER; 70 mem. asscns.

Die Unternehmensverbände im Lande Bremen eV (Federation of Employers' Associations in the Land of Bremen): Schillerstr. 10, 28195 Bremen; tel. (421) 368020; fax (421) 3680249; Pres. Dr MANFRED AHLSDORFF; Dir EBERHARD SCHODDE; 16 mem. asscns.

Landesvereinigung der Unternehmensverbände in Hamburg eV (Federation of Employers' Associations in Hamburg): Kapstadring 10, 22297 Hamburg; tel. (40) 63785000; Pres. Dr HELLMUT KRUSE; Gen. Man. JÜRGEN MEINEKE; 30 mem. asscns.

Vereinigung der Hessischen Unternehmerverbände eV (Federation of Employers' Associations in Hesse): Emil-von-Behring-Str. 4, 60439 Frankfurt a.M.; tel. (69) 958080; fax (69) 95808126; e-mail vhu@unternehmerverbaende.de; internet www.unternehmerverbaende.de; f. 1947; Pres. Prof. DIETER WEIDEMANN; Dir and Sec. VOLKER FASBENDER; 51 mem. asscns.

Vereinigung der Unternehmensverbände für Mecklenburg-Vorpommern e.V. (Federation of Employers' Associations of Mecklenburg-West Pomerania): Eckdrift 93, 19061 Schwerin; tel. (385) 6356100; fax (385) 6356151; internet www.bildungswerk-wirtschaft.de; Pres. KLAUS HERING; Dir Dr THOMAS KLISCHAN; 22 mem. asscns.

Unternehmensverbände Niedersachsen eV (Federation of Employers' Associations in Lower Saxony): Schiffgraben 36, 30175 Hannover; tel. (511) 8505243; fax (511) 8505268; e-mail uvn@uvn-online.de; internet www.uvn-online.de; Pres. Dr KURT EIGLMEIER; Dir GERNOT PREUSS; 60 mem. asscns.

Landesvereinigung der Arbeitgeberverbände Nordrhein-Westfalen eV (North Rhine-Westphalia Federation of Employers' Associations): Postfach 300643, 40406 Düsseldorf; Uerdingerstr. 58–62, 40474 Düsseldorf; tel. (211) 45730; fax (211) 4573209; e-mail arbeitgebernrw@arbeitgebernrw.de; Pres. Dr Ing. JOCHEN F. KIRCHHOFF; Dir Dr HANSJÖRG DÖPP; 82 mem. asscns.

Landesvereinigung Rheinland-Pfälzischer Unternehmerverbände eV (Federation of Employers' Associations in the Rhineland Palatinate): Hölderlinstr. 1, 55131 Mainz; tel. (6131) 55750; fax (6131) 557539; internet www.lvu.de; f. 1963; Pres. Dr EBERHARD SCHWARZ; 29 mem. asscns.

Vereinigung der Saarländischen Unternehmensverbände (Federation of Employers' Associations in Saarland): Harthweg 15, 66119 Saarbrücken; tel. (681) 954340; fax (681) 5847386; internet www.vsu.de; Pres. Dr WALTER KOCH; Dir Dr HEIKO JÜTTE; 19 mem. asscns.

Vereinigung der Sächsischen Wirtschaft ev (VSW) (Federation of Employers' Associations in Saxony): Postfach 300200, 01131 Dresden; Washingtonstr. 16, 01139 Dresden; tel. (351) 255930; fax (351) 2559378; internet www.wirtschaftsverbaende-sachsen.de; Pres. MANFRED KREUTEL; Gen. Man. Dr ANDREAS WINKLER; 30 mem. asscns.

Landesvereinigung der Arbeitgeber-und-Wirtschaftsverbände Sachsen-Anhalt e.V. (Provincial Federation of Employers' and Managers' Associations of Saxony-Anhalt): Postfach 4249, 39017 Magdeburg; Humboldtstr. 14, 39112 Magdeburg; tel. (391) 625450; fax (391) 6254570; Pres. Dr ROLF BROSE; Dir Dr JOCHEN STEINECKE; 18 mem. asscns.

Vereinigung der Schleswig-Holsteinischen Unternehmensverbände eV (Federation of Employers' Associations in Schleswig-Holstein): Adolf-Steckel-Str. 17, 24768 Rendsburg; tel. (4331) 14200; fax (4331) 142020; Pres. Prof. Dr HANS HEINRICH DRIFTMANN; Dir JÜRGEN MEINEKE; 36 mem. asscns.

Verband der Wirtschaft Thüringens e.V. (Association of Thuringian Management): Postfach 329, 99007 Erfurt; Lossiusstr. 1, 99094 Erfurt; tel. (361) 67590; fax (361) 6759222; Pres. Dipl. Ing. WALTER BOTSCHATZKI; Dir LOTAR SCHMIDT; 37 mem. asscns.

UTILITIES

Electricity

Bewag AG: 12432 Berlin; tel. (30) 26711077; fax (30) 26714667; e-mail bewag@bewag.com; internet www.bewag.de; f. 1884; supplies

Berlin; promotes development of urban utilization of renewable energy resources.

E.ON Energie AG: Brienner Str. 40, 80333 München; tel. (800) 2030408; fax (800) 3888883; e-mail info@eon-energie.de; internet www.eon-energie.de; f. 2000 by merger of Bayernwerk AG and Preussenelektra AG; Jt Chairs of Bd ULRICH HARTMANN, Prof. Dr WILHELM SIMSON.

Energie Baden-Württemberg (EnBW): Durlacher Allee 93; tel. (800) 999; e-mail info@enbw.com; internet www.enbw.com.

Hamburgische Electricitäts-Werke AG (HEW): Überseering 12, 22297 Hamburg; tel. (40) 63960; (40) 63862770; e-mail hew@hew.de; internet www.hew.de; 73% owned by regional Govt; supplies Hamburg region.

RWE Energie AG: Postfach 103165, 45031 Essen; Kruppstr. 5, 45128 Essen; tel. (201) 1851; fax (201) 1854313; internet www.rweenergie.de; Pres. DIETMAR KUHNT; CEO MANFRED REMMEL.

Vereinigte Elektrizitätswerke Westfalen AG (VEW): Postfach 105056, 44047 Dortmund; Rheinlanddamm 24, 44139 Dortmund; tel. (231) 4381; e-mail info@vew.de; internet www.vew.de; partly state-owned; serves North Rhine-Westphalia.

Vereinigte Energiewerke AG (VEAG): Chaussestr. 23, 10115 Berlin; tel. (30) 51512521; fax (30) 51502220; e-mail info@veag.de; internet www.veag.de; serves eastern Germany.

Vereinigung Deutscher Elektrizitätswerk eV (VDEW): Stresemannallee 23, 60596 Frankfurt a.M.; tel. (69) 63041; fax (69) 6304289; internet www.strom.de; asscn of electricity supply cos; Dir-Gen. Dr EBERHARD MELLER.

Gas

Bundesverband der Deutschen Gas- und Wasserwirtschaft eV (BGW): Euskirchener Str. 80, Bonn; tel. (228) 520010; internet www.bgw.de; asscn of gas and water cos.

GASAG Berliner Gaswerke AG: 10703 Berlin; tel. (30) 78720; fax (30) 78723044; e-mail service@gasag.de; internet www.gasag.de; Chair. Supervisory Bd Dr KARL KAUERMANN.

Gasversorgung Süddeutschland GmbH (GVS): Stuttgart; internet www.gvs-erdgas.de; f. 1961; Chair. Supervisory Bd GERHARD WIDDER.

Ruhrgas AG: Huttropstr. 60, 45138 Essen; tel. (201) 1843857; fax (201) 1843171; e-mail info@ruhrgas.com; internet www.ruhrgas.de; f. 1926; Chair. FRIEDRICH SPÄTH.

Vereinigte Elektrizitätswerke Westfalen AG (VEW): Postfach 105056, 44047 Dortmund; Rheinlanddamm 24, 44139 Dortmund; tel. (231) 4381; e-mail info@vew.de; internet www.vew.de; partly state-owned; supplies gas (and electricity, see above) to North Rhine-Westphalia.

TRADE UNIONS

Following German unification in October 1990, the trade unions of the former GDR were absorbed into the member unions of the DGB (see below).

Deutscher Gewerkschaftsbund (DGB): Postfach 101026, 40001 Düsseldorf; Hans-Böckler-Str. 39, 40476 Düsseldorf; tel. (211) 43010; fax (211) 4301471; internet www.dgb.de; f. 1949; Pres. DIETER SCHULTE; Vice-Pres. URSULA ENGELEN-KEFER.

The following unions, with a total of 8,310,783 members (December 1998), are affiliated to the DGB:

Industriegewerkschaft Bauen-Agrar-Umwelt (Building and Construction Trade): Olof-Palme-Str. 19, 60439 Frankfurt a.M.; tel. (69) 957370; fax (69) 95737800; e-mail presse@igbau.de; internet www.igbau.de; Pres. KLAUS WIESEHÜGEL; 539,744 mems (Dec. 2000).

Industriegewerkschaft Bergbau, Chemie, Energie (IG BCE) (Mining, Chemical and Energy): Postfach 3047, 30030 Hannover; Königsworther Platz 6, 30167 Hannover; tel. (511) 76310; fax (511) 7631713; e-mail abt.internationales.europa@igbce.de; internet www.igbce.de; Pres. HUBERTUS SCHMOLDT; 890,000 mems (Dec. 2000).

Gewerkschaft der Eisenbahner Deutschlands (Railwaymen): Weilburger Str. 24; 60326 Frankfurt a.M.; tel. (69) 7536204; fax (69) 7536223; e-mail gdad.hansen@t-online.de; Pres. NORBERT HANSEN; 352,161 mems (Dec. 1998).

Gewerkschaft Erziehung und Wissenschaft (Education and Sciences): Reifenbergerstr. 21, 60489 Frankfurt a.M.; tel. (69) 789730; fax (69) 78973201; Pres. Dr DIETER WUNDER; 281,326 mems (Dec. 1998).

*Gewerkschaft Handel, Banken und Versicherungen (Commerce, Banks and Insurance): Kanzlerstr. 8, 40472 Düsseldorf; tel. (211) 90400; fax (211) 9040888; f. 1973; Pres. MARGRET MÖNIG-RAANE; 471,333 mems (Dec. 1998).

Gewerkschaft Holz und Kunststoff (Wood and Plastic-work): Sonnenstr. 10, 40227 Düsseldorf; tel. (211) 77030; fax (211) 7703201;

e-mail 106443.1070@compuserve.com; f. 1945; Pres. GISBERT SCHLEMMER; 145,128 mems (Dec. 1998).

Gewerkschaft Leder (Leather): Willi-Bleicher-Str. 20, 70174 Stuttgart; tel. (711) 295555; fax (711) 293345; Pres. WERNER DICK; 25,000 mems (Dec. 1994).

*Industriegewerkschaft Medien (Media): Postfach 102451, 70020 Stuttgart; Friedrichstr. 15, 70174 Stuttgart; tel. (711) 20180; fax (711) 2018262; internet www.igmedien.de; Pres. DETLEF HENSCHE; 180,000 mems. (Nov. 1999).

IG Metall—die Gewerkschaft in Produktion und Dienstleistung der Bereiche Metall-Elektro, Textil-Bekleidung, Holz-Kunststoff (Metal Workers' Union): Lyoner Str. 32, 60519 Frankfurt a.M.; tel. (69) 66930; fax (69) 66932843; e-mail presse.igm@igmetall.de; internet www.igmetall.de; Chair. KLAUS ZWICKEL; 2.7m. mems (1999).

Gewerkschaft Nahrung-Genuss-Gaststätten (Food, Delicacies and Catering): Haubachstr. 76, 22765 Hamburg; tel. (40) 380130; fax (40) 3892637; e-mail hauptverwaltung@ngg.net; internet www.gewerkschaft-ngg.de; f. 1949; Pres. FRANZ-JOSEF MÖLLENBERG; 260,000 mems (Jan. 2000).

*Gewerkschaft Öffentliche Dienste, Transport und Verkehr (Public Services and Transport Workers' Union): Theodor-Heuss-Str. 2, 70174 Stuttgart; tel. (711) 20970; fax (711) 2097462; Chair. HERBERT MAI; 1,582,776 mems (Dec. 1998).

Gewerkschaft der Polizei (Police Union): Forststr. 3A, 40721 Hilden; tel. (211) 71040; fax (211) 7104222; f. 1950; Chair. NORBERT SPINRATH; Sec. W. DICKE; 193,578 mems (Dec. 1998).

*Deutsche Postgewerkschaft (Post and Telecommunications Union): Rhonestr. 2, 60528 Frankfurt a.M.; tel. (69) 66950; fax (69) 666941; internet www.dpg-hv.de; Pres. KURT VAN HAAREN; 474,094 mems (Dec. 1998).

Gewerkschaft Textil-Bekleidung (Textiles and Clothing): Ross Str. 94, 40476 Düsseldorf; tel. (211) 43090; fax (211) 4309505; Pres. WILLI ARENS; 234,240 mems (Dec. 1994).

The following are the largest unions outside the DGB:

DBB—Beamtenbund und Tarifunion (Federation of Civil Servants): Peter-Hensen-Str. 5–7, 53175 Bonn; tel. (228) 8110; fax (228) 811171; e-mail post@dbb.de; internet www.dbb.de; f. 1918; Pres. ERHARD GEYER; 1.2m. mems (2000).

*Deutsche Angestellten-Gewerkschaft (DAG) (Clerical, Technical and Administrative Workers): Johannes-Brahms-Platz 1, 20355 Hamburg; tel. (40) 3491501; fax (40) 34915400; e-mail info@dag.de; internet www.dag.de; f. 1945; Chair. ROLAND ISSEN; 501,009 mems (1996).

* The amalgamation of these service sector unions was scheduled to take place in 2001.

Transport

RAILWAYS

In 1997 the total length of track in Germany was 44,823 km.

Deutsche Bahn AG (German Railways): Holzmarktstr. 17, 10179 Berlin; tel. (30) 2970; fax (30) 29726131; internet www.bahn.de; f. 1994 following merger of Deutsche Bundesbahn and Deutsche Reichsbahn; state-owned (transfer to private-sector ownership pending); Chair. HARTMUT MEHDORN.

Metropolitan Railways

Berliner Verkehrsbetriebe (BVG) (Berlin Transport Authority): Potsdamer Str. 188, 10773 Berlin; tel. (30) 2560; fax (30) 2164186; e-mail bvg@bvg.de; internet www.bvg.de; f. 1929; operates approximately 143.3 km of underground railway; also runs tram and bus services; Dirs RÜDIGER VORM WALDE, Dr HANS-HEINO DUBENKROPP, Dr JOACHIM NIKLAS, HILMAR SCHMIDT-KOHLHAS.

Stadtwerke München GmbH, Unternehmensbereich Verkehr: 80287 München; tel. (89) 21912400; fax (89) 21912405; e-mail koenig.herbert@swm.de; underground (85 km), tramway (71 km), omnibus (402 km); Man. HERBERT KÖNIG.

Association

Verband Deutscher Verkehrsunternehmen (VDV) (Association of German Transport Undertakings): Kamekestr. 37–39, 50672 Köln; tel. (221) 579790; fax (221) 514272; e-mail info@vdv.de; internet www.vdv.de; f. 1895; public transport, freight transport by rail; Pres. Dr DIETER LUDWIG; Exec. Dir Prof. Dr ADOLF MÜLLER-HELLMANN.

ROADS

In January 1998 there were 11,309 km of motorway, 41,419 km of other main roads and 178,346 km of secondary roads. There were some 641,866 km of classified roads in January 1996.

INLAND WATERWAYS

There are 7,467 km of navigable inland waterways, including the Main–Danube Canal, linking the North Sea and the Black Sea, which was opened in September 1992. Inland shipping accounts for about 20% of total freight traffic.

Associations

Bundesverband der Deutschen Binnenschiffahrt eV: Dammstr. 15–17, 47119 Duisburg; tel. (203) 800060; fax (203) 8000621; f. 1948; central Inland Waterway Association to further the interests of operating firms; Pres. WILHEIM MÜNNING; 5 Mans.

Bundesverband Öffentlicher Binnenhäfen eV: Hammer Landstr. 3, 41460 Neuss; tel. (2131) 21624; fax (2131) 908282; e-mail boeb@binnenhafen.de; internet www.binnenhafen.de; Chair. ERICH STAAKE.

Bundesverband der selbstständigen Abteilung Binnenschiffahrt eV: Hochkreuzallee 89, 53175 Bonn; tel. (228) 318162; fax (228) 318163; Man. Dir ANDREA BECKSCHÄFER.

Deutsche Binnenreederei Binnenschiffahrt Spedition Logistik GmbH: Alt Stralau 55–58, 10245 Berlin; tel. (30) 293760; fax (30) 29376201; e-mail reichelt@online-now-de; internet www.binnenreederei.de; f. 1949; Dir-Gen. HANS-WILHELM DÜNNER.

Hafenschiffahrtsverband Hamburg eV: Mattentwiete 2, 20457 Hamburg; tel. (40) 361280; fax (40) 36128292.

Verein für europäische Binnenschiffahrt und Wasserstrassen eV (VBW): Dammstr. 15–17, 47119 Duisburg; tel. (203) 8000627; fax (203) 8000628; e-mail vbw-eubinsch@t-online.de; represents all branches of the inland waterways; Pres. Prof. D. SCHRÖDER; Dir G. DÜTEMEYER.

SHIPPING

The principal seaports for freight are Bremen, Hamburg, Rostock-Überseehafen and Wilhelmshaven. Some important shipping companies are:

Argo Reederei Richard Adler & Söhne: Postfach 107529, 28075 Bremen; tel. (421) 363070; fax (421) 321575; Finland, UK; Propr MAX ADLER.

Aug. Bolten, Wm. Miller's Nachfolger GmbH & Co: Mattentwiete 8, 20457 Hamburg; tel. (40) 36011; fax (40) 3601423; e-mail management@aug-bolten.de; internet www.aug-bolten.de; tramp; Man. Dir DIETER OSTENDORF.

Bugsier- Reederei- und Bergungs-Gesellschaft mbH & Co: Postfach 112273, 20422 Hamburg; Johannisbollwerk 10, 20459 Hamburg; tel. (40) 311110; fax (40) 313693; salvage, towage, tugs, ocean-going heavy lift cranes, submersible pontoons, harbour tugs; Man. Dirs B. J. SCHUCHMANN, J. W. SCHUCHMANN, A. HUETTMANN.

Christian F. Ahrenkiel GmbH & Co. KG: Postfach 100220, An der Alster 45, 20099 Hamburg; tel. (40) 248380; fax (40) 24838346; e-mail info@ahrenkiel.net; internet www.ahrenkiel.net; shipowners, operators and managers.

DAL Deutsche Afrika-Linien GmbH & Co: Palmaille 45, 22767 Hamburg; tel. (40) 380160; fax (40) 38016663; Europe and South Africa; Man. Dirs H. VON RANTZAU, Dr E. VON RANTZAU.

Deutsche Seereederei Rostock GmbH: Rostock; tel. (381) 4580; fax (381) 4582215; container ships, general cargo ships, bulk carriers, cargo trailer ships, railway ferries, special tankers.

Döhle, Peter, Schiffahrts-KG (GmbH & Co): Postfach 500440, 22767 Hamburg; Palmaille 33, 22767 Hamburg; tel. (40) 381080; fax (40) 38108255; internet www.doehle.de; Man. Dir JOCHEN DÖHLE; shipbrokers, chartering agent, shipowners.

Egon Oldendorff: Fünfhausen 1, 2400 Lübeck; tel. (451) 15000; fax (451) 73522; Dirs H. OLDENDORFF, G. ARNDT, W. DRABERT, T. WEBER, U. BERTHEAU.

Ernst Russ GmbH: Alsterufer 10, 20354 Hamburg; tel. (40) 414070; fax (40) 41407111; f. 1893; worldwide.

F. Laeisz Schiffahrtsgesellschaft mbH & Co: Postfach 111111, 20411 Hamburg; Trostbrücke 1, 20457 Hamburg; tel. (40) 368080; fax (40) 364876; e-mail info@laeiszline.de; internet www.laeiszline.de; f. 1983; Dirs NIKOLAUS W. SCHÜES, GERHARD HEYENGA, H. NIKOLAUS SCHÜES.

Fisser & v. Doornum GmbH & Co: Postfach 130365, Feldbrunnenstr. 43, 20148 Hamburg; tel. (40) 441860; fax (40) 4108050; f. 1879; tramp; Man. Dirs CHRISTIAN FISSER, Dr MICHAEL FISSER.

Hamburg Südamerikanische Dampfschiffahrts-Gesellschaft KG: Ost-West-Str. 59–61, 20457 Hamburg; tel. (40) 37050; fax (40) 37052400; e-mail central@hsdgham.hamburg-sued.com; internet www.hamburg-sued.com; f. 1871; worldwide service.

Hapag-Lloyd AG: Ballindamm 25, 20095 Hamburg; tel. (40) 30010; fax (40) 336432; f. 1970; North, Central and South America, Middle East, Asia, Australasia; Chair. BERND WREDE; Dir ALBRECHT METZE.

John T. Essberger GmbH & Co: Postfach 500429, Palmaille 49, 22767 Hamburg; tel. (40) 380160; fax (40) 38016579; f. 1924; Man. Dirs Dr E. VON RANTZAU, H. VON RANTZAU.

Oldenburg-Portugiesische Dampfschiffs-Rhederei GmbH & Co KG: Postfach 110869, 20408 Hamburg; Kajen 10, 20459 Hamburg; tel. (40) 361580; fax (40) 36158200; f. 1882; Spain, Portugal, Madeira, North Africa, Canary Islands; Man. Dirs G. KEMPF, J. BERGMANN.

Rhein-, Maas und See-Schiffahrtskontor GmbH: Krausstr. 1A, 47119 Duisburg; tel. (203) 8040; fax (203) 804-330; e-mail rms-team@rheinmaas.de; internet www.rheinmaas.de; f. 1948.

Sloman Neptun Schiffahrts-AG: Postfach 101469, 28014 Bremen; Langenstr. 44, 28195 Bremen; tel. (421) 17630; fax (421) 1763-200; f. 1873; Scandinavia, North-western Europe, Mediterranean, North Africa; gas carriers; agencies, stevedoring; Mans SVEN-MICHAEL EDYE, DIRK LOHMANN.

Walther Möller & Co: Thedestr. 2, 22767 Hamburg; tel. (40) 3803910; fax (40) 38039199; e-mail chartering@wmco.de.

Shipping Organizations

Verband Deutscher Küstenschiffseigner (German Coastal Shipowners' Association): Hamburg-Altona; tel. (40) 313435; fax (40) 315925; f. 1896; Pres. PETER TH. HAUSEN; Man. KLAUS KÖSTER.

Verband Deutscher Reeder eV (German Shipowners' Association): Postfach 305580, 20317 Hamburg; Esplanade 6, 20354 Hamburg; tel. (40) 350970; fax (40) 35097211; Pres. FRANK LEONHARDT; Man. Dir Dr BERND KRÖGER.

Zentralverband der Deutschen Seehafenbetriebe eV (Federal Association of German Seaport Operators): Hamburg; tel. (40) 366377; fax (40) 366377; e-mail zds-seehafen@t-online.de; f. 1932; Chair. PETER DIETRICH; 246 mems.

CIVIL AVIATION

There are three international airports in the Berlin region and further international airports at Köln-Bonn, Dresden, Düsseldorf, Frankfurt, Hamburg, Hannover, Leipzig, München and Stuttgart. Plans were under way in 2000 for the construction of a major new international airport to serve Berlin.

Aero Lloyd Flugreisen Luftverkehrs-KG: Postfach 2029, Lessingstr. 7–9, 61440 Oberursel; tel. (6171) 62501 fax (6171) 625109; f. 1981; charter services; Gen. Mans Dr W. SCHNEIDER, WOLFGANG JOHN.

Condor Flugdienst GmbH: Am Greunen Weg 3, 65440 Kelsterbach; tel. (6107) 9390; fax (6107) 939440; internet www.condor.de; f. 1955, wholly-owned subsidiary of Lufthansa; charter and inclusive-tour services; Man. Dirs DIETER HEINEN, Dr RUDOLF TEWES, MANFRED SCHWABENBAUER.

Deutsche Lufthansa AG: Von-Gablenz-Str. 2–6, 50679 Köln; tel. (221) 8260; fax (221) 8263818; f. 1953; extensive world-wide network; Chair. Supervisory Bd Dr WOLFGANG RÖLLER; Chair. Exec. Bd JÜRGEN WEBER.

Germania Flug-GmbH: Flughafen Berlin Tegel, Gebäude Z3, 13405 Berlin; tel. (30) 41015540; fax (30) 41013500; f. 1978; charter and inclusive-tour services; Man. Dr HENRICH BISCHOFF.

Hapag-Lloyd Flug-GmbH: Postfach 420240, Flughafenstr. 10, 30855 Langenhagen; tel. (511) 97270; fax (511) 9727739; e-mail info@hlf.de; internet www.hlf.de; f. 1972; charter and scheduled passenger services; Man. Dirs WOLFGANG KURTH, DIETER SCHENK.

LTU Lufttransport-Unternehmen GmbH: Flughafen, Halle 8, 40474 Düsseldorf; tel. (211) 9418888; fax (211) 9418881; f. 1955; charter and scheduled services; Man. Dir PETER HASLEBACHER.

Lufthansa Cargo AG: Langer Kornweg 34, 65441 Kelsterbach; tel. (6107) 777615; fax (6107) 777888; f. 1993; wholly-owned subsidiary of Lufthansa; freight-charter world-wide; Man. Dirs WALTER GEHL, JEAN-PETER JANSEN, STEFAN LAUER.

Lufthansa Cityline GmbH: Flughafen Köln-Bonn, Heinrich-Steinmann-Str., 51147 Köln; tel. (2203) 5960; fax (2203) 596801; scheduled services; Man. Dir GEORG STEINBACHER.

Tourism

Germany's tourist attractions include spas, summer and winter resorts, mountains, medieval towns and castles, and above all a variety of fascinating cities. The North and Baltic Sea coasts, the Rhine Valley, the Black Forest, the mountains of Thuringia, the Erzgebirge and Bavaria are the most popular areas. In 1998 there were 54,247 hotels and guesthouses in Germany, with 2,404,688 beds available for tourists. The total number of foreign visitors was 16,137,100 in 1999, compared with 15,593,800 in 1998.

Deutsche Zentrale für Tourismus eV (DZT) (German National Tourist Board): Beethovenstr. 69, 60325 Frankfurt a.M.; tel. (69) 974640; fax (69) 751903; e-mail gnto-fra@compuserve.com; internet www.germany-tourism.de; f. 1948; Dir URSULA SCHÖRCHER.

GHANA

Introductory Survey

Location, Climate, Language, Religion, Flag, Capital

The Republic of Ghana lies on the west coast of Africa, with Côte d'Ivoire to the west and Togo to the east. It is bordered by Burkina Faso to the north. The climate is tropical, with temperatures generally between 21°C and 32°C (70°–90°F) and average annual rainfall of 2,000 mm (80 ins) on the coast, decreasing inland. English is the official language, but there are eight major national languages. Many of the inhabitants follow traditional beliefs and customs. Christians comprise an estimated 42% of the population. The national flag (proportions 3 by 2) has three equal horizontal stripes, of red, yellow and green, with a five-pointed black star in the centre of the yellow stripe. The capital is Accra.

Recent History

Ghana was formed as the result of a UN-supervised plebiscite in May 1956, when the British-administered section of Togoland, a UN Trust Territory, voted to join the Gold Coast, a British colony, in an independent state. Ghana was duly granted independence, within the Commonwealth, on 6 March 1957, and thus became the first British dependency in sub-Saharan Africa to achieve independence under majority rule. Dr Kwame Nkrumah, the Prime Minister of the former Gold Coast since 1952, became Prime Minister of the new state. Ghana became a republic on 1 July 1960, with Nkrumah as President. In 1964 the Convention People's Party, led by Nkrumah, was declared the sole authorized party.

In February 1966 Nkrumah, whose repressive policies and financial mismanagement had caused increasing resentment, was deposed by a military coup, whose leaders established a governing National Liberation Council (NLC), led by Gen. Joseph Ankrah. In April 1969, following disputes within the NLC, Ankrah was replaced by Brig. (later Lt-Gen.) Akwasi Afrifa, and a new Constitution was introduced. Power was returned in October to an elected civilian Government, led by Dr Kofi Busia. However, in reaction to increasing economic and political difficulties, the army again seized power in January 1972, under the leadership of Lt-Col (later Gen.) Ignatius Acheampong. Some improvement in Ghana's economic situation was achieved by the military, which announced in 1977 that it intended to relinquish power to a new government following a general election to take place in 1979. These plans, however, were forestalled in July 1978 by Acheampong's deputy, Lt-Gen. Frederick Akuffo, who assumed power in a bloodless coup. Tensions within the army became evident in May 1979, when junior military officers staged an unsuccessful coup attempt. The alleged leader of the conspirators, Flight-Lt Jerry Rawlings, was imprisoned, but was subsequently released by other officers. On 4 June he and his associates successfully seized power, amid popular acclaim, established the Armed Forces Revolutionary Council (AFRC), led by Rawlings, and introduced measures to eradicate corruption. Acheampong and Akuffo were among nine senior officers who were convicted on charges of corruption and executed.

The AFRC indicated that its assumption of power was temporary, and the elections took place in June 1979, as scheduled, although the return to civilian rule was postponed until September. The People's National Party (PNP), led by Dr Hilla Limann, emerged with the largest number of parliamentary seats and formed a coalition Government with support from the smaller United National Convention. Dr Limann took office as President in September. However, dissatisfaction with measures taken by the Government to improve the economy provoked widespread strikes and riots.

On 31 December 1981 Rawlings seized power for a second time, and established a governing Provisional National Defence Council (PNDC), with himself as Chairman. The Council of State was abolished, the Constitution suspended, the legislature dissolved and political parties banned. In 1982 city and district councils were replaced by People's Defence Committees (PDC), which were designed to allow popular participation in local government. In 1984 the PDC were redesignated as Committees for the Defence of the Revolution (CDR).

The PNDC's policies initially received strong support, but discontent with the regime and with the apparent ineffectiveness of its economic policies was reflected by a series of coup attempts and widespread student unrest; between 1984 and 1987 some 34 people were executed for their alleged involvement in plots to overthrow the Government. In August 1986 a former government minister and presidential candidate, Victor Owusu, was arrested for alleged subversion. In June 1987 it was announced that several people had been arrested and that weapons had been seized, following the discovery of a further conspiracy to overthrow the PNDC. In November the Government detained a further seven people, including leaders of two opposition movements, the New Democratic Movement (NDM) and the Kwame Nkrumah Revolutionary Guards (KNRG).

In July 1987 the PNDC announced that elections for district assemblies, scheduled for mid-1987, were to be postponed until late 1988, and that the ban on political parties was to remain. By April 1988 more than 89% of the electorate had been registered to vote in the forthcoming elections. In that month there was an extensive government reshuffle, in which a new post to co-ordinate the work of the CDR was created. During 1988 the number of districts was increased from 65 to 110. Elections for the district assemblies were held in stages between December 1988 and February 1989. Although one-third of the 7,278 members of the district assemblies were appointed by the PNDC, the establishment of the assemblies was envisaged as the first stage in the development of a new political system of national democratic administration.

On 24 September 1989 a coup attempt was staged, led by a close associate of Rawlings, Maj. Courage Quashigah. Shortly afterwards the Commander of the Armed Forces was dismissed, and Rawlings himself assumed control of the armed forces until June 1990. In October 1989 five senior members of the security forces, including Quashigah, were arrested on charges of conspiring to assassinate Rawlings. The predominance of the Ewe ethnic group in government positions and other important posts, which had provoked discontent among other factions, was initially considered to be the cause of the revolt, although a board of inquiry into the allegations of treason concluded that most of the conspirators were motivated by personal grievances and ambition. In January 1990 five more arrests were made in connection with the coup attempt. In August the human rights organization, Amnesty International, criticized the continued detention of Quashigah and six other members of the security forces, claiming that they were imprisoned for political dissension.

In July 1990, in response to pressure from Western aid donors to introduce further democratic reforms, the PNDC announced that a National Commission for Democracy (NCD) would organize a series of regional debates to consider Ghana's political and economic future. (Ten such debates took place between July and October 1992.) In August a newly-formed political organization, the Movement for Freedom and Justice (MFJ), criticized the NCD, claiming that it was too closely associated with the PNDC, and also demanded the abolition of legislation prohibiting political associations, the release of all political prisoners, the cessation of press censorship and the holding of a national referendum on the restoration of a multi-party system. In September the MFJ accused the PNDC of intimidation, after its inaugural meeting was suppressed by security forces. In October the PNDC pledged to accept the conclusions of any national consensus on future democracy in the country.

In December 1990 Rawlings announced proposals for the introduction of a constitution by the end of 1991; the PNDC was to consider recommendations presented by the NCD, and subsequently to convene a consultative body to determine constitutional reform. However, the MFJ, the Christian Council of Ghana and the Ghana Bar Association objected to the proposals, on the grounds that no definite schedule for political reform had been presented, and that no criteria had been established for the composition of the consultative body.

In March 1991 the NCD presented a report on the democratic process, which recommended the election of an executive President for a fixed term, the establishment of a legislature and the creation of the post of Prime Minister. Rawlings announced that the PNDC would consider the report and submit recommendations to a national consultative body later that year. In May, however, the PNDC endorsed the restoration of a multi-party system and approved the NCD's recommendations, although it was emphasized that the formation of political associations remained prohibited. The MFJ immediately disputed the veracity of the PNDC's announcement, causing the state-controlled press to accuse the MFJ of planning subversive activity. Later in May the Government announced the establishment of a 260-member Consultative Assembly, which was to present a draft constitution to the PNDC by the end of 1991. The Government appointed a nine-member committee of constitutional experts, who were to submit recommendations for a draft constitution to the Consultative Assembly by the end of July.

In June 1991 the Government reiterated denials that a number of political prisoners were detained in Ghana. In the same month the PNDC announced an amnesty for political exiles, which did not, however, include persons who were implicated in acts of subversion against the Government. In August the committee of constitutional experts submitted a series of recommendations for reform, which included the establishment of a parliament and a council of state. It was proposed that the President, who would also be Commander-in-Chief of the Armed Forces, would be elected by universal suffrage for a four-year term of office, while the leader of the party that commanded a majority in the legislature would be appointed as Prime Minister. However, the subsequent review of the draft Constitution by the Consultative Assembly was impeded by opposition demands for a boycott, on the grounds that the number of government representatives in the Assembly was too high. Later in August Rawlings announced that presidential and legislative elections were to take place in late 1992.

In December 1991 the Government established an Interim National Electoral Commission (INEC), which was to be responsible for the demarcation of electoral regions and the supervision of elections and referendums. In January 1992 the Government extended the allocated period for the review of the draft Constitution to the end of March 1992. In March Rawlings announced a programme for transition to a multi-party system, which was to be completed on 7 January 1993. Later in March 1992 the Government granted an amnesty to 17 prisoners who had been convicted of subversion, including Quashigah.

At the end of March 1992 the Consultative Assembly approved the majority of the constitutional recommendations that had been submitted to the PNDC. However, the proposed creation of the post of Prime Minister was rejected by the Assembly; executive power was to be vested in the President, who would appoint a Vice-President. Opposition groups subsequently objected to a provision in the draft Constitution that members of the Government be exempt from prosecution for human rights violations allegedly committed during the PNDC's rule. At a national referendum on 28 April, however, the draft Constitution was approved by 92% of votes cast, with 43.7% of the electorate voting.

On 18 May 1992 the Government introduced legislation permitting the formation of political associations; political parties were henceforth required to apply to the INEC for legal recognition, although emergent parties were not permitted to use names or slogans associated with 21 former political organizations that remained proscribed, and individual monetary contributions to political parties were restricted. Later in May the High Court rejected an application for an injunction against the legislation by opposition leaders, who claimed that it was biased in favour of the PNDC. At the end of May it was reported that some 63 people had been killed in clashes between the Gonja and Nawuri ethnic groups in northern Ghana.

In June 1992 a number of political associations were established, many of which were identified with supporters of former President Nkrumah; six opposition movements, including the People's National Convention (PNC), led by ex-President Limann, were subsequently granted legal recognition. In the same month a coalition of pro-Government organizations, the National Democratic Congress (NDC), was formed to contest the forthcoming elections on behalf of the PNDC. However, an existing alliance of Rawlings' supporters, the Eagle Club, refused to join the NDC, and created its own political organization, the Eagle Party (later known as the EGLE—Every Ghanaian Living Everywhere—Party). In July Rawlings denied that he was associated with the Eagle Club, and rejected the

EGLE Party's nomination as its candidate for the presidential election. In August the Government promulgated a new electoral code, which included a provision that in the event that no presidential candidate received more than 50% of votes cast the two candidates with the highest number of votes would contest a second round within 21 days. In September Rawlings officially retired from the air force (although he retained the post of Commander-in-Chief of the Armed Forces in his capacity as Head of State), in compliance with a stipulation in the new Constitution, and accepted a nomination to contest the presidential election as a candidate of the NDC. The NDC, the EGLE Party and the National Convention Party (NCP) subsequently formed a pro-Government electoral coalition, known as the Progressive Alliance.

In October 1992 legislation that permitted indefinite detention without trial was repealed. However, new legislation, providing for the detention of individuals suspected of certain crimes for a period of up to 14 days, was promulgated, and a special review court, empowered to extend the detention period, was established. Later in October the High Court dismissed an application by the MFJ for an injunction to prevent Rawlings from contesting the presidential election, on the grounds that he was not a Ghanaian national (his father was British), and that he remained accountable for charges of treason in connection with the coups that he had led.

Rawlings was elected President on 3 November 1992, securing 58.3% of votes cast. The four opposition parties that had presented candidates, the PNC, the New Patriotic Party (NPP), the National Independence Party (NIP) and the People's Heritage Party (PHP), claimed that there had been widespread electoral malpractice, although international observers maintained that, despite isolated irregularities, the election had been conducted fairly. Later in November the NPP, the PNC, the NIP and the PHP withdrew from the forthcoming legislative elections (scheduled for 8 December), in protest at the Government's refusal to comply with their demands for the compilation of a new electoral register and the investigation of alleged misconduct during the presidential election. As a result, the legislative elections were postponed until 22 December, and subsequently by a further week, and the nomination of new candidates permitted. In December the opposition claimed that many of its members had left Ghana, as a result of widespread intimidation by the Government. In the legislative elections, which took place on 29 December, the NDC secured 189 of the 200 seats in the Parliament, while the NCP obtained eight seats, the EGLE Party one seat and independent candidates the remaining two. According to official figures, however, only 29% of the electorate voted in the elections.

On 7 January 1993 Rawlings was sworn in as President of what was designated the Fourth Republic, the PNDC was dissolved and the new Parliament was inaugurated. Later in January the NPP, the PNC, the NIP and the PHP formed an alliance, known as the Inter-party Co-ordinating Committee, and announced that they were to act as an official opposition to the Government, despite their lack of representation in the Parliament. At the end of January Rawlings began to submit nominations for members of the Council of Ministers and the Council of State for approval by the Parliament. However, he announced that members of the existing Government were to remain in office in an interim capacity, pending the appointment of a Council of Ministers and other officials. The opposition subsequently criticized the delay in the formation of a new government, and protested that the new Constitution did not permit members of the former PNDC to remain in office. In March the nomination of a number of ministers was approved by the Parliament. Later that month legislation was promulgated to exempt from prosecution perpetrators of offences that had been committed under the auspices of the former PNDC Government.

In April 1993 elections took place for the regional seats in the Council of State. In May a 17-member Council of Ministers, which included several ministers who had served in the former PNDC administration, was inaugurated. Substantial pledges of assistance for Ghana, made in July at a meeting of donor nations, under the aegis of the World Bank, indicated Western support for the new Government. In the same month the Supreme Court upheld a motion by the NPP that certain existing legislation was in contravention of the Constitution. In August the NPP announced that it was prepared to recognize the legitimacy of the Government. In October the Minister of Justice, who, in his capacity as public prosecutor, had failed to win several trials in the Supreme Court, resigned after a state-owned newspaper questioned his competence. In November a 20-member National Security Council, chaired by the Vice-President, Kow Nkensen Arkaah, was inaugurated. In December the PHP, the NIP and a faction of the PNC, all of which comprised supporters of ex-President Nkrumah, merged to form a new organization, known as the People's Convention Party (PCP).

In February 1994 long-standing hostility between the Konkomba ethnic group and the land-owning Nanumba intensified into clashes in the Northern Region in which some 500 people were killed, following demands by the Konkomba for traditional status that would entitle them to own land. The Government subsequently dispatched troops and imposed a state of emergency in seven districts for a period of three months, although skirmishes continued in the region, and subsequently involved several other ethnic groups. Some 6,000 Konkomba were reported to have fled to Togo. In March 12 people were killed at Tamale, the capital of the Northern Region, when security forces fired on demonstrators belonging to the Dagomba ethnic group, who had allegedly attacked a number of Konkomba.

In March 1994 a minor government reorganization was effected. Later that month elections to the District Assemblies took place, except in those districts subject to the state of emergency. In April the Government instigated negotiations between representatives of the various groups involved in the conflict in the Northern Region. In the same month the authorities claimed that reported threats to kill Quashigah (the instigator of the coup attempt in 1989) and editors of two privately-owned newspapers were part of a conspiracy to destabilize the Government. In May a further minor reorganization of the Government took place. Meanwhile, the state of emergency in the Northern Region (where a total of 1,000 people had been killed, and a further 150,000 displaced) was extended for one month. In early June, however, the factions involved in the hostilities signed a peace agreement that provided for the imposition of an immediate cease-fire and renounced violence as a means of settling disputes over land-ownership. The Government subsequently announced that troops were to be permanently stationed in the Northern Region in order to prevent further conflict, and established a negotiating team that was to attempt to resolve the inter-ethnic differences. The state of emergency was subsequently extended until early August, when the Government announced that order had been restored in the Northern Region.

In September 1994 five civilians, who had allegedly conspired to overthrow the Government, were charged with treason. In October two men were arrested by security forces, after attempting to transport armaments illicitly to the Northern Region; further arrests followed, in connection with violent incidents in which several people had been killed. Following a joint rally of the NPP, the PNC and the PCP in November, the parties announced that they would present a single candidate to contest the presidential election in 1996.

In March 1995 the Government imposed a curfew in the Northern Region following renewed ethnic violence, in which about 100 people were killed. In April a joint commission, comprising prominent members of the Konkomba and Nanumba, was established, in an effort to resolve the conflict. Meanwhile, the imposition, in February, of value-added tax (VAT) under the budget for 1995 prompted widespread protests, while civil servants threatened to initiate strike action; a series of demonstrations, which was organized by a grouping of opposition leaders, Alliance for Change, culminated in May, when five people were killed in clashes between government supporters and protesters. (The Government subsequently agreed to suspend VAT, although it was reintroduced, at a lower rate, in 1999.) Later in May the National Executive Committee of the NCP decided to withdraw the party from the government coalition, claiming that the NDC had dominated the alliance. However, Arkaah, a member of the NCP, announced that he was to retain the office of Vice-President (despite rumours of ill-feeling between Arkaah and the President, which had been prevalent for several months) on the grounds that his mandate remained valid. In July the long-serving Minister of Finance, Kwesi Botchwey, resigned, apparently in response to the failure to introduce VAT; a minor reorganization of the Council of Ministers ensued. At a by-election in the same month, a joint candidate of the PNC, NPP, NCP and PCP secured the vacant seat. In October the Chairman of the NCP resigned, following dissent within the party. In November the Commission on Human Rights and Administrative Justice (CHRAJ) commenced investigations into allegations of corruption on the part of government ministers and civil servants. In early 1996 opposition parties demanded the resignation of Rawlings, following an incident in which the President allegedly assaulted Arkaah. Rawlings reshuffled his Council of Ministers in March.

In April 1996 presidential and parliamentary elections were scheduled for 10 December, although this was later changed to 7 December to meet constitutional requirements. A consolidation of the opposition parties took place prior to the deadline for the nomination of candidates in September. In May Kwame Pianim, prospective presidential candidate for the NPP, was disqualified from the elections on the grounds of his conviction for treason in 1982. In the same month the Popular Party for Democracy and Development (PPDD) announced its merger with the PCP, and announced its support for unity with the NPP. In June Thomas Appiah resigned for personal reasons as Chairman of the NCP and Vice-Chairman of the PCP. In July the NCP announced that it had removed Kow Nkensen Arkaah as its leader, following his selection as presidential candidate by the PCP. In August the NPP and PCP announced the formation of an electoral coalition, the Great Alliance; it was subsequently announced that John Kufuor, of the NPP, was to be the Great Alliance's presidential candidate, with Arkaah, of the PCP, as the candidate for the vice-presidency. The NCP stated that it would support the NDC in the forthcoming elections, while the PNC announced its intention to contest the elections alone, with Edward Mahama as its presidential candidate. In September the NDC nominated Rawlings as its presidential candidate. By 18 September, the official deadline for the nomination of candidates, only the Great Alliance, the Progressive Alliance (the NDC, the EGLE party and the Democratic People's Party—DPP) and the PNC had succeeded in having their nomination papers accepted. In October the NCP, which, according to the Electoral Commission (EC), had not presented the appropriate papers, declared its intention to take legal action against the Commission. The EC denied accusations that it had shown bias against the NCP. The selection of common candidates provoked a lengthy dispute between the NPP and the PCP. In late October at least 20 people were wounded in clashes between NDC and NPP militants in Tamale and Kibi. In November a network of independent Domestic Election Observers was created to oversee the December elections. The resignation of the Minister of the Interior in October was followed, in November, by the resignations of the Minister of Trade and Industry and the Presidential Aide on Cocoa Affairs, following corruption allegations against them.

In the presidential election, which duly took place on 7 December 1996, Rawlings was re-elected by 57.2% of votes cast, while Kufuor secured 39.8% of the votes. In the parliamentary elections the NDC's representation was reduced to 133 seats, while the NPP won 60 seats, the PCP five and the PNC one seat. Voting was postponed in one constituency in Ashanti, because of a legal dispute concerning the eligibility of candidates. (The seat was subsequently won by the NPP in a by-election in June 1997.) Despite opposition claims of malpractice, international observers declared that the elections had been conducted fairly, and an electoral turn-out of 76.8% was reported. Following the announcement of the election results, about 15 people were injured in clashes between NDC and opposition supporters in Bimbila, south-east of Tamale. At the end of December the PCP announced that the Great Alliance had broken down. On 7 January 1997 Rawlings was sworn in as President.

The appointment of a new Council of Ministers led to a protracted dispute between the NDC and the opposition, prompting a series of parliamentary boycotts by the NPP, which insisted that all ministerial appointees be approved by the parliamentary appointments committee prior to assuming their duties. In February 1997 opposition parties sought a ruling from the Supreme Court to prevent Kwame Peprah, the reappointed Minister of Finance, from presenting the budget. Owing to the NDC's parliamentary majority, however, procedures were approved to allow those ministers who had been retained from the previous Government to avoid the vetting process. The majority of ministerial appointments had been made by April, although a number of posts were not filled until June. In early June the Supreme Court ruled that all presidential nominees for ministerial positions had to be approved by Parliament, even if they had served in the previous Government. Following the ruling, the NPP withdrew from the chamber on several occasions when ministers attempted to address Parliament. The Government subsequently announced that it was prepared to submit all ministers to vetting procedures.

In September 1997 it was reported that three people had been killed, and more than 1,000 displaced, in the Brong-Ahafo Region, following inter-ethnic skirmishes, which had been prompted by a dispute over land-ownership. In January 1998 four people were killed, and 26 injured, in an outbreak of violence between opposing Muslim factions in the Brong-Ahafo Region; 57 people were subsequently arrested. In September 1998 108 people were arrested in Kumasi, in the Ashanti Region, following violent clashes between rival Muslim sects.

Following further accusations of government corruption, Rawlings dismissed a Minister of State in February 1998, after a committee of inquiry discovered lapses of propriety regarding a sea defence project for which the Minister was responsible. In August the NCP and the PCP merged to form the Convention Party. An earlier attempt by the party to register as the Convention People's Party (CPP) had been rejected on the grounds that the use of the name of a proscribed party was unconstitutional. (This decision was reversed in 2000, however, when the Convention Party was permitted to adopt the name and logo of Nkrumah's former party.) In October the NPP nominated Kufuor to stand again as its presidential candidate, in elections due to be held in 2000. In November 1998 Rawlings effected a government reshuffle. At an NDC congress in December 1998 the position of 'Life Chairman' of the party was created for Rawlings, who then confirmed he would comply with the terms of the Constitution and not attempt to stand for a third term as President. In April 1999 Rawlings announced that the incumbent Vice-President, John Evans Atta Mills, was to contest the election on behalf of the NDC.

In March 1999 ECOMOG forces in Sierra Leone arrested a Ghanaian officer, Capt. James Owoo, who had allegedly been involved in attempts to remove the PNDC administration in the 1980s. He was subsequently taken to Accra where he was charged with conspiring to overthrow the Rawlings Government in 1998. In June 1999, owing to dissatisfaction within the NDC at the changes carried out at the party congress and at Rawlings' pronouncement regarding his successor, a disaffected group of party members broke away to form a new political organization, the National Reform Party (NRP). Rawlings carried out three government reshuffles in late 1999 and early 2000. In April 2000 Rawlings granted amnesty to some 1,000 prisoners, including two former army officers convicted of participating in subversive activities in the 1980s. At the end of April Mills was elected unopposed as the NDC presidential candidate for the forthcoming election.

In August 2000 it was announced that the forthcoming presidential and parliamentary elections would take place on 7 December. Seven parties had submitted candidates by the closure of nominations for the presidency in mid-September. In addition to Mills, the candidates included Kufuor, representing the NPP, Mahama, for the PNC, and George Hagan, for the CPP. The EGLE Party and the DPP announced their support for Mills.

In early October 2000 attacks on the offices of two independent newspapers in Accra were widely condemned by the Ghana Journalists Association, the Government and opposition parties. Additionally, two journalists were briefly detained in early November on charges related to the theft of a computer diskette from the offices of the NDC, while a third journalist was also arrested for allegedly making libellous remarks made about Rawlings on a television broadcast.

Isolated outbreaks of violence occurred between supporters of the NPP and the NDC in early November 2000, prompting traditional chiefs to organize a 'peace conference' later that month. The conference, which was attended by representatives of all the political parties contesting the elections, accused politicians of making inflammatory statements, but was criticized by opposition groups for failing to apportion sufficient blame to the President. The leadership of the NDC and the NPP subsequently urged their supporters to desist from acts of violence. In early December the Supreme Court reversed an EC decision that only those with new photographic identity cards would be allowed to vote in the forthcoming elections, ruling that old forms of identification, bearing thumbprints, would also be accepted. Opposition parties criticized the ruling; the NPP claimed it would enable the NDC to manipulate the electoral process. The EC had earlier admitted that the electoral register included some 1.5m. non-existent voters. Meanwhile, the former

campaign manager of the NPP, who had defected from the party in mid-November, alleged that it was intending to instigate electoral fraud.

An estimated 62% of the electorate voted in the elections on 7 December 2000 (although, as a result of the inaccurate voters' register, it was claimed that the real rate of participation could have been as high as 80%). OAU observers subsequently declared the elections to have been held in an orderly and fair manner. In Bawku, in the Upper East Region, at least 10 people died in inter-ethnic clashes following the closure of the polls, although it was reported that this violence was largely unrelated to the elections. In the elections to the 200-seat Parliament the NPP won 100 seats, while the NDC obtained 92 seats, the PNC three, the CPP one, and independent candidates four. The NPP, becoming the largest parliamentary party for the first time, gained an unprecedented degree of support in rural areas, as well as in its traditional urban strongholds. In the presidential election Kufuor won 48.2% of the valid votes cast, compared with the 44.5% secured by Mills. As no candidate had been successful in gaining an absolute majority of votes, a second round of voting, between Kufuor and Mills, was scheduled for 28 December.

In late December 2000 there were reports of isolated violent incidents of a politically-motivated nature across Ghana. Although the second round of the presidential election proceeded largely without incident on 28 December, minor disruptions to voting were reported; in one incident, in a suburb of Accra, a ballot box and voters' list were destroyed when 10 people raided a polling station. It was also reported that an NPP deputy had been stabbed in Accra by uniformed men, who had also fired on two of his supporters. Kufuor was elected to the presidency, with 56.9% of the valid votes cast, while Mills secured 43.1%. Mills conceded defeat on 30 December, and Rawlings congratulated Kufuor on his victory. The NPP attributed their victory to discontent with corruption in the former administration and its reluctance to implement economic and structural reforms. Although Kufuor stated that officials of the outgoing regime would not be persecuted, he proposed the establishment of an organization to investigate human rights abuses allegedly perpetrated following the coup led by Rawlings in 1981.

On 7 January 2001 Kufuor was inaugurated as President; on the following day it was announced that Rawlings had accepted a goodwill ambassadorial post at the UN for one year. President Kufuor announced the appointment of 11 ministers on 11 January, including his brother, Kwame Addo Kufuor, as Minister of Defence. On 22 January Kufuor completed the formation of his new Council of Ministers, naming a further 12 ministers and four ministers of state. The Government notably included one member from each of the CPP, the NRP and the PNC. However, the NDC criticized as unconstitutional Kufuor's decision to allow his ministerial nominees to exercise executive authority prior to their approval by Parliament and announced that the case would be brought before the Supreme Court.

The stated priority of the new Government was the creation of wealth, which was to be encouraged by greater promotion of the private sector and through the eradication of corruption within the government and in the parastatal sector. To this effect Vice-President Alhaji Aliu Mahama announced that a code of conduct for ministers and government appointees, to be prepared in conjunction with organizations from civil society, would be implemented. Additionally, Kufuor rejected symbols of the Rawlings era, including the throne used by the outgoing President, and announced that the presidential jet, which Rawlings had controversially purchased in 1999, was to be sold. In February 2001 it was announced that members of the military were to be forbidden from celebrating the anniversaries of the coups staged by Rawlings in 1979 and 1981, and that their participation in quasi-political organizations, supportive of either the NDP or NPP, was also to be prohibited. In that month the Government announced that the price of petroleum was to be gradually doubled in order to reduce the state debt, although wages were also to be increased, to reduce the impact of the rise. As concern about violent crime continued to grow, the Government declared a two-week amnesty, during which citizens could surrender unlicensed weapons and ammunition to the state, without fear of prosecution. Also in February Kufuor ordered the suspension of the heads of six public-sector financial institutions, to enable an investigation into allegations of embezzlement to be conducted. The Minister of Youth and Sports, Mallam Ali Yussif Issah, the sole ministerial representative of the PNC in the Government, resigned in mid-March after allegedly losing a suitcase containing US $46,000 intended as a bonus for the national football team.

Following a military coup in Burkina Faso in October 1987, which was condemned by the Ghanaian Government, links between the two countries were temporarily strained, but improved following meetings between Rawlings and Capt. Blaise Compaoré, the Burkinabè leader, in early 1988. In December 1989, however, Ghana was accused by Burkina Faso of involvement in an attempt to overthrow the Burkinabè Government. In January 1990 120 Ghanaians were deported from Burkina Faso without official explanation. In March 1998 Ghana and Burkina Faso agreed to establish a joint commission to manage water resources. Tensions had previously arisen over Burkinabè plans to build hydroelectric dams on a major tributary of the Volta river. Further agreements on co-operation were signed in August during a visit to Ghana by Compaoré. Compaoré attended Kufuor's presidential inauguration in January 2001, and the two Presidents met during an official visit by Kufuor to Burkina Faso in March.

In 1986 relations between Ghana and Togo became strained, following subversive activity by Ghanaian dissidents based in Togo, and an attempted coup in Togo, which was allegedly initiated from Ghanaian territory. The common border between the two countries was closed for several months from October. Between December 1988 and January 1989 more than 130 Ghanaians were deported from Togo, where they were alleged to be residing illegally. In October 1991 the Governments of Ghana and Togo signed an agreement on the free movement of goods and persons between the two countries. In October 1992, however, Ghana denied claims by the Togolese Government that it was implicated in subversive activity by Togolese dissidents based in Ghana. In November Rawlings formally protested to the Togolese Government, after five Ghanaians were killed by Togolese security forces on the border between the two countries.

In March 1993 the Rawlings administration denied allegations, made by the Togolese Government, of Ghanaian complicity in an armed attack on the residence of Togo's President. In January 1994 relations with Togo deteriorated further, following an attempt to overthrow the Togolese Government, which the Togolese authorities claimed had been staged by armed dissidents based in Ghana. The Ghanaian Chargé d'affaires in Togo was arrested, and Togolese forces killed 12 Ghanaians and attacked a customs post and several villages near the border. Ghana, however, denied the accusations of involvement in the coup attempt, and threatened to retaliate against further acts of aggression. In May allegations by the Togolese Government that Ghana was responsible for bomb attacks in Togo, owing to a lack of border security, led to further tension between the two nations. In August the Togolese Government protested to Ghana, following an article in a privately-owned Ghanaian newspaper to the effect that Togolese rebels based in Ghana were preparing to launch an offensive to overthrow the Eyadéma administration. Later that year, however, relations between the two countries improved, and in November full diplomatic links were formally restored. In December Togo's border with Ghana (which had been closed in January 1994) was reopened. In July 1995 discussions between Eyadéma and Rawlings resulted in an agreement providing for the reconstitution of Ghanaian-Togolese joint commissions. In August the Togolese Government denied involvement in the assassination of a political opponent who had taken refuge in Ghana. In February 1996 both Parliaments established friendship groups. By the end of 1996 some 48,000 Togolese refugees were estimated to have received payment for voluntary repatriation. Eyadéma and Rawlings met again in Accra in May 1998, amid an easing of relations between the two countries. In August a joint operation was mounted to arrest a group of armed men from Ghana who had attacked military posts in Togo. In August 1999, following recent Togolese incursions into Ghanaian territory and airspace, delegations from the two countries met in Ghana for talks, after which both sides expressed their desire for peace and harmony between the two countries. In September the Ghanaian Government proposed that the Ghana-Togo border demarcation commission resume its work. In January 2001 President Kufuor's first state visit was to Togo, provoking criticism from pro-democracy protesters, who noted that the visit coincided with celebrations to mark the 34th anniversary of the coup that brought Eyadéma to power. Kufuor stated that his Government would be vigilant in preventing attacks on Togo from Ghanaian territory.

During the conflict in Liberia, which commenced in December 1989 (see Liberia, Vol. II), Ghana contributed troops to the Monitoring Group (ECOMOG) of the Economic Community of West African States (ECOWAS, see p. 170). As Chairman of the ECOWAS Conference of Heads of State and Government, Rawlings mediated prolonged negotiations between the warring Liberian factions in the mid-1990s. Ghana granted temporary asylum to some 2,000 Liberian war refugees in May 1996, but insisted that no more could be accepted in the future. By mid-1997, however, some 17,000 Liberian refugees had arrived in Ghana. In August Rawlings was the first foreign leader to visit Liberia following its return to civilian rule. In January 1999 Ghanaian ECOMOG troops began to leave Liberia. Meanwhile, in June 1997 Ghana, together with Côte d'Ivoire, Guinea and Nigeria, became a member of the 'committee of four', which was established by ECOWAS to monitor the situation in Sierra Leone, following the staging of a military coup in the previous month; troops were dispatched to participate in a peace-keeping force. It was reported in February 1998 that Ghana had opposed the use of force by the Nigerian contingent of this peace-keeping unit to overthrow the military government in Sierra Leone. Following the reinstatement of the democratically-elected Government in March, ECOMOG units remained in the country and continued to launch attacks against rebel forces, which still retained control of a number of areas. In August 2000 it was estimated that 775 Ghanaian troops were stationed in Sierra Leone.

Government

Under the terms of the Constitution, which was approved by national referendum on 28 April 1992, Ghana has a multi-party political system. Executive power is vested in the President, who is the Head of State and Commander-in-Chief of the Armed Forces. The President is elected by direct universal suffrage for a maximum of two four-year terms of office. Legislative power is vested in a 200-member unicameral Parliament, which is elected by direct universal suffrage for a four-year term. The President appoints a Vice-President, and nominates a Council of Ministers, subject to approval by the Parliament. The Constitution also provides for a 25-member Council of State, principally comprising regional representatives and presidential nominees, and a 20-member National Security Council, chaired by the Vice-President, which act as advisory bodies to the President.

Ghana has 10 regions, each headed by a Regional Minister, who is assisted by a regional co-ordinating council. The regions constitute 110 administrative districts, each with a District Assembly, which is headed by a District Chief Executive. Regional colleges, which comprise representatives selected by the District Assemblies and by regional Houses of Chiefs, elect a number of representatives to the Council of State.

Defence

At 1 August 2000 Ghana had total armed forces of 7,000 (army 5,000, navy 1,000 and air force 1,000). The defence budget for 2000 was 190,000m. cedis. The headquarters of the Defence Commission of the OAU is in Accra.

Economic Affairs

In 1998, according to estimates by the World Bank, Ghana's gross national product (GNP), measured at average 1996–98 prices, was US $7,269m., equivalent to $390 per head (or $1,735 on an international purchasing-power parity basis). During 1990–98, it was estimated, GNP per head increased, in real terms, at an average annual rate of 1.4%, while the population increased at an average annual rate of 3.1% over the same period. GNP was estimated at $7,400m. in 1999, equivalent to $390 per head. Ghana's gross domestic product (GDP) increased, in real terms, at an average annual rate of 4.3% in 1990–99; GDP increased by 4.7% in 1998 and by an estimated 4.4% in 1999.

Agriculture (including forestry and fishing) contributed an estimated 35.6% of GDP in 1999. An estimated 57.1% of the labour force were employed in the sector in that year. The principal cash crops are cocoa beans (Ghana being one of the world's leading producers, and exports of which accounted for 29.9% of total exports in 1998), coffee, bananas, cassava, oil palm, coconuts, limes, kola nuts and shea-nuts (karité nuts). Timber production is also important, with the forestry sector accounting for 3.8% of GDP in 1997 and 9.4% of total export earnings in 1998. Fishing satisfies more than three-quarters of domestic requirements. During 1990–99, according to the World

Bank, agricultural GDP increased at an annual average rate of 3.4%; agricultural GDP increased by an estimated 4.9% in 1999. In early 2001 the government announced plans to make Ghana self-sufficient in rice production.

Industry (including mining, manufacturing, construction and power) contributed an estimated 25.3% of GDP in 1999, and employed 12.8% of the working population in 1984. According to the World Bank, industrial GDP increased at an average annual rate of 4.8% in 1990–99, and increased by an estimated 6.9% in 1999.

Mining contributed 5.7% of GDP in 1997, and employed 0.5% of the working population in 1984. Gold and diamonds are the major minerals exported, although Ghana also exploits large reserves of bauxite and manganese ore. According to IMF figures, the GDP of the mining sector increased by an average of 5.1% per year in 1993–97, and by 5.6% in 1997.

Manufacturing contributed an estimated 8.9% of GDP in 1999, and employed 10.9% of the working population in 1984. The most important sectors are food processing, textiles, vehicles, cement, paper, chemicals and petroleum. According to the World Bank, manufacturing GDP increased at an average annual rate of 3.2% in 1990–98, and increased by an estimated 6.0% in 1999.

The Akosombo and Kpong hydroelectric plants supply 90% of Ghana's electricity; thermal power provides an alternative source of energy. Low rainfall resulted in a severe energy crisis in 1998, however, prompting the Government to accelerate plans for the further development of thermal power. The construction of a nuclear reactor at Kwabenya, near Accra, was completed in January 1995. In August 1999 the Governments of Ghana, Benin, Togo and Nigeria agreed jointly to finance the West African Gas Pipeline (WAGP), which was to supply natural gas from Nigeria to the three recipient countries. The project was scheduled to be completed in 2001. Imports of mineral fuels comprised 4.8% of the total value of imports in 1998. Electricity is exported to Benin and Togo.

The services sector contributed an estimated 39.1% of GDP in 1999, and engaged 26.1% of the working population in 1984. According to the World Bank, the GDP of the services sector increased at an average annual rate of 5.0% in 1990–99, and increased by 6.0% in 1998 and by estimated 2.2% in 1999.

In 1999 Ghana recorded a visible trade deficit of US $1,111.5m., while there was a deficit of $766.0m. on the current account of the balance of payments. In 1998 the principal source of imports was the USA (11.7%); other major sources were the United Kingdom and Germany. Switzerland was the principal market for exports (taking 23.6% of the total) in that year; other important purchasers were the United Kingdom, the Netherlands and Germany. The principal exports in 1998 were gold (which accounted for 37.5% of total export earnings), cocoa beans and timber and timber products. The principal imports in 1998 were machinery and transport equipment and food and live animals.

Ghana's overall budget deficit for 1998 was 1,393,000m. cedis (equivalent to 8.1% of GDP). Ghana's external debt totalled US $6,884m. at the end of 1998, of which $5,570m. was long-term public debt. In the same year the cost of debt-servicing was equivalent to 28.4% of exports of goods and services. In 1990–99 the average annual rate of inflation was 25.7%. Consumer prices increased by 12.4% in 1999 and by 25.2% in 2000. In 1995 some 41,000 people were registered as unemployed in Ghana.

Ghana is a member of the Economic Community of West African States (ECOWAS, see p. 170), of the International Cocoa Organization (ICCO, see p. 304) and of the International Coffee Organization (ICO, see p. 304).

Although Ghana's economy has made steady progress since the transfer to civilian rule in 1992, it remains vulnerable to unfavourable weather conditions and to fluctuations in international commodity prices. In May 1999 the IMF approved a three-year Enhanced Structural Adjustment Facility, equivalent to US $209.4m., to support the Government's economic reform programme. During 1999–2000, however, government finances were severely strained by a sustained fall in prices for Ghana's two major export commodities, gold and cocoa (which had declined in value by almost 50% between 1998 and late 2000), and by an increase in the price of petroleum, sales of which were subsidized by the state. The cedi depreciated by 51.7% against the US dollar in 2000 and foreign reserves remained low at the end of the year. Economic concerns were widely regarded as being a major factor in ensuring the election to the presidency, in December 2000, of John Kufuor, who was perceived to be a proponent of greater economic reform, liberalization and privatization. In March 2001 the Government raised petroleum prices by 64%, with the intention of doubling prices by the end of the year. However, it was feared that a proposed compensatory increase in wages would result in a higher rate of inflation. In March Ghana announced that it would seek assistance under the World Bank's Heavily Indebted Poor Countries (HIPC) initiative. Targets for 2001 included an annual GDP growth rate of 4% and a rate of inflation of 25%.

Social Welfare

The Government provides hospitals and medical care at nominal rates, and there is a government pension scheme. In 1992 government health facilities included 49 general hospitals and about 300 rural health clinics; religious missions operated 41 hospitals and 64 clinics, while there were an additional 400 private clinics. In that year there were about 800 physicians and 11,000 nurses working in the public sector, with about 300 physicians working in private practice. In 1998 the Government allocated 131,500m. cedis for health services (3.9% of total expenditure) and 250,295m. cedis for social security and welfare (equivalent to 7.5% of total expenditure).

Education

Education is officially compulsory for eight years between the ages of six and 14. Primary education begins at the age of six and lasts for six years. Secondary education, beginning at the age of 12, lasts for a further seven years, comprising a first cycle lasting four years and a second cycle of three years. Following four years of junior secondary education, pupils are examined to determine admission to senior secondary school courses, or to technical and vocational courses. In 1994 primary enrolment was equivalent to 79% of children in the relevant age-group (boys 84%; girls 74%), while the comparable ratio for secondary enrolment in 1991 was 36% (boys 44%; girls 28%). It was estimated that 52,000 students were enrolled in higher education in 1992, with about 10,700 students attending the country's five universities. Tertiary institutions also included 38 teacher-training colleges, seven diploma-awarding colleges, 21 technical colleges and six polytechnics. Expenditure on education by the central Government in 1998 was 608,000m. cedis (18.2% of total spending). According to UNESCO estimates, the average rate of adult illiteracy in 1995 was 36.1% (males 25.3%; females 46.6%).

Public Holidays

2001: 1 January (New Year's Day), 6 March (Independence Day and Eid al-Adha*, Feast of the Sacrifice), 13–16 April (Easter), 1 May (Labour Day), 1 July (Republic Day), 7 December (National Farmers' Day), 17 December* (Eid al-Fitr, end of Ramadan), 25–26 December (Christmas).

2002: 1 January (New Year's Day), 23 February* (Eid-al-Adha, Feast of the Sacrifice), 6 March (Independence Day), 29 March–1 April (Easter), 1 May (Labour Day), 1 July (Republic Day), 6 December (National Farmers' Day and Eid-al-Fitr*, end of Ramadan), 25–26 December (Christmas).

* These holidays are dependent on the Islamic lunar calendar and may vary by one or two days from the dates given.

Weights and Measures

The metric system is in force.

Statistical Survey

Source (except where otherwise stated): Central Bureau of Statistics, POB 1098, Accra; tel. (21) 66512.

Area and Population

AREA, POPULATION AND DENSITY

Area (sq km)	238,537*
Population (census results)	
1 March 1970	8,559,313
11 March 1984	
Males	6,063,848
Females	6,232,233
Total	12,296,081
Population (UN estimates at mid-year)†	
1997	18,656,000
1998	19,162,000
1999	19,678,000
Density (per sq km) at mid-1999	82.5

* 92,100 sq miles.
† Source: UN, *World Population Prospects: The 1998 Revision.*

POPULATION BY REGION (1991 estimates)

Ashanti	2,485,800
Brong-Ahafo	1,433,000
Central	1,359,900
Eastern	2,003,200
Greater Accra	1,696,200
Northern	1,389,100
Upper East	921,200
Upper West	526,400
Volta	1,433,000
Western	1,374,500
Total	14,622,200

Principal ethnic groups (1991 estimates, percentage of total population): Akan 52.4, Mossi 15.8, Ewe 11.9, Ga-Adangme 7.8, Guan 11.9, Gurma 3.3, Yoruba 1.3.

PRINCIPAL TOWNS (population at 1984 census)

Accra (capital). . .	867,459	Takoradi . . .	61,484
Kumasi . . .	376,249	Cape Coast . .	57,224
Tamale . . .	135,952	Sekondi . . .	31,916
Tema	131,528		

BIRTHS AND DEATHS (UN estimates, annual averages)

	1980–85	1985–90	1990–95
Birth rate (per 1,000) . .	45.0	43.1	40.1
Death rate (per 1,000) . .	13.1	11.9	10.6

Expectation of life (UN estimates, years at birth, 1990–95): 58.0 (males 56.3; females 59.7).

Source: UN, *World Population Prospects: The 1998 Revision.*

ECONOMICALLY ACTIVE POPULATION (1984 census)

	Males	Females	Total
Agriculture, hunting, forestry and fishing	1,750,024	1,560,943	3,310,967
Mining and quarrying . . .	24,906	1,922	26,828
Manufacturing	198,430	389,988	588,418
Electricity, gas and water . .	14,033	1,404	15,437
Construction	60,692	3,994	64,686
Trade, restaurants and hotels .	111,540	680,607	792,147
Transport, storage and communications	117,806	5,000	122,806
Financing, insurance, real estate and business services . .	19,933	7,542	27,475
Community, social and personal services	339,665	134,051	473,716
Total employed	2,637,029	2,785,451	5,422,480
Unemployed	87,452	70,172	157,624
Total labour force	2,724,481	2,855,623	5,580,104

Source: ILO, *Yearbook of Labour Statistics.*

Mid-1999 (estimates in '000): Agriculture, etc. 5,340; Total 9,350 (Source: FAO).

Agriculture

PRINCIPAL CROPS ('000 metric tons)

	1997	1998	1999
Maize	996	1,035	1,014
Millet	144	172	160
Sorghum	333	387	302
Rice (paddy)	197	194	210
Sugar cane	140	147	140*
Cassava (Manioc) . . .	7,000	7,227	7,845
Yams	2,408	2,634	3,249
Taro (Coco yam) . . .	1,530	1,597	1,707
Onions	35	38	39*
Tomatoes	220	216	215*
Green chillies and peppers . .	235	300	270*
Eggplants (Aubergines)* . .	6	6	6
Pulses*	16	16	15
Oranges	257	270	270*
Lemons and limes* . . .	30	30	30
Mangoes*	4	4	4
Bananas	15	15	15*
Plantains	1,818	1,893	2,046
Pineapples*	35	35	35
Palm kernels	34*	40*	40*
Groundnuts (in shell) . .	154	212	190*
Coconuts	295	310	305*
Coffee (green)	3	8	8*
Cocoa beans	322	409	398†
Tobacco (leaves) . . .	2	2	3*

* FAO estimate(s).   † Unofficial figure.
Source: FAO.

LIVESTOCK ('000 head, year ending September)

	1997	1998	1999*
Horses*	2	2	2
Asses*	13	13	13
Cattle	1,260	1,273	1,285
Pigs	353	352	350
Sheep	2,467	2,516	2,565
Goats	2,634	2,739	2,800
Poultry	15,964	17,467	18,000

* FAO estimates.
Source: FAO.

LIVESTOCK PRODUCTS ('000 metric tons)

	1997	1998	1999
Beef and veal	12	14	14
Mutton and lamb	6	7	7
Goat meat	6	7	7
Pig meat	8	8	8
Poultry meat	15	16	16
Other meat*	90	90	90
Cows' milk	33	33	33
Hen eggs	17	19	19
Cattle hides	2	2	2

* FAO estimates.

Source: FAO.

Forestry

ROUNDWOOD REMOVALS ('000 cubic metres, excl. bark)

	1996	1997	1998
Sawlogs, veneer logs and logs for sleepers	1,166	1,189	1,138
Other industrial wood . . .	89	89	89
Fuel wood	20,678	20,678	20,678
Total	21,933	21,956	21,905

Source: FAO, *Yearbook of Forest Products*.

SAWNWOOD PRODUCTION ('000 cubic metres, incl. railway sleepers)

	1996	1997	1998
Coniferous (softwood). . .	54	—	—
Broadleaved (hardwood) . .	550	575	590
Total	604	575	590

Source: FAO, *Yearbook of Forest Products*.

Fishing

('000 metric tons, live weight)

	1996	1997	1998
Capture	477.0	446.8	442.7
Freshwater fishes . . .	73.6	70.0	74.5
Bigeye grunt	13.6	19.8	12.1
Jack and horse mackerels .	10.9	17.5	16.6
Round sardinella . . .	118.4	49.4	56.0
Madeiran sardinella . .	13.6	14.2	15.5
Other sardinellas . . .	20.1	36.0	33.3
European anchovy . . .	98.3	82.7	44.6
Skipjack tuna	19.6	27.7	34.2
Yellowfin tuna	12.2	16.5	17.8
Chub mackerel	15.6	19.9	30.2
Aquaculture	0.6*	0.4	0.4*
Total catch	477.6	447.2	443.1

* FAO estimate.

Source: FAO, *Yearbook of Fishery Statistics*.

Mining

('000 metric tons, unless otherwise indicated)

	1995	1996*	1997*
Gold ('000 kilograms)† . . .	51.3	48.3	53.5
Diamonds ('000 carats) . .	622.7	714.3	585.5
Manganese ore‡	100.0	266.8	333.4
Bauxite	513.0	383.4	500.7

* Estimates.

† Figures refer to the metal content of ores.

‡ Figures refer to gross weight. The estimated manganese content was 101,000 metric tons in 1996.

Source: IMF, *Ghana: Selected Issues* (January 1999).

Industry

SELECTED PRODUCTS ('000 metric tons, unless otherwise indicated)

	1994	1995	1996
Groundnut oil*	25	21	17
Coconut oil*	6	6	6
Palm oil*	100	100	105
Palm kernel oil*	9	9	9
Motor spirit (petrol)* . . .	215	218	218
Kerosene*	125	127	128
Diesel and gas oil* . . .	214	215	215
Cement	1,350†	1,400†	1,575
Aluminium (unwrought)‡§ . .	140.7	135.4	137.0
Electric energy (million kWh)* .	6,155	6,159	6,036

1997: ('000 metric tons): Groundnut oil 20, Coconut oil 7, Palm oil 92, Palm kernel oil 10.

1998: ('000 metric tons): Groundnut oil 28, Coconut oil 7, Palm oil 111, Palm kernel oil 12.

1999: ('000 metric tons): Groundnut oil 25, Coconut oil 7, Palm oil 105*, Palm kernel oil 12.

* Provisional or estimated figures.

† Data from US Bureau of Mines.

‡ Primary metal only.

§ Data from *World Metal Statistics* (London).

Sources: FAO; UN, *Industrial Commodity Statistics Yearbook*.

Finance

CURRENCY AND EXCHANGE RATES

Monetary Units

100 pesewas = 1 new cedi.

Sterling, Dollar and Euro Equivalents (29 December 2000)

£1 sterling = 10,658.6 cedis;

US $1 = 7,142.9 cedis;

€1 = 6,646.4 cedis;

100,000 cedis = £9.382 = $14.000 = €15.046.

Average Exchange Rate (cedis per US $)

1998   2,314.15

1999   2,647.32

2000   5,321.68

GENERAL BUDGET ('000 million new cedis)

Revenue*	1995	1996	1997
Tax revenue	1,138.5	1,710.6	2,070.0
Taxes on income, profits and			
capital gains	275.0	433.3	606.4
Individual	80.8	131.1	225.1
Corporate	157.2	242.3	293.1
Other unallocated taxes on			
income	37.0	59.9	88.3
Domestic taxes on goods			
and services	503.7	732.4	833.4
General sales, turnover or			
value-added tax	210.1	329.6	407.4
Excises (excl. petroleum)	69.6	112.6	111.6
Petroleum revenue	224.0	290.2	314.3
Taxes on international trade			
and transactions	359.9	544.9	630.2
Import duties	202.6	267.2	364.3
Export duties	157.2	277.7	265.9
Non-tax revenue	446.1	287.0	376.7
Total	**1,584.6**	**1,997.5**	**2,446.7**

Expenditure†	1993	1994‡	1995‡
General public services	83.9	145.4	93.6
Defence	39.5	30.9	34.5
Public order and safety	30.8	23.9	42.9
Education	179.2	207.6	258.7
Health	56.6	58.6	73.6
Social security and welfare	57.8	112.3	138.8
Housing and community amenities	12.4	16.8	48.7
Other community and			
social services	10.1	20.6	—
Economic services	129.7	137.3	199.3
Agriculture, forestry and fishing	28.4	26.8	18.5
Mining, manufacturing and			
construction	11.0	18.5	24.6
Utilities	7.0	12.8	21.5
Transport and communications	79.5	75.5	116.7
Other economic services	3.8	3.7	18.0
Other purposes	162.7	338.9	342.7
Interest payments	134.8	230.1	328.8
Sub-total	**762.7**	**1,092.3**	**1,232.8**
Special efficiency payments§	50.8	64.0	51.4
Total	**813.5**	**1,156.3**	**1,284.2**
Current	694.3	n.a.	n.a.
Capital	135.3	n.a.	n.a.
Adjustment for payment arrears‖	−16.0	n.a.	n.a.

* Excluding grants received ('000 million new cedis): 280.1 in 1995; 291.1 in 1996; 262.2 in 1997. Also excluded are the proceeds from the divestiture of state-owned enterprises ('000 million new cedis): 106.2 in 1995; 143.5 in 1996; 105.7 in 1997.
† Excluding lending minus repayments ('000 million new cedis): 8.0 in 1993; 8.3 in 1994; 15.8 in 1995. Also excluded is capital expenditure resulting from foreign financing ('000 million new cedis): 286.9 in 1993; 456.0 in 1994; 564.8 in 1995.
‡ Excluding unallocable expenditure.
§ Including provision for redeployment, retraining and relocation of public-sector employees.
‖ Minus sign indicates an increase in arrears.

Source: IMF, *Ghana: Selected Issues* (January 1999).

INTERNATIONAL RESERVES (US $ million at 31 December)

	1997	1998	1999
Gold*	n.a.	78.8	78.9
IMF special drawing rights	3.4	59.7	18.2
Reserve position in IMF	23.4	24.5	56.5
Foreign exchange	n.a.	292.8	379.1
Total	**n.a.**	**455.8**	**532.7**

* National valuation.

Source: IMF, *International Financial Statistics*.

MONEY SUPPLY ('000 million new cedis at 31 December)

	1997	1998	1999
Currency outside banks	981.82	1,083.63	1,186.14
Deposits of non-financial public			
enterprises	6.32	3.17	2.76
Demand deposits at deposit money			
banks	776.54	982.53	939.25
Total money (incl. others)	**1,767.26**	**2,073.12**	**2,129.41**

Source: IMF, *International Financial Statistics*.

COST OF LIVING (Consumer Price Index; base: 1995 = 100)

	1997	1998	1999
All items	187.4	214.8	241.5

Source: IMF, *International Financial Statistics*.

NATIONAL ACCOUNTS ('000 million new cedis at current prices)

National Income and Product

	1995	1996	1997
GDP in purchasers'			
values	**7,418.0**	**10,633.1**	**14,113.4**
Net factor income from abroad	−155.1	−220.0	273.9
Gross national product	**7,262.9**	**10,413.1**	**13,839.5**
Less Consumption of fixed capital	359.8	560.5	996.7
National income in market			
prices	**6,903.1**	**9,852.6**	**12,842.8**

Source: IMF, *International Financial Statistics*.

Expenditure on the Gross Domestic Product

	1995	1996	1997
Government final consumption			
expenditure	921.7	1,345.0	1,743.8
Private final consumption			
expenditure	6,108.1	8,800.3	11,267.0
Increase in stocks	5.4	6.2	127.3
Gross fixed capital			
formation	1,028.1	1,464.2	3,338.2
Total domestic expenditure	**8,063.3**	**11,615.7**	**16,476.3**
Exports of goods and			
services	1,898.9	2,537.6	2,794.6
Less Imports of goods and services	2,544.2	3,520.1	5,157.5
GDP in purchasers' values	**7,418.0**	**10,633.1**	**14,113.4**
GDP at constant 1990 prices	**2,530.3**	**2,661.1**	**2,796.7**

Source: IMF, *International Financial Statistics*.

Gross Domestic Product by Economic Activity

	1995	1996	1997
Agriculture and livestock	2,351.0	3,440.0	3,848.7
Forestry and logging	211.0	297.0	477.2
Fishing	444.0	680.0	724.2
Mining and quarrying	371.0	536.0	719.8
Manufacturing	723.0	979.0	1,277.5
Electricity, water and gas	206.0	302.0	425.7
Construction	582.0	856.0	1,199.6
Transport, storage and communications	303.0	423.0	580.4
Wholesale and retail trade	465.0	654.0	917.0
Finance, real estate and business services	302.6	430.0	586.6
Public administration, defence and other government services	825.0	1,124.0	1,377.0
Other community, social and personal services	185.0	249.0	341.6
Private non-profit services	72.0	97.0	133.2
GDP at factor cost	7,040.6	10,067.0	12,608.5
Indirect taxes, *less* subsidies	712.0	1,272.0	1,504.9
GDP in purchasers' values	7,752.6	11,339.0	14,113.4

Source: IMF, *Ghana: Selected Issues* (January 1999).

BALANCE OF PAYMENTS (US $ million)

	1997	1998	1999
Exports of goods f.o.b.	1,489.9	2,090.8	2,116.6
Imports of goods f.o.b.	−2,128.2	−2,896.5	−3,228.1
Trade balance	−638.3	−805.7	−1,111.5
Exports of services	164.9	440.9	467.8
Imports of services	−505.0	−612.8	−610.5
Balance on goods and services	−978.4	−977.6	−1,254.2
Other income received	26.7	26.7	15.0
Other income paid	−158.1	−163.0	−146.8
Balance on goods, services and income	−1,109.8	−1,113.9	−1,386.0
Current transfers received	576.5	751.0	637.8
Current transfers paid	−16.4	−17.1	−17.8
Current balance	−549.7	−380.0	−766.0
Capital account (net)	−1.0	−1.0	−1.0
Direct investment from abroad	82.6	55.7	17.0
Other investment assets	33.1	87.9	183.1
Other investment liabilities	378.1	372.2	191.7
Net errors and omissions	83.7	−27.0	327.3
Overall balance	26.7	107.8	−47.9

Source: IMF, *International Financial Statistics*.

External Trade

PRINCIPAL COMMODITIES (US $ million)

Imports	1996	1997	1998
Food and live animals	267.4	361.1	536.2
Rice	53.8	46.5	106.0
Mineral fuels, lubricants, etc.	55.4	341.8	159.5
Crude petroleum	21.5	139.1	97.1
Petroleum products	30.6	200.7	52.0
Chemicals	100.7	110.6	100.7
Machinery and transport equipment	876.7	1,270.8	1,293.0
Passenger cars (incl. buses)	127.7	114.5	154.9
Lorries and trucks	134.7	224.0	229.8
Miscellaneous manufactured articles	105.9	116.1	40.3
Total (incl. others)	2,839.7	3,033.6	3,329.8

Exports	1996	1997	1998
Cocoa beans	494.7	384.8	541.6
Cocoa products	73.2	92.7	78.2
Timber and timber products	147.8	170.5	171.0
Gold	681.6	545.1	679.4
Electricity	58.2	67.6	40.9
Total (incl. others)	1,698.0	1,753.7	1,811.6

Source: Ministry of Trade and Industry, Accra.

PRINCIPAL TRADING PARTNERS (US $ million)

Imports	1996	1997	1998
Belgium	68.1	87.7	136.7
China, People's Repub.	96.7	76.0	105.8
France	123.6	118.5	129.2
Germany	341.6	237.6	277.4
India	72.2	61.7	77.5
Italy	108.6	130.3	152.7
Japan	176.0	167.0	159.9
Korea, Republic	59.8	68.3	110.2
Netherlands	108.9	146.6	153.2
Nigeria	262.5	163.6	44.9
South Africa	48.1	70.5	90.6
Spain	82.1	77.4	102.2
United Kingdom	453.1	472.8	383.8
USA	360.7	395.2	390.0
Total (incl. others)	2,839.7	3,033.6	3,329.8

Exports	1996	1997	1998
Belgium	32.3	35.3	65.4
France	60.5	80.5	77.8
Germany	142.6	117.8	93.8
Italy	44.8	49.7	57.0
Japan	58.4	75.1	55.3
Netherlands	165.3	211.8	202.4
South Africa	6.1	3.2	41.3
Spain	31.3	31.9	31.9
Switzerland	486.3	437.1	418.0
Togo	19.0	14.9	60.0
United Kingdom	369.5	284.4	364.5
USA	49.2	33.8	69.2
Total (incl. others)	1,639.8	1,586.1	1,770.6

Source: Ministry of Trade and Industry, Accra.

Transport

RAILWAYS (traffic)

	1996
Passengers carried ('000)	2,100
Freight carried ('000 metric tons)	857
Passenger-km (million)	208
Net ton-km (million)	152.8

Source: *Railway Directory*.

ROAD TRAFFIC ('000 motor vehicles in use at 31 December)

	1994	1995*	1996*
Passenger cars	90.0	90.0	90.0
Lorries and vans	44.7	45.0	45.0

* Estimates.

Source: International Road Federation, *World Road Statistics*.

SHIPPING

Merchant Fleet (registered at 31 December)

	1996	1997	1998
Number of vessels . . .	195	206	205
Total displacement ('000 grt) . .	134.7	129.7	115.5

Source: Lloyd's Register of Shipping.

International Sea-borne Freight Traffic
(estimates, '000 metric tons)

	1991	1992	1993
Goods loaded	2,083	2,279	2,424
Goods unloaded	2,866	2,876	2,904

Source: UN Economic Commission for Africa, *African Statistical Yearbook*.

CIVIL AVIATION (traffic on scheduled services)

	1995	1996	1997
Kilometres flown (million) . .	5	6	6
Passengers carried ('000) . .	186	197	211
Passenger-km (million) . .	611	655	702
Total ton-km (million) . .	86	91	99

Source: UN, *Statistical Yearbook*.

Tourism

ARRIVALS BY NATIONALITY

	1995	1996	1997
Côte d'Ivoire	13,750	14,657	15,646
France	10,334	11,016	11,759
Germany	13,799	14,709	15,702
Liberia	7,500	7,995	8,534
Netherlands	6,924	7,380	7,878
Nigeria	39,254	41,842	44,667
Togo	8,560	9,124	9,739
United Kingdom	24,762	26,395	28,177
USA	18,864	20,108	21,465
Total (incl. others)* . . .	286,000	304,860	325,434

* Includes Ghanaian nationals resident abroad: 77,850 in 1995; 82,984 in 1996; 88,585 in 1997.

Source: World Tourism Organization, *Yearbook of Tourism Statistics*.

Receipts from tourism (US $ million): 233 in 1995; 248 in 1996; 266 in 1997 (Source: mainly UN, *Statistical Yearbook*).

Communications Media

	1995	1996	1997
Radio receivers ('000 in use) . .	4,000	4,250	4,400
Television receivers ('000 in use) .	1,600	1,650	1,730
Telephones ('000 main lines in use)	63	78	106
Telefax stations (number in use) .	5,000*	n.a.	n.a.
Mobile cellular telephones (subscribers)	6,200	12,766	21,866
Daily newspapers			
Number	4	4	n.a.
Average circulation ('000 copies)	310*	250	n.a.

* Provisional or estimated figures.

Sources: UNESCO, *Statistical Yearbook*; UN, *Statistical Yearbook*.

Education

(1989/90, unless otherwise indicated)

	Institutions	Teachers	Students
Pre-primary	4,735	15,152	323,406
Primary (public only)[1] . . .	12,134	71,863	2,154,646
Secondary			
General (public only) . . .	n.a.	39,903[2]	841,722[3]
Teacher training . . .	38[4]	1,001	15,723
Vocational (public only) . .	205[5]	1,247	22,578[3]
University	5[6]	700[7]	10,700[6]

[1] 1994/95 figures.
[2] 1990/91 figure.
[3] 1991/92 figure.
[4] 1988 figure.
[5] 1988/89 figure.
[6] 1992 figure.
[7] Excluding the University of Ghana.

Source: mainly UNESCO, *Statistical Yearbook*.

1992: *Primary* 10,623 institutions, 1,800,000 students (estimate); *Junior secondary* 5,136 institutions, 569,000 students (estimate); *Senior secondary* 404 institutions, 147,000 students (estimate); *Higher* 52,000 students.

Source: African Development Bank.

Directory

The Constitution

Under the terms of the Constitution of the Fourth Republic, which was approved by national referendum on 28 April 1992, Ghana has a multi-party political system. Executive power is vested in the President, who is Head of State and Commander-in-Chief of the Armed Forces. The President is elected by universal adult suffrage for a term of four years, and appoints a Vice-President. The duration of the President's tenure of office is limited to two four-year terms. It is also stipulated that, in the event that no presidential candidate receives more than 50% of votes cast, a new election between the two candidates with the highest number of votes is to take place within 21 days. Legislative power is vested in a 200-member uni-cameral Parliament, which is elected by direct adult suffrage for a four-year term. The Council of Ministers is appointed by the President, subject to approval by the Parliament. The Constitution also provides for a 25-member Council of State, principally comprising presidential nominees and regional representatives, and a 20-member National Security Council (chaired by the Vice-President), both of which act as advisory bodies to the President.

The Government

HEAD OF STATE

President and Commander-in-Chief of the Armed Forces: JOHN AGYEKUM KUFUOR (inaugurated 7 January 2001).

Vice-President: Alhaji ALIU MAHAMA.

COUNCIL OF MINISTERS
(March 2001)

A coalition of the New Patriotic Party (NPP), the Convention People's Party (CPP) and the National Reform Party (NRP).

Minister of Presidential Affairs and Chief of Staff: JAKE OBETSEBI-LAMPTEY (NPP).

Minister of Governmental Affairs and Chair. of National Planning Commission: JOSEPH HENRY MENSAH (NPP).

Minister of Communication: OWUSU AGYAPONG (NPP).

Minister of Defence: KWAME ADDO KUFUOR (NPP).

Minister of Education: CHRISTOPHER AMEYAW-AKUMFI (NPP).

Minister of Manpower Development and Employment: CECILIA BANNERMAN (NRP).

Minister of the Environment, Science and Technology: DOMINIC FOBIH (NPP).

Minister of Finance: YAW OSAFU-MARFO (NPP).

Minister of Agriculture: Maj. (retd) COURAGE QUARSHIGAH (NPP).

Minister of Foreign Affairs: HACKMAN OWUSU-AGYEMAN (NPP).

Minister of Health: RICHARD ANANE (NPP).

Minister of the Interior: Alhaji MALIK YAKUBU ALHASSAN (NPP).

Minister of Justice and Attorney-General: NANA AKUFO ADDO (NPP).

Minister of Lands, Forestry and Mines: KWEKU AFRIYIE (NPP).

Minister of Local Government and Rural Development: KWADWO BAAH-WIREDU (NPP).

Minister of Energy: ALBERT KAN-DAPAAH (NPP).

Minister of Women's Affairs: GLADYS ASMAH (NPP).

Minister of Economic Planning and Regional Co-operation: KWESI NDUOM (CPP).

Minister of Roads and Transportation: K. ADJEI-DAKO (NPP).

Minister of Trade and Industry: KOFI KONADU APRAKU (NPP).

Minister of Works and Housing: KWAMENA BARTELS (NPP).

Minister of Youth and Sports: (vacant).

Minister of Tourism: HAWA YAKUBU (NPP).

There are also four Ministers of State.

REGIONAL MINISTERS
(March 2001)

Ashanti: S. K. BOAFO.
Brong Ahafo: ERNEST K. DEBRAH.
Central: ISAAC EDUMADZE.
Eastern: OSAFO MENSAH.
Greater Accra: Sheikh I. C. QUAYE.
Northern: BEN SALIFU.
Upper East: MOKTAR SAHANOON.
Upper West: SALIFU MAHAMI.
Volta: KWASI OWUSA-YEBOAH.
Western: JOSEPH BOAHENE AIDOO.

MINISTRIES

Office of the President: POB 1627, Osu, Accra.

Ministry of Agriculture: POB M37, Accra; tel. (21) 665421; fax (21) 663250; e-mail mofa@africaonline.com.gh.

Ministry of Communication: POB M41, Accra; tel. (21) 228011; fax (21) 229786.

Ministry of Defence: Burma Camp, Accra; tel. (21) 777611; fax (21) 773951.

Ministry of Economic Planning and Regional Co-operation: Accra.

Ministry of Education: POB M45, Accra; tel. (21) 665421; fax (21) 664067.

Ministry of Energy: POB M212, Accra; tel. (21) 667151; fax (21) 668262.

Ministry of the Environment, Science and Technology: POB M232, Accra; tel. (21) 662626; fax (21) 666828; e-mail barnes@africaonline.com.gh.

Ministry of Finance: POB M40, Accra; tel. (21) 665441; fax (21) 667069; internet www.finance.gov.gh.

Ministry of Foreign Affairs: POB M53, Accra; tel. (21) 664951; fax (21) 665363.

Ministry of Governmental Affairs: Parliament House, Accra; tel. (21) 664716.

Ministry of Health: POB M44, Accra; tel. (21) 662014; fax (21) 666808.

Ministry of the Interior: POB M42, Accra; tel. (21) 665421; fax (21) 667450.

Ministry of Justice: POB M60, Accra.

Ministry of Lands, Forestry and Mines: POB M212, Accra; tel. (21) 665421; fax (21) 666801.

Ministry of Local Government and Rural Development: POB M50, Accra; tel. (21) 665421; fax (21) 661015.

Ministry of Manpower Development and Employment: POB M84, Accra; tel. (21) 665797; fax (21) 662683.

Ministry of Presidential Affairs: Accra.

Ministry of Roads and Transportation: POB 38, Accra; tel. (21) 223908; fax (21) 234522.

Ministry of Tourism: POB 4386, Accra; tel. (21) 666701; fax (21) 666182.

Ministry of Trade and Industry: POB M85, Accra; tel. (21) 665421; fax (21) 664115; e-mail gatewayl@ghana.com.

Ministry of Women's Affairs: Accra.

Ministry of Works and Housing: POB M43, Accra; tel. (21) 665421; fax (21) 663268.

Ministry of Youth and Sports: POB 1272, Accra; tel. (21) 665421; fax (21) 663927.

President and Legislature

PRESIDENT

Presidential Election, First Ballot, 7 December 2000

Candidate				Votes	% of votes
JOHN AGYEKUM KUFUOR (NPP)	.	.	.	3,131,739	48.17
JOHN EVANS ATTA MILLS (NDC)	.	.	.	2,895,575	44.54
EDWARD MAHAMA (PNC)	.	.	.	189,659	2.92
GEORGE HAGAN (CPP)	.	.	.	115,641	1.78
AUGUSTUS (GOOSIE) TANOH (NRP)	.	.	.	78,629	1.21
DAN LARTEY (GCPP)	.	.	.	67,504	1.04
CHARLES WEREKO-BROBBY (UGM)	.	.	.	22,123	0.34
Total	.	.	.	6,500,870	100.00

Second Ballot, 28 December 2000

Candidate				Votes	% of votes
JOHN AGYEKUM KUFUOR (NPP)	.	.	.	3,631,263	56.90
JOHN EVANS ATTA MILLS (NDC)	.	.	.	2,750,124	43.10
Total	.	.	.	6,381,387	100.00

PARLIAMENT

Speaker: PETER ALA ADJETEY.

Legislative Election, 7 December 2000

Party	Seats
New Patriotic Party (NPP)	100
National Democratic Congress (NDC)	92
People's National Convention (PNC)	3
Convention People's Party (CPP)	1
Independents	4
Total	**200**

COUNCIL OF STATE

Chairman: (vacant).

Political Organizations

Convention People's Party (CPP): 825/3 Mango Tree Ave, Asylum Down, POB 10939, Accra-North; tel. (21) 221776; f. 1998 as Convention Party by merger of the National Convention Party (f. 1992) and the People's Convention Party (f. 1993); present name adopted in 2000; Nkrumahist; Chair. ABUBAKAR ALHASSAN; Sec.-Gen. B. K. NKETSIAH.

Democratic People's Party (DPP): 698/4 Star Ave, Kokomlemle, Accra; tel. (21) 221671; f. 1992; Chair. DANIEL K. G. MARKIN; Sec.-Gen. LAWRENCE K. HONU.

EGLE (Every Ghanaian Living Everywhere) Party: Kokomlemle, Accra; f. 1992 as the Eagle Party; Chair. NANA YAW BOAKYE OFORI ATTA; Sec.-Gen. SAM PEE YALLEY.

Ghana Democratic Republican Party (GDRP): C39/5 Onyaa Cres., opposite Nima Police Station, Accra; tel. (21) 226230; f. 1992; Chair. KOFI AMOAH; Sec.-Gen. NII ODARTEY-LAWSON.

Great Consolidated People's Party (GCPP): Citadel House, POB 3077, Accra; tel. (21) 229721; f. 1996; Nkrumahist; Chair. DAN LARTEY; Sec.-Gen. NICHOLAS MENSAH.

National Democratic Congress (NDC): 641/4 Ringway Close, Kokomlemle, POB 5825, Accra-North; tel. (21) 224905; internet www.ndc.org.gh; f. 1992; party of fmr Pres. Jerry Rawlings; Chair. Alhaji ISSIFU ALI; Sec.-Gen. Alhaji HUUDU YAHAYA.

National Reform Party (NRP): 21 Mango Tree Ave, Asylum Down, POB 19403, Accra; tel. (21) 228578; f. 1999 by a breakaway group from the NDC; Chair. PETER GAMELI KPORDUGBE; Sec.-Gen. KYERETWIE OPOKU.

New Patriotic Party (NPP): POB 3456, Accra; tel. (21) 227951; fax (21) 224418; e-mail npp@africanonline.com.gh; internet www.nppghana.com; f. 1992 by supporters of the fmr Prime Minister, Kofi Busia, and J. B. Danquah; Chair. SAMUEL ARTHUR ODOI-SYKES; Sec.-Gen. DAN BOTWE.

People's National Convention (PNC): Kokomlemle, near Sadisco, Accra; tel. (21) 226528; f. 1992; Nkrumahist; Chair. (vacant); Sec.-Gen. NII NOI DOWUON.

United Ghana Movement (UGM): 1 North Ridge Cres., Accra; tel. (21) 225581; fax (21) 231390; e-mail info@ugmghana.org; internet www.ugmghana.org; f. 1996 by a breakaway group from the NPP; Chair. NII ARMAH TAGOE; Sec.-Gen. ERIC DUTENYA KWABLA.

Diplomatic Representation

EMBASSIES AND HIGH COMMISSIONS IN GHANA

Algeria: 22 Josif Broz Tito Ave, POB 2747, Accra; tel. (21) 776719; fax (21) 776828; e-mail amb.dz.acc@n.c.s.com.gh; Ambassador: HASSANE RABEHI.

Benin: 19 Volta St, Second Close, Airport Residential Area, POB 7871, Accra; tel. (21) 774860; fax (21) 774889; Ambassador: SÉDJORO THÉOPHILE HOUESSINON.

Brazil: 24 Sir Arku Korsah Rd, Roman Ridge Ambassadorial Area, POB CT 3859, Accra; tel. (21) 774921; fax (21) 778566; e-mail brasemb@ighmail.com; Ambassador: PAULO AMÉRICO V. WOLOWSKI.

Bulgaria: 3 Kakramadu Rd, East Cantonments, POB 3193, Accra; tel. (21) 772404; fax (21) 774231; e-mail bulembgh@ghana.com; Chargé d'affaires: GEORGE MITEV.

Burkina Faso: 772/3, Asylum Down, off Farrar Ave, POB 651, Accra; tel. (21) 221988; e-mail ambafaso@ghana.com; Ambassador: EMILE GOUBA.

Canada: No. 42, Independence Ave, POB 1639, Accra; tel. (21) 228555; fax (21) 773792; e-mail accra@dfait-maeci.gc.ca; High Commissioner: JANET GRAHAM.

China, People's Republic: 6 Agostino Neto Rd, Airport Residential Area, POB 3356, Accra; tel. (21) 777073; fax (21) 774527; e-mail chinaemb@ghana.com; Ambassador: LU YONGSHOU.

Côte d'Ivoire: F710/2 18th Lane, off Cantonments Rd, POB 3445, Christiansborg, Accra; tel. (21) 774611; fax (21) 773516; Ambassador: AMON TANOE EMMANUEL.

Cuba: 20 Amilcar Cabral Rd, Airport Residential Area, POB 9163 Airport, Accra; tel. (21) 775868; Ambassador: JUAN CARRETERO.

Czech Republic: C260/5, Kanda High Rd No. 2, POB 5226, Accra-North; tel. (21) 223540; fax (21) 225337; e-mail accraczemb@ighmail.com; Ambassador: JINDŘICH JUNEK.

Denmark: 67 Dr Isert Rd, 8th Ave Extension, North Ridge, POB C596, Accra; tel. (21) 253473; fax (21) 228061; e-mail accamb@accamab.um.dk; Ambassador: OLE BLICHER-OLSEN.

Egypt: 27 Noi Fetreke St, Roman Ridge, POB 2508, Accra; tel. and fax (21) 776795; Ambassador: ABDEL MOHEIM AHMED TALAAT.

Ethiopia: 6 Adiembra Rd, East Cantonments, POB 1646, Accra; tel. (21) 775928; fax (21) 776807; e-mail ethioemb@ghana.com; Ambassador: Dr KUWANG TUTILAM.

France: 12th Rd, off Liberation Ave, POB 187, Accra; tel. (21) 774480; fax (21) 778321; e-mail ambaccra@africaonline.com.gh; internet www.amba-france-gh.org; Ambassador: JEAN-MICHEL BERRIT.

Germany: Valdemosa Lodge, Ridge St No. 6, North Ridge, POB 1757, Accra; tel. (21) 221311; fax (21) 221347; e-mail geramb@ghana.com; Ambassador: CHRISTIAN NAKONZ.

Guinea: 11 Osu Badu St, Dzorwulu, POB 5497, Accra-North; tel. (21) 777921; fax (21) 760961; Ambassador: DORE DIALE DRUS.

Holy See: 8 Drake Ave, Airport Residential Area, POB 9675, Accra; tel. (21) 777759; fax (21) 774019; Apostolic Nuncio: Most Rev. GEORGE KOCHERRY, Titular Archbishop of Othona.

India: 9 Ridge Rd, Roman Ridge, POB 3040, Accra; tel. (21) 775601; fax (21) 772176; e-mail indiahc@ghana.com; High Commissioner: DILJIT SINGH PANNUN.

Iran: 12 Arusah St, Roman Ridge, POB 12673, Accra-North; tel. and fax (21) 777043; Ambassador: KIUMARS FOTUHI-QIYAM.

Italy: Jawaharlal Nehru Rd, POB 140, Accra; tel. (21) 775621; fax (21) 777056; e-mail ambital@africaonline.com.gh; Ambassador: GIANCARLO IZZO.

Japan: 5th Ave Extension, West Cantonments, POB 1637, Accra; tel. (21) 765060; fax (21) 762553; Ambassador: SHOSUKE ITO.

Korea, Democratic People's Republic: 139 Nortei Ababio Loop, Ambassadorial Estate, POB 13874, Accra; tel. (21) 777825; Ambassador: (vacant).

Korea, Republic: 3 Abokobi Rd, East Cantonments, POB 13700, Accra-North; tel. (21) 776157; Ambassador: HWANG PU-HONG.

Lebanon: F864/1 off Cantonments Rd, OSU, POB 562, Accra; tel. (21) 776727; fax (21) 764290; e-mail lebanon@ighmail.com; Ambassador: CHARBEL AOUN.

Liberia: 10 West Cantonments, off Jawaharlal Nehru Rd, POB 895, Accra; tel. (21) 775641; Ambassador: ELWOOD GREAVES.

Libya: 14 Sixth St, Airport Residential Area, POB 9665, Accra; tel. (21) 774820; Secretary of People's Bureau: Dr FATIMA MAGAME.

Mali: Agostino Neto Rd, Airport Residential Area, POB 1121, Accra; tel. (21) 666423; Ambassador: MUPHTAH AG HAIRY.

Netherlands: 89 Liberation Rd, Thomas Sankara Circle, POB 3248, Accra; tel. (21) 773644; fax (21) 773655; Ambassador: HELN C. R. M. PRINCEN.

Niger: E104/3 Independence Ave, POB 2685, Accra; tel. (21) 224962; Ambassador: OUMAROU YOUSSOUFOU.

Nigeria: Josif Broz Tito Ave, POB 1548, Accra; tel. (21) 776158; High Commissioner: T. A. OLU-OTUNLA.

Pakistan: 11 Ring Rd East, Danquah Circle, POB 1114, Accra; tel. (21) 776059; High Commissioner: Dr ABDUL KABIR.

Poland: 2 Akosombo St, Airport Residential Area, POB 2552, Accra; tel. (21) 775972; fax (21) 776108; Chargé d'affaires a.i.: KAZIMIERZ MAURER.

Russia: F856/1, Ring Rd East, POB 1634, Accra; tel. (21) 775611; fax (21) 772699; e-mail russia@ghana.com; Ambassador: PAVEL D. PAVLOV.

Saudi Arabia: 10 Noi Fetreke St, Roman Ridge, Airport Residential Area, POB 670, Accra; tel. (21) 774311; Chargé d'affaires a.i.: ANWAR ABDUL FATTAH ABDRABBUH.

South Africa: 10 Klottey Cres., Labone North, POB 298, Accra; tel. (21) 762380; fax (21) 762381; e-mail sahcgh@africaonline.com.gh; High Commissioner: JOSIAH MOTSEPE.

Spain: Drake Ave Extension, Airport Residential Area, POB 1218, Accra; tel. (21) 774004; fax (21) 776217; e-mail spainemb@ghana.com; Ambassador: FERNANDO CORRAL.

Switzerland: 9 Water Rd, North Ridge Area, POB 359, Accra; tel. (21) 228125; fax (21) 223583; Ambassador: PETER SCHWEIZER.

Togo: Togo House, near Cantonments Circle, POB C120, Accra; tel. (21) 777950; fax (21) 777961; Ambassador: ASSIONGBOR FOLIVI.

United Kingdom: Osu Link, off Gamel Abdul Nasser Ave, POB 296, Accra; tel. (21) 221665; fax (21) 7010655; e-mail high.commission@ accra.mail.fco.gov.uk; High Commissioner: IAN W. MACKLEY.

USA: Ring Road East, POB 194, Accra; tel. (21) 228440; fax (21) 776008; internet usembassy.state.gov/ghana; Ambassador: KATHRYN DEE ROBINSON.

Yugoslavia: 35 Senchi St, Airport Residential Area, POB 1629, Accra; tel. (21) 775761; e-mail yuambacc@ghana.africaonline .com.gh; Ambassador: LAZAR COVIĆ.

Judicial System

The civil law in force in Ghana is based on the Common Law, doctrines of equity and general statutes which were in force in England in 1874, as modified by subsequent Ordinances. Ghanaian customary law is, however, the basis of most personal, domestic and contractual relationships. Criminal Law is based on the Criminal Procedure Code, 1960, derived from English Criminal Law, and since amended. The Superior Court of Judicature comprises a Supreme Court, a Court of Appeal, a High Court and a Regional Tribunal; Inferior Courts include Circuit Courts, Circuit Tribunals, Community Tribunals and such other Courts as may be designated by law.

Supreme Court: Consists of the Chief Justice and not fewer than nine other Justices. It is the final court of appeal in Ghana and has jurisdiction in matters relating to the enforcement or interpretation of the Constitution.

Chief Justice: E. K. WIREDU (acting).

Court of Appeal: Consists of the Chief Justice and not fewer than five Judges of the Court of Appeal. It has jurisdiction to hear and determine appeals from any judgment, decree or order of the High Court.

High Court: Comprises the Chief Justice and not fewer than 12 Justices of the High Court. It exercises original jurisdiction in all matters, civil and criminal, other than those for offences involving treason. Trial by jury is practised in criminal cases in Ghana and the Criminal Procedure Code, 1960, provides that all trials on indictment shall be by a jury or with the aid of Assessors.

Circuit Courts: Exercise original jurisdiction in civil matters where the amount involved does not exceed C100,000. They also have jurisdiction with regard to the guardianship and custody of infants, and original jurisdiction in all criminal cases, except offences where the maximum punishment is death or the offence of treason. They have appellate jurisdiction from decisions of any District Court situated within their respective circuits.

District Courts: To each magisterial district is assigned at least one District Magistrate who has original jurisdiction to try civil suits in which the amount involved does not exceed C50,000. District Magistrates also have jurisdiction to deal with all criminal cases, except first-degree felonies, and commit cases of a more serious nature to either the Circuit Court or the High Court. A Grade I District Court can impose a fine not exceeding C1,000 and sentences of imprisonment of up to two years and a Grade II District Court may impose a fine not exceeding C500 and a sentence of imprisonment of up to 12 months. A District Court has no appellate jurisdiction, except in rent matters under the Rent Act.

Juvenile Courts: Jurisdiction in cases involving persons under 17 years of age, except where the juvenile is charged jointly with an adult. The Courts comprise a Chairman, who must be either the District Magistrate or a lawyer, and not fewer than two other members appointed by the Chief Justice in consultation with the Judicial Council. The Juvenile Courts can make orders as to the protection and supervision of a neglected child and can negotiate with parents to secure the good behaviour of a child.

National Public Tribunal: Considers appeals from the Regional Public Tribunals. Its decisions are final and are not subject to any further appeal. The Tribunal consists of at least three members and not more than five, one of whom acts as Chairman.

Regional Public Tribunals: Hears criminal cases relating to prices, rent or exchange control, theft, fraud, forgery, corruption or any offence which may be referred to them by the Provisional National Defence Council.

Special Military Tribunal: Hears criminal cases involving members of the armed forces. It consists of between five and seven members.

Religion

At the 1960 census the distribution of religious groups was: Christians 42.8%, traditional religions 38.2%, Muslims 12.0%, unclassified 7.0%.

CHRISTIANITY

Christian Council of Ghana: POB 919, Accra; tel. (21) 776678; fax (21) 776725; f. 1929; advisory body comprising member churches and two affiliated organizations (1996); Gen. Sec. Rev. ROBERT ABOAGYE-MENSAH.

The Anglican Communion

Anglicans in Ghana are adherents of the Church of the Province of West Africa, comprising 12 dioceses, of which seven are in Ghana.

Archbishop of the Province of West Africa and Bishop of Koforidua: Most Rev. ROBERT GARSHONG ALLOTEY OKINE, POB 980, Koforidua; tel. (81) 2329.

Bishop of Accra: Rt Rev. JUSTICE OFEI AKROFI, Bishopscourt, POB 8, Accra; tel. and fax (21) 669125.

Bishop of Cape Coast: Rt Rev. KOBINA ADDUAH QUASHIE, Bishopscourt, POB A233, Adisadel Estates, Cape Coast; tel. and fax (42) 2637.

Bishop of Kumasi: Rt Rev. DANIEL YINKAH SARFO, Bishop's Office, POB 144, Kumasi; tel. and fax (51) 24117; e-mail kumangli@ africaonline.com.gh.

Bishop of Sekondi: (vacant), POB 85, Sekondi; tel. (21) 6048; fax (21) 669125.

Bishop of Sunyani: Rt Rev. THOMAS AMPAH BRIENT, Bishop's House, POB 23, Sunyani; fax (61) 7023; e-mail deegyab@ighmail.com.

Bishop of Tamale: Rt Rev. EMMANUEL ARONGO, POB 110, Tamale NR; tel. (71) 2018; fax (71) 22849.

The Roman Catholic Church

Ghana comprises three archdioceses and 15 dioceses. At 31 December 1998 there were 2,172,490 adherents in the country, equivalent to 9.7% of the total population.

Ghana Bishops' Conference: National Catholic Secretariat, POB 9712, Airport, Accra; tel. (21) 500491; fax (21) 500493; e-mail dscncs@africaonline.com.gh; f. 1960; Pres. Most Rev. PETER K. APPIAH-TURKSON, Archbishop of Cape Coast.

Archbishop of Accra: Most Rev. DOMINIC KODWO ANDOH, Chancery Office, POB 247, Accra; tel. (21) 222728; fax (21) 231619.

Archbishop of Cape Coast: Most Rev. PETER KODWO APPIAH-TURKSON, Archbishop's House, POB 112, Cape Coast; tel. (42) 33471; fax (42) 33473.

Archbishop of Tamale: Most Rev. GREGORY EBO KPIEBAYA, Gumbehini Rd, POB 163, Tamale; tel. (71) 22425; fax (71) 22425.

Other Christian Churches

African Methodist Episcopal Zion Church: POB MP522, Mamprobi, Accra; tel. (21) 669200; e-mail amezion@africaonline.com.gh; f. 1898; Pres. Rt Rev. WARREN M. BROWN.

Christian Methodist Episcopal Church: POB 3906, Accra; Pres. Rev. YENN BATA.

Evangelical-Lutheran Church of Ghana: POB KN197, Kaneshie; tel. (21) 223487; fax (21) 220947; e-mail elcga@africaonline .com.gh; Pres. Rt Rev. Dr PAUL KOFI FYNN; 26,000 mems.

Evangelical-Presbyterian Church: POB 18, Ho, Volta Region; tel. (91) 755; fax (91) 8275; f. 1847; Moderator Rev. JAPHET YAO LEDO; 295,000 mems.

Ghana Baptist Convention: POB 1979, Kumasi; tel. (51) 5215; f. 1963; Pres. Rev. FRED DEEGBE; Sec. Rev. FRANK ADAMS; 63,200 mems.

Ghana Mennonite Church: POB 5485, Accra; fax (21) 220589; f. 1957; Moderator Rev. MICHAEL BADASU; Sec. ISAAC K. QUARTEY; 4,800 mems.

Methodist Church of Ghana: E252/2, Liberia Rd, POB 403, Accra; tel. (21) 228120; fax (21) 227008; e-mail mcghqs@africaonline .com.gh; Pres. Rt Rev. Dr SAMUEL ASANTE ANTWI;
Sec. Rev. MACLEAN AGYIRI KUMI; 341,000 mems.

Presbyterian Church of Ghana: POB 1800, Accra; tel. (21) 662511; fax (21) 665594; f. 1828; Moderator Rt Rev. ANTHONY ANTWI BEEKO; Sec. Rev. Dr D. N. A. KPOBI; 422,500 mems.

Seventh-day Adventists: POB 1016, Accra; tel. (21) 223720; fax (21) 227024; e-mail waumsda1@ghana.com; 1943; Pres. P. O. MENSAH; Sec. SETH A. LARMIE.

The African Methodist Episcopal Church, the F'Eden Church and the Religious Society of Friends (Quakers) are also active in Ghana.

ISLAM

There is a substantial Muslim population in the Northern Region. The majority are Malikees.

Ghana Muslim Representative Council: Accra.

Chief Imam: CHEICK USMAN NUBUSHARABUTU.

The Press

DAILY NEWSPAPERS

Daily Graphic: Graphic Rd, POB 742, Accra; tel. (21) 228911; fax (21) 669886; e-mail graphic@ghana.com; internet www.graphic.com.gh; f. 1950; state-owned; Editor ELVIS D. ARYEH; circ. 100,000.

The Ghanaian Times: New Times Corpn, Ring Rd West, POB 2638, Accra; tel. (21) 228282; fax (21) 229398; e-mail newtimes@ghana.com; f. 1958; state-owned; Editor CHRISTIAN AGGREY; circ. 45,000.

PERIODICALS

Weekly

Bombshell: Crossfire Publications, POB 376, Sakumono, Accra; tel. (21) 234750; fax (21) 233172; Editor BEN ASAMOAH.

Business and Financial Times: POB 2157, Accra; tel. and fax (21) 223334; e-mail bft@ighmail.com; internet www.financialtimesghana.com; f. 1989; Man. Editor JOHN HANSON; Editor WALLY ODOOM; circ. 20,000.

Champion: POB 6828, Accra-North; tel. (21) 229079; Man. Dir MARK D. N. ADDY; Editor FRANK CAXTON WILLIAMS; circ. 300,000.

Christian Chronicle: Accra; English; Editor GEORGE NAYKENE.

The Crusading Guide: POB 8523, Accra-North; tel. (21) 763339; fax (21) 761541; Editor KWEKU BAAKO Jr.

The Democrat: Democrat Publications, POB 13605, Accra; tel. (21) 76804; Editor L. K. NYAHO.

The Dispatch: 1 Dade Walk, North Labone, POB C1945, Cantonments, Accra; tel. (21) 763339; e-mail ephson@usa.net; Editor BEN EPHSON.

Echo: POB 5288, Accra; f. 1968; Sun.; Man. Editor M. K. FRIMPONG; circ. 40,000.

Entertaining Eye: Kad Publications, POB 125, Darkuman-Accra; Editor NANA KWAKYE YIADOM; circ. 40,000.

Evening Digest: News Media Ltd, POB 7082, Accra; tel. (21) 221071; Editor P. K. ANANTITETTEH.

Experience: POB 5084, Accra-North; Editor ALFRED YAW POKU; circ. 50,000.

Free Press: Tommy Thompson Books Ltd, POB 6492, Accra; tel. (21) 225994; independent; English; Editor EBEN QUARCOO.

Ghana Life: Ghana Life Publications, POB 11337, Accra; tel. (21) 229835; Editor NIKKI BOA-AMPONSEM.

Ghana Palaver: Palaver Publications, POB 15744, Accra-North; tel. (21) 232495; f. 1994; Editor BRUCE QUANSAH.

Ghanaian Chronicle: General Portfolio Ltd, Private Mail Bag, Accra-North; tel. (21) 227789; fax (21) 775895; e-mail chronicle@africaonline.com.gh; internet www.ghanaian-chronicle.com; Editor EBO QUANSAH; circ. 60,000.

Ghanaian Dawn: Dawn Publications, POB 721, Mamprobi, Accra; Editor MABEL LINDSAY.

The Ghanaian Voice: Newstop Publications, POB 514, Mamprobi, Accra; tel. 226943; e-mail voice@aspcc.africaonline.co.gh; Editor DAN K. ANSAH; circ. 100,000.

The Gossip: Gossip Publications, POB 5355, Accra-North; Editor C. A. ACHEAMPONG.

Graphic Showbiz: Graphic Rd, POB 742, Accra; tel. (21) 228911; fax (21) 669886; e-mail graphic@ghana.com; state-owned; Editor LEE ACCORLEY.

Graphic Sports: Graphic Rd, POB 742, Accra; tel. (21) 228911; e-mail graphic@ghana.com; state-owned; Editor JOE AGGREY; circ. 60,000.

The Guide: Western Publications Ltd, POB 8253, Accra-North; tel. (21) 232760; Editor KWEKU BAAKO Jnr.

High Street Journal: POB 7974, Accra-North; tel. (12) 239835; fax (12) 239837; e-mail hsjaccra@ghana.com; Editor SHEIKH ABUTIATE.

The Independent: Clear Type Press Bldg Complex, off Graphic Rd, POB 4031, Accra; tel. and fax (12) 661091; internet www.africaonline.com.gh/independent; f. 1989; Editor KABRAL BLAY AMIHERE.

The Mirror: Graphic Rd, POB 742, Accra; tel. (21) 228911; fax (21) 669886; f. 1953; state-owned; Sat.; Editor E. N. V. PROVENCAL; circ. 90,000.

The New Ghanaian: Tudu Publishing House, POB 751, Tamale; tel. (71) 22579; Editor RAZAK EL-ALAWA.

New Nation: POB 6828, Accra-North; Editor S. N. SASRAKU; circ. 300,000.

Private Eye: Kad Life Books Channels, POB 125, Accra; tel. (21) 230684; Editor AWUKU AGYEMANG-DUAH.

Public Agenda: P. A. Communications, POB 5564, Accra-North; tel. (21) 238821; fax (21) 231687; e-mail isodec@ghana.com; f. 1994; Editor YAO GRAHAM; circ. 12,000.

Sporting News: POB 5481, Accra-North; f. 1967; Man. Editor J. OPPONG-AGYARE.

The Standard: Standard Newspapers & Magazines Ltd, POB 765, Accra; tel. (21) 220165; Roman Catholic; Editor ISAAC FRITZ ANDOH; circ. 10,000.

Statesman: Kinesic Communications, POB 846, Accra; tel. and fax (21) 233242; official publ. of the New Patriotic Party; Editor HARUNNA ATTAH.

The Weekend: Newstop Publications, POB 514, Mamprobi, Accra; tel. and fax (21) 226943; Editor EMMANUEL YARTEY; circ. 40,000.

Weekly Events: Clear Type Image Ltd, 29 Olympic Street (Enterprise House), Kokomlemle, POB 7634, Accra-North; tel. (21) 223085; Editor JORIS JORDAN DODOO.

Weekly Insight: Militant Publications Ltd, POB K272, Accra New Town, Accra; tel. (21) 660148; fax (21) 774338; e-mail insight93@yahoo.com; f. 1993; independent; English; Editor KWESI PRATT Jnr.

Weekly Spectator: New Times Corpn, Ring Road West, POB 2638, Accra; tel. (21) 228282; fax (21) 229398; state-owned; f. 1963; Sun.; Editor WILLIE DONKOR; circ. 165,000.

Other

Africa Flamingo: Airport Emporium Ltd, POB 9194, Accra; monthly; Editor FELIX AMANFU; circ. 50,000.

African Observer: POB 1171, Kaneshie, Accra; tel. (012) 231459; bi-monthly; Editor STEVE MALLORY.

African Woman: Ring Rd West, POB 1496, Accra; monthly.

AGI Newsletter: c/o Asscn of Ghana Industries, POB 8624, Accra-North; tel. (21) 777283; e-mail agi@ighmail.com; f. 1974; quarterly; Editor (vacant); circ. 1,500.

Akwansosem: Ghana Information Services, POB 745, Accra; tel. (21) 228011; quarterly; in Akuapim Twi, Asanti Twi and Fante; Editor KATHLEEN OFOSU-APPIAH.

Armed Forces News: General Headquarters, Directorate of Public Relations, Burma Camp, Accra; tel. (21) 776111; f. 1966; quarterly; Editor ADOTEY ANKRAH-HOFFMAN; circ. 4,000.

Boxing and Football Illustrated: POB 8392, Accra; f. 1976; monthly; Editor NANA O. AMPOMAH; circ. 10,000.

Business and Financial Concord: Sammy Tech Consult Enterprise, POB 5677, Accra-North; tel. (21) 232446; fortnightly; Editor KWABENA RICHARDSON.

Business Watch: POB C3447, Cantonents, Accra; tel. (21) 233293; internet www.africaonline.com.gh/bwatch; monthly; Editor BEN DWUMMAH-ADU (acting).

Chit Chat: POB 7043, Accra; monthly; Editor ROSEMOND ADU.

Christian Messenger: Presbyterian Book Depot Bldg, POB 3075, Accra; tel. and fax (21) 662415; f. 1883; English; every two weeks; also **The Presbyterian** (in Twi and Ga); quarterly; Editor G. B. K. OWUSU; circ. 40,000.

Drum: POB 1197, Accra; monthly; general interest.

Ghana Journal of Science: Ghana Science Asscn, POB 7, Legon; tel. (21) 500253; monthly; Editor Dr A. K. AHAFIA.

Ghana Official News Bulletin: Information Services Dept, POB 745, Accra; English; political, economic, investment and cultural affairs.

Ideal Woman (Obaa Sima): POB 5737, Accra; tel. (21) 221399; f. 1971; fortnightly; Editor KATE ABBAM.

Insight and Opinion: POB 5446, Accra; quarterly; Editorial Sec. W. B. OHENE.

Legon Observer: POB 11, Legon; fax (21) 774338; f. 1966; publ. by Legon Society on National Affairs; fortnightly; Chair. J. A. DADSON; Editor EBOW DANIEL.

Police News: Police HQ, Accra; monthly; Editor S. S. APPIAH; circ. 20,000.

The Post: Ghana Information Services, POB 745, Accra; tel. (21) 228011; f. 1980; monthly; current affairs and analysis; circ. 25,000.

Radio and TV Times: Ghana Broadcasting Corpn, Broadcasting House, POB 1633, Accra; tel. (21) 221161; f. 1960; quarterly; Editor SAM THOMPSON; circ. 5,000.

The Scope: POB 8162, Tema; monthly; Editor EMMANUEL DOE ZIORKLUI; circ. 10,000.

Students World: POB M18, Accra; tel. (21) 774248; fax (21) 778715; e-mail aframpub@ighmail.com; f. 1974; monthly; educational; Man. Editor ERIC OFEI; circ. 10,000.

The Teacher: Ghana National Asscn of Teachers, POB 209, Accra; tel. (21) 221515; fax (21) 226286; f. 1931; quarterly; circ. 30,000.

Truth and Life: Gift Publications, POB 11337, Accra-North; monthly; Editor Pastor KOBENA CHARM.

Uneek: POB 230, Achimota, Accra; tel. (21) 543853; fax (21) 231355; e-mail uneekgh@yahoo.com; internet www.africaonline.com.gh/uneek; monthly; leisure, culture; CEO and Editor FRANCIS ADAMS.

The Watchman: Watchman Gospel Ministry, POB GP 4521, Accra; tel. (21) 502011; fax (21)507428; e-mail sonlife@africaonline.com.gh; fortnightly; Pres. and CEO DIVINE P. KUMAH; Chair. Dr E. K. OPUNI.

NEWS AGENCIES

Ghana News Agency: POB 2118, Accra; tel. (21) 665136; fax 669841; e-mail ghnews@ncs.com.gh; f. 1957; Gen. Man. SAM B. QUAICOE; 10 regional offices and 110 district offices.

Foreign Bureaux

Associated Press (AP) (USA): Accra; Bureau Chief P. K. COBINAH-ESSEM.

Xinhua (New China) News Agency (People's Republic of China): 2 Seventh St, Airport Residential Area, POB 3897, Accra; tel. (21) 772042.

Deutsche Presse-Agentur (Germany) and Reuters (UK) are also represented.

PRESS ASSOCIATION

Ghana Journalists Association: POB 4636, Accra; tel. (21) 234692; fax (21) 234694; e-mail info@ghanamedia.com; internet www.ghanamedia.com/gja; Pres. GIFTY AFFENYI-DADZIE.

Publishers

Advent Press: POB 0102, Osu, Accra; tel. (21) 777861; f. 1937; Gen. Man. EMMANUEL C. TETTEH.

Adwinsa Publications (Ghana) Ltd: Advance Press Bldg, 3rd Floor, School Rd, POB 92, Legoh Accra; tel. (21) 221654; f. 1977; general, educational; Man. Dir KWABENA AMPONSAH.

Afram Publications: 9 Ring Rd East, POB M18, Accra; tel. (21) 774248; fax (21) 778715; e-mail aframpub@ighmail.com; f. 1974; textbooks and general; Man. Dir ERIC OFEI.

Africa Christian Press: POB 30, Achimota; tel. (21) 244147; fax (21) 220271; e-mail acpbooks@ghana.com; f. 1964; religious, fiction, theology, children's, leadership; Gen. Man. RICHARD A. B. CRABBE.

Allgoodbooks Ltd: POB AN10416, Accra-North; tel. (21) 665629; fax (21) 302993; e-mail allgoodbooks@hotmail.com; f. 1968; children's; Man. MARY ASIRIFI.

Asempa Publishers: POB 919, Accra; tel. (21) 233084; fax (21) 235140; e-mail asempa@ncs.com.gh; f. 1970; religion, social issues, African music, fiction, children's; Gen. Man. Rev. EMMANUEL B. BORTEY.

Baafour and Co: POB K189, Accra New Town; f. 1978; general; Man. B. KESE-AMANKWAA.

Benibengor Book Agency: POB 40, Aboso; fiction, biography, children's and paperbacks; Man. Dir J. BENIBENGOR BLAY.

Black Mask Ltd: 17 Watson Ave, Adabraka, Accra; tel. (21) 234577; f. 1979; textbooks, plays, novels, handicrafts; Man. Dir YAW OWUSU ASANTE.

Editorial and Publishing Services: POB 5743, Accra; general, reference; Man. Dir M. DANQUAH.

Educational Press and Manufacturers Ltd: POB 9184, Airport-Accra; tel. (21) 220395; f. 1975; textbooks, children's; Man. G. K. KODUA.

Encyclopaedia Africana Project: POB 2797, Accra; tel. (21) 776939; fax (21) 779228; e-mail eap@africaonline.com.gh; internet www.endarkenment.com/eap; f. 1962; reference; Dir GRACE BANSA.

Frank Publishing Ltd: POB MB414, Accra; tel. (21) 240711; f. 1976; secondary school textbooks; Man. Dir FRANCIS K. DZOKOTO.

Ghana Publishing Corpn: Assembly Press Ltd, POB 124, Accra; tel. (21) 664338; fax (21) 664330; e-mail asspcom@africaonline.com.gh; internet www.africaonline.com.gh/Assembly; f. 1965; state-owned; textbooks and general fiction and non-fiction; Man. Dir F. K. NYARKO.

Ghana Universities Press: POB GP4219, Accra; tel. (21) 500300; fax (21) 501930; f. 1962; scholarly and academic; Dir K. M. GANU.

Golden Wings Publications: 26 Mantse Kwao St, POB 1337, Accra; educational and children's; Man. Editor GREGORY ANKRAH.

Miracle Bookhouse: POB 7487, Accra-North; tel. (21) 226684; f. 1977; general; Man. J. APPIAH-BERKO.

Moxon Paperbacks: POB M160, Accra; tel. (21) 761175; fax (21) 777971; f. 1967; travel and guide books, fiction and poetry, Africana, telephone directory; Man. Dir JAMES MOXON.

Sam-Woode Ltd: A.979/15 Dansoman High Street, POB 12719, Accra-North; tel. (21) 305287; fax (021) 310482; e-mail samwoode@ghana.com; educational and children's; Chair. KWESI SAM-WOODE.

Sedco Publishing Ltd: Sedco House, 5 Tabon St, North Ridge, POB 2051, Accra; tel. (21) 221332; fax (21) 220107; e-mail sedco@africaonline.com.gh; f. 1975; educational; Man. Dir COURAGE K. SEGBAWU.

Sheffield Publishing Co: Accra; tel. (21) 667480; fax (21) 665960; f. 1970; religion, politics, economics, science, fiction; Publr RONALD MENSAH.

Unimax Publishers Ltd: 42 Ring Rd South Industrial Area, POB 10722, Accra-North; tel. (21) 227443; fax (21) 225215; e-mail unimax@africanonline.com.gh; representative of Macmillan (UK); atlases, educational and children's; Man. Dir EDWARD ADDO.

Waterville Publishing House: POB 195, Accra; tel. (21) 663124; f. 1963; general fiction and non-fiction, textbooks, paperbacks, Africana; Man. Dir H. W. O. OKAI.

Woeli Publishing Services: POB NT601, Accra New Town; tel. and fax (21) 229294; f. 1984; children's, fiction, academic; Dir W. A. DEKUTSEY.

PUBLISHERS' ASSOCIATIONS

Ghana Book Development Council: POB M430, Accra; tel. (21) 229178; f. 1975; govt-financed agency; promotes and co-ordinates writing, production and distribution of books; Exec. Dir D. A. NIMAKO.

Ghana Book Publishers' Association: POB LT471, Laterbiokorshie, Accra; tel. (21) 229178; fax (21) 220271; e-mail acpbooks@ghana.com; Sec. E. B. BORTEY.

Private Newspaper Publishers' Association of Ghana (PRINPAG): POB 125, Darkuman, Accra; Chair. NANA KOFI KOOMSON; Gen. Sec. K. AGYEMANG DUAH.

Broadcasting and Communications

TELECOMMUNICATIONS

Ghana Telecom: Telecom House, nr Kwame Nkrumah Circle, Accra-North; tel. (21) 221001; fax (21) 221002; e-mail administrator@ghanatel.net; internet www.ghanatel.net; f. 1995; 30% transferred to private ownership in 1997; Dir-Gen. JOSEPH AGGREY-MENSAH; Man. Dir ADNAN ROFIEE.

ACG Telesystems (Westel) Ghana Ltd: Dr Isert Rd, 7th Ave Ext., Ridge PMB, Accra-North; tel. (21) 232308; fax (21) 232309; e-mail btaylor@acg.com.gh; f. 1997; owned jointly by Ghana National Petroleum Corpn and Western Wireless Corpn (USA); Man. Dir WILLIAM TAYLOR.

BROADCASTING

There are internal radio broadcasts in English, Akan, Dagbani, Ewe, Ga, Hausa and Nzema, and an external service in English and French. There are three transmitting stations, with a number of relay stations. There is a total of eight main colour television transmitters. The Ghana Broadcasting Corporation operates two national networks, Radio 1 and Radio 2, which broadcast from Accra. There is also an FM station in Accra (known as Radio GAR), a regional FM station at Bolgatanga and a community FM station at Apam, as well as an external service which broadcasts in English and French.

Ghana Broadcasting Corporation: Broadcasting House, POB 1633, Accra; tel. (21) 221161; fax (21) 221153; e-mail gbc@ghana.com; internet www.gbc.com.gh; f. 1935; Dir-Gen. Dr KOFI FRIMPONG; Dir of TV Prof. MARK DUODU; Dir of Radio CRIS TACKIE.

Finance

(cap. = capital; res = reserves; dep. = deposits; m. = million; brs = branches; amounts in cedis)

BANKING

The commercial banking sector comprised nine commercial banks, four development banks and four merchant banks in 1998. There were also 130 rural banks and several non-banking financial institutions.

Central Bank

Bank of Ghana: POB 2674, Accra; tel. (21) 666902; fax (21) 662996; e-mail secretary@bog.gov.gh; internet www.bog.gov.gh; f. 1957; bank of issue; cap. 100,000m., res 100,504m., dep. 656,228m. (Dec. 1998); Chair. and Gov. KWABENA DUFFUOR.

Commercial and Development Banks

Agricultural Development Bank: Cedi House, Liberia Rd, POB 4191, Accra; tel. (21) 662758; fax (21) 662846; e-mail adb@ africaonline.com.gh; internet www.ghanaclassifieds.com/adb; f. 1965; 79% state-owned; credit facilities for farmers and commercial banking; cap. and res 77,658.4m., dep. 119,463.0m. (Dec. 1997); Chair. Nathan Quao; Man. Dir S. A. Welbeck; 34 brs.

Ghana Commercial Bank Ltd: POB 134, Accra; tel. (21) 664914; fax (21) 662168; e-mail gcbmail@ncs.com.gh; f. 1953; 59.1% state-owned; cap. 20,000m., res 96,399m., dep. 662,012m. (Dec. 1998); Man. Dir A. A. Tannor; 134 brs.

Leasafric Ghana Ltd: 7 Main St, Tesano, POB C2430, Accra; tel. (21) 240140; fax (21) 228375; e-mail leasafric@africaonline.com.gh; cap. 893m. (Dec. 1996); Chair. John Kobina Rishcardson; Man. Dir Seth K. Dei.

National Investment Bank Ltd (NIB): 37 Kwame Nkrumah Ave, POB 3726, Accra; tel. (21) 669301; fax (21) 240030; f. 1963; 86.5% state-owned; provides long-term investment capital, jt venture promotion, consortium finance man. and commercial banking services; cap. 3,259.7m., dep. 58,867.5m. (Dec. 1997); Chair. Togbe Kwao Anipati; Man. Dir Steve Dadzie; 11 brs.

NTHC Ltd: Martco House, Okai Mensah Link, off Kwame Nkrumah Ave, POB KIA 9563, Airport, Accra; tel. (21) 238492; fax (21) 229975; e-mail nthc@ghana.com; internet www.nthcghana.com; fmrly National Trust Holding Co. Ltd; f. 1976 to provide stockbrokerage services, asset management and financial advisory services; cap. 500m. (2000); Chair. Benjamin Adu-Amankwa; Man. Dir Paul Effah Oteng (acting).

Prudential Bank Ltd: 34 Kwame Nkrumah Ave, PMB GPO, Accra; tel. (21) 226322; fax (21) 226803; e-mail prudential@ghana.com; internet www.prudentialbank-ghana.com; f. 1996; Chair. John Sackah Addo; Man. Dir Stephen Sekyere-Abankwa.

SSB Bank Ltd: POB 13119, Accra; tel. (21) 221726; fax (21) 220713; e-mail ssb@ncs.com.gh; internet www.ssb.com.gh; f. 1976 as Social Security Bank; cap. 6,735m., dep. 488,318m. (Dec. 1999); Chair. Francis E. Y. Attipoe; Man. Dir Pryce Koyo Thompson.

Trust Bank Ghana Ltd: Re-Insurance House, 68 Kwame Nkrumah Ave, POB 1862, Accra; tel. (21) 240049; fax (21) 240056; e-mail trust@ghana.com; f. 1996; cap. 10,000m., res 5,347.2m., dep. 60,078.9m. (Dec. 1998); Chair. Alex Awuku; Man. Dir Jean-Marie Marquebreucq; 6 brs.

Merchant Banks

CAL Merchant Bank Ltd: 45 Independence Ave, POB 14596, Accra; tel. (21) 221056; fax (21) 231913; e-mail calbank@calbank-gh.com; internet www.africaonline.com.gh/Cal; f. 1990 as Continental Acceptances Ltd; cap. 1,121.0m., res 16,695.2m., dep. 45,795.2m. (Dec. 1998); Chair. Louis Casely-Hayford; Man. Dir Jude Kofi Bucknor.

Ecobank Ghana Ltd (EBG): 19 Seventh Ave, Ridge West, Private Mail Bag, GPO, Accra; tel. (21) 229532; fax (21) 667127; e-mail ecobank@ghana.com; internet www.ghanaclassifieds.com/ecobank; f. 1989; 93.7% owned by Ecobank Transnational Inc (Togo, operating under the auspices of the Economic Community of West African States); cap. 18,200m., res 24,098.2m., dep. 277,105.8m. (Dec. 1998); Chair. Edward Patrick Larbi Gyampoh; Man. Dir Jean N. Aka.

First Atlantic Merchant Bank Ltd: Atlantic Place, 1 Seventh Ave, Ridge West, POB C1620, Cantonments, Accra; tel. (21) 231433; fax (21) 231399; e-mail fambl@ghana.com; f. 1994; cap. 2,000m., res 2,563.9m., dep. 35,307.6m. (Dec. 1998); Chair. Sam Jonah; Man. Dir Jude Arthur.

Merchant Bank (Ghana) Ltd: Merban House, 44 Kwame Nkrumah Ave, POB 401, Accra; tel. (21) 666331; fax (21) 667305; e-mail merban_services@ighmail.com; internet www.merbankgh.com; f. 1972; cap. 5,000m., res 12,497m., dep. 166,828m. (Dec. 1998); Chair. Dr John Richardson; Man. Dir Chris N. N. Nartey; 5 brs.

Foreign Banks

Barclays Bank of Ghana Ltd (UK): Barclays House, High St, POB 2949, Accra; tel. (21) 664901; fax (21) 667420; e-mail barclays.ghana@barclays.com; internet www.africa.barclays.com/ghana.htm; f. 1971; 10% state-owned; cap. 1,000m., res 57,628m., dep. 485,302m. (Dec. 1998); Chair. Nana Wereko Ampem; Man. Dir K. Quansah; 26 brs.

Stanbic Bank Ghana: POB CT2344, Cantonments, Accra; tel. (21) 250066; fax (21) 2344685; e-mail stanbic@ghana.com; internet www.stanbic.ghana.com.gh; f. 1999; subsidiary of the Standard Bank of South Africa Ltd; Man. Dir J. P. Standing; 1 br.

Standard Chartered Bank Ghana Ltd (UK): 3rd Floor, Accra, High St Building, POB 768, Accra; tel. (21) 664591; fax (21) 667751; e-mail dzaney@scb.ghana.nhs.compuserve.com; f. 1896 as Bank of British West Africa; cap. 2,649m., res 124,315m., dep. 1,028,931m. (Dec. 1999); Chair. David Andoh; CEO Vishnu Mohan; 28 brs.

STOCK EXCHANGE

Ghana Stock Exchange (GSE): Cedi House, 5th Floor, Liberia Rd, POB 1849, Accra; tel. (21) 669908; fax (21) 669913; e-mail stockex@ghana.com; internet www.gse.com.gh; 52 mems; Man. Dir Yeboa Amoah.

INSURANCE

Ghana Union Assurance Co Ltd: POB 1322, Accra; tel. (21) 664421; fax (21) 664988; e-mail gua@ghana.com; f. 1973; insurance underwriting; Man. Dir Kwadwo Duku.

The Great African Insurance Co Ltd: POB 12349, Accra North; tel. (21) 227459; fax (21) 228905; f. 1980; Man. Dir Kwasi Akoto.

The State Insurance Company of Ghana Ltd: POB 2363, Accra; tel. (21) 666961; fax (21) 662205; f. 1962 as State Insurance Corporation of Ghana, renamed as above 1995; state-owned, privatization pending in 2001; all classes of insurance; Man. Dir Victor Kusi Yeboah.

Social Security and National Insurance Trust: Pension House, POB M149, Accra; tel. (21) 667742; fax (21) 662226; f. 1972; covers over 650,000 contributors; Dir-Gen. Eric Adjei.

Vanguard Assurance Co Ltd: Insurance Hall, Derby House, Derby Ave, POB 1868, Accra; tel. (21) 666485; fax (21) 668610; f. 1974; general accident, marine, motor and life insurance; Man. Dir Nana Awuah-Darko Ampem; 7 brs.

Several foreign insurance companies operate in Ghana.

Trade and Industry

GOVERNMENT AGENCIES

Divestiture Implementation Committee: F35/5 Ring Road East, North Labone, POB CT102, Cantonments, Accra; tel. (21) 772049; fax (21) 228428; e-mail dicgh@ncs.com.gh; internet www.ghana.com.gh/dic; f. 1988; Exec. Sec. Emmanuel Agbodo.

Food Production Corporation: POB 1853, Accra; f. 1971; state corpn providing employment for youth in large-scale farming enterprises; controls 76,900 ha of land (16,200 ha under cultivation); operates 87 food farms on a co-operative and self-supporting basis, and rears poultry and livestock.

Ghana Export Promotion Council (GEPC): POB M146, Accra; tel. (21) 228813; fax (21) 668263; e-mail gepc@ghana.com; internet www.exportghana.org; f. 1974; Exec. Sec. Tawia Akyea.

Ghana Food Distribution Corporation: POB 4245, Accra; tel. (21) 228428; f. 1971; buys, stores, preserves, distributes and retails foodstuffs through 10 regional centres; Man. Dir E. H. K. Amankwa.

Ghana Free Zones Board: POB M626, Accra; tel. (21) 670532; fax (21) 670536; e-mail freezone@africaonline.com.gh; internet www.ghanaclassifieds.com/gfzb; f. 1996; approves establishment of cos in export processing zones; Exec. Sec. George Aboagye.

Ghana Industrial Holding Corporation (GIHOC): POB 2784, Accra; tel. (21) 664998; f. 1967; controls and manages state enterprises, including steel, paper, bricks, paint, electronics, metals, canneries, distilleries and boat-building factories; also has three subsidiary cos and four jt ventures; dissolution approved by law in 1993; Chair. J. E. K. Moses; Man. Dir J. K. Williams.

Ghana Investment Promotion Centre (GIPC): POB M193, Accra; tel. (21) 665125; fax (21) 663801; e-mail gipc@ghana.com; internet www.gipc.org.gh; f. 1981; negotiates new investments, approves projects, registers foreign capital and decides extent of govt participation; Chair. P. V. Obeng.

Ghana National Trading Corporation (GNTC): POB 67, Accra; tel. (21) 664871; f. 1961; organizes exports and imports of selected commodities; over 500 retail outlets in 12 admin. dists.

Ghana Standards Board: c/o POB MB245, Accra; tel. (21) 500065; fax (21) 500092; e-mail gsblib@ghana.com; f. 1967; establishes and promulgates standards; promotes standardization, industrial efficiency and development and industrial welfare, health and safety; operates certification mark scheme; 403 mems; Dir. Kwasi Nkansa.

Ghana Trade and Investment Gateway Project (GHATIG): POB M47, Accra; tel. 663439; fax 665423; e-mail gateway1@ghana.com; promotes private investment and trade, infrastructural development of free trade zones and export processing zones.

National Board for Small-scale Industries: Ministry of Trade and Industry, POB M85, Accra; f. 1985; promotes small and medium-scale industrial and commercial enterprises by providing credit, advisory services and training.

State Farms Corporation: Accra; undertakes agricultural projects in all regions but Upper Region; Man. Dir E. N. A. Thompson (acting).

State Housing Company: POB 2753, Accra; f. 1982 by merger; oversees govt housing programme; privatization pending in 2001.

CHAMBER OF COMMERCE

Ghana National Chamber of Commerce: POB 2325, Accra; tel. (21) 662427; fax (21) 662210; e-mail gncc@ncs.com.gh; f. 1961; promotes and protects industry and commerce, organizes trade fairs; 2,500 individual mems and 8 mem. chambers; Pres. Ato Ampiah; CEO Sal D. Amegavie.

INDUSTRIAL AND TRADE ASSOCIATIONS

Best Fibres Development Board: POB 1992, Kumasi; f. 1970; promotes the commercial cultivation of best fibres and their processing, handling and grading.

Federation of Associations of Ghanaian Exporters (FAGE): POB M124, Accra; tel. (21) 232554; fax (21) 232726; e-mail fage@ighmail.com; internet www.ghana-exporter.org; non-governmental, not-for-profit organization for exporters of non-traditional exports; over 2,500 mems.

Ghana Cocoa Board (COCOBOD): POB 933, Accra; tel. (21) 221212; fax (21) 667104; e-mail cocobod@africaonline.comigh; f. 1985; monopoly purchaser of cocoa until 1993; responsible for purchase, grading and export of cocoa, coffee and shea nuts; also encourages production and scientific research aimed at improving quality and yield of these crops; controls all exports of cocoa; CEO John Newman.

Ghana Timber Export Development Board: POB 515, Takoradi; tel. (31) 22921; fax (31) 23339; e-mail timbod@ghana.com; internet www.ghana-timber.demon.co.uk; f. 1985; promotes the development of the timber industry and the sale and export of timber; CEO Douglas Asamany.

Grains and Legumes Development Board: POB 4000, Kumasi; tel. (51) 4231; f. 1970; state-controlled; promotes and develops production of cereals and leguminous vegetables.

Minerals Commission: 9 Switch Rd, Residential Area, Cantonments, POB M248, Accra; tel. (21) 772783; fax (21) 773324; e-mail mincom@ncs.com.gh; f. 1984; supervises, promotes and co-ordinates the minerals industry; CEO Kofi Ansah.

EMPLOYERS' ORGANIZATION

Ghana Employers' Association: 122 Kojo Thompson Rd, POB 2616, Accra; tel. (21) 678455; fax (21) 678405; e-mail geadmin@ghanaemployers.org; internet www.ghanaemployers.org; f. 1959; 400 mems; Pres. Ato Ampiah; Vice-Pres. Charles Mensah.

Affiliated Bodies

Association of Ghana Industries: Trade Fair Centre, POB 8624, Accra-North; tel. and fax (21) 779793; e-mail agi@ghana.com; internet www.agi.org.gh; f. 1957; Pres. Prince Kofi Kludjeson; Exec. Dir Andrew E. Quayson; 320 mems.

Ghana Booksellers' Association: POB 10367, Accra-North; tel. (21) 773002; fax (21) 773242; Pres. Sampson Brako; Gen. Sec. Fred J. Reimmer.

Ghana Chamber of Mines: POB 991, Accra; tel. (21) 760652; fax (21) 760653; e-mail info@ghanachamines.com; internet www.ghanachamines.com; f. 1928; Pres. James Ananam; Exec. Dir Keith Baptist.

Ghana Electrical Contractors' Association: POB 1858, Accra.

Ghana National Association of Teachers: POB 209, Accra; tel. (21) 221515; fax (21) 226286; f. 1931; Pres. G. N. Naaso; Gen. Sec. Paul Osei-Mensah.

Ghana National Contractors' Association: c/o J. T. Osei and Co, POB M11, Accra.

Ghana Timber Association (GTA): POB 1020, Kumasi; tel. and fax (51) 25153; f. 1952; promotes, protects and develops timber industry; Chair. Tetteh Nanor.

UTILITIES

Electricity

Electricity Company of Ghana (ECG): Electro-Volta House, POB 521, Accra; tel. (21) 664941; fax (21) 666262; e-mail ecgho@gh.com; privatization pending in 2001; Man. Dir Musa B. Adam.

Ghana Atomic Energy Commission: POB 80, Legon, Accra; tel. (21) 400310; fax (21) 400807; e-mail secgaec@ncs.com.gh; f. 1963; promotes, develops and utilizes nuclear techniques; construction of a research reactor at Kwabenya, near Accra, which was begun in 1964, was completed in 1995; Chair. F. K. A. Allotey.

Volta River Authority: Electro-Volta House, POB MB77, Accra; tel. (21) 664941; fax (21) 662610; e-mail orgsrv@accra.vra.com; f. 1965; controls the generation and distribution of electricity; Chair. and CEO E. A. K. Kalitsi.

Water

Ghana Water Co Ltd: POB M194, Accra; tel. (21) 666781; f. 2001 to provide, distribute and conserve water supplies for public, domestic and industrial use, and to establish, operate and control sewerage systems; Man. Dir Charles Adjei.

CO-OPERATIVES

In 1998 there were 11,154 registered co-operative societies, grouped into four sectors: industrial, financial, agricultural and marine.

Department of Co-operatives: POB M150, Accra; tel. (21) 666212; fax (21) 772789; f. 1944; govt-supervised body, responsible for registration, auditing and supervision of co-operative socs; Registrar R. Buachie-Aphram.

Ghana Co-operatives Council Ltd: POB 4034, Accra; tel. (21) 232195; f. 1951; co-ordinates activities of all co-operative socs; comprises five active nat. asscns and two central organizations; Sec.-Gen. Thomas Andoh.

The five national associations and two central organizations include the Ghana Co-operative Marketing Asscn Ltd, the Ghana Co-operative Credit Unions Asscn Ltd, the Ghana Co-operative Distillers and Retailers Asscn Ltd, and the Ghana Co-operative Poultry Farmers Asscn Ltd.

TRADE UNIONS

Ghana Trades Union Congress (GTUC): Hall of Trade Unions, POB 701, Accra; tel. (21) 662568; fax (21) 667161; f. 1945; 17 affiliated unions; Chair. Interim Man. Cttee E. K. Aboagye; Sec.-Gen. Christian Appiah-Agyei.

Transport

RAILWAYS

Ghana has a railway network of 1,300 km, which connects Accra, Kumasi and Takoradi.

Ghana Railway Corporation: POB 251, Takoradi; tel. (31) 22181; fax (31) 23797; f. 1977; responsible for the operation and maintenance of all railways; privatization pending in 2001; Man. Dir M. K. Arthur.

ROADS

In 1996 Ghana had an estimated total road network of 37,800 km, including 30 km of motorways, 5,230 km of main roads, and 9,620 km of secondary roads; some 24.1% of the road network was paved. A five-year Road Sector Expenditure Programme, costing US $259m., commenced in 1995.

Ghana Highway Authority: POB 1641, Accra; tel. (21) 666591; fax (21) 665571; f. 1974 to plan, develop, administer and maintain trunk roads and related facilities; CEO B. L. T. Sakibu.

State Transport Company: Ring Rd West, POB 7384, Accra; tel. (21) 221912; f. 1965; fmrly State Transport Corporation; long-distance coach services; Man. Dir Lt-Col Akyea-Mensah.

SHIPPING

The two main ports are Tema (near Accra) and Takoradi, both of which are linked with Kumasi by rail. A project to upgrade facilities at both ports, at a cost of US $365m., was to commence in 1998. In 1996 some 6.7m. metric tons of goods were handled at the two ports.

Ghana Ports and Harbour Authority: POB 150, Tema; tel. (22) 202631; fax (22) 202812; e-mail ghpa@ghana.com; holding co for the ports of Tema and Takoradi; privatization pending in 2001; Dir Gen. K. T. Dovlo.

Alpha (West Africa) Line Ltd: POB 451, Tema; operates regular cargo services to west Africa, the UK, the USA, the Far East and northern Europe; shipping agents; Man. Dir Ahmed Edgar Collingwood Williams.

Black Star Line Ltd: 4th Lane, Kuku Hill Osu, POB 248, Accra; tel. (21) 2888; fax (21) 2889; f. 1957; state-owned; transfer to private sector pending in 1998; operates passenger and cargo services to Europe, the UK, Canada, the USA, the Mediterranean and West Africa; shipping agents; Chair. Magnus Addico; Man. Dir Capt. V. N. Attuquayefio.

Bunktrad Shipping and Trading Ltd: 4th Floor, Trust Towers, POB 14801, Accra; tel. (21) 238401; fax (21) 236121; e-mail bunktrad@africaonline.com.gh; charters tankers; Dir Sam Sackley.

Holland West-Afrika Lijn NV: POB 269, Accra; cargo services to and from North America and the Far East; shipping agents.

Liner Agencies and Trading (Ghana) Ltd: POB 214, Tema; tel. (22) 202987; fax (22) 202989; e-mail enquiries@liner-agencies.com; internet www.liner-agencies.com; international freight services; shipping agents; Dir J. Ossei-Yaw.

Remco Shipping Lines Ltd: POB 3898, Accra; tel. (21) 224609.

Scanship (Ghana) Ltd: CFAO Bldg, High St, POB 1705, Accra; tel. (21) 664314; shipping agents.

Association

Ghana Shippers' Council: Enterprise House, 5th Floor, High St, POB 1321, Accra; tel. (21) 666915; fax (21) 668768; e-mail scouncil@shippers-gh.com; internet www.ghanashipperscouncil.org; f. 1974; represents interests of 15,000 registered Ghanaian shippers; also provides cargo-handling and allied services; CEO KOFI MBIAH.

CIVIL AVIATION

The main international airport is at Kotoka (Accra). There are also airports at Kumasi, Sunyani and Tamale. The construction of a dedicated freight terminal at Kotoka Airport was completed in 1994. In 2000 592,276 passengers and 46,085 metric tons of freight passed through Kotoka Airport.

Ghana Civil Aviation Authority: PMB, Kotoka International Airport, Accra; tel. (21) 776171; fax (21) 773293; e-mail centre-gcaa@ighmail.com; internet www.gcaa.com.gh; f. 1986.

Gemini Airlines Ltd: America House, POB 7328, Accra-North; tel. (21) 665785; f. 1974; operates weekly cargo flight between Accra and London; Dir V. OWUSU; Gen. Man. P. F. OKINE.

Ghana Airways Ltd.: Ghana Airways House, Ghana Airways Avenue, POB 1636, Accra; tel. (21) 773321; fax (21) 773316; e-mail ghanaairways@ighmail.com; internet www.ghana-airways.com; f. 1958; state-owned; transfer to private sector pending in 1999; operates regional services and international routes to West African, Asian and European destinations, and to the USA and South Africa; Chair. of Bd VICTORIA ADDY; CEO (vacant).

Tourism

Ghana's attractions include fine beaches, game reserves, traditional festivals, and old trading forts and castles. In 1996 a 15-year Integrated National Tourism Development Plan was initiated, under which annual tourist arrivals were targeted to exceed 1m. by 2020. In 1997 325,434 tourists visited Ghana, with revenue from tourism totalling US $266m.

Ghana Tourist Board: POB 3106, Accra-North; tel. (21) 238330; fax (21) 231779; e-mail gtb@africaonline.com.gh; internet www.africaonline.com.gh/Tourism; f. 1968; Exec. Dir DOREEN OWUSU-FIANKO (acting).

Ghana Association of Tourist and Travel Agencies: Ramia House, Kojo Thompson Rd, POB 7140, Accra; tel. (21) 228933; Pres. JOSEPH K. ANKUMAH; Sec. JOHNNIE MOREAUX.

Ghana Tourist Development Co Ltd: POB 8710, Accra; tel. (21) 776109; fax (21) 772093; f. 1974; develops tourist infrastructure, incl. hotels, restaurants and casinos; operates duty-free shops; Man. Dir ALFRED KOMLADZEI.

GREECE

Introductory Survey

Location, Climate, Language, Religion, Flag, Capital

The Hellenic Republic lies in south-eastern Europe. The country consists mainly of a mountainous peninsula between the Mediterranean Sea and the Aegean Sea, bounded to the north by Albania, the former Yugoslav republic of Macedonia and Bulgaria, and to the east by Turkey. To the south, east and west of the mainland lie numerous Greek islands, of which the largest is Crete. The climate is Mediterranean, with mild winters and hot summers. The average temperature in the capital is 28°C (82°F) in July and 9°C (48°F) in January. The language is Greek, of which there are two forms—the formal language (katharevoussa) and the language commonly spoken and taught in schools (demotiki). Almost all of the inhabitants profess Christianity, and the Greek Orthodox Church, to which about 97% of the population adhere, is the established religion. The national flag (proportions 3 by 2) displays nine equal horizontal stripes of blue and white, with a white cross throughout a square canton of blue at the upper hoist. The capital is Athens.

Recent History

The liberation of Greece from the German occupation (1941–44) was followed by a civil war, which lasted until 1949. The Communist forces were defeated, and the constitutional monarchy re-established. King Konstantinos (Constantine) acceded to the throne on the death of his father, King Paul, in 1964. A succession of weak governments and conflicts between the King and his ministers, and an alleged conspiracy involving military personnel who supported the Centre Union Party, culminated in a coup, led by right-wing army officers, in April 1967. An attempted counter-coup, led by the King, failed, and he went into exile. Col Georgios Papadopoulos emerged as the dominant personality in the new regime, becoming Prime Minister in December 1967 and Regent in March 1972. The regime produced nominally democratic constitutional proposals, but all political activity was banned and its opponents were expelled from all positions of power or influence.

Following an abortive naval mutiny, Greece was declared a republic in June 1973; Papadopoulos was appointed President in July. Martial law was ended, and a civilian Cabinet was appointed in preparation for a general election to be held by the end of that year. A student uprising at the Athens Polytechnic in November was violently suppressed by the army, and another military coup overthrew Papadopoulos. Lt-Gen. Phaidon Ghizikis was appointed President, and a mainly civilian Cabinet, led by Adamantios Androutsopoulos, was installed, but effective power lay with a small group of officers and the military police under Brig.-Gen. Demetrios Ioannides. As a result of the failure of the military junta's attempt to overthrow President Makarios of Cyprus, and its inability to prevent the Turkish invasion of the island (see chapter on Cyprus), the Androutsopoulos Cabinet collapsed in July 1974. President Ghizikis summoned from exile a former Prime Minister, Konstantinos Karamanlis, who was invited to form a civilian Government of National Salvation. Martial law was ended, the press was released from state control and political parties, including the Communists, were allowed to operate freely. A general election in November resulted in a decisive victory for Karamanlis's Nea Dimokratia (New Democracy—ND) party, which won 220 of the 300 parliamentary seats. A referendum in December rejected proposals for a return to constitutional monarchy, and in June 1975 a new republican Constitution, providing for a parliamentary democracy, was promulgated. In the same month Prof. Konstantinos Tsatsos, a former cabinet minister, was elected President by the Parliament (Vouli).

In the general election of November 1977 ND was re-elected with a reduced majority. In May 1980 Karamanlis was elected President; Georgios Rallis subsequently assumed the leadership of ND and was appointed Prime Minister. Rallis encountered considerable opposition from the increasingly popular Panellinion Socialistikon Kinema (Panhellenic Socialist Movement—PASOK). In the general election of October 1981 PASOK gained an absolute majority in Parliament. The PASOK leader, Andreas Papandreou, became Prime Minister of the first socialist

Government in Greek history, which was initially committed to withdrawal from the European Community (EC, now the European Union—EU—see p. 181), to the removal of US military bases from Greek territory and to the implementation of an extensive programme of domestic reform. By the end of 1982 the Government had extended the franchise, legalized civil marriage and divorce, and restructured the university system, although plans to 'socialize' industry were scaled down, following widespread opposition.

In March 1985 Papandreou unexpectedly withdrew support for President Karamanlis's candidature for a further five-year term in office. The Prime Minister planned to amend the 1975 Constitution, proposing to relieve the President of all executive power, making the Head of State's functions largely ceremonial. Karamanlis resigned in protest, and Parliament elected Christos Sartzetakis, a judge, as President, in a vote that was widely considered to be unconstitutional. A general election was held in June 1985 to enable the Government to secure support for the proposed constitutional changes. PASOK was returned to power, winning 161 seats in the 300-member Parliament; ND secured 126 seats. In October the Government introduced a stringent programme of economic austerity, provoking widespread industrial unrest, which continued throughout 1986. In March 1986, despite considerable opposition from ND, Parliament approved a series of constitutional amendments limiting the influence of the President, whose executive powers were transferred to the legislature (see The Constitution).

In May 1987, in response to numerous accusations made by ND of mismanagement and corruption on the part of the Government, Papandreou sought and won a parliamentary vote of confidence in his Government. Opposition to the Government's economic austerity programme had continued in 1987 and in November Papandreou was forced to modify the programme. Despite a series of disruptive strikes by teachers and doctors in June 1988, a parliamentary motion expressing 'no confidence' in the Government was defeated. However, the Government suffered a serious reverse in November, when several leading members of the Cabinet were implicated in a major financial scandal involving alleged embezzlement from the Bank of Crete, and were forced to resign.

In January 1989 the Elliniki Aristera (Greek Left Party—EAR), led by Leonidas Kyrkos, formed an electoral alliance with the 'Exterior' faction of the Kommunistiko Komma Ellados (Communist Party of Greece—KKE), under the leadership of Charilaos Florakis, to create the Coalition of the Left and Progress (Synaspismos), commonly referred to as the Left Coalition. At a general election in June ND won the largest proportion of the votes cast, but failed to attain an overall majority in Parliament. Following the failure of both ND and PASOK to reach an agreement with the Left Coalition to form a coalition government, President Sartzetakis empowered the Left Coalition to seek a coalition agreement. The Left Coalition unexpectedly agreed to form an interim administration with ND, on the condition that the ND leader, Konstantinos Mitsotakis, renounced his claim to the premiership. Accordingly, Tzannis Tzannetakis, an ND deputy for Athens, was appointed Prime Minister in a new Cabinet, which included two Communist ministers. The unprecedented Conservative-Communist coalition announced its intention to govern for only three months, during which time it would aim to implement a *katharsis* (campaign of purification) of Greek politics. Accordingly, the administration resigned in early October, having initiated investigations into the involvement of officials of the former socialist Government, including Papandreou, in a number of scandals involving banking, armaments and financial transactions. The President of the Supreme Court, Yannis Grivas, was subsequently appointed Prime Minister in an interim Cabinet composed of non-political personalities, which was to oversee the year's second general election. However, the result of the election, conducted in November, was again inconclusive (ND won 46% of the total votes cast, PASOK 41% and the Left Coalition 11%). The political crisis was temporarily resolved in mid-November, when the three parties agreed to form a coalition that would administer the country pending the results of a further poll, to be conducted in April 1990. Xenofon Zolotas, a former Governor of the Bank of Greece, was appointed Prime Minister to lead the interim Cabinet. However, following a dispute over military promotions in February 1990, the Government collapsed, and the same non-political individuals who had overseen the November 1989 election were reinstated to govern until the new general election. Attempts by Parliament in February and March 1990 to elect a head of state by the required majority were unsuccessful, owing largely to a decision taken by ND representatives to abstain from voting, following the refusal of their candidate, Karamanlis, to take part in the election. A general election, conducted in April, finally resolved the parliamentary deadlock. ND secured 150 seats in the 300-seat Parliament. Following the announcement of the results, Mitsotakis secured the support of Konstantinos Stefanopoulos, the leader (and the one elected parliamentary representative) of the Komma Dimokratikis Ananeosis (Party of Democratic Renewal—DIANA), thereby enabling him to form the first single-party Government since 1981. In May 1990 Karamanlis took office as President for a five-year term, following his election by 153 of the 300 members of Parliament. Stefanopoulos formally rejoined ND in June.

The failure of the interim administrations to reach a consensus on comprehensive economic programmes, and the unpopularity of austerity measures introduced by the new Government, led to widespread industrial unrest. Throughout 1990 appeals by trade unions for general strikes were regularly supported by more than 1m. workers, seriously disrupting public services and industry. Despite apparent public dissatisfaction with many policies instigated by the new administration, ND were successful in municipal elections held in October. In November reforms to the electoral law, providing for a modified form of proportional representation, in which political parties wishing to appoint representatives to Parliament would require a minimum of 3% of the national vote in a general election, were finally ratified. The new electoral system, which also incorporated procedural disincentives to the formation of political alliances to contest elections, was vehemently criticized by left-wing parties as unconstitutional.

In March 1991 Andreas Papandreou and three of his former ministers were tried on charges of complicity in large-scale embezzlement from the Bank of Crete during their terms of office. Papandreou, who refused to attend court proceedings (on the grounds that his indictment had been politically motivated), was tried *in absentia* and without legal representation; in January 1992 he was acquitted of all charges, while two of the former ministers received minor sentences (the third had died during the trial).

In August 1991 Mitsotakis effected a comprehensive reorganization of the Cabinet (including the removal of his daughter from the post of Under-Secretary to the Prime Minister), in response to public criticism of family involvement in politics. In April 1992 the Prime Minister successfully sought a vote of confidence from Parliament, following the dismissal of the Minister of Foreign Affairs, Antonis Samaras, and Mitsotakis's assumption of the portfolio, in order to co-ordinate personally the Greek response to attempts by the former Yugoslav republic of Macedonia (FYRM) to achieve international recognition as the independent Republic of Macedonia (see below). As part of a cabinet reorganization effected in August (which included the controversial reappointment of the Prime Minister's daughter to her previous post), Michalis Papakonstantinou, a staunch defender of national territorial integrity, was allocated the foreign affairs portfolio. Ministerial disaffection with what was perceived as Mitsotakis's moderate stance regarding the FYRM, and with the Government's policy of economic austerity, increased in late 1992, but was curtailed somewhat following the Prime Minister's dismissal and reorganization of the entire Cabinet in early December. Industrial unrest continued throughout 1992 and 1993, in response to privatization plans and further austerity measures.

In September 1993 two ND deputies resigned, in response to an appeal for support by Politiki Anixi (Political Spring—POLAN), a centre-right party that had been established in July by Antonis Samaras. The consequent loss of Mitsotakis's one-seat majority in Parliament obliged him to offer the Government's resignation and to call an early general election. At the election, conducted in October, PASOK obtained 46.9% of the total votes cast and 170 of the 300 parliamentary seats, while ND received 39.3% of the votes and 111 seats, and POLAN

secured 4.9% of the votes and 10 seats. At the end of October Mitsotakis resigned as leader of ND.

Papandreou's victory in the general election provoked immediate concern among members of the EU, owing to the anti-European attitude that the PASOK leader had adopted during his previous tenure of office. In his first policy statement, however, Papandreou gave assurances of his commitment to European integration. In May 1994 Papandreou, contrary to his post-election commitment to revoke the privatization programme, announced his intention to generate revenue through the sale of a minority share in the state telecommunications company. (The sale was formally approved by Parliament in November, although it was postponed, owing to depressed world markets.) Following a reduction in electoral support for PASOK in elections to the European Parliament in June (the party received 37.6% of the votes cast), Papandreou undertook a reorganization of the Cabinet.

In May 1994 Parliament recommended that Mitsotakis by tried for his alleged involvement in the illegal monitoring of opposition leaders' telephone conversations during the 1990 election campaign. In September 1994 Parliament voted to charge Mitsotakis and two of his former ministers with bribery, in relation to the sale of a state-owned cement company in 1992; in January 1995, however, Parliament supported a proposal by Papandreou to suspend the trial.

In March 1995 Stefanopoulos was elected President by 181 of the 300 members of Parliament, having failed to secure the required two-thirds' majority in two earlier rounds of voting. Stefanopoulos, a candidate jointly favoured by PASOK and POLAN, took office on 10 March. From mid-1995 tensions within the governing PASOK became increasingly evident. In August a deputy was expelled from the party as a result of his suggestion that the Prime Minister should resign and his public criticism of the considerable political influence and ambitions of Papandreou's wife, Dimitra Liani-Papandreou, who had been appointed Chief of Staff in October 1993. In September 1995 a minor reorganization of the Cabinet was undertaken following the resignation of the Minister of Industry, Energy and Technology and of Commerce, Konstantinos Simitis, citing interference in his policies by senior PASOK officials, mainly supporters of the party Secretary-General, Apostolos-Athanasios (Akis) Tsohatzopoulos (a close associate of Papandreou), who were opposed to extensive economic reform. Simitis, together with Theodhoros Pangalos, who had resigned from the party's executive committee earlier in the month, Vasiliki (Vasso) Papandreou, a former EU Commissioner (who refused to accept a place in the Cabinet in the reorganization) and Paraskevas Avgerinos, a former Minister of EU Affairs, constituted a group of 'dissident' PASOK deputies (referred to as the Group of Four) who urged the resignation of Papandreou, in view of his failing health, and further reforms to modernize the party. In November Papandreou was admitted to hospital suffering from pneumonia. His prime ministerial duties were assumed by Tsohatzopoulos, who had joined the Cabinet in September and was replaced as Secretary-General of PASOK in October. While Papandreou's condition remained critical throughout December, vigorous internal discussions ensued within PASOK regarding his successor. In January 1996 the opposition parties expressed their concern at the power vacuum resulting from Papandreou's confinement. A parliamentary motion of 'no confidence' in the Government was defeated; however, senior PASOK members subsequently strengthened their resolve to settle the issue. On 15 January Papandreou submitted his resignation as Prime Minister, although he remained leader of PASOK. Three days later Simitis was elected to the premiership, having won the support of 86 of the 167 members of the PASOK parliamentary party (compared with 75 by his nearest opponent, Tsohatzopoulos) in a second round of voting. Simitis awarded Pangalos the foreign affairs portfolio but retained Tsohatzopoulos and Gerasimos Arsenis (another supporter of Papandreou who had also contested the leadership election) in the Cabinet in an attempt to unite the party. However, the majority of former Papandreou associates were replaced by pro-European ministers who supported Simitis's desire for economic reform.

Almost immediately after assuming the premiership in January 1996, Simitis was confronted by a sharp escalation in hostilities with Turkey (see below). Following his acceptance of a US-brokered compromise to defuse the situation, Simitis was vigorously condemned by all opposition parties. In February the Prime Minister dismissed the Chief of Staff of the Greek Armed Forces, Adm. Christos Lyberis, owing to the latter's disclosure of government deliberations concerning the use of military force against Turkey during the Aegean crisis.

In March 1996 the delayed privatization of the state telecommunications company was initiated, with an offer of 8% of the company's equity. The share issue was reportedly oversubscribed, despite a public demonstration of opposition by company employees in February. Also in March legislation (adopted by the PASOK administration in April 1994) to renationalize property owned by the exiled monarch, King Konstantinos, and to remove his family's citizenship, was ruled by the Supreme Court to be unconstitutional; however, in June 1997 the Supreme Court upheld the 1994 law. In April 1998 the King presented his case to the European Court of Human Rights, and in November 2000 the Court ruled that the legislation had violated the King's rights, and that the two parties had six months to reach agreement on compensation.

Following the death of Papandreou in June 1996, Simitis was elected leader of PASOK at a party congress, with 53.5% of the votes cast, defeating his closest rival, Tsohatzopoulos, who represented the populist faction of the party. None the less, in August Simitis announced that an early general election was to be held (not due by law until October 1997), in order to obtain a firm mandate for his Government to pursue the reforms needed to achieve European economic and monetary union (EMU) targets, and for the Government's implementation of its proposed foreign affairs policies. In the poll, which was held on 22 September 1996, PASOK won 162 of the 300 parliamentary seats, with 41.5% of the votes cast, securing victory over ND which, having conducted a populist campaign, including commitments of financial assistance to farmers and pensioners and a tougher foreign policy stance, took 108 seats (38.2%). Support for POLAN declined substantially, and the party lost all 10 of the seats gained at the previous election. Key ministers in the new PASOK administration were retained from the outgoing Cabinet, in particular to ensure continuity in foreign policy and management of the economy. Following ND's electoral defeat, Miltiades Evert resigned as party leader, but was re-elected to the position the following month. In March 1997 Konstantinos Karamanlis (a nephew of his namesake, the former President and ND party leader) was elected leader of ND, despite his lack of experience in government.

Meanwhile, labour unrest continued in late 1996 and early 1997, and a general strike took place in November 1996, observed by 3m. workers, to protest against new austerity measures. Despite increasing criticism from former supporters, both within and outside the party's parliamentary group, who accused him of abandoning PASOK's commitment to protecting low-income workers, Simitis continued to implement unpopular austerity policies in accordance with his commitment to meeting the 'convergence' criteria of EMU. A further general strike, in protest at pay and conditions, was widely observed in October 1997. In December Simitis expelled three deputies from PASOK's parliamentary group for voting against budget proposals for 1998, which were subsequently passed by a considerable margin by Parliament.

Industrial action continued to cause disruption in 1998. A parliamentary vote in favour of curbing collective bargaining rights and reducing benefits at loss-making state corporations, combined with the announcement of restricted wage increases at state enterprises, resulted in two weeks of strikes, which culminated in a rally in Athens in early February. Road blockades, erected by farmers in mid-January, were removed in mid-February, after an attempt to gain higher government subsidies failed. In May a widely observed general strike was organized in protest at privatization plans and the implementation of further austerity measures. Also in May employees at the Ionian and Popular Bank of Greece went on strike in protest at the Bank's proposed privatization; they were supported by transport and shipyard workers who also held stoppages, despite a court ruling declaring all the strikes illegal. The response to the strikes, in particular the use of riot police, caused divisions within the Government; however, at the end of June, after six weeks, the strike ended and the privatization programme was approved.

Following a defeat sustained by PASOK at the local elections, held in October, a minor cabinet reorganization was effected. Four new ministers entered the Cabinet and Konstantinos Geitonas, formerly the Minister of Health and Welfare, was transferred to the newly created role of Minister to the Prime Minister. In late November, in response to criticism of its austerity programme (introduced to ensure entry to EMU in

2001), the Government sought and won a parliamentary vote of confidence, by 163 votes to 136. Simitis had threatened to expel PASOK deputies from the party if they failed to support the motion.

In February 1999 it emerged that Abdullah Ocalan, the leader of the proscribed Kurdistan Workers' Party (Partiya Karkeren Kurdistan—PKK), who was wanted in Turkey on a number of terrorist charges, had been given refuge at the Greek embassy in Kenya before being captured by the Turkish authorities. Kenya officially denounced Greece for allowing Ocalan to enter the country in a diplomatic aircraft, without informing the Kenyan authorities of his presence there. Kurdish groups demonstrated at Greek embassies across Europe, and in Greece the Ministers of the Interior, Public Administration and Decentralization, of Foreign Affairs and of Public Order were forced to resign, prompting a cabinet reorganization. Three senior cabinet ministers changed portfolio, including Vasiliki (Vasso) Papandreou, formerly Minister of Development, who was appointed Minister of the Interior, Public Administration and Decentralization, and three deputy ministers were promoted, including Georgios Papandreou (the son of the late Andreas Papandreou), who replaced Theodoros Pangalos as Minister of Foreign Affairs. Simitis was re-elected unopposed as leader of PASOK at a party congress in March.

Industrial action continued in 1999. In January student demonstrations, in protest at an educational reform law affecting the university entrance system, escalated into riots in Athens. Moreover, in July the appointment of a new management team at Olympic Airways, with the aim of making the airline profitable within two years, led to stoppages over fears of widespread redundancies.

At the beginning of February 2000 Prime Minister Simitis announced that an early general election was to be held on 9 April. On 9 February Stefanopoulos was re-elected President by 269 of the 300 members of Parliament, defeating his sole opponent, Leonidas Kyrkos of the Left Coalition; Stefanopoulos was the first incumbent President of Greece to be re-elected to the post. In the April general election PASOK, again led by Simitis, was returned to office, after winning 43.8% of the votes cast and 158 parliamentary seats, thus narrowly defeating ND, which obtained 42.7% of the votes and 125 seats. The KKE won 5.2% of the ballot and 11 seats, and the Coalition of the Left and Progress secured 3.2% and six seats. On 12 April Simitis formed a new Government, the principal portfolios remaining with their previous incumbents.

In September 2000 82 people were killed when a ferry sank off the island of Paros. The boat's captain and four crewmen were charged with manslaughter and lesser charges, and in November the Vice-President of Minoan Flying Dolphins, the shipping company that owned the ferry, committed suicide. The sinking emphasized the problem of regulating the competitive Greek coastal-shipping industry, and public concern over the safety of Greece's ageing passenger fleet led the Government temporarily to withdraw 65 ferries and a cruise ship from service.

In November 2000 Simitis dismissed Theodoros Pangalos, by this time Minister of Culture, from the Government, after Pangalos expressed criticism of a number of government policies, including a new draft bill on labour-market reform, which included plans to introduce a 38-hour working week with deregulated working hours, in order to help businesses to cope with seasonal demand. Pangalos was replaced by Evangelos Venizelos. In December the Greek General Confederation of Labour staged a 24-hour strike in protest at the planned labour reforms.

Throughout 1991 numerous dissident attacks against 'capitalist' (and particularly US) military and commercial targets in Greece were carried out. In July 1992 the November 17 Revolutionary Organization claimed responsibility for an unsuccessful attempt to assassinate the Minister of Finance, in which a member of the public died. In December an ND deputy was shot and injured by the same group, in protest against alleged corruption within the Government, and against recent economic initiatives. Activity by dissident groups, in particular the November 17 organization and the Revolutionary People's Struggle (ELA), was evident throughout 1994, with attacks against foreign companies and other targets. In July the November 17 group claimed responsibility for the assassination of a Turkish diplomat. A series of measures to combat terrorism was announced by the Government in September, following a bomb attack on a police vehicle. In February 1996 an unsuccessful attack on the US embassy in Athens was believed by police to have been perpetrated by November 17 activists. In May 1997 three November 17 insurgents shot and killed a shipowner in Piraeus. In December a bomb was discovered outside the office of the Minister of Development; a similar device was placed outside the offices of a Canadian gold-mining company. In January 1998 the police arrested more than 15 suspected members of the Fighting Guerrilla Faction, a left-wing group believed to be responsible for a number of bombings, including an attack on the offices of Alitalia, the Italian airline, in 1997. In late January and February 1998 there were several explosions at the offices of US companies in Greece; these were thought to be related to US action in Iraq (see chapter on Iraq), although an anti-tank rocket attack on a US bank was believed to have been carried out by the November 17 group. During May an incendiary attack was carried out at the office of the Minister of Press and Mass Media and an explosive device was found at the office of the Minister of Transport and Communications; there were also explosions at the Ionian and Popular Bank of Greece and Olympic Airways. A bomb that exploded at the Athens office of Barclays Bank was attributed to a group entitled the Autonomous Cells of Rebel Action, which also claimed responsibility for an explosion in June. Dissident activities continued throughout 2000 and into 2001. In June 2000 the British defence attaché, Brig. Stephen Saunders, was assassinated by the November 17 group, which claimed that Saunders had helped to co-ordinate the NATO bombing of the Serbian province of Kosovo and Metohija, Yugoslavia, in 1999—a claim that was denied by British officials. The group also claimed responsibility for a series of attacks in April–May 1999 (see below). Saunders' murder led to international concern that Greece was failing to co-operate fully with international anti-terrorist efforts, although in July 2000 a series of anti-terrorist initiatives were agreed between Greece and the United Kingdom. In November, however, the ELA claimed responsibility for four bomb attacks in Athens and in January 2001 a member of Parliament was injured in Piraeus in an attack that was attributed to November 17.

Greece became a full member of the EC (now EU) in January 1981, having signed the treaty of accession in 1979. Although originally critical of Greece's membership, the PASOK Government confined itself to seeking modification of the terms of accession, in order to take into account the under-developed Greek economy, and gave qualified assent to concessions proposed by the EC in 1983. In July 1992 the Greek Parliament voted overwhelmingly to ratify the Treaty on European Union (see p. 181).

Following his accession to power in 1996, Simitis adopted a new approach in foreign relations, promoting Greece as a regional leader both politically and economically. In June 1997 Greece hosted a conference in Thessaloníki (Salonika) for ministers responsible for foreign affairs from Balkan states to discuss methods of improving regional co-operation and security. This was followed in November in Crete by the first summit of leaders of 'South-East European' countries, which was attended by representatives from Greece, Turkey, Albania, Bulgaria, the FYRM, Romania, Yugoslavia and Bosnia and Herzegovina. Agreement was reached to establish a standing secretariat to help resolve outstanding regional disputes. In May 1999 the sixth Balkan forum was held in Thessaloníki, and in November Greece announced a five-year programme of aid to assist economic recovery in South-Eastern Europe.

Relations with Turkey have been characterized by long-standing disputes concerning Cyprus (q.v.) and sovereignty over the continental shelf beneath the Aegean Sea. The difficulties in relations with Turkey were exacerbated by the unilateral declaration of an 'independent' Turkish-Cypriot state in Cyprus in November 1983 (the 'Turkish Republic of Northern Cyprus'— 'TRNC'), together with various minor sovereignty disputes over islands in the Aegean Sea, which led to Greece's withdrawal from military exercises of the North Atlantic Treaty Organization (NATO—see p. 241) in August 1984 and to a boycott of manoeuvres in subsequent years. In March 1987 a disagreement between Greece and Turkey over petroleum-prospecting rights in disputed areas of the Aegean Sea almost resulted in military conflict. In January 1988, however, the Greek and Turkish Prime Ministers, meeting in Davos, Switzerland, agreed that the two countries' premiers should meet annually in order to improve bilateral relations (the Davos meeting was the first formal contact between Greek and Turkish Heads of Government for 10 years), and that joint committees should be established to negotiate peaceful solutions to disputes.

In 1994, however, the issue of the demarcation of territorial waters in the Aegean Sea re-emerged as a major source of tension between the two countries. Greece's right to extend its territorial waters from six to 12 nautical miles, as enshrined in the international Convention on the Law of the Sea (see p. 226), was strongly condemned by Turkey, which feared the loss of shipping access, via the Aegean Sea, to international waters. The Turkish Government insisted that any expansion of territorial waters on the part of Greece would be considered an act of aggression, to which Turkey would retaliate. The dispute intensified prior to the scheduled entry into force of the Convention, in mid-November, with both countries conducting concurrent military exercises in the Aegean. In early 1995 the Greek Government obstructed an agreement to establish a customs union between Turkey and the EU until, in March, it secured a defined agreement from the EU regarding a timetable for accession negotiations with Cyprus. The concern surrounding the international Convention on the Law of the Sea re-emerged in June, when the Greek Parliament ratified the treaty. The Greek Government was criticized by some opposition politicians for not immediately enforcing the Convention, while Turkey reiterated its stance and conducted further military exercises in the region. In early 1996 tensions between the two countries were exacerbated by conflicting claims of sovereignty over Imia (Kardak), a group of small, uninhabited islands in the Aegean Sea. By late January Greek and Turkish military vessels were patrolling the islands and attempts were made to raise the respective national flags on the territory. The new PASOK administration, despite considerable criticism from ND, complied with a petition by the US Government to withdraw all military vessels and troops from the area and to remove the national flags, in order to end the threat of military action.

In February 1996 opposition by the Greek Government delayed the implementation of a financial protocol of the EU-Turkey customs union, which was to provide assistance amounting to ECU 375m. Greece claimed that Turkey's aggressive action in the Aegean violated the terms of the customs-union agreement. While the new Greek Prime Minister, Konstantinos Simitis, resolved to pursue a more constructive foreign-policy stance towards Turkey, a series of incidents throughout 1996 involving alleged violations of Greek airspace by Turkish aircraft and confrontations between Greek and Turkish patrol vessels in the Aegean precluded any improvement in relations. In July Greece finally withdrew its opposition to Turkey's participation in an EU-Mediterranean assistance programme, in response to a joint statement by EU Heads of Government urging an end to Turkey's 'hostile policy' towards Greece; however, the block on funds from the customs-union agreement remained in effect. In August, following an escalation in inter-communal tension in Cyprus, Greece reassured the Greek Cypriot authorities of its full support, and the Greek armed forces were placed on full alert. In November Greece announced an extensive programme to modernize the Greek military infrastructure, which, it insisted, was necessary to counter the perceived threat of military action by Turkey, yet which contributed to international concern at the escalating militarization of the region.

In April 1997 the Greek Deputy Minister of Foreign Affairs met his Turkish counterpart in Malta, under EU auspices, and it was agreed to establish two committees of independent experts who would communicate through the EU to explore ways of improving relations between the two countries. At a NATO summit in Madrid, Spain, in July Simitis and the Turkish President, Süleyman Demirel, held direct talks (the first such meeting for three years), which led to an agreement, known as the Madrid Declaration, in which they pledged not to use violence or the threat of violence in resolving the countries' bilateral disputes. However, relations remained strained, particularly concerning Greek support of Cyprus's application for membership of the EU; Turkey threatened integration with the 'TRNC' should Cyprus be admitted to the organization. Further tension was caused by frequent alleged violations of Greek airspace by Turkish military aircraft, in particular the reported harassment of an aircraft carrying the Greek Minister of Defence from Cyprus to Greece, following joint military exercises with Greek Cypriot forces. These incidents and a near-collision between Greek and Turkish warships in October threatened the agreement reached in Madrid. In November, however, Simitis held a meeting with the Turkish Prime Minister, Mesut Yılmaz, at which Simitis accepted an invitation to visit Ankara and it was agreed to explore confidence-building measures. Turkey, however, continued to advocate dialogue on all issues, whereas Greece reaffirmed its commitment to a gradual approach, insisting that Turkey accept international arbitration for disputes over sovereignty in the Aegean as a prerequisite both to official talks and to the lifting of Greece's veto on EU financial aid to Turkey. In November Greece threatened to oppose Turkey's participation in a planned EU enlargement conference in London, unless Turkey abandoned its attempts to prevent EU accession talks with Cyprus, which were due to begin in April 1998, and threatened to veto the admission to the EU of all the South-East European countries if Cyprus were rejected.

At a NATO summit in early December 1997 an agreement was signed, under which Greece and Turkey would share control of military flights in the Aegean under NATO's new military command structure (although this agreement had yet to be endorsed by the political leaders of each country). Later that month, however, Turkey resumed its violations of Greek airspace over the Aegean. In late December Turkey expelled a Greek diplomat for engaging in intelligence-gathering operations and Greece responded with the retaliatory expulsion of a Turkish diplomat.

As Cyprus began accession talks with the EU in March 1998, Greece reiterated its intention to veto the admission of Eastern European countries if Cyprus were not included, and its refusal to lift its veto on EU financial aid to Turkey. In early June the NATO Secretary-General, Javier Solana, announced that Greece and Turkey had agreed to continue talks regarding confidence-building measures and to activate a 1988 agreement providing for a flight moratorium over the Aegean in July and August; however, Greece later expressed doubts about the durability of the agreement. In an attempt to improve relations with Turkey, in August Greece attempted to persuade Cyprus to cancel its proposed purchase of an anti-aircraft missile system, suggesting that its deployment could be delayed by a dialogue on arms reduction. Turkey later welcomed the decision, taken at the end of December, not to deploy the missile system in Cyprus; despite Turkey's insistence that it was not a suitable alternative location, missiles were deployed on Crete in March 1999.

In July 1999 talks were held in New York, USA, between the Greek and Turkish Ministers of Foreign Affairs; discussions were limited to relatively minor issues and were reported to have been positive. Around the same time, however, Greece alleged that two Turkish military aircraft had intercepted a Greek aircraft carrying the Minister of Transport to Cyprus and had forced it briefly to alter course. Relations between the two countries improved in late August when Greece offered both financial and material assistance to Turkey, following a severe earthquake in the north-west of that country; Greece also announced its intention to lift its veto on EU financial aid to Turkey. Turkey reciprocated Greece's provision of emergency assistance when an earthquake struck Athens in early September. Later in that month the Mayor of İstanbul visited Athens, where he held talks with the city's Mayor, and in November it was announced that jointly operated train services were to be introduced between Greece and Turkey. At an EU summit, held in Helsinki, Finland, in December, a diplomatic impasse was finally ended when Greece formally lifted its objections to Turkey's membership of the EU, although an EU offer for Turkey to join included conditions concerning the resolution of both the Cyprus issue and of its dispute with Greece in the Aegean. The notable improvement in relations between Greece and Turkey was evident in late January 2000 when the Greek Minister of Foreign Affairs, Georgios Papandreou, visited Ankara for talks with his Turkish counterpart and the Turkish Prime Minister, in the first official visit by a Greek Minister of Foreign Affairs to Turkey since 1962. During negotiations, the Cyprus situation was discussed and Turkey raised the possibility of military co-operation between the two countries. In addition, a number of agreements, regarding matters such as investment, crime and tourism, were signed by the two sides. In early February 2000 the *rapprochement* between Greece and Turkey continued with an official visit to Athens by the Turkish Minister of Foreign Affairs, during which further co-operation agreements (primarily relating to economic affairs) were signed. In October 2000, however, relations were strained once again, when Greece withdrew from a joint NATO military exercise in the Aegean Sea, after it accused Turkey of preventing Greek airplanes from flying over the disputed islands of Limnos and Ikaria.

In August 1985 Greece and Albania reopened their borders, which had remained closed since 1940, and Greece formally annulled claims to North Epirus (southern Albania), where there is a sizeable Greek minority. In August 1987 the Greek Government put a formal end to a legal vestige of the Second World War by proclaiming that it no longer considered Greece to be at war with Albania. In April 1988 relations between Greece and Albania improved significantly when the two countries signed an agreement to promote trade between their border provinces. During the early 1990s, however, bilateral relations were severely strained by persisting concerns relating to the treatment of ethnic Greeks residing in Albania (numbering an estimated 300,000), the illegal immigration of several thousand Albanians seeking work opportunities or political asylum in Greece and the efforts of the Greek Government to secure their return. In March 1996 President Stefanopoulos signed a treaty of friendship and co-operation with Albania's President Berisha. Several issues appeared to have been resolved, with Albania agreeing to provide Greek-language education in schools serving the ethnic Greek population and Greece declaring its willingness to issue temporary work permits for at least 150,000 seasonal workers from Albania.

Following a revolt in southern Albania in March 1997, the Greek Government obtained guarantees from Albania for the security of the ethnic Greek population and negotiated with rebel leaders to ensure stability. Greece contributed 700 men to a multinational force led by Italy, which was established with a mandate to facilitate the distribution of humanitarian aid. Albanian banditry became a security problem in June and July, especially on the island of Corfu, where naval frigates clashed with Albanian pirates. In August Greece agreed to legitimize the status of tens of thousands of illegal Albanian immigrants by granting them temporary work permits in exchange for assistance from the Albanians in combating cross-border crime. During April 1998 the two countries signed a military-training accord; plans were later announced for joint military exercises and Greece pledged to provide military reconstruction aid to Albania. In August the establishment was announced of a free border zone between the two countries to take effect in 2000; citizens of either country living in this area were to be given special entry documents for both Greece and Albania. In May 1999 a new border crossing was opened between Greece and Albania and in September ministers from both countries called for increased co-operation between the two police forces.

Attempts after 1991 by the FYRM to achieve international recognition as an independent state were strenuously opposed by the Greek Government, which insisted that 'Macedonia' was a purely geographical term (delineating an area that included a large part of northern Greece) and expressed fears that the adoption of such a name could imply ambitions on the Greek province of Macedonia and might foster a false claim to future territorial expansion. In early 1993 the Greek administration withdrew its former objection to the use of the word 'Macedonia', and its derivatives, as part of a fuller name for the new republic. At the end of March the Greek Government accepted a UN proposal that the title 'the former Yugoslav republic of Macedonia' should be used temporarily and agreed to hold direct talks with the FYRM to consider confidence-building measures. In late 1993 the newly elected PASOK Government strongly criticized recognition of the FYRM by several EU members and, despite assurances that it would adopt a more conciliatory attitude, in February 1994 the Government condemned a decision by the USA (the final member of the UN Security Council to do so) to recognize the FYRM. At an emergency meeting in mid-February, the Cabinet agreed to prevent any movement of goods, other than humanitarian aid, into the FYRM via the northern Greek port of Thessaloníki. The initiative was widely criticized by the international community as effectively constituting an illegal trade embargo, and the EU ministers responsible for foreign affairs urged Greece to revoke the measures, which, it was determined, violated EU law. Intensive negotiations with the Greek authorities failed to resolve the issue and in mid-April the European Commission commenced legal proceedings against Greece at the Court of Justice of the European Communities. In April 1995 a preliminary opinion of the Court determined that the embargo was not in breach of Greece's obligations under the Treaty of Rome. In September the ministers responsible for foreign affairs of Greece and the FYRM, meeting in New York, under UN auspices, signed an interim accord to normalize relations between the two countries, which included recognition of the existing international border. Under the terms of the agreement, Greece was to grant access to the port facilities at Thessaloníki and to remove all obstructions to the cross-border movement of people and goods following a period of 30 days, during which the FYRM was to approve a new state flag (removing the symbolic Vergina sun). The measures were successfully implemented by mid-October; a few days later agreement was concluded on the establishment of liaison offices in the two countries' capitals. Negotiations were to be pursued regarding the issue of a permanent name for the FYRM, which would be acceptable to both sides. In March 1997 the Greek Minister of Foreign Affairs visited the FYRM for the first time since its independence from Yugoslavia.

During the conflict in the former Yugoslavia, Greece pursued an active involvement in efforts to promote a peaceful political settlement in the region. In contrast to most of its European partners, Greece maintained close relations with the Yugoslav Government and advocated the removal of the UN-imposed trade embargo against Serbia and Montenegro. Greece's stance, which was shared notably by Bulgaria and Russia, contributed to a strengthening of relations between these countries.

In late 1998 Greece advocated a diplomatic (rather than a military) solution to the ethnic conflict in the Yugoslav province of Kosovo and Metohija, and in March 1999 declared that it would not participate in the newly launched NATO air offensive against Serb targets. Insurgent activity, in protest at the NATO action, increased in Greece during 1999; in April a bomb in an Athens hotel resulted in one person being killed and another seriously injured. In May rocket attacks, attributed to the November 17 Revolutionary Organization, were launched on the residences of the Dutch and German ambassadors to Greece and on three foreign banks in Athens. Public opinion in Greece was, in general, strongly opposed to NATO and a three-day visit by US President Bill Clinton, planned for November, was rearranged as a 24-hour visit later in the month, following a series of protests (including two bombing incidents). During Clinton's stay demonstrations escalated into riots in Athens, and around the same time Greece withdrew from a proposed anti-terrorism pact with the USA, without proffering any reason for doing so.

In July 2000 Germany and Greece became involved in a diplomatic dispute, after a Greek court took steps to expropriate German assets to compensate the families of victims of Nazi war crimes. The court's action followed a demand by the Greek Supreme Court in April that Germany pay DM 55m. in compensation to residents of the village of Distomo, in central Greece, where Nazi occupiers killed over two hundred people in June 1944. Germany filed a caveat in response to the court's decision, effectively delaying proceedings until October 2001.

Government

Under the Constitution of June 1975, the President is Head of State and is elected by Parliament for a five-year term. The President appoints the Prime Minister and, upon his recommendation, the other members of the Cabinet. In March 1986 Parliament approved a series of constitutional amendments, divesting the President of his executive powers and transferring them to the legislature (see The Constitution). The unicameral Parliament has 300 members, directly elected by universal adult suffrage for four years. Greece comprises 13 regions, including Greater Athens, and is divided into 51 administrative divisions.

Defence

Greece returned to the military structure of the North Atlantic Treaty Organization (NATO, see p. 241) in 1980, after an absence of six years. Military service is compulsory for all men between 18 and 40 years of age, and lasts 19–21 months. In 1978 women were given the right to volunteer for military service of 30–50 days' basic training and for specialized training. In 1998 a law was passed providing for the conscription of women (for four days a year) to assist in the defence of the border regions. At 1 August 2000 the armed forces numbered 159,170, of whom 98,321 were conscripts, and consisted of an army of 110,000 (including a national guard of 34,000), a navy of 19,000 and an air force of 30,170; in addition, there was a coast guard and customs force of 4,000. The USA occupied two military bases in Greece with a total of 420 troops stationed there in August 2000. Budget estimates for 2000 allocated 1,160,000m. drachmae to defence. In 2000 Greece committed 3,500 troops to the proposed joint EU rapid reaction force, which was to be ready for deployment by 2003.

Economic Affairs

In 1998, according to estimates by the World Bank, Greece's gross national product (GNP), measured at average 1996–98 prices, was US $123,394m., equivalent to $11,740 per head. During 1990–98, it was estimated, GNP per head increased, in real terms, at an average rate of 1.2% per year. Over the same period the population grew at an average annual rate of 0.5%. In 1999 GNP totalled an estimated $124,000m., equivalent to $11,770 per head (or $14,595 per head on an international purchasing-power parity basis). Greece's gross domestic product (GDP) increased, in real terms, at an average annual rate of 1.9% in 1990–99. According to the IMF, GDP increased by 3.1% in 1998, 3.4% in 1999 and 3.9% in 2000.

Agriculture (including hunting, forestry and fishing) contributed 7.6% of GDP in 1998 and engaged 17.8% of the employed labour force. The principal cash crops are fruit and vegetables (which, together, accounted for about 12.4% of total export earnings in 1998), cereals, sugar beets and tobacco. Agricultural GDP decreased at an average annual rate of 3.7% in 1994–97.

Industry (including mining, manufacturing, power and construction) provided 22.8% of GDP in 1998 and engaged 23.0% of the employed labour force. During 1990–95 industrial GDP declined at an average annual rate of 0.4%. However, following the International Olympic Committee's—IOC, see p. 218—announcement, in 1997, that the 2004 Olympic Games would be held in Athens, public expenditure on infrastructure projects stimulated growth in the construction industry. The sector recorded an increase of 10% in 1998.

Mining and quarrying contributed 0.6% of GDP in 1998 and engaged 0.5% of the employed labour force. Mineral fuels and lubricants, iron and steel, and aluminium and aluminium alloys are the major mineral/metal exports. Lignite, magnesite, silver ore and marble are also mined. In addition, Greece has small reserves of uranium and natural gas.

Manufacturing provided 11.1% of GDP in 1998 and engaged 14.6% of the employed labour force. The most important branches in 1995, measured by output in factor values, were food products (accounting for 20.1% of the total), metals and metal products (12.3%), textiles and clothing (11.0%), petroleum refining (10.5%) and chemicals (9.5%). Manufacturing production increased each year from 1994, and increased by 3.4% in 1998, compared with 1.0% in 1997.

Energy is derived principally from petroleum and lignite. Petroleum and petroleum products accounted for 7.0% of the total cost of imports in 1998. Greece is exploiting an offshore petroleum deposit in the north-eastern Aegean Sea. Hydroelectric and solar power resources are also being developed.

The services sector contributed 69.7% of GDP in 1998 and engaged 59.2% of the employed labour force. Tourism is an important source of foreign exchange in Greece. In 1998 visitor arrivals totalled 10.9m. and receipts from the tourist sector amounted to US $5,186m., compared with $3,771m. in 1997. During 1990–94 GDP from the services sector increased at an average annual rate of 0.6%.

In 1999 Greece recorded a visible trade deficit of US $17,946.5m., and there was a deficit of $5,101.5m. on the current account of the balance of payments. In 1998 the principal source of imports (16.3%) was Italy, closely followed by Germany (15.3%); other major sources were France, the United Kingdom and the Netherlands. The principal market for exports in 1998 was Germany (18.4%); other major purchasers were Italy, the United Kingdom and France. The principal exports in 1998 were clothing, fruit and vegetables, petroleum and petroleum products and non-ferrous metals. The principal imports were petroleum and petroleum products, road vehicles and parts, textiles and electrical machinery.

In 1999 there was a projected budgetary deficit of 2,182,000m. drachmae (equivalent to 1.7% of GDP). Greece's total public external debt was 8,330,000m. drachmae at the end of 1997. In 1999 the cost of debt-servicing was equivalent to 9% of GDP. In 1990–98 the average annual rate of inflation was 10.9%; consumer prices increased by 5.5% in 1997, by 4.8% in 1998 and by 2.6% in 1999. According to the IMF, 11.8% of the labour force were unemployed in 2000.

Greece is a member of the European Union (EU—see p. 181), the Organisation for Economic Co-operation and Development (OECD—see p. 247) and the Black Sea Economic Co-operation group (see p. 265).

The priority of the Simitis Government was to ensure the admittance of Greece to full EU economic and monetary union (EMU) by 2001. Progress towards this aim was improved considerably by Greece's admission to the European exchange rate mechanism (ERM) in March 1998, which increased investor confidence and necessitated a 13.8% devaluation of the hitherto overvalued drachma, making exports more competitive. A reform programme, comprising reductions in public spending and an acceleration in the privatization programme, was announced in conjunction with the ERM entry, in order to offset the effects of devaluation on inflation and the budgetary deficit. High interest rates were imposed to combat inflationary pressures, although this adversely affected government attempts to reduce debt-financing costs. However, a significant decline was achieved in both the budgetary deficit and public-sector debt in 1998 and, again, in 1999. In November 1999 the EU removed Greece from its list of countries with excessive deficits. The projected budgetary deficit for 1999 met the target for EMU entry and in February–March 2000 a rate of inflation of 2% was recorded, thereby qualifying Greece for full EMU membership. After submitting its application in March, on 19 June Greece received a formal invitation to join EMU from 1 January 2001. Greece duly became a member of EMU at the beginning of 2001, thereby becoming the 12th member country in the so-called 'euro-zone'. Although Greece did not satisfy the requirement stipulated in the Maastricht Treaty that the ratio of government debt to GDP be less than 60%, the Government aimed to achieve this objective by the end of the decade. In 2000 Greece's public-sector debt was equivalent to 103.9% of GDP, and it was projected to reach some 98.2% of GDP in 2001. Moreover, the budget for 2001 predicted a budgetary surplus of 0.5%—the first surplus for some decades—and GDP growth of 4.0%.

Social Welfare

There is a state social insurance scheme for wage-earners, while voluntary or staff insurances provide for salaried staff. Every citizen is entitled to an old-age pension and sickness benefit. In 1996 Greece had 356 hospital establishments, with 502 beds per 100,000 inhabitants. In that year there were 205 physicians per 100,000 population working in the country. Of total projected expenditure by the central Government in 1999, some 2,225,000m. drachmae (15.6%) was allocated to health, social welfare and insurance.

Education

Education is available free of charge at all levels, and is officially compulsory for all children between the ages of six and 15 years. Primary education begins at the age of six and lasts for six years. Secondary education, beginning at the age of 12, is generally for six years, divided into two equal cycles. In 1997 primary enrolment included 99.9% of children in the relevant age-group, and the comparable ratio at secondary schools was 91.4%. In 1994 enrolment in tertiary education was equivalent to 38.1% of the relevant age-group. In 1997/98 some 172,559 students were enrolled in institutions of higher education. Between 1951 and 1981 the average rate of adult illiteracy declined from 72% to 10%. At the 1991 census the rate was only 4.8% (males 2.3%; females 7.0%). In 1999 projected budgetary expenditure on education was 1,304,000m. drachmae (9.2% of total expenditure).

The vernacular language (demotiki) has replaced the formal version (katharevoussa) in secondary education.

Public Holidays

2001: 1 January (New Year's Day), 6 January (Epiphany), 26 February (Clean Monday), 25 March (Independence Day), 13–16 April (Greek Orthodox Easter), 1 May (Labour Day), 4 June (Whit Monday), 15 August (Assumption of the Virgin Mary), 28 October ('Ochi' Day, anniversary of Greek defiance of Italy's 1940 ultimatum), 25–26 December (Christmas).

2002: 1 January (New Year's Day), 6 January (Epiphany), 18 March (Clean Monday), 25 March (Independence Day), 1 May (Labour Day), 3–6 May (Greek Orthodox Easter), 24 June (Whit Monday), 15 August (Assumption of the Virgin Mary), 28 October ('Ochi' Day, anniversary of Greek defiance of Italy's 1940 ultimatum), 25–26 December (Christmas).

Weights and Measures

The metric system is in force.

Statistical Survey

Source (unless otherwise stated): National Statistical Service of Greece, Odos Lykourgou 14–16, 101 66 Athens; tel. (1) 3289530; fax (1) 3241102; e-mail info@statistics.gr; internet www.statistics.gr.

Area and Population

AREA, POPULATION AND DENSITY

Area (sq km)	131,957*
Population (census results)†	
5 April 1981	9,740,417
17 March 1991	
Males	5,055,408
Females	5,204,492
Total	10,259,900
Population (official estimates at mid-year)	
1996	10,475,878
1997	10,498,836
1998	10,516,366
Density (per sq km) at mid-1998	79.7

* 50,949 sq miles.
† Including armed forces stationed abroad, but excluding foreign forces stationed in Greece.

PRINCIPAL TOWNS (population at 1991 census)

Athinai (Athens,		Iraklion . . .	. 116,178
the capital) . .	772,072	Larissa . . .	. 113,090
Thessaloniki		Volos . . .	. 77,192
(Salonika) . .	383,967	Kavala . . .	. 58,025
Piraeus . . .	182,671	Serres . . .	. 50,390
Patras . . .	153,344	Canea . . .	. 50,077

BIRTHS, MARRIAGES AND DEATHS

	Registered live births		Registered marriages		Registered deaths	
	Number	Rate (per 1,000)	Number	Rate (per 1,000)	Number	Rate (per 1,000)
1992 . .	104,081	10.1	48,631	4.7	98,231	9.5
1993 . .	101,799	9.8	62,195	6.0	97,419	9.4
1994 . .	103,763	9.9	56,813	5.4	97,807	9.4
1995 . .	101,495	9.7	63,987	6.1	100,158	9.6
1996 . .	100,718	9.6	45,408	4.3	100,740	9.6
1997 . .	102,038	9.7	60,535	5.8	99,738	9.5
1998 . .	100,894	9.4	55,489	5.5	102,668	9.5
1999* . .	116,038	10.9	n.a.	6.4	104,190	9.8

* Provisional figures. (Source: UN, *Population and Vital Statistics Report* and *Monthly Bulletin of Statistics*.)

Expectation of life (years at birth, 1998): Males 75.3; Females 80.5.

ECONOMICALLY ACTIVE POPULATION
(sample surveys, '000 persons aged 14 years and over, April–June)*

	1996	1997	1998†
Agriculture, hunting, forestry and fishing	786.1	765.0	704.2
Mining and quarrying . . .	17.2	17.3	18.3
Manufacturing	576.1	558.7	577.9
Electricity, gas and water. . .	40.7	40.7	35.3
Construction and public works	251.8	249.0	282.3
Trade, restaurants and hotels. .	858.0	872.5	917.0
Transport, storage and communications . . .	254.0	246.7	244.8
Finance, insurance, banking and business services . . .	248.5	257.0	290.6
Other services	839.4	847.3	896.8
Total employed . . .	3,871.9	3,854.1	3,967.2
Unemployed	446.4	440.4	478.5
Total labour force . . .	4,318.3	4,294.4	4,445.7
Males	2,637.4	2,612.0	2,692.9
Females	1,680.9	1,682.4	1,752.8

* Including members of the regular armed forces, but excluding persons on compulsory military service.
† '000 persons aged 15 years and over.

Agriculture

PRINCIPAL CROPS ('000 metric tons)

	1997	1998	1999
Wheat	1,991	2,058	2,064
Rice (paddy)	214	209	161
Barley	348	358	320
Maize	2,025	1,816	1,950
Rye	36	41	31
Oats	88	83	114
Potatoes	883	876	867
Dry beans	25	22	22*
Other pulses	18	20	20*
Sunflower seed	36	40	41†
Olives	1,879	2,068	1,938†
Cabbages	212	209	210*
Tomatoes	2,013	2,085	2,098
Cucumbers and gherkins . .	174	152	160*
Aubergines	74	74	80*
Green peppers*	100	110	n.a.
Onions (dry)	161	167	160*
Watermelons	671	662	685
Melons	163	161	165*
Grapes	1,213	1,216†	1,200*
Sugar beets	2,798	1,996	2,389
Apples	373	358	318
Pears	77	71	66†
Peaches and nectarines . .	588	528	1,000†
Oranges	1,011	814	1,118
Lemons and limes . . .	164	183	182
Apricots	40	38	70†
Almonds	43	35	46
Tobacco (leaves) . . .	137	137	140
Cotton (lint)†	370	382	384†

* FAO estimates(s).   † Unofficial estimate(s).

Source: FAO, *Production Yearbook*.

LIVESTOCK ('000 head, year ending 30 September)

	1997	1998	1999
Horses .	33	33*	33*
Mules .	39	35*	35*
Asses .	83	80*	80*
Cattle .	580	596	577
Pigs. .	987	938	933
Sheep .	8,896	8,952	8,756†
Goats .	5,570	5,878	5,520

Chickens (million): 28 in 1997; 28* in 1998; 28* in 1999.

* FAO estimate.   † Unofficial estimate.

Source: FAO.

LIVESTOCK PRODUCTS ('000 metric tons)

	1997	1998	1999
Beef and veal .	70	69	67
Mutton and lamb .	89	93	80†
Goat meat .	54	56	47†
Pig meat .	142	143	138
Horse meat .	3	3	3
Poultry meat .	158	148	153
Other meat .	13	10	10
Cows' milk .	739	769	760†
Sheep's milk.	722	630†	670*
Goats' milk .	523	448†	450*
Cheese .	224	229	230
Butter .	5	5	5†
Poultry eggs .	115	119	112
Honey .	14	14	14
Wool: greasy.	9	10	10
Cattle and buffalo hides .	13	13	13
Sheepskins* .	19	18	17
Goatskins .	10	10	10

* FAO estimate(s).   † Unofficial estimate.

Source: FAO.

Forestry

ROUNDWOOD REMOVALS ('000 cubic metres, excl. bark)

	1996	1997	1998
Sawlogs, veneer logs and logs for sleepers .	467	403	360
Pulpwood .	105	105	135
Other industrial wood .	102	n.a.	n.a.
Fuel wood .	1,338	1,236	1,197
Total .	2,012	1,744	1,692

Source: FAO, *Yearbook of Forest Products.*

SAWNWOOD PRODUCTION (FAO estimates, '000 cubic metres)

	1996	1997	1998
Coniferous (softwood). .	210	81	85
Broadleaved (hardwood) .	127	49	52
Total .	337	130	137

Source: FAO, *Yearbook of Forest Products.*

Fishing

('000 metric tons, live weight)

	1996	1997	1998
Capture .	162.4	170.9	128.2
Freshwater fishes .	16.5	16.0	21.8
Bogue .	6.7	6.0	4.2
Mediterranean horse mackerel	8.0	7.2	4.4
European pilchard (sardine) .	18.9	20.1	17.7
European anchovy .	15.1	14.6	17.1
Chub mackerel .	6.5	5.6	2.2
Mediterranean mussel .	12.6	24.1	6.4
Aquaculture .	39.9	48.8	59.9
Barramundi (giant sea perch)	11.7	15.2	18.5
Dorada .	13.8	18.0	22.0
Mediterranean mussel .	10.2	11.0	14.5
Total catch .	202.3	219.7	188.2

Note: Figures exclude aquatic plants and aquatic mammals.

Source: FAO, *Yearbook of Fishery Statistics.*

Mining

('000 metric tons, unless otherwise indicated)

	1994	1995	1996
Lignite .	56,741	57,662	59,781
Crude petroleum .	500	435	493
Iron ore*†‡ .	810	800	810
Bauxite .	2,201	2,165	2,166
Zinc concentrates§ .	17.2*	14.5*	7.2*
Lead concentrates§ .	19.9*	20.4*	8.4*
Silver ore (metric tons)*§ .	45	45	16
Magnesite .	512.4	556.8	532.5
Salt (unrefined)‡ .	192	200	140
Kaolin .	77	95	58‖
Gypsum .	630	692	759‖
Marble ('000 cu m) .	890	585	737
Natural gas (petajoules) .	2	2	2

1997 ('000 metric tons, unless otherwise indicated): Bauxite 1,828; Zinc 17.8§; Lead 193.2§; Silver (metric tons) 36§; Salt (unrefined) 200‡.

* Figures refer to the metal content of ores and concentrates.
† Estimate(s).
‡ Data from the US Bureau of Mines.
§ Data from *World Metal Statistics.*
‖ Source: National Statistical Service of Greece.

Source: UN *Industrial Commodity Statistics Yearbook.*

Industry

SELECTED PRODUCTS
('000 metric tons, unless otherwise indicated)

	1994	1995	1996
Edible fats .	42	44	44
Olive oil (crude) .	329	360	398
Raw sugar .	307	249	287
Wine .	164	193	192
Beer ('000 hectolitres) .	4,376	4,025	3,766
Cigarettes (million) .	32,843	39,291	38,269
Cotton yarn (pure) .	122	122	116
Woven cotton fabrics—pure and mixed (metric tons) .	30,145	26,066	19,668
Wool yarn—pure (metric tons) .	5,044	7,652	7,554
Woven woollen fabrics—pure and mixed (metric tons) .	434	618	1,118
Yarn of artificial material (metric tons) .	15,460	19,948	21,025
Fabrics of artificial fibres (metric tons) .	9,178	9,946	11,513
Footwear—excl. rubber and plastic ('000 pairs) .	6,058	6,382	6,009
Rubber and plastic footwear ('000 pairs) .	3,986	3,463	3,294
Paper and paperboard .	395	408	340
Sulphuric acid .	623	759	773
Hydrochloric acid (21° Bé) .	25	42	45
Nitric acid (54% or 36.3° Bé) .	407	437	462

— continued	1994	1995	1996
Polyvinyl chloride . . .	83	77	95
Liquefied petroleum gas . .	441	479	392
Naphthas . . .	549	732	943
Motor spirit (petrol) . .	3,595	3,491	3,455
Jet fuels . .	1,394	1,816	1,969
Distillate fuel oils . .	3,349	3,130	4,023
Residual fuel oils . .	4,738	5,490	6,742
Cement . .	12,774	13,116	13,559
Crude steel (incl. alloys) . .	848	939	847
Aluminium (unwrought) . .	146.4	153.6	147.6
Electric energy (million kWh) .	33,464	33,949	35,464

Finance

CURRENCY AND EXCHANGE RATES

Monetary Units
100 lepta (singular: lepton) = 1 drachma (plural: drachmae).

Sterling, Dollar and Euro Equivalents (29 December 2000)
£1 sterling = 545.6 drachmae;
US $1 = 365.6 drachmae;
€1 = 340.2 drachmae;
1,000 drachmae = £1.833 = $2.735 = €2.939.

Average Exchange Rate (drachmae per US $)
1998	295.53
1999	305.65
2000	365.40

Note: Greece became a member of the euro area on 1 January 2001, since when a fixed exchange rate of €1 = 340.75 drachmae has been in operation.

BUDGET ('000 million drachmae)*

Revenue	1997	1998†	1999‡
Ordinary budget	8,467.3	9,528.0	10,030.0
Tax revenue	7,600.9	8,829.2	9,088.5
Direct taxes	2,767.0	3,587.3	3,474.0
Personal income tax . .	1,297.5	1,585.4	1,441.0
Corporate income tax . .	641.7	1,017.5	968.3
Indirect taxes . . .	4,833.9	5,241.9	5,614.5
Consumption taxes. . .	1,767.0	1,854.1	1,894.0
Transaction taxes . .	2,923.6	3,246.9	3,550.5
Value-added tax . .	2,448.6	2,720.7	3,000.0
Stamp duty . .	257.5	292.0	300.0
Non-tax revenue . . .	866.4	698.8	941.5
Capital receipts . . .	474.7	408.2	537.5
Investment budget . . .	719.0	913.0	1,060.0
Receipts from European Union .	698.0	890.0	1,030.0
SAGAP§.	819.0	810.0	973.0
Total	10,005.3	11,251.0	12,063.0

Expenditure	1997	1998†	1999‡
Defence	941	1,018	1,046
Education	1,128	1,217	1,304
Health, social welfare and insurance	2,051	2,229	2,225
Agriculture	1,166	1,242	1,456
Interest payments‖ . . .	3,027	3,051	3,160
Other purposes . . .	4,195	4,602	5,028
Total‖	12,509	13,358	14,218
Ordinary budget	10,064	10,667	11,050
Investment budget . . .	1,626	1,881	2,195
SAGAP§.	819	810	973

* Figures refer to the budgetary transactions of the central Government, excluding the operations of social security funds and public entities (such as hospitals, educational institutions and government agencies) with individual budgets.
† Provisional.
‡ Projected.
§ Special Account for Guarantees of Agricultural Products.
‖ Excluding capitalized interest ('000 million drachmae): 33 in 1997; 27 in 1998; 27 (projected) in 1999.

Source: IMF, *Greece: Selected Issues* (December 1999).

INTERNATIONAL RESERVES (US $ million at 31 December)*

	1998	1999	2000
Gold†	685.3	781.8	753.2
IMF special drawing rights . .	0.5	5.2	12.0
Reserve position in IMF . .	269.6	391.1	296.8
Foreign exchange . . .	17,188.3	17,726.0	13,115.5
Total	18,143.7	18,904.1	14.177.5

* Figures exclude deposits made with the European Monetary Institute.
† Gold reserves are valued at market-related prices.

Source: IMF, *International Financial Statistics*.

MONEY SUPPLY ('000 million drachmae at 31 December)

	1997	1998	1999
Currency outside banks . . .	2,239.2	2,284.3	2,798.7
Private-sector deposits at Bank of Greece	570.7	568.4	643.1
Demand deposits at commercial banks	2,221.5	2,708.5	3,748.1
Total money	5,031.3	5,561.2	7,190.0

Source: IMF, *International Financial Statistics*.

COST OF LIVING (Consumer Price Index; base: 1990 = 100)

	1997	1998	1999
Food	198.0	206.7	211.6
Fuel and light	173.3	167.2	153.6
Clothing	208.1	220.0	228.6
Rent	286.1	304.5	318.4
All items (incl. others) . . .	218.5	229.0	235.0

Source: ILO, *Yearbook of Labour Statistics*.

NATIONAL ACCOUNTS
(million drachmae at current prices)
Expenditure on the Gross Domestic Product*

	1997	1998	1999
Government final consumption expenditure	5,018,900	5,505,600	5,734,400
Private final consumption expenditure	23,905,900	25,742,100	27,124,700
Increase in stocks . . .	64,500	107,500	−67,500
Gross fixed capital formation . .	6,612,400	7,758,300	8,566,700
Total domestic expenditure .	35,601,700	39,113,500	41,358,300
Exports of goods and services . .	6,432,000	7,123,400	7,690,700
Less Imports of goods and services .	8,929,900	10,364,400	10,901,800
GDP in purchasers' values . .	33,103,800	35,872,500	38,147,200
GDP at constant 1995 prices .	28,857,500	29,738,200	30,737,300

* Figures are rounded to the nearest 100 million drachmae.

Source: IMF, *International Financial Statistics*.

Gross Domestic Product by Economic Activity

	1996	1997*	1998*
Agriculture, hunting, forestry and fishing	2,386,665	2,387,701	2,451,667
Mining and quarrying . . .	182,844	190,725	199,318
Manufacturing	3,512,020	3,636,006	3,611,072
Electricity, gas and water. . .	583,182	597,063	647,329
Construction.	1,891,239	2,415,977	2,929,430
Wholesale and retail trade .	4,091,971	4,544,294	4,979,965
Transport, storage and communication	1,628,177	1,797,743	1,986,258
Finance, insurance and real estate†	5,044,271	5,585,064	6,011,523
Public administration and defence	1,849,646	2,071,335	2,201,533
Other services	6,153,433	6,809,155	7,417,804
Sub-total	27,323,448	30,035,063	32,435,899
Less Imputed bank service charge	832,290	986,272	1,079,680
Less Other adjustments . . .	195,038	202,879	257,257
GDP at factor cost	26,296,120	28,845,912	31,098,962
Indirect taxes, *less* subsidies .	3,382,354	3,875,900	4,487,238
GDP in purchasers' values .	29,678,474	32,721,812	35,586,200

* Figures are provisional.

† Including imputed rents of owner-occupied dwellings.

BALANCE OF PAYMENTS (US $ million)

	1997	1998	1999
Exports of goods f.o.b. . . .	6,427.8	6,671.5	8,546.9
Imports of goods f.o.b. . . .	−23,666.7	−23,305.1	−26,493.4
Trade balance	−17,239.0	−16,633.5	−17,946.5
Exports of services . . .	10,119.2	11,188.4	16,494.3
Imports of services . . .	−3,669.0	−4,380.4	−9,242.0
Balance on goods and services	−10,788.8	−9,825.6	−10,694.2
Other income received . .	1,255.3	1,533.7	2,553.4
Other income paid . . .	−2,823.5	−3,072.2	−3,229.6
Balance on goods, services and income	−12,357.0	−11,364.1	−11,370.4
Current transfers received . .	7,553.8	8,206.7	7,200.6
Current transfers paid . . .	−40.2	−489.4	−931.6
Current balance	−4,843.5	−3,646.9	−5,101.5
Direct investment (net) .	1,617.0	337.9	33.4
Portfolio investment (net). .	1,605.0	12,058.2	6,452.2
Other investment assets . .	−8,505.5	−6,402.4	−4,801.9
Other investment liabilities .	5,513.2	2,643.3	4,042.0
Net errors and omissions . .	−1,227.0	−135.4	131.0
Overall balance . . .	−5,840.8	4,854.7	755.1

Source: Bank of Greece.

External Trade

PRINCIPAL COMMODITIES (US $ million)

Imports c.i.f.	1996	1997	1998
Food and live animals . .	3,410.1	3,222.1	3,242.1
Meat and meat preparations .	856.5	837.0	848.8
Fresh, chilled or frozen meat .	815.8	797.4	810.1
Dairy products and birds' eggs .	578.9	532.3	543.9
Beverages and tobacco. .	578.9	524.6	550.8
Crude materials (inedible) except fuels	934.2	916.9	863.5
Mineral fuels, lubricants, etc. .	2,500.2	2,117.9	2,172.1
Petroleum, petroleum products, etc.	2,378.7	1,979.0	2,013.0
Crude petroleum oils, etc. .	2,014.9	1,577.0	1,669.0
Chemicals and related products	3,496.5	3,384.2	3,579.4
Medicinal and pharmaceutical products	937.2	984.1	1,056.1
Artificial resins, plastic materials, etc.	692.2	650.3	655.9

Imports c.i.f. — *continued*	1996	1997	1998
Basic manufactures . . .	5,213.2	5,090.3	5,122.0
Paper, paperboard and manufactures	784.9	728.8	803.0
Textile yarn, fabrics, etc. . .	1,181.7	1,149.4	1,128.8
Iron and steel	939.3	880.6	870.3
Non-ferrous metals . . .	528.3	645.6	550.7
Machinery and transport equipment	8,597.6	8,067.5	9,361.5
Machinery specialized for particular industries . .	932.7	969.6	991.7
General industrial machinery, equipment and parts . .	1,119.0	1,125.8	1,172.4
Office machines and automatic data-processing equipment .	513.4	541.7	600.0
Telecommunications and sound equipment	847.9	850.9	1,183.3
Other electrical machinery, apparatus, etc. . . .	1,086.1	1,018.4	1,227.8
Road vehicles and parts* . .	2,478.0	2,385.5	2,593.9
Passenger motor cars (excl. buses)	1,459.8	1,380.6	1,518.9
Other transport equipment* . .	1,080.6	670.5	1,137.5
Ships, boats and floating structures	943.3	538.7	613.4
Miscellaneous manufactured articles	3,522.1	3,441.6	3,539.3
Clothing and accessories (excl. footwear)	952.3	975.4	1,030.5
Total (incl. others)	28,419.0	26,970.7	28,753.6

* Excluding tyres, engines and electrical parts.

Exports f.o.b.	1996	1997	1998
Food and live animals . . .	2,016.9	1,926.8	2,036.6
Fish and fish preparations . .	208.0	236.3	253.7
Cereals and cereal preparations	225.7	256.0	164.1
Vegetables and fruit . . .	1,298.1	1,127.0	1,336.9
Fresh, chilled, frozen or simply preserved vegetables. . .	272.2	247.5	279.0
Fresh or dried fruit and nuts (excl. oil nuts) . . .	472.0	438.2	459.2
Preserved fruit and fruit preparations	360.9	296.4	411.4
Beverages and tobacco. . .	720.2	670.1	579.6
Tobacco and manufactures . .	505.5	511.0	434.5
Unmanufactured tobacco (incl. refuse)	353.5	355.1	330.2
Unstripped tobacco . .	301.9	290.7	266.4
Crude materials (inedible) except fuels	861.2	675.7	566.6
Textile fibres and waste . .	511.1	348.2	260.4
Cotton	497.5	334.9	250.4
Raw cotton (excl. linters) .	464.3	311.7	227.7
Mineral fuels, lubricants, etc. .	1,000.2	926.4	724.0
Petroleum, petroleum products, etc.	973.1	897.6	695.7
Refined petroleum products. .	866.5	815.4	600.7
Gasoline and other light oils	296.1	304.5	210.0
Residual fuel oils . .	348.4	316.5	233.7
Animal and vegetable oils, fats and waxes	758.7	406.7	350.0
Fixed vegetable oils and fats .	756.9	403.7	346.2
Soft fixed vegetable oils. .	754.6	402.4	344.6
Olive oil.	738.4	378.3	308.2
Chemicals and related products	566.7	606.0	660.0
Basic manufactures . . .	2,356.2	2,258.4	2,288.4
Textile yarn, fabrics, etc. . .	507.2	466.7	541.0
Textile yarn . . .	242.6	224.6	247.8
Non-metallic mineral manufactures	490.0	482.9	402.8
Lime, cement, etc. . . .	383.9	375.4	302.6
Cement	269.3	253.3	197.1
Iron and steel	338.9	293.2	304.1
Non-ferrous metals . . .	550.3	592.6	613.7
Aluminium	383.6	424.1	456.7
Worked aluminium and aluminium alloys . .	303.5	339.7	351.0

Exports f.o.b. — *continued*	1996	1997	1998
Machinery and transport equipment	960.7	983.0	1,110.7
Electrical machinery, apparatus, etc.	396.0	423.0	464.4
Miscellaneous manufactured articles	2,365.6	2,484.4	2,273.2
Clothing and accessories (excl. footwear)	1,878.5	1,980.3	1,813.9
Women's, girls' and infants' outer garments of non-knitted textile fabrics	257.8	428.3	209.1
Knitted or crocheted outer garments and accessories (excl. gloves, stockings, etc.), non-elastic	683.1	606.6	631.9
Knitted or crocheted undergarments (incl. foundation garments of non-knitted fabrics)	593.5	533.1	615.5
Cotton undergarments, non-elastic	552.7	493.0	556.8
Non-textile clothing and accessories, and headgear of all materials	252.1	308.4	256.0
Fur clothing (not including headgear) and other articles made of furskins; artificial fur and articles made thereof	240.8	298.1	246.1
Total (incl. others)	11,879.7	11,167.1	10,765.2

Source: UN, *International Trade Statistics Yearbook.*

PRINCIPAL TRADING PARTNERS (US $ million)*

Imports c.i.f.	1996	1997	1998
Austria	329.5	278.4	293.9
Belgium-Luxembourg	1,011.7	974.8	1,023.8
Bulgaria	368.3	414.9	383.4
China, People's Republic	461.7	475.0	492.9
Denmark	381.6	399.0	415.0
Egypt	617.7	456.9	375.0
Finland	224.2	231.2	321.6
France	2,280.4	2,393.2	2,500.6
Germany	4,147.0	3,800.4	4,410.0
Iran	500.0	510.2	609.5
Italy	4,973.3	4,540.1	4,688.7
Japan	909.8	879.3	929.6
Korea, Republic	635.4	505.8	594.3
Netherlands	1,821.2	1,671.3	1,821.2
Russia	694.2	632.6	488.1
Saudi Arabia	390.5	495.2	456.6
Spain	978.3	946.5	1,054.6
Sweden	415.0	461.0	575.5
Switzerland	474.8	475.1	472.3
Turkey	231.3	295.7	362.6
United Kingdom	1,921.6	1,748.2	1,846.7
USA	940.8	921.4	1,138.9
Total (incl. others)	28,418.9	26,970.6	28,753.6

Exports f.o.b.	1996	1997	1998
Albania	322.9	251.8	192.6
Austria	151.3	121.2	129.2
Belgium-Luxembourg	183.4	174.7	163.8
Bulgaria	312.1	319.7	440.7
Cyprus	417.0	371.4	410.0
Egypt	86.9	104.0	117.1
France	598.5	483.9	496.6
Germany	2,207.2	2,078.9	1,981.8
Gibraltar	123.0	79.4	32.7
Israel	128.8	130.2	122.8
Italy	1,597.8	1,425.4	1,276.7
Lebanon	189.7	107.3	113.0
Macedonia, former Yugoslav Republic	232.1	273.4	260.1
Malta	110.6	111.7	105.0
Netherlands	304.8	280.5	324.5
Romania	173.8	176.6	218.5
Russia	360.5	419.8	267.9
Spain	380.5	226.0	285.2
Sweden	142.3	139.8	142.9
Turkey	354.0	437.1	338.1
Ukraine	138.5	130.6	80.0
United Kingdom	706.4	719.7	722.9
USA	454.8	488.8	479.9
Yugoslavia	168.5	202.8	187.0
Total (incl. others)	11,879.6	11,167.0	10,765.1

* Imports by country of first consignment; exports by country of consumption.

Source: UN, *International Trade Statistics Yearbook.*

Transport

RAILWAYS (estimated traffic)

	1996	1997	1998
Passenger-kilometres (million)	1,752	1,783	1,559
Net ton-kilometres (million)	350	330	399

ROAD TRAFFIC (motor vehicles in use at 31 December)

	1996	1997	1998
Passenger cars	2,339,421	2,500,099	2,675,676
Buses and coaches	25,096	25,622	26,320
Goods vehicles	914,827	951,785	987,357
Motorcycles	517,890	570,965	633,765

SHIPPING

Merchant fleet (at 1 July)

	1996		1997	
	Vessels	Gross reg. tons	Vessels	Gross reg. tons
Cargo boats	823	14,691,256	667	11,830,912
Passenger boats	521	1,028,624	524	1,099,670
Tankers	425	14,753,083	398	12,679,572
Others	340	101,738	338	97,920

1998 (at 31 December): 1,545 vessels; 25,224,543 gross registered tons (Source: Lloyd's Register of Shipping, *World Fleet Statistics*).

Freight traffic

	1994	1995	1996
Vessels entered ('000 net reg. tons)	68,785	73,059	87,867
Goods loaded ('000 metric tons)*	21,087	21,940	21,356
Goods unloaded ('000 metric tons)*	33,048	38,573	38,549

* International sea-borne shipping.

CIVIL AVIATION
(domestic and foreign flights of Olympic Airways)

	1996	1997	1998
Kilometres flown ('000) . .	65,847	68,415	67,606
Passenger-kilometres ('000) .	8,533,168	9,260,651	8,561,153
Freight ton-kilometres ('000) .	118,738	129,100	112,615
Mail ton-kilometres ('000) . .	12,669	14,662	20,265

Tourism

	1996	1997	1998
Number of visitors* . . .	9,233,295	10,070,325	10,916,046
Receipts (US $ million) . .	3,723.1	3,770.6	5,186.0

* Including cruise passengers.

Source: partly World Tourism Organization, *Yearbook of Tourism Statistics*.

TOURISTS BY COUNTRY OF ORIGIN
(foreign citizens, excluding cruise passengers)

Country	1996	1997	1998
Austria	359,604	388,118	450,195
Belgium-Luxembourg . .	213,567	229,310	273,674
Denmark	298,959	344,261	292,532
France	462,732	426,678	486,201
Germany	1,907,863	1,994,670	2,136,515
Italy	491,081	533,303	659,688
Netherlands	452,179	464,144	548,339
Sweden	448,257	472,481	467,617
Switzerland	256,425	295,731	289,387
United Kingdom	1,687,999	1,711,942	2,044,243
USA	222,130	240,555	219,362
Yugoslavia (former) . . .	231,496	198,999	201,633
Total (incl. others) . . .	9,233,295	10,070,325	10,916,046

Communications Media

	1995	1996	1997
Radio receivers ('000 in use) . .	4,389	4,424	4,481
Television receivers ('000 in use) .	2,223	2,289	2,357
Telephones ('000 main lines in use)	5,163	5,329	5,431
Telefax stations in use (estimates)*	30,000	40,000	n.a.
Mobile cellular telephones (subscribers)*	273,000	550,000	937,700
Daily newspapers			
Number	132	140	122
Average circulation ('000 copies)	1,423	1,516	1,389

1998: Telephones ('000 main lines in use) 5,536.
Books* (titles published): 4,225 in 1996.

* Sources: UN, *Statistical Yearbook*, and UNESCO, *Statistical Yearbook*.

Education

(1997/98)

	Institutions	Teachers	Students
Pre-primary	5,700	8,785	139,987
Primary	6,695	45,814	646,528
Secondary:			
General	3,205	52,508	664,190
Technical, vocational and ecclesiastical .	640	13,249	154,756
Higher:			
Universities	18	9,472	110,621
Technical	14	6,009	57,678
Vocational and ecclesiastical .	n.a.	560	4,260

Directory

The Constitution

A new Constitution for the Hellenic Republic came into force on 11 June 1975. The main provisions of this Constitution, as subsequently amended, are summarized below.

Greece shall be a parliamentary democracy with a President as Head of State. All powers are derived from the people and exist for the benefit of the people. The established religion is that of The Eastern Orthodox Church of Christ.

EXECUTIVE AND LEGISLATIVE

The President

In March 1986 a series of amendments to the Constitution was approved by a majority vote of Parliament, which relieved the President of his executive power and transferred such power to the legislature, thus confining the Head of State to a largely ceremonial role.

The President is elected by Parliament for a period of five years. The re-election of the same person shall be permitted only once. The President represents the State in relations with other nations, is Supreme Commander of the armed forces and may declare war and conclude treaties. The President shall appoint the Prime Minister and, on the Prime Minister's recommendation, the other members of the Government. The President shall convoke Parliament once every year and in extraordinary session whenever he deems it reasonable. In exceptional circumstances the President may preside over the Cabinet, convene the Council of the Republic, and suspend Parliament for a period not exceeding 30 days. In accordance with the amendment of March 1986, the President was deprived of the right to dismiss the Prime Minister, his power to call a referendum was limited, and the right to declare a state of emergency was transferred to Parliament. The President can now dissolve Parliament only if the resignation of two Governments in quick succession demonstrates the absence of political stability. If no party has a majority in Parliament, the President must offer an opportunity to form a government to the leader of each of the four biggest parties in turn, strictly following the order of their parliamentary strengths. If no party leader is able to form a government, the President may try to assemble an all-party government; failing that, the President must appoint a caretaker cabinet, led by a senior judge, to hold office until a fresh election takes place. The Constitution continues to reserve a substantial moderating role for the President, however, in that he retains the right to object to legislation and may request Parliament to reconsider it or to approve it with an enlarged majority.

The Government

The Government consists of the Cabinet which comprises the Prime Minister and Ministers. The Government determines and directs the general policy of the State in accordance with the Constitution and the laws. The Cabinet must enjoy the confidence of Parliament and may be removed by a vote of no confidence. The Prime Minister is to be the leader of the party with an absolute majority in Parliament, or, if no such party exists, the leader of the party with a relative majority.

The Council of the Republic

The Council of the Republic shall be composed of all former democratic Presidents, the Prime Minister, the leader of the Opposition and the parliamentary Prime Ministers of governments which have enjoyed the confidence of Parliament, presided over by the President. It shall meet when the largest parties are unable to form a government with the confidence of Parliament and may empower the President to appoint a Prime Minister who may or may not be a member of Parliament. The Council may also authorize the President to dissolve Parliament.

Parliament

Parliament is to be unicameral and composed of not fewer than 200 and not more than 300 deputies elected by direct, universal and secret ballot for a term of four years. Parliament shall elect its own President, or Speaker. It must meet once a year for a regular session of at least five months. Bills passed by Parliament must be ratified by the President and the President's veto can be nullified by an absolute majority of the total number of deputies. Parliament may impeach the President by a motion signed by one-third and passed by two-thirds of the total number of deputies. Parliament is also empowered to impeach present or former members of the Government. In these cases the defendant shall be brought before an *ad hoc* tribunal presided over by the President of the Supreme Court

and composed of 12 judges. Certain legislative work, as specified in the Constitution, must be passed by Parliament in plenum, and Parliament cannot make a decision without an absolute majority of the members present, which under no circumstances shall be less than one-quarter of the total number of deputies. The Constitution provides for certain legislative powers to be exercised by not more than two Parliamentary Departments. Parliament may revise the Constitution in accordance with the procedure laid down in the Constitution.

THE JUDICIAL AUTHORITY

Justice is to be administered by courts of regular judges, who enjoy personal and functional independence. The President, after consultations with a judicial council, shall appoint the judges for life. The judges are subject only to the Constitution and the laws. Courts are divided into administrative, civil and penal and shall be organized by virtue of special laws. They must not apply laws which are contrary to the Constitution. The final jurisdiction in matters of judicial review rests with a Special Supreme Tribunal.

Certain laws, passed before the implementation of this Constitution and deemed not contrary to it, are to remain in force. Other specified laws, even if contrary to the Constitution, are to remain in force until repealed by further legislation.

INDIVIDUAL AND SPECIAL RIGHTS

All citizens are equal under the Constitution and before the law, having the same rights and obligations. No titles of nobility or distinction are to be conferred or recognized. All persons are to enjoy full protection of life, honour and freedom, irrespective of nationality, race, creed or political allegiance. Retrospective legislation is prohibited and no citizen may be punished without due process of law. Freedom of speech, of the Press, of association and of religion are guaranteed under the Constitution. All persons have the right to a free education, which the state has the duty to provide. Work is a right and all workers, irrespective of sex or other distinction, are entitled to equal remuneration for rendering services of equal value. The right of peaceful assembly, the right of a person to property and the freedom to form political parties are guaranteed under the Constitution. The exercise of the right to vote by all citizens over 18 years of age is obligatory. No person may exercise his rights and liberties contrary to the Constitution.

MOUNT ATHOS

The district of Mount Athos shall, in accordance with its ancient privileged status, be a self-governing part of the Greek State and its sovereignty shall remain unaffected.

The Government

HEAD OF STATE

President: KONSTANTINOS STEFANOPOULOS (took office 10 March 1995; re-elected 9 February 2000).

THE CABINET
(March 2001)

Prime Minister: KONSTANTINOS (COSTAS) SIMITIS.

Minister of the Interior, Public Administration and Decentralization: VASILIKI (VASSO) PAPANDREOU.

Minister of National Defence: APOSTOLOS-ATHANASIOS (AKIS) TSOHATZOPOULOS.

Minister of Foreign Affairs: GEORGIOS PAPANDREOU.

Minister of the National Economy and of Finance: IOANNIS PAPANTONIOU.

Minister of Development: NIKOS CHRISTODOULAKIS.

Minister of the Environment, Physical Planning and Public Works: KONSTANTINOS (COSTAS) LALIOTIS.

Minister of Education and Religious Affairs: PETROS EPHTHIMIOU.

Minister of Agriculture: GEORGIOS ANOMERITIS.

Minister of Labour and Social Affairs: ATHANASIOS GIANNITSIS.

Minister of Health and Welfare: ALEKOS PAPADOPOULOS.

Minister of Justice: MICHALIS STATHOPOPUOLOS.

Minister of Culture: EVANGELOS VENIZELOS.

Minister of Merchant Marine: CHRISTOS PAPOUTSIS.

Minister of Public Order: MIKHAIL KHRISOKHOIDHIS.

Minister of Macedonia and Thrace: GEORGIOS PASCHALIDIS.

Minister of the Aegean: NIKOS SIFOUNAKIS.

Minister of Transport and Communications: CHRISTOS VERELIS.

Minister of Press and Mass Media: DIMITRIS REPPAS.

Minister of State: MILITIADES PAPAOIANNOU.

MINISTRIES

Office of the President: Odos Vas. Georgiou 7, 106 74 Athens; tel. (1) 7283111; fax (1) 7248938.

Office of the Prime Minister: Leoforos Vassilissis Sophias 15, 106 74 Athens; tel. (1) 3393502; fax (1) 3393500; e-mail mail@ primeminister.gr; internet www.primeminister.gr.

Ministry of the Aegean: Leoforos Syngrou 49, 117 43 Athens; tel. (1) 9225240; fax (1) 9216204; e-mail webmaster@ypai.aegean.gr; internet www.ypai.aegean.gr.

Ministry of Agriculture: Odos Acharnon 2–6, Athens; tel. (1) 5245587; fax (1) 5240475; e-mail webmaster@minagric.gr; internet www.minagr.gr.

Ministry of Culture: Odos Bouboulinas 20, 106 82 Athens; tel. (1) 8201637; fax (1) 8201373; e-mail w3admin@culture.gr; internet www.culture.gr.

Ministry of Development: Odos Mihalakopoulou 80, 115 28 Athens; tel. (1) 7708615; fax (1) 7788279.

Ministry of Education and Religious Affairs: Odos Metropoleos 15, 105 57 Athens; tel. (1) 3230461; fax (1) 3248264; e-mail edu_ref@ypepth.gr; internet www.ypepth.gr.

Ministry of the Environment, Physical Planning and Public Works: Odos Amaliados 17, 115 23 Athens; tel. (1) 6431461; fax (1) 6432589; e-mail minister@minenv.gr; internet www.minenv.gr.

Ministry of Finance: Odos Karageorgi Servias 10, 105 62 Athens; tel. (1) 8477116; fax (1) 3238657; e-mail gsis@di.uoia.gr; www.mof.glk.gr/.

Ministry of Foreign Affairs: Odos Zalokosta 2, 106 71 Athens; tel. (1) 3610581; fax (1) 3624195; e-mail mfa@mfa.gr; internet www.mfa.gr.

Ministry of Health and Welfare: Odos Aristotelous 17, 104 33 Athens; tel. (1) 5232820; fax (1) 5231707; e-mail info@ypyp.gr; internet www.health.gov.gr.

Ministry of the Interior, Public Administration and Decentralization: Odos Stadiou 27, 101 83 Athens; tel. (1) 3221915; fax (1) 3240631; e-mail kominatos@ypes.gr; internet www.ypes.gr.

Ministry of Justice: Odos Mesogeion 96, 115 27 Athens; tel. (1) 7751303; fax (1) 7759879.

Ministry of Labour and Social Affairs: Odos Pireos 40, 104 37 Athens; tel. (1) 5291111; fax (1) 5249805; e-mail postmaster@www .labor-ministry.gr; internet www.labor-ministry.gr.

Ministry of Macedonia and Thrace: Aghiou Dimitriou Str., 541 23 Thessaloníki; tel. (31) 264321; fax (31) 263332; e-mail webmaster@ mathra.gr; internet www.mathra.gr/.

Ministry of Merchant Marine: Odos Gregoriou Lambraki 150, Piraeus; tel. (1) 4121211; fax (1) 4134286; e-mail yen@yen.gr.

Ministry of National Defence: Stratopedo Papagou, Holargos, Athens; tel. (1) 6552001; fax (1) 6443832; e-mail epyetha@mod.gr; internet www.mod.gr.

Ministry of National Economy: Plateia Syntagmatos, 105 63 Athens; tel. (1) 3230931; fax (1) 3232218; e-mail info@ypetho.gr.

Ministry of Press and Mass Media: Odos Zalokosta 10, 106 71 Athens; tel. (1) 3630911; fax (1) 3609682; e-mail press01@otenet.gr; internet www.minpress.gr.

Ministry of Public Order: P. Khanellopoulou 4, 101 77 Athens; tel. (1) 6928510; fax (1) 6921675; e-mail ydt@otenet.gr; internet www.ydt.gr.

Ministry of Transport and Communications: Odos Xenofontos 13, 101 91 Athens; tel. (1) 3251211; fax (1) 3239039; e-mail yme@ otenet.gr.

Legislature

VOULI

Parliament: Parliament Bldg, Syntagma Sq., 101 80 Athens; tel. (1) 3288434; fax (1) 3310013; e-mail www.parliament.gr/en/ contact.htm; internet www.parliament.gr.

President of Parliament: APOSTOLOS KAKLAMANIS.

General Election, 9 April 2000

	Seats	Percentage of Votes
Panhellenic Socialist Movement (PASOK)	158	43.8
New Democracy (ND)	125	42.7
Communist Party (KKE)	11	5.2
Coalition of the Left and Progress	6	3.2
Democratic Social Movement (DHKKI)	—	2.7
Others	—	2.4
Total	**300**	**100.0**

Political Organizations

Coalition of the Left and Progress (Synaspismos): Pl. Elefthrias 1, 10553 Athens; tel. (1) 3378400; fax (1) 3217003; internet www.syn.gr; f. 1989 as an alliance of the nine political groups comprising the Greek Left Party and the Communist Party of Greece ('of the Exterior'); in 1991 the hard-line conservative faction of the Communist Party withdrew from the alliance; however, the Coalition continued to command considerable support from the large reformist faction of the KKE; transformed into a single party in 1992; Pres. NIKOS KONSTANTOPOULOS.

Communist Party of Greece (KKE) (Kommunistiko Komma Ellados): Leoforos Irakliou 145, Perissos, 142 31 Athens; tel. (1) 2592111; fax (1) 2592286; internet www.kke.gr/; f. 1918; banned 1947, reappeared 1974; Gen. Sec. ALEKA PAPARIGA.

Democratic Social Movement (DIKKI): Odos Halkokondili 9, 106 77 Athens; tel. (1) 3829051; fax (1) 3839047; e-mail dikki@otenet.gr; internet www.dikki.gr/; f. 1995; leftist party; opposes further integration with the EU; Leader DIMITRIS TSOVOLAS.

Democratic Socialist Party (KODISO): Odos Mavromichali 9, 106 79 Athens; tel. (1) 3602716; fax (1) 3625901; f. 1979 by former EDIK deputies; favours membership of the EU and political wing of NATO, decentralization and a mixed economy; Pres. CH. PROTOPAPAS.

Greek National Political Union (EPEN): Athens; tel. (1) 3643760; fax (1) 8943100; f. 1984; right-wing; Leader CHRYSSANTHOS DIMITRIADIS.

Hellenic Liberal Party: Athens; tel. (1) 3606111; f. 1910; aims to revive political heritage of fmr Prime Minister, Eleftherios Venizelos; 6,500 mems; Pres. NIKITAS VENIZELOS.

Liberal Party: Athens; f. 1999; Founder STEFANOS MANOS.

New Democracy Party (ND) (Nea Dimokratia): Odos Rigillis 18, 106 74 Athens; tel. (1) 7290071; fax (1) 7214327; e-mail valinak@ otenet.gr; internet www.nd.gr; f. 1974 by Konstantinos Karamanlis; a broadly-based centre-right party which advocates social reform in the framework of a liberal economy; supports European integration and enlargement; led and completed Greece's accession into the EU; Pres. Dr KONSTANTINOS AL. KARAMANLIS; Dir-Gen. IOANNIS VARTHOLOMEOS.

Panhellenic Socialist Movement (PASOK) (Panellinion Socialistikon Kinima): Odos Charilaou Trikoupi 50, Athens; tel. (1) 3232049; internet www.pasok.gr; f. 1974; incorporates Democratic Defence and Panhellenic Liberation Movement resistance organizations; supports social welfare, decentralization and self-management, aims at a Mediterranean socialist development through international cooperation; 500 local organizations, 30,000 mems; Leader KONSTANTINOS (COSTAS) SIMITIS; Sec.-Gen. KONSTANTINOS SKANDALIDES.

Political Spring (POLAN) (Politiki Anixi): Odos Aiolou 11, 105 55 Athens; tel. (1) 3254355-9; fax (1) 3249429; internet www .politikianixi.gr; f. 1993; centre-right; Leader ANTONIS SAMARAS.

Union of Democratic Centre Party (EDIK) (Enossi Dimokratikou Kentrou): Odos Charilaou Trikoupi 18, 106 79 Athens; tel. (1) 3612792; fax (1) 3634412; e-mail edik@edik.gr; internet www.edik.gr; f. 1974; democratic socialist party, merging Centre Union (f. 1961 by Georgios Papandreou) and New Political Forces (f. 1974 by Prof. Ioannis Pesmazoglou and Prof. G. A. Mangakis); favours a united Europe; Chair. Prof. NEOKLIS SARRIS.

Other parties include the People's Militant Unity Party (f. 1985 by PASOK splinter group), the Progressive Party (f. 1979, right-wing), the (Maoist) Revolutionary Communist Party of Greece (EKKE), the Panhellenic Unaligned Party of Equality (PAKI, f. 1988; Leader KHARALAMBOS ALOMA TAMONTSIDES), Olympianism Party (pacifist, Leader GIORGIOS ZOE), and the left-wing United Socialist Alliance of Greece (ESPE, f. 1984).

Dissident organizations include the left-wing 17 November Revolutionary Organization (f. 1975; opposed to Western capitalism and the continuing existence of US military bases in Greece), the 1 May Revolutionary Organization, the Revolutionary People's Struggle (ELA), People's Revolutionary Solidarity, the Anti-State Struggle group, the Christos Tsoutsouvis Revolutionary Organization, the Revolutionary Praxis, Fighting Guerilla Faction and Autonomous Cells of Rebel Action.

Diplomatic Representation

EMBASSIES IN GREECE

Albania: Odos Karachristou 1, Kolonaki, 115 21 Athens; tel. (1) 7234412; fax (1) 7231972; Ambassador: KASTRIOT ROBO.

Algeria: Leoforos Vassileos Konstantinou 14, 116 35 Athens; tel. (1) 7564191; fax (1) 7018681; e-mail ambdzath@otenet.gr; Ambassador: KAMEL HOUHOU.

Argentina: Leoforos Vassilissis Sofias 59, Athens; tel. (1) 7224753; fax (1) 7227568; Ambassador: JORGE DE BELAUSTEGUI.

Armenia: Leoforos Sygrou 159, 171 21 Athens; tel. (1) 9345727; fax (1) 9318100; e-mail armemb@hol.gr; Ambassador: ARMEN PETROSSIAN.

Australia: Odos Dimitriou Soutsou 37/Odos Tsoha, Athens; tel. (1) 6447303; e-mail ausembgr@hol.gr; internet www.ausemb.gr; Ambassador: ROSS BURNS.

Austria: Leoforos Alexandras 26, 106 83 Athens; tel. (1) 8257230; fax (1) 8219823; e-mail austria@ath.forthnet.gr; Ambassador: Dr RENÉ POLLITZER.

Belgium: Odos Sekeri 3, 106 71 Athens; tel. (1) 3617886; fax (1) 3604289; e-mail athens@diplobel.org; Ambassador: CLAUDE RIJMENANS.

Brazil: Plateia Philikis Etairias 14, 106 73 Athens; tel. (1) 7213039; Ambassador: ALCIDES DA COSTA GUIMARÃES FILHO.

Bulgaria: Odos Stratigou Kallari 33A, Palaio Psychiko, 154 52 Athens; tel. (1) 6478105; fax (1) 6478130; Ambassador: BRANIMIR PETROV.

Canada: Odos Ioannou Ghennadiou 4, 115 21 Athens; tel. (1) 7254011; Ambassador: DEREK R. T. FRASER.

Chile: Leoforos Vasilissis Sofias 25, 106 74 Athens; tel. (1) 7252574; fax (1) 7252536; e-mail embachilegr@ath.forthnet.gr; Ambassador: MARCIA COVARRUBIAS.

China, People's Republic: Odos Krinon 2A, Paleo Psychiko, 154 52 Athens; tel. (1) 6723282; fax (1) 6723819; Ambassador: ZHEN JIANGUO.

Colombia: Vrasida 3, 115 28 Athens; tel. (1) 7236848; fax (1) 7246270; Ambassador: ENRIQUE GAVIRIA-LIEVANO.

Congo, Democratic Republic: Athens; tel. (1) 6847013; Ambassador: BOMOLO LOKOKA.

Cuba: Odos Sofokleou 5, Filothei, 152 37 Athens; tel. (1) 6842807; fax (1) 6849590; Ambassador: ANA MARÍA GONZÁLEZ SUÁREZ.

Cyprus: Odos Herodotou 16, 106 75 Athens; tel. (1) 7232727; fax (1) 7231927; Ambassador: KHARALAMBOS CHRISTOFOROU.

Czech Republic: Odos Georgiou Seferis 6, Palaio Psychiko, 154 52 Athens; tel. (1) 6713755; fax (1) 6710675; e-mail athens@embassy.mzv.cz; Ambassador: VLADIMÍR ZAVÁZAL.

Denmark: Leoforos Vassilissis Sofias 11, 106 71 Athens; tel. (1) 3608315; fax (1) 3636163; e-mail athamb@athamb.um.dk; Ambassador: HANS GRUNNET.

Egypt: Leoforos Vassilissis Sofias 3, 106 71 Athens; tel. (1) 3618612; fax (1) 3603538; e-mail emthens@hol.gr; Ambassador: MOHAMED EL-AMIR KHALIL.

Estonia: Patriarchou Ioakeim 48, 106 76 Athens; tel. (1) 7229803; fax (1) 7229804; e-mail estemb@otenet.gr; Chargé d'affaires a.i.: KATRIN KANARIK.

Finland: Odos Eratosthenous 1, 116 35 Athens; tel. (1) 7010444; Ambassador: ARTO TANNER.

France: Leoforos Vassilissis Sofias 7, 106 71 Athens; tel. (1) 3391000; fax (1) 3391009; e-mail ambafran@hol.gr; internet www.ambafran.gr; Ambassador: JEAN-MAURICE RIPERT.

Georgia: Odos Agiou Dimitriou 24, 154 52 Paleo Psihio, Athens; tel. (1) 6716737; fax (1) 6716722; Ambassador: ALEKSANDRE CHIKVAIDZE.

Germany: Odos Karaoli and Dimitriou 3, 106 75 Athens; tel. (1) 7285111; fax (1) 7251205; e-mail boathens@compulink.gr; internet www.germanembassy.gr; Ambassador: KARL-HEINZ ALBERT KUHNA.

Holy See: POB 65075, Odos Mavili 2, Palaio Psychiko, 154 52 Athens; tel. (1) 6743598; fax (1) 6742849; e-mail nunate@mail .otenet.gr; Apostolic Nuncio: Most Rev. PAUL FOUAD TABET, Titular Archbishop of Sinna.

Honduras: Piraeus; tel. (1) 4118850; fax (1) 4116105; Chargé d'affaires a.i.: TEODOLINDA BANEGAS DE MAKRIS.

Hungary: Odos Kalvou 16, Palaio Psychiko, 154 52 Athens; tel. (1) 6725337; Ambassador: ISTVÁN PATAKI.

India: Odos Kleanthous 3, 106 74 Athens; tel. (1) 7216227; fax (1) 7211252; Ambassador: AFTAB SETH.

Indonesia: Odos Papanastasidu 55, Palaio Psychiko, 154 52 Athens; tel. (1) 6712737; Ambassador: SAMSUBAHRI SIREGAR.

Iran: Odos Kalari 16, Palaio Psychiko, Athens; tel. (1) 6471436; Ambassador: MAHDI KHANDAGH ABADI.

Iraq: Odos Mazaraki 4, Palaio Psychiko, Athens; tel. (1) 6715012; Ambassador: FETAH AL-KHEZREJI.

Ireland: Leoforos Vassileos Konstantinou 7, Athens; tel. (1) 7232771; fax (1) 7240217; Ambassador: EAMON RYAN.

Israel: Odos Marathonodromou 1, Palaio Psychiko, 154 52 Athens; tel. (1) 6719530; fax (1) 6479510; Ambassador: DAVID SASSON.

Italy: Odos Sekeri 2, 106 74 Athens; tel. (1) 3617260; fax (1) 3617330; Ambassador: ENRICO PIETROMARCHI.

Japan: 21st Floor, Athens A Tower, Leoforos Messoghion 2–4, Pirgas Athinon, 115 27 Athens; tel. (1) 7758101; fax (1) 7758206; Ambassador: MOTOI OKUBO.

Jordan: Odos Panagi Zervou 30, Palaio Psychiko, 154 10 Athens; tel. (1) 6474161; fax (1) 6470578; Ambassador: AMJAD MAJALI.

Korea, Republic: Odos Eratosthenous 1, 116 35 Athens; tel. (1) 7012122; Ambassador: NAM KYUN PARK.

Kuwait: Odos Marathonodromou 27, Palaio Psychiko, 154 52 Athens; tel. (1) 6473593; fax (1) 6875875; Ambassador: ALI FAHED AZ-ZAID.

Lebanon: 6, Odos Maritou 25, Palaio Psychiko, 154 52 Athens; tel. (1) 6755873; fax (1) 6755612; e-mail grlibemb@otenet.gr; Ambassador: WILLIAM HABIB.

Libya: Odos Vironos 13, Palaio Psychiko, 154 52 Athens; tel. (1) 6472120; Secretary of the People's Bureau: AYAD M. TAYARI.

Mexico: Plateia Philikis Etairias 14, 106 73 Athens; tel. (1) 7294780; fax (1) 7294783; e-mail embamex2@compulink.gr; Ambassador: ARIEL BUIRA.

Morocco: Odos Mousson 14, Palaio Psychiko, 154 52 Athens; tel. (1) 6744209; fax (1) 6749480; Ambassador: NOUREDDINE SEFIANI.

Netherlands: Leoforos Vassileos Konstantinou 5–7, 106 74 Athens; tel. (1) 7239701; fax (1) 7248900; e-mail nlgovath@dutchembassy.gr; internet www.dutchembassy.gr/; Ambassador: P. R. BROUWER.

New Zealand: Leoforos Kifissias 268, 152 32 Halandri, Athens; tel. (1) 6874700; fax (1) 6874444; e-mail costas.cotsilinis@gr.pwcglobal .com; Ambassador: PETER BENNETT.

Norway: Leoforos Vassilissis Sofias 23, 106 74 Athens; tel. (1) 7246173; fax (1) 7244989; e-mail norwemba@netplan.gr; Ambassador: JAN WESSEL HEGG.

Pakistan: Odos Loukianou 6, Kolonaki, 106 75 Athens; tel. (1) 7290122; fax (1) 7247231; Ambassador: AMIN JAN NAIM.

Peru: Leoforos Vassilissis Sofias 105, Athens; tel. (1) 6411221; fax (1) 6411321; Ambassador: MARTÍN YRIGOYEN-YRIGOYEN.

Poland: Odos Chryssanthemon 22, Palaio Psychiko, 154 52 Athens; tel. (1) 6716917; Ambassador: JANUSZ LEWANDOWSKI.

Portugal: Leoforos Vassilissis Sofias 23, 106 74 Athens; tel. (1) 7290096; fax (1) 7245122; e-mail embportg@otenet.gr; Ambassador: ANTÓNIO SYDER SANTIAGO.

Romania: Odos Emmanuel Benaki 7, Palaio Psychiko, Athens; tel. (1) 6728875; fax (1) 6728883; Ambassador: DAN RĂDULESCU.

Russia: Odos Nikiforou Litra 28, Palaio Psychiko, Athens; tel. (1) 6725235; Ambassador: MICHAEL BOTCHARNIKOV.

Saudi Arabia: Odos Marathonodromou 71, Palaio Psychiko, 154 52 Athens; tel. (1) 6716911; Ambassador: Sheikh ABDULLAH ABDUL-RAHMAN AL-MALHOOQ.

Slovakia: Odos Georgiou Seferis 4, Palaio Psychiko, 154 52 Athens; tel. (1) 6776757; fax (1) 6776760; e-mail zuateny@compulink.gr; Ambassador: MILAN DUBČEK.

South Africa: Leoforos Kifissias 60, 151 25 Athens; tel. (1) 6106645; fax (1) 6106640; e-mail embassy@southafrica.gr; internet www .southafrica.gr; Ambassador: DAVID JACOBS.

Spain: Odos D. Areapagitou 21, 117 42 Athens; tel. (1) 9213123; fax (1) 9214264; e-mail emb-esp@otenet.gr; Ambassador: JAVIER JIMÉNEZ-UGARTE.

Sweden: Leoforos Vassileos Konstantinou 7, 106 74 Athens; tel. (1) 7290421; fax (1) 7229953; e-mail ambassaden.athens@foreign .ministry.se; Ambassador: BJÖRN ELMÉR.

Switzerland: Odos Iassiou 2, 115 21 Athens; tel. (1) 7230364; Ambassador: CHARLES STEINHÄUSLIN.

Syria: Odos Marathonodromou 79, Palaio Psychiko, Athens; tel. (1) 6725577; Ambassador: SHAHIN FARAH.

Thailand: Odos Taigetou 23, Palaio Psychiko, 154 52 Athens; tel. (1) 6717969; fax (1) 6479508; Ambassador: SUKHUM RASMIDATTA.

Tunisia: Odos Anthéon 2, Palaio Psychiko, 154 52 Athens; tel. (1) 6717590; fax (1) 6713432; e-mail tunisie@otenet.gr; Ambassador: ALI HACHANI.

Turkey: Odos Vassileos Gheorghiou B 8, 106 74 Athens; tel. (1) 7245915; fax (1) 7229597; e-mail turkembgr@hol.gr; Ambassador: ALI TUYGAN.

Ukraine: Odos Stefanu Delta 2–4, 152 37 Athens; tel. (1) 6718957; fax (1) 6855363.

United Kingdom: Odos Ploutarchou 1, 106 75 Athens; tel. (1) 7272600; fax (1) 7272734; e-mail britania@hol.gr; internet www .british-embassy.gr; Ambassador: DAVID MADDEN.

USA: Leoforos Vassilissis Sofias 91, 106 60 Athens; tel. (1) 7212951; fax (1) 7226724; internet www.usembassy.gr; Ambassador: R. NICH-OLAS BURNS.

Uruguay: Odos Likavitou I G, 106 72 Athens; tel. (1) 3613549; Ambassador: ULYSSES PEREIRA REVERBEL.

Venezuela: Athens; tel. (1) 7708769; Ambassador: OLGA LUCILA CAR-MONA.

Yugoslavia: Leoforos Vassilissis Sofias 106, Athens; tel. (1) 7774344; Ambassador: DRAGMIR VUČIĆEVIĆ.

Judicial System

The Constitution of 1975 provides for the establishment of a Special Supreme Tribunal. Other provisions in the Constitution provided for a reorganization of parts of the judicial system to be accomplished through legislation.

SUPREME ADMINISTRATIVE COURTS

Special Supreme Tribunal: Odos Patision 30, Athens; has final jurisdiction in matters of constitutionality.

Council of State: Odos Panepistimiou 47, 105 64 Athens; tel. (1) 3223830; fax (1) 3231154; has appellate powers over acts of the administration and final rulings of administrative courts; has power to rule upon matters of judicial review of laws.

President: VASSILIS BOTOPOULOS.

SUPREME JUDICIAL COURT

Supreme Civil and Penal Court: Leoforos Alexandros 121, 115 22 Athens; tel. (1) 6411506; fax (1) 6433799; e-mail areios@otenet.gr; supreme court in the State, having also appellate powers; consists of six sections, four Civil and two Penal, and adjudicates in quorum.

President: STEPHANOS MATHIAS.

COURTS OF APPEAL

There are 12 Courts of Appeal with jurisdiction in cases of Civil and Penal Law of second degree, and, in exceptional penal cases, of first degree.

COURTS OF FIRST INSTANCE

There are 59 Courts of First Instance with jurisdiction in cases of first degree, and in exceptional cases, of second degree. They function both as Courts of First Instance and as Criminal Courts. For serious crimes the Criminal Courts function with a jury.

In towns where Courts of First Instance sit there are also Juvenile Courts. Commercial Tribunals do not function in Greece, and all commercial cases are tried by ordinary courts of law. There are, however, Tax Courts in some towns.

OTHER COURTS

There are 360 Courts of the Justice of Peace throughout the country. There are 48 Magistrates' Courts (or simple Police Courts).

In all the above courts, except those of the Justice of Peace, there are District Attorneys. In Courts of the Justice of Peace the duties of District Attorney are performed by the Public Prosecutor.

Religion

CHRISTIANITY

The Eastern Orthodox Church

The Orthodox Church of Greece: Odos Ioannou Gennadiou 14, 115 21 Athens; tel. (1) 7218381; f. 1850; 78 dioceses, 8,335 priests, 84 bishops, 9,025,000 adherents (1985).

The Greek branch of the Holy Eastern Orthodox Church is the officially established religion of the country, to which nearly 97% of the population profess adherence. The administrative body of the Church is the Holy Synod of 12 members, elected by the bishops of the Hierarchy.

Primate of Greece: Archbishop CHRISTODOULOS of Athens.

Within the Greek State there is also the semi-autonomous Church of Crete, composed of seven Metropolitans and the Holy Archbishopric of Crete. The Church is administered by a Synod consisting of the seven Metropolitans under the Presidency of the Archbishop; it is under the spiritual jurisdiction of the Oecumenical Patriarchate of Constantinople, which also maintains a degree of administrative control.

Archbishop of Crete: Archbishop TIMOTHEOS (whose See is in Heraklion).

There are also four Metropolitan Sees of the Dodecanese, which are spiritually and administratively dependent on the Oecumenical Patriarchate and, finally, the peninsula of Athos, which constitutes the region of the Holy Mountain (Mount Athos) and comprises 20 monasteries. These are dependent on the Oecumenical Patriarchate of Constantinople, but are autonomous and are safeguarded constitutionally.

The Roman Catholic Church

Latin Rite

Greece comprises four archdioceses (including two directly responsible to the Holy See), four dioceses and one Apostolic Vicariate. At December 1998 there were an estimated 56,038 adherents in the country.

Bishop's Conference: Conferentia Episcopalis Graeciae, Odos Homirou 9, 106 72 Athens; tel. (1) 3624311; fax (1) 3618632; f. 1967; Pres. Most Rev. NIKOLAOS FÓSKOLOS, Archbishop of Athens.

Archdiocese of Athens: Archbishopric, Odos Homirou 9, 106 72 Athens; tel. (1) 3624311; fax (1) 3618632; Archbishop Most Rev. NIKOLAOS FÓSKOLOS.

Archdiocese of Rhodes: Archbishopric, Odos I. Dragoumi 5A, 851 00 Rhodes; tel. (241) 21845; fax (241) 26688; Apostolic Administrator Most Rev. NIKOLAOS FÓSKOLOS (Archbishop of Athens).

Metropolitan Archdiocese of Corfu, Zante and Cefalonia: Archbishopric, Montzenikhov 3, 491 00 Kerkyra; tel. and fax (661) 30277; Archbishop Mgr ANTONIOS VARTHALITIS.

Metropolitan Archdiocese of Naxos, Andros, Tinos and Mykonos: Archbishopric, 842 00 Tinos; tel. (283) 22382; fax (283) 24769; e-mail karcntam@thn.forthnet.gr; also responsible for the suffragan diocese of Chios; Archbishop Mgr NIKOLAOS PRINTESIS

Apostolic Vicariate of Salonika (Thessaloníki): Leoforos Vassilissis Olgas 120A, 546 45 Thessaloníki; tel. (31) 835780; Apostolic Administrator Archbishop Mgr VARTHALITIS of Corfu.

Byzantine Rite

Apostolic Exarchate for the Byzantine Rite in Greece: Odos Akarnon 246, 112 53 Athens; tel. (1) 8670170; fax (1) 8677039; e-mail pliarion@hol.gr; 2 parishes (Athens and Jannitsa, Macedonia); 7 secular priests, 2,300 adherents (Dec. 1997); Exarch Apostolic Mgr ANARGHYROS PRINTESIS, Titular Bishop of Gratianopolis.

Armenian Rite

Exarchate for the Armenian Catholics in Greece: Odos René Piot 2, 117 44 Athens; tel. (1) 9014089; fax (1) 9012109; 600 adherents (Dec. 1997); Exarch Archpriest NICHAN KARAKEHEYAN.

Protestant Church

Greek Evangelical Church (Reformed): Odos Markon Botsari 24, 117 41 Athens; tel. (1) 9222684; e-mail info@gec.gr; internet www.gec.gr; f. 1858; comprises 30 organized churches; 5,000 adherents (1996); Moderator Rev. JOANNIS YPHANTIDES.

ISLAM

The law provides as religious head of the Muslims a Chief Mufti; the Muslims in Greece possess a number of mosques and schools.

JUDAISM

The Jewish population of Greece, estimated in 1943 at 75,000 people, was severely reduced as a result of the German occupation. In 1994 there were about 5,000 Jews in Greece.

Central Board of the Jewish Communities of Greece: Odos Voulis 36, 105 57 Athens; tel. (1) 3244315; fax (1) 3313852; e-mail hhkis@hellasnet.gr; f. 1945; officially recognized representative body of the communities of Greece; Pres. MOSES KONSTANTINIS.

Jewish Community of Athens: Odos Melidoni 8, 105 53 Athens; tel. (1) 3252823; fax (1) 3220761; e-mail isrkath@hellasnet.gr; Rabbi JACOB D. ARAR.

Jewish Community of Larissa: Odos Kentavrou 27, Larissa; tel. (41) 220762; Rabbi ÉLIE SABETAI.

Jewish Community of Thessaloníki: Odos Tsimiski 24, 546 24 Thessaloníki; tel. (31) 275701; e-mail jct1@compulink.gr; Pres. ANDREAS SEFIHA; Rabbi ITZHAK DAYAN.

The Press

PRINCIPAL DAILY NEWSPAPERS

Morning papers are not published on Mondays, nor afternoon papers on Sundays. Afternoon papers are more popular than morning ones; in 1990 about 73,644 papers were sold each morning and up to 784,474 each afternoon.

Athens

Acropolis: Leoforos Ionias 166, 111 44 Athens; tel. (1) 2114594; fax (1) 2114594; f. 1881; morning; Independent-Conservative; Acropolis

Publications SA; Publr G. LEVIDES; Dir MARNIS SKOUNDRIDAKIS; circ. 50,819.

Apogevmatini (The Afternoon): Odos Phidiou 12, 106 78 Athens; tel. (1) 6430011; fax (1) 3609876; f. 1956; independent; Publr GEORGIOS HATZIKONSTANTINOU; Editor P. KARAYANNIS; circ. 67,257.

Athens Daily Post: Odos Stadiou 57, Athens; tel. (1) 3249504; f. 1952; morning; English; Owner G. SKOURAS.

Athens News: Odos Christou Lada 3, 102 37 Athens; tel. (1) 3333161; fax (1) 3231384; e-mail athnews@dolnet.gr; internet athensnews.dolnet.gr; f. 1952; morning; English; Publr CHRISTOS D. LAMBRAKIS; circ. 6,500.

Athlitiki Icho (Athletics Echo): Odos Aristonos 5-7, 104 41 Athens; tel. (1) 5232201; fax (1) 5232433; f. 1945; morning; Editor K. GEORGALAS; circ. 40,000.

Avgi (Dawn): Odos Ag. Konstantiou 12, 104 31 Athens; tel. (1) 5231831; fax (1) 5231830; e-mail editors@telephos.gr; internet www.avgi.org/nea-avgi/main_page.asp; f. 1952; morning; independent newspaper of the left; Dir and Editor L. VOUTSAS; circ. 5,400.

Avriani (Tomorrow): Odos Dimitros 11, 177 78 Athens; tel. (1) 3424090; fax (1) 3452190; f. 1980; evening; Publr GEORGE KOURIS; circ. 51,317.

Dimokratikos Logos (Democratic Speech): Odos Dimitros 11, 177 78 Athens; tel. (1) 3424023; fax (1) 3452190; f. 1986; morning; Dir and Editor KOSTAS GERONIKOLOS; circ. 7,183.

Eleftheri Ora: Odos Akademias 32, 106 72 Athens; tel. (1) 3621868; fax (1) 3603258; f. 1981; evening; Editor G. MIHALOPOULOS; circ. 1,026.

Eleftheros Typos (Free Press): Iroos Matsi, Ano Kalamaki, Athens; tel. (1) 9942431; f. 1983; evening; Dir and Editor CH. PASALARIS; circ. 167,186.

Eleftherotypia (Press Freedom): Odos Minoou 10–16, 117 43 Athens; tel. (1) 9296001; fax (1) 9028311; internet www.enet.gr/online/online_p1.jsp; f. 1974; evening; Publr CHR. TEGOPOULOS; Dir S. FYNDANIDIS; circ. 115,000.

Estia (Vesta): Odos Anthimou Gazi 7, 105 61 Athens; tel. (1) 3230650; fax (1) 3243071; e-mail estianews@otenet.gr; f. 1894; afternoon; Publr and Editor KOINONIA ASTIKOU DIKAIOU; circ. 60,000.

Ethnos (Nation): Odos Benaki 152, Metamorfosi Chalandriou, 152 35 Athens; tel. (1) 6580640; fax (1) 6396515; internet www.ethnos.gr/; f. 1981; evening; Publr GEORGE BOBOLAS; Dir TH. KALOUDIS; circ. 84,735.

Express: Odos Halandriou 39, Paradissos Amaroussiou, 151 25 Athens; tel. (1) 6850200; fax (1) 6852202; internet www.kapatel.gr/express/; f. 1963; morning, financial; Publr Hellenews Publications; Editor D. G. KALOFOLIAS; circ. 28,000.

Filathlos: Odos Dimitros 11, 177 78 Athens; tel. (1) 3424090; f. 1982; morning; Dir NICK KARAGIANNIDIS; Publr and Editor G. A. KOURIS; circ. 40,000.

Imerissia (Daily): Odos Benaki & Ag. Nektariou, Metamorfosi Chalandriou, 152 35 Athens; tel. (1) 6061729; fax (1) 6016563; e-mail imerissia@pegasus.gr; internet www.pegasus.gr; f. 1947; morning; Publr PETROS ANTONIADIS; Man. Editor ANONIS DALIPIS; circ. 26,000.

Kathimerini (Every Day): Odos Sokrateous 57, Athens; tel. (1) 5231001; fax (1) 5247685; internet www.kathimerini.gr/; f. 1919; morning; Conservative; Editor A. KARKAYANNIS; circ. 34,085.

Kerdos (Profit): Leoforos Kifissias 178, Halandri, 152 31 Athens; tel. (1) 6473384; fax (1) 6472003; f. 1985; morning; Publr TH. LIAKOUNAKOS; Man. Editor SERAFIM KONSTANDINIDIS; circ. 18,000.

Messimvrini (Midday): El Venizelou 10, 106 71 Athens; tel. (1) 3646019; fax (1) 3636125; f. 1980; evening; Publr and Dir PANOS LOUKAKOS; circ. 17,451.

Naftemporiki (Daily Journal): Odos Lenorman 205, 104 42 Athens; tel. (1) 5130605; fax (1) 5146013; internet www.naftemporiki.gr; f. 1923; morning; non-political journal of finance, commerce and shipping; Dir N. ATHANASSIADIS; circ. 35,000.

Ora Gia Spor (Time for Sport): Athens; tel. (1) 9251200; fax (1) 9226167; f. 1991; sport; Editor EVANGELOS SEMBOS.

Rizospastis (Radical): Odos Irakliou 145, Perissos, 142 31 Athens; tel. (1) 2522002; fax (1) 2529480; internet www.rizospastis.gr/wwwengine; f. 1974; morning; pro-Soviet Communist; Dir T. TSIGAS; Editor G. TRIKALINOS; circ. 28,740.

Ta Nea (News): Odos Christou Lada 3, 102 37 Athens; tel. (1) 3250611; fax (1) 3228797; internet ta-nea.dolnet.gr/; f. 1944; liberal; evening; Dir L. KARAPANAYIOTIS; Editor CHRISTOS LAMBRAKIS; circ. 135,000.

Vradyni (Evening Press): Athens; tel. (1) 5231001; f. 1923; evening; right-wing; Gen. Man. H. ATHANASIADOU; circ. 71,914.

Patras

Peloponnesos: Maizonos 206, 262 22 Patras; tel. (61) 312530; fax (61) 312535; f. 1886; independent conservative; Publr and Editor S. DOUKAS; circ. 7,000.

Thessaloníki

Ellinikos Vorras (Greek North): Odos Grammou-Vitsi 19, 551 34 Thessaloníki; tel. (31) 416621; f. 1935; morning; Publr TESSA LEVANTIS; Dir N. MERGIOS; circ. 14,467.

Thessaloníki: Odos Monastiriou 85, 546 27 Thessaloníki; tel. (31) 521621; f. 1963; evening; Propr Publishing Co of Northern Greece SA; Dir LAZAROS HADJINAKOS; Editor KATERINA VELLIDI; circ. 36,040.

SELECTED PERIODICALS

Agora (Market): Leoforos Kifissias 178, Halandri, 151 31 Athens; tel. (1) 6473384; fax (1) 6477893; f. 1987; fortnightly; politics, finance; Dir ANT. KEFALAS; circ. 20,000.

Aktines: Odos Karytsi 14, 105 61 Athens; tel. (1) 3235023; f. 1938; monthly; current affairs, science, philosophy, arts; aims to promote a Christian civilization; Publr Christian Union; circ. 10,000.

Athèmes: Athens; monthly; French; cultural; Chief Editor EMMANUEL ADELY; circ. 5,000.

The Athenian: Athens; tel. (1) 3222802; fax (1) 3223052; e-mail the-athenian@hol.gr; internet www.hol.gr; f. 1974; monthly; English; Publr KONSTANTINOS GEROU; Editor JOANNA STAVROPOULOS; circ. 14,000.

Auto Express: Odos Halandriou 39, Halandri, 152 32 Athens; tel. (1) 6816906; fax (1) 6825858; Dir D. KALOFOLIAS; circ. 18,828.

Computer Gia Olous (Computers for All): Syngrou 44, 117 42 Athens; tel. (1) 9238672; fax (1) 9216847; monthly; Editor GEORGE CHRISTOPOULOS.

Deltion Diikiseos Epichiriseon Euro-Unial (Business Administration Bulletin Euro-Unial): Odos Rhigillis 26, 106 74; Athens; tel. (1) 7235736; fax (1) 7240000; e-mail busadmibul@otenet.gr; monthly; Editor I. PAPAMICHALAKIS; circ. 26,000.

Demosiografiki (Journalism): Procopiou 7–9, 171 24 Athens; tel. (1) 9731338; fax (1) 3816738; e-mail hazzynic@yahoo.com; f. 1987; quarterly; Dir JOHN MENOÚNOS; circ. 4,000.

Ekonomicos Tachydromos (Financial Courier): Odos Christou Lada 3, 102 37 Athens; tel. (1) 3333630; fax (1) 3238740; e-mail oikonomikos@dolnet.gr; f. 1926; weekly; illustrated magazine; Man. Editor DENIS ANTIPAS; circ. 23,000.

Elle: Odos Kleisthenous 213, 153 44 Athens; tel. (1) 6062531; fax (1) 6062648; e-mail magelle@compulink.gr; f. 1988; monthly; women's magazine; Editor FLORA TZIMAKA; circ. 57,120 (1997).

Epiloghi: Odos Stadiou 4, 105 64 Athens; tel. (1) 3238427; fax (1) 3235160; e-mail epilogi@mail.hol.gr; f. 1962; weekly; economics; Editor GEORGE MALOUHOS.

Greece's Weekly for Business and Finance: Athens; tel. (1) 7707280; weekly; English; finance; Dir V. KORONAKIS.

Gynaika (Women): Odos Fragoklissias 7, Marousi, 151 25 Athens; tel. (1) 6199149; fax (1) 6104707; f. 1950; monthly; fashion, beauty, cookery, social problems, news; Publr CHRISTOS TERZOPOULOS; circ. 45,000.

Hellenews: Odos Halandriou 39, Marousi, 151 25 Athens; tel. (1) 6899400; fax (1) 6899430; weekly; English; finance and business; Publr Hellenews Publications; Editor J. M. GERMANOS.

Idaniko Spiti (Ideal Home): Odos St Nectarios, 152 35 Athens; tel. (1) 6061777; fax (1) 6011044; e-mail pa@pegasus.gr; internet www.idanikospiti.gr; f. 1990; monthly; interior decoration; Editor ANNA SAKLARIDOU; circ. 44,201 (1997).

Klik: Odos Fragoklisias 7, 151 25 Athens; tel. (1) 6897945; fax (1) 6899153; internet www.klik.gr/; f. 1987; monthly; popular music, media and fashion; Editor PETROS COSTOPOULOS.

Marie Claire: Odos Stadiou 24, 105 64 Athens; tel. (1) 3333654; fax (1) 3227770; e-mail marieclaire@dolnet.gr; monthly; women's magazine.

Men: Odos Fragoklisias 7, 151 25 Athens; tel. (1) 6826680; fax (1) 6824730; internet www.men.gr/index.htm; six a year; men's fashion and general interest.

Oikonomiki Viomichaniki Epitheorissis (Industrial Review): Odos Zalokosta 4, 106 71 Athens; tel. (1) 3626360; fax (1) 3626388; e-mail editor@oikonomiki.gr; internet www.oikonomiki.gr; f. 1934; monthly; industrial and economic review; Publr A. C. VOVOLINI-LASKARIDIS; Editor D. KARAMANOS; circ. 25,000.

48 Ores (48 Hours): Leoforos Alexandras 19, 114 73 Athens; tel. (1) 6430313; fax (1) 6461361; weekly; Dir and Editor SP. KARATZAFERIS; circ. 9,127.

Pantheon: Odos Christou Lada 3, 102 37 Athens; tel. (1) 3230221; fax (1) 3228797; fortnightly; Publr and Dir N. THEOFANIDES; circ. 23,041.

Politika Themata: Odos Ypsilantou 25, 106 75 Athens; tel. (1) 7218421; weekly; Publr J. CHORN; Dir C. KYRKOS; circ. 2,544.

Pontiki (Mouse): Odos Massalias 10, 106 81 Athens; tel. (1) 3609531; weekly; humour; Dir and Editor K. PAPAIOANNOU.

Ptisi (Flight and Space): Odos Helioupoleos 2–4, 172 37 Athens; tel. (1) 9792500; fax (1) 9792528; e-mail tpress@techlink.gr; internet www.techlink.gr; f. 1975; monthly; Editor COSTAS CAVATHAS; circ. 68,000 (1997).

Radiotileorassi (Radio-TV): Odos Mourouzi 16, 106 74 Athens; tel. (1) 7224811; weekly; circ. 134,626.

Technika Chronika (Technical Times): Odos Karageorgi Servias 4, 105 62 Athens; tel. (1) 3234751; f. 1952; monthly; general edition on technical and economic subjects; Editor D. ROKOS; circ. 12,000.

Tilerama: Odos Voukourestiou 18, 106 71 Athens; tel. (1) 3607160; fax (1) 3607032; f. 1977; weekly; radio and television; circ. 189,406.

To Vima (Tribune): Odos Christou Lada 3, 102 37 Athens; tel. (1) 3333103; fax (1) 3239097; f. 1922; weekly; liberal; Dir and Editor STAVROS R. PSYCHARIS; circ. 250,000.

La Tribune héllenique: Athens; every two months; French; politics, economics; Dir THEODORE BENAKIS; circ. 3,000.

NEWS AGENCIES

Athens News Agency (ANA): Odos Tsoha 36, 115 21 Athens; tel. (1) 6400560; fax (1) 6400581; e-mail ape@ana.gr; internet www.ana.gr; f. 1895; correspondents in leading capitals of the world and towns throughout Greece; Gen. Dir ANDREAS CHRISTODOULIDES.

Foreign Bureaux

Agence France-Presse (AFP): Athens; tel. (1) 3633388; Bureau Chief JEAN-PIERRE ALTIER.

Agencia EFE (Spain): Athens; tel. (1) 3635826; Bureau Chief D. MARÍA-LUISA RUBIO; Correspondent JUAN JOSÉ FERNÁNDEZ ELORRIAGA.

Agenzia Nazionale Stampa Associata (ANSA) (Italy): Odos Kanari 9, 106 71 Athens; tel. (1) 3605285; fax (1) 3635367; Correspondent FRANCESCO INDRACCOLO.

Associated Press (AP) (USA): Leoforos Amalias 52, 105 52 Athens; tel. (1) 3310802; fax (1) 3310804.

Deutsche Presse-Agentur (dpa) (Germany): Miniati 1, 116 36 Athens; tel. (1) 9247774; fax (1) 9222185; Correspondent HILDEGARD HÜLSENBECK.

Informatsionnoye Telegrafnoye Agentstvo Rossii—Telegrafnoye Agentstvo Suverennykh Stran (ITAR—TASS) (Russian Federation): Odos Gizi 39, Palaio Psychiko, 15 452 Athens; tel. and fax (1) 6713069; Bureau Chief VLADIMIR V. MALYSHEV.

Novinska Agencija Tanjug (Yugoslavia): Evrou 94–96, Ambelokipi, Athens; tel. (1) 7791545.

Reuters Hellas SA (United Kingdom): 7th Floor, Kolokotroni 1/ Leoforos Stadiou, 105 62 Athens; tel. (1) 3647610; fax (1) 3604490; Man. Dir WILLIAM CAIRLEY.

Rossiiskoye Informatsionnoye Agentstvo—Novosti (RIA—Novosti) (Russian Federation): Odos Irodotou 9, 138 Athens; tel. (1) 7291016; Bureau Chief BORIS KOROLYOV; Correspondent J. KURIZIN.

Xinhua (New China) News Agency (People's Republic of China): Odos Amarilidos 19, Palaio Psychiko, Athens; tel. (1) 6724997; Bureau Chief XIE CHENGHAO.

PRESS ASSOCIATIONS

Enosis Antapokriton Xenou Tipou (Foreign Press Association of Greece): Odos Akademias 23, 106 71 Athens; tel. (1) 3637318; fax (1) 3605035.

Enosis Syntakton Imerission Ephimeridon Athinon (Journalists' Union of Athens Daily Newspapers): Odos Akademias 20, 106 71 Athens; tel. (1) 3632601; fax (1) 3632608; f. 1914; Pres. DIMITRIOS MATHIOPOULOS; Gen. Sec. MANOLIS MATHIOUDAKIS; 1,400 mems.

Enosis Syntakton Periodikou Tipou (Journalists' Union of the Periodical Press): Odos Valaoritou 9, 106 71 Athens; tel. (1) 3636039; fax (1) 3644967; e-mail espt@magazinepress.gr; internet www magazinepress.gr; Pres. ATHENESE PAPANDROPOULOS; 600 mems.

Publishers

Agkyra Publications: Leoforos Kifisou 85, Egaleo, 122 41 Athens; tel. (1) 3455276; fax (1) 3474732; f. 1890; general; Man. Dir DIMITRIOS PAPADIMITRIOU.

Akritas: Odos Efessou 24, 171 21 Athens; tel. (1) 9334685; fax (1) 9311436; e-mail akritaspublications@ath.forthnet.gr; f. 1979; history, spirituality, children's books.

D. I. Arsenidis & Co: Odos Akademias 57, 106 79 Athens; tel. (1) 3629538; fax (1) 3618707; biography, literature, children's books, history, philosophy, social sciences; Man. Dir JOHN ARSENIDIS.

Boukoumanis Editions: Odos Mavromichali 1, 106 79 Athens; tel. (1) 3618502; fax (1) 3630669; f. 1967; history, politics, sociology, psychology, belles-lettres, educational, arts, children's books, ecology; Man. ELIAS BOUKOUMANIS.

Dorikos Publishing House: Odos Charalabou Sotiriou 9–11, 114 72 Athens; tel. (1) 6454726; fax (1) 3301866; f. 1958; literature, fiction, history, politics; Editor ROUSSOS VRANAS.

Ekdotike Athenon, SA: Odos Omirou 11, 106 72 Athens; tel. (1) 3608911; fax (1) 3606157; f. 1961; history, archaeology, art; Man. Dirs GEORGE A. CHRISTOPOULOS, JOHN C. BASTIAS.

G. C. Eleftheroudakis, SA: Odos Panepistimiou 17, 105 64 Athens; tel. (1) 3314180; fax (1) 3239821; e-mail elebooks@netor.gr; f. 1915; general, technical and scientific; Man. Dir VIRGINIA ELEFTHEROU-DAKIS-GREGOU.

Exandas Publrs: Odos Didotou 57, 106 81 Athens; tel. (1) 3804885; fax (1) 3813065; e-mail exandas@otenet.gr; internet www .exandasbooks.gr; f. 1974; fiction, literature, social sciences; Pres. MAGDA N. KOTZIA.

Govostis Publishing, SA: Zoodohou Pigis 21, 106 81 Athens; tel. (1) 3815433; fax (1) 3816661; e-mail cotsos@compulink.gr; f. 1926; arts, fiction, politics; Pres. COSTAS GOVOSTIS.

Denise Harvey: Katounia, 340 05 Limmi, Evia; tel. and fax (227) 31154; f. 1972; modern Greek literature and poetry, belles-lettres, theology, translations, selected general list (English and Greek); Man. Dir DENISE HARVEY.

Hestia-I.D. Kollaros & Co, SA: Odos Solonos 60, 106 72 Athens; tel. (1) 3615077; fax (1) 3606759; f. 1885; literature, history, politics, architecture, philosophy, travel, religion, psychology, textbooks, general; Gen. Dir MARINA KARAITIDIS.

Kastaniotis Editions, SA: Odos Zalogou 11, 106 78 Athens; tel. (1) 3301208; fax (1) 3822530; e-mail kastaniotis@ath.forthnet.gr; f. 1969; arts, fiction, social sciences; Man. Dir ATHANASIOS KASTANIOTIS.

Kritiki Publishing: Odos Koletti 25, 106 77 Athens; tel. (1) 3622390; fax (1) 3621367; e-mail biblia@kritiki.gr; internet www .kritiki.gr; f. 1987; economics, politics, literature, philosophy, business/management, popular science; Pres. THEMIS MINOGLOU.

Kronos: Odos Egnatia 33, 546 26 Thessaloníki; tel. (31) 532077; fax (31) 538158; Dir TH. GIOTAS.

Lambrakis Press, SA: Odos Christou Lada 3, 102 37 Athens; tel. (1) 3333555; fax (1) 3228797; internet www.dolnet.gr; newspapers and magazines; 18 titles.

Livani Publishing Org.: Odos Solonos 98, 106 80 Athens; tel. (1) 3610589; fax (1) 3617791; e-mail glykeria@livanis.gr; general; Publr A. A. LIVANI.

Minoas Ilias Konstantaropoulos & Co, OE: Odos Possidonos 1, 141 21 Athens; tel. (1) 2776814; fax (1) 2711056; e-mail info@ minoas.gr; internet www.minoas.gr; f. 1954; fiction, art, history; Man. Dir YANNIS KONSTANTAROPOULOS.

Odos Panos: Odos Didotou 39, 106 08 Athens; tel. and fax (1) 3616782; internet www.odospanos-cigaret.gr; poetry, drama, biography.

Papazissis Publishers: Nikitara 2, 106 78 Athens; tel. (1) 3822496; fax (1) 3809150; e-mail papazisi@otenet.gr; internet www.papzisi.gr; f. 1929; economics, politics, law, history, school books; Man. Dir VICTOR PAPAZISSIS.

Patakis Publications: Odos Valtetsiou 14, 106 80 Athens; tel. (1) 3638362; fax (1) 3628950; art, reference, literature, educational, philosophy, psychology, sociology, religion, music, children's books, educational toys, CD-Rom and audiobooks; Pres. STEFANOS PATAKIS.

Pontiki Publications SA: Odos Massalias 10, 106 80 Athens; tel. (1) 3609531; fax (1) 3645406; f. 1979; govt, history, political science; Man. Dir KOSTAS TABANIS.

John Sideris: Odos Stadiou 44, 105 64 Athens; tel. (1) 3229638; fax (1) 3245052; f. 1898; school textbooks, general; Man. J. SIDERIS.

J. G. Vassiliou: Odos Hippokratous 15, 106 79 Athens; tel. (1) 3623382; fax (1) 3623580; f. 1913; fiction, history, philosophy, dictionaries and children's books; Pres. J. VASSILIOU.

Government Publishing House

Government Printing House: Odos Kapodistriou 34, 104 32 Athens; tel. (1) 5248320.

PUBLISHERS' FEDERATIONS

Hellenic Federation of Publishers and Booksellers: Odos Themistokleus 73, 106 83 Athens; tel. (1) 3300924; fax (1) 3301617; e-mail poev@otenet.gr; f. 1961; Pres. GEORGE DARDANOS; Gen. Sec. STEFANOS VASILOPOULOS.

Publishers' and Booksellers' Association of Athens: Odos Themistokleus 73, 106 83 Athens; tel. (1) 3303268; fax (1) 3823222; Pres. VASSILIS CHATZIAKOVOU; Sec. ELENI KAVIAKI.

Broadcasting and Communications

TELECOMMUNICATIONS

National Telecommunications Commission (NTC): Leoforos Kifissias 60, 151 25 Athens; tel. (1) 6805040; fax (1) 6805049;

e-mail alouk@eet.gr; internet www.eet.gr; regulatory body; Chair. EMMANOUIL GIACOUMAKIS.

Organismos Telepikoinonion tis Elladas, SA (OTE) (Hellenic Telecommunications Organization): Leoforos Kifissias 99, 151 24 Maroussi, Athens; tel. (1) 8827015; fax (1) 6115825; e-mail ote@ ote.gr; internet www.ote.gr; f. 1949; owned 51% by the Government, 49% by public shareholders; 5.6m. lines in service; Chair. and Chief Exec. NIKOS MANASSIS; Man. Dir GEORGE SYMEONIDIS.

COSMOTE: Leoforos Kifissias 44, 151 25 Athens; tel. (1) 6177700; fax (1) 6177594; e-mail customercare@cosmote.gr; internet www.cosmote.gr; 59% owned by OTE, 18%-owned by Telenor (Norway), 7% owned by WR Com (based in Cyprus); the remaining 16% of shares were offered for tender in Oct. 2000; mobile services; Man. Dir NIKOS MANASSIS.

Maritel: Odos Egaleo 8, 185 45 Piraeus; tel. (1) 4599500; fax (1) 4599600; e-mail maritel@maritel.gr; internet www.maritel.gr; OTE subsidiary; marine telecommunications; Chair. THEODOROS VENIAMIS; Man. Dir MICHALIS MICHAELIDES.

Panafon Hellenic Telecom SA: Leoforos Messoghion 2, 115 27 Athens; tel. (1) 7483601; e-mail webmaster@panafon.gr; internet www.panafon.gr; 55%-owned by Vodafone Europe Holdings BV (United Kingdom); mobile telecommunications; Chair. JULIAN HORN-SMITH; Chief Exec. GEORGE KORONIAS.

Telestet Hellas SA: Leoforos Alex. Papagoy 8, 157 71 Athens; tel. (1) 7772033; internet www.telestet.gr; 75%-owned by STET International; mobile network; Man. Dir GIACINTO CICCHESE.

RADIO

Elliniki Radiophonia Tileorassi (ERT, SA) (Greek Radio-Television): Leoforos Messoghion 432, 153 42 Athens; tel. (1) 6066835; fax (1) 6009325; e-mail pxristofylakou@ert.gr; state-controlled since 1938; Chair. and Man. Dir PANAGHIOTIS PANAGHIOTOU.

Elliniki Radiophonia-ERA (Greek Radio): POB 60019, Leoforos Messoghion 432, 153 42 Aghia Paraskevi, Athens; tel. (1) 6066815; fax (1) 6009425; e-mail ijanetakos@ert.gr; Dir YANNIS TZANNETAKOS.

Macedonia Radio Station: Odos Angelaki 2, 546 21 Thessaloníki; tel. (31) 299400; fax (31) 299451; e-mail ert3rd@compulink.gr; internet www.ert3.gr.

TELEVISION

A television network of 17 transmitters is in operation. The State's monopoly of television broadcasting ended in 1990, and by 1998 there were 17 private broadcasters.

State stations

Elliniki Radiophonia Tileorassi (ERT, SA) (Greek Radio-Television): (see Radio).

Elliniki Tileorassi (Greek Television) **1 (ET1):** Leoforos Messoghion 136, 115 27 Athens; tel. (1) 7758824; fax (1) 7797776; e-mail kalavanos@ert.gr; Dir-Gen. KONSTANTINOS ALAVANOS.

ET2: Leoforos Messoghion 136, 115 25 Athens; tel. (1) 7701911; fax (1) 7797776; Dir-Gen. PANAYOTIS PANAYOTOU.

ET3: Aggelaki 2, 546 21 Thessaloníki; tel. (31) 299610; fax (31) 299655; e-mail pr@ert3.gr; internet www.ert3.gr; Dir-Gen. MICHALIS ALEXANDRIDIS.

Private stations

Antenna TV: Leoforos Kifissias 10–12, 151 25 Maroussi, Athens; tel. (1) 688600; fax (1) 6834349; e-mail webmaster@antenna.gr; internet www.antenna.gr; Chair. M. X. KYRIAKOU.

Channel Seven-X: Leoforos Kifissias 64, Athens; tel. (1) 68976042; fax (1) 6897608.

City Channel: Leoforos Kastoni 14, 41223 Larissa; tel. (41) 232839; fax (41) 232013.

Mega Channel: Leoforos Messoghion 117, 115 26 Athens; tel. (1) 6903000; fax (1) 6983600; e-mail ngeorgiou@megatv.com; internet www.megatv.com; f. 1989; Man. Dir ELIAS TSIGAS.

Neo Kanali SA: Pireos 9-11, 105 52 Athens; tel. (1) 5238230; fax (1) 5247325.

Serres TV: Nigritis 27, 62124 Serres.

Skai TV: Phalereos & Ethnarchou 2, Macaroiu, N. Phaliro.

Star Channel: Dimitras 37, 1178 Tayros, Athens; tel. (1) 3450626; fax (1) 3452190.

Tele City: Praxitelous 58, 17674 Athens; tel (1) 9429222; fax (1) 9413589.

Teletora: Lycabetous 17, 10672 Athens; tel. (1) 3617285; fax (1) 3638712.

Traki TV: Central Square, 67100 Xanthi; tel. (541) 20670; fax (541) 27368.

TRT: Odos Zachou 5, 38333 Volos; tel. (421) 288013; fax (421) 36888.

TV Macedonia: Nea Egnatia 222, 54642 Thessaloníki; tel. (31) 850512; fax (31) 850513.

TV Plus: Athens; tel. (1) 9028707; fax (1) 9028310.

TV-100: Odos Aggelaki 16, 54621 Thessaloníki; tel. (31) 265828; fax (31) 267532.

Finance

(cap. = capital; p.u. = paid up; res = reserves; dep. = deposits; dre = drachmae; m. = million; br. = branch)

BANKING

Central Bank

Bank of Greece: Leoforos E. Venizelos 21, 102 50 Athens; tel. (1) 3201111; fax (1) 3232239; e-mail bogsecr@ath.forthnet.gr; f. 1927; state bank of issue; cap. dre 13,905.4m., res dre 114,970.2m., dep. dre 7,801,693.3m. (Dec. 1997); Gov. LUKAS PAPADEMOS; 27 brs.

Commercial Banks

Agricultural Bank of Greece: Odos Panepistimiou 23, 105 64 Athens; tel. (1) 3230521; fax (1) 3234386; f. 1929; wholly owned by State; cap. dre 360,007.0m., res dre 119,027.8m., dep. dre 3,542,985.5m. (Dec. 1999); Gov. and Chair. PETROS LAMBROU; 437 brs.

Alpha Bank: Stadiou 40, 102 52 Athens; tel. (1) 3260000; fax (1) 3265438; e-mail secretariat@alpha.gr; internetwww.alpha.gr; f. 1879, renamed 2000; cap. dre 253,714.5m., res dre 265,303.2m., dep. dre 6,793,088.2m. (Dec. 2000); Chair. and Gen. Man. YANNIS S. COSTOPOULOS; 418 brs.

Bank of Attica: Odos Omirou 23, 106 72 Athens; tel. (1) 3646910; fax (1) 3646115; e-mail info@bankofattica.gr; internet www .bankofattica.gr; f. 1925; affiliated to the Commercial Bank of Greece; cap. dre 4,742.1m., res dre 44,563.8m., dep. dre 277,930.1m. (Dec. 1999); Chair. SOULIS-CHRISTOS APOSTOLOPOULOS; 39 brs.

Commercial Bank of Greece: Odos Sophokleous 11, 102 35 Athens; tel. (1) 3284000; fax (1) 3253746; e-mail pubrel@combank.gr; internet www.combank.gr; f. 1907; cap. dre 140,995.5m., res dre 450,411.2m., dep. dre 3,808,503.5m. (Dec. 1999); Chair. and Chief Exec. YANNIS STOURNARAS; Gen. Man. GEORGE MICHELIS; 380 brs.

EFG Eurobank Ergasias SA: Odos Othonos 8, 105 57 Athens; tel. (1) 3337000; fax (1) 3233866; internet www.eurobank.gr; f. 1990 as Euromerchant Bank SA (Eurobank), renamed EFG Eurobank in 1997, and as above in 2000; merged with Bank of Athens and Bank of Crete in 1999, and with Ergobank in 2000; cap. dre 16,500m., res dre 6,980m., dep. dre 263.327m. (Dec. 1996); Pres. X. NIKITAS; Man. Dir NIKOLAS NANOPOULOS; 5 brs.

Egnatia Bank: Odos Danaidon 4, 546 26 Thessaloníki; tel. (31) 598600; fax (31) 598675; e-mail pr@egnatiabank.gr; internet www.egnatiabank.gr; f. 1991; merged with Bank of Central Greece in 1999; Pres. VASSILLOS THEOCHARAKIS; Man. Dir and Gen. Man. VASSILLIS KELTSOPOULOS; 49 brs.

General Bank of Greece SA: Odos Panepistimiou 9, 102 29 Athens; tel. (1) 3327000; fax (1) 3222271; f. 1937 as Bank of the Army Share Fund, renamed General Hellenic Bank in 1966, and as above in 1998; cap. dre 16,972.1m., res dre 24,348.3m., dep. dre 527,077.9m. (Dec. 1999); Chair. JOHN MANOS; Gen. Man. JOHN MOUZGELAS; 95 brs.

Laiki Bank (Hellas) SA: Odos Panepistimiou 16, 106 72 Athens; tel. (1) 3550000; fax (1) 3243141; f. 1992 as European Popular Bank, renamed as above in 2000; cap. dre 15,250m., res dre 13,421.8m., dep. dre 259,735.6m. (Dec. 1999); Chair. KIKIS LAZARIDES; Dep. Gen. Man. CHRISTOS STYLANIDES; 13 brs.

National Bank of Greece, SA: Odos Aeolou 86, 102 32 Athens; tel. (1) 3441000; fax (1) 3346550; internet www.ethniki.gr; f. 1841; cap. dre 236,226.2m., res dre 494,444.5m., dep. dre 11,768,266.7m. (Dec. 1999); Gov. THEODOROS KARATZAS; 610 brs.

Piraeus Bank, SA: Leoforos Amalias 20, 105 57 Athens; tel. (1) 3335000; fax (1) 3335080; internet www.piraeusbank.gr; f. 1916; merged with Macedonia Thrace Bank and Xiosbank in June 2000; cap. dre 148,760.8m., res 254,984.2m., dep. dre 1,032,304.1m. (Dec. 1999); Chair. M. SALLAS; Man. Dir D. WATSON; 36 brs.

Piraeus Prime Bank, SA: Leoforos Vassilissis Sofias 75, 115 21 Athens; tel. (1) 7250323; fax (1) 7210134; f. 1981 as Banque Franco-Hellenique de Commerce International et Maritime SA, renamed Credit Lyonnais Grèce 1994 and as above 1998; cap. dre 8,300m., res dre 5,075.7m., dep. dre 69,149.9m. (Dec. 1997); Pres. ALFRED BOUCKAERT; Man. Dir BAUDOUIN MERLET; 1 br.

Telesis Investment Bank, SA: Odos Fragoklissias 5, 151 25 Maroussi, Athens; tel. (1) 6196960; fax (1) 619191; e-mail telesisbk@ telesis.gr; f. 1990 as Dorian Bank, renamed as above in 2000; cap. dre 41,720.0m., res dre 40,870.6m., dep. dre 98,849.2m. (Dec. 1999); Chair. MARINA EFRAIMOGLU; 3 brs.

Development Banks

Hellenic Industrial Development Bank, SA: Leoforos Syngrou 87, 117 45 Athens; tel. (1) 9241425; fax (1) 9241513; f. 1964; state-owned limited liability banking company; the major Greek institution in the field of industrial investment; cap. dre 245,890.0m., res dre 44,424.3m., dep. dre 502,897.6m. (Dec. 1996); Chair. and Gov. GEORGE KASMAS; 11 brs.

National Investment Bank for Industrial Development, SA: Leoforos Amalias 12-14, 105 57 Athens; tel. (1) 3242651; fax (1) 3296211; f. 1963; cap. dre 8,971.8m., res dre 44,572.4m., dep. dre 447,259.0m. (Dec. 1999); long-term loans, equity participation, promotion of co-operation between Greek and foreign enterprises; Chair. THEODORE KARATZAS; Man. Dir DEMETRIOS PAVLAKIS.

STOCK EXCHANGE

Athens Stock Exchange: Odos Sophokleous 10, 105 59 Athens; tel. (1) 3211301; fax (1) 3213938; internet www.ase.gr; f. 1876; Pres. PANAYOTIS ALEXAKIS; Vice-Pres. THEODOROS PANTOLAKIS.

PRINCIPAL INSURANCE COMPANIES

Agrotiki Hellenic Insurance Co: Leoforos Syngrou 163, 171 21 Athens; tel. (1) 9379100; fax (1) 9358924; Gen. Man. TR. LISIMACHOU.

Alpha Insurance: Leoforos Kifissias 44, 151 25 Maroussi, Athens; tel. (1) 6162000; fax (1) 6162810; f. 1940; Chair. PHOTIS P. COSTOPOULOS; Gen. Man. JOHN L. GALANOPOULOS.

Apollon Insurance Co: Leoforos Syngrou 39, 117 43 Athens; tel. (1) 9236362; fax (1) 9236916; f. 1976; Gen. Man. E. PANANIDIS.

Aspis Pronia General Insurance SA: Leoforos Kifissias 62, 151 25 Maroussi, Athens; tel. (1) 6804480; fax (1) 6898990; f. 1941; Pres. and Chief Exec. PAUL PSOMIADES.

Astir: Odos Merlin 6, 106 71 Athens; tel. (1) 3604111; fax (1) 3633333; f. 1930; Gen. Man. B. CHARDALIAS.

Atlantiki Enosis: Odos Messoghion 71, 115 26 Athens; tel. (1) 7799211; fax (1) 7794446; f. 1970; Gen. Man. N. LAPATAS.

Dynamis, SA: Leoforos Syngrou 106, 117 41 Athens; tel. (1) 9227255; fax (1) 9237768; f. 1977; Man. Dir NIKOLAS STAMATOPOULOS.

Egnatia Co: Odos Fragon 1, 546 26 Thessaloníki; tel. (31) 523325; fax (31) 523555; Rep. P. MIGAS.

Emporiki: Odos Philhellinon 6, 105 57 Athens; tel. (1) 3240093; fax (1) 3223835; f. 1940; Chair. PHOTIS P. KOSTOPOULOS; Exec. Dir MICHAEL P. PSALIDAS.

Estia Insurance and Reinsurance Co, SA: Odos Parnonos 3, 151 25 Maroussi, Athens; tel. (1) 6127540; fax (1) 6127559; f. 1943; Chair. ALKIVIADIS CHIONIS; Gen. Man. D. GIANNIOS.

Ethniki Hellenic General Insurance Co: Odos Karageorgi Servias 8, 102 10 Athens; tel. (1) 3299000; fax (1) 3236101; f. 1891; Gen. Man. C. PHILIPOU.

Eurogroup Insurance and Reinsurance Co: Leoforos Syngrou 247, 171 22 Athens; tel. (1) 9425094; fax (1) 9411919.

Galaxias: Leoforos Syngrou 40–42, 117 42 Athens; tel. (1) 9241082; fax (1) 9241698; f. 1967; Gen. Man. I. TSOUPRAS.

Geniki Epagelmatiki: Odos Panepistimiou 56, 106 78 Athens; tel. (1) 3636910; fax (1) 3606848; f. 1967; Gen. Man. A. FILIPPATOS.

Gothaer Hellas, SA: Odos Michalakopoulou 174, 115 27 Athens; tel. (1) 7750801; fax (1) 7757094; Gen. Man. S. GALANIS.

Hellas: Leoforos Kifissias 119, 151 24 Marousi; tel. (1) 6124286; fax (1) 8027189; f. 1973; Gen. Man. N. NARDIS.

Hellenic Reliance General Insurances, SA: Leoforos Kifissias 304, 152 32 Halandri; tel. (1) 6843733; fax (1) 6843734; f. 1990; Man. Dir S. F. TRIANTAFYLLAKIS.

Hellenobretanniki General Insurances, SA: Leoforos Messogion 2–4, 115 27 Athens; tel. (1) 7755301; fax (1) 7714768; f. 1988.

Helvetia General Insurance Co: Leoforos Kifissias 124, 115 26 Athens; tel. (1) 6980840; fax (1) 6923446; f. 1943; Gen. Man. J. DELENDAS.

Horizon Insurance Co, SA: Leoforos Amalias 26A, 105 57 Athens; tel. (1) 3227932; fax (1) 3225540; f. 1965; Gen. Mans THEODORE ACHIS, CHR. ACHIS.

Hydrogios: Odos Solonos 137, 176 75 Athens; tel. (1) 9401300; fax (1) 9407072; Gen. Man. A. KASKARELIS.

Ikonomiki: Odos Kapodistriou 38, 104 32 Athens; tel. (1) 5243374; fax (1) 5234962; f. 1968; Gen. Man. D. NIKOLAIDIS.

Imperial Hellas, SA: Leoforos Syngrou 253, 171 22 Athens; tel. (1) 9426352; fax (1) 9426202; f. 1971; Gen. Man. G. JANIS.

Interamerican Hellenic Life Insurance Co: Interamerican Plaza, Leoforos Kifissias 117, 151 80 Maroussi, Athens; tel. (1) 6191111; fax (1) 6191877; e-mail tzoumass@interamerican.gr; f. 1971; Pres. and Man. Dir DIMITRI KONTOMINAS.

Interamerican Property and Casualty Insurance Co: Leoforos Kifissias 117, 151 80 Maroussi, Athens; tel. (1) 6191111; fax (1) 8060820; e-mail tzoumas@interamerican.gr; f. 1974; Man. Dir C. BERTSIAS.

Kykladiki: Leoforos Syngrou 80–88, 117 41 Athens; tel. (1) 9247664; fax (1) 9247344; f. 1919; Gen. Man. PAN. KATSIKOSTAS.

National Insurance Institution of Greece: Odos Agiou Konstantinou 6, 104 31 Athens; tel. (1) 5223300; fax (1) 5239754; Rep. J. KYRIAKOS.

Olympic-Victoria General Insurance Co, SA: Odos Tsimiski 21, 546 22 Thessaloníki; tel. (31) 239331; fax (31) 239264; f. 1972; Man. Dir G. ANDONIADIS.

Panellinios: Leoforos Syngrou 171, 171 21 Athens; tel. (1) 9352003; fax (1) 9352451; f. 1918; Gen. Man. A. VALYRAKIS.

Pegasus Insurance Co: Odos Stadiou 5, 105 62 Athens; tel. (1) 3227357; fax (1) 3246728; Gen. Man. M. PARASKAKIS.

Phoenix-General Insurance Co of Greece, SA: Odos Omirou 2, 105 64 Athens; tel. (1) 3295111; fax (1) 3239135; f. 1928; general insurance; Rep. G. KOTSALOS.

Poseidon: Odos Karaiskou 163, 185 35 Piraeus; tel. (1) 4522685; fax (1) 4184337; f. 1972; Gen. Man. THANOS J. MELAKOPIDES.

Proodos: Leoforos Syngrou 198, 176 71 Kallithea; tel. (1) 9593302; fax (1) 9592992; f. 1941; Gen. Man. P. KARALIS.

Propontis–Merimna A.E.A.: Odos Agiou Konstantinou 6, 104 31 Athens; tel. (1) 5223300; fax (1) 5239754; f. 1917; Man. Dirs E. BALAHILL, M. ARTAVANIS.

Sideris Insurance Co, SA: Odos Lekka 3–5, 105 63 Athens; tel. (1) 3224484; fax (1) 3231066; Dir G. SIDERIS.

Syneteristiki: Leoforos Syngrou 367, 175 64 Athens; tel. (1) 9491280; fax (1) 9403148; Gen. Man. D. ZORBAS.

United Insurance Co SA: Leoforos Kifissias 250–254, 152 31 Athens; tel. (1) 6742411; fax (1) 6741826; e-mail united@atheneos.com; f. 1977; Pres. D. DASKALOPOULOS; Man. Dir P. ATHENEOS.

A large number of foreign insurance companies also operate in Greece.

Insurance Association

Association of Insurance Companies: Odos Xenophontos 10, 105 57 Athens; tel. (1) 3334100; fax (1) 3334149; e-mail eaee@eaee.gr; internet www.eaee.gr; 149 mems; Gen. Dir MARGARITA ANTONAKI.

Trade and Industry

GOVERNMENT AGENCY

Organismos Anasinkrotiseos Epicheiriseon (Industrial Reconstruction Organization): Athens; f. 1982; reconstruction and sale of Greek businesses under state receivership.

CHAMBERS OF COMMERCE

Athens Chamber of Commerce and Industry: Odos Akademias 7, 106 71 Athens; tel. (1) 3625342; fax (1) 3618810; e-mail info@acci.gr; internet www.acci.gr; f. 1919; Pres. JOHN KOCPRALOS; Sec.-Gen. DRACOULIS FOUNDOUKAKOS; 55,000 mems.

Athens Chamber of Small and Medium-sized Industries: Odos Akademias 18, 106 71 Athens; tel. (1) 3680700; fax (1) 3614726; e-mail info@acsmi.gr; f. 1940; Pres. G. KYRIOPOULOS; Sec.-Gen. ATH. PAVLOU; c. 60,000 mems.

Handicraft Chamber of Piraeus: Odos Karaiscou 111, 185 32 Piraeus; tel. (1) 4174152; f. 1925; Pres. KONSTANTINOS MOSCHOLIOS; Sec.-Gen. PANTELIS ANTONIADIS; 18,500 mems.

Piraeus Chamber of Commerce and Industry: Odos Loudovikou 1, 185 31 Piraeus; tel. (1) 4177241; fax (1) 4178680; f. 1919; Pres. GEORGE KASSIMATIS; Sec.-Gen. KONSTANTINOS SARANTOPOULOS.

Thessaloníki Chamber of Commerce and Industry: Odos Tsimiski 29, 546 24 Thessaloníki; tel. (31) 224438; fax (31) 230237; f. 1919; Pres. PANTELIS KONSTANTINIDIS; Sec.-Gen. EMMANUEL VLACHOYANNIS; 14,500 mems.

INDUSTRIAL AND TRADE ASSOCIATIONS

Association of Industries of Northern Greece: Morihovou 1, 546 35 Thessaloníki; tel. (31) 539817; fax (31) 546244; f. 1914; Pres. NIKOLAOS EFTHIMIADES.

Federation of Greek Industries (SEV): Odos Xenophontos 5, 105 57 Athens; f. 1907; Chair. ELEFTHERIOS ANTONAKOPOULOS; 950 mems.

Hellenic Cotton Board: Leoforos Syngrou 150, 176 71 Athens; tel. (1) 9225011; fax (1) 9249656; f. 1931; state organization; Pres. P. K. MYLONAS.

Hellenic Organization of Small and Medium-sized Industries and Handicrafts: Odos Xenias 16, 115 28 Athens; tel. (1) 7491370;

fax (1) 7491146; e-mail interel@eommex.gr; Pres. GEORGE FRANTZES-
KAKIS.

UTILITIES
Electricity

Public Power Corpn (DEH): Odos Xalkokondyli 30, 104 32
Athens; tel. (1) 5230301; fax (1) 5238445; e-mail webmaster@dei.gr;
internet www.dei.gr; f. 1950; generating capacity 9,372 MW; generation, transmission and distribution of electricity in Greece; Chair.
G. BIRDIMIRIS; Gen. Man. A. PAPATHANASIOU.

Gas

Public Gas Corpn (DEPA): Leoforos Messoghian 207, 115 25
Athens; tel. (1) 6749106; fax (1) 6749504; e-mail dimep@otenet.gr;
internet www.depa.gr; owned by Public Petroleum Corpn (DEH);
began gas imports 1997; initially for industrial use.

Water

In 1980 a law was passed under which Municipal Enterprises
for Water Supply and Sewerage (DEYA) were created to manage
drinking water and sewerage throughout Greece. Since then some
90 DEYA have been established.

**The Hellenic Union of Municipal Enterprises for Water
Supply and Sewerage (EDEYA):** Odos Anthimou Gaza 3, 441
22 Larissa; internet www.edeya.gr; f. 1989; 67 mems; co-ordinates
activities of DEYA and represents them to the Government.

TRADE UNIONS

There are about 5,000 registered trade unions, grouped together in
82 federations and 86 workers' centres, which are affiliated to the
Greek General Confederation of Labour.

Greek General Confederation of Labour (GSEE): Odos Patis-
sion 69, Athens; tel. (1) 8834611; fax (1) 8229802; f. 1918; Pres.
CHRISTOS PROTOPAPAS; Gen. Sec. IOANNIS THEONAS; 700,000 mems.

Pan-Hellenic Federation of Seamen's Unions (PNO): Livanos
Bldg, Akti Miaouli 47–49, 185 36 Piraeus; tel. (1) 4292960; fax (1)
4293040; f. 1920; confederation of 14 marine unions; Pres. YANNIS
CHELAS; Gen. Sec. JOHN HALAS.

Transport

RAILWAYS

A five-year programme to upgrade the Greek rail network was
initiated in 1996, supported by 350m. drachmae from EU structural
funds. The major undertaking was to electrify the 500-km
Athens–Thessaloníki line and to extend services to the Bulgarian
border. Construction of a 26.3-km electrified extension to the
Athens–Piraeus line, in order to provide a three-line urban railway
system for Athens, was scheduled to be completed by October 1998.

Ilektriki Sidirodromi Athinon–Pireos (ISAP) (Athens–Piraeus
Electric Railways): Odos Athinas 67, 105 52 Athens; tel. (1) 3248311;
fax (1) 3223935; internet www.isap.gr; 26 km of electrified track;
Man. Dir KOSTAS M. VASSILIADIS.

Organismos Sidirodromon Ellados (OSE) (Hellenic Railways
Organization Ltd): Odos Karolou 1–3, 104 37 Athens; tel. (1)
5248395; fax (1) 5243290; f. 1971; state railways; total length of
track: 2,600 km (1995); Chair. CHR. PAPAGEORGIOU; Dir Gen. A. LAZ-
ARIS.

ROADS

In 1995 there were an estimated 116,440 km of roads in Greece. Of
this total, an estimated 9,120 km were main roads, and 420 km
were motorways.

INLAND WATERWAYS

There are no navigable rivers in Greece.

Corinth Canal: built 1893; over six km long, links the Corinthian
and Saronic Gulfs; shortens the journey from the Adriatic to the
Piraeus by 325 km; spanned by three single-span bridges, two for
road and one for rail; can be used by ships of a maximum draught
of 22 ft and width of 60 ft.

SHIPPING

In 1998 the Greek merchant fleet totalled 1,545 vessels amounting
to 25,224,543 grt. Greece controls one of the largest merchant
fleets in the world. The principal ports are Piraeus, Patras and
Thessaloníki.

Union of Greek Shipowners: Akti Miaouli 85, 185 38 Piraeus;
Pres. JOHN GOUMAS.

Port Authorities

Port of Patras: Patras Port Authority, Central Port Office, Patras;
tel. (61) 341002; fax (61) 327136; Harbour Master Capt. NIKOLAS
RAFAILOVITS.

Port of Piraeus: Port of Piraeus Authority, Odos Merarchias 2,
185 35 Piraeus; tel. (1) 4520910; fax (1) 4520852; Gen. Man. SPIROS
STALIAS; Harbour Master Capt. EMMANUEL PELOPONNESIOS.

Port of Thessaloníki: Thessaloníki Port Authority, POB 10467,
541 10 Thessaloníki; tel. (31) 593911; fax (31) 510500; e-mail
secretariat@thpa.gr; internet www.thpa.gr; Chief Exec. SOTIRIS I.
THEOFANIS; Gen. Man. D. PAPADOPOULOS.

Among the largest shipping companies are:

Anangel Shipping Enterprises, SA: Akti Miaouli 25, 185 10
Piraeus; tel. (1) 4224500; fax (1) 4224819; Man. Dir J. PLATSIDAKIS.

Attika Shipping Co: Odos Voucourestion 16, 10671 Athens; tel.
(1) 3609631; fax (1) 3601439; Dir G. PRIOVOLOS.

Bilinder Marine Corpn, SA: Odos Igias 1–3 and Akti Themisto-
kleos, 185 36 Piraeus; tel. (1) 4287300; fax (1) 4287355; Gen. Man.
V. ARMOGENI.

Ceres Hellenic Shipping Enterprises Ltd: Akti Miaouli 69, 185
37 Piraeus; tel. (1) 4591000; fax (1) 4283552; e-mail chse@ceres.gr;
Dir NICK FISTES.

Chandris (Hellas) Inc: POB 80067, Akti Miaouli 95, 185 38
Piraeus; tel. (1) 4290300; fax (1) 4290256; e-mail chandris@
19080845.multimessage.com; Man. Dirs A. C. PIPERAS, M. G.
SKORDIAS.

Costamare Shipping Co, SA: Odos Zephyrou 60 and Leoforos
Syngrou, 175 64 Athens; tel. (1) 9390000; fax (1) 9409051; Pres.
Capt. V. C. KONSTANTAKOPOULOS; Man. Dir Capt. G. SARDIS.

European Navigation Inc: Odos Artemissiou 2 and Fleming Sq.,
166 75 Athens; tel. (1) 8981581; fax (1) 8946777; Dir P. KARNESSIS.

Glafki (Hellas) Maritime Co: Odos Mitropoleos 3, 105 57 Athens;
tel. (1) 3244991; fax (1) 3228944; Dirs M. FRAGOULIS, G. PANAGIOTOU.

Golden Union Shipping Co, SA: Odos Aegales 8, 185 45 Piraeus;
tel. (1) 4329900; fax (1) 4627933; Man. Dir THEODORE VENIAMIS.

M. Koutlakis and Co Ltd: Makras Stoas 5, 185 31 Piraeus; tel.
(1) 4129428; fax (1) 4178755; Dir M. KOUTLAKIS.

Laskaridis Shipping Co Ltd: Odos Chimaras 5, 151 25 Maroussi,
Athens; tel. (1) 6899090; fax (1) 6806762; e-mail athens@laskship
.cc.cwmail.com; Man. Dirs P. C. LASKARIDIS, A. C. LASKARIDIS.

Marmaras Navigation Ltd: Odos Filellinon 4–6, Okeanion Bldg,
185 36 Piraeus; tel. (1) 4294226; fax (1) 4294304; Dir D. DIAMANTIDES.

Minoan Lines Shipping SA: Odos 25 August 17, 712 02 Iraklion;
tel. (81) 330301; fax (81) 330308; internet www.minoan.gr; Pres.
KONSTANTINOS KLIRONOMAS.

Naftomar Shipping and Trading Co Ltd: Leoforos Alkyonidon
243, 166 73 Voula; tel. (1) 9670220; fax (1) 9670237; e-mail naftomar
@naftomar.gr; Man. Dir RIAD ZEIN.

Strintzis Lines Maritime S.A.: Odos Akti Possidonos 26, 185 31
Piraeus; (1) 4225000; fax (1) 4225265; Man. Dir G. STRINTZIS.

Thenamaris (Ships Management) Inc: Odos Athinas 16, Kav-
ouri, 166 71 Athens; tel. (1) 8969111; fax (1) 8969653; e-mail
sg.gd@thenamaris.gr; Dir K. MARTINOS.

Tsakos Shipping and Trading, SA: Leoforos Syngrou 367, Faliro,
175 64 Athens; tel. (1) 9380700; fax (1) 9480710; Dirs P. N. TSAKOS,
E. SAROGLOU.

United Shipping and Trading Co of Greece, SA: Odos Iassonos
6, 185 37 Piraeus; tel. (1) 4283660; fax (1) 4283630; Dir CH. TSAKOS.

Varnima Corporation International, SA: Odos Irodou Attikou
12A, 151 24 Maroussi, Athens; tel. (1) 8093000; fax (1) 8093222;
e-mail john_k@attglobal.net; Gen. Man. S. V. SPANOUDAKIS.

CIVIL AVIATION

There are international airports at Athens, Thessaloníki, Alexan-
droupolis, Corfu, Lesbos, Andravida, Rhodes, Kos and Heraklion/
Crete, and 24 domestic airports (of which 13 are authorized to
receive international flights). Construction of a new international
airport at Spata, some 25 km east of Athens, was finally approved
in 1995. The airport was expected to become operational in 2000,
with a handling capacity of 16m. passengers per year.

Cronus Airlines: Leoforos Vauliogmenis 500, 174 56 Alimos; tel. (1) 9956400; fax (1) 9956405; f. 1995; charter services to the United Kingdom, East Africa and Middle East; Chair. IOANNIS TH. MANETAS.

Olympic Airways, SA: Leoforos Syngrou 96–100, 117 41 Athens; tel. (1) 9269111; fax (1) 9267154; e-mail olyair10@otenet.gr; internet www.olympic-airways.gr; f. 1957; state-owned, 49% privatization projected by June 2001; domestic services linking principal cities and islands in Greece, and international services to Singapore, Thailand, South Africa and the USA, and throughout Europe and the Middle East; Chair. and Chief Exec. DIONYSIOS KALOFONOS.

Olympic Aviation: Leoforos Syngrou 96–100, 117 41 Athens; tel. (1) 9269111; fax (1) 9884059; wholly owned subsidiary of Olympic Airways; independent operator of scheduled domestic and regional services; Chair. STERGIOS PAPASIS; Chief Exec. PETROS STEFANOU.

Tourism

The sunny climate, the natural beauty of the country and its great history and traditions attract tourists to Greece. There are numerous islands and many sites of archaeological interest. The number of tourists visiting Greece increased from 1m. in 1968 to 10.9m. in 1998. Receipts from tourism, which totalled US $120m. in 1968, reached $5,186m. in 1998.

Ellinikos Organismos Tourismou (EOT) (Greek National Tourist Organization): Odos Amerikis 2B, 105 64 Athens; tel. (1) 3223111; fax (1) 3252895; Pres. IOANNIS STEFANIDES; Vice-Pres. IOANNIS ROUBATIS.

GRENADA

Introductory Survey

Location, Climate, Language, Religion, Flag, Capital

Grenada, a mountainous, heavily-forested island, is the most southerly of the Windward Islands, in the West Indies. The country also includes some of the small islands known as the Grenadines, which lie to the north-east of Grenada. The most important of these are the low-lying island of Carriacou and its neighbour, Petit Martinique. The climate is semi-tropical, with an average annual temperature of 28°C (82°F) in the lowlands. Annual rainfall averages about 1,500 mm (60 ins) in the coastal area and 3,800 mm to 5,100 mm (150–200 ins) in mountain areas. Most of the rainfall occurs between June and December. The majority of the population speak English, although a French patois is sometimes spoken. According to the census of 1991, 82% of Grenada's population were of African descent, while 13% were of mixed ethnic origins. Most of the population profess Christianity, and the main denominations are Roman Catholicism (to which 53% of the population adhered at the time of the 1991 census) and Anglicanism (about 14% of the population). The national flag (proportions 2 by 1) consists of a diagonally-quartered rectangle (yellow in the upper and lower segments, green in the right and left ones) surrounded by a red border bearing six five-pointed yellow stars (three at the upper edge of the flag, and three at the lower edge). There is a red disc, containing a large five-pointed yellow star, in the centre, and a representation of a nutmeg (in yellow and red) on the green segment near the hoist. The capital is St George's.

Recent History

Grenada was initially colonized by the French but was captured by the British in 1762. British control was recognized in 1783 by the Treaty of Versailles. Grenada continued as a British colony until 1958, when it joined the Federation of the West Indies, remaining a member until the dissolution of the Federation in 1962. Full internal self-government and statehood in association with the United Kingdom were achieved in March 1967. During this period, the political life of Grenada was dominated by Herbert Blaize, the leader of the Grenada National Party (GNP), and Eric Gairy, a local trade union leader, who in 1950 founded the Grenada United Labour Party (GULP), with the support of an associated trade union. Gairy became Premier after the elections of 1967 and again after those of 1972, which he contested chiefly on the issue of total independence. Grenada became independent, within the Commonwealth, on 7 February 1974, with Gairy as Prime Minister. Domestic opposition to Gairy was expressed in public unrest, and the formation by the three opposition parties—the GNP, the United People's Party and the New Jewel Movement (NJM)—of the People's Alliance, which contested the 1976 general elections and reduced GULP's majority in the Lower House.

The rule of Sir Eric Gairy, as he became in June 1977, was regarded by the opposition as increasingly autocratic and corrupt, and on 13 March 1979 he was replaced in a bloodless coup by the leader of the left-wing NJM, Maurice Bishop. The new People's Revolutionary Government (PRG) suspended the 1974 Constitution and announced the imminent formation of a People's Consultative Assembly to draft a new constitution. Meanwhile, Grenada remained a monarchy, with the British Queen as Head of State, represented in Grenada by a Governor-General. During 1980–81 there was an increase in repression, against a background of mounting anti-Government violence and the PRG's fears of an invasion by US forces.

By mid-1982 relations with the USA, the United Kingdom and the more conservative members of the Caribbean Community and Common Market (CARICOM—see p. 142) were becoming increasingly strained: elections had not been arranged, restrictions against the privately-owned press had been imposed, many detainees were still awaiting trial, and Grenada was aligning more closely with Cuba and the USSR. Cuba was contributing funds and construction workers for the airport at Point Salines, a project which further strengthened the US Government's conviction that Grenada was to become a centre for Soviet manoeuvres in the area.

In March 1983 the armed forces were put on alert, in response to renewed fears that the USA was planning to invade. (The USA strenuously denied any such plans.) In June Bishop sought to improve relations with the USA, and announced the appointment of a commission to draft a new constitution. This attempt at conciliation was denounced by the more left-wing members of the PRG as an ideological betrayal. A power struggle developed between Bishop and his deputy, Bernard Coard, the Minister of Finance and Planning. In October Bishop was placed under house arrest, allegedly for his refusal to share power with Coard. The commander of the People's Revolutionary Army (PRA), Gen. Austin Hudson, subsequently announced that Bishop had been expelled from the NJM. On 19 October thousands of Bishop's supporters stormed the house, freed Bishop, and demonstrated outside the PRA headquarters. PRA forces responded by firing into the crowd. Later in the day, Bishop, three of his ministers and two trade unionists were executed by the PRA. The Government was replaced by a 16-member Revolutionary Military Council (RMC), led by Gen. Austin and supported by Coard and one other minister. The remaining NJM ministers were arrested and imprisoned, and a total curfew was imposed.

Regional and international outrage at the assassination of Bishop, in addition to fears of a US military intervention, were so intense that after four days the RMC relaxed the curfew, reopened the airport and promised a swift return to civilian rule. However, the Organisation of Eastern Caribbean States (OECS, see p. 309) resolved to intervene in an attempt to restore democratic order, and asked for assistance from the USA, which readily complied. (It is unclear whether the decision to intervene preceded or followed a request for help to the OECS by the Grenadian Governor-General, Sir Paul Scoon.) On 25 October 1983 some 1,900 US military personnel invaded the island, accompanied by 300 troops from Jamaica, Barbados and member countries of the OECS. Fighting continued for some days, and the USA gradually increased its troop strength, with further reinforcements waiting off shore with a US naval task force. The RMC's forces were defeated, while Coard, Austin and others who had been involved in the coup were detained.

On 9 November 1983 Scoon appointed a non-political interim Council to assume responsibility for the government of the country until elections could be held. Nicholas Brathwaite, a former Commonwealth official, was appointed Chairman of this Council in December. The 1974 Constitution was reinstated (although the country did not rejoin the East Caribbean Supreme Court), and an electoral commission was created. By mid-December the USA had withdrawn all its forces except 300 support troops who were to assist the 430 members of Caribbean forces remaining on the island. A 550-member police force, trained by the USA and the United Kingdom, was established, including a paramilitary body that was to be the new defence contingent.

Several political parties that had operated clandestinely or from exile during the rule of the PRG re-emerged and announced their intention of contesting the elections for a new House of Representatives. Sir Eric Gairy returned to Grenada in January 1984 to lead GULP, but stated that he would not stand as a candidate himself. In May three former NJM ministers formed the Maurice Bishop Patriotic Movement (MBPM) to contest the elections. A number of centrist parties emerged or re-emerged, including Blaize's GNP. Fears that a divided opposition would allow GULP to win a majority of seats in the new House resulted in an agreement by several of these organizations, in August 1984, to form the New National Party (NNP), led by Blaize.

At the general election held in December 1984 the NNP achieved a convincing victory by winning 14 of the 15 seats in the House of Representatives, with 59% of the popular votes. Both GULP (which won 36% of the votes cast) and the MBPM claimed that the poll had been fraudulent, and the one successful GULP candidate, Marcel Peters, initially refused to take his seat in protest. He subsequently accepted the seat, but was expelled from the party and formed the Grenada Democratic Labour Party (GDLP). Blaize became Prime Minister. US and

Caribbean troops remained in Grenada, at Blaize's request, until September 1985.

The trial of 19 detainees (including Coard, his wife, Phyllis, and Gen. Austin), accused of murder and conspiracy against Bishop and six of his associates, opened in November 1984. However, repeated adjournments postponed the trial of 18 of the detainees until April 1986. One of the detainees agreed to give evidence for the State in return for a pardon. Eventually, verdicts on 196 charges of murder and conspiracy to murder were returned by the jury in December. Fourteen of the defendants were sentenced to death, three received prison sentences of between 30 and 45 years, and one was acquitted.

Internal differences gradually led to the disintegration of the NNP. In 1986 its parliamentary strength was reduced to 12 seats, following the resignation of two members who subsequently formed the Democratic Labour Congress (DLC). Three more government members resigned in April 1987, and joined forces with the DLC and the GDLP in July to form a united opposition, with six seats in the House of Representatives. In October they formally launched a new party, the National Democratic Congress (NDC), led by George Brizan, who had earlier been appointed parliamentary opposition leader. In January 1989 Brizan resigned as leader of the NDC in order to allow the election of Nicholas Brathwaite (head of the interim Government of 1983–84) to that post.

During 1988–89 the actions of the Blaize Government, under provisions of the controversial Emergency Powers Act of 1987, gave rise to concerns both within the opposition and among regional neighbours. Deportation orders and bans were enforced by the administration against prominent left-wing politicians and journalists from the region, and a variety of books and journals were proscribed.

Meanwhile, a deterioration in Blaize's health coincided with a growing challenge to his administration from within the NNP during 1988. In January 1989 Blaize was replaced as party leader by his cabinet colleague, Dr Keith Mitchell, although he remained Prime Minister. In July, however, following allegations of corruption by the NDC, Blaize announced the dismissal of Mitchell and the Chairman of the NNP, accusing them of violating the principles of cabinet government. Amid uncertainty as to whether the Blaize faction had formed a separate party, two more members of the Government resigned, thus reducing support for the Blaize Government to only five of the 15 members of the House of Representatives. Blaize did not officially announce the formation of a new party, the National Party (TNP), until late August, by which time he had advised the acting Governor-General to prorogue Parliament. (The Government thereby avoided being defeated in a motion of 'no confidence', the immediate dissolution of Parliament and the prospect of an early general election.) The term of the Parliament was due to expire at the end of December, and a general election had to be held within three months. However, Blaize died in mid-December, and the Governor-General appointed Ben Jones, Blaize's former deputy and the new leader of TNP, as Prime Minister. At the general election, held in March 1990, no party achieved an absolute majority in the House of Representatives. The NDC won seven of the 15 seats, GULP won four, while TNP and the NNP won only two each. The NDC achieved a working majority in Parliament when one of GULP's successful candidates announced his defection to the NDC. Brathwaite subsequently became Prime Minister and appointed a new Cabinet.

In July 1991 the Court of Appeal upheld the original verdicts that had been imposed in 1986 on the defendants in the Bishop murder trial, and further pleas for clemency were rejected. Preparations for the imminent hanging of the 14, however, provoked international outrage, and in August Brathwaite announced that the death sentences were to be commuted to terms of life imprisonment. His decision (which was contrary to prevailing public opinion on Grenada) was considered to have been influenced by intense pressure from politicians and human rights organizations, together with the potential detrimental effect on the country's important tourist industry.

A series of strikes by public-sector and port workers during 1992–93 caused considerable disruption, and prompted the approval by Parliament in mid-1993 of legislation aimed at restricting the right of trade unions to take industrial action.

Brathwaite resigned as leader of the NDC in September 1994 and was succeeded by George Brizan. In February 1995 Brathwaite resigned as Prime Minister, and was succeeded by Brizan. At the general election held in June, the NNP secured eight of the 15 seats in the House of Representatives, while the NDC's representation was reduced to five seats. The remaining two seats were secured by GULP. Dr Keith Mitchell, leader of the NNP, became Prime Minister and appointed a Cabinet. The NNP subsequently undertook negotiations with GULP in an attempt to strengthen its single-seat majority and to secure the two-thirds' majority required to amend the Constitution. In July Francis Alexis resigned as deputy leader of the NDC, alleging that an NDC member of Parliament had been unfairly treated by the party prior to the election. In November he and three other former NDC members announced the formation of a new opposition group, the Democratic Labour Party (DLP).

The appointment in August 1996 of Daniel (later Sir Daniel) Williams to the post of Governor-General provoked considerable controversy because of Williams' connections with the NNP (he had been deputy leader of the party during the 1980s) and his previous role as a cabinet minister in the Government of Herbert Blaize. Opposition members staged a walk-out at his inauguration ceremony, a protest that led to Brizan, the Leader of the Opposition, being suspended from the House of Representatives for one month.

Concern that the Government was attempting to restrict media freedom was heightened during 1996, following a series of apparently politically-motivated personnel changes at the state-owned Grenada Broadcasting Corporation. Local and regional press associations criticized the appointment, in April, of a senior NNP official as chief news editor and the dismissal, in July, of four experienced journalists (for allegedly failing to report an event staged by the ruling party). In January 1997 the Chairman of the corporation was similarly dismissed for failing to broadcast the budget debate in its entirety.

In late February 1997 Mitchell removed the Minister of Health, Housing and the Environment, Grace Duncan, from the post of Deputy Prime Minister, announcing the abolition of the deputy premiership. Earlier in the month Duncan had boycotted the NNP's annual convention, citing minor grievances with the Prime Minister. Duncan was dismissed in mid-July for making what were termed 'vulgar' remarks about Mitchell and for disclosing confidential information about government affairs, as well as allegedly disseminating misinformation, to the media. The dismissed minister subsequently stated that she had warned Mitchell of an internal party plot to undermine his administration. Meanwhile, in May GULP joined with the NDC, TNP, DLP and MBPM to announce a strategy of co-operation in opposing the Government on major national issues, accusing Mitchell of a lack of consultation and of 'growing dictatorship'. In the previous month an opposition motion of 'no confidence' in the Government had been rejected by the House of Representatives. At the end of June the establishment was announced of an eighth political party, the Grenada Progressive Party, led by Prescott Williams.

In March 1997 the Government's Mercy Committee rejected a request made by the Conference of Churches of Grenada for the release, on the grounds of their deteriorating physical and mental health, of Phyllis Coard and another of those serving terms of life imprisonment for the murder of Maurice Bishop. None the less, the Committee gave assurances that the detainees' medical requirements would receive attention, and that conditions at the prison where they were being held would be improved. Also in March Mitchell announced plans for the establishment of a national commission to investigate the 1979–83 revolutionary period.

Sir Eric Gairy, the founder and leader of GULP, died in August 1997. A lengthy power struggle within the party ensued, but a convention to elect Gairy's successor was eventually held in April/May 1998; in a controversial vote, Herbert Preudhomme (a former Deputy Prime Minister) narrowly defeated his opponent, who subsequently launched a protest against alleged electoral fraud.

In January 1998 Mitchell announced a cabinet reorganization and the creation of a new ministry, of Carriacou and Petit Martinique affairs, to be headed by Elvin Nimrod. In September the NDC and GULP announced that they had begun a working dialogue to seek to unseat the Government. In late November the Minister of Foreign Affairs, Raphael Fletcher, resigned from the Government and NNP in order to join GULP, citing his 'growing disenchantment and disagreement' with Mitchell. His resignation resulted in the dissolution of Parliament on 2 December; a general election was called for January 1999, although constitutionally it was not due until mid-2000. The

DLP and GULP agreed to contest the election together in an informal alliance known as United Labour.

At the general election held on 18 January 1999 (in which 56.5% of the electorate voted), the NNP achieved a comprehensive victory, receiving 62.2% of total votes cast and obtaining all of the 15 seats in the House of Representatives. The NDC won 24.9% of the votes, while the United Labour alliance received only 11.6%. Keith Mitchell retained his position as Prime Minister and appointed a new Cabinet. Several ministers retained their portfolios, while Mitchell himself replaced Fletcher as Minister of Foreign Affairs. The NNP's return to power constituted the first time in the country's history that a political party had been given two successive terms in government. In its electoral campaign the party had highlighted its recent successes in maintaining strong economic growth and reducing unemployment.

In late September and early October 1999 two leading journalists were arrested on separate charges of alleged criminal libel. One of the detainees was the editor of *Grenada Today*, George Worme, who had published a letter accusing Mitchell of having bribed voters during the last election campaign. Opposition parties, human rights organizations and media associations claimed that the Government was seeking to intimidate independent journalists. In November 2000 the Grenada High Court ruled that the charge brought against Worme was unconstitutional, since it violated his right to free expression.

Also in early October 1999 Bernard Coard, the former Deputy Prime Minister serving a term of life imprisonment with 16 others for the 1983 murder of Prime Minister Maurice Bishop and a number of his associates (see above), read a statement issued from the prison. In the statement Coard, for the first time, accepted full responsibility for the crimes; it was, however, unclear as to whether he was speaking on behalf of all 17 prisoners.

On 1 November 1999 Mitchell announced a cabinet reorganization in which he ceded the Foreign Affairs and Finance portfolios to Mark Isaac and Anthony Boatswain, respectively. The Minister of Agriculture, Lands, Forestry and Fisheries, Michael Baptiste, was demoted to junior minister. On 5 June 2000 Mitchell dismissed Baptiste from the Government, after Baptiste was reported to have openly criticized Mitchell's running of the country. Mitchell reportedly offered Baptiste the opportunity to remain as an NNP member of Parliament, or to join the opposition. Baptiste opted for the latter and became the sole opposition member in the House of Representatives (he subsequently became a member of GULP).

On 6 September 2000 three diplomats from the People's Republic of China, including the ambassador to Trinidad and Tobago, were deported from Grenada after they were accused of making statements that 'constituted interference in the internal affairs of Grenada'. The delegation were staying on the island for three days as guests of the Grenada–China Friendship Society, a non-political organization recently formed by Baptiste, which aimed to promote closer links between the two countries. From 1983 Grenada has maintained diplomatic relations with the Republic of China (Taiwan) instead of the People's Republic of China.

In October 2000 proposed government changes to Grenada's labour laws were condemned by the Trades Union Council (TUC) and opposition parties. The proposals followed labour unrest in April and May when teachers staged a series of stoppages following a dispute over pay, and port workers voted in favour of strike action after negotiations over new contracts broke down. Furthermore, on 12 May the Technical and Allied Workers' Union organized a national rally to protest at the allegedly unfair dismissal of 26 employees of the Grenada Broadcasting Network.

In December 2000 the World Bank approved US $10m. in loan and credit support to Grenada to strengthen its response to, and preparedness for, natural disasters; the funds were also intended to finance road reconstruction and flood control programmes.

In January 2001 the Minister of Foreign Affairs, Mark Isaac, was dismissed, reportedly following his decision to re-establish diplomatic relations with Libya without first gaining cabinet approval. He was succeeded by Elvin Nimrod. In March Raymond Anthony replaced Lawrence Joseph as Attorney-General and was also appointed Minister of Legal Affairs, a portfolio hitherto held by Nimrod. Joseph was appointed Minister of Labour and Local Government. At the same time, Nimrod was given the international trade portfolio.

In January 2001 a new opposition party, the United Labour Congress (ULC) was formed, following the merger of GULP and the People's Progressive Action. Michael Baptiste was appointed the ULC's interim leader and Kenny Lalsingh its interim Chairman pending a formal launch later in the year.

As a member of the OECS, Grenada has been involved in discussions concerning the possible formation of a political union. In 1988 Grenada, Dominica, Saint Lucia and Saint Vincent and the Grenadines decided to proceed with their own plans for a political union. In late 1990 it was agreed that a Windward Islands Regional Constituent Assembly (RCA) would be convened to discuss the economic and political feasibilities of creating a federation. In late 1992 members of Grenada's House of Representatives fully endorsed a continuation of progress towards political unity. In 1995 the newly-elected Mitchell Government expressed its commitment to increased political and economic integration between the four countries.

In May 1996 Grenada signed two treaties with the USA, relating to mutual legal assistance and extradition, as part of a regional campaign to combat drugs-trafficking. Improved relations with Cuba, which had been severely strained since 1983, resulted in offers of assistance with education, health and agriculture in Grenada in early 1997. Prime Minister Mitchell led a delegation to Cuba in April of that year; at the same time an aircraft of Cuba's national airline, carrying representatives of the Cuban Government, landed at Point Salines for the first time since the downfall of the revolution. In August 1998 President Fidel Castro Ruz of Cuba visited Grenada at Mitchell's invitation, provoking protest from GULP and the DLP, which demanded the release of political prisoners from Cuban jails and the implementation by Cuba of certain human rights agreements. Diplomatic relations between Grenada and Cuba (which had been suspended in 1983) were restored in December 1999. In 2000 Grenada also restored diplomatic relations with Libya (suspended in 1983) and established diplomatic relations with Belarus.

Government

Grenada has dominion status within the Commonwealth. The British monarch is Head of State and is represented locally by a Governor-General. Executive power is held by the Cabinet, led by the Prime Minister. Parliament comprises the Senate, made up of 13 Senators appointed by the Governor-General on the advice of the Prime Minister and the Leader of the Opposition, and the 15-member House of Representatives, elected by universal adult suffrage. The Cabinet is responsible to Parliament.

Defence

A regional security unit was formed in late 1983, modelled on the British police force and trained by British officers. A paramilitary element, known as the Special Service Unit and trained by US advisers, acts as the defence contingent and participates in the Regional Security System, a defence pact with other East Caribbean states.

Economic Affairs

In 1999, according to estimates by the World Bank, Grenada's gross national product (GNP), measured at average 1997–99 prices, was US $335m., equivalent to US $3,450 per head (or US $5,847 per head on an international purchasing-power parity basis). In 1990–98, it was estimated the country's GNP per head increased, in real terms, by an annual average of 1.8%. Over the same period Grenada's population increased at an average rate of 0.4% per year. Gross domestic product (GDP) increased, in real terms, at an average annual rate of 3.6% in 1990–99. Real GDP increased by 4.2% in 1997, by 7.3% in 1998 and by an estimated 8.2% in 1999; growth was projected at 5.3% for 2000.

Agriculture (including hunting, forestry and fishing) contributed 7.5% of GDP in 1999. The sector engaged 13.8% of the employed labour force in 1998. Grenada, known as the Spice Island of the Caribbean, is the largest producer of nutmeg after Indonesia (which produces some 75% of the world's total), and in 1987 it supplied 23% of the world's nutmeg. In 1999, according to preliminary IMF data, sales of nutmeg and mace (the pungent red membrane around the nut) accounted for 36.2% of Grenada's domestic export earnings. The other principal cash crops are bananas and other fruit and cocoa. Exports of bananas were suspended in early 1997 by the Windward Islands Banana Development and Exporting Company (WIBDECO) because of poor quality, but were permitted to resume in late 1998, following a rehabilitation programme. Nevertheless, exports of bananas were still greatly reduced in 1999, although some recovery in the sector was anticipated in 2000. In 1996 a US company conducted a feasibility study into the development of large-scale vanilla cultivation on Grenada. Livestock production, for domestic consumption, is important on Carriacou. There are extensive timber reserves on the island of Grenada; forestry development is strictly controlled and involves a programme of reafforestation. Exports of fish contributed 6.7% of domestic export earnings in 1999. Agricultural GDP declined at an average annual rate of 1.1% in 1990–99. The sector's GDP contracted by 0.9% in 1997, and by a further 1.2% in 1998, owing to a reduction in output of cocoa and bananas. However, agricultural GDP grew by some 10.0% in 1999, largely owing to increased production of nutmeg, mace and bananas.

Industry (mining, manufacturing, construction and utilities) provided 20.8% of GDP in 1999, and engaged 23.9% of the employed labour force in 1998. The mining sector accounted for only 0.2% of employment in 1998 and 0.5% of GDP in 1999. In 1996 a US company announced plans to conduct exploration for oil and gas deposits off the southern coast of Grenada. Manufacturing, which contributed 6.8% of GDP in 1999 and employed 7.4% of the working population in 1998, consists mainly of the processing of agricultural products and of cottage industries producing garments and spice-based items. A nutmeg oil distillation plant commenced production in 1995, and exports of the oil earned some EC $2m. in that year. From the late 1990s the electronic component sector gained in significance. Exports from this sector accounted for almost one-third (30.6%) of total merchandise exports. Rum, soft drinks, paints and varnishes, household paper products and the tyre-retreading industries are also important. Manufacturing GDP increased by an average of 6.1% per year in 1990–99. The sector's GDP increased by 5.3% in 1997, by 14.1% in 1998 and by 12.1% in 1999. Overall, industrial GDP increased by an average of 5.9% annually in 1990–99.

Grenada is dependent upon imports for its energy requirements, and in 1999 mineral fuels, lubricants, etc. accounted for 7.2% of the total cost of imports.

The services sector contributed 71.6% of GDP in 1999, when the hotels and restaurants sector accounted for some 8.4% of GDP. Tourism receipts totalled around EC$251.5m. in 1999. Since 1984 the number of stop-over arrivals and cruise-ship visitors has more than doubled. In 1998 the tourism industry recovered after experiencing several difficulties in 1997; in 1999, however, total visitor arrivals declined by 3.9%, to 376,535. The decrease was partly as a result of a 8.6% fall in cruise-ship arrivals. Stop-over arrivals, however, increased by 8.2% in 1999. Of total stop-over visitors (excluding non-resident Grenadians) in 1999, 32.5% were from the USA, 20.1% from Caribbean countries and 24.5% from the United Kingdom. The GDP of the services sector increased at an average annual rate of 5.9% in 1990–99.

In 1999 Grenada recorded a visible trade deficit of EC $345.4m. and there was a deficit of EC $137.9m. on the current account of the balance of payments. In 1998 the principal source of imports was the USA, accounting for 39.3% of the total. The USA is also the principal market for exports, taking 36.6% of the total in 1998. Trinidad and Tobago provided 22.2% of imports and received 3.0% of Grenada's exports in 1998. The principal exports are agricultural, notably nutmeg. The principal imports in 1999 were machinery and transport equipment, foodstuffs, and basic manufactures. The trade deficit is partly offset by earnings from tourism, capital receipts and remittances from Grenadians working abroad.

In 1999 there was a current budgetary surplus of EC $50.3m. and an overall deficit of EC $32.5m. Grenada's total external debt was US $182.8m. at the end of 1998, of which US $113.0m. was long-term public debt. In 1998 the cost of debt-servicing was equivalent to 5.0% of the value of exports of goods and services. The average annual rate of inflation was 2.2% in 1990–99, and consumer prices increased by 1.2% in 1997, by 1.4% in 1998 and by just 0.3% in 1999. According to government figures, an estimated 11% of the labour force were unemployed at the end of 2000.

Grenada is a member of CARICOM (see p. 142), and secured limited protection for some of its products when tariff barriers within the organization were removed in 1988. It is also a member of the Economic Commission for Latin America and the Caribbean (ECLAC, see p. 30), the Organization of American States (OAS, see p. 261), the Organisation of Eastern Caribbean States (OECS, see p. 309) and is a signatory of the Cotonou Agreement, the successor arrangement to the Lomé Conventions between the African, Caribbean and Pacific (ACP) countries and the European Union (see p. 208).

Grenada's economy remains largely dependent upon agriculture, which is vulnerable to adverse weather conditions and infestation by pests. Furthermore, the economy's susceptibility to the fluctuations in international commodity prices was demonstrated in 1990, when the price of nutmeg on the world market decreased by 30%, following the breakdown of Grenada's cartel agreement with Indonesia (signed in 1987). The two countries have since concluded several informal agreements in an attempt to stabilize the world nutmeg market through closer co-operation. From 1997 a decline in production of nutmeg in Indonesia resulted in higher prices on the external market, stimulating a significant increase in Grenada's output. In 1999 the country earned US $14.9m. from exports of nutmeg, compared with US $8.7m. in 1998. Nutmeg production was expected to increase in 2000; however, a fall in world prices was predicted, as production levels also were projected to increase in Indonesia.) The need for further economic diversification has recently been underscored by the potential loss of preferential access to European markets for banana producers of the ACP countries.

In the late 1990s the Government attempted to diversify the economy partly through the expansion of the 'offshore' financial sector. Since the introduction of legislation in 1997, some 900 'offshore' financial companies (including 21 banks) have been registered in Grenada; in September 1999 the creation of a regulatory body, the International Business and Finance Corporation, was announced. In January 2000, moreover, the Government established the Grenada International Financial Services Authority (GIFSA) to regulate the international financial services sector. In the same year, following Grenada's inclusion on international money-laundering and tax havens blacklists and the collapse (and subsequent government takeover) of an 'offshore' bank, the Government introduced measures to strengthen the GIFSA. These included redoubling efforts to combat money-laundering and drugs-trafficking; the establishment of a bank supervision department to ensure that all financial institutions operated within the norms of the sector; and a review of all existing legislation governing the financial services sector to comply with the requirements of the Organisation for Economic Co-operation and Development by March 2001. As part of this effort, in this month the Government revoked the licences of 17 'offshore' banks.

The most promising sector of the economy is tourism, from which revenue more than doubled between 1990 and 1999. Growth in the tourism sector has, in turn, stimulated the construction sector, the GDP of which expanded by some 5.0% in 1999. However, growth in the sector was expected to slow in 2000, as major construction projects neared completion. Some 95% of taxpayers were effectively exempted from personal income tax obligations after April 1996, when the Government raised significantly the income threshold for liability for this tax. In 1999 the IMF urged the Grenadian Government to tighten fiscal policy in order to improve the state of public finances (which continue to suffer from sizeable internal and external debts), warning that otherwise the high economic growth of recent years would become unsustainable. Growth in GDP of 5.0%–6.0% was forecast for 2000.

Social Welfare

There was no system of social security payments in Grenada prior to 1979. New initiatives launched in that year included the Youth for Reconstruction Programme, to provide basic paramedical services and assistance to the elderly and disabled, a national milk distribution programme and the establishment of community-directed day care centres. A National Insurance Scheme was inaugurated in 1983. In 1997 there was one hospital bed for every 178 people and one physician per 1,244 inhabitants. There are three main hospitals in St. George's, St. Andrew's and on Carriacou, as well as six local health centres, all in the main towns. The Ministry of Health and the Environment also finances free weekly clinics in each district. A psychiatric hospital, destroyed by military action in 1983, was rebuilt with US financial aid. Projected budgetary expenditure on health was EC $27.5m. in 1997 (equivalent to 13.3% of total recurrent expenditure).

Education

Education is free and compulsory for children between the ages of five and 16 years. Primary education begins at five years of age and lasts for seven years. Secondary education, beginning at the age of 12, lasts for a further five years. In 1995 a total of 23,256 children received public primary education in 57 schools. There were 19 public secondary schools, with 7,260 pupils registered, in that year. Technical Centres have been established in St Patrick's, St David's and St John's, and the Grenada National College, the Mirabeau Agricultural School and the Teachers' Training College have been incorporated into the Technical and Vocational Institute in St George's. The Extra-Mural Department of the University of the West Indies has a branch in St George's. A School of Medicine has been established at St George's University (SGU), where a School of Arts and Sciences was also founded in 1997, while there is a School of Fishing at Victoria. The rate of adult literacy was estimated at around 96% in the late 1990s. In 1997 the World Bank agreed to finance a US $7.6m. loan for improvements to schools. Projected budgetary expenditure on education was EC $25m. in 1998 (equivalent to 11.5% of total recurrent expenditure).

Public Holidays

2001: 1 January (New Year's Day), 7 February (Independence Day), 13 April (Good Friday), 16 April (Easter Monday), 7 May (Labour Day), 4 June (Whit Monday), 14 June (Corpus Christi), 6–7 August (Emancipation Holidays), 25 October (Thanksgiving Day), 25–26 December (Christmas).

2002: 1 January (New Year's Day), 7 February (Independence Day), 29 March (Good Friday), 1 April (Easter Monday), 6 May (Labour Day), 20 May (Whit Monday), 30 May (Corpus Christi), 5–6 August (Emancipation Holidays), 25 October (Thanksgiving Day), 25–26 December (Christmas).

Weights and Measures

The metric system is in use.

Statistical Survey

Source (unless otherwise stated): Central Statistical Office, Ministry of Finance, Lagoon Rd, St George's; tel. 440-2731; fax 440-4115.

AREA AND POPULATION

Area: 344.5 sq km (133.0 sq miles).

Population: 89,088 at census of 30 April 1981; 94,806 (males 46,637; females 48,169) at census of 12 May 1991 (excluding 537 persons in institutions and 33 persons in the foreign service); 100,100 (official estimate) at mid–1998.

Density (mid–1998): 290.6 per sq km.

Principal Town: St George's (capital), population 4,439 (1991 census).

Births and Deaths (1996): Registered live births 2,096 (birth rate 21.3 per 1,000); Registered deaths 782 (death rate 7.9 per 1,000).

Expectation of Life (years at birth, 2000): 71 (males 68; females 73). Source: *Population Reference Bureau.*

Employment (employees only, 1998): Agriculture, hunting, forestry and fishing 4,794; Mining and quarrying 58; Manufacturing 2,579; Electricity, gas and water 505; Construction 5,163; Wholesale and retail trade 6,324; Restaurants and hotels 1,974; Transport, storage and communications 2,043; Financing, insurance and real estate 1,312; Public administration, defence and social security 1,879; Community services 3,904; Other services 2,933; Activities not adequately defined 1,321; Total employed 34,789 (males 20,733; females 14,056).

AGRICULTURE, ETC.

Principal Crops (FAO estimates, '000 metric tons, 1999): Roots and tubers 4; Pulses 1; Coconuts 7; Vegetables 3; Sugar cane 7; Apples 1; Plums 1; Oranges 1; Grapefruit and pomelos 2; Other citrus fruits 1; Avocados 2; Mangoes 2; Bananas 4; Plantains 1; Other fruits 3; Cocoa beans 1 (unofficial figure). Source: FAO.

Official Estimates ('000 lb, 1999): Cocoa beans 2,073; Bananas 1,248; Nutmeg 5,876; Mace 459. Source: IMF, *Grenada: Statistical Annex* (August 2000).

Livestock (FAO estimates, '000 head, 1999): Cattle 4; Pigs 5; Sheep 13; Goats 7; Asses 1. Source: FAO.

Livestock Products (FAO estimates, '000 metric tons, 1999): Meat 1; Cows' milk 1; Hen eggs 1. Source: FAO.

Fishing (metric tons, live weight, 1998): Capture 1,718 (Groupers 52, Bigeye scads 53, Other scads 101, Common dolphinfish 153; Wahoos 59, Blackfin tuna 236, Yellowfish tuna 351, Atlantic sailfish 154, Atlantic blue marlin 61, Other marine fishes 165); Total catch 1,718. Source: FAO, *Yearbook of Fishery Statistics.*

INDUSTRY

Production (1994): Rum 3,000 hectolitres; Beer 24,000 hectolitres; Wheat flour 4,000 metric tons (1996); Cigarettes 15m.; Electricity 95 million kWh (1996). Source: mainly UN, *Industrial Commodity Statistics Yearbook.*

FINANCE

Currency and Exchange Rates: 100 cents = 1 Eastern Caribbean dollar (EC $). *Sterling, US Dollar and Euro Equivalents* (29 December 2000): £1 sterling = EC $4.029; US $1 = EC $2.700; €1 = EC $2.512; EC $100 = £24.82 = US $37.04 = €39.80. *Exchange Rate:* Fixed at US $1 = EC $2.70 since July 1976.

Budget (EC $ million 1999): *Revenue:* Tax revenue 232.0 (Taxes on income and profits 38.6, Taxes on property 7.1, Taxes on domestic goods and services 44.3, Taxes on international trade and transactions 142.0); Other current revenue 38.7; Capital revenue 3.6; Total 274.3, excluding grants received (17.8). *Expenditure:* Current expenditure 220.4 (Personal emoluments 119.4, Goods and services 30.2, Interest payments 23.0, Transfers and subsidies 47.8); Capital expenditure 104.2; Total 324.6.
Source: Eastern Caribbean Central Bank, *Report and Statement of Accounts.*

2000 (projections, EC $ million): *Revenue:* Total 297.5 (Recurrent 297.5; Capital 0), excl. grants (30.1). *Expenditure:* Total 357.9 (Recurrent 242.9; Capital 115.0).

International Reserves (US $ million at 31 December 1999): IMF special drawing rights 0.00; Foreign exchange 50.84; Total 50.84. Source: IMF, *International Financial Statistics.*

Money Supply (EC $ million at 31 December 1999): Currency outside banks 64.75; Demand deposits at deposit money banks 126.28; Total money 191.03. Source: IMF, *International Financial Statistics.*

Cost of Living (Consumer Price Index; base: 1995 = 100): 103.3 in 1997; 104.7 in 1998; 105.0 in 1999. Source: IMF, *International Financial Statistics.*

Expenditure on the Gross Domestic Product (EC $ million at current prices, 1999): Government final consumption expenditure 147.5; Private final consumption expenditure 695.8; Gross fixed capital formation 391.3; Increase in stocks 14.0; *Total domestic expenditure* 1,248.6; Exports of goods and services, *less* Imports of goods and services –228.2; *GDP in purchasers' values* 1,020.4. Source: IMF, *International Financial Statistics.*

Gross Domestic Product by Economic Activity (EC $ million at current prices, 1999): Agriculture, hunting, forestry and fishing 67.2; Mining and quarrying 4.1; Manufacturing 60.5; Electricity and water 41.5; Construction 79.3; Wholesale and retail trade 93.7; Restaurants and hotels 74.5; Transport and communications 201.1; Finance and insurance 77.9; Real estate 29.1; Government services 139.0; Other community, social and personal services 22.6; *Sub-total* 890.4; *Less* Imputed bank service charge 56.7; *GDP at factor cost* 833.8. Source: Eastern Caribbean Central Bank, *Statistical Digest 2000.*

Balance of Payments (EC $ million, 1999): Exports of goods f.o.b. 152.96; Imports of goods f.o.b. –498.35; *Trade balance* –345.39; Exports of services 428.86; Imports of services –217.81; *Balance on goods and services* –134.34; Other income received 11.53; Other income paid –90.67; *Balance on goods, services and income* –213.48; Current transfers received 96.07; Current transfers paid –20.44; *Current balance* –137.85; Capital account (net) 74.22; Direct investment from abroad 125.17; Portfolio investment liabilities 2.03; Portfolio investment assets –0.96; Other investment liabilities 62.64; Other investment assets –85.09; Net errors and omissions –29.27; *Overall balance* –10.89. Source: Eastern Caribbean Central Bank, *Balance of Payments 2000.*

EXTERNAL TRADE

Principal Commodities (US $ million, preliminary, 1999): *Imports:* Food and live animals 45.2; Crude materials (inedible) except fuels 5.9; Mineral fuels, lubricants, etc. 16.6; Chemicals 15.6; Basic manufactures 44.8; Machinery and transport equipment 66.0; Miscellaneous manufactured articles 31.1; Total (incl. others) 230.4 (excl. unrecorded imports). *Exports:* Cocoa 1.4; Nutmeg 14.9; Mace 1.9; Fish 3.1; Paper products 1.7; Flour 3.3; Electronic components 14.2; Total (incl. others) 46.4 (excl. re-exports 3.3). Source: IMF, *Grenada: Statistical Annex* (August 2000).

Principal Trading Partners (EC $ million, 1998): *Imports c.i.f.:* Antigua and Barbuda 8.1; Barbados 14.1; Canada 17.3; Netherlands 7.2; Trinidad and Tobago 122.3; United Kingdom 52.0; USA 216.4; Total (incl. others) 550.1. *Exports f.o.b.:* Antigua and Barbuda 2.2; Barbados 6.0; Canada 1.5; Dominica 3.3; France 2.7; French West Indies 2.9; Germany 5.5; Jamaica 1.8; Netherlands 14.6; Republic of Ireland 6.4; Saint Lucia 8.6; Saint Vincent and the Grenadines 1.5; Trinidad and Tobago 3.4; United Kingdom 3.2; USA 41.1; Total (incl. others) 112.3. Source: OECS, *External Merchandise Trade Annual Report 1998.*

TRANSPORT

Road Traffic (1991): Motor vehicles registered 8,262.

Shipping: *Merchant Fleet* (registered at 31 December 1998): 5 vessels (total displacement 887 grt). Source: Lloyd's Register of Shipping, *World Fleet Statistics. International Sea-borne Freight Traffic* (estimates, '000 metric tons, 1995): Goods loaded 21.3; Goods unloaded 193.0. *Ship Arrivals* (1991): 1,254. *Fishing vessels* (registered, 1987): 635.

Civil Aviation (aircraft arrivals, 1995): 11,310.

TOURISM

Visitor Arrivals: 368,417 in 1997; 391,680 in 1998; 376,535 (125,291 stop-overs, 243,042 cruise-ship passengers, 8,202 excursionists) in 1999. Source: Eastern Caribbean Central Bank, *Balance of Payments 2000.*

Cruise-ship Calls: 328 in 1998.

Receipts from Tourism (EC $ million): 219.1 in 1997; 231.7 in 1998; 251.5 in 1999. Source: Eastern Caribbean Central Bank, *Balance of Payments 2000*.

COMMUNICATIONS MEDIA

Radio Receivers (1997): 57,000 in use*.

Television Receivers (1997): 33,000 in use*.

Telephones (1997): 27,000 main lines in use†.

Telefax Stations (1996): 270 in use†.

Mobile Cellular Telephones (1997): 976 subscribers†.

Non-Daily Newspapers (1996): 4; circulation 14,000*.

* Source: UNESCO, *Statistical Yearbook*.

† Source: UN, *Statistical Yearbook*.

EDUCATION

Pre-primary (1994): 74 schools; 158 teachers; 3,499 pupils.

Primary (1995): 57 schools; 849 teachers; 23,256 pupils.

Secondary (1995): 19 schools; 381 teachers; 7,260 pupils.

Higher (excluding figures for the Grenada Teachers' Training College, 1993): 66 teachers; 651 students.

Directory

The Constitution

The 1974 independence Constitution was suspended in March 1979, following the coup, and almost entirely restored between November 1983, after the overthrow of the Revolutionary Military Council, and the elections of December 1984. The main provisions of this Constitution are summarized below:

The Head of State is the British monarch, represented in Grenada by an appointed Governor-General. Legislative power is vested in the bicameral Parliament, comprising a Senate and a House of Representatives. The Senate consists of 13 Senators, seven of whom are appointed on the advice of the Prime Minister, three on the advice of the Leader of the Opposition and three on the advice of the Prime Minister after he has consulted interests which he considers Senators should be selected to represent. The Constitution does not specify the number of members of the House of Representatives, but the country consists of 15 single-member constituencies, for which representatives are elected for up to five years, on the basis of universal adult suffrage.

The Cabinet consists of a Prime Minister, who must be a member of the House of Representatives, and such other ministers as the Governor-General may appoint on the advice of the Prime Minister.

There is a Supreme Court and, in certain cases, a further appeal lies to Her Majesty in Council.

The Government

Head of State: HM Queen ELIZABETH II (succeeded to the throne 6 February 1952).

Governor-General: Sir DANIEL WILLIAMS (appointed 8 August 1996).

THE CABINET
(April 2001)

Prime Minister and Minister of National Security and Information: Dr KEITH MITCHELL.

Minister of Finance, Trade, Industry and Planning: ANTHONY BOATSWAIN.

Minister of Foreign Affairs and International Trade, and of Carriacou and Petit Martinique Affairs: Sen. ELVIN NIMROD.

Minister of Health and the Environment: CLARICE MODESTE-CURWEN.

Minister of Education: AUGUSTINE JOHN.

Minister of Youth, Sports and Community Development: ADRIAN MITCHELL.

Minister of Agriculture, Lands, Forestry and Fisheries: CLARIS CHARLES.

Minister of Tourism, Civil Aviation, Social Security, Gender and Family Affairs: BRENDA HOOD.

Minister of Housing, Social Services, Culture and Co-operatives: CUTHBERT BRIAN McQUEEN.

Minister of Communications, Works and Public Utilities: Sen. GREGORY BOWEN.

Minister of Transport: OLIVER ARCHIBALD.

Minister of Implementation: JOSLYN WHITEMAN.

Minister of Labour and Local Government: Sen. LAWRENCE JOSEPH.

Attorney-General and Minister of Legal Affairs responsible for Labour: Sen. RAYMOND ANTHONY.

MINISTRIES

Office of the Governor-General: Government House, St George's; tel. 440-2401; fax 440-6688.

Office of the Prime Minister: Ministerial Complex, 6th floor, St George's; tel. 440-2255; fax 440-4116; e-mail gndpm@caribsurf.com.

Ministry of Agriculture, Lands, Forestry and Fisheries: Ministerial Complex, 2nd and 3rd Floors, St George's; tel. 440-2708; fax 440-4191; e-mail grenfish@caribsurf.com.

Ministry of Carriacou and Petit Martinique Affairs: Beauséjour, Carriacou; tel. 443-6026; fax 443-6040.

Ministry of Communications, Works and Public Utilities: Ministerial Complex, 4th Floor, St George's; tel. 440-2181; fax 440-4122; e-mail ministerworks@caribsurf.com.

Ministry of Education: Young St, St George's; tel. 440-2166; fax 440-6650; e-mail mail@mined.edu.gd.

Ministry of Finance, Trade, Industry and Planning: Financial Complex, Lagoon Rd, St George's; tel. 440-2731; fax 440-4115; e-mail plandev@caribsurf.com.

Ministry of Foreign Affairs and International Trade: Ministerial Complex, 4th floor, Botanical Gardens, St. George's; tel. 440-2640; fax 440-4184; e-mail faffgnd@caribsurf.com.

Ministry of Health and the Environment: Ministerial Complex, 1st and 2nd Floors, Botanical Gardens, St. George's; tel. 440-2649; fax 440-4127; e-mail min_healthgrenada@caribsurf.com.

Ministry of Housing, Social Services, Culture and Co-operatives: Ministerial Complex, 1st and 2nd Floors, Botanical Gardens, St. George's; tel. 440-6917; fax 440-6924.

Ministry of Implementation: Ministerial Complex, 6th Floor, St George's; tel. 440-2255; fax 440-4116.

Ministry of Information: Ministerial Complex, 6th Floor, Botanical Gardens, St George's; tel. 440-2255; fax 440-4116.

Ministry of Labour and Local Government: St George's.

Ministry of Legal Affairs: Church St, St George's; tel. 440-2050; fax 440-6630; e-mail legalaffairs@caribsurf.com.

Ministry of National Security: Botanical Gardens, St George's; tel. 440-2255.

Ministry of Tourism, Civil Aviation, Social Security, Gender and Family Affairs: Ministerial Complex, 4th Floor, Botanical Gardens, St George's; tel. 440-0366, fax 440-0443; e-mail mot@caribsurf.com; internet www.spiceisle.com.users.mot.

Ministry of Transport: Young St, St. George's.

Ministry of Youth, Sports and Community Development: Ministerial Complex, 2nd Floor, Botanical Gardens, St George's; tel. 440-6917; fax 440-6924.

Legislature

PARLIAMENT

Houses of Parliament: Church St, St George's; tel. 440-2090; fax 440-4138.

Senate

President: Sen. Dr JOHN WATTS.

There are 13 appointed members.

House of Representatives

Speaker: Sir CURTIS STRACHAN.

General Election, 18 January 1999

	Votes	%	Seats
New National Party (NNP)	25,897	62.2	15*
National Democratic Congress (NDC)	10,399	24.9	–
United Labour*†	4,853	11.6	–
Others	455	1.1	–
Total	41,604	100.0	15

* In June 2000 the NNP's parliamentary representation was reduced to 14 seats after one of its deputies, Michael Baptiste, joined the opposition. As a consequence, United Labour gained one seat in the House of Representatives.

† Informal electoral alliance composed of the Grenada United Labour Party (GULP) and the Democratic Labour Party (DLP).

Political Organizations

Democratic Labour Party (DLP): St George's; f. 1995 by former members of the NDC; Leader Dr FRANCIS ALEXIS; Dep. Leader WAYNE FRANCIS.

Grenada Progressive Party: f. 1997; Leader PRESCOTT WILLIAMS.

Maurice Bishop Patriotic Movement (MBPM): St George's; f. 1984 by former members of the New Jewel Movement; socialist; Leader TERRENCE MARRYSHOW.

National Democratic Congress (NDC): St George's; f. 1987 by former members of the NNP and merger of Democratic Labour Congress and Grenada Democratic Labour Party; centrist; Leader TILLMAN THOMAS; Dep. Leader JOAN PURCELL.

The National Party (TNP): St George's; f. 1989 by Prime Minister Herbert Blaize and his supporters, following a split in the New National Party; Chair. GEORGE McGUIRE; Leader BEN JONES.

New National Party (NNP): St George's; f. 1984, following merger of Grenada Democratic Movement, Grenada National Party and National Democratic Party; centrist; Chair. LAWRENCE JOSEPH; Leader Dr KEITH MITCHELL; Dep. Leader GREGORY BOWEN.

United Labour Congress (ULC): St George's; f. 2001 following merger of Grenada United Labour Party (GULP, f. 1950) and People's Progressive Action Party; Chair. KENNY LALSINGH (acting); Leader MICHAEL BAPTISTE (acting).

United Republican Party (URP): St George's; f. 1993 by Grenadians residing in New York, USA; Leader ANTONIO LANGDON.

Diplomatic Representation

EMBASSIES AND HIGH COMMISSION IN GRENADA

China (Taiwan): Archibald Ave, POB 36, St George's; tel. 440-3054; e-mail rocemgnd@caribsurf.com; Ambassador: DAVID Y. L. LIN.

Cuba: St George's; Ambassador: HUMBERTO RIVERO.

United Kingdom: British High Commission, 14 Church St, St George's; tel. 440-3222; fax 440-4939; e-mail bhcgrenada@caribsurf.com (High Commissioner resident in Barbados).

USA: POB 54, St George's; tel. 444-1173; fax 444-4820; e-mail usemb_gd@caribsurf.com; internet www.spiceisle.com/homepages/usemb_gd/embinfo (Ambassador resident in Barbados).

Venezuela: Archibald Ave, POB 201, St George's; tel. 440-1721; fax 440-6657; Ambassador: TEOFILO LABRADOR.

Judicial System

Justice is administered by the West Indies Associated States Supreme Court, composed of a High Court of Justice and a Court of Appeal. The Itinerant Court of Appeal consists of three judges and sits three times a year; it hears appeals from the High Court and the Magistrates' Court. The Magistrates' Court administers summary jurisdiction.

In 1988 the OECS excluded the possibility of Grenada's readmittance to the East Caribbean court system until after the conclusion of appeals by the defendants in the Maurice Bishop murder trial (see Recent History). Following the conclusion of the case in 1991, Parliament voted to rejoin the system, thus also restoring the right of appeal to the Privy Council in the United Kingdom.

Attorney-General: ERROL THOMAS.

Puisne Judges: LYLE K. ST PAUL, BRIAN KEITH ALLEYNE.

Registrar of the Supreme Court: SANDRA BELFON.

President of the Court of Appeal: C. M. DENNIS BYRON.

Office of the Attorney-General: St George's; tel. 440-2050.

Religion

CHRISTIANITY

The Roman Catholic Church

Grenada comprises a single diocese, suffragan to the archdiocese of Castries (Saint Lucia). The Bishop participates in the Antilles Episcopal Conference (based in Port of Spain, Trinidad and Tobago). At 31 December 1998 there were an estimated 54,686 adherents in the diocese.

Bishop of St George's in Grenada: Rt Rev. SYDNEY ANICETUS CHARLES, Bishop's House, Morne Jaloux, POB 375, St George's; tel. 443-5299; fax 443-5758; e-mail bissac@caribsurf.com.

The Anglican Communion

Anglicans in Grenada are adherents of the Church in the Province of the West Indies, and represented 14% of the population at the time of the 1991 census. The country forms part of the diocese of the Windward Islands (the Bishop, the Rt Rev. SEHON GOODRIDGE, resides in Kingstown, Saint Vincent).

Other Christian Churches

The Presbyterian, Methodist, Plymouth Brethren, Baptist, Salvation Army, Jehovah's Witness, Pentecostal (7.2% of the population in 1991) and Seventh-day Adventist (8.5%) faiths are also represented.

The Press

NEWSPAPERS

Bernacle: Tyrell St, St George's; tel. 440-5151; monthly; Editor IAN GEORGE.

Business Eye: Young St, St George's; tel. 440-3425.

The Consumer: Melville St, POB 232, St George's; tel. 440-2305; weekly.

The Grenada Guardian: Upper Lucas St, St George's; tel. 444-3823; fax 444-2873; weekly; organ of GULP.

The Grenada Informer: Market Hill, POB 622, St George's; tel. 440-5762; fax 440-4119; e-mail movanget@caribsurf.com; f. 1985; weekly; Editor CARLA BRIGGS; circ. 6,000.

Grenada Times: Market Hill, POB 622, St George's; tel. 440-5762; fax 440-4117; weekly; Editor JEROME MCBARNETT.

Grenada Today: St John's St, POB 142, St George's; tel. 440-4401; internet www.belgrafix.com/gtoday98.htm; weekly; Editor GEORGE WORME.

The Grenadian Voice: 10 Melville St, POB 633, St George's; tel. 440-1498; fax 440-4117; e-mail gvoice@caribsurf.com; internet www.spiceisle.com/gvoice; weekly; Editor LESLIE PIERRE; circ. 3,000.

Government Gazette: St George's; weekly; official.

PRESS ASSOCIATION

Press Association of Grenada: St George's; f. 1986; Pres. LESLIE PIERRE.

Inter Press Service (IPS) (Italy) is also represented.

Publishers

Anansi Publications: Hillsborough St, St George's; tel. 440-0800; e-mail aclouden@caribsurf.com.

Grenada Publishers Ltd: Torchlight, Melville St, St George's; tel. 440-2305.

Broadcasting and Communications

TELECOMMUNICATIONS

Cable and Wireless Grenada Ltd: POB 119, The Carenage, St. George's; tel. 440-1000; fax 440-4134; e-mail gndinfo@caribsurf.com; internet www.candw.gd; f. 1989; 30% govt-owned; Chair. NICK KOUMARIANOS; Man. DAVID WRIGHT.

Grenada Postal Corporation: Burns Point, St George's; tel. 440-2526; fax 440-4271; Chair. CUTHBERT JOHN; Man. LEO ROBERTS.

Grenada Telecommunications Ltd (Grentel): POB 119, St George's; tel. 444-2202; fax 444-4848; internet www.spiceisle.com; Gen. Man. NEVILLE CALLISTE.

BROADCASTING

Grenada Broadcasting Network: Observatory Rd, POB 535, St George's; tel. 440-2446; fax 440-4180; e-mail gbn@caribsurf.com; internet www2.spiceisle.com; f. 1972; 60% privately-owned, 40% govt-owned; Chair. KEN GORDON; Man. Dir HAMLET MARK.

Radio

Spice Capitol Radio FM 90: Springs, St George's; tel. 440-0162.

The Harbour Light of the Windwards: Carriacou; tel. and fax 443-7628; e-mail hbrlight@caribsurf.com; Station Man. RANDY CORNELIUS; Chief Engineer JOHN MCPHERSON.

Television

Television programmes from Trinidad and from Barbados can be received on the island.

Grenada Broadcasting Corporation (Television): Morne Jaloux, POB 535, St. George's; tel. 444-5522; fax 444-5054; govt-owned; Man. Dir CECIL BENJAMIN; Programme Dir ANDRÉ JEROME.

Finance

(cap. = capital; res = reserves; dep. = deposits; amounts in Eastern Caribbean dollars)

The Eastern Caribbean Central Bank (see p. 310), based in Saint Christopher, is the central issuing and monetary authority for Grenada.

Eastern Caribbean Central Bank—Grenada Office: NIS Bldg, Melville St, St George's; tel. 440-3016; fax 440-6721.

BANKING

Grenada Bank of Commerce Ltd: Corner of Cross and Halifax Sts, POB 4, St George's; tel. 440-3521; fax 440-4153; e-mail gbcltd@caribsurf.com; f. 1983; 10% govt-owned; cap. 7.4m., res 8.8m., dep. 227.4m. (Dec. 1999); Chair. PETER JULY; Gen. Man. MORRIS MATHLIN.

Grenada Co-operative Bank Ltd: 8 Church St, POB 135, St George's; tel. 440-2111; fax 440-6600; e-mail co-opbank@caribsurf.com; f. 1932; Man. Dir and Sec. G. V. STEELE; brs in St Andrew's and St Patrick's.

Grenada Development Bank: POB 734, Melville St, St George's; tel. 440-2382; fax 440-6610; e-mail gdbbank@caribsurf.com; f. 1976, following merger; Chair. ARNOLD CRUICKSHANK; Man. PATRICK LA ROSE.

National Commercial Bank of Grenada Ltd: NCB House, POB 857, Grand Anse, St George's; tel. 444-2265; fax 444-5500; e-mail ncbgnd@caribsurf.com; internet www.ncbgrenada.com; f. 1979; 51% owned by Republic Bank Ltd, Port of Spain; cap. 15.0m., res 8.1m., dep. 333.1m. (Sept. 1999); Chair. RONALD HARFORD; Man. Dir MICHAEL B. ARCHIBALD; 9 brs.

Foreign Banks

Bank of Nova Scotia (Canada): Granby and Halifax Sts, POB 194, St George's; tel. 440-3274; fax 440-4173; Man. B. ROBINSON; 3 brs.

Barclays Bank PLC (UK): Church and Halifax Sts, POB 37, St George's; tel. 440-3232; fax 440-4103; Man. IVAN BROWNE; 3 sub-brs in Carriacou, Grenville and Grand Anse.

Caribbean Commercial Bank (Trinidad and Tobago): St George's; 1 br.

INSURANCE

Several foreign insurance companies operate in Grenada and the other islands of the group. Principal locally-owned companies include the following:

Grenada Insurance and Finance Co Ltd: Young St, POB 139, St George's; tel. 440-3004.

Grenada Motor and General Insurance Co Ltd: Scott St, St George's; tel. 440-3379.

Grenadian General Insurance Co Ltd: Corner of Young and Scott Sts, POB 47, St George's; tel. 440-2434; fax 440-6618.

Trade and Industry

CHAMBERS OF COMMERCE

Grenada Chamber of Industry and Commerce, Inc: DeCaul Bldg, Mt Gay, POB 129, St George's; tel. 440-2937; fax 440-6621; e-mail gcic@caribsurf.com; internet www.spiceisle.com/homepages/gcic; f. 1921, incorporated 1947; 180 mems; Pres. AZAM RAHAMAN; Exec. Dir CHRISTOPHER DERIGGS.

Grenada Manufacturing Council: POB 129, St George's; tel. 440-2937; fax 440-6627; e-mail gcic@caribsurf.com; f. 1991 to replace Grenada Manufacturers' Asscn; Chair. CHRISTOPHER DEALLIE.

INDUSTRIAL AND TRADE ASSOCIATIONS

Grenada Cocoa Association: Scott St, St George's; tel. 440-2234; fax 440-1470; f. 1987, following merger; changed from co-operative to shareholding structure in late 1996; Chair. LAWRENCE GRENADE; Gen. Man. KEN-MARTIN WHITEMAN.

Grenada Co-operative Banana Society: Scott St, St George's; tel. 440-2486; fax 440-4199; f. 1955; a statutory body to control production and marketing of bananas; Exec. Chair. DANIEL LEWIS; Gen. Man. JOHN MARK (acting).

Grenada Co-operative Nutmeg Association: POB 160, St George's; tel. 440-2117; fax 440-6602; f. 1947; processes and markets all the nutmeg and mace grown on the island; to include the production of nutmeg oil; Chair. BYRON CAMPBELL; Man. (vacant).

Grenada Industrial Development Corporation: Frequente Industrial Park, Frequente, St David's; tel. 444-1035; fax 444-4828; e-mail gidc@caribsurf.com; internet www.spiceisle.com/users/gidc; f. 1985; Chair. RUPERT AGOSTINI; Man. TERENCE MOORE.

Marketing and National Importing Board: Young St, St George's; tel. 440-1791; fax 440-4152; e-mail mnib.com@mailcaribsurf.com; f. 1974; govt-owned; imports basic food items, incl. sugar, rice and milk; Chair. ANTHONY BOATSWAIN; Man. FITZROY JAMES.

EMPLOYERS' ORGANIZATION

Grenada Employers' Federation: Mt Gay, POB 129, St George's; tel. 440-1832; 60 mems.

There are several marketing and trading co-operatives, mainly in the agricultural sector.

UTILITIES

Public Utilities Commission: St George's.

Electricity

Grenada Electricity Services Ltd (Grenlec): POB 381, Halifax St, St George's; tel. 440-2097; fax 440-4106; e-mail grenlec@caribsurf.com; internet elec.carilec.com.lc/grenlec; generation and distribution; 90% privately-owned, 10% govt-owned; Chair. G. ROBERT BLANCHARD; Gen. Man. NIGEL D. WARDLE.

Water

National Water and Sewerage Authority: The Carenage, St George's; tel. 440-2155; fax 440-4107; Chair. NELSON LOUISON; Man. LEROY NECKLES.

TRADE UNIONS

Grenada Trade Union Council (GTUC): Green St, POB 405, St George's; tel 440-3733; Pres. C. ERIC PIERRE; Gen. Sec. CLARIS CHARLES.

Commercial and Industrial Workers' Union: Bains Alley, St George's; tel. 440-3423; 492 mems; Pres. A. DE BOURG.

Grenada Union of Teachers (GUT): Marine Villa, St George's; f. 1913; Pres. CLARIS CHARLES; 1,300 mems.

Seamen and Waterfront Workers' Union: The Carenage, POB 154, St George's; tel. 440-2573; f. 1952; Pres. ALBERT JULIEN; Gen. Sec. ERIC PIERRE; 350 mems.

Technical and Allied Workers' Union (TAWU): Green St, POB 405, St George's; tel. 440-2231; fax 440-5878; f. 1958; Pres. Sen. CHESTER HUMPHREY.

Bank and General Workers' Union (BGWU): St George's; tel. 440-3563; Pres. DEREK ALLARD.

Grenada Manual, Maritime and Intellectual Workers' Union (GMMIWU): St George's; Pres. (vacant); Vice-Pres. RAYMOND ANTHONY.

Grenada Media Workers' Association: St George's; Pres. RAY ROBERTS.

Public Workers' Union (PWU): POB 420, St George's; tel. 440-2203; f. 1931; Pres. LAURET CLARKSON; Exec. Sec. ALVIN ST JOHN.

Transport

RAILWAYS

There are no railways in Grenada.

ROADS

In 1996 there were approximately 1,040 km (646 miles) of roads, more than half of which were suitable for motor traffic. Public transport is provided by small private operators, with a system covering the entire country. In 1996 a concessionary loan worth some US $29m. was secured from the Government of Japan for a project to improve the road between St George's and St Andrew's.

SHIPPING

The main port is St George's, with accommodation for two ocean-going vessels of up to 500 ft. A number of shipping lines call at St George's. Grenville, on Grenada, and Hillsborough, on Carriacou, are used mostly by small craft.

Grenada Ports Authority: POB 494, The Carenage, St George's; tel. 440-7678; fax 440-3418; e-mail grenport@caribsurf.com; internet www.grenadaports.com; Chair. WALTER ST JOHN; Man. AMBROSE PHILLIP.

CIVIL AVIATION

The Point Salines International Airport, 10 km (6 miles) from St George's, was opened in October 1984, and has scheduled flights to most East Caribbean destinations, including Venezuela, and to the United Kingdom and North America. Work on an EC $30m.-project to renovate and expand the airport was scheduled to begin in early 2000. There is an airfield at Pearls, 30 km (18 miles) from St George's, and Lauriston Airport, on the island of Carriacou, offers regular scheduled services to Grenada, Saint Vincent and Palm Island (Grenadines of Saint Vincent).

Grenada is a shareholder in the regional airline, LIAT (see under Antigua and Barbuda). In 1987 Air Antilles (based in Saint Lucia) was designated as the national carrier.

Grenada Airports Authority: Point Salines Int. Airport, POB 385, St George's; f. 1985; tel. 444-4101; fax 444-4838; e-mail gaa@caribsurf.com; Chair. MICHAEL MCINTYRE; Gen. Man. DONALD MCPHAIL.

Tourism

Grenada has the attractions of both white sandy beaches and a scenic, mountainous interior with an extensive rain forest. There are also sites of historical interest, and the capital, St George's, is a noted beauty spot. In 1999 there were 376,535 tourist arrivals, of which 243,042 were cruise-ship passengers, and tourism earned some EC \$252m. There were approximately 1,670 hotel rooms in 1996. In 1997 a joint venture between the Government of Grenada and the Caribbean Development Bank to upgrade and market some 50 unprofitable hotels was implemented. In addition, the Ministry of Tourism, in conjunction with the Board of Tourism and the Hotel Association, announced a 10-year development plan to increase hotel capacity from its present level to 2,500 rooms.

Grenada Board of Tourism: POB 293, Burns Point, St George's; tel. 440-2279; fax 440-6637; e-mail gbt@caribsurf.com; internet www.grenada.org; f. 1991; Chair. LYDEN RAMDHANNY; Dir WILLIAM JOSEPH.

Grenada Hotel Association Ltd: POB 440, St George's; tel. 444-1353; fax 444-4847; e-mail grenhota@caribsurf.com; internet www.grenadahotelsinfo.com; f. 1961; Pres. ESTHER NOEL; Dirs LEO GARBUTT, AUGUSTUS CRUICKSHANK.

GUATEMALA

Introductory Survey

Location, Climate, Language, Religion, Flag, Capital

The Republic of Guatemala lies in the Central American isthmus, bounded to the north and west by Mexico, with Honduras and Belize to the east and El Salvador to the south. It has a long coastline on the Pacific Ocean and a narrow outlet to the Caribbean Sea. The climate is tropical in the lowlands, with an average temperature of 28°C (83°F), and more temperate in the central highland area, with an average temperature of 20°C (68°F). The official language is Spanish, but more than 20 indigenous languages are also spoken. Almost all of the inhabitants profess Christianity: the majority are Roman Catholics, while about 10% are Protestants. The national flag (proportions 8 by 5) has three equal vertical stripes, of blue, white and blue, with the national coat of arms (depicting a quetzal, the 'bird of freedom', and a scroll, superimposed on crossed rifles and sabres, encircled by a wreath) in the centre of the white stripe. The capital is Guatemala City.

Recent History

Under Spanish colonial rule, Guatemala was part of the Viceroyalty of New Spain. Independence was obtained from Spain in 1821, from Mexico in 1824 and from the Federation of Central American States in 1838. Subsequent attempts to revive the Federation failed and, under a series of dictators, there was relative stability, tempered by periods of disruption. A programme of social reform was begun by Juan José Arévalo (President in 1944–50) and his successor, Col Jacobo Arbenz Guzmán, whose policy of land reform evoked strong opposition from landowners. In 1954 President Arbenz was overthrown in a coup led by Col Carlos Castillo Armas, who invaded the country with US assistance. Castillo became President but was assassinated in July 1957. The next elected President, Gen. Miguel Ydigoras Fuentes, took office in March 1958 and ruled until he was deposed in March 1963 by a military coup, led by Col Enrique Peralta Azurdia. He assumed full powers as Chief of Government, suspended the Constitution and dissolved the legislature. A Constituent Assembly, elected in 1964, introduced a new Constitution in 1965. Dr Julio César Méndez Montenegro was elected President in 1966, and in 1970 the candidate of the Movimiento de Liberación Nacional (MLN), Col (later Gen.) Carlos Araña Osorio, was elected President. Despite charges of fraud in the elections of March 1974, Gen. Kjell Laugerud García of the MLN took office as President in July.

President Laugerud sought to discourage extreme right-wing violence and claimed some success, although it was estimated that 50,000–60,000 people were killed in political violence between 1970 and 1979. In March 1978 Gen. Fernando Romeo Lucas García was elected President. The guerrilla movement increased in strength in 1980–1981, while the Government was accused of the murder and torture of civilians and, particularly, persecution of the country's indigenous Indian inhabitants, who comprise 60% of the population.

In the presidential elections of March 1982, from which the left-wing parties were absent, the Government's candidate, Gen. Angel Aníbal Guevara, was declared the winner; however, the elections were denounced as fraudulent by the other presidential candidates. Guevara was prevented from taking office in July by a coup on 23 March, in which a group of young right-wing military officers installed Gen. José Efraín Ríos Montt (a candidate in the 1974 presidential elections) as leader of a three-man junta. Congress was closed, and the Constitution and political parties suspended. In June Gen. Ríos Montt dissolved the junta and assumed the presidency. He attempted to fight corruption, reorganized the judicial system and disbanded the secret police. The number of violent deaths diminished. However, after initially gaining the support of the national university, the Roman Catholic Church and the labour unions and hoping to enter into dialogue with the guerrillas, who refused to respond to an amnesty declaration in June, Ríos Montt declared a state of siege, and imposed censorship of the press, in July. In addition, the war against the guerrillas intensified, and a civil defence force of Indians was established. The efficiency and ruthlessness of the army increased. Whole villages were burnt, and many inhabitants killed, in order to deter the Indians from supporting the guerrillas. Ríos Montt's increasingly corporatist policies alienated all groups, and his fragile hold on power was threatened in 1982 by several attempted coups, which he managed to forestall.

The US administration was eager to renew sales of armaments and the provision of economic and military aid to Guatemala, which had been suspended in 1977 as a result of serious violations of human rights. In January 1983 the US Government, satisfied that there had been a significant decrease in such violations during Ríos Montt's presidency, announced the resumption of arms sales to Guatemala. However, independent reports claimed that the situation had deteriorated, and revealed that 2,600 people had been killed during the first six months of Ríos Montt's rule. In March the army was implicated in the massacre of 300 Indian peasants at Nahulá, and there was a resurgence in the activity of both left- and right-wing 'death squads'. The President declared a 30-day amnesty for guerrillas and political exiles, and lifted the state of siege. Furthermore, he announced the creation of an electoral tribunal to oversee a proposed transfer from military rule to civilian government. In April the army launched a new offensive, which made significant gains against the guerrillas. The Government's pacification programme comprised three phases of aid programmes, combined with the saturation of the countryside by anti-guerrilla units. The 'guns and beans' policy provided food and medicine in exchange for recruitment to the Patrullas de Autodefensa Civil (PAC), a pro-Government peasant militia. (By 1985 these self-defence patrols numbered 900,000 men.) The 'roofs, bread and work' phase involved the development of 'model villages', and the 'Aid Programme for Areas in Conflict' was an ambitious rural development scheme.

By mid-1983 opposition to the President was widespread. On 8 August Gen. Oscar Humberto Mejía Victores, the Minister of Defence, led a successful coup against President Ríos Montt. The new President announced the abolition of the secret tribunals and ended press censorship. A 90-day amnesty for guerrillas was announced in October and subsequently extended throughout 1984. Urban and rural terrorism continued to escalate, however, and in November 1983 the Government was accused of directing a campaign of kidnappings against the Roman Catholic Church. Following the murder in northern Guatemala of six US aid workers, the USA suspended the US $50m. in aid to Guatemala in 1984. Israel continued to supply weapons to Guatemala, and Israeli military advisers were reported to be active in the country. In accordance with the President's assurance of electoral reform, elections for a Constituent Assembly were held in July 1984, at which the centre groups, including the newly formed Unión del Centro Nacional (UCN), obtained the greatest number of votes. Under the system of proportional representation, however, the right-wing coalition of the MLN and the Central Auténtica Nacionalista (CAN) together obtained a majority of seats in the Assembly.

Guatemala's new Constitution was promulgated in May 1985. Elections for the presidency, the National Congress and 331 mayoralties were scheduled be held in November. Prior to the elections, there was a substantial increase in rebel activity and political assassinations by 'death squads'. Furthermore, in September violent protests, led by students and trade unionists, erupted in reaction to a series of price increases.

Eight candidates participated in the presidential election in November 1985, but the main contest was between Jorge Carpio Nicolle, the candidate of the UCN, and Mario Vinicio Cerezo Arévalo, the candidate of the Partido Democracia Cristiana Guatemalteca (PDCG). As neither of the leading candidates obtained the requisite majority, a second round of voting was held in December, when Cerezo secured 68% of the votes cast. The PDCG formed the majority party in the new National Congress and won the largest proportion of mayoralties. Cerezo was believed to enjoy the support of the US administration, which increased its allocation of economic aid and resumed military aid to Guatemala, in support of the new civilian Government.

Immediately prior to the transfer of power in January 1986, the outgoing military Government decreed a general amnesty to encompass those suspected of involvement in abuses of human rights since March 1982. In the following month, however, in an attempt to curb the continuing violence and to improve the country's poor record for the observance of human rights, the notorious Department of Technical Investigations was dissolved and replaced by a new criminal investigations unit. Violence continued unabated, however, with 700 killings reported in the first six months of 1986. Cerezo claimed that not all murders were politically motivated, while his relations with the armed forces remained precarious. Meanwhile, a grouping of relatives of victims of repression, the Grupo de Apoyo Mutuo (GAM) attracted increasing support, and in August about 3,000 demonstrators took part in a protest to demand information on the fate of the thousands of *'desaparecidos'* ('disappeared'). In April 1987 the creation of a government commission to investigate disappearances was announced. Nevertheless, by mid-1988 there were frequent reports of torture and killings by right-wing 'death squads' as discontent with the Government's liberal policies increased. In September 1989 the Consejo Nacional de Desplazados de Guatemala (CONDEG) was created to represent the 1m. refugees who had fled their homes since 1980. According to the UN Commission for Human Rights almost 3,000 complaints of human rights abuses were lodged in 1989.

In August 1987 a peace plan for the region was signed in Guatemala City by the Presidents of Costa Rica, El Salvador, Guatemala, Honduras and Nicaragua. Although the plan was principally concerned with the conflicts in Nicaragua and El Salvador, it also referred to the long-standing guerrilla war in Guatemala. Subsequently, a Commission of National Reconciliation (CNR) was formed in compliance with the terms of the accord. In October representatives of the Guatemalan Government and the main guerrilla grouping, the Unidad Revolucionaria Nacional Guatemalteca (URNG), met in Spain to discuss the question of peace in Guatemala. The negotiations ended without agreement. Right-wing pressure on the Government, and an attempted coup in May 1988, forced Cerezo to postpone further negotiations with the URNG. Despite evident right-wing opposition to the policies of Cerezo, the PDCG won 140 mayoralties out of 272 at municipal elections held in April. These were Guatemala's first elections in which voting was not compulsory, and, consequently, the level of participation was low (only an estimated 40% of the electorate). After another coup plot was discovered in July, Cerezo rejected the URNG's proposal for a truce.

During 1989 guerrilla activity by groups from both the right and the left intensified. Many political figures and labour leaders fled the country after receiving death threats from paramilitary groups. In January a new leftist group emerged, the Comando Urbano Revolucionario, which joined the URNG guerrillas. Meanwhile, Cerezo refused to negotiate with the URNG for as long as its members remained armed. In September the URNG made further proposals for negotiations, following the signing of the Tela Agreement (the Central American peace plan accord, see p. 1199), but these were rejected. A major counter-insurgency operation was launched by the Government in December. In the same month, Cerezo accused the ruling party in El Salvador of supplying weapons to the right-wing death squads of Guatemala.

In May 1989 another coup attempt was foiled without bloodshed. During August and September a secret right-wing military organization perpetrated a series of terrorist attacks in an attempt to destabilize the Government. At the same time, the ruling party was undergoing a political crisis, following its internal presidential primary elections in August. The PDCG's choice of presidential candidate had been split between Alfonso Cabrera Hidalgo, the party's Secretary-General and former Minister of Foreign Affairs, and René de León Schlotter, the leader of the party's left wing and Minister of Urban and Rural Development. The most likely compromise candidate, Danilo Barillas, had been assassinated a short while before the selection procedure, allegedly by the extreme right, which, by provoking disunity within the PDCG, hoped to give an advantage to its own candidates. The former military ruler, Gen. José Efraín Ríos Montt, also presented his candidacy for the presidential election that was to take place one year later. He was supported by the moderate Partido Institucional Democrático (PID) and the Frente de Unidad Nacional (FUN) and secured considerable public support. However, in October 1990 his candidacy was declared invalid on constitutional grounds (under the Constitution, anyone taking part in, or benefiting from, a military coup was disqualified from participating in elections).

In August 1989 Cerezo and his Mexican counterpart held a meeting, aimed at resolving the refugee problem and at establishing collaboration against drugs-trafficking in the region. As Mexico had begun implementing measures to combat the problem of drugs-trafficking within its borders, with some success, Guatemala was consequently developing as a new centre for heroin production and cocaine transhipments from Central America to the USA. Local efforts to confront the problem were largely ineffective, and a US $1m. programme dedicated mainly to the aerial spraying of poppy fields, financed by the USA, was hampered by ground-level retaliatory attacks.

Despite Cerezo's promise to restrict the unlawful activities of the armed forces and right-wing death squads, the number of politically-motivated assassinations and 'disappearances' escalated in 1990. In March the US ambassador was recalled, in protest at the President's continued failure to curb the growing incidence of human rights violations. In the same month the URNG and the CNR began discussions in Oslo, Norway, with a view to resolving the problem of reincorporating the armed movements into the country's political process. In June representatives of the CNR and of nine political parties, including the ruling PDCG, met for further talks with the URNG in Madrid, Spain. As a result of these negotiations, the URNG pledged not to disrupt the presidential and legislative elections scheduled for November, and agreed to participate in a constituent assembly to reform the Constitution.

In the presidential election of November 1990 none of the presidential candidates obtained an absolute majority in the first round, leading to a second ballot on 6 January 1991 between the two leading candidates, Jorge Serrano Elías of the Movimiento de Acción Solidaria (MAS) and Jorge Carpio Nicolle of the UCN. Serrano, a former member of the 1982 Ríos Montt Government, who secured the support of right-wing opinion, received 68% of the votes cast. The MAS failed to secure a majority in the legislative elections, however, and in an effort to offset the imbalance in Congress, Serrano invited members of the Plan por el Adelantamiento Nacional (PAN) and the Partido Socialista Democrático (PSD) to participate in the formation of a coalition Government.

In April 1991 a fresh round of direct talks between the URNG and the Government was begun in Mexico City. The initial meeting, resulted in an agreement on negotiating procedures and an agenda for further talks. However, in an attempt to destabilize the Government's efforts at national reconciliation, members of the state security forces, believed to be acting independently of their superiors, launched a campaign of violence, directing death threats against leaders of trade unions and human rights organizations, and murdering a PSD politician. These actions indicated a clear division within the military between those favouring a negotiated settlement and those regarding the talks merely as a political platform for the rebels. In late 1991 the ombudsman, Ramiro de León Carpio, secured the resignation of the Director of the National Police, Col. Mario Enrique Paíz Bolanos, who was alleged to be responsible for the use of torture. Further peace talks at the end of the year failed to produce any agreement.

Negotiations between the Government and the URNG, which took place in Mexico City in August 1992, led to concessions by the Government, which agreed to curb the expansion of the PAC. These self-defence patrols played a major role in the army's counter-insurgency campaign and were widely accused of human rights violations. The URNG, which maintained that *campesinos* (peasants) were forcibly enlisted into the PAC, included in its conditions for a peace agreement the immediate dissolution of the patrols. In November the Government accepted renewed proposals by the URNG for the establishment of a commission on past human rights violations, but only on the pre-condition that the rebels sign a definitive peace accord. In January 1993 Serrano announced his commitment to the negotiation and signing of a peace agreement with the URNG within 90 days. In the event that an agreement was not reached, Serrano pledged that a cease-fire would be implemented at the end of that period, provided that the URNG demonstrate its commitment to the peace process. In response, the URNG called for a 50% reduction in the size of the armed forces, and repeated demands for the immediate dissolution of the PAC and the dismissal of military officials implicated in human rights violations. The Government rejected these proposals. Talks stalled in March, owing principally to government demands that the

URNG disarm as a precondition to the implementation of procedures for the international verification of human rights in Guatemala. Negotiations were suspended in May, owing to the prevailing constitutional crisis (see below).

In June 1993 the URNG announced a unilateral cease-fire as a gesture of goodwill to the incoming President Ramiro de León Carpio. Government proposals announced in July, which aimed to involve all sectors of society in a Permanent Forum for Peace addressing social, economic and human rights problems independently of simultaneous cease-fire negotiations with the URNG, were rejected by the rebels. In August, in a concession to the URNG, de León announced the reform of the Estado Mayor Presidencial, a military body widely accused of human rights offences. However, in the following month the army announced that it would be resuming military operations against the rebels, which had been suspended in June. In October the Government presented a revised peace plan to the UN, providing for the creation of a Permanent Forum for Peace and renewed cease-fire negotiations with a view to an eventual amnesty for the URNG; the plan was, however, rejected by the rebels. Preliminary talks were finally resumed in Mexico in January 1994.

In May 1992 fears of a possible military coup were raised by a series of bombings and bomb threats in the capital. The campaign was widely recognized as the activity of right-wing elements of the military and the private sector, which aimed to force the Government to abandon its plans to implement tax reforms and to cease negotiations with the URNG. In July the Minister of the Interior, Fernando Hurtado Prem, was forced to resign amidst allegations of police brutality. The decision followed the violent dispersal by anti-riot police of some 500 *campesinos* who had gathered outside the Palacio Nacional to demand the resolution of a land dispute.

In October 1992 the Government signed an accord for the return from Mexico of an estimated 40,000 Guatemalan refugees. The refugees were promised land, security guarantees and a three-year exemption from military service. The flow of refugees from Mexico was stimulated in early 1994 by large numbers fleeing the Amerindian uprising in the Mexican state of Chiapas (see Chapter on Mexico, Vol II). However, by the end of 1994 few returnees had received the land that had been promised to them, and many had suffered attacks and intimidation by the security forces.

In May 1993 unrest at economic austerity measures escalated as public confidence in the Government declined. In that month a rally attended by some 10,000 people was staged in the capital to demand Serrano's resignation. With the MAS no longer able to effect a constructive alliance in Congress and the country's stability in jeopardy, on 25 May Serrano, with the support of the military, suspended parts of the Constitution and dissolved Congress and the Supreme Court. A ban was imposed on the media and Serrano announced that he would rule by decree pending the drafting of a new constitution by a constituent assembly, which was to be elected within 60 days. In addition to civil unrest, Serrano cited widespread corruption (which, he alleged, permeated all state institutions) as the motive for his actions. The constitutional coup provoked almost unanimous international condemnation, with the USA immediately suspending in excess of US $30m. in aid. Such pressure, in addition to overwhelming domestic opposition, led the military to reappraise its position and, opting to effect a return to constitutional rule, it forced the resignation of Serrano, who relinquished his post on 1 June and subsequently fled to El Salvador. He was later granted political asylum in Panama. The Minister of National Defence, Gen. José Domingo García Samayoa, assumed control of the country, pending the election of a new president. An attempt by Vice-President Gustavo Adolfo Espina Salguero to assume the presidency was prevented by a legislative boycott of his ratification. He was later ruled ineligible for the post by the Constitutional Court.

On 3 June 1993 the entire Cabinet, excluding García and the Minister of the Interior, Francisco Perdomo Sandoval, resigned. On the same day the Attorney-General presented charges, including those of violation of the Constitution, abuse of authority and embezzlement, against Serrano, Espina and Perdomo, all of whom were reported to have left the country. On 5 June, following an order by the Constitutional Court, Congress reconvened and conducted elections for a new president. The Instancia Nacional de Consenso (INC), a broad coalition of political parties, business leaders and trade unions which had been instrumental in removing Serrano from office, proposed

three candidates, of whom Ramiro de León Carpio, the former human rights ombudsman, was elected President in an uncontested second round of voting. He was inaugurated on the following day to complete the remainder of Serrano's term, which was due to end in January 1996. The USA subsequently restored its aid programme to Guatemala.

In August 1993, as an initial measure in a campaign to eradicate corruption from state institutions and restore dwindling public confidence in his Government, de León requested the voluntary resignation of Congress and the Supreme Court. The request caused a serious division in the legislature, which separated into two main factions, the Gran Grupo Parlamentario (GGP), which included some 70 members of the MAS, UCN, PAN and the Frente Republicano Guatemalteco (FRG) and supported the dismissal of 16 deputies identified by the INC as corrupt, and a group of 38 deputies, including members of the PDCG and independents, who supported the voluntary resignation of all 116 deputies. In September, following the suspension of a congressional session by the President of Congress, Fernando Lobo Dubón (a member of the PDCG), the GGP defied the decision and elected a new President of Congress. Although Lobo was temporarily reinstated by the Constitutional Court, the GGP threatened to boycott any further sessions convened by him. In order to resolve the deadlock, de León requested the Supreme Electoral Tribunal to put the issue to a referendum on 28 November. However, in early November the Constitutional Court upheld a Supreme Court injunction of the previous month, suspending the referendum.

In mid-November 1993, following the mediatorial intervention of the Bishops' Conference of Guatemala, a compromise was reached between the Government and the legislature, involving a series of constitutional reforms which were summarily approved by Congress in order to be put to a referendum on 30 January 1994. The constitutional reforms were subsequently approved by the referendum, although fewer than 20% of the electorate participated in the voting, reflecting popular concern that more extensive reforms were necessary. The reforms took effect in early April, and fresh legislative elections were to be held in mid-August. The new Congress, which was to serve until 14 January 1996, was to appoint the members of a new, enlarged Supreme Court. Other reforms included a reduction in the terms of office of the President, legislature and municipal authorities (from five to four years), and of the Supreme Court justices (from six to five years), and a reduction in the number of seats in Congress. In April 1994 a climate of escalating violence and instability, characterized by attacks on legislators and foreign citizens, and by the assassination of the President of the Constitutional Court, prompted de León to place the army in charge of internal security.

In January 1994 preliminary talks, held in Mexico, between the Government and the URNG resulted in an agreement on the resumption of formal peace negotiations, to be based on the agenda agreed in Mexico in April 1991. In March agreement was reached on a timetable aimed at achieving a definitive peace agreement by the end of the year. In addition, a general human rights agreement was signed, providing guarantees, including a government commitment to eliminate illegal security corps, strengthen national human rights institutions and cease obligatory military recruitment. Agreement was also reached on the establishment of a UN human rights mission to verify the implementation of the accord. Further talks in Oslo, Norway, resulted in the signing, in June, of agreements on the resettlement of people displaced by the civil war (estimated to number some 1m.), and on the establishment of a Commission for Historical Clarification (Comisión para el Esclarecimiento Histórico—CEH) to investigate human rights violations committed during the 33-year conflict. The role of the CEH, the creation of which was strongly opposed by the security forces, would be to report on past violations but would not extend to initiating legal proceedings against offenders.

In August 1994 the URNG withdrew from the peace negotiations and accused the Government of failing to observe the human rights provisions agreed in March. Guerrilla activity subsequently escalated in late August. Talks resumed in November, but remained deadlocked until February 1995, when a new timetable for negotiations, achieved with the mediation of the UN, was announced. The new agenda, which was formally agreed by the Government and the URNG in March, provided for a cease-fire agreement by June and the signing of a definitive peace accord in August. In March the issue of the identity and rights of indigenous peoples was finally resolved. The principal remaining issues to be discussed included agrarian and other socio-economic reform, the role of the armed forces, the resettlement of displaced people and the incorporation of URNG guerrillas into civilian life. However, talks continued beyond the agreed deadline, and throughout 1995, without agreement on the substantive issues. In September, in an attempt to lend impetus to the peace process, the Government announced the demobilization of the approximately 24,000-strong paramilitary force, the Comisionados Militares. However, in the following month a military patrol killed 11 people in an attack on a resettlement area for refugees returning from Mexico at Xamán in the department of Alta Verapaz. The incident prompted the resignation of the Minister of National Defence.

At the legislative election held in August 1994 only some 20% of the electorate exercised their vote, again reflecting widespread scepticism at the extent to which the reforms instigated by de León would serve to rid Guatemalan institutions of corruption. Of the 80 seats in the new legislature (reduced from 116), the FRG secured 32, the PAN 24, the PDCG 13, the UCN seven, the MLN three and the Unión Democrática (UD) one. Despite winning the greatest number of seats, the FRG, led by Gen. (retd) José Efraín Ríos Montt, was excluded from the 12-member congressional directorate by an alliance of the PAN, PDCG, MLN and UD. However, in December the PDCG transferred its allegiance to the FRG and Ríos Montt was subsequently elected President of Congress. His inauguration in January 1995 provoked demonstrations by human rights organizations, which considered him responsible for the deaths of as many as 15,000 civilians as a result of counter-insurgency operations conducted during his period as *de facto* ruler in 1982–83.

In September 1994 the UN General Assembly formally announced the establishment of the Human Rights Verification Mission in Guatemala (MINUGUA), as envisaged in the March 1994 agreement between the Government and the URNG. The mission, which was to comprise 220 human rights observers, 60 police and 10 military officers, began arriving in November.

In March 1995 Guatemala's record on human rights came under particular scrutiny. At the beginning of the month the USA announced that it had suspended all remaining military aid to the country, in protest at the Government's failure to investigate cases involving the murder or disappearance of US citizens in Guatemala. In March MINUGUA issued its first report. The document drew attention to human rights abuses perpetrated by the security forces and the PAC, and the Government's failure to investigate such incidents was once again condemned.

In June 1995 Ríos Montt formally requested registration as a candidate in the forthcoming presidential election, despite the constitutional provision precluding the candidacy of anyone who had previously come to power by means of a coup, as Ríos Montt had done in 1982. In August the Supreme Electoral Tribunal confirmed that he was not eligible to stand for election and in the same month the Supreme Court ruled that he should be suspended from his position as President of Congress for a period of four months to answer charges of abuse of authority and violation of the Constitution. The charges concerned an attempt by Ríos Montt and several other FRG deputies to impeach the magistrates of the Supreme Electoral Tribunal without first securing congressional approval.

The presidential and legislative elections on 12 November 1995 were notable for the return to the electoral process, for the first time for more than 40 years, of the left wing, which was represented by the Frente Democrático Nueva Guatemala (FDNG). In addition, the URNG, which had boycotted all previous elections, declared a unilateral cease-fire to coincide with the electoral campaign and urged people to exercise their vote. As no candidate received the necessary 50% of the votes to win the presidential election outright, the two leading candidates, Alvaro Enrique Arzú Irigoyen of the PAN and Alfonso Portillo of the FRG, contested a second round of voting on 7 January 1996, at which Arzú secured a narrow victory with 51.22% of the votes cast. At the legislative election the PAN secured 43 of the total of 80 seats in Congress, the FRG won 21, the Alianza Nacional (AN) nine, the FDNG six, and the MLN obtained the remaining seat.

Shortly after assuming office on 14 January 1996, Arzú implemented a comprehensive reorganization of the military high command, replacing those officers who were not in favour of a negotiated peace settlement. In late February Arzú met the high command of the URNG in Mexico City, the first direct meeting between a Guatemalan President and the rebels since

the early 1970s. In March Congress ratified the International Labour Organization's Convention on the rights of indigenous peoples. However, the document, which had been before Congress since 1992 and had encountered strong opposition from landed interests, had been amended by Congress, prompting protests by Indian organizations. On 20 March the URNG announced an indefinite unilateral cease-fire. Arzú responded immediately by ordering the armed forces to suspend counter-insurgency operations.

On 6 May 1996 the Government and the URNG signed an agreement on agrarian and socio-economic issues. The accord, which aimed to address the problem of widespread poverty by establishing a more efficient and equitable agrarian structure, provided for the introduction of a new agrarian bank (which would supply funds for *campesinos* to purchase property), the establishment of a land registry to define ownership and the introduction of a land tax. The Government also undertook to double expenditure on health and education over the next four years. In response, the URNG suspended its 'war-tax' (protection money extorted from landowners and businesses). In that month Congress approved legislation limiting the right of public-sector employees to strike. A demonstration by trade unions in protest at the legislation was dispersed by the security forces. In the following month Congress adopted legislation that made members of the armed forces accountable to civilian courts for all but strictly military crimes.

In September 1996 the Government and the URNG signed an agreement in Mexico City on the strengthening of civilian power and the role of the armed forces. Under the terms of the accord, all military and intelligence services were to be placed under the authority of the Government. The police force was to be reorganized, with the creation of a new National Civilian Police force (Policía Nacional Civil—to number at least 20,000 by the end of 1999), which would replace the existing units. The armed forces were to be reduced in size by one-third in 1997 and were to relinquish responsibility for internal security. Also confirmed in the accord was the abolition of the PAC. By early December the demobilization of the PAC, estimated to number some 202,000 members, was officially concluded. Later that month a general amnesty law was approved by Congress. Whilst the law did not exonerate former combatants for human rights violations, the rebels expressed concern that the amnesty was too extensive and that atrocities committed by the armed forces would go unpunished. Human rights groups announced plans to take legal action to have the law annulled.

On 29 December 1996 the Government and the URNG signed the definitive peace treaty in Guatemala City, bringing to an end some 36 years of civil war, during which an estimated 140,000 people had died. The demobilization of URNG guerrillas, estimated to number some 3,250, was to be supervised by MINUGUA. Earlier in the year the URNG had established a 44-member political council to prepare for the reconstitution of the organization as a broad-based political party. Demobilization began in March 1997, and was completed in early May.

In February 1997 the Commission for Historical Clarification was appointed. The Commission was to begin operating in August for a period of 10 months. In March Congress approved legislation providing for the privatization of state-owned companies, prompting widespread protest by trade unionists. In late March the UN General Assembly renewed the mandate of MINUGUA for a further year to monitor the implementation of the peace treaty. In June the URNG registered as a political party in formation and elected a transitional leadership committee to conduct the transformation of the movement. Elections to a provisional executive committee were held in August.

In July 1997 the first contingent of 1,200 agents of the new National Civilian Police force began operating. In December the demobilization of the PMA was concluded. In accordance with the terms of the peace treaty, more than 15,000 members of the armed forces had been demobilized by the end of 1997.

In February 1998, in an effort to curb rising violent crime, the Government began the deployment of an additional 10,000 troops and police throughout the country. In April the UN Human Rights Commission removed Guatemala from the list of countries under its observation. The decision did not affect the operations of MINUGUA, which continued to monitor the fulfilment of the peace accords. In June MINUGUA released a report detailing the rising incidence of crime in Guatemala and criticizing the Government's failure to control the activities of paramilitary vigilante groups and the apparent inability of the justice system to deal with cases of serious crime.

In April 1998 the auxiliary bishop of the metropolitan diocese of Guatemala City, Juan José Gerardi Conedera, was murdered. Gerardi had been a founder, in 1989, of the Roman Catholic Church's Oficina de Derechos Humanos del Arzobispado (ODHA—Archbishopric's Human Rights Office), and a prominent critic of the armed forces. Days before his death Gerardi had presented a report by the ODHA documenting human rights abuses committed during the civil conflict, of which army personnel were found responsible for some 80%. Although two civilian suspects were subsequently detained in connection with Gerardi's murder, the Church and human rights groups expressed the widely-held belief that the real perpetrators had been members of the armed forces. In July, in what the Church and human rights groups interpreted as a further attempt to conceal the truth, a priest, Mario Orantes Nájera (who had been the first to discover Gerardi's body), was arrested. He was formally charged with Gerardi's murder in October. In November, in a report commissioned by the Church, former chief prosecutor Acisclo Valladares Molina asserted that the murder revealed all the signs of an extrajudicial execution. In February 1999 the presiding judge in the case, Henry Monroy, ordered the release of Orantes on grounds of insufficient evidence. However, in March Monroy withdrew from the case after allegedly receiving threats against his life. In October the state prosecutor investigating the murder, Celvin Galindo, also resigned after receiving death threats. Galindo, who went into exile in the USA, subsequently questioned the ability and political will of the Government to resolve the case, in view of the alleged military involvement in the murder.

In August 1999, in what was widely regarded as a test case for the judicial system, 25 members of the armed forces convicted of the massacre in 1995 of 11 civilians in Xamán, Alta Verapaz, received minimum sentences of five years' imprisonment. The case was the first in which military personnel accused of killing civilians had been tried by a civilian court and the decision, which provoked public outrage, served greatly to undermine confidence in the courts' ability to administer justice in the remaining 625 cases of massacres attributed to the security forces. By contrast, in late 1998 death sentences had been passed on three members of the PAC found guilty of participating in massacres of civilians. In December 1999 MINUGUA issued a report stating that commitments made by the Arzú administration under the 1996 peace treaty to reduce the influence of the military remained unfulfilled. It asserted that, contrary to the treaty, the armed forces had increased its presence in some rural areas, and that the Government had failed to order the dissolution of the presidential guard, which was to have been replaced by a unit under civilian control. In late 2000 the UN Secretary-General, Kofi Annan, recommended that MINUGUA's mandate be renewed for a further year. According to MINUGUA, the number of extra-judicial executions doubled between 1996 and 2000 and in the latter year the incidence of death threats increased significantly. In September 2000 a human rights worker was abducted and interrogated regarding his investigation into massacres by the security forces during the civil war.

In February 1999 the Commission for Historical Clarification published its report in which it attributed more than 93% of human rights violations committed during the civil conflict to the armed forces and state paramilitaries. Furthermore, it described counter-insurgency operations during the period 1981–83 as 'genocide' against the Mayan people. It also concluded that the USA had financed and trained Guatemalan forces responsible for atrocities. The report recommended that compensation be provided for the families of victims, that prosecutions be brought against those suspected of crimes against humanity and that a purge of the armed forces be implemented. In response the Government described the Commission's findings as 'controversial' and did not express any intention of pursuing its recommendations.

In late 1999 the Guatemalan Nobel Peace Prize winner, Rigoberta Menchú, filed a case in Spain against former generals Ríos Montt, Lucas García and Mejía Victores, and other military officers, for the crimes of genocide, state terrorism and torture; however, in December 2000 the Spanish National High Court ruled that it was not competent to investigate the case. In August 2000 the Government accepted responsibility for 44 cases of human rights violations being investigated by the Inter-American Commission on Human Rights and, in early 2001, paid compensation for those deaths involving street children. In December 2000 the Commission also ruled that the military

was responsible for the torture and murder of guerrilla leader Efraín Bamaca Velásquez. In the same month the ODHA filed a case against Ríos Montt for human rights violations during his regime.

The URNG formally registered as a political party in December 1998. The application followed the approval by Congress in October of constitutional reforms provided for in the 1996 peace accords. The reforms, which concerned the rights of indigenous peoples, the role of the armed forces and the police, and the strengthening of the courts, remained to be ratified in a referendum. At the referendum, conducted on 16 May 1999, 55.6% of participating voters rejected the constitutional amendments. However, the turn-out was extremely low, with only 18.6% of the 4m. registered voters taking part, and observers attributed the result to a lack of information and to mistrust of the political establishment by the electorate rather than to the rejection of the peace accords themselves. The Government, for its part, pledged that the peace process would not be affected by the result. At presidential and legislative elections, conducted on 7 November, the voter turnout, at some 40%, was greatly improved. As no candidate received the necessary 50% of the votes to win the presidential election outright, the two leading candidates, Alfonso Antonio Portillo Cabrera of the FRG and Oscar Berger Perdomo of the PAN, contested a second round of voting on 26 December, in which Portillo secured victory with 68.3% of the votes cast. Of the 113 seats in the legislature (enlarged from 80 seats) the FRG secured an outright majority with 63 seats, while the PAN won 37, the Alianza Nueva Nación nine, the PDCG two, and the Partido Liberal Progresista and La Organización Verde each obtained one seat. The new Government assumed office in January 2000.

In June 2000 a political crisis ensued after it was revealed that illegal modifications had been made to legislation setting the tax on alcoholic beverages after it had been approved by Congress. The Supreme Court appointed a judge to investigate those believed to be responsible: 23 FRG deputies and the President of Congress, Ríos Montt. On 5 March 2001 the parliamentary immunity of those accused was removed by the Supreme Court and Ríos Montt was ordered to resign the congressional presidency, while five of the 23 deputies were ordered to give up their seats. Ríos Montt, nevertheless, refused to comply with the Supreme Court's order (a position supported by President Portillo). Later in the month it was announced that a government inquiry into Ríos Montt's role in the affair was to be held. In mid-March two deputies defected from the FRG to join the Unidad Nacional de Esperanza, a coalition established by the former presidential candidate Alvaro Colom Caballero, thus reducing the FRG's legislative majority to 61.

Until the return to civilian government in 1986, Guatemala remained steadfast in its claims to the neighbouring territory of Belize, a former British dependency. In protest at the United Kingdom's decision to grant independence to Belize, in accordance with a UN General Assembly resolution of November 1980, Guatemala severed diplomatic relations with the United Kingdom. However, Guatemala's new Constitution, which took effect in January 1986, did not include Belize in its delineation of Guatemalan territory. In December full diplomatic relations were resumed. The removal of economic sanctions and trade restrictions from Belize in late 1986 opened the way to Guatemalan investment in that territory and to the possibility of joint development projects.

In May 1988 discussions were held in Miami, USA, between representatives of Guatemala, Belize and the United Kingdom. The participants decided to establish a permanent Joint Commission to formulate a draft treaty to resolve Guatemala's claims to Belize. In October the Commission announced the establishment of three subcommissions, to be responsible for drafting the treaty; the delimitation of the border; and the creation of a joint development zone, with the co-operation of the United Kingdom and the European Community (EC, now European Union—EU). Approval of the treaty was to be decided by referendums, to be held in both Guatemala and Belize.

In September 1991 Guatemala and Belize signed an accord under the terms of which Belize pledged to legislate to reduce its maritime boundaries and to allow Guatemala access to the Caribbean Sea and use of its port facilities. In return, President Serrano officially announced his country's recognition of Belize as an independent state and established diplomatic relations. The Belizean legislature approved the Maritime Areas Bill in January 1992. Serrano's decision to recognize Belize, made without consulting Congress and without holding a referendum, provoked protests from the opposition, who claimed that Serrano's actions were unconstitutional. In November 1992 Guatemala's Constitutional Court rejected a request by opposition deputies to declare Serrano's actions unconstitutional. In an address to the nation, Serrano subsequently confirmed that Guatemala maintained its territorial claim on Belize. At the end of November Congress voted to ratify Serrano's decision to recognize Belize.

In April 1993 Guatemala and Belize signed a non-aggression pact, affirming their intent to refrain from the threat or use of force against each other, and preventing either country from being used as a base for aggression against the other. In July the Belizean Prime Minister, Manuel Esquivel, reportedly suspended the September 1991 accord, stating that it involved too many concessions on the part of Belize and that the issue should be put to a referendum. In September the United Kingdom announced that the British garrison, which had been stationed in Belize since the mid-1970s, was to be withdrawn by October 1994.

In March 1994, Guatemala formally reaffirmed its territorial claim to Belize, prompting the Belizean Minister of Foreign Affairs to seek talks with the British Government regarding assistance with national defence. Concern was also expressed by the Standing Committee of Ministers of Foreign Affairs of the Caribbean Community and Common Market (CARICOM—see p. 142), which reaffirmed its support for Belizean sovereignty. In September 1996 the Ministers of Foreign Affairs of Guatemala and Belize conducted preliminary talks in New York, USA, concerning a resumption of negotiations on the territorial dispute. In August 1997 President Arzú ordered an increased military presence on the border with Belize following reports of incursions by Belizean troops into Guatemalan territory. In 2000 Guatemala continued to propose that international arbitration be sought to resolve the issue, while Belize maintained that the matter should be settled through bilateral negotiations.

In November 1998 a joint Guatemalan–Belizean commission was established to deal with immigration and cross-border traffic. In August 2000 a panel of negotiators was established at the headquarters of the Organization of American States (see p. 261) in Washington, DC, to supervise the process of bilateral negotiations. In November the two countries agreed to initiate joint patrols of the unofficial common border. However, during 2000 there were various alleged incursions of Belizean soldiers into the proximity zone between the two countries.

Government

Guatemala is a republic comprising 22 departments. Under the 1986 Constitution (revised in 1994), legislative power is vested in the unicameral National Congress, with 113 members elected for four years by universal adult suffrage. Of the total seats, 91 are filled by departmental representation and 22 according to national listing. Executive power is held by the President (also directly elected for four years), assisted by a Vice-President and an appointed Cabinet.

Defence

In August 2000 the armed forces totalled 31,400, of whom 29,200 were in the army (including 23,000 conscripts), 1,500 in the navy (including 650 marines) and 700 in the air force. In addition, there were paramilitary forces of 19,000. Military service is by selective conscription for 30 months. In September 1996, as part of the ongoing peace process, the Government signed an agreement with the rebel URNG whereby the armed forces were to be placed under the control of the Government. Under the terms of the accord, the armed forces were reduced in number by one-third in 1997. This reduction included the disbanding of the Policía Militar Ambulante (Mobile Military Police), which was completed in late 1997.The accord also provided for the abolition of the Patrullas de Autodefensa Civil (PAC), which were demobilized in late 1996. Defence expenditure in 2000 was budgeted at US $123m.

Economic Affairs

In 1998, according to estimates by the World Bank, Guatemala's gross national product (GNP), measured at average 1996–98 prices, was US $17,759m., equivalent to $1,640 per head (or $3,474 per head on an international purchasing-power parity basis). During 1990–98, it was estimated, GNP per head increased, in real terms, at an average rate of 1.5% per year. Over the same period, the population increased by an average of 3.0% per year. Guatemala's gross domestic product (GDP) increased,

in real terms, by an average of 4.2% per year in 1990–99 and by 3.5% in 1999.

Agriculture, including forestry and fishing, contributed an estimated 23.1% of GDP in 1999. In 1998 an estimated 47.4% of the labour force were employed in this sector. The principal cash crops are coffee (which accounted for 22.7% of export earnings in 1998), sugar cane and bananas. Exports of shrimps are also significant. During 1990–99 agricultural GDP increased, in real terms, by an estimated average of 2.7% per year. Growth in agricultural GDP was an estimated 2.2% in 1999.

Industry, including mining, manufacturing, construction and power, contributed an estimated 20.1% of GDP in 1999. This sector employed 18.1% of the working population in 1995. Industrial GDP increased by an estimated average of 4.1% per year in 1990–99. Growth in industrial GDP was an estimated 4.1% in 1999.

Mining contributed an estimated 0.6% of GDP in 1998 and employed 0.1% of the working population in 1995. The most important mineral export is petroleum, although this accounted for only 2.4% of total export earnings in 1998. In addition, copper, antimony, lead, zinc and tungsten are mined on a small scale. There are also deposits of nickel, gold and silver.

Guatemala's industrial sector is the largest in Central America. Manufacturing contributed an estimated 13.4% of GDP in 1999 and employed 13.6% of the working population in 1995. The main branches of manufacturing, measured by gross value of output, are food-processing, textiles, plastic products, paper and paper products, pharmaceuticals and industrial chemicals. Manufacturing GDP increased by an average of 2.8% per year in 1989–99. Growth in manufacturing GDP was an estimated 2.6% in 1999. Guatemala's clothing assembly, or *maquila*, manufacturing sector expanded by 34% in 1998 and employed some 80,000 workers.

Energy is derived principally from mineral fuels and, to a lesser extent, hydroelectric power. Guatemala is a marginal producer of petroleum, with an average output of about 22,000 b/d in 1998. Imports of petroleum and petroleum products comprised 7.4% of the value of total imports in 1998. In late 1998 80% of the capital of the state-owned Empresa Eléctrica de Guatemala was sold to foreign investors for US $520m. At the same time, the Instituto Nacional de Electrificación was sold for $100m.

In 1999 the services sector contributed an estimated 56.8% of GDP, and in 1995 it employed 23.8% of the working population. The GDP of the services sector increased by an average of 4.9% per year in 1990–99, rising by an estimated 3.7% in 1999.

In 1999 Guatemala recorded a visible trade deficit of US $1,445.1m., and there was a deficit of $1,025.9m. on the current account of the balance of payments. In 1998 the principal source of imports (42.2%) was the USA; other major suppliers were Mexico, El Salvador and Japan. The USA was also the principal market for exports (taking 32.6% of exports in that year); other significant purchasers were El Salvador, Honduras, Costa Rica, Germany and Mexico. The main exports in 1998 were coffee, sugar, bananas and petroleum. The principal imports were raw materials for industry, non-durable consumer goods, capital goods for industry, durable consumer goods, capital goods for transport and fuels and lubricants.

In 1998 there was a budgetary deficit of 1,565.9m. quetzales, equivalent to some 1.3% of GDP. At the end of 1999 Guatemala's total external debt stood at US $4,061m. In that year the cost of debt-servicing totalled $386m. In 1990–99 the average annual rate of inflation was 12.1%. Consumer prices increased by an average of 5.2% in 1999 and by 6.0% in 2000. An estimated 7.5% of the labour force were unemployed in 1999.

Guatemala is a member of the Central American Common Market (CACM, see p. 147). In 2000 Guatemala, El Salvador and Honduras signed a free-trade agreement with Mexico, which promised greater market access and increased bilateral trade.

In 1991 the Government adopted a structural adjustment programme in order to address the serious fiscal imbalances and external debt problems that had characterized the previous decade. The resultant economic recovery enabled the Government to resume relations with international credit agencies and to clear debt arrears. However, low tax revenue was a major problem, forcing the Government to borrow heavily, keeping interest rates high, discouraging investment and impeding growth. In 1995 the legislature approved a series of reforms to the tax system, which, in turn, facilitated a new stand-by agreement with the International Monetary Fund. The signing of the peace accord in December 1996, which signalled the end of the civil conflict, improved Guatemala's economic prospects significantly. It was envisaged that expenditure of US $2,500m. would be required to implement the accord. In January 1997 international donors pledged $1,900m. in loans and donations towards the Government's reconstruction programme. However, the funding was contingent upon the Government significantly increasing tax revenues. Significant increases were expected following the creation of an independent tax superintendency in 1998. Furthermore, in October the Government undertook to introduce a series of fiscal reforms and established a Fiscal Pact Preparatory Committee. However, as a result of the destruction caused by 'Hurricane Mitch' in November 1998, the curtailment of external credit from banks owing to instability in the international financial markets, and declining international prices for Guatemala's principal exports of coffee and sugar, economic growth slowed significantly in 1999. The incoming Government of Alfonso Portillo made the Fiscal Pact a priority. The agreement, signed in May 2000 by government and opposition representatives and business and community leaders, comprised eight distinct areas: fiscal balance of payments, state revenue, tax administration, public spending, public debt, public property, supervision and control mechanisms, and fiscal decentralization. One of the Pact's principal aims was to increase tax revenue to 12% of GDP by 2002, either through an increased rate of value-added tax (VAT) or more effective collection of VAT. GDP growth of some 3.0% was envisaged in both 2000 and 2001. An annual inflation rate of 7.5% was forecast for 2001.

Social Welfare

Social security is compulsory, and all employers with five or more workers are required to enrol with the State Institute of Social Security. Benefits are available to registered workers for industrial accidents, sickness, maternity, disability, widowhood and hospitalization. In 1995 Guatemala had 58 private hospitals, with a total of 1,657 beds, and in 1997 there were an estimated 93.3 physicians and 27.0 nurses per 100,000 inhabitants working in the health service. In 1986 a vaccination programme to benefit more than 1m. children was begun, in a campaign to combat infant mortality. According to preliminary figures, in 1997 budgetary expenditure on health was 882.2m. quetzales (8.1% of total spending).

Education

Elementary education is free and, in urban areas, compulsory between seven and 14 years of age. Primary education begins at the age of seven and lasts for six years. Secondary education, beginning at 13 years of age, lasts for up to six years, comprising two cycles of three years each. In 1999 there were 9,607 pre-primary schools, 17,905 primary schools and 3,118 secondary schools. In 1997 enrolment at primary schools was equivalent to 73.8% of children in the relevant age-group (males 77.4%; females 70.2%). The comparable figure for secondary education in that year was 34.9% (males 38.1%; females 31.7%). There are five universities. In 1981 a 'national literacy crusade' was launched by the Government, but in 1998, according to estimates by the UNDP, the average rate of adult illiteracy was 32.7% (males 25.1%; females 40.3%). In 1997 budgetary expenditure on education was an estimated 1,670.5m. quetzales (15.3% of total spending).

Public Holidays

2001: 1 January (New Year's Day), 6 January (Epiphany), 13–16 April (Easter), 1 May (Labour Day), 30 June (Anniversary of the Revolution), 15 August (Assumption, Guatemala City only), 15 September (Independence Day), 12 October (Columbus Day), 20 October (Revolution Day), 1 November (All Saints' Day), 24–25 December (Christmas), 31 December (New Year's Eve).

2002: 1 January (New Year's Day), 6 January (Epiphany), 29 March–1 April (Easter), 1 May (Labour Day), 30 June (Anniversary of the Revolution), 15 August (Assumption, Guatemala City only), 15 September (Independence Day), 12 October (Columbus Day), 20 October (Revolution Day), 1 November (All Saints' Day), 24–25 December (Christmas), 31 December (New Year's Eve).

Weights and Measures

The metric system is in official use.

Statistical Survey

Sources (unless otherwise stated): Banco de Guatemala, 7a Avda 22-01, Zona 1, Apdo 365, Guatemala City; tel. 230-6222; fax 253-4035; internet www.banguat.gob.gt; Dirección General de Estadística, Edif. América 4°, 8a Calle 9-55, Zona 1, Guatemala City; tel. 232-6136; fax 232-4790; e-mail info-ine@ine.gob.gt; internet www.ine.gob.gt/indexbak.htm.

Area and Population

AREA, POPULATION AND DENSITY

Area (sq km)	
Land	108,429
Inland water	460
Total	108,889*
Population (census results)†	
26 March 1981	
Males	3,015,826
Females	3,038,401
Total	6,054,227
17 April 1994	8,322,051
Population (official estimates at mid-year)	
1998	10,799,132
1999	11,088,372
2000	11,385,334
Density (per sq km) at mid-2000	104.6

* 42,042 sq miles.
† Excluding adjustments for underenumeration, estimated to have been 13.7% in 1981.

DEPARTMENTS (estimated population at mid-2000)

Alta Verapaz	.	814,300	Petén . . .		333,389
Baja Verapaz	.	203,430	Quetzaltenango	.	678,251
Chimaltenango	.	427,602	Quiché . .	.	588,831
Chiquimula	.	313,150	Retalhuleu .	.	241,921
El Progreso .	.	143,197	Sacatepéquez	.	259,265
Escuintla	.	483,768	San Marcos .	.	844,486
Guatemala	.	2,578,526	Santa Rosa .	.	319,814
Huehuetenango	.	879,987	Solola . .	.	307,791
Izabal	.	333,956	Suchitepéquez	.	403,609
Jalapa .	.	270,055	Totonicapán .	.	361,303
Jutiapa .	.	385,909	Zacapa . .	.	212,794

PRINCIPAL TOWNS (estimated population at mid-2000)

Guatemala City	.	1,015,303	San Juan		
Mixco .	.	440,065	Sacatepéquez	.	137,136
Villa Nueva .	.	363,574	Jalapa .	.	115,493
San Pedro Carcha		159,574	Escuintla	.	113,320
Coban . .	.	156,086	Totonicapán .	.	103,173
Quetzaltenango	.	148,108			

BIRTHS, MARRIAGES AND DEATHS

	Registered live births		Registered marriages		Registered deaths	
	Number	Rate (per 1,000)	Number	Rate (per 1,000)	Number	Rate (per 1,000)
1991 . .	359,904	38.0	44,440	4.7	66,703	7.0
1992 . .	363,648	37.3	46,795	4.8	64,837	6.7
1993 . .	370,138	36.9	45,736	4.6	64,515	6.4
1994 . .	381,497	37.0	48,356	4.7	74,761	7.2
1995 . .	371,091	34.9	49,701	4.7	65,159	6.1
1996 . .	377,723	34.6	47,428	4.3	60,618	5.5
1997 . .	387,862	36.9	51,908	4.9	67,691	6.4
1998 . .	362,165	33.5	51,459	4.8	69,322	6.4

Expectation of life (UNDP estimates, years at birth, 1998): 64.4 (males 61.7; females 67.6).

ECONOMICALLY ACTIVE POPULATION
(official estimates for 1995)

	Males	Females	Total
Agriculture, forestry, hunting and fishing	1,767,791	30,436	1,798,227
Mining and quarrying . . .	3,052	43	3,095
Manufacturing	329,033	91,895	420,928
Construction	126,234	664	126,898
Electricity, gas, water and sanitary services	9,023	262	9,285
Commerce	155,122	70,818	225,940
Transport, storage and communications	75,563	1,814	77,377
Services	163,945	207,462	371,407
Activities not adequately described	48,408	13,493	61,901
Total	**2,678,171**	**416,887**	**3,095,058**

Agriculture

PRINCIPAL CROPS ('000 metric tons)

	1997	1998	1999
Sugar cane	17,687.0	18,189.4	16,350.0
Cotton (lint)	1.4	2.8†	2.8*
Maize	860.9	1,068.8	1,109.1
Rice	21.9	30.7	38.7
Dry beans	72.7	83.6	93.3
Wheat	23.0	5.0†	3.0†
Coffee*	248.5	235.0	293.5
Bananas	730.0*	880.0*	732.5
Plantains*	55.0	53.0	52.0

* FAO estimate(s).   † Unofficial figure.

Source: FAO.

LIVESTOCK ('000 head, year ending September)

	1997	1998	1999
Horses*	118.0	118.0	118.0
Cattle	2,337.0†	2,330.0†	2,300.0*
Sheep*	551.1	551.2	551.3
Pigs	801.5	825.6	825.0*
Goats*	109.2	109.2	109.3

Chickens* (million): 23 in 1997; 24 in 1998; 24 in 1999.

* FAO estimate(s).   † Unofficial figure.

Source: FAO.

LIVESTOCK PRODUCTS ('000 metric tons)

	1997	1998	1999
Beef and veal	54.4	54.5	47.0†
Pig meat	17.0	17.0	17.6*
Poultry meat	114.5	120.2	129.0†
Cheese*	11.1	11.1	11.1
Hen eggs*	108.9	109.0	109.0
Cattle hides*	7.5	7.6	7.6

* FAO estimates.   † Unofficial figure.

Source: FAO.

Forestry

ROUNDWOOD REMOVALS ('000 cubic metres, excl. bark)

	1996	1997	1998
Sawlogs, veneer logs and logs for sleepers	251	159	159
Other industrial wood . . .	42	42	42
Fuel wood	12,794	12,794	12,794
Total	13,087	12,995	12,995

Source: FAO, *Yearbook of Forest Products*.

SAWNWOOD PRODUCTION

('000 cubic metres, incl. railway sleepers)

	1996	1997	1998
Coniferous (softwood) . . .	263	263	263
Broadleaved (hardwood) . .	92	92	92
Total	355	355	355

Source: FAO, *Yearbook of Forest Products*.

Fishing

('000 metric tons, live weight)

	1996	1997	1998
Capture	7.7	6.9	10.8
Penaeus shrimps . . .	0.7	0.7	2.0
Pacific seabobs . . .	2.2	0.4	1.3
Aquaculture	3.4	4.4	3.1
Nile tilapia . . .	n.a.	n.a.	1.0
Other tilapias . . .	1.5	1.8	0.5
Penaeus shrimps . . .	1.4	2.0	1.4
Total catch	11.1	11.3	14.0

Source: FAO, *Yearbook of Fishery Statistics*.

Mining

SELECTED PRODUCTS ('000 metric tons, unless otherwise indicated)

	1995	1996	1997
Crude petroleum . . .	467	729	975
Antimony ore (metric tons) . .	665	880	880
Limestone	1,407	1,280	1,500
Sand, silica and quartz . .	107	67	81
Gravel and crushed stone . .	1,063	1,233	1,000

Source: UN, *Industrial Commodity Statistics Yearbook*.

Industry

SELECTED PRODUCTS

('000 metric tons, unless otherwise indicated)

	1997	1998	1999
Cement	1,315	1,330	1,885
Sugar	613	580	899
Electricity (million kWh) . .	4,132	n.a.	n.a.
Cigarettes (million) . . .	2,198	4,184	4,376

Finance

CURRENCY AND EXCHANGE RATES

Monetary Units

100 centavos = 1 quetzal.

Sterling, Dollar and Euro Equivalents (29 December 2000)

£1 sterling = 11.536 quetzales;
US $1 = 7.731 quetzales;
€1 = 7.194 quetzales;
1,000 quetzales = £86.68 = $129.35 = €139.01.

Average Exchange Rate (quetzales per US dollar)

1998	6.3947
1999	7.3856
2000	7.7632

BUDGET (million quetzales)

Revenue*	1996	1997	1998
Current revenue .	8,544.7	10,153.0	12,550.0
Taxation	8,144.0	9,382.5	11,623.3
Taxes on income, profits and capital gains . . .	2,003.7	2,299.5	2,392.2
Individual . . .	245.5	189.7	210.6
Corporate . . .	1,182.1	1,091.5	1,364.6
Domestic taxes on goods and services	4,429.5	5,365.2	7,310.3
Sales or turnover taxes .	3,437.3	4,208.9	5,299.1
Excises	863.7	1,004.1	1,674.7
Taxes on international trade and transactions . .	1,501.6	1,537.6	1,685.1
Customs duties . .	1,501.6	1,537.6	1,682.1
Other current revenue . .	400.7	770.5	926.7
Entrepreneurial and property income	185.2	66.0	402.0
Administrative fees, nonindustrial and incidental sales	26.3	495.2	289.7
Contributions to government employee pension and welfare funds within Government . . .	187.5	204.6	213.2
Capital revenue			34.7
Total	8,445.1	9,627.7	11,856.2

Expenditure	1995	1996	1997†
General public services . . .	2,033.7	2,384.9	n.a.
Internal security . . .	289.2	n.a.	n.a.
Defence	842.9	1,074.3	n.a.
Education	1,352.0	1,433.0	1,670.5
Health	718.6	723.7	882.2
Social security and welfare . .	599.8	632.5	837.2
Housing and community services	505.1	669.4	1,084.5
Social funds	403.1	406.5	772.4
Economic services . . .	1,105.1	1,113.7	n.a.
Agriculture	205.6	190.6	n.a.
Transportation and communications . . .	797.1	849.0	n.a.
Total (incl. others) . . .	8,096.9	8,936.6	10,916.9

* Excluding grants received (million quetzales): 53.7 in 1996; 55.3 in 1997; 92.93 in 1998.
† Estimates.

1998 (million quetzales): Expenditure 13,515.0 (incl. lending minus repayments 29.01).

Sources: IMF, *Guatemala: Recent Economic Developments*; IMF, *Government Finance Statistics Yearbook*.

1999 (million quetzales): Revenue 14,735.7 (incl. grants received 188.2); Expenditure (incl. lending minus repayments) 18,728.1.
2000 (million quetzales): Revenue 15,953.3 (incl. grants received 112.4); Expenditure (incl. lending minus repayments) 18,916.1.

Source: IMF, *International Financial Statistics*.

INTERNATIONAL RESERVES (US $ million at 31 December)

	1998	1999	2000
Gold*	9.1	9.1	9.1
IMF special drawing rights . .	12.2	11.5	9.8
Foreign exchange . . .	1,322.9	1,177.7	1,736.6
Total	1,344.2	1,198.3	1,755.5

* Valued at US $42.22 per troy ounce.

Source: IMF, *International Financial Statistics.*

MONEY SUPPLY (million quetzales at 31 December)

	1998	1999	2000
Currency outside banks . .	5,632.5	7,752.8	7,218.7
Demand deposits at deposit money banks	7,866.9	7,614.1	12,579.7
Total money (incl. others) . .	13,613.5	15,467.6	20,060.9

Source: IMF, *International Financial Statistics.*

COST OF LIVING
(Consumer Price Index; base: 1990 = 100)

	1997	1998	1999
Food	244.4	255.7	261.3
Clothing	189.6	200.1	207.0
Rent	232.5	255.0	278.0
All items (incl. others) . .	249.8	266.4	280.2

Source: ILO, *Yearbook of Labour Statistics.*

NATIONAL ACCOUNTS
Expenditure on the Gross Domestic Product
(million quetzales at current prices)

	1997	1998	1999
Government final consumption expenditure	5,391	6,733	7,729
Private final consumption expenditure	93,804	105,119	114,769
Increase in stocks . . .	−1,540	−1,424	−2,810
Gross fixed capital formation .	16,302	20,785	23,801
Total domestic expenditure .	113,957	131,213	143,489
Exports of goods and services .	19,370	22,532	25,103
Less Imports of goods and services	25,454	32,618	35,015
GDP in purchasers' values .	107,873	121,127	133,577

Source: IMF, *International Financial Statistics.*

Gross Domestic Product by Economic Activity
(million quetzales at constant 1958 prices)

	1996	1997*	1998†
Agriculture, hunting, forestry and fishing	1,035.2	1,064.2	1,098.3
Mining and quarrying . . .	19.6	24.4	29.4
Manufacturing	601.2	617.4	639.2
Electricity, gas and water . .	93.2	101.9	112.0
Construction	133.3	152.9	161.8
Trade, restaurants and hotels .	374.2	396.3	426.2
Transport, storage and communications	1,064.6	1,104.6	1,160.8
Finance, insurance and real estate	213.7	225.9	245.1
Ownership of dwellings . .	203.0	210.4	217.6
General government services . .	314.7	330.9	347.7
Other community, social and personal services . . .	250.7	259.5	268.8
Total	4,303.4	4,488.4	4,706.9

* Preliminary figures.   † Estimates.

BALANCE OF PAYMENTS (US $ million)

	1997	1998	1999
Exports of goods f.o.b. . .	2,602.9	2,846.9	2,780.6
Imports of goods f.o.b. . . .	−3,542.7	−4,255.7	−4,225.7
Trade balance	−939.8	−1,408.8	−1,445.1
Exports of services . . .	588.8	639.9	699.5
Imports of services . . .	−650.5	−791.8	−790.7
Balance on goods and services	−1,001.5	−1,560.7	−1,536.3
Other income received . .	72.4	91.4	76.2
Other income paid . . .	−311.1	−275.1	−280.7
Balance on goods, services and income	−1,240.2	−1,744.4	−1,740.8
Current transfers received . .	628.8	742.9	754.4
Current transfers paid . . .	−22.1	−37.6	−39.5
Current balance	−633.5	−1,039.1	−1,025.9
Capital account (net) . . .	85.0	71.0	68.4
Direct investment from abroad .	84.4	672.8	154.6
Portfolio investment assets .	−18.1	−11.6	−26.0
Portfolio investment liabilities .	249.7	65.8	136.5
Other investment assets . .	221.2	241.7	199.9
Other investment liabilities .	200.2	168.0	172.5
Net errors and omissions . .	40.7	66.8	195.0
Overall balance	229.6	235.4	−125.0

Source: IMF, *International Financial Statistics.*

External Trade

PRINCIPAL COMMODITIES (US $ million)

Imports c.i.f.	1996	1997	1998
Food and live animals	369.6	414.0	422.8
Cereals and cereal preparations	176.8	147.0	105.0
Wheat and meslin (unmilled)	84.8	54.8	12.0
Crude materials (inedible) except fuels	63.3	91.9	98.7
Mineral fuels, lubricants, etc.	466.7	412.6	385.7
Petroleum, petroleum products, etc.	423.4	366.3	343.7
Crude petroleum oils, etc.	128.1	126.4	90.9
Refined petroleum products	288.9	231.8	244.4
Gasoline and other light oils	123.7	33.4	79.0
Animal and vegetable oils, fats and waxes	49.7	58.2	84.2
Chemicals and related products	528.3	684.7	756.9
Medicinal and pharmaceutical products	107.4	124.6	161.8
Medicaments (incl. veterinary)	86.3	100.3	128.6
Essential oils, perfume materials and cleansing preparations	53.1	86.0	110.8
Manufactured fertilizers	67.2	94.8	68.1
Artificial resins, plastic materials, etc.	99.4	135.5	146.8
Products of polymerizations, etc.	82.7	117.1	127.5
Basic manufactures	500.8	672.3	898.6
Paper, paperboards and manufactures	117.2	161.5	204.1
Paper and paperboard (not cut to size or shape)	84.2	107.2	130.6
Iron and steel	116.9	154.6	253.0
Universals, plates and sheets	55.7	78.4	115.4
Machinery and transport equipment	921.3	1,187.4	1,600.1
Power-generating machinery and equipment	46.8	78.0	118.5
Machinery specialized for particular industries	113.0	159.0	219.8
Office machines and automatic data-processing equipment	71.2	90.9	112.9
Telecommunications and sound equipment	85.3	122.6	160.7
Road vehicles and parts	371.5	408.7	590.3
Passenger motor cars (excl. buses)	157.1	158.8	252.4
Lorries and special motor vehicles	126.1	143.4	187.5
Lorries and trucks	125.7	142.8	185.8
Miscellaneous manufactured articles	222.3	298.7	365.6
Total (incl. others)	3,146.3	3,852.0	4,650.9

Exports f.o.b.	1996	1997	1998
Food and live animals	1,139.2	1,323.2	1,463.8
Cereals and cereal preparations	53.2	77.4	67.8
Vegetables and fruit	251.8	248.5	317.3
Fresh or simply preserved vegetables	54.0	53.3	64.9
Fresh or dried fruit and nuts (excl. oil nuts)	185.5	182.1	237.5
Bananas and plantains	156.3	152.5	194.7
Sugar, sugar preparations and honey	228.9	278.1	336.8
Sugar and honey	222.0	272.1	332.3
Raw beet and cane sugars	202.1	255.4	316.7
Coffee, tea, cocoa and spices	514.8	629.9	625.6
Coffee and coffee substitutes	473.1	589.6	586.8
Coffee (incl. husks and skins) and substitutes containing coffee	473.0	589.6	586.7

Exports f.o.b. — *continued*	1996	1997	1998
Beverages and tobacco	38.2	52.0	59.2
Crude materials (inedible) except fuels	146.0	136.3	122.1
Crude rubber	48.7	38.7	27.5
Natural rubber and gums	48.6	38.7	27.5
Mineral fuels, lubricants, etc.	65.8	98.7	61.7
Petroleum, petroleum products, etc.	65.8	98.7	61.6
Crude petroleum oils, etc.	60.5	96.5	58.3
Chemicals and related products	236.7	263.4	292.7
Medicinal and pharmaceutical products	74.4	68.6	85.3
Medicaments (incl. veterinary)	70.3	64.7	81.8
Essential oils, perfume materials and cleansing preparations	69.4	84.2	100.5
Soap, cleansing and polishing preparations	36.0	41.9	55.0
Basic manufactures	232.9	261.9	321.8
Textile yarn, fabrics, etc.	50.3	45.5	73.3
Iron and steel	58.2	69.3	74.2
Machinery and transport equipment	37.4	52.6	62.3
Miscellaneous manufactured articles	118.9	133.3	175.0
Clothing and accessories (excl. footwear)	38.7	43.9	60.5
Total (incl. others)	2,030.8	2,344.1	2,581.7

PRINCIPAL TRADING PARTNERS (US $ million)

Imports c.i.f.	1996	1997	1998
Aruba	107.0	127.4	69.2
Brazil	42.8	38.9	62.0
Canada	56.2	72.1	56.1
Costa Rica	62.0	108.0	163.2
El Salvador	128.8	228.5	334.8
Germany	99.6	114.2	131.7
Honduras	44.0	65.6	96.1
Italy	38.5	52.2	45.1
Japan	99.3	130.0	209.2
Korea, Republic	27.8	26.3	46.8
Mexico	322.5	438.4	485.1
Netherlands	46.5	24.8	40.7
Panama	79.8	111.9	153.8
Spain	40.9	44.0	51.6
United Kingdom	31.5	43.1	51.5
USA	1,409.4	1,613.6	1,962.8
Venezuela	165.3	180.5	152.7
Total (incl. others)	3,146.2	3,851.9	4,650.8

Exports f.o.b.	1996	1997	1998
Belgium	27.3	36.2	30.7
Canada	37.7	51.2	53.9
Chile	13.5	26.8	11.8
Costa Rica	99.8	111.9	120.0
El Salvador	258.0	310.9	320.1
France	21.6	20.6	20.7
Germany	102.6	113.5	111.0
Honduras	140.2	177.3	215.9
Italy	21.2	27.0	29.7
Japan	42.1	53.3	57.4
Korea, Republic	2.8	5.1	52.8
Mexico	80.0	77.0	105.3
Netherlands	29.4	39.7	37.2
Nicaragua	79.9	83.2	92.6
Panama	46.3	42.6	67.7
Peru	29.5	13.2	48.5
Russian Federation	19.6	0.1	71.1
Sweden	21.5	22.3	19.4
United Kingdom	18.3	14.0	28.5
USA	746.7	841.2	841.8
Venezuela	12.5	34.6	26.7
Total (incl. others)	2,030.7	2,344.1	2,581.7

Source: UN, *International Trade Statistics Yearbook*.

Transport

RAILWAYS (traffic)

	1994	1995	1996
Passenger-km (million) . . .	991	0	0
Freight ton-km (million) . . .	25,295	14,242	836

Source: UN, *Statistical Yearbook*.

ROAD TRAFFIC ('000 motor vehicles in use)

	1994	1995	1996
Passenger cars	102.0	102.0	102.0
Commercial vehicles	97.0	97.0	97.0

Source: IRF, *World Road Statistics*.

SHIPPING
Merchant Fleet (registered at 31 December)

	1996	1997	1998
Number of vessels	5	5	5
Total displacement ('000 grt) . .	0.8	0.8	0.8

Source: Lloyd's Register of Shipping, *World Fleet Statistics*.

International Sea-borne Freight Traffic ('000 metric tons)

	1992	1993	1994
Goods loaded	2,176	1,818	2,096
Goods unloaded	3,201	3,025	3,822

CIVIL AVIATION (traffic on scheduled services)

	1995	1996	1997
Kilometres flown (million) . .	6	6	5
Passengers carried ('000) . .	300	300	508
Passenger-km (million) . . .	500	530	368
Total ton-km (million) . . .	70	71	77

Source: UN, *Statistical Yearbook*.

Tourism

TOURIST ARRIVALS BY COUNTRY OF ORIGIN

	1997	1998	1999
Canada	16,603	19,721	19,149
Costa Rica	18,393	21,408	25,556
El Salvador	108,506	133,683	272,747
France	12,937	14,814	14,584
Germany	18,895	20,805	18,069
Honduras	30,520	37,433	59,545
Italy	17,752	18,003	17,225
Mexico	63,557	61,387	54,901
Nicaragua	13,821	15,621	30,497
Spain	15,525	14,928	18,289
USA	162,528	168,851	182,597
Total (incl. others) . . .	576,362	636,276	822,695

Tourism receipts (US $ million): 167 in 1996; 325 in 1997; 394 in 1998.

Communications Media

	1995	1996	1997
Radio receivers ('000 in use) . .	750	800	835
Television receivers ('000 in use) .	600	620	640
Daily newspapers: number . .	5	7	n.a.
Telephones ('000 main lines in use)	286	338	430
Telefax stations (number in use) .	n.a.	10,000	n.a.
Mobile cellular telephones (subscribers)	29,999	43,421	64,194

Sources: UN, *Statistical Yearbook*, and UNESCO, *Statistical Yearbook*.

Education

(1999)

	Institutions	Teachers	Students
Pre-primary .	9,607	11,813	308,240
Primary	17,905	47,811	1,825,088
Secondary	3,118	20,543	305,818
Tertiary	1,462	13,105	146,291

Directory

The Constitution*

In December 1984 the Constituent Assembly drafted a new Constitution (based on that of 1965), which was approved in May 1985 and came into effect in January 1986. A series of amendments to the Constitution were approved by referendum in January 1994 and came into effect in April 1994. The Constitution's main provisions are summarized below:

Guatemala has a republican representative democratic system of government and power is exercised equally by the legislative, executive and judicial bodies. The official language is Spanish. Suffrage is universal and secret, obligatory for those who can read and write and optional for those who are illiterate. The free formation and growth of political parties whose aims are democratic is guaranteed. There is no discrimination on grounds of race, colour, sex, religion, birth, economic or social position or political opinions.

The State will give protection to capital and private enterprise in order to develop sources of labour and stimulate creative activity.

Monopolies are forbidden and the State will limit any enterprise which might prejudice the development of the community. The right to social security is recognized and it shall be on a national, unitary, obligatory basis.

Constitutional guarantees may be suspended in certain circumstances for up to 30 days (unlimited in the case of war).

CONGRESS

Legislative power rests with Congress, which is made up of 113 deputies, 91 of whom are elected according to departmental representation. The remaining 22 deputies are elected by national listing. Congress meets on 15 January each year and ordinary sessions last four months; extraordinary sessions can be called by the Permanent Commission or the Executive. All Congressional decisions must be taken by absolute majority of the members, except in special cases laid down by law. Deputies are elected for four years; they may be re-elected after a lapse of one session, but only once. Congress is responsible for all matters concerning the President and Vice-President and their execution of their offices; for all electoral matters; for all matters concerning the laws of the Republic; for approving the budget and decreeing taxes; for declaring war; for conferring honours, both civil and military; for fixing the coinage and the system of weights and measures; for approving, by two-thirds' majority, any international treaty or agreement affecting the law, sovereignty, financial status or security of the country.

PRESIDENT

The President is elected by universal suffrage, by absolute majority for a non-extendable period of four years. Re-election or prolongation of the presidential term of office are punishable by law. The President is responsible for national defence and security, fulfilling the Constitution, leading the armed forces, taking any necessary steps in time of national emergency, passing and executing laws, international policy, nominating and removing Ministers, officials and diplomats, co-ordinating the actions of Ministers of State. The Vice-President's duties include presiding over Congress and taking part in the discussions of the Council of Ministers.

ARMY

The Guatemalan Army is intended to maintain national independence, sovereignty and honour, territorial integrity and peace within the Republic. It is an indivisible, apolitical, non-deliberating body and is made up of land, sea and air forces.

LOCAL ADMINISTRATIVE DIVISIONS

For the purposes of administration the territory of the Republic is divided into 22 Departments and these into 330 Municipalities, but this division can be modified by Congress to suit interests and general development of the Nation without loss of municipal autonomy. Municipal authorities are elected every four years.

JUDICIARY

Justice is exercised exclusively by the Supreme Court of Justice and other tribunals. Administration of Justice is obligatory, free and independent of the other functions of State. The President of the Judiciary, judges and other officials are elected by Congress for five years. The Supreme Court of Justice is made up of 13 judges. The President of the Judiciary is also President of the Supreme Court. The Supreme Court nominates all other judges. Under the Supreme Court come the Court of Appeal, the Administrative Disputes Tribunal, the Tribunal of Second Instance of Accounts, Jurisdiction Conflicts, First Instance and Military, the Extraordinary Tribunal of Protection. There is a Court of Constitutionality presided over by the President of the Supreme Court.

* Under the terms of an accord, signed with the URNG in September 1996, concerning civilian power and the role of the armed forces, the Government undertook to revise the Constitution to relieve the armed forces of responsibility for internal security. This role was assumed by a new National Civilian Police force from mid-1997.

The Government

HEAD OF STATE

President: ALFONSO ANTONIO PORTILLO CABRERA (took office 14 January 2000).

Vice-President: JUAN FRANCISCO REYES LÓPEZ.

CABINET
(April 2001)

Minister of Foreign Affairs: GABRIEL ORELLANA ROJAS.

Minister of the Interior: BYRON BARRIENTES.

Minister of National Defence: Brig.-Gen. EDUARDO ARÉVALO LACS.

Minister of Public Finance: EDUARDO WEYMANN FUENTES.

Minister of Economy: MARCO ANTONIO VENTURA.

Minister of Public Health and Social Welfare: MARIO BOLAÑOS.

Minister of Communications, Transport and Public Works: LUIS RABBE.

Minister of Agriculture, Livestock and Food: JORGE ROLANDO ESCOTO MARROQUÍN.

Minister of Education: MARIO ROLANDO TORRES.

Minister of Employment and Social Security: JUAN FRANCISCO ALFARO MIJANGOS.

Minister of Energy and Mines: RAÚL EDMUNDO ARCHILA SERRANO.

Minister of Culture and Sport: OTILIA LUX DE COTI.

Minister of the Environment: HAROLDO QUEJ CHEN.

MINISTRIES

Ministry of Agriculture, Livestock and Food: Edif. Monja Blanca, 7 Avda 12-90, Zona 13, Guatemala City; tel. 362-4764; fax 332-8302; e-mail magadest@intelnet.net.gt; internet www.maga.gob.gt.

Ministry of Communications, Transport and Public Works: Palacio Nacional, 6a Calle y 7a Avda, Zona 1, Guatemala City; tel. 22-1212; fax 28-1613.

Ministry of Culture and Sport: 24a Calle 3-81, Zona 1, Guatemala City; tel. 230-0718; fax 230-0758.

Ministry of Economy: 8a Avda 10-43, Zona 1, Guatemala City; tel. 238-3330; internet www.mineco.gob.gt.

Ministry of Education: Palacio Nacional, 6a Calle y 7a Avda, Zona 1, Guatemala City; tel. 22-0162; fax 253-7386; internet www.mineduc.gob.gt.

Ministry of Employment and Social Security: Edif. NASA, 14 Calle 5-49, Zona 1, Guatemala City; tel. 230-1361; fax 251-3559; internet www.mintrabajo.gob.gt.

Ministry of Energy and Mines: Diagonal 17, 29–78, Zona 11, Guatemala City; tel. 276-0679; fax 276-3175; e-mail informatica@mem.gob.gt; internet www.mem.gob.gt.

Ministry of Environment: Edif. Plaza Robi 3°, 5a Calle 4-31, Zona 1, 01001 Guatemala; tel. 230-1719; fax 230-1718.

Ministry of Foreign Affairs: 2a Avda 4-17, Zona 10, Guatemala City; tel. 332-1900; fax 332-0805; e-mail webmaster@minex.gob.gt; internet www.minex.gob.gt.

Ministry of the Interior: Palacio Nacional, 6a Calle y 7a Avda, Zona 1, Guatemala City; tel. 22-1212; fax 251-5368.

Ministry of National Defence: Palacio Nacional, 6a Calle y 7a Avda, Zona 1, Guatemala City; tel. 22-1212; fax 28-1613; internet www.mindef.mil.gt.

Ministry of Public Finance: Edif. de Fianzas, Centro Cívico, 8a Avda y Calle 21, Zona 1, Guatemala City; tel. 251-1380; fax 251-0987; internet www.minfin.gob.gt.

Ministry of Public Health and Social Welfare: Palacio Nacional, 6a Calle y 7a Avda, Zona 1, Guatemala City; tel. 22-1212; fax 22-2736.

President and Legislature

PRESIDENT

Election, 7 November 1999

	Percentage of votes cast
Alfonso Antonio Portillo Cabrera (FRG) . . .	47.8
Oscar Berger Perdomo (PAN)	30.3
Alvaro Colom Caballeros (ANN)	12.3
Acisclo Valladares Molina (PLP)	3.1
Juan Francisco Bianchi Castillo (ARDE) . .	2.1
Ana Catalina Soberanis Reyes (FDNG) . .	1.3
José Enrique Asturias Rudeke (LOV) . . .	1.1
Danilo Julián Roca Barillas (UCN) . . .	1.0
Total (incl. others)	100.0

Since none of the candidates achieved the required 50% of the votes necessary to win outright, a second round of voting was held on 26 December 1999. At this election Alfonso Antonio Portillo Cabrera (FRG) received 68.3% of the valid votes cast, while Oscar Berger Perdomo (PAN) won the remaining 31.7%.

CONGRESO NACIONAL

President: Gen. (retd) José Efraín Ríos Montt.

Vice-Presidents: César Leonel Soto Arango, Zury Mayté Ríos-Montt Sosa de López-Villatoro, Luis Alfonso Rosales Marroquín.

Election, 7 November 1999

	Seats
Frente Republicano Guatemalteco (FRG)	63
Partido de Avanzada Nacional (PAN)	37
Alianza Nueva Nación (ANN)	9
Partido Democracia Cristiana Guatemalteca (PDCG) . .	2
Partido Liberal Progresista (PLP)	1
La Organización Verde (LOV)	1
Total	113

Political Organizations

Acción Reconciliadora Democrática (ARDE): 4a Avda 14-53, Zona 1, Guatemala City; tel. 232-0591; fax 251-4076; centre-right; Sec.-Gen. Herlindo Alvarez del Cid.

Alianza Democrática: 6 Avda 15-41, Zona 1, Guatemala City; tel. 591-4158; f. 1992; centre party; Leader Leopoldo Urrutia.

Alianza Nueva Nación (ANN): electoral alliance comprising:

Desarrollo Integral Auténtico (DIA): 12a Calle 'A' 2-18, Zona 1, Guatemala City; tel. 232-8044; e-mail morlain@guate.net; left-wing party; Sec.-Gen. Francisco Rolando Morales Chávez.

Unidad de Izquierda Democrática (UNID): Guatemala City; left-wing party.

Unidad Revolucionaria Nacional Guatemalteca (URNG): (see below).

Alianza Popular Cinco (AP5): 6a Avda 3-23, Zona 1, Guatemala City; tel. 231-6022; Sec.-Gen. Max Orlando Molina Narciso.

Central Auténtica Nacionalista (CAN): 15a Avda 4-31, Zona 1, Guatemala City; tel. 251-2992; f. 1980 from the CAO (Central Arañista Organizado); Leader Héctor Mayora Dawe; Sec.-Gen. Jorge Roberto Arana España.

Comité Guatemalteca de Unidad Patriota (CGUP): f. 1982; opposition coalition consisting of:

Frente Democrático Contra la Represión (FDCR): Leader Rafael García.

Frente Popular 31 de Enero (FP-31): f. 1980; left-wing amalgamation of student, peasant and trade union groups.

Frente de Avance Nacional (FAN): 3a Calle 'A' 1-66, Zona 10, Guatemala City; tel. 231-8036; right-wing group; Sec.-Gen. Federico Abundio Maldonado Gularte.

Frente Cívico Democrático (FCD): Guatemala City; Leader Jorge González del Valle.

Frente Demócrata Guatemalteco: Leader Clemente Marroquín Rojas.

Frente Democrático Nueva Guatemala (FDNG): left-wing faction of Partido Revolucionario; Pres. Jorge González del Valle; Sec.-Gen. Rafael Arriaga.

Frente Republicano Guatemalteco (FRG): 3 Calle 5-50, Zona 1, Guatemala City; tel. 238-2756; internet www.frg.com.gt; f. 1988; right-wing group; leader Gen. (retd) José Efraín Ríos Montt.

Frente de Unidad Nacional (FUN): 6a Avda 5-18, Zona 12, Guatemala City; tel. 271-4048; f. 1971; nationalist group; Leader Gabriel Girón Ortiz.

Fuerza Demócrata Popular: 11a Calle 4-13, Zona 1, Guatemala City; tel. 251-5496; f. 1983; democratic popular force; Sec. Lic. Francisco Reyes Ixcamey.

Fuerza Nueva: Leader Carlos Rafael Soto.

La Organización Verde (LOV): 5 Calle A 0-64, Zona 3, Guatemala City; tel. 230-3946; electoral coalition comprising:

Unidad Social Demócrata.

Unión Democrática (UD): Of. 4, 13°, Avda Reforma 12-01, Zona 10, Guatemala City; tel. 331-8573; e-mail chea@infovia.com.gt; f. 1983; Sec.-Gen. José Luis Chea Urruela.

Movimiento de los Descamisados (MD): Avda J. R. Barrios L. 896 Sta Luisa, Zona 6, Guatemala City; Sec.-Gen. Enrique Morales Pérez.

Movimiento Humanista de Integración Demócrata: Guatemala City; f. 1983; Leader Victoriano Alvarez.

Movimiento de Liberación Nacional (MLN): 2a Avda 38-11, Zona 8, Guatemala City; tel. 22-6528; e-mail mln@wepa.com.gt; internet www.wepa.com.gt/mln; f. 1960; extreme right-wing; 95,000 mems; Leader Lic. Mario Sandóval Alarcón; Sec.-Gen. Ulysses Charles Dent Weissenberg.

Movimiento 20 de Octubre: Leader Marco Antonio Villamar Contreras.

Pantinamit: f. 1977; represents interests of Indian population; Leader Fernando Tezahuic Tohón.

Partido de Avanzada Nacional (PAN): 7 Avda 10-38, Zona 9, Guatemala City; tel. 334-1702; internet www.pan.org.gt; Leader Alvaro Enrique Arzú Irigoyen; Gen. Sec. Héctor Cifuentes Mendoza.

Partido Democracia Cristiana Guatemalteca (PDCG): Avda Elena 20-66, Zona 3, Guatemala City; tel. 251-7804; f. 1955; 130,000 mems; Sec.-Gen. Luis Alfonso Cabrera Hidalgo.

Partido Demócrata Guatemalteco (PDG): Guatemala City; Sec.-Gen. Jorge Antonio Reyna Castillo.

Partido Institucional Democrático (PID): Guatemala City; f. 1965; 60,000 mems; moderate conservative; Sec.-Gen. Oscar Humberto Rivas García; Dir Donaldo Alvarez Ruiz.

Partido Libertador Progresista (PLP): 5a Calle 5-44, Zona 1, Guatemala City; tel. 232-5548; e-mail plp@intelnet.net.gt; f. 1990; Sec.-Gen. Ismael Muñoz Pérez.

Partido Petenero: Guatemala City; f. 1983; defends regional interests of El Petén.

Partido Progresista (PP): 1a Calle 6-77, Zona 2, Guatemala City; Sec.-Gen. José Ramón Fernández González.

Partido Reformador Guatemalteco (PREG): 3a Calle 9-59, Zona 1, Guatemala City; tel. 22-8759; Sec.-Gen. Miguel Angel Montepeque Contreras.

Partido Revolucionario de los Trabajadores Centro-americanos (PRTC): Guatemala City.

Partido Social Cristiano (PSC): P. Savoy, Of. 113, 8°, 8a Calle 9-41, Zona 1, Guatemala City; tel. 274-0577; f. 1983; Sec.-Gen. Alfonso Alonzo Barillas.

Partido Socialista Democrático (PSD): Guatemala City; f. 1978; Sec.-Gen. Sergio Alejandro Pérez Cruz.

Partido de Unificación Anticomunista (PUA): Guatemala City; right-wing party; Leader Leonel Sisniega Otero.

Unidad Nacional de Esperanza (UNE): Guatemala City; f. 2001; Founder and Pres. Alvaro Colom Caballero.

Unidad Nacionalista Organizada (UNO): Calzada Aguilar Batres 17-14, Zona 11, Guatemala City; Sec.-Gen. Mario Roberto Armando Ponciano Castillo.

Unión del Centro Nacional (UCN): 12a Calle 2-45, Zona 1, Guatemala City; tel. 253-6211; fax 253-4038; f. 1984; centre party; Sec.-Gen. Edmond Mulet.

Unión Reformista Social (URS): 5a Calle 'A' 0-64, Zona 3, Guatemala City; Sec.-Gen. Marcos Emilio Recinos Alvarez.

In February 1982 the principal guerrilla groups unified to form the **Unidad Revolucionaria Nacional Guatemalteca (URNG)** (Guatemalan National Revolutionary Unity): 11 Avda 11-56, Zona 2, Guatemala City; tel. and fax 254-0572; e-mail prensaurng@guate .net; internet www.urng.com; has links with the PSD. The political wing of the URNG was the **Representación Unitaria de la Oposición Guatemalteca (RUOG)**. At the end of 1996 the URNG consisted of:

Ejército Guerrillero de los Pobres (EGP): f. 1972; draws main support from Indians of western highlands; works closely with the **Comité de Unidad Campesina (CUC)** (Committee of Peasant Unity) and radical Catholic groups; mems 4,000 armed, 12,000 unarmed.

Fuerzas Armadas Rebeldes (FAR): formed early 1960s; originally military commission of CGTG; associated with the CNT and CONUS trade unions; based in Guatemala City, Chimaltenango and El Petén; Commdr JORGE ISMAEL SOTO GARCÍA ('PABLO MONSANTO').

Organización del Pueblo en Armas (ORPA): f. 1979; military group active in San Marcos province; originally part of FAR; Commdr RODRIGO ASTURIAS ('GASPAR ILOM').

Partido Guatemalteco del Trabajo (PGT): communist party; divided into three armed factions: PGT-Camarilla (began actively participating in war in 1981); PGT-Núcleo de Conducción y Dirección; PGT-Comisión Nuclear; Gen. Sec. RICARDO ROSALES ('CARLOS GONZÁLEZ').

In December 1996 the Government and the URNG signed a definitive peace treaty, bringing the 36-year conflict to an end. The demobilization of the URNG guerrillas began in March 1997 and was completed by early May. In June the URNG registered as a political party in formation. In August the movement held elections to a provisional executive committee. The URNG applied for formal recognition as a political party in October 1998 and was formally registered in December. In May 1999 the URNG formed an alliance, the Alianza Nueva Nación, with the FDNG (which later withdrew from the alliance), the UNID and the DIA in order to contest legislative elections, scheduled to be held in November 1999.

Diplomatic Representation

EMBASSIES IN GUATEMALA

Argentina: 2a Avda 11-04, Zona 10, Apdo 112, Guatemala City; tel. 332-6419; fax 332-1654; e-mail embargen@concyt.gob.gt; Ambassador: FELIX CORDOVA MOYANO.

Austria: Edif. Plaza Marítima, 4°, 6a Avda 20-25, Zona 10, Guatemala City; tel. 368-1134; fax 333-6180; Ambassador: GABRIEL KRAMARICS.

Belgium: Avda de la Reforma 13-70, Zona 9, Apdo 3725, Guatemala City; tel. 225-6633; Ambassador: MICHEL DELFOSSE.

Belize: Edif. El Reformador, Suite 801, Avda de la Reforma 1-50, Zona 9, Guatemala City; tel. 334-5531; fax 334-5536; e-mail embelguate@guate.net; Ambassador: MOISES CAL.

Bolivia: 12a Avda 15-37, Zona 10, Guatemala City; Chargé d'affaires a.i.: Dr JOSÉ GABINA VILLANUEVA G.

Brazil: 18a Calle 2-22, Zona 14, Apdo 196-A, Guatemala City; tel. 337-0949; fax 337-3475; e-mail brasilgua@gua.gbm.net; Ambassador: SÉRGIO DAMASCENO VIEIRA.

Canada: Edif. Edyma Plaza, 8°, 13a Calle 8-44210, Guatemala City; tel. 333-6102; fax 333-6153; Ambassador: DANIEL LIVERMORE.

Chile: 14 Calle 15-21, Zona 13, Guatemala City; tel. 334-8273; fax 334-8276; e-mail echile.gu@intelnet.net.gt; Ambassador: H. E. JORGE MOLINA VALDIVIESO.

China (Taiwan): 4a Avda 'A' 13–25, Zona 9, Apdo 1646, Guatemala City; tel. 339-0711; fax 332-2668; e-mail embajada@micro.com.gt; Ambassador: ANDREW J. S. WU.

Colombia: Edif. Gemini 10, 12a Calle, 1a Avda, Zona 10, Guatemala City; tel. 335-3602; fax 335-3603; e-mail embajada.col@gold.guate.net; Ambassador: ANGELA ROBAYO BELLO.

Costa Rica: 3°, Of. 320, Avda de la Reforma 8-60, Zona 9, Guatemala City; tel. 331-9604; fax 332-1520; e-mail embarica@intelnet.net.gt; Ambassador: YOLANDA INGIANNA-MAINIERI.

Cuba: 13 Calle 5-72, Zona 10, Guatemala City; tel. 333-7679; fax 337-3282; Ambassador: PASTOR RODRÍGUEZ VALIENTE.

Dominican Republic: Vista Hermosa, 5°, 18 Avda 1-50, Zona 15, Guatemala City; tel. 369-3580; fax 365-7966; Ambassador: ROBERTO VICTORIA.

Ecuador: 4 Avda 12-04, Zona 14, Guatemala City; tel. 337-2994; fax 368-1831; e-mail embecuad@guate.net; Ambassador: EDUARDO CABEZAS MOLINA.

Egypt: Edif. Cobella 5°, 5 Avda 10-84, Zona 14, Apdo 502, Guatemala City; tel. 333-6296; fax 368-2808; Ambassador: MOHAMED ALI AFIFI.

El Salvador: 4a Avda 13-60, Zona 10, Guatemala City; tel. 366-6147; fax 366-2234; e-mail emsalva@pronet.net.gt; Ambassador: SALVADOR JOSÉ TRIGUEROS HIDALGO.

Finland: 2A Calle 18-37, Zona 15, Apdo 2, Guatemala City; tel. 365-9270; fax 365-8375; e-mail imesland@infovia.com.gt; Ambassador: RISTO VALTHEIM.

France: Edif. Marbella, 16a Calle 4-53, Zona 10, Guatemala City; tel. 337-3639; fax 337-3180; e-mail ambfrguate@pronet.net.gt; Ambassador: SERGE PINOT.

Germany: Edif. Plaza Marítima, 20 Calle 6-20, Zona 10, Guatemala City; tel. 333-6903; fax 337-0031; Ambassador: Dr JOACHIM NEUKIRCH.

Holy See: 10a Calle 4-47, Zona 9, Guatemala City (Apostolic Nunciature); tel. 332-4274; fax 334-1918; e-mail nuntius@gua.net; Apostolic Nuncio: Most Rev. RAMIRO MOLINER INGLÉS, Titular Archbishop of Sarda.

Honduras: 9a Avda 16-34, Zona 10, Guatemala City; tel. 368-0842; fax 337-3921; e-mail embhon@infovia.com.gt; Ambassador: YOLANDA PALAU DE FERNÁNDEZ.

Israel: 13a Avda 14-07, Zona 10, Guatemala City; tel. 333-4624; fax 333-6950; e-mail esrembgu@guaweb.net; Ambassador: SCHLOMO COHEN.

Italy: 5a Avda 8-59, Zona 14, Guatemala City; tel. 337-4557; fax 337-0795; e-mail embitaly@guatenet.net.gt; Ambassador: ALESSANDRO SERAFINI.

Japan: Edif. Torre Internacional, 10531, Avda La Reforma 16-85, Zona 10, Guatemala City; tel. 331-9666; fax 331-5462; Ambassador: HISATO MURAYAMA.

Korea, Republic: Edif. El Reformador, 7°, Avda La Reforma 1-50, Zona 9, Apdo 1649, Guatemala City; tel. 334-5480; fax 334-5481; Ambassador: TAE SHIK CHUNG.

Mexico: 15 Calle 3-20, Zona 10, Guatemala City; tel. 333-7254; fax 333-7615; Ambassador: SALVADOR ARRIOLA BARRENECHEA.

Nicaragua: 10a Avda 14-72, Zona 10, Guatemala City; tel. 368-0785; fax 337-4264; e-mail embanic-guat@intco.com.gt; Ambassador: FRANCISCO JAVIER RAMOS SÁNCHEZ.

Norway: Edif. Murano Center 15°, Of. 1501, 14 Calle 3-51, Zona 10, Apdo 1764, Guatemala City; tel. 366-5908; fax 366-5928; Ambassador: ARNE AASHEM.

Panama: Centro Empresarial Torre II, Of. 702, 5a Avda 15-45, Zona 10, Guatemala City; tel. 333-7176; fax 337-2446; Ambassador: ALONSO ROY.

Spain: 6a Calle 6-48, Zona 9, Guatemala City; tel. 334-3757; fax 332-2456; Ambassador: VÍCTOR LUIS FAGILDE GONZÁLEZ.

Sweden: 8a Avda 15-07, Zona 10, Guatemala City; tel. 333-6536; fax 333-7607; e-mail swedish-emb@gua.gbm.net; Ambassador: STAFFAN WRIGSTAD.

Switzerland: Torre Internacional, 14°, 16 Calle 0-55, Zona 10, 01010 Guatemala City; tel. 367-5520; fax 367-5811; e-mail swissemgua@c.net.gt; Ambassador: CHRISTIAN HAUSWIRTH.

United Kingdom: Edif. Torre Internacional, 11°, Avda La Reforma 16-00, Zona 10, Guatemala City; tel. 367-5425; fax 367-5430; e-mail embassy@infovia.com.gt; Ambassador: ANDREW J. F. CAIE.

USA: Avda de la Reforma 7-01, Zona 10, Guatemala City; tel. 331-1541; fax 331-6660; Ambassador: DONALD J. PLANTY.

Uruguay: Edif. Plaza Marítima, 5°, Of. 5-3, 6a Avda 20-25, Zona 10, Guatemala City; tel. 337-0229; fax 333-7553; e-mail uruguate@guate.net; Ambassador: ALFREDO MENINI TERRA.

Judicial System

Corte Suprema: Centro Cívico, Guatemala City.

There are 13 members of the Supreme Court, appointed by the Congress.

President of the Supreme Court: JOSÉ ROLANDO QUESADA FERNÁNDEZ.

Civil Courts of Appeal: 10 courts, 5 in Guatemala City, 2 in Quezaltenango, 1 each in Jalapa, Zacapa and Antigua. The two Labour Courts of Appeal are in Guatemala City.

Judges of the First Instance: 7 civil and 10 penal in Guatemala City, 2 civil each in Quezaltenango, Escuintla, Jutiapa and San Marcos, 1 civil in each of the 18 remaining Departments of the Republic.

Religion

Almost all of the inhabitants profess Christianity, with a majority belonging to the Roman Catholic Church. In recent years the Protestant Churches have attracted a growing number of converts.

CHRISTIANITY

The Roman Catholic Church

For ecclesiastical purposes, Guatemala comprises two archdioceses, 10 dioceses and the Apostolic Vicariates of El Petén and Izabal. At 31 December 1998 adherents represented about 81.8% of the total population.

Bishops' Conference: Conferencia Episcopal de Guatemala, Secretariado General del Episcopado, Km 15, Calzada Roosevelt 4-54, Zona 7, Mixco, Apdo 1698, Guatemala City; tel. 593-1831; fax 593-1834; e-mail ceg@quetzal.net; internet www.iglesiacatolica.org.gt; f. 1973; Pres. VíCTOR HUGO MARTíNEZ CONTRERAS, Archbishop of Los Altos, Quetzaltenango-Totonicapán.

Archbishop of Guatemala City: PRóSPERO PEñADOS DEL BARRIO, Arzobispado, 7a Avda 6-21, Zona 1, Apdo 723, Guatemala City; tel. 232-1071; fax 238-0004.

Archbishop of Los Altos, Quetzaltenango—Totonicapán: VíCTOR HUGO MARTíNEZ CONTRERAS, Arzobispado, 11a Avda 6-27, Zona 1, Apdo 11, Quezaltenango; tel. (961) 2840; fax (961) 6049.

The Anglican Communion

Guatemala comprises one of the five dioceses of the Iglesia Anglicana de la Región Central de América.

Bishop of Guatemala: Rt Rev. ARMANDO GUERRA SORIA, Avda Castellana 40–06, Zona 8, Apdo 58-A, Guatemala City; tel. 272-0852; fax 472-0764; e-mail diocesis@infovia.com.gt; diocese founded 1967.

Protestant Churches

The Baptist Church: Convention of Baptist Churches of Guatemala, 12a Calle 9–54, Zona 1, Apdo 322, Guatemala City; tel. 22-4227; f. 1946; Pres. Lic. JOSé MARROQUíN R.

Church of Jesus Christ of Latter-day Saints: 12a Calle 3–37, Zona 9, Guatemala City; 17 bishoprics, 9 chapels; Regional Rep. GUILLERMO ENRIQUE RITTSCHER.

Lutheran Church: Consejo Nacional de Iglesias Luteranas, Apdo 1111, Guatemala City; tel. 22-3401; 3,077 mems; Pres. Rev. DAVID RODRíGUEZ U.

Presbyterian Church: Iglesia Evangélica Presbiteriana Central, 6a Avda 'A' 4–68, Zona 1, Apdo 655, Guatemala City; tel. 232-0791; fax 232-2832; f. 1882; 36,000 mems; Pastor: Rev. JOSé RAMIRO BOLAñOS RIVERA.

Union Church: 12 Calle 7–37, Plaza España, Zona 9, Apdo 150-A, Guatemala City; tel. 331-6904; fax 362-3961; e-mail unionchurch@guate.net; f. 1943; Pastor: W. KARL SMITH; Youth Pastor: BRENT C. WILLIAMS.

BAHÁ'Í FAITH

National Spiritual Assembly of the Bahá'ís: 3a Calle 4–54, Zona 1, Guatemala City; tel. 232-9673; fax 232-9673; e-mail aenguate@emailgua.com; mems resident in 464 localities; Sec. MARVIN E. ALVARADO E.

The Press

PRINCIPAL DAILIES

Al Día: Avda La Reforma 6–64, Zona 9, Guatemala City; tel. 339-0870; fax 339-1276; f. 1996; Pres. LIONEL TORIELLO NáJERA; Dir GERARDO JIMéNEZ ARDóN.

Diario de Centroamérica: 18a Calle 6–72, Zona 1, Guatemala City; tel. 22-4418; f. 1880; morning; official; Dir LUIS MENDIZáBAL; circ. 15,000.

La Hora: 9a Calle 'A' 1–56, Zona 1, Apdo 1593, Guatemala City; tel. 232-6864; fax 251-7084; e-mail lahora@tikal.net.gt; f. 1920; evening; independent; Dir OSCAR MARROQUíN ROJAS; circ. 18,000.

Impacto: 9a Calle 'A' 1-56, Apdo 1593, Guatemala City; tel. 22-6864; fax 251-7084; daily.

La Nación: 1a Avda 11-12, Guatemala City.

El Periódico: 15a Avda 24–51, Zona 13, Guatemala City; tel. 362-0242; fax 332-9761; e-mail periodic@gold.guate.net; f. 1996; morning; independent; Pres. JOSé RUBéN ZAMORA; Editors JUAN LUIS FONT, SYLVIA GEREDA; circ. 50,000.

Prensa Libre: 13a Calle 9–31, Zona 1, Apdo 2063, Guatemala City; tel. 230-5096; fax 251-8768; e-mail econtrer@infovia.com.gt; internet www.prensalibre.com; f. 1951; morning; independent; Gen. Man. EDGAR CONTRERAS MOLINA; Editor GONZALO MARROQUíN GODOY; circ. 120,000.

Siglo Veintiuno: 7a Avda 11-63, Zona 9, Guatemala City; tel. 360-6704; fax 331-9145; e-mail buzon21@sigloxxi.com; internet www.sigloxxi.com; f. 1990; morning; Pres. LIONEL TORIELLO NáJERA; circ. 65,000.

La Tarde: 14a Avda 4-33, Guatemala City.

PERIODICALS

AGA: 9a Calle 3–43, Zona 1, Guatemala City; monthly; agricultural.

Crónica Semanal: Edif. Torre Profesional II, Of. 312, 6a Avda 0-60, Guatemala City; tel. 235-2155; fax 235-2360; f. 1988; weekly; politics, economics, culture; Publr FRANCISCO PéREZ.

Gerencia: La Asociación de Gerentes de Guatemala, Edif. Aseguradora General, 7°, 10a Calle 3-17, Guatemala City; tel. 231-1644; fax 231-1646; f. 1967; monthly; official organ of the Association of Guatemalan Managers; Editor MARGARITA SOLOGUREN.

El Industrial: 6a Ruta 9-21, Zona 4, Guatemala City; monthly; official organ of the Chamber of Industry.

Inforpress Centroamericana: Guatemala City; f. 1972; weekly; Spanish; regional political and economic news and analysis; Dir ARIEL DE LEóN.

Panorama Internacional: 13a Calle 8-44, Zona 9, Apdo 611-A, Guatemala City; tel. 233-6367; fax 233-6203; weekly; politics, economics, culture.

PRESS ASSOCIATIONS

Asociación de Periodistas de Guatemala (APG): 14a Calle 3-29, Zona 1, Guatemala City; tel. 232-1813; fax 238-2781; e-mail apg@terra.com.gt; f. 1947; Pres. SALVADOR BONINI; Sec. MARIO DOMíN-GUEZ VALIENTE.

Cámara Guatemalteca de Periodismo (CGP): Guatemala City; Pres. EDUARDO DíAZ REINA.

Círculo Nacional de Prensa (CNP): Guatemala City; Pres. ISRAEL TOBAR ALVARADO.

NEWS AGENCIES

Inforpress Centroamericana: 7a Avda 2-05, Zona 1, Guatemala City; tel. and fax 221-0301; e-mail inforpre@guate.net; internet www.worldcom.nl/CAR; f. 1972; independent news agency; publishes two weekly news bulletins, in English and Spanish.

Foreign Bureaux

ACAN-EFE (Central America): Edif. El Centro, 8°, Of. 8-21, 9a Calle y 7a Avda, Zona 1, Of. Guatemala City; tel. 251-9454; fax 251-9484: Man. ANA CAROLINA ALPíREZ A.

Agenzia Nazionale Stampa Associata (ANSA) (Italy): Torre Norte, Edif. Geminis 10, Of. 805, 12a Calle 1-25, Zona 10, Guatemala City; tel. 235-3039; Chief ALFONSO ANZUETO LóPEZ.

Deutsche Presse-Agentur (dpa) (Germany): 5a Calle 4-30, Zona 1, Apdo 2333, Guatemala City; tel. 251-7505; fax 251-7505; Correspondent JULIO CéSAR ANZUETO.

Inter Press Service (IPS) (Italy): Edif. El Centro, 3°, Of. 13, 7a Avda 8-56, Zona 1, Guatemala City; tel. 253-8837; fax 251-4736; Correspondent GEORGE RODRíGUEZ-OTEIZA.

United Press International (UPI) (USA): 6a Calle 4-17, Zona 1, Guatemala City; tel. and fax 251-4258; Correspondent AMAFREDO CASTELLANOS.

Publishers

Ediciones América: 12a Avda 14-55B, Zone 1, Guatemala City; tel. 251-4556; Man. Dir RAFAEL ESCOBAR ARGüELLO.

Ediciones Gama: 5a Avda 14-46, Zone 1, Guatemala City; tel. 234-2331; Man. Dir SARA MONZóN DE ECHEVERRíA.

Ediciones Legales 'Commercio e Industria': 12a Avda 14-78, Zone 1, Guatemala City; tel. 253-5725; Man. Dir LUIS EMILIO BARRIOS.

Editorial del Ministerio de Educación: 15a Avda 3-22, Zona 1, Guatemala City.

Editorial Nueva Narrativa: Edif. El Patio, Of. 106, 7a Avda 7-07, Zona 4, Guatemala City; Man. Dir MAX ARAúJO A.

Editorial Oscar de León Palacios: 6a Calle 'A' 10-12, Zone 11, Guatemala City; tel. 272-1636; educational texts; Man. Dir OSCAR DE LEóN CASTILLO.

Editorial Palo de Hormigo: O Calle 16-40, Zone 15, Col. El Maestro, Guatemala City; tel. 369-2080; fax 369-8858; e-mail juanfercif@hotmail.com; f. 1990; Man. Dir JUAN FERNANDO CIFUENTES.

Editorial Universitaria: Edif. de la Editorial Universitaria, Universidad de San Carlos de Guatemala, Ciudad Universitaria, Zona 12, Guatemala City; tel. and fax 476-9628; literature, social sciences, health, pure and technical sciences, humanities, secondary and university educational textbooks; Editor RAúL FIGUEROA SARTI.

F & G Editores: 30 Avda 'B' 4-50, Zona 7, Jardines de Tikal I, Guatemala City; fax 474-0214; e-mail fgeditor@guate.net; internet www.fygeditores.com; f. 1990 as Figueroa y Gallardo, changed name in 1993; law, literature and social sciences; Editor RAúL FIGUEROA SARTI.

Piedra Santa: 5a Calle 7-55, Zona 1, Guatemala City; tel. 220-1524; fax 323-9053; f. 1947; children's literature, text books; Man. Dir IRENE PIEDRA SANTA.

Seminario de Integración Social Guatemalteco: 11a Calle 4-31, Zona 1, Guatemala City; tel. 22-9754; f. 1956; sociology, anthropology, social sciences, educational textbooks.

Broadcasting and Communications

TELECOMMUNICATIONS

Superintendencia de Telecomunicaciones de Guatemala: Edif. Murano Center, 16°, 14a Calle 3-51, Zona 10, Guatemala City; tel. 366-5880; fax 366-5890; e-mail supertel@sit.gob.gt; internet www.sit.gob.gt; Superintendent José Romeo Orellana.

Empresa Guatemalteca de Telecomunicaciones (Guatel): Guatemala City; internet www.guatel.com.gt; 95% share transferred to private ownership in 1998; Dir Alfredo Guzmán.

BROADCASTING

Dirección General de Radiodifusión y Televisión Nacional: Edif. Tipografía Nacional, 3°, 18 de Septiembre 6-72, Zona 1, Guatemala City; tel. 253-2539; f. 1931; government supervisory body; Dir-Gen. Enrique Alberto Hernández Escobar.

Radio

There are five government and six educational stations, including:

La Voz de Guatemala: 18a Calle 6-72, Zona 1, Guatemala City; tel. 253-2539; government station; Dir Arturo Soto Echeverría.

Radio Cultural TGN: 4a Avda 30-09, Zona 3, Apdo 601, Guatemala City; tel. 471-4378; fax 440-0260; e-mail ssywulka@guate.net; f. 1950; religious and cultural station; programmes in Spanish and English, Cakchiquel and Kekchí; Dir Esteban Sywulka; Man. Anthony Wayne Berger.

There are some 80 commercial stations, of which the most important are:

Emisoras Unidas de Guatemala: 4a Calle 6-84, Zona 13, Guatemala City; tel. 440-5133; fax 440-5159; e-mail rboileau@tikal.net.gt; f. 1964; Pres. Jorge Edgardo Archila Marroquín; Vice-Pres. Rolando Archila Marroquín.

Radio Cinco Sesenta: 14a Calle 4-73, Zona 11, Guatemala City; Dir Edna Castillo Obregón.

Radio Continental: Guatemala City; Dir Roberto Vizcaíno R.

Radio Nuevo Mundo: 6a Avda 10-45, Zona 1, Apdo 281, Guatemala City; fax 232-2036; f. 1947; Man. Alfredo González Gamarra.

Radio Panamericana: 1a Avda 35-48, Zona 7, Guatemala City; Dir Jaime J. Paniagua.

La Voz de las Américas: 11a Calle 2-43, Zona 1, Guatemala City; Dir Augusto López S.

Television

Canal 3—Radio-Televisión Guatemala, SA: 30a Avda 3-40, Zona 11, Apdo 1367, Guatemala City; tel. 292-2491; fax 294-7492; f. 1956; commercial station; Pres. Lic. Max Kestler Farnés; Vice-Pres. J. F. Villanueva.

Canal 5—Televisión Cultural y Educativa, SA: 4a Calle 18-38, Zona 1, Guatemala City; tel. 238-1781; fax 232-7003; f. 1980; cultural and educational programmes; Dir Alfredo Herrera Cabrera.

Teleonce: 20a Calle 5-02, Zona 10, Guatemala City; tel. 368-2595; fax 337-0861; f. 1968; commercial; Gen. Dir Juan Carlos Ortiz.

Televisiete, SA: Blvr Vista Hermosa 18-07, Zona 15, Apdo 1242, Guatemala City; tel. 369-0033; fax 369-1393; f. 1988; commercial station channel 7; Dir Abdón Rodríguez Zea.

Trecevisión, SA: 3a Calle 10-70, Zona 10, Guatemala City; tel. 26-3266; commercial; Dir Ing. Pedro Melgar R.; Gen. Man. Gilda Valladares Ortiz.

Finance

(cap. = capital; p.u. = paid up; res = reserves; dep. = deposits; m. = million; brs = branches; amounts in quetzales)

BANKING

Superintendencia de Bancos: 9a Avda 22-00, Zona 1, Apdo 2306, Guatemala City; tel. 232-0001; fax 232-5301; e-mail sibcos@guate .net; internet www.sib.gob.gt; f. 1946; Superintendent Roberto A. Gutiérrez Nájera.

Central Bank

Banco de Guatemala: 7a Avda 22-01, Zona 1, Apdo 365, Guatemala City; tel. 230-6222; fax 253-4035; internet www.banguat.gob.gt; f. 1946; cap. and res 603.2m., dep. 12,040.6m. (Dec. 1997); Pres. Lizardo Arturo Sosa López; Man. Edwin Giovanni Verbena de León; 8 brs.

State Commercial Bank

Crédito Hipotecario Nacional de Guatemala: 7a Avda 22-77, Zona 1, Apdo 242, Guatemala City; tel. 230-6542; fax 238-2041;

e-mail mercchn@bancared.net.gt; internet www.bancared.com.gt; f. 1930; government-owned; Pres. Fabián Pira Arrivillaga; Gen. Man. Sergio Durini Cárdenas; 35 agencies.

Private Commercial Banks
Guatemala City

Banco Agrícola Mercantil, SA: 7a Avda 7-30, Zona 9, Guatemala City; tel. 362-3141; fax 251-0780; e-mail interbam@guate.net; internet www.bamguatemala.com; f. 1948; cap. 84.1m., res 2.5m., dep. 974.1m. (Dec. 1996); Gen. Man. Alfonso Villa de Voto; 2 brs, 8 agencies.

Banco del Agro, SA: 9a Calle 5-39, Zona 1, Apdo 1443, Guatemala City; tel. 251-4026; fax 232-4566; e-mail info@banagro.com.gt; internet www.banagro.com.gt; f. 1956; cap. 10.0m., res 19.4m., dep. 374.9m. (June 1991); Pres. José María Valdés García; Gen. Man. Héctor Estuardo Pivaral; 41 brs.

Banco del Café, SA: Avda de la Reforma 9-30, Zona 9, Apdo 831, Guatemala City; tel. 361-3645; fax 331-1418; e-mail mercadeo@ bancafe.com.gt; internet www.bancafe.com.gt; f. 1978; total assets 6.63m. (1999); merged with Multibanco in 2000; Pres. Eduardo Manuel González Rivera; Asst Gen. Man. Ingo Haberland Haesloop.

Banco de Comercio: Edif. Centro Operativo, 6a Avda 8-00, Zona 9, Guatemala City; tel. 339-0504; fax 339-0555; internet www .bancared.gt; f. 1991; 33 brs.

Banco del Ejército, SA: 7a Avda 3-73, Zona 9, Apdo 1797, Guatemala City; tel. 362-7042; fax 362-7108; e-mail baneje@gua.net; internet www.banejer.com.gt; f. 1972; cap. 72.2m., res 22.2m., dep. 735.9m. (Dec. 1997); Pres. Col Guido Fernando Abdala Peñagos; 14 brs.

Banco de Exportación, SA: Avda de la Reforma 11-49, Zona 10, Guatemala City; tel. 231-9861; fax 232-2879; e-mail infbanex@ banex.net.gt; internet www.banex.net.gt; f. 1985; cap. 71.8m., res 30.0m., dep. 731.3m. (Dec. 1993); Pres. Dr Francisco Mansilla Córdova; Man. Ing. Rafael Viejo Rodríguez.

Banco Industrial, SA (BAINSA): Edif. Centro Financiero, Torre 1, 7a Avda 5-10, Zona 4, Apdo 744, Guatemala City; tel. 234-5111; fax 232-1712; f. 1964 to promote industrial development; total assets 7.91m. (1999); Pres. Juan Miguel Torrebiarte Lantzendorffer; Gen. Man. Lic. Norberto Rodolfo Castellanos Díaz.

Banco Inmobilario, SA: 7a Avda 11-59, Zona 9, Apdo 1181, Guatemala City; tel. 332-1950; fax 332-2325; e-mail info@bancoinmob .com.gt; internet www.bcoinmob.com.gt; f. 1958; cap. 45.0m., res 6.2m., dep. 532.3m. (June 1992); Pres. Emilio Antonio Peralta Portillo; Man. Marco Antonio Ovando; 15 brs.

Banco Internacional, SA: Torre Internacional, Avda Reforma 15-85, Zona 10, Apdo 2588, Guatemala City; tel. 366-6666; fax 366-6743; e-mail binter60@gua.gbm.net; internet www.bcointer.com.gt; f. 1976; cap. 50.0m., res 15.4m., dep. 822.6m. (Dec. 1997); Pres. Juan Skinner-Klée; Gen. Man. José Manuel Requejo Sánchez; 28 brs.

Banco del Quetzal, SA: Edif. Plaza El Roble, 7a Ave 6-26, Zona 9, Apdo 1001-A, Guatemala City; tel. 231-8333; fax 232-6937; f. 1984; cap. 37.4m., dep. 342.7m. (July 1994); Pres. Lic. Mario Roberto Leal Pivaral; Gen. Man. Alfonso Villa Devoto.

Banco Reformador, SA: 7a Avda 7-24, Zona 9, Guatemala City; tel. 362-0888; fax 362-0847; cap. 1,720; merged with Banco de la Construcción in 2000; 60 brs.

Banco SCI: Edif. SCI Centre, Avda La Reforma 9-76, Zona 9, Guatemala City; tel. 331-7515; fax 331-2262; e-mail atencion@sci .net.gt; internet www.sci.com.gt; f. 1967.

Banco de los Trabajadores: 8a Avda 9-41, Zona 1, Apdo 1956, Guatemala City; tel. 22-4651; fax 251-8902; f. 1966; deals with loans for establishing small industries as well as normal banking business; Pres. Lic. César Amilcar Bárcenas; Gen. Man. Lic. Oscar H. Andrade Elizondo.

Banco Uno: Edif. Unicentro, 1°, Blvd Los Próceres, 18 Calle 5-56, Zona 10, Guatemala City; tel. 366-1818; e-mail bancouno@gua .pibnet.com; internet www.bancared.com.gt/Uno.

G & T Continental: 7a Avda 1-86, Zona 4, Guatemala City; tel. 331-2333; fax 332-9083; and Plaza Continental, 6a Avda 9-08, Zona 9, Guatemala City; tel. 339-2001; fax 339-2091; e-mail gfc@email .continet.com.gt; internet www.gyt.com.gt; f. 2000 following merger of Banco Continental and Banco Granai y Townson; total assets 11.4m. (2000); 130 brs.

Quezaltenango

Banco de Occidente, SA: 7a Ave 11-15, Zona 1, Quezaltenango; tel. (961) 53-1333; fax (961) 30-0970; e-mail occidente@occidente.com.gt; internet www.occidente.com.gt; f. 1881; total assets 12.45m. (1999); Pres. Dr Luis Beltranena Valladares; Gen. Man. Ing. José E. Ascoli Cáceres; 29 brs.

State Development Bank

Banco Nacional de Desarrollo Agrícola—BANDESA: 9a Calle 9-47, Zona 1, Apdo 350, Guatemala City; tel. 253-5222; fax 253-

7927; f. 1971; agricultural development bank; Pres. Minister of Agriculture, Livestock and Food; Gen. Man. GUSTAVO ADOLFO LEAL CASTELLANOS.

Finance Corporations

Corporación Financiera Nacional (CORFINA): 11a Avda 3-14, Zona 1, Guatemala City; tel. 253-4550; fax 22-5805; f. 1973; provides assistance for the development of industry, mining and tourism; Pres. Lic. SERGIO A. GONZÁLEZ NAVAS; Gen. Man. Lic. MARIO ARMANDO MARTÍNEZ ZAMORA.

Financiera Guatemalteca, SA (FIGSA): 1a Avda 11-50, Zona 10, Apdo 2460, Guatemala City; tel. 232-1423; fax 231-0873; f. 1962; investment agency; Pres. CARLOS GONZÁLEZ BARRIOS; Gen. Man. Ing. ROBERTO FERNÁNDEZ BOTRÁN.

Financiera Industrial y Agropecuaria, SA (FIASA): Plaza Continental, 3°, 6a Avda 9-08, Zona 9, Guatemala City; tel. 239-1951; fax 239-2089; f. 1968; private development bank; medium- and long-term loans to private industrial enterprises in Central America; cap. 2.5m., res 27.1m. (Dec. 1994); Pres. JORGE CASTILLO LOVE; Gen. Man. Lic. ALEJANDRO MEJÍA AVILA.

Financiera Industrial, SA (FISA): Centro Financiero, Torre 2, 7a Avda 5-10, Zona 4, Apdo 744, Guatemala City; tel. 232-1750; fax 231-1773; f. 1981; cap. 3m., res 6.2m. (Aug. 1991); Pres. CARLOS ARÍAS MASSELLI; Gen. Man. Lic. ELDER F. CALDERÓN REYES.

Financiera de Inversión, SA: 11a Calle 7-44, Zona 9, Guatemala City; tel. 332-4020; fax 332-4320; f. 1981; investment agency; cap. 15.0m. (June 1997); Pres. Lic. MARIO AUGUSTO PORRAS GONZÁLEZ; Gen. Man. Lic. JOSÉ ROLANDO PORRAS GONZÁLEZ.

Foreign Bank

Lloyds TSB Group PLC: Edif. Gran Vía, 6a Avda 9-51, Zona 9, Guatemala City; tel. 332-7580; fax 332-7641; f. 1959; cap. 18.7m., dep. 79.5m. (2000); Man. N. M. A. HUBBARD; 10 brs.

Banking Association

Asociación de Banqueros de Guatemala: Edif. Quinta Montúfar, 2°, 12a Calle 4-74, Zona 9, Guatemala City; tel. 231-8211; fax 231-9477; f. 1961; represents all state and private banks; Pres. Ing. RAFAEL VIEJO RODRÍGUEZ.

STOCK EXCHANGE

Guatemala Stock Exchange: 4a Calle 6-55, Zona 9, Guatemala City; tel. 234-2479; fax 231-4509; f. 1987; the exchange is commonly owned (one share per associate) and trades stocks from private companies, government bonds, letters of credit and other securities.

INSURANCE
National Companies

Aseguradora General, SA: 10a Calle 3-17, Zona 10, Guatemala City; tel. 332-5933; fax 334-2093; f. 1968; Pres. JUAN O. NIEMANN; Man. ENRIQUE NEUTZE A.

Aseguradora Guatemalteca, SA: Edif. Torre Azul, 10°, 4a Calle 7-53, Zona 9, Guatemala City; tel. 361-0206; fax 361-1093; aseguate@ guate.net; f. 1978; Pres. Gen. CARLOS E. PINEDA CARRANZA; Man. CÉSAR A. RUANO SANDOVAL.

Cía de Seguros Generales Granai & Townson, SA: 2a Ruta, 2-39, Zona 4, Guatemala City; tel. 334-1361; fax 332-2993; f. 1947; Pres. ERNESTO TOWNSON R.; Exec. Man. MARIO GRANAI FERNÁNDEZ.

Cía de Seguros Panamericana, SA: Avda de la Reforma 9-00, Zona 9, Guatemala City; tel. 232-5922; fax 231-5026; f. 1968; Pres. JOHN ROBERTS; Gen. Man. Lic. SALVADOR ORTEGA.

Cía de Seguros El Roble, SA: Torre 2, 7a Avda 5-10, Zona 4, Guatemala City; tel. 332-1702; fax 332-1629; f. 1973; Pres. FEDERICO KÖNG VIELMAN; Man. Ing. RICARDO ERALES CÓBAR.

Comercial Aseguradora Suizo-Americana, SA: 7a Avda 7-07, Zona 9, Apdo 132, Guatemala City; tel. 332-0666; fax 331-5495; f. 1946; Pres. WILLIAM BICKFORD B.; Gen. Man. MARIO AGUILAR.

Departamento de Seguros y Previsión del Crédito Hipotecario Nacional: 7a Avda 22-77, Zona 1, Centro Cívico, Guatemala City; tel. 250-0271; fax 253-8584; f. 1935; Pres. FABIÁN PIRA; Man. SERGIO DURINI.

Empresa Guatemalteca Cigna de Seguros, SA: Edif. Plaza Marítima 10, 6a Avda 20-25, Zona 10, Guatemala City; tel. 337-2285; fax 337-0121; f. 1951; Gen. Man. Lic. RICARDO ESTRADA DARDÓN.

La Seguridad de Centroamérica, SA: Avda de la Reforma 12-01, Zona 10, Guatemala City; tel. 231-7566; fax 231-7580; f. 1967; Pres. EDGARDO WAGNER D.; Vice-Pres. RICARDO CAU MARTÍNEZ.

Seguros Alianza, SA: Edif. Etisa, 6°, Plazuela España, Zona 9, Guatemala City; tel. 331-5475; fax 331-0023; f. 1968; Pres. LUIS FERNANDO SAMAYOA; Gen. Man. DAVID LEMUS PIVARAL.

Seguros de Occidente, SA: 7a Calle 'A' 7-14, Zona 9, Guatemala City; tel. 231-1222; fax 234-1413; f. 1979; Pres. Lic. PEDRO AGUIRRE; Gen. Man. CARLOS LAINFIESTA.

Seguros Universales, SA: 4a Calle 7-73, Zona 9, Apdo 1479, Guatemala City; tel. 334-0733; fax 332-3372; e-mail tato@ universales.net; f. 1962; Manager PEDRO NOLASCO SICILIA.

Insurance Association

Asociación Guatemalteca de Instituciones de Seguros (AGIS): Edif. Torre Profesional I, Of. 411, 4°, 6a Avda 0-60, Zona 4, Guatemala City; tel. 235-1657; fax 235-2021; f. 1953; 12 mems; Pres. ENRIQUE NUETZE A.; Man. Lic. FERNANDO RODRÍGUEZ TREJO.

Trade and Industry

DEVELOPMENT ORGANIZATIONS

Comisión Nacional Petrolera: Diagonal 17, 29-78, Zona 11, Guatemala City; tel. 276-0680; fax 276-3175; f. 1983; awards petroleum exploration licences.

Consejo Nacional de Planificación Económica: 9a Calle 10-44, Zona 1, Guatemala City; tel. 251-4549; fax 253-3127; e-mail mrayo@ns.concyt.gob.gt; f. 1954; prepares and supervises the implementation of the national economic development plan; Sec.-Gen. MARIANO RAYO MUÑOZ.

Corporación Financiera Nacional (CORFINA): see under Finance (Finance Corporations).

Empresa Nacional de Fomento y Desarrollo Económico de El Petén (FYDEP): 11a Avda 'B' 32-46, Zona 5, Guatemala City; tel. 231-6834; f. 1959; attached to the Presidency; economic development agency for the Department of El Petén; Dir FRANCISCO ANGEL CASTELLANOS GÓNGORA.

Instituto de Fomento de Hipotecas Aseguradas (FHA): Edif. Aristos Reforma, 2°, Avda Reforma 7-62, Zona 9, Guatemala City; tel. 362-9434; fax 362-9492; e-mail fha@guate.net; internet www.fha.centroamerica.com; f. 1961; insured mortgage institution for the promotion of house construction; Pres. HOMERO AUGUSTO GONZÁLEZ BARILLAS; Man. Lic. JOSÉ SALVADOR SAMAYOA AGUILAR.

Instituto Nacional de Administración Pública (INAP): 5a Avda 12-65, Zona 9, Apto 2753, Guatemala City; tel. 26-6339; f. 1964; provides technical experts to assist all branches of the Government in administrative reform programmes; provides in-service training for local and central government staff; has research programmes in administration, sociology, politics and economics; provides postgraduate education in public administration; Gen. Man. Dr ARIEL RIVERA IRÍAS.

Instituto Nacional de Transformación Agraria (INTA): 14a Calle 7-14, Zona 1, Guatemala City; tel. 28-0975; f. 1962 to carry out agrarian reform; current programme includes development of the 'Faja Transversal del Norte'; Pres. Ing. NERY ORLANDO SAMAYOA; Vice-Pres Ing. SERGIO FRANCISCO MORALES-JUÁREZ, ROBERTO EDMUNDO QUIÑÓNEZ LÓPEZ.

CHAMBERS OF COMMERCE AND INDUSTRY

Comité Coordinador de Asociaciones Agrícolas, Comerciales, Industriales y Financieras (CACIF): Edif. Cámara de Industria de Guatemala, 6a Ruta 9-21, Zona 4, Guatemala City; tel. 231-0651; co-ordinates work on problems and organization of free enterprise; mems: 6 chambers; Pres. JORGE BRIZ; Sec.-Gen. RAFAEL POLA.

Cámara de Comercio de Guatemala: 10a Calle 3-80, Zona 1, Guatemala City; tel. 28-2681; fax 251-4197; f. 1894; Gen. Man. EDGARDO RUIZ.

Cámara de Industria de Guatemala: 6a Ruta 9-21, 12°, Zona 4, Apdo 214, Guatemala City; tel. 334-0850; fax 334-1090; f. 1958; Pres. JUAN JOSÉ URRUELA KONG; Gen. Man. CARLOS PERALTA.

INDUSTRIAL AND TRADE ASSOCIATIONS

Asociación de Agricultores Productores de Aceites Esenciales: 6a Calle 1-36, Zona 10, Apdo 272, Guatemala City; tel. 234-7255; f. 1948; essential oils producers' asscn; 40 mems; Pres. FRANCISCO RALDA; Gen. Man. CARLOS FLORES PAGAZA.

Asociación de Azucareros de Guatemala (ASAZGUA): Edif. Tívoli Plaza, 6a Calle 6-38, Zona 9, Guatemala City; fax 231-8191; f. 1957; sugar producers' asscn; 19 mems; Gen. Man. Lic. ARMANDO BOESCHE.

Asociación de Exportadores de Café: 11a Calle 5-66, 3°, Zona 9, Guatemala City; coffee exporters' asscn; 37 mems; Pres. EDUARDO GONZÁLEZ RIVERA.

Asociación General de Agricultores: 9a Calle 3-43, Zona 1, Guatemala City; f. 1920; general farmers' asscn; 350 mems; Pres. DAVID ORDÓÑEZ; Man. PEDRO ARRIVILLAGA RADA.

Asociación Nacional de Avicultores (ANAVI): Edif. Galerías Reforma, Torre 2, 9°, Of. 904, Avda de la Reforma 8-60, Zona 9, Guatemala City; tel. 231-1381; fax 234-7576; f. 1964; national asscn of poultry farmers; 60 mems; Pres. Lic. FERNANDO ROJAS; Dir Dr MARIO A. MOTTA GONZÁLEZ.

Asociación Nacional de Fabricantes de Alcoholes y Licores (ANFAL): Km 16½, Carretera Roosevelt, Zona 10, Apdo 2065, Guatemala City; tel. 292-0430; f. 1947; distillers' asscn; Pres. FELIPE BOTRÁN MERINO; Man. Lic. JUAN GUILLERMO BORJA MOGOLLÓN.

Asociación Nacional del Café—Anacafé: Edif. Etisa, Plazuela España, Zona 9, Guatemala City; tel. 236-7180; fax 234-7023; f. 1960; national coffee asscn; Pres. WILLIAM STIXRUD.

Cámara del Agro: 15a Calle 'A' 7-65, Zona 9, Guatemala City; tel. 26-1473; f. 1973; Man. CÉSAR BUSTAMANTE ARAÚZ.

Consejo Nacional del Algodón: 11a Calle 6-49, Zona 9, Guatemala City; tel. 234-8390; fax 234-8393; f. 1964; consultative body for cultivation and classification of cotton; 119 mems; Pres. ROBERTO MARTÍNEZ R.; Man. ALFREDO GIL SPILLARI.

Gremial de Huleros de Guatemala: Edif. Centroamericano, Of. 406, 7a Avda 7-78, Zona 4, Guatemala City; tel. 231-4917; f. 1970; rubber producers' guild; 125 mems; Pres. JOSÉ LUIS RALDA; Man. Lic. CÉSAR SOTO.

UTILITIES

Electricity

Empresa Eléctrica de Guatemala, SA: 6a Avda 8-14, Zona 1, Guatemala City; tel. 230-3050; fax 253-1746; f. 1972; state electricity producer; 80% share transferred to private ownership in 1998; Pres. RICARDO CASTILLO SINIBALDI.

Instituto Nacional de Electrificación (INDE): Edif. La Torre, 7a Avda 2-29, Zona 9, Guatemala City; tel. (2) 34-5711; fax (2) 34-5811; f. 1959; former state agency for the generation and distribution of hydroelectric power; principal electricity producer; privatized in 1998; Pres. GUILLERMO RODRÍGUEZ.

CO-OPERATIVES

Instituto Nacional de Cooperativas (INACOP): 4a Calle 4-37, Zona 9, 01001 Guatemala City; tel. 234-1097; fax 234-7536; technical and financial assistance in planning and devt of co-operatives; Man. CÉSAR AGUSTO MASSELLA BARRERA.

TRADE UNIONS

Frente Nacional Sindical (FNS) (National Trade Union Front): Guatemala City; f. 1968 to achieve united action in labour matters; affiliated are two confederations and 11 federations, which represent 97% of the country's trade unions and whose General Secretaries form the governing council of the FNS. The affiliated organizations include:

  Comité Nacional de Unidad Sindical Guatemalteca— CONUS: Leader MIGUEL ANGEL SOLÍS; Sec.-Gen. GERÓNIMO LÓPEZ DÍAZ.

  Confederación General de Sindicatos (General Trade Union Confederation): 18a Calle 5-50, Zona 1, Apdo 959, Guatemala City.

  Confederación Nacional de Trabajadores (National Workers' Confederation): Guatemala City; Sec.-Gen. MIGUEL ANGEL ALBIZÚREZ.

  Consejo Sindical de Guatemala (Guatemalan Trade Union Council): 18a Calle 5-50, Zona 1, Apdo 959, Guatemala City; f. 1955; admitted to ICFTU and ORIT; Gen. Sec. JAIME V. MONGE DONIS; 30,000 mems in 105 affiliated unions.

  Federación Autónoma Sindical Guatemalteca (Guatemalan Autonomous Trade Union Federation): Guatemala City; Gen. Sec. MIGUEL ANGEL SOLÍS.

  Federación de Obreros Textiles (Textile Workers' Federation): Edif. Briz, Of. 503, 6a Avda 14-33, Zona 1, Guatemala City; f. 1957; Sec.-Gen. FACUNDO PINEDA.

  Federación de Trabajadores de Guatemala (FTG) (Guatemalan Workers' Federation): 5a Calle 4-33, Zona 1, Guatemala City; tel. 22-6515; Promoter ADRIAN RAMÍREZ.

A number of unions exist without a national centre, including the Union of Chicle and Wood Workers, the Union of Coca-Cola Workers and the Union of Workers of the Enterprise of the United Fruit Company.

Central General de Trabajadores de Guatemala (CGTG): 3a Avda 12-22, Zona 1, Guatemala City; tel. 232-9234; fax 251-3212; f. 1987; Sec.-Gen. JOSÉ E. PINZÓN SALAZAR.

Central Nacional de Trabajadores (CNT): 9a Avda 4-29, Zona 1, Apdo 2472, Guatemala City; f. 1972; cover all sections of commerce, industry and agriculture including the public sector; clandestine since June 1980; Sec.-Gen. JULIO CELSO DE LEÓN; 23,735 mems.

Unidad de Acción Sindical y Popular (UASP): f. 1988; broad coalition of leading labour and peasant organizations; includes:

  Comité de la Unidad Campesina (CUC) (Committee of Peasants' Unity).

Confederación de Unidad Sindical de Trabajadores de Guatemala (CUSG): 5a Calle 4-33, Zona 1, Guatemala City; tel. 22-6515; f. 1983; Sec.-Gen. FRANCISCO ALFARO MIJANGOS.

Federación Nacional de Sindicatos de Trabajadores del Estado de Guatemala (Fenasteg): Sec. ARMANDO SÁNCHEZ.

Sindicato de Trabajadores de la Educación Guatemaltecos (STEG).

Sindicato de Trabajadores de la Industria de la Electricidad (STINDE).

Sindicato de Trabajadores del Instituto Guatemalteco de Seguro Social (STIGSS).

Unidad Sindical de Trabajadores de Guatemala (UNSI-TRAGUA).

Transport

RAILWAYS

In 1998 there were 1,390 km of railway track in Guatemala, of which some 102 km were plantation lines.

Ferrocarriles de Guatemala—FEGUA: 9a Avda 18-03, Zona 1, Guatemala City; tel. 232-7720; fax 238-3039; e-mail feguarivera@ hotmail.com; f. 1968; 50-year concession to rehabilitate and operate railway awarded in 1997 to the US Railroad Devt Corpn; 782 km from Puerto Barrios and Santo Tomás de Castilla on the Atlantic coast to Tecún Umán on the Mexican border, via Zacapa, Guatemala City and Santa María. Branch lines: Santa María–San José; Las Cruces–Champerico. From Zacapa another line branches southward to Anguiatú, on the border with El Salvador; owns the ports of Barrios (Atlantic) and San José (Pacific); first 65-km section, Guatemala City—El Chile, and a further 300-km section, extending to Barrios, reopened in 1999; Administrator RENÉ MINERA PÉREZ.

ROADS

In 1999 there were an estimated 14,021 km of roads, of which 3,081 km were paved. The Guatemalan section of the Pan-American highway is 518.7 km long and totally asphalted. In 1997 the privately-owned Palin–Escuintla toll road opened.

SHIPPING

Guatemala's major ports are Puerto Barrios and Santo Tomás de Castilla, on the Gulf of Mexico, San José and Champerico on the Pacific Ocean, and Puerto Quetzal, which was redeveloped in the late 1990s.

Armadora Marítima Guatemalteca, SA: 14a Calle 8-14, Zona 1, Apdo 1008, Guatemala City; tel. 230-4686; fax 253-7464; cargo services; Pres. and Gen. Man. L. R. CORONADO CONDE.

Empresa Portuaria 'Quetzal': Edif. Torre Azul, 1°, 4a Calle 7-53, Zona 9, Guatemala City; tel. 334-7101; fax 334-8172; e-mail pquetzal@terra.com.gt; internet www.puerto-quetzal.gob.gt; port and shipping co; Man. LEONEL MONTEJO.

Empresa Portuaria Nacional Santo Tomás de Castilla: Edif. Mini, 6a Avda 1-27, Zone 4, Guatemala City; tel. 232-3685; fax 232-6894; Man. ENRIQUE SALAZAR.

Flota Mercante Gran Centroamericana, SA: Edif. Canella, 5°, 1a Calle 7-21, Zona 9, Guatemala City; tel. 231-6666. 1959; services from Europe (in association with WITASS), Gulf of Mexico, US Atlantic and East Coast Central American ports; Pres. R. S. RAMÍREZ; Gen. Man. J. E. A. MORALES.

Líneas Marítimas de Guatemala, SA: Edif. Plaza Marítima, 8°, 6a Avda 20-25, Zona 10, Guatemala City; tel. 237-0166; cargo services; Pres. J. R. MATHEAU ESCOBAR; Gen. Man. F. HERRERÍAS.

Several foreign lines link Guatemala with Europe, the Far East and North America.

CIVIL AVIATION

There are two international airports, 'La Aurora' in Guatemala City and at Santa Elena Petén.

Aerolíneas de Guatemala—AVIATECA: Avda Hincapié 12-22, Aeropuerto 'La Aurora', Zona 13, Guatemala City; tel. 231-8261; fax 231-7412; internet www.flylatinamerica.com; f. 1945; internal services and external services to the USA, Mexico, and within Central America; transferred to private ownership in 1989; Pres. Ing. JULIO OBOLS GOMES; Gen. Man. ENRIQUE BELTRONERA.

Aeroquetzal: Avda Hincapié y 18a Calle, Lado Sur, Aeropuerto 'La Aurora', Zona 13, Guatemala City; tel. 231-8282; fax 232-1491; scheduled domestic passenger and cargo services, and external services to Mexico.

Aerovías: Avda Hincapié 4 y 18a Calle, Aeropuerta 'La Aurora', Zona 13, Guatemala City; tel. 232-5686; fax 234-7470; operates scheduled and charter cargo services; Pres. FERNANDO ALFONSO CASTILLO R.; Vice-Pres. NELSON C. PUENTE.

Aviones Comerciales de Guatemala (Avcom): Avda Hincapié, Aeropuerto 'La Aurora', Zona 13, Guatemala City; tel. 231-5821; fax 232-4946; domestic charter passenger services.

Tourism

As a result of violence in the country, the annual total of tourist arrivals declined from 504,000 in 1979, when tourist receipts were US $201m., to 192,000 in 1984 (receipts $56.6m.). After 1985, however, the number of arrivals recovered and were recorded as some 853,072 in 2000, when receipts were an estimated $751m.

Instituto Guatemalteco de Turismo (INGUAT) (Guatemala Tourist Commission): Centro Cívico, 7a Avda 1-17, Zona 4, Guatemala City; tel. 331-1333; fax 331-8893; e-mail inguat@guate.net; internet www.guatemala.travel.com.gt; f. 1967; policy and planning council: 11 mems representing the public and private sectors; Pres. ALEJANDRO BOTRÁN; Dir MARIANO BELTRANENA FALLA.

Asociación Guatemalteca de Agentes de Viajes (AGAV) (Guatemalan Association of Travel Agents): 6a Avda 8-41, Zona 9, Apdo 2735, Guatemala City; tel. 231-0320; Pres. MARÍA DEL CARMEN FERNÁNDEZ O.

GUINEA

Introductory Survey

Location, Climate, Language, Religion, Flag, Capital

The Republic of Guinea lies on the west coast of Africa, with Sierra Leone and Liberia to the south, Senegal and Guinea-Bissau to the north, and Mali and Côte d'Ivoire inland to the east. The climate on the coastal strip is hot and moist, with temperatures ranging from about 32°C (90°F) in the dry season to about 23°C (73°F) in the wet season (May–October). The interior is higher and cooler. The official language is French, but Soussou, Manika and six other national languages are widely spoken. Most of the inhabitants are Muslims, but some follow traditional animist beliefs. Around 2% are Roman Catholics. The national flag (proportions 3 by 2) consists of three equal vertical stripes, of red, yellow and green. The capital is Conakry.

Recent History

The Republic of Guinea (formerly French Guinea, part of French West Africa) became independent on 2 October 1958, after 95% of voters rejected the Constitution of the Fifth Republic under which the French colonies became self-governing within the French Community. The new state was the object of punitive reprisals by the outgoing French authorities: all aid was withdrawn, and the administrative infrastructure destroyed. The Parti démocratique de Guinée—Rassemblement démocratique africain (PDG—RDA) became the basis for the construction of new institutions. Its leader, Ahmed Sekou Touré, became President, and the PDG—RDA the sole political party.

Sekou Touré, formerly a prominent trade unionist, pursued vigorous policies of socialist revolution. Opposition was ruthlessly crushed, and Sekou Touré perpetuated rumours of a 'permanent conspiracy' by foreign powers to overthrow his regime. By 1983 almost 2m. Guineans were estimated to have fled the country. Several coup attempts were alleged during the 1960s, and an abortive invasion by Portuguese troops and Guinean exiles in 1970 prompted the execution of many of those convicted of involvement.

All private trade was forbidden in 1975: transactions were conducted through official co-operatives under the supervision of an 'economic police'. In August 1977 demonstrations by women in Conakry, in protest against the abolition of the traditional market and the abuse of power by the 'economic police', provoked rioting in other towns, as a result of which three state governors were killed. Sekou Touré subsequently disbanded the 'economic police', and allowed limited private trading to recommence in July 1979. Meanwhile, in November 1978 it was announced that the functions of the PDG—RDA and the State were to be merged, and the country was renamed the People's Revolutionary Republic of Guinea. There was, none the less, a general move away from rigid Marxism and a decline in relations with the USSR, as Guinea sought a political and economic *rapprochement* with its African neighbours, with France and with other Western powers. In December 1978 Valéry Giscard d'Estaing made the first visit by a French President to independent Guinea.

At legislative elections in January 1980 voters endorsed the PDG—RDA's list of 210 candidates for a new Assemblée nationale (to replace the former Assemblée législative). In May 1982 Sekou Touré was returned unopposed to the presidency for a fourth seven-year term of office, reportedly receiving 100% of the votes cast. He made his first official visit to France in September of that year.

In January 1984 a plot to overthrow the Government was disclosed when a group of mercenaries was arrested in southern Senegal. Thousands of Guineans were reportedly detained, accused of complicity in the affair. In March Sekou Touré died while undergoing surgery in the USA. On 3 April, before a successor had been chosen by the ruling party, the armed forces seized power in a bloodless coup. A Comité militaire de redressement national (CMRN) was appointed, headed by Col (later Gen.) Lansana Conté, hitherto commander of the Boké region. The PDG—RDA and the legislature were dissolved, and the Constitution was suspended. The CMRN pledged to restore democracy and to respect human rights; some 250 political

prisoners were released, and a relaxation of press restrictions was announced. In May the country was renamed the Second Republic of Guinea. The Prime Minister, Col Diarra Traoré, toured the region to rally support from Guinea's neighbours, and also visited Europe in an effort to attract foreign investment and to consolidate relations, particularly with France. By mid-1984 an estimated 200,000 Guinean exiles had returned to the country.

Trials of former associates of Sekou Touré, most of whom had been detained since the coup, began in November 1984. In December President Conté assumed the posts of Head of Government and Minister of Defence; the post of Prime Minister was abolished, and Traoré was demoted to a lesser post. In July 1985 Traoré attempted to seize power while Conté was out of the country. Troops loyal to Conté suppressed the revolt, and Traoré was arrested, along with members of his family and more than 200 suspected sympathizers. A series of attacks was subsequently aimed at the Malinke ethnic group, of which both Traoré and the late President Sekou Touré were members. In May 1987 it was announced that 58 people, including nine former government ministers, had been sentenced to death in secret trials for crimes committed under Sekou Touré or following the 1985 coup attempt. The announcement did little to allay international suspicions that many detainees had already been executed in the aftermath of the abortive coup, and in December 1987 Conté admitted that Traoré had died in the hours following his arrest. In January 1988 an amnesty was announced for 67 political prisoners, including Sekou Touré's widow and son.

In October 1985 Conté began to implement radical economic reforms, demanded by the World Bank and IMF as preconditions for the provision of structural aid. In December the Council of Ministers was reorganized to include a majority of civilians. In late 1989 Conté announced that, following a national referendum on a proposed new constitution, a joint civilian and military Comité transitoire de redressement national (CTRN) would replace the CMRN. After a transitional period of not more than five years, civilian rule would be established, with an executive and legislature directly elected within a two-party system. The draft Constitution of what was designated the Third Republic was endorsed by 98.7% of the 97.4% of the electorate who voted in a referendum on 23 December 1990; the 36-member CTRN was inaugurated in February 1991 under Conté's chairmanship.

In November 1990, meanwhile, Conté appealed to political exiles to return to Guinea. Alpha Condé, the leader of the Rassemblement populaire guinéen (RPG—an unofficial political organization whose activities the authorities had suppressed), returned to Guinea in May 1991, after a long period of exile. Three arrests were made when security forces dispersed a meeting of Condé's supporters, and a ban was subsequently imposed on unauthorized meetings and demonstrations. In June one person was killed when security forces opened fire on demonstrators outside the police headquarters in Conakry, to where Condé had been summoned in connection with the seizure of allegedly subversive materials. Condé was subsequently granted political asylum in Senegal.

In October 1991 Conté announced that an 'organic law' authorizing the registration of an unlimited number of political parties would come into effect in April 1992, and that legislative elections would be held before the end of 1992. The Constitution was promulgated on 23 December 1991, and in January 1992 Conté ceded the presidency of the CTRN (whose membership was, at the same time, reduced to 15), in conformity with the constitutional separation of the powers of the executive and the legislature. In February most military officers and all those who had returned from exile after the 1984 coup (known as *Guinéens de l'extérieur*) were removed from the Council of Ministers.

The 'organic law' entered into force on 3 April 1992, whereupon 17 political parties, including the RPG, were legalized; Condé returned to Guinea in June. However, a lack of cohesion among opposition parties undermined attempts to persuade the Government to convene a national conference in advance of elections. Moreover, it was rumoured that the pro-Conté Parti pour l'unité et le progrès (PUP), established by prominent *Guinéens de l'extérieur*, was benefiting from state funds. Conté reportedly escaped an assassination attempt in October, when gunmen opened fire on the vehicle in which he was travelling. In December the Government postponed indefinitely the legislative elections, which had been scheduled for the end of that month. Subsequent indications that the parliamentary elections would not take place until after a presidential election caused resentment among the opposition, which had hoped to present a single candidate (from the party that had performed best in the legislative elections) for the presidency.

In September 1993 the Government banned all street demonstrations, following violent incidents when police opened fire on anti-Government protesters in Conakry, as a result of which, according to official figures, 18 people were killed. In October, at the first meeting between Conté and opposition leaders since the legalization of political parties, it was agreed to establish an independent electoral commission. Controversy subsequently arose regarding the composition of the electoral commission, as well as the Government's decision to place it under the jurisdiction of the Minister of the Interior and Security.

In October 1993 the Supreme Court approved eight candidates for the presidential election, scheduled for 5 December. Among Conté's main rivals were Condé, Mamadou Boye Bâ of the Union pour la nouvelle République (UNR) and Siradiou Diallo of the Parti pour le renouveau et le progrès (PRP). Opposition candidates subsequently demanded that the election be postponed, citing irregularities in the compilation of electoral lists as well as delays in the issuing of voting cards and in the appointment of the electoral commission. In late November the Government postponed the election until 19 December. At least four deaths were recorded in pre-election violence involving PUP supporters and opposition activists, and there were six deaths in Conakry as voting proceeded as scheduled. Although several opposition candidates were reported to have withdrawn prior to the election, the official rate of participation by voters was high, at 78.5%. Preliminary results indicated that Conté had secured an absolute majority of the votes cast, thus obviating the need for a second round of voting. Opposition claims that the poll had been fraudulent and the result manipulated in favour of Conté intensified when the Supreme Court annulled the outcome of voting in the Kankan and Siguiri prefectures (in both of which Condé had won more than 95% of the votes), owing to irregularities in the conduct of the polls. According to the official results of the election, confirmed by the Court in early January 1994, Conté was elected with 51.7% of the votes cast; Condé took 19.6% of the votes, Bâ 13.4% and Diallo 11.9%.

Conté, who had resigned from the army in order to contest the election as a civilian, was inaugurated as President on 29 January 1994. His stated priorities included the strengthening of national security and the promotion of economic growth. A major restructuring of the Council of Ministers was implemented in August.

In May 1994 Bâ, asserting his lack of confidence in the Guinean opposition, announced the UNR's intention to support Conté as the country's legitimately elected Head of State. However, relations between the Government and the opposition remained generally strained, and the RPG in particular alleged the harassment of its supporters by the security forces. The announcement that there would be no facilities abroad to allow expatriate Guineans to vote in the forthcoming legislative elections (following violent disturbances at polling stations abroad at the presidential election) provoked criticism by opposition parties and by members of the electoral commission, who stated that this act of disenfranchisement contravened both the Constitution and the electoral code. Consequently the UNR withdrew its support for Conté.

In December 1994 the Government announced new measures aimed at combating organized crime and other serious offences. As well as the creation of a special police unit to counter banditry, the enforcement of the death penalty was envisaged, together with stricter policies governing immigration and asylum for refugees—the Conté administration frequently attributed the increase in insecurity to the presence of large numbers of refugees (see below) in Guinea. In January 1996 human rights organizations expressed concern at the recent rejection of appeals against six death sentences.

Meanwhile, in February 1995 Conté readopted his military title. The legislative election finally took place on 11 June. Prior to the elections opposition leaders alleged that efforts were being made to prevent campaigning in areas where support for the opposition was likely to be strong. They also denounced the use of portraits of Conté on PUP campaign materials, protesting that the President was constitutionally required to distance himself from party politics. A total of 846 candidates, from 21 parties, contested the 114 seats in the Assemblée nationale. As preliminary results indicated that the PUP had won an overwhelming majority in the legislature, the so-called 'radical' opposition (the RPG, the PRP and the UNR) protested that voting had been conducted fraudulently, stating that they would take no further part in the electoral process and announcing their intention to boycott the assembly. According to the final results, which were verified by the Supreme Court in July (whereupon the Assemblée nationale officially superseded the CTRN), the PUP won 71 seats—having taken 30 of the 38 single-member constituencies and 41 of the 76 seats allocated by a system of national proportional representation. Eight other parties won representation, principal among them the RPG, which took 19 seats, the PRP and the UNR, both of which won nine seats. Some 63% of the registered electorate were reported to have voted. At municipal elections in late June the PUP won control of 20 of the country's 36 municipalities, while the RPG, the PRP and the UNR, which had presented a co-ordinated campaign, took 10. The opposition again protested of electoral fraud. In July the three 'radical' opposition parties joined with nine other organizations in a Coordination de l'opposition démocratique (Codem), which indicated its willingness to enter into a dialogue with the authorities. At a meeting with a representative of Codem, the Minister of the Interior, Alsény René Gomez, rejected the incidences of alleged fraud presented by Codem as inconsequential. Representatives of all the elected parties, none the less, attended the official inauguration of the Assemblée nationale, on 30 August. Boubacar Biro Diallo, of the PUP, was elected as the new parliament's Speaker.

In February 1996 Conté was reportedly seized as he attempted to flee the presidential palace during a mutiny by disaffected elements of the military, and was held by rebels for some 15 hours until he made concessions including a doubling of salaries and immunity from prosecution for those involved in the uprising. The Minister of Defence, Col Abdourahmane Diallo, was dismissed, and Conté assumed personal responsibility for defence. It was estimated that about 50 people were killed and at least 100 injured as rebels clashed with forces loyal to Conté. As many as 2,000 soldiers, including members of the Presidential Guard, were believed to have joined the rebellion. Despite Conté's undertaking that there would be no punitive action, several officers were arrested shortly afterwards, and Conté and Gomez stated that any legal proceedings would be a matter for the judiciary.

In late February 1996 Codem withdrew from a parliamentary commission investigating the circumstances surrounding the coup attempt, in protest at Conté's allusions to opposition links with anti-Government elements within the military. The initial recommendations of the commission included a complete separation of the political and military elements in national life; the need to restore discipline within the armed forces was also stated. In March it was announced that eight members of the military, including four senior officers, had been charged with undermining state security in connection with the coup attempt. A reinforcement of security measures followed the assassination of the commander of the military camp where the February rebellion had begun. Calm was quickly restored, and Conté left his barracks for the first time since early February to meet President Alpha Oumar Konaré of Mali, who arrived in Conakry to discuss terms for the release into Guinean custody of one of the alleged perpetrators of the coup attempt, who had taken refuge in the Malian embassy. (In the following month, however, Mali recalled its ambassador from Conakry, protesting that Guinean forces had stormed the embassy to arrest the officer.)

The armed forces Chief of Staff and the military Governor of Conakry, both of whom had been regarded as close associates of Conté, were replaced in April 1996, apparently in accordance with the President's expressed commitment to a restructuring of both the civilian and military administration. In July Conté announced (for the first time under the Third Republic) the appointment of a Prime Minister. The premiership was assigned to a non-partisan economist, Sydia Touré. A comprehensive reorganization of the Government included the departure of Gomez and the division of the Ministry of the Interior into two separate departments (one responsible for territorial administration and decentralization, the other for security), as well as the appointment of a new Minister of Justice. During August 1996 40 of those detained in connection with the February mutiny were released from custody; charges remained against three suspects, including Cmmdr Joseph Gbago Zoumanigui, allegedly a main conspirator, who was believed to have fled the country. Touré announced that his Government's priorities were to be economic recovery and the combating of institutionalized corruption. A new financing programme was agreed with the IMF in January 1997. In the following month Touré relinquished control of the economy portfolio to his two ministers-delegate, who now became Minister of Planning and Co-operation and Minister of the Economy and Finance.

In June 1997 it was announced that a State Security Court was to be established to deal with matters of exceptional jurisdiction, and that its first task would be to try the alleged leaders of the 1996 mutiny. The establishment of the court provoked strong criticism both by the opposition parties and the Guinean lawyers' association, which expressed particular concern that there was no constitutional provision for such a court, that its members were to be personally appointed by Conté, and that the mutiny trial was to be held in camera. The political opposition again warned that Conté should beware of reneging on his earlier pledge that there would be no reprisals for those involved in the rebellion.

The Ministers of Security and of Planning and Co-operation left the Government in October 1997, as part of a reorganization of portfolios in which a new Minister of the Interior and Decentralization, Zaïnoul Abidine Sanoussi, was appointed. Dorank Assifat Diasseny, hitherto Minister of Territorial Administration and Decentralization, was transferred to the higher education and scientific research portfolio, but shortly afterwards was appointed Minister of National Defence (thereby becoming the first civilian to hold this post since the 1984 *coup d'état*).

In a report published in October 1997 the Association guinéenne des droits de l'homme accused the Guinean security forces of the systematic ill-treatment of detainees. The association expressed particular concern at the continued detention of civilians related to the suspects in the 1996 mutiny, and at the detention without trial, in solitary confinement, of Liberian and Sierra Leonean nationals. In November 1997 it was revealed that 53 soldiers, in custody since the mutiny, had in a joint letter to the Assemblée nationale alleged that they had been tortured following their arrest.

A total of 96 defendants were brought before the State Security Court in February 1998, to answer charges related to the attempted coup of 1996; hearings were immediately adjourned, after defence lawyers complained that they had had no access to their clients for the past four months. Hearings resumed in March, but were further adjourned, following reports that defence lawyers were refusing to represent their clients, whose rights were, they alleged, being infringed by the State Security Court. The Court reconvened in September; 38 of the accused received custodial sentences ranging from seven months to 15 years, some with hard labour (Zoumanigui was sentenced *in absentia*), while 51 defendants were acquitted.

In March 1998 Bâ and two other UNR deputies were arrested, following the deaths of nine people as a result of violence in a suburb of Conakry. The authorities alleged that Islamist extremists were implicated in the unrest, although other observers stated that ethnic rivalries had exacerbated confrontations between members of the security forces and residents whose homes were threatened with demolition. The brief detention, in early April, of two RPG deputies who had attended a political rally in eastern Guinea further exacerbated tensions, and Codem deputies boycotted the opening ceremony of the new session of the Assemblée nationale. Bâ was released in June, and in September his two UNR colleagues resumed their seats in the legislature, having been released from custody. In October the Speaker of the Assemblée nationale was suspended from the PUP, after he denounced what he termed 'atrocious and inhuman torture' of detainees; Diallo subsequently issued a further statement regretting the PUP's 'insolent contempt for the law'.

Meanwhile, Codem denounced proposals for the establishment of an Haut conseil aux affaires électorales (HCE), which was to act in conjunction with the Ministry of the Interior and Decentralization in preparing and supervising the forthcoming presidential election. The 68-member HCE was to comprise representatives of the presidential majority, as well as opposition delegates, ministerial representatives and members of civic society. The opposition again alleged that the PUP

was abusing the state apparatus in support of Conté, and that a ban on public demonstrations would disadvantage other candidates. Conté was challenged by four candidates, including Mamadou Boye Bâ, representing the Union pour le progrès et le renouveau (formed in September 1998 by a merger of the UNR and the PRP), and Alpha Condé (who had been out of the country since April 1997, owing to fears for his safety), for the RPG. Despite violent incidents during the election campaign, voting proceeded as scheduled on 14 December 1998. However, the arrest of Condé two days after the poll, near the border with Côte d'Ivoire, on the grounds that he was seeking to leave the country illegally and was plotting against the state, provoked further violence. By the end of the month at least 12 people were reported to have been killed as a result of violence in Conakry, Kankan, Siguiri and Baro. In late December Condé was formally charged with having recruited mercenaries with the aim of overthrowing the Conté regime. Meanwhile, opposition representatives denounced the conduct of the election as fraudulent, and withdrew from the HCE. The official results, as issued by the HCE on 17 December, and confirmed by the Supreme Court two weeks later, confirmed a decisive victory for Conté, with 56.1% of the valid votes cast. Bâ took 24.6% and Condé 16.6%. The rate of participation by registered voters was 71.4%.

At his inauguration, on 30 January 1999, Conté emphasized that his administration would ensure the defence of individual freedoms and security, and gave an undertaking that all abuses, including those committed by the security forces, would be severely punished. In March Lamine Sidimé, hitherto Chief Justice of the Supreme Court, was appointed Prime Minister of a new Government. (The position of Chief Justice remained vacant in early 2001.) Ibrahima Kassory Fofana was reappointed Minister of the Economy and Finance, although it had been widely rumoured that he would himself be awarded the premiership. An apparent purge of the military high command, in mid-March, included the removal from office of former Chief of Staff Col Oumar Sanko; 18 officers were dismissed, accused of high treason, and 13 retired early, on the grounds of what were termed 'serious faults' arising from the 1996 mutiny.

Impending local government elections were postponed in early June 1999. In mid-June Codem denounced government proposals to extend the mandate of the President of the Republic from five years to seven, although assurances were given that, if adopted, the measure would take effect from the presidential election due in 2003, and would not be applied retroactively.

Opposition groups and human rights organizations campaigned throughout 1999 and 2000 for the release of Alpha Condé and other activists arrested at the time of the 1998 presidential election. Condé's defence counsel withdrew from the case in February 1999, citing serious violations of the rule of law and exercise of legal practice on the part of the authorities. Lawyers complained in particular of being denied free access to their client, who was being held in solitary confinement, and that a French defence lawyer had been denied entry to Guinea. However, the lawyers resumed their defence in April. In July it was announced that Condé's trial would begin in September; however, a decree published in August stating that the RPG leader would be tried by the State Security Court provoked further controversy. Moreover, it was reported that Condé would not be allowed foreign lawyers. In the event, Condé's trial was further delayed, and his lawyers protested that neither the defence nor the prosecution had received any documentation relating to the trial. Trials of other opposition activists were pursued in the mean time. In March 1999 13 RPG officials were sentenced to four months' imprisonment, convicted of disturbing public order, but were released at the President's behest; 15 others were sentenced *in absentia* to five years' detention.

Rumours of disaffection in some quarters of the military circulated in mid-1999: in August it was reported that dissident Guinean soldiers in Sierra Leone were planning an offensive against the Conté regime, with the support of Sierra Leonean rebel elements. In December the Government banned a march planned by Codem in order to protest against the continued detention of Condé. In that month a senior journalist at *L'Indépendant Plus* was briefly detained by the police, following the newspaper's publication of allegations relating to official corruption.

In January 2000 a major government reshuffle was announced, in which several senior ministers were dismissed. In February members of the Assemblée nationale, including PUP deputies, urged the President to release Condé, noting that

Condé possessed parliamentary immunity from prosecution. In mid-April the trial of Condé and his 47 co-defendants began, on charges that included plotting to kill President Conté, hiring mercenaries and threatening state security. However, following the rejection of their appeal that the trial be abandoned, the defence lawyers withdrew from the case, and a further postponement ensued. The defendants subsequently alleged that they had been tortured while in detention. The case reopened in early May, but was again postponed, as the defendants rejected the defence lawyers appointed by the court. At the reopening of the trial in late May Condé refused to speak; the case was adjourned until August to allow the defence to prepare their case.

Conté carried out a further ministerial reshuffle in June 2000. The Ministry of Security was abolished and the portfolio was incorporated into the Ministry of Territorial Administration and Decentralization. Eight parties presented candidates in the delayed local elections, which were held on 25 June. Legislative elections, which had been scheduled for the same date, were postponed. With the exception of isolated clashes between PUP and opposition supporters in Conakry, voting was reported to have occurred in a peaceful atmosphere. However, before the announcement of the results, a series of clashes between the security forces and UPR members resulted in at least five deaths and many more injuries. According to the final results, the PUP and its allies gained control of 33 of the 38 constituencies.

In September 2000 Condé was sentenced to five years' imprisonment, despite prosecution demands for a life sentence, while seven other defendants were given custodial sentences of between 18 months and three years; 40 other defendants were acquitted. Two days prior to the conclusion of the trial, President Conté had accused Condé of having instigated fighting on Guinea's borders with Sierra Leone and Liberia.

In early September 2000 an armed rebellion in the forest region of south-east Guinea reportedly resulted in at least 40 deaths. Instability subsequently intensified in regions near the borders with Sierra Leone and Liberia, with incidences of cross-border attacks on Guinean civilians and the military becoming increasingly common. An attack on Macenta, near the Liberian border, in mid-September led to 35 deaths, according to official figures; an official of the UN High Commissioner for Refugees (UNHCR) was killed and another representative of the organization was reportedly taken hostage. Fighting between armed groups and Guinean soldiers was reported to have led to some 360 deaths between early September and mid-October.

The Government attributed the upsurge in violence to forces supported by the Governments of Liberia and Burkina Faso, and to members of the Sierra Leonean rebel group, the Revolutionary United Front (RUF, see Sierra Leone chapter, vol. II), in alliance with Guinean dissidents. In October 2000 a previously unknown organization, the Rassemblement des forces démocratiques de Guinée (RFDG), claimed responsibility for the armed attacks, which, it stated, were an attempt to overthrow President Conté. The reputed spokesman for the rebel group, Mohamed Lamine Fofona, refused to name the leader of the RFDG, but refuted suggestions that it was led by the son of former President Sekou Touré and denied claims that it was linked with overseas groups. The Guinean authorities rejected the existence of the RFDG. Following an attack on the town of Forécariah, the local Governor expelled some 32,000 refugees from the region, many of whom were subject to further attacks, particularly following a speech made by Conté, in which he accused refugees from Sierra Leone and Liberia of forming alliances with rebel groups seeking to destabilize Guinea.

Meanwhile, the Assemblée nationale failed to reconvene, as planned, on 25 September 2000. The Government announced that the delayed legislative elections would be held on 26 November, and that the new parliamentary session would open in January 2001. However, Codem declared that it would not participate in elections until national security had been re-established.

In mid-November 2000 an attack on two villages in Kindia prefecture was attributed to forces associated with the RUF. Later that month a series of cross-border attacks in Guéckédou prefecture were reportedly conducted by former members of a faction of a now-dissolved Liberian dissident group, the United Liberation Movement of Liberia for Democracy (ULIMO), ULIMO-K (see chapter on Liberia, vol. II), which President Conté had previously supported.

In November 2000 Conté appointed Mamadou Cellou Diallo, hitherto Minister of Planning and Co-operation, to a newly-created ministerial position, entitled Adviser to the Presidency of the Republic, in charge of Relations with the Republican Institutions. Also in that month Conté issued a decree postponing the legislative elections indefinitely. In December, almost exactly two years after the arrest of Alpha Condé, the human rights organization, Amnesty International, issued a report in which they called for the immediate and unconditional release of Condé and 47 other detainees in Guinea. The report also questioned the independence of the State Security Court.

In early December 2000 an attack on Guéckédou, near to the 'Parrot's Beak' area of Guinea, which borders on both Sierra Leone and Liberia, led to at least 86 deaths, according to the Government, and the almost complete destruction of the city. It was announced that the Guinean armed forces had killed 150 rebels while repelling a subsequent attack on nearby Kissidougou. The Government estimated that some 94,000 people had been displaced as a result of fighting in the region. By the end of the month increased instability in south-east Guinea had forced aid agencies to withdraw indefinitely. Jean-Marie Doré, the leader of the UPG, accused the Guinean army of using indiscriminate violence in attacks on civilians and claimed that Conté was attempting to destroy the country.

In early January 2001 Conté dismissed Diassény as Minister at the Presidency, in charge of National Defence; he was, however, retained as a cabinet member, receiving the title of Minister, Special Adviser at the Presidency. The defence portfolio thus came under Conté's direct control. In mid-January a number of opposition parties met with the PUP and its allies in a national political dialogue initiated by Conté, although Codem declared that the release of Condé was a precondition to further discussions.

Rebel attacks around Guéckédou continued throughout January 2001. Meanwhile, reports that Guinean planes had launched minor air offensives on rebel-held border areas of Sierra Leone emerged. In late January reports that Fofana had been arrested remained unsubstantiated. In late January and early February more than 130 deaths were reported in a series of attacks around Macenta. Allegations persisted that an unofficial alliance between former ULIMO-K rebels and Guinean government forces had broken down, with the result that ULIMO-K forces were now attacking Guinean military and civilian targets. A rebel attack on Nongoa, a garrison town close to the 'Parrot's Beak' region, in early March, forced an estimated 10,000 people to disperse northwards.

Meanwhile, in February 2001 the death penalty, which had been suspended in 1984, was officially restored, and four of five defendants sentenced to death in 1995 were executed by firing squad (the fifth had died in detention). In early March a series of explosions at an army munitions dump in Conakry killed at least 42 people and injured 60 others, according to reports. The Government blamed the explosions on a handling error and announced that it would recompense the medical expenses of the injured. Condé was released from prison in May.

Relations with both the Government of France and with private French interests strengthened considerably in the 1990s: official assistance from, and trade with, France is of great importance to the Guinean economy, as is French participation in the mining sector and in newly-privatized organizations. However, the progress of the trial of the RPG leader, Alpha Condé, remained a source of concern to the French authorities, and during his visit to Guinea in July 1999, President Jacques Chirac sought assurances from the Government that the trial would be 'transparent'. A meeting of the joint commission for Franco-Guinean co-operation took place in Conakry in November 1999. However, in mid-2000 a meeting of francophone parliamentarians called on Guinea's donor countries to suspend assistance in protest at the conduct of the Condé trial. As a member of the Organization of the Islamic Conference (see p. 266) Guinea has also forged links with other Islamic states, notably signing several co-operation agreements with Iran in the 1990s.

In August 1990 Guinean armed forces were deployed along the border with Liberia, following a series of violent incursions by deserters from the Liberian army. Guinean army units also participated in the ECOMOG cease-fire monitoring group, deployed in Liberia in that month (see the Economic Community of West African States—ECOWAS, p. 170). In April 1991 it was announced that a Guinean contingent was to be dispatched to Sierra Leone to assist that country in repelling violations of its territory by Charles Taylor's National Patriotic Front of Liberia (NPFL). In October 1992 the Guinean Government admitted that Liberian forces were being trained in Guinea; it was stated that those receiving instruction were to constitute the first Liberian government forces following an eventual restoration of peace in that country. Efforts were undertaken from early 1994 to reinforce security along Guinea's borders, following incursions by fighters of both the NPFL and the anti-Taylor ULIMO.

Following the *coup d'état* in Sierra Leone in April 1992, ex-President Momoh was granted asylum in Guinea, despite Conté's expressed wish to establish 'normal' relations with the new regime of Capt. Valentine Strasser. Strasser also took refuge in Guinea after he was deposed in January 1996. Close co-operation was developed with the new regime of President Ahmed Tejan Kabbah from March 1996. Kabbah made several visits to Guinea and, in turn, fled to Guinea in May 1997, establishing a government-in-exile, following the seizure of power in Sierra Leone by forces led by Maj. Johnny Paul Koroma. Military reinforcements were deployed to protect Guinea's border, and 1,500 Guinean troops were dispatched in support of the Nigerian-led ECOMOG force in Sierra Leone. Guinea joined other members of the international community in condemning the subversion of constitutional order in Sierra Leone, and became a member of the 'Committee of Four' (with Côte d'Ivoire, Ghana and Nigeria) charged with ensuring the implementation of decisions and recommendations pertaining to the situation in Sierra Leone.

The Liberian Government delivered a formal note of protest to Guinea in April 1999, in response to what it termed an invasion from Guinea of the border town of Voinjama, in Lofa County, by a rebel group, which had briefly held hostage aid workers and foreign diplomats before being repelled by the Liberian armed forces. The Guinean Government denied the accusations, reiterating that Guinea was committed to the pursuit of peace. In August, however, the Liberian Government declared a state of emergency, again claiming that an invasion force had entered Liberia from Guinea. The border between the two countries was closed with immediate effect. Guinea again denied involvement, and urged international observers to visit the border area to verify that incursions were not originating from Guinea. In late August ECOWAS ministers responsible for foreign affairs agreed to establish a commission in an effort to resolve the issue of border insecurity in this region. In the following month Guinea protested to the Organization of African Unity, the UN and ECOWAS, after 28 people were allegedly killed in attacks by Liberian troops on villages in the Macenta region. None the less, at an extraordinary summit meeting of eight ECOWAS leaders in mid-September Presidents Conté and Taylor made pledges of good neighbourliness and non-aggression. The summit condemned the attacks, without apportioning blame. The functions of the Mano River Union (MRU—see p. 309) were to be reactivated, with its members—Guinea, Liberia and Sierra Leone—directed to exchange information on suspected perpetrators of subversive activities, and to establish a joint committee on border security. The summit also urged the international community to assist in addressing the humanitarian crisis resulting from the attacks.

Liberia reopened the border with Guinea in February 2000, and in April the ministers responsible for security of the three member states of the MRU agreed to allow reciprocal inspections of border areas. Military officials from the three countries met in May, in order to consider strategies for peace in the region. None the less, in July the Liberian Government reported renewed fighting in the Lofa region, following an attack by rebel groups allegedly based in Guinea. The Liberian Government, which dispatched reinforcements to the area, threatened to attack the bases of the rebel groups in Guinea, and accused the Guinean authorities of complicity with the rebels. Guinea again denied any involvement in the attacks and accused the Liberian Government of deliberate misinformation. In August President Taylor expressed his Government's continued commitment to work towards a peaceful settlement within the framework of the MRU, while reaffirming his determination to defend Liberian territory from attack.

Relations between Guinea and Liberia deteriorated as tensions in the border region intensified from September 2000. In that month Guinean soldiers were reported to have entered the residence of the Liberian ambassador in Conakry, removing the Liberian flag, while the Liberian consul-general was declared *persona non grata* for acts that the Guinean Government described as being incompatible with his status. Additionally, Liberia accused the authorities in Conakry of obstructing attempts to evacuate Liberian nationals from the unstable border regions of Guinea. In early October tripartite discussions were held between Guinea, Liberia and Sierra Leone. Later that month, however, Taylor repeated charges that Guinea was aiding alleged dissidents in the north of Liberia, and announced an increased military deployment along the joint border, while Guinean authorities issued similar accusations against the Liberian Government.

In November 2000 ECOWAS dispatched a technical committee to investigate armed incursions between the MRU nations. In the following month ECOWAS announced that a peace-keeping force, comprising 1,676 troops from Mali, Niger, Nigeria and Senegal, would be deployed along Guinea's borders with Liberia and Sierra Leone in February 2001, with an initial mandate of six months. However, the force had still not been established by late April.

In January 2001 Liberia accused the Guinean Government of having supported the recent shelling of towns in its Foya district and recalled its ambassador from Conakry. Also in January Liberia announced that it would deploy an infantry battalion at the border with Guinea, in response to Guinea's announcement that it would strengthen its military presence in border regions. In late January the Liberian Government protested to ECOWAS and to the UN following an attack on its embassy in Conakry. In February Taylor reiterated allegations, initially made in the previous month, that Guinea permitted dissidents to launch cross-border attacks on Foya and Kolahun in northern Liberia. The Liberian Government accused Guinea of launching further air and artillery attacks on Voinjama in late February, while a US-based group, Human Rights Watch, claimed that Guinean shellfire had killed at least 41 civilians in Sierra Leone since September 2000. In March 2001 Liberia demanded the closure of the Guinean and Sierra Leonean embassies in Monrovia.

The protracted conflicts in Liberia and Sierra Leone have resulted in the presence in Guinea of large numbers of refugees—variously estimated to number 5%–15% of the total population. UNHCR assessed the total number of refugees in Guinea at 501,500 at the end of 1999, compared with 482,500 at the beginning of that year. Following the installation of elected organs of government in Liberia, under the presidency of Charles Taylor, in 1997, UNHCR facilitated a programme for the voluntary repatriation of refugees. By mid-1999 some 80,000 refugees had left Guinea for Liberia. However, repatriations were effectively halted from August, as a result of the closure of the Guinea–Liberia border (see above). Meanwhile, continuing insecurity in Sierra Leone during 1999 was unlikely to expedite the return of some 366,000 refugees from Guinean territory. UNHCR and the International Committee of the Red Cross were forced to restrict their operations in southern Guinea from September 2000. Refugee camps increasingly came under attack from rebel groups, Guinean armed forces and civilians, who seemed to regard the refugee population as a source of instability; in October some 4,000 refugees were reported to have fled from a camp at Farmoriah. In January 2001 armed men, believed to be members of ULIMO—K, reportedly infiltrated refugee camps sheltering Sierra Leoneans in south-eastern Guinea.

Regional instability has created considerable uncertainty regarding the actual number and whereabouts of refugees in Guinea. As clashes intensified, in October 2000 UNHCR began an operation to transfer some 210,000 refugees, and 70,000 displaced Guineans, to more stable regions in the north. However, renewed violence forced relief agencies to suspend almost entirely their aid programmes within Guinea between November 2000 and late February 2001. In February 2001 the United Nations High Commissioner for Refugees, Ruud Lubbers, announced that the Guinean authorities had agreed, when circumstances permitted, to open a 'humanitarian corridor' to allow refugees to leave the conflict zones around Kissidougou for safer regions to the north, although President Kabbah of Sierra Leone suggested the establishment of a route to the south, which would allow refugees to return directly to Sierra Leone. Meanwhile, it was estimated that some 400,000 refugees were beyond reach of aid, with tens of thousands more caught between rival warring factions.

Renewed conflict in mid-March 2001 again caused a suspension of aid supplies to the most troubled regions. In late March a UNHCR mission discovered that large areas of the 'Parrot's Beak' region were deserted, at least six refugee camps around Nongoa had been destroyed, and some 187 metric tons of food aid from the UN World Food Programme had been looted. Meanwhile, the Guinean army was reportedly refusing humanitarian groups permission to enter 'Parrot's Beak' and preventing refugees from leaving. UNHCR estimated that some 59,000 refugees had returned from Guinea to Sierra Leone between September 2000 and late March 2001, including 40,000 by boat and 13,000 by foot, while several thousand were believed to have travelled through RUF-held areas of Sierra Leone. However, more than 135,000 refugees remained isolated in camps in the 'Parrot's Beak' region, including some 30,000–40,000 in Kolomba, at the southernmost point of the region.

Government

Under the terms of the Constitution promulgated on 23 December 1991, and amended by an 'organic law' of 3 April 1992, the President of the Republic, who is Head of State, is elected for five years by universal adult suffrage, in the context of a multi-party political system. The 114-member Assemblée nationale, which holds legislative power, is elected by universal suffrage with a five-year mandate. The mandate of the first elected Assemblée nationale expired in June 2000; legislative elections scheduled for that month were postponed until November and subsequently indefinitely. The President of the Republic is also Head of Government, and in this capacity appoints the other members of the Council of Ministers.

Local administration is based on eight administrative entities—the city of Conakry and seven administrative regions—each under the authority of an appointed Governor; the country is sub-divided into 34 regions (prefectures), including Conakry, which is divided into five communes. In January 2001, a number of prefectures in the south and south-east of Guinea, which were subject to repeated dissident attacks, were amalgamated under a military administration.

Defence

In August 2000 Guinea's active armed forces totalled 9,700, comprising an army of 8,500, a navy of 400 and an air force of 800. Paramilitary forces comprised a Republican Guard of 1,600 and a 1,000-strong gendarmerie, as well as a reserve 'people's militia' of 7,000. Military service is compulsory (conscripts were estimated at some 7,500 in 2000) and lasts for two years. The defence budget for 2000 was estimated at 90,000m. FG.

Economic Affairs

In 1998, according to estimates by the World Bank, Guinea's gross national product (GNP), measured at average 1996–98 prices, was US $3,777m., equivalent to $530 per head (or $1,722 on an international purchasing-power parity basis). During 1990–98, it was estimated, GNP per head increased, in real terms, at an average annual rate of 2.1%. Over the same period the population increased by an annual average of 3.0%. GNP was estimated at $3,700m. in 1999, equivalent to $510 per head. Guinea's gross domestic product (GDP) increased, in real terms, at an average annual rate of 4.2% in 1990–99; according to the IMF, GDP increased by 4.5% in 1998 and by 3.3% in 1999.

Agriculture (including hunting, forestry and fishing) contributed an estimated 23% of GDP in 1999. About 84.2% of the labour force were employed in the agricultural sector in that year. The principal cash crops are fruits, oil palm, groundnuts and coffee. Important staple crops include cassava, rice and other cereals and vegetables. The attainment of self-sufficiency in rice and other basic foodstuffs remains a priority. The food supply is supplemented by the rearing of cattle and other livestock. The Government has made efforts towards the commercial exploitation of Guinea's forest resources (forests cover about two-thirds of the country's land area) and substantial fishing stocks. During 1990–99 agricultural GDP increased by an estimated annual average of 4.5%; growth of 5.2% was recorded in 1998.

Industry (including mining, manufacturing, construction and power) contributed an estimated 36% of GDP in 1999. Less than 2% of the employed labour force were engaged in the industrial sector at the time of the 1983 census. Industrial GDP increased by an estimated annual average of 4.5% in 1990–99; growth of 4.9% was recorded in 1998.

Measured at constant 1994 prices, mining contributed 16.3% of GDP in 1998. Only 0.7% of the employed labour force were engaged in the sector in 1983. Guinea is the world's foremost exporter of bauxite and the second largest producer of bauxite ore, possessing between one-quarter and one-third of known reserves of the mineral. In 1998, according to estimates published by the IMF, exports of bauxite and alumina provided

59.9% of export earnings. Gold and diamonds are also mined: recorded exports of these contributed, respectively, an estimated 17.7% and 7.2% of total export revenue in 1998. The eventual exploitation of valuable reserves of high-grade iron ore at Mt Nimba, near the border with Liberia, is envisaged, although political instability in the region from 1999 seemed likely to delay such development. Of Guinea's other known mineral deposits, only granite is exploitable on a commercial scale. The GDP of the mining sector increased by 3.6% in 1998.

The manufacturing sector remains largely undeveloped, contributing only an estimated 4% of GDP in 1999. In 1983 only 0.6% of the employed labour force were engaged in the manufacturing sector. Other than the country's one alumina smelter, most industrial companies are involved in import-substitution, including the processing of agricultural products and the manufacture of construction materials. Manufacturing GDP increased by an annual average of 3.6% in 1990–98; growth of 5.2% was recorded in 1998.

Electricity generation is, at present, insufficient to meet demand, and power failures outside the mining and industrial sectors (in which the largest operators generate their own power supplies) have been frequent. However, Guinea possesses considerable hydroelectric potential. The 75-MW Garafiri dam project was inaugurated in 1999, and a further major scheme, at Kaléta, is scheduled for completion in 2002. In the mean time, some 600,000 metric tons of hydrocarbons are imported annually, and in 1996 imports of petroleum products accounted for 5.5% of the value of total imports.

The services sector contributed an estimated 41% of GDP in 1999. During 1990–99 the average rate of growth in the sector's GDP was estimated at 3.2% per year; growth of 4.3% was recorded in 1998.

In 1999 Guinea recorded a visible trade surplus of US $94.5m., while there was a deficit of $151.6m. on the current account of the balance of payments. Of the countries which reported trade with Guinea to the IMF, the principal suppliers of imports in 1998 were France (which supplied 24.8% of the total) and the USA (9.8%); other major suppliers were the Belgo-Luxembourg Economic Union, Côte d'Ivoire and the People's Republic of China. The principal markets for exports in the same year were the USA (which took an estimated 16.4% of exports) and the Belgo-Luxembourg Economic Union (13.7%); other major purchasers included Spain, Ireland, France and Ukraine. Ukraine is notable as a market for Guinean bauxite. The principal exports in 1998 were bauxite, gold, alumina and diamonds. The principal imports included machinery and mechanical appliances, mineral products and prepared foodstuffs.

In 1998 Guinea's overall budget deficit was estimated at 192,650m. FG, equivalent to 4.1% of GDP in that year. A budget deficit of 116,310m. FG was forecast for 1999. The country's total external debt was US $3,546m. at the end of 1998, of which $3,126m. was long-term public debt. In that year the cost of debt-servicing was equivalent to 19.5% of the value of exports of goods and services. Annual inflation averaged 5.3% in 1991–98; consumer prices increased by an annual average of 5.1% in 1998.

Guinea is a member of the Economic Community of West African States (ECOWAS, see p. 170), of the Gambia River Basin Development Organization (OMVG, see p. 308), of the International Coffee Organization (see p. 304), of the West Africa Rice Development Association (WARDA, see p. 306) and of the Mano River Union (see p. 309).

Guinea's potential for the attainment of wealth is substantial, owing to its valuable mineral deposits, water resources and generally favourable climate; however, the economy remains over-dependent on revenue from bauxite reserves and on external assistance, the country's infrastructure is vastly inadequate and its manufacturing base narrow. Since 1985 economic liberalization measures have been undertaken, as advocated by the IMF and the World Bank, and by the late 1990s, despite frequent difficulties in implementing reforms, growth in overall GDP was considerable; success had been achieved in reducing the rate of inflation, foreign-exchange reserves had increased, as had private investment in the economy. The depression in world mineral prices during 1999 resulted in a sharp decline in revenue from sales of bauxite and alumina, and also hampered efforts to sell a majority stake in the Friguia alumina plant to private interests. Meanwhile, the IMF expressed concern at weaknesses particularly in fiscal revenue collection, and annual funding under the Enhanced Structural Adjustment Facility (ESAF) originally agreed in early 1997 was delayed until the end of 1999, when support under the Poverty Reduction and

Growth Facility (the successor to the ESAF) was granted. Budget revenue was again lower than envisaged in 2000, partly owing to a decline in traditional exports. None the less, GDP growth of 4.5% was projected for that year. Ongoing insecurity in neighbouring Liberia and Sierra Leone, which initially led to the presence in Guinea of large numbers of refugees, and which has subsequently seriously undermined the political and social stability of Guinea, has, furthermore, adversely affected the country's economy, with agriculture output reportedly being particularly reduced in consequence. The large-scale transfer of capital to Mali from Guinea was reported in December 2000, in response not only to the political situation, but also as a result of increased crime. In October 2000 the Government stated that unrest in the border regions with Sierra Leone and Liberia had cost Guinea some US $15m.–$18m. annually since 1989. In addition to humanitarian aid granted to relieve the consequences of continued violence in border regions from late 2000, Guinea was to receive development aid from Germany and the Banque arabe pour le développement économique en Afrique. In December 2000 the IMF and the World Bank announced that Guinea would also be a recipient of some $880m. in debt relief as part of the Heavily Indebted Poor Countries (HIPC) initiative. Guinea was also among 19 countries to be granted debt relief by France. The preservation of political stability, and thus the maintenance of investor confidence (as well as donor support), was to remain essential to the pursuit of economic reform.

Social Welfare

Wages are fixed according to the Government Labour Code. A maximum working week of 48 hours is in force for industrial workers. In 1995, according to estimates by the World Health Organization, there were 13.0 physicians and 55.7 nurses per 100,000 population. The extension of basic health care to low-income groups forms a significant element of the Government's structural adjustment efforts. Private medical care has been legally available since 1984. Budget estimates for 1998 allocated 16,400m. FG to health (representing 2.5% of total budgetary expenditure).

Education

Education is provided free of charge at every level in state institutions. Primary education, which begins at seven years of age and lasts for six years, is officially compulsory. In 1997, however, enrolment at primary schools was equivalent to only 54% of children in the relevant age-group (boys 68%; girls 41%). As part of government plans to extend the provision of basic education, it was aimed to increase the rate of primary enrolment to 53% by 2000. Secondary education, from the age of 13, lasts for seven years, comprising a first cycle (collège) of four years and a second (lycée) of three years. Enrolment at secondary schools in 1997 was equivalent to only 14% of children in the appropriate age-group (boys 20%; girls 7%). There are universities at Conakry and Kankan, and other tertiary institutions at Maneah, Boké and Faranah. In 1993, according to the national literacy service, the average rate of adult illiteracy was 72% (males 61%; females 83%). UNESCO estimated average adult illiteracy at 64.1% in 1995 (males 50.0%; females 78.0%). Private schools, which had been banned for 23 years under the Sekou Touré regime, were legalized in 1984. Budget estimates for 1998 allocated 75,600m. FG to education (equivalent to 11.5% of total budgetary expenditure).

Public Holidays

2001: 1 January (New Year's Day), 16 April (Easter Monday), 1 May (Labour Day), 4 June* (Mouloud, birth of Muhammad), 27 August (Anniversary of Women's Revolt), 28 September (Referendum Day), 2 October (Republic Day), 1 November (All Saints' Day), 22 November (Day of 1970 Invasion), 17 December* (Id al-Fitr, end of Ramadan), 25 December (Christmas).

2002: 1 January (New Year's Day), 1 April (Easter Monday), 1 May (Labour Day), 24 May* (Mouloud, birth of Muhammad), 27 August (Anniversary of Women's Revolt), 28 September (Referendum Day), 2 October (Republic Day), 1 November (All Saints' Day), 22 November (Day of 1970 Invasion), 6 December* (Id al-Fitr, end of Ramadan), 25 December (Christmas).

* These holidays are determined by the Islamic lunar calendar and may vary by one or two days from the dates given.

Weights and Measures

The metric system is in force.

Statistical Survey

Source (unless otherwise stated): Service de la Statistique Générale, Conakry; tel. 44-21-48.

Area and Population

AREA, POPULATION AND DENSITY

Area (sq km)	245,857*
Population (census results)	
4–17 February 1983	4,533,240†
31 December 1996‡	
Males	3,496,150
Females	3,668,673
Total	7,164,823
Density (per sq km) at census of 1996	29.1

* 94,926 sq miles.
† Excluding adjustment for underenumeration.
‡ Provisional figure, including refugees from Liberia and Sierra Leone (estimated at 640,000).

PRINCIPAL TOWNS (population at 1996 census)

Conakry (capital)	1,091,483	Kankan . . .	261,341
Kindia. . .	287,607	Labé . . .	249,515
N'Zérékoré. . .	282,772		

BIRTHS AND DEATHS (UN estimates, annual averages)

	1980–85	1985–90	1990–95
Birth rate (per 1,000). . .	51.3	47.3	44.1
Death rate (per 1,000) . .	23.8	22.0	19.4

Expectation of life (UN estimates, years at birth, 1990–95): 44.5 (males 44.0; females 45.0).

Source: UN, *World Population Prospects: The 1998 Revision.*

ECONOMICALLY ACTIVE POPULATION
(persons aged 10 years and over, census of 1983, provisional)

	Males	Females	Total
Agriculture, hunting, forestry and fishing	856,971	566,644	1,423,615
Mining and quarrying . . .	7,351	4,890	12,241
Manufacturing	6,758	4,493	11,251
Electricity, gas and water .	1,601	1,604	3,205
Construction.	5,475	3,640	9,115
Trade, restaurants and hotels. .	22,408	14,901	37,309
Transport, storage and communications . . .	17,714	11,782	29,496
Finance, insurance, real estate and business services . . .	2,136	1,420	3,556
Community, social and personal services	82,640	54,960	137,600
Activities not adequately defined* .	101,450	54,229	155,679
Total labour force	1,104,504	718,563	1,823,067

* Includes 18,244 unemployed persons (not previously employed), whose distribution by sex is not available.

Source: ILO, *Yearbook of Labour Statistics.*

Mid-1999 (estimates in '000): Agriculture, etc. 3,094; Total labour force 3,674 (Source: FAO).

Agriculture

PRINCIPAL CROPS ('000 metric tons)

	1997	1998	1999
Maize	85	89	89*
Millet*	10	10	10
Sorghum	5†	5*	5*
Rice (paddy)	716	764	750
Other cereals* . . .	111	118	118
Sweet potatoes . . .	135*	135	135*
Cassava (Manioc) . .	732	812	812*
Yams	95*	89	89*
Taro (Coco yam) . .	27	29	29*
Pulses*	60	60	60
Coconuts*	18	18	18
Cotton (lint)	10	16	16*
Vegetables	476*	476	476*
Sugar cane* . . .	220	220	220
Citrus fruits* . . .	215	215	215
Bananas	150*	150	150*
Plantains	430*	429	429*
Mangoes	75*	85	85*
Pineapples	67*	72	72*
Other fruits* . . .	46	46	46
Palm kernels* . . .	52	52	52
Groundnuts (in shell) . .	158	174	174*
Coffee (green) . . .	20†	21	21*
Cocoa beans† . . .	6	9	5
Tobacco (leaves)* . .	2	2	2

* FAO estimate(s). † Unofficial figure(s).

Source: FAO.

LIVESTOCK ('000 head, year ending September)

	1997	1998	1999
Cattle	2,291	2,337	2,368
Sheep	650	669	687
Goats	788	820	864
Pigs.	51	53	54
Horses*	3	3	3
Asses*	2	2	2
Poultry	7,600	8,700	8,900

* FAO estimates.

Source: FAO.

LIVESTOCK PRODUCTS (FAO estimates, '000 metric tons)

	1997	1998	1999
Beef and veal . . .	15	15	15
Poultry meat . . .	3	3	3
Mutton and lamb . .	2	2	2
Goat meat	3	3	3
Other meat . . .	5	6	6
Cows' milk	57	59	62
Goats' milk	5	5	5
Sheep's milk . . .	2	2	2
Poultry eggs . . .	8	8	8
Cattle hides . . .	2	3	3

Source: FAO.

Forestry

ROUNDWOOD REMOVALS ('000 cubic metres, excl. bark)

	1996	1997	1998
Sawlogs, veneer logs and logs for sleepers	170	160	138
Other industrial wood . . .	507	511	512
Fuel wood	7,950	7,980	8,000
Total	8,627	8,651	8,650

Source: FAO, *Yearbook of Forest Products.*

SAWNWOOD PRODUCTION ('000 cubic metres, incl. railway sleepers)

	1996	1997	1998
Total (all broadleaved) . . .	85	25	26

Source: FAO, *Yearbook of Forest Products.*

Fishing

('000 metric tons, live weight)

	1996	1997	1998
Freshwater fishes	2.8	3.6	4.0
Sea catfishes.	3.6	2.5	2.6
Bobo croaker	3.4	2.8	2.8
West African croakers . .	2.9	2.2	2.6
Porgies and seabreams . .	3.8	3.6	3.0
Mullets	1.9	1.2	1.5
Jack and horse mackerels . .	3.6	1.5	7.1
Sardinellas	6.1	4.2	6.3
Bonga shad	26.1	29.5	27.9
Total catch (incl. others) . .	63.4	62.4	69.8

Source: FAO, *Yearbook of Fishery Statistics.*

Mining

	1995	1996	1997
Bauxite ('000 metric tons)* . .	17,733	18,393	18,392
Diamonds ('000 carats)† . . .	365	205	200

* Source: *World Metal Statistics* (London).
† Data from the US Bureau of Mines.

Source: UN, *Industrial Commodity Statistics Yearbook.*

Gold (mineral content of ore, metric tons): 7.0 in 1996; 7.1 in 1997; 13.1 in 1998 (Source: Gold Fields Mineral Services Ltd, *Gold Survey 1999*).

Industry

SELECTED PRODUCTS ('000 metric tons, unless otherwise indicated)

	1995	1996	1997
Salted, dried or smoked fish* . .	11.0	10.8*	10.8*
Raw sugar*†	19	19	19
Alumina (calcined equivalent)‡ .	616	640	640
Electric energy (million kWh) .	537*	541	n.a.

* Data from FAO.
† Provisional or estimated figures.
‡ Data from the US Bureau of Mines.

Source: UN, *Industrial Commodity Statistics Yearbook.*

Palm oil (unrefined): 55 (estimate) in 1997; 50 in 1998; 50 (estimate) in 1999 (Source: FAO).

Finance

CURRENCY AND EXCHANGE RATES

Monetary Units
100 centimes = 1 franc guinéen (FG or Guinean franc).

Sterling, Dollar and Euro Equivalents (29 December 2000)
£1 sterling = 2,808.7 Guinean francs;
US $1 = 1,882.3 Guinean francs;
€1 = 1,751.5 Guinean francs;
10,000 Guinean francs = £3.560 = $5.313 = €5.710.

Average Exchange Rate (Guinean francs per US $)
1997   1,095.3
1998   1,236.8
1999   1,387.4

BUDGET ('000 million Guinean francs)

Revenue*	1996	1997	1998
Mining-sector revenue . . .	106.8	123.0	126.4
Special tax on mining products .	101.5	116.1	116.7
Other revenue	291.8	353.0	370.4
Tax revenue	266.0	320.5	337.5
Taxes on income and profits .	43.5	46.0	48.1
Personal	26.0	26.1	26.1
Corporate	8.9	9.5	9.5
Taxes on domestic production and trade	166.2	200.6	217.4
Value-added tax (VAT)† .	58.0	108.8	96.4
Excise surcharge . .	11.1	9.0	8.5
Petroleum excise tax . .	66.7	63.9	66.3
Taxes on international trade .	56.3	74.0	71.9
Import duties . . .	49.6	71.1	67.8
Total	398.6	475.9	496.7

Expenditure‡	1996	1997	1998
Current expenditure . . .	350.7	377.4	388.1
Wages and salaries . .	173.4	171.7	181.2
Other goods and services .	75.0	83.9	89.8
Subsidies and transfers . .	50.3	54.3	53.0
Interest payments . .	52.1	67.4	64.1
Public investment programme .	288.6	341.5	250.4
Domestically financed . .	48.7	39.7	41.4
Externally financed . .	239.9	301.7	209.0
Restructing of banking system .	–	6.0	13.6
Sub-total	639.4	724.9	652.1
Adjustment for payments arrears§	–9.1	56.6	66.9
Total (cash basis) . . .	630.3	781.5	719.0

* Excluding grants received ('000 million Guinean francs): 122.5 in 1996; 127.8 in 1997; 127.8 in 1998.
† VAT, introduced in August 1996, replaced the turnover tax. Includes VAT (turnover tax before 1996) on imports.
‡ Excluding lending minus repayments ('000 million Guinean francs): 1.5 in 1997; 3.9 in 1998.
§ Minus sign indicates an increase in arrears.
Source: IMF, *Guinea: Statistical Appendix* (February 2000).

INTERNATIONAL RESERVES (US $ million at 31 December)

	1997	1998	1999
IMF special drawing rights . .	2.66	1.43	1.29
Reserve position in IMF . . .	0.10	0.11	0.10
Foreign exchange	118.88	235.17	198.29
Total	121.63	236.71	199.68

Source: IMF, *International Financial Statistics.*

MONEY SUPPLY (million Guinean francs at 31 December)

	1996	1997	1998
Currency outside banks . .	154,420	191,635	209,682
Demand deposits at commercial banks	112,590	130,430	144,030
Total (incl. others) . . .	273,465	331,666	360,682

Source: IMF, *International Financial Statistics.*

COST OF LIVING
(Consumer Price Index; base: 1991 = 100)

	1996	1997	1998
Food	141.2	140.7	154.7
Fuel and light . . .	120.0	123.3	124.9
Clothing.	117.0	124.0	123.0
Housing.	124.3	126.0	129.5
All items (incl. others) . .	134.2	136.8	143.8

Source: IMF, *Guinea: Statistical Appendix* (February 2000).

NATIONAL ACCOUNTS

Expenditure on the Gross Domestic Product
('000 million Guinean francs at current prices)

	1996	1997	1998
Government final consumption expenditure . . .	325.5	345.0	337.4
Private final consumption expenditure . . .	3,135.9	3,282.0	3,625.0
Increase in stocks . . .	65.0	57.0	59.0
Gross fixed capital formation . .	607.7	674.1	738.6
Total domestic expenditure .	4,134.1	4,358.1	4,760.0
Exports of goods and services .	739.8	844.1	1,010.8
Less Imports of goods and services	898.7	936.5	1,093.0
GDP in purchasers' values . .	3,975.1	4,265.8	4,677.7
GDP at constant 1994 prices .	3,663.2	3,840.5	4,012.5

Gross Domestic Product by Economic Activity
('000 million Guinean francs at constant 1994 prices)

	1996	1997	1998
Agriculture, hunting, forestry and fishing	746.2	784.3	824.8
Mining and quarrying . .	588.9	608.4	630.3
Manufacturing	140.0	146.3	153.9
Electricity, gas and water. .	18.1	19.2	20.8
Construction.	309.1	328.3	350.6
Trade	1,013.9	1,065.6	1,116.8
Transport	216.2	226.6	243.6
Administration	187.7	175.9	166.1
Other services . . .	321.5	336.9	356.1
GDP at factor cost . . .	3,541.6	3,691.4	3,863.0
Indirect taxes	121.6	149.1	149.6
GDP in purchasers' values . .	3,663.2	3,840.5	4,012.5

Source: IMF, *Guinea: Statistical Appendix* (February 2000).

BALANCE OF PAYMENTS (US $ million)

	1997	1998	1999
Exports of goods f.o.b. . . .	630.1	693.0	677.9
Imports of goods f.o.b. . . .	−512.5	−572.0	−583.4
Trade balance	117.6	121.0	94.5
Exports of services . . .	110.7	110.8	113.2
Imports of services . . .	−321.6	−382.7	−342.1
Balance on goods and services .	−93.3	−150.9	−134.4
Other income received . .	7.8	9.0	24.7
Other income paid . . .	−121.3	−133.5	−106.9
Balance on goods, services and income	−206.9	−275.5	−216.6
Current transfers received . .	131.4	116.2	80.1
Current transfers paid . .	−15.6	−24.3	−15.1
Current balance . . .	−91.1	−183.6	−151.6
Direct investment from abroad .	17.3	17.8	63.4
Portfolio investment assets . .	−	−82.7	−20.0
Other investment assets . . .	−99.1	−14.6	0.7
Other investment liabilities . .	−7.5	87.5	73.1
Net errors and omissions . .	49.8	17.8	−45.0
Overall balance . . .	−130.6	−157.8	−79.5

Source: IMF, *International Financial Statistics.*

External Trade

PRINCIPAL COMMODITIES (US $ million)

Imports c.i.f.	1996	1997	1998*
Vegetable products . . .	72.1	80.4	54.2
Prepared foodstuffs; beverages and tobacco .	52.5	58.1	76.9
Mineral products. .	92.0	83.8	85.8
Products of the chemical or allied industries, plastics and rubber	64.8	67.2	61.9
Textiles and textile articles . .	28.6	27.2	23.4
Base metals and articles thereof	42.5	44.1	43.7
Machinery and mechanical appliances	111.5	112.9	126.8
Vehicles, vessels and other transport equipment . .	55.5	33.9	40.4
Total (incl. others) . . .	583.7	572.5	571.8

Exports f.o.b.	1996	1997	1998*
Bauxite	309.0	322.6	324.3
Alumina	103.0	94.5	100.2
Diamonds	42.2	56.8	51.2
Gold	82.2	79.8	125.3
Coffee	13.5	31.6	23.3
Fish	27.5	35.8	38.5
Total (incl. others) . . .	612.7	660.0	709.2

* Estimates.

Source: IMF, *Guinea: Statistical Appendix* (February 2000).

PRINCIPAL TRADING PARTNERS (percentage of trade)*

Imports f.o.b.						1996	1997	1998
Austria .	.	.	.	.	.	0.3	0.2	1.8
Belgium-Luxembourg		.	.	.		8.1	9.2	7.9
Canada .	.	.	.	.	.	1.2	0.5	1.4
China, People's Repub.		.	.			2.1	3.8	5.6
Côte d'Ivoire	.	.	.	.		14.0	6.3	6.6
France (incl. Monaco)		.	.	.		16.2	25.0	24.8
Germany	.	.	.	.		1.6	2.1	2.5
Hong Kong	.	.	.	.		2.1	1.9	4.0
India .	.	.	.	.	.	3.6	1.1	1.0
Italy .	.	.	.	.	.	3.2	3.9	4.1
Japan .	.	.	.	.	.	4.4	4.2	3.0
Netherlands .	.	.	.	.		2.9	2.8	3.9
Nigeria .	.	.	.	.		1.5	0.6	0.5
Senegal .	.	.	.	.		1.4	1.4	1.8
Singapore .	.	.	.	.		0.5	1.0	1.1
South Africa .	.	.	.	.		0.1	2.6	2.3
Spain .	.	.	.	.	.	2.2	2.9	3.3
Switzerland .	.	.	.	.		0.3	0.4	1.3
United Kingdom	.	.	.	.		1.8	4.1	2.7
USA .	.	.	.	.	.	6.6	8.3	9.8

Exports f.o.b.				1996	1997	1998
Belgium-Luxembourg		.	.	4.3	6.7	13.7
Cameroon	.	.	.	3.0	3.8	3.8
Canada .	.	.	.	7.7	3.1	2.2
Côte d'Ivoire	.	.	.	–	–	1.0
France (incl. Monaco)		.	.	8.5	12.8	6.9
Germany	.	.	.	4.1	3.6	3.5
Ireland .	.	.	.	10.4	11.1	12.2
Italy .	.	.	.	5.3	3.3	1.9
Netherlands .	.	.	.	0.4	0.1	1.3
Norway .	.	.	.	2.4	2.5	0.7
Spain .	.	.	.	10.9	17.5	12.4
Switzerland .	.	.	.	1.3	0.6	–
Ukraine .	.	.	.	–	–	6.7
United Kingdom .	.	.	.	3.0	4.1	0.4
USA .	.	.	.	33.2	23.1	16.4

* Data are compiled on the basis of reporting by Guinea's trading partners. Non-reporting countries include, notably, the countries of the former USSR, with the exception of Ukraine in 1998 only.

Source: IMF, *Guinea: Statistical Appendix* (February 2000).

Transport

RAILWAYS (estimated traffic)

	1991	1992	1993
Freight ton-km (million) . .	660	680	710

Source: UN Economic Commission for Africa, *African Statistical Yearbook*.

ROAD TRAFFIC (estimates, motor vehicles in use)

	1994	1995	1996
Passenger cars .	.	.	13,160	13,720	14,100
Lorries and vans .	.	.	18,000	19,400	21,000

Source: IRF, *World Road Statistics*.

SHIPPING
Merchant Fleet (registered at 31 December)

	1996	1997	1998
Number of vessels .	.	.	25	30	30
Total displacement ('000 grt) .	.	6.7	9.0	11.2

Source: Lloyd's Register of Shipping, *World Fleet Statistics*.

International Sea-borne Freight Traffic (Port of Conakry, '000 metric tons)

	1998	1999
Goods loaded .	.	.	.	.	2,194	2,089
Goods unloaded .	.	.	.	.	1,680	1,851

Source: Poste d'Expansion Economique, Conakry.

CIVIL AVIATION (traffic on scheduled services)

	1995	1996	1997
Kilometres flown (million)	.	.	1	1	1
Passengers carried ('000) .	.	.	30	31	31
Passenger-km (million)	.	.	48	50	50
Total ton-km (million)	.	.	5	5	5

Source: UN, *Statistical Yearbook*.

Tourism

FOREIGN VISITOR ARRIVALS

	1997	1998
Belgium .	.	.	.	.	.	1,026	1,386
France .	.	.	.	.	.	3,009	4,550
Germany	.	.	.	.	.	788	846
Italy .	.	.	.	.	.	1,469	1,850
Lebanon .	.	.	.	.	.	495	1,765
United Kingdom .	.	.	.	.		974	1,080
Total (incl. others)	.	.	.	.		17,000	23,000

Receipts from tourism (US $ million): 6 in 1996; 5 in 1997.

Source: World Tourism Organization, *Yearbook of Tourism Statistics*.

Communications Media

	1995	1996	1997
Radio receivers ('000 in use) .	.	325	350	357
Television receivers ('000 in use) .	.	65	75	85
Telephones ('000 main lines in use) .		11	16	20
Telefax stations (number in use) .	.	n.a.	1,000	2,018
Mobile cellular telephones (subscribers) .	. . .	950	950	2,868
Non-daily newspapers:				
Number .	.	.	.	n.a.	1	n.a.
Average circulation ('000 copies) .		n.a.	20	n.a.

Sources: UNESCO, *Statistical Yearbook*; UN, *Statistical Yearbook*.

Education

(1997/98, unless otherwise indicated)

	Institu-tions	Teachers	Students		
			Males	Females	Total
Pre-primary .	202*	594	n.a.	n.a.	30,857
Primary .	3,723	13,883	425,644	249,088	674,732
Secondary:					
General .	n.a.	5,099	114,212	39,449	153,661
Teacher training	n.a.	194†	288‡	271‡	559‡
Vocational	n.a.	1,114§	3,009‡	1,637‡	4,646‡
Tertiary* .	n.a.	307	780	1,098	1,878

* 1996/97 figure(s). † 1993/94 figure. ‡ 1995/96 figure. § 1992/93 figure.
Source: UNESCO, *Statistical Yearbook*.

Directory

The Constitution

The Constitution (*Loi fondamentale*) of the Third Republic of Guinea was adopted in a national referendum on 23 December 1990 and promulgated on 23 December 1991. An 'organic law' of 3 April 1992, providing for the immediate establishment of an unlimited number of political parties, countermanded the Constitution's provision for the eventual establishment of a two-party political system. There was to be a five-year period of transition, overseen by a Comité transitoire de redressement national (CTRN), to civilian rule, at the end of which executive and legislative authority would be vested in organs of state elected by universal adult suffrage in the context of a multi-party political system. The CTRN was dissolved following the legislative elections of June 1995.

The Constitution defines the clear separation of the powers of the executive, the legislature and the judiciary. The President of the Republic, who is Head of State, must be elected by an absolute majority of the votes cast, and a second round of voting is held should no candidate obtain such a majority at a first round. The duration of the presidential mandate is five years, and elections are by universal adult suffrage. Any candidate for the presidency must be aged between 40 and 70 years, must not be a serving member of the armed forces, and must be proposed by a political party. The President is Head of Government, and is empowered to appoint ministers and to delegate certain functions. The legislature is the 114-member Assemblée nationale. One-third of the assembly's members are elected as representatives of single-member constituencies, the remainder being appointed from national lists, according to a system of proportional representation. The legislature is elected, by universal suffrage, with a five-year mandate

The Government

HEAD OF STATE

President: Gen. Lansana Conté (took office 4 April 1984; elected 19 December 1993; re-elected 14 December 1998).

COUNCIL OF MINISTERS
(March 2001)

President of the Republic and President of the Council of Ministers: Gen. Lansana Conté.

Prime Minister: Lamine Sidimé.

Adviser to the Presidency of the Republic, in charge of Relations with the Republican Institutions: El Hadj Thierno Mamadou Cellou Diallo.

Minister at the Presidency, in charge of Foreign Affairs: Hadja Mawa Bangoura Camara.

Minister, Special Adviser at the Presidency: Dorank Assifat Diassény.

Minister of Justice, Keeper of the Seals: Abou Camara.

Minister of Territorial Administration, Decentralization and Security: Moussa Solano.

Minister of the Economy and Finance: Cheick Ahmadou Camara.

Minister of Trade, Industry and Small- and Medium-sized Enterprises: Mariama Déo Balde.

Minister of Mines, Geology and the Environment: Ibrahima Soumah.

Minister of Agriculture and Livestock: Jean Paul Sarr.

Minister of Fishing and Aquaculture: Mansa Moussa Sidibé.

Minister of Water and Energy: Niankoye Fassou Sagno.

Minister of Public Works and Transport: Cellou Dalein Diallo.

Minister of Town Planning and Housing: Blaise Foromo.

Minister of Communications: Mamady Condé.

Minister of Pre-university and Civil Education: Germain Doualamou.

Minister of Technical Education and Professional Training: Fodé Almamy Sylla.

Minister of Higher Education and Scientific Research: Eugène Camara.

Minister of Public Health: Dr Mamadou Saliou Diallo.

Minister of Youth, Sports and Culture: Abdel Kader Sangaré.

Minister of Tourism, Hotels and Handicrafts: Sylla Koumba Diakité.

Minister of Employment and the Civil Service: Lamine Kamara.

Minister of Social Affairs, Women's Promotion and Children's Affairs: Mariama Aribot.

Minister, Secretary-General of the Presidency: El Hadj Fodé Bangoura.

Secretary-General of the Government: El Hadj Ousmane Sanoko.

MINISTRIES

Office of the Prime Minister: BP 5141, Conakry; tel. 41-52-83; fax 41-52-82.

Ministry of Agriculture and Livestock: Cité du Port, BP 576, Conakry; tel. 41-11-81; fax 41-11-69.

Ministry of Communications: BP 617, Conakry; tel. 41-50-01; fax 41-47-97; e-mail com@sutelgui.net.gn.

Ministry of the Economy and Finance: BP 579, Conakry; tel. 45-17-95; fax 42-21-02.

Ministry of Employment and the Civil Service: blvd du Commerce, Conakry; tel. 41-59-65.

Ministry of Fishing and Aquaculture: BP 307, Conakry; tel. 41-12-58; fax 41-35-28.

Ministry of Foreign Affairs: BP 2519, Conakry; tel. 41-16-33; fax 41-16-21.

Ministry of Higher Education and Scientific Research: BP 964, Conakry; tel. 41-48-94; fax 41-20-12.

Ministry of Justice: face Immeuble 'La Paternelle', Conakry; tel. 45-29-06.

Ministry of Mines, Geology and the Environment: BP 295, Conakry; tel. 41-38-33; fax 41-49-13.

Ministry of Pre-university and Civil Education: BP 2201, Conakry; tel. 41-19-05.

Ministry of Public Health: BP 585, Conakry; tel. 41-20-32; fax 41-41-38.

Ministry of Public Works and Transport: BP 715, Conakry; tel. 41-36-39; fax 41-35-77.

Ministry of Social Affairs, Women's Promotion and Children's Affairs: BP 527, Conakry; tel. 41-20-15; fax 41-46-60.

Ministry of Technical Education and Professional Training: BP 2201, Conakry; tel. 41-44-84; fax 41-33-54.

Ministry of Territorial Administration, Decentralization and Security: près de la Gendarmerie Nationale, BP 3495, Conakry; tel. 41-15-10; fax 45-45-07.

Ministry of Tourism, Hotels and Handicrafts: Conakry; tel. 41-49-94.

Ministry of Town Planning and Housing: BP 846, Conakry; tel. 41-46-87; fax 41-46-88.

Ministry of Trade, Industry and Small- and Medium-sized Enterprises: BP 468, Conakry; tel. 44-26-06; fax 44-49-90.

Ministry of Water and Energy: Conakry.

Ministry of Youth, Sports and Culture: BP 262, Conakry; tel. 41-19-59; fax 41-19-26.

President and Legislature

PRESIDENT

Election, 14 December 1998

Candidate	% of votes
Lansana Conté (PRP)	56.11
Mamadou Boye Bâ (UPR)	24.62
Alpha Condé (RPG)	16.58
Jean-Marie Doré (UPG)	1.72
Charles-Pascal Tolno (PPG)	0.95
Total	**100.00**

ASSEMBLÉE NATIONALE*

Speaker: El Hadj BOUBACAR BIRO DIALLO.
General election, 11 June 1995

Party									Seats
PUP	.	.	.	.	.	.	.	.	71
RPG	.	.	.	.	.	.	.	.	19
PRP†	.	.	.	.	.	.	.	.	9
UNR†	.	.	.	.	.	.	.	.	9
UPG	.	.	.	.	.	.	.	.	2
Djama	.	.	.	.	.	.	.	.	1
PDG—AST	.	.	.	.	.	.	.	.	1
PDG—RDA	.	.	.	.	.	.	.	.	1
UNP	.	.	.	.	.	.	.	.	1
Total	.	.	.	.	.	.	.	.	**114**

* The five-year mandate of the Assemblée nationale elected on 11 June 1995 expired in June 2000. Legislative elections, scheduled to take place on 26 November 2000, were postponed indefinitely.
† The Parti pour le renouveau et le progrès (PRP) and the Union pour la nouvelle République (UNR) merged in September 1998 to form the Union pour le progrès et le renouveau (UPR).

Advisory Council

Conseil Economique et Social: Immeuble FAWAZ, Corniche Sud, Coléaah, Commune de Matam, BP 2947, Conakry; tel. 45-31-23; fax 45-31-24; f. 1997; 45 mems; Pres. MICHEL KAMANO; Sec.-Gen. MAMADOU BOBO CAMARA.

Political Organizations

There were 46 officially registered parties in mid-2000, of which the following were the most important.

Parti démocratique africain (PDA): Pres. MARCEL CROSS.

Parti démocratique de Guinée—Ahmed Sekou Touré (PDG—AST): f. 1994, following split from PDG—RDA.

Parti démocratique de Guinée—Rassemblement démocratique africain (PDG—RDA): f. 1946, revived 1992; Leader El Hadj ISMAËL MOHAMED GASSIM GUSHEIN.

Parti Djama: Leader MOHAMED MANSOUR KABA.

Parti du peuple de Guinée (PPG): socialist; Leader CHARLES-PASCAL TOLNO.

Parti de l'unité et du progrès (PUP): supports Pres. Conté; Sec.-Gen. ABOUBACAR SAMPAORÉ.

Rassemblement populaire guinéen (RPG): Leaders ALPHA CONDÉ, AHMED TIDIANE CISSÉ.

Union des forces républicaines (UFR): Conakry; f. 1992; social-liberal party; Pres. SIDIYA TOURÉ; Sec.-Gen. BAKARY ZOUMANIGUI.

Union pour le progrès de Guinée (UPG): Sec.-Gen. JEAN-MARIE DORÉ.

Union pour le progrès et le renouveau (UPR): f. 1998 by merger of the Parti pour le renouveau et le progrès and the Union pour la nouvelle République; Pres. SIRADIOU DIALLO.

Union nationale pour le progrès (UNP): Leader PAUL LOUIS FABER.

Note: The **Coordination de l'opposition démocratique (Codem)** was established in July 1995, under the leadership of MAMADOU BOYE BÂ, as an alliance of 12 opposition groups. Leading mems include the UPR and the RPG.

Diplomatic Representation

EMBASSIES IN GUINEA

Algeria: Commune de Kaloum, face Etat Major de la Gendarmerie Nationale, BP 1004, Conakry; tel. 44-15-03; fax 41-15-08.

Canada: BP 99, Conakry; tel. 46-23-95; fax 46-42-35; e-mail cnaky@dfait-maeci.gc.ca; Ambassador: DENIS BRIAND.

China, People's Republic: Quartier Donka, Cité Ministérielle, Commune de Dixinn, BP 714, Conakry; tel. 41-48-35; Ambassador: XU MENGSHUI.

Congo, Democratic Republic: Quartier Almamya, ave de la Gare, Commune du Kaloum, BP 880, Conakry; tel. 45-15-01.

Cuba: Corniche-Nord, Coronthie, Commune du Kaloum, BP 71, Conakry; tel. 44-42-68; fax 41-50-76; Ambassador: LUIS DELGADO PÉREZ.

Egypt: Corniche-Sud, BP 389, Conakry; tel. and fax 41-23-94; e-mail ambassadeegypte.conakry@arobase.eti-bull.net; Ambassador: NOFAL ES-SAYED.

France: Immeuble Chavanel, blvd du Commerce, BP 570, Conakry; tel. 41-16-05; fax 41-27-08; e-mail amb.fr.conakry@eti-bull.net; Ambassador: DENIS BAUER.

Germany: 2e blvd, Commune de Kaloum, BP 540, Conakry; tel. 41-15-06; fax 45-22-17; e-mail diplogerma@eti-bull.net; internet www.amb-allemagne.org.gn; Ambassador: PIUS A. FISCHER.

Ghana: Immeuble Ex-Urbaine et la Seine, BP 732, Conakry; tel. 44-15-10; Ambassador: Air Vice-Marshal J. E. A. KOTEI.

Guinea-Bissau: Quartier Bellevue, Commune de Dixinn, BP 298, Conakry.

Iran: Commune de Dixinn, BP 310, Conakry; tel. 41-15-98; Ambassador: JAVAD ROWSHAN ZAMIR QOROQI.

Japan: Lanseboundji, Corniche Sud, Commune de Matam, BP 895, Conakry; tel. 41-36-07; fax 41-25-75; Ambassador: KEIICHI KITABAN.

Korea, Democratic People's Republic: BP 723, Conakry; Ambassador: PAK CHANG SUK.

Liberia: Cité Ministérielle, Donka, Commune de Dixinn, BP 18, Conakry; tel. 42-26-71; Chargé d'affaires: SIAKA FAHNBULLEH.

Libya: Commune de Kaloum, BP 1183, Conakry; tel. 41-41-72.

Mali: La Minière, Commune de Dixinn, BP 299, Conakry; tel. 41-15-39.

Morocco: Cité des Nations, Villa 12, Commune du Kaloum, BP 193, Conakry; tel. 41-36-86; fax 41-38-16; Ambassador: MOHAMED TOUHAMI.

Nigeria: Corniche Sud, Quartier de Matam, BP 54, Conakry; tel. 41-43-75; Ambassador: PETER N. OYEDELE.

Russia: BP 329, Conakry; tel. and fax 41-27-77; e-mail ambrus-gui@mirinet.net.gn; Ambassador: IGOR I. STUDENNIKOV.

Saudi Arabia: près de l'hôtel Camayenne, Commune de Dixinn, BP 611, Conakry; tel. 41-24-86; Chargé d'affaires: ABDULLAH NASSER AL CHARIF.

Senegal: BP 842, Conakry; tel. and fax 44-44-13; Ambassador: MAKHILY GASSAMA.

Sierra Leone: Quartier Bellevue, face aux cases présidentielles, Commune de Dixinn, BP 625, Conakry; tel. 44-50-08; Ambassador: Commdr MOHAMED DIABY.

Togo: ave de la République, Immeuble Kaloum, Commune du Kaloum, BP 3633, Conakry; tel. 41-47-72.

Ukraine: Cité des Nations, BP 1350, Conakry; tel. 79-46-90; fax 45-37-95.

USA: rue KA 038, BP 603, Conakry; tel. 41-15-20; fax 41-15-22; e-mail amemconakry.adm@eti-bull.net; internet www.eti-bull.net/usembassy; Ambassador: TIMBERLAKE FOSTER.

Yugoslavia: BP 1154, Conakry; tel. 46-42-65; e-mail ambyugui@leland-gn.org; Ambassador: DANILO MILIĆ.

Judicial System

The Constitution of the Third Republic embodies the principle of the independence of the judiciary, and delineates the competences of each component of the judicial system, including the Higher Magistrates' Council, the Supreme Court, the High Court of Justice and the Magistrature. A restructuring of the judicial system is being undertaken, with international financial and technical support, as part of the programme of structural adjustment.

President of the Supreme Court: (vacant).

Director of Public Prosecutions: ANTOINE IBRAHIM DIALLO.

Note: A State Security Court was established in June 1997, with exceptional jurisdiction to try, 'in times of peace and war', crimes against the internal and external security of the State. Members of the court are appointed by the President of the Republic. There is no constitutional provision for the existence of such a tribunal.

President of the State Security Court: Commdr SAMA PANNIVAL BANGOURA.

Religion

It is estimated that 85% of the population are Muslims and 8% Christians, while 7% follow animist beliefs.

ISLAM

National Islamic League (NIL): Conakry; f. 1988; Sec.-Gen. El Hadj AHMED TIDIANE TRAORÉ.

CHRISTIANITY

The Anglican Communion

Anglicans in Guinea are adherents of the Church of the Province of West Africa, comprising 12 dioceses. The diocese of Guinea and Guinea-Bissau (as the diocese of Guinea) was established in 1985 as the first French-speaking diocese in the Province. The Archbishop of the Province is the Bishop of Koforidua, Ghana.

Bishop of Guinea and Guinea-Bissau: (vacant), Cathédrale Toussaint, BP 1187, Conakry; tel. 45-13-23.

The Roman Catholic Church

Guinea comprises one archdiocese and two dioceses. At 31 December 1998 Roman Catholics in Guinea comprised about 2.0% of the total population.

Bishops' Conference: Conférence Episcopale de la Guinée, BP 2016, Conakry; tel. and fax 41-32-70; e-mail dhewara@eti.met.gn; Pres. Most Rev. ROBERT SARAH, Archbishop of Conakry.

Archbishop of Conakry: Most Rev. ROBERT SARAH, Archevêché, BP 2016, Conakry; tel. and fax 41-32-70; e-mail dhewara@eti.met.gn.

The Press

Regulatory Authority

Conseil National de la Communication (CNC): Conakry; f. 1991; regulates the operations of the press, and of radio and television; regulates political access to the media; nine mems; two meetings each week; Pres. EMILE TOMPAPA.

Newspaper and Periodicals

L'Evénement de Guinée: BP 796, Conakry; tel. 44-33-91; monthly; independent; f. 1993; Dir BOUBACAR SANKARELA DIALLO.

Fonike: BP 341, Conakry; sport and general; Dir IBRAHIMA KALIL DIARE.

Horoya (Liberty): Coléah, BP 191, Conakry; tel. 41-34-75; fax 45-10-16; e-mail horoya@leland-gn.org; govt daily; Dir OUSMANE CAMARA.

L'Indépendant: route du Palais du Peuple, BP 2427, Conakry; tel. 41-57-62; fax 41-43-19; e-mail indepdt@mirinet.net.gn; weekly; also L'Indépendant Plus; Publr ABOUBACAR SYLLA; Editor-in-Chief SALIOU SAMB.

Journal Officiel de Guinée: BP 156, Conakry; fortnightly; organ of the Govt.

La Lance: route du Palais du Peuple, BP 2427, Conakry; tel. and fax 41-23-85; e-mail lalance@mirinet.net.gn; internet www.mirinet .net.gn/lynx/lce; weekly; general information; Dir SOULEYMANE DIALLO.

Le Lynx: Immeuble Baldé Zaïre Sandervalia, BP 4968, Conakry; tel. 41-23-85; fax 41-23-85; e-mail le-lynx@mirinet.net.gn; internet www.mirinet.net.gn/lynx; f. 1992; weekly; satirical; Editor SOULEYMAN E. DIALLO.

L'Observateur: Conakry; independent; Dir SEKOU KONE.

L'Oeil: Conakry; independent; weekly; Dir of Publishing ISMAËL BANGOURA.

Le Scribe: 124 rue MO-268, BP 1305, Conakry; tel. 22-75-87; e-mail lescribe@mirinet.net.gn; f. 1997; evangelical Christian magazine; Dir JOSEPH SOURO CAMARA; Editor-in-Chief PIERRE CAMARA.

3-P Plus (Parole-Plume-Papier); 7e ave Bis Almamyah, BP 5122, Conakry; tel. 45-22-32; fax 45-29-31; e-mail 3p-plus@mirinet.net.gn; internet www.mirinet.net.gn/3p_plus; journal of arts and letters; 6 a year; Dir MOHAMED SALIFOU KEÏTA.

NEWS AGENCY

Agence Guinéenne de Presse: BP 1535, Conakry; tel. 46-54-14; f. 1960; Man. Dir MOHAMED CONDÉ.

PRESS ASSOCIATION

Association Guinéenne des Editeurs de la Presse Indépendante (AGEPI): Conakry; f. 1991; an asscn of independent newspaper publ; Chair. BOUBACAR SANKARELA DIALLO.

Publishers

Editions du Ministère de l'Education Nationale: Direction nationale de la recherche scientifique, BP 561, Conakry; tel. 44-19-50; f. 1959; general and educational; Dir Prof. KANTÉ KABINÉ.

Editions SKK: Conakry; Propr SIDIKI KUBÉLÉ KEITA.

Broadcasting and Communications

TELECOMMUNICATIONS

Regulatory Bodies

Direction Nationale des Postes et Télécommunications: Conakry; tel. 41-13-31; fax 45-31-16; e-mail koly@leland-gn.org; f. 1997; regulates transport, postal and telecommunications services; Dir. KOLY CAMARA.

Comité National de Coordination des Télécommunications (CNCT): BP 5000, Conakry; tel. 41-40-79; fax 45-31-16; Exec. Sec. SEKOU BANGOURA.

Service Providers

Intercel: BP 965, Conakry; tel. 45-24-08; fax 41-52-60; e-mail fdick@sotelgui.net.gn; mobile cellular telephone operator; Dir FRANÇOIS DICK.

Société des Télécommunications de Guinée (SOTELGUI): BP 2066, Conakry; tel. 41-10-28; fax 45-02-01; e-mail marzuki@sotelgui .net.gn; f. 1993; privatized 1995; internet www.leland-gn.org; 60% owned by Telkom Malaysia; 40% state-owned; also provides mobile cellular services; 51,020 subscribers (1998); Dir El Hadj MARZUKI ABDULLAH.

Spacetel Guinée SA: BP 835, Conakry; tel. and fax 12-66-00-11; e-mail aboukhalil@spacetelguinee.com; f. 1994; mobile cellular telephone operator; operates with a range of 50km around Conakry; 5,000 subscribers (1998); Chair. ABOU KHALIL.

BROADCASTING

Regulatory Authority

Conseil National de la Communication (CNC): see above.

Radio

Radiodiffusion-Télévision Guinéenne (RTG): BP 391, Conakry; tel. 44-22-05; broadcasts in French, English, Créole-English, Portuguese, Arabic and local languages; Dir-Gen. JUSTIN MOREL.

The establishment of a network of rural radio stations is in progress.

Television

Radiodiffusion-Télévision Guinéenne (RTG): (see Radio); transmissions in French and local languages; one channel; f. 1977.

Finance

(cap. = capital; res = reserves; m. = million; brs = branches; amounts in Guinean francs)

BANKING

Central Bank

Banque Centrale de la République de Guinée (BCRG): 3 blvd du Commerce, BP 692, Conakry; tel. 41-26-51; fax 41-48-98; f. 1960; bank of issue; Gov. IBRAHIMA CHÉRIF BAH; Dep. Gov. FODÉ SOUMAH.

Commercial Banks

Banque Internationale pour le Commerce et l'Industrie de la Guinée, SA (BICI—GUI): ave de la République, BP 1484, Conakry; tel. 41-45-15; fax 41-39-62; f. 1985; 51% state-owned; cap. and res 15,830m., total assets 197,815m. (Dec. 1998); transfer to private ownership pending; Pres. IBRAHIMA SOUMAH; Man. Dir JEAN-PIERRE BAJON-ARNAL; 11 brs.

Banque Populaire Maroco-Guinéenne (BPMG): ave de la République, BP 4400, Conakry 1; tel. 41-23-60; fax 41-32-61; f. 1991; 35% owned by Crédit Populaire du Maroc (Morocco), 20% state-owned, cap. and res 708m., total assets 28,345m. (Dec. 1996); Dir AMRANI SIDI MOHAMED; 3 brs.

Ecobank Guinée: ave de la République, BP 5687, Conakry; tel. 45-34-23; fax 45-42-41; e-mail ecobank@mirinet-net.com; activities commenced 1999; wholly owned by Ecobank Transnational Inc. (operating under the auspices of the Economic Community of West African States); Man. Dir KUMLAN ADJARHO OWEH.

First American Bank of Guinea: Blvd du Commerce, angle 9ème Ave, BP 4540, Conakry; tel. 41-34-32; fax 41-35-29; f. 1994; jt-owned by Mitan Capital Ltd, Grand Cayman and El Hadj Haidara Abdourahmane Chérif, Mali.

International Commercial Bank: 4e ave Boulbinet, K.A. 020, Bât. 346, BP 3547, Conakry; tel. 41-25-89; fax 41-54-50.

Société Générale de Banques en Guinée: Immeuble Boffa, BP 1514, Conakry 1; tel. 45-60-00; fax 41-25-65; f. 1985; 48% owned by Société Générale (France); cap. and res 7,892m., total assets 101,555m. (Dec. 1998); Pres. ROGER SERVONNET; Man. Dir JEAN-CLAUDE ROBERT.

Union Internationale de Banque en Guinée (UIBG): 6e ave de la République, angle 5e blvd, BP 324, Conakry; tel. 41-43-09; fax 41-42-77; f. 1987; 68% owned by Crédit Lyonnais Global Banking (France); cap. and res 2,224m., total assets 36,726m. (Dec. 1998); Pres. ALPHA AMADOU DIALLO; Man. Dir CHARLES ROSSNER.

Islamic Bank

Banque Islamique de Guinée: 6e ave de la République, BP 1247, Conakry; tel. 41-50-86; fax 41-50-71; e-mail bigconakry@ eti-bull.net; f. 1983; 68.5% owned by Dar al-Maal al-Islami (DMI

Trust); cap. and res 1,514m., total assets 21,046m. (Dec. 1998); Pres. ADERRAOUF BENESSAIAH; Man. Dir ABDELMAJID BENJELLOUN.

INSURANCE

Société Guinéenne d'Assurance Mutuelle (SOGAM): Conakry; tel. 41-50-57; fax 41-25-57.

Société Nouvelle d'Assurance de Guinée (SONAG): BP 3363, Conakry; tel. 41 49 77; fax 41-43-03.

Union Guinéenne d'Assurances et de Réassurances (UGAR): Place des Martyrs, BP 179, Conakry; tel. 41-48-41; fax 41-17-11; f. 1989; 40% owned by AXA (France), 35% state-owned; cap. 2,000m.; Man. Dir RAPHAËL Y. TOURÉ.

Trade and Industry

GOVERNMENT AGENCIES

Centre de Promotion et de Développement Miniers (CPDM): BP 295, Conakry; tel. 41-15-44; fax 41-49-13; e-mail cpdm@mirinet .net.gn; f. 1995; promotes investment and co-ordinates devt strategy in mining sector; Dir MORCIRÉ SYLLA.

Entreprise Nationale Import-Export (IMPORTEX): BP 152, Conakry; tel. 44-28-13; state-owned import and export agency; Dir MAMADOU BOBO DIENG.

Office de Promotion des Investissements Privés-Guichet Unique (OPIP): BP 2024, Conakry; tel. 41-49-85; fax 41-39-90; e-mail dg@opip.org.gn; internet www.mirinet.net.gn/opip; f. 1992; promotes private investment; Dir-Gen. DIANKA KOEVOGUI.

DEVELOPMENT ORGANIZATIONS

Agence Française de Développement (AFD): 5e ave, Conakry; tel. 41-25-69; fax 41-28-74; e-mail 3621.debroisee@afd.fr; fmrly Caisse Française de Développement; Dir in Guinea EMMANUEL DE-BROISE.

Mission Française de Coopération: BP 570, Conakry; tel. 41-43-56; administers bilateral aid; Dir in Guinea ANDRÉ BAILLEUL.

CHAMBERS OF COMMERCE

Chambre d'Agriculture de Guinée: Conakry; tel. 42-28-81.

Chambre de Commerce, d'Industrie et d'Artisanat de Guinée: BP 545, Conakry; tel. 46-42-16; fax 41-42-17; f. 1995; Pres. OUSMANE BALDE; Sec.-Gen. MOHAMED SAID FOFANA; 70 mems.

Chambre Economique de Guinée: BP 609, Conakry.

TRADE AND EMPLOYERS' ASSOCIATIONS

Association des Commerçants de Guinée: BP 2468, Conakry; tel. 41-30-37; fax 45-31-66; Sec.-Gen. OUMAR CAMARA.

Association des Femmes Entrepreneurs de Guinée (AFEG): BP 790, Conakry; fax 41-32-06.

Conseil National du Patronat Guinéen: c/o Hann & Cie, BP 431, Conakry; tel. 41-36-51; fax 44-37-12; f. 1992; Pres. MAMADOU SYLLA.

Fédération Patronale de l'Agriculture et de l'Elévage (FEPAE): BP 5684, Conakry; tel. 22-95-56; fax 41-54-36; Pres. MAMDOU SYLLA; Sec.-Gen. MAMADY CAMARA.

Groupement des Importateurs Guinéens (GIG): BP 970, Conakry; tel. 42-18-18; fax 42-19-19; Pres. FERNAND BANGOURA.

UTILITIES

Electricity

Barrage Hydroélectrique de Garafiri: BP 1770, Conakry; tel. 41-50-91; inaugurated 1999.

Entreprise Nationale d'Electricité de Guinée (ENELGUI): BP 322, Conakry; tel. 41-42-43; fax 41-17-51; production of electricity; Man. Dir BOKARY SYLLA.

Société Guinéenne d'Electricité (SOGEL): Conakry; f. 1994; majority ownership held jtly by Hydro-Québec (Canada), Électricité de France and SAUR (France), 33% owned by ENELGUI; production, transport and distribution of electricity.

Water

Service National d'Aménagement des Points d'Eau (SNAPE): BP 2064, Conakry; tel. 41-18-93; fax 41-50-58; e-mail snape@ mirinet.net.gn; supplies water in rural areas.

Société Nationale des Eaux de Guinée (SONEG): BP 150, Conakry; tel. and fax 41-43-81; f. 1988; national water co; Dir-Gen. OUSMAN ARIBOT.

TRADE UNIONS

Confédération Nationale des Travailleurs de Guinée (CNTG): Bourse du Travail, Corniche Sud 004, BP 237, Conakry; tel. and fax 41-50-44; f. 1984; Sec.-Gen. MOHAMED SAMBA KÉBÉ.

Organisation Nationale des Syndicats Libres de Guinée (ONSLG): BP 4033, Conakry; tel. 41-52-17; fax 43-02-83; 27,000 mems (1996).

Union Syndicale des Travailleurs de Guinée (USTG): BP 1514, Conakry; tel. 41-25-65; fax 41-25-58; 26,000 mems (1996).

Transport

RAILWAYS

There are 1,086 km of railways in Guinea, including 662 km of 1-m gauge track from Conakry to Kankan in the east of the country, crossing the Niger at Kouroussa. The contract for the first phase of the upgrading of this line was awarded to a Slovak company in early 1997. Three lines for the transport of bauxite link Sangaredi with the port of Kamsar in the west, via Boké, and Conakry with Kindia and Fria, a total of 383 km.

Office National des Chemins de Fer de Guinée (ONCFG): BP 589, Conakry; tel. 44-46-13; fax 41-35-77; f. 1905; Man. Dir MOREL MARGUERITE CAMARA.

Chemin de Fer de Boké: BP 523, Boké; operations commenced 1973.

Chemin de Fer Conakry–Fria: BP 334, Conakry; operations commenced 1960; Gen. Man. A. CAMARA.

Chemin de Fer de la Société des Bauxites de Kindia: BP 613, Conakry; tel. 41-38-28; operations commenced 1974; Gen. Man. K. KEITA.

ROADS

In 1996 there were an estimated 30,500 km of roads, including 4,300 km of main roads and 7,960 km of secondary roads; about 5,030 km of the road network were paved. An 895-km cross-country road links Conakry to Bamako, in Mali, and the main highway connecting Dakar (Senegal) to Abidjan (Côte d'Ivoire) also crosses Guinea. The road linking Conakry to Freetown (Sierra Leone) forms part of the Trans West African Highway, extending from Morocco to Nigeria.

La Guinéenne-Marocaine des Transports (GUIMAT): Conakry; f. 1989; owned jtly by Govt of Guinea and Hakkam (Morocco); operates national and regional transport services.

Société Générale des Transports de Guinée (SOGETRAG): Conakry; f. 1985; 63% state-owned; bus operator.

SHIPPING

Conakry and Kamsar are the international seaports. Conakry handled 3.9m. metric tons of foreign trade in 1999, while in 1994 some 12m. tons of bauxite were transported to Kamsar for shipment.

Getma Guinea SA: 60 blvd du Commerce, BP 1648, Conakry; tel. 41-42-78; fax 41-42-73; e-mail contact@getma.com; internet www.getma.com; f. 1978; marine transportation.

Port Autonome de Conakry (PAC): BP 805, Conakry; tel. 41-27-28; fax 41-26-04; e-mail pac@eti-bull.net; internet www.eti-bull.net/pac; haulage, porterage; Gen. Man. ALIOU DIALLO.

Société Navale Guinéenne (SNG): BP 522, Conakry; tel. 44-29-55; fax 41-39-70; f. 1968; state-owned; shipping agents; Dir-Gen. NOUNKÉ KEITA.

SOAEM: BP 3177, Conakry; tel. 41-25-90; fax 41-20-25; e-mail soaem.gn@mirinet.net.gn.

SOTRAMAR: Kamsar; e-mail sotramar@sotramar.com; f. 1971; exports bauxite from mines at Boké through port of Kamsar.

CIVIL AVIATION

There is an international airport at Conakry-Gbessia, and smaller airfields at Labé, Kankan and Faranah. Facilities at Conakry have been upgraded, at a cost of US $42.6m.; the airport handled some 300,000 passengers in 1999.

Air Dabia: 7e Ave, Almamya, Conakry; tel. 45-39-05; fax 45-35-27; private; two weekly flights to Banjul, The Gambia.

Air Guinée: 6 ave de la République, BP 12, Conakry; tel. 44-46-02; e-mail air-guinee@mirinet.net.gn; f. 1960; transfer pending to one-third private ownership; regional and internal services; Dir-Gen. Sekou Sangare.

Guinée Air Service: Aéroport Conakry-Gbessia; tel. 41-27-61.

Guinée Inter Air: Aéroport Conakry-Gbessia; tel. 41-37-08.

Société de Gestion et d'Exploitation de l'Aéroport de Conakry (SOGEAC): BP 3126, Conakry; tel. 46-48-03; f. 1987; manages Conakry-Gbessia international airport; 51% state-owned.

Tourism

Some 23,000 tourists visited Guinea in 1998; receipts from tourism in 1997 totalled US \$5m. Under a major tourism development project announced in 1995, 186 tourist sites were to be renovated, and access to them improved, and it was planned to increase the number of hotel beds from less than 800 to 25,000 by 1999.

Office National du Tourisme: Immeuble al-Iman, 6e ave de la République, BP 1275, Conakry; tel. 45-51-63; fax 45-51-64; e-mail ontour@leland-gn.org; internet www.mirinet.net.gn/ont; f. 1997; Dir-Gen. Ibrahim A. Diallo.

GUINEA-BISSAU

Introductory Survey

Location, Climate, Language, Religion, Flag, Capital

The Republic of Guinea-Bissau lies on the west coast of Africa, with Senegal to the north and Guinea to the east and south. The climate is tropical, although maritime and Sahelian influences are felt. The average temperature is 20°C (68°F). The official language is Portuguese, of which the locally spoken form is Creole (Crioulo). Other dialects are also widely spoken. The principal religious beliefs are animism and Islam. There is a small minority of Roman Catholics and other Christian groups. The national flag (proportions 2 by 1) has two equal horizontal stripes, of yellow over light green, and a red vertical stripe, with a five-pointed black star at its centre, at the hoist. The capital is Bissau.

Recent History

Portuguese Guinea (Guiné) was colonized by Portugal in the 15th century. Nationalist activism began to emerge in the 1950s. Armed insurgency commenced in the early 1960s, and by 1972 the Partido Africano da Independência da Guiné e Cabo Verde (PAIGC) was in control of two-thirds of the country. The independence of the Republic of Guinea-Bissau was unilaterally proclaimed in September 1973, with Luis Cabral (the brother of the founder of the PAIGC, Amílcar Cabral) as President of the State Council. Hostilities ceased following the military coup in Portugal in April 1974, and on 10 September Portugal recognized the independence of Guinea-Bissau under the leadership of Luis Cabral.

The PAIGC regime introduced measures to establish a single-party socialist state. At elections in December 1976 and January 1977 voters chose regional councils from which a new National People's Assembly was later selected. In 1978 the Chief State Commissioner, Francisco Mendes, died; he was succeeded by Commander João Vieira, hitherto State Commissioner for the Armed Forces and President of the National People's Assembly.

The PAIGC initially supervised both Cape Verde and Guinea-Bissau, the Constitutions of each remaining separate but with a view to eventual unification. These arrangements were terminated in November 1980, when President Cabral was deposed in a coup organized by Vieira, who was installed as Chairman of the Council of the Revolution. Diplomatic relations between Guinea-Bissau and Cape Verde were restored after the release of Cabral from detention in 1982. In May 1982 President Vieira removed several left-wing ministers from the Government and appointed Vítor Saúde Maria, Vice-Chairman of the Council of the Revolution and former Minister of Foreign Affairs, as Prime Minister.

In 1983 Vieira established a commission to examine plans for the revision of the Constitution and the electoral code. In March 1984 Vieira dismissed Saúde Maria from the premiership. Although his removal from office was attributed to his alleged involvement in a coup plot, it appeared that the principal reason for Saúde Maria's dismissal was his opposition to the proposed constitutional changes, which would accord more power to the President. In late March Vieira formally assumed the role of Head of Government, and elections to regional councils took place. In May the National People's Assembly, which had been dissolved following the 1980 coup, was re-established, and the Council of the Revolution was replaced by a 15-member Council of State, selected from among the members of the Assembly. Vieira was subsequently elected as President of the Council of State and Head of State. The National People's Assembly immediately ratified the new Constitution, and formally abolished the position of Prime Minister.

In August 1985 Vieira initiated a campaign against corruption, during which many senior officials were dismissed or arrested. This campaign apparently provoked a military coup attempt in November, led by Col Paulo Correia, the First Vice-President of the Council of State, and other senior army officers. Six people who had been implicated in the coup attempt subsequently died in prison. Of the 53 surviving defendants, 12 alleged plotters were sentenced to death and 41 imprisoned in July 1986. Correia and five other defendants were executed, but the other death sentences were commuted. During 1988 and

1989 a number of those convicted of involvement in the coup were pardoned, and by January 1990 all the remaining detainees who had been implicated in the plot had been released.

In November 1986 the PAIGC endorsed proposals for the liberalization of the economy and re-elected Vieira as party Secretary-General for a further four years. In February 1987 Vieira appointed Dr Vasco Cabral, hitherto Minister of Justice, as Permanent Secretary of the Central Committee of the PAIGC, in an attempt to reinforce party support for the programme of economic liberalization.

In early 1989 it was announced that the PAIGC had established a six-member national commission to revise the Constitution. Regional elections took place in early June, at which 95.8% of those who voted (about 50% of the registered electorate) endorsed the single PAIGC list. In mid-June the Regional Councils, in turn, elected the National People's Assembly, which subsequently elected the Council of State, of which Vieira was re-elected President. In January 1990 Vieira announced the creation of two commissions to review, respectively, the programme and statutes of the PAIGC and the laws governing land ownership.

In April 1990 Vieira announced his approval, in principle, of the introduction of a multi-party political system. In October a draft programme for the transition to a multi-party system was discussed at a national conference. In December the Central Committee of the PAIGC agreed to the adoption of a multi-party system, following a period of transition, and the holding of a presidential election in 1993. In May 1991 a series of constitutional amendments ending one-party rule were approved by the National People's Assembly, terminating the political monopoly of the PAIGC. In addition, all links between the PAIGC and the armed forces were severed, and the introduction of a free-market economy was guaranteed. New legislation in October accorded greater freedom to the press and permitted the formation of new trade unions. In November the Frente Democrática (FD) became the first opposition party to obtain official registration.

In December 1991 a major government reshuffle took place, in which the office of Prime Minister was restored. Carlos Correia was appointed to the post. In late 1991 and early 1992 three further opposition parties obtained legal status: the Resistência da Guiné-Bissau—Movimento Bah-Fatah (RGB—MB), led by Domingos Fernandes Gomes; the Frente Democrática Social (FDS), led by Rafael Barbosa; and the Partido Unido Social Democrático (PUSD), led by Vítor Saúde Maria. Following a split in the FDS, a further party, the Partido para a Renovação Social (PRS), was established in January 1992 by the former Vice-Chairman of the FDS, Koumba Yala. In the same month four opposition parties—the PUSD, FDS, RGB—MB and the Partido da Convergência Democrática (PCD), led by Vítor Mandinga—agreed on the establishment of a 'democratic forum', whose demands included the dissolution of the political police, the creation of an electoral commission and an all-party consultation on the setting of election dates. In March 1992 some 30,000 people attended an opposition demonstration in Bissau, the first such mass-meeting to be permitted by the Government. The demonstrators were protesting against alleged government corruption and violations of human rights by the security forces. In the same month it was announced that presidential and legislative elections would take place in November and December, respectively.

In May 1992 a dissident group, known as the 'Group of 121', broke away from the PAIGC to form the Partido de Renovação e Desenvolvimento (PRD). The PRD advocated the establishment of a transitional government, pending elections, and the disbanding of the political police. In mid-May the leader of the RGB—MB, Domingos Fernandes Gomes, returned from exile in Portugal and, with the leaders of the FD, PCD, FDS and the PUSD, met Vieira to discuss further democratic reform.

In July 1992, following threats by the 'democratic forum' that it would form a parallel government and boycott elections if the PAIGC did not seek consensus with the opposition on electoral issues, the Government agreed to establish a multi-party national transition commission to organize and oversee the democratic process. In late July the leader of the Frente da Luta para a Libertação da Guiné (FLING), François Kankoila Mendy, returned from The Gambia after a 40-year exile. Two further opposition parties—the Partido Democrático do Progresso (PDP), led by Amine Michel Saad, and the Movimento para a Unidade e a Democracia (MUDE), led by Filinto Vaz Martins—were legalized in August. In November 1992 the Government announced the postponement of presidential and legislative elections until March 1993. The delay arose from a disagreement concerning the sequence in which the elections should take place. Contrary to government plans, the opposition parties demanded that the legislative elections precede the presidential election.

Legislation preparing for the transition to a multi-party democracy was approved by the National Assembly in February 1993, and in the following month a commission was appointed to supervise the forthcoming elections. However, reports in March of a coup attempt against the Government threatened to disrupt the transition to democracy. Initial reports indicated that Maj. Robalo de Pina, commander of the Forças de Intervenção Rápida (an élite guard responsible for presidential security), had been assassinated in what appeared to be an army rebellion, provoked by disaffection at poor standards of pay and living conditions. Some 50 people were arrested, including the leader of the PRD, João da Costa. Opposition politicians claimed that the incident had been contrived by the Government in an effort to discredit the opposition. Da Costa and nine other PRD detainees were released in June pending trial, but were forbidden to engage in political activity. In May, following a further split in the FDS, a new political party, the Partido da Convenção Nacional (PCN), was formed. In July Vieira announced that multi-party presidential and legislative elections would be held in March 1994. In August 1993 da Costa was rearrested for allegedly violating the conditions of his parole, prompting renewed accusations by opposition politicians that the Government's actions were politically motivated. Following a threatened boycott of the National Electoral Commission by the opposition, da Costa was conditionally released. He was subsequently tried, but was acquitted in February 1994.

One week before the designated date of the elections, Vieira announced their postponement, owing to financial and technical difficulties. In May 1994 it was announced that the elections would be held in July. In early May six opposition parties, the FD, FDS, MUDE, PDP, PRD and the Liga Guineense de Protecção Ecológica (LIPE), formed a coalition, the União para a Mudança (UM).

The elections took place on 3 July 1994, although voting was extended for two days, owing to logistical problems. The PAIGC secured a clear majority in the National People's Assembly, winning 62 of the 100 seats, but the results of the presidential election were inconclusive, with Vieira winning 46.3% of the votes, while his nearest rival, Koumba Yala of the PRS, secured 21.9% of the votes. As no candidate had obtained an absolute majority the two leading candidates contested a second round of polling on 7 August. Despite receiving the combined support of all the opposition parties, Yala was narrowly defeated, securing 48.0% of the votes, compared with Vieira's 52.0%. Yala contested the results, accusing the PAIGC of electoral fraud and claiming that the state security police had conducted a campaign of intimidation against opposition supporters. Yala's claims were, however, rejected, and on 20 August he accepted the results of the election while affirming that the PRS would not participate in the new Government. International observers later declared the elections to have been free and fair. Vieira was inaugurated as President on 29 September 1994 and appointed Manuel Saturnino da Costa (the Secretary-General of the PAIGC) as Prime Minister in late October. The Council of Ministers was appointed in November, comprising solely members of the PAIGC.

In April 1995 the FD, FDS, MUDE, PDP and the PRD reconstituted the UM coalition, and elected João da Costa as President and Amine Saad as Secretary-General. The LIPE, which had two representatives in the legislature and was a member of the original UM coalition, did not join the new organization, which was granted legal status in November. In August legal status was granted to a new party, the Partido Social Democrático (PSD), which was formed by dissidents from the RGB—MB.

Guinea-Bissau attained membership of the Union économique et monétaire ouest-africaine (UEMOA, see p. 211) in March 1997 and entered the Franc Zone in April. The national currency was replaced, over a three-month transitional period, by the franc CFA, and the Banque centrale des états de l'Afrique de l'ouest (BCEAO) assumed the central banking functions of the Banco Central da Guiné-Bissau.

In May 1997, in order to address what Vieira described as a serious political crisis that was undermining the functioning of the State, da Costa was dismissed. Carlos Correia was subsequently appointed Prime Minister, and a new 14-member Council of Ministers was inaugurated in June. On 11 October Correia was dismissed, bringing to an end an institutional crisis that had lasted since his inauguration as Prime Minister in June. The legislative process had been obstructed by opposition deputies who claimed that, by omitting to consult those parties represented in the legislature on Correia's appointment, Vieira had acted unconstitutionally. In October the Supreme Court ruled that Vieira had indeed contravened the Constitution. Following consultations with party leaders, Vieira reappointed Correia on 13 October, with the full support of the main opposition parties.

In January 1998, following the seizure in Guinea-Bissau of a cache of weapons, a number of officers of the armed forces were arrested on charges of supplying arms to separatists from the Senegalese region of Casamance. In February the Chief of Staff of the Armed Forces, Brig. Ansumane Manè, was dismissed for his alleged implication in these activities.

In March 1998, following protest by opposition parties at delays in the organization of legislative elections, an independent national elections commission was established. The elections were due to be held in July. In April a new political party, the União Nacional para a Democracia e o Progresso (UNDP), led by former Minister of the Interior Abubacar Baldè, was established. In the same month Brig. Ansumane Manè publicly accused the Minister of Defence and a group of officers of the armed forces of involvement in arms-trafficking to the Casamance separatists, a practice which, he maintained, was long-established and continued with the acquiescence of Vieira. Vieira was re-elected President of the PAIGC in May, while Paulo Medina was elected to the new post of Permanent Secretary; the post of Secretary-General was abolished.

In June 1998 rebel troops, led by Brig. Ansumane Manè, seized control of the Bra military barracks in the capital, as well as other strategic locations in the city, including the international airport. Manè subsequently formed a 'military junta for the consolidation of democracy, peace and justice' and demanded the resignation of Vieira and his administration. With the support of Senegalese and Guinean soldiers, troops loyal to the Government attempted unsuccessfully to regain control of rebel-held areas of the city, and heavy fighting ensued. Over the following days more than 3,000 foreign nationals were evacuated from the capital to Senegal. An estimated further 200,000 residents of Bissau fled the city, prompting fears of a humanitarian disaster, with the hostilities preventing aid organizations from distributing emergency food and medical supplies to the refugees. Fighting continued into July, with many members of the Guinea-Bissau armed forces reportedly defecting to the side of the rebels.

On 26 July 1998, following mediation by a delegation from the lusophone commonwealth body, the Comunidade dos Países de Língua Portuguesa (CPLP, see below), the Government and the rebels agreed to implement a truce. On 25 August representatives of the Government and the rebels met, under the auspices of the CPLP and the Economic Community of West African States (ECOWAS, see p. 170), on Sal island, Cape Verde, where agreement was reached to transform the existing truce into a cease-fire. The accord provided for the reopening of the international airport and for the deployment of international forces to maintain and supervise the cease-fire. In September talks between the Government and the rebels resumed in Abidjan, Côte d'Ivoire. However, the rebels' demand that all Senegalese and Guinean forces be withdrawn from the country as a prerequisite to a definitive peace agreement was rejected by the Government. The rebels, in turn, rejected a proposal for the establishment by Senegal of a buffer zone within Guinea-Bissau territory along the border with Casamance. In October the rebels agreed to a government proposal for the creation of a demilitarized zone separating the opposing forces in the capital. However, before the proposal could be formally endorsed, the cease-fire collapsed as fighting erupted in the capital and several other towns. On 20 October the Government imposed a nationwide curfew, and on the following day Vieira declared a unilateral cease-fire. By that time almost all of the government troops had joined forces with the rebels, who were thought to control some 99% of the country. On 23 October Brig. Manè agreed to conform to a 48-hour truce to allow Vieira to clarify his proposals for a negotiated peace settlement, and agreement was subsequently reached for direct talks to be held in Banjul, The Gambia. At the talks, which took place on 29 October, the rebels confirmed that they would not seek Vieira's resignation. Further talks, held, under the aegis of ECOWAS, in Abuja, Nigeria, resulted in the signing of a peace accord on 1 November. Under the terms of the accord, the two sides reaffirmed the cease-fire of 25 August, and resolved that the withdrawal of Senegalese and Guinean troops from Guinea-Bissau be conducted simultaneously with the deployment of an ECOMOG (ECOWAS Cease-fire Monitoring Group) interposition force, which would guarantee security on the border with Senegal. It was also agreed that a government of national unity would be established, to include representatives of the rebel junta, and that presidential and legislative elections would be held no later than March 1999. In November 1998 agreement was reached on the composition of a Joint Executive Commission to implement the peace accord. The Commission approved the structure of the new government, which was to comprise 10 ministers and seven secretaries of state. On 3 December Francisco José Fadul was appointed Prime Minister, and later that month Vieira and Manè reached agreement on the allocation of portfolios to the two sides. The first contingent of 100 ECOMOG troops arrived in late December.

In January 1999 Fadul announced that presidential and legislative elections would not take place in March as envisaged in the Abuja accord, and would not be conducted until the end of the year. Also in January agreement was reached between the Government, the rebel military junta and ECOWAS on the strength of the ECOMOG interposition force, which was to comprise some 710 troops. Agreement was also reached on a timetable for the withdrawal of Senegalese and Guinean troops from the country. However, at the end of January hostilities resumed in the capital resulting in numerous fatalities and the displacement of some 250,000 residents. On 9 February talks between the Government and the rebels produced agreement on a cease-fire and provided for the immediate withdrawal of Senegalese and Guinean troops. On 20 February the new Government of National Unity was announced. The disarmament of rebel troops and those loyal to the President, as provided for under the Abuja accord, began in early March. The withdrawal of Senegalese and Guinean troops was completed that month following an extension of the deadline, from 28 February to 16 March, owing to logistical problems. In April a report was released by the National People's Assembly exonerating Manè of charges of trafficking arms to the Casamance rebels. While the report, which had been due for release in June 1998 when hostilities began, called for the reinstatement of Manè as Chief of Staff of the Armed Forces, it revealed that Vieira's presidential guard had been heavily implicated in the arms-trafficking.

In early May 1999 Vieira announced that presidential and legislative elections would take place on 28 December. However, on 7 May, to widespread condemnation by the international community, Vieira was overthrown by the rebel military junta. Fighting had erupted in Bissau on the previous day when rebel troops seized stockpiles of weapons that had been at Bissau airport since the disarmament of the rival forces in March. The rebels, who claimed that their actions had been prompted by Vieira's refusal to allow his presidential guard to be disarmed, surrounded the presidential palace and forced its surrender. Vieira subsequently took refuge at the Portuguese embassy, where on 10 May he signed an unconditional surrender. The President of the National People's Assembly, Malam Bacai Sanha, was appointed acting President of the Republic pending a presidential election. The Government of National Unity remained in office. At a meeting of the ruling bodies of the PAIGC that month, Vieira was replaced as party President in an interim capacity by Manuel Saturnino da Costa. At a meeting in late May of representatives of the Government, the military junta and the political parties, agreement was reached that Vieira should stand trial for his involvement in arms-trafficking to the Casamance separatists and for political and economic crimes relating to his terms in office. Vieira agreed to stand trial, but only after receiving medical treatment abroad, after which, he pledged, he would return to Guinea-Bissau. At a meeting of ECOWAS foreign ministers held in Togo that month Vieira's overthrow was condemned and demands were made for

him to be permitted to leave Guinea-Bissau. It was also decided that ECOMOG forces would be withdrawn from the country; the last ECOMOG troops left in early June. That month Vieira was permitted to seek medical treatment in France, but instead went into exile in Portugal where he was offered political asylum. Also in June Sanha announced that presidential and legislative elections would take place by 28 November. In July constitutional amendments were introduced limiting the tenure of presidential office to two terms and abolishing the death penalty. It was also stipulated that the country's principal offices of state could only be held by Guinea-Bissau nationals born of Guinea-Bissau parents.

In September 1999 an extraordinary congress of the PAIGC voted to expel Vieira from the party. Also expelled were the former Prime Minister Carlos Correia and five ministers from his administration, while the incumbent Minister of Defence and Freedom Fighters, Francisco Benante, was appointed President of the party. In October a mass grave was discovered containing the bodies of 22 people thought to have been executed during the Vieira regime. An earlier such discovery, of 14 bodies, had been made in the previous month. Later in October the Attorney-General, Amine Michel Saad, announced that he had sufficient evidence to prosecute Vieira for crimes against humanity and expressed his intention to seek Vieira's extradition from Portugal.

Presidential and legislative elections took place on 28 November 1999, with voting extended for a further day owing to logistical problems. As no candidate received the necessary 50% of the votes to win the presidential election outright, the leading candidates, Koumba Yala of the PRS and Malam Bacai Sanha of the PAIGC, were to contest a second round of voting in January 2000. Of the 102 seats in the enlarged legislature, the PRS secured 38, the RGB—MB 28, the PAIGC 24, Aliança Democrática four, the UM three, the PSD three, and the FDS and the UNDP one each. In that month former President Luis Cabral returned from Portugal to Guinea-Bissau for the first time since he was exiled following his removal from power by Vieira in a military coup in 1980.

In December 1999 thousands of soldiers, who had fought in support of the military junta to oust Vieira, protested in the capital to demand the payment of salary arrears and war allowances. The soldiers returned to barracks following promises of payment by the Government. In November the World Bank had announced that it was to finance a three-year, US $25m. plan to demobilize and reintegrate the thousands of former civilians who had taken up arms in the recent conflict.

At the second round of the presidential election, conducted on 16 January 2000, Yala secured victory with 72% of the votes cast. Yala assumed power on 17 February and installed a new Council of Ministers, which included members of several former opposition parties, later that month. Caetano N'Tchama of the PRS was appointed Prime Minister. The election was subsequently judged by international observers to have been 'free and fair'. In April Fernando Correia was appointed Minister of Defence to replace Lt-Col Veríssimo Correia Seabra. In May it was reported that tensions were increasing between Yala and certain elements in the army, who viewed the head of the military junta, Gen. Ansumane Manè, as the rightful leader of the country, on the grounds that it was he who had ousted Vieira from power. The refusal of Lamine Sagna, the commander of the national navy, to resign, following his dismissal by Yala (Sagna had allegedly received bribes in return for the release of a Korean fishing boat that had entered Guinea-Bissau's waters illegally) further exacerbated the tensions. However, Sagna subsequently agreed to stand down following an agreement by Yala to co-operate and communicate further with the military. Also in that month a new political party, the Aliança Socialista da Guiné-Bissau (ASG) was formed, under the leadership of the former Chairman of the national human rights commission, Fernando Gomes.

In September 2000 four government ministers (all members of the RGB—MB) were dismissed by N'Tchama, apparently as a result of a disagreement with the PRS over the terms of the coalition agreement. However, later that month, following negotiations between the two parties, the ministers were reinstated in order to prevent a crisis within the coalition, as no party was able to command a majority. In October Yala appointed a State Council, comprising members of all parliamentary political parties, which was to have an advisory role.

Demonstrations organized by the PAIGC, in support of demands for the resignation of the coalition Government, took place in Bissau in November 2000. In late November Manè declared himself Commander-in-Chief of the armed forces, following renewed violence in Bissau, instigated by soldiers loyal to Manè. However, government troops quickly suppressed the insurgency, and a number of opposition leaders were arrested. Manè fled the capital, and was subsequently shot dead by the security forces. A parliamentary inquiry was later established to determine the causes of Manè's death.

In January 2001 the Minister for Education, Science and Technology, João José Silva Monteiro, and the Minister for War Veterans, Iancuba Indajai, were dismissed. A minor government reshuffle later that month was prompted by the resignation, in protest at the earlier dismissals, of a number of RGB—MB ministers, who claimed that they had not been consulted by N'Tchama, in violation of the coalition agreement. The RGB—MB subsequently withdrew from the coalition Government (formed with the PRS) as a gesture of solidarity with the ministers. On 19 March Yala dismissed N'Tchama in an attempt to increase stability in the minority Government; the former Deputy Prime Minister and Minister of Foreign Affairs, Faustino Fadut Imbali, was appointed in his place and subsequently formed a new Government. However it was reported that Imbali's appointment was not supported by a number of opposition parties.

Relations with Portugal deteriorated in October 1987, when six Portuguese vessels were seized for alleged illegal fishing in Guinea-Bissau's territorial waters. Portugal retaliated by suspending non-medical aid, but revoked its decision in early November, after the vessels were released. A few days later, however, the head of security at the embassy of Guinea-Bissau in Lisbon requested political asylum and disclosed the presence of explosive devices in the embassy, which, he alleged, were to be used to eliminate members of the then-exiled opposition movement, RGB—MB (see above). These allegations were vehemently denied by the Government of Guinea-Bissau. A four-day visit by the Portuguese Prime Minister, Aníbal Cavaco Silva, in 1989 signified a distinct improvement in relations between the two countries. In July 1996 Vieira made an official visit to Portugal, during which agreement was reached on improved bilateral relations, particularly in the area of defence. In the same month Guinea-Bissau was among the five lusophone African nations which, along with Brazil and Portugal, officially established the Comunidade dos Países de Língua Portuguesa (CPLP), a lusophone grouping intended to benefit each member state by means of joint co-operation in technical, cultural and social matters.

In 1989 a dispute arose between Guinea-Bissau and Senegal over the demarcation of maritime borders, which had been based on a 1960 agreement between the former colonial powers, Portugal and France. Guinea-Bissau began proceedings against Senegal in the International Court of Justice (ICJ) after rejecting an international arbitration tribunal's ruling in favour of Senegal. President Abdou Diouf of Senegal met President Vieira in Dakar, the Senegalese capital, in August. Guinea-Bissau requested direct negotiations with Senegal, and enlisted the aid of President Mubarak of Egypt, then the President of the Organization of African Unity (OAU), and President Soares of Portugal as mediators.

In January 1990 Guinea-Bissau again urged the OAU, Portugal and also France to help in achieving a peaceful solution to the dispute. Guinea-Bissau and Senegal came close to armed conflict in May, following a Senegalese military incursion into Guinea-Bissau territory. The Senegalese detachment was subsequently withdrawn. In August some 300 nationals of Guinea-Bissau fled the Senegalese region of Casamance, following clashes between the Senegalese army and Casamance separatists. In September more than 1,600 Senegalese sought refuge in Guinea-Bissau, having fled the Casamance region. In November 1991 the ICJ ruled that the 1960 agreement regarding the demarcation of maritime borders between Guinea-Bissau and Senegal remained valid. In December 1992, in retaliation for the deaths of two Senegalese soldiers at the hands of Casamance separatists, the Senegalese air force and infantry bombarded alleged Casamance separatist bases in the São Domingos area of Guinea-Bissau. The reprisals resulted in the death of two civilians. In response, the Government of Guinea-Bissau protested to the Senegalese authorities against the violation of Guinea-Bissau's borders and air space, and denied Senegalese claims that it was providing support for the rebels. The Senegalese Government offered assurances that there would be no repetition of the incident. In March, in an apparent attempt

to convince Senegal that it did not support the rebels, the Government handed over Abbé Augustin Diamacouné Senghor, one of the exiled leaders of the Casamance separatists, to the Senegalese authorities.

In October 1993 the Presidents of Guinea-Bissau and Senegal signed an agreement in Dakar, providing for the joint management and exploitation of the countries' maritime zones. Petroleum resources were to be divided, with Senegal receiving an 85% share and Guinea-Bissau the remaining 15%. Fishing resources were to be divided according to the determination of a joint management agency. The agreement was renewable after a period of 20 years. In December 1995 the legislature authorized the ratification of the October 1993 accord. In the previous month the ICJ announced that Guinea-Bissau had halted all proceedings regarding the border dispute with Senegal.

In February 1995 the Senegalese air force bombarded a village in Guinea-Bissau, close to the border with Senegal. Despite an acknowledgement by the Senegalese authorities that the bombing had occurred as the result of an error, the Senegalese armed forces conducted a similar attack later in the same month, when another border village came under artillery fire. In March, in an attempt to achieve a *rapprochement* between the two countries, President Diouf visited Guinea-Bissau to provide a personal apology for the two recent incidents and to offer a commitment that Senegal would respect Guinea-Bissau's sovereignty. In September, following a meeting at Gabú, in Guinea-Bissau, between representatives of both Governments, agreement was reached to strengthen co-operation and establish regular dialogue concerning security on the countries' joint border. However, a further attack by the Senegalese air force in October prompted the Guinea-Bissau legislature to form a commission of inquiry to investigate such border incidents. In November Prime Minister da Costa paid a three-day visit to Senegal, aimed at strengthening co-operation between the two countries. In June 1996 a meeting held at Kolda, in Senegal, between ministerial delegations from Guinea-Bissau and Senegal resulted in renewed commitments to improved collaboration on security.

In April 2000 there were renewed reports of a number of incidents on the border between Senegal and Guinea-Bissau. Five people were alleged to have been killed as a result of bombardments in the border region of Casamance; however, the Senegalese Government denied accusations that its troops had entered Guinea-Bissau, and in May requested assistance from Guinea-Bissau to resolve the Casamance conflict. Also in that month, calls by the Senegalese President, Abdoulaye Wade, for the presence of UN military observers along the border between the two countries, were rejected by Yala. However, in July Yala agreed to provide assistance to Senegal, in the hope of finding a rapid solution to the separatist conflict in that country. On 5 August an agreement was signed by Yala and Wade ordering the immediate re-opening of the border between the two countries; moreover, the agreement provided for the establishment of a joint military force to patrol the border area. It was also agreed that a joint commission would be set up to 'identify and return' cattle and other goods allegedly stolen by Guinea-Bissau citizens in the area.

Government

Under the terms of the 1984 Constitution (revised in 1991, 1996 and 1999), Guinea-Bissau is a multi-party state, although the formation of parties on a tribal or geographical basis is prohibited. Legislative power is vested in the National People's Assembly, which comprises 102 members, elected by universal adult suffrage for a term of four years. Executive power is vested in the President of the Republic, who is Head of State and who governs with the assistance of an appointed Council of Ministers, led by the Prime Minister. The President is elected by universal adult suffrage for a term of five years.

Defence

In August 2000 the armed forces totalled 9,250 men (army 6,800, navy 350, air force 100 and paramilitary gendarmerie 2,000). Expenditure on defence in 2000 was budgeted at an estimated US $3m.

Economic Affairs

In 1998, according to estimates by the World Bank, Guinea-Bissau's gross national product (GNP), measured at average 1996–98 prices, was US $184m., equivalent to $160 per head (or $573 on an international purchasing-power parity basis).

During 1990–98, it was estimated, GNP per head decreased, in real terms, at an average rate of 1.3% per year. Over the same period the population increased by an average of 2.5% per year. In 1999 GNP was estimated at $195m. ($160 per head). Guinea-Bissau's gross domestic product (GDP) increased, in real terms, at an average annual rate of 1.1% in 1990–98. Real GDP rose by 4.8% in 1997 but declined by an estimated 27.7% in 1998.

Agriculture (including forestry and fishing) contributed 62.4% of GDP in 1998, according to IMF estimates. An estimated 83.1% of the labour force were employed in the sector in 1999. The main cash crops are cashew nuts (exports of which were valued at some US $50m. in 1999/2000) and cotton. Other crops produced include rice, roots and tubers, groundnuts, maize, millet and sorghum. Livestock and timber production are also important. The fishing industry is developing rapidly; earnings from fishing exports and the sale of fishing licences now represent the country's second largest source of export revenue (revenue from fishing licences reached 9,100m. francs CFA in 1997). According to the World Bank, agricultural GDP increased, in real terms, by an average of 4.0% per year in 1990–98. Agricultural GDP declined by an estimated 17.3% in 1998.

Industry (including mining, manufacturing, construction and power) employed an estimated 4.1% of the economically active population at mid-1994 and provided an estimated 12.7% of GDP in 1998. According to the World Bank, industrial GDP decreased, in real terms, by an average of 1.4% per year in 1990–98. Industrial GDP declined by an estimated 12.7% in 1998.

The mining sector is underdeveloped, although Guinea-Bissau possesses large reserves of bauxite and phosphates. Drilling of three offshore petroleum wells began in November 1989.

The sole branches of the manufacturing sector are food-processing, brewing and timber- and cotton-processing, while there are plans to develop fish-processing. Manufacturing contributed 7% of GDP in 1997. According to the World Bank, manufacturing GDP increased, in real terms, by an average of 0.1% per year in 1990–98.

Energy is derived principally from thermal and hydroelectric power. Imports of petroleum and petroleum products comprised an estimated 9.8% of the value of total imports in 1998.

Services employed an estimated 19.4% of the economically active population at mid-1994 and provided an estimated 24.9% of GDP in 1998. According to the World Bank, the combined GDP of the service sectors decreased, in real terms, at an average rate of 1.4% per year in 1990–98. It declined by an estimated 40.0% in 1998.

In 1998 Guinea-Bissau recorded a trade deficit of US $13.6m. and there was a deficit of $30.3m. on the current account of the balance of payments. In 1998 the principal source of imports was the Netherlands (38.8%); other major suppliers were Portugal and the People's Republic of China. In that year India was the principal market for exports (85.9%). The principal exports in 1998 were cashew nuts and cotton. The principal imports in that year were food and live animals, petroleum and petroleum products, electrical equipment and machinery, and transport equipment.

In 1998 there was an estimated budgetary deficit of 19,700m. francs CFA (including grants from abroad and net lending), equivalent to 16.4% of GDP. Guinea-Bissau's total external debt was US $964.43m. at the end of 1998, of which $873.1m. was long-term public debt. In that year the cost of debt-servicing was equivalent to 25.6% of the total value of exports of goods and services. In 1990–98 the average annual rate of inflation was 41.5%. Consumer prices increased by an average of 6.5% in 1998, but fell by 0.7% in 1999.

Guinea-Bissau is a member of the Economic Community of West African States (ECOWAS, see p. 170) and of the West African organs of the Franc Zone (see p. 210).

Guinea-Bissau is one of the world's poorest countries. Its economy is largely dependent on the traditional rural sector, which employs the vast majority of the labour force and produces primarily for subsistence. Since the late 1980s Guinea-Bissau has evolved from a rigidly controlled command economy into a largely free-market economy. The economy remains very dependent on foreign financing, which accounts for more than 50% of budget revenue. Guinea-Bissau joined the Union économique et monétaire ouest-africaine in March 1997 and entered the Franc Zone in April, when the Guinea peso was replaced by the franc CFA as the unit of currency. The economy received a serious reverse following the military uprising of June 1998. The extensive destruction of public buildings and private business prem-

ises, and the displacement of some 400,000 people, imposed a serious burden on the country's underdeveloped infrastructure, necessitating appeals for humanitarian aid. Real GDP declined by an estimated 27.7% in that year and the crisis resulted in the accumulation of substantial government payment obligations. Following the overthrow of President Vieira in May 1999, the Government urged the international community to continue with economic aid. In September the IMF awarded US $3m. in emergency aid in support of the Government's reconstruction and economic recovery programme. In January 2000 the IMF approved emergency assistance of $2m., which, it was hoped, would assist the economic recovery programme. In December the IMF and the World Bank's International Development Association awarded some $790m. in debt-service relief as part of the enhanced Heavily Indebted Poor Countries Initiative. Moreover, a three-year Poverty Reduction and Growth Facility, worth some $18m., was awarded by the IMF in support of the Government's 2000–03 programme of economic reform. The programme's principal objectives included improved access to social services and education, greater fiscal transparency, a decrease in the rate of inflation, the demobilization of the military and the reform of the civil service. GDP was projected to increase by some 9.3% in 2000 and by 8.5% in 2001.

Social Welfare

Medical services are limited, owing to a severe shortage of facilities. The Government aims to establish one regional hospital in each of the eight regions. In 1981 there were 1,532 hospital beds. In the early 1990s there were 18 physicians per 100,000 population and 45 nurses per 100,000 population working in the country. Of total budgetary expenditure by the central Government in 1987, 2,638.0m. pesos (5.4%) was for health services, and a further 4,272.7m. pesos (8.8%) for social security and welfare. In January 1989 the Government announced that hospital treatment would no longer be provided free of charge. In mid-2000 the African Development Bank provided US $500,000 in funding for an emergency health programme.

Education

Education is officially compulsory only for the period of primary schooling, which begins at seven years of age and lasts for six years. Secondary education, beginning at the age of 13, lasts for up to five years (a first cycle of three years and a second of two years). In 1988 the total enrolment at primary and secondary schools was equivalent to 38% of the school-age population (males 49%; females 27%). In 1994 enrolment at primary schools was equivalent to 62% of children in the relevant age-group (males 79%; females 45%). In 1988 enrolment at secondary schools was equivalent to 7% (males 9%; females 4%). Expenditure on education by the central Government in 1989 was 5,051m. pesos (2.7% of total spending). In 1997 the International Development Association approved a credit of US $14.3m. for a project to expand and upgrade the education system. Mass literacy campaigns have been introduced: according to UNESCO estimates, however, the average rate of adult illiteracy in 1995 was still very high, at 68.5% (males 52.5%; females 83.7%). In January 1991 President Vieira announced plans for the establishment of the country's first university.

Public Holidays

2001: 1 January (New Year), 20 January (Death of Amílcar Cabral), 6 March* (Tabaski, Feast of the Sacrifice), 8 March (International Women's Day), 1 May (Labour Day), 3 August (Anniversary of the Killing of Pidjiguiti), 24 September (National Day), 14 November (Anniversary of the Movement of Readjustment), 17 December* (Korité, end of Ramadan), 25 December (Christmas Day).

2002: 1 January (New Year), 20 January (Death of Amílcar Cabral), 23 February* (Tabaski, Feast of the Sacrifice), 8 March (International Women's Day), 1 May (Labour Day), 3 August (Anniversary of the Killing of Pidjiguiti), 24 September (National Day), 14 November (Anniversary of the Movement of Readjustment), 6 December* (Korité, end of Ramadan), 25 December (Christmas Day).

* Religious holidays, which are dependent on the Islamic lunar calendar, may differ by one or two days from the dates shown.

Weights and Measures

The metric system is used.

Statistical Survey

Area and Population

AREA, POPULATION AND DENSITY

Area (sq km)	36,125*
Population (census results)	
16–30 April 1979	753,313
1 December 1991	
Males	476,210
Females	507,157
Total	983,367
Population (UN estimates at mid-year)	
1997	1,136,000
1998	1,161,000
1999	1,187,000
Density (per sq km) at mid-1999	32.9

* 13,948 sq miles.

POPULATION BY REGION (1991 census)

Bafatá	143,377
Biombo	60,420
Bissau	197,610
Bolama/Bijagos	26,691
Cacheu	146,980
Gabú	134,971
Oio	156,084
Quinara	44,793
Tombali	72,441
Total	983,367

PRINCIPAL TOWNS (population at 1979 census)

Bissau (capital) . .	109,214	Catió	5,170
Bafatá . . .	13,429	Cantchungo† . .	4,965
Gabú* . . .	7,803	Farim . . .	4,468
Mansôa . . .	5,390		

* Formerly Nova Lamego. † Formerly Teixeira Pinto.

BIRTHS AND DEATHS (UN estimates, annual averages)

	1980–85	1985–90	1990–95
Birth rate (per 1,000) . . .	44.7	43.9	43.3
Death rate (per 1,000) . .	25.1	23.1	21.4

Expectation of life (UN estimates, years at birth, 1990–95): 43.5 (males 41.8; females 45.2).

Source: UN, *World Population Prospects: The 1998 Revision*.

ECONOMICALLY ACTIVE POPULATION
('000 persons at mid-1994)

	Males	Females	Total
Agriculture, etc.	195	175	370
Industry	15	5	20
Services	80	14	94
Total	290	194	484

Source: UN Economic Commission for Africa, *African Statistical Yearbook*.

Mid-1999 (estimates in '000): Agriculture, etc. 457; Total 550 (Source: FAO).

Agriculture

PRINCIPAL CROPS ('000 metric tons)

	1997	1998	1999
Rice (paddy)*	125*	130	130
Maize	9†	9*	9
Millet	29†	30*	30*
Sorghum*	19	21	21
Roots and tubers* . .	77	78	78
Groundnuts (in shell)* .	18	18	18
Coconuts*	44	44	44
Palm kernels* . . .	8	8	8
Vegetables and melons* .	25	25	25
Plantains* . . .	36	36	36
Other fruits* . . .	36	36	36
Sugar cane* . . .	6	6	6
Cashew nuts* . . .	38	38	38
Cotton (lint)* . . .	1	1	1

* FAO estimate(s).   † Unofficial figure.

Source: FAO.

LIVESTOCK (FAO estimates, '000 head, year ending September)

	1997	1998	1999
Cattle	510	520	520
Pigs	335	340	340
Sheep	275	280	280
Goats	305	315	315

Source: FAO.

LIVESTOCK PRODUCTS (FAO estimates, '000 metric tons)

	1997	1998	1999
Beef and veal . . .	4	4	4
Pig meat	10	10	10
Cows' milk . . .	13	13	13
Goats' milk . . .	3	3	3

Source: FAO.

Forestry

ROUNDWOOD REMOVALS ('000 cubic metres, excluding bark)

	1996	1997	1998
Sawlogs, veneer logs and logs for sleepers*	40	40	40
Other industrial wood . .	121	124	127
Fuel wood†	422	422	422
Total	583	586	589

* Assumed to be unchanged since 1971.
† Assumed to be unchanged since 1979.

Source: FAO, *Yearbook of Forest Products*.

SAWNWOOD PRODUCTION
('000 cubic metres, including railway sleepers)

	1996	1997	1998
Total*	16	16	16

* Assumed to be unchanged since 1971.

Source: FAO, *Yearbook of Forest Products*.

Fishing

(metric tons, live weight)

	1996	1997	1998
Freshwater fishes	250	250	200
Meagre	482	500	486
Croakers and drums	1,020	1,055	1,025
Mullets	3,050	3,155	3,065
Natantian decapods	1,100	1,140	1,107
Total catch (incl. others)	7,000	7,250	7,000

Source: FAO, *Yearbook of Fishery Statistics.*

Industry

SELECTED PRODUCTS

	1996	1997	1998
Vegetable oils (million litres)	4.3	4.1	n.a.
Electric energy (million kWh)	47.6	48.2	40.1

Source: IMF, *Guinea-Bissau: Statistical Annex* (October 1999).

Finance

CURRENCY AND EXCHANGE RATES

Monetary Units

100 centimes = 1 franc de la Communauté financière africaine (CFA).

Sterling, Dollar and Euro Equivalents (29 December 2000)

£1 sterling = 1,051.93 francs CFA;
US $1 = 704.95 francs CFA;
€1 = 655.96 francs CFA;
10,000 francs CFA = £9.506 = $14.185 = €15.245.

Average Exchange Rate (francs CFA per US $)

1998	589.95
1999	615.70
2000	711.98

Note: An exchange rate of 1 French franc = 50 francs CFA, established in 1948, remained in force until January 1994, when the CFA franc was devalued by 50%, with the exchange rate adjusted to 1 French franc = 100 francs CFA. This relationship to French currency remained in effect with the introduction of the euro on 1 January 1999. From that date, accordingly, a fixed exchange rate of €1 = 655.957 francs CFA has been in operation. Following Guinea-Bissau's admission in March 1997 to the Union économique et monétaire ouest-africaine, the country entered the Franc Zone on 17 April. As a result, the Guinea peso was replaced by the CFA franc, although the peso remained legal tender until 31 July. The new currency was introduced at an exchange rate of 1 franc CFA = 65 Guinea pesos. At 31 March 1997 the exchange rate in relation to US currency was $1 = 36,793.3 Guinea pesos.

BUDGET (million francs CFA)

Revenue*	1997	1998
Tax revenue	12,456.5	4,514.8
Income taxes	1,992.8	857.7
Business profits	1,290.1	460.9
Individuals	624.6	381.7
Consumption taxes	2,400.1	461.2
On imports	2,363.8	432.6
General sales tax	—	588.5
Taxes on international trade and transactions	7,290.5	2,265.6
Import duties	2,583.8	1,356.8
Export duties	2,466.3	214.3
Port service charges	2,240.5	694.5
Other taxes	759.1	256.5
Non-tax revenue	11,515.5	2,079.1
Entrepreneurial and property income	584.2	110.4
Fees and duties	9,189.8	899.9
Fishing licences	8,994.9	763.9
Total	23,972.0	6,593.9

Expenditure†	1997	1998
Current expenditure	17,069.9	22,683.2
Wages and salaries	4,873.6	5,663.7
Goods and services	6,134.1	5,563.5
Transfers	4,441.6	3,294.1
Scheduled external interest payments	1,620.5	8,161.9
Capital expenditure	27,882.6	7,499.8
Total	44,952.4	30,183.1

* Excluding grants received ('000 million francs CFA): 20.0 in 1997; 3.9 in 1998.

† Excluding net lending ('000 million francs CFA): 20.6 in 1997; −0.1 in 1998.

Source: IMF, *Guinea-Bissau: Statistical Annex* (October 1999).

CENTRAL BANK RESERVES (US $ million at 31 December)

	1997	1998	1999
IMF special drawing rights	0.06	0.03	0.08
Foreign exchange	33.65	35.73	35.21
Total	33.70	35.76	35.28

Source: IMF, *International Financial Statistics.*

MONEY SUPPLY (million francs CFA at 31 December)

	1997	1998	1999
Currency outside banks	20,137	17,642	24,186
Demand deposits at deposit money banks	16,431	14,476	14,476
Total money (incl. others)	36,625	32,194	39,420

Source: IMF, *International Financial Statistics.*

COST OF LIVING (Consumer Price Index; base: 1995 = 100)

	1997	1998	1999
Food, beverages and tobacco	224.7	239.4	237.7

Source: IMF, *International Financial Statistics.*

NATIONAL ACCOUNTS (million francs CFA at current prices)

Expenditure on the Gross Domestic Product

	1995	1996	1997
Government final consumption expenditure	10,033	10,891	18,118
Private final consumption expenditure	117,485	132,206	141,323
Increase in stocks	154	5,624	27
Gross fixed capital formation	22,373	21,248	21,278
Total domestic expenditure	150,045	169,969	180,746
Exports of goods and services	16,051	17,304	38,370
Less Imports of goods and services	42,122	47,932	60,154
GDP in purchasers' values	123,974	139,340	158,961

Source: IMF, *International Financial Statistics.*

Gross Domestic Product by Economic Activity (estimates)

	1997	1998
Agriculture, hunting, forestry and fishing . .	84,094	74,831
Mining and quarrying		
Manufacturing	17,250	11,134
Electricity, gas and water		
Construction	6,307	4,071
Trade, restaurants and hotels. . . .	36,601	23,624
Transport, storage and communications . .	3,614	2,333
Finance, insurance, real estate, etc. . . .		
Community, social and personal services (excl. government)	1,389	897
Government services	4,751	3,067
GDP at factor cost	154,006	119,956
Indirect taxes	2,744	1,357
GDP at market prices	156,750	121,313

Source: IMF, *Guinea-Bissau: Statistical Annex* (October 1999).

BALANCE OF PAYMENTS (US $ million)

	1995	1996	1997
Exports of goods f.o.b. . . .	23.90	21.61	48.86
Imports of goods f.o.b. . . .	−59.34	−56.80	−62.49
Trade balance	−35.44	−35.19	−13.63
Exports of services . . .	5.69	6.96	8.00
Imports of services	−29.91	−29.25	−26.15
Balance on goods and services	−59.66	−57.48	−31.78
Other income paid	−21.09	−18.65	−14.30
Balance on goods, services and income	−80.75	−76.13	−46.08
Current transfers received . .	31.42	15.70	15.80
Current transfers paid . . .	−1.32	—	—
Current balance	−50.65	−60.43	−30.28
Capital account (net). . . .	49.20	40.70	32.20
Other investment assets . . .	—	—	−5.80
Other investment liabilities . .	−28.25	−12.30	7.83
Net errors and omissions . . .	−11.26	−11.44	−15.87
Overall balance	−40.96	−43.46	−11.92

Source: IMF, *International Financial Statistics*.

External Trade

PRINCIPAL COMMODITIES (US $ million)

Imports c.i.f.	1996	1997	1998*
Food and live animals . . .	25.1	31.1	17.1
Rice	13.9	22.2	10.2
Sugar	1.4	0.7	0.5
Oil	2.2	2.1	0.6
Dairy products	2.0	2.5	2.7
Beverages and tobacco . . .	4.0	6.7	1.5
Other consumer goods . . .	4.6	8.5	1.7
Durable consumer goods . .	1.6	3.0	0.5
Non-durable consumer goods . .	2.2	4.1	0.6
Petroleum and petroleum products	9.3	9.5	6.2
Diesel fuel and gasoline . .	6.5	6.6	6.0
Construction materials . . .	7.7	8.5	1.2
Transport equipment. . . .	9.4	12.5	4.1
Passenger vehicles	2.5	3.3	1.6
Freight vehicles	5.8	7.8	2.0
Electrical equipment and machinery	6.5	8.5	4.5
Total (incl. others)	68.9	88.6	63.1

* Provisional figures.

Exports f.o.b.	1996	1997	1998*
Cotton	1.3	0.1	1.5
Cashew nuts.	18.6	45.6	22.4
Fish.	0.7	0.5	0.5
Shrimp	0.6	0.4	0.5
Wood products	0.8	1.2	0.5
Logs	0.5	0.4	0.3
Total (incl. others) . . .	21.6	48.5	26.7

* Provisional figures.

Source: IMF, *Guinea-Bissau: Statistical Annex* (October 1999).

PRINCIPAL TRADING PARTNERS

Imports (percentage of trade)	1996	1997	1998*
China, People's Repub. . . .	n.a.	n.a.	24.8
Japan	3.6	5.9	n.a.
Netherlands	n.a.	n.a.	38.8
Portugal	n.a.	n.a.	27.8
Senegal	n.a.	n.a.	2.0
USA	7.2	2.5	n.a.

* Provisional figures. Data cover only imports recorded by customs.

Exports (percentage of trade)	1996	1997	1998*
India	86.1	94.0	85.9
Thailand	n.a.	2.6	n.a.

* Provisional figures.

Source: IMF, *Guinea-Bissau: Statistical Annex* (October 1999).

Transport

ROAD TRAFFIC (motor vehicles in use, estimates)

	1994	1995	1996
Passenger cars	5,940	6,300	7,120
Commercial vehicles . . .	4,650	4,900	5,640

Source: International Road Federation, *World Road Statistics*.

SHIPPING
Merchant Fleet (registered at 31 December)

	1996	1997	1998
Number of vessels . . .	21	21	23
Total displacement (grt) . .	5,891	5,617	6,079

Source: Lloyd's Register of Shipping, *World Fleet Statistics*.

International Sea-Borne Freight Traffic
(UN estimates, '000 metric tons)

	1991	1992	1993
Goods loaded	40	45	46
Goods unloaded	272	277	283

Source: UN Economic Commission for Africa, *African Statistical Yearbook*.

CIVIL AVIATION (traffic on scheduled services)

	1995	1996	1997
Kilometres flown (million) . .	1	1	—
Passengers carried ('000) . .	21	21	21
Passenger-km (million) . .	10	10	10
Total ton-km (million) . .	1	1	1

Source: UN, *Statistical Yearbook*.

Communications Media

	1994	1995	1996
Radio receivers ('000 in use) . .	42	45	47
Telephones ('000 main lines in use)	9	9	8
Telefax stations (number in use) .	480	500	500
Daily newspapers:			
Number	1	1	1
Average circulation ('000 copies)	6	6	6

1997: Radio receivers 49,000 in use; Telephones 8,000 main lines in use.

Sources: UNESCO, *Statistical Yearbook*; UN, *Statistical Yearbook*.

Education

(1988)

	Insti-tutions	Teachers	Students		
			Males	Females	Total
Pre-primary . . .	5	43	384	370	754
Primary . . .	632*	3,065*	50,744	28,291	79,035
Secondary:					
General . .	n.a.	617†	3,588	1,917	5,505
Teacher training. .	n.a.	33	137	39	176
Vocational . .	n.a.	74	593	56	649
Tertiary . . .	n.a.	n.a.	380	24	404

* 1987 figures.   † 1986 figure.

Primary (1994/95): 100,369 students (63,415 males; 36,954 females).

Source: UNESCO, *Statistical Yearbook*.

Directory

The Constitution

A new Constitution for the Republic of Guinea-Bissau was approved by the National People's Assembly on 16 May 1984 and amended in May 1991, November 1996 and July 1999 (see below). The main provisions of the 1984 Constitution were:

Guinea-Bissau is an anti-colonialist and anti-imperialist Republic and a State of revolutionary national democracy, based on the people's participation in undertaking, controlling and directing public activities. The Partido Africano da Independência da Guiné e Cabo Verde (PAIGC) shall be the leading political force in society and in the State. The PAIGC shall define the general bases for policy in all fields.

The economy of Guinea-Bissau shall be organized on the principles of state direction and planning. The State shall control the country's foreign trade.

The representative bodies in the country are the National People's Assembly and the regional councils. Other state bodies draw their powers from these. The members of the regional councils shall be directly elected. Members of the councils must be more than 18 years of age. The National People's Assembly shall have 150 members, who are to be elected by the regional councils from among their own members. All members of the National People's Assembly must be over 21 years of age.

The National People's Assembly shall elect a 15-member Council of State, to which its powers are delegated between sessions of the Assembly. The Assembly also elects the President of the Council of State, who is also automatically Head of the Government and Commander-in-Chief of the Armed Forces. The Council of State will later elect two Vice-Presidents and a Secretary. The President and Vice-Presidents of the Council of State form part of the Government, as do Ministers, Secretaries of State and the Governor of the National Bank.

The Constitution can be revised at any time by the National People's Assembly on the initiative of the deputies themselves, or of the Council of State or the Government.

Note: Constitutional amendments providing for the operation of a multi-party political system were approved unanimously by the National People's Assembly in May 1991. The amendments stipulated that new parties seeking registration must obtain a minimum of 2,000 signatures, with at least 100 signatures from each of the nine provinces. (These provisions were adjusted in August to 1,000 and 50 signatures, respectively.) In addition, the amendments provided for the National People's Assembly (reduced to 100 members) to be elected by universal adult suffrage, for the termination of official links between the PAIGC and the armed forces, and for the operation of a free-market economy. Multi-party elections took place in July 1994.

In November 1996 the legislature approved a constitutional amendment providing for Guinea-Bissau to seek membership of the Union économique et monétaire ouest-africaine and of the Franc Zone.

In July 1999 constitutional amendments were introduced limiting the tenure of presidential office to two terms and abolishing the death penalty. It was also stipulated that the country's principal offices of state could only be held by Guinea-Bissau nationals born of Guinea-Bissau parents.

The Government

HEAD OF STATE

President of the Republic and Commander-in-Chief of the Armed Forces: KOUMBA YALA (assumed power 17 February 2000).

COUNCIL OF MINISTERS
(March 2001)

The Government comprises members of the Partido para a Renovação Social (PRS), the Partido da Convergência Democrática (PCD), the Foro Cívico da Guiné/Social Democracia (FCG/SD), the Partido Social Democrático (PSD), the Resistência da Guiné-Bissau—Movimento Bah-Fatah (RGB—MB) and Independents.

Prime Minister: FAUSTINO FADUT IMBALI (Ind.).

Minister of Internal Administration: ANTÓNIO ARTUR SANHA (PRS).

Minister of Defence: LUCIO SOARES (Ind.).

Minister of Media and Parliamentary Issues, with responsibility for the Council of Ministers, and Government Spokesperson: JOAQUIM BALDE (PSD).

Minister of Foreign Affairs: ANTONIETA ROSA GOMES (FCG/SD).

Minister of Social Infrastructure: CARLITOS BARAI (PRS).

Minister of Justice: DIONISIO CABI (PRS).

Minister of the Economy and Finance: RUI DUARTE DE BARROS (Ind.).

Minister of Agriculture and Forestry: ALAMARA NHASSE (PRS).

Minister of Social Solidarity, Employment and the Fight against Poverty: FILOMENA MASCARENHAS TIPOTE (PRS).

Minister of Fisheries and the Sea: OSCAR BALDE (RGB—MB).

Minister of Natural Resources and Energy: JULIO BALDE (PCD).

Minister of Public Administration and Labour: CARLOS PINTO PEREIRA (PCD).

Minister of Education, Science and Technology: GERALDO MARTINS (PCD).

Minister of Public Health: FRANCISCO DIAS (Ind.).

There are, in addition, seven Junior Ministers.

MINISTRIES

All of the ministries are located in Bissau.

Office of the Prime Minister: Avda Unidade Africana, CP 137, Bissau; tel. 211308; fax 201671.

Ministry of Agriculture and Forestry: Avda Amílcar Cabral, CP 102, Bissau; tel. 202251; fax 201157.

Ministry of Defence: Amura, Bissau; tel. 213297.

Ministry of the Economy and Finance: CP 67, Avda 3 de Agosto, Bissau; tel. 215193; fax 214586.

Ministry of Education, Science and Technology: Rua Areolino Cruz, Bissau; tel. 202244.

Ministry of Fisheries and the Sea: Bissau.

Ministry of Foreign Affairs: Rua General Omar Torrijo, Bissau; tel. 202752; fax 202378.

Ministry of Internal Administration: Avda Unidade Africana, Bissau; tel. 201527.

Ministry of Justice: Avda Amílcar Cabral, CP 17, Bissau; tel. 202187.

Ministry of Media and Parliamentary Issues: Bissau.

Ministry of Natural Resources and Energy: Bissau.

Ministry of Public Administration and Labour: Bissau.

Ministry of Public Health: CP 50, Bissau; tel. 201107; fax 201701.

Ministry of Social Infrastructure: CP 14, Bissau; tel. 202466; fax 201137.

Ministry of Social Solidarity, Employment and the Fight against Poverty: Bissau.

President and Legislature

PRESIDENT

Presidential Election, First Ballot, 28 November 1999

Candidate	% of Votes
KOUMBA YALA (PRS)	38.8
MALAM BACAI SANHA (PAIGC)	23.4
FAUSTINO IMBALI (PUSD/RGB—MB)	8.2
FERNANDO GOMES (Independent)	7.0
JOÃO TATIS SÁ (Independent)	6.5
ABUBACAR BALDÈ (UNDP)	5.4
Total (incl. others)	**100.0**

Second Ballot, 16 January 2000

Candidate	% of Votes
KOUMBA YALA (PRS)	72.0
MALAM BACAI SANHA (PAIGC)	28.0
Total	**100.0**

NATIONAL PEOPLE'S ASSEMBLY
General Election, 28 November 1999

	Seats
Partido para a Renovação Social (PRS).	38
Resistência da Guiné-Bissau—Movimento Bah-Fatah (RGB–MB)	28
Partido Africano da Independência da Guiné e Cabo Verde (PAIGC)	24
Aliança Democrática (AD)	4
União para a Mudança (UM)	3
Partido Social Democrático (PSD)	3
Frente Democrática Social (FSD)	1
União Nacional para a Democracia e o Progresso (UNDP)	1
Total (incl. others)	102

Political Organizations

Aliança Democrática (AD): c/o National People's Assembly, Bissau.

Aliança Socialista da Guiné-Bissau (ASG): Bissau; f. 2000; Leader FERNANDO GOMES.

Foro Cívico da Guiné/Social Democracia (FCG/SD): Bissau; Leader ANTONIETA ROSA GOMES.

Frente Democrática Social (FDS): c/o National People's Assembly, Bissau; f. 1991; legalized in Dec. 1991; Leader RAFAEL BARBOSA.

Frente da Luta para a Libertação da Guiné (FLING): Bissau; f. 1962 as an external opposition movement; legally registered in May 1992; Leader FRANÇOIS KANKOILA MENDY.

Liga Guineense de Protecção Ecológica (LIPE): Bairro Missirá 102, CP 1290, Bissau; tel. and fax 252309; f. 1991; ecology party; Pres. Alhaje BUBACAR DJALÓ.

Partido Africano da Independência da Guiné e Cabo Verde (PAIGC): CP 106, Bissau; f. 1956; fmrly the ruling party in both Guinea-Bissau and Cape Verde; although Cape Verde withdrew from the PAIGC following the coup in Guinea-Bissau in Nov. 1980, Guinea-Bissau has retained the party name and initials; Pres. FRANCISCO BENANTE; Perm. Sec. FLAVIO PROENÇA.

Partido da Convergência Democrática (PCD): Bissau; Leader VÍTOR MANDINGA.

Partido para a Renovação Social (PRS): c/o National People's Assembly, Bissau; f. 1992 by four mems of the Frente Democrática Social; officially registered in Oct. 1992; Leader (vacant).

Partido Social Democrático (PSD): c/o National People's Assembly, Bissau; f. 1995 by breakaway faction of RGB–MB; Leader JOAQUIM BALDÉ; Sec.-Gen. GASPAR FERNANDES.

Partido Unido Social Democrático (PUSD): Bissau; f. 1991; officially registered in Jan. 1992; Leader (vacant).

Resistência da Guiné-Bissau—Movimento Bah-Fatah (RGB–MB): c/o National People's Assembly, Bissau; f. 1986 in Lisbon, Portugal, as Resistência da Guiné-Bissau—Movimento Bafatá; adopted present name prior to official registration in Dec. 1991; maintains offices in Paris (France), Dakar (Senegal) and Praia (Cape Verde); Chair. HELDER VAZ LOPES.

União para a Mudança (UM): c/o National People's Assembly, Bissau; f. 1994 as coalition to contest presidential and legislative elections, re-formed April 1995; comprises following parties:

Frente Democrática (FD): Bissau; f. 1991; officially registered in Nov. 1991; Pres. CANJURA INJAI; Sec.-Gen. MARCELINO BATISTA.

Movimento para a Unidade e a Democracia (MUDE): Bissau; officially registered in Aug. 1992; Leader FILINTO VAZ MARTINS.

Partido Democrático do Progresso (PDP): Bissau; f. 1991; officially registered in Aug. 1992; Pres. of Nat. Council AMINE MICHEL SAAD.

Partido de Renovação e Desenvolvimento (PRD): Bissau; f. 1992 as the 'Group of 121' by PAIGC dissidents; officially registered in Oct. 1992; Leaders MANUEL RAMBOUT BARCELOS, AGNELO REGALA.

União Nacional para a Democracia e o Progresso (UNDP): c/o National People's Assembly, Bissau; f. 1998; Leader ABUBACAR BALDÉ.

Diplomatic Representation
EMBASSIES IN GUINEA-BISSAU

Brazil: Rua São Tomé, Bissau; tel. 201327; fax 201317; Ambassador: LUIZ FERNANDO NAZARETH.

China (Taiwan): Avda Amílcar Cabral 35, CP 66, Bissau; tel. 201501; fax 201466.

Cuba: Rua Joaquim N'Com 1, Bissau; tel. 213579; Ambassador: DIOSDADO FERNÁNDEZ GONZÁLEZ.

Egypt: Avda Omar Torrijos, Rua 15, CP 72, Bissau; tel. 213642; Ambassador: MOHAMED REDA FARAHAT.

France: Avda 14 de Novembro, Bairro de Penha, Bissau; tel. 201610; fax 253142; Ambassador: BERNARD LE TOURNEAU.

Guinea: Rua 14, no. 9, CP 396, Bissau; tel. 212681; Ambassador: MOHAMED LAMINÉ FODÉ.

Libya: Rua 16, CP 362, Bissau; tel. 212006; Representative: DOKALI ALI MUSTAFA.

Portugal: Rua Cidade de Lisboa 6, Apdo 276, Bissau; tel. 201261; fax 201269; Ambassador: FRANCISCO HENRIQUES DA SILVA.

Russia: Avda 14 de Novembro, Bissau; tel. 251036; fax 251050; Ambassador: VIKTOR M. ZELENOV.

Senegal: Avda Omar Torrijos 43A, Bissau; tel. 211561; Ambassador: MAMADOU NIANG.

USA: CP 297, 1067 Bissau; tel. 252273; fax 252282; Ambassador: PEGGY BLACKFORD.

Judicial System

Judges of the Supreme Court are appointed by the Conselho Superior da Magistratura.

President of the Supreme Court: MAMADU SALIU DJALO PIRES.

Religion

According to the 1991 census, 45.9% of the population are Muslims, 39.7% are animists and 14.4% are Christians, mainly Roman Catholics.

CHRISTIANITY
The Roman Catholic Church

Guinea-Bissau comprises a single diocese, directly responsible to the Holy See. The Bishop participates in the Episcopal Conference of Senegal, Mauritania, Cape Verde and Guinea-Bissau, currently based in Senegal. At 31 December 1998 there were an estimated 135,252 adherents in the country.

Bishop of Bissau: JOSÉ CÂMNATE NA BISSIGN, CP 20, Avda 14 de Novembro, 1001 Bissau; tel. 251057; fax 251058.

The Anglican Communion

Anglicans in Guinea-Bissau are adherents of the Church of the Province of West Africa, comprising 12 dioceses.

Bishop of Guinea and Guinea-Bissau: (vacant), BP 1187, Conakry, Guinea.

The Press

Baguerra: Bissau; owned by the Partido da Convergência Democrática.

Banobero: Bissau; weekly; Dir FERNANDO JORGE PEREIRA.

Correio-Bissau: Bissau; weekly; f. 1992; Editor-in-Chief JOÃO DE BARROS; circ. 9,000.

Journal Nô Pintcha: Bissau; daily; Dir Sra CABRAL; circ. 6,000.

NEWS AGENCY

Agência Noticiosa da Guinea (ANG): CP 248, Bissau; tel. 212151.

Broadcasting and Communications
TELECOMMUNICATIONS

Guiné-Telecom: Bissau; 49% state-owned.

RADIO AND TELEVISION

An experimental television service began transmissions in 1989. Regional radio stations were to be established at Bafatá, Cantchungo and Catió in 1990. In 1990 Radio Freedom, which broadcast on behalf of the PAIGC during Portuguese rule and had ceased operations in 1974, resumed transmissions.

Radiodifusão Nacional da República da Guiné-Bissau: CP 191, Bissau; govt-owned; broadcasts in Portuguese on short-wave, MW and FM; Dir FRANCISCO BARRETO.

Rádio Bombolom: f. 1996; independent; Dir AGNELO REGALA.

Rádio Pidjiguiti: f. 1995; independent.

Finance

(cap. = capital; res = reserves; m. = million; brs = branches;
amounts in francs CFA unless otherwise indicated)

BANKING

Central Bank

Banque Centrale des Etats de l'Afrique de l'Ouest (BCEAO):
Avda Amílcar Cabral, CP 38, Bissau; tel. 215548; fax 201305; HQ
in Dakar, Senegal; f. 1955; bank of issue for the mem states of the
Union économique et monétaire ouest-africaine (UEMOA, com-
prising Benin, Burkina Faso, Côte d'Ivoire, Guinea-Bissau, Mali,
Niger, Senegal and Togo); cap. and res 806,918m., total assets
4,084,464m.; (Dec. 1998); Gov. CHARLES KONAN BANNY; Dir in Guinea-
Bissau LUÍS CÂNDIDO LOPES RIBEIRO.

Other Banks

Banco Internacional da Guiné-Bissau: Avda Amílcar Cabral,
CP 74, 1064 Bissau; tel. 201256; fax 201033; e-mail bigb@sol
.gtelecom.gw; f. 1989; cap. 3,260m. Guinea pesos (Dec. 1993); 26%
state-owned, 25% by Guinea-Bissau enterprises and private
interests, 49% by Crédito Predial Português (Portugal); Chair. FIL-
INTO E. BARROS; Gen. Man. JOSÉ ANTÓNIO TAVARES DA CRUZ.

Banco Totta e Açores (Portugal): Rua 19 de Setembro 15, CP 618,
Bissau; tel. 214794; fax 201591; Gen. Man. CARLOS MADEIRA.

Caixa de Crédito da Guiné: Bissau; govt savings and loan institution.

Caixa Económica Postal: Avda Amílcar Cabral, Bissau; tel.
212999; postal savings institution.

STOCK EXCHANGE

In 1998 a regional stock exchange, the Bourse Régionale des Valeurs
Mobilières, was established in Abidjan, Côte d'Ivoire, to serve the
member states of the UEMOA.

INSURANCE

In 1979 it was announced that a single state-owned insurer was to
replace the Portuguese company Ultramarina.

Trade and Industry

The Government has actively pursued a policy of small-scale industrialization to compensate for the almost total lack of manufacturing
capacity. Following independence, it adopted a comprehensive programme of state control, and in 1976 acquired 80% of the capital of
a Portuguese company, **Ultramarina**, a large firm specializing in
a wide range of trading activities, including ship-repairing and
agricultural processing. The Government also held a major interest
in the **CICER** brewery (until its privatization in 1996) and created
a joint-venture company with the Portuguese concern **SACOR** to
sell petroleum products. Since 1975 three fishing companies have
been formed with foreign participation: **GUIALP** (with Algeria),
Estrela do Mar (with the former USSR) and **SEMAPESCA** (with
France), all of which were awaiting divestment in 1998. In December
1976 **SOCOTRAM**, an enterprise for the sale and processing of
timber, was inaugurated. It operates a factory in Bissau for the
production of wooden tiles and co-ordinates sawmills and carpentry
shops throughout the country. In 1998 SOCOTRAM was in the
process of being divested through separate sales of its regional
operational divisions. The restructuring of several further public

enterprises was proceeding in the late 1990s, as part of the Government's programme to attract private investment.

**Empresa Nacional de Pesquisas e Exploração Petrolíferas e
Mineiras (PETROMINAS):** Rua Eduardo Mondlane 58, Bissau;
tel. 212279; state-owned; regulates all prospecting for hydrocarbons
and other minerals; Dir-Gen. ANTÓNIO CARDOSO.

CHAMBER OF COMMERCE

Associação Comercial, Industrial e Agrícola da Guiné-Bissau:
Bissau; f. 1987; Pres. CANJURA INJAI.

UTILITIES

Electricity and Water

EAGB: Bissau; operated under contract by private management co.

TRADE UNION

União Nacional dos Trabalhadores da Guiné (UNTG): 13 Avda
Ovai di Vievra, CP 98, Bissau; tel. 212094; Pres. DEFEJADO LIMA DA
COSTA; Sec.-Gen. MÁRIO MENDES CORREA.

Legislation permitting the formation of other trade unions was
approved by the National People's Assembly in 1991.

Transport

RAILWAYS

There are no railways in Guinea-Bissau. In March 1998 Guinea-
Bissau and Portugal signed an agreement providing for the construction of a railway linking Guinea-Bissau with Guinea.

ROADS

In 1996, according to International Road Federation estimates,
there were about 4,400 km of roads, of which 453 km were paved. A
major road rehabilitation scheme is proceeding, and an international
road, linking Guinea-Bissau with The Gambia and Senegal, is
planned. In 1989 the Islamic Development Bank granted more than
US $2m. towards the construction of a 111-km road linking north
and south and a 206-km road between Guinea-Bissau and Guinea.

SHIPPING

Under a major port modernization project, the main port at Bissau
was to be renovated and expanded, and four river ports were to be
upgraded to enable barges to load and unload at low tide. The total
cost of the project was estimated at US $47.4m., and finance was
provided by the World Bank and Arab funds. In 1986 work began
on a new river port at N'Pungda, which was to be partly funded by
the Netherlands.

CIVIL AVIATION

There is an international airport at Bissau, which there are plans
to expand, and 10 smaller airports serving the interior.

Transportes Aéreos da Guiné-Bissau (TAGB): Aeroporto
Osvaldo Vieira, CP 111, Bissau; tel. 201277; fax 251536; f. 1977;
domestic services and flights to France, Portugal, the Canary Islands
(Spain), Guinea and Senegal; Dir Capt. EDUARDO PINTO LOPES .

Air Bissau: CP 111, Bissau; tel. 251063; fax 251008.

Tourism

Centro de Informação e Turismo: CP 294, Bissau; state tourism
and information service.

GUYANA

Introductory Survey

Location, Climate, Language, Religion, Flag, Capital

The Co-operative Republic of Guyana lies on the north coast of South America, between Venezuela to the west and Suriname to the east, with Brazil to the south. The narrow coastal belt has a moderate climate with two wet seasons, from April to August and from November to January, alternating with two dry seasons. Inland, there are tropical forests and savannah, and the dry season lasts from September to May. The average annual temperature is 27°C (80°F), with average rainfall of 1,520 mm (60 ins) per year inland, rising to between 2,030 mm (80 ins) and 2,540 mm (100 ins) on the coast. English is the official language but Hindi, Urdu and Amerindian dialects are also spoken. The principal religions are Christianity (which is professed by about 50% of the population), Hinduism (about 33%) and Islam (less than 10%). The national flag (proportions 5 by 3 when flown on land, but 2 by 1 at sea) is green, with a white-bordered yellow triangle (apex at the edge of the fly) on which is superimposed a black-bordered red triangle (apex in the centre). The capital is Georgetown.

Recent History

Guyana was formerly British Guiana, a colony of the United Kingdom, formed in 1831 from territories finally ceded to Britain by the Dutch in 1814. A new Constitution, providing for universal adult suffrage, was introduced in 1953. The elections of April 1953 were won by the left-wing People's Progressive Party (PPP), led by Dr Cheddi Bharat Jagan. In October, however, the British Government, claiming that a communist dictatorship was threatened, suspended the Constitution. An interim administration was appointed. The PPP split in 1955, and in 1957 some former members founded a new party, the People's National Congress (PNC), under the leadership of Forbes Burnham. The PNC drew its support mainly from the African-descended population, while PPP support came largely from the (Asian-descended) 'East' Indian community.

A revised Constitution was introduced in December 1956 and fresh elections were held in August 1957. The PPP won and Dr Jagan became Chief Minister. Another Constitution, providing for internal self-government, was adopted in July 1961. The PPP won the elections in August and Dr Jagan was appointed premier in September. In the elections of December 1964, held under the system of proportional representation that had been introduced in the previous year, the PPP won the largest number of seats in the Legislative Assembly, but not a majority. A coalition Government was formed by the PNC and The United Force (TUF), with Burnham as Prime Minister. This coalition led the colony to independence, as Guyana, on 26 May 1966.

The PNC won elections in 1968 and in 1973, although the results of the latter, and every poll thenceforth until the defeat of the PNC in 1992, were disputed by the opposition parties. Guyana became a co-operative republic on 23 February 1970, and Arthur Chung was elected non-executive President in March. In 1976 the PPP, which had boycotted the National Assembly since 1973, offered the Government its 'critical support'. Following a referendum in July 1978 that gave the Assembly power to amend the Constitution, elections to the Assembly were postponed for 15 months. The legislature assumed the role of a constituent assembly, established in November 1978, to draft a new constitution. In October 1979 elections were postponed for a further year. In October 1980 Forbes Burnham declared himself executive President of Guyana, and a new Constitution was promulgated.

Internal opposition to the PNC Government had increased after the assassination in June 1980 of Dr Walter Rodney, leader of the Working People's Alliance (WPA). The Government was widely believed to have been involved in the incident; an official inquest into Rodney's death was finally ordered in November 1987, but in 1988 it produced a verdict, rejected by the opposition, of death by misadventure. All opposition parties except the PPP and TUF urged their supporters to boycott the December 1980 elections to the National Assembly. The PNC, under Burnham, received 77.7% of the votes, according to official results, and won 41 of the 53 elective seats, although allegations of substantial electoral malpractice were made, both within the country and by international observers. None the less, Burnham was formally inaugurated as President in January 1981.

In 1981 arrests and trials of opposition leaders continued, and in 1982 the Government's relations with human rights groups, and especially the Christian churches, deteriorated further. Editors of opposition newspapers were threatened, political violence increased, and the Government was accused of interference in the legal process. Industrial unrest and public discontent continued in 1983, as Guyana's worsening economic situation increased opposition to the Government, and led to growing disaffection within the trade union movement and the PNC. There were more strikes in 1984, and in December Burnham announced some concessions, including a rise in the daily minimum wage (virtually the only increase since 1979).

Burnham died in August 1985 and was succeeded as President by Desmond Hoyte, hitherto the First Vice-President and Prime Minister. President Hoyte's former posts were assumed by Hamilton Green, previously the First Deputy Prime Minister. At a general election in December the PNC won 78% of the votes and 42 of the elective seats in the National Assembly. Hoyte was declared President-elect. Opposition groups, including the PPP and WPA, denounced the poll as fraudulent. In January 1986 five of the six opposition parties formed the Patriotic Coalition for Democracy (PCD).

During 1988 the opposition expressed fears about the independence of the judiciary. The opposition also claimed that the Government's continued recourse to the laws of libel against its critics was an abuse of the legal system. Social unrest and industrial disruption in 1988 continued to hamper government efforts to reform the economy, while the Government's hold on power was further compromised, following a division within the trade union movement. Seven unions withdrew from the Trades Union Congress (TUC) in September, alleging that elections for TUC officials were weighted in favour of PNC-approved candidates. The seven independent unions formed a separate congress, the Federation of Independent Trade Unions in Guyana (FITUG), in October. However, the Government refused to negotiate with the FITUG, accusing it of being politically motivated. Furthermore, the severity of austerity measures contained in the budget of March 1989, which included a devaluation of the currency, prompted a six-week strike in the sugar and bauxite industries.

Outside the formal opposition of the political parties, the Government also experienced pressure from members of the Guyana Human Rights Association, business leaders and prominent religious figures. This culminated, in January 1990, in the formation of a movement for legal and constitutional change, Guyanese Action for Reform and Democracy (Guard), which initiated a series of mass protests, urging the Government to accelerate the process of democratic reform. To counter this civic movement, the PNC began mobilizing its own newly-established Committees to Re-elect the President (Creeps). Guard accused the Creeps of orchestrating violent clashes at Guard's rallies, and of fomenting racial unrest in the country in an attempt to regain support from the Afro-Guyanese population.

In October 1990 the former US President, Jimmy Carter, visited President Hoyte to discuss matters related to electoral reform. It was agreed that a new electoral register would be compiled. However, the date of the forthcoming general election was postponed, following the approval of legislation by the PNC in January 1991, extending the term of office of the National Assembly by two months after its official dissolution date of 2 February 1991. In March a further two-month extension of the legislative term provoked the resignation of TUF and PPP members from the National Assembly (in addition to the WPA members, who had resigned a month earlier). Similar extensions followed in May and July, owing to alleged continuing problems relating to electoral reforms. The National Assembly was finally dissolved in late September. The publication of the revised electoral register in that month, however, revealed widespread inaccuracies, including the omission of an estimated 100,000 eligible voters. In November several opposition parties announced a boycott of the general election, which had been rescheduled for mid-December. However, on 28 November Hoyte declared a state of emergency in order to legitimize a further postponement of the election (which, according to the Constitution, was due to take place by 28 December). Legislation restoring the opposition seats in the National Assembly followed, and the Assembly was reconvened. In mid-December the state of emergency was extended until June 1992. A further revised electoral register was published in that month, and was finally approved by the Elections Commission in August. The election took place on 5 October and resulted in a narrow victory for the PPP in alliance with the CIVIC movement (a social and political movement of businessmen and professionals), which secured 32 of the 65 elective seats in the National Assembly (53.5% of the votes), while the PNC secured 31 (42.3% of the votes). The result, which signified an end to the PNC's 28-year period in government, provoked riots by the mainly Afro-Guyanese PNC supporters in Georgetown, in which two people were killed. International observers were, however, satisfied that the elections had been fairly conducted, and on 9 October Dr Cheddi Bharat Jagan took office as President. On the following day Jagan appointed Samuel Hinds, an industrialist who was not a member of the PPP, as Prime Minister.

Following a joint conference in September 1993, the unions belonging to the TUC and the FITUG agreed to reunify as the TUC. In May 1994 a strike, organized by four public-sector unions in support of demands for pay increases, was ended after 10 days when the Government agreed to a 35% increase in the minimum wage.

At municipal and local government elections held in August 1994, the first to be contested since 1970, the PPP/CIVIC alliance secured control of 49 of the 71 localities concerned. However, the important post of mayor of Georgetown was won by former PPP member Hamilton Green, representing Good and Green Georgetown, a party founded specifically to contest the election in the capital.

In December 1994 the National Assembly approved a proposal, drafted by the PPP, for the creation of a select parliamentary committee to review the Constitution, with a view to adopting reforms prior to the next general election, due in 1997. However, the PNC, whose support would be required to gain the two-thirds' majority necessary for constitutional amendments, voted against the proposal, favouring instead the appointment of a constituent assembly.

In August 1995 a serious environmental incident resulted in the temporary closure of Omai Gold Mines Ltd (OGML). The company, which began production in the Omai District of Essequibo province in 1993, was responsible for an increase of some 400% in Guyana's gold production in subsequent years and was Guyana's largest foreign investor. However, in August 1995 a breach in a tailings pond (a reservoir where residue from the gold extraction process is stored) resulted in the spillage of some 3.5m. cu m of cyanide-tainted water, of which a large volume flowed into the Omai river, a tributary of the Essequibo river. Environmental warnings were issued to residents of the Essequibo region, and the National Assembly approved a resolution to close the mine for an indefinite period pending an inquiry into the incident. In January 1996 a government-appointed commission of inquiry recommended that OGML be permitted to resume operations subject to the prior implementation of certain environmental safeguards. OGML resumed operations in the following month.

In February 1996, amid growing public concern at an increase in criminal violence, Guyana resumed judicial executions with the hanging of a convicted murderer. The execution, the first for more than five years, provoked protest from human rights organizations.

In March 1997, following the death of Dr Cheddi Bharat Jagan, Prime Minister Hinds succeeded to the Presidency, in accordance with the provisions of the Constitution. Hinds subsequently appointed Janet Jagan, the widow of the former President, to the post of Prime Minister. In September the PPP/CIVIC alliance formally adopted Jagan as its presidential candidate for the forthcoming general election.

At the general election of 15 December 1997 delays in the verification of votes prompted protest by PNC supporters who accused the Government of electoral fraud, and 11 protesters were injured during clashes with the security forces. With some 90% of the votes counted, the Chairman of the Elections Commission, Doudnauth Singh, declared that Jagan had established an unassailable lead, and on 19 December she was inaugurated as President. Singh's actions were strongly criticized as being premature by opposition parties, and the PNC expressed its intention to appeal to the High Court to have Jagan's appointment annulled. In the following days PNC supporters began a series of public demonstrations in protest at the alleged electoral fraud and at Jagan's appointment. On 31 December the final election results were declared. With two legislative seats remaining to be decided by the National Congress of Local Democratic Organs (see The Constitution), the PPP/CIVIC alliance secured 34 seats, the PNC won 26, and TUF, the Alliance for Guyana and the Guyana Democratic Party each obtained one seat. (In February 1998 the remaining two seats were declared to have been won by the PPP/CIVIC alliance.)

In January 1998, in the light of continued unrest being fomented by opposition supporters, the Government accepted a proposal by private-sector leaders for an international audit of the election to be conducted. The PNC, however, rejected the proposal and demanded instead the holding of fresh elections. In mid-January, in rejection of an appeal by the PNC, the Chief Justice ruled that it was beyond the jurisdiction of the High Court to prohibit Jagan from exercising her presidential functions pending a judicial review of the election. The ruling provoked serious disturbances in Georgetown, which, in turn, prompted the Government to introduce a one-month ban on public assemblies and demonstrations in the capital. Nevertheless, public protests by PNC supporters continued in defiance of the ban, resulting in confrontation with the security forces. However, in mid-January, following mediation by a three-member CARICOM commission, headed by a former Minister of Foreign Affairs of Barbados, Sir Henry Forde, it was announced that an agreement (the Herdmanston Agreement) had been signed by Jagan and PNC leader Desmond Hoyte, which provided for the organization of fresh elections within 36 months and the creation of a constitutional commission to make recommendations on constitutional reform, subsequently to be submitted to a national referendum and a National Assembly vote. The agreement also made provision for an independent audit of the December election, and in February the PPP/CIVIC alliance and the PNC agreed on the legal procedures necessary for the audit, which was to be conducted by a CARICOM electoral team, to be authorized. Meanwhile, although the PNC had submitted the names of 22 deputies who would represent the party in an emergency, the PNC continued to boycott the National Assembly. In early June the CARICOM commission upheld the published results of the December poll, declaring that there had been only minor procedural irregularities. While both the PPP and the PNC were bound to abide by the findings of the commission (under the terms of the Herdmanston Agreement), Hoyte continued publicly to question the legitimacy of the Jagan administration. Later in the month, mounting political frustration, arising from the National Assembly's informing the PNC that its deputies had effectively forfeited their legislative seats (having failed to attend six consecutive sittings), erupted onto the streets of Georgetown. PNC supporters congregated in the capital, where violent demonstrations against the Government escalated into riot conditions that were dispersed by the security forces with rubber bullets and tear gas. However, renewed CARICOM mediation between the PPP and the PNC, at the CARICOM annual summit in Saint Lucia in early July, produced fresh commitments from both sides to restore peaceful political dialogue, renew discussions on constitutional reform and reinstate full legislative participation. Legislation designed to enable the PNC deputies to recover their seats in the legislature was subsequently formulated by both sides, and the PNC (with the exception of Hoyte—who continued to deny the legitimacy of Jagan's authority) rejoined the National Assembly on 14 July.

In August 1998 the National Assembly announced a 14-member select committee on constitutional reform, entrusted with establishing the terms of reference and composition of a national reform commission. The select committee comprised eight members of the PPP/CIVIC alliance, four from the PNC and one each from the TUF and the AFG. In January 1999 the 20-member Constitutional Reform Commission was created, comprising representatives of the country's principal political parties and community groups. The Commission had until the end of July 1999 to formulate recommendations for constitutional reform. Also in January, Ronald Gajraj, a former head of the national police commission, relieved the Prime Minister of the home affairs portfolio, following mounting concern at a recent sharp increase in violent crimes in the business community.

In February 1999 Hoyte, who had alleged that the PPP/ CIVIC alliance was not interested in achieving a lasting political solution, announced that the PNC was to withdraw from discussions and was to resume public protests. In response, President Jagan warned that she would not 'succumb to unreasonableness and uncompromising stances'. In March, however, Maurice King, the facilitator appointed by CARICOM, announced that Hoyte and Jagan had agreed to meet privately, and in May the parties agreed to resume dialogue.

In April 1999 the Constitutional Reform Commission began public consultations. The PPP/CIVIC alliance submitted proposals suggesting that the country should be renamed the Republic of Guyana, and that the President should be limited to two consecutive terms of office. The PPP/CIVIC also proposed the deletion of the clause in the Constitution whereby the President is empowered to dissolve the National Assembly should he/she be censured by the Assembly. These proposals were subsequently adopted in the report published by the Commission in July. The Commission further proposed that the President should no longer have the power to dismiss a public officer in the public interest, and the President and Cabinet should be collectively responsible to the National Assembly and should resign if defeated in a vote of 'no confidence'.

In late April 1999 the Guyana Public Service Union (GPSU) called a general strike after the Government had offered a pay rise of between 3% and 4.5% in response to the union's demand for an increase of at least 40%. Other public-sector unions later joined the GPSU in taking industrial action, and much of the country was paralysed. Tension was exacerbated following the serving of legal summonses to three prominent union leaders for having organized protest marches in defiance of a government ban, while in mid-May the police opened fire (with pellet guns) on an allegedly violent crowd of strikers, injuring 17 people. After 56 days of industrial action, an agreement was finally reached between the unions and the authorities in late June, which granted public-sector workers an interim pay rise of 4.6% prior to the full settlement of their claim by an arbitration tribunal. Many members of the GPSU were reported to be dissatisfied with the agreement, and the headquarters of the union were subsequently attacked, while the Minister for Public Service, George Fung-On, was assaulted in his car. In September the arbitration tribunal awarded public-sector workers an increase of 31.6% in 1999 and 26.7% in 2000. The Government, however, announced that it would only be bound by the tribunal's findings if it could be proved that the tribunal had followed the correct procedures, and it also warned the unions that the cost of the pay rises might necessitate redundancies.

In early August 1999 President Jagan announced her retirement on the grounds of ill health. Jagan was replaced as President by the erstwhile Minister of Finance, Bharrat Jagdeo. The appointment of Jagdeo, whose relative youth (he was 35 years of age at the time of his appointment), reported willingness to reach across the political divide, and strong background in economics all contributed to his popularity, was widely welcomed in Guyana and by the international community. Jagdeo, who announced that he was to continue the largely market-orientated policies of the Jagan administration, reappointed Samuel Hinds as Prime Minister (Hinds had earlier resigned in accordance with the requirements of the Constitution), and announced that there was to be no cabinet reorganization in the immediate future. There was, however, controversy at the absence of Hoyte and other PNC representatives from the President's inauguration ceremony; Hoyte, who had refused to recognize Jagan as President, was reported to have declined to recognize any successor nominated by her. In late November Saisnarine Kowlessar, the head of the University of Guyana's Department of Management, was appointed Minister in the Office of the President with responsibility for Finance, a portfolio previously held by the President. The President also appointed Geoffrey Da Silva as the new Minister of Trade, Industry and Tourism, replacing Michael Shree Chan, who had retired on the grounds of ill health.

In December 1999 the National Assembly approved the establishment of a committee to supervise the revision of the Constitution prior to the legislative elections scheduled for mid-January 2001. Two 'task forces' were also established by the National Assembly; one was to deal with electoral reform and the other was to establish an Ethnic Relations Commission. In

June 2000 a political consensus was reached on the proposed electoral reform. In the following month, the National Assembly approved legislation making the electoral reform task force a permanent institution (to be known as the Guyana Elections Commission—GECOM). In August legislation allowing for the creation of the Ethnic Relations Commission was passed (although it was not officially established until December). In October the legislature unanimously approved a constitutional amendment establishing a mixed system of proportional representation combining regional constituencies and national candidate lists. Also approved was the abolition of the Supreme Congress of the People of Guyana and the National Congress of Local Democratic Organs. On the same day Winslow Martin Zephyr was elected as the new Speaker of the National Assembly, following the death earlier in the month of Derek Jagan.

However, on 17 November 2000 GECOM announced that the elections that, according to the Herdmanston Agreement, were to be held on 17 January 2001, were to be postponed, owing to delays in the enactment of the proposed reform. A dispute had arisen between the Government and the PNC over the number of parliamentary seats that were to be allocated by region. (In early December a new election date of 19 March 2001 was announced.) GECOM proposed that an all-party committee would be established to decide who was to rule the country in January–March. The PPP/CIVIC alliance immediately declared its intention to continue to govern until March, while the opposition insisted that the Government should resign on 17 January and that an interim coalition Government should be formed. Nevertheless, in December all parties agreed to refer the matter to an all-party committee. The PPP/CIVIC was to remain in office, but agreed to limit its powers.

In mid-January 2001 a constitutional crisis arose when a high court judge, Claudette Singh, declared the December 1997 elections to be null and void: she ruled that the legislature had acted illegally in making the possession of a voter identification card a prerequisite for voting, and alleged that there had been instances of electoral fraud. However, later in the month she ruled that the Government should remain in office until the March ballot, although no legislation, other than that necessary for the election, should be passed. Temporary validity was granted to legislation passed after December 1997. GECOM and the PPP/CIVIC declared their intention to appeal against the ruling on voter cards.

The general and regional elections of 19 March 2001 were preceded by demonstrations over the late distribution of voter identification cards (despite the announcement, in mid-February, that voters would be allowed to use other forms of identification). The elections, which were contested by 11 political parties, were overseen by an international delegation led by former US President, Jimmy Carter. The PPP/CIVIC gained 53.0% of the votes cast. The party also obtained a majority in the National Assembly, with 34 seats; while the PNC (which contested the elections as the PNC/Reform) won 27 seats, the Guyana Action Party, in alliance with the WPA, gained two seats, while Rise, Organize and Rebuild Guyana Movement and TUF each secured one seat. Some 89.9% of the registered electorate participated. International observers declared the elections to be generally free and fair, and on 23 March Jagdeo was officially declared President-elect. However, the PNC/Reform alleged that there had been a number of breaches of electoral procedure and successfully obtained a High Court injunction postponing the presidential inauguration. In subsequent violent demonstrations three people were injured. In late March the Chief Justice refused a further request to stay the proceedings, and ordered an immediate declaration of the official results. On 31 March Bharrat Jagdeo was sworn in as President. A new Cabinet was announced in early April. Further protests greeted the reappointment of PPP member Roger Luncheon to head the civil service. Earlier in March Jagdeo and Hoyte, the PNC/Reform's leader and presidential candidate, had issued a joint statement pledging to co-operate on the drafting of a new constitution.

Guyana has border disputes with its neighbours, Venezuela and Suriname, although relations with Brazil have continued to improve through trade and military agreements. Suriname restored diplomatic representation in Guyana in 1979 and bilateral meetings were resumed at the end of the year. In 1983 relations improved further as a result of increased trade links between the countries. In late 1998 it was announced that a joint border commission, created to negotiate the settlement of a territorial dispute between Suriname and Guyana, was to be revived, after a two-year suspension. The two countries were also expected to conclude an agreement on fishing rights. However, in May 2000 Suriname formally claimed that Guyana had violated its territorial integrity by granting the concession to the Canadian-based company, CGX Energy Inc., to explore for petroleum and gas. In June the two countries initiated negotiations to settle the dispute.

In 1962 Venezuela renewed its claim to 130,000 sq km (50,000 sq miles) of land west of the Essequibo river (nearly two-thirds of Guyanese territory). The area was accorded to Guyana in 1899, on the decision of an international tribunal, but Venezuela based its claim on a papal bull of 1493, referring to Spanish colonial possessions. The Port of Spain Protocol of 1970 put the issue in abeyance until 1982. Guyana and Venezuela referred the dispute to the UN in 1983, and, after a series of UN efforts and a visit to Venezuela by President Hoyte, the two countries agreed to a mutually acceptable intermediary, suggested by the UN Secretary-General, in August 1989. In March 1999 Guyana and Venezuela established a joint commission, the High Level Binational Commission, which was intended to expedite the resolution of the territorial dispute and to promote mutual co-operation. However, in September the Venezuelan Government alleged that the Guyanese authorities had granted concessions to petroleum companies within the disputed areas, and in October President Chávez of Venezuela, speaking on the 100th anniversary of the international tribunal's decision, announced his Government's intention to reopen its claim to the territory. Reports of Venezuelan troop movements near the border area caused alarm in Guyana, but were described by the Venezuelan authorities as part of a campaign against drugs-traffickers. In December an agreement was reached between the two countries on co-operation in the fisheries sector. In January 2000 the Guyanese Government approved a donation of US \$100,000 to Venezuela to assist humanitarian efforts following the severe flooding in that country. Early in 2000 Guyana signed an agreement with the US-based Beal Aerospace Corpn to build the world's first private satellite-launching facility in the disputed territory of Essequibo. However, following objections by Venezuela and financial difficulties, the company abandoned the project. Nevertheless, in January 2001 Venezuela announced an oil exploration project in the same disputed zone.

During the early 1990s Hoyte committed Guyana to closer integration with the Caribbean Community and Common Market (CARICOM, see p. 142), and CARICOM played an active role in attempts to achieve a peace agreement between the PPP and PNC in the late 1990s. In 2000 President Jagdeo led negotiations on entry into the World Trade Organization (see p. 292).

Government

Under the 1980 Constitution, legislative power is held by the unicameral National Assembly, with 65 members: 53 elected for five years by universal adult suffrage, on the basis of proportional representation, and 12 regional representatives. In the elections of March 2001 the regional constituency lists were combined with the national candidate lists. Executive power is held by the President, who leads the majority party in the Assembly and holds office for its duration. The President appoints and heads a Cabinet, which includes the Prime Minister, and may include Ministers who are not elected members of the Assembly. The Cabinet is collectively responsible to the National Assembly. Guyana comprises 10 regions, each having a regional democratic council that returns a representative to the National Assembly.

Defence

In August 2000 the Combined Guyana Defence Force consisted of some 1,600 men (of whom 1,400 were in the army, 100 were in the air force and some 100 in the navy). One-third of the combined forces are civilian personnel. A paramilitary force, the People's Militia, totalled 1,500. Defence expenditure was budgeted at \$ G950m. for 2000.

Economic Affairs

According to estimates by the World Bank, in 1998 Guyana's gross national product (GNP), measured at average 1996–98 prices, was US \$661m., equivalent to \$780 per head (or \$3,139 per head on an international purchasing-power parity basis). During 1990–98, it was estimated, GNP per head increased, in real terms, at an average rate of 10.7% per year. Over the same period, the population increased at an average annual rate of 0.9%. Guyana's gross domestic product (GDP) increased, in real terms, by an average of 5.7% per year during 1989–99, and increased by an estimated 3.0% in 1999. GDP was estimated to have increased by 3.9% in 2000.

Agriculture (including forestry and fishing) provided an estimated 41.7% of GDP in 1999, according to preliminary figures, and employed an estimated 18.7% of the economically active population in 1998. The principal cash crops are sugar cane (sugar providing an estimated 27.0% of the value of total domestic exports in 1999, although this figure fell slightly in 2000) and rice (14.1% in 1999). The sugar industry alone accounted for an estimated 15.8% of GDP in 1999, and, it was estimated, employed about 24,000 people at peak season. Sugar production levels in 1999 were the highest since 1978. Vegetables and fruit are cultivated for the local market, and livestock-rearing is being developed. Fishing (particularly for shrimp) is also important, and accounted for an estimated 6.2% of GDP in 1999. In the late 1990s the Government initiated a project to develop a sustainable fishing industry. Agricultural production increased at an average annual rate of 5.7% during 1989–99. Agricultural GDP declined, in real terms, by 6.5% in 1998, but increased by an estimated 13.4% in 1999.

Timber resources in Guyana are extensive and underdeveloped. According to FAO estimates, some 77% of the country's total land area consisted of forest and woodland in 1994. In 1999 timber shipments provided an estimated 7.4% of total domestic exports, compared with 2.4% in the previous year. Although foreign investment in Guyana's largely undeveloped interior continues to be encouraged by the Government, there is much popular concern at the extent of the exploitation of the rainforest. Timber production, which increased rapidly in the early and mid-1990s, declined by 24% in 1998, owing to the economic crisis in East Asia. However the forestry sector recovered in the following year.

Industry (including mining, manufacturing and construction) provided an estimated 21.9% of GDP in 1999, and engaged 24.0% of the employed labour force at the time of the 1980 census. Industrial GDP increased at an average annual rate of 9.4% in 1989–99. Industrial GDP decreased, in real terms, by 0.9% in 1998 and by an estimated 1.5% in 1999.

Mining contributed an estimated 13.6% of GDP in 1999, and employed 4.8% of the total working population in 1980. Bauxite, which is used for the manufacture of aluminium, is one of Guyana's most valuable exports, and accounted for an estimated 15.3% of total domestic exports in 1999, although this figure fell slightly in 2000. The registered production of gold (accounting for an estimated 21.5% of domestic exports in 1999) increased considerably during the late 1980s and 1990s, reaching a peak in production in 1998. However, owing to high production costs and poor ore quality, productivity declined in 1999 and 2000, although gold exports increased significantly in the later year. In 2000 the gold industry was estimated to directly employ some 32,000 people. There are also significant diamond resources and some petroleum reserves. In 2000 Mazaruni Granite Products Ltd initiated a US \$34m. development and modernization programme of granite production. The GDP of the mining sector was estimated to have increased by an average of 7.3% per year in 1990–99. The sector's GDP increased, in real terms, by 2.7% in 1998 and by 8.4% in 1999. In 2000 a seven-year programme was initiated to develop and regenerate one of the principal bauxite mining towns, Linden, through the promotion of non-bauxite enterprises.

Manufacturing accounted for an estimated 3.6% of GDP in 1999, and, according to the 1980 census, employed 14.4% of the total working population. The main activities are the processing of bauxite, sugar, rice and timber. Manufacturing GDP increased at an average annual rate of 11.5% in 1989–99. Manufacturing GDP decreased by 8.6% in 1998, but increased by an estimated 13.0% in 1999.

Energy requirements are almost entirely met by imported hydrocarbon fuels. In 1999, according to preliminary figures, fuels and lubricants constituted 16.1% of the total value of imports (mainly from Venezuela and Trinidad and Tobago).

The services sector contributed an estimated 36.4% of GDP in 1999, and engaged 43.2% of the employed labour force in 1980. The GDP of the services sector increased by an average of 3.5% per year in 1989–99. Services GDP increased, in real terms, by 1.3% in 1998, but decreased by an estimated 0.8% in 1999.

In 1999 Guyana recorded a visible trade deficit of US $25.2m. and a deficit of US $75.2m. on the current account of the balance of payments. In 1998 the principal source of imports was the USA (26.6%). Trinidad and Tobago and the United Kingdom are other important suppliers of imports. In 1998 Canada was the principal market for exports (26.9% of total exports); the United Kingdom, Trinidad and Tobago and the Netherlands are also significant recipients. The principal exports are sugar, gold, bauxite and rice, and the principal imports are capital goods and consumer goods.

In 1999 the overall budget deficit was an estimated $ G2,791m. (equivalent to 2.6% of GDP). According to World Bank estimates, by the end of 1999 Guyana's external debt totalled US $1,688m. The cost of debt-servicing in 1999 was US $106m. Urban consumer prices increased by 4.6% in 1998 and by 7.5% in 1999. In 2000 the annual rate of inflation was an estimated 6.1%. An estimated 12% of the labour force were unemployed in 1992.

Guyana is a founder member of CARICOM (see p. 142). It is also a member of the UN Economic Commission for Latin America and the Caribbean (ECLAC, see p. 30) and of the International Sugar Organization (see p. 305).

In 1988, in response to serious economic decline, the Government introduced an extensive recovery programme of adjustment measures and structural reforms, Funds were made available under two Enhanced Structural Adjustment Facilities (ESAF), approved by the IMF in 1990 and in 1994. In 1996 negotiations with the 'Paris Club' of creditor nations and Trinidad and Tobago resulted in the cancellation of 67% of Guyana's bilateral debt with five creditor nations (a total reduction of US $395m.). In 1998, however, Guyana was severely affected by a substantial period of drought, resulting from aberrant climatic conditions (associated with the periodic warming of the tropical Pacific Ocean, known as El Niño), which undermined the production of export crops, thus diminishing foreign exchange earnings and exacerbating the economic difficulties arising from a decline in world gold prices. As a consequence, real GDP in 1998 declined by 1.5%, while the rate of inflation in that year increased to 4.6%. In July 1998 the Government secured a new three-year ESAF with the IMF, and in May 1999 the IMF and the World Bank declared that Guyana had become eligible for some US $410m. in nominal debt-service relief under the Initiative for Highly Indebted Poor Countries (HIPC Initiative). It was hoped that the estimated 24% reduction in the external debt burden would permit increased budgetary spending on education and social welfare. However, following industrial action by public-sector workers in mid-1999 (see Recent History), the Government was obliged to grant salary increases of 26.6%, effective from January 2000, thereby reducing the funds available for development expenditure; the decision was criticized by the IMF. In an attempt to stimulate development, the first Jagdeo administration sought to attract foreign investment in Guyana and to restore investor confidence, damaged by the political and social unrest of the late 1990s. However, in 2000 the country faced falling prices for its export commodities and rising prices for its imports. Nevertheless, economic growth of 3.5% was forecast for 2001.

Social Welfare

Health services are provided by the Government, partly through the National Insurance Scheme, by non-governmental organiza-tions, by the private sector, and by state-owned companies for their work force. The 1994 version of the National Health Plan identified as a priority the control of malaria, acute respiratory infections and sexually transmitted diseases, while the National Development Strategy of 1997 emphasized health promotion and improved access to health services, in particular for geographically isolated Amerindian communities. In 1998, according to IMF estimates, there was one hospital bed per 236 inhabitants. In 1997 there were 18.1 physicians per 100,000 inhabitants and 84.2 nurses per 100,000 inhabitants. In 1997, as well as the Georgetown Public Hospital, the Government operated three specialist hospitals, four regional hospitals, 18 district hospitals, 39 health posts and 194 health centres. In addition, there were six private hospitals and five company hospitals. In 1996 the Government spent $ G2.88m. on health, equivalent to 6.3% of the national budget.

Education

Education is officially compulsory, and is provided free of charge, for eight years between six and 14 years of age. Primary education begins at six years of age and lasts for at least six years. Secondary education, beginning at 12 years of age, lasts for up to five years, comprising a first cycle of three years and a second cycle of two years. Gross primary enrolment in 1997 was equivalent to an estimated 92.8% of children in the relevant age-group (boys 92.6%; girls 93.0%). Gross secondary enrolment in that year was equivalent to an estimated 74.9% of children in the relevant age-group (boys 73.4%; girls 76.4%). There are also 14 technical, vocational, special and higher educational institutions. These include the University of Guyana in Georgetown and a teacher training college. In 1998, according to estimates by the UNDP, the average rate of adult illiteracy was only 1.8% (males 1.2%; females 2.3%), one of the lowest in the Western hemisphere. Expenditure on education by the central Government in 1996 was estimated at $ G4,590m., and represented 10.0% of total government expenditure in that year.

Public Holidays

2001: 1 January (New Year's Day), 23 February (Mashramani, Republic Day), 6 March (Id al-Adha, feast of the Sacrifice*), 13 April (Good Friday), 16 April (Easter Monday), 1 May (Labour Day), 5 May (Indian Heritage Day), 4 June (Yum an-Nabi, birth of the Prophet*), 2 July (Caribbean Day), 6 August (Freedom Day), 17 December (Id al-Fitr, end of Ramadan*), 25–26 December (Christmas).

2002: 1 January (New Year's Day), 23 February (Mashramani, Republic Day, and Id al-Adha, feast of the Sacrifice*), 29 March (Good Friday), 1 April (Easter Monday), 1 May (Labour Day), 5 May (Indian Heritage Day), 24 May (Yum an-Nabi, birth of the Prophet*), 1 July (Caribbean Day), 5 August (Freedom Day), 6 December (Id al-Fitr, end of Ramadan*), 25–26 December (Christmas).

* These holidays are dependent on the Islamic lunar calendar and may vary by one or two days from the dates given.

In addition, the Hindu festivals of Holi Phagwah (usually in March) and Divali (October or November) are celebrated. These festivals are dependent on sightings of the moon and their precise date is not known until two months before they take place.

Weights and Measures

The metric system has been introduced.

Statistical Survey

Source (unless otherwise stated): Bank of Guyana, 1 Church St and Ave of the Republic, POB 1003, Georgetown; tel. 226-3261; fax 227-2965; e-mail communications@bankofguyana.org.gy; internet www.bankofguyana.org.gy.

AREA AND POPULATION

Area: 214,969 sq km (83,000 sq miles).

Population: 758,619 (males 375,481, females 382,778) at census of 12 May 1980; 701,704 (males 344,928, females 356,776) at census of 12 May 1991; 782,000 in 1999 (official estimate).

Density (1999): 3.6 per sq km.

Ethnic Groups (official estimates, 1999): 'East' Indians 51%, Africans 41%, Portuguese and Chinese 2%, Amerindians 6%, Others less than 1%.

Regions (estimated population, 1986): Barima–Waini 18,500; Pomeroon–Supenaam 42,000; Essequibo Islands–West Demerara 102,800; Demerara–Mahaica 310,800; Mahaica–Berbice 55,600; East Berbice–Corentyne 149,000; Cuyuni–Mazaruni 17,900; Potaro–Siparuni 5,700; Upper Takutu–Upper Essequibo 15,300; Upper Demerara–Berbice 38,600.

Births and Deaths (official estimates): Birth rate 24.9 per 1,000 in 1995–2000, 17.9 per 1,000 in 2000; Crude death rate 7.4 per 1,000 in 1995–2000, 8.4 per 1,000 in 2000.

Expectation of Life (official estimates, years at birth, 2000): 64.1 (males 61.1; females 67.2).

Economically Active Population (persons between 15 and 65 years of age, 1980 census): Agriculture, forestry and fishing 48,603; Mining and quarrying 9,389; Manufacturing 27,939; Electricity, gas and water 2,772; Construction 6,574; Trade, restaurants and hotels 14,690; Transport, storage and communications 9,160; Financing, insurance, real estate and business services 2,878; Community, social and personal services 57,416; Activities not adequately defined 15,260; Total employed 194,681 (males 153,645; females 41,036); Unemployed 44,650 (males 26,439, females 18,211); Total labour force 239,331 (males 180,084, females 59,247). *Mid-1998* (estimates): Agriculture, etc. 68,000; Total labour force 364,000 (Source: FAO, *Production Yearbook*).

AGRICULTURE, ETC.

Principal Crops (FAO estimates, '000 metric tons, 1999): Rice (paddy) 600 (unofficial figure); Maize 3; Roots and tubers 42; Coconuts 56; Sugar cane 3,000 (unofficial figure) Pulses 2; Vegetables 7; Oranges 3; Bananas 11; Plantains 14. Source: FAO.

Livestock (FAO estimates, '000 head, year ending September 1999): Cattle 220; Pigs 20; Sheep 130; Goats 79; Chickens 11,600. Source: FAO.

Livestock Products (FAO estimates, '000 metric tons, 1999): Beef and veal 3; Mutton and lamb 1; Pig meat 1; Poultry meat 12; Cows' milk 13; Hen eggs 7. Source: FAO.

Forestry ('000 cubic metres, 1998): Roundwood removals: Sawlogs, veneer logs and logs for sleepers 410, Pulpwood 2, Other industrial wood 19, Fuel wood 11, Total 442; Sawnwood production: Total 57. Source: FAO, *Yearbook of Forest Products*.

Fishing ('000 metric tons, live weight, 1998): Capture 57.0 (Marine fishes 38.3, Atlantic seabob 17.2); Aquaculture 0.2 (FAO estimate); Total catch 57.2. Source: FAO, *Yearbook of Fishery Statistics*.

MINING

Production (preliminary figures, 1999): Bauxite 2,215,281 metric tons; Gold 414,905 troy oz.

INDUSTRY

Selected Products (preliminary figures, 1996): Raw sugar 257,000 metric tons; Rum 237,000 hectolitres; Beer 112,000 hectolitres; Cigarettes 400.2m.; Electric energy 328m. kWh. Sources: UN, *Industrial Commodity Statistics Yearbook*; IMF, *Guyana: Statistical Appendix* (February 1998).

FINANCE

Currency and Exchange Rates: 100 cents = 1 Guyana dollar ($ G). *Sterling, US Dollar and Euro Equivalents* (30 November 2000): £1 sterling = $ G262.51; US $1 = $ G184.75; €1 = $ G160.44; $ G1,000 = £3.809 = US $5.413 = €6.233. *Average Exchange Rate:* ($ G per US $): 142.4 in 1997; 150.5 in 1998; 178.0 in 1999.

Budget (estimates, $ G million, 1999): *Revenue:* Tax revenue 33,647 (Income tax 13,618, Property tax 607, Consumption tax 12,297, Taxes on international trade 4,590, Other tax 2,535); Other current revenue 2,388; Total 36,033, excl. grants received (5,320). *Expendi-*

ture: Current expenditure 32,922 (Personnel emoluments 11,821, Other goods and services 6,215, Interest 9,455, Transfers 5,430); Capital expenditure 11,222; Total (incl. lending minus repayments) 44,144. Source: IMF, *Guyana: Statistical Annex* (January 2001).

International Reserves (US $ million at 31 December 1999): IMF special drawing rights 1.27, Foreign exchange 276.01; Total 277.28. Source: IMF, *International Financial Statistics*.

Money Supply ($ G million at 31 December 1999): Currency outside banks 13,394, Demand deposits at commercial banks 9,949; Total money (including also private-sector deposits at the Bank of Guyana) 23,350. Source: IMF, *International Financial Statistics*.

Cost of Living (Urban Consumer Price Index; base: 1995 = 100): 110.9 in 1997; 116.0 in 1998; 124.7 in 1999. Source: IMF, *International Financial Statistics*.

Expenditure on the Gross Domestic Product (estimates, $ G million at current prices, 1998): Government final consumption expenditure 19,114; Private final consumption expenditure 70,843; Gross fixed capital formation 31,144; *Total domestic expenditure* 121,101; Exports of goods and services 103,920; *Less* Imports of goods and services, 116,557; *GDP in purchasers' values* 108,465. Source: IMF, *Guyana: Recent Economic Developments* (June 1999).

Gross Domestic Product by Economic Activity (estimates, $ G million at current factor cost, 1999): Agriculture (incl. forestry and fishing) 42,536; Mining and quarrying 13,923; Manufacturing (incl. power) 3,681; Construction 4,771; Distribution 4,268; Transport and communication 7,138; Rented dwellings 3,848; Financial services 3,387; Other services 1,570; Government 16,976; GDP at factor cost 102,098; Indirect taxes, *less* subsidies 18,570; GDP at market prices 120,668.

Balance of Payments (US $ million, 1999): Exports of goods f.o.b. 525.0; Imports of goods c.i.f. –550.2; *Trade balance* –25.2; Exports of services (net) –31.1; *Balance on goods and services* –56.3; Other income received (net) –57.9; *Balance on goods, services and income* –114.2; Current transfers received (net) 39.0; *Current balance –* 75.2; Capital transfer 15.5; Government long-term capital (net) 34.9; Private long-term capital (net) 48.0; Short-term capital (net) –27.0; Net errors and omissions –0.6; *Overall balance* –4.4.

EXTERNAL TRADE

Principal Commodities (preliminary figures, US $ million, 1999): *Imports c.i.f.*: Capital goods 135.5; Consumer goods 174.9; Fuel and lubricants 88.5; Other intermediate goods 151.0; Total (incl. others) 550.2. *Exports f.o.b.*: Bauxite 77.2; Sugar 136.2; Rice 71.1; Gold 108.7; Shrimps 29.2; Timber 37.3, Total (incl. others, excl. re-exports) 504.7.

Principal Trading Partners (estimates, US $ million, 1998): *Imports:* Cuba 17; Netherlands 12; Trinidad and Tobago 121; United Kingdom 43; USA 160; Total (incl. others) 601. *Exports:* Canada 141; Netherlands 13; Trinidad and Tobago 14; United Kingdom 108; Total (incl. others) 525.

TRANSPORT

Road Traffic ('000 vehicles in use, 1993): Passenger cars 24.0; Commercial vehicles 9.0. Source: UN, *Statistical Yearbook*.

Shipping (international sea-borne freight traffic, estimates in '000 metric tons, 1990): Goods loaded 1,730; Goods unloaded 673. Source: UN, *Monthly Bulletin of Statistics. Merchant Fleet* (at 31 December 1998): Vessels 62; Displacement 16,260 grt. Source: Lloyd's Register of Shipping, *World Fleet Statistics*.

Civil Aviation (traffic on scheduled services, 1997): Kilometres flown (million) 3; passengers carried ('000) 126; passenger-km (million) 248; total ton-km (million) 26. Source: UN, *Statistical Yearbook*.

TOURISM

Visitor Arrivals ('000): 102.0 in 1996; 93.0 in 1997; 80.0 in 1998.

Tourist Receipts (US $ million): 46 in 1996; 39 in 1997; 60 in 1998. Source: World Bank, *World Development Indicators*.

COMMUNICATIONS MEDIA

Radio Receivers (1997): 420,000 in use*.

Television Receivers (1997): 46,000 in use*.

Telephones (1997): 55,000 main lines in use†.

Telefax Stations (1990): 195 in use†.

Mobile Cellular Telephones (1997): 1,400 subscribers†.

Daily Newspapers (1996): 2; estimated circulation 42,000*.

Non-daily Newspapers (1988): 6 (estimate); estimated circulation 84,000*.

Book Production (school textbooks, 1996): 1 title.

* Source: UNESCO, *Statistical Yearbook*.
† Source: UN, *Statistical Yearbook*.

EDUCATION

Pre-primary (1997/98): Institutions 305; Teachers 1,976; Students 33,366.

Primary (1997/98): Institutions 418; Teachers 3,710; Students 100,998.

General Secondary (1997/98): Institutions 416; Teachers 3,028; Students 61,253.

Special Education (1997/98): Institutions 6; Teachers 28; Students 585.

Technical and Vocational (1997/98): Institutions 6; Teachers 168; Students 3,307.

Teacher Training (1997/98): Institutions 1; Teachers 70; Students 1,235.

University (1997/98): Institutions 1; Teachers 383; Students 4,671.

Private Education (1997/98): Institutions 5; Teachers 138; Students 1,590.

Source: Ministry of Education, Georgetown.

Directory

The Constitution*

Guyana became a republic, within the Commonwealth, on 23 February 1970. A new Constitution was promulgated on 6 October 1980. Its main provisions are summarized below:

The Constitution declares the Co-operative Republic of Guyana to be an indivisible, secular, democratic sovereign state in the course of transition from capitalism to socialism. The bases of the political, economic and social system are political and economic independence, involvement of citizens and socio-economic groups, such as co-operatives and trade unions, in the decision-making processes of the State and in management, social ownership of the means of production, national economic planning and co-operativism as the principle of socialist transformation. Personal property, inheritance, the right to work, with equal pay for men and women engaged in equal work, free medical attention, free education and social benefits for old age and disability are guaranteed. Individual political rights are subject to the principles of national sovereignty and democracy, and freedom of expression to the State's duty to ensure fairness and balance in the dissemination of information to the public. Relations with other countries are guided by respect for human rights, territorial integrity and non-intervention.

THE PRESIDENT

The President is the supreme executive authority, Head of State and Commander-in-Chief of the armed forces, elected for a term of office, usually of five years' duration, with no limit on re-election. The successful presidential candidate is the nominee of the party with the largest number of votes in the legislative elections. The President may prorogue or dissolve the National Assembly (in the case of dissolution, fresh elections must be held immediately) and has discretionary powers to postpone elections for up to one year at a time for up to five years. The President may be removed from office on medical grounds, or for violation of the Constitution (with a two-thirds' majority vote of the Assembly), or for gross misconduct (with a three-quarters' majority vote of the Assembly if allegations are upheld by a tribunal).

The President appoints a First Vice-President and Prime Minister who must be an elected member of the National Assembly, and a Cabinet of Ministers, which may include non-elected members and is collectively responsible to the legislature. The President also appoints a Leader of the Opposition, who is the elected member of the Assembly deemed by the President most able to command the support of the opposition.

THE LEGISLATURE

The legislative body is a unicameral National Assembly of 65 members; 53 members are elected by universal adult suffrage in a system of proportional representation, 10 members are elected by the 10 Regional Democratic Councils and two members are elected by the National Congress of Local Democratic Organs. The Assembly passes bills, which are then presented to the President, and may pass constitutional amendments.

LOCAL GOVERNMENT

Guyana is divided into 10 Regions, each having a Regional Democratic Council elected for a term of up to five years and four months, although it may be prematurely dissolved by the President. Local councillors elect from among themselves deputies to the National Congress of Democratic Organs. This Congress and the National Assembly together form the Supreme Congress of the People of Guyana, a deliberative body which may be summoned, dissolved or prorogued by the President and is automatically dissolved along with the National Assembly.

OTHER PROVISIONS

Impartial commissions exist for the judiciary, the public service and the police service. An Ombudsman is appointed, after consultation between the President and the Leader of the Opposition, to hold office for four years.

* In October 2000 several amendments to the Constitution were approved by the National Assembly. These included the introduction of a mixed system of proportional representation, combining regional constituencies and national candidate lists, and the abolition of the Supreme Congress of the People of Guyana and of the National Congress of Local Democratic Organs. In January 2001 the High Court ruled that the 1997 election of the legislature was null and void. However, it granted temporary validity to legislation passed after December 1997.

The Government

HEAD OF STATE

President: BHARRAT JAGDEO (sworn in 11 August 1999; re-elected 19 March 2001).

CABINET
(May 2001)

Prime Minister: SAMUEL A. HINDS.

Minister of Agriculture: NAVIN CHANDARPAL.

Minister of Amerindian Affairs: CAROLYN RODRIGUES.

Minister of Culture, Youth and Sports: GAIL TEIXEIRA.

Minister of Education: Dr HENRY JEFFREY.

Minister of Finance: SAISNARINE KOWLESSAR.

Minister of Fisheries, Crops and Livestock: SATYADEOW SAWH.

Minister of Foreign Affairs: RUDY INSANALLY.

Minister of Foreign Trade in the Ministry of Foreign Affairs: CLEMENT ROHEE.

Minister of Health: Dr LESLIE RAMSAMMY.

Minister of Home Affairs: RONALD GAJRAJ.

Minister of Housing and Water: SHAIK BAKSH.

Minister of Human Services, Social Security and Labour: Dr DALE BISNAUTH.

Minister in the Ministry of Human Services, Social Security and Labour: BIBI SHADICK.

Minister of Information: BHARRAT JAGDEO.

Minister of Local Government: HARRY PERSAUD NOKTA.

Minister in the Ministry of Local Government: CLINTON COLLYMORE.

Minister of Parliamentary Affairs in the Office of the President: REEPU DAMAN PERSAUD.

Minister of Planning and Economic Development: (vacant).

Minister of Public Service Management: Dr JENNIFER WESTFORD.

Minister of Tourism and Industry: (vacant).

Minister of Transport and Hydraulics: CARL ANTHONY XAVIER.

Attorney-General: (vacant).

Secretary to the Cabinet: Dr ROGER LUNCHEON.

MINISTRIES

Office of the President: New Garden St and South Rd, Georgetown; tel. 225-1330; fax 226-3395.

Office of the Prime Minister: Wights Lane, Georgetown; tel. 227-3101; fax 226-7563.

Office of Amerindian Affairs: see Ministry of Public Works and Communications.

Ministry of Agriculture: POB 1001, Regent and Vlissingen Rds, Georgetown; tel. 227-5527; fax 227-3638; e-mail guyagri@hotmail.com; internet www.sdnp.org.gy/minagri.

Ministry of Culture, Youth and Sports: 71 Main St, North Cummingsburg; tel. 226-0142; fax 226-5067.

Ministry of Education: 26 Brickdam, Stabroek, POB 1014, Georgetown; tel. 226-3094; fax 225-8511; internet www.sdnp.org.gy/minedu.

Ministry of Finance: Main and Urquhart Sts, Georgetown; tel. 227-1114; fax 226-1284.

Ministry of Fisheries, Crops and Livestock: Regent and Vlissengen Rds, Georgetown; tel. 225-8310; fax 227-2928; e-mail minfcl@sdnp.org.gy; internet www.sdnp.org.gy/minagri.

Ministry of Foreign Affairs: Takuba Lodge, 254 South Rd and New Garden St, Georgetown; tel. 226-1606; fax 225-9192; e-mail minfor@sdnp.org.gy; internet www.minfor.gov.gy.

Ministry of Health: Brickdam, Stabroek, Georgetown; tel. 226-1560; fax 225-6958; internet www.sdnp.org.gy/moh.

Ministry of Home Affairs: 6 Brickdam, Stabroek, Georgetown; tel. 225-7270; fax 226-2740.

Ministry of Housing and Water: Homestretch Ave, Durban Park; tel. 225-4991.

Ministry of Human Services, Social Security and Labour: 1 Water and Cornhill Sts, Stabroek, Georgetown; tel. 225-7073; fax 227-1308; e-mail nrdocgd@sdnp.org.gy; internet www.sdnp.org.gy/mohss.

Ministry of Information: Area B, Homestretch Ave, Durban Park, Georgetown; tel. 227-1101; fax 226-4003; internet www.sdnp .org.gy/mininfo.

Ministry of Legal Affairs and Office of Attorney-General: 95 Carmichael St, Georgetown; tel. 225-3607; fax 225-0732.

Ministry of Local Government: De Winkle Bldgs, Fort St, Kingston, Georgetown; tel. 225-8621.

Ministry of Planning and Economic Development: Georgetown.

Ministry of Public Service Management: Wight's Lane, Kingston, Georgetown; tel. 227-2365; fax 225-6954.

Ministry of Tourism and Industry: 229 South Rd, Lacytown, Georgetown; tel. 226-2505; fax 225-4310; e-mail mtti@sdnp.org.gy; internet www.sdnp.org.gy/mtti.

Ministry of Transport and Hydraulics: Georgetown.

President and Legislature

NATIONAL ASSEMBLY

Speaker: WINSLOW MARTIN ZEPHYR.

Election, 19 March 2001

Party	No. of seats		
	Regional	National	Total
People's Progressive Party/ CIVIC (PPP/CIVIC) . . .	11	23	34
People's National Congress/ Reform (PNC/Reform) . .	13	14	27
Guyana Action Party/Working People's Alliance (GAP/WPA)	1	1	2
Rise, Organize and Rebuild Guyana Movement (ROAR) .	—	1	1
The United Force (TUF) . .	—	1	1
Total	**25**	**40**	**65**

Under Guyana's system of proportional representation, the nominated candidate of the party receiving the most number of votes was elected to the presidency. Thus, on 23 March the candidate of the PPP/CIVIC alliance, BHARRAT JAGDEO, was declared President-elect, defeating HUGH DESMOND HOYTE of the PNC/Reform alliance. JAGDEO was inaugurated as President on 31 March.

Political Organizations

CIVIC: New Garden St, Georgetown; social/political movement of businessmen and professionals; allied to PPP; Leader SAMUEL ARCHIBALD ANTHONY HINDS.

God Bless Guyana (GBG): Georgetown; Leader HARDAT SINGH.

Guyana Action Party (GAP): Georgetown; allied to WPA; Leader PAUL HARDY.

Guyana Democratic Party (GDP): Georgetown; f. 1996; Leaders ASGAR ALLY, NANDA K. GOPAUL.

Guyana Labour Party (GLP): Georgetown; f. 1992 by members of Guyanese Action for Reform and Democracy.

Guyana National Congress (GNC): Georgetown.

Guyana People's Party (GPP): Georgetown; f. 1996; Leader MAX MOHAMED.

Guyana Republican Party (GRP): Paprika East Bank, Essequibo; f. 1985; right-wing; Leader LESLIE PRINCE (resident in the USA).

Guyana's Alliance for Progress: 199 Charlotte Street, Georgetown; tel. 227-8845; e-mail guyanasalliance@yahoo.com; internet guyanese.webjump.com.

Horizon and Star (HAS): Georgetown.

Jutice For All Party (JFAP): 73 Robb and Wellington Sts, Lacytown, Georgetown; tel. 226-5462; fax 227-3050; e-mail sharma@ guyana.net.gy; internet www.jfa-gy.com; Leader CHANDRANARINE SHARMA.

National Democratic Front (NDF): Georgetown; Leader JOSEPH BACCHUS.

National Front Alliance: Georgetown.

National Independence Party: Georgetown; Leader SAPHIER HUSSIEN.

National Republican Party (NRP): Georgetown; f. 1990 after a split with URP; right-wing; Leader ROBERT GANGADEEN.

Patriotic Coalition for Democracy (PCD): Georgetown; f. 1986 by five opposition parties; the PCD campaigns for an end to alleged

electoral malpractices; principal offices, including the chair of the collective leadership, rotate among the parties; now comprises the following three parties:

Democratic Labour Movement (DLM): 34 Robb and King Sts, 4th Floor, Lacytown, POB 10930, Georgetown; f. 1983; democratic-nationalist; Pres. PAUL NEHRU TENNASSEE.

People's Democratic Movement (PDM): Stabroek House, 10 Croal St, Georgetown; tel. 226-4707; fax 226-3002; f. 1973; centrist; Leader LLEWELLYN JOHN.

People's Progressive Party (PPP): Freedom House, 41 Robb St, Lacytown, Georgetown; tel. 227-2095; fax 227-2096; e-mail ppp@ guyana.net.gy; internet www.pppcivic.org; f. 1950; Marxist-Leninist; allied to CIVIC; Leader JANET JAGAN; Gen. Sec. DONALD RAMOTAR.

People's National Congress/Reform (PNC/Reform): Congress Place, Sophia, POB 10330, Georgetown; tel. 225-7852; fax 225-6055; e-mail pnc@guyana-pnc.org; internet www.guyana-pnc.org; f. 1955 after a split with the PPP; Reform wing established in 2000; PNC Leader HUGH DESMOND HOYTE; PNC Chair ROBERT CORBIN; Reform Leader STANLEY MING; Reform Chair. JEROME KHAN.

People's Republic Party: POB 10162, Georgetown; e-mail info@ peoplesrepublicparty.com; internet www.mins.net/prp; Chair HARRY DAS.

People's Unity Party of Guyana (PUP): POB 10-1223, Georgetown; e-mail peter@ramsaroop.com; internet www. peoplesunityparty.com; f. 1999; Leader PETER R. RAMSAROOP.

Rise, Organize and Rebuild Guyana Movement (ROAR): 186 Parafield, Leonora, West Coast Demerara, POB 101409, Georgetown; tel. 068-2452; e-mail guyroar@hotmail.com; internet www .jaiag.com; f. 1999.

The United Force (TUF): 95 Robb and New Garden Sts, Bourda, Georgetown; tel. 226-2596; fax 225-2973; e-mail manzoornadir@ yahoo.com; internet tuf.homestead.com/index.htm; f. 1960; right-wing; advocates rapid industrialization through govt partnership and private capital; Leader MANZOOR NADIR.

United People's Party: 77 Winter Place, Brickdam, Georgetown; tel. 227-5217; fax 227-5166; e-mail unitedguyana@yahoo.com; internet upp.webjump.com.

United Republican Party (URP): Georgetown; f. 1985; right-wing; advocates federal govt; Leader Dr LESLIE RAMSAMMY.

United Workers' Party (UWP): Georgetown; f. 1991; Leader WINSTON PAYNE.

Working People's Alliance (WPA): Walter Rodney House, Lot 80, Croal St, Stabroek, Georgetown; tel. 225-6624; internet www.saxakali.com/wpa; originally popular pressure group, became political party 1979; independent Marxist; allied to GAP; Collective Leadership: EUSI KWAYANA, Dr CLIVE THOMAS, Dr RUPERT ROOPNARINE, WAZIR MOHAMED.

Diplomatic Representation

EMBASSIES AND HIGH COMMISSIONS IN GUYANA

Brazil: 308 Church St, Queenstown, POB 10489, Georgetown; tel. 225-7970; fax 226-9063; e-mail bragetown@solutions2000.net; Ambassador: CLAUDIO LYRA.

Canada: High and Young Sts, POB 10880, Georgetown; tel. 227-2081; fax 225-8380; e-mail grgtn@dfait-maecl.gc.ca; High Commissioner: JACQUES CRÊTE.

China, People's Republic: 108 Duke St, Kingston, Georgetown; tel. 227-1651; Ambassador: WANG FUYUAN.

Colombia: 306 Church and Peter Rose Sts, Queenstown, POB 10185, Georgetown; tel. 227-1410; fax 225-8198; e-mail embcolguy@ solutions2000.net; Ambassador: Dr LUIS GUILLERMO MARTÍNEZ FERNÁNDEZ.

Cuba: 40 High St, Kingston, Georgetown; tel. 226-6732; Ambassador: RICARDO GARCIA DIAZ.

India: Bank of Baroda Bldg, 10 Ave of the Republic, POB 101148, Georgetown; tel. 226-3996; fax 225-7012; High Commissioner: Dr PRAKASH V. JOSHI.

Korea, Democratic People's Republic: 82 Premniranjan Place, Georgetown; tel. 226-0266; Ambassador: JON HYON CHAN.

Russia: 3 Public Rd, Kitty, Georgetown; tel. 226-9773; fax 227-2975; Ambassador: TAHIR BYASHIMOVICH DURDIYEV.

Suriname: 304 Church St, POB 10508, Georgetown; tel. 226-7844; Ambassador: HUMPHREY ABDUL RAFIK HASRAT.

United Kingdom: 44 Main St, POB 10849, Georgetown; tel. 226-5881; fax 225-3555; e-mail consular@georgetown.mail.fco.gov.uk; internet www.britain-un-guyana.org; High Commissioner: EDWARD GLOVER.

USA: Duke and Young Sts, Kingston, Georgetown; tel. 225-4900; fax 225-8497; Ambassador: RONALD GODARD.

Venezuela: 296 Thomas St, Georgetown; tel. 226-1543; Ambassador: JEAN-FRANÇOIS PULVENIS.

Judicial System

The Judicature of Guyana comprises the Supreme Court of Judicature, which consists of the Court of Appeal and the High Court (both of which are superior courts of record), and a number of Courts of Summary Jurisdiction.

The Court of Appeal, which came into operation in 1966, consists of the Chancellor as President, the Chief Justice, and such number of Justices of Appeal as may be prescribed by the National Assembly.

The High Court of the Supreme Court consists of the Chief Justice as President of the Court and Puisne Judges. Its jurisdiction is both original and appellate. It has criminal jurisdiction in matters brought before it on indictment. A person convicted by the Court has a right of appeal to the Guyana Court of Appeal. The High Court of the Supreme Court has unlimited jurisdiction in civil matters and exclusive jurisdiction in probate, divorce and admiralty and certain other matters. Under certain circumstances, appeal in civil matters lies either to the Full Court of the High Court of the Supreme Court, which is composed of not less than two judges, or to the Guyana Court of Appeal.

A magistrate has jurisdiction to determine claims where the amount involved does not exceed a certain sum of money, specified by law. Appeal lies to the Full Court.

Chancellor of Justice: CECIL KENNARD.

Chief Justice: DESIRÉE BERNARD.

High Court Justice: CLAUDETTE SINGH.

Attorney-General: CHARLES RAMSON.

Religion

CHRISTIANITY

Guyana Council of Churches: 26 Durban St, Lodge, Georgetown; tel. 225-3020; e-mail bishopedghill@hotmail.com; f. 1967 by merger of the Christian Social Council (f. 1937) and the Evangelical Council (f. 1960); 15 mem. churches, 1 assoc. mem.; Chair. Bishop JUAN A. EDGHILL; Sec. Rev. KEITH HALEY.

The Anglican Communion

Anglicans in Guyana are adherents of the Church in the Province of the West Indies, comprising eight dioceses. The Archbishop of the Province is the Bishop of the North Eastern Caribbean and Aruba, resident in St John's, Antigua. The diocese of Guyana also includes French Guiana and Suriname. In 1986 the estimated membership in the country was 125,000.

Bishop of Guyana: Rt Rev. RANDOLPH OSWALD GEORGE, Austin House, 49 High St, Georgetown 1; tel. 226-4183; fax 226-3353.

The Baptist Church

The Baptist Convention of Guyana: POB 10149, Georgetown; tel. 226-0428; Chair. Rev. ALFRED JULIEN.

The Lutheran Church

The Lutheran Church in Guyana: Lutheran Courts, POB 88, New Amsterdam; tel. and fax (3) 6479; e-mail lcg@guyana.net.gy; f. 1947; 11,000 mems; Pres. Rev. ROY K. THAKURDYAL.

The Roman Catholic Church

Guyana comprises the single diocese of Georgetown, suffragan to the archdiocese of Port of Spain, Trinidad and Tobago. At 31 December 1998 adherents of the Roman Catholic Church comprised about 10.9% of the total population. The Bishop participates in the Antilles Episcopal Conference Secretariat, currently based in Port of Spain, Trinidad.

Bishop of Georgetown: G. BENEDICT SINGH, Bishop's House, 27 Brickdam, POB 10720, Stabroek, Georgetown; tel. 226-4469; fax 225-8519; e-mail rcbishop@networksgy.com.

Other Christian Churches

Other denominations active in Guyana include the African Methodist Episcopal Church, the African Methodist Episcopal Zion Church, the Church of God, the Church of the Nazarene, the Ethiopian Orthodox Church, the Guyana Baptist Mission, the Guyana Congregational Union, the Guyana Presbyterian Church, the Hallelujah Church, the Methodist Church in the Caribbean and the Americas, the Moravian Church and the Presbytery of Guyana.

HINDUISM

Hindu Religious Centre: Maha Sabha, 162 Lamaha St, POB 10576, Georgetown; tel. 225-7443; f. 1934; Hindus account for about one-third of the population; Pres. RAMRAJ JAGNANDAN; Gen. Sec. CHRISHNA PERSAUD.

ISLAM

The Central Islamic Organization of Guyana (CIOG): M.Y.O. Bldg, Woolford Ave, Thomas Lands, POB 10245, Georgetown; tel. 225-8654; fax 225-7313; e-mail ciog@sdnp.org.gy; internet www.ali.on.ca/ciog; Pres. Alhaji FAZEEL M. FEROUZ: Gen. Sec. MUJTABA NASIR.

Guyana United Sad'r Islamic Anjuman: 157 Alexander St, Kitty, POB 10715, Georgetown; tel. 226-9620; f. 1936; 120,000 mems; Pres. Haji A. H. RAHAMAN; Sec. YACOOB HUSSAIN.

The Press

DAILIES

Guyana Chronicle: 2A Lama Ave, Bel Air Park, POB 11, Georgetown; tel. 226-3243; fax 227-5208; e-mail khan@guyana.net.gy; internet www.guyanachronicle.com; f. 1881; govt-owned; also produces weekly *Sunday Chronicle* (tel. 226-3243); Editor-in-Chief SHARIEF KHAN; circ. 23,000 (weekdays), 43,000 (Sundays).

Stabroek News: 46–47 Robb St, Lacytown, Georgetown; tel. 225-7473; fax 225-4637; e-mail stabroeknews@stabroeknews.com; internet www.stabroeknews.com; f. 1986; also produces weekly *Sunday Stabroek*; liberal independent; Editor-in-Chief DAVID DE CAIRES; circ. 24,000 (weekdays), 40,000 (Sundays).

WEEKLIES AND PERIODICALS

The Catholic Standard: 293 Oronoque St, Queenstown, POB 10720, Georgetown; tel. 226-1540; f. 1905; weekly; Editor COLIN SMITH; circ. 10,000.

Diocesan Magazine: 144 Almond and Oronoque Sts, Queenstown, Georgetown; quarterly.

Guyana Business: 156 Waterloo St, POB 10110, Georgetown; tel. 225-6451; f. 1889; organ of the Georgetown Chamber of Commerce and Industry; quarterly; Editor C. D. KIRTON.

Guyana Review: 143 Oronoque St, POB 10386, Georgetown; tel. 226-3139; fax 227-3465; e-mail guyrev@networksgy.com; internet www.guyanareview.com; f. 1993; monthly.

Guynews: Georgetown; monthly.

Kaieteur News: 24 Saffon St, Charlestown; tel. 225-8452; fax 225-8473; f. 1994; independent weekly; Editor W. HENRY SKERRETT; circ. 30,000.

Mirror: Lot 8, Industrial Estate, Ruimveldt, Greater Georgetown; tel. 226-2471; fax 226-2472; internet www.mirrornews.org; owned by the New Guyana Co Ltd; Sundays and Wednesdays; Editor JANET JAGAN; circ. 25,000.

New Nation: Congress Place, Sophia, Georgetown; tel. 226-7891; f. 1955; organ of the People's National Congress; weekly; Editor FRANCIS WILLIAMS; circ. 26,000.

The Official Gazette of Guyana: Guyana National Printers Ltd, Lot 1, Public Road, La Penitence; weekly; circ. 450.

Ratoon: Georgetown; monthly.

Thunder: Georgetown; f. 1950; organ of the People's Progressive Party; quarterly; Editor RALPH RAMKARRAN; circ. 5,000.

NEWS AGENCY

Guyana Information Services: Office of the President, New Garden St and South Rd, Georgetown; tel. 226-3389; fax 226-4003; f. 1993; Dir MILTON DREPAUL.

Foreign Bureaux

Inter Press Service (Italy): Georgetown; tel. 225-3213.

United Press International (UPI) (USA): Georgetown; tel. 226-5153.

Xinhua (New China) News Agency (People's Republic of China): 52 Brickdam, Stabroek, Georgetown; tel. 226-9965.

Associated Press (USA) and Informatsionnoye Telegrafnoye Agentstvo RossiiTelegrafnoye Agentstvo Suverennykh Stran (ITAR-TASS) (Russia) are also represented.

PRESS ASSOCIATION

Guyana Press Association: Georgetown; revived in 1990; Pres. ENRICO WOOLFORD.

Publishers

Guyana Free Press: POB 10386, Georgetown; tel. 226-3139; fax 227-3465; e-mail guyrev@networksgy.com; books and learned journals.

Guyana National Printers Ltd: 1 Public Rd, La Penitence, POB 10256, Greater Georgetown; tel. 225-3623; e-mail gnpl@guyana.net.gy; f. 1939; govt-owned printers and publishers; privatization pending; Chair. DESMOND N. MOHAMED.

Guyana Publications Inc.: 46/47 Robb St, Lacytown, Georgetown; tel. 225-7473; fax 225-4637.

Broadcasting and Communications

TELECOMMUNICATIONS

Caribbean Wireless Telecom (CWT): Georgetown; f. 1999; intends to launch a mobile cellular telephone service by 2001; CEO EARL SINGH.

Guyana Telephones and Telegraph Company (GT & T): 79 Brickdam, POB 10628, Georgetown; tel. 226-7840; fax 226-2457; internet www.gtt.co.gy; f. 1991; formerly state-owned Guyana Telecommunications Corpn; 80% ownership by Atlantic Tele-Network (USA); Gen. Man. SONITA JAGAN; Chair. CORNELIUS PRIOR.

BROADCASTING

Radio

Guyana Broadcasting Corporation (GBC): Broadcasting House, 44 High St, POB 10760, Georgetown; tel. 225-8734; fax 225-8756; f. 1979; operates channels GBC 1 (Coastal Service) and GBC 2 (National Service); Gen. Man. DAVID DE GROOT (acting).

Radio Roraima: Georgetown.

Voice of Guyana: Georgetown.

Television

Guyana Television: 68 Hadfield St, Georgetown; tel. 226-9231; f. 1993; fmrly Guyana Television Corporation; govt-owned; limited service; Dir A. BREWSTER.

Two private stations relay US satellite television programmes.

Finance

(dep. = deposits; m. = million; brs = branches;
amounts in Guyana dollars)

BANKING

Central Bank

Bank of Guyana: 1 Church St and Ave of the Republic, POB 10280, Georgetown; tel. 226-3250; fax 227-2965; e-mail boglib@guyana.net.gy; internet www.bankofguyana.org.gy; f. 1965; cap. 1,000m., res 10,138m., dep. 86,717m. (Dec. 1998); central bank of issue; acts as regulatory authority for the banking sector; Gov. DOLLY S. SINGH; Dir LESLIE GLEN.

Commercial Banks

Demerara Bank Ltd: 230 Camp and South Sts, Georgetown; tel. 225-50610; fax 225-0601; e-mail banking@demerarabank.com; internet www.demerarabank.com; f. 1994; cap. 450m., res 52m., dep. 4,949m. (Sept. 1998); Chair. YESU PERSAUD; Man. AHMED M. KHAN.

Guyana Bank for Trade and Industry Ltd: 47–48 Water St, POB 10280, Georgetown; tel. 226-68431; fax 227-1612; e-mail banking@gbtibank.com; f. 1987 to absorb the operations of Barclays Bank; dep. $G 19,490m., res $G 1,789m., total assets $G 23,961m. (1998); CEO R. K. SHARMA; 6 brs.

Guyana National Co-operative Bank: 1 Lombard and Cornhill Sts, POB 10400, Georgetown; tel. 225-7810; fax 226-0231; f. 1970; merged with Guyana Co-operative Agricultural and Industrial Development Bank in 1995; state-owned; Gen. Man. ROSALIE A. ROBERTSON; 11 brs.

National Bank of Industry and Commerce (NBIC): 38–40 Water St, POB 10440, Georgetown; tel. 226-4091; fax 227-2921; 51% govt-owned; 17.5% owned by National Insurance Scheme; Man. Dir CONRAD PLUMMER; 5 brs.

Foreign Banks

Bank of Baroda (India): 10 Regent St and Ave of the Republic, POB 10768, Georgetown; tel. 226-4005; fax 225-1691; f. 1908; Chief Man. P. SAVID.

Bank of Nova Scotia (Canada): 104 Carmichael St, Georgetown; tel. 225-9222; fax 225-9309; e-mail bns.guyana@scotiabank.com; Man. FARRIED SULLIMAN; 5 brs.

Citizens' Bank Ltd (Jamaica): 201 Camp and Charlotte Sts, Lacytown, Georgetown; tel. 226-1705; fax 227-8251; internet citizens-carib.com/guyana.htm; f. 1994; Chair. DENNIS LALOR.

INSURANCE

In mid-1999 there were six insurance companies licensed to operate in Guyana.

Demerara Mutual Life Assurance Society Ltd: Demerara Life Bldg, 61–62 Robb St and Ave of the Republic, POB 10409, Georgetown; tel. 225-8991; fax 225-8288; f. 1891; Chair. RICHARD B. FIELDS; Gen. Man. EAWAN E. DEVONISH.

Diamond Fire and General Life: Georgetown; f. 2000; privately owned; cap. $G 100m.

Guyana Co-operative Insurance Service: 46 Main St, Georgetown; tel. 225-9153; f. 1976; 67% share offered for private ownership in 1996; Chair. G. A. LEE; Gen. Man. PAT BENDER.

Guyana and Trinidad Mutual Life Insurance Co Ltd: Lots 27–29, Robb and Hincks Sts, Georgetown; tel. 225-7910; fax 225-9397; e-mail gtmgroup@guyana.net.org; f. 1925; Chair. HAROLD B. DAVIS; Man. Dir R. E. CHEONG; affiliated company: Guyana and Trinidad Mutual Fire Insurance Co Ltd.

Hand-in-Hand Mutual Fire and Life Group: 1–4 Ave of the Republic, POB 10188, Georgetown; tel. 225-0462; fax 225-7519; f. 1865; fire and life insurance; Chair. J. A. CHIN; Gen. Man. K. A. EVELYN.

Insurance Association

Insurance Association of Guyana: 54 Robb St, Bourda, POB 10741, Georgetown; tel. 226-3514; f. 1968.

STOCK EXCHANGE

In July 1989 the Government announced that it intended to establish a national securities exchange, with a view to becoming a member of the proposed regional stock exchange.

Trade and Industry

GOVERNMENT AGENCIES

Guyana Agency for the Environment: Georgetown; tel. 225-7523; fax 225-7524; f. 1988; formulates, implements and monitors policies on the environment; Dir Dr WALTER CHIN.

Guyana Marketing Corporation: 87 Robb and Alexander Sts, Georgetown; tel. 226-8255; fax 227-4114; e-mail newgmc@networksgy.com; Chair. CHANDRABALLI BISHESWAR; Gen. Man. ROXANNE GREENIDGE.

Guyana Public Communications Agency: Georgetown; tel. 227-2025; f. 1989; Exec. Chair. KESTER ALVES.

Trade and Investment Agency: Office of the President, New Garden St and South Rd, Georgetown; f. 2001; Chair. BHARRAT JAGDEO; CEO GEOFF DA SILVA.

DEVELOPMENT ORGANIZATIONS

Guyana Office for Investment (Go-Invest): 190 Camp and Church Sts, Georgetown; tel. 225-0658; fax 225-0655; e-mail goinvest@sdnp.org.gy; internet www.goinvest.gov.gy; f. 1994; provision of investment promotion service for foreign and local cos; under control of the Office of the President; Dir. KHELLAWAN LALL.

State Planning Commission: 229 South St, Lacytown, Georgetown; tel. 226-8093; fax 227-2499; Chief Planning Officer CLYDE ROOPCHAND.

Institute of Private Enterprise Development (IPED): Georgetown; f. 1986 to help establish small businesses; total loans provided $G771m.; total jobs created 52,002; Chair. YESU PERSAUD.

CHAMBER OF COMMERCE

Georgetown Chamber of Commerce and Industry: 156 Waterloo St, Cummingsburg, POB 10110, Georgetown; tel. 225-5846; fax 226-3519; f. 1889; 122 mems; Pres. JOHN S. DE FREITAS; Chief Exec. G. C. FUNG-ON.

INDUSTRIAL AND TRADE ASSOCIATIONS

Bauxite Industry Development Company Ltd: 71 Main St, Georgetown; tel. 225-7780; fax 226-7413; f. 1976; Chair. J. I. F. BLACKMAN.

Guyana Rice Development Board: 117 Cowan St, Georgetown; tel. 225-8717; fax 225-6486; e-mail grdb@gol.net.gy; internet www.cra.cc/grdb; f. 1994 to assume operations of Guyana Rice Export Board and Guyana Rice Grading Centre; Chair. and CEO CHARLES KENNARD.

Livestock Development Co Ltd: 58 High St, Georgetown; tel. 226-1601.

EMPLOYERS' ORGANIZATIONS

Consultative Association of Guyanese Industry Ltd: 157 Waterloo St, POB 10730, Georgetown; tel. 226-4603; f. 1962; 193 mems, 3 mem. asscns, 159 assoc. mems; Chair. DAVID KING; Exec. Dir DAVID YANKANA.

Forest Products Association of Guyana: 157 Waterloo St, Georgetown; tel. 226-9848; f. 1944; 47 mems; Pres. L. J. P. WILLEMS; Exec. Officer WARREN PHOENIX.

Guyana Manufacturers' Association Ltd: 62 Main St, Cummingsburg, Georgetown; tel. 227-4295; fax 227-0670; f. 1967; 190 members; Pres. KIM KISSOON; Exec. Sec. TREVOR SHARPLES.

Guyana Rice Producers' Association: Lot 104, Regent St, Lacytown, Georgetown; tel. 226-4411; f. 1946; *c.* 35,000 families; Pres. BUDRAM MAHADEO.

UTILITIES
Electricity

Guyana Power and Light Inc: 40 Main St, POB 10390, Georgetown; tel. 225-4618; fax 227-1978; f. 1999; fmrly Guyana Electricity Corpn.; 50% state-owned; 50% owned by the Commonwealth Devt Corpn and the Electricity Supply Bd International; Chair. ADAM HEDAYAT; CEO NOEL HATCH.

Water

Guyana Water Authority (GUYWA): Georgetown; CEO KARAN SINGH.

CO-OPERATIVE SOCIETIES

Chief Co-operatives Development Officer: Ministry of Human Services and Social Security, 1 Water and Cornhill Sts, Georgetown; tel. 225-8644; fax 225-3477; f. 1948; L. MILLER.

In October 1996 there were 1,324 registered co-operative societies, mainly savings clubs and agricultural credit societies, with a total membership of 95,950.

TRADE UNIONS

Trades Union Congress (TUC): Critchlow Labour College, Woolford Ave, Non-pareil Park, Georgetown; tel. 226-1493; fax 227-0254; f. 1940; national trade union body; 22 affiliated unions; merged with the Federation of Independent Trade Unions in Guyana in 1993; Pres. LAURIE LEWIS; Gen. Sec. JOSEPH H. POLLYDORE.

Amalgamated Transport and General Workers' Union: 46 Urquhart St, Georgetown; tel. 226-6243; Pres. RICHARD SAMUELS.

Clerical and Commercial Workers' Union (CCWU): Clerico House, 140 Quamina St, South Cummingsburg, POB 101045, Georgetown; tel. 227-0611; Gen. Sec. BIRCHMORE PHILADELPHIA.

Federative Union of Government Employees (FUGE): Georgetown.

General Workers' Union: 79 New North Rd, Georgetown; tel. 226-4879; f. 1954; terminated affiliation to People's National Congress in 1989; Pres. NORRIS WITTER; Gen. Sec. EDWIN JAMES; 3,000 mems.

Guyana Agricultural and General Workers' Union (GAWU): 104–106 Regent St, Lacytown, Georgetown; tel. 227-2091; fax 227-2093; e-mail gawu@networksgy.com; allied to the PPP; Pres. KOMAL CHAND; Gen. Sec. SEEPAUL NARINE; 20,000 mems.

Guyana Bauxite Supervisors' Union: Linden; Gen. Sec. LINCOLN LEWIS.

Guyana Labour Union: 198 Camp St, Georgetown; tel. 227-1196; Pres.-Gen. HUGH DESMOND HOYTE; 6,000 mems.

Guyana Mine Workers' Union: 56 Wismar St, Wismar; tel. (4) 2822; Pres. ASHTON ANGEL; Gen. Sec. CHRISTOPHER JAMES; 5,800 mems.

Guyana Postal and Telecommunication Workers' Union: 310 East St, POB 10352, Georgetown; tel. 226-5255; fax 225-1633; Pres. MAUREEN WALCOTT-FORTUNE; Gen. Sec. DIAN PRINCE-JOHNSON.

Guyana Public Service Union (GPSU): 160 Regent Rd and New Garden St, Georgetown; tel. 226-1770; Pres. PATRICK YARDE; Gen. Sec. RANDOLPH KIRTON; 11,600 mems.

Guyana Teachers' Union: Georgetown.

National Association of Agricultural, Commercial and Industrial Employees: 64 High St, Kingston, Georgetown; tel. 227-2301; f. 1946; Pres. B. KHUSIEL; *c.* 2,000 mems.

Printing Industry and Allied Workers' Union: Georgetown; Gen. Sec. LESLIE REECE.

University of Guyana Workers' Union: Turkeyen, Georgetown; supports Working People's Alliance; Pres. Dr CLIVE THOMAS; Chair. AL CREIGHTON.

Transport

RAILWAY

There are no public railways in Guyana.

Linmine Railway: Mackenzie, Linden; tel. (4) 2279; fax (4) 6795; bauxite transport; 15 km of line, Coomara to Linden; Superintendent O. BARNWELL.

ROADS

The coastal strip has a well-developed road system. In 1996 there were an estimated 7,970 km (4,859 miles) of paved and good-weather roads and trails.

SHIPPING

Guyana's principal ports are at Georgetown and New Amsterdam. The port at Linden serves for the transportation of bauxite products. A ferry service is operated between Guyana and Suriname. Communications with the interior are chiefly by river, although access is hindered by rapids and falls. There are 1,077 km (607 miles) of navigable rivers. The main rivers are the Mazaruni, the Potaro, the Essequibo, the Demerara and the Berbice. By 2002 a bridge was to be constructed across the Berbice River to link the west bank with the town of New Amsterdam, accessible only by ferry. In 2000 the Brazilian Government announced that it would finance the construction of both a deep-water port and another river bridge.

Transport and Harbours Department: Battery Rd, Kingston, Georgetown; tel. 225-9350; e-mail t&hd@solutions2000.net; Gen. Man. IVOR B. ENGLISH; Harbour Master STEPHEN THOMAS.

Shipping Association of Guyana Inc: 24 Water St, Georgetown; tel. 226-1505; fax 226-1881; e-mail ferna@guyana.net.gy; f. 1952; Pres. CHRISTOPHER FERNANDES; Sec. and Man. W. V. BRIDGEMOHAN; members:

Guyana National Industrial Company Inc.: 2–9 Lombard St, Charlestown, POB 10520, Georgetown; tel. 225-8428; fax 225-8526; metal foundry, ship building and repair, agents for a number of international transport cos; Man. Dir and CEO CLAUDE SAUL.

Guyana National Shipping Corporation Ltd: 5–9 Lombard St, La Penitence, POB 10988, Georgetown; tel. 226-1732; fax 225-3815; e-mail gnsc@guyana.net.gy; internet www.gnsc.com; govt-owned; Exec. Chair. DESMOND MOHAMED; Man. Dir M. F. BASCOM.

John Fernandes Ltd: 24 Water St, POB 10211, Georgetown; tel. 225-6294; fax 226-1881; e-mail chris@jf-ltd.com; ship agents, pier operators and stevedore contractors; Man. Dir C. J. FERNANDES.

CIVIL AVIATION

The main airport is Timehri International, 42 km (26 miles) from Georgetown. By 1998 there were some 94 airstrips.

Guyana Airways 2000: 32 Main St, POB 10223, Georgetown; tel. 225-7337; fax 226-0032; internet www.turq.com/guyana/guyanair .html; f. 1939 as British Guiana Airways; renamed as Guyana Airways Corpn 1963; state-owned until 1999 when 51% share sold and renamed as above; operates internal scheduled services and external services to the USA, Canada, Curaçao, Brazil, Barbados and Trinidad and Tobago; Chair. ANTHONY MEKDECI.

There is a weekly flight, via Georgetown, from Caracas (Venezuela) to Port of Spain (Trinidad and Tobago) and Suriname.

Tourism

Despite the beautiful scenery in the interior of the country, Guyana has limited tourist facilities, and began encouraging tourism only in the late 1980s. In the 1990s Guyana began to develop its considerable potential as an eco-tourism destination. However, tourist arrivals declined towards the end of the decade. The total number of visitors to Guyana in 1998 was 80,000. Tourism receipts totalled US $60m. in 1998.

Tourism and Hospitality Association of Guyana: 157 Waterloo Street, Georgetown; tel. 225-0807; fax 225-0817; e-mail thag@ networksgy.com; internet www.exploreguyana.com; f. 1992; Exec. Dir INDIRA ANANDJIT.

HAITI

Introductory Survey

Location, Climate, Language, Religion, Flag, Capital

The Republic of Haiti occupies the western part of the Caribbean island of Hispaniola (the Dominican Republic occupies the remaining two-thirds) and some smaller offshore islands. Cuba, to the west, is less than 80 km away. The climate is tropical but the mountains and fresh sea winds mitigate the heat. Temperatures vary little with the seasons, and the annual average in Port-au-Prince is about 27°C (80°F). The rainy season is from May to November. The official languages are French and Creole. About 70% of the population belong to the Roman Catholic Church, the country's official religion, and other Christian churches are also represented. The folk religion is voodoo, a fusion of beliefs originating in West Africa involving communication with the spirit-world through the medium of trance. The national flag (proportions variable) has two equal vertical stripes, of dark blue and red. The state flag (proportions 5 by 3) has, in addition, a white rectangular panel, containing the national coat of arms (a palm tree, surmounted by a Cap of Liberty and flanked by flags and cannons), in the centre. The capital is Port-au-Prince.

Recent History

Haiti was first colonized in 1659 by the French, who named the territory Saint-Domingue. French sovereignty was formally recognized by Spain in 1697. Following a period of internal unrest, a successful uprising, begun in 1794 by African-descended slaves, culminated in 1804 with the establishment of Haiti as an independent state, ruled by Jean-Jacques Dessalines, who proclaimed himself Emperor. Hostility between the negro population and the mulattos continued throughout the 19th century until, after increasing economic instability, the USA intervened militarily and supervised the government of the country from 1915 to 1934. Mulatto interests retained political ascendancy until 1946, when a negro President, Dumarsais Estimé, was installed following a military coup. Following the overthrow of two further administrations, Dr François Duvalier, a country physician, was elected President in 1957.

The Duvalier administration soon became a dictatorship, maintaining its authority by means of a notorious private army, popularly called the Tontons Macoutes (Creole for 'Bogeymen'), who used extortion and intimidation to crush all possible opposition to the President's rule. In 1964 Duvalier became President-for-Life, and at his death in April 1971 he was succeeded by his 19-year-old son and designated successor Jean-Claude Duvalier.

At elections held in February 1979 for the 58-seat National Assembly, 57 seats were won by the official government party, the Parti de l'Unité Nationale. The first municipal elections for 25 years, which took place in 1983, were overshadowed by allegations of electoral fraud and Duvalier's obstruction of opposition parties. No opposition candidates were permitted to contest the elections for the National Assembly held in February 1984.

In April 1985 Duvalier announced a programme of constitutional reforms, including the eventual appointment of a Prime Minister and the formation of political parties, subject to certain limiting conditions. In September Roger Lafontant, the minister most closely identified with the Government's acts of repression, was dismissed. However, protests organized by the Roman Catholic Church and other religious groups gained momentum, and further measures to curb continued disorder were adopted in January 1986. The university and schools were closed indefinitely, and radio stations were forbidden to report on current events. Duvalier imposed a state of siege and declared martial law.

In February 1986, following intensified public protests, Duvalier and his family fled from Haiti to exile in France, leaving a five-member National Council of Government (Conseil National Gouvernemental—CNG), led by the Chief of Staff of the army, Gen. Henri Namphy, to succeed him. The interim military-civilian Council appointed a new Cabinet. The National Assembly was dissolved, and the Constitution was suspended. Later in the month, the Tontons Macoutes were disbanded. Prisoners from Haiti's largest gaol were freed under a general amnesty. However, renewed rioting occurred to protest against the inclusion in the new Government of known supporters of the former dictatorship. In March 1986 there was a cabinet reshuffle. The new, three-member, CNG comprised Gen. Namphy, Col (later Brig.-Gen.) Williams Régala and Jacques François.

In April 1986 Gen. Namphy announced a proposed timetable for elections to restore constitutional government by February 1988. The first of these elections, to select 41 people (from 101 candidates) who would form part of the 61-member Constituent Assembly that was to revise the Constitution, took place in October 1986. However, the level of participation at the election was only about 5%.

The new Constitution was approved by 99.8% of voters in a referendum held on 29 March 1987. An estimated 50% of the electorate voted. An independent Provisional Electoral Council (Conseil Electoral Provisoire—CEP) was appointed to supervise the presidential and legislative elections, which were scheduled for 29 November.

On 29 November 1987 the elections were cancelled three hours after voting had begun, owing to renewed violence and killings, for which former members of the Tontons Macoutes were believed to be responsible. The Government dissolved the CEP and took control of the electoral process. In December a new CEP was appointed by the Government, and elections were rescheduled for 17 January 1988. Leslie Manigat of the Rassemblement des Démocrates Nationalistes et Progressistes (RDNP), with 50.3% of the total votes cast, was declared the winner of the presidential election. Legislative and municipal elections were held concurrently. Opposition leaders alleged that there had been extensive fraud and malpractice.

The Manigat Government took office in February 1988, but was overthrown by disaffected members of the army in June. Gen. Namphy, whom Manigat had attempted to replace as army Chief of Staff, assumed the presidency and appointed a Cabinet comprising members of the armed forces. The Constitution of 1987 was abrogated, and Duvalier's supporters returned to prominence, as did the Tontons Macoutes.

On 18 September 1988 Gen. Namphy was ousted in a coup, led by Brig.-Gen. Prosper Avril (who became President), who advocated the introduction of radical reforms. In November an independent electoral body, the Collège Electoral d'Haïti (CEDA), was established to supervise future elections, to draft an electoral law and to ensure proper registration of voters.

In March 1989 President Avril partially restored the Constitution of 1987 and restated his intention to hold democratic elections. In the following month the Government survived two coup attempts by the Leopard Corps, the country's élite anti-subversion squadron, and the Dessalines battalion, based in Port-au-Prince. Both battalions were subsequently disbanded.

In September 1989 Avril published a timetable for elections that had been drafted by the CEP. It provided for local and regional elections to be held in April 1990, followed by national and legislative elections, in two rounds, in July and August. The presidential election, also in two rounds, was scheduled to take place in October and November 1990. (These arrangements were revised under the interim presidency of Ertha Pascal-Trouillot—see below.)

In early January 1990, during the President's absence abroad on official business, the Rassemblement National, a broadly-based opposition coalition including conservative and left-wing political organizations, initiated a series of strikes and demonstrations to protest against the Government's economic policies. On 20 January, following his return to Haiti, Avril imposed a 30-day state of siege and a series of restrictions on political activity; however, these lasted only a few days. At the same time it was announced that all political prisoners had been released.

Avril resigned as President in March 1990, in response to sustained popular and political opposition, together with diplomatic pressure from the USA. Before entering temporary exile in the USA, Avril ceded power to the Chief of the General Staff, Gen. Hérard Abraham, who subsequently transferred authority to Ertha Pascal-Trouillot, a member of the Supreme Court. As

President of a civilian interim Government, Pascal-Trouillot shared power with a 19-member Council of State, whose principal function was to assist in preparations for the elections that were to be held later in the year. In May a new CEP was established. In September the CEP announced the postponement, until mid-December, of the elections, owing to a delay in the arrival of necessary funds and materials from donor countries.

The presidential and legislative elections took place on 16 December 1990. Preliminary results indicated an overwhelming victory in the presidential election for Fr Jean-Bertrand Aristide, a left-wing Roman Catholic priest representing the Front National pour le Changement et la Démocratie (FNCD), who secured some 67% of the votes cast. His closest rival was Marc Bazin, the candidate of the centre-right Mouvement pour l'Instauration de la Démocratie en Haïti (MIDH), who obtained about 14% of the poll. However, the results of the concurrent first round of legislative voting were less decisive. Aristide's FNCD won five of the 27 seats in the Senate, and 18 (of 83) seats in the Chamber of Deputies, while the Alliance Nationale pour la Démocratie et le Progrès (ANDP) secured 16 seats in the lower house. Seven other seats in the Chamber of Deputies were distributed among other political parties.

In January 1991, one month before Aristide was due to be sworn in as President, a group of army officers, led by Roger Lafontant, seized control of the presidential palace, and forced Pascal-Trouillot to announce her resignation. However, the army remained loyal to the Government and arrested Lafontant and his associates. A low turn-out in the second round of legislative voting, on 20 January 1991, was attributed to popular unease as a result of the recent coup attempt. The most successful party, the FNCD, won a further nine seats in the Chamber of Deputies, and an additional eight in the Senate, thereby failing to secure an overall majority in the two legislative chambers.

Aristide was inaugurated as President on 7 February 1991. The new Head of State subsequently initiated proceedings to secure the extradition from France of ex-President Duvalier to face charges that included embezzlement, abuse of power and murder. Aristide also undertook the reform of the armed forces (in July Gen. (later Lt-Gen.) Raoul Cédras replaced Gen. Hérard Abraham as Commander-in-Chief.). In February the new President nominated one of his close associates, René García Préval, as Prime Minister.

In April 1991 Ertha Pascal-Trouillot was arrested on charges of complicity in the attempted coup three months previously. She was initially released, pending the completion of investigations, and in September left the country. In July Roger Lafontant was found guilty of organizing the attempted coup and sentenced to life imprisonment.

On 30 September 1991 a military junta, led by Gen. Cédras, overthrew the Government. Following diplomatic intervention by the USA, France and Venezuela, Aristide was allowed to go into exile. The coup received international condemnation, and an almost immediate economic embargo was imposed on Haiti by the Organization of American States (OAS, see p. 261). Many hundreds of people were reported to have been killed during the coup, including the imprisoned Lafontant. On 7 October military units assembled 29 members of the legislature and coerced them into approving the appointment of Joseph Nerette as interim President, and several days later a new Cabinet was announced. The OAS, however, continued to recognize Aristide as the legitimate President.

During the following months the OAS attempted to negotiate a settlement. However, the two sides remained deadlocked over the conditions for Aristide's return, the main obstacles being Aristide's insistence that Cédras be imprisoned or exiled, and the legislature's demands for an immediate repeal of the OAS embargo and a general amnesty. In February 1992, following OAS-supervised talks in Washington, DC, between Aristide and members of a Haitian legislative delegation, an agreement was signed providing for the installation of René Théodore, leader of the Mouvement pour la Reconstruction Nationale, as Prime Minister,. He was to govern in close consultation with the exiled Aristide and facilitate his return. Aristide undertook to respect all decisions taken by the legislature since the coup of September 1991, and agreed to a general amnesty for the police and armed forces. The economic embargo imposed by the OAS was to be revoked on ratification of the agreement by the legislature. However, in mid-March 1992 politicians opposed to the accord were reportedly coerced into withdrawing from a joint session

of the Senate and the Chamber of Deputies, leaving it inquorate. In late March, following an appeal by interim President Nerette, the Supreme Court declared the agreement null and void, on the grounds that it violated the Constitution by endangering the country's sovereignty. In response, the OAS increased economic sanctions against Haiti.

In May 1992, following a tripartite summit meeting involving the legislature, the Government and the armed forces, an agreement providing for a 'consensus government' was ratified by the Senate. The agreement envisaged the appointment of a new Prime Minister and a multi-party government of national consensus to seek a solution to the political crisis and negotiate an end to the economic embargo. In June the legislature, in the absence of the FNCD (which boycotted the sessions) approved the nomination of Marc Bazin, of the MIDH, to be Prime Minister. Under the terms of the tripartite agreement, the presidency was left vacant, ostensibly to allow for Aristide's return, although commentators suggested that this was purely a political manoeuvre by the military-backed Government and that such an eventuality was unlikely. A Cabinet, comprising members of most major parties (with the significant exception of the FNCD), was installed, with the army retaining control of the interior and defence. The appointment of the new Government provoked world-wide condemnation.

In July 1992 a 10-member 'presidential commission', headed by Fr Antoine Adrien, was appointed by Aristide to hold negotiations with what he termed the 'real forces' in Haiti, referring to the armed forces and the wealthy élite. In September the Government agreed to allow the presence of an 18-member OAS commission in Haiti to help to guarantee human rights, reduce violence and assess progress towards a resolution of the prevailing political crisis. In February 1993 a further agreement was reached with the OAS and the UN on sending another international civil commission comprising some 200 representatives.

In April 1993 the joint envoy of the UN and the OAS, Dante Caputo, visited Haiti to present a series of proposals for the restoration of democratic rule in Haiti. These provided for the resignation of the military high command in return for a full amnesty for those involved in the coup of 1991, and for the establishment of a government of consensus and the eventual reinstatement of Aristide. A sum of US $1,000m. in economic aid was to become available once democracy was restored. However, the proposals were rejected by Cédras.

In early June 1993 the USA imposed sanctions against Haiti. Shortly afterwards Bazin resigned as Prime Minister. His position was believed to have become untenable following the refusal of several cabinet ministers to respect his demand for their resignation, and the withdrawal of the support in the legislature of the Parti National Progressiste Révolutionnaire (PANPRA)—which deprived the Government of a parliamentary majority. In late June, following the imposition of a world-wide petroleum and arms embargo by the UN Security Council, Cédras agreed to attend talks with Aristide on Governor's Island, New York, under the auspices of the UN and the OAS. On 3 July the so-called Governor's Island peace accord was signed, delineating a 10-point agenda for Aristide's reinstatement. Under the terms of the accord the embargo was to be revoked following the installation of a new Prime Minister (to be appointed by Aristide), Cédras would retire and a new Commander-in-Chief of the armed forces would be appointed by Aristide, who would return to Haiti by 30 October. The accord was approved by Haiti's main political parties, and a six-month political 'truce' was agreed to facilitate the transition. Legislation providing for a series of political and institutional reforms, as required under the terms of the accord, was to be enacted, including provision for the transfer of the police force to civilian control.

In August 1993 the legislature ratified the appointment by Aristide of Robert Malval as Prime Minister. The UN Security Council subsequently suspended its petroleum and arms embargo. In September a concerted campaign of political violence and intimidation by police auxiliaries, known as 'attachés', threatened to undermine the Governor's Island accord. Demands made by Malval that the attachés be disbanded were ignored by the chief of police, Col Joseph Michel François. With the upsurge of a Duvalierist tendency, largely embodied by the attachés, a new political party, the Front Revolutionnaire pour l'Avancement et le Progrès d'Haïti (FRAPH), was founded in opposition to any attempt to reinstate Aristide. In late September the UN Security Council approved a resolution providing for the immediate deployment of a lightly-armed United Nations

Mission In Haiti (UNMIH, renamed United Nations Support Mission in Haiti in June 1996, United Nations Transition Mission in Haiti in July 1997, and United Nations Civilian Police Mission in Haiti (MIPONUH) in November 1997). A new unarmed mission, the International Civilian Support Mission in Haiti, superseded MIPONUH in March 2000, comprising 150 members, to advise in the creation of a new police force and the modernization of the army. The new mission's mandate ended on 6 February 2001.

In October 1993, in violation of the Governor's Island accord, Cédras and François refused to resign their posts, asserting that the terms of the amnesty offered by Aristide were not sufficiently broad. In that month the campaign of political violence by the attachés escalated. A US vessel transporting members of the UNMIH was prevented from docking at Port-au-Prince, and its arrival prompted violent demonstrations of defiance by the attachés. Several days later the Minister of Justice, Guy Malary, was assassinated. In response, the US Government ordered six warships into Haitian territorial waters to enforce the reimposed UN embargo. As a result of the instability, the UN/OAS international civil commission and other foreign government personnel were evacuated to the Dominican Republic.

In December 1993 Malval officially resigned as Prime Minister, although he remained in office pending the appointment of a successor. In discussions with the US Government held earlier in the month, Malval announced a new initiative for a National Salvation Conference, involving multi-sector negotiations (to include the military) on a return to democratic rule. However, Aristide rejected the proposals, proposing instead a National Reconciliation Conference, excluding the military, which took place in Miami, USA, in mid-January 1994. Following the military regime's failure to meet the revised UN deadline of 15 January to comply with the terms of the Governor's Island accord, in late January the USA unilaterally imposed further sanctions denying officers of the military regime access to assets held in the USA and cancelling their travel visas. In that month members of the UN/OAS international civil commission began to return to Haiti.

In February 1994 a 13-member faction of the Senate—including eight members elected in January 1993 in partial legislative elections condemned as illegal by the USA and UN and widely regarded as an attempt by the military regime to legitimize its rule—appointed Bernard Sansaricq as President of the Senate. However, the incumbent President of the Senate, Firmin Jean-Louis, did not relinquish his position and continued to be recognized by the international community. In the same month Aristide twice rejected peace plans drafted by the USA, demanding instead the implementation of the Governor's Island accord.

In April 1994 the US Government abandoned its attempts to effect a compromise solution to the crisis in Haiti in favour of the implementation of more rigorous economic sanctions with a view to forcing the military regime to relinquish power. In late April the USA proposed a resolution to the UN Security Council endorsing the implementation of extended sanctions. On 6 May the UN Security Council approved a resolution introducing sanctions banning all international trade with Haiti, excluding food and medicine, reducing air links with the country and preventing members of the regime from gaining access to assets held outside Haiti.

In early 1994 the 13-member faction of the Senate led by Bernard Sansaricq declared the presidency of the Republic vacant, invoking Article 149 of the Constitution, which provides that, in case of prolonged absence by the Head of State, the position may be assumed by the President of the Court of Cassation. In May, with the support of the armed forces, the 13 senators and 30 members of the Chamber of Deputies—not a sufficient number to form a quorum—appointed the President of the Court of Cassation, Emile Jonassaint, provisional President of the Republic. He subsequently appointed a new Cabinet. The appointment of the Jonassaint administration was denounced as illegal by the international community and by the outgoing acting Prime Minister, Robert Malval. In the following month, the USA increased sanctions against Haiti. Jonassaint's appointment also revealed a division within the three-man junta at the head of the military regime—namely Cédras, François and the Chief of Staff of the army, Brig.-Gen. Philippe Biamby. François reportedly opposed the move and did not attend the inauguration ceremony.

In July 1994 the Haitian junta issued an order providing for the expulsion of the UN/OAS international civil commission. The order was immediately condemned by the UN Security Council. On 31 July the UN Security Council passed a resolution authorizing 'all necessary means' to remove the military regime from power. The terms of the resolution also provided for a UN peace-keeping force to be deployed once stability had been achieved, to remain in Haiti until February 1996, when Aristide's presidential term expired. In August the UN officially abandoned efforts to effect a peaceful solution to the crisis in Haiti. In the same month leaders of the Caribbean Community and Common Market (CARICOM, see p. 142) agreed to support a US-led military invasion.

On 19 September 1994 a nominally multinational force comprised almost entirely of US troops began a peaceful occupation of Haiti. The occupation followed the diplomatic efforts of a mission led by former US President Jimmy Carter, which resulted in a compromise agreement, thus narrowly avoiding a full-scale invasion. Under the terms of the agreement, the Haitian security forces were to co-operate with the multilateral force in effecting a transition to civilian rule. All sanctions were to be lifted and the military junta granted 'early and honourable retirement' following legislative approval of a general amnesty law, or by 15 October at the latest (the date when Aristide was to return from exile to resume his presidency). The agreement did not, however, require the junta's departure from Haiti, nor did it address the reform of the security forces. In late September the legislature began a joint session to discuss the draft amnesty law. Those legislators elected illegally in January 1993 were replaced by legislators returning from exile in the USA. Following the occupation, acts of violence by the Haitian police against supporters of Aristide led to a modification of the rules of operation of the multinational force, allowing for intervention to curb the violence. In late September the USA announced the suspension of its unilateral sanctions, although the Haitian military's assets in the USA remained frozen. A few days later the UN Security Council approved a resolution ending all sanctions against Haiti with effect from the day after the return to Haiti of Aristide.

In early October 1994 Aristide signed a decree authorizing legislation, approved by the legislature that month, for the amnesty of those involved in the coup of September 1991. Cédras and Biamby promptly went into exile in Panama, whilst François was reported to have already fled to the Dominican Republic where he was granted asylum. Later that month the USA formally ended its freeze on the assets of the Haitian military regime, estimated to be worth some US $79m. On 12 October Robert Malval resumed office as interim Prime Minister following the resignation of the Jonassaint administration. Aristide returned to Haiti on 15 October to resume his presidency and on 25 October appointed Smarck Michel as premier. He also appointed Gen. Jean-Claude Duperval provisional Commander-in-Chief of the armed forces and Gen. Bernardin Poisson Chief of Staff of the army.

A new Cabinet, comprising mainly members of the pro-Aristide Organisation Politique Lavalas (OPL), was inaugurated on 8 November 1994. In mid-November Gen. Poisson succeeded Gen. Duperval as Commander-in-Chief of the armed forces. Later that month the legislature approved the separation of the police from the army, by which time some 3,000 of the Haitian armed forces, selected as free from accusations of human rights abuses, had undergone a rapid training course under the supervision of US and Canadian instructors to form part of a 4,000-strong interim police force. The remaining 1,000 recruits were returned refugees who had been trained for the purpose while at the refugee camp at Guantánamo, Cuba (see below).

In December 1994 the formation of a new CEP, responsible for organizing and supervising the forthcoming legislative, local and municipal elections, was completed. However, owing to procedural delays the elections were thought unlikely to be held until mid-1995, leaving a period of legislative inactivity, between the end of the current legislative term, ending in January 1995, and the inauguration of a new legislature, at a time when reform would be vital to the successful transition to peaceful civilian rule. In mid-December 1994 Aristide authorized the creation of a national commission of truth and justice to investigate past human rights violations, and ordered the reduction of the armed forces to 1,500 (from an estimated combined army and police force of 7,000–7,500). In the following month two commissions were established for the restructuring of the armed forces and the new civilian police force.

In January 1995 US military commanders certified that the situation in Haiti was sufficiently stable to enable the transfer of authority to the UN. On 30 January the UN Security Council adopted a resolution authorizing the deployment of a UN force of 6,000 troops and 900 civil police to succeed the incumbent multinational force. The UN force, entitled (like that deployed in 1993) the United Nations Mission in Haiti (UNMIH), was to be led by a US commander and include some 2,400 US troops. It was to be responsible for reducing the strength of the army and training both the army and the 4,000-strong (subsequently increased to 6,000) civilian police force, as well as maintaining the 'secure and stable' environment.

On 31 March 1995, against a background of increasing violence and criticism at the inadequacy of the interim police force, authority was officially transferred from the multinational force to the UNMIH. The security situation deteriorated further in April, revealing widespread discontent at high prices, unemployment and the planned privatization of state enterprises. In late April Aristide announced that, following the election of the new legislature, he would seek a constitutional amendment providing for the abolition of the armed forces. (The armed forces were subsequently disbanded, although the constitutional amendment providing for their official abolition could not be approved until the end of the new legislative term.)

The first round of legislative, local and municipal elections (including elections to 18 of the 27 seats in the Senate, all 83 seats in the Chamber of Deputies, 125 mayorships and 555 local councils) were held on 25 June 1995. Owing to administrative failures and isolated incidents of violence and intimidation, voting continued into the following day. Despite the extension, thousands of intending voters were unable to participate, and a further, complementary poll was to be scheduled. The widespread irregularities prompted several opposition parties to demand the annulment of the elections and the dissolution of the CEP, which many perceived as too closely associated with the OPL, the party with majority representation in the Government. The official election results, which were released in mid-July, indicated that all of the 21 seats so far decided had been won by the Plateforme Politique Lavalas (PPL), a three-party electoral alliance comprising the OPL, the Mouvement pour l'Organisation du Pays and the Pati Louvri Baryè. The results were rejected by the majority of opposition parties, which announced a boycott of the electoral process. Continued criticism of the CEP by the opposition led to the resignation of the President of the CEP, Anselme Rémy, in late July.

In early August 1995 the FNCD, MIDH and PANPRA withdrew their respective representatives from the Government, in protest at the absence of a resolution to the electoral dispute. The Minister of Culture, Jean-Claude Bajeux, of the Congrès National des Movements Démocratiques (KONAKOM) resisted his party's demand that he resign, and remained the sole opposition member in the Cabinet. On 13 August, following successive postponements, the complementary elections, for voters who had been denied the opportunity to vote on 25 June, were conducted in 21 districts. A further 17 seats were decided, all of which were won by the PPL. In late August the US Government presented a plan aimed at resolving the electoral dispute. However, its proposals, which included the annulment of the first round elections in many areas, were rejected by the CEP. The second round of voting was held on 17 September, despite the boycott that was maintained by the main opposition parties, and resulted in further large gains for the PPL, which won 17 of the 18 contested seats in the 27-member Senate and 68 seats in the 83-member Chamber of Deputies. The remaining contested seats were won mainly by independent candidates.

In October 1995 Michel resigned as Prime Minister, and was succeeded by the Minister of Foreign Affairs, Claudette Werleigh. She indicated that the new administration intended to retain control of strategic state enterprises, which Michel had planned to sell, and would seek a national debate on the issue of privatization.

In November 1995, despite extensive popular support for Aristide to continue in office for a further three years (to compensate for those years spent in exile), the President confirmed that he would leave office in February 1996. At a presidential election held on 17 December 1995, which was boycotted by all the main opposition parties except KONAKOM, the candidate endorsed by Aristide, René Préval (Prime Minister between February and September 1991), was elected with some 87.9% of the votes cast. He was inaugurated as President on 7 February 1996, and later that month the legislature approved the appointment of

Rosny Smarth as Prime Minister. A new Cabinet was sworn in on 6 March.

The months following the inauguration of the Smarth administration were marked by a high incidence of violence in the capital. Seven members of the civilian police force were murdered over a three-month period, in what was interpreted by Préval as an attempt by anti-democratic forces to destabilize the Government. In mid-August 1996, against a background of unrest and general hostility towards government economic policy, in particular plans for the privatization of state enterprises, a series of armed attacks were conducted against public buildings, including the parliament building and the central police headquarters. The attacks followed the arrest that month, at the headquarters of the right-wing Mobilisation pour le Développement National (MDN), of some 20 former officers of the armed forces who were accused of plotting against the Government. On 20 August two leading members of the MDN were murdered by unidentified gunmen. Opposition politicians accused the Government of responsibility for the killings, and evidence emerged implicating members of the presidential guard in the murders. In mid-September, on the advice of the US Government, Préval dismissed the head of the presidential guard and initiated a reorganization of the unit, which was conducted with the assistance of some 30 US security agents who were sent to protect the President.

In November 1996, as a result of diverging interests within the PPL, Aristide officially established a new political party, La Fanmi Lavalas (FL), which, it was anticipated, would promote his candidacy for the next presidential election. Aristide had openly expressed his opposition to Préval's adoption of economic policies proposed by the International Monetary Fund (IMF), notably the privatization of state enterprises. At the end of the year a series of strikes were conducted by employees in the education, health and transport sectors in support of salary demands and in protest at price rises and poor working conditions. In mid-January 1997 a general strike, in support of demands for the resignation of the Smarth administration and the reversal of the planned divestment of state enterprises, received considerable support.

On 6 April 1997 partial legislative elections were held for nine of the 27 seats in the Senate and two seats in the Chamber of Deputies, as well as elections to local councils. The elections were boycotted by many opposition parties, and less than 5% of the electorate participated in the poll. Of the legislative seats contested only two, in the Senate, were decided, both of which were secured by candidates of the FL. The OPL, the majority party in the governing coalition, alleged that members of the CEP had manipulated the election results in favour of Aristide's party, and demanded the resignation of the CEP and the conduct of a fresh ballot. OAS observers of the poll supported the claims of electoral irregularities, and, following strong international pressure the CEP postponed the second round of the elections, scheduled for 25 May, until mid-June (they were subsequently postponed indefinitely). The OPL had announced that it would boycott the second round elections.

In the light of mounting popular opposition, on 9 June 1997 Smarth resigned from office, although he remained Prime Minister in a caretaker capacity pending the appointment of a replacement. Smarth criticized the CEP for failing to annul the results of the April elections and thus perpetuating the electoral impasse. In the following month Préval nominated Ericq Pierre as Smarth's replacement, but his nomination was rejected by the Chamber of Deputies. In September supporters of Aristide announced the formation of a new 25-member Anti-Neoliberal Bloc in the lower house. In the light of Préval's failure to nominate a candidate for Prime Minister who was acceptable to the legislature, on 20 October Smarth announced that he was to cease his role as caretaker Prime Minister and recommended that his Cabinet resign. Several ministers complied with this request and in late October Préval redesignated their portfolios to remaining cabinet members.

In early November 1997, in an effort to resolve the political crisis, Préval nominated Hervé Y. Denis, an economist and former Minister of Information, Culture and Co-ordination in the Government of Robert Malval, as Prime Minister. In addition, Préval announced the establishment of an electoral commission, comprising three independent legal experts, to resolve the electoral deadlock, and the resignation of six of the nine members of the CEP. The OPL, however, continued to demand the annulment of the April elections and the replacement of the entire CEP. In January 1998 the legislature formally announced its decision to reject the nomination of Denis. The FL subsequently rejected a proposal by the OPL for the creation of a body to mediate in the legislature and thus facilitate the appointment of a new Prime Minister.

In March 1998, following negotiations with the Anti-Neoliberal Bloc, the OPL (renamed the Organisation du Peuple en Lutte in February) withdrew its demands for the annulment of the April 1997 elections as a precondition for the approval of a new Prime Minister, and proposed three candidates. However, Préval subsequently renominated Denis: his candidacy was rejected by the legislature for a second time in April. In July Préval finally agreed to replace the CEP. Préval subsequently received the support of the OPL for the nomination of the incumbent Minister of National Education, Jacques Édouard Alexis, for Prime Minister. Conversely, the Anti-Neoliberal Bloc opposed the nomination of Alexis, who, it maintained, favoured the structural adjustment policies advocated by the IMF. In August the FL announced that it had formally gone into opposition to the Préval administration.

In November 1998 the Senate voted to extend the legislature's current term to October 1999; under electoral legislation adopted in 1995, the term of office of legislators elected in that year's delayed vote had been shortened by one year in order to restore the constitutional timetable of elections, and was thus due to end in January 1999. In December 1998 Alexis was finally declared eligible to assume the office of Prime Minister, subject to his nomination being approved by the legislature (which did not occur until November 2000). The decision had been delayed by a report by the state auditing board, subsequently declared inaccurate, which found irregularities in Alexis' tenure as Minister of National Education. On 11 January 1999 Préval announced that he would no longer recognize the legislature, rejecting the Senate's earlier decision to extend its mandate, and declared that he would install a new government by presidential decree. In mid-January Préval withdrew parliamentary funding prompting the legislature to seek a Supreme Court ruling on the constitutionality of the 1995 electoral law. Préval also entered into consultations with opposition parties in an effort to reach agreement on the composition of a new CEP. In February the Supreme Court postponed indefinitely a decision concerning the electoral law.

On 25 March 1999 Préval appointed by decree a new Cabinet headed by Alexis and including representatives of five small opposition parties that had negotiated an agreement with the President to end the political impasse. The OPL, which had ceased negotiations following the murder, in early March, of one of its leaders, was not included in the new administration. The party, which alleged that the killing had been perpetrated by supporters of Aristide, also stated that it would boycott any elections organized by the new CEP, which was appointed in that month. In May the Supreme Court refused to rule on the legality of Préval's decision to end the funding of the outgoing parliament. The OPL subsequently announced that it had accepted that the parliamentary term had ended and that it would participate in the forthcoming elections. In June the CEP announced that it would disregard the results of the flawed partial legislative elections of April 1997, and presented draft electoral legislation that envisaged the holding of legislative elections in November and December 1999. Préval criticized the CEP's decision concerning the 1997 elections, but in July 1999 he signed a decree annulling them. A new electoral law set 28 November as a provisional date for the first round of legislative and local elections. In August, however, the CEP announced that, for logistical and financial reasons, it had postponed the first round of elections; a new date of 19 December was announced in the following month. However, this too was postponed, as was a further date of 21 March. The delays in holding the ballot prompted violent protests in the capital, in support of demands for the dismissal of the CEP. In January 2000 the remaining US troops stationed in Haiti were withdrawn.

On 21 May 2000 the first round of legislative and municipal elections was held, in which an estimated 60% of the electorate participated. Opposition parties alleged that the results had been manipulated in favour of the FL, claims supported by OAS observers, and demanded the annulment of the election and the conduct of a fresh ballot. The CEP rejected these claims, but in mid-June the CEP President, Léon Manus, fled to the Dominican Republic, claiming that he had received death threats following his refusal to validate the first-round results. His flight prompted demonstrations by Aristide supporters, demanding the publication of the results. According to official first-round results, the FL won 16 of the 19 contested seats in the Senate, and 26 of the 83 seats in the lower house. The results were criticized as inaccurate by the UN, the OAS and numerous foreign governments. Nevertheless, a second round of voting went ahead on 9 July (postponed from 25 June). Opposition protests and a boycott by the 15-party opposition coalition, the Convergence Démocratique (CD) resulted in a low voter turn-out (an estimated 10%) and a high incidence of violence, with 10 separate bombs killing two people and wounding a further 17. According to official results, the FL won 72 seats in the Chamber of Deputies and 18 of the 19 seats contested in the 27-seat upper house (the Pati Louvri Baryè won one seat). The party also gained control of some 80% of the local councils. In September Préval announced that elections to the presidency and to renew the remaining eight senate seats would be held in November. The CD immediately announced its intention to boycott the elections.

In mid-October 2000 it was revealed that an attempt by members of the police force to overthrow the Government had been uncovered. The seven police officers accused of planning the coup fled to the Dominican Republic, and were subsequently granted asylum in Ecuador. The Government reacted by dismissing several senior police officers. In November a court sentenced Gen. Cédras and 36 other senior army officers to life imprisonment with hard labour, *in absentia*, for their role in the murders of 15 people in the shanty town of Raboteau in May 1994.

At the presidential election of 26 November 2000, Aristide was elected with some 91.7% of the votes cast; the remaining six candidates all won less than 2.0% of the ballot. According to official estimates some 60.5% of the electorate voted, although opposition leaders claimed a far lower participation. The only official observer mission, from CARICOM, estimated a 30% voter turn-out. The FL also won the remaining eight seats in the concurrently-held election in the Senate.

In December 2000 an eight-member Transition Committee was established to oversee the smooth transfer of power to Aristide, who was to take office on 7 February 2001. However, in January 2001 the CD announced the formation of an alternative, provisional Government, known as the Front Alternatif, headed by Gérard Gourgue, with the intention of holding fresh elections within two years. The announcement provoked widespread violent demonstrations by Aristide supporters. Discussions between the President-elect and opposition leaders in early February ended without agreement. Two days after his inauguration, President Aristide named Jean-Marie Chérestal, a former Minister of Finance, as Prime Minister, and in early March a new Cabinet was appointed. The new Government included the former MIDH premier, Marc Bazin, and Stanley Théard, a government minister under Duvalier. The CD responded by calling for a month of anti-Government protests. In the same month, in an attempt to end the political impasse, Aristide appointed a new nine-member CEP to investigate the results of the disputed May 2000 elections. The CD was not represented on the Council. In mid-March the new Minister of Foreign Affairs and Relations, Joseph Antonio, announced that legislative elections would be held one year early, in November 2002. Three days later violent protests broke out in Port-au-Prince, in which three people died and dozens were injured. Government supporters attempted to burn down the CD's headquarters and demanded the arrest of the Front Alternatif leader, Gérard Gourgue. On 21 March, in a widely-condemned move, the Senate passed a resolution calling for Gourgue's arrest. Aristide subsequently called for a truce and dialogue between the two sides.

International relations, although improved after 1971, continued to be strained because of Haiti's unpopular political regimes and government corruption. Relations between Haiti and its neighbour on the island of Hispaniola, the Dominican Republic, have traditionally been tense because of the use of the border area by anti-Government guerrillas, smugglers and illegal emigrants, resulting in the periodic closure of the border. Relations between the Dominican Republic and Haiti deteriorated in mid-1991, following a unilateral decision by President Balaguer of the Dominican Republic to repatriate all illegal Haitian residents aged under 16 or over 60, thus placing a considerable burden on Haiti's resources. In March 1996, following an official visit to the Dominican Republic by Préval, the first by a Haitian President since 1935, a joint communiqué was issued establishing a bilateral commission to promote improved co-operation between the two countries. In February 1997, following a rash of repatriations of Haitian refugees from the Dominican Republic, a further communiqué was signed outlining new conditions for the process of repatriation. In June 1998, following an official visit to Haiti by the President of the Dominican Republic, Leonel Fernández Reyna, agreement was reached to establish joint border patrols to combat the traffic of drugs and other contraband between the two countries. In November 1999 Préval submitted a formal protest to the Dominican Republic following a spate of summary deportations of Haitians from the neighbouring country; according to human rights observers, some 8,000 Haitians were forcibly repatriated in the first three weeks of that month. Following a direct meeting between representatives of the two Governments, a protocol was signed in early December limiting the repatriations. Relations between the two countries were strained in November 2000 following the Dominican Republic's refusal to extradite the police officers accused of planning a coup against the Préval Government in the previous month (see above). In January 2001 some 7,500 Haitians were forcibly repatriated from the Dominican Republic.

Following the coup of 30 September 1991, the USA came under international criticism for its forced repatriation of Haitian refugees fleeing the repressive military regime. In November, following an appeal by the Haitian Refugee Center in Miami, USA, a US federal judge in Florida ordered a temporary halt to the repatriation. More than 10,000 refugees were taken into custody by the US coastguard in the period following the coup, the majority of whom were transported to a specially provided camp at the US naval base at Guantánamo, Cuba. However, at the end of January 1992 the US Supreme Court annulled the federal judge's ruling, and repatriation resumed. While a small percentage of refugees were considered for political asylum, the US Government insisted that the majority were economic refugees and therefore not eligible for asylum. In May President George Bush issued an executive order providing for refugees who were intercepted at sea by the US coastguard to be repatriated immediately without any evaluation being made of their right to asylum. The decision, which was condemned by human rights groups, was overturned in July by an appeals court in New York. However, in August the US Supreme Court suspended the appeals court decision, and the executive order stood pending a definitive ruling by the Supreme Court itself. In mid-August fears for the safety of repatriated Haitians were redoubled when Haitian security forces immediately detained some 150 refugees on their return. The policy of President Bush concerning Haitian immigration continued under the presidency of Bill Clinton, despite promises to the contrary made during his election campaign. In January 1993, in response to concern that his election victory might encourage a considerable increase in Haitians seeking refuge, Clinton urged them not to flee Haiti and promised renewed efforts to find a democratic solution to the crisis. In June 1993 the US Supreme Court ruled to uphold the executive order of May 1992, continued under the Clinton administration, which provided for the forcible repatriation of Haitian refugees intercepted at sea.

In April 1994 Aristide announced that he was to abrogate a treaty signed in 1981 under the terms of which the USA was authorized to forcibly repatriate Haitian refugees intercepted at sea. In May, following concerted pressure by US groups, including a 40-strong black caucus in the US Congress, the US Government reversed its policy regarding Haitian refugees, agreeing to resume hearings for all asylum applications—to be conducted at screening centres established later on the British dependent territory of the island of Grand Turk and off the shore of Jamaica. The new policy prompted a renewed exodus of thousands of refugees forcing a further change of US policy in July under which refugees granted asylum were henceforth to be held indefinitely in 'safe havens' outside the USA. In January 1995, following a failed attempt, which included financial incentives, to persuade Haitian refugees at Guantánamo to return voluntarily to Haiti, the US Government ordered the immediate forcible repatriation of nearly all Haitians at the camp. In the same month a repatriation accord was signed with the Bahamas providing for the return of some 10,000 refugees to Haiti by the end of 1995.

Government

The Constitution, approved by referendum in March 1987, provided for a bicameral legislature, comprising a 77-member Chamber of Deputies (later enlarged to 83 members) and a 27-member Senate. The Chamber of Deputies was elected for a term of four years, while the Senate was elected for a term of six years with one-third renewed every two years. Both houses were elected by universal adult suffrage. Executive power was held by the President, who was elected by universal adult suffrage for a five-year term and could not stand for immediate re-election. The President selected a Prime Minister from the political party commanding a majority in the legislature. The Prime Minister chose a Cabinet in consultation with the President. However, the Constitution was interrupted by successive coups, in June and September 1988 and September 1991. A return to constitutional rule was finally effected in October 1994, following the intervention of a US-led multinational force and the reinstatement of the exiled President Aristide.

There are nine Départements, subdivided into arrondissements and communes.

Defence

In November 1994, following the return to civilian rule, measures providing for the separation of the armed forces from the police force were approved by the legislature. In December President Aristide ordered the reduction of the armed forces to 1,500. In that month two commissions were established for the restructuring of the armed forces and the formation of a new 4,000-strong civilian police force (later enlarged to 6,000). In 1995 the armed forces were effectively dissolved, although officially they remained in existence pending an amendment to the Constitution providing for their abolition. In August 2000 the civilian police force numbered an estimated 5,300. There was also a coast guard of 30. The security budget for 2000 was an estimated US $49m.

Economic Affairs

In 1998, according to estimates by the World Bank, Haiti's gross national product (GNP), measured at average 1996–98 prices, was US $3,163m., equivalent to $410 per head (or $1,379 per head on an international purchasing-power parity basis). During 1990–98, it was estimated, GNP per head declined, in real terms, by an average of 3.7% per year. Over the same period the population increased at an average annual rate of 2.4%. Haiti's gross domestic product (GDP) decreased, in real terms, at an average annual rate of 1.3% in 1989–99. Real GDP increased by 2.4% in 1998/99 and by 1.2% in 1999/2000.

Agriculture (including hunting, forestry and fishing) contributed an estimated 31.0% of GDP in 1998/99, measured at constant 1975/76 prices. About 63.0% of the total labour force were engaged in agricultural activities in 1998. The principal cash crop is coffee (which accounted for 4.1% of export earnings in 1997/98). The export of oils for cosmetics and pharmaceuticals is also important. The main food crops are sugar, bananas, maize, sweet potatoes and rice. During 1989–99, according to the World Bank, the real GDP of the agricultural sector decreased at an average annual rate of 3.2%; agricultural GDP increased by 2.2% in 1997/98 and by an estimated 1.1% in 1998/99.

Industry (including mining, manufacturing, construction and power) contributed 21.6% of GDP at constant prices in 1998/99. About 8.8% of the employed labour force were engaged in the sector in 1990. According to the World Bank, industrial GDP declined at an average annual rate of 1.1% in 1989–99; it increased by 6.1% in 1997/98 and by an estimated 4.9% in 1998/99.

Mining contributed 0.2% of GDP at constant prices in 1998/99. About 1% of the employed labour force were engaged in extractive activities in 1990. Marble, limestone and calcareous clay are mined. There are also unexploited copper, silver and gold deposits.

Manufacturing contributed 7.4% of GDP at constant prices in 1998/99. Some 35,000 people were engaged in the sector in mid-2000. The most important branches in 1996, measured by value added, were food products, textiles (including apparel, leather and fur products and footwear), chemicals (including rubber and plastic products) and tobacco. Manufacturing GDP decreased by an average of 11.8% per year in 1989–99; manufacturing GDP increased by 1.9% in 1997/98 and by an estimated 2.4% in 1998/99.

Energy is derived principally from local timber and charcoal. One-third of the country's public electricity comes from the Péligre hydroelectric plant. Imports of fuel products accounted for 10.0% of the value of merchandise imports in 1997/98.

The services sector contributed 47.4% of GDP at constant prices in 1998/99 and engaged 22.8% of the employed labour force in 1990. According to the World Bank, the GDP of the services sector declined by an average of 0.2% per year in

1989–99. However, it increased by 1.9% in 1997/98 and by an estimated 1.8% in 1998/99.

In 1998/99 Haiti recorded a visible trade deficit of US $469.7m., and there was a deficit of $59.6m. on the current account of the balance of payments. In 1999/2000 the trade deficit was estimated at US $498.8m., with a current account deficit of $57.6m. In 1998 the principal source of imports (60%) was the USA; the USA was also the principal market for exports (87%) in that year. Other significant trading partners were France, Canada, Japan and the Dominican Republic. The principal exports in 1997/98 were manufactured articles (86.1%) and coffee. The principal imports in that year were food and live animals (37.2%), manufactured goods and machinery and transport equipment. In 2000 smuggling was estimated to have accounted for two-thirds of Haiti's imports.

In the financial year ending 30 September 1998 there was a budgetary deficit of 776.5m. gourdes (equivalent to 1.2% of GDP). At the end of 1998 Haiti's total external debt was US $1,048m., of which $980m. was long-term public debt. In that year the cost of debt-servicing was equivalent to 8.2% of the total value of exports of goods and services. The annual rate of inflation averaged 22.6% in 1990–98. Consumer prices increased by an annual average of 8.7% in 1999 and by 13.7% in 2000. Some 70% of the labour force were estimated to be unemployed in 1997.

Haiti is a member of the International Coffee Organization (see p. 304) and the Latin American Economic System (SELA, see p. 308). In July 1999 Haiti was granted full membership of the Caribbean Community and Common Market (CARICOM, see p. 142). Haiti is also a signatory of the European Union's Lomé Convention (which expired in February 2000 and was replaced by the Cotonou Agreement in June—see p. 208).

In terms of average income, Haiti is the poorest country in the Western hemisphere, and there is extreme inequality of wealth. The suspension of all non-humanitarian aid and the imposition of successive, and increasingly severe, economic sanctions by the international community, following the military coup of September 1991, had devastating effects on the Haitian economy, serving to exacerbate the extreme poverty endured by the majority of the population. Following the return to civilian rule in late 1994, sanctions were ended and preparations made for the release of aid and new loans. At a meeting of donor nations in Paris in January 1995 measures were agreed for the implementation of an Emergency Economic Recovery Programme, subject to the conclusion of a stand-by agreement with the IMF. However, structural adjustment measures stipulated by the IMF, notably the divestment of public enterprises and the rationalization of the civil service, were not approved by the legislature until late 1996. The IMF subsequently approved a three-year credit of US $131m. under an Enhanced Structural Adjustment Facility (ESAF), which, in turn, facilitated access to further multilateral development aid totalling in excess of $1,000m. However, owing to a parliamentary crisis (see Recent History) the majority of the reforms were not implemented, thus obstructing the disbursement of development aid. By the time of the expiry of the ESAF in October 1999 the bulk of the IMF financing had not been drawn. Furthermore, in November the Alexis administration, which was inaugurated in March of that year, revealed that international agencies had almost entirely failed to honour promises to finance its $311m. short-term economic action plan, initiated in May, which aimed to create employment, improve living conditions and restore public confidence. In 1999 economic activity slowed as a result of the effects on agricultural output of the destruction caused in September 1998 by 'Hurricane Georges'. Economic growth slowed further in 1999/2000, exacerbated by the ongoing political impasse, which continued to impede investment and private-sector confidence, as well as the implementation of the necessary structural adjustments that would allow economic development. Foreign reserves fell by an estimated 20% in 2000. The main source of growth was the continued expansion of exports, principally from the textile sector. In January the European Union suspended payment of almost $70m. in aid to Haiti, and the Inter-American Development Bank was withholding $220m.-worth of loans. On taking office in March 2001, the new Aristide Government appealed for financial aid to recommence. However, international confidence in Haiti's democratic process had to be restored before aid could be resumed.

Social Welfare

Industrial and commercial workers are provided with free health care. In 1995 Haiti had 50 hospital establishments. In the public sector in the same year there were an estimated 641 physicians, 95 dentists and 928 nurses in the country. In mid-1999 there were more than 300 Cuban physicians working in Haiti. Public health received an allocation of 89.5m. gourdes in the Government's budget for 1984/85. Religious and other voluntary groups provide medical services in rural areas and in Port-au-Prince.

Education

Education is provided by the State, by the Roman Catholic Church and by other religious organizations, but many schools charge for tuition, books or uniforms. Teaching is based on the French model, and French is used as the language of instruction. Primary education, which normally begins at six years of age and lasts for six years, is officially compulsory. Secondary education usually begins at 12 years of age and lasts for a further six years, comprising two cycles of three years each. In 1997 primary enrolment included only 19.4% of children in the relevant age-group (18.9% of boys; 19.9% of girls). Enrolment at secondary schools in 1997 was equivalent to only 34.2% of children in the relevant age-group (35.2% of boys; 33.2% of girls). In 1985, according to estimates by UNESCO, the average rate of adult illiteracy was 62.4% (males 59.9%; females 64.7%), the highest national level in the Western hemisphere. The rate was even higher in rural areas (about 85%), where Creole is the popular language. Some basic adult education programmes, with instruction in Creole, were created in an attempt to redress the problem of adult illiteracy. By 1998, according to UNDP estimates, the rate had fallen to 52.2% (males 49.9%; females 54.4%). Higher education is provided by 18 vocational training centres and 42 domestic science schools, and by the Université d'Etat d'Haïti, which has faculties of law, medicine, dentistry, science, agronomy, pharmacy, economic science, veterinary medicine and ethnology. Government expenditure on education in 1990 was 216m. gourdes, equivalent to 20.0% of total government expenditure.

Public Holidays

2001: 1 January (Independence Day), 2 January (Heroes of Independence), 26 February (Shrove Monday, half-day), 27 February (Shrove Tuesday), 13 April (Good Friday), 14 April (Pan-American Day), 1 May (Labour Day), 18 May (Flag Day), 22 May (National Sovereignty), 15 August (Assumption), 24 October (United Nations Day), 2 November (All Souls' Day, half-day), 18 November (Army Day and Commemoration of the Battle of Vertières), 5 December (Discovery Day), 25 December (Christmas Day).

2002: 1 January (Independence Day), 2 January (Heroes of Independence), 11 February (Shrove Monday, half-day), 12 February (Shrove Tuesday), 29 March (Good Friday), 14 April (Pan-American Day), 1 May (Labour Day), 18 May (Flag Day), 22 May (National Sovereignty), 15 August (Assumption), 24 October (United Nations Day), 2 November (All Souls' Day, half-day), 18 November (Army Day and Commemoration of the Battle of Vertières), 5 December (Discovery Day), 25 December (Christmas Day).

Weights and Measures

Officially the metric system is in force but many US measures are also used.

Statistical Survey

Sources (unless otherwise stated): Banque de la République d'Haïti, angle rue du Magasin d'État et rue des Miracles, BP 1570, Port-au-Prince; tel. 299-1000; fax 299-1145; e-mail webmaster@brh.net; internet www.brh.net; Ministère des Finances, Port-au-Prince.

Area and Population

AREA, POPULATION AND DENSITY

Area (sq km)	27,750*
Population (census results)†	
31 August 1971	4,329,991
30 August 1982	
Males	2,448,370
Females	2,605,422
Total	5,053,792
Population (official estimates at mid-year)‡	
1998	6,682,785
1999	6,774,081
2000	7,180,294
Density (per sq km) at mid-2000	258.7

* 10,714 sq miles.
† Excluding adjustment for underenumeration.
‡ Provisional figures.

DEPARTMENTS (population estimates, 2000)

Artibonite . . .	1,013,779	North-West . .	420,971
Central . . .	490,790	South . . .	653,398
Grande-Anse . .	641,399	South-East . .	457,013
North	759,318	West	2,494,862
North-East . .	248,764	**Total** . . .	7,180,294

PRINCIPAL TOWNS (estimated population at mid-1996)

Port-au-Prince (capital) .	884,472	Delmas . . .	240,429
Carrefour	290,204	Cap-Haïtien . .	102,233

Source: UN, *Demographic Yearbook*.

BIRTHS AND DEATHS (World Bank estimates)

	1996	1997	1998
Crude birth rate (per 1,000) . .	32	32	31
Crude death rate (per 1,000) . .	12	13	13

Source: World Bank, *World Development Indicators*.

Expectation of life (estimates, years at birth, 1998): 54.0 (males 51.5; females 56.4) (Source: UNDP, *Human Development Report*).

ECONOMICALLY ACTIVE POPULATION
(official estimates, persons aged 10 years and over, mid-1990)

	Males	Females	Total
Agriculture, hunting, forestry and fishing	1,077,191	458,253	1,535,444
Mining and quarrying . .	11,959	12,053	24,012
Manufacturing . . .	83,180	68,207	151,387
Electricity, gas and water .	1,643	934	2,577
Construction	23,584	4,417	28,001
Trade, restaurants and hotels.	81,632	271,338	352,970
Transport, storage and communications . . .	17,856	2,835	20,691
Financing, insurance, real estate and business services	3,468	1,589	5,057
Community, social and personal services	81,897	73,450	155,347
Activities not adequately defined .	33,695	30,280	63,975
Total employed . . .	1,416,105	923,356	2,339,461
Unemployed	191,333	148,346	339,679
Total labour force . . .	1,607,438	1,071,702	2,679,140

Source: ILO, *Yearbook of Labour Statistics*.

Mid-1998 (estimates in '000): Agriculture, etc. 2,168; Total labour force 3,418 (Source: FAO, *Production Yearbook*).

Agriculture

PRINCIPAL CROPS ('000 metric tons)

	1997*	1998	1999*
Rice (paddy)	160	101	100
Maize	230	206	250
Sweet potatoes . . .	160	170	172
Dry beans	50	35	36
Sugar cane	1,100	1,000	1,000
Bananas	250	288	290
Coffee (green) . . .	27	27	28
Cocoa beans	4	5	5

* FAO estimates.
Source: FAO.

LIVESTOCK ('000 head, year ending September)

	1997	1998	1999
Horses*	490	490	490
Mules*	80	80	80
Asses*	210	210	210
Cattle	1,270	1,300	1,300*
Pigs	600	800	800*
Sheep	161†	138	138*
Goats	1,445†	1,618†	1,619*

Chickens (million): 4* in 1997; 5 in 1998; 5* in 1999.
* FAO estimate(s).   † Unofficial figure(s).
Source: FAO.

LIVESTOCK PRODUCTS ('000 metric tons)

	1997	1998	1999
Beef and veal	28	31	31†
Goat meat	5*	5*	5†
Pig meat	25	27	27†
Horse meat	5	5	5
Poultry meat	6	8	8
Cows' milk†	37†	37†	38
Goats' milk	20	20	20
Hen eggs†	4	4	4
Cattle hides	4	5	5

* Unofficial figures.   † FAO estimate(s).
Source: FAO.

Forestry

ROUNDWOOD REMOVALS ('000 cubic metres, excl. bark)

	1996	1997	1998
Sawlogs, veneer logs and logs for sleepers* . . .	224	224	224
Other industrial wood* . .	15	15	15
Fuel wood	6,245	6,362	6,158
Total	6,484	6,601	6,397

* Annual output assumed to be unchanged since 1971.
Source: FAO, *Yearbook of Forest Products*.

SAWNWOOD PRODUCTION
(FAO estimates, '000 cubic metres, incl. railway sleepers)

	1996	1997	1998
Coniferous (softwood) . . .	8	8	8
Broadleaved (hardwood) . . .	6	6	6
Total	14	14	14

Source: FAO, *Yearbook of Forest Products.*

Fishing

(FAO estimates, metric tons, live weight)

	1996	1997	1998
Freshwater fishes . .	500	500	450
Marine fishes . . .	4,000	4,000	4,000
Caribbean spiny lobster . .	190	210	200
Inshore shrimps	150	150	160
Stromboid conchs . . .	400	380	350
Total catch	5,245	5,311	5,219

Source: FAO, *Yearbook of Fishery Statistics.*

Industry

SELECTED PRODUCTS
(metric tons, unless otherwise indicated, year ending 30 September)

	1999/2000
Edible oils	38,839.6
Butter	2,972.2
Margarine	2,387.4
Cornflour	104,542.6
Soap	30,069.9
Detergent	4,506.1
Beer ('000 cases of 24 bottles) . .	784.5
Beverages ('000 cases of 24 bottles)	1,807.7
Rum ('000 750ml bottles) . . .	2,009.5
Electric energy (million kWh) . .	697.6

Finance

CURRENCY AND EXCHANGE RATES

Monetary Units
  100 centimes = 1 gourde.

Sterling, Dollar and Euro Equivalents (29 December 2000)
  £1 sterling = 33.611 gourdes;
  US $1 = 22.524 gourdes;
  €1 = 20.959 gourdes;
  1,000 gourdes = £29.75 = $44.40 = €47.71.

Average Exchange Rate (gourdes per US $)
  1998   16.766
  1999   16.938
  2000   21.171

Note: The official rate of exchange was maintained at US $1 = 5 gourdes until September 1991, when the central bank ceased all operations at the official rate, thereby unifying the exchange system at the 'floating' free market rate.

BUDGET (million gourdes, year ending 30 September)

Revenue	1995/96	1996/97	1997/98
Current receipts	3,178	4,770	5,252
Internal receipts . . .	2,678	3,731	4,174
Income tax	485	688	630
General sales tax . .	619	1,271	1,420
Excises	495	705	855
Other domestic receipts . .	235	1,056	1,225
Customs	499	1,039	1,078
Transfers from public enterprises .	238	57	119
Total	3,417	4,828	5,371

Expenditure	1995/96	1996/97	1997/98
Current expenditure . . .	4,459	4,217	4,828
Wages and salaries . . .	2,083	2,689	2,815
Operations	895	1,242	1,434
Subsidies	622	272	243
Interest on public debt . .	211	374	437
External debt . . .	143	206	215
Internal debt . . .	68	168	222
Other current expenditure . .	648	−360	−101
Capital expenditure . . .	145	874	1,219
Total*	4,604	5,084	6,036

* Including net lending (million gourdes): 0.0 in 1995/96; −7.0 in 1996/97; −11 in 1997/98.

Source: IMF, *Haiti: Statistical Annex* (October 1999).

INTERNATIONAL RESERVES (US $ million at 31 December)*

	1995	1996	1997
IMF special drawing rights . .	0.5	0.1	0.1
Reserve position in IMF . . .	0.1	0.1	0.1
Foreign exchange . . .	105.2	107.8	77.0
Total	105.8	107.9	77.2

* Excluding gold (valued at market-related prices, US $ million): 6.6 in 1989.

Source: IMF, *International Financial Statistics.*

MONEY SUPPLY (million gourdes at 31 December)*

	1998	1999	2000
Currency outside banks . .	3,905.4	4,927.1	5,773.4
Demand deposits at commercial banks	2,544.2	3,241.3	3,306.0
Total money (incl. others) . .	6,650.9	8,422.8	9,241.1

* Beginning in September 1997, data are based on an improved sectorization of the accounts.

Source: IMF, *International Financial Statistics.*

COST OF LIVING
(Consumer Price Index, year ending 30 September; base: 1991 = 100)

	1991/92	1992/93	1993/94
Food	119.0	134.3	182.0
Clothing and footwear . .	114.4	134.0	186.4
Furnishings	117.8	154.7	190.1
Housing, heating and light .	108.3	138.9	204.9
Services	112.5	137.5	226.7
All items	115.6	137.3	186.9

All items (base: 1995 = 100): 160.8 in 1998; 174.8 in 1999; 198.7 in 2000 (Source: IMF, *International Financial Statistics*).

NATIONAL ACCOUNTS (million gourdes, year ending 30 September)
Expenditure on the Gross Domestic Product (at current prices)

	1997/98	1998/99	1999/2000
Final consumption expenditure .	60,543	68,808	78,559
Increase in stocks . . . }	7,596	8,924	10,069
Gross fixed capital formation . }			
Total domestic expenditure .	68,139	77,732	88,628
Exports of goods and services .	7,799	9,017	9,933
Less Imports of goods and services	16,883	19,460	21,765
GDP in purchasers' values . .	59,055	67,289	76,797
GDP at constant 1976 prices .	4,634	n.a.	n.a.

Source: IMF, *International Financial Statistics.*

Gross Domestic Product by Economic Activity
(at constant 1975/76 prices)

	1996/97*	1997/98†	1998/99†
Agriculture, hunting, forestry and fishing	1,373	1,403	1,418
Mining and quarrying . . .	9	9	10
Manufacturing	324	330	338
Electricity, gas and water . .	42	42	43
Construction	514	562	598
Trade, restaurants and hotels. .	607	623	635
Transport, storage and communication . . .	97	98	105
Government services . . .	820	829	826
Finance, insurance, real estate and business services . .	357	366	374
Other services	211	216	231
Sub-total	4,354	4,478	4,578
Import duties	161	174	184
GDP in purchasers' values .	4,515	4,653	4,762

* Provisional figures.
† Estimates.

BALANCE OF PAYMENTS
(US $ million, year ending 30 September)

	1995/96	1996/97	1997/98
Exports of goods f.o.b. . . .	82.5	205.4	299.3
Imports of goods f.o.b. . . .	−498.6	−559.6	−640.7
Trade balance	−416.1	−354.2	−341.4
Exports of services . . .	109.1	173.7	180.0
Imports of services . . .	−283.3	−331.5	−380.6
Balance on goods and services	−590.3	−512.0	−542.0
Other income paid . . .	−9.9	−13.6	−11.7
Balance on goods, services and income	−600.2	−525.6	−553.7
Current transfers received . .	462.5	477.9	515.6
Current balance . . .	−137.7	−47.7	−38.1
Direct investment from abroad .	4.1	4.0	10.8
Other investment assets . .	−4.6	21.6	86.8
Other investment liabilities .	68.4	35.9	95.5
Net errors and omissions . .	19.4	16.0	−120.5
Overall balance . . .	−50.4	29.8	34.5

Source: IMF, *International Financial Statistics.*

External Trade

PRINCIPAL COMMODITIES
(US $ million, year ending 30 September)

Imports c.i.f.	1995/96	1996/97	1997/98
Food and live animals . . .	343.0	318.4	301.5
Mineral fuels, lubricants, etc. . .	79.4	74.9	80.8
Machinery and transport equipment	125.0	111.5	125.8
Raw materials	7.9	17.2	22.5
Manufactured goods . . .	130.6	154.4	223.2
Total (incl. others) . . .	687.9	706.6	811.5

Exports f.o.b.	1995/96	1996/97	1997/98
Coffee	6.9	13.0	11.6
Essential oils	5.7	2.9	3.7
Light manufactures . . .	126.6	159.4	244.9
Total (incl. others) . . .	147.7	195.5	284.3

Source: IMF, *Haiti: Statistical Annex* (October 1999).

PRINCIPAL TRADING PARTNERS*
(US $ million, year ending 30 September)

Imports c.i.f.	1989/90	1990/91	1991/92
Belgium	3.4	3.7	2.9
Canada	22.0	31.9	15.2
France	24.5	32.4	17.2
Germany, Federal Republic .	14.6	19.2	10.0
Japan	23.6	31.2	17.7
Netherlands	11.2	13.9	8.7
United Kingdom . . .	5.6	6.7	4.2
USA	153.1	203.2	126.7
Total (incl. others) . . .	332.2	400.5	277.2

Exports f.o.b.†	1989/90	1990/91	1991/92
Belgium	15.9	19.5	6.0
Canada	4.5	4.7	2.3
France	17.4	21.6	6.1
Germany, Federal Republic .	5.4	6.6	2.4
Italy	16.5	20.7	8.7
Japan	2.4	2.9	0.9
Netherlands	3.4	4.3	1.4
United Kingdom . . .	2.3	2.3	0.7
USA	78.3	96.3	39.7
Total (incl. others) . . .	163.7	198.7	74.7

* Provisional.
† Excluding re-exports.

Source: Administration Générale des Douanes.

Transport

ROAD TRAFFIC ('000 motor vehicles in use)

	1994	1995	1996
Passenger cars	30.0	49.0	59.0
Commercial vehicles . . .	30.0	29.0	35.0

Source: UN, *Statistical Yearbook.*

SHIPPING
Merchant Fleet (registered at 31 December)

	1996	1997	1998
Number of vessels	6	7	5
Total displacement ('000 grt) . .	1.0	1.6	1.3

Source: Lloyd's Register of Shipping, *World Fleet Statistics*.

International Sea-borne Freight Traffic ('000 metric tons)

	1988	1989	1990
Goods loaded	164	165	170
Goods unloaded	684	659	704

Source: UN, *Monthly Bulletin of Statistics*.

CIVIL AVIATION
International flights, 1995: Passengers arriving 367,900; Passengers departing 368,330.

Tourism

TOURISM ARRIVALS BY COUNTRY OF ORIGIN

	1996	1997	1998
Canada	14,783	15,825	15,489
Dominican Republic	7,373	7,319	7,905
France	7,471	7,179	6,984
USA	96,253	94,783	93,978
Total (incl. others) . . .	150,147	148,735	146,837

Receipts from tourism (US $ million): 81 in 1996; 80 in 1997; 58 in 1998.
Source: World Tourism Organization, *Yearbook of Tourism Statistics*.

Communications Media

	1995	1996	1997
Radio receivers ('000 in use) . .	380	400	415
Television receivers ('000 in use) .	35	36	38
Telephones ('000 main lines in use)*	60	60	60

Daily newspapers: 4 in 1996 (total circulation 20,000 copies).
Book production: 340 titles published in 1995.
* Estimates.
Sources: UNESCO, *Statistical Yearbook*; UN, *Statistical Yearbook*.

Education

(1994/95)

	Institutions	Teachers	Students
Pre-primary	n.a.	n.a.	230,391*
Primary	10,071	30,205	1,110,398
Secondary	1,038	15,275	195,418
Tertiary	n.a.	654*	6,288*

* 1990/91 figures.

Directory

The Constitution

The Constitution of the Republic of Haiti, which was approved by the electorate in a referendum held in March 1987, provided for a system of power-sharing between a President (who may not serve two consecutive five-year terms), a Prime Minister, a bicameral legislature and regional assemblies. Prominent former supporters of ex-President Jean-Claude Duvalier were to be barred from elective office for 10 years. Authority was to be distributed regionally. The army and the police were no longer to be a combined force. The death penalty was abolished, and there was to be an independent judiciary. Official status was given to the Creole language spoken by Haitians and to the folk religion, voodoo (vaudou). The Constitution was suspended after a military *coup d'état* in June 1988, but was partially restored in March 1989. It was fully restored when the military ruler, Brig.-Gen. Prosper Avril, fled in March 1990 and an interim President was appointed, pending a presidential election in December 1990. Fr Jean-Bertrand Aristide was elected President, but was deposed in September 1991 by a military coup. In October a new President and Government were installed by the army, which claimed that it was acting in accordance with the Constitution. In June 1992 the presidency was declared to be vacant, but in May 1994 a pro-military faction of the Senate declared the head of the Supreme Court, Émile Jonassaint, provisional President. Following US mediation and threat of invasion, international peace-keeping forces (initially a nominally multinational force comprised almost entirely of US troops) began to arrive on the island on 19 September. Lt-Gen. Raoul Cédras, the Commander-in-Chief of the armed forces, resigned on 10 October, and Jonassaint resigned on the following day. On 15 October President Aristide returned to Haiti, to begin the restoration of constitutional government. He declared the army dissolved in April 1995. The constitutional amendment formally abolishing it was due to be passed by the legislature elected in May and July 2000.

The Government

HEAD OF STATE

President: JEAN-BERTRAND ARISTIDE (assumed office on 7 February 2001).

CABINET
(April 2001)

Prime Minister: JEAN-MARIE CHÉRESTAL.

Minister of Agriculture and the Environment: SÉBASTIEN HILAIRE.

Minister of the Civil Service: WEBSTER PIERRE.

Minister of Commerce and Industry: STANLEY THÉARD.

Minister of Culture and Communications: GUY PAUL.

Minister of Economy and Finance: GUSTAVE FAUBERT.

Minister of Foreign Affairs and Religion: JOSEPH ANTONIO.

Minister for Haitians Residing Abroad: LESLIE VOLTAIRE.

Minister of the Interior: HENRI-CLAUDE MÉNARD.

Minister of Justice: GARY LISSADE.

Minister of Labour and Social Affairs: EUDES SAINT-PREUX CRAAN.

Minister of National Education, Youth and Sport: GEORGES MERISIER.

Minister of Planning and External Co-operation: MARC BAZIN.

Minister of Public Health: HENRI-CLAUDE VOLTAIRE.

Minister of Public Works: ERNST LARAQUE.

Minister of Tourism: MARTINE DEVERSON.

Minister of Women's Affairs and Rights: GINETTE LUBIN.

Secretary of State for Labour: RONALD JOSEPH.

Secretary of State for Population: JEAN ANDRE.

Secretary of State for Public Security: GÉRARD DUBREUIL.

Secretary of State for Tourism: MARTINE DEVERSON.

Secretary of State for Youth, Sports and Civic Service: EVANS LESCOUFLAIR.

Secretary of State for Finance: JOCELERME PRIVERT.

MINISTRIES

Office of the President: Palais National, Champ de Mars, Port-au-Prince; tel. 222-3024.

Office of the Prime Minister: Villa d'Accueil, Delmas 60, Musseau, Port-au-Prince; tel. 245-0007; fax 245-1624.

Ministry of Agriculture and the Environment: Rte Nationale 1, Damien, Port-au-Prince; tel. 222-3596.

Ministry of the Civil Service: Port-au-Prince.

Ministry of Commerce and Industry: rue Légitime 26, Champ-de-Mars, Port-au-Prince; tel. 222-1628; fax 223-8402.

Ministry of Culture and Communications: rue Roy 31, Port-au-Prince; tel. 222-7357.

Ministry of Economy and Finance: Palais des Ministères, Port-au-Prince; tel. 222-0724.

Ministry of Foreign Affairs and Religion: blvd Harry S Truman, Cité de l'Exposition, Port-au-Prince; tel. 222-8482; fax 223-1668.

Ministry for Haitians Residing Abroad: rue Duncombe 37, Port-au-Prince; tel. 245-1116; fax 245-3400.

Ministry of the Interior: Palais des Ministères, Port-au-Prince; tel. 222-6490; fax 223-5742.

Ministry of Justice: ave Charles Sumner 19, Port-au-Prince; tel. 245-1626.

Ministry of Labour and Social Affairs: rue de la Révolution 16, Port-au-Prince; tel. 222-1244.

Ministry of National Education, Youth and Sport: rue Audain, Port-au-Prince; tel. 222-1036; fax 223-7887.

Ministry of Planning and External Co-operation: Palais des Ministères, Port-au-Prince; tel. 222-4148; fax 223-4193.

Ministry of Public Health: Palais de Ministères, Port-au-Prince; tel. 222-1583; fax 222-4066.

Ministry of Public Works: Palais des Ministères, BP 2002, Port-au-Prince; tel. 222-2164; fax 223-4586.

Ministry of Tourism: Port-au-Prince.

Ministry of Women's Affairs and Rights: Champ de Mars, Port-au-Prince; tel. 222-1479.

President and Legislature

PRESIDENT

Presidential Election, 26 November 2000

Candidates	% of votes
JEAN-BERTRAND ARISTIDE (FL)	91.7
JEAN-ARNOLD DUMAS	2.0
EVAN NICOLAS	1.6
SERGE SYLVAIN	1.3
CALIXTE DORISCA	1.3
JACQUES PHILIPPE DORCE	1.1
PAUL ARTHUR FLEURIVAL	1.0
Total (incl. others)	100.0

LEGISLATURE

Sénat
(Senate)

President: YVON NEPTUNE.

Elections, 21 May, 9 July and 26 November 2000

	Seats
La Fanmi Lavalas (FL)	26
Pati Louvri Baryè (PLB)	1
Total	27

Chambre des Députés
(Chamber of Deputies)

President: PIERRE PAUL COTIN.

Elections, 21 May, 9 July and 26 November 2000

	Seats
La Fanmi Lavalas (FL)	73
Mouvement Chrétien pour Batir une Nouvelle Haïti (MOCHRENA)	3
Espace de Concertation	2
Pati Louvri Baryè (PLB)	2
Koordinasyon Resistans Grandans (KOREGA-ESCANP)	1
Organisation du Peuple en Lutte (OPL)	1
Independent	1
Total	**83**

Political Organizations

Alliance pour l'Avancement d'Haïti (ALAH): BP 13350, Station de Delmas, Port-au-Prince; tel. 245-0446; fax 257-4804; f. 1975; Leader REYNOLD GEORGES.

Congrès National des Mouvements Démocratiques (KONAKOM): f. 1987; social democratic; Leader VICTOR BENOÎT.

Convergence Démocratique (CD): f. 2000; coalition of 15 anti-Lavalas parties; Leaders SERGE GILLES, EVANS PAUL.

Espace de Concertation: f. 1999; centre-left coalition; Leader EVANS PAUL.

La Fanmi Lavalas: f. 1996; formed a coalition with the MOP, the OPL and the PLB; Leader JEAN-BERTRAND ARISTIDE.

Jeunesse Pouvoir Populaire (JPP): f. 1997; Leader RENÉ CIVIL.

Konfederasyon Inite Demokratik (KID): f. 1986; Leader EVANS PAUL.

Koordinasyon Resistans Grandans (KOREGA-ESCANP): regionally based; radical left; Leader Fr JOACHIM SAMEDI.

Mobilisation pour le Développement National (MDN): c/o CHISS, 33 rue Bonne Foi, BP 2497, Port-au-Prince; tel. 222-3829; e-mail info@mdnhaiti.org; internet www.mdnhaiti.org; f. 1986; Pres. HUBERT DE RONCERAY; Sec. Gen. MAX CARRE.

Mouvement Chrétien pour Batir une Nouvelle Haïti (MOCHRENA): f. 1991; Leader LUC MESADIEUX.

Mouvement Démocratique pour la Libération d'Haïti (MODELH): Leader FRANÇOIS LATORTUE.

Mouvement pour l'Instauration de la Démocratie en Haïti (MIDH): 114 ave Jean Paul II, Port-au-Prince; tel. 245-8377; f. 1986; centre-right; Pres. MARC BAZIN.

Mouvement pour l'Organisation du Pays (MOP): f. 1946; centre party; Leader JEAN MOLIÈRE.

Mouvement Patriotique pour le Sauvetage National (MPSN): f. 1998; right-wing coalition; Leader HUBERT DE RONCERAY.

Mouvement pour la Reconstruction Nationale (MRN): f. 1991; Leader RENÉ THÉODORE.

Organisation du Peuple en Lutte (OPL): f. 1991 as Organisation Politique Lavalas; name changed as above 1998; Leaders GÉRARD PIERRE-CHARLES, SAUVEUR PIERRE-ÉTIENNE.

Parti Agricole et Industrie National (PAIN): Leader LOUIS DEJOIE.

Parti des Démocrates Haïtiens (PADEMH): Leader JEAN-JACQUES CLARK PARENT.

Parti Démocratique et Chrétien d'Haïti (PDCH): f. 1979; Christian Democrat party; Leader JOACHIN PIERRE.

Parti pour un Développement Alternatif (PADH): Leader GÉRARD DALVIUS.

Parti National Progressiste Révolutionnaire (PANPRA): f. 1989; social-democratic; mem. of Socialist International; Leader SERGE GILLES.

Parti Populaire National: f. 1999; Leader BEN DUPUY.

Parti Social Chrétien d'Haïti (PSCH): Leader GRÉGOIRE EUGÈNE.

Pati Louvri Baryè (PLB): f. 1992; Leader RENAUD BERNARDIN.

Rassemblement des Démocrates Chrétiens (RDC): Leader EDDY VOLEL.

Rassemblement des Démocrates Nationalistes et Progressistes (RDNP): f. 1979; centre party; Sec.-Gen. LESLIE FRANÇOIS MANIGAT.

Union Démocrates Patriotiques (UDP): Leader ROCKEFELLER GUERRE.

Diplomatic Representation

EMBASSIES IN HAITI

Argentina: 8 rue Mangones, Berthe, Pétionville, BP 1755, Port-au-Prince; tel. 257-5725; fax 257-8227; Ambassador: JOSÉ MARÍA BERRO MADERO.

Brazil: 37 rue Lamarre, Pétionville, BP 15845, Port-au-Prince; tel. 256-0900; fax 510-6111; Ambassador: ANTÔNIO FERREIRA DA ROCHA.

Canada: 18 route de Delmas, BP 826, Port-au-Prince; tel. 223-2358; fax 223-8720; Ambassador: GILLES BERNIER.

Chile: 384 route de Delmas, entre rues 42 et 44, Port-au-Prince; Ambassador: LUCHO LARRAÍN CRUZ.

China (Taiwan): 16 rue Leon Nau, Pétionville, BP 655, Port-au-Prince; tel. 256-8063; fax 256-8067; e-mail ambrde@aen2.net; Ambassador: MICHEL LU CHING-LONG.

Colombia: Complexe 384, No 7, route de Delmas, entre rues 42 et 44, Port-au-Prince; tel. 246-2599; fax 246-5595; Ambassador: GUILLERMO TRIANA AYALA.

Cuba: Port-au-Prince; Ambassador: OSCAR COET BLACKSTOCK.

Dominican Republic: rue Panaméricaine 121, BP 56, Pétionville, Port-au-Prince; tel. 257-0383; fax 257-9215; Ambassador: ALBERTO EMILIO DESPRADEL CABRAL.

Ecuador: BP 2531, Port-au-Prince; tel. 222-4576; Chargé d'affaires: ADOLFO ALVAREZ.

France: 51 place des Héros de l'Indépendance, BP 1312, Port-au-Prince; tel. 222-0951; fax 223-9858; Ambassador: YVES GAUDEUL.

Germany: 2 impasse Claudinette, Bois Moquette, Pétionville, BP 1147, Port-au-Prince; tel. 257-7280; fax 257-4131; e-mail germanem@haitiworld.com; Ambassador: JULIUS GEORG LUY.

Holy See: rue Louis Pouget, Morne Calvaire, BP 326, Port-au-Prince; tel. 257-6308; fax 257-3411; e-mail nonciature@haitiworld.com; Apostolic Nuncio: Most Rev. LUIGI BONAZZI, Titular Archbishop of Atella.

Japan: Villa Bella Vista 2, impasse Tulipe, Desprez, Port-au-Prince; tel. 245-3333; fax 245-8834; Ambassador: HISANOBU HASAMA.

Mexico: Delmas 60, 2, BP 327, Port-au-Prince; tel. 257-8100; fax 256-6528; e-mail embmxhai@yahoo.com; Ambassador: CARLOS FERRER.

Spain: 54 rue Pacot, State Liles, BP 386, Port-au-Prince; tel. 245-4410; fax 245-3901; Ambassador: RAFAEL MATOS GONZÁLEZ DE CAREAGA.

USA: 5 blvd Harry S Truman, BP 1761, Port-au-Prince; tel. 223-5511; fax 223-5515; Ambassador: BRIAN DEAN CURRAN.

Venezuela: blvd Harry S Truman, Cité de l'Exposition, BP 2158, Port-au-Prince; tel. 222-0973; Ambassador: IRMA ANTONINI.

Judicial System

Law is based on the French Napoleonic Code, substantially modified during the presidency of François Duvalier.

Courts of Appeal and Civil Courts sit at Port-au-Prince and the three provincial capitals: Gonaïves, Cap Haïtien and Port de Paix. In principle each commune has a Magistrates' Court. Judges of the Supreme Court and Courts of Appeal are appointed by the President.

Supreme Court: Port-au-Prince; tel. 222-3212; Pres. PRADEL JEAN (acting).

Religion

Roman Catholicism and the folk religion voodoo (vaudou) are the official religions. There are various Protestant and other denominations.

CHRISTIANITY

The Roman Catholic Church

For ecclesiastical purposes, Haiti comprises two archdioceses and seven dioceses. At 31 December 1998 adherents represented some 66.9% of the population.

Bishops' Conference: Conférence Episcopale de Haïti, angle rues Piquant et Lamarre, BP 1572, Port-au-Prince; tel. 222-5194; fax 223-5318; e-mail cehd@haitiworld.com; f. 1977; Pres. Rt Rev. HUBERT CONSTANT, Bishop of Fort-Liberté.

Archbishop of Cap-Haïtien: Most Rev. FRANÇOIS GAYOT, Archevêché, rue 19–20 H, CP 22, Cap-Haïtien; tel. 262-0071; fax 262-0593.

Archbishop of Port-au-Prince: Most Rev. FRANÇOIS-WOLFF LIGONDÉ, Archevêché, rue Dr Aubry, BP 538, Port-au-Prince; tel. 222-2043.

The Anglican Communion

Anglicans in Haiti fall under the jurisdiction of a missionary diocese of Province II of the Episcopal Church in the USA.

Bishop of Haiti: Rt Rev. JEAN ZACHE DURACIN, Eglise Episcopale d'Haïti, BP 1309, Port-au-Prince; fax 257-3412; e-mail epihaiti@globalsud.net.

Protestant Churches

Baptist Convention: BP 20, Cap-Haïtien; tel. 262-0567; f. 1964; Pres. Rev. MOÏSE JOËL DORSINVILLE.

Lutheran Church: Petite Place Cuzeau, BP 13147, Delmas, Port-au-Prince; tel. 246-3179; f. 1975; Minister BEN BICHOTTE.

Other denominations active in Haiti include Methodists and the Church of God 'Eben-Ezer'.

The Press

DAILIES

Le Matin: 88 rue du Quai, BP 367, Port-au-Prince; tel. 222-2040; f. 1908; French; independent; circ. 5,000.

Le Nouvelliste: 198 rue du Centre, BP 1316, Port-au-Prince; tel. 223-2114; fax 223-2313; f. 1898; evening; French; independent; Dir MAX CHAUVET; circ. 6,000.

PERIODICALS

Haïti en Marche: 8 ruelle Cheriez, Port-au-Prince; tel. 245-1910; fax 513-5688; internet www.haitienmarche.com; weekly; Editor MARCUS GARCIA.

Haïti Progrès: 11 rue Capois, Port-au-Prince; tel. 222-6513; internet www.haiti-progres.com; weekly; Dir BEN DUPUY.

Haïti Observateur: 98 ave John Brown, Port-au-Prince; tel. 228-0782; weekly; Editor LEO JOSEPH.

Le Messager du Nord-Ouest: Port de Paix; weekly.

Le Moniteur: BP 214 bis, Port-au-Prince; tel. 222-1744; 2 a week; French; the official gazette; circ. 2,000.

Optique: French Institute, BP 1316, Port-au-Prince; monthly; arts.

Le Septentrion: Cap-Haïtien; weekly; independent; Editor NELSON BELL; circ. 2,000.

NEWS AGENCIES

Agence Haïtienne de Presse (AHP): 6 rue Fernand, Port-au-Prince; tel. 245-7222; fax 245-5836; e-mail ahp@haitiworld.com; internet www.ahphaiti.org; Dir-Gen. VENEL REMARAIS.

Haiti On Line (HOL): 40 bis rue Lamarre, Pétionville; tel. (Miami, USA) (305) 385-3539; fax (305) 418-7541; internet www.haitionline.com; f. 1996; Dir YVES RENAUD.

Foreign Bureaux

Agence France-Presse (AFP): 72 rue Pavée, BP 62, Port-au-Prince; tel. 222-3469; fax 222-3759; Bureau Chief DOMINIQUE LEVANTI.

Agencia EFE (Spain): Port-au-Prince; tel. 255-9517; Correspondent HEROLD JEAN-FRANÇOIS.

Associated Press (AP) (USA): BP 2443, Port-au-Prince; tel. 257-4240; Correspondent MIKE NORTON.

Inter Press Service (Italy): 16 rue Malval, Turgeau, BP 19046, Port-au-Prince; tel. 245-9393; fax 245-9292; e-mail ipshaiti@haitiweb.net; Correspondent IVES-MARIE CHANEL.

Prensa Latina (Cuba): Port-au-Prince; tel. 246-5149; Correspondent JACQUELÍN TELEMAQUE.

United Press International (UPI) (USA): Port-au-Prince; tel. 223-6565; Correspondent ROOSEVELT JEAN-FRANÇOIS.

Publishers

Editions des Antilles: route de l'Aéroport, Port-au-Prince.

Editions Caraïbes S.A.: 57, rue Pavée, BP 2013, Port-au-Prince; tel. 222-0032; Man. PIERRE J. ELIE.

Editions du Soleil: BP 2471, rue du Centre, Port-au-Prince; tel. 222-3147; education.

L'Imprimeur Deux: Le Nouvelliste, 198 rue du Centre, Port-au-Prince.

Maison Henri Deschamps—Les Entreprises Deschamps Frisch, SA: 25 rue Dr Martelly Seïde, BP 164, Port-au-Prince; tel. 223-2215; fax 223-4976; e-mail entreprisesdeschamps@globelsud.net; f. 1898; education and literature; Man. Dir JACQUES DESCHAMPS, Jr; CEO PETER J. FRISCH.

Natal: Imprimerie, rue Barbancourt, Port-au-Prince; Dir ROBERT MALVAL.

Théodore: Imprimerie, rue Dantes Destouches, Port-au-Prince.

Broadcasting and Communications

TELECOMMUNICATIONS

Conseil National des Télécommunications (CONATEL): 16 ave Marie Jeanne, Cité de l'Exposition, BP 2002, Port-au-Prince; tel. 222-0300; fax 222-0579; f. 1969; govt communications licensing authority; Dir-Gen. JEAN ARY CÉANT.

Télécommunications d'Haïti (Téléco): Blvd Jean-Jacques Dessalines, BP 814, Port-au-Prince; tel. 245–2200; fax 223-0002; scheduled for privatization; Dir-Gen. (vacant).

BROADCASTING

Radio

Radio Antilles International: 175 rue du Centre, BP 2335, Port-au-Prince; tel. 223-0696; f. 1984; independent; Dir-Gen. JACQUES SAMPEUR.

Radio Cacique: 5 Bellevue, BP 1480, Port-au-Prince; tel. 245-2326; f. 1961; independent; Dir JEAN-CLAUDE CARRIÉ.

Radio Caraïbes: 19 rue Chavannes, Port-au-Prince; tel. 223-0644; f. 1973; independent.

Radio Galaxie: 17 rue Pavée, Port-au-Prince; independent; Dir YVES JEAN-BART.

Radio Haïti Inter: Delmas 66A, 522, en face de Delmas 91, BP 737, Port-au-Prince; tel. 257-3111; f. 1935; independent; Dir MICHÈLE MONTAS.

Radio Lakansyel: 285 route de Delmas, Port-au-Prince; tel. 246-2020; independent; Dir ALEX SAINT-SURIN.

Radio Lumière: Côte-Plage 16, BP 1050, Port-au-Prince; f. 1959; tel. 234-0330; f. 1959; Protestant; independent.

Radio Magic Stéreo: 346 route de Delmas, Port-au-Prince; tel. 245-5404; independent; Dir FRITZ JOASSIN.

Radio Metropole: 8 Delmas 52, BP 62, Port-au-Prince; tel. 246-2626; fax 246-3130; f. 1970; independent; Dir-Gen. RICHARD WIDMAIER.

Radio Nationale d'Haïti: 174 rue du Magasin de l'Etat, BP 1143, Port-au-Prince; tel. 223-5712; fax 223-5911; govt-operated; Dir-Gen. MICHEL FAVARD.

Radio Plus: 85 rue Pavée, BP 1174, Port-au-Prince; tel. 222-1588; independent; Dir LIONEL BÉNJAMIN.

Radio Port-au-Prince: Stade Sylvio Cator, BP 863, Port-au-Prince; f. 1979; independent; Dir GEORGE L. HÉRARD.

Radio Signal FM: 127 rue Louverture, Petionville, BP 391, Port-au-Prince; tel. 298-4370; fax 298-4372; e-mail signalfm@netcourrier.com; f. 1991; independent; Dir-Gen. ANNE-MARIE ISSA.

Radio Soleil: BP 1362, Archevêché de Port-au-Prince; tel. 222-3062; fax 222-3516; f. 1978; Catholic; independent; educational; broadcasts in Creole and French; Dir Fr ARNOUX CHÉRY.

Radio Solidarité: Port-au-Prince; Dir VENEL REMARAIS.

Radio Superstar: 38 rue Safran, Delmas 68, Port-au-Prince; tel. 257-7219; independent; Dir ALBERT CHANCY.

Radio Tropic FM: 6 ave John Brown, Port-au-Prince; tel. 223-6565; independent; Dir GUY JEAN.

Radio Vision 2000: Port-au-Prince; internet www.radiovision2000.com; Dir LÉOPOLD BERLANGER.

Television

PVS Antenne 16: 137 rue Monseigneur Guilloux, Port-au-Prince; tel. and fax 222-1277; f. 1988; independent; Dir-Gen. RAYNALD DELERME.

Télé Haïti: blvd Harry S Truman, BP 1126, Port-au-Prince; tel. 222-3887; fax 222-9140; f. 1959; independent; pay-cable station with 33 channels; in French, Spanish and English; Dir MARIE CHRISTINE MOURRAL BLANC.

Télévision Nationale d'Haïti: Delmas 33, BP 13400, Port-au-Prince; tel. 246-2952; fax 246-0693; e-mail info@haiticulture.net; internet www.haiticulture.net/tnh/index.htm; f. 1979; govt-owned; cultural; 4 channels in Creole, French and Spanish; administered by four-mem. board; Dir RAYNALD LOUIS.

Trans-America: ruelle Roger, Gonaïves; f. 1990; tel 74-0113; independent; Dir-Gen. HÉBERT PELISSIER.

TVA: rue Liberté, Gonaïves; independent; cable station with three channels; Dir-Gen. GÉRARD LUC JEAN-BAPTISTE.

Finance

(cap. = capital; m. = million; res = reserves; dep. = deposits;
amounts in gourdes; brs = branches)

BANKING

Central Bank

Banque de la République d'Haïti: angle rues du Magasin de
l'Etat et des Miracles, BP 1570, Port-au-Prince; tel. 299-1000; fax
299-1145; e-mail brh_adm@brh.net; internet www.brh.net; f. 1911;
bank of issue; cap. and res 6.5m., dep. 204m. (May 1994); Pres. FRITZ
JEAN; Gen. Dir ROLAND PIERRE.

Commercial Banks

Banque Commerciale d'Haïti: Champ de Mars, Port-au-Prince;
tel. 222-3931.

Banque Nationale de Crédit: angle rues du Quai et des Miracles,
BP 1320, Port-au-Prince; tel. 299-4081; fax 222-3331; f. 1979; cap.
25m., dep. 729.9m. (Sept. 1989); Pres. EDOUARD RACINE; Gen. Man.
SOCRATE L. DEVIME.

Banque Populaire Haïtienne: angle rues des Miracles et du
Centre, Port-au-Prince; tel. 222-1800; fax 222-4389; f. 1955; state-
owned; cap. and res 84m., dep. 210m. (July 1994); Dir-Gen. REGI-
NALD MONDÉSIR.

**Banque de Promotion Commerciale et Industrielle SA (PRO-
MOBANK):** ave John Brown et rue Lamarre, BP 2323, Port-au-
Prince; tel. 299-8000; fax 223-0982; e-mail marketing@mail
.promobank.net; f. 1974 as B.N.P. Haïti, name changed as above
1994; cap. 60.4m., res 16.4m., dep. 1,183.4m. (Dec. 1998); Pres.
GILBERT BIGIO; Gen. Man. JEAN PERRE.

Banque de l'Union Haïtienne: angle rues du Quai et Bonne Foi,
BP 275, Port-au-Prince; tel. 222-1300; fax 223-2852; f. 1973; cap.
30.1m., res 6.2m., dep. 1,296.7m. (Sept. 1997); Pres. OSWALD J.
BRANDT II; 11 brs.

Capital Bank: 149-151 rue des Miracles, BP 2464, Port-au-Prince;
tel. 222-2830; fax 222-2898; frmly Banque de Crédit Immobilier,
SA; Pres. BERNARD ROY; Gen. Man. LILIANE C. DOMINIQUE.

Sogebank, SA (Société Générale Haïtienne de Banque, SA):
rue des Miracles, BP 1315, Port-au-Prince; tel. 222-4800; fax 222-
5366; f. 1986; cap. 79.5m.; Pres. JEAN CLAUDE NADAL; Dir-Gen.
CHARLES CLERMONT; 7 brs.

Sogebel: route de l'Aéroport, BP 2409, Port-au-Prince; tel. 229-
5353; fax 229-5352; f. 1988; cap. 15.1m., dep. 249.9m.; Gen. Man.
CLAUDE PIERRE-LOUIS; 2 brs.

Unibank: 94 place Geffard, BP 46, Port-au-Prince; tel. 299-2300;
fax 299-2332; e-mail info@unibank.net; f. 1993; cap. 100m., res
17.5m., dep. 3,366m. (Sept. 1999); Pres. F. CARL BRAUN; Dir-Gen.
FRANCK HELMCKE; 20 brs.

Foreign Banks

Bank of Nova Scotia (Canada): 360 blvd J.J. Dessalines, BP 686,
Port-au-Prince; tel. 222-4462; fax 222-9340; Dir-Gen. CLAUDE E.
MARCEL; Man. B. A. THEARD; 3 brs.

Banque Nationale de Paris (France): ave John Brown et rue
Lamarre, Port-au-Prince; tel. 222-2300; fax 222-6720; Dir-Gen.
MARCEL GARCÍA; 2 brs.

Citibank, NA (USA): 242 route de Delmas, BP 1688, Port-au-
Prince; tel. 246-2600; fax 246-0985; Vice-Pres. GLADYS M. COUPET.

Development Bank

Banque Nationale de Développement Agricole: Port-au-Prince;
tel. 222-1969; Dir-Gen. YVES LEREBOURS.

INSURANCE

National Companies

L'Atout Assurance, SA: 77 rue Lamarre, Port-au-Prince; tel. 223-
9378; Dir JEAN EVEILLARD.

Compagnie d'Assurances d'Haïti, SA (CAH): étage Dynamic
Entreprise, route de l'Aéroport, BP 1489, Port-au-Prince; tel. 246-
0700; fax 246-0236; f. 1978; Pres. PHILIPPE R. ARMAND.

Excelsior Assurance, SA: rue 6, no 24, Port-au-Prince; tel. 245-
8881; fax 245-8598; Dir-Gen. EMMANUEL SANON.

Générale d'Assurance, SA: Champ de Mars, Port-au-Prince; tel.
222-5465; fax 222-6502; f. 1985; Dir-Gen. ROLAND ACRA.

Haïti Sécurité Assurance, SA: 16 rue des Miracles, BP 1754,
Port-au-Prince; tel. 223-2118; Dir-Gen. WILLIAM PHIPPS.

International Assurance, SA (INASSA): angle rues des Miracles
et Pétion, Port-au-Prince; tel. 222-1058; Dir-Gen. RAOUL MÉROVÉ-
PIERRE.

Multi Assurances, SA: route de l'Aéroport, Port-au-Prince; tel.
246-0700; fax 246-0236; Dir-Gen. PHILIPPE ARMAND.

National Assurance, SA (NASSA): 153 rue des Miracles, BP 532,
Port-au-Prince; tel. 223-1058; fax 223-1821; Dir-Gen. FRITZ DUPUY.

Office National d'Assurance Vieillesse (ONA): Champ de Mars,
Port-au-Prince; tel. 222-1655; Dir-Gen. MARGARETH LAMUR.

Société de Commercialisation d'Assurance, SA (SOCOMAS):
autoroute de Delmas, BP 636, Port-au-Prince; tel. 249-3090; Dir-
Gen. JEAN DIDIER GARDÈRE.

Foreign Companies

Les Assurances Léger, SA (France): 40 rue Lamarre, BP 2120,
Port-au-Prince; tel. 222-3451; fax 223-8634; Pres. GÉRARD N. LÉGER.

Cabinet d'Assurances Fritz de Catalogne (USA): angle rues du
Peuple et des Miracles, BP 1644, Port-au-Prince; tel. 222-6695; fax
223-0827; Dir FRITZ DE CATALOGNE.

Capital Life Insurance Company Ltd (Bahamas): angle rues du
Peuple et des Miracles, BP 1644, Port-au-Prince; tel. 222-6695; fax
223-0827; Agent FRITZ DE CATALOGNE.

Dupuy & Merové-Pierre (USA): angle rues des Miracles et Pétion
153, Port-au-Prince; tel. 223-1058; fax 223-1821; agents for Cigna
International La Nationale d'Assurance SA; Dirs FRITZ DUPUY, RAOUL
MÉROVÉ-PIERRE.

Groupement Français d'Assurances (France): autoroute de
Delmas, Port-au-Prince; tel. 249-0433; fax 222-6677; internet
www.ine.gov./sector/index.htm; Agent ALBERT A. DUFORT.

National Western Life Insurance (USA): 13 rue Pie XII, Cité de
l'Exposition, Port-au-Prince; tel. 223-0734; Agent VORBE BARRAU
DUPUY.

Preservatrices Foncières Assurances (France): angle rues du
Magasin de l'Etat et Eden, Place Geffrard 266, étage Stecher, Port-
au-Prince; tel. 222-4210; Agent PHILIPPE GATION.

Union des Assurances de Paris (UAP) (France): autoroute de
Delmas, Port-au-Prince; tel. 223-7652; Agent YVES GARDÈRE.

Insurance Association

Association des Assureurs d'Haïti: c/o Les Assurances Léger,
SA, 40 rue Lamarre, BP 2120, Port-au-Prince; tel. 223-2137; fax
223-8634; Dir GÉRARD N. LÉGER.

Trade and Industry

GOVERNMENT AGENCY

**Centre de Promotion des Investissements et des Exporta-
tions Haïtiennes (PROMINEX):** angle rue Lamarre et ave John
Brown, Port-au-Prince; tel. 222-6381; Pres. CLAUDE LEVY.

DEVELOPMENT ORGANIZATIONS

Fonds de Développement Industriel (FDI): Immeuble PROMO-
BANK, 4e Étage, ave John Brown et rue Lamarre, BP 2597, Port-au-
Prince; tel. 222-7852; fax 222-8301; f. 1981; Dir ROOSEVELT SAINT-DIC.

**Société Financière Haïtienne de Développement, SA
(SOFIHDES):** 11 blvd Harry S Truman, BP 1399, Port-au-Prince;
tel. 222-8904; fax 222-8997; f. 1983; industrial and agro-industrial
project financing, accounting, data processing, management consultancy; cap. 7.5m. (1989); Dir-Gen. FAUBERT GUSTAVE; 1 br.

CHAMBERS OF COMMERCE

Chambre de Commerce et d'Industrie d'Haïti (CCIH): blvd
Harry S Truman, Cité de l'Exposition, BP 982, Port-au-Prince; tel.
223-0786; fax 222-0281; e-mail ccih@compa.net; internet www
.intervision2000.com/iv2-trop/index.html; f. 1895; Pres. OLIVIER
NADAL; Exec. Dir MICHAÈLE BERROUET FIGNOLÉ.

**Chambre de Commerce et d'Industrie Haïtiano-Américaine
(HAMCHAM):** First National City Bank, route de Delmas, BP
13486, Delmas, Port-au-Prince; tel. 246-2600; fax 246-0985; f. 1979;
Pres. GLADYS COUPET.

**Chambre de Commerce et d'Industrie des Professions du
Nord:** Boîte Postale 244, Cap-Haïtien; tel. 262-2360; fax 262-2895.

**Chambre Franco-Haïtienne de Commerce et d'Industrie
(CFHCI):** Le Plaza Holiday Inn, rue Capois, Champ de Mars, Port-
au-Prince; tel. 223-8404; fax 223-8131; f. 1987; Pres. PATRICK VICTOR;
Sec. AXAN ABELLARD.

INDUSTRIAL AND TRADE ORGANIZATIONS

Association des Industries d'Haïti (ADIH): 199 route de Delmas,
entre Delmas 31 et 33, étage Galerie 128, BP 2568, Port-au-Prince;
tel. 246-4509; fax 246-2211; f. 1980; Pres. RICHARD COLES; Exec. Dir
MARLÈNE SAM.

**Association Nationale des Distributeurs de Produits Pétrol-
iers (ANADIPP):** Centre Commercial Dubois, route de Delmas,
Bureau 401, Port-au-Prince; tel. 246-1414; fax 245-0698; f. 1979;
Pres. MAURICE LAFORTUNE.

Association Nationale des Importateurs et Distributeurs de Produits Pharmaceutiques (ANIDPP): c/o Maison Nadal, rue du Fort Per, Port-au-Prince; tel. 222-1418; fax 222-4767; Pres. BERNARD CRAAN.

Association des Producteurs Agricoles (APA): BP 1318, Port-au-Prince; tel. 246-1848; fax 246-0356; f. 1985; Pres. REYNOLD BONNEFIL.

Association des Producteurs Nationaux (APRONA): c/o Mosaïques Gardère, ave Hailé Sélassié, Port-au-Prince; tel. and fax 249-4433; Pres. FRANTZ GARDÈRE.

Association des Exportateurs de Café (ASDEC): c/o USMAN, ave Somoza/Delmas, BP B-65, Port-au-Prince; tel. 222-2627; fax 222-1394; Pres. FRITZ BRANDT.

UTILITIES
Electricity

Electricité d'Haïti: rue Dante Destouches, Port-au-Prince; tel. 222-4600; state energy utility company; Dir ROSEMOND PRADEL.

Péligre Hydroelectric Plant: Artibonite Valley.

Saut-Mathurine Hydroelectric Plant: Les Cayes.

TRADE UNIONS

Centrale Autonome des Travailleurs Haïtiens (CATH): 93 rue des Casernes, Port-au-Prince; tel. 222-4506; f. 1980; Sec. Gen. FIGNOLE SAINT-CYR.

Centrale des Travailleurs Haïtiens (CTH): f. 1989; Sec.-Gen. JEAN-CLAUDE LEBRUN.

Confédération Ouvriers Travailleurs Haïtiens (KOTA): 155 rue des Césars, Port-au-Prince.

Confédération Nationale des Educateurs Haïtiens (CNEH): rue Berne 21, Port-au-Prince; tel. 245-1552; fax 245-9536; f. 1986.

Fédération Haïtienne de Syndicats Chrétiens (FHSC): BP 416, Port-au-Prince; Pres. LÉONVIL LEBLANC.

Fédération des Ouvriers Syndiques (FOS): angle rues Dr Aubry et des Miracles 115, BP 371, Port-au-Prince; tel. 222-0035; f. 1984; Pres. JOSEPH J. SÉNAT.

Organisation Générale Indépendante des Travailleurs et Travailleuses d'Haïti (OGITH): 121, 2e étage, angle route Delmas et Delmas 11, Port-au-Prince; tel. 249-0575; f. 1988; Gen. Sec. JEAN-PHILIPPE GESNER.

Syndicat des Employés de l'EDH (SEEH): c/o EDH, rue Joseph Janvier, Port-au-Prince; tel. 222-3367.

Union Nationale des Ouvriers d'Haïti—UNOH: Delmas 11, 121 bis, Cité de l'Exposition, BP 3337, Port-au-Prince; f. 1951; Pres. MARCEL VINCENT; Sec.-Gen. FRITZNER ST VIL; 3,000 mems from 8 affiliated unions.

A number of unions are non-affiliated and without a national centre, including those organized on a company basis.

Transport

RAILWAYS

The only remaining railway was used to transport sugar cane, but it closed during the early 1990s.

ROADS

In 1996, according to International Road Federation estimates, there were 4,160 km (2,585 miles) of roads, of which 24.3% was paved. All-weather roads from Port-au-Prince, to Cap-Haïtien, on the northern coast, and to Les Cayes, in the south, were completed by the 1980s, with finance from the World Bank. Another, connecting Port-au-Prince with the southern town of Jacmel, was built and financed by France.

SHIPPING

Many European and American shipping lines call at Haiti. The two principal ports are Port-au-Prince and Cap-Haïtien. There are also 12 minor ports.

Autorité Portuaire Nationale: blvd La Saline, BP 616, Port-au-Prince; tel. 222-1942; fax 223-2440; e-mail jjulio@mail.com; f. 1978; Dir-Gen. JULIO JULIEN.

CIVIL AVIATION

The international airport, situated 8 km (5 miles) outside Port-au-Prince, is the country's principal airport, and is served by many international airlines linking Haiti with the USA and other Caribbean islands. There is an airport at Cap-Haïtien, and smaller airfields at Jacmel, Jérémie, Les Cayes and Port-de-Paix.

Air Haïti: Aéroport International, Port-au-Prince; tel. 246-3311; f. 1969; began cargo charter operations 1970; scheduled cargo and mail services from Port-au-Prince to Cap-Haïtien, San Juan (Puerto Rico), Santo Domingo (Dominican Republic), Miami and New York (USA); Gen. Man. Mr GONZALES.

Caribintair: Aéroport International, Port-au-Prince; tel. 246-0778; scheduled domestic service and charter flights to Santo Domingo (Dominican Republic) and other Caribbean destinations.

Haiti Air Freight, SA: Aéroport International, CP 170, Port-au-Prince; tel. 246-2572; fax 246-0848; cargo carrier operating scheduled and charter services from Port-au-Prince and Cap-Haïtien to Miami (USA) and Puerto Rico.

Haïti Trans Air: Aéroport International, BP 2526, Port-au-Prince; tel. 246-0418; fax 238938; scheduled flights to Miami and New York (USA); Pres. CHARLES H. VOIGHT.

Tourism

Tourism was formerly Haiti's second largest source of foreign exchange. In 1985/86 the number of visitors totalled 208,092. As a result of subsequent political instability, the number of cruise ships visiting Haiti declined considerably, causing a sharp decline in the number of tourist arrivals; visitors to Haiti in 1994 totalled 70,200. With the restoration of democracy in late 1994, the development of the tourism industry was identified as a priority by the Government. In 1998 stop-over tourists totalled 146,837, while cruise-ship excursionists numbered 246,221.

Secrétariat d'Etat au Tourisme: 8 rue Légitime, Champ de Mars, Port-au-Prince; tel. 223-5631; fax 223-5380; e-mail tourisme@set-haiti.org; internet www.haititourisme.com; Secretary of State for Tourism MARYSE PÉNETTE KEDAR.

Association Haïtienne des Agences de Voyages: rue des Miracles 17, Port-au-Prince; tel. 222-8855; fax 222-2054.

Association Touristique d'Haïti: rue Lamarre, Choucoune Plaza, Pétionville, BP 2562, Port-au-Prince; tel. 257-4647; fax 257-4134; Pres. DOMINIQUE CARVONIS; Exec. Dir GILIANE CÉSAR JOUBERT.

HONDURAS

Introductory Survey

Location, Climate, Language, Religion, Flag, Capital

The Republic of Honduras lies in the middle of the Central American isthmus. It has a long northern coastline on the Caribbean Sea and a narrow southern outlet to the Pacific Ocean. Its neighbours are Guatemala to the west, El Salvador to the south-west and Nicaragua to the south-east. The climate ranges from temperate in the mountainous regions to tropical in the coastal plains: temperatures in the interior range from 15°C (59°F) to 24°C (75°F), while temperatures in the coastal plains average about 30°C (86°F). There are two rainy seasons in upland areas, May–July and September–October. The national language is Spanish. Almost all of the inhabitants profess Christianity, and the overwhelming majority are adherents of the Roman Catholic Church. The national flag (proportions 2 by 1) has three horizontal stripes, of blue, white and blue, with five blue five-pointed stars, arranged in a diagonal cross, in the centre of the white stripe. The capital is Tegucigalpa.

Recent History

Honduras was ruled by Spain from the 16th century until 1821 and became a sovereign state in 1838. From 1939 the country was ruled as a dictatorship by Gen. Tiburcio Carías Andino, leader of the Partido Nacional (PN), who had been President since 1933. In 1949 Carías was succeeded as President by Juan Manuel Gálvez, also of the PN. In 1954 the leader of the Partido Liberal (PL), Dr José Ramón Villeda Morales, was elected President, but was immediately deposed by Julio Lozano Díaz, himself overthrown by a military Junta in 1956. The Junta organized elections in 1957, when the PL secured a majority in Congress and Villeda was re-elected President. He was overthrown in 1963 by Col (later Gen.) Oswaldo López Arellano, the Minister of Defence, who, following elections held on the basis of a new Constitution, was appointed President in June 1965.

A presidential election in March 1971 was won by Dr Ramón Ernesto Cruz Uclés, the PN candidate. In December 1972, however, Cruz was deposed in a bloodless coup, led by former President López. In March 1974, at the instigation of the Consejo Superior de las Fuerzas Armadas (Supreme Council of the Armed Forces), President López was replaced as Commander-in-Chief of the Armed Forces by Col (later Gen.) Juan Melgar Castro, who was appointed President in April 1975. President Melgar was forced to resign by the Consejo Superior de las Fuerzas Armadas in August 1978, and was replaced by a military Junta. The Commander-in-Chief of the Armed Forces, Gen. Policarpo Paz García, assumed the role of Head of State, and the Junta promised that elections would take place.

Military rule was ended officially when, in April 1980, elections to a Constituent Assembly were held. The PL won 52% of the votes but was unable to assume power. Gen. Paz was appointed interim President for one year. At a general election in November 1981 the PL, led by Dr Roberto Suazo Córdova, gained an absolute majority in the National Assembly. Suazo was sworn in as President in January 1982. However, real power lay in the hands of Col (later Gen.) Gustavo Alvarez Martínez, who was appointed Head of the Armed Forces in the same month. In November Gen. Alvarez became Commander-in-Chief of the Armed Forces, having brought about an amendment to the Constitution in that month, whereby the posts of President and Commander-in-Chief of the Armed Forces, which had been merged under the rule of the military Junta, were separated. During 1982 and 1983 Gen. Alvarez suppressed increasing political unrest by authorizing the arrests of trade union activists and left-wing sympathizers; 'death squads' were allegedly also used to eliminate 'subversive' elements of the population. In March 1984 Gen. Alvarez was deposed as Commander-in-Chief of the Armed Forces by a group of army officers.

At the November 1985 presidential election the leading candidate of the PN, Rafael Leonardo Callejas Romero, obtained 42% of the individual votes cast, but the leading candidate of the PL, José Simeón Azcona del Hoyo (who had obtained only 27% of the individual votes cast), was declared the winner because, in accordance with a new electoral law, the combined votes of the PL's candidates secured the requisite majority of 51% of the total votes cast.

In February 1988 a report by the human rights organization Amnesty International gave evidence of an increase in violations of human rights by the armed forces and by right-wing 'death squads'. In August of that year, and again in 1989, the Inter-American Court of Human Rights (an organ of the Organization of American States—OAS, see p. 261) found the Honduran Government guilty of the 'disappearances' of Honduran citizens between 1981 and 1984, and ordered that compensation be paid to the families involved. In January 1989 Gen. Alvarez was killed by left-wing guerrillas in Tegucigalpa. The PL gained a majority of seats in the National Assembly at legislative elections held in November, while Callejas of the PN won the concurrent presidential election, receiving 51% of the votes cast. Callejas assumed office in January 1990. The new administration promptly adopted economic austerity measures, which provoked widespread social unrest.

In May 1991 units of the armed forces were implicated in the massacre of nine farmers during a dispute over land ownership. In the following month Amnesty International published a report alleging the mistreatment, torture and killing of detainees by members of the Honduran security forces, and the International Confederation of Free Trade Unions accused the security forces of complicity in the assassinations of several trade union organizers during 1990 and early 1991. In January 1992 the Government announced the creation of a special commission to investigate numerous accusations of corruption against government officials.

In March 1993, in response to increasing pressure by human rights organizations and criticism by the State Department of the USA, the Government established a special commission to investigate allegations of human rights violations by the armed forces and to evaluate the need for a reform of the security forces and the judiciary. In its report, the commission recommended the replacement of the armed forces' much-criticized secret counter-intelligence organization, the División Nacional de Investigaciones (DNI), with a body under civilian control. Other recommendations included the establishment of a fully independent Public Ministry office headed by a democratically-elected Attorney-General.

At presidential and legislative elections held in November 1993, Carlos Roberto Reina Idiaquez, the candidate of the PL, was elected President, winning 52% of the votes cast. The PL also obtained a clear majority in the National Assembly, with 71 seats, while the PN secured 55 seats and the Partido Innovación y Unidad—Social Democracia (PINU) won the remaining two seats. Legislation replacing the DNI with a new ministry, the Dirección de Investigación Criminal (DIC), was approved in December 1993. On taking office in January 1994 Reina, a former President of the Inter-American Court of Human Rights, expressed his commitment to the reform of the judicial system, which had failed to act effectively against those responsible for human rights violations. In addition he promised to redefine the role of the armed forces, reducing its size and sphere of influence. In that month, following the release by the National Commission for the Protection of Human Rights of a report incriminating the armed forces in the disappearance of 184 people in the previous decade, the head of the Commission, Leo Valladares Lanza, demanded the resignation of the Commander-in-Chief of the Armed Forces, Gen. Luis Alonso Discua Elvir. At the time of the disappearances Discua had been the Commander of Battalion 3-16, the army intelligence unit widely regarded as responsible for the murder of left-wing political activists. As a result of the report, the Supreme Court ordered an investigation of the allegations.

In April 1994 an apparent attempt to assassinate Reina was thwarted when one of three Nicaraguan hired assassins revealed the plot to the Honduran authorities. The Nicaraguans reportedly had been offered US $400,000 by a Honduran, Luis Hernández Sosa, to conduct the killing. Reina dismissed suggestions of a political motive for the attempt, attributing it instead to the work of criminals opposed to his efforts to suppress drugs-trafficking in Honduras. In that month demonstrations were organized in the capital in protest at the deterioration of living standards caused by the Government's economic austerity policies. Demonstrations also occurred in the department of Copán where peasant organizations blocked the Pan-American Highway in support of demands for Reina to honour election commitments to reduce the severity of the economic policies of the previous administration.

In May 1994 the National Assembly approved a proposal for a reform of the Constitution to abolish compulsory military service (the amendment was ratified by the National Assembly in April 1995). Also approved was the transfer of the police from military to civilian control. In that month measures initiated by the Callejas administration for the establishment of a Public Ministry were officially completed. The new ministry was to be supervised by the DIC, which was inaugurated in January 1995. The DNI was officially disbanded in June 1994.

In July 1994, following protracted demonstrations in the capital, 4,000 members of indigenous organizations occupied the National Assembly building and succeeded in securing an agreement with the Government granting rights and social assistance to the country's indigenous community, including the creation of the first indigenous municipality in Yamaranguila, Intibucá. The following months were characterized by growing social and political tension, including several bomb attacks. Concern was raised by human rights organizations that the climate of instability was being fomented by the armed forces in an attempt to stem the rapid diminution of its powers. In August however, Reina conceded the temporary reintroduction of compulsory conscription in order to fill some 7,000 vacancies which the armed forces complained were impairing military efficiency. In the same month Reina ordered an investigation into charges of corruption and drugs-trafficking in the air force. Widespread concern at the possibility that growing tension between the Government and the armed forces might result in a military coup prompted Gen. Discua to issue a public statement denying any such intentions and reaffirming military support for the civilian authorities. In mid-August an increase in the incidence of crime and violent demonstrations resulting from the accumulating effect of austerity measures, a worsening energy crisis and food shortages, forced the Government to declare a state of national emergency and to deploy the armed forces to maintain order.

In November 1994 public-sector unions organized strikes in protest at low pay, poor working conditions and the Government's failure to honour earlier pay agreements. The disputes were resolved, however, following government promises of concessions. In late November corruption charges were filed by the public prosecutor's office against former President Callejas and 12 of his former ministers.

In July 1995 sustained protests by members of indigenous organizations, in support of demands that the Government honour its commitments of July 1994 to the indigenous community, culminated in a 2,000-strong demonstration in the capital. The protests resulted in renewed pledges by the Government to provide social assistance and grant land titles to the indigenous population. In September the PL, PN, PINU and Partido Demócrata Cristiano de Honduras (PDCH) established the Consejo Nacional de Convergencia (National Convergence Council) in order to seek a consensus on political, social and economic issues.

In July 1995, in an unprecedented development in the Government's efforts to investigate past human rights violations, a civilian court issued indictments against 10 senior officers of the security services who had been involved in the activities of Battalion 3-16 during the 1980s. The charges concerned the kidnapping, torture and attempted murder in 1982 of six left-wing students. However, the officers refused to appear in court, invoking an amnesty granted in 1991 which, they claimed, afforded them immunity from prosecution. In October a warrant was issued for the arrest of several of the officers, who promptly went into hiding. In January 1996 the Supreme Court ruled that the officers were not entitled to protection under the 1991 amnesty law, overturning an earlier decision by the Court of Appeal. Information concerning the activities of Battalion 3-16, which had been financed and trained by the US Central Intelligence Agency, was sought from the US Government by Valladares to support the prosecution of this and other human rights cases.

In January 1996 Col. Mario Raúl Hung Pacheco succeeded Gen. Discua as Commander-in-Chief of the Armed Forces, and was subsequently promoted to the rank of General. In the following month, in an apparent demonstration of his control over the military high command, Reina ignored the nominations for a new Minister of National Defence and Public Security proposed by Gen. Hung, appointing his own candidate instead. In the following month a grenade was thrown into the grounds of the presidential residence, prompting speculation that the armed forces had been responsible for the attack.

In mid-1996 there was widespread protest at the Government's policies of wage restraint and the implementation of public-sector redundancies. Public-sector workers conducted strikes in support of demands for salary increases, a reform of the labour code and price controls. Following negotiations, the Government granted concessions, including payments totalling US $12.2m. in answer to salary demands.

In July 1996 the Human Rights Defence Committee (Codeh) claimed that the extra judicial execution of five former military intelligence agents had occurred in recent months, and alleged that the killings were the responsibility of military officers who were attempting to prevent evidence of human rights violations from coming to light. Later that month four officers of the armed forces were arrested for allegedly conspiring to overthrow the Commander-in-Chief of the Armed Forces. Gen. Hung, however, dismissed the incident, claiming that it merely reflected the discontent within the ranks at low pay and reductions in the defence budget.

In early October 1996 a bomb exploded, without causing injury, at the parliament building in the capital. A further device was defused outside the headquarters of the PL. Responsibility for the attacks was claimed later that month by a previously unknown organization describing itself as 'Hambre' (Hunger), which claimed to be acting in response to recent rises in fuel prices. However, the President of Codeh, Ramón Custodio, expressed the popular suspicion that the attacks had been perpetrated by the armed forces in an attempt to pressurize the civilian authorities into reversing the decline in military influence in the country. In mid-October, Custodio's home in San Pedro Sula was the target of a grenade attack. A further such attack was conducted in early November on a central court building in Tegucigalpa, resulting in one fatality. In response, the Government deployed some 3,000 troops to patrol the capital and San Pedro Sula. An organization known as 'Justa C.' claimed responsibility for the attack and issued death threats to several judges involved in the investigation of cases concerning official corruption and human rights abuses by the armed forces.

In early 1997 the legislature approved a constitutional reform providing for control of the police force to be transferred from the military to the civilian authorities. The Fuerza de Seguridad Pública, which had been under military control since 1963 and was widely suspected of perpetrating human rights abuses, was to be replaced by a new force, the Policía Nacional. The official transfer occurred in May 1998. Nevertheless, reports of human rights abuses continued. In June 2000 a local human rights group, Casa Alianza, reported that an alleged 'social cleansing' programme by the police and security forces had resulted in the death of some 302 street children since January 1998.

In February 1997 demonstrations by thousands of public-sector employees, who were protesting in support of demands for salary increases, culminated in violent clashes between demonstrators and the security forces. As a result of sustained unrest the Government subsequently signed a social pact with labour leaders, which included commitments to increased social spending and price controls on basic goods. In May, following the killing of two ethnic minority leaders in the previous month, more than 3,000 members of the indigenous community conducted a march from the western departments of Copán and Ocotepeque to the capital to protest outside the presidential palace. As a result, Reina signed an agreement to conduct a full investigation into the killings and to accelerate the distribution of some 7,000 ha of land to the indigenous community. However, the killing of a further two ethnic minority leaders later that month led to accusations by human rights groups that attempts were being made to eliminate minority autonomous organizations. In March 2000 four leaders of the Chortí people were shot and killed by a landowner's private security guards.

In October 1997 the National Assembly unanimously approved a constitutional amendment providing for the reduction of the legislature from 128 to 80 seats. The legislation would have to be ratified by the succeeding National Assembly, following the forthcoming general election. At the general election held on 30 November Carlos Roberto Flores Facussé, the candidate of the ruling PL, was elected President, winning 52.7% of the votes cast; Alba Nora Gúnera de Melgar, the PN candidate, took 42.7% of the votes. The PL also obtained a majority in the National Assembly, with 67 seats, while the PN secured 55 seats, the PINU won three, the PDCH two and the left-wing Partido de Unificación Democrática obtained the remaining seat. In December Flores announced his intention to conduct a restructuring of the armed forces. He was inaugurated on 27 January 1998.

In September 1998 the National Assembly approved a constitutional amendment abolishing the post of Commander-in-Chief of the Armed Forces and transferring its responsibilities to the Minister of National Defence and Public Security. The amendment was ratified in the following session of the National Assembly, in January 1999. In October 1998, in the wake of a serious escalation in the incidence of violent crime in Tegucigalpa and San Pedro Sula, and in response to increasing pressure, in particular from business groups concerned at the effect of growing public insecurity on investment, Flores deployed the armed forces to reinforce the efforts of the police in those two cities.

In November 1998, in the wake of the devastation caused by 'Hurricane Mitch', which struck the country in late October, causing losses estimated at US $5,000m., Flores declared a state of emergency and imposed a curfew in order to combat widespread looting. At least 6,600 people were estimated to have died, with a further 8,052 people reported missing, as a result of the storms, which left some 2.13m. homeless and caused widespread damage to the country's infrastructure, as well as destroying principal export crops.

In January 1999 Flores conducted a major cabinet reorganization in an apparent attempt to eradicate corruption and inefficiency. Later in that month the National Assembly ratified the constitutional amendment placing the armed forces directly under civilian control. The military's ruling body, the Consejo Superior de las Fuerzas Armadas, was also disbanded. Edgardo Dumas Rodríguez was subsequently appointed to the defence portfolio. In July, acting on intelligence reports of a plot by senior-ranking military officers to overthrow the Government, Flores implemented a number of changes to the military high command. Notably, the Head of the Joint Chiefs of Staff, Col Eugenio Romero Eucedo, who was suspected of being one of the principal instigators of the coup plot, was replaced by the head of the presidential guard, Col Daniel López Carballo, who was considered to be loyal to the presidency. The plot itself was believed to have been prompted by resentment in the officer corps at the determination of Dumas to exert civilian control over the armed forces, and in particular at his plans to investigate military expenditure and supervise the armed forces' extensive business activities.

In January 2001 Dumas resigned as Minister of National Defence, citing personal reasons. He was replaced by Enrique Flores Valeriano, hitherto the Minister of the Interior and Justice. At the same time, Hernán Corrales Padilla, PDCH leader and Minister of International Co-operation, relinquished his ministerial post in order to prepare for legislative and presidential elections, scheduled to be held in November. In mid-December the PL confirmed that its presidential nominee would be Rafael Pineda Ponce, the President of the Asamblea Nacional. Luis Cosenza was chosen as the PN's candidate; however, it was expected that he would be replaced by his ally, Ricardo Maduro, once a dispute over Maduro's nationality (he was born in Panama) had been resolved.

From the early 1980s former members of the Nicaraguan National Guard, regarded by the left-wing Sandinista Government of Nicaragua as counter-revolutionaries ('Contras'), established bases in Honduras, from which they conducted raids across the border between the two countries, allegedly with support from the Honduran armed forces. In 1983, when Honduran foreign policy was controlled by the pro-US Gen. Alvarez (the Commander-in-Chief of the Armed Forces), US involvement in Honduras increased substantially. In February 1983 the USA and Honduras initiated 'Big Pine', a series of joint military manoeuvres on Honduran territory; these exercises continued throughout the 1980s, thus enabling the USA to construct permanent military installations in Honduras. In return for considerable military assistance from the USA, the Honduran Government permitted US military aid to be supplied to the Contras based in Honduras.

Following the overthrow of Gen. Alvarez in 1984, public opposition to the US military presence in Honduras increased,

causing a temporary deterioration in relations between Honduras and the USA. In 1985 the USA declined to enter into a security pact with Honduras, but confirmed that it would take 'appropriate' measures to defend Honduras against any Communist aggression. In August of that year the Honduran Government announced that it would prevent the US Government from supplying further military aid to the Contras through Honduras. However, following a visit by President Azcona to the USA in 1986, the supply of aid was believed to have resumed.

In 1986 relations with Nicaragua deteriorated sharply, when Honduran troops were mobilized in an attempt to curb alleged border incursions by Nicaraguan government forces. In December, however, following revelations that the USA had secretly sold weapons to the Government of Iran and that the proceeds had been used to finance the activities of the Contra rebels, President Azcona requested the departure of the Contras from Honduras.

In August 1987 Honduras, Costa Rica, El Salvador, Guatemala and Nicaragua signed a Central American peace plan, known as the 'Esquipulas agreement', the crucial provisions of which were the implementation of simultaneous cease-fires in Nicaragua and El Salvador, a halt to foreign assistance to rebel groups, democratic reform in Nicaragua, a ban on the use of foreign territory as a base for attack, and the establishment of national reconciliation commissions in each of the Central American nations. However, the commitment of the Honduran Government to the accord appeared to be only partial. Claiming that it no longer permitted the Nicaraguan Contras to maintain bases on its territory, the Honduran Government opposed a clause in the agreement providing for the establishment of a committee to monitor the dismantling of Contra bases in Honduras.

In March 1988 several thousand US troops were temporarily deployed in Honduras, in response to an incursion into Honduran territory by the Nicaraguan army. Further violations of the border between Honduras and Nicaragua occurred during that year, as Nicaraguan troops forced at least 12,000 Contra rebels, based in the border area, into Honduras. In November President Azcona declared his opposition to the presence of the Contras in his country. In the following month it was announced that the International Court of Justice (ICJ) would consider an application that had been submitted by the Nicaraguan Government in 1986, in which Nicaragua contended that Honduras had breached international law by allowing the Contras to operate from its territory. In response, the Honduran Government threatened to withdraw support from the Esquipulas agreement.

In February 1989 a summit meeting of the five Central American Presidents was convened at Costa del Sol, El Salvador. An agreement was reached whereby the Nicaraguan Contra forces encamped in Honduras would demobilize, while President Ortega of Nicaragua guaranteed that free and fair elections would take place in his country by February 1990. At a further summit meeting, held in August at Tela, Honduras, the conditions for the demobilization of the Contras were expanded. The Honduran Government agreed to the establishment by the UN and the OAS of an international commission to oversee the voluntary repatriation or removal to a third country of the rebel forces by December 1989; in return, the Nicaraguan Government agreed to abandon the action that it had initiated against Honduras at the ICJ.

Despite these initiatives towards peace, the Contra rebels continued to launch attacks against Nicaraguan troops during the latter part of t1989, maintaining their positions in Honduras beyond the December deadline. In February 1990, following national elections in Nicaragua, the outgoing President Ortega of Nicaragua ordered his forces to observe an immediate unilateral cease-fire with the Contras. The rebel units officially disbanded and left Honduras in June.

In June 1995 Honduras and Nicaragua signed an accord providing for the visible demarcation of each country's territorial waters in the Gulf of Fonseca, and the establishment of a joint naval patrol to police the area. The agreement followed frequent disputes concerning fishing rights in the Gulf, which occurred as a consequence of inefficient demarcation. Despite the agreement, however, conflict continued, and the demarcation process did not begin until May 1998. In early 2000 there was an exchange of gunfire between Honduran and Nicaraguan patrol boats in the Gulf (where jurisdiction was shared with El Salvador).

In December 1999 a further dispute arose with Nicaragua, prompting it to sever commercial ties with, and impose import taxes on, Honduras, in direct contravention of Central American free-trade undertakings. The dispute stemmed from the Caribbean Sea Maritime Limits Treaty, which Honduras had signed with Colombia in 1986 and had finally ratified in late November 1999, thereby formally recognizing a frontier with Colombia the demarcation of which granted Colombia territorial rights to areas of the Caribbean historically claimed by Nicaragua. In February 2000, following OAS mediation, the two countries agreed to establish a maritime exclusion zone in the disputed area. In the following month, representatives of Honduras and Nicaragua met in Washington, DC, where they signed an accord on joint patrols in the Caribbean, pending a ruling by the ICJ, and on combined operations in the Gulf of Fonseca. Agreement was also reached on the withdrawal of forces from the land border area. However, in February 2001 bilateral relations deteriorated after the Nicaraguan defence minister accused Honduras of violating the March 2000 accords by carrying out military exercises in the area.

A long-standing dispute between Honduras and El Salvador, regarding the demarcation of the two countries' common border and rival claims to three islands in the Gulf of Fonseca, caused hostilities to break out between the two countries in 1969. Although armed conflict soon subsided, the Honduran and Salvadorean Governments did not sign a peace treaty until 1980. In 1982 the Honduran armed forces were engaged against guerrilla forces in El Salvador, indicating an improvement in Honduran–Salvadorean relations. Honduran troops were also reportedly responsible for the deaths of several hundred Salvadorean refugees in Honduras during that year. In 1986, however, the Governments of Honduras and El Salvador agreed that their conflicting territorial claims should be examined by the ICJ. During 1989 several border clashes occurred between Honduran and Salvadorean troops. In September 1992 the ICJ awarded Honduras sovereignty over some two-thirds of the disputed mainland territory and over one of the disputed islands in the Gulf of Fonseca. However, in subsequent years disputes continued to arise concerning the legal rights of those people resident in the reallocated territory, particularly with regard to land ownership. Following protracted negotiation, a convention governing the acquired rights and nationality of those people was finally signed by the Presidents of both countries in January 1998. An agreement was also signed providing for the demarcation of the countries' common border to be undertaken within one year. By September 2000 232.5 km of the 374 km border had been demarcated.

In November 1991 the Presidents of Honduras and El Salvador signed an agreement to establish a free-trade zone on their common border, and subsequently to seek economic union. In May 1992 the Governments of Honduras, El Salvador and Guatemala agreed to promote trade and investment between the three countries. A further agreement, concluded by Honduras, El Salvador and Guatemala in October of that year, provided for the eventual establishment of a Central American political federation.

Government

Under the provisions of the Constitution approved by the National Assembly in 1982, the President is elected by a simple majority of the voters. The President holds executive power and has a single four-year mandate. Legislative power is vested in the National Assembly, with 128 members elected by universal adult suffrage for a term of four years. The country is divided into 18 local Departments.

In October 1997 the National Assembly approved a constitutional amendment providing for the reduction of the legislature from 128 to 80 members. In order to be adopted, the amendment would have to be ratified by the succeeding National Assembly, which was elected in November 1997.

Defence

Military service is voluntary. Active service lasts eight months, with subsequent reserve training. In August 2000 the armed forces totalled 8,300 men, of whom 5,500 were in the army, 1,000 in the navy and 1,800 in the air force. Paramilitary forces numbered 6,000 men. In 2000 government expenditure on defence was budgeted at 520m. lempiras. In 1990 US military aid to Honduras was almost halved, compared with the previous year, to US $20.2m. By 2000 annual assistance from the USA had been reduced to $0.5m. In 2000 some 820 US troops were based in Honduras.

Economic Affairs

In 1998, according to estimates by the World Bank, Honduras' gross national product (GNP), measured at average 1996–98 prices, was US $4,564m., equivalent to $740 per head (or $2,338 per head on an international purchasing-power parity basis). During 1990–98, it was estimated, GNP per head increased, in real terms, at an average annual rate of 1.4%. Over the same period the population increased at an average annual rate of 3.3%. Honduras' gross domestic product (GDP) increased, in real terms, at an average annual rate of 3.2% in 1990–99; GDP increased by 2.9% in 1998, but declined by 1.9% in 1999.

Agriculture (including hunting, forestry and fishing) contributed an estimated 16.2% of GDP and employed 35.1% of the economically active population in 1999. The principal cash crop is coffee (which contributed an estimated 20.7% of all export earnings in 1999). However, in 2000 exports were reduced as part of a world-wide plan to improve coffee prices. Banana production decreased during the 1990s and, following the destruction of more than 70% of the total crop as a result of 'Hurricane Mitch', in 1999 bananas contributed only an estimated 3.0% of all export earnings. Furthermore, in June 2000 one of the principal banana corporations, Chiquita Brands, announced a substantial reduction in its operations in the country following hurricane damage and a downturn in the market. The main subsistence crops include maize, plantains, beans, rice, sugar cane and citrus fruit. Exports of shellfish make a significant contribution to foreign earnings (supplying 15.5% of total export earnings in 1999), and timber production is also important. Agricultural GDP increased at an average annual rate of 1.8% during 1990–99, but declined by 2.9% in 1998 and by an estimated 8.7% in 1999.

Industry (including mining, manufacturing, construction and power) contributed an estimated 31.9% of GDP and employed 22.0% of the economically active population in 1999. Industrial GDP increased at an average annual rate of 3.6% during 1990–99; it increased by 4.2% in 1998 and by an estimated 4.0% in 1999.

Mining contributed an estimated 2.0% of GDP and employed 0.2% of the economically active population in 1999. Lead, zinc and silver are the major mineral exports. Gold, copper and low-grade iron ore are also mined. In addition, small quantities of petroleum derivatives are exported. Until the end of the 1990s, when new funding was announced, the gold, silver and other mineral deposits had remained unexplored. The GDP of the mining sector increased by an average of 6.4% per year in 1991–98, and by an estimated 7.4% in 1998.

Manufacturing contributed an estimated 19.6% of GDP and employed 16.4% of the economically active population in 1999. In 1998 the most important branches, measured by gross value of output, were food products, beverages (including beer), cigarettes, apparel and wood products. In 2000 the successful *maquiladora* (assembly plant) sector employed some 100,000 local workers. Manufacturing GDP increased at an average annual rate of 3.8% during 1989–99, by 3.4% in 1998 and by an estimated 2.6% in 1999.

Energy is derived principally from hydroelectric power, which accounted for some 55% of energy consumption in the late 1990s. Imports of mineral fuels and lubricants accounted for an estimated 9.4% of the value of total imports in 1999. Fuel wood remains a prime source of domestic energy. In 2001 the US company, AES Corporation, announced plans to construct a US $650m. natural gas plant that would supply some 800MW of electricity to Honduras and other countries in the region. The plant was to be completed by 2003.

The services sector contributed an estimated 51.9% of GDP and engaged 42.9% of the working population in 1999. The GDP of the services sector increased by an average of 3.7% per year in 1990–99, and by 5.6% in 1998; however, in 1999 the sector's contribution to GDP decreased by an estimated 0.2%.

In 1999 Honduras recorded a visible trade deficit of US $709.1m., while there was a deficit of $536.8m. on the current account of the balance of payments. Workers' remittances from abroad totalled about $409m. in 2000. In 1999 the principal source of imports (43.7%) was the USA; other major suppliers were Guatemala, El Salvador and Mexico. The USA was also the principal market for exports (36.6%) in that year; other significant purchasers were El Salvador, Guatemala and Nicaragua. The principal exports in 1999 were coffee and shellfish. The principal imports in 1999 were crude materials for industry, non-durable consumer goods and capital goods for industry.

In 1999 there was a budgetary deficit of 3,576m. lempiras (equivalent to 4.7% of GDP in that year). Honduras' external debt totalled US $5,356m. at the end of 1999. In that year the cost of debt-servicing was $367m. The annual rate of inflation averaged 19.1% in 1990–99. Consumer prices increased by an annual average of 11.7% in 1999. Some 3.7% of the labour force were unemployed in 1999; however, it was estimated that more than 35% of the work-force were underemployed.

Honduras is a member of the Central American Common Market (CACM, see p. 147).

In terms of average income, Honduras is among the poorest nations in the Western hemisphere, with some 80% of the population living below the poverty line. In October 1998 the Honduran economy was devastated by the effects of 'Hurricane Mitch'. Much of the country's infrastructure was destroyed, and as many as 2.13m. people left homeless. Losses in agricultural production were estimated at US $200m. for 1998, rising to more than $500m. for 1999, while the total cost to the economy of the hurricane damage was estimated at $5,000m. In May 1999 the Consultative Group for Honduras of international financial agencies and donor countries agreed to provide $2,800m. for the reconstruction process. In March the IMF approved a three-year Enhanced Structural Adjustment Facility (ESAF) totalling $215m. in support of the Government's economic programme for 1999–2001. In the following month the 'Paris Club' of creditor governments agreed to suspend Honduras' bilateral debt-service payments for a period of three years, and offered a 67% reduction in its debt of $1,170m. on the condition that it complied with the terms of the ESAF. These included commitments by the Government to reduce public expenditure, rationalize state bureaucracy, and sustain its privatization programme. The successful implementation of these measures also facilitated further debt relief under the Heavily Indebted Poor Countries (HIPC) initiative of the World Bank, to which Honduras was admitted in December 1999. In July 2000 the IMF and the World Bank announced that the country's debt service payments would be reduced by $900m. over 20 years. However, in December the IMF suspended a $22m. disbursement to the Honduran Government owing to the lack of progress in its privatization programme. An attempt to sell the state telecommunications company, Hondutel, had failed in October and the Asamblea Nacional had failed to pass legislation that would enable the sale of the national energy company, ENEE (Empresa Nacional de Energía Eléctrica). In 2000 the economy grew by 4.7%, in part owing to the continuing growth in the *maquiladora* sector and investment in the post-hurricane reconstruction programme. Forecasts for 2001 put economic growth at 3.5%, based on an expected increase in private-sector investment and the receipt of further credits for reconstruction, in addition to proceeds from the divestment of state assets.

Social Welfare

The state-run system of social security provides benefits for sickness, maternity, orphans, unemployment and accidents. It also provides family and old-age allowances. The Labour Code affords guarantees for employees. In 1991 the Government announced plans to transfer the provision of some social welfare services to the private sector. In 1997 there were 83.2 physicians per 100,000 inhabitants and 25.5 nurses per 100,000 inhabitants. In 1998 there were 63 hospitals (of which 35 were private), 1,092 health centres and 5,720 hospital beds, cots and incubators. The 1995 budget allocated 1,071.5m. lempiras to the health sector.

Education

Primary education, beginning at seven years of age and lasting for six years, is officially compulsory and is provided free of charge. Secondary education, which is not compulsory, begins at the age of 13 and lasts for up to five years, comprising a first cycle of three years and a second of two years. On completion of the compulsory period of primary education, every person is required to teach at least two illiterate adults to read and write. In 1998, according to estimates by the UNDP, adult illiteracy averaged 26.6% (males 26.6%; females 26.5%). In 1998 the enrolment at primary schools included 87.5% of children in the relevant age-group (males 86.4%; females 88.6%), while enrolment at secondary schools in that year was equivalent to only 36.0% of children in the appropriate age-group (males 34.1%; females 37.9%). There are seven universities, including the Autonomous National University in Tegucigalpa. For 1995 the education budget was 1,353m. lempiras (16.5% of total government expenditure). In December 2000 the Inter-American Development Bank (IDB) approved a US $29.6m. loan to expand and reform the education system.

Public Holidays

2001: 1 January (New Year's Day), 13–16 April (Easter), 14 April (Pan-American Day/Bastilla's Day), 1 May (Labour Day), 15 September (Independence Day), 3 October (Morazán Day), 12 October (Discovery Day), 21 October (Army Day), 25 December (Christmas).

2002: 1 January (New Year's Day), 29 March–1 April (Easter), 14 April (Pan-American Day/Bastilla's Day), 1 May (Labour Day), 15 September (Independence Day), 3 October (Morazán Day), 12 October (Discovery Day), 21 October (Army Day), 25 December (Christmas).

Weights and Measures

The metric system is in force, although some old Spanish measures are used, including: 25 libras = 1 arroba; 4 arrobas = 1 quintal (46 kg).

Statistical Survey

Source (unless otherwise stated): Department of Economic Studies, Banco Central de Honduras—BANTRAL,
6a y 7a Avda, 1a Calle, Apdo 3165, Tegucigalpa; tel. 237-2270; fax 238-0376.

Area and Population

AREA, POPULATION AND DENSITY

Area (sq km) .	112,492*
Population (census results)†	
6 March 1974 .	2,656,948
29 May 1988	
Males .	2,110,106
Females .	2,138,455
Total .	4,248,561
Population (official estimates at mid-year)	
1998 .	6,179,700
1999 .	6,385,000
2000 .	6,597,100
Density (per sq km) at mid-2000 .	58.6

* 43,433 sq miles.
† Excluding adjustments for underenumeration, estimated to have been 10% at the 1974 census.

PRINCIPAL TOWNS (estimated population, '000 at mid-2000)

Tegucigalpa	. .	1,037.6	Siguatepeque . . .	51.0
San Pedro Sula	. .	471.0	Puerto Cortés . . .	35.6
El Progreso	. .	109.4	Juticalpa . . .	33.3
La Ceiba	. .	107.2	Santa Rosa de	
Choluteca .	. .	96.9	Copán . . .	27.8
Comayagua .	. .	73.2	Tela . . .	26.3
Danlí .	. .	64.4	Olanchito . . .	22.9

BIRTHS AND DEATHS (World Bank estimates, annual averages)

	1997	1998	1999
Birth rate (per 1,000). . . .	32.6	31.9	31.1
Death rate (per 1,000) . . .	5.7	5.5	5.3

Expectation of life (estimates, years at birth, 1998): 69.6; Males 67.7, Females 72.5 (Source: UNDP, *Human Development Report*).

ECONOMICALLY ACTIVE POPULATION
('000 persons aged 10 years and over, September 1999)

	Males	Females	Total
Agriculture, hunting, forestry and fishing	732.5	73.6	806.1
Mining and quarrying . .	2.3	1.5	3.8
Manufacturing . . .	180.2	196.6	376.9
Electricity, gas and water .	6.6	1.6	8.2
Construction	114.3	3.5	117.8
Trade, restaurants and hotels .	182.3	306.8	489.1
Transport, storage and communications . . .	51.8	4.2	56.0
Financing, insurance, real estate and business services . .	31.2	18.7	49.9
Community, social and personal services . . .	170.8	220.3	391.1
Total employed . . .	**1,472.1**	**826.9**	**2,299.0**
Unemployed	56.7	32.6	89.3
Total labour force . . .	**1,528.7**	**859.6**	**2,388.3**

Source: ILO, *Yearbook of Labour Statistics*.

Agriculture

PRINCIPAL CROPS ('000 metric tons)

	1997	1998	1999
Rice (paddy). . . .	50	28	13
Maize	610	471	478
Sorghum	96	90	71
Dry beans	75	73	53
Sugar cane . . .	3,637	3,779	3,756
Pineapples . . .	68*	73	70
Bananas	946	862	861
Plantains	231	218	250
Coffee (green) . . .	163	173	185
Tobacco	4	4	4

* FAO estimate.
Source: FAO.

LIVESTOCK ('000 head)

	1997	1998	1999
Cattle	2,061	2,200	2,061
Pigs*	670	700	798
Horses*	176	177	178
Mules*	69	69	70

Poultry (FAO estimates, million): 17 in 1997; 17 in 1998; 18 in 1999.
* FAO estimates.
Source: FAO.

LIVESTOCK PRODUCTS ('000 metric tons)

	1997	1998	1999
Beef and veal	26	28	21*
Pig meat	15	16	17
Poultry meat	58	54	59
Cows' milk	524	605	674
Hen eggs	40	41†	41†

* Unofficial figure.   † FAO estimate.
Source: FAO.

Forestry

ROUNDWOOD REMOVALS ('000 cubic metres, excluding bark)

	1996	1997	1998
Sawlogs, veneer logs and logs for sleepers .	645	711	789
Other industrial wood . .	1	8	6
Fuel wood	6,038	6,209	6,381
Total	**6,684**	**6,928**	**7,176**

Source: FAO, *Yearbook of Forest Products*.

SAWNWOOD PRODUCTION
('000 cubic metres, incl. railway sleepers)

	1996	1997	1998
Coniferous (softwood) . .	321	357	352
Broadleaved (hardwood) . .	1	22	17
Total	**322**	**379**	**369**

Source: FAO, *Yearbook of Forest Products*.

Fishing

('000 metric tons, live weight)

	1996	1997	1998
Capture*	14.9	17.3	14.9
Yellowfin tuna* . . .	1.9	1.9	1.9
Caribbean spiny lobster .	0.5	1.0	0.3
Penaeus shrimps . .	1.3	2.6	1.9
Stromboid conchs . .	0.5	3.0	3.0
Cuttlefish, bobtail squids .	3.1	2.1	2.1
Octopuses, etc. . . .	1.0	0.5	0.5
Aquaculture*	10.1	9.3	8.1
Total catch* . . .	25.0	26.6	23.0

Note: Figures exclude crocodiles, recorded by number rather than weight. The number of spectacled caimans caught was: 6,000 in 1996.

* FAO estimates.

Source: FAO, *Yearbook of Fishery Statistics*.

Mining

(metal content)

	1998	1999	2000
Lead ('000 metric tons) . .	6	5	4
Zinc ('000 metric tons) . .	41	41	36
Silver (metric tons) . .	60	54	51

Industry

SELECTED PRODUCTS

	1996	1997	1998
Raw sugar ('000 quintales) .	5,007	5,311	5,445
Cement ('000 bags of 42.5 kg) .	22,324	25,126	24,141
Cigarettes ('000 packets of 20) .	105,437	130,141	190,722
Beer ('000 12 oz bottles) .	237,612	293,899	279,382
Soft drinks ('000 12 oz bottles) .	1,147,189	1,319,886	1,218,911
Wheat flour ('000 quintales) .	2,173	2,262	2,300
Fabric ('000 yards) . . .	24,053	30,695	62,460
Other alcoholic drinks ('000 litres)	7,081	7,298	7,864
Vegetable oil and butter ('000 lb)	110,542	131,307	132,867

Finance

CURRENCY AND EXCHANGE RATES

Monetary Units
100 centavos = 1 lempira.

Sterling, Dollar and Euro Equivalents (29 December 2000)
£1 sterling = 22.593 lempiras;
US $1 = 15.141 lempiras;
€1 = 14.088 lempiras;
1,000 lempiras = £44.26 = $66.05 = €70.98.

Average Exchange Rate (lempiras per US $)
1998   13.3850
1999   14.2132
2000   14.8392

BUDGET (million lempiras)

Revenue	1997	1998	1999*
Current revenue . . .	10,374.4	13,214.2	14,621.5
Taxes	8,652.1	11,973.0	13,538.1
Direct taxes . . .	2,512.3	3,377.4	2,891.6
Income tax . . .	2,293.3	3,110.2	2,646.7
Property tax . . .	219.0	267.2	244.9
Indirect taxes . . .	6,138.0	8,593.4	10,643.9
Exports . . .	88.3	72.3	7.9
Imports . . .	2,067.8	2,043.2	1,977.1
Non-tax revenue . .	1,422.1	943.4	741.7
Transfers . . .	300.2	297.8	341.7
Other revenue (incl. capital revenue)	3.4	3.2	0.0
Total . . .	10,377.8	13,217.4	14,621.5

Expenditure	1997	1998	1999*
Current expenditure . .	10,072.2	11,182.3	12,359.0
Consumption expenditure .	5,421.8	6,692.5	8,177.5
Interest	2,697.8	2,314.3	1,700.4
Internal debt . .	1,090.9	647.8	562.0
External debt . .	1,606.9	1,666.5	1,138.4
Transfers . . .	1,952.6	2,175.5	2,481.1
Capital expenditure . .	2,912.8	3,569.2	5,601.1
Real investment . .	1,661.2	1,811.9	2,294.1
Transfers . . .	1,243.2	1,730.0	3,306.6
Net lending . . .	740.9	540.0	237.6
Total . . .	13,725.9	15,291.5	18,197.7

* Estimates.

CENTRAL BANK RESERVES (US $ million at 31 December)

	1998	1999	2000
Gold*	6.25	6.28	5.99
IMF special drawing rights . .	0.07	0.94	0.10
Foreign exchange . .	818.00	1,244.80	1,301.70
Reserve position in IMF . .	—	11.84	11.24
Total	824.32	1,263.86	1,319.03

* National valuation.

Source: IMF, *International Financial Statistics*.

MONEY SUPPLY (million lempiras at 31 December)

	1997	1998	1999
Currency outside banks . .	3,315	3,744	4,714
Demand deposits at commercial banks	4,287	4,841	5,666
Total money (incl. others) . .	8,294	9,344	11,050

Source: IMF, *International Financial Statistics*.

COST OF LIVING (Consumer Price Index; base: 1990 = 100)

	1997	1998	1999
Food	419.7	468.9	505.9
Fuel and power . . .	382.0	374.0	340.0
Clothing and Footwear . .	363.5	420.0	474.7
Rent	326.2	362.3	401.4
All items	378.4	430.2	480.4

Source: ILO, *Labour Statistics Yearbook*.

NATIONAL ACCOUNTS (million lempiras at current prices)
Expenditure on the Gross Domestic Product

	1997	1998	1999
Government final consumption expenditure	5,118	7,086	8,766
Private final consumption expenditure	40,528	45,781	51,609
Increase in stocks	3,994	910	2,980
Gross fixed capital formation	15,354	20,702	23,748
Total domestic expenditure	64,994	74,479	87,103
Exports of goods and services	28,217	33,054	32,672
Less Imports of goods and services	31,775	37,301	43,212
GDP in purchasers' values	61,436	70,232	76,563
GDP at constant 1978 prices	6,693	6,890	6,760

Source: IMF, *International Financial Statistics*.

Gross Domestic Product by Economic Activity

	1997	1998*	1999†
Agriculture, hunting, forestry and fishing	12,439	11,515	10,635
Mining and quarrying	920	1,102	1,325
Manufacturing	9,535	11,186	12,916
Electricity, gas and water	2,946	3,093	3,208
Construction	2,464	2,905	3,516
Wholesale and retail trade	6,264	7,360	8,365
Transport, storage and communications	2,464	2,985	3,423
Finance, insurance and real estate	4,882	6,490	6,960
Owner-occupied dwellings	2,941	3,478	3,990
Public administration and defence	3,162	3,596	4,153
Other services	5,207	6,372	7,261
GDP at factor cost	53,224	60,082	65,752
Indirect taxes, *less* subsidies	8,212	10,150	10,811
GDP in purchasers' values	61,436	70,232	76,563

* Preliminary figures. † Estimates.

BALANCE OF PAYMENTS (US $ million)

	1997	1998	1999
Exports of goods f.o.b.	1,856.5	2,016.5	1,848.9
Imports of goods f.o.b.	−2,150.4	−2,339.6	−2,558.0
Trade balance	−293.9	−323.1	−709.1
Exports of services	334.9	370.0	431.5
Imports of services	−360.9	−395.0	−497.6
Balance on goods and services	−319.9	−348.1	−775.2
Other income received	70.0	105.5	102.9
Other income paid	−281.8	−266.2	−228.5
Balance on goods, services and income	−531.7	−508.8	−900.8
Current transfers received	306.8	268.6	365.4
Current transfers paid	−47.3	−76.7	−1.4
Current balance	−272.2	−316.9	−536.8
Capital account (net)	14.6	47.6	75.2
Direct investment from abroad	121.5	84.0	230.0
Financial derivatives liabilities	—	−25.8	−16.8
Other investment assets	−53.4	−61.7	−135.0
Other investment liabilities	175.2	264.2	273.2
Net errors and omissions	196.5	6.7	52.5
Overall balance	182.2	−1.9	−57.7

Source: IMF, *International Financial Statistics*.

External Trade

PRINCIPAL COMMODITIES (US $ million)

Imports c.i.f.	1997	1998*	1999*
Consumer goods	567.6	681.4	749.5
Non-durable	325.2	397.4	476.0
Durable	242.4	284.0	273.5
Crude materials and intermediate products	732.5	730.3	791.3
For agriculture	98.2	95.6	80.8
For industry	634.3	634.7	710.5
Mineral fuels and lubricants	233.7	214.4	256.4
Construction materials	78.7	102.8	116.0
Capital goods	449.0	669.5	700.9
For agriculture	53.5	69.0	85.2
For industry	241.3	390.6	399.4
For transport	154.2	209.9	216.3
Total (incl. others)	2,148.6	2,499.6	2,727.8

Exports f.o.b.	1997	1998*	1999*
Bananas	212.0	175.7	37.7
Coffee	326.3	429.8	258.1
Zinc	53.8	36.3	39.4
Shellfish	179.1	188.7	193.2
Melons	39.3	43.8	47.0
Soaps and detergents	36.9	37.2	38.7
Total (incl. others)	1,445.7	1,576.8	1,248.8

* Preliminary figures.

PRINCIPAL TRADING PARTNERS (US $ million)

Imports c.i.f.*	1997	1998	1999
Brazil	24.2	23.5	30.9
Colombia	16.0	16.1	28.0
Costa Rica	56.6	87.9	97.8
El Salvador	113.4	156.4	180.4
Germany	33.4	33.5	46.4
Guatemala	151.1	232.5	224.7
Japan	76.4	117.1	107.2
Mexico	115.2	118.7	136.6
Netherlands	9.7	35.1	27.6
Nicaragua	21.1	24.9	38.0
Spain	20.1	26.7	30.6
USA	1,033.0	1,165.8	1,193.3
Venezuela	28.5	31.8	29.3
Total (incl. others)	2,148.6	2,499.6	2,727.8

* Preliminary figures.

Exports f.o.b.*	1997	1998	1999
Belgium	65.7	70.4	47.8
Costa Rica	28.1	24.6	27.3
El Salvador	61.0	83.3	83.3
France	14.5	15.6	12.1
Germany	120.6	124.4	42.9
Guatemala	57.8	88.7	72.9
Italy	41.7	30.9	24.8
Japan	43.2	66.7	55.6
Netherlands	15.6	14.9	16.1
Nicaragua	66.1	65.7	73.7
Spain	49.1	44.3	38.4
United Kingdom	52.7	32.9	12.6
USA	666.2	626.3	457.4
Total (incl. others)	1,445.7	1,576.8	1,248.7

* Preliminary figures.

Transport

ROAD TRAFFIC (motor vehicles in use)

	1997	1998	1999
Passenger cars	80,145	84,334	90,114
Commercial vehicles	231,048	267,381	295,749
Motorcycles and bicycles	25,829	28,622	31,568

SHIPPING

Merchant Fleet (registered at 31 December)

	1996	1997	1998
Number of vessels	1,408	1,339	1,465
Total displacement ('000 grt)	1,197.8	1,053.0	1,083.2

Source: Lloyd's Register of Shipping, *World Fleet Statistics*.

International Sea-borne Freight Traffic ('000 metric tons)

	1988	1989	1990
Goods loaded	1,328	1,333	1,316
Goods unloaded	1,151	1,222	1,002

Source: UN, *Monthly Bulletin of Statistics*.

CIVIL AVIATION (traffic on scheduled services)

	1993	1994	1995
Kilometres flown (million)	4	5	5
Passengers carried ('000)	409	449	474
Passenger-km (million)	362	323	341
Total ton-km (million)	50	42	33

Source: UN, *Statistical Yearbook*.

Tourism

VISITOR ARRIVALS BY COUNTRY OF ORIGIN

	1996	1997	1998
Canada	7,711	9,300	8,025
Costa Rica	10,509	12,516	12,665
El Salvador	20,778	29,291	32,534
Germany	6,602	6,919	6,321
Guatemala	23,949	32,915	30,393
Mexico	7,698	9,285	10,185
Nicaragua	29,174	34,734	39,285
USA	107,389	118,357	127,303
Total (incl. others)	263,317	306,646	321,149

Receipts from tourism (US $ million): 115 in 1996; 120 in 1997; 164 in 1998.

Sources: World Tourism Organization, *Yearbook of Tourism Statistics*; World Bank, *World Development Indicators*.

Communications Media

	1995	1996	1997
Radio receivers ('000 in use)	2,310	2,380	2,450
Television receivers ('000 in use)	500	550	570
Telephones ('000 main lines in use)	161	190	234
Daily newspapers	6	6	6
Weekly newspapers	2	n.a.	3

Sources: partly UN, *Statistical Yearbook,* and UNESCO, *Statistical Yearbook*.

Education

(1998)

	Insti-tutions	Teachers	Students
Pre-primary	2,401	3,184	89,537
Primary	8,743	32,519	1,077,333
Secondary	917	14,357	183,245
University level	10	5,088	76,573

Directory

The Constitution

Following the elections of April 1980, the 1965 Constitution was revised. The new Constitution was approved by the National Assembly in November 1982, and amended in 1995. The following are some of its main provisions:

Honduras is constituted as a democratic Republic. All Hondurans over 18 years of age are citizens.

THE SUFFRAGE AND POLITICAL PARTIES

The vote is direct and secret. Any political party which proclaims or practises doctrines contrary to the democratic spirit is forbidden. A National Electoral Council will be set up at the end of each presidential term. Its general function will be to supervise all elections and to register political parties. A proportional system of voting will be adopted for the election of Municipal Corporations.

INDIVIDUAL RIGHTS AND GUARANTEES

The right to life is declared inviolable; the death penalty is abolished. The Constitution recognizes the right of habeas corpus and arrests may be made only by judicial order. Remand for interrogation may not last more than six days, and no-one may be held incommunicado for more than 24 hours. The Constitution recognizes the rights of free expression of thought and opinion, the free circulation of information, of peaceful, unarmed association, of free movement within and out of the country, of political asylum and of religious and educational freedom. Civil marriage and divorce are recognized.

WORKERS' WELFARE

All have a right to work. Day work shall not exceed eight hours per day or 44 hours per week; night work shall not exceed six hours per night or 36 hours per week. Equal pay shall be given for equal work. The legality of trade unions and the right to strike are recognized.

EDUCATION

The State is responsible for education, which shall be free, lay, and, in the primary stage, compulsory. Private education is liable to inspection and regulation by the State.

LEGISLATIVE POWER

Deputies are obliged to vote, for or against, on any measure at the discussion of which they are present. The National Assembly has power to grant amnesties to political prisoners; approve or disapprove of the actions of the Executive; declare part or the whole of the Republic subject to a state of siege; declare war; approve or withhold approval of treaties; withhold approval of the accounts of public expenditure when these exceed the sums fixed in the budget; decree, interpret, repeal and amend laws, and pass legislation fixing the rate of exchange or stabilizing the national currency. The National Assembly may suspend certain guarantees in all or part of the Republic for 60 days in the case of grave danger from civil or foreign war, epidemics or any other calamity. Deputies are elected in the proportion of one deputy and one substitute for every 35,000 inhabitants, or fraction over 15,000. Congress may amend the basis in the light of increasing population.

EXECUTIVE POWER

Executive power is exercised by the President of the Republic, who is elected for four years by a simple majority of the people. No President may serve more than one term.

JUDICIAL POWER

The Judiciary consists of the Supreme Court, the Courts of Appeal and various lesser tribunals. The nine judges and seven substitute judges of the Supreme Court are elected by the National Assembly for a period of four years. The Supreme Court is empowered to declare laws unconstitutional.

THE ARMED FORCES

The armed forces are declared by the Constitution to be essentially professional and non-political. The President exercises military power through a Commander-in-Chief who is designated for a period of three years by the National Assembly, and may be dismissed only by it by a two-thirds' majority.

LOCAL ADMINISTRATION

The country is divided into 18 Departments for purposes of local administration, and these are subdivided into 290 autonomous Municipalities; the functions of local offices shall be only economic and administrative.

The Government

HEAD OF STATE

President: CARLOS ROBERTO FLORES FACUSSÉ (assumed office 27 January 1998).
Vice-President: GLADYS AIDA CABALLERO.

CABINET
(April 2001)

Minister of the Interior and Justice: VERA SOFIA RUBÍ.

Minister in the Office of the President: GUSTAVO ADOLFO ALFARO ZELAYA.

Minister of Foreign Affairs: ROBERTO FLORES BERMÚDEZ.

Minister of Industry and Commerce: OSCAR KAFATI.

Minister of Finance: GABRIELA NÚÑEZ LÓPEZ.

Minister of National Defence: ENRIQUE FLORES VALERIANO.

Minister of Public Security: GAUTAMA FONSECA ZUNIGA.

Minister of Labour and Social Welfare: ROSA AMÉRICA MIRANDA DE GALO.

Minister of Health: PLUTARCO CASTELLANOS.

Minister of Public Education: RAMÓN CÁLIX FIGUEROA.

Minister of Public Works, Transport and Housing: TOMÁS R. LOZANO REYES.

Minister of Culture, Art and Sports: HERMÁN ALLAN PADGETT.

Minister of Agriculture and Livestock: GUILLERMO ALVARADO DOWNING.

Minister of Natural Resources and Environment: SILVIA XIOMARA GÓMEZ DE CABALLERO.

Minister of Tourism: ANA DEL SOCORRO ABARCA DE PERDOMO.

Minister of International Co-operation: GLENDA GALLARDO.

MINISTRIES

Office of the President: Palacio José Cecilio del Valle, Blvd Juan Pablo II, Tegucigalpa; tel. 232-6282; fax 231-0097.

Ministry of Agriculture and Livestock: Tegucigalpa.

Ministry of Culture, Art and Sports: Avda La Paz, Apdo 3287, Tegucigalpa; tel. 236-9643; fax 236-9532; e-mail binah@ sdnhon.org.hn; internet www.sdnhon.org.hn/miembros/cultura.

Ministry of Finance: 5a Avda, 3a Calle, Tegucigalpa; tel. 22-1278; fax 238-2309.

Ministry of Foreign Affairs: Centro Cívico Gubernamental, Antigua Casa Presidencial, Blvd Fuerzas Armadas, Tegucigalpa; tel. 234-1922; fax 234-1484; internet www.sre.hn.

Ministry of Health: 4a Avda, 3a Calle, Tegucigalpa; tel. 22-1386; fax 238-4141; internet www.paho-who.hn/ssalud.htm.

Ministry of Industry and Commerce: Edif. Salame, 5a Avda, 4a Calle, Tegucigalpa; tel. 238-2025; fax 237-2836.

Ministry of the Interior and Justice: Palacio de los Ministerios, 2°, Tegucigalpa; tel. 237-1130; fax 237-1121; e-mail dgaatm@ sdnhon.org.hn; internet www.sdnhon.org.hn/~dgaatm.

Ministry of International Co-operation: Tegucigalpa.

Ministry of Labour and Social Welfare: 2a y 3a Avda, 7a Calle, Comayagüela, Tegucigalpa; tel. 22-8526; fax 22-3220.

Ministry of National Defence and Public Security: 5a Avda, 4a Calle, Tegucigalpa; tel. 22-8560; fax 238-0238.

Ministry of Natural Resources and Environment: 100 ms al sur del Estadio Nacional, Apdo 1389, Tegucigalpa; tel. 239-4296; fax 232-6250; e-mail oss@serna.gob.hn; internet www.serna.gob.hn.

Ministry of Public Education: 1a Avda, 2a y 3a Calle 201, Comayagüela, Tegucigalpa; tel. 22-8517; fax 237-4312.

Ministry of Public Works, Transport and Housing: Barrio La Bolsa, Comayagüela, Tegucigalpa; tel. 233-7690; fax 25-2227.

Ministry of Tourism: Edif. Salame, 5a Avda, 4a Calle, Tegucigalpa; tel. 238-2025; fax 237-2836.

President and Legislature

PRESIDENT

Election, 30 November 1997

Candidate		Votes cast	% of votes
CARLOS ROBERTO FLORES FACUSSÉ (PL)	. .	1,039,567	52.70
ALBA NORA GÚNERA DE MELGAR (PN)	. .	843,154	42.74
OLBAN F. VALLADARES (PINU)	. .	41,463	2.10
ARTURO CORRALES ALVÁREZ (PDCH)	. .	24,717	1.25
MATÍAS FUNES (PUD)	. .	23,745	1.20
Total	. . . .	1,972,646	100.00

ASAMBLEA NACIONAL

President: RAFAEL PINEDA PONCE.

General Election, 30 November 1997

Party		Votes cast	% of votes	Seats
Partido Liberal (PL)	. .	940,575	49.55	67
Partido Nacional (PN)	. .	789,015	41.56	55
Partido Innovación y Unidad—Social Democracia (PINU)	.	78,495	4.13	3
Partido Demócrata Cristiano de Honduras (PDCH)	. .	49,650	2.62	2
Partido de Unificación Democrática (PUD)	. .	40,658	2.14	1
Total*	. . . .	1,898,393	100.00	128

* There were, in addition, 108,635 blank votes and 55,431 spoiled votes.

Political Organizations

Asociación para el Progreso de Honduras (APROH): right-wing grouping of business interests and members of the armed forces; Vice-Pres. MIGUEL FACUSSÉ; Sec. OSWALDO RAMOS SOTO.

Francisco Morazán Frente Constitucional (FMFC): f. 1988; composed of labour, social, political and other organizations.

Frente Patriótico Hondureño (FPH): left-wing alliance comprising:

> **Partido de Acción Socialista de Honduras (PASOH):** Leaders MARIO VIRGILIO CARAS, ROGELIO MARTÍNEZ REINA.

> **Partido Comunista de Honduras—Marxista-Leninista (PCH—ML):** f. 1954; gained legal status 1981; linked with DNU; Leader RIGOBERTO PADILLA RUSH.

Partido Demócrata Cristiano de Honduras (PDCH): legally recognized in 1980; Pres. EFRAÍN DÍAZ ARRIVILLAGA; Leader Dr HERNÁN CORRALES PADILLA.

Partido Innovación y Unidad—Social Democracia (PINU): 29 Avda de Comayaguela 912, Apdo 105, Tegucigalpa; tel. 237-1357; fax 237-4245; f. 1970; legally recognized in 1978; Leader OLBAN F. VALLADARES.

Partido Liberal (PL): Col. Miramonte atrás del supermercado La Colonia, No 1, Tegucigalpa; tel. 232-0520; fax 232-0797; internet www.partido-liberal.hn; f. 1891; factions within the party include the Alianza Liberal del Pueblo, the Movimiento Florista (Leader CARLOS ROBERTO FLORES FACUSSÉ), and the Movimiento Liberal Democrático Revolucionario (Pres. JORGE ARTURO REINA); Pres. CARLOS ROBERTO FLORES FACUSSÉ; Sec.-Gen. ROBERTO MICHELETTI BAIN.

Partido Nacional (PN): Paseo el Obelisco, Comayaguela, Tegucigalpa; tel. 237-7310; fax 237-7365; f. 1902; traditional right-wing party; internal opposition tendencies include Movimiento Democratizador Nacionalista (MODENA), Movimiento de Unidad y Cambio (MUC), Movimiento Nacional de Reivindicación Callejista (MONARCA) and Tendencia Nacionalista de Trabajo; Pres. CARLOS URBIZO; Sec. MARIO AGUILAR GONZÁLEZ.

Partido de Unificación Democrática (PUD): f. 1993; left-wing coalition comprising Partido Revolucionario Hondureño, Partido Renovación Patriótica, Partido para la Transformación de Honduras and Partido Morazanista.

Pueblo Unido en Bloque por Honduras (PuebloH): Tegucigalpa; f. 1999; Leader RAMÓN CUSTODIO.

Unión Revolucionaria del Pueblo (URP): f. 1980 following split in Communist Party; peasant support.

The Dirección Nacional Unificada—Movimiento Revolucionario Hondureño (DNU—MRH) comprises the following guerrilla groups:

Fuerzas Populares Revolucionarias (FRP) Lorenzo Zelaya.
Frente Morazanista para la Liberación de Honduras (FMLH).
Froylan Turcios.
Movimiento Popular de Liberación Cinchonero (MPLC).
Movimiento de Unidad Revolucionaria (MUR).
Partido Revolucionario de los Trabajadores Centroamericanos de Honduras (PRTCH).

Other guerrilla forces include the **Alianza por Acción Anticomunista (AAA)** and the **Frente Popular de Liberación, Nueve de Mayo (FPL)**.

Diplomatic Representation

EMBASSIES IN HONDURAS

Argentina: Avda José María Medina 417, Col. Rubén Darío, Apdo 3208, Tegucigalpa; tel. 232-3376; fax 231-0376; Ambassador: ADRIÁN GUILLERMO MIRSON.

Belize: Hotel Honduras Maya, Apdo 1586, Tegucigalpa; tel. 220-5070; fax 220-5071; Chargé d'Affaires a.i.: RICHARD CLARK VINELLI REISMAN.

Brazil: Col. La Reforma, Calle La Salle 1309, Apdo 341, Tegucigalpa; tel. 236-5867; fax 236-5873; e-mail brastegu@hondudata.com; Ambassador: RUBEM AMARAL, Jr.

Chile: Edif. Interamericana frente Los Castaños, Blvd Morazán, Apdo 222, Tegucigalpa; fax 232-8853; Ambassador: GERMÁN CARRASCO.

China (Taiwan): Col. Lomas del Guijarro, Calle Eucaliptos 3750, Apdo 3433, Tegucigalpa; tel. 231-1484; fax 232-7645; e-mail giohon@datum.hn; Ambassador: CHING-YEN CHANG.

Colombia: Edif. Palmira, 4°, Col. Palmira, Apdo 468, Tegucigalpa; tel. 232-9709; fax 232-8133; Ambassador: GERMÁN RAMÍREZ BULLA.

Costa Rica: Residencial El Triángulo, Lomas del Guijarro, 1a Calle 3451, Apdo 512, Tegucigalpa; tel. 232-1768; fax 232-1876; e-mail embacori@sigmanet.hn; Chargé d'Affaires a.i.: MÁXIMO SUÁREZ ULLOA.

Dominican Republic: Col. La Granja 402, 4a Calle entre 4a y 5a Avda Comayagüela, Apdo 1460, Tegucigalpa; Ambassador: JUAN EMILIO CANÓ DE LA MOTA.

Ecuador: Col. Palmira, Avda Juan Lindo 122, Apdo 358, Tegucigalpa; tel. 236-5980; fax 236-6929; Ambassador: Dr JOSÉ IGNACIO JIJÓN FREILE.

El Salvador: Col. San Carlos, Calzada República del Uruguay 219, Apdo 1936, Tegucigalpa; tel. 236-8045; fax 236-9403; Ambassador: Dr VICENTE MACHADO SALGADO.

France: Col. Palmira, Avda Juan Lindo, Apdo 3441, Tegucigalpa; tel. 236-6800; fax 236-8051; Ambassador: GILLES VIDAL.

Germany: Edif. Paysen, 3°, Blvd Morazán, Apdo 3145, Tegucigalpa; tel. 232-3161; fax 232-9518; Ambassador: ANDREAS KULICK.

Guatemala: Col. Palmira, Avda Juan Lindo 313, Apdo 34-C, Tegucigalpa; tel. 232-5018; Ambassador: EUNICE LIMA.

Holy See: Palacio de la Nunciatura Apostólica, Col. Palmira 412, Apdo 324, Tegucigalpa; tel. 236-6613; fax 232-8280; e-mail nunciatureateg@hondudata.com; Apostolic Nuncio: Most Rev. GEORGE PANIKULAM, Titular Archbishop of Arpaia.

Israel: Edif. Palmira, Col. Palmira, Apdo 1187, Tegucigalpa; Ambassador: SHIMON AGOUR.

Italy: Col. Reforma 2602, Avda Principal, Apdo 9093, Tegucigalpa; tel. 236-6810; fax 236-5659; e-mail ambtegus@cablecolor.hn; Ambassador: Dr MARIO ALBERTO MONTECALVO.

Japan: Col. Reforma, 2a Avda, Plaza del Guanacaste, Apdo 125-C, Tegucigalpa; Ambassador: KIICHI ITABASHI.

Mexico: Avda República de México 2402, Apdo 769, Tegucigalpa; tel. 232-4039; fax 232-4224; Ambassador: BENITO ANDION SANCHO.

Nicaragua: Col. Tepeyac, Bloque M-1, 1130, Apdo 392, Tegucigalpa; tel. 232-7224; fax 231-1412; Ambassador: Dr JOSÉ RENÉ GUTIÉRREZ HUETE.

Panama: Edif. Palmira, Col. Palmira, Apdo 397, Tegucigalpa; tel. 231-5441; fax 231-5441; Ambassador: JULIO E. GÓMEZ AMADOR.

Peru: Col. La Reforma, Calle Principal 2618, Tegucigalpa; tel. 221-0596; fax 236-6070; e-mail embaperu@netsys.hn; Chargé d'Affaires a.i.: CARLOS ALBERTO YRIGOYEN FORNO.

Spain: Col. Matamoros, Calle Santander 801, Apdo 3223, Tegucigalpa; tel. 236-6875; fax 236-8682; Ambassador: CARLOS GÓMEZ-MÚGICA SANZ.

United Kingdom: Edif. Palmira, 3°, Col. Palmira, Apdo 290, Tegucigalpa; tel. 232-0612; fax 232-5480; Ambassador: DAVID A. OSBORNE.

USA: Avda La Paz, Apdo 26-C, Tegucigalpa; tel. 232-3120; fax 232-0027; Ambassador: JAMES F. CREAGAN.

Uruguay: Edif. Palmira, 4°, Col. Palmira, Apdo 329, Tegucigalpa; Ambassador: ALFREDO MENINI TERRA.

Venezuela: Col. Rubén Darío, entre Avda Las Minitas y Avda Rubén Darío, Casa 2321, Tegucigalpa; Ambassador: JESÚS ELÍAS M.

Judicial System

Justice is administered by the Supreme Court (which has nine judges), five Courts of Appeal, and departmental courts (which have their own local jurisdiction).

Tegucigalpa has two Courts of Appeal which have jurisdiction (1) in the department of Francisco Morazán, and (2) in the departments of Choluteca Valle, El Paraíso and Olancho.

The Appeal Court of San Pedro Sula has jurisdiction in the department of Cortés. That of Comayagua has jurisdiction in the departments of Comayagua, La Paz and Intibucá; that of Santa Bárbara in the departments of Santa Bárbara, Lempira and Copán.

Supreme Court: Edif. Palacio de Justicia, contiguo Col. Miraflores, Centro Cívico Gubernamental, Tegucigalpa; tel. 233-9208; fax 233-6784.

President of the Supreme Court of Justice: OSCAR ARMANDO AVILA.

Attorney-General: EDMUNDO ORELLANA.

Religion

The majority of the population are Roman Catholics; the Constitution guarantees toleration to all forms of religious belief.

CHRISTIANITY
The Roman Catholic Church

Honduras comprises one archdiocese and six dioceses. At 31 December 1998 some 90.3% of the population were adherents.

Bishops' Conference: Conferencia Episcopal de Honduras, Los Laureles, Comayagüela, Apdo 3121, Tegucigalpa; tel. 229-1111; fax 229-1144; e-mail ceh@sdnhon.org.hn; f. 1929; Pres. Cardinal OSCAR ANDRÉS RODRÍGUEZ MARADIAGA, Archbishop of Tegucigalpa.

Archbishop of Tegucigalpa: Cardinal OSCAR ANDRÉS RODRÍGUEZ MARADIAGA, Arzobispado, 3a-2a Avda 1113, Apdo 106, Tegucigalpa; tel. 237-0353; fax 222-2337.

The Anglican Communion

Honduras comprises a single missionary diocese, in Province IX of the Episcopal Church in the USA.

Bishop of Honduras: Rt Rev. LEOPOLD FRADE, Apdo 586, San Pedro Sula; tel. 556-6155; fax 556-6467; e-mail episcopal@mayanet.hn.

The Baptist Church

Baptist Convention of Honduras: Apdo 2176, Tegucigalpa; tel. and fax 236-6717; Pres. TOMÁS MONTOYA.

BAHÁ'Í FAITH

National Spiritual Assembly: Sendero de los Naranjos 2801, Col. Castaños, Apdo 273, Tegucigalpa; tel. 232-6124; fax 231-1343; e-mail bahaihon@globenet.hn; mems resident in 667 localities.

The Press

DAILIES

El Faro Porteño: Puerto Cortés.

La Gaceta: Tegucigalpa; f. 1830; morning; official govt paper; Dir MARCIAL LAGOS; circ. 3,000.

El Heraldo: Avda los Próceres, Frente Instituto del Tórax, Barrio San Felipe, Apdo 1938, Tegucigalpa; tel. 236-6000; fax 21-0778; f. 1979; morning; independent; Dir JOSÉ FRANCISCO MORALES CÁLIX; circ. 45,000.

El Nuevo Día: 3a Avda, 11–12 Calles, San Pedro Sula; tel. 52-4298; fax 57-9457; e-mail elndia@hondutel.hn; f. 1994; morning; independent; Pres. ABRAHAM ANDONIE; Editor ARMANDO CERRATO; circ. 20,000.

El Periódico: Carretera al Batallón, Tegucigalpa; tel. 234-3086; fax 234-3090; f. 1993; morning; Pres. EMIN ABUFELE; Editor OSCAR ARMANDO MARTÍNEZ.

La Prensa: 3a Avda, 6a–7a Calles No 34, Apdo 143, San Pedro Sula; tel. 53-3101; fax 53-0778; e-mail laprensa@simon.intertel.hn; internet www.laprensahn.com; f. 1964; morning; independent; Pres. JORGE CANAHUATI LARACH; Editor NELSON EDGARDO FERNÁNDEZ; circ. 62,000.

El Tiempo: Altos del Centro Comercial Miramontes, Col. Miramontes, Tegucigalpa; tel. 231-0418; internet www.tiempo.hn; f. 1970; liberal; Dir MANUEL GAMERO; circ. 42,000.

El Tiempo: 1a Calle, 5a Avda 102, Santa Anita, Apdo 450, San Pedro Sula; tel. 53-3388; fax 53-4590; e-mail tiempo@simon.intertel.hn; internet www.tiempo.hn; f. 1960; morning; left-of-centre; Pres. JAIME ROSENTHAL OLIVA; Editor MANUEL GAMERO; circ. 35,000.

La Tribuna: Col. Santa Bárbara, Comayagüela, Apdo 1501, Tegucigalpa; tel. 233-1138; fax 233-1188; e-mail tribuna@david.intertel.hn; internet www.latribuna.hn; f. 1977; morning; independent; Dir ADÁN ELVIR FLORES; Pres. CARLOS ROBERTO FLORES FACUSSÉ; circ. 45,000.

PERIODICALS

Cambio Empresarial: Apdo 1111, Tegucigalpa; tel. 237-2853; fax 237-0480; monthly; economic, political, social; Editor JOAQUÍN MEDINA OVIEDO.

El Comercio: Cámara de Comercio e Industrias de Tegucigalpa, Blvd Centroamérica, Apdo 3444, Tegucigalpa; tel. 232-4200; fax 232-0759; f. 1970; monthly; commercial and industrial news; Dir-Gen. Lic. HÉCTOR MANUEL ORDÓÑEZ.

Cultura para Todos: San Pedro Sula; monthly.

Espectador: San Pedro Sula; weekly.

Extra: Tegucigalpa; tel. 237-2533; f. 1965; monthly; independent; current affairs; Editor VICENTE MACHADO VALLE.

Hablemos Claro: Edif. Abriendo Brecha, Blvd Suyapa, Tegucigalpa; tel. 232-8058; fax 239-7008; e-mail abrecha@hondutel.hn; f. 1990; weekly; Editor RODRIGO WONG ARÉVALO; circ. 15,000.

Hibueras: Apdo 955, Tegucigalpa; Dir RAÚL LANZA VALERIANO.

Presente: Tegucigalpa; monthly.

Revista Ideas: Tegucigalpa; 6 a year; women's interest.

Revista Prisma: Tegucigalpa; quarterly; cultural; Editor MARÍA LUISA CASTELLANOS.

Sucesos: Tegucigalpa; monthly.

Tribuna Sindical: Tegucigalpa; monthly.

PRESS ASSOCIATION

Asociación de Prensa Hondureña: 6a Calle (altos), Barrio Guanacaste, Apdo 893, Tegucigalpa; tel. 237-8345; f. 1930; Pres. MIGUEL OSMUNDO MEJA ERAZO.

FOREIGN NEWS AGENCIES

Agence France-Presse (AFP) (France): Tegucigalpa; Correspondent WINSTON CÁLIX.

Agencia EFE (Spain): Edif. Jiménez Castro, 5°, Of. 505, Tegucigalpa; tel. 22-0493; Bureau Chief ARMANDO ENRIQUE CERRATO CORTÉS.

Agenzia Nazionale Stampa Associata (ANSA) (Italy): Edif. La Plazuela, Barrio La Plazuela, Tegucigalpa; tel. 237-7701; Correspondent RAÚL MONCADA.

Deutsche Presse-Agentur (dpa) (Germany): Edif. Jiménez Castro, Of. 203, 4a Calle y 5a Avda, No 405, Apdo 3522, Tegucigalpa; tel. 237-8570; Correspondent WILFREDO GARCÍA CASTRO.

Inter Press Service (IPS) (Italy): Apdo 228, Tegucigalpa; tel. 232-5342; Correspondent JUAN RAMÓN DURÁN.

Reuters (United Kingdom): Edif. Palmira, frente Honduras Maya, 5°, Col. Palmira, Tegucigalpa; tel. 231-5329.

United Press International (UPI) (USA): c/o El Tiempo, Altos del Centro Comercial Miramontes, Col. Miramontes, Tegucigalpa; tel. 231-0418; Correspondent VILMA GLORIA ROSALES.

Publishers

Compañía Editora Nacional, SA: 5A Calle Oriente, No 410, Tegucigalpa.

Editora Cultural: 6A Avda Norte, 7a Calle, Comayagüela, Tegucigalpa.

Editorial Nuevo Continente: Tegucigalpa; tel. 22-5073; Dir LETICIA SILVA DE OYUELA.

Editorial Paulino Valladares, Carlota Vda de Valladares: 5a Avda, 5a y 6a Calle, Tegucigalpa.

Guaymuras: Apdo 1843, Tegucigalpa; tel. 237-5433; fax 237-4931; f. 1980; Dir ISOLDA ARITA MELZER; Admin. ROSENDO ANTÚNEZ.

Industria Editorial Lypsa: Apdo 167-C, Tegucigalpa; tel. 22-9775; Man. JOSÉ BENNATON.

Universidad Nacional Autónoma de Honduras: Blvd Suyapa, Tegucigalpa; tel. 231-4601; fax 231-4601; f. 1847.

Broadcasting and Communications

TELECOMMUNICATIONS

Comisión Nacional de Telecomunicaciones (Conatel): Apdo 15012, Tegucigalpa; tel. 221-3500; fax 221-0578; e-mail nhernandez@conatel.hn; Pres. NORMAN ROY HERNÁNDEZ D.; Exec. Sec. WALTER DAVID SANDOVAL.

Empresa Hondureña de Telecomunicaciones (Hondutel): Apdo 1794, Tegucigalpa; tel. 237-9802; fax 237-1111; scheduled for privatization in 2001; Gen. Man. ROBERTO MICHELLETTI BAIN.

BROADCASTING

Radio

Radio América: Col. Alameda, frente a la Droguería Mandofer, Apdo 259, Tegucigalpa; commercial station; tel. 232-7028; fax 231-4180; f. 1948; 13 relay stations; Pres. MANUEL ANDONIE FERNÁNDEZ; Gen. Man. BERNARDINO RIVERA.

Radio Nacional de Honduras: Zona El Olvido, Apdo 403, Tegucigalpa; tel. 238-5478; fax 237-9721; f. 1976; official station, operated by the Govt; Dir ROY ARTHURS LEYLOR.

Radio Tegucigalpa: Edif. Landa Blanca, Calle La Fuente, Tegucigalpa; tel. 238-3880; f. 1982; Dir NERY ARTEAGA; Gen. Man. ANTONIO CONDE MAZARIEGOS.

La Voz de Centroamérica: 9a Calle, 10a Avda 64, Apdo 120, San Pedro Sula; tel. 52-7660; fax 57-3257; f. 1955; commercial station; Gen. Man. NOEMI SIKAFFY.

La Voz de Honduras: Blvd Suyapa, Apdo 642, Tegucigalpa; commercial station; 23 relay stations; Gen. Man. NOEMI VALLADARES.

Television

Centroamericana de Televisión, Canal 7 y 4: Edif. Televicentro, Blvd Suyapa, Apdo 734, Tegucigalpa; tel. 239-2081; fax 232-0097; f. 1959; Pres. JOSÉ RAFAEL FERRARI; Gen. Man. RAFAEL ENRIQUE VILLEDA.

Compañía Televisora Hondureña, SA: Blvd Suyapa, Apdo 734, Tegucigalpa; tel. 232-7835; fax 232-0097; f. 1959; main station Channel 5; nine relay stations; Gen. Man. JOSÉ RAFAEL FERRARI.

Corporación Centroamericana de Comunicaciones, SA de CV: 9a Calle, 10A Avda 64, Barrio Guamilito, Apdo 120, San Pedro Sula; tel. 557-5033; fax 557-3257; e-mail info@vicatv.hn; internet www.vicatv.hn; f. 1986; Pres. BLANCA SIKAFFY.

Voz y Imagen de Centro América: 9a Calle, 10A Avda 64, Barrio Guamilito, Apdo 120, San Pedro Sula; tel. 52-7660; fax 57-3257; Channels 9, 2 and 13; Pres. BLANCA SIKAFFY.

Telesistema Hondureño, SA, Canal 3: Edif. Televicentro, Blvd Suyapa, Apdo 734, Tegucigalpa; tel. 232-7064; fax 232-5019; f. 1967; Pres. MANUEL VILLEDA TOLEDO; Gen. Man. RAFAEL ENRIQUE VILLEDA.

Telesistema Hondureño, Canal 7: Col. Tara, Apdo 208, San Pedro Sula; tel. 53-1229; fax 57-6343; f. 1967; Pres. MANUEL VILLEDA TOLEDO; Dir JOSÉ RAFAEL FERRARI.

Trecevisión: Apdo 393, Tegucigalpa; subscriber TV; one relay station in San Pedro Sula; Gen. Man. F. PON AGUILAR.

Finance

(cap. = capital; res = reserves; dep. = deposits;
m. = million; brs = branches;
amounts in lempiras unless otherwise stated)

BANKING

Central Bank

Banco Central de Honduras—BANTRAL: Avda Juan Ramón Molina, 7a Avda y 1a Calle, Apdo 3165, Tegucigalpa; tel. 237-2270; fax 237-1876; internet www.bch.hn; f. 1950; bank of issue; cap. 63.7m., res 373.5m., dep. 4,762.2m. (Dec. 1992); Pres. VICTORIA ASFURA DE DÍAZ; Vice Pres. DANIEL ALFREDO FIGUEROA; 4 brs.

Commercial Banks

Banco Atlántida, SA (BANCATLAN): Blvd Centroamérica, Plaza Bancatlán, Apdo 3164, Tegucigalpa; tel. 232-1050; fax 232-6120; e-mail webmaster@bancatlan.hn; internet www.bancatlan.hn; f. 1913; cap. 500.0m., res 170.3m., dep. 5,121.0m. (Dec. 2000); Exec. Pres. GUILLERMO BUESO; Exec. Vice-Pres SALVADOR GÓMEZ, ROLANDO FUNES, JUDITH B. DE SALAZAR; 17 brs.

Banco del Comercio, SA (BANCOMER): 6a Avda, Calle SO 1-2, Apdo 160, San Pedro Sula; tel. 54-3600; Pres. RODOLFO CÓRDOBA PINEDA; 4 brs.

Banco Continental, SA (BANCON): Edif. Continental, 3a Avda 7, entre 2a y 3a Calle, Apdo 390, San Pedro Sula; tel. 239-2288; fax 239-0388; f. 1974; cap. 100m., res 14.3m., dep. 304.5m. (Dec. 1994); Pres. JAIME ROSENTHAL OLIVA; 6 brs.

Banco de las Fuerzas Armadas, SA (BANFFAA): Centro Comercial Los Castaños, Blvd Morazán, Apdo 877, Tegucigalpa; tel. 232-0164; fax 232-4728; e-mail webmaster@banffaa.hn; internet www.banffaa.hn; f. 1979; cap. 10m., res 33.2m., dep. 428.1m. (Dec. 1992); Pres. ROBERTO LÁZARUS LOZANO; Gen. Man. CARLOS RIVERA XATRUCH; 15 brs.

Banco Futuro: Edif. La Plazuela, 3a y 4a Calle, 4a Avda 1205, Tegucigalpa; tel. 237-4000; fax 237-1835; internet www.futuro.hn.

Banco Grupo El Ahorro Hondureño (BGA): Avda Colón 714, Apdo 3185, Tegucigalpa; tel. 237-5161; fax 237-4638; e-mail bancahorro@bancahorro.hn; internet www.bancahorro.hn; f. 2000, following a merger of Banco del Ahorro Hondureño and Banco La Capitalizadora Hondureña; cap. 648m., dep. 366m.; 125 brs.

Banco de Honduras, SA: Blvd Suyapa, Col. Loma Linda Sur, Tegucigalpa; tel. 232-6122; fax 232-6167; f. 1889; total assets 15,106m. (1999); Gen. Man. PATRICIA FERRO; 3 brs.

Banco Mercantil, SA: Blvd Suyapa, frente a Emisoras Unidas, Apdo 116, Tegucigalpa; tel. 232-0006; fax 232-3137; internet www.bamernet.hn; Pres. JOSÉ LAMAS; Gen. Man. JACOBO ATALA.

Banco de Occidente, SA (BANCOCCI): 6a Avda, Calle 2-3, Apdo 3284; tel. 237-0310; fax 237-0486; e-mail boccipan@pty.com; f. 1951; cap. and res 69m., dep. 606m. (June 1994); Pres. and Gen. Man. JORGE BUESO ARIAS; Vice-Pres. EMILIO MEDINA R.; 6 brs.

Banco Sogerin, SA: 8a Avda, 1a Calle, Apdo 440, San Pedro Sula; tel. 550-3888; fax 550-2001; e-mail sogelba@hondutel.hn; f. 1969; cap. and res 150.8m., dep. 857.9m. (Dec. 2000); Pres. and Gen. Man. EDMOND BOGRÁN ACOSTA; 31 brs.

Banco de los Trabajadores, SA (BANCOTRAB): 3a Avda, 13a Calle, Paseo El Obelisco, Comayagüela, Apdo 3246, Tegucigalpa; tel. 237-8723; f. 1967; cap. and res US \$6.6m., dep. \$43.1m. (Dec. 1992); Pres. ROLANDO DEL CID VELÁSQUEZ; 13 brs.

Development Banks

Banco Centroamericano de Integración Económica: Edif. Sede BCIE, Blvd Suyapa, Apdo 772, Tegucigalpa; tel. 228-2182; fax 228-2183; internet www.bcie.org; f. 1960 to finance the economic development of the Central American Common Market and its mem. countries; mems Costa Rica, El Salvador, Guatemala, Honduras, Nicaragua; cap. and res US \$1,005.7m. (June 1999); Exec. Pres. ALEJANDRO ARÉVALO.

Banco Financiera Centroamericana, SA (FICENSA): Edif. La Interamericana, Blvd Morazán, Apdo 1432, Tegucigalpa; tel. 238-1661; fax 238-1630; f. 1974; private org. providing finance for industry, commerce and transport; total assets 11,023m. (1999); Pres. OSWALDO LÓPEZ ARELLANO; Gen. Man. ROQUE RIVERA RIBAS.

Banco Hondureño del Café, SA (BANHCAFE): Calle República de Costa Rica, Blvd Juan Pablo II, Apdo 583, Tegucigalpa; tel. 232-8370; fax 232-8332; e-mail bcafeinf@hondutel.hn; f. 1981 to help finance coffee production; owned principally by private coffee producers; cap. 63.1m., res 110.3m., dep. 1,174.8m. (Dec. 2000); Pres. RAMÓN DAVID RIVERA; Gen. Man. RENÉ ARDÓN MATUTE; 50 brs.

Banco Municipal Autónomo (BANMA): 6a Avda, 6a Calle, Tegucigalpa; tel. 22-5963; fax 237-5187; f. 1963; Pres. JUSTO PASTOR CALDERÓN; 2 brs.

Banco Nacional de Desarrollo Agrícola (BANADESA): 4a Avda y 5a Avda, 13a y 14a Calles, Apdo 212, Tegucigalpa; tel. 237-2201; fax 237-5187; f. 1980; govt development bank (transfer to private ownership pending); loans to agricultural sector; cap. 34.5m., res 42.7m., dep. 126.9m. (March 1993); Pres. GUSTAVO A. ZELAYA CHÁVEZ; 34 brs.

Financiera Nacional de la Vivienda—FINAVI: Apdo 1194, Tegucigalpa; f. 1975; housing development bank; Exec. Pres. Lic. ELMAR LIZARDO.

Foreign Bank

Lloyds TSB Bank PLC: Edif. Europa, Col. San Carlos, Calle República de México, Avda Ramón Ernesto Cruz, Apdo 3136, Tegucigalpa; tel. 236-6864; fax 236-6417; e-mail lloydstsb@honduras.hn; Man. G. JOHNS.

Banking Association

Asociación Hondureña de Instituciones Bancarias (AHIBA): Blvd Suyapa contiguo a CANNON, Apdo 1344, Tegucigalpa; tel. 235-6770; fax 239-0191; f. 1956; 22 mem. banks; Pres. JACOBO ATALA Z.; Exec. Sec. GUILLERMO MATAMOROS.

STOCK EXCHANGE

Bolsa Hondureña de Valores: Edif. Martínez Valenzuela, 1°, 2a Calle, 3a Avda, San Pedro Sula; tel. 553-4410; fax 553-4480; e-mail bhvsps@bhv.hn2.com; Gen. Man. MARCO TULIO LÓPEZ PEREIRA.

INSURANCE

American Home Assurance Co: Edif. Los Castaños, 4°, Blvd Morazán, Apdo 3220, Tegucigalpa; tel. 232-3938; fax 232-8169; f. 1958; Mans LEONARDO MOREIRA, EDGAR WAGNER.

Aseguradora Hondureña, SA: Edif. El Planetario, 4°, Col. Lomas de Guijarro Sur, Calle Madrid, Avda Paris, Apdo 312, Tegucigalpa; tel. 232-2729; fax 231-0982; e-mail gerencia@asegurahon.hn; f. 1954; Pres. JOSÉ MARÍA AGURCIA; Gen. Man. GERARDO CORRALES.

Compañía de Seguros El Ahorro Hondureño, SA: Edif. Trinidad, Avda Colón, Apdo 3643, Tegucigalpa; tel. 237-8219; fax 237-4780; e-mail elahorro@seguroselahorro.hn; f. 1917; Pres. JORGE A. ALVARADO.

Interamericana de Seguros, SA: Col. Los Castaños, Apdo 593, Tegucigalpa; tel. 232-7614; fax 232-7762; f. 1957; Pres. CAMILO ATALA FARAJ; Gen. Man. LUIS ATALA FARAJ.

Pan American Life Insurance Co (PALIC): Edif. PALIC, Avda República de Chile 804, Tegucigalpa; tel. 220-5757; fax 232-3907; e-mail palic@david.intertel.hn; f. 1944; Gen. Man. ALBERTO AGURCIA.

Previsión y Seguros, SA: Edif. Maya, Col. Palmira, Apdo 770, Tegucigalpa; tel. 231-2127; fax 232-5215; f. 1982; Pres. Gen. HÉCTOR CASTRO CABUS; Gen. Man. P. M. ARTURO BOQUÍN OSEJO.

Seguros Atlántida: Edif. Sonisa, Costado Este Plaza Bancatlán, Tegucigalpa; tel. 232-4014; fax 232-3688; e-mail morellana@bancatlan.hn; f. 1986; Pres. GUILLERMO BUESO; Gen. Man. JUAN MIGUEL ORELLANA.

Seguros Continental, SA: 3A Avda 2 y 3, 7a Calle, Apdo 320, San Pedro Sula; tel. 52-0880; fax 52-2750; f. 1968; Pres. JAIME ROSENTHAL OLIVA; Gen. Man. MARIO R. SOLÍS.

Seguros Crefisa: Edif. Ficensa, 1°, Blvd Morazán, Apdo 3774, Tegucigalpa; tel. 238-1750; fax 238-1714; e-mail ggerencia@crefisa.hn; internet www.crefisa.hn; f. 1993; Pres. OSWALDO LÓPEZ ARELLANO; Gen. Man. MARIO BATRES PIÑEDA.

Insurance Association

Cámara Hondureña de Aseguradores (CAHDA): Edif. Los Jarros, Blvd Morazán, Local 313, Apdo 3290, Tegucigalpa; tel. 239-0342; fax 232-6020; e-mail cahda@gbm.hn; f. 1974; Man. JOSÉ LUIS MONCADA RODRÍGUEZ.

Trade and Industry

GOVERNMENT AGENCIES

Fondo Hondureño de Inversión Social (FHIS): Tegucigalpa; internet www.fhis.hn; social investment fund; Gen. Man. MANUEL ZELAYA ROSALES.

Fondo Social de la Vivienda (FOSOVI): Col. Florencia, Tegucigalpa; tel. 239-1605; social fund for housing, urbanization and devt; Gen. Man. MARIO MARTÍ.

Secretaria Técnica del Consejo Superior de Planificación Económica (CONSUPLANE): Edif. Bancatlán, 3°, Apdo 1327, Comayagüela, Tegucigalpa; tel. 22-8738; f. 1965; national planning office; Exec. Sec. FRANCISCO FIGUEROA ZÚÑIGA.

DEVELOPMENT ORGANIZATIONS

Consejo Hondureño de la Empresa Privada (COHEP): Edif. COHEP contiguo a Plaza Visión, Calle Yoro, Col. Tepeyac, Apdo 3240, Tegucigalpa; tel. 235-3336; fax 235-3344; e-mail presidencia@cohep.com; f. 1968; comprises 23 private enterprises; Pres. Dr JULIETTE HANDAL DE CASTILLO.

Corporación Financiera de Olancho: f. 1977 to co-ordinate and manage all financial aspects of the Olancho forests project; Pres. RAFAEL CALDERÓN LÓPEZ.

Corporación Hondureña de Desarrollo Forestal (COHDEFOR): Salida Carretera del Norte, Zona El Carrizal, Comayagüela, Apdo 1378, Tegucigalpa; tel. 22-8810; fax 22-2653; f. 1974; semi-autonomous org. exercising control and man. of the forestry industry; transfer of all sawmills to private ownership was proceeding in 1991; Gen. Man. PORFIRIO LOBO S.

Dirección General de Minas e Hidrocarburos (General Directorate of Mines and Hydrocarbons): Blvd Miraflores, Apdo 981, Tegucigalpa; tel. 232-7848; fax 232-7848; Dir-Gen. MIGUEL VILLEDA VILLELA.

Instituto Hondureño del Café (IHCAFE): Apdo 40-C, Tegucigalpa; tel. 237-3131; f. 1970; coffee devt programme; Gen. Man. FERNANDO D. MONTES M.

Instituto Hondureño de Mercadeo Agrícola (IHMA): Apdo 727, Tegucigalpa; tel. 235-3193; fax 235-5719; f. 1978; agricultural devt agency; Gen. Man. TULIO ROLANDO GIRÓN ROMERO.

Instituto Nacional Agrario (INA): Col. La Almeda, 4a Avda, entre 10a y 11a Calles, No 1009, Apdo 3391, Tegucigalpa; tel. 232-8400; fax 232-8398; agricultural devt programmes; Exec. Dir ANÍBAL DELGADO FIALLOS.

CHAMBERS OF COMMERCE

Cámara de Comercio e Industrias de Cortés: 17a Avda, 10a y 12a Calle, Apdo 14, San Pedro Sula; tel. 53-0761; f. 1931; 812 mems; Pres. ROBERTO REYES SILVA; Dir LUIS FERNANDO RIVERA.

Cámara de Comercio e Industrias de Tegucigalpa: Blvd Centroamérica, Apdo 3444, Tegucigalpa; tel. 232-4200; fax 232-0759; e-mail camara@ccit.hn; internet www.ccit.hn; Pres. ANTONIO TAVEL OTERO.

Federación de Cámaras de Comercio e Industrias de Honduras (FEDECAMARA): Edif. Castañito, 2°, Col. Castaño, Sur, 6a Avda, Calle Jamaica, Apdo 3393, Tegucigalpa; tel. 232-6083; fax 232-1870; e-mail fedecamara@sigmanet.hn; internet www.sieh.org; f. 1948; 1,200 mems; Pres. SERGIO EVENOR BONILLA; Exec. Dir DANILO ROMERO MARTÍNEZ.

INDUSTRIAL AND TRADE ASSOCIATIONS

Asociación de Bananeros Independientes (ANBI) (National Association of Independent Banana Producers): San Pedro Sula; tel. 22-7336; f. 1964; 62 mems; Pres. Ing. JORGE ALBERTO ALVARADO; Sec. CECILIO TRIMINIO TURCIOS.

Asociación Hondureña de Productores de Café (Coffee Producers' Association): 10a Avda, 6a Calle, Apdo 959, Tegucigalpa.

Asociación Nacional de Exportadores de Honduras (ANEXHON) (National Association of Exporters): Tegucigalpa; comprises 104 private enterprises; Pres. Dr RICHARD ZABLAH.

Asociación Nacional de Industriales (ANDI) (National Association of Manufacturers): Blvd Los Próceres 505, Apdo 20-C, Tegucigalpa; Pres. HÉCTOR BULNES; Exec. Sec. DORCAS DE GONZALES.

Asociación Nacional de Pequeños Industriales (ANPI) (National Association of Small Industries): Apdo 730, Tegucigalpa; Pres. JUAN RAFAEL CRUZ.

Federación Nacional de Agricultores y Ganaderos de Honduras (FENAGH) (Farmers and Livestock Breeders' Association): Tegucigalpa; tel. 231-1392; Pres. ROBERTO GALLARDO LARDIZÁBAL.

Federación Nacional de Cooperativas Cañeras (Fenacocal) (National Federation of Sugar Cane Co-operatives): Tegucigalpa.

UTILITIES

Electricity

Empresa Nacional de Energía Eléctrica—ENEE (National Electrical Energy Co): 7a Calle, 1a Avda, Apdo 99, Tegucigalpa; tel. 238-5977; fax 237-9881; e-mail eneeger@enee.gn; internet www.enee.hn; f. 1957; state-owned electricity co; scheduled for privatization in 2001; Pres. XIOMARA GOMEZ.

TRADE UNIONS

Asociación Nacional de Empleados Públicos de Honduras (ANDEPH) (National Association of Public Employees of Honduras): Plaza Los Dolores, Tegucigalpa; tel. 237-4393; Pres. OSCAR MARTÍNEZ.

Confederación de Trabajadores de Honduras—CTH (Workers' Confederation of Honduras): Edif. FARAJ, 5°, Avda Lempira, Barrio La Fuente, Apdo 720, Tegucigalpa; tel. 238-7859; fax 237-4243; f. 1964; affiliated to CTCA, ORIT, CIOSL, FIAET and ICFTU; Pres. JOSÉ ANGEL MEZA; Sec.-Gen. FRANCISCO GUERRERO NÚÑEZ; 200,000 mems; comprises the following federations:

> **Federación Central de Sindicatos Libres de Honduras (FECESITLIH)** (Honduran Federation of Free Trade Unions): 1a Avda, 1a Calle 102, Apdo 621, Comayagüela, Tegucigalpa; tel. 237-5601; Pres. JOSÉ ANGEL MEZA.
>
> **Federación Sindical de Trabajadores Nacionales de Honduras (FESITRANH)** (Honduran Federation of Farmworkers): 10a Avda, 11a Calle, Barrio Los Andes, San Pedro Sula; tel. 57-2539; f. 1957; Pres. MARIO QUINTANILLA.
>
> **Sindicato Nacional de Motoristas de Equipo Pesado de Honduras (SINAMEQUIPH)** (National Union of HGV Drivers): Tegucigalpa; tel. 237-4243; Pres. ERASMO FLORES.

Central General de Trabajadores de Honduras (CGTH) (General Confederation of Labour of Honduras): Calle Real de Comayagüela, Apdo 1236, Tegucigalpa; tel. 237-4398; attached to Partido Demócrata Cristiano; Sec.-Gen. FELICITO AVILA.

Federación Auténtica Sindical de Honduras (FASH): 1a Avda, 11a Calle 1102, Comayagüela, Tegucigalpa.

Federación de Trabajadores del Sur (FETRASUR) (Federation of Southern Workers): Choluteca.

Federación Unitaria de Trabajadores de Honduras (FUTH): 2a Avda entre 11a y 12a Calle, Casa 1127, frente a BANCAFE, Apdo 1663, Comayagüela, Tegucigalpa; tel. 237-6349; f. 1981; linked to left-wing electoral alliance Frente Patriótico Hondureño; Pres. HÉCTOR HERNÁNDEZ FUENTES; 45,000 mems.

Frente de Unidad Nacional Campesino de Honduras (FUNA-CAMH): f. 1980; group of farming co-operatives and six main peasant unions as follows:

Asociación Nacional de Campesinos Hondureños (ANACH) (National Association of Honduran Farmworkers): 3a Avda, entre 9a y 10a Calle, Barrio Barandillas, San Pedro Sula; tel. 53-1884; f. 1962; affiliated to ORIT; Pres. ANTONIO JULÍN MÉNDEZ; 80,000 mems.

Federación de Cooperativas Agropecuarias de la Reforma Agraria de Honduras (FECORAH): Barrio Guanacaste, Casa 1702, Tegucigalpa; tel. 237-5391; Pres. JOSÉ NAHUM CÁLIX.

Frente Nacional de Campesinos Independientes de Honduras.

Unión Nacional de Campesinos (UNC) (National Union of Farmworkers): 1a Avda, Comayagüela, Tegucigalpa; tel. 238-2435; linked to CLAT; Pres. MARCIAL REYES CABALLERO; c. 25,000 mems.

Unión Nacional de Campesinos Auténticos de Honduras (UNCAH).

Unión Nacional de Cooperativas Populares de Honduras (UNACOOPH).

Transport

RAILWAYS

The railway network is confined to the north of the country and most lines are used for fruit cargo.

Ferrocarril Nacional de Honduras (National Railway of Honduras): 1a Avda entre 1a y 2a Calle, Apdo 496, San Pedro Sula; tel. and fax 552-8001; f. 1870; govt-owned; 595 km of track; Gen. Man. M. A. QUINTANILLA.

Tela Railroad Co: La Lima; tel. 56-2037; Pres. RONALD F. WALKER; Gen. Man. FREDDY KOCH.

Vaccaro Railway: La Ceiba; tel. 43-0511; fax 43-0091; fmrly operated by Standard Fruit Co.

ROADS

In 1998 there were an estimated 14,602 km of roads in Honduras, of which 2,644 km were paved. Some routes have been constructed by the Instituto Hondureño del Café and COHDEFOR in order to facilitate access to coffee plantations and forestry development areas. In November 2000 the World Bank approved a US $66.5m. loan to repair roads and bridges damaged or destroyed by 'Hurricane Mitch' in 1998.

Dirección General de Caminos: Barrio La Bolsa, Comayagüela, Tegucigalpa; tel. 225-1703; fax 225-2469; f. 1915; Dir KATHYA M. PASTOR; highways board.

SHIPPING

The principal port is Puerto Cortés on the Caribbean coast, which is the largest and best-equipped port in Central America. Other ports include Tela, La Ceiba, Trujillo/Castilla, Roatán, Amapala and San Lorenzo; all are operated by the Empresa Nacional Portuaria. There are several minor shipping companies. A number of foreign shipping lines call at Honduran ports.

Empresa Nacional Portuaria (National Port Authority): Apdo 18, Puerto Cortés; tel. 55-0192; fax 55-0968; f. 1965; has jurisdiction over all ports in Honduras; a network of paved roads connects Puerto Cortés and San Lorenzo with the main cities of Honduras, and with the principal cities of Central America; Gen. Man. ROBERTO VALENZUELA SIMÓN.

CIVIL AVIATION

Local airlines in Honduras compensate for the deficiencies of road and rail transport, linking together small towns and inaccessible districts. There are four international airports: Golosón airport in La Ceiba, Ramón Villeda Morales airport in San Pedro Sula, Toncontín airport in Tegucigalpa, and Juan Manuel Gálvaz airport in Roatán. In 2001 it was announced that San Francisco Airport, USA, was to invest some US $150m. in the four airports over two years. In 2000 plans for a new airport inside the Copán Ruinas archaeological park, 400 km west of Tegucigalpa, were announced.

Honduras Airways: Tegucigalpa; f. 1994; operates domestic flights and scheduled services to the USA.

Isleña Airlines: Avda San Isidro, frente al Parque Central, Apdo 402, La Ceiba; tel. 43-2683; fax 43-2632; e-mail islena@caribe.hn; internet www.caribe.hn; domestic service and service to Guatemala, Nicaragua and the Cayman Islands; Pres. and CEO ARTURO ALVARADO WOOD.

Líneas Aéreas Nacionales, SA (LANSA): La Ceiba; f. 2001; scheduled international services and flights within Central America.

Tourism

Tourists are attracted by the Mayan ruins, the fishing and boating facilities in Trujillo Bay and Lake Yojoa, near San Pedro Sula, and the beaches on the northern coast. There is an increasing eco-tourism industry. Honduras received 321,149 tourists in 1998, when tourism receipts totalled US $164m.

Instituto Hondureño de Turismo: Edif. Europa, 5°, Col. San Carlos, Apdo 3261, Tegucigalpa; tel. 222-2124; fax 222-6621; e-mail tourisminfo@iht.hn; internet www.letsgohonduras.hn; f. 1972; dept of the Secretaría de Cultura y Turismo; Dir-Gen. RICARDO MARTÍNEZ.

HUNGARY

Introductory Survey

Location, Climate, Language, Religion, Flag, Capital

The Republic of Hungary (known as the Hungarian People's Republic between August 1949 and October 1989) lies in eastern Europe, bounded to the north by Slovakia, to the east by Ukraine and Romania, to the south by Yugoslavia (the Serbian province of Vojvodina) and Croatia, and to the west by Slovenia and Austria. Its climate is continental, with long, dry summers and severe winters. Temperatures in Budapest are generally between –3°C (27°F) and 28°C (82°F). The language is Hungarian (Magyar). There is a large Romany community (numbering between 500,000 and 700,000 people), and also Croat, German, Romanian, Serbian, Slovak, Slovene and Jewish minorities. Most of the inhabitants profess Christianity, and the largest single religious denomination is the Roman Catholic Church, representing about 65% of the population. Other Christian groups are the Calvinists (20%), the Lutheran Church (5%) and the Hungarian Orthodox Church. The national flag (proportions 3 by 2) consists of three equal horizontal stripes, of red, white and green. The capital is Budapest.

Recent History

Although Hungary co-operated with Nazi Germany before the Second World War and obtained additional territory when Czechoslovakia was partitioned in 1938 and 1939, when it sought to break the alliance in 1944, the country was occupied by German forces. In January 1945 Hungary was liberated by Soviet troops and signed an armistice, restoring the pre-1938 frontiers. It became a republic in February 1946. Meanwhile, land distribution, instituted in 1945, continued. Nationalization measures began in December 1946, despite opposition from the Roman Catholic Church under Cardinal József Mindszenty. In the 1947 elections the Communists became the largest single party, with 22.7% of the vote. By the end of that year the Communist Party had emerged as the leading political force. The Communists merged with the Social Democrats to form the Hungarian Workers' Party in June 1948. A People's Republic was established in August 1949.

Mátyás Rákosi became the leading figure as First Secretary of the Workers' Party. Opposition was subsequently removed by means of purges and political trials. Rákosi became Prime Minister in 1952 but, after the death of Stalin one year later, was replaced by the more moderate Imre Nagy, and a short period of liberalization followed. Rákosi, however, remained as First Secretary of the party, and in 1955 forced Nagy's resignation. András Hegedüs, sponsored by Rákosi, was appointed Prime Minister. Dissension between the Rákosi and Nagy factions increased in 1956; in July Rákosi was forced to resign but was replaced by a close associate, Ernő Gerő.

The consequent discontent provoked demonstrations against Communist domination, and in October 1956 fighting broke out. Nagy was reinstated as Prime Minister, renounced membership of the Warsaw Pact and promised various other controversial reforms. In November Soviet troops, stationed in Hungary under the 1947 peace treaty, intervened, and the uprising was suppressed. A new Soviet-supported Government, led by János Kádár, was installed. Some 20,000 participants in the uprising were arrested, of whom 2,000 were subsequently executed, including Nagy and four associates. Many opponents of the regime were deported to the USSR. Kádár, who was appointed the leader of the renamed Hungarian Socialist Workers' Party (HSWP), held the premiership until January 1958, and from September 1961 to July 1965.

The 13th HSWP Congress, held in March 1985, re-elected Kádár leader of the party, with the new title of General Secretary of the Central Committee. The Congress reaffirmed the Party's commitment to the country's economic reforms, which had been introduced in 1968. The legislative election in June 1985 was the first to be held under the revised electoral law, giving voters a wider choice of candidates under the system of mandatory multiple nominations. In June 1987 Pál Losonczi was replaced in the largely ceremonial post of President of the Presidential Council by Károly Németh, a leading member of

the HSWP. Károly Grósz, a member of the Politburo, was appointed Chairman of the Council of Ministers.

At a special ideological conference of the HSWP, held in May 1988, major changes in party personnel and policy were approved. Kádár was replaced as General Secretary of the Central Committee by Károly Grósz. Kádár was promoted to the newly created and purely ceremonial post of HSWP President, but lost his membership of the Politburo. About one-third of the members of the Central Committee (in particular, conservative associates of Kádár) were removed and replaced by younger politicians. The new Politburo included Rezső Nyers, who had been largely responsible for the economic reforms initiated in 1968, but who had been removed from the Politburo in 1975. Grósz declared his commitment to radical economic and political change, although he excluded the immediate possibility of a multi-party political system. In June 1988 Dr Brunó Ferenc Straub, who was not a member of the HSWP, was elected to the post of President of the Presidential Council, in succession to Károly Németh. In November Miklós Németh, a prominent member of the HSWP, replaced Grósz as Chairman of the Council of Ministers.

Following Grósz's appointment as leader of the HSWP, there was a relaxation of censorship laws and independent political groups were formally established. In January 1989 the right to strike was fully legalized. In the same month the National Assembly enacted two laws guaranteeing the right to demonstrate freely and to form associations and political parties independent of the HSWP.

In February 1989 the HSWP agreed to support the transition to a multi-party system and to abandon the clause in the Constitution upholding the party's leading role in society. In the following month an estimated 100,000 people took part in a peaceful anti-Government demonstration in Budapest, in support of demands for democracy, free elections, the withdrawal of Soviet troops from Hungary, and an official commemoration of the 1956 uprising and of the execution of Imre Nagy in 1958.

During 1989 there was increasing evidence of dissension within the HSWP between conservative and reformist members. (At least 100,000 members had tendered their resignation between late 1987 and early 1989.) In April Grósz was re-elected General Secretary of the Party, and the Politburo was replaced by a smaller body. In May the Council of Ministers declared its independence from the HSWP. In the same month Kádár was relieved of his post as President of the HSWP and of his membership of the Central Committee of the party, officially for health reasons. In June a radical restructuring of the HSWP was effected, following increasing dissatisfaction among members with Grósz's leadership: while Grósz remained as General Secretary of the party, the newly elected Chairman, Rezső Nyers, effectively emerged as the Party's leading figure.

In June 1989 discussions were initiated between the HSWP and representatives of opposition groups regarding the holding of multi-party elections, changes to the presidential structure, amendments to the Constitution and economic reforms. Evidence of the opposition's increasing strength was provided at a provincial by-election in July, when a joint candidate of three main opposition groups, the centre-right Hungarian Democratic Forum (HDF), the liberal Alliance of Free Democrats (AFD) and the Federation of Young Democrats (FYD), defeated a candidate of the HSWP, thus becoming the first opposition deputy since 1947 to win representation in the legislature. Four of five further by-elections were won by opposition candidates in July–September 1989.

At the 14th HSWP Congress, held in October 1989, delegates voted to dissolve the Party and to reconstitute it as the Hungarian Socialist Party (HSP), with Nyers as Chairman. The HSP initially failed to attract a large membership, however, and in December HSWP activists declared that their party had not been dissolved, and that it still retained a membership of around 80,000. Gyula Thürmer was elected the HSWP President.

On 23 October 1989 (the anniversary of the 1956 uprising) the Republic of Hungary was proclaimed. In preparation the

National Assembly approved fundamental amendments to the Constitution, including the removal of the clause guaranteeing one-party rule. A new electoral law was approved, and the Presidential Council was replaced by the post of President of the Republic. Mátyás Szűrös, the President of the National Assembly (Speaker), was named President of the Republic, on an interim basis.

Hungary's first free multi-party elections since 1945 were held, in two rounds, on 25 March and 8 April 1990. The elections were held under a mixed system of proportional and direct representation and were contested by a total of 28 parties and groups. The HDF received the largest share of the total votes cast (42.7%) and won 165 of the 386 seats in the National Assembly. The Independent Smallholders' Party (ISP, which advocated the restoration to its original owners of land collectivized after 1947) and the Christian Democratic People's Party (CDPP), both of which contested the second round of the election in alliance with the HDF, secured 43 and 21 seats, respectively. The AFD obtained the second-largest proportion of the total votes (23.8%), winning 92 seats in the Assembly. The FYD, which was closely aligned with the AFD, obtained 21 seats. The HSP, with 8.5% of the votes, secured 33 seats in the legislature. The HSWP failed to secure the 4% of the votes required for representation.

A coalition Government was formed in May 1990, comprising members of the HDF (which held the majority of posts), together with members of the ISP, the CDPP and three independents. József Antall, the Chairman of the HDF, had earlier been elected to chair the new Council of Ministers. Among the declared aims of the new Government was withdrawal from the Warsaw Pact (the defence grouping of the Soviet bloc), membership of the European Community (now European Union—EU—see p. 181) and a full transition to a Western-style market economy. In August Árpád Göncz, a writer and member of the AFD, was elected President of the Republic by an overwhelming majority of the legislature. In May Gyula Horn, the Minister of Foreign Affairs in the outgoing Government, had replaced Nyers as leader of the HSP.

At elections in September and October 1990, designed to replace the Soviet-style council system with a system of multi-party self-governing local bodies, a coalition of the AFD and the FYD won control of Budapest and many other cities, while in rural areas independent candidates gained an overwhelming majority of the votes. The governing coalition's poor result was attributed, in large part, to its failure to redress the recent sharp increase in the rates of inflation and unemployment.

In mid-1991 the National Assembly approved legislation to compensate the former owners of land and property that had been expropriated between 1939 and 1989. Legislation was approved by parliament in November that would allow prosecution for the crimes of murder and treason committed between 1944 and 1990. However, Göncz refused to give assent to the bill, and in March 1992 the Constitutional Court ruled that such retroactive legislation, which held individuals responsible for the crimes of the former Communist regime, was inadmissible. Nevertheless, in May the National Assembly approved legislation to compensate for persons killed, imprisoned or deported, or whose property had been expropriated, for political reasons during the period 1939–89. Further legislation was approved in early 1993 allowing for prosecutions in connection with crimes committed under the Communist regime.

In February 1992 the Chairman of the ISP, József Törgyán, announced that his party was withdrawing from the government coalition, in protest at what he claimed to be a lack of political influence. However, most of the ISP's deputies in the National Assembly refused to withdraw their support for the Government, thus causing a rift in the Party. In April as many as 20,000 people were reported to have attended an anti-Government demonstration organized by Törgyán in Budapest. The split in the Party was formalized in June, when party members who remained loyal to Antall suspended Törgyán as their Chairman, and elected László Horváth to chair what subsequently became the United Historic Smallholders' Party.

Meanwhile, in June 1992 a public disagreement arose between Antall and Göncz over alleged government interference in the state radio and television corporations and other branches of the mass media. During 1992–93 many senior media figures resigned or were dismissed, and in October 1993 some 10,000 people demonstrated in Budapest to demand press freedom.

In September 1992 some 50,000 people demonstrated in Budapest against extreme right-wing figures, including the Vice-Chairman of the HDF, István Csurka; the Government's failure to censure Csurka prompted widespread criticism. At an HDF congress in January 1993 Antall avoided a threatened revolt and possible split in the party by accepting the election of six right-wing extremists to the party's presidium. In May Lajos Für resigned from his position as Secretary-General of the HDF, claiming that he had not been able to maintain the unity of the party, which was divided between supporters of Csurka and centrists led by Antall. In July, however, Csurka was expelled from the HDF for his increasingly unacceptable views. (He subsequently founded the Hungarian Justice and Life Party—HJLP.) Antall died in December; he was succeeded as Prime Minister by Dr Péter Boross, an independent and hitherto the Minister of the Interior, who had acted as premier while Antall was receiving medical treatment. In February 1994 Für was elected Chairman of the HDF. In that month an investigation was initiated into alleged financial irregularities at the Ministry of Defence.

Legislative elections, which took place on 8 and 29 May 1994, resulted in a clear parliamentary majority for the HSP, which received 33.0% of the votes cast for regional party lists and won 209 of the National Assembly's 386 seats. The AFD won 19.8% of the votes and 70 seats, while the HDF won only 11.7% of the votes and 37 seats. The Independent Smallholders' and Peasants' Party (ISPP—formerly the ISP), the CDPP and the FYD won, respectively, 26, 22 and 20 seats. Csurka's HJLP attracted only 1.6% of the votes at the first round and did not proceed to the second. Horn announced that the HSP would be willing to form a government with the AFD, and the two parties signed a coalition agreement (whereby the HSP was to control the majority of posts in the Council of Ministers, while the AFD would have right to veto government decisions) in late June. With 279 seats in the National Assembly, the coalition held the two-thirds' majority necessary to institute constitutional reforms. Horn was invested as Prime Minister in July. At municipal elections in December the HSP won 32.3% of the votes and the AFD 15.7%.

In June 1994 129 Hungarian Radio employees, who had been dismissed in March, ostensibly for economic reasons, were reinstated; their dismissal had prompted mass demonstrations and widespread accusations that the Government sought to use the state radio service for propaganda purposes, since many of those dismissed had been known for their anti-Government views. In July, however, the directors of Hungarian Radio and Hungarian Television were dismissed, having been accused of favouring the former HDF administration. In October the Constitutional Court declared government interference in the media to be unlawful. In January 1995 László Bekesi, the HSP Minister of Finance, resigned, following disagreements with Horn regarding economic reform. In the same month the Director of the State Property Agency was dismissed, following his alleged mismanagement of hotel privatization. In late February Dr Lajos Bokros of the HSP was designated Minister of Finance; at the same time Horn appointed Tamás Suchman, also of the HSP, to the newly created post of Minister for Privatization, under the jurisdiction of the Ministry of Finance, and appointed a new president of the central bank. Economic austerity measures, adopted in March, prompted strong domestic criticism; the ministers responsible for public health and for national security (both members of the HSP) resigned shortly after the programme was announced, and some 10,000 people joined a demonstration in Budapest to denounce the measures.

In early May 1995 the National Assembly approved legislation that was designed to accelerate the privatization process. On 19 June Göncz was re-elected President of the Republic by an overwhelming majority in the National Assembly. In late June the HSP Minister of Trade and Industry, who had criticized the privatization of parts of the energy sector, was dismissed; he was replaced by Imre Dunai, a technocrat with no party affiliation. At the end of June the Constitutional Court ruled that elements of the austerity programme announced in March (specifically those relating to welfare provisions) were unconstitutional. Accordingly, in late July the National Assembly approved new adjustments, including increases in fuel prices and reductions in government expenditure, in an attempt to mitigate losses arising from the judgment.

The economic programme continued to cause dissent within the Government. The HSP Minister of Labour tendered her resignation in early October 1995, in protest at the social consequences of the austerity measures. In late November, following a ruling by the Constitutional Court against the validity of further provisions of the austerity programme, Bokros submitted his resignation, although this was rejected by Horn. In mid-February 1996, however, Bokros again tendered his resignation (which was accepted by Horn), citing a lack of support from other government members. A banker, Péter Medgyessy, who had been Deputy Chairman and Chairman of the Planning and Economic Committee in the administration of Miklós Németh, was appointed the new Minister of Finance.

Division was reported in the HDF in early March 1996, following the election of Sándor Lezsák to the party leadership. Denouncing what they regarded as an increasingly nationalistic tendency in the party, a faction led by Iván Szabó (who had been Minister of Finance in the HDF Government) broke away to form a new organization, the Hungarian Democratic People's Party.

In August 1996 Imre Dunai resigned from the post of Minister of Industry and Trade, ostensibly on grounds of ill health; it was reported that he had opposed the proposed increases in fuel prices. Dunai was replaced by Tamás Suchman (who retained responsibility for the privatization portfolio). Later in August the Government announced that increases in fuel prices were to be postponed, pending an independent review of the energy industry. (In January 1997 the Government finally increased fuel prices, although by far less than originally envisaged.)

In October 1996 the Government removed the directors of the Hungarian Privatization and State Holding Company (ÁPV Rt—formed in 1995 by the amalgamation of the State Property Agency and State Holding Company), after it emerged that they had endorsed payments made to a lawyer who had not been formally contracted, in contravention of the body's internal regulations. Horn subsequently announced the dismissal of Suchman from the Government, on the grounds that, as Minister for Privatization, he was responsible for ÁPV Rt's violation of regulations. In January 1997 the HDF proposed a motion expressing 'no confidence' in Horn in the National Assembly, on the grounds that he was ultimately responsible for the unauthorized payments made by ÁPV Rt. In February a parliamentary investigative committee attributed responsibility to the Government for the irregularities. (In June eight officials were charged with fraud or mismanagement in connection with the operations of ÁPV Rt.) In March two members of the National Intelligence Bureau were dismissed, after it emerged that the service had conducted unauthorized investigations of several prominent HSP members (who were suspected of having connections with organized-crime groups).

Following a NATO summit meeting, which took place in Madrid, Spain, in July 1997, Hungary was invited to enter into discussions regarding its application for membership of the Organization; it was envisaged that Hungary (together with the Czech Republic and Poland) would be formally admitted to NATO by April 1999. In August 1997 the Government announced that a national referendum on the country's entry into NATO would be conducted on 16 November.

In September 1997 Horn rejected demands that he resign from office by a committee that had been established to investigate the past of senior politicians; the committee claimed that Horn had served with a paramilitary force that had restored Communist power following the 1956 rebellion, and that he had suppressed political opposition through the security services.

At the national referendum, which took place on 16 November 1997 as scheduled, Hungary's accession to NATO was approved by 85.3% of the votes cast, with 49% of the electorate participating in the referendum. The National Election Committee ratified the results of the referendum (despite objections by a pacifist movement, which claimed that the low rate of voter participation invalidated the results). It had also been planned to submit to the electorate amendments to legislation regulating foreign land ownership. However, owing to controversy over the wording of the proposals, the National Assembly approval their removal from the referendum in early November. In December the HDF established an electoral alliance with the Federation of Young Democrats—Hungarian Civic Party (FYD—HCP, which had been reconstituted from the FYD) and the Hungarian Christian Democratic Federation, a newly formed association of breakaway members of the CDPP.

The first round of the legislative election, which was contested by 26 parties, took place on 10 May 1998: the HSP secured 32.3% of the votes cast, while the FYD—HCP won 28.2% of the votes, and the ISPP 13.8%. Following a second round of voting on 24 May, however, the FYD—HCP, with 147 seats, obtained

the highest representation in the National Assembly; the HSP received 134 seats, the ISPP 48, the AFD 24, the HDF 18 and the HJLP 14. The defeat of the HSP was widely attributed to discontent with social and economic conditions, and the increasing rate of crime. At the inaugural session of the new legislature in June, a member of the FYD—HCP, János Áder, was elected President of the National Assembly. In the same month, following inter-party negotiations, the FYD—HCP signed an agreement with the HDF and the ISPP, providing for the formation of a new coalition government. (The FYD—HCP and ISPP also agreed to contest in alliance the forthcoming presidential election in 2000.) In early July the Chairman of the FYD—HCP, Viktor Orbán, was elected to the office of Prime Minister by the National Assembly, which subsequently approved the installation of a new Council of Ministers, comprising 11 representatives of the FYD—HCP, four of the ISPP (later renamed the Independent Smallholders' and Civic Party—ISCP), one of the HDF and one of the Hungarian Christian Democratic Federation. The new Government presented a programme for the reduction of crime and the improvement of social and economic conditions.

In September 1998, following the resignation of Horn from the leadership of the HSP, in response to the Party's electoral defeat, a former minister, László Kovács, was elected Chairman. Local government elections were conducted in October: it was reported that the three government coalition parties had received 39.6% of the votes cast, while the HSP and AFD won 35.1% of the votes. In December a constitutional amendment that would have empowered the Council of Ministers, rather than the legislature, to approve the deployment of foreign troops in Hungary and Hungarian troops abroad (thereby facilitating Hungary's participation in NATO) failed to obtain the requisite two-thirds' majority in the National Assembly. Later in December the HSP and AFD deputies boycotted the legislature, in protest at government proposals for the appointment of new management boards of the state media supervisory bodies. In February 1999 the National Assembly approved Hungary's membership of NATO by an overwhelming majority, and the country formally joined NATO in the following month. In December Orbán replaced the Minister of Economic Affairs and the Minister of National Cultural Heritage in a government reorganization. At an FYD–HCP congress in January 2000, László Kövér, hitherto the Minister without Portfolio responsible for National Security, replaced Orbán as leader of the party; he was to resign from the Council of Ministers later that year.

In the presidential election, held on 5 June 2000, Ferenc Mádl, the sole candidate, gained 251 votes out of a possible 386 in the first round of voting. As he had failed to obtain the requisite two-thirds' majority, a second round of voting was held on 6 June. However, this ballot, too, proved inconclusive and a final round of voting was held on the same day. Mádl took office on 4 August.

In May 2000 the Minister of Transport, Telecommunications and Water Management, Kálmán Katona, was dismissed, after having threatened to resign, as the result of plans to transfer responsibility for the telecommunications industry to the Office of the Prime Minister. Katona was replaced by László Nogradi. In November, however, Nogradi resigned, following a car accident that had resulted in the death of the driver of another vehicle; he was replaced by János Fónagy. In the same month Ferenc Ligetvari, environment minister from June (following the resignation of Pál Pepó, who faced allegations of financial misconduct), was dismissed in relation to an embezzlement scandal. Béla Turi-Kovács was appointed as his successor. Further government changes were announced in December. Mihály Varga was nominated to succeed Zsigmond Járai as Minister of Finance from March 2001, when Járai was to become Governor of the National Bank, and István Mikola was appointed to replace Árpád Gogl as Minister of Health from the beginning of 2001, when Gogl was to become Director of the National Health Institute.

In January 2001 a power struggle within the leadership of the ISCP resulted in the expulsion of a deputy, László Csucs, from the National Assembly and the dismissal of the Chairman of the Budapest branch of the Party. Csucs and four disaffected deputies subsequently attempted to remove József Törgyán from the leadership of the ISCP while he was on an official visit overseas. Upon his return, the four deputies resigned from the ISCP, thereby reducing the Party's representation in the National Assembly from 47 deputies to 43. In February Törgyán resigned from his position as Minister of Agriculture and Rural Development, amid mounting criticism of his ministerial conduct. András Vonza was appointed as his successor in March.

There has been considerable activism within Hungary by the country's ethnic minorities for the protection of their rights. In July 1993 the National Assembly adopted legislation guaranteeing the cultural, civil and political rights of 12 minority groups and prohibiting all forms of ethnic discrimination. Following the approval of this legislation, minority-rights activists launched a new campaign to change Hungary's electoral law, with the aim of securing the direct representation of ethnic groups in the legislature. In the 1994 municipal elections, ethnic minorities were able to elect their own local ethnic authorities, with consultative roles on cultural and educational issues affecting the community. In April 1995 the Roma of Hungary elected their own governing body. The National Autonomous Authority of the Romany Minority (the first such body in the former Eastern bloc) was to be empowered to administer funds and deliberate issues affecting the Roma. All of its 53 seats were won by the Lungo Drom Alliance, led by Florian Farkas. In February 1995 Hungary signed the Council of Europe's Convention on the Protection of National Minorities. However, an increase in overt nationalism among the parties of the right became an issue of considerable concern during the 1990s.

In the late 1980s the Hungarian Government made successive diplomatic efforts in an attempt to improve the treatment of the 1.7m. ethnic Hungarians in Romania. In August 1996 Hungary and Romania finalized a bilateral treaty (which was formally signed in September), guaranteeing the inviolability of the joint border between the two countries and the rights of ethnic minorities. (However, the Hungarian opposition protested at the failure of the treaty to recognize the right to autonomy of the ethnic Hungarian community in Romania.) In February 1997 the Ministers of Defence of Hungary and Romania signed a co-operation agreement, providing for the protection and exchange of military secrets between the two countries, and the establishment of a joint military unit, which would be deployed in peace-keeping operations. In May President Göncz made an official visit to Romania (the first by a Hungarian Head of State). In January 2000 an environmental disaster in Romania, caused by a cyanide spill at the Baia Mare gold mine, poisoned the Tisza river, which flows through Hungary, prompting tensions between the two countries. In February a joint Hungarian–Romanian committee of experts was formed with the EU, to assess the ecological damage resulting from the accident. The mine subsequently accepted full responsibility for the disaster and compensation was to be awarded.

Apart from issues arising from the presence of a large ethnic Hungarian minority in Slovakia (numbering almost 570,000 in late 1993), relations between Hungary and Slovakia have been strained by a dispute over the Gabčíkovo-Nagymaros hydroelectric project (a joint Hungarian-Czechoslovak scheme initiated in 1977), involving the diversion of a 222-km stretch of the River Danube and the construction of a twin-dam system. In May 1989 the Hungarian Government suspended work on the project in response to pressure from environmentalists, and in November it announced that it was abandoning the scheme. Czechoslovakia decided, in July 1991, to proceed unilaterally with the project; the resumption of work, in February 1992, prompted the Hungarian Government to abrogate the 1977 treaty with effect from May 1992. In April 1993 the two countries agreed to refer the case to the International Court of Justice (ICJ) and to operate a temporary water-management scheme in the mean time.

In March 1995 (despite protests by nationalists within Hungary against concessions made by the Government) Horn and his Slovak counterpart, Vladimír Mečiar, signed a Treaty of Friendship and Co-operation in which the two countries undertook to guarantee the rights of ethnic minorities and recognized the inviolability of their joint border. However, its ratification was subsequently delayed, owing to differing interpretations of its provisions with regard to the protection of national minorities. An amendment to the treaty, approved by the Slovak legislature in March 1996, rejected the concept of autonomy for the Hungarian minority in Slovakia, prompting protests from the Hungarian opposition. Nevertheless, the treaty came into effect in May, following its ratification by the Slovak President.

In August 1997 discussions between Horn and the Slovak Prime Minister, Vladimír Mečiar, resulted in an agreement that a joint committee be established to monitor the standard of human rights of ethnic Hungarians resident in Slovakia and the Slovak community in Hungary; however, there was subsequent dissent over the composition of the proposed committee. In September relations between Hungary and Slovakia became strained, after Horn rejected a suggestion by Mečiar that a voluntary repatriation programme for the respective ethnic communities in the two countries be initiated. Later in September the ICJ concluded proceedings regarding the dispute between Hungary and Slovakia over the Gabčíkovo-Nagymaros hydroelectric project, ruling that both countries had contravened international law: Hungary had breached the terms of the agreement by withdrawing from the project, while the former Czechoslovakia had continued work without the permission of the Hungarian Government. Both Hungary and Slovakia were required to pay compensation for damages incurred, and to resume negotiations regarding the further implementation of the agreement. Hungarian and Slovak delegations were subsequently established to conduct discussions on the ruling of the ICJ. Following continued negotiations between the two countries, in March 1998 a draft agreement regarding the planned location of a new dam on the River Danube was signed. However, the Hungarian Government subsequently declared that the agreement would not be implemented until a study into possible damage to the environment was conducted. In July the newly installed coalition Government announced that the draft agreement formulated by the previous administration was invalid, and that it intended to reconsider the decision to proceed with the construction of the dam. In December 1999 Hungary submitted an 800-page document to the Slovak Government, in which it renounced any claim to a share of the hydroelectric energy produced by the dam project, but requested an increase in the flow of common water along the Danube, in order to maintain the ecological balance. In February 2001 Slovakia accepted that it had no legal means to compel Hungary to proceed with the project, but stated that it would seek compensation from the Hungarian Government.

Hungary pursues an active foreign policy, and relations with many Western nations improved steadily from the late 1980s. In November 1990 Hungary was the first Eastern European country to become a member of the Council of Europe (see p. 165). Hungary's associate membership of the EU came into effect on 1 February 1994, and in April of that year Hungary became the first post-Communist state to apply for full EU membership. In March 1996 Hungary was admitted to the Organisation for Economic Co-operation and Development (see p. 247). From December 1995 US troops belonging to the NATO-controlled Implementation Force in Bosnia and Herzegovina (IFOR) were stationed at an air base at Taszar, in south-western Hungary; a second base was subsequently established at the southern town of Pécs. In May 1996 the Government indicated that it would be willing for US troops to remain in Hungary, following the withdrawal of peace-keeping forces from Bosnia and Herzegovina. Hungary contributed some 450 troops to IFOR in 1996, and continued to support its replacement Stabilization Force (SFOR, see p. 244). Hungary was formally admitted to NATO in March 1999 (see above). During the NATO bombardment of Yugoslavia (which commenced later that month—see chapter on Yugoslavia) the Government allowed NATO forces to use Hungarian military bases and airspace.

Government

Legislative power is held by the unicameral National Assembly (Országgyűlés), comprising 386 members, who are elected for four years by universal adult suffrage under a mixed system of proportional and direct representation. The President of the Republic (Head of State) is elected by the National Assembly for a term of five years. The President, who is also Commander-in-Chief of the Armed Forces, may be re-elected for a second term. The Council of Ministers, the highest organ of state administration, is elected by the Assembly on the recommendation of the President. For local administrative purposes Hungary is divided into 19 counties and the capital city (with 22 districts). A 53-member National Autonomous Authority of the Romany Minority, elected in April 1995, is empowered to administer funds disbursed by the central Government.

Defence

Military service starts at the age of 18 years. The period of military service was reduced from one year to nine months in November 1997. The total regular forces in August 2000 numbered 43,790 (including 22,900 conscripts): army 23,500, air force 11,500 and centrally controlled personnel 8,790. Paramilitary forces comprised 12,000 border guards, as well as 2,000 members of the internal security forces. In March 1999 Hungary became a member of NATO. Government expenditure on defence in 1999 was 182,000m. forint.

Economic Affairs

In 1998, according to estimates by the World Bank, Hungary's gross national product (GNP), measured at average 1996–98 prices, was US $45,660m., equivalent to $4,510 per head (or $9,832 per head on an international purchasing-power parity basis). During 1990–98, it was estimated, GNP per head increased, in real terms, at an average annual rate of 0.9%. Over the same period the population decreased at an average annual rate of 0.3%. Hungary's gross domestic product (GDP) declined, in real terms, at an average annual rate of 0.2% during 1990–99; real GDP grew by an estimated 3.8% in 1999.

Agriculture (including forestry and fishing) contributed an estimated 5.7% of GDP in 1998. About 7.1% of the employed labour force were engaged in the sector in 1999. The principal crops are wheat, maize, sugar beets, barley and potatoes. Viticulture is also important. During 1990–97, according to the World Bank, agricultural GDP declined at an average annual rate of 3.8%. Growth in agricultural GDP was estimated at 13.6% in 1996, and at 1.5% in 1997; however, growth declined by some 1.5% in 1998, and there was a particularly poor harvest in 1999, when wheat production declined by some 54%, owing to weather damage.

Industry (including mining, manufacturing, construction, and power) contributed an estimated 33.7% of GDP in 1998, and engaged 34.0% of the employed labour force in 1999. According to the World Bank, industrial GDP increased at an average annual rate of 1.1% in 1990–97. Growth in industrial GDP was estimated at 10% in 1997 and at 8% in 1998. Industrial production (excluding construction) increased by 11.1% in 1997 and by 12.4% in 1998.

Mining and quarrying accounted for only 0.4% of GDP in 1997, and engaged 0.6% of the employed labour force in 1999. Hungary's most important mineral resources are lignite, brown coal and natural gas. Petroleum, bauxite and hard coal are also exploited. During 1990–98 the output of the mining sector declined at an average annual rate of 11.1%. Production fell by 8.4% in 1997 and by 20.4% in 1998.

The manufacturing sector contributed an estimated 24.7% of GDP in 1998, and engaged 24.4% of the employed labour force in 1999. In 1995 the principal branches of the sector, in terms of their contribution to gross production, were food products (accounting for 22.6% of the total), machinery and electrical equipment (13.2%), metals and metal products (11.9%) and chemicals (10.6%). According to the World Bank, manufacturing GDP increased at an average annual rate of 6.5% in 1990–99. Growth in manufacturing GDP was estimated at 13.0% in 1997 and 10.3% in 1998.

In 1998 some 12% of Hungary's energy supply was from electricity generated by nuclear power. Further supply is derived from coal, petroleum and natural gas. Mineral fuels represented 6.6% of the value of total imports in 1998.

The services sector has a significant role in the Hungarian economy, contributing an estimated 60.6% of GDP in 1998, and engaging 58.9% of the employed labour force in 1999. According to the World Bank, the GDP of the services sector increased at an average rate of 0.3% per year in 1990–97. Growth in GDP of the services sector was estimated at 4.3% in 1998. In 1996 it was estimated that the tourist sector contributed about 20% of GDP and 30% of export earnings.

In 1999 Hungary recorded a visible trade deficit of US $2,191m., and there was a deficit of $2,101m. on the current account of the balance of payments. In 1998 the principal source of imports was Germany (accounting for 28.2% of the total); other major sources were Austria, Italy and Russia. Germany was also the principal market for exports in that year (36.6%); other important purchasers were Austria, the Netherlands and the USA. The principal exports in 1998 were machinery and transport equipment, food and live animals, basic manufactures, miscellaneous manufactured articles (most notably clothing and accessories) and chemical products. The main imports in that year were machinery and transport equipment (most notably road vehicles and parts), basic manufactures, chemical products, miscellaneous manufactured articles and mineral fuels.

Hungary's overall budgetary deficit in 2000 was an estimated 449,300m. forint. The country's total external debt at the end of 1998 was estimated to be US $28,580m., of which $15,941m. was long-term public debt. In that year the cost of debt-servicing was equivalent to 27.3% of the value of exports of goods and services. The annual rate of inflation averaged 22.8% in 1990–98; consumer prices increased by an average of 14.3% in 1998, by 10.0% in 1999 and by an estimated 9.7% in 2000. The average rate of unemployment was 7.0% of the labour force in 1999, and in 2000 the unemployment rate declined to 6.4%.

Hungary is a member (as a 'Country of Operations') of the European Bank for Reconstruction and Development (EBRD, see p. 176). Hungary became an associate member of the European Union (EU, see p. 181) in February 1994, and subsequently applied for full EU membership. In March 1996 Hungary was admitted to the Organisation for Economic Co-operation and Development (OECD, see p. 247). Hungary's free-trade agreement with the European Free Trade Association (EFTA, see p. 178) took effect from October 1993.

In 1990 the Hungarian Government pledged to effect a full transition to a Western-style market economy, and to this end initiated a comprehensive programme of liberalization measures. However, the programme's implementation caused increasingly high levels of inflation and unemployment, a large external debt and a deficit on the current account of the balance of payments. In 1994 the new administration announced a series of devaluations of the forint, a widening and acceleration of the privatization programme, and controversial reductions in expenditure on social security and welfare. By the end of 1997 the Government's policy of fiscal discipline, in conjunction with rapid progress in the programme of large-scale privatization and progressive reductions in real income, had resulted in a decline in the public-sector deficit and the rate of inflation. The high level of foreign investment, with a consequent increase in industrial output and exports, contributed to a strong overall growth in the economy. In early 1998 the IMF announced that it had ended its stand-by credit arrangement with Hungary, on the grounds that the country no longer required external financial assistance. In July the new coalition Government indicated that it intended to continue the previous administration's policies for economic stabilization. In 1999 continued strong growth in the economy was generated, in part, by a substantial increase in exports, despite the negative impact of the Russian economic crisis (which particularly affected Hungary's agricultural exports), and the conflict in Yugoslavia in March–June (which damaged the tourism and trade sectors). With the country continuing to benefit from the high inflow of foreign capital, the rate of inflation further declined, while improvements in the budgetary and current-account deficits were also recorded. In December it was announced that, as a result of the success in achieving economic stabilization, Hungary would be one of the first of the applicant nations to be admitted to the EU, and was expected to be granted full membership in 2003. By 1999 around 70% of Hungary's international trade was conducted with EU countries, while exports to Russia had declined significantly. This reorientation of trade was largely the result of the expansion of the technologically-advanced machinery industry, particularly in the automotive, electronics and informatics sectors. However, demand for such products began to slow in the second half of 2000, when trade with Russia began to display a marked revival. In that year the primary concern of both the EU and the Bretton Woods institutions remained reform of Hungary's health-care sector, which was among the least-developed of the OECD countries.

Social Welfare

The national insurance scheme is based largely on non-state contributions. Employers and employees pay health insurance and pension contributions. The Health Insurance Act, passed in July 1992, made health insurance obligatory.

The implementation of the five-day working week was completed by 1985. There is a guaranteed minimum wage (of 25,500 forint per month at June 2000), and employment is non-discriminatory. A uniform system of retirement pensions was introduced in 1975: workers draw between 33% and 75% of their earnings, according to the number of years of service. Male workers are usually entitled to retirement pensions at the age of 60 and women at 55.

In January 1989 unemployment benefit was introduced. There are also invalidity pensions, widows' pensions and orphans' allowances. Social insurance covers sickness benefits. Most medical consultation and treatment is free, although a small charge is generally made for medicines, and between 15% and 50% for medical appliances. In 1989 private medical practice was authorized. The social insurance scheme also covers maternity benefits. Women are entitled to 24 weeks' maternity leave on full pay. In 1999 there were 362 physicians per 100,000 of the population, and some 83,992 hospital beds in use in Hungary. The rate of infant mortality was 8.4 per 1,000 live births in 1999. In 2000 life expectancy was 66 years for men and 75 years for women. Of total expenditure by the central Government in 1998, 265,400m. forint (6.0%) was for health, and a further 1,329,000m. forint (29.9%) was for social security and welfare. Expenditure by local government in 1997 included 205,200m. forint (18.2% of total spending) for health and 140,800m. forint (12.5%) for social security and welfare. In 1998 the Government introduced comprehensive pension reforms, supported by the World Bank, whereby employees would be legally obliged to pay 25% of pension contributions to private pension schemes. In 1999 the real monthly pension stood at 29,600 forint. In that year, according to the IMF, there were 2,423,000 pensioners. The Government introduced child-care benefits in 1999, including family allowance and schooling support.

Education

Children under the age of three years attend crèches (bölcsődék), and those between the ages of three and six years attend kindergartens (óvodák). Education is compulsory between the ages of six and 16 years. Primary education begins at six years of age, with the basic school (általános iskola), and continues until the age of 14. In 1997 primary enrolment included 98% of children in the relevant age-group, while the comparable ratio for secondary education was 97%. In southern Hungary bilingual schools have been established to promote the languages of the national minorities. The majority of children continue with their education after 16 years of age. The most popular types of secondary school are the grammar school (gimnázium) and the secondary vocational school (szakközépiskola). The gimnázium provides a four-year course of mainly academic studies, although some vocational training does feature on the curriculum. The szakközépiskola offers full vocational training together with a general education, emphasis being laid on practical work. Apprentice training schools (szakmunkásképző intézetek) are attached to factories, agricultural co-operatives, etc., and lead to full trade qualifications. Further educational reform is being directed at revising the curricula and the method of assessing pupils. In 1999–2000 the system of higher education underwent a major transformation, as a result of which, from 1 January 2000, there were 30 state-run universities and colleges, 26 church universities and colleges and six colleges run by various foundations. In 1995 an estimated 23.8% of the relevant age-group continued into tertiary education (males 21.8%; females 26.0%). Expenditure on education in 1998 was some 381,200m. forint (equivalent to 8.6% of total government expenditure). In 1998 the adult literacy rate for those over the age of 15 years was 99.3%.

Public Holidays

2001: 1 January (New Year's Day), 15 March (anniversary of 1848 uprising against Austrian rule), 16 April (Easter Monday), 1 May (Labour Day), 20 August (Constitution Day), 23 October (Day of the Proclamation of the Republic), 25–26 December (Christmas).

2002: 1 January (New Year's Day), 15 March (anniversary of 1848 uprising against Austrian rule), 1 April (Easter Monday), 1 May (Labour Day), 20 August (Constitution Day), 23 October (Day of the Proclamation of the Republic), 25–26 December (Christmas).

Weights and Measures

The metric system is in force.

Statistical Survey

Source (unless otherwise stated): Központi Statisztikai Hivatal (Hungarian Central Statistical Office), 1525 Budapest, Keleti Károly u. 5–7; tel. (1) 345-6136; fax (1) 345-6378; e-mail erzsebet.veto@office.ksh.hu; internet www.ksh.hu.

Area and Population

AREA, POPULATION AND DENSITY

Area (sq km)	93,030*
Population (census results)	
1 January 1980.	10,709,463
1 January 1990	
Males	4,984,904
Females	5,389,919
Total	10,374,823
Population (official estimates at 1 January)	
1998	10,135,400
1999	10,091,789
2000	10,043,224
Density (per sq km) at 1 January 2000	108.0

* 35,919 sq miles.

Languages (1990 census): Magyar (Hungarian) 98.5%; German 0.4%; Slovak 0.1%; Romany 0.5%; Croatian 0.2%; Romanian 0.1%.

ADMINISTRATIVE DIVISIONS (1 January 2000)

	Area (sq km)	Resident Population ('000)	Density (per sq km)	County Town (with population)*
Counties:				
Bács-Kiskun .	8,445	533	63	Kecskemét (105,464)
Baranya .	4,430	401	90	Pécs (158,607)
Békés. .	5,631	392	70	Békéscsaba (63,958)
Borsod-Abaúj-Zemplén .	7,247	730	101	Miskolc (173,629)
Csongrád .	4,263	418	98	Szeged (159,133)
Fejér . .	4,359	424	97	Székesfehérvár (105,293)
Győr-Moson-Sopron .	4,089	425	104	Győr (127,275)
Hajdú-Bihar .	6,211	542	87	Debrecen (205,032)
Heves. .	3,637	323	89	Eger (57,891)
Jász-Nagykun-Szolnok .	5,582	411	74	Szolnok (76,875)
Komárom-Esztergom .	2,265	312	138	Tatabánya (72,054)
Nógrád .	2,544	217	85	Salgótarján (44,404)
Pest . .	6,393	1,033	162	Budapest† (1,838,753)
Somogy .	6,036	330	55	Kaposvár (66,826)
Szabolcs-Szatmár-Bereg .	5,937	570	96	Nyíregyháza (112,882)
Tolna . .	3,703	244	66	Szekszárd (35,358)
Vas . .	3,337	266	80	Szombathely (82,074)
Veszprém .	4,613	372	81	Veszprém (62,631)
Zala . .	3,784	293	77	Zalaegerszeg (61,033)
Capital City				
Budapest† .	525	1,812	3,451	—
Total . .	93,030	10,043	108	—

* At 1 January 1999.

† Budapest has separate County status. The area and population of the city are not included in the larger County (Pest) which it administers.

PRINCIPAL TOWNS (population at 1 January 1999)

Budapest (capital) .	1,838,753		Nyíregyháza . .	112,882
Debrecen . . .	205,032		Kecskemét. . .	105,464
Miskolc . . .	176,629		Székesfehérvár. .	105,293
Szeged . . .	159,133		Szombathely . .	82,074
Pécs	158,607		Szolnok . .	76,875
Győr	127,275		Tatabánya . . .	72,054

Budapest (population in 2000): 1,811,552.

BIRTHS, MARRIAGES AND DEATHS

	Registered live births		Registered marriages		Registered deaths	
	Number	Rate (per 1,000)	Number	Rate (per 1,000)	Number	Rate (per 1,000)
1993 . .	117,033	11.4	54,099	5.3	150,244	14.6
1994 . .	115,598	11.3	54,114	5.3	146,889	14.3
1995 . .	112,054	11.0	53,463	5.2	145,431	14.2
1996 . .	105,272	10.3	48,930	4.8	143,130	14.0
1997 . .	100,350	9.9	46,905	4.6	139,434	13.7
1998 . .	97,301	9.6	44,915	4.4	140,870	13.9
1999 . .	94,645	9.4	45,465	4.5	143,210	14.2
2000* .	97,500	9.7	48,000	4.8	135,500	13.5

* Preliminary figures.

Expectation of Life (years at birth, 1999): Males 66.3; females 75.1.

ECONOMICALLY ACTIVE POPULATION
(labour force surveys, '000 persons aged 15 years to 74 years)

	1997	1998	1999
Agriculture, hunting, forestry and fishing	287.9	278.8	270.4
Mining and quarrying . . .	27.2	25.7	24.4
Manufacturing	864.1	912.1	928.9
Electricity, gas and water supply .	97.4	96.5	89.8
Construction.	219.2	230.0	253.0
Wholesale and retail trade; repair of motor vehicles, motorcycles, and personal and household goods	496.8	472.2	517.5
Hotels and restaurants . . .	120.9	121.6	133.2
Transport, storage and communications . . .	310.0	301.9	308.3
Financial intermediation . . .	83.3	81.8	80.9
Real estate, renting and business activities	146.3	163.0	183.9
Public administration and defence; compulsory social security	293.8	294.3	301.9
Education	296.9	305.5	306.9
Health and social work . . .	232.1	237.8	239.2
Other community, social and personal service activities . .	167.5	171.8	169.8
Private household with employed persons	0.8	1.5	2.0
Extra-territorial organizations and bodies.	2.1	3.0	1.4
Activities not adequately defined .	0.1	0.2	—
Total employed*	3,646.3	3,697.7	3,811.5
Unemployed	348.8	313.0	284.7
Total labour force	3,995.1	4,010.7	4,096.2
Males	2,257.6	2,230.9	2,273.8
Females	1,737.5	1,779.8	1,822.4

Source: partly ILO, *Yearbook of Labour Statistics*.

2000: Total employed* 3,849; Unemployed 263; Total labour force 4,112.

* Excluding persons on child care leave.

Agriculture

PRINCIPAL CROPS ('000 metric tons)

	1997	1998	1999
Wheat	5,259	4,899	2,638
Rice (paddy)	7	7	7
Barley	1,330	1,305	1,042
Maize	6,828	6,143	7,149
Rye	153	129	81
Oats	138	132	178
Potatoes	1,140	1,148	1,199
Pulses	120	142	119
Sunflower seed	540	718	793
Rapeseed	145	73	328
Sugar beet	3,691	3,361	2,934
Grapes	717	720	570
Apples	500	482	443
Tobacco (leaves)	11	13	14*

* FAO estimate.
Source: FAO.

LIVESTOCK ('000 head, year ending September)

	1997	1998	1999
Cattle	909	871	873
Pigs	5,289	4,931	5,479
Sheep	872	858	909
Goats	108	108	108
Horses	70	72	72
Chickens	27,827	30,983	30,557
Ducks	1,533	1,553	2,378
Geese	1,089	1,136	1,074
Turkeys	1,986	1,993	1,986

Source: FAO.

LIVESTOCK PRODUCTS ('000 metric tons)

	1997	1998	1999
Beef and veal	55	47	45*
Mutton and lamb . . .	2	3	3†
Pig meat	581	570	664*
Poultry meat	402	452	400*
Cows' milk	1,989	2,107	2,073
Sheep's milk	19	25	25*
Goats' milk	10	10	10*
Butter	13	16	15†
Cheese	91	89	93
Hen eggs	188	188	177
Other poultry eggs . . .	3	3	3*
Honey	16	17	16
Wool:			
greasy	3	3	3
clean†	1	1	n.a.
Cattle hides	4*	3*	4*

* FAO estimate(s).   † Unofficial figures.
Source: FAO.

Forestry

ROUNDWOOD REMOVALS ('000 cu metres, excl. bark)

	1996	1997	1998
Sawlogs, veneer logs and logs for			
sleepers	1,226	1,192	1,168
Pulpwood	375	360	363
Other industrial wood . . .	199	780	765
Fuel wood	1,853	1,909	1,871
Total	3,653	4,241	4,167

Source: FAO, *Yearbook of Forest Products.*

SAWNWOOD PRODUCTION ('000 cu metres)

	1996	1997	1998
Coniferous (softwood) . . .	102	110	103
Broadleaved (hardwood) . . .	183	207	195
Total	285	317	298

Source: FAO, *Yearbook of Forest Products.*

Fishing

(metric tons, live weight)

	1996	1997	1998
Capture	7,606	7,406	7,265
Common carp	2,717	2,255	3,373
Silver carp	862	1,483	731
Other cyprinids	2,210	2,231	1,895
European eel	579	124	182
Aquaculture	8,080	9,334	10,222
Common carp	5,788	6,420	7,069
Silver carp	1,007	1,703	1,943
Total catch	15,686	16,740	17,487

Source: FAO, *Yearbook of Fishery Statistics.*

Mining

('000 metric tons, unless otherwise indicated)

	1996	1997	1998
Hard coal	962	924	877
Brown coal	6,538	6,552	6,004
Lignite	7,575	8,089	7,610
Crude petroleum	1,477	1,360	1,258
Bauxite	1,056	743	909
Natural gas (million cu metres) .	4,872	4,689	4,340

Industry

SELECTED PRODUCTS ('000 metric tons, unless otherwise indicated)

	1996	1997	1998
Crude steel	2,060	1,819	1,940
Cement	2,747	2,811	2,999
Nitrogenous fertilizers* . .	274.8	262.1	224.9
Refined sugar	555.5	487.2	439.4
Buses (number)	967	1,951	1,232
Leather footwear ('000 pairs) .	12,295	11,868	11,649
Electric power (million kWh) .	34,978	35,305	37,023
Television receivers ('000)† .	706	963	1,703
Radio receivers ('000) . .	310	528	2,328

* Production in terms of nitrogen.
† Including video monitors and video projectors.

Finance

CURRENCY AND EXCHANGE RATES

Monetary Units
100 fillér = 1 forint.

Sterling, Dollar and Euro Equivalents (29 December 2000)
£1 sterling = 424.87 forint;
US $1 = 284.73 forint;
€1 = 264.94 forint;
1,000 forint = £2.354 = $3.512 = €3.774.

Average Exchange Rate (forint per US dollar)
1998	214.402
1999	237.146
2000	282.179

BUDGET ('000 million forint)*

Revenue†	1996	1997	1998
Tax revenue	2,328.8	2,780.2	3,221.8
Taxes on income, profits and			
capital gains . . .	516.4	588.9	694.8
Individual	389.4	424.5	477.5
Corporate	126.9	164.2	217.3
Social security contributions .	718.7	916.6	1,069.0
Domestic taxes on goods and			
services	807.1	1,034.7	1,241.2
General sales, turnover or			
value-added taxes . .	515.1	674.8	796.9
Excises	222.1	267.5	320.6
Import duties	248.7	161.3	131.6
Other current revenue . .	373.5	400.0	434.8
Entrepreneurial and property			
income	173.1	203.7	151.3
Administrative fees and			
charges, non-industrial and			
incidental sales . . .	135.8	111.0	164.3
Capital revenue	9.2	15.1	26.3
Total	**2,711.5**	**3,195.3**	**3,682.9**

Expenditure‡	1996	1997	1998
General public services . .	129.1	156.1	226.7
Defence	63.3	105.9	102.1
Public order and safety . .	103.3	142.4	169.6
Education	255.0	321.2	381.2
Health	142.5	207.4	265.4
Social security and welfare .	1,032.0	1,217.5	1,329.0
Housing and community amenities	51.9	51.7	68.9
Recreational, cultural and			
religious affairs and services .	82.2	62.7	79.5
Economic affairs and services . .	331.5	357.2	460.0
Agriculture, forestry, fishing and			
hunting	117.2	111.6	157.0
Transport and communications .	128.0	145.0	184.7
Other purposes	769.2	1,034.7	1,367.2
Interest payments . . .	557.9	831.3	779.0
Sub-total	**2,960.1**	**3,656.8**	**4,449.6**
Adjustment	-0.3	—	-0.1
Total	**2,959.8**	**3,656.8**	**4,449.5**
Current	2,698.9	3,305.1	4,037.5
Capital	260.9	351.6	412.0

* Figures refer to the consolidated operations of the central Government, comprising the State Budget, the Pension Fund, the Health Insurance Fund and six extrabudgetary funds.
† Excluding grants received ('000 million forint): 19.3 in 1996; 24.6 in 1997; 78.6 in 1998.
‡ Excluding lending minus repayments ('000 million forint): -237.5 in 1996; -216.4 in 1997; -64.8 in 1998.

Source: IMF, *Government Finance Statistics Yearbook*.

INTERNATIONAL RESERVES (US $ million at 31 December)

	1998	1999	2000
Gold*	29	29	28
IMF special drawing rights . .	1	4	12
Reserve position in IMF . .	79	243	263
Foreign exchange	9,239	10,707	10,915
Total	**9,348**	**10,983**	**11,218**

* National valuation.
Source: IMF, *International Financial Statistics*.

MONEY SUPPLY (million forint at 31 December)

	1997	1998	1999
Currency outside banks . .	562,600	667,000	845,300
Demand deposits at commercial			
and savings banks . . .	961,300	1,121,900	1,274,700
Total money (incl. others) . .	**1,528,300**	**1,789,200**	**2,123,400**

Source: IMF, *International Financial Statistics*.

COST OF LIVING (Consumer Price Index; base: 1990 = 100)

	1997	1998	1999
Food	419.4	479.8	493.7
Fuel and light	899.3	1,060.3	1,160.0
Clothing and footwear . .	394.4	450.0	497.7
All items (incl. others) . .	**452.9**	**517.7**	**569.5**

NATIONAL ACCOUNTS ('000 million forint at current prices)
Expenditure on the Gross Domestic Product

	1996	1997	1998
Government final consumption			
expenditure . . .	703.6	900.8	1,024.6
Private final consumption			
expenditure . . .	4,389.8	5,270.1	6,282.6
Increase in stocks* . . .	399.9	467.9	607.8
Gross fixed capital formation . .	1,475.5	1,898.9	2,384.6
Total domestic expenditure .	**6,968.8**	**8,537.7**	**10,299.6**
Exports of goods and services .	2,678.7	3,885.6	5,105.9
Less Imports of goods and services	2,753.6	3,882.6	5,318.2
GDP in purchasers' values .	**6,893.9**	**8,540.7**	**10,087.4**
GDP at constant 1995 prices .	**5,689.3**	**5,949.4**	**6,238.5**

Source: IMF, *International Financial Statistics*.

Gross Domestic Product by Economic Activity

	1995	1996	1997
Agriculture, hunting, forestry and			
fishing	333.0	402.4	445.1
Mining and quarrying*† . .	22.9	25.9	33.9
Manufacturing*	1,111.1	1,360.9	1,804.5
Electricity, gas and water† . .	162.5	204.6	285.3
Construction	227.8	260.7	345.9
Trade, restaurants and hotels .	655.7	804.6	1,017.4
Transport, storage and			
communications . . .	442.8	556.1	736.2
Finance, insurance, real estate			
and business services . .	965.1	1,276.0	1,446.9
Government services (incl. non-			
profit institutions) . . .	832.7	967.5	1,212.0
Other community and social			
services	179.2	202.7	228.8
Sub-total	**4,932.9**	**6,061.3**	**7,556.0**
Net taxes on commodities . .	900.4	1,051.5	1,226.5
Less Imputed bank service charge .	219.2	218.8	241.8
GDP in purchasers' values .	**5,614.0**	**6,893.9**	**8,540.7**

* The activities of the Hungarian Oil and Gas Company are included in manufacturing.
† The operations of eight coal-mining enterprises are included in electricity.

BALANCE OF PAYMENTS (US $ million)

	1997	1998	1999
Exports of goods f.o.b. . . .	19,640	20,747	21,846
Imports of goods f.o.b. . . .	−21,602	−23,101	−24,037
Trade balance	**−1,962**	**−2,354**	**−2,191**
Exports of services . . .	5,733	5,921	5,650
Imports of services . . .	−3,465	−4,141	−4,266
Balance on goods and services	**306**	**−574**	**−806**
Other income received . .	1,382	1,111	775
Other income paid . . .	−2,808	−2,990	−2,417
Balance on goods, services and			
income	**−1,120**	**−2,453**	**−2,448**
Current transfers received . .	335	379	590
Current transfers paid . .	−197	−231	−243
Current balance . . .	**−982**	**−2,304**	**−2,101**
Capital account (net) . . .	117	189	29
Direct investment abroad . .	−433	−478	−250
Direct investment from abroad .	2,167	2,037	1,951
Portfolio investment assets . .	−134	−93	−75
Portfolio investment liabilities .	−914	1,925	2,065
Financial derivatives assets .	12	185	852
Financial derivatives liabilities .	−4	−38	−899
Other investment assets . .	−584	−507	−1,151
Other investment liabilities .	549	−13	2,176
Net errors and omissions . .	32	49	−261
Overall balance . . .	**−175**	**951**	**2,335**

Source: IMF, *International Financial Statistics*.

External Trade

Note: Beginning in 1997, Hungary's customs territory includes the country's industrial free zones.

PRINCIPAL COMMODITIES (distribution by SITC, million forint)

Imports c.i.f.	1996	1997	1998
Food and live animals . .	107,407	147,780	183,608
Crude materials (inedible)			
except fuels	91,972	110,719	136,927
Mineral fuels, lubricants, etc.	334,446	378,717	361,302
Petroleum, petroleum products, etc.	158,117	173,371	161,338
Gas (natural and manufactured) .	129,555	155,688	159,902
Chemicals and related products	342,584	447,313	565,446
Organic chemicals . . .	62,523	81,896	87,327
Medicinal and pharmaceutical			
products	70,766	90,657	121,172
Basic manufactures . .	548,480	782,511	1,056,034
Paper, paperboard and			
manufactures	78,065	99,921	128,129
Textile yarn, fabrics, etc. . .	140,300	189,361	250,717
Iron and steel	66,490	102,230	147,008
Non-ferrous metals . . .	77,777	117,538	128,878
Other metal manufactures . .	76,592	120,297	182,817
Machinery and transport			
equipment	753,657	1,664,015	2,566,694
Power-generating machinery and			
equipment	23,107	207,026	355,915
Machinery specialized for			
particular industries . .	83,787	119,687	179,789
General industrial machinery,			
equipment and parts . .	115,826	209,174	320,716
Office machines and automatic			
data-processing machines .	61,348	241,598	319,846
Telecommunications and sound			
equipment	94,247	215,448	336,457
Other electrical machinery,			
apparatus, etc. . . .	186,859	414,162	600,755
Road vehicles and parts (excl.			
tyres, engines and electrical			
parts)	151,613	215,332	385,384
Miscellaneous manufactured			
articles	266,320	391,471	593,037
Clothing and accessories (excl.			
footwear)	59,772	71,665	95,706
Total (incl. others) . . .	2,468,050	3,961,164	5,511,511

Exports f.o.b.	1996	1997	1998
Food and live animals . .	318,233	414,337	470,124
Meat and meat preparations . .	122,418	148,309	145,637
Cereals and cereal preparations .	27,811	77,850	103,735
Vegetables and fruit . . .	89,000	100,190	111,045
Beverages and tobacco . .	49,196	48,392	49,945
Crude materials (inedible)			
except fuels	90,357	102,006	113,477
Mineral fuels, lubricants, etc. .	81,272	94,098	93,134
Petroleum, petroleum products, etc.	59,960	65,341	64,980
Chemicals and related products	222,608	305,822	346,986
Organic chemicals . . .	45,018	63,169	72,489
Medicinal and pharmaceutical			
products	47,253	70,384	72,964
Plastics in primary forms . .	57,307	76,295	84,754
Basic manufactures . .	355,095	476,309	613,358
Textile yarn, fabrics, etc. . .	44,899	55,139	73,271
Non-metallic mineral			
manufactures	41,277	58,459	71,795
Iron and steel	56,342	65,944	80,358
Non-ferrous metals . . .	55,093	80,902	91,418
Other metal manufactures . .	66,520	92,414	126,855
Machinery and transport			
equipment	511,217	1,611,425	2,564,268
Power-generating machinery and			
equipment	23,752	283,701	601,241
Machinery specialized for			
particular industries . .	41,206	58,732	76,429
General industrial machinery,			
equipment and parts . .	58,549	88,347	125,587
Office machines and automatic			
data-processing machines .	7,295	318,797	522,323
Telecommunications and sound			
equipment	47,089	230,355	371,889
Other electrical machinery,			
apparatus, etc. . . .	227,761	408,412	533,377
Road vehicles and parts (excl.			
tyres, engines and electrical			
parts)	84,699	203,211	302,915
Miscellaneous manufactured			
articles	357,250	478,948	649,656
Furniture and parts; bedding,			
mattresses, etc. . . .	42,056	65,242	92,315
Clothing and accessories (excl.			
footwear)	168,420	208,684	273,871
Footwear	48,965	61,837	76,404
Total (incl. others) . . .	2,001,654	3,566,839	4,934,502

PRINCIPAL TRADING PARTNERS (million forint)*

Imports c.i.f.	1996	1997	1998
Austria	233,492	417,948	529,447
Belgium and Luxembourg . .	62,775	95,922	141,068
Brazil	26,579	33,599	41,570
Czech Republic and Slovakia . .	132,697	170,026	210,415
France	104,543	172,482	267,354
Germany	582,182	1,067,936	1,555,129
Italy	199,848	291,062	415,994
Japan	54,919	130,304	211,842
Netherlands	77,765	102,430	139,099
Poland	45,441	67,102	98,677
Russia	307,802	362,938	355,867
Spain	n.a.	51,443	87,199
Sweden	42,967	48,635	65,053
Switzerland and Liechtenstein .	53,402	68,212	92,761
Ukraine	n.a.	52,456	48,239
United Kingdom	80,558	135,698	187,821
USA	86,492	148,719	212,456
Total (incl. others) . . .	2,468,050	3,961,164	5,511,511

Exports f.o.b.	1996	1997	1998
Austria	212,539	406,172	524,913
Belgium and Luxembourg . .	43,298	88,657	131,715
Czech Republic and Slovakia .	82,726	109,415	151,265
France	73,952	134,343	187,757
Germany	580,085	1,328,988	1,805,434
Italy	160,154	218,619	283,553
Netherlands	53,414	100,065	233,641
Poland	59,230	95,428	113,467
Romania	42,365	60,115	121,273
Russia	118,426	180,907	140,231
Slovenia	n.a.	54,050	51,630
Spain	n.a.	53,458	81,487
Sweden	20,989	27,484	45,061
Switzerland and Liechtenstein .	26,907	42,868	57,034
Ukraine	n.a.	46,900	46,893
United Kingdom	58,386	119,098	175,932
USA	70,912	114,931	224,740
Total (incl. others)	2,001,654	3,566,839	4,934,502

* Imports by country of production; exports by country of last consignment.

Transport

RAILWAYS (traffic)

	1996	1997	1998
Passengers carried (million) . .	157.4	156.7	157.0
Passenger-kilometres (million) .	8,582	8,669	8,884
Net ton-kilometres (million) .	7,634	8,149	8,150

ROAD TRAFFIC (motor vehicles in use at 31 December)

	1996	1997	1998
Passenger cars . . .	2,434,241	2,297,115	2,365,000
Buses and coaches . . .	21,790	18,616	19,386
Lorries and vans	332,203	315,242	325,300
Motorcycles	157,500	137,983	137,983

Source: IRF, *World Road Statistics*.

SHIPPING
Merchant Fleet (registered at 31 December)

	1996	1997	1998
Number of vessels . . .	10	6	2
Total displacement ('000 grt) .	50.2	26.7	15.3

Source: Lloyd's Register of Shipping, *World Fleet Statistics*.

Inland Waterways (traffic)

	1996	1997	1998
Freight carried ('000 metric tons) .	2,108	2,074	2,390
Freight ton-km (million) . . .	2,482	1,644	1,561

CIVIL AVIATION (traffic)

	1996	1997	1998
Passengers carried . . .	1,859,000	2,001,000	2,188,000
Passenger-km ('000) . . .	2,774,900	3,049,200	3,038,000
Cargo carried: metric tons . .	15,000	18,000	15,000
Cargo ton-km	44,200,000	49,700,000	42,100,000

Tourism

	1998	1999	2000
Tourists arrivals ('000) . . .	33,624	28,803	31,141
Tourist receipts (US $ million) .	2,504	2,203	n.a.

TOURISTS BY COUNTRY OF ORIGIN
('000 arrivals, including visitors in transit)

	1996	1997	1998
Austria	5,757	5,750	5,936
Bulgaria	380	350	352
Czech Republic and Slovakia . .	4,642	5,689	5,845
Germany	3,831	3,843	3,852
Poland	640	631	540
Romania	4,365	3,914	1,197
Russia	1,182	163	147
Total (incl. others) . . .	39,833	37,315	33,624

Communications Media

	1995	1996	1997
Radio receivers ('000 in use) .	6,500*	7,000*	7,010
Television receivers ('000 in use) .	4,375*	4,400*	4,420
Main telephone lines in use . .	1,893,000†	2,651,000	3,095,000
Mobile cellular telephone subscribers	143,000†	265,000†	473,100
Book titles	n.a.	8,835	8,911
Daily newspapers* . . .	41	40	n.a.
Average daily circulation* . .	2,022,000	1,895,000	n.a.

* Source: UNESCO, *Statistical Yearbook*.
† Source: UN, *Statistical Yearbook*.
1998: Main telephone lines in use 3,385,000; Mobile cellular telephone subscribers 1,034,000; Book titles 10,626.
1999: Main telephone lines in use 3,605,000; Mobile cellular telephone subscribers 1,620,000; Book titles 9,731.

Education

(1999/2000, estimates, unless otherwise indicated)

	Institu-tions	Teach-ers	Students		
			Males	Females	Total
Pre-primary . .	4,643	31,409	188,565	177,139	365,704
Primary . .	3,696	82,829	491,101	469,500	960,601
Secondary:					
General . .	1,533	14,155	57,641	87,569	145,210
Teacher-training*	n.a.	n.a.	159	1,045	1,104
Vocational .	990	26,512	195,268	162,035	357,303
Higher:					
Universities, etc.. . .	30	12,804	53,520†	52,761†	88,479
Other . .	59	8,338	23,167†	33,716†	83,037

* Estimated figures for full-time teacher-training.
† 1998/99 figure.

Directory

The Constitution

A new Constitution was introduced on 18 August 1949, and the Hungarian People's Republic was established two days later. The Constitution was amended in April 1972 and December 1983. Further, radical amendments were made in October 1989. Shortly afterwards, the Republic of Hungary was proclaimed.

The following is a summary of the main provisions of the Constitution, as amended in October 1989.

GENERAL PROVISIONS

The Republic of Hungary is an independent, democratic constitutional state in which the values of civil democracy and democratic socialism prevail in equal measures. All power belongs to the people, which they exercise directly and through the elected representatives of popular sovereignty.

Political parties may, under observance of the Constitution, be freely formed and may freely operate in Hungary. Parties may not directly exercise public power. No party has the right to guide any state body. Trade unions and other organizations for the representation of interests safeguard and represent the interests of employees, members of co-operatives and entrepreneurs.

The State safeguards the people's freedom, the independence and territorial integrity of the country as well as the frontiers thereof, as established by international treaties. The Republic of Hungary rejects war as a means of settling disputes between nations and refrains from applying force against the independence or territorial integrity of other states, and from threats of violence.

The Hungarian legal system adopts the universally accepted rules of international law. The order of legislation is regulated by an Act of constitutional force.

The economy of Hungary is a market economy, availing itself also of the advantages of planning, with public and private ownership enjoying equal right and protection. Hungary recognizes and supports the right of undertaking and free competition, limitable only by an Act of constitutional force. State-owned enterprises and organs pursuing economic activities manage their affairs independently, in accordance with the mode and responsibility as provided by law.

The Republic of Hungary protects the institutions of marriage and the family. It provides for the indigent through extensive social measures, and recognizes and enforces the right of each citizen to a healthy environment.

GOVERNMENT

National Assembly

The highest organ of state authority in the Republic of Hungary is the National Assembly, which exercises all the rights deriving from the sovereignty of the people and determines the organization, direction and conditions of government. The National Assembly enacts the Constitution and laws, determines the state budget, decides the socio-economic plan, elects the President of the Republic and the Council of Ministers, directs the activities of ministries, decides upon declaring war and concluding peace and exercises the prerogative of amnesty.

The National Assembly is elected for a term of four years and members enjoy immunity from arrest and prosecution without parliamentary consent. It meets at least twice a year and is convened by the President of the Republic or by a written demand of the Council of Ministers or of one-fifth of the Assembly's members. It elects a President, Deputy Presidents and Recorders from among its own members, and it lays down its own rules of procedure and agenda. As a general rule, the sessions of the National Assembly are held in public.

The National Assembly has the right of legislation which can be initiated by the President of the Republic, the Council of Ministers or any committee or member of the National Assembly. Decisions are valid only if at least half of the members are present, and they require a simple majority. Constitutional changes require a two-thirds majority. Acts of the National Assembly are signed by the President of the Republic.

The National Assembly may pronounce its dissolution before the expiry of its term, and in the event of an emergency may prolong its mandate or may be reconvened after dissolution. A new National Assembly must be elected within three months of dissolution and convened within one month of polling day.

Members of the National Assembly are elected on the basis of universal, equal and direct suffrage by secret ballot, and they are accountable to their constituents, who may recall them. All citizens of 18 years and over have the right to vote, with the exception of those who are unsound of mind, and those who are deprived of their civil rights by a court of law.

President of the Republic

The President of the Republic is the Head of State of Hungary. He/she embodies the unity of the nation and supervises the democratic operation of the mechanism of State. The President is also the Commander-in-Chief of the Armed Forces. The President is elected by the National Assembly for a period of five years, and may be re-elected for a second term. Any citizen of Hungary qualified to vote, who has reached 35 years of age before the day of election, may be elected President.

The President may issue the writ for general or local elections, convene the National Assembly, initiate legislation, hold plebiscites, direct local government, conclude international treaties, appoint diplomatic representatives, ratify international treaties, appoint higher civil servants and officers of the armed forces, award orders and titles, and exercise the prerogative of mercy.

Council of Ministers

The highest organ of state administration is the Council of Ministers, responsible to the National Assembly and consisting of the Prime Minister and other Ministers who are elected by the National Assembly on the recommendation of the President of the Republic. The Council of Ministers directs the work of the ministries (listed in a special enactment) and ensures the enforcement of laws and the fulfilment of economic plans; it may issue decrees and annul or modify measures taken by any central or local organ of government.

Local Administration

The local organs of state power are the county, town, borough and town precinct councils, whose members are elected for a term of four years by the voters in each area. Local councils direct economic, social and cultural activities in their area, prepare local economic plans and budgets and supervise their fulfilment, enforce laws, supervise subordinate organs, maintain public order, protect public property and individual rights, and direct local economic enterprises. They may issue regulations and annul or modify those of subordinate councils. Local Councils are administered by an Executive Committee elected by and responsible to them.

JUDICATURE

Justice is administered by the Supreme Court of the Republic of Hungary, county and district courts. The Supreme Court exercises the right of supervising in principle the judicial activities and practice of all other courts.

All judicial offices are filled by election; Supreme Court, county and district court judges are all elected for an indefinite period; the President of the Supreme Court is elected by the National Assembly. All court hearings are public unless otherwise prescribed by law, and those accused are guaranteed the right of defence. An accused person must be considered innocent until proved guilty.

Public Prosecutor

The function of the Chief Public Prosecutor is to supervise the observance of the law. He is elected by the National Assembly, to whom he is responsible. The organization of public prosecution is under the control of the Chief Public Prosecutor, who appoints the public prosecutors.

RIGHTS AND DUTIES OF CITIZENS

The Republic of Hungary guarantees for its citizens the right to work and to remuneration, the right of rest and recreation, the right to care in old age, sickness or disability, the right to education, and equality before the law; women enjoy equal rights with men. Discrimination on grounds of sex, religion or nationality is a punishable offence. The State also ensures freedom of conscience, religious worship, speech, the press and assembly. The right of workers to organize themselves is stressed. The freedom of the individual, and the privacy of the home and of correspondence are inviolable. Freedom for creative work in the sciences and the arts is guaranteed.

The basic freedoms of all workers are guaranteed and foreign citizens enjoy the right of asylum.

Military service (with or without arms) and the defence of their country are the duties of all citizens.

The Government

HEAD OF STATE

President of the Republic: FERENC MÁDL (elected 6 June 2000; took office 4 August 2000).

COUNCIL OF MINISTERS

(March 2001)

A coalition of the Federation of Young Democrats—Hungarian Civic Party (FYD—HCP), the Independent Smallholders' and Civic Party (ISCP) and the Hungarian Democratic Forum (HDF).

Prime Minister: VIKTOR ORBÁN (FYD—HCP).

Minister of Agriculture and Rural Development: ANDRÁS VONZA (ISCP).

Minister of Defence: JÁNOS SZABÓ (ISCP).

Minister of Economic Affairs: Dr GYÖRGY MATOLCSY (FYD—HCP).

Minister of Education: ZOLTÁN POKORNI (FYD—HCP).

Minister of Health: ISTVÁN MIKOLA (FYD—HCP).

Minister of Home Affairs: SÁNDOR PINTÉR (FYD—HCP).

Minister of Justice: IBOLYA DÁVID (HDF).

Minister of Environmental Protection: Dr BÉLA TURI-KOVÁCS (ISCP).

Minister of National Cultural Heritage: ZOLTÁN ROCKENBAUER (FYD—HCP).

Minister of Social and Family Affairs: PÉTER HARRACH.

Minister of Youth and Sport: TAMÁS DEUTSCH (FYD—HCP).

Minister of Transport and Water Management: Dr JÁNOS FÓNAGY (FYD—HCP).

Minister of Foreign Affairs: JÁNOS MARTONYI (FYD—HCP).

Minister of Finance: MIHÁLY VARGA (FYD—HCP).

Minister without Portfolio responsible for the Co-ordination of EU (PHARE) Programme: IMRE BOROS (ISCP).

Minister without Portfolio responsible for National Security: ERVIN DEMETER (FYD—HCP).

MINISTRIES

Office of the President: 1055 Budapest, Kossuth Lajos tér 3–5; tel. (1) 441-4103.

Office of the Prime Minister: 1055 Budapest, Kossuth Lajos tér 1–3; tel. (1) 441-4000; fax (1) 268-3050; internet www.kancellaria. gov.hu.

Ministry of Agriculture and Rural Development: 1055 Budapest, Kossuth Lajos tér 11; tel. (1) 301-4000; fax (1) 302-0408; internet www.fvm.hu/aindex.html.

Ministry of Defence: 1055 Budapest, Balaton u. 7–11; tel. (1) 236-5111; fax (1) 311-0182; internet www.h-m.hu.

Ministry of Economic Affairs: 1055 Budapest, Honvéd u. 13–15; tel. (1) 302-2355; fax (1) 374-2700; internet www.gm.hu.

Ministry of Education: 1055 Budapest, Szalay u. 10–14; tel. (1) 302-0600; fax (1) 302-2002; internet www.mkm.hu.

Ministry of Environmental Protection: 1011 Budapest, POB 351, Fő u. 44–50; tel. (1) 457-3300; fax (1) 201-2846; e-mail schreier .katalin@ktmolam2.ktm.hu; internet www.ktm.hu.

Ministry of Finance: 1051 Budapest, József Nádor tér 2–4; tel. (1) 318-2066; fax (1) 318-2570; internet www.meh.hu.

Ministry of Foreign Affairs: 1027 Budapest, Bem rkp. 47; tel. (1) 458-1000; fax (1) 212-5981; internet www.mfa.gov.hu.

Ministry of Health: 1051 Budapest, Arany János u. 6–8; tel. (1) 332-3100; fax (1) 302-0925; internet www.nepjoleti.gov.hu.

Ministry of Home Affairs: 1051 Budapest, József Attila u. 2–4; tel. (1) 331-3700; fax (1) 118-2870; internet www.b-m.hu.

Ministry of Justice: 1055 Budapest, Kossuth Lajos tér 4; tel. (1) 441-3003; internet www.im.hu.

Ministry of National Cultural Heritage: 1077 Budapest, Wesse-lényi u. 20–22; tel. (1) 484-7100; fax (1) 484-7172; internet www.nkom.hu.

Ministry of Social and Family Affairs: 1051 Budapest, Roosevelt tér 7/8; tel. (1) 302-2100; fax (1) 332-8128.

Ministry of Transport and Water Management: 1077 Budapest, Dob u. 75–81, POB 87; tel. (1) 322-0220; fax (1) 322-8695; internet www.meh.hu.

Ministry of Youth and Sport: 1054 Budapest, Hold u. 1; tel. (1) 311-9080; fax (1) 269-0188; internet www.ism.hu/start.htm.

Legislature

ORSZÁGGYÜLÉS

(National Assembly)

National Assembly: 1055 Budapest, Kossuth Lajos tér 4; tel. (1) 112-0600; fax (1) 153-0533; internet www.mkogy.hu.

President of the National Assembly: JÁNOS ÁDER.

Deputy Presidents: KATALIN SZILI, GEZA GYIMOTHY, FERENC WEKLER.

General election, 10 and 24 May 1998

	% of votes	Seats
Federation of Young Democrats—		
Hungarian Civic Party (FYD—HCP) .	38.34	147
Hungarian Socialist Party (HSP) . . .	34.72	134
Independent Smallholders' and Peasants'		
Party (ISPP)	12.44	48
Alliance of Free Democrats (AFD) . . .	6.22	24
Hungarian Democratic Forum (HDF) .	4.44	18
Hungarian Justice and Life Party (HJLP)	3.63	14
Other	0.21	1
Total	**100.00**	**386**

Political Organizations

Agrarian Association (Agrarszövetség): Budapest; Chair. TAMÁS NAGY.

Alliance for Eastern Hungary: Budapest; f. 2000; right-wing; Leaders ATTILA SZABÓ, SÁNDOR CSEN.

Alliance of Free Democrats—AFD (Szabad Demokraták Szövet-sége—SzDSz): 1143 Budapest, Girella u. 3; tel. (1) 223-2050; fax (1) 221-0579; e-mail zsolt.udvarvolgyi@szdsz.hu; internet www.szdsz .hu; f. 1988; 19,000 mems (2000); Chair. GÁBOR DEMSZKY.

Christian Democratic People's Party—CDPP (Keresztényde-mokrata Néppárt—KDNP): 1126 Budapest, Nagy Jenő u. 5; tel. (1) 175-0333; fax (1) 155-5772; e-mail kulugy@kdnp.hu; internet www.kdnp.hu; re-formed 1989; Chair. GYÖRGY GICZY.

Entrepreneurs' Party: Budapest; mem. of Olive Branch 2000 (f. 2000) grouping.

Federation of Young Democrats—Hungarian Civic Party—FYD—HCP (Magyar Polgári Párt—FIDESZ): 1062 Budapest, Lendvay u. 28; tel. (1) 269-5353; fax (1) 269-5343; e-mail sajto@ fidesz.parlament.hu; internet www.fidesz.hu; f. 1988 as the Federa-tion of Young Democrats; renamed April 1995; 10,000 mems; Leader LÁSZLÓ KÖVÉR.

Green Party of Hungary: Budapest; Chair. ZOLTÁN MEDVECZKY.

Hungarian Christian Democratic Federation—MKDSZ: f. 1997 by breakaway members of the Christian Democratic People's Party; allied to the Federation of Young Democrats—Hungarian Civic Party; Chair. LÁSZLÓ SURJAN.

Hungarian Civic Co-operation Association (Magyar Polgari Egyuettmuekoedes Egyesuelet): Budapest; f. 1996; Chair. GYÖRGY GRANASZTOI; Gen. Sec. ZOLTÁN VESZELOVSZKI.

Hungarian Democratic Forum—HDF (Magyar Demokrata Fórum—MDF): 1027 Budapest, Bem tér 3; 1539 Budapest, POB 579; tel. (1) 212-2819; fax (1) 212-2856; internet www.mdf.hu; f. 1988; centre-right; formed Olive Branch 2000 initiative in Feb. 2000; 25,000 mems (Dec. 1995); Chair. IBOLYA DÁVID.

Hungarian Democratic People's Party—HDPP (Magyar Demo-krata Néppárt—MDN): Budapest; f. 1996 by former mems of HDF; moderate; mem. of Olive Branch 2000 (f. 2000) grouping; Chair. ERZSÉBET PUSZTAI.

Hungarian Justice and Life Party—HJLP (Magyar Igazság és Élet Párt—MIEP): c/o Office of Deputies, 1085 Budapest, Széchenyi rakpart 19; tel. (1) 268-5199; fax (1) 268-5197; internet www.miep.hu; f. 1993; Chair. ISTVÁN CSURKA.

Hungarian Social Democratic Party—HSDP (Magyarországi Szociáldemokrata Párt—MSzDP): 1074 Budapest, Dohány u. 76, POB 1067; tel. and fax (1) 342-3547; f. 1890; absorbed by Communist Party in 1948; revived 1988; affiliated with the Social Democratic Youth Movement; 3,000 mems (Dec. 1997); Chair. LÁSZLÓ KAPOLYI.

Hungarian Socialist Party—HSP (Magyar Szocialista Párt—MSzP): 1081 Budapest, Köztársaság tér 26; tel. (1) 210-0046; fax (1) 210-0081; internet www.mszp.hu; f. 1989 to replace the Hungarian Socialist Workers' Party; 40,000 mems (Dec. 1999); Chair. LÁSZLÓ KOVÁCS.

Hungarian Workers' Party—HWP (Magyar Munkáspárt—MMP): 1082 Budapest, Baross út 61; tel. (1) 334-2721; fax (1) 313-

5423; e-mail mpzoo@matavnet.hu; internet www.munkaspart.hu; f. 1956 as Hungarian Socialist Workers' Party; dissolved and replaced by Hungarian Socialist Party (see above) in 1989; re-formed in 1989 as Hungarian Socialist Workers' Party, name changed as above 1992; approx. 30,000 mems (Oct. 1992); Pres. Dr GYULA THÜRMER.

Independent Smallholders' and Civic Party—ISCP (Független Kisgazda-, Földmunkás- és Polgári Párt—FKgP): 1056 Budapest, Belgrád rkp. 24; tel. and fax (1) 3181824; internet www.fkgp.hu; f. 1988 as the Independent Smallholders' Party, name subsequently changed to the Independent Smallholders' and Peasants' Party; 60,000 mems; Chair. Dr JÓZSEF TÖRGYÁN.

Liberal Civic Alliance—Entrepreneurs' Party: Budapest; Chair. PÉTER ZWACK.

Lungo Drom Alliance: ethnic Roma party; Leader FLORIAN FARKAS.

Movement for Hungarian Unity: Budapest; f. 1995; nationalist; Pres. IMRE POZSGAY.

National Alliance for Hungary: Salgotarjan; f. 1995; nationalist.

Peace Party of Hungarian Gypsies (Magyar Ciganyok Bekepartja): Budapest; f. 1993; Leader ALBERT HORVÁTH.

United Historic Smallholders' Party—UHSP (Egyesült Kisgazdapárt—Történelmi Tagozat—EKgP–TT): Budapest; f. 1992 as the 'Historical Section' of the Independent Smallholders' Party (now the ISCP); renamed 1993; Chair. JÁNOS SZABÓ; Gen. Sec. ANTAL BELAFI.

World National People's Rule Party: Budapest; f. 1993; right-wing; Chair. ALBERT SZABÓ.

Diplomatic Representation

EMBASSIES IN HUNGARY

Afghanistan: 1021 Budapest, Budakeszi út 55D, P5, 111.2; tel. (1) 176-7742; Chargé d'affaires: SAYED IBRAHIM GAILANI.

Albania: 1068 Budapest, Bajza u. 26; tel. (1) 122-7251; Ambassador: ISUF BASHKURTI.

Algeria: 1014 Budapest, Dísz tér 6; tel. (1) 175-9884; Ambassador: BACHIR ROUIS.

Argentina: 1023 Budapest, Vérhalom u. 12-16B; tel. (1) 122-8467; Ambassador: GUILLERMO JORGE MCGOUGH.

Australia: 1126 Budapest, Királyhágó tér 8i9; tel. (1) 201-8899; fax (1) 201-9792; internet www.ausembbp.hu; Ambassador: LEO CRUISE.

Austria: 1068 Budapest, Benczúr u. 16; tel. (1) 269-6700; fax (1) 269-6702; Ambassador: Dr ERICH KUSSBACH.

Belgium: 1015 Budapest, Toldy Ferenc u. 13; tel. (1) 201-1571; fax (1) 175-1566; Ambassador: MICHEL CARLIER.

Brazil: 1062 Budapest, Délibáb u. 30; tel. (1) 351-0060; fax (1) 351-0066; e-mail hunbrem@ind.eunet.hu; Ambassador LUCIANO OZORIO ROSA.

Bulgaria: 1062 Budapest, Andrássy út 115; tel. (1) 322-0824; fax (1) 322-5215; e-mail bgembhu@ibm.net; Ambassador: CHRISTO HALATCHEV.

Cambodia: Budapest; tel. (1) 155-1128; fax (1) 155-1128; Ambassador: UNG SEAN.

Canada: 1121 Budapest, Budakeszi út 32; tel. and fax (1) 275-1210; Ambassador: RODNEY IRWIN.

Chile: 1061 Budapest, Józsefhegyi út 28–30; tel. (1) 212-0061; fax (1) 212-0059; Ambassador: CELSO ENRIQUE MORENO LAVAL.

China, People's Republic: 1068 Budapest, Benczúr u. 17; tel. (1) 122-4872; Ambassador: ZHAO XIDI.

Colombia: 1025 Budapest, Józsefhegyi út 28-30 G-6; tel. (1) 325-7617; fax (1) 325-7618; e-mail embajada.budapest@colombia.hu; Ambassador: BELARMINO PINILLA.

Costa Rica: Budapest; tel. (1) 1851-431; Ambassador: JORGE EDOARDO VILLAFRANCA NÚÑEZ.

Croatia: 1125 Budapest, Nógradi út 28B; tel. (1) 155-1522; fax (1) 175-4336; Ambassador: Dr ALEKSANDAR SOLC.

Cuba: 1026 Budapest, Harangvirá utca 7; tel. (1) 200-8916; fax (1) 200-8045; e-mail embacuba.bud@mail.matav.hu; Ambassador: CARLOS TREJO SOSA.

Cyprus: Budapest, Budakeszi út 55D, P7, 6th Floor; tel. (1) 266-1330; fax (1) 200-8769.

Czech Republic: 1064 Budapest, Rozsa utca 61; tel. (1) 351-0539; fax (1) 351-9189; e-mail budapest@embassy.mzv.cz; Ambassador: RUDOLF JINDRÁK.

Denmark: 1122 Budapest, Határőr út 37; tel. (1) 155-7320; fax (1) 175-3803; Ambassador: ERIK SKOV.

Ecuador: 1021 Budapest, Budakeszi u. 55D, P8, V/1; tel. (1) 200-8918; fax (1) 200-8682; e-mail mecuahun@mail.elender.hu; Ambassador: CARLOS BORJA MARTÍNEZ.

Egypt: 1016 Budapest, Bérc u. 16; tel. (1) 466-8060; e-mail 113060.2173@compuserve.com; Ambassador: OSSAMA HAGGAG.

Finland: 1118 Budapest, Kelenhegyi út 16A; tel. (1) 385-0700; fax (1) 385-0843; e-mail sanomat.bud@formin.fi; Ambassador: HANNU HALINEN.

France: 1062 Budapest, Lendvay u. 27; tel. (1) 332-4980; fax (1) 311-8291; e-mail ambasfn-presse@matavnet.hu; internet www .ambafrance.hu; Ambassador: PAUL POUPADE.

Germany: 1143 Budapest, Stefánia út 101–103; tel. (1) 467-3500; fax (1) 467-3505; Ambassador: WILFRIED GRUBER.

Greece: 1063 Budapest, Szegfű u. 3; tel. (1) 122-8004; Ambassador: NIKOLAOS KALANTZIANOS.

Holy See: 1126 Budapest, Gyimes út 1–3; tel. (1) 355-8979; fax (1) 355-6987; Apostolic Nuncio: Most Rev. KARL-JOSEF RAUBER, Titular Archbishop of Iubaltiana.

India: 1025 Budapest, Búzavirág u. 14; tel. (1) 325-7742; fax (1) 325-7745; Ambassador: LAKSHMI PURI.

Indonesia: 1068 Budapest, Városligeti fasor 26; tel. (1) 342-8508; fax (1) 322-8669; Ambassador: HASSAN ABDULDJALIL.

Iran: 1062 Budapest, Délibáb u. 29; tel. (1) 251-3755; fax (1) 251-2271; Ambassador: Dr MORTEZA SAFFARI NATANZI.

Iraq: 1146 Budapest, Hermina u. 7; tel. (1) 343-0071; fax (1) 343-0072; Ambassador: JAHEED RABAH AHMEED.

Israel: 1026 Budapest, Fullánk u. 8; tel. (1) 2000-781; fax (1) 2000-783; e-mail isremb@alarmix.hu; Ambassador: JOEL ALON.

Italy: 1143 Budapest, Stefánia út 95; tel. (1) 343-6065; fax (1) 343-6058; e-mail ambital@pronet.hu; Ambassador: GIOVAN BATTISTA VERDERAME.

Japan: 1125 Budapest, Zalai út 7; tel. (1) 275-1275; fax (1) 275-1281; Ambassador: YOSHITOMO TANAKA.

Kazakhstan: 1025 Budapest, II ker., Kapy út 59; tel. (1) 275-1300; fax (1) 275-2092; e-mail kazak@euroweb.hu; Ambassador: TULEUTAI SULEIMENOV.

Korea, Republic: 1062 Budapest, Andrássy út 109; tel. (1) 351-1179; fax (1) 351-1182; Ambassador: HAN HWA-GHIL.

Libya: 1143 Budapest, Stefánia út 111; tel. (1) 122-6076; Head of People's Bureau: OMAR MUFTAH DALLAL.

Mexico: 1023 Budapest, Vérhalom u. 12–16; tel. (1) 326-0487; fax (1) 326-0485; Ambassador: JORGE CHEN.

Mongolia: 1022 Budapest II, k. Bogár u. 14/C; tel. (1) 115-9625; fax (1) 135-9532; Ambassador: DERGELDALIYN DZAMBADZANCAN.

Morocco: 1026 Budapest, Törökvész Lejtö 12A; tel. (1) 275-1467; fax (1) 275-1437; e-mail sifamabudap@attglobal.net; Ambassador: SAAD BADDOU.

Netherlands: 1022 Budapest, Füge út 5–7; tel. (1) 326-5301; fax (1) 326-5978; Ambassador: E. F. NIEHE.

New Zealand: Budapest; tel. (1) 131-2144; fax (1) 131-0593; Chargé d'affaires: TAMÁS TAKATSY.

Norway: 1015 Budapest, Ostrom u. 13, POB 32; tel. (1) 212-9400; fax (1) 212-9410; e-mail norwegian.embassy@pronet.hu; Ambassador: BJORN FRODE ØSTERN.

Peru: 1122 Budapest, Tóth Lörinc u. 5 ; tel. (1) 155-4019; fax (1) 155-1019; Ambassador: BERTHA VEGA PÉREZ.

Philippines: 1025 Budapest II, Jozsefhegyi út 28–30; tel. (1) 212-3897; fax (1) 212-2945; Ambassador: FRANKLIN M. EBDALIN.

Poland: 1068 Budapest, Városligeti fasor 16; tel. (1) 342-5566; fax (1) 351-1722; Ambassador: GRZEGORZ LUBCZYK.

Portugal: 1020 Budapest, Romer Flóris u. 58; tel. (1) 316-2645; fax (1) 316-2642; Ambassador: Dr ANTÓNIO BAPTISTA MARTINS.

Romania: 1146 Budapest, Thököly út 72; tel. (1) 352-0271; fax (1) 343-6035; Ambassador: PETRU CORDOS.

Russia: 1062 Budapest, Bajza u. 35; tel. (1) 332-0911; Ambassador: VALERY MUSATOV.

Slovakia: 1143 Budapest, Stefánia út 22-24; tel. (1) 251-1700; fax (1) 251-1460; Chargé d'affaires: JURAJ PALACKA.

Slovenia: 1025 Budapest, Cseppkö u. 68; tel. (1) 438-5600; fax (1) 325-9187; Ambassador: IDA MOČIVNIK.

Spain: 1067 Budapest, Eötvös u. 11B; tel. (1) 3429-992; fax (1) 3510-572; Ambassador: FERNANDO PERPINÁ-ROBERT.

Sweden: 1146 Budapest, Ajtósi Dürer sor 27A; tel. (1) 460-6020; fax (1) 460-6021; e-mail ambassaden.budapest@foreign.ministry.se; Ambassador: STAFFAN CARLSSON.

Switzerland: 1143 Budapest, Stefánia út 107; tel. (1) 343-9491; Ambassador: RUDOLF WEIERSMUELLER.

Syria: 1026 Budapest, Harangvirág u. 3; tel. (1) 176-7186; Ambassador: (vacant).

Thailand: 1025 Budapest, Verecke út 79; tel. (1) 325-9892; fax (1) 325-9886; Ambassador: PRADAP PIBULSONGGRAM.

Tunisia: 1021 Budapest, Budakeszi út 55D; tel. (1) 200-8929; fax (1) 200-8931; Chargé d'affaires: ABDELWAHEB BOUZOUITA.

Turkey: 1014 Budapest, Úri u. 45; tel. (1) 3445025; fax (1) 3445143; e-mail budapest@turkishembassy.hu; Ambassador: BEDRETTIN TUN-ABAS.

Ukraine: 1125 Budapest, Nogradi u. 8; tel. (1) 155-2443; fax (1) 202-2287; Ambassador: DMYTRO TKACH.

United Kingdom: 1051 Budapest, Harmincad u. 6; tel. (1) 266-2888; fax (1) 266-0907; e-mail info@britemb.hu; internet www .britishembassy.hu; Ambassador: NIGEL THORPE.

USA: 1054 Budapest, Szabadság tér 12; tel. (1) 475-4400; fax (1) 475-4764; internet www.usis.hu; Ambassador: PETER F. TUFO.

Uruguay: 1023 Budapest 2, Vérhalom u. 12–16; tel. and fax (1) 326-0459; e-mail urupest@euroweb.hu; Ambassador: HOMERO DIEGO MARTÍNEZ LAWLOR.

Venezuela: 1023 Budapest, Vérhalom u. 12–16; tel. (1) 326-0460; fax (1) 326-0450; Ambassador: JORGE A. GONZÁLEZ.

Viet Nam: 1068 Budapest 2, Benczúr u. 18; tel. (1) 142-9943; Ambassador: TRAN VAN DAO.

Yemen: 1025 Budapest, Józsefhegyi út 28-30; tel. (1) 115-3844; Ambassador: (vacant).

Yugoslavia: 1068 Budapest, Dózsa György út 92B; tel. (1) 142-0566; fax (1) 251-1283; Chargé d'affaires: BRANISAL NOVAKOVIĆ.

Judicial System

The system of court procedure in Hungary is based on an Act that came into effect in 1953 and has since been updated frequently. The system of jurisdiction is based on the local courts (district courts in Budapest, city courts in other cities), labour courts, county courts (or the Metropolitan Court) and the Supreme Court. In the legal remedy system of two instances, appeals against the decisions of city and district courts can be lodged with the competent county court and the Metropolitan Court of Budapest respectively. Against the judgment of first instance of the latter, appeal is to be lodged with the Supreme Court. The Chief Public Prosecutor and the President of the Supreme Court have the right to submit a protest on legal grounds against the final judgment of any court.

By virtue of the 1973 Act, effective 1974 and modified in 1979, the procedure in criminal cases is differentiated for criminal offences and for criminal acts. In the first instance, criminal cases are tried, depending on their character, by a professional judge; where justified by the magnitude of the criminal act, by a council composed of three members, a professional judge and two lay assessors, while in major cases the court consists of five members, two professional judges and three lay assessors. In the Supreme Court, second instance cases are tried only by professional judges. The President of the Supreme Court is elected by the National Assembly. Judges are appointed by the President of the Republic for an indefinite period. Assessors are elected by the local municipal councils.

In the interest of ensuring legality and a uniform application of the law, the Supreme Court exercises a principled guidance over the jurisdiction of courts. In the Republic of Hungary judges are independent and subject only to the Law and other legal regulations.

The Minister of Justice supervises the general activities of courts. the Chief Public Prosecutor is elected by the National Assembly. The Chief Public Prosecutor and the Prosecutor's Office provide for the consistent prosecution of all acts violating or endangering the legal order of society, the safety and independence of the state, and for the protection of citizens.

The Prosecutors of the independent prosecuting organization exert supervision over the legality of investigations and the implementation of punishments, and assist with specific means in ensuring that legal regulations should be observed by state, economic and other organs and citizens, and they support the legality of court procedures and decisions.

President of the Supreme Court: PÁL SOLT.

Chief Public Prosecutor: PÉTER POLT.

Constitutional Court: 1015 Budapest, Donáti u. 35-45; tel. (1) 212-1160; fax (1) 212-1170; internet www.mkab.hu; Pres. Dr JÁNOS NÉMETH.

Religion

CHRISTIANITY

Ecumenical Council of Churches in Hungary (Magyarországi Egyházak Ökumenikus Tanácsa): 1026 Budapest, Bimbó u. 127; tel. (1) 394-4847; fax (1) 394-1210; e-mail oikoumene@lutheran.hu; internet oikoumene.lutheran.hu; f. 1943; member churches: Baptist, Bulgarian Orthodox, Evangelical Lutheran, Hungarian Orthodox, Methodist, Reformed Church, Romanian Orthodox and Serbian Orthodox; Pres. Bishop Dr MIHÁLY MÁRKUS; Gen. Sec. Dr TIBOR GÖRÖG.

The Roman Catholic Church

In 1994 Hungary comprised four archdioceses, nine dioceses (including one for Catholics of the Byzantine rite) and one territorial abbacy (directly responsible to the Holy See). At 31 December 1997 the Church had 6,240,688 adherents in Hungary.

Bishops' Conference: Magyar Katolikus Püspöki Konferencia, 1071 Budapest, Városligeti fasor 45; tel. (1) 342-6959; fax (1) 342-6957; e-mail pkt@katolikus.hu; f. 1969; Pres. Dr ISTVÁN SEREGÉLY, Archbishop of Eger.

Latin Rite

Archbishop of Eger: Dr ISTVÁN SEREGÉLY, 3301 Eger, Széchenyi u. 1, POB 80; tel. (36) 313-259; fax (36) 320-508; e-mail egersek@ektf.hu.

Archbishop of Esztergom-Budapest: Cardinal Dr LÁSZLÓ PASKAI, Primate of Hungary, 1014 Budapest, Uri u. 62; tel. (1) 202-5611; fax (1) 202-5458; e-mail paskai@communio.hcbc.hu.

Archbishop of Kalocsa-Kecskemét: Dr BALÁZS BÁBEL, 6301 Kalocsa, POB 29, Szentháromság tér 1; tel. and fax (78) 462-166; e-mail kalocsa@communio.hcbc.hu.

Archbishop of Veszprém: Dr GYULA MÁRFI, 8200 Veszprém, Vár u. 16-18; tel. (88) 426-088; fax (88) 426-287.

Byzantine Rite

Bishop of Hajdúdorog: SZILÁRD KERESZTES, 4401 Nyiregyháza, Bethlen u. 5, POB 60; tel. (42) 317-397; fax (42) 314-734; 253,000 adherents (Dec. 1992); the Bishop is also Apostolic Administrator of the Apostolic Exarchate of Miskolc, with an estimated 25,000 Catholics of the Byzantine rite (Dec. 1997).

Protestant Churches

Baptist Union of Hungary (Magyarországi Baptista Egyház): 1068 Budapest, Benczur u. 31; tel. (1) 343-0618; fax (1) 352-9707; e-mail baptist.convention@mail.datanet.hu; f. 1846; 11,500 mems; Pres. Rev. KÁLMÁN MÉSZÁROS; Gen.-Sec. Rev. KORNÉL MÉSZÁROS.

Evangelical Lutheran Church in Hungary (Magyarországi Evangélikus Egyház): 1085 Budapest, Üuöi u. 24; tel. (1) 317-5567; fax (1) 317-0872; e-mail orszagos@lutheran.hu; 430,000 mems (1992); Presiding Bishop IMRE SZEBIK; Dir KÁROLY HAFENSCHER.

Hungarian Methodist Church (Magyarországi Metodista Egyház): 1032 Budapest, Kiscelli u. 73; tel. (1) 250-1536; fax (1) 250-1536; e-mail kiscelli@matavnet.hu; Superintendent Dr ISTVÁN CSERNÁK.

Reformed Church in Hungary—Presbyterian (Magyarországi Református Egyház): 1146 Budapest, Abonyi u. 21; tel. (1) 343-7870; e-mail rch@mail.elender.hu; 2m. mems (1987); 1,306 churches; Pres. of Gen. Synod Bishop Dr GUSZTÁV BÖLCSKEI.

Unitarian Church in Hungary (Magyarországi Unitárius Egyház): 1055 Budapest V, Nagy Ignác u. 4; tel. (1) 111-2801; Bishop Rev. MARTIN BENCZE.

The Eastern Orthodox Church

Hungarian Orthodox Church (Magyar Orthodox Egyház): 1052 Budapest, Petőfi tér 2.1.2.; tel. (1) 318-4813; Administrator Archpriest Dr FERIZ BERKI.

Romanian Orthodox Church in Hungary (Magyarországi Román Ortodox Egyház): 5700 Gyula, Groza park 2; tel. (66) 61-281; Bishop PÁL ÁRDELEÁN.

Serbian Orthodox Diocese (Szerb Görögkeleti Egyházmegye): 2000 Szentendre, POB 22; Bishop Dr DANILO KRISTIC.

The Russian (6,000 mems) and Bulgarian Orthodox Churches are also represented.

BUDDHISM

Hungarian Buddhist Mission (Magyarországi Buddhista Misszió): 1386 Budapest, Postafiók 952; tel. (36) 138-52098; e-mail amm@dakiniland.net; internet www.dharma.hu; Rep. Dr LAJOS PRESSING.

Hungarian Zen Buddhist Community (Magyarországi Csan Buddhista Közösség): Budapest; Leader FÁRAD LOTFI.

ISLAM

There are about 3,000 Muslims in Hungary.

Hungarian Islamic Community (Magyar Iszlám Közösség): Budapest; tel. (1) 177-7602; Leader Dr BALÁZS MIHÁLFFY.

JUDAISM

The Jewish community in Hungary is estimated to number between 100,000 and 120,000 people. Some 80% of Hungary's Jewish community resides in Budapest.

Federation of Jewish Communities in Hungary (Magyarországi Zsidó Hitközségek Szövetsége): 1075 Budapest, Sip u. 12, Budapesti Zsidó Hitközség (Jewish Community of Budapest); tel.

(1) 342-1335; fax (1) 342-1790; e-mail bzsh@mail.matav.hu; 80,000 mems; 40 active synagogues; Orthodox and Conservative; Man. Dir GUSZTÁV ZOLTAI; Chief Rabbi of Hungary Dr JÓZSEF SCHWEITZER.

The Press

In 1996 there were 40 dailies, with an average daily circulation of 1,895,000. Budapest dailies circulate nationally. The most popular are: *Népszabadság, Nemzeti Sport* and *Népszava. Népszabadság,* the most important daily, was formerly the central organ of the Hungarian Socialist Workers' Party, but is now independent. Most daily newspapers were partially foreign-owned.

PRINCIPAL DAILIES

Békéscsaba

Békés Megyei Hírlap (Békés County News): 5601 Békéscsaba, Munkácsy u. 4; tel. (66) 446-242; fax (66) 441-020; internet www.bmhirlap.hu; f. 1945; Editor-in-Chief ZOLTÁN ÁRPÁSI; circ. 49,000.

Budapest

Blikk: Budapest; f. 1994; colour tabloid.

Magyar Hírlap (Hungarian Journal): 1087 Budapest, Kerepesi út 29B; tel. (1) 210-0050; fax (1) 210-3737; internet www .magyarhirlap.hu; f. 1968; 100% foreign-owned; Editor-in-Chief MÁTYÁS VINCE; circ. 75,000.

Magyar Nemzet (Hungarian Nation): 1073 Budapest, Erzsébet krt 9–11; tel. (1) 141-4320; internet www.magyarnemzet.com; 45% foreign-owned; Editor-in-Chief TIBOR PETHŐ; circ. 70,000.

Mai Nap (Today): 1145 Budapest, Szugló u. 14; tel. (1) 470-1382; fax (1) 470-1351; e-mail info@mainap.hu; f. 1988; Editor-in-Chief FERENC KÖSZEGI; circ.100,000.

Metro: 1106 Budapest, Fehér út 10, 21-es épület; tel. (1) 431-6464; fax (1) 431-6465; e-mail info@metro.hu; internet www.metro.hu; Editor IZBÉKI GÁBOR.

NAPI Gazdaság (World Economy): 1135 Budapest, Csata u. 32; tel. (1) 350-4349; fax (1) 350-1117; e-mail napi@mail.eleuder.hu; internet www.napi.hu; Editor-in-Chief ADÁM DANKÓ; circ. 16,000.

Nemzeti Sport (National Sport): 1141 Budapest, Szugló u. 83-85; tel. (1) 460-2600; fax (1) 460-2612; Editor-in-Chief TAMÁS SZEKERES; circ. 140,000.

Népszabadság (People's Freedom): 1960 Budapest, Bécsi út 122-124; tel. (1) 436-4500; fax (1) 387-8699; e-mail eotvosp@ nepszabadsag.hu; internet www.nepszabadsag.hu; f. 1942; independent; Editor-in-Chief PÁL EÖTVÖS; circ. 200,000.

Népszava (Voice of the People): 1022 Budapest, Törökvész u. 30A; tel. (1) 202-7788; fax (1) 202-7798; e-mail online@nepszava.hu; internet www.nepszava.hu; f. 1873; Editor ANDRÁS KERESZTY; circ. 120,000.

Pest Megyei Hírlap (Pest County Journal): Budapest; tel. (1) 138-2399; Editor-in-Chief Dr ANDRÁS BÁRD; circ. 43,000.

Pesti Hírlap (Pest Journal): 1051 Budapest, Október 6 u. 8; tel. (1) 117-6162; fax (1) 117-6029; f. 1993; Editor-in-Chief ANDRÁS BENCSIK; circ. 50,000.

Üzlet (Business): Budapest; tel. (1) 111-8260; Editor-in-Chief IVÁN ÉRSEK.

Debrecen

Hajdú-Bihari Napló (Hajdú-Bihar Diary): 4024 Debrecen, Dósa nádor tér 10; tel. (52) 413-395; fax (52) 412-326; e-mail naplo@ iscomp.hu; internet www.naplo.hu; f. 1944; Editor-in-Chief ZSOLT PORCSIN; circ. 60,000.

Dunaújváros

A Hírlap (The Journal): 2400 Dunaújváros, Városháza tér 1; tel. (25) 16-010; Editor-in-Chief CSABA D. KISS.

Eger

Heves Megyei Hírlap (Heves County Journal): 3301 Eger, Barkóczy u. 7; tel. (36) 13-644; e-mail hmhirlap@axels.hu; internet www.agria.hu/hmhirlap; Editor-in-Chief LEVENTE KAPOSI; circ. 33,000.

Győr

Kisalföld: 9021 Győr, Újlak u. 4/a; tel. (96) 504-444; fax (96) 504-414; e-mail kisalfoldmail.matav.hu; internet www.kisalfold.hu; Editor-in-Chief NYERGES CSABA.

Kaposvár

Somogyi Hírlap (Somogy Journal): 7401 Kaposvár, Latinca Sándor u. 2A; tel. (82) 11-644; internet www.somogyihirlap.hu; Editor-in-Chief Dr IMRE KERCZA; circ. 59,000.

Kecskemét

Petőfi Népe: 6000 Kecskemét, Szabadság tér 1A; tel. (76) 481-391; internet www.petofinepe.hu; Editor-in-Chief Dr DÁNIEL LOVAS; circ. 60,000.

Miskolc

Déli Hírlap (Midday Journal): 3527 Miskolc, Bajcsy-Zsilinszky út 15; tel. (46) 42-694; Editor-in-Chief DEZSŐ BEKES; circ. 20,000.

Észak-Magyarország (Northern Hungary): 3527 Miskolc, Bajcsy-Zsilinszky út 15; tel. (46) 341-888; internet www.eszak.hu/eszako .2/; Editor-in-Chief LÁSZLÓ GÖRÖMBÖLYI; circ. 45,000.

Nyíregyháza

Kelet-Magyarország (Eastern Hungary): 4401 Nyíregyháza, Zrínyi u. 3–5; tel. (42) 11-277; Editor-in-Chief Dr SÁNDOR ÁNGYAL; circ. 80,000.

Pécs

Új Dunántúli Napló: 7601 Pécs, Hunyadi út 11; tel. (72) 15-000; internet 195.184.19.151/index.php3; Editor-in-Chief JENŐ LOMBOSI; circ. 84,000.

Salgótarján

Új Nógrád (New Nógrád): 3100 Salgótarján, Palócz Imre tér 4; tel. (32) 10-589; Editor-in-Chief LÁSZLÓ SULYOK; circ. 23,000.

Szeged

Délvilág (Southern World): 6740 Szeged, Tanácsköztársaság út 10; tel. (62) 14-911; internet www.delvilag.hu; Editor-in-Chief ISTVÁN NIKOLÉNYI; circ. 20,000.

Délmagyarország (Southern Hungary): 6740 Szeged, Stefánia 10; tel. (62) 481-281; internet www.delmagyar.szeged.hu; Editor-in-Chief IMRE DLUSZTUS; circ. 70,000.

Székesfehérvár

Fejér Megyei Hirlap (Fejér County Journal): 8003 Székesfehérvár, Honvéd u. 8; tel. (22) 12-450; Editor-in-Chief JÁNOS Á. SZABÓ; circ. 52,000.

Szekszárd

Tolna Megyei Népújság (Tolna News): 7100 Szekszárd, Liszt Ferenc tér 3; tel. (74) 16-211; Editor-in-Chief GYÖRGYNÉ KAMARÁS; circ. 32,000.

Szolnok

Új Néplap (New People's Paper): 5001 Szolnok, Kossuth tér 1, I. Irodaház; tel. (56) 42-211; internet www.ujneplap.hu; Editor-in-Chief JÓZSEF HAJNAL; circ. 46,000.

Szombathely

Vas Népe (Vas People): 9700 Szombathely, Berzsenyi tér 2; tel. (94) 12-393; Editor-in-Chief SÁNDOR LENGYEL; circ. 65,000.

Tatabánya

24 Óra (24 Hours): 2800 Tatabánya, Fö tér 4; tel. (34) 514-012; fax (34) 514-011; e-mail szerk.kom@axels.hu; internet www.24ora.hu; Editor-in-Chief FERENC SZTRAPÁK; circ. 23,000.

Veszprém

Napló (Diary): 8201 Veszprém, Szabadság tér 15; tel. (80) 27-444; Editor-in-Chief ELEMÉR BALOGH; circ. 58,000.

Zalaegerszeg

Zalai Hírlap (Zala Journal): 8901 Zalaegerszeg, Ady Endre u. 62; tel. (92) 12-575; Editor-in-Chief JÓZSEF TARSOLY; circ. 71,000.

WEEKLIES

Élet és Irodalom (Life and Literature): 1089 Budapest, Rezsö tér 15; tel. (1) 210-2157; fax (1) 269-9241; e-mail es@es.hu; internet www.es.hu; f. 1957; literary and political; Editor ZOLTÁN KOVÁCS; circ. 16,000.

Élet és Tudomány (Life and Science): 1088 Budapest, Bródy Sándor u 16; tel. and fax (1) 138-2472; f. 1946; popular science; Editor-in-Chief Dr HERCZEG JÁNOS; circ. 20,000.

Evangélikus Élet (Evangelical Life): 1085 Budapest, Üllői út. 24; tel. and fax (1) 117-1108; f. 1933; Evangelical–Lutheran Church newspaper; Editor MIHÁLY TÓTH-SZÖLLŐS; circ. 12,000.

Heti Világgazdaság (World Economy Weekly): 1124 Budapest, Németvölgy u. 62-64; tel. (1) 3555-411; fax (1) 3555-693; internet www.hvg.hu; f. 1979; Editor-in-Chief IVÁN LIPOVECZ; circ. 141,000.

Képes Újság (Illustrated News): 1085 Budapest, Gyulai Pál u. 14; tel. (1) 113-7660; f. 1960; Editor MIHÁLY KOVÁCS; circ. 400,000.

Ludas Matyi: Budapest; tel. (1) 133-5718; satirical; Editor JÓZSEF ÁRKUS; circ. 352,000.

L'udové Noviny (People's News): 1065 Budapest, Nagymező u. 49; tel. (1) 131-9184; in Slovak, for Slovaks in Hungary; Editor PÁL KONDÁCS; circ. 1,700.

Magyar Mezőgazdaság (Hungarian Agriculture): 1355 Budapest, Kossuth Lajos tér 11; tel. (1) 112-2433. 1946; Editor-in-Chief Dr KÁROLY FEHÉR; circ. 24,000.

Magyar Nők Lapja (Hungarian Women's Journal): 1022 Budapest, Törökvész út 30A; tel. (1) 212-4020; fax (1) 326-8264; e-mail noklapja@ noklapja.ekh.hu; f. 1949; Editor-in-Chief LILI ZÉTÉNYI; circ. 550,000.

Magyarország (Hungary): Budapest; tel. (1) 138-4644; f. 1964; news magazine; Editor DÉNES GYAPAY; circ. 200,000.

Narodne Novine (People's News): 1396 Budapest, POB 495; tel. (1) 112-4869; f. 1945; for Yugoslavs in Hungary; in Serbo-Croat and Slovene; Chief Editor MARKO MARKOVIĆ; circ. 2,800.

Neue Zeitung (New Paper): 1391 Budapest, Lendvay u. 22, POB 224; tel. (1) 302-6877; e-mail neueztg@mail.elender.hu; f. 1957; for Germans in Hungary; Editor JOHANN SCHUTH; circ. 4,500.

Rádió és Televízióújság (Radio and TV News): 1801 Budapest; tel. (1) 138-8114; fax (1) 138-7349; f. 1924; Editor MÁRTA BÓDAY; circ. 300,000.

Reform: Budapest; tel. and fax (1) 122-4240; f. 1988; popular tabloid; 50% foreign-owned; Editor PÉTER TŐKE; circ. 300,000.

Reformátusok Lapja: 1395 Budapest, POB 424; tel. (1) 117-6809; fax (1) 117-8386; f. 1957; Reformed Church paper for the laity; Editor-in-Chief and Publr ATTILA P. KOMLÓS; circ. 30,000.

Szabad Föld (Free Earth): 1087 Budapest, Könyves Kálmán krt 76; tel. and fax (1) 133-6794; f. 1945; Editor GYULA ÉCK; circ. 720,000.

Szövetkezet (Co-operative): 1054 Budapest, Szabadság tér 14; tel. (1) 131-3132; National Council of Hungarian Consumer Co-operative Societies; Editor-in-Chief ATTILA KOVÁCS; circ. 85,000.

Tallózó: 1133 Budapest, Visegrádi u. 110-112; tel. and fax (1) 149-8707; f. 1989; news digest; Editor-in-Chief GYÖRGY ANDAI; circ. 35,000.

Tőzsde Kurir (Hungarian Stock Market Courier): Budapest; tel. (1) 122-3273; fax (1) 142-8356; business; Editor-in-Chief ISTVÁN GÁBOR BENEDEK.

Új Ember (New Man): 1053 Budapest, Kossuth Lajos u. 1; tel. (1) 117-3661; fax (1) 117-3471; f. 1945; religious weekly; Editor LÁSZLÓ RÓNAY; circ. 70,000.

OTHER PERIODICALS

(Published monthly unless otherwise indicated)

Állami Gazdaság (State Farming): General Direction of State Farming, 1054 Budapest, Akadémia u. 1–3; tel. (1) 112-4617; fax (1) 111-4877; f. 1946; Editor P. GÖRGÉNYI.

Beszeloe (The Speaker): 1364 Budapest, POB 143; tel. and fax (1) 302-1271; e-mail beszelo@mailc3.hu; culture and criticism; Editor-in-Chief ILONA KISS.

Business Partner Hungary: 1081 Budapest, Csokonai u. 3; tel. (1) 303-9586; fax (1) 303-9582; e-mail nemeth@kopdat.hu; internet www.kopdat.hu; f. 1986; every two months; English and German; economic journal published by Economic, Research Marketing and Computing Co Ltd (KOPINT-DATORG); Head of Dept ILONA NÉMETH.

Egyházi Krónika (Church Chronicle): 1052 Budapest, Petőfi tér 2.1.2; tel. and fax (1) 318-4813; f. 1952; every 2 months; Eastern Orthodox Church journal; Editor Archpriest Dr FERIZ BERKI.

Elektrotechnika (Electrical Engineering): 1055 Budapest, Kossuth Lajos tér 6–8; tel. (1) 353-0117; fax (1) 353-4069; e-mail lernyei .mee@mtesz.hu; f. 1908; organ of Electrotechnical Association; Editor Dr JÁNOS BENCZE; circ. 6,500.

Élelmezési Ipar (Food Industry): 1372 Budapest, POB 433; tel. (1) 214-6691; fax (1) 214-6692; e-mail mail.mete@mtesz.hu; internet www.mtesz.hu; f. 1947; Scientific Society for Food Industry; Editor Dr ISTVÁN TÓTH-ZSIGA.

Energia és Atomtechnika (Energy and Nuclear Technology): 1055 Budapest, Kossuth Lajos tér 6–8; tel. (1) 153-2751; fax (1) 156-1215; f. 1947; every two months; Scientific Society for Energy Economy; Editor-in-Chief Dr G. BŐKI.

Energiagazdálkodás (Energy Economy): 1055 Budapest, Kossuth Lajos tér 6; tel. (1) 153-2751; fax (1) 153-3894; Scientific Society for Energetics; Editor Dr ANDOR ANESINI.

Ezermester (The Handyman): Budapest; tel. (1) 132-1987. 1957; do-it-yourself magazine; Editor JÓZSEF PERÉNYI; circ. 50,000.

Gép (Machinery): 1027 Budapest, Fő u. 68; tel. (1) 135-4175; fax (1) 153-0818; f. 1949; Scientific Society of Mechanical Engineering; Editor Dr KORNÉL LEHOFER.

Hungarian Business Herald: Budapest; tel. and fax (1) 186-6143; f. 1970; quarterly review published in English and German by the Ministry of Industry and Trade; Editor-in-Chief Dr GERD BIRÓ; circ. 4,000.

Hungarian Travel Magazine: Budapest, Múzeum u. 11; tel. (1) 138-4643; quarterly in English and German; illustrated journal of the Tourist Board for visitors to Hungary; Man. Editor JÚLIA SZ. NAGY.

Ipar-Gazdaság (Industrial Economy): 1371 Budapest, POB 433; tel. (1) 202-1083; f. 1948; Editor Dr TAMÁS MÉSZÁROS; circ. 4,000.

Jogtudományi Közlöny (Law Gazette): 1535 Budapest, POB 773; 1015 Budapest, Donáti u. 35-45; tel. (1) 355-0330; fax (1) 355-0441; e-mail jogtud@mkab.hu; f. 1866; legal and administrative sciences; Editor-in-Chief Dr IMRE VÖRÖS; circ. 1,000.

Kortárs (Contemporary): 1426 Budapest, POB 108; tel. (1) 342-1168; e-mail kortars@elender.hu; internet www.elender.hu/kortars; f.1957; literary gazette; Editor-in-Chief IMRE KIS PINTÉR; circ. 5,000.

Közgazdasági Szemle (Economic Review): 1112 Budapest, Budaörsi u. 43–45; tel. (1) 319-3165; fax (1) 319-3166; f. 1954; published by Cttee for Economic Sciences of Hungarian Academy of Sciences; Editor KATALIN SZABÓ; circ. 3,000.

Made in Hungary: 1426 Budapest, POB 3; economics and business magazine published in English by Hungarian News Agency (MTI); Editor GYÖRGY BLASITS.

Magyar Hirek (Hungarian News): 1068 Budapest, Benczúr u. 15; tel. (1) 122-5616; fax (1) 122-2421; every 2 weeks; illustrated magazine primarily for Hungarians living abroad; Editor GYÖRGY HALÁSZ; circ. 70,000.

Magyar Jog (Hungarian Law): 1054 Budapest, Szemere u. 10; tel. (1) 311-4880; fax (1) 311-4013; f. 1953; law; Editor-in-Chief Dr JÁNOS NÉMETH; circ. 2,200.

Magyar Közlöny (Official Gazette): 1055 Budapest, Bajcsy Zs. u. 78; tel. (1) 112-1236; Editor Dr ELEMÉR KISS; circ. 90,000.

Magyar Tudomány (Hungarian Science): Hungarian Academy of Sciences, 1051 Budapest, Nádor u. 7; tel. and fax (1) 317-9524; e-mail matud@hefka.iif.hu; internet www.matud.hu; f. 1842; multidisciplinary science review; Editors GYÖRGY ENYEDI, MIKLÓS HERNÁDI, ZSUZSA SZENTGYORGYI.

Pedagógusok Lapja (Teachers' Review): 1068 Budapest, Városligeti fasor 10; tel. (1) 322-8464; e-mail psz-seh@mail.matav.hu; internet www.deltasoft.hu/pszseh; f. 1945; published by the Hungarian Union of Teachers; Editor-in-Chief ÁROK ANTAL; circ. 10,000.

Református Egyház (Reformed Church): 1146 Budapest, Abonyi u. 21; tel. (1) 343-7870; f. 1949; official journal of the Hungarian Reformed Church; Editor-in-Chief LAJOS TÓTH; circ. 1,300.

Statisztikai Szemle (Statistical Review): 1525 Budapest, POB 51; tel. (1) 487-4343; fax (1) 487-4344; e-mail statszemle@ksh.gov.hu; internet www.ksh.hu/statszml; f. 1923; Editor-in-Chief Dr LÁSZLÓ HUNYADI; circ. 800.

Technika (Technology): 1027 Budapest, Fö u. 68; tel. (1) 201-7083; fax (1) 201-8564; f. 1957; official journal of the Hungarian Academy of Engineering; monthly in Hungarian, annually in English, German and Russian; Editor-in-Chief MARGIT WELLEK; circ. 15,000.

Turizmus (Tourism): 1088 Budapest, Múzeum u. 11; tel. (1) 266-5853; fax (1) 338-4293; e-mail turizmus@mail.matav.hu; Editor ZSOLT SZEBENI; circ. 8,000.

Új Élet (New Life): 1075 Budapest, Síp u. 12; tel. (1) 322-2829; every 2 weeks; for Hungarian Jews; Editor Dr PÉTER KARDOS; circ. 5,000.

Új Technika (New Technology): Budapest; tel. (1) 155-7122; f. 1967; popular industrial quarterly; circ. 35,000.

Vigilia: 1364 Budapest, POB 48; tel. (1) 317-7246; fax (1) 317-7682; e-mail vigilia@hcbc.hu; internet www.hcbc.hu/vigilia; f. 1935; Catholic; Editor LÁSZLÓ LUKÁCS; circ. 4,000.

NEWS AGENCIES

Hungarian News Agency (Magyar Távirati Iroda—MTI): 1016 Budapest, Naphegy tér 8; tel. (1) 175-6722; fax (1) 175-3973; internet www.mti.hu; f. 1880; 19 brs in Hungary; 14 bureaux abroad; Dir-Gen. KÁROLY ALEXA.

Foreign Bureaux

Agence France-Presse (AFP): 1016 Budapest, Naphegy u. 29; tel. (1) 356-8416; fax (1) 201-9161; e-mail afpbud@elender.hu; Correspondent ESZTER SZÁMADÓ.

Agenzia Nazionale Stampa Associata (ANSA) (Italy): Budapest; tel. (1) 135-2323; Bureau Chief GAETANO ALIMENTI.

Associated Press (AP) (USA): 1122 Budapest, Maros u. 13; tel. (1) 156-9129; Correspondent ALEX BANDY.

Informatsionnoye Telegrafnoye Agentstvo Rossii—Telegrafnoye Agentstvo Suverennykh Stran (ITAR—TASS) (Russia): 1023 Budapest, Vérhalom u. 12–16; Correspondent YEVGENII POPOV.

Reuters (United Kingdom): 1088 Budapest, Rákóczi út 1–3, East-West Business Centre; tel. (1) 266-2410; fax (1) 266-2030; Chief Correspondent MITYA NEW.

Rossiyskoye Informatsionnoye Agentstvo—Novosti (RIA-Novosti) (Russia): Budapest; tel. (1) 132-0594; fax (1) 142-3325; Bureau Chief A. POPOV.

Tlačová agentúra Slovenskej republiky (TASR) (Slovakia): 1026 Budapest, Garas út 24B; tel. and fax (1) 135-1843; Bureau Chief PETER KLENKO.

Xinhua (New China) News Agency (People's Republic of China): Budapest; tel. (1) 176-7548; fax (1) 176-2571; Chief Correspondent ZHOU DONGYAO.

PRESS ASSOCIATIONS

Hungarian Newspaper Publishers' Association: 1034 Budapest, Bécsi út 122-124; tel. (1) 368-8674; fax (1) 388-6707; e-mail mle.peto@mail.matav.hu; f. 1990; Gen. Sec. JÁNOS PETŐ; 40 mems.

National Association of Hungarian Journalists (Magyar Újságírók Országos Szövetsége—MUOSZ): 1062 Budapest, Andrássy út 101; tel. (1) 322-1699; fax (1) 322-1881; f. 1896; Gen. Sec. GÁBOR BENCSIK; 7,000 mems.

Publishers

PRINCIPAL PUBLISHING HOUSES

Akadémiai Kiadó: 1117 Budapest, Prielle Kornélia u. 19–35; tel. (1) 204-3978; fax (1) 204-3979; e-mail spj@akkrt.hu; f. 1828; humanities, social, natural and technical sciences, dictionaries, periodicals; Hungarian and English; Man. Dir PÉTER JÁNOSÓS.

Corvina Kiadó Kft.: 1051 Budapest, Vörösmarty tér 1; tel. (1) 318-4347; fax (1) 318-4410; e-mail corvina@mail.matav.hu; f. 1955; Hungarian works translated into foreign languages, art and educational books, fiction and non-fiction, tourist guides, cookery books and musicology; Man. Dir ISTVÁN BART.

EMB Music Publisher Ltd: Budapest tel. (1) 318-4228; fax (1) 338-2752; e-mail musicpubl@emb.hu; internet www.emb.hu; f. 1950; music publishing and books on musical subjects; Dir ISTVÁN HOMOLYA.

Európa Könyvkiadó: 1055 Budapest, Kossuth Lajos tér 13–15; tel. (1) 131-2700; fax (1) 131-4162; f. 1945; world literature translated into Hungarian; Man. LEVENTE OSZTOVITS.

Gondolat Könyvkiadó Vállalat: Budapest; tel. (1) 138-3358; fax (1) 138-4540; f. 1957; popular scientific publications on natural and social sciences, art, encyclopaedic handbooks; Dir GYÖRGY FEHÉR.

Helikon Kiadó: 1053 Budapest, Papnövelde u. 8; tel. (1) 117-4865; fax (1) 117-4865; bibliophile books; Dir KATALIN BERGER.

Képzőművészeti Kiadó: Budapest; tel. (1) 251-1527; fax (1) 251-1527; fine arts; Man. Dr ZOLTÁN KEMENCZEI.

Kossuth Kiadó Rt.: 1043 Budapest, Csányi László u. 36; tel. (1) 370-0607; fax (1) 370-0602; e-mail rt@kossuted.hu; f. 1944; social sciences, educational and philosophy publications, information technology books; Man. ANDRÁS SÁNDOR KOCSIS.

Közgazdasági és Jogi Könyvkiadó Rt: Budapest; tel. (1) 112-6430; fax (1) 111-3210; f. 1955; business, economics, law, sociology, psychology, tax, politics, education, dictionaries; Man. Dir DAVID G. YOUNG.

Magvető Könyvkiadó: 1806 Budapest, POB 123; tel. (1) 235-5032; e-mail magveto@lira.hu; f. 1955; literature; Dir GÉZA MORCSÁNYI.

Medicina Könyvkiadó Rt: 1054 Budapest, Zoltan u. 8; tel. (1) 112-2650; fax (1) 112-2450; f. 1957; books on medicine, sport, tourism; Dir BORBÁLA FARKASVÖLGYI.

Mezőgazda Kiadó: 1165 Budapest, Koronafürt u. 44; tel. (1) 407-6575; fax (1) 407-7571; ecology, natural sciences, environmental protection, food industry; Man. Dr LAJOS LELKES.

Móra Ferenc Ifjúsági Kiadó Rt.: 1134 Budapest, Váci út 19; tel. (1) 320-4740; fax (1) 320-5382; e-mail mora_kiado@elender.hu; f. 1950; youth and children's books; Man. Dr JÁNOS CS. TÓTH.

Műszaki Könyvkiadó: 1033 Budapest III, Szentendre út 89–93; tel. (1) 437-2405; fax (1) 437-2404; e-mail lakatosz@muszakikiado.hu; internet www.muszakikiado.hu; f. 1955; scientific and technical, vocational and general text books; Man. SÁNDOR BÉRCZI.

Nemzeti Tankönyvkiadó Rt. (National Textbook Publishing House): 1143 Budapest, Szobránc u. 6-8; tel. (1) 460-1800; fax (1) 460-1869; e-mail public@ntk.hu; internet www.ntk.hu; f. 1949; school and university textbooks, pedagogical literature and language books; Man. ISTVÁN ÁBRAHÁM.

Népszava Lapés Könyvkiadó Vállalat: 1553 Budapest, Rákóczi u. 54; tel. (1) 122-4810; National Confederation of Hungarian Trade Unions; Man. Dr JENŐ KISS.

Statiqum Kiadó és Nyomda Kft: 1033 Budapest, Kaszásdülő u. 2; tel. (1) 250-0311; fax (1) 168-8635; f. 1991; publications on statistics, system-management and computer science; Dir BENEDEK BELECZ.

Szépirodalmi Könyvkiadó: Budapest; tel. (1) 122-1285; f. 1950; modern and classical Magyar literature; Man. SÁNDOR Z. SZALAI.

Zrinyi Kiadó: 1087 Budapest, Kerepesi u. 29B; tel. (1) 133-9165; military literature; Man. MÁTÉ ESZES.

CARTOGRAPHERS

Cartographia—Hungarian Company for Mapping: 1590 Budapest, POB 80; tel. (1) 363-3639; fax (1) 363-4639; f. 1954; Dir Dr ÁRPÁD PAPP-VÁRY.

Department of Lands and Mapping (Földügyi és Térképészeti Főosztály): 1055 Budapest, Kossuth Lajos tér 11; tel. (1) 331-3736; fax (1) 301-4691; e-mail laszlo.niklasz@fvm.hu; f. 1967; Gen. Man. GÉZA APAGYI.

PUBLISHERS' ASSOCIATION

Hungarian Publishers' and Booksellers' Association (Magyar Könyvkiadók és Könyvterjesztők Egyesülése): Budapest; tel. (1) 343-2540; fax (1) 343-2541; e-mail mkke@mkke.hu; f. 1795; most leading Hungarian publishers are members of the Association; Pres. ISTVÁN BART; Sec.-Gen. PÉTER ZENTAI.

WRITERS' UNION

Association of Hungarian Writers (Magyar Írószövetség): 1062 Budapest, Bajza u. 18; tel. (1) 322-8840; f. 1945; Pres. BÉLA POMOGÁTS.

Broadcasting and Communications

TELECOMMUNICATIONS

Matáv: 1541 Budapest, Krisztina Krt 6–8; tel. (1) 212-2872; fax (1) 201-1201; telecommunications co; f. 1991; 59% owned by Deutsche Telekom (Germany); Chief Exec. EMIL TOMKA.

RADIO

Hungarian Radio (Magyar Rádió): 1800 Budapest, Bródy Sándor u. 5–7; tel. (1) 328-8388; fax (1) 328-7004; internet www.radio.hu; f. 1924; stations: Radio Kossuth, Radio Petőfi, Radio Bartók (mainly classical music); 8 regional studios; external broadcasts in English, German, Hungarian, Romanian, Russian, Slovak and Serbo-Croat; Pres. ISTVÁN SZIJARTO (acting).

Radio C: Budapest; f. 2001; Roma radio station; Man. GYÖRGY KERENYI.

Radio Danubius: f. 1986; privatized 1998; broadcasts news, music and information in Hungarian 24 hours a day; transmitting stations in Budapest, Lake Balaton region, Sopron, Szeged and Debrecen; Dir JÓZSEF LÁSZLÓ.

TELEVISION

Hungarian Television (Magyar Televízió): 1810 Budapest, Szabadság tér 17; tel. (1) 353-3200; fax (1) 373-4133; e-mail mtvintrel@intrel.mtv.hu; internet www.mtv.hu; f. 1957; first channel, MTV 1, terrestrial, broadcasts 19 hours a day and the second channel, MTV 2, satellite, 24 hours a day, colour transmissions; 100 high-capacity relay stations; Pres. Dr LÁSZLÓ ZSOLT SZABÓ.

Finance

(cap. = capital; res = reserves; dep. = deposits; m. = million; amounts in forint, unless otherwise stated)

Under economic reforms, introduced in 1987, three banks were established to assume the commercial banking activities of the National Bank of Hungary: the Hungarian Credit Bank, the Commercial and Credit Bank and the Budapest Bank. The already existing Hungarian Foreign Trade Bank and the National Savings and Commercial Bank also became fully chartered financial institutions. In 1998 there were seven large commercial banks, the other two being the Central European International Bank (which until 1997 operated as an 'offshore' bank) and the Post Bank and Savings Bank Corporation; all of these institutions (with the exception of the Post Bank) were in private ownership. At the end of 1998 there were a total of 36 commercial banks, of which 28 were foreign- or jointly-owned banks, and an additional seven specialized financial institutions. There were also 241 savings co-operatives.

Responsibility for bank supervision is divided between the National Bank of Hungary and the State Banking Supervision Agency. Under new legislation, introduced in January 1997, the supervision of the banking system was reorganized, and the supervisory responsibilities of the National Bank were restricted to areas relating to the operation of monetary policy and the foreign exchange system.

BANKING

Central Bank

National Bank of Hungary (Magyar Nemzeti Bank): 1850 Budapest, Szabadság tér 8–9; tel. (1) 302-3000; fax (1) 332-3913; internet www.mnb.hu; f. 1924; cap. 10,000m., res 56,216m., dep. 1,970,965m.

(Dec. 1999); issue of banknotes; transacts international payments business; supervises banking system; Pres. ZSIGMOND JÁRAI; 23 brs.

Commercial Banks

ABN Amro (Magyar) Bank RT: 1133 Budapest, Pozsonyi út 77-79; tel. (1) 465-7200; fax (1) 359-0250; f. 1987 as Magyar Hitel Bank RT; name changed in 1997; cap. 33,053m., res 1,825m., dep. 294,424m. (Dec. 1998); Chief Exec. C. MICHIEL HELFRICH.

Bank Austria Creditanstalt Hungary RT: 1054 Budapest, Akadémia u. 17; tel. (1) 269-0812; fax (1) 353-4959; f. 1990; cap. 6,828m., res 5,462m., dep. 192,253m. (Dec. 1998); Chair. Dr ALARICH FENYVES; Chief Exec. Dr MATTHIAS KUNSCH.

Bank of Hungarian Savings Co-operatives Ltd (Magyar Takarékszövetkezeti Bank Rt): 1122 Budapest, Pethényi köz 10; 1064 Budapest, POB 62; tel. (1) 202-3777; fax (1) 356-2649; e-mail mtblcsf@matavnet.hu; f. 1989; cap. 4,237m., res 212m., dep. 88,700m. (1998); Pres. Dr FRIEDBERT MALT; Gen. Man. Dr ZSOLT HERNÁDI.

BNP Paribas Bank (Hungaria) RT: 1055 Budapest, Honvéd utca 20; tel. (1) 374-6300; fax (1) 269-3967; f. 1991; cap. 3,500m., res 2,329m., dep. 58,153m. (Dec. 1999); Chair. Dr HANS-JÜRGEN HAAS-WITTMÜSS; Gen. Man. GUY ROSA.

Budapest Bank Ltd: 1054 Budapest, Honvèd u. 10; tel. (1) 328-1700; fax (1) 269-2417; e-mail info@bbrt.hu; internet www.bbrt.hu; f. 1987; cap. 19,337m., res 5,189m., dep. 246,680m. (Dec. 1999); privatized in 1995; Chief Exec. RICHARD PELLY; 75 brs.

Central-European International Bank Ltd (CIB): 1027 Budapest, Medve út. 4–14, POB 394; tel. (1) 212-1330; fax (1) 212-4200; e-mail cib@cib.hu; internet www.cib.hu; f. 1979; merged with CIB Hungária Bank Rt in 1998; cap. 23,500m., res 11,298m., dep. 372,937m. (Dec. 1999); Chair. LUIGI VERCELLINI; Pres. and Chief Exec. GYÖRGY ZDEBORSKY.

Citibank Rt: 1051 Budapest, Szabadság tér 7, Bank Center, Citibank Tower; tel. (1) 374-5000; fax (1) 374-5100; internet www.citibank.hu; f. 1985; merged with Europai Kereskedelmi Bank RT in 1999; cap. 13,004.6m., res 4,786m., dep. 165,739m. (Dec. 1999); Chief Exec. and Gen. Man. MARK T. ROBINSON.

Commercial and Credit Bank Ltd (Kereskedelmiés Hitelbank Rt): 1051 Budapest, Vigadó tér 1; tel. (1) 328-9000; fax (1) 328-9696; e-mail khbinfo@khb.hu; internet www.khb.hu; f. 1986; cap. 25,756m., res 2,546m., dep. 501,530m. (Dec. 1999); Chair. Dr ISTVÁN SZALKAI; 123 brs.

Commerzbank (Budapest) Rt: 1054 Budapest, Széchenyi rkp. 8, POB 1070; tel. (1) 374-8100; fax (1) 269-4530; e-mail commerzbank@commerzbank.hu; f. 1993; cap. 2,466.9m., res 5,856.1m., dep. 113,034.0m. (Dec. 1998); Chair. of Sup. Bd ANDREAS DE MAIZIÈRE; Chief Exec. and Man. Dir HANS VON ROSENBERG LIPINSKY.

Erste Bank Hungary Rt: 1054 Budapest, Hold u. 16; tel. (1) 373-2400; fax (1) 373-2499; internet www.erstebank.hu; f. 1987 as Mezobank Rt; name changed 1998; cap. 7,237m., dep. 150,889m. (Dec. 1999); Chair. REINHARD ORTNER; 55 brs.

European Commercial Bank Ltd (Európai Kereskedelmi Bank Rt—EKB): 1056 Budapest, Váci út 81; tel. (1) 328-4800; fax (1) 328-4801; e-mail szentmiklossy@ekb.hu; internet www.ekb.hu; f. 1990; cap. 3,262m. (Dec. 1996); Chair. and Chief Exec. ANDRÁS FELKAI; 6 brs.

General Banking and Trust Co. Ltd (Általános Értékforgalmi Bank Rt): 1055 Budapest, Marko u. 9; tel. (1) 269-1473; fax (1) 269-1442; e-mail esebok@gbt.hu; internet www.gbt.hu; f. 1922; 50% share owned by Gazprom Bank (Russia); cap. 76.9m., res 24.3m., dep. 699.1m. (Dec. 1999); Chair. MEGDET RAHIMKULOV; 11 brs.

Hungarian Credit Bank Ltd (ABN AMRO—Magyar—Bank Rt): 1853 Budapest, Szabadság tér 5–6; tel. (1) 269-2122; fax (1) 269-2245; f. 1987; cap. 14,000m. (Dec. 1991); activities include venture financing, securities trading, real estate investments; 89 brs; privatized in 1996; Chair. and Chief Exec. Dr ISTVÁN TÖRÖCSKEI; 89 brs.

Hungarian Development Bank Ltd: 1051 Budapest, Nador u. 31; tel. (1) 428-1400; fax (1) 428-1490; e-mail bank@mfb.hu; internet www.mfb.hu; f. 1991 as an investment company; cap. 25,980.0m., res 24,389.6m., dep. 115,580m. (Dec. 1999); Chair. Dr PÉTER PATONAI.

Hungarian Foreign Trade Bank Ltd (Magyar Külkereskedelmi Bank Rt): 1056 Budapest, V. Vaci u. 38; tel. (1) 269-0922; fax (1) 269-0959; e-mail exterbank@mkb.hu; internet www.mkb.hu; f. 1950; commercial banking; 85.0% owned by the Bayerische Landesbank Girozentrale; cap. 11,520m., res 45,523m., dep. 516,601m. (Dec. 1999); 29 brs; Chair. and Chief Exec. TAMÁS ERDEI.

HYPO Vereinsbank Hungária Rt: 1065 Budapest, Nagymezö u. 44; tel. (1) 301-5100; fax (1) 269-0398; e-mail gcsaki@mail.hypo.de; internet www.hypovereinsbank.hu; f. 1993; dep. 64,111m. (Dec. 1998); Chief Exec. Dr GÜNTHER ÖPPITZ.

ING Bank Rt: 1061 Budapest, Andrássy út 9; tel. (1) 235-8700; fax (1) 322-2288; f. 1992 as NMB Bank; owned by ING Bank NV (Amsterdam); cap. 15,758m., res 5,281m., dep. 134,648m. (Dec. 1998); Man. Dir RANDOLPH S. KOPPA.

Inter-Európa Bank Ltd: 1054 Budapest, Szabadság tér 15, POB 65; tel. (1) 373-6000; fax (1) 269-2526; e-mail ieb@ieb.hu; internet www.ieb.hu; f. 1981 as INTERINVEST; associated mem. of San Paolo Group; cap. 6,608.6m., res 2,233.8m., dep. 93,336.5m. (Dec. 1999); Chair. Dr PÉTER MEDGYESSY; Man. Dir EZIO SALVAI; 18 brs.

Konzumbank RT: 1054 Budapest, Tüköry u. 4, POB 300; tel. (1) 374-7300; fax (1) 374-7355; e-mail info@konzumbank.hu; internet www.konzumbank.hu; f. 1986; cap. 5,031m., res 2,273m., dep. 52,329m. (Dec. 1999); Chair. LÁSZLÓ BARANYAI.

National Savings and Commercial Bank Ltd—NSB Ltd (Országos Takarékpénztár és Kereskedelmi Bank Rt—OTP Rt): 1051 Budapest, Nádor u. 16; tel. (1) 353-1444; fax (1) 312-6858; f. 1949; cap. 28,000m., res 80,196m., dep. 1,573,744m. (Dec. 1999); savings deposits, credits, foreign transactions; privatized in late 1996; 380 brs; Chair. and Chief Exec. Dr SÁNDOR CSÁNYI; 380 brs.

Post Bank and Savings Bank Corporation (Postabank és Takarékpénztár Rt): 1132 Budapest, Váci út 48; tel. (1) 318-0855; fax (1) 317-1369; e-mail info@postabank.hu; internet www.postabank.hu; f. 1988; state-owned; cap. 20,021m., res 20,165m., dep. 248,090m. (Dec. 1998); Chair. LÁSZLÓ MADARASZ; 63 brs.

Raiffeisen Bank Rt: 1054 Budapest, Akademia u. 6, POB 173; tel. (1) 484-4100; fax (1) 484-4444; e-mail info@raiffeisen.hu; internet www.raiffeisen.hu; f. 1986 as Unicbank Rt; name changed in 1999; cap. 10,564.8m., res 6,449.9m., dep. 190,035.6m. (Dec. 1999); Man. Dir Dr PÉTER FELCSUTI; 30 brs.

Specialized Financial Institutions

Hungarian Export-Import Bank Ltd (Magyar Export-Import Bank Rt): 1065 Budapest, Nagymezö u. 46-48; tel. (1) 269-0580; fax (1) 269-4476; e-mail eximh@eximbank.hu; internet www.eximbank.hu; cap. 7,100m., res 400m., dep. 55,605m. (Dec. 1999); Pres. Dr KÁLMÁN MIZSEI; Gen. Man. Dr IVÁN NYÍRI.

Kvantum Investment Bank Ltd: 1117 Budapest, Budafoki út 79; tel. (1) 464-4085; fax (1) 161-3457; Pres. JÁNOS ERÖS; Gen. Man. LÁSZLÓ HAÁS.

Merkantil Bank Ltd: 1051 Budapest, József Attila u. 24; tel. (1) 118-2688; fax (1) 117-2331; f. 1988; affiliated to Commercial and Creditbank Ltd; cap. 1,100m.; Chair. and Chief Exec. ÁDÁM KOLOSSVÁRY.

Opel Bank Hungary: 1027 Budapest, Kapás u. 11-15; tel. (1) 457-9110; Gen. Man. JARI ARJAVALTA.

Porsche Bank Hungaria AG.: 1139 Budapest, Fay u. 27; tel. (1) 465-4701; fax (1) 465-4711; e-mail r.walker@porschebank.hu; Pres. PÁL ANTALL.

Rákóczi Regional Development Bank Ltd (Rákóczi Regionális Fejlesztési Bank Rt): 3530 Miskolc, Mindszent tér 1; tel. (46) 510-300; fax (46) 510-396; e-mail central@rakoczibank.hu; internet www.rakoczibank.hu; f. 1992; Gen. Man. KORNÉL KOSZTICZA.

Other Financial Institution

Central Corporation of Banking Companies (Pénzintézeti Központ): 1093 Budapest, Lónyay u. 38; tel. (1) 117-1255; fax (1) 215-9963; f. 1916; banking, property, rights and interests, deposits, securities, and foreign exchange management; cap. 11,127m., res 3,548m., dep. 12,289m.; Chair. and Chief Exec. PÉTER KIRÁLY; 3 brs.

STOCK EXCHANGE

Budapest Stock Exchange (Budapesti Értéktőzsde): 1052 Budapest, Deák Ferenc u. 5; tel. (1) 429-6700; fax (1) 429-6800; e-mail info@bse.hu; internet www.bse.hu; Pres. ANDRÁS SIMOR; Chief Exec. MÁRIA DUNAVÖLGYI.

COMMODITY EXCHANGE

Budapest Commodity Exchange (Budapesti Árutőzsde): 1134 Budapest, Róbert Károly krt. 61–65; tel. (1) 465-6979; fax (1) 465-6981; e-mail bce@bce-bat.com; internet www.bce-bat.com; Chair. ATTILA KOVÁCS.

INSURANCE

In July 1986 the state insurance enterprise was divided into two companies, one of which retained the name of the former Állami Biztosító. By 1995 13 insurance companies had been established.

Atlasz Travel Insurance Company (Atlasz Utazási Biztosító): 1052 Budapest, Deák F. u. 23; tel. (1) 118-1999; fax (1) 117-1529; f. 1988; cap. 1,000m.; Gen. Man. GÁBOR DARVAS.

Garancia Insurance Company (Garancia Biztosító Rt): 1054 Budapest, Vadász u. 12; tel. (1) 269-2533; fax (1) 269-2549; f. 1988; cap. 4,050m.; Gen. Man. and Chief Exec. Dr ZOLTÁN NAGY; 25 brs.

Hungária Insurance Company (Hungária Biztosító Rt): 1054 Budapest, Bajcsy u. 52; tel. (1) 301-6565; fax (1) 301-6100; f. 1986; handles international insurance, industrial and commercial insurance and motor-car, marine, life, household, accident and liability insurance; cap. 4,266m.; Chair. and Chief Exec. Dr MIHÁLY PATAI.

Insurance Company (AB-AEGON Általános Biztosító Rt): 1091 Budapest, Üllői St 1; tel. (1) 218-1866; fax (1) 217-7065; f. 1949 as Állami Biztosító, reorganized 1986, present name since 1992; handles pensions, life and property insurance, insurance of agricultural plants, co-operatives, foreign insurance, etc.; Gen. Man. Dr GÁBOR KEPECS.

Trade and Industry

GOVERNMENT AGENCY

Hungarian Privatization and State Holding Company (ÁPV Rt): 1133 Budapest, Pozsonyi út 56; tel. (1) 237-4400; fax (1) 237-4100; e-mail apvrt@apvrt.hu; f. 1995 by merger of the State Property Agency and the State Holding Company; Chair. GYULA GANSPERGER.

NATIONAL CHAMBERS OF COMMERCE AND AGRICULTURE

Hungarian Chamber of Agriculture (Magyar Agrárkamara): 1036 Budapest, Lajos u. 160-162; tel. (1) 368-6890; fax (1) 250-5138; e-mail agota@kozpont.agrarkamara.hu; Pres. MIKLÓS CSIKAI.

Hungarian Chamber of Commerce and Industry (Magyar Kereskedelmi és Iparkamara): 1372 Budapest V, POB 452; tel. (1) 368-6890; fax (1) 250-5138; e-mail mkik@mail.mkik.hu; f. 1850; central organization of the 20 Hungarian county chambers of commerce and industry; based on a system of compulsory membership; over 400,000 mems. Pres. Dr LAJOS TOLNAY; Sec.-Gen. PÉTER DUNAI.

REGIONAL CHAMBERS OF COMMERCE

Bács-Kiskun County Chamber of Commerce: 6000 Kecskemét, Árpád krt 4, POB 228; tel. (76) 501-500; fax (76) 501-538; e-mail bkmkik@mail.datanet.hu; internet www.tradehu.com; f. 1994; Chair. JÓZSEF GAÁL; Sec. LÁSZLÓ LEITNER.

Békés County Chamber of Commerce and Industry: 5600 Békéscsaba, Penza ltp. 5; tel. (66) 451-775; fax (66) 324-976; e-mail bmkik@elender.hu; internet www.bmkik.ini.hu; Chair. TAMÁS HÓDSÁGI; Sec. ZSOLT TÓTH.

Borsod-Abaúj-Zemplén County Chamber of Commerce and Industry (Borsod-Abaúj-Zemplén Kereskedelmi és Iparkamara): 3525Miskolc, Szentpáli u. 1; tel. (46) 328-539; fax (46) 328-722; e-mail bokik@mail.bokik.hu; internet www.bokik.hu; f. 1990; membership of 1,100 cos; Pres. TAMÁS BIHALL; Sec. ANNA BAÁN-SZILÀGYI.

Budapest Chamber of Industry and Commerce (Budapesti Kereskedelmi és Iparkamara): 1016 Budapest, Krisztina krt. 99; tel. (1) 488-2173; fax (1) 488-2180; e-mail nemzetkozi@bkik.hu; internet www.bkik.hu; f. 1850; Chair. LÁSZLÓ KOJI; Sec.-Gen. PÉTER RÉVÉSZ.

Csongrád County Chamber of Commerce and Industry : 6721 Szeged, Tisza L. krt. 2–4; tel. (62) 423-451; fax (62) 426-149; e-mail csmkik@tiszanet.hu; internet www.tiszanet.hu/kamara; Chair. ISTVÁN SZERI; Sec. LAJOS HORVÁTH.

Fejér County Chamber of Commerce and Industry (Fejér Megyei Kereskedelmi és Iparkamara): 8000 Székesfehérvár, Petőfi u. 5; tel. (22) 327-627; fax (22) 510-312; Chair. JENŐ RADETZKY; Sec.-Gen. Dr MIKLÓS SISKA.

Győr-Moson-Sopron County Chamber of Commerce and Industry: 9001 Győr, Király u. 20; tel. (96) 318-485; fax (96) 319-650; Chair. PÉTER JANCSÓ; Dir JÓZSEF VÁPÁR.

Hajdú-Bihar County Chamber of Commerce and Industry: 4025 Debrecen, Petőfi tér 10; tel. (52) 500-721; fax (52) 500-720; Chair. FERENC MIKLÓSSY; Sec. Dr EVA SKULTÉTI.

Heves County Chamber of Commerce and Industry: 3300 Eger, Deák F. út 51; tel. (36) 429-612; fax (36) 312-989; Chair. JÓZSEF GYETVAI; Sec.-Gen. GÁBOR FÜLÖP.

Jász-Nagykun-Szolnok County Chamber of Commerce and Industry: 5000 Szolnok, Verseghy Park 8; tel. (56) 510-610; fax (56) 370-005; e-mail kamara@jnszmkik.hu; internet www.jnszmkik.hu; Chair. Dr ANDRÁS SZIRÁKI; Sec. Dr IMRE KERÉKGYÁRTÓ.

Komárom-Esztergom County Chamber of Commerce and Industry: 2800 Tatabánya, Előd vezér u. 17; tel. (34) 316-259; fax (34) 316-259; Chair. Dr ISTVÁN HORVÁTH; Sec. ZOLTÁN BÁTOR.

Nógrád County Chamber of Commerce and Industry: 3100 Salgótarján, Alkotmàny u. 9A; tel. (32) 520-860; fax (32) 520-862; e-mail nklk@nklk.hu; internet www.ccinograd.com; Chair. FODOR ERZSÉBET KOVÁCS; Sec. Dr ERZSÉBET KURUCZ.

Pécs-Baranya County Chamber of Commerce and Industry: 7625 Pécs, Dr Majorossy I. u. 36; tel. (72) 211-592; fax (72) 211-604; Chair. GYULA HIGI; Sec. TAMÁS SÍKFŐI.

Pest County Chamber of Commerce and Industry (Pest Megyei Kereskedelmi és Iparkamara): 1056 Budapest, Vàci u. 40; tel. (1)

317-7666; fax (1) 317-7755; e-mail titkarsag@pmkik.hu; internet www.pmkik.hu; Chair. Dr ZOLTÁN VERECZKEY; Sec.-Gen. Dr LAJOS KUPCSOK.

Somogy County Chamber of Commerce (Somogyi Kereskedelmi és Iparkamara): 7400 Kaposvár, Anna u. 6; tel. (82) 501-000; fax (82) 319-428; e-mail skik@skik.hu; internet www.sominfo.hu/skik; Chair. JÓZSEF VARGA; Dep. Pres. LAJOS HORVÁTH.

Szabolcs-Szatmár-Bereg County Chamber of Commerce and Industry: 4400 Nyíregyháza, Szarvas u. 1–3; tel. (42) 416-074; fax (42) 311-750; Chair. Dr JÁNOS VERES; Sec. Dr IMRE JAKAB.

Tolna County Chamber of Commerce and Industry: 7100 Szekszárd, Arany J. u. 23–25; tel. (74) 411-661; fax (74) 411-456; e-mail rostasrostas@tmkik.hu; Chair. Dr KÁLMÁN BERTHA; Sec. ILONA ROSTAS.

Vas County Chamber of Commerce and Industry (Vas Megyei Kereskedelmi és Iparkamara): 9700 Szombathely, Honvéd tér 2; tel. (94) 312-356; fax (94) 316-936; e-mail vmkik@vmkik.hu; internet www.vmkik.hu; Chair. VINCE KOVÁCS; Sec.-Gen. SÁNDOR KISS.

Veszprém County Chamber of Commerce and Industry: 8200 Veszprém, Budapest út 3; tel. (88) 429-008; fax (88) 412-150; e-mail vkik@infornax.hu; Chair. KÁROLY HENGER; Dir TAMÁS CSABAI.

Zala County Chamber of Commerce and Industry (Zalai Kereskedelmi és Iparkamara): 8900 Zalaegerszeg, Petőfi u. 24; tel. (92) 550-510; fax (92) 550-525; e-mail zmkik@zmkik.hu; Chair. IMRE FARKAS; Sec.-Gen. ISTVÁN TÓTH.

INDUSTRIAL AND TRADE ASSOCIATIONS

HUNICOOP Foreign Trade Company Ltd for Industrial Co-operation: 1367 Budapest 5, POB 111; tel. (1) 267-1477; fax (1) 267-1482; agency for foreign companies in Hungary, export and import.

Interco-operation Co Ltd for Trade Promotion: 1085 Budapest, POB 136; tel. (1) 118-9966; fax (1) 118-2161; establishment and carrying out of co-operation agreements, representation of foreign companies, brands, marketing and distribution, joint ventures and import-export deals.

Hungarian Industrial Association (Magyar Iparszövetség—OKISz): 1146 Budapest, Thököly u. 58–60; tel. (1) 343-5570; fax (1) 343-5521; e-mail okisz@okiszinfo.hu; internet www.okiszinfo.hu; safeguards interests of over 2,000 member enterprises (all private); Pres. LÁSZLÓ HÖRÖMPÖLY.

National Co-operative Council (Országos Szövetkezeti Tanács—OSzT): 1054 Budapest, Szabadság tér 14; tel. (1) 312-7467; fax (1) 311-3647; f. 1968; Pres. TAMÁS FARKAS; Sec. Dr JÓZSEF PÁL.

National Federation of Agricultural Co-operators and Producers (Mezőgazdasági Szövetkezők és Termelők Országos Szövetsege—MOSZ): 1054 Budapest, Akadémia u. 1–3; tel. and fax (1) 353-2552; e-mail mosz@mail.tvnet.hu; internet www.msztorz.hu; f. 1990; frmly Termelő szövetkezetek Országos Tanácsa (TOT) (National Council of Agricultural Co-operatives); Pres. TAMÁS NAGY; Sec.-Gen. GÁBOR HORVÁTH; est. 1,300 mem. orgs.

National Federation of Consumer Co-operatives (Általános Fogyasztási Szövetkezetek Országos Szövetsége—ÁFEOSz): 1054 Budapest, Szabadság tér 14; tel. (1) 153-4222; fax (1) 111-3647; safeguards interests of Hungarian consumer co-operative societies; organizes co-operative wholesale activities; Pres. Dr PÁL BARTUS; 800,000 mems.

UTILITIES
Electricity

Hungarian Energy Office: 1081 Budapest, Köztársaság tér 7; tel. (1) 317-4089; fax (1) 317-1330; e-mail hivatal.energia@eh .ikm.x400gw.itb.hu; f. 1994; regulation and supervision of activities performed by gas and electricity companies, price regulation and protection of consumer interest; Pres. GYÖRGY HATVANI.

Hungarian Power Companies Ltd (Magyar Villamos Müvek Rt—MVM Rt): 1255 Budapest, POB 77; 1011 Budapest, Vám u. 5–7; tel. (1) 201-5455; fax (1) 202-1246; Hungarian national electricity wholesaler and power-system controller; all 6 distributors and 6 (of 8) power-plant companies privatized in 1995–97; Chair. GYULA LENGYEL.

National Power Grid Company Ltd: 1054 Budapest, Szabadsajto út 5.

Paks Nuclear Plant Ltd (Paksi Atomeromu v Pav): 7031 Paks, POB 71; tel. (75) 311222; fax (75) 355-1332; internet www.npp.hu; f. 1992; electrical energy production; Plant Man. SÁNDOR NAGY; 2,800 employees.

Gas

Degaz—Delalfoldi Gazszolgaltato Rezvenytarsasag: 6724 Szeged, Pulcz u. 44; tel. (62) 472-572; fax (63) 324-943; public gas supply and services; 1,327 employees.

Hungarian Oil and Gas Company Ltd (MOL—Magyar Olaj és Gáziparirt Rt): 1117 Budapest, Október huszonharmadika u. 18; tel. (1) 209-0000; fax (1) 209-0005; e-mail webmaster@mol.hu; internet www.mol.hu; f. 1991 by merger of part of the National Oil and Gas Trust and a technical development co; privatized in 1995, with the state retaining a 25% stake; 19,648 employees; Chair. (vacant); Chief Exec. GYÖRGY MOSONYI.

TRADE UNIONS

Since 1988, and particularly after the restructuring of the former Central Council of Hungarian Trade Unions (SzOT) as the National Confederation of Hungarian Trade Unions (MSzOSz) in 1990, several new union federations have been created. Several unions are affiliated to more than one federation, and others are completely independent.

Trade Union Federations

Association of Hungarian Free Trade Unions (Magyar Szabad Szakszervezetek Szövetsége): Budapest; f. 1994; 200,000 mems.

Autonomous Trade Union Confederation (Autonóm Szakszervezetek Svövetsége): 1068 Budapest, Benczúr út 45; tel. (1) 342-1776; Pres. LAJOS FŐCZE.

Principal affiliated unions include:

Federation of Hungarian Chemical Industry Workers' Unions (Magyar Vegyipari Dolgozók Szakszervezeti Szövetsége): 1068 Budapest, Benczúr út 45; tel. (1) 342-1778; fax (1) 342-9978; f. 1906; Pres. LAJOS FŐCZE; 42,000 mems.

Democratic Confederation of Free Trade Unions (Függelten Szakszervezetek Demokratikus Ligája—FSzDL): 1146 Budapest, Thököly út 156; tel. (1) 251-2300; fax (1) 251-2288; e-mail liga@telnet.hu; f. 1988; Pres. ISTVÁN GASKÓ; 98,000 mems.

Principal affiliated unions include:

Democratic Trade Union of Scientific Workers (Tudományos Dolgozók Demokratikus Szakszervezete—TDDSz): 1068 Budapest, Városligeti fasor 38; tel. (1) 142-8438; f. 1988; Chair. PÁL FORGACS.

Federation of Unions of Intellectual Workers (Értelmiségi Szakszervezeti Tömörülés—ÉSzT): 1068 Budapest, Városligeti fasor 10; tel. (1) 122-8456; Pres. Dr LÁSZLÓ KIS; Gen. Sec. Dr GÁBOR BÁNK.

Forum for the Co-operation of Trade Unions (Szakszervezetek Együttmüködési Fóruma—SzEF): 1068 Budapest VIII, Puskin u. 4; tel. (1) 138-2651; fax (1) 118-7360; f. 1990; Pres. Dr ENDRE SZABÓ.

Principal affiliated unions include:

Federation of Hungarian Public Service Employees' Unions (Közszolgálati Szakszervezetek Szövetsége): 1081 Budapest, Kiss Jozsef u. 8 II em; tel. (1) 313-5436; fax (1) 133-7223; f. 1945; Pres. PÉTER MICHALKO; Vice-Pres. Dr JUDIT BÁRDOS, Dr CSILLA NOVÁK.

National Confederation of Hungarian Trade Unions (Magyar Szakszervezetek Országos Szövetsége—MSzOSz): 1415 Budapest, VI. Dózsa György út 84B; tel. (1) 352-1815; fax (1) 342-1799; f. 1898, reorganized 1990; Pres. Dr LÁSZLÓ SÁNDOR; Dep. Pres. FERENC RABI; 405,000 mems in 41 mem. orgs.

Principal affiliated unions include:

Commercial Employees' Trade Union (Kereskedelmi Alkalmazottak Szakszervezete): 1066 Budapest, Jókai u. 6; tel. (1) 131-8970; fax (1) 132-3382; f. 1900; Pres. Dr JÓZSEF SÁLING; 160,000 mems.

Confederation of Iron and Metallurgical Industry Workers' Unions (Vas- és Fémipari Dolgozók Szakszervezeti Szövetsége): 1086 Budapest, Magdolna u. 5–7; tel. (1) 210-0130; fax (1) 333-8327; e-mail vasasszaksz@mail.datanet.hu; f. 1877; Pres. KÁROLY SZŐKE; 135,000 mems.

Federation of Agricultural, Forestry and Water Supply Workers' Unions (Mezőgazdasági, Erdészeti és Vizügyi Dolgozók Szakszervezeti Szövetsége—MEDOSZ): 1066 Budapest, Jókai u. 2; tel. (1) 301-9050; fax (1) 331-4568; e-mail medosz.mat@matavnet.hu; f. 1906; Pres. (vacant); Gen. Sec. Dr ANDRÁS BERECZKY; 16,086 mems.

Federation of Building, Wood and Building Industry Workers' Unions (Épitő-, Fa-és Épitőanyagipari Dolgozók Szakszervezeteinek Szövetsége): Budapest; tel. (1) 122-9426; fax (1) 142-4395; f. 1906; Pres. JÁNOS NAGYMIHALY; Vice-Pres. ANTAL MIHALUSZ; 140,000 mems.

Federation of Chemical Workers' Unions of Hungary, Confederation Founding Section (Magyar Vegyipari Dolgozók Szakszervezeti Szövetsége, össz-szövetségi alapitó tagozata): Budapest; tel. (1) 342-1778; fax (1) 342-9975; Gen. Sec. GYÖRGY PASZTERNÁK; 12,000 mems.

Federation of Communal Service Workers' Unions (Kommunális Dalgozók Szakszervezete): 1068 Budapest, Benczur u. 43; tel. (1) 111-6950; Gen. Sec. ZSOLT PÉK; 28,000 mems.

Federation of Hungarian Artworkers' Unions (Müvészeti Szakszervezetek Szövetsége): 1068 Budapest, Városligeti fasor 38; tel. (1) 342-8927; fax (1) 342-8372; e-mail eji@mail.datanet.hu; f. 1957; Pres. LÁSZLÓ GYIMESI; 32,000 mems.

Federation of Local Industry and Municipal Workers' Unions (Helyiipari és Városgazdasági Dolgozók Szövetségének): 1068 Budapest, Benczúr u. 43; tel. (1) 111-6950; f. 1952; Pres. JÓZSEFNÉ SVEVER; Gen. Sec. PÁL BAKÁNYI; 281,073 mems.

Federation of Mineworkers' Unions (Bányaipari Dolgozók Szakszervezete): 1068 Budapest, Városligeti fasor 46–48; tel. (1) 322-1226; fax (1) 342-1942; f. 1913; Pres. ANTAL SCHALKHAMMER; Vice-Pres. Dr JÁNOS HORN; 80,000 mems.

Federation of Municipal Industries and Service Workers' Unions (Települési Ipari és Szolgáltatási Dolgozók Szakszervezete): 1068 Budapest, Benczur u. 43; tel. (1) 111-6950; Gen. Sec. ZOLTÁN SZIKSZAI; 20,000 mems.

Federation of Postal and Telecommunications Workers' Unions (Postai és Hirközlési Dolgozók Szakszervezeti Szövetsége): 1146 Budapest, Cházár András u. 13; tel. (1) 142-8777; fax (1) 121-4018; f. 1945; Pres. ENIKŐ HESZKY-GRICSER; 69,900 mems.

Federation of Transport Workers' Unions (Közlekedési Dolgozók Szakszervezeteinek Szövetségé): 1081 Budapest, Köztársaság tér 3; tel. (1) 113-9046; f. 1898; Pres. ISTVÁN TRENKA; 8,000 mems.

Hungarian Federation of Food Industry Workers' Unions (Magyar Élelmezésipari Dolgozók Szakszervezeteinek Szövetsége): 1068 Budapest, Városligeti fasor 44; tel. (1) 122-5880; fax (1) 142-8568; f. 1905; Pres. GYULA SÓKI; Gen. Sec. BÉLA VANEK; 226,243 mems.

Hungarian Graphical Workers' Union (Nyomdaipari Dolgozók Szakszervezete): 1085 Budapest, Kölcsey u. 2; tel. (1) 266-0065; fax (1) 266-0028; f. 1862; Pres. ANDRÁS BÁRSONY; Vice-Pres JÁNOS ACZÉL, EMIL SZELEI; 17,000 mems.

Hungarian Union of Teachers (Magyar Pedagógusok Szakszervezete): 1068 Budapest, Városligeti fasor 10; tel. (1) 122-8456; fax (1) 142-8122; f. 1945; Gen. Sec. ISTVÁNNÉ SZÖLLŐSI; 200,000 mems.

Hungarian Union of Textile Workers (Magyar Textilipari Dolgozók Szakszervezete): 1068 Budapest, Rippl-Rónai u. 2; tel. (1) 428-196; fax (1) 122-5414; f. 1905; Pres. (vacant); Gen. Sec. TAMÁS KELETI; 70,241 mems.

Textile Workers' Union (Textilipari Dolgozók Szakszervezete): 1068 Budapest, Rippl Rónai u. 2; tel. (1) 112-3868; fax (1) 342-8169; Gen. Sec. TAMÁS KELETI; 39,500 mems.

Union of Health Service Workers (Egészségügyben Dolgozók Szakszervezeteinek Szövetsége): 1051 Budapest, Nádor u. 32, POB 36; tel. (1) 110-645; f. 1945; Pres. Dr ZOLTÁN SZABÓ; Gen. Sec. Dr PÁLNÉ KÁLLAY; 280,536 mems.

Union of Leather Industry Workers (Bőripari Dolgozók Szakszervezete): 1062 Budapest, Bajza u. 24; tel. (1) 342-9970; f. 1868; Gen. Sec. TAMÁS LAJTOS; 12,000 mems.

Union of Clothing Workers (Ruházatipari Dolgozók Szakszervezete ()): 1077 Budapest, Almássy tér 2; tel. (1) 342-3702; fax (1) 122-6717; f. 1892; Gen. Sec. TAMÁS WITTICH; 22,000 mems.

Transport

RAILWAYS

In 1991 the total rail network in Hungary amounted to 10,607 km. Some 157m. passengers were carried in 1998. There is an underground railway in Budapest, which had a network of 23 km in 1989; in that year 296m. passengers were carried. Since 1996 PHARE, the EU's programme for the economic reconstruction of Eastern Europe, has financed a number of modernization projects of the rail network.

Hungarian State Railways Ltd (Magyar Államvasutak—MÁV): 1940 Budapest, Andrássy út 73–75; tel. (1) 322-0660; fax (1) 342-8596; f. 1868; transformed into joint-stock co in 1993; total network 7,600 km, including 2,360 km of electrified lines (1998); Pres. GYULA TAKÁCSY; Gen. Dir MÁRTON KUKELY.

Railway of Győr–Sopron–Ebenfurt (Győr–Sopron–Ebenfurti-Vasut—Gysev-RÖeEE): 9400 Sopron, Matyas Kiraly u. 19; Hungarian-Austrian-owned railway; 101 km in Hungary, 65 km in Austria, all electrified; transport of passengers and goods; Dir-Gen. Dr JÁNOS BERÉNYI.

ROADS

At the end of 1998 the road network totalled 188,203 km, including 438 km of motorways, 29,630 km of main or national roads and 23,199 km of secondary roads. There are extensive long-distance bus services. Road passenger and freight transport is provided by the state-owned Volán companies and by individual operators. In

1996 a section of a 42-km motorway was opened between Győr and Hegyeshalom. The road was eventually to extend from Budapest to Vienna (Austria).

Hungarocamion: 1442 Budapest, POB 108; tel. (1) 257-3600; fax (1) 256-6755; international road freight transport company; 17 offices in Europe and the Middle East; fleet of 1,100 units for general and specialized cargo; Gen. Man. GABRIELLA SZAKÁL; 3,800 employees.

Centre of Volán Enterprises (Volán Vállalatok Központja): 1391 Budapest, Erzsébet krt 96, POB 221; tel. (1) 112-4290; centre of 25 Volán enterprises for inland and international road freight and passenger transport, forwarding, tourism; fleet of 17,000 lorries, incl. special tankers for fuel, refrigerators, trailers, 8,000 buses for regular passenger transport; 3 affiliates, offices and joint-ventures in Europe; Head ELEMER SASLICS.

SHIPPING AND INLAND WATERWAYS

At the end of 1994 the Hungarian river merchant fleet comprised 199 vessels, with a capacity totalling 223,718 dwt. At 31 December 1998 the ocean merchant fleet comprised only two vessels, with a combined displacement of 15,285 grt.

Hungarian Shipping Co (MAHART—Magyar Hajózási Rt): 1366 Budapest, POB 58; tel. (1) 118-1880; fax (1) 138-2421; carries passenger traffic on the Danube and Lake Balaton; cargo services on the Danube and its tributaries, Lake Balaton, and also Mediterranean and ocean-going services; operates port of Budapest (container terminal, loading, storage, warehousing, handling and packaging services); ship-building and ship-repair services; Pres. and Dir-Gen. ANDRÁS FÁY.

MAFRACHT International Shipping, Forwarding and Agency Ltd Co: 1364 Budapest 4, POB 105; tel. (1) 266-1208; fax (1) 266-1329; shipping agency.

CIVIL AVIATION

The Ferihegy international airport is 16 km from the centre of Budapest. Ferihegy-2 opened in 1985. In 1999 a new passenger terminal opened. Balatonkiliti airport, near Siófok in western Hungary, reopened to international traffic in 1989. Public internal air services resumed in 1993, after an interval of 20 years, between Budapest and Nyíregyháza, Debrecen, Szeged, Pécs, Szombathely and Győr.

Air Traffic and Airport Administration (Légiforgalmi és Repülőtéri Igazgatóság): 1675 Budapest, POB 53; tel. (1) 291-8722; fax (1) 157-6982; f. 1973; controls civil air traffic and operates Ferihegy and Siófok Airports; Dir-Gen. TAMÁS ERDEI.

General Directorate of Civil Aviation (Légügyi Főigazgatóság): 1400 Budapest, Dob u. 75–81, POB 87; tel. (1) 342-2544; fax (1) 322-2848; controls civil aviation; Dir-Gen. ÖDÖN SKONDA.

Hungarian Airlines (Magyar Légiközlekedési Részvénytársaság—MALÉV Rt): 1051 Budapest, Roosevelt tér 2, POB 122; tel. (1) 235-3535; fax (1) 266-2685; f. 1946; regular services from Budapest to Europe, North Africa, North America, Asia and the Middle East; Pres. FERENC SZARVAS; Chief Exec. FERENC KOVÁCS.

LinAir Hungarian Regional Airlines: 1675 Budapest, POB 53; tel. (1) 296-7092; fax (1) 296-7891; e-mail info@linair.hu; internet www.linair.hu; f. 1994; regional carrier; Man. Dir TAMÁS KOVÁCS.

Tourism

Tourism has developed rapidly and is an important source of foreign exchange. Lake Balaton is the main holiday centre for boating, bathing and fishing. Hungary's cities have great historical and recreational attractions. The annual Budapest Spring Festival is held in March. Budapest has numerous swimming pools watered by thermal springs, which are equipped with modern physiotherapy facilities. Revenue from tourism in 1999 totalled about US $2,500m., a slight decrease from the previous year, owing to the conflict in the neighbouring Federal Republic of Yugoslavia. By 2000 there were already signs of regeneration of the tourist industry. There were 31.1m. foreign visitors in 2000, compared with 28.8m. in 1999.

Association of Hungarian Travel Agencies: 1364 Budapest, POB 267; tel. (1) 318-6866; fax (1) 318-4977; f. 1973; Gen. Sec. CSABO CSÓK.

Hungarian Travel Agency (IBUSZ—Idegenforgalmi, Beszerzési, Utazási és Szállítási Rt): 1364 Budapest, Ferenciek tér 5; tel. (1) 118-6866; fax (1) 117-7723; f. 1902; has 118 brs throughout Hungary; Gen. Man. Dr ERIKA SZEMENKÁR.

Tourinform: 1052 Budapest, Sütö u. 2; tel. (1) 317-9800; fax (1) 317-9656; e-mail tourinform@mail.hungarytourism.hu; internet www.hungarytourism.hu.

Tourism Office of Budapest: 1364 Budapest, POB 215; tel. (1) 266-0479; fax (1) 266-7477; e-mail info@budapestinfo.hu; internet www.budapestinfo.hu; Dir LÁSZLÓ FEKETE.

ICELAND

Introductory Survey

Location, Climate, Language, Religion, Flag, Capital

The Republic of Iceland comprises one large island and numerous smaller ones, situated near the Arctic Circle in the North Atlantic Ocean. The main island lies about 300 km (190 miles) south-east of Greenland, about 1,000 km (620 miles) west of Norway and about 800 km (500 miles) north of Scotland. The Gulf Stream keeps Iceland warmer than might be expected, with average temperatures ranging from 10°C (50°F) in the summer to 1°C (34°F) in winter. Icelandic is the official language. Almost all of the inhabitants profess Christianity: the Evangelical Lutheran Church is the established church and embraces about 88% of the population. The civil flag (proportions 25 by 18) displays a red cross, bordered with white, on a blue background, the upright of the cross being towards the hoist; the state flag (proportions 16 by 9) bears the same design, but has a truncated triangular area cut from the fly. The capital is Reykjavík.

Recent History

Iceland became independent on 17 June 1944, when the Convention that linked it with Denmark, under the Danish crown, was terminated. Iceland became a founder member of the Nordic Council (see p. 237) in 1952, and has belonged to both NATO (see p. 241) and the Council of Europe (see p. 165) since 1949. Membership of the European Free Trade Association (EFTA, see p. 178) was formalized in 1970.

From 1959 to 1971 Iceland was governed by a coalition of the Independence Party (IP) and the Social Democratic Party (SDP). Following the general election of June 1971, Olafur Jóhannesson, the leader of the Progressive Party (PP), formed a coalition Government with the left-wing People's Alliance (PA) and the Union of Liberals and Leftists. At the general election held in June 1974 voters favoured right-wing parties, and in August the IP and the PP formed a coalition Government, led by the IP leader, Geir Hallgrímsson. Failure adequately to address economic difficulties resulted in a decline in the coalition's popularity, however, and prompted the Government's resignation in June 1978, following extensive election gains by the PA and the SDP. Disagreements over economic measures, and over the PA's advocacy of Icelandic withdrawal from NATO, led to two months of negotiations before a new government could be formed. In September Jóhannesson formed a coalition of the PP with the PA and the SDP, but this Government, after addressing immediate economic necessities, resigned in October 1979, when the SDP withdrew from the coalition. An interim administration was formed by Benedikt Gröndal, the SDP leader. The results of a general election, held in December, were inconclusive, and in February 1980 Gunnar Thoroddsen of the IP formed a coalition with the PA and the PP.

In June 1980 Vigdís Finnbogadóttir, a non-political candidate who was favoured by left-wing groups because of her opposition to the US military airbase at Keflavík, achieved a narrow victory in the election for the mainly ceremonial office of President. She took office on 1 August 1980, becoming the world's first popularly-elected female Head of State. The coalition Government lost its majority in the Lower House of the Althingi/Alþingi (Parliament) in September 1982, and a general election took place in April 1983. The IP received the largest share (38.7%) of the votes cast, but two new parties, the Social Democratic Alliance (SDA) and the Women's List (WL), together won almost 13% of the votes cast. A centre-right coalition was formed by the IP and the PP, with Steingrímur Hermannsson (the PP leader and former Minister of Fisheries and Communications) as Prime Minister. In May 1985 the Althingi unanimously approved a resolution declaring the country a 'nuclear-free zone', i.e. banning the entry of nuclear weapons.

A general election for an enlarged, 63-seat Althingi was held in April 1987. Both parties of the outgoing coalition suffered losses: the IP's representation decreased from 24 to 18 seats, and the PP lost one of its 14 seats. The right-wing Citizens' Party (CP, which had been formed only one month earlier by Albert Guðmundsson, following his resignation from the Ministry of Energy and Industry and from the IP) won seven

seats. Ten seats were won by the SDP, which included former members of the SDA (disbanded in 1986). A coalition of the IP, the PP and the SDP was formally constituted in July 1987. Thorsteinn Pálsson, the leader of the IP since November 1983 and the Minister of Finance in the outgoing Cabinet, was appointed Prime Minister.

In June 1988 President Finnbogadóttir (who had begun a second term in office, unopposed, in August 1984) was elected for a third term, receiving more than 90% of the votes cast. This was the first occasion on which an incumbent President seeking re-election had been challenged. In August 1992 the President began a fourth term of office, her candidacy being unopposed.

In September 1988 the SDP and the PP withdrew from the Pálsson Government, following disagreements over economic policy. Later that month, the PP leader, Steingrímur Hermannsson, became Prime Minister in a centre-left coalition with the SDP and the PA. The new Government committed itself to a series of devaluations of the króna, and introduced austerity measures, with the aim of lowering the rate of inflation and stimulating the fishing industry.

Following the resignation of Guðmundsson from the leadership of the CP in January 1989, relations between this party and the left improved, and in September a new Government, based on a coalition agreement between the PP, the SDP, the PA, the CP and the Association for Equality and Social Justice, was formed. Hermannsson, who remained as Prime Minister, affirmed that the new Government would not change its policies, emphasizing the need to reduce inflation and to stimulate economic growth, as well as reiterating an earlier declaration of the Althingi that no nuclear weapons would be located in Iceland.

In March 1991 Davíð Oddsson, the mayor of Reykjavík, successfully challenged Pálsson for the leadership of the IP. At a general election in April the IP emerged as the largest single party, securing 26 seats (with 38.6% of the votes cast), mostly at the expense of the CP. Although the incumbent coalition would have retained an overall majority of seats, the SDP decided to withdraw from the coalition, chiefly as a result of the failure to reach agreement on Iceland's position in the discussions between EFTA and the European Community (EC, now European Union, EU, see p. 181) with regard to the creation of a European Economic Area (EEA, see p. 202). A new coalition Government was formed in late April by the IP and the SDP, with Oddsson as Prime Minister; the new administration promised economic liberalization and a strengthening of links with the USA and Europe (although no application for membership of the EC was envisaged), but was faced with a deteriorating economic situation.

In 1991 Iceland's Constitution was amended, ending the system whereby the Althingi was divided into an Upper House (one-third of the members) and a Lower House.

Although the IP secured the largest number of seats (25, with 37% of the votes cast) at a general election in April 1995, the SDP obtained only seven seats, three fewer than in the previous election. Later in the month a new coalition Government was formed, comprising the IP and the PP, with Oddsson continuing as Prime Minister, and Halldór Ásgrímsson, the leader of the PP, being named Minister of Foreign Affairs. Since both parties in the coalition opposed the Common Fisheries Policy of the EU, it was considered unlikely that Iceland would apply for full membership of the EU in the near future.

Following the decision by Finnbogadóttir not to seek re-election as President in 1996, the principal candidates were Ólafur Ragnar Grímsson, a former leader of the PA (who had previously opposed Iceland's membership of NATO), Pétur Hafstein, a justice in the Supreme Court, and Guðrún Agnarsdóttir of the WL. In the election, held on 29 June 1996, Grímsson secured 41% of the votes cast, while Hafstein won 29% and Agnarsdóttir gained 26%. Grímsson duly took office as President in August. He began a second term of office in August 2000, his candidacy being unopposed.

At a general election held on 8 May 1999 the IP obtained the largest share of the votes cast (40.7%) and won 26 seats, thereby remaining the party with the largest representation in the

Althingi. An electoral grouping entitled The Alliance, which was composed of the PA, the SDP, the People's Movement and the WL, received 26.8% of the votes and won 17 seats, while the PP won 18.4% (12 seats). Two new parties also secured seats in the Althingi: the Left-Green Movement, established by three former PA deputies, obtained 9.1% of the votes cast (six seats), while the Liberal Party, founded by the former IP minister Sverrir Hermannsson, won 4.2% (two seats). A new coalition Government, which, once again, comprised the IP and the PP, and which continued to be led by Oddsson, took office at the end of the month.

The importance of fishing to Iceland's economy, and fears of excessive exploitation of the fishing grounds near Iceland by foreign fleets, caused the Icelandic Government to extend its territorial waters to 12 nautical miles (22 km) in 1964 and to 50 nautical miles (93 km) in 1972. British opposition to these extensions resulted in two 'cod wars'. In October 1975 Iceland unilaterally introduced a fishing limit of 200 nautical miles (370 km), both as a conservation measure and to protect Icelandic interests. The 1973 agreement on fishing limits between Iceland and the United Kingdom expired in November 1975, and failure to reach a new agreement led to the third and most serious 'cod war'. Casualties occurred, and in February 1976 Iceland temporarily severed diplomatic relations with the United Kingdom, the first diplomatic break between two NATO countries. In June the two countries reached an agreement, and in December the British trawler fleet withdrew from Icelandic waters. In June 1979 Iceland declared its exclusive rights to the 200-mile fishing zone. Following negotiations between the EC and EFTA on the creation of the EEA, an agreement was reached (in October 1991) allowing tariff-free access to the EC for 97% of Iceland's fisheries products by 1997, while Iceland was to allow EC vessels to catch 3,000 metric tons of fish per year in its waters, in return for some access to EC waters. The EEA agreement was ratified by the Althingi in January 1993 and entered into force in January 1994.

In August 1993 a dispute developed between Iceland and Norway over fishing rights in an area of the Barents Sea fished by Iceland, over which Norway claimed jurisdiction. The dispute continued throughout 1994, and in June the Norwegian coastguards cut the nets of Icelandic trawlers fishing for cod in the disputed region. Iceland's case was weakened in January 1995, when Canada officially recognized Norway's sovereign rights over the disputed area (a fisheries protection zone extending 200 km around the Svalbard archipelago). A similar dispute arose in August 1996 between Iceland and Denmark over fishing rights in an area of the Atlantic Ocean between Iceland and Greenland (a self-governing province of Denmark). The Danish Government claimed that an agreement had been concluded in 1988 to allow fishing boats that were in possession of a licence issued in Greenland to operate in the area. Iceland, however, denied the existence of such an agreement, and announced that Danish boats would not be permitted to fish in the disputed area.

Iceland strongly criticized the moratorium on commercial whaling, imposed (for conservation purposes) by the International Whaling Commission (IWC, see p. 300) in 1986, and continued to catch limited numbers of whales for scientific purposes until 1989, when it halted whaling, following appeals by environmental organizations for an international boycott of Icelandic products. In 1991 Iceland announced its withdrawal from the IWC (with effect from June 1992), claiming that certain species of whales were not only too plentiful to be in danger of extinction, but were also threatening Iceland's stocks of cod and other fish. In 1994 a report, commissioned by the Government, recommended that limited hunting be resumed in the future. In March 1999 the Althingi voted to end the self-imposed 10-year ban on whaling and requested the Government to implement the ruling, urging a resumption of hunting as soon as possible. In September 2000 the Prime Minister reportedly announced that Iceland would apply to rejoin the IWC in 2001; he did not specify a timetable for the resumption of hunting.

Government

According to the Constitution, executive power is vested in the President (elected for four years by universal adult suffrage) and the Cabinet, consisting of the Prime Minister and other ministers appointed by the President. In practice, however, the President performs only nominally the functions ascribed in the Constitution to this office, and it is the Cabinet alone which holds real executive power. Legislative power is held jointly by the President and the unicameral Althingi (Parliament), with 63 members elected by universal suffrage for four years (subject

to dissolution by the President), using a system of proportional representation in eight multi-member constituencies. The Cabinet is responsible to the Althingi. For the purposes of local government Iceland is divided into 124 municipalities; in 2001 the municipalities were in a process of amalgamation that was expected to last several years.

Defence

Apart from a 120-strong coastguard, Iceland has no defence forces of its own, but it is a member of NATO (see p. 241). There are units of US forces at Keflavík air base, which is used for observation of the North Atlantic Ocean, under a bilateral agreement made in 1951 between Iceland and the USA. The airfield at Keflavík is a base for the US airborne early warning system. In August 2000 a total of 1,640 US military personnel (navy 960, air force 600, marines 80) were stationed in Iceland, together with a 16-strong naval contingent from the Netherlands.

Economic Affairs

In 1998, according to estimates by the World Bank, Iceland's gross national product (GNP), measured at 1996–98 prices, was US $7,626m., equivalent to $27,830 per head (or $24,774 per head on an international purchasing-power parity basis). During 1990–98, it was estimated, GNP per head increased, in real terms, at an average annual rate of 1.5%. Over the same period the population increased at an average annual rate of 1.0%. Estimated GNP in 1999 was $8,109m. ($29,280 per head). Iceland's gross domestic product (GDP) increased, in real terms, at an average annual rate of 2.3% during 1990–99; GDP increased by 4.5% in 1998 and by 4.3% in 1999.

Agriculture (including fishing) contributed some 9.4% of GDP in 1997; 8.9% of the employed labour force were engaged in the agricultural sector in 1999. The principal agricultural products are dairy produce and lamb, although these provided less than 1% of export earnings in 1997. Marine products accounted for 72.7% of total export earnings in 1998. A cod quota system is in place to avoid the depletion of fish stocks through over-fishing as happened in previous years. During 1990–99 agricultural GDP (including fishing) declined at an average annual rate of 1.6%; agricultural GDP (excluding fishing) increased at an average annual rate of 1.1% over the same period, while the GDP of the fishing sector declined by 2.3% per year. Agricultural GDP (excluding fishing) increased, in real terms, by 3.2% in 1998 and 3.9% in 1999; the GDP of the fishing sector declined by 8.0% in 1998 and by 1.6% in 1999.

Industry (including mining, manufacturing, construction and power) contributed 28.2% of GDP in 1997. In 1999 23.1% of the employed labour force were engaged in the industrial sector. Mining activity is negligible. During 1990–97 industrial GDP increased at an average annual rate of 1.6%; industrial GDP increased by 6.6% in 1996 and by 6.7% in 1997.

Manufacturing contributed 16.7% of GDP in 1997, and employed 22.4% of the labour force in 1999. The most important sectors, measured by gross value of output (excluding fish processing, which dominates the sector), are the production of aluminium, diatomite, fertilizer, cement and ferro-silicon. Fish processing contributed 4.9% of GDP in 1997; however, the GDP of the fish-processing sector declined by 5.3% in 1998 and by 1.1% in 1999. Manufacturing GDP (including fish processing) increased, in real terms, at an average annual rate of 2.4% in 1990–99; it increased by 4.1% in 1998 and by 4.9% in 1999.

Services contributed 62.4% of GDP in 1997 and employed 68.0% of the labour force in 1999. GDP from services increased, in real terms, at an annual average rate of 2.6% during 1990–97; it increased by 6.1% in 1996 and by 5.1% in 1997.

Iceland is potentially rich in hydroelectric and geothermal power, but both energy sources are significantly underexploited. Hydroelectric power has promoted the development of the aluminium industry while geothermal energy provides nearly all the country's heating and hot water. Imports of mineral fuels and lubricants comprised 4.8% of the value of merchandise imports in 1998.

In 1999 Iceland recorded a visible trade deficit of US $308m. and there was a deficit of $600m. on the current account of the balance of payments. In 1999 the principal sources of imports were Germany (11.8%), the USA (10.9%) and Norway (10.4%); the principal market for exports was the United Kingdom (19.7%), followed by the USA (14.7%) and Germany (13.1%). In the same year EU member countries provided 60.0% of Iceland's merchandise imports and took 64.2% of exports. The principal imports in 1998 were road vehicles, electrical machinery, apparatus and appliances and industrial machinery and equipment. The principal exports in the same year were marine products (including animal feeds) and non-ferrous metals.

In 1998 there was a budgetary surplus of 2,800m. krónur, equivalent to 0.5% of GDP. Iceland's net external debt was equivalent to 56.3% of GDP at the end of 1998; the cost of debt-servicing was equivalent to an estimated 21.0% of export earnings in the same year. The annual rate of inflation averaged 3.0% in 1990–99; consumer prices increased by 3.4% in 1999 and by 5.0% in 2000. In July 2000 1.1% of the total labour force were unemployed.

Iceland is a member of the Nordic Council (see p. 237), the Nordic Council of Ministers (see p. 237), the European Free Trade Association (EFTA, see p. 178) and the Organisation for Economic Co-operation and Development (OECD, see p. 247). Although Iceland is not a member of the European Union (EU, see p. 181), it joined the EU's Schengen Agreement (see p. 194) along with Denmark, Finland and Sweden (all EU members) by virtue of its membership in the Nordic passport union (Norway also joined).

During the late 1990s the Icelandic economy expanded rapidly, partly as a result of the recovery of the fishing industry but largely owing to the diversification of the economy through extensive deregulation and restructuring begun in the early 1990s. The tourism sector has expanded rapidly while significant biotechnology and information technology industries have been developed. The financial sector has benefited from the liberalization of capital flows and a series of privatizations. The privatization programme initiated in 1991 continued with the partial transfer to the private sector of Iceland Telecom scheduled for 2001. However, the rapid expansion of the economy (as well as the high international price for petroleum) led to an increase in inflation. Although economic growth was predicted to slow (partly as a result of the decrease in fishing quotas, owing to lower stock estimates), thus easing inflationary pressures, the announcement of lower stock estimates in June and July 2000 led to the rapid depreciation of the currency and the temporary closure of the interbank foreign exchange market; interest rates were raised to protect the krona from further decline, leaving little flexibility to control inflation. Continuing strong consumer confidence also led to a large deficit on the current account of the balance of payments, which was equivalent to about 7% of GDP in 2000, owing to increased purchases of imported consumer goods. However, the Government presided over a budgetary surplus of 3% in 2000, much of which was allocated to reduce public indebtedness and to improve pension provision. Iceland has benefited greatly from its membership of the European Economic Area (see p. 202) but is reluctant to join the EU, owing to the potentially adverse effects of the Common Fisheries Policy on the Icelandic fishing industry. However, the Government was likely to be under increased pressure in the future to establish some form of link with the European single currency, the euro, to protect certain industries, notably tourism, from the effects of currency fluctuations.

Social Welfare

There is a comprehensive system of social security and social assistance, providing a wide range of insurance benefits, including old-age and invalidity pensions, family allowances, maternity grants, widows' and widowers' benefits, occupational accident benefits, etc. The scheme is mainly financed by the Government. Pensions and health insurance now apply to all residents in Iceland. Accident insurance applies to all wage and salary earners and self-employed persons—unless they request exemption—and unemployment insurance to skilled and unskilled workers and seamen. In 2000 there were 950 physicians and surgeons, 2,243 nurses and 285 dentists working in Iceland. In that year the country had 12 general hospitals, with about 1,200 short-term beds. Of total expenditure by the central Government in 2000, 47,942m. krónur (24.8%) was for health, while a further 40,660m. krónur (21.0%) was for social security and welfare.

Education

Education is compulsory and free for 10 years between six and 16 years of age (primary and lower secondary levels). Upper secondary education begins at 16 years of age and usually lasts for four years. In 1999 89% of 16-year-olds were continuing their education at a secondary school. Iceland has 10 institutions providing tertiary-level education, including two non-university institutions. Expenditure on education by all levels of government in 1998 was 33,428m. krónur, representing 15.0% of total public expenditure. Local communities finance compulsory education.

Public Holidays

2001: 1 January (New Year's Day), 12 April (Maundy Thursday), 13 April (Good Friday), 16 April (Easter Monday), 19 April (First Day of Summer), 1 May (Labour Day), 24 May (Ascension Day), 4 June (Whit Monday), 17 June (National Day), 6 August (Bank Holiday), 24–26 December (Christmas), 31 December (New Year's Eve).

2002: 1 January (New Year's Day), 28 March (Maundy Thursday), 29 March (Good Friday), 1 April (Easter Monday), 25 April (First Day of Summer), 1 May (Labour Day), 9 May (Ascension Day), 20 May (Whit Monday), 17 June (National Day), 5 August (Bank Holiday), 24–26 December (Christmas), 31 December (New Year's Eve).

Weights and Measures

The metric system is in force.

Statistical Survey

Sources (unless otherwise stated): Statistics Iceland, Skuggasundi 3, 150 Reykjavík; tel. 5609800; fax 5628865; e-mail statice@statice.is; internet www.statice.is; National Economic Institute of Iceland, Reykjavík; tel. 5699500; internet www.ths.is; Seðlabanki Íslands (Central Bank of Iceland), Kalkofnsvegur 1, 150 Reykjavík; tel. 5699600; internet www.sedlabanki.is.

AREA AND POPULATION

Area: 103,000 sq km (39,769 sq miles).

Population: 204,578 at census of 1 December 1970; 275,264 (males 137,874; females 137,390) at 1 December 1998; 278,717 (males 139,518; females 139,199) at 1 December 1999.

Density (per sq km): 2.7 (1999).

Principal Town: Reykjavík (capital), population 109,763 at 1 December 1999.

Births, Marriages and Deaths (1999): Live births 4,100 (birth rate 14.8 per 1,000); Marriages 1,560 (marriage rate 5.6 per 1,000); Deaths 1,901 (death rate 6.9 per 1,000).

Expectation of Life (years at birth, 1998/99): Males 77.5; Females 81.4.

Employment (1999): Agriculture and fishing 13,700; Manufacturing 23,600; Electricity and water supply 1,200; Construction 10,600; Trade, restaurants and hotels 27,100; Transport, storage and communications 11,600; Finance, real estate and business services 16,800; Public administration, education, health services and other services not specified 48,700; Total 153,300.

AGRICULTURE, ETC.

Principal Crops (metric tons, 1999): cereals 0.5; potatoes 9.0; cabbages 0.7; tomatoes 1.0; cucumbers and gherkins 1.0; other vegetables 0.7.
Source: partly FAO.

Livestock ('000 head, 1999): Cattle 74.5; Sheep 490.5; Horses 77.3; Pigs 3.9; Poultry 160.6.

Livestock Products (metric tons, 1999): Mutton and lamb 8,644; Beef 3,664; Pig meat 4,706; Milk ('000 litres, processed) 107,196; Wool (unwashed) 1,000; Sheepskins 2,030*; Eggs 2,000.
* FAO estimate.
Source: partly FAO.

Fishing ('000 metric tons, live weight, 1999): Atlantic cod 260.6; Saithe 44.7; Haddock 30.7; Atlantic redfishes 110.3; Capelin 703.7; Atlantic herring 298.4; Shrimp 43.0; Total (incl. others) 1,732.7.

INDUSTRY

Selected Products ('000 metric tons, unless otherwise indicated, 1999): Frozen fish 141.5 (1999, demersal catch); Salted, dried or smoked fish 72.5 (1996); Cement 117.8; Ferro-silicon 67.8; Aluminium (unwrought) 170.1; Electric energy 7,185 million kWh.

FINANCE

Currency and Exchange Rates: 100 aurar (singular: eyrir) = 1 new Icelandic króna (plural: krónur). *Sterling, Dollar and Euro Equivalents* (29 December 2000): £1 sterling = 126.39 krónur; US $1 = 84.70 krónur; €1 = 78.81 krónur; 1,000 krónur = £7.912 = $11.806 = €12.688. *Average Exchange Rate* (krónur per US $): 70.958 in 1998; 72.335 in 1999; 78.616 in 2000.

Budget (million krónur, 1997): *Revenue:* Tax revenue 132,415 (Taxes on income, profits and capital gains 32,745, Social security contributions 14,353, Taxes on property 6,895, Domestic taxes on goods and services 76,035); Other current revenue 21,211 (Entrepreneurial and property income 9,435, Administrative fees and charges, non-industrial and incidental sales 8,866); Capital revenue 1,574; Total 136,369. *Expenditure:* General public services 8,846; Public order and safety 6,875; Education 15,526; Health 36,916; Social security and welfare 36,064; Housing and community amenities 1,081; Recreational, cultural and religious affairs and services 4,592; Economic affairs and services 25,097 (Agriculture, forestry, fishing and hunting 8,915, Transport and communications 11,597); Other purposes 17,993 (Interest payments 15,606); Total 152,990 (current 141,904, capital 11,087), excluding lending minus repayments (347). Note: Figures refer to consolidated operations of the central Government, comprising budgetary accounts and social security funds. Source: IMF, *Government Finance Statistics Yearbook*.

1998 (million krónur): Total revenue 220,800; Total expenditure 218,000.

1999 (estimates, million krónur): Total revenue 225,900; Total expenditure 243,800.

2000 (estimates, million krónur): Total revenue 276,300; Total expenditure 256,400.

Note: Figures for 1998–2000 refer to transactions of the public sector (including local government units). Source: Central Bank of Iceland.

International Reserves (US $ million at 31 December 2000): Reserve position in IMF 24.2; Foreign exchange 364.6; Total 388.9. Figures exclude gold, which was valued at US $2.8m. in 1998. Source: IMF, *International Financial Statistics*.

Money Supply (million krónur at 31 December 1998): Currency outside banks 6,322; Demand deposits at commercial and savings banks 51,852; Total money 56,878. Source: IMF, *International Financial Statistics*.

Cost of Living (consumer price index for Reykjavík; average of monthly figures; base: May 1988 = 100): 183.3 in 1998; 189.6 in 1999; 199.1 in 2000.

Gross domestic product in purchasers' values (million krónur at current prices): 529,949 in 1997; 577,407 in 1998; 624,606 (provisional) in 1999.

Expenditure on the Gross Domestic Product (million krónur at current prices, 1999): Government final consumption expenditure 143,119; Private final consumption expenditure 367,252; Increase in stocks 139; Gross fixed capital formation 142,164; *Total domestic expenditure* 652,674; Exports of goods and services 214,363; *Less* Imports of goods and services 242,432; *Gross domestic product* 624,606.

GDP by Economic Activity (million krónur at current prices, 1997): Agriculture 8,351; Fishing 33,748; Manufacturing 74,828; Electricity and water supply 18,278; Construction 33,684; Trade, restaurants and hotels 55,635; Transport, storage and communication 34,975; Finance, insurance, real estate and business services 88,381; Other private services 21,420; Government services 63,212; Private non-profit institutions serving households 16,318; *Sub-total* 448,828; Statistical discrepancies 14,460; *Less* Imputed bank service charges 21,837; *GDP at factor cost* 441,451; Indirect taxes 93,504; *Less* Subsidies 10,276; *GDP in purchasers' values* 524,679.

Balance of Payments (US $ million, 1999): Exports of goods f.o.b. 2,009, Imports of goods f.o.b. −2,317, *Trade balance* −308; Exports of services 952, Imports of services −1,044, *Balance on goods and services* −400; Other income received 112, Other income paid −303, *Balance on goods, services and income* −591; Current transfers received 5, Current transfers paid −14, *Current balance* −600; Capital account (net) n.a., Direct investment abroad −104, Direct investment from abroad 64, Portfolio investment assets −428, Portfolio investment liabilities 1,031, Financial derivatives assets 60, Financial derivatives liabilities −57, Other investment assets −172, Other investment liabilities 525, Net errors and omissions −244, *Overall balance* 75. Source: IMF, *International Financial Statistics*.

EXTERNAL TRADE

Principal Commodities (distribution by SITC, million krónur, 1998): *Imports c.i.f.:* Fish, crustaceans, molluscs and preparations thereof 4,500; Metalliferous ores and metal scrap 5,683; Petroleum and petroleum products 8,391; Medicinal and pharmaceutical products 4,242; Paper, paperboard and articles thereof 4,365; Textile yarn, etc. 3,875; Iron and steel 3,639; Machinery specialized for particular industries 7,546; General industrial machinery and equipment 9,556; Office machines and computers 6,244; Telecommunications equipment, etc. 6,423; Electrical machinery, apparatus and appliances 12,934; Road vehicles 16,881; Other transport equipment 8,299; Furniture, mattresses, cushions, etc. 3,785; Apparel and clothing accessories 6,437; Total (incl. others) 176,072. *Exports f.o.b.:* Fish, crustaceans, molluscs and preparations thereof 85,292; Animal feeds (excl. unmilled cereals) 11,954; Animal oils and fats 4,634; Iron and steel 3,241; Non-ferrous metals 18,422; Total (incl. others) 136,592.

Principal Trading Partners (million krónur, country of consignment, 1999): *Imports c.i.f.:* Australia 4,728.7; Denmark 14,723.8; France 6,940.0; Germany 21,580.3; Italy 6,139.6; Japan 10,091.8; Netherlands 9,455.3; Norway 18,957.0; Spain 3,555.7; Sweden 11,327.1; UK 16,719.6; USA 19,866.9; Total (incl. others) 182,321.5. *Exports f.o.b.:* Denmark 6,678.7; France 7,513.6; Germany 18,964.5; Japan 7,296.6; Netherlands 8,710.6; Norway 6,929.8; Portugal 6,959.3; Spain 7,503.8; Switzerland 5,370.3; UK 28,478.6; USA 21,355.7; Total (incl. others) 144,928.1.

TRANSPORT

Road Traffic (registered motor vehicles at 1 January 2000): Passenger cars 151,409; Buses and coaches 1,621; Goods vehicles 17,807; Motorcycles 1,508 (1999).

Shipping: *Merchant fleet* (registered vessels, 1 January 2000): Fishing vessels 841 (displacement 184,698 grt); Passenger ships, tankers and other vessels 138 (displacement 31,693 grt). *International freight traffic* ('000 metric tons, 1994): Goods loaded 1,162; Goods unloaded 1,733.

Civil Aviation (scheduled external Icelandic traffic, '000, 1996): Kilometres flown 22,526, Passenger-kilometres 2,801,000, Cargo ton-kilometres 52,655, Mail ton-kilometres 1,987.

TOURISM

Foreign Visitors by Country of Origin (1999): Denmark 25,138, France 13,533, Germany 31,684, Norway 22,579, Sweden 26,815, UK 31,466, USA 44,709; Total (incl. others) 262,605.

Receipts from Tourists (million krónur): 26,336 in 1998; 27,852 in 1999.

COMMUNICATIONS MEDIA

Radio Receivers (1999): 110,889 licensed.

Television Receivers (1999): 106,372 licensed.

Telephones (1999): 160,900 in use.

Telefax Stations (1993): 4,100 in use (Source: UN, *Statistical Yearbook*).

Mobile Cellular Telephones (subscribers, 1999): 172,600.

Books (production, 1999): 1,866 titles (incl. new editions).

Daily Newspapers (1999): 3 (combined circulation 100,000 copies per issue).

EDUCATION

Institutions (1999): Pre-primary 252; Primary and secondary (lower level) 192; Secondary (higher level) 39; Tertiary (universities and colleges) 8.

Teachers (incl. part-time, 1999): Pre-primary 3,257; Primary and secondary (lower level) 4,196; Secondary (higher level) 1,516; Tertiary 1,431.

Students (1999): Pre-primary 14,761; Primary 31,282; Secondary (lower level) 11,748; Secondary (higher level) 20,388; Tertiary 10,064.

Directory

The Constitution

The Constitution came into force on 17 June 1944, when Iceland became an independent Republic. The main provisions of the Constitution, including subsequent amendments, are summarized below:

GOVERNMENT

The President is elected for four years by universal suffrage. All those qualified to vote who have reached the age of 35 years are eligible for the Presidency.

Legislative power is vested jointly in the President of the Republic and the Althingi (Alþingi—Parliament). Executive power is vested in the President. The authority vested in the President shall be exercised through the Cabinet. The President appoints the Ministers to the Cabinet under the auspices of the Prime Minister, or the Prime Minister-elect when a new Cabinet is being assembled. The President may be dismissed only if a resolution supported by three-quarters of the Althingi is approved by a plebiscite.

The Althingi is composed of 63 Members, elected by the people by secret ballot on the basis of proportional representation, for four years, in eight multi-member constituences. The franchise for general elections to the Althingi is universal above the age of 18. Every national having the right to vote and an unblemished reputation is eligible to be elected to the Althingi, except for the Judges of the Supreme Court. Seats that fall vacant between legislative elections are filled by substitutes elected at the same time as titular Members.

The Althingi is convened by the President for a regular session every year on 1 October and continues in session until the same date next year, unless the election period of its Members has elapsed earlier or it has been dissolved. The President may adjourn meetings of the Althingi, but not for more than two weeks not more than once a year. The President may dissolve the Althingi. Elections must then be held within two months and the Althingi must reassemble within eight months. Sessions are held in one chamber and its meetings are public. The Althingi elects a President, who presides over its proceedings.

Legislative bills are either submitted to the Althingi by the President of the Republic through his/her Ministers or by individual Members of the Althingi. Bills must be given three readings in the Althingi and be approved by a simple majority before they are submitted to the President. If the President disapproves a bill it nevertheless becomes valid, but must be submitted to a plesbiscite.

Each Member of the Althingi has the right to request, subject to the permission of the Althingi, information from a Minister or an answer, orally or in writing, regarding a public matter, by tabling a question or requesting a report. Ministers are responsible to the Althingi and may be impeached by that body, in which case they are tried by the Court of Impeachment.

LOCAL GOVERNMENT

Iceland is divided into 124 municipalities which have definite geographical boundaries and cover the entire island. In each municipality there is a municipal council elected every four years. All citizens over the age of 18 years are eligible to vote. In larger municipalities councillors are elected by proportional representation and frequently on party political lines. In the smallest rural areas councillors are usually elected on an individual basis. Municipal councils are enacted to set their own property rates and local income taxes, within certain limits determined by law. A municipal executive council (elected every year) is in charge of the chief administration, including municipal finances, budgeting, personnel and legal matters. Executive councils may also take charge of infrastructural investments and public works.

The Government

HEAD OF STATE

President: ÓLAFUR RAGNAR GRÍMSSON (took office 1 August 1996; began a second term in August 2000).

THE CABINET

(March 2001)

A coalition of the Independence Party (IP) and the Progressive Party (PP).

Prime Minister and Minister of the Statistical Bureau of Iceland: DAVÍÐ ODDSSON (IP).

Minister for Foreign Affairs and External Trade: HALLDÓR ÁSGRÍMSSON (PP).

Minister of Finance: GEIR H. HAARDE (IP).

Minister of Fisheries: ÁRNI M. MATHIESEN (IP).

Minister of Justice and Ecclesiastical Affairs: SÓLVEIG PÉTURSDÓTTIR (IP).

Minister of Agriculture: GUÐNÍ ÁGÚSTSSON (PP).

Minister for the Environment: SIV FRIDLEIFSDÓTTIR (PP).

Minister of Industry and Commerce: VALGERÐUR SVERRISDÓTTIR (PP).

Minister of Education, Science and Culture: BJÖRN BJARNASON (IP).

Minister of Social Affairs: PÁLL PÉTURSSON (PP).

Minister of Communications: STURLA BÖDVARSSON (IP).

Minister of Health and Social Security: INGIBJORG PALMADÓTTIR (PP).

MINISTRIES

Office of the President: Stadastaður, Soleyjargata 1, 150 Reykjavík; tel. 5404400; fax 5624802; e-mail forseti@forseti.is.

Prime Minister's Office: Stjórnarráðshúsinu v/Laekjargötu, 150 Reykjavík; tel. 5609400; fax 5624014; e-mail postur@for.stjr.is; internet www.stjr.is/for.

Ministry of Agriculture: Sölvhólsgata 7, 150 Reykjavík; tel. 5609750; fax 5521160; e-mail postur@lan.stjr.is; internet www.stjr.is/lan.

Ministry of Communications: Hafnarhúsinu við Tryggvagötu, 150 Reykjavík; tel. 5609630; fax 5621702; e-mail postur@sam.stjr.is; internet www.sam.stjr.is.

Ministry of Education, Science and Culture: Sölvhólsgata 4, 150 Reykjavík; tel. 5609500; fax 5623068; e-mail postur@mrn.stjr.is; internet www.mrn.stjr.is.

Ministry for the Environment: Vonarstraeti 4, 150 Reykjavík; tel. 5609600; fax 5624566; e-mail postur@umh.stjr.is; internet www.stjr.is/umh.

Ministry of Finance: Arnarhváli, 150 Reykjavík; tel. 5609200; fax 5628280; e-mail postur@fjr.stjr.is; internet www.stjr.is/fjr.

Ministry of Fisheries: Skúlagötu 4, 150 Reykjavík; tel. 5609670; fax 5621853; e-mail sjavar@hafro.is; internet www.stjr.is/sjr.

Ministry for Foreign Affairs: Raudarárstíg 25, 150 Reykjavík; tel. 5609900; fax 5622373; e-mail external@utn.stjr.is; internet www.mfa.is.

Ministry of Health and Social Security: Laugavegi 116, 150 Reykjavík; tel. 5609700; fax 5519165; e-mail postur@htr.stjr.is; internet www.stjr.is/htr.

Ministry of Industry and Commerce: Arnarhváli, 150 Reykjavík; tel. 5609070; fax 5621289; e-mail postur@ivr.stjr.is; internet www.stjr.is/ivr.

Ministry of Justice and Ecclesiastical Affairs: Arnarhváli, 150 Reykjavík; tel. 5609010; fax 5527340; e-mail postur@dkm.stjr.is; internet www.stjr.is/dkm.

Ministry of Social Affairs: Hafnarhúsinu við Tryggvagötu, 150 Reykjavík; tel. 5609100; fax 5524804; e-mail postur@fel.stjr.is.

President and Legislature

PRESIDENT

Presidential Election, 29 June 1996

	Number of votes cast	% of votes
ÓLAFUR RAGNAR GRÍMSSON	68,370	40.9
PÉTUR K. HAFSTEIN	48,863	29.2
GUÐRÚN AGNARSDÓTTIR	43,578	26.0
ÁSTTHÓR MAGNÚSSON	4,422	2.6

ALTHINGI

(Alþingi)

Althingi: v/Austurvöll, 150 Reykjavík; tel. 5630500; fax 5630520; e-mail parlsec@althingi.is; internet www.althingi.is.

Speaker of the Althingi: HALLDÓR BLÖNDAL.

Secretary-General (Clerk) of the Althingi: FRIDRIK ÓLAFSSON.

General Election, 8 May 1999

	% of votes	Seats
Independence Party	40.7	26
The Alliance*	26.8	17
Progressive Party	18.4	12
Left-Green Movement	9.1	6
Liberal Party	4.2	2
Others	0.8	—
Total	**100.0**	**63**

* The Alliance (Samfylkinginn) comprises the People's Alliance, the Social Democratic Party, the People's Movement and the Women's List.

Political Organizations

Althýdubandalag (People's Alliance—PA): Austurstraeti 10, 101 Reykjavík; tel. 5517500; fax 5517599; f. 1956 by amalgamation of a section of the Social Democratic Party and the Socialist Unity Party, reorganized as a socialist party 1968; twin goals of socialism and national independence; Chair. MARGRÉT FRÍMANNSDÓTTIR; Parliamentary Leader SVAVAR GESTSSON; Gen. Sec. HEIMIR MÁR PÉTURSSON.

Althýduflokkurinn (Social Democratic Party—SDP): Althýdu-husið, Hverfisgata 8–10, 101 Reykjavík; tel. 5529244; fax 5629155; f. 1916 with a moderate socialist programme; emphasizes greater equality in the distribution of wealth and income; Chair. JÓN BALDVIN HANNIBALSSON; Parliamentary Leader ÖSSUR SKARPHÉDINSSON.

Framsóknarflokkurinn (Progressive Party—PP): Hverfisgata 33, POB 453, 121 Reykjavík; tel. 5404300; fax 5404301; e-mail framsokn @framsokn.is; internet www.framsokn.is; f. 1916 with a programme of social liberalism and co-operation; Chair. HALLDÓR ÁSGRÍMSSON; Parliamentary Leader KRISTINN H. GUNNARSSON; Sec.-Gen. EGILL HEIÐAR GÍSLASON.

Frjálslyndi flokkurinn (Liberal Party): c/o v/Austurvöll, 150 Reykjavík; tel. 5630500; fax 5630520; formed by Sverrir Hermannsson, former member of the IP and cabinet minister; Leader SVERRIR HERMANNSSON.

Samtök um kvennalista (Women's List—WL): Hverfisgata 8–10, 101 Reykjavík; tel. 5513725; fax 5629155; e-mail kvennalistinn@ kvennalistinn.is; internet www.centrum.is/kvennalistinn/; f. 1983; a non-hierarchical feminist movement to promote the interests of women and children; parliamentary leadership rotates.

Sjálfstædisflokkurinn (Independence Party—IP): Háaleitisbraut 1, 105 Reykjavík; tel. 5151700; fax 5151717; e-mail xd@xd.is; internet www.xd.is; f. 1929 by an amalgamation of the Conservative and Liberal Parties; its programme is social reform within the framework of private enterprise and the furtherance of national and individual independence; Leader DAVÍÐ ODDSSON.

Thjóðvaki—hreyfing folksins (Awakening of the Nation—People's Movement): Hafnarstraeti 7, 101 Reykjavík; tel. 5528100; fax 5627060; f. 1994; founded by dissident mems of the SDP; Leader JÓHANNA SIGURÐARDÓTTIR.

Vinstrihreyfing-Grænt frambod (Left-Green Movement): c/o v/Austurvöll, 150 Reykjavík; tel. 5630500; fax 5630520; e-mail vg@vg.is; internet www.vg.is; founded by dissident members of the PA, the Women's Party, the Greens and independent left-wingers.

Diplomatic Representation

EMBASSIES IN ICELAND

China, People's Republic: Viðimelur 29, POB 580, Reykjavík; tel. 5526751; fax 5626110; Ambassador: WANG RONGHUA.

Denmark: Hverfisgata 29, 101 Reykjavík; tel. 5621230; fax 5623316; e-mail rekamb@rekamb.um.dk; Ambassador: FLEMMING MØRCH.

Finland: Túngata 30, 101 Reykjavík; tel. 5100100; fax 5623880; e-mail finamb@li.is; Ambassador: TIMO H. KOPONEN.

France: Túngata 22, 101 Reykjavík; tel. 5517621; fax 5628177; Ambassador: LOUIS BARDOLLET.

Germany: Laufásvegur 31, POB 400, 121 Reykjavík; tel. 5301100; fax 5301101; e-mail germanembassy@islandia.is; Ambassador: Dr REINHART W. EHNI.

Norway: Fjólugata 17, 101 Reykjavík; tel. 5520700; fax 5529553; e-mail noramb@simnet.is; internet www.noregur.is; Ambassador: KIELL H. HALVORSEN.

Russia: Garðastraeti 33, 101 Reykjavík; tel. 5515156; fax 5620633; Ambassador: ANATOLY S. ZAYTSEV.

Sweden: Box 8136, 128 Reykjavík; tel. 5201230; fax 5201235; e-mail sveamb@itn.is; Ambassador: HERMAN AF TROLLE.

United Kingdom: Laufásvegur 31, 101 Reykjavík; POB 460, 121 Reykjavík; tel. 5505100; fax 5505105; e-mail britemb@centrum.is; Ambassador: JOHN HOWARD CULVER.

USA: Laufásvegur 21, 101 Reykjavík; tel. 5629100; fax 5629139; Ambassador: BARBARA J. GRIFFITHS.

Judicial System

All cases are heard in Ordinary Courts except those specifically within the jurisdiction of Special Courts. The Ordinary Courts include both a lower division of urban and rural district courts presided over by the district magistrates, and the Supreme Court.

Justices of the Supreme Court are appointed by the President and cannot be dismissed except by the decision of a court. The Justices elect the Chief Justice for a period of two years.

SUPREME COURT

Dómhúsið v. Arnarhól, 150 Reykjavík; tel. 5103030; fax 5623995; e-mail haestirettur@haestirettur.is; internet www.haestirettur.is.

Chief Justice: PÉTUR KR. HAFSTEIN.

Justices: ARNLJÓTUR BJÖRNSSON, GUÐRÚN ERLENDSDÓTTIR, GARÐAR GÍSLASON, GUNNLAUGUR CLAESSEN, HJÖRTUR TORFASON, HRAFN BRAGASON, MARKÚS SIGURBJÖRNSSON, HARALDUR HENRYSSON.

Religion

CHRISTIANITY

Protestant Churches

Tjodkirkja Islands (Evangelical Lutheran Church of Iceland): Biskupsstofa, Laugavegur 31, 150 Reykjavík; tel. 5351500; fax 5513284; e-mail kirkjan@kirkjan.is; internet www.kirkjan.is; the national Church, endowed by the State; about 88% of the population are members; Iceland forms one diocese, Reykjavík, with two suffragan sees; 284 parishes and 138 pastors; Bishop KARL SIGURBJÖRNSSON.

Fríkirkjan í Reykjavík (The Congregational Church in Reykjavík): POB 1671, 121 Reykjavík; tel. 5527270; fax 5527287; e-mail hjorturm@frikirkian.is; f. 1899; Free Lutheran denomination; 5,500 mems; Head HJORTUR M. JOHANNSSON.

Óhádi söfnudurinn (Independent Congregation): Reykjavík; Free Lutheran denomination; 1,100 mems; Head Rev. THÓRSTEINN RAGNARSSON.

Seventh-day Adventists: Suðurhlid 36, 105 Reykjavík; tel. 5887800; fax 5887808; e-mail sda@mmedia.is; internet www.sda.is.

The Roman Catholic Church

Iceland comprises a single diocese, directly responsible to the Holy See. At 31 December 1997 there were an estimated 2,950 adherents in the country (just over 1% of the total population).

Bishop of Reykjavík: Most Rev. Dr JÓHANNES M. GIJSEN, Hávallagötu 14, POB 489, 121 Reykjavík; tel. 5525388; fax 5623878.

The Press

PRINCIPAL DAILIES

Althýdublaðið (The Labour Journal): Hverfisgata 8–10, 101 Reykjavík; tel. 5625566; fax 5629244; f. 1919; organ of the Social Democratic Party; Editor HRAFN JÖKULSSON; circ. 4,000.

DV (Dagblaðið-Visir): Thverholt 11, POB 5380, 105 Reykjavík; tel. 5505000; fax 5505020; f. 1981; independent; Editors JÓNAS KRISTJÁNSSON, OLI BJÖRN KÁRASON; circ. 44,000.

Dagur-Tíminn: Strandgata 31, POB 58, 600 Akureyri; tel. 4606100; fax 4627639; f. 1918, restructured 1996; organ of the Progressive Party; Editor STEFÁN JÓN HAFSTEIN.

Morgunblaðið (Morning News): Kringlan 1, POB 3040, 103 Reykjavík; tel. 5691100; fax 5691181; e-mail mbl@mbl.is; internet www.mbl.is; f. 1913; independent; Editors MATTHÍAS JOHANNESSEN, STYRMIR GUNNARSSON; circ. 53,000.

WEEKLIES

Austri: Tjarnarbraut 19, POB 173, 700 Egilsstaðir; tel. 4711984; e-mail austri@eldhorn.is; local newspaper; f. 1979; Editor JÓN KRISTJÁNSSON; circ. 2,000.

Einherji: Siglufjorður; organ of the Progressive Party.

Fiskifréttir: POB 1120, 121 Reykjavík; tel. 5155500; fax 5155599; e-mail fiskifrettir@frodi.is; f. 1983; weekly; for the fishing industry; Editor GUÐJÓN EINARSSON; circ. 6,000.

Helgarpósturinn (Weekend Post): Borgartúni 27, 101 Reykjavík; tel. 5522211; fax 5522311; f. 1994; independent; Editor PÁLL VILHJÁLMSSON; circ. 10,000.

Íslendingur-Ísafold (Icelander-Icecountry): Kaupangi v/Mýrarveg, 600 Akureyri; tel. 4621500; f. 1915; for North and East Iceland; Editor STEFÁN SIGTRYGGSSON.

Séð & Heyrt: Seljavegur 2, 101 Reykjavík; tel. 5155652; fax 5155599; e-mail bjarni@frodi.is; showbusiness and celebrities; Editors BJARNI BRYNJOLFSSON, KRISTJAN THORVALDSSON; circ. 23,000.

Siglfirðingur: Siglufjorður; organ of the Independence Party.

Skagablaðið: Skólabraut 21, 300 Akranesi; tel. 4314222; fax 4314122; f. 1984; local newspaper; Editor SIGURÐUR SVERRISSON; circ. 1,500.

Suðurnesjafréttir: Hafnargötu 28, 230 Keflavík; tel. 4213800; fax 4213802; f. 1992; local newspaper; Editors EMIL PÁLL JÓNSSON, HALLDÓR LEVI BJÖRNSSON; circ. 6,500.

Sunnlenska Fréttablaðið: Austurvegi 1, 800 Selfoss; tel. 4823074; fax 4823084; f. 1991; local newspaper; Editor BJARNI HARÐARSON; circ. 6,300.

Vestfirska Fréttablaðið: Fjarðastraeti 16, 400 Ísafjörður; tel. 4564011; fax 4565225; f. 1975; local newspaper; Editors HLYNUR THÓR MAGNÚSSON, GÍSLI HJARTARSON; circ. 2,000.

Vikan: Seljavegur 8, 101 Reykjavík; tel. 5155500; fax 5155592; e-mail johanna@frodi.is; Editors JOHANNA HARDARDOTTIR, HRUND HAUKSDÓTTIR; circ 13,000–17,000.

Vikublaðið (The Weekly Paper): Austurstraeti 10A, 101 Reykjavík; tel. 5528655; fax 5517599; f. 1992; organ of People's Alliance; Editor FRIÐRIK THÓR GUÐMUNDSSON; circ. 3,000–4,000.

Víkurblaðið: Heðinsbraut 1, 640 Húsavík; tel. 4641780; fax 4641399; f. 1979; local newspaper; Editor JÓHANNES SIGURJÓNSSON; circ. 1,300.

Víkurfréttir: Grundarvegur 23, 260 Reykjanesbær; tel. 4214717; fax 4212777; e-mail pket@vf.is; internet www.vf.is; f. 1983; local newspaper; Editor PÁLL KETILSSON; circ. 6,500.

OTHER PERIODICALS

Ægir: Skerpla, Suðurlandsbraut 10, Reykjavík; tel. 5681225; fax 5681224; f. 1905; published by the Fisheries Association of Iceland in co-operation with Athygli ehf Publishing; monthly; Editors BJARNI KR. GRÍMSSON, JÓHANN ÓLAFUR HALLDÓRSSON; circ. 2,500.

Æskan og ABC (The Youth and ABC): Eiríksgötu 5, 101 Reykjavík; tel. 5510248; fax 5510248; f. 1897; 9 a year; children's magazine; Editor KARL HELGASON.

Atlantica: Nóatún 17, 105 Reykjavík; tel. 5115700; fax 5115701; e-mail iceland@icenews.is; internet www.icenews.is; 6 a year; in-flight magazine of Icelandair; Editor HARALDUR J. HAMAR.

AVS (Arkitektur, verktækni og skipulag): Garðastræti 17, 101 Reykjavík; tel. 5616577; fax 5616571; e-mail skipark@centrum.is; f, 1979; 4 a year; architecture and environment; Editor GESTUR ÓLAFSSON; circ. 6,000.

Bændablaðið: POB 7080, 127 Reykjavík; tel. 5630300; fax 5623058; e-mail ath@bi.bondi.is; f. 1995; fortnightly; organ of the Icelandic farmers' union; Editor ASKELL THÓRISSON; circ. 6,400.

Bíllinn: Myrargata 26, 101 Reykjavík; tel. 5526090; fax 5529490; f. 1982; 3–4 a year; cars and motoring equipment; Editor LEÓ M. JÓNSSON; circ. 4,000.

Bleikt og Blátt: Seljavegur 2, 101 Reykjavík; tel. 5155500; fax 5155599; e-mail bogb@frodi.is; f. 1989; 6 a year; sex education, communication between men and women; Editor DAVÍÐ THOR JÓNSSON; circ. 11,000.

Eiðfaxi: Dligglivogur 10, POB 8133, 128 Reykjavík; tel. 5882525; fax 5882528; e-mail eidfaxi@eidfaxi.is; internet www.eidfaxi.is; f. 1977; monthly; horse-breeding and horsemanship; Man. Dir GYÐA GERÐARSDÓTTIR; Editors JENS EINARSSON, HULDA G. GEIRSDÓTTIR; circ. 7,000.

Fasteignablaðið: Sídumúli 10, 108 Reykjavík; tel. 5888844; fax 5888843; monthly; real estate; Editor DAVÍÐ JÓNSSON; circ. 60,000.

Fjármálatíðindi: Kalkofnsvegur 1, 150 Reykjavík; tel. 5699600; fax 5699605; e-mail publish@centbk.is; internet www.sedlabanki.is; 2 a year; economic journal published by the Central Bank; circ. 1,300.

Freyr, búnaðarblað: Baendahöllin við Hagatorg, POB 7080, 127 Reykjavík; tel. 5630300; fax 5623058; e-mail bbl@bi.bondi.is; internet www.bondi.is; monthly; agriculture; Editors ASKELL THORISSON, MATTHIAS EGGERTSSON; circ. 1,900.

Frjáls Verslun (Free Trade): Borgartún 23, 105 Reykjavík; tel. 5617575; fax 5618646; f. 1939; 10 a year; business magazine; Editor JÓN G. HAUKSSON; circ. 6,000–9,000.

Gestgjafinn: Seljavegur 2, 101 Reykjavík; tel. 5155500; fax 5155599; e-mail gestgjafinn@frodi.is; f. 1981; 12 a year; food and wine; Editor SOLVEIG BALDURSDOTTIR; circ. 13,000–16,000.

Hagtíðindi (Monthly Statistics): published by Statistics Iceland, Skuggasund 3, 150 Reykjavík; tel. 5609800; fax 5628865; e-mail statice@statice.is; internet www.statice.is; f. 1916; monthly; Dir-Gen. HALLGRIMUR SNORRASON; circ. 1,000.

Hár og Fegurð (Hair and Beauty Magazine): Skúlagata 54, 105 Reykjavík; tel. and fax 5628141; e-mail pmelsted@vortex.is; internet www.vortex.is/fashion; f. 1980; 3 a year; hair, beauty, fashion; Editor PÉTUR MELSTEÐ.

Heilbrigðismál: Skógarhlíð 8, 105 Reykjavík; tel. 5621414; fax 5621417; f. 1949; quarterly; public health; Editor JÓNAS RAGNARSSON; circ. 6,000.

Heima Er Bezt: Grensasvegi 14, 128 Reykjavík; tel. 5882400; fax 5888994; e-mail heb@skjaldborg.is; f. 1951; monthly; literary; Editor GUÐJÓN BALDVINSSON; circ. 3,500.

Heimsmynd: Aðalstræti 4, 101 Reykjavík; tel. 5622020; fax 5622029; f. 1986; 10 a year; general interest; Editor KARL BIRGISSON; circ. 8,000.

Hús og Híbýli: Seljavegur 2, 101 Reykjavík; tel. 5155500; fax 5155599; e-mail hogh@frodi.is; f. 1978; 12 a year; architecture, family and homes; Editor ELÍN ALBERTSDÓTTIR; circ. 13,000–16,000.

Húsfreyjan (The Housewife): Túngata 14, 101 Reykjavík; tel. 5517044; f. 1950; quarterly; the organ of the Federation of Icelandic Women's Societies; Editor HRAFNHILDUR VALGARÐS; circ. 4,000.

Iceland Business: Nóatún 17, 105 Reykjavík; tel. 5115700; fax 5115701; e-mail iceland@icenews.is; internet www.icenews.is; f. 1994; 5 a year, in English; Publr HARALDUR J. HAMAR.

Iceland Review: Nóatún 17, 105 Reykjavík; tel. 5115700; fax 5115701; e-mail iceland@icenews.is; internet www.icenews.is; f. 1963; quarterly, in English; general; Editor HARALDUR J. HAMAR.

Innflutningur (Import): Héðinsgata 1–3, 105 Reykjavík; tel. 5813411; fax 5680211; f. 1991; 3–4 a year; Editor SÓLVEIG BALDURSDÓTTIR; circ. 5,000.

Ithróttablaðið: Seljavegur 2, 101 Reykjavík; tel. 5155500; fax 5155599; f. 1939; 6 a year; sport; Editor JÓHANN ARNASON; circ. 6,000.

Lisin að lifa: Hverfisgata 105, 101 Reykjavík; tel. 5882111; fax 5882114; e-mail feb@islandia.is; f. 1986; 4 a year; for elderly people; Editor SU BJÖRGUINS; circ. 13,000–15,000.

Mannlíf: Seljavegur 2, 101 Reykjavík; tel. 5155500; fax 5155599; e-mail mannlif@frodi.is; f. 1984; 10 a year; general interest; Editors GERDUR KRISTNÝ GUDJÖNSDÓTTIR; circ. 16,000.

Myndbönd mánaðarins (Videos of the Month): Ármúli 15, 108 Reykjavík; tel. 5811280; fax 5811286; f. 1993; monthly; Editor GUÐBERGUR ÍSLEIFSSON; circ. 26,000.

Ný menntamál: Lágmúli 7, 108 Reykjavík; tel. 5531117; e-mail hannes@ismennt.is; f. 1983; quarterly; educational issues; Editor HANNES ÍSBERG; circ. 6,500.

NýttLíf: Seljavegur 2, 101 Reykjavík; tel. 5155660; fax 5155599; e-mail nyttlif@frodi.is; f. 1978; 11 a year; fashion; Editor GULLVEIG SÆMUNDSDÓTTIR; circ. 13,000–17,000.

Peningamál: Kalkofnsvegi 1, 150 Reykjavik; tel. 5699600; fax 5699608; e-mail sedlabanki@sedlabanki.is; internet www.sedlabanki.is; f. 1999; quarterly bulletin published by the Central Bank; circ. 1,600.

Sjávarfréttir: POB 1120, 121 Reykjavík; tel. 5155500; fax 5155599; e-mail fiskifrettir@frodi.is; f. 1973; yearly; ship registry, statistics on Icelandic fisheries; Editor GUDJÓN EINARSSON; circ. 5,500.

Skutull (Harpoon): Fjarðarstræti 2, 400 Isafjörður; tel. 4563948; fax 4565148; e-mail stapi@simnet.is; f. 1923; monthly; organ of the Social Democratic Party; Editor GÍSLI HJARTARSON.

Stúdentablaðið: Stúdentaheimilinu v/Hringbraut, 101 Reykjavík; tel. 5700850; fax 5700855; e-mail shi@hi.is; internet www.shi.hi.is; f. 1924; 8 issues during the academic year; students' interests; Editor SIGTRYGGUR MAGNASON; circ. 7,500.

Sveitastjórnarmál: Háaleitisbraut 11, 128 Reykjavík; tel. 5813711; fax 5687866; f. 1941; 24 a year; publ. by the Asscn of Icelandic Municipalities: Editor UNNAR STEFÁNSSON; circ. 3,400.

Uppeldi: Bolholt 4, 105 Reykjavík; tel. 5680170; fax 5677215; f. 1988; quarterly; Editor KRISTÍN ELFA GUÐNADÓTTIR; circ. 10,000.

Úrval (Digest): Thverholt 11, 105 Reykjavík; tel. 5505000; fax 5505999; f. 1942; bi-monthly; Editor SIGURÐUR HREIÐARSSON; circ. 6,500.

Veiðimaðurinn (Hunter): Hédinshúsið, Seljavegur 2, 101 Reykjavík; tel. 5155500; fax 5155599; e-mail frodi@frodi.is; f. 1984; 3 a year; fishing and hunting; Editor GYLFI PALSSON; circ. 5,000–7,000.

Vera: Vesturgata 3B, 101 Reykjavík; tel. 5522188; fax 5527560; e-mail vera@vera.is; internet www.vera.is; f. 1982; 6 a year; feminist issues; Editor ELÍSABET THORGEIRSDÓTTIR.

Víkingur (Seaman): Borgartún 18, 105 Reykjavík; 10 a year; Editor SIGURJÓN VALDIMARSSON.

Vinnan (Work): Grensásvegur 16A, 108 Reykjavík; tel. 5813044; fax 5680093; e-mail arnar@gsi.is; 6 a year; f. 1943; publ. by Icelandic Federation of Labour; Editor Dr GUÐMUNDUR ARNASON; circ. 5,000.

NEWS AGENCIES
Foreign Bureaux

Agence France-Presse (AFP): Garðastræti 13, 101 Reykjavík; tel. 5510586; Correspondent GÉRARD LEMARQUIS.

United Press International (UPI) (USA): Reykjavík; tel. 5539816; Correspondent BERNARD SCUDDER.

PRESS ASSOCIATION

Samtök bæjar- og héraðsfréttablaða (Asscn of Local Newspapers): Bæjarhraun 16, 220 Hafnarfjörður; tel. 5651945; fax 5650745; represents 15 newspapers; Pres. FRÍÐA PROPPE.

Publishers

Bjartur & Salka: Bræðraborgarstig 9, 101 Reykjavík; tel. 5621828; fax 5628360; e-mail snar@itn.is; f. 1989; contemporary fiction; Dir SNÆBJÖRN ARNGRÍMSSON.

Bifröst: Skjaldborg/Birtingur, bokaklubbur, c/o Gudjon Baldvinsson, Grensasvegi 14, 128 Reykjavík; tel. 5882400; fax 5888994; e-mail heb@skjaldborg.is; f. 1988; spiritual, self-help, new age; Dir GUÐMUNDUR EINARSSON.

Bókaútgáfa Æskunnar: Eiríksgata 5, 101 Reykjavík; tel. and fax 5510248; Editor KARL HELGASON.

Bókaútgáfan Bjartur: Braeðraborgarstígur 9, 101 Reykjavík; tel. 5621826; fax 5628360; f. 1989; contemporary fiction; Man. Dir SNAEBJÖRN ARNGRÍMSSON.

Bókaútgáfan Björk: Birkivöllum 30, 800 Selfoss; tel. 4821394; fax 4823894; f. 1941; children's; Dir ERLENDUR DANIELSSON.

Bókaútgáfan Hólar: Byggðavegi 101B, 600 Akureyri; tel. 4622515; fax 5871180; f. 1995; general; Dir JÓN HJALTASON.

Edda, Publishing and Media House: Suðurlandsbruat 12, 108 Reykjavík; tel. 5152500; fax 5152505; e-mail mm@mm.is; internet www.edda.is; Gen. Dir HALLDÓR GUÐMUNDSSON.

   Almenna bókafélagið: Suðurlandsbraut 12, 108 Reykjavík; tel. 5503000; fax 5503033; general; Publ. Dir BJARNI ÞORSTEINSSON.

   Forlagið: Suðurlandsbraut 12, 108 Reykjavík; tel. 5152500; fax 5152505; e-mail forlag@mm.is; f. 1984; general; Publ. Dir KRISTJÁN B. JONASSON.

   Iceland Review, bókadeild: Nóatún 17, 105 Reykjavík; tel. 5115700; fax 5503033; e-mail arnike@mm.is; Dir ÁRNI KR. EINARSSON.

   Mál og menning: Laugavegi 18, 101 Reykjavík; tel. 5152500; fax 5152505; e-mail info@mm.is; internet www.mm.is; f. 1937; Dir HALLDÓR GUÐMUNDSSON.

   Vaka-Helgafell: Síðumúli 6, 108 Reykjavík; tel. 5503000; fax 5503033; e-mail vaka@vaka.is; f. 1942; general, fiction, non-faction; Dir PÉTUR MÁR ÓLAFSSON.

Fjölvi–Vasa: Njorvasundi 15A, 104 Reykjavík; tel. 5688433; fax 5688142; e-mail fjolvi@mmedia.is; f. 1966; general; Dir ÞORSTEINN THORARENSEN.

Frjáls fjölmiðlun: Thverholt 11, POB 5380, 105 Reykjavík; tel. 5505000; fax 5505999; f. 1981; fiction in translation, romance; Gen. Man. EYJÓLFUR SVEINSSON.

Fróði Publishing House: Seljavegi 2, 101 Reykjavík; tel. 5155500; fax 5155599; e-mail frodi@frodi.is; internet www.frodi.is; Dir MAGNÚS HREGGVIÐSSON.

   Fróði Ltd: Seljavegi 2, 101 Reykjavík; tel. 5155500; fax 5155599; e-mail frodi@frodi.is; internet www.frodi.is; f. 1989; general, magazines; Dir MAGNÚS HREGGVIÐSSON.

   Iðunn: Seljavegi 2, 101 Reykjavík; tel. 5155579; e-mail idunn@idunn.is; internet www.frodi.is; f. 1945; general; Dir. JÓN KARLSSON.

Háskólaútgáfan (University Publishing): Háskóli Íslands v/Suðurgötu, 101 Reykjavík; tel. 5254009; fax 5521331; e-mail uh@rhi.hi.is; f. 1988; non-fiction, science, culture, history; Man. Dir JÖRUNDUR GUÐMUNDSSON.

Hið íslenska bókmenntafélag: Siðumúli 21, POB 8935, 128 Reykjavík; tel. 5889060; fax 5889095; e-mail hib@islandia.is; internet www.arctic.is/hib; f. 1816; general; Pres. SIGURÐUR LÍNDAL; Dir SVERRIR KRISTINSSON.

Hið íslenska Fornritafélag: Siðumúli 21, POB 8935, 128 Reykjavík; tel. 5889060; fax 5889095; e-mail hib@islandia.is; internet www.arctic.is/hib; f. 1928; Pres. J. NORDAL.

Hörpuútgáfan: Stekkjarholti 8–10, POB 25, 300 Akranes; tel. 4312860; fax 4313309; e-mail bragi@horpuutgafan.is; f. 1960; fiction, general; Dir BRAGI ÞORÐARSON.

Islendingasagnaútgáfan—Muninn: POB 488, 222 Hafnarfjörður; tel. 8985868; fax 5655868; muninn@isl.is; f. 1945; poetry, fiction, children's, general non-fiction; Dir BENEDIKT KRISTJÁNSSON.

JPV Forlag: Lynghálsi 10, 110 Reykjavík; tel. 5250400; fax 5250410; e-mail johann@gen.is; f. 2000; general, Dir JÓHANN PÁLL VALDIMARSSON.

Krydd í tilveruna: Bakkasel 10, 109 Reykjavík; tel. 5575444; fax 5575466; f. 1989; mainly cookery; Dir ANTON ÖRN KJAERNSTED.

Leiðarljós: Sólbrekku, Hellum, 355 Snæfellsbær; tel. 4356810; fax 4356801; e-mail leidar@centrum.is; f. 1995; self-help, spiritual, non-fiction; Dir GUÐRÚN BERGMANN.

Mál og mynd: Bræðraborgarstig 9, 101 Reykjavík; tel. 5528866; fax 5528870; e-mail malogmynd@centum.is; non-fiction; Dir ÍVAR GISSURARSON.

Námsgagnastofnun (National Centre for Educational Materials): Laugavegí 166, 105 Reykjavík; tel. 5528088; fax 5624137; e-mail simi@nams.is; f. 1979; Dir INGIBJÖRG ÁSGEIRSDÓTTIR.

Nýja bókafélagið: Kringlunni 7, 108 Reykjavík; tel. 5111777; fax 5111770; f. 1999; general; Dir JAKOB ASGEIRSSON.

Ormstunga: Lynghálsi 10, 110 Reykjavík; tel. 5250407; fax 5250408; e-mail books@ormstunga.is; internet www.ormstunga.is; f. 1992; Icelandic and foreign fiction; Dir GÍSLI MÁR GÍSLASON.

PP Forlag: Ármula 29, 108 Reykjavík; tel. 5687054; fax 5250408; e-mail pilot@islandia.is; f. 1997; general; Dir SIGRÚN HALLDÓRSDÓTTIR.

Reykholt: POB 8950, 128 Reykjavík; tel. 5888821; fax 5888380; f. 1987; general; Dir REYNIR JÓHANNSSON.

Samhjálp Hvitasunnumanna: Hverfisgötu 42, 101 Reykjavík; tel. 5611000; fax 5610050; e-mail samhjalp@samhjalp.is; religious, pentacostal; Dir ÓLI ÁGÚSTSSON.

Setberg: Freyjugötu 14, POB 619, 101 Reykjavík; tel. 5517667; fax 5526640; f. 1950; fiction, cookery, juvenile, picture books, activity books and children's books; Dir ARNBJÖRN KRISTINSSON.

Skálholtsútgáfan: Laugavegi 31, 101 Reykjavík; tel. 5521090; fax 5621595; e-mail kirkbok@ismennt.is; f. 1981; non-fiction, Christian church; Man. Dir EDDA MÖLLER.

Skjaldborg Ltd: Grensásvegi 14, POB 8427, 108 Reykjavík; tel. 5882400; fax 5888994; e-mail skjaldborg@skjaldborg.is; general; Dir BJÖRN EIRÍKSSON.

Sögufélagið: Fischersundi 3, 101 Reykjavík; tel. 5514620; f. 1902; non-fiction, history; Dir RAGNHEIÐUR ÞORLÁKSDÓTTIR.

Stofnun Arna Magnussonar: Arnagarður v/ Suðurgotu, 101 Reykjavík; tel. 5254010; fax 5254035; e-mail rosat@hi.is; internet www.am.hi.is; f. 1972; non-fiction; Dir VÉSTEINN ÓLASON.

Þjóðsaga: Kringlunni 7, 108 Reykjavík; tel. 5331277; fax 5331270; e-mail pbk@hansa.is; non-fiction; Dir PÁLL BRAGI KRISTJÁNSSON.

Æskan: Stangarhyl 4, 110 Reykjavík; tel. 5305400; fax 5305407; e-mail bara@aeskan.is; general, children's books, magazines; Dir ÓLAFUR LOFTSSON.

PUBLISHERS' ASSOCIATION

Félag íslenskra bókaútgefenda (Icelandic Publishers' Asscn): Barónsstíg 5, 101 Reykjavík; tel. 5118020; fax 5115020; e-mail baekur@mmedia.is; internet this.is/baekur; f. 1889; Pres. SIGURDUR SVAVARSSON; Man. VILBORG HARÐARDÓTTIR.

Broadcasting and Communications
TELECOMMUNICATIONS

The local telecommunications market was deregulated, in accordance with European rules, on 1 January 1998.

Post and Telecom Administration: Smiðjuvegur 68–70, 200 Kópavogur; tel. 5101500; fax 5101509; e-mail pta@pta.is.

Hallo!–Frjáls fjarskipti hf: Skúlagötu 19, 101 Reyakjvík; provides mobile telecommunications.

Iceland Telecom Ltd: Austurvöllur, 150 Reykjavík; tel. 5506000; fax 5506009; e-mail simi@simi.is; internet www.simi.is; f. 1998; operation of telecommunications; also operation of Skyggnir, earth station for satellite telecommunications; scheduled for partial privatization in 2001; Pres. and CEO THORARINN V. THORARINSSON.

IMC Island ehf: Skólavörðustíg 12, 101 Reykjavík; provides mobile telecommunications.

Íslandssími: Borgartún 30, 105 Reykjavík; f. 1999; provides mobile telecommunications; specializes in corporate, fixed line and internet operations; Chief Exec. EYTHOR ARNALDS.

Landssími Íslands hf: Thorvaldssensstræti 4, 150 Reykjavík; provides mobile telecommunications.

Lina.Net ehf: Skúlagötu 19, 101 Reykjavík; provides mobile telecommunications.

Nordial á Islandi hf: Köllunarklettsvegi 2, 104 Reykjavík; provides international service.

Tal hf: Síðumúla 28, 108 Reykjavík; mobile telephone operator; controlled 26% of mobile calls in 2000.

BROADCASTING

Ríkisútvarpið (Icelandic National Broadcasting Service): Broadcasting Centre, Efstaleiti 1, 150 Reykjavík; tel. 5153000; fax 5153010; e-mail isradio@ruv.is; internet www.ruv.is; f. 1930; Dir-Gen. MARKÚS ÖRN ANTONSSON; Chair. of Programme Board GUNNLAUGUR SÆVAR GUNNLAUGSSON.

Radio

Ríkisútvarpið: Radio Division, Efstaleiti 1, 150 Reykjavík; tel. 5153000; fax 5153010; f. 1930; Dir of Radio DORA INGVADOTTIR.

Programme 1 has two long-wave, three medium-wave and 77 FM transmitters broadcasting 127 hours a week.

Programme 2 has 67 FM transmitters broadcasting 168 hours a week.

Akraneskaupstaður: Stillholt 16–18, 300 Akranes; broadcasts only in Akranes; Dir BJÖRN LÁRUSSON.

Almiðlun ehf: Trönuhraun 6, 220 Hafnarfjörður; tel. 5651766; fax 5651796; broadcasts in Hafnarfjörður and Reykjavík area; Dir HALLDÓR ÁRNI SVEINSSON.

Bjarni Jónasson: Brekkugata 1, 900 Vestmannaeyjar; tel. 4811534; fax 4813475; broadcasts only in Vestmannaeyjar; Dir BJARNI JONASSON.

Búðarhreppur: Hafnargata 12, 750 Fáskrúðsfjörður; broadcasts only in Fáskrúðsfjörður.

Evrópsk Fjölmiðlun: Hlaðbae 11, 110 Reykjavík; tel. 5676111; Dir ERÍKUR SIGURBJÖRNSSON.

Fínn Miðill hf: Aðalstræti 6, 101 Reykjavík; tel. 5116500; fax 5116501.

Fjölbrautarskóli Norðurlands vestra: 550 Sauðárkrókur; broadcasts only in Sauðárkrókur.

Frostið ehf: Ráðhústorg 1, 600 Akureyri; broadcasts only in Akureyri; Dir DAVÍÐ RÚNAR GUNNARSSON.

Hallbjörn Hjartarson: Brimnesi, 545 Skagaströnd; tel. 4522960; e-mail kantrybar@islandia.is; broadcasts in Skaga-strönd, Blönduós and Sauðárkrókur; Dir HALLBJÖRN HJARTARSON.

Húsavíkurkaupstaður: Ketilsbraut 9, 640 Húsavík; tel. 4642277; broadcast in Húsavík; Dir EINAR BJÖRNSSON.

Íslenska Útvarpsfélagið hf (Icelandic Broadcasting Corporation): Lyngháls 5, 110 Reykjavík; tel. 5156000; fax 5156860; f. 1986; privately-owned; Pres. HREGGVIÐUR JÓNSSON.

   Bylgjan: Lyngháls 5, 110 Reykjavík; tel. 5156300; fax 5156830.

Kristilega útvarpsstöðin Lindin: Krókháls 4A, 110 Reykjavík; tel. 5671030; e-mail lindin@lindin.is; Dir MICHAEL E. FITZGERALD.

Suðurnesjabrosið hf: Hafnargarta 15, 230 Keflavík; tel. 4216300; fax 4216301; broadcasts only in Reykjanesbær; Dir RAGNAR ORN STEFÁNSSON.

Útvarp Vestmannaeyjar: Brekkugata 1, 900 Vestmannaeyjar; tel. 4811534; fax 4813475; broadcasts only in Vestmannaeyjar; Dir BJARNI JÓNASSON.

Útvarpsklúbburinn Sköpun: Bolholt 6, 105 Reykjavík; Dir SVERRIR JÚLÍUSSON.

Vila–Árna Útvarp: Skipholt 6, 355 Ólafsvík; tel. 4361334; fax 4361379; Dir VILHELM ARNASON.

Television

Ríkisútvarpið–Sjónvarp (Icelandic National Broadcasting Service—Television): Efstaleiti 1, 150 Reykjavík; tel. 5153000; fax 5153010; e-mail isradio@ruv.is; internet www.ruv.is; f. 1966; covers 99% of the population; broadcast daily, total 70 hours a week; Dir Gen. MARKÚS ÖRN ANTONSSON; Man. Dir BJARNI GUÐMUNDSSON.

Aksjón ehf: Strandgötu 31, 600 Akureyri; tel. 4611050; fax 4612356; e-mail aksjon@nett.is; broadcasts only in Akureyri; Dir GÍSLI GUNNLAUGSSON.

Almiðlun ehf: Trönuhraun 6, 220 Hafnarfjörður; tel. 5651766; fax 5651796; broadcasts only in Hafnarfjörður; Dir HALLDÓR ÁRNI SVEINSSON.

Fjölsýn: Strandvegur 47, 900 Vestmannaeyjar; tel. 4811300; fax 4812643; e-mail sigit@eyjar.is; broadcasts only in Vesstmannaeyjar; Dir OMAR GUÐMUNDSSON.

Húsvísk Fjölmiðlun hf: Héðinsbraut 1, 640 Húsavík; tel. 4641780; fax 4641785; broadcasts only in Húsavík; Dir OMAR GUÐMUNDSSON.

Íslenska Útvarpsfélagið hf (Icelandic Broadcasting Corporation): Lyngháls 5, 110 Reykjavík; tel. 5156000; fax 5156860; f. 1986; privately-owned 'pay-TV' station; Pres. HREGGVIÐUR JÓNSSON.

Íslenska Sjónvarpsfélagið hf: Skipholti 19, 105 Reykjavík.

Kristniboðskirkjan: Grensásvegur 8, 108 Reykjavík; tel. 5683131; fax 5683741; broadcasts only in the Reykjavík area; religious; Dir EIRÍKUR SIGURBJÖRNSSON.

Skjávarp ehf: Víkurbruat 4, 780 Höfn Hornarfirði; tel. 4700700; Dir AGÚST ÓLAFSSON.

Stöð 3: Krokhals 6, 112 Reykjavík; tel. 5335600; fax 5335699; f. 1996; Dir MAGNÚS KRISTJÁNSSON.

Sunnlensk fjömiðlun hf: Eyrarvegur 2, 800 Selfoss; tel. 4823840; fax 4833758; broadcasts only in Selfoss; Dir EINAR SIGURÐSSON.

Villa Video: Skipholt 6, 335 Ólafsvík; tel. 4361563; fax 4361379; broadcasts only in Ólafsvík; Dir VILHELM ÁRNASON.

The US Navy operates a radio station (24 hours a day), and a cable television service (80 hours a week), on the NATO base at Keflavík.

Finance

(cap. = capital; p.u. = paid up; res = reserves; dep. = deposits; m. = million; kr = krónur; brs = branches)

BANKING

Since the 1980s Iceland's banking and finance system has undergone substantial transformation. In 1989–90 the number of commercial banks was reduced from seven to three, by amalgamating four banks to form Íslandsbanki as the only remaining major commercial bank in private ownership. The 27 savings banks operate a commercial bank, Icebank, which functions as a central banking institution. In January 1995 full liberalization of foreign exchange regulations on the movement of capital was realized.

Central Bank

Seðlabanki Íslands (Central Bank of Iceland): Kalkofnsvegur 1, 150 Reykjavík; tel. 5699600; fax 5699605; e-mail sedlabanki@sedlabanki.is; internet www.sedlabanki.is; f. 1961 to take over central banking activities of Landsbanki Íslands; cap. and res 18,682m. kr, dep. 50,232m. kr (Dec. 1999); Chair. of Bd of Govs BIRGIR ÍSL. GUNNARSSON.

Commercial Banks

Búnaðarbanki Íslands (Agricultural Bank of Iceland): Austurstraeti 5, 155 Reykjavík; tel. 5256000; fax 5256189; e-mail intdiv@bi.is; internet www.bi.is; f. 1929; 85% state-owned; independent bank, incorporated and partially transferred to the private sector in 1998; cap. 5,434.5m. kr, res 119.1m. kr, dep. 80,374.6m. kr (Dec. 1998); Chair. PÁLMI JÓNSSON; Man. Dirs STEFÁN PÁLSSON, JÓN ADÓLF GUÐJÓNSSON, SÓLON R. SIGURÐSSON; 35 brs.

Icebank Ltd (Sparisjóðabanki Íslands hf): Rauðarárstígur 27, POB 5220, 125 Reykjavík; tel. 5404000; fax 5404001; e-mail icebank@icebank.spar.is; www.icebank.is; f. 1986; central bank of the 27 Icelandic savings banks and wholly owned by them; cap. 602.8m. kr, res 338.6m. kr, dep. 38,537.9m. kr (Dec. 1999); Chair. HALLGRÍMUR JÓNSSON; Man. Dir SIGURÐUR HAFSTEIN; 55 brs.

Íslandsbanki hf: Kirkjusandur, 155 Reykjavík; tel. 5608000; fax 5608522; upplysingar@isbank.is; internet www.isbank.is; f. 1990 by merger of four banks; cap. 3,877.5m. kr, res 1,076.5m. kr, dep. 96,593.1m. kr (Dec. 1998); Chair. KRISTJÁN RAGNARSSON; Group Man. Dir VALUR VALSSON; 32 brs.

Landsbanki Íslands hf (National Bank of Iceland Ltd): Austurstraeti 11, 155 Reykjavík; tel. 5606600; fax 5529882; internet www.landsbanki.is; f. 1885; 68% state-owned; incorporated and partially transferred to the private sector in 1988; cap. and res 11,391m. kr, dep. 77,821m. kr (Dec. 1999); Chair. Bd Dir HELGI S. GUÐMUNDSSON; Group Man. Dir and CEO HALLDÓR J. KRISTJANSSON; 62 brs.

Investment Bank

Fjárfestingarbanka atvinnulífsins (FBA) (Icelandic Investment Bank): Ármúla 13A, 108 Reykjavík; tel. 5805000; fax 5805099; internet www.fba.is; f. 1998 through the merger of the Fisheries Investment Fund (f. 1905), the Industrial Loan Fund (f. 1935), the Industrial Development Fund and the Export Credit Fund; specializes in financing industrial projects and venture capital; 51% state-owned; Chief Exec. BJARNI ARMANSSON.

STOCK EXCHANGE

Iceland Stock Exchange: Kalkofnsvegur 1, 150 Reykjavík; tel. 5699775; fax 5699777; e-mail stefan@vi.is; internet www.invest.is/sectors/E/companies/ise.html; f. 1985; Pres. STEFAN HALLDORSSON; Chair. EIRIKUR GUDNASON.

INSURANCE

Tryggingastofnun Ríkisins (State Social-Security Institution): Laugavegi 114, 150 Reykjavík; tel. 5604400; fax 5624535; f. 1936; Man. Dir KARL STEINAR GUÐNASON; Chair. of Tryggingaráð (Social-Security Board) BOLLI HÉÐINSSON.

Private Insurance Companies

Alþjóða líftryggingarfélagið hf: Lágmúla 5, 108 Reykjavík; tel. 5401400; fax 5401401; e-mail alif@alif.is; internet www.alif.is.

Bátatrygging Breiðafjarðar: Smiðjustíg 3, 340 Stykkishólmi; tel. 4381117; fax 4381500.

Iceland Insurance Co Ltd: Ármúla 3, 108 Reykjavík; tel. 5605060; fax 5605100; e-mail info@vis.is; f. 1989; Chair. KJARTAN GUNNARSSON; Man. Dir AXEL GÍSLASON.

Íslensk Endurtrygging hf (Icelandic Reinsurance Co Ltd): Suðurlandsbraut 6, 108 Reykjavík; tel. 5331200; fax 5331201; f. 1939; Gen. Man. BJARNI THORDARSON.

Líftryggingafélag Íslands hf: Ármúla 3, 108 Reykjavík; tel. 5605060; fax 5605100; internet www.lif.is.

Samábyrgðin hf (Icelandic Mutual Fishing Craft Insurance): Lágmúli 9, 108 Reykjavík; tel. 5681400; fax 5584645; f. 1909; Man. Dir PÁLL SIGURDSSON.

Sameinaða líftryggingarfélagið hf: Sigtún 42, POB 5180, 125 Reykjavík; tel. 5695400; fax 5815455.

Sjóvá-Almennar tryggingar hf (Marine-General Insurance Co): Kringlan 5, POB 3200, 123 Reykjavík; tel. 5692500; fax 5813718; f. 1988; all branches except life; Chair. BENEDIKT SVEINSSON; Gen. Mans EINAR SVEINSSON, ÓLAFUR B. THORS.

Trygging hf: Aðalstræti 6, 101 Reykjavík; tel. 5152000; fax 5152020.

Tryggingamiðstöðin hf: Aðalstræti 6, 101 Reykjavík; tel. 5152000; fax 5152020; internet www.tmhf.is.

Vátryggingafélag Íslands hf: Ármúla 3, 108 Reykjavík; tel. 5605060; fax 5605100; e-mail upplysingar@vis.is; internet www.vis.is.

Vélbátaábyrgðarfélag Ísfirðinga: Kringlan 5, 103 Reykjavík; tel. 5692500; fax 5813718.

Vélbátaábyrgðarfélagið Grótta: Síðumúla 29, 108 Reykjavík; tel. 5536800; fax 5536812.

Viðlagatrygging Íslands: Laugavegi 162, 105 Reykjavík; tel. 5529677; fax 5629675.

Vörður—Vátryggingafélag: Skipagötu 9, 600 Akureyri; tel. 4648000; fax 4648001; e-mail oli@vordur.is.

Supervisory Authority

Fjármálaeftirlitið: Suðurlandsbraut 32, 108 Reykjavík; tel. 5252700; fax 5252727; e-mail fme@fme.is; internet www.fme.is; f. 1974 as Vátryggingaeftirlitið; present name adotped 1999; Man. Dir PÁLL GUNNAR PÁLSSON.

Trade and Industry

GOVERNMENT AGENCIES

Orkustofnun (National Energy Authority): Grensásvegi 9, 108 Reykjavík; tel. 5696000; fax 5688896; e-mail os@os.is; internet www.os.is; f. 1967; advises the Minister of Industry and Commerce on matters concerning energy; studies Icelandic energy resources and energy uses; Dir Gen. THORKELL HELGASON.

Trade Council of Iceland: POB 1000, 121 Reykjavík; tel. 5114000; fax 5114040; e-mail icetrade@icetrade.is; internet www.icetrade.is; provides information on Icelandic exporters and products; Man. Dir JÓN ASBERGSSON.

CHAMBER OF COMMERCE

Verslunarrád Íslands (Iceland Chamber of Commerce): Hús verslunarinnar, 103 Reykjavík; tel. 5107100; fax 5686564; e-mail mottaka@chamber.is; internet www.chamber.is; f. 1917; Chair. BOGI PALSSON; Gen. Sec. VILHJÁLMUR EGILSSON; 370 mems.

INDUSTRIAL AND TRADE ASSOCIATIONS

Fiskifélag Íslands (Fisheries Association): Reykjavík; tel. 5510500; fax 5527969; e-mail fi@fiskifelag.is; internet www.fiskifelag.is; f. 1911; conducts technical and economic research and services for fishing vessels and for fishing industry; Man. PETUR BJARNASON.

Landssamband Íslenzkra Utvegsmanna (Fishing Vessel Owners' Federation): POB 893, Reykjavík; tel. 5509500; fax 5509501; e-mail fridrik@liu.is; f. 1939; Chair. K. RAGNARSSON; Man. FRIÐRIK JÓN ARNGRÍMSSON.

SÍF Ltd (Union of Icelandic Fish Producers Ltd): Fjarðargata 13–15, POB 20, 222 Hafnarfjörður; tel. 5508000; fax 5508001; e-mail sif@sif.is; f. 1932; exporting salted fish and fish products; Gen. Man. GUNNAR ÖRN KRISTJÁNSSON.

EMPLOYERS' ORGANIZATIONS

Samtök atvinnulífsins (Confederation of Icelandic Employers): Garðastræti 41, POB 520, 121 Reykjavík; tel. 5115000; fax 5115050; e-mail jonina.gissurardottir@sa.is; f. 1934; Chair. FINNUR GEIRSSON; Man. Dir ARI EDWALD.

Samtök Iðnaðarins (Federation of Icelandic Industries—FII): Hallveigarstig 1, POB 1450, 121 Reykjavík; tel. 5115555; fax 5115566; e-mail mottaka@si.is; internet www.si.is; f. 1993 by merger of Federation of Icelandic Industries (f. 1933), Federation of Icelandic Crafts and Industries (f. 1932) and four other employers' organizations; Chair. VILMUNDUR JOSEFSSON; Gen. Man SVEINN HANNESSON; 2,500 mems.

UTILITIES
Electricity

Hitaveita Suðurnesja (Suðurnes Regional Heating Corpn): Brekkustíg 36, POB 225, 260 Nardvík; f. 1974; produces and distributes hot-water heating and electricity for the Suðurnes region.

Landsvirkjun (National Power Company): Háaleitisbraut 68, 103 Reykjavík; tel. 5159000; fax 5159007; e-mail landsvirkjun@lv.is; internet www.landsvirkjun.is; f. 1965; generates, transmits, sells and distributes electric power wholesale to public distribution systems and industrial enterprises; Chair. JOHANNES GEIR SIGURGEIRSSON; Man. Dir FRIDRIK SOPHUSSON.

Orkubú Vestfjarda (Vestfjords Power Company): Stakkanesi 1, 400 Isafjördur; f. 1977; produces, distributes and sells electrical energy in the Vestfjords area.

Rafmagnsveitur RíkisinsRARIK (Iceland State Electricity): Rauðarárstíg 10, 105 Reykjavík; tel. 5605500; fax 5605600; internet www.rarik.is; f. 1947; produces, procures, distributes and sells electrical energy; also provides consultancy services.

TRADE UNIONS

Althýðusamband Íslands (ASÍ) (Icelandic Federation of Labour): Grensásvegi 16A, POB 8720, 128 Reykjavík; tel. 5813044; fax 5680093; e-mail skrifst@asi.is; f. 1916; affiliated to ICFTU, the European Trade Union Confederation and the Council of Nordic Trade Unions; Chair. GRÉTAR THORSTEINSSON; Gen. Sec. ARI SKÚLASON; 65,000 mems.

Menningar- og Fraeðslusamband Althýðu (MFA) (Workers' Educational Association): Grensásveg 16A, 108 Reykjavík; tel. 5331818; fax 5331819; e-mail ieg@asi.is; internet www.asi.is; Chair. HAUKUR HARDARSON; Gen. Sec. INGIBJORG E. GUDMUNDSDOTTIR.

Bandalag Starfsmanna Ríkis og Baeja (BSRB) (Municipal and Government Employees' Association): Grettisgötu 89, 105 Reykjavík; tel. 5626688; fax 5629106; e-mail bsrb@tv.is; f. 1942; Chair. ÖGMUNDUR JÓNASSON; 16,855 mems.

Blaðamannafélag Íslands (Union of Icelandic Journalists): Síðumúla 23, Reykjavík; tel. 5539155; fax 5539177; e-mail bi@press.is; internet www.press.is; f. 1897; Chair. HJÁLMAR JÓNSSON; 400 mems.

Transport

RAILWAYS

There are no railways in Iceland.

ROADS

Much of the interior is uninhabited and the main road follows the coastline. Regular motor coach services link the main settlements. At 31 December 1998 Iceland had 12,681 km of roads, of which 4,304 km were main roads.

Bifreiðastöð Íslands hf (BSÍ) (Iceland Motor Coach Service): Umferðarmiðstöðinni, Vatnsmýrarveg 10, 101 Reykjavík; tel. 5522300; fax 5529973; f. 1936; 45 scheduled bus lines throughout Iceland; also operates sightseeing tours and excursions; Chair. ÓSKAR SIGURJÓNSSON; Man. Dir GUNNAR SVEINSSON.

SHIPPING

Heavy freight is carried by coastal shipping. The principal seaport for international shipping is Reykjavík.

Port Authority

Port of Reykjavík: Hafnarhusi, Tryggvagotu 17, 121 Reykjavík; tel. 5528900; fax 5258990; e-mail hofnin@rhofn.rvk.is; internet www.rvk.is/hofnin; Harbour Master JÓN A. INGÓLFSSON.

Principal Companies

Eimskip (Iceland Steamship Co Ltd): Pósthússtraeti 2, POB 220, 101 Reykjavík; tel. 5257000; fax 5257009; e-mail info@eimskip.com; internet www.eimskip.com; f. 1914 as Eimskipafélag Íslands; transportation and logistics services incl. ground operation, warehousing, coastal service, trucking and intermodal transportation between Iceland and the UK, Scandinavia, the Baltic, the rest of Europe, the USA and Canada; Man. Dir HÖRÐUR SIGURGESTSSON.

Nesskip hf: POB 175, 172 Seltjarnarnes; tel. 5625055; fax 5612052; e-mail nesskip@nesskip.is; internet www.nesskip.is; f. 1974; bulk cargo shipping services to the USA, Canada, Russia, Scandinavia, the Baltic countries and other parts of Europe; agency and chartering for vessels in all Icelandic ports; Chair. E. SVEINSSON; Man. Dir G. ÁSGEIRSSON.

Samskip hf: Holtabakki v/Holtaveg, 104 Reykjavík; tel. 5698300; fax 5698327; e-mail samskip@samskip.is; internet www.samskip.is; services to Europe, USA, and the Far East; Dir ÓLAFUR ÓLAFSSON.

CIVIL AVIATION

Air transport is particularly important to Iceland and is used both for the transport of people and to transport agricultural produce from remote districts. More than 90% of passenger traffic between Iceland and other countries is by air. There are regular air services between Reykjavík and outlying townships. There is an international airport at Keflavík, 47 km from Reykjavík.

Air Atlanta Icelandic: Atlanta House, POB 80, 270 Mosfellsbaer; tel. 5667700; fax 5667766; e-mail admin@atlanta.is; internet www.atlanta.is; f. 1986; scheduled and charter international and domestic flights; Chair. THORA GUDMUNDSDOTTIR JOHANNSSON.

Air Iceland: Reykjavík Airport, 101 Reykjavík; tel. 5703000; fax 5703001; e-mail jonkarl@airiceland.is; internet www.airiceland.is;

f. 1959; scheduled, regional flights; 96%-owned by Icelandair; Chair. SIGURDUR HELGASON; Gen. Man. JÓN KARL ÓLAFSSON.

Icelandair (Flugleiðir hf): Reykjavík Airport, 101 Reykjavík; tel. 5050300; fax 5050350; e-mail pr@icelandair.is; internet www.icelandair.net; f. 1973 as the holding company for the two principal Icelandic airlines, Flugfélag Íslands (f. 1937) and Loftleiðir (f. 1944); in 1979 all licences, permits and authorizations previously held by Flugfélag Íslands and Loftleiðir were transferred to it; network centred in Reykjavík, to nine domestic airfields, and scheduled external services to more than 20 international destinations in northern Europe and the USA; Pres. and CEO SIGURÐUR HELGASON.

Tourism

Iceland's main attraction for tourists lies in the rugged beauty of the interior, with its geysers and thermal springs. In 1999 there were 262,605 tourist arrivals, an increase of more than 30,000 visitors compared with 1998.

Iceland Tourist Board: Laekjargata 3, 101 Reykjavík; tel. 5527488; fax 5624749; internet www.icetourist.is; Gen. Man. MAGNÚS ODDSSON.

INDIA

Introductory Survey

Location, Climate, Language, Religion, Flag, Capital

The Republic of India forms a natural sub-continent, with the Himalaya mountain range to the north. Two sections of the Indian Ocean—the Arabian Sea and the Bay of Bengal—lie to the west and east, respectively. India's neighbours are Tibet (the Xizang Autonomous Region of the People's Republic of China), Bhutan and Nepal to the north, Pakistan to the north-west and Myanmar (formerly Burma) to the north-east, while Bangladesh is surrounded by Indian territory except for a short frontier with Myanmar in the east. Near India's southern tip, across the Palk Strait, is Sri Lanka. India's climate ranges from temperate to tropical, with an average summer temperature on the plains of approximately 27°C (85°F). Annual rainfall varies widely, but the summer monsoon brings heavy rain over much of the country in June and July. The official language is Hindi, spoken by about 30% of the population. English is used as an associate language for many official purposes. The Indian Constitution also recognizes 17 regional languages, of which the most widely spoken are Telugu, Bengali, Marathi, Tamil, Urdu and Gujarati. In addition, many other local languages are used. According to the 1991 census, about 82% of the population are Hindus and 11% Muslims. There are also Christians, Sikhs, Buddhists, Jains and other minorities. The national flag (proportions 3 by 2) has three equal horizontal stripes, of saffron, white and green, with the Dharma Chakra (Wheel of the Law), in blue, in the centre of the white stripe. The capital is New Delhi.

Recent History

After a prolonged struggle against British colonial rule, India became independent, within the Commonwealth, on 15 August 1947. The United Kingdom's Indian Empire was partitioned, broadly on a religious basis, between India and Pakistan. The principal nationalist movement that had opposed British rule was the Indian National Congress (later known as the Congress Party). At independence the Congress leader, Jawaharlal Nehru, became India's first Prime Minister. Sectarian violence, the movement of 12m. refugees, the integration of the former princely states into the Indian federal structure and a territorial dispute with Pakistan over Kashmir presented major problems to the new Government.

India became independent as a dominion, with the British monarch as Head of State, represented by an appointed Governor-General. In November 1949, however, the Constituent Assembly approved a republican Constitution, providing for a president (with mainly ceremonial functions) as head of state. Accordingly, India became a republic on 26 January 1950, although remaining a member of the Commonwealth. France transferred sovereignty of Chandernagore to India in May 1950, and ceded its four remaining Indian settlements in 1954.

The lack of effective opposition to Congress policies expedited industrialization and social reform. In December 1961 Indian forces overran the Portuguese territories of Goa, Daman and Diu, which were immediately annexed by India. Border disputes with the People's Republic of China escalated into a brief military conflict in 1962. Nehru died in May 1964 and was succeeded by Lal Bahadur Shastri. India and Pakistan fought a second war over Kashmir in 1965. Following mediation by the USSR, Shastri and President Ayub Khan of Pakistan signed a joint declaration, aimed at a peaceful settlement of the Kashmir dispute, on 10 January 1966. Shastri died on the following day, however, and Nehru's daughter, Indira Gandhi, became Prime Minister.

Following the presidential election of August 1969, when two factions of Congress supported different candidates, the success of Indira Gandhi's candidate split the party. The Organization (Opposition) Congress, led by Morarji Desai, emerged in November, but at the next general election to the lower house of the legislature, the Lok Sabha (House of the People), held in March 1971, Indira Gandhi's wing of Congress won 350 of the 515 elective seats.

Border incidents led to a 12-day war with Pakistan in December 1971. The Indian army rapidly occupied East Pakistan, which India recognized as the independent state of Bangla-

desh. Indira Gandhi and President Zulfikar Ali Bhutto of Pakistan held a summit conference at Shimla in June–July 1972, when the two leaders agreed that their respective forces should respect the cease-fire line in Kashmir, and that India and Pakistan should resolve their differences through bilateral negotiations or other peaceful means. In 1975 the former protectorate of Sikkim became the 22nd state of the Indian Union, leading to tensions in India's relations with Nepal.

A general election to the Lok Sabha was held in March 1977, when the number of elective seats was increased to 542. The election resulted in victory for the Janata (People's) Party, chaired by Morarji Desai, who became Prime Minister. The Janata Party and an allied party, the Congress for Democracy, together won 298 of the 540 seats where polling took place. Congress obtained 153 seats. In January 1978 Indira Gandhi became leader of a new breakaway political group, the Congress (Indira) Party, known as Congress (I).

In 1979 the Government's ineffectual approach to domestic problems provoked a wave of defections by Lok Sabha members of the Janata Party. Many joined Raj Narain, who formed a new party, the Lok Dal, the policies of which were based on secularism. Congress (I) lost its position as official opposition party after defections from its ranks to the then official Congress Party by members who objected to Indira Gandhi's perceived authoritarianism. The resignation of Desai's Government in July was followed by the departure from the Janata Party of Charan Singh, who became the leader of the Lok Dal and, shortly afterwards, Prime Minister in a coalition with both Congress parties. When Congress (I) withdrew its support, Singh's 24-day administration collapsed, and Parliament was dissolved. A general election to the Lok Sabha was held in January 1980. Congress (I) received 42.7% of the total votes and won an overwhelming majority (352) of the elective seats. The Janata Party won only 31 seats, while the Lok Dal secured 41 seats. Indira Gandhi was reinstated as Prime Minister. Presidential rule was imposed in nine states, hitherto governed by opposition parties, in February. At elections to state assemblies in June, Congress (I) won majorities in eight of them.

By-elections in June 1981 for the Lok Sabha and state assemblies were notable because of the overwhelming victory that Rajiv Gandhi, the Prime Minister's son, obtained in the former constituency of his late brother (killed in an air crash in 1980) and because of the failure of the fragmented Janata Party to win any seats. In February 1983 Rajiv Gandhi became a General Secretary of Congress (I).

Indira Gandhi's Government faced serious problems, as intercommunal disturbances in several states (particularly Assam and Meghalaya) continued in 1982–83, with violent protests against the presence of Bengali immigrants. Election defeats in Andhra Pradesh, Karnataka and Tripura represented a series of set-backs for Indira Gandhi. Disturbances occurred in Jammu and Kashmir during local elections in 1983 and 1984. Alleged police corruption and the resurgence of caste violence (notably in Bihar and Gujarat) caused further problems for the Government.

There was also unrest in the Sikh community of Punjab, despite the election to the Indian presidency in July 1982 of Giani Zail Singh, the first Sikh to hold the position. Demands were made for greater religious recognition, for the settlement of grievances over land and water rights, and over the sharing of the state capital at Chandigarh with Haryana; in addition, a minority called for the creation of a separate Sikh state ('Khalistan'). In October 1983 the state was brought under presidential rule. However, the violence continued, and followers of an extremist Sikh leader, Jarnail Singh Bhindranwale, established a terrorist stronghold inside the Golden Temple (the Sikh holy shrine) at Amritsar. The Government sent in troops to dislodge the terrorists and the assault resulted in the death of Bhindranwale and hundreds of his supporters, and serious damage to surrounding buildings. A curfew was imposed, and army personnel blockaded Amritsar.

In October 1984 Indira Gandhi was assassinated by militant Sikh members of her personal guard. Her son, Rajiv Gandhi, was immediately sworn in as Prime Minister, despite his lack of ministerial experience. The widespread communal violence that erupted throughout India, resulting in more than 2,000 deaths, was curbed by prompt government action. Congress (I) achieved a decisive victory in elections to the Lok Sabha in December. Including the results of the January 1985 polling, the party received 49.2% of the total votes and won 403 of the 513 contested seats.

In February 1986 there were mass demonstrations and strikes throughout India in protest at government-imposed increases in the prices of basic commodities. The opposition parties united against Rajiv Gandhi's policies, and Congress (I) suffered considerable reversals in the indirect elections to the upper house of the legislature, the Rajya Sabha (Council of States) in March. In April Rajiv Gandhi attempted to purge Congress (I) of critics calling themselves 'Indira Gandhi loyalists', and, in a major government reorganization, he appointed Sikhs to two senior positions. The Prime Minister survived an assassination attempt by three Sikhs in October.

In June 1986 Laldenga, the leader of the Mizo National Front (MNF), signed a peace agreement with Rajiv Gandhi, thus ending Mizoram's 25 years of rebellion. The accord granted Mizoram limited autonomy in the drafting of local laws, independent trade with neighbouring foreign countries and a general amnesty for all Mizo rebels. Laldenga led an interim coalition government until February 1987, when the MNF won an absolute majority at elections to the state assembly. In that month Mizoram and Arunachal Pradesh were officially admitted as the 23rd and 24th states of India, and in May the Union Territory of Goa became India's 25th state.

During 1987 Congress (I) experienced serious political setbacks. It sustained defeats in a number of state elections, and political tensions were intensified by an open dispute between the Prime Minister and the outgoing President, Giani Zail Singh. Public concern was aroused by various accusations of corruption and financial irregularities made against senior figures in the ruling party. Notable among these scandals was the 'Bofors affair', in which large payments were allegedly made to Indian agents by a Swedish company in connection with its sales of munitions to the Indian Government. The Prime Minister denied any involvement, and a committee of inquiry subsequently exonerated him of any impropriety. Several ministers resigned from the Government, among them the Minister of Defence, Vishwanath Pratap (V. P.) Singh, who was also, with three other senior politicians, expelled from Congress (I) in July for 'anti-party activities'. V.P. Singh soon emerged as the leader of the Congress (I) dissidents, and in October formed a new political group, the Jan Morcha (People's Front), advocating more radical social change.

In 1988 a more confrontational style was adopted by the central administration towards non-Congress (I) state governments, and presidential rule was imposed in states suffering political instability. The opposition forces attained a degree of unity when four major centrist parties, the Indian National Congress (S), the Jan Morcha, the Janata Party and the Lok Dal, and three major regional parties formed a coalition National Front (Rashtriya Morcha), to oppose Congress (I) at the next election. Three of the four centrist parties formed a new political grouping, the Janata Dal (People's Party), which was to work in collaboration with the National Front. V.P. Singh, who was widely regarded as Rajiv Gandhi's closest rival, was elected President of the Janata Dal.

At the general election to the Lok Sabha held in November 1989, Congress (I) lost its overall majority. Of the 525 contested seats, it won 193, the Janata Dal and its electoral allies in the National Front won 141 and three, respectively, and the right-wing Hindu nationalist Bharatiya Janata Party (BJP) won 88. In early December, after the National Front had been promised the support of the communist parties and the BJP, V.P. Singh was sworn in as the new Prime Minister. He appointed Devi Lal, the populist Chief Minister of Haryana and President of Lok Dal (B), as Deputy Prime Minister, and a Kashmiri Muslim, Mufti Mohammed Sayeed, as Minister of Home Affairs. This latter appointment was widely seen as a gesture of reconciliation to the country's Muslims and as reaffirmation of the Government's secular stance. A few weeks later V.P. Singh's Government won a vote of confidence in the Lok Sabha, despite the abstention of all the Congress (I) members. In January 1990 the Government ordered the mass resignation of all the state Governors; the President then appointed new ones. In February elections were held to 10 state assemblies, all formerly controlled

by Congress (I). Congress (I) lost power in eight of the 10 assemblies and there was a notable increase in support for the BJP.

In July 1990 Devi Lal was dismissed from his post as Deputy Prime Minister, for nepotism, disloyalty and for making unsubstantiated accusations of corruption against ministerial colleagues. In August there were violent demonstrations in many northern Indian states against the Government's populist decision to implement the recommendations of the 10-year-old Mandal Commission and to raise the quota of government and public-sector jobs reserved for deprived sections of the population. In October the Supreme Court directed the Government to halt temporarily the implementation of the quota scheme, in an attempt to curb the caste violence.

In October 1990 the BJP withdrew its support for the National Front, following the arrest of its President, Lal Krishna Advani, as he led a controversial procession of Hindu devotees to the holy town of Ayodhya, in Uttar Pradesh, to begin the construction of a Hindu temple on the site of a disused ancient mosque. V.P. Singh accused the BJP leader of deliberately inciting intercommunal hatred by exhorting Hindu extremists to join him in illegally tearing down the mosque. Paramilitary troops were sent to Ayodhya, and thousands of Hindu activists were arrested, in an attempt to prevent a Muslim–Hindu confrontation. However, following repeated clashes between police and crowds, Hindu extremists stormed and slightly damaged the mosque and laid siege to it for several days.

In November 1990 one of the Prime Minister's leading rivals in the Janata Dal, Chandra Shekhar (with the support of Devi Lal), formed his own dissident faction, known as the Janata Dal (Socialist) or Janata Dal (S) (which merged with the Janata Party in April 1991 to become the Samajwadi Party). The Lok Sabha convened for a special session, at which the Government overwhelmingly lost a vote of confidence. V.P. Singh immediately resigned, and the President invited Rajiv Gandhi, as leader of the party holding the largest number of seats in the Lok Sabha, to form a new government. Rajiv Gandhi refused the offer, in favour of Chandra Shekhar. Although the strength of the Janata Dal (S) in the Lok Sabha comprised only about 60 deputies, Congress (I) had earlier offered it unconditional parliamentary support. On 10 November 1990 Chandra Shekhar was sworn in as Prime Minister. Devi Lal became Deputy Prime Minister and President of the Janata Dal (S). Shekhar won a vote of confidence in the Lok Sabha and a new Council of Ministers was appointed. Although Shekhar succeeded in initiating talks between the two sides in the Ayodhya dispute, violence between Hindus and Muslims increased throughout India in December.

In January 1991 the Prime Minister imposed direct rule in Tamil Nadu, claiming that this was necessitated by the increased activity of Sri Lankan Tamil militants in the state, which had led to the breakdown of law and order. In the resultant riots more than 1,000 arrests were made. The Government suffered a further set-back in February. Five members of the Council of Ministers were forced to resign when they lost their seats in the Lok Sabha for violating India's anti-defection laws: they had left the Janata Dal to join the Janata Dal (S). The fragility of the parliamentary alliance between the Janata Dal (S) and Congress (I) became apparent in March, when the Congress (I) deputies boycotted Parliament, following the revelation that Rajiv Gandhi's house had been kept under police surveillance. In an unexpected counter-move, Chandra Shekhar resigned, but accepted the President's request that he remain as head of an interim Government until the holding of a fresh general election.

As the general election, which was scheduled to take place over three days in late May 1991, approached, it seemed likely that no party would win an outright majority and that the political stalemate would continue. On 21 May, however, after the first day's polling had taken place, Rajiv Gandhi was assassinated, by members of the Tamil separatist group, the Liberation Tigers of Tamil Eelam (LTTE), while campaigning in Tamil Nadu. Consequently, the remaining elections were postponed until mid-June. The final result gave Congress (I) 227 of the 511 seats contested, the BJP, which almost doubled its share of the vote compared with its performance in the 1989 general election, won 119 seats, and the Janata Dal, the popularity of which had considerably declined, gained only 55 seats. P.V. Narasimha Rao, who had been elected as acting President of Congress (I) following Rajiv Gandhi's assassination, assumed the premiership and appointed a new Council of Ministers. The new Government's main priority on assuming power was to attempt to solve the country's severe economic crisis, caused by an enormous foreign debt, high inflation, a large deficit on the current account of the balance of payments, and an extreme shortage of foreign exchange reserves. The new Minister of Finance, Dr Manmohan Singh (an experienced economist and former Governor of the Reserve Bank of India), launched a far-reaching programme of economic liberalization and reform, including the dismantling of bureaucratic regulations and the encouragement of private and foreign investment. In late September the Government announced the adoption of the recommendations of the Mandal Commission that 27% of government jobs and institutional places be reserved for certain lower castes, in addition to the 22.5% already reserved for 'untouchable' castes and tribal people. (In November 1992 the Supreme Court ruled that non-Hindus, such as Christians and Sikhs, who were socially disadvantaged were also entitled to job reservations.)

After a brief reconciliatory period in the latter half of 1991, Narasimha Rao's Government began to be faced with problems, both from opposition agitation and from within its own ranks. In January 1992 the BJP increased communal tension between Hindus and Muslims by hoisting the national flag on Republic Day in Srinagar, the capital of Kashmir (see below). In mid-1992 efforts were also made by the BJP to use the contentious issue of the Ayodhya site (the Ram Janmabhoomi/Babri Masjid—Hindu temple/Muslim mosque—dispute, see above) to embarrass the Government. In May a major financial scandal involving the Bombay Stock Exchange was uncovered. It was alleged that several members of the Council of Ministers were amongst the beneficiaries, allegations that prompted the resignation of the Minister of State for Commerce. In July, however, the Congress (I) candidate, Dr Shankar Dayal Sharma, was elected, with no serious opposition, to the presidency.

Following the collapse of talks in November 1992 between the Vishwa Hindu Parishad (VHP) (World Hindu Council) and the All India Babri Masjid Action Committee regarding the Ayodhya dispute, the VHP and the BJP appealed for volunteers to begin the construction of a Hindu temple on the site of the existing mosque in early December. As thousands of Hindu militants assembled in Ayodhya, thousands of paramilitary troops were dispatched to the town in an attempt to avert any violence. Despite the armed presence, however, the temple/ mosque complex was stormed by the Hindu volunteers, who proceeded to tear down the remains of the ancient mosque. This highly inflammatory action provoked widespread communal violence throughout India (Bombay, or Mumbai as it was later renamed, being one of the worst-affected areas), which resulted in more than 1,200 deaths, and prompted world-wide condemnation, notably from the neighbouring Islamic states of Pakistan and Bangladesh, where violent anti-Hindu demonstrations were subsequently held. The central Government also strongly condemned the desecration and demolition of the holy building and pledged to rebuild it. The leaders of the BJP, including L. K. Advani and the party's President, Dr Murli Manohar Joshi, and the leaders of the VHP were arrested, the BJP Chief Minister of Uttar Pradesh resigned, the state legislature was dissolved and Uttar Pradesh was placed under President's rule. The security forces took full control of Ayodhya, including the disputed complex, meeting with little resistance. The Government banned five communal organizations, including the VHP and two Muslim groups, on the grounds that they promoted disharmony among different religious communities. Throughout India stringent measures were taken by the security forces to suppress the Hindu/Muslim violence, which lasted for about one week. In mid-December the Government established a commission of inquiry into the events leading to the demolition of the mosque at Ayodhya. In an attempt to avert any further acts of Hindu militancy, the central Government dismissed the BJP administrations in Madhya Pradesh, Rajasthan and Himachal Pradesh and placed these three states under presidential rule. Narasimha Rao's various actions were given implicit approval later that month when a motion of 'no confidence' presented by the BJP against the Government was soundly defeated. In late December the Government announced plans to acquire all the disputed areas in Ayodhya. The acquired land would be made available to two trusts, which would be responsible for the construction of a new Hindu temple and a new mosque and for the planned development of the site.

There was a resurgence in Hindu/Muslim violence in India's commercial centre, Mumbai, and in Ahmedabad in January

1993, however, necessitating the imposition of curfews and the dispatch of thousands of extra paramilitary troops to curb the serious unrest. In an apparent attempt to restore public confidence in the Government, Narasimha Rao carried out an extensive reshuffle of the Council of Ministers in mid-January. Despite a government ban on communal rallies, thousands of Hindu militants attempted to converge on the centre of New Delhi to attend a mass rally organized by the BJP in late February. In an effort to prevent the proposed rally taking place, thousands of BJP activists were arrested throughout India and the crowds that did gather in the capital were dispersed by the security forces using batons and tear gas. In March there were a number of bomb explosions in Mumbai, which caused about 250 casualties. The Government claimed that the explosions were linked with Pakistan intelligence agencies.

In July 1993 Narasimha Rao narrowly survived a vote of 'no confidence', which was moved in the Lok Sabha by virtually all the opposition parties. The following month the Prime Minister suffered a blow to his political prestige when the Government was forced to abandon two proposed bills (aimed at the BJP, in particular), which would have banned political parties from using religious appeals in campaigns. However, in November in the state assembly elections in the four northern states where BJP state administrations had been dismissed by the central Government in December 1992 following the Ayodhya crisis, the BJP regained power in only one state, Rajasthan, while Congress (I) obtained outright majorities in Himachal Pradesh and Madhya Pradesh. These results appeared to highlight a definite decline in the popularity of the BJP. In December 1993 Congress (I)'s political standing was strengthened when a small faction of the Janata Dal led by Ajit Singh merged with the ruling party, thus giving the latter a parliamentary majority.

The following year, 1994, was, for the most part, a period of relative political stability. The extensive economic reforms continued to show positive results and Narasimha Rao's premiership appeared fairly secure, with the opposition suffering from fragmentation (particularly the Janata Dal) and with no serious challenges from within Congress (I) itself. In mid-1994, however, the opposition deputies boycotted parliamentary proceedings for three weeks in protest at what they regarded as lack of effective action following an official inquiry into the 1992 securities scandal in order to understate the involvement of Congress (I) ministers. The popularity and strength of the ruling Congress (I) appeared to have declined considerably by the end of 1994, when the party suffered crushing defeats in elections to the state assemblies in Andhra Pradesh and Karnataka (former strongholds of Congress (I)); it was also defeated in state elections in Sikkim. In late December the Government's image was enhanced to some extent when three ministers were finally forced to resign over their alleged roles in corruption scandals (the Prime Minister had earlier been reluctant to dismiss them). Shortly afterwards, the Minister for Human Resource Development, Arjun Singh, who was widely viewed as Narasimha Rao's main rival within Congress (I), resigned from his post, citing his dissatisfaction and frustration at the Government's perceived incompetence regarding corruption, the Bombay Stock Exchange scandal, the Ayodhya crisis and the investigation into Rajiv Gandhi's assassination. In January 1995, with important state elections rapidly approaching, Narasimha Rao attempted to quell increasing dissent within his Government and party by suspending Arjun Singh from the working committee of Congress (I) for 'anti-party activities'; in the following month the rebel politician was expelled from the party. In May Singh, together with Narain Dutt Tewari, recruited dissident members of Congress (I) in many states and formed a new breakaway party, known as the All India Indira Congress (Tewari); the party merged with Congress (I), however, in December 1996.

Congress (I) enjoyed mixed results in the state elections held in February/March 1995. In an apparent attempt to bolster his political standing, Narasimha Rao reshuffled and enlarged the Council of Ministers in mid-September. In January 1996, however, accusations of corruption came to the fore in Indian politics when the Central Bureau of Investigation charged seven leading politicians, including L.K. Advani of the BJP, Devi Lal and Arjun Singh, and sought the prosecution of three Union ministers (who subsequently resigned) for allegedly accepting bribes of large amounts of money from a Delhi-based industrialist, Surendra Jain. The sheer scale of the scandal (known as the Hawala— illegal money transfer—case), with regard to the size of the sums involved and the number of people implicated, led to widespread public disillusionment with politicians in general. The BJP attempted to implicate Narasimha Rao in the scandal by releasing a purported statement by Jain alleging that payments were made to the Prime Minister; these accusations were promptly denied by Narasimha Rao. The Prime Minister was also faced with more serious and potentially more damaging difficulties concerning the prosecution, on charges of cheating and criminal conspiracy, of a flamboyant faith healer and 'godman', Chandraswami, who had been consulted by generations of political leaders, including Narasimha Rao himself. At the end of January another high-ranking political figure, the President of the Janata Dal, S.R. Bommai, was implicated in the scandal; Bommai subsequently resigned from his post. In February Congress (I)'s hopes of retaining power in the forthcoming general election appeared increasingly fragile when three more ministers resigned from the Council of Ministers after their names had been linked to the Hawala case.

The results of the general election, which was held over three days at the end of April and early May 1996, gave no party or group an overall majority. The largest party in terms of seats was the BJP, which won 160 seats, and with the support of the Shiv Sena and other smaller allies could count on an overall legislative strength of 194 seats. Congress (I) gained 136 seats. The National Front (comprising the Janata Dal and its allies) and Left Front (representing the two major communist parties) together obtained 179 seats, with the remainder won by minor parties and independents. On 15 May, as soon as the electoral position was clear, the President asked the BJP under its new parliamentary leader, Atal Bihari Vajpayee, to form the new Government and to prove its majority support within two weeks. Given the antagonism felt towards the BJP by the majority of other political parties, the latter proved impossible, and Vajpayee resigned on 28 May in anticipation of his Government's inevitable defeat in a parliamentary vote of confidence. In the mean time, the National and Left Fronts had merged to form an informal coalition known as the United Front (UF), which comprised a total of 13 parties, with the Janata Dal, the Samajwadi Party, the two communist parties and the regional Dravida Munnetra Kazhagam (DMK) and Telugu Desam as its major components. With Congress (I) prepared to lend external support, the UF was able to form a Government at the end of May. A former Chief Minister of Karnataka, H. D. Deve Gowda, was selected to lead the UF and the new Government.

In September 1996 Narasimha Rao resigned from the leadership of Congress (I) after he was ordered to stand trial for his alleged involvement in the Chandraswami case; the party presidency was assumed by the veteran politician, Sitaram Kesri. Later that month separate charges of forgery and criminal conspiracy (dating back to the former Prime Minister's tenure of the external affairs ministry in the 1980s) were made against the beleaguered Narasimha Rao; he resigned in December 1996 as Congress (I)'s parliamentary leader and was replaced in the following month by Kesri.

At the end of March 1997 Deve Gowda was faced with a serious political crisis when Congress (I) threatened to withdraw its parliamentary support for the UF Government. On 11 April the Prime Minister resigned following the defeat of the UF administration in a vote of confidence (by 158 votes to 292). A few days later Inder Kumar Gujral, the Minister of External Affairs in the outgoing Government, was chosen by the UF to replace Deve Gowda as leader of the coalition. On 22 April Gujral was sworn in as Prime Minister and appointed a new Council of Ministers. In May Sonia Gandhi, the widow of the former Prime Minister Rajiv Gandhi, joined Congress (I) as a 'primary member', and in the following month Kesri was re-elected President of the party in Congress (I)'s first contested leadership poll since 1977. In June 1997 the ruling coalition was faced with another high-level corruption case when the President of the Janata Dal and Chief Minister of Bihar, Laloo Prasad Yadav, was forced to resign from his posts prior to his arrest on several counts of conspiracy in an animal fodder scandal. Yadav subsequently formed a breakaway faction of his party, known as the Rashtriya Janata Dal, and Sharad Yadav was elected as the new President of the Janata Dal. In July Kocheril Raman Narayanan was elected, almost unanimously, as India's new President; this appointment was particularly notable in that Narayanan was the first Indian President to originate from a Dalit (or 'untouchable') background. In September former Prime Minister Narasimha Rao was charged in a Delhi court with corruption and criminal conspiracy. In the

same month a five-year investigation into the destruction of the mosque at Ayodhya in 1992 led to charges of criminal conspiracy and incitement to riot being filed against senior BJP and religious leaders, including L. K. Advani and the leader of Shiv Sena, Balashaheb 'Bal' Thackeray.

The UF Government looked increasingly insecure in late November 1997 when Congress (I) threatened to withdraw its parliamentary support unless the Tamil Nadu-based DMK, which was alleged to be indirectly implicated in the 1991 assassination of Rajiv Gandhi, was expelled from the coalition. Prime Minister Gujral rejected Congress (I)'s demand, and was consequently forced to resign on 28 November when Congress (I) withdrew its support for the Government, as earlier threatened. This constituted the third government collapse in less than two years. In early December President Narayanan dissolved the Lok Sabha following the inability of both Congress (I) and the BJP to form an alternative coalition government. It was announced that Gujral would retain the premiership in an acting capacity pending the holding of a fresh general election in early 1998.

During December 1997 Congress (I) suffered a series of internal splits and defections in at least six states. In an apparent attempt to halt the fragmentation of the ailing party, in late December Sonia Gandhi agreed to campaign on behalf of Congress (I) in the run-up to the general election. After a low-key start Sonia Gandhi gained in confidence and popularity during the campaign and attracted ever-larger crowds; she steadfastly refused, however, to stand for actual parliamentary office. Sonia Gandhi's deceased husband was, once again, in the forefront of political news at the end of January 1998, when 26 Tamil militants implicated in the murder of Rajiv Gandhi were sentenced to death by a court in Chennai (Madras). (In May 1999, however, the Supreme Court in New Delhi acquitted 19 defendants and commuted the sentences of three others.)

In the general election, which was held in February/March 1998, the BJP and its regional allies established themselves as the pre-eminent force in Indian politics. The BJP emerged as the largest party, with 182 of the 545 seats in the Lok Sabha, but failed to win an overall majority. Congress (I) secured 142 seats, and shortly after the election Sonia Gandhi replaced Kesri as the party's President. On 19 March President Narayanan appointed the parliamentary leader of the BJP, Atal Bihari Vajpayee (who had briefly held the premiership in mid-1996), as Prime Minister and asked him to form a stable coalition government and to seek a legislative vote of confidence within the next 10 days. This he did (by 274 votes to 261) on 28 March, with the support of the All-India Anna Dravida Munnetra Kazhagam (AIADMK), the Telugu Desam (which eventually left the UF) and a number of other minor groups. None the less, it was apparent from the very outset that Vajpayee's 14-party coalition Government had a fragile hold on power and that the Prime Minister would be required to use both skill and tact to retain his position.

In May 1998 the Government shocked both India and the rest of the world by ordering the carrying out of a series of underground nuclear test explosions. This provocative action was at first greeted with massive popular enthusiasm, but Pakistan's retaliatory tests and a rapid realization of the negative international consequences (particularly the imposition of economic sanctions by the USA) soon led to a more measured domestic assessment.

In early July 1998, in the face of strong opposition from several groups, the Government was forced to defer a parliamentary bill proposing the reservation of one-third of seats in the Lok Sabha and in state legislatures for women (male deputies again prevented the introduction of the Women's Reservation Bill in December). In August the Government approved draft bills providing for the creation of three new states (Uttaranchal, Vananchal and Chhattisgarh), but deferred another proposed piece of legislation to confer full statehood on Delhi.

In November 1998 Congress (I) showed a strong revival in its popularity at the expense of the BJP when it removed the ruling party from power in state elections to Rajasthan and Delhi (both traditionally BJP strongholds) and unexpectedly retained its majority in the elections to the legislature in Madhya Pradesh. Congress (I)'s resurgence was variously ascribed to Sonia Gandhi's rising popularity, a reaction to the BJP's inefficiency and public anger at the soaring prices of basic commodities (notably onions, India's most basic staple after rice).

In early December 1998 tens of thousands of Christians throughout India held a day of protest against alleged Hindu persecution, which, they claimed, had escalated considerably since the assumption of power by the BJP in March. Later in the month widespread disruption was caused by a one-day nation-wide strike called by various trade unions in protest against the Government's economic policies. At the end of December a fresh outbreak of violence against Christians by Hindu zealots was reported in Gujarat; further incidents were reported in January 1999. In that month the murder of an Australian Christian missionary and his two young sons by a mob in a village in Orissa was widely condemned both internationally and within India itself. Five alleged activists from a militant Hindu organization, called Bajrang Dal, were among those arrested in connection with the attack. The Government, under pressure not to appear to be condoning Hindu extremism, ordered a high-level judicial inquiry into the murders. In October 2000 a 13-year-old boy was sentenced to 14 years' imprisonment for his participation in the attack. The trial of the 14 others accused of the murders was scheduled to take place in December.

In early April 1999 Prime Minister Vajpayee rejected demands by the BJP's troublesome coalition partner the AIADMK (whose controversial leader, Jayaram Jayalalitha, was faced with ongoing investigations into corruption allegations) to reinstate the Chief of Staff of the Navy and to dismiss the Minister of Defence, George Fernandes; the following day the two AIADMK ministers resigned from the Government. The President resolved the resultant political stalemate by forcing Vajpayee to seek a parliamentary vote of confidence. The Government narrowly lost the motion (by 270 votes to 269) and the President then invited Sonia Gandhi to assemble a new coalition. Following her failure to do so, the Lok Sabha was dissolved on 26 April and fresh elections were called. Vajpayee and his Government remained in power, in an acting capacity, pending the holding of the polls.

In May 1999 Congress (I)'s erstwhile parliamentary leader, Sharad Pawar, who had earlier publicly criticized Sonia Gandhi's foreign (Italian) origins, announced the formation of a breakaway party, entitled the Nationalist Congress Party (NCP); the NCP absorbed the Indian National Congress (S) in the following month. The outbreak of hostilities between Indian and Pakistani troops in the Kargil area of Kashmir in mid-1999 (see below) had a very positive effect on the nationalist BJP's standing and, in particular, on that of Vajpayee, who, as acting Prime Minister, was widely perceived to have responded with dignity, firmness and commendable restraint in the face of Pakistani provocation. The fact that India, in effect, emerged victorious from the Kargil crisis (in forcing a Pakistani retreat) had a major impact on the public's perception of the acting Government.

The BJP contested the general election, held in September–October 1999, at the head of a 24-member alliance, known as the National Democratic Alliance (NDA), which comprised numerous and diverse minor regional and national parties with little shared ideology. The NDA won an outright majority in the Lok Sabha, with 299 of the 545 seats, while Congress (I) and its electoral allies obtained 134 seats. Although Sonia Gandhi won both of the seats that she herself contested in Karnataka and Uttar Pradesh, her lack of political experience, her weak grasp of Hindi and her foreign birth all contributed to Congress (I)'s worst electoral defeat since India's independence. Following his appointment as leader of the NDA, Vajpayee was sworn in as Prime Minister for a third term at the head of a large coalition Government.

Shortly after its return to power, the BJP-led administration was faced with widespread problems caused by a devastating cyclone, which struck the eastern state of Orissa at the end of October 1999, leaving more than 10,000 people dead and up to 1.5m. people homeless. A massive and costly relief programme was launched and large amounts of foreign aid were urgently requested. The authorities were much criticized, however, for their slow response to the tragedy, and in December the Chief Minister of Orissa resigned amid continuing criticism of his administration's handling of the aftermath of the cyclone.

Despite protests organized by Hindu fundamentalists and threats of sabotage, the head of the Roman Catholic Church, Pope John Paul II, carried out a peaceful state visit of India, amid tight security, in early November 1999. During the pontiff's meetings with senior Indian politicians, he broached the subject of the recent upsurge in anti-Christian persecution and called for greater religious tolerance (while asserting the freedom to proselytize).

The induction of four additional ministers into the Government in late November 1999 (including the creation of a Ministry of Information Technology, reflecting the growing importance of this sector to the Indian economy) appeared to contradict the Minister of Finance's publicly-stated resolve to reduce administrative costs. In late December the Government again attempted unsuccessfully to introduce the Women's Reservation Bill in the Lok Sabha; the lower house descended into chaos when opposition deputies staged a rowdy demonstration against the controversial legislation. In early February 2000 the former Chief Justice, M. N. Venkatachaliah, was appointed as chairman of a new national commission, which was to review the Constitution.

In February and March 2000 state elections were held. Overall, regional parties fared better than Congress (I) and the BJP. At the end of March biennial elections for one-third of the members of the Rajya Sabha took place. The BJP increased its membership from 43 to 47, giving the ruling National Democratic Alliance a total of 99 seats. Congress (I) lost four seats, reducing its total to 58 members. At the end of May a government reorganization took place.

In mid-May 2000 the Government introduced three items of legislation in the Lok Sabha to establish the states of Chhattisgarh, Jharkhand and Uttaranchal, and amended versions were finally passed by the Lok Sabha and Rajya Sabha in August. The three new states came into being in November.

In June 2000 the Chief Minister of Bihar, Rabri Devi, and her husband were charged with corruption. In July a threat to arrest the leader of the Shiv Sena, Bal Thackeray, for his alleged role in the 1992–93 communal riots, led to violent conflict on the streets. Although Thackeray was duly arrested, a Mumbai court dismissed the case on account of the fact that the case was too old and fell outside the country's statute of limitations. Vajpayee rejected the resignations of three ministers over the decision to prosecute Thackeray, and forced the Minister of Law, Justice and Company Affairs, Ram Jethmalani, to resign after he opposed the Supreme Court.

In late August 2000 the Minister of Power, Ranjaram Kumaramangalam, died. A month later the Council of Ministers was partially reorganized and expanded to 76 members. The Council of Ministers was reorganized again in November. In mid-November Sonia Gandhi was re-elected President of Congress (I). In October the former Prime Minister, P. V. Narasimha Rao, was convicted of corruption. He was sentenced to three years' imprisonment and was fined Rs. 100,000. In early October the former Chief Minister of Tamil Nadu, Jayaram Jayalalitha, was convicted of corruption and sentenced to three years' imprisonment. In the same month the Central Bureau of Investigation filed charges against three Indian businessmen, the Hinduja brothers, for allegedly accepting bribes in the 'Bofors' affair (see above). The businessmen were later ordered to appear before a New Delhi court in mid-January 2001. The hearing was adjourned until the end of February.

Indian identity was a contentious issue during 2000. In March the BJP conceded to pressure from Congress (I) and some BJP allies to order the Government of Gujarat to rescind its decision to remove the ban on civil servants becoming members of the RSS. In June violent attacks against Christians resumed. In an attempt to show that the Government was taking the problem seriously, Vajpayee met a delegation of bishops to discuss the renewed violence. Nevertheless, in July Indian Christians protested across South India, demanding protection against the attacks. In October the leader of the RSS urged the Government to replace 'foreign' churches with a national church and to expel all Christian missionaries. The RSS campaign caused embarrassment for the Government, in particular Vajpayee, who requested the newly-appointed BJP President, Bangaru Laxman, to declare that the views of the RSS did not represent those of the BJP.

In early December 2000 communal tension between Hindus and Muslims increased, following Vajpayee's statement that the construction of the Ram Janmabhoomi, the Hindu temple, in Ayodhya was an expression of 'national sentiment that has yet to be realized' and part of the 'unfinished agenda' of his Government. Although the Prime Minister later attempted to diminish his remarks, declaring that he did not support the destruction of the Muslim Babri Masjid, the opposition demanded an immediate apology and forced the abrupt adjournment of the Lok Sabha and Rajya Sabha. Opposition members also called for the resignation of three ministers, including L. K. Advani, who were charge-sheeted by the Central Bureau of Investigation in a case relating to the demolition of the Babri Masjid. Vajpayee rejected the demand, and a week after the remarks were made the opposition in the Lok Sabha presented a censure motion requesting the removal of the three ministers and the resignation of the Prime Minister. The motion was rejected in the Lok Sabha. The Government was defeated in the Rajya Sabha. The Prime Minister confirmed that the Government would abide by the judgment of the Supreme Court with regard to the three ministers. In the mean time tension between Hindus and Muslims was exacerbated by Bal Thackeray's statement in his party's journal that Muslims in India should be disenfranchised.

In January–February 2001 the largest ever Hindu gathering, the Maha Kumbh Mela took place, centring on Allahabad, Uttar Pradesh, at the confluence of the Rivers Ganges and Yamuna, and the mythical River Saraswati. The 42-day festival (which takes place every 12 years) attracted more than 100m. people. In January plans for a negotiated settlement over the religious site in Ayodhya suffered a set-back when the All India Babri Masjid Action Committee ruled out negotiations with the VHP. VHP leaders convened a religious parliament, the Dharma Sansad, at the Maha Kumbh festival. The Dharma Sansad stated that all obstacles impeding the obstruction of the temple should be removed by the relevant organizations by 12 March 2002. In February 2001 an Indian high court ruled that nearly 40 people could be brought to trial in connection with the destruction of the mosque in Ayodhya, and that senior BJP leaders would not be among the defendants.

In mid-October 2000 the Supreme Court approved the continuation of work on the controversial Sardar Sarovar dam, on the Narmada River in Gujarat. Construction stopped in 1994, when environmental activists, representing the tens of thousands of people whom the dam would displace, lodged a case against the authorities. The World Bank had withdrawn its funding, citing environmental concerns, in 1993. Campaigners against the project claimed that the authorities had failed to provide an acceptable rehabilitation and resettlement programme.

All levels of government faced large-scale problems during 2000 and 2001. Severe drought affected Andhra Pradesh, Gujarat and Rajasthan in 2000. In January 2001 a devastating earthquake occurred in Gujarat, the epicentre being in the coastal town of Bhuj. More than 30,000 people were killed and over 1m. people were made homeless. The central Government and the Government of Gujarat were criticized for their tardy reaction to the disaster, a delay that reportedly led to greater loss of life. In March the revelation of an alleged false arms deal involving senior officials led to the resignation of the BJP President, Bangaru Laxman and of the Minister of Defence, George Fernandes. The entire Government came under pressure from the opposition to resign.

Regional issues have always played and continue to play an important role in Indian political affairs. In 1986 the Gurkhas (of Nepalese stock) in West Bengal launched a campaign for a separate autonomous homeland in the Darjeeling region and the recognition of Nepali as an official language. The violent separatist campaign, led by the Gurkha National Liberation Front (GNLF), was prompted by the eviction of about 10,000 Nepalis from the state of Meghalaya, where the native residents feared that they were becoming outnumbered by immigrants. When violent disturbances and a general strike were organized by the GNLF in June 1987, the central Government agreed to hold tripartite talks with the GNLF's leader, Subhas Ghising, and the Chief Minister of West Bengal. The Prime Minister rejected the GNLF's demand for an autonomous Gurkha state, but Ghising agreed to the establishment of a semi-autonomous Darjeeling Hill Development Council. Under the formal peace agreement, the GNLF was to cease all agitation and to surrender weapons, while the state government was to release all GNLF detainees. The Government agreed to grant Indian citizenship to all Gurkhas born or domiciled in India. Elections to the Darjeeling Hill Development Council were held in November. The GNLF won 26 of the 28 elective seats (the 14 remaining members of the Council were to be nominated) and Ghising was elected Chairman of the Council. However, the GNLF continued to demand the establishment of a fully autonomous Gurkha state. In 1992 a constitutional amendment providing for the recognition of Nepali as an official language was adopted.

In December 1985 an election for the state assembly in Assam was won by the Asom Gana Parishad (AGP) (Assam People's Council), a newly-formed regional party. This followed the signing, in August, of an agreement between the central Govern-

ment and two groups of Hindu activists, concluded after five years of sectarian violence, which limited the voting rights of immigrants (mainly Bangladeshis) to Assam. When the accord was announced, Bangladesh stated that it would not take back Bengali immigrants from Assam and denied that it had allowed illegal refugees to cross its borders into Assam. Another disaffected Indian tribal group, the Bodos of Assam, demanded a separate state of Bodoland within India. In February 1989 the Bodos, under the leadership of the All Bodo Students' Union (ABSU), intensified their separatist campaign by organizing strikes, bombings and violent demonstrations. The central Government dispatched armed forces to the state. In August the ABSU agreed to hold peace talks with the state government and central government officials. The ABSU agreed to suspend its violent activities, while the Assam government agreed to suspend emergency security measures. The situation became more complicated in 1989, when a militant Maoist group, the United Liberation Front of Assam (ULFA), re-emerged. The ULFA demanded the outright secession of the whole of Assam from India. In 1990 the ULFA claimed responsibility for about 90 assassinations, abductions and bombings. In November, when the violence began to disrupt the state's tea industry, the central Government placed Assam under direct rule, dispatched troops to the state and outlawed the ULFA. By late December the unrest seemed to have been substantially quelled. In the state elections in 1991 the AGP was defeated, and a Congress (I) ministry took power. In September, following the breakdown of prolonged talks with the ULFA, the Government launched a new offensive against the ULFA guerrillas and declared the entire state a disturbed area. The ULFA suffered a serious set-back in mid-1992 when a large number of its leading members surrendered to the authorities. Meanwhile, following the suspension of violence by the ABSU, the Bodo Security Force (BSF) assumed the leading role in the violent campaign for a separate state of Bodoland. The separatist campaign was intensified in 1992 with indiscriminate killings, abductions, bomb explosions and large-scale extortion. The BSF was outlawed by the central Government in November. At a tripartite meeting attended by the Minister of State for Home Affairs, the Chief Minister of Assam and the President of the ABSU in Guwahati in February 1993, a memorandum was signed providing for the establishment of a 40-member Bodoland Autonomous Council, which would be responsible for the socio-economic and cultural affairs of the Bodo people. However, attacks leading to substantial loss of life were made by Bodo and ULFA activists in the second half of the 1990s both on the security forces and on non-tribal groups in the area. In March 2000 the Government and Bodo militants agreed to a cease-fire. Peace negotiations were under way, and in September the cease-fire was extended by one year. However, violence between the state government and the ULFA continued. Elsewhere in north-eastern India, violence, both intertribal (particularly against ethnic Bengali settlers) and anti-Government, continued during this period in Tripura, Bihar, Mizoram, Manipur and Nagaland.

In September 1985 there was a temporary improvement in the unstable situation in Punjab when an election for the state assembly was held, following an agreement between the central Government and the main Sikh party, the Shiromani Akali Dal (SAD). The election was peaceful and resulted in a victory for the SAD, which assumed power after two years of presidential rule. Part of the 1985 agreement was the proposed transfer of Chandigarh, since 1966 the joint capital of Punjab and Haryana, to Punjab alone. In return, Haryana was to benefit from the completion of the Sutlej-Yamuna canal, to bring irrigation water from Punjab to the dry south of the state, and the transfer of several Hindi-speaking border villages from Punjab to Haryana. Four commissions were established to organize the transfer, but all failed, and by early 2000 the transfer had still not taken place. In January 1986 Sikh extremists re-established a stronghold inside the Golden Temple complex at Amritsar and Hindu–Sikh violence continued throughout the year. In mid-1986 the extremists separated from the ruling moderate SAD (Longowal) and formed several militant factions. In 1987 Rajiv Gandhi reimposed President's rule in Punjab. Despite the resumption of discussions between the Government and the moderate Sikh leaders, the violence continued. In November 1991 more than 50,000 extra troops were deployed in Punjab (bringing the total number of army, paramilitary and police forces in the state to about 200,000) as part of an intensification of operations against Sikh separatists in the run-up to the state elections and parliamentary by-elections, which were held in mid-February 1992. Congress (I) won 12 of the 13 parliamentary seats in Punjab and gained an overall majority in the state legislature. The elections, which brought to an end five years of presidential rule, were, however, boycotted by the leading factions of the SAD and attracted an extremely low turn-out. The Congress (I) state government that was formed under the leadership of Beant Singh, therefore, lacked any real credibility. Despite the continuing violence between the separatists and the security forces, the large turn-out in the municipal elections in September (the first in 13 years) afforded some hope that normality was returning to Punjab. Local council elections, held in January 1993 (the first in 10 years), also attracted a substantial turn-out. The security situation improved steadily in the course of 1993 and political activity revived. In late August 1995, however, violence erupted in Punjab again when Beant Singh was killed in a powerful car-bomb explosion detonated by suspected Sikh extremists in Chandigarh. This seemed to have been an isolated act of terrorism. The national elections in April/May 1996 were conducted smoothly in the Punjab, and gave the mainstream SAD a convincing victory in the state's parliamentary constituencies. The incumbent Congress (I) administration was routed by an SAD/BJP electoral alliance in state elections held in February 1997; in contrast to the 1992 state elections, turn-out was high. In both the 1998 and 1999 parliamentary elections the SAD again established an electoral alliance with the BJP, and was awarded representation in Vajpayee's consecutive administrations.

In mid-2000 ethnic tensions in the southern states of Karnataka and Tamil Nadu were exacerbated following the kidnapping of the renowned South Indian actor, Rajkumar, by the notorious Tamil criminal, Veerappan, at the end of July. In return for Rajkumar's release, Veerappan demanded financial compensation for the Tamil people affected by the 1991 ethnic riots, recognition of Tamil as one of the languages used in government business in Karnataka and the release of prisoners held in the state, charged under an anti-terrorist law. The abduction caused outbursts of violence by supporters of Rajkumar in Karnataka. The state Governments of Karnataka and Tamil Nadu sent a mediator to negotiate with Veerappan and eventually agreed to meet the conditions set by the abductor. Although the high courts in the two states agreed to the early release of 51 of Veerappan's allies, in November the Supreme Court in New Delhi overruled the decision. A week later Rajkumar was unexpectedly released. Officials denied that they had paid a ransom, and Veerappan remained at large.

In 1986 India and Bangladesh signed an agreement on measures to prevent cross-border terrorism. In 1988 the two countries established a joint working committee to examine methods of averting the annual devastating floods in the Ganges delta. In 1992 the Indian Government, under the provisions of an accord signed with Bangladesh in 1974, formally leased the Tin Bigha Corridor (a small strip of land covering an area of only 1.5 ha) to Bangladesh for 999 years. India maintained sovereignty over the Corridor, but the lease gave Bangladesh access to its enclaves of Dahagram and Angarpota. The transfer of the Corridor occasioned protests from right-wing quarters in India, who also made an issue over the presence in Delhi and other cities of illegal immigrants from Bangladesh and claimed that the Bangladesh Government had done little to protect its Hindu minority. In December 1996 India signed an 'historic' treaty with Bangladesh, which was to be in force for 30 years, regarding the sharing of the Ganges waters. In October 2000 India and Bangladesh began negotiations on border-related issues.

Relations between India and Nepal deteriorated in 1989, when India decided not to renew the two treaties determining trade and transit, insisting that a common treaty covering both issues be negotiated. Nepal refused, stressing the importance of keeping the treaties separate on the grounds that Indo-Nepalese trade issues are negotiable, whereas the right of transit is a recognized right of land-locked countries. India responded by closing most of the transit points through which Nepal's trade is conducted. The dispute was aggravated by Nepal's acquisition of Chinese-made military equipment, which, according to India, violated the Treaty of Peace and Friendship of 1950. However, in June 1990 India and Nepal signed an agreement restoring trade relations and reopening the transit points. Chandra Shekhar visited Kathmandu in February 1991 (the first official visit to Nepal by an Indian Prime Minister since 1977), shortly after it was announced that the first free elections in Nepal were to be held in May. In June 1997 the Indian Prime Minister, Inder Kumar Gujral, made a visit to Nepal and announced the opening of a transit route through north-east India between Nepal and Bangladesh. Gujral and the Nepalese Prime Minister, Lokendra Bahadur Chand, also agreed that there should be a review of the 1950 treaty between the two countries. Relations between India and Nepal were strained as a result of rumours that an Indian film actor had made derogatory remarks about Nepal in a television interview in December 2000. The allegations, strongly denied by the actor, provoked a week of violent protests in Nepal, including attacks on Indians and their businesses. The Nepalese Government temporarily ordered a ban on the actor's films. Once it became known that the television station had no knowledge of such an interview and that the allegations were untrue, the violence ceased and relations returned to normal.

Relations with Pakistan had deteriorated in the late 1970s and early 1980s, owing to Pakistan's potential capability for the development of nuclear weapons and as a result of major US deliveries of armaments to Pakistan. The Indian Government believed that such deliveries would upset the balance of power in the region and precipitate an arms race. Pakistan's President, Gen. Mohammad Zia ul-Haq, visited India in 1985, when he and Rajiv Gandhi announced their mutual commitment not to attack each other's nuclear installations and to negotiate the sovereignty of the disputed Siachen glacier region in Kashmir. Pakistan continued to demand a settlement of the Kashmir problem in accordance with earlier UN resolutions, prescribing a plebiscite under the auspices of the UN in the two parts of the state, now divided between India and Pakistan. India argued that the problem should be settled in accordance with the Shimla agreement of 1972, which required that all Indo-Pakistani disputes be resolved through bilateral negotiations. The Indian decision to construct a barrage on the River Jhelum in Jammu and Kashmir, in an alleged violation of the 1960 Indus Water Treaty, also created concern in Pakistan. In December 1988 Rajiv Gandhi visited Islamabad for discussions with Pakistan's Prime Minister, Benazir Bhutto. The resulting agreements included a formal pledge not to attack each other's nuclear installations. Relations reached a crisis in late 1989, when the outlawed Jammu and Kashmir Liberation Front (JKLF) and several other militant Muslim groups intensified their campaigns of civil unrest, strikes and terrorism, demanding an independent Kashmir or unification with Pakistan. The Indian Government sent in troops and placed the entire Srinagar valley under curfew. Pakistan denied India's claim that the militants were trained and armed in Pakistan-held Kashmir (known as Azad Kashmir). In January 1990 Jammu and Kashmir was placed under Governor's rule, and in July under President's rule. Tension was eased in December, following discussions between the Ministers of External Affairs of both countries. Violence between the Indian security forces and the militant groups, however, continued during 1991–92. Throughout 1993 and in early 1994, the Government's approach to the Kashmir crisis was a combination of a tough military policy and generally fruitless attempts to engage in dialogue. In December 1994 Pakistan was successful in securing the passage of a resolution condemning reported human rights abuses by Indian security forces in Kashmir at a summit meeting of the Organization of the Islamic Conference (OIC, see p. 266). (In the same month Pakistan's decision to close down its consulate in Mumbai, amid claims of Indian support for acts of terrorism in Karachi, provided a further indication of the growing rift between the two countries.) By 1996 the total death toll resulting from the conflict in Jammu and Kashmir, including civilians, security force personnel and militants, was estimated at up to 20,000. The situation in Kashmir improved somewhat, however, when elections for the national parliamentary seats were held in the troubled state shortly after the general election in April/May 1996. There was a reasonably high turn-out, although there were widespread complaints that the security forces had pressurized voters into going to the polling stations. Following the successful holding of elections to the Lok Sabha, state elections were conducted in Jammu and Kashmir in September (the first to be held since 1987) and attracted a turn-out of more than 50%, despite being boycotted by the majority of the separatist groups and being dismissed as a sham by the Pakistani Government. The moderate Jammu and Kashmir National Conference, led by Dr Farooq Abdullah, won the majority of seats in the state assembly, and, on assuming power, immediately offered to instigate talks with the separatist leaders.

Meanwhile, in June 1994 the Indian army had begun to deploy a new missile, named the Prithvi, which had the capacity to reach most of Pakistan. While the 'arms race' between the two countries continued, with claims on both sides concerning the other's missile programmes, talks (which had been suspended since 1994) were resumed in March 1997, both at official and at ministerial level. Of most significance were the negotiations between India and Pakistan's Foreign Secretaries, which took place in Islamabad in June. These talks resulted in an agreement to establish a series of working parties to consider groups of issues, which were to be considered separately from each other. One such group of issues specifically related to Jammu and Kashmir. Tension increased in September when a large-scale outbreak of artillery exchanges along the Line of Control (LoC) resulted in about 40 civilian deaths. The Indian Prime Minister and his Pakistani counterpart kept in contact using a new telephone 'hotline' in an attempt to prevent hostilities from escalating. After a hiatus of more than one year (during which time both countries carried out controversial nuclear test explosions—see above), Indo-Pakistan talks at foreign secretary level regarding Kashmir and other issues were resumed in Islamabad in October 1998. In February 1999 relations appeared to improve considerably when Prime Minister Vajpayee made an historic bus journey (inaugurating the first passenger bus service between India and Pakistan) over the border to Lahore. Following his welcome by the Pakistani Prime Minister, Mohammad Nawaz Sharif, the two leaders held a summit meeting (the first to be conducted in Pakistan for 10 years), at the end of which they signed the Lahore Declaration, which, with its pledges regarding peace and nuclear security, was patently designed to allay world-wide fears of a nuclear 'flashpoint' in South Asia, and committed the two sides to working towards better relations and to implementing a range of confidence-building measures. The contentious subject of Jammu and Kashmir was, however, largely avoided.

Despite the apparent *rapprochement* between India and Pakistan, in April 1999 both countries carried out separate tests on their latest missiles, which were capable of carrying nuclear warheads. In early May the situation deteriorated drastically when the Indian army discovered that Islamic guerrilla groups, allegedly reinforced by regular Pakistani troops (this was later confirmed), had occupied strategic positions on the Indian side of the LoC in the Kargil area of Kashmir. Air strikes launched by the Indian air force at the end of the month failed to dislodge the so-called 'infiltrators', and the army was forced to wage an expensive and lengthy campaign, during which more than 480 Indian soldiers were killed and two Indian military aircraft were shot down. In mid-July, however, Indian military dominance combined with US diplomatic pressure led to a Pakistani withdrawal. In August there was renewed tension when India shot down a Pakistani naval reconnaissance aircraft near Pakistan's border with Gujarat, killing all 16 personnel on board; Pakistan retaliated the following day by opening fire on Indian military aircraft in the same area.

In October/November 1999 there was a notable increase in terrorist incidents in Kashmir, and Indian and Pakistani forces were reported to have resumed skirmishes across the LoC. Relations between the two countries worsened in early November after the success of Vajpayee in promoting the official condemnation of the new Pakistani military regime by the Commonwealth heads of government, following the military coup in Pakistan in mid-October, led by Gen. Pervez Musharraf. In December the Indian Government stated that it would not resume dialogue with Pakistan until the latter halted 'cross-border terrorism'.

In late December 1999 the Kashmir conflict came to international attention when a group of five Islamic fundamentalists hijacked an Indian Airlines aircraft and held its 155 passengers captive at Qandahar airport in southern Afghanistan for one week. The hijackers, who killed one of the hostages, demanded a large ransom payment and the release of 36 Muslim militants being held in Indian prisons who supported the Kashmiri separatist movement. Under increasing domestic pressure to prioritize the safety of the hostages, the Indian Government agreed to release three of the prisoners in exchange for the safe return of the captive passengers and crew. Despite Indian accusations of complicity, the Pakistani Government denied any links with the hijackers. In early January 2000 Prime Minister Vajpayee stated that India would 'work towards getting Pakistan declared a terrorist state'.

In April 2000 there were indications that the Indian Government was willing to re-establish dialogue with Kashmiri militants. Leaders of the All-Party Hurriyat Conference, an organization that to an extent, acted as the political voice for some of the militant groups, were released in April and May. In June the Kashmir state assembly adopted a resolution demanding that the state return to the constitutional position it had held between 1947 and 1953, which would in effect have given it autonomy within the Indian Union. The Vajpayee Government rejected the resolution. In July one of the main militant groups, the Hizbul Mujahideen, declared a three-month cease-fire. The gesture obtained a quick and positive response from the Indian Government: the Indian Army suspended all offensive operations against the Kashmiri militants for the first time in 11 years. Other militant groups, however, denounced the cessation of hostilities as a betrayal and continued their violent campaign, in an attempt to disrupt the peace process. The Hizbul Mujahideen ended the cease-fire at the beginning of August because the Indian Government opposed a tripartite discussion including representatives of Pakistan. As a result, Pakistan appeared rather moderate and India somewhat intransigent. Vajpayee accused Pakistan of orchestrating the events, of encouraging divisions among militant leaders and of turning the Kashmir issue into a pan-Islamic movement.

Following the collapse of the cease-fire, violence in the region intensified. In September security in the area was heightened. India continued to oppose entering negotiations with Pakistan as long as the latter supported Kashmiri insurgents. According to Kashmiri authorities, between January and mid-October 2000 more than 2,000 people had been killed in sectarian violence. In November the Chief Minister of Jammu and Kashmir, Dr Farooq Abdullah, announced the instigation of a judicial inquiry into the killing of 36 unarmed Sikhs in March and the killing of five alleged militants a few days later by Indian security forces. In the same month the Indian Government declared the suspension of combat operations against Kashmiri militants during the holy Muslim month of Ramadan. The unilateral cease-fire began at the end of November; Indian security forces were allowed to retaliate if fired upon. The majority of national parties and foreign governments supported the cessation of hostilities. The All-Party Hurriyat Conference welcomed the development and offered to enter negotiations with Pakistani authorities in order to prepare for tripartite discussions. The Hizbul Mujahideen and other militant groups, however, rejected the offer and continued their campaign of violence. In early December Pakistan declared that its armed forces would exercise maximum restraint along the LoC and extended an invitation to the All-Party Hurriyat Conference to participate in joint preparations for the establishment of tripartite negotiations. A few days later Pakistan proposed that tripartite dialogue begin after Ramadan, pending which the All-Party Hurriyat Conference should participate in bilateral dialogue with the Indian Government and Pakistani authorities, respectively. India reiterated that it was prepared to enter dialogue with Pakistan once the violence ended.

In mid-December 2000 the Indian Government extended the cease-fire for a further month; despite several incidents of violence, there had been relative peace along the LoC. At the same time, Pakistan announced the partial withdrawal of forces deployed along the LoC. Kashmiri militants, however, extended their violent campaign against the cease-fire to the Red Fort in Old Delhi, where three people were shot dead. At the end of December India agreed to issue passports to a delegation of All-Party Hurriyat Conference leaders to allow them to visit Pakistan; however, by February 2001 the applications had not been processed. In mid-January the Indian high commissioner to Pakistan visited Gen. Musharraf. This meeting signified the first contact at such a high political level since the military coup in Pakistan in 1999. The two officials urged an early resumption of negotiations on the Kashmir question. Violence escalated in January 2001; nevertheless, the Council of Ministers extended the cease-fire by another month until 26 February. In February, despite continuing violence, the Indian Council of Ministers extended the unilateral cease-fire for a further three months. Separatist groups continued to dismiss the offer. In mid-January the first phase of Panchayat elections took place. The All-Party Hurriyat Conference boycotted the local elections. The eight-phase process was due to be completed in March.

Relations with Pakistan appeared to improve following the earthquake in Gujarat in January 2001, when Pakistan offered humanitarian relief to India and the leaders of the two countries thus established contact.

Since 1983 India's relations with Sri Lanka have been dominated by conflicts between the island's Sinhalese and Tamil communities, in which India has sought to arbitrate. In July 1987 Rajiv Gandhi and the Sri Lankan President, Junius Jaye-wardene, signed an accord aimed at settling the conflict. An Indian Peace-Keeping Force (IPKF) was dispatched to Sri Lanka but encountered considerable resistance from the Tamil separatist guerrillas. Following the gradual implementation of the peace accord, the IPKF troops completed their withdrawal in March 1990. Violence flared up again, however, and the flow of Sri Lankan refugees into Tamil Nadu increased considerably. By late 1991 the number of Sri Lankans living in refugee camps in the southern Indian state was estimated at more than 200,000. The assassination of Rajiv Gandhi in May 1991, by members of the LTTE, completed India's disenchantment with the latter organization. Measures were subsequently taken by the state government in Tamil Nadu to suppress LTTE activity within the state, and also to begin the process of repatriating refugees. The repatriation programme (allegedly conducted on a voluntary basis) proved a slow and difficult process. In May 1992 the LTTE was officially banned in India. In December 1998 the Indian Prime Minister and Sri Lankan President signed a bilateral free-trade agreement, which finally came into effect in March 2000.

During 1981 there was an improvement in India's relations with the People's Republic of China. Both countries agreed to attempt to find an early solution to their Himalayan border dispute and to seek to normalize relations. China was displeased, however, when, in February 1987, Arunachal Pradesh was granted full statehood, and in that year both sides accused each other of troop concentrations on the disputed frontier and of border violations. A joint working group to negotiate the border dispute met in July 1989. The first meeting of the Sino-Indian joint group on trade was held in September and considerable progress was made in arranging for an expansion of commercial contacts. The joint working group for settlement of the border dispute met again in August 1990, and agreed to a mechanism whereby their military personnel were to meet periodically, to maintain peace in the border region. In February 1991 a major breakthrough occurred when a draft protocol for 1991/92, including the proposed resumption of border trade between the two countries for the first time in three decades, was signed. All six border posts had been closed since the brief border war in 1962. In December 1991 the Chinese Prime Minister, Li Peng, made an official visit to India (the first such visit to India by a Chinese Prime Minister for 31 years), during which a memorandum on the resumption of bilateral border trade was signed. Bilateral border trade was actually resumed between India and China in July 1992. At the fourth meeting of the joint group on trade, held in Beijing in January 1993, a protocol was signed by the two sides, agreeing to open more border posts for trade, to expand the scope of traded commodities and to encourage mutual investment in each other's countries. In December 1994 it was announced that India and China had agreed to hold joint military exercises in 1995 along the border in the Himalayan region of Ladakh. Sino-Indian relations were further strengthened as a result of a three-day visit to India conducted by the Chinese President, Jiang Zemin, in November 1996 (the first visit by a Chinese Head of State to India). Despite the gradual improvement in relations, however, India has frequently indicated that it is unhappy with the nuclear asymmetry between the two countries and with what it perceives as China's willingness to transfer missiles and missile technology to Pakistan. Sino-Indian relations deteriorated following India's 1998 nuclear tests, partly because China believed that India was using a fabricated threat from China to justify its actions. In June 1999 the Indian Minister of External Affairs visited Beijing to restore Sino-Indian dialogue. In 2000 relations improved. During border negotiations in November, India and China exchanged detailed maps of the middle sector of the Line of Actual Control: a significant step towards resolving differences. In January 2001 a senior Chinese official, Li Peng, visited India in an effort further to improve bilateral relations. China was increasingly wary of India's active interest in South-East Asia. The former Premier had a brief meeting with Vajpayee about the border issue and China's alleged depositing of cheap goods in the Indian market.

Prior to its disintegration in December 1991, the USSR was a major contributor of economic and military assistance to India. In early 1992 both Russia and Ukraine agreed to maintain arms supplies to India, and in February an Indo-Russian trade and payments protocol was signed. The President of Russia, Boris Yeltsin, made an official visit to India in 1993, during which he signed an Indo-Russian Treaty of Friendship and Co-operation. In October 1996 India and Russia signed a defence co-operation agreement (later extended to 2010), and in December India signed a US $1,800m.-contract to purchase 40 fighter aircraft from Russia. In June 1998 Russia defied a G-8 ban on exporting nuclear technology to India by agreeing to supply the latter with two nuclear reactors. In November 1999 India and Russia signed a defence agreement regarding their joint manufacture of military aircraft and submarines. In October 2000 the newly-elected Russian President, Vladimir Putin, visited India. The two countries signed a declaration of 'strategic partnership', which involved co-operation on defence, economic matters and international terrorism issues. India signed a contract to purchase 50 Sukhoi-30 fighter aircraft from Russia, with a licence to manufacture around 150 more. The deal, reportedly worth more than US$3,000m., was finalized in December. In February 2001 India agreed to buy 310 T-90 Russian tanks, at an estimated cost of $700m.

Following the collapse of India's long-time ally the USSR in December 1991, the Indian Government sought to strengthen its ties with the USA. In January 1992 discussions were held between Indian and US officials regarding military co-operation and ambitious joint defence projects. However, the USA remains concerned about the risks of nuclear proliferation in the South Asia region as a whole, and has yet to achieve a mutual understanding with India as regards this issue (India has repeatedly refused to sign the Nuclear Non-Proliferation Treaty—NPT). In addition, despite India's recent adoption of a programme of economic liberalization, conflicts over trade and related issues have arisen between the USA and India. During a visit to India by the US Secretary of Defense in January 1995, a 'landmark' agreement on defence and security co-operation was signed by the two countries.

In mid-1996, in a move that provoked widespread international condemnation, India decided not to be party to the Comprehensive Test Ban Treaty (CTBT), which it had earlier supported, so long as the existing nuclear powers were unwilling to commit themselves to a strict timetable for full nuclear disarmament. In May 1998 India's controversial decision to explode five nuclear test devices and to claim thereby its new status as a nuclear-weapons state, led to a rapid escalation in the arms race with Pakistan (which responded with its own series of nuclear tests). The USA, with limited support from other countries, subsequently imposed economic sanctions on both India and Pakistan until such time as they had signed the NPT and the CTBT and taken steps to reverse their nuclear programmes. Immediately after the tests, India announced a self-imposed moratorium on further testing (which still held in early 2000) and launched itself into intense diplomatic activity. During 1998–99 the USA lifted some of the sanctions imposed on India and Pakistan, whilst reiterating its requests that the two countries sign the CTBT and exercise restraint in their respective missile programmes to ensure peace in South Asia. The US President, Bill Clinton, made an official six-day state visit to India in March 2000 (the first by a US President since 1978). President Clinton appeared to endorse India's position that the Kashmir issue was a local matter and did not directly concern the international community. India indicated that it would maintain a moratorium on further nuclear tests. In September Vajpayee visited the USA. He continued to assert that consensus among Indian ministers had to be reached before a decision on the CTBT could be made. In mid-January 2001 India successfully test-fired its Agni-II intermediate ballistic missile for the second time. Vajpayee declared that the test was necessary for India's national security; however, the move was criticized by Pakistan, Japan and the United Kingdom and caused concern in China.

Government

India is a federal republic. Legislative power is vested in Parliament, consisting of the President and two Houses. The Council of States (Rajya Sabha) has 245 members, most of whom are indirectly elected by the state assemblies for six years (one-third retiring every two years), the remainder being nominated by the President for six years. The House of the People (Lok Sabha) has 543 elected members, serving for five years (subject to dissolution). A small number of members of the Lok Sabha may be nominated by the President to represent the Anglo-Indian community, while the 543 members are directly elected by universal adult suffrage in single-member constituencies. The President is a constitutional Head of State, elected for five years by an electoral college comprising elected members of both Houses of Parliament and the state legislatures. The President exercises executive power on the advice of the Council of Ministers, which is responsible to Parliament. The President appoints the Prime Minister and, on the latter's recommendation, other ministers.

India contains 28 self-governing states, each with a Governor (appointed by the President for five years), a legislature (elected for five years) and a Council of Ministers headed by the Chief Minister. Bihar, Jammu and Kashmir, Karnataka, Maharashtra and Uttar Pradesh have bicameral legislatures, the other 23 state legislatures being unicameral. Each state has its own legislative, executive and judicial machinery, corresponding to that of the Indian Union. In the event of the failure of constitutional government in a state, presidential rule can be imposed by the Union. There are also six Union Territories and one National Capital Territory, administered by Lieutenant-Governors or Administrators, all of whom are appointed by the President. The Territories of Delhi and Pondicherry also have elected chief ministers and state assemblies.

Defence

At 1 August 2000 the total strength of India's armed forces was 1,303,000: an army of 1,100,000, a navy of 53,000 and an air force of 150,000. Active paramilitary forces totalled 1,069,000 men, including the 174,000-strong Border Security Force (based mainly in the troubled state of Jammu and Kashmir). Military service is voluntary, but, under the amended Constitution, it is the fundamental duty of every citizen to perform national service when called upon. The proposed defence budget for 2000/01 was estimated at Rs 420,913.9m. (equivalent to 10.9% of total expenditure). In February 2001 the Government announced an increase of 13.8% in defence expenditure for 2001/02.

Economic Affairs

In 1998, according to estimates by the World Bank, India's gross national product (GNP), measured at average 1996–98 prices, was US $427,407m., equivalent to $440 per head (or $2,060 per head on an international purchasing-power parity basis). During 1990–98, it was estimated, GNP per head increased, in real terms, at an average annual rate of 4.3%. Over the same period, the population increased by an average of 2.0% per year. In 1999 GNP totalled an estimated $442,200m. (equivalent to $450 per head). India's gross domestic product (GDP) increased, in real terms, at an average annual rate of 6.1% in 1990–99. According to the Asian Development Bank (ADB), real GDP growth reached 6.8% in 1998/99 and 6.4% in 1999/2000.

Agriculture (including forestry and fishing) contributed an estimated 28% of GDP in 1999. About 60.1% of the economically active population were employed in agriculture in 1999. The principal cash crops are cotton (cotton fabrics and yarn accounted for 7.8% of total export earnings in 1999/2000), tea, rice, spices and cashew nuts. Coffee and jute production are also important. The average annual growth rate in the output of the agricultural sector was 3.8% in 1990–99. According to estimates by the ADB, agricultural GDP increased by 7.2% in 1998/99. In 1999/2000, however, the growth rate declined to 1.3%.

Industry (including mining, manufacturing, power and construction) contributed an estimated 25% of GDP in 1999. About 19.4% of the working population were employed in the industrial sector in 1991. Industrial GDP increased at an average annual rate of 6.7% in 1990–99. According to the ADB, the rate of growth of the GDP of the industrial sector reached an estimated 4.0% in 1998/99. Industrial production growth increased to 7.8% in 1999/2000. In terms of output, India ranks among the 12 leading industrial nations in the world.

Mining contributed an estimated 2.1% of GDP in 1998/99, and employed 0.6% of the working population in 1991. Iron ore and cut diamonds are the major mineral exports. Coal, limestone, zinc and lead are also mined. In 1999 India was the third largest coal producer in the world after the People's Republic of China and the USA. Mining GDP increased by an average annual rate of 3.3% during 1994–99.

Manufacturing contributed an estimated 16% of GDP in 1999, and employed 10.0% of the working population in 1991. The GDP of the manufacturing sector increased at an average annual rate of 8.0% during 1990–98. Manufacturing GDP rose by 4.0% in 1998/99 and by 9.3% in 1999/2000. In 1995 the most important branches, measured by gross value of output, were food products (accounting for 13.9% of the total), textiles (11.0%), iron and steel (9.5%) and industrial chemicals (9.0%).

In late 1998 India had a total generating capacity of 81,000 MW. In 1996 thermal plants accounted for an estimated 81% of total power generation and hydroelectric plants (often dependent on monsoons) for 17%; the remaining 2% was contributed by nuclear power. Imports of mineral fuels, lubricants, etc. comprised 22.2% of the cost of total imports in 1999/2000.

The services sector, which is dominated by the rapidly expanding data-processing business and the growing tourism industry, contributed an estimated 46% of GDP in 1999, and engaged 20.5% of the economically active population in 1991. The GDP of the services sector increased by an average of 7.7% per year in 1990–99; the rate of growth reached 8.3% in 1998/99 and 8.6% in 1999/2000.

In 1999 India recorded a trade deficit of US $8,029m., and there was a deficit of $2,784m. on the current account of the balance of payments. In 1998/99 the principal source of imports (an estimated 8.7%) and the principal market for exports (an estimated 21.8%) was the USA. Other major trading partners were Japan, the United Kingdom and Germany. The principal exports in 1999/2000 were gems and jewellery, chemicals and related products, engineering products and ready-made garments. The principal imports were mineral fuels and lubricants, pearls, precious and semi-precious stones, chemicals and non-electrical machinery.

In the financial year ending 31 March 2000 there was a projected budgetary deficit of Rs 817,700m. In 1997, according to the UN, India's total official development assistance stood at US $1,678.2m. (of which $903.4m. was in the form of grants and $774.8m. was in the form of loans). India's total external debt was $98,232m. at the end of 1998, of which $85,207m. was long-term public debt. In that year the cost of debt-servicing was equivalent to 20.6% of earnings from the exports of goods and services. The average annual rate of inflation was an estimated 9.6% in 1990–99; consumer prices rose by 8.2% in 1997/98 and by 8.9% in 1998/99. In rural India the number of people wholly unemployed comprise about 6% of the potential labour force for adult males, but the proportion is around 23% when account is taken of underemployment.

India is a member of the Asian Development Bank (ADB, see p. 131), of the UN's Economic and Social Commission for Asia and the Pacific (see p. 28) and of the South Asian Association for Regional Co-operation (SAARC, see p. 279).

The process of wide-ranging economic reform initiated in 1991, including trade and investment liberalization, industrial deregulation, disinvestment by the Government in public enterprises and their gradual privatization, financial and tax reforms, etc., has continued despite several changes in government. By 2000 a variety of sectors—including power, coal, telecommunications, postal services, transport (with the exception of the railways) and insurance—had been opened up to private (domestic and foreign) investment. In May of that year the Government announced the partial privatization of Air-India (60% to private companies, of which up to 26% was available to foreign investors). The airline was put on sale at the end of September and attracted much international interest. The Government was expected to make a decision on the sale of Maruti Udyog, India's largest car manufacturer, in early 2001. Despite these and other developments, privatization and disinvestment in India continued to progress at a very slow pace. The impact of economic sanctions imposed by the USA, Japan and a number of other countries on India in response to the latter's conduct of nuclear tests in May 1998 proved to be much less serious than initially anticipated. The general robustness of the Indian economy was also highlighted in mid-1999, when a serious border conflict with Pakistan in the Kashmir region (necessitating large amounts of supplementary defence expenditure) left it relatively unscathed. A major area of concern in 2000 remained the rise in India's fiscal deficit, which was largely due to the conflict with Pakistan in Kargil in 1999, the cyclone in Orissa and the inert disinvestment programme. The earthquake in Gujarat was likely further to exacerbate fiscal deficit and hinder plans to boost economic growth. A second area of concern in early 2001 was the possibility of a decline in export growth, as a result of the deceleration in the economy of the USA (a major purchaser of India's goods), while the Indian rupee had depreciated less than other regional currencies, thereby rendering India's exports less competitive. In April 2001, moreover, in order to comply with the regulations of the World Trade Organization (WTO), further restrictions on imports were to be removed, thus presenting local manufacturers with a greater challenge. The late 1990s, however, witnessed India's rapid emergence as a 'software superpower'; in 2000 software exports constituted the country's single largest export item, earning, according to the National Association of Software and Service Companies (Nasscom), an estimated US $3,900m. in 1999/2000. Nasscom forecast software exports to reach $50,000m. by 2008. The rapidly-expanding industry presented increasing employment opportunities. Nevertheless, concern grew over the high number of qualified information technology professionals leaving the country for better-paid work elsewhere.

Social Welfare

Health programmes are primarily the responsibility of the state governments, but the Union Government provides finance for improvements in public health services. The structure of the health system is based on a network of primary health centres. In 1984 India had 297,228 physicians (3.9 per 10,000 population), 9,598 dentists, 170,870 nursing personnel and 258,445 midwifery personnel. In 1993 there were an estimated 1,364 people per hospital bed. Various national health programmes aim to combat leprosy, malaria, polio and tuberculosis. Smallpox was declared eradicated in 1977. In December 1998 more than 120m. children under the age of five throughout India were immunized against polio in the world's largest public health campaign. The family planning programme was launched in 1952 and the emphasis now is on advice and education through Family Welfare Centres. In 1999–2001 India suffered from several natural disasters: a cyclone in Orissa, severe drought and famine in Andhra Pradesh, Gujarat and Rajasthan, and an earthquake in the state of Gujarat. The catastrophes raised the risk of disease and poverty. The earthquake left over 1m. people homeless. The resultant lack of clean water, proper shelter and basic sanitation led to an increase in cases of typhoid, cholera and gastroenteritis. Proposed budgetary expenditure on social services by the central Government in the financial year 2000/01 was 166,236.7m. rupees (4.3% of total government spending); however, this was likely to increase in order to fund humanitarian relief.

Education

Education is primarily the responsibility of the individual state governments. Elementary education for children between the ages of six and 14 years is theoretically compulsory in all states except Nagaland and Himachal Pradesh. There are facilities for free primary education (lower and upper stages) in all the states. Enrolment at the first level of education in 1996 was equivalent to 101% of children aged six to 10 years (110% of boys; 90% of girls). Secondary enrolment in 1996 was equivalent to 49% of those aged 11 to 17 (59% of boys; 39% of girls). India had a total of 228 universities and institutions with university status in 1998/99, and some 11,089 university and affiliated colleges. University enrolment was 7.42m. in 1998/99. In 1995, according to UNESCO estimates, the rate of adult illiteracy in India averaged 47.9% (males 34.5%; females 62.3%). Budgetary expenditure on education in 1995/96 was 23,800m. rupees (1.4% of total spending).

Public Holidays

The public holidays observed in India vary locally. The dates given below apply to Delhi. As religious feasts depend on astronomical observations, holidays are usually declared at the beginning of the year in which they will be observed. It is not possible, therefore, to indicate more than the month in which some of the following holidays will occur.

2001: 1 January (New Year's Day), 26 January (Republic Day), 6 March (Id ul-Zuha, Feast of the Sacrifice), 9 March (Holi), 26 March (Muharram, Islamic New Year), 6 April (Mahavir Jayanti), 13 April (Good Friday), 16 April (Easter Monday), 7 May (Buddha Purnima), 4 June (Birth of the Prophet), 15 August (Independence Day), 2 October (Mahatma Gandhi's Birthday), 26 October (Dussehra), 15 November (Diwali), 30 November (Guru Nanak Jayanti), 17 December (Id al-Fitr, end of Ramadan), 25–26 December (Christmas).

2002: 1 January (New Year's Day), 26 January (Republic Day), 23 February (Id ul-Zuha, Feast of the Sacrifice), March (Holi), 15 March (Muharram, Islamic New Year), 29 March (Good Friday), 1 April (Easter Monday), April (Mahavir Jayanti), April/May (Buddha Purnima), 24 May (Birth of the Prophet), 15 August (Independence Day), August/September (Janmashtami), September/October (Dussehra), 2 October (Mahatma Gandhi's birthday), November (Diwali, Guru Nanak Jayanti), 6 December (Id al-Fitr, end of Ramadan), 25–26 December (Christmas).

Weights and Measures

The metric system has been officially introduced. The imperial system is also still in use, as are traditional Indian weights and measures, including:

    1 tola = 11.66 grams
    1 seer = 933.1 grams
    1 maund = 37.32 kg
    1 lakh = (1,00,000) = 100,000
    1 crore = (1,00,00,000) = 10,000,000

Statistical Survey

Source (unless otherwise stated): Central Statistical Organization, Ministry of Statistics and Programme Implementation, Sardar Patel Bhavan, Patel Chowk, New Delhi 110 001; tel. (11) 3732150; fax (11) 3342384; e-mail doscc@bol.net.in; internet www.nic.in/stat.

Area and Population

AREA, POPULATION AND DENSITY*

Area (sq km)	3,287,263†
Population (census results)	
1 March 1991‡§	846,302,688
1 March 2001‖ ¶	
Males	531,277,078
Females	495,738,169
Total	1,027,015,247
Population (official estimates at mid-year)	
1996	939,540,000
1997	955,220,000
1998	970,933,000
Density (per sq km) at March 2001	324

* Including Sikkim (incorporated into India on 26 April 1975) and the Indian-held part of Jammu and Kashmir.
† 1,269,219 sq miles.
‡ Excluding adjustment for underenumeration, estimated at 1.5%.
§ Including estimate for the Indian-held part of Jammu and Kashmir.
‖ Provisional results.
¶ Including estimates for certain areas in the states of Gujarat and Himachal Pradesh where the census could not be conducted, owing to recent natural disasters.
Source: Registrar General of India.

STATES AND TERRITORIES

	Capital	Area (sq km)	Population March 1981	Population March 1991
States				
Andhra Pradesh	Hyderabad .	275,045	53,551,026	66,508,008
Arunachal Pradesh[1] .	Itanagar .	83,743	631,839	864,558
Assam .	Dispur .	78,438	18,041,248	22,414,322
Bihar† .	Patna .	94,163	69,914,734	64,530,465
Chhattisgarh .	Raipur .	135,000	n.a.	17,615,000*
Goa[5] .	Panaji .	3,702	1,007,749	1,169,793
Gujarat .	Gandhinagar .	196,024	34,085,799	41,309,582
Haryana .	Chandigarh[2]	44,212	12,922,119	16,463,648
Himachal Pradesh .	Shimla .	55,673	4,280,818	5,170,877
Jammu and Kashmir[3]	Srinagar .	222,236	5,987,389	7,718,700*
Jharkhand† .	Ranchi .	79,714	n.a.	21,844,000*
Karnataka .	Bangalore .	191,791	37,135,714	44,977,201
Kerala .	Thiruvananthapuram (Trivandrum)	38,863	25,453,680	29,098,518
Madhya Pradesh† .	Bhopal .	308,346	52,178,844	48,566,170
Maharashtra .	Mumbai (Bombay) .	307,713	62,782,818	78,937,187
Manipur .	Imphal .	22,429	1,420,953	1,837,149
Meghalaya .	Shillong .	22,429	1,335,819	1,774,778
Mizoram[4] .	Aizawl .	21,081	493,757	689,756
Nagaland .	Kohima .	16,579	774,930	1,209,546
Orissa .	Bhubaneswar .	155,707	26,370,271	31,659,736
Punjab .	Chandigarh[2]	50,362	16,788,915	20,281,969
Rajasthan .	Jaipur .	342,239	34,261,862	44,005,990
Sikkim .	Gangtok .	7,096	316,385	406,457
Tamil Nadu .	Chennai (Madras) .	130,058	48,408,077	55,858,946
Tripura .	Agartala .	10,486	2,053,058	2,757,205
Uttaranchal† .	Dehradun .	55,845	n.a.	7,045,000*
Uttar Pradesh† .	Lucknow	238,566	110,862,512	132,067,187
West Bengal .	Kolkata (Calcutta)	88,752	54,580,647	68,077,965

— continued	Capital	Area (sq km)	Population March 1981	Population March 1991
Territories				
Andaman and Nicobar Islands .	Port Blair .	8,249	188,741	280,661
Chandigarh[2] .	Chandigarh .	114	451,610	642,015
Dadra and Nagar Haveli	Silvassa .	491	103,676	138,477
Daman and Diu[5]	Daman .	112	78,981	101,586
Delhi .	Delhi .	1,483	6,220,406	9,420,644
Lakshadweep .	Kavaratti .	32	40,249	51,707
Pondicherry .	Pondicherry .	492	604,471	807,785

* Estimate.
† Chhattisgarh, Jharkhand and Uttaranchal (formerly parts of Madhya Pradesh, Uttar Pradesh and Bihar respectively) were granted statehood in November 2000; figures for area and population have been adjusted accordingly.

[1] Arunachal Pradesh was granted statehood in February 1987.
[2] Chandigarh forms a separate Union Territory, not within Haryana or Punjab. As part of a scheme for a transfer of territory between the two states, Chandigarh was due to be incorporated into Punjab on 26 January 1986, but the transfer was postponed.
[3] The area figure refers to the whole of Jammu and Kashmir State, of which 78,114 sq km (Azad Kashmir) is occupied by Pakistan. The population figures refer only to the Indian-held part of the territory.
[4] Mizoram was granted statehood in February 1987.
[5] Goa was granted statehood in May 1987. Daman and Diu remain a Union Territory.

Source: *Census of India*, 1981 and 1991.

PRINCIPAL TOWNS (population at 1991 census*)

Greater Mumbai (Bombay) . .	9,925,891	Thiruvanananthapuram (Trivandrum) .	699,872
Delhi . . .	7,206,704	Gwalior . . .	690,765
Kolkata (Calcutta) .	4,399,819	Jodhpur . . .	666,279
Chennai (Madras) .	3,841,396	Nashik . . .	656,925
Bangalore . .	3,302,296	Hubli-Dharwar .	648,298
Hyderabad . .	3,145,939	Faridabad Complex. .	617,717
Ahmedabad . .	2,954,526	Rajkot . . .	612,458
Kanpur (Cawnpore) . .	1,879,420	Mysore . . .	606,755
Nagpur . . .	1,624,752	Solapur . . .	604,215
Lucknow . .	1,619,115	Ranchi . . .	599,306
Pune (Poona) . .	1,566,651	Srinagar . . .	594,775†
Surat . . .	1,505,872	Bareilly . . .	590,661
Jaipur (Jeypore) .	1,458,183	Guwahati . . .	584,342
Indore . . .	1,091,674	Kochi (Cochin) . .	582,588
Bhopal . . .	1,062,771	Aurangabad . .	573,272
Vadodara (Baroda) .	1,061,598	Kota . . .	537,371
Ludhiana . .	1,042,740	Pimpri-Chinchwad .	517,083
Kalyan . . .	1,014,557	Chandigarh . .	510,565
Haora (Howrah) .	950,435	Jalandhar . .	509,510
Madurai . .	940,989	Gorakhpur . .	505,566
Varanasi (Banaras) .	932,399	Aligarh . . .	480,520
Patna . . .	917,243	Jamshedpur . .	478,950
Agra . . .	891,790	Guntur . . .	471,051
Coimbatore . .	816,321	Kozhikode (Calicut)	456,618
Allahabad . .	806,486	Ghaziabad . .	454,156
Thane (Thana) . .	803,389	Warangal . . .	447,653
Jabalpur (Jubbulpore) . .	764,586	Raipur . . .	438,639
Meerut . . .	753,778	Moradabad . .	429,214
Visakhapatnam (Vizag) .	752,037	Durgapur . . .	425,836
		Amravati . . .	421,576
Amritsar . . .	708,835	Bikaner . . .	416,289
Vijayawada (Vijayavada) .	701,827	Bhubaneswar . .	411,542
		Kolhapur . . .	406,370
		Cuttack . . .	403,418

PRINCIPAL TOWNS (population at 1991 census*) — *continued*

Ajmer	402,700	Ujjain		362,633
Bhavnagar	402,338	Jamnagar		350,544
Bhilainagar	395,360	Bokaro Steel City		333,683
Bhiwandi	392,214	Rajahmundry		324,881
Tiruchirapalli	387,223	Bhatpara		315,976
Saharanpur	374,945	Jhansi		313,491
Ulhasnagar	369,077	New Mumbai		
Salem	366,712	(Bombay)		307,724

* Figures refer to the city proper in each case. For urban agglomerations, the following populations were recorded: Greater Mumbai (Bombay) 12,596,243; Kolkata (Calcutta) 11,021,918; Delhi 8,419,084; Chennai (Madras) 5,421,985; Hyderabad 4,344,437; Bangalore 4,130,288; Ahmedabad 3,312,216; Pune (Poona) 2,493,987; Kanpur 2,029,889; Lucknow 1,669,204; Nagpur 1,664,006; Surat 1,518,950; Jaipur (Jeypore) 1,518,235; Kochi (Cochin) 1,140,605; Vadodara (Baroda) 1,126,824; Indore 1,109,056; Coimbatore 1,100,746; Patna 1,099,647; Madurai 1,085,914; Visakhapatnam (Vizag) 1,057,118; Varanasi (Banaras) 1,030,863; Agra 948,063; Jabalpur (Jubbulpore) 888,916; Meerut 849,799; Vijayawada (Vijayavada) 845,756; Allahabad 844,546; Thiruvananthapuram (Trivandrum) 826,225; Dhanbad 815,005; Kozhikode (Calicut) 801,190; Asansol 763,939; Jamshedpur 763,939; Nashik 725,341; Gwalior 717,780; Tiruchirapalli 711,862; Durg-Bhilainagar 685,474; Rajkot 654,490; Mysore 653,345; Solapur 620,846; Bareilly 617,350; Ranchi 614,795; Aurangabad 592,709; Salem 578,291; Chandigarh 575,829; Ghaziabad 511,759; Warangal 467,757; Kannur 463,962; Raipur 462,694; Moradabad 443,701; Cuttack 440,295; Mangalore 426,341; Kolhapur 418,538; Bhavnagar 405,225; Belgaum 402,412; Pondicherry 401,437; Rajahmundry 401,397. † 1981 census figure.

Capital: New Delhi, population 301,297 at 1991 census.

BIRTHS AND DEATHS

(estimates, based on Sample Registration Scheme)

	1996	1997	1998
Birth rate (per 1,000)	27.4	27.2	26.4
Death rate (per 1,000)	8.9	8.9	9.0

Expectation of life (UN estimates, years at birth, 1990–95): 60.3 (males 60.5; females 60.6) (Source: UN, *World Population Prospects: The 1998 Revision*).

ECONOMICALLY ACTIVE POPULATION

(persons aged five years and over, 1991 census, excluding Jammu and Kashmir)

	Males	Females	Total
Agriculture, hunting, forestry and fishing	139,361,719	51,979,110	191,340,829
Mining and quarrying	1,536,919	214,356	1,751,275
Manufacturing	23,969,433	4,702,046	28,671,479
Construction	5,122,468	420,737	5,543,205
Trade and commerce	19,862,725	1,433,612	21,296,337
Transport, storage and communications	7,810,126	207,620	8,017,746
Other services	23,995,194	5,316,428	29,311,622
Total employed	221,658,584	64,273,909	285,932,493
Marginal workers	2,705,223	25,493,654	28,198,877
Total labour force	224,363,807	89,767,563	314,131,370

Unemployment (work applicants at 31 December, '000 persons aged 14 years and over): 36,742 (males 28,722, females 8,020) in 1995; 37,430 (males 29,050, females 8,380) in 1996; 39,140 (males 30,107; females 9,033) in 1997; 40,089 (males 30,563; females 9,526) in 1998; 40,371 (males 30,438; females 9,933) in 1999 (Source: ILO, *Yearbook of Labour Statistics*).

Agriculture

PRINCIPAL CROPS ('000 metric tons, year ending 30 June)

	1997/98	1998/99	1999/2000*
Rice (milled)	82,540	86,000	89,480
Sorghum (Jowar)	7,530	8,710	8,860
Cat-tail millet (Bajra)	7,640	7,030	5,660
Maize	10,820	10,680	11,470
Finger millet (Ragi)	2,090	2,810	2,380
Small millets	640	760	620
Wheat	66,350	70,780	75,570
Barley	1,680	1,470	1,460
Total cereals	179,290	188,240	195,500
Chick-peas (Gram)	6,130	6,680	5,080
Pigeon-peas (Tur)	1,850	2,770	2,790
Dry beans, dry peas, lentils and other pulses	4,990	5,350	5,510
Total food grains	192,260	203,040	208,880
Groundnuts (in shell)	7,370	9,170	5,310
Sesame seed	570	560	650
Rapeseed and mustard	4,700	5,780	5,950
Linseed	240	270	290
Castor beans	830	840	900
Total edible oil seeds (incl. others)	21,320	25,210	20,870
Cotton lint†	10,850	12,178	13,000
Jute‡	9,960	8,692	8,500
Kenaf (Mesta)‡	1,060	1,003	1,000
Tea (made)	811	850	800
Sugar cane:			
production gur	27,950	29,570	30,000
production cane	279,540	295,730	300,000
Tobacco (leaves)	650	670	660
Potatoes	17,650	22,490	22,500

* Provisional figures.
† Production in '000 bales of 170 kg each.
‡ Production in '000 bales of 180 kg each.

Source: Directorate of Economics and Statistics, Ministry of Agriculture and Ministry of Commerce (for tea).

LIVESTOCK ('000 head, year ending September)

	1997	1998	1999
Cattle	209,489	212,121*	214,877*
Sheep	56,472	57,100*	57,600*
Goats	120,560	121,362*	122,530*
Pigs	15,411	16,005*	16,005†
Horses†	990	990	990
Asses†	1,000	1,000	1,000
Mules†	200	200	200
Buffaloes	91,784	90,909*	92,090*
Camels†	1,030	1,030	1,030

Chickens (million): 343† in 1997; 375* in 1998; 383† in 1999.

* Unofficial figure.   † FAO estimate(s).

Source: FAO.

LIVESTOCK PRODUCTS ('000 metric tons)

	1997	1998	1999
Beef and veal	1,378	1,401	1,421
Buffalo meat.	1,403	1,380	1,410
Mutton and lamb	222	226	228
Goat meat	458	462	466
Pig meat	533	543	543
Poultry meat	527	540	559
Cows' milk	29,576	35,500*	36,000*
Buffaloes' milk	38,393	35,850*	38,000*
Goats' milk	3,128	3,150*	3,180*
Butter and ghee .	1,470*	1,600*	1,750*
Hen eggs	1,612*	1,683*	1,733*
Wool:			
greasy.	44	44†	44†
clean .	30*	30†	n.a.
Cattle and buffalo hides (fresh)	953	942	954
Sheepskins (fresh)	51	51	52
Goatskins (fresh).	126	127	128

* Unofficial figure.   † FAO estimate(s).

Source: FAO.

Forestry

ROUNDWOOD REMOVALS ('000 cu metres, excl. bark)

	1996	1997	1998
Sawlogs, veneer logs and logs for sleepers*	18,350	18,350	18,350
Pulpwood†	1,208	1,208	1,208
Other industrial wood	5,413	5,506	5,598
Fuel wood	265,333	269,857	274,334
Total	290,304	294,921	299,490

* Assumed to be unchanged since 1985.
† Assumed to be unchanged since 1978.

Source: FAO, *Yearbook of Forest Products.*

SAWNWOOD PRODUCTION
(FAO estimates, '000 cu metres, incl. railway sleepers)

	1983	1984	1985
Coniferous sawnwood	2,091	2,286	2,500
Broadleaved sawnwood	12,404	13,621	14,960
Total	14,495	15,907	17,460

1986–98: Annual production as in 1985.

Source: FAO, *Yearbook of Forest Products.*

Fishing

('000 metric tons, live weight)

	1996	1997	1998
Capture .	3,474.1	3,517.1	3,214.8
Bombay-duck (Bummalo)	185.1	213.1	179.8
Croakers and drums	299.6	313.2	272.2
Indian oil-sardine (sardinella)	136.7	212.1	209.1
Indian mackerel	293.5	190.4	171.0
Aquaculture .	1,783.5	1,862.3	2,029.6
Roho labeo	491.7	519.3	570.1
Mrigal carp	460.0	480.0	520.0
Catla .	475.0	510.0	550.0
Total catch .	5,257.6	5,379.4	5,244.4

Source: FAO, *Yearbook of Fishery Statistics.*

Mining

('000 metric tons, unless otherwise indicated)

	1997/98	1998/99	1999/2000
Coal	297,000	292,270	299,996
Lignite .	23,064	23,419	21,847
Iron ore*	75,723	72,230	73,475
Manganese ore* .	1,642	1,538	1,565
Bauxite .	6,112	6,610	6,854
Chalk (Fireclay)	450	470	369
Kaolin (China clay)	791	741	752
Dolomite	3,003	2,922	2,835
Gypsum	2,195	2,267	3,288
Limestone	110,000	113,213	127,891
Crude petroleum.	33,828	32,722	32,011
Sea salt .	12,600	12,369	n.a.
Chromium ore*	1,511	1,418	1,696
Phosphorite	1,219	1,262	1,136
Kyanite .	6.0	6.1	6.5
Magnesite	374	350	330
Steatite .	475	482	528
Copper ore* .	4,500	4,225	3,108
Lead concentrates*	61.0	62.8	62.9
Zinc concentrates*	293	350	360
Mica—crude (metric tons)	1,697	1,484	1,273
Gold (kilograms) .	2,636	2,683	2,442
Diamonds (carats)	30,994	34,579	40,666
Natural gas (million cu m)†	19,703	25,706	19,984

* Figures refer to gross weight. The estimated metal content is: Iron 63%; Manganese 40%; Chromium 30%; Copper 1.2%; Lead 70%; Zinc 60%.
† Figures refer to gas utilized.

Source: Indian Bureau of Mines.

Industry

SELECTED PRODUCTS ('000 metric tons, unless otherwise indicated)

	1997/98	1998/99	1999/2000
Refined sugar*	13,248	14,299	17,470
Cotton cloth (million sq metres)	20,032	13,106	13,755
Jute manufactures	1,463	1,389	n.a.
Paper and paper board	4,296	4,450	5,089
Soda ash	1,567	1,459	1,540
Fertilizers	13,656	13,624	14,274
Petroleum products	61,300	68,496	85,894
Cement	82,872	90,500	100,240
Pig-iron (saleable)	3,427	2,991	n.a.
Finished steel	22,654	25,124	25,966
Aluminium (metric tons)	548,880	542,005	618,682
Diesel engines (number)	1,946,400	2,221,194	2,927,538
Sewing machines (number)	96,756	63,932	59,808
Radio receivers (number) .	32,400	1,700	n.a.
Television receivers (number) .	2,370,000	2,460,300	2,561,600
Electric fans (number)	8,040,000	7,950,000	8,150,000
Passenger cars and multipurpose vehicles	535,655	527,022	759,488
Commercial vehicles (number)	160,894	135,891	173,521
Motor cycles, mopeds and scooters (number)	3,072,667	3,374,508	3,778,011
Bicycles (number)	9,765,600	10,615,400	13,733,700

* Figures relate to crop year (beginning November) and are in respect of cane sugar only.

Finance

CURRENCY AND EXCHANGE RATES

Monetary Units
100 paise (singular: paisa) = 1 Indian rupee.

Sterling, Dollar and Euro Equivalents (29 December 2000)
£1 sterling = 69.76 rupees;
US $1 = 46.75 rupees;
€1 = 43.50 rupees;
1,000 Indian rupees = £14.33 = $21.39 = €22.99.

Average Exchange Rate (rupees per US $)
1998	41.259
1999	43.055
2000	44.942

BUDGET (million rupees, year ending 31 March)

Revenue	1998/99	1999/2000*	2000/01†
Tax revenue .	1,293,168.0	1,534,271.6	1,786,957.9
Customs .	406,682.7	478,000.0	535,720.0
Union excise duties	532,461.6	610,000.0	694,330.0
Corporation tax	245,291.1	299,150.0	400,400.0
Income tax	57,549.0	101,325.0	118,163.2
Non-tax revenue .	1,105,722.6	1,268,117.6	1,307,531.8
Interest receipts	300,619.8	391,225.4	410,965.4
Dividends and profits	94,104.0	93,108.7	112,044.0
General services	59,511.8	64,443.1	68,132.0
Economic services	622,627.7	687,140.2	689,508.8
Total (incl. others) .	**3,004,833.0**	**3,475,544.3**	**3,865,688.8**

Expenditure	1998/99	1999/2000*	2000/01†
General services .	1,353,829.2	1,659,610.5	1,816,650.6
Organs of state	13,846.4	16,496.3	14,591.7
Fiscal services .	28,538.5	30,623.1	32,970.5
Interest payments and debt-servicing	778,823.9	964,033.0	1,056,422.8
Administrative services.	83,675.7	93,425.6	99,619.7
Pensions and miscellaneous general services .	136,945.5	182,676.7	192,132.0
Defence services	311,999.2	372,355.8	420,913.9
Social services	136,832.2	163,449.0	166,236.7
Economic services	990,952.7	1,060,646.7	1,122,148.5
Agriculture and related activities	150,916.2	167,428.4	157,576.3
Rural development .	51,613.3	51,302.7	45,471.4
Irrigation and flood control .	2,588.6	3,113.4	3,852.0
Special areas programmes .	8,537.0	16,571.8	34,798.1
Energy	24,845.4	32,839.4	35,410.3
Industry and minerals .	103,232.1	131,244.5	117,145.1
Transport .	321,798.5	379,740.1	412,405.8
Communications	215,886.1	221,033.6	245,091.8
Science, technology and the environment	29,283.0	32,561.5	39,589.2
General economic services .	82,252.5	24,811.3	30,808.5
Grants in aid and contributions	510,808.9	578,260.8	746,769.8
Grants in aid to state governments	250,961.6	293,866.5	405,463.7
Grants in aid to Union Territories	7,477.1	8,530.2	8,774.4
Payment of states' share of Union excise duties .	246,650.6	269,580.0	324,870.0
Technical and economic co-operation with other countries	5,719.6	6,284.0	7,661.7
Disbursements by Union Territories .	12,410.0	13,577.3	13,883.2
Total .	**3,004,833.0**	**3,475,544.3**	**3,865,688.8**

* Revised estimates.   † Estimates.

Source: Government of India, Annual Budget Papers, 2000/01.

INTERNATIONAL RESERVES (US $ million at 31 December)

	1997	1998	1999
Gold* .	2,880	2,492	2,403
IMF special drawing rights .	77	83	4
Reserve position in IMF .	287	300	671
Foreign exchange .	24,324	26,958	31,992
Total .	**27,568**	**29,833**	**35,070**

* National valuation (8,880 rupees per troy ounce in 1997; 9,215 rupees per ounce in 1998; 9,085 rupees per ounce in 1999).

Source: IMF, *International Financial Statistics*.

MONEY SUPPLY
(million rupees, last Friday of year ending 31 March)

	1997/98	1998/99*	1999/2000
Currency with the public .	1,460,040	1,689,440	1,887,050
Demand deposits with banks .	1,179,360	1,363,880	1,488,060
Other deposits with Reserve Bank	35,410	37,960	31,090
Total money .	**2,674,810**	**3,091,280**	**3,406,200**

* Revised figures.
Source: Reserve Bank of India.

COST OF LIVING
(Consumer Price Index for Industrial Workers; base: 1990 = 100)

	1997	1998	1999
Food (incl. beverages) .	199.0	228.8	232.5
Fuel and light .	177.8	193.3	205.6
Clothing (incl. footwear) .	184.9	192.8	199.3
Rent .	161.0	201.1	236.3
All items (incl. others) .	**192.5**	**217.7**	**228.0**

Source: ILO, *Yearbook of Labour Statistics*.

NATIONAL ACCOUNTS
('000 million rupees at current prices, year ending 31 March)

National Income and Product

	1996/97	1997/98	1998/99
Domestic factor incomes* .	11,026	12,339	14,465
Consumption of fixed capital .	1,347	1,505	1,659
Gross domestic product at factor cost .	**12,373**	**13,844**	**16,124**
Indirect taxes .	1,626	1,711	1,944
Less Subsidies .	1,247	1,312	1,502
GDP in purchasers' values .	**13,620**	**15,156**	**17,626**
Factor income from abroad . *Less* Factor income paid abroad	−131	−132	−150
Gross national product .	**13,489**	**15,024**	**17,476**
Less Consumption of fixed capital	1,347	1,505	1,659
National income in market prices .	**12,142**	**13,519**	**15,818**
Other current transfers from abroad .	442	439	435
Less Other current transfers paid abroad .	2	2	3
National disposable income .	**12,582**	**13,957**	**16,250**

* Compensation of employees and the operating surplus of enterprises.

Expenditure on the Gross Domestic Product

	1996/97	1997/98	1998/99
Government final consumption expenditure	1,456	1,715	2,164
Private final consumption expenditure	8,924	9,721	11,161
Increase in stocks	−158	101	65
Gross fixed capital formation	3,139	3,439	3,780
Total domestic expenditure	13,361	14,976	17,170
Exports of goods and services	1,449	1,652	1,971
Less Imports of goods and services	1,610	1,843	2,225
Statistical discrepancy	421	371	711
GDP in purchasers' values	13,620	15,156	17,626

Gross Domestic Product by Economic Activity
(provisional estimates, at current factor cost)

	1996/97	1997/98	1998/99
Agriculture	3,475.0	3,527.5	4,286.8
Forestry and logging	135.4	151.4	184.4
Fishing	150.6	195.6	222.2
Mining and quarrying	272.1	329.3	332.5
Manufacturing	2,152.9	2,301.5	2,509.1
Electricity, gas and water	298.5	336.0	381.0
Construction	629.1	784.5	922.4
Trade, restaurants and hotels	1,970.9	1,904.7	2,134.2
Transport, storage and communications	923.7	977.0	1,130.4
Banking and insurance	770.1	840.3	951.8
Real estate and business services	621.0	735.3	866.3
Public administration and defence	646.4	798.9	1,008.2
Other services	807.0	962.5	1,194.3
Total	12,852.6	13,844.5	16,123.8

BALANCE OF PAYMENTS (US $ million)

	1997	1998	1999
Exports of goods f.o.b.	35,702	34,076	37,528
Imports of goods f.o.b.	−45,730	−44,828	−45,556
Trade balance	−10,028	−10,752	−8,029
Exports of services	9,111	11,691	14,443
Imports of services	−12,443	−14,540	−17,441
Balance on goods and services	−13,360	−13,601	−10,997
Other income received	1,484	1,806	1,919
Other income paid	−5,002	−5,443	−5,629
Balance on goods, services and income	−16,878	−17,238	−14,707
Current transfers received	13,975	10,402	11,958
Current transfers paid	−62	−67	−35
Current balance	−2,965	−6,903	−2,784
Direct investment abroad	−113	−48	−79
Direct investment from abroad	3,577	2,635	2,169
Portfolio investment liabilities	2,556	−601	2,317
Other investment assets	−4,743	−3,239	−1,455
Other investment liabilities	8,357	9,837	6,203
Net errors and omissions	−1,348	1,390	293
Overall balance	5,321	3,071	6,664

Source: IMF, *International Financial Statistics*.

OFFICIAL DEVELOPMENT ASSISTANCE (US $ million)

	1995	1996	1997
Bilateral donors	1,024.3	1,013.6	909.6
Multilateral donors	719.6	922.7	768.6
Total	1,743.9	1,936.3	1,678.2
Grants	994.7	1,024.7	903.4
Loans	749.2	911.6	774.8
Per caput assistance (US $)	1.9	2.1	1.8

Source: UN, *Statistical Yearbook for Asia and the Pacific*.

External Trade

PRINCIPAL COMMODITIES
(million rupees, year ending 31 March)

Imports c.i.f.	1997/98	1998/99	1999/2000
Manufactured fertilizers	31,370	33,694	46,680
Metalliferous ores and metal scrap	27,440	29,271	36,828
Mineral fuels, lubricants, etc.	303,410	269,190	454,210
Organic chemicals	65,410 ⎫	112,900	124,760
Inorganic chemicals	44,460 ⎭		
Artificial resins, plastic materials, etc.	25,740	28,430	30,600
Pearls, precious and semi-precious stones	124,210	158,200	232,960
Iron and steel	52,900	41,276	37,608
Non-ferrous metals	34,200	25,130	23,570
Non-electrical machinery	214,940	123,650	117,015
Transport equipment	39,070	26,795	29,865
Electronic goods	83,910	91,303	114,046
Total (incl. others)	1,541,760	1,783,319	2,045,827

Source: Ministry of Commerce.

Exports f.o.b.	1997/98	1998/99	1999/2000
Marine products	44,868	41,929	50,234
Tea and maté	18,763	23,020	n.a.
Oil cakes	34,352	19,121	15,862
Cotton fabrics, yarn, etc.	121,320	110,492	126,717
Ready-made garments	144,050	172,763	189,437
Carpets	15,260	22,870	26,280
Leather and leather manufactures	60,610	69,870	66,660
Gems and jewellery	198,670	249,450	330,890
Iron ore	17,700	16,084	11,636
Engineering products	164,830	160,070	189,470
Chemicals and related products	163,380	175,220	205,160
Petroleum products	13,110	3,760	1,300
Ores and minerals (excluding iron ore, mica and coal)	20,440	37,590	39,290
Man-made textiles	29,910	28,095	33,330
Electronic goods and computer software	28,230	21,150	24,540
Total (incl. others)	1,301,010	1,397,531	1,629,249

Source: Ministry of Commerce.

PRINCIPAL TRADING PARTNERS
(million rupees, year ending 31 March)

Imports c.i.f.	1996/97	1997/98	1998/99*
Australia	46,761	55,210	62,810
Bahrain	31,880	22,530	19,630
Belgium	79,935	99,160	105,980
Canada	11,120	15,640	15,600
France	27,268	29,650	30,560
Germany	100,503	93,980	89,980
Iran	31,040	23,530	20,440
Italy	35,052	34,250	46,030
Japan	77,654	79,710	100,310
Korea, Republic	31,368	37,230	49,030
Kuwait	85,370	85,460	63,180
Malaysia	39,320	43,810	66,060
Netherlands	17,536	16,550	19,660
Russia	27,570	32,360	28,490
Saudi Arabia	98,322	93,220	78,880
Singapore	37,748	44,510	57,400
Switzerland	40,020	98,130	120,800
United Arab Emirates	61,630	66,150	72,520
United Kingdom	75,781	90,810	107,930
USA	130,840	138,140	153,190
Total (incl. others)	1,389,190	1,541,760	1,760,950

Exports f.o.b.	1996/97	1997/98	1998/99*
Australia	13,680	16,290	16,400
Bangladesh	30,848	29,230	41,680
Belgium	38,790	45,180	54,580
Canada	12,531	16,100	20,060
France	25,424	28,230	35,440
Germany	67,204	71,490	79,290
Hong Kong	66,122	71,800	79,240
Italy	35,150	41,450	44,820
Japan	71,209	70,560	69,450
Korea, Republic . . .	18,406	17,380	11,540
Malaysia	18,855	18,210	13,370
Netherlands	30,259	29,870	32,850
Russia	28,800	35,420	30,380
Saudi Arabia	20,490	25,650	32,530
Singapore	34,700	28,980	21,880
Spain	15,080	16,440	21,520
Switzerland	10,640	13,660	13,600
Thailand	15,871	12,780	13,450
United Arab Emirates . .	52,398	62,900	77,950
United Kingdom . . .	72,665	79,560	80,280
USA	232,717	252,830	308,420
Total (incl. others) . . .	1,188,173	1,301,010	1,416,040

* Provisional figures.

Source: Ministry of Commerce.

Transport

RAILWAYS (million, year ending 31 March)

	1997/98	1998/99*	1999/2000
Passengers	4,348	4,415	4,635
Passenger-km	379,897	391,885	420,449
Freight (metric tons) . . .	445.5	420.9	456.4
Freight (metric ton-km) . . .	286,771	281,094	305,513

* Revised figures.

Source: Railway Board, Ministry of Railways.

ROAD TRAFFIC ('000 motor vehicles in use at 31 March)

	1996	1997	1998*
Private cars, jeeps and taxis . .	4,204	4,662	5,088
Buses and coaches . . .	449	488	512
Goods vehicles	2,031	2,260	2,413
Motor cycles and scooters . . .	23,252	25,693	27,919
Others	3,847	4,128	4,526
Total	33,783	37,231	40,458

* Provisional figures.

Source: Transport Research Division, Ministry of Surface Transport.

SHIPPING
Merchant Fleet (registered at 31 December)

	1996	1997	1998
Vessels	920	941	947
Displacement ('000 grt) . .	7,127.2	6,934.3	6,777.1

Source: Lloyd's Register of Shipping, *World Fleet Statistics*.

International Sea-Borne Traffic (year ending 31 March)

	1997/98	1998/99	1999/2000
Vessels* ('000 nrt):			
Entered	47,052	47,719	49,270
Cleared	45,369	38,414	33,253
Freight† ('000 metric tons):			
Loaded	61,173	62,970	n.a.
Unloaded	117,329	140,700	n.a.

* Excluding minor and intermediate ports.
† Including bunkers.
Sources: Transport Research Division, Ministry of Surface Transport; Directorate General of Commercial Intelligence and Statistics.

CIVIL AVIATION (traffic)

	1997/98	1998/99	1999/2000
Kilometres flown ('000) . . .	175,308	187,046	193,417
Passenger-km ('000)	23,353,980	23,909,446	24,623,528
Freight ton-km ('000)	482,148	517,102	532,611
Mail ton-km ('000) . . .	21,048	28,707	33,838

Source: Directorate General of Civil Aviation.

Tourism

FOREIGN VISITORS BY COUNTRY OF ORIGIN*

	1997	1998	1999
Australia	50,647	57,807	73,041
Canada	78,570	80,111	82,892
CIS	32,190	29,493	34,620
France	91,423	97,898	85,891
Germany	105,979	93,993	85,033
Italy	53,854	54,058	50,677
Japan	99,729	89,565	79,373
Malaysia	60,401	47,496	52,613
Netherlands	44,843	54,227	48,826
Singapore	52,004	54,328	53,310
Sri Lanka	122,080	118,292	120,072
United Kingdom . . .	360,567	376,513	345,085
USA	244,239	244,687	251,925
Total (incl. others) . . .	1,973,647	1,974,815	2,024,131

* Figures exclude nationals of Bangladesh and Pakistan. Including these, the total was 2,374,094 in 1997, 2,358,629 in 1998 and 2,481,928 in 1999.

Source: Ministry of Tourism.

Visitor arrivals: 2,620,000 in 2000.

Receipts from tourism (million rupees): 119,508 in 1998; 130,418 in 1999; 144,086 in 2000.

Communications Media

	1995	1996	1997
Television receivers ('000 in use)	47,000	57,700	63,000
Radio receivers ('000 in use) . .	111,000	113,500	116,000
Main telephone lines ('000)* .	9,795.3	11,978	14,543
Telefax stations ('000 in use) . .	70	70	100*
Daily newspapers . . .	4,236	4,453	4,719
Non-daily newspapers and other periodicals*	32,702	n.a.	n.a.

* Year ending 31 March.

Daily newspapers: 4,719 in 1997; 4,890 in 1998; 5,157 in 1999.
1998: 21,593,700 main telephone lines; 1,070,709 mobile cellular telephone subscribers.
1999: 41,498 non-daily newspapers and other periodicals.
1999/2000 (year ending 31 March): 26,510,000 main telephone lines; 2,090,000 mobile cellular telephone subscribers.

Sources: Ministry of Communications; Registrar of Newspapers for India; Ministry of Information and Broadcasting; UNESCO, *Statistical Yearbook*; UN, *Statistical Yearbook*.

Education

(1998/99)

	Institutions	Teachers	Students
Primary	626,737	1,903,539	110,985,877
Middle	190,166	1,277,904	40,353,358
Secondary (High school) . . } Higher secondary (New pattern) }	112,438	1,747,878	27,767,449

Source: Planning, Monitoring and Statistics Division, Department of Education, Ministry of Human Resources Development.

Directory

The Constitution

The Constitution of India, adopted by the Constituent Assembly on 26 November 1949, was inaugurated on 26 January 1950. The Preamble declares that the People of India solemnly resolve to constitute a Sovereign Democratic Republic and to secure to all its citizens justice, liberty, equality and fraternity. There are 397 articles and nine schedules, which form a comprehensive document.

UNION OF STATES

The Union of India comprises 28 states, six Union Territories and one National Capital Territory. There are provisions for the formation and admission of new states.

The Constitution confers citizenship on a threefold basis of birth, descent, and residence. Provisions are made for refugees who have migrated from Pakistan and for persons of Indian origin residing abroad.

FUNDAMENTAL RIGHTS AND DIRECTIVE PRINCIPLES

The rights of the citizen contained in Part III of the Constitution are declared fundamental and enforceable in law. 'Untouchability' is abolished and its practice in any form is a punishable offence. The Directive Principles of State Policy provide a code intended to ensure promotion of the economic, social and educational welfare of the State in future legislation.

THE PRESIDENT

The President is the head of the Union, exercising all executive powers on the advice of the Council of Ministers responsible to Parliament. He is elected by an electoral college consisting of elected members of both Houses of Parliament and the Legislatures of the States. The President holds office for a term of five years and is eligible for re-election. He may be impeached for violation of the Constitution. The Vice-President is the ex officio Chairman of the Rajya Sabha and is elected by a joint sitting of both Houses of Parliament.

THE PARLIAMENT

The Parliament of the Union consists of the President and two Houses: the Rajya Sabha (Council of States) and the Lok Sabha (House of the People). The Rajya Sabha consists of 245 members, of whom a number are nominated by the President. One-third of its members retire every two years. Elections are indirect, each state's legislative quota being elected by the members of the state's legislative assembly. The Lok Sahba has 543 members elected by adult franchise; not more than 13 represent the Union Territories and National Capital Territory. Two members are nominated by the President to represent the Anglo-Indian community.

GOVERNMENT OF THE STATES

The governmental machinery of states closely resembles that of the Union. Each of these states has a governor at its head appointed by the President for a term of five years to exercise executive power on the advice of a council of ministers. The states' legislatures consist of the Governor and either one house (legislative assembly) or two houses (legislative assembly and legislative council). The term of the assembly is five years, but the council is not subject to dissolution.

LANGUAGE

The Constitution provides that the official language of the Union shall be Hindi. (The English language will continue to be an associate language for many official purposes.)

LEGISLATION—FEDERAL SYSTEM

The Constitution provides that bills, other than money bills, can be introduced in either House. To become law, they must be passed by both Houses and receive the assent of the President. In financial affairs, the authority of the Lower House is final. The various subjects of legislation are enumerated on three lists in the seventh schedule of the Constitution: the Union List, containing nearly 100 entries, including external affairs, defence, communications and atomic energy; the State List, containing 65 entries, including local government, police, public health, education; and the Concurrent List, with over 40 entries, including criminal law, marriage and divorce, labour welfare. The Constitution vests residuary authority in the Centre. All matters not enumerated in the Concurrent or State Lists will be deemed to be included in the Union List, and in the event of conflict between Union and State Law on any subject enumerated in the Concurrent List the Union Law will prevail. In time of emergency Parliament may even exercise powers otherwise exclusively vested in the states. Under Article 356, 'If the President on receipt of a report from the government of a state or otherwise is satisfied that a situation has arisen in which the Government of the state cannot be carried on in accordance with the provisions of this Constitution, the President may by Proclamation: (a) assume to himself all or any of the functions of the government of the state and all or any of the powers of the governor or any body or authority in the state other than the Legislature of the state; (b) declare that the powers of the Legislature of the state shall be exercisable by or under the authority of Parliament; (c) make such incidental provisions as appear to the President to be necessary': provided that none of the powers of a High Court be assumed by the President or suspended in any way. Unless such a Proclamation is approved by both Houses of Parliament, it ceases to operate after two months. A Proclamation so approved ceases to operate after six months, unless renewed by Parliament. Its renewal cannot be extended beyond a total period of three years. An independent judiciary exists to define and interpret the Constitution and to resolve constitutional disputes arising between states, or between a state and the Government of India.

OTHER PROVISIONS

Other Provisions of the Constitution deal with the administration of tribal areas, relations between the Union and states, inter-state trade and finance.

AMENDMENTS

The Constitution is flexible in character, and a simple process of amendment has been adopted. For amendment of provisions concerning the Supreme Courts and the High Courts, the distribution of legislative powers between the Union and the states, the representation of the states in Parliament, etc., the amendment must be passed by both Houses of Parliament and must further be ratified by the legislatures of not less than half the states. In other cases no reference to the state legislatures is necessary.

Numerous amendments were adopted in August 1975, following the declaration of a state of emergency in June. The Constitution (39th Amendment) Bill laid down that the President's reasons for proclaiming an emergency may not be challenged in any court. Under the Constitution (40th Amendment) Bill, 38 existing laws may not be challenged before any court on the ground of violation of fundamental rights. Thus detainees under the Maintenance of Internal Security Act could not be told the grounds of their detention and were forbidden bail and any claim to liberty through natural or common law. The Constitution (41st Amendment) Bill provided that the President, Prime Minister and state Governors should be immune from criminal prosecution for life and from civil prosecution during their term of office.

In November 1976 a 59-clause Constitution (42nd Amendment) Bill was approved by Parliament and came into force in January 1977. Some of the provisions of the Bill are that the Indian Democratic Republic shall be named a 'Democratic Secular and Socialist Republic'; that the President 'shall act in accordance with' the advice given to him by the Prime Minister and the Council of Ministers, and, acting at the Prime Minister's direction, shall be empowered for two years to amend the Constitution by executive order, in any way beneficial to the enforcement of the whole; that the term of the Lok Sabha and of the State Assemblies shall be extended from five to six years; that there shall be no limitation on the constituent power of Parliament to amend the Constitution, and that India's Supreme Court shall be barred from hearing petitions challenging constitutional amendments; that strikes shall be forbidden in the public services and the Union Government have the power to deploy police or other forces under its own superintendence and control in any state. Directive Principles are given precedence over Fundamental Rights: 10 basic duties of citizens are listed, including the duty to 'defend the country and render national service when called upon to do so'.

The Janata Party Government, which came into power in March 1977, promised to amend the Constitution during the year, so as to 'restore the balance between the people and Parliament, Parliament and the judiciary, the judiciary and the executive, the states and the centre, and the citizen and the Government that the founding fathers of the Constitution had worked out'. The Constitution (43rd Amendment) Bill, passed by Parliament in December 1977, the Constitution (44th Amendment) Bill, passed by Parliament in December 1977 and later redesignated the 43rd Amendment, and the Constitution (45th Amendment) Bill, passed by Parliament in December 1978 and later redesignated the 44th Amendment, reversed most of the changes enacted by the Constitution (42nd Amendment) Bill. The 44th Amendment is particularly detailed on emergency provisions: An emergency may not be proclaimed unless 'the security of India or any part of its territory was threatened by war or external aggression or by armed rebellion.' Its introduction must be approved by a two-thirds majority of Parliament within a month, and after six months the emergency may be continued only with the approval of Parliament. Among the provisions left unchanged after these Bills were a section subordinating Fundamental Rights to Directive Principles and a clause empowering the central Government to deploy armed forces under its control in any state without the state government's consent. In May 1980 the Indian Supreme Court repealed sections 4 and 55 of the 42nd Amendment Act, thus curtailing Parliament's power to enforce directive principles and to amend the Constitution. The death penalty was declared constitutionally valid.

The 53rd Amendment to the Constitution, approved by Parliament in August 1986, granted statehood to the Union Territory of Mizoram; the 55th Amendment, approved in December 1986, granted statehood to the Union Territory of Arunachal Pradesh; and the 57th Amendment, approved in May 1987, granted statehood to the Union Territory of Goa (Daman and Diu remain, however, as a Union Territory). The 59th Amendment, approved in March 1988, empowered the Government to impose a state of emergency in Punjab, on the grounds of internal disturbances. In December 1988 the minimum voting age was lowered from 21 to 18 years. The 71st Amendment, approved in August 1992, gave official language status to Nepali, Konkani and Manipuri. In August 2000 legislation to permit the establishment of three new states, Chhattisgarh, Jharkhand and Uttaranchal, was approved by Parliament.

THE PANCHAYAT RAJ SCHEME

This scheme is designed to decentralize the powers of the Union and State Governments. It is based on the Panchayat (Village Council) and the Gram Sabha (Village Parliament) and envisages the gradual transference of local government from state to local authority. Revenue and internal security will remain state responsibilities at present. By 1978 the scheme had been introduced in all the states except Meghalaya, Nagaland and 23 out of 31 districts in Bihar. The Panchayat operated in all the Union Territories except Lakshadweep, Mizoram (which became India's 23rd state in February 1987) and Pondicherry. The 72nd Amendment, approved in late 1992, provided for direct elections to the Panchayats, members of which were to have a tenure of five years.

The Government

President: Dr Kocheril Raman Narayanan (sworn in 25 July 1997).
Vice-President: Krishan Kant (sworn in 21 August 1997).

COUNCIL OF MINISTERS
(May 2001)

A coalition of the Bharatiya Janata Party (BJP), the Biju Janata Dal (BJD), the Dravida Munnetra Kazhagam (DMK), the Shiv Sena (SS), the Shiromani Akali Dal (SAD), Jammu and Kashmir National Conference, the Marumalarchi Dravida Munnetra Kazhagam (MDMK), the Janata Dal (United) (JD–U) and Independents (Ind.).

Prime Minister*: Atal Bihari Vajpayee (BJP).
Minister of Home Affairs: Lal Krishna Advani (BJP).
Minister of External Affairs and Defence: Jaswant Singh (BJP).
Minister of Finance: Yashwant Sinha (BJP).
Minister of Health and Family Welfare: Dr C. P. Thakur (BJP).
Minister of Tourism (with additional charge of Department of Culture): Ananth Kumar (BJP).
Minister of Environment and Forests: T. R. Baalu (DMK).
Minister of Urban Development and Poverty Alleviation: Jagmohan (BJP).
Minister of Labour: Dr Satya Narayan Jatiya (BJP).
Minister of Heavy Industries and Public Enterprises: Manohar Joshi (SS).
Minister of Human Resource Development, of Ocean Development and of Science and Technology: Dr Murli Manohar Joshi (BJP).
Minister of Law, Justice and Company Affairs (with additional charge of Shipping): Arun Jaitley (BJP).
Minister of Power: Suresh Prabhakar Prabhu (SS).
Minister of Parliamentary Affairs and of Information Technology: Pramod Mahajan (BJP).
Minister of Commerce and Industry: Murasoli Maran (DMK).
Minister of Petroleum and Natural Gas: Ram Naik (BJP).
Minister of Tribal Affairs: Juel Oram (BJP).

Minister of Communications: Ram Vilas Paswan (JD–U).
Minister of Information and Broadcasting: Sushma Swaraj (BJP).
Minister of Rural Development: M. Venkaiah Naidu (BJP).
Minister of Chemicals and Fertilizers: Sukhdev Singh Dhindsa (SAD).
Minister of Textiles: Kashiram Rana (BJP).
Minister of Consumer Affairs and Public Distribution: Shanta Kumar (BJP).
Minister of Civil Aviation: Sharad Yadav (JD–U).
Minister of Water Resources: Arjun Sethi (BJP).
Minister of Youth Affairs and Sports: Uma Bharati (BJP).
Minister of Agriculture and Railways: Nitish Kumar (JD–U).
Minister of Mines: Sunderlal Patwa (BJP).

Ministers of State with Independent Charge

Minister of State for Social Justice and Empowerment: Maneka Gandhi (Ind.).
Minister of State for Road Transport and Highways: Maj.-Gen. B. C. Khanduri (BJP).
Minister of State for Non-Conventional Energy Sources: K. Kannapan (MDMK).
Minister of State for Steel: B. K. Tripathy (BJD).
Minister of State for Small-scale Industries and Agro and Rural Industries: Vasundhara Raje (BJP).
Minister of State for Coal: N. T. Shanmugham (PMK).
Minister of State for Disinvestment (with additional charge of Statistics and Programme Implementation): Arun Shourie (BJP).

There are, in addition, 38 Ministers of State without independent charge.

* The Prime Minister is also in charge of ministries and departments not allotted to others.

MINISTRIES

President's Office: Rashtrapati Bhavan, New Delhi 110 004; tel. (11) 3015321; fax (11) 3017290; internet www.goidirectory.nic.in.
Vice-President's Office: 6 Maulana Azad Rd, New Delhi 110 011; tel. (11) 3016344; fax (11) 3018124.
Prime Minister's Office: South Block, New Delhi 110 011; tel. (11) 3013040; fax (11) 3016857; internet www.pmindia.nic.in.
Ministry of Agriculture: Krishi Bhavan, Dr Rajendra Prasad Rd, New Delhi 110 001; tel. (11) 3382651; fax (11) 3386004.
Ministry of Atomic Energy: South Block, New Delhi 110 011; tel. (11) 3011773; fax (11) 3013843.
Ministry of Chemicals and Fertilizers: Shastri Bhavan, New Delhi 110 001; tel. (11) 3383695; fax (11) 3386222.
Ministry of Civil Aviation: Rajiv Gandhi Bhavan, Safdarjung Airport, New Delhi 110 023; tel. (11) 4610358; fax (11) 4610354; e-mail web@civilav.delhi.nic.in; internet www.civilaviation.nic.in.
Ministry of Civil Supplies, Consumer Affairs and Public Distribution: Krishi Bhavan, New Delhi 110 001; tel. (11) 3384882; fax (11) 3388302.
Ministry of Coal: Shram Shakti, Rafi Marg, New Delhi 110 001; tel. (11) 3384884; fax (11) 3387738; e-mail secy.moc@sb.nic.in; internet www.coal.nic.in.
Ministry of Commerce and Industry: Udyog Bhavan, New Delhi 110 011; tel. (11) 3012107; fax (11) 3014335; internet www.commin.nic.in.
Ministry of Communications: Sanchar Bhavan, 20 Asoka Rd, New Delhi 110 001; tel. (11) 3719898; fax (11) 3782344.
Ministry of Consumer Affairs and Public Distribution: Krishi Bhavan, New Delhi 110 011; internet www.fcamin.nic.in.
Ministry of Defence: South Block, New Delhi 110 011; tel. (11) 3012380; internet www.mod.nic.in.
Ministry of Disinvestment: 132 Yojana Bhavan, Sansad Marg, New Delhi 110 001; tel. (11) 3711094; fax (11) 3710492.
Ministry of Electronics: Electronics Niketan, 6 CGO Complex, New Delhi 110 003; tel. (11) 4364041; fax (11) 4363134.
Ministry of Environment and Forests: Paryavaran Bhavan, CGO Complex Phase II, Lodi Rd, New Delhi 110 003; tel. (11) 4360721; fax (11) 4360678; e-mail secy@menf.delhi.nic.in; internet www.envfor.nic.in.
Ministry of External Affairs: South Block, New Delhi 110 011; tel. (11) 3012318; fax (11) 3010700; internet www.meadev.gov.in.
Ministry of Finance: North Block, New Delhi 110 001; tel. (11) 3012611; fax (11) 3012477; e-mail jsdea@finance.delhi.nic.in; internet www.finmin.nic.in.

Ministry of Food: 45 Krishi Bhavan, New Delhi 110 001; tel. (11) 3382437; fax (11) 3782213.

Ministry of Food-Processing Industries: Panchsheel Bhavan, Khelgaon Marg, New Delhi 110 049; tel. (11) 6493225; fax (11) 6493228.

Ministry of Health and Family Welfare: Nirman Bhavan, New Delhi 110 011; tel. (11) 3018863; fax (11) 3014252; e-mail secyhlth@mohfw.delhi.nic.in; internet www.mohfw.nic.in.

Ministry of Heavy Industries and Public Enterprises: Udyog Bhavan, New Delhi 110 011; tel. (11) 3012433; fax (11) 3011770.

Ministry of Home Affairs: North Block, New Delhi 110 001; tel. (11) 3011989; fax (11) 3015750; e-mail mhaweb@mhant.delhi.nic.in; internet www.mha.nic.in.

Ministry of Human Resource Development: Shastri Bhavan, New Delhi 110 001; tel. (11) 3386995; fax (11) 3384093.

Ministry of Information and Broadcasting: Shastri Bhavan, New Delhi 110 001; tel. (11) 3382639; fax (11) 3383513; internet www.mib.nic.in.

Ministry of Information Technology: Electronics Niketan, 6, CGO Complex, Lodi Rd, New Delhi 110 003; tel. (11) 4364041; internet www.mit.gov.in.

Ministry of Labour: Shram Shakti Bhavan, Rafi Marg, New Delhi 110 001; tel. (11) 3710265; fax (11) 3711708; e-mail labour@lisd.delhi.nic.in; internet www.labour.nic.in.

Ministry of Law, Justice and Company Affairs: Shastri Bhavan, Dr Rajendra Prasad Rd, New Delhi 110 001; tel. (11) 3384777; fax (11) 3387259; e-mail lawmin@caselaw.delhi.nic.in; internet www.nic.in/lawmin/.

Ministry of Mines and Minerals: Rm 114.C, Shastri Bhavan A-wing, New Delhi 110 011; tel. (11) 3385173; fax (11) 3386402; e-mail dom@sb.nic.in; internet www.nic.in/mines.

Ministry of Non-Conventional Energy Sources: Block 14, CGO Complex, New Delhi 110 003; tel. (11) 4361481; fax (11) 4361298; e-mail secymnes@ren02.nic.in; internet www.mnes.nic.in.

Ministry of Ocean Development: Block 12, CGO Complex, Lodi Rd, New Delhi 110 003; tel. (11) 4360874; fax (11) 4360779.

Ministry of Parliamentary Affairs: Parliament House, New Delhi 110 001; tel. (11) 3017663; fax (11) 3017726; e-mail parlmin@sansad.nic.in; internet www.mpa.nic.in.

Ministry of Personnel, Public Grievances and Pensions: North Block, New Delhi 110 001; tel. (11) 3014848; fax (11) 3012432; e-mail pgweb@arpg.delhi.nic.in; internet www.persmin.nic.in.

Ministry of Petroleum and Natural Gas: Shastri Bhavan, New Delhi 110 001; tel. (11) 3383501; fax (11) 3384787; e-mail dspdi.png@sb.nic.in; internet www.petroleum.nic.in.

Ministry of Planning and Programme Implementation: Sardar Patel Bhavan, Patel Chowk, New Delhi 110 001; tel. (11) 3732150; fax (11) 3732067.

Ministry of Power: Shram Shakti Bhavan, New Delhi 110 001; tel. (11) 3710271; fax (11) 3717519; internet www.powermin.nic.in.

Ministry of Railways: Rail Bhavan, Raisina Rd, New Delhi 110 001; tel. (11) 3384010; fax (11) 3384481; internet www.indianrailway.com.

Ministry of Rural Development: Krishi Bhavan, New Delhi 110 001; tel. (11) 3384467; fax (11) 3782502; e-mail arunbhat@rural.delhi.nic.in; internet www.rural.nic.in.

Ministry of Science and Technology: Technology Bhavan, New Mehrauli Rd, New Delhi 110 016; tel. (11) 6511439; fax (11) 6863847; internet www.mst.nic.in.

Ministry of Small-scale Industries and Agro and Rural Industries: Udyog Bhavan, New Delhi, 110 011; tel. (11) 3013045; internet www.ssi.nic.in.

Ministry of Social Justice and Empowerment: Shastri Bhavan, Dr Rajendra Prasad Rd, New Delhi 110 001; tel. (11) 3382683; fax (11) 3384918; e-mail secywel@sb.nic.in; internet www.socialjustice.nic.in.

Ministry of Steel: Udyog Bhavan, New Delhi 110 011; tel. (11) 3015489; fax (11) 3013236; e-mail dvs@ub.nic.in; internet www.nic.in/steel.

Ministry of Surface Transport: Parivahan Bhavan, 1 Sansad Marg, New Delhi 110 001; tel. (11) 3714938; fax (11) 3714324; internet www.nic.in/most.

Ministry of Textiles: Udyog Bhavan, New Delhi 110 011; tel. (11) 3011769; fax (11) 3013711; e-mail textiles@ub.delhi.nic.in; internet www.texmin.nic.in.

Ministry of Tourism: Transport Bhavan, Parliament St, New Delhi 110 001; tel. (11) 3711792; fax (11) 3710518.

Ministry of Tribal Affairs: Rm 212.D, Shastri Bhavan, New Delhi; tel. (11) 3381652; e-mail dirtdb.wel@sb.nic.in; internet www.tribal.nic.in.

Ministry of Urban Development and Poverty Alleviation: Nirman Bhavan, New Delhi 110 011; tel. (11) 3018495; fax (11) 3014459; e-mail secyurban@alpha.nic.in; internet www.urbanindia.nic.in.

Ministry of Water Resources: Shram Shakti Bhavan, Rafi Marg, New Delhi 110 001; tel. (11) 3710305; fax (11) 3710253; internet www.wrmin.nic.in.

Ministry of Youth Affairs and Sports: Shastri Bhavan, Dr Rajendra Prasad Rd, New Delhi 110 001; tel. (11) 3382897; fax (11) 3387418; internet www.yas.nic.in.

Legislature

PARLIAMENT

Rajya Sabha
(Council of States)

Most of the members of the Rajya Sabha are indirectly elected by the State Assemblies for six years, with one-third retiring every two years. The remaining members are nominated by the President.

Chairman: KRISHAN KANT.

Deputy Chairman: NAJMA HEPPTULLAH.

Distribution of Seats, January 2001

Party	Seats
Congress (I)	57
Janata Dal	6
Communist Party of India—Marxist	15
Telugu Desam	13
Bharatiya Janata Party	47
Samajwadi Party	9
Rashtriya Janata Dal	10
Dravida Munnetra Kazhagam	9
Shiromani Akali Dal	5
Biju Janata Dal	3
Tamil Maanila Congress	3
Asom Gana Parishad	2
Muslim League	2
Forward Bloc	1
All-India Anna Dravida Munnetra Kazhagam	5
Communist Party of India	6
Jammu and Kashmir National Conference (F)	3
Shiv Sena	5
Bahujan Samaj Party	4
Revolutionary Socialist Party	3
Jharkhand Mukti Morcha	2
Indian National Lok Dal	2
Independents and others	22
Nominated	11
Total	**245**

Lok Sabha
(House of the People)

Speaker: GANTI MOHAN CHANDRA BALAYOGI.

General Election, 5, 11, 18 and 25 September and 3 October 1999

Party	Seats
National Democratic Alliance	299
Bharatiya Janata Party	182
Dravida Munnetra Kazhagam	12
Marumalarchi Dravida Munnetra Kazhagam	4
Pattali Makkal Katchi	5
Janata Dal (United)	20
Shiv Sena	15
Shiromani Akali Dal	2
Indian National League	4
Himachal Vikash Congress	1
Telugu Desam	29
Biju Janata Dal	10
Trinamool Congress	8

General Election, 5, 11, 18 and 25 September and 3 October 1999 – *continued*

Party	Seats
Sikkim Democratic Front	1
Manipur State Congress Party	1
Jammu and Kashmir National Conference	4
M.G.R. Anna D.M. Kazhagam	1
Congress (I) and allies	134
Congress (I)	112
Rashtriya Janata Dal	7
All-India Anna Dravida Munnetra Kazhagam	10
Muslim League Kerala State Committee	2
Rashtriya Lok Dal	2
Kerala Congress (M)	1
Bahujan Samaj Party	14
Comunist Party of India	4
Communist Party of India—Marxist	32
Samajwadi Party	26
Nationalist Congress Party	7
Revolutionary Socialist Party	3
Asom Gana Parishad	1
Peasants' and Workers' Party of India	1
Janata Dal (Secular)	1
Independents and others	20
Nominated	2*
Vacant	1
Total	**545**

* Nominated by the President to represent the Anglo-Indian community.

State Governments

(May 2001)

ANDHRA PRADESH
(Capital—Hyderabad)

Governor: Dr CHAKRAVARTY RANGARAJAN.

Chief Minister: N. CHANDRABABU NAIDU (Telugu Desam).

Legislative Assembly: 294 seats (Telugu Desam 180, Congress—I 90, Communist—CPI—M 2, Bharatiya Janata Party 12, independents and others 9, vacant 1).

ARUNACHAL PRADESH
(Capital—Itanagar)

Governor: ARVIND DAVE.

Chief Minister: MUKUT MITHI (Congress—I).

Legislative Assembly: 60 seats (Congress—I 53, Nationalist Congress Party 4, Arunachal Congress 1, independents 2).

ASSAM
(Capital—Dispur)

Governor: Lt-Gen. (retd) S. K. SINHA.

Chief Minister: TARUN GOGOI (Congress—I).

Legislative Assembly: 126 seats (Congress—I 70, Asom Gana Parishad 20, Bharatiya Janata Party 8, Nationalist Congress Party 3, All-India Trinamool Congress 1, independents and others 23, vacant 1).

BIHAR
(Capital—Patna)

Governor: VINOD CHANDRA PANDE.

Chief Minister: RABRI DEVI (RJD).

Legislative Assembly: 243 seats (Rashtriya Janata Dal 114, Bharatiya Janata Party 35, Congress—I 12, Samata Party 29, Janata Dal (United) 18, Bahujan Samaj Party 5, Communist—CPI 6, Communist—CPI—M 2, Communist—Marxist-Leninist (Liberation) 6, independents and others 16).

Legislative Council: 96 seats.

CHHATTISGARH
(Capital—Raipur)

Governor: DINESH NANDAN SAHAYA.

Chief Minister: AJIT JOGI (Congress—I).

Legislative Assembly: 90 seats (Congress—I 48, Bharatiya Janata Party 38, Bahujan Samaj Party 2, others 2). To be confirmed.

GOA
(Capital—Panaji)

Governor: MOHAMMAD FAZAL.

Chief Minister: MANOHAR PARRIKAR (Bharatiya Janata Party).

Legislative Assembly: 40 seats (Congress—I 10, Maharashtrawadi Gomantak Party 12, Bharatiya Janata Party 5, United Goans Party 3, independents and others 10).

GUJARAT
(Capital—Gandhinagar)

Governor: SUNDAR SINGH BHANDARI.

Chief Minister: KESHUBHAI PATEL (Bharatiya Janata Party).

Legislative Assembly: 182 seats (Bharatiya Janata Party 116, Rashtriya Janata Party 4, Congress—I 55, Janata Dal 3, independents and others 4).

HARYANA
(Capital—Chandigarh)

Governor: BABU PRAMANAND.

Chief Minister: OM PRAKASH CHAUTALA (Indian National Lok Dal).

Legislative Assembly: 90 seats (Congress—I 21, Indian National Lok Dal 46, Haryana Vikas Party 2, Bharatiya Janata Party 6, National Congress Party 1, Republican Party of India 1, Bahujan Samaj Party 1, independents and others 12).

HIMACHAL PRADESH
(Capital—Shimla)

Governor: SURAJ BHAN.

Chief Minister: PREM KUMAR DHUMAL (Bharatiya Janata Party).

Legislative Assembly: 68 seats (Congress—I 31, Bharatiya Janata Party 28, Himachal Vikas Congress 4, independents 1, vacant 4).

JAMMU AND KASHMIR
(Capitals—(Summer) Srinagar, (Winter) Jammu)

Governor: GIRISH CHANDRA SAXENA.

Chief Minister: Dr FAROOQ ABDULLAH (Jammu and Kashmir National Conference).

Legislative Assembly: 87 seats (Jammu and Kashmir National Conference 55, Bharatiya Janata Party 8, Congress—I 7, Janata Dal 5, Bahujan Samaj Party 4, All India Indira Congress (Tewari) 1, Communist—CPI—M 1, Awami League 1, independents 2, others 3).

Legislative Council: 36 seats.

JHARKHAND
(Capital—Ranchi)

Governor: PRABHAT KUMAR.

Chief Minister: BABULAL MARANDI (Bharatiya Janata Party).

Legislative Assembly: 81 seats (Bharatiya Janata Party 32, Congress—I 11, Jharkhand Mukti Morcha 12, Rashtriya Janata Dal 9, Samata Party 4, Janata Dal—U 4, others 9). To be confirmed.

KARNATAKA
(Capital—Bangalore)

Governor: V. S. RAMA DEVI.

Chief Minister: SOMANAHALLI MALLIAM KRISHNA (Congress—I).

Legislative Assembly: 224 seats Congress—I 132, Bharatiya Janata Party 44, Janata Dal (Secular) 19, Janata Dal (United) 9, independents and others 20).

Legislative Council: 75 seats.

KERALA
(Capital—Thiruvananthapuram)

Governor: SUKHDEV SINGH KANG.

Chief Minister: A. K. ANTHONY (Congress—I).

Legislative Assembly: 140 seats (Congress—I 62, Communist—CPI—M 23, Muslim League 16, Kerala Congress (M) 9, Communist—CPI 7, Janata Dal (S) 3, Nationalist Congress Party 2, Kerala Congress 2, Kerala Congress (Joseph) 2, Revolutionary Socialist Party 2, independents and others 12).

MADHYA PRADESH
(Capital—Bhopal)

Governor: Dr BHAI MAHAVIR.

Chief Minister: DIGVIJAY SINGH (Congress—I).

Legislative Assembly: 230 seats (Congress—I 126, Bharatiya Janata Party 80, Bahujan Samaj Party 9, Samajwadi Party 4, independents and others 11).

MAHARASHTRA
(Capital—Mumbai)

Governor: Dr P. C. ALEXANDER.

Chief Minister: VILASRAO DESMUKH (Congress—I).

Legislative Assembly: 288 seats (Congress—I 75, Shiv Sena 69, Nationalist Congress Party 58, Bharatiya Janata Party 56, Janata Dal (Secular) 2, Peasants' and Workers' Party 5, Bharatiya Bahujan Mahasangh 3, Communist—CPI—M 2, Samajwadi Party 2, independents and others 16).

Legislative Council: 78 seats.

MANIPUR
(Capital—Imphal)

Governor: VED P. MARWAH.

Chief Minister: W. NIPAMACHA SINGH (Manipur State Congress).

Legislative Assembly: 60 seats (Congress—I 11, Manipur Peoples' Party 1, Manipur State Congress Party 32, Federal Party 6, Bharatiya Janata Party 6, Samata Party 1, Nationalist Congress Party 1, Janata Dal (Secular) 1, independents 1).

MEGHALAYA
(Capital—Shillong)

Governor: M. M. JACOB.

Chief Minister: E. K. MAULONG.

Legislative Assembly: 60 seats (Congress—I 16, Nationalist Congress Party 9, United Democratic Party 20, Bharatiya Janata Party 3, People's Democratic Movement 3, Hills State People's Democratic Party 3, independents and others 6).

MIZORAM
(Capital—Aizawl)

Governor: VED P. MARWAH (acting).

Chief Minister: ZORAMTHANGA (Mizo National Front).

Legislative Assembly: 40 seats (Mizo National Front 21, Congress—I 6, Mizo People's Conference 12, others 1).

NAGALAND
(Capital—Kohima)

Governor: OM PRAKASH SHARMA.

Chief Minister: S. C. JAMIR (Congress—I).

Legislative Assembly: 60 seats (Congress—I 53, independents and others 10).

ORISSA
(Capital—Bhubaneswar)

Governor: M. M. RAJENDRAN.

Chief Minister: NAVEEN PATNAIK (Biju Janata Dal).

Legislative Assembly: 147 seats (Biju Janata Dal 68, Bharatiya Janata Party 38, Congress—I 26, Jharkhand Mukti Morcha 3, Communist—CPI 1, Communist—CPI—M 1, Janata Dal (Secular) 1, All-India Trinamool Congress 1, independents 8).

PUNJAB
(Capital—Chandigarh)

Governor: Lt-Gen. (retd) J. F. R. JACOB.

Chief Minister: PRAKASH SINGH BADAL (Shiromani Akali Dal).

Legislative Assembly: 117 seats (Shiromani Akali Dal 75, Congress—I 14, Bharatiya Janata Party 18, Communist—CPI 2, Akali Dal (Mann) 1, Bahujan Samaj Party 1, independents 6).

RAJASTHAN
(Capital—Jaipur)

Governor: ANSHUMAN SINGH.

Chief Minister: ASHOK GEHLOT (Congress—I).

Legislative Assembly: 200 seats (Congress—I 150, Bharatiya Janata Party 33, Janata Dal 3, Communist—CPI—M 1, Bahujan Samaj Party 2, independents and others 8, vacant 3).

SIKKIM
(Capital—Gangtok)

Governor: CHAUDHURY RANDHIR SINGH.

Chief Minister: PAWAN KUMAR CHAMLING (Sikkim Democratic Front).

Legislative Assembly: 32 seats (Sikkim Democratic Front 25, Sikkim Sangram Parishad 7).

TAMIL NADU
(Capital—Chennai)

Governor: M. S. FATHIMA BEEVI.

Chief Minister: JAYARAM JAYALALITHA (AIADMK).

Legislative Assembly: 234 seats (AIADMK 123, Dravida Munnetra Kazhagam 31, Tamil Maanila Congress 23, Pattali Makkal Katchi 20, Congress—17, Communist—CPI—M 6, Communist—CPI 5, Bharatiya Janata Party 4, Forward Bloc 1, independents and others 5).

TRIPURA
(Capital—Agartala)

Governor: Lt-Gen. (retd) K. M. SETH.

Chief Minister: MANIK SARKAR (Communist—CPI—M).

Legislative Assembly: 60 seats (Communist—CPI—M 38, Congress—I 13, Tripura Upajati Juba Samity 4, independents and others 5).

UTTARANCHAL
(Capital—Dehradun)

Governor: SURJIT SINGH BARNALA.

Chief Minister: NITYANAND SWAMY (Bharatiya Janata Party).

Legislative Assembly: 31 seats (Bharatiya Janata Party 17, Samajwadi Party 3, Congress—I 1, Bahujan Samaj Party 1, others 9). To be confirmed.

UTTAR PRADESH
(Capital—Lucknow)

Governor: VISHNU KANT SHASTRI.

Chief Minister: RAJNATH SINGH (Bharatiya Janata Party).

Legislative Assembly: 403 seats (Bharatiya Janata Party 158, Samajwadi Party 107, Bahujan Samaj Party 47, Congress—I 13, Loktantric Congress 20, Janatantric Bahujan Samaj Party 19, Janata Dal (R) 3, Janata Dal 3, Communist—CPI—M 4, Bharatiya Kisan Kamgar Party 8, independents and others 21).

Legislative Council: 108 seats.

WEST BENGAL
(Capital—Kolkata)

Governor: VIREN J. SHAH.

Chief Minister: BUDDHADEV BHATTACHARYA (Communist—CPI—M).

Legislative Assembly: 294 seats (Communist—CPI—M 143, All-India Trinamool Congress 60, Congress—I 26, Forward Bloc 25, Revolutionary Socialist Party 17, Communist—CPI 7, independents and others 16).

UNION TERRITORIES

Andaman and Nicobar Islands (Headquarters—Port Blair): Lt-Gov.: I. P. GUPTA.

Chandigarh (Headquarters—Chandigarh): Administrator: Lt. Gen (retd) J. F. R. JACOB. Chandigarh was to be incorporated into Punjab state on 26 January 1986, but the transfer was postponed indefinitely.

Dadra and Nagar Haveli (Headquarters—Silvassa): Administrator: O. P. KELKAR.

Daman and Diu (Headquarters—Daman): Administrator: O. P. KELKAR.

Lakshadweep (Headquarters—Kavaratti): Administrator: CHAMAN LAL.

Pondicherry (Capital—Pondicherry): Lt-Gov.: Dr RAJANI RAI. Chief Minister: P. SHANMUGAM (Congress—I). Assembly: 30 seats (Congress—I 11, DMK 7, Pattali Makkal Katchi 4, AIADMK 3, Tamil Maanila Congress 2, Bharatiya Janata Party 1, independents 2).

NATIONAL CAPITAL TERRITORY

Delhi (Headquarters—Delhi): Lt-Gov.: VIJAY KUMAR KAPOOR. Chief Minister: SHEILA DIXIT (Congress—I). Assembly: 70 seats (Congress—I 51, Bharatiya Janata Party 15, Janata Dal 2, independents 2, vacant 1).

Political Organizations

MAJOR NATIONAL POLITICAL ORGANIZATIONS

All India Congress Committee (I): 24 Akbar Rd, New Delhi 110 011; tel. (11) 3019080; f. 1978, as Indian National Congress (I), as a breakaway group under Indira Gandhi; Pres. SONIA GANDHI; Gen. Secs AMBIKA SONI, MOHSINA KIDWAI, MOTILAL VORA, OSCAR FERNANDES, PRABHA RAO, SUSHIL SHINDE; 35m. mems (1998).

Bahujan Samaj Party (Majority Society Party): c/o Lok Sabha, New Delhi; promotes the rights of the *Harijans* ('Untouchables') of India; Leader KANSHI RAM; Gen. Sec. Ms MAYAWATI.

Bharatiya Janata Party (BJP) (Indian People's Party): 11 Ashok Rd, New Delhi 110 001; tel. (11) 3382234; fax (11) 3782163; e-mail bjpco@del3.vsnl.net.in; internet www.bjp.org; f. 1980 as a breakaway group from Janata Party; radical right-wing Hindu party; Pres. K. JANA KRISHNAMURTHY; Vice-Pres. J. P. MATHUR; Gen. Secs NARENDRA MODI, SANGHA PRIYA GAUTAM, SUMITRA MAHAJAN, M. V. NAIDU; 10.5m. mems.

Communist Party of India (CPI): Ajoy Bhavan, Kotla Marg, New Delhi 110 002; tel. (11) 3235546; fax (11) 3235543; e-mail cpi@vsnl.com; internet www.cpofindia.org; f. 1925; advocates the establishment of a socialist society led by the working class, and ultimately of a communist society; nine-mem. central secretariat; Gen. Sec. ARDHENDU BHUSHAN BARDHAN; 555,010 mems (2000).

Communist Party of India—Marxist (CPI—M): A. K. Gopalan Bhavan, 27–29 Bhai Vir Singh Marg, New Delhi 110 001; tel. (11) 3747435; fax (11) 3747483; e-mail cpim@vsnl.com; internet www.del.vsnl.net.in/cpim; f. 1964 as pro-Beijing breakaway group from the CPI; declared its independence of Beijing in 1968 and is managed by a central committee of 73 mems and a politburo of 17 mems; Leaders JYOTI BASU, PRAKASH KARAT, SITARAM YECHURY, SOMNATH CHATTERJEE; Gen. Sec. HARKISHAN SINGH SURJEET; 717,645 mems (1998).

Janata Dal (People's Party): 7 Jantar Mantar Rd, New Delhi 110 001; tel. (11) 3368833; fax (11) 3368138; f. 1988 as a merger of parties within the Rashtriya Morcha; advocates non-alignment, the eradication of poverty, unemployment and wide disparities in wealth, and the protection of minorities; 136-mem. National Executive; Pres. SHARAD YADAV; Sec.-Gen. Dr BAPU KALDATE; split into two factions in July 1999—Janata Dal (United), headed by SHARAD YADAV, and Janata Dal (Secular), headed by H. D. DEVE GOWDA.

Nationalist Congress Party (NCP): 10 Dr Bishambhar Das Marg, New Delhi 110001; tel. (11) 3314417; fax (11) 3352112; f. 1999 as breakaway faction of Congress (I); Pres. SHARAD PAWAR; Gen. Sec. TARIQ ANWAR.

MAJOR REGIONAL POLITICAL ORGANIZATIONS

Akhil Bharat Hindu Mahasabha: Hindu Mahasabha Bhavan, Mandir Marg, New Delhi 110 001; tel. (11) 3342087; fax (11) 3363105; f. 1915; seeks the establishment of a democratic Hindu state; Pres. DINESH CHANDRA TYAGI; Gen. Sec. Dr MADANLAL GOYAL; 525,000 mems.

All-India Anna Dravida Munnetra Kazhagam (AIADMK) (All-India Anna Dravidian Progressive Asscn): Lloyd's Rd, Chennai 600 004; f. 1972; breakaway group from the DMK; Chair. (vacant); Gen. Sec. C. JAYARAM JAYALALITHA.

All India Forward Bloc: 28 Gurudwara Rakabganj Rd, New Delhi 110 001; tel. and fax (11) 3714131; e-mail dbiswas@sansad.nic.in; f. 1940 by Netaji Subhash Chandra Bose; socialist aims, including nationalization of major industries, land reform and redistribution, and the establishment of a union of socialist republics through revolution; Chair. D. D. SHASTRI; Gen. Sec. DEBABRATA BISWAS; 900,000 mems (1999).

All India Trinamool Congress: 125-D, Parliament House, New Delhi 110 001; tel. (11) 3034355; Leader MAMATA BANERJEE.

Asom Gana Parishad (AGP) (Assam People's Council): Golaghat, Assam; f. 1985; draws support from the All-Assam Gana Sangram Parishad and the All-Assam Students' Union (Pres. KESHAB MAHANTA; Gen. Sec. ATUL BORA); advocates the unity of India in diversity and a united Assam; Pres. PRAFULLA KUMAR MOHANTA; a breakaway faction formed a new central exec. committee under PULAKESH BARUA in April 1991.

Dravida Munnetra Kazhagam (DMK): Anna Arivalayam, Teynampet, Chennai 600 018; f. 1949; aims at full autonomy for states (primarily Tamil Nadu) within the Union, to establish regional languages as state languages and English as the official language pending the recognition of regional languages as official languages of the Union; Pres. MUTHUVEL KARUNANIDHI; Gen. Sec. K. ANBAZHAGAN; more than 4m. mems.

Indian National Lok Dal: c/o Rajya Sabha, New Delhi.

Jammu and Kashmir National Conference (JKNC): Mujahid Manzil, Srinagar 190 002; tel. 71500; fmrly All Jammu and Kashmir National Conference, f. 1931, renamed 1939, reactivated 1975; state-based party campaigning for internal autonomy and responsible self-govt; Pres. Dr FAROOQ ABDULLAH; Gen. Sec. SHEIKH NAZIR AHMAD; 1m. mems.

Jharkhand Mukti Morcha: c/o Rajya Sabha, New Delhi.

Pattali Makkal Katchi: Chennai; Leader Dr RAMADAS.

Peasants' and Workers' Party of India: Mahatma Phule Rd, Naigaum, Mumbai 400 014; f. 1949; Marxist; seeks to nationalize all basic industries, to promote industrialization, and to establish a unitary state with provincial boundaries drawn on a linguistic basis; Gen. Sec. DAJIBA DESAI; c. 10,000 mems.

Rashtriya Loktantrik Morcha (National Democratic Front): New Delhi; f. 1998; Convenor MULAYAM SINGH YADAV; includes:

Rashtriya Janata Dal (RJD) (National People's Party): New Delhi; f. 1997 as a breakaway group from Janata Dal; Leader LALOO PRASAD YADAV.

Samajwadi Party (Socialist Party): New Delhi; f. 1991 by the merger of the Janata Dal (S) and the Janata Party; National Pres. MULAYAM SINGH YADAV; Gen. Sec. AMAR SINGH.

Republican Party of India (RPI): Ensa Hutments, I Block, Azad Maidan, Fort, Mumbai 400 001; tel. (22) 2621888; main aim is to realize the aims and objects set out in the preamble to the 1950 Constitution; Pres. PRAKASH RAO AMBEDKAR; Gen. Sec. RAMDAS ATHAVALE; 100,000 mems.

Revolutionary Socialist Party: c/o Lok Sabha, New Delhi.

Samata Party: 220 VP House, Rafi Marg, New Delhi 110 001; tel. (11) 3017172; fax (11) 3793397; f. 1994; Pres. (vacant).

Shiromani Akali Dal: Baradan Shri Darbar Sahib, Amritsar; f. 1920; merged with Congress Party 1958–62; Sikh party composed of several factions both moderate and militant; seeks the establishment of an autonomous Sikh state of 'Khalistan'; Pres. (Shiromani Akali Dal—Badal) PRAKASH SINGH BADAL; Sec.-Gen. (Shiromani Akali Dal—Badal) GURDEV SINGH DHINDSA.

Shiv Sena: Shiv Sena Bhavan, Ram Ganesh Gadkari Chowk, Dadar, Mumbai 400 028; tel. (22) 4309128; e-mail senabhavan@shivsena.org; internet www.shivsena.org; f. 1966; militant Hindu group; Pres. BALASHAHEB 'BAL' THACKERAY.

Tamil Maanila Congress: c/o Lok Sabha, New Delhi; Pres. G. K. MOOPANAR; Gen. Sec. PETER ALPHONS.

Tamil Rajiv Congress: Chennai; Pres. K. RAMAMURTHY.

Telugu Desam (Telugu Nation): 3-5-910, Himayatnagar, Hyderabad 500 029; tel. (842) 237290; f. 1982; state-based party (Andhra Pradesh); campaigns against rural poverty and social prejudice; Pres. N. CHANDRABABU NAIDU.

Diplomatic Representation

EMBASSIES AND HIGH COMMISSIONS IN INDIA

Afghanistan: 5/50F Shanti Path, Chanakyapuri, New Delhi 110 021; tel. (11) 6886625; fax (11) 6875439; Ambassador: MASOOD KHALILI.

Algeria: B-3/61 Safdarjung Enclave, New Delhi 110 029; tel. (11) 6185057; fax (11) 6185062; e-mail embalg@nda.vsnl.net.in; Ambassador: ABDELHAMID SENOUCI BEREKSI.

Argentina: B-8/9 Vasant Vihar, Paschmi Marg, New Delhi 110 057; tel. (11) 6141345; fax (11) 6886501; e-mail eindi@giasdl01.vsnl.net.in; Ambassador: GERARDO M. BIRITOS.

Australia: 1/50-G Shanti Path, Chanakyapuri, New Delhi 110 021; tel. (11) 6888223; fax (11) 6885199; High Commissioner: ROBERT STEPHEN LAURIE.

Austria: EP/13 Chandragupta Marg, Chanakyapuri, New Delhi 110 021; tel. (11) 6889037; fax (11) 6886929; e-mail aedelhi@del2.vsnl.net.in; Ambassador: Dr HERBERT TRAXL.

Bangladesh: 56 Ring Rd, Lajpat Nagar-III, New Delhi 110 024; tel. (11) 6834065; fax (11) 6839237; High Commissioner: MOSTAFA FAROQUE MOHAMMAD.

Belarus: D-6/23 Vasant Vihar, New Delhi 110 057; tel. (11) 6151202; fax (11) 6151203; e-mail embelind@del6.vsnl.net.in; Ambassador: ULADZIMIR A. SAKALOVSKY.

Belgium: 50N, Shanti Path, Chanakyapuri, New Delhi 110 021; tel. (11) 6889851; fax (11) 6885821; e-mail ambabel@del2.vsnl.net.in; Ambassador: GUY TROUVEROY.

Bhutan: Chandragupta Marg, Chanakyapuri, New Delhi 110 021; tel. (11) 6889807; fax (11) 6876710; Ambassador: Lyonpo DAGO TSHERING.

Bosnia and Herzegovina: 57 Poorvi Marg, Vasant Vihar, New Delhi 110 057; tel. (11) 6147415; fax (11) 6143042; Ambassador: NOVAK TODOROVIĆ.

Brazil: 8 Aurangzeb Rd, New Delhi 110 011; tel. (11) 3017301; fax (11) 3793684; e-mail brasindi@giasdl01.vsnl.net.in; Ambassador: VERA BARROUIN MACHADO.

Brunei: A-42 Vasant Marg, Vasant Vihar, New Delhi 110 057; tel. (11) 6148340; fax (11) 6142101; High Commissioner: Dato' Paduka Haji ABDUL MOKTI Haji MOHAMMAD DAUD.

Bulgaria: 16/17 Chandragupta Marg, Chanakyapuri, New Delhi 110 021; tel. (11) 6115550; fax (11) 6876190; e-mail bedg.bulgrin@aworld.net.in; Ambassador: EDVIN SUGAREV.

Burkina Faso: G-5, Anand Niketan, New Delhi 110 021; tel. (11) 4671678; fax (11) 4671745; e-mail emburnd@bol.net.in; Ambassador ALBERT E. KIEMDE.

Cambodia: New Delhi; tel. (11) 6495092; fax (11) 6495093; Ambassador: SIM SUONG.

Canada: N-14 Panchsheel Park, New Delhi 110 017; tel. (11) 6876500; fax (11) 6876579; e-mail domcan.delhi@delhi01.x400.gc.ca; High Commissioner: PETER S. SUTHERLAND.

Chile: 146 Jorbagh, New Delhi 110 003; tel. (11) 4617123; fax (11) 4617102; e-mail embchile@giasdl01.vsnl.net.in; Ambassador: MANUAL CARDENAS.

China, People's Republic: 50D Shanti Path, Chanakyapuri, New Delhi 110 021; tel. (11) 6871585; fax (11) 6885486; Ambassador: ZHOU GANG.

Colombia: 82D Malcha Marg, Chanakyapuri, New Delhi 110 021; tel. (11) 6110773; fax (11) 6112486; Ambassador: MARÍA CLARA BETANCUR.

Congo, Democratic Republic: B-39 Soami Nagar, New Delhi 110 017; tel. (11) 6222796; fax (11) 6227226; Ambassador: KITENGE NKUMBI KASDNGO.

Croatia: 70 Ring Rd, Lajpat Nagar-III, New Delhi 110 024; tel. (11) 6924761; fax (11) 6924763; e-mail croemnd@del1.vsnl.net.in; Ambassador: Dr ZORAN ANDRIĆ.

Cuba: E-1/9 Vasant Vihar, New Delhi 110 057; tel. (11) 6143849; fax (11) 6143806; e-mail embcuind@ndf; Ambassador: OLGA CHAMERO TRIAS.

Cyprus: 106 Jor Bagh, New Delhi 110 003; tel. (11) 4697503; fax (11) 4628828; e-mail cyprus@del3.vsnl.net.in; High Commissioner: REA YIORDAMLIS.

Czech Republic: 50M Niti Marg, Chanakyapuri, New Delhi 110 021; tel. (11) 6110205; fax (11) 6886221; e-mail newdelhi@embassy.mzv.cz; Ambassador: IVAN JESTŘÁB.

Denmark: 11 Aurangzeb Rd, New Delhi 110 011; tel. (11) 3010900; fax (11) 3010961; e-mail denmark@vsnl.com; internet www.denmarkindia.com; Ambassador: BIRGIT STORGAARD MADSEN.

Egypt: 1/50M Niti Marg, Chanakyapuri, New Delhi 110 021; tel. (11) 6114096; fax (11) 6885355; e-mail egypt@del2.vsnl.net.in; Ambassador: GEHAD MADI.

Ethiopia: 7/50G Satya Marg, Chanakyapuri, New Delhi 110 021; tel. (11) 6119513; fax (11) 6875731; e-mail delethem@bol.net.in; Ambassador: DESTA ERIFO.

Finland: E–3 Nyaya Marg, Chanakyapuri, New Delhi 110 021; tel. (11) 6115258; fax (11) 6886713; e-mail sanomat.NDE@formin.fi; internet www.finembindia.com; Ambassador: BENJAMIN BASSIN.

France: 2/50E Shanti Path, Chanakyapuri, New Delhi 110 021; tel. (11) 6118790; fax (11) 6872305; Ambassador: BERNARD DE MONTFERRAND.

Germany: 6 Block 50G, Shanti Path, Chanakyapuri, New Delhi 110 021; tel. (11) 6871831; fax (11) 6873117; e-mail german@del3.vsnl.net.in; internet www.germanembassy-india.org; Ambassador: HEIMO RICHTER.

Ghana: 50-N Satya Marg, Chanakyapuri, New Delhi 110 021; tel. (11) 6883298; fax (11) 6883202; High Commissioner: (vacant).

Greece: 16 Sundar Nagar, New Delhi 110 003; tel. (11) 4617800; fax (11) 4601363; e-mail hellemb@del2.vsnl.net.in; Ambassador: YANNIS-ALEXIS ZEPOS.

Holy See: 50C Niti Marg, Chanakyapuri, New Delhi 110 021 (Apostolic Nunciature); tel. (11) 6889184; fax (11) 6874286; e-mail nuntius@bol.net.in; Pro-Nuncio: Most Rev. LORENZO BALDISSERI, Titular Archbishop of Diocletiana.

Hungary: Plot 2, 50M Niti Marg, Chanakyapuri, New Delhi 110 021; tel. (11) 6114737; fax (11) 6886742; e-mail huembdel@giasdl01.vsnl.net.in; Ambassador: ANDRAS DALLOS.

Indonesia: 50A Chanakyapuri, New Delhi 110 021; tel. (11) 6118642; fax (11) 6884402; e-mail iembassy@giasdl01.vsnl.net.in; Ambassador: GATOT SUWARDI.

Iran: 5 Barakhamba Road, New Delhi 110 001; tel. (11) 3329600; fax (11) 3325493; Ambassador: MIR MAHMOUD-MOUSSAVI KHAMENEH.

Iraq: 169–171 Jor Bagh, New Delhi 110 003; tel. (11) 4618011; fax (11) 4631547; Ambassador: SALAH ABDUL KADER MAHMOOD.

Ireland: 13 Jor Bagh, New Delhi 110 003; tel. (11) 4626733; fax (11) 4697053; Ambassador: PHILIP McDONOGH.

Israel: 3 Aurangzeb Rd, New Delhi 110 011; tel. (11) 3013238; fax (11) 3014298; e-mail israelem@vsnl.com; Ambassador: DAVID APHEK.

Italy: 50E Chandragupta Marg, Chanakyapuri, New Delhi 110 021; tel. (11) 6114355; fax (11) 6873889; e-mail italemb@nde.vsnl.net.in; internet www.italembdelhi.com; Ambassador: BENEDETTO AMARI.

Japan: Plots 4–5, 50G Shanti Path, Chanakyapuri, New Delhi 110 021; tel. (11) 6876581; fax (11) 6885587; Ambassador: HIROSHI HIRABAYASHI.

Jordan: 1/21 Shanti Niketan, New Delhi 110 021; tel. (11) 6889857; fax (11) 6883763; e-mail jordemb@ndf.vsnl.net.in; Ambassador: HUSHAN MUHAISEN.

Kazakhstan: 4 Olof Palme Marg, Vasant Vihar, New Delhi 110 057; tel. (11) 6144779; fax (11) 6144778; e-mail embaskaz@giasdl01.vsnl.net.in; Ambassador: ASKAR O. SHAKIROV.

Kenya: E-66 Vasant Marg, Vasant Vihar, New Delhi 110 057; tel. (11) 6146537; fax (11) 6146550; High Commissioner: L. O. AMAYO.

Korea, Democratic People's Republic: D-14 Maharani Bagh, New Delhi 110 065; tel. (11) 6829644; fax (11) 6829645; Ambassador: PAK MYONG GU.

Korea, Republic: 9 Chandragupta Marg, Chanakyapuri, POB 5416, New Delhi 110 021; tel. (11) 6885412; fax (11) 6884840; Ambassador: LEE CHONG-MOO.

Kuwait: 5A Shanti Path, Chanakyapuri, New Delhi 110 021; tel. (11) 4100791; fax (11) 6881115; Ambassador: ABDULLAH AHMED AL-MURAD.

Kyrgyzstan: B-8/25 Vasant Vihar, New Delhi 110 057; tel. (11) 6141682; fax (11) 6140372; e-mail kyrghyz@del3.vsnl.net.in; Ambassador: OSMONAKUN IBRAIMOV.

Laos: E53 Panchshila Park, New Delhi 110 017; tel. (11) 6497447; fax (11) 6495812; Ambassador: KIDENG THAMMAVONG.

Lebanon: 10 Sardar Patel Marg, Chanakyapuri, New Delhi 110 021; tel. (11) 3013174; fax (11) 3015555; e-mail lebanemb@giasdl01.vsnl.net.in; Ambassador: Dr JEAN DANIEL.

Libya: 22 Golf Links, New Delhi 110 003; tel. (11) 4697717; fax (11) 4633005; Secretary of People's Bureau: NURI EL-FITURI AL-MADANI.

Malaysia: 50M Satya Marg, Chanakyapuri, New Delhi 110 021; tel. (11) 6111291; fax (11) 6881538; e-mail hcom@del2.vsnl.net.in; High Commissioner: Dato' S. K. CHOO.

Mauritius: 5 Kautilya Marg, Chanakyapuri, New Delhi 110 021; tel. (11) 3011112; fax (11) 3019925; e-mail mhcnd@giasdl01.vsnl.net.in; High Commissioner: ROHIT NARAINSING GUTTEE.

Mexico: B-33 Friends Colony (West), New Delhi 110 065; tel. (11) 6932860; fax (11) 6932864; Ambassador: PEDRO GONZALEZ-RUBIO.

Mongolia: 34 Archbishop Makarios Marg, New Delhi 110 021; tel. (11) 4631728; fax (11) 4633240; e-mail embassy.mongolia@gems.vsnl.net.in; Ambassador: OIDOVYN NYAMDAVAA.

Morocco: 33 Archbishop Makarios Marg, New Delhi 110 003; tel. (11) 4636920; fax (11) 4636925; e-mail sifamand@giasl01.vsnl.net.in; Ambassador: (vacant).

Myanmar: 3/50F Nyaya Marg, Chanakyapuri, New Delhi 110 021; tel. (11) 6889007; fax (11) 6877942; e-mail myandeli@nda.vsnl.net.in; Ambassador: U TIN LATT.

Namibia: D-6/24 Vasant Vihar, New Delhi 110 057; tel. (11) 6144772; fax (11) 6146120; e-mail nhcdelhi@del2.vsnl.net.in; High Commissioner: JOEL KAAPANDA.

Nepal: Barakhamba Rd, New Delhi 110 001; tel. (11) 3329969; fax (11) 3326857; e-mail rned.ramjnki@axcess.net.in; Ambassador: Dr BHEKH B. THAPA.

Netherlands: 6/50F Shanti Path, Chanakyapuri, New Delhi 110 021; tel. (11) 6884951; fax (11) 6884956; e-mail nlembas@giasdl01.vsnl.net.in; Ambassador: P. F. C. KOCH.

New Zealand: 50N Nyaya Marg, Chanakyapuri, New Delhi 110 021; tel. (11) 6883170; fax (11) 6883165; e-mail nzhc@ndf.vsnl.net.in; High Commissioner: ADRIAN SIMCOCK.

Nigeria: 21 Olof Palme Marg, Vasant Vihar, New Delhi 110 057; tel. (11) 6146211; fax (11) 6146647; e-mail nigeria.nhc@axcess.net.in; High Commissioner: HABIB OMOKHAGBOR ELABOR.

Norway: 50C Shanti Path, Chanakyapuri, New Delhi 110 021; tel. (11) 6873532; fax (11) 6873814; e-mail noramb@vsnl.com; Ambassador: JON WESTBORG.

Oman: 16 Olof Palme Marg, New Delhi 110 057; tel. (11) 6144798; fax (11) 6146478; Ambassador: KHALIFA BIN ALI BIN ESSA AL-HARTHY.

Pakistan: 2/50G Shanti Path, Chanakyapuri, New Delhi 110 021; tel. (11) 4676004; fax (11) 6872339; High Commissioner: ASHRAF JEHANGIR QAZI.

Peru: D-6/13C, Vasant Vihar, New Delhi 110 057; tel. (11) 6144085; fax (11) 6146427; e-mail lepru@vsnl.com; Ambassador: CARLOS HIGUERAS-RAMOS.

Philippines: 50N Nyaya Marg, Chanakyapuri, New Delhi 110 021; tel. (11) 6889091; fax (11) 6876401; e-mail phndelhi@del2.vsnl.net.in; Ambassador: JOSÉ P. DEL ROSARIO, Jr.

Poland: 50M Shanti Path, Chanakyapuri, New Delhi 110 021; tel. (11) 6889211; fax (11) 6871914; Ambassador: JAN KRZYSZTOF MROZIEWICZ.

Portugal: 13 Sundar Nagar, New Delhi 110 003; tel. (11) 4601262; fax (11) 4601252; e-mail embportin@ndf.vsnl.net.in; internet www.embportindia.com; Ambassador: MANUEL MARCELO CURTO.

Qatar: G-5 Anand Niketan, New Delhi 110 021; tel. (11) 6117988; fax (11) 6886080; Ambassador: MUBARAK RASHID M. AL-BOAININ.

Romania: A-52 Vasant Marg, Vasant Vihar, New Delhi 110 057; tel. (11) 6140447; fax (11) 6140611; e-mail emrond@hotmail.com; Ambassador: PETRU PETRA.

Russia: Shanti Path, Chanakyapuri, New Delhi 110 021; tel. (11) 6873799; fax (11) 6876823; Ambassador: ALEKSANDER KADAKIN.

Saudi Arabia: D-12, New Delhi South Extension Part II, New Delhi 110 049; tel. (11) 6252470; fax (11) 6259333; Ambassador: A. REHMAN N. ALOHALY.

Senegal: 30 Paschimi Marg, Vasant Vihar, New Delhi 110 057; tel. (11) 6143720; fax (11) 6145809; Ambassador: AHMED EL MANSOUR DIOP.

Singapore: E-6 Chandragupta Marg, Chanakyapuri, New Delhi 110 021; tel. (11) 6885659; fax (11) 6886798; e-mail singhnd@giasdl01.vsnl.net.in; High Commissioner: KWOK PUN WONG.

Slovakia: 50M Niti Marg, Chanakyapuri, New Delhi 110 021; tel. (11) 6889071; fax (11) 6877941; e-mail skdelhi@giasdl01.vsnl.net.in; Ambassador: LADISLAV VOLKO.

Somalia: A-17, Defence Colony, New Delhi 110 024; tel. (11) 4619559; Ambassador: MOHAMED OSMAN OMAR.

South Africa: B-18 Vasant Marg, Vasant Vihar, New Delhi 110 057; tel. (11) 6149411; fax (11) 6143605; e-mail highcommissioner@sahc-india.com; High Commissioner: M. E. NKOANA MASHABANE.

Spain: 12 Prithviraj Rd, New Delhi 110 011; tel. (11) 3792085; fax (11) 3793375; Ambassador: ALBERTO ESCUDERO CLARAMUNT.

Sri Lanka: 27 Kautilya Marg, Chanakyapuri, New Delhi 110 021; tel. (11) 3010201; fax (11) 3015295; e-mail lankacom@del2.vsnl.net.in; High Commissioner: SENAKA BANDARANAYAKE.

Sudan: Plot No. 3, Shanti Path, Chanakyapuri, New Delhi 110 021; tel. (11) 6873785; fax (11) 6883758; Ambassador: AWED EL KARIM FADLALLA.

Sweden: Nyaya Marg, Chanakyapuri, New Delhi 110 021; tel. (11) 6875760; fax (11) 6885401; e-mail embassy.new.delhi@sida.se; Ambassador: K. G. ENGSTROM.

Switzerland: Nyaya Marg, Chanakyapuri, New Delhi 110 021; tel. (11) 6878372; fax (11) 6873093; e-mail swienidel@vsnl.com; Ambassador: Dr WALTER B. GYGER.

Syria: D-5/8, Vasant Vihar, New Delhi 110 057; tel. (11) 6140285; fax (11) 6143107; Ambassador: (vacant).

Tanzania: 10/1 Sarv Priya Vihar, New Delhi 110 016; tel. (11) 6853046; fax (11) 6968408; High Commissioner: AHMED K. M. KIWIANUKA.

Thailand: 56N Nyaya Marg, Chanakyapuri, New Delhi 110 021; tel. (11) 6118103; fax (11) 6872029; e-mail thaiemb@nda.vsnl.net.in; Ambassador: THAWATJAI THAVISRI.

Trinidad and Tobago: 131 Jor Bagh, New Delhi 110 003; tel. (11) 4618186; fax (11) 4624581; e-mail hcreptt@giasdl01.vsnl.net.in; High Commissioner: TEDWIN HERBERT (acting).

Tunisia: 23 Olof Palme Marg, Vasant Vihar, New Delhi 110 057; tel. (11) 6145346; fax (11) 6145301; e-mail embtun@nde.vsnl.net.in; Ambassador: MOHAMED SAHBI BASLI.

Turkey: 50N Nyaya Marg, Chanakyapuri, New Delhi 110 021; tel. (11) 6889054; fax (11) 6881409; e-mail temdelhi@telz.vsnl.net.in; Ambassador: YUSUF BULUC.

Turkmenistan: 1/13 Shanti Niketan, New Delhi 110 021; tel. (11) 6118409; fax (11) 6118332; e-mail turkmind@del3.vsnl.net.in; Ambassador: ASHIR ATAEV.

Uganda: B-3/26 Vasant Vihar, New Delhi 110 057; tel. (11) 6144413; fax (11) 6144405; e-mail ughcom@ndb.vsnl.net.in; High Commissioner: JOSEPH TOMUSANGE.

Ukraine: 46 Paschimi Marg, Vasant Vihar, New Delhi 110 057; tel. (11) 6146041; fax (11) 6146043; e-mail embassy@bol.net.in; Ambassador: VALENTYN V. ADOMAITIS.

United Arab Emirates: EP–12 Chandragupt Marg, New Delhi 110 021; tel. (11) 6872937; fax (11) 6873272; Ambassador: AHMED ABDULLAH AL-MUSALLY.

United Kingdom: Shanti Path, Chanakyapuri, New Delhi 110 021; tel. (11) 6872161; fax (11) 6872882; e-mail bhcndpa@del2.vsnl.net.in; internet www.ukinindia.org; High Commissioner: Sir ROBERTSON YOUNG.

Uruguay: A 16/2 Vasant Vihar, New Delhi 110 057; tel. (11) 6151991; fax (11) 6144306; e-mail uruind@del3.vsnl.net.in; Ambassador: ENRIQUE ANCHORDOQUI.

USA: Shanti Path, Chanakyapuri, New Delhi 110 021; tel. (11) 4198000; fax (11) 4190060; Ambassador: RICHARD F. CELESTE.

Uzbekistan: D-4/6 Vasant Vihar, New Delhi 110 057; tel. (11) 6149026; fax (11) 6143246; Ambassador: IBRAHIM MAVLANOV.

Venezuela: N-114 Panchshila Park, New Delhi 110 017; tel. (11) 6496913; fax (11) 6491686; e-mail embavene@del2.vsnl.net.in; Ambassador: WALTER MARQUEZ.

Viet Nam: 17 Kautilya Marg, Chanakyapuri, New Delhi 110 021; tel. (11) 3018059; fax (11) 3017714; e-mail sqdelhi@del3.vsnl.net.in; Ambassador: PHAM SY TAM.

Yemen: 41 Paschimi Marg, Vasant Vihar, New Delhi 110 057; tel. (11) 6151705; fax (11) 6144383; Ambassador: IBRAHIM ABDULLA I. SAIDI.

Yugoslavia: 3/50G Niti Marg, Chanakyapuri, New Delhi 110 021; tel. (11) 6873661; fax (11) 6885535; e-mail zvezda@del2.vsnl.net.in; Ambassador: Dr CEDOMIR STRABAC.

Zambia: C-79 Anand Niketan, New Delhi 110 021; tel. (11) 4101289; fax (11) 4101520; e-mail zambiand@nde.vsnl.net.in; High Commissioner: S. K. MUBUKWANU.

Zimbabwe: B-8 Anand Niketan, New Delhi 110 021; tel. (11) 6885060; fax (11) 6886073; High Commissioner: LUCIA MUVINGI.

Judicial System
THE SUPREME COURT

The Supreme Court, consisting of a Chief Justice and not more than 25 judges appointed by the President, exercises exclusive jurisdiction in any dispute between the Union and the states (although there are certain restrictions where an acceding state is involved). It has appellate jurisdiction over any judgment, decree or order of the High Court where that Court certifies that either a substantial question of law or the interpretation of the Constitution is involved. The Supreme Court can enforce fundamental rights and issue writs covering habeas corpus, mandamus, prohibition, quo warranto and certiorari. The Supreme Court is a court of record and has the power to punish for its contempt.

Provision is made for the appointment by the Chief Justice of India of judges of High Courts as ad hoc judges at sittings of the Supreme Court for specified periods, and for the attendance of retired judges at sittings of the Supreme Court. The Supreme Court has advisory jurisdiction in respect of questions which may be referred to it by the President for opinion. The Supreme Court is also empowered to hear appeals against a sentence of death passed by a State High Court in reversal of an order of acquittal by a lower court, and in a case in which a High Court has granted a certificate of fitness.

The Supreme Court also hears appeals which are certified by High Courts to be fit for appeal, subject to rules made by the Court. Parliament may, by law, confer on the Supreme Court any further powers of appeal.

The judges hold office until the age of 65 years.

Supreme Court: New Delhi; tel. (11) 3388942; fax (11) 3383792; internet www.caselaw.delhi.nic.in\sc-cl.

Chief Justice of India: Dr ADARSH SEIN ANAND.

Judges of the Supreme Court: S. P. BHARUCHA, BRIJESH KUMAR, S. RAJENDRA BABU, A. P. MISRA, SYED SHAH MOHAMMED QUADRI, KALLUPURACKAL T. THOMAS, DORAISWAMY RAJU, Y. K. SABHARWAL, BHUPINDER NATH KIRPAL, BISHWANATH AGARWAL, VISHESHWAR NATH KHARE, RUMA PAL, S. N. VARIAVA, SHIVRAJ V. PATIL, K. G. BALAKRISHNAN, G. B. PATTANAIK, MANHARLAL BHIKHALAL SHAH, DEBAPRIYA MOHAPATRA, UMESH CHANDRA BANERJEE, RAMESH CHANDRA LAHOTI, SANTOSH HEGDE, RAM PRAKASH SETHI, S. N. PHUKAN.

Attorney-General: SOLI J. SORABJEE.

HIGH COURTS

The High Courts are the Courts of Appeal from the lower courts, and their decisions are final except in cases where appeal lies to the Supreme Court.

LOWER COURTS

Provision is made in the Code of Criminal Procedure for the constitution of lower criminal courts called Courts of Session and Courts of Magistrates. The Courts of Session are competent to try all persons duly committed for trial, and inflict any punishment authorized by the law. The President and the local government concerned exercise the prerogative of mercy.

The constitution of inferior civil courts is determined by regulations within each state.

Religion
INDIAN FAITHS

Buddhism: The Buddhists in Ladakh (Jammu and Kashmir) are followers of the Dalai Lama. Head Lama of Ladakh: KAUSHAK SAKULA, Dalgate, Srinagar, Kashmir. In 1991 there were 6.3m. Buddhists in India, representing 0.80% of the population.

Hinduism: 672.6m. Hindus (1991 census), representing 82.4% of the population.

Islam: Muslims are divided into two main sects, Shi'as and Sunnis. Most of the Indian Muslims are Sunnis. At the 1991 census Islam had 95.2m. adherents (11.2% of the population).

Jainism: 3.4m. adherents (1991 census), 0.4% of the population.

Sikhism: 16.3m. Sikhs (comprising 2.0% of the population at the 1991 census), the majority living in the Punjab.

Zoroastrians: More than 120,000 Parsis practise the Zoroastrian religion.

CHRISTIANITY

According to the 1991 census, Christians represented 2.3% of the population in India.

National Council of Churches in India: Christian Council Lodge, Civil Lines, POB 205, Nagpur 440 001, Maharashtra; tel. (712) 531312; fax (712) 520554; e-mail nccindia@nagpur.dot.net.in; internet www.ncci.org; f. 1914; mems: 26 reformed and three orthodox churches, 14 regional Christian councils, 14 All-India ecumenical orgs and seven related agencies; represents c. 8m. mems; Pres. Most Rev. VINOD PETER; Gen. Sec. Rev. Dr IPE JOSEPH.

Orthodox Churches

Malankara Orthodox Syrian Church: Catholicate Palace, Devalokam, Kottayam 686 038, Kerala; tel. 578500; c. 2.5m. mems (1995); 22 bishops, 21 dioceses, 1,340 parishes; Catholicos of the East and Malankara Metropolitan: HH BASELIUS MARTHOMA MATHEWS II; Asscn Sec. A. K. THOMAS.

Mar Thoma Syrian Church of Malabar: Mar Thoma Sabha Office, Poolatheen, Tiruvalla 689 101, Kerala; tel. (473) 630449; fax (473) 630327; c. 800,000 mems (1997); Metropolitan: Most Rev. Dr ALEXANDER MAR THOMA; Sec. Very Rev. A. C. KURIAN.

The Malankara Jacobite Syrian Orthodox Church is also represented.

Protestant Churches

Church of North India (CNI): CNI Bhavan, 16 Pandit Pant Marg, New Delhi 110 001; tel. (11) 3716513; fax (11) 3716901; e-mail gscni@nda.vsnl.net.in; internet www.cnisynod.org; f. 1970 by merger of the Church of India (fmrly known as the Church of India, Pakistan, Burma and Ceylon), the Council of the Baptist Churches in Northern India, the Methodist Church (British and Australasian Conferences), the United Church of Northern India (a union of Presbyterians and Congregationalists, f. 1924), the Church of the Brethren in India, and the Disciples of Christ; comprises 26 dioceses; c. 1.2m. mems (1999); Moderator Most Rev. VINOD A. R. PETER, Bishop of Nagpur; Gen. Sec. Dr VIDYA SAGAR LALL.

Church of South India (CSI): CSI Centre, 5 Whites Rd, Chennai 600 014; tel. (44) 8521566; fax (44) 8523528; e-mail csi@vsnl.com; internet www.csisynod.org; f. 1947 by merger of the Weslyan Methodist Church in South India, the South India United Church (itself a union of churches in the Congregational and Presbyterian/Reformed traditions) and the four southern dioceses of the (Anglican) Church of India; comprises 21 dioceses (incl. one in Sri Lanka); c. 2.8m. mems (2000); Moderator Most Rev. K. J. SAMUEL, Bishop of Kerala; Gen. Sec. Rev. G. DYVASIRVADAM.

Methodist Church in India: Methodist Centre, 21 YMCA Rd, Mumbai Central, Mumbai 400 008; tel. and fax (22) 3074137; e-mail gensecmci@vsnl.com; f. 1856 as the Methodist Church in Southern Asia; 600,000 mems (1998); Gen. Sec. Rev. TARANATH S. SAGAR.

Samavesam of Telugu Baptist Churches: C. A. M. Compound, Nellore 524 003, Andhra Pradesh; tel. (861) 24177; f. 1962; comprises 856 independent Baptist churches; 578,295 mems (1995); Gen. Sec. Rev. Dr S. BENJAMIN.

United Evangelical Lutheran Churches in India: 1 First St, Haddows Rd, Chennai 600 006; tel. (44) 6421575; fax (44) 6421870; f. 1975; 11 constituent denominations: Andhra Evangelical Lutheran Church, Arcot Lutheran Church, Evangelical Lutheran Church in Madhya Pradesh, Gossner Evangelical Lutheran Church, India Evangelical Lutheran Church, Jeypore Evangelical Lutheran Church, Northern Evangelical Lutheran Church, North Western Gossner Evangelical Lutheran Church, South Andhra Lutheran Church, Good Samaritan Evangelical Lutheran Church and Tamil Evangelical Lutheran Church; c. 1.3m. mems; Pres. Rev. C. S. R. TOPNO; Exec. Sec. Dr K. RAJARATNAM.

Other denominations active in the country include the Assembly of the Presbyterian Church in North East India, the Bengal-Orissa-Bihar Baptist Convention (6,000 mems), the Chaldean Syrian Church of the East, the Convention of the Baptist Churches of Northern Circars, the Council of Baptist Churches of North East India, the Council of Baptist Churches of Northern India, the Hindustani Convent Church and the Mennonite Church in India.

The Roman Catholic Church

India comprises 24 archdioceses and 142 dioceses. These include four archdioceses and 20 dioceses of the the Syro-Malabar rite, and one archdiocese and three dioceses of the Syro-Malankara rite. The archdiocese of Goa and Daman is also the seat of the Patriarch of the East Indies. The remaining archdioceses are metropolitan sees.

In 1999 there were an estimated 16.3m. adherents of the Roman Catholic faith in the country.

Catholic Bishops' Conference of India (CBCI): CBCI Centre, 1 Ashok Place, Goledakkhana, New Delhi 110 001; tel. (11) 3344470; fax (11) 3364615; e-mail cbci@nda.vsnl.net.in; f. 1944; Pres. Most Rev. CYRIL MAR BASELIOS MALANCHARUVIL, Archbishop of Thiruvananthapuram; Sec.-Gen. Most Rev. Dr OSWALD GRACIAS, Archbishop of Agra.

Latin Rite

Conference of Catholic Bishops of India—Latin Rite (CCBI—LR): CCBI Secretariat, Divya Deepti Sadan, 2nd Floor, 9–10 Bhai Vir Singh Marg, POB 680, New Delhi 110 001; tel. (11) 3364222; fax (11) 3364343; e-mail ccbi@vsnl.net; f. 1994; Pres. Most Rev. HENRY SEBASTIAN D'SOUZA, Archbishop of Calcutta.

Patriarch of the East Indies: Most Rev. RAUL NICOLAU GONSALVES (Archbishop of Goa and Daman), Paço Patriarcal, POB 216, Altinho, Panjim, Goa 403 001; tel. (832) 223353; fax (832) 224139.

Archbishop of Agra: Most Rev. Dr OSWALD GRACIAS, Cathedral House, Wazirpura Rd, Agra 282 003; tel. (562) 351318; fax (562) 353939; e-mail abpossie@sancharnet.in.

Archbishop of Bangalore: Most Rev. IGNATIUS PAUL PINTO, Archbishop's House, 75 Miller's Rd, Bangalore 560 046; tel. (80) 3330438; fax (80) 3330838; e-mail bgarchdi@bgl.vsnl.net.in.

Archbishop of Bhopal: Most Rev. PASCHAL TOPNO, Archbishop's House, 33 Ahmedabad Palace Rd, Bhopal 462 001; tel. (755) 540829; fax (755) 544737; e-mail adbhopal@vsnl.com.

Archbishop of Bombay (Mumbai): Cardinal IVAN DIAS, Archbishop's House, 21 Nathalal Parekh Marg, Fort, Mumbai 400 001; tel. (22) 2021093; fax (22) 2853872; e-mail bombaydiocese@vsnl.com.

Archbishop of Calcutta (Kolkata): Most Rev. HENRY SEBASTIAN D'SOUZA, Archbishop's House, 32 Park St, Kolkata 700 016; tel. (33) 2471960; fax (33) 2474666; e-mail archbishop@cal.indiax.com.

Archbishop of Chennai (Madras) and Mylapore: Most Rev. JAMES MASILAMONY ARUL DAS, Archbishop's House, 21 San Thome High Rd, Chennai 600 004; tel. (44) 4941102; fax (44) 4941999.

Archbishop of Cuttack-Bhubaneswar: Most Rev. RAPHAEL CHEENATH, Archbishop's House, Satya Nagar, Bhubaneswar 751 007; tel. (674) 502234; fax (674) 501817.

Archbishop of Delhi: Most Rev. VINCENT M. CONCESSAO, Archbishop's House, 1 Ashok Place, Goledakkhana, New Delhi 110 001; tel. (11) 3343457; fax (11) 3746575; e-mail archbish@ndf.vsnl.net.in.

Archbishop of Guwahati: Most Rev. THOMAS MENAMPARAMPIL, Archbishop's House, POB 100, Guwahati 781 001; tel. (361) 547664; fax (361) 520588; e-mail bishop@gw1.vsnl.net.in; internet www.catholicindia.org/guwahati.htm.

Archbishop of Hyderabad: Most Rev. SAMININI ARULAPPA, Archbishop's House, Sardar Patel Rd, Secunderabad 500 003; tel. (40) 7805545; fax (40) 7805104.

Archbishop of Imphal: Most Rev. JOSEPH MITTATHANY, Archbishop's House, POB 35, Imphal 795 001; tel. (385) 221170; fax (385) 220193.

Archbishop of Madurai: Most Rev. MARIANUS AROKIASAMY, Archbishop's House, K. Pudur, Madurai 625 007; tel. (452) 563330; fax (452) 566630.

Archbishop of Nagpur: Most Rev. ABRAHAM VIRUTHAKULANGARA, Archbishop's House, 25 Kamptee Rd, Mohan Nagar, Nagpur 440 001; tel. (712) 533239; fax (712) 527906; e-mail abpabrah@nagpur.dot.net.in.

Archbishop of Patna: Most Rev. BENEDICT JOHN OSTA, Archbishop's House, Bankipore, Patna 800 004; tel. (612) 673811; fax (612) 664816; e-mail archbishop@satyam.net.in.

Archbishop of Pondicherry and Cuddalore: Most Rev. Dr S. MICHAEL AUGUSTINE, Archbishop's House, Cathedral St, POB 193, Pondicherry 605 001; tel. (413) 334748; fax (413) 339911.

Archbishop of Ranchi: Most Rev. TELESPHORE P. TOPPO, Archbishop's House, Purulia Rd, POB 5, Ranchi 834 001; tel. (651) 204728; fax (651) 300844.

Archbishop of Shillong: Most Rev. DOMINIC JALA, Archbishop's House, POB 37, Shillong 793 003; tel. (364) 23355; fax (364) 211306.

Archbishop of Verapoly: Most Rev. DANIEL ACHARUPARAMBIL, Latin Archbishop's House, POB 2581, Kochi 682 031; tel. (484) 372892; fax (484) 360911; e-mail vpoly@vsnl.com.

Syro-Malabar Rite

Major Archbishop of Ernakulam-Angamaly: Cardinal MAR VARKEY VITHAYATHIL, Major Archbishop's House, Ernakulam, POB 2580, Kochi 682 031; tel. (484) 352629; fax (484) 366028; e-mail abperang@md3.vsnl.net.in.

Archbishop of Changanacherry: Most Rev. JOSEPH MAR POWATHIL, Archbishop's House, POB 20, Changanacherry 686 101; tel. (481) 420379; fax (481) 422540; e-mail abpchry@md2.vsnl.net.in.

Archbishop of Tellicherry: Most Rev. GEORGE VALIAMATTAM, Archbishop's House, POB 70, Tellicherry 670 101; tel. and fax (497) 231058.

Archbishop of Trichur: Most Rev. JACOB THOOMKUZHY, Archbishop's House, Trichur 680 005; tel. (487) 333325; fax (487) 338204.

Syro-Malankara Rite

Archbishop of Thiruvananthapuram: Most Rev. CYRIL MAR BASELIOS MALANCHARUVIL, Archbishop's House, Pattom, Thiruvananthapuram 695 004; tel. (471) 541643; fax (471) 541635.

BAHÁ'Í FAITH

National Spiritual Assembly: Bahá'í House, 6 Canning Rd, POB 19, New Delhi 110 001; tel. (11) 3386458; fax (11) 3782178; e-mail nsaindia@bahaindia.org; internet www.bahaindia.org; c. 2m. mems; Sec.-Gen. R. N. SHAH; Exec. Sec. A. K. MERCHANT.

The Press

Freedom of the Press was guaranteed under the 1950 Constitution. In 1979 a Press Council was established (its predecessor was abolished in 1975), the function of which was to uphold the freedom of the press and maintain and improve journalistic standards.

The growth of a thriving press has been inhibited by cultural barriers caused by religious, social and linguistic differences. Consequently the English-language press, with its appeal to the educated middle-class urban readership throughout the states, has retained its dominance. The English-language metropolitan dailies are some of the widest circulating and most influential newspapers. The main Indian language dailies, by paying attention to rural affairs, cater for the increasingly literate non-anglophone provincial population. Most Indian-language papers have a relatively small circulation.

The majority of publications in India are under individual ownership (74% in 1995), and they claim a large part of the total circulation (49% in 1995). The most powerful groups, owned by joint stock companies, publish most of the large English dailies and frequently have considerable private commercial and industrial holdings. Four of the major groups are as follows:

Times of India Group (controlled by family of the late ASHOK JAIN): dailies: *The Times of India, Economic Times*, the Hindi *Navbharat Times*, the *Maharashtra Times* (Mumbai); periodicals: the English fortnightlies *Femina* and *Filmfare*.

Indian Express Group (controlled by the RAMNATH GOENKA family): publishes nine dailies including the *Indian Express*, the Marathi *Lokasatta*, the Tamil *Dinamani*, the Telugu *Andhra Prabha*, the Kannada *Kannada Prabha* and the English *Financial Express*; six periodicals including the English weeklies *Indian Express* (Sunday edition), *Screen*, the Telugu *Andhra Prabha Illustrated Weekly* and the Tamil *Dinamani Kadir* (weekly).

Hindustan Times Group (controlled by the K. K. BIRLA family): dailies: the *Hindustan Times* (Delhi, Lucknow and Patna), *Pradeep* (Patna) and the Hindi *Hindustan* (Delhi and Patna); periodicals: the weekly *Overseas Hindustan Times* and the Hindi monthly *Nandan* and *Kadambini* (New Delhi).

Ananda Bazar Patrika Group (controlled by AVEEK SARKAR and family): dailies: the *Ananda Bazar Patrika* (Kolkata) and the English *The Telegraph*; periodicals include: *Business World*, Bengali fortnightly *Desh*, Bengali monthly *Anandamela*, Bengali monthly *Anandalok* and the Bengali monthly *Sananda*.

PRINCIPAL DAILIES
Delhi (incl. New Delhi)

The Asian Age: New Delhi; tel. (11) 3712543; fax (11) 3755514; internet www.asianageonline.com; f. 1994; morning; English; also publ. from Bangalore, Bhubaneswar, Mumbai, Kolkata and London; Editor-in-Chief M. J. AKBAR; circ. 83,700 (New Delhi and Mumbai).

Business Standard: Pratap Bhavan, 5 Bahadur Shah Zafar Marg, New Delhi 110 002; tel. (11) 3720202; fax (11) 3720201; e-mail editor@business-standard.com; internet www.business-standard .com; morning; English; also publ. from Kolkata, Bangalore, Chennai and Mumbai; Editor T. N. NINAN; combined circ. 67,300.

Daily Milap: 8A Bahadur Shah Zafar Marg, New Delhi 110 002; tel. (11) 3317737; fax (11) 3319166; e-mail info@milap.com; internet www.milap.com; f. 1923; Urdu; nationalist; Man. Editor PUNAM SURI; Chief Editor NAVIN SURI; circ. 31,250.

Daily Pratap: Pratap Bhavan, 5 Bahadur Shah Zafar Marg, New Delhi 110 002; tel. (11) 3317938; fax (11) 3318276; f. 1919; Urdu; Editor K. NARENDRA; circ. 26,700.

Delhi Mid Day: World Trade Tower, Barakhamba Lane, New Delhi 110 001; tel. (11) 3715581; fax (11) 3350491; e-mail delhimidday@ hotmail.com; f. 1989; Editor JOHN DAYAL.

The Economic Times: 7 Bahadur Shah Zafar Marg, New Delhi 110 002; tel. (11) 3302000; fax (11) 3323346; internet www.economic

times.com; f. 1961; English; also publ. from Kolkata, Ahmedabad, Bangalore, Hyderabad, Chennai and Mumbai; Editor (Delhi) ARINDAM SENGUPTA; combined circ. 534,200, circ. (Delhi) 107,900.

Financial Express: Bahadur Shah Zafar Marg, New Delhi 110 002; tel. (11) 3311111; e-mail feletters@express2.indexp.co.in; internet www.financialexpress.com; f. 1961; morning; English; also publ. from Ahmedabad (in Gujarati), Mumbai, Bangalore, Kolkata, Kochi and Chennai; Editor SANJAYA BARU; combined circ. 60,000.

The Hindu: INS Bldg, Rafi Marg, New Delhi 110 001; tel. (11) 3715426; fax (11) 3718158; f.1878; morning; English; also publ. from Bangalore, Coimbatore, Hyderabad, Chennai, Madurai, Thiruvananthapuram and Visakhapatnam; Editor N. RAVI; combined circ. 720,550.

Hindustan: 18/20 Kasturba Gandhi Marg, New Delhi 110 001; tel. (11) 3361234; fax (11) 3704645; f. 1936; morning; Hindi; also publ. from Lucknow and Patna; Editor AJAY UPADHYAY; circ. (Delhi) 97,700, (Patna) 292,700, (Lucknow) 90,200.

The Hindustan Times: 18/20 Kasturba Gandhi Marg, New Delhi 110 001; tel. (11) 3361234; fax (11) 3704589; internet www.hindus tantimes.com; f. 1923; morning; English; also publ. from Patna and Lucknow; Editor VIR SANGHVI; circ. (Delhi) 566,600, combined circ. 594,100.

Indian Express: Bahadur Shah Zafar Marg, New Delhi 110 002; tel. (11) 3311111; fax (11) 3716037; internet www.indianexpress.com; f. 1953; English; also publ. from 7 other towns; Man. Editor VIVEK GOENKA; Editor-in-Chief SHEKHAR GUPTA; combined circ. 688,878, circ. (New Delhi, Jammu and Chandigarh) 140,400.

Janasatta: 9/10 Bahadur Shah Zafar Marg, New Delhi 110 002; f. 1983; Hindi; tel. (11) 3311111; fax (11) 3310089; also publ. from Kolkata, Chandigarh and Mumbai; Editor-in-Chief PRABHASH JOSHI; circ. (New Delhi and Chandigarh) 33,900, combined circ. 78,700.

National Herald: Herald House, Bahadur Shah Zafar Marg, New Delhi 110 002; tel. (11) 3319014; fax (11) 3313458; f. 1938; English; nationalist; also publ. from Lucknow; Editor-in-Chief K. V. S. RAMA SARMA; combined circ. 80,000.

Navbharat Times: 7 Bahadur Shah Zafar Marg, New Delhi 110 002; tel. (11) 3302000; fax (11) 3323346; f. 1947; Hindi; also publ. from Mumbai; Editor RAMESH CHANDRA; combined circ. 490,000, circ. (Delhi) 323,800.

The Pioneer: Link House, 3 Bahadur Shah Zafar Marg, New Delhi 110 002; tel. (11) 3755271; fax (11) 3755275; e-mail pioneer@ del2.vsnl.net.in; internet www.dailypioneer.com; f. 1865; also publ. from Lucknow; Editor CHANDAN MITRA combined circ. 154,000, circ. (Delhi) 78,000.

Punjab Kesari: Romesh Bhavan, 2 Printing Press Complex, nr Wazirpur DTC Depot, Ring Rd, Delhi 110 035; tel. (11) 7194459; fax (11) 7194470; e-mail ashwanik@nda.vsnl.net.in; Hindi; also publ. from Jalandhar and Ambala; Editor ASHWINI KUMAR; circ. 274,000 (Delhi).

Rashtriya Sahara: Amba Deep, Kasturba Gandhi Marg, New Delhi 110 001; tel. (11) 3755316; fax (11) 3755317; morning; Hindi; also publ. from Lucknow and Gorakhpur; Resident Editor NISHIT JOSHI; circ. 121,900 (New Delhi), 116,600 (Lucknow).

Sandhya Times: 7 Bahadur Shah Zafar Marg, New Delhi 110 002; tel (11) 3302000; fax (11) 3323346; f. 1979; Hindi; evening; Editor SAT SONI; circ. 77,000.

The Statesman: Rajiv Gandhi Circus, New Delhi 110 001; tel. (11) 3315911; fax (11) 3315295; f. 1875; English; also publ. from Kolkata and Siliguri; Editor-in-Chief C. R. IRANI; combined circ. 184,200.

The Times of India: 7 Bahadur Shah Zafar Marg, New Delhi 110 002; tel. (11) 3302000; fax (11) 3323346; internet www.timesofindia .com; f. 1838; English; also publ. from Mumbai, Kolkata, Bangalore, Ahmedabad, Lucknow and Patna; Man. Editor RAMESH CHANDRA; circ. (Delhi and Kolkata) 546,200, combined circ. 1,429,300.

Andhra Pradesh
Hyderabad

Deccan Chronicle: 36 Sarojini Devi Rd, Hyderabad 500 003; tel. (40) 7803930; fax (40) 7805256; f. 1938; English; Editor-in-Chief M. J. AKBAR; Editor A. T. JAYANTI; circ. 139,100.

Eenadu: Somajiguda, Hyderabad 500 082; tel. (40) 3318181; fax (40) 3318555; e-mail eenadu@hd2.vsnl.net.in; f. 1974; Telugu; also publ. from 14 other towns; Chief Editor RAMOJI RAO; combined circ. 900,000.

Newstime: 6-3-570 Somajiguda, Hyderabad 500 482; tel. (40) 318181; fax (40) 318555; f. 1984; also publ. from Vijaywada and Visakhapatnam; Editor RAMOJI RAO; circ. 60,000.

Rahnuma-e-Deccan: 5-3-831, Goshamahal, Hyderabad 500 012; tel. (40) 4732225; fax (40) 4616991; f. 1949; morning; Urdu; independent; Gen. Man. MIR ALI HYDER HUSSAINI; Chief Editor SYED VICA-RUDDIN; circ. 20,000.

Siasat Daily: Jawaharlal Nehru Rd, Hyderabad 500 001; tel. (40) 4603666; fax (40) 4603188; e-mail siasat@hd1.vsnl.net.in; internet www.siasat.com; f. 1949; morning; Urdu; Editor ZAHID ALI KHAN; circ. 45,812.

Vijayawada

Andhra Jyoti: Andhra Jyoti Bldg, POB 712, Vijayawada 520 010; tel. (866) 474532; f. 1960; Telugu; also publ. from Hyderabad, Visakhapatnam and Tirupati; Editor NANDURI RAMAMOHAN RAO; combined circ. 78,600.

Andhra Prabha: 16-1-28, Kolandareddy Rd, Poornanandampet, Vijayawada 520 003; tel. (866) 571351; internet www.andhraprabha .com; f. 1935; Telugu; also publ. from Bangalore, Hyderabad, Chennai and Visakhapatnam; Editor V. V. DEEKSHITULU; combined circ. 24,100.

New Indian Express: 16-1-28, Kolandareddy Rd, Poornanandampet, Vijayawada 520 003; tel. (866) 571351; English; also publ. from Bangalore, Belgaum, Kochi, Kozhikode, Thiruvananthapuram, Madurai, Chennai, Hyderabad, Visakhapatnam, Coimbatore and Bhubaneswar; Man. Editor MANOJ KUMAR SONTHALIA; Editor (Andhra Pradesh) P. S. SUNDARAM; combined circ. 310,800.

Assam
Guwahati

Asomiya Pratidin: Maniram Dewan Rd, Guwahati 781 003; tel. (361) 540420; fax (361) 524634; e-mail protidin@gw1.vsnl.net.in; morning; Assamese; circ. 92,533.

Assam Tribune: Tribune Bldgs, Maniram Dewan Rd, Chandmari, Guwahati 781 003; tel. (361) 661357; fax (361) 666398; e-mail webmaster@assamtribune.com; internet www.assamtribune.com; f. 1939; English; Man. Dir and Editor P. G. BARUAH; circ. 52,000.

Dainik Agradoot: Agradoot Bhavan, Dispur, Guwahati 781 006; tel. (361) 561923; fax (361) 560655; e-mail agradoot@gwldot.net.in; f. 1995; Assamese; Editor K. S. DEKA; circ. 50,500.

Dainik Assam: Tribune Bldgs, Maniram Dewan Rd, Chandmari, Guwahati 781 003; tel. (361) 541360; fax (361) 516356; e-mail webmaster@assamtribune.com; internet www.assamtribune.com; f. 1965; Assamese; Editor ANIL BARUAH; circ. 18,000.

The North East Daily: Maniram Dewan Rd, Chandmari, Guwahati 781 003; tel. (361) 524594; fax (361) 524634; e-mail protidin@gw1.vsnl.net.in; Assamese; circ. 34,891.

Jorhat

Dainik Janambhumi: Nehru Park Rd, Jorhat 785 001; tel. (376) 320033; fax (376) 321713; f. 1972; Assamese; Editor DEVA KR. BORAH; circ. 29,000.

Bihar
Patna

Aryavarta: Mazharul Haque Path, Patna 800 001; tel. (612) 230716; fax (612) 222350; e-mail aryavart@dte.vsnl.net.in; morning; Hindi; Editor BHAKTISHWAR JHA.

Hindustan Times: Buddha Marg, Patna 800 001; tel. (612) 223434; fax (612) 226120; f. 1918; morning; English; also publ. from New Delhi and Lucknow; Editor V. N. NARAYANAN; circ. 27,500.

Indian Nation: Mazharul Haque Path, Patna 800 001; tel. (612) 237780; fax (612) 222350; e-mail aryavart@dte.vsnl.net.in; morning; English; Editor BHAKTISHWAR JHA.

The Times of India: Times House, Fraser Rd, Patna 800 001; tel. (612) 226301; fax (612) 233525; also publ. from New Delhi, Mumbai, Ahmedabad, Bangalore and Lucknow; Man. Editor RAMESH CHANDRA; circ. 27,600.

Ranchi (now in Jharkhand)

Ranchi Express: 55 Baralal St, Ranchi 834 001; tel. (651) 206320; fax (651) 203466; f. 1963; Hindi; Editor AJAY MAROO; circ. 82,200.

Goa
Panaji

Gomantak: Gomantak Bhavan, St Inez, Panaji, Goa 403 001; tel. (832) 422700; fax (832) 422701; f. 1962; morning; Marathi and English edns; Editor LAXMAN T. JOSHI; circ. 20,400 (Marathi), 6,200 (English).

Navhind Times: Navhind Bhavan, Rua Ismail Gracias, POB 161, Panaji, Goa 403 001; tel. (832) 224033; fax (832) 224258; e-mail navhind@goa1.dot.net.in; f. 1963; morning; English; Editor ARUN SINHA; circ. 35,102.

Gujarat
Ahmedabad

Gujarat Samachar: Gujarat Samachar Bhavan, Khanpur, Ahmedabad 380 001; tel. (79) 5504010; fax (79) 5502000; f. 1930; morning; Gujarati; also publ. from Surat, Rajkot, Baroda, Mumbai and New York; Editor SHANTIBHAI SHAH; combined circ. 861,200.

Indian Express: Janasatta Bldg, Mirzapur Rd, Ahmedabad; tel. (79) 5507028; fax (79) 5507708; f. 1968; English; also publ. in 19 other towns throughout India; Man. Editor VIVEK GOENKA; Chief Editor SHEKHAR GUPTA; circ. (Ahmedabad and Vadodara) 45,000.

Lokasatta—Janasatta: Mirzapur Rd, POB 188, Ahmedabad 380 001; tel. (79) 5507307; fax (79) 5507708; f. 1953; morning; Gujarati; also publ. from Rajkot and Vadodara; Man. Editor VIVEK GOENKA; combined circ. 23,700.

Sandesh: Sandesh Bhavan, Gheekanta Rd, Ahmedabad 380 001; tel. (79) 5624241; fax (79) 5624392; e-mail sandesh@adl.vsnl.net.in; f. 1923; Gujarati; also publ. from Baroda, Rajkot and Surat; Editor FALGUNBHAI C. PATEL; combined circ. 657,300.

The Times of India: 139 Ashram Rd, POB 4046, Ahmedabad 380 009; tel. (79) 6582151; fax (79) 6583758; f. 1968; English; also publ. from Mumbai, Delhi, Bangalore, Patna and Lucknow; Resident Editor KAMLENDRA KANWAR; circ. (Ahmedabad) 100,550.

Western Times: 'Western House', Marutnandan Complex, Madalpur, Ahmedabad 380 006; tel. (79) 6576037; fax (79) 6577421; e-mail western@icenet.net.in; f. 1967; English and Gujarati edns; also publ. (in Gujarati) from Mehsana, Surendranagar, Godhra, Charotar-Nadiad, South Gujarat, Gandhinagar, Baroda and Bharuch; Man. Editor NIKUNJ PATEL; Editor RAMU PATEL; circ. (Ahmedabad) 25,364 (English), 39,359 (Gujarati); circ. 27,775 (Mehsana), 27,675 (Godhra), 21,545 (Charotar-Nadiad), 24,620 (Baroda), 27,645 (South Gujarat), 21,620 (Gandhinagar).

Bhuj

Kutchmitra: Kutchmitra Bhavan, nr Indirabai Park, Bhuj 370 001; tel. (2832) 52090; fax (2832) 50271; f. 1947; Propr Saurashtra Trust; Editor KIRTI KHATRI; circ. 34,161.

Rajkot

Jai Hind: Jai Hind Press Bldg, Babubhai Shah Marg, POB 59, Rajkot 360 001; tel. (281) 440511; fax (281) 448677; e-mail jaihind@satyam.net.in; f. 1948; morning and evening (in Rajkot as *Sanj Samachar*); Gujarati; also publ. from Ahmedabad; Editor Y. N. SHAH; combined circ. 152,196.

Phulchhab: Phulchhab Bhavan, Phulchhab Chowk, Rajkot 360 001; tel. (281) 444611; fax (281) 448751; f. 1950; morning; Gujarati; Propr Saurashtra Trust; Editor DINESH RAJA; circ. 103,700.

Surat

Gujaratmitra and Gujaratdarpan: Gujaratmitra Bhavan, nr Old Civil Hospital, Sonifalia, Surat 395 003; tel. (261) 478703; fax (261) 478700; e-mail gujaratmitra@satyam.net.in; f. 1863; morning; Gujarati; Editor B. P. RESHAMWALA; circ. 88,624.

Jammu and Kashmir
Jammu

Himalayan Mail: Srinagar; f. 1996; English.

Kashmir Times: Residency Rd, Jammu 180 001; tel. (191) 543676; fax (191) 542028; e-mail kashmirtimes@vsnl.com; internet www.kashmirtimes.com; f. 1955; morning; English and Hindi; Editor PRABODH JAMWAL; circ. 67,500.

Srinagar

Srinagar Times: Badshah Bridge, Srinagar; f. 1969; Urdu; Editor GULAM MUHAMMAD SOFI; circ. 14,000.

Karnataka
Bangalore

Deccan Herald: 75 Mahatma Gandhi Rd, Bangalore 560 001; tel. (80) 5588999; fax (80) 5587179; internet www.deccanherald.com; f. 1948; morning; English; also publ. from Hubli-Dharwar; Editor-in-Chief K. N. HARI KUMAR; combined circ. 182,700.

Kannada Prabha: Express Bldgs, 1 Queen's Rd, Bangalore 560 001; tel. (80) 2866893; fax (80) 2866617; e-mail bexpress@bgl.vsnl.net.in; internet www.kannadaprabha.com; f. 1967; morning; Kannada; also publ. from Belgaum and Hyderabad; Editor Y. N. KRISHNAMURTHY; circ. 114,800.

New Indian Express: 1 Queen's Rd, Bangalore 560 001; tel. (80) 2256893; fax (80) 2256617; f. 1965; English; also publ. from Kochi, Hyderabad, Chennai, Madurai, Vijayawada and Vizianagaram; Man. Editor MANOJ KUMAR SONTHALIA; Editor SHEKHAR GUPTA; combined circ. 310,800.

Prajavani: 75 Mahatma Gandhi Rd, Bangalore 560 001; tel. (80) 5587292; fax (80) 5587675; internet www.prajavani.net; f. 1948; morning; Kannada; also publ. from Hubli-Dharwar; Editor-in-Chief K. N. HARIKUMAR; combined circ. 341,800.

Hubli-Dharwar

Samyukta Karnataka: Koppikar Rd, Hubli 580 020; tel. (836) 364303; fax (836) 362760; e-mail info@samyuktakarnataka.com; internet www.samyuktakarnataka.com; f. 1933; Kannada; also publ.

from Bangalore and Gulburga; Man. Editor K. SHAMA RAO; combined circ. 189,800.

Manipal

Udayavani: Udayavani Bldg, Press Corner, Manipal 576 119; tel. (8252) 70845; fax (8252) 70563; f. 1970; Kannada; Editor T. SATISH U. PAI; circ. 154,700.

Kerala
Kottayam

Deepika: POB 7, Kottayam 686 001; tel. (481) 566706; fax (481) 567947; e-mail deepika@md2.vsnl.net.in; internet www.deepika .com; f. 1887; Malayalam; independent; also publ. from Kannur, Kochi, Thiruvananthapuram and Thrissur; Dir GEORGE JACOB; combined circ. 150,000.

Malayala Manorama: K. K. Rd, POB 26, Kottayam 686 001; tel. (481) 563646; fax (481) 562479; e-mail editor@malayalamanorama .com; internet www.malayalamanorama.com; f. 1888; also publ. from Kozhikode, Thiruvananthapuram, Palakkad, Kannur, Kollam, Thrissur and Kochi; morning; Malayalam; Man. Dir and Editor MAMMEN MATHEW; Chief Editor K. M. MATHEW; combined circ. 1,146,300.

Kozhikode

Deshabhimani: 11/127 Convent Rd, Kozhikode 673 032; tel. (495) 77286; f. 1946; morning; Malayalam; publ. by the CPI—M; also publ. from Kochi and Thiruvananthapuram; Chief Editor S. RAMACHANDRAN PILLAI; combined circ. 160,200.

Mathrubhumi: Mathrubhumi Bldgs, K. P. Kesava Menon Rd, POB 46, Kozhikode 673 001; tel. (495) 366655; fax (495) 366656; e-mail mathrelt@md2.vsnl.net.in; f. 1923; Malayalam; Editor R. GOPALAKRISHNAN; also publ. from Thiruvananthapuram, Kannur, Thrissur, Kottayam and Kochi; combined circ. 754,600.

Thiruvananthapuram

Kerala Kaumudi: POB 77, Pettah, Thiruvananthapuram 695 024; tel. (471) 461050; fax (471) 461985; e-mail sreeni@giasmd01.vsnl .net.in; internet www.keralakaumudi.com; f. 1911; Malayalam; also publ. from Kollam, Alappuzha, Kochi, Kannur and Kozhikode; Editor-in-Chief M. S. MANI; combined circ. 141,200.

Thrissur

Express: POB 15, Trichur 680 001; tel. 25800; f. 1944; Malayalam; Editor K. BALAKRISHNAN; circ. 68,200.

Madhya Pradesh
Bhopal

Dainik Bhaskar: 6 Dwarka Sadan, Habibganj Rd, Bhopal 462 011; tel. (755) 551601; f. 1958; morning; Hindi; also publ. from Indore, Raipur, Jhansi, Bhopal, Bilaspur and Gwalior; Chief Editor R. C. AGARWAL; circ. 87,300 (Bhopal), 43,500 (Gwalior), 26,500 (Bilaspur), 134,300 (Indore), 70,300 (Raipur).

Indore

Naidunia: 60/1 Babu Labhchand Chhajlani Marg, Indore 452 009; tel. (731) 763111; fax (731) 763120; e-mail naidunia@edi.com; internet www.naidunia.com; f. 1947; morning; Hindi; Chief Editor ABHAY CHHAJLANI; circ. 128,900.

Raipur (now in Chhattisgarh)

Deshbandhu: Deshbandhu Complex, Ramsagarpara Layout, Raipur 492 001; tel. (771) 534911; fax (771) 534955; Hindi; also publ. from Jabalpur, Satna, Bilaspur and Bhopal; Chief Editor LALIT SURJAN; circ. 53,600 (Raipur), 19,300 (Satna), 24,240 (Bhopal), 19,637 (Jabalpur), 27,300 (Bilaspur).

Maharashtra
Kolhapur

Pudhari: 2318, 'C' Ward, Kolhapur 416 002; tel. (231) 22251; fax (231) 22256; f. 1974; Marathi; Editor P. G. JADHAV; circ. 146,000.

Mumbai

Afternoon Despatch and Courier: 6 Nanabhai Lane, Fort, Mumbai 400 001; tel. (22) 2871616; fax (22) 2870371; e-mail aftnet@ bom2.vsnl.net.in; internet www.afternoondc.com; evening; English; Editor BEHRAM CONTRACTOR; circ. 65,800.

The Daily: Asia Publishing House, Mody Bay Estate, Calicut St, Mumbai 400 038; tel. (22) 2653104; fax (22) 2619773; f. 1981; Editor RAJIV BAJAJ; circ. 38,700.

The Economic Times: Times of India Bldg, Dr Dadabhai Naoroji Rd, Mumbai 400 001; tel. (22) 2620271; fax (22) 2620144; e-mail etbom@timesgroup.com; internet www.economictimes.com; f. 1961; also publ. from New Delhi, Kolkata, Ahmedabad, Hyderabad, Chennai and Bangalore; English; Exec. Editor JAIDEEP BOSE; combined circ. 351,900, circ. (Mumbai) 121,200.

Financial Express: Express Towers, Nariman Point, Mumbai 400 021; tel. (22) 2022627; fax (22) 2886402; e-mail iemumbai@express .indexp.co.in; internet www.financialexpress.com; f. 1961; morning; English; also publ. from New Delhi, Bangalore, Kolkata, Coimbatore, Kochi, Ahmedabad (Gujarati) and Chennai; Man. Editor VIVEK GOENKA; combined circ. (English) 29,400.

The Free Press Journal: Free Press House, 215 Free Press Journal Rd, Nariman Point, Mumbai 400 021; tel. (22) 2874566; fax (22) 2874688; e-mail freepress@bom2.vsnl.net.in; f. 1930; English; also publ. from Indore; Man. Editor G. L. LAKHOTIA; combined circ. 87,000.

Indian Express: Express Towers, Nariman Point, Mumbai 400 021; tel. (22) 2022627; fax (22) 2022139; f. 1940; English; also publ. from Pune and Nagpur; Man. Editor VIVEK GOENKA; Chief Editor SHEKHAR GUPTA; combined circ. 189,300.

Inquilab: 156 D. J. Dadajee Rd, Tardeo, Mumbai 400 034; tel. (22) 4942586; fax (22) 4936571; e-mail azizk@mid-day.mailserve.net; internet www.inquilab.com; f. 1938; morning; Urdu; Editor FUZAIL JAFFEREY; circ. 34,522.

Janmabhoomi: Janmabhoomi Bhavan, Janmabhoomi Marg, Fort, POB 62, Mumbai 400 001; tel. (22) 2870831; fax (22) 2874097; e-mail bhoomi@bom3.vsnl.net.in; f. 1934; evening; Gujarati; Propr Saurashtra Trust; Editor KUNDAN VYAS; circ. 62,000.

Lokasatta: Express Towers, Nariman Point, Mumbai 400 021; tel. (22) 2022627; fax (22) 2022139; internet www.loksatta.com; f. 1948; morning (incl. Sunday); Marathi; also publ. from Pune, Nagpur and Ahmednagar; Editor AROON TIKEKAR; combined circ. 384,300.

Maharashtra Times: Dr Dadabhai Naoroji Rd, POB 213, Mumbai 400 001; tel. (22) 2620271; fax (22) 2620144; f. 1962; Marathi; Editor KUMAR KETKAR; circ. 186,100.

Mid-Day: 64 Sitaram Mills Compound, N. M. Joshi Marg, Lower Parel, Mumbai 400 011; tel. (22) 3054545; fax (22) 3054861; e-mail mid-day@giasbm01.vsnl.net.in; internet www.mid-day.com; f. 1979; daily and Sunday; English; Editor AYAZ MEMON; circ. 134,100.

Mumbai Samachar: Red House, Syed Abdulla Brelvi Rd, Fort, Mumbai 400 001; tel. (22) 2045531; fax (22) 2046642; f. 1822; morning and Sunday; Gujarati; political, social and commercial; Editor PINKY DALAL; circ. 128,800.

Navakal: 13 Shenviwadi, Khadilkar Rd, Girgaun, Mumbai 400 004; tel. (22) 353585; f. 1923; Marathi; Editor N. Y. KHADILKAR; circ. 298,900.

Navbharat Times: Dr Dadabhai Naoroji Rd, Mumbai 400 001; tel. (22) 2620382; f. 1950; Hindi; also publ. from New Delhi, Jaipur, Patna and Lucknow; circ. (Mumbai) 168,200.

Navshakti: Free Press House, 215 Nariman Point, Mumbai 400 021; tel. (22) 2874566; f. 1932; Marathi; Editor D. B. JOSHI; circ. 65,000.

Sakal: Sakal Bhavan, Plot No. 42-B, Sector No. 11, CBD Belapur, Navi Mumbai 400 614; tel. (22) 7574327; fax (22) 7574280; f. 1970; daily; Marathi; also publ. from Pune, Nasik and Kolhapur; Editor RADHAKRISHNA NARVEKAR; combined circ. 438,500.

The Times of India: The Times of India Bldg, Dr Dadabhai Naoroji Rd, Mumbai 400 001; tel. (22) 2620271; fax (22) 2620144; e-mail toieditorial@timesgroup.com; internet www.timesofindia.com; f. 1838; morning; English; also publ. from Delhi, Ahmedabad, Bangalore, Patna and Lucknow; Exec. Man. Editor DILEEP PADGAONKAR; circ. (Mumbai and Pune) 607,100, combined circ. 1,429,300.

Nagpur

Hitavada: Wardha Rd, Nagpur 440 012; tel. (712) 523155; fax (712) 535093; e-mail hitavada@nagpur.net.in; f. 1911; morning; English; Man. Editor BANWARILAL PUROHIT; Editor V. PHANSHIKAR; circ. 53,500.

Lokmat: Lokmat Bhavan, Wardha Rd, Nagpur 440 012; tel. (712) 523527; fax (712) 526923; also publ. from Jalgaon, Ahmednagar, Solapur, Nasik and Aurangabad; Marathi; **Lokmat Samachar** (Hindi) publ. from Nagpur and Aurangabad; **Lokmat Times** (English) publ. from Nagpur and Aurangabad; Editor VIJAY DARDA; combined circ. 273,700.

Nava Bharat: Nava Bharat Bhavan, Cotton Market, Nagpur 440 018; tel. (712) 726677; f. 1938; morning; Hindi; also publ. from Bhopal, Jabalpur, Bilaspur, Indore and Raipur; Editor-in-Chief R. G. MAHESWARI; combined circ. 443,200.

Tarun Bharat: 28 Farmland, Ramdaspeth, Nagpur 440 010; tel. (712) 525052; e-mail ibharat@nagpur.dot.net.in; f. 1941; Marathi; independent; also publ. from Mumbai and Solapur; Gen. Man. RAMDAS MULEY; Editor SUDHIR PATHAK; circ. 56,166 (Nagpur).

Pune

Kesari: 568 Narayan Peth, Pune 411 030; tel. (20) 4459250; fax (20) 4451677; f. 1881; Marathi; also publ. from Solapur, Kolhapur, Chiplun, Ahmednagar and Sangli; Editor ARVIND VYANKATESH GOKHALE; combined circ. 150,000.

Sakal: 595 Budhwar Peth, Pune 411 002; tel. (20) 4455500; fax (20) 4450583; e-mail sakal@giaspn01.vsnl.net.in; f. 1932; daily; Marathi;

also publ. from Mumbai, Nashik, Aurangabad and Kolhapur; Editor ANANT DIXIT; Man. Dir PRATAP PAWAR; combined circ. 573,000.

Orissa
Bhubaneswar

Dharitri: B-26, Industrial Estate, Bhubaneswar 751 010; tel. (674) 580101; fax (674) 580795; e-mail dharitri@mail.com; internet www.dharitri.com; evening and morning; Oriya; Editor TATHAGATA SATPATHY; circ. 134,540.

Pragativadi: 178-B, Mancheswar Industrial Estate, Bhubaneswar 751 010; tel. (674) 580298; fax (674) 582636; e-mail pragativadi@yahoo.com; circ. 117,547.

Cuttack

Prajatantra: Prajatantra Bldgs, Behari Baug, Cuttack 753 002; tel. (671) 603071; fax (671) 603063; f. 1947; Oriya; Editor BHARTRUHARI MAHTAB; circ. 118,400.

Samaj: Cuttack; tel. (671) 20994; fax (671) 601044; f. 1919; Oriya; circ. 124,000.

Punjab
Chandigarh

The Tribune: Sector 29C, Chandigarh 160 020; tel. (172) 655065; fax (172) 655054; e-mail tribunet@ch1.dot.net.in; internet www.tribuneindia.com; f. 1881 (English edn), f. 1978 (Hindi and Punjabi edns); Editor (all edns) HARI JAISINGH; Editor (Hindi edn) VIJAY SAIGHAL; Editor (Punjabi edn) G. S. BHULLAR; circ. 217,100 (English), 82,100 (Hindi), 79,000 (Punjabi).

Jalandhar

Ajit: Ajit Bhavan, Nehru Garden Rd, Jalandhar 144 001; tel. 55960; f. 1955; Punjabi; Man. Editor S. BARJINDER SINGH; circ. 187,500.

Hind Samachar: Civil Lines, Jalandhar 144 001; tel. (181) 280104; fax (181) 280113; f. 1948; morning; Urdu; also publ. from Ambala Cantt; Editor VIJAY KUMAR CHOPRA; Jt Editor AVINASH CHOPRA; combined circ. 45,048.

Jag Bani: Civil Lines, Jalandhar 144 001; tel. (181) 280104; fax (181) 280113; f. 1978; morning; Punjabi; Editor VIJAY KUMAR CHOPRA; Jt Editor AVINASH CHOPRA; circ. 173,742.

Punjab Kesari: Civil Lines, Jalandhar 144 001; tel. (181) 280104; fax (181) 280113; f. 1965; morning; Hindi; also publ. from Delhi and Ambala; Editor VIJAY KUMAR CHOPRA; Jt Editor AVINASH CHOPRA; combined circ. 816,413.

Rajasthan
Jaipur

Rajasthan Patrika: Kesargarh, Jawahar Lal Nehru Marg, Jaipur 302 004; tel. (141) 561582; fax (141) 566011; e-mail info@rajasthan_patrika.com; internet www.rajasthan_patrika.com; f. 1956; Hindi edn also publ. from Jodhpur, Bikaner, Udaipur, Bangalore and Kota; Editor MOTI CHAND KOCHAR; combined circ. (Hindi) 493,100.

Rashtradoot: M.I. Rd, POB 30, Jaipur 302 001; tel. (141) 372634; fax (141) 373513; f. 1951; Hindi; also publ. from Kota, Udaipur, Ajmer and Bikaner; CEO SOMESH SHARMA; Chief Editor RAJESH SHARMA; circ. 368,482 (Jaipur), 76,763 (Kota), 45,250 (Bikaner), 38,023 (Udaipur), 27,514 (Ajmer).

Tamil Nadu
Chennai (Madras)

Daily Thanthi: 46 E.V.K. Sampath Rd, POB 467, Chennai 600 007; tel. (44) 5387731; fax (44) 5380069; f. 1949; Tamil; also publ. from Bangalore, Coimbatore, Cuddalore, Erode, Madurai, Nagercoil, Salem, Tiruchi, Tirunelveli, Pondicherry and Vellore; Gen. Man. D. RAJIAH; Editor R. THIRUVADI; combined circ. 584,713.

Dinakaran: 106/107 Kutchery Rd, Mylapore, POB 358, Chennai 600 004; tel. (44) 4941006; fax (44) 4951008; e-mail dinakaran@dinakaran.com; internet www.dinakaran.com; f. 1977; Tamil; also publ. from Madurai, Tiruchirapalli, Vellore, Tirunelveli, Salem and Coimbatore; Man. Dir K. KUMARAN; Editor D. PAULRAJ; combined circ. 351,872.

Dinamalar: 20/1, Casa Major Rd, Egmore, Chennai 600 002; tel. (44) 8267106; f. 1951; Tamil; also publ. from Coimbatore, Erode, Madurai, Pondicherry, Tiruchirapalli, Tirunelveli and Vellore; Editor R. KRISHNAMOORTHY; combined circ. 429,500.

Dinamani: Express Estates, Mount Rd, Chennai 600 002; tel. (44) 8520751; fax (44) 8524500; e-mail express@giasmd01.vsnl.net.in; internet www.dinamani.com; f. 1934; morning; Tamil; also publ. from Madurai, Coimbatore and Bangalore; Editor T. SAMBANDAM; combined circ. 187,800.

Financial Express: Vasanthi Medical Center, 30/20 Pycrofts Garden Rd, Chennai 600 006; tel. (44) 8231112; fax (44) 8231489; internet www.financialexpress.com; f. 1961; morning; English; also publ. from Mumbai, Ahmedabad (in Gujarati), Bangalore, Kochi,

Kolkata and New Delhi; Man. Editor VIVEK GOENKA; combined circ. 32,594.

The Hindu: Kasturi Bldgs, 859/860 Anna Salai, Chennai 600 002; tel. (44) 8589060; fax (44) 8545703; e-mail wsvcs@thehindu.co.in; internet www.the-hindu.com; f. 1878; morning; English; independent; also publ. from Bangalore, Coimbatore, New Delhi, Visakhapatnam, Hyderabad, Thiruvananthapuram and Madurai; Publr S. RANGARAJAN; Editor N. RAVI; combined circ. 720,549.

The Hindu Business Line: Kasturi Bldgs, 859/860 Anna Salai, Chennai 600 002; tel. (44) 8589060; fax (44) 8545703; internet www.hindubusinessline.com; f. 1994; morning; English; also publ. from Bangalore, Hyderabad, Madurai, Coimbatore, New Delhi, Visakhapatnam and Thiruvananthapuram; Publr S. RANGARAJAN; Editor N. RAM; combined circ. 34,312.

Murasoli: 93 Kodambakkam High Rd, Chennai 600 034; tel. (44) 470044; f. 1960; organ of the DMK; Tamil; Editor S. SELVAM; circ. 54,000.

New Indian Express: Express Estates, Anna Salai, Chennai 600 002; tel. (44) 8461818; fax (44) 8461830; e-mail newexpress@vsnl.com; internet www.newindpress.com; f. 1932 as Indian Express; morning; English; also publ. from 7 other cities; Man. Editor MANOJ KUMAR SONTHALIA; combined circ. 324,161.

Tripura
Agartala

Dainik Sambad: 11 Jagannath Bari Rd, POB 2, Agartala 799 001; tel. (381) 226676; fax (381) 224845; f. 1966; Bengali; morning; Editor BHUPENDRA CHANDRA DATTA BHAUMIK.

Uttar Pradesh
Agra

Amar Ujala: Sikandra Rd, Agra 282 007; tel. (562) 321600; fax (562) 322181; e-mail amarujal@nde.vsnl.net.in; internet www.amarujala.org; f. 1948; Hindi; also publ. from Bareilly, Allahabad, Jhansi, Kanpur, Moradabad, Chandigarh and Meerut; Editor AJAY K. AGARWAL; Dep. Gen. Man. L. K. SHRIMALI; circ. 132,000 (Agra), 92,500 (Bareilly), 42,500 (Moradabad), 163,000 (Meerut), 128,000 (Kanpur), 54,000 (Allahabad), 12,500 (Jhansi), 184,500 (Chandigarh).

Allahabad

Amrita Prabhat: 10 Edmonstone Rd, Allahabad 211 001; tel. (532) 600654; f. 1977; Hindi; Editor TAMAL KANTI GHOSH; circ. 44,000.

Northern India Patrika: 10 Edmonstone Rd, Allahabad 211 001; tel. (532) 52665; f. 1959; English; Editor MANAS MUKUL DAS; circ. 46,000.

Kanpur

Dainik Jagran: 2 Sarvodaya Nagar, Kanpur 208 005; tel. (512) 216161; fax (512) 216972; e-mail jpl@jagran.com; internet www.jagran.com; f. 1942; Hindi; also publ. from 10 other cities; Editor NARENDRA MOHAN; combined circ. 1,058,000.

Vyapar Sandesh: 26/104 Birhana Rd, Kanpur 208 001; tel. (512) 352066; f. 1958; Hindi; commercial news and economic trends; Editor HARI SHANKAR SHARMA; circ. 17,000.

Lucknow

National Herald: Lucknow; f. 1938 Lucknow, 1968 Delhi; English; Editor-in-Chief K. V. S. RAMA SHARMA.

The Pioneer: 20 Vidhan Sabha Marg, Lucknow 226 001; tel. (522) 2812820; fax (522) 2812814; f. 1865; English; also publ. from New Delhi; Publr DIPAK MUKERJI; Editor CHANDAN MITRA; combined circ. 136,000.

Swatantra Bharat: 1st Floor, Suraj Deep Complex, 1 Jopling Rd, Lucknow 226 001; tel. (522) 209301; fax (522) 209308; e-mail sbharat@lw1.vsnl.net.in; f. 1947; Hindi; also publ. from Kanpur; Editor K. K. SRIVASTAVA; circ. 66,058 (Lucknow), 48,511 (Kanpur).

Varanasi

Aj: Aj Bhavan, Sant Kabir Rd, Kabirchaura, Varanasi 221 001; tel. (542) 393981; fax (542) 393989; f. 1920; Hindi; also publ. from Gorakhpur, Patna, Allahabad, Ranchi, Agra, Bareilly, Lucknow, Jamshedpur, Dhanbad and Kanpur; Editor SHARDUL VIKRAM GUPTA; circ. 46,700 (Agra), 39,500 (Allahabad), 41,200 (Gorakhpur), 156,500 (Kanpur), 19,800 (Jamshedpur), 52,100 (Lucknow), 141,500 (Patna), 38,500 (Ranchi), 182,400 (Varanasi), 28,300 (Bareilly).

West Bengal
Kolkata (Calcutta)

Aajkaal: 96 Raja Rammohan Sarani, Kolkata 700 009; tel. (33) 3509803; fax (33) 3500877; e-mail aajkaal@cal.vsnl.net.in; f. 1981; morning; Bengali; Chief Editor PRATAP K. ROY; circ. 160,500.

Ananda Bazar Patrika: 6 Prafulla Sarkar St, Kolkata 700 001; tel. (33) 2374880; fax (33) 2253241; internet www.anandabazar.com; f. 1922; morning; Bengali; Editor AVEEK SARKAR; circ. 692,400.

Bartaman: 76A Acharya J.C. Bose Rd, Kolkata 700 014; tel. (33) 2443907; fax (33) 2441215; f. 1984; also publ. from Siliguri; Editor BARUN SENGUPTA; circ. 435,600.

Business Standard: Church Lane, Kolkata 700 001; tel. (33) 278000; fax (33) 2253241; f. 1975; morning; also publ. from New Delhi, Bangalore, Chennai and Mumbai; English; Editor T. N. NINAN; combined circ. 67,300.

The Economic Times: 105/7A, S. N. Banerjee Rd, Kolkata 700 014; tel. (33) 294232; fax (33) 292400; English; also publ. from Ahmedabad, Delhi, Bangalore, Chennai, Hyderabad and Mumbai; circ. (Kolkata) 47,800.

Financial Express: 83 B. K. Pal Ave, Kolkata 700 005; morning; English; also publ. from Mumbai, Ahmedabad, Bangalore, Coimbatore, Kochi, Chennai and New Delhi; Man. Editor VIVEK GOENKA; combined circ. 29,400.

Ganashakti: 74A A. J. C. Bose Rd, Kolkata 700 016; tel. (33) 2458950; fax (33) 2448090; e-mail mail@ganashakti.co.in; internet www.ganashakti.com; f. 1967; morning; Bengali; Editor DIPEN GHOSH; circ. 120,700.

Himalchuli: 7 Old Court House St, Kolkata 700 001; tel. (33) 207618; fax (33) 206663; f. 1982; Nepali; Editor S. C. TALUKDAR; circ. 42,494.

Sambad Pratidin: 20 Prafulla Sarkar St, Kolkata 700 072; tel. (33) 2253707; fax (33) 2252536; e-mail pratidin@cal2.vsnl.net.in; internet www.sangbadpratidin.com; morning; Bengali; Editor SWAPAN SADHAN BASU; circ. 258,100.

Sandhya Aajkaal: 96 Raja Rammohan Sarani, Kolkata 700 009; tel. (33) 3509803; fax (33) 3500877; evening; Bengali; Chief Editor PRATAP K. ROY; circ. 18,400.

Sanmarg: 160C Chittaranjan Ave, Kolkata 700 007; tel. (33) 2414800; fax (33) 2415087; e-mail sanmarg@vsnl.com; f. 1948; Hindi; Editor RAMAWATAR GUPTA; circ. 94,833.

The Statesman: Statesman House, 4 Chowringhee Sq., Kolkata 700 001; tel. (33) 2257070; fax (33) 2250118; f. 1875; morning; English; independent; also publ. from New Delhi and Siliguri; Editor-in-Chief C. R. IRANI; combined circ. 184,200.

The Telegraph: 6 Prafulla Sarkar St, Kolkata 700 001; tel. (33) 2374880; fax (33) 2253240; e-mail thetelegraphindia@newscom.com; f. 1982; English; Editor AVEEK SARKAR; circ. 249,500.

Uttar Banga Sambad: 7 Old Court House St, Kolkata 700 001; tel. (33) 2207618; fax (33) 2206663; f. 1980; Bengali; Editor S. C. TALUKDAR; circ. 102,366.

Vishwamitra: 74 Lenin Sarani, Kolkata 700 013; tel. (33) 2441139; fax (33) 2446393; e-mail vismtra@cal2.vsnl.net.in; f. 1916; morning; Hindi; commercial; Editor PRAKASH CHANDRA AGRAWALLA; combined circ. 96,310.

SELECTED PERIODICALS

Delhi and New Delhi

Alive: Delhi Press Bldg, E-3, Jhandewala Estate, Rani Jhansi Rd, New Delhi 110 055; tel. (11) 3529557; fax (11) 3625020; f. 1940; monthly; English; political and cultural; Editor VISHWA NATH; circ. 10,000.

Bal Bharati: Patiala House, Publications Division, Ministry of Information and Broadcasting, Delhi 110 001; tel. (11) 387038; f. 1948; monthly; Hindi; for children; Editor SHIV KUMAR; circ. 30,000.

Biswin Sadi: B-1, Nizamuddin West, New Delhi 110 013; tel. (11) 4626556; f. 1937; monthly; Urdu; Editor Z. REHMAN NAYYAR; circ. 32,000.

Business Today: F-26 Connaught Place, New Delhi 110 001; tel. (11) 3315801; fax (11) 3318385; e-mail btoday@giasdl01.vsnl.net.in; internet www.business-today.com; fortnightly; English; Editor ANAND P. RAMAN; circ. 112,600.

Careers Digest: 21 Shankar Market, Delhi 110 001; tel. (11) 44726; f. 1963; monthly; English; Editor O. P. VARMA; circ. 35,000.

Catholic India: CBCI Centre, 1 Ashok Place, Goldakkhana, New Delhi 110 001; tel. (11) 3344470; fax (11) 3364615; e-mail cbci@nda.vsnl.net.in; quarterly.

Champak: Delhi Press Bldg, E-3, Jhandewala Estate, Rani Jhansi Rd, New Delhi 110 055; tel. (11) 3529557; fax (11) 3625020; f. 1969; fortnightly (Hindi, English, Gujarati and Marathi edns); monthly (Kannada edn); children; Editor VISHWA NATH; combined circ. 122,400.

Children's World: Nehru House, 4 Bahadur Shah Zafar Marg, New Delhi 110 002; tel. (11) 3316970; fax (11) 3721090; e-mail cbtnd@vsnl.com; internet www.childrensbooktrust.com; f. 1968; monthly; English; Editor NAVIN MENON; circ. 25,000.

Competition Refresher: 2767, Bright House, Daryaganj, New Delhi 110 002; tel. (11) 3282226; fax (11) 3269227; e-mail psbright@ndf.vsnl.net.in; internet www.brightcareers.com; f. 1984; monthly; English; Chief Editor D. S. PHULL; Publr and Man. Dir PRITAM SINGH BRIGHT; circ. 162,529.

Competition Success Review: 604 Prabhat Kiran Bldg, Rajendra Place, Delhi 110 008; tel. (11) 5712898; fax (11) 5754647; monthly; English; f. 1964; Editor S. K. SACHDEVA; circ. 271,800.

Computers Today: Marina Arcade, G-59 Connaught Circus, New Delhi 110 001; tel. (11) 3736233; fax (11) 3725506; e-mail ctoday @india-today.com; f. 1984; Editor J. SRIHARI RAJU; circ. 38,800.

Cricket Samrat: L-1, Kanchan House, Najafgarh Rd, Commercial Complex, nr Milan Cinema, New Delhi 110 015; tel. (11) 5191175; fax (11) 5469581; f. 1978; monthly; Hindi; Editor ANAND DEWAN; circ. 189,200.

Employment News: Government of India, East Block IV, Level 5, R. K. Puram, New Delhi 110 066; tel. (11) 6193316; f. 1976; weekly; Hindi, Urdu and English edns; Gen. Man. and Chief Editor N. N. SHARMA; Editor RANJANA DEV SARMAH; combined circ. 550,000.

Filmi Duniya: 16 Darya Ganj, New Delhi 110 002; tel. (11) 3278087; fax (11) 3279341; f. 1958; monthly; Hindi; Chief Editor NARENDRA KUMAR; circ. 146,700.

Filmi Kaliyan: 4675-B/21 Ansari Rd, New Delhi 110 002; tel. (11) 3272080; f. 1969; monthly; Hindi; cinema; Editor-in-Chief V. S. DEWAN; circ. 82,400.

Global Travel Express: 26F Rajiv Gandhi Chowk (Connaught Place), New Delhi 110 001; tel. (11) 3312329; f. 1993; monthly; English; travel and tourism; Chief Editor HARBHAJAN SINGH; Editor GURINDER SINGH; circ. 28,499.

Grih Shobha: Delhi Press Bldg, E-3 Jhandewala Estate, Rani Jhansi Rd, New Delhi 110 055; tel. (11) 3529557; fax (11) 3625020; f. 1979; monthly; Kannada, Marathi, Hindi and Gujarati edns; women's interests; Editor VISHWA NATH; circ. 112,700 (Kannada), 65,600 (Gujarati), 157,500 (Marathi), 328,000 (Hindi).

India Perspectives: Room 149B 'A' Wing, Shastri Bhavan, New Delhi 110 001; tel. (11) 3389471; f. 1988; Editor BHARAT BHUSHAN.

India Today: F 14/15, Connaught Place, New Delhi 110 001; tel. (11) 3315801; fax (11) 3316180; e-mail letters.editor@intoday.com; internet www.india-today.com; f. 1975; English, Tamil, Telugu, Malayalam and Hindi; weekly; Editor PRABHU CHAWLA; Editor-in-Chief AROON PURIE; circ. 430,000 (English), 287,500 (Hindi), 77,600 (Tamil), 80,700 (Malayalam), 68,700 (Telugu).

Indian Observer: 26F Rajiv Gandhi Chowk (Connaught Place), New Delhi 110 001; tel. (11) 3312329; f. 1964; fortnightly; English; Editor HARBHAJAN SINGH; circ. 36,000.

Indian Railways: 411 Rail Bhavan, Raisina Rd, New Delhi 110 001; tel. (11) 3383540; fax (11) 3384481; f. 1956; monthly; English; publ. by the Ministry of Railways (Railway Board); Editor MANOHAR D. BANERJEE; circ. 12,000.

Journal of Industry and Trade: Ministry of Commerce, Delhi 110 011; tel. (11) 3016664; f. 1952; monthly; English; Man. Dir A. C. BANERJEE; circ. 2,000.

Junior Science Refresher: 2769, Bright House, Daryaganj, New Delhi 110 002; tel. (11) 3282226; fax (11) 3269227; e-mail psbright@ndf.vsnl.net.in; internet www.brightcareers.com; f. 1987; monthly; English; Chief Editor D. S. PHULL; Publr and Man. Dir PRITAM SINGH BRIGHT; circ. 109,563.

Kadambini: Hindustan Times House, Kasturba Gandhi Marg, New Delhi 110 001; tel. (11) 3704581; fax (11) 3704600; f. 1960; monthly; Hindi; Editor RAJENDRA AWASTHY; circ. 100,000.

Krishak Samachar: Bharat Krishak Samaj, Dr Panjabrao Deshmukh Krishak Bhavan, A-1 Nizamuddin West, New Delhi 110 013; tel. (11) 4619508; e-mail ffi@mantraonline.com; f. 1957; monthly; English and Hindi edns; agriculture; Editor Dr. KRISHAN BIR CHAUDHARY; circ. (English) 6,000, (Hindi) 17,000.

Kurukshetra: Ministry of Rural Development, Room No. 655/661, 'A' Wing, Nirman Bhavan, New Delhi 110 011; tel. (11) 3015014; fax (11) 3386879; monthly; English; rural development; Editor P. V. RAO; circ. 14,000.

Mainstream: 145/1D Shahpur Jat, 1st Floor, nr Asiad Village, New Delhi 110 049; tel. (11) 6497188; English; weekly; politics and current affairs; Editor SUMIT CHAKRAVARTTY.

Mayapuri: A-5, Mayapuri Phase 1, New Delhi 110 064; tel. (11) 5141439; fax (11) 5138596; e-mail mayapuri@hotmail.com; f. 1974; weekly; Hindi; cinema; Editor A. P. BAJAJ; circ. 146,144.

Mukta: Delhi Press Bldg, E-3 Jhandewala Estate, Rani Jhansi Rd, New Delhi 110 055; tel. (11) 3529557; fax (11) 3625020; f. 1979; monthly; Hindi, Gujarati and Marathi edns; youth; Editor VISHWA NATH; circ. 322,722.

Nandan: Hindustan Times House, Kasturba Gandhi Marg, New Delhi 110 001; tel. (11) 3361234; fax (11) 3704600; e-mail jaiprakashbharti/edth/del/htl@hindustantimes.com; f. 1963 monthly; Hindi; Editor Jai Prakash Bharti; circ. 125,000.

New Age: 15 Kotla Rd, Delhi 110 055; tel. (11) 3230762; fax (11) 3235543; e-mail cpindia@del2.vsnl.net.in; f. 1953; main organ of the Communist Party of India; weekly; English; Editor Shameem Faizee; circ. 215,000.

Organiser: 29 Rani Jhansi Marg, New Delhi 110 055; tel. (11) 7526977; fax (11) 7514876; f. 1947; weekly; English; Editor Seshadri Chari; circ. 44,100.

Outlook: AB-10 Safdarjung Enclave, New Delhi 110 029; tel. (11) 6191421; fax (11) 6191420; e-mail outlook@outlookindia.com; internet www.outlookindia.com; f. 1995; weekly; Editor-in-Chief Vinod Mehta; circ. 221,124.

Panchjanya: Sanskriti Bhavan, Deshbandhu Gupta Marg, Jhandewala, New Delhi 110 055; tel. (11) 3514244; fax (11) 3558613; e-mail panch@nde.vsnl.net.in; f. 1947; weekly; Hindi; general interest; nationalist; Chair. S. N. Bansal; Editor Tarun Vijay; circ. 59,300.

Proven Trade Contacts: POB 5730, New Delhi 110 055; tel. (11) 3526402; fax (11) 3625666; e-mail tc@narang.com; internet www.narang.com/ptc; f. 1992; monthly; medical/surgical/scientific/pharmaceutical trade promotion; circ. 10,000.

Punjabi Digest: 209 Hemkunt House, 6 Rajendra Place, POB 2549, New Delhi 110 008; tel. (11) 5715225; f. 1971; literary monthly; Gurmukhi; Chief Editor Sardar J. B. Singh; circ. 84,200.

Rangbhumi: 5A/15 Ansari Rd, Darya Ganj, Delhi 110 002; tel. (11) 3274667; f. 1941; Hindi; films; Editor S. K. Gupta; circ. 30,000.

Sainik Samachar: Block L-1, Church Rd, New Delhi 110 001; tel. (11) 3019668; f. 1909; pictorial fortnightly for India's armed forces; English, Hindi, Urdu, Tamil, Punjabi, Telugu, Marathi, Kannada, Gorkhali, Malayalam, Bengali, Assamese and Oriya edns; Editor P. K. Pattayanak; circ. 20,000.

Saras Salil: Delhi Press Bldg, E-3, Jhandewala Estate, Rani Jhansi Rd, New Delhi 110 055; tel. (11) 3529557; fax (11) 3625020; f. 1993; fortnightly; Hindi; Editor Vishwa Nath; circ. 1,101,171.

Sarita: Delhi Press Bldg, E-3, Jhandewala Estate, Rani Jhansi Rd, New Delhi 110 055; tel. (11) 3529557; fax (11) 3625020; f. 1945; fortnightly; Hindi; family magazine; Editor Vishwa Nath; circ. 138,989.

Shama: 13/14 Asaf Ali Rd, New Delhi 110 002; tel. (11) 3232674; fax (11) 3235167; f. 1939; monthly; Urdu; art and literature; Editors M. Yunus Dehlvi, Idrees Dehlvi, Ilyas Dehlvi; circ. 58,000.

Suman Saurabh: Delhi Press Bldg, E-3 Jhandewala Estate, Rani Jhansi Rd, New Delhi 110 055; tel. (11) 3529557; fax (11) 3625020; f. 1983; monthly; Hindi; youth; Editor Vishwa Nath; circ. 44,831.

Sushama: 13/14 Asaf Ali Rd, New Delhi 110 002; tel. (11) 3232674; fax (11) 3235167; f. 1959; monthly; Hindi; art and literature; Editors Idrees Dehlvi, Ilyas Dehlvi, Yunus Dehlvi; circ. 30,000.

Trade Union Record: 24 Canning Lane, New Delhi 110 001; tel. (11) 3387320; fax (11) 3386427; f. 1930; fortnightly; English and Hindi edns; Editor Santosh Kumar.

Vigyan Pragati: PID Bldg, Dr K. S. Krishnan Marg, New Delhi 110 012; tel. (11) 5785647; fax (11) 5731353; f. 1952; monthly; Hindi; popular science; Editor Deeksha Bist; circ. 100,000.

Woman's Era: Delhi Press Bldg, E-3, Jhandewala Estate, Rani Jhansi Rd, New Delhi 110 055; tel. (11) 3529557; fax (11) 3625020; f. 1973; fortnightly; English; women's interests; Editor Vishwa Nath; circ. 85,267.

Yojana: Yojana Bhavan, Sansad Marg, New Delhi 110 001; tel. (11) 3710473; f. 1957; monthly; English, Tamil, Bengali, Marathi, Gujarati, Assamese, Malayalam, Telugu, Kannada, Punjabi, Urdu, Oriya and Hindi edns; Chief Editor Dr J. Bhagyalakshmi; circ. more than 100,000.

Andhra Pradesh
Hyderabad

Andhra Prabha Illustrated Weekly: 591 Lower Tank Bund Rd, Express Centre, Domalaguda, Hyderabad 500 029; tel. (40) 233586; f. 1952; weekly; Telugu; Editor Potturi Venkateswara Rao; circ. 21,800.

Secunderabad

Andhra Bhoomi Sachitra Vara Patrika: 36 Sarojini Devi Rd, Secunderabad 500 003; tel. (842) 7802346; fax (842) 7805256; f. 1977; weekly; Telugu; Editor T. Venkatram Reddy; circ. 48,300.

Vijayawada

Andhra Jyoti Sachitra Vara Patrika: Vijayawada 520 010; tel. (866) 474532; f. 1967; weekly; Telugu; Editor Puranam Subramanya Sarma; circ. 59,000.

Bala Jyoti: Labbipet, Vijayawada 520 010; tel. (866) 474532; f. 1980; monthly; Telugu; Assoc. Editor A. Sasikant Satakarni; circ. 12,500.

Jyoti Chitra: Andhra Jyoti Bldgs, Vijayawada 520 010; tel. (866) 474532; f. 1977; weekly; Telugu; Editor T. Kutumba Rao; circ. 20,100.

Swati Saparivara Patrika: Anil Bldgs, Suryaraopet, POB 339, Vijayawada 520 002; tel. (866) 431862; fax (866) 430433; e-mail swati@md3.vsnl.net.in; f. 1984; weekly; Telugu; Editor Vemuri Balaram; circ. 236,831.

Vanita Jyoti: Labbipet, POB 712, Vijayawada 520 010; tel. (866) 474532; f. 1978; monthly; Telugu; Asst Editor J. Satyanarayana; circ. 13,100.

Assam
Guwahati

Agradoot: Agradoot Bhavan, Dispur, Guwahati 781 006; tel. (361) 561923; fax (361) 560655; e-mail agradoot@gwldot.net.in; f. 1971; bi-weekly; Assamese; Editor K. S. Deka; circ. 41,212.

Asam Bani: Tribune Bldg, Guwahati 781 003; tel. (361) 661356; fax (361) 540594; e-mail dileepchandan@yahoo.com; internet www.assamtribune.com; f. 1955; weekly; Assamese; Editor Dileep Chandan; circ. 14,000.

Sadin: Maniram Dewan Rd, Chandmari, Guwahati 781 003; tel. (361) 524594; fax (361) 524634; e-mail protidin@gw1.vsnl.net.in; weekly; Assamese; circ. 60,161.

Bihar
Patna

Anand Digest: Govind Mitra Rd, Patna 800 004; tel. (612) 656557; fax (612) 225192; f. 1981; monthly; Hindi; family magazine; Editor Dr S. S. Singh; circ. 44,500.

Balak: Govind Mitra Rd, POB 5, Patna 800 004; tel. (612) 650341; f. 1926; monthly; Hindi; children's; Editor S. R. Saran; circ. 32,000.

Gujarat
Ahmedabad

Akhand Anand: Anand Bhavan, Relief Rd, POB 123, Ahmedabad 380 001; tel. (79) 357482; f. 1947; monthly; Gujarati; Pres. Anand Amin; Editor Prakash N. Shah; circ. 10,000.

Chitralok: Gujarat Samachar Bhavan, Khanpur, POB 254, Ahmedabad 380 001; tel. (79) 5504010; fax (79) 5502000; f. 1952; weekly; Gujarati; films; Man. Editor Shreyans S. Shah; circ. 20,000.

Sakhi: Sakhi Publications, Jai Hind Press Bldg, nr Gujarat Chamber, Ashram Rd, Navrangpura, Ahmedabad 380 009; tel. (79) 6581734; fax (79) 6587681; f. 1984; fortnightly; Gujarati; women's; Man. Editor Nita Y. Shah; Editor Y. N. Shah; circ. 10,000.

Shree: Gujarat Samachar Bhavan, Khanpur, Ahmedabad 380 001; tel. (79) 5504010; fax (79) 5502000; f. 1964; weekly; Gujarati; women's; Editor Smrutiben Shah; circ. 20,000.

Stree: Sandesh Bhavan, Gheekanta, POB 151, Ahmedabad 380 001; tel. (79) 5624241; fax (79) 5624392; e-mail sandesh@adl.vsnl.net.in; 1962; weekly; Gujarati; Jt Editors Ritaben Patel, Lilaben Patel; circ. 62,700.

Zagmag: Gujarat Samachar Bhavan, Khanpur, Ahmedabad 380 001; tel. (79) 22821; f. 1952; weekly; Gujarati; for children; Editor Bahubali S. Shah; circ. 38,000.

Rajkot

Amruta: Jai Hind Publications, Jai Hind Press Bldg, Babubhai Shah Marg, Rajkot 360 001; tel. (281) 440513; fax (281) 448677; f. 1967; weekly; Gujarati; films; Editor Y. N. Shah; circ. 27,000.

Niranjan: Jai Hind Publications, Jai Hind Press Bldg, Babubhai Shah Marg, Rajkot 360 001; tel. (281) 440517; fax (281) 448677; f. 1972; fortnightly; Gujarati; children's; Editor N. R. Shah; circ. 15,000.

Parmarth: Jai Hind Publications, Jai Hind Press Bldg, Babubhai Shah Marg, Rajkot 360 001; tel. (281) 440511; fax (281) 448677; monthly; Gujarati; philosophy and religion; Editor Y. N. Shah; circ. 30,000.

Phulwadi: Jai Hind Publications, Jai Hind Press Bldg, Babubhai Shah Marg, Rajkot 360 001; tel. (281) 440513; fax (281) 448677; f. 1967; weekly; Gujarati; for children; Editor Y. N. Shah; circ. 27,000.

Karnataka
Bangalore

Mayura: 75 Mahatma Gandhi Rd, Bangalore 560 001; tel. (80) 5588999; fax (80) 5587179; f. 1968; monthly; Kannada; Editor-in-Chief K. N. Hari Kumar; circ. 49,800.

New Leader: 93 North Rd, St Mary's Town, Bangalore 560 005; f. 1887; weekly; English; Editor Rt Rev. Herman D'Souza; circ. 10,000.

Prajamata: North Anjaneya Temple Rd, Basavangudi, Bangalore 560 004; tel. (80) 602481; f. 1931; weekly; Kannada; news and current affairs; Chief Editor G. V. Anji; circ. 28,377.

Sudha: 66 Mahatma Gandhi Rd, Bangalore 560 001; tel. (80) 5588999; fax (80) 5587179; f. 1965; weekly; Kannada; Editor-in-Chief K. N. HARI KUMAR; circ. 112,700.

Manipal

Taranga: Udayavani Bldg, Press Corner, Manipal 576 119; tel. (8252) 70845; fax (8252) 70563; e-mail taranga@manipalpress.com; internet www.udayavani.com; f. 1983; weekly; Kannada; Exec. Editor SANDHYA S. PAI; circ. 121,400.

Kerala
Kottayam

Balarama: MM Publications Ltd, POB 226, Erayilkadavu, Kottayam 686 001; tel. (481) 563721; fax (481) 564393; e-mail vanbal@satyam.net.in; f. 1972; children's weekly; Malayalam; Chief Editor BINA MATHEW; Senior Man. V. SAJEEV GEORGE; circ. 246,792.

Malayala Manorama: K. K. Rd, POB 26, Kottayam 686 001; tel. (481) 563646; fax (481) 562479; e-mail editor@malayalamanorama.com; internet www.malayalamanorama.com; f. 1937; weekly; Malayalam; also publ. from Kozhikode; Man. Dir and Editor MAMMEN MATHEW; Chief Editor MAMMEN VARGHESE; combined circ. 1,163,300.

Manorajyam: Manorajyam Bldg, M. C. Rd, Kottayam 686 039; tel. (481) 61203; f. 1967; weekly; Malayalam; Publr R. KALYANARAMAN; circ. 50,900.

Vanitha: MM Publications Ltd, POB 226, Erayilkadavu, Kottayam 686 001; tel. (481) 563721; fax (481) 564393; e-mail mmpubls@md3.vsnl.net.in; f. 1975; women's fortnightly; Malayalam; Chief Editor Mrs K. M. MATHEW; Senior Man. V. SAJEEV GEORGE; circ. 369,200.

The Week: Malayala Manorama Co Ltd, K. K. Rd, POB 26, Kottayam 686 001; tel. (481) 563646; fax (481) 562479; e-mail editor@theweek.com; internet www.the_week.com; f. 1982; weekly; English; current affairs; Chief Editor MAMMEN MATHEW; circ. 163,400.

Kozhikode

Arogya Masika: Mathrubhumi Bldgs, K. P. Kesava Menon Rd, Kozhikode 673 001; tel. (495) 366655; fax (495) 366656; e-mail mathrclt@md2.vsnl.net.in; monthly; Malayalam; health; Man. Editor P. V. CHANDRAN; circ. 100,100.

Chitrabhumi: Mathrubhumi Bldgs, K. P. Kesava Menon Rd, Kozhikode 673 001; tel. (495) 366655; fax (495) 366656; weekly; Malayalam; films; Editor M. T. VASUDEVAN NAIR; circ. 36,100.

Grihalakshmi: Mathrubhumi Bldgs, K. P. Kesava Menon Rd, POB 46, Kozhikode 673 001; tel. (495) 366655; fax (495) 366656; e-mail mathrclt@md2.vsnl.net.in; internet www.mathrubhumi.com; f. 1979; monthly; Malayalam; women's; Editor K. K. SREEDHARAN NAIR; circ. 72,100.

Mathrubhumi Illustrated Weekly: Mathrubhumi Bldgs, K. P. Kesava Menon Rd, POB 46, Kozhikode 673 001; tel. (495) 366655; fax (495) 56656; f. 1923; weekly; Malayalam; Editor M. T. VASUDEVAN NAIR; circ. 49,100.

Sports Masika: Mathrubhumi Bldgs, K. P. Kesava Menon Rd, Kozhikode 673 001; tel. (495) 366655; fax (495) 366656; monthly; Malayalam; sport; Exec. Editor V. RAJAGOPAL; circ. 85,000.

Quilon

Karala Sabdam: Thevally, Quilon 691 009; tel. (474) 72403; fax (474) 740710; f. 1962; weekly; Malayalam; Man. Editor B. A. RAJAKRISHNAN; circ. 66,600.

Nana: Therally, Quilon 691 009; tel. 2403; weekly; Malayalam; Man. Editor B. A. RAJAKRISHNAN; circ. 50,500.

Thiruvananthapuram

Kalakaumudi: Kaumudi Bldgs, Pettah, Thiruvananthapuram 695 024; tel. (471) 443531; fax (471) 442895; e-mail kalakaumudi@vsnl.com; f. 1975; weekly; Malayalam; Chief Editor M. S. MANI; Gen. Man. ABRAHAM EAPEN; circ. 73,000.

Vellinakshatram: Kaumudi Bldgs, Pettah, Thiruvananthapuram 695 024; tel. (471) 443531; fax (471) 442895; e-mail kalakaumudi@vsnl.com; internet www.vellinakshatram.com; f. 1987; film weekly; Malayalam; Editor PRASAD LAKSHMANAN; Man. Editor SUKUMARAN MANI; circ. 55,000.

Madhya Pradesh
Bhopal

Krishak Jagat: 14 Indira Press Complex, M. P. Nagar, POB 37, Bhopal 462 011; tel. (755) 768452; fax (755) 510334; e-mail krishjag@bom6.vsnl.net.in; internet www.krishakjagatindia.com; f. 1946; weekly; Hindi; agriculture; Chief Editor VIJAY KUMAR BONDRIYA; Editor SUNIL GANGRADE; circ. 100,000.

Maharashtra
Mumbai (Bombay)

Abhiyaan: Abhiyaan Press and Publications Ltd, 4A/B, Government Industrial Estate, Charkop, Kandivli (W), Mumbai 400 067; tel. (22) 8687515; fax (22) 8680991; f. 1986; weekly; Gujarati; Dir DILIP PATEL; Editor VINOD PANDYA; circ. 140,900.

Arogya Sanjeevani: C-14 Royal Industrial Estate, 5-B Naigaum Cross Rd, Wadala, Mumbai 400 031; tel. (22) 4138723; fax (22) 4133610; e-mail woman@bom3.vsnl.net.in; f. 1990; quarterly; Hindi; Editor VAIDYA MISHRA; circ. 52,900.

Auto India: Nirmal, Nariman Point, Mumbai 400 021; tel. (22) 2883946; fax (22) 2883940; e-mail editor@auto-india.com; f. 1994; monthly; Editor RAJ WARRIOR; circ. 79,700.

Bhavan's Journal: Bharatiya Vidya Bhavan, Mumbai 400 007; tel. (22) 3634462; fax (22) 3630058; f. 1954; fortnightly; English; literary; Man. Editor J. H. DAVE; Editor S. RAMAKRISHNAN; circ. 25,000.

Blitz News Magazine: Saiman House, off Sayani Rd, Prabhadevi, Mumbai 400 025; tel. (22) 4372474; fax (22) 4229048; f. 1941; weekly; English; Editor-in-Chief M. J. AKBAR; combined circ. 419,000.

Bombay Samachar: Red House, Sayed Brelvi Rd, Mumbai 400 001; tel. (22) 2045531; fax (22) 2046642; f. 1822; weekly; Gujarati; Editor JEHANBUX D. DARUWALA; circ. 136,400.

Business India: Nirmal, 14th Floor, Nariman Point, Mumbai 400 021; tel. (22) 2024422; fax (22) 2875671; f. 1978; fortnightly; English; Publr ASHOK ADVANI; circ. 95,700.

Business World: 25–28 Atlanta, 2nd Floor, Nariman Point, Mumbai 400 021; tel. (22) 2851352; fax (22) 2870310; f. 1980; weekly; English; Man. Editor PARTHASARATHI SWAMI; Exec. Editor P. G. MATHAI; circ. 89,500.

Chitralekha: 62 Vaju Kotak Marg, Fort, Mumbai 400 001; tel. (22) 2614730; fax (22) 2615895; e-mail advertise@chitralekha.com; f. 1950 (Gujarati), f. 1989 (Marathi); weekly; Gujarati and Marathi; Editors BHARAT SHELANI, GYANESH MAHARAO; circ. 251,059 (Gujarati), 112,239 (Marathi).

Cine Blitz Film Monthly: 17/17H Cawasji Patel St, Fort, Mumbai 400 001; tel. (22) 2044143; fax (22) 2047984; f. 1974; English; Editor RITA K. MEHTA; circ. 184,100.

Dalal Street: DSJ Communications Ltd, 105 Shreyas Bldg, New Link Rd, Andheri (W), Mumbai 400 057; tel. (22) 6293293; fax (22) 6291105; f. 1985; fortnightly; investment; Editor PRATAP PADODE.

Debonair: Maurya Publications (Pvt) Ltd, 20/21, Juhu Centaur Hotel, Juhu Tara Rd, POB 18292, Mumbai 400 049; tel. (22) 6116632; fax (22) 6152677; e-mail maurya@debonairindia.com; f. 1972; monthly; English; Publr CHAITANYA PRABHU; CEO JOSEPH MASCARENHAS; circ. 110,000.

Economic and Political Weekly: Hitkari House, 284 Shahid Bhagatsingh Rd, Mumbai 400 001; tel. (22) 2696073; fax (22) 2696072; e-mail epw@vsnl.com; internet www.epw.org; f. 1966; English; Editor KRISHNA RAJ; circ. 132,800.

Femina: Times of India Bldg, Dr Dadabhai Naoroji Rd, Mumbai 400 001; tel. (22) 2620271; fax (22) 2620985; e-mail femina@toi.com; internet www.feminaindia.com; f. 1959; fortnightly; English; Editor SATHYA SARAN; circ. 154,000.

Filmfare: Times of India Bldg, Dr Dadabhai Naoroji Rd, Mumbai 400 001; tel. (22) 2620271; fax (22) 2620144; internet www.filmfare.com; f. 1952; fortnightly; English; Editor KHALID MOHAMED; circ. 196,200.

G: 62 Vaju Kotak Marg, Fort, Mumbai 400 001; tel. (22) 2614730; fax (22) 2615395; e-mail advertise@chitralekha.com; f. 1989; monthly; English; Editor BHAWNA SOMAYA; circ. 61,437.

Gentleman: Teritex Business Service Centre, B-201 Teritex Bldg, opp. Chandivli Petrol Pump, Saki Vihar Rd, Saki Naka Andheri (East), Mumbai 400 072; tel. (22) 8571490; fax (22) 8572447; e-mail gent@bom3.vsnl.net.in; internet www.wbiznetgroup.com; f. 1980; monthly; English; Editor PREMNATH NAIR (acting).

Indian PEN: Theosophy Hall, 40 New Marine Lines, Mumbai 400 020; tel. (22) 2032175; e-mail ambika.sirkar@gems.vsnl.net.in; f. 1934; quarterly; organ of Indian Centre of the International PEN; Editor RANJIT HOSKOTE.

Janmabhoomi-Pravasi: Janmabhoomi Bhavan, Janmabhoomi Marg, Fort, POB 62, Mumbai 400 001; tel. (22) 2870831; fax (22) 2874097; e-mail bhoomi@bom3.vsnl.net.in; f. 1939; weekly; Gujarati; Propr Saurashtra Trust; Editor KUNDAN VYAS; circ. 104,700.

JEE: 62 Vaju Kotak Marg, Fort, Mumbai 400 001; tel. (22) 2614730; fax (22) 2615895; e-mail advertise@chitralekha.com; fortnightly; Gujarati and Marathi; Editor MADHURI KOTAK; circ. 92,160 (Gujarati), 30,150 (Marathi).

Meri Saheli: C-14 Royal Industrial Estate, 5-B Naigaum Cross Rd, Wadala, Mumbai 400 031; tel. (22) 4182797; fax (22) 4133610; e-mail woman@bom3.vsnl.net.in; f. 1987; monthly; Hindi; Editor HEMA MALINI; circ. 296,100.

Movie: Mahalaxmi Chambers, 5th Floor, 22 Bhulabhai Desai Rd, Mumbai 400 026; tel. (22) 4935636; fax (22) 4938406; f. 1981; monthly; English; Editor DINESH RAHEJA; circ. 70,700.

New Woman: C-14 Royal Industrial Estate, 5-B Naigaum Cross Rd, Wadala, Mumbai 400 031; tel. (22) 4138723; fax (22) 4133610; e-mail woman@bol.net.in; f. 1996; monthly; English; Editor HEMA MALINI; circ. 79,658.

Onlooker: Free Press House, 215 Free Press Journal Marg, Nariman Point, Mumbai 400 021; tel. (22) 2874566; f. 1939; fortnightly; English; news magazine; Exec. Editor K. SRINIVASAN; circ. 61,000.

Reader's Digest: Orient House, Adi Marzban Path, Ballard Estate, Mumbai 400 001; tel. (22) 2617291; fax (22) 2613347; f. 1954; monthly; English; Publr and Editor ASHOK MAHADEVAN; circ. 389,378.

Savvy: Magna Publishing Co Ltd, Magna House, 100/E Old Prabhadevi Rd, Prabhadevi, Mumbai 400 025; tel. (22) 4362270; fax (22) 4306523; e-mail savvy@magnamags.com; internet www.magnamags.com; f. 1984; monthly; English; Editor SAIRA MENEZES; circ. 99,500.

Screen: D-2, Podar Chambers, Mathuradas Mill Compound, Ideal Industrial Estate, Lower Parel (W), Mumbai 400 013; tel. (22) 4046420; fax (22) 4920657; f. 1951; film weekly; English; Editor UDAYA TARA NAYAR; circ. 90,000.

Society: Magna Publishing Co Ltd, Magna House, 100/E Old Prabhadevi Rd, Prabhadevi, Mumbai 400 025; tel. (22) 4362270; fax (22) 4306523; f. 1979; monthly; English; Editor LALITHA GOPALAN; circ. 67,200.

Star and Style: Maurya Publications (Pvt) Ltd, 20/21, Juhu Centaur Hotel, Juhu Tara Rd, POB 18292, Mumbai 400 049; tel. (22) 6116632; fax (22) 6152677; e-mail maurya@bom3.vsnl.net.in; f. 1965; bimonthly; English; film; Publr/Editor NISHI PREM; circ. 60,000.

Stardust: Magna Publishing Co Ltd, Magna House, 100/E Old Prabhadevi Rd, Prabhadevi, Mumbai 400 025; tel. (22) 4362270; fax (22) 4306523; e-mail stardust@bom1.vsnl.net.in; f. 1985; monthly; English; Editor SONALI KOTNIS; circ. 308,000.

Vyapar: Janmabhoomi Bhavan, Janmabhoomi Marg, POB 62, Fort, Mumbai 400 001; tel. (22) 2870831; fax (22) 2874097; e-mail rajeshbhayani@hotmail.com; f. 1949 (Gujarati), 1987 (Hindi); Gujarati (2 a week) and Hindi (weekly); commerce; Propr Saurashtra Trust; Editor RAJESH M. BHAYANI; circ. 33,300 (Gujarati), 19,500 (Hindi).

Yuvdarhsan: c/o Warsha Publications Pvt Ltd, Warsha House, 6 Zakaria Bunder Rd, Sewri, Mumbai 400 015; tel. (22) 441843; f. 1975; weekly; Gujarati; Editor and Man. Dir R. M. BHUTTA; circ. 18,600.

Nagpur

All India Reporter: AIR Ltd, Congress Nagar, POB 209, Nagpur 440 012; tel. (712) 534321; fax (712) 526283; e-mail air@allindiareporter.com; internet www.allindiareporter.com; f. 1914; weekly and monthly; English; law journals; Chief Editor V. R. MANOHAR; circ. 55,500.

Rajasthan

Jaipur

Balhans: Kesargarh, Jawahar Lal Nehru Marg, Jaipur 302 004; tel. (141) 561582; fax (141) 566011; e-mail ads@rajasthanpatrika.com; internet www.rajasthanpatrika.com; fortnightly; Hindi; circ. 60,200.

Itwari Patrika: Kesargarh, Jawahar Lal Nehru Marg, Jaipur 302 004; tel. (141) 561582; fax (141) 566011; weekly; Hindi; circ. 18,200.

Rashtradoot Saptahik: HO, M.I. Rd, POB 30, Jaipur 302 001; tel. (141) 372634; fax (141) 373513; f. 1983; Hindi; also publ. from Kota and Bikaner; Chief Editor and Man. Editor RAJESH SHARMA; CEO SOMESH SHARMA; combined circ. 167,500.

Tamil Nadu

Chennai (Madras)

Aishwarya: 325 N. S. K. Salai, Chennai 600 024; tel. (44) 422064; f. 1990; weekly; Tamil; general; Editor K. NATARAJAN; circ. 20,000.

Ambulimama: 82 Defence Officers Colony, Ekkatuthangal, Chennai 600 097; e-mail chandamama@vsnl.com; f. 1947; children's monthly; Tamil; Editor B. VISWANATHA REDDI; circ. 65,000.

Ambuli Ammavan: 82 Defence Officers Colony, Ekkatuthangal, Chennai 600 097; e-mail chandamama@vsnl.com; f. 1970; children's monthly; Malayalam; Editor B. VISWANATHA REDDI; circ. 12,000.

Ananda Vikatan: 757 Anna Salai, Chennai 600 002; tel. (44) 8524054; fax (44) 8523819; e-mail editor@vikatan.com; internet www.vikatan.com; f. 1924; weekly; Tamil; Editor and Man. Dir S. BALASUBRAMANIAN; circ. 374,051.

Aval Vikatan: 757 Anna Salai, Chennai 600 002; tel. (44) 8524054; fax (44) 8523819; e-mail editor@vikatan.com; internet www

.vikatan.com; f 1998; fortnightly; Tamil; Editor B. SRINIVASAN; circ. 165,718.

Chandamama: 82 Defence Officers Colony, Ekkatuthangal, Chennai 600 097; e-mail chandamama@vsnl.com; f. 1947; children's monthly; Hindi, Gujarati, Telugu, Kannada, English, Sanskrit, Bengali, Assamese; Editor B. VISWANATHA REDDI; combined circ. 420,000.

Chandoba: 82 Defence Officers Colony, Ekkatuthangal, Chennai 600 097; e-mail chandamama@vsnl.com; f. 1952; children's monthly; Marathi; Editor B. VISWANATHA REDDI; circ. 93,000.

Chutti Vikatan: 757 Anna Salai, Chennai 600 002; tel. (44) 8524054; fax (44) 8523819; e-mail editor@vikatan.com; internet www.vikatan.com; f. 1999; monthly; Tamil; Editor B. SRINIVASAN; Man. Dir S. BALASUBRAMANIAN; circ. 75,000.

Devi: 727 Anna Salai, Chennai 600 006; tel. (44) 8521428; f. 1979; weekly; Tamil; Editor B. RAMACHANDRA ADITYAN; circ. 136,500.

Dinamani Kadir: Express Estate, Mount Rd, Chennai 600 002; tel. (44) 8520751; fax (44) 8524500; weekly; Editor G. KASTURI RANGAN (acting); circ. 55,000.

Frontline: Kasturi Bldgs, 859/860 Anna Salai, Chennai 600 002; tel. (44) 8589060; fax (44) 8545703; f. 1984; fortnightly; English; Publr S. RANGARAJAN; Editor N. RAM; circ. 67,225.

Hindu International Edition: 859/860 Anna Salai, Chennai 600 002; tel. (44) 8413344; fax (44) 8415325; f. 1975; weekly; English; Editor N. RAVI; circ. 3,000.

Jahnamamu (Oriya): 82 Defence Officers Colony, Ekkatuthangal, Chennai 600 097; e-mail chandamama@vsnl.com; f. 1972; children's monthly; Editor B. VISWANATHA REDDI; circ. 111,000.

Junior Vikatan: 757 Anna Salai, Chennai 600 002; tel. (44) 8524054; fax (44) 8523819; e-mail editor@vikatan.com; internet www.vikatan.com; f. 1983; 2 times a week; Tamil; Editor and Man. Dir S. BALASUBRAMANIAN; circ. 250,000.

Kalai Magal: POB 604, Chennai 600 004; tel. (44) 843099; f. 1932; monthly; Tamil; literary and cultural; Editor R. NARAYANASWAMY; circ. 10,200.

Kalkandu: 306 Purasaivakkam High Rd, Chennai 600 010; f. 1948; weekly; Tamil; Editor P. V. PARTHASARTHY; circ. 55,000.

Kalki: 47 Jawaharlal Nehru Rd, Ekkatuthangal, Chennai 600 097; tel. (44) 2345621; e-mail kalkiweekly@vsnl.com; internet www.kalkiweekly.com; f. 1941; weekly; Tamil; literary and cultural; Editor SEETHA RAVI; circ. 58,000.

Kumudam: 151 Purasawalkam High Rd, Chennai 600 010; tel. (44) 6422146; fax (44) 6425041; e-mail kumudam@giasmd0l.vsnl.net.in; f. 1947; weekly; Tamil; Editor Dr S. A. P. JAWAHAR PALANIAPPAN; circ. 399,100.

Kungumam: 93A Kodambakkam High Rd, Chennai 600 034; tel. (44) 8268177; f. 1978; weekly; Tamil; Editor PARASAKTHI; circ. 124,700.

Malaimathi: Chennai; f. 1958; weekly; Tamil; Editor P. S. ELANGO; circ. 48,100.

Muththaram: 93A Kogambakkam High Rd, Chennai 600 034; tel. (44) 476306; f. 1980; weekly; Tamil; Editor Sri PARASAKTHI; circ. 27,400.

Pesum Padam: 325 N. S. K. Salai, Chennai 600 024; tel. (44) 422064; f. 1942; monthly; Tamil; films; Man. Editor K. NATARAJAN; circ. 34,700.

Picturpost: 325 N. S. K. Salai, Chennai 600 024; tel. (44) 422064; f. 1943; monthly; English; films; Man. Editor K. NATARAJAN; circ. 11,000.

Rajam: 325 N. S. K. Salai, Chennai 600 024; tel. (44) 422064; f. 1986; monthly; Tamil; women's interests; Man. Dir and Editor K. NATARAJAN; circ. 32,677.

Rani Muthu: 1091 Periyar E.V.R. High Rd, Chennai 600 007; tel. (44) 5324771; e-mail rani.chen@gems.vsnl.net.in; f. 1969; fortnightly; Tamil; Editor A. MA. SAMY; circ. 79,117.

Rani Weekly: 1091 Periyar E.V.R. High Rd, Chennai 600 007; tel. (44) 5324771; e-mail rani.chen@gems.vsnl.net.in; f. 1962; Tamil; Editor A. MA. SAMY; circ. 194,400.

Sportstar: Kasturi Bldgs, 859/860 Anna Salai, Chennai 600 002; tel. (44) 8413344; fax (44) 8415325; f. 1978; weekly; English; Publr S. RANGARAJAN; Editor N. RAM; circ. 75,400.

Thuglak: 46 Greenways Rd, Chennai 600 028; tel. (44) 4936913; fax (44) 4936915; f. 1970; weekly; Tamil; Editor CHO S. RAMASWAMY; circ. 149,100.

Vellore

Madha Jothidam: 3 Arasamaram St, Vellore 632 004; f. 1949; monthly; Tamil; astrology; Editor and Publr A. K. THULASIRAMAN; circ. 8,000.

Uttar Pradesh
Allahabad

Alokpaat: Mitra Prakashan (Pvt) Ltd, 281 Muthiganj, Allahabad 211 003; tel. (532) 606693; fax (532) 601156; f. 1986; monthly; Bengali; Editor ALOKE MITRA; circ. 33,700.

Manohar Kahaniyan: Mitra Prakashan (Pvt) Ltd, 281 Muthiganj, Allahabad 211 003; tel. (532) 606693; fax (532) 601156; f. 1940; monthly; Hindi; Editor ALOKE MITRA; circ. 301,200.

Manorama: Mitra Parkashan (Pvt) Ltd, 281 Muthiganj, Allahabad 211 003; tel. (532) 606694; fax (532) 606379; f. 1924 (Hindi), 1986 (Bengali); fortnightly (Hindi), monthly (Bengali); Editor ALOKE MITRA; circ. 176,000 (Hindi), 33,000 (Bengali).

Maya: Mitra Prakashan (Pvt) Ltd, 281 Muthiganj, Allahabad 211 003; tel. (532) 606694; fax (532) 601156; f. 1929; fortnightly; Hindi; Editor ALOKE MITRA; circ. 175,200.

Nutan Kahaniyan: 15 Sheo Charan Lal Rd, Allahabad 211 003; tel. (532) 400612; f. 1975; Hindi; monthly; Chief Editor K. K. BHARGAVA; circ. 167,500.

Satyakatha: Mitra Prakashan (Pvt) Ltd, 281 Muthiganj, Allahabad 211 003; tel (532) 606693; fax (532) 606379; f. 1974; monthly; Hindi; Editor ALOKE MITRA; circ. 98,100.

West Bengal
Kolkata (Calcutta)

All India Appointment Gazette: 7 Old Court House St, Kolkata 700 001; tel. (33) 2206663; fax (33) 2296548; f. 1973; 2 a week; English; Editor S. C. TALUKDAR; circ. 158,900.

Anandalok: 6 Prafulla Sarkar St, Kolkata 700 001; tel. (33) 2374880; fax (33) 2253240; f. 1975; fortnightly; Bengali; film; Editor DULENDRA BHOWMIK; circ. 50,000.

Anandamela: 6 Prafulla Sarkar St, Kolkata 700 001; tel. (33) 2216600; fax (33) 2253240; f. 1975; monthly; Bengali; juvenile; Editor DEBASHIS BANDOPADHYAY; circ. 48,500.

Contemporary Tea Time: 1/2 Old Court House Corner, POB 14, Kolkata 700 001; tel. (33) 2200099; fax (33) 2435753; e-mail calcutta@ctl.co.in; f. 1988; quarterly; English; tea industry; Exec. Editor GITA NARAYANI; circ. 5,000.

Desh: 6 Prafulla Sarkar St, Kolkata 700 001; tel. (33) 274880; f. 1933; fortnightly; Bengali; literary; Editor AMITABHA CHOUDHURY; circ. 70,700.

Investment Preview: 7 Old Court House St, Kolkata 700 001; tel. (33) 2206663; fax (33) 296548; f. 1992; weekly; English; Editor S. C. TALUKDAR; circ. 53,845.

Khela: 96 Raja Rammohan Sarani, Kolkata 700 009; tel. (33) 3509803; f. 1981; weekly; Bengali; sports; Editor ASOKE DASGUPTA; circ. 18,300.

Naba Kallol: 11 Jhamapookur Lane, Kolkata 700 009; tel. (33) 354294; f. 1960; monthly; Bengali; Editor P. K. MAZUMDAR; circ. 26,400.

Neetee: 4 Sukhlal Johari Lane, Kolkata; f. 1955; weekly; English; Editor M. P. PODDAR.

Prabuddha Bharata (Awakened India): 5 Dehi Entally Rd, Kolkata 700 014; tel. (33) 2440898; fax (33) 2450050; e-mail advaita@vsnl.com; internet www.advaitaonline.com; f. 1896; monthly; art, culture, religion and philosophy; Publr SWAMI BODHASARANANDA; circ. 8,000.

Sananda: 6 Prafulla Sarkar St, Kolkata 700 001; tel. (33) 2374880; fax (33) 2253241; f. 1986; monthly; Bengali; Editor APARNA SEN; circ. 88,000.

Saptahik Bartaman: 76A J. C. Bose Rd, Kolkata 700 014; tel. (33) 2448208; fax (33) 2441215; f. 1988; weekly; Bengali; Editor BARUN SENGUPTA; circ. 118,500.

Screen: P-5, Kalakar St, Kolkata 700 070; f. 1960; weekly; Hindi; Editor M. P. PODDAR; circ. 58,000.

Statesman: Statesman House, 4 Chowringhee Sq., Kolkata 700 001; tel. (33) 2257070; fax (33) 2250118; f. 1875; overseas weekly; English; Editor-in-Chief C. R. IRANI.

Suktara: 11 Jhamapooker Lane, Kolkata 700 009; tel. (33) 355294; f. 1948; monthly; Bengali; juvenile; Editor M. MAJUMDAR; circ. 35,200.

NEWS AGENCIES

Press Trust of India Ltd: 4 Parliament St, New Delhi 110 001; tel. (11) 3716621; fax (11) 3718714; f. 1947, re-established 1978; Chair. Prof. E. V. CHITNIS; Gen. Man. M. K. RAZDAN.

United News of India (UNI): 9 Rafi Marg, New Delhi 110 001; tel. (11) 3715898; fax (11) 3716211; e-mail uninet@del2.vsnl.net.in; f. 1961; Indian language news in Hindi and Urdu; English wire service; World TV News Service (UNISCAN); photograph service; graphics service; special services covering banking and business;

brs in 90 centres in India; Chair. SHOBHA SUBRAHMANYAN; Gen. Man. and Chief Editor VIRENDER MOHAN.

Foreign Bureaux

Agence France-Presse (AFP): 410 Surya Kiran Bldg, 19 Kasturba Gandhi Marg, New Delhi 110 001; tel. (11) 3712963; fax (11) 3311105; Bureau Chief PASCAL TAILLANDIER.

Agencia EFE (Spain): 72 Jor Bagh, New Delhi 110 003; tel. (11) 4618092; fax (11) 4649114; Correspondent ISABEL CALLEJA SOLERA.

Agenzia Nazionale Stampa Associata (ANSA) (Italy): C-179 Defence Colony, New Delhi 110 024; tel. (11) 4615004; fax (11) 4640190; e-mail natale@giasdl01.vsnl.net.in; Bureau Chief BENIAMINO NATALE.

Associated Press (AP) (USA): 6B Jor Bagh Lane, New Delhi 110 003; tel. (11) 4628506; fax (11) 4616870; Bureau Chief ARTHUR MAX.

Deutsche Presse-Agentur (dpa) (Germany): 39 Golf Links, New Delhi 110 003; tel. (11) 4617792; fax (11) 4635772; e-mail dpadelhi@del2.vsnl.net.in; Chief Rep. JÜRGEN HEIN.

Informatsionnoye Telegrafnoye Agentstvo Rossii—Telegrafnoye Agentstvo Suverennykh Stran (ITAR—TASS) (Russia): E-5/4 Vasant Vihar, New Delhi 110 057; tel. (11) 6886232; fax (11) 6876233; Bureau Chief LEONID KOTOV.

Inter Press Service (IPS) (Italy): 49 (F.F.) Defence Colony Market, New Delhi 110 024; tel. (11) 4634154; fax (11) 4624725.

Islamic Republic News Agency (IRNA) (Iran): New Delhi; tel. (11) 6446866; fax (11) 6221529; Bureau Chief MOHD FAZELI.

Jiji Tsushin (Japan): New Delhi; tel. (11) 6879432; fax (11) 6113578; Correspondent RYOGO HORI.

Kyodo News Service (Japan): PTI Bldg, 1st Floor, 4 Parliament St, New Delhi 110 001; tel. (11) 3711954; fax (11) 3718756; Bureau Chief SHINGO KINIWA.

Reuters (UK): 1 Kautilya Marg, Chanakyapuri, New Delhi 110 021; tel. (11) 3012024; fax (11) 3014043; e-mail delhi.newsroom@reuters.com; Bureau Chief MYRA MACDONALD.

United Press International (UPI) (USA): 706, Sector 7B, Chandigarh 160 019; tel. (172) 772365; fax (172) 772366; e-mail hsnanda@ch1.dot.net.in; Bureau Chief HARBAKSH SINGH NANDA.

Xinhua (New China) News Agency (People's Republic of China): 50D, Shanti Path, Chanakyapuri, New Delhi 110 021; tel. (11) 601886; Chief YAN FENG.

The following agencies are also represented: Associated Press of Pakistan, A. P. Dow Jones, Bloomberg Business News, Depthnews, Knight-Ridder Financial News, Middle East News Agency and Viet Nam News Agency.

CO-ORDINATING BODIES

Press Information Bureau: Shastri Bhavan, Dr Rajendra Prasad Rd, New Delhi 110 001; tel. (11) 3383643; f. 1946 to co-ordinate press affairs for the govt; represents newspaper managements, journalists, news agencies, parliament; has power to examine journalists under oath and may censor objectionable material; Prin. Information Officer N. J. KRISHNA.

Registrar of Newspapers for India: Ministry of Information and Broadcasting, West Block 8, Wing 2, Ramakrishna Puram, New Delhi 110 066; tel. (11) 608788; f. 1956 as a statutory body to collect press statistics; maintains a register of all Indian newspapers; Registrar VIVEKANANDA RAY.

PRESS ASSOCIATIONS

All-India Newspaper Editors' Conference: 36–37 Northend Complex, Rama Krishna Ashram Marg, New Delhi 110 001; tel. (11) 3364519; fax (11) 3716665; f. 1940; c. 400 mems; Pres. VISHWA BANDHU GUPTA; Secs MANAK CHOPRA, BISHAMBER NEWAR.

All India Small and Medium Newspapers' Federation: 26-F Rajiv Gandhi Chowk (Connaught Place), New Delhi 110 001; tel. (11) 3326000; c. 9,000 mems; Pres. HARBHAJAN SINGH; Gen. Secs B. C. GUPTA, B. M. SHARMA.

The Foreign Correspondents' Club of South Asia: AB-19 Mathura Rd, New Delhi 110 001; tel. (11) 3388535; 210 mems; Pres. S. VENKATANARAYAN; Man. KIRAN KAPUR.

Indian Federation of Working Journalists: A-4/199 Basant Lane, Nr Railway Central Hospital, New Delhi 110 001; tel. (11) 3348894; fax (11) 3348871; f. 1950; 27,000 mems; Pres. K. VIKRAM RAO; Sec.-Gen. PARMANAND PANDEY.

Indian Journalists' Association: New Delhi; Pres. VIJAY DUTT; Gen. Sec. A. K. DHAR.

Indian Languages Newspapers' Asscn: Janmabhoomi Bhavan, Janmabhoomi Marg, POB 10029, Fort, Mumbai 400 001; tel. (22) 2870537; f. 1941; 320 mems; Pres. VIJAY KUMAR BONDRIYA; Hon. Gen. Secs PRADEEP G. DESHPANDE, KRISHNA SHEWDIKAR, LALIT SHRIMAL.

Indian Newspaper Society: INS Bldg, Rafi Marg, New Delhi 110 001; tel. (11) 3715401; fax (11) 3723800; e-mail indnews@nde.vsnl.net.in; f. 1939; 685 mems; Pres. VIJAY KUMAR CHOPRA; Sec.-Gen. P. K. LAHIRI.

National Union of Journalists (India): 7 Jantar Mantar Rd, 2nd Floor, New Delhi 110 001; tel. (11) 3368610; fax (11) 3369664; e-mail nujindia@ndf.vsnl.in; internet www.education.vsnl.com/nujindia; f. 1972; 12,000 mems; Pres. SHYAM KHOSLA; Sec.-Gen. P. K. ROY.

Press Club of India: 1 Raisina Rd, New Delhi 110 001; tel. 3719844; f. 1948; 3,500 mems; Pres. W. D. MATHUR; Sec. Gen. FARAZ AHMED.

Press Council of India: Faridkot House, Ground Floor, Copernicus Marg, New Delhi 110 001; established under an Act of Parliament to preserve the freedom of the press and maintain and improve the standards of newspapers and news agencies in India; 28 mems; Chair. Justice P. V. SAWANT; Sec. REVA KHETRAPAL.

Press Institute of India: Sapru House Annexe, Barakhamba Rd, New Delhi 110 001; tel. (11) 3318066; fax (11) 3311975; e-mail presinst@reno2.nic.in; f. 1963; 29 mem. newspapers and other orgs; Chair. NARESH MOHAN; Dir AJIT BHATTACHARJEA.

Publishers

Delhi and New Delhi

Affiliated East-West Press (Pvt) Ltd: G-1/16 Ansari Rd, Daryaganj, New Delhi 110 002; tel. (11) 3264180; fax (11) 3260538; e-mail affiliat@vsnl.com; textbooks and reference books; Dirs SUNNY MALIK, KAMAL MALIK.

Allied Publishers Ltd: 13/14 Asaf Ali Rd, New Delhi 110 002; tel. (11) 3239001; fax (11) 3235967; e-mail aplnd@del2.vsnl.net.in; academic and general; Man. Dir S. M. SACHDEV.

Amerind Publishing Co (Pvt) Ltd: Oxford Bldg, N-56 Connaught Circus, New Delhi 110 001; tel. (11) 3314957; fax (11) 3322639; f. 1970; offices at Kolkata, Mumbai and New York; scientific and technical; Dirs MOHAN PRIMLANI, GULAB PRIMLANI.

Arnold Heinman Publishers (India) Pvt Ltd: AB/9 Safdarjung Enclave, 1st Floor, New Delhi 110 029; tel. (11) 6883422; fax (11) 6877571; f. 1969 as Arnold Publishers (India) Pvt Ltd; literature and general; Man. Dir G. A. VAZIRANI.

Atma Ram and Sons: 1376 Kashmere Gate, POB 1429, Delhi 110 006; tel. (11) 2523082; f. 1909; scientific, technical, humanities, medical; Man. Dir S. PURI; Dir Y. PURI.

B.I. Publications Pvt Ltd: 13 Daryaganj, New Delhi 110 002; tel. (11) 3274443; fax (11) 3261290; e-mail bigroup@del3.vsnl.net.in; f. 1959; academic, general and professional; Man. Dir R. D. BHAGAT.

S. Chand and Co Ltd: Ram Nagar, POB 5733, New Delhi 110 055; tel. (11) 7772080; fax (11) 7777446; e-mail schandco@giasdl01.vsnl.net.in; internet www.schandgroup.com; f. 1917; educational and general in English and Hindi; also book exports and imports; Man. Dir RAJENDRA KUMAR GUPTA.

Children's Book House: A-4 Ring Rd, South Extension Part I, POB 3854, New Delhi 110 049; tel. (11) 4636030; fax (11) 4636011; e-mail neeta@giasdl01.vsnl.net.in; internet www.neetaprakashan.com; f. 1952; educational and general; Dir R. S. GUPTA.

Children's Book Trust: Nehru House, 4 Bahadur Shah Zafar Marg, New Delhi 110 002; tel. (11) 3316970; fax (11) 3721090; e-mail cbtnd@vsnl.com; internet www.childrensbooktrust.com; f. 1957; children's books in English and other Indian languages; Editor C. G. R. KURUP; Gen. Man. RAVI SHANKAR.

Concept Publishing Co: A/15-16, Commercial Block, Mohan Garden, New Delhi 110 059; tel. (11) 5648039; fax (11) 5648053; e-mail publishing@conceptpub.com; f. 1975; geography, rural and urban development, education, sociology, economics, anthropology, agriculture, religion, history, law, philosophy, information sciences, ecology; Man. Dir ASHOK KUMAR MITTAL; Man. Editor D. N. GULATI.

Frank Bros and Co (Publishers) Ltd: 4675A Ansari Rd, 21 Darya Ganj, New Delhi 110 002; tel. (11) 3263393; fax (11) 3269032; e-mail fbros@ndb.vsnl.net.in; f. 1930; children's and educational books; Chair. R. C. GOVIL.

Global Business Press: GT Rd, 18–19 Dilshad Garden, Delhi 110 095; tel. (11) 2297792; fax (11) 2282332; business, management and computers; Dir SHEKHAR MALHOTRA.

Heritage Publishers: 32 Prakash Apartments, 5 Ansari Rd, Darya Ganj, New Delhi 110 002; tel. (11) 3266258; fax (11) 3263050; e-mail heritage@nda.vsnl.net.in; f. 1973; social sciences, art and architecture, technical, medical, scientific; Propr and Dir B. R. CHAWLA.

Hind Pocket Books (Pvt) Ltd: 18–19 Dilshad Garden, Delhi 110 095; tel. (11) 2297792; fax (11) 2282332; f. 1958; fiction and non-fiction paperbacks in English, Hindi, Punjabi, Malayalam and Urdu; Chair DINANATH MALHOTRA; Exec. Dir SHEKHAR MALHOTRA.

Hindustan Publishing Corpn (India): 4805/24 Bharat Ram Rd, Daryaganj, New Delhi 110 002; tel. (11) 3254401; fax (11) 6193511; e-mail hpc@hpc.cc; internet www.hpc.cc; archaeology, pure and applied sciences, geology, sociology, anthropology, economics; Man. Partner P. C. KUMAR.

Kali for Women: B1/8 Hauz Khas, New Delhi 110 016; tel. (11) 6852530; fax (11) 6864497; e-mail kaliw@del2.vsnl.net.in; women's studies, social sciences, humanities, general non-fiction, fiction, etc.; Heads of Organization URVASHI BUTALIA, RITU MENON.

Lalit Kala Akademi: Rabindra Bhavan, New Delhi 110 001; tel. (11) 3387241; fax (11) 3782485; e-mail lka@lalitkala.org.in; internet www.lalitkala.org.in; books on Indian art; Exec. Editor SHARDA GUPTA.

Lancers Books: POB 4236, New Delhi 110 048; tel. (11) 6241617; fax (11) 6992063; e-mail lanbooks@aol.com; f. 1977; politics (with special emphasis on north-east India), defence; Propr S. KUMAR.

Madhuban Educational Books: 576 Masjid Rd, Jangpura, New Delhi 110 014; tel. (11) 4314605; fax (11) 4310879; e-mail orders@vikas.gobookshopping.com; internet www.gobookshopping.com; f. 1969; school books, children's books; Chair. and Man. Dir CHANDER M. CHAWLA.

Motilal Banarsidas Publishers (Pvt) Ltd: 41 U.A. Bungalow Rd, Jawahar Nagar, Delhi 110 007; tel. (11) 3911985; fax (11) 3930689; e-mail gloryindia@poboxes.com; internet www.mlbdbooks.com; f. 1903; Indology, in English and Sanskrit; Man. Dir N. P. JAIN; 7 brs.

Munshiram Manoharlal Publishers Pvt Ltd: 54 Rani Jhansi Rd, POB 5715, New Delhi 110 055; tel. (11) 3671668; fax (11) 3612745; e-mail mrml@mantraonline.com; f. 1952; Indian art, architecture, archaeology, religion, music, law, medicine, dance, dictionaries, travel, history, politics, numismatics, Buddhism, philosophy, sociology, etc.; Publishing Dir DEVENDRA JAIN; Dir ASHOK JAIN.

National Book Trust: A-5 Green Park, New Delhi 110 016; tel. (11) 6564020; fax (11) 6851795; e-mail nbtindia@ndb.vsnl.net.in; f. 1957; autonomous organization established by the Ministry of Human Resources Development to produce and encourage the production of good literary works; Chair. Dr SITAKANT MAHAPATRA; Dir NIRMAL KANTHI BHATACHARJEE.

National Council of Educational Research and Training (NCERT): Sri Aurobindo Marg, New Delhi 110 016; tel. (11) 6851070; fax (11) 6868419; e-mail dirc@glasdlo1.vsnl.net.in; f. 1961; school textbooks, teachers' guides, research monographs, journals, etc.; Dir Prof. A. K. SHARMA.

Neeta Prakashan: A-4 Ring Rd, South Extension Part I, POB 3853, New Delhi 110 049; tel. (11) 4636010; fax (11) 4636011; e-mail neeta@giasdl01.vsnl.net.in; internet www.neetaprakashan.com; f. 1960; educational, children's, general; Dir RAKESH GUPTA.

New Age International Pvt Ltd: 4835/24 Ansari Rd, Daryaganj, New Delhi 110 002; tel. (11) 3278348; fax (11) 3267437; e-mail del.nail@axcess.net.in; f. 1966; science, engineering, technology, management, humanities, social science; Dir A. R. KUNDAJI.

Oxford and IBH Publishing Co (Pvt) Ltd: 66 Janpath, New Delhi 110 001; tel. (11) 3324578; fax (11) 3710090; e-mail oxford@vsnl.com; f. 1964; science, technology and reference in English; Dir VIJAY PRIMLANI; Man. Dir MOHAN PRIMLANI.

Oxford University Press: YMCA Library Bldg, 1st Floor, Jai Singh Rd, POB 43, New Delhi 110 001; tel. (11) 3273841; fax (11) 3277812; e-mail mk@oupin.com; f. 1912; educational, scientific, medical, general and reference; Man. Dir MANZAR KHAN.

Penguin Books India (Pvt) Ltd: 11 Community Centre, Panchsheel Park, New Delhi 110 017; tel. (11) 6494401; fax (11) 6494403; e-mail penguin@del2.vsnl.net.in; f. 1987; Indian literature and general non-fiction in English; Chair. MICHAEL LYNTON; CEO and Publr DAVID DAVIDAR.

People's Publishing House (Pvt) Ltd: 5E Rani Jhansi Rd, New Delhi 110 055; tel. (11) 7524701; f. 1947; Marxism, Leninism, peasant movt; Dir SHAMEEM FAIZEE.

Pitambar Publishing Co Pvt Ltd: 888 East Park Rd, Karol Bagh, New Delhi 110 005; tel. (11) 3670067; fax (11) 3676058; e-mail pitambar@bol.net.in; internet www.pitambar.com; academic, children's books, textbooks and general; Man. Dir ANAND BHUSHAN; 5 brs.

Prentice-Hall of India (Pvt) Ltd: M-97 Connaught Circus, New Delhi 110 001; tel. (11) 3321779; fax (11) 3717179; e-mail phi@phindia.com; internet www.phindia.com; f. 1963; university-level text and reference books; Man. Dir A. K. GHOSH.

Pustak Mahal: 10B Netaji Subhas Marg, Daryaganj, New Delhi 110 002; tel. (11) 3272783; fax (11) 3260518; e-mail delaad37@giasdl01.vsnl.net.in; children's, general, computers, religious, encyclopaedia; Man. Dir RAM AVTAR GUPTA; Dir (Production) VINOD KUMAR GUPTA.

Rajkamal Prakashan (Pvt) Ltd: 1B Netaji Subhas Marg, New Delhi 110 002; tel. (11) 3274463; fax (11) 3278144; f. 1946; Hindi; literary; also literary journal and monthly trade journal; Man. Dir ASHOK MAHESHWARI.

Rajpal and Sons: 1590 Madrasa Rd, Kashmere Gate, Delhi 110 006; tel. (11) 2965483; fax (11) 2967791; e-mail orienpbk @ndb.vsnl.net.in; f. 1891; humanities, social sciences, art, juvenile; Hindi; Chair VISHWANATH MALHOTRA.

RIS (Research and Information System) Publications: Zone IV-B, Fourth Floor, India Habitat Centre, Lodhi Rd, New Delhi 110 003; tel. (11) 4617403; fax (11) 4628068; e-mail risnodec@ del2.vsnl.net.in; f. 1983; current and economic affairs involving non-aligned and developing countries; Dir-Gen. Dr V. R. PANCHAMUKHI.

Rupa & Co: 7/16 Ansari Rd, Daryaganj, POB 7017, New Delhi 110 002; tel. (11) 3278586; fax (11) 3277294; e-mail del.rupaco@ axcess.net.in; internet www.rupaandco.com; f. 1936; Chief Exec. R. K. MEHRA.

Sage Publications India Pvt Ltd: 32 M-Block Market, Greater Kailash-1, POB 4215, New Delhi 110 048; tel. (11) 6485884; fax (11) 6472426; e-mail sageind@nda.vsnl.net.in; internet www.indiasage .com; f. 1981; social science, development studies, business and management studies; Man. Dir TEJESHWAR SINGH.

Sahitya Akademi: Rabindra Bhavan, 35 Ferozeshah Rd, New Delhi 110 001; tel. (11) 3386626; fax (11) 3382428; e-mail secy@ndb.vsnl.net.in; internet www.sahitya-akademi.org; f. 1956; bibliographies, translations, monographs, encyclopaedias, literary classics, etc.; Pres. RAMAKANTA RATH; Sec. Dr K. SATCHIDANANDAN.

Scholar Publishing House (P) Ltd: 85 Model Basti, New Delhi 110 005; tel. (11) 3541299; fax (11) 3676565; e-mail scholar@ vsnl.com; internet www.scholargroup.com; f. 1968; educational; Man. Dir Y. P. RANADE.

Shiksha Bharati: Madrasa Rd, Kashmere Gate, Delhi 110 006; tel. (11) 2969812; fax (11) 2967791; f. 1955; textbooks, creative literature, popular science and juvenile in Hindi and English; Editor MEERA JOHRI.

Sterling Publishers (Pvt) Ltd: L-10 Green Park Extension, New Delhi 110 016; tel. (11) 6191874; fax (11) 6192008; e-mail ghai@nda.vsnl.net.in; internet www.sterlingpublishers.com; f. 1965; academic books on the humanities and social sciences, children's books, computer books, management books, paperbacks; Chair. and Man. Dir S. K. GHAI; Gen. Man. A. J. SEHGAL.

Tata McGraw-Hill Publishing Co Ltd: 7 West Patel Nagar, New Delhi 110 008; tel. (11) 5819304; fax (11) 5819302; e-mail info_india@mcgraw-hill.com; internet www.tatamcgrawhill.com; f. 1970; engineering, computers, sciences, medicine, management, humanities, social sciences; Chair. Dr F. A. MEHTA; Man. Dir Dr N. SUBRAHMANYAM.

Vikas Publishing House (Pvt) Ltd: 576 Masjid Rd, Jangpura, New Delhi 110 014; tel. (11) 4314605; fax (11) 4310879; e-mail orders@vikas.gobookshopping.com; internet www.gobookshopping .com; f. 1969; computers, management, commerce, sciences, engineering, textbooks; Chair. and Man. Dir CHANDER M. CHAWLA.

A. H. Wheeler & Co Ltd: 411 Surya Kiran Bldg, 19 K. G. Marg, New Delhi 110 001; tel. (11) 3312629; fax (11) 3357798; e-mail wheelerpub@mantraonline.com; f. 1958; textbooks, reference books, computer science and information technology, electronics, management, telecommunications, social sciences, etc.; Exec. Pres. ALOK BANERJEE.

Chennai (Madras)

Higginbothams Ltd: 814 Anna Salai, POB 311, Chennai 600 002; tel. (44) 8520640; fax (44) 8528101; e-mail higginbothams@vsnl.com; f. 1844; general; Dir S. CHANDRASEKHAR.

B. G. Paul and Co: 4 Francis Joseph St, Chennai; f. 1923; general, educational and oriental; Man. K. NILAKANTAN.

T. R. Publications Pvt Ltd: PMG Complex, 2nd Floor, 57 South Usman Rd, T. Nagar, Chennai 600 017; tel. (44) 4340765; fax (44) 4348837; e-mail trgeetha@giasmd01.vsnl.net.in; internet www .trpubs.com; Chief Exec. S. GEETHA.

Kolkata (Calcutta)

Academic Publishers: 12/1A Bankim Chatterjee St, POB 12341, Kolkata 700 073; tel. (33) 2414857; fax (33) 2413702; e-mail acabooks@cal.vsnl.net.in; f. 1958; textbooks, management, medical, technical; Man. Partner B. K. DHUR.

Advaita Ashrama: 5 Dehi Entally Rd, Kolkata 700 014; tel. (33) 2164000; fax (33) 2450050; e-mail advaita@vsnl.com; internet www.advaitaonline.com; f. 1899; religion, philosophy, spiritualism, Vedanta; publication centre of Ramakrishna Math and Ramakrishna Mission; Publication Man. Swami BODHASARANANDA.

Allied Book Agency: 18A Shyama Charan De St, Kolkata 700 073; tel. (33) 312594; general and academic; Dir B. SARKAR.

Ananda Publishers (Pvt) Ltd: 45 Beniatola Lane, Kolkata 700 009; tel. (33) 2414352; fax (33) 2253240; e-mail ananda@ cal3.vsnl.net.in; literature, general; Dir A. SARKAR; Gen. Man. D. N. BASU.

Assam Review Publishing Co: 27A Waterloo St, 1st Floor, Kolkata 700 069; tel. (33) 2482251; fax (33) 2158293; e-mail teknokom@ satyam.net.in; f. 1926; publrs of *Tea Plantation Directory* and *Tea News*; Partners G. L. BANERJEE, S. BANERJEE.

Book Land (Pvt) Ltd: Kolkata; tel. (33) 2414158; economics, politics, history and general; Dir SUBHANKAR BASU.

Chuckervertty, Chatterjee and Co Ltd: 15 College Sq., Kolkata 700 073; tel. (33) 2416425; Man. Dir MALA MAZUMDAR.

Eastern Law House (Pvt) Ltd: 54 Ganesh Chunder Ave, Kolkata 700 013; tel. (33) 2374989; fax (33) 2150491; e-mail elh@cal.vsnl .net.in; f. 1918; legal, commercial and accountancy; Dir ASOK DE; br. in New Delhi.

Firma KLM Private Ltd: 257B B. B. Ganguly St, Kolkata 700 012; tel. (33) 2374391; fax (33) 2217294; e-mail fklm@satyam.net.in; f. 1950; Indology, scholarly in English, Bengali, Sanskrit and Hindi, alternative medicine; Man. Dir R. N. MUKHERJI.

Intertrade Publications (India) (Pvt) Ltd: 55 Gariahat Rd, POB 10210, Kolkata 700 019; tel. (33) 474872; f. 1954; economics, medicine, law, history and trade directories; Man. Dir Dr K. K. ROY.

A. Mukherjee and Co (Pvt) Ltd: 2 Bankim Chatterjee St, Kolkata 700 073; tel. (33) 311406; fax (33) 7448172; f. 1940; educational and general in Bengali and English; Man. Dir RAJEEV NEOGI.

Naya Prokash: 206 Bidhan Sarani, POB 11468, Kolkata 700 006; tel. (33) 2414709; fax (33) 5382897; e-mail npsales@cal2.vsnl.net.in; f. 1960; agriculture, horticulture, Indology, history, political science; Man. Dir BHUBANI MITRA; Senior Partner BARIN MITRA.

New Era Publishing Co: 31 Gauri Bari Lane, Kolkata 700 004; f. 1944; Propr Dr P. N. MITRA; Man. S. K. MITRA.

W. Newman and Co Ltd: 3 Old Court House St, Kolkata 700 069; tel. (33) 2489436; f. 1854; general; Man. K. M. BANTIA.

Punthi Pustak: 136/4B Bidhan Sarani, Kolkata 700 004; tel. (33) 558473; religion, history, philosophy; Propr S. K. BHATTACHARYA.

Renaissance Publishers (Pvt) Ltd: 15 Bankim Chatterjee St, Kolkata 700 012; f. 1949; politics, philosophy, history; Man. Dir J. C. GOSWAMI.

Saraswati Library: 206 Bidhan Sarani, Kolkata 700 006; tel. (33) 345492; f. 1914; history, philosophy, religion, literature; Man. Partner B. BHATTACHARJEE.

M. C. Sarkar and Sons (Pvt) Ltd: 14 Bankim Chatterjee St, Kolkata 700 073; tel. (33) 312490; f. 1910; reference; Dirs SUPRIYA SARKAR, SAMIT SARKAR.

Visva-Bharati: 6 Acharya Jagadish Bose Rd, Kolkata 700 017; tel. (33) 2479868; f. 1923; literature; Dir ASHOKE MUKHOPADHYAY.

Mumbai (Bombay)

Allied Publishers Ltd: 15 J. N. Heredia Marg, Ballard Estate, Mumbai 400 001; tel. (22) 2617926; fax (22) 2617928; e-mail alliedpl@bom4.vsnl.net.in; f. 1934; economics, politics, history, philosophy, science, mathematics; Man. Dir S. M. SACHDEV.

Bharatiya Vidya Bhavan: Munshi Sadan, Kulapati K. M. Munshi Marg, Mumbai 400 007; tel. (22) 4950916; fax (22) 3630058; e-mail brbhavan@bom7.vsnl.net.in; f. 1938; art, literature, culture, education, philosophy, religion, history of India; various periodicals in English, Hindi, Sanskrit and other Indian languages; Pres. R. VENKATARAMAN; Sec.-Gen. S. RAMAKRISHNAN.

Blackie and Son (Pvt) Ltd: Blackie House, 103–105 Walchand Hirachand Marg, POB 381, Mumbai 400 001; tel. (22) 261410; f. 1901; educational, scientific and technical, general and juvenile; Man. Dir D. R. BHAGI.

Himalaya Publishing House: 'Ramdoot', Dr Bhalerao Marg (Kelewadi), Girgaon, Mumbai 400 004; tel. (22) 3800170; fax (22) 3877178; e-mail himpub@bomb5.vsnl.net.in; f. 1976; textbooks and research work; Dir MEENA PANDEY; CEO D. P. PANDEY.

India Book House Ltd: 412 Tulsiani Chambers, Nariman Point, Mumbai 400 021; tel. (22) 2840626; fax (22) 2835099; e-mail ibhltd@bom2.vsnl.net.in; Man. Dir DEEPAK MIRCHANDANI.

International Book House (Pvt) Ltd: Indian Mercantile Mansions (Extension), Madame Cama Rd, Mumbai 400 001; tel. (22) 2021634; fax (22) 2851109; e-mail ibh@vsnl.com; internet www.intbh.com; f. 1941; general, educational, scientific and law; Man. Dir S. K. GUPTA; Exec. Dir SANJEEV GUPTA.

Jaico Publishing House: 127 Mahatma Gandhi Rd, opposite Mumbai University, Mumbai 400 023; tel. (22) 2676702; fax (22) 2656412; e-mail jaicopub@giasbm01.vsnl.net.in; f. 1947; general paperbacks, management, computer and engineering books, etc.; imports scientific, medical, technical and educational books; Man. Dir ASHWIN J. SHAH.

Popular Prakashan (Pvt) Ltd: 35c Pandit Madan Mohan Malaviya Marg, Tardeo, Popular Press Bldg, opp. Roche, Mumbai 400 034; tel. (22) 4941656; fax (22) 4952627; e-mail popular@ bom7.vsnl.net.in; f. 1968; sociology, biographies, religion, philosophy, fiction, arts, music, current affairs, medicine, history, politics and administration in English and Marathi; Man. Dir R. G. BHATKAL.

Somaiya Publications (Pvt) Ltd: 172 Mumbai Marathi Granthasangrahalaya Marg, Dadar, Mumbai 400 014; tel. (22) 4130230; fax (22) 2047297; e-mail somaiyabooks@rediffmail.com; internet www.somaiya.com; f. 1967; economics, sociology, history, politics, mathematics, sciences, language, literature, education, psychology, religion, philosophy, logic; Chair. Dr S. K. SOMAIYA; Chief Editor AVINASH S. PANDIT.

Taraporevala, Sons and Co (Pvt) Ltd D.B.: 210 Dr Dadabhai Naoroji Rd, Fort, Mumbai 400 001; tel. (22) 2071433; f. 1864; Indian art, culture, history, sociology, scientific, technical and general in English; Chief Exec. R. J. TARAPOREVALA.

N. M. Tripathi (Pvt) Ltd: 164 Shamaldas Gandhi Marg, Mumbai 400 002; tel. (22) 2013651; f. 1888; general in English and Gujarati; Chair. N. M. TRIVEDI; Man. Dir KARTIK R. TRIPATHI.

Other Towns

Bharat Bharati Prakashan & Co: Western Kutchery Rd, Meerut 250 001; tel. 663698; f. 1952; textbooks; Man. Dir SURENDRA AGARWAL.

Bharati Bhawan: Thakurbari Rd, Kadamkuan, Patna 800 003; tel. (612) 671356; fax (612) 670010; e-mail bbpdpat@giascl01.vsnl.com; f. 1942; educational and juvenile; Man. Partner TARIT KUMAR BOSE.

Bishen Singh Mahendra Pal Singh: 23A New Connaught Place, POB 137, Dehra Dun 248 001; tel. (135) 655748; fax (135) 650107; e-mail bsmps@del2.vsnl.net.in; internet www.bishensinghbooks .com; f. 1957; botany, forestry, agriculture; Dirs GAJENDRA SINGH GAHLOT, ABHIMANYU GAHLOT.

Catholic Press: Ranchi 834 001, Bihar; f. 1928; books and periodicals; Dir WILLIAM TIGGA.

Chugh Publications: 2 Strachey Rd, POB 101, Allahabad; tel. (532) 623063; sociology, economics, history, general; Propr RAMESH KUMAR CHUGH.

Geetha Book House: K. R. Circle, Mysore 570 001; tel. (821) 33589; f. 1959; general; Dirs M. GOPALA KRISHNA, M. GURURAJA RAO.

Kalyani Publishers: 1/1 Rajinder Nagar, Civil Lines, Ludhiana, Punjab 141 008; tel. (161) 745756; fax (161) 745872; textbooks; Dir USHA RAJ KUMAR.

Kitabistan: 30 Chak, Allahabad 211 003; tel. (532) 653219; f. 1932; general, agriculture, govt publs in English, Hindi, Urdu, Farsi and Arabic; Partners A. U. KHAN, SULTAN ZAMAN.

Krishna Prakashan Media (P) Ltd: (Unit) Goel Publishing House, 11 Shivaji Rd, Meerut 250 001; tel. (121) 642946; fax (121) 645855; textbooks; Man. Dir SATYENDRA KUMAR RASTOGI; Dir ANITA RASTOGI.

The Law Book Co (Pvt) Ltd: 18B Sardar Patel Marg, Civil Lines, POB 1004, Allahabad 211 001; tel. (532) 624905; fax (532) 420852; e-mail bagga1@nae.vsnl.net.in; f. 1929; legal texts in English; Dir ANIL BAGGA; Man. Dir L. R. BAGGA.

Macmillan India Ltd: 315/316 Raheja Chambers, 12 Museum Rd, Bangalore 560 001; tel. (80) 5587878; fax (80) 5588713; e-mail rberi@bgl.vsnl.net.in; school and university books in English; general; Pres. and Man. Dir RAJIV BERI; Dir (Technical) DEBASHISH BANERJEE.

Navajivan Publishing House: PO Navajivan, Ahmedabad 380 014; tel. (79) 7540640; f. 1919; Gandhiana and related social science; in English, Hindi and Gujarati; Man. Trustee JITENDRA DESAI; Sales Man. KAPIL RAWAL.

Nem Chand and Bros: Civil Lines, Roorkee 247 667; tel. (1332) 72258; fax (1332) 73258; f. 1951; engineering textbooks and journals.

Orient Longman Ltd: 3-6-272 Himayat Nagar, Hyderabad 500 029; tel. (40) 3224305; fax (40) 3222900; e-mail orlongco@hd2.dot .net.in; f. 1948; educational, technical, general and children's in English and almost all Indian languages; Chair. SHANTA RAMESHWAR RAO; Dirs Dr NANDINI RAO, J. KRISHNADEV RAO.

Publication Bureau: Panjab University, Chandigarh 160 014; tel. (172) 541782; f. 1948; textbooks, academic and general; Man. H. R. GROVER.

Publication Bureau: Punjabi University, Patiala 147 002; tel. (175) 282461; university-level text and reference books; Head of Bureau Dr HAZARA SINGH.

Ram Prasad and Sons: Hospital Rd, Agra 282 003; tel. (562) 367904; fax (562) 360906; e-mail ea_08@yahoo.com; f. 1905; agricultural, arts, history, commerce, education, general, pure and applied science, economics, sociology; Dirs R. N., B. N., Y. N. and RAVI AGARWAL; Man. S. N. AGARWAL; br. in Bhopal.

Government Publishing House

Publications Division: Ministry of Information and Broadcasting, Govt of India, Patiala House, New Delhi 110 001; tel. (11) 3387983; fax (11) 3386879; f. 1941; culture, art, literature, planning and development, general; also 21 periodicals in English and several Indian languages; Dir SURINDER KAUR.

PUBLISHERS' ASSOCIATIONS

Bombay Booksellers' and Publishers' Association: No. 25, 6th Floor, Bldg No. 3, Navjivan Commercial Premises Co-op Society Ltd, Dr Bhadkamkar Marg, Mumbai 400 008; tel. (22) 3088691; f. 1961; 400 mems; Pres. K. M. VARGHESE; Gen. Sec. ALI I. KAZI.

Delhi State Booksellers' and Publishers' Association: 3026/7H Shiv Chowk, (South Patel Nagar) Ranjit Nagar, New Delhi 110 008; tel. (11) 5772748; fax (11) 5786769; f. 1943; 400 mems; Pres. Dr S. K. BHATIA; Sec. S. K. JAIN.

Federation of Educational Publishers in India: 19 Rani Jhansi Rd, New Delhi 110 055; tel. (11) 3522697; f. 1987; 14 affiliated asscns; 157 mems; Pres. Dr Y. P. RANADE; Sec.-Gen. KAMAL ARORA.

Federation of Indian Publishers: Federation House, 18/1-C Institutional Area, nr JNU, New Delhi 110 067; tel. (11) 6964847; fax (11) 6864054; e-mail fipl@satyam.net.in; internet www.federation ofindianpublishers.com; 18 affiliated asscns; 159 mems; Pres. S. BALWANT; Hon. Gen. Sec. SHAKTI MALIK.

Akhil Bharatiya Hindi Prakashak Sangh: A-2/1, Krishan Nagar, Delhi 110 051; tel. (11) 2219398; f. 1954; 400 mems; Pres. INDER SENGAR; Gen. Sec. ARUN KUMAR SHARMA.

All Assam Publishers' and Booksellers' Association: College Hostel Rd, Panbazar, Guwahati 780 001; tel. (361) 634790; fax (361) 513886; Pres. NABIN BARUAH; Sec. J. N. DUTTA BARUAH.

All India Urdu Publications' and Booksellers' Association: 437 Matia Mahal, Delhi 110 006; tel. (11) 3265480; fax (11) 3257189; e-mail aakif@del3.vsnl.net.in; internet www.aakif.com; f. 1988; 150 mems; Pres. Dr KHALIQ ANJUM; Gen. Sec. S. M. ZAFAR ALI.

Booksellers' and Publishers' Association of South India: 8, II Floor, Sun Plaza, G. N. Chetty Rd, Chennai 600 006; 158 mems; Pres. S. CHANDRASEKAR; Sec. RAVI CHOPRA.

Gujarati Sahitya Prakashak Vikreta Mandal: Navajivan Trust, P.O. Navajivan, Ahmedabad 380 014; tel. (79) 7540635; 125 mems; Pres. JITENDRA DESAI; Sec. K. N. MADRASI.

Karnataka Publishers' Association: 88 Mysore Rd, Bangalore 560 018; tel. (80) 601638; Pres. Prof. H. R. DASEGOWDA; Sec. S. V. SRINIVASA RAO.

Kerala Publishers' and Booksellers' Association: Piaco Bldg, Jew St, Kochi 682 011; 30 mems; Pres. D. C. KIZHAKEMURI; Sec. E. K. SEKHAR.

Marathi Prakashak Parishad: c/o Saraswati Granth Bhandar, Amber Chambers, Appa Balwant Chowk, Pune 411 002; tel. (212) 4451219; fax (212) 4454086; 100 mems; Pres. A. G. KULK.

Orissa Publishers' and Booksellers' Association: Binodbihari, Cuttack 753 002; tel. (671) 620637; f. 1973–74; 280 mems; Pres. KRISHNA CHANDRA BEHERA; Sec. BHIKARI CHARAN MOHAPATRA.

Paschimbanga Prakasak Sabha: 206 Bidhan Sarani, Kolkata 700 006; tel. (33) 3504534; fax (33) 2413852; Pres. J. SEN; Gen. Sec. T. SAHA.

Publishers' Association of West Bengal: 6-B, Ramanath Mazumder St, Kolkata 700 009; tel. (33) 325580; 164 mems; Pres. MOHIT KUMAR BASU; Gen. Sec. SHANKARI BHUSAN NAYAK.

Publishers' and Booksellers' Association of Bengal: 93 Mahatma Gandhi Rd, Kolkata 700 007; tel. (33) 2411993; f. 1912; 4,500 mems; Pres. HIMANGSHU BANDOPADHYAY; Gen. Sec. CHITTA SINGHA ROY.

Punjabi Publishers' Association: Satnam Singh, Singh Brothers, Bazar Mai Sewan, Amritsar 143 006; tel. (183) 45787; Sec. SATNAM SINGH.

Vijayawada Publishers' Association: 27-1-68, Karl Marx Rd, Vijayawada 520 002; tel. (866) 433353; fax (866) 426348; 41 mems; Pres. DUPATI VIJAY KUMAR; Sec. U. N. YOGI.

Federation of Publishers' and Booksellers' Associations in India: 2nd Floor, 84 Darya Ganj, New Delhi 110 002; tel. (11) 3272845; fax (11) 3281227; 16 affiliated asscns; 550 mems; Pres. S. C. SETHI; Sec. K. P. R. NAIR.

Publishers' and Booksellers' Guild: 5A Bhawani Dutta Lane, Kolkata 700 073; tel. (33) 2413680; fax (33) 2418248; e-mail guild@cal2.vsnl.net.in; f. 1975; 38 mems; organizes annual Calcutta Book Fair; Pres. PRABIR KUMAR MAZUMDAR; Sec. KALYAN SHAH.

UP Publishers' and Booksellers' Association: 111-A/243 Ashok Nagar, Kanpur 208 012; asscn for Uttar Pradesh state.

Broadcasting and Communications

TELECOMMUNICATIONS

Telecom Regulatory Authority of India (TRAI): 16th Floor, Jawahar Vyapar Bhavan 1, Tolstoy Marg, New Delhi 110 001; tel.

(11) 3357815; fax (11) 3738708; e-mail trai@del2.vsnl.net.in; internet www.trai.gov.in; f. 1998; Chair. S. S. SODHI; Vice-Chair. BAL KRISHAN ZUTSHI.

Bharti Telenet Ltd: Indore; f. 1998; India's first privately-owned telephone network; Exec. Dir BHAGWAN KHURANA.

Ericsson: POB 10912, New Delhi 110 066.

ITI (Indian Telephone Industries) Ltd: 45/1 Magrath Rd, Bangalore 560 025; tel. (80) 5566366; fax (80) 5593188; f. 1948; mfrs of all types of telecommunication equipment, incl. telephones, automatic exchanges and long-distance transmission equipment; also produces optical fibre equipment and microwave equipment; will manufacture all ground communication equipment for the 22 earth stations of the Indian National Satellite; in conjunction with the Post and Telegraph Department, a newly designed 2,000-line exchange has been completed; Chair. and Man. Dir J. K. GUPTA.

Mahanagar Telephone Nigam Ltd (MTNL): Jeevan Bharati Tower, 124 Connaught Circus, New Delhi 110 001; tel. (11) 3732212; fax (11) 3317344; internet www.mtnl.net.in; f. 1986; 66% state-owned; owns and operates telephone networks in Mumbai and Delhi; Chair. S. RAJAGOPALAN.

Videsh Sanchar Nigam Ltd (VSNL): M. G. Rd, Fort, Mumbai 400 001; tel. (22) 2624020; fax (22) 2624027; e-mail helpdesk@giaspn01.vsnl.net.in; internet www.vsnl.com; f. 1986; 65% state-owned; held monopoly on international telecommunications services since 1994, scheduled to end in 2002; Chair. and Man. Dir AMITABH KUMAR.

BROADCASTING

Prasar Bharati (Broadcasting Corpn of India): New Delhi; autonomous body; oversees operations of state-owned radio and television services; f. 1997; Chief Exec. R. R. SHAH.

Radio

All India Radio (AIR): Akashvani Bhavan, Parliament St, New Delhi 110 001; tel. (11) 3710006; fax (11) 3714061; broadcasting is controlled by the Ministry of Information and Broadcasting and is primarily govt-financed; operates a network of 199 stations and 313 transmitters (grouped into four zones—north, south, east and west), covering 98.8% of the population and over 90% of the total area of the country; Dir-Gen. Dr O. P. KEJRIWAL.

The News Services Division of AIR, centralized in New Delhi, is one of the largest news organizations in the world. It has 42 regional news units, which broadcast 314 bulletins daily in 24 languages and 38 dialects. One hundred and three bulletins in 19 languages are broadcast in the Home Services, 137 regional bulletins in 72 languages and dialects, and 65 bulletins in 24 languages in the External Services.

Television

Doordarshan India (Television India): Mandi House, Doordarshan Bhavan, Copernicus Marg, New Delhi 110 001; tel. (11) 3387786; fax (11) 3386507; f. 1976; broadcasting is controlled by the Ministry of Information and Broadcasting and is govt-financed; programmes: 280 hours weekly; 4 All-India channels, 11 regional language satellite channels, 4 state networks and 1 international channel; Dir-Gen. K. S. SARMA; Chief Exec. K. C. C. RAJA.

In December 2000 74.8% of the country's area and 87.9% of the population were covered by the TV network. There were 1,107 transmitters in operation in that month. By 1999 47 programme production centres and nine relay centres had been established.

Satellite television was introduced in India by a Hong Kong company, Star TV, in 1991. By mid-1993 Star TV attracted an audience of about 18.8m. in India. In July 1992 the Government announced that it would permit broadcasting time to private companies on a second state channel (the Metro Channel) broadcast to major Indian cities. In August 1993 Doordarshan India launched five new satellite television channels; three of the channels were taken off the air, however, in February 1994 following the introduction of a new satellite television policy. Doordarshan International Channel commenced broadcasting (three hours daily) in March 1995; the service was extended to 18 hours daily in November 1996. In 1997 legislation was introduced to license private broadcasters and to impose a 49% limit on foreign ownership of television channels.

Finance

(cap. = capital; p.u. = paid up; res = reserves; dep. = deposits; m. = million; brs = branches; amounts in rupees)

BANKING
State Banks

Reserve Bank of India: Central Office Bldg, Shahid Bhagat Singh Rd, POB 406, Mumbai 400 023; tel. (22) 2661602; fax (22) 2661784; e-mail rbiprd@giasbm01.vsnl.net.in; internet www.rbi.org.in; f. 1934; nationalized 1949; sole bank of issue; cap. 50m., res 65,000m., dep. 691,192.3m. (Dec. 1999); Gov. Dr BIMAL JALAN; Dep. Govs Dr Y. V. REDDY, JAGDISH CAPOOR, S. P. TALWAR; 4 offices and 14 brs.

State Bank of India: Madame Cama Rd, POB 10121, Mumbai 400 021; tel. (22) 2022426; e-mail gm@mumbai.cobom.sbi.co.in; internet www.sbi.co.in; f. 1955; cap. p.u. 5,263m., dep. 1,690,419.3m. (March 1999); 7 associates, 7 domestic subsidiaries/affiliates, 3 foreign subsidiaries, 4 jt ventures abroad; Chair. JANAKI BALLABH; Man. Dir VEPA KAMESAM; 9,050 brs (incl. 52 overseas brs and rep. offices in 31 countries).

State-owned Commercial Banks

Fourteen of India's major commercial banks were nationalized in 1969 and a further six in 1980. They are managed by 15-mem. boards of directors (two directors to be appointed by the central Government, one employee director, one representing employees who are not workmen, one representing depositors, three representing farmers, workers, artisans, etc., five representing persons with special knowledge or experience, one Reserve Bank of India official and one Government of India official). The Department of Banking of the Ministry of Finance controls all banking operations.

There were 65,408 branches of public-sector and other commercial banks in December 1999.

Aggregate deposits of all scheduled commercial banks amounted to Rs 8,419,670m. in March 2000.

Allahabad Bank: 2 Netaji Subhas Rd, Kolkata 700 001; tel. (33) 2209258; fax (33) 2214048; e-mail albfd@giascl01.vsnl.net.in; internet www.allahabadbank.com/; f. 1865; nationalized 1969; cap. p.u. 2,467m., res 6,430.9m., dep. 176,421m. (March 2000); Chair. and Man. Dir B. SAMAL; 1,861 brs.

Andhra Bank: Andhra Bank Bldgs, Saifabad, 5-9-11 Secretariat Rd, Hyderabad 500 004; tel. (40) 243929; fax (40) 3242026; e-mail andhrabank.fedho@gnhyd; internet www.andhrabankindia.com; f. 1923; nationalized 1980; cap. p.u. 3,479.5m., res 2,318.1m., dep. 144,180m. (March 2000); Chair. and Man. Dir B. VASANTHAN; 980 brs and 87 extension counters.

Bank of Baroda: 1st Floor, Mackinnon Mackenzie Bldg, 4 Shoorji Vallabhdas Marg, Ballard Pier, 10046, Mumbai 400 001; tel. (22) 2610341; fax (22) 2620408; e-mail bobio@calva.com; internet www.bankofbaroda.com; f. 1908; nationalized 1969; cap. 2,943.3m., res 29,402.7m., dep. 513,081.9m. (March 2000); Chair. and Man. Dir P. S. SHENOY; 2,522 brs in India, 37 brs overseas.

Bank of India: Express Towers, Nariman Point, POB 234, Mumbai 400 021; tel. (22) 2023020; fax (22) 2022831; e-mail cmdboi@bom5.vsnl.net.in; internet www.bankofindia.com; f. 1906; nationalized 1969; cap. 6,383.9m., res and surplus 18,726.6m., dep. 477,439m. (March 2000); Chair. and Man. Dir K. V. KRISHNAMURTHY; 2,515 brs in India, 19 brs overseas.

Bank of Maharashtra: 'Lokmangal', 1501 Shivajinagar, Pune 411 005; tel. (212) 5532731; fax (212) 5533246; e-mail bomcocmd@vsnl.com; internet www.bank-of-maharashtra.com; f. 1935; nationalized 1969; cap. 3,305.1m., res 2,139.4m., dep. 134,065.5m. (March 2000); Chair. and Man. Dir S. C. BASU; 1,155 brs.

Canara Bank: 112 Jayachamarajendra Rd, POB 6648, Bangalore 560 002; tel. (812) 2221581; fax (812) 2222704; e-mail canbank@blr.vsnl.net.in; internet www.canbankindia.com; f. 1906; nationalized 1969; cap. 5,778.7m., res 20,180.1m., dep. 480,013.6m. (March 2000); Chair. and Man. Dir R. J. KAMATH; 2,348 brs in India, 1 br. overseas.

Central Bank of India: Chandermukhi, Nariman Point, Mumbai 400 021; tel. (22) 2026428; fax (22) 2044336; f. 1911; nationalized 1969; cap. 18,054.5m., res and surplus 7,666m., dep. 358,717.1m. (March 2000); Chair. and Man. Dir K. C. CHOWDHARY; 3,084 brs.

Corporation Bank: Mangaladevi Temple Rd, POB 88, Mangalore 575 001; tel. (824) 426416; fax (824) 441208; e-mail rmd@corpbank.co.in; internet www.corpbank.com; f. 1906; nationalized 1980; cap. 1,199.3m., res 10,247.6m., dep. 142,796.3m. (March 2000); Chair. and Man. Dir K. CHERIAN VARGHESE; Exec. Dir N. S. GUJRAL; 651 brs.

Dena Bank: Maker Towers 'E', 7th–10th Floor, Cuffe Parade, Colaba, POB 6058, Mumbai 400 005; tel. (22) 2189151; fax (22) 2181612; internet www.denabank.com; f. 1938 as Devkaran Nanjee Banking Co Ltd; nationalized 1969; cap. 2,068.2m., res and surplus 4,898.7m., dep. 117,953.5m. (March 1999); Chair. and Man. Dir A. G. JOSHI; 1,134 brs.

Indian Bank: 31 Rajaji Salai, POB 1866, Chennai 600 001; tel. (44) 514151; fax (44) 5231285; e-mail indbank@giasmd01.vsnl.net.in; internet www.indian-bank.com; f. 1907; nationalized 1969; cap. 25,039.6m., res 3,946.7m., dep. 191,135m. (March 2000); Chair. and Man. Dir RANJANA KUMAR; Exec. Dir M. B. N. RAO; 1,424 brs.

Indian Overseas Bank: 762 Anna Salai, POB 3765, Chennai 600 002; tel. (44) 8523880; fax (44) 8523395; e-mail iobfx@vsnl.com; internet www.iob.com; f. 1937; nationalized 1969; cap. 3,336m., res

4,162m., dep. 243,177m. (March 2000); Chair. and Man. Dir R. V. SHASTRI; Exec. Dir S. C. GUPTA; 1,419 brs.

Oriental Bank of Commerce: Harsha Bhavan, E Block, Connaught Place, POB 329, New Delhi 110 001; tel. (11) 3323444; fax (11) 3321514; e-mail obc@obcindia.com; internet www.obcindia.com; f. 1943; nationalized 1980; cap. 1,925.4m., res 12,356.8m., dep. 220,952.1m. (March 2000); Chair. and Man. Dir B. D. NARANG; 533 brs.

Punjab and Sind Bank: 21 Bank House, Rajendra Place, New Delhi 110 008; tel. (11) 5720849; fax (11) 5751765; internet www.punjabandsindbank.com; f. 1908; nationalized 1980; cap. 2,430.6m., res 1,307.4m., dep. 94,966m. (March 1999); Chair. and Man. Dir SURINDER SINGH KOHLI; Exec. Dir M. S. KAPUR; 811 brs.

Punjab National Bank: 7 Bhikaiji Cama Place, Africa Ave, New Delhi 110 066; tel. (11) 6185981; fax (11) 6193315; e-mail pnbibd@ndf.vsnl.net.in; internet www.pnbindia.com; f. 1895; nationalized 1969; merged with New Bank of India in 1993; cap. 2,122.4m., res 20,603.5m., dep. 474,832.3m. (March 2000); Chair. and Man. Dir S. S. KOHLI; Exec. Dir K. R. CHABRIA; 4,200 brs.

Syndicate Bank: POB 1, Manipal 576 119; tel. (8252) 71181; fax (8252) 70266; e-mail idcb@syndicatebank.com; internet www .syndicatebank.com; f. 1925 as Canara Industrial and Banking Syndicate Ltd; name changed as above 1964; nationalized 1969; cap. 4,718.3m., res 5,764.8m., dep. 236,554.2m. (March 2000); Chair. and Man. Dir D. T. PAI; Exec. Dir J. Y. DIWANJI; 1,702 brs.

UCO Bank: 10 Biplabi Trailokya Maharaj Sarani (Brabourne Rd), POB 2455, Kolkata 700 001; tel. (33) 2254120; fax (33) 2253986; e-mail hoidiv.calcutta@ucobank.wiprobt.ems.vsnl.net.in; internet www.ucobank.com; f. 1943 as United Commercial Bank Ltd; nationalized 1969; name changed as above 1985; cap. 22,645.2m., res 3,881.8m., dep. 183,600m. (March 2000); Chair. and Man. Dir V. P. SHETTY; Exec. Dir M. M. VAISH; 1,797 brs.

Union Bank of India: Union Bank Bhavan, 239 Vidhan Bhavan Marg, Nariman Point, Mumbai 400 021; tel. (22) 2023060; fax (22) 2025238; e-mail union@bom3.vsnl.net.in; internet www .unionbankofindia.com; f. 1919; nationalized 1969; cap. 3,380m., res 14,088m., dep. 311,054m. (March 2000); Chair. and Man. Dir V. LILADHAR; 2,087 brs.

United Bank of India: 16 Old Court House St, Kolkata 700 001; tel. (33) 2487471; fax (33) 2485852; e-mail utbihoc@giascl1.vsnl .net.in; f. 1950; nationalized 1969; cap. 18,108.7m., res 1,589.4m., dep. 167,877.0m. (March 2000); Chair. and Man. Dir BISWAJIT CHOUDHURI; Exec. Dir G. R. SUNDARAVADIVEL; 1,319 brs.

Vijaya Bank: 41/2 Mahatma Gandhi Rd, Bangalore 560 001; tel. (80) 5584066; fax (80) 5588853; e-mail vijbank@bgl.vsnl.net.in; internet www.vijayabank.com; f. 1931; nationalized 1980; cap. 2,592.4m., res 1,878.4m., dep. 115,928.8m. (March 2000); Chair. and Man. Dir N. R. NATARAJAN; 842 brs.

Principal Private Banks

Bank of Madura Ltd: 'Karumuttu Nilayam', 758 Anna Salai, POB 5225, Chennai 600 002; tel. (44) 8523456; fax (44) 8523868; e-mail mdsaab34@giasmd01.vsnl.net.in; internet www.bankofmadura .com; f. 1943; cap. 117.7m., res 2,093.3m., dep. 36,310.4m. (March 2000); Chair. Dr K. M. THIAGARAJAN; Gen. Mans V. NACHIAPPAN, S. KATHIRESAN; 276 brs.

The Bank of Rajasthan Ltd: C-3 Sardar Patel Marg, Jaipur 302 001; tel. (141) 381222; fax (141) 381123; e-mail borit@jp1.dot.net.in; f. 1943; cap. p.u. 179.4m., res 1,690.4m., dep. 30,131.6m. (March 1999); Chair. PRAVIN KUMAR TAYAL; Man. Dir K. M. BHATTACHARYA; 307 brs.

Benares State Bank Ltd (BSB): S-20/52 A-K Varuna Bridge, Varanasi 221 002; tel. (542) 348681; fax (542) 348680; f. 1946; cap. 621.1m., res 36.5m., dep. 7,849.8m. (March 1999); Chair. H. DINESH NAYAK; 105 brs.

Bharat Overseas Bank Ltd: Habeeb Towers, 756 Anna Salai, Chennai 600 002; tel. (44) 8525686; fax (44) 8524700; e-mail bobl@md3.vsnl.net.in; f. 1973; cap. 3,722.4m., res 4,562.9m., dep. 6,876.1m. (March 2000); Chair. G. KRISHNAMURTHY; Dep. Gen. Man. G. CHANDRAN; 77 brs.

Bombay Mercantile Co-operative Bank Ltd: 78 Mohammed Ali Rd, Mumbai 400 003; tel. (22) 3425961; fax (22) 3433385; e-mail bmcb@bom5.vsnl.net.in; f. 1939; cap. 126m., res 1,696.6m., dep. 27,756.3m. (March 2000); Chair. A. R. KIDWAI; Man. Dir SHAMIM KAZIM; 52 brs.

The Catholic Syrian Bank Ltd: St Mary's College Rd, POB 502, Trichur 680 020; tel. (487) 333020; fax (487) 333435; e-mail csbho@md2.vsnl.net.in; internet www.casybank.com; f. 1920; cap. 99.9m., res 401.8m., dep. 22,029.8m. (March 1999); Chair. and CEO A. SOLOMON; Gen. Man. JOHN J. ALAPATT; 267 brs.

Centurion Bank Ltd: 1201 Raheja Centre, Free Press Journal Marg, Nariman Point, Mumbai 400 021; tel. (22) 2047234; fax (22) 2845860; e-mail cblho@bom3.vsnl.net.in; internet www.centurion

bank.com; f. 1995; cap. 1,524.7m., res 215.9m., dep. 47,048.3m. (March 2000); Chair. DEV AHUJA; Man. Dir V. SRINIVASAN.

City Union Bank Ltd: 149 TSR (Big) St, Kumbakonam 612 001; tel. (435) 432322; fax (435) 431746; e-mail cub@vsnl.com; internet www.cityunion.com; f. 1904; cap. 240.0m., res 797.4m., dep. 13,405m. (March 2000); Chair. V. NARYANAN; Chief Gen. Man. K. VENKATARAMAN; 109 brs.

The Federal Bank Ltd: Federal Towers, POB 103, Alwaye 683 101; tel. (484) 624061; fax (484) 622566; e-mail fednri@md2.vsnl.net.in; internet www.federal-bank.com; f. 1931; cap. 217.1m., res and surplus 3,311m., dep. 67,820.7m. (March 2000); Chair. K. P. PADMAKUMAR; 399 brs.

Global Trust Bank Ltd: 303-48-3 Sardar Patel Rd, Secunderabad 500 003; tel. (40) 7819333; fax (40) 7815879; e-mail ask@global trustbank.com; internet www.globaltrustbank.com; f. 1994; cap. p.u. 1,214m., res 4,064.3m., dep. 65,975.1m. (March 2000); Chair. and Man. Dir RAMESH GELLI; Exec. Dir SRIDHAR SUBASRI; 72 brs.

ICICI Bank: ICICI Towers, 4th Floor, South Tower, Bandra–Kurla Complex, Bandra (East), Mumbai 400 051; tel. (22) 6531414; fax (22) 6531167; e-mail sinorhn@icicibank.com; internet www .icicibank.com; f. 1994; cap. 1,968.2m., res and surplus 9,526.9m., dep. 98,660.2m. (March 2000); Man. Dir and CEO H. N. SINOR; 86 brs.

IndusInd Bank Ltd: IndusInd House, 425 Dadasaheb Bhadkamkar Marg, Lamington Rd, nr Opera House, Mumbai 400 004; tel. (22) 3859901; fax (22) 3859913; e-mail glob@indusind.com; internet www.indusind.com; f. 1994; cap. 1,590.1m., res 3,742.8m., dep. 65,459.6m. (March 2000); Chair. ARJUN ASRANI; Man. Dir K. R. MAHESWARI; 28 brs.

Jammu and Kashmir Bank Ltd: Zum Zum Bldg, Ram Bagh, Srinagar 190 015; tel. (194) 430730; fax (194) 430247; e-mail jkbgm@nde.vsnl.net.com; internet www.jammuandkashmirbank .com; f. 1938; cap. p.u. 480.1m., res 3,805.5m., dep 94,220.9m. (March 2000); Chair. and CEO M. Y. KHAN; 389 brs.

The Karnataka Bank Ltd: POB 716, Kodialbail, Mangalore 575 003; tel. (824) 440751; fax (824) 441212; internet www .thekarnatakabankltd.com; f. 1924; cap. 135m., dep. 51,741.7m. (March 2000); Chair. and CEO Mr ANANTHAKRISHNA; 346 brs.

The Karur Vysya Bank Ltd: Erode Rd, POB 21, Karur 639 002; tel. (4324) 32520; fax (4324) 30202; e-mail kvbid@giasmd01.vsnl.net.in; f. 1916; cap. 60.0m., res 1,886.2m., dep. 30,906.1m. (March 2000); Chair. A. D. NAVANEETHAN; Sr Gen. Man. V. DEVARAJAN; 206 brs.

Lakshmi Vilas Bank Ltd: Kathaparai, Salem Rd, POB 2, Karur 639 006; tel. (4324) 20051; fax (4324) 20068; e-mail lbvho.cppd@ gninet.global.net.in; internet www.lakshmivilasbankltd.com; f. 1926; cap. 115.1m., res 897.2m., dep. 15,910.1m. (March 1999); Chair. K. R. SHENOY; Gen. Man. R. MUNISWAMY; 205 brs.

The Sangli Bank Ltd: Rajwada Chowk, POB 158, Sangli 416 416; tel. (233) 73611; fax (233) 77156; f. 1916; cap. p.u. 60.2m., dep. 7,303.6m. (March 1995); Chair. and CEO SURESH D. JOSHI; Gen. Man. Dr V. PRASANNA BHAT; 178 brs.

The South Indian Bank Ltd: SIB House, Mission Quarters, Thrissur 680 001, Kerala; tel. (487) 420020; fax (487) 442021; e-mail head@southindianbank.com; internet www.southindianbank .com; f. 1929; cap. 355.2m., res 1,513.4m., dep. 38,853.6m. (March 2000); Chair. and CEO A. SETHUMADHAVAN; 365 brs.

Tamilnad Mercantile Bank Ltd: 57 Victoria Extension Rd, Tuticorin 628 002; tel. (461) 321932; fax (461) 322994; f. 1921 as Nadar Bank, name changed as above 1962; cap. 2.8m., res 2,262.3m., dep. 26,646m. (March 2000); Chair. S. KRISHNAMURTHY; 142 brs.

The United Western Bank Ltd: 172/4 Raviwar Peth, Shivaji Circle, POB 2, Satara 415 001; tel. (2162) 20517; fax (2162) 23374; internet www.uwbankindia.com; f. 1936; cap. 298.9m., res and surplus 1,967.7m., dep. 43,488.4m. (March 2000); Chair. and Chief Exec. P. N. JOSHI; Gen. Man. V. G. PALKAR; 203 brs.

The Vysya Bank Ltd: 72 St Marks Rd, Bangalore 560 001; tel. (80) 2272021; fax (80) 2272220; internet www.vysyabanka.com; f. 1930; cap. 171.9m., res 4,206m., dep. 65,104m. (March 1999); Chair. K. R. RAMAMOORTHY; Exec. Dir G. LAXMINARAYANA; 492 brs.

Foreign Banks

ABN AMRO Bank NV (Netherlands): 14 Veer Nariman Rd, POB 97, Mumbai 400 023; tel. (22) 2042331; CEO FERGUS FLEMING; 6 brs.

Abu Dhabi Commercial Bank (UAE): Rehmat Manzil, 75-B Veer Nariman Rd, Mumbai 400 020; tel. (22) 2830235; fax (22) 2870686; Chief Exec. KHALIFA MOHAMMAD HUSSEIN; 1 br.

American Express Bank Ltd (USA): 7th Floor, Maker Chambers IV, 211 Nariman Point, Mumbai 400 021; tel. (22) 2833293; fax (22) 2872968; Country Head STEVE MARTIN; 4 brs.

ANZ Grindlays Bank (UK): 90 Mahatma Gandhi Rd, POB 725, Mumbai 400 023; tel. (22) 271295; fax (22) 2619903; Country Head ANUROOP SINGH; 39 brs.

Banca Nazionale del Lavoro Spa (Italy): 67 Maker Chambers VI, 6th Floor, Nariman Point, Mumbai 400 021; tel. (22) 2047763; fax (22) 2023482; Rep. L. S. AGARWAL.

Bank Muscat SAOG (Oman): 29 Empire Infantry, Infantry Rd, Bangalore 560 001; tel. (80) 2867755; fax (80) 2862214; e-mail bmiimgt@bgl.vsnl.net.in; CEO SAMIT GHOSH; 1 br.

Bank of America NA (USA): Express Towers, POB 10080, Nariman Point, Mumbai 400 021; tel. (22) 2852882; fax (22) 2029016; CEO HUGH L. MCCOLL, Jr; 3 brs.

Bank of Bahrain and Kuwait BSC: Jolly Maker Chambers II, Ground Floor, POB 11692, 225 Nariman Point, Mumbai 400 021; tel. (22) 2823698; fax (22) 2044458; Gen. Man. and CEO K. S. KRISHNAKUMAR; 2 brs.

Bank of Ceylon: 1090 Poonamallee High Rd, Chennai 600 084; tel. (44) 6420972; fax (44) 5325590; e-mail ceybank@md3 .vsnl.net.in; internet www.bocindia.com; Asst Vice-Pres. B. KARTHIK; Country Man. N. V. MOORTHY.

Bank of Nova Scotia (Canada): Mittal Tower B, Nariman Point, Mumbai 400 021; tel. (22) 2832822; fax (22) 2873125; Sr Vice-Pres. and CEO (India) DOUGLAS H. STEWART; Vice-Pres. and Man. BHASKAR DESAI; 3 brs.

Bank of Tokyo-Mitsubishi Ltd (Japan): Jeevan Prakash, Sir P. Mehta Rd, Mumbai 400 001; tel. (22) 2660564; fax (22) 2661787; Regional Rep. for India and Gen. Man. KUNIHIKO NISHIHARA; 4 brs.

Barclays Bank PLC (UK): 21–23 Maker Chambers VI, 2nd Floor, Nariman Point, Mumbai 400 021; tel. (22) 2044353; fax (22) 2043238; CEO AJAY SONDHI; 2 brs.

BNP Paribas (France): French Bank Bldg, 4th Floor, 62 Homji St, Fort, POB 45, Mumbai 400 001; tel. (22) 2660822; fax (22) 2660144; e-mail bnp@giasbm01.vsnl.net.in; internet www.bnpparibas.com; Chief Exec. and Country Man. JONATHAN LYON; 8 brs.

Chase Manhattan Bank: Mafatlal Centre, 9/F, Nariman Point, Mumbai 400 021; tel. (22) 2855666; fax (22) 2027772; Man. Dir and Sr Country Officer (India and South Asia) ANIL BHALLA; 1 br.

Chinatrust Commercial Bank (Taiwan): 21-A Janpath, New Delhi 110 001; tel. (11) 3356001; fax (11) 3731815; e-mail ctcbindd@ndf.vsnl.net.in; internet www.chinatrustindia.com; Gen. Man. and CEO ROBERT C. F. WANG; 1 br.

Citibank, NA (USA): Sakhar Bhavan, 230 Backbay Reclamation, Nariman Point, Mumbai 400 021; tel. (22) 2025499; internet www .citibank.com/india; CEO NANOO PAMNANI; 11 brs.

Commerzbank AG (Germany): Free Press House, 215 Free Press Journal Rd, Nariman Point, Mumbai 400 021; tel. (22) 2885510; fax (22) 2885524; Gen. Mans G. SHEKHAR, PETER KENYON-MUIR; 2 brs.

Crédit Agricole Indosuez (France): Ramon House, 169 Backbay Reclamation, Mumbai 400 020; tel. (22) 2045104; fax (22) 2049108; Sr Country Officer ALAIN BUTZBACH; Gen. Man. NIRENDU MAZUMDAR.

Crédit Lyonnais (France): Scindia House, 1st Floor, Narottam Morarjee Marg, Ballard Estate, Mumbai 400 038; tel. (22) 2612313; fax (22) 2612603; Chief Exec. and Country Man. JEAN-YVES LE PAULMIER; 4 brs.

Deutsche Bank AG (Germany): DB House, Hazarimal Somani Marg, Fort, POB 1142, Mumbai 400 001; tel. (22) 2074720; fax (22) 2075047; CEO JAVAD SHIRAZI; 5 brs.

Development Bank of Singapore Ltd: Maker Chambers IV, 12th Floor, Nariman Point, Mumbai 400 021; tel. (22) 2826991; fax (22) 2875602; 1 br.

Dresdner Bank (Germany): Hoechst House, Nariman Point, Mumbai 400 021; tel. (22) 2850009; 2 brs.

Fuji Bank Ltd (Japan): Maker Chambers III, 1st Floor, Jamnalal Bajaj Rd, Nariman Point, Mumbai 400 021; tel. (22) 2886638; fax (22) 2886640; CEO (India) and Gen. Man. TATSUJI TAMAKA; 1 br.

Hongkong and Shanghai Banking Corpn Ltd (Hong Kong): 52-60 Mahatma Gandhi Rd, POB 128, Mumbai 400 001; tel. (22) 2674921; fax (22) 2658309; internet www.hongkongbank.com; CEO ZARIR J. CAMA; 21 brs.

ING Bank (Netherlands): Hoechst House, 7th Floor, 193 Backbay Reclamation, Nariman Point, Mumbai 400 005; tel. (22) 2029876; fax (22) 2046134; Country Head PRADEEP SAXENA; 2 brs.

Mashreq Bank PSC (United Arab Emirates): Air-India Bldg, Nariman Point, Mumbai 400 021; tel. (22) 2026096; fax (22) 2831278; CEO SUNEIL KUCCHAL.

Oman International Bank SAOG (Oman): 201 Raheja Centre, Free Press Journal Marg, Nariman Point, Mumbai 400 021; tel. (22) 2837733; fax (22) 2875626; e-mail oibind@bom3.vsnl.net.in; Country Man. ABDUL GHAFOOR AL-BULUSHI; 2 brs.

Sanwa Bank Ltd (Japan): Mercantile House, Upper Ground Floor, 15 Kasturba Gandhi Marg, New Delhi 110 001; tel. (11) 3318008; fax (11) 3315162; Gen. Man. NOBUO OJI.

Société Générale (France): Maker Chambers IV, Bajaj Marg, Nariman Point, POB 11635, Mumbai 400 021; tel. (22) 2870909;

fax (22) 2045459; e-mail sgbombay@giasbm01.vsnl.net.in; CEO R. KERNEIS; 4 brs.

Sonali Bank (Bangladesh): 'Apeejay House', 15 Park St, Kolkata 700 016; tel. (33) 247998; Dep. Gen. Man. SIRAJUDDIN AHMED; 1 br.

Standard Chartered Bank (UK): New Excelsior Bldg, 4th Floor, A. K. Naik Marg, POB 1806, Mumbai 400 001; tel. (22) 2075409; fax (22) 2072550; e-mail vkrishn@scbindia.mhs.compuserve .com; Chief Exec. HARPAL DUGGAL; 19 brs.

State Bank of Mauritius Ltd: 101, Raheja Centre, 1st Floor, Free Press Journal Marg, Nariman Point, Mumbai 400 021; tel. (22) 2842965; fax (22) 2842966; Gen. Man. and CEO P. THONDRAYEN; 2 brs.

Sumitomo Bank (Japan): 15/F Jolly Maker Chamber No. 2, 225 Nariman Point, Mumbai 400 021; tel. (22) 2880025; fax (22) 2880026; CEO and Gen. Man. KOZO OTSUBO.

Union Bank of Switzerland: Mumbai.

Banking Organizations

Indian Banks' Association: Stadium House, 6th Floor, Block 3, Veer Nariman Rd, Churchgate, Mumbai 400 020; tel. (22) 2844999; fax (22) 2835638; 172 mems; Chair. S. S. KOHLI; Sec. K. C. CHOWDHARY.

Indian Institute of Bankers: 'The Arcade', World Trade Centre, 2nd Floor, East Wing, Cuffe Parade, Mumbai 400 005; tel. (22) 2187003; fax (22) 2185147; e-mail iibgen@bom5.vsnl.net.in; internet www.iib.org.in; f. 1928; 343,202 mems; Pres. G. G. VAIDYA; Chief Sec. R. H. SARMA.

National Institute of Bank Management: NIBM Post Office, Kondhwe Khurd, Pune 411 048; tel. (20) 6833080; fax (20) 6834478; e-mail nibmweb@nibm.ernet.in; internet www.nibmindia.com; f. 1969; Dir Dr GANTI SUBRAHMANYAM.

DEVELOPMENT FINANCE ORGANIZATIONS

Agricultural Finance Corporation Ltd: Dhanraj Mahal, 1st Floor, Chhatrapati Shivaji Maharaj Marg, Mumbai 400 001; tel. (22) 2028924; fax (22) 2028966; e-mail afcl@vsnl.com; internet www.afcindia.com; f. 1968 by a consortium of 45 public- and private-sector commercial banks including development finance institutions to help increase the flow of investment and credit into agriculture and rural development projects; provides project consultancy services to commercial banks, Union and State govts, public-sector corps, the World Bank, the ADB, FAO, the International Fund for Agricultural Development and other institutions and to individuals; undertakes techno-economic and investment surveys in agriculture and agro-industries etc.; 3 regional offices and 9 br. offices; cap. p.u. 150m., res and surplus 25.5m. (March 2000); Chair. Dr. P. V. SHENOI; Man. Dir A. M. ALAM.

Export-Import Bank of India: Centre 1, Floor 21, World Trade Centre, Cuffe Parade, Mumbai 400 005; tel. and fax (22) 2182572; e-mail eximind@vsnl.com; internet www.eximbankindia.com; f. 1982; cap. 4,999.9m., res 8,352.1m., dep. 34,239.9m. (March 1999); offices in Bangalore, Chennai, Kolkata, New Delhi, Pune, Ahmedabad, Johannesburg, Budapest, Rome, Singapore and Washington, DC; Man. Dir Y. B. DESAI; Exec. Dir T. C. VENKAT SUBRAMANIAN.

Housing Development Finance Corpn Ltd (HDFC): Ramon House, 169 Backbay Reclamation, Mumbai 400 020; tel. (22) 2820282; fax (22) 2046758; e-mail library@hdfcindia.com; internet www.hdfcindia.com; provides loans to individuals and corporate bodies; Chair. DEEPAK S. PAREKH; Man. Dir ADITYA PURI; 69 brs.

Industrial Credit and Investment Corpn of India Ltd: ICICI Towers, Bandra-Kurla Complex, Mumbai 400 051; tel. (11) 6531414; fax (11) 6531122; internet www.icici.com; f. 1955 to assist industrial enterprises by providing finance in both rupee and foreign currencies in the form of long- or medium-term loans or equity participation, guaranteeing loans from other private investment sources, furnishing managerial, technological and administration advice to industry; also offers suppliers' and buyers' credit, export development capital, asset credit, technology finance, instalment sale and equipment leasing facilities, and infrastructure finance; zonal offices at Mumbai, Kolkata, Chennai, New Delhi, Vadodara, Pune, Bangalore, Hyderabad and Coimbatore; development office at Guwahati (Assam); equity share cap. 4,781.4m., res 41,921.8m. (March 1998); Chair. and Man. Dir K. V. KAMATH.

Industrial Development Bank of India (IDBI): IDBI Tower, WTC Complex, Cuffe Parade, Colaba, Mumbai 400 005; tel. (22) 2189111; fax (22) 2180411; e-mail s.koshy@idbi.co.in; internet www.idbi.com; f. 1964, reorg. 1976; 72.1% govt-owned; India's premier financial institution for providing direct finance, refinance of industrial loans and bills, finance to large- and medium-sized industries, and for extending financial services, such as merchant banking and forex services, to the corporate sector; 5 zonal offices and 38 br. offices; cap. 6,600m., res 83,650m., dep. 410,828.9m. (March 2000); Chair. and Man. Dir GIAN PRAKASH GUPTA; Dep. Gen. Man. SUSAN KOSHY.

Small Industries Development Bank of India: 10/10 Madan Mohan Malviya Marg, Lucknow 226 001; tel. (522) 209517; fax (522) 209514; e-mail snairan@sidbi.com; internet www.sidbi.com; f. 1990; wholly-owned subsidiary of Industrial Development Bank of India; promotes, finances and develops small-scale industries; cap. p.u. 4,500m., res 24,240m. (March 2000); Chair. Dr SAILENDRA NARAIN; 39 offices.

Industrial Finance Corpn of India Ltd: IFCI Tower, 61 Nehru Place, New Delhi 110 019; tel. (11) 6487444; fax (11) 6488471; e-mail ifci@giasd01.vsnl.net.in; internet www.ifciltd.com; f. 1948 to provide medium- and long-term finance to cos and co-operative socs in India, engaged in manufacture, preservation or processing of goods, shipping, mining, hotels and power generation and distribution; promotes industrialization of less developed areas, and sponsors training in management techniques and development banking; cap. p.u. 4,569.9m., res 6,482.2m. (March 2000); Chair. and Man. Dir P. V. NARASIMHAN; Exec. Dirs S. P. BANERJEE, H. C. SHARMA; 11 regional offices and 6 other offices.

Industrial Investment Bank of India: A. G. Towers, 2nd Floor, 125/1 Park St, Kolkata 700 017; tel. (33) 2291351; fax (33) 2295240; Chair. and Man. Dir Dr G. GOSWAMI.

National Bank for Agriculture and Rural Development: Plot no. C-24, G Block, Bandra-Kurla Complex, Bangra (E), Mumbai 400 051; tel. (22) 6530071; e-mail nabpro@bom7.vsnl.net.in; internet www.nabard.org; f. 1982 to provide credit for agricultural and rural development through commercial, co-operative and regional rural banks; cap. p.u. 20,000m., res 29,479m. (March 2000); held 50% each by the cen. Govt and the Reserve Bank; Chair. Y. C. NANDA; Man. Dir SAROJ K. KALIA; 17 regional offices, 10 sub-offices and 5 training establishments.

STOCK EXCHANGES

There are 24 stock exchanges (with a total of more than 6,250 listed companies) in India, including:

National Stock Exchange of India Ltd: 'A' Wing, Mahindra Towers, 1st Floor, Worli, Mumbai 400 018; tel. (22) 4960525; fax (22) 4935631; e-mail postmaster@nse.co.in; internet www.nseindia.com; f. 1994; Man. Dir RAVI NARAIN.

Ahmedabad Share and Stock Brokers' Association: Manek Chowk, Ahmedabad 380 001; tel. (79) 347149; fax (79) 340117; f. 1894; 299 mems; Pres. V. G. GAJJAR; Exec. Dir RAJIV DESAI.

Bangalore Stock Exchange Ltd: 51 Stock Exchange Towers, 1st Corss, J. C. Rd, Bangalore 560 027; tel. (812) 2995234; fax (80) 2995242; e-mail edbgse@blr.vsnl.net.in; 234 mems; Pres. JAGDISH V. AHUJA; Exec. Dir K. KAMALA.

Calcutta Stock Exchange Association Ltd: 7 Lyons Range, Kolkata 700 001; tel. (33) 2206928; fax (33) 2104486; internet www.cse-india.com; f. 1908; 910 mems; Pres. KAMAL PAREKA; Sec. P. K. RAY.

Delhi Stock Exchange Association Ltd: DSE House, 3/1 Asaf Ali Rd, New Delhi 110 002; tel. (11) 3292170; fax (11) 3292174; e-mail exedir@dseindia.org.in; f. 1947; 379 mems; Pres. SUDHIR JOSHI; Exec. Dir S. S. SODHI.

Ludhiana Stock Exchange Association Ltd: Feroze Gandhi Market, Ludhiana 141 001; tel. (161) 412316; fax (161) 404748; e-mail lse@satyam.net.in; f. 1981; 301 mems; Pres. R. C. SINGAL; Gen. Man. H. S. SIDHU.

Madras Stock Exchange Ltd: Exchange Bldg, 11 Second Line Beach, POB 183, Chennai 600 001; tel. (44) 5221085; fax (44) 5244897; e-mail mseed@md3.vsnl.net.in; f. 1937; 168 mems; Pres. M. S. NARAYANASAMY; Exec. Dir SHAJI CHERIAN.

Mangalore Stock Exchange: Rama Bhavan Complex, 4th Floor, Kodialbail, Mangalore 575 003; tel. (824) 440581; fax (824) 440736; 146 mems; Pres. RAMESH RAI; Exec. Dir UMESH P. MASKERI.

Mumbai Stock Exchange: Phiroze Jeejeebhoy Towers, 25th Floor, Dalal St, Fort, Mumbai 400 001; tel. (22) 2655861; fax (22) 2655726; e-mail webmaster@bseindia.com; internet www.bseindia.com; f. 1875; 638 mems; Pres. (vacant); Exec. Dir. A. N. JOSHI; Sec. A. A. TIRODKAR.

Thiruvananthapuram Stock Exchange: Thiruvananthapuram; Dir JOSE JOHN.

Uttar Pradesh Stock Exchange Association Ltd: 14/113 Civil Lines, Kanpur 208 001; tel. (512) 293115; fax (512) 293175; e-mail upse@lw1.vsnl.net.in; 500 mems; Pres. H. K. GARG; Exec. Dir Dr J. N. GUPTA.

The other recognized stock exchanges are: Hyderabad, Madhya Pradesh (Indore), Cochin, Pune, Guwahati, Jaipur, Bhubaneswar (Orissa), Coimbatore, Saurashtra, Meerut, Vadodara and Magadh (Patna).

INSURANCE

In January 1973 all Indian and foreign insurance companies were nationalized. The general insurance business in India is now trans-acted by only four companies, subsidiaries of the General Insurance Corpn of India, formed under the 1972 General Insurance Business Nationalisation Act. The Insurance Regulatory Development Authority Bill, approved by the legislature in December 1999, established a regulatory authority for the insurance sector and henceforth permitted up to 26% investment by foreign companies in new domestic, private-sector insurance companies.

General Insurance Corpn of India (GIC): 'Suraksha', 170 J. Tata Rd, Churchgate, Mumbai 400 020; tel. (22) 2833046; fax (22) 2855423; e-mail sengupt@gic.nic.in; internet www.gic.nic.in; f. 1973 by the reorg. of 107 private non-life insurance cos (incl. brs of foreign cos operating in the country) as the four subsidiaries listed below; Chair. D. SENGUPTA; Man. Dir M. K. TANDON.

National Insurance Co Ltd: 3 Middleton St, Kolkata 700 071; tel. (33) 2472130; fax (33) 2402369; e-mail poddar-an@national.nic.in; internet www.national.nic.in; Chair. and Man. Dir A. N. PODDAR; 19 regional offices, 254 divisional offices and 690 branch offices.

New India Assurance Co Ltd: New India Assurance Bldg, 87 Mahatma Gandhi Rd, Fort, Mumbai 400 001; tel. (22) 2674617; fax (22) 2652811; f. 1919; Chair./Man. Dir D. SENGUPTA; 21 regional offices, 315 divisional offices, 827 branch offices and 32 overseas offices.

The Oriental Insurance Co Ltd: Oriental House, A-25/27 Asaf Ali Rd, New Delhi 110 002; tel. (11) 3279221; fax (11) 3263175; e-mail bdbanerjee@oriental.nic.in; Chair. and Man. Dir B. D. BANERJEE.

United India Insurance Co Ltd: 24 Whites Rd, Chennai 600 014; tel. (44) 8520161; fax (44) 8525280; e-mail knb@united.nic.in; internet www.united.nic.in; Chair. and Man. Dir K. N. BHANDARI.

Life Insurance Corpn of India (LIC): 'Yogakshema', Jeevan Bima Marg, Mumbai 400 021; tel. (22) 2021383; fax (22) 2020274; e-mail liccreos@bom3.vsnl.net.in; internet www.licindia.com; f. 1956; controls all life insurance business; Chair. G. N. BAJPAI; Man. Dirs A. RAMAMURTHY and N. C. SHARMA; 2,048 brs and three overseas offices.

Trade and Industry
GOVERNMENT AGENCIES AND DEVELOPMENT ORGANIZATIONS

Coal India Ltd: 10 Netaji Subhas Rd, Kolkata 700 001; tel. (33) 2488099; fax (33) 2483373; internet www.coalindia.nic.in; cen. govt holding co with eight subsidiaries; responsible for almost total (more than 90%) exploration for, planning and production of coal mines; owns 498 coal mines throughout India; marketing of coal and its products; cap. p.u. Rs72,205.4m. (March 1999); Chair. P. K. SENGUPTA; 660,000 employees (1995).

Cotton Corpn of India Ltd: Plot No. 3A, Sector No. 10, CBD Belapur, Navi Mumbai 400 614; tel. (22) 7579217; fax (22) 7576030; e-mail ccimum@bom7.vsnl.net.in; internet www.cotcorp.com; f. 1970 as an agency in the public sector for the purchase, sale and distribution of home-produced cotton and imported cotton staple fibre; exports staple cotton; cap. p.u. Rs230m., res and surplus Rs2,115.0m. (March 1999); Chair. and Man. Dir VISHWA NATH.

Export Credit Guarantee Corpn of India Ltd: Express Towers, 10th Floor, Nariman Point, Mumbai 400 021; tel. (22) 2845472; fax (22) 2045253; e-mail ecgcedp@bom2.vsnl.net.in; f. 1957 to insure for risks involved in exports on credit terms and to supplement credit facilities by issuing guarantees, etc.; cap. Rs2,900m., res Rs2,337m. (March 1999); Chair. and Man. Dir B. B. SHARMA; 23 brs.

Fertilizer Corpn of India Ltd: 'Madhuban', 55 Nehru Place, New Delhi 110 019; tel. (11) 6444971; fax (11) 6416694; e-mail fci@fci.hub.nic.in; f. 1961; fertilizer factories at Sindri (Bihar), Gorakhpur (Uttar Pradesh), Talcher (Orissa) and Ramagundam (Andhra Pradesh), producing nitrogenous and some industrial products; cap. Rs7,317.4m. (March 1999); Chair. and Man. Dir Dr U. K. SEN.

Food Corpn of India: 16–20 Barakhamba Lane, New Delhi 110 001; tel. (11) 3413871; fax (11) 3413231; f. 1965 to undertake trading in food grains on a commercial scale but within the framework of an overall govt policy; to provide farmers an assured price for their produce; to supply food grains to the consumer at reasonable prices; also purchases, stores, distributes and sells food grains and other foodstuffs and arranges imports and handling of food grains and fertilizers at the ports; distributes sugar in a number of states and has set up rice mills; cap. p.u. Rs13,474.5m. (March 1999); Chair. BHURE LAL; Man. Dir P. R. DASGUPTA; 65,131 employees.

Handicrafts and Handlooms Exports Corpn of India Ltd: 5th Floor, Jawahar Vyapar Bhavan Annexe, 1 Tolstoy Marg, New Delhi 110 001; tel. (11) 3701086; fax (11) 3701051; e-mail hhecco.wyapar@eaxcess.net.in; internet www.hhecworld.com; f. 1958; govt undertaking dealing in export of handicrafts, handloom goods, ready-to-wear clothes, carpets, jute, leather and precious jewellery, and import of bullion and raw silk; promotes exports and trade development; cap. p.u. Rs108.2m., res and surplus Rs23.6m. (March 1999); Chair. and Man. Dir K. K. SINHA

Housing and Urban Development Corpn Ltd: HUDCO Bhavan, India Habitat Centre, Lodhi Rd, New Delhi 110 003; tel. (11) 4648160; fax (11) 4625308; internet www.hudcoindia.com; f. 1970; to finance and undertake housing and urban development programmes including the establishment of new or satellite towns and building material industries; cap. p.u. Rs3,960m., res and surplus Rs3,995m. (March 1999); 21 brs; Chair. and Man. Dir V. SURESH; Sec. GOPAL KRISHAN.

India Trade Promotion Organisation (ITPO): Pragati Bhavan, Pragati Maidan, Lal Bahadur Shastri Marg, New Delhi 110 001; tel. (11) 3371540; fax (11) 3318142; e-mail itpo@giasdl10.vsnl.net.in; internet www.indiatrade promotion.org; f. 1992 following merger; promotes selective development of exports of high quality products; arranges investment in export-orientated ventures undertaken by India with foreign collaboration; organizes trade fairs; operates Trade Information Centre; cap. p.u. Rs2.5m., res and surplus Rs1,541.8m. (March 1999); brs in Bangalore, Mumbai, Kolkata, Kanpur and Chennai, and in Frankfurt, New York, Tokyo and Dubai; Chair. and Man. Dir RATHI VIJAY JHA.

Jute Corpn of India Ltd: 1 Shakespeare Sarani, Kolkata 700 071; tel. (33) 2828831; fax (33) 2826938; e-mail jutecorp@vsnl.net.in; f. 1971; objects: (i) to undertake price support operations in respect of raw jute; (ii) to ensure remunerative prices to producers through efficient marketing; (iii) to operate a buffer stock to stabilize raw jute prices; (iv) to handle the import and export of raw jute; (v) to promote the export of jute goods; cap. p.u. Rs50m. (March 1999); Chair. and Man. Dir A. K. KHASTAGIR.

Minerals and Metals Trading Corpn of India Ltd (MMTC): Scope Complex, Core-1, 7 Institutional Areas, Lodi Rd, New Delhi 110 003; tel. (11) 4362200; fax (11) 4360724; e-mail cpmr@mmtclimited.com; internet www.mmtclimited.com; f. 1963; export of iron and manganese ore, ferro-manganese, finished stainless steel products, engineering, agricultural and marine products, textiles, leather items, chemicals and pharmaceuticals, mica, coal and other minor minerals; import of steel, non-ferrous metals, rough diamonds, fertilizers, etc. for supply to industrial units in the country; cap. p.u. Rs500m., res Rs6,628m. (March 1999); 9 regional offices and 16 sub-regional offices in India; foreign offices in Japan, the Republic of Korea, Jordan and Romania; Chair. and Man. Dir SHIV DAYAL KAPOOR; 3,246 employees.

National Co-operative Development Corpn: 4 Siri Institutional Area, Hauz Khas, New Delhi 110 016; tel. (11) 6567475; fax (11) 6962370; e-mail dirmis@ncdc.delhi.nic.in; internet www.ncdc.nic.in; f. 1963 to plan, promote and finance country-wide programmes through co-operative societies for the production, processing, marketing, storage, export and import of agricultural produce, foodstuffs and notified commodities; also programmes for the development of poultry, dairy, fish products, coir, handlooms, distribution of consumer articles in rural areas and minor forest produce in the co-operative sector; 15 regional and state directorates; Pres. NITISH KUMAR; Man. Dir P. K. MISHRA.

National Industrial Development Corpn Ltd: Chanakya Bhavan, Africa Ave, New Delhi 110 021; tel. (11) 4670153; fax (11) 6876166; e-mail nidc123@del2.vsnl.net.in; internet www.exploreindia.com/nidc; f. 1954; consultative engineering, management and infrastructure services to cen. and state govts, public and private sector enterprises, the UN and overseas investors; cap. p.u. Rs17.9m. (March 1999); Chair. and Man. Dir PRANAB GHOSH.

National Mineral Development Corpn Ltd: Khanij Bhavan, 10-3-311/A Castle Hills, Masab Tank, POB 1352, Hyderabad 500 028; tel. (40) 3538713; fax (40) 3538711; internet www.nmdc-india.com; f. 1958; cen. govt undertaking; to exploit minerals (excluding coal, atomic minerals, lignite, petroleum and natural gas) in public sector; may buy, take on lease or otherwise acquire mines for prospecting, development and exploitation; iron ore mines at Bailadila-11C, Bailadila-14 and Bailadila-5 in Madhya Pradesh, and at Donimalai in Karnataka State; new 5m. metric ton iron ore mine under construction at Bailadila-10/11A; diamond mines at Panna in Madhya Pradesh; research and development laboratories and consultancy services covering all aspects of mineral exploitation at Hyderabad; investigates mineral projects; cap. p.u. Rs1,321.6m., res and surplus Rs8,188.6m. (March 2000); Chair. and Man. Dir P. R. TRIPATHI.

National Productivity Council: Utpadakta Bhavan, Lodi Rd, New Delhi 110 003; tel. (11) 4643778; fax (11) 4615002; e-mail npc@ren02.nic.in; internet www.npcindia.org; f. 1958 to increase productivity and to improve quality by improved techniques which aim at efficient and proper utilization of available resources; autonomous body representing national orgs of employers and labour, govt ministries, professional orgs, local productivity councils, small-scale industries and other interests; 12 regional directorates, 2 regional offices; 75 mems; Chair. AJIT KUMAR; Dir-Gen. K. SRINIVASAN.

National Research Development Corpn: 20–22 Zamroodpur Community Centre, Kailash Colony Extension, New Delhi 110 048; tel. (11) 6417821; fax (11) 6460506; e-mail nrdc@giasd101.vsnl.net.in; internet www.nrdcindia.com; f. 1953 to stimulate development and commercial exploitation of new inventions with financial and technical aid; finances development projects to set up demonstration units in collaboration with industry; exports technology; cap. p.u. Rs39.2m., res and surplus Rs39.4m. (March 1999); Man. Dir N. K. SHARMA.

National Seeds Corpn Ltd: Beej Bhavan, Pusa, New Delhi 110 012; tel. (11) 5712292; fax (11) 5766462; e-mail nsc@vsnl.com; f. 1963 to improve and develop the seed industry; cap. p.u. Rs206.2m., res and surplus Rs173.7m. (March 1999); Chair. and Man. Dir P. D. SUDHAKAR.

The National Small Industries Corpn Ltd: NSIC Bhavan, Okhla Industrial Estate, New Delhi 110 020; tel. (11) 6834697; fax (11) 6848218; e-mail nsicttc@gias0101.vsnl.net.in; internet www.nic.in/nsic; f. 1955 to aid, advise, finance, protect and promote the interests of small industries; establishes and supplies machinery for small industries in other developing countries on turn-key basis; cap. p.u. Rs1,099.9m. (March 1997); all shares held by the Govt; Chair. and Man. Dir M. AHMED.

PEC Ltd: 'Hansalaya', 15 Barakhamba Rd, New Delhi 110 001; tel. (11) 3316372; fax (11) 3314797; e-mail pec@pecltd.org; internet www.pecltd.org; f. 1971; export of engineering, industrial and railway equipment; undertakes turn-key and other projects and management consultancy abroad; countertrade, trading in agrocommodities, construction materials (steel, cement, clinkers, etc.) and fertilizers; cap. p.u. Rs15m., res and surplus Rs178.2m. (March 1999); Chair. and Man. Dir A. K. SRIVASTAVA.

Rehabilitation Industries Corpn Ltd: 25 Mirza Ghalib St, Kolkata 700 016; tel. (33) 2441185; fax (33) 2451085; f. 1959 to create employment opportunities through multi-product industries, ranging from consumer goods to engineering products and services, for refugees from Bangladesh and migrants from Pakistan, repatriates from Myanmar and Sri Lanka, and other immigrants of Indian extraction; cap. p.u. Rs47.6m. (March 1999); Chair. and Man. Dir R. P. THAKRAL.

State Farms Corpn of India Ltd: Farm Bhavan, 14–15 Nehru Place, New Delhi 110 019; tel. (11) 6446903; fax (11) 6226898; e-mail sfci@vsnl.net; f. 1969 to administer the central state farms; activities include the production of quality seeds of high-yielding varieties of wheat, paddy, maize, bajra and jowar; advises on soil conservation, reclamation and development of waste and forest land; consultancy services on farm mechanization; auth. cap. Rs241.9m., res and surplus Rs357.0m. (March 2000); Chair. BHASKAR BARUA; Man. Dir K. ARYA.

State Trading Corpn of India Ltd: Jawahar Vyapar Bhavan, Tolstoy Marg, New Delhi 110 001; tel. (11) 3701100; fax (11) 3701123; e-mail stcofindia@gems.vsnl.net.in; internet www.stcindia.com; f. 1956; govt undertaking dealing in exports and imports; cap. p.u. Rs300m., res and surplus Rs4,154.4m. (March 1999); 18 regional brs and 9 offices overseas; Chair. and Man. Dir S. M. DEWAN; 1,930 employees (1994).

Steel Authority of India Ltd (SAIL): Ispat Bhavan, Lodi Rd, POB 3049, New Delhi 110 003; tel. (11) 4367481; fax (11) 4367015; e-mail sail.co@vsnl.co; internet www.sail.co.in; f. 1973 to provide co-ordinated development of the steel industry in the public sector; integrated steel plants at Bhilai, Bokaro, Durgapur, Rourkela; alloys steel plants at Durgapur and Salem; subsidiaries: Visvesvaraya Iron and Steel Ltd (Karnataka), Indian Iron and Steel Co (West Bengal) and Maharashtra Elektrosmelt Ltd; combined crude steel capacity is 12.5m. metric tons annually; equity cap. Rs41,304m., res and surplus Rs19,314.4m. (March 2000); Chair. and Man. Dir ARVIND PANDE; Dir (Finance) V. S. JAIN; 160,000 employees (2000).

Tea Board of India: 14 B. T. M. Sarani (Brabourne Rd), POB 2172, Kolkata 700 001; tel. (33) 251411; fax (33) 2251417; provides financial assistance to tea research stations; sponsors and finances independent research projects in universities and tech. institutions to supplement the work of tea research establishments; also promotes tea production and export; Chair. NABA KRISHNA DAS.

CHAMBERS OF COMMERCE

Associated Chambers of Commerce and Industry of India (ASSOCHAM): 11 Community Centre, Zamrudpur, New Delhi 110 048; tel. (11) 6292310; fax (11) 6451981; e-mail assocham@sansad.nic.in; internet www.assocham.org; f. 1920; a central org. of 350 chambers of commerce and industry and industrial asscns representing more than 90,000 cos throughout India; 6 promoter chambers, 125 ordinary mems, 48 patron mems and 467 corporate associates; Pres. RAGHU MODY; Sec.-Gen. JAYANT BHUYAN.

Federation of Indian Chambers of Commerce and Industry (FICCI): Federation House, Tansen Marg, New Delhi 110 001; tel. (11) 3738760; fax (11) 3320714; e-mail ficci.bisnet@gems.vsnl.net.in;

internet www.bisnetindia.com; f. 1927; 500 ordinary mems, 53 corporate mems, 1,349 assoc. mems, 190 cttee mems; Pres. CHIRAYUR AMIN; Sec.-Gen. Dr AMIT MITRA.

ICC India: Federation House, Tansen Marg, New Delhi 110 001; tel. (11) 3738760; fax (11) 3320714; e-mail iccindia@del2.vsnl .net.in; internet www.bisnetindia/iccindia/; f. 1929; 35 org. mems, 453 assoc. mems, 8 patron mems, 118 cttee mems; Pres. ARUNACHALAM VELLAYAN; Exec. Dir G. D. AWASTHI.

Associated Chambers of Commerce and Industry of Uttar Pradesh: 2/122 Vijaya Khand, Gomti Nagar, Lucknow 226 016; tel. (522) 301956; fax (522) 301958; e-mail asochmup@lw1.vsnl.net.in; 495 mems; Pres. U. K. MODI; Sec.-Gen. R. K. JAIN.

Bengal Chamber of Commerce and Industry: 6 Netaji Subhas Rd, Kolkata 700 001; tel. (33) 2203733; fax (33) 2201289; e-mail bencham@cal3.vsnl.net.in; f. 1853; 242 mems; Pres. S. B. GANGULY; Sec. PRADIP DAS GUPTA.

Bengal National Chamber of Commerce and Industry: 23 R. N. Mukherjee Rd, Kolkata 700 001; tel. (33) 2482951; fax (33) 2487058; e-mail bncci@bncci.com; internet www.bncci.com; f. 1887; 500 mems, 35 affiliated industrial and trading asscns; Pres. B. N. KUMAR; Sec. D. P. NAG.

Bharat Chamber of Commerce: 9 Park Mansions, 2nd Floor, 57-A Park Street, Kolkata, 700 016; tel. (33) 2299591; fax (33) 2294947; f. 1900; c. 500 mems; Pres. H. M. BANGAR; Sec. K. SARMA.

Bihar Chamber of Commerce: Khem Chand Chaudhary Marg, POB 71, Patna 800 001; tel. (612) 670535; fax (612) 689505; e-mail secgen@dte.vsnl.net.in; f. 1926; 800 ordinary mems, 125 org. mems, 10 life mems; Pres. HARIHAR NATH; Sec.-Gen. S. P. GUPTA.

Bombay Chamber of Commerce and Industry: Mackinnon Mackenzie Bldg, 4 Shoorji Vallabhdas Rd, Ballard Estate, POB 473, Mumbai 400 001; tel. (22) 2614681; fax (22) 2621213; e-mail bccm@ giasbm01.vsnl.net.in; internet www.bombaychamber.com; f. 1836; 824 ordinary mems, 526 assoc. mems, 75 hon. mems; Pres. K. K. NOHRIA; Exec. Dir L. A. D'SOUZA.

Calcutta Chamber of Commerce: 18H Park St, Stephen Court, Kolkata 700 071; tel. (33) 2290758; fax (33) 2298961; 450 mems; Pres. HEMANT KANORIA; Sec. SATISH JHUNJHUNWALA.

Chamber of Commerce and Industry (Regd): O.B 31, Rail Head Complex, Jammu 180 012; tel. (191) 455151; fax (191) 430000; 1,069 mems; Pres. RAM SAHAI; Sec. Gen. RAJENDRA MOTIAL.

Cochin Chamber of Commerce and Industry: Bristow Rd, Willingdon Island, POB 503, Kochi 682 003; tel. (484) 668349; fax (484) 668651; e-mail chamber@md2.vsnl.net.in; internet www .cochinchamber.com; f. 1857; 168 mems; Pres. A. K. ATAL; Sec. EAPEN KALAPURAKAL.

Council of EU Chambers of Commerce in India: 3rd Floor, Y.B. Chavan Centre, Gen. J. Bhosale Marg, Mumbai 400 021; tel. (22) 2854563; fax (22) 2854564; e-mail ceuc@bom3.vsnl.net.in; 240 mems; Pres. JASU SHAH; Sec. C. H. IYER.

Federation of Andhra Pradesh Chambers of Commerce and Industry: 11-6-841, Red Hills, POB 14, Hyderabad 500 004; tel. (40) 3393658; fax (40) 3395083; e-mail fapcci@hd1.vsnl.net.in; f. 1917; 2,400 mems; Pres. E. J. S. RAO; Sec. K. NARAYANA RAO.

Federation of Karnataka Chambers of Commerce and Industry: Kempegowda Rd, Bangalore 560 009; tel. (80) 2262355; fax (80) 2251826; e-mail fkcci@mantraonline.com; f. 1916; 2,150 mems; Pres. K. RAMASWAMY; Sec. C. MANOHAR.

Federation of Madhya Pradesh Chambers of Commerce and Industry: Udyog Bhavan, 129A Malviya Nagar, Bhopal 462 003; tel. (755) 551451; fax (755) 551451; f. 1975; 500 ordinary mems, 58 asscn mems; Pres. RANJIT VITHALDAS; Sec.-Gen. PRAFULLA MAHESHWARI.

Goa Chamber of Commerce: Goa Chamber Bldg, Rua de Ormuz, POB 59, Panjim 403 001; tel. (832) 224223; fax (832) 223420; f. 1908; more than 373 mems; Pres. DATTARAJ V. SALGAOCAR; Sec. O. L. DA LAPA-SOARES.

Gujarat Chamber of Commerce and Industry: Shri Ambica Mills, Gujarat Chamber Bldg, Ashram Rd, POB 4045, Ahmedabad 380 009; tel. (79) 6582301; fax (79) 6587992; e-mail bis@ gujaratchamber.org; internet www.gujaratchamber.org; f. 1949; 7,745 mems; Pres. RATANPRAKASH A. GUPTA; Sec.-Gen. BIPIN D. PATEL.

Indian Chamber of Commerce: India Exchange, 4 India Exchange Place, Kolkata 700 001; tel. (33) 2203243; fax (33) 2204790; e-mail icccal@giascl.01.vsnl.net.in; internet www .allindia.com/icc; f. 1925; 342 ordinary mems, 46 assoc. mems, 10 corporate group mems, 17 affiliated asscns; Pres. C. K. DHANUKA; Sec.-Gen. NAZEEB ARIF.

Indian Chamber of Commerce and Industry: Four Square House, 49 Community Centre, New Friends Colony, New Delhi 110 065; tel. (11) 6921741; fax (11) 6840775; e-mail godfrey@del2 .vsnl.net.in; Pres. L. K. MODI; Hon. Sec. R. P. SWAMI.

Indian Merchants' Chamber: IMC Bldg, IMC Marg, Churchgate, Mumbai 400 020; tel. (22) 2025438; fax (22) 2048508; e-mail imc@imcnet.org; internet www.imcnet.org; f. 1907; 185 asscn mems, 2,700 mem. firms; Pres. PRADEEP B. CHINAI; Sec. P. N. MOGRE.

Indo-American Chamber of Commerce: 1C Vulcan Insurance Bldg, Veer Nariman Rd, Mumbai 400 020; tel. (22) 2821413; fax (22) 2046141; e-mail iacc@vsnl.com; 2,700 mems; Pres. AMIT KUMAR SEN; Sec.-Gen. SUBRAMANIAM AYYAR; 4 regional offices, 8 br. offices and 1 rep. office in USA.

Indo-French Chamber of Commerce and Industry: B-5 Venkatesh Chambers, Prescot Rd, Mumbai 400 001; tel. (22) 2064660; fax (22) 2064619; e-mail ifcci@lwbbs.net; f. 1977; 600 mems; Pres. BINAY KUMAR; Exec. Dir FRANCIS CLEMENT DE LA FORGE.

Indo-German Chamber of Commerce: Maker Towers 'E', 1st Floor, Cuffe Parade, Mumbai 400 005; tel. (22) 2186131; fax (22) 2180523; e-mail bombay@indo-german.com; internet www.indo -german.com; f. 1956; 6,000 mems; Pres. SURAT L. MEHTA; Dir-Gen. Dr G. KRUEGER.

Karnataka Chamber of Commerce and Industry: Karnataka Chamber Bldg, J. C. Nagar, Hubli 580 020; tel. (836) 365223; fax (836) 360933; e-mail kccihbl@blr.vsnl.net.in; internet www .kccihubli.com; f. 1928; 2,500 mems; Pres. D. S. GUDDODAGI; Hon. Sec. D. R. KHOBARE.

Madhya Pradesh Chamber of Commerce and Industry: Chamber Bhavan, Sanatan Dharam Mandir Marg, Gwalior 474 009; tel. (751) 332916; fax (751) 323844; f. 1906; 1,705 mems; Pres. V. K. GANGWAL; Hon. Sec. VIRENDRA BAPNA.

Madras Chamber of Commerce and Industry: Karumuttu Centre, 634 Anna Salai, Chennai 600 035; tel. (44) 4349452; fax (44) 4349164; e-mail mascham@md3.vsnl.net.in; internet www.mcci-india.com; f. 1836; 286 mem. firms, 47 assoc., 14 affiliated, 11 honorary, 3 others; Pres. L. SABARETNAM; Sec. R. SUBRAMANIAN.

Maharashtra Chamber of Commerce and Industry: Oricon House, 6th Floor, 12 K. Dubhash Marg, Fort, Mumbai 400 001; tel. (22) 2855859; fax (22) 2855861; e-mail maharashtrachamber @vsnl.com; f. 1927; 1,954 mems; Pres. KHUSHALCHANDRA PODDAR; Sec.-Gen. DILIP SALVEKAR.

Mahratta Chamber of Commerce, Industries and Agriculture: Tilak Rd, POB 525, Pune 411 002; tel. (20) 4440371; fax (20) 4447902; e-mail mccipune@vsnl.com; internet www.mcciapune.com; f. 1934; 1,450 mems; Pres. ARUN FIRODIA; Sec.-Gen. D. K. ABHYANKAR.

Merchants' Chamber of Commerce: 15B Hemanta Basu Sarani, Kolkata 700 001; tel. (33) 2483123; fax (33) 2488657; e-mail mercham@cal.vsnl.net.in; f. 1901; 600 mems; Pres. RAVI TODI; Exec. Dir R. K. SEN.

Merchants' Chamber of Uttar Pradesh: 14/76 Civil Lines, Kanpur 208 001; tel. (512) 291306; fax (512) 210238; f. 1932; 180 mems; Pres. J. K. LOHIA; Sec. P. N. DIXIT.

North India Chamber of Commerce and Industry: 9 Gandhi Rd, Dehra Dun, Uttar Pradesh; tel. (935) 23479; f. 1967; 105 ordinary mems, 29 asscn mems, 7 mem. firms, 91 assoc. mems; Pres. DEV PANDHI; Hon. Sec. ASHOK K. NARANG.

Oriental Chamber of Commerce: 6A Dr Rajendra Prasad Sarani (Clive Row), Kolkata 700 001; tel. (33) 2202120; fax (33) 2203609; f. 1932; 255 ordinary mems, 3 assoc. mems; Pres. Dr SYED AHMED FEROZIE; Sec. KAZI ABU ZOBER.

PHD Chamber of Commerce and Industry: PHD House, Thapar Floor, 4/2 Siri Institutional Area, opp. Asian Games Village, POB 130, New Delhi 110 016; tel. (11) 6863801; fax (11) 6863135; e-mail phdcci@del2.vsnl.net.in; f. 1905; 1,585 mems, 92 asscn mems; Pres. SUSHIL ANSAL; Sec.-Gen. H. S. TANDON.

Rajasthan Chamber of Commerce and Industry: Rajasthan Chamber Bhavan, M.I. Rd, Jaipur 302 003; tel. (141) 565163; fax (141) 561419; e-mail rajcham@jpl.vsnl.net.in; internet www .rajchamber.com; 1,000 mems; Pres. S. K. MANSINGHKA; Hon. Sec.-Gen. Dr K. L. JAIN.

Southern India Chamber of Commerce and Industry: Indian Chamber Bldgs, 6 Esplanade, POB 1208, Chennai 600 108; tel. (44) 5342228; fax (44) 5341876; e-mail sicci@md3.vsnl.net.in; f. 1909; 1,000 mems; Pres. R. MUTHU; Sec. J. PRASAD DAVIDS.

Upper India Chamber of Commerce: 14/113 Civil Lines, POB 63, Kanpur 208 001; tel. (512) 543905; fax (512) 210684; f. 1888; 127 mems; Pres. DILIP BHARGAVA; Sec. S. P. SRIVASTAVA.

Utkal Chamber of Commerce and Industry Ltd: Barabati Stadium, Cuttack 753 005; tel. (671) 301211; fax (671) 302059; f. 1964; 225 mems; Pres. Dr S. K. TAMOTIA; Sec. SHASHI SEKHAR SAMAL.

Uttar Pradesh Chamber of Commerce: 15/197 Civil Lines, Kanpur 208 001; tel. 211696; f. 1914; 200 mems; Pres. Dr B. K. MODI; Sec. AFTAB SAMI.

INDUSTRIAL AND TRADE ASSOCIATIONS

Ahmedabad Textile Mills' Association: Ashram Rd, Navrangpura, POB 4056, Ahmedabad 380 009; tel. (79) 6582273; fax (79)

6588574; f. 1891; 29 mems; Pres. SAMVEG A. LALBHAI; Sec.-Gen. ABHINAVA SHUKLA.

All India Federation of Master Printers: A-370, 2nd Floor, Defence Colony, New Delhi 110 024; tel. (11) 4601571; fax (11) 4601570; f. 1953; e-mail aifmp@hotmail.com; 46 affiliates, 700 mems; Pres. V. K. MALIK; Hon. Gen. Sec. GOVIND BHARGAVA.

All India Manufacturers' Organization (AIMO): Jeevan Sahakar, 4th Floor, Sir P.M. Rd, Fort, Mumbai 400 001; tel. (22) 2661016; fax (22) 2660838; f. 1941; 800 mems; Pres. KAMALKUMAR R. DUJODWALA; Hon. Gen. Sec. SURESH DEORA.

All India Plastics Manufacturers' Association: AIPMA House, A-52, St No. 1, MIDC, Andheri (East), Mumbai 400 093; tel. (22) 8217324; fax (22) 8216390; e-mail aipma@bom2.vsnl.net.in; internet www.aipma.org; f. 1947; 2,318 mems; Pres. ARVIND M. MEHTA; Hon. Sec. SURESH D. ATRE.

All India Shippers' Council: Federation House, Tansen Marg, New Delhi 110 001; tel. (11) 3738760; fax (11) 3320714; f. 1967; 200 mems; Chair. RAMU S. DEORA; Sec. M. Y. REDDY.

Association of Man-made Fibre Industry of India: Resham Bhavan, 78 Veer Nariman Rd, Mumbai 400 020; tel. (22) 2040009; fax (22) 2049172; f. 1954; 7 mems; Pres. P. S. SHARMA; Sec. S. K. MARATHE.

Automotive Component Manufacturers' Association of India: 203–205 Kirti Deep Bldg, Nangal Raya Business Centre, New Delhi 110 046; tel. (11) 5501669; fax (11) 5593189; e-mail acma@vsnl.com; internet www.indianauto.com; 398 mems; Pres. L. GANESH; Exec. Dir VISHNU MATHUR.

Automotive Tyre Manufacturers' Association: PHD House, opp. Asian Games Village, Siri Fort Institutional Area, New Delhi 110 016; tel. (11) 6851187; fax (11) 6864799; e-mail atma@nda .vsnl.net.in; 10 mems; Chair. ONKAR S. KANWAR; Dir-Gen. D. RAVINDRAN.

Bharat Krishak Samaj (Farmers' Forum, India): Dr Panjabrao Deshmukh Krishak Bhavan, A-1 Nizamuddin West, New Delhi 110 013; tel. (11) 4619508; fax (11) 4619509; e-mail ffi@mantraonline .com; f. 1954; national farmers' org.; 5m. ordinary mems, 70,000 life mems; Chair. Dr BAL RAM JAKHAR; Exec. Chair./Gen. Sec. Dr KRISHAN BIR CHAUDHARY.

Bombay Metal Exchange Ltd: 88/90, Gulalwadi, Kika St, 1st Floor, Mumbai 400 004; tel. (22) 2421964; fax (22) 2422640; e-mail bme@bom8.vsnl.net.in; promotes trade and industry in non-ferrous metals; 460 mems; Pres. ASHOK G. BAFNA; Sec. T. S. B. IYER.

Bombay Shroffs Association: 233 Shaikh Memon St, Mumbai 400 002; tel. (22) 3425588; f. 1910; 410 mems; Pres. SEVANTILAL P. SHAH; Hon. Secs RAMESH S. SURA, VASANTLAL M. CHOKSI.

Calcutta Flour Mills Association: 25/B Shakespeare Sarani, Kolkata 700 017; tel. (33) 2476723; fax (33) 2209748; f. 1932; 28 mems; Chair. D. N. JATIA; Hon. Sec. R. BHAGAT.

Calcutta Tea Traders' Association: 6 Netaji Subhas Rd, Kolkata 700 001; tel. (33) 2201574; fax (33) 2201289; f. 1886; 1,490 mems; Chair. G. BHALLA; Sec. J. KALYANA SUNDARAM.

Cement Manufacturers' Association: Vishnu Kiran Chambers, 2142-47 Gurudwara Rd, Karol Bagh, New Delhi 110 005; tel. (11) 5763026; fax (11) 5738476; e-mail cmand@nda.vsnl.net.in; 57 mems; 121 major cement plants; Pres. T. M. M. NAMBIAR; Sec.-Gen. R. PARTHA SARATHY.

Confederation of Indian Industry (CII): 23 Institutional Area, Lodi Rd, New Delhi 110 003; tel. (11) 4629994; fax (11) 4626149; e-mail cii@ciionline.org; internet www.ciionline.org; f. 1974; 3,800 mem. cos; Pres. ARUN BHARAT RAM; Dir-Gen. TARUN DAS.

Consumer Electronics and Television Manufacturers' Association (CETMA): J-13, Jangpura Extension, New Delhi 110 014; tel. (11) 4327777; fax (11) 4321616; Pres. RAJEEV KARWAL; Sec.-Gen. SURESH KHANNA.

East India Cotton Association: Cotton Exchange Bldg, 9th Floor, 175 Kalbadevi Rd, Marwari Bazar, Mumbai 400 002; tel. (22) 2404876; fax (22) 2405578; e-mail eica@bom8.vsnl.net.in; f. 1921; 411 mems; Pres. SURESH A. KOTAK; P. K. C. SHARMA.

Electronic Component Industries Association (ELCINA): ELCINA House, 422 Okhla Industrial Estate, New Delhi 110 020; tel. (11) 6928053; fax (11) 6923440; e-mail elcina@del2.vsnl.net.in; internet www.elcina.com; f. 1967; Pres. K. VIJAY KUMAR GUPTA; Sec.-Gen. SOMNATH CHATTERJEE.

Federation of Gujarat Industries: Federation Bldg, Sampatrao Colony, R. C. Dutt Rd, Baroda 390 007; tel. (265) 311101; fax (265) 339054; e-mail fgi@zaverchand.co.in; internet www.zaverchand .co.in/federationofgujarat/; f. 1918; 450 mems; Pres. RAMESH AGRAWAL; Sec.-Gen. Dr PARESH RAVAL.

Federation of Hotel and Restaurant Associations of India: B-82 Himalaya House, 23 K. G. Marg, New Delhi 110 001; tel. (11) 3323770; fax (11) 3318781; e-mail fhrai@vsnl.com; internet www.fhrai.com; Pres. SANTOSH R. SHETTY; Sec.-Gen. SHYAM SURI.

Federation of Indian Export Organisations: PHD House, 3rd Floor, Siri Institutional Area, Hauz Khas, New Delhi 110 016; tel. (11) 6851310; fax (11) 6863087; e-mail fieo@nda.vsnl.net.in; f. 1965; 5,900 mems; Pres. K. K. JAIN; Dir-Gen. RANJIT LALL.

The Fertiliser Association of India: 10 Shaheed Jit Singh Marg, New Delhi 110 067; tel. (11) 6517305; fax (11) 6960052; e-mail fai@vsnl.com; internet www.fadinap.org/india/; f. 1955; 1,796 mems; Chair. AJAY SHRIRAM; Dir-Gen. PRATAP NARAYAN.

Grain, Rice and Oilseeds Merchants' Association: Grainseeds House, 72/80 Yusef Meheralli Rd, Mumbai 400 003; tel. (22) 3754021; f. 1899; 1,200 mems; Pres. HIRJI NANJI KENIA.

Indian Drug Manufacturers' Association: 102B Poonam Chambers, Dr A. B. Rd, Worli, Mumbai 400 018; tel. (22) 4944624; fax (22) 4950723; e-mail idma@giasbm01.vsnl.net.in; 600 mems; Pres. N. H. ISRANI; Sec.-Gen. I. A. ALVA.

Indian Electrical and Electronics Manufacturers' Association (IEEMA): 501 Kakad Chambers, 132 Dr Annie Besant Rd, Worli, Mumbai 400 018; tel. (22) 4936528; fax (22) 4932705; e-mail mumbai@ieema.org; internet www.ieema.org; f. 1948; 400 mems; Pres. RAJESH JAIN; Sec.-Gen. SUNIL P. MORE.

Indian Jute Mills Association: Royal Exchange, 6 Netaji Subhas Rd, Kolkata 700 001; tel. (33) 2209918; fax (33) 2205643; e-mail ijma@cal2.vsnl.net.in; sponsors and operates export promotion, research and product development; regulates labour relations; 33 mems; Chair. SANJAY KAJARIA; Dir Gen. S. K. BHATTACHARYA.

Indian Leather Industries Association: India Exchange, 4 India Exchange Place, 7th Floor, Kolkata 700 001; tel. (33) 2207763; fax (33) 2203973; 70 mems; Pres. S. S. KUMAR; Exec. Dir S. K. GUPTA.

Indian Machine Tool Manufacturers' Association: 17 Nangal Raya Commercial Complex, New Delhi 110 046; tel. (11) 5592814; fax (11) 5599882; e-mail imtma@del2.vsnl.net.in; internet www .imtex.org; 400 mems; Pres. SHRINIVAS G. SHIRGURKAR; Sec. A. MUKHERJEE.

Indian Mining Association: 6 Netaji Subhas Rd, Kolkata 700 001; tel. (33) 263861; f. 1892; 50 mems; Sec. K. MUKERJEE.

Indian Mining Federation: 135 Biplabi Rash Behari Basu Rd, 2nd Floor, Kolkata 700 001; tel. (33) 2428975; f. 1913; 40 mems; Chair. V. K. ARORA; Sec. S. K. GHOSE.

Indian Motion Picture Producers' Association: IMPPA House, Dr Ambedkar Rd, Bandra (West), Mumbai 400 050; tel. (22) 6486344; fax (22) 6480757; f. 1938; 1,700 mems; SHAKTI SAMANTA; Sec. SHASHANK JARE.

Indian National Shipowners' Association: 22 Maker Tower, F, Cuffe Parade, Mumbai 400 005; tel. (22) 2182103; fax (22) 2182104; e-mail insamum@vsnl.com; f. 1929; 30 mems; Pres. ROHET N. TOLANI; CEO B. V. NILKUND.

Indian Oilseed & Produce Exporters' Association: 78/79 Bajaj Bhavan, Nariman Point, Mumbai 400 021; tel. (22) 2023225; fax (22) 2029236; e-mail iopea@bom3.vsnl.net.in; internet www.iopea.org; f. 1956; 350 mems; Chair. TUSHAR TANNA; Sec. A. N. SUBRAMANIAN.

Indian Paper Mills Association: India Exchange, 8th Floor, India Exchange Place, Kolkata 700 001; tel. (33) 2203242; fax (33) 2204495; f. 1939; 37 mems; Pres. K. K. KHEMKA; Sec. B. GHOSH.

Indian Refractory Makers' Association: 5 Lala Lajpat Rai Sarani, 4th Floor, Kolkata 700 020; tel. (33) 2810868; fax (33) 2408357; e-mail irma@giascl01.vsnl.net.in; internet www.irmaindia .com; 85 mems; Chair. C. D. KAMATH; Exec. Dir P. DAS GUPTA.

Indian Soap and Toiletries Makers' Association: 614 Raheja Centre, Free Press Journal Marg, Mumbai 400 021; tel. (22) 2824115; fax (22) 2853649; e-mail istma@bom3.vsnl.net.in; 38 mems; Pres. B. V. PATEL; Sec.-Gen. V. P. MENON.

Indian Sugar Mills Association: 'Sugar House', 39 Nehru Place, New Delhi 110 019; tel. (11) 6472554; fax (11) 6472409; e-mail sugarmil@nda.vsnl.net.in; f. 1932; 200 mems; Pres. TILAK DHAR; Dir-Gen. S. L. JAIN.

Indian Tea Association: Royal Exchange, 6 Netaji Subhas Rd, Kolkata 700 001; tel. (33) 2102474; fax (33) 2434301; e-mail ita@cal2.vsnl.net.in; f. 1881; 63 mem. cos; 490 tea estates; Chair. R. S. JHAWAR; Sec.-Gen. D. CHAKRABARTI.

Indian Woollen Mills' Federation: Churchgate Chambers, 7th Floor, 5 New Marine Lines, Mumbai 400 020; tel. (22) 2624372; fax (22) 2624675; e-mail iwmf@bom3.vsnl.net.in; f. 1963; 50 mems; Chair. ARUN K. CHURIWAL; Sec.-Gen. A. C. CHAUDHURI.

Industries and Commerce Association: ICO Association Rd, POB 70, Dhanbad 826 001; tel. (326) 303147; fax (326) 303787; f. 1933; 70 mems; Pres. B. N. SINGH; Sec. K. R. CHAKRAVARTY.

Jute Balers' Association: 12 India Exchange Place, Kolkata 700 001; tel. (33) 2201491; f. 1909; 300 mems; Chair. NIRMAL KUMAR BHUTORIA; Sec. SUJIT CHOUDHURY.

Maharashtra Motor Parts Dealers' Association: 13 Kala Bhavan, 3 Mathew Rd, Mumbai 400 004; tel. (22) 3614468; 375 mems; Pres. J. C. UNADKAT; Sec. J. R. CHANDAWALLA.

Millowners' Association, Mumbai: Elphinstone Bldg, 10 Veer Nariman Rd, Fort, POB 95, Mumbai 400 001; tel. (22) 2040411; fax (22) 2832611; f. 1875; 25 mem. cos; Chair. HIREN M. SHAH; Sec.-Gen. V. Y. TAMHANE.

Mumbai Motor Merchants' Association Ltd: 304 Sukh Sagar, N. S. Patkar Marg, Mumbai 400 007; tel. (22) 8112769; 409 mems; Pres. S. TARLOCHAN SINGH ANAND; Gen. Sec. S. BHUPINDER SINGH SETHI.

Mumbai Textile Merchants' Mahajan: 250 Sheikh Memon St, Mumbai 400 002; tel. (22) 2065750; fax (22) 2000311; f. 1881; 1,900 mems; Pres. SURENDRA TULSIDAS SAVAI; Hon. Secs DHIRAJ S. KOTHARI, RAJESH B. PATEL.

National Association of Software and Service Companies (NASSCOM): International Youth Centre, Uma Shankar Dixit Marg, Chanakyapuri, New Delhi 110 021; tel. (11) 3015416; fax (11) 3015452; e-mail nasscom@nasscom.org; internet www.nasscom.org; more than 650 mems; Pres. (vacant).

Organisation of Pharmaceutical Producers of India (OPPI): Cook's Blg, 1st Floor, 324 Dr Dadabhoy Naoroji Rd, Fort, Mumbai 400 001; tel. (22) 2045509; fax (22) 2044705; e-mail oppi@bom3.vsnl.net.in; internet www.indiaoppi.com; 61 ordinary mems, 6 associate mems; Pres. H. R. KHUSROKHAN; Sec.-Gen. R. D. JOSHI.

Society of Indian Automobile Manufacturers: Core 4B, 5th Floor, India Habitat Centre, Lodhi Rd, New Delhi 110 003; tel. (11) 4647810; fax (11) 4648222; e-mail siamsoc@bol.net.in; f. 1960; 33 mems; Pres. VENU SRINIVASAN; Exec. Dir RAJAT NANDI.

Southern India Mills' Association: Racecourse, Coimbatore 641 018, Tamil Nadu; tel. (422) 211391; fax (422) 217160; f. 1933; 347 mems; Chair. B. K. K. VANAVARAYAR; Sec. P. R. SUBRAMANIAN.

Surgical Manufacturers and Traders' Association: 60 Darya Ganj, New Delhi 110 002; tel. (11) 3271027; Pres. ASHOK SARIN; Sec. RAVI AWASTHI.

Synthetic and Art Silk Mills' Association Ltd: 3rd Floor, Sasmira Bldg, Sasmira Marg, Worli, Mumbai 400 025; tel. (22) 4945372; fax (22) 4938350; e-mail sasma_100@pacific.net.in; f. 1939; 150 mems; Chair. V. S. CHALKE; Sec. K. A. SAMUEL.

Telecom Equipment Manufacturers' Association of India (TEMA): PHD House, 4th Floor, R. K. Dalmia Wing, opp Asian Games Village, New Delhi 110 016; tel. (11) 6859621; fax (11) 6859620; e-mail tema@del2.vsnl.net.in; internet www.india-times.com/tema; Exec. Sec. VINOD TULI.

Travel Agents' Association of India: 2D Lawrence and Mayo House, 276 Dr D. N. Rd, Mumbai 400 001; tel. (22) 2074022; fax (22) 2074559; e-mail travels@bom2.vsnl.net.in; 1,600 mems; Pres. PRADIP MADHAVJI; Hon. Sec.-Gen. SHUBHADA JOSHI.

United Planters' Association of Southern India (UPASI): Glenview, POB 11, Coonoor 643 101; tel. (423) 30270; fax (423) 32030; e-mail upasi@vsnl.com; f. 1893; 1,100 mems; Pres. E. R. JOSEPH; Sec.-Gen. K. J. JOSEPH.

EMPLOYERS' ORGANIZATIONS

Council of Indian Employers: Federation House, Tansen Marg, New Delhi 110 001; tel. (11) 3738760; fax (11) 3320714; f. 1956; comprises:

All India Organisation of Employers (AIOE): Federation House, Tansen Marg, New Delhi 110 001; tel. (11) 3738760; fax (11) 3320714; f. 1932; 210 mems (incl. 158 associate mems); Pres. N. SRINIVASAN; Sec.-Gen. Dr AMIT MITRA.

Employers' Federation of India (EFI): Army and Navy Bldg, 148 Mahatma Gandhi Rd, Mumbai 400 023; tel. (22) 2844232; fax (22) 2843028; f. 1933; 28 asscn mems, 176 ordinary mems, 18 hon. mems; Pres. ARVIND R. DOSHI; Sec.-Gen. S. K. NANDA.

Standing Conference of Public Enterprises (SCOPE): SCOPE Complex, 1st Floor, Core No. 8, 7 Lodi Rd, New Delhi 110 003; tel. (11) 4360101; fax (11) 4361371; e-mail mahakeem@nicsco.delhi.nic.in; f. 1973; representative body of all central public enterprises in India; advises the Govt and public enterprises on matters of major policy and co-ordination; trade enquiries, regarding imports and exports of commodities, carried out on behalf of mems; 198 mems; Chair. ARUN PRASADA; Sec.-Gen. M. A. HAKEEM.

Employers' Association of Northern India: 14/113 Civil Lines, POB 344, Kanpur 208 001; tel. (512) 210513; f. 1937; 190 mems; Chair. RAJIV KEHR; Sec.-Gen. P. DUBEY.

Employers' Federation of Southern India: Karumuttu Centre, 1st Floor, 498 Anna Salai, Chennai 600 035; tel. (44) 4349452; fax (44) 4349164; f. 1920; 463 mems; Pres. C. B. ABYSHEKAR; Sec. N. KANNAN.

UTILITIES

Electricity

Central Electricity Regulatory Authority (CERC): New Delhi; responsible for technical co-ordination and supervision of electricity programmes; advises Ministry of Power on all technical, financial and economic issues; Chair. S.L. RAO.

Bombay Suburban Electric Supply Ltd: 6th Floor, Nagin Mahal, 82 Veer Nariman Rd, Mumbai 400 020; tel. (22) 2043287; fax (22) 2041280; internet www.bses.com; f. 1929; has monopoly in supply of electricity to Mumbai; Chair. and Man. Dir R. V. SHAHI.

Calcutta Electricity Supply Corpn Ltd (CESC): CESC House, Chouringhee Sq., Kolkata 700 001; tel. (33) 2256040; fax (33) 2256334; f. 1978; generation and supply of electricity; Chair. R. P. GOENKA; Man. Dir SUMANTRA BANERJEE.

Damodar Valley Corpn: DVC Towers, VIP Rd, Kolkata 700 054; tel. (33) 3551935; fax (33) 3551937; e-mail dvchq@wb.nic.in; f. 1948 to administer the first multipurpose river valley project in India, the Damodar Valley Project, which aims at unified development of irrigation, flood control and power generation in West Bengal and Bihar; operates nine power stations, incl. thermal, hydel and gas turbine; power generating capacity 2,761.5 MW (1999); Chair. J. C. JETLI.

Essar Power Ltd: Essar House, Mahalaxmi, Mumbai 400 034; tel. (22) 4950606; fax (22) 4954787; Chair. S. N. RUIA.

National Hydroelectric Power Corporation: Sector 33, Faridabad 121 003; f. 1975; Chair and Man. Dir YOGENDRA PRASAD.

National Thermal Power Corporation Ltd: Core-7, SCOPE Complex, Lodi Rd, New Delhi 110 003; tel. (11) 4360100; fax (11) 4361018; e-mail pr@ntpcn.ernet.in; internet www.ntpc.net; f. 1975; operates 11 coal-fired and five gas-fired power stations throughout India; Chair. and Man. Dir C. P. JAIN; 24,000 employees.

Noida Power Co Ltd: A-46, Sector 26, Noida, Uttar Pradesh 201 301; tel. (11) 8520567; fax (11) 8533542; f. 1922; distribution of electricity; Chair. and Man. Dir USHA CHATRATH; CEO P. NEOGI.

Nuclear Power Corporation of India Ltd: Commerce Center-1, World Trade Centre, Cuffe Parade, Mumbai 400 005; tel. (22) 2182171; fax (22) 2180109; internet www.npcil.org; Chair. and Man. Dir V. K. CHATURVEDI.

Power Grid Corporation of India Ltd: B-9, Qutab Institutional Area, Katwaria Sarai, New Delhi 110 016; tel. (11) 6560121; fax (11) 6560039; internet www.powergridindia.com; f. 1989; responsible for formation of national power grid; Chair. and Man. Dir R. P. SINGH.

Tata Power Co Ltd: Bombay House, 24 Homi Mody St, Mumbai 400 001; tel. (22) 2048331; fax (22) 2040505; generation, transmission and distribution of electrical energy; Chair. RATAN N. TATA; Man. Dir ADI J. ENGINEER.

Thana Electric Supply Co Ltd: Asian Bldg, 1st Floor, 17 Ramji Kamani Marg, Ballard Estate, Mumbai 400 001; tel. (22) 2615444; fax (22) 2611069; e-mail thanaele@bom2.vsnl.net.in; f. 1927; Man. Dir SURESH S. MEMMADY.

Gas

Gas Authority of India Ltd: 16 Bhikaji Cama Place, R. K. Puram, Delhi 110 066; tel. (11) 6172580; fax (11) 6185941; e-mail name@gail.com.in; internet www.nic.in/gail; f. 1984; 80% state-owned; transports, processes and markets natural gas; constructing gas-based petrochemical complex; Chair. and Man. Dir C. R. PRASAD; 1,513 employees.

Water

Brihanmumbai Municipal Corporation (Hydraulic Engineers' Department): Municipal Corporation Offices, Ground Floor, Annex Bldg, Mahapalika Marg, Mumbai 400 001; tel. (22) 2620025; fax (22) 2700532; Head Eng. S. N. TURKAR.

Calcutta Municipal Corporation (Water Supply Department): 5 S. N. Banerjee Rd, Kolkata 700 013; tel. (33) 2444518; fax (33) 2442578; f. 1870; Chief Municipal Eng. DIBYENDU ROY CHOWDHURY.

Chennai Metropolitan Water Supply and Sewerage Board: No. 1 Pumping Station Rd, Chintadripet, Chennai 600 002; tel. (44) 8525717; fax (44) 831243; f. 1978; Chair. and Man. Dir SANTHA SHEELA NAIR.

Delhi Water Supply and Sewage Disposal Undertaking: Varunalaya Phase II, Jhandewalan, New Delhi 110 005; tel. (11) 7535944; fax (11) 7535939; part of the Delhi Municipal Corporation (f. 1957).

TRADE UNIONS

Indian National Trade Union Congress (INTUC): 4 Bhai Veer Singh Marg, New Delhi 110 001; tel. (11) 3747768; fax (11) 3364244; e-mail intuchq@del3.vsnl.net.in; f. 1947; 3,796 affiliated unions with a total membership of 6,464,024; affiliated to ICFTU; 25 state brs and 29 nat. feds; Pres. G. SANJEEVA REDDY; Gen. Sec. SUBRATA MUKHERJEE.

Indian National Cement Workers' Federation: Mazdoor Karyalaya, Congress House, Mumbai 400 004; tel. (22) 3871809; fax (22) 3870981; 49,000 mems; 38 affiliated unions; Pres. H. N. TRIVEDI; Gen. Sec. N. NANJAPPAN.

Indian National Chemical Workers' Federation: Tel Rasayan Bhavan, Tilak Rd, Dadar, Mumbai 400 014; tel. (22) 4121742; fax (22) 4130950; 35,000 mems; Pres. RAJA KULKARNI; Gen. Sec. R. D. BHARADWAJ.

Indian National Electricity Workers' Federation: 392 Sector 21-B, Faridabad 121 001; tel. (129) 215089; fax (129) 215868; 276,113 mems; 151 affiliated unions; Pres. D. P. PATHAK; Gen. Sec. S. L. PASSEY.

Indian National Metal Workers' Federation: 35 K Rd, Jamshedpur 831 001; tel. (657) 431475; Pres. N. K. BHATT; Gen. Sec. S. GOPESHWAR.

Indian National Mineworkers' Federation: Imperial House, 13 Ganesh Chandra Ave, Kolkata 700 013; tel. (33) 260987; fax (33) 2159644; f. 1949; 351,454 mems in 139 affiliated unions; Pres. RAJENDRA P. SINGH; Gen. Sec. S. Q. ZAMA.

Indian National Paper Mill Workers' Federation: 6/B, LIGH, Barkatpura, Hyderabad 500 027; tel. (40) 7564706; Pres. G. SANJEEVA REDDY; Gen. Sec. R. CHANDRASEKHARAN.

Indian National Port and Dock Workers' Federation: 15 Coal Dock Rd, Kolkata 700 043; tel. (33) 455929; f. 1954; 18 affiliated unions; 81,000 mems; Pres. JANAKI MUKHERJEE; Gen. Sec. G. KALAN.

Indian National Sugar Mills Workers' Federation: A-176, Darulsafa Marg, Lucknow 226 001; tel. (522) 247638; 100 affiliated unions; 40,000 mems; Pres. ASHOK KUMAR SINGH; Gen. Sec. P. K. SHARMA.

Indian National Textile Workers' Federation: 27 Burjorji Bharucha Marg, Mumbai 400 023; tel. (22) 261577; f. 1948; 400 affiliated unions; 363,790 mems; Pres. P. L. SUBBIAH; Gen. Sec. SACHIN AHIR.

Indian National Transport Workers' Federation: Bus Mazdoor Karyalaya, L/1, Hathital Colony, Jabalpur 482 001; tel. (761) 429210; 263 affiliated unions; 327,961 mems; Pres. D. B. PILWAIKAR; Gen. Sec. K. S. VERMA.

National Federation of Petroleum Workers: Tel Rasayan Bhavan, Tilak Rd, Dadar, Mumbai 400 014; tel. (22) 4121742; fax (22) 4130950; f. 1959; 22,340 mems; Pres. RAJA KULKARNI; Gen. Sec. S. N. SURVE.

Bharatiya Mazdoor Sangh: Ram Naresh Bhavan, Tilak Gali, Pahar Ganj, New Delhi 110 055; tel. (11) 7524212; fax (11) 7520654; f. 1955; 3,507 affiliated unions with a total membership of 3,116,564 mems; 24 state brs; 28 nat. feds; Pres. RAMAN GIRDHAR SHAH; Gen. Sec. HASUBHAI DAVE.

Centre of Indian Trade Unions: BTR Bhavan, 13-A Rouse Ave, New Delhi 110 002; tel. (11) 3221206; fax (11) 3221284; e-mail citu@vsnl.net.in; f. 1970; 3,250,000 mems; 24 state and union territory brs; 3,900 affiliated unions, 10 nat. federations; Pres. E. BALANANDAN; Gen. Sec. M. K. PANDHE.

Assam Chah Karmachari Sangha: POB 13, Dibrugarh 786 001; tel. 20870; 13,553 mems; 20 brs; Pres. G. C. SARMAH; Gen. Sec. A. K. BHATTACHARYA.

All-India Trade Union Congress (AITUC): 24 Canning Lane, New Delhi 110 001; tel. (11) 3387320; fax (11) 3386427; e-mail aitucong@bol.net.in; f. 1920; affiliated to WFTU; 3m. mems, 3,000 affiliated unions; 26 state brs, 10 national federations; Pres. J. CHITHARANJAN; Gen. Sec. K. L. MAHENDRA.

Major affiliated unions:

Annamalai Plantation Workers' Union: Valparai, Via Pollachi, Tamil Nadu; over 21,000 mems.

Zilla Cha Bagan Workers' Union: Mal, Jalpaiguri, West Bengal; 15,000 mems; Pres. NEHAR MUKHERJEE; Gen. Sec. BIMAL DAS GUPTA.

United Trades Union Congress (UTUC): 249 Bepin Behari Ganguly St, Kolkata 700 012; tel. (33) 275609; f. 1949; 584,523 mems from 413 affiliated unions; 10 state brs and 6 nat. feds; Pres. P. C. JOHN; Gen. Sec. S. R. SEN GUPTA.

Major affiliated unions:

All India Farm Labour Union: Patna; c. 35,000 mems; Pres. MAHENDRA SINGH TIKAIT.

Bengal Provincial Chatkal Mazdoor Union: Kolkata; textile workers; 28,330 mems.

Hind Mazdoor Sabha (HMS): 'Shrama-Sadhana', 57 D. V. Pradhan Rd, Hindu Colony, Dadar (East), Mumbai 400 014; tel. (22) 4144336; fax (22) 4102759; e-mail mki@vsnl.com; f. 1948; affiliated to ICFTU; 4.8m. mems from 2,700 affiliated unions; 20 state councils; 18 nat. industrial feds; Pres. A. SUBRAMANIAM; Gen. Sec. UMRAOMAL PUROHIT.

Major affiliated unions:

Colliery Mazdoor Congress (Coalminers' Union): Pres. MADHU DANDAVATE; Gen. Sec. JAYANTA PODDER.

Mumbai Port Trust Dock and General Employees' Union: Pres. Dr SHANTI PATEL; Gen. Sec. S. K. SHETYE.

South Central Railway Mazdoor Union: 7C Railway Bldg, Accounts Office Compound, Secunderabad 500 371; tel. (40) 7821351; e-mail scrmu@hotmail.com; internet www.scrmu.org; f. 1966; 89,150 mems; Pres. K. S. N. MURTHY; Gen. Sec. N. SUNDARESAN; 135 brs.

Transport and Dock Workers' Union: Gen. Sec. MANOHAR KOTWAL.

West Bengal Cha Mazdoor Sabha: Cha Shramik Bhavan, Jalpaiguri 735 101, West Bengal; tel. (3561) 31140; fax (3561) 30349; f. 1947; 55,000 mems; Pres. Prof. SUSHIL ROY; Gen. Sec. SAMIR ROY.

Western Railway Employees' Union: Pres. JAGDISH AJMERA; Gen. Sec. UMRAOMAL PUROHIT.

Confederation of Central Government Employees and Workers: 4B/6 Ganga Ram Hospital Marg, New Delhi 110 060; tel. (11) 587804; 1.2m. mems; Pres. S. MADHUSUDAN; Sec.-Gen. S. K. VYAS.

Affiliated union:

National Federation of Post, Telephone and Telegraph Employees (NFPTTE): C-1/2 Baird Rd, New Delhi 110 001; tel. (11) 322545; f. 1954; 221,880 mems (est.); Pres. R. G. SHARMA; Gen. Sec. O. P. GUPTA.

All India Bank Employees' Association (AIBEA): 3B Lall Bazar St, 1st Floor, Kolkata 700 001; tel. (33) 2489371; fax (33) 2486072; e-mail aibea@cal2.vsnl.net.in; 27 state units, 710 affiliated unions, 525,000 mems; Pres. SURESH D. DHOPESWARKAR; Gen. Sec. TARAKESWAR CHAKRABORTI.

All India Defence Employees' Federation (AIDEF): Survey No. 81, Elphinstone Rd, Khadki, Pune 411 003; tel. (212) 318761; 350 affiliated unions; 400,000 mems; Pres. SAMUEL AUGUSTINE; Gen. Sec. D. LOBO.

All India Port and Dock Workers' Federation: 9 Second Line Beach, Chennai 600 001; tel. (44) 5224222; fax (44) 5225983; f. 1948; 100,000 mems in 34 affiliated unions; Pres. S. R. KULKARNI; Gen. Sec. S. C. C. ANTHONY PILLAI.

All India Railwaymen's Federation (AIRF): 4 State Entry Rd, New Delhi 110 055; tel. (11) 3343493; fax (11) 3363167; f. 1924; 1,031,248 mems (1999); 16 affiliated unions; Pres. UMRAOMAL PUROHIT; Gen. Sec. J. P. CHAUBEY.

National Federation of Indian Railwaymen (NFIR): 3 Chelmsford Rd, New Delhi 110 055; tel. (11) 3734013; f. 1952; 20 affiliated unions; 907,485 mems (1997); Pres. MAHINDRA PRATAP; Gen. Sec. M. RAGHAVAIAH.

Transport

RAILWAYS

India's railway system is the largest in Asia and the fourth largest in the world. In 1999/2000 the total length of Indian railways exceeded 62,809 route-km. The network carried 12m. passengers and more than 1m. metric tons of freight traffic per day. The Government exercises direct or indirect control over all railways through the Railway Board. India's largest railway construction project of the 20th century, the 760-km Konkan railway line (which took seven years and almost US $1,000m. to build), was officially opened in January 1998.

A 16.45-km underground railway, which carries more than 1m. people daily, was completed in Kolkata in 1995.

Ministry of Railways (Railway Board): Rail Bhavan, Raisina Rd, New Delhi; tel. (11) 3384010; fax (11) 3381453; internet www.indianrailway.com; Chair. ASHOK KUMAR.

Zonal Railways

The railways are grouped into 15 zones:

Central: Chhatrapati Shivaji Terminus (Victoria Terminus), Mumbai 400 001; tel. (22) 2621230; fax (22) 2624555; e-mail gmcr@bom2.vsnl.net.in; internet www.cr-mumbai.com; Gen. Man. RAJENDRA NATH.

East Central: Hajipur; tel. (6224) 74728; fax (6224) 74738; f. 1996; Gen. Man. I. I. M. S. RANA.

East Coast: Bhubaneswar 751 023; tel. (674) 300773; fax (674) 300196; e-mail bishtbms@hotmail.com; internet webind.com/eastcoastrailway; f. 1996; Gen. Man. B. M. S. BISHT.

Eastern: 17 Netaji Subhas Rd, Kolkata 700 001; tel. (33) 2027596; fax (33) 2480370; Gen. Man. IQBAL INDER MOHAN SINGH RANA.

North Central: Allahabad; tel. (532) 624530; fax (532) 624841; e-mail secyncr@hotmail.com; f. 1996; Gen. Man. V. K. GARG; Chief Public Relations Officer and Sec. B. P. AWASTHI.

North Eastern: Gorakhpur 273 012; tel. (551) 201041; fax (551) 201842; e-mail gmner@nda.vsnl.net.in; Gen. Man. S. N. PANDEY.

North Western: Jaipur; tel. (141) 360695; fax (141) 200322; Gen. Man. AJIT KISHORE.

Northeast Frontier: Maligaon, Guwahati 781 011; tel. (361) 570422; fax (361) 571124; f. 1958; Gen. Man. RAJENDRA NATH.

Northern: Baroda House, Kasturba Gandhi Marg, New Delhi 110 001; tel. (11) 3387227; fax (11) 3384503; e-mail nragm@vsnl.com; Gen. Man. SUBHAS P. MEHTA.

South Central: Rail Nilayam, Secunderabad 500 371; tel. (40) 834234; fax (40) 833203; internet www.scrailway.gov.in; Gen. Man. N. KRITHIVASAN.

South Eastern: Garden Reach Rd, Kidderpore, Kolkata 700 043; tel. (33) 4793532; fax (33) 497826; internet www.serailway.com; Gen. Man. R. K. THOOMAL.

South Western: Bangalore; tel. (80) 2205773; fax (80) 2282787; f. 1996; Gen. Man. K. B. WARIYAR.

Southern: Park Town, Chennai 600 003; tel. (44) 5353157; fax (44) 5351439; internet www.srailway.com; Gen. Man. AJIT KISHORE.

West Central: Jabalpur; tel. (761) 327444; fax (761) 328133; e-mail osdwcr@yahoo.com; f. 1996; Gen. Man. R. K. THOOPAL; Sec. KARTIC CHAUHAN.

Western: Churchgate, Mumbai 400 020; tel. (22) 2014421; fax (22) 2017631; internet www.westernrailwayindia.com; Gen. Man. V. D. GUPTA.

ROADS

In December 2000 there were an estimated 3.15m. km of roads in India, 57,704 km of which were national highways. About 50% of the total road network was paved. In January 1999 the Government launched the ambitious 500,000m. rupee-National Highways Road Development project, which included plans to build an east-west corridor linking Silchar with Porbandar and a north-south corridor linking Kashmir with Kanyakumari, as well as a circuit of roads linking the four main cities of Mumbai, Chennai, Kolkata and New Delhi.

Ministry of Surface Transport (Roads Wing): Transport Bhavan, 1 Parliament St, New Delhi 110 001; tel. (11) 3715159; responsible for the construction and maintenance of India's system of national highways, with a total length of 57,737 km in 2001, connecting the state capitals and major ports and linking with the highway systems of neighbouring countries. This system includes 172 national highways which constitute the main trunk roads of the country.

Border Roads Development Board: f. 1960 to accelerate the economic development of the north and north-eastern border areas; it has constructed 28,342 km and improved 32,885 km of roads, and maintains about 16,872 km in the border areas.

National Highways Authority of India: 1 Eastern Ave, Maharani Bagh, New Delhi 110 065; tel. (11) 6317965; fax (11) 6924383; e-mail nhai@vsnl.com; internet www.nhai.org; f. 1995; planning, designing, construction and maintenance of national highways; under Ministry of Surface Transport; Chair. DEEPAK DASGUPTA.

INLAND WATERWAYS

About 14,500 km of rivers are navigable by power-driven craft, and 3,700 km by large country boats. Services are mainly on the Ganga and Brahmaputra and their tributaries, the Godavari, the Mahanadi, the Narmada, the Tapti and the Krishna.

Central Inland Water Transport Corpn Ltd: 4 Fairlie Place, Kolkata 700 001; tel. (33) 2202321; fax (33) 2436164; e-mail ciwtc@cal3.vsnl.net.in; internet www.ciwtc.com; f. 1967; inland water transport services in Bangladesh and the north-east Indian states; also shipbuilding and repairing, general engineering, dredging, lightering of ships and barge services; Chair. and Man. Dir S. C. DUA.

SHIPPING

In March 2000 India was 17th on the list of principal merchant fleets of the world. In mid-2000 the fleet had 515 ships, with a total displacement of 7.07m. grt. There were some 102 shipping companies operating in India in January 2000. The major ports are Chennai, Haldia, Jawaharlal Nehru (at Nhava Sheva near Mumbai), Kandla, Kochi, Kolkata, Mormugao, Mumbai, New Mangalore, Paradip (Paradeep), Tuticorin and Visakha (Visakhapatnam).

Chennai (Madras)

South India Shipping Corpn Ltd: Chennai House, 7 Esplanade Rd, POB 234, Chennai 600 108; tel. (44) 5341441; fax (44) 5340948; Chair. J. H. TARAPORE; Man. Dir F. G. DASTUR.

Kolkata (Calcutta)

India Steamship Co Ltd: India Steamship House, 21 Hemanta Basu Sarani, POB 2090, Kolkata 700 001; tel. (33) 2481171; fax (33) 2488133; e-mail india.steamship@gems.vsnl.net.in; f. 1928; cargo services; Chair. K. K. BIRLA; Man. Dir L. M. S. RAJWAR; br in Delhi.

Surrendra Overseas Ltd: Apeejay House, 15 Park St, Kolkata 700 016; tel. (33) 2172372; fax (33) 2179596; e-mail solcal@apeejaygroup.com; internet www.apeejaygroup.com; shipowners; Chair. JIT PAUL.

Mumbai (Bombay)

Century Shipping Ltd: 12th Floor, Earnest House, 194 Nariman Point, Mumbai 400 021; tel. (22) 2022734; fax (22) 2027274; Chair. B. K. BIRLA; Pres. N. M. JAIN.

Chowgule & Co (Pvt) Ltd: Bakhtawar, 3rd Floor, Nariman Point, POB 11596, Mumbai 400 021; tel. (22) 2026822; fax (22) 2024845; f. 1963; Chair. VISHWASRAO DATTAJI CHOWGULE; Man. Dir SHIVAJIRAO DATTAJI CHOWGULE.

Essar Shipping Ltd: Essar House, 11 Keshavrao Khadye Marg, Mahalaxmi, Mumbai 400 034; tel. (22) 4950606; fax (22) 4950607; f. 1975; Chair. S. N. RUIA; Man. Dir B. S. KUMAR.

The Great Eastern Shipping Co Ltd: Ocean House, 134/A Dr Annie Besant Rd, Worli, Mumbai 400 018; tel. (22) 4922100; fax (22) 4925900; internet www.greatship.com; f. 1948; cargo services; Exec. Chair. K. M. SHETH; Man. Dir BHARAT SHETH; br. in New Delhi.

Shipping Corpn of India Ltd: Shipping House, 245 Madame Cama Rd, Mumbai 400 021; tel. (22) 2026666; fax (22) 2026905; e-mail scicmd@giasbm01.vsnl.net.in; f. 1961 as a govt undertaking; Chair. and Man. Dir P. K. SRIVASTAVA; brs in Kolkata, New Delhi, Chennai and London.

Tolani Shipping Co Ltd: 10A Bakhtawar, Nariman Point, Mumbai 400 021; tel. (22) 2026878; fax (22) 2870697; Chair. and Man. Dir Dr N. P. TOLANI.

Varun Shipping Co Ltd: 3rd Floor, Laxmi Bldg, 6 Shoorji Vallabhdas Marg, Ballard Estate, Mumbai 400 001; tel. (22) 2658114; fax (22) 2621723; f. 1971; Chair. DILIP D. KHATAU; Man. Dir ARUN MEHTA.

CIVIL AVIATION

There are five main international airports and 90 domestic airports and 27 civil enclaves. By mid-1998 nine airports (in Mumbai, Delhi, Chennai, Kolkata, Hyderabad, Ahmedabad, Goa, Bangalore and Thiruvananthapuram) had been identified for expansion/upgrading.

Airports Authority of India: Rajiv Gandhi Bhavan, Safdarjung Airport, New Delhi 110 003; tel. (11) 4632950; fax (11) 4632990; manages the international and domestic airports; Chair. D. V. GUPTA.

Air-India: Air-India Bldg, 218 Backbay Reclamation, Nariman Point, Mumbai 400 021; tel. (22) 2024142; fax (22) 2048521; e-mail airindpr@bom3.vsnl.net.in; internet www.airindia.com; f. 1932 as Tata Airlines; renamed Air-India in 1946; in 1953 became a state corpn responsible for international flights; services to 46 online stations (incl. 2 cargo stations) and 84 offline offices throughout the world; Chair. RAVINDRA GUPTA; Man. Dir MICHAEL P. MASCARENHAS; plans to merge with Indian Airlines by 2001.

Alliance Air-Airline Allied Services: 1st Floor, Domestic Arrival Terminal, Indira Gandhi International Airport, Palam, New Delhi 110 037; tel. (11) 5662458; fax (11) 5662006; e-mail aaslmd@del2.vsnl.net.in; internet www.allianceair-india.com/; f. 1996; 100% owned by Indian Airlines; scheduled passenger services to regional destinations; Man. Dir ANIL GOYAL.

Archana Airways: 41A Friends Colony (East), Mathura Rd, New Delhi 110 065; tel. (11) 6842001; fax (11) 6847762; f. 1991; commenced operations 1993; scheduled and charter passenger services to domestic destinations; Dir/Chair. A. K. BHARTIYA; Man. Dir N. K. BHARTIYA.

Blue Dart Express: 88–89 Old International Terminal, Meenambakkam Airport, Chennai 600027; tel. (44) 2334995; fax (44) 2349067; e-mail bdal@md2.vsnl.net.in; internet www.bluedart.com; f. 1983 as Blue Dart Courier Services; name changed as above in 1990; air express transport co; Chair. TUSHAR K. JANI; Chief Exec. NITEEN GUPTE.

Continental Aviation: E-4/130 Arera Colony, Bhopal 462 016; tel. (755) 566625; fax (755) 563447; domestic passenger services; Gen. Man. SAM VERMA.

East West Airlines: 18 New Kantwadi Rd, Bandra, Mumbai 400 050; tel. (22) 6436678; fax (22) 6431724; f. 1992; private co; services to 33 major domestic destinations; Chair. NASIR A. WAHID; Man. Dir (vacant).

Elbee Airlines: SM House, 11 Sahakar House, Vile Parla East, Mumbai 400 057; tel. (22) 8237006; fax (22) 8227201; e-mail elbeebom@bom4.vsnl.net.in; internet www.elbeenet.com/elbeeair.htm; f. 1994; scheduled and charter cargo services to domestic destinations; Chief Exec. ASHIS NAIN.

Gujarat Airways Ltd: Vanijya Bhavan, Race Course, Vadodara 390 007; tel. (265) 330864; fax (265) 339628; e-mail info@

gujaratairways.com; internet www.gujaratairways.com; f. 1994; commenced operations 1995; scheduled services to domestic destinations; Chair. G. N. PATEL; Man. Dir R. C. SHARMA.

Indian Airlines: Airlines House, 113 Gurudwara Rakabganj Rd, New Delhi 110 001; tel. (11) 3718951; fax (11) 3711014; internet www.nic.in/indian-airlines; f. 1953; state corpn responsible for regional and domestic flights; services to 63 cities throughout India and to 16 destinations in the Middle East and the Far East; Chair. and Man. Dir SUNIL ARORA.

Jagson Airlines: 12E Vandana Bldg, 11 Tolstoy Marg, New Delhi 110 001; tel. (11) 3721594; fax (11) 3324693; e-mail jagson@id.eth.net; f. 1991; scheduled and charter passenger services to domestic destinations; Chair. JAGDISH GUPTA; Man. Dir PRADEEP GUPTA.

Jet Airways (India) Ltd: S. M. Centre, 1st Floor, Andheri-Kurla Rd, Andheri (East), Mumbai 400 059; tel. (22) 8505080; fax (22) 8505631; internet www.jetairways.com; f. 1992; commenced operations 1993; private co; scheduled passenger services to domestic and regional destinations; Chair. and Man. Dir NARESH GOYAL; Exec. Dir SAROJ K. DATTA.

NEPC Airlines: 36 Wallajah Rd, Chennai 600 002; tel. (44) 848075; fax (44) 447353; f. 1994; private co; passenger services to domestic destinations; Chair. and Man. Dir RAVI PRAKASH KHEMKA.

Sahara Airlines: 7th Floor, Ambadeep Bldg, 14 Kasturba Gandhi Marg, New Delhi 110 001; tel. (11) 3326851; fax (11) 3326858; e-mail ukbose@saharaairline.com; internet www.saharaairline.com; f. 1991, as Sahara India Airlines; commenced operations 1993; private co; scheduled passenger and cargo services to domestic destinations; Chair. SUBRATA R. SAHARA; Dir PARVEZ DAMANIA.

TransBharat Aviation: 201 Laxmi Bhavan, 72 Nehru Place, Delhi 110 019; tel. (11) 6419600; fax (11) 3313353; f. 1990; commenced operations 1991; charter services throughout India.

UP Airways Ltd: Roopali House, A-2 Defence Colony, New Delhi 110 024; tel. (11) 4638201; fax (11) 4646292; e-mail sgsimpex@del3.vsnl.net.in; private co; charter services to domestic destinations; Chair. and Man. Dir SUBHASH GULATI; Chief Exec. Capt. H. S. BEDI.

Tourism

The tourist attractions of India include its scenery, its historic forts, palaces and temples, and its rich variety of wild life. Tourist infrastructure has recently been expanded by the provision of more luxury hotels and improved means of transport. In 2000 there were about 2.62m. foreign visitors to India, and revenue from tourism totalled an estimated 144,086m. rupees.

Ministry of Tourism: Transport Bhavan, Parliament St, New Delhi 110 001; tel. (11) 3717890; fax (11) 3710518; formulates and administers govt policy for promotion of tourism; plans the organization and development of tourist facilities; operates tourist information offices in India and overseas; Dir-Gen. ATUL SINHA.

India Tourism Development Corpn Ltd: SCOPE Complex, Core 8, 6th Floor, 7 Lodi Rd, New Delhi 110 003; tel. (11) 4360303; fax (11) 4360233; e-mail itdcscope@usa.net; f. 1966; operates Ashok Group of hotels (largest hotel chain owner), resort accommodation, tourist transport services, duty-free shops and a travel agency and provides consultancy and management services; Chair. and Man. Dir ASHA MURTHY.

INDONESIA

Introductory Survey

Location, Climate, Language, Religion, Flag, Capital

The Republic of Indonesia consists of a group of about 17,500 islands (including rocks, reefs, sandbanks, etc.), lying between the mainland of South-East Asia and Australia. The archipelago is the largest in the world, and it stretches from the Malay peninsula to New Guinea. The principal islands are Java, Sumatra, Kalimantan (comprising more than two-thirds of the island of Borneo), Sulawesi (Celebes), Irian Jaya (also known as West Papua, comprising the western part of the island of New Guinea), Maluku (the Moluccas) and West Timor (comprising part of the island of Timor). Indonesia's only land frontiers are with Papua New Guinea, to the east of Irian Jaya, with the Malaysian states of Sarawak and Sabah, which occupy northern Borneo, and with East Timor, to the east of West Timor. The climate is tropical, with an average annual temperature of 26°C (79°F) and heavy rainfall during most seasons. Rainfall averages 706 mm (28 ins) annually in Indonesia, although there are large variations throughout the archipelago; the heaviest annual rainfall (2,286 mm or 90 ins) is along the equatorial rain belt, which passes through Sumatra, Borneo and Sulawesi. The official language is Bahasa Indonesia (a form of Malay); there are an estimated 583 other languages and dialects spoken in the archipelago, including Javanese, Sundanese, Arabic and Chinese. An estimated 88% of the inhabitants profess adherence to Islam. About 10% of the population are Christians, while most of the remainder are either Hindus or Buddhists. The national flag (proportions 3 by 2) has two equal horizontal stripes, of red and white. The capital is Jakarta, on the island of Java.

Recent History

Indonesia was formerly the Netherlands East Indies (except for the former Portuguese colony of East Timor, see below). Dutch occupation began in the 17th century and gradually extended over the whole archipelago. Nationalist opposition to colonial rule began in the early 20th century. During the Second World War the territory was occupied by Japanese forces from March 1942. On 17 August 1945, three days after the Japanese surrender, a group of nationalists proclaimed the independence of Indonesia. The first President of the self-proclaimed republic was Dr Sukarno, a leader of the nationalist movement since the 1920s. The declaration of independence was not recognized by the Netherlands, which attempted to restore its pre-war control of the islands. After four years of intermittent warfare and negotiations between the Dutch authorities and the nationalists, agreement was reached on a formal transfer of power. On 27 December 1949 the United States of Indonesia became legally independent, with Sukarno continuing as President. Initially, the country had a federal Constitution which gave limited self-government to the 16 constituent regions. In August 1950, however, the federation was dissolved, and the country became the unitary Republic of Indonesia. The 1949 independence agreement excluded West New Guinea (subsequently Irian Jaya, or West Papua), which remained under Dutch control until October 1962; following a brief period of UN administration, however, it was transferred to Indonesia in May 1963.

Sukarno followed a policy of extreme nationalism, and his regime became increasingly dictatorial. His foreign policy was sympathetic to the People's Republic of China but, under his rule, Indonesia also played a leading role in the Non-aligned Movement (see p. 318). Inflation and widespread corruption eventually provoked opposition to Sukarno's regime; in September–October 1965 there was an abortive military coup, in which the Partai Komunis Indonesia (PKI—Indonesian Communist Party) was strongly implicated. A mass slaughter of alleged PKI members and supporters ensued. In March 1966 Sukarno was forced to transfer emergency executive powers to military commanders, led by Gen. Suharto, Chief of Staff of the Army, who outlawed the PKI. In February 1967 Sukarno transferred full power to Suharto. In March the Majelis Permusyawaratan Rakyat (MPR—People's Consultative Assembly) removed Sukarno from office and named Suharto acting President. He became Prime Minister in October 1967 and, following his election by the MPR, he was inaugurated as President in

March 1968. In July 1971, in the first general election since 1955, the government-sponsored Sekretariat Bersama Golongan Karya (Joint Secretariat of Functional Groups), known as Golkar, won a majority of seats in the Dewan Perwakilan Rakyat (Dewan—House of Representatives). Suharto was re-elected to the presidency in March 1973.

Under Suharto's 'New Order', real power passed from the legislature and the Cabinet to a small group of army officers and to the Operation Command for the Restoration of Order and Security (Kopkamtib), the internal security organization. Left-wing movements were suppressed, and a liberal economic policy adopted. A general election in May 1977 gave Golkar a majority in the legislature, and Suharto was re-elected President (unopposed) in March 1978. Despite criticism of the Government (most notably a petition signed by 50 prominent citizens in 1980), Golkar won an increased majority in the elections in May 1982, although the campaign was marred by considerable violence. In March 1983 Suharto was re-elected, again unopposed, as President.

During 1984 Suharto's attempt to introduce legislation requiring all political, social and religious organizations to adopt *pancasila*, the five-point state philosophy (belief in a supreme being; humanitarianism; national unity; democracy by consensus; social justice), as their only ideology encountered opposition, particularly from the Petition of 50 (the signatories of the 1980 protest). Serious rioting and a series of bombings and arson attempts in and around Jakarta were allegedly instigated by Muslim opponents of the proposed legislation, and many Muslims were tried and sentenced to long terms of imprisonment. A law concerning mass organizations was enacted in June 1985, and all the political parties had accepted Pancasila by July. At the April 1987 general election, despite persistent international allegations of corruption and of abuses of human rights, particularly in East Timor (see below), Golkar won 299 of the 500 seats in the Dewan. Moreover, for the first time, the party achieved an overall majority of seats in each of Indonesia's 27 provinces.

In February 1988 new legislation reaffirmed the 'dual (i.e. military and socio-economic) function' of the Indonesian Armed Forces (ABRI). Shortly afterwards, Gen. Try Sutrisno (hitherto Chief of Staff of the Army) replaced Gen. L. B. (Benny) Murdani as Commander-in-Chief of the Armed Forces. In March Suharto was again re-elected unopposed as President. At the subsequent vice-presidential election, in a departure from previous procedure, Suharto did not recommend a candidate, but encouraged the MPR to choose one. However, Lt-Gen. (retd) Sudharmono, the Chairman of Golkar, and Dr Jailani Naro, the leader of the Partai Persatuan Pembangunan (PPP—United Development Party), were both nominated for the post, and Gen. Suharto was obliged to indicate his preference for Sudharmono before Naro withdrew his candidacy and Sudharmono was elected unopposed. ABRI disapproved of Sudharmono's appointment as, under his chairmanship of Golkar, there had been a shift away from military dominance in the grouping and he was suspected of having left-wing sympathies. In October Sudharmono resigned as Chairman of Golkar and was replaced by Gen. (retd) Wahono, who was acceptable both to ABRI and the developing bureaucratic élite.

In early 1989 tension arising from land disputes produced social unrest in three areas of Java and on the island of Sumbawa (east of Bali and Lombok), in Nusa Tenggara. The most serious incident took place in February in southern Sumatra, where between 30 and 100 people were killed as a result of clashes between the armed forces and dissenting villagers. The first student demonstrations since 1978 were held to protest against the Government's expropriation of land without sufficient indemnification for those subject to relocation. The armed forces did not attempt to suppress the student protests. This implicit criticism of the regime and discussions about democratization and reform had been encouraged by speculation over Suharto's successor, which had begun as a result of comments made by Suharto in the previous April. In early May 1989, however, Suharto warned officials to dismiss the topic of the succession and in September, when the Partai Demokrasi Indonesia (PDI—Indonesian Democratic Party) announced that it would support his candidacy, it appeared likely that he would seek election for a sixth term. In August 1990 a group of 58 prominent Indonesians, comprising many of the original Petition of 50, issued a public demand to Suharto to retire from the presidency at the end of his current term of office and to permit greater democracy in Indonesia.

During 1991, in response to the growing demand for political *keterbukaan* (openness), several new organizations were formed to promote freedom of expression and other democratic values. In late 1991 this assertiveness by political groupings was paralleled by a climate of labour unrest. During this period, arrests and the alleged intimidation of activists were instrumental in curbing expressions of dissent. In an attempt to control student unrest, political campaigns were banned on university campuses. In September Suharto removed several of the most outspoken members of Golkar from the list of candidates to contest the legislative elections, scheduled to take place on 9 June 1992.

The Government had, for some time, been seeking to win the support of the Muslim electorate in preparation for the presidential elections in 1993. In 1989 Suharto promoted legislation whereby decisions by Islamic courts no longer required confirmation by civil courts, and in December 1990 the President opened the symposium of the newly-formed Association of Indonesian Muslim Intellectuals (ICMI), an organization which united a broad spectrum of Islamic interests. In 1991 Suharto made his first pilgrimage to Mecca, acceded to Islamic demands for certain educational reforms and supported the establishment of an Islamic bank. ABRI was opposed to the establishment of ICMI because it regarded the polarization of politics by religion as a threat to stability. During 1990 the nature of ABRI's dual function had been queried from within the armed forces, with some support evinced for a reduction of its political role. However, pressure from ABRI was widely believed to have led to Suharto's gestures towards democratization.

In March 1992 Indonesia's largest Islamic organization, Nahdlatul Ulama (Council of Scholars), held the first large rally of its kind in Indonesia since 1966. Attendance at the gathering (which was ostensibly organized in support of the Constitution and the state ideology but was effectively a display of support for the organization) was limited to 200,000 by the Government. In February and April, however, meetings of the Democratic Forum (also led by the Chairman of Nahdlatul Ulama, Abdurrahman Wahid) were banned.

During the strictly-monitored four-week campaign period leading to elections for the Dewan, for local government bodies and for district councils, political parties were prohibited from addressing religious issues, the question of the dominant role of the ethnic Chinese community in the economy, or any subject that might present a threat to national unity. The opposition parties did, however, exploit the increasing public resentment about the rapidly-expanding businesses of Suharto's children (some of whom had been awarded monopoly rights, which hindered economic development). The Forum for the Purification of People's Sovereignty (formed in 1991) urged the voters to boycott the elections, in an effort to elicit reforms from the Government, and also criticized the extent of the President's powers. Members of the Petition of 50 also refused to vote.

On 9 June 1992 90.4% of the electorate participated in the election to the Dewan, which resulted in a further victory for Golkar (although its share of the votes declined to 68%, compared with 73% in 1987). Golkar secured 282 of the 400 elective seats, while 62 seats were won by the PPP (a gain of one seat compared with 1987) and 56 seats (compared with 40) by the PDI, which had mobilized almost 3m. supporters at a rally in Jakarta in the week prior to the election.

In October 1992 Suharto accepted nominations by Golkar, the PPP, the PDI and ABRI for a sixth term of office as President. His victory in the presidential election, due to take place in March 1993, was thus assured. Public attention then focused on the vice-presidency. Owing to the increasing public debate over ABRI's active involvement in political affairs and, in particular, concern over whether the appointment of 100 members of ABRI to the Dewan remained justifiable, it was deemed important that ABRI consolidate its position through the election to the vice-presidency of its own principal candidate, Sutrisno. Suharto, however, was rumoured to support the prospective candidacy of the Minister of State for Research and Technology, Prof. Dr Ir Bucharuddin Jusuf (B. J.) Habibie, an influential Muslim leader and the then Chairman of ICMI.

Other prominent contenders included Gen. Rudini (the Minister of Home Affairs) and Maj.-Gen. Wismoyo Arismunandar (the Commander of the Strategic Reserve Command—Kostrad—and Suharto's brother-in-law). In a manifestation of greater political openness, the merits of the prospective candidates were discussed in the local press. Sutrisno was subsequently endorsed as a vice-presidential candidate by the PDI, the PPP, ABRI and, finally, Golkar. At a meeting of the MPR on 10 and 11 March Suharto and Sutrisno were duly elected to the posts of President and Vice-President respectively.

Suharto's new Government, which was announced in mid-March 1993, comprised 22 new appointees in the 41-member Cabinet. ABRI representation was reduced from 11 to eight members and the influential Rudini and Murdani were excluded from the Cabinet. Those primarily responsible for the country's economic policy since 1988, Prof. Dr Johannes B. Sumarlin, Adrianus Mooy and Radius Prawiro (all western-educated Christians) were replaced, leaving only three Christians in the Cabinet; several members of ICMI were included in the new list, thus advancing the faction led by Habibie, who was unpopular with ABRI, partly owing to his interference in arms purchases. Suharto announced that the new Government would pursue the aim of greater democracy and openness; the immigration blacklist was swiftly reduced from 17,000 names to less than 9,000. In mid-1993 Suharto met a prominent member of the Petition of 50, revoked a travel ban on all dissidents and established a National Council on Human Rights.

In October 1993 at the party Congress the Minister of Information, Harmoko, became the first civilian to be elected to the chairmanship of Golkar. In an unprecedented move Suharto had openly endorsed Harmoko's candidacy; it was widely speculated that this was to prevent ABRI from supporting its own candidate and effectively denying the President a choice, as was the case in the election of Sutrisno to the vice-presidency. Also at the Congress Suharto's family entered active national politics; his son, Bambang Trihatmodjo, and daughter, Siti Hardijanti Rukmana (known as Mbak Tutut), who had both been appointed to the MPR in 1992, were elected to positions of responsibility within Golkar.

In July 1993 the incumbent Chairman of the PDI, Soerjadi, was re-elected to the post at a fractious party Congress. The Government invalidated the election of Soerjadi, who had incurred Suharto's displeasure by campaigning during the June 1992 elections for a limited presidential term of office, and appointed a 23-member 'caretaker board' pending new elections. An extraordinary Congress of the PDI ended inconclusively in early December owing to the unexpected candidacy for the chairmanship of Megawati Sukarnoputri, the daughter of former President Sukarno. Despite government pressure to elect Budi Hardjono, a senior party official, Megawati received overwhelming support from the participants of the Congress. The 'caretaker board' prevented a vote from taking place and the PDI delegates were dispersed at midnight as the government-issued licence to hold a congress expired. Later that month, amid accusations of official interference, the Government ordered the holding of a new PDI Congress, at which Megawati was elected Chairman.

In June 1993 the USA imposed a deadline of February 1994 for Indonesia to improve workers' rights or lose trade privileges under the Generalized System of Preferences. In an attempt to avoid sanctions, the Government adopted reforms to the only officially recognized trade union, the Serikat Pekerja Seluruh Indonesia (All Indonesia Workers' Union), introduced a substantial increase in the minimum wage and revoked the controversial 1986 Labour Law which allowed the intervention of the armed forces in labour disputes. Indonesia suffered a subsequent increase in industrial unrest as workers went on strike accusing employers of failing to pay the new minimum wage and demanding improved working conditions. In February 1994 the independent Serikat Buruh Sejahtera Indonesia (SBSI—Indonesian Prosperous Labour Union), which had had its application for registration formally rejected in June 1993, appealed for a one-hour national work stoppage. Two days prior to the strike the General Secretary of the SBSI, Muchtar Pakpahan, was arrested and charged with inciting hatred against the Government (although he was released in the following month). In April 1994 riots broke out in Medan, Sumatra, over workers' demands for improved factory conditions and the implementation of the new minimum wage, and rapidly degenerated into attacks on Chinese property and business executives. The attacks on Chinese companies reflected a widely-held perception that the ethnic Chinese had benefited disproportionately from the country's rapid economic growth. Three members of the SBSI surrendered to the authorities in May and admitted to having organized the protest. Further strikes broke out later in the month in other parts of north Sumatra. In August Pakpahan was rearrested. He was given a three-year prison sentence in November for inciting labour unrest (which was later extended to four years). By that time, it was estimated that the majority of factories had complied with the provision of the new minimum wage.

In January 1995 it was announced by the armed forces that 300 members of the PDI were to be investigated for links to the 1965 coup attempt, following allegations that many members had relatives or contacts in the banned PKI. This apparent attempt to discredit the opposition grouping was followed in May by a ban on the presence of Megawati at the commemoration, in June, of the 25th anniversary of the death of her father, Sukarno, ostensibly because it might provoke outbreaks of violence but more probably because the occasion might have fostered support for the PDI.

Throughout 1995 the Indonesian authorities attempted to ascribe social unrest to communist subversion, asserting that a communist revival remained a threat to national security. In September the Chief of Staff of the Armed Forces named several prominent dissidents, including Muchtar Pakpahan (whose conviction for incitement had been overturned by the Supreme Court in that month), as members of 'formless organizations,' which, he claimed, infiltrated pressure groups to promote the resurgence of communism. In November 300 people were arrested in Java as subversives, who were allegedly using the tactics of the PKI.

In July 1995, in response to widespread condemnation of Indonesia's human rights violations, Suharto announced that three prisoners detained for their complicity in the 1965 coup attempt would be released to coincide with the 50th anniversary of independence in August. The administration also subsequently announced that the code ET (which stood for *Eks Tahanan Politik*—former political prisoner) was to be removed from identity papers following the anniversary. The measure affected about 1.3m. citizens, most of whom had been arrested following the 1965 coup attempt, but released without trial; ET status had subjected them to certain restrictions (for example, in employment) and to widespread discrimination. The Government also revoked legislation requiring a permit for political gatherings, although the security forces still had to be notified. This display of liberality was, however, tempered by a new campaign against press freedom and political dissent.

In October 1995 30 members of an extreme right-wing group, the Islamic State of Indonesia, were arrested in western Java for attempting to overthrow 'the unitary state of Indonesia'. There were fears that Suharto's apparent attempt to balance the influence of the armed forces with an emphasis on Islam would create religious disharmony. Critics blamed the ICMI-sponsored newspaper *Republika* and its magazine *Ummat* for fomenting religious passions, leading to outbreaks of violence. Social unrest was also caused, however, by a disparity in living standards; in January 1996 in Bandung, West Java, thousands took part in demonstrations against the disproportionately wealthy ethnic Chinese.

In December 1995 Suharto implemented an unprecedented mid-term cabinet reorganization, in which Prof. Dr Satrio Budiardjo Yudono was dismissed and the Ministry of Trade, over which he had presided, was merged with the Ministry of Industry. This dismissal of one of Habibie's protégés, the day before Habibie's re-election to the chairmanship of the increasingly powerful ICMI, was widely interpreted as a signal from Suharto for Habibie to restrain his political ambitions. The accusations of financial irregularities and nepotism levelled against the Minister of Communications, Haryanto Dhanutirto (also a close associate of Habibie), were similarly interpreted.

In early 1996 there were limited moves to create greater political freedom. In January the Government abolished permit requirements for political meetings (police permission was still necessary for public gatherings and demonstrations). In March a group of political activists established an Independent Election Monitoring Committee, which was immediately declared unconstitutional by the Government. In April the Government restored voting rights to 1,157,820 people who had been associated with the PKI, leaving a further 20,706 still ineligible to vote. The Government's increasing concern over potential opposition to Golkar in the 1997 elections, however, resulted in a return

to more authoritarian practices. In May 1996 Sri Bintang Pamungkas, an outspoken member of the PPP expelled from the Dewan in March 1995, received a custodial sentence of 34 months for insulting Suharto; he remained free, however, pending an appeal. In the same month Pamungkas formed a new political organization, the Partai Uni Demokrasi Indonesia (PUDI—United Democratic Party of Indonesia), which ABRI and the Government refused to recognize. In December the High Court upheld the verdict against Pamungkas, who subsequently appealed to the Supreme Court.

In June 1996 the Government responded to the increasing popularity of Megawati's leadership of the PDI, and consequent potential threat to Golkar: government supporters within the PDI organized a party congress in the northern Sumatran town of Medan, which removed Megawati as leader of the party, and installed a former Chairman, Soerjadi. PDI members loyal to Megawati (who contested the legitimacy of the congress) organized demonstrations in her support throughout the country during July, and occupied the PDI headquarters in Jakarta. At the end of July members of Soerjadi's PDI faction and the armed forces acted to remove Megawati and her supporters forcibly from the PDI headquarters, prompting mass rioting in Jakarta. Violent clashes ensued between protesters and the security forces, in which five people were killed, 149 injured and 23 accounted missing, according to an official report (although the PDI claimed that the actual figures were higher). Sporadic rioting continued in the following days, during which security forces were instructed to shoot demonstrators on sight. Following the riots, the Government declared the minor, Marxist-influenced Partai Rakyat Demokrasi (PRD) to be responsible for the disturbances, and renewed its campaign against communism, claiming that the PRD was the PKI's successor. Among those arrested in connection with the riots were Budiman Sujatmiko, the Chairman of the PRD, and the trade union leader, Muchtar Pakpahan, whose trials commenced in December. In April 1997 Sujatmiko was convicted of subversion and sentenced to three years' imprisonment. Sujatmiko announced that he and four other PRD members who were also given custodial sentences would appeal against the verdict. In September the Government disbanded the PRD, declaring it to be a proscribed organization.

In an attempt to inhibit opposition efforts in the 1997 legislative elections, Suharto, in October 1996, ordered ABRI to suppress all political dissent. The Government's continued lack of commitment to its stated policy of political openness was demonstrated when, in November, it declared that it would take action against non-governmental organizations which violated Indonesian law and the *pancasila* ideology. In December the Dewan ratified legislation granting the Government extensive powers to revoke the broadcasting permits of private television and radio stations. In the same month a government decree banned mass rallies during the 1997 election campaign. In February 1997 the Government announced that all election campaign speeches, including those broadcast on television and radio, were to be vetted to ensure their adherence to the *pancasila*.

Repressive measures against Megawati's faction of the PDI continued; in September 1996 the Government declared Megawati's new party headquarters in eastern Jakarta to be illegal and it was closed by the military. Candidates nominated by Megawati's faction for the 1997 parliamentary elections were omitted from the final list of candidates in January 1997. In April thousands of supporters of Megawati rallied outside the Dewan to demand the right to contest the general election. In March Pamungkas was arrested for promoting a boycott of the legislative elections and two PUDI officials were also detained.

Prior to the general election, which was held on 29 May 1997, the Government permitted a campaign period of 25 days during which no two parties were permitted to campaign simultaneously in the same region. Despite these precautions and a heavy security presence, there was extensive localized pre-election violence. In the worst incident 125 people were killed when a shopping centre was set alight during clashes between supporters of Golkar and the PPP in the provincial capital of Kalimantan, Banjarmasin; more than 150 others were killed in various other incidents across the country. Following the election, riots in Madura, as a result of PPP claims that ballots had not been counted, resulted in an unprecedented repeat of voting at 86 polling stations on 4 June. The final results of the election, which continued to attract allegations of electoral fraud, revealed that Golkar had secured 74.3% of the vote (compared with 68.1% in 1992) giving it control of 325 seats, the PPP had won 89 seats, while Soerjadi's PDI had secured only 11 seats (compared with 56 in 1992).

Social unrest, which had been widespread in 1996, continued throughout 1997, as a result of religious tension, income disparity between social and ethnic groups and the repercussions of the transmigration programme initiated in 1971. The worst violence began in West Kalimantan in December 1996 as indigenous Dayak tribesmen massacred hundreds of Madurese transmigrants following an attack by Muslim youths on local schoolgirls. Despite a peace agreement in February 1997, fighting continued into March and thousands were displaced as they sought refuge from the attacks. In September six people died and there was extensive damage to property in two days of rioting which took place in Ujung Pandang (now Makassar), South Sulawesi, following the murder of a Muslim girl by an ethnic Chinese youth.

In June 1997 Harmoko was replaced as Minister of Information by the retiring Army Chief of Staff, Gen. Raden Hartono, and allocated a newly-created special affairs portfolio. In October Harmoko was also elected Speaker of the Dewan. Gen. Wiranto, the head of Kostrad, was appointed Army Chief of Staff and subsequently replaced Gen. Feisal as Commander-in-Chief of the Armed Forces in February 1998. Following four such military reorganizations in 1996, an extensive military reorganization took place in August 1997 in which commanders regarded as loyal to Suharto gained promotions.

In August 1997 the two principal Muslim leaders, Abdurrahman Wahid and Amien Rais, the leader of the second largest Islamic grouping, Muhammadiyah, were excluded from the list of 500 civilian and military appointees to the MPR. Amien Rais had been forced to resign from a board of experts in ICMI in February for publicly criticizing the controversial Freeport mine in Irian Jaya (West Papua, see below).

Following a massive decline in the value of the Indonesian currency between August and October 1997, Suharto was forced to accept a rescue programme from the International Monetary Fund (IMF) to restore confidence in the country's economy. However, Suharto subsequently failed to implement reforms required by the IMF that he feared would provoke social and political unrest and adversely affect his family and friends, who had long benefited from control of lucrative monopolies and tariff protection of their businesses. In December widespread rumours of Suharto's ill health provoked a further crisis of confidence in the Indonesian economy, owing to continuing uncertainty concerning the succession to the presidency. At the end of the month an unprecedented gathering of Muslim leaders and intellectuals took place, including members of ICMI; the participants rejected Suharto's leadership and rallied around Amien Rais, who had already offered himself as a presidential candidate. Wahid, although absent from the meeting, subsequently joined Amien Rais and Megawati (who had entered an informal alliance) in calling for Suharto's resignation. Megawati also, in a largely symbolic gesture since the President had to be a nominee of a party represented in the MPR, presented herself as a presidential candidate. In January 1998 Suharto, who was subject to unprecedented criticism for his mishandling of the economy and tolerance of corruption, delivered an unrealistic budget which failed to comply with IMF stipulations. A further rapid decline of the currency and massive price increases of staple foodstuffs ensued, causing incidents of rioting and then widespread buying and hoarding of basic commodities. Following meetings with foreign leaders and IMF representatives, Suharto was forced to announce a second budget in which he agreed to measures which, if implemented, would seriously harm the interests of his family and friends. At the end of January, however, despite opposition to his candidacy, Suharto declared his acceptance of Golkar's nomination for the presidency (announced in October) thus assuring his victory in the presidential election scheduled to be held on 10 March 1998. He indicated that of the 13 contenders for the vice-presidency he would support Habibie's candidacy, despite the minister's unpopularity with ABRI and his reputation for extravagant expenditure on high-technology projects. His failure formally to endorse a successor, however, continued to exacerbate political and economic turmoil.

At the presidential election (held, as scheduled, on 10 March 1998) Suharto was re-elected unopposed. Following his re-election, Suharto endorsed the nomination of Habibie as the new Vice-President, and on 14 March Suharto announced the appointment of a new, 36-member Cabinet, which included a

number of members of his immediate circle of friends and family. (Prior to his re-election, Suharto had also appointed his son-in-law, Lt-Gen. Prabowo Subianto, as Commander of Kostrad.) Suharto's appointment of such a Cabinet defied the recommendations of the IMF (which had expressed concern over the privileges that continued to be enjoyed by Suharto's friends and family) and further exacerbated popular discontent within the country. Following Suharto's re-election, student protests in support of calls for the President's resignation and for fundamental political and economic reforms increased. On 5 May riots erupted in Jakarta, precipitated by the announcement of a 70% increase in the price of fuel. During the following days violence and unrest spread throughout the archipelago. On 12 May six students were shot dead by military snipers during a student protest at Trisakti University in Jakarta, and violence in the city reached a peak on 14 May. It was initially estimated that during 12–15 May 500 people were killed in the capital while a further 700 perished elsewhere; however, a report published by Indonesia's leading human rights group in early June stated that at least 1,188 people had died in Jakarta alone. Thousands of buildings and vehicles were also destroyed, and a number of those who died were looters trapped inside burning buildings. Indonesia's ethnic-Chinese minority was the particular target for much of the violence that occurred in May: an uncertain number of Chinese were murdered, numerous Chinese women were raped, and Chinese homes and businesses were looted and burned. On 21 May, following days of violence and sustained popular and political pressure to step down (including an unprecedented demand for his resignation by Harmoko on 18 May, and the resignation of the 14 economic ministers in the Cabinet), Suharto announced his resignation as President. Vice-President Habibie was sworn in immediately as Suharto's successor, and subsequently appointed a new 'reform Cabinet', which, however, included a number of ministers from the previous administration. The new President also announced the release of a number of political prisoners (including Muchtar Pakpahan and Sri Bintang Pamungkas), encouraged government departments to sever ties with enterprises owned by Suharto's family, and supported Gen. Wiranto in his dismissal of Suharto's son-in-law, Lt.-Gen. Prabowo, from his position in Kostrad (it was subsequently announced that Prabowo had been formally dismissed from the army following an investigation into his conduct as Commander of the unit, and was also to face a court martial). Early in his presidency, Habibie also announced that elections would be held in 1999; new political parties began to be formed in anticipation of fresh electoral laws. On 1 June 1998 an investigation into the assets of former President Suharto and other government officials was announced, and later the same month Habibie expelled 41 members of the MPR, including several close associates of Suharto, on account of alleged corruption, nepotism and collusion. (Seven members of Suharto's family were ousted from their seats in the MPR the following month.) Despite such moves, however, Habibie was considered by many to be under the control of Suharto, and there were repeated demands from student groups and other opposition organizations for Habibie to relinquish the presidency and for a transitional government to be installed.

Discontent and rioting continued across the archipelago throughout the latter half of 1998, fuelled by dissatisfaction at the pace of change under the new administration and by severe food shortages, as well as by increasing tension among different ethnic and religious groups. A four-day special session of the MPR was convened in Jakarta on 10 November, and on 13 November at least 16 people were killed and more than 400 injured when students and civilians clashed with soldiers outside the building where the MPR session was being held; the violence was the worst since the riots in May. Further riots occurred in Jakarta on 22 November, in which at least another 14 people died during clashes between Muslims and Catholics; churches and Christian schools were also attacked.

On 3 November 1998 a report was published containing the findings of a panel appointed by the Government to investigate the riots in May. While the report gave no single figure for the number of people killed or injured, the panel found that elements of the military had acted as provocateurs during the riots (with particular suspicion falling on a unit led by Lt-Gen. Prabowo) and concluded that the riots had been 'created as part of a political struggle at the level of the élite'. The panel recommended that further investigations be carried out into the causes of the violent unrest. (Contrary to earlier official statements, the report also found that a number of rapes had taken place during the riots.) On 9 December former President Suharto faced questioning at the Higher Prosecutor's Office over allegations of corruption; two former cabinet ministers, including Suharto's close associate, Mohammad (Bob) Hasan, were also summoned for questioning. In early December 1998 Amnesty International published a report criticizing the human rights record of the Habibie Government.

On 3 December 1998 it was announced that a legislative election would be held on 7 June 1999; it was further announced that the MPR (including 200 additional delegates) would convene on 29 August to elect a new President. In early December 1998 a large demonstration was held in Jakarta by supporters of Megawati, effectively marking the beginning of electoral campaigning, and in early January 1999 it was reported that Golkar representatives had hinted at the possibility of entering a coalition with unspecified opposition parties. On 27 January a number of changes to the electoral laws were announced in advance of the forthcoming election: in accordance with a new electoral system combining both district and proportional voting, seats in the Dewan were to be allocated proportionally, but only parties fielding candidates in a substantial number of districts would be permitted to contest the election. (Although, by the end of December, more than 100 parties were reported to have applied to be registered to participate in the election, the new legislation was expected to result in a far smaller number of parties qualifying to stand.) It was further announced that civil servants were no longer to be obliged to support Golkar, that the number of seats in the Dewan allocated to the military was to be reduced from 75 to 38 and that the membership of the MPR was to be reduced from 1,000 to 700 (500 of whom would comprise the members of the Dewan while, of the remainder, 135 were to be elected by the provincial assemblies and 65 appointed by the Komite Pemilihan Umum—General Election Committee).

Violent unrest continued across the archipelago throughout January and February 1999: at least 159 people were killed during clashes between Muslims and Christians on the island of Ambon, in the province of Maluku, while a number of others died in outbreaks of violence elsewhere, prompting a call for national unity from President Habibie. Although the campaigning for the forthcoming legislative election dominated the political agenda during the first half of 1999, the Habibie Government continued to pursue an extensive programme of reform during this period. Amongst new laws passed were several that benefited the provinces, including one providing for the election of district heads (*bupati*) by the district assemblies. In April the Subversion Law, introduced under the Suharto administration in 1963 and previously applied in the suppression of political dissidents, was repealed by the MPR (although some of the prohibitions covered by the law were retained). In May a presidential decree was announced in which Habibie removed a ban on the use and teaching of the Mandarin Chinese language and also outlawed discrimination on the grounds of ethnic origin. Two significant changes also took place in the armed forces in the first half of 1999: following a reshuffle of military personnel in January, in April the police force—part of the Indonesian military since 1962—was formally separated from the armed forces (although it remained under the control of the Ministry of Defence); and the armed forces resumed their revolutionary-era name, Tentara Nasional Indonesia (TNI—the Indonesian National Defence Forces), in place of the Suharto-era name, ABRI (the Armed Forces of the Republic of Indonesia). The Government remained under considerable public pressure during this period, however, to investigate the accumulation of wealth by the Suharto family during the years of Suharto's presidency, and there was considerable popular dissatisfaction at the progress of the official investigation: although several members of Suharto's family had been questioned, at mid-1999 only Suharto's youngest son, Hutomo 'Tommy' Mandala Putra, faced prosecution. Concerns also remained that the former President continued to exercise undue political influence.

President Habibie was nominated as the sole presidential candidate of the Golkar party on 14 May 1999, despite concerns expressed by some elements of the party that Habibie's close association with former President Suharto could have a potential negative impact on the party's electoral performance. On 18 May the three leading opposition parties—Megawati's Partai Demokrasi Indonesia Perjuangan (PDI—P, Indonesian Democratic Struggle Party), Abdurrahman Wahid's Partai Kebangkitan Bangsa (PKB, National Awakening Party), and Amien

Rais's Partai Amanat Nasional (PAN, National Mandate Party)—agreed to form an informal electoral alliance against Golkar; however, the alliance exhibited instability from an early stage. The election campaign was formally opened on 19 May, and proceeded with only minimal incidents of violent disruption, with 48 parties competing for a share of the vote. The election was held as scheduled on 7 June; approximately 118m. people voted (a turn-out of 91%). A delay of about seven weeks before the results of the poll were announced led to some accusations of suspected irregularities; however, the delay was widely accepted to be a consequence of infrastructural difficulties and inexperience. As expected, Megawati's PDI—P led the polls, winning 34% of the votes cast (154 seats); the second largest share of the vote was unexpectedly won by Golkar, who secured 20% of votes cast (120 seats), performing poorly in the cities but achieving a strong result in the outer islands. Abdurrahman Wahid's PKB secured 59 seats, while Amien Rais's PAN won just 7% of the vote (35 seats). Some 14 other smaller parties also won seats in the MPR, with a combined share of the vote totalling about 7%. Despite allegations made by a number of minor parties of irregularities in the election process, the results were finally endorsed by President Habibie on 3 August. In the context of the election results, Megawati and Habibie emerged initially as the main candidates for the presidency, which was originally scheduled to be decided in November. On 20 October, however, following the rejection of his presidential record by the MPR in a secret ballot, Habibie withdrew his candidacy just hours before the vote (which had been rescheduled to take place on that day) was due to be held. Expectations that Megawati would be elected President increased immediately; however, Megawati failed to win the contest, receiving 313 votes compared with the 373 secured by Abdurrahman Wahid, the only other serious candidate for the presidency, who had received the endorsement of a number of Islamic parties as well as the support of the Golkar party following the withdrawal of Habibie from the contest. The announcement of Wahid's victory provoked outrage from Megawati's supporters, and violent protests ensued in Jakarta and elsewhere on Java, as well as on the island of Bali. On 21 October the MPR voted to appoint Megawati as Vice-President. The new Cabinet was announced on 26 October, and reflected the conciliatory and inclusive approach of the new President: it included both Islamist and nationalist representatives, as well as representatives of non-Javanese groups (reportedly including Acehnese, Bugis, Irianese (West Papuan), Batak, Sumatran and Balinese minorities), and an ethnic Chinese was appointed as chief economic minister. Gen. Wiranto, who was appointed Co-ordinating Minister for Political Affairs and Security, was replaced as Minister of Defence by the former Minister of Education and Culture, Yuwono Sudarsono, the first civilian to hold the post. Wiranto was replaced as Commander-in-Chief of the TNI by Adm. Widodo Adi Sutjipto.

On 27 October 1999 the newly-appointed Attorney-General, Marzuki Darusman, announced that the investigation into the allegations of corruption made against former President Suharto—which had been closed under the Habibie Government on the alleged grounds of lack of evidence—was to be reopened. The apparent commitment of the new administration to addressing the issue of corruption was further emphasized in November, when Wahid urged the investigation of three government ministers in relation to allegations of corruption. One of the ministers reportedly implicated, the Co-ordinating Minister for People's Welfare and the Eradication of Poverty and leader of the PPP, Hamzah Haz, resigned from the Cabinet in late November.

In the months following Wahid's election to the presidency, further violent unrest took place across the archipelago. Particularly serious ethnic violence continued on the island of Ambon in Maluku province where, according to official estimates in December 1999, more than 750 people had died and many thousands more had fled the region, since the outbreak of the most recent series of violent clashes between Muslims and Christians in the region in January of that year. (Aid agencies, however, estimated the total number of dead to be much higher.) In mid-December President Wahid and Vice-President Megawati (who was subject to harsh criticism for her failure to address the crisis, despite having been charged by Wahid with special responsibility for Maluku) visited the strife-torn region and urged an end to the conflict. Later the same month hundreds more troops were sent to Ambon to supplement the 2,500 already deployed in Maluku, following a further escalation of the violence and the occurrence of dozens more deaths. Although the predominantly Muslim northern districts of Maluku were formally separated as the new province of North Maluku in late 1999, this failed to dispel the tension, and in December violence flared on other islands in the region, with at least 265 people reported killed in clashes between Christians and Muslims on the island of Halmahera at the end of the month.

On 31 January 2000 Indonesia's National Human Rights Commission released a report containing the results of its investigation into the role of the Indonesian armed forces in human rights abuses in the former Indonesian province of East Timor (see below). Thirty-three military officers, including the former Commander-in-Chief of the armed forces, Gen. Wiranto, were implicated by the report. In response to the Commission's conclusions, President Wahid demanded Wiranto's resignation from his post of Co-ordinating Minister for Political Affairs and Security. Over the following two weeks, Wahid repeated his public calls for Wiranto to resign from the Cabinet; Wiranto, however, continued openly to defy Wahid's demands. In mid-February Wahid suspended Wiranto from his position; Wiranto was to maintain his ministerial rank, although his portfolio was allocated to the Minister of Home Affairs, Gen. (retd) Suryadi Sudirja, pending an investigation into the conclusions contained in the Commission's report. Wiranto resigned in mid-May. In January, meanwhile, a reorganization took place within the TNI, in which officers loyal to Wiranto were apparently removed from positions of influence. A second reorganization of senior military personnel was announced in February, in which Maj.-Gen. Agus Wirahadikusumah, who was reportedly committed to Wahid's policy of disengaging the military from Indonesian politics, was appointed as the head of Kostrad. In August doubts concerning the commitment of the Indonesian Government to the trial of military personnel suspected of involvement in gross human rights violations in East Timor were provoked when the MPR introduced a constitutional amendment that excluded military personnel from prosecution for crimes committed prior to the enactment of the relevant legislation, an amendment that was feared by many international observers seriously to threaten the possibility of the prosecution of members of the Indonesian military believed responsible for recent human rights abuses in the territory. These doubts were compounded in early September, when Gen. Wiranto's name was not included on a list, announced by the Attorney-General's office, of 19 suspects named in connection with such violations.

In late April 2000 President Wahid dismissed from the Cabinet the Minister of State for Investment and Development of State Enterprises, Laksamana Sukardi of the PDI—P, and the Minister of Trade and Industry, Yusuf Kalla of the pro-Habibie wing of Golkar; Wahid subsequently suggested that both Ministers were guilty of corruption. In July Wahid faced fierce criticism from the Dewan when he refused to explain the reasons for his dismissal of the two Ministers. Meanwhile, general misgivings about Wahid's style of government also increased during 2000. On 9 August, apparently in response to increasing criticism of his leadership from within the Indonesian legislature, Wahid announced that he was to delegate the daily administration of the Government to Vice-President Megawati. The President stated, however, that he was to retain overall control, and that Megawati was to be accountable to him. It was subsequently speculated by many observers that Wahid's announcement had been intended to safeguard his own position during the 12-day session of the MPR held on 7–18 August, in the context of widespread dissatisfaction with the President's record among the members of the legislative body. The announcement of the apparent power-sharing arrangement appeared to placate the MPR, which was rumoured previously to have considered the possibility either of requesting that Wahid step down or of removing him from office in a special session of the legislature. In the event, however, amendments to the Constitution passed by the MPR in August included articles defining explicitly the authority of the Dewan, particularly in relation to the body's questioning and investigating of government activities; legislation was also passed to extend military representation in the MPR until 2009, four years after the date at which the military had been scheduled to lose its remaining 38 seats in the chamber. On 23 August President Wahid announced the formation of a new 26-member Cabinet. The incoming Cabinet included considerably fewer representatives of Megawati's PDI—P, reportedly resulting in serious tensions between the President and the Vice-President. Two of the most influential cabinet posts were allocated to Wahid loyalists: Susilo Bambang Yudhoyono was appointed Co-ordinating Minister for Political Affairs, Security and Social Welfare, while Rizal Ramli was designated Co-ordinating Minister for the Economy, Finance and Industry, replacing Kwik Kian Gie, who had resigned in advance of the reorganization.

On 31 August 2000 the trial of former President Suharto was adjourned for a fortnight after the former President, who in early August had been formally charged with corruption arising from his 30 years in power, failed to appear in court to hear the charges against him. Following claims by Suharto's lawyers that their client was seriously ill and not fit to stand trial, the judge allowed the defence team two weeks in which to prepare the testimony of the former President's 23 doctors, detailing the defendant's condition. In late September all corruption charges against Suharto were dismissed after an independent team of doctors declared that the former President was mentally and physically unfit to stand trial, provoking violent protests on the streets of Jakarta. In early November, however, the Jakarta High Court ruled that the trial was to resume. In mid-September, meanwhile, President Wahid announced that he had ordered the arrest of Suharto's youngest son, Hutomo ('Tommy') Mandala Putra in connection with a series of bomb threats and explosions in Jakarta in August and September in which supporters of Suharto and his family were suspected of involvement. In one attack in mid-September at least 15 people were killed when a bomb exploded in the basement of the Jakarta Stock Exchange. (In the previous month, three people were killed in a bomb attack on the residence of the Philippine ambassador to Jakarta; President Wahid, however, suggested that this explosion was connected with political tensions in the Philippines.) In late September Hutomo Mandala Putra was sentenced to 18 months' imprisonment after being convicted on an unrelated charge of fraudulent activity; however, he subsequently evaded arrest and went into hiding.

In early September 2000 the Dewan appointed a committee to investigate two financial scandals with which President Wahid had been linked. The first of the two scandals involved the irregular diversion of US $4.1m. from the funds of the Badan Urusan Logistic (BULOG—the National Logistics Agency), whilst the second concerned a donation of US $2m. made by Sultan Hassanal Bolkiah of Brunei. Although, initially, there appeared to be no compelling evidence implicating Wahid in these scandals, the President's refusal to be questioned on either matter provoked intense frustration among legislators. The commission reported the findings of its investigation into President Wahid's involvement in the scandals in late January 2001, concluding that Wahid 'could be suspected of playing a role' in the theft of BULOG funds by his personal masseur and that the President had been deliberately inconsistent in his explanations of how the donation from Sultan Hassanal Bolkiah (originally intended for social welfare) had been spent; however, the commission failed to present conclusive evidence that Wahid had personally benefited from either situation. Following the presentation of the committee's report, thousands of protesters demanding the resignation of the President clashed with police in violent demonstrations in Jakarta. In early February the Dewan, in response to the commission's conclusions, voted by 393 votes to four for the formal censure of Wahid over his alleged involvement in the scandals. According to Indonesian law, Wahid was given three months to respond to the motion of censure and to explain his actions to the Dewan. If, three months after the original memorandum of censure, the members of the Dewan should remain unsatisfied by the President's response, a further warning could be issued after which Wahid would be given 30 days to act before a vote could be held to remove him from office. Following the issue of the original memorandum of censure, however, the President continued to deny any wrongdoing, and dismissed the course of action taken by the Dewan as being based on an interpretation of events rather than on the facts of the case. He also rejected demands for his resignation—voiced by numerous prominent political figures, including Wahid's former ally, Amien Rais—and stated his intention to complete his term of presidential office. In the days following the censure of the President, tens of thousands of pro-Wahid demonstrators took to the streets in Surabaya and other centres in East Java (President Wahid's home province), and protesters set fire to the regional offices of Golkar, which had supported the vote to censure Wahid. Later the same month Wahid offered himself for questioning by police investigating the two scandals. Also in February, following his censure by the Dewan, Wahid dismissed the Minister for Justice and Human Rights Affairs, Yusril Ihza Mahendra, allegedly for disloyalty.

The escalation of communal violence across the archipelago, together with separatist tensions in individual regions such as Aceh and Irian Jaya (also known as West Papua —see below), continued to be one of the principal challenges facing the Wahid Government throughout much of 2000 and early 2001. In 2000 some of the worst such violence again occurred in the provinces of Maluku and North Maluku, arising from an ongoing conflict between the region's Christian and Muslim populations. By mid-2000 more than 4,000 people were reported to have been killed and some 300,000 displaced as a result of the violence. In one attack in June at least 116 people, including 108 Christians, were believed to have been killed in the village of Duma in North Maluku, and in the same month up to 600 Christians fleeing the violence were reported to have drowned when the ship on which they were travelling sank off the island of Halmahera. In late June President Wahid declared a state of civil emergency in the provinces of Maluku and North Maluku, in a vain attempt to curb the escalation of violence in the region. Later the same month, it was announced that around 1,400 of the 10,200 members of the armed forces in the region were to be replaced because they had become involved in the conflict, and in the case of at least one outbreak of serious violence it was reported that evidence had emerged of the military's collusion with elements of the militant Muslim paramilitary organization, Laskar Jihad, which had travelled to the region to participate in the campaign of violence, thus supporting the view of many observers that the Indonesian military was allowing Muslim attacks on Christians to take place. In December 18 people were reported to have been killed and more than 80 others injured in a series of bombings of Christian Churches in nine towns and cities across Indonesia, including Jakarta, on Christmas Eve. No group claimed responsibility for the explosions, which were condemned by President Wahid as an attempt to destabilize his Government by inciting religious hatred and fear among the Christian and Muslim communities. The attacks prompted concerns about the possibility of the spread to the capital of religious violence similar to that raging in Maluku. In February 2001 violence also broke out in the province of Central Kalimantan, where fierce resentment of Madurese transmigrants remained rife among the indigenous Dayak tribespeople. At least 428 Madurese were murdered by native Dayaks, and many of the victims were beheaded in accordance with traditional Dayak practices; many thousands more fled their homes. The failure of the armed forces to control the violence—the legacy of a resettlement programme begun under the Suharto Government in the 1970s—and to protect Madurese refugees in their care led to further allegations of the military's complicity in ethnic violence.

On 1 January 2001 new legislation took effect devolving increased financial and administrative control to Indonesia's regional governments. (The central Government was meanwhile to retain control over justice, defence, foreign affairs and monetary policy.) The day after the introduction of the new legislation, the Minister of State for State Administrative Reforms, Ryaas Rasyid, resigned from his post, reportedly because of his frustration at the inadequacy of the Government's preparations for the implementation of the new decentralization policy, which was intended to defuse separatist tensions across the archipelago; the Cabinet Secretary, Marsilam Simandjuntak, was appointed as Rasyid's temporary replacement.

During 1974, meanwhile, several parties emerged within the small Portuguese colony of East Timor, with aims ranging from full independence to integration with Indonesia or Australia. Indonesia, which had never presented a claim to East Timor, initially showed little interest in the territory. In 1975 Portuguese forces withdrew from the colony, and the territory's capital, Dili, was occupied by the forces of the left-wing Frente Revolucionária do Timor Leste Independente (Fretilin), which advocated independence for East Timor. To prevent Fretilin from gaining full control of the territory, Indonesian troops intervened and established a provincial government. In July 1976 East Timor was declared the 27th province of Indonesia. Human rights organizations subsequently claimed that as many as 200,000 people, from a total population of 650,000, might have been killed by the Indonesian armed forces during the annexation. The Indonesian Government, however, ignored widespread international condemnation of the invasion. The UN meanwhile continued officially to recognize Portugal as the administrative power in East Timor. In February 1983 the UN Commission on Human Rights adopted a resolution affirming East Timor's right to independence and self-determination. In November 1990

the Indonesian Government rejected proposals by the military commander of Fretilin, José Alexandre (Xanana) Gusmão, for unconditional peace negotiations aimed at ending the armed struggle in East Timor. In August 1992 the UN General Assembly adopted its first resolution condemning Indonesia's violations of human rights in East Timor.

The downfall of President Suharto in May 1998 and the subsequent accession to the presidency of Habibie raised hopes, both internationally and within East Timor itself, that independence for the territory might be granted in the near future. In August it was announced that Indonesia and Portugal had agreed to hold discussions on the possibility of 'wide-ranging' autonomy for East Timor. On 27 January 1999, however, the Indonesian Government unexpectedly announced that, if the East Timorese were to vote to reject Indonesia's proposals for autonomy, it would consider granting independence to the province. Although the Government was initially opposed to a referendum on the issue of independence for East Timor, it signed an agreement with Portugal on 5 May, giving its assent to a process of 'popular consultation' to take the form of a UN-supervised poll to determine the territory's future status. The referendum proceeded on 30 August, and resulted in an overwhelming rejection by 78.5% of voters of the Indonesian Government's proposals for autonomy and in an endorsement of independence for East Timor. Following the announcement of the result of the referendum, which led to a rapid deterioration in the security situation in East Timor, in late September Indonesia and Portugal reiterated their agreement for the transfer of authority in East Timor to the UN. Also in late September the Indonesian armed forces formally relinquished responsibility for security in the territory to the UN peace-keeping force, the International Force for East Timor (Interfet); the last Indonesian troops left East Timor in late October. On 19 October the result of the referendum was ratified by the Indonesian MPR, thus permitting East Timor's accession to independence to proceed. (See chapter on East Timor, p. 1387.) In September 2000 Indonesia faced outrage from the UN and the international community following the murder of three UN aid workers by pro-Jakarta militias in West Timor. The Indonesian Government came under strong criticism for its failure to control the militia groups, which were believed by many to be receiving the support of the Indonesian military. Indonesia subsequently refused to co-operate with a planned UN investigation into the killings.

In the mid-1970s dissent re-emerged in Aceh, which, at the end of the war of independence, had held the status of a full province of the Republic of Indonesia but which had subsequently had this status removed before being made a special territory (Daerah Istimewa) with considerable autonomy in religious and educational affairs. The dissent was provoked by the exploitation by the central Government of Aceh's natural resources and the subsequent lack of benefits from these operations received by the region itself. A sense of the erosion of Aceh's autonomy was heightened by the migration and transmigration of other Indonesians into the region and by the increasing power of the central Government, and in 1976 the Gerakan Aceh Merdeka (GAM—Free Aceh Movement) was formed by Hasan di Tiro, who declared independence in 1977. This small rebellion was swiftly suppressed by the armed forces; however, Tiro later established a government-in-exile in Sweden.

In 1989 opposition to the central Government rose again, this time led by the National Liberation Front Aceh Sumatra. The region was made a 'military operations zone' in 1990, thus allowing the armed forces far greater freedom to counter the uprising. By mid-1991 the rebellion had been largely suppressed; however, it was estimated that about 1,000 Acehnese had been killed in the process, as a result of the use of excessive and indiscriminate force by the military. The number of deaths continued to rise in subsequent years, and in 1993 Amnesty International estimated that about 2,000 Acehnese had been killed since 1989, with hundreds of others having 'disappeared'.

Aceh's status as a 'military operations zone' was revoked in June 1998, following the downfall of President Suharto in May, and an apology for past military excesses was made by Gen. Wiranto. The subsequent intended withdrawal of Indonesian troops from the province was suspended, however, following rioting in Aceh in September. Decentralization measures introduced by President Habibie failed to defuse resentment in the province, and public opinion in Aceh became increasingly sympathetic towards the notion of independence. Violence continued to escalate in the province throughout 1999: in January at least 15 people were killed during military operations, and in May at least 42 Acehnese were killed during raids carried out by the armed forces on suspected GAM hideouts. The discovery of several mass graves of people killed by the armed forces during security operations further exacerbated tension in the province. Violence continued to escalate following the legislative elections of 9 June as GAM guerrillas intensified their campaign for independence for Aceh. On 23 July at least 56 Acehnese villagers were killed by the military in an attack on the village of Beutong Ateuh in western Aceh, and by late August 200 Acehnese were reported to have been killed by the Indonesian armed forces since the initiation in June of a renewed military campaign in an attempt by the central Government to suppress the uprising.

In early November 1999, following the rejection by legislators in the provincial assembly of demands for the holding of a referendum on self-determination for Aceh, a provincial government building in western Aceh was set on fire during a demonstration by 5,000 protesters. While much of the ongoing widespread violence in the province was attributed to the separatist movement, it was believed by observers that some unrest was initiated by so-called 'provocateurs' acting to destabilize the province and undermine the separatist movement. On 4 November the newly-appointed President of Indonesia, Abdurrahman Wahid, unexpectedly stated that the holding of a referendum in Aceh was a possibility; these remarks were confirmed by the President several days later. In late November, however, Wahid made it clear that the suggested poll would not include the option of independence, but would instead offer Aceh a broad degree of autonomy. Wahid's proposals angered the TNI, which, in the wake of the vote in favour of independence in East Timor in August, reportedly feared that, unless brought under control, the separatist movement in Aceh could potentially incite rebellion across the archipelago and contribute to national disintegration. The offer of increased autonomy, rather than independence, also failed to satisfy Acehnese separatists, and violence continued throughout the province. In May 2000 the Indonesian Government and Acehnese rebel negotiators agreed upon a cease-fire, which took effect from 2 June. Also in May 2000 24 junior soldiers and one civilian were sentenced to various terms of imprisonment for the murder in July 1999 of 58 Acehnese in Beutong Aceh; however, the trial was criticized by both Acehnese community groups, which had demanded the death penalty for the accused, and by human rights lawyers, who urged the holding of a wider trial of crimes against humanity in the province. In September 2000 the cease-fire was extended by three months to January 2001. Violence continued throughout the province, however, and it was estimated by Acehnese human rights groups that more than 1,000 civilians had died in clashes between the Indonesian military and Acehnese rebels during 2000. In December thousands of Acehnese protesters rallied peacefully in Banda Aceh, demanding independence for the province. However, it was reported that at least 34 (and possibly as many as 200, according to human rights groups) unarmed civilians had been killed in the days preceding the rally as the result of military action to target Acehnese en route to the demonstration. On the day after the protest, Acehnese separatists withdrew from peace talks with the Indonesian Government, stating that they would resume negotiations only when the military ceased killing Acehnese civilians. In January 2001 peace talks between the Indonesian Government and Acehnese separatists recommenced. In the same month the cease-fire was extended to February.

In May 1977 there was a rebellion in the province of Irian Jaya (also known as West Papua), annexed to Indonesia in 1963 (see above). The rebellion was said to have been organized by the Organisasi Papua Merdeka (OPM—Free Papua Movement), which seeks unification with Papua New Guinea. Fighting continued until December 1979, when Indonesia and Papua New Guinea finalized a new border administrative agreement. Frequent border incidents followed, however, and in early 1984 fighting broke out in Jayapura, the capital of Irian Jaya. As a result, about 10,000 refugees fled over the border into Papua New Guinea. In October 1984 Indonesia and Papua New Guinea signed a five-year agreement establishing a joint border security committee; by the end of 1985 Indonesians were continuing to cross into Papua New Guinea, but a limited number of repatriations took place in 1986. There was also concern among native Irian Jayans (who are of Melanesian origin) at the introduction of large numbers of Javanese into the province,

under the Government's transmigration scheme. This was interpreted as an attempt to reduce the Melanesians to a minority and thus to stifle opposition. In 1986 it was announced that the Government intended to resettle 65m. people over a 20-year period, in spite of protests from human rights and conservation groups that the scheme would cause ecological damage and interfere with the rights of the native Irian Jayans. Relations with Papua New Guinea improved when the Prime Minister, Paias Wingti, visited Suharto in January 1988. However, a series of cross-border raids by the Indonesian armed forces in October and November, in an attempt to capture Melanesian separatists operating on the border, led to renewed tension between the two countries. In October 1990 the Governments of Indonesia and Papua New Guinea renewed the basic accord on border arrangements; which included an agreement on the formation of a joint defence committee and a formal commitment to share border intelligence. In early September 1992 the two countries agreed to facilitate the passage of border trade, and in the following month an Indonesian consulate was established in Vanimo.

In March 1991 the leader of the OPM, Melkianus Salossa (who had been arrested in Papua New Guinea in May 1990 and deported to Indonesia), was sentenced to life imprisonment. In May 1992 Indonesian troops crossed into Papua New Guinea to destroy an OPM camp at Wutung, prior to the legislative elections in Indonesia in June. In October 1993 clashes were reported in Irian Jaya between government troops and separatist rebels; the armed forces were alleged to have killed 73 inhabitants of a neighbouring village. In late February 1994 it was reported that the OPM had proposed entering into peace talks with the Indonesian Government.

In April 1995 the Australian Council for Overseas Aid (ACFOA) alleged that 37 Irian Jayans had been killed by security forces near the Freeport copper and gold mine between June 1994 and February 1995. In August the ACFOA's claims were reiterated by non-governmental organizations, which lodged a complaint with the National Commission on Human Rights in Jakarta about summary executions, arbitrary detentions and torture in the province between mid-1994 and mid-1995. In November 1995 four members of ABRI were arrested in an investigation into the killing in May of 11 unarmed civilians at a prayer meeting. Also in November the Overseas Private Investment Corporation (a US government agency) cancelled political risk insurance valued at US $100m. for Freeport (a subsidiary of a US enterprise), citing environmental concerns. Freeport's perceived responsibility for the situation in Irian Jaya arose from its role as civil administrator in the area of the mine and also because the indigenous inhabitants' campaigns against Freeport's indiscriminate exploitation of natural resources in the area often resulted in their being killed by security forces as suspected members of the OPM.

In December 1995 clashes between Indonesian forces and the OPM intensified, forcing hundreds of refugees to cross into Papua New Guinea. In January 1996, in an attempt to raise awareness of their cause, the OPM kidnapped 26 hostages, including seven Europeans. The various issues that the OPM hoped to highlight included the claim that ABRI had been responsible for killing 43,000 indigenous inhabitants of Irian Jaya since 1977. The movement's demands included autonomy for Irian Jaya, the withdrawal of Indonesian troops and compensation for the relatives of those killed. A number of the hostages were released by the OPM. In May, however, 11 hostages (including six Europeans) remained captive. Following the rejection of a negotiated settlement by the OPM, an operation to effect their rescue was instigated by ABRI, during which eight OPM soldiers were killed; two Indonesian hostages were killed by their captors, while the other nine hostages were safely rescued.

Four people were killed in riots in Jayapura in March 1996, which had been precipitated by the return of the remains of Thomas Wainggai (a resistance leader who had died while serving a 20-year custodial sentence for subversion) for burial. Riots near the Grasberg mine in the same month were the result of problems similar to those experienced by residents in the Freeport area (relating principally to the lack of any benefit from the mining project to the local community and to the potential impact of the project on the local environment). There were also tensions among the local Irianese, Indonesians from other provinces and commercial operators. In April Freeport agreed to allocate 1% of revenue over a period of 10 years to community development programmes for tribal groups living around the mine, and to tighten environmental safeguards. In October armed clashes between Indonesian troops and the OPM resulted in the death of a separatist.

In July 1998, following the resignation of President Suharto in May and his subsequent replacement by President Habibie, troops clashed with pro-independence demonstrators in Jayapura. Two people were reported to have been killed in the violence, and a further five were reportedly killed during an outbreak of violence on the island of Biak in July. In early October the Government revoked the status of Irian Jaya as a 'military operations zone' following the conclusion of a cease-fire agreement with the OPM in late September; however, the move was not followed by the withdrawal of troops from the region. In February 1999 Irian Jayan tribal leaders raised the issue of independence for the province at a meeting with President Habibie. (A referendum on self-determination for the province had been promised by the Indonesian Government prior to the territory's annexation in 1963; however, whilst a vote was eventually held in 1969, only tribal chiefs selected by Jakarta were allowed to participate and the result was widely discredited.) The independence movement in the province continued to strengthen throughout 1999, and was encouraged by the achievements of the East Timorese independence movement (see above). In early December independence demonstrations took place throughout Irian Jaya. Protests held in Jayapura reportedly took place without any incidents of violence, although at least three protesters were reported to have been killed by the Indonesian armed forces during independence demonstrations held in the town of Timika. Later the same month a delegation from the Dewan visited the province and announced that the administration of the newly-elected President Abdurrahman Wahid had agreed to the popular demand that the province's name be changed from Irian Jaya to West Papua, although it was emphasized that this decision should not be construed as implying the Government's approval of any moves towards the province's secession from Indonesia. (It was subsequently reported, however, that the proposed change had failed to receive the requisite approval of the Indonesian legislature.)

In late May–early June 2000 the Papuan People's Congress was held in Jayapura. The Congress, which was attended by a reported 4,000 people, concluded with the adoption of a five-point resolution reinstating a declaration of independence for West Papua originally made in 1961, before the province's annexation to Indonesia. The declaration was, however, immediately rebuffed by the Indonesian Government. In early October between 30 and 40 people were killed and many others injured in clashes between police and West Papuan separatists in the town of Wamena when police attempted to remove a Morning Star independence flag being flown by the separatists. Although President Wahid had previously decreed that the flying of the Morning Star flag was allowed, provided that the flag was flown alongside, and slightly lower than, the Indonesian flag, following the violence the Government introduced a ban on the flying of the flag. In November and early December the Indonesian military took severe action against separatists; seven people were shot dead by the armed forces in an outbreak of violence in the town of Merauke, and dozens of separatist sympathizers, including the pro-independence leader, Theys Eluay, were arrested. On 1 December pro-independence supporters rallied in the province to mark the 39th anniversary of the first unilateral declaration of West Papua's independence. The rallies were largely peaceful, but in the town of Fakfak two demonstrators were shot dead by police. In early 2001 the Indonesian Government continued its refusal to consider the possibility of independence for the province. In January, however, it was reported that special autonomy for West Papua might be implemented by May of that year.

Under Suharto, Indonesia's foreign policy was one of non-alignment, although the country maintained close relations with the West. As a member of the Association of South East Asian Nations (ASEAN), Indonesia supported the organization's opposition to Viet Nam's military presence in Cambodia and played a prominent role in attempts to find a political solution to the situation in Cambodia (see p. 890). The Indonesian Minister of Foreign Affairs and his French counterpart were appointed Co-Chairmen of the Paris International Conference on Cambodia, which first met in August 1989. In 1997, following Second Prime Minister Hun Sen's assumption of sole power in Cambodia, Indonesia led ASEAN attempts to resolve the crisis.

In July 1985 Indonesia and the People's Republic of China signed a memorandum of understanding on the resumption of direct trade links, which had been suspended since 1967. In April 1988 the Indonesian Government indicated its readiness to re-establish full diplomatic relations with China, subject to an assurance that the latter would not seek to interfere in Indonesia's internal affairs; previously, Suharto had insisted that China acknowledge its alleged complicity in the 1965 attempted coup. Diplomatic relations were finally restored in August 1990, following an Indonesian undertaking to settle financial debts incurred with China by the Sukarno regime. In November Suharto visited China and Viet Nam (the first Indonesian leader to do so since 1964 and 1975 respectively). Suharto subsequently announced that former Indonesian communists living in exile would be permitted to return home, although they risked imprisonment. In 1995 China extended claims to territorial waters within Indonesia's exclusive economic zone, consequently threatening Indonesia's natural gas resources, in particular those situated in the region of the Natuna Islands. An extensive Indonesian military exercise in September 1996, which concluded at the Natuna Islands, was perceived as a demonstration of the archipelago's strength to China. Also in September as many as 50 Chinese fishing vessels were detained by Indonesia and later expelled.

Bilateral relations between Indonesia and China suffered a reverse in 1998 following the violence perpetrated against ethnic Chinese Indonesians at the time of the fall of Suharto in May. China issued a strong diplomatic protest at the violence, and gave prominent coverage in the state-controlled media to reports of the rapes, arson and murders. Following his accession to the presidency, President Habibie publicly expressed his sympathy for the plight of the ethnic Chinese victims of violence. Subsequently, in May 1999, as part of an ongoing programme of general reform, Habibie lifted a ban that had existed on the use and teaching of the Mandarin Chinese language within Indonesia. In early December the newly-appointed President of Indonesia, Abdurrahman Wahid, made an official visit to China; Wahid was believed by observers to attach considerable importance to the improvement of relations with China.

In December 1989 Indonesia and Australia concluded a temporary agreement providing for joint exploration for petroleum and gas in the Timor Gap, which had been a disputed area since 1978. However, no permanent sea boundary was approved. The validity of the Timor Gap agreement was challenged by Portugal, which instituted proceedings at the International Court of Justice (ICJ), on the grounds that the agreement infringed Portuguese sovereignty and interests; however, in June 1995 the ICJ rejected the case on the grounds that it would affect a country that was not represented, as Indonesia did not recognize the ICJ's jurisdiction. In June 1993 the East Timorese resistance began proceedings in the High Court of Australia to overturn legislation confirming the Timor Gap agreement on the grounds that Australia was bound by international law, which did not recognize Indonesia's annexation of East Timor. In April 1990 Indonesia and Australia restored defence co-operation links, following a four-year disruption. In September 1994 Vice-President Sutrisno became the first high-ranking Indonesian official to visit Australia since Suharto's last visit in 1975.

In July 1995 Indonesia withdrew the nomination of Lt-Gen. Herman Mantiri, a former Chief of the General Staff, as ambassador to Australia, owing to widespread protests there concerning his defence of the actions of the Indonesian armed forces in the 1991 Dili massacre. Relations with Australia were also strained by Australia's decision to allow 18 East Timorese refugees to remain in the country following their arrival by boat in May (although they were not granted political asylum), by several incidents involving the burning of the Indonesian flag in Australian cities in protest at Indonesia's occupation of East Timor, and by Australia's decision to investigate claims of new evidence about the killing of six Australia-based journalists during the annexation of East Timor in 1975. The Indonesian Government claimed that the journalists had died in cross-fire, while eyewitnesses stated that they had been executed by Indonesian troops. In June 1996 an Australian government report concluded that the journalists had been killed by the Indonesian army. A report published by the International Commission of Jurists, a human rights organization based in Switzerland, in 1998 concluded that Indonesian troops had killed the journalists in order to conceal Indonesia's invasion of East Timor, and in October of that year it was announced that Australia was to reopen a judicial inquiry into the killings. In late 2000 newly-declassified documents provided conclusive evidence that Australian officials had been aware of Indonesia's plans to invade East Timor. Meanwhile, in December 1995 Indonesia signed a treaty with Australia to enhance defence links, committing the two countries to consultation in the event of a threat to security. In September 1996 Indonesia and Australia reached an agreement (to be formally approved) on the delineation of their maritime boundaries, and in October the Australia-Indonesia Development Area was created to develop economic links between the two countries. In March 1997 Indonesia and Australia signed a treaty defining permanent maritime boundaries between the two countries, whilst retaining the Timor Gap agreement. (Indonesia later ceased to be a party to the Timor Gap agreement when it relinquished control of the territory in October 1999.)

Following the downfall of Suharto in May 1998, relations between Indonesia and Australia continued to be affected by the issue of East Timor. In January 1999 the Indonesian Government expressed its 'deep regret' at Australia's announcement earlier the same month that it was to change its policy on East Timor and actively to promote 'self-determination' in the territory. Following the vote in favour of independence held in East Timor in August 1999, Australia committed 4,500 peace-keeping troops to the International Force for East Timor (Interfet), which was formed by the UN to restore order in the territory following the violence perpetrated by pro-Jakarta militias after the announcement of the result of the poll. A military co-operation agreement between Indonesia and Australia, which had been signed four years previously, was reported in October to have been cancelled as a result of the Indonesian Government's displeasure at Australia's leading involvement in the peace-keeping operation. In 2000 relations between Indonesia and Australia continued to be strained. President Wahid repeatedly postponed his visit to Australia. In December, however, a ministerial delegation from Jakarta visited Canberra to prepare for a visit by President Wahid, subsequently rescheduled for April 2001. In November 2000 the Australian ambassador to Indonesia, John McCarthy, was physically attacked by a pro-Jakarta mob in Makassar, Sulawesi. The Australian Government accepted the Indonesian Government's apology for the incident.

In October 1996 Indonesia and Malaysia agreed to submit disputed claims to the islands of Ligitan and Sipadan to the ICJ, and in August 1997 the two countries agreed to postpone talks on the issue of the islands, pending a ruling by the Court. In February 1997 Malaysia closed its border with Indonesia on the island of Borneo for one week, owing to increased racial tension and riots in West Kalimantan. The forced repatriation in early 1998 of thousands of Indonesian workers from Malaysia as a result of the regional economic crisis placed a strain on relations between the two countries. Relations were further strained in October when the Indonesian Government condemned the treatment received in custody by the former Malaysian Deputy Prime Minister and Minister of Finance, Anwar Ibrahim (see chapter on Malaysia), breaking with a tradition amongst ASEAN countries of non-interference in the internal affairs of other member countries.

In March 1996 the USA ended a ban on military training for members of ABRI, which had been imposed after the Dili massacre in 1991. In early June 1997, however, it was announced that President Suharto had cancelled Indonesia's participation in US military training programmes in response to the recent condemnation by the US House of Representatives of abuses of human rights committed by Indonesian armed forces in East Timor; the planned purchase by Indonesia of a number of US military aircraft was also cancelled. In November 1999 the newly-appointed President of Indonesia, Abdurrahman Wahid, made an official visit to the USA. In October 2000, however, relations between Indonesia and the USA deteriorated markedly as the result of a combination of factors, including the perceived 'interference' in Indonesian domestic political affairs of the recently-appointed US ambassador to Indonesia, Robert Gelbard, US criticism of Indonesia's failure to control pro-Jakarta militias in West Timor following the murder of three UN workers by militia members in September, and Indonesian perceptions of US bias towards Israel in the Middle East conflict. In late October and early November Muslim groups rallied outside the US embassy in Jakarta, calling for 'jihad', threats were made against US citizens in Indonesia, US companies in the country were attacked and it was reported that the Indonesian Government had requested Gelbard's immediate removal and replacement. In late October the USA closed its embassy

in Jakarta for two weeks, and in early November the US Government warned citizens to defer all non-essential travel to the archipelago.

In September 1994 a 220-strong medical detachment from the Indonesian army joined the UN Protection Force in Bosnia and Herzegovina (UNPROFOR), in the first mission of its kind to Europe. Indonesia's international standing was further enhanced when, in January 1995, it replaced Pakistan as the non-permanent Asian representative on the UN Security Council for a period of two years. In October 1997 Indonesia proposed that two permanent seats for the representation of Asia be established on the Council. In October 1994 Indonesia underscored its pivotal regional role through hosting its fifth informal meeting to resolve peacefully the dispute over the conflicting claims of six Asian countries to sovereignty over parts of the South China Sea, particularly the Spratly Islands. Moreover, in November the Asia-Pacific Economic Co-operation (APEC, see p. 128) summit meeting took place in Bogor. Indonesia had been one of the founding members of APEC, which had been established in 1989.

On 16 November 1994 the United Nations Convention on the Law of the Sea came into effect and immediately led to recognition of Indonesia's status as an archipelago and the country's sovereignty over all of the waters between its islands. Enforcement of the convention increased Indonesia's territorial waters by more than 3m. sq km.

In August 1995 Queen Beatrix of the Netherlands, the former colonial power in Indonesia, visited Indonesia (the first Dutch monarch to do so for 24 years) and spoke of her regret for the suffering caused by Dutch rule. Bilateral relations were strained from 1992, when Indonesia rejected Dutch aid because it was linked to progress on human rights.

In September and October 1997 President Suharto apologized to neighbouring countries when thick smog, caused by fires started in land-clearance operations in southern Sumatra and central and southern Kalimantan, affected Malaysia, Singapore and parts of the Philippines and Thailand. In late 1999 the newly-appointed President of Indonesia, Abdurrahman Wahid, made a tour of neighbouring ASEAN countries.

In October 1998 it was reported that Indonesia and Portugal were to open representative offices in each other's capital cities in January 1999. In May 1999 the two countries signed an agreement allowing for total independence for East Timor if the East Timorese people voted to reject autonomy proposals offered by the Indonesian Government in a UN-supervised referendum scheduled for August. In late December, with the issue of the status of East Timor resolved following a vote in favour of independence at the referendum in August, Indonesia and Portugal formally re-established full diplomatic relations.

In August 2000 it was reported that President Wahid had announced his intention to visit Iraq in the near future, and had expressed his desire to develop Indonesia's relations with Iraq and other Muslim countries. In June of the same year President Wahid made an official visit to Iran, and in October Indonesia and Pakistan signed a memorandum of understanding relating to the promotion of bilateral ties. In January 2001 the Prime Minister of India made a four-day visit to Indonesia, following a visit to India by President Wahid in February 2000.

Government

The highest authority of the State is the Majelis Permusyawaratan Rakyat (MPR—People's Consultative Assembly), with 700 members (reduced from 1,000 in 1999) who serve for five years. The MPR includes all 500 members of the Dewan Perwakilan Rakyat (House of Representatives), the country's legislative organ. The Dewan has 38 members appointed from Tentara Nasional Indonesia (TNI—the Indonesian National Defence Forces) and 462 directly-elected representatives. The remaining 200 seats in the MPR comprise 135 members elected by provincial assemblies and 65 members appointed by the Komite Pemilihan Umum (General Election Committee). Executive power rests with the President, elected for five years by the MPR. He governs with the assistance of an appointed Cabinet, which is responsible to him.

There are 32 provinces, and local government is through a three-tier system of provincial, regency and village assemblies. Each province is headed by a Governor, who is elected to a five-year term of office by the Provincial Assembly. Provincial Governors must be confirmed by the President, who also approves the election of the Governor of Jakarta, which is designated as a 'special district', as are Aceh and Yogyakarta.

Defence

In August 2000 the total strength of the armed forces was 297,000 men: army an estimated 230,000, navy an estimated 40,000 and air force 27,000. There were also paramilitary forces, comprising an estimated 195,000 police, 12,000 marine police and an estimated 40,000 trainees of KAMRA (People's Security). Military service is selective and lasts for two years. Defence expenditure for 2000 was budgeted at an estimated Rp. 18,900,000m.

Economic Affairs

In 1998, according to estimates by the World Bank, Indonesia's gross national product (GNP), measured at average 1996–98 prices, was US $130,600m., equivalent to $640 per head (or $2,407 per head on an international purchasing-power parity basis). During 1990–98, it was estimated, GNP per head increased, in real terms, at an average rate of 4.0% per year. Over the same period the population grew by an average of 1.9% per year. Indonesia's gross domestic product (GDP) increased, in real terms, by an average of 4.7% per year in 1990–99. GDP declined by an estimated 13.0% in 1998, before increasing by an estimated 0.3% in 1999.

Agriculture, forestry and fishing contributed 19.5% of GDP in 1999, and engaged 43.2% of the employed labour force in the same year. Principal crops for domestic consumption were rice, cassava and maize. Once self-sufficient in rice, Indonesia was obliged to import supplies during the 1990s. In the late 1990s Indonesia remained a major exporter of rubber and palm oil. Other principal cash crops were coffee, spices, tea, cocoa, tobacco, bananas, coconuts and sugar cane. The fishing sector contributed an estimated 1.7% of GDP in 1996. In 1995 an estimated 61% of Indonesia's land area was covered by tropical rain forests. In 1985 a ban on the export of logs was announced, although processed wood products remained a significant export commodity. In 1992 this ban was replaced by an export tax. During 1990–98, according to the World Bank, agricultural GDP increased by an estimated average of 2.6% per year. The GDP of the sector decreased by 0.7% in 1998, before expanding by 2.1% in 1999.

Industry (including mining, manufacturing, construction and power) engaged 17.8% of the employed labour force in 1999, and provided 43.3% of GDP in the same year. During 1990–98, according to the World Bank, industrial GDP increased by an average of 7.8% per year. The GDP of the sector decreased by 14.0% in 1998, but increased by 1.9% in 1999.

Mining engaged only 0.8% of the employed labour force in 1999, but contributed 10.1% of GDP in the same year. Indonesia's principal mineral resource is petroleum, and the country remained the world's leading exporter of liquefied natural gas in 1994. In 1999 Indonesia produced 440.5m. barrels of crude petroleum and 3,068.3m. barrels of natural gas. In 1992 Indonesia became the world's second largest producer of tin. Bauxite, nickel, copper, gold, silver and coal are also mined. During 1991–96 mining and quarrying GDP increased by an average of 4.9% per year. The GDP of the sector expanded by 6.3% in 1996 and by 2.1% in 1997, but decreased by 2.8% in 1998 and by 1.7% in 1999.

Manufacturing contributed 25.4% of GDP in 1999, and engaged 12.9% of the employed labour force in the same year. Apart from petroleum refineries, the main branches of the sector (in terms of output) in 1996 were food products (contributing 13.1% of the total), textiles (11.6%), transport equipment (8.7%) and electrical machinery (7.4%). According to the World Bank, manufacturing GDP increased by an estimated average of 8.8% per year in 1990–98. Manufacturing GDP decreased by 11.4% in 1998, before increasing by 2.6% in 1999.

During the 1980s Indonesia broadened the base of its energy supplies to include gas, coal, hydroelectricity and geothermal energy, in addition to the traditional dependence on petroleum. In 1996, of the total 73,794m. kWh of electricity produced, thermal plants accounted for 81.4%, hydropower for 15.0% and geothermal output for 3.6%. In 1998 imports of petroleum and its products comprised 10.0% of the value of merchandise imports.

Services (including trade, transport and communications, finance and tourism) provided an estimated 37.3% of GDP in 1999, and engaged 38.9% of the employed labour force in the same year. Tourism is normally one of the principal sources of foreign exchange. Revenue from the 4.6m. visitors in 1998 totalled US $3,459m., having declined from a total of $5,321m. from 5.2m. visitors in 1997. According to the World Bank, the GDP of the services sector expanded by an estimated average of 5.4% per year in 1990–98. The sector's GDP decreased by 16.5% in 1998 and by a further 1.0% in 1999.

In 1999 Indonesia recorded a visible trade surplus of US $20,644m. In the same year a surplus of $5,785m. was recorded on the current account of the balance of payments. In 1999 the principal source of imports (12.1%) and principal market for exports (21.4%) was Japan. Other major suppliers were the USA, Singapore, Australia, Germany and the Republic of Korea; other major purchasers were the USA, Singapore, the Republic of Korea, the People's Republic of China and the Netherlands. The principal exports in 1998 were machinery and transport equipment, petroleum and petroleum products, natural and manufactured gas, wood and wood products (particularly plywood), clothing and textiles. In the same year the principal imports were machinery, transport and electrical equipment, and chemical and mineral products.

The draft budget for 2001/02 projected a deficit of Rp. 52,110,000m. Indonesia's total external debt totalled US $150,875m. at the end of 1998, of which $66,944m. was long-term public debt. In that year the cost of debt-servicing was equivalent to 33.0% of revenue from exports of goods and services. The annual rate of inflation averaged 8.4% in 1990–97. Consumer prices rose by an average of 58.5% in 1998 and by 20.5% in 1999. The inflation rate was estimated to have declined to 6.8% in 2000. In 1999, according to official figures, 6.4% of the labour force were unemployed. Other sources, however, suggested a rate of about 15%, while the level of underemployment remained very high.

Indonesia is a member of the Association of South East Asian Nations (ASEAN—see p.134), the Asian Development Bank (ADB—see p. 131), the Asia-Pacific Economic Co-operation forum (APEC—see p. 128) and the Organization of the Petroleum Exporting Countries (OPEC—see p. 269). As a member of ASEAN, Indonesia signed an accord in January 1992, pledging to establish a free trade zone, to be known as the ASEAN Free Trade Area (AFTA), within 15 years (subsequently reduced to 10 years), beginning in January 1993.

The rapid financial deregulation from 1988, which resulted in a massive rise in the number of banks and an unsustainable expansion of bank credit and offshore borrowing, increased Indonesia's vulnerability to the currency crisis which affected South-East Asia in the second half of 1997. In August the Government was forced to allow the flotation of the currency, which constituted an effective devaluation, causing widespread unemployment and hardship. A US $43,000m. IMF programme to restore confidence in the economy was agreed in October, but President Suharto failed to honour the conditions of the agreement. Although a second agreement with the IMF and a revised budget were endorsed by Suharto in January 1998, the rupiah subsequently continued to fall sharply against other currencies, while the value of shares on the Jakarta Stock Exchange also registered a steep decline. Also in January 1998 the Indonesian Banking Restructuring Agency (IBRA) was established to address the problems of the country's banking sector, which remained in disarray. The importance of the IBRA was emphasized in 1999 following a scandal involving Bank Bali, from which funds had allegedly been transferred to a company linked to the former ruling party, Golkar. The scandal resulted in delays in the disbursement of loans, estimated to total US $4,600m., from the IMF, the World Bank and the ADB. Suspension of the IMF support programme in March 1998, meanwhile, weakened international confidence in the country's economy; but a new agreement with the IMF was subsequently concluded. A sharp reduction in government subsidies on fuel, energy and public transport was announced in May 1998, resulting in a dramatic increase in prices. The ensuing riots led to the resignation of President Suharto. In late June a third revision of the IMF rescue programme was agreed. Subsequently, restrictions on foreign investment in the banking sector and other industries were relaxed, and the planned privatization of a number of state-owned companies was announced. Approved foreign direct investment was reported to have declined by more than 50% in 1998, while GDP contracted sharply. During 1999, however, the economy began to recover Although unemployment remained high, a marginal expansion in GDP was recorded, inflation was reduced dramatically, interest rates were lowered and the currency appreciated. The appointment of President Wahid in October 1999 appeared initially to restore a degree of international confidence in the Indonesian economy. In February 2000 international donors pledged US $4,700m. in loans and grants to finance the country's budget, while in the same month the IMF approved a three-year US $5,000m. extended fund facility to support the Government's economic and structural reforms. Meeting in Japan in October, the Consultative Group for Indonesia (CGI—a donor grouping chaired by the World Bank and incorporating IMF representatives) pledged aid totalling US $4,800m., as well as technical assistance grants amounting to $530m. However, the steady deterioration during 2000 of international and domestic confidence in both the style of leadership of Wahid and in the commitment of his administration to the implementation of economic reforms, combined with increasing concerns about Indonesia's volatile domestic political situation, seriously undermined the economy, leading to a severe decline in the value of the rupiah, which continued in the first quarter of 2001. In January 2000, meanwhile, the banking sector also provided serious cause for concern when an independent audit revealed that the central bank might be subject to far greater losses and liabilities than previously acknowledged, thus prompting calls for the recapitalization of the bank. In November 2000, following a state audit of the bank, it was concluded that Rp. 84,500,000m. of central bank loans extended during the regional economic crisis in 1997 and 1998 were unrecoverable; the audit also found that of Rp.144,500,000m. of central bank funds, up to Rp. 130,000,000m. had been misused. GDP was estimated to have increased by 4.5% in 2000. In October 2000 the Government announced its forecast of 4.5% economic growth for 2001. The draft budget for 2001/02 focused on the rehabilitation of Indonesia's financial sector, the repayment of debts and the introduction of a greater level of control over spending for the archipelago's outer provinces. In early 2001, however, the economic outlook remained extremely uncertain, as the economy of the USA (a major purchaser of Indonesia's exports) began to decelerate and as international prices for petroleum (one of the country's principal exports) began to weaken. Moreover, the restoration of political stability in the country, as well as the demonstration by the Government of its commitment to the full implementation of wide-ranging economic and structural reforms and to the establishment of a transparent and accountable financial system, continued to be of paramount importance.

Social Welfare

Certain members of the population benefit from a state insurance scheme. Benefits include life insurance and old-age pensions. In addition, there are two social insurance schemes, administered by state corporations, providing pensions and industrial accident insurance. In 1997 Indonesia had 1,090 hospitals (with a total of 121,996 beds). In 1995 there were 7,076 public health centres in Indonesia. In March 1996 there were 30,402 physicians working in the country and 138,974 nurses and midwives. In the 1999/2000 budget, according to provisional data, Rp. 4,488,200m. , equivalent to 2.2% of total expenditure, was allocated to health, family planning and welfare.

Education

Education is mainly under the control of the Ministry of Education and Culture, but the Ministry of Religious Affairs is in charge of Islamic religious schools at the primary level. In 1987 primary education, beginning at seven years of age and lasting for six years, was made compulsory. In 1993 it was announced that compulsory education was to be expanded to nine years. Secondary education begins at 13 years of age and lasts for six years, comprising two cycles of three years each. Primary enrolment in 1994 included 97% of children in the relevant age-group (males 99%; females 95%). In the same year enrolment at secondary level included 42% of the relevant population (males 45%; females 39%). In 1997/98, according to preliminary data, there were 1,391 universities. In 1994 enrolment at tertiary level was equivalent to 11.1% of the relevant population (males 13.5%; females 8.6%). In 1999/2000, according to provisional data, the Government allocated Rp. 7,742,700m., representing 3.8% of total expenditure, to education. In 1995, according to UNESCO estimates, the average rate of adult illiteracy was 16.3% (males 10.3%; females 22.1%).

Public Holidays

2001: 1 January (New Year's Day), 24 January (Chinese New Year), 6 March* (Id al-Adha, Feast of the Sacrifice), 26 March* (Muharram, Islamic New Year), 13 April (Good Friday), 16 April (Easter Monday), 7 May (Vesak Day), 24 May (Ascension Day), 4 June* (Mouloud, Prophet Muhammad's Birthday), 17 August (Independence Day), 15 October* (Ascension of the Prophet Muhammad), 17 December* (Id al-Fitr, end of Ramadan), 25 December (Christmas Day).

2002: 1 January (New Year's Day), 12 February (Chinese New Year), 23 February* (Id al-Adha, Feast of the Sacrifice), 15 March* (Muharram, Islamic New Year), 29 March (Good Friday), 1 April (Easter Monday), 9 May (Ascension Day), 24 May* (Mouloud, Prophet Muhammad's Birthday), 26 May (Vesak Day), 17 August (Independence Day), 4 October* (Ascension of the Prophet Muhammad), 6 December* (Id al-Fitr, end of Ramadan), 25 December (Christmas Day).

* These holidays are dependent on the Islamic lunar calendar and may vary by one or two days from the dates given.

Weights and Measures

The metric system is in force.

Statistical Survey

Source (unless otherwise stated): Badan Pusat Statistik (Central Bureau of Statistics/Statistics Indonesia), Jalan Dr Sutomo 6–8, Jakarta 10710; tel. (21) 3507057; fax (21) 3857046; e-mail bpshq@bps.go.id; internet www.bps.go.id.

Note: Unless otherwise stated, figures for East Timor (occupied by Indonesia between July 1976 and October 1999) are not included in the tables.

Area and Population

AREA, POPULATION AND DENSITY

Area (sq km)	1,922,570*
Population (census results)	
31 October 1980	146,934,948
31 October 1990	
Males	89,076,606
Females	89,554,590
Total	178,631,196
Population (official estimates at 31 December)	
1994	191,390,500
1995	194,440,100
1996	197,483,200
Density (per sq km) at 31 December 1996. . . .	102.7

* 742,308 sq miles.

Population (estimate at mid-1998): 204,420,000.

ISLANDS (estimated population at 31 December 1996)*

	Area (sq km)	Popula-tion	Density (per sq km)
Jawa (Java) and Madura . . .	127,499	116,379,200	912.8
Sumatera (Sumatra)	482,393	41,840,700	86.7
Sulawesi (Celebes)	191,800	14,019,800	73.1
Kalimantan	547,891	10,807,900	19.7
Nusa Tenggara†	67,502	7,348,600	108.9
Bali	5,633	2,924,400	519.2
Maluku (Moluccas) . . .	77,871	2,141,700	27.5
Irian Jaya (West Papua) . .	421,981	2,020,900	4.8
Total	1,922,570	197,483,200	102.7

* Figures refer to provincial divisions, each based on a large island or group of islands but also including adjacent small islands.
† Comprising most of the Lesser Sunda Islands, principally Flores, Lombok, Sumba, Sumbawa and part of Timor.

PRINCIPAL TOWNS (estimated population at 31 December 1996)

Jakarta (capital)	9,341,400
Surabaya	2,743,400
Bandung	2,429,000
Medan	1,942,000
Palembang	1,394,300
Semarang	1,366,500
Ujung Pandang (Makassar)	1,121,300
Malang	775,900
Padang	739,500
Banjarmasin	544,700
Surakarta	518,600
Pontianak	459,100
Yogyakarta (Jogjakarta)	421,000

BIRTHS AND DEATHS (UN estimates, annual averages)

	1980–85	1985–90	1990–95
Birth rate (per 1,000) . . .	32.2	28.2	24.6
Death rate (per 1,000) . . .	11.2	9.4	8.4

Expectation of life (UN estimates, years at birth, 1990–95): 62.6 (males 61.0; females 64.5).

Source: UN, *World Population Prospects: The 1998 Revision.*

Birth rate (per 1,000): 23.3 in 1996; 22.9 in 1997; 22.5 in 1998. Source: UN, *Statistical Yearbook for Asia and the Pacific.*

Death rate (per 1,000): 7.6 in 1996; 7.5 in 1997; 7.5 in 1998. Source: UN, *Statistical Yearbook for Asia and the Pacific.*

EMPLOYMENT (persons aged 15 years and over)

	1997	1998	1999
Agriculture, hunting, forestry and fishing	34,789,927	39,414,765	38,378,133
Mining and quarrying . . .	875,280	674,597	725,739
Manufacturing	11,008,951	9,933,622	11,515,955
Electricity, gas and water. . .	233,237	147,849	188,321
Construction.	4,184,970	3,521,682	3,415,147
Trade, restaurants and hotels .	16,953,006	16,814,233	17,529,099
Transport, storage and communi-cations	4,125,429	4,153,707	4,206,067
Financing, insurance, real estate and business services . .	656,724	617,722	633,744
Public services	12,574,844	12,394,272	12,224,654
Activities not adequately defined .	3,161	—	—
Total employed	85,405,529	87,672,449	88,816,859

Agriculture

PRINCIPAL CROPS ('000 metric tons, incl. East Timor)

	1997	1998	1999
Rice (paddy)	49,377	49,200	50,866
Maize	8,771	10,169	9,204
Potatoes.	813	998	827
Sweet potatoes	1,847	1,928	1,928*
Cassava (Manioc) . . .	15,134	14,696	15,422
Other roots and tubers . .	331	350	349*
Dry beans*	870	900	900
Soybeans	1,357	1,306	1,383
Groundnuts (in shell)† . .	983	930	990
Coconuts	14,710†	13,000*	13,000*
Copra*	1,360	1,120	n.a.
Palm kernels	1,190	1,303	1,490†
Cabbages	1,339	1,459	1,401
Tomatoes	279	334	324
Pumpkins, squash and gourds* .	145	150	150
Cucumbers and gherkins* . .	310	310	310
Aubergines (Eggplants)* . .	145	150	150
Chillies and peppers (green) . .	348	374	497
Onions (dry)	606	559	805
Garlic	102	84	63
Green beans	186	186	172
Carrots	227	333	265
Other vegetables* . . .	1,552	1,583	1,568
Sugar cane	27,764	27,180†	21,400†
Oranges.	693	614	614*
Avocados	130	131	122
Mangoes	1,088	600	802
Pineapples	386	327	257
Bananas	3,057	3,177	3,166
Papayas	361	490	380
Other fruits and berries* . .	2,419	2,419	2,419*
Cashew nuts.	67	69	69*
Coffee (green)	454	455	417†
Cocoa beans	307	330†	350†
Tea (made)	149	152	152*
Tobacco (leaves)	137	138	138*
Natural rubber	1,549	1,564	1,687†

* FAO estimate(s).   † Unofficial figure(s).

Source: FAO.

LIVESTOCK ('000 head, incl. East Timor; year ending September)

	1997	1998	1999*
Cattle	12,031	12,239	12,239
Sheep	7,700	8,151	8,151
Goats	14,308	15,198	15,198
Pigs	8,589	10,069	10,069
Horses	582	740†	740
Buffaloes	3,114	3,145	3,145

Chickens (million): 1,002 in 1997; 889 in 1998; 1,000* in 1999.
Ducks (million): 30 in 1997; 28† in 1998; 28* in 1999.

* FAO estimate(s).   † Unofficial figure(s).

Source: FAO.

LIVESTOCK PRODUCTS ('000 metric tons, incl. East Timor)

	1997	1998	1999
Beef and veal	355	354	354
Buffalo meat	47	46	45
Mutton and lamb	42	34	37
Goat meat	66	48	47
Pig meat	666	759	759
Poultry meat	900	618	695
Cows' milk	424	375	384
Sheep's milk	93	98	98
Goats' milk	232	232	232
Hen eggs	613	393	406
Other poultry eggs	155	137	140
Wool (greasy)	23	24	24
Cattle and buffalo hides	42	42	42*
Sheepskins	10	8	8
Goatskins	15	11	11

Note: Figures for meat refer to inspected production only, i.e. from animals slaughtered under government supervision.

* FAO estimate.

Source: FAO.

Forestry

ROUNDWOOD REMOVALS ('000 cubic metres, excluding bark)

	1996	1997	1998
Sawlogs, veneer logs and logs for sleepers:			
Coniferous	333	333	n.a.
Non-coniferous	32,250	32,250	21,444
Pulpwood	11,547	11,547	11,547
Other industrial wood	3,112	3,158	3,204
Fuel wood	152,515	154,772	157,023
Total	199,757	202,060	193,218

Source: FAO, *Yearbook of Forest Products.*

SAWNWOOD PRODUCTION
('000 cubic metres, including railway sleepers)

	1996	1997	1998
Coniferous (softwood)	138	138	n.a.
Broadleaved (hardwood)	7,200	7,100	2,545
Total	7,338	7,238	2,545

Source: FAO, *Yearbook of Forest Products.*

Fishing

('000 metric tons, live weight)

	1996	1997	1998
Capture	3,557.6	3,791.0	3,698.9
Scads	251.3	276.9	268.0
Goldstripe sardinella	157.1	156.9	161.2
Bali sardinella	88.6	138.6	86.1
'Stolephorus' anchovies	161.8	183.6	166.5
Skipjack tuna	182.1	187.2	203.8
Indian mackerels	188.9	201.4	197.1
Aquaculture	733.1	662.5	696.9
Common carp	178.4	146.7	184.0
Milkfish	162.1	142.7	147.9
Total catch	4,290.7	4,453.6	4,395.7

Note: Figures exclude aquatic plants ('000 metric tons): 161.5 (capture 13.5, aquaculture 148.0) in 1996; 126.0 (capture 11.0, aquaculture 115.0) in 1997; 133.9 (capture 16.7, aquaculture 117.2) in 1998. Also excluded are crocodiles, recorded by number rather than by weight. The number of crocodiles caught was: 250 in 1997; 11,647 in 1998.

Source: FAO, *Yearbook of Fishery Statistics.*

Mining

('000 metric tons, unless otherwise indicated)

	1997	1998	1999
Crude petroleum (million barrels)	484.0	480.1	440.5
Natural gas (million barrels)	3,166.0	2,978.9	3,068.3
Bauxite	808.7	620.5	1,116.3
Coal	54,608.4	60,321.0	64,602.1
Nickel ore†	2,830.0	3,233.4	3,235.3
Copper concentrate†	1,817.9	2,640.0	2,645.2
Tin ore (metal content, metric tons)	55.2	54.0	47.8
Gold (kg)‡	89,978.6	124,018.7	129,032.0
Silver (kg)‡	279,160.5	348,973.8	292,331.0

† Figures refer to gross weight. The estimated metal content was: Nickel 3.1%; Copper 44%.
‡ Including gold and silver in copper concentrate.

Industry

SELECTED PRODUCTS ('000 metric tons, unless otherwise indicated)

	1994	1995	1996
Refined sugar	2,224	2,202	2,564
Cigarettes (million) . .	36,421	38,768	n.a.
Veneer sheets ('000 cubic metres) .	50	50	50
Plywood ('000 cubic metres) .	9,836	9,500	9,575
Newsprint	150	243	267
Other printing and writing paper .	992	1,061	1,236
Other paper and paperboard* . .	1,823	2,121	2,618
Nitrogenous fertilizers† . .	2,357	2,428	2,986
Jet fuel	686	838	1,167
Motor spirit (petrol) . .	5,264	4,942	7,155
Naphthas	1,138	1,115	1,673
Kerosene	6,694	6,193	6,894
Distillate fuel oils . .	13,200‡	13,300‡	14,400
Residual fuel oils . .	11,000‡	11,600‡	10,200
Lubricating oils . . .	253	236	240
Liquefied petroleum gas .	3,122	2,941	3,179
Rubber tyres ('000)§ . .	20,842	12,033	n.a.
Cement	24,564	23,136	n.a.
Aluminium (unwrought)‖¶	221.9	228.1	223.2
Tin (unwrought, metric tons)‡‖¶	39,000	44,218	48,960
Radio receivers ('000). .	3,372	n.a.	n.a.
Passenger motor cars ('000)** .	95	127	n.a.
Electric energy (million kWh)‡	64,351‡	68,399‡	73,794
Gas from gasworks (terajoules) .	15,065	19,807	21,000

* Data from the FAO.
† Production in terms of nitrogen.
‡ Provisional or estimated production.
§ For road motor vehicles, excluding bicycles and motorcycles.
‖ Primary metal production only.
¶ Data from *World Metal Statistics*.
** Vehicles assembled from imported parts.

Source: UN, *Industrial Commodity Statistics Yearbook*.

Palm oil ('000 metric tons): 4,008 in 1994; 4,480 in 1995; 4,899 in 1996; 5,385 in 1997; 5,902 in 1998; 6,250 (unofficial figure) in 1999. Source: FAO.

Raw sugar (centrifugal, '000 metric tons): 2,421 in 1994; 2,105 in 1995; 2,094 in 1996; 2,190 in 1997; 1,932 (unofficial figure) in 1998; 2,140 (unofficial figure) in 1999. Source: FAO.

Finance

CURRENCY AND EXCHANGE RATES

Monetary Units
100 sen = 1 rupiah (Rp.).

Sterling, Dollar and Euro Equivalents (29 December 2000)
£1 sterling = 14,317.7 rupiah;
US $1 = 9,595.0 rupiah;
€1 = 8,928.1 rupiah;
100,000 rupiah = £6.984 = $10.422 = €11.201.

Average Exchange Rate (rupiah per US $)
1998	10,013.6
1999	7,855.2
2000	8,421.8

BUDGET ('000 million rupiah, year ending 31 March)

Revenue	1997/98	1998/99	1999/2000*
Tax revenue	101,493.2	143,701.8	171,296.8
Taxes on income, profits, etc. .	64,947.3	97,297.4	118,164.4
General sales, turnover or VAT	25,198.8	27,728.7	33,087.1
Excises	5,101.2	7,730.3	10,381.2
Taxes on international trade .	3,127.2	6,956.6	5,025.3
Import duties . .	2,998.7	2,316.4	4,177.0
Export duties . .	128.5	4,640.2	848.3
Other current revenue . .	10,782.3	12,200.0	17,131.7
Profit receipts . . .	2,340.7	3,428.3	5,430.4
Other	8,441.6†	8,771.7	11,701.3
Total	**112,275.5**	**155,901.8**	**188,428.5**

Expenditure	1997/98	1998/99	1999/2000*
Current expenditure . . .	73,921.1	125,900.0	155,880.3
Personnel (central govt.) . .	17,269.0	22,656.2	32,105.5
Pensions . . .	4,225.0	5,310.0	9,205.0
Material	8,999.3	9,838.6	9,971.3
Armed forces . . .	1,825.4	2,671.9	2,117.8
Transfers to regions . .	11,060.5	13,074.2	17,341.2
Interest on external debt .	11,262.9	24,650.0	20,615.0
Gross interest costs of bank restructuring	0.0	8,384.8	22,230.4
Subsidies	21,120.9	41,799.3	47,024.6
Petroleum . . .	9,814.3	28,606.6	35,839.1
Food	10,598.7	6,426.7	5,415.4
Other	11,306.6	13,192.7	11,185.5
Other	2,383.1	2,825.0	4,474.5
Development expenditure (including net lending) . .	44,651.0	55,252.0	49,020.0
General public services . .	1,011.2	1,083.4	924.5
Education	5,145.0	7,072.9	7,742.7
Health, family planning and welfare	2,051.3	4,150.0	4,488.2
Housing and water supply . .	1,333.4	2,435.9‡	2,121.9‡
Other community and social services	1,581.6	2,261.4	2,568.3
Manpower and transmigration	1,368.3	1,933.8	2,058.1
Economic services . . .	17,564.0	23,506.0	16,038.1
Agriculture and irrigation§ .	3,268.5	7,126.0‖	3,604.6‖
Electricity	4,448.9	5,829.3	3,799.4
Transport and tourism . .	7,711.7	8,756.4	6,361.4
Trade and co-operatives¶ . .	998.8	895.3**	1,642.6**
Regional, business and environment	7,045.9	11,456.7	15,607.3
Regional development . .	6,019.0	10,558.3	11,648.7
Investment through banking system	381.4	256.7	3,171.1
Total	**118,572.1**	**181,152.0**	**204,900.3**

* Figures are provisional.
† Including privatization proceeds.
‡ Excluding credit for low-cost housing.
§ Excluding fertilizer subsidies.
‖ Excluding farming loans and credit for plantation.
¶ Excluding bank restructuring costs.
** Excluding co-operatives credit and loans for primary-level co-operatives' members.

Source: IMF, *Indonesia: Statistical Appendix* (October 2000).

INTERNATIONAL RESERVES (US $ million at 31 December)

	1997	1998	1999
Gold*	809	803	812
IMF special drawing rights . .	499	312	—
Reserve position in IMF . .	—	—	200
Foreign exchange . . .	16,088	22,401	26,245
Total	**17,396**	**23,516**	**27,257**

* Valued at market-related prices.

Source: IMF, *International Financial Statistics*.

MONEY SUPPLY ('000 million rupiah at 31 December)

	1997	1998	1999
Currency outside banks . .	28,424	41,394	58,353
Demand deposits at deposit money banks	40,232	45,717	55,327
Total money (incl. others) . .	**68,785**	**87,301**	**114,562**

Source: IMF, *International Financial Statistics*.

COST OF LIVING (Consumer Price Index; base: 1990 = 100)

	1995	1996	1997
Food (incl. beverages) . . .	156.3	171.1	186.2
All items (incl.others) . .	**153.2**	**165.3**	**176.2**

Source: ILO, *Yearbook of Labour Statistics*.

All items (base: 1995 = 100): 115.2 in 1997; 181.7 in 1998; 218.9 in 1999. (Source: IMF, *International Financial Statistics*).

NATIONAL ACCOUNTS ('000 million rupiah at current prices)

National Income and Product

	1990	1991	1992
Domestic factor incomes* . .	172,393	201,118	229,946
Consumption of fixed capital . .	9,784	11,380	13,045
Gross domestic product (GDP) at factor cost	182,177	212,498	242,991
Indirect taxes, *less* subsidies . .	13,420	15,004	17,795
GDP in purchasers' values . .	195,597	227,502	260,786
Net factor income from abroad .	−9,614	−10,899	−12,213
Gross national product (GNP)	185,983	216,603	248,573
Less Consumption of fixed capital .	9,784	11,380	13,045
National income in market prices	176,199	205,223	235,528

* Compensation of employees and the operating surplus of enterprises. The amount is obtained as a residual.

Source: UN, *National Accounts Statistics*.

Expenditure on the Gross Domestic Product

	1997	1998	1999
Government final consumption expenditure	42,952	54,416	72,631
Private final consumption expenditure	387,171	644,539	811,681
Gross capital formation . .	199,301	197,470	146,224
Total domestic expenditure	629,424	896,425	1,030,536
Exports of goods and services . .	174,871	506,245	390,560
Less Imports of goods and services	176,600	413,058	301,654
GDP in purchasers' values .	627,695	989,612	1,119,442
GDP at constant 1993 prices .	433,247	376,893	378,053

Source: IMF, *Indonesia: Statistical Appendix* (October 2000).

Gross Domestic Product by Economic Activity

	1997	1998	1999
Agriculture, forestry and fishing .	101,009	173,913	218,044
Mining and quarrying . . .	55,562	133,353	112,638
Manufacturing	168,179	238,064	284,804
Electricity, gas and water. . .	7,835	11,235	13,369
Construction.	46,679	61,756	73,418
Trade, hotels and restaurants. .	99,582	167,244	183,627
Transport and communications	38,531	51,937	66,077
Finance, insurance and real estate	42,920	54,966	55,098
Government services	32,128	40,641	56,745
Other services (including business services)	35,274	56,503	55,622
Total	627,696	989,611	1,119,442

Source: IMF, *Indonesia: Statistical Appendix* (October 2000).

BALANCE OF PAYMENTS (US $ million)

	1997	1998	1999
Exports of goods f.o.b. . .	56,298	50,371	51,242
Imports of goods f.o.b. . .	−46,223	−31,942	−30,598
Trade balance	10,075	18,429	20,644
Exports of services . . .	6,941	4,479	4,579
Imports of services . . .	−16,607	−11,961	−11,553
Balance on goods and services.	409	10,947	13,670
Other income received . .	1,855	1,910	1,891
Other income paid . . .	−8,187	−10,099	−11,690
Balance on goods, services and income	−5,923	2,758	3,871
Current transfers received . .	1,034	1,338	1,914
Current balance . . .	−4,889	4,096	5,785
Direct investment abroad. .	−178	−44	−72
Direct investment from abroad .	4,677	−356	−2,745
Portfolio investment liabilities .	−2,632	−1,878	−1,792
Other investment liabilities . .	−2,470	−7,360	−1,332
Net errors and omissions . .	−2,645	1,849	2,128
Overall balance . . .	−8,137	−3,693	1,972

Source: IMF, *International Financial Statistics*.

External Trade

PRINCIPAL COMMODITIES (distribution by SITC, US $ million)

Imports c.i.f.	1996	1997	1998
Food and live animals . . .	3,926.6	2,979.8	2,611.7
Cereals and cereal preparations .	2,002.5	1,106.1	1,567.9
Wheat and meslin (unmilled) .	1,050.4	776.6	630.5
Rice	766.4	109.0	861.2
Crude materials (inedible) except fuels	3,441.3	2,958.8	2,349.1
Pulp and waste paper . . .	704.6	616.5	612.8
Textile fibres and waste . . .	1,261.3	1,034.0	976.0
Cotton	980.6	818.9	763.7
Raw cotton (excl. linters) . .	980.1	816.0	762.3
Mineral fuels, lubricants, etc.	3,775.0	4,142.0	2,752.4
Petroleum, petroleum products, etc.	3,746.2	4,094.9	2,724.3
Crude petroleum oils, etc. .	1,519.0	1,467.1	1,058.3
Refined petroleum products .	2,086.2	2,451.7	1,611.7
Gas oils	963.6	1,173.1	893.2
Chemicals and related products	5,876.9	5,768.9	4,030.0
Organic chemicals . . .	2,226.8	2,222.9	1,491.5
Plastic materials, etc. . . .	1,166.4	1,067.7	730.9
Products of polymerization, etc..	740.8	695.2	433.0
Basic manufactures . . .	6,844.7	6,715.4	4,671.0
Textile yarn, fabrics, etc. . . .	1,288.4	1,172.9	1,036.6
Iron and steel	2,370.8	2,286.4	1,478.6
Non-ferrous metals . . .	905.4	825.0	521.6
Other metal manufactures . .	813.3	957.5	683.7
Machinery and transport equipment	17,458.6	17,499.8	9,902.9
Power-generating machinery and equipment	1,968.6	1,877.0	1,154.5
Internal combustion piston engines and parts . .	727.5	725.1	237.7
Machinery specialized for particular industries . . .	4,118.4	3,959.4	2,702.2
Textile and leather machinery .	740.4	783.9	731.5
General industrial machinery, equipment and parts . .	3,629.2	3,682.3	2,394.3
Heating and cooling equipment and parts	944.1	857.5	505.5
Mechanical handling equipment	909.8	905.7	577.6
Telecommunications and sound equipment	1,766.3	1,778.8	504.8

Imports c.i.f. — *continued*	1996	1997	1998
Other electrical machinery, apparatus, etc.	1,868.4	2,110.7	1,228.4
Road vehicles and parts*	2,673.5	2,593.0	940.0
Parts and accessories for cars, buses, lorries, etc.*	1,359.5	1,297.2	388.0
Miscellaneous manufactured articles	1,215.0	1,164.8	763.5
Total (incl. others)	42,928.5	41,679.8	27,336.9

* Excluding tyres, engines and electrical parts.

Source: UN, *International Trade Statistics Yearbook*.

Exports f.o.b.	1996	1997	1998
Food and live animals	3,764.5	3,531.5	3,717.5
Fish, crustaceans and molluscs	1,676.9	1,619.4	1,614.5
Crustaceans and molluscs (fresh, chilled, frozen or salted)	1,063.6	1,045.9	1,038.0
Coffee, tea, cocoa and spices	1,275.8	1,285.1	1,516.3
Crude materials (inedible) except fuels	5,081.2	4,357.9	3,719.3
Crude rubber (incl. synthetic and reclaimed)	1,922.9	1,501.4	1,110.1
Natural rubber and gums	1,920.1	1,498.9	1,106.3
Natural rubber (other than latex)	1,872.9	1,467.0	1,087.2
Metalliferous ores and metal scrap	2,034.3	1,737.5	1,474.9
Ores and concentrates of non-ferrous base metals	2,019.1	1,718.2	1,453.3
Copper ores and concentrates	1,747.7	1,497.4	1,307.5
Mineral fuels, lubricants, etc.	12,860.9	13,153.9	9,429.4
Coal, coke and briquettes	1,123.7	1,491.4	1,349.6
Coal, lignite and peat	1,121.0	1,485.1	1,346.6
Petroleum, petroleum products, etc.	7,243.3	6,822.4	4,264.3
Crude petroleum oils, etc.	5,711.9	5,480.0	3,348.7
Refined petroleum products	1,502.1	1,283.1	694.6
Gas (natural and manufactured)	4,494.0	4,840.2	3,815.5
Petroleum gases, etc., in the liquefied state	4,494.0	4,840.2	3,815.5
Animal and vegetable oils, fats and waxes	1,567.8	2,282.1	1,520.7
Fixed vegetable oils and fats	1,343.7	2,196.0	1,152.5
Fixed vegetable oils, fluid or solid, crude, refined or purified	1,338.4	2,174.9	1,152.1
Chemicals and related products	1,723.6	1,869.4	2,086.6
Basic manufactures	10,887.9	9,778.8	8,832.6
Wood and cork manufactures (excl. furniture)	4,839.8	4,445.3	2,714.4
Veneers, plywood, etc.	3,985.9	3,729.2	2,207.3
Plywood of wood sheets	3,595.4	3,410.6	2,078.0
Paper, paperboard, etc.	947.4	939.6	1,439.9
Textile yarn, fabrics, etc.	2,856.9	2,268.9	2,358.0
Woven fabrics of man-made fibres*	1,150.7	854.3	905.6
Machinery and transport equipment	4,994.1	4,620.1	4,654.7
Telecommunications and sound equipment	2,068.2	1,752.8	1,360.6
Other electrical machinery, apparatus, etc.	1,085.6	1,084.3	1,060.8
Miscellaneous manufactured articles	8,613.8	6,876.0	6,603.6
Clothing and accessories (excl. footwear)	3,654.7	2,952.9	2,681.3
Footwear	2,135.0	1,477.2	1,156.7
Footwear with leather soles	1,662.4	1,145.6	898.6
Jewellery, goldsmiths' and silversmiths' wares, etc.	528.2	703.4	1,661.7
Total (incl. others)	49,814.8	53,443.7	48,847.6

* Excluding narrow or special fabrics.

Source: UN, *International Trade Statistics Yearbook*.

PRINCIPAL TRADING PARTNERS (US $ million)*

Imports c.i.f.	1997†	1998	1999
Australia	2,426.7	1,760.5	1,460.4
Belgium/Luxembourg	339.5	276.8	178.3
Brazil	352.3	203.5	n.a.
Canada	682.4	504.2	421.2
China, People's Republic	1,518.0	906.3	1,242.2
France	1,016.5	568.1	371.6
Germany	2,628.7	2,365.7	1,398.5
India	697.4	293.0	n.a.
Iran	444.2	175.0	n.a.
Italy	917.9	480.4	276.9
Japan	8,252.3	4,292.4	2,913.3
Korea, Republic	2,321.8	1,527.8	1,330.1
Malaysia	864.8	626.6	605.6
Netherlands	565.9	338.4	346.7
Russia	287.3	30.4	n.a.
Singapore	3,410.9	2,542.8	2,525.9
Sweden	482.0	235.4	156.0
Switzerland	335.3	228.0	n.a.
Thailand	866.7	842.0	933.4
United Kingdom	1,084.4	920.3	511.2
USA	5,440.9	3,517.3	2,839.0
Total (incl. others)	41,679.8	27,336.9	24,003.3

Exports f.o.b.	1997†	1998	1999
Australia	1,517.4	1,533.5	1,484.8
Belgium/Luxembourg	795.7	876.5	696.5
China, People's Republic	2,229.3	1,832.0	2,008.9
France	499.3	547.3	503.2
Germany	1,465.7	1,401.3	1,233.9
Hong Kong	1,785.1	1,865.0	1,330.0
Italy	826.1	858.8	655.5
Japan	12,485.0	9,116.0	10,397.2
Korea, Republic	3,462.2	2,567.8	3,319.8
Malaysia	1,357.2	1,358.5	1,335.9
Netherlands	1,842.4	1,512.3	1,543.6
Philippines	794.1	707.4	694.7
Saudi Arabia	579.3	505.9	n.a.
Singapore	5,467.9	5,718.3	4,930.5
Spain	888.1	868.7	741.6
Thailand	848.4	942.5	812.7
United Arab Emirates	745.8	653.6	n.a.
United Kingdom	1,238.1	1,143.1	1,176.1
USA	7,148.1	7,031.0	6,896.5
Total (incl. others)	53,443.6	48,847.6	48,665.4

* Imports by country of production; exports by country of consumption. Figures include trade in gold.

† Source: *Statistical Yearbook of Indonesia*.

Transport

RAILWAYS (traffic)

	1996	1997	1998*
Passengers embarked (million)	154	159	169
Passenger-km (million)	15,223	15,518	16,340
Freight loaded ('000 tons)	18,481	19,186	20,290
Freight ton-km (million)	4,700	5,030	5,368

* Estimates.

Source: Indonesian State Railways.

ROAD TRAFFIC (motor vehicles registered at 31 December)

	1996	1997	1998*
Passenger cars	2,409,088	2,653,662	2,734,769
Lorries and trucks	1,434,783	1,551,038	1,564,512
Buses and coaches	595,419	598,476	625,364
Motor cycles	10,090,805	12,028,475	12,718,199

* Estimates.

Source: State Police of Indonesia.

SHIPPING

Merchant Fleet (registered at 31 December)

	1996	1997	1998
Number of vessels . . .	2,348	2,383	2,359
Displacement ('000 grt) . .	2,972.6	3,195.0	3,252.1

Source: Lloyd's Register of Shipping, *World Fleet Statistics*.

Sea-borne Freight Traffic ('000 metric tons)

	1996	1997	1998*
International:			
Goods loaded	132,693	131,289	131,210
Goods unloaded	74,178	67,196	67,209
Domestic:			
Goods loaded	160,953	147,769	147,979
Goods unloaded	141,150	148,055	148,148

CIVIL AVIATION (traffic on scheduled services)

	1996	1997	1998*
Kilometres flown (million) . .	190	193	142
Passengers carried ('000) . .	11,571	11,635	7,891
Passenger-km (million) . .	20,551	21,190	13,883
Total ton-km (million) . .	2,552	2,596	1,691

* Preliminary data.

Source: *Statistical Yearbook of Indonesia*.

Tourism

FOREIGN VISITORS BY COUNTRY OF ORIGIN

	1997	1998	1999
Australia	539,156	394,543	531,211
France	107,843	70,396	78,613
Germany	185,976	141,314	169,083
Japan	706,942	469,409	606,102
Korea, Republic	246,307	177,852	220,440
Malaysia	481,713	491,597	440,212
Netherlands	144,622	81,507	86,022
Philippines	50,925	104,192	46,177
Singapore	1,376,377	1,446,660	1,332,877
Taiwan	404,929	281,959	349,247
United Kingdom	142,161	137,600	138,296
USA	171,707	150,042	151,763
Total (incl. others) . . .	5,185,243	4,606,416	4,727,520

Receipts from tourism (US $ million): 5,321 in 1997; 3,459 in 1998.

Communications Media

	1995	1996	1997
Television receivers ('000 in use) .	13,000	13,500	13,750
Radio receivers ('000 in use) . .	29,500	31,000	31,500
Telephones ('000 main lines in use)	3,291*	4,186	4,982
Telefax stations (number in use)*†	85,000	125,000	185,000
Mobile cellular telephones			
(subscribers)*	210,643	562,517	916,173
Daily newspapers:			
Number of titles	74	69	n.a.
Average circulation ('000) . .	4,701	4,665	n.a.
Non-daily newspapers:			
Number of titles	90	94	n.a.
Average circulation ('000) . .	3,895	4,696	n.a.

Telephones ('000 main lines in use): 4,736† in 1999‡.

* Source: UN, *Statistical Yearbook*.
† Estimate(s).
‡ Source: Badan Pusat Statistik (Statistics Indonesia), Jakarta.

Source (unless otherwise indicated): UNESCO, *Statistical Yearbook*.

Education

(1997/98*)

	Institutions	Teachers	Pupils and Students
Primary schools	151,064	1,158,616	25,689,693
General junior secondary schools .	21,157	434,722	7,956,506
General senior secondary schools .	8,241	219,783	2,864,633
Vocational senior secondary schools	4,006	127,270	1,862,060
Universities	1,391	181,545	2,051,001

* Preliminary data.

Source: Ministry of Education and Culture.

Directory

The Constitution

Indonesia had three provisional Constitutions: in August 1945, February 1950 and August 1950. In July 1959 the Constitution of 1945 was re-enacted by presidential decree. The General Elections Law of 1969 supplemented the 1945 Constitution, which has been adopted permanently by the Majelis Permusyawaratan Rakyat (MPR—People's Consultative Assembly). The following is a summary of its main provisions, with subsequent amendments:

GENERAL PRINCIPLES

The 1945 Constitution consists of 37 articles, four transitional clauses and two additional provisions, and is preceded by a preamble. The preamble contains an indictment of all forms of colonialism, an account of Indonesia's struggle for independence, the declaration of that independence and a statement of fundamental aims and principles. Indonesia's National Independence, according to the text of the preamble, has the state form of a Republic, with sovereignty residing in the People, and is based upon five fundamental principles, the *pancasila*:

1. Belief in the One Supreme God.
2. Just and Civilized Humanity.
3. The Unity of Indonesia.
4. Democracy led by the wisdom of deliberations (*musyawarah*) and consensus among representatives.
5. Social Justice for all the people of Indonesia.

STATE ORGANS

Majelis Permusyawaratan Rakyat—MPR (People's Consultative Assembly)

Sovereignty is in the hands of the People and is exercised in full by the MPR as the embodiment of the whole Indonesian People. The MPR is the highest authority of the State, and is to be distinguished from the legislative body proper (Dewan Perwakilan Rakyat, see below), which is incorporated within the MPR. The MPR, with a total of 700 members (reduced from 1,000 in 1999), is composed of the 500 members of the Dewan, 135 members elected by provincial assemblies and 65 members appointed by the Komite Pemilihan Umum (General Election Committee). Elections to the MPR are held every five years. The MPR sits at least once every five years, and its primary competence is to determine the Constitution and the broad lines of the policy of the State and the Government. It also elects the President and Vice-President, who are responsible for implementing that policy. All decisions are taken unanimously in keeping with the traditions of *musyawarah*.

The President

The highest executive of the Government, the President, holds office for a term of five years and may be re-elected once. As Mandatory of the MPR he must execute the policy of the State according to the Decrees determined by the MPR during its Fourth General and Special Sessions. In conducting the administration of the State, authority and responsibility are concentrated in the President. The Ministers of the State are his assistants and are responsible only to him.

Dewan Perwakilan Rakyat (House of Representatives)

The legislative branch of the State, the Dewan Perwakilan Rakyat, sits at least once a year. It has 500 members: 38 nominated by the President (from the armed forces) and 462 directly elected. Every statute requires the approval of the Dewan. Members of the Dewan have the right to submit draft bills which require ratification by the President, who has the right of veto. In times of emergency the President may enact ordinances which have the force of law, but such Ordinances must be ratified by the Dewan during the following session or be revoked.

Dewan Pertimbangan Agung—DPA (Supreme Advisory Council)

The DPA is an advisory body assisting the President who chooses its members from political parties, functional groups and groups of prominent persons.

Mahkamah Agung (Supreme Court)

The judicial branch of the State, the Supreme Court and the other courts of law are independent of the Executive in exercising their judicial powers.

Badan Pemeriksa Keuangan (State Audit Board)

Controls the accountability of public finance, enjoys investigatory powers and is independent of the Executive. Its findings are presented to the Dewan.

The Government

HEAD OF STATE

President: ABDURRAHMAN WAHID (inaugurated 20 October 1999).
Vice-President: MEGAWATI SUKARNOPUTRI.

CABINET
(May 2001)

Co-ordinating Minister for Political Affairs, Security and Social Welfare: Lt-Gen. (retd) AGUM GUMELAR.

Co-ordinating Minister for the Economy, Finance and Industry: Dr RIZAL RAMLI.

Minister of Home Affairs and Regional Autonomy: Gen. (retd) SURYADI SUDIRJA.

Minister of Foreign Affairs: Dr ALWI SHIHAB.

Minister of Defence: Prof. Dr MOHAMMAD MAHFUD MAHMODIN.

Minister of Maritime Exploration: ROCHIMIN DAHURI.

Minister for Justice and Human Rights Affairs, Acting Minister of State for State Administrative Reforms and Cabinet Secretary: MARSILAM SIMANDJUNTAK.

Minister of Finance and State Enterprises Development: PRIJADI PRAPTO SUBARDJO.

Minister of Industry and Trade: LUHUT BINSAR PANJAITAN.

Minister of Agriculture and Forestry: Prof Dr Ir BUNGARAN SARAGIH.

Minister of Mines and Mineral Resources: Dr Ir PURNOMO YUSGIANTORO.

Minister of Transportation and Telecommunication: BUDI MULYAWAN SUYITNO.

Minister of Manpower and Transmigration: Ir AL HILAL HAMDI.

Minister of National Education: Dr YAHYA MUHAIMIN.

Minister of Health and Social Welfare: Dr AHMAD SUYUDI.

Minister of Religious Affairs: Drs KIAI Haji MUHAMMAD TOLKHAKH HASAN.

Minister of Settlement and Territorial Development: Ir ERNA WITULAR.

Minister of Culture and Tourism: Drs I. GDE ARDIKA.

Minister of State for Research and Technology: Dr A. S. HIKAM.

Minister of State for Co-operatives and Small- and Medium-Sized Businesses: Drs ZARKASIH NUR.

Minister of State for the Environment: Dr A. SONNY KERAF.

Minister of State for Women's Affairs: Dra KHOFIFAH INDAR PARAWANSA.

Junior Minister for Agriculture and Forestry: MARZUKI USMAN.

Junior Minister for Eastern Indonesian Development: MANUEL KAISIEPO.

Junior Minister for National Economy Restructuring: (vacant).

Officials with the rank of Minister of State:
Attorney-General: BAHARUDIN LOPA.
State Secretary: DJOHAN EFFENDI.

MINISTRIES

Office of the President: Istana Merdeka, Jakarta; tel. (21) 3840946.

Office of the Vice-President: Jalan Merdeka Selatan 6, Jakarta; tel. (21) 363539.

Office of the Attorney-General: Jalan Sultan Hasanuddin 1, Kebayoran Baru, Jakarta; tel. (21) 7208557; fax (21) 7392576.

Office of the Cabinet Secretary: Jalan Veteran 18, Jakarta Pusat; tel. (21) 3810973.

Office of the Co-ordinating Minister for Political Affairs, Security and Social Welfare: Jalan Medan Merdeka Barat 15, Jakarta 10110; tel. (21) 3849453; fax (21) 3450918.

Office of the Co-ordinating Minister for the Economy, Finance and Industry: Jalan Taman Suropati 2, Jakarta 10310; tel. (21) 3849063; fax (21) 334779.

Office of the State Secretary: Jalan Veteran 17, Jakarta 10110; tel. (21) 3849043; fax (21) 3452685; internet www.ri.go.id.

Ministry of Agriculture and Forestry: Jalan Harsono R.M. 3, Ragunan, Pasar Minggu, Jakarta Selatan 12550; tel. (21) 7804086; fax (21) 7804237.

Ministry of Defence: Mabes TNI Cilangkap, Jakarta Timur; tel. (21) 3842679; fax (21) 3806711; internet www.dephan.go.id.

Ministry of Finance and State Enterprises Development: Jalan Lapangan Banteng Timur 2-4, Jakarta 10710; tel. (21) 3814324; fax (21) 353710; internet www.depkeu.go.id.

Ministry of Foreign Affairs: Jalan Taman Pejambon 6, Jakarta 10110; tel. (21) 366014; fax (21) 3805511; internet www.dfa-deplu .go.id.

Ministry of Health and Social Welfare: Jalan H. R. Rasuna Said, Block X5, Kav. 4-9, Jakarta 12950; tel. (21) 5201587; fax (21) 5201591.

Ministry of Home Affairs and Regional Autonomy: Jalan Merdeka Utara 7, Jakarta Pusat 10110; tel. (21) 3842222; fax (21) 372812.

Ministry of Industry and Trade: Jalan Jenderal Gatot Subroto, Kav. 52–53, 2nd Floor, Jakarta Selatan; tel. (21) 5256458; fax (21) 5229592; e-mail men-indag@dprin.go.id.

Ministry of Justice and Human Rights Affairs: Jalan H. R. Rasuna Said, Kav. 4–5, Kuningan, Jakarta Pusat; tel. (21) 5253004; fax (21) 5253095.

Ministry of Manpower and Transmigration: Jalan Jenderal Gatot Subroto, Kav. 51, Jakarta Selatan 12950; tel. (21) 5255683; fax (21) 515669; internet www.depnaker.go.id.

Ministry of Mines and Mineral Resources: Jalan Merdeka Selatan 18, Jakarta 10110; tel. (21) 3804242; fax (21) 3847461; internet www.dipu.com.

Ministry of National Education: Jalan Jenderal Sudirman, Senayan, Jakarta Pusat; tel. (21) 5731618; fax (21) 5736870.

Ministry of Religious Affairs: Jalan Lapangan Banteng Barat 3–4, Jakarta Pusat; tel. (21) 3811436; fax (21) 380836; internet www.depag.go.id.

Ministry of Transportation and Telecommunication: Jalan Merdeka Barat 8, Jakarta 10110; tel. (21) 3456332; fax (21) 3451657.

Office of the Minister of State for Co-operatives and Small- and Medium-Sized Businesses: Jalan H. R. Rasuna Said, Kav. 3–5, POB 177, Jakarta Selatan 12940; tel. (21) 5204366; fax (21) 5204383.

Office of the Minister of State for the Environment: Jalan D. I. Panjaitan, Kebon Nanas Lt. II, Jakarta 134110; tel. (21) 8580103; fax (21) 8580101.

Office of the Minister of State for Research and Technology: Jalan M. H. Thamrin 8, Jakarta Pusat; tel. (21) 324767; fax (21) 328169.

Office of the Minister of State for Women's Affairs: Jalan Medan Merdeka Barat 15, Jakarta 10110; tel. (21) 3805563; fax (21) 3805562; e-mail birum@menperta.go.id.

OTHER GOVERNMENT BODIES

Supreme Advisory Council: Jalan Merdeka Utara 15, Jakarta; tel. (21) 362369; Chair. Gen. (retd) ACHMAD TIRTOSUDIRO; Sec.-Gen. SUTOYO.

Badan Pemeriksa Keuangan–BPK (State Audit Board): Jalan Gatot Subroto 31, Jakarta; tel. (21) 584081; internet www.bpk.go.id; Chair. Prof. Dr SATRIO BUDIHARDJO JUDONO; Vice-Chair. Drs BAMBANG TRIADJI.

Legislature

MAJELIS PERMUSYAWARATAN RAKYAT–MPR
(People's Consultative Assembly)

Jalan Gatot Subroto 6, Jakarta; tel. (21) 5801322: fax (21) 5734526; e-mail sumpr@jakarta.wasantara.net.id; internet mpr.wasantara .net.id.

The Majelis Permusyawaratan Rakyat (MPR–People's Consultative Assembly) consists of the 500 members of the Dewan Perwakilan Rakyat (House of Representatives) and 200 other appointees (reduced from 500 in 1999), including regional delegates and representatives of various professions.

Speaker: Dr AMIEN RAIS.

	Seats
Members of the Dewan Perwakilan Rakyat	500
Regional representatives	135
Professional representatives	65
Total	**700**

Dewan Perwakilan Rakyat
(House of Representatives)

Jalan Gatot Subroto 16, Jakarta; tel. (21) 586833; e-mail humas -dpr@dpr.go.id; internet www.dpr.go.id.

Following the election of June 1999 the Dewan Perwakilan Rakyat (House of Representatives) comprised 500 members; of these, 462 were directly elected (increased from 425) and 38 were nominated by the President from the armed forces (reduced from 75).

Speaker: Ir AKBAR TANDJUNG.

General Election, 7 June 1999

	Seats
Partai Demokrasi Indonesia Perjuangan (PDI–P)	154
Golongan Karya (Golkar)	120
Partai Persatuan Pembangunan (PPP)	59
Partai Kebangkitan Bangsa (PKB)	51
Partai Amanat Nasional (PAN)	35
Partai Bulan Bintang (PBB)	13
Partai Keadilan (PK)	6
Partai Keadilan dan Persatuan (PKP)	6
Partai Demokrasi Kasih Bangsa (PDKB)	3
Partai Nahdlatul Umat (PNU)	3
Partai Bhinneka Tunggal Ika	3
Partai Demokrasi Indonesia (PDI)	2
Others	7
Appointed members*	38
Total	**500**

* Members of the political wing of the Indonesian National Defence Forces (TNI).

Political Organizations

Prior to 1998, electoral legislation permitted only three organizations (Golkar, the PDI and PPP) to contest elections. Following the replacement of President Suharto in May 1998, political restrictions were relaxed and new parties were allowed to form (with the only condition being that all parties must adhere to the *pancasila* and reject communism); by early 1999, more than 200 new political parties were reported to have been established.

Barisan Nasional (National Front): Jakarta; f. 1998; committed to ensuring that Indonesia remains a secular state; Sec.-Gen. RACHMAT WITOELAR.

Chinese Indonesian Reform Party: Jakarta; f. 1998.

Indonesian National Unity: Jakarta; f. 1995 by fmr mems of Sukarno's National Party; seeks full implementation of 1945 Constitution; Chair. SUPENI.

Indonesian Reform Party (PPI): Jakarta; f. 1998; Gen. Chair. CHANDRA KUWATLI; Sec.-Gen. Dr H. ACE MULYADI.

Islamic Indonesian Party (PII): Jakarta; f. 1998; Pres. SUUD BAJEBER; Sec.-Gen. SYAIFUL MUNIR.

National Brotherhood Foundation: Jakarta; f. 1995; Chair. KHARIS SUHUD.

New Indonesian National Party: Jakarta; f. 1998.

Partai Amanat Nasional (PAN) (National Mandate Party): c/o Dewan Perwakilan Rakyat, Jalan Gatot Subroto 16, Jakarta; f. 1998; aims to achieve democracy, progress and social justice, to limit the length of the presidential term of office and to increase autonomy in the provinces; Gen. Chair. Dr AMIEN RAIS; Sec.-Gen. FAISAL BASRI.

Partai Bhinneka Tunggal Ika: c/o Dewan Perwakilan Rakyat, Jalan Gatot Subroto 16, Jakarta.

Partai Bulan Bintang (PBB) (Cresent Moon and Star Party): c/o Dewan Perwakilan Rakyat, Jalan Gatot Subroto 16, Jakarta; f. 1998; Leader YUSRIL IHZA MAHENDRA.

Partai Demokrasi Indonesia (PDI) (Indonesian Democratic Party): Jalan Diponegoro 58, Jakarta 10310; tel. (21) 336331; fax (21) 5201630; f. 1973 by the merger of five nationalist and Christian parties; Chair. SOERJADI (installed to replace Megawati Sukarnoputri as leader of the party in a government-orchestrated coup in 1996).

Partai Demokrasi Indonesia Perjuangan (PDI–P) (Indonesian Democratic Struggle Party): c/o Dewan Perwakilan Rakyat, Jalan Gatot Subroto 16, Jakarta; established by Megawati Sukarnoputri, fmr leader of the Partai Demokrasi Indonesia (PDI–see above), following her removal from the leadership of the PDI by the Government in 1996; Chair. MEGAWATI SUKARNOPUTRI.

Partai Demokrasi Kasih Bangsa (PDKB) (The Nation Compassion Democratic Party): Secretariat, Kompleks Widuri Indah Blok A-4, Jalan Palmerah Barat 353, Jakarta Selatan 12210; tel. and fax (21) 5330973.

Partai Golongan Karya (Golkar) (Functional Group): Jalan Anggrek Nellimurni, Jakarta 11480; tel. (21) 5302222; fax (21) 5303380; f. 1964; reorg. 1971; 23m. mems (1999); Co-ordinator of Advisors Haji HARMOKO; Pres. and Chair. Ir AKBAR TANDJUNG; Sec.-Gen. TUSWANDI.

Partai Keadilan (PK) (Justice Party): c/o Dewan Perwakilan Rakyat, Jalan Gatot Subroto 16, Jakarta; internet www.keadilan.or.id; f. 1998; Islamic; Pres. Dr NUR MAHMUDI ISMA'IL; Sec.-Gen. LUTHFI HASAN ISHAAQ.

Partai Keadilan dan Persatuan (PKP) (Justice and Unity Party): c/o Dewan Perwakilan Rakyat, Jalan Gatot Subroto 16, Jakarta; f. 1999; Gen. Chair. EDI SUDRADJAT.

Partai Kebangkitan Bangsa (PKB) (National Awakening Party): Jakarta; Islamic; f. 1998; Chair. of Exec. Council KIAI Haji MA'RUF AMIN; Chair. of Advisory Council Haji MATORI ABDUL JALIL.

Partai Kebangkitan Umat (PKU) (Islamic Awakening Party): c/o Dewan Perwakilan Rakyat, Jalan Gatot Subroto 16, Jakarta; f. 1998 by clerics and members of the Nahdlatul Ulama, with the aim of promoting the adoption of Islamic law in Indonesia.

Partai Nahdlatul Umat (PNU): c/o Dewan Perwakilan Rakyat, Jalan Gatot Subroto 16, Jakarta; Islamic party.

Partai Pembauran (Assimilation Party): Jakarta; f. 1998; Chinese.

Partai Persatuan Pembangunan (PPP) (United Development Party): Jalan Diponegoro 60, Jakarta 10310; tel. (21) 336338; fax (21) 3908070; f. 1973 by the merger of four Islamic parties; Leader: HAMZAH HAZ; Sec.-Gen. ALI MARWAN HANAN.

Partai Rakyat Demokrasi (PRD) (People's Democratic Party): Jakarta; Chair. BUDIMAN SUJATMIKO.

Partai Tionghoa Indonesia (The Indonesian-Chinese Party): Jakarta; f. 1998; Chinese.

Partai Uni Demokrasi Indonesia (PUDI) (Democratic Union Party of Indonesia): Jakarta; e-mail sribintangpamungkas@e-mail.com; f. 1996; Chair. Sri BINTANG PAMUNGKAS.

Other groups with political influence include:

Nahdlatul Ulama (Council of Scholars): Jalan H. Agus Salim 112, Jakarta Pusat; tel. (21) 336250; largest Muslim organization; 30m. mems; Chair. AHMAD HASYIM.

Muhammadiyah: Jalan Menteng Raya 62, Jakarta Pusat; tel. (21) 3903024; fax (21) 3141582; second largest Muslim organization; f. 1912; 28m. mems; Chair. (vacant).

Syarikat Islam: Jalan Taman Amir Hamzah Nomor 2, Jakarta; tel. (21) 31906037.

Ikatan Cendekiawan Muslim Indonesia (ICMI) (Association of Indonesian Muslim Intellectuals): Gedung BPPT, Jalan M.H. Thamrin 8, Jakarta; tel. (21) 3410382; f. 1990 with government support; Chair. ACHMAD TIRTOSUDIRO; Sec.-Gen. ADI SASONO.

Masyumi Baru: Jalan Pangkalan Asem 12, Cempaka Putih Ba, Jakarta Pusat; tel. (21) 4225774; fax (21) 7353077; Sec.-Gen. RIDWAN SAIDI.

The following groups remain in conflict with the Government:

Gerakan Aceh Merdeka (GAM) (Free Aceh Movement): based in Aceh; f. 1976; seeks independence from Indonesia; Leader HASAN DI TIRO; Military Commdr TEUNGKU ABDULLAH SYAFIIE.

National Liberation Front Aceh Sumatra: based in Aceh; f. 1989; seeks independence from Indonesia.

Organisasi Papua Merdeka (OPM) (Free Papua Movement): based in Irian Jaya (West Papua); f. 1963; seeks unification with Papua New Guinea; Chair. MOZES WEROR; Leader KELLY KWALIK.

Papua Presidium Council: based in Irian Jaya (West Papua); seeks independence from Indonesia; Chair. THEYS ELUAY.

Diplomatic Representation

EMBASSIES IN INDONESIA

Afghanistan: Jalan Dr Kusuma Atmaja 15, Jakarta; tel. (21) 333169; Chargé d'affaires: ABDUL GHAFUR BAHER.

Algeria: Jalan H. R. Rasuna Said, Kav. 10-1, Kuningan, Jakarta 12950; tel. (21) 5254719; fax (21) 5254654; Ambassador: SOUFIANE MIMOUNI.

Argentina: Menara Mulia, Suite 1901, Jalan Jenderal Gatot Subroto Kav. 9–11, Jakarta 12930; tel. (21) 5265661; fax (21) 5265664; e-mail embargen@cbn.net; Ambassador: JOSÉ LUIS MIGNINI.

Australia: Jalan H. R. Rasuna Said, Kav. C15-16, Jakarta 12940; tel. (21) 25505555; fax (21) 5227101; internet www.austembjak.or.id; Ambassador: JOHN McCARTHY.

Austria: Jalan Diponegoro 44, Jakarta 10310; tel. (21) 338101; fax (21) 3904927; e-mail auambjak@rad.net.id; Ambassador: Dr VIKTOR SEGALLA.

Bangladesh: Jalan Denpasar Raya 3, Block A-13 Kav. 10, Kuningan, Jakarta 12950; tel. (21) 5221574; fax (21) 5261807; e-mail bdootjak@rad.net.id; Ambassador: Maj.-Gen. Dr M. AFSARUL QADER.

Belgium: Deutsche Bank Bldg, 16th Floor, Jalan Imam Bonjol 80, Jakarta 10310; tel. (21) 3162030; fax (21) 3162035; e-mail jakarta@diplobel.org; Ambassador: LUK DARRAS.

Brazil: Menara Mulia, Suite 1602, Jalan Jenderal Gatot Subroto, Kav. 9, Jakarta 12930; tel. (21) 3904056; fax (21) 3101374; Ambassador: JADIEL FERREIRA DE OLIVEIRA.

Brunei: Wisma BCA, 8th Floor, Jalan Jenderal Sudirman, Kav. 22–23, Jakarta Selatan 12920; tel. (21) 5712124; fax (21) 5712205; Ambassador: Dato' Paduka Haji AWANG YAHYA BIN Haji HARRIS.

Bulgaria: Jalan Imam Bonjol 34–36, Jakarta 10310; tel. (21) 3904049; fax (21) 3904049; Ambassador: GATYU GATEV.

Canada: Wisma Metropolitan I, 5th Floor, Jalan Jenderal Sudirman, Kav. 29, POB 8324/JKS, Jakarta 12920; tel. (21) 5250709; fax (21) 5712251; e-mail jkrta.gr@jkrta01.x400.gc.ca; Ambassador: KEN J. SUNQUIST.

Chile: Bina Mulia Bldg, 7th Floor, Jalan H. R. Rasuna Said, Kav. 10, Kuningan, Jakarta 12950; tel. (21) 5201131; fax (21) 5201955; Ambassador: FERNANDO COUSIÑO.

China, People's Republic: Jalan Jenderal Sudirman 69, Jakarta; tel. (21) 714897; fax (21) 7207782; Ambassador: CHEN SHIQIU.

Colombia: Central Plaza Bldg, 16th Floor, Jalan Jenderal Sudirman, Kav. 48, Jakarta; tel. (21) 516446; fax (21) 5207717; Ambassador: LUIS FERNANDO ANGEL.

Croatia: Menara Mulia, Suite 2101, Jalan Gatot Subroto, Kav. 9–11, Jakarta 12930; tel. (21) 5257822; fax (21) 5204073; e-mail croemb@rad.net.id; internet www.croatemb.or.id; Ambassador: BORIS MITROVIĆ.

Czech Republic: Jalan Gereja Theresia 20, POB 1319, Jakarta Pusat; tel. (21) 3904075; fax (21) 336282; e-mail Jakarta embassy .MZV.CZ; internet www.czech-embassy.or.id; Ambassador: MILAN ŠARAPATKA.

Denmark: Menara Rajawali, 25th Floor, Jalan Mega Kuningan, Lot 5.1, Jakarta 12950; tel. (21) 5761478; fax (21) 5761535; e-mail dkemb9@cbn.net.id; internet www.emb-denmark.or.id; Ambassador: MICHAEL STERNBERG.

Egypt: Jalan Teuku Umar 68, Jakarta 10350; tel. (21) 331141; fax (21) 3105073; Ambassador: AHMAD NABIL ELSALAWY.

Finland: Menara Rajawali, 9th Floor, Jalan Mega Kuningan, Kawasan Mega Kuningan, Jakarta 12950; tel. (21) 5761650; fax (21) 5761631; e-mail sanomat.jak@formin.fi; Ambassador: HANNU HIMANEN.

France: Jalan M. H. Thamrin 20, Jakarta 10310; tel. (21) 3142807; fax (21) 3143338; Ambassador: GÉRARD CROS.

Germany: Jalan M. H. Thamrin 1, Jakarta 10310; tel. (21) 323908; fax (21) 3143338; Ambassador: WALTER LEWALTER.

Holy See: Jalan Merdeka Timur 18, POB 4227, Jakarta Pusat (Apostolic Nunciature); tel. (21) 3841142; fax (21) 3841143; Apostolic Nuncio: Most Rev. RENZO FRATINI, Titular Archbishop of Botriana.

Hungary: 36 Jalan H. R. Rasuna Said, Kav. X/3, Kuningan, Jakarta 12950; tel. (21) 5203459; fax (21) 5203461; Ambassador: LAJOS TAMÁS.

India: Jalan H. R. Rasuna Said, Kav. S/1, Kuningan, Jakarta 12950; tel. (21) 5204150; fax (21) 5204160; e-mail eoiisi@indo.net.id; Ambassador: M. VENKATRAMAN.

Iran: Jalan Hos Cokroaminoto 110, Menteng, Jakarta Pusat; tel. (21) 331391; fax (21) 3107860; Ambassador: SEYED MOHSEN NABAVI.

Iraq: Jalan Teuku Umar 38, Jakarta 10350; tel. (21) 4214067; fax (21) 4214066; Chargé d'affaires: MUSTAFA MUHAMMAD TAWFIQ.

Italy: Jalan Diponegoro 45, Jakarta 10310; tel. (21) 337445; fax (21) 337422; e-mail italemba@rad.net.id; internet www.italambjkt.or.id; Ambassador: ALESSANDRO MEROLA.

Japan: Jalan M. H. Thamrin 24, Jakarta 10350; tel. (21) 324308; fax (21) 325460; Ambassador: TAIZO WATANABE.

Jordan: Jalan Denpasar Raya, Blok A XIII, Kav. 1–2, Jakarta 12950; tel. (21) 5204400; fax (21) 5202447; Ambassador: LU'AY KHASHMAN.

Korea, Democratic People's Republic: Jalan H. R. Rasuna Said, Kav. X.5, Jakarta; tel. (21) 5210181; Ambassador: KIM PYONG HONG.

Korea, Republic: Jalan Jenderal Gatot Subroto 57, Jakarta Selatan; tel. (21) 5201915; fax (21) 514159; Ambassador: KIM JAE-SUP.

Kuwait: Jalan Denpasar Raya, Blok A XII, Kuningan, Jakarta 12950; tel. (21) 5202477; fax (21) 5204359; Ambassador: JASEM M. J. AL-MUBARAKI.

Laos: Jalan Patra Kuningan XIV 1-A, Kuningan, Jakarta 12950; tel. (21) 5229602; fax (21) 5229601; e-mail laoemjkt@cabi.net.id; Ambassador: SOMPHET KHOUSAKOUN.

Libya: Jalan Pekalongan 24, Jakarta; tel. (21) 335308; fax (21) 335726; Chargé d'affaires a.i.: TAJEDDIN A. JERBI.

Malaysia: Jalan H. R. Rasuna Said, Kav. X/6, Kuningan, Jakarta 12950; tel. (21) 5224947; fax (21) 5224974; e-mail mwjakarta@indosat.net.id; Ambassador: Datuk RASTAM MOHAMMAD ISA.

Mexico: Menara Mulia, Suite 2306, Jalan Gatot Subroto, Kav. 9–11, Jakarta 12930; tel. (21) 5203980; fax (21) 5203978; Ambassador: SERGIO LEY-LÓPEZ.

Morocco: Suite 512, 5th Floor, South Tower, Kuningan Plaza, Jalan H. R. Rasuna Said C-11-14, Jakarta 12940; tel. (21) 5200773; fax (21) 5200586; Ambassador: HASSAN FASSI-FIHRI.

Myanmar: Jalan Haji Agus Salim 109, Jakarta Selatan; tel. (21) 320440; fax (21) 327204; Ambassador: U NYUNT TIN.

Netherlands: Jalan H. R. Rasuna Said, Kav. S/3, Kuningan, Jakarta 12950; tel. (21) 5251515; fax (21) 5700734; e-mail nlgovjak@ibm.net; internet www.neth-embassy-jakarta.org; Ambassador: Baron S. VAN HEEMSTRA.

New Zealand: BRI II Bldg, 23rd Floor, Jalan Jenderal Sudirman, Kav. 44–46, Jakarta; tel. (21) 5709460; fax (21) 5709457; e-mail nzembjak@cbn.net.id; Ambassador: MICHAEL GREEN.

Nigeria: Jalan Tamam Patra xiv/11–11A, Kuningan Timur, POB 3649, Jakarta Selatan 12950; tel. (21) 5260922; fax (21) 5260924; e-mail embnig@centrin.net.id; Ambassador: SAIDU MOHAMMED.

Norway: Bina Mulia Bldg, 4th Floor, Jalan H. R. Rasuna Said, Kav. 10, Jakarta 12950; tel. (21) 5251990; fax (21) 5207365; Ambassador: SJUR TORGERSEN.

Pakistan: Jalan Teuku Umar 50, Jakarta 10350; tel. (21) 350576; e-mail pakjkt@rad.net.id; Ambassador: MATAHAR HUSEIN.

Papua New Guinea: Panin Bank Centre, 6th Floor, Jalan Jenderal Sudirman 1, Jakarta 10270; tel. (21) 7251218; fax (21) 7201012; e-mail kdujkt@tbn.net.id; Ambassador: TARCY ERI.

Peru: Menara Rajawali, 12th Floor, Jalan Mega Kuningan Lot 5.1, Kawasan Mega, Kuningan, Jakarta 12950; tel. (21) 5761820; fax (21) 5761825; e-mail embaperu@cbn.net.id; Ambassador: ELARD ESCALA.

Philippines: Jalan Imam Bonjol 6–8, Jakarta 10310; tel. (21) 3100334; fax (21) 3151167; e-mail phjkt@indo.net.id; Ambassador: LEONIDES T. CADAY.

Poland: H. R. Rasuna Said, Kav. X Blok IV/3, Jakarta Selatan 12950; tel. (21) 2525948; fax (21) 2525958; Ambassador: KRZYSZTOF SZUMSKI.

Qatar: Jakarta; tel. (21) 5277751; fax (21) 5277753.

Romania: Jalan Teuku Cik Ditiro 42A, Menteng, Jakarta Pusat; tel. (21) 3106240; fax (21) 3907759; Ambassador: DUMITRU TANCU.

Russia: Jalan H. R. Rasuna Said, Blok X/7, Kav. 1–2, Jakarta; tel. (21) 5222912; Ambassador: NIKOLAI SOLOVIYEV.

Saudi Arabia: Jalan M. T. Haryono Kav. 27, Cawang Atas, Jakarta Timur; tel. (21) 8011533; fax (21) 8011527; Ambassador: ABDULLAH A. ALIM.

Singapore: Jalan H. R. Rasuna Said, Blok X/4, Kav. 2, Kuningan, Jakarta 12950; tel. (21) 5201489; fax (21) 5201486; Ambassador: EDWARD LEE.

Slovakia: Jalan Prof. Mohammed Yamin 29, POB 1368, Jakarta Pusat; tel. (21) 3101068; fax (21) 3101180; e-mail slovemby@indo.net.id; Ambassador: MILAN LAJČIAK.

South Africa: Suite 705, Wisma GKBI, Jalan Jenderal Sudirman 28, Jakarta 10210; tel. (21) 5740660; fax (21) 5740661; e-mail saembjak@centrin.net.id; internet www.saembassy-jakarta.or.id; Ambassador: N. M. MASHABANE.

Spain: Jalan H. Agus Salim 61, Jakarta 10350; tel. (21) 335937; fax (21) 325996; Ambassador: ANTONIO SÁNCHEZ JARA.

Sri Lanka: Jalan Diponegoro 70, Jakarta 10320; tel. (21) 3161886; fax (21) 3107962; e-mail lankaemb@vision.net.id; Ambassador: TISSA DIAS BANDARANAYAKE.

Sudan: Wisma Bank Dharmala, 7th Floor, Suite 01, Jalan Jenderal Sudirman, Kav. 28, Jakarta 12920; tel. (21) 5212099; fax (21) 5212077; e-mail sudanijk@centrin.net.id; Ambassador: HASSAN IBRAHIM GADELKARIM.

Sweden: Menara Rajawali, 9th Floor, Jalan Mega Kuningan, Lot 51, Kawasan Mega Kuningan, Jakarta 12950; POB 2824, Jakarta 10001; tel. (21) 5762690; fax (21) 5762691; e-mail sweden@cbn.net.id; internet www.swedemb-jakarta.com; Ambassador: HARALD SANDBERG.

Switzerland: Jalan H. R. Rasuna Said X-3/2, Kuningan 12950 Jakarta Selatan; tel. (21) 5256061; fax (21) 5202289; e-mail swiemjak@rad.net.id; Ambassador: GÉRARD FONJALLAZ.

Syria: Jalan Karang Asem I/8, Jakarta 12950; tel. (21) 515991; Ambassador: NADIM DOUAY.

Thailand: Jalan Imam Bonjol 74, Jakarta 10310; tel. (21) 3904052; fax (21) 3107469; e-mail thaijkt@indo.net.id; Ambassador: SOMPHAND KOKILANON.

Tunisia: Wisma Dharmala Sakti, Jalan Jenderal Sudirman 32, Jakarta 10220; tel. (21) 5703432; fax (21) 5700016; Ambassador: MOHAMED GHERIB.

Turkey: Jalan H. R. Rasuna Said, Kav. 1, Kuningan, Jakarta 12950; tel. (21) 516258; fax (21) 5226056; Ambassador: SEVINÇ DALYANOĞLU.

Ukraine: Simprug Permata 1, No. 39, Jakarta 12220; tel. (21) 7205356; fax (21) 7266969.

United Arab Emirates: Jalan Prof. Dr Satrio Kav. 16-17, Jakarta 12950; tel. (21) 5206518; fax (21) 5206526; e-mail uaeemb@rad.net; Ambassador: MOHAMMED SULTAN ALSOWAIDI.

United Kingdom: Jalan M. H. Thamrin 75, Jakarta 10310; tel. (21) 3156264; fax (21) 3926263; e-mail postmaster@jakarta.mail.fco.gov.uk; internet www.britain-in-indonesia.or.id; Ambassador: RICHARD GOZNEY.

USA: Jalan Merdeka Selatan 4-5, Jakarta 10110; tel. (21) 3442211; fax (21) 3862259; internet www.usembassyjakarta.org; Ambassador: SKIP BOYCE.

Venezuela: Menara Mulia, 20th Floor, Suite 2005, Jalan Jenderal Gatot Subroto, Kav. 9–11, Jakarta Selatan 12930; tel. (21) 5227547; fax (21) 5227549; Ambassador: VASCO ALTUVE FEBRES.

Viet Nam: Jalan Teuku Umar 25, Jakarta; tel. (21) 3100358; fax (21) 3100359; Ambassador: NGUYEN DANG QUANG.

Yemen: Jalan Yusuf Adiwinata 29, Jakarta; tel. (21) 3904074; fax (21) 4214946; Ambassador: ABDUL WAHAD FARAH.

Yugoslavia: Jalan Hos Cokroaminoto 109, Jakarta 10310; tel. (21) 3143560; fax (21) 3143613; e-mail ambajaka@rad.net.id; Chargé d'affaires: DUSAN STOJKOVIC.

Judicial System

There is one codified criminal law for the whole of Indonesia. In December 1989 the Islamic Judicature Bill, giving wider powers to Shariah courts, was approved by the Dewan Perwakilan Rakyat (House of Representatives). The new law gave Muslim courts authority over civil matters, such as marriage. Muslims may still choose to appear before a secular court. Europeans are subject to the Code of Civil Law published in the State Gazette in 1847. Alien orientals (i.e. Arabs, Indians, etc.) and Chinese are subject to certain parts of the Code of Civil Law and the Code of Commerce. The work of codifying this law has started, but, in view of the great complexity and diversity of customary law, it may be expected to take a considerable time to achieve.

Supreme Court (Mahkamah Agung): Jalan Merdeka Utara 9–13, Jakarta 10110; tel. (21) 3843348; fax (21) 3811057; the final court of appeal.

Chief Justice: Prof. BAGIR MANAN.

Deputy Chief Justice: TAUFIK.

High Courts in Jakarta, Surabaya, Medan, Makassar, Banda Aceh, Padang, Palembang, Bandung, Semarang, Banjarmasin, Menado, Denpasar, Ambon and Jayapura deal with appeals from the District Courts.

District Courts deal with marriage, divorce and reconciliation.

Religion

All citizens are required to state their religion. According to a survey in 1985, 86.9% of the population were Muslims, while 9.6% were Christians, 1.9% were Hindus, 1.0% were Buddhists and 0.6% professed adherence to tribal religions.

Five national religious councils—representing the Islamic, Catholic, Protestant, Hindu and Buddhist religious traditions—were established to serve as liaison bodies between religious adherents and the Government and to advise the Government on the application of religious principles to various elements of national life.

ISLAM

In 1993 nearly 90% of Indonesians were Muslims. Indonesia has the world's largest Islamic population.

Majelis Ulama Indonesia (MUI) (Indonesian Ulama Council): Komp. Masjid Istiqlal, Jalan Taman Wijaya Kesuma, Jakarta 10710; tel. (21) 3455471; fax (21) 3855412; Central Muslim organization; Chair. (vacant).

CHRISTIANITY

Persekutuan Gereja-Gereja di Indonesia (Communion of Churches in Indonesia): Jalan Salemba Raya 10, Jakarta 10430; tel. (21) 3908119; fax (21) 3150457; e-mail pgi@bit.net.id; f. 1950; 70 mem. churches; Chair. Rev. Dr SULARSO SOPATER; Gen. Sec. Rev. Dr JOSEPH M. PATTIASINA.

The Roman Catholic Church

Indonesia comprises eight archdioceses and 26 dioceses. At 31 December 1997 there were an estimated 5,686,450 adherents in Indonesia (excluding the territory of East Timor), representing 2.7% of the population.

Bishops' Conference: Konferensi Waligereja Indonesia (KWI), Jalan Cut Meutia 10, POB 3044, Jakarta 10002; tel. (21) 336422; fax (21) 3918527; e-mail kwi@parokinet.org; f. 1973; Pres. Rt Rev. JOSEPH SUWATAN, Bishop of Manado.

Archbishop of Ende: Most Rev. ABDON LONGINUS DA CUNHA, Keuskupan Agung, POB 210, Jalan Katedral 5, Ndona-Ende 86312, Flores; tel. (381) 21176; fax (381) 21606.

Archbishop of Jakarta: Cardinal JULIUS RIYADI DARMAATMADJA, Keuskupan Agung, Jalan Katedral 7, Jakarta 10710; tel. (21) 3813345; fax (21) 3855681.

Archbishop of Kupang: Most Rev. PETER TURANG, Keuskupan Agung Kupang, Jalan Thamrin, Oepoi, Kupang 85111, Timor NTT; tel. and fax (0380) 33331.

Archbishop of Medan: Most Rev. ALFRED GONTI PIUS DATUBARA, Jalan Imam Bonjol 39, POB 1191, Medan 20152, Sumatra Utara; tel. (61) 4516647; fax (61) 4145745; e-mail mar39@indosat.net.id.

Archbishop of Merauke: Most Rev. JACOBUS DUIVENVOORDE, Keuskupan Agung, Jalan Mandala 30, Merauke 99602, Irian Jaya (West Papua); tel. (971) 21011; fax (971) 21311.

Archbishop of Pontianak: Most Rev. HIERONYMUS HERCULANUS BUMBUN, Keuskupan Agung, Jalan A. R. Hakin 92A, POB 1119, Pontianak 78011, Kalimantan Barat; tel. (561) 732382; fax (561) 738785; e-mail kap@pontianak.wasantara.net.id.

Archbishop of Semarang: Most Rev. IGNATIUS SUHARYO HARDJOATMODJO), Keuskupan Agung, Jalan Pandanaran 13, Semarang 50244; tel. (24) 411780; fax (24) 414741.

Archbishop of Makassar: Most Rev. JOHANNES LIKU ADA', Keuskupan Agung, Jalan Thamrin 5–7, Makassar 90111, Sulawesi Selatan; tel. (411) 315744; fax (411) 326674; e-mail pseupg@indosat.net.id.

Other Christian Churches

Protestant Church in Indonesia (Gereja Protestan di Indonesia): Jalan Medan Merdeka Timur 10, Jakarta 10110; tel. (21) 3519003; fax (21) 34830224; consists of 10 churches of Calvinistic tradition; 2,789,155 mems, 3,841 congregations, 1,965 pastors (1998); Chair. Rev. Dr D. J. LUMENTA.

Numerous other Protestant communities exist throughout Indonesia, mainly organized on a local basis. The largest of these (1985 memberships) are: the Batak Protestant Christian Church (1,875,143); the Christian Church in Central Sulawesi (100,000); the Christian Evangelical Church in Minahasa (730,000); the Christian Protestant Church in Indonesia (210,924); the East Java Christian Church (123,850); the Evangelical Christian Church in Irian Jaya (West Papua—360,000); the Evangelical Christian Church of Sangir-Talaud (190,000); the Indonesian Christian Church/Huria Kristen Indonesia (316,525); the Javanese Christian Churches (121,500); the Kalimantan Evangelical Church (182,217); the Karo Batak Protestant Church (164,288); the Nias Protestant Christian Church (250,000); the Protestant Church in the Moluccas (575,000); the Simalungun Protestant Christian Church (155,000); and the Toraja Church (250,000).

BUDDHISM

All-Indonesia Buddhist Association: Jakarta.
Indonesian Buddhist Council: Jakarta.

HINDUISM

Hindu Dharma Council: Jakarta.

The Press

In August 1990 the Government announced that censorship of both the local and foreign press was to be relaxed and that the authorities would refrain from revoking the licences of newspapers that violated legislation governing the press. In practice, however, there was little change in the Government's policy towards the press. In June 1994 the Government revoked the publishing licences of three principal news magazines, *Tempo*, *Editor* and *DeTik*. Following the resignation of President Suharto in May 1998, the new Government undertook to allow freedom of expression. *DeTik* magazine subsequently resumed publication under the new name, *DeTak*, in July; *Tempo* magazine resumed publication in October.

PRINCIPAL DAILIES

Bali

Harian Pagi Umum (Bali Post): Jalan Kepudang 67A, Denpasar 80232; f. 1948; daily (Indonesian edn), weekly (English edn); Editor K. NADHA; circ. 25,000.

Irian Jaya (West Papua)

Berita Karya: Jayapura.
Cendrawasih Post: Jayapura; Editor RUSTAM MADUBUN.

Teropong: Jalan Halmahera, Jayapura.

Java

Angkatan Bersenjata: Jalan Kramat Raya 94, Jakarta Pusat; tel. (21) 46071; fax (21) 366870.

Bandung Post: Jalan Lodaya 38A, Bandung 40264; tel. (22) 305124; fax (22) 302882; f. 1979; Chief Editor AHMAD SAELAN; Dir AHMAD JUSACC.

Berita Buana: Jalan Tahah Abang Dua 33–35, Jakarta, 10110; tel. (21) 5487175; fax (21) 5491555; f. 1970; relaunched 1990; Indonesian; circ. 150,000.

Berita Yudha: Jalan Letjenderal Haryono MT22, Jakarta; tel. (21) 8298331; f. 1971; Indonesian; Editor SUNARDI; circ. 50,000.

Bisnis Indonesia: Wisma Bisnis Indonesia, Jalan Letjenderal S. Parman, Kav. 12, Slipi, Jakarta; tel. (21) 5305869; fax (21) 5305868; f. 1985; Indonesian; Editor SUKAMDANI S. GITOSARDJONO; circ. 60,000.

Harian Indonesia (Indonesia Rze Pao): Jalan Toko Tiga Seberang 21, POB 4755, Jakarta 11120; tel. (21) 6295984; fax (21) 6297830; f. 1966; Chinese; Editor W. D. SUKISMAN; Dir HADI WIBOWO; circ. 42,000.

Harian Terbit: Jalan Pulogadung 15, Kawasan Industri Pulogadung, Jakarta 13920; tel. (21) 4602953; fax (21) 4602950; f. 1972; Indonesian; Editor H. R. S. HADIKAMAJAYA; circ. 125,000.

Harian Umum AB: CTC Bldg, 2nd Floor, Kramat Raya 94, Jakarta Pusat; f. 1965; official armed forces journal; Dir GOENARSO; Editor-in-Chief N. SOEPANGAT; circ. 80,000.

The Indonesia Times: Jalan Pulo Lentut 12, Jakarta Timur; tel. (21) 4611280; fax (21) 375012; f. 1974; English; Editor TRIBUANA SAID; circ. 35,000.

Indonesian Observer: Wisma Indovision, 9th Floor, Jalan Raya Panjang Blok Z/III, Green Garden, Jakarta 11520; tel. (21) 5825568; fax (21) 5813984; internet www.indonesian-observer.com; f. 1955; English; independent; Editor TAUFIK DARUSMAN; circ. 25,000.

Jakarta Post: Jalan Palmerah Selatan 15, Jakarta 10270; tel. (21) 5300476; fax (21) 5309066; internet www.thejakartapost.com; f. 1983; English; Gen. Man. RAYMOND TORUAN; Chief Editor SUSANTO PUDJOMARTONO; circ. 50,000.

Jawa Pos: Jalan Kembang Jepun 167–169, Surabaya; tel. (31) 830774; fax (31) 830996; f. 1949; Indonesian; Chief Editor DAHLAN ISKAN; circ. 120,000.

Kedaulatan Rakyat: Jalan P. Mangkubumi 40–42, Yogyakarta; tel. (274) 65685; fax (274) 63125; f. 1945; Indonesian; independent; Editor IMAN SUTRISNO; circ. 50,000.

Kompas: Jalan Palmerah Selatan 26–28, Jakarta; tel. (21) 5483008; fax (21) 5305868; f. 1965; Indonesian; Editor Drs JAKOB OETAMA; circ. 523,453.

Media Indonesia Daily: Jalan Pilar Mas Raya Kav. A-D, Kedoya Selatan, Kebon Jeruk, Jakarta 11520; tel. (21) 5812088; fax (21) 5812105; e-mail redaksi@mediaindonesia.co.id; internet www .mediaindo.co.id; f. 1989; fmrly Prioritas; Indonesian; Publr SURYA PALOH; Editor DJAFAR H. ASSEGAFF; circ. 2,000.

Merdeka: Jalan Raya Kebayoran Lama 17, Jakarta Selatan 12210; tel. (21) 5556059; fax (21) 5556063; f. 1945; Indonesian; independent; Dir and Chief Editor B. M. DIAH; circ. 130,000.

Neraca: Jalan Jambrut 2–4, Jakarta; tel. (21) 323969; fax (21) 3101873.

Pelita (Torch): Jalan Jenderal Sudirman 65, Jakarta; f. 1974; Indonesian; Muslim; Editor AKBAR TANJUNG; circ. 80,000.

Pewarta Surabaya: Jalan Karet 23, POB 85, Surabaya; f. 1905; Indonesian; Editor RADEN DJAROT SOEBIANTORO; circ. 10,000.

Pikiran Rakyat: Jalan Asia-Afrika 77, Bandung 40111; tel. (22) 51216; f. 1950; Indonesian; independent; Editor BRAM M. DARMAPRAWIRA; circ. 150,000.

Pos Kota: Yayasan Antar Kota, Jalan Gajah Mada 100, Jakarta 10130; tel. (21) 6290874; f. 1970; Indonesian; Editor H. SOFYAN LUBIS; circ. 500,000.

Republika: Jalan Warung Buncit Raya 37, Jakarta 12510; tel. (21) 7803747; fax (21) 7800420; f. 1993; organ of ICMI; Chief Editor PARNI HADI.

Sinar Pagi: Jalan Letjenderal Haryono MT22, Jakarta Selatan.

Suara Karya: Jalan Bangka II/2, Kebayoran Baru, Jakarta Selatan; tel. (21) 7991352; fax (21) 7995261; f. 1971; Indonesian; Editor SYAMSUL BASRI; circ. 100,000.

Suara Merdeka: Jalan Pandanaran 30, Semarang 50241; tel. (24) 412660; fax (24) 411116; f. 1950; Indonesian; Publr Ir BUDI SANTOSO; Editor SUWARNO; circ. 200,000.

Suara Pembaruan: Jalan Dewi Sartika 136/D, Cawang, Jakarta 13630; tel. (21) 8013208; fax (21) 8007262; e-mail koransp@suarapembaruan.com; f. 1987; licence revoked in 1986 as Sinar Harapan (Ray of Hope); Publr Dr ALBERT HASIBUAN.

Surabaya Post: Jalan Taman Ade Irma Nasution 1, Surayaba; tel. (31) 45394; fax (31) 519585; f. 1953; independent; Publr Mrs Tuty Azis; Editor Imam Pujono; circ. 115,000.

Wawasan: Komplek Pertokoan Simpang Lima, Blok A 10, Semarang 50241; tel. (24) 4150858; fax (24) 4510025; e-mail waspada@indosat.net.id; internet www.waspada.co.id; f. 1986; Indonesian; Chief Editor H. Prabudi Said; circ. 65,000.

Kalimantan

Banjarmasin Post: Jalan Haryono MT 54–143, Banjarmasin; tel. (511) 54370; fax (511) 66123; e-mail bpost@Indomedia.com; internet www.indomedia.com/bpost/; f. 1971; Indonesian; Chief Editor H. Basuki Subianto; circ. 50,000.

Gawi Manuntung: Jalan Pangeran Samudra 97B, Banjarmasin; f. 1972; Indonesian; Editor M. Ali Sri Indradjaya; circ. 5,000.

Harian Umum Akcaya: Jalan Veteran 1, Pontianak.

Lampung Post: Jalan Pangkal Pinang, Lampung.

Manuntung: Jalan Jenderal Sudirman RT XVI 82, Balikpapan 76144; tel. (542) 35359.

Maluku

Pos Maluku: Jalan Raya Pattimura 19, Ambon; tel. (911) 44614.

Suara Maluku: Komplek Perdagangan Mardikas, Block D3/11A, Ternate; tel. (911) 44590.

Riau

Riau Pos: Pekanbaru, Riau; circ. 40,000.

Sulawesi

Bulletin Sulut: Jalan Korengkeng 38, Lt II Manado, 95114, Sulawesi Utara.

Cahaya Siang: Jalan Kembang II 2, Manado, 95114, Sulawesi Utara; tel. (431) 61054; fax (431) 63393.

Fajar (Dawn): Makassar; circ. 35,000.

Manado Post: Jalan Yos Sudarso 73, Manado.

Pedoman Rakyat: Jalan H. A. Mappanyukki 28, Makassar; f. 1947; independent; Editor M. Basir; circ. 30,000.

Suluh Merdeka: Jalan Haryane MT, POB 1105, Manado, 95110.

Tegas: Jalan Mappanyukki 28, Makassar; tel. (411) 3960.

Sumatra

Analisa: Jalan Jenderal A. Yani 37–43, Medan; tel. (61) 326655; fax (61) 514031; f. 1972; Indonesian; Editor Soffyan; circ. 75,000.

Harian Haluan: Jalan Damar 59 C/F, Padang; f. 1948; Editor-in-Chief Rivai Marlaut; circ. 40,000.

Harian Umum Nasional Waspada: Jalan Brigjenderal 1 Katamso, Medan 20151; tel. (61) 4150858; fax (61) 4510025; e-mail waspada@indosat.net.id; internet www.waspada.co.id; f. 1947; Indonesian; Editor-in-Chief H. Prabudi Said.

Mimbar Umum: Merah, Medan; tel. (61) 517807; f. 1947; Indonesian; independent; Editor Mohd Lud Lubis; circ. 55,000.

Serambi Indonesia: Jalan T. Nyak Arief 159, Lampriek, Banda Aceh.

Sinar Indonesia Baru: Jalan Brigjenderal Katamso 66, Medan 20151; tel. (61) 512530; fax (61) 510150; f. 1970; Indonesian; Chief Editor G. M. Panggabean; circ. 150,000.

Suara Rakyat Semesta: Jalan K. H. Ashari 52, Palembang; Indonesian; Editor Djadil Abdullah; circ. 10,000.

Waspada: Jalan Jenderal Sudirman, cnr Jalan Brigjenderal Katamso 1, Medan 20151; tel. (61) 550858; fax (61) 510025; f. 1947; Indonesian; Chief Editor Ani Idrus; circ. 60,000 (daily), 55,000 (Sunday).

PRINCIPAL PERIODICALS

Amanah: Jalan Garuda 69, Kemayoran, Jakarta; tel. (21) 410254; fortnightly; Muslim current affairs; Indonesian; Man. Dir Maskun Iskandar; circ. 180,000.

Berita Negara: Jalan Pertjetakan Negara 21, Kotakpos 2111, Jakarta; tel. (21) 4207251; fax (21) 4207251; f. 1951; 2 a week; official gazette.

Bobo: PT Gramedia, Jalan Kebahagiaan 4-14, Jakarta 11140; tel. (21) 6297809; fax (21) 6390080; f. 1973; weekly; children's magazine; Editor Tineke Latumeten; circ. 240,000.

Bola: Yayasan Tunas Raga, Jalan Palmerah Selatan 17, Jakarta 10270; tel. and fax (21) 5483008; 2 a week; Tue. and Fri.; sports magazine; Indonesian; Editor Sumohadi Marsis; circ. 715,000.

Buana Minggu: Jalan Tanah Abang Dua 33, Jakarta Pusat 10110; tel. (21) 364190; weekly; Sunday; Indonesian; Editor Winoto Partho; circ. 193,450.

Business News: Jalan H. Abdul Muis 70, Jakarta 10160; tel. (21) 3848207; fax (21) 3454280; f. 1956; 3 a week (Indonesian edn), 2 a week (English edn); Chief Editor Sanjoto Sastromihardjo; circ. 15,000.

Citra: Gramedia Bldg, Unit 11, 5th Floor, Jalan Palmerah Selatan 24-26, Jakarta 10270; tel. (21) 5483008; fax (21) 5494035; f. 1990; weekly; TV and film programmes, music trends and celebrity news; circ. 239,000.

Depthnews Indonesia: Jalan Jatinegara Barat III/6, Jakarta 13310; tel. (21) 8194994; fax (21) 8195501; f. 1972; weekly; publ. by Press Foundation of Indonesia; Editor Sumono Mustoffa.

Dunia Wanita: Jalan Brigjenderal, Katamso 1, Medan; tel. (61) 4150858; fax (61) 4510025; e-mail waspada@indosat.net.id; f. 1949; fortnightly; Indonesian; women's tabloid; Chief Editor Dr Rayati Syafrin; circ. 10,000.

Economic Review: c/o Bank BNI, Strategic Planning Division, Jalan Jenderal Sudirman, Kav. 1, POB 2955, Jakarta 10220; tel. (21) 5728606; fax (21) 5728456; f. 1966; 4 a year; English.

Ekonomi Indonesia: Jalan Merdeka, Timur 11–12, Jakarta; tel. (21) 494458; monthly; English; economic journal; Editor Z. Achmad; circ. 20,000.

Eksekutif: Jalan R. S. Fatmawati 21, Jakarta 12410; tel. (21) 7502513; fax (21) 7502676.

Femina: Jalan H. R. Rasuna Said, Blok B, Kav. 32–33, Jakarta Selatan; tel. (21) 513816; fax (21) 513041; f. 1972; weekly; women's magazine; Publr Sofjan Alisjahbana; Editor Widarti Gunawan; circ. 130,000.

Forum: Kebayoran Centre, 12A–14, Jalan Kebayoran Baru, Welbak, Jakarta 12240; tel. (21) 7255625; fax (21) 7255645.

Gadis Magazine: Jalan H. R. Rasuna Said, Blok B, Kav. 32–33, Jakarta 12910; tel. (21) 5253816; fax (21) 5262131; e-mail gadis@indosat.net.id; internet www.gadis-online.com; f. 1973; every 10 days; Indonesian; teen lifestyle magazine; Editor-in-Chief Petty S. F.; circ. 100,000.

Gamma: Jakarta; f. 1999; by fmr employees of *Tempo* and *Gatra*.

Gatra: Gedung Gatra, Jalan Kalibata Timur IV/15, Jakarta 12740; tel. (21) 7973535; fax (21) 79196941; e-mail gatra@gatra.com; internet www.gatra.com; f. 1994 by fmr employees of *Tempo* (banned 1994–1998); Gen. Man. and Editor-in-Chief Widi Yarmanto.

Gugat (Accuse): Surabaya; politics, law and crime; weekly; circ. 250,000.

Hai: Gramedia, Jalan Palmerah Selatan 22, Jakarta 10270; tel. (21) 5483008; fax (21) 6390080; f. 1973; weekly; youth magazine; Editor Arswendo Atmowiloto; circ. 70,000.

Indonesia Business News: Wisma Bisnis Indonesia, Jalan Letjenderal S. Parman, Kav. 12, Slipi, Jakarta 11410; tel. (21) 5304016; fax (21) 5305868; English.

Indonesia Business Weekly: Jalan Letjenderal S. Parman, Kav. 12, Slipi, Jakarta 11410; tel. (21) 5304016; fax (21) 5305868; English; Editor Taufik Darusman.

Indonesia Magazine: 20 Jalan Merdeka Barat, Jakarta; tel. (21) 352015; f. 1969; monthly; English; Chair. G. Dwipayana; Editor-in-Chief Hadely Hasibuan; circ. 15,000.

Intisari (Digest): Jalan Palmerah Selatan 24–26, Gedung Unit II, 5th Floor, Jakarta 10270; tel. (21) 5483008; fax (21) 5494035; e-mail intisari@indomedia.com; internet www.indomedia.com/intisari; f. 1963; monthly; Indonesian; popular science, health, crime and general interest; Editors Al. Heru Kustara, Irawati; circ. 141,000.

Jakarta Jakarta: Gramedia Bldg, Unit II, 5th Floor, Jalan Palmerah Selatan No. 24–26, Jakarta 10270; tel. (21) 5483008; fax (21) 5494035; f. 1985; weekly; food, fun, fashion and celebrity news; circ. 70,000.

Keluarga: Jalan Sangaji 11, Jakarta; fortnightly; women's and family magazine; Editor S. Dahono.

Majalah Ekonomis: POB 4195, Jakarta; monthly; English; business; Chief Editor S. Arifin Hutabarat; circ. 20,000.

Majalah Kedokteran Indonesia (Journal of the Indonesian Medical Asscn): Jalan Kesehatan 111/29, Jakarta 11/16; f. 1951; monthly; Indonesian, English.

Manglé: Jalan Lodaya 19–21, 40262 Bandung; tel. (22) 411438; f. 1957; weekly; Sundanese; Chief Editor Drs Oejang Darajatoen; circ. 74,000.

Matra: Grafity Pers, Kompleks Buncit Raya Permai, Kav. 1, Jalan Warung, POB 3476, Jakarta; tel. (21) 515952; f. 1986; monthly; men's magazine; general interest and current affairs; Editor-in-Chief (vacant); circ. 100,000.

Mimbar Kabinet Pembangunan: Jalan Merdeka-Barat 7, Jakarta; f. 1966; monthly; Indonesian; publ. by Dept of Information.

Mutiara: Jalan Dewi Sartika 136D, Cawang, Jakarta Timur; general interest; Publr H. G. Rorimpandey.

Nova: PT Gramedia, Jalan Kebahagiaan 4-14, Jakarta 11140; tel. (21) 6297809; fax (21) 6390080; weekly; Sunday; women's interest; Indonesian; Editor EVIE FADJARI; circ. 220,000.

Oposisi: Jakarta; weekly; politics; circ. 400,000.

Otomotif: Gramedia Bldg, Unit II, 5th Floor, Jalan Palmerah Selatan 24–26, Jakarta 10270; tel. (21) 5490666; fax (21) 5494035; e-mail iklanmjl@ub.net.id; f. 1990; weekly; automotive specialist tabloid; circ. 215,763.

Peraba: Bintaran Kidul 5, Yogyakarta; weekly; Indonesian and Javanese; Roman Catholic; Editor W. KARTOSOEHARSONO.

Pertani PT: Jalan Pasar Minggu, Kalibata, POB 247/KBY, Jakarta Selatan; tel. (21) 793108; f. 1974; monthly; Indonesian; agricultural; Pres. Dir Ir RUSLI YAHYA.

Petisi: Surabaya; weekly; Editor CHOIRUL ANAM.

Rajawali: Jakarta; monthly; Indonesian; civil aviation and tourism; Dir R. A. J. LUMENTA; Man. Editor KARYONO ADHY.

Selecta: Kebon Kacang 29/4, Jakarta; fortnightly; illustrated; Editor SAMSUDIN LUBIS; circ. 80,000.

Simponi: Jakarta; f. 1994 by former employees of *DeTik* (banned 1994–98).

Sinar Jaya: Jakarta Selatan; fortnightly; agriculture; Chief Editor Ir SURYONO PROJOPRANOTO.

Swasembada: Gedung Chandra Lt 2, Jalan M. H. Thamrin 20, Jakarta 10310; tel. (21) 3103316.

Tempo: Gedung Tempo, 8th Floor, Jalan H.R. Rasuna Said, Kav. C-17, Kuningan, Jakarta 12940; tel. (21) 5201022; fax (21) 5200092; f. 1971; weekly; Editor-in-Chief BAMBANG HARYMURTI.

Tiara: Gramedia Bldg, Unit 11, 5th Floor, Jalan Palmerah Selatan 24–26, Jakarta 10270; tel (21) 5483008; fax (21) 5494035; f. 1990; fortnightly; lifestyles, features and celebrity news; circ. 47,000.

Ummat: Jakarta; Islamic; sponsored by ICMI.

NEWS AGENCIES

Antara (Indonesian National News Agency): Wisma Antara, 19th and 20th Floors, 17 Jalan Merdeka Selatan, POB 1257, Jakarta 10110; tel. (21) 364768; fax (21) 3843052; f. 1937; 2,784 commercial, 11 radio, five television and 86 newspaper subscribers in 1994; 27 brs in Indonesia, seven overseas brs; nine bulletins in Indonesian and seven in English; monitoring service of stock exchanges worldwide; photo service; Editor-in-Chief BUDIARTO DANUJAYA; Gen. Man. PARNI HADI.

Kantorberita Nasional Indonesia (KNI News Service): Jalan Jatinegara Barat III/6, Jakarta Timur 13310; tel. (21) 811003; fax (21) 8195501; f. 1966; independent national news agency; foreign and domestic news in Indonesian; Dir and Editor-in-Chief Drs SUMONO MUSTOFFA; Exec. Editor HARIM NURROCHADI.

Foreign Bureaux

Agence France-Presse (AFP): Jalan Indramayu 18, Jakarta Pusat 10310; tel. (21) 3336082; fax (21) 3809186; Chief Correspondent PASCAL MALLET.

Agenzia Nazionale Stampa Associata (ANSA) (Italy): Jalan Petogogan 1 Go-2 No, 13 Kompleks RRI, Kebayoran Baru, Jakarta Selatan; tel. (21) 7391996; fax (21) 7392247; Correspondent HERYTNO PUJOWIDAGDO.

Associated Press (AP) (USA): Deutsche Bank Bldg, 14th Floor, No. 1403–1404, Jalan Imam Bonjol 80, Jakarta 10310; tel. (21) 39831269; fax (21) 39831270; e-mail gspencer@ap.org; Chief of Bureau GEOFF SPENCER.

Central News Agency Inc (CNA) (Taiwan): Jalan Gelong Baru Timur 1-13, Jakarta Barat; tel. and fax (21) 5600266; Bureau Chief WU PIN-CHIANG.

Informatsionnoye Telegrafnoye Agentstvo Rossii—Telegrafnoye Agentstvo Suverennykh Stran (ITAR—TASS) (Russia): Jalan Surabaya 7 Menteng, Jakarta Pusat 10310; tel. and fax (21) 3155283; e-mail ab1952@indosat.net.id; Correspondent ANDREY ALEKSANDROVICH BYTCHKOV.

Inter Press Service (IPS) (Italy): Gedung Dewan Pers, 4th Floor, Jalan Kebon Sirih 34, Jakarta 10110; tel. (21) 3453131; fax (21) 3453175; Chief Correspondent ABDUL RAZAK.

Jiji Tsushin (Japan): Jalan Raya Bogor 109B, Jakarta; tel. (21) 8090509; Correspondent MARGA RAHARJA.

Kyodo Tsushin (Japan): Skyline Bldg, 11th Floor, Jalan M. H. Thamrin 9, Jakarta 10310; tel. (21) 345012; Correspondent MASAYUKI KITAMURA.

Reuters (United Kingdom): Wisma Antara, 6th Floor, Jalan Medan Merdeka Selatan 17, Jakarta 10110; tel. (21) 3846364; fax (21) 3448404; Bureau Chief JONATHAN THATCHER.

United Press International (UPI) (USA): Wisma Antara, 14th Floor, Jalan Medan Merdeka Selatan 17, Jakarta; tel. (21) 341056; Bureau Chief JOHN HAIL.

Xinhua (New China) News Agency (People's Republic of China): Jakarta.

PRESS ASSOCIATIONS

Alliance of Independent Journalists (AJI): Jakarta; f. 1994; unofficial; aims to promote freedom of the press; Sec.-Gen. AHMAD TAUFIK.

Persatuan Wartawan Indonesia (Indonesian Journalists' Asscn): Gedung Dewan Pers, 4th Floor, Jalan Kebon Sirih 34, Jakarta 10110; tel. (21) 353131; fax (21) 353175; f. 1946; government-controlled; 5,041 mems (April 1991); Chair. TARMAN AGAM; Gen. Sec. H. SOFJAN LUBIS.

Serikat Penerbit Suratkabar (SPS) (Indonesian Newspaper Publishers' Asscn): Gedung Dewan Pers, 6th Floor, Jalan Kebon Sirih 34, Jakarta 10110; tel. (21) 3459671; fax (21) 3862373; e-mail sps-pst@dnet.net.id; internet www.dnet.net.id/sps; f. 1946; Exec. Chair. Drs S. L. BATUBARA; Sec.-Gen. Drs AMIR E. SIREGAR.

Yayasan Pembina Pers Indonesia (Press Foundation of Indonesia): Jalan Jatinegara Barat III/6, Jakarta 13310; tel. (21) 8194994; f. 1967; Chair. SUGIARSO SUROYO, MOCHTAR LUBIS.

Publishers

Jakarta

Aries Lima/New Aqua Press PT: Jalan Rawagelan II/4, Jakarta Timur; tel. (21) 4897566; general and children's; Pres. TUTI SUNDARI AZMI.

Aya Media Pustaka PT: Wijaya Grand Centre C/2, Jalan Dharmawangsa III, Jakarta 12160; tel. (21) 7206903; fax (21) 7201401; children's; Dir Drs ARIANTO TUGIYO.

PT Balai Pustaka: Jalan Gunung Sahari Raya 4, POB 1029, Jakarta 10710; tel. and fax (21) 3855733; e-mail bp1917@hotmail.com; f. 1917; children's, school textbooks, literary, scientific publs and periodicals; Dir R. SISWADI.

Bhratara Niaga Media PT: Jalan Oto Iskandardinata III/29F, Jakarta 13340; tel. (21) 8502050; fax (21) 8191858; f. 1986; fmrly Bhratara Karya Aksara; university and educational textbooks; Man. Dir AHMAD JAYUSMAN.

Bina Rena Pariwara PT: Jalan Pejaten Raya 5-E, Pasar Minggu, Jakarta 12510; tel. (21) 7261179; fax (21) 7901938; fax (21) 7901939; f. 1988; financial, social science, economic, Islamic, children's; Dir Dra YULIA HIMAWATI.

Bulan Bintang PT: Jalan Kramat Kwitang 1/8, Jakarta 10420; tel. (21) 3901651; fax (21) 3107027; f. 1954; Islamic, social science, natural and applied sciences, art; Pres. AMRAN ZAMZAMI; Man. Dir FAUZI AMELZ.

Bumi Aksara PT: Jalan Sawo Raya 18, Rawamanguu, Jakarta 13220; tel. (21) 4717049; fax (21) 4700989; f. 1990; university textbooks; Dir H. AMIR HAMZAH.

Cakrawala Cinta PT: Jalan Minyak I/12B, Duren Tiga, Jakarta 12760; tel. (21) 7990725; fax (21) 7974076; f. 1984; science; Dir Drs M. TORSINA.

Centre for Strategic and International Studies (CSIS): Jalan Tanah Abang III/23–27, Jakarta 10160; tel. (21) 3865532; fax (21) 3847517; e-mail csis@pacific.net.id; f. 1971; political and social sciences; Dir Dr DAOED JOESOEF.

Cipta Adi Pustaka: Graha Compaka Mas Blok C 22, Jalan Cempaka Putih Raya, Jakarta Pusat; tel. (21) 4213821; fax (21) 4269315; f. 1986; encyclopedias; Dir BUDI SANTOSO.

Dian Rakyat PT: Jalan Rawagelas I/4, Kaw. Industri Pulo Gadung, Jakarta; tel. (21) 4604444; fax (21) 4609115; f. 1966; general; Dir H. MOHAMMED AIS.

Djambatan PT: Jalan Wijaya I/39, Jakarta 12170; tel. (21) 7203199; fax (21) 7227989; f. 1954; children's, textbooks, social sciences, fiction; Dir SJARIFUDIN SJAMSUDIN.

Dunia Pustaka Jaya: Jalan Rawa Bambu Rt. 003/07 38, Komp. BATAN, Pasar Minggu, Jakarta Selatan 12520; tel. (21) 7891875; fax (21) 3909320; f. 1971; fiction, religion, essays, poetry, drama, criticism, art, philosophy and children's; Man. A. RIVAI.

EGC Medical Publications: Jalan Agung Jaya III/2, Sunter Agung Podomoro, Jakarta 14350; tel. (21) 686351; fax (21) 686352; f. 1978; medical and public health, nursing, dentistry; Dir IMELDA DHARMA.

Elex Media Komputindo: Jalan Palmerah Selatan 22, Kompas–Gramedia Bldg 6th Floor, Jakarta 10270; tel. (21) 5483008; fax (21) 5326219; e-mail sekr_bukuanakln@elexmedia.co.id; f. 1985; computing and technology; Dir TEDDY SURIANTO.

Erlangga PT: Jalan H. Baping 100, Ciracas, Jakarta 13740; tel. (21) 8717006; fax (21) 8717011; e-mail mahameru@rad.net.id; f. 1952; secondary school and university textbooks; Man. Dir GUNAWAN HUTAURUK.

Gaya Favorit Press: Jalan H. R. Rasuna Said, Blok B, Kav. 32–33, Jakarta 12910; tel. (21) 5209370; fax (21) 5209366; f. 1971; fiction, popular science and children's; Vice-Pres. MIRTA KARTOHADIPRODJO; Man. Dir WIDARTI GUNAWAN.

Gema Insani Press: Jalan Kalibata Utara II/84, Jakarta 12740; tel. (21) 7984391; fax (21) 7984388; e-mail gipnet@indosat.net.id; internet www.gemainsani.co.id; f. 1986; Islamic; Dir UMAR BASYAR-AHIL.

Ghalia Indonesia: Jalan Pramuka Raya 4, Jakarta 13140; tel. (21) 8584330; fax (21) 8502334; f. 1972; children's and general science, textbooks; Man. Dir LUKMAN SAAD.

Gramedia Widyasarana Indonesia: Jalan Palmerah Selatan 22, Lantai IV, POB 615, Jakarta 10270; tel. (21) 5483008; fax (21) 5300545; f. 1973; university textbooks, general non-fiction, children's and magazines; Gen. Man. ALFONS TARYADI.

Gunung Mulia PT: Jalan Kwitang 22–23, Jakarta 10420; tel. (21) 3901208; fax (21) 3901633; e-mail bpkgm@centrin.net.id; f. 1951; general, children's, Christian; Dirs BUDI ARLIANTO, Rev. Dr SOE-TARMAN.

Hidakarya Agung PT: Jalan Kebon Kosong F/74, Kemayoran, Jakarta Pusat; tel. (21) 4241074; Dir MAHDIARTI MACHMUD.

Ichtiar: Jalan Majapahit 6, Jakarta Pusat; tel. (21) 3841226; f. 1957; textbooks, law, social sciences, economics; Dir JOHN SEMERU.

Indira PT: Jalan Borobudur 20, Jakarta 10320; tel. (21) 882754; f. 1953; general science and children's; Man. Dir BAMBANG P. WAH-YUDI.

Kinta CV: Jalan Kemanggisan Ilir V/110, Pal Merah, Jakarta Barat; tel. (21) 5494751; f. 1950; textbooks, social science, general; Man. Drs MOHAMAD SALEH.

LP 3 ES: Jalan Letjen. S. Parman 81, Jakarta 11420; tel. (21) 5674211; fax (21) 5683785; e-mail lp3es@indo.net.id; f. 1971; general; Dir IMAM AHMAD.

Masagung Group: Gedung Idayu, Jalan Kwitang 13, POB 2260, Jakarta 10420; tel. (21) 3154890; fax (21) 3154889; f. 1986; general, religious, textbooks, science; Pres. H. ABDURRAHMAN MASAGUNG.

Midas Surya Grafindo PT: Jalan Kesehatan 54, Cijantung, Jakarta 13760; tel. (21) 8400414; fax (21) 8400270; f. 1984; children's; Dir Drs FRANS HENDRAWAN.

Mutiara Sumber Widya PT: Jalan Kramat II 55, Jakarta; tel. (21) 3926043; fax (21) 3160313; f. 1951; textbooks, Islamic, social sciences, general and children's; Pres. FADJRAA OEMAR.

Penebar Swadya PT: Jalan Gunung Sahari III/7, Jakarta Pusat; tel. (21) 4204402; fax (21) 4214821; agriculture, animal husbandry, fisheries; Dir Drs ANTHONIUS RIYANTO.

Penerbit Universitas Indonesia: Jalan Salemba Raya 4, Jakarta; tel. (21) 335373; f. 1969; science; Man. S. E. LEGOWO.

Pradnya Paramita PT: Jalan Bunga 8–8A, Matraman, Jakarta 13140; tel. (21) 8504944; e-mail pradnya@centrin.net.id; f. 1973; children's, general, educational, technical and social science; Pres. Dir WILLY LALUYAN.

Pustaka Antara PT: Jalan Taman Kebon Sirih III/13, Jakarta Pusat 10250; tel. (21) 3156994; fax (21) 322745; e-mail nacelod@indonet.id; f. 1952; textbooks, political, Islamic, children's and general; Man. Dir AIDA JOESOEF AHMAD.

Pustaka Binaman Pressindo: Bina Manajemen Bldg, Jalan Menteng Raya 9–15, Jakarta 10340; tel. (21) 2300313; fax (21) 2302047; e-mail pustaka@bit.net.id; f. 1981; management; Dir Ir MAKFUDIN WIRYA ATMAJA.

Pustaka Sinar Harapan PT: Jalan Dewi Sartika 136D, Jakarta 13630; tel. (21) 8093208; fax (21) 8091652; f. 1981; general science, fiction, comics, children's; Dir ARISTIDES KATOPPO.

Pustaka Utma Grafiti PT: Jalan Utan Kayu 68EFG, Utan Kayu Utara, Jakarta 13120; tel. (21) 8567502; fax (21) 8573387; f. 1981; social sciences, humanities and children's books; Dir ZULKIFLY LUBIS.

Rajagrafindo Persada PT: Jalan Pelepah Hijau IV TN-1 14–15, Kelapa Gading Permai, Jakarta 14240; tel. (21) 4529409; fax (21) 4520951; f. 1980; general science and religion; Dir Drs ZUBAIDI.

Rineka Cipta PT: Blok B/5, Jalan Jenderal Sudirman, Kav. 36A, Bendungan Hilir, Jakarta 10210; tel. (21) 5737646; fax (21) 5711985; f. 1990 by merger of Aksara Baru (f. 1972) and Bina Aksara; general science and university texts; Dir Drs SUARDI.

Rosda Jayaputra PT: Jalan Kembang 4, Jakarta 10420; tel. (21) 3904984; fax (21) 3901703; f. 1981; general science; Dir H. ROZALI USMAN.

Sastra Hudaya: Jalan Kalasan 1, Jakarta Pusat; tel. (21) 882321; f. 1967; religious, textbooks, children's and general; Man. ADAM SALEH.

Tintamas Indonesia: Jalan Kramat Raya 60, Jakarta 10420; tel. and fax (21) 3911459; f. 1947; history, modern science and culture, especially Islamic; Man. Miss MARHAMAH DJAMBEK.

Tira Pustaka: Jalan Cemara Raya 1, Kav. 10D, Jaka Permai, Jaka Sampurna, Bekasi 17145; tel. (21) 8841277; fax (21) 8842736; f. 1977; translations, children's; Dir ROBERT B. WIDJAJA.

Widjaya: Jalan Pecenongan 48C, Jakarta Pusat; tel. (21) 3813446; f. 1950; textbooks, children's, religious and general; Man. DIDI LUTHAN.

Yasaguna: Jalan Minangkabau 44, POB 422, Jakarta Selatan; tel. (21) 8290422; f. 1964; agricultural, children's, handicrafts; Dir HILMAN MADEWA.

Bandung

Alma'arif: Jalan Tamblong 48–50, Bandung; tel. (22) 4207177; f. 1949; textbooks, religious and general; Man. H. M. BAHARTHAH.

Alumni PT: Jalan Bukit Pakar Timur II/109, Bandung 40197; tel. (22) 2501251; fax (22) 2503044; f. 1968; university and school textbooks; Dir EDDY DAMIAN.

Angkasa: Jalan Merdeka 6, POB 1353 BD, Bandung 40111; tel. (22) 4204795; fax (22) 439183; Dir H. FACHRI SAID.

Armico: Jalan Madurasa Utara 10, Cigereleng, Bandung 40253; tel. (22) 5202234; fax (22) 5201972; f. 1980; school textbooks; Dir Ir ARSIL TANJUNG.

Citra Aditya Bakti PT: Jalan Geusanulun 17, Bandung 40115; tel. (22) 438251; fax (22) 438635; f. 1985; general science; Dir Ir IWAN TANUATMADJA.

Diponegoro Publishing House: Jalan Mohammad Toha 44–46, Bandung 40252; tel. and fax (22) 5201215; e-mail dpnegoro@indosat.net.id; f. 1963; Islamic, textbooks, fiction, non-fiction, general; Man. H. A. DAHLAN.

Epsilon Group: Jalan Marga Asri 3, Margacinta, Bandung 40287; tel. (22) 7567826; f. 1985; school textbooks; Dir Drs BAHRUDIN.

Eresco PT: Jalan Megger Girang 98, Bandung 40254; tel. (22) 5205985; fax (22) 5205984; f. 1957; scientific and general; Man. Drs ARFAN ROZALI.

Ganeca Exact Bandung: Jalan Kiaracondong 167, Pagauban, Bandung 40283; tel. (22) 701519; fax (22) 775329; f. 1982; school textbooks; Dir Ir KETUT SUARDHARA LINGGIH.

Mizan Pustaka PT: Jalan Yodkali 16, Bandung 40124; tel. (22) 700931; e-mail info@mizan.com; internet www.mizan.com; f. 1983; Islamic and general books; Pres. Dir HAIDAR BAGIR; Man. Dir PUTUT WIDJANARKO.

Penerbit ITB: Jalan Ganesa 10, Bandung 40132; tel. and fax (22) 2504257; e-mail itbpress@bdg.centrin.net.id; f. 1971; academic books; Dir EMMY SUPARKA; Chief Editor SOFIA MANSOOR-NIKSOLIHIN.

Putra A. Bardin: Jalan Ganesya 4, Bandung; tel. (22) 2504319; f. 1998; textbooks, scientific and general; Dir NAI A. BARDIN.

Remaja Rosdakarya PT: Jalan Ciateul 34–36, POB 284, Bandung 40252; tel. (22) 5200287; fax (22) 5202529; textbooks and children's fiction; Pres. ROZALI USMAN.

Sarana Panca Karyam PT: Jalan Kopo 633 KM 13/4, Bandung 40014; f. 1986; general; Dir WIMPY S. IBRAHIM.

Tarsito PT: Jalan Guntur 20, Bandung 40262; tel. (22) 304915; fax (22) 314630; academic; Dir T. SITORUS.

Flores

Nusa Indah: Jalan El Tari, Ende 86318, Flores; tel. (381) 21502; fax (381) 22373; f. 1970; religious and general; Dir HENRI DAROS.

Kudus

Menara Kudus: Jalan Menara 4, Kudus 59315; tel. (291) 371143; fax (291) 36474; f. 1958; Islamic; Man. CHILMAN NAJIB.

Medan

Hasmar: Jalan Letjenderal Haryono M.T. 1, POB 446, Medan 20231; tel. (61) 24181; f. 1962; primary school textbooks; Dir HAS-BULLAH LUBIS; Man. AMRAN SAID RANGKUTI.

Impola: Jalan H.M. Joni 46, Medan 20217; tel. (61) 711415; f. 1984; school textbooks; Dir. PAMILANG M. SITUMORANG.

Islamiyah: Jalan Sutomo 328–329, Kotakpos 11, Medan; tel. (61) 25426; f. 1954.

Madju: Jalan Amaliun 37, Medan 20215; tel. (61) 711990; fax (61) 717753; f. 1950; textbooks, children's and general; Pres. H. MOHAMED ARBIE; Man. Dir Drs ALFIAN ARBIE.

Masco: Jalan Sisingamangaraja 191, Medan 20218; tel. (61) 713375; f. 1992; school textbooks; Dir P. M. SITUMORANG.

Monora: Jalan Letjenderal Jamin Ginting 583, Medan 20156; tel. (61) 812667; fax (61) 812669; f. 1968; school textbooks; Dir CHAIRIL ANWAR.

Semarang

Aneka Ilmu: Jalan Raya Semarang Demak Km. 8.5, Sayung, Demak; tel. (24) 580335; fax (24) 582903; f. 1983; general and school textbooks; Dir H. SUWANTO.

Efhar COY PT: Jalan Dorang 7, Semarang; tel. (24) 511172; fax (24) 551540; f. 1976; gen. textbooks; Dir H. DARADJAT HARAHAP.

Intan Pariwara: Jalan Beringin, Klaten Utara, Kotak Pos III, Kotif Klaten, Jawa-Tengah; tel. (272) 22441; fax (272) 22021; school textbooks; Pres. SOETIKNO.

Mandira PT: Jalan Letjenderal M.T. Haryono 501, Semarang 50241; tel. (24) 316150; fax (24) 415092; f. 1962; Dir Ir A. HARIYANTO.

Mandira Jaya Abadi PT: Jalan Letjenderal M.T. Haryono 501, Semarang 50241; tel. (24) 519547; fax (24) 542189; f. 1981; Dir Ir A. HARIYANTO.

Solo

Pabelan PT: Jalan Raya Pajang, Kertasura KM 8, Solo 57162; tel. (271) 743975; fax (271) 714775; f. 1983; school textbooks; Dir AGUNG SASONGKO.

Tiga Serangkai PT: Jalan Dr Supomo 23, Solo; tel. (271) 714344; fax (271) 713607; f. 1977; school textbooks; Dir ABDULLAH.

Surabaya

Airlangga University Press: Kampus C, Jalan Mulyorejo, Surabaya; tel. (31) 5992246; fax (31) 5992248; academic; Dir Drs SOEDHARTO.

Bina Ilmu PT: Jalan Tunjungan 53E, Surabaya 60275; tel. (31) 5323214; fax (31) 5315421; f. 1973; school textbooks, Islamic; Pres. ARIEFIN NOOR.

Bintang: Jalan Potroagung III/41C, Surabaya; tel. (31) 3770687; fax (31) 3715941; school textbooks; Dir AGUS WINARNO.

Grip PT: Jalan Rungkut Permai II/C–11, Surabaya; tel. (31) 22564; f. 1958; textbooks and general; Man. Mrs SURIPTO.

Jaya Baya: Jalan Embong Malang 69H, POB 250, Surabaya 60001; tel. (31) 41169; f. 1945; religion, philosophy and ethics; Man. TADJIB ERMADI.

Marfiah: Jalan Kalibutuh 131, Surabaya; tel. (31) 46023; reference and primary school textbooks; Man. S. WAHYUDI.

Sinar Wijaya: Jalan Raya Sawo VII/58, Bringin-Lakarsantri, Surabaya; tel. (31) 706615; general; Dir DULRADJAK.

Yogyakarta

Andi Publishers: Jalan Beo 38–40, Yogyakarta 55281; tel. (274) 561881; fax (274) 588282; e-mail andi_pub@indo.net.id; f. 1980; Christian, computing, business, management and technical; Dir J. H. GONDOWIJOYO.

BPFE PT: Jalan Gambiran 37, Yogyakarta 55161; tel. (274) 373760; fax (274) 380819; f. 1984; university textbooks; Dir Drs INDRIYO GITOSUDARMO.

Centhini Yayasan: Gg. Bekisar UH V/716 E–1, Yogyakarta 55161; tel. (274) 383148; f. 1984; Javanese Culture; Chair. H. KARKONO KAMAJAYA.

Gadjah Mada University Press: Jalan Grafika 1, Campus UGM, Bulaksumur, Yogyakarta 55231; tel. (274) 902727; fax (274) 561037; f. 1971; university textbooks; Dir Drs H. SUKAMTO.

Indonesia UP: Gg. Bekisar UH V/716 E–1, Yogyakarta 55161; tel. (274) 383148; f. 1950; general science; Dir H. KARKONO KAMAJAYA.

Kanisius Publr: Jalan Cempaka 9, Deresan, POB 1125, Yogyakarta 55281; tel. (274) 588783; fax (274) 563349; e-mail office@kanisius.co.id; internet www.kanisius.co.id; f. 1922; children's, textbooks, Christian and general; Man. E. SURONO.

Kedaulatan Rakyat PT: Jalan P. Mangkubumi 40–42, Yogyakarta; tel. (274) 2163; Dir DRONO HARDJUSUWONGSO.

Penerbit Tiara Wacana Yogya: Jalan Kaliurang KM 7, 8 Kopen 16, Banteng, Yogyakarta 55581; tel. and fax (274) 880683; f. 1986; university textbooks and general science; Dir SITORESMI PRABUNINGRAT.

Government Publishing House

Balai Pustaka PT (Persero) (State Publishing and Printing House): Jalan Gunung Sahari Raya 4, Jakarta Pusat; tel. (21) 3451616; fax (21) 3841714; history, anthropology, politics, philosophy, medical, arts and literature; Pres. Dir Dr ZAKARA IDRIS.

PUBLISHERS' ASSOCIATION

Ikatan Penerbit Indonesia (IKAPI) (Asscn of Indonesian Book Publishers): Jalan Kalipasir 32, Jakarta 10330; tel. (21) 3141907; fax (21) 3146050; e-mail sekretariat@ikapi.or.id; internet www.ikapi.or.id; f. 1950; 631 mems (Jan. 2000); Pres. ARSELAN HARAHAP; Sec.-Gen. SAHAR L. HASSAN.

Broadcasting and Communications

TELECOMMUNICATIONS

Directorate-General of Posts and Telecommunications

(Postel): Gedung Depparpostel, Jalan Medan Merdeka Barat 17, Jakarta 10110; tel. (21) 3838501; fax (21) 3860754; Dir Gen. SASMITO DIRDJO; Dep. Dir. Gen. R. SAKSONO SOEDARSO.

PT Indosat (Persero) Tbk: Jalan Medan Merdeka Barat 21, POB 2905, Jakarta 10110; tel. (21) 3802614; fax (21) 3458155; e-mail sant@indosat.com; internet www.indosat.com; telecommunications; partially privatized in 1994; Pres. HARI KARTANA.

PT Satelit Palapa Indonesia (SATELINDO): Jalan Daan Mogot Km 11, Jakarta 11710; POB 1220, Jakarta 11012; tel. (21) 5451745; fax (21) 5451748; Gen. Man. IWAN KRISNADI.

PT Telekomunikasi Indonesia Tbk (TELKOM): Corporate Office, Jalan Japati No. 1, Bandung 40133; tel. (22) 4521510; fax (22) 440313; internet www.telkom.co.id; domestic telecommunications; 24.2% of share capital was transferred to the private sector in 1995; CEO ASMAN AKHIR NASUTION.

BROADCASTING

Regulatory Authority

Directorate-General of Radio, Television and Film: Jalan Merdeka Barat 9, Jakarta 10110; Dep. Dir M. ARSYAD SUBIK.

Radio

Radio Republik Indonesia (RRI): Jalan Medan Merdeka Barat 4–5, Jakarta 10160; tel. (21) 3849091; fax (21) 367132; f. 1945; 49 stations; Dir ARSYAD SUBIK; Dep. Dirs FACHRUDDIN SOEKARNO (Overseas Service), ABDUL ROCHIM (Programming), SUKRI (Programme Development), SAZLI RAIS (Administration), CHAERUL ZEN (News).

Voice of Indonesia: Medan Merdeka Barat 4–5, POB 1157, Jakarta; tel. (21) 3456811; foreign service; daily broadcasts in Arabic, English, French, German, Bahasa Indonesia, Japanese, Bahasa Malaysia, Mandarin, Spanish and Thai.

Television

In March 1989 Indonesia's first private commercial television station began broadcasting to the Jakarta area. In 1996 there were five privately-owned television stations in operation.

PT Cakrawala Andalas Televisi (ANTEVE): Sentra Mulia, 18th Floor, Jalan H. R. Rasuna Said, Kav. X-6 No. 8, Jakarta 12940; tel. (21) 5222086; fax (21) 5222087; e-mail ancorcom@uninet.net.id; f. 1993; private channel; broadcasting to ten cities; Pres. Dir H.R. AGUNG LAKSONO; Gen. Man. CEO NENNY SOEMAWINATA.

PT Rajawali Citra Televisi Indonesia (RCTI): Jalan Raya Pejuangan 3, Kebon Jeruk, Jakarta 11000; tel. (21) 5303540; fax (21) 5493852; f. 1989; first private channel; 20-year licence; Pres. Dir M. S. RALIE SIREGAR; Vice-Pres. ALEX KUMARA.

PT Surya Citra Televisi (SCTV): Wisma Indovision, 19th Floor, Jalan Panjang Blok Z/111, Green Garden, Jakarta 11520; tel. (21) 5825858; fax (21) 5828555; e-mail pr@sctv.co.id; internet www.sctv.co.id; f. 1990; private channel broadcasting nationally; Pres. Dir Dr Ir AGUS MULYANTO.

PT Televisi Pendidikan Indonesia (TPI): Jalan Pintu II—Taman Mini Indonesia Indah, Pondok Gede, Jakarta Timur 13810; tel. (21) 8412473; fax (21) 8412470; f. 1991; private channel funded by commercial advertising; Pres. Dir SITI HARDIJANTI RUKMANA.

Televisi Republik Indonesia (TVRI): TVRI Senayan, Jalan Gerbang Pemuda, Senayan, Jakarta; tel. (21) 5733135; fax (21) 5732408; f. 1962; state-controlled; Man. Dir AZIS HUSEIN.

Finance

(cap. = capital; auth. = authorized; p.u. = paid up;
res = reserves; dep. = deposits; m. = million; brs = branches;
amounts in rupiah)

BANKING

In December 1996 there were 9,276 banks, with 14,956 branches, in operation in Indonesia, including seven state commercial banks, 27 regional government banks, 164 private national banks and 41 foreign and joint-venture banks. At the end of March 1995 total bank deposits stood at 167,123,000m. rupiahs. A programme of extensive reform of the banking sector was in the process of being implemented in 1999, under the auspices of the Indonesian Bank Restructuring Agency (IBRA, see p. 2007). In March the Government announced plans to close 38 private domestic banks, to nationalize seven and to recapitalize a further nine. In addition, four of the state-owned banks had been merged into a single new institution, Bank Mandiri, in the previous year.

Central Bank

Bank Indonesia: Jalan M. H. Thamrin 2, Jakarta 10110; tel. (21) 3817187; fax (21) 3501867; e-mail humasbi@bi.go.id; internet www.bi.go.id; f. 1828; nationalized as central bank in 1953; cap.

7,628,000m., dep. 87,445,000m. (March 1999); Gov. Dr SYAHRIL SABIRIN; Dep. Gov. MIRANDA S. GOELTOM; 42 brs.

State Banks

In late December 1997 the Government announced that four of the state-owned banks—Bank Bumi Daya, Bank Dagang Negara, Bank Ekspor Impor Indonesia and Bank Pembangunan Indonesia—were to merge; the four banks subsequently merged into a single new institution, PT Bank Mandiri, which was established in July 1999.

PT Bank Mandiri (Persero): Plaza Mandiri, Jalan Jenderal Gatot Subroto, Kav. 36-38, Jakarta 12190; tel. (21) 5265045; fax (21) 5263640; internet www.bankmandiri.co.id; f. 1999 as a result of the merger of four state-owned banks—PT Bank Bumi Daya, PT Bank Dagang Negara, PT Bank Ekspor Impor Indonesia and PT Bank Pembangunan Indonesia; Pres. Commissioner BINHADI; Pres. Dir E. C. W. NELOE.

PT Bank Negara Indonesia (Persero) Tbk: Jalan Jenderal Sudirman, Kav. 1, POB 2955, Jakarta 10001; tel. (21) 2511946; fax (21) 2511113; e-mail hin@bni.co.id; internet www.bni.co.id; f. 1946; commercial bank; specializes in credits to the industrial sector; cap. 2,187,162m., dep. 75,028,735m. (Dec. 1999); Pres. Dir WIDIODO SUKARMAN; 585 local brs, 6 overseas brs.

PT Bank Rakyat Indonesia (Persero): Jalan Jenderal Sudirman, Kav. 44–46, POB 94, Jakarta 10210; tel. (21) 2510244; fax (21) 2510303; f. 1895, present name since 1946; commercial and foreign exchange bank; specializing in agricultural smallholdings and rural development; scheduled for transfer to the public sector; cap. 1,000,000m., res 748,853m., dep. 29,907,957m. (Dec. 1997); Pres. and Dir DJOKOSANTOSO MOELJONO; 324 brs.

PT Bank Tabungan Negara (Persero): Gedung Menara BTN, Jalan Gajah Mada 1, Jakarta 10130; tel. (21) 6336789; fax (21) 6336801; e-mail dtrs-sti@btn.co.id; internet www.btn.co.id; f. 1964; commercial bank; scheduled to become a subsidiary of Bank Negara Indonesia; cap. 1,250,000m., dep. 8,081,998m. (Dec. 1997); Pres. Dir TITO SOETALAKSANA; 48 brs.

Commercial Banks

PT ANZ Panin Bank: Panin Bank Centre, Jalan Jenderal Sudirman (Senayan), Jakarta 10270; tel. (21) 5750300; fax (21) 5727447; internet www.anz.com/indonesia/; f. 1990 as Westpac Panin Bank; 85%-owned by the Australia and New Zealand Banking Group Ltd; cap. 50,000m., dep. 972,000m. (Dec. 2000); Pres. Dir SCOTT ARMSTRONG.

PT Bank Arta Pratama: Jalan Pangeran Jayakarta 115, Jakarta 10730; POB 1551, Jakarta; tel. (21) 6262658; fax (21) 6262625; f. 1967 as Bank Arta Pusara; total assets 2,073,000m. (June 1998); Pres. Dir SUDIANTORO; Chair. SUGIANTO KUSUMA; 35 brs.

Bank Artha Graha: Bank Artha Graha Tower, Jalan Jenderal Sudirman, Kav. 52–53, Jakarta 12920; tel. (21) 5152168; fax (21) 5152162; e-mail agraha@rad.net.id; f. 1967; cap. 75,000m., dep. 340,344m. (Dec. 1993); Pres. Dir ANTON B. S. HUDYANA; Chair. T. B. SILALAHI; 21 brs.

PT Bank Bali: Bank Bali Tower, 18th Floor, Jalan Jenderal Sudirman, Kav. 27, Jakarta 12920; tel. (21) 5237899; fax (21) 2500811; internet www.bankbali.co.id; f. 1954; cap. 340,520m., res 274,686m., dep. 10,239,355m. (Dec. 1998); Pres. Commissioner Prof. Dr J. B. MARLIN; 118 brs.

PT Bank Central Asia: Wisma BCA, 5th Floor, Jalan Jenderal Sudirman, Kav. 22–23, Jakarta 12920; tel. (21) 5711250; fax (21) 5701865; f. 1957; placed under the supervision of the Indonesian Bank Restructuring Agency in May 1998; cap. 1,471,993m., res 30,585,306m., dep. 86,802,979m. (Dec. 1999); Chair. SUDONO SALIM; 442 brs.

PT Bank Central Dagang: Menara BCD, Ground & 1st Floor, Jalan Jenderal Sudirman, Kav. 26, Jakarta 12920; tel. (21) 2506288; fax (21) 2506280; f. 1969; cap. 20,000m., res 533m., dep. 685,874m. (Dec. 1996); Chair. SAM HANDOYO; Pres. Dir HINDARTO HOVERT TANTULAR; 11 brs.

Bank Crédit Lyonnais Indonesia: Menara Mulia, Suite 2501, Jalan Jenderal Gatot Subroto, Kav. 9–11, Jakarta 12930; tel. (21) 2520234; fax (21) 2520123; f. 1989; cap. 50,000m., dep. 689,442m. (Dec. 1997); Pres. Dir P. A. MUYL; 2 brs.

PT Bank Danamon Indonesia Tbk: Wisma Bank Danamon, Jalan Jenderal Sudirman, Kav. 45, Jakarta 12930; tel. (21) 5770551; fax (21) 5770704; f. 1956; placed under the supervision of the Indonesian Bank Restructuring Agency in April 1998; cap. 1,120,189m., res 300,028m., dep. 17,587,267m. (Dec. 1996); Chair. PETER B. STOCK; Pres. UNTUNG PURWITO; 737 brs.

PT Bank Dharmala: Wisma Bank Dharmala, Jalan Jenderal Sudirman, Kav. 28, Jakarta 12920; tel. (21) 5212211; fax (21) 5212251; f. 1989 as PT Bank Dharmala Nugraha; cap. 180,000m., dep. 1,093,501m. (Dec. 1996); Pres. SUHANDA WIRAATMADJA; Chair. SUYANTO GONDOKUSUMO; 22 brs.

PT Bank Duta: Jalan Kebon Sirih 12, POB 265 KBY, Jakarta 10110; tel. (21) 3800900; fax (21) 3801005; internet www.bankduta .co.id; f. 1966; placed under the control of Bank Indonesia in September 1990, owing to 'improper foreign exchange dealings'; cap. 140,597m., res 4,832m., dep. 2,209,879m. (Dec. 1990); Chair. SONNI DWI HARSONO; Pres. MUCHTAR MANDALA; 40 brs.

PT Bank Fuji International Indonesia: Plaza B11, 24th Floor, Tower 2, Jalan M. H. Thamrin 51, Jakarta 10350; tel. (21) 3925222; fax (21) 3926354; f. 1989; cap. 144,375m., res 25,908m., dep. 1,431,883m. (Dec. 1998); Pres. Dir TAKAO ENDO.

Bank Internasional Indonesia (BII): Plaza BII, Jalan M. H. Thamrin, Kav. 22, Jakarta 10350; tel. (21) 2300888; fax (21) 2301494; e-mail bii-info@idola.net.id; internet www.bii.co.id; cap. 13,054,668m., res 1,307,238m., dep. 26,101,065m. (Dec. 1999); Chair. (vacant); Pres. Dir (vacant); 194 brs.

PT Bank LTCB Central Asia: Bank Central Asia Bldg, Jalan Jenderal Sudirman, Kav. 22–23, Jakarta 12920; tel. (21) 5712562; fax (21) 5710639; f. 1989; 75%-owned by Long-Term Credit Bank of Japan Ltd; cap. 50,000m., dep. 51,718m. (Dec. 1996); Pres. SHUICHI TAKENAKA; 442 brs.

PT Bank Mashill Utama: Plaza Mashill, 1st–6th Floor, Jalan Jenderal Sudirman, Kav. 25, Jakarta 12920; tel. (21) 5221995; fax (21) 5221985; f. 1988; cap. 188,260m., res 10,000m., dep. 901,534m. (Dec. 1997); Chair. KARTA WIDJAJA; Pres. Dir A. T. WINDOE; 31 brs.

PT Bank Mayapada Internasional: Arthaloka Bldg, Ground & 1st Floor, Jalan Jenderal Sudirman, Kav. 2, Jakarta 10220; tel. (21) 2511588; fax (21) 2511539; e-mail mayapada@cbn.net.id; f. 1989; cap. 182,000m., dep. 765,524m. (Dec. 1999); Chair. J. K. WONSONO; Pres. Dir HARYONO TJAHJARIJADI; 5 brs, 7 sub-brs.

PT Bank Muamalat Indonesia (BMI): Arthaloka Bldg, Jalan Jenderal Sudirman 2, Jakarta 10220; tel. (21) 2511414; fax (21) 2511453; Indonesia's first Islamic bank; cap. 165,593m. (July 2000); Pres. Dir A. RIAWAN AMIN; Chair. ABBAS ADHAR.

PT Bank Niaga: Graha Niaga, Jalan Jenderal Sudirman, Kav. 58, Jakarta 12190; tel. (21) 2505252; fax (21) 2505205; e-mail caniaga@attglobal.net; internet www.bankniaga.com/; f. 1955; cap. 359,270m., res 557,805m., dep. 12,614,890m. (Dec. 1999); Pres. and CEO RUDY CAPELLE; Chair. NASRUDIN SUMINTAPURA; 76 brs.

Bank NISP Tbk: Jalan Taman Cibeunying Selatan 31, Bandung 40114; tel. (22) 7234123; fax (22) 7100466; e-mail nisp@banknisp .com; internet www.banknisp.com; f. 1941; cap. 274,611m., dep. 2,740,549m. (Dec. 1999); Pres. Dir PRAMUKTI SURJAUDAJA; Chair. KARMAKA SURJANDAJA; 69 brs.

PT Bank Nusa National: Kodel House, Jalan H. R. Rasuna Said, Kav. B4, Jakarta 12920; tel. (21) 5221533; fax (21) 5221529; f. 1998 as a result of the merger of PT Bank Nusa International, PT Bank Nasional, PT Bank Nasional Komersil and PT Bank Angkasa.

PT Bank Sakura Swadharma: Wisma BNI, 19th Floor, Jalan Jenderal Sudirman, Kav. 1, POB 1658 JKP, Jakarta 10001; tel. (21) 5701401; fax (21) 5701398; f. 1989 as PT Bank Mitsui Swadharma; 85%-owned by Sakura Bank Ltd; cap. 50,000m., dep. 530,901m. (Dec. 1998); Pres. Dir YOSHIO UCHINO.

PT Bank Sanwa Indonesia: Bank Bali Tower, 4th–5th Floor, Jalan Jenderal Sudirman, Kav. 27, Jakarta 12920; tel. (21) 2500401; fax (21) 2500410; f. 1989 as PT Sanwa Indonesia Bank; cap. 150,000m., dep. 1,132,839 (Dec. 1998); Pres. Dir MAKOTO KANEKO; Chair. RYOSUKE TAMAKOSHI.

PT Bank Sumitomo Indonesia: New Summitmas Bldg, 10th Floor, Jalan Jenderal Sudirman, Kav. 61–62, Jakarta 12069; tel. (21) 5227011; fax (21) 5227022; f. 1989; cap. 56,075m., dep. 353,978m. (Dec. 1995); Pres. Dir RYOICHI HASEGAWA; 1 br.

PT Bank Surya Tbk: Bank Surya Bldg, Jalan M.H. Thamrin, Kav. 9, Jakarta Pusat; tel. (21) 2302933; fax (21) 3902470; f. 1969; cap. 111,000m., dep. 1,305,290m. (Dec. 1996); Chair. H. SUDWIKATMONO; Pres. Dir A. K. ARIAWAN; 13 local brs, 1 overseas br; operations suspended 1998.

PT Bank Tiara Asia: Wisma Bank Tiara, Jalan M.T. Haryono, Kav. 16, Jakarta 12810; tel. (21) 8310210; fax (21) 8310250; f. 1989; placed under the supervision of the Indonesian Bank Restructuring Agency in April 1998; cap. 185,000m., dep. 1,880,211m. (Dec. 1996); Chair. Haji RADEN PANDI MOHAMMED NOER; Pres. Dir IGNATIUS HERRY WIBOWO; 34 brs.

PT Bank Universal: Plaza Setiabudi, 2nd Floor, Jalan H. R. Rasuna Said, Kav. 62, Jakarta 12920; tel. (21) 5210550; fax (21) 5210588; e-mail bankuniversal@bu.astra.co.id; internet www .bankuniversal.astra.co.id; f. 1990; cap. 849,196m., res 4,734,630m., dep. 9,099,995m. (Dec. 1999); Pres. Dir STEPHEN Z. SATYAHADI; Chair. THEODORE PERMADI RACHMAT; 69 brs.

PT Lippo Bank: Asia Tower Bldg, 19th Floor, Jalan Diponegoro Bulever 101, Lippo Village, Karawaci-Tangerang 15810; tel. (21) 5460555; fax (21) 5460718; internet www.lippobank.co.id; f. 1948; cap. 1,593,354m., res 925,716m., dep. 18,549,197m. (Dec. 1998); Chair. MOCHTAR T. RIADY; Pres. Dir and CEO IAN CLYNE; 310 brs.

PT Pan Indonesia Tbk (Panin Bank): Panin Bank Centre, Jalan Jenderal Sudirman, Senayan, Jakarta 10270; tel. (21) 2700545; fax (21) 2700340; e-mail panin@panin.co.id; internet www.panin.co.id; f. 1971; cap. 2,873,244m., dep. 6,578,181m. (Dec. 1999); Chair. FUADY MOURAD; Pres. H. ROSTIAN SJAMSUDIN; 106 brs, 2 overseas brs.

PT Pesona Kriyadana: Jalan Pecenongan 84, POB 1471, Jakarta 10120; tel. (21) 3458103; fax (21) 3451617; f. 1974; fmrly Overseas Express Bank, Bank Utama; cap. 85,000m., res 16,039m., dep. 1,944,241m. (Dec. 1995); Chair. A. SUBOWO; Pres. Dir JANPIE SIAHAAN; 8 brs.

PT Prima Express Bank: Jalan Roa Malaka Selatan 67, Jakarta 11230; tel. (21) 2601433; fax (21) 6906540; e-mail primex@rad.net.id; f. 1956; cap. and res 34,998m., dep. 1,134,557m. (Dec. 1999); Pres. MICHAEL HUTABARAT; Dirs JACKING EDYANTO WIJAYA, HADI CHRISTIANTO WIJAYA, SERIAN WIJATNO; 16 brs, 7 sub-brs.

PT Tamara Bank: Jalan Asemka 31, POB 1435, Jakarta 11110; tel. (21) 2600180; fax (21) 2600090; internet www.indoexchange.com/tamara-bank/; f. 1957; cap. 142,830m., res 17,854m., dep. 1,725,131m. (Dec. 1997); Chair. SOEMITRO; Pres. Dir SETIJONO PUDJOWARSITO; 64 brs.

PT United City Bank Tbk (Unibank): Midplaza Bldg, 7th Floor, Jalan Jenderal Sudirman, Kav. 10–11, Jakarta 10220; tel. (21) 5735750; fax (21) 5735751; f. 1967 as Bank Permata Sari; cap. 114,750m., res 21,630m., dep. 965,623m. (Dec. 1997); Chair. SUKANTO TANOTO; Pres. Dir ODANG KARIANA; 9 brs.

Foreign Banks

ABN AMRO Bank NV (Netherlands): Jalan Ir H. Juanda 23–24, POB 2950, Jakarta 10029; tel. (21) 2312777; fax (21) 2313222; Man. C. J. DE KONING.

Bangkok Bank Public Company Ltd (Thailand): Jalan M. H. Thamrin 3, Jakarta 10110; POB 4165, Jakarta 11041; tel. (21) 3808065; fax (21) 3853881; f. 1968; Gen. Man. SAKSITH TEJASAKULSIN.

Bank of America NA (USA): Jakarta Stock Exchange Bldg Tower 1, 22nd Floor, Jalan Jenderal Sudirman, Kav. 52–53, Jakarta 12190; POB 4931 JKTM, Jakarta 12049; tel. (21) 5158100; fax (21) 5151407; e-mail rahul.goswamy@bankofamerica.com; f. 1968; Man. Dir and Country Man. RAHUL GOSWAMY.

Bank of Tokyo-Mitsubishi Ltd (Japan): Midplaza Bldg, 1st–3rd Floors, Jalan Jenderal Sudirman, Kav. 10–11, POB 2711, Jakarta 10220; tel. (21) 5706185; fax (21) 5731927; Gen. Man. HIDEYUKI ABE.

The Chase Manhattan Bank, NA (USA): Chase Plaza, 4th Floor, Jalan Jenderal Sudirman, Kav. 21, POB 311/JKT, Jakarta 12920; tel. (21) 5710088; fax (21) 5703690; Vice-Pres. and Sr Officer PETER NICE.

Citibank, NA (USA): Landmark Bldg, Jalan Jenderal Sudirman 1, Jakarta 12910; tel. (21) 5782007; fax (21) 5789303; f. 1912; Vice-Pres JAMES F. HUNT, EDWIN GERUNGAN, ROBERT THORNTON.

Deutsche Bank, AG (Germany): Deutsche Bank Bldg, Jalan Iman Bonjol 80, Jakarta 10310; POB 1135, Jakarta 10011; tel. (21) 331092; fax (21) 335252; Gen. Man. HEINZ POEHLSEN.

Hongkong and Shanghai Banking Corpn Ltd (Hong Kong): 1–4/F, World Trade Centre, Jalan Jenderal Sudirman, Kav. 29–31, Jakarta 12920; POB 2307, Jakarta 10023; tel. (21) 5211010; fax (21) 5211103; CEO P. C. L. HOLBERTON; 6 brs.

Standard Chartered Bank (United Kingdom): Wisma Standard Chartered Bank, Jalan Jenderal Sudirman, Kav. 33-A, Jakarta 10220; POB 57 JKWK, Jakarta 10350; tel. (21) 2513333; fax (21) 5721234; Chief Exec. DAVID HAWKINS; 4 brs.

Banking Association

The Association of Indonesian National Private Commercial Banks (Perhimpunan Bank-Bank Umum Nasional Swasta—PERBANAS): Jalan Karet Kuningan, Setiabudi, Jakarta 12940; tel. (21) 5223038; fax (21) 5223037; f. 1952; 94 mems; Chair. GUNARNI SOEWORO; Sec.-Gen. WIBOWO NGASERIN.

STOCK EXCHANGES

At the end of January 2000 278 companies were listed on the Jakarta Stock Exchange, and market capitalization was 410,520,769m. rupiah.

Bursa Paralel: PT Bursa Paralel Indonesia, Gedung Bursa, Jalan Medan Merdeka Selatan 14, Jakarta; tel. (21) 3810963; fax (21) 3810989; f. 1987.

Jakarta Stock Exchange (JSX): PT Bursa Efek Jakarta, Jakarta Stock Exchange Bldg, 4th Floor, Jalan Jenderal Sudirman, Kav. 52–53, Jakarta 12190; tel. (21) 5150515; fax (21) 5150330; PT Bursa Efek Jakarta, the managing firm of the JSX was transferred to the private sector in April 1992; 197 securities houses constitute the members and the shareholders of the exchange, each company owning one share; Dir HARRY WIGUNA.

Surabaya Stock Exchange: PT Bursa Efek Surabaya, 5th Floor, Gedung Medan Pemuda, Jalan Pemuda 27–31, Surabaya 60271; tel.

(31) 5340888; fax (31) 5342888; e-mail helpdesk@bes.co.id; f. 1989; Chair. NATAKOESOEMAH.

Regulatory Authority

Badan Pengawas Pasar Modal (BAPEPAM) (Capital Market Supervisory Agency): Jalan Medan Merdeka Selatan 14, Jakarta 10110; POB 1439; tel. (21) 365509; fax (21) 361460; Chair. BACELIUS RURU; Exec. Sec. M. IRSAN NASARUDIN.

INSURANCE

In August 1996 there were 163 insurance companies, comprising 98 non-life companies, 56 life companies, four reinsurance companies and five social insurance companies.

Insurance Supervisory Authority of Indonesia: Directorate of Financial Institutions, Ministry of Finance, Jalan Dr Wahidin, Jakarta 10710; tel. (21) 3451210; fax (21) 3849504; Dir SOPHAR L. TORUAN.

Selected Life Insurance Companies

PT Asuransi AIA Indonesia: Bank Panin Senayan, 7th and 8th Floors, Jalan Jenderal Sudirman, Senayan, Jakarta 10270; tel. (21) 5721388; fax (21) 5721389; f. 1975; Pres. Dir HARRY HARMAIN DIAH.

PT Asuransi Allianz Aken Life: Summitmas II, 20th Floor, Jalan Jenderal Sudirman, Kav. 61–62, Jakarta 12190; tel. (21) 2526690; fax (21) 2526580; e-mail azaken@ibm.net; internet www.allianz .com; Pres. Dir Dr PETER ENARES.

Asuransi Jiwa Bersama Bumiputera 1912: Wisma Bumiputera, Lt. 17–21, Jalan Jenderal Sudirman, Kav. 75, Jakarta 12910; tel. (21) 5703812; fax (21) 5712837; Pres. Drs H. SUGUARTO; Dir H. SURATNO HADISUWITO.

PT Asuransi Jiwa Buana Putra: Jalan Salemba Tengah 23, Jakarta Pusat; tel. (21) 3908835; fax (21) 3908810; f. 1974; Pres. SUBAGYO SUTJITRO; Dir H. M. FATHONI SUSILO.

PT Asuransi Jiwa Bumiputera John Hancock: Plaza Mashill, 7th Floor, Jalan Jenderal Sudirman, Kav. 25, Jakarta 12920; tel. (21) 5228857; fax (21) 5228819; e-mail iby@pacific.net.id; internet www.jhancock.co.id; life insurance and pension schemes; CEO DAVID W. COTTRELL.

PT Asuransi Jiwa Central Asia Raya: Komp. Duta Merlin, Blok A 6–7, Jalan Gajah Mada 3–5, Jakarta 10130; tel. (21) 6338512; fax (21) 6346972; Man. Dir DJONNY WIGUNA.

PT Asuransi Jiwasraya: Jalan H. Juanda 34, POB 240, Jakarta 10120; tel. (21) 3845031; fax (21) 3862344; f. 1959; Dir H. R. SUDRADJAT DJAJAKUSUMAH.

PT Asuransi Jiwa 'Panin Putra': Jalan Pintu Besar Selatan 52A, Jakarta 11110; tel. (21) 672586; fax (21) 676354; f. 1974; Pres. Dir SUJONO SOEPENO; Chair. NUGROHO TJOKROWIRONO.

PT Asuransi Jiwa Pura Nusantara: Wisma Bank Dharnala, Lt. 20–21, Jalan Jenderal Sudirman, Jakarta 12920; tel. (21) 5211990; fax (21) 5212001; Dir MURNIATY KARTONO.

PT Asuransi Lippo Life: Menara Matahari Lippo Life Bldg, Lt. 7, Jalan Bulevar Palem Raya 7, Lippo Karawaci, Tangerang 15811; tel. (21) 5475433; fax (21) 5475401; f. 1983; life insurance, pensions, healthcare.

PT Asuransi Panin Life: Panin Bank Plaza, 5th Floor, Jalan Palmerah Utara 52, Jakarta 11480; tel. (21) 5484870; fax (21) 5484570; Pres. NUGROHO TJOKROWIRONO; Dir SUJONO SUPENO.

Bumi Asih Jaya Life Insurance Co Ltd: Jalan Matraman Raya 165–167, Jakarta 13140; tel. (21) 8509850 fax (21) 8509669; f. 1967; Chair. D. S. SINAGA; Pres. K. M. SINAGA.

Bumiputera 1912 Mutual Life Insurance Co: Wisma Bumiputera, 18th–21st Floors, Jalan Jenderal Sudirman, Kav. 75, Jakarta 12910; tel. (21) 5782717; f. 1912; Pres. SUGIARTO.

Koperasi Asuransi Indonesia: Jalan Iskandarsyah I/26, Jakarta; tel. (21) 7207879; fax (21) 7207451; Dir H. J. V. SUGIMAN.

Selected Non-Life Insurance Companies

PT Asuransi Bina Dharma Arta: Wisma Dharmala Sakti, Lt. 8, Jalan Jenderal Sudirman, Kav. 32, Jakarta 10220; tel. (21) 5708157; fax (21) 5708166; Pres. SUYANTO GONDOKUSUMO; Dir SUHANDA WIRAATMADJA.

PT Asuransi Bintang Tbk: Jalan R. S. Fatmawati 32, Jakarta 12430; tel. (21) 7504872; fax (21) 7506197; internet www.bintang .co.id; f. 1955; general insurance; Dirs ARIYANTI SULIYANTO, M. IQBAL, DJUNAIDI MAHARI.

PT Asuransi Buana Independen: Jalan Pintu Besar Selatan 78, Jakarta 11110; tel. (21) 6904331; fax (21) 6263005; Exec. Vice-Pres. SUSANTY PURNAMA.

PT Asuransi Central Asia: Komp. Duta Meolin, Blok A 4–5, Jalan Gajah Mada 3–5, Jakarta 10130; tel. (21) 373073; fax (21) 3848526; Pres. ANTHONY SALIM; Dir TEDDY HAILAMSAH.

PT Asuransi Danamon: Gedung Danamon Asuransi, Jalan H. R. Rasuna Said, Kav. C10, Jakarta 12920; tel. (21) 516512; fax (21) 516832; Chair. USMAN ADMADJAJA; Pres. Dir OTIS WUISAN.

PT Asuransi Dayin Mitra: Gateway Bldg, 1st Floor, Jalan Letjen. S. Parman, Kav. 91, Jakarta 11420; tel. (21) 5668237; fax (21) 5668382; f. 1982; general insurance; Man. Dir LARSOEN HAKER.

PT Asuransi Indrapura: Jakarta; tel. (21) 5703729; fax (21) 5705000; f. 1954; Presiding Dir ROBERT TEGUH.

PT Asuransi Jasa Indonesia: Jalan Letjenderal M. T. Haryono, Kav. 61, Jakarta 12780; tel. (21) 7994508; Pres. Dr Ir BAMBANG SUBIANTO; Dir AMIR IMAM POERO.

PT Asuransi Parolamas: Jalan Teluk Betung 56, Jakarta 10230; tel. (21) 3144032; fax (21) 3145152; Pres. TJUT RUKMA; Dir Drs SYARIFUDDIN HARAHAP.

PT Asuransi Ramayana: Jalan Kebon Sirih 49, Jakarta 10343; tel. (21) 337148; fax (21) 334825; f. 1956; Chair. R. G. DOERIAT; Pres. Dir F. WIDYASANTO.

PT Asuransi Tri Pakarta: Jalan Paletehan I/18, Jakarta 12160; tel. (21) 711850; fax (21) 7394748; Pres. Drs M. MAINGGOLAN; Dir HUSNI RUSTAM.

PT Asuransi Wahana Tata: Jalan H. R. Rasuna Said, Kav. 12, Jakarta 12920; tel. (21) 5203145; fax (21) 5203146; Chair. S. SUGIARSO; Pres. RUDY WANANDI.

PT Lloyd Indonesia: Jalan Tiang Bendera 34-1, Jakarta 11230; tel. (21) 677195; Dir JOHNY BASUKI.

Berdikari Insurance Company: Jalan Merdeka Barat 1, Jakarta 10002; tel. (21) 375048; fax (21) 370586; Pres. Maj.-Gen. BUSTANUL ARIFIN.

PT Maskapai Asuransi Indonesia (MAI): Jalan Sultan Hasanuddin 53–54, Kebayoran Baru, Jakarta Selatan 12160; tel. (21) 7204250; fax (21) 7256980; Pres. IGNATIUS SOEBIAKTO.

PT Maskapai Asuransi Jasa Tania: Gedung Agro Bank, Lt. 4, Jalan Teuku Cik Ditiro 14, Jakarta 10350; tel. (21) 3101912; fax (21) 323089; Pres. H. R. SUTEDJIO; Dir Drs H. ABELLAH.

PT Maskapai Asuransi Timur Jauh: Jalan Medan Merdeka Barat 1, Jakarta Pusat; tel. (21) 370266; f. 1954; Pres. Dir BUSTANIL ARIFIN; Dirs V. H. KOLONDAM, SOEBAKTI HARSONO.

PT Pan Union Insurance: Panin Bank Plaza, Lt. 6, Jalan Palmerah Utara 52, Jakarta 11480; tel. (21) 5480669; fax (21) 5484047; e-mail paninins@cbn.net.id; Chair. CHANDRA R. GUNAWAN; Pres. NIZARWAN HARAHAP.

PT Perusahaan Maskapai Asuransi Murni: Jalan Roa Malaka Selatan 21–23, Jakarta Barat; tel. (21) 679968; f. 1953; Dirs HASAN DAY, HOED IBRAHIM, R. SOEGIATNA PROBOPINILIH.

PT Pool Asuransi Indonesia: Blok A–IV Utara, Jalan Muara Karang Raya 293, Jakarta 14450; tel. (21) 6621946; fax (21) 6678021; f. 1958; Pres. BAMBANG GUNAWAN TANUJAYA; Dir TANDJUNG SUSANTO.

PT Tugu Pratama Indonesia: Wisma Tugu, Jalan H. R. Rasuna Said, Kav. C-8-9, Jakarta 12940; tel. (21) 8299575; fax (21) 8291170; f. 1981; general insurance; Chair. F. ABDA'OE; Pres. SONNI DWI HARSONO.

Joint Ventures

PT Asuransi AIU Indonesia: Jalan K. H. Hasyim Ashari 35, Jakarta 10130; tel. (21) 3865467; fax (21) 3865504; Pres. Dir PETER MEYER; Vice-Pres. NANI KAUDIN.

PT Asuransi Jayasraya: Jalan M. H. Thamrin 9, Jakarta; tel. (21) 324207; Dirs SUPARTONO, SADAO SUZUKI.

PT Asuransi Jiwa EKA Life: Wisma EKA Jiwa, 8th Floor, Jalan Mangga Dua Raya, Jakarta 10730; tel. (21) 6257808; fax (21) 6257837; e-mail ekalife@uninet.net.id; Chair RAMON G. MADRID; Pres. G. SULISTIYANTO.

PT Asuransi Mitsui Marine Indonesia: Menara Thamrin, 14th Floor, Jalan M. H. Thamrin, Kav. 3, Jakarta 10340; tel. (21) 2303432; fax (21) 2302930; Pres. Dir S. AOSHIMA; Vice-Pres. PUTU WIDNYANA.

PT Asuransi Royal Indrapura: Jakarta Stock Exchange Bldg, 29th Floor, Jalan Jenderal Sudirman, Kav. 52–53, Jakarta 12190; tel. (21) 5151222; fax (21) 5151771; Pres. Dir Ir MINTARTO HALIM; Man. Dir MORAY B. MARTIN.

Insurance Association

Dewan Asuransi Indonesia (Insurance Council of Indonesia): Jalan Majapahit 34, Blok V/29, Jakarta 10160; tel. (21) 363264; fax (21) 354307; f. 1957; Chair. MUNIR SIAMSOEDDIN; Gen. Sec. SOEDJIWO.

Trade and Industry

GOVERNMENT AGENCIES

Agency for Strategic Industries (BPIS): Jakarta; f. 1989; co-ordinates for production of capital goods.

Badan Pengkajian dan Penerapan Teknologi—BPPT (Agency for the Assessment and Application of Technology): Jalan M. H. Thamrin 8, Jakarta 10340; tel. (21) 3162222; e-mail webmaster@bppt.go.id; internet www.bppt.go.id.

Badan Penyehatan Perbankan Nasional—BPPN (Indonesian Bank Restructuring Agency—IBRA): Jakarta; internet www.bppn.go.id; f. 1998 to restructure the banking sector; Chair. EDWIN GERUNGAN; Sr Deputy Chair. ARWIN RASYID.

Badan Tenaga Nuklir Nasional—BATAN (National Nuclear Energy Agency): Jalan Kuningan Barat, Mampang Prapatan, Jakarta 12710; tel. (21) 5251109; fax (21) 5251110; e-mail ppink@batan.go.id; internet www.batan.go.id.

Badan Urusan Logistic—BULOG (National Logistics Agency): Jalan Jenderal Gatot Subroto 49, POB 2345, Jakarta 12950; tel. and fax (21) 5256482; e-mail rotu03@bulog.go.id; internet www.bulog.go.id; Chair. RIZAL RAMLI.

National Agency for Export Development (NAFED): Jalan Gajah Mada 8, Jakarta; tel. (21) 3841072; fax (21) 3848380.

National Economic Council: Jakarta; f. 1999; 13-member council formed to advise the President on economic policy; Chair. EMIL SALIM; Sec.-Gen. Sri MULYANI INDRAWATI.

DEVELOPMENT ORGANIZATIONS

Badan Koordinasi Penanaman Modal (BKPM) (Investment Co-ordinating Board): Jalan Jenderal Gatot Subroto 44, POB 3186, Jakarta 12190; tel. (21) 5252008; fax (21) 5254945; e-mail sysadm@bkpm.go.id; internet www.bkpm.go.id; f. 1976.

Badan Perencanaan Pembangunan Nasional—Bappenas (National Planning Development Board): Jalan Taman Suropati 2, Jakarta 10310; tel. (21) 336207; fax (21) 3145374; e-mail admin@bappenas.go.id; internet www.bappenas.go.id; formulates Indonesia's national economic development plans.

Commercial Advisory Foundation in Indonesia (CAFI): Jalan Probolinggo 5, Jakarta 10350; tel. (21) 3156013; fax (21) 3156014; f. 1958; information, economic regulations bulletin, consultancy and translation services; Chair. JOYCE SOSROHADIKOESOEMO; Man. Dir LEILA RIDWAN SOSROHADIKOESOEMO.

CHAMBER OF COMMERCE

Kamar Dagang dan Industri Indonesia (KADIN) (Indonesian Chamber of Commerce and Industry): Chandra Bldg, 3rd–5th Floors, Jalan M. H. Thamrin 20, Jakarta 10350; tel. (21) 324000; fax (21) 3150241; f. 1969; 27 regional offices throughout Indonesia; Chair. Ir ABURIZAL BAKRIE; Sec.-Gen. Ir IMAN SUCIPTO UMAR.

INDUSTRIAL AND TRADE ASSOCIATIONS

Association of Indonesian Automotive Industries (GAIKINDO): Jalan H.O.S. Cokroaminoto 6, Jakarta 10350; tel. (21) 3102754; fax (21) 332100.

Association of Indonesian Beverage Industries (ASRIM): Jalan M. Ikhwan Mais 8, Jakarta Pusat; tel. (21) 3841222; fax (21) 3842294.

Association of Indonesian Coal Industries (ABBI): Perum Batu Bara Bldg, Jalan Supomo 10, Jakarta Selatan; tel. (21) 8295608.

Association of Indonesian Coffee Exporters (AICE): Jalan R. P. Soeroso 20, Jakarta 10330; tel. (21) 3106765; fax (21) 3144115; Chair. OESMAN SOEDARGO.

Association of Indonesian Heavy Equipment Industries (HINABI): c/o PT Traktor Nusantara, Jalan Pulogadung 32, Jakarta 13930; tel. (21) 4703932; fax (21) 4713940.

Association of Indonesian Tea Producers (ATI): Jalan Sindangsirna 4, Bandung 40153; tel. (22) 2038966; fax (22) 231455.

Association of State-Owned Companies: CTC Bldg, Jalan Kramat Raya 94–96, Jakarta; tel. (21) 346071; co-ordinates the activities of state-owned enterprises; Pres. ODANG.

Electric and Electronic Appliance Manufacturers' Association: Jalan Pangeran, Blok 20/A-1D, Jakarta; tel. (21) 6480059.

GINSI (Importers' Asscn of Indonesia): Bank Niaga Bldg, 1st Floor, Jalan M. H. Thamrin 55, Jakarta 10350; tel. (21) 3911057; fax (21) 3911060; f. 1956; 2,921 mems (1996); Chair. AMIRUDIN SAUD; Sec.-Gen. D. KADARSYAH.

Indonesian Cocoa Association (AKI): Jalan Brawijaya VII/5, Kebayoran Baru, Jakarta 12160; tel. (21) 771721; fax (21) 7203487.

Indonesian Cement Association: Graha Purnayudha, Jalan Jenderal Sudirman, Jakarta; tel. (21) 5207603; fax (21) 5207188.

Indonesian Exporters' Federation: Menara Sudirman, 8th Floor, Jalan Jenderal Sudirman, Kav. 60, Jakarta 12190; tel. (21) 5226522; fax (21) 5203303; Chair. HAMID IBRAHIM GANIE.

Indonesian Footwear Association (APRISINDO): Gedung Langlang Asia Ruang A, Jalan Daan Mogot 151, Jakarta Barat

11510; tel. (21) 5664157; fax (21) 5604671; e-mail aprisindo@vision .net.id; Chair. ANTON J. SUPIT.

Indonesian Furniture Industry and Handicraft Association (ASMINDO): Gedung Manggala Wanabakti Blok IV, 5th Floor, Room 501A–502A, Jalan Jenderal Gatot Subroto, Senayan Jakarta 10270; tel. (21) 5700249; fax (21) 5704619.

Indonesian Nutmeg Exporters' Association: Jalan Hayam Wuruk 103, Jakarta; tel. (21) 6297432.

Indonesian Palm Oil Producers' Association: Jalan Pulo Mas IIID/1, Jakarta; tel. (21) 4892635; Chair. NUKMAN NASUTION.

Indonesian Precious Metals Association: Jalan Wahid Hasyim 45, Jakarta; tel. (21) 3841771.

Indonesian Pulp and Paper Association: Jalan Cimandiri 6, Jakarta 10330; tel. (21) 326084; fax (21) 3140168.

Indonesian Textile Association (API): Panin Bank Centre, 3rd Floor, Jalan Jenderal Sudirman 1, Jakarta Pusat 10270; tel. (21) 7396094; fax (21) 7396341; f. 1974; Sec.-Gen. DANANG D. JOEDONAGORO.

Indonesian Tobacco Association: Jalan H. Agus Salim 85, Jakarta 10350; tel. (21) 3140627; fax (21) 325181; Pres. H. A. ISMAIL.

Masyarakat Perhutanan Indonesia (MPI) (Indonesian Forestry Community): Gedung Manggala Wanabakti, 9th Floor, Wing B/Blok IV, Jalan Jenderal Gatot Subroto, Jakarta Pusat 10270; tel. (21) 5733010; fax (21) 5732564; f. 1974; nine mems; Pres. M. HASAN.

National Board of Arbitration (BANI): Jalan Merdeka Timur 11, Jakarta; f. 1977; resolves company disputes; Chair. Prof. R. SUBEKTI.

Rubber Association of Indonesia (Gapkindo): Jalan Cideng Barat 62A, Jakarta; tel. (21) 3846813; fax (21) 3846811; Exec. Dir SUHARTO HONGGOKUSUMO.

Shippers' Council of Indonesia: Jalan Kramat Raya 4–6, Jakarta; Pres. R. S. PARTOKUSUMO.

UTILITIES
Electricity

PT Perusahaan Umum Listrick Negara (PLN): Jalan Trunojoyo, Blok 1/35, Kebayaran Baru, Jakarta Selatan 12610; tel. (21) 7395522; fax (21) 7711330; state-owned electricity co; Pres. Dir ADI SATRIYA.

Gas

PT Perusahaan Pertambangan Minyak dan Gas Bumi Negara (PERTAMINA): Jalan Merdeka Timur 1, Jakarta 10110; tel. (21) 3815111; fax (21) 363585; f. 1957; state-owned petroleum and natural gas mining enterprise; Pres. Dir MARTIONO HADIANTO.

Perusahaan Gas Negara (PGN) (Public Gas Corporation): Jakarta; monopoly of domestic gas distribution; Pres. Dir QOYUM TJANDRANEGARA.

Water

PDAM DKI Jakarta (PAM JAYA): Jalan Penjernihan 11, Pejompongan, Jakarta; tel. (21) 5704250; fax (21) 5711796; f. 1977; responsible for the water supply and sewerage systems of Jakarta; Pres. Dir Ir H. RAMA BOEDI.

PDAM Kodya Dati II Bandung: Jalan Badaksinga 10, Bandung 40132; tel. (22) 2509030; fax (22) 2508063; f. 1974; responsible for the water supply and sewerage systems of Bandung; Pres. Dir Ir IBRAHIM SURIAMIHARDJA.

PDAM Tirtanadi Medan: Jalan Sisingamangaraja 1, Medan 20212; tel. (61) 571666; fax (61) 572771; f. 1979; manages the water supply of Medan and nearby towns and cities; Man. Dir Ir KUMALA SIREGAR.

CO-OPERATIVES

In 1996 there were 48,391 primary and secondary co-operatives in Indonesia; membership of primary co-operatives was 27,006,000 in the same year.

Indonesian Co-operative Council: Jakarta; Pres. Sri EDY SWASONO.

TRADE UNIONS

Serikat Buruh Sejahtera Indonesia (SBSI) (Indonesian Prosperity Trade Union Central Board): Jakarta; f. 1998; application for official registration rejected in May 1998; 1,228,875 mems in 168 branches in 27 provinces throughout Indonesia; Gen. Chair. MUCHTAR PAKPAHAN; Gen. Sec. SUNARTY.

Federasi Serikat Pekerja Seluruh Indonesia (FSPSI) (Federation of All Indonesian Trades Unions): Jalan Raya Pasar Minggu Km 17 No. 9, Jakarta 12740; tel. (21) 7974359; fax (21) 7974361; f. 1973, renamed 1995; sole officially recognized National Trade Union Centre; comprises 18 national industrial unions; 5.1m. mems

in February 1999; Gen. Chair. JACOB NUWA WEA; Gen. Sec. SJUKUR SARTO.

Transport

Directorate General of Land Transport and Inland Waterways: Ministry of Transportation and Telecommunication, Jalan Medan Merdeka Barat 8, Jakarta 10110; tel. (21) 3456332; fax (21) 3451657; Dir-Gen. SOEJONO.

RAILWAYS

There are railways on Java, Madura and Sumatra, totalling 6,458 km in 1996, of which 125 km were electrified.

In 1995 a memorandum of understanding was signed by a consortium of European, Japanese and Indonesian companies for the construction of a subway system in Jakarta, which was expected to cost US $1,300m. and be completed in 2001.

Perusahan Umum Kereta Api (PERUMKA): Jalan Perintis Kermedekaan 1, Bandung 40117, Java; tel. (22) 430031; fax (22) 430062; six regional offices; transferred to the private sector in 1991; Chief Dir Drs ANWAR SUPRIADI.

ROADS

There is an adequate road network on Java, Sumatra, Sulawesi, Kalimantan, Bali and Madura, but on most of the other islands traffic is by jungle track or river boat. In 1997 the road network in Indonesia totalled 342,700 km; 27,357 km were main roads and 40,490 km were secondary roads. About 158,670 km of the network were paved.

Directorate General of Highways: Ministry of Public Works, Jalan Pattimura 20, Kebayoran Baru, Jakarta Selatan 12110; tel. (21) 7262805; fax (21) 7260769; Dir-Gen. Ir SURYATIN SASTROMIJOYO.

SHIPPING

The Ministry of Communications controls 349 ports and harbours, of which the four main ports of Tanjung Priok (near Jakarta), Tanjung Perak (near Surabaya), Belawan (near Medan) and Makassar (formerly Ujung Pandang, in South Sulawesi) have been designated gateway ports for nearly all international shipping to deal with Indonesia's exports and are supported by 15 collector ports. Of the ports and harbours, 127 are classified as capable of handling ocean-going shipping.

Directorate General of Sea Communications: Ministry of Communications, Jalan Medan Merdeka Barat 8, Jakarta 10110; tel. (21) 3456332; Dir-Gen. SOENTORO.

Indonesian National Ship Owners' Association (INSA): Jalan Gunung Sahari 79, Jakarta Pusat; tel. (21) 414908; fax (21) 416388; Pres. H. HARTOTO HADIKUSUMO.

Shipping Companies

Indonesian Oriental Lines, PT Perusahaan Pelayaran Nusantara: Jalan Raya Pelabuhan Nusantara, POB 2062, Jakarta 10001; tel. (21) 494344; Pres. Dir A. J. SINGH.

PT Jakarta Lloyd: Jalan Agus Salim 28, Jakarta Pusat 10340; tel. (21) 331301; fax (21) 333514; f. 1950; services to USA, Europe, Japan, Australia and the Middle East; Pres. Dir Drs M. MUNTAQA.

PT Karana Line: Jalan Kali Besar Timur 30, POB 1081, Jakarta 11110; tel. (21) 6907381; fax (21) 6908365; Pres. Dir BAMBANG EDIYANTO.

PT Pelayaran Bahtera Adhiguna (Persero): Jalan Kalibesar Timur 10–12, POB 4313, Jakarta 11043; tel. (21) 6912613; fax (21) 6901450; f. 1971; Pres. H. DJAJASUDHARMA.

PT Pelayaran Nasional Indonesia (PELNI): Jalan Gajah Mada 14, Jakarta 10130; tel. (21) 6334342; fax (21) 3854130; state-owned; national shipping co; Pres. Dir ISNOOR HARYANTO.

PT Pelayaran Samudera Admiral Lines: Jalan Gunung Sahari 79–80, Jakarta 10610; POB 1476, Jakarta 10014; tel. (21) 4247908; fax (21) 4206267; e-mail admiral@uninet.net.id; Pres. Dir DJOKO SOETOPO.

PT (Persero) Pann Multi Finance: Pann Bldg, Jalan Cikini IV/ 11, POB 3377, Jakarta 10330; tel. (21) 322003; fax (21) 322980; state-controlled; Pres. Dir W. NAYOAN; Dir HAMID HADIJAYA.

PT Perusahaan Pelayaran Gesuri Lloyd: Gesuri Lloyd Bldg, Jalan Tiang Bendera IV 45, Jakarta 11230; tel. (21) 6904000; fax (21) 6904190; e-mail gesuri@pacific.net.id; internet www.gesuri i.co.id; f. 1963; Pres. FRANKIE NURIMBA.

PT Perusahaan Pelayaran 'Nusa Tenggara': Kantor Pusat, Jalan Raya Pelabuhan Benoa, POB 3069, Denpasar 80222, Bali; tel. (361) 723608; fax (361) 722059; e-mail ntship@indo.net.id; Man. Dir KETUT DERESTHA.

PT Perusahaan Pelayaran Samudera 'Samudera Indonesia': Jalan Kali Besar Barat 43, POB 1244, Jakarta; tel. (21) 671093;

fax (21) 674242; Chair. and Dir Soedarpo Sastrosatomo; Exec. Dir Randy Effendi.

PT Perusahaan Pelayaran Samudera Trikora Lloyd: Bank Bumi Daya Bldg, 2nd and 3rd Floors, Jalan Malaka 1, Jakarta 11230; POB 4076, Jakarta 11001; tel. (21) 6907751; fax (21) 6907757; f. 1964; Pres. Dir Ganesha Soegiharto; Man. Dir P. R. S. van Heeren.

PT Perusahaan Pertambangan Minyak dan Gas Bumi Negara (PERTAMINA): Directorate for Shipping, Harbour and Communication, Jalan Yos Sudarso 32–34, POB 327, Tanjung Priok, Jakarta; tel. (21) 4301086; fax (21) 4301492; state-owned; tanker services; Pres. and Chair. Dr Ibnu Sutowo.

CIVIL AVIATION

The first stage of a new international airport, the Sukarno-Hatta Airport, at Cengkareng, near Jakarta, was opened in April 1985, to complement Halim Perdanakusuma Airport, which was to handle charter and general flights only. A new terminal was opened at Sukarno-Hatta in December 1991, vastly enlarging airport capacity. Construction of an international passenger terminal at the Frans Kaisepo Airport, in Irian Jaya (West Papua), was completed in 1988. Other international airports include Ngurah Rai Airport at Denpasar (Bali), Polonia Airport in Medan (North Sumatra), Juanda Airport, near Surabaya (East Java), Sam Ratulangi Airport in Manado (North Sulawesi) and Hasanuddin Airport, near Makassar (formerly Ujung Pandang, South Sulawesi). There are a total of 72 airports, six of which are capable of accommodating wide-bodied aircraft. Domestic air services link the major cities, and international services are provided by the state airline, PT Garuda Indonesia, by its subsidiary, PT Merpati Nusantara Airlines, and by numerous foreign airlines. In December 1990 it was announced that private airlines equipped with jet-engined aircraft would be allowed to serve international routes.

In September 2000 Indonesia had 10 domestic airlines, three of which served international routes; licences had also been awarded to a further two new airlines which had yet to begin operations.

Directorate-General of Air Communications: Jalan Arief Rahman Hakim 3, Jakarta 10340; tel. (21) 3914235; fax (21) 3914239; Dir-Gen. Zainuddin Sikado.

Air Wagon International Airlines: Jakarta; f. 2000; domestic services.

Bayu Indonesia: Jakarta; f. 2000; international services.

PT Bouraq Indonesia Airlines (BOU): Jalan Angkasa 1–3, POB 2965, Jakarta 10720; tel. (21) 6295289; fax (21) 6298651; f. 1970; private company; scheduled regional and domestic passenger and cargo services linking Jakarta with points in Java, Borneo, Sulawesi, Bali, Timor and Tawau (Malaysia); Pres. J. A. Sumendap; Exec. Vice-Pres. G. B. Rungkat.

Dirgantara Air Service (DAS): POB 6154, Jakarta 13610; tel. (21) 8097243; fax (21) 8094348; charter services from Jakarta, Barjarmas and Pontianak to destinations in West Kalimantan; Chair. Makki Perdanakusuma.

PT Garuda Indonesia: Garuda Indonesia Bldg, Jalan Merdeka Selatan 13, Jakarta 10110; tel. (21) 2311801; fax (21) 2311962; internet www.garuda.co.id; f. 1949; state airline; operates scheduled domestic, regional and international services to destinations in Europe, the USA, the Middle East, Australasia and the Far East; Pres. Abdulgani.

Indonesian Airlines: Jakarta; f. 2000; domestic services.

Lion Mentari Airlines: Jakarta; f. 2000; domestic and international services.

PT Mandala Airlines: Jalan Garuda 76, POB 3706, Jakarta 10620; tel. (21) 4206646; fax (21) 4249494; f. 1969; privately-owned; scheduled regional and domestic passenger and cargo services; Pres. V. Subageo; Vice-Pres. Zaidun Bhakti.

PT Merpati Nusantara Airlines: Jalan Angkasa, Blok 15 Kav. 2–3, Jakarta 10720; tel. (21) 6548888; fax (21) 6540620; e-mail lt13@indosat.net.id; f. 1962; subsidiary of PT Garuda Indonesia; domestic and regional services to Australia and Malaysia; Pres. Dir Wahyu Hidayat.

Pelita Air Service: Jalan Abdul Muls 52–56A, Jakarta 10160; tel. (21) 2312030; fax (21) 2312216; internet www.pelita-air.co.id; f. 1970; domestic services; Dir Soeratman.

Tourism

Indonesia's tourist industry is based mainly on the islands of Java, famous for its volcanic scenery and religious temples, and Bali, renowned for its scenery and Hindu-Buddhist temples and religious festivals. Lombok, Sumatra and Sulawesi are also increasingly popular. Domestic tourism within Indonesia has also increased significantly. In 1999 4.7m. foreign tourists visited Indonesia, compared with 4.6m. in 1998 and 5.2m. in 1997. Foreign exchange earnings from tourism declined from US $5,321m. in 1997 to US $3,459m. in 1998.

Department of Culture and Tourism: Jalan Medan Merdeka Barat 16–19, Jakarta Pusat; tel. (21) 3838805; fax (21) 3848245; internet www.indonesiatourisminfo.com; f. 1957; Chair. I. Gede Ardika.

Indonesia Tourism Promotion Board: Wisma Nugra Santana, 9th Floor, Jalan Jenderal Sudirman 7–8, Jakarta 10220; tel. (21) 5704879; fax (21) 5704855; e-mail itpb@cbn.net.id; internet www.goindo.com; private body; promotes national and international tourism; Chair. Pontjo Sutowo; CEO Gatot Soemartono.

IRAN

Introductory Survey

Location, Climate, Language, Religion, Flag, Capital

The Islamic Republic of Iran lies in western Asia, bordered by Azerbaijan and Turkmenistan to the north, by Turkey and Iraq to the west, by the Persian (Arabian) Gulf and the Gulf of Oman to the south, and by Pakistan and Afghanistan to the east. The climate is one of great extremes. Summer temperatures of more than 55°C (131°F) have been recorded, but in the winter the great altitude of much of the country results in temperatures of –18°C (0°F) and below. The principal language is Farsi (Persian), spoken by about 50% of the population. Turkic-speaking Azerbaijanis form about 27% of the population, and Kurds, Arabs, Balochis and Turkomans form less than 25%. The great majority of Persians and Azerbaijanis are Shi'i Muslims, while the other ethnic groups are mainly Sunni Muslims. There are also small minorities of Christians (mainly Armenians), Jews and Zoroastrians. The Bahá'í faith, which originated in Iran, has been severely persecuted. The national flag (proportions 7 by 4) comprises three unequal horizontal stripes, of green, white and red, with the emblem of the Islamic Republic of Iran (the stylized word Allah) centrally positioned in red, and the inscription 'Allaho Akbar' ('God is Great') written 11 times each in white Kufic script on the red and green stripes. The capital is Tehran.

Recent History

Iran, called Persia until 1935, was formerly a monarchy, ruled by a Shah (Emperor). In 1927 Reza Khan, a Cossack officer, seized power in a military coup, and was subsequently elected Shah, adopting the title Reza Shah Pahlavi. In 1941 British and Soviet forces occupied Iran, and the Shah (who favoured Nazi Germany) was forced to abdicate in favour of his son, Muhammad Reza Pahlavi. British and US forces left Iran in 1945, but Soviet forces remained in the north-west of the country (Azerbaijan province) until 1946. The United Kingdom retained considerable influence through the Anglo-Iranian Oil Co, which controlled much of Iran's extensive petroleum reserves. In March 1951, however, the Majlis (National Consultative Assembly) approved the nationalization of the petroleum industry, despite British and other Western opposition. The leading advocate of nationalization, Dr Muhammad Mussadeq, who became Prime Minister in May 1951, was deposed in August 1953 in a military *coup d'état*, engineered by the US and British intelligence services.

The Shah gradually increased his personal control of government following the coup, assuming dictatorial powers in 1963 with the so-called 'White Revolution'. Large estates were redistributed to small farmers, and women were granted the right to vote in elections, provoking opposition from landlords and the conservative Muslim clergy. In 1965 Prime Minister Hassan Ali Mansur was assassinated, reportedly by a follower of Ayatollah Ruhollah Khomeini, a Shi'ite Muslim fundamentalist religious leader strongly opposed to the Shah. (Khomeini had been deported in 1964 for his opposition activities, and was living in exile in Iraq.) Amir Abbas Hoveida held the office of Prime Minister until 1977.

Between 1965 and 1977 Iran enjoyed political stability and considerable economic growth, based on substantial petroleum revenues which funded a high level of expenditure on defence equipment and infrastructure projects. From late 1977, however, public opposition to the regime increased dramatically, largely in response to a declining economy and the repressive nature of the Shah's rule. By the end of 1978 anti-Government demonstrations and strikes were widespread, involving both left-wing and liberal opponents of the Shah, as well as Islamist activists. The most effective opposition came from supporters of Ayatollah Khomeini, who was now based in France. The growing unrest forced the Shah to leave Iran in January 1979. Khomeini arrived in Tehran on 1 February and effectively took power 10 days later. A 15-member Islamic Revolutionary Council was formed to govern the country, in co-operation with a Provisional Government, and on 1 April Iran was declared an Islamic republic. Supreme authority was vested in the Wali Faqih, a religious leader (initially Khomeini) appointed by the Shi'ite clergy. Executive power was to be vested in a President, to which post Abolhasan Bani-Sadr was elected in January 1980, with some 75% of the votes cast. Elections to a 270-member Majlis (National—later Islamic—Consultative Assembly) took place in two rounds in March and May. The Islamic Republican Party (IRP), which was identified with Khomeini and traditionalist Muslims, won some 60 seats, but subsequently gained considerable support among other deputies.

In November 1979 Iranian students seized 63 hostages in the US embassy in Tehran. The original purpose of the siege was in support of a demand for the return of the Shah (then in the USA) to Iran to face trial. The Shah died in Egypt in July 1980, by which time Iran had made other demands, notably for a US undertaking not to interfere in its affairs. Intense diplomatic activity finally resulted in the release of the 52 remaining hostages in January 1981.

The hostage crisis had forced the resignation of the moderate Provisional Government, and during 1980 it became clear that a rift was developing between President Bani-Sadr and his modernist allies on the one hand, and the IRP and traditionalist elements on the other. Clashes between supporters of the two groups escalated in June 1981 into sustained fighting between members of the Mujahidin-e-Khalq (an Islamist guerrilla group that supported Bani-Sadr) and troops of the Revolutionary Guard Corps. The Majlis voted to impeach the President, who was subsequently dismissed by Khomeini. Bani-Sadr fled to France, as did the leader of the Mujahidin, Massoud Rajavi. A presidential election in July resulted in victory for the Prime Minister, Muhammad Ali Rajani. He was succeeded as Prime Minister by Muhammad Javar Bahunar. Meanwhile, conflict between the Mujahidin-e-Khalq and government forces intensified. In August both the President and Prime Minister were killed in a bomb attack attributed to the Mujahidin. A further presidential election, held in October, was won by Hojatoleslam Ali Khamenei. Mir Hussein Moussavi was appointed Prime Minister.

Two ministers resigned and three more were dismissed in August 1983. The outgoing ministers were right-wing 'bazaaris', members of the merchant class, who opposed policies of nationalization and land reform advocated by technocrats in the Government. Moussavi's attempts to implement such economic reforms were continually obstructed by the predominantly conservative, clerical Majlis. Elections to the second Majlis in April and May 1984 resulted in a clear win for the IRP. The elections were boycotted by the sole opposition party to have a degree of official recognition, Nehzat-Azadi (Liberation Movement of Iran), led by Dr Mehdi Bazargan (who had been Prime Minister of the Provisional Government from February to November 1979), in protest at the allegedly undemocratic conditions prevailing in Iran. During 1985 there were reports of anti-Government demonstrations and rioting in Tehran and other cities, precipitated by austere economic conditions and dissatisfaction with the conduct of the war with Iraq (see below).

Three candidates, including the incumbent, contested the August 1985 presidential election. The Council of Guardians (responsible for the supervision of elections) had rejected almost 50 others, among them Bazargan, who opposed the continuation of the war with Iraq. Khamenei was elected President for a second four-year term, with 85.7% of the votes cast. Despite some opposition in the Majlis, Hussein Moussavi was reconfirmed as Prime Minister in October.

For most of the 1980s Iran's domestic and foreign policy was dominated by the war with Iraq. In September 1980, ostensibly to assert a claim of sovereignty over the disputed Shatt al-Arab waterway, Iraqi forces invaded Iran along a 500-km front, apparently anticipating a rapid military victory. Iranian forces offered strong resistance, and a conflict of attrition developed. Iran began a counter-offensive in early 1982; by June it had forced Iraq to withdraw from Iranian territory, and Iranian troops subsequently entered Iraq. In October 1983 Iran launched a series of offensives across its northern border with Iraq, thus threatening Iraq's only remaining outlet for petroleum exports, the Kirkuk pipeline. Iraq intensified its aerial attacks on Iranian towns and on Iran's petroleum industry, centred on Kharg Island in the Persian (Arabian) Gulf. In February–March 1984 a further Iranian offensive led to the capture of the marshlands around the man-made Majnoun Islands in southern Iraq, the site of extensive petroleum resources. From May Iraq began attacking tankers using the Kharg Island oil terminal, and Iran retaliated by targeting Saudi Arabian and Kuwaiti tankers in the Gulf.

In March 1985 an estimated 50,000 Iranian troops were committed to a mass offensive on the southern front. The army crossed the Tigris river, but was repelled by Iraqi forces, with heavy casualties on both sides, and Iraq renewed aerial bombardment of Iranian cities. In April the UN Secretary-General, Javier Pérez de Cuéllar, visited both Tehran and Baghdad, but failed to establish a basis for peace negotiations. Iran insisted that only the removal of the Iraqi President, Saddam Hussain, in conjunction with agreement by Iraq to pay war reparations, could bring an end to the hostilities. Between August 1985 and January 1986 Iraq made some 60 air raids on Kharg Island, impeding petroleum shipments from the terminal. Attacks on tankers and other commercial vessels in the Gulf were increased by both Iran and Iraq during 1986, and Iran frequently intercepted merchant vessels, confiscating goods believed to be destined for Iraq.

In January 1986 Iraq claimed to have recaptured most of the Majnoun Islands, and in February Iranian troops crossed the Shatt al-Arab and occupied the disused Iraqi port of Faw and part of the surrounding peninsula, thus threatening Iraq's only access to the Gulf; an Iraqi counter-offensive failed to dislodge an estimated 30,000 Iranian troops. Iraqi forces were diverted by a second offensive by Iran into Iraqi Kurdistan, several hundred kilometres to the north. In May Iraq made its first armed incursion into Iran since 1982, occupying the area around Mehran; however, Iranian troops forced a withdrawal within two months. Also in May 1986 an Iraqi air raid on Tehran (the first since June 1985) initiated a new wave of reciprocal attacks, continuing into 1987, on urban and industrial centres. By early 1987 Iranian forces had advanced to within 10 km of the Iraqi city of Basra, although further offensives failed to capture the city.

Although Iran was virtually diplomatically isolated by the war, in late 1986 it emerged that the USA, despite its active discouragement of arms sales to Iran by other countries, had begun secret negotiations with the country in 1985 and had made shipments of weapons, allegedly in exchange for Iranian assistance in securing the release of US hostages held by Shi'ite groups in Lebanon, and an Iranian undertaking to relinquish involvement in international terrorism. Meanwhile, Iran had begun to attack Kuwaiti shipping, and neutral vessels using Kuwait, in retaliation for Kuwait's support for Iraq. In mid-1987 the USA agreed to reregister 11 Kuwaiti tankers under the US flag, thus entitling them to US naval protection. The United Kingdom, France, the Netherlands, Belgium and Italy subsequently dispatched minesweepers to the Gulf region.

Iraq recaptured the Faw peninsula in April 1988, forcing Iranian forces to withdraw across the Shatt al-Arab. In June Iraq retook Majnoun Island and the surrounding area. In July an Iran Air passenger flight, allegedly mistaken for an attacking fighter jet, was shot down by a US aircraft carrier in the Strait of Hormuz; all 290 passengers and crew were killed. In that month Iraqi troops crossed into Iranian territory for the first time since 1986, capturing the border town of Dehloran, and the last Iranian troops on Iraqi territory were dislodged.

On 18 July 1988 Iran unexpectedly announced its unconditional acceptance of UN Security Council Resolution 598, adopted one year earlier. This urged an immediate cease-fire, the withdrawal of military forces to international boundaries, and the co-operation of Iran and Iraq in mediation efforts to achieve a peace settlement. A cease-fire came into effect on 20 August, and UN-sponsored peace negotiations began shortly afterwards in Geneva, Switzerland. In the same month a UN Iran-Iraq Military Observer Group (UNIIMOG) was deployed in the region. However, the negotiations soon became deadlocked in disputes regarding the sovereignty of the Shatt al-Arab, the exchange of prisoners of war, and the withdrawal of armed forces to within international boundaries. Hopes of a comprehensive peace settlement were raised by a meeting of the Iranian and Iraqi Ministers of Foreign Affairs in Geneva in July 1990, but were swiftly overshadowed by Iraq's invasion of Kuwait in August. On 16 August Saddam Hussain sought an immediate, formal peace with Iran, accepting all the claims that

Iran had pursued since the declaration of a cease-fire (including the reinstatement of the Algiers Agreement of 1975, dividing the Shatt al-Arab waterway). Iraq immediately began to redeploy troops from the border with Iran to Kuwait. Prisoner exchanges took place, and in September 1990 Iran and Iraq restored diplomatic relations. In February 1991 the withdrawal of all armed forces to internationally recognized boundaries was confirmed by UNIIMOG, whose mandate was terminated shortly afterwards.

Iran condemned Iraq's invasion of Kuwait, and observed the economic sanctions imposed by the UN on Iraq. However, it was unequivocal in its condemnation of the deployment of the US-led multinational force in the Gulf region. Relations between Iran and Iraq deteriorated after the liberation of Kuwait in February 1991. Iran protested strongly against the suppression of the Shi'a-led rebellion in southern and central Iraq, and the accompanying destruction of Shi'a shrines in the region, and renewed its demand for the resignation of Saddam Hussain. Iraq, in turn, accused Iran of supporting the rebellion. Thus, there was little further progress in implementing the terms of Resolution 598 until October 1993, when high-level bilateral talks were reported to have recommenced on the exchange of remaining prisoners of war. (See below for further details of relations between Iran and Iraq.)

Elections to the Majlis in April and May 1988 apparently provided a stimulus to reformist elements in the Government (identified with Hashemi Rafsanjani, since 1980 the Speaker of the Majlis, and Prime Minister Moussavi) by producing an assembly strongly representative of their views. (The elections were the Islamic Republic's first not to be contested by the IRP, which had been dissolved in 1987.) In June 1988 Rafsanjani was re-elected as Speaker and Moussavi was overwhelmingly endorsed as Prime Minister. In February 1989, however, Ayatollah Khomeini referred explicitly to a division in the Iranian leadership between 'reformers' (who sought a degree of Western participation in Iran's post-war reconstruction) and 'conservatives' (who opposed such involvement), and declared that he would never permit the 'reformers' to prevail. His intervention was reportedly prompted by the decision of Rafsanjani to contest the presidential election scheduled for mid-1989. In March and April prominent 'reformers' within the leadership, including Ayatollah Ali Hossein Montazeri (who had been designated as successor to Khomeini by the Council of Experts in 1985), resigned.

Ayatollah Khomeini died on 3 June 1989. In an emergency session on 4 June the Council of Experts elected President Khamenei to succeed Khomeini as Iran's spiritual leader (Wali Faqih). The presidential election, scheduled to take place in mid-August, was brought forward to 28 July, to be held simultaneously with a referendum on proposed amendments to the Constitution. Both 'conservatives' and 'reformers' within the leadership apparently united in support of Rafsanjani's candidacy for the presidency, and Rafsanjani (opposed only by Abbas Sheibani, a former government minister widely regarded as a 'token' candidate) secured an overwhelming victory, with 95.9% of the votes cast. A similar proportion of voters approved the constitutional amendments, the most important of which was the abolition of the post of Prime Minister (and a consequent increase in power for the President).

Rafsanjani appointed a Government balancing 'conservatives', 'reformers' and technocrats, and its endorsement by the Majlis, in August 1989, was viewed as a mandate for Rafsanjani to conduct a more conciliatory policy towards the West, despite the opposition of some 'conservative' elements. Popular protests against food shortages and high prices in early 1990 demonstrated the urgent need for economic reform. In October, with the co-operation of Ayatollah Khamenei, Rafsanjani was able to prevent the election of many powerful 'conservatives' to the Council of Experts. Elections to the fourth Majlis were held in April and May 1992. Of those who applied to contest the elections, about one-third (mostly considered to be opponents of Rafsanjani) were disqualified by the Council of Guardians. It was thus estimated that about 70% of the newly-elected deputies were supporters of, or likely to align themselves with, Rafsanjani. However, while the President appeared to have succeeded in marginalizing the 'conservatives', he remained constrained, not least by the fact that economic reform was lowering the living standards of the traditional constituency of the Islamic regime, the urban lower classes. Serious rioting reported in several cities during April and May was attributed by some observers to dissatisfaction with the Government's economic programme.

The extent to which Rafsanjani had lost popular support became clear when he stood for re-election to the presidency on 11 June 1993. Competing against three ostensibly 'token' candidates, Rafsanjani received 63.2% of the votes from a low electoral turn-out of 56%. An attempt was made on Rafsanjani's life at a rally in Tehran in February 1994. Responsibility for the attack was later claimed by the self-styled 'Free Officers of the Revolutionary Guards'. Later that month the President was obliged to appoint a new Minister of Culture and Islamic Guidance after Ayatollah Khamenei approved the appointment of the incumbent minister, Ali Larijani, to replace the President's brother, Muhammad Hashemi, as Director-General of the national broadcasting authority. Muhammad Hashemi Rafsanjani had for several months been criticized by 'conservatives' within the Majlis for mismanagement and for encouraging what were deemed 'immoral' broadcasts. (However, in August 1995 the President's brother was appointed Vice-President in charge of Executive Affairs and War Reconstruction.) Rafsanjani's opponents in the Majlis sought, meanwhile, to modify economic reforms proposed by the Government. In May 1994 the Government indicated that it would proceed more cautiously with a plan to reduce economic subsidies applied to basic commodities. In November, after almost a year of debate, the Majlis approved the Government's second five-year economic plan.

In August 1995 the official news agency cited members of the special commission for monitoring political parties as stating that political parties, associations and groups were free to conduct political activities in Iran on condition that they honoured the country's Constitution. It was subsequently reported, however, that Nehzat-Azadi had been refused formal registration as a political party, despite its hitherto quasi-legal status. Earlier in the month representatives of Nehzat-Azadi had criticized new electoral legislation granting the Council of Guardians the power to approve election candidates. In December Iranian officials were reported to have indicated that political parties would be authorized to contest future elections.

Legislative elections (to the fifth Majlis) in 1996 provided an important measure of the shifting balance of power between 'reformers', or 'liberals', and 'conservatives' in Iranian politics. The first round of voting, on 8 March, produced results in about 140 of the total 270 seats; turn-out by voters was put at about 77%. Candidates of the Servants of Iran's Construction, a pro-Rafsanjani faction formed to contest the elections, were reported to have won some 70% of the seats. However, the 'conservative' Society of Combatant Clergy, with the unofficial patronage of Ayatollah Khamenei, claimed that its candidates had achieved an equally conclusive victory. After the second round of voting, on 19 April, unofficial sources suggested that the Society of Combatant Clergy would command the loyalty of 110–120 deputies in the new Majlis, and the Servants of Iran's Construction that of 90–100 deputies.

In March 1997 Rafsanjani was appointed Chairman of the Committee to Determine the Expediency of the Islamic Order (which arbitrates in disputes between the Majlis and the Council of Guardians) for a further five-year term, indicating that he would continue to play an influential role in political life upon the imminent expiry of his presidential mandate. In early May the Council of Guardians approved four candidatures for the presidential election (a further 234 were rejected). Early expectations were that Ali Akbar Nateq Nouri, the Majlis Speaker (who apparently enjoyed the support of virtually all the members of the Society of Combatant Clergy), would secure an easy victory. However, in the days prior to the election, which took place on 23 May, Sayed Muhammad Khatami (a presidential adviser and former Minister of Culture and Islamic Guidance) emerged as a strong contender. Regarded as a 'liberal', Khatami—supported by the Servants of Iran's Construction, as well as by intellectuals, women's and youth groups, and the business classes—took some 69.1% of the total votes cast, ahead of Nateq Nouri, with 24.9%. The rate of participation by voters was more than 88%. (Nateq Nouri was re-elected Speaker of the Majlis in June.)

Taking office in August 1997, President Khatami emphasized his commitment to fostering sustained and balanced growth in the political, economic, cultural and educational spheres, as well as freedom of and respect for the individual and rights of the nation, in the context of the rule of law. In foreign affairs, the President undertook to promote the principle of mutual respect, but pledged that Iran would stand up to any power

seeking to subjugate Iranian sovereignty. Notable among the 'moderate' appointees in Khatami's first Council of Ministers were Ata'ollah Mohajerani (a former Vice-President) as Minister of Culture and Islamic Guidance, and Abdollah Nuri as Minister of the Interior (a post he had previously held in 1989–93). Kamal Kharrazi (hitherto Iran's ambassador to the UN) replaced the veteran Ali Akbar Velayati as Minister of Foreign Affairs, while Qorbanali Dorri Najafabadi became Minister of Information. Hassan Habibi was retained by Khatami as First Vice-President. Six further Vice-Presidents included Muhammad Hashemi Rafsanjani, who remained as Vice-President in Charge of Executive Affairs; Ma'sumeh Ebtekar, as Vice-President and Head of the Organization for the Protection of the Environment, was the first woman to be appointed to such a senior government post since the Islamic Revolution. In November Khatami appointed a new Committee for Ensuring and Supervising the Implementation of the Constitution.

In the months following his election, President Khatami appeared conciliatory towards the West, and also urged more tolerance of dissent in Islamic societies among groups who remained 'within the framework of law and order'. Khamenei, meanwhile, continued to denounce the West's military and cultural ambitions, particularly those of the USA and Israel. The divergent messages of Iran's political and spiritual leaders were widely interpreted by Western commentators as indicative of conflict between the country's 'moderate' and 'conservative' factions. Although Khatami pledged his allegiance to Khamenei as Iran's spiritual leader, the new President's assumption of office appeared to revive long-standing rivalries among the senior clergy. The focus of opposition to Khamenei was seemingly Ayatollah Montazeri (Khomeini's designated successor prior to March 1989), who openly criticized Khamenei's authority and demanded that Khatami be allowed to govern without interference. In November 1997 police used tear gas to disperse a violent demonstration in Qom by supporters of Khamenei, who had gathered to denounce Montazeri and one of his allies, Ayatollah Azari Qumi. Protests in support of Khamenei persisted in Qom, Tehran and elsewhere until Khamenei intervened to end them; he none the less demanded that Montazeri be tried for treason, and that all those who questioned his authority be prosecuted in accordance with the law. Montazeri's supporters claimed in subsequent months that the Ayatollah was being held under house arrest. Khamenei expressed unprecedentedly vociferous criticism of Montazeri in May 1998, after the latter's supporters distributed tracts in Esfahan urging his release; a subsequent pro-Khamenei demonstration there was reportedly attended by some 200,000 of his followers.

Although it was frequently emphasized that there was no rift between 'conservatives' and 'moderates' (Khamenei denounced reports of tensions within the regime as Western propaganda), the arrest on corruption charges, in April 1998, of the mayor of Tehran, Gholamhossein Karbaschi, was widely interpreted as evidence of the extent of rivalries. the detention of Karbaschi, a popular 'moderate', was apparently the culmination of investigations into the conduct of municipal affairs, as a result of which several of the mayor's aides had already been arrested. Earlier in the year the Minister of the Interior, Abdollah Nuri, had criticized Ayatollah Muhammad Yazdi, the 'conservative' Head of the Judiciary (an influential member of the Committee to Determine the Expediency of the Islamic Order appointed by, and responsible only to, Khamenei), for what he alleged to be the persecution of the mayor, and Karbaschi's arrest was denounced by several government members. Consultations (at Khamenei's behest) between Khamenei, Khatami, Yazdi, Majlis Speaker Nateq Nouri and former President Rafsanjani failed to prevent a rally by some 2,000 supporters of Karbaschi at the University of Tehran, and clashes between 'moderate' and 'conservative' students reportedly resulted in about 100 arrests. Karbaschi was freed from detention, pending trial, and in May it was reported that the Ministry of the Interior had authorized the registration of the Servants of Iran's Construction as a political party (styled the Servants of Construction Party), with Karbaschi as its Secretary-General. Karbaschi's trial, on charges including involvement in the misappropriation of funds, receipt of bribes and the abuse of public property, opened in June; the televised proceedings received widespread publicity. He was sentenced in late July to five years' imprisonment, convicted of embezzlement, squandering state property and mismanagement (but acquitted of bribery charges). Following an appeal, in December the duration of the custodial sentence was reduced to two years; a punishment of 60 lashes, suspended at the time of sentencing, was commuted to a fine of IR 10m. (in addition to one of IR 1,000m. imposed in July), and a 20-year prohibition from holding public office was reduced to 10 years. A further appeal failed to overturn Karbaschi's conviction, and he began his custodial sentence in May 1999. However, he received a presidential pardon and was released in late January 2000 (shortly before the legislative elections).

In June 1998, meanwhile, as Karbaschi's trial proceeded, the Majlis voted to dismiss Nuri as Minister of the Interior. Impeachment had been initiated by a group of 'conservative' deputies who charged that Nuri had made provocative statements via the media, and questioned his support for Karbaschi; the minister's opponents further maintained that he had permitted dissident rallies and had also failed to counter unrest involving supporters of Ayatollah Montazeri in late 1997. Khatami, who had opposed Nuri's impeachment, appointed Abdolvahed Musavi-Lari (also regarded as a relative 'moderate') to the Ministry of the Interior, and later named Nuri as Vice-President in charge of Development and Social Affairs. In August 1998 it was reported that Khamenei had ceded control of the police forces to Musavi-Lari. (Under the Constitution, the forces are under the jurisdiction of the Wali Faqih, but by convention responsibility is transferred to the Minister of the Interior; however, Khamenei had declined to accord Nuri control of the police.)

During 1998 the Khatami administration apparently moved to formalize its support base. In addition to the registration of the Servants of Construction as a political party, the Islamic Iran Solidarity Party was authorized by the Ministry of the Interior early in the year. Vice-President Ma'sumeh Ebtekar was among the leaders of the Islamic Iran Participation Front, inaugurated in December. However, at elections to the Council of Experts in October, 'conservatives' retained overwhelming control of the assembly, with an estimated 60% of the 86 seats being won by candidates of the 'radical' right wing; the Council of Guardians had rejected the candidacies of most 'reformists'. None the less, candidates of a 'centrist' grouping apparently associated with ex-President Rafsanjani took about 10% of the seats on the Council. The rate of participation by voters, at 46.3%, was significantly lower than that recorded at the 1997 presidential election.

The Minister of Information, Qorbanali Dorri Najafabadi, resigned in February 1999, after it was admitted that agents of his ministry had (allegedly without his knowledge) been responsible for the murders of five intellectuals and dissident writers (among them Dariush Foruhar, leader of the unauthorized but officially-tolerated Iranian People's Party) in late 1998. He was replaced by Ali Yunesi, who had led an investigative commission into the murders. In June 1999 it was reported that a former deputy minister of information, who had been one of four intelligence agents arrested and charged in connection with the crimes, had committed suicide while in custody.

Iran's first local government elections since the Islamic Revolution took place in February 1999, when some 60% of the electorate voted for 200,000 council seats. The elections resulted in considerable success for 'reformist' candidates, notably in Tehran, Shiraz and Esfahan; 'conservatives' secured control of councils in their strongholds of Qom and Mashad. Marked successes were recorded by female candidates, who won a total of about 300 seats. In subsequent weeks 'conservative' elements challenged the election of many 'reformist' councillors: among those whose victories were overturned was former Minister of the Interior Abdollah Nuri. Meanwhile, it was reported that the process of electing a successor to Karbaschi as mayor of Tehran was being hampered by opponents of the 'reformists', and it was not until June that Morteza Alviri, an adviser to Khatami, was chosen to head the city. The local elections were regarded as an important indicator of the likely progress towards elections to the Majlis, due in early 2000: while electoral support for 'reformist' and 'liberal' candidates was apparently strong, it was anticipated that 'conservative' elements would make strenuous efforts to restrict the influence of the legislature.

In April 1999 the Mujahidin-e-Khalq claimed responsibility for the assassination, in Tehran, of the deputy chief of staff of the armed forces, Lt-Gen. Ali Sayyad Shirazi. In the same month Mohsen Kadivar, a prominent reformist cleric, was sentenced to 18 months' imprisonment by the Special Clerical Court. Kadivar, who had openly questioned the validity of one of the central tenets of post-Revolutionary Iran, had been arrested in February on charges of disseminating false information and confusing

public opinion. In May an attempt by 'conservatives' in the Majlis to impeach the Minister of Culture and Islamic Guidance, Ata'ollah Mohajerani (a close associate of Khatami), was narrowly defeated. Mohajerani was accused by his detractors, who cited in particular what was perceived as his liberal policy towards the media, of failing to uphold revolutionary and Islamic principles.

The issue of press censorship had, meanwhile, increasingly become a focus of the political rivalries between 'conservatives' and 'reformists'. During 1998 several prominent journals had been closed, and their journalists prosecuted, and Khamenei had personally sought action against publications that abused freedom of speech to weaken Islamic beliefs. In July 1999 the Majlis endorsed draft amendments to legislation governing the press that would, in effect, curb the activities of the 'liberal' press, notably by requiring journalists to disclose sources of information. Immediately *Salam*, a 'reformist' newspaper with close links to President Khatami, was ordered by the Special Clerical Court to close. The newspaper had recently published a document produced by the deputy information minister whose suicide had been reported in June (see above) advocating stricter controls on the reformist media. The new press restrictions provoked what were reportedly the most serious street disturbances in Tehran since the Revolution. The day after the closure of *Salam* was ordered, a small demonstration by students at the University of Tehran was dispersed with considerable violence by police. Hours later security forces, aided by militant vigilantes of the Ansar-e Hezbollah, raided student dormitories on the university campus. The authorities later stated that one student had been killed, although students claimed that there had been as many as eight deaths. Mass protests erupted, and subsequently degenerated into rioting in Tehran and other cities that attracted much coverage by the international media. After five days the protests were quelled, with some 1,400 arrests made, by security forces and right-wing vigilantes. President Khatami meanwhile urged the students to respect law and order, emphasizing that the unrest could jeopardize his reforms. For his part, Khamenei blamed the violence on Iran's external enemies. The Supreme Council for National Security (led by Khatami) announced that two senior police officials had been dismissed, and that the chief of police, whose removal from office had been sought by the protesters, had been reprimanded. Following an appearance before a closed session of the Majlis in August, it was reported that the chief of police had informed the legislature that almost 100 police-officers had been arrested for their role in the campus raid. At the end of August it was announced that Tehran's head of police had been dismissed. Meanwhile, in early August the ban on *Salam* was extended to five years, and the journal's publisher (who had in late July been convicted on charges including defamation and publication of a classified document) was given a suspended 42-month prison sentence, fined and banned from publishing for three years. Also in August Muhammad Yazdi was succeeded, upon retirement, as Head of the Judiciary by Ayatollah Mahmoud Hashemi Shahrudi. Yazdi's immediate appointment to the Council of Guardians suggested that he was likely to continue to play a prominent role on behalf of the right wing in Iranian political life. In mid-September it was reported that four alleged leaders of the July riots had been sentenced to death; 45 defendants were given terms of imprisonment and fined, and a further 20 were acquitted. (However, the death sentences of the four student leaders were commuted to 15 years' imprisonment at the end of April 2000.)

In subsequent months the 'conservative' authorities continued to make strenuous efforts to curb the activities of the 'reformist' press. At the end of October 1999 Abdollah Nuri was brought before the Special Clerical Court, accused in his capacity as editor of the 'liberal' *Khordad* daily of (among other charges) insulting Islamic sanctities, publishing reports contrary to religious fundamentals, and refuting the values of Ayatollah Khomeini. Many observers regarded the charges against Nuri as a clear attempt to prevent his standing for election to the Majlis, where, if elected, he was likely to be a strong contender for the post of Speaker. In November Nuri was convicted on 15 charges and sentenced to five years' imprisonment; he was also fined IR 15m., and the closure of *Khordad* was ordered. An appeal lodged with the Supreme Court was rejected in January 2000, on the grounds that the court had no constitutional authority to overturn a verdict of the Special Clerical Court.

As anticipated, the process of scrutinizing candidates by the Council of Guardians, in preparation for elections to the Majlis scheduled for February 2000, resulted in the disqualification of many known 'reformist' candidates, on grounds principally of disloyalty to Islam, to Iran's Constitution or spiritual leader. ('Conservative' deputies had, in late 1999, introduced legislation giving the Council extensive powers to vet election candidates.) However, it appeared that the 'reformist' wing had had some success in presenting lesser-known candidates, who were approved as eligible to seek election by the Guardians. Nevertheless, while there were indications, as the election approached, that the sixth Majlis might include sufficient numbers of 'liberals' and 'moderates' to present the first real challenge to the 'conservative' majority, the extent of the success achieved by 'reformist' and 'moderate' candidates of the Islamic Iran Participation Front and the Servants of Construction was not widely predicted. An estimated 80% of Iran's registered electorate participated in the poll on 18 February 2000. Among those who secured notable victories were Muhammad Reza Khatami (brother of the President and head of the Participation Front's political bureau), who in Tehran took the highest number of votes of all candidates, Ali Reza Nuri (brother of the imprisoned former Minister of the Interior) and Jamileh Kadivar (the wife of Ata'ollah Mohajerani and sister of dissident cleric Mohsen Kadivar). 'Conservative' candidates, meanwhile, were overwhelmingly defeated in Mashad, Esfahan, Shiraz and Tabriz. There was a marked increase in the proportion of Majlis seats won by women, while the number of clerics in the new assembly declined. The Council of Guardians ordered the recount of almost one-third of the votes cast in Tehran, following allegations of irregularities; however, Ayatollah Khamenei intervened to prevent a complete recount of ballots for all 30 Tehran seats. Principal among those whose election was initially in doubt was former President Rafsanjani, who had narrowly secured election to one of the capital's seats; however, Rafsanjani resigned his seat in late May, thereby relinquishing his ambition to become the new Speaker of the Majlis. Meanwhile, a second round of voting, for 66 undecided seats, proceeded on 5 May (having been postponed from April by the Council of Guardians). At the end of May the incoming Majlis elected Mahdi Karrubi, the candidate of the Servants of Construction, as Speaker, a post which he had previously held in 1989–92.

The outcome of the first round of legislative voting appeared to exacerbate the struggle for political dominance between 'conservative' and 'reformist' elements. While the opening, in late February 2000, of the trial of 20 police-officers and security officials (among them the former Tehran chief of police), on charges of involvement in the attacks on students that had preceded the violent unrest of July 1999, was interpreted as an expression of the State's likely response to acts of provocation by forces that might seek to foment further unrest, conservative elements of the Revolutionary Guards Corps issued a statement in mid-April 2000 that was interpreted as a warning that a 'reformist' victory would not be tolerated. For its part, the judiciary pursued its actions against the 'reformist' press: a new press law, endorsed by the outgoing, conservative-controlled Majlis, made criticism of the Constitution illegal and increased judicial powers to close newspapers. The Majlis also approved legislation effectively depriving the legislature of authority to call to account security organizations under the control of Ayatollah Khamenei. In mid-March Sayed Hajjarian, a prominent 'reformer', manager of the daily *Sobh Emruz* and one of President Khatami's leading political advisers, was seriously wounded in a gun attack which some claimed had been perpetrated by forces linked to the intelligence service. In mid-May five men were found guilty of having carried out the attempted assassination and sentenced to terms of imprisonment ranging from three to 15 years; three others were acquitted.

By mid-2000 it was estimated that 'reformist' or 'liberal' deputies held some 200 of the seats in the new Majlis, with the remaining 90 occupied by 'conservatives'. (In November the Majlis decided to hold by-elections in mid-2001—the time of the scheduled presidential election—for 18 seats where the results of earlier voting had been annulled.) However, while 'reformist' deputies acted swiftly to draft legislation to replace the previous year's restrictive press law, as well as proposals to curb the powers of the Council of Guardians, Muhammad Reza Khatami, who was elected in mid-June 2000 to the position of First Deputy Speaker of the Majlis, indicated that change would proceed at a moderate pace. At the end of July the first conference of the Islamic Iran Participation Front elected Muhammad Reza Khatami as party Secretary-General.

At the end of June 2000 it was announced that Ayatollah Khamenei had dismissed as Chief of Police Brig.-Gen. Heyedat Loftian, who was regarded by many 'reformists' as responsible for the assault that had prompted the violent clashes involving students and security forces one year earlier. Loftian's replacement was Brig.-Gen. Muhammad Baqer Qalibaf. Demonstrations took place in Tehran in early July 2000 to mark the anniversary of the unrest; the protests (which targeted not only 'anti-reformist' forces, but also what was perceived as the slow pace of reform under President Khatami) again degenerated into clashes involving demonstrators and Ansar-e Hezbollah militants, and many arrests were made. Shortly afterwards the former Tehran chief of police, Brig.-Gen. Farhad Nazari, and 17 co-defendants were acquitted on charges arising from the police invasion of student dormitories in July 1999; two police-officers received custodial sentences, having been convicted on relatively minor charges. Meanwhile, at least two people were reported to have died during protests against water and electricity shortages held in several cities at the beginning of July 2000.

In early August 2000 Ayatollah Khamenei acted to block the new legislature's efforts to amend the press law by issuing a decree instructing the Majlis not to debate the proposed changes (which were intended primarily to make it more difficult for the judiciary to imprison journalists), on the grounds that such reforms would endanger state security and religious faith. Khamenei's intervention, which illustrated the restrictions that the 'reformist'-dominated Majlis was likely to encounter in implementing its legislative programme, appeared to sanction a more vigorous campaign against the 'liberal' interests in subsequent months. At the end of August a police-officer was killed, and about 100 people were injured, in four days of violent clashes between 'pro-reform' students and Ansar-e Hezbollah militants in the western town of Khorramabad. The confrontations occurred as two 'reformists', including the dissident cleric Mohsen Kadivar, were prevented by the militants from addressing an annual student congress. (Kadivar had been released from prison in July, although he had been informed of the possibility of indictment on further 'yet unknown' political charges.) In early November the Council of Guardians rejected for a second time the proposed relaxation of the press law; the amendments were thus submitted for jurisdiction by the Committee to Determine the Expediency of the Islamic Order. It was reported in that month that some 30 'pro-reform' publications had been closed down by the authorities since April, some of which had reopened under new names to seek to overcome previous closures. Meanwhile, in mid-September it was announced that Khamenei had dismissed the uncompromising chief of security police, Brig.-Gen. Muhammad Reza Naqdi, after a number of officers under his command were convicted of torture in a case in which Naqdi had been implicated.

Meanwhile, the State Plan and Budget Organization was merged in mid-June 2000 with the Organization for Administrative and Employment Affairs; Muhammad Reza Aref, hitherto Minister of Posts, Telegraphs and Telephones, was accorded responsibility for the new Organization of Administration and Planning within the Council of Ministers, while Vice-Presidents Muhammad Ali Najafi and Muhammad Baqerian, the respective heads of the former organizations, were redesignated Advisers to the President with the rank of Vice-President. In early October the Majlis voted to reject Khatami's nomination as Minister of Posts, Telegraphs and Telephones of Nasrollah Jahangard, who had been responsible for the portfolio in an acting capacity since June, owing to what was considered his poor management record.

In early October 2000 it was reported that Ata'ollah Mohajerani, the 'liberal' Minister of Culture and Islamic Guidance (whom 'conservatives' in the fifth Majlis had narrowly failed to impeach in 1999) had tendered his resignation. However, President Khatami apparently delayed official acceptance of his resignation until mid-December 2000, when Mohajerani was redesignated Chairman of the Organization for the Dialogue of Civilizations, a post which, many observers noted, would involve him in cultural rather than political affairs. Ahmad Masjed Jame'i, reputedly more of a 'conservative' than Mohajerani, was appointed as his successor on a temporary basis, and was confirmed in this post in mid-January 2001, when the Majlis endorsed this and other recent ministerial nominations. Earlier in December 2000 it had been announced that the Ministries of Agriculture and of Construction Jihad had been merged to create a new Ministry of Agriculture Jihad, while those of Industries and of Mines and Metals had been merged to form a Ministry of Industries and Mines. In early November 2000 the trial opened in Tehran of a group of prominent 'reformists', accused of 'acting against national security and propagandizing against the regime' by attending a conference on political reform in Iran, held in Berlin, Germany, in April. Among the accused were a dissident cleric, Hassan Yousefi Eshkevari, whose separate trial before the Special Clerical Court in October on charges including apostasy had provoked considerable controversy, the 'reformist' politician Jamileh Kadivar, and a well-known investigative journalist, Akbar Ganji. The severity of the sentences, pronounced in mid-January 2001, against seven of the defendants, who were condemned to custodial terms of between four and 10 years (Ganji received the maximum prison term, followed by five years' internal exile), was condemned by 'reformist' politicians within Iran; three others received suspended sentences, while six were acquitted. Appeals were immediately lodged by all those convicted. The outcome of Eshkevari's trial had not been disclosed, although there were unconfirmed reports that he had been sentenced to death. A focus of Ganji's investigations in recent months had been the deaths of dissident intellectuals in late 1998 (see above). While the journalist had amassed what he alleged was evidence of the involvement of senior members of the 'conservative' establishment in the murders, the authorities maintained that the assassinations had been instigated by 'rogue' agents of the Ministry of Information. The trial of 18 people, including senior intelligence officers, accused of involvement in the murders began before a military court in Tehran in late December 2000. (The court had recently announced that former Minister of Information Najafabadi had no case to answer.) Although all but two of the accused were said by the authorities to have confessed to involvement, hearings were boycotted by relatives of the victims, who regarded the trial, held in camera, as an attempt to conceal the true circumstances surrounding the deaths. At the end of January 2001 three intelligence agents were condemned to death, having been convicted of perpetrating the killings; five received life sentences, and seven others custodial terms of up to 10 years (the other defendants were acquitted). Meanwhile, as the trial began of a 'reformist' former Deputy Minister of the Interior accused of vote-rigging in the 2000 Majlis elections and incitement to violence in Khorramabad in August of that year, more than 150 Majlis deputies signed a letter, read out in the assembly and published in several 'pro-reform' newspapers, accusing the judiciary of harassing political and social activists and warning Ayatollah Hashemi Shahrudi that those responsible to him would be in breach of the law if they failed to co-operate with the Majlis in exercise its rights of supervision and investigation.

In mid-December 2000 the Council of Guardians declared that the presidential election would take place on 8 June 2001. It remained uncertain at this stage whether Khatami, who in late November had stated publicly that he had been unable to enforce the rights and freedoms enshrined in the Constitution, and had done insufficient to prevent the judiciary's punitive actions against the 'reformist' press and 'liberal' activists, would seek re-election; he did, however, subsequently declare his candidacy.

Relations with the USA since the end of the Iran–Iraq War have continued to be characterized by mutual suspicion. The USA, alleging that Iran is pursuing a programme of military expansion, has expressed particular concern over the nature of nuclear co-operation between the People's Republic of China, Russia and Iran, and has sought to persuade its Western allies to reduce economic and technical assistance to, and direct investment in, Iran. Iran maintains that it is not engaged in the development of weapons of mass destruction, while the Chinese and Russian Governments have strenuously denied involvement in non-civilian nuclear projects in Iran. In May 1994 US pressure was evident when the World Bank announced that it would approve no new loans to Iran in the foreseeable future. In July bomb attacks against Jewish targets in the United Kingdom and Argentina prompted the USA to accuse Iran—which it alleged to have been responsible for the attacks—of seeking to disrupt the Middle East peace process.

In April 1995 US efforts to isolate Iran internationally culminated in the announcement that all US companies and their overseas subsidiaries would be banned from investing in, or trading with, Iran. It was subsequently conceded that US oil companies active in the Caucasus and Central Asia would be allowed to participate in exchange deals with Iran in order to facilitate the marketing of petroleum from countries of the former USSR. Russia refused to support the embargo, but announced in May that it would henceforth separate the civilian and military components of an agreement to supply Iran with a nuclear reactor, to be constructed at Bushehr. In mid-1996 the US Congress approved legislation (termed the Iran-Libya Sanctions Act—ILSA) to penalize companies operating in US markets that were investing US \$40m. (subsequently amended to \$20m.) or more in energy projects in prescribed countries deemed to be sponsoring terrorism. Like the trade embargo imposed on Iran in 1995, however, these so-called secondary economic sanctions received little international support. In December 1996 Iran and Russia concluded an extensive co-operation agreement. In September 1997, furthermore, a consortium comprising French, Malaysian and Russian energy companies signed a contract with the Iranian National Oil Company to invest some \$2,000m. in the development of natural gas in Iranian waters in the Persian Gulf. Threats of sanctions were effectively averted in May 1998, when the US administration agreed to waive penalties for which the Secretary of State deemed the companies involved to be liable. This decision apparently facilitated further foreign investment in Iran, most notably in hydrocarbons projects, in 1998–2000.

Khatami's election to the Iranian presidency prompted speculation regarding prospects for an improvement in relations with the USA and other Western countries. A notable development was the designation by the USA, in October 1997, of the opposition Mujahidin-e-Khalq as one of 30 proscribed terrorist organizations. (Members of these groups would be denied visas for entry to the USA and would be banned from fund-raising on US territory.) In December Khatami expressed his desire to engage in a 'thoughtful dialogue' with the American people. In what was interpreted as a major concession, US President Bill Clinton stated subsequently that the USA would not require Iran (or any other Islamic state) to modify its attitude towards the Middle East peace process. The cautious *rapprochement* continued in January 1998, when Khatami made a widely-publicized address, via a US cable and satellite television news network, emphasizing the need to develop closer cultural links between Iran and the USA; that he did not urge direct political dialogue was generally interpreted as a compromise between 'moderates' in his administration and the regime's 'conservatives', most notably Khamenei, who continued vociferously to reject the possibility of any normalization of relations with the USA. In March President Clinton was reported to have marked the Iranian New Year for the first time with a broadcast to Iran, and in April the US Department of State modified its warning against travel to Iran, recommending instead that visits to the country be deferred. Also in April, a report by the US Department of State assessed Iran to have been the country 'most active' in sponsoring terrorism during 1997.

The announcement, in July 1998, that Iran had successfully test-fired a new ballistic missile, *Shehab-3*, capable of striking targets at a distance of 1,300 km, caused renewed tensions. (The missile could potentially target Israel and also US forces in the Gulf.) US concerns regarding what it perceived as Iran's efforts to acquire weapons of mass destruction remained a principal cause of mutual suspicion, and there was continuing evidence of efforts by the Clinton administration to block trading agreements deemed to assist Iran's military programme. Ukraine announced, following a visit by the US Secretary of State in early March, that it would not proceed with an agreement to supply turbines for the Bushehr reactor; however, Russia, stating that the Bushehr plant was in conformity with standards prescribed by the International Atomic Energy Agency for the prevention of nuclear weapons' proliferation, subsequently declared its willingness to provide the equipment.

The USA was among countries to condemn the arrest, revealed in June 1999, of 13 Jews in Shiraz and Esfahan, on charges of espionage on behalf of Israel and the USA. At the beginning of July 2000, after a closed trial in Shiraz, 10 of the defendants were convicted and given custodial sentences of between four and 13 years. US officials subsequently criticized the Iranian authorities for their failure to release any of the imprisoned Jews on appeal, although their sentences were reduced to terms of between two and nine years in September. In September 1999, meanwhile, the US House of Representatives approved non-proliferation legislation requiring the imposition of sanctions against any country aiding Iran in the development of weapons of mass destruction. Furthermore, while the Clinton administration continued to extend the prospect of further co-operation, indications that this might be contingent upon Iranian assistance in investigations into the bombing of a US military housing complex in Saudi Arabia in 1996 (see below) were not well received in Iran, which had consistently denied involvement. In October, none the less, the opposition National Council of Resistance was designated by the USA as a terrorist organization.

Addressing the American-Iranian Council in Washington, DC, in mid-March 2000, US Secretary of State Madeleine Albright announced an end to restrictions on imports from Iran of several non-hydrocarbons items. This substantive step towards the normalization of relations was in recognition of what the US administration regarded as trends towards democracy under President Khatami. Albright furthermore offered what amounted to an apology for the role played by the USA in the *coup d'état* of 1953, as well as for US support for Iraq in the Iran–Iraq War. Such concessions were, however, accompanied by the assertion that Iran had done little to modify its support for what Albright termed international terrorism and its efforts to develop nuclear weaponry. In April 2000 the USA imposed sanctions on the Iranian Ministry of Defence and on three industrial organizations alleged by the US authorities to have been involved in the transfer of missile technology; Iran denied the claims. In the following month, despite US objections, the World Bank approved the release of two loans to Iran (the first new lending since 1994—see Economic Affairs, below). Open meetings and other contacts involving Iranian and US officials at the UN Millennium Summit in New York in early September 2000, and a lecture tour undertaken later that month by the Iranian Minister of Foreign Affairs, Kamal Kharrazi, appeared to reinforce expectations of a further *rapprochement*. Early indications that the new administration of George W. Bush, inaugurated in January 2001, was reviewing US policy on sanctions were welcomed by the Iranian Government, and it was widely expected that ILSA, due for review in August, would not be renewed.

The European Union (EU, see p. 181), pursued a policy of 'critical dialogue' with Iran during the 1990s, despite US pressure as well as tensions between Iran and certain EU members. A lengthy period of strained relations with the United Kingdom, in particular, developed after Ayatollah Khomeini issued a *fatwa* (edict) in February 1989, imposing a death penalty against a British writer, Salman Rushdie, for material deemed offensive to Islam in his novel *The Satanic Verses*. 'Critical dialogue' was suspended in April 1997, after a German court ruled that the Iranian authorities had ordered the assassination of four prominent members of the dissident Democratic Party of Iranian Kurdistan in Berlin in September 1992. Germany announced the withdrawal of its ambassador to Tehran and expelled four Iranian diplomats, while other EU members similarly withdrew their representatives. Although EU ministers responsible for foreign affairs swiftly agreed to a return of their ambassadors, Iran's reluctance to readmit the German envoy prevented the normalization of relations for several months. Khatami's installation as President and the subsequent appointment of a new Council of Ministers in August 1997 apparently eased tensions, and in November a compromise arrangement was finally reached allowing the readmission of all ambassadors from EU countries. In February 1998, furthermore, EU foreign ministers effectively resumed 'critical dialogue' by an agreement to resume senior-level ministerial contacts with Iran. Following a meeting between Kharrazi and the British Secretary of State for Foreign and Commonwealth Affairs, Robin Cook, at the UN headquarters in New York in September, the Iranian Minister of Foreign Affairs confirmed that the Iranian Government had no intention of threatening the life of Rushdie or anyone associated with his work, nor would it encourage or assist any attempt to do so; the Government also dissociated itself from any reward offered in connection with the *fatwa*. However, 'conservative' clerics maintained that the *fatwa* issued by Ayatollah Khomeini was irrevocable, and the Qom-based 15 Khordad Foundation subsequently increased its financial reward offered for the writer's murder. Relations between Iran and the United Kingdom were, none the less, upgraded to ambassadorial level in May 1999. President Khatami became the first Iranian Head of State to visit the West since the Islamic Revolution when, in March, he travelled to Italy and the Vatican; Khatami also made an official visit to France in October, while in the previous month President Thomas Klestil of Austria made the first visit to Iran by an EU Head of State since the Revolution. Kharrazi visited the United Kingdom in January 2000; however, a visit to Iran by Robin

Cook, scheduled for May, was delayed until July and was again postponed in late June, shortly before the anticipated delivery of sentences in the Shiraz espionage trial (see above), although British officials denied that these and subsequent postponements were linked to events in Iran. Meanwhile, relations with Germany remained under some strain following the imposition in January 1998 of a death sentence on a German national convicted of sexual relations with a Muslim woman; the Supreme Court overturned the sentence in February 1999, and in a retrial in October the defendant was convicted and fined in respect of a lesser offence. By this time new charges related to alleged espionage had been imposed, but these charges were dismissed in January 2000. (The German national was released at the same time as an Iranian held on spying charges in Germany.) In July a visit to Germany by President Khatami (the first by an Iranian leader for more than 30 years) provoked widespread protests by Iranian dissidents resident there.

Relations between Iran and Saudi Arabia were frequently strained after the Islamic Revolution of 1979. A period of particularly hostile relations, following the deaths of 275 Iranian pilgrims as a result of fierce clashes with Saudi security forces in the Islamic holy city of Mecca during the *Hajj* (annual pilgrimage) in July 1987 culminated in the suspension of diplomatic relations in April 1988. Links were restored in March 1991. Allegations of Iranian involvement in the bombing of a US military housing complex at al-Khobar, Saudi Arabia, in June 1996 again strained relations for several months. Some improvement was apparent during the first half of 1997, and the installation of the new Government in Iran, in August, facilitated further *rapprochement*. There was considerable speculation that the improvement in relations reflected the desire of the two countries, as the region's principal petroleum producers, to co-operate in maintaining world oil prices and in efforts to curtail over-production by members of the Organization of the Petroleum Exporting Countries (see p. 269). An Iranian delegation led by former President Rafsanjani began a 10-day visit to Saudi Arabia in February 1998, at the end of which the formation of a joint ministerial committee for bilateral relations was announced, and several co-operation agreements were signed following a visit to Iran by the Saudi Minister of State for Foreign Affairs in May. The signing of a Saudi-Iranian security agreement was announced in April 2001.

The Khatami administration has also sought improved relations with Saudi Arabia's fellow members of the Co-operation Council for the Arab States of the Gulf (GCC, see p. 160), although a long-standing territorial dispute with the United Arab Emirates (UAE) remains to be resolved. In March 1992 Iran occupied those parts of the Abu Musa islands and the Greater and Lesser Tunbs that had remained under the control of Sharjah, in the UAE, since the original occupation in 1971. In December 1994 the UAE announced its intention to refer the dispute to the International Court of Justice in the Hague, the Netherlands. In early 1995 Iran was reported to have deployed air defence systems on Abu Musa and the Greater and Lesser Tunbs, prompting the USA to warn of a potential threat to shipping. In November talks between Iran and the UAE aimed at facilitating ministerial-level negotiations on the disputed islands ended in failure. Relations deteriorated further in the first half of 1996, after Iran opened an airport on Abu Musa and a power station on Greater Tunb. In 1997 the UAE protested that Iran was repeatedly violating the emirates' territorial waters. Talks in March were inconclusive, and in June the UAE protested to Iran and the UN at Iran's construction of a pier on Greater Tunb. Following a meeting with the UAE's Minister of Foreign Affairs during the eighth conference of the Organization of the Islamic Conference (OIC, see p. 266), held in Tehran in December 1997, President Khatami emphasized his willingness to discuss bilateral issues directly with President Zayed bin Sultan an-Nayhan of the UAE. Although the latter was reported to be cautious about Iran's attempts at *rapprochement*, in the following month UAE officials expressed willingness to enter into negotiations. None the less, both countries continued to assert their sovereignty over the three areas.

Iran hosts the largest refugee population in the world. At the end of 1999, according to the office of the UN High Commissioner for Refugees, there were 1,835,700 refugees in the country, of whom 1,325,700 were from Afghanistan and 510,000 from Iraq.

Victories achieved by the Sunni fundamentalist Taliban in the Afghan civil war in September 1996 prompted Iran, which supported the Government of President Burhanuddin Rabbani, to express fears for its national security, and to accuse the USA of interference in Afghanistan's internal affairs. In June 1997 the Taliban accused Iran of espionage and ordered the closure of the Iranian embassy in Kabul and the withdrawal of all Iranian diplomats. Iran retaliated by halting all trade across its land border with Afghanistan, prompting Taliban protests that the ban violated international law. In August 1998 10 Iranian diplomats and an Iranian journalist based in the city of Mazar-i-Sharif were reported to have been captured and killed by Taliban militia. By mid-September, as it emerged that nine of the missing Iranian nationals had been murdered by members of Taliban as they stormed Mazar-i-Sharif, 500,000 Iranian troops had reportedly been placed on full military alert in readiness for open conflict with Afghanistan. In mid-October, in an attempt to defuse the crisis, Taliban agreed to free all Iranian prisoners being held in Afghanistan and to punish those responsible for the killing of the nine Iranian diplomats.

In September 1997 Iraq opened a border crossing with Iran, thereby permitting, for the first time since the outbreak of the Iran–Iraq War, Iranian pilgrims to visit Shi'ite Muslim shrines on its territory. At the end of the month, however, Iranian aircraft violated the air exclusion zone over southern Iraq in order to bomb two bases of the Mujahidin-e-Khalq in that country (prompting Iraqi aircraft also to enter the zone). Vice-President Taha Yassin Ramadan of Iraq, attending the OIC conference in Tehran in December 1997, was the most senior Iraqi official to visit Iran since 1979. President Khatami subsequently expressed the hope that problems between the two countries could be resolved 'through negotiation and understanding'. During a visit to Iran by Iraq's Minister of Foreign Affairs in January 1998, it was agreed to establish joint committees with the aim of expediting prisoner exchanges, facilitating pilgrimages for Iranians to traditional Shi'a shrines in Iraq, and addressing other contentious issues. Exchanges of prisoners of war were reported at intervals in 1998–2000, despite periodic mutual accusations of failure to comply with obligations in this respect. In August 1999, according to Iranian statistics, some 55,438 Iranian and 39,417 Iraqi detainees had been exchanged since 1981. During late 2000 some improvement in bilateral relations was apparent: in mid-October Kharrazi became the first Iranian foreign minister to visit Iraq for a decade. Kharrazi described the talks as 'positive', and the two countries agreed to reactivate a 1975 border and security agreement that had been in abeyance since 1980. In November 2000 a bilateral transport and communications accord was signed. However, there were unconfirmed reports in October that Iran's Supreme Council for National Security was to suspend all high-level contacts with the Iraqi Government, following a series of mortar attacks on targets in Tehran apparently perpetrated by the Iraqi-based Mujahidin-e-Khalq.

Closer relations were developed with Turkey during the 1990s, despite periodic tensions arising particularly from Turkish allegations of Iranian support for the Kurdish separatist Partya Karkeren Kurdistan (PKK) in its conflict with the armed forces in south-eastern Turkey (q.v.). In 1997 Iran was a founder member of the Istanbul-based Developing Eight (D-8, see p. 307) group of Islamic countries. Meanwhile, considerable political and economic advantage has been perceived arising from Iran's potential as a transit route for hydrocarbons from the former Soviet republics of Central Asia, and since the early 1990s Iran has sought to strengthen its position in Central Asia through bilateral economic, security and cultural agreements as well as institutions such as the Tehran-based Economic Co-operation Organization (see p. 175).

In June 2000 President Khatami made a state visit to the People's Republic of China, during which both countries undertook to strengthen co-operation in trade and economic affairs and to engage in a dialogue with regard to social and cultural issues. Khatami also visited Japan in November. In September Iran and Algeria agreed to resume diplomatic relations; Algeria had severed links in 1993, accusing the Iranian Government of sponsoring armed Islamist groups in their conflict with the Algerian military regime.

Government

Legislative power is vested in the Islamic Consultative Assembly (Majlis), with 290 members. The chief executive of the administration is the President. The Majlis and the President are both elected by universal adult suffrage for a term of four years. A 12-member Council of Guardians supervises elections and ensures that legislation is in accordance with the Constitution and with Islamic precepts. The Committee to Determine the Expediency of the Islamic Order, created in February 1988 and formally incorporated into the Constitution in July 1989, rules on legal and theological disputes between the Majlis and the Council of Guardians. The executive, legislative and judicial wings of state power are subject to the authority of the Wali Faqih (supreme religious leader).

Iran is divided into 28 provinces, each with an appointed Governor. Elections for some 200,000 local council seats (the first local elections since the 1979 Revolution) took place in February 1999.

Defence

In August 2000 Iran's regular armed forces were estimated to total 513,000: army 325,000, Revolutionary Guard Corps (Pasdaran Inquilab) some 125,000, navy 18,000, air force around 45,000. There were some 350,000 army reserves. Paramilitary forces comprised an estimated 200,000 volunteers of the Basij and some 40,000 under the command of the Ministry of the Interior. There is a 21-month period of compulsory military service. Defence expenditure for the Iranian year ending 20 March 2001 was budgeted at IR 13,100,000m.

Economic Affairs

In 1998, according to estimates by the World Bank, Iran's gross national product (GNP), measured at average 1996–98 prices, was US $102,242m., equivalent to $1,650 per head (or $5,121 per head on an international purchasing-power parity basis). During 1990–98, it was estimated, GNP per head increased in real terms by an average of 1.8% per year. Over the same period the population increased by an average of 1.9% per year. GNP in 1999 totalled an estimated $110,500m., equivalent to $1,760 per head. According to official estimates, the country's gross domestic product (GDP) increased, in real terms, at an average annual rate of 4.3% between 1990/91 and 1999/2000 (Iranian years ending 20 March). GDP increased by 2.0% in 1998/99, and by an estimated 3.3% in 1999/2000.

Agriculture (including forestry and fishing) contributed an estimated 20.9% of GDP in 1999/2000. About 23.0% of the employed labour force were engaged in agriculture at the time of the 1996 census. The principal cash crops are fresh and dried fruit and nuts, which accounted for 19.6% of non-petroleum export earnings in 1998/99. The principal subsistence crops are wheat, barley, sugar beet and sugar cane. Imports of cereals comprised some 6.1% of the value of total imports in 1998/99. Agricultural GDP increased by an average of 4.3% per year between 1990/91 and 1999/2000; the sector's GDP increased by 9.5% in 1998/99, but declined by an estimated 0.3% in 1999/2000, owing to the effects of the worst drought for three decades.

Industry (including mining, manufacturing, construction and power) contributed an estimated 31.2% of GDP in 1999/2000, and engaged 30.7% of the employed labour force at the 1996 census. During 1990/91–1999/2000 industrial GDP increased by an average of 3.4% per year; growth was estimated at 2.3% in 1999/2000.

Mining (including petroleum refining) contributed an estimated 9.1% of GDP in 1999/2000, and engaged 0.8% of the working population in 1996. Metal ores are the major non-hydrocarbon mineral exports, and coal, magnesite and gypsum are also mined. The sector is dominated by petroleum and natural gas, which together contributed an estimated 8.4% of GDP in 1999/2000. In January 2000 Iran's reserves of petroleum were estimated at 89,700m. barrels, sufficient to maintain the 1999 level of production for almost 70 years. However, since 1999 several important discoveries of petroleum have been made, leading to estimates in late 2000 that reserves might be closer to 130,000m. barrels. With effect from February 2001, Iran's production quota within the Organization of the Petroleum Exporting Countries (OPEC, see p. 269), was 3.70m. barrels per day. Iran's reserves of natural gas (23,000,000m. cu m in January 2000) are the second largest in the world, after those of Russia. The GDP of the mining sector increased by an average of 0.7% per year in 1990/91–1999/2000; mining GDP was estimated to have declined by 0.8% in 1999/2000.

Manufacturing (excluding petroleum refining) contributed about 16.9% of GDP in 1999/2000, and engaged 17.5% of the employed labour force in 1996. The most important sectors, in terms of value added, are textiles, food processing and transport equipment. The sector's GDP increased by an average of 5.3% per year in 1990/91–1999/2000, with growth in 1999/2000 estimated at 2.5%.

Principal sources of energy are natural gas and coal. Imports of mineral fuels and lubricants comprised 1.3% of the value of total imports in 1998/99.

The services sector contributed an estimated 48.0% of GDP in 1999/2000, and engaged 44.5% of the employed labour force in 1996. During 1990/91–1999/2000 the GDP of the services sector increased by an average of 4.8% per year; the sector's GDP increased by an estimated 4.3% in 1999/2000.

In the year ending March 2000 Iran recorded a visible trade surplus of US $6,215m., and there was a surplus of $4,726m. on the current account of the balance of payments. In 1998/99 the principal source of imports was Germany (which supplied 11.6% of total imports); other major suppliers included Italy and Japan. The principal markets for exports in that year were the United Kingdom and Japan (which took, respectively, 16.8% and 15.7% of total exports); Italy, the United Arab Emirates and Greece were also important markets for Iranian exports. Other than petroleum and natural gas, Iran's principal exports in 1999/2000 were carpets, pistachios and other nuts and fruits, and iron and steel. Exports of petroleum and gas comprised 82.5% of the value of total exports in 1999/2000. The principal imports in 1998/99 were machinery and transport equipment, basic manufactures, chemicals, and food and live animals.

For the financial year ending 20 March 2000 Iran recorded a budget surplus estimated at IR 4,301,000m., equivalent to 1.0% of GDP. Iran's total external debt was US $14,391m. at the end of 1998, of which $7,679m. was long-term public debt. In that year the cost of debt-servicing was equivalent to 20.3% of the value of exports of goods and services. At the end of 1999 the country's total external debt was estimated at $16,300m. The annual rate of inflation averaged 25.6% in 1990/91–1999/2000. Consumer prices increased by an average of 20.4% in 1999/2000. Some 12.5% of the total labour force were estimated to be unemployed at the end of 2000.

Iran is a member of OPEC, of the Economic Co-operation Organization (ECO, see p. 175), of the Developing Eight (D-8, see p. 307) group of Islamic countries, and was admitted to the Group of 15 developing countries (G-15) in mid-2000.

Notable weaknesses in the Iranian economy include the Government's dependence on revenue from the petroleum sector, high rates of unemployment and inflation, and disparities in the distribution of income. Additional strain has, moreover, been placed on domestic resources by the presence in Iran of some 2m. refugees from Afghanistan and Iraq. The extent of Iran's reliance on the oil sector was clearly demonstrated during 1998/99, as the rapid decline in international petroleum prices entailed a decline of some 40% in revenue from petroleum sales and caused a marked deterioration in the balance of payments: deficits were recorded on trade and on the current account for the first time since 1993/94. However, the strong recovery in petroleum prices from mid-1999 strengthened government revenue and resulted in renewed payments' surpluses. A major emphasis of the Third Five Year Development Plan (TFYDP), which took effect in March 2000, was to be the reduction of Iran's dependence on the oil sector as the principal generator of wealth. President Khatami advocated as fundamental to the Plan the restructuring of the state portfolio and the elimination of monopolies, together with wide-ranging tax reforms. A priority was to be job-creation, with a target of some 765,000 new posts annually. A partial flotation of the rial was also planned, with subsidized rates to be retained only for transactions in essential commodities. Growth under the plan was forecast at some 6% annually (subsequent government estimates for 2000/01 were in the region of 5%), and major new oil and gas discoveries from 1999 enhanced confidence that the Plan's ambitious objectives might be realized. In its draft budget for 2001/2002, announced in late 2000, the Government projected a 25% increase in public expenditure, almost one-half of which was to be used to stimulate economic growth and create new jobs. Following the licensing in 1999/2000 of four private non-bank credit institutions, the TFYDP allowed for the private ownership of banks for the first time since the Revolution. In addition, a return to international capital markets was planned, with an envisaged Eurobond issue valued at US $300m.–$500m. scheduled for late 2000. Meanwhile, a stabilization fund established in March of that year, into which were paid petroleum revenues exceeding budgeted income, was forecast to reach US $8,000m. by March 2001; one-half of its value was to be reserved for use in the event of a future decline in international oil prices below budgeted levels, while the remainder was intended for private sector development and export promotion. In spite of ongoing efforts by the USA to deter foreign investment in the Iranian economy (see Recent History), the recovery in petroleum prices resulted in enhanced foreign interest in impor-

tant new petroleum and natural gas schemes, and the Khatami administration's economic programme was further strengthened in May 2000 by a decision by the World Bank (also despite US objections) to resume lending (with a total of $230m. for sanitation and health care schemes) for the first time since 1994. Meanwhile, the installation in mid-2000 of a new Majlis with a 'reformist' majority was expected to expedite Khatami's economic liberalization measures, although there were indications by early 2001 that short-term policy might be motivated less by ideology than by the imminence of the presidential election, scheduled for June.

Social Welfare

Under Article 29 of the 1979 Constitution, the Government has a duty to provide every citizen with insurance benefits covering illness, unemployment and retirement. In 1997/98 there were 54,812 physicians, 10,178 dentists and 7,412 pharmacists working in the country. In that year there were 96,148 hospital beds. Of total budgeted expenditure by the central Government in the financial year 1999/2000, according to preliminary figures, IR 4,066,000m. (3.6%) was for health and nutrition, and a further IR 11,774,000m. (10.5%) was for other social services (excluding education).

Education

Primary education is officially compulsory, and is provided free of charge, for five years between six and 10 years of age, although this has not been fully implemented in rural areas. Secondary education, from the age of 11, lasts for up to seven years, comprising a first cycle of three years and a second of four years. In 1996 the total enrolment at primary and secondary schools was equivalent to 86% of the school-age population (90% of boys; 83% of girls). In 1996 primary enrolment included 90% of children in the relevant age-group (91% of boys; 88% of girls), while enrolment at secondary schools was equivalent to 59% of the appropriate age-group. There are 37 universities, including 16 in Tehran. There were 625,380 students enrolled at Iran's universities and equivalent institutions in 1997/98, in addition to the 666,529 students enrolled at the Islamic Azad University in 1998/99. In 1997/98 the rate of illiteracy among the population aged 15 and above was 20.3% for males and 34.1% for females. Expenditure on education by the central Government in the financial year 1999/2000, according to provisional figures, was IR 17,484,000m. (15.6% of total spending).

Public Holidays

The Iranian year 1380 runs from 21 March 2001 to 20 March 2002, and the year 1381 from 21 March 2002 to 20 March 2003.

2001: 25 January* (Martyrdom of Imam Sadeq), 10 February* (Birth of Imam Reza), 11 February (Victory of the Islamic Revolution), 6 March* (Qorban, Feast of the Sacrifice), 14 March* (Qadir-e-Khom), 20 March (Day of Oil Industry Nationalization), 21–24 March (Nowrooz, Iranian New Year), 1 April (Islamic Republic Day), 2 April* (Sizdah-bedar, 13th and final day of Nowrooz celebrations), 3 April* (Tasooay-e-Hosseini), 4 April* (Ashooray-e-Hosseini), 3 May* (Qiyam-e-Khoonin), 13 May* (Arbain-e-Hosseini), 21 May* (Flight of Prophet Muhammad), 4 June (Death of Imam Khomeini and Birth of Prophet Muhammad*), 9 June* (Birth of Imam Ali), 1 October* (Mabas), 15 October* (Birth of Imam Mahdi), 8 December* (Martyrdom of Imam Ali), 17 December* (Fetr, end of Ramadan).

2002: 14 January* (Martyrdom of Imam Sadeq), 30 January* (Birth of Imam Reza), 11 February (Victory of the Islamic Revolution), 23 February* (Qorban, Feast of the Sacrifice), 3 March* (Qadir-e-Khom), 20 March (Day of Oil Industry Nationalization), 21–24 March (Nowrooz, Iranian New Year), 23 March* (Tasooay-e-Hosseini), 24 March* (Ashooray-e-Hosseini), 1 April (Islamic Republic Day), 2 April* (Sizdah-bedar, 13th and final day of Nowrooz celebrations), 22 April* (Qiyam-e-Khoonin), 2 May* (Arbain-e-Hosseini), 10 May* (Flight of Prophet Muhammad), 24 May* (Birth of Prophet Muhammad), 29 May* (Birth of Imam Ali), 4 June (Death of Imam Khomeini), 20 September* (Mabas), 4 October* (Birth of Imam Mahdi), 27 November* (Martyrdom of Imam Ali), 6 December*† (Fetr, end of Ramadan).

* These holidays are dependent on the Islamic lunar calendar and may vary by one or two days from the dates given.

Weights and Measures

The metric system is in force, but some traditional units are still in general use.

Statistical Survey

The Iranian year runs from 21 March to 20 March.

Source (except where otherwise stated): Statistical Centre of Iran, POB 14155-6133, Dr Fatemi Ave, Cnr Rahiye Moayeri, Opposite Sazeman-e-Ab, Tehran 14144; tel. (21) 8965061; fax (21) 8963451; e-mail sci@sci.or.ir; internet www.sci.or.ir.

Area and Population

AREA, POPULATION AND DENSITY

Area (sq km)	1,648,000*
Population (census results)†	
1 October 1991	55,837,163
25 October 1996	
Males	30,515,159
Females	29,540,329
Total	60,055,488
Population (official estimate at mid-year)	
1997	60,940,000
1998	61,836,000
1999	62,746,000
Density (per sq km) at mid-1999	38.1

* 636,296 sq miles.
† Excluding adjustment for underenumeration.

PROVINCES (1996 census)*

Province (Ostan)	Population	Provincial capital
Tehran (Teheran)	11,176,139	Tehran (Teheran)
Markazi (Central)	1,228,812	Arak
Gilan	2,241,896	Rasht
Mazandaran	4,028,296	Sari
East Azarbayejan	3,325,540	Tabriz
West Azarbayejan	2,496,320	Orumiyeh
Bakhtaran (Kermanshah) . .	1,778,596	Bakhtaran
Khuzestan	3,746,772	Ahwaz
Fars	3,817,036	Shiraz
Kerman	2,004,328	Kerman
Khorasan	6,047,661	Mashad
Esfahan	3,923,355	Esfahan
Sistan and Baluchestan . .	1,722,579	Zahedan
Kordestan	1,346,383	Sanandaj
Hamadan	1,677,957	Hamadan
Chaharmahal and Bakhtiari . .	761,168	Shahr-e-Kord
Lorestan	1,584,434	Khorramabad
Ilam	487,886	Ilam
Kohgiluyeh and Boyerahmad .	544,356	Yasuj
Bushehr	743,675	Bushehr
Zanjan	1,036,873	Zanjan
Semnan	501,447	Semnan
Yazd	750,769	Yazd
Hormozgan	1,062,155	Bandar-e-Abbas
Ardabil	1,168,011	Ardabil
Qom	853,044	Qom
Total	**60,055,488**	—

* On 1 January 1997 the legislature approved a law creating a new province, Qazvin (with its capital in the city of Qazvin). In June 1997 the Council of Ministers approved draft legislation to establish another new province, Golestan (with its capital in the city of Gorgan), by dividing the existing province of Mazandaran.

PRINCIPAL TOWNS (population at 1996 census)

Tehran (Teheran,		Rasht . . .	417,748
the capital) .	6,758,845	Mehrshahr . .	413,299*
Mashad (Meshed) .	1,887,405	Hamadan . .	401,281
Esfahan (Isfahan) .	1,266,072	Kerman . .	384,991
Tabriz . .	1,191,043	Arak . .	380,755
Shiraz . .	1,053,025	Ardabil (Ardebil) .	340,386
Karaj . .	940,968	Yazd . .	326,776
Ahwaz . .	804,980	Qazvin . .	291,117
Qom . .	777,677	Zanjan . .	286,295
Bakhtaran		Sanandaj . .	277,808
(Kermanshah) .	692,986	Bandar-e-Abbas .	273,578
Orumiyeh . .	435,200	Khorramabad .	272,815
Zahedan . . .	419,518	Eslamshahr	
		(Islam Shahr) .	265,450

* Estimated population at 1 October 1994 (Source: UN, *Demographic Yearbook*).

BIRTHS AND DEATHS (UN estimates, annual averages)

	1980–85	1985–90	1990–95
Birth rate (per 1,000) . . .	46.1	40.2	30.0
Death rate (per 1,000) . . .	10.5	7.9	6.4

Expectation of life (UN estimates, years at birth, 1990–95): 67.2 (males 66.5; females 68.0).

Source: UN, *World Population Prospects: The 1998 Revision*.

1991: Registered live births 1,885,649 (birth rate 33.8 per 1,000); Registered deaths 461,443 (death rate 8.3 per 1,000).

1994: Registered live births 1,304,255 (birth rate 21.9 per 1,000); Registered deaths 175,438 (death rate 2.9 per 1,000).

Note: Registration is incomplete.

ECONOMICALLY ACTIVE POPULATION
(persons aged 6 years and over, 1996 census)

	Males	Females	Total
Agriculture, hunting and forestry .	3,024,380	294,156	3,318,536
Fishing	38,418	309	38,727
Mining and quarrying . .	115,185	4,699	119,884
Manufacturing . . .	1,968,806	583,156	2,551,962
Electricity, gas and water supply .	145,239	5,392	150,631
Construction.	1,634,682	15,799	1,650,481
Wholesale and retail trade; repair of motor vehicles, motorcycles and personal and household goods	1,804,143	38,146	1,842,289
Hotels and restaurants . .	82,293	2,485	84,778
Transport, storage and communications . . .	955,271	17,541	972,792
Financial intermediation . .	139,286	13,586	152,872
Real estate, renting and business activities	137,039	12,051	149,090
Public administration and defence; compulsory social security	1,519,449	98,651	1,618,100
Education	581,597	459,459	1,041,056
Health and social work . .	184,242	118,897	303,139
Other community, social and personal service activities . .	183,246	41,159	224,405
Private households with employed persons	57,037	4,933	61,970
Extra-territorial organizations and bodies.	660	220	880
Central departments and offices .	30,389	2,563	32,952
Activities not adequately defined .	204,808	52,220	257,028
Total employed . . .	**12,806,170**	**1,765,402**	**14,571,572**

Unemployed ('000 persons, 1996 census): 1,455 (males 1,183; females 272).

1997/98 ('000 persons): Total employed 14,803; Unemployed 2,037; Total labour force 16,840.

Agriculture

PRINCIPAL CROPS ('000 metric tons)

	1997	1998	1999
Wheat	10,045	11,955	8,673
Rice (paddy)	2,350	2,771	2,348
Barley	2,499	3,301	1,999
Maize	915	941	700*
Potatoes	3,284	3,430	3,433
Dry beans	139	183	183†
Chick-peas	267	249	171
Lentils	83	95	95†
Soybeans	142	138	140*
Tomatoes	2,547	3,204	3,490
Pumpkins, squash and gourds	500*	500†	500†
Cucumber and gherkins	1,038	1,302	1,367
Onions (dry)	1,157	1,210	1,677
Other vegetables	3,911	3,900	3,900
Watermelons	2,174	2,473	2,179
Melons	926	1,168	1,055
Grapes	2,125	2,315	2,342
Dates	877	918	908
Apples	1,998	1,944	2,137
Pears	207	187	187†
Peaches and nectarines	218	267	267†
Plums	110	118	118†
Oranges	1,706	1,749	1,866
Tangerines, mandarins, clementines and satsumas	684	727	727†
Lemons and limes	940	891	972
Other citrus fruits	154	155	155
Apricots	225	243	243†
Other fruits and berries	1,641	1,648	1,648
Sugar cane	2,059	1,970	2,200†
Sugar beets	4,754	4,987	5,500†
Almonds	74	112	112†
Pistachios	112	314	131
Tea (made)	69	60	60†
Tobacco (leaves)	24	23	23†
Cotton (lint)*	132	139	151

* Unofficial figure.   † FAO estimate.

Source: FAO.

LIVESTOCK ('000 head, year ending September)

	1997	1998	1999
Horses*	250	250	250
Mules*	137	137	137
Asses*	1,400	1,400	1,400
Cattle	8,638	8,785	8,047
Buffaloes	465	474	474
Camels	143	143	175*
Sheep	52,117	53,245	53,900
Goats	26,000	25,757	25,757

Chickens* (million): 210 in 1997; 230 in 1998; 230 in 1999.

* FAO estimate(s).

Source: FAO.

LIVESTOCK PRODUCTS ('000 metric tons)

	1997	1998	1999
Beef and veal	298	315	295
Buffalo meat	11	11	11
Mutton and lamb	301	309	293
Goat meat	105	109	104
Poultry meat	717	719	748
Other meat	6	6	6
Cows' milk	3,897	4,095	4,403
Buffaloes' milk	190*	169	176
Sheep's milk	412	463	549
Goats' milk	396	398	396
Cheese	197	204	213
Butter	121	128	139
Poultry eggs	470	498	538
Honey†	8	8	8
Wool (greasy)	57	63	74
Cattle hides	43	45	42
Sheepskins	56	58	55
Goatskins	19	20	19

* Unofficial figure.   † FAO estimate.

Source: FAO.

Forestry

ROUNDWOOD REMOVALS ('000 cubic metres, excl. bark)

	1996	1997	1998
Sawlogs, veneer logs and logs for sleepers	371	409	341
Pulpwood	525	536	448
Other industrial wood	4,007	4,007	4,007
Fuel wood	1,997	1,997	1,997
Total	6,900	6,949	6,793

Source: FAO, *Yearbook of Forest Products*.

SAWNWOOD PRODUCTION
('000 cubic metres, incl. railway sleepers)

	1996	1997	1998
Total (all broadleaved)	144	141	129

Source: FAO, *Yearbook of Forest Products*.

Fishing

('000 metric tons, live weight)

	1996	1997	1998
Capture	351.7	349.9	366.9
Silver carp	17.5	15.8	11.6
Other cyprinids	28.4	29.1	34.5
Caspian shads	57.0	60.4	85.0
Longtail tuna	16.5	17.9	19.4
Yellowfin tuna	28.5	19.9	20.0
Aquaculture	30.0	30.3	33.2
Common carp	7.0	16.3	16.4
Silver carp	16.8	5.4	5.5
Total catch	381.7	380.2	400.1

Source: FAO, *Yearbook of Fishery Statistics*.

Production of caviar (metric tons, year ending 20 March): 281 in 1988/89; 310 in 1989/90; 233 in 1990/91.

Mining

CRUDE PETROLEUM
('000 barrels per day, year ending 20 March)

	1997/98	1998/99	1999/2000
Total production	3,623	3,666	3,373

Source: Ministry of Oil.

NATURAL GAS (million cu metres, year ending 20 March)*

	1997/98	1998/99	1999/2000†
Consumption (domestic)‡ . . .	47,600	51,500	58,700
Flared	11,500	11,100	10,800
Regional uses and wastes. . .	10,400	9,900	10,500
Total production	69,500	72,500	80,000

* Excluding gas injected into oil wells.
† Estimates.
‡ Includes gas for household, commercial, industrial, generator and refinery consumption.

Source IMF, *Islamic Republic of Iran: Statistical Appendix* (September 2000).

OTHER MINERALS ('000 metric tons, year ending 20 March)

	1997/98	1998/99	1999/2000
Iron ore*	6,300	6,000	6,000
Copper ore*	117.2	119.0†	120.0
Lead ore*	18.2	13.0	14.0
Zinc ore*	76.5	82.0	80.0
Chromium ore	169.0	211.6	254.7
Magnesite†	40	40	40
Fluorspar (Fluorite) . . .	20†	20	20
Barite (Barytes)	181.2	180.0	170.0
Salt (unrefined)	450†	500†	500
Gypsum (crude)	8,900†	9,000	n.a.

* Figures refer to the metal content of ores.
† Estimate.

Source: US Geological Survey.

Hard coal ('000 metric tons, year ending 20 March): 1,135 in 1996/97 (Source: UN, *Industrial Commodity Statistics Yearbook*).

Industry

PETROLEUM PRODUCTS
('000 metric tons, year ending 20 March)

	1994/95*	1995/96*	1996/97
Liquefied petroleum gas . . .	3,100	3,710	3,750
Naphtha	300	400	420
Motor spirit (petrol) . . .	6,200	6,300	6,400
Aviation gasoline	100	100	100
Kerosene	4,500	4,600	4,655
White spirit	300	300	300
Jet fuel	1,200	1,250	1,300
Gas-diesel (distillate fuel) oil . .	14,400	14,500	14,600
Residual fuel oils . . .	14,100	14,100	14,100
Lubricating oils	610	610	610
Petroleum bitumen (asphalt) . .	2,100	2,200	2,100

* Provisional or estimated figures.

Source: UN, *Industrial Commodity Statistics Yearbook*.

OTHER PRODUCTS (year ending 20 March)*

	1994/95	1995/96	1996/97
Refined sugar ('000 metric tons) .	1,052	1,151	1,597
Cigarettes (million) . . .	7,939	9,787	11,860
Paints ('000 metric tons) . . .	36	32	33
Cement ('000 metric tons) .	16,250	16,904	17,426
Refrigerators ('000) . . .	629	638	887
Gas stoves ('000). . . .	215	243	n.a.
Telephone sets ('000) . . .	218	161	89
Radios and recorders ('000) .	138	33	48
Television receivers ('000) .	360	253	433
Motor vehicles (assembled) ('000) .	69	92	n.a.
Footwear (million pairs) . . .	17.6	15.8	16.1
Carpets and rugs ('000 sq m) . .	28,064	25,369	28,970

* Figures refer to production in large-scale manufacturing establishments with 50 workers or more.

Source: mainly UN, *Industrial Commodity Statistics Yearbook*.

Production of Electricity (million kWh, year ending 20 March): *Ministry of Energy:* 77,086 in 1994/95; 80,044 in 1995/96; 85,825 in 1996/97; 92,310 in 1997/98; 97,863 in 1998/99; 107,148 in 1999/2000. *Private Sector:* 4,933 in 1994/95; 4,925 in 1995/96; 5,026 in 1996/97; 5,434 in 1997/98; 5,550 in 1998/99; 5,670 in 1999/2000.

Finance

CURRENCY AND EXCHANGE RATES

Monetary Units
100 dinars = 1 Iranian rial (IR).

Sterling, Dollar and Euro Equivalents (29 December 2000)
£1 sterling = 3,376.7 rials;
US $1 = 2,262.9 rials;
€1 = 2,105.7 rials;
10,000 Iranian rials = £2.961 = $4.419 = €4.749.

Average Exchange Rate (rials per US $)
1998   1,751.86
1999   1,752.93
2000   1,764.43

Note: In March 1993 the multiple exchange rate system was unified, and since then the exchange rate of the rial has been market-determined. The foregoing information refers to the base rate, applicable to receipts from exports of petroleum and gas, payments for imports of essential goods and services, debt-servicing costs and imports related to large national projects. There is also an export rate, set at a mid-point of US $1 = 3,007.5 rials in May 1995, which applies to receipts from non-petroleum exports and to all other official current account transactions not effected at the base rate. The weighted average of the basic and export rates was estimated to be US $1 = 2,194.0 rials in 1996 and $1 = 2,779.5 rials in 1997. It was reported in September 1999 that the export rate would be abolished in March 2000, and that thereafter most transactions would be conducted at a 'floating' exchange rate. The free-market rate in December 1999 was about 8,100 rials per US dollar.

BUDGET ('000 million rials, year ending 20 March)*

Revenue	1998/99	1999/2000†	2000/01‡
Oil and gas revenues . . .	22,530	51,408	82,961
Non-oil revenues	40,351	60,663	67,251
Taxation	18,686	25,831	33,961
Income and wealth taxes . .	12,675	16,584	21,845
Corporate taxes . .	7,922	10,048	12,899
Public corporations . .	3,827	4,944	6,099
Private corporations . .	4,095	5,105	6,800
Taxes on wages and salaries	1,698	2,469	3,400
Taxes on other income . .	2,199	2,914	4,120
Import taxes . . .	4,432	5,805	6,900
Customs duties . .	2,558	3,046	3,771
Order registration fees .	1,846	2,532	3,000
Taxes on consumpton and sales	1,579	3,442	5,216
Non-tax revenues . . .	12,734	22,686	16,810
Services and sales of goods .	3,373	5,300	8,626
Other revenues§ . . .	9,361	17,386	8,184
Special revenues	8,931	12,146	16,481
Total	62,881	112,071	150,212

Expenditure‖	1997/98	1998/99	1999/2000‡
General services	5,777	6,469	8,062
National defence	6,548	8,144	8,660
Social services	27,490	31,151	33,752
Education	14,159	16,344	17,484
Health and nutrition	3,458	3,694	4,066
Social security and welfare } Other social services	9,404	10,767	11,774
Economic services	13,792	13,920	21,252
Agriculture	1,587	1,591	1,799
Water resources	1,863	1,444	3,500
Petroleum, fuel and power	6,214	6,803	8,301
Transport and communication	3,086	3,156	4,303
Other economic services	1,042	926	3,349
Other expenditure§	9,952	11,373	24,933
Foreign exchange obligations	7,216	5,077	3,095
Special expenditures	6,397	8,666	12,146
Total	**76,842**	**84,843**	**111,900**
Current	44,498	53,632	65,129
Capital	19,061	17,655	31,530

2000/01 (forecasts, '000 million rials): Total expenditure and net lending 136,761 (current expenditure 89,096).

* Figures refer to the consolidated accounts of the central Government, comprising the General Budget, the operations of the Social Security Organization and special (extrabudgetary) revenue and expenditure.
† Provisional figures.
‡ Forecasts.
§ Including operations of the Organization for Protection of Consumers and Producers, a central government unit with its own budget.
‖ Excluding lending minus repayments ('000 million rials): −330 in 1997/98; −187 in 1998/99.

Source: IMF, mainly *Islamic Republic of Iran: Statistical Appendix* (September 2000).

INTERNATIONAL RESERVES (US $ million at 31 December)*

	1993	1994	1995
Gold (national valuation)	229	242	252
IMF special drawing rights	144	143	134
Total	**373**	**385**	**386**

* Excluding reserves of foreign exchange, for which no figures are available since 1982 (when the value of reserves was US $5,287m.).

1996 (US $ million at 31 December): IMF special drawing rights 345.
1997 (US $ million at 31 December): IMF special drawing rights 330.
1998 (US $ million at 31 December): IMF special drawing rights 2.
1999 (US $ million at 31 December): IMF special drawing rights 139.

Source: IMF, *International Financial Statistics*.

MONEY SUPPLY ('000 million rials at 20 December)

	1997	1998	1999
Currency outside banks	11,271	14,050	16,652
Non-financial public enterprises' deposits at Central Bank	2,642	4,662	5,304
Demand deposits at commercial banks	41,064	48,732	59,996
Total money	**54,977**	**67,444**	**81,952**

Source: IMF, *International Financial Statistics*.

COST OF LIVING (Consumer Price Index in urban areas, year ending 20 March; base: 1990/91 = 100)

	1997/98	1998/99	1999/2000
Food, beverages and tobacco	568.4	709.6	867.2
Clothing	487.8	521.8	564.1
Housing, fuel and light	489.5	589.4	700.9
All items (incl. others)	**538.2**	**645.6**	**777.4**

Source: Bank Markazi Jomhouri Islami Iran.

NATIONAL ACCOUNTS
('000 million rials at current prices, year ending 20 March)
National Income and Product

	1997/98	1998/99	1999/2000*
Domestic factor incomes†	231,379.8	271,709.9	348,963.1
Consumption of fixed capital	46,284.9	55,885.8	67,733.6
Gross domestic product (GDP) at factor cost	**277,664.8**	**327,595.7**	**416,696.7**
Indirect taxes } *Less* Subsidies	165.8	741.5	1,471.7
GDP in purchasers' values	**277,830.6**	**328,337.2**	**418,168.4**
Factor income from abroad } *Less* Factor income paid abroad	−2,793.4	−1,776.8	−2,365.3
Gross national product (GNP)	**275,037.2**	**326,560.4**	**415,803.1**
Less Consumption of fixed capital	46,284.9	55,885.8	67,733.6
National income in market prices	**228,752.3**	**270,674.6**	**348,069.5**

* Provisional figures.
† Compensation of employees and the operating surplus of enterprises.

Source: Bank Markazi Jomhouri Islami Iran.

Expenditure on the Gross Domestic Product

	1997/98	1998/99	1999/2000
Government final consumption expenditure	38,365	43,792	56,296
Private final consumption expenditure	172,350	212,784	265,498
Increase in stocks*	−9,829	−412	−3,957
Gross fixed capital formation	69,232	72,446	92,619
Total domestic expenditure	**270,118**	**328,610**	**410,456**
Exports of goods and services	36,374	27,144	53,964
Less Imports of goods and services	28,661	27,416	46,252
GDP in purchasers' values	**277,831**	**328,338**	**418,168**
GDP at constant 1982/83 prices†	**15,203**	**15,508**	**16,024**

* Including statistical discrepancy.
† Including adjustment for changes in terms of trade ('000 million rials): −1,503.8 in 1997/98; −1,572.8 in 1998/99; −1,487.3 in 1999/2000.

Source: mainly IMF, *International Financial Statistics*.

Gross Domestic Product by Economic Activity (at factor cost)

	1997/98	1998/99	1999/2000*
Agriculture, hunting, forestry and fishing	55,819.8	72,421.5	86,996.7
Mining and quarrying†	33,640.3	23,549.1	37,784.0
Manufacturing†	44,316.8	57,179.5	70,664.7
Electricity, gas and water	4,801.1	5,960.7	7,421.1
Construction	11,060.7	11,071.4	14,082.8
Trade, restaurants and hotels	47,031.8	58,183.3	76,802.0
Transport, storage and communications	22,389.3	27,487.4	34,386.7
Finance, insurance, real estate and business services	28,536.6	34,332.6	44,759.0
Government services	27,005.7	30,975.5	35,652.2
Other services	5,603.7	6,842.1	8,627.9
Sub-total	**278,205.8**	**328,003.1**	**417,177.1**
Less Imputed bank service charge	541.0	407.4	480.4
Total	**277,664.8**	**327,595.7**	**416,696.7**

* Provisional figures.
† Refining of petroleum is included in mining and excluded from manufacturing.

Source: Bank Markazi Jomhouri Islami Iran.

BALANCE OF PAYMENTS (US $ million, year ending 20 March)

	1997/98	1998/99	1999/2000*
Exports of goods f.o.b.	18,381	13,118	19,726
Petroleum and gas	15,471	9,933	16,270
Non-petroleum and gas exports	2,910	3,185	3,456
Imports of goods f.o.b.	−14,123	−14,286	−13,511
Trade balance	4,258	−1,168	6,215
Exports of services	1,192	1,793	1,350
Imports of services	−3,371	−2,761	2,908
Balance on goods and services	2,079	−2,136	4,657
Other income received	466	230	156
Other income paid	−725	−731	−431
Balance on goods, services and income	1,820	−2,637	4,382
Unrequited transfers (net)	393	497	344
Current balance	2,213	−2,140	4,726
Long-term capital (net)	−3,554	−1	−2,397
Short-term capital (net)	−1,268	2,271	−677
Net errors and omissions	−1,096	−1,702	193
Overall balance	−3,705	−1,572	−1,845

* Provisional figures.

Source: Bank Markazi Jomhouri Islami Iran.

External Trade

PRINCIPAL COMMODITIES (US $ million, year ending 20 March)

Imports c.i.f. (distribution by SITC)*	1996/97	1997/98	1998/99
Food and live animals	2,581	2,508	1,583
Cereals and cereal preparations	1,881	1,705	878
Sugar, sugar preparations and honey	335	405	23
Crude materials (inedible) except fuels	770	647	596
Mineral fuels, lubricants, etc.	377	265	186
Animal and vegetable oils and fats	602	434	654
Vegetable oils and fats	580	420	633
Chemicals	1,931	1,890	1,774
Chemical elements and compounds	571	494	458
Medicinal and pharmaceutical products	448	n.a.	n.a.
Plastic materials, etc.	385	403	413
Basic manufactures	3,704	2,720	2,520
Paper, paperboard, etc.	569	392	266
Textile yarn, fabrics, etc	304	324	310
Iron and steel	2,049	1,290	1,287
Machinery and transport equipment	4,205	5,045	6,348
Non-electric machinery	2,325	2,672	3,501
Electrical machinery, apparatus, etc.	1,184	1,444	1,521
Transport equipment	696	929	1,326
Miscellaneous manufactured articles	353	384	538
Scientific instruments, watches, etc.	217	271	380
Total (incl. others)	15,117	14,196	14,323

* Including registration fee, but excluding defence-related imports.
† Provisional figures.

1999/2000 (US $ million): Total imports c.i.f. 13,290.
Source: IMF, *Islamic Republic of Iran: Statistical Appendix* (September 2000).

Exports f.o.b.*	1997/98	1998/99	1999/2000
Agricultural and traditional goods	1,250.7	1,412.3	1,478.0
Carpets	635.7	570.1	691.2
Fruit and nuts (fresh and dried)	337.5	591.9	517.3
Pistachios	197.3	416.0	315.1
Animal skins and hides, and leather	101.3	54.0	55.5
Metal ores	45.1	12.8	36.2
Industrial manufactures	1,579.8	1,588.2	1,847.7
Chemical products	101.9	139.7	83.3
Footwear	61.6	47.1	42.7
Textile manufactures	41.0	17.8	40.9
Copper bars, sheets and wire	41.2	28.2	85.1
Domestic appliances and sanitary ware	48.3	5.6	—
Iron and steel	183.9	138.6	219.4
Hydrocarbons (gas)	152.1	183.4	150.7
Total	2,875.6	3,013.3	3,361.9

* Excluding exports of petroleum (US $ million): 19,271 in 1996/97; 15,464† in 1997/98.

Source: Bank Markazi Jomhouri Islami Iran.

PRINCIPAL TRADING PARTNERS
(US $ million, year ending 20 March)

Imports c.i.f.	1996/97	1997/98	1998/99
Argentina	798	833	632
Australia	741	522	358
Austria	172	265	267
Azerbaijan	252	n.a.	n.a.
Belgium	926	457	899
Brazil	349	294	472
Canada	449	616	311
China, People's Republic	242	n.a.	n.a.
France	437	675	556
Germany	2,100	1,854	1,660
India	231	n.a.	n.a.
Italy	675	795	1,188
Japan	844	882	1,005
Korea, Republic	445	552	687
Netherlands	268	296	362
Russia	644	704	549
Spain	252	263	410
Switzerland	812	531	326
Thailand	405	173	162
Turkey	284	289	272
United Arab Emirates	473	562	759
United Kingdom	685	681	574
Total (incl. others)	15,117	14,196	14,323

Exports f.o.b.	1996/97	1997/98	1998/99
Azerbaijan	200.0	213.4	n.a.
Belgium	28.6	236.0	177
Brazil	11.8	351.7	n.a.
China, People's Republic	73.6	543.4	350
France	721.2	683.9	445
Germany	570.2	427.5	434
Greece	1,118.5	988.9	651
Hong Kong	673.4	248.5	n.a.
India	721.8	530.9	365
Italy	1,821.9	1,630.9	1,122
Japan	3,835.4	2,787.3	2,060
Korea, Republic	1,716.4	1,280.2	648
Russia	48.9	250.0	n.a.
Singapore	585.8	694.5	514
Spain	748.2	633.7	n.a.
Sweden	7.1	220.1	n.a.
Taiwan	69.4	376.1	n.a.
Thailand	39.4	252.1	n.a.
Turkey	706.3	545.9	497
United Arab Emirates	695.4	775.4	885
United Kingdom	3,907.6	3,037.2	2,204
Total (incl. others)	22,391.0	18,380.8	13,118

Source: Bank Markazi Jomhouri Islami Iran and IMF, *Islamic Republic of Iran: Statistical Appendix* (September 2000).

Transport

RAILWAYS (traffic)

	1995	1996	1997
Passenger-km (million) . . .	7,294	7,044	6,103
Freight ton-km (million) . . .	11,865	13,638	14,400

Source: UN, *Statistical Yearbook*.

ROAD TRAFFIC (estimates, '000 motor vehicles in use)

	1994	1995	1996
Passenger cars	1,636	1,714	1,793
Lorries and vans. . . .	626	657	692
Motor-cycles and mopeds . .	2,262	2,381	2,566

Source: International Road Federation, *World Road Statistics*.

SHIPPING

Merchant Fleet (registered at 31 December)

	1996	1997	1998
Number of vessels . . .	414	417	382
Displacement ('000 grt) . .	3,566.8	3,553.0	3,347.4

Source: Lloyd's Register of Shipping, *World Fleet Statistics*.

International Sea-borne Freight Traffic
('000 metric tons)

	1994	1995	1996
Goods loaded	128,026	132,677	140,581
Crude petroleum and petroleum products	123,457	127,143	134,615
Goods unloaded	20,692	22,604	27,816
Petroleum products . .	6,949	7,240	7,855

CIVIL AVIATION (traffic on scheduled services)

	1995	1996	1997
Kilometres flown (million) . .	40	50	70
Passengers carried ('000) . .	6,291	7,610	9,804
Passenger-km (million) . .	5,634	6,634	8,852
Total ton-km (million) . .	621	708	901

Tourism

	1995	1996	1997
Tourist arrivals ('000) . . .	452.1	567.3	739.7
Tourism receipts (US $ million)	190	244	327

Source: UN, *Statistical Yearbook*.

Communications Media

	1994	1995	1996
Radio receivers ('000 in use) . .	15,550	15,580	16,600
Television receivers ('000 in use) .	4,076	4,300	4,500
Telephones ('000 main lines in use)*	4,320	5,090	5,825
Telefax stations (number in use)*	30,000	n.a.	n.a.
Mobile cellular telephones (subscribers)*	9,200	15,902	59,967
Book production:			
Titles	10,753	13,031	15,073
Copies ('000)	n.a.	87,756	87,861
Daily newspapers:			
Number	12	27	32
Average circulation ('000 copies)	1,154†	1,446	1,651

1997: Radio receivers ('000 in use) 17,000; Television receivers 4,610; Telephones ('000 main lines in use)* 6,513; Mobile cellular telephones (subscribers)* 238,942.

* Twelve months ending March following the year stated.
† UN estimate.
Sources: UNESCO, *Statistical Yearbook*; UN, *Statistical Yearbook*.
Periodicals (number): 403 in 1994; 623 in 1995.

Education

(1996/97, unless otherwise indicated)

	Insti-tutions	Teachers	Students		
			Males	Females	Total
Pre-primary . . .	3,322	6,025	99,842	95,339	195,181
Primary . . .	63,101	298,755	4,885,665	4,352,728	9,238,393
Secondary:					
General* . . .	n.a.	228,889	3,974,141	3,310,470	7,284,611
Teacher-training* . .	n.a.	538	13,605	7,605	21,210
Vocational* . .	n.a.	19,880	262,952	84,056	347,008
Higher:					
Universities, etc. . .	n.a.	28,343	237,510	129,786	367,296
Distance-learning . .	n.a.	3,380	73,615	59,320	132,935
Others	n.a.	8,304	58,782	20,057	78,839

* 1994/95 figures. Figures for all categories of secondary education in 1996/97 were: Teachers 280,309; Students 8,776,792 (males 4,711,559; females 4,065,233).
† Excluding private universities.
Source: UNESCO, *Statistical Yearbook*.

Directory

The Constitution

A draft constitution for the Islamic Republic of Iran was published on 18 June 1979. It was submitted to a 'Council of Experts', elected by popular vote on 3 August 1979, to debate the various clauses and to propose amendments. The amended Constitution was approved by a referendum on 2–3 December 1979. A further 45 amendments to the Constitution were approved by a referendum on 28 July 1989.

The Constitution states that the form of government of Iran is that of an Islamic Republic, and that the spirituality and ethics of Islam are to be the basis for political, social and economic relations. Persians, Turks, Kurds, Arabs, Balochis, Turkomans and others will enjoy completely equal rights.

The Constitution provides for a President to act as chief executive. The President is elected by universal adult suffrage for a term of four years. Legislative power is held by the Majlis (Islamic Consultative Assembly), with 290 members (effective from the 2000 election) who are similarly elected for a four-year term. Provision is made for the representation of Zoroastrians, Jews and Christians.

All legislation passed by the Islamic Consultative Assembly must be sent to the Council for the Protection of the Constitution (Article 94), which will ensure that it is in accordance with the Constitution and Islamic legislation. The Council for the Protection of the Constitution consists of six religious lawyers appointed by the Faqih (see below) and six lawyers appointed by the High Council of the Judiciary and approved by the Islamic Consultative Assembly. Articles 19–42 deal with the basic rights of individuals, and provide for equality of men and women before the law and for equal human, political, economic, social and cultural rights for both sexes.

The press is free, except in matters that are contrary to public morality or insult religious belief. The formation of religious, political and professional parties, associations and societies is free, provided they do not negate the principles of independence, freedom, sovereignty and national unity, or the basis of Islam.

The Constitution provides for a Wali Faqih (religious leader) who, in the absence of the Imam Mehdi (the hidden Twelfth Imam), carries the burden of leadership. The amendments to the Constitution that were approved in July 1989 increased the powers of the Presidency by abolishing the post of Prime Minister, formerly the Chief Executive of the Government.

The Government

WALI FAQIH (RELIGIOUS LEADER)

Ayatollah SAYED ALI KHAMENEI.

HEAD OF STATE

President: Hojatoleslam Dr SAYED MUHAMMAD KHATAMI (assumed office 3 August 1997).

First Vice-President: HASSAN IBRAHIM HABIBI.

Vice-President in charge of Executive Affairs: MUHAMMAD HASHEMI RAFSANJANI.

Vice-President in charge of Legal and Parliamentary Affairs: Hojatoleslam MUHAMMAD ALI SADUQI.

Vice-President and Head of the Iranian Atomic Energy Organization: GHOLAMREZA AGHAZADEH.

Vice-President and Head of the Organization for the Protection of the Environment: MA'SUMEH EBTEKAR.

Vice-President and Head of the Physical Education Organization: SAYED MOSTAFA HASHEMI-TABA.

Advisers to the President with the rank of Vice-President: MUHAMMAD BAQERIAN, MUHAMMAD ALI NAJAFI.

COUNCIL OF MINISTERS
(May 2001)

Minister of Foreign Affairs: KAMAL KHARRAZI.

Minister of Education: HOSSEIN MOZAFAR.

Minister of Culture and Islamic Guidance: AHMAD MASJED JAME'I.

Minister of Information: Hojatoleslam ALI YUNESI.

Minister of Commerce: MUHAMMAD SHARI'ATMADARI.

Minister of Health: MUHAMMAD FARHADI.

Minister of Posts, Telegraphs and Telephones: AHMAD MOTAMEDI.

Minister of Justice: Hojatoleslam MUHAMMAD ISMAÏL SHOUSHTARI.

Minister of Defence and Logistics: ALI SHAMKHANI.

Minister of Roads and Transport: (vacant).

Minister of Higher Education: MOSTAFA MO'IN.

Minister of Industries and Mines: ESHAQ JAHANGIRI.

Minister of Labour and Social Affairs: HOSSEIN KAMALI.

Minister of the Interior: Hojatoleslam SAYED ABDOLVAHED MUSAVI-LARI.

Minister of Agricultural Jihad: MAHMUD HOJJATI.

Minister of Housing and Urban Development: ALI ABD AL-ALIZADEH.

Minister of Energy: HABIBOLLAH BITARAF.

Minister of Oil: BIZAM NAMDAR-ZANGENEH.

Minister of Economic Affairs and Finance: HOSSEIN NAMAZI.

Minister of Co-operatives: MORTEZA HAJI.

Head of the Presidential Office: MUHAMMAD ALI ABTAHI.

Head of the Organization of Administration and Planning: MUHAMMAD REZA AREF.

MINISTRIES

All ministries are in Tehran.

Office of the President: Tehran; e-mail khatami@president.ir; internet www.president.ir.

Ministry of Agricultural Jihad: 20 Malaei Ave, Vali-e-Asr Sq, Tehran; tel. (21) 8895354; fax (21) 8904357; e-mail intaffairs@jahad.net.

Ministry of Commerce: Vali-e-Asr Ave, Tehran; tel. (21) 8893620; fax (2) 896504; e-mail irantradepoint@irtp.com; internet www.irtp.com.

Ministry of Co-operatives: 16 Bozorgmehr St, Vali-e-Asr Ave, Tehran 14169; tel. (21) 6400938; fax (21) 6417041.

Ministry of Culture and Higher Education: Ostad Nejatollahi St, Sepand St, Tehran; tel. (21) 8141; fax (21) 896395; e-mail mche@mche.or.ir; internet www.mche.or.ir.

Ministry of Culture and Islamic Guidance: Baharestan Sq., Tehran; tel. (21) 32411; fax (21) 3117535; e-mail ershad@neda.net.

Ministry of Defence and Logistics: Shahid Yousuf Kaboli St, Sayed Khandan Area, Tehran; tel. (21) 21401; fax (21) 864008; e-mail vds@isiran.com.

Ministry of Economic Affairs and Finance: Sour Israfil St, Babe Homayoon Ave, Tehran; tel. (21) 3251; fax (21) 390528.

Ministry of Education: Si-e-Tir St, Emam Khomeini Sq., Tehran; tel. (21) 32421; fax (21) 675503.

Ministry of Energy: North Palestine St, Tehran; tel. (21) 890001; fax (21) 8801995; e-mail webmaster@moe.or.ir.

Ministry of Foreign Affairs: Shahid Abd al-Hamid Mesri St, Ferdowsi Ave, Tehran; tel. (21) 3211; fax (21) 3212763; e-mail matbuat@mfa.gov.ir; internet www.mfa.gov.ir.

Ministry of Health and Medical Education: POB 15655-415, 371 Shariati Ave, Averezi Station, Tehran 16139; tel. (21) 767631; fax (21) 7676733; e-mail webmaster@damavand.mohem.gov.ir; internet www.mohem.gov.ir.

Ministry of Housing and Urban Development: Shahid Khoddami St, Vanak Sq., Tehran; tel. (21) 877711; fax (21) 8776634; e-mail hud@icic.gov.ir.

Ministry of Industries and Mines: Tehran.

Ministry of Information: POB 16765-1947, Tehran; tel. (21) 233031; fax (21) 23305.

Ministry of the Interior: Jahad Sq., Fatemi St, Tehran; tel. (21) 61311; fax (21) 650912.

Ministry of Justice: Panzdah-e-Khordad Sq., Tehran; tel. (21) 8191; fax (21) 3113143.

Ministry of Labour and Social Affairs: Azadi Ave, Tehran; tel. (21) 930050; fax (21) 931066.

Ministry of Oil: Hafez St, Taleghani Ave, Tehran; tel. (21) 6152738; fax (21) 6152823; e-mail webmaster@nioc.org; internet www.nioc.org.

Ministry of Posts, Telegraphs and Telephones: POB 11365-931, Dr Shariati Ave, Tehran 16314; tel. (21) 864796; fax (21) 866023; e-mail webmaster@195.146.32.12; internet www.iranpac.net.ir.

Ministry of Roads and Transport: 49 Taleghani Ave, Spahbod Gharani St, Tehran; tel. (21) 6460583; fax (21) 6407991.

President and Legislature

PRESIDENT

Election, 23 May 1997

Candidates	Votes	%
SAYED MUHAMMAD KHATAMI	20,088,338	69.1
ALI AKBAR NATEQ NOURI	7,233,568	24.9
SAYED REZA ZAVAREI	771,463	2.7
MUHAMMAD MUHAMMADI REYSHAHRI	742,599	2.6
Spoilt votes	240,994	0.8
Total	29,076,962	100.0

MAJLIS-E-SHURA E ISLAMI—ISLAMIC CONSULTATIVE ASSEMBLY

A first round of voting in elections to the sixth Majlis took place on 18 February 2000; and a second, for 66 undecided seats, on 5 May. Successful candidates in both rounds of voting were, for the most part, associated with either the 'conservative' tendency or its 'reformist' counterpart that are generally held to characterize Iranian political life. However, a significant number of independent candidates, who might ally themselves with either of the two principal tendencies, also contested the elections successfully. The sixth Majlis was notable as the first in which 'reformist' or 'liberal' candidates were estimated to have gained a working majority.

Speaker: Hojatoleslam MAHDI KARRUBI.

First Deputy Speaker: MUHAMMAD REZA KHATAMI.

Second Deputy Speaker: BEZHAD NABAVI.

SHURA-YE ALI-YE AMNIYYAT-E MELLI—SUPREME COUNCIL FOR NATIONAL SECURITY

Formed in July 1989 to co-ordinate defence and national security policies, the political programme and intelligence reports, and social, cultural and economic activities related to defence and security. The Council is chaired by the President and includes two representatives of the Wali Faqih, the Head of the Judiciary, the Speaker of the Majlis, the Chief of Staff, the General Command of the Armed Forces, the Minister of Foreign Affairs, the Minister of the Interior, the Minister of Information and the Head of the Plan and Budget Organization.

MAJLIS-E KHOBREGAN—COUNCIL OF EXPERTS

Elections were held on 10 December 1982 to appoint a Council of Experts which was to choose an eventual successor to the Wali Faqih (then Ayatollah Khomeini) after his death. The Constitution provides for a three- or five-man body to assume the leadership of the country if there is no recognized successor on the death of the Wali Faqih. The Council comprises 86 clerics. Elections to a third term of the Council were held on 23 October 1998.

Speaker: Ayatollah ALI MESHKINI.

First Deputy Speaker: Hojatoleslam ALI AKBAR HASHEMI RAFSANJANI.

Second Deputy Speaker: Ayatollah IBRAHIM AMINI NAJAFABADI.

Secretaries: Hojatoleslam HASSAN TAHERI-KHORRAMABADI, Ayatollah QORBANALI DORRI NAJAFABADI.

SHURA-E-NIGAHBAN—COUNCIL OF GUARDIANS

The Council of Guardians, composed of six qualified Muslim jurists appointed by Ayatollah Khomeini and six lay Muslim lawyers, appointed by the Majlis from among candidates nominated by the Head of the Judiciary, was established in 1980 to supervise elections and to examine legislation adopted by the Majlis, ensuring that it accords with the Constitution and with Islamic precepts.

Chairman: Ayatollah MUHAMMAD MUHAMMADI GUILANI.

SHURA-YE TASHKHIS-E MASLAHAT-E NEZAM— COMMITTEE TO DETERMINE THE EXPEDIENCY OF THE ISLAMIC ORDER

Formed in February 1988, by order of Ayatollah Khomeini, to arbitrate on legal and theological questions in legislation passed by the Majlis, in the event of a dispute between the latter and the supervisory Council of Guardians. Its permanent members, defined in March 1997, are Heads of the Legislative, Judiciary and Executive Powers, the jurist members of the Council of Guardians and the Minister or head of organization concerned with the pertinent arbitration.

Chairman: Hojatoleslam ALI AKBAR HASHEMI RAFSANJANI.

HEY'AT-E PEYGIRI-YE QANUN ASASI VA NEZARAT BAR AN—COMMITTEE FOR ENSURING AND SUPERVISING THE IMPLEMENTATION OF THE CONSTITUTION

Formed by President Khatami in November 1997; members are appointed for a four-year term.

Members: Dr GUDARZ EFTEKHAR-JAHROMI; MUHAMMAD ISMAÏL SHOUSHTARI; SAYED ABDOLVAHED MUSAVI-LARI; Dr HOSSEIN MEHRPUR; Dr MUHAMMAD HOSSEIN HASHEMI.

Political Organizations

Numerous political organizations were registered in the late 1990s, following the election of President Khatami, among them several political tendencies that had formed within the Majlis. The following organizations appeared to have achieved considerable success at elections to the sixth Majlis in early 2000:

Chekad-e Azadandishan (Freethinkers' Front).

Hezb-e E'tedal va Towse'eh (Moderation and Development Party).

Hezb-e Hambastegi-ye Iran-e Islami (Islamic Iran Solidarity Party).

Hezb-e Kargozaran-e Sazandegi (Servants of Construction Party): Sec.-Gen. GHOLAMHOSSEIN KARBASCHI.

Jam'iyat-e Isargaran (Society of Self-sacrificing Devotees).

Jebbeh-ye Masharekat-e Iran-e Islami (Islamic Iran Participation Front): Leader (vacant).

Majma'-e Niruha-ye Khat-e Imam (Assembly of the Followers of the Imam's Line).

Most of the following organizations are opposed to the Iranian Government:

Anzar-e Hezbollah: f. 1995; seeks to gain access to the political process for religious militants.

Democratic Party of Iranian Kurdistan: e-mail pdkiran@club-internet.fr; internet www.pdk-iran.org; f. 1945; seeks autonomy for Kurdish area; mem. of the National Council of Resistance; 54,000 mems; Sec.-Gen. MUSTAPHA HASSANZADEH.

Fedayin-e-Khalq (Warriors of the People): urban Marxist guerrillas; Spokesman FARRAKH NEGAHDAR.

Fraksion-e Hezbollah: f. 1996 by deputies in the Majlis who had contested the 1996 legislative elections as a loose coalition known as the Society of Combatant Clergy; Leader ALI AKBAR HOSSAINI.

Hezb-e-Komunist Iran (Communist Party of Iran): e-mail cpi@cpiran.org; internet www.cpiran.org; f. 1979 by dissident mems of Tudeh Party; Sec.-Gen. 'AZARYUN'.

Komala: e-mail komala@cpiran.org; internet www.cpiran.org/En/Komala; f. 1969; Kurdish wing of the Communist Party of Iran; Marxist-Leninist; First Sec. IBRAHIM ALIZADEH.

Mujahidin-e-Khalq (Holy Warriors of the People): Islamic guerrilla group; since June 1987 comprising the National Liberation Army; mem. of the National Council of Resistance; Leaders MASSOUD RAJAVI and MARYAM RAJAVI (in Baghdad, 1986–).

National Democratic Front: e-mail ndfi@azadi-iran.org; internet www.azadi-iran.org; f. March 1979; Leader HEDAYATOLLAH MATINE-DAFTARI (in Paris, January 1982–).

National Front (Union of National Front Forces): comprises Iran Nationalist Party, Iranian Party, and Society of Iranian Students; Leader Dr KARIM SANJABI (in Paris, August 1978–).

Nehzat-Azadi (Liberation Movement of Iran): f. 1961; emphasis on basic human rights as defined by Islam; Gen. Sec. Dr IBRAHIM YAZDI; Principal Officers Prof. SAHABI, S. SADR, Dr SADR, Eng. SABAGHIAN, Eng. TAVASSOLI.

Pan-Iranist Party: extreme right-wing; calls for a Greater Persia; Leader Dr MOHSEN PEZESHKPOUR.

Sazmane Peykar dar Rahe Azadieh Tabaqe Kargar (Organization Struggling for the Freedom of the Working Class): Marxist-Leninist.

Tudeh Party (Communist): e-mail mardom@tudehpartyiran.org; internet www.tudehpartyiran.org; f. 1941; declared illegal 1949; came into open 1979, banned again April 1983; First Sec. Cen. Cttee ALI KHAVARI.

The National Council of Resistance (NCR) was formed in Paris in October 1981 by former President ABOLHASAN BANI-SADR and the Council's current leader, MASSOUD RAJAVI, the leader of the Mujahidin-e-Khalq in Iran. In 1984 the Council comprised 15 opposition groups, operating either clandestinely in Iran or from exile abroad. BANI-SADR left the Council in 1984 because of his objection to RAJAVI's growing links with the Iraqi Government. The French Government asked RAJAVI to leave Paris in June 1986 and he is now based in Baghdad, Iraq. On 20 June 1987 RAJAVI, Secretary of the NCR, announced the formation of a National Liberation Army

(10,000–15,000-strong) as the military wing of the Mujahidin-e-Khalq. There is also a National Movement of Iranian Resistance, based in Paris. Dissident members of the Tudeh Party founded the Democratic Party of the Iranian People in Paris in February 1988.

Diplomatic Representation

EMBASSIES IN IRAN

Afghanistan: Dr Beheshi Ave, Corner of 4th St, Pakistan St, Tehran; tel. (21) 8735600; Ambassador: MOHAMMAD KHEIRKHAH.

Albania: Tehran; Ambassador: GILANI SHEHU.

Angola: Tehran; Ambassador: MANUEL BERNARDO DE SOUSA.

Argentina: 3rd and 4th Floor, 7 Argentina Sq., Tehran; tel. (21) 8718294; fax (21) 8712583; Chargé d'affaires: EDUARDO LIONEL DE'AUP.

Armenia: 1 Ostad Shahriar St, Razi St, Jomhouri Islami Ave, Tehran 11337; tel. (21) 674833; fax (21) 670657; Ambassador: YAHAN BAIBOURDIAN.

Australia: POB 15875-4334, No. 13, 23rd St, Shahid Khaled al-Islambuli Ave, Tehran 15138; tel. (21) 8724456; fax (21) 8720484; Ambassador: STUART HUME.

Austria: 3rd Floor, 78 Argentine Sq., Tehran; tel. (21) 8710753; fax (21) 8710778; Ambassador: Dr HELMUTH WERNER EHRLICH.

Azerbaijan: Shahid Lavasani Ave, Shahid Salekhi Ave, 30 Vatanpur St, Tehran; tel. (21) 2280063; fax (21) 2284929; e-mail azaremb@www.dci.co.ir; Ambassador: ABBASALI K. HASANOV.

Bahrain: 248 Africa Ave, Cnr of Zoubin Alley, Tehran; tel. (21) 2263381; fax (21) 2269112; Chargé d'affaires: RAMSEY JALAL.

Bangladesh: POB 11365-3711, Gandhi Ave, 5th St, Building No. 14, Tehran; tel. (21) 8772979; fax (21) 8778295; e-mail banglaemb@neda.net; Ambassador: TUFAIL K. HAIDER.

Belarus: No. 18, Ghem-Magham Farahani Ave, 6th St, Ground Floor, Tehran; tel. (21) 8731601.

Belgium: POB 11365-115, 3 Babak Alley, Shabdiz St, Shahid Fayyaz Bakhsh Ave, Tehran 19659; tel. (21) 2009507; Ambassador: GUILLAUME METTEN.

Bosnia and Herzegovina: No. 485, Aban Alley, 4th St, Iran Zamin Ave, Shahrak-e-Ghods, Tehran; tel. (21) 8092728.

Brazil: Vanak Sq., 58 Vanak Ave, Tehran 19964; tel. (21) 8035175; fax (21) 8083348; e-mail emb_brazil@yahoo.com; Ambassador: CLAUDIO LUIZ DOS SANTOS ROCHA.

Brunei: No. 41–43, Moshiri St, Giti Blvd, Golestan Blvd, Africa Ave, Tehran; tel. (21) 2043918.

Bulgaria: POB 11365-7451, Vali-e-Asr Ave, Dr Abbaspour Ave, Nezami-e-Ganjavi St, No. 82, Tehran; tel. (21) 8775662; Ambassador: STEFAN POLENDAKOV.

Canada: POB 11365-4647, 57 Shahid Sarafraz St, Ostad Motahhari Ave; tel. (21) 8732623; fax 8733202; Ambassador: MICHEL DE SALABERRY.

Chad: Tehran.

China, People's Republic: 13 Narenjestan 7th, Pasdaran Ave, Tehran; tel. (21) 2291240; Ambassador: SUN BIGAN.

Colombia: 5 Faryar St, Hedayat St, Darrous, Tehran; tel. (21) 2558957; Ambassador: RAFAEL CANAL SANDOVAL.

Congo, Democratic Republic: Tehran; tel. (21) 222190; Chargé d'affaires: N'DJATE ESELE SASA.

Croatia: No. 25, 1st Behestan, Pasdaran St, Tehran; tel. (21) 2589923.

Cuba: 10 Taban Alley, Naft-e-Jonobi, Mirdamad, Tehran; tel. (21) 2257809; Ambassador: ENRIQUE TRUJILLO RAPALLO.

Cyprus: 55 Shahid Sartip Reza Saeidi, Farmanieh Ave, Tehran; tel. (21) 2299795; fax (21) 2299794; Ambassador: GEORGIOS VIRYDES.

Czech Republic: POB 11365-4457, Mirza-ye Shirazi Ave, Ali Mirza Hassani St, No. 15, Tehran; tel. (21) 8716720; fax (21) 8717858; Chargé d'affaires: Eng. JIŘÍ DOLEŽAL.

Denmark: POB 19395-5358, 18 Dashti Ave, Tehran 19148; tel. (21) 261363; fax (21) 2030007; e-mail ambadane.teheran@inet.uni2.dk; internet www.inet.uni2.dk/home/ambadane.teheran; Ambassador: HUGO ØESTERGAARD-ANDERSEN.

Ethiopia: Tehran; Ambassador: MOHAMMED HASAN KAHIM.

Finland: Cnr of Nilou St, Vanaq Sq., Vali-e-Asr Ave, Tehran; tel. (21) 8889151; fax (21) 2210948; Ambassador: A. KOISTINEN.

France: 85 Neauphle-le-Château Ave, Tehran; tel. (21) 6706005; Ambassador: PHILIPPE DE SUREMAIN.

Gambia: Tehran; Ambassador: OMAR JAH.

Georgia: POB 19575-379, Elahiyeh, Tehran; tel. (21) 2211470; fax (21) 2206848; e-mail georgia@apadana.com; Ambassador: JEMSHID GIUNASHVILI.

Germany: POB 11365-179, 320–324 Ferdowsi Ave, Tehran; tel. (21) 3114111; fax (21) 3119883; Ambassador: Dr RÜDIGER REYELS.

Ghana: Tehran; Ambassador: Mr AL-HASSAN.

Greece: POB 11365-8151, Africa Ave, Esfandiar St No. 43, Tehran 19686; tel. (21) 2050533; Ambassador: DIMITRI TSIKOURIS.

Guinea: POB 11365-4716, Ave Shariati, Ave Malek, No. 10, Tehran; tel. (21) 7535744; fax (21) 7535743; Ambassador: ALPHA IBRAHIMA SOW.

Holy See: Apostolic Nunciature, POB 11365-178, Razi Ave, No. 97, Neauphle-le-Château Ave, Tehran; tel. (21) 6403574; fax (21) 6419442; e-mail apnun-thr@ravan.com; Apostolic Nuncio: Most Rev. ANGELO MOTTOLA, Titular Archbishop of Cercina.

Hungary: POB 6363-19395, Darrous, Hedayat Sq, Shadloo St, No. 15, Tehran; tel. (21) 2550460; fax (21) 2550503; Ambassador: Dr ISTVÁN VÁSÁRY.

India: POB 15875-4118, 46 Mir-Emad St, Cnr of 9th St, Dr Behesti Ave, Tehran; tel. (21) 855102; fax (21) 855973; Ambassador: S. K. ARORA.

Indonesia: POB 11365-4564, Ghaem Magham Farahani Ave, No. 210, Tehran; tel. (21) 8716865; Ambassador: BAMBANG SUDARSONO.

Iraq: Karamian Alley, No. 17, Pol-e-Roomi, Dr Shariati Ave, Tehran; tel. (21) 2218386; Chargé d'affaires: ABD AS-SATTAR AR-RAWI.

Ireland: Farmaniyeh Ave, North Kamraniyeh St, Bonbast Nahid St, No. 8, Tehran 19369; tel. (21) 2297918; fax (21) 2286933; Ambassador: THOMAS D. LYONS.

Italy: POB 11365-7863, 81 Neauphle-le-Château Ave, Tehran; tel. (21) 6496955; fax (21) 6496961; Ambassador: LUDOVICO ORTONA.

Japan: POB 11365-814, Bucharest Ave, Corner of 5th St, Tehran; tel. (21) 8713396; Ambassador: UKERU MAGOSAKI.

Jordan: No. 147, Corner of 4th Alley, Mahestan St, Phase 1, Sharak-e-Ghods, Tehran; tel. (21) 8082466; fax (21) 2007160; Ambassador NUH ALI SALMAN.

Kazakhstan: Darrus, Hedayat St, Masjed, No. 4, Tehran; tel (21) 2565933; fax (21) 2546400; e-mail kazembir@apadana.com; Ambassador: VYACHESLAV GIZZATOV.

Kenya: 60 Hormoz Satari St, Africa Ave, Tehran; tel. (21) 8790795; fax (21) 2270160; Ambassador: SALIM JUMA.

Korea, Democratic People's Republic: 349 Vahid Dastjerdi Ave, Africa Ave, Tehran; tel. (21) 8783341; Ambassador: KIM JONG NAM.

Korea, Republic: No. 37, Ahmad Ghasir Ave, Tehran; tel. (21) 8751125; fax (21) 8737917; Ambassador: SHIN JANG-BUM.

Kuwait: No. 323/2, Vahid Dastjerdi Ave, Tehran; tel. (21) 8785997; Ambassador: ABDULLAH ABD AL-AZIZ AD-DUWAYKH.

Kyrgyzstan: No. 12, Norinjistan 5th, Pasdaran, Tehran; tel. (21) 2281720.

Laos: Tehran; Ambassador: CHANPHENG SIHAPHOM.

Lebanon: No. 31, Kalantari St, Ghantari Ave, Tehran; tel. (21) 8908451; fax (21) 8907345; Ambassador: ADNAN MANSOUR.

Libya: Ostad Motahhari Ave, No. 163, Tehran; tel. (21) 8742815; Sec.-Gen. Committee of People's Bureau: MAHDI AL-MABIRASH.

Malaysia: 72 Fereshteh Ave, Tehran; tel. (21) 2009275; fax (21) 2009143; Ambassador: MUHAMMAD KHALIS.

Mexico: POB 15875-4636, No. 41, Golfam St, Africa Expressway, Tehran; tel. (21) 2057586; fax (21) 2225375; Ambassador: ANTONIO DUEÑAS PULIDO.

Mongolia: Tehran; Ambassador: L. KHASHOAT.

Morocco: No. 47, Armachan Sharghi St, Africa Ave, Tehran; tel. (21) 2059707; fax (21) 2051872; Ambassador: JAMAL EDDINE GHAZI.

Mozambique: Tehran; Ambassador: MURADE ISAC MIGUIGY MURARGY.

Myanmar: Tehran; Ambassador: U SAW HLAING.

Namibia: Tehran; Ambassador: MWAILEPENI T. P. SHITILIFA.

Nepal: Tehran; Ambassador: Gen. ARJUN NARSING RONA.

Netherlands: POB 11365-138, Darrous, Shahrzad Blvd, Kamasaie St, 1st East Lane, No. 33, Tehran 19498; tel. (21) 2567005; fax (21) 2566990; e-mail nlambiran@dpi.net.ir; Ambassador: R. A. MOLLINGER.

New Zealand: POB 15875-4313, 34 North Golestan Complex, Cnr of 2nd Park Alley and Sosan St, Aghdasiyeh St, Niavaran, Tehran; tel. (21) 2800289; fax (21) 2831673; e-mail <newzealand@mavara.com; Ambassador: WARWICK ALEXANDER HAWKER.

Niger: Tehran.

Nigeria: No. 11, 31st St, Shahid Khalid Islambuli Ave, Tehran; tel. (21) 8774936; Ambassador: ADO SANUSI.

Norway: POB 19395-5398, Pasdaran Ave, Kouhestan 8, Ekhtiarieh Shomali 412, Tehran; tel. (21) 2291333; fax (21) 2292776; Ambassador: SVEIN AASS.

Oman: No. 12, Tandis Alley, Africa Ave, Tehran; tel. (21) 2056831; Chargé d'affaires a.i.: RASHID BIN MUBARAK BIN RASHID AL-ODWALI.

Pakistan: Dr Fatemi Ave, Jamshidabad Shomali, Mashal St, No. 1, Tehran; tel. (21) 934332; Ambassador: JAVID HUSSEIN.

Philippines: No. 49, Golazin St, Africa Ave, Tehran; tel. (21) 2056196; fax (21) 2046239; Ambassador ERNESTO V. LLAMAS.

Poland: Africa Ave, Piruz St, No. 1/3, Tehran; tel. (21) 8787262; Ambassador: WITOLD WASZCZYKOWSKI.

Portugal: No. 13, Rouzbeh Alley, Darrous, Hedayat St, Tehran; tel. (21) 2543237; fax (21) 8777834; Ambassador: Dr MANUEL MARCELO CURTO.

Qatar: Africa Ave, Golazin Ave, Parke Davar, No. 4, Tehran; tel. (21) 2051255; Ambassador: ALI ABDULLAH ZAID AL-MAHMOOD.

Romania: Fakhrabad Ave 12, Baharestan Ave, Tehran; tel. (21) 7509309; fax (21) 7509841; Ambassador: NICOLAE STAN.

Russia: 39 Neauphle-le-Château Ave, Tehran; tel. (21) 6701161; Ambassador: KONSTANTIN SHUVALOV.

Saudi Arabia: No. 1, Niloufar, Boustan, Pasdaran Ave, Tehran; tel. (21) 2050081; fax (21) 2050083; Ambassador: JAMIL BIN ABDULLAH AL-JISHI.

Senegal: No. 7, Piroze Sharghi St, Africa Ave, Tehran; tel. (21) 8783596.

Sierra Leone: No. 10, Malek St, Off Dr Shariati Ave, Tehran; tel. (21) 7502819.

Slovakia: POB 11365-4451, No. 24, Babak Markazi St, Africa Ave, Tehran; tel. (21) 8791058; fax (21) 2271057; Chargé d'affaires a.i.: ALEXANDER BAJKAI.

Slovenia: No. 10, 7th St, Khalid Islamboli Ave, Tehran; tel. (21) 8716873.

South Africa: POB 11365-7476, 5 Yekta St, Vali-e-Asr Ave, Tehran; tel. (21) 2702866; fax (21) 2716191; e-mail saemb@irost.com; Ambassador: MZOLISI MABUDE.

Spain: 76 Sarv St, Africa Ave, Tehran; tel. (21) 8714575; fax (21) 8724581; Ambassador: LEOPOLDO STAMPA PIÑEIRO.

Sri Lanka: 6 Arash St, Africa Ave, Tehran; tel. (21) 2053902; fax (21) 2052688; Chargé d'affaires a.i.: N. KARUNADASA.

Sudan: No. 39, Babak B'ahrami Alley, Zafar St, Africa Ave, Tehran; tel. (21) 8781183; fax (21) 295008; Ambassador: Dr ABDEL RAHANA MOHAMMED SAID.

Sweden: POB 19575-458, 2 Nastaran St, Pasdaran Ave, Tehran; tel. (21) 2296802; fax (21) 2286021; Ambassador: MATS MARLING.

Switzerland: POB 19395-4683, 13/1 Boustan Ave, Elahieh, 19649 Tehran; tel. (21) 268227; fax 269448; Ambassador: TIM GULDIMANN.

Syria: 19 Iraj St, Africa Ave, Tehran; tel. (21) 2059031; Ambassador: AHMAD AL-HASSAN.

Tajikistan: Tehran.

Tanzania: Tehran.

Thailand: POB 11495-111, Baharestan Ave, Parc Amin ed-Doleh, No. 4, Tehran; tel. (21) 7531433; fax (21) 7532022; Ambassador: MAHADI WIMANA.

Tunisia: No. 12, Shahid Dr Lavasani, Tehran; tel. (21) 2704161; Ambassador: Dr NOUREDDINE AL-HAMDANI.

Turkey: Ferdowsi Ave, No. 314, Tehran; tel. (21) 3115299; fax (21) 3117928; Ambassador: TURAN MORALI.

Turkmenistan: No. 39, 5th Golestan St, Pasdaran Ave, Tehran; tel. (21) 2542178; Ambassador: MURAT NAZAROV.

Ukraine: 101 Vanaq Sq, Tehran 487; tel. (21) 8005650; fax (21) 8007130; Chargé d'affaires: IVAN G. MAYDAN.

United Arab Emirates: No. 355, Vahid Dastjerdi Ave, Vali-e-Asr Ave, Tehran; tel. (21) 8781333; Ambassador: AHMAD MUHAMMAD BORHEIMAH.

United Kingdom: POB 11365-4474, 143 Ferdowsi Ave, Tehran 11344; tel. (21) 6705011; fax (21) 6708021; e-mail britemb@neda.net; Ambassador: NICHOLAS W. BROWNE.

Uruguay: 45 Shabnam Alley, Atefi Shargi St, Africa Ave, Tehran; tel. (21) 2052030; Ambassador: JOAQUIN PIRIZ JORGE.

Uzbekistan: No. 6, Nastaran Alley, Boostan St, Pasdaran Ave; tel. (21) 2299158.

Venezuela: POB 15875-4354, No. 26, Tandis St, Africa Ave, Tehran; tel. (21) 8715185; fax (21) 622840; Ambassador: Dr HERNÁN CALCU-RIAN.

Viet Nam: No. 180, Dr Lavasani St, Pasdaran Ave, Tehran; tel. (21) 2293530; Ambassador: VUXNAN ANG.

Yemen: No. 17, Giti Blvd, Golestan Blvd, Africa Ave, Tehran; tel. (21) 2048619; Chargé d'affaires a.i.: Dr AHMAD MUHAMMAD ALI ABDULLAH.

Yugoslavia: POB 11365-118, Vali-e-Asr Ave, Fereshteh Ave, Bossni Alley, No. 12, 19659 Tehran; tel. (21) 2044126; fax (21) 2044978; Chargé d'affaires: STOJAN GLIGORIĆ.

Judicial System

In August 1982 the Supreme Court revoked all laws dating from the previous regime which did not conform with Islam. In October 1982 all courts set up prior to the Islamic Revolution were abolished. In June 1987 Ayatollah Khomeini ordered the creation of clerical courts to try members of the clergy opposed to government policy. A new system of *qisas* (retribution) was established, placing the emphasis on speedy justice. Islamic codes of correction were introduced in 1983, including the dismembering of a hand for theft, flogging for fornication and violations of the strict code of dress for women, and stoning for adultery. In 1984 there was a total of 2,200 judges. The Supreme Court has 16 branches.

Head of the Judiciary: Ayatollah SAYED MAHMOUD HASHEMI SHAH-RUDI.

SUPREME COURT

Chief Justice: Hojatoleslam MUHAMMAD MUHAMMADI GUILANI.

Prosecutor-General: Hojatoleslam MORTEZA MOQTADAI.

Religion

According to the 1979 constitution, the official religion is Islam of the Ja'fari sect (Shi'ite), but other Islamic sects, including Zeydi, Hanafi, Maleki, Shafe'i and Hanbali, are valid and will be respected. Zoroastrians, Jews and Christians will be recognized as official religious minorities. According to the 1976 census, there were then 310,000 Christians (mainly Armenian), 80,000 Jews and 30,000 Zoroastrians.

ISLAM

The great majority of the Iranian people are Shi'a Muslims, but there is a minority of Sunni Muslims. Persians and Azerbaijanis are mainly Shi'i, while the other ethnic groups are mainly Sunni.

CHRISTIANITY
The Roman Catholic Church

At 31 December 1998 there were an estimated 11,550 adherents in Iran, comprising 5,350 of the Chaldean Rite, 2,200 of the Armenian Rite and 4,000 of the Latin Rite.

Armenian Rite

Bishop of Esfahan: (vacant), Armenian Catholic Bishopric, Khiaban Ghazzali 22, Tehran; tel. (21) 677204; fax (21) 8715191.

Chaldean Rite

Archbishop of Ahwaz: HANNA ZORA, Archbishop's House, POB 61956, Naderi St, Ahwaz; tel. (61) 24890.

Archbishop of Tehran: RAMZI GARMOU, Archevêché, Forsat Ave 91, Tehran 15819; tel. (21) 8823549.

Archbishop of Urmia (Rezayeh) and Bishop of Salmas (Shahpour): THOMAS MERAM, Khalifagari Kaldani Katholiq, POB 338, Orumiyeh 57135; tel. (441) 22739.

Latin Rite

Archbishop of Esfahan: IGNAZIO BEDINI, Consolata Church, POB 11365-445, 75 Neauphle-le-Château Ave, Tehran; tel. (21) 673210; fax (21) 6494749.

The Anglican Communion

Anglicans in Iran are adherents of the Episcopal Church in Jerusalem and the Middle East, formally inaugurated in January 1976. The Rt Rev. HASSAN DEHQANI-TAFTI, the Bishop in Iran from 1961 to 1990, was President-Bishop of the Church from 1976 to 1986. He was succeeded by the Bishop of Jerusalem during 1986–96 and the Bishop of Egypt from 1996 to 2000.

Bishop in Iran and President of the Episcopal Church in Jerusalem and the Middle East: Rt Rev. IRAJ KALIMI MOTTAHEDEH, St Luke's Church, POB 81465-135, Abbas-abad Rd, Esfahan; tel. (31) 231435; diocese founded 1912.

Presbyterian Church

Synod of the Evangelical (Presbyterian) Church in Iran: Assyrian Evangelical Church, Khiaban-i Hanifnejad, Khiaban-i Aramanch, Tehran; Moderator Rev. ADEL NAKHOSTEEN.

ZOROASTRIANS

There are about 30,000 Zoroastrians, a remnant of a once widespread sect. Their religious leader is MOUBAD.

OTHER COMMUNITIES

Communities of Armenians, and somewhat smaller numbers of Jews (an estimated 30,000 in 1986), Assyrians, Greek Orthodox

Christians, Uniates and Latin Christians are also found as officially recognized faiths. The Bahá'í faith, which originated in Iran, has about 300,000 Iranian adherents, although at least 10,000 are believed to have fled since 1979 in order to escape persecution. The Government banned all Bahá'í institutions in August 1983.

The Press

Tehran dominates the media, as many of the daily papers are published there, and the bi-weekly, weekly and less frequent publications in the provinces generally depend on the major metropolitan dailies as a source of news. A press law announced in August 1979 required all newspapers and magazines to be licensed and imposed penalties of imprisonment for insulting senior religious figures. Offences against the Act will be tried in the criminal courts. Under the Constitution the press is free, except in matters that are contrary to public morality, insult religious belief or slander the honour and reputation of individuals. Since the late 1990s the press has been the target of an intense judicial campaign to curb its freedoms.

PRINCIPAL DAILIES

Abrar (Rightly Guided): 26 Shahid Denesh Kian Alley, Below Zartasht St, Vali-e-Asr Ave, Tehran; tel. (21) 8848270; fax (21) 8849200; f. 1985 after closure of *Azadegan* by order of the Prosecutor-General; morning; Farsi; circ. 75,000.

Aftab-e-Yazd (Sun of Yazd): Tehran; f. 2000; pro-reform; Editor MOJTABA VAHEDI; circ. 100,000.

Alik: POB 11365-953, Jomhoori Islami Ave, Alik Alley, Tehran 11357; tel. (21) 676671; f. 1931; afternoon; political and literary; Armenian; Propr A. AJEMIAN; circ. 3,400.

Bahari Iran: Khayaban Khayham, Shiraz; tel. (71) 33738.

Ettela'at (Information): Ettela'at Bldg, Mirdamad Ave, South Naft St, Tehran 15499; tel. (21) 29999; fax (21) 2258022; internet www.ettela'at.com; f. 1925; evening; Farsi; political and literary; operates under the direct supervision of Wilayat-e-Faqih (religious jurisprudence); Editor S. M. DOAEI; circ. 500,000.

Fath: Tehran; pro-reform; publication suspended in 2000.

Hayat-e No (New Life): Tehran; f. 2000; pro-reform; Man. Dir SAYED HADI KHAMENEI.

Iran News: 41 Lida St, Vali-e-Asr Ave, North Vanak Sq, Tehran; tel. (21) 8880231; fax (21) 8786475; e-mail irannews@www.dci.co.ir; English.

Kayhan (Universe): Ferdowsi Ave, Tehran; tel. (21) 3110251; e-mail kayhan@ofogh.net; internet www.kayhannews.com; f. 1941; evening; Farsi; political; also publishes *Kayhan International* (f. 1959; daily; English; Editor HAMID NAJAFI), *Kayhan Arabic* (f. 1980; daily; Arabic), *Kayhan Persian* (f. 1942; daily; Persian), *Kayhan Havaie* (f. 1950; weekly for Iranians abroad; Farsi), *Zan-e-Ruz* (Woman Today; f. 1964; weekly; Farsi), *Kayhan Varzeshi* (World of Sport; f. 1955; weekly; Farsi), *Kayhan Bacheha* (Children's World; f. 1956; weekly; Farsi), *Kayhan Farhangi* (World of Culture; f. 1984; monthly; Farsi); owned and managed by Mostazafin Foundation from October 1979 until 1 January 1987, when it was placed under the direct supervision of Wilayat-e-Faqih (religious jurisprudence); Chief Editor HOSSEIN SHARIATMADARI; circ. 350,000.

Khorassan: Meshed; Head Office: Khorassan Daily Newspapers, 14 Zohre St, Mobarezan Ave, Tehran; f. 1948; Propr MUHAMMAD SADEGH TEHERANIAN; circ. 40,000.

Khordad: Tehran; pro-reform; publication suspended in 1999.

Neshat: Tehran; pro-reform; publication suspended in 1999.

Rahnejat: Darvazeh Dowlat, Isfahan; political and social; Propr N. RAHNEJAT.

Ressallat (The Message): Tehran; tel. (21) 8902642; fax (21) 8900587; organ of right-wing group of the same name; political, economic, social; Propr Ressallat Foundation; Man. Dir MORTEZA NABAVI; circ. 100,000.

Salam: 2 Shahid Reza Nayebi Alley, South Felestin St, Tehran; tel. (21) 6495831; fax (21) 6495835; f. 1991; Farsi; political, cultural, economic, social; Editor MUHAMMAD MUSAVI KHOIENI. (Closure ordered July 1999.)

Sobh Emruz: Tehran; pro-reform; publication suspended in 2000; Man. SAYED HAJJARIAN.

Tehran Times: 32 Bimeh Alley, Nejatullahi Ave, Tehran 15998; tel. (21) 8810293; fax (21) 8808214; f. 1979; independent; English; Man. Dir ABBAS SALIMI NAMIN.

PRINCIPAL PERIODICALS

Acta Medica Iranica: Faculty of Medicine, Tehran Medical Sciences Univ., Poursina St, Tehran 14-174; tel. (21) 6112743; fax (21)

6404377; f. 1960; quarterly; English; Editors-in-Chief A. R. DEHPOUR, M. SAMINI; circ. 2,000.

Akhbar-e-Pezeshki: 86 Ghaem Magham Farahani Ave, Tehran; weekly; medical; Propr Dr T. FORUZIN.

Ashur: Ostad Motahhari Ave, 11-21 Kuhe Nour Ave, Tehran; tel. (21) 622117; f. 1969; Assyrian; monthly; Founder and Editor Dr W. BET-MANSOUR; circ. 8,000.

Auditor: 77 Ferdowsi Ave North, Tehran; quarterly; financial and managerial studies.

Ayandeh: POB 19575-583, Niyavaran, Tehran; tel. (21) 283254; fax (21) 6406426; monthly; Iranian literary, historical and book review journal; Editor Prof. IRAJ AFSHAR.

Bulletin of the National Film Archive of Iran: POB 5158, Baharestan Sq., Tehran 11365; tel. 311242. 1989; English periodical; Editor M. H. KHOSHNEVIS.

Daneshmand: POB 15875-3649, Tehran; tel. (21) 8741323; f. 1963; monthly; scientific and technical magazine; Editor-in-Chief A. R. KARAMI.

Daneshkadeh Pezeshki: Faculty of Medicine, Tehran Medical Sciences University; tel. (21) 6112743; fax (21) 6404377; f. 1947; 10 a year; medical magazine; Propr Dr HASSAN AREFI; circ. 1,500.

Donaye Varzesh: Khayyam Ave, Ettela'at Bldg, Tehran; tel. (21) 3281; fax (21) 3115530; weekly; sport; Editor G. H. SHABANI; circ. 200,000.

Echo of Islam: POB 14155-3899, Tehran; tel. (21) 8758296; fax (21) 892725; e-mail editor-in-chief@www.iran-itf.com; internet www.iran-itf.com/echoofislam.html; monthly; English; published by the Islamic Thought Foundation; Man. Dir MUHAMMAD BEHESHTI; Editor-in-Chief MUHAMMAD SH. SHAKIB.

Ettela'at Elmi: 11 Khayyam Ave, Tehran; tel. (21) 3281; fax (21) 3115530; f. 1985; fortnightly; sciences; Editor Mrs GHASEMI; circ. 75,000.

Ettela'at Haftegi: 11 Khayyam Ave, Tehran; tel. (21) 3281; fax (21) 3115530; f. 1941; general weekly; Editor F. JAVADI; circ. 150,000.

Ettela'at Javanan: POB 15499-51199, Ettela'at Bldg, Mirdamad Ave, South Naft St, Tehran; tel. (21) 29999; fax (21) 2258022; f. 1966; weekly; youth; Editor M. J. RAFIZADEH; circ. 120,000.

Farhang-e-Iran Zamin: POB 19575-583, Niyavaran, Tehran; tel. (21) 283254; annual; Iranian studies; Editor Prof. IRAJ AFSHAR.

Film International, Iranian Film Quarterly: POB 11365-875, Tehran; tel. (21) 6709373; fax (21) 6719971; e-mail filmmag@apadana.com; f. 1993; quarterly; English; Editor HOUSHANG GOLMAKANI; circ 20,000.

Iran Press Digest (Economic): POB 11365-5551, Hafiz Ave, 4 Kucheh Hurtab, Tehran; tel. (21) 668114; weekly; Editor J. BEHROUZ.

Iran Press Digest (Political): POB 11365-5551, Hafiz Ave, 4 Kucheh Hurtab, Tehran; tel. (21) 668114; weekly.

Iranian Cinema: POB 5158, Baharestan Sq., Tehran 11365; tel. 311242; f. 1985; annually; English; Editor B. REYPOUR.

Javaneh: POB 15875-1163, Motahhari Ave, Cnr Mofatteh St, Tehran; tel. (21) 839051; published by Soroush Press; quarterly.

JIDA: POB 14185-518, Tehran; tel. (21) 8269591; fax 8269592; e-mail IDA@apadna.com; f. 1963; four a year; journal of the Iranian Dental Association; Editor-in-Chief Dr ALI KOWSARI.

Kayhan Bacheha (Children's World): Shahid Shahsheragi Ave, Tehran; tel. (21) 310251. 1956; weekly; Editor AMIR HOSSEIN FARDI; circ. 150,000.

Kayhan Varzeshi (World of Sport): Ferdowsi Ave, Tehran; tel. (21) 310251. 1955; weekly; Dir MAHMAD MONSETI; circ. 125,000.

Mahjubah: POB 14155-3897, Tehran; tel. (21) 8000067; fax (21) 8001453; e-mail tjamshid@chamran.ut.ac.ir; Islamic family magazine; published by the Islamic Thought Foundation.

Music Iran: 1029 Amiriye Ave, Tehran; f. 1951; monthly; Editor BAHMAN HIRBOD; circ. 7,000.

Negin: Vali Asr Ave, Adl St 52, Tehran; monthly; scientific and literary; Propr and Dir M. ENAYAT.

Salamate Fekr: M.20, Kharg St, Tehran; tel. (21) 223034; f. 1958; monthly; organ of the Mental Health Soc.; Editors Prof. E. TCHEHRAZI, ALI REZA SHAFAI.

Soroush: POB 15875-1163, Motahhari Ave, Corner Mofatteh St, Tehran; tel. (21) 830771; f. 1972; two monthly magazines in Farsi, one for children and one for adolescents; Editor MEHDI FIROOZAN.

Zan-e-Ruz (Woman Today): Ferdowsi Ave, Tehran; tel. (21) 3911570; fax (21) 3911569; e-mail kayhan@istn.irost.com; internet www.irost.com/kayhan; f. 1964; weekly; women's; circ. over 60,000. (Closure ordered April 1999.)

NEWS AGENCIES

Islamic Republic News Agency (IRNA): POB 764, 873 Vali-e-Asr Ave, Tehran; tel. (21) 8902050; fax (21) 8905068; e-mail irna@

irna.com; internet www.irna.com; f. 1936; Man. Dir FEREYDOUN VERD-INEZHAD; Deputy Man. Dir MUHAMMAD TAQI ROWGHANIHA.

Foreign Bureaux

Agence France-Presse (AFP): POB 15115-513, Office 207, 8 Vanak Ave, Vanak Sq., Tehran 19919; tel. (21) 8777509; fax (21) 8886289; Correspondent CHRISTOPHE DE ROQUEFEUIL.

Agenzia Nazionale Stampa Associata (ANSA) (Italy): Khiabane Shahid Bahonar (Niavaran) Kuche Mina No. 16, Tehran 19367; tel. (21) 276930; Chief of Bureau LUCIANO CAUSA.

Informatsionnoye Telegrafnoye Agentstvo Rossii—Telegrafnoye Agentstvo Suverennykh Stran (ITAR—TASS) (Russia): Kehyaban Hamid, Kouche Masoud 73, Tehran.

Kyodo Tsushin (Japan): No. 23, First Floor, Couche Kargozar, Couche Sharsaz Ave, Zafar, Tehran; tel. (21) 220448; Correspondent MASARU IMAI.

Reuters (UK): POB 15875-1193, Tehran; tel. (21) 847700.

Xinhua (New China) News Agency (People's Republic of China): 75 Golestan 2nd St, Pasdaran Ave, Tehran; tel. (21) 241852; Correspondent CHEN MING.

Publishers

Amir Kabir Book Publishing and Distribution Co: POB 11365-4191, Jomhouri Eslami St, Esteghlal Sq, Tehran; tel. (21) 6463487; fax (21) 390752; f. 1948; historical, social, literary and children's books; Dir H. ANWARY.

Ebn-e-Sina: Meydane 25 Shahrivar, Tehran; f. 1957; educational publishers and booksellers; Dir EBRAHIM RAMAZANI.

Eghbal Printing & Publishing Organization: 15 Booshehr St, Dr Shariati Ave, Tehran; tel. (21) 768113; f. 1903; Man. Dir DJAVAD EGHBAL.

Iran Chap Co: Mirdamad Ave, South Naft St, Tehran; tel. (21) 29999; fax (21) 2258022; e-mail iranchap@hotmail.com; f. 1966; newspapers, books, magazines, book binding, colour printing and engraving; Man. Dir M. DOAEI.

Iran Exports Publication Co Ltd: POB 14335-746, 27 Eftekhar St, Vali-e-Asr Ave, Tehran 15956; tel. (21) 8801800; fax (21) 8900547; f. 1987; business and trade.

Ketab Sara: Tehran; Chair. SADEGH SAMII.

Khayyam: Jomhoori Islami Ave, Tehran; Dir MUHAMMAD ALI TARAGHI.

Majlis Press: Ketab-Khane Majlis-e-Showray-e Eslami No. 1 and the Documentation Centre, POB 11365-866, Baharestan Sq., Tehran; tel. (21) 3130919; fax (21) 3124339; e-mail frelations@majlis .com; f. 1923; Ketab Khane Majlis-e-Showray-e Eslami No. 2, Imam Khomeini Ave, Tehran 13174; tel. (21) 6135335; fax (21) 3124339; f. 1950; arts. humanities, social sciences, politics, Iranian and Islamic studies; Dir SAYED MUHAMMAD ALI AHMADI ABHARI.

Sahab Geographic and Drafting Institute: POB 11365-617, 30 Somayeh St, Hoquqi Crossroad, Dr Ali Shariati Ave, Tehran 16517; tel. (21) 7535907; fax (21) 7535876; maps, atlases, and books on geography, science, history and Islamic art; Man. Dir MUHAMMAD-REZA SAHAB.

Scientific and Cultural Publications Co: Ministry of Culture and Higher Education, 64th St, Sayyed Jamal-ed-Din Asad Abadi Ave; tel. (21) 8048037; f. 1974; Iranian and Islamic studies and scientific and cultural books; Pres. SAYED JAVAD AZHARS.

Tehran University Press: 16 Kargar Shomali Ave, Tehran; tel. (21) 8012076; fax (21) 8012077; f. 1944; university textbooks; Man. Dir Dr M. SHEKARCI.

Broadcasting and Communications

TELECOMMUNICATIONS

Telecommunications Company of Iran (TCI): POB 3318, Dr Ali Shariati Ave, Tehran; tel. (21) 8849899; fax (21) 869085; Chair. and Man. Dir Dr SAYED ABDOLLAH MIRTAHERI.

BROADCASTING

Islamic Republic of Iran Broadcasting (IRIB): POB 19395-3333, Vali-e-Asr Ave, Jame Jam St, Tehran; tel. (21) 21961; fax (21) 213910; e-mail webmaster@irib.com; internet www.irib.com; semi-autonomous authority, affiliated with the Ministry of Culture and Islamic Guidance; non-commercial; operates five national television and three national radio channels, as well as local provincial radio stations throughout the country; Dir-Gen. Dr ALI LARIJANI.

Radio

Radio Network 1 (Voice of the Islamic Republic of Iran): there are three national radio channels: Radio Networks 1 and 2 and

Radio Quran, which broadcasts recitals of the Quran (Koran) and other programmes related to it; covers whole of Iran and reaches whole of Europe, the Central Asian republics of the CIS, whole of Asia, Africa and part of USA; medium-wave regional broadcasts in local languages; Arabic, Armenian, Assyrian, Azerbaijani, Balochi, Bandari, Dari, Farsi, Kurdish, Mazandarani, Pashtu, Turkoman, Turkish and Urdu; external broadcasts in English, French, German, Spanish, Turkish, Arabic, Kurdish, Urdu, Pashtu, Armenian, Bengali, Russian and special overseas programme in Farsi; 53 transmitters.

Television

Television (Vision of the Islamic Republic of Iran): 625-line, System B; Secam colour; two production centres in Tehran producing for two networks and 28 local TV stations.

Finance

(cap. = capital; res = reserves; dep. = deposits;
brs = branches; m. = million; amounts in rials)

BANKING

Banks were nationalized in June 1979 and a revised commercial banking system was introduced consisting of nine banks (subsequently expanded to 10). Three banks were reorganized, two (Bank Tejarat and Bank Mellat) resulted from mergers of 22 existing small banks, three specialize in industry and agriculture and one, the Islamic Bank (now Islamic Economy Organization), set up in May 1979, was exempt from nationalization. The tenth bank, the Export Development Bank, specializes in the promotion of exports. A change-over to an Islamic banking system, with interest (forbidden under Islamic law) being replaced by a 4% commission on loans, began on 21 March 1984. All short- and medium-term private deposits and all bank loans and advances are subject to Islamic rules. A partial liberalization of the banking sector is planned by the Khatami administration.

Although the number of foreign banks operating in Iran has fallen dramatically since the Revolution, some 30 are still represented.

Central Bank

Bank Markazi Jomhouri Islami Iran (Central Bank): POB 11365-8551, Ferdowsi Ave, Tehran; tel. (21) 3110231; fax (21) 3115674; e-mail G.SecDept@cbi.iranet.net; internet www.cbi .iranet.net; f. 1960; Bank Markazi Iran until Dec. 1983; issuing bank, government banking; cap. 250,000m., res 261,320m., dep. 66,338,697m. (March 1999); Gov. Dr MOHSEN NOURBAKHSH.

Commercial Banks

Bank Keshavarzi (Agricultural Bank): POB 14155-6395, 129 Patrice Lumumba Ave, Jalal al-Ahmad Expressway, Tehran 1445; tel. (21) 8250135; fax (21) 8262313; e-mail info@agri-bank .com; internet www.agri-bank.com; f. 1979 by merger; state-owned; cap. 419,458m., dep. 3,593,882m. (Dec. 1999); Man. Dir Dr JALAL RASOULOF; 1,630 brs.

Bank Mellat (Nation's Bank): Head Office Bldg, 327 Taleghani Ave, Cnr Forsat St, Tehran 15817; tel. (21) 82961; fax (21) 82962700; f. 1980 by merger of 10 fmr private banks; state-owned; cap. 605,000m., dep. 18,063,013m.; total assets 26,657,248m. (March 1998); Chair. and Man. Dir S. MANOUCHEHRI; 1,885 brs.

Bank Melli Iran (The National Bank of Iran): POB 11365-171, Ferdowsi Ave, Tehran; tel. (21) 3231; fax (21) 3912813; f. 1928; present name since 1943; state-owned; cap. 1,145,000m., res 18,475m., dep. 29,369,389m. (March 1998); CEO and Man. Dir FREIDOUN TOHIDI MOGHADAM; 2,998 brs in Iran, 21 abroad.

Bank Refah Kargaran: POB 15714, 40 Shirazi St, Mollasadra Ave, Tehran; tel. (21) 8042926; fax (21) 8042926; f. 1960; state-owned; cap. 55,000m., dep. 1,278,224m. (March 1996); Man. Dir J. SABER KHIABANI; 461 brs.

Bank Saderat Iran (The Export Bank of Iran): POB 15745-631, Bank Saderat Tower, 43 Somayeh Ave, Tehran; tel. (21) 832699; fax (21) 8839539; f. 1952; state-owned; cap. 948,000m., res. 12,491m., dep. 570,502m. (March 1999); Chair. and Man. Dir Sayed SHARIF RAZAVI; 3,291 brs in Iran, 23 abroad.

Bank Sepah (Army Bank): POB 9569, Imam Khomeini Sq, Tehran 11364; tel. (21) 3111091; fax (21) 2255267; f. 1925; state-owned; cap. 400,000m., res 5,888m., dep. 18,075,212m. (March 1999); Chair. and Man. Dir VALIOLLAH SAIF; 1,480 brs in Iran, 4 abroad.

Bank Tejarat (Commercial Bank): POB 11365-5416, 130 Taleghani Ave, Nejatoullahie, Tehran 15994; tel. (21) 81041; fax (21) 8828215; f. 1979 by merger of 12 banks; state-owned; cap. 571,120m., res 41,099m., dep. 19,042,295m. (March 1999); Man. Dir and Chair. S. A. MILANI; 1,800 brs in Iran, 3 abroad.

Islamic Economy Organization (formerly Islamic Bank of Iran): Ferdowsi Ave, Tehran; f. February 1980; cap. 2,000m.; provides interest-free loans and investment in small industry.

Development Banks

Bank Sanat va Madan (Bank of Industry and Mines): POB 15875-4456, 593 Hafiz Ave, Tehran; tel. (21) 8903271; fax (21) 8899294; e-mail bankim@iran-bim.com; f. 1979 as merger of the following: Industrial Credit Bank (ICB), Industrial and Mining Development Bank of Iran (IMDBI), Development and Investment Bank of Iran (DIBI), Iranian Bankers Investment Company (IBICO); cap. 1,280,000m., res 36,257m., total assets 2,447,396m. (1996); Chair. and Man. Dir ABDORAHMAN NADIMI BOUSHEHRI.

Export Development Bank of Iran: POB 15875-5964, 129 Khaled Eslamboli St, Tehran 15139; tel. (21) 8725140; fax (21) 8716979; e-mail kohzadi@edbi.iranet.net; internet www.edbi.iranet.net; cap. 280,000m., res. 19,122m., dep. 1,149,830m. (March 2000); Chair and Man. Dir Dr NOWROOZ KOHZADI; 22 brs.

Housing Bank

Bank Maskan (Housing Bank): POB 11365-5699, 247 Ferdowsi Ave, Tehran; tel. (21) 675021; f. 1980; state-owned; cap. 140,000m., dep. 7,996,390m., total assets 9,838,667m. (March 2000); provides mortgage and housing finance; 630 brs; Chair. and Man. Dir AHMAD FARSHCHIAN.

Regulatory Authority

Supreme Council of Banks: Tehran; comprises two bankers and five ministerial appointees; regulates internal affairs of all Iranian banks; Chair. Dr HOSSEIN NEMAZI.

STOCK EXCHANGE

Tehran Stock Exchange: 228 Hafez Ave, Tehran 11389; tel. (21) 6708385; fax (21) 6700155; e-mail stock@neda.net; internet www.neda.net/tse; f. 1966; Sec.-Gen. AHMAD MIRMOTAHARI.

INSURANCE

The nationalization of insurance companies was announced in June 1979.

Bimeh Alborz (Alborz Insurance Co): POB 4489-15875, Alborz Bldg, 234 Sepahbod Garani Ave, Tehran; tel. (21) 8803773; fax (21) 8803771; f. 1959; state-owned insurance company; all types of insurance; Man. Dir ALI FATHALI.

Bimeh Asia (Asia Insurance Co): POB 15815-1885, Asia Insurance Bldg, 297-299 Taleghani Ave, Tehran; tel. (21) 8898110; fax (21) 8898113; all types of insurance; Man. Dir MASOUM ZAMIRI.

Bimeh Dana (Dana Insurance Co): 25 Fifteenth Ave, Gandi St, Tehran; tel. (21) 8770971; fax 8770812; life, personal accident and health insurance; Chair. and Man. Dir. ALI FARHANDI.

Bimeh Iran (Iran Insurance Co): POB 14155-6363, Dr Fatemi Ave, No. 107, Tehran; tel. (21) 8864698; fax (21) 8864669; all types of insurance; Man. Dir ALI MUSAREZA.

Bimeh Markazi Iran (Central Insurance of Iran): POB 19395-5588, 72 Africa Ave, Tehran 19157; tel. (21) 2050001; fax (21) 2054099; e-mail cent-ir@kanoon.net; supervises the insurance market and tariffs for new types of insurance cover; the sole state reinsurer for domestic insurance companies, which are obliged to reinsure 50% of their direct business in life insurance and 25% of business in non-life insurance with Bimeh Markazi Iran; Pres. ABDOLNASSER HEMMATI.

Trade and Industry

CHAMBER OF COMMERCE

Iran Chamber of Commerce, Industries and Mines: 254 Taleghani Ave, Tehran; tel. (21) 8846031; fax (21) 8825111; e-mail info@iccim.org; internet www.iccim.org; supervises the affiliated 32 Chambers in the provinces; Pres. ALINAQI KHAMOUSHI.

INDUSTRIAL AND TRADE ASSOCIATIONS

National Iranian Industries Organization (NIIO): POB 14155-3579, 133 Dr Fatemi Ave, Tehran; tel. (21) 656031-40; fax (21) 658070; f. 1979; owns 400 factories in Iran.

National Iranian Industries Organization Export Co (NECO): POB 14335-589, No. 8, 2nd St, Ahmad Ghasir Ave, Tehran 15944; tel. (21) 8733564; fax (21) 8732586.

STATE HYDROCARBONS COMPANIES

Iranian Offshore Oil Co (IOOC): POB 15875-4546, 339 Dr Beheshti Ave, Tehran; tel. (21) 8714102; fax (21) 8717420; wholly owned subsidiary of NIOC; f. 1980; development, exploitation and production of crude petroleum, natural gas and other hydrocarbons in all offshore areas of Iran in the Persian Gulf and the Caspian Sea; Chair. M. AGAZADEH; Dir S. A. JALILIAN.

National Iranian Gas Co (NIGC): Man. Dir MUHAMMAD MUHAMMADNEZHAD.

National Iranian Oil Co (NIOC): POB 1863, Taleghani Ave, Tehran; tel. (21) 6151; internet www.nioc.org; state organization controlling all 'upstream' activities in the petroleum and natural gas industries; incorporated April 1951 on nationalization of petroleum industry to engage in all phases of petroleum operations; in February 1979 it was announced that, in future, Iran would sell petroleum direct to the petroleum companies, and in September 1979 the Ministry of Oil assumed control of the National Iranian Oil Company, and the Minister of Oil took over as Chairman and Managing Director; Chair. of Board and Gen. Man. Dir BIZAM NAMDAR-ZANGENEH (Minister of Oil).

National Iranian Oil Refining and Distribution Co (NIORDC): POB 15815-3499, NIORDC Bldg, 140 Ostad Nejatollahi Ave, Tehran; tel. (21) 8801001; fax (21) 6152142; f. 1992 to assume responsibility for refining, pipeline distribution, engineering, construction and research in the petroleum industry from NIOC; Chair. and Man. Dir GHOLAMREZA AQAZADEH.

CO-OPERATIVES

Central Organization for Co-operatives of Iran: Ministry of Co-operatives, 16 Bozorgmehr St, Vali-e-Asr Ave, Tehran 14169; tel. (21) 6400938; fax (21) 6417041; f. 1993; 9m. mems in 48,000 co-operative societies.

Central Organization for Rural Co-operatives of Iran (CORC): Tehran; Man. Dir SAYED HASSAN MOTEVALLI-ZADEH.

The CORC was founded in 1963, and the Islamic Government of Iran has pledged that it will continue its educational, technical, commercial and credit assistance to rural co-operative societies and unions. At the end of the Iranian year 1363 (1984/85) there were 3,104 Rural Co-operative Societies with a total membership of 3,925,000 and share capital of 25,900m. rials. There were 181 Rural Co-operative Unions with 3,097 members and capital of 7,890m. rials.

Transport

RAILWAYS

Iranian Islamic Republic Railways: POB 13185-1498, Shahid Kalantari Bldg, Railway Sq., Tehran; tel. (21) 5641686; fax (21) 5647086; e-mail rail-rai@neda.net; f. 1934; affiliated with Ministry of Roads and Transport; Pres. Deputy Minister of Roads and Transport; Man. Dir Eng. MAHMOUD RAHMATI.

In 1999 the Iranian railway system comprised 6,300 km of standard 1,435 mm gauge, 146 km of electrified lines, and 94 km of wide 1,676 mm gauge. The system includes the following main routes:

Trans-Iranian Railway runs 1,392 km from Bandar Turkman on the Caspian Sea in the north, through Tehran, and south to Bandar Imam Khomeini on the Persian Gulf.

Southern Line links Tehran to Khorramshahr via Qom, Arak, Dorood, Andimeshk and Ahwaz; 937 km.

Northern Line links Tehran to Gorgan via Garmsar, Firooz Kooh and Sari; 499 km.

Tehran–Kerman Line via Kashan, Yazd and Zarand; 1,106 km.

Tehran–Tabriz Line linking with the Azerbaijan Railway; 736 km.

Tabriz–Djulfa Electric Line: 146 km.

Garmsar–Meshed Line connects Tehran with Meshed via Semnan, Damghan, Shahrud and Nishabur; 812 km. A line is under construction to link Meshed with Sarakhs on the Turkmen border. A 768-km line linking Meshed with Bafq is also under construction.

Qom–Zahedan Line when completed will be an intercontinental line linking Europe and Turkey, through Iran, with India. Zahedan is situated 91.7 km west of the Baluchistan frontier, and is the end of the Pakistani broad gauge railway. The section at present links Qom to Kerman via Kashan, Sistan, Yazd, Bafq and Zarand; 1,005 km. A branch line from Sistan was opened in 1971 via Isfahan to the steel mill at Zarrin Shahr; 112 km. A broad-gauge (1,976-mm) track connects Zahedan and Mirjaveh, on the border with Pakistan; 94 km.

Zahedan–Quetta (Pakistan) Line: 685 km; not linked to national network.

Ahwaz–Bandar Khomeini Line connects Bandar Khomeini with the Trans-Iranian railway at Ahwaz; this line is due to be double-tracked; 112 km.

Azerbaijan Railway extends from Tabriz to Djulfa (146.5 km), meeting the Caucasian railways at the Azerbaijani frontier. Electrification works for this section have been completed and the electrified line was opened in April 1982. A standard gauge railway line (139 km) extends from Tabriz (via Sharaf–Khaneh) to the Turkish frontier at Razi.

Bandar Abbas–Bafq: construction of a 730-km double-track line to link Bandar Abbas and Bafq commenced in 1982. The first phase, linking Bafq to Sirjan (260 km), was opened in May 1990, and the second phase was opened in March 1995. The line provides access to the copper mines at Sarcheshmeh and the iron ore mines at Gole-Gohar.

Bafq–Chadormalou: a 130-km line connecting Bafq to the Chadormalou iron-ore mines is under construction.

Chadormalou–Tabas: a 220-km line is under construction.

A passenger service running from Dushanbe (Tajikistan) to Tehran, via Uzbekistan and Turkmenistan, was scheduled to begin in early 2001.

Underground Railway

In May 1995 the Tehran Urban and Suburban Railway Co concluded agreements with three Chinese companies for the completion of the Tehran underground railway, on which work had originally commenced in 1977. It was reported that about 80% of the work on two lines (one, 34 km in length, running north to south, and a second, 20 km in length, running east to west) had been completed. A 31-km suburban line, linking Tehran with the satellite city of Karaj, was inaugurated in February 1999, while phased sections of the urban lines were to enter service from the end of that year.

Tehran Urban and Suburban Railway Co (Metro): POB 4661, 37 Mir Emad St, Tehran 15878; tel. (21) 8740144; fax (21) 8740114; e-mail tusrc@dpi.net.ir; Chair. and Man. Dir MOHSEN HASHEMI.

ROADS

In 1997 there were an estimated 165,724 km of roads, including 712 km of motorways, 24,662 km of highways, main or national roads and 54,141 km of secondary or regional roads; about 50% of the road network was paved. There is a paved highway (A1, 2,089 km) from Bazargan on the Turkish border to the Afghanistan border. The A2 highway runs 2,473 km from the Iraqi border to Mir Javeh on the Pakistan border.

Ministry of Roads and Transport: (see Ministries, above).

INLAND WATERWAYS

Principal waterways:

Lake Rezaiyeh (Lake Urmia): 80 km west of Tabriz in North-West Iran; and Karun river flowing south through the oilfields into the Shatt al-Arab, thence to the head of the Persian Gulf near Abadan.

Lake Rezaiyeh: From Sharafkhaneh to Golmankhaneh there is a twice-weekly service of tugs and barges for transport of passengers and goods.

Karun River: Regular cargo service is operated by the Mesopotamia-Iran Corpn Ltd. Iranian firms also operate daily motor-boat services for passengers and goods.

SHIPPING

Persian Gulf: The main oil terminal is at Kharg Island. The principal commercial non-oil ports are Bandar Shahid Rajai (which was officially inaugurated in 1983 and handles 9m. of the 12m. tons of cargo passing annually through Iran's Persian Gulf ports), Bandar Khomeini, Bushehr, Bandar Abbas and Chah Bahar. A project to develop Bandar Abbas port, which predates the Islamic Revolution and was originally to cost IR 1,900,000m., is now in progress. Khorramshahr, Iran's biggest port, was disabled in the war with Iraq, and Bushehr and Bandar Khomeini also sustained war damage, which has restricted their use. In August 1988 the Iranian news agency (IRNA) announced that Iran was to spend US $200m. on the construction of six 'multi-purpose' ports on the Arabian and Caspian Seas, while ports which had been damaged in the war were to be repaired.

Caspian Sea: Principal ports Bandar Anzali (formerly Bandar Pahlavi) and Bandar Nowshahr.

Ports and Shipping Organization: 751 Enghelab Ave, Tehran; tel. (21) 8809280; fax (21) 8804100; affiliated with Ministry of Roads and Transport; Man. Dir MOKHTAR KALANTARY.

Principal Shipping Companies

Irano–Hind Shipping Co: POB 15875-4647, Sedaghat St, Vali-e-Asr Ave, Tehran; tel. (21) 2058095; fax (21) 2057739; joint venture between the Islamic Republic of Iran and the Shipping Corpn of India; Chair. Capt. P. P. RADHAKRISHNAN.

Islamic Republic of Iran Shipping Lines (IRISL): POB 15875-4646, 675 North East Corner of Vali-e-Asr Sq., Tehran; tel. (21) 8893801; fax (21) 889413; internet www.irisl.net; f. 1967; affiliated with the Ministry of Commerce; liner services between the Persian (Arabian) Gulf and Europe, the Far East and South America and between the Caspian Sea and Central Asia; Chair. ALI ASHRAF AFKHAMI.

National Iranian Tanker Co: POB 16765-947, 67–8 Atefis St, Africa Ave, Tehran; tel. (21) 2229093; fax (21) 2223011; Chair. and Man. Dir MUHAMMAD SOURI.

CIVIL AVIATION

The two main international airports are Mehrabad (Tehran) and Abadan. An international airport was opened at Isfahan in July 1984 and the first international flight took place in March 1986. Work on a new international airport, 40 km south of Tehran, abandoned in 1979, resumed in the mid-1980s, and work on three others, at Tabas, Ardebil and Ilam was under way in mid-1990. The airports at Urumiyeh, Ahwaz, Bakhtaran, Sanandaz, Abadan, Hamadan and Shiraz were to be modernized and smaller ones constructed at Lar, Lamard, Rajsanjan, Barm, Kashan, Maragheh, Khoy, Sirjan and Abadeh. In early 1995 the Economic Co-operation Organization (ECO) agreed to establish a regional airline (Eco Air), based in Tehran. Construction of Imam Khomeini airport in Tehran, anticipated to be one of the largest airports in the world, was due to begin in 1998.

Civil Aviation Organization (CAO): Tehran; affiliated with Ministry of Roads and Transport; Head BEHZAD MAZAHERI.

Iran Air (Airline of the Islamic Republic of Iran): POB 13185-755, Iran Air Bldg, Mehrabad Airport, Tehran; tel. (21) 979111; fax (21) 6003248; f. 1962; serves the Middle East and Persian (Arabian) Gulf area, Europe, Asia and the Far East; Man. Dir AHMAD REZA KAZEMI.

Iran Air Tours: 191 Motahari Ave, Dr Moffateh Rd, Tehran 15879; tel. (21) 8708390; fax (21) 8555884; f. 1992; serves Middle East; Chair. A. M. KHALILI.

Iran Asseman Airlines: POB 141748, Mehrabad Airport, Tehran 13145-1476; tel. (21) 6484198; fax (21) 6404318; f. after Islamic Revolution as result of merger of Air Taxi Co (f. 1958), Pars Air (f. 1969), Air Service Co (f. 1962) and Hoor Asseman; Man. Dir ALI ABEDZADEH; domestic routes and charter services.

Kish Air: POB 19395-4639, 215 Africa Highway, Tehran 19697; tel. (21) 4665639; fax (21) 4665221; internet www.itto.org/transport/kishair; f. 1991 under the auspices of the Kish Development Organization; serves Persian Gulf area, Frankfurt, London and Paris; Pres. Capt. Y. KHALILI.

Mahan Air: Kerman; f. 1993; domestic routes and regular flights to Damascus, Syria.

Saha Airline: POB 13445-956, Tehran 13873; tel. (21) 6696200; fax (21) 6698016; f. 1990; operates passenger and cargo charter domestic flights and services to Europe, Asia and Africa; Man. Dir Capt. A. SAEDI.

Tourism

Tourism was adversely affected by political upheaval following the Revolution. Iran's chief attraction for tourists is its wealth of historical sites, notably Esfahan, Rasht, Tabriz, Susa and Persepolis. Some 1,007,597 international tourist arrivals were recorded in 1998, compared with 326,048 in 1994. Receipts from tourism in 1997 totalled US $327m. Tourism centres are currently administered by the State, through the Ministry of Culture and Islamic Guidance, although in late 1997 the ministry indicated its intention to transfer all tourism affairs to the private sector.

Iran National Tourist Organization (INTO): Tehran; internet www.iran-tourism.com; f. 1979; affiliated with Ministry of Culture and Islamic Guidance; Man. Dir. ABDOLLAH HOSSEINI.

IRAQ

Introductory Survey

Location, Climate, Language, Religion, Flag, Capital

The Republic of Iraq is an almost land-locked state in western Asia, with a narrow outlet to the sea on the Persian (Arabian) Gulf. Its neighbours are Iran to the east, Turkey to the north, Syria and Jordan to the west, and Saudi Arabia and Kuwait to the south. The climate is extreme, with hot, dry summers, when temperatures may exceed 43°C (109°F), and cold winters, especially in the highlands. Summers are humid near the Persian Gulf. The official language is Arabic, spoken by about 80% of the population; about 15% speak Kurdish, while there is a small Turkoman-speaking minority. Some 95% of the population are Muslims, of whom more than 50% belong to the Shi'i sect. However, the regime that came to power in 1968 has been dominated by members of the Sunni sect. The national flag (proportions 3 by 2) has three equal horizontal stripes, of red, white and black, with three five-pointed green stars on the central white stripe. The inscription 'Allahu Akhbar' ('God is Great') was added to the flag in January 1991. The capital is Baghdad.

Recent History

Iraq was formerly part of Turkey's Ottoman Empire. During the First World War (1914–18), when Turkey was allied with Germany, the territory was captured by British forces. In 1920 Iraq was placed under a League of Nations mandate, administered by the United Kingdom. In 1921 Amir Faisal ibn Hussain, a member of the Hashimi (Hashemite) dynasty of Arabia, was proclaimed King of Iraq, and his brother, Abdullah, was proclaimed Amir (Emir) of neighbouring Transjordan (later renamed Jordan), also administered by the United Kingdom under a League of Nations mandate. The two new monarchs were sons of Hussain (Hussein) ibn Ali, the Sharif of Mecca, who had proclaimed himself King of the Hijaz (now part of Saudi Arabia) in 1916. The British decision to nominate Hashemite princes to be rulers of Iraq and Transjordan was a reward for Hussain's co-operation in the wartime campaign against Turkey. After prolonged negotiations, a 25-year Anglo-Iraqi Treaty of Alliance was signed in 1930. The British mandate ended on 3 October 1932, when Iraq became fully independent.

During its early years the new kingdom was faced with Kurdish revolts (1922–32) and with border disputes in the south. The leading personality in Iraqi political life under the monarchy was Gen. Nuri as-Said, who became Prime Minister in 1930 and held the office for seven terms over a period of 28 years. He strongly supported Iraq's close links with the United Kingdom and with the West in general.

After the death of King Faisal I in 1933, the Iraqi monarchy remained pro-British in outlook, and in 1955 Iraq signed the Baghdad Pact, a British-inspired agreement on collective regional security. However, following the overthrow of King Faisal II (the grandson of Faisal I) during a military revolution on 14 July 1958, which brought to power a left-wing nationalist regime headed by Brig. (later Lt-Gen.) Abd al-Karim Kassem, the 1925 Constitution was abolished, the legislature was dissolved, and in March 1959 Iraq withdrew from the Baghdad Pact. Kassem, who had maintained a precarious and increasingly isolated position, opposed by pan-Arabists, Kurds and other groups, was assassinated in February 1963 in a coup by members of the armed forces. The new Government of Col (later Field Marshal) Abd as-Salem Muhammad Aref was more pan-Arab in outlook, and sought closer relations with the United Arab Republic (Egypt). Following his death in March 1966, President Aref was succeeded by his brother, Maj.-Gen. Abd ar-Rahman Muhammad Aref, who was ousted on 17 July 1968 by members of the Arab Renaissance (Baath) Socialist Party. Maj.-Gen. (later Field Marshal) Ahmad Hassan al-Bakr, a former Prime Minister, became President and Prime Minister, and supreme authority was vested in the Revolutionary Command Council (RCC), of which President al-Bakr was also Chairman.

Relations with the Syrian Government deteriorated after a younger generation of Baathists seized power in Syria in 1970. A bitter rivalry existed thereafter between Syrian and Iraqi Baathists. Relations improved in October 1978, when President Hafiz al-Assad of Syria visited Baghdad.

On 16 July 1979 the Vice-Chairman of the RCC, Saddam Hussain, who had long exercised real power in Iraq, replaced al-Bakr as RCC Chairman and as President of Iraq. Shortly afterwards several members of the RCC were executed for their alleged part in a coup plot. The suspicion of Syrian implication in the attempted putsch resulted in the suspension of discussions concerning political and economic union between the two countries.

During 1979 the Iraqi Communist Party broke away from the National Progressive Front (NPF), an alliance of Baathists, Kurdish groups and Communists, claiming that the Baathists were conducting a 'reign of terror'. In February 1980 Saddam Hussain announced a National Charter, reaffirming the principles of non-alignment. In June elections took place (the first since the 1958 revolution) for a 250-member, legislative National Assembly; these were followed in September by the first elections to a 50-member Kurdish Legislative Council in the Kurdish Autonomous Region (which had been established in 1970).

Saddam Hussain retained his positions as Chairman of the RCC and Regional Secretary of the Baath Party following its regional Congress in June 1982. A subsequent purge throughout the administration consolidated his control. Kurdish rebels became active in northern Iraq, occasionally supporting Iranian forces in the war with Iraq (see below). Another threat was posed by the Supreme Council of the Islamic Revolution in Iraq (SCIRI), formed in the Iranian capital, Tehran in November 1982 by the exiled Shi'ite leader Muhammad Baqir al-Hakim. None the less, the majority of Iraq's Shi'ite community was not attracted by the Islamist fundamentalism of Ayatollah Khomeini of Iran, remaining loyal to Iraq and its Sunni President, while Iranian-backed militant groups (such as the Shi'ite fundamentalist Ad-Da'wa al-Islamiya group, which made numerous attempts to assassinate Saddam Hussain) were ineffective.

In the second half of the 1980s Saddam Hussain consolidated his control over the country and secured the loyalty of Iraq's Shi'ite community. In 1988, as a reward for its role in the war against Iran, the President announced political reforms, including the introduction of a multi-party system, and in January 1989 declared that these would be incorporated into a new permanent constitution. In April 1989 elections took place to the 250-seat National Assembly, in which one-quarter of the candidates were members of the Baath Party and the remainder either independent or members of the NPF. More than 50% of the newly-elected deputies were reported to be Baathists. In July the National Assembly approved a new draft constitution, under the terms of which a 50-member Consultative Assembly was to be established; both institutions would assume the duties of the RCC, which would be abolished after a presidential election.

During the 1980s representatives of Iraq's 2.5m.–3m. Kurds demanded greater autonomy. Resources were repeatedly diverted from the war with Iran to control Kurdish insurgency in the north-east of the country. Saddam Hussain sought an accommodation with the Kurds, and a series of discussions began in December 1983, after a cease-fire had been agreed with Jalal Talibani, the leader of the main Kurdish opposition party in Iraq, the Patriotic Union of Kurdistan (PUK). The discussions did not, however, include the other main Kurdish group, the Democratic Party of Kurdistan (DPK), led by Masoud Barzani. Negotiations collapsed in May 1984, and armed conflict resumed in Kurdistan in January 1985 between PUK guerrillas and government troops, with Kurdish and Iranian forces repeatedly collaborating in raids against Iraqi military and industrial targets.

During February 1988 DPK and PUK guerrillas (assisted by Iranian forces) made inroads into government-controlled territory in Iraqi Kurdistan. In March the Iraqi Government retaliated by using chemical weapons against the Kurdish town of Halabja. In May the DPK and the PUK announced the formation of a coalition of six organizations to continue the struggle for Kurdish self-determination and to co-operate militarily with Iran. The cease-fire in the Iran–Iraq War in August allowed Iraq to launch a new offensive to overrun guerrilla bases near the borders with Iran and Turkey, again allegedly employing chemical weapons. Kurdish civilians and fighters fled across the borders, and by mid-September there were reported to be more than 200,000 Kurdish refugees in Iran and Turkey. In that month, with the army effectively in control of the border with Turkey, the Iraqi Government offered a full amnesty to all Iraqi Kurds inside and outside the country, excluding only Jalal Talibani. It also began to evacuate inhabitants of the Kurdish Autonomous Region to the interior of Iraq, as part of a plan to create a 30-km uninhabited 'security zone' along the whole of Iraq's border with Iran and Turkey. By October 1989, despite international censure of the evacuation programme, the 'security zone' was reported to be in place, prompting the PUK to announce a nation-wide urban guerrilla campaign against the Government. In September elections had proceeded to the legislative council of the Kurdish Autonomous Region.

Relations with Iran, precarious for many years, descended into full-scale war in September 1980. Iraq had become increasingly dissatisfied with the 1975 Algiers Agreement, which had defined the southern border between Iran and Iraq as the mid-point of the Shatt al-Arab waterway, and also sought the withdrawal of Iranian forces from Abu Musa and the Tunb islands, which Iran had occupied in 1971. The Iranian Revolution of 1979 exacerbated these grievances, and conflict soon developed as Iran accused Iraq of encouraging Arab demands for autonomy in Iran's Khuzestan ('Arabistan') region. Suspicion within Iraq's Sunni leadership of Shi'ite Iran under Ayatollah Khomeini was fuelled by Iranian backing for the SCIRI and other Iraqi groups opposed to Saddam Hussain. Border tensions in mid-1980 escalated into more extensive fighting after Iran ignored Iraqi demands for the withdrawal of Iranian forces from the border area of Zain ul-Qos, in Diali province, which Iraq maintained should have been returned under the 1975 agreement. In September 1980 Iraq abrogated the Algiers Agreement, and Iraqi forces advanced into Iran. Fierce Iranian resistance led to military deadlock until mid-1982, when Iranian counter-offensives led to the retaking of the port of Khorramshahr and the withdrawal of Iraqi troops from territory occupied in 1980. In July 1982 the Iranian army crossed into Iraq. (For a fuller account of the Iran–Iraq War (1980–88), see the chapter on Iran.)

In 1984 the balance of military power in the war with Iran moved in Iraq's favour, and its financial position improved as the USA and the USSR provided aid. Iraq and the USA re-established full diplomatic relations (which had been severed by Iraq following the Arab–Israeli war of 1967) in November 1984. In April 1985 the UN Secretary-General, Javier Pérez de Cuéllar, visited both Tehran and Baghdad in an attempt to establish a basis for the commencement of peace negotiations: Iraq insisted that it was interested only in a permanent cease-fire and immediate, direct negotiations with Iran, while Iran continued to demand the removal of Saddam Hussain, an Iraqi admission of responsibility for starting the war, and the payment of reparations.

Iraqi forces began to recapture land occupied by Iran in early 1988, and in July they crossed into Iran for the first time since 1986. In that month Iran announced its unconditional acceptance of UN Security Council Resolution 598, and by August a cease-fire was in force, monitored by the UN Iran-Iraq Military Observer Group (UNIIMOG). However, negotiations on the full implementation of the Resolution had made little progress by the time of Iraq's invasion of Kuwait in August 1990, at which point Saddam Hussain abruptly sought a formal peace agreement with Iran, by accepting all the claims that Iran had pursued since the cease-fire, including the reinstatement of the Algiers Agreement of 1975. (See the chapter on Iran for details of subsequent relations between Iran and Iraq.)

In mid-1990 the Iraqi Government criticized countries (principally Kuwait and the United Arab Emirates) that had persistently produced petroleum in excess of the quotas imposed by the Organization of the Petroleum Exporting Countries (OPEC, see p. 269). Iraq also accused Kuwait of violating the Iraqi border in order to secure petroleum resources, and demanded that Kuwait waive Iraq's debt repayments. On the eve of an OPEC ministerial meeting, held in Geneva, Switzerland, in July, Iraq mustered troops on its border with Kuwait. Direct negotiations between Iraq and Kuwait, with the aim of resolving their disputes over territory and Iraq's war debt, failed, and on 2 August Iraqi forces invaded Kuwait, taking control of the country and establishing a provisional 'free government'. On 8 August Iraq announced its formal annexation of Kuwait. The UN Security Council responded to Iraq's action by unanimously adopting, on the day of the invasion, Resolution 660, which demanded the immediate and unconditional withdrawal of Iraqi forces from Kuwait. Subsequent resolutions imposed mandatory economic sanctions against Iraq and occupied Kuwait (No. 661), and declared Iraq's annexation of Kuwait to be null and void (662). On 7 August, at the request of King Fahd of Saudi Arabia, the US Government dispatched troops and aircraft to Saudi Arabia, in order to secure the country's border with Kuwait against a possible Iraqi attack: other countries quickly lent their support to what was designated 'Operation Desert Shield', and a multinational force was formed to defend Saudi Arabia. Meanwhile, at a meeting of the League of Arab States (the Arab League, see p. 232) on the day after the invasion, 14 of the 21 members condemned the invasion and demanded an unconditional withdrawal by Iraq; one week later 12 member states voted to send an Arab deterrent force to the region of the Persian (Arabian) Gulf. However, there were widespread demonstrations of popular support for Iraq, notably among the Palestinian population of Jordan and in the Maghreb states.

Diplomatic efforts to achieve a peaceful solution to the Gulf crisis all foundered on Iraq's refusal to withdraw its forces from Kuwait. In November 1990 the UN Security Council adopted a resolution (No. 678) which permitted member states to use 'all necessary means' to enforce the withdrawal of Iraqi forces from Kuwait if they had not left by 15 January 1991. 'Operation Desert Storm'—in effect, war with Iraq—began on the night of 16–17 January, with air attacks on Baghdad by the multinational force. The Iraqi air force offered little effective resistance, and by the end of January the allied force had achieved air supremacy. Iraq launched *Scud* missiles against Saudi Arabia and Israel, but considerable diplomatic pressure was brought to bear upon Israel to prevent it from retaliating—which, since it would have been politically impossible for any Arab state to fight alongside Israel against Iraq, would have severely undermined the multinational force. In February Iraq formally severed diplomatic relations with Egypt, France, Italy, Saudi Arabia, Syria, the United Kingdom and the USA. In that month two Soviet-sponsored peace plans were accepted by Iraq but rejected by the US-led coalition (on the grounds that the proposals did not comply with UN Security Council resolutions on unconditional withdrawal from Kuwait). During the night of 23–24 February the multinational force began a ground offensive for the liberation of Kuwait: Iraqi troops were quickly defeated and surrendered in large numbers. A cease-fire was declared by the US Government on 28 February. Iraq agreed to renounce its claim to Kuwait, to release prisoners of war, and to comply with all pertinent UN Security Council resolutions. UN Security Council Resolution 687, adopted in April, provided for the establishment of a commission to demarcate the border between Iraq and Kuwait. The resolution also linked the removal of sanctions imposed on Iraq following its invasion of Kuwait to the elimination of non-conventional weaponry, to be certified by a UN Special Commission (UNSCOM), and also required that Iraq accept proposals for the establishment of a war reparation fund to be derived from Iraqi petroleum reserves.

Within Iraq the war was followed by domestic unrest: in March 1991 rebel forces, including Shi'ite Muslims and disaffected soldiers, were reported to have taken control of Basra and other southern cities, but the rebellion was soon crushed by troops loyal to Saddam Hussain. In the north Kurdish separatists overran a large area of Kurdistan. The various Kurdish factions, allied since 1988 in the Kurdistan Iraqi Front (KIF), claimed that the objective of the northern insurrection was the full implementation of a 15-article peace plan concluded between Kurdish leaders and the Iraqi Government in 1970. Lacking military support from the UN-authorized multinational force, the Kurdish guerrillas were unable to resist the onslaught of the Iraqi armed forces, which were redeployed northwards as soon as they had crushed the uprising in southern Iraq, and an estimated 1m.–2m. Kurds fled before the Iraqi army across the northern mountains into Turkey and Iran. UN Security Council Resolution 688, adopted in April 1991, condemned the repression of Iraqi civilians, most recently in the Kurdish-populated areas, and insisted that Iraq allow immediate access by international humanitarian organizations to all those in need of assistance. This allowed the institution of an international repatriation and relief effort—co-ordinated by a multinational task force, designated 'Provide Comfort', which was immediately established in south-east Turkey to provide relief to displaced persons and to enforce the security both of the refugees and of the humanitarian effort in designated 'safe havens' on Iraqi territory north of latitude 36°N. A second phase of 'Operation Provide Comfort', which began in July, had only a limited role in humanitarian operations (responsibility for which had been assumed by the UN, under the terms of a memorandum of understanding with the Iraqi Government), its role being principally to deter further Iraqi aggression against the Kurds.

A second air exclusion zone, south of latitude 32°N, was established by France, Russia, the United Kingdom and the USA in August 1992, with the aim of protecting southern Iraqi Shi'ite communities and the inhabitants of Iraq's southern marshlands. The UN Secretary-General subsequently indicated UN Security Council support for the measure. In December 1992 a combat aircraft shot down an Iraqi fighter which had allegedly entered the exclusion zone, and subsequent Iraqi military activity within the exclusion zone provoked attacks by Western forces on targets in southern Iraq in January 1993. (A ban imposed by the Iraqi Government on UN flights into the country was cited as further justification for the attacks.) Further air raids by Western forces on targets in northern and southern Iraq took place in late January. In May, in response to the deployment of Iraqi armed forces close to the northern exclusion zone, the USA warned Iraq that it might suffer military reprisals in the event of any incursion into the Kurdish-held north. In June the USA launched an attack against intelligence headquarters in Baghdad, in retaliation for Iraq's role in an alleged conspiracy to assassinate former US President George Bush in Kuwait in April. In July Iraqi armed forces were reported to have renewed the Government's offensive against the inhabitants of the marshlands of southern Iraq. In May 1996 government forces were reported to have launched a major offensive against the Shi'a opposition and tribes in Basra governorate. Further fighting was reported in September and at the end of the year there were armed clashes between the security forces and the Shi'a opposition throughout the southern regions. In April 1998 the Iran-based SCIRI claimed that a renewed offensive against the Shi'a opposition in the southern regions had resulted in the execution of some 60 Shi'ites during March.

Meanwhile, in April 1991 the PUK leader, Jalal Talibani, announced that President Saddam Hussain had agreed in principle to implement the provisions of the Kurdish peace plan of 1970. However, negotiations subsequently became deadlocked over the delineation of the Kurdish Autonomous Region, in which Kurdish groups wished the city of Kirkuk to be included. In October, in the absence of any negotiated agreement on an 'autonomous Kurdistan', the Iraqi Government withdrew all services from the area, effectively subjecting it to an economic blockade. The KIF proceeded to organize elections, in May 1992, to a 105-member Kurdish national assembly, and for a paramount Kurdish leader. The outcome of voting, in which virtually the entire electorate (of some 1.1m.) participated, was that the DPK and the PUK were entitled to an almost equal number of seats. None of the smaller Kurdish parties achieved representation, and the DPK and the PUK subsequently agreed to share equally the seats in the new Assembly. The election for an overall Kurdish leader was deemed inconclusive, with Masoud Barzani, the leader of the DPK, receiving 47.5% of the votes cast, and Jalal Talibani 44.9%.

In December 1993 armed conflict broke out between militants of the PUK and the Islamic League of Kurdistan, also known as the Islamic Movement of Iraqi Kurdistan (IMIK). Following mediation by the Iraqi National Congress (INC—a broad coalition of opposition groups), the two parties signed a peace agreement in February 1994. However, more serious armed conflict between partisans of the PUK and DPK led, in May, to the division of the northern Kurdish-controlled enclave into two zones. The two parties concluded a peace agreement in June, but fighting resumed in August; further peace accords, in November and December, proved short-lived. In January 1995, as fighting broke out again, Saddam Hussain offered to mediate in the dispute, prompting the Government of the United Kingdom to warn that the conflict might provide the Iraqi regime with a pretext to reassert control over the north. In June the IMIK withdrew from the INC, and in July there was renewed fighting between PUK and DPK forces. As a result of this resumption of factional hostilities, scheduled elections to the Kurdish national assembly were postponed. Peace negotiations under the auspices of the USA began in Dublin, Ireland, in August 1995 but collapsed in the following month. Subsequent

negotiations in the Iranian capital in October led to the signing of an agreement by the DPK and PUK to hold elections to the Kurdish national assembly in May 1996. US-sponsored talks resumed in northern Iraq in November.

Tensions had been heightened in March and April 1995 as Turkish armed forces attacked bases of the Kurdistan Workers' Party (Partiya Karkeren Kurdistan—PKK) in the Kurdish enclave; Turkish troops again crossed the border into northern Iraq in July. Subsequently Turkey's continued support for the DPK in its efforts to expel PKK fighters from the Kurdish enclave was believed by some observers to have encouraged the PUK to seek support from Iran. The USA and Turkey were concerned at reports later in the year that the armed wing of the Iranian-based SCIRI had begun to deploy inside the Kurdish enclave. None the less, in February 1996 Turkey and NATO agreed to continue 'Operation Provide Comfort', which had become controversial in Turkey owing to the presence of PKK bases in the Kurdish enclave.

In early 1996 the PUK leader, Jalal Talibani, offered to participate in peace negotiations with the DPK, and to take part in new elections to the Kurdish national assembly. Meanwhile, the USA continued to try to mediate an agreement between the DPK and the PUK on the demilitarization of the Arbil region. However, hostilities between the DPK and the PUK escalated in August, as the PUK contested the DPK's monopoly of duties levied on Turkish traders. Further US-sponsored peace talks failed, and at the end of the month the deployment of Iraqi armed forces inside the Kurdish area of northern Iraq, where they assisted DPK forces in retaking the PUK-held Kurdish towns of Arbil and Sulaimaniya, provoked a new international crisis. In early September the USA unilaterally launched retaliatory 'limited' air-strikes on air defence and communications targets in southern Iraq, and at the same time extended the southern air exclusion zone from latitude 32°N to latitude 33°N (thereby incorporating some southern suburbs of Baghdad). Turkey, which had refused to allow the use of its air bases for the US operation, deployed some 20,000 troops to reinforce its border with Iraq. Also in early September the DPK captured the towns of Degala, Koy Sinjaq and Sulaimaniya, thereby gaining control of all three Kurdish provinces. The Iraqi Government subsequently announced the restoration of Iraqi sovereignty over Kurdistan, and offered an amnesty to its Kurdish opponents. In late September the DPK formed a DPK-led coalition administration comprising, among others, the IMIK, the Kurdistan Communist Party and representatives of the northern Assyrian and Turkoman communities. In October PUK fighters were reported to have recaptured much of the territory they had ceded to the DPK, and to be approaching the town of Arbil, having regained control of Sulaimaniya and Halabja. The PUK claimed that it would not, however, attempt to recapture Arbil because the town remained under the protection of Iraqi armed forces. Concern that Iran's alleged involvement in the conflict would provoke direct Iraqi intervention in the north prompted renewed diplomatic efforts on the part of the USA and Turkey, and US-sponsored peace talks in Ankara, Turkey, in late October resulted in a truce agreement; further talks took place in November.

A new air surveillance programme, 'Northern Watch', began in January 1997, following the termination of 'Operation Provide Comfort'. The new operation, based in south-east Turkey, was to be conducted by British, Turkish and US forces: France had announced that it would not participate, since the 'Northern Watch' mandate contained no provision for the supply of humanitarian aid.

In May 1997 as many as 50,000 Turkish troops entered northern Iraq, where, apparently in co-operation with the DPK, they launched a major offensive against PKK bases. The incursion was condemned by Iraq and by Iran and Syria. The UN Secretary-General, Kofi Annan, demanded the withdrawal of Turkish troops from the area, expressing concern that their presence might obstruct the supply of food to the Kurdish enclave. Some 15,000 Turkish troops, again supported by DPK units, launched a further offensive against PKK bases in northern Iraq in September.

In March 1997 the DPK had withdrawn from the US-sponsored peace negotiations. Although the DPK and the PUK continued to affirm their commitment to the pursuit of peace, each accused the other of violating the cease-fire. In early October Turkish, British and US representatives met the leaders of the two parties in an attempt to defuse escalating tensions in northern Iraq. Diplomatic efforts failed, and in mid-

October, as Turkey began to withdraw its armed forces from northern Iraq (and as a US naval aircraft carrier was ordered to the Gulf, in response to an escalation of tensions between Iraq and Iran, to deter both countries from violating the northern and southern air exclusion zones) the PUK launched its strongest military assault against the DPK for a year, targeting several strategic points along the 1996 cease-fire line. The DPK alleged that the offensive had been orchestrated by Iran and conducted with PKK support. PUK and DPK representatives subsequently attended US-led negotiations in Turkey, resulting in a new cease-fire. However, fighting resumed later in the month; claims by the PUK that Turkey was assisting the DPK, which claimed to have regained most of the territory lost to the PUK during the recent hostilities, were denied by the Turkish Government, which insisted that its military campaign was directed solely against the PKK. By mid-1998 a fragile cease-fire between the PUK and the DPK appeared to be enduring and the two organizations agreed to exchange prisoners and to seek to co-operate in other areas. In September the USA brokered a formal peace agreement between the two parties: the accord, signed in Washington, DC, by Masoud Barzani on behalf of the DPK and Jalal Talibani for the PUK, provided for Kurdish legislative elections in 1999 (these did not take place, however), a unified regional administration, the sharing of local revenues, an end to hostilities and co-operation in implementing the 'oil-for-food' programme (see below) to benefit the Kurdish population. A new Kurdish coalition government was appointed by the Kurdish national assembly in December 1999. It was reported to comprise members of the DPK, the Kurdistan Independent Labour Party, the Assyrian Democratic Movement and the Turkoman community. While no substantive progress was made subsequently in establishing formal, cohesive administrative structures in the Kurdish regions, officials of the US Department of State reported, following a visit to northern Iraq in February 2000, that Kurdish leaders had agreed to work quickly towards the implementation of the 1998 agreement.

Meanwhile, some 7,000 Turkish troops were reported to have crossed into northern Iraq in early February 1998, as the crisis between the Iraqi Government and the UN regarding weapons inspections deepened (see below), in order to prevent an influx of Kurdish refugees into south-east Turkey in the event of US air-strikes against Iraqi territory. In February 1999 the capture by Turkish forces, in Nairobi, Kenya, of the PKK leader, Abdullah Ocalan (see the chapter on Turkey), provoked demonstrations by Kurds in northern Iraq and world-wide; some 4,000 Turkish troops again entered northern Iraq in pursuit of PKK sympathizers. However, the Turkish armed forces were subsequently reported to have halted their campaign against the PKK in northern Iraq. In November PKK fighters were reported to have attacked positions held by the DPK, and late in the month Iraq accused Turkey of having strengthened its forces in northern Iraq. In December Turkey accused Iraq of lending support to the PKK.

Following Iraq's defeat by the US-led coalition forces, Saddam Hussain strengthened his control over the country by placing family members and close supporters in the most important government positions. In September 1991 the Baath Party held its 10th Congress—the first such Congress since 1982—at which Saddam Hussain was re-elected Secretary-General of the Party's powerful Regional Command. Saddam Hussain attempted to bolster his domestic popularity through continued defiant rhetoric and confrontation with the UN over the dispatching of UN inspectors to monitor the elimination of Iraq's weapons of mass destruction, as stipulated by UN Security Council Resolution 687 (adopted in April 1991). In May 1994, facing a deepening economic crisis, Saddam Hussain personally assumed the post of Prime Minister. In January 1995 a comprehensive reorganization of military ranks took place, apparently the consequence of an unsuccessful military *coup d'état* in the same month. In March another attempted coup—organized this time by the former head of Iraqi military intelligence and supported by Kurdish insurgents in the north and Shi'ite rebels in the south—was reported to have been suppressed. A further reorganization of military personnel resulted in the appointment of a new Chief of the General Staff in April 1995. Reports of a mutiny by the armed forces at the Abu Ghraid army base, near Baghdad, in June were strongly denied by the Government. However, it appeared that an uprising had been organized by members of the Sunni Dulaimi clan, with the support of the élite 14 July battalion of the Iraqi army. A new Minister of Defence and a new Chief of the General Staff were appointed

in July. In an apparent attempt to re-establish domestic and international recognition of Saddam Hussain's mandate, a meeting of the RCC was convened in September at which an interim amendment of the Constitution was approved whereby the elected Chairman of the RCC would automatically assume the Presidency of the Republic, subject to the approval by the National Assembly and endorsement by national plebiscite. Saddam Hussain's candidature was duly approved by the National Assembly, and the referendum proceeded on 15 October, at which 99.96% of the votes cast (in a turn-out of 99.47%) endorsed the President's continuing in office. The result of the referendum was declared null and void in a statement issued by nine Iraqi opposition groups. In December 1996 Saddam Hussain's older son, Uday, survived an assassination attempt, but sustained serious injuries. Both the Sunni Dulaimi clan and Ad-Da'wa al-Islamiya claimed responsibility for the attack, although it was widely reported that the shooting was engineered by a former army officer whose uncle had been executed in 1990 after denouncing the Iraqi regime. In March 1997 an Iraqi opposition source alleged that Saddam Hussain had ordered the execution of 197 prisoners in retaliation for the attack on his son. In the previous month it had been reported that the President's other son, Qusay, had twice been targeted by assassins, but had escaped injury on both occasions.

The first elections to the Iraqi National Assembly since 1989 took place on 24 March 1996, when 689 candidates (all of whom had received the prior approval of a government selection committee) contested 220 of the Assembly's 250 seats: the remaining 30 seats were reserved for representatives of the Autonomous Regions of Arbil, D'hok and As-Sulaimaniya and were filled by presidential decree. It was estimated that some 90% of Iraq's electorate had participated in the elections. The INC, based in London, United Kingdom, and other groups opposed to the Government denounced the elections from abroad. In October the Baath Party elected two new members to its Regional Command.

Reports emerged in late 1997 that a number of senior military officers and Baath Party members had been executed, as had an estimated 800 prisoners suspected of belonging to opposition organizations. Many mid-level and senior Baath Party officials were apparently replaced in a political purge that was thought to have been organized in order to dilute the influence of increasingly powerful provincial party groups.

In April 1998, in his annual report on Iraq, the Special Rapporteur of the UN Commission on Human Rights, Max van der Stoel, asserted that at least 1,500 people had been executed in Iraq during 1997, mainly for political reasons. Iraqi officials dismissed the report as 'a mere repetition of the same allegations and false accusations'. Van der Stoel later denounced the assassination of two senior Shi'a religious leaders, Ayatollah Murtada al-Burujirdi and Grand Ayatollah Mirza Ali al-Gharawi, killed in April and June respectively; and expressed fears that the murders were part of a systematic attack on the independent leadership of Iraq's Shi'a Muslims. The Iraqi Government denied any involvement in the murders, attributing them instead to 'malicious foreign-based elements'. In a new report submitted in November 1998 the UN Special Rapporteur referred to the Iraqi Government as 'one of the most repressive regimes in the world since the end of the Second World War'. The report accused the Government of continuing with a policy of forcibly deporting Kurds from the Kirkuk region, and, elsewhere, identified the plight of internally displaced persons was as one of Iraq's most pressing humanitarian concerns. In February 1999 the killing of the leader of Iraq's Shi'a community, Grand Ayatollah Muhammad Sadiq as-Sader, provoked demonstrations in Baghdad and other cities. Despite claims by the INC that the unrest marked the beginning of an uprising against the Iraqi regime, it was reported that the demonstrations had been brutally suppressed by units of the Iraqi Special Republican Guards, whose members are mainly Sunni Muslims. In April the Iraqi authorities announced that four men had been executed for the murder of the Grand Ayatollah. While many observers claimed that as-Sader had been murdered by government agents, there was also speculation that he might have been killed by other Shi'a who regarded him as a 'lackey' of the Government.

Several Western-based Arabic newspapers reported in early 2000 that the Iraqi authorities had foiled a coup attempt: accounts of the circumstances surrounding the alleged plot varied, with some sources claiming that about 40 officers of the

Republican Guard had been executed for their part in an attempt to assassinate Saddam Hussein.

Elections took place on 27 March 2000 for 220 seats in the National Assembly. Official results stated that 165 seats had been won by members of the Baath Party, and the remaining 55 elective seats by independent candidates; a further 30 independents were nominated by the Government to fill the 30 seats reserved for representatives of the Kurdish areas of the north, where the Iraqi authorities stated it was impossible to organize elections since the region remained 'occupied' by the USA. Saddam Hussein's eldest son, Uday, was elected to the legislature for the first time, having reportedly received the highest number of votes of any candidate. Some 88.6% of the eligible electorate were reported to have participated in the polls. The new National Assembly was inaugurated in early April, when (despite recent speculation that the President's son would assume the post of Speaker) Sa'adoun Hammadi, who had held the office since 1996, was re-elected as Speaker. Throughout 2000 there was speculation that Saddam Hussein's son Qusay, who was reported to have been appointed deputy commander of the army and commander of the northern military region, had become the Iraqi leader's designated successor. Western-based media claimed in September and again in January 2001 that Saddam Hussein was in poor health, although the Iraqi authorities denied such reports.

In early May 2000 the SCIRI claimed to have perpetrated a rocket attack on presidential offices in Baghdad, in which there were said to have been a number of casualties; there were reports that Saddam Hussein had been scheduled to meet with his sons at the presidential palace at the time of the attack.

Shahib al-Malki retired as Minister of Justice at the beginning of July 2000 and was replaced by Mundhir Ibrahim ash-Shawi. There were further significant changes to the Council of Ministers in mid-April 2001, when Deputy Prime Minister Tareq Aziz assumed the foreign affairs portfolio on an interim basis: the outgoing Minister of Foreign Affairs, Muhammad Saeed as-Sahaf, became Minister of Culture and Information.

Issues of the maintenance of sanctions originally imposed under UN Security Council Resolution 661 and of Iraqi non-compliance with its obligations under Resolution 687 with regard to its weapons capabilities remained inextricably linked in the decade following the Gulf conflict. Security Council Resolution 692, adopted in May 1991, provided for the establishment of the UN Compensation Commission (UNCC) for victims of Iraqi aggression (both governments and individuals), to be financed by a levy (subsequently fixed at 30%) on Iraqi petroleum revenues. In August the Security Council adopted Resolution 706 (subsequently approved in Resolution 712 in September), proposing that Iraq should be allowed to sell petroleum worth up to US $1,600m. over a six-month period, the revenue from which would be paid into an escrow account controlled by the UN. Part of the sum thus realized was to be made available to Iraq for the purchase of food, medicines and supplies for essential civilian needs. Iraq rejected the terms proposed by the UN for the resumption of exports of petroleum, and in February 1992 withdrew from further negotiations. In April the UN reiterated its demand that Iraq should comply with the terms of Security Council Resolutions 706 and 712 before resuming petroleum exports. In October the UN Security Council adopted Resolution 778, permitting the confiscation of oil-related Iraqi assets to the value of up to $500m.

UN Security Council Resolution 707, adopted in August 1991, condemned Iraq's failure to comply with UN weapons inspectors, and demanded that Iraq disclose details of all non-conventional weaponry, that it allow members of UNSCOM and of the International Atomic Energy Agency (IAEA, see p. 76) unrestricted access to necessary areas and records, and that it halt all nuclear activities. Resolution 715, adopted in October, established the terms under which UNSCOM was to inspect Iraq's weapons capabilities. In October 1993 the Iraqi Government agreed to UN demands that it should release details of its weapons suppliers, and in November accepted the provisions for long-term weapons-monitoring contained in Resolution 715. However, it was clear by the end of the year that neither the Security Council nor the US Government would be willing to allow even a partial easing of sanctions until Iraq had demonstrated a sustained commitment to the dismantling of its weapons systems. Moreover, the US Government reiterated that Iraq must first also comply with all other relevant UN resolutions, recognize the newly-demarcated border with Kuwait and cease the repression of its Kurdish and southern Shi'ite communities.

In February 1994 the head of UNSCOM, Rolf Ekeus, stated, following talks with senior Iraqi officials, that Iraq had agreed to co-operate with UN weapons inspectors under Resolution 715. Thereafter, the Iraqi Government engaged in a campaign of diplomacy to obtain the removal of economic sanctions, and in July the first signs emerged of a division within the UN Security Council regarding their continuation. Russia, France and the People's Republic of China were all in favour of acknowledging Iraq's increased co-operation with UN agencies, but were unable to obtain the agreement of the other permanent members of the Council—the USA and the United Kingdom. Tensions mounted in October when, as Ekeus announced that a system for monitoring Iraqi defence industries was ready to begin operating, there was a large movement of Iraqi forces towards the border with Kuwait, apparently to draw attention to Iraq's demands for swift action to ease the sanctions. The response principally of the US and British military was swift, with additional naval vessels and forces deployed to the region, and Iraqi forces began to withdraw northward. The Security Council adopted a resolution (No. 949) demanding that the withdrawal of all Iraqi forces recently transferred to southern Iraq be completed immediately, and stipulating that Iraq must not 'utilize its military or any other forces in a hostile or provocative manner to threaten its neighbours or the UN operations in Iraq'. In November the Iraqi National Assembly voted to recognize Kuwait within the border defined by the UN in April 1992.

In January 1995 the UN Secretary-General, Boutros Boutros-Ghali, offered to resume dialogue with Iraq on a partial removal of the economic sanctions. The UN Security Council subsequently renewed the sanctions in force against Iraq for a further 60 days; however, France and Russia were reported to have argued for a partial easing of sanctions, provided that Iraq co-operated fully with UN weapons inspection. The sanctions were renewed for a further 60 days in March. Iraqi attempts to secure an end to the sanctions had suffered a serious reverse from February, when the head of UNSCOM announced that the Iraqi authorities had failed satisfactorily to account for material (known to have been imported in 1988) used in the manufacture of biological weapons. In April 1995 the Iraqi Government rejected as a violation of its sovereignty a revised UN proposal (contained in Security Council Resolution 986) for the partial resumption of exports of Iraqi petroleum to generate funds for humanitarian supplies under what was designated an 'oil-for-food' programme. After a further renewal of the economic sanctions in July, the Iraqi Minister of Foreign Affairs, Muhammad Saeed as-Sahaf, insisted that UNSCOM should complete its report and promote an end to the sanctions by the end of August if it wished to avoid the complete cessation of co-operation from the Iraqi authorities; however, the Government subsequently adopted a less confrontational stance. Sanctions continued to be renewed at 60-day intervals.

In January 1996 it was announced that talks between the UN and Iraq on the sale of Iraqi petroleum, on the basis of Resolution 986, were to recommence. In May Iraq accepted the UN's terms governing a resumption of crude petroleum sales. At the insistence of the USA and the United Kingdom, the terms stipulated that Iraq should not be involved in the distribution to the Kurdish governorates of humanitarian aid purchased with funds realized. The memorandum of understanding signed by Iraq and the UN permitted Iraq to sell some 700,000 barrels per day (b/d) of petroleum over a period of six months, after which the UN would review the situation before deciding whether sales should continue for a further six months. Of every US $1,000m. realized through the sales, $300m. would be paid into the UN reparations fund; $30m.–$50m. would contribute to the costs of UN operations in Iraq; and $130m.–$150m. would go towards funding UN humanitarian operations in Iraq's Kurdish governorates. Remaining revenues would be used for the purchase and distribution, under close UN supervision, of humanitarian goods in Iraq. While Iraq heralded the memorandum of understanding as the beginning of the dismantlement of the sanctions regime, the position of the UN remained that the embargo on sales of Iraqi petroleum would not be fully revoked until all of the country's weapons of mass destruction had been accounted for and disposed of.

In March 1996 the UN renewed the sanctions in force against Iraq for a further 60 days. The head of UNSCOM had reported to the Security Council his concern that Iraq might still be engaged in the development of prohibited weapons systems, and might be concealing biological missile warheads from the UN inspectorate. Incidents of non-co-operation between the Iraqi authorities and UN weapons inspection teams were reported at intervals. In July the UN sanctions committee announced procedures governing renewed sales of Iraqi petroleum; however, these terms required unanimous approval by the UN Security Council, and their endorsement was delayed by the USA's insistence on more stringent monitoring. A revised version was approved in August. In September, however, the implementation of Resolution 986 was postponed indefinitely, in response to the deployment of Iraqi armed forces inside the Kurdish 'safe haven' in northern Iraq (see above).

In October 1996 UNSCOM rejected Iraq's 'full, final and complete disclosures on its weapons programmes'. The US Treasury was reported at this time to have granted its approval for the opening of an escrow account with the New York branch of the Banque Nationale de Paris, but the implementation of Resolution 986 was now dependent on the satisfaction of the UN Secretary-General with stability in northern Iraq and the approval by the UN sanctions committee of a formula fixing the value of Iraqi crude petroleum to be sold. Despite signs of renewed co-operation, in April 1997 Rolf Ekeus reiterated concerns that Iraq was not fully co-operating with UNSCOM weapons inspectors. Relations between Iraq and UNSCOM deteriorated in June after the Security Council accused Iraq of obstructing inspection flights over Iraqi territory; Iraq subsequently denied UNSCOM access to three military sites. The UN reported renewed co-operation by Iraq in July, following the inauguration of Richard Butler as the new head of UNSCOM. In October, however, Butler's initial report to the UN Security Council asserted that although some progress had been made in inspecting Iraqi missiles, Iraq had failed to produce a credible account of its biological, chemical and nuclear warfare programmes and was continuing to hinder UNSCOM's work. Subsequently, within the UN Security Council, the USA and the United Kingdom proposed a resolution to prohibit Iraqi officials considered to be responsible for obstructing weapons inspections from leaving the country. France and Russia objected to the draft resolution but approved a revised version to impose a travel ban on Iraqi officials in April 1998 should non-co-operation with UNSCOM continue.

In October 1997 Iraq's RCC criticized the high proportion of UNSCOM personnel supplied by the USA, claiming that they were opposed to the removal of sanctions. Iraq demanded that all such personnel should leave the country by 5 November; the deadline was subsequently extended by one week, in order to allow a UN mission to travel to Baghdad to attempt to resolve the dispute. When negotiations failed, the UN Security Council unanimously adopted a resolution (No. 1137) that immediately activated the travel ban on Iraqi officials. The resolution also stipulated that Iraq should retract its decision to expel US personnel and stated that further Iraqi intransigence regarding weapons inspections would result in the suspension of the 60-day sanctions review until April 1998 and, furthermore, possibly provoke military action. Iraq refused to withdraw its demand and US weapons inspectors were forced to leave the country. In response to the escalating crisis, the USA and the United Kingdom ordered military reinforcements to the region. Tensions appeared to ease in mid-November, after the Iraqi Deputy Prime Minister, Tareq Aziz, met the Russian Minister of Foreign Affairs, Yevgenii Primakov, who affirmed that Russia would continue to promote the removal of economic sanctions on condition that Iraq complied with Resolution 1137. UNSCOM weapons inspectors were permitted to return to Iraq soon afterwards, but renewed Iraqi co-operation with UNSCOM was short-lived, as Iraqi officials refused to allow UNSCOM the unconditional access which it sought to areas designated as presidential palaces. In mid-December Richard Butler, accompanied by British, French and Russian commissioners, held talks in Baghdad with Tareq Aziz. Although Aziz expressed satisfaction at the presence of representatives of countries other than the USA, no progress was achieved, and in response to the apparent impasse the USA reiterated its unilateral threat of military action in order to force Saddam Hussain to capitulate to UN demands.

The confrontation over weapons inspections deepened in January 1998, when Iraq prohibited inspections by an UNSCOM team led by a former US marine officer, Scott Ritter, claiming that Ritter was spying for the US Central Intelligence Agency (CIA); the inspection team subsequently left Iraq. Meanwhile, the UN Security Council issued a statement deploring Iraq's failure to provide UNSCOM with 'full, unconditional and imme-

diate access to all sites'. It was evident, none the less, that while the USA and United Kingdom continued to advocate increased coercion with regard to Iraq, the People's Republic of China, France and Russia were more amenable to the offsetting US dominance within UNSCOM. Richard Butler returned to Iraq, where he apparently agreed to Russian proposals to include experts from each of the permanent members of the Security Council, and from Germany, in forthcoming technical talks with Iraqi officials on the subject of weapons production records, thereby 'diluting' the presence of US personnel. However, Iraq maintained that it would be prepared to discuss UNSCOM access only following completion of the technical talks. The USA, supported by the United Kingdom, indicated that it was prepared to mount a military response to Iraq's continued non-co-operation, and the US Secretary of State, Madeleine Albright, and Secretary of Defense, William Cohen, led US diplomatic efforts to secure international and support for possible military action against Iraq. However, China, France and Russia opposed the use of force. In view of threatened air-strikes against Iraq, Russia's Deputy Minister of Foreign Affairs, Viktor Posuvalyuk, held extensive talks with Iraqi officials in Baghdad in late January and early February. The Russian President, Boris Yeltsin, maintained that Russia would veto any Security Council resolution authorizing military attacks on Iraq, and warned that US military strikes could have serious international repercussions. Furthermore, it became apparent that there was little regional support for military action against Iraq: only Kuwait announced its approval of force if diplomatic efforts should fail; Saudi Arabia and Bahrain refused to authorize military attacks from their territories, while Egypt and Syria notably signalled their disapproval of military strikes against Iraq. Meanwhile, senior representatives of the Arab League, Russia, Turkey and France met in Baghdad in early February in an attempt to defuse the crisis. In mid-February the five permanent members of the UN Security Council approved a compromise formula whereby a group of diplomats, specially appointed by the UN Secretary-General in consultation with experts from UNSCOM and the IAEA, would be allowed unconditional and unrestricted access to the eight so-called presidential sites. The Secretary-General, Kofi Annan, travelled to Baghdad in order to discuss the compromise, which was accepted by Iraq following a meeting between Annan and Saddam Hussain; a new memorandum of understanding governing inspections was subsequently signed by Tareq Aziz and Kofi Annan, thus averting the immediate threat of military action. In early March the UN Security Council unanimously approved a resolution (No. 1154) endorsing the memorandum of understanding and warning of 'extreme consequences' should Iraq renege on the agreement. Inspection teams returned to Iraq shortly afterwards, and members of the special group began visiting the presidential sites later in the month. In April, in his six-monthly report to the Security Council, the head of UNSCOM concluded that there had been no progress in the disarmament verification process since October 1997, and that the destruction of Iraq's chemical and biological weapons was incomplete. (Furthermore, an annex to a report issued by the head of the special group had assessed that the presidential sites contained 'very little equipment, documentation or other material' and had 'undergone extensive evacuation'.) Iraq, however, insisted that all of its weapons of mass destruction had been destroyed and requested the complete and comprehensive removal of sanctions. US and British opposition frustrated Russian attempts to secure a vote on a draft resolution proposing an end to weapons inspections, in view of an IAEA report concluding that it had failed to uncover evidence of a nuclear weapons programme in Iraq, and in late April the UN Security Council, in response to the Butler's report, voted not to review the sanctions in force against Iraq. The USA began in May to withdraw military reinforcements deployed in the region at the height of the inspections crisis.

Richard Butler visited Baghdad in June 1998, where during talks with the Deputy Prime Minister, Tareq Aziz, significant progress was reportedly made on plans for the verification of Iraqi disarmament and the eventual removal of sanctions. Later in the month the UNSCOM head was reported to have informed the UN Security Council that US military tests on weaponry dismantled as part of the inspection process had shown that Iraq had loaded missile warheads with a chemical weapon component prior to the Gulf conflict. (Subsequent tests on the samples by French and Swiss scientists reportedly disclosed evidence of a decontaminant used to destroy agents of biological warfare.) The IAEA again reported in July that it had no evidence that Iraq was concealing nuclear weapons, but considered that Iraq lacked 'full transparency' in its disclosures to inspectors. In August negotiations between Butler and Aziz collapsed: Iraq rejected UNSCOM proposals for the acceleration of the inspection programme, reportedly insisting that UNSCOM should report to the Security Council that Iraq had eliminated its weapons of mass destruction, and reiterated demands for a restructuring of UNSCOM to overcome the perceived US dominance. Iraq suspended arms inspections, and Saddam Hussain announced new terms and conditions for their resumption including the establishment of a new executive bureau to supervise UNSCOM's operations. This effectively halted inspections of new sites, while UNSCOM continued existing monitoring without the co-operation of the Iraqi authorities. The UN Security Council voted later in August to renew the sanctions regime for a further 60 days, but in September unanimously adopted a resolution (No. 1194) condemning Iraq's action of the previous month, demanding that Iraq co-operate fully with UNSCOM, and suspending indefinitely the review of the sanctions regime. The Iraqi Government announced in response that it was suspending all co-operation with UNSCOM indefinitely. Meanwhile, the apparent desire of the US administration to avoid a confrontation such as that earlier in the year prompted the resignation of Scott Ritter from UNSCOM.

Reporting to the Security Council in October 1998, Richard Butler asserted that while Iraq was close to fulfilling its obligations with regard to missiles and chemical weapons programmes, UNSCOM remained concerned about the country's capacity for biological warfare. At the end of the month there was a serious deterioration in relations between Iraq and UNSCOM: following a joint meeting, chaired by Saddam Hussain, of the RCC and Baath Party leaders, Iraq announced the suspension of all co-operation until the UN Security Council cancelled the sanctions regime, dismissed Butler as head of UNSCOM, and restructured the inspection body so as to ensure its neutrality. (UNSCOM inspectors were not expelled, however, and the IAEA was to be permitted to continue its operations in Iraq.) The suspension of co-operation was endorsed by the Iraqi National Assembly in early November. Shortly afterwards the UN Security Council unanimously adopted a resolution (No. 1205) demanding that Iraq immediately and unconditionally resume co-operation with UNSCOM; the British-drafted resolution made no mention of military reprisals, to which the People's Republic of China, France and Russia remained strongly opposed. The USA, meanwhile, sought support within the UN Security Council and among Arab states for further military action against Iraq, and the US and British military enforcements were again dispatched to the Gulf region. Egypt, Saudi Arabia and Syria, while they opposed the threat of force, urged Iraq to resume co-operation. In mid-November, as the USA and United Kingdom reportedly prepared to carry out air-strikes against Iraqi targets, Iraq announced that UNSCOM would be permitted unconditionally to resume the weapons inspection programme; inspectors subsequently returned to Iraq and resumed their monitoring programme.

However, Iraq's relations with UNSCOM deteriorated once again in early December 1998, after a weapons inspection team was denied access to the Baath Party headquarters in Baghdad: the inspection was part of a new series of what were termed 'challenge inspections' by UNSCOM officers. In a report to the UN Security Council mid-December, Butler assessed that Iraq had failed to comply with its undertaking of the previous month regarding full co-operation with UNSCOM, and on the night of 16–17 December, following the withdrawal from Iraq of UNSCOM and IAEA personnel, the USA and the United Kingdom commenced a campaign of air-strikes against Iraqi targets; the operation, designated 'Desert Fox' was terminated on 20 December, with the USA and United Kingdom claiming to have caused significant damage to Iraqi military installations. France, Russia and China contended that the military action had been undertaken without UN Security Council authorization; however, the USA and the United Kingdom maintained that Resolution 1154, adopted in March, provided sufficient authorization. Following the attacks, Iraq, which accused the head of UNSCOM of having deliberately provided the USA and the United Kingdom with a pretext for military action, remained implacably opposed to the resumption of weapons inspections by UNSCOM. In January 1999 US and Iraqi fighter aircraft clashed in the air exclusion zone over southern Iraq. Throughout the month ground-launched attacks on US aircraft engaged in policing the zone (in retaliation for which US aircraft launched

attacks on Iraqi defence sites) appeared to confirm speculation that Iraq was pursuing a more confrontational policy of refusing to recognize the air exclusion zone. In late February and early March US and British armed forces carried out further air attacks on Iraqi air defence and other military sites in response to alleged violations of the air exclusion zone, and in retaliation for further alleged ground-launched attacks. The Iraqi authorities claimed that on at least one occasion the US and British forces had attacked civilian targets. In March the People's Republic of China urged the USA and the United Kingdom to halt the air-strikes against Iraq, moreover claiming, as did Russia, that the air exclusion zones were illegal since they had never been authorized by the UN. By mid-1999 US and British aircraft had reportedly made more than 200 multi-missile air-strikes against Iraq since mid-December 1998. US and British aircraft continued to attack Iraqi air defence targets during the second half of 1999, throughout 2000, and into 2001.

The new US administration of George W. Bush, which assumed office in January 2001, swiftly demonstrated its resolve to maintain an uncompromising stance with regard to Iraq. In mid-February US and British fighter aircraft launched their first attack since Operation Desert Fox of December 1998 on air defence targets near Baghdad, in what the US President described as a 'routine mission' to enforce the northern and southern air exclusion zones. In justification of the assaults, the USA and United Kingdom cited a recent increased threat to their military aircraft operating in the exclusion zones from Iraqi missile defences. Iraq protested that the air-strikes had targeted residential areas of Baghdad, while there were Western media reports that three people had been killed, and more than 30 injured, in the initial attacks. The air-strikes were widely condemned by Arab states (other than Kuwait and Saudi Arabia), as well as by France, Russia and the People's Republic of China.

The campaign of air-strikes conducted against Iraqi targets in December 1998 was regarded as marking the collapse of UNSCOM's mission. In January 1999, in order to establish the basis for a new approach to Iraq, the UN created three panels—to consider the question of Iraq's disarmament, to examine the issue of Kuwaiti prisoners of war, and to review the humanitarian situation—which reported in March. The panel on disarmament proposed the reform of UNSCOM, in ways, it was claimed, that would reduce the influence on it of the USA and the United Kingdom. Nevertheless, the panel concluded that there were outstanding issues in almost every weapons category and urged a reinforced, continuous monitoring and verification programme. Iraq was deemed by the second panel not to have supplied adequate information to the UN regarding the fate of Kuwaiti prisoners of war. The humanitarian panel reported that Iraq had fallen into deep poverty since 1991, and recommended, *inter alia*, that the country should be permitted to export as much oil as possible in order to finance purchases under the oil-for-food programme. Iraq denounced the proposals of all three panels, declaring that they provided pretexts for continued aggression by the country's enemies.

Diplomatic initiatives undertaken by the Netherlands and the United Kingdom from early 1999 with the aim of drafting a proposal, acceptable to all the permanent members of the Security Council, to establish a successor body to UNSCOM, culminated, in December, in the adoption by the Security Council of a resolution (No. 1284) that modified the regime in force for monitoring Iraqi weapons systems. Under the new resolution UNSCOM was to be replaced by a UN Monitoring, Verification and Inspection Commission (UNMOVIC). The resolution provided for the suspension of the economic sanctions in force against Iraq for renewable 120-day periods, provided that Iraq co-operated fully with the new weapons inspectorate and the IAEA throughout such periods. The resolution also effectively removed restrictions on the maximum amount of petroleum that Iraq was permitted to sell under the oil-for-food programme. Resolution 1284 was not approved unanimously, with the People's Republic of China, France and Russia, together with Malaysia (a non-permanent member) abstaining. Iraq's immediate response was to state that it would not co-operate with UNMOVIC; it was notable, however, that the Government did not categorically reject the resolution at this time. Iraq was opposed to the UN Secretary-General's proposed appointment of Rolf Ekeus, Butler's predecessor as head of UNSCOM, to chair UNMOVIC, and in January 2000 China, Russia and France formally objected to the nomination. In late January the Security Council unanimously endorsed the appointment of

Hans Blix, a former Director-General of the IAEA, as head of UNMOVIC. Meanwhile, IAEA personnel undertook the first routine inspection of Iraqi facilities since their withdrawal in December 1998.

UNMOVIC's 17 members, appointed in March 2000, included representatives of 10 countries in addition to those of the five permanent members of the Security Council. Earlier in the month Blix had emphasized in his first report to the Security Council that, should Iraq permit the return of weapons inspectors, UNMOVIC would resume 'surprise' or 'challenge' inspections of Iraqi sites. In mid-March Iraq's deputy premier, Tareq Aziz, decisively rejected the terms of Resolution 1284. In subsequent months the Iraqi Government repeated at frequent intervals that it would never admit UNMOVIC to enter the country, and in early September Hans Blix was prevailed upon to amend a report to the UN Security Council in which he had asserted that weapons inspectors were ready to return to Iraq: the reworded document, asserting that UNMOVIC could conduct a number of preparatory inspection activities 'if and when' inspectors were permitted to enter Iraq, was accepted by all permanent members of the Security Council later in the month. In early March 2001 it was reported that a recent UNMOVIC assessment had concluded that Iraq may still have the ability to build and use biological and chemical weapons, and may have stocks of mustard gas, biological weapons and anthrax, and also that Iraq could have the capability to deliver *Scud* missiles. Meanwhile, mid-January the Iraqi Government requested that the UN Secretary-General order an inquiry into the use by the multinational force of depleted uranium as a weapons component during the Gulf conflict, in view of the high incidence of cancers and birth deformities within the Iraqi population since 1991.

Exports of Iraqi crude petroleum, under the terms of Resolution 986, recommenced in December 1996, whereupon Turkish officials reported that Iraq was pumping 350,000 b/d of crude petroleum through the Kirkuk–Yumurtalik pipeline. The first supplies of food purchased with the revenues from these exports arrived in Iraq in March 1997, resulting in an increase in basic food rations. In June the oil-for-food agreement was extended for a further six months, but Iraq suspended its petroleum exports shortly afterwards, protesting that it had not received sufficient humanitarian aid from the UN. Iraq submitted a new distribution plan, which was approved by the UN, and exports of petroleum recommenced in mid-August. (Owing to the previous interruption of exports, the UN Security Council modified the terms of the original oil-for-food agreement, permitting Iraq an extra 30 days to sell its first tranche of oil but contracting the time limit for sales of the second tranche by 30 days.) In December the UN renewed the sales agreement for another six months, but the following day exports were again halted at Iraq's request: Iraq once again criticized the UN for inefficient delivery of humanitarian supplies and drafted another revised distribution plan. Exports of petroleum resumed in January 1998, following UN approval of the new plan. In February the UN Security Council raised the maximum permitted revenue from exports of petroleum to US $5,200m. in the six months to the end of July, of which Iraq would be permitted to spend some $3,550m. on humanitarian goods. The remainder would be used to finance reparations and UN operations in the country. However, Iraq stated that without rehabilitation of its oil sector it would be unable to export more than $4,000m.-worth of oil every six months. In March UN technicians conducted an assessment of the Iraqi oil sector, reporting that Iraq was currently able to export oil to the value of only $3,000m. every six months, and that it would only be able to maintain this level of exports if it was allowed to import essential spare parts. The UN Secretary-General therefore requested the Security Council to allow Iraq to divert $300m. of oil revenues in order to carry out repairs to oil production facilities, and to reduce the value of permitted Iraqi exports under the revised agreement to $4,000m. every six months; Iraq was required to submit a new aid distribution programme before the revised agreement could take effect. The new plan, which was submitted in May and approved by the UN Secretary-General at the end of the month, provided for oil sales worth $4,500m. over the following six months, of which $3,100m. was to be allocated for humanitarian supplies and urgent infrastructural repairs, while the remainder would finance war reparations. In June the UN Security Council approved a resolution allowing Iraq to purchase spare parts to the value of $300m. for the oil sector. In November the Security Council renewed the oil-for-food agree-

ment, allowing Iraq to sell $5,200m.-worth of oil over six months. (Owing to low world petroleum prices for oil at that time and infrastructural inadequacy, however, it appeared unlikely that Iraqi oil sales would raise more than $3,000m. during the period.) In May 1999 the oil-for-food programme was extended for a sixth phase. In October the UN Security Council unanimously adopted a resolution (No. 1242) permitting Iraq to sell $3,040m.-worth of oil in addition to the quota agreed in May, with the intention of compensating for a shortfall in oil revenues in the two previous sale periods. However, Iraq's request to spend a further $300m. on equipment for the oil industry was not granted. In November, as the six-month sale period expired, Iraq rejected a proposal by the UN Security Council that the oil-for-food programme should be extended for a further two weeks, pending the revision of the programme's terms of reference. Iraq then temporarily suspended its exports of oil, causing world prices to rise to their highest levels since 1990 and prompting speculation that Iraq was seeking to expose divisions that were known to exist within the Security Council regarding the future policy towards Iraq. In December the Security Council voted unanimously to extend the oil-for-food programme for a further six months. In late March 2000, in response to a report in which Kofi Annan recommended that Iraq be allowed to purchase increased quantities of parts and equipment to offset permanent damage to its oil industry, the UN Security Council unanimously approved a resolution permitting Iraq to make such purchases to the value of US $600m. over six months. The oil-for-food programme was extended for further six-month periods in June and December. Prior to the latter extension, Iraq had briefly suspended petroleum exports, causing a sharp increase in international oil prices.

In mid-February 2000 two senior UN officials working in Iraq—the UN Humanitarian Co-ordinator in Iraq (responsible for the oil-for-food programme), Hans von Sponeck, and the head of World Food Programme operations in Iraq, Jutta Burghardt—resigned in protest at the hardship inflicted on the Iraqi people by the continuing sanctions regime. (The previous oil-for-food co-ordinator, Denis Halliday, had resigned in 1998 after similarly denouncing the failure of the operation of UN sanctions). Tun Myat, who took up office as UN Humanitarian Co-ordinator in Baghdad at the end of April, rejected criticism of the oil-for-food programme but undertook to try to improve its management. Throughout 2000 there was evidence of continued polarization among the five permanent members of the UN Security Council regarding the maintenance of the sanctions regime, while there were reports that Kofi Annan might himself favour a move towards so-called 'smarter sanctions'—targeting specific individuals rather than the entire Iraqi population. Furthermore, the international community became increasingly vocal in its condemnation of the humanitarian consequences of a decade of sanctions. In mid-March, in spite of the objections of the UN sanctions committee, a British parliamentarian led an aid mission by road from the Jordanian capital, Amman, to Baghdad, delivering medicines to the headquarters of the Iraqi Red Crescent Society, and in early April a member of the Italian and European parliaments chartered an aircraft from Amman to Jordan, in direct contravention of the UN embargo on air travel to Iraq. In August President Hugo Chàvez Friàs of Venezuela became the first democratically-elected head of state to visit Iraq since the Gulf conflict, travelling overland from Iran in order to avoid violating the air embargo. In late September medical personnel and members of the French cultural and sporting establishment made a much-publicized three-day visit to Iraq, aboard an aircraft chartered by a French non-governmental organization: the French authorities insisted that the flight did not require prior authorization by the UN sanctions committee since its mission was humanitarian. In subsequent months numerous missions of intellectuals, politicians and writers made similar international flights into Iraq, in demonstrations of their opposition to the maintenance of the sanctions regime. In late June two employees of the UN Food and Agriculture Organization in Baghdad had been shot dead, and seven injured, by an assailant (who claimed to be acting alone) protesting at the impact of sanctions on the Iraqi population.

Meanwhile, following the reopening in mid-August 2000 of Baghdad's Saddam International airport (for the first time since 1991), several foreign airlines announced their intention to begin commercial scheduled flights to Iraq: notable among these was the Russian carrier Aeroflot, which signed a memorandum of understanding with the Iraqi authorities in October 2000 (no date was specified for the resumption of flights), while the

Egyptian President Hosni Mubarak stated in the same month that he would not object to the resumption of flights from Egypt should any private airline chose to operate services. In August a rail link between Baghdad and Aleppo, Syria, was reopened after an interval of some 20 years. Furthermore, in November Iraq began to transport crude petroleum from Iraq to Syria, via a pipeline not used since the early 1980s (the oil-for-food agreement permitted oil exports only via two designated outlets); the new route was assessed as having the capacity to more than double Iraqi oil sales from their existing level of 150,000 b/d. However, while Saddam Hussain insisted that the sanctions regime was beginning to disintegrate, the new US administration under President George W. Bush, who assumed office in January 2001, emphasized its commitment to ensuring the maintenance of the sanctions regime pending the full implementation of Resolution 1284.

At the end of September 2000 the UN Security Council approved the payment to Kuwait of US $15,900m. in compensation for lost production and sales of petroleum as a result of the 1990–91 occupation. However, it was agreed to reduce the levy on Iraq's petroleum revenues destined for reparations under the oil-for-food programme from 30% to 25%: France and Russia had hitherto delayed a decision by the UNCC on the payment, and earlier in September Russia warned of its inclination to oppose Kuwaiti claims to reparations unless the levy on Iraqi oil revenues was reduced to 20%.

In September 2000 Iraq reiterated allegations that Kuwait was stealing Iraqi petroleum by drilling in an area near the Iraq–Kuwait border. Iraq also accused both Kuwait and Saudi Arabia of inflicting (through the maintenance of the sanctions regime) suffering on the Iraqi population, and alleged that Saudi Arabia was appropriating Iraqi petroleum transported under the oil-for-food programme. In September and again in October reports of Iraqi troop movements near the Iraq–Kuwait demilitarized zone prompted Kuwait to reinforce security arrangements in the border area. None the less, a general improvement was perceived in Iraq's relations with other Arab states in the latter part of 2000. Iraq's Minister of Foreign Affairs, Muhammad Saeef as-Sahaf, undertook a regional tour in late October, visiting Egypt, Jordan, Libya, Qatar and Yemen. In the same month Iraq was represented at a summit meeting of the Arab League for the first time since 1990, as RCC member Izzat Ibrahim ad-Duri attended the emergency session convened to discuss the Israeli–Palestinian crisis that had erupted at the end of September 2000. In early November the Jordanian Prime Minister, Ali Abu ar-Ragheb, became the highest ranking Arab leader to visit Iraq since the Gulf crisis. Reciprocal visits by Iraqi and Egyptian delegations culminated in an agreement, in early January 2001, to establish a joint free-trade zone, and Syria subsequently indicated its interest in joining such a trading arrangement.

In October 1998 the US Congress approved the Iraq Liberation Act, which allows the US President to provide up to US $97m. in military assistance to Iraqi opposition groups in exile. In April 1999 11 opposition groups gathered in London, United Kingdom, where they undertook to reform the moribund INC and to prepare by July a plan of campaign against Saddam Hussain's regime. Although the two main Kurdish factions, the DPK and the PUK, attended the meeting, the SCIRI and the Iraqi Communist Party did not participate. Two new organizations were created at the meeting: a collegiate leadership of seven members (six members were nominated, with the remaining place reserved for a representative of the SCIRI), and a five-member committee charged with contacting all opposition groups. In November, delegates to a national assembly of the INC, held in New York, USA, elected a 65-member central council and a new, seven-member collegiate leadership.

Government

Executive power rests with the President and a Revolutionary Command Council (RCC). In September a national referendum approved an interim amendment of the Constitution whereby the elected Chairman of the RCC would automatically assume the Presidency of the Republic, subject to the approval by the National Assembly and endorsement by national plebiscite. Considerable influence is exercised by the Regional Command of the Baath Party, while the routine administration of the country is undertaken by an appointed Council of Ministers. Legislative responsibility is shared between the RCC and the National Assembly, with 250 members elected by universal adult suffrage for four years. (At each of the legislative elections held in 1996 and in 2000 only 220 seats were elective; the remaining 30 seats—reserved for representatives of the Kurdish regions—were filled by government nominees.) The country is divided into 18 governorates (including three Autonomous Regions).

Defence

Military service is compulsory for all men at the age of 18 years, and lasts between 18 months and two years, extendable in wartime. In August 2000 the armed forces totalled an estimated 429,000 regular members: the army had an estimated total strength of 375,000 (including an estimated 100,000 recalled reserves); the air force had a strength of some 35,000, the navy an estimated 2,000, and an air defence command an estimated strength of 17,000. Paramilitary forces comprised security troops, border guards and *fedayeen* ('martyrs'), with strengths estimated, respectively, at 15,000, 20,000 and 10,000–15,000. Defence expenditure in 1999 was estimated at US $1,400m.

Economic Affairs

In 1996, according to estimates by the *Middle East Economic Digest* of London, Iraq's gross domestic product (GDP), measured in current prices, was US $11,500m., equivalent to about $596 per head. According to the same source, GDP declined by about 15% in 1996, compared with 1995. Over the period 1990–98 the population increased by an average of 3.0% per year, according to estimates by the World Bank.

Agriculture (including forestry and fishing) contributed 46.9% of GDP in 1995, compared with 15.3% in 1989—i.e. prior to the invasion of Kuwait. An estimated 10.6% of the labour force were employed in agriculture in 1999. Dates are the principal cash crop. Other crops include wheat, barley, maize, sugar beet and cane, and melons. Production of eggs and poultry meat is also important. During 1990–99, according to FAO data, agricultural production declined by an average of 4.1% per year; output declined by 14.1% in 1999. Output of cereals fell from 3.45m. metric tons in 1990 to an estimated 1.60m. metric tons in 1999; preliminary FAO estimates for 2000 assessed cereals production at only 0.8m. metric tons.

Industry (including mining, manufacturing, construction and power) employed 19.1% of the labour force in 1987; the sector provided only 1.1% of GDP in 1995 (compared with 37.9% in 1989).

Mining (including production of crude petroleum and gas) employed 1.3% of the labour force in 1987. The sector contributed less than 0.1% of GDP in 1994 (compared with 17.9% in 1989), and by 1995 its contribution was negative. Iraq had proven reserves of 112,500m. barrels of petroleum at the end of 1999, as well as 3,110,000m. cu m of natural gas. Reserves of phosphates, sulphur, gypsum and salt are also exploited.

Manufacturing employed 7.4% of the labour force in 1987, and contributed 0.7% of GDP in 1995 (compared with 12.3% in 1989). Measured by the value of output, chemical, petroleum, coal, rubber and plastic products accounted for 35.2% of manufacturing activity in 1986. Other important branches of the sector in that year were food products (providing 15.8% of manufacturing output), non-metallic mineral products (12.6%) and textiles (6.1%). In the immediate aftermath of the war with the multinational force, all of Iraq's electrically-powered installations were reported to have ceased functioning, as a result of the destruction of power plants, etc. By late 1991 a drastic decline in industrial output had been observed, with further hundreds of industrial projects having ceased, owing to the continued trade embargo, and a consequent steep rise in unemployment.

Energy is derived principally from hydroelectric power, and there is also an oil-fired power station.

The services sector employed 19.1% of the labour force in 1987, and contributed 52.2% of GDP in 1995 (compared with 46.7% in 1989). In 1996, according to the *Middle East Economic Digest*, Iraq recorded a trade surplus of US $300m. In that year, according to the same source, the current account of the balance of payments was estimated to be in balance. Crude petroleum was by far the most important export before the imposition of economic sanctions(see below). According to the IMF, the value of Iraq's imports in 1999 was ID 479.1m.

In a six-month emergency reconstruction budget, announced in mid-1991, planned expenditure in the general consolidated budget was reduced from ID 14,596m. to ID 13,876m., while investment budget expenditure was reduced from ID 2,340m. to ID 1,660m. The Iraqi Government estimated that, at 1 January 1991, its total external debt stood at ID 13,118m. (US $42,320m.); and that the servicing of the debt over the period 1991–95 would cost ID 23,388m. ($75,450m.). These estimates did not, however, take into account loans made to Iraq during the Iran–Iraq War by Saudi Arabia and Kuwait. The *Middle East Economic Digest* estimated that in 1996 the average rate of inflation was 450%, compared with inflation averaging 24.4% per year in 1985–89.

Iraq is a member of the Arab Fund for Economic and Social Development (see p. 125), the Council of Arab Economic Unity (p. 163),the Organization of Arab Petroleum Exporting Countries (p. 264), the Organization of the Petroleum Exporting Countries (p. 269) and the Arab Co-operation Council (p. 306).

Revenues accruing to Iraq through the oil-for-food sales (permitted since early December 1996 in accordance with UN Security Council Resolution 986, see Recent History) are governed by stringent restrictions. Under the terms of Resolution 986, Iraq was initially permitted to sell petroleum to the value of US $2,000m. over a six-month period (subsequently extended). Of this, only about $1,200m. was available to the Iraqi Government, exclusively for the purchase of humanitarian goods under the supervision of the UN. In February 1998 the UN Security Council increased the maximum permitted revenue from exports of petroleum to $5,200m. in the six months to 31 July. This increase was subsequently renewed, but Iraq was not able to take full advantage of it owing to the urgent need for rehabilitation of parts of its oil production sector. This need was acknowledged in June, when the UN Security Council adopted a resolution permitting Iraq to import equipment to the value of $300m. for the sector. In late 1998 it was estimated that Iraq's oil production capacity was declining by 4%–6% annually. Revenues were, furthermore, undermined by the decline at that time in international prices for petroleum. In October the UN Security Council adopted a resolution permitting Iraq to sell additional oil valued at $3,040m., with the intention of compensating for a shortfall in oil revenues in the two previous sale periods. In December the UN Security Council effectively removed restrictions on the value of Iraqi petroleum exports. In March 2000 the Security Council unanimously approved a resolution permitting Iraq to make further purchases of parts and equipment for the oil industry to the value of $600m. over six months. The oil-for-food programme was extended for further six-month periods in June and December.

According to an official UN report compiled in March 1991, Iraq's war with the multinational force 'wrought near apocalyptic results on the economic infrastructure', relegating Iraq to a 'pre-industrial age but with all the disabilities of post-industrial dependency on an intensive use of energy and technology'. The damage to the infrastructure has been reflected in every sector, with recovery undoubtedly obstructed by more than a decade of international sanctions. The failure of irrigation and drainage systems, owing to lack of fuel and spare parts, compounded by the inability of farmers to obtain pesticides and fertilizers, have resulted in very poor harvests, while reduced production of animal feed has resulted in a significant decrease in livestock and livestock products. The consequences for the Iraqi population of the resultant food shortages have been particularly severe. Upon his resignation in September 1998, the first co-ordinator of the UN oil-for-food programme, instituted in 1996, estimated that 4,000–5,000 Iraqi children were dying each month as a result of contaminated water supplies, poor sanitation, malnutrition and inadequate health facilities. His successor resigned in February 2000, as did the head of World Food Programme operations, in protest at what they considered to be the consequences of the sanctions regime and the inadequacy of the humanitarian programme to meet the basic requirements of the Iraqi people. In August 1999 a report by the UN Children's Fund (UNICEF) claimed that infant mortality rates in areas under Iraqi government control had more than doubled since the imposition of economic sanctions in 1990. UNICEF claimed that in some parts of Iraq that were outside government control infant mortality rates had fallen. (Iraqi claims that the increases were the result of the sanctions regime were countered by the US administration, which accused the Iraqi authorities of inadequate ordering and distribution of supplies.) A report issued by the International Committee of the Red Cross in February 2000 stated that infant mortality had risen threefold since the imposition of sanctions in 1990, and that the death rate among children under five years of age was at least five times greater than the level prior to the Gulf crisis; a report published in the United Kingdom in the medical journal, *The Lancet*, in May 2000 similarly attributed a more than doubling of child mortality rates since the imposition of sanctions to malnutrition, to shortages of power and water in hospitals, and to increases in the incidence of communicable diseases.

Social Welfare

A limited Social Security Scheme was introduced in 1957 and extended in 1976. Benefits are given for old age, sickness, unemployment, maternity, marriage and death. Health services are provided free of charge. More than US $1,500m. was spent on building more than 30 new hospitals under the 1981–85 Five-Year Plan, providing about 11,500 beds. By the end of 1986, as a result of these additions, Iraq had 228 hospital establishments, with a total of 32,166 beds. In 1998, according to WHO data, Iraq had 55 physicians per 100,000 population and 236 nursing personnel per 100,000 population. Owing to the impact of sanctions, however, Iraq lacks funds to pay for adequate medical provisions. In September 1997 the Iraqi Government stated that hospitals could operate at only 30% of capacity.

Education

Education is provided free of charge, and primary education, beginning at six years of age and lasting for six years, has been made compulsory in an effort to reduce illiteracy. (In 1995 an estimated 42% of Iraqi adults were illiterate.) Enrolment at primary schools of children in the relevant age-group reached 100% in 1978, but the proportion had fallen to 76% by 1995 (males 81%; females 71%). Secondary education begins at 12 years of age and lasts for up to six years, divided into two cycles of three years each. Enrolment at secondary schools in 1995 was equivalent to 42% of children in the appropriate age-group (males 51%; females 32%). There are 47 teacher-training institutes, 19 technical institutes and eight universities. In the 1991/92 academic year 46,250 students were reported to have enrolled in courses of higher education.

Public Holidays

2001: 1 January (New Year's Day), 6 January (Army Day), 8 February (14 Ramadan Revolution, anniversary of the 1963 *coup d'état*), 6 March* (Id al-Adha, Feast of the Sacrifice), 26 March* (Islamic New Year), 4 April* (Ashoura), 4 June* (Mouloud, Birth of Muhammad), 14 July (Republic Day, anniversary of the 1968 *coup d'état*), 17 July (Baath Revolution Day), 8 August (Peace Day, anniversary of the cease-fire announcement in the war with Iran), 15 October* (Leilat al-Meiraj, ascension of Muhammad), 17 December* (Id al-Fitr, end of Ramadan).

2002: 1 January (New Year's Day), 6 January (Army Day), 8 February (14 Ramadan Revolution, anniversary of the 1963 *coup d'état*), 23 February* (Id al-Adha, Feast of the Sacrifice), 15 March* (Islamic New Year), 24 March* (Ashoura), 24 May* (Mouloud, Birth of Muhammad), 14 July (Republic Day, anniversary of the 1968 *coup d'état*), 17 July (Baath Revolution Day), 8 August (Peace Day, anniversary of the cease-fire announcement in the war with Iran), 4 October* (Leilat al-Meiraj, ascension of Muhammad), 6 December* (Id al-Fitr, end of Ramadan).

* These holidays are dependent on the Islamic lunar calendar and may vary by one or two days from the dates given.

Weights and Measures

The metric system is in force. Local measurements are also used, e.g. 1 meshara or dunum = 2,500 sq metres (0.62 acre).

Statistical Survey

Source (unless otherwise indicated): Central Statistical Organization, Ministry of Planning, Karradat Mariam, ash-Shawaf Sq., Baghdad; tel. (1) 537-0071.

Area and Population

AREA, POPULATION AND DENSITY*

Area (sq km)	438,317†
Population (census results)	
17 October 1987	16,335,199
17 October 1997	
Males	10,940,764
Females	11,077,219
Total	22,017,983
Density (per sq km) in October 1997	50.2

* No account has been taken of the reduction in the area of Iraq as a result of the adjustment to the border with Kuwait that came into force on 15 January 1993.

† 169,235 sq miles. This figure includes 924 sq km (357 sq miles) of territorial waters but excludes the Neutral Zone, of which Iraq's share is 3,522 sq km (1,360 sq miles). The Zone lies between Iraq and Saudi Arabia, and is administered jointly by the two countries. Nomads move freely through it but there are no permanent inhabitants.

GOVERNORATES (population at 1987 census)

	Area* (sq km)	Popu-lation	Density (per sq km)
Nineveh	37,698	1,479,430	39.2
Salah ad-Din	29,004	726,138	25.0
At-Ta'meem	10,391	601,219	57.9
Diala	19,292	961,073	49.8
Baghdad	5,159	3,841,268	744.6
Al-Anbar	137,723	820,690	6.0
Babylon	5,258	1,109,574	211.0
Karbala	5,034	469,282	93.2
An-Najaf	27,844	590,078	21.2
Al-Qadisiya	8,507	559,805	65.8
Al-Muthanna	51,029	315,816	6.2
Thi-Qar	13,626	921,066	67.6
Wasit	17,308	564,670	32.6
Maysan	14,103	487,448	34.6
Al-Basrah (Basra) . .	19,070	872,176	45.7
Autonomous Regions:			
D'hok	6,120	293,304	47.9
Irbil (Arbil)	14,471	770,439	53.2
As-Sulaimaniya . . .	15,756	951,723	60.4
Total	437,393	16,335,199	37.3

* Excluding territorial waters (924 sq km).

PRINCIPAL TOWNS (estimated population, 1970)

Baghdad (capital) .	1,984,142	An-Najaf . . .	147,855
Al-Basrah (Basra) .	333,684	Al-Hillah (Hilla) .	103,544
Al-Mawsil (Mosul) .	310,313	As-Sulaimaniya .	103,091
Kirkuk . . .	191,294	Irbil (Arbil) . .	101,779

BIRTHS AND DEATHS (UN estimates, annual averages)

	1980–85	1985–90	1990–95
Birth rate (per 1,000) . . .	41.0	40.3	38.4
Death rate (per 1,000) . .	8.4	7.2	10.4

Expectation of life (UN estimates, years at birth, 1990–95): 58.6 (males 58.6; females 60.1).

Source: UN, *World Population Prospects: The 1998 Revision*.

Registered live births (1992) 502,415 (birth rate 26.4 per 1,000); Registered deaths (1990) 76,683 (death rate 4.4 per 1,000). Note: Registration is incomplete.

ECONOMICALLY ACTIVE POPULATION*
(persons aged 7 years and over, 1987 census)

	Males	Females	Total
Agriculture, forestry and fishing .	422,265	70,741	493,006
Mining and quarrying . . .	40,439	4,698	45,137
Manufacturing	228,242	38,719	266,961
Electricity, gas and water . .	31,786	4,450	36,236
Construction	332,645	8,541	341,186
Trade, restaurants and hotels .	191,116	24,489	215,605
Transport, storage and communications	212,116	12,155	224,271
Financing, insurance, real estate and business services . . .	16,204	10,811	27,015
Community, social and personal services	1,721,748	233,068	1,954,816
Activities not adequately defined .	146,616	18,232	167,848
Total labour force . . .	3,346,177	425,904	3,772,081

* Figures exclude persons seeking work for the first time, totalling 184,264 (males 149,938, females 34,326), but include other unemployed persons.

Source: ILO, *Yearbook of Labour Statistics*.

Mid-1999 (estimates in '000): Agriculture, etc. 653; Total 6,171 (Source: FAO).

Agriculture

PRINCIPAL CROPS ('000 metric tons)

	1997	1998	1999*
Wheat	1,063†	1,214†	800
Rice (paddy)	244†	300†	240
Barley	778†	859†	500
Maize	121†	133†	100
Potatoes*	400	420	330
Dry broad beans* . .	18	19	10
Sunflower seed . . .	67†	70†	45
Sesame seed . . .	14†	14†	8
Olives*	13	14	12
Cabbages*	21	21	12
Tomatoes*	850	865	500
Cauliflower*	33	34	22
Pumpkins, etc.* . . .	60	62	39
Cucumbers and gherkins* .	340	344	215
Aubergines (Eggplants)* .	153	155	95
Chillies and peppers (green)* .	30	32	19
Onions (dry)* . . .	70	74	50
Carrots*	10	11	7
Other vegetables* . .	722	740	473
Watermelons* . . .	440	455	400
Melons*	220	226	210
Grapes*	300	305	290
Dates	625†	630*	545
Sugar cane* . . .	70	71	68
Apples*	80	86	80
Peaches and nectarines* .	25	26	25
Plums*	30	31	30
Oranges*	310	316	300
Tangerines, etc.* . .	40	43	39
Lemons and limes* . .	15	16	15
Apricots*	30	32	30
Other fruits and berries* .	90	94	84
Tobacco (leaves)* . .	3	3	2
Cotton (lint) . . .	9†	9*	9

† FAO estimate(s).   * Unofficial figure.

Source: FAO.

LIVESTOCK ('000 head, year ending September)

	1997	1998*	1999*
Horses*	47	48	46
Mules*	12	13	11
Asses*	380	385	375
Cattle	1,300†	1,320	1,100
Buffaloes	62†	64	60
Camels*	7	8	8
Sheep	6,584†	6,700	6,000
Goats	1,466†	1,500	1,300
Poultry*	18,500	20,000	18,000

* FAO estimates.   † Unofficial figure.

Source: FAO.

LIVESTOCK PRODUCTS ('000 metric tons)

	1997	1998	1999
Beef and veal*	44	45	39
Buffalo meat*	2	2	2
Mutton and lamb	19	20	18
Goat meat*	8	8	7
Poultry meat*	41	44	39
Cows' milk*	300	315	278
Buffalo milk*	28	26	25
Sheep's milk	155	156	148
Goats' milk	53	53	47
Cheese	30	30	28
Butter	8	8	7
Hen eggs*	23	24	23
Wool (greasy)*	12	13	11
Cattle and buffalo hides	5	5	5
Sheepskins	4	4	3
Goatskins	2	2	2

* FAO estimates.

Source: FAO.

Forestry

ROUNDWOOD REMOVALS ('000 cubic metres, excl. bark)

	1996	1997	1998
Sawlogs, veneer logs and logs for sleepers	20	20	25
Other industrial wood	30	30	34
Fuel wood	15	111	118
Total	65	161	177

Source: FAO, *Yearbook of Forest Products*.

SAWNWOOD PRODUCTION ('000 cu m, incl. railway sleepers)

	1996	1997	1998
Total (all broadleaved)	8	8	12

Source: FAO, *Yearbook of Forest Products*.

Fishing

(FAO estimates, '000 metric tons, live weight)

	1996	1997	1998
Capture	30.7	31.3	22.6
Common carp	5.5	4.2	2.3
Other cyprinids	7.7	4.8	1.7
Other freshwater fishes	5.8	11.6	5.1
Marine fishes	11.7	10.8	13.5
Aquaculture (Common carp)	2.5	3.4	0.6
Total catch	33.2	34.7	23.2

Source: FAO, *Yearbook of Fishery Statistics*.

Mining

('000 metric tons, unless otherwise indicated)

	1995	1996	1997
Crude petroleum	36,089	36,260	n.a.
Natural gas (petajoules)	124	126	141
Native sulphur*	250†	250	250
Natural phosphates*	1,000†	1,000	1,000
Salt (unrefined)*	250	250†	250
Gypsum (crude)*	450	450†	n.a.

* Data from the US Bureau of Mines. Data on natural phosphates refer to gross weight. The estimated phosphoric acid content was 30%.
† Provisional or estimated figure.

Source: UN, *Industrial Commodity Statistics Yearbook*.

Industry

SELECTED PRODUCTS
('000 metric tons, unless otherwise indicated)

	1994	1995	1996
Naphtha	500*	500*	500
Motor spirit (petrol)	2,970*	2,990*	3,000
Kerosene	1,120*	1,130*	1,135
Jet fuel	1,110*	1,120*	1,130
Gas-diesel (distillate fuel) oil	6,880*	6,900*	6,920
Residual fuel oils	9,000*	9,000*	9,000
Lubricating oils	200*	200*	200
Paraffin wax	100	100	105
Petroleum bitumen (asphalt)	420*	420*	425
Liquefied petroleum gas:			
from natural gas plants	700*	1,560*	1,590
from petroleum refineries	600*	600*	600
Cement†	15,000	18,000	n.a.
Electric energy (million kWh)	28,000*	29,000*	29,660

* Provisional or estimated figure.
† Estimates by the US Bureau of Mines.

Cigarettes: 5,794 million in 1992.
Footwear (excluding rubber): 4,087,000 pairs in 1992.

Source: UN, *Industrial Commodity Statistics Yearbook*.

Finance

CURRENCY AND EXCHANGE RATES
Monetary Units
  1,000 fils = 20 dirhams = 1 Iraqi dinar (ID).

Sterling, Dollar and Euro Equivalents (29 December 2000)
  £1 sterling = 463.86 fils;
  US $1 = 310.86 fils;
  €1 = 289.25 fils;
  100 Iraqi dinars = £215.58 = \$321.69 = €345.72.

Exchange Rate
  From February 1973 to October 1982 the Iraqi dinar was valued at US \$3.3862. Since October 1982 it has been valued at \$3.2169. The dinar's average value in 1982 was \$3.3513. The aforementioned data refer to the official exchange rate. There is, in addition, a special rate for exports and also a free-market rate. The unofficial exchange rate was \$1 = 1,800 dinars in September 2000.

BUDGET ESTIMATES (ID million)

Revenue	1981	1982
Ordinary	5,025.0	8,740.0
Economic development plan	6,742.8	7,700.0
Autonomous government agencies	7,667.8	n.a.
Total	19,434.9	n.a.

Petroleum revenues (estimates, US $ million): 9,198 in 1981; 10,250 in 1982; 9,650 in 1983; 10,000 in 1984; 11,900 in 1985; 6,813 in 1986; 11,300 in 1987.

Expenditure	1981	1982
Ordinary	5,025.0	8,740.0
Economic development plan	6,742.0	7,700.0
Autonomous government agencies. . . .	7,982.4	n.a.
Total	19,750.2	n.a.

1991 (ID million): General consolidated state budget expenditure 13,876; Investment budget expenditure 1,660.

CENTRAL BANK RESERVES (US $ million at 31 December)

	1975	1976	1977
Gold	168.0	166.7	176.1
IMF special drawing rights . .	26.9	32.5	41.5
Reserve position in IMF . .	31.9	31.7	33.4
Foreign exchange	2,500.5	4,369.8	6,744.7
Total	2,727.3	4,600.7	6,995.7

IMF special drawing rights (US $ million at 31 December): 132.3 in 1981; 81.9 in 1982; 9.0 in 1983; 0.1 in 1984; 7.2 in 1987.
Reserve position in IMF (US $ million at 31 December): 130.3 in 1981; 123.5 in 1982.
Note: No figures for gold or foreign exchange have been available since 1977.
Source: IMF, *International Financial Statistics*.

COST OF LIVING (Consumer Price Index; base: 1990 = 100)

	1991*
Food.	363.9
Fuel and light	135.4
Clothing	251.1
Rent.	107.0
All items (incl. others)	286.5

* May to December only.
Source: ILO, *Yearbook of Labour Statistics*.

NATIONAL ACCOUNTS (ID million at current prices)
National Income and Product

	1989	1990	1991
Compensation of employees . .	6,705.2	7,855.4	8,989.9
Operating surplus	11,866.0	12,936.6	10,405.2
Domestic factor incomes .	18,571.2	20,792.0	19,395.1
Consumption of fixed capital . .	1,836.7	2,056.3	1,918.2
Gross domestic product (GDP) at factor cost. . . .	20,407.9	22,848.3	21,313.3
Indirect taxes	1,035.0	1,024.8	485.6
Less Subsidies	417.1	576.3	1,859.2
GDP in purchasers' values. .	21,025.8	23,296.8	19,939.7
Net factor income from the rest of the world	-704.3	-773.9	-650.5
Gross national product .	20,321.5	22,522.9	19,289.2
Less Consumption of fixed capital .	1,836.7	2,056.3	1,918.2
National income in market prices	18,484.8	20,466.6	17,371.0
Net current transfers from abroad	-149.3	-49.3	122.8
National disposable income .	18,335.5	20,417.3	17,493.8

Source: UN, *National Accounts Statistics*.

Expenditure on the Gross Domestic Product

	1989	1990	1991
Government final consumption expenditure	5,990.1	6,142.0	7,033.3
Private final consumption expenditure	11,232.4	11,760.5	9,611.1
Increase in stocks . . .	-2,317.5	-976.9	-520.0
Gross fixed capital formation . .	6,305.5	6,220.0	3,289.1
Total domestic expenditure .	21,210.5	23,145.6	20,453.5
Exports of goods and services . .	4,482.6	4,305.4	547.8
Less Imports of goods and services	4,667.3	4,154.2	1,061.6
GDP in purchasers' values. .	21,025.8	23,296.8	19,939.7

Source: UN, *National Accounts Statistics*.

Gross Domestic Product by Economic Activity

	1993	1994	1995
Agriculture, hunting, forestry and fishing	45,463	302,265	1,255,760
Mining and quarrying . . .	92	179	-2,090
Manufacturing	6,214	51,183	19,077
Electricity, gas and water* . .	277	442	1,498
Construction.	4,758	6,022	11,913
Trade, restaurants and hotels* .	33,757	126,629	712,987
Transport, storage and communications . . .	19,191	106,036	514,104
Finance, insurance and real estate†	8,047	31,387	79,686
Government services‡ . . .	8,650	11,487	59,050
Other services	1,691	6,227	37,110
Sub-total	128,139	641,857	2,689,096
Less Imputed bank service charge	5,142	11,851	30,399
GDP at factor cost . .	122,997	630,006	2,658,697
Indirect taxes, *less* subsidies . .	-10,855	-17,832	-106,934
GDP in purchasers' values .	112,142	612,174	2,551,763

* Gas distribution is included in trade.
† Including imputed rents of owner-occupied dwellings.
‡ Including domestic services of households.
Source: UN, *National Accounts Statistics*.

External Trade

PRINCIPAL COMMODITIES (ID million)

Imports c.i.f.	1976	1977*	1978
Food and live animals . .	159.6	154.0	134.5
Cereals and cereal preparations	70.0	79.9	74.9
Sugar, sugar preparations and honey.	37.2	24.1	10.2
Crude materials (inedible) except fuels . . .	33.7	20.5	25.1
Chemicals	58.5	47.4	58.7
Basic manufactures . .	293.3	236.7	285.2
Textile yarn, fabrics, etc. . .	44.3	69.4	72.7
Iron and steel	127.5	44.3	73.2
Machinery and transport equipment . . .	557.4	625.8	667.4
Non-electric machinery . .	285.4	352.5	368.1
Electrical machinery, apparatus, etc.	106.9	120.2	160.5
Transport equipment. . . .	165.2	153.1	138.8
Miscellaneous manufactured articles	33.2	49.4	51.7
Total (incl. others)	1,150.9	1,151.3	1,244.1

* Figures are provisional. Revised total is ID 1,323.2 million.

Total imports (official estimates, ID million): 1,738.9 in 1979; 2,208.1 in 1980; 2,333.8 in 1981.
Total imports (IMF estimates, ID million): 6,013.0 in 1981; 6,309.0 in 1982; 3,086.2 in 1983; 3,032.4 in 1984; 3,285.7 in 1985; 2,773.0 in 1986; 2,268.7 in 1987; 2,888.8 in 1988; 3,077.1 in 1989; 2,028.5 in 1990; 131.5 in 1991; 187.3 in 1992; 165.6 in 1993; 155.0 in 1994; 206.8 in 1995; 176.3 in

1996; 285.0 in 1997; 449.9 in 1998; 479.1 in 1999 (Source: IMF, *International Financial Statistics*).

Total exports (ID million): 5,614.6 (crude petroleum 5,571.9) in 1977; 6,422.7 (crude petroleum 6,360.5) in 1978; 12,522.0 (crude petroleum 12,480.0) in 1979.

Exports of crude petroleum (estimates, ID million): 15,321.3 in 1980; 6,089.6 in 1981; 5,982.4 in 1982; 5,954.8 in 1983; 6,937.0 in 1984; 8,142.5 in 1985; 5,126.2 in 1986; 6,988.9 in 1987; 7,245.8 in 1988.

Source: IMF, *International Financial Statistics*.

PRINCIPAL TRADING PARTNERS (US $ million)

Imports c.i.f.	1988	1989	1990
Australia	153.4	196.2	108.7
Austria	n.a.	1.1	50.9
Belgium and Luxembourg	57.6	68.2	68.3
Brazil	346.0	416.4	139.5
Canada	169.9	225.1	150.4
China, People's Republic	99.2	148.0	157.9
France	278.0	410.4	278.3
Germany	322.3	459.6	389.4
India	32.3	65.2	57.5
Indonesia	38.9	122.7	104.9
Ireland	150.4	144.9	31.6
Italy	129.6	285.1	194.0
Japan	533.0	621.1	397.2
Jordan	164.3	210.0	220.3
Korea, Republic	98.5	123.9	149.4
Netherlands	111.6	102.6	93.8
Romania	113.3	91.1	30.1
Saudi Arabia	37.2	96.5	62.5
Spain	43.4	129.0	40.5
Sri Lanka	50.1	33.5	52.3
Sweden	63.0	40.6	64.8
Switzerland	65.7	94.4	126.6
Thailand	22.3	59.2	68.9
Turkey	874.7	408.9	196.0
USSR	70.7	75.7	77.9
United Kingdom	394.6	448.5	322.1
USA	979.3	1,001.7	658.4
Yugoslavia	154.5	182.0	123.1
Total (incl. others)	5,960.0	6,956.2	4,833.9

Exports f.o.b.	1988	1989	1990*
Belgium and Luxembourg	147.5	249.6	n.a.
Brazil	1,002.8	1,197.2	n.a.
France	517.4	623.9	0.8
Germany	122.0	76.9	1.7
Greece	192.5	189.4	0.3
India	293.0	438.8	14.7
Italy	687.1	549.7	10.6
Japan	712.1	117.1	0.1
Jordan	28.4	25.2	101.6
Netherlands	152.9	532.3	0.2
Portugal	120.8	125.8	n.a.
Spain	370.0	575.7	0.7
Turkey	1,052.6	1,331.0	83.5
USSR	835.7	1,331.7	8.9
United Kingdom	293.1	167.0	4.4
USA	1,458.9	2,290.8	0.2
Yugoslavia	425.4	342.0	10.4
Total (incl. others)	10,268.3	12,333.7	392.0

* Excluding exports of most petroleum products.

Source: UN, *International Trade Statistics Yearbook*.

Transport

RAILWAYS (traffic)

	1995*	1996†	1997†
Passenger-km (million)	2,198	1,169	1,169
Freight ton-km (million)	1,120	931	956

* Source: UN, *Statistical Yearbook*.
† Source: Railway Gazette International, *Railway Directory*.

ROAD TRAFFIC ('000 motor vehicles in use)

	1993	1994	1995
Passenger cars	672.4	678.5	680.1
Commercial vehicles	309.3	317.2	319.9

Source: UN, *Statistical Yearbook*.

SHIPPING

Merchant Fleet (registered at 31 December)

	1996	1997	1998
Number of vessels	113	102	99
Total displacement ('000 grt)	856.9	572.0	511.1

Source: Lloyd's Register of Shipping, *World Fleet Statistics*.

CIVIL AVIATION (revenue traffic on scheduled services)

	1991	1992	1994*
Kilometres flown (million)	0	0	0
Passengers carried ('000)	28	53	31
Passenger-km (million)	17	35	20
Freight ton-km (million)	0	3	2

* Figures for 1993 unavailable.
Source: UN, *Statistical Yearbook*.

Tourism

ARRIVALS AT FRONTIERS OF VISITORS FROM ABROAD*

Country of nationality	1994	1995	1996
Bahrain	261	934	1,717
India	2,899	4,015	1,338
Jordan	60,460	26,253	19,192
Lebanon	2,740	3,913	3,942
Pakistan	5,082	7,034	7,749
Saudi Arabia	n.a.	3,240	6,380
Yemen	2,418	4,114	2,188
Total (incl. others)	89,384	60,540	51,330

* Including same-day visitors.

Source: World Tourism Organization, *Yearbook of Tourism Statistics*.

Communications Media

	1995	1996	1997
Radio receivers ('000 in use) . .	4,500	4,700	4,850
Television receivers ('000 in use) .	1,600	1,700	1,750
Daily newspapers			
Number	4*	4	n.a.
Average circulation ('000 copies)	530*	407	n.a.

* Estimate.

Source: UNESCO, *Statistical Yearbook*.

Telephones ('000 main lines in use, year ending 30 June): 675 (estimate) in 1994/95; 675 in 1995/96; 675 in 1996/97 (Source: UN, *Statistical Yearbook*).

Education

(1995/96)

	Insti-tutions	Teachers	Students Males	Students Females	Students Total
Pre-primary . . .	571	4,841	43,889	41,135	85,024
Primary . . .	8,145	145,455	1,602,071	1,301,852	2,903,923
Secondary:					
General . . .	n.a.	52,393	631,457	406,025	1,037,482
Teacher training .	n.a.	1,392	9,414	14,120	23,534
Vocational . .	n.a.	8,511	81,917	17,488	99,405

Source: UNESCO, *Statistical Yearbook*.

Directory

The Constitution

The following are the principal features of the Provisional Constitution, issued on 22 September 1968:

The Iraqi Republic is a popular democratic and sovereign state. Islam is the state religion.

The political economy of the State is founded on socialism.

The State will protect liberty of religion, freedom of speech and opinion. Public meetings are permitted under the law. All discrimination based on race, religion or language is forbidden. There shall be freedom of the Press, and the right to form societies and trade unions in conformity with the law is guaranteed.

The Iraqi people is composed of two main nationalities: Arabs and Kurds. The Constitution confirms the nationalistic rights of the Kurdish people and the legitimate rights of all other minorities within the framework of Iraqi unity.

The highest authority in the country is the Council of Command of the Revolution (or Revolutionary Command Council—RCC), which will promulgate laws until the election of a National Assembly. The Council exercises its prerogatives and powers by a two-thirds majority.

Two amendments to the Constitution were announced in November 1969. The President, already Chief of State and Head of the Government, also became the official Supreme Commander of the Armed Forces and President of the RCC. Membership of the latter body was to increase from five to a larger number at the President's discretion.

Earlier, a Presidential decree replaced the 14 local government districts by 16 governorates, each headed by a governor with wide powers. In April 1976 Tikrit (Salah ad-Din) and Karbala became separate governorates, bringing the number of governorates to 18, although three of these are designated Autonomous Regions.

The 15-article statement which aimed to end the Kurdish war was issued on 11 March 1970. In accordance with this statement, a form of autonomy was offered to the Kurds in March 1974, but some of the Kurds rejected the offer and fresh fighting broke out. The new Provisional Constitution was announced in July 1970. Two amendments were introduced in 1973 and 1974, the 1974 amendment stating that 'the area whose majority of population is Kurdish shall enjoy autonomy in accordance with what is defined by the Law'.

The President and Vice-President are elected by a two-thirds majority of the Council. The President, Vice-President and members of the Council will be responsible to the Council. Vice-Presidents and Ministers will be responsible to the President.

Details of a new, permanent Constitution were announced in March 1989. The principal innovations proposed in the permanent Constitution, which was approved by the National Assembly in July 1990, were the abolition of the RCC, following a presidential election, and the assumption of its duties by a 50-member Consultative Assembly and the existing National Assembly; and the incorporation of the freedom to form political parties. The new, permanent Constitution is to be submitted to a popular referendum for approval.

In September 1995 an interim constitutional amendment was endorsed by the RCC whereby the elected Chairman of the RCC will assume the Presidency of the Republic subject to the approval of the National Assembly and endorsement by national referendum.

In July 1973 President Bakr announced a National Charter as a first step towards establishing the Progressive National Front. A National Assembly and People's Councils are features of the Charter. A law to create a 250-member National Assembly and a 50-member Kurdish Legislative Council was adopted on 16 March 1980, and the two Assemblies were elected in June and September 1980 respectively.

The Government

HEAD OF STATE

President and President of the Revolutionary Command (RCC): SADDAM HUSSAIN (assumed power 16 July 1979; confirmed in office by national referendum 15 October 1995).

Vice-Presidents: TAHA YASSIN RAMADAN, TAHA MOHI ED-DIN MARUF.

Vice-President of the RCC: IZZAT IBRAHIM AD-DUR.

COUNCIL OF MINISTERS
(May 2001)

Prime Minister: SADDAM HUSSAIN.

Deputy Prime Minister and Acting Minister of Foreign Affairs: TAREQ AZIZ.

Deputy Prime Minister: MUHAMMAD HAMZAH AZ-ZUBAYI.

Deputy Prime Minister and Minister of Finance: HIKMAT MIZBAN IBRAHIM.

Minister of Trade: MUHAMMAD MAHDI SALIH.

Minister of Justice: MUNDHIR IBRAHIM ASH-SHAWI.

Minister of Defence: Gen. SULTAN HASHIM AHMAD.

Minister of Oil: Gen. AMIR MUHAMMAD RASHID.

Minister of Health: UMEED MADHAT MUBARAK.

Minister of Labour and Social Affairs: Gen. SAADI TUMA ABBAS.

Minister of Irrigation and acting Minister of the Interior: MAHMOUD DIYAB AL-AHMAD.

Minister of Agriculture: ABDULLAH HAMEED MAHMOUD SALEH.

Minister of Transport and Communications: Dr AHMAD MURTADA AHMAD KHALIL.

Minister of Industry and Minerals: ADNAN ABD AL-MAJID JASSIM.

Minister of Higher Education and Scientific Research: HUMAM ABD AL-KHALIQ ABD AL-GHAFUR.

Minister of Education: FAHD SALIM ASH-SHAKRAH.

Minister of Awqaf (Religious Endowments) and Religious Affairs: Dr ABD AL-MUNIM AHMAD SALIH.

Minister of Information: MUHAMMAD SAEED AS-SAHAF.

Minister of Culture: HAMID YUSUF HAMADI.

Minister of Housing and Construction: MAAN ABDULLAH SARSAM.

Minister of State for Military Industrialization: ABD AT-TAWAB MULLAH HOWEICH.

Minister of State for Foreign Affairs: Dr NAJI SABRI AHMAD.

Minister of State for Military Affairs: Gen. ABD AL-JABBAR KHALIL ASH-SHANSHAL.

Ministers of State: ARSHAD MUHAMMAD AHMAD MUHAMMAD AZ-ZIBARI, ABD AL-WAHHAB UMAR MIRZA AL-ATRUSHI, SAMAL MAJID FARAJ.

President of the Planning Committee: HASSAN ABD AL-MONIM AL-KHATAB.

Director of the State Electricity Organization: FAISAL SAHBAN.

MINISTRIES

Office of the President: Presidential Palace, Karradat Mariam, Baghdad.

Ministry of Agriculture: Khulafa St, Khullani Sq., Baghdad; tel. (1) 887-3251.

Ministry of Awqaf (Religious Endowments) and Religious Affairs: North Gate, St opposite College of Engineering, Baghdad; tel. (1) 888-9561.

Ministry of Culture and Information: Nr an-Nusoor Sq., fmrly Qasr as-Salaam Bldg, Baghdad; tel. (1) 551-4333.

Ministry of Defence: North Gate, Baghdad; tel. (1) 888-9071.

Ministry of Education: POB 258, Baghdad; tel. (1) 886-0000.

Ministry of Finance: Khulafa St, Nr ar-Russafi Sq., Baghdad; tel. (1) 887-4871.

Ministry of Foreign Affairs: Opposite State Org. for Roads and Bridges, Karradat Mariam, Baghdad; tel. (1) 537-0091.

Ministry of Health, Labour and Social Affairs: Khulafa St, Khullani Sq., Baghdad; tel. (1) 887-1881.

Ministry of Industry and Minerals: Nidhal St, Nr Sa'adoun Petrol Station, Baghdad; tel. (1) 887-2006.

Ministry of Oil: POB 6178, al-Mansour, Baghdad; tel. (1) 443-0749.

Ministry of Planning: Karradat Mariam, ash-Shawaf Sq., Baghdad; tel. (1) 537-0071.

Ministry of Trade: Khulafa St, Khullani Sq., Baghdad; tel. (1) 887-2682.

Ministry of Transport and Communications: Nr Martyr's Monument, Karradat Dakhil, Baghdad; tel. (1) 776-6041.

Legislature

NATIONAL ASSEMBLY

Speaker: Dr SA'ADOUN HAMMADI.

Elections to the 220 elective seats of the fifth National Assembly took place on 27 March 2000. According to official results, candidates of the ruling Baath Party were reported to have successfully contested 165 of the Assembly's seats, while independent candidates were returned to the remaining 55 elective seats. The remaining 30 seats of the Assembly that are reserved for representatives of the Kurdish Autonomous Regions were filled by government-appointed independents.

KURDISH AUTONOMOUS REGION

Executive Council: Chair. MUHAMMAD AMIN MUHAMMAD (acting).

Legislative Council: Chair. AHMAD ABD AL-QADIR AN-NAQSHABANDI.

In May 1992, in the absence of a negotiated autonomy agreement with the Iraqi Government, the KIF (see below) organized elections to a 105-member Kurdish National Assembly. The DPK and the PUK were the only parties to achieve representation in the new Assembly and subsequently agreed to share seats equally between them. Elections held at the same time as those to the National Assembly, to choose an overall Kurdish leader, were inconclusive and were to be held again at a later date.

Political Organizations

National Progressive Front: Baghdad; f. July 1973, when Arab Baath Socialist Party and Iraqi Communist Party signed a joint manifesto agreeing to establish a comprehensive progressive national and nationalistic front. In 1975 representatives of Kurdish parties and organizations and other national and independent forces joined the Front; the Iraqi Communist Party left the National Progressive Front in mid-March 1979; Sec.-Gen. NAIM HADDAD (Baath).

> **Arab Baath Socialist Party:** POB 6012, al-Mansour, Baghdad; revolutionary Arab socialist movement founded in Damascus in 1947; has ruled Iraq since July 1968, and between July 1973 and March 1979 in alliance with the Iraqi Communist Party in the National Progressive Front; founder MICHEL AFLAQ; Regional Command Sec.-Gen. SADDAM HUSSAIN; Deputy Regional Command Sec.-Gen. IZZAT IBRAHIM; 18-mem. Regional Command; approx. 100,000 mems.

> **Kurdistan Revolutionary Party:** f. 1972; succeeded Democratic Kurdistan Party; admitted to National Progressive Front 1974; Sec.-Gen. ABD AS-SATTAR TAHER SHAREF.

There are several illegal opposition groups, including:

Ad-Da'wa al-Islamiya (Voice of Islam): f. 1968; based in Tehran; mem. of the Supreme Council of the Islamic Revolution in Iraq (see below); guerrilla group; Leader Sheikh AL-ASSEFIE.

Iraqi Communist Party: Baghdad; f. 1934; became legally recognized in July 1973 on formation of National Progressive Front; left National Progressive Front March 1979; proscribed as a result of its support for Iran during the Iran–Iraq War; First Sec. AZIZ MUHAMMAD.

Umma (Nation) Party: f. 1982; opposes Saddam Hussain's regime; Leader SAAD SALEH JABR.

There is also a breakaway element of the Arab Baath Socialist Party represented on the Iraqi National Joint Action Cttee (see below); the Democratic Gathering (Leader SALEH DOUBLAH); the Iraqi Socialist Party (ISP; Leader Gen. HASSAN AN-NAQUIB); the Democratic Party of Kurdistan (DPK; f. 1946; Leader MASOUD BARZANI); the Patriotic Union of Kurdistan (PUK; f. 1975; Leader JALAL TALIBANI); the Socialist Party of Kurdistan (SPK; f. 1975; Leader RASSOUL MARMAND); the United Socialist Party of Kurdistan (USPK; Leader MAHMOUD OSMAN), a breakaway group from the PUK; the Kurdistan People's Democratic Party (KPDP; Leader SAMI ABD AR-RAHMAN); the Kurdish Workers' Party (PKK); the Islamic League of Kurdistan (ILK, also known as the Islamic Movement of Iraqi Kurdistan (IMIK)); the Kurdish Hezbollah (Party of God); f. 1985; Leader Sheikh MUHAMMAD KALED), a breakaway group from the DPK and a member of the Supreme Council of the Islamic Revolution in Iraq (SCIRI), which is based in Tehran under the leadership of the exiled Iraqi Shi'ite leader, Hojatoleslam MUHAMMAD BAQIR AL-HAKIM, and has a military wing, the Badr Brigade; the Iraqi National Accord (INA; Leader SALAH ESH-SHEIKHLI); and Hizb al-Watan or Homeland Party (Leader MISHAAN AL-JUBOURI).

Various alliances of political and religious groups have been formed to oppose the regime of Saddam Hussain in recent years. They include the Kurdistan Iraqi Front (KIF; f. 1988), an alliance of the DPK, the PUK, the SPK, the KPDP and other, smaller Kurdish groups; the Iraqi National Joint Action Cttee, formed in Damascus in 1990 and grouping together the SCIRI, the four principal Kurdish parties belonging to the KIF, Ad-Da'wa al-Islamiya, the Movement of the Iraqi Mujahidin (based in Teheran; Leaders Hojatoleslam MUHAMMAD BAQIR AL-HAKIM and SAID MUHAMMAD AL-HAIDARI), the Islamic Movement in Iraq (Shi'ite group based in Teheran; Leader Sheikh MUHAMMAD MAHDI AL-KALISI), Jund al-Imam (Imam Soldiers; Shi'ite; Leader ABU ZAID), the Islamic Action Organization (based in Tehran; Leader Sheikh TAQI MODARESSI), the Islamic Alliance (based in Saudi Arabia; Sunni; Leader ABU YASSER AL-ALOUSI), the Independent Group, the Iraqi Socialist Party, the Arab Socialist

Movement, the Nasserite Unionist Gathering and the National Reconciliation Group. There is also the London-based Iraqi National Congress (INC), which has sought to unite the various factions of the opposition. At a conference held in London in April 1999 a new collegiate leadership, under SALAH ESH-SHEIKHLI of the INA, was appointed. In November some 300 delegates to a national assembly, held in New York, USA, elected a 65-member central council and a new, seven-member collegiate leadership (AYAD ALLAWI, INA; RIYAD AL-YAWAR, independent; Sharif ALI BIN AL-HUSSAIN, Movement for Constitutional Monarchy; AHMAD CHALABI, independent; Sheikh MOHAMMED MOHAMMED ALI, independent; LATIF RASHID, PUK; HOSHYAR AZ-ZIBARI, DPK). In September 1992 the KPDP, the SPK and the Kurdish Democratic Independence Party were reported to have merged to form the Kurdistan Unity Party (KUP).

Diplomatic Representation

EMBASSIES IN IRAQ

Albania: Baghdad; Ambassador: GYLANI SHEHU.

Algeria: ash-Shawaf Sq., Karradat Mariam, Baghdad; tel. (1) 537-2181; Ambassador: AL-ARABI SI AL-HASSAN.

Argentina: POB 2443, Hay al-Jamia District 915, St 24, No. 142, Baghdad; tel. (1) 776-8140; Ambassador: GERÓNIMO CORTES-FUNES.

Australia: POB 661, Masba 39B/35, Baghdad; tel. (1) 719-3434; Ambassador: P. LLOYD (embassy temporarily closed).

Bahrain: POB 27117, al-Mansour, Hay al-Watanabi, Mahalla 605, Zuqaq 7, House 4/1/44, Baghdad; tel. (1) 542-3656; Ambassador: ABD AR-RAHMAN AL-FADHIL.

Bangladesh: 75/17/929 Hay Babel, Baghdad; tel. (1) 719-6367; Ambassador: MUFLEH R. OSMARRY.

Belgium: Hay Babel 929/27/25, Baghdad; tel. (1) 719-8297; Ambassador: MARC VAN RYSSELBERGHE.

Brazil: 609/16 al-Mansour, Houses 62/62–1, Baghdad; tel. (1) 541-1365; Ambassador: MAURO SERGIO CONTO.

Bulgaria: POB 28022, Ameriya, New Diplomatic Quarter, Baghdad; tel. (1) 556-8197; Ambassador: ASSEN ZLATANOV.

Canada: 47/1/7 al-Mansour, Baghdad; tel. (1) 542-1459; Ambassador: DAVID KARSGAARD.

Central African Republic: 208/406 az-Zawra, Harthiya, Baghdad; tel. (1) 551-6520; Chargé d'affaires: RENÉ BISSAYO.

Chad: POB 8037, 97/4/4 Karradat Mariam, Baghdad; tel. (1) 537-6160; Ambassador: MAHAMAT DJIBER AHNOUR.

China, People's Republic: New Embassy Area, International Airport Rd, Baghdad; tel. (1) 556-2741; fax (1) 541-7628; Ambassador: ZHANG WEIQIU.

Cuba: St 7, District 929 Hay Babel, al-Masba Arrasat al-Hindi; tel. 776-5324; Ambassador: LUIS MARISY FIGUEREDO.

Czech Republic: Dijlaschool St, No. 37, Mansour, Baghdad; tel. (1) 541-7136; fax (1) 543-0275; Chargé d'affaires: MIROSLAV BELICA.

Djibouti: POB 6223, al-Mansour, Baghdad; tel. (1) 551-3805; Ambassador: ABSEIA BOOH ABDULLA.

Finland: POB 2041, Alwiyah, Baghdad; tel. (1) 776-6271; Ambassador: (vacant).

Greece: 63/3/913 Hay al-Jamia, al-Jadiriya, Baghdad; tel. (1) 776-6572; Ambassador: EPAMINONDAS PEYOS.

Holy See: POB 2090, as-Sa'adoun St 904/2/46, Baghdad (Apostolic Nunciature); tel. (1) 719-5183; fax (1) 224-5411; Apostolic Nuncio: Most Rev. GIUSEPPE LAZZAROTTO, Titular Archbishop of Numana.

Hungary: POB 2065, Abu Nuwas St, az-Zuwiya, Baghdad; tel. (1) 776-5000; Ambassador: TAMÁS VARGA; also represents Italian interests.

India: POB 4114, House No. 6, Zuqaq 25, Mahalla 306, Hay al-Magrib, Baghdad; tel. (1) 422-2014; fax (1) 422-9549; Ambassador: ARIF QAMARAIN.

Indonesia: 906/2/77 Hay al-Wahda, Baghdad; tel. (1) 719-8677; Ambassador: A. A. MURTADHO.

Iran: Karradat Mariam, Baghdad; Ambassador: Chargé d'affaires: HOSSEIN NIKNAM.

Ireland: 913/28/101 Hay al-Jamia, Baghdad; tel. (1) 776-8661; Ambassador: PATRICK MCCABE.

Japan: 929/17/70 Hay Babel, Masba, Baghdad; tel. (1) 719-5156; fax (1) 719-6186.

Jordan: POB 6314, House No. 1, St 12, District 609, al-Mansour, Baghdad; tel. (1) 541-2892; Ambassador: HMROUD AL-QATARNAH.

Korea, Republic: 915/22/278 Hay al-Jamia, Baghdad; tel. (1) 776-5496; Ambassador: BONG RHUEM CHEI.

Libya: Baghdad; Head of the Libyan People's Bureau: ABBAS AHMAD AL-MASSRATI (acting).

Malaysia: 6/14/929 Hay Babel, Baghdad; tel. (1) 776-2622; Ambassador: K. N. Nadarajah.

Malta: 2/1 Zuqaq 49, Mahalla 503, Hay an-Nil, Baghdad; tel. (1) 772-5032; Chargé d'affaires a.i.: Nader Salem Rizzo.

Mexico: 601/11/45 al-Mansour, Baghdad; tel. (1) 719-8039; Chargé d'affaires: Víctor M. Delgado.

Morocco: POB 6039, Hay al-Mansour, Baghdad; tel. (1) 552-1779; Ambassador: Muhammad Auragh.

Netherlands: POB 2064, 29/35/915 Jadiriya, Baghdad; tel. (1) 776-7616; Ambassador: Dr N. van Dam.

New Zealand: POB 2350, 2D/19 az-Zuwiya, Jadiriya, Baghdad; tel. (1) 776-8177; Ambassador: (vacant).

Nigeria: POB 5933, 2/3/603 Mutanabi, al-Mansour, Baghdad; tel. (1) 542-1750; Ambassador: A. G. Abdullahi.

Oman: POB 6180, 213/36/15 al-Harthiya, Baghdad; tel. (1) 551-8198; Ambassador: Khalifa bin Abdulla bin Salim al-Homaidi.

Pakistan: 14/7/609 al-Mansour, Baghdad; tel. (1) 541-5120; fax (1) 542-8707; Ambassador: Manzar Shafiq.

Philippines: Hay Babel, Baghdad; tel. (1) 719-3228; Ambassador: Ronaldo Baronca.

Poland: POB 2051, 30 Zuqaq 13, Mahalla 931, Hay Babel, Baghdad; tel. (1) 719-0296; Ambassador: Krzysztof Slominski.

Portugal: POB 2123, 66/11 al-Karada ash-Sharqiya, Hay Babel, Sector 925, St 25, No. 79, Alwiya, Baghdad; tel. (1) 718-7524; Ambassador: (vacant).

Qatar: 152/406 Harthiya, Hay al-Kindi, Baghdad; tel. (1) 551-2186; Ambassador: Muhammad Rashid Khalifa al-Khalifa.

Romania: Arassat al-Hindia, Hay Babel, Zuqaq 31, Mahalla 929, No 452/A, Baghdad; tel. (1) 776-2860; Chargé d'affaires: Gheorghe Tsarlescu.

Russia: 4/5/605 al-Mutanabi, Baghdad; tel. (1) 541-4749; Ambassador: Aleksandr Petrovich Chevin.

Senegal: 569/5/10, Hay al-Mansour Baghdad; tel. (1) 542-0806; Ambassador: Doudou Diop.

Slovakia: POB 238, Jamiyah St, No. 94, Jadiriyah, Baghdad; tel. (1) 776-7367.

Somalia: 603/1/5 al-Mansour, Baghdad; tel. (1) 551-0088; Ambassador: Issa Ali Mohammed.

Spain: POB 2072, ar-Riyad Quarter, District 908, Street No. 1, No. 21, Alwiya, Baghdad; tel. (1) 719-2852; Ambassador: Juan López de Chicheri.

Sri Lanka: POB 1094, House No. 22, Zukak 29, Mahalla 903, Hay al-Karada, Baghdad; tel. (1) 719-3040; Ambassador: N. Navaratnarajah.

Sudan: 38/15/601 al-Imarat, Baghdad; tel. (1) 542-4889; Ambassador: Ali Adam Muhammad Ahmad.

Sweden: 15/41/103 Hay an-Nidhal, Baghdad; tel. (1) 719-5361; Ambassador: Henrik Amneus.

Switzerland: POB 2107, Hay Babel, House No. 41/5/929, Baghdad; tel. (1) 719-3091.

Thailand: POB 6062, 1/4/609, al-Mansour, Baghdad; tel. (1) 541-8798; Ambassador: Cheuy Suetrong.

Tunisia: POB 6057, Mansour 34/2/4, Baghdad; tel. (1) 551-7786; Ambassador: Larbi Hantous.

Turkey: POB 14001, 2/8 Waziriya, Baghdad; tel. (1) 422-2768; Ambassador: Sönmez Köksal.

Uganda: 41/1/609 al-Mansour, Baghdad; tel. (1) 551-3594; Ambassador: Swaib M. Musoke.

United Arab Emirates: al-Mansour, 50 al-Mansour Main St, Baghdad; tel. (1) 551-7026; Ambassador: Hilal Sa'id Hilal az-Zu'abi.

Venezuela: al-Mansour, House No. 12/79/601, Baghdad; tel. (1) 552-0965; Ambassador: Freddy Rafael Alvarez Yanes.

Viet Nam: 29/611 Hay al-Andalus, Baghdad; tel. (1) 551-1388; Ambassador: Tran Ky Long.

Yemen: Jadiriya 923/28/29, Baghdad; tel. (1) 776-0647; Ambassador: Muhammad Abdullah ash-Shami.

Yugoslavia: POB 2061, 16/35/923 Hay Babel, Jadiriya, Baghdad; tel. (1) 776-7887; fax (1) 217-1069; Chargé d'affaires a.i.: Jovan Kostić.

Judicial System

Courts in Iraq consist of the following: The Court of Cassation, Courts of Appeal, First Instance Courts, Peace Courts, Courts of Sessions, *Shari'a* Courts and Penal Courts.

The Court of Cassation: This is the highest judicial bench of all the Civil Courts; it sits in Baghdad, and consists of the President and a number of vice-presidents and not fewer than 15 permanent judges, delegated judges and reporters as necessity requires. There are four bodies in the Court of Cassation, these are: (*a*) the General body, (*b*) Civil and Commercial body, (*c*) Personal Status body, (*d*) the Penal body.

Courts of Appeal: The country is divided into five Districts of Appeal: Baghdad, Mosul, Basra, Hilla, and Kirkuk, each with its Court of Appeal consisting of a president, vice-presidents and not fewer than three members, who consider the objections against the decisions issued by the First Instance Courts of first grade.

Courts of First Instance: These courts are of two kinds: Limited and Unlimited in jurisdiction.

Limited Courts deal with Civil and Commercial suits, the value of which is 500 Iraqi dinars and less; and suits, the value of which cannot be defined, and which are subject to fixed fees. Limited Courts consider these suits in the final stage and they are subject to Cassation.

Unlimited Courts consider the Civil and Commercial suits irrespective of their value, and suits the value of which exceeds 500 Iraqi dinars with first grade subject to appeal.

First Instance Courts consist of one judge in the centre of each *Liwa*, some *Qadhas* and *Nahiyas*, as the Minister of Justice judges necessary.

Courts of Sessions: There is in every District of Appeal a Court of Sessions which consists of three judges under the presidency of the President of the Court of Appeal or one of his vice-presidents. It considers the penal suits prescribed by Penal Proceedings Law and other laws. More than one Court of Sessions may be established in one District of Appeal by notification issued by the Minister of Justice mentioning therein its headquarters, jurisdiction and the manner of its establishment.

Shari'a Courts: A *Shari'a* Court is established wherever there is a First Instance Court; the Muslim judge of the First Instance Court may be a *Qadhi* to the *Shari'a* Court if a special *Qadhi* has not been appointed thereto. The *Shari'a* Court considers matters of personal status and religious matters in accordance with the provisions of the law supplement to the Civil and Commercial Proceedings Law.

Penal Courts: A Penal Court of first grade is established in every First Instance Court. The judge of the First Instance Court is considered as penal judge unless a special judge is appointed thereto. More than one Penal Court may be established to consider the suits prescribed by the Penal Proceedings Law and other laws.

One or more Investigation Court may be established in the centre of each *Liwa* and a judge is appointed thereto. They may be established in the centres of *Qadhas* and *Nahiyas* by order of the Minister of Justice. The judge carries out the investigation in accordance with the provisions of Penal Proceedings Law and the other laws.

There is in every First Instance Court a department for the execution of judgments presided over by the Judge of First Instance if a special president is not appointed thereto. It carries out its duties in accordance with the provisions of Execution Law.

Religion

ISLAM

About 95% of the population are Muslims, more than 50% of whom are Shi'ite. The Arabs of northern Iraq, the Bedouins, the Kurds, the Turkomans and some of the inhabitants of Baghdad and Basra are mainly of the Sunni sect, while the remaining Arabs south of the Diyali belong to the Shi'i sect.

CHRISTIANITY

There are Christian communities in all the principal towns of Iraq, but their principal villages lie mostly in the Mosul district. The Christians of Iraq comprise three groups: (*a*) the free Churches, including the Nestorian, Gregorian and Syrian Orthodox; (*b*) the churches known as Uniate, since they are in union with the Roman Catholic Church, including the Armenian Uniates, Syrian Uniates and Chaldeans; (*c*) mixed bodies of Protestant converts, New Chaldeans and Orthodox Armenians.

The Assyrian Church

Assyrian Christians, an ancient sect having sympathies with Nestorian beliefs, were forced to leave their mountainous homeland in northern Kurdistan in the early part of the 20th century. The estimated 550,000 members of the Apostolic Catholic Assyrian Church of the East are now exiles, mainly in Iraq, Syria, Lebanon and the USA. Their leader is the Catholicos Patriarch, His Holiness Mar Dinkha IV.

The Orthodox Churches

Armenian Apostolic Church: Bishop Avak Asadourian, Primate of the Armenian Diocese of Iraq, POB 2280, Younis as-Saba'awi Sq.,

Baghdad; tel. (1) 885-1853; fax (1) 885-1857; nine churches (four in Baghdad); 18,000 adherents, mainly in Baghdad.

Syrian Orthodox Church: about 12,000 adherents in Iraq.

The Greek Orthodox Church is also represented in Iraq.

The Roman Catholic Church

Armenian Rite

At 31 December 1998 the archdiocese of Baghdad contained an estimated 2,000 adherents.

Archbishop of Baghdad: Most Rev. PAUL COUSSA, Archevêché Arménien Catholique, Karrada Sharkiya, POB 2344, Baghdad; tel. (1) 719-1827.

Chaldean Rite

Iraq comprises the patriarchate of Babylon, five archdioceses (including the patriarchal see of Baghdad) and five dioceses (all of which are suffragan to the patriarchate). Altogether, the Patriarch has jurisdiction over 21 archdioceses and dioceses in Iraq, Egypt, Iran, Lebanon, Syria, Turkey and the USA, and the Patriarchal Vicariate of Jerusalem. At 31 December 1998 there were an estimated 190,650 Chaldean Catholics in Iraq (including 151,000 in the archdiocese of Baghdad).

Patriarch of Babylon of the Chaldeans: His Beatitude RAPHAËL I BIDAWID, POB 6112, Patriarcat Chaldéen Catholique, Baghdad; tel. (1) 887-9604; fax (1) 884-9967.

Archbishop of Arbil: Most Rev. JACQUES ISHAQ, Archevêché Catholique Chaldéen, Ainkawa, Arbil; tel. (665) 24701.

Archbishop of Baghdad: the Patriarch of Babylon (see above).

Archbishop of Basra: Most Rev. DJIBRAIL KASSAB, Archevêché Chaldéen, POB 217, Ahsar-Basra; tel. (40) 210323.

Archbishop of Kirkuk: Most Rev. ANDRÉ SANA, Archevêché Chaldéen, Kirkuk; tel. (50) 213978.

Archbishop of Mosul: Most Rev. GEORGES GARMO, Archevêché Chaldéen, Mayassa, Mosul; tel. (60) 762022; fax (60) 772460.

Latin Rite

The archdiocese of Baghdad, directly responsible to the Holy See, contained an estimated 3,000 adherents at 31 December 1999.

Archbishop of Baghdad: Most Rev. PAUL DAHDAH, Archevêché Latin, Hay al-Wahda—Mahalla 904, rue 8, Imm. 44, POB 35130, Baghdad; tel. (1) 719-9537; fax (1) 717-2471.

Melkite Rite

The Greek-Melkite Patriarch of Antioch (MAXIMOS V HAKIM) is resident in Damascus, Syria.

Patriarchal Exarchate of Iraq: Rue Asfar, Karrada Sharkiya, Baghdad; tel. (1) 719-1082; 600 adherents (31 December 1995); Exarch Patriarchal: Archimandrite NICOLAS DAGHER.

Syrian Rite

Iraq comprises two archdioceses, containing an estimated 53,500 adherents at 31 December 1998.

Archbishop of Baghdad: Most Rev. ATHANASE MATTI SHABA MATOKA, Archevêché Syrien Catholique, Baghdad; tel. (1) 719-1850; fax (1) 719-0168.

Archbishop of Mosul: Most Rev. CYRILLE EMMANUEL BENNI, Archevêché Syrien Catholique, Mosul; tel. (60) 762160.

The Anglican Communion

Within the Episcopal Church in Jerusalem and the Middle East, Iraq forms part of the diocese of Cyprus and the Gulf. Expatriate congregations in Iraq meet at St George's Church, Baghdad (Hon. Sec. GRAHAM SPURGEON). The Bishop in Cyprus and the Gulf is resident in Cyprus.

JUDAISM

Unofficial estimates assess the present size of the Jewish community at 2,500, almost all residing in Baghdad.

OTHERS

About 30,000 Yazidis and a smaller number of Turkomans, Sabians and Shebeks reside in Iraq.

Sabian Community: Head Sheikh DAKHIL, Nasiriyah; 20,000 adherents; Mandeans, mostly in Nasiriyah.

Yazidis: Leader TASHIN BAIK, Ainsifni; 30,000 adherents.

The Press

DAILIES

Al-Baath ar-Riyadhi: Baghdad; sports; Propr and Editor UDAY SADDAM HUSSAIN.

Babil (Babylon): Baghdad; f. 1991; Propr and Editor UDAY SADDAM HUSSAIN.

Baghdad Observer: POB 624, Karantina, Baghdad; f. 1967; tel. (1) 416-9341; English; state-sponsored; Editor-in-Chief NAJI AL-HADITHI; circ. 22,000.

Al-Iraq: POB 5717, Baghdad; f. 1976; Kurdish; formerly *Al-Ta'akhi*; organ of the National Progressive Front; Editor-in-Chief SALAHUDIN SAEED; circ. 30,000.

Al-Jumhuriya (The Republic): POB 491, Waziriya, Baghdad; f. 1963, refounded 1967; Arabic; Editor-in-Chief SAMI MAHDI; circ. 150,000.

Al-Qadisiya: Baghdad; organ of the army.

Ar-Riyadhi (Sportsman): POB 58, Jadid Hassan Pasha, Baghdad; f. 1971; Arabic; published by Ministry of Youth; circ. 30,000.

Tariq ash-Sha'ab (People's Path): as-Sa'adoun St, Baghdad; Arabic; organ of the Iraqi Communist Party; Editor ABD AR-RAZZAK AS-SAFI.

Ath-Thawra (Revolution): POB 2009, Aqaba bin Nafi's Square, Baghdad; tel. (1) 719-6161; f. 1968; Arabic; organ of Baath Party; Editor-in-Chief HAMEED SAEED; circ. 250,000.

WEEKLIES

Alif Baa (Alphabet): POB 8063, Ministry of Education Bldg, Baghdad; tel. (1) 886-2948; fax (1) 884-3799; Arabic; Editor-in-Chief AMIR AL-HILOU; circ. 25,000.

Al-Idaa'a wal-Television (Radio and Television): Iraqi Broadcasting and Television Establishment, Karradat Mariam, Baghdad; tel. (1) 537-1161; radio and television programmes and articles; Arabic; Editor-in-Chief KAMIL HAMDI ASH-SHARQI; circ. 40,000.

Majallati: Children's Culture House, POB 8041, Baghdad; Arabic; children's newspaper; Editor-in-Chief RAAD BENDER; circ. 35,000.

Ar-Rased (The Observer): Baghdad; Arabic; general.

Sabaa Nisan: Baghdad; f. 1976; Arabic; organ of the General Union of the Youth of Iraq.

Sawt al-Fallah (Voice of the Peasant): Karradat Mariam, Baghdad; f. 1968; Arabic; organ of the General Union of Farmers Societies; circ. 40,000.

Waee ul-Ummal (The Workers' Consciousness): Headquarters of General Federation of Trade Unions in Iraq, POB 2307, Gialani St, Senak, Baghdad; Arabic; Iraq Trades Union organ; Chief Editor KHALID MAHMOUD HUSSEIN; circ. 25,000.

PERIODICALS

Afaq Arabiya (Arab Horizons): POB 2009, Aqaba bin Nafi's Sq., Baghdad; monthly; Arabic; literary and political; Editor-in-Chief Dr MOHSIN J. AL-MUSAWI.

Al-Aqlam (Pens): POB 4032, Adamiya, Baghdad; tel. (1) 443-3644; f. 1964; publ. by the Ministry of Culture and Information; monthly; Arabic; literary; Editor-in-Chief Dr ALI J. AL-ALLAQ; circ. 7,000.

Bagdad: Dar al-Ma'mun for Translation and Publishing, POB 24015, Karradat Mariam, Baghdad; tel. (1) 538-3171; fortnightly; French; cultural and political.

Al-Funoon al-Ida'iya (Fields of Broadcasting): Cultural Affairs House, Karradat Mariam, Baghdad; quarterly; Arabic; supervised by Broadcasting and TV Training Institute; engineering and technical; Chief Editor MUHAMMAD AL-JAZA'RI.

Gilgamesh: Dar al-Ma'mun for Translation and Publishing, POB 24015, Karradat Mariam, Baghdad; tel. (1) 538-3171; quarterly; English; cultural.

Hurras al-Watan: Baghdad; Arabic.

L'Iraq Aujourd'hui: POB 2009, Aqaba bin Nafi's Sq., Baghdad; f. 1976; bi-monthly; French; cultural and political; Editor NADJI AL-HADITHI; circ. 12,000.

Iraq Oil News: POB 6178, al-Mansour, Baghdad; tel. (1) 541-0031; f. 1973; monthly; English; publ. by the Information and Public Relations Div. of the Ministry of Oil.

The Journal of the Faculty of Medicine: College of Medicine, University of Baghdad, Jadiriya, Baghdad; tel. (1) 93091; f. 1935; quarterly; Arabic and English; medical and technical; Editor Prof. YOUSUF D. AN-NAAMAN.

Majallat al-Majma' al-'Ilmi al-'Iraqi (Journal of the Academy of Sciences): POB 4023, Waziriya, Baghdad; tel. (1) 422-1733; fax (1) 425-4523; f. 1950; quarterly; Arabic; scholarly magazine on Arabic Islamic culture; Editor-in-Chief Dr NAJIH M. K. EL-RAWI.

Majallat ath-Thawra az-Ziraia (Magazine of Iraq Agriculture): Baghdad; quarterly; Arabic; agricultural; published by the Ministry of Agriculture and Irrigation.

Al-Maskukat (Coins): Dept of Antiquities and Heritage, Karkh, Salihiya St, Baghdad; tel. (1) 884-0875; f. 1969; annually; numismatics; Chair. of Ed. Board RABI' AL-QAISI.

Al-Masrah wal-Cinema: Iraqi Broadcasting, Television and Cinema Establishment, Salihiya St, Baghdad; monthly; Arabic; artistic, theatrical and cinema.

Al-Mawrid: POB 2009, Aqaba bin Nafi's Sq., Baghdad; f. 1971; monthly; Arabic; cultural.

Al-Mu'allem al-Jadid: Ministry of Education, al-Imam al-A'dham St, A'dhamaiya, Nr Antar Sq., Baghdad; tel. (1) 422-2594. 1935; quarterly; Arabic; educational, social, and general; Editor-in-Chief KHALIL I. HAMASH; circ. 190,000.

An-Naft wal-Aalam (Oil and the World): Ministry of Oil, POB 6178, Baghdad; f. 1973; monthly; Arabic; Editor-in-Chief Gen. AMIR MUHAMMAD RASHID.

Sawt at-Talaba (The Voice of Students): al-Maghreb St, Waziriya, Baghdad; f. 1968; monthly; Arabic; organ of National Union of Iraqi Students; circ. 25,000.

As-Sina'a (Industry): POB 5665, Baghdad; every 2 months; Arabic and English; publ. by Ministry of Industry and Minerals; Editor-in-Chief ABD AL-QADER ABD AL-LATIF; circ. 16,000.

Sumer: Dept of Antiquities and Heritage, Karkh, Salihiya St, Baghdad; tel. (1) 884-0875; f. 1945; annually; archaeological, historical journal; Chair. of Ed. Board RABI AL-QAISI.

Ath-Thaqafa (Culture): Place at-Tahrir, Baghdad; f. 1970; monthly; Arabic; cultural; Editor-in-Chief SALAH KHALIS; circ. 5,000.

Ath-Thaqafa al-Jadida (The New Culture): Baghdad; f. 1969; monthly; pro-Communist; Editor-in-Chief SAFA AL-HAFIZ; circ. 3,000.

At-Turath ash-Sha'abi (Popular Heritage): POB 2009, Aqaba bin Nafi's Sq., Baghdad; monthly; Arabic; specializes in Iraqi and Arabic folklore; Editor-in-Chief LUTFI AL-KHOURI; circ. 15,000.

Al-Waqai al-Iraqiya (Official Gazette of Republic of Iraq): Ministry of Justice, Baghdad; f. 1922; Arabic and English weekly editions; circ. Arabic 4,000, English 400; Dir HASHIM N. JAAFER.

PRESS ORGANIZATIONS

The General Federation of Journalists: POB 6017, Baghdad; tel. (1) 541-3993.

Iraqi Journalists' Union: POB 14101, Baghdad; tel. (1) 537-0762.

NEWS AGENCIES

Iraqi News Agency (INA): POB 3084, 28 Nissan Complex—Baghdad, Sadoun; tel. (1) 8863024. 1959; Dir-Gen. UDAI EL-TAIE.

Foreign Bureaux

Agence France-Presse (AFP): POB 190, Apt 761-91-97, Baghdad; tel. (1) 551-4333; Correspondent FAROUQ CHOUKRI.

Agenzia Nazionale Stampa Associata (ANSA) (Italy): POB 5602, Baghdad; tel. (1) 776-2558; Correspondent SALAH H. NASRAWI.

Associated Press (AP) (USA): Hay al-Khadra 629, Zuqaq No. 23, Baghdad; tel. (1) 555-9041; Correspondent SALAH H. NASRAWI.

Deutsche Presse-Agentur (dpa) (Germany): POB 5699, Baghdad; Correspondent NAJHAT KOTANI.

Informatsionnoye Telegrafnoye Agentstvo Rossii—Telegrafnoye Agentstvo Suverennykh Stran (ITAR—TASS) (Russia): 67 Street 52, Alwiya, Baghdad; Correspondent ANDREI OSTALSKY.

Reuters (UK): House No. 8, Zuqaq 75, Mahalla 903, Hay al-Karada, Baghdad; tel. (1) 719-1843; Correspondent SUBHY HADDAD.

Xinhua (New China) News Agency (People's Republic of China): al-Mansour, Adrus District, 611 Small District, 5 Lane No. 8, Baghdad; tel. (1) 541-8904; Correspondent ZHU SHAOHUA.

Publishers

National House for Publishing, Distribution and Advertising: Ministry of Culture and Information, POB 624, al-Jumhuriya St, Baghdad; tel. (1) 425-1846. 1972; publishes books on politics, economics, education, agriculture, sociology, commerce and science in Arabic and other Middle Eastern languages; sole importer and distributor of newspapers, magazines, periodicals and books; controls all advertising activities, inside Iraq as well as outside; Dir-Gen. M. A. ASKAR.

Afaq Arabiya Publishing House: POB 4032, Adamiya, Baghdad; tel. (1) 443-6044; fax (1) 444-8760; publisher of literary monthlies, *Al-Aqlam* and *Afaq Arabiya*, periodicals, *Foreign Culture, Art, Folklore,* and cultural books; Chair. Dr MOHSIN AL-MUSAWI.

Dar al-Ma'mun for Translation and Publishing: POB 24015, Karradat Mariam, Baghdad; tel. (1) 538-3171; publisher of newspapers and magazines including: the *Baghdad Observer* (daily newspaper), *Bagdad* (monthly magazine), *Gilgamesh* (quarterly magazine).

Al-Hurriyah Printing Establishment: Karantina, Sarrafia, Baghdad; tel. (1) 69721; f. 1970; largest printing and publishing

establishment in Iraq; state-owned; controls *Al-Jumhuriyah* (see below).

Al-Jamaheer Press House: POB 491, Sarrafia, Baghdad; tel. (1) 416-9341; fax (1) 416-1875; f. 1963; publisher of a number of newspapers and magazines, *Al-Jumhuriyah, Baghdad Observer, Alif Baa, Yord Weekly*; Pres. SAAD QASSEM HAMMOUDI.

Al-Ma'arif Ltd: Mutanabi St, Baghdad; f. 1929; publishes periodicals and books in Arabic, Kurdish, Turkish, French and English.

Al-Muthanna Library: Mutanabi St, Baghdad; f. 1936; booksellers and publishers of books in Arabic and oriental languages; Man. ANAS K. AR-RAJAB.

An-Nahdah: Mutanabi St, Baghdad; politics, Arab affairs.

Kurdish Culture Publishing House: Baghdad; f. 1976; attached to the Ministry of Culture and Information.

Ath-Thawra Printing and Publishing House: POB 2009, Aqaba bin Nafi's Sq., Baghdad; tel. (1) 719-6161; f. 1970; state-owned; Chair. TAREQ AZIZ.

Thnayan Printing House: Baghdad.

Broadcasting and Communications

TELECOMMUNICATIONS

Iraqi Telecommunications and Posts: POB 2450, Karrada Dakhil, Baghdad; tel. (1) 718-0400; fax (1) 718-2125; Dir-Gen. Eng. MEZHER M. HASAN.

BROADCASTING

State Enterprise for Communications and Post: f. 1987 from State Org. for Post, Telegraph and Telephones, and its subsidiaries.

State Organization for Broadcasting and Television: Broadcasting and Television Bldg, Salihiya, Karkh, Baghdad; tel. (1) 537-1161.

Iraqi Broadcasting and Television Establishment: Salihiya, Baghdad; tel. (1) 884-4412; fax (1) 541-0480; f. 1936; radio broadcasts began 1936; home service broadcasts in Arabic, Kurdish, Syriac and Turkoman; foreign service in French, German, English, Russian, Azeri, Hebrew and Spanish; there are 16 medium-wave and 30 short-wave transmitters; Dir-Gen. SABAH YASEEN.

Radio

Idaa'a Baghdad (Radio Baghdad): f. 1936; 22 hours daily.

Idaa'a Sawt al-Jamahir: f. 1970; 24 hours.

Other stations include **Idaa'a al-Kurdia, Idaa'a al-Farisiya** (Persian).

Radio Iraq International: POB 8145, Baghdad.

Television

Baghdad Television: Ministry of Culture and Information, Iraqi Broadcasting and Television Establishment, Salihiya, Karkh, Baghdad; tel. (1) 537-1151; f. 1956; government station operating daily on two channels for 9 hours and 8 hours respectively; Dir-Gen. Dr MAJID AHMAD AS-SAMARRIE.

Kirkuk Television: f. 1967; government station; 6 hours daily.

Mosul Television: f. 1968; government station; 6 hours daily.

Basra Television: f. 1968; government station; 6 hours daily.

Missan Television: f. 1974; government station; 6 hours daily.

Kurdish Television: f. 1974; government station; 8 hours daily.

There are 18 other TV stations operating in the Iraqi provinces.

Finance

(cap. = capital; dep. = deposits; res = reserves;
brs = branches; m. = million; amounts in Iraqi dinars)

All banks and insurance companies, including all foreign companies, were nationalized in July 1964. The assets of foreign companies were taken over by the State. In May 1991 the Government announced its decision to end the State's monopoly in banking, and by mid-1992 three private banks had commenced operations.

BANKING

Central Bank

Central Bank of Iraq: POB 64, Rashid St, Baghdad; tel. (1) 886-5171; f. 1947 as National Bank of Iraq; name changed as above 1956; has the sole right of note issue; cap. and res 125m. (Sept. 1988); Gov. SUBHI N. FRANKOOL; brs in Mosul and Basra.

Nationalized Commercial Banks

Rafidain Bank: New Banks St, Baghdad; tel. (1) 415-8001; f. 1941; state-owned; cap. 2,000m., res 1,702.3m., dep. 453,678m., total assets 503,145.1m. (Dec. 1998); Pres. DHIA HABIB AL-KHAYYOON; 152 brs in Iraq, 9 brs abroad.

Rashid Bank: BOP 7177, Haifa St, Baghdad; tel. (1) 885-3411; f. 1988; state-owned; cap. 1,000m., res 1.5m., dep. 236.1m. (1999); Chair. and Gen. Man. FAIQ M. AL-OBAIDY; 133 brs.

Private Commercial Banks

Baghdad Bank: POB 64, Rashid St, Baghdad; tel. (1) 717-5007; fax (1) 717-3487; f. 1992; cap. 100m.; Chair. HASSAN AN-NAJAFI.

Commercial Bank of Iraq SA: POB 5639, 902/14/13 Al-Wahda St, Baghdad; tel. (1) 707-0049, fax (1) 718-4312; f. 1992; cap. 800m. (1998); Chair. MUHAMMAD H. DRAGH.

Specialized Banks

Al-Ahli Bank for Agricultural Investment and Financing: Al-Huria Sq., Al-Ahh, Baghdad.

Agricultural Co-operative Bank of Iraq: POB 2421, Rashid St, Baghdad; tel. (1) 886-4768; fax (1) 886-5047; f. 1936; state-owned; cap. 295.7m., res 14m., dep. 10.5m., total assets 351.6m. (Dec. 1988); Dir-Gen. HDIYA H. AL-KHAYOUN; 32 brs.

Industrial Bank of Iraq: POB 5825, as-Sinak, Baghdad; tel. (1) 887-2181; fax (1) 888-3047; f. 1940; state-owned; cap. 59.7m., dep. 77.9m. (Dec. 1988); Dir-Gen. BASSIMA ABD AL-HADDI ADH-DHAHIR; 5 brs.

Investment Bank of Iraq: POB 3724, 102/91/24 Hay as-Sadoon, Alwiya, Baghdad; tel. (1) 718-4624; fax (1) 719-8505; f. 1993; cap. 300m., res 39.2m. (Dec. 1998); Chair. THAMIR R. SHAIKHLY; Man. Dir MOWAFAQ HASAN MAHMOOD.

Iraqi Islamic Bank SA: POB 940, Al-Kahiay, Bab Al-Muathem, Baghdad; tel. (1) 414-0694.

Iraqi Middle East Investment Bank: POB 10379, Bldg 65, Hay Babel, 929 Arasat al-Hindiya, Baghdad; tel. (1) 717-3745; f. 1993; cap., res and dep. 3,254.8m. (1998).

Real Estate Bank of Iraq: POB 8118, 29/222 Haifa St, Baghdad; tel. (1) 885-3212; fax (1) 884-0980; f. 1949; state-owned; gives loans to assist the building industry; cap. 800m., res 11m., total assets 2,593.6m. (Dec. 1988); acquired the Co-operative Bank in 1970; Dir-Gen. ABD AR-RAZZAQ AZIZ; 18 brs.

INSURANCE

Iraq Life Insurance Co: POB 989, Aqaba bin Nafi's Sq., Khalid bin al-Waleed St, Baghdad; tel. (1) 719-2184; f. 1959; state-owned; Chair. and Gen. Man. TARIQ KHALIL IBRAHIM.

Iraq Reinsurance Co: POB 297, Aqaba bin Nafi's Sq., Khalid bin al-Waleed St, Baghdad; tel. (1) 719-5131; fax (1) 791497; f. 1960; state-owned; transacts reinsurance business on the international market; total assets 93.2m. (1985); Chair. and Gen. Man. K. M. AL-MUDARIES.

National Insurance Co: POB 248, National Insurance Co Bldg, Al-Khullani St, Baghdad; tel. (1) 885-3026; fax (1) 886-1486; f. 1950; cap. 20m.; all types of general and life insurance, reinsurance and investment; Chair. and Gen. Man. MUHAMMAD HUSSAIN JAAFAR ABBAS.

STOCK EXCHANGE

Capital Market Authority: Baghdad; Chair. MUHAMMAD HASSAN FAG EN-NOUR.

Trade and Industry

CHAMBERS OF COMMERCE

Federation of Iraqi Chambers of Commerce: Mustansir St, Baghdad; tel. (1) 886-1811; fax (1) 886-0283; f. 1969; all Iraqi Chambers of Commerce are affiliated to the Federation; Chair. ZUHAIR A. AL-YOUNIS; Sec.-Gen. FALIH A. AS-SALEH.

INDUSTRIAL AND TRADE ASSOCIATIONS

In 1987 and 1988, as part of a programme of economic and administrative reform, to increase efficiency and productivity in industry and agriculture, many of the state organizations previously responsible for various industries were abolished or merged, and new state enterprises or mixed-sector national companies were established to replace them.

Military Industries Commission (MIC): Baghdad; attached to the Ministry of Defence; Chair. ABD AT-TAWAB ABDULLAH MULLAH HAWAISH.

State enterprises include the following:

Iraqi State Enterprise for Cement: f. 1987 by merger of central and southern state cement enterprises.

National Co for Chemical and Plastics Industries: Dir-Gen. RAJA BAYYATI.

The Rafidain Co for Building Dams: f. 1987 to replace the State Org. for Dams.

State Enterprise for Battery Manufacture: f. 1987; Dir-Gen. ADEL ABBOUD.

State Enterprise for Construction Industries: f. 1987 by merger of state orgs for gypsum, asbestos, and the plastic and concrete industries.

State Enterprise for Cotton Industries: f. 1988 by merger of State Org. for Cotton Textiles and Knitting, and the Mosul State Org. for Textiles.

State Enterprise for Drinks and Mineral Water: f. 1987 by merger of enterprises responsible for soft and alcoholic drinks.

State Enterprise for the Fertilizer Industries: f. by merger of Basra-based and central fertilizer enterprises.

State Enterprise for Import and Export: f. 1987 to replace the five state organizations responsible to the Ministry of Trade for productive commodities, consumer commodities, grain and food products, exports and imports.

State Enterprise for Leather Industries: f. 1987; Dir-Gen. MUHAMMAD ABD AL-MAJID.

State Enterprise for Sugar Beet: f. 1987 by merger of sugar enterprises in Mosul and Sulaimaniya.

State Enterprise for Textiles: f. 1987 to replace the enterprise for textiles in Baghdad, and the enterprise for plastic sacks in Tikrit.

State Enterprise for Tobacco and Cigarettes.

State Enterprise for Woollen Industries: f. by merger of state orgs for textiles and woollen textiles and Arbil-based enterprise for woollen textiles and women's clothing.

AGRICULTURAL ORGANIZATIONS

The following bodies are responsible to the Ministry of Agriculture and Irrigation:

State Agricultural Enterprise in Dujaila.

State Enterprise for Agricultural Supplies: Dir-Gen. MUHAMMAD KHAIRI.

State Enterprise for Developing Animal Wealth.

State Enterprise for Fodder.

State Enterprise for Grain Trading and Processing: Dir-Gen. ZUHAIR ABD AR-RAHMAN.

State Enterprise for Poultry (Central and Southern Areas).

State Enterprise for Poultry (Northern Area).

State Enterprise for Sea Fisheries: POB 260, Basra; Baghdad office: POB 3296, Baghdad; tel. (1) 92023; fleet of 3 fish factory ships, 2 fish carriers, 1 fishing boat.

PEASANT SOCIETIES

General Federation of Peasant Societies: Baghdad; f. 1959; has 734 affiliated Peasant Societies.

EMPLOYERS' ORGANIZATION

Iraqi Federation of Industries: Iraqi Federation of Industries Bldg, al-Khullani Sq., Baghdad; f. 1956; 6,000 mems; Pres. HATAM ABD AR-RASHID.

UTILITIES

Electricity

State Enterprise for Generation and Transmission of Electricity: f. 1987 from State Org. for Major Electrical Projects; Dir SALAH YUSUF KUZAYR.

PETROLEUM AND GAS

Ministry of Oil: POB 6178, al-Mansour City, Baghdad; tel. (1) 551-0031; solely responsible until mid-1989 for petroleum sector and activities relevant to it; since mid-1989 these responsibilities have been shared with the Technical Corpn for Special Projects of the Ministry of Industry and Military Industrialization (Ministry of Industry and Minerals from July 1991); the Ministry was merged with INOC in 1987; the state organizations responsible to the ministry for petroleum refining and gas processing, for the distribution of petroleum products, for training personnel in the petroleum industry, and for gas were simultaneously abolished, and those for northern and southern petroleum, for petroleum equipment, for petroleum and gas exploration, for petroleum tankers, and for petroleum projects were converted into companies, as part of a plan to reorganize the petroleum industry and make it more efficient; Minister of Oil Gen. AMIR MUHAMMAD RASHID.

Iraq National Oil Co (INOC): POB 476, al-Khullani Sq., Baghdad; tel. (1) 887-1115. in 1964 to operate the petroleum industry at home and abroad; when Iraq nationalized its petroleum industry, structural changes took place in INOC, and it became solely responsible for exploration, production, transportation and marketing of Iraqi crude petroleum and petroleum products. INOC was merged with the Ministry of Oil in 1987, and the functions of some of the organizations under its control were transferred to newly-created ministerial departments or to companies responsible to the ministry.

Iraqi Oil Drilling Co: f. 1990.

Iraqi Oil Tankers Co: POB 37, Basra; tel. (40) 319990; fmrly the State Establishment for Oil Tankers; re-formed as a company in 1987; responsible to the Ministry of Oil for operating a fleet of 17 oil tankers; Chair. MUHAMMAD A. MUHAMMAD.

National Co for Distribution of Oil Products and Gas: POB 3, Rashid St, South Gate, Baghdad; tel. (1) 888-9911; fmrly a state organization; re-formed as a company in 1987; fleet of 6 tankers; Dir-Gen. ALI H. IJAM.

National Co for Manufacturing Oil Equipment: fmrly a state organization; re-formed as a company in 1987.

National Co for Oil and Gas Exploration: INOC Building, POB 476, al-Khullani Sq., Baghdad; fmrly the State Establishment for Oil and Gas Exploration; re-formed as a company in 1987; responsible for exploration and operations in difficult terrain such as marshes, swamps, deserts, valleys and in mountainous regions; Dir-Gen. RADHWAN AS-SAADI.

Northern Petroleum Co (NPC): POB 1, at-Ta'meem Governorate; f. 1987 by the merger of the fmr Northern and Central petroleum organizations to carry out petroleum operations in northern Iraq; Dir-Gen. GHAZI SABIR ALI.

Southern Petroleum Co (SPC): POB 240, Basra; fmrly the Southern Petroleum Organization; re-formed as the SPC in 1987 to undertake petroleum operations in southern Iraq; Dir-Gen. ASRI SALIH (acting).

State Co for Oil Marketing (SCOM): Man.-Dir ZEIN SADDAM AT-TIKRITI.

State Co for Oil Projects (SCOP): POB 198, Oil Compound, Baghdad; tel. (1) 416-8040; fax (1) 286-9432; fmrly the State Org. for Oil Projects; re-formed as a company in 1987; responsible for construction of petroleum projects, mostly inside Iraq through direct execution, and also for design supervision of the projects and contracting with foreign enterprises, etc.; Dir-Gen. Dr TALA'AT HATTAB.

State Enterprise for Oil and Gas Industrialization in the South: f. 1988 by merger of enterprises responsible for the gas industry and petroleum refining in the south.

State Enterprise for Petrochemical Industries.

State Establishment for Oil Refining in the Central Area: Dir-Gen. KAMIL AL-FATLI.

State Establishment for Oil Refining in the North: Dir-Gen. TAHA HAMOUD.

State Establishment for Pipelines: Dir-Gen. SABAH ALI JOUMAH.

TRADE UNIONS

General Federation of Trade Unions of Iraq (GFTU): POB 3049, Tahrir Sq., Rashid St, Baghdad; tel. (1) 887-0810; fax (1) 886-3820; f. 1959; incorporates six vocational trade unions and 18 local trade union federations in the governorates of Iraq; the number of workers in industry is 536,245, in agriculture 150,967 (excluding peasants) and in other services 476,621 (1986); GFTU is a member of the International Confederation of Arab Trade Unions and of the World Federation of Trade Unions; Pres. FADHIL MAHMOUD GHAREB.

Union of Teachers: Al-Mansour, Baghdad; Pres. Dr ISSA SALMAN HAMID.

Union of Palestinian Workers in Iraq: Baghdad; Sec.-Gen. SAMI ASH-SHAWISH.

There are also unions of doctors, pharmacologists, jurists, artists, and a General Federation of Iraqi Women (Chair. MANAL YOUNIS).

Transport

RAILWAYS

The metre-gauge line runs from Baghdad, through Khanaqin and Kirkuk, to Arbil. The standard gauge line covers the length of the country, from Rabia, on the Syrian border, via Mosul, to Baghdad (534 km), and from Baghdad to Basra and Umm Qasr (608 km), on the Arabian Gulf. A 404-km standard-gauge line linking Baghdad to Husaibah, near the Iraqi-Syrian frontier, was completed in 1983.

The 638-km line from Baghdad, via al-Qaim (on the Syrian border), to Akashat, and the 252-km Kirkuk–Baiji–Haditha line, which was designed to serve industrial projects along its route, were opened in 1986. The 150-km line linking the Akashat phosphate mines and the fertilizer complex at al-Qaim was formally opened in January 1986 but had already been in use for two years. Lines totalling some 2,400 km were planned at the beginning of the 1980s, but by 1988 only 800 km had been constructed. All standard-gauge trains are now hauled by diesel-electric locomotives, and all narrow-gauge (one-metre) line has been replaced by standard gauge (1,435 mm). As well as the internal service, there is a regular international service between Baghdad and İstanbul. Passenger rail services between Mosul and Aleppo, Syria, resumed in August 2000 after an interruption of almost 20 years. A rapid transit transport system is to be established in Baghdad, with work to be undertaken as part of the 1987–2001 development plan for the city.

Responsibility for all railways, other than the former Iraq Republic Railways (see below), and for the design and construction of new railways, which was formerly the province of the New Railways Implementation Authority, was transferred to the newly created State Enterprise for Implementation of Transport and Communications Projects.

State Enterprise for Iraqi Railways: Baghdad Central Station Bldg, Damascus Sq., Baghdad; tel. (1) 543-4404; fax (1) 884-0480; fmrly the Iraqi Republic Railways, under the supervision of State Org. for Iraqi Railways; re-formed as a State Enterprise in 1987, under the Ministry of Transport and Communications; total length of track (1996): 2,029 km, consisting of 1,496 km of standard gauge, 533 km of one-metre gauge; Dir-Gen. GHASSAN ABD AR-RAZAQ AL-ANI.

New Railways Implementation Authority: POB 17040, al-Hurriya, Baghdad; tel. (1) 537-0021; est. to design and construct railways to augment the standard-gauge network and to replace the metre-gauge network; Sec.-Gen. R. A. AL-UMARI.

ROADS

At the end of 1996, according to the International Road Federation, there was an estimated total road network of 47,400 km, of which approximately 40,760 km were paved.

The most important roads are: Baghdad–Mosul–Tel Kotchuk (Syrian border), 521 km; Baghdad–Kirkuk–Arbil–Mosul-Zakho (border with Turkey), 544 km; Kirkuk–Sulaimaniya, 160 km; Baghdad–Hilla–Diwaniya–Nasiriya–Basra, 586 km; Baghdad–Kut-Nasirya, 186 km; Baghdad–Ramadi–Rurba (border with Syria), 555 km; Baghdad–Kut–Umara–Basra–Safwan (border with Kuwait), 660 km; Baghdad–Baqaba–Kanikien (border with Iran). Most sections of the six-lane 1,264-km international Express Highway, linking Safwan (on the Kuwaiti border) with the Jordanian and Syrian borders, had been completed by June 1990. Studies have been completed for a second, 525-km Express Highway, linking Baghdad and Zakho on the Turkish border. The estimated cost of the project is more than US $4,500m. and is likely to preclude its implementation in the immediate future. An elaborate network of roads was constructed behind the war front with Iran in order to facilitate the movement of troops and supplies during the 1980–88 conflict.

Iraqi Land Transport Co: Baghdad; f. 1988 to replace State Organization for Land Transport; fleet of more than 1,000 large trucks; Dir Gen. AYSAR AS-SAFI.

Joint Land Transport Co: Baghdad; joint venture between Iraq and Jordan; operates a fleet of some 750 trucks.

State Enterprise for Implementation of Expressways: f. 1987; Dir-Gen. FAIZ MUHAMMAD SAID.

State Enterprise for Passenger Transport: Dir Gen. THABIT MAHMUD GHARIB.

State Enterprise for Roads and Bridges: POB 917, Karradat Mariam, Karkh, Baghdad; tel. (1) 32141; responsible for road and bridge construction projects to the Ministry of Housing and Construction.

SHIPPING

The ports of Basra and Umm Qasr are usually the commercial gateway of Iraq. They are connected by various ocean routes with all parts of the world, and constitute the natural distributing centre for overseas supplies. The Iraqi State Enterprise for Maritime Transport maintains a regular service between Basra, the Gulf and north European ports. There is also a port at Khor az-Zubair, which came into use during 1979.

At Basra there is accommodation for 12 vessels at the Maqal Wharves and accommodation for seven vessels at the buoys. There is one silo berth and two berths for petroleum products at Muftia and one berth for fertilizer products at Abu Flus. There is room for eight vessels at Umm Qasr. There are deep-water tanker terminals at Khor al-Amaya and Faw for three and four vessels respectively. The latter port, however, was abandoned during the early part of the Iran–Iraq War.

For the inland waterways, which are now under the control of the General Establishment for Iraqi Ports, there are 1,036 registered river craft, 48 motor vessels and 105 motor boats.

General Establishment for Iraqi Ports: Maqal, Basra; tel. (40) 413211; f. 1987, when State Org. for Iraqi Ports was abolished; Dir-Gen. ABD AR-RAZZAQ ABD AL-WAHAB.

State Enterprise for Iraqi Water Transport: POB 23016, Airport St, al-Furat Quarter, Baghdad; f. 1987 when State Org. for Iraqi Water Transport was abolished; responsible for the planning, supervision and control of six nat. water transportation enterprises, incl.:

> **State Enterprise for Maritime Transport (Iraqi Line):** POB 13038, al-Jadiriya al-Hurriya Ave, Baghdad; tel. (1) 776-3201; Basra office: 14 July St, POB 766, Basra; tel. 210206; f. 1952; Dir-Gen. JABER Q. HASSAN; Operations Man. M. A. ALI.

Shipping Company

Arab Bridge Maritime Navigation Co: Aqaba, Jordan; tel. (03) 316307; fax (03) 316313; f. 1987; joint venture by Egypt, Iraq and Jordan to improve economic co-operation; an expansion of the company that established a ferry link between the ports of Aqaba, Jordan, and Nuweibeh, Egypt, in 1985; cap. US $6m.; Chair. NABEEH AL-ABWAH.

CIVIL AVIATION

There are international airports near Baghdad, at Bamerni, and at Basra. Baghdad's Saddam International Airport reopened after postwar refurbishment in August 2000. However, international air links have been virtually halted by the UN embargo imposed in 1990. Internal flights, connecting Baghdad to Basra and Mosul, recommenced in November of that year. Civilian, as well as military, airports sustained heavy damage during the war with the multinational force in 1991.

National Co for Civil Aviation Services: al-Mansour, Baghdad; tel. (1) 551-9443; f. 1987 following the abolition of the State Organization for Civil Aviation; responsible for the provision of aircraft, and for airport and passenger services.

Iraqi Airways Co: Saddam International Airport, Baghdad; tel. (1) 887-2400; fax (1) 887-5808; f. 1948; Dir-Gen. AYAD ABD AL-KARIM HAMAM.

IRELAND

Introductory Survey

Location, Climate, Language, Religion, Flag, Capital

The Republic of Ireland consists of 26 of the 32 counties which comprise the island of Ireland. The remaining six counties, in the north-east, form Northern Ireland, which is part of the United Kingdom. Ireland lies in the Atlantic Ocean, about 80 km (50 miles) west of Great Britain. The climate is mild and equable, with temperatures generally between 0°C (32°F) and 21°C (70°F). Irish is the official first language, but its use as a vernacular is now restricted to certain areas, collectively known as the Gaeltacht, mainly in the west of Ireland. English is universally spoken. Official documents are printed in English and Irish. The vast majority of the inhabitants profess Christianity: of these about 95% are Roman Catholics and 5% Protestants. The national flag (proportions 2 by 1) consists of three equal vertical stripes, of green, white and orange. The capital is Dublin.

Recent History

The whole of Ireland was formerly part of the United Kingdom. In 1920 the island was partitioned, the six north-eastern counties remaining part of the United Kingdom, with their own government. In 1922 the 26 southern counties achieved dominion status, under the British Crown, as the Irish Free State. The dissolution of all remaining links with Great Britain culminated in 1937 in the adoption, by plebiscite, of a new constitution, which gave the Irish Free State full sovereignty within the Commonwealth. Formal ties with the Commonwealth were ended in 1949, when the 26 southern counties became a republic. The partition of Ireland remained a contentious issue, and in 1969 a clandestine organization, calling itself the Provisional Irish Republican Army (IRA—see Northern Ireland, Vol. II), initiated a violent campaign to achieve reunification.

In the general election of February 1973, the Fianna Fáil party, which had held office, with only two interruptions, since 1932, was defeated. Jack Lynch, who had been Prime Minister since 1966, resigned, and Liam Cosgrave formed a coalition between his own party, Fine Gael, and the Labour Party. The Irish Government remained committed to power-sharing in the six counties, but opposed any British military withdrawal from Northern Ireland (see Northern Ireland, Vol. II).

Following the assassination of the British Ambassador to Ireland by the Provisional IRA in July 1976, the Irish Government introduced stronger measures against terrorism. Fianna Fáil won the general election of June 1977 and Jack Lynch again became Prime Minister. In December 1979 Lynch resigned as Prime Minister and was succeeded by Charles Haughey. In June 1981, following an early general election, Dr Garret FitzGerald, a former Minister for Foreign Affairs, became Prime Minister in a coalition government between his own party, Fine Gael, and the Labour Party. However, the rejection by the Dáil of the coalition's budget proposals precipitated a further general election in February 1982. Haughey was returned to power, with the support of three members of the Workers' Party and two independents. The worsening economic situation, however, made the Fianna Fáil Government increasingly unpopular, and in November Haughey lost the support of the independents over proposed reductions in public expenditure. In the subsequent general election Fianna Fáil failed to gain an overall majority, and in December FitzGerald took office as Prime Minister in a coalition with the Labour Party.

During 1986 FitzGerald's coalition lost support, partly due to the formation of a new party, the Progressive Democrats, by disaffected members of Fianna Fáil. In June a controversial government proposal to end a 60-year constitutional ban on divorce was defeated by national referendum, and shortly afterwards, as a result of a series of defections, the coalition lost its parliamentary majority. In January 1987 the Labour Party refused to support Fine Gael's budget proposals envisaging reductions in planned public expenditure, and the coalition collapsed. Fianna Fáil, led by Haughey, won 81 of the 166 seats in the Dáil at the general election held in February. Fianna Fáil formed a minority government, which commenced upon a programme of unprecedented economic austerity.

In May 1989, following the Government's sixth parliamentary defeat over a minor policy issue, Haughey called a general election for 15 June. Fine Gael and the Progressive Democrats subsequently concluded an electoral pact to oppose Fianna Fáil. Although the Haughey administration had achieved significant economic improvements, severe reductions in public expenditure and continuing problems of unemployment and emigration adversely affected Fianna Fáil's electoral support, and it obtained only 77 of the 166 seats in the Dáil, while Fine Gael won 55 seats and the Progressive Democrats six seats.

At the end of June 1989 the Dáil reconvened to elect the Prime Minister. The Progressive Democrats voted in favour of Alan Dukes, the leader of Fine Gael, in accordance with their pre-election pact, and Haughey was defeated by 86 votes to 78. Dukes and Dick Spring, the leader of the Labour Party, also failed to be elected. Haughey was forced to resign (on the insistence of the opposition parties, who claimed that his remaining as Prime Minister would be unconstitutional), although he continued to lead an interim administration. After nearly four weeks of negotiations, however, Fianna Fáil formed an 'alliance' with the Progressive Democrats and included two of the latter's members in a new cabinet. In mid-July 1989 Haughey became Prime Minister in an Fianna Fáil–Progressive Democrats coalition.

In October 1991 the Government, whose popularity had been adversely affected by economic recession, won a vote of confidence in the Dáil by 84 votes to 81. The motion of 'no confidence' had been introduced following a series of financial scandals involving public officials. Although members of Fianna Fáil were critical of Haughey's management of these affairs, they were reluctant to precipitate a general election, owing to the party's decline in popularity. The narrow government victory was secured with the support of the Progressive Democrats, following an agreement between Fianna Fáil and the Progressive Democrats on a programme of tax reforms. In November 1991, however, a group of Fianna Fáil deputies proposed a motion demanding Haughey's removal as leader of the party. Albert Reynolds, the Minister for Finance and a former close associate of Haughey, and Padraig Flynn, the Minister for the Environment, announced their intention of supporting the motion, and were immediately dismissed from office. In the event the attempt to depose Haughey was defeated by a substantial majority of the Fianna Fáil parliamentary grouping.

In January 1992 a former Minister for Justice, Seán Doherty, alleged that, contrary to Haughey's previous denials, the Prime Minister had been aware of the secret monitoring, in 1982, of the telephone conversations of two journalists perceived to be critical of the Government. The Progressive Democrats made its continued support of the Government (without which a general election would have been necessary) conditional on Haughey's resignation. In February Reynolds was elected as leader of Fianna Fáil and assumed the office of Prime Minister, following Haughey's resignation. Reynolds extensively reshuffled the Cabinet, but retained the two representatives of the Progressive Democrats, in an attempt to preserve the coalition Government.

In June 1992 the leader of the Progressive Democrats, Desmond O'Malley, criticized Reynolds' conduct as Minister for Industry and Commerce in a parliamentary inquiry, which had been established in June 1991 to investigate allegations of fraud and political favouritism in the beef industry during 1987–88. In October 1992, in his testimony to the inquiry, the Prime Minister accused O'Malley of dishonesty. Following Reynolds' refusal to withdraw the allegations, in early November the Progressive Democrats left the coalition, and the Government was defeated on the following day in a motion of 'no confidence', proposed in the Dáil by the Labour Party. It was subsequently announced that a general election was to take place on 25 November, concurrently with three constitutional referendums on abortion. Fianna Fáil suffered a substantial loss of support, securing only 68 of the 166 seats in the Dáil (compared with 77 seats in 1989). Fine Gael also obtained a reduced number of seats (45, compared with 55 in 1989). In contrast, the Labour

Party attracted substantial support, more than doubling its number of seats (33, compared with 15 in 1989), while the Progressive Democrats increased its representation from six seats in 1989 to 10. In the concurrent referendums on abortion two of the proposals (on the right to seek an abortion in another European Community (EC, now European Union, EU, see p. 181) state and the right to information on abortion services abroad) were approved by about two-thirds of the votes cast. The third proposal—on the substantive issue of abortion, permitting the operation only in cases where the life (not merely the health) of the mother was threatened—was rejected, also by a two-thirds' majority.

Since no party had secured an overall majority in the general election, an extended period of consultations ensued, during which the four major parties negotiated on the composition of a governing coalition. In January 1993 Fianna Fáil and the Labour Party reached agreement on a joint policy programme and formed a coalition Government, which took office on 12 January. Albert Reynolds retained the premiership, while Dick Spring received the foreign affairs portfolio, as well as the post of Deputy Prime Minister. In June the Government began the introduction of a number of important social reforms. The Dáil approved legislation to provide for the legalized sale of prophylactics and the decriminalization of homosexual acts between consenting adults over the age of 17 years

In November 1994 serious differences arose within the coalition Government over the insistence by Fianna Fáil that the Attorney-General, Harry Whelehan, be appointed to a senior vacancy that had arisen in the High Court. Although such promotions accorded with past precedent, Whelehan's conservative record on social issues, particularly in relation to abortion, was unacceptable to the Labour Party, whose specific objection to Whelehan's appointment was based on his alleged obstruction, as Attorney-General, of the processing of an extradition warrant for a Roman Catholic priest sought by the authorities in Northern Ireland on charges of the sexual abuse of children. (During the seven months taken to process the extradition request, the accused had returned voluntarily to Northern Ireland, where he was tried and imprisoned.) It was alleged by the Labour Party that the transfer of Whelehan to the presidency of the High Court was intended by Fianna Fáil to protect him from public accountability for his conduct as Attorney-General. However, Reynolds and the Fianna Fáil members of the Cabinet approved the appointment in the absence of the Labour Party ministers.

On 15 November 1994 Reynolds admitted to the Dáil that there was no satisfactory explanation for the delay in processing the extradition warrant, but denied that the matter affected the suitability of Whelehan for judicial office. On the following day, after consultations with the new Attorney-General, Reynolds conceded that there had been unnecessary delays in the extradition procedure, and that Whelehan's promotion had been ill-advised. Spring, however, accused Reynolds of having earlier deliberately withheld information, and Whelehan of having lied. The Labour Party withdrew from the coalition, and on the following day the Government resigned. Reynolds, while remaining as Prime Minister of a 'caretaker' Government, relinquished the Fianna Fáil leadership on 19 November and was succeeded by the Minister for Finance, Bertie Ahern. Whelehan, meanwhile, resigned as President of the High Court.

The desire of all the major political parties to avoid immediate general elections led to protracted efforts to form a new coalition administration. Discussions between Spring and Ahern, however, failed to produce an agreement. Following extensive negotiations between the Labour Party and other parties, a new coalition, led by John Bruton, who had assumed the leadership of Fine Gael in late 1990, and with Spring as the Deputy Prime Minister and Minister for Foreign Affairs, took office on 15 December 1994. A third coalition partner, the Democratic Left, obtained the social welfare portfolio.

In November 1995 a referendum on the termination of the constitutional ban on divorce resulted in a narrow majority (50.3% to 49.7%) in favour of legalizing the dissolution of marriage. The proposal was supported by all the major political parties, but strongly opposed by the Roman Catholic Church. The outcome of the referendum was the subject of an unsuccessful legal challenge in the Supreme Court in 1996, and the first divorce under the revised constitutional arrangements was granted in January 1997 (although legislation to implement the reform did not come into effect until February).

In November 1996 the Minister for Transport, Energy and Communications, Michael Lowry, resigned following allegations that he had received personal financial gifts from an Irish business executive, Ben Dunne. Alan Dukes was named as Lowry's successor. During 1997 an inquiry into other political donations by Dunne, chaired by Justice Brian McCracken, revealed that payments totalling some IR£1.3m. had been made to the former Irish Prime Minister, Charles Haughey, during his term in office. Haughey later admitted the allegations, although insisting that he had no knowledge of the donations until he resigned his premiership; however, McCracken's report, published in August, condemned Haughey's earlier misleading evidence given to the tribunal and recommended further legal investigation. The Government, at that time led by Bertie Ahern of Fianna Fáil following a general election (see below), endorsed the results of the inquiry and agreed to establish a new tribunal to investigate further payments made to politicians and the sources of specific 'offshore' bank accounts that had been used by Haughey. In December 1998 it was revealed that a tax liability on some IR£2m. of personal financial gifts received by Haughey, including those made by Dunne, had been cancelled by the Revenue Commission. Opposition criticism of the decision intensified following the disclosure that the tax appeals commissioner responsible for the concession was a brother-in-law of Ahern. Ahern denied that he had influenced the decision.

In May 1997 the Prime Minister called a general election, relying on strong economic growth figures and the negative impact of allegations concerning financial donations to former Fianna Fáil leader Charles Haughey to secure victory for Fine Gael's coalition with the Labour Party and Democratic Left, despite public opinion polls revealing a significant shortfall in support for the Government over the opposition Fianna Fáil. In the election, which was conducted on 6 June, none of the main political parties secured an overall majority in the Dáil. Fine Gael increased its representation from 45 seats to 54, having won 27.9% of the first-preference votes cast, while Fianna Fáil secured 77 seats with 39.3% of the votes. Support for the Labour Party, however, declined substantially and the party won just 17 seats (compared with 33 in the 1992 parliament). Sinn Féin won its first ever seat in the Dáil at the election. John Bruton conceded that he could not form a majority coalition administration, and Bertie Ahern, the Fianna Fáil leader, undertook to form a new government, in alliance with the Progressive Democrats, which had won four parliamentary seats, and with the support of independents. A new administration, with Ahern as Prime Minister, was formally approved in the Dáil at the end of June.

In September 1997 Mary Robinson, a liberal human rights lawyer, who had been elected President in November 1990, as an independent candidate with the support of the Labour Party and the Workers' Party, resigned her position in order to assume her new functions as the United Nations High Commissioner for Human Rights. All the main parties put forward candidates to contest the ensuing presidential election; however, internal divisions within Fianna Fáil were revealed following the failure of Albert Reynolds, the former Prime Minister, to secure that party's nomination. Controversy arose during the election campaign when private documents were supplied to a newspaper, with the intention of undermining support for the Fianna Fáil candidate, Dr Mary McAleese, by emphasizing her sympathies with the republican movement. A former Fine Gael political adviser was later arrested in connection with the leaked information. In the election, conducted on 30 October, McAleese won 45.2% of the first-preference votes cast, compared with 29.3% for Mary Banotti of Fine Gael. McAleese was inaugurated on 11 November, and became the country's first President to be from Northern Ireland. In early November the Labour Party leader, Dick Spring, resigned, owing to his party's poor electoral performances. He was replaced by Ruairí Quinn, who had been Minister for Finance in the previous Fine Gael-Labour Party administration.

In January 1999 the Government was undermined by revelations of a financial scandal involving its Commissioner to the EU, Padraig Flynn. It was alleged that, in 1989, Flynn, who held the environment portfolio at that time, had misappropriated a political donation made to his party, Fianna Fail, by a property developer. In October Ahern and three former finance ministers were required to give evidence to the public accounts committee of the Dáil.

In mid-October 1999 the Irish Nurses' Organization began an indefinite strike in support of demands for salary increases and improved working conditions. The Government refused to concede to the demands stating that they amounted to a 35% increase in basic salary, a figure far higher than that stipulated in the 'Partnership 2000' agreement between the unions, businesses and the Government under which unions had agreed to voluntary pay restraint in exchange for tax cuts and an influence on economic policy. It was feared that a concession to the nurses would precipitate similar demands from other unions. Following negotiations between union and government representatives the nurses agreed to suspend the strike and return to work pending a vote on the Labour Court's proposed IR£20m. settlement package and in early November the members of the four nursing unions voted to accept the Labour Court's proposals. Over the following months there were further incidences of industrial action by public-sector workers, who expressed their discontent at rising consumer prices and unsatisfactory working conditions and staffing levels. Nevertheless, in March 2000 the Irish Congress of Trade Unions (ICTU) accepted the Programme for Prosperity and Fairness (PPF—the successor to 'Partnership 2000'), which had been negotiated by businesses, unions and the Government, and provided for cumulative pay rises over 33 months in exchange for productivity and 'no strike' agreements. Meanwhile, in late January Ahern effected a cabinet reorganization, following the resignation of David Andrews, the Minister of Foreign Affairs. He was replaced by Brian Cowen, who had held the health portfolio.

During 2000 independent judicial inquiries investigating corruption among politicians continued to implicate many senior political figures. In January at a tribunal chaired by Justice Michael Moriarty, which was investigating payments made to the former Prime Minister, Haughey, and the use of 'offshore' bank accounts, the revelation that Denis Foley, a Fianna Fáil deputy, had held up to IR£100,000 in such accounts prompted Foley's resignation from the Dáil's Public Accounts Committee and, the following month, from the Fianna Fáil parliamentary party. In late May Foley was suspended from the Dáil for 14 days for breach of parliamentary procedure after admitting he had failed to declare that he held money in 'offshore' accounts before voting on a motion to extend the terms of reference to the McCracken inquiry (see above) into payments to politicians. Meanwhile, in mid-April 2000 Frank Dunlop, a political lobbyist and former government press secretary, admitted to an inquiry into planning irregularities in Dublin, headed by Justice Feargus Flood, that in 1991 he had paid a total of IR£112,000 to 15 Dublin county councillors on behalf of a property developer in order to ensure a favourable decision. Dunlop also testified that Fine Gael leader, Bruton, was aware that a member of Fine Gael had demanded IR£250,000 from Dunlop to secure that member's vote in favour of the decision. Furthermore, Bruton was also accused by Liam Lawlor, a Fianna Fáil deputy, who himself admitted that he had received political contributions from Dunlop for 'legitimate electoral purposes', of benefiting from the decision. Bruton vehemently denied both accusations and both Fianna Fáil and Fine Gael announced they were to launch internal investigations to ascertain whether any of their members had received such payments. Days later the Deputy Prime Minister, Mary Harney, denied allegations which appeared in a newspaper claiming that two Fianna Fáil politicians, one of whom was suspected to be Prime Minister Ahern had, in 1989, both received IR£50,000 from a business executive in return for their assistance with a major retail project. Ahern subsequently publicly confirmed he was indeed the subject of the story but denied any involvement in the matter.

Upon resumption of the Flood inquiry in mid-May 2000, Dunlop claimed that a current Fianna Fáil deputy had received 'on-going' payments for his assistance with planning matters. Fine Gael concurrently revealed the results of their internal investigation into the matter and disclosed it was satisfied that, except in the case of three of its current members where evidence was inconclusive, any payments received by Fine Gael members had not influenced their voting intentions. In late May the Moriarty tribunal heard that between 1979 and 1996 Haughey had received payments totalling IR£8.5m., a much larger figure than had previously been acknowledged, and it was announced that Haughey would appear before the tribunal in July as a witness. In early June Lawlor, who had resigned from the Dáil's Members' Interests Committee in April, resigned from Fianna Fáil following the publication of a report by the Fianna Fáil's Standards in Public Life Committee, which described him as 'uncooperative and contradictory' in his dealings with its inves-

tigation. In late June separate criminal proceedings against Haughey were indefinitely postponed after a Dublin court ruled that pre-trial publicity, including remarks made by Harney in a newspaper interview, could have influenced potential jury members and would prevent Haughey from receiving a fair hearing. In July Haughey duly appeared before the Moriarty tribunal and continued to give evidence to the inquiry during late 2000 despite mounting fears regarding his health. In mid-January 2001 Lawlor was sentenced to three months imprisonment for failing to comply with a High Court order to give evidence regarding the use of his credit cards to the Flood tribunal. Lawlor was released after serving seven days of the sentence but subsequently resigned from several parliamentary commissions. Later that month the Dáil voted in favour of a government motion that stipulated that Lawlor would be forced to resign if he failed to co-operate fully with the inquiry.

The Minister of Finance's decision in late May 2000 to nominate Hugh O'Flaherty, a former Supreme Court judge, for the position of Vice-President of the European Investment Bank (EIB), provoked widespread opposition criticism. O'Flaherty had resigned in April 1999, rather than face impeachment proceedings in the Dáil, after the Chief Justice criticized his interference in a criminal case, which resulted in the early release of a prisoner. Many observers attributed the comprehensive defeat of the Fianna Fáil candidate by an independent at a parliamentary by-election held in South Tipperary in late June 2000 to the controversy surrounding the O'Flaherty decision and the continuing inquiries into corruption. Just days after the by-election defeat the Fianna Fáil-Progressive Democrats coalition narrowly defeated a motion of 'no confidence', which had been proposed by the opposition, by 84 votes to 80. On the day prior to the defeat of the motion Ahern had appeared before the Moriarty tribunal and had faced accusations that he and other senior party members had withheld details of an internal party investigation into political donations in 1996 from the inquiry. In late August the Government's credibility was further diminished when O'Flaherty withdrew his nomination to the EIB, ostensibly owing to a perceived lack of support from the bank's other European directors. O'Flaherty's nomination had, however, been the subject of intense media criticism and also a legal challenge in the Supreme Court by a university lecturer.

During late 2000 the Government and employers' organizations came under increasing pressure from trade unions to review the PPF as rising inflation threatened to eradicate the benefits of pay rises agreed under the programme. Several unions organized industrial action in protest at the lack of government action, most notably the Association of Secondary Teachers in Ireland (ASTI), which had denounced the PPF as inadequate. ASTI members staged a series of strikes, which severely disrupted classes and forced the closure of several schools. In early December the ICTU executive endorsed compensatory measures to offset the impact of inflation, which had been negotiated by unions and businesses. However, negotiations between the Government and ASTI members broke down later that month: ASTI members recommenced industrial action in mid-January 2001 but agreed to suspend their strike during negotiations with the Labour Court, which began later that month. However, the Labour Court's ruling, which was issued in mid-March, failed to satisfy ASTI who subsequently staged a one-day strike, prompting a public rebuke from Ahern.

Meanwhile, in late January 2001 Fine Gael deputies passed a motion of 'no confidence' in their leader Bruton, who resigned as leader of the party with immediate effect. He was replaced the following month by Michael Noonan, a former Minister of Health.

Regular discussions between the British and Irish heads of government, initiated in May 1980, led to the formation in November 1981 of an Anglo-Irish Intergovernmental Council, intended to meet at ministerial and official levels. Consultations between the United Kingdom and Ireland on the future of Northern Ireland resulted in November 1985 in the signing of the Anglo-Irish Agreement, which provided for regular participation in Northern Ireland affairs by the Irish Government on political, legal, security and cross-border matters. The involvement of the Government of Ireland was to be through an Intergovernmental Conference. The Agreement maintained that no change in the status of Northern Ireland would be made without the assent of the majority of its population. The terms of the Agreement were approved by both the Irish and the British Parliaments, despite strong opposition by many Protestants in Northern Ireland.

Under the provisions of the Anglo-Irish Agreement, the Irish Government pledged co-operation in the implementation of new measures to improve cross-border security, in order to suppress IRA operations. It also promised to participate in the European Convention on the Suppression of Terrorism, which it signed in February 1986 and ratified in December 1987, when legislation amending the 1965 Extradition Act came into effect. In the same month the Government introduced controversial measures (without consulting the British Government) granting the Irish Attorney-General the right to approve or reject warrants for extradition of suspected IRA terrorists to the United Kingdom. In January 1988, however, the Irish Supreme Court ruled that members of the IRA could not be protected from extradition to Northern Ireland on the grounds that their offences were politically motivated. In December, however, the Irish Attorney-General refused to grant the extradition of an alleged terrorist who had been repatriated to Ireland in November, following a similar refusal by the Belgian authorities. The Irish decision was based on allegations that the accused man would not receive a fair trial in the United Kingdom because publicity had prejudiced his case.

Relations between the Irish and British Governments in 1988 were also strained when Irish confidence in the impartiality of the British legal system was severely undermined by proposed legislation to combat terrorism in Northern Ireland and by the decision, in January, not to prosecute members of the Royal Ulster Constabulary (RUC) allegedly implicated in a policy of shooting terrorist suspects, without attempting to apprehend them, in Northern Ireland in 1982. Difficult relations with the United Kingdom did not, however, present a threat to the Anglo-Irish Agreement, and the co-ordination between the Garda Síochána (Irish police force) and the RUC, established under the agreement, resulted in an unprecedentedly high level of co-operation on cross-border security. In February 1989 a permanent joint consultative assembly, comprising 25 British and 25 Irish MPs, was established. The representatives were selected in October. The assembly's meetings, the first of which began in February 1990, were to take place twice a year, alternately in Dublin and London.

In July 1990 an IRA member who had been charged with terrorist offences in the United Kingdom, lost his appeal against extradition in the High Court in Dublin. It was the first case to be considered under the 1987 Extradition Act, based on the European Convention on the Suppression of Terrorism. In November the Supreme Court upheld the ruling, and the alleged terrorist, Desmond Ellis, was extradited to stand trial in the United Kingdom. In November 1991 the Supreme Court upheld the extradition to the United Kingdom of an IRA member convicted of murder, who had escaped from detention in Belfast. At the same time, however, the Supreme Court overturned an order for extradition to the United Kingdom of two other IRA members who had similarly escaped, ruling that their convictions of possession of non-automatic fire-arms did not constitute an extraditable offence. This prompted assurances from the Minister of Justice that this omission in the legislation on extradition would be rectified. The Irish Government, however, also requested changes in British legislation to ensure that defendants could be tried in the United Kindom only for the offences for which they had been extradited. In January 1994 the Irish Cabinet approved draft legislation to remove the argument of 'political offence', and subsequent exemption from extradition, to persons charged with the use or possession of non-automatic weapons.

In January 1990 the British Secretary of State for Northern Ireland, Peter Brooke, launched an initiative to convene meetings between representatives from the major political parties in Northern Ireland, and the British and Irish Governments, to discuss devolution in Northern Ireland. In response to demands from Northern Ireland's Unionist parties, the Irish and British Governments publicly stated that they were prepared to consider an alternative to the Anglo-Irish Agreement. In March the Irish Supreme Court rejected an attempt by Ulster Unionists to have the Anglo-Irish Agreement declared contrary to Ireland's Constitution, which claims jurisdiction over Northern Ireland. In May the Unionists agreed to hold direct discussions with the Irish Government, a concession previously withheld because it lent credence to the Irish claim to a right to be involved in Northern Ireland's affairs. Disagreement remained, however, on the timing and conditions of Ireland's entry to the talks. Following extensive negotiations, discussions between the Northern Ireland parties, which were a prelude to the inclusion of

the Irish Government, commenced in June 1991. They were suspended several times but did reach the inclusion of the Irish Government in April and September 1992. The principal point of contention was the Unionists' demand that Ireland hold a referendum on Articles 2 and 3 of its Constitution, which lay claim to the territory of Northern Ireland. Ireland was unwilling to make such a concession except as part of an overall settlement. With no progress made on this question, nor on the subject of Ireland's role in the administration of Northern Ireland, the negotiations formally ended in November, and the Anglo-Irish Conference, which had been temporarily suspended, resumed.

At the end of October 1993 the new Irish Prime Minister, Albert Reynolds and his British counterpart, John Major, issued a joint statement setting out the principles on which future negotiations were to be based. The statement emphasized the precondition that Sinn Féin permanently renounce violence before being admitted to the negotiations. In December the Prime Ministers made a joint declaration, known as the 'Downing Street Declaration', which provided a specific framework for a peace settlement. The Declaration referred to the possibility of a united Ireland and accepted the legitimacy of self-determination, but insisted on majority consent within Northern Ireland. While the Sinn Féin and Unionist parties considered their response to the Declaration, Reynolds received both groups' conditional support for his proposal to establish a 'Forum for Peace and Reconciliation', which was to encourage both sides to end violent action. In January 1994 the Irish Cabinet relaxed a ban (that had operated since 1976) forbidding the broadcast of interviews and speeches by persons deemed to be paramilitary supporters.

In April 1994 the IRA declared a temporary cease-fire over the Easter period. Despite a subsequent resumption of operations negotiations culminated in an announcement on 31 August by the IRA that it had ceased all military operations. This was followed in October by a similar suspension on the part of its counterpart loyalist organizations. In late 1994 and early 1995 the Irish authorities granted early release to more than 15 prisoners convicted of IRA terrorist offences. Inter-governmental talks were maintained, resulting in the publication, in February 1995, of a 'Joint Framework' document, in which the Irish Government undertook to support the withdrawal of the Republic's constitutional claim to jurisdiction over Northern Ireland. The document's proposals, which included detailed arrangements for cross-border institutions and economic programmes which would operate on an all-island basis (see Northern Ireland, Vol. II), were stated by the British Government to be intended to provide a basis for public discussion and not as a definitive statement of government policy.

During 1995 the Irish Government expressed its increasing concern at the delay in initiating substantive all-party negotiations on the formulation of a permanent settlement of the conflict in Northern Ireland, largely owing to the insistence of the British Government that the IRA decommission its weapons as a precondition to such talks Joint proposals in August by the British and Irish Governments for the formation of an international panel to consider the merits of decommissioning paramilitary weaponry in Northern Ireland received the full support of the US Government.. The international panel, under the chairmanship of George Mitchell (a former US Senator and close political associate of President Clinton), began work in December, in a series of private meetings with representatives of the contending political interests. Its findings, announced in January 1996, recommended that the decommissioning of arms should take place in parallel with all-party talks, and that their destruction should be monitored by an independent commission. The British and Irish Governments accepted the recommendations of the report, but new controversy arose over proposals by the British Cabinet to hold elections for a Northern Ireland assembly, which was to provide the framework for all-party negotiations. Although broadly acceptable to Unionist interests, this plan was rejected outright by Northern Ireland's Social Democratic and Labour Party (SDLP) and Sinn Féin, and declared unacceptable by the Irish Government.

In February 1996, following a bomb explosion in London, the IRA announced that the cease-fire had been terminated. Official contacts with Sinn Féin were suspended by the British and Irish Governments, pending acceptable assurances that the IRA had discontinued all violence. Multi-party meetings, which commenced in June without Sinn Féin participation, were overshadowed in July by violent confrontations in Northern Ireland between the RUC and nationalists opposed to the routing of loyalist parades through predominantly nationalist districts. The Irish Government formally protested to the British Government over the conduct of the RUC, both in failing to re-route the processions and in its methods of suppressing the ensuing public disorders. The multi-party talks were suspended in March 1997, pending the outcome of a general election in the United Kingdom. In May a meeting of the Irish Prime Minister, Bruton with the newly-elected British premier, Anthony (Tony) Blair, and the new Secretary of State for Northern Ireland, Dr Marjorie Mowlam, generated speculation that significant progress could be achieved in furthering a political agreement. In June the two Governments announced a new initiative to proceed with the decommissioning of paramilitary weapons, on the basis of the Mitchell report, at the same time as pursuing political negotiations for a constitutional settlement. In early July the newly-elected Irish Prime Minister, Bertie Ahern, confirmed his commitment to the peace initiative during a meeting with Blair in London, and declared his support for the efforts of the British administration to prevent violence during the sectarian marching season in Northern Ireland. On 19 July the IRA announced a restoration of its cease-fire. A few days later the Irish and British Governments issued a joint statement that all-party negotiations would commence in mid-September with the participation of Sinn Féin. At the same time, however, the Unionist parties rejected the measures for weapons decommissioning that had been formulated by the two Governments. At the end of July the Irish Government restored official contacts with Sinn Féin and resumed the policy of considering convicted IRA activists for early release from prison.

In September 1997 Sinn Féin endorsed the so-called Mitchell principles, which committed participants in the negotiations to accepting the outcome of the peace process and renouncing violence as a means of punishment or resolving problems, providing for the party's participation in all-party talks when they resumed in the middle of that month. However, the Unionist parties failed to attend the opening session of the talks, owing partly to a statement by the IRA undermining Sinn Féin's endorsement of the Mitchell principles. A procedural agreement to pursue negotiations in parallel with the decommissioning of weapons (which was to be undertaken by a separate commission, the Independent International Commission on Decommissioning (IICD), led by Gen. John de Chastelain of Canada) was signed by all the main parties later in September. Substantive negotiations commenced in October but were adjourned in mid-December without agreement on an agenda for the next session of discussions. In mid-January 1998 the two Governments published a document outlining a framework for negotiations and specified that they hoped to achieve a settlement by May.

In March 1998 Mitchell set a deadline of 9 April for the conclusion of the peace talks. On 10 April the two Governments and eight political parties involved in the talks signed a comprehensive political accord, the Good Friday (or Belfast) Agreement, at Stormont Castle. Immediately thereafter the two Governments signed a new British-Irish Agreement, replacing the Anglo-Irish Agreement of November 1985, committing them to put the provisions of the multi-party agreement into effect, subject to approval of the Good Friday Agreement by a referendum to be held in the whole of Ireland in May. The peace settlement provided for changes to the Irish Constitution and to British constitutional legislation to enshrine the principle that a united Ireland could be achieved only with the consent of the majority of the people of both Ireland and Northern Ireland. Under the terms of the Good Friday Agreement the new Northern Ireland Assembly was to have devolved legislative powers over areas of social and economic policy, while security, justice, taxation and foreign policy were to remain under the authority of the British Government. Executive authority was to be discharged by an Executive Committee, comprising a First Minister, Deputy First Minister and as many as 10 ministers of government departments. The Assembly, which was to be elected in June, was to operate in transitional mode, without legislative or executive powers, until the establishment of the North/South and British-Irish institutions. In addition, provision was made for the release of paramilitary prisoners affiliated to organizations that established a complete and unequivocal cease-fire. All qualifying prisoners were to be released within two years of the commencement of the scheme, which was due to begin in June. The decommissioning of paramilitary weapons was to be completed within two years of the approval by referendum of the Good Friday Agreement. On 22 April the Dáil overwhelmingly approved the peace agreement. At referendums held simultaneously on 22 May the people of Ireland and Northern Ireland voted in support of the Good Friday Agreement. In Ireland 94.4% voted to allow the Government to become party to the agreement, while in Northern Ireland 71.1% voted to approve the accord.

Elections to the 108-member Northern Ireland Assembly were conducted on 25 June 1998; the Assembly convened for the first time in July.and elected the leader of the Ulster Unionist Party (UUP), David Trimble, as Northern Ireland's First Minister to head the Executive Committee. The peace process was threatened with disruption by sectarian violence in July and by the detonation of an explosive device in August in Omagh, Northern Ireland; the device was planted by a Republican splinter group, the Real IRA. Later that month Ahern announced a series of anti-terrorist measures, including restrictions on the right to silence and an extension to the maximum period of detention allowable for suspected terrorists, in an effort to facilitate convictions against terrorists based in Ireland

Progress in the peace process continued to be obstructed throughout late 1998 by a dispute between Unionists and Sinn Féin concerning the decommissioning of paramilitary weapons, with Trimble insisting that the admittance of Sinn Féin representatives to the Executive Committee be conditional on progress in the demilitarization of the IRA. As a result of the dispute the deadlines for the formation both of the Executive Committee and the North/South body (specified as 21 October by the Good Friday Agreement), and for the devolution of powers to the new Northern Ireland institutions (envisaged for 10 March 1999) were not met. Despite strenuous efforts to end the impasse, a new April deadline was also not met. An 'absolute' deadline for the devolution of powers was subsequently set for 30 June 1999, after which date, Blair asserted, he would suspend the Northern Ireland Assembly if agreement had not been reached. On 25 June the two Prime Ministers presented a compromise plan which envisaged the immediate establishment of the Executive Committee prior to the surrender of paramilitary weapons, with the condition that Sinn Féin guarantee that the IRA complete decommissioning by May 2000. Negotiations continued beyond the June deadline but effectively collapsed in mid-July and a review of the peace process, headed by George Mitchell, began in early September. In November Mitchell succeeded in producing an agreement providing for the devolution of powers to the Executive Committee. The agreement followed a statement by the IRA that it would appoint a representative to enter discussions with the IICD. At a meeting of the ruling council of the UUP held in late November Trimble persuaded his party to vote in favour of the agreement. On 29 November 1999 the Northern Ireland Assembly convened to appoint the 10-member Executive Committee. On 2 December power was officially transferred from Westminster to the new Northern Ireland executive at Stormont Castle. On the same day, in accordance with the Good Friday Agreement, the Irish Government removed from the Constitution the Republic's territorial claim over Northern Ireland.

In mid-December 1999 the Cabinet of the Republic attended the inaugural meeting, in Armagh, of the North/South Ministerial Council. The British-Irish Council met for the first time later that month. However, in late January 2000 Adams dismissed the possibility of imminent IRA decommissioning and a report by the IICD confirmed that there had been no disarmament. With the prospect of the collapse of the peace process the British and Irish Governments engaged in intensive negotiations. On 1 February the IRA released a statement giving assurances that its cease-fire would not be broken and expressing support for the peace process. On 4 February the IRA were given until 11 February to begin decommissioning. However, it failed to comply and legislation came into effect on that day suspending the new executive, legislative and co-operative institutions and returning Northern Ireland to direct rule. The IRA subsequently announced its withdrawal from discussions with the IICD, raising serious doubts about the future of its cease-fire. In addition, Adams refused to participate in any further review of the peace process until the suspended institutions had been restored. At a republican rally held at the end of February Adams announced that Sinn Féin had abandoned its special role of attempting to persuade the IRA to decommission.

Direct talks between the Irish and British Governments and the principle parties resumed in early May 2000 with the British Government pledging to restore the Northern Ireland institutions on 22 May and postpone the deadline for decommissioning until June 2001 subject to a commitment by the IRA on the arms issue. On 6 May the IRA responded by offering to 'initiate a process that will completely and verifiably put arms beyond use'. On 30 May power was once again transferred from Westminster to the new Northern Ireland institutions. However, the issue of IRA weapons decommissioning continued to severely threaten the peace process during late 2000 and early 2001 (see chapter on Northern Ireland). In November 2000 the British House of Lords approved legislation, which would enable members of the Irish Parliament to stand for election to the Northern Ireland Assembly as well as to the British lower chamber of Parliament, the House of Commons, but prohibited the holding of office in both Northern Ireland and the Republic of Ireland.

Ireland became a member of the EC (now the EU) in 1973. In May 1987 the country affirmed its commitment to the EC when, in a referendum, 69.9% of Irish voters supported adherence to the Single European Act, which provided for closer economic and political co-operation between EC member-states (including the creation of a single Community market by 1993). In December 1991, during the EC summit conference at Maastricht, in the Netherlands, Ireland agreed to the far-reaching Treaty on European Union. Ireland secured a special provision within the Treaty (which was signed by all parties in February 1992), guaranteeing that Ireland's constitutional position on abortion would be unaffected by any future EC legislation. The four major political parties in Ireland united in support of the ratification of the Treaty prior to a referendum on the issue, which took place in June. Despite opposition, from both pro- and anti-abortion campaigners, to the special provision within the Treaty and the threat to Ireland's neutrality inherent in the document's proposals for a common defence policy, ratification of the Treaty was endorsed by 68.7% of the votes cast (57.3% of the electorate participated in the referendum). In a referendum conducted in May 1998, 62% of Irish voters endorsed the Amsterdam Treaty, which had been signed by EU ministers in October 1997, amending the Treaty on European Union.

Government

Legislative power is vested in the bicameral National Parliament, comprising the Senate (with restricted powers) and the House of Representatives. The Senate (Seanad Éireann) has 60 members, including 11 nominated by the Prime Minister (Taoiseach) and 49 indirectly elected for five years. The House of Representatives (Dáil Éireann) has 166 members (Teachtaí Dála), elected by universal adult suffrage for five years (subject to dissolution) by means of the single transferable vote, a form of proportional representation.

The President (Uachtarán) is the constitutional Head of State, elected by direct popular vote for seven years. Executive power is effectively held by the Cabinet, led by the Prime Minister, who is appointed by the President on the nomination of the Dáil. The President appoints other Ministers on the nomination of the Prime Minister with the previous approval of the Dáil. The Cabinet is responsible to the Dáil.

Defence

At 1 August 2000 the regular armed forces totalled 11,460. The army comprised 9,300, the navy 1,100 and the air force 1,060. There was also a reserve of 14,800. Defence was allocated IR£595m. (3.1% of total expenditure) in the 2000 budget. Military service is voluntary.

Economic Affairs

In 1998, according to estimates by the World Bank, Ireland's gross national product (GNP), measured at average 1996–98 prices, was US $69,322m., equivalent to $18,710 per head (or $17,991 on an international purchasing-power parity basis). During 1990–98, it was estimated, GNP per head increased, in real terms, at an average rate of 6.1% per year. Over the same period, the population increased by an average of 0.8% per year. In 1999 GNP was estimated at $71,400m. ($19,160 per head). Ireland's gross domestic product (GDP) increased, in real terms, by an average of 6.6% per year in 1990–99. GDP rose by 10.7% in 1997, by 8.6% in 1998 and by 9.8% in 1999.

Agriculture (including forestry and fishing) contributed an estimated 4.1% of GDP (at factor cost) in 1999. An estimated 7.8% of the working population were employed in the sector in 2000. Beef and dairy production dominate Irish agriculture (in 1999 meat and meat preparations accounted for 2.7% of total exports while dairy products and birds' eggs accounted for 1.5%). Principal crops include barley, sugar beet, potatoes and wheat.

Agricultural GDP increased by an average of 0.5% per year during 1991–97, and by an estimated 1.4% in 1997.

Industry (comprising mining, manufacturing, construction and utilities) provided an estimated 37.0% of GDP in 1999, and employed an estimated 28.5% of the working population in 2000. Industrial GDP increased by an average of 9.6% per year during 1991–97, by 16.2% in 1995, 8.3% in 1996 and by an estimated 15.2% in 1997.

Mining (including quarrying and turf production) provided employment to 0.4% of the working population in 1997. Ireland possesses substantial deposits of lead-zinc ore and recoverable peat, both of which are exploited. Natural gas, mainly from the Kinsale field, and small quantities of coal are also extracted. A significant natural gas deposit discovered in 1999 was expected to yield sufficient gas to meet more than half of the country's current average demand. Offshore reserves of petroleum have been located and several licences awarded to foreign-owned enterprises to undertake further exploration. During 1980–90 mining production decreased by an annual average of 1.7%.

Manufacturing was estimated to employ 20.3% of the working population in 1997. The manufacturing sector comprises many high-technology, largely foreign-owned, capital-intensive enterprises. The electronics industry accounted for 32.6% of the value of exports in 1996. During 1992–96 manufacturing production increased by an average of 10.1% per year.

Energy is derived principally from petroleum, which provided 51% of total requirements in 1996, while coal provided 18%, natural gas 18%, peat 11%, and hydroelectric power 2%. In 1999 imports of mineral fuels were 2.8% (by value) of total merchandise imports.

Service industries (including commerce, finance, transport and communications, and public administration) contributed an estimated 58.9% of GDP in 1999, and employed 63.7% of the working population in 2000. The financial sector is of increasing importance to Ireland. An International Financial Services Centre in Dublin was opened in 1990; by September 1999 more than 485 companies were participating in the Centre, many of which were foreign concerns attracted by tax concessions offered by the Irish Government. Tourism is one of the principal sources of foreign exchange. Revenue from the tourism and travel sector amounted to IR£2,502m. in 1999. The GDP of the services sector increased by an average of 4.3% per year during 1991–97, and by an estimated 6.2% in 1997.

In 1999, according to IMF statistics, Ireland recorded a visible trade surplus of US $24,178m. and there was a surplus of $595m. on the current account of the balance of payments. In that year the principal source of imports (33.1%) was the United Kingdom; other major sources were the USA (16.7%), Germany (6.2%), and Japan (5.8%). The United Kingdom was also the principal market for exports (22.0%); other major purchasers were the USA (15.4%), Germany (11.9%), France (8.4%) and the Netherlands (6.2%). In 1999 principal imports included office equipment and other electrical machinery, chemical products, road vehicles and parts and other manufactured items. Principal exports included electronic goods, chemicals and beef and dairy products.

In 2000 it was projected that there would be a budgetary surplus of IR£2,444m. The 1999 budget recorded a surplus of IR£1,513m. (equivalent to 1.7% of GDP). At the end of 1996 Ireland's total national debt was estimated to be IR£29,912m., and in that year the cost of servicing the debt amounted to an estimated IR£2,560m. In 1994 the ratio of debt interest to GNP was 2.4%. The annual rate of inflation averaged 2.2% in 1990–99. The rate decreased from 2.4% in 1998 to 1.6% in 1999, but increased to 5.6% in 2000. An estimated 4.3% of the labour force were unemployed in 2000, compared with 10.3% in 1997.

Ireland became a member of the European Community (EC, now European Union, EU, see p. 181) in 1973, and of the EC's Exchange Rate Mechanism (ERM) in 1979.

Between 1993–99 the Irish economy enjoyed an unprecedentedly high rate of growth with GDP increasing by an annual average of 7.9%. This was attributable to a number of factors including prudent fiscal and monetary management, an expanding, well-qualified labour force and social partnership agreements between the Government, businesses and trade unions, providing for guaranteed pay rises in return for productivity and 'no strike' agreements. In addition government policies offering financial incentives to foreign-owned enterprises resulted in a substantial increase in direct foreign investment and steady expansion, particularly in the financial services and electronic manufacturing industries. (By 1998 Ireland had become the world's second largest exporter of computer software, after the USA.) Ireland was one of 11 EU countries to adopt the single European currency, the euro, on 1 January 1999. The economy continued to grow during 2000, however both the EU and the IMF expressed their growing concern at the continued sharp rise in the rate of inflation, which was attributed to a large increase in excise duty, high petroleum prices and the weakness of the euro. By November inflation had reached over 6%—the highest rate since 1985—and threatened the future of the most recent social partnership agreement, the Programme for Prosperity and Fairness (PPF), which had been finalized in March 2000. Despite earlier pledges to the contrary, the Government agreed to renegotiate the PPF later that month following the exertion of pressure by Irish trade unions (see Recent History). A series of anti-inflationary measures were announced in the 2001 budget along with significant tax reductions and public spending increases, which were aimed at restricting wage demands and addressing shortages in the labour market and infrastructural deficiencies.. Inflation declined during early 2001, however, in February the EU reprimanded the Irish Government over its 'inflationary' budget and made a formal recommendation that it take countervailing measures to realign the budget with the EU's economic policy guidelines. The Irish Government rejected the censure on the grounds that the inflationary factors in the economy were largely external and would be unaffected by domestic fiscal policy. Nevertheless, Ireland remained Europe's fastest-growing economy, budget surpluses were at record levels, the country's debts were the second lowest in the EU, Ireland was allocating 1% of GNP per year to a public pension fund to address the effects of demographic changes on pension liabilities and unemployment was predicted to continue to decline.

Social Welfare

Social welfare benefits in Ireland may be grouped broadly in three categories: contributory (social) insurance payments, which are made on the basis of pay-related social insurance contributions; non-contributory (social assistance) payments, which are made on the basis of claimants' satisfying the criteria of a means test; and universal services, such as child benefit and free travel. Child benefit is payable to all households for each child.

Social insurance is compulsory for both employees and the self-employed. The social insurance scheme provides for orphans' benefits, widows'/widowers', retirement and old-age pensions; unemployment, disability, maternity, invalidity, death grants and occupational injury, dental and optical benefits. The cost of the social insurance scheme is shared by the employer, the employee, the self-employed and the State. Varying rates of social insurance are payable, and the rate payable determines the range of benefits available. Private-sector employees contribute the highest rate and have cover for all benefits; the contributions of the self-employed provide funds for old age, maternity and adoptive benefits, and survivors' benefits and orphans' contributory allowance; permanent and pensionable employees in the state sector have cover mainly for widows'/widowers' (contributory) pensions, orphans' (contributory) allowance and limited occupational injury benefits.

People of inadequate means who are not entitled to benefit under these contributory schemes may receive non-contributory pensions or other benefits from the State or other public funds. These benefits include one-parent family payments, old-age and blindness pensions, carers' allowance, orphans' (non-contributory) pension, supplementary welfare allowance, unemployment assistance and family income supplement. The central Government's budgetary expenditure on social welfare services in 2000 was projected at IR£5,384m. (equivalent to 27.9% of total expenditure).

Health services are provided by eight health boards, administered by the Department of Health and Children. There are two categories of entitlement, with people on low incomes qualifying for the full range of health services free of charge, and people on higher incomes qualifying for fewer free services.

Drugs and medicines are available free of charge to all people suffering from specified long-term ailments. Hospital in-patient and out-patient services are free of charge to all children under 16 years of age, suffering from specified long-term ailments. Immunization and diagnostic services, as well as hospital services, are free of charge to everyone suffering from an infectious disease. A maintenance allowance is also payable in certain cases. The central Government's budgetary expenditure on health was projected at IR£4,037m. in 2000 (20.9% of total spending). In addition, there are various community welfare services for the chronically sick, the elderly, the disabled and families under stress. In 1995 Ireland had 104 publicly-funded hospitals, with a total of 13,557 beds. In 1998 there were 219.0 physicians per 100,000 of the population.

Education

The State in Ireland has constitutional responsibility for the national education system. Irish schools are owned, not by the State, but by community groups, traditionally religious groups. It is in general an aided system: the State does not itself operate the schools (with a few minor exceptions) but assists other bodies, usually religious, to do so.

Education in Ireland is compulsory for nine years between six and 15 years of age. Primary education may begin at the age of six and lasts for six years. Aided primary schools account for the education of 98.5% of children in the primary sector, who attend until the age of 12, when they transfer to a post-primary school. Post-primary education lasts for up to six years, comprising a junior cycle of three years and a senior cycle of two or three years. The Junior Certificate examination is taken after three years in post-primary (second-level) education. By 1997 some 92% of 16-year-olds were participating in full-time, post-compulsory education. In 1998/99 there were 14 technical colleges providing a range of craft, technical, professional and other courses. There are four universities: the University of Dublin (Trinity College); the National University of Ireland (comprising the University Colleges of Cork, Dublin and Galway); and the Dublin City University and the University of Limerick (former National Institutes of Higher Education, which obtained university status in 1989).

In the 2000 budget IR£2,871m. (equivalent to 14.9% of total expenditure) was allocated to education.

Public Holidays

2001: 1 January (New Year), 19 March (for St Patrick's Day), 13 April (Good Friday), 16 April (Easter Monday), 7 May (May Day Holiday), 4 June (June Bank Holiday), 6 August (August Bank Holiday), 29 October (October Bank Holiday), 25–26 December (Christmas).

2002: 1 January (New Year), 18 March (for St Patrick's Day), 29 March (Good Friday), 1 April (Easter Monday), 6 May (May Day Holiday), 3 June (June Bank Holiday), 5 August (August Bank Holiday), 28 October (October Bank Holiday), 25–26 December (Christmas).

Weights and Measures

The metric system of weights and measures is the primary system in force, but the imperial system is still used in a number of limited activities.

Statistical Survey

Source (unless otherwise stated): Central Statistics Office, Skehard Rd, Cork; tel. (21) 359000; fax (21) 359090; e-mail information@cso.ie; internet www.cso.ie.

Area and Population

AREA, POPULATION AND DENSITY

Area (sq km)	70,273*
Population (census results)	
21 April 1991	3,525,719
28 April 1996	
Males	1,800,232
Females	1,825,855
Total	3,626,087
Population (preliminary estimates at April)	
1998	3,704,900
1999	3,744,700
2000	3,786,900
Density (per sq km) at April 2000	53.9

* 27,133 sq miles.

ADMINISTRATIVE DIVISIONS (1996 census)

Province/County	Area (sq km)	Population	Density (per sq km)
Connaught	17,711	433,231	24.5
Galway	6,148	188,854	30.7
Leitrim	1,590	25,057	15.8
Mayo	5,586	111,524	20.0
Roscommon . . .	2,548	51,975	20.4
Sligo	1,838	55,821	30.4
Leinster	19,801	1,924,702	97.2
Carlow	897	41,616	46.4
Dublin	922	1,058,264	1,147.8
Kildare	1,695	134,922	79.6
Kilkenny	2,073	75,336	36.3
Laoighis	1,720	52,945	30.8
Longford	1,091	30,166	27.6
Louth	826	92,166	111.6
Meath	2,342	109,732	46.9
Offaly	2,001	59,117	29.5
Westmeath	1,840	63,314	34.4
Wexford	2,367	104,371	44.1
Wicklow	2,027	102,683	50.7
Munster	24,674	1,033,903	41.9
Clare	3,450	94,006	27.2
Cork	7,500	420,510	56.1
Kerry	4,807	126,130	26.2
Limerick	2,756	165,042	59.9
Tipperary	4,305	133,535	31.0
Waterford	1,857	94,680	51.0
Ulster (part) . . .	8,088	234,251	29.0
Cavan	1,932	52,944	27.4
Donegal	4,861	129,994	26.7
Monaghan	1,295	51,313	39.6
Total	70,273	3,626,087	51.6

PRINCIPAL TOWNS
(population, including suburbs or environs, at 1996 census)

Dublin (capital)*	. 952,700	Galway	. . .	57,400
Cork . . .	. 180,000	Waterford	. . .	44,200
Limerick .	. 79,100			

* Greater Dublin area, including Dún Laoghaire (population 55,540 in 1991).

BIRTHS, MARRIAGES AND DEATHS

	Registered live births		Registered marriages		Registered deaths	
	Number	Rate (per 1,000)	Number	Rate (per 1,000)	Number	Rate (per 1,000)
1992 . .	51,584	14.5	16,636	4.7	30,780	8.7
1993 . .	49,456	13.8	16,824	4.7	31,656	8.9
1994 . .	47,929	13.4	16,621	4.6	30,744	8.6
1995 . .	48,530	13.5	15,604	4.3	31,494	8.8
1996 . .	50,390	13.9	16,174	4.5	31,514	8.7
1997 . .	52,311	14.3	15,631	4.3	31,605	8.6
1998 . .	53,551	14.5	16,783	4.5	31,352	8.5
1999 . .	53,354	14.2	18,526	4.9	31,683	8.5

Expectation of life (1999): Males 73.3; Females 78.3 (Source: World Health Organization, *World Health Report 2000*).

IMMIGRATION AND EMIGRATION (preliminary figures, '000)

	1998	1999	2000
Immigrants	44.0	47.5	42.3
Emigrants	21.2	29.0	22.3

ECONOMICALLY ACTIVE POPULATION
(estimates, '000 persons, quarterly (March-May) labour force survey)

	1998	1999	2000
Agriculture, forestry and fishing .	135.0	135.9	130.9
Mining and quarrying . . .			
Manufacturing	302.9	308.9	309.9
Electricity, gas and water . .			
Construction	126.2	142.1	166.3
Wholesale and retail trade . .	211.4	223.3	253.8
Hotels and restaurants . .	98.1	102.6	109.0
Transport, storage and communication	89.9	96.0	100.8
Financial and other business services	171.8	195.8	212.1
Public administration and defence	70.7	74.4	77.8
Education and health . .	206.9	220.4	234.7
Other services	84.7	91.8	93.4
Total employed	1,494.5	1,591.1	1,670.7
Males	899.9	947.3	989.9
Females	594.6	643.9	680.8
Total unemployed	126.6	96.9	74.9

Agriculture

PRINCIPAL CROPS ('000 metric tons)

	1997	1998	1999
Wheat	725	673	597
Oats	132	119	136
Barley	1,087	1,073	1,278
Potatoes	472	482	559
Sugar beet	1,648	1,640	1,712

LIVESTOCK ('000 head)

	1998	1999	2000*
Cattle	7,795	7,751	7,323
Sheep	8,373	7,998	7,638
Pigs	1,819	1,787	n.a.

* Provisional figures.

LIVESTOCK PRODUCTS ('000 metric tons)

	1997	1998	1999
Beef and veal	563	586	637
Mutton and lamb	75	83	86
Pig meat	220	240	252
Poultry meat	127	126	126
Cows' milk	5,306	5,141	5,170
Butter	150	141	146
Cheese	101	100	114
Dry milk (excl. whey)	140	132	129
Hen eggs	30	26	29
Cattle hides*	69	68	74
Sheepskins*	17	17	17

* FAO estimates.

Forestry

ROUNDWOOD REMOVALS ('000 cubic metres, excluding bark)

	1998	1999	2000
Sawlogs, veneer logs and logs for sleepers	1,495	1,531	1,759
Pulpwood	852	966	961
Fuel wood	16	11	10
Total	2,363	2,508	2,730

SAWNWOOD PRODUCTION ('000 cubic metres, including railway sleepers)

	1996	1997	1998
Coniferous (softwood)	670	632	565
Broadleaved (hardwood)	17	10	10
Total	687	642	575

Source: FAO, *Yearbook of Forest Products*.

Fishing

SEA FISH (landings in metric tons)

	1997	1998	1999
European plaice	1,698	1,731	1,424
Atlantic cod	5,706	5,294	3,860
Haddock	6,230	6,572	4,898
Megrim	3,063	3,383	3,162
Whiting	9,392	7,762	7,643
Dogfish	2,382	2,403	1,645
Atlantic herring	57,155	58,248	45,334
Atlantic mackerel	53,084	67,310	59,609
Horse mackerel	75,002	74,253	58,201
Total fish (incl. others)	261,429	294,898	250,696
Crabs	8,037	7,970	8,550
Norway lobster (Dublin Bay prawn)	3,454	3,998	4,603
Mussels	5,506	5,660	8,563
Total shellfish (incl. others*)	29,704	29,946	36,594
Total catch	291,133	324,843	287,290

* Excludes oysters, clams and farmed mussels.

INLAND FISH (catch in metric tons)

	1997	1998	1999
Atlantic salmon	570	624	515
Total catch (incl. others)	736	895	765

Mining

('000 metric tons, unless otherwise indicated)

	1997	1998	1999
Natural gas (terajoules)	90,635	67,470	44,587
Lead*	45.1	36.5	44.1
Zinc*	194.8	181.0	199.3
Silver (kilograms)*	13,284	10,824	n.a.

* Figures refer to the metal content of ores mined.

Peat ('000 metric tons, excluding peat for horticultural use): 4,767 in 1992; 3,288 in 1993.

Industry

SELECTED PRODUCTS
('000 metric tons, unless otherwise indicated)

	1994	1995	1996
Flour	212	212	190
Margarine	n.a.	36	54
Cigarettes (million)	7,000	7,500	7,500
Woven woollen fabrics (sq. m)	n.a.	700,000	900,000
Motor spirit (petrol)	354	382	379
Distillate fuel oils	840	814	765
Residual fuel oils	819	785	793
Electric energy (million kWh)	n.a.	17,556	18,845

Source: mainly UN, *Industrial Commodity Statistics Yearbook*.

1997: Margarine 12,600 metric tons; Woven woollen fabric 900,000 sq. m; Cigarettes (million) 461; Electric energy 19,551 kWh.
1998: Woven woollen fabric 800,000 sq. m; Electric energy 20,485m. kWh.
1999: Electric energy 21,278m. kWh.

Finance

CURRENCY AND EXCHANGE RATES

Monetary Units:
100 pence (singular: penny) = 1 Irish pound (IR£ or punt).

Sterling, Dollar and Euro Equivalents (29 December 2000)
£1 sterling = IR£1.2630;
US $1 = 84.64 pence;
€1 = 78.76 pence;
IR£100 = £79.18 sterling = $118.15 = €126.97.

Average Exchange Rate (US $ per Irish pound)
1998   1.4257
1999   1.3528
2000   1.1698

Note: Since the introduction of the euro, with Irish participation, on 1 January 1999, a fixed exchange rate of €1 = 78.7564 pence has been in operation.

BUDGET (IR£ million)

Revenue	1998	1999	2000*
Tax revenue	16,129	18,559	21,321
Customs	160	136	164
Excise	2,822	3,198	3,357
Capital taxes	305	509	786
Income tax	5,737	6,323	7,177
Corporation tax	2,065	2,710	3,061
Motor vehicle duties	8	10	10
Stamp duties	540	719	872
Value-added tax	4,270	4,878	5,883
Employment and training levy	222	77	11
Non-tax revenue	370	434	420
Total	16,499	18,993	21,741

Expenditure	1998	1999	2000*
Debt service	2,410	2,198	2,028
Agriculture, fisheries and forestry	673	702	846
Defence	511	536	595
Justice (incl. police)	847	881	1,002
Education	2,445	2,648	2,871
Social welfare	4,754	4,943	5,384
Health	3,079	3,598	4,037
Industry and labour	583	658	758
Total (incl. others)	16,574	17,741	19,297

* Projections.

GOLD RESERVES AND CURRENCY IN CIRCULATION
(IR£ million at 31 December)

	1998	1999	2000*
Official gold reserves	88	43	47
Coin and bank notes in circulation	3,040	3,662	5,434

* At November 2000.

COST OF LIVING
(Consumer Price Index; base: November 1996 = 100)

	1998	1999	2000
Food	106.1	109.6	113.7
Alcoholic drink	104.8	108.7	114.0
Tobacco	108.0	112.7	130.5
Clothing and footwear	87.2	81.1	76.5
Fuel and light	99.0	100.8	109.9
Housing	102.6	91.5	100.0
Durable household goods	100.3	99.7	100.0
Other goods	103.6	105.7	109.7
Transport	102.4	105.3	114.0
Services and related expenditure	104.7	109.7	116.0
All items	103.1	104.8	110.7

NATIONAL ACCOUNTS (IR£ million at current prices)
National Income and Product

	1997	1998	1999†
Gross domestic product at factor cost	47,142	53,910	61,263
Net factor income from the rest of the world*	−6,332	−7,389	−9,984
Gross national product at factor cost	40,810	46,521	51,297
Less Consumption of fixed capital	5,179	6,107	7,114
Net national product at factor cost	35,630	40,414	44,166
of which:			
Compensation of employees	22,384	25,221	28,347
Other domestic income	13,246	15,193	15,819
Indirect taxes, less subsidies	5,618	6,671	7,789
Net national product at market prices	41,249	47,086	51,954
Consumption of fixed capital	5,179	6,107	7,114

National Income and Product — *continued*

	1997	1998	1999†
Gross national product at market prices	46,428	53,193	59,068
Less Net factor income from the rest of the world*	−6,332	−7,389	−9,984
Gross domestic product at market prices	52,760	60,582	69,052
Balance of exports and imports of goods and services*	−6,253	−7,225	−9,438
Available resources	46,507	53,357	59,614
of which:			
Private consumption expenditure	27,900	31,219	34,743
Government consumption expenditure	7,274	7,978	8,753
Gross fixed capital formation	10,650	13,275	16,175
Increase in stocks	683	886	−57

* Excludes transfers between Ireland and the rest of the world.
† Preliminary figures.

Gross Domestic Product by Economic Activity (at factor cost)

	1997	1998	1999*
Agriculture, forestry and fishing	2,853	2,808	2,583
Mining, manufacturing, electricity, gas, water and construction	17,793	20,904	23,524
Public administration and defence	2,037	2,234	2,333
Transport, communications and trade	7,916	9,043	10,278
Other services	17,739	21,209	24,800
Sub-total	48,338	56,198	63,518
Adjustment for financial services	−1,621	−1,970	−2,296
Discrepancy	426	−318	41
Total	47,142	53,910	61,263

* Preliminary.

BALANCE OF PAYMENTS (US $ million)

	1997	1998	1999
Exports of goods f.o.b.	55,293	78,562	66,989
Imports of goods f.o.b.	−36,668	−53,172	−42,811
Trade balance	18,625	25,390	24,178
Exports of services	6,186	16,735	14,683
Imports of services	−15,195	−29,626	−26,076
Balance on goods and services	9,616	12,499	12,785
Other income received	7,353	25,430	24,991
Other income paid	−17,059	−38,800	−38,467
Balance on goods, services and income	−90	−870	−691
Current transfers received	3,083	7,428	5,311
Current transfers paid	−1,128	−5,543	−4,026
Current balance	1,866	1,016	595
Capital account (net)	871	1,218	593
Direct investment abroad	−1,008	−4,955	−5,415
Direct investment from abroad	2,743	11,035	19,091
Portfolio investment assets	−716	−66,738	−82,487
Portfolio investment liabilities	−2,505	54,735	67,370
Other investment assets	−48,337	−25,211	−37,382
Other investment liabilities	42,340	35,821	37,148
Net errors and omissions	3,639	−3,709	−1,487
Overall balance	−1,109	3,212	−1,973

Source: IMF, *International Financial Statistics*.

External Trade

PRINCIPAL COMMODITIES (distribution by SITC, IR£ million)

Imports c.i.f.	1997	1998	1999
Food and live animals	1,656.3	1,831.8	2,006.8
Crude materials (inedible) except fuels	448.2	514.3	525.6
Mineral fuels, lubricants, etc.	897.6	793.9	969.8
Petroleum, petroleum products, etc.	700.3	579.9	744.5
Chemicals and related products	3,210.6	3,418.3	3,873.1
Organic chemicals	769.3	970.0	1,149.0
Medicinal and pharmaceutical products	591.9	733.3	879.4
Artificial resins and plastic materials, etc.	340.8	354.1	338.6
Basic manufactures	2,682.1	2,968.0	2,991.7
Paper, paperboard, etc.	558.4	606.0	606.4
Textile yarn, fabrics, etc.	446.3	491.9	436.5
Machinery and transport equipment	11,750.5	15,797.2	17,855.6
Machinery specialized for particular industries	713.4	1,047.9	794.6
General industrial machinery, equipment and parts	691.3	879.9	920.1
Office machines and automatic data-processing equipment	4,807.8	6,262.1	6,565.5
Parts and accessories for office machines, etc.	1,777.1	2,646.0	3,146.4
Telecommunications and sound equipment	674.9	913.7	1,611.4
Other electrical machinery, apparatus, etc.	2,520.7	3,436.2	4,013.0
Road vehicles and parts (excl. tyres, engines and electrical parts)	1,525.5	2,189.8	2,337.0
Passenger motor cars (excl. buses)	1,075.8	1,573.0	1,688.9
Miscellaneous manufactured articles	3,122.8	3,483.6	3,827.7
Clothing and accessories (excl. footwear)	719.5	834.2	861.4
Total (incl. others)*	25,882.1	31,278.1	34,682.1

* Including transactions not classified by commodity.

Exports f.o.b.	1997	1998	1999
Food and live animals	3,624.5	3,896.1	4,310.0
Meat and meat preparations	1,064.9	1,166.9	1,393.6
Fresh, chilled or frozen meat	909.9	1,000.9	1,207.2
Dairy products and birds' eggs	828.4	802.6	793.4
Crude materials (inedible) except fuels	607.6	583.3	627.0
Chemicals and related products	8,933.0	14,299.0	16,609.3
Organic chemicals	4,038.6	7,833.3	8,942.4
Organo-inorganic and heterocyclic compounds	3,394.5	6,965.0	7,602.2
Heterocyclic compounds (incl. nucleic acids)	2,970.0	6,306.1	6,978.7
Basic manufactures	1,378.2	1,420.4	1,425.1
Machinery and transport equipment	13,359.9	16,888.3	20,383.5
Office machines and automatic data-processing equipment	8,079.3	10,191.2	11,718.1
Automatic data-processing machines and units	5,142.9	6,210.5	6,918.7
Electrical machinery, apparatus, etc.	2,943.2	3,317.4	4,031.4
Miscellaneous manufactured articles	4,760.4	5,280.8	5,807.4
Professional, scientific and controlling instruments and apparatus	870.4	1,098.6	1,092.1
Total (incl. others)*	35,336.4	45,144.6	52,537.2

* Including transactions not classified by commodity.

PRINCIPAL TRADING PARTNERS (IR£ million)*

Imports c.i.f.	1997	1998	1999
Belgium-Luxembourg	306.0	365.3	463.0
China, People's Republic	322.0	503.6	513.2
France	1,254.4	1,222.5	1,433.2
Germany	1,561.5	1,942.7	2,157.1
Italy	499.5	605.1	753.4
Japan	1,784.9	2,184.0	2,006.6
Korea, Republic	348.1	502.1	609.8
Netherlands	849.2	971.2	1,050.5
Singapore	1,415.7	1,536.2	1,352.0
Taiwan	356.6	583.1	716.5
United Kingdom	8,945.4	10,605.8	11,483.5
USA	3,876.9	5,010.9	5,784.7
Total (incl. others)	25,882.1	31,278.1	34,682.1

Exports f.o.b.	1997	1998	1999
Belgium-Luxembourg	1,767.9	2,871.0	2,747.0
France	2,845.4	3,791.5	4,435.7
Germany	4,428.5	6,530.9	6,276.6
Italy	1,161.9	1,525.6	1,991.2
Japan	1,117.0	1,170.9	1,534.0
Malaysia	313.6	255.4	644.3
Netherlands	2,515.4	2,492.9	3,272.3
Spain	912.0	1,210.5	1,439.4
Sweden	563.7	857.7	861.4
Switzerland	601.5	910.6	1,265.8
United Kingdom	8,706.4	10,175.8	11,534.6
USA	3,977.3	6,097.8	8,066.5
Total (incl. others)	35,336.4	45,144.6	52,537.2

* Imports by country of origin; exports by country of final destination.

Transport

RAILWAYS (traffic, '000)

	1997	1998	1999
Passengers carried	28,913	32,291	32,561
Passenger train-km	11,348	11,289	11,132
Freight tonnage	2,916	2,683	2,901
Freight train-km	4,187	4,117	4,067

ROAD TRAFFIC (licensed motor vehicles at 31 December)

	1997	1998	1999
Passenger cars	1,134,429	1,196,901	1,269,245
Lorries and vans	158,158	170,866	188,814
Buses and coaches	16,186	17,353	19,640
Motorcycles and mopeds	24,424	24,398	26,677

SHIPPING

Merchant Fleet (registered at 31 December)

	1996	1997	1998
Number of vessels	164	165	150
Total displacement (grt)	218,990	235,008	183,809

Source: Lloyd's Register of Shipping, *World Fleet Statistics*.

Sea-borne Freight Traffic ('000 metric tons)*

	1997	1998	1999
Goods loaded	10,737	11,260	12,202
Goods unloaded	25,593	28,694	30,726

* Figures refer to vessels engaged in both international and coastal trade.

CIVIL AVIATION

	1994	1995	1996
Passengers carried ('000) . . .	9,316	10,568	11,956
Freight (incl. mail) carried (tons) .	104,263	124,144	146,681
Total aircraft movements . . .	199,653	204,850	228,167
scheduled	113,011	120,884	136,667
non-scheduled	86,642	83,966	91,500

Tourism

FOREIGN TOURIST ARRIVALS BY ORIGIN ('000)*

	1997	1998	1999
Great Britain	3,025	3,383	3,558
France	253	274	281
Germany	302	309	303
Netherlands	132	134	139
Other continental Europe . .	488	545	609
USA	711	791	861
Canada	52	63	82
Other areas	201	216	233
Total	5,164	5,716	6,068

* Excluding visitors from Northern Ireland and excursionists.

Communications Media

	1998	1999	2000
Television licences*	1,015,668	1,037,845	964,989†
Telephone lines	1,507,470	1,634,131	1,737,794
Daily newspapers	6	6	6

* Sales of licences.
† To November 2000.

Radio receivers (1997, estimate): 2,550,000 in domestic use.

Television receivers (1997, estimate): 1,470,000 in domestic use.

Daily newspapers (1996): 6 (estimated circulation 543,000).

Non-daily newspapers (1996): 77 (estimated circulation 1,561,000).

Book production (1985): 2,679 titles (including 2,051 pamphlets).

Source: UNESCO, *Statistical Yearbook*.

Education

(1998/99)

	Institutions	Teachers (full-time)	Students (full-time)
National schools* . . .	3,303	21,500	452,533
Secondary schools . . .	432	12,180	211,369
Vocational schools . . .	245	5,497	97,998
Comprehensive schools . .	16	520	8,532
Community schools . . .	66	2,609	44,152
Teacher (primary) training colleges	3	14	454
Technology colleges† . .	14	2,560	43,476
Universities and institutes .	10	3,084	63,737

* National schools are state-aided primary schools.
† Comprising 12 Institutes of Technology, Dublin Institute of Technology, and the Hotel Training and Catering College, Killybegs.

Directory

The Constitution

The Constitution took effect on 29 December 1937. Ireland became a republic on 18 April 1949. The following is a summary of the Constitution's main provisions:

TITLE OF THE STATE

The title of the State is Éire or, in the English language, Ireland.

NATIONAL STATUS*

The Constitution declares that Ireland is a sovereign, independent, democratic State. It affirms the inalienable, indefeasible and sovereign right of the Irish nation to choose its own form of government, to determine its relations with other nations, and to develop its life, political, economic and cultural, in accordance with its own genius and traditions.

The Constitution applies to the whole of Ireland, but, pending the reintegration of the national territory, the laws enacted by the Parliament established by the Constitution have the same area and extent of application as those of the Irish Free State.

THE PRESIDENT

At the head of the State is the President, elected by direct suffrage, who holds office for a period of seven years. The President, on the advice of the Government or its head, summons and dissolves Parliament, signs and promulgates laws and appoints judges; on the nomination of the Dáil, the President appoints the Prime Minister (Taoiseach) and, on the nomination of the Prime Minister with the previous approval of the Dáil, the President appoints the other members of the Government. The supreme command of the Defence Forces is vested in the President, its exercise being regulated by law.

In addition, the President has the power to refer certain Bills to the Supreme Court for decision on the question of their constitutionality; and also, at the instance of a prescribed proportion of the members of both Houses of Parliament, to refer certain Bills to the people for decision at a referendum.

The President, in the exercise and performance of certain of his or her constitutional powers and functions, has the aid and advice of a Council of State.

PARLIAMENT

The Oireachtas, or National Parliament, consists of the President and two Houses, viz. a House of Representatives called Dáil Éireann, and a Senate, called Seanad Éireann. The Dáil consists of 166 members, who are elected for a five-year term by adult suffrage on the system of proportional representation by means of the single, transferable vote. Of the 60 members of the Senate, 11 are nominated by the Prime Minister, six are elected by the universities, and 43 are elected from five panels of candidates established on a vocational basis, representing: national language and culture, literature, art, education and such professional interests as may be defined by law for the purpose of this panel; agriculture and allied interests, and fisheries; labour, whether organized or unorganized; industry and commerce, including banking, finance, accountancy, engineering and architecture; and public administration and social services, including voluntary social activities.

A maximum period of 90 days is afforded to the Senate for the consideration or amendment of Bills sent to that House by the Dáil, but the Senate has no power to veto legislation.

EXECUTIVE

The Executive Power of the State is exercised by the Government, which is responsible to the Dáil and consists of not fewer than seven and not more than 15 members. The head of the Government is the Prime Minister.

FUNDAMENTAL RIGHTS

The State recognizes the family as the natural, primary and fundamental unit group of Society, possessing inalienable and imprescriptible rights antecedent and superior to all positive law. It acknowledges the right to life of the unborn and, with due regard to the equal right to life of the mother, guarantees in its laws to defend and vindicate that right. It acknowledges the right and duty of parents to provide for the education of their children, and, with due regard to that right, undertakes to provide free education. It pledges itself also to guard with special care the institution of marriage.

The Constitution contains special provision for the recognition and protection of the fundamental rights of citizens, such as personal liberty, free expression of opinion, peaceable assembly, and the formation of associations and unions.

Freedom of conscience and the free practice and profession of religion are, subject to public order and morality, guaranteed to every citizen. No religion may be endowed or subjected to discriminatory disability. Since December 1972, when a referendum was taken on the issue, the Catholic Church has no longer enjoyed a special, privileged position.

SOCIAL POLICY

Certain principles of social policy intended for the general guidance of Parliament, but not cognizable by the courts, are set forth in the Constitution. Among their objects are the direction of the policy of the State towards securing the distribution of property so as to subserve the common good, the regulation of credit so as to serve the welfare of the people as a whole, the establishment of families in economic security on the land, and the right to an adequate means of livelihood for all citizens.

The State pledges itself to safeguard the interests, and to contribute where necessary to the support, of the infirm, the widow, the orphan and the aged, and shall endeavour to ensure that citizens shall not be forced by economic necessity to enter occupations unsuited to their sex, age or strength.

AMENDMENT OF THE CONSTITUTION

No amendment to the Constitution can be effected except by the decision of the people given at a referendum.

* Under the terms of the Good Friday Agreement, signed in April 1998 and approved by referendum in May, provision was made for a change to the Constitution to enshrine the principle that a united Ireland could be achieved only with the agreement and consent of the majority of the people of both Ireland and Northern Ireland. Accordingly, Articles 2 and 3 of the Constitution, which lay claim to the territory of Northern Ireland, were removed on 2 December 1999.

The Government

HEAD OF STATE

Uachtarán (President): Dr MARY McALEESE (assumed office 11 November 1997).

THE CABINET
(April 2001)

A coalition of Fianna Fáil (FF) and the Progressive Democrats (PD).

Taoiseach (Prime Minister): BERTIE AHERN (FF).

Tánaiste (Deputy Prime Minister) and Minister for Enterprise, Trade and Employment: MARY HARNEY (PD).

Minister for the Marine and Natural Resources: FRANK FAHEY (FF).

Minister for Foreign Affairs: BRIAN COWEN (FF).

Minister for Public Enterprise: MARY O'ROURKE (FF).

Minister for Defence: MICHAEL SMITH (FF).

Minister for Agriculture, Food and Rural Development: JOE WALSH (FF).

Minister for Finance: CHARLES McCREEVY (FF).

Minister for Health and Children: MICHEÁL MARTIN (FF).

Minister for the Environment and Local Government: NOEL DEMPSEY (FF).

Minister for Social, Community and Family Affairs: DERMOT AHERN (FF).

Minister for Arts, Heritage, Gaeltacht and the Islands: SÍLE DE VALERA (FF).

Minister for Justice, Equality and Law Reform: JOHN O'DONOGHUE (FF).

Minister for Tourism, Sport and Recreation: JAMES McDAID (FF).

Minister for Education and Science: MICHAEL J. WOODS (FF).

MINISTRIES

Office of the President: Áras an Uachtaráin, Phoenix Park, Dublin 8; tel. (1) 6171000; fax (1) 6171001; e-mail webmaster@aras.irlgov.ie; internet www.irlgov.ie/aras.

Department of the Taoiseach: Government Bldgs, Upper Merrion St, Dublin 2; tel. (1) 6224888; fax (1) 6789791; e-mail webmaster@ taoiseach.irlgov.ie; internet www.irlgov.ie/taoiseach.

Department of Agriculture, Food and Rural Development: Kildare St, Dublin 2; tel. (1) 6072000; fax (1) 6616263; e-mail infodaff@indigo.ie; internet www.irlgov.ie/daff.

Department of Arts, Heritage, Gaeltacht and the Islands: Dún Aimhirgin, 43–49 Mespil Rd, Dublin 4; tel. (1) 6473000; fax (1) 6670826; e-mail eolas@ealga.ie; internet www.irlgov.ie/ealga.

Department of Defence: Coláiste Caoimhín, Mobhí Rd, Dublin 9; tel. (1) 8042000; fax (1) 8377993; e-mail webmaster@ defence.irlgov.ie; internet www.irlgov.ie/defence.

Department of Education and Science: Marlborough St, Dublin 1; tel. (1) 8734700; fax (1) 8786712; e-mail webmaster@educ.irlgov.ie; internet www.irlgov.ie/educ.

Department of Enterprise, Trade and Employment: Kildare St, Dublin 2; tel. (1) 6312121; fax (1) 3612827; e-mail webmaster@ entemp.ie; internet www.entemp.ie.

Department of the Environment and Local Government: Custom House, Dublin 1; tel. (1) 8882479; fax (1) 8882576; e-mail press-office@environ.irlgov.ie; internet www.environ.ie.

Department of Finance: Government Bldgs, Upper Merrion St, Dublin 2; tel. (1) 6767571; fax (1) 6789936; e-mail webmaster@ finance.irlgov.ie; internet www.irlgov.ie/finance.

Department of Foreign Affairs: 80 St Stephen's Green, Dublin 2; tel. (1) 4780822; fax (1) 4781484; e-mail library1@iveagh.irlgov.ie; internet www.irlgov.ie/iveagh.

Department of Health and Children: Hawkins House, Hawkins St, Dublin 2; tel. (1) 6354000; fax (1) 6354001; e-mail queries@ health.irlgov.ie; internet www.doh.ie.

Department of Justice, Equality and Law Reform: 72–76 St Stephen's Green, Dublin 2; tel. (1) 6028202; fax 6615461; e-mail pagemaster@justice.irlgov.ie; internet www.irlgov.ie/justice.

Department of the Marine and Natural Resources: Leeson Lane, Dublin 2; tel. (1) 6785444; fax (1) 6618214; e-mail minister@ marine.irlgov.ie; internet www.irlgov.ie/marine.

Department for Public Enterprise: 44 Kildare St, Dublin 2; tel. (1) 6041090; fax (1) 6041185; e-mail webmaster@dpe.ie; internet www.irlgov.ie/tec.

Department of Social, Community and Family Affairs: Áras Mhic Dhiarmada, Store St, Dublin 1; tel. (1) 6797777; fax (1) 7043868; e-mail webweaver@welfare.eirmail400.ie; internet www.dscfa.ie.

Department of Tourism, Sport and Recreation: Kildare St, Dublin 2; tel. (1) 6313800; fax (1) 6611201; e-mail web_master@tourism-sport.irlgov.ie; internet www.irlgov.ie/tourism-sport.

Legislature

OIREACHTAS (NATIONAL PARLIAMENT)

Parliament comprises two Houses—Dáil Éireann (House of Representatives), with 166 members (Teachtaí Dála), elected for a five-year term by universal adult suffrage, and Seanad Éireann (Senate), with 60 members serving a five-year term, of whom 11 are nominated by the Taoiseach (Prime Minister) and 49 elected (six by the universities and 43 from specially constituted panels).

Dáil Éireann

Speaker: SÉAMUS PATTISON.

General Election, 6 June 1997

Party					Votes*	% of votes*	Seats
Fianna Fáil	.	.	.	.	703,682	39.33	77
Fine Gael	.	.	.	.	499,936	27.95	54
Labour Party	.	.	.	.	186,044	10.40	17
Progressive Democrats	.	.			83,765	4.68	4
Democratic Left	.	.	.		44,901	2.51	4
Others	.	.	.	.	270,657	15.13	10
Total	.	.	.	.	**1,788,985**	**100.00**	**166**

* The election was conducted by means of the single transferable vote. Figures refer to first-preference votes.

Seanad Éireann

Speaker: BRIAN MULLOLY.

Election, August 1997 (11 non-affiliated members nominated)

Party	Seats at election
Fianna Fáil	29
Fine Gael	16
Labour	4
Progressive Democrats	4
Others	7

Political Organizations

Christian Solidarity Party: 52 Foxrock Ave, Foxrock, Dublin 18; tel. (1) 2891040; fax (1) 2891042; e-mail comharcriostai@tinet.ie; Pres. and Leader Dr GERARD CASEY; Nat. Sec. PATRICK SMYTH.

Comhaontas Glas (Green Party): 5A Upper Fownes St, Temple Bar, Dublin 2; tel. (1) 6790012; fax (1) 6797168; e-mail greenpar@iol.ie; internet www.greenparty.ie; fmrly The Ecology Party; advocates a humane, ecological society, freedom of information and political decentralization; Nat. Co-ordinator MARY BOWERS.

Communist Party of Ireland: James Connolly House, 43 East Essex St, Dublin 2; tel. and fax (1) 6711943; e-mail cpi@indigo.ie; internet www.communistpartyofireland.ie; f. 1933; advocates a united, socialist, independent Ireland; Chair. EUGENE McCARTAN; Gen. Sec. JAMES STEWART.

Democratic Left: 69 Middle Abbey St, Dublin 1; tel. (1) 8729550; fax (1) 8729238; e-mail dlhead@indigo.ie; internet www.connect.ie/ users/dl; f. 1992; democratic socialist; Leader PROINSIAS DE ROSSA; Gen. Sec. JOHN GALLAGHER.

Fianna Fáil (Republican Party): 13 Upper Mount St, Dublin 2; tel. (1) 6761551; fax (1) 6785690; e-mail info@fiannafail.ie; internet www.fiannafail.ie; f. 1926; centrist; Pres. and Leader BERTIE AHERN; Gen. Sec. MARTIN MACKIN.

Fine Gael (United Ireland Party): 51 Upper Mount St, Dublin 2; tel. (1) 6198444; fax (1) 6625046; e-mail finegael@finegael.com; internet www.finegael.ie; f. 1933; centrist; Pres. and Leader MICHAEL NOONAN; Gen. Sec. TOM CURRAN.

The Labour Party: 17 Ely Place, Dublin 2; tel. (1) 6612615; fax (1) 6612640; e-mail head_office@labour.ie; internet www .labour.ie; f. 1912; Leader RUAIRÍ QUINN; Gen. Sec. MIKE ALLAN.

Muintir na hÉireann Pairti: 58 The Palms, Roebuck Rd, Dublin 14; tel. and fax (1) 2831484; e-mail muintir@indigo.ie; f. 1995; Christian conservative; Leader RICHARD GREENE.

Progressive Democrats: 25 South Frederick St, Dublin 2; tel. (1) 6794399; fax (1) 6794757; e-mail info@progressivedemocrats.ie; internet www.progressivedemocrats.ie; f. 1985 by fmr mems of Fianna Fáil; conservative; Leader MARY HARNEY; Gen. Sec. JOHN HIGGINS.

Sinn Féin (Ourselves Alone): 44 Parnell Sq., Dublin 1; tel. (1) 8726100; fax (1) 8733441; e-mail sinnféin@iol.ie; internet www .sinnfein.ie; f. 1905; advocates the termination of British rule in Northern Ireland; seeks the establishment of a democratic socialist republic in a reunified Ireland; Pres. GERRY ADAMS; Chair. MITCHEL McLAUGHLIN.

The Workers' Party: 23 Hill St, Dublin 1; tel. (1) 8740716; fax (1) 8748702; e-mail pqloc@indigo.ie; internet www.workers-party.org; f. 1905; fmrly Sinn Féin The Workers' Party; aims to establish a unitary socialist state on the island of Ireland; Pres. TOM FRENCH; Gen. Sec. PAT QUEARNEY.

Diplomatic Representation

EMBASSIES IN IRELAND

Argentina: 15 Ailesbury Drive, Dublin 4; tel. (1) 2691546; fax (1) 2600404; e-mail argembsy@indigo.ie; Ambassador: VICTOR E. BEAUGÉ.

Australia: Fitzwilton House, 2nd Floor, Wilton Terrace, Dublin 2; tel. (1) 6761517; fax (1) 6785185; e-mail david.keys@dfat.gov.au; internet www.australianembassy.ie; Ambassador: ROBERT G. HALVERSON.

Austria: 15 Ailesbury Court, 93 Ailesbury Rd, Dublin 4; tel. (1) 2694577; fax (1) 2830860; e-mail austroam@iol.ie; Ambassador: Dr PAUL LEIFER.

Belgium: 2 Shrewsbury Rd, Dublin 4; tel. (1) 2692082; fax (1) 2838488; e-mail dublin@diplobel.org; Ambassador: Baron ALAIN GUILLAUME.

Brazil: Europa House, Harcourt St, Dublin 2; tel. (1) 4756000; fax (1) 4751341; Ambassador: ARMANDO SÉRGIO FRAZÃO.

Bulgaria: 22 Burlington Rd, Dublin 4; tel. (1) 6603293; fax (1) 6603915; bgemb@tinet.ie; Chargé d'affaires a.i.: PETER POPTCHEV.

Canada: 65–68 St Stephen's Green, Dublin 2; tel. (1) 4781988; fax (1) 4781285; e-mail cdnembsy@iol.ie; Ambassador: RONALD A. IRWIN.

China, People's Republic: 40 Ailesbury Rd, Dublin 4; tel: (1) 2691707; fax (1) 2839938; Ambassador: ZHANG XIAOKANG.

Cyprus: 71 Lower Leeson St, Dublin 2; tel. (1) 6763060; fax 6763099; e-mail embassyofcyprusdub@eircom.net; Ambassador: Dr NICHOLAS EMILIOU.

Czech Republic: 57 Northumberland Rd, Ballsbridge, Dublin 4; tel. (1) 6681135; fax (1) 6681660; Ambassador: PETR KOLÁŘ.

Denmark: 121–122 St Stephen's Green, Dublin 2; tel. (1) 4756404; fax (1) 4784536; e-mail embassy@denmark.ie; internet www .denmark.ie; Ambassador: K. ERIK TYGESEN.

Egypt: 12 Clyde Rd, Ballsbridge, Dublin 4; tel. (1) 6606566; fax (1) 6683745; e-mail embegypt@indigo.ie; Ambassador: HASSAN SALEM.

Estonia: 24 Merlyn Park, Dublin 4; tel. (1) 2691552; fax (1) 2605119; e-mail asjur@gofree.indigo.ie; Chargé d'affaires a.i.: TRIIN PARTS.

Finland: Russell House, Stokes Place, St Stephen's Green, Dublin 2; tel. (1) 4781344; fax (1) 4783727; Ambassador: TIMO JALKANEN.

France: 36 Ailesbury Rd, Ballsbridge, Dublin 4; tel. (1) 2601666; fax (1) 2830178; Ambassador: HENRI BENOÎT DE COIGNAC.

Germany: 31 Trimleston Ave, Booterstown, Blackrock, Co Dublin; tel. (1) 2693011; fax (1) 2693946; e-mail germany@indigo.ie; Ambassador: Dr GOTTFRIED HAAS.

Greece: 1 Upper Pembroke St, Dublin 2; tel. (1) 6767254; fax (1) 6618892; e-mail dubgremb@tinet.ie; Ambassador: MARIA ZOGRAFOU.

Holy See: 183 Navan Rd, Dublin 7 (Apostolic Nunciature); tel. (1) 8380577; fax (1) 8380276; e-mail nuncioirl@eircom.net; Apostolic Nuncio: Most Rev. GIUSEPPE LAZZAROTO, Titular Archbishop of Numana.

Hungary: 2 Fitzwilliam Place, Dublin 2; tel. (1) 6612902; fax (1) 6612880; Ambassador: Dr GÉZA PÁLMAI.

India: 6 Leeson Park, Dublin 6; tel. (1) 4970843; fax (1) 4978074; Ambassador: CHOKILA IYER.

Iran: 72 Mount Merrion Ave, Blackrock, Co Dublin; tel. (1) 2880252; fax (1) 2834246; Ambassador: HASSAN TAHERIAN.

Israel: 122 Pembroke Rd, Dublin 4; tel. (1) 6680303; fax (1) 6680418; e-mail info@embisrael.iol.ie; Ambassador: MARK SOFER.

Italy: 63–65 Northumberland Rd, Dublin 4; tel. (1) 6601744; fax (1) 6682759; e-mail italianembassy@eircom.net; internet homepage .eircom.net/~italianembassy; Ambassador: Dr FERDINANDO ZEZZA.

Japan: Nutley Bldg, Merrion Centre, Nutley Lane, Dublin 4; tel. (1) 2694244; fax (1) 2838726; e-mail general@japanembassy.ie; Ambassador: KAZUKO YOKOO.

Korea, Republic: Clyde House, 15 Clyde Rd, Ballsbridge, POB 2101, Dublin 4; tel. (1) 6608800; fax (1) 6608716; Ambassador: KI HO CHANG.

Mexico: 43 Ailesbury Rd, Dublin 4; tel. (1) 2600699; fax (1) 2600411; e-mail embasmex@indigo.ie; Ambassador: DANIEL DULTZIN DUBIN.

Morocco: 53 Raglan Rd, Ballsbridge, Dublin 4; tel. (1) 6609449; fax (1) 6609468; e-mail sifamdub@indigo.ie; Chargé d'affaires a.i.: AÏCHA EL KABBAJ.

Netherlands: 160 Merrion Rd, Dublin 4; tel. (1) 2693444; fax (1) 2839690; e-mail info@netherlandsembassy.ie; internet www .netherlandsembassy.ie; Ambassador: LOUIS PETER VAN VLIET.

Nigeria: 56 Leeson Park, Dublin 6; tel. (1) 6604366; fax (1) 6604092; Ambassador: ELIAS NATHAN.

Norway: 34 Molesworth St, Dublin 2; tel. (1) 6621800; fax (1) 6621890; e-mail noremb@indigo.ie; Ambassador: LIV MØRCH FINBORUD.

Poland: 5 Ailesbury Rd, Dublin 4; tel. (1) 2830855; fax (1) 2698309; e-mail polembas@iol.ie; internet www.polishembassy.ie; Ambassador: JANUSZ SKOLIMOWSKI.

Portugal: Knocksinna House, Knocksinna, Foxrock, Dublin 18; tel. (1) 2894416; fax (1) 2892849; e-mail ptembassydublin@tinet.ie; Ambassador: JOÃO DE VALLERA.

Romania: 47 Ailesbury Rd, Dublin 4; tel. (1) 2692852; fax (1) 2692122; e-mail romemb@iol.ie; Chargé d'affaires a.i.: Dr GEORGE MAIOR.

Russia: 186 Orwell Rd, Dublin 14; tel. (1) 4922048; fax (1) 4923525; Ambassador: EVGUENI NICKOLAEVICH MIKHAILOV.

Slovakia: 20 Clyde Rd, Ballsbridge, Dublin 4; tel. (1) 6600012; fax (1) 6600014; Chargé d'affaires a.i.: MARCEL PEŠKO.

South Africa: Alexander House, Earlsfort Terrace, Dublin 2; tel. (1) 6615553; fax (1) 6615590; e-mail saembdub@iol.ie; Ambassador: PIERRE DIETRICHSEN.

Spain: 17A Merlyn Park, Dublin 4; tel. (1) 2691640; fax (1) 2691854; Ambassador: JOSÉ MARÍA SANZ PASTOR.

Sweden: 13–17 Dawson St, Dublin 2; tel. (1) 6715822; fax (1) 6796718; e-mail swedembdublin@eircom.net; Ambassador: PETER OSVALD.

Switzerland: 6 Ailesbury Rd, Dublin 4; tel. (1) 2692515; fax (1) 2830344; e-mail vertretnng@dub.rep.admin.ch; Ambassador: WILLY HOLD.

Turkey: 11 Clyde Rd, Dublin 4; tel. (1) 6685240; fax (1) 6685014; e-mail turkemb@iol.ie; Ambassador: S. GÜNALTAY SIBAY.

United Kingdom: 29 Merrion Rd, Dublin 4; tel. (1) 2053700; fax (1) 2053885; internet www.britishembassy.ie; Ambassador: Sir IVOR ROBERTS.

USA: 42 Elgin Rd, Ballsbridge, Dublin 4; tel. (1) 6687777; fax (1) 6689946; internet www.usembassy.ie; Ambassador: MICHAEL J. SULLIVAN.

Judicial System

Justice is administered in public by judges appointed by the President on the advice of the Government. The judges of all courts are completely independent in the exercise of their judicial functions. The jurisdiction and organization of the courts are dealt with in the Courts (Establishment and Constitution) Act, 1961, and the Courts (Supplemental Provisions) Acts, 1961 to 1981.

Attorney-General: MICHAEL MCDOWELL.

SUPREME COURT

The Supreme Court: Four Courts, Dublin 7; tel. (1) 8886000; fax (1) 8732332; internet www.courts.ie; consisting of the Chief Justice and seven other judges, has appellate jurisdiction from all decisions of the High Court. The President of Ireland may, after consultation with the Council of State, refer a bill which has been passed by both Houses of the Oireachtas (other than a money bill or certain others), to the Supreme Court to establish whether it or any other provisions thereof are repugnant to the Constitution.

Chief Justice: RONAN KEANE.

Judges:

SUSAN GAGEBY DENHAM, JOHN MURRAY, FRANCIS MURPHY, HUGH GEOGHEGAN, CATHERINE MCGUINNESS, ADRIAN HARDIMAN, NIAL FENNELLY.

COURT OF CRIMINAL APPEAL

The Court of Criminal Appeal, consisting of the Chief Justice or an ordinary judge of the Supreme Court and two judges of the High Court, deals with appeals by persons convicted on indictment, where leave to appeal has been granted. The Court has jurisdiction to review a conviction or sentence on the basis of an alleged miscarriage of justice. The Director of Public Prosecutions may appeal against an unduly lenient sentence. The decision of the Court of Criminal Appeal is final unless the Court or Attorney-General or the Director of Public Prosecutions certifies that a point of law involved should, in the public interest, be taken to the Supreme Court.

HIGH COURT

The High Court: Four Courts, Dublin 7; tel. (1) 8886592; fax (1) 8725669; internet www.courts.ie; consists of the President of the High Court and 21 ordinary judges, has full original jurisdiction in, and power to determine, all matters and questions whether of law or fact, civil or criminal. The High Court on circuit acts as an appeal court from the Circuit Court. The Central Criminal Court sits as directed by the President of the High Court to try criminal cases outside the jurisdiction of the Circuit Court. The duty of acting as the Central Criminal Court is assigned, for the time being, to a judge of the High Court.

President: FREDERICK MORRIS.

Judges:

MELLA CARROLL, ROBERT BARR, RICHARD JOHNSON, VIVIAN LAVAN, PAUL J. P. CARNEY, DECLAN BUDD, DERMOT KINLEN, BRIAN MCCRACKEN, MARY LAFFOY, MICHAEL MORIARTY, PETER KELLY, THOMAS C. SMYTH, DIARMUID B. D. O'DONOVAN, PHILIP O'SULLIVAN, KEVIN C. O'HIGGINS, JOHN QUIRKE, MATTHEW P. SMITH, NICHOLAS KEARNS, IARFHLAITH O'NEILL, AINDRIAS OCAOIMH, JOSEPH FINNEGAN, RODERICK MURPHY, DANIEL HERBERT, PAUL BUTLER, LIAM MCKECHNIE.

CIRCUIT AND DISTRICT COURTS

The civil jurisdiction of the Circuit Court is limited to IR£30,000 in contract and tort and in actions founded on hire-purchase and credit-sale agreements and to a rateable value of IR£200 in equity, and in probate and administration, but where the parties consent the jurisdiction is unlimited. In criminal matters the Court has jurisdiction in all cases except murder, rape, treason, piracy and allied offences. One circuit court judge is permanently assigned to each of the circuits outside Dublin with the exception of Cork, which has three judges. Dublin has ten permanent judges. In addition there are eight permanently unassigned judges. The President of the

District Court is ex officio an additional Judge of the Circuit Court. The Circuit Court acts as an appeal court from the District Court, which has a summary jurisdiction in a large number of criminal cases where the offence is not of a serious nature. In civil matters the District Court has jurisdiction in contract and tort (except slander, libel, seduction, slander of title, malicious prosecution and false imprisonment) where the claim does not exceed IR£5,000 and in actions founded on hire-purchase and credit-sale agreements.

All criminal cases except those dealt with summarily by a justice in the District Court are tried by a judge and a jury of 12 members. Juries are also used in some civil cases in the High Court. In a criminal case 10 members of the jury may, in certain circumstances, agree on a verdict, and in a civil case the agreement of nine members is sufficient.

Religion

CHRISTIANITY

The organization of the churches takes no account of the partition of Ireland into two separate political entities; both the Republic of Ireland and Northern Ireland are subject to a unified ecclesiastical jurisdiction. The Roman Catholic Primate of All Ireland and the Church of Ireland (Protestant Episcopalian) Primate of All Ireland have their seats in Northern Ireland, at Armagh, and the headquarters of the Presbyterian Church in Ireland is at Belfast, Northern Ireland.

At 31 December 1998 adherents to the Roman Catholic Church represented some 77% of the population. In 1999 there were 284,704 adherents to the Presbyterian Church and 55,839 to the Methodist Church. In 1996 there were 346,015 adherents to the Church of Ireland.

Irish Council of Churches: Inter-Church Centre, 48 Elmwood Ave, Belfast, BT9 6AZ, Northern Ireland; tel. (28) 90382750; fax (1232) 381737; e-mail icpep@mail.com; internet www.irishchurches.org; f. 1922 (present name adopted 1966); nine mem. churches; Pres. Rev. Canon I. M. ELLIS (Church of Ireland); Gen. Sec. Dr R. D. STEVENS.

The Roman Catholic Church

Ireland (including Northern Ireland) comprises four archdioceses and 22 dioceses.

Archbishop of Armagh and Primate of All Ireland: Most Rev. SEÁN B. BRADY, Ara Coeli, Cathedral Rd, Armagh, BT61 7QY, Northern Ireland; tel. (28) 37522045; fax (28) 37526182.

Archbishop of Cashel and Emly: Most Rev. DERMOT CLIFFORD, Archbishop's House, Thurles, Co Tipperary; tel. (504) 21512; fax (504) 22680; e-mail cashelemly@eircom.net.

Archbishop of Dublin and Primate of Ireland: Cardinal DESMOND CONNELL, Archbishop's House, Drumcondra, Dublin 9; tel. (1) 8373732; fax (1) 8369796.

Archbishop of Tuam: Most Rev. MICHAEL NEARY, Archbishop's House, St Jarlath's, Tuam, Co Galway; tel. (93) 24166; fax (93) 28070.

Numerous Roman Catholic religious orders are strongly established in the country. These play an important role, particularly in the spheres of education, health and social welfare.

Church of Ireland
(The Anglican Communion)

Ireland (including Northern Ireland) comprises two archdioceses and 10 dioceses.

Central Office of the Church of Ireland: Church of Ireland House, Church Ave, Dublin 6; tel. (1) 4978422; fax (1) 4978821; e-mail office@rcbdub.org; internet www.ireland.anglican.org/rcb.html; 410,000 mems (1999); Chief Officer and Sec. to the Representative Church Body R. H. SHERWOOD.

Archbishop of Armagh and Primate of All Ireland and Metropolitan: Most Rev. Lord EAMES, The See House, Cathedral Close, Armagh, BT61 7EE, Northern Ireland; tel. (28) 37527144; fax (28) 37527823; e-mail archbishop@armagh.anglican.org.

Archbishop of Dublin and Primate of Ireland and Metropolitan: Most Rev. WALTON N. F. EMPEY, The See House, 17 Temple Rd, Milltown, Dublin 6; tel. (1) 4977849; fax (1) 4976355.

Other Christian Churches

Association of Baptist Churches: 117 Lisburn Rd, Belfast, BT9 7AF, Northern Ireland; tel. (28) 90663108; fax (28) 90663616; e-mail buofi@aol.com; Pres. RAYMOND PITT; Sec. Pastor W. COLVILLE.

Church of Jesus Christ of Latter-day Saints (Mormon): The Willows, Glasnevin, Dublin 11; tel. (1) 8306899; fax (1) 8304638.

Greek Orthodox Church in Ireland: Sacred Church of the Annunciation, 46 Arbour Hill, Dublin 7; Very Rev. IRENEU CRACIUN.

Lutheran Church in Ireland: Lutherhaus, 24 Adelaide Rd, Dublin 2; tel. (1) 6766548; Pastor Rev. FRITZ-GERT MAYER.

Methodist Church in Ireland: 1 Fountainville Ave, Belfast, BT9 6AN, Northern Ireland; tel. (28) 90324554; fax (28) 90239467; e-mail mci@iol.ie; Sec. Rev. EDMUND T. I. MAWHINNEY.

Moravian Church in Ireland: 25 Church Rd, Gracehill, Ballymena, BT42 2NL, Northern Ireland; tel. (28) 25653141; f. 1749; Chair. of Conf. Rev. V. D. LAUNDER.

Non-Subscribing Presbyterian Church of Ireland: 102 Carrickfergus Rd, Larne, Co Antrim, Northern Ireland; tel. (28) 28272600; Clerk to Gen. Synod Rev. Dr JOHN W. NELSON.

Presbyterian Church in Ireland: Church House, Fisherwick Place, Belfast, BT1 6DW, Northern Ireland; tel. (28) 90322284; fax (28) 90236609; e-mail clerk@presbyterianireland.org; Moderator of Gen. Assembly Rt Rev. H. A. DUNLOP; Clerk of Assembly and Gen. Sec. Very Rev. Dr S. HUTCHINSON.

The Religious Society of Friends: Swanbrook House, Bloomfield Ave, Morehampton Rd, Dublin 4; tel. and fax (1) 6683684; Registrar VALERIE O'BRIEN.

Salvation Army: POB 2098, Dublin Central Mission, Lower Abbey St, Dublin 1; tel. (1) 8740987; fax (1) 8747478; Divisional Dir Maj. HOWARD SERCOMBE.

BAHÁ'Í FAITH

National Spiritual Assembly: 24 Burlington Rd, Dublin 4; tel. (1) 6683150; fax (1) 6689632; e-mail nsairl@iol.ie; internet www.bahai.ie.

ISLAM

The Muslim population of the Republic of Ireland was enumerated at 3,875 in the 1991 census. The number of adherents was estimated to total 9,000 in 1996, inclusive of Northern Ireland.

Islamic Cultural Centre of Ireland: 19 Roebuck Rd, Clonskeagh, Dublin 14; tel. (1) 2080000; fax (1) 2080001; e-mail iccislam@eircom.net; Imam SHAIKH HUSSEIN HALAWA.

Islamic Foundation of Ireland: 163 South Circular Rd, Dublin 8; tel. (1) 4533242; fax (1) 4532785; e-mail ifi@indigo.ie; Imam YAHYA MUHAMMAD AL-HUSSEIN.

JUDAISM

The Jewish community was estimated to number 1,200 in 1996.

Chief Rabbi: (vacant), Herzog House, Zion Rd, Rathgar, Dublin 6; tel. (1) 4923751; fax (1) 4924680; e-mail irishcom@iol.ie.

The Press

A significant feature of the Irish press is the number of weekly newspapers published in provincial centres.

DAILIES
Cork

Evening Echo: Academy St, Cork; tel. (21) 272722; fax 275112; f. 1892; Editor BRIAN FEENEY; circ. 27,000.

Irish Examiner: Academy St, POB 21, Cork; tel. (21) 272722; fax 275112; e-mail features@examiner.ie; internet www.examiner.ie; f. 1841; Editor BRIAN LOONEY; circ. 57,000.

Dublin

Evening Herald: Independent House, 90 Middle Abbey St, Dublin 1; tel. (1) 8731666; fax (1) 8731787; e-mail herald.news@independent.ie; f. 1891; Editor GERARD O'REGAN; circ. 115,000.

Irish Independent: Independent House, 90 Middle Abbey St, Dublin 1; tel. (1) 7055333; fax (1) 8720304; internet www.independent.ie; f. 1905; Editor VINCENT DOYLE; circ. 163,000.

The Irish Times: 10–16 D'Olier St, POB 74, Dublin 2; tel. (1) 6792022; fax (1) 6793910; e-mail itemail@irish-times.com; internet www.ireland.com; f. 1859; Editor CONOR BRADY; circ. 105,000.

The Star: Star House, 62A Terenure Rd North, Dublin 6; tel. (1) 4901228; fax (1) 4902193; Editor GERARD O'REAGAN; circ. 85,000.

PRINCIPAL WEEKLY NEWSPAPERS

An Phoblacht/Republican News: 58 Parnell Sq., Dublin 1; tel. (1) 8733611; fax (1) 8733074; e-mail aprn@irlnet.com; internet www.irlnet.com/aprn; f. 1970; Editor MARTIN SPAIN; circ. 28,000.

Anglo-Celt: Anglo-Celt Pl., Cavan; tel. (49) 31100; fax (49) 32280; internet www.unison.ie/anglo_celt; f. 1846; Fri.; Editor J. F. O'HANLON; circ. 16,000.

Argus: Park St, Dundalk, Co Louth; tel. (42) 31500; fax (42) 31643; internet www.unison.ie/the_argus; f. 1835; Thurs.; Editor KEVIN MULLIGAN; circ. 9,300.

Clare Champion: Barrack St, Ennis, Co Clare; tel. (65) 6828105; fax (65) 6820374; e-mail editor@clarechampion.ie; internet www .clarechampion.ie; f. 1903; Thurs.; Editor GERRY COLLISON; circ. 20,000.

Connacht Tribune: 15 Market St, Galway; tel. (91) 567251; fax (91) 567970; e-mail stephenco@eircom.net; internet www.con -telegraph.ie; f. 1909; Fri.; Editor J. CUNNINGHAM; circ. 29,900.

Connaught Telegraph: Ellison St, Castlebar, Co Mayo; tel. (94) 21711; fax (94) 24007; e-mail conntel@tinet.ie; f. 1828; Wed.; Editor TOM GILLESPIE; circ. 16,000.

Donegal Democrat: Donegal Rd, Ballyshannon, Co Donegal; tel. (72) 51201; fax (72) 51945; f. 1919; Fri.; Editor JOHN BROMLEY; circ. 18,000.

Drogheda Independent: 9 Shop St, Drogheda, Co Louth; tel. (41) 9838658; fax (41) 9834271; internet www.unison.ie/ drogheda_independent; f. 1884; Thurs.; Editor PAUL MURPHY; circ. 14,000.

Dundalk Democrat: 3 Earl St, Dundalk, Co Louth; tel. (42) 9334058; fax (42) 9331399; f. 1849; Sat.; Editor PETER E. KAVANAGH; circ. 16,000.

Dungarvan Leader and Southern Democrat: 78 O'Connell St, Dungarvan, Co Waterford; tel. (58) 41203; fax (58) 45301; Wed.; Editor COLM J. NAGLE; circ. 13,000.

Dungarvan Observer and Munster Industrial Advocate: Shandon, Dungarvan, Co Waterford; tel. (58) 41205; fax (58) 41559; e-mail observer@indigo.ie; Editor JAMES A. LYNCH; circ. 11,000.

Echo and South Leinster Advertiser: Mill Park Rd, Enniscorthy, Co Wexford; tel. (54) 33231; fax (54) 33506; f. 1902; Wed.; Editor JAMES GAHAN; circ. 22,000.

The Guardian: The People Newspapers Ltd, Castle Hill, Enniscorthy, Co Wexford; tel. (54) 33833; fax (54) 35910; e-mail dasherin@ hotmail.com; f. 1881; Wed.; Man. Dir G. WALSH; circ. 36,000.

Iris Oifigiuil (Official Irish Gazette): 4–5 Harcourt Rd, Dublin 2; tel. (1) 6613111; fax (1) 4752760; f. 1922; Publs Man. BRIAN O'CONNELL.

The Kerryman/The Corkman: Clash Industrial Estate, Tralee, Co Kerry; tel. (66) 21666; fax (66) 21608; internet www.unison.ie/ corkman; f. 1904; Thurs.; Editor GERARD COLLERAN; circ. 35,000.

Kilkenny People: 34 High St, Kilkenny; tel. (56) 21015; fax (56) 21414; e-mail info@kilkennypeople.ie; internet www.kilkennypeople .ie; f. 1892; weekly; Editor JOHN KERRY KEANE; circ. 17,000.

Leinster Express: Dublin Rd, Portlaoise, Co Laois; tel. (502) 21666; fax (502) 20491; e-mail lexpress@indigo.ie; internet www.unison.ie/ leinster_express; f. 1831; weekly; Man. Editor TEDDY FENNELLY; circ. 18,500.

Leinster Leader: 19 South Main St, Naas, Co Kildare; tel. (45) 897302; fax (45) 897647; e-mail iain@iol.ie; internet www.unison.ie/ leinster_leader; f. 1880; Wed.; Editor MICHAEL SHEERAN; circ. 15,000.

Leitrim Observer: St George's Terrace, Carrick-on-Shannon, Co Leitrim; tel. (78) 20025; fax (78) 20112; internet www.unison.ie/ leitrim_observer; f. 1889; Wed.; Editor ANTHONY HICKEY; circ. 10,000.

Limerick Chronicle: 54 O'Connell St, Limerick; tel. (61) 71315233; fax (61) 71314804; f. 1766; Tues.; Editor BRENDAN HALLIGAN; circ. 7,000.

Limerick Leader: 54 O'Connell St, Limerick; tel. (61) 71214500; fax (61) 71314804; e-mail admin@limerick-leader.ie; internet www.limerick-leader.ie; f. 1889; 4 a week; Editor BRENDAN HALLIGAN; circ. 26,000 (weekend edn).

Limerick Post: Town Hall, Rutland St, Limerick; tel. (61) 71413322; fax (61) 71417684; e-mail news@limerickpost.ie; internet www.limerickpost.ie; f. 1986; Thurs.; Editor BILLY RYAN; circ. 36,500.

Longford Leader: Market Sq., Longford; tel. (43) 45241; fax (43) 41489; e-mail ads@longford-leader.iol.ie; internet www.rmbi.ie; f. 1897; Wed.; Editor EUGENE MCGEE; circ. 25,000.

Longford News: Earl St, Longford; tel. (43) 45627; fax (43) 41549; e-mail infor@longford-news.iol.ie; internet www.unison.ie/ longford_news; Wed.; Editor PAUL HEALY; circ. 24,000.

Mayo News: The Fairgreen, Westport, Co Mayo; tel. (98) 25311; fax (98) 26108; e-mail mayonews@anu.ie; internet www.mayonews.ie; f. 1892; Wed.; Man. Editor SEÁN STAUNTON; circ. 35,000.

Meath Chronicle and Cavan and Westmeath Herald: 12 Market Sq., Navan, Co Meath; tel. (46) 79600; fax (46) 23565; e-mail info@meath-chronicle.ie; internet www.meath-chronicle.ie; f. 1897; Sat.; Editor KEN DAVIS; circ. 18,000.

Midland Tribune: Emmet St, Birr, Co Offaly; tel. (509) 20003; fax (509) 20588; e-mail midtrib@iol.ie; internet www.unison.ie/ midland_tribune; f. 1881; Wed.; Editor JOHN O'CALLAGHAN; circ. 16,000.

The Munster Express: 37 The Quay and 1–3 Hanover St, Waterford; tel. (51) 872141; fax (51) 873452; e-mail munster@iol.ie; internet www.munster-express.ie; f. 1859; 2 a week; Editor K. J. WALSH; circ. 19,000.

Nationalist and Leinster Times: 42 Tullow St, Carlow; tel. (503) 70100; fax (503) 31442; e-mail news@leinster-times.ie; f. 1883; weekly; Editor E. COFFEY; circ. 17,000.

Nationalist Newspaper: Queen St, Clonmel, Co Tipperary; tel. (52) 22211; fax (52) 25248; f. 1890; Thurs.; Editor TOM CORR; circ. 16,000.

The Northern Standard: The Diamond, Monaghan; tel. (47) 81867; fax (47) 72257; e-mail garysmyth@eircom.net; f. 1839; Fri.; Editor MARTIN SMYTH; circ. 15,000.

Offaly Express: Bridge St, Tullamore, Co Offaly; tel. (506) 21744; fax (506) 51930; e-mail lexpress@indigo.ie; internet www.rmbi.ie; weekly; Editor JOHN WHELAN; circ. 18,000 (with Leinster Express).

Roscommon Champion: Abbey St, Roscommon; tel. (903) 25051; fax (903) 25053; f. 1927; weekly; Editor PAUL HEALY; circ. 10,000.

Roscommon Herald: Boyle, Co Roscommon; tel. (79) 62622; fax (79) 62926; e-mail roherald@indigo.ie; internet www.unison.ie/ roscommon_herald; f. 1859; weekly; Editor CHRISTINA MCHUGH; circ. 17,000.

Sligo Champion: Wine St, Sligo; tel. (71) 69222; fax (71) 69040; e-mail sales@sligochampion.ie; internet www.unison.ie/ sligo_champion; f. 1836; Wed.; Editor S. FINN; circ. 15,300.

Southern Star: Ilen St, Skibbereen, Co Cork; tel. (28) 21200; fax (28) 21071; e-mail info@southernstar.ie; f. 1889; Sat.; Editor LIAM O'REGAN; circ. 16,000.

Sunday Business Post: 80 Harcourt St, Dublin 2; tel. (1) 6026000; fax (1) 6796496; e-mail sbpost@iol.ie; internet www.sbpost.ie; Editor DAMIEN KIBERD; circ. 42,000.

Sunday Independent: Independent House, 90 Middle Abbey St, Dublin 1; tel. (1) 7055333; fax (1) 7055779; e-mail sunday.letters@ independent.ie; internet www.independent.ie; f. 1905; Editor AENGUS FANNING; circ. 334,000.

Sunday Tribune: 15 Lower Baggot St, Dublin 2; tel. (1) 6615555; fax (1) 6615302; e-mail editorial@tribune.ie; internet www .tribune.ie; f. 1980; Editor MATT COOPER; circ. 89,000.

Sunday World: Newspaper House, 18 Rathfarnham Rd, Terenure, Dublin 6; tel. (1) 4063500; fax (1) 4901838; e-mail news@ sundayworld.com; internet www.sundayworld.com; f. 1973; Editor COLM MACGINTY; circ. 308,786.

Tipperary Star: Friar St, Thurles, Co Tipperary; tel. (504) 21122; fax (504) 21110; e-mail info@tipperarystar.ie; internet www .tipperarystar.ie; f. 1909; Wed.; Editor MICHAEL DUNDON; circ. 10,000.

Tuam Herald: Dublin Rd, Tuam, Co Galway; tel. (93) 24183; fax (93) 24478; e-mail editor@tuamherald.ie; f. 1837; Wed.; Editor DAVID BURKE; circ. 11,000.

Tullamore Tribune: Church St, Tullamore, Co Offaly; tel. (506) 46768; fax (506) 21927; e-mail tulltrib@eircom.net; f. 1978; Wed.; Editor G. J. SCULLY; circ. 10,000.

Waterford News & Star: 25 Michael St, Waterford; tel. (51) 874951; fax (51) 855281; e-mail editor@waterford-news.ie; f. 1848; Thurs.; Editor P. DOYLE; circ. 16,000.

Western People: Francis St, Ballina, Co Mayo; tel. (96) 21188; fax (96) 70208; e-mail wpeople@iol.ie; internet www.westernpeople.ie; f. 1883; Tues.; Editor TERENCE REILLY; circ. 24,000.

Westmeath Examiner: 19 Dominick St, Mullingar, Co Westmeath; tel. (44) 48426; fax (44) 40640; e-mail newsdesk@westmeath-examiner.ie; internet www.westmeath-examiner.ie; f. 1882; weekly; Man. Dir MARTIN NALLY; circ. 14,000.

Wicklow Times: 1 Eglinton Rd, Bray, Co Wicklow; tel. (1) 2869111; fax (1) 2869074; e-mail wicklowtimes@tinet.ie; fortnightly; Man. Editor SHAY FITZMAURICE; cir. 30,500.

SELECTED PERIODICALS

Banking Ireland: 50 Fitzwilliam Sq., Dublin 2; tel. (1) 6764587; fax (1) 6619781; f. 1898; quarterly; journal of the Inst. of Bankers in Ireland; Editor GERRY LAWLOR; circ. 15,500.

Business & Finance: 50 Fitzwilliam Sq., Dublin 2; tel. (1) 6764587; fax (1) 6619781; e-mail belenos@tinet.ie; internet www .businessandfinance.ie; f. 1964; weekly; Man. Editor JOHN MCGEE; circ. 11,000.

History Ireland: POB 695, James's St PO, Dublin 8; tel. (1) 4535730; fax (1) 4533234; e-mail historyireland@connect.ie; quarterly; Jt Editors HIRAM MORGAN, TOMMY GRAHAM.

Hot Press: 13 Trinity St, Dublin 2; tel. (1) 6795077; fax (1) 6795097; e-mail hotpress@iol.ie; internet www.hot-press.com; fortnightly; music, leisure, current affairs; Editor NIALL STOKES; circ. 21,000.

In Dublin: 3–7 Camden Place, Dublin 2; tel. (1) 4784322; fax (1) 4781055; f. 1976; fortnightly; listings and reviews of entertainments, restaurants; also news and current affairs; Editor ALANNA GALLAGHER; circ. 16,000.

Ireland Afloat: 2 Lower Glenageary Rd, Dún Laoghaire, Co Dublin; tel. (1) 2846161; fax (1) 2846192; e-mail info@afloat.ie; internet www.afloat.ie; monthly; sailing and boating; Man. Editor DAVID O'BRIEN; circ. 10,000.

Ireland's Own: Channing House, Rowe St, Wexford; tel. (53) 40140; f. 1902; weekly; family interest; Editors GERRY BREEN, PHILIP MURPHY; circ. 50,000.

The Irish Catholic: 55 Lower Gardiner St, Dublin 1; tel. (1) 8555619; fax (1) 8364805; e-mail icn@indigo.ie; weekly; Editor DAVID QUINN; circ. 30,000.

Irish Computer: CPG House, Glenageary Office Park, Dún Laoghaire, Co Dublin; tel. (1) 2847777; fax (1) 2847584; f. 1977; monthly; Editor DECLAN McCOLGAN; circ. 7,400.

Irish Farmers' Journal: Irish Farm Centre, Bluebell, Dublin 12; tel. (1) 4199500; fax (1) 4520876; e-mail editdept@farmersjournal.ie; f. 1948; weekly; Editor MATTHEW DEMPSEY; circ. 75,000.

Irish Field: 11–15 D'Olier St, POB 711, Dublin 2; tel. (1) 6792022; fax (1) 6791885; e-mail irish-field@irish-times.ie; f. 1870; weekly; horse racing, breeding and equine leisure; Man. Editor VALENTINE LAMB; circ. 11,788.

Irish Historical Studies: c/o Dept of Modern History, Trinity College, Dublin 2; tel. (1) 6081020; e-mail wvaughan@tcd.ie; 2 a year; Editors Dr CIARAN BRADY, Dr DAVID HAYTON.

Irish Journal of Medical Science: Royal Academy of Medicine in Ireland, 6 Kildare St, Dublin 2; tel. (1) 6767650; fax (1) 6611684; e-mail secretary@rami.iol.ie; quarterly; organ of the Royal Academy of Medicine; Editor THOMAS WALSH.

Irish Law Times (including Irish Law Log): Round Hall Sweet & Maxwell, Brehon House, 4 Upper Ormond Quay, Dublin 7; tel. (1) 8730101; fax (1) 8720078; e-mail terri.mcdonnell@itps.co.uk; f. 1983; 20 a year; Editor RAYMOND BYRNE.

Irish Medical Journal: 10 Fitzwilliam Place, Dublin 2; tel. (1) 6767273; fax (1) 6612758; e-mail imj@imj.ie; internet www.imj.ie; 10 a year; journal of the Irish Medical Org.; Editor Dr JOHN MURPHY; circ. 7,500.

The Irish Skipper: Taney Hall, Eglinton Terrace, Dublin 14; tel. (1) 2960000; fax (1) 2960383; e-mail gmills@maccommunications.ie; monthly; journal of the commercial fishing and aquaculture industries; Editor GILLIAN MILLS.

Irish University Review: Rm J210, University College, Belfield, Dublin 4; fax (1) 7061174; 2 a year; literature, history, fine arts, politics, cultural studies; Editor ANTHONY ROCHE.

Management: 52 Glasthule Rd, Sandycove, Co Dublin; tel. (1) 2800000; fax (1) 2801818; f. 1954; monthly; Editor SANDRA O'CONNELL; circ. 9,000.

Motoring Life: Cyndale Enterprises Ltd, 48 North Great George's St, Dublin 1; tel. (1) 8780444; fax (1) 8787740; f. 1946; monthly; Editor KEVIN FENIX; circ. 9,000.

PC Live!: Prospect House, 3 Prospect Rd, Glasnevin, Dublin 9; tel. (1) 8824444; fax (1) 8300888; e-mail info@scope.ie; internet www.techcentral.ie; monthly; computers and the internet; Editor STEPHEN CAWLEY; circ. 18,000.

Phoenix: 44 Lower Baggot St, Dublin 2; tel. (1) 6611062; fax (1) 6624532; e-mail phoenix@indigo.ie; internet www.phoenix-magazine .com; f. 1983; fortnightly; news and comment; Editor PADDY PRENDIVILLE; circ. 22,000.

RTE Guide: Radio Telefís Éireann, Donnybrook, Dublin 4; tel. (1) 2083146; fax (1) 2083085; weekly; programmes of the Irish broadcasting service; Editor HEATHER PARSONS; circ. 168,600.

Sportsworld: 48 North Great George's St, Dublin 1; tel. (1) 8780444; fax (1) 8787740; monthly; Editor DAVID GUINEY; circ. 23,000.

Studies: 35 Lower Leeson St, Dublin 2; tel. (1) 6766785; fax (1) 6762984; fax (1) 6762984; e-mail studies@s-j.ie; internet www .studiesirishreview.ie; f. 1912; quarterly review of letters, history, religious and social questions; Editor Fr NOEL BARBER.

U Magazine: 2 Clanwilliam Court, Lower Mount St, Dublin 2; tel. (1) 6623158; fax (1) 6619757; f. 1979; monthly; Editor ANNETTE O'MEARA; circ. 20,750.

Woman's Way: 2 Clanwilliam Court, Lower Mount St, Dublin 2; tel. (1) 6623158; fax (1) 6628719; f. 1963; weekly; Editor CELINE NAUGHTON; circ. 67,000.

The Word: Divine Word Missionaries, Donamon, Roscommon, tel. and fax (903) 62608; e-mail wordeditor@eircom.net; f. 1953; monthly; Catholic general interest; Editor Rev. THOMAS CAHILL; circ. 24,500.

NEWS AGENCIES

Ireland International News Agency: 51 Wellington Quay, Dublin 2; tel. (1) 6712442; fax (1) 6796586; e-mail iina@indigo.ie; Chair. TOM McPHAIL; Man. Dir DIARMAID MacDERMOTT.

Foreign Bureaux

Agenzia Nazionale Stampa Associata (ANSA) (Italy): 56 Greenfield Park, Knocklyon, Dublin 24; tel. (1) 4941389; fax (1) 4941300; e-mail enzo@iol.ie; Bureau Chief ENZO FARINELLA.

Informatsionnoye Telegrafnoye Agentstvo Rossii–Telegrafnoye Agentstvo Suverennykh Stran (ITAR–TASS) (Russia): 59 Glenbrook Park, Dublin; tel. (1) 2885513; Chief of Bureau EVGENY KLESHKOV.

Reuters Ireland: Kestrel House, Clanwilliam Place, Lower Mount St, Dublin 2; tel. (1) 5001550; fax (1) 5001551; Chief Correspondent KEITH WEIR.

Rossiiskoye Informatsionnoye Agentstvo—Novosti (RIA—Novosti) (Russia) is also represented.

PRESS ORGANIZATIONS

National Newspapers of Ireland: Clyde Lodge, 15 Clyde Rd, Dublin 4; tel. (1) 6689099; fax (1) 6689872; e-mail nni@ cullencommunications.ie; Chair. GAVIN O'REILLY; Co-ordinating Dir FRANK CULLEN.

Regional Newspapers Association of Ireland: Sheridan House, 33 Parkgate St, Dublin 8; tel. (1) 6779049; fax (1) 6779144; e-mail michelle@rnan.ie; internet www.rnan.ie; f. 1917; 37 mems; Pres. JACK DAVIS; CEO NEVILLE GALLOWAY.

Publishers

Anvil Books Ltd: 45 Palmerston Rd, Dublin 6; tel (1) 4973628; fax (1) 4968263; f. 1964; Irish history and biography, folklore, children's fiction (10 years and above); Dirs R. DARDIS, M. DARDIS.

Attic Press Ltd: Crawford Business Park, Crosses Green, Cork; tel. (21) 4321725; fax (21) 4315329; e-mail corkunip@ucc.ie; internet www.iol.ie/~atticirl; imprint of Cork University Press; Dirs SARA WILBOURNE, Prof. DES CLARKE.

Boole Press Ltd: Olympia House, 61–63 Dame St, POB 6271, Dublin 2; tel. (1) 6081507; fax (1) 6082282; e-mail jmiller@tcd.ie; f. 1979; scientific, technical, medical, scholarly; Man. Dir P. McKEEVER.

Butterworth Ireland Ltd: 26 Upper Ormond Quay, Dublin 7; tel. (1) 8731555; fax (1) 8731876; e-mail ircustomer@butterworths.co.uk; taxation and law; Chair. S. STOUT.

Comhairle Bhéaloideas Éireann (Folklore of Ireland Council): c/o Dept of Irish Folklore, University College, Belfield, Dublin 4; tel. (1) 693244; Editor Prof. SÉAMUS O'CATHÁIN.

Cork University Press: Crawford Business Park, Crosses Green, Cork; tel. (21) 4902980; fax (21) 4315329; e-mail corkunip@ucc.ie; internet www.corkuniversitypress.com; f. 1925; academic; Man. Dir SARA WILBOURNE.

Dominican Publications: 42 Parnell Sq., Dublin 1; tel. (1) 8731355; fax (1) 8731760; e-mail dompubs@iol.ie; f. 1897; religious affairs in Ireland and the developing world, pastoral-liturgical aids; Man. Rev. AUSTIN FLANNERY.

Dundalgan Press (W. Tempest) Ltd: Francis St, Dundalk, Co Louth; tel. (42) 9334013; fax (42) 9332351; e-mail info@dundalgen.ie; f. 1859; history and biography; Man. Dir GERARD GORMLEY.

C J Fallon: POB 1054, Lucan Rd, Palmerstown, Dublin 20; tel. (1) 6166400; fax (1) 6166499; e-mail cjfallon@iol.ie; internet www .cjfallon.ie; f. 1927; educational; Man. Dir H. J. McNICHOLAS.

Four Courts Press: Fumbally Lane, Dublin 8; tel. (1) 4534668; fax (1) 4534672; e-mail info@four-courts-press.ie; internet www.four .courts-press.ie; f. 1970; philosophy, theology, Celtic and Medieval studies, art, literature, modern history; Dirs MICHAEL ADAMS, MARTIN HEALY, GERARD O'FLAHERTY.

Gallery Press: Loughcrew, Oldcastle, Co Meath; tel. and fax (49) 8541779; e-mail gallery@indigo.ie; f. 1970; poetry, plays, prose by Irish authors; Editor PETER FALLON.

Gill and Macmillan Ltd: Goldenbridge, Inchicore, Dublin 8; tel. (1) 4531005; fax (1) 4541688; internet www.gillmacmillan.ie; f. 1968; literature, biography, history, mind, body and spirit, social sciences, theology, philosophy and textbooks; Man. Dir M. H. GILL.

Goldsmith Press: Newbridge, Co Kildare; tel. (45) 433613; fax (45) 434648; e-mail de@iol.ie; internet www.irishpoems.com; f. 1972; poetry, Irish art, plays, foreign language, general; Dirs DESMOND EGAN, VIVIENNE ABBOTT.

Irish Academic Press: 44 Northumberland Rd, Dublin 4; tel. (1) 6688244; fax (1) 6601610; e-mail info@iap.ie; internet www.iap.ie; f. 1974; academic, mainly history and Irish studies; Dirs FRANK CASS, MICHAEL ZAIDNER, STEWART CASS; Man. Ed. LINDA LONGMORE.

Lilliput Press: 62/63 Sitric Rd, Arbour Hill, Dublin 7; tel. (1) 6711647; fax (1) 6711233; e-mail lilliput@indigo.ie; internet indigo.ie/~lilliput; ecology and environment, literary criticism, biography, Irish history, general; Publr ANTONY FARRELL.

Mentor Books: 43 Furze Rd, Sandyford Industrial Estate, Dublin 18; tel. (1) 2952112; fax (1) 2952114; e-mail all@mentorbooks.ie; internet www.mentorbooks.ie; educational, general; Man. Dir DANIEL MCCARTHY.

Mercier Press Ltd: 5 French Church St, Cork; tel. (21) 4275040; fax (21) 4274969; e-mail books@mercier.ie; internet www.mercier.ie; f. 1946; Irish folklore, history, literature, art, politics, humour, music, religious; Chair. GEORGE EATON; Man. Dir JOHN F. SPILLANE.

O'Brien Educational Ltd: 20 Victoria Rd, Dublin 6; tel. (1) 4923333; fax (1) 4922777; e-mail books@obrien.ie; internet www.obrien.ie; f. 1974; biography, reference, children's, reference; Man. Dir MICHAEL O'BRIEN.

Poolbeg Press Ltd: 123 Baldoyle Industrial Estate, Dublin 13; tel. (1) 8321477; fax (1) 8321430; e-mail poolbeg@iol.ie; f. 1976; general, poetry, politics, children's; Man. Dir PHILIP MACDERMOTT.

Round Hall Ltd: 43 Fitzwilliam Place, Dublin 2; tel. (1) 6625301; fax (1) 6625302; e-mail enquiries@roundhall.ie; law books and journals; Dir ELANOR MCGARRY.

Royal Irish Academy: 19 Dawson St, Dublin 2; tel. (1) 6762570; fax (1) 6762346; e-mail admin@ria.ie; internet www.ria.ie; f. 1785; humanities and sciences; Exec. Sec. PATRICK BUCKLEY; Editor RACHEL MCNICHOLL.

Sáirséal–Ó Marcaigh: 13 Bóthar Chríoch Mhór, Dublin 11; tel. and fax (1) 8378914; books in Irish; Dirs AINGEAL Ó MARCAIGH, CAOIMHÍN Ó MARCAIGH.

Sporting Books: 4 Sycamore Rd, Mount Merrion, Co Dublin; tel. (1) 2887914; fax (1) 2885779; sports; Publr RAYMOND SMITH.

Town House/Country House: Trinity House, Charleston Rd, Dublin 6; tel. (1) 4972399; fax (1) 4970927; e-mail books@townhouse.ie; fiction, biography, art, environmental, general; Dirs TREASA COADY, JIM COADY.

Veritas Publications: 7–8 Lower Abbey St, Dublin 1; tel. (1) 8788177; fax (1) 8786507; e-mail publications@veritas.ie; internet www.veritas.ie; f. 1900; religious and educational; Dir MAURA HYLAND.

Wolfhound Press: 68 Mountjoy Sq., Dublin 1; tel. (1) 8740354; fax (1) 8720207; internet www.wolfhound.ie; f. 1974; literature, biography, art, children's, fiction, history; Publr SÉAMUS CASHMAN.

Woodtown Music Publications Ltd: Teach an Dáma, Stráid an Dáma, Dublin 2; tel. and fax (1) 6793664; f. 1966; original works by Irish composers; Chair. GARECH DE BRÚN.

Government Publishing House

Stationery Office: Government Supplies Agency, 4–5 Harcourt Rd, Dublin 2; tel. (1) 6613111; fax (1) 4780645.

PUBLISHERS' ASSOCIATION

Irish Book Publishers' Association: 43–44 Temple Bar, Dublin 2; tel. (1) 6707393; fax (1) 6707642; e-mail cle@iol.ie; internet www.publishingireland.com; f. 1970; 54 mems; Pres. SARA WILBOURNE; Exec. Dir ORLA MARTIN.

Broadcasting and Communications

TELECOMMUNICATIONS

Office of the Director of Telecommunications Regulation: Abbey Court, Irish Life Centre, Lower Abbey St, Dublin 1; tel. (1) 8049600; fax (1) 8049680; internet www.odtr.ie; f. 1997 as the regulatory authority for Ireland's telecommunication sector. Issues licences to service providers; manages the interconnection of telecommunications networks; approves equipment and oversees national telephone numbering; Dir ETAIN DOYLE.

Cable and Wireless Ltd: 1 Airton Rd, Tallaght, Dublin 24; tel. (1) 4346333; fax (1) 4346339; e-mail info@candw.ie; internet www.candw.ie; independent telecommunications services provider; supplies telecommunications equipment including video-conferencing systems and paging devices; Man. Dir EDDIE BRENNAN; Gen. Man. PAT MACGRATH.

EIRCELL: Unit 9, Richview Office Park, Dublin 14; tel. (1) 2037777; fax (1) 2037778; e-mail custcare@circell.ie; internet www.eircell.ie; a subsidiary of Vodafone Ltd (UK), providing national mobile telecommunications services.

eircom plc: St Stephen's Green West, Dublin 2; tel. (1) 6714444; fax (1) 6716916; e-mail press-office@eircom.ie; internet www.eircom.ie; f. 1984; frmly Telecom Éireann; nationalized body responsible for the provision of national and international telecommunications services, including mobile services; partially privatized in 1999; Chair. RAY MCSHARRY; CEO ALFIE KANE.

> **eircom net:** Unit B, East Point Business Park, Fairview, Dublin 3; tel. (1) 7010011; fax (1) 7010185; e-mail info@eircom.net;

internet www.eircom.net; f. 1996 to provide internet services to both business and private customers; Gen. Man. FINTAN LAWLEE.

ESAT Telecom: 1 Grand Canal Quay, Dublin 2; internet www.esat.ie; private telecommunication company; purchased by British Telecommunications PLC in January 2000; Chair. and Chief Exec. DENIS O'BRIEN.

BROADCASTING

The Radio and Television Act of 1988 provided for the establishment of an independent television station, an independent national radio service and a series of local radio stations (see below).

The Independent Radio and Television Commission (IRTC): Marine House, Clanwilliam Place, Dublin 2; tel (1) 6760966; fax (1) 6760948; e-mail info@irtc.ie; internet www.irtc.ie; f. 1988; established by the Govt to ensure the creation, development and monitoring of independent broadcasting in Ireland; operations are financed by levies paid by franchised stations; Chair. NIALL STOKES; CEO MICHAEL O'KEEFFE.

Broadcasting Complaints Commission: POB 913, Dublin 2, tel. (1) 6767571; f. 1997; responsible for acting upon complaints relating to material broadcast by RTE and local radio stations; Chair. RAY MURPHY.

Radio

Radio Telefís Éireann (RTE): Donnybrook, Dublin 4; tel. (1) 2083111; fax (1) 2083080; internet www.rte.ie; national broadcasting corpn, f. 1960; financed by net licence revenue and sale of advertising time, which is limited to 10% of transmission time; governed by Authority of nine mems, appointed by the GOA; operates six radio networks, Radio 1 (news, music, drama and variety shows), 2FM (popular music), Lyric FM (music, arts and culture), Raidió na Gaeltachta (see below), Radio OneWorld (multicultural programmes), and Radio Ceolnet (an internet only channel broadcasting traditional Irish music); Chair. of Authority Prof. FARREL CORCORAN; Dir-Gen. BOB COLLINS; Dir of Programmes (Radio) HELEN SHAW.

> **Raidió na Gaeltachta:** Casla, Connemara, Co Galway; tel. (91) 506677; fax (91) 506666; e-mail rnag@rte.ie; f. 1972; broadcasts a minimum of 115 hours per week in Irish language; financed by RTE; Controller TOMAS MAC CONIOMAIRE.

100-102 Today FM: 124 Upper Abbey St, Dublin 1, tel. (1) 8049000; fax (1) 8049099; e-mail 100-102@todayfm.com; internet www.todayfm.com; f. 1998; national, independent station; Chair. JOHN MCCOLGAN.

Dublin's 98 FM: The Malt House, Grand Canal Quay, Dublin 2; tel. (1) 6708989; fax (1) 6708969; e-mail online@98fm.ie; internet www.98fm.ie; provides news service to independent local radio stations under contract from the IRTC; Chair. DENIS O'BRIEN; Head of News JOHN KEOGH.

There are also local radio stations operating under the supervision of the Independent Radio and Television Commission.

Television

Radio Telefís Éireann (RTE): (see above); operates three television channels (RTE 1, Network 2 and TG4—an Irish language television service that began transmissions in November 1996; Chair. of Authority Prof. FARREL CORCORAN; Dir-Gen. BOB COLLINS: Dir of Programmes (Television) JOE MULHOLLAND.

TV3: Dublin; e-mail info@tv3; internet www.tv3.ie; f. 1998; first national, commercial, independent television network; Man. Dir and CEO RICK HETHERINGTON; Dir of Programming MATTHEW SALWAY.

Finance

(cap. = capital; p.u. = paid up; res = reserves;
dep. = deposits; m. = million; brs = branches;
amounts in Irish pounds (IR£) or euros (€) unless otherwise stated)

BANKING

Ireland participates in the European System of Central Banks which consists of the European Central Bank and the national central banks of all 15 EU Member States.

Central Bank

Bank Ceannais na hÉireann (Central Bank of Ireland): POB 559, Dame St, Dublin 2; tel. (1) 6716666; fax (1) 6716561; e-mail en@centralbank.ie; internet www.centralbank.ie; f. 1942; bank of issue; cap. and res €2,510m., dep. €7,015m. (Dec. 1999); Gov. MAURICE O'CONNELL; Dir-Gen. Dr PÁDRAIG MCGOWAN.

Principal Banks

ACCBANK PLC: Charlemont Place, Dublin 2; tel. (1) 4184000; fax (1) 4184444; e-mail info@accbank.ie; internet www.accbank.ie; f. 1927; state-owned; provides banking services to personal customers, small businesses, farmers and corporate entities; total assets €3,065m. (Dec. 1999); Chair. P. O'Connor; CEO C. Darling; 49 brs.

AIB Capital Markets PLC: AIB International Centre, IFSC, Dublin 1; tel. (1) 8740222; fax (1) 8741610; e-mail grouppa@iol.ie; internet www.aib.ie/capitalmarkets; f. 1966; merchant banking and investment management; cap. p.u. IR£ 8m., dep. IR£ 1,105m. (Dec. 1997); Chair. and Man. Dir Michael D. Buckley.

AIB Group: POB 452, Bankcentre, Ballsbridge, Dublin 4; tel. (1) 6600311; fax (1) 6609508; internet www.aib.ie; f. 1966; fmrly Allied Irish Banks PLC; cap. and res €2,201m., dep. €55,241m. (Dec. 1999); Chair. Lochlann Quinn; CEO Michael Buckley; 900 brs and offices.

Anglo Irish Bank Corporation PLC: 18–21 St Stephen's Green, Dublin 2; tel. (1) 6162000; fax (1) 6611852; e-mail anglo@iol.ie; internet www.angloirishbank.ie; f. 1964; cap. and res IR£ 261.1m., dep. IR£ 7,056.9m. (Sept. 1999); Chair. Anthony O'Brien; CEO Seán P. Fitzpatrick.

Anglo Irish Corporate Bank Ltd: Stephen Court, 18–21 St Stephen's Green, Dublin 2; tel. (1) 6162000; fax (1) 6611852; wholly-owned subsidiary of Anglo Irish Bank Corporation PLC; Chair. Seán P. Fitzpatrick.

Ansbacher Bankers Ltd: 18–21 St Stephen's Green, Dublin 2; tel. (1) 6613699; fax (1) 6618408; f. 1950; wholly-owned subsidiary of Anglo Irish Bank Corporation PLC; Chair. Seán P. Fitzpatrick.

Bank of Ireland Asset Management: 26 Fitzwilliam Place, Dublin 2; tel. (1) 6616433; fax (1) 6616688; f. 1966; investment management; auth. cap. 10m.; CEO William R. Cotter.

Bank of Ireland Group: Lower Baggot St, Dublin 2; tel. (1) 6615933; fax (1) 6615193; e-mail customer.care@ho.boi.ie; internet www.bankofireland.ie; f. 1783; cap. and res €1,769m., dep. €54,340m. (March 2000); Gov. Laurence Crowley; CEO Maurice A. Keane; 358 brs.

Bank of Scotland (Ireland) Ltd: 65-68 St Stephen's Green, Dublin 2; tel. (1) 4083500; fax (1) 4753220; e-mail info@bankofscotland.ie; internet www.bankofscotland.ie; f. 1965 as Equity Bank Ltd, name changed in 2000; cap. and res €80.4m., dep. €1,317.8m. (Feb. 2000); Chief Exec. Mark Duffy; 2 brs.

Barclays Bank PLC: 47/48 St Stephen's Green, Dublin 2; tel. (1) 6611777; fax (1) 6623141; internet www.barclays.com; total assets 569m. (Dec. 1996); Country Dir Paul Shovlin.

Bear Stearns Bank PLC: Harcourt Centre, Charlotte Way, Dublin 2; tel. (1) 4026200; fax (1) 4026237; e-mail plambert@bear.com; internet www.bearstearns.com; f. 1996; cap. and res. US $40.0m., dep. US $520.1m. (June 1998); Chair. Samuel Molinard.

BNP Paribas Dublin: 5 George's Dock, Dublin 1; tel. (1) 6125000; fax (1) 6125100; e-mail dublin.desk@bnpparibas.com; Chair. G. Lohier; Gen. Man. Michel de Vibraye.

BW Bank Ireland PLC: POB 4566, 6 George's Dock, IFSC, Dublin 1; tel. (1) 6701812; fax (1) 6701817; e-mail banking@bwbank.ie; f. 1994; cap. and res €94.6m., dep. €2,305.5m. (Dec. 1999); Chair. Dieter Maier; Man. Dir Bryan Higgins.

Chase Manhattan Bank (Ireland) PLC: Chase Manhattan House, International Financial Services Centre, Dublin 1; tel. (1) 6123000; fax (1) 6123123; internet www.chase.com; cap. and res US $30.1m., dep. US $597.4m. (Dec. 1997); in Sept. 2000 Chase Manhattan and J. P. Morgan agreed to merge to form J. P. Morgan Chase and Co; Man. Dir Frank Gaynor.

DePfa-Bank Europe PLC: 3 Harbourmaster Pl., IFSC, Dublin 1; tel. (1) 6071600; fax (1) 8290213; e-mail information@depfa.ie; internet www.depfa.com; cap. DM 500.2m., res DM 37,539.6m. (Dec. 1998); Chair. Gerhard Bruckermann; Man. Dir Dermot Cahillane.

Dresdner Bank (Ireland) PLC: La Touche House, IFSC, Dublin 1; tel. (1) 8181100; fax (1) 8181199; internet www.dresdner-bank.ie; f. 1995; commercial; subsidiary of Dresdner Bank (AG), Germany; total assets US $7,075.1m. (Dec. 1998); Gen. Mans Werner Schwanberg, Thomas Kiefer.

G E Capital Woodchester Bank Ltd: Woodchester House, Golden Lane, Dublin 8; tel. (1) 4780000; fax (1) 4781082; f. 1972; merchant banking; cap. and res IR£ 18.6m., dep. IR£ 1,070.2m. (Dec. 1997); Chair. Craig McKinney; 11 brs.

Guinness and Mahon (Ireland) Ltd: 56–59 St Stephen's Green, Dublin 2; tel. (1) 7095200; fax (1) 7095210; f. 1836; cap. and res IR£ 5.7m., dep. IR£ 69.3m. (Dec. 1996); Chair. and Man. Dir Brian McConnell.

GZ-Bank Ireland PLC: Trade Centre, IFSC, Dublin 1; tel. (1) 6700715; fax (1) 8290298; f. 1994 as SGZ (Ireland) PLC, name changed in 2000; e-mail info@gz-bank.ie; cap. €153.4., dep. €1,166.6m. (Dec. 1999); Man. Dirs Andreas Neugebauer, Mark Jacob.

ICC Bank PLC: 72–74 Harcourt St, Dublin 2; tel. (1) 4155555; fax (1) 6717797; e-mail info@icc.ie; internet www.icc.ie; f. 1933; privatized in 2000; industrial and commercial financing; cap. and res IR£ 40.4m., dep. IR£ 2,177.0m. (Oct. 1999); Chair. Phil Flynn; Man. Dir Michael Quinn; 6 brs.

IIB Bank Ltd: 91 Merrion Sq., Dublin 2; tel. (1) 6619744; fax (1) 6785034; e-mail info@iib-bank.ie; internet www.iib-bank.ie; f. 1973; subsidiary of Kredietbank NV, Belgium; merchant banking; cap. and res €221.2m., dep. €6,319.9m. (Dec. 1998); Chair. Patrick C. McEvoy; CEO Edward A. Marah.

Irish Life and Permanent PLC: Lower Abber St, Dublin 1; tel (1) 6615577; fax (1) 6615828; f. 1884 as Irish Temperance Building Society, name changed in 1999; e-mail info@irishpermanent.ie; internet www.irishpermanent.ie; cap and res IR£ 53.7m., dep. IR£ 5,887.9m. (Dec. 1998).

Lombard & Ulster Banking Ltd: Ulster Bank Group Centre, George's Quay, Dublin 2; tel. (1) 6085000; fax (1) 6085001; e-mail info@lombard.ie; internet www.lombard.ie; f. 1971; subsidiary of Ulster Bank Ltd; cap. p.u. 2.8m. (Dec. 1996); Chair. M. Rafferty; CEO B. Kingston; 13 brs.

National Irish Bank: 7/8 Wilton Terrace, Dublin 2; tel. (1) 6385000; fax (1) 6385198; f. 1986; subsidiary of National Australia Bank Group; cap. and res IR£ 1,715.6m. (Sept. 1998); Chair. Sir David Fell; CEO Don Price; 61 brs.

Pfizer International Bank Europe: La Touche House, IFSC, Dublin 1; tel. (1) 6700277; fax (1) 6700466; f. 1985; cap. US $410,000., dep. US $80.8m. (Nov. 1998); Pres. Frank E. Salerno; Man. Dir B. Michael Senior.

Rabobank Ireland Plc: George's Dock House, IFSC, Dublin 1; tel. (1) 6076100; fax (1) 6701724; e-mail liz.mansfield@dub.rabobank.com; internet www.rabobank-ireland.ie; f. 1994; corporate and investment banking; owned by Rabobank Nederland; cap. and res guilders 759.1m., dep. guilders 27,956.2m. (Dec. 1999); Chair. Wouter J. Kolff; Man. Dir Fergus Murphy.

Rheinhyp Bank Europe Plc: POB 4343, Commerzbank House, Guild St, 1 IFSC, Dublin 1; tel. (1) 6491600; fax (1) 6491659; e-mail rheinhyp@indigo.ie; f. 1994 as RHEINHYP Europe Plc, name changed in 1995; total assets €2,033m. (Dec. 1999); Chair. Dr Karsten von Köller; Man. Dir Christian Ferchland.

SGZ-Bank Ireland Plc: POB 4720, Trade Centre, International Financial Services Centre, Dublin 1; tel. (1) 6700715; fax (1) 8290298; e-mail sgz@iol.ie; f. 1994 as SGZ (Ireland) Plc, name changed in 1995; total assets DM 6,100m. (Dec. 1999); Gen. Mans Mark Jacob, Andreas Neugebauer.

Ulster Bank Ltd: 33 College Green, Dublin 2; tel. (1) 6777623; fax (1) 6775035; subsidiary of National Westminster Bank PLC (United Kingdom); cap. and res 115.9m., dep. 7,767.2m. (Dec. 1997); Chair. Sir George Quigley; CEO M. J. Wilson; 205 brs.

Ulster Bank Markets Ltd: Ulster Bank Group Centre, George's Quay, Dublin 2; tel. (1) 6084000; fax (1) 6084288; e-mail admin@ulsterbank.com; internet www.ulsterbank.com; f. 1973; subsidiary of Ulster Bank Ltd; total assets 5,061m. (Nov. 1998); Chair. Martin Rafferty; CEO Patrick M. McMahon.

UniCredito Italiano Bank (Ireland) PLC: La Touche House, IFSC, Dublin 1; tel. (1) 6702000; fax (1) 6702100; e-mail enquiry@creditodublin.ie; f. 1996 as Credito Italiano Bank (Ireland) PLC, name changed in 1999; cap. and res €413.2m., dep. €2,268.1m. (Dec. 1999); Chair. Brian J. Hillery; Man. Dir Franco Schepes.

Westdeutsche Landesbank (Ireland) PLC: 2 Harbourmaster Place, IFSC, Dublin 1; tel. (1) 6127199; fax (1) 6127107; e-mail info@westlb.ie; f. 1978 as Standard Chartered Bank Ireland Ltd, name changed in 1996; cap. and res DM 234.1m., dep DM 2,745.1m. (Dec. 1998); Chair. Dr W. A. Prautzsch; Man. Dir T. Kaiser.

Savings Banks

An Post Savings and Investments: College House, Townsend St, Dublin 2; tel. (1) 7057200; fax (1) 7057292; internet www.anpost.ie; f. 1861; dep. 3,040m. (Dec. 1994); Dir Terry Reynolds; 1,356 brs.

TSB Bank: TSB Corporate Centre, Blackrock, Co Dublin; tel. (1) 2124000; fax (1) 2124001; e-mail info@tsbbank.ie; internet www.tsbbank.ie; f. 1992; total assets IR£ 2,028.1m. (Dec. 1999); Chair. Finbarr Golden; CEO Harry W. Lorton; 80 brs.

Banking Associations

The Institute of Bankers in Ireland: Nassau House, Nassau St, Dublin 2; tel. (1) 6793311; fax (1) 6793504; e-mail instbank@indigo.ie; f. 1898; 15,000 mems; Pres. Martin J. Wilson; CEO Anthony Walsh.

Irish Bankers' Federation: Nassau House, Nassau St, Dublin 2; tel. (1) 6715311; fax (1) 6796680; e-mail ibf@ibf.ie; more than 50 mems; Pres. John Collins; Dir-Gen. James A. Bardon.

Irish Banks' Information Service: Nassau House, Nassau St, Dublin 2; tel. (1) 6715299; fax (1) 6796680; e-mail ibis@ibisis.iol.ie; internet www.iol.ie/ibis; Chair. Kevin Kelly; Man. Felix O'Regan.

STOCK EXCHANGE

The Irish Stock Exchange: 28 Anglesea St, Dublin 2; tel. (1) 6174200; fax (1) 6776045; f. 1799 as the Dublin Stock Exchange;

amalgamated in 1973 with the United Kingdom stock exchanges to form The International Stock Exchange of the United Kingdom and the Republic of Ireland; separated from The International Stock Exchange in 1995; operates independently under the supervision of the Central Bank of Ireland; Chair. D. KINGSTON; CEO TOM HEALY; 99 mems.

INSURANCE
Principal Companies

AXA PMPA Insurance Ltd: Wolfe Tone House, Wolfe Tone St, Dublin 1; tel. (1) 8721000; fax (1) 8721633; f. 1967; CEO G. P. N. HEALY.

Canada Life Assurance (Ireland) Ltd: Canada Life House, Temple Rd, Blackrock, Co Dublin; tel. (1) 2102000; fax (1) 210220; internet www.canadalife.ie; f. 1903; Man. Dir D. A. GALLAGHER.

Eagle Star Insurance: Eagle Star House, Ballsbridge Park, Dublin 2; tel. (1) 6770666; fax (1) 6670644; f. 1919; Man. Dir IAN C. STUART.

Eagle Star Life Assurance Co (Ireland) Ltd: Eagle Star House, Frascati Rd, Blackrock, Co Dublin; tel. (1) 2831301; fax (1) 2831578; f. 1950; Man. Dir M. J. BRENNAN.

Hansard Europe Ltd: POB 43, Enterprise House, Frascati Rd, Blackrock, Co Dublin; tel. (1) 2112800; fax (1) 2112850.

Hibernian Group PLC: Haddington Rd, Dublin 4; tel. (1) 6078000; fax (1) 6608730; f. 1908; life and general; Chair. J. P. CULLITON; CEO A. D. DALY.

Irish Life PLC: Irish Life Centre, Lower Abbey St, Dublin 1; tel. (1) 7042000; fax (1) 7041900; f. 1939; financial services; Chair. CONOR MCCARTHY; Man. Dir DAVID WENT.

Lifetime Assurance Co Ltd: Lifetime House, Lower Baggot St, Dublin 2; tel. (1) 7039500; fax (1) 6620811; f. 1987; life; Chair. HENRY J. BYRNE; Man. Dir ROY KEENAN.

New Ireland Assurance Co PLC: 11–12 Dawson St, Dublin 2; tel. (1) 6172000; fax (1) 6172800; e-mail info@newireland.ie; internet www.newireland.ie; f. 1924; Chair. and Man. Dir JOHN F. CASEY.

Royal & SunAlliance: 13–17 Dawson St, Dublin 2; tel. (1) 6771851; fax (1) 6717625; Gen. Man. PAUL DONALDSON.

Standard Life Assurance Co: 90 St Stephen's Green, Dublin 2; tel. (1) 6397000; fax (1) 6397262; f. 1834; life assurance, pensions, investments and annuities; Gen. Man. ALAN S. ASHE.

Zurich Insurance Co: Eagle Star House, Ballsbridge Park, Ballsbridge, Dublin 4; tel. (1) 6670666; fax (1) 6670644; property, liability, motor; Man. P. A. CASSIDY.

Insurance Associations

Insurance Institute of Ireland: 39 Molesworth St, Dublin 2; tel. (1) 6772582; fax (1) 6772621; e-mail iii@iol.ie; internet www.insurance-institute.ie; f. 1885; Pres. BILL HANNAN; CEO DENIS HEVEY; 4,000 mems.

Irish Brokers' Association: 87 Merrion Sq., Dublin 2; tel. (1) 6613067; fax (1) 6619955; e-mail iba@iol.ie; internet www.irishbrokers.com; Pres. KIERAN KELLY; 600 mems.

Irish Insurance Federation: Insurance House, 39 Molesworth St, Dublin 2; tel. (1) 6761820; fax (1) 6761943; e-mail fed@iif.ie; Pres. JOHN O'HANRON; CEO MICHAEL KEMP.

Trade and Industry

GOVERNMENT AGENCIES

An Post (The Post Office): General Post Office, Dublin 1; tel. (1) 7057000; fax (1) 8723553; e-mail press-office@anpost.ie; internet www.anpost.ie; f. 1984; provides national postal, savings and agency services through c. 2,000 outlets; Chair. STEPHEN O'CONNOR; CEO JOHN HYNES.

FÁS—Foras Áiseanna Saothair (Training and Employment Authority): 27–33 Upper Baggot St, Dublin 4; tel. (1) 6070500; fax (1) 6070600; e-mail info@fas.ie; internet www.fas.ie; f. 1988; responsible for the provision of specific skills training, apprenticeships and traineeships, employment programmes; supports co-operative and community enterprise; offers an industrial advisory service; public recruitment service at all levels of occupations; Chair. BRIAN GEOGHEGAN; Dir-Gen. JOHN J. LYNCH.

FORFÁS: Wilton Park House, Wilton Place, Dublin 2; tel. (1) 6073000; fax (1) 6073030; e-mail forfas@forfas.ie; internet www.forfas.ie; f. 1993 to provide advice and to co-ordinate national industrial and technological policy; co-ordinates Enterprise Ireland and IDA Ireland (see below); Chair. TOM TONER; Chief Exec. JOHN TRAVERS.

National Economic and Social Council—NESC: First Floor, Frederick House, 19 South Frederick St, Dublin 2; tel. (1) 6713155; fax (1) 6713589; e-mail info@nesc.ie; internet www.nesc.ie; f. 1973; analyses and reports on strategic issues relating to the efficient development of the economy and the achievement of social justice; Dir Dr SÍLE O'CONNOR.

DEVELOPMENT ORGANIZATIONS

Enterprise Ireland: Wilton Park House, Wilton Place, Dublin 2; tel. (1) 8082000; fax (1) 8082020; internet www.enterprise-ireland.com; brings together An Bord Tráchtála, Forbairt and the in-company training activities of FAS (see above); Chair. PATRICK J. MOLLOY; CEO DAN FLINTER.

An Bord Tráchtála (Irish Trade Board): Merrion Hall, Strand Rd, Sandymount, Dublin 4; tel. (1) 2066000; fax (1) 2066400; internet www.irish-trade.ie; f. 1991; assists Irish firms to establish sustainable markets in Ireland and abroad; 23 overseas offices; Chair. SEÁN MURRAY; CEO OLIVER TATTAN.

Forbairt: Wilton Park House, Wilton Place, Dublin 2; tel. (1) 8082000; fax (1) 8082020; f. 1993; state-sponsored organization responsible for encouraging technological development of Irish industry; Chair. EILEEN O'MARA WALSH; CEO DAN FLINTER.

Industrial Development Agency (IDA Ireland): Wilton Park House, Wilton Place, Dublin 2; tel. (1) 6034000; fax (1) 6034040; e-mail idaireland@ida.ie; internet www.idaireland.com; f. 1993; state-sponsored organization responsible for the encouragement of foreign investment in Irish industrial development; administers financial incentive schemes; 19 overseas offices; Chair. DENIS HANRAHAN; CEO KIERAN MCGOWAN.

Irish Productivity Centre: IPC House, 42–47 Lower Mount St, Dublin 2; tel. (1) 6623233; fax (1) 6623300; e-mail finnob@ipc.ie; aims to increase industrial productivity in Ireland; its council is composed of representatives from the Irish Business and Employers' Confed. and the Irish Congress of Trade Unions in equal numbers; offers consultancy services and practical assistance to Irish cos; Chair. S. MCCARTHY; CEO TOM MCGUINNESS.

Teagasc (Agriculture and Food Development Authority): 19 Sandymount Ave, Dublin 4; tel. (1) 6376000; fax (1) 6688023; e-mail pr@hq.teagasc.ie; internet www.teagasc.ie; f. 1988; provides advisory, research, educational and training services to agri-food sector and rural communities; Chair. Dr TOM O'DWYER; Nat. Dir Dr LIAM DOWNEY.

CHAMBERS OF COMMERCE

The Chambers of Commerce of Ireland: 22 Merrion Sq., Dublin 2; tel. (1) 6612888; fax (1) 6612811; e-mail chambers@iol.ie; internet www.chambersireland.ie; f. 1923; represents c. 10,000 businesses and 40 direct corporate mems; Pres. PHILIP O'REILLY; Chief Exec. SIMON NUGENT.

Cork Chamber of Commerce: Fitzgerald House, Summerhill North, Cork; tel. (21) 4509044; fax (21) 4508568; e-mail info@corkchamber.ie; internet www.corkchamber.ie; f. 1819; Pres. JOHN CASHELL; Chief Exec. MICHAEL GEARY.

Dublin Chamber of Commerce: 7 Clare St, Dublin 2; tel. (1) 6614111; fax (1) 6766043; e-mail info@dubchamber.ie; internet www.dubchamber.ie; f. 1783; Pres. JIM RUANE.

INDUSTRIAL AND TRADE ASSOCIATIONS

Construction Industry Federation: Construction House, Canal Rd, Dublin 6; tel. (1) 4977487; fax (1) 4966953; e-mail cif@indigo.ie; 33 asscns representing 3,000 mems; Pres. JOE TIERNAN; Dir-Gen. LIAM B. KELLEHER.

Irish Creamery Milk Suppliers' Association (ICMSA): John Feely House, 15 Upper Mallow St, Limerick; tel. (61) 314677; fax (61) 315737; e-mail icmsa@eircom.net; f. 1950; Pres. FRANK ALLEN; Gen. Sec. CIARAN DOLAN.

Irish Farmers' Association (IFA): Irish Farm Centre, Bluebell, Dublin 12; tel. (1) 4500266; fax (1) 4551043; e-mail ifapress@indigo.ie; Pres. TOM PARLON; Gen. Sec. MICHAEL BERKEREY.

Irish Fishermen's Organisation Ltd: Cumberland House, Fenian St, Dublin 2; tel. (1) 6612400; fax (1) 6612424; f. 1974; Chair. J. V. MADDOCK; Sec.-Gen. J. F. DOYLE.

Irish Grain and Feed Association: 18 Herbert St, Dublin 2; tel. (1) 6760680; fax (1) 6616774; e-mail igfa@cereal.iol.ie; Pres. S. GORMLEY; Dir S. A. FUNGE.

EMPLOYERS' ORGANIZATIONS

Irish Business and Employers Confederation (IBEC): Confederation House, 84–86 Lower Baggot St, Dublin 2; tel. (1) 6601011; fax (1) 6601717; internet www.iol.ie/ibec; f. 1993; represents c. 7,000 cos and orgs; Pres. RICHARD BURROW; Dir-Gen. JOHN DUNNE.

Irish Exporters Association: 28 Merrion Sq., Dublin 2; tel. (1) 6612182; fax (1) 6612315; e-mail iea@irishexporters.ie; internet www.irishexporters.ie; Pres. BRENDAN FARRELL; CEO JOHN WHELAN.

UTILITIES
Electricity
Electricity Supply Board: Lower Fitzwilliam St, Dublin 2; tel. (1) 6765831; fax (1) 6760727; internet www.esb.ie; f. 1927, reorg. 1988; operates 26 generating stations and manages the transmission and distribution of Ireland's electricity; Chair. W. M. McCann; CEO K. O'Hara.

Gas
Bord Gáis Éireann (BGE) (The Irish Gas Board): POB 51, Gasworks Rd, Co Cork; tel. (21) 4524000; fax (21) 4524240; internet www.bordgais.com; f. 1976; natural gas transmission and distribution; Chair. Michael N. Conlon; CEO Gerry Walsh.

Water
Dept of the Environment: Custom House, Dublin 1; tel. (1) 8882479; fax (1) 8882576; e-mail press-office@environ.irlgov.ie; internet www.environ.ie; responsiblity for water supply.

CO-OPERATIVES
Irish Co-operative Organisation Society Ltd: 84 Merrion Sq., Dublin 2; tel. (1) 6764783; fax (1) 6624502; f. 1894 to co-ordinate the co-operative movement; three operating divisions; offices in Dublin, Cork, Sligo and Brussels, Belgium; Pres. Dessie Boylan; Dir-Gen. John Tyrrell; mems: 130 co-operatives representing c. 175,000 farmers.

Irish Dairy Board: Grattan House, Lower Mount St, Dublin 2; tel. (1) 6619599; fax (1) 6612778; e-mail idb@idb.ie; internet www .idb.ie; f. 1961, reorg. 1973 as a famers' co-operative; principal exporter of Irish dairy products; Chair. Thomas Cleary; Man. Dir Noel Cawley.

TRADE UNIONS
Central Organization
Irish Congress of Trade Unions (ICTU): 31–32 Parnell Sq., Dublin 1; tel. (1) 8897777; fax (1) 8872012; e-mail congress@ictu.ie; internet www.ictu.ie; f. 1894; represents 738,000 workers in 63 affiliated unions in the Republic and Northern Ireland (1999); Gen. Sec. Peter Cassells.

Principal Trade Unions Affiliated to the ICTU
*__Amalgamated Engineering and Electrical Union, AEU Section:__ 26–34 Antrim Rd, Belfast, Northern Ireland, BT15 2AA; tel. (28) 90743271; f. 1992 by merger; Irish Rep. P. Williamson; 24,472 mems (2000).

*__Amalgamated Transport and General Workers' Union:__ Transport House, 102 High St, Belfast, Northern Ireland, BT1 2DL; tel. (28) 90232381; fax (28) 90240133; Irish Regional Sec. M. O'Reilly; 48,541 mems (2000).

Association of Higher Civil and Public Servants: 4 Warner's Lane, Dartmouth Rd, Dublin 6; tel. (1) 6686077; fax (1) 6680380; e-mail info@ahcps.ie; Gen. Sec. S. Ó Riordáin; 2,400 mems (2000).

Association of Secondary Teachers, Ireland (ASTI): ASTI House, Winetavern St, Dublin 8; tel. (1) 6040160; fax (1) 6719280; e-mail info@asti.ie; internet www.asti.ie; Gen. Sec. C. Lennon; 16,500 mems (2000).

*__Association of Teachers and Lecturers:__ c/o University of Ulster, 11b Coleraine Campus, Coleraine; Irish Rep. P. Quinn.

Building and Allied Trades' Union: Arus Hibernia, 13 Blessington St, Dublin 7; tel. (1) 8301911; fax (1) 8304869; Gen. Sec. Patrick O'Shaughnessy; 9,030 mems (2000).

Civil and Public Service Union: 19–20 Adelaide Rd, Dublin 2; tel. (1) 6765394; Gen. Sec. B. Horan; 13,600 mems (2000).

Communications Workers' Union: Áras Ghaibréil, 575 North Circular Rd, Dublin 1; tel. (1) 8366388; fax (1) 8365582; f. 1922; Gen. Sec. Con Scanlon; 19,600 mems (2000).

Electricity Supply Board Officers' Association: 43 East James's Place, Lower Baggot St, Dublin 2; tel. (1) 6767444; fax (1) 6789226; f. 1959; Gen. Sec. Willie Cremins; 2,020 mems (2000).

Federated Union of Government Employees: 32 Parnell Sq., Dublin 1; tel. (1) 8787057; 1,300 mems (2000).

*__Graphical, Paper and Media Union:__ 107 Clonskeagh Rd, Dublin 6; tel. (1) 2697788; fax (1) 2839977; Irish Rep. E. A. Kirkpatrick; 7,499 mems (2000).

Irish Bank Officials' Association: 93 St Stephen's Green, Dublin 2; tel. (1) 4755908; fax (1) 4780567; e-mail iboa@eircom.net; ; Gen. Sec. Ciaran Ryan; 16,807 mems (2000).

Irish Medical Organization: 10 Fitzwilliam Place, Dublin 2; tel. (1) 6767273; fax (1) 6612758; e-mail imo@iol.ie; CEO George McNeice; 4,300 mems (2000).

Irish Municipal, Public and Civil Trade Union (IMPACT): Nerney's Court, Dublin 1; tel. (1) 8171500; fax (1) 8171501; e-mail bharbor@impact.ie; internet www.impact.ie; f. 1991; Gen. Sec. Peter McLoone; 40,000 mems (2000).

Irish National Teachers' Organization: 35 Parnell Sq., Dublin 1; tel. (1) 8722533; fax (1) 8722462; e-mail info@into.ie; internet www.into.ie; f. 1868; Gen. Sec.Joe O'Toole; 28,330 mems (2000).

Irish Nurses' Organization: 11 Fitzwilliam Place, Dublin 2; tel. (1) 6760137; fax (1) 6610466; e-mail libinfo@ino.ie; Gen. Sec. Liam Doran; 27,391 mems (2000).

*__National Union of Journalists (Irish Executive Council):__ Liberty Hall, 9th Floor, Dublin 1; tel. (1) 8053258; fax (1) 8749250; e-mail liberty.hall@nuj.ie; Irish Rep. E. Ronayne; 3,833 mems (2000).

Prison Officers' Association: 18 Merrion Sq., Dublin 2; tel. (1) 6625495; Gen. Sec. John Clinton; 3,000 mems (2000).

Public Service Executive Union: 30 Merrion Sq., Dublin 2; tel. (1) 6767271; fax (1) 6615777; e-mail pseu@iol.ie; f. 1890; Gen. Sec. D. Murphy; 8,000 mems (2000).

Services, Industrial Professional and Technical Union (SIPTU): Liberty Hall, Dublin 1; tel. (1) 8749731; fax (1) 8749368; e-mail siptu@iol.ie; f. 1990; Gen. Pres. Des Geraghty; Gen. Sec. John McDonnell; 201,002 mems (2000).

Teachers' Union of Ireland: 73 Orwell Rd, Rathgar, Dublin 6; tel. (1) 4922588; fax (1) 4922953; e-mail tui@aonad.iol.ie; internet www.tui.ie; f. 1955; Gen. Sec. James Dorney; 10,593 mems (2000).

Technical, Engineering and Electrical Union: 5 Cavendish Row, Dublin 1; tel. (1) 8747047; fax (1) 8747048; f. 1992; Gen. Sec. Owen Wills; 30,396 mems (2000).

*__Transport Salaried Staffs' Association:__ Nerney's Court, off Temple St, Dublin 1; tel. (1) 8743467; fax (1) 8745662; f. 1897; Sec. Rodger Hannon; 1,812 mems (2000).

*__Ulster Teachers' Union:__ 94 Malone Rd, Belfast BT9 5HP; tel. (28) 90662216; Gen. Sec. Ray Calvin.

*__Union of Construction, Allied Trades and Technicians:__ 56 Parnell Sq. West, Dublin 1; tel. (1) 8731599; Regional Sec. Jim Moore; 13,760 mems (2000).

Union of Retail, Bar and Administrative Workers (MANDATE): O'Lehane House, 9 Cavendish Row, Dublin 1; tel. (1) 8746321; fax (1) 8729581; e-mail mandate@mandate.ie; f. 1994; Gen. Sec. Owen Nulty; 37,892 mems (2000).

*These unions have their head office in the United Kingdom. Membership figures relate jointly to the Republic of Ireland and Northern Ireland.

Unions not Affiliated to the ICTU
Chartered Institute of Journalists (Irish Region): EETPU Section, 5 Whitefriars, Aungier St, Dublin 2; tel. (1) 4784141; fax (1) 4750131; e-mail wims@journalism.com; internet www.cioj.dircon .co.uk; Chair. (Ireland) James Wims.

National Bus and Rail Union: 54 Parnell Sq., Dublin 1; tel. (1) 8730411; fax (1) 8730137; Gen. Sec. Peter Bunting.

Transport
Córas Iompair Éireann (CIE) (The Irish Transport Co): Heuston Station, Dublin 8; tel. (1) 6771871; fax (1) 7032276; f. 1945, reorg. 1986; state corpn operating rail and road transport services; three operating cos: Iarnród Éireann (Irish Rail), Bus Éireann (Irish Bus) and Bus Atha Cliath (Dublin Bus); Chair. Brian A. Joyce; CEO Michael P. McDonnell.

RAILWAYS
In 1996 there were 1,872 km of track, of which 37 km were electrified. Railway services are operated by Iarnród Éireann.

Iarnród Éireann (Irish Rail): Connolly Station, Dublin 1; tel. (1) 8363333; fax (1) 8364760; e-mail info@irishrail.ie; internet www .irishrail.ie; f. 1987; division of CIE; Chair. Michael P. McDonnell; Man. Dir Joe Meagher.

INLAND WATERWAYS
The Grand and Royal Canals and the canal link into the Barrow Navigation system are controlled by CIE. The Grand Canal and Barrow are open to navigation by pleasure craft, and the rehabilitation and restoration of the Royal Canal is proceeding. The River Shannon, which is navigable from Limerick to Lough Allen, includes stretches of the Boyle, Suck, Camlin, and Inny Rivers, the Erne Navigation, and the Shannon-Erne Waterway. The total length of Irish navigable waterways is about 700 km. A further 10 km of the Suck and Boyle Rivers were due to be opened to navigation in 1998/99.

ROADS

At 31 December 1996 there were an estimated 92,500 km of roads, of which 5,270 km were main roads. About 94% of all roads were surfaced.

National Roads Authority: St Martin's House, Waterloo Rd, Dublin 4; tel. (1) 6602511; fax (1) 6680009; internet www.nra.ie; f. 1994; responsible for the planning, supervision and maintenance of nat. road network; Chair. LIAM CONNELLAN; CEO MICHAEL TOBIN.

SHIPPING

The principal sea ports are Dublin, Dún Laoghaire, Cork, Waterford, Rosslare, Limerick, Foynes, Galway, New Ross, Drogheda, Dundalk, Fenit and Whiddy Island.

Arklow Shipping Ltd: North Quay, Arklow, Co Wicklow; tel. (402) 39901; fax (402) 39902; Man. Dir JAMES S. TYRELL; 9 carriers.

Dublin Shipping Ltd: Shrewsbury House, Cabinteely, Dublin 18; tel. (1) 2350122; fax (1) 2847612; Chair. D. R. HUSSEY; Man. Dir EUGENE GIBNEY; 3 tankers.

Irish Continental Group PLC: Ferryport, Alexandra Rd, POB 19, Dublin 1; tel. (1) 6075628; fax (1) 8552268; e-mail info@icg.ie; internet www.icg.ie; controls Irish Ferries, operating passenger vehicle and roll-on/roll-off freight ferry services between Ireland, the United Kingdom and continental Europe; Chair. T. TONER; Man. Dir E. ROTHWELL.

Irish Ferries: Ferryport, Alexandra Rd, POB 19, Dublin 1; tel. (1) 8552222; fax (1) 8552272; e-mail info@irishferries.ie; internet www.irishferries.ie; drive-on/drive-off car ferry and roll-on/roll-off freight services between Ireland, the United Kingdom and continental Europe, operating up to 109 sailings weekly; Group Man. Dir E.ROTHWELL.

Stena Line: Ferry Terminal, Dún Laoghaire Harbour, Co Dublin; tel. (1) 2047700; fax (1) 2047620; e-mail info.ie@stenaline.com; internet www.stenaline.ie; services between Dún Laoghaire and Dublin Port and Holyhead including high-speed catamaran, Rosslare and Fishguard, Belfast and Stranraer, passengers, drive-on/drive-off car ferry, roll-on/roll-off freight services.

Associations

Irish Chamber of Shipping: 5 Clanwilliam Sq., Grand Canal Quay, Dublin 2; tel. (1) 6618211; fax (1) 6618270; e-mail bks@iol.ie; Pres. ALEX MULLIN; Dir B. W. KERR.

Irish Ship Agents' Association: Ormonde House, 26 Harbour Row, Cobh, Co Cork; tel. (21) 813180; fax (21) 811849; e-mail isaa@tinet.ie; Pres.WILL LENNON; Sec. Lt-Commdr LIAM SMITH.

CIVIL AVIATION

There are international airports at Shannon, Dublin, Cork and Knock (Horan International), but only Shannon and Knock are used for transatlantic flights. The national airline is Aer Lingus.

Aer Rianta (Irish Airports Authority): Dublin Airport, Dublin; tel. (1) 8141111; fax (1) 8445113; internet www.aer-rianta.com; state-controlled; responsible for the management and development of Dublin, Shannon and Cork airports; also operates seven hotels in Ireland and manages duty-free retail shops in several overseas locations; Chair. NOEL HANLON; CEO JOHN BURKE.

Airlines

Aer Lingus Group PLC: Dublin Airport, Dublin; tel. (1) 7052222; fax (1) 7053832; internet www.aerlingus.ie; f. 1936, reorg. 1993; state-owned; domestic and international scheduled services; Chair. BERNIE CAHILL; CEO GARRY CULLEN.

Aer Turas Teoranta: Corballis Park, Dublin Airport, Dublin; tel. (1) 8444131; fax (1) 8446049; e-mail aerturasdublin@tinet.ie; f. 1962; world-wide cargo and passenger charter services; Chair. JOHN J. HARNETT; CEO PATRICK J. COUSINS.

Ryanair: Dublin Airport, Dublin; tel. (1) 8444489; fax (1) 8444402; internet www.ryanair.ie; f. 1985; scheduled and charter passenger services; Chair. DAVID BONDERMAN; CEO MICHAEL O'LEARY.

Tourism

Intensive marketing campaigns have been undertaken in recent years to develop new markets for Irish tourism. In addition to many sites of historic and cultural interest, the country has numerous areas of natural beauty, notably the Killarney Lakes and the west coast. In 1999 a total of 6.07m. foreign tourists (excluding residents of Northern Ireland and excursionists) visited the Republic.

Bord Fáilte Éireann (Irish Tourist Board): Baggot St Bridge, Dublin 2; tel. (1) 6024000; fax (1) 6024100; e-mail user@irishtouristboard.ie; internet www.ireland.travel.ie; f. 1955; Chair. MARK MORTELL; Chief Exec. JOHN DULLY.

Dublin Regional Tourism Authority Ltd: Suffolk St, Dublin 2; tel. (1) 6057700; fax (1) 6057757; e-mail reservations@dublintourism.ie; internet www.visitdublin.com; Chair. MICHAEL FLOOD; CEO FRANK MAGEE.

Irish Tourist Industry Confederation: Alliance House, Adelaide St, Dún Laoghaire, Co Dublin; tel. (1) 2844222; fax (1) 2804218; represents all major commercial tourism interests; Chair. DAVID BUNWORTH; CEO BRENDAN LEAHY.

Irish Travel Agents' Association: Heaton House, 3rd Floor, 32 South William St, Dublin 2; tel. (1) 6794089; fax (1) 6719897; e-mail info@itaa.ie; internet www.itaa.ie; f. 1971; 340 mems; Pres. FERGUS KILKELLY; CEO BRENDAN MORAN.

ISRAEL

Introductory Survey

Location, Climate, Language, Religion, Flag, Capital

The State of Israel lies in western Asia, occupying a narrow strip of territory on the eastern shore of the Mediterranean Sea. The country also has a narrow outlet to the Red Sea at the northern tip of the Gulf of Aqaba. All of Israel's land frontiers are with Arab countries, the longest being with Egypt to the west and with Jordan to the east. Lebanon lies to the north, and Syria to the north-east. The climate is Mediterranean, with hot, dry summers, when the maximum temperature in Jerusalem is generally between 30°C and 35°C (86°F to 95°F), and mild, rainy winters, with a minimum temperature in the city of about 5°C (41°F). The climate is sub-tropical on the coast but more extreme in the Negev Desert, in the south, and near the shores of the Dead Sea (a lake on the Israeli-Jordanian frontier), where the summer temperature may exceed 50°C (122°F). The official language of Israel is Hebrew, spoken by about two-thirds of the population, including most Jews. About 15% of Israeli residents, including Muslim Arabs, speak Arabic (which is also the language spoken by the inhabitants of the Occupied Territories and the Emerging Palestinian Autonomous Areas), while many European languages are also spoken. About 79% of the population profess adherence to Judaism, the officially recognized religion of Israel, while about 15% are Muslims. The national flag (proportions 11 by 8) has a white background, with a six-pointed blue star composed of two overlapping triangles (the 'Shield of David') between two horizontal blue stripes near the upper and lower edges. Although the Israeli Government has designated the city of Jerusalem (part of which is Jordanian territory annexed by Israel in 1967) as the country's capital, this is not recognized by the UN, and most foreign governments maintain their embassies in Tel-Aviv.

Recent History

The Zionist movement, launched in Europe in the 19th century, aimed at the re-establishment of an autonomous community of Jews in their historical homeland of Palestine (the 'Promised Land'). The growth of Zionism was partly due to the insecurity felt by Jewish minorities in many European countries as a result of racial and religious discrimination and persecution, known as anti-semitism.

Palestine, long inhabited by Arabs, became a part of Turkey's Ottoman Empire in the 16th century. During the First World War the Arabs under Ottoman rule rebelled. Palestine was occupied by British forces in 1917–18, when the Turks withdrew. In November 1917 the British Foreign Secretary, Arthur Balfour, declared British support for the establishment of a Jewish national home in Palestine, on condition that the rights of 'the existing non-Jewish communities' there were safeguarded. This so-called Balfour Declaration was confirmed by the governments of other countries then at war with Turkey. British occupation of Palestine continued after the war, when the Ottoman Empire was dissolved. In 1920 the territory was formally placed under British administration by a League of Nations mandate, which incorporated the Balfour Declaration. British rule in Palestine was hampered by the conflict between the declared obligations to the Jews and the rival claims of the indigenous Arab majority. In accordance with the mandate, Jewish settlers were admitted to Palestine (whose population in 1919 was almost entirely Arab), but only on the basis of limited annual quotas. There was serious anti-Jewish rioting by Arabs in 1921 and again in 1929. Attempts to restrict immigration led to Jewish-sponsored riots in 1933. The extreme persecution of Jews by Nazi Germany caused an increase in the flow of Jewish immigrants, both legal and illegal, which intensified the unrest in Palestine. In 1937 a British proposal to establish separate Jewish and Arab states, while retaining a British-mandated area, was accepted by most of the Zionists but rejected by the Arabs, and by the end of that year hostilities between the two communities had descended into open conflict. A British scheme offering eventual independence for a bi-communal Palestinian state was postponed because of the Second World War. During the war the Nazis caused the deaths of an estimated 6m. Jews in central and eastern Europe, more than one-third of the world's total Jewish population.

The enormity of the Holocaust greatly increased international sympathy for Jewish claims to a homeland in Palestine.

After the war there was strong opposition by Palestinian Jews to continued British occupation. Numerous terrorist attacks were made by Jewish groups against British targets. In November 1947 the UN approved a plan for the partition of Palestine into two states, one Jewish (covering about 56% of the area) and one Arab. The plan was, however, rejected by Arab states and by the leadership of the Palestinian Arabs. Meanwhile, the conflict between the two communities in Palestine escalated into full-scale war.

On 14 May 1948 the United Kingdom terminated its Palestine mandate, and Jewish leaders immediately proclaimed the State of Israel, with David Ben-Gurion as Prime Minister. Although the new state had no agreed frontiers, it quickly received wide international recognition. Neighbouring Arab countries sent forces into Palestine in an attempt to crush Israel. Fighting continued until January 1949, when cease-fire agreements left Israel in control of 75% of Palestine, including West Jerusalem. The *de facto* territory of Israel was thus nearly one-third greater than the area assigned to the Jewish state under the UN partition plan. Most of the remainder of Palestine was controlled by Jordanian forces. This area, known as the West Bank (or, to Israelis, as Judaea and Samaria), was annexed by Jordan in December 1949 and fully incorporated in April 1950. No independent Arab state was established in Palestine, and the independence of Israel was not recognized by any Arab government until 1980.

When the British mandate ended the Jewish population of Palestine was about 650,000 (or 40% of the total). The new state of Israel encouraged further Jewish immigration: the Law of Return, adopted in July 1950, established a right of immigration for all Jews, and resulted in a rapid influx of Jewish settlers. Many former Arab residents of Palestine, meanwhile, had become refugees in neighbouring countries, mainly Jordan and Lebanon. About 400,000 Arabs had evacuated their homes prior to May 1948, and a similar number fled subsequently. In 1964 exiled Palestinian Arabs formed the Palestine Liberation Organization (PLO), with the aim, at that time, of overthrowing Israel.

Israel launched an attack on Egypt in October 1956, occupying the Gaza Strip (part of Palestine under Egyptian occupation since 1949) and the Sinai Peninsula. After pressure from the UN and the USA, Israeli forces evacuated these areas in 1957, when a UN Emergency Force (UNEF) was established in Sinai. In 1967 the United Arab Republic (Egypt) secured the withdrawal of UNEF from its territory. Egyptian forces immediately reoccupied the garrison at Sharm esh-Sheikh, near the southern tip of Sinai, and closed the Straits of Tiran to Israeli shipping, effectively (as in 1956) blockading the Israeli port of Eilat. In retaliation, Israeli forces attacked Egypt, Jordan and Syria, swiftly making substantial territorial gains. The so-called Six-Day War left Israel in possession of all Jerusalem, the West Bank area of Jordan, the Sinai Peninsula in Egypt, the Gaza Strip and the Golan Heights in Syria. East Jerusalem was almost immediately integrated into the State of Israel, while the other conquered areas were regarded as Occupied Territories.

Ben-Gurion resigned in June 1963 and was succeeded by Levi Eshkol. Three of the parties in the ruling coalition merged to form the Israel Labour Party in 1968. On the death of Eshkol in 1969, Golda Meir was elected Prime Minister. A cease-fire between Egypt and Israel was arranged in August 1970, but other Arab states and Palestinian Arab guerrilla (mainly PLO) groups continued hostilities. Another war between the Arab states and Israel began on 6 October 1973, as Arab forces invaded Israeli-held territory on Yom Kippur (the Day of Atonement), the holiest day of the Jewish year. Egyptian forces crossed the Suez Canal and reoccupied part of Sinai, while Syrian troops launched an offensive on the Golan Heights. Having successfully countered these advances, Israel made cease-fire agreements with Egypt and Syria on 24 October.

Gen. Itzhak Rabin succeeded Golda Meir as Prime Minister of a Labour Alignment coalition in 1974. In May 1977 the Labour Alignment was defeated in a general election, and the

Likud (Consolidation) bloc, led by Menachem Begin of the Herut (Freedom) Party, formed a Government with the support of minority parties.

In November 1977 the Egyptian President, Anwar Sadat, visited Israel, indicating tacit recognition of the State of Israel. In September 1978 President Jimmy Carter of the USA, President Sadat and Prime Minister Begin met at the US presidential retreat at Camp David, Maryland, and concluded two agreements: a 'framework for peace in the Middle East', providing for autonomy for the West Bank and Gaza Strip after a transitional period of five years; and a 'framework for the conclusion of a peace treaty between Egypt and Israel'. In February 1980 Egypt was the first Arab country to grant diplomatic recognition to Israel. However, approval by the Israeli Knesset (parliament) in that year of legislation stating explicitly that Jerusalem should be forever the undivided capital of Israel, and Israel's formal annexation of the Golan Heights in 1981, subsequently impeded prospects of agreement on Palestinian autonomy.

Israel's phased withdrawal from Sinai was completed in April 1982. In June Israeli forces, under 'Operation Peace for Galilee', advanced through Lebanon and surrounded West Beirut, trapping 6,000 PLO fighters. Egypt withdrew its ambassador from Tel-Aviv in protest. Diplomatic efforts resulted in the evacuation of 14,000–15,000 PLO and Syrian fighters from Beirut to various Arab countries. In September Lebanese Phalangists massacred Palestinian refugees in the Sabra and Chatila camps in Beirut. An official Israeli inquiry found that Israel's leaders were indirectly responsible through negligence; Gen. Ariel Sharon was forced to resign as Minister of Defence. Talks between Israel and Lebanon culminated in an agreement, in May 1983, declaring an end to hostilities and envisaging the withdrawal of all foreign forces from Lebanon within three months. Syria rejected this, leaving some 30,000 troops and 7,000 PLO fighters in the Beka'a valley and northern Lebanon. Israel thus refused to withdraw its troops, although these were redeployed south of Beirut in September, and were reduced from 30,000 to 10,000 by the end of the year.

The Government's prestige had been damaged by the Beirut massacre and by a capitulation to wage demands by Israel's doctors. In August 1983 Itzhak Shamir succeeded Begin as leader of the Likud bloc and Prime Minister. Economic difficulties further undermined the Government during the second half of the year, and the Labour Party forced a general election in July 1984. Neither the Labour Alignment nor Likud could form a viable coalition, so President Chaim Herzog invited the Labour leader, Shimon Peres, to form a government of national unity with Likud.

Responsibility for policing the occupied southern area of Lebanon fell increasingly on the Israeli-controlled 'South Lebanon Army' (SLA). Israel's own forces completed a withdrawal in June 1985, leaving a narrow buffer zone on the Lebanese side of the border effectively controlled by the SLA. During 1986 rocket attacks on settlements in northern Israel were resumed by Palestinian guerrillas. Israel responded with air assaults on Palestinian targets in southern Lebanon. Meanwhile, the Shi'ite fundamentalist Hezbollah intensified attacks on SLA positions within the buffer zone. The conflict escalated following the abduction, in July 1989, of a local Shi'a Muslim leader by Israeli agents; and again in February 1992, after the assassination by the Israeli air force of the Hezbollah Secretary-General, Sheikh Abbas Moussawi.

From 1984 numerous attempts were made to resolve the most urgent problem in the Middle East—the desire of Palestinians for an independent state. There was virtual deadlock because the PLO would not recognize Israel's right to exist, while Israel refused to participate in direct talks with the PLO, which it regarded as a terrorist organization. Repeated proposals by King Hussein of Jordan for an international peace conference were rejected by Israel, on the grounds that this would involve a PLO delegation. In December 1987 demonstrations and civil disobedience against Israeli rule in the Gaza Strip intensified and spread to the other Occupied Territories. Israeli attempts to crush the *intifada* (uprising) were condemned by world opinion for their severity.

In July 1988 King Hussein abrogated Jordan's legal and administrative responsibilities in the West Bank, and declared that he would no longer represent the Palestinians in any international conference on the Palestinian question. This undermined Israel's Palestine policy, and strengthened the PLO's negotiating position as the sole legitimate representative of the Palestinian people. In November the PLO declared an independent Palestinian State (notionally the West Bank and Gaza Strip), and endorsed UN Security Council Resolution 242 (of November 1967), thereby implicitly granting recognition to Israel. In December Yasser Arafat, the Chairman of the PLO, stated explicitly that the Palestine National Council accepted two States, a Palestinian State and a Jewish State, Israel. He presented a peace initiative, including proposals for a UN-sponsored international conference, the establishment of a UN peace-keeping force to supervise Israeli withdrawal from the Occupied Territories, and a comprehensive settlement based on UN Security Council Resolutions 242 and 338 (of October 1973). The USA refused to accept the PLO proposals, but it did open a dialogue with the organization. However, Prime Minister Itzhak Shamir (the Likud leader had assumed the Israeli premiership in October 1986, in accordance with the 1984 coalition agreement) would not negotiate, distrusting the PLO's undertaking to abandon violence. Instead, he appeared to favour the introduction of limited self-rule for the Palestinians of the West Bank and Gaza Strip, as outlined in the 1978 Camp David accords. At the general election in November 1988, as in 1984, neither Likud nor Labour secured enough seats in the Knesset to form a coalition with groups of smaller parties. Eventually, another Government of national unity was formed, under Shamir, with Shimon Peres as Deputy Prime Minister and Minister of Finance.

In April 1989 Shamir presented a peace proposal that would include a reaffirmation by Egypt, Israel and the USA of the Camp David accords, and plans for the holding of free democratic elections in the West Bank and Gaza for Palestinian delegates who could negotiate self-rule under Israeli authority. The proposals, precluding direct talks with the PLO, were unacceptable to the PLO, which did not consider that elections could establish the basis for a political settlement. In September, none the less, President Hosni Mubarak of Egypt invited clarification of Shamir's plans and offered to convene an Israeli-Palestinian meeting in Cairo. This was rejected by Likud ministers, on the grounds that it would entail direct contact with PLO delegates. In November Israel provisionally accepted a proposal by the US Secretary of State, James Baker, for a preliminary meeting to discuss the holding of elections in the West Bank and Gaza, on condition that Israel would not be required to negotiate with the PLO and that the talks would concern only Israel's election proposals. However, the PLO continued to demand a direct role, and the Baker initiative foundered.

The fragile Likud-Labour coalition was endangered in early 1990 by disputes and dismissals, and in March the Knesset adopted a motion of 'no confidence' in Prime Minister Shamir. Shimon Peres attempted unsuccessfully to form a new coalition, and in June, after several weeks of political bargaining, Shamir was able to form a new Government. In a policy document Shamir emphasized the right of Jews to settle in all parts of 'Greater Israel', his opposition to the creation of an independent Palestinian state, and his refusal to negotiate with the PLO—or with any Palestinians other than those resident in the Occupied Territories (excluding East Jerusalem). The new Government was a narrow, right-wing coalition of Likud and five small parties, with three independent members of the Knesset.

In March 1990 US President George Bush opposed the granting to Israel of a loan of some US $400m. for the housing of Soviet Jewish immigrants, since Israel would not guarantee to refrain from constructing new settlements in the Occupied Territories. Violence erupted throughout Israel and the Occupied Territories in May. The PLO's refusal to condemn the violence caused the USA to suspend its dialogue with the organizations and to veto a UN Security Council resolution urging that international observers be dispatched to the Occupied Territories. In June Shamir invited President Hafiz al-Assad of Syria to peace negotiations, and the UN Secretary-General's special envoy also visited Israel for discussions. However, Shamir rejected US proposals for direct talks between Israeli and Palestinian delegations.

Iraq's invasion of Kuwait in August 1990 brought about an improvement in US-Israeli relations: it was imperative, if a coalition of Western and Arab powers opposed to Iraq was to be maintained, that Israel should not become actively involved in the conflict. In October some 17 Palestinians were shot dead by Israeli police, following clashes with Jewish worshippers. International outrage at the shootings resulted in a UN Security Council vote to send an investigative mission; Israel, however, agreed only to receive a UN emissary. Iraqi missile attacks on Israel in January 1991, shortly after the US-led multinational force had begun its offensive against Iraq, threatened the cohesion of the force. US diplomatic efforts, and the installation in Israel of US air defence systems, averted an immediate Israeli response. Meanwhile, widespread support for Iraq among Palestinians increased the Israeli Government's insistence that Shamir's own peace plan, formulated in 1989, could be the only basis for dialogue.

In March 1991 President Bush identified the resolution of the Arab–Israeli conflict as among his administration's priorities. By August intensive diplomacy by US Secretary of State James Baker had secured the agreement of the Israeli, Syrian, Egyptian, Jordanian and Lebanese Governments, and of Palestinian representatives, to attend a regional peace conference, the terms of reference for which would be a comprehensive peace settlement based on UN Security Council Resolutions 242 and 338. An initial, 'symbolic' session was held in Madrid, Spain, in October. However, subsequent talks soon became deadlocked over procedural issues. Israel, wary of making any gesture that might be construed as recognition of Palestinian independence, repeatedly questioned the status of the Palestinian-Jordanian delegation and the right of the Palestinian component to participate separately in negotiations; furthermore, Israel's refusal to halt construction of new settlements in the Occupied Territories continually jeopardized the peace process. In February 1992, immediately prior to the fourth session of peace talks, to be held in Washington, DC, Baker demanded a complete halt to Israel's settlement-building programme as a precondition for the granting of loan guarantees to the value of US \$10,000m. for the housing of Jewish immigrants from the former USSR.

The right-wing minority members of the Israeli Government, opposed to participation by Israel in the peace conference, threatened to withdraw from the coalition if funds were not made available for the settlement programme. In December 1991 the Government's majority in the Knesset was reduced when the Minister of Agriculture (a member of the right-wing nationalist Tzomet Party) resigned in protest at the Prime Minister's opposition to electoral reform. The majority was lost entirely in January 1992, when two other right-wing nationalist groups, Moledet and Tehiya, left the coalition. Their withdrawal was a deliberate attempt to obstruct the third session of the Middle East peace conference, in Moscow, Russia, where delegates had begun to address the granting of transitional autonomy to Palestinians in the West Bank and Gaza Strip. A general election was subsequently scheduled for June, with Itzhak Shamir heading a minority administration meanwhile.

A fifth round of negotiations was held in Washington, DC, in April 1992. Procedural issues were resolved, and, during talks with the Palestinian component of the Palestinian-Jordanian delegation, Israeli representatives presented proposals for the holding of municipal elections in the West Bank and Gaza Strip, and for the transfer of control of health-care provision there to Palestinian authorities. The Palestinian delegation did not reject the proposals outright, although they fell far short of the Palestinians' aim of full legislative control of the Occupied Territories. No progress was made in the meetings between Israeli and Syrian delegations on the issue of the Golan Heights.

In May 1992 the first multilateral negotiations between the parties to the Middle East peace conference commenced; however, the sessions were boycotted by Syria and Lebanon, considering them futile until progress had been made in the bilateral negotiations. Various combinations of delegations in several cities attended discussions concerning regional economic co-operation; regional arms control; Palestinian refugees; water resources; and environmental issues. Israel boycotted the meetings on Palestinian refugees and regional economic development after the USA approved Palestinian proposals to allow exiles (i.e. non-residents of the Occupied Territories) to be included in the Palestinian delegations to these two sessions.

In the June 1992 general election the Labour Party won 44 of the 120 seats in the Knesset, and Likud 32. Meretz—an alliance of Ratz, Shinui and the United Workers' Party, which had won 12 seats—confirmed its willingness to form a coalition government with the Labour Party. However, even with the support of the two Arab parties—the Democratic Arab Party and Hadash—which together held five seats in the Knesset, such a coalition would have a majority of only two votes over the so-called 'right bloc' (Likud, Tzomet, Moledet and Tehiya) and the religious parties which had allied themselves with Likud in the previous legislature. Itzhak Rabin (who had replaced Shimon Peres as Chairman of the Labour Party earlier in the year) was accordingly obliged to solicit support among

the religious parties. His Government, presented to the Knesset in July, was an alliance of Labour, Meretz and the ultra-orthodox Shas; the coalition held a total of 62 Knesset seats, and also commanded the unofficial support of the two Arab parties.

Most international observers regarded the installation of the Labour-led coalition as having improved the prospects of the Middle East peace process. However, at the conclusion of a sixth round of bilateral negotiations between Israeli, Syrian, Lebanese and Palestinian-Jordanian delegations in September 1992, no breakthrough was reported. In October, in a clear gesture of support for the new Government, the USA granted Israel the loan guarantees that it had hitherto withheld. Multilateral negotiations on regional economic co-operation, in which an Israeli delegation participated, took place in Paris, France, in October; a seventh round of bilateral negotiations convened in Washington in October–November, and multilateral talks on the issue of refugees were held in Ottawa, Canada, in November. Nevertheless, no tangible progress was achieved.

An eighth round of bilateral negotiations between Israeli and Arab delegations commenced in Washington in December 1992. However, the talks were quickly overtaken by events in the Occupied Territories (where there had been several weeks of violent confrontations involving Palestinians and the Israeli security forces), which led to the withdrawal of the Arab participants. In mid-December, in response to the deaths in the Occupied Territories of five members of the Israeli security forces, and to the abduction and murder by the Islamic Resistance Movement (Hamas) of an Israeli policeman, the Government ordered the deportation to Lebanon of 413 alleged Palestinian supporters of Hamas. The Lebanese authorities refused to co-operate in this action, leaving the deportees stranded in the territory between Israel's self-declared southern Lebanese security zone and Lebanon proper. The expulsions provoked international outrage, and intense diplomatic pressure was placed on Israel to revoke the deportation order. The UN Security Council unanimously approved a resolution (No. 799) condemning the deportations and demanding the return of the deportees to Israel. At the end of December the Israeli Government asserted that only 10 of the deportees had been unjustifiably expelled and would be permitted to return to Israel. Meanwhile, the Palestinian delegation to the eighth round of bilateral negotiations indicated that it would not resume talks until all of the deportees had been readmitted to Israel. In February 1993 the Israeli Government reportedly indicated its willingness to allow about 100 of the deportees to return, but insisted that the remainder should serve a period of exile lasting at least until the end of the year. The ninth round of bilateral negotiations was formally suspended; although the Security Council welcomed the Israeli Government's decision to permit the return of 100 deportees, Palestinians party to the peace talks insisted on full implementation of Resolution 799 as a precondition for resumed discussions. In March, amid a sharp escalation in violence between Palestinians and the Israeli security forces in the Occupied Territories, Israel sealed off the West Bank and the Gaza Strip indefinitely.

The suspended ninth round of bilateral negotiations in the Middle East peace process resumed in Washington in April 1993. The Palestinian delegation apparently agreed to attend the sessions following pressure by Arab governments, and after Israel had agreed to allow Faisal Husseini, the nominal leader of the Palestinian delegation, to participate. (Israel had previously refused this concession because Husseini was a resident of East Jerusalem, the status of which Israel regarded as distinct from that of the West Bank, the Gaza Strip and the Golan Heights.) Israel was also reported to have undertaken no longer to resort to punitive deportations, and, with the USA, to have reaffirmed its commitment to Resolutions 242 and 338 as the terms of reference for the peace process. However, no substantive progress was achieved by the talks.

In May 1993 Ezer Weizman was inaugurated as President; Weizman, the leader of the Yahad party, had been elected by the Knesset in March. Also in March Likud members had chosen Binyamin Netanyahu to replace Shamir as Likud leader.

A 10th round of bilateral negotiations, convened in Washington in June 1993, achieved no progress on a statement of principles concerning Palestinian self-rule in the Occupied Territories, now regarded as the key element in the Middle East peace process. However, it was agreed to establish a committee to pursue this issue. Meanwhile, no progress was made on the issues of contention between the Israeli delegation and its Syrian, Lebanese and Jordanian counterparts. At the end of

July Israeli armed forces mounted the most intensive air and artillery attacks on targets in Lebanon since 'Operation Peace for Galilee' in 1982, in retaliation for attacks by Hezbollah fighters on settlements in northern Israel.

The opening of the 11th round of bilateral negotiations, in Washington at the end of August 1993, was eclipsed by an unexpected breakthrough in negotiations between Israel and the PLO, which culminated in the signing, on 13 September, of a Declaration of Principles on Palestinian self-rule in the Occupied Territories. The agreement, which entailed mutual recognition by Israel and the PLO, had been elaborated during a series of secret negotiations mediated by Norwegian diplomacy (and was therefore commonly known as the Oslo accords). The Declaration of Principles established a detailed timetable for Israel's disengagement from the Occupied Territories, and stipulated that a permanent settlement of the Palestinian question should be in place by December 1998. From 13 October 1993 Palestinian authorities were to assume responsibility for education and culture, health, social welfare, direct taxation and tourism in the Gaza Strip and the Jericho area of the West Bank, and a transitional period of Palestinian self-rule was to begin on 13 December.

Although Prime Minister Rabin secured ratification of the Declaration of Principles, and of Israel's recognition of the PLO, by the Knesset on 23 September 1993, there was widespread opposition to it from the right-wing. The PLO Central Council, meeting in the Tunisian capital, approved the accord on 11 October. However, the conclusion of the agreement aggravated divisions in the Palestinian liberation movement. Within the PLO some senior officials, hitherto loyal to Yasser Arafat's leadership, now declared their opposition to him, while dissident groups, such as the Democratic Front for the Liberation of Palestine (DFLP), denounced the Declaration of Principles as treason. Meanwhile, the reaction to the Declaration of Principles by the other Arab Governments engaged in peace negotiations with Israel was mixed. King Hussein of Jordan welcomed the agreement, and immediately agreed an agenda for direct discussions with Israel; this was also ratified by the Knesset on 23 September. Talks took place in Washington between Crown Prince Hassan of Jordan and Shimon Peres, Israel's Minister of Foreign Affairs, in October. Despite reports of subsequent secret negotiations, King Hussein insisted, during visits to Egypt and Syria in November, that Jordan would not conclude a separate peace agreement with Israel. Lebanon, meanwhile, feared that the divisions provoked by the Declaration of Principles within the Palestinian movement might lead to renewed conflict on Lebanese territory. It remained unclear whether Syria—which neither condemned nor welcomed the agreement—would continue to support those Palestinian groups opposed to Arafat's position.

Also in September 1993 the resignation of Aryeh Der'i of the ultra-orthodox Shas, as Minister of the Interior, following allegations of corruption, provoked the withdrawal from the Government of other Shas ministers, thus reducing the coalition to an alliance between the Labour Party and Meretz (and the Government's majority in the Knesset to only two). Protracted negotiations failed to achieve the return of Shas to the governing coalition, and were eventually superseded by an agreement with Yi'ud, a breakaway group from the Tzomet Party, which signed a coalition agreement in July 1994.

Itzhak Rabin and Yasser Arafat held their first meeting in the context of the Declaration of Principles in Cairo on 6 October 1993. A joint PLO-Israeli liaison committee subsequently met for the first time on 13 October, with delegations headed, respectively, by Mahmud Abbas and Shimon Peres. It was agreed that the committee should meet at frequent intervals to monitor the implementation of the Declaration of Principles. A technical committee also held three meetings during October in the Egyptian resort of Taba: its task was to define the precise details of Israel's military withdrawal from the Gaza Strip and Jericho, scheduled to take place between 13 December 1993 and 13 April 1994. However, it proved impossible satisfactorily to negotiate the details of Israel's withdrawal by December 1993, largely because of a failure to agree on security arrangements for border crossings between the Gaza Strip and Jericho and Jordan and Egypt.

Following meetings in Damascus between the US Secretary of State, Warren Christopher, and Syria's President Assad and Minister of Foreign Affairs in December 1993, Syria announced its willingness to resume bilateral talks with Israel. In January 1994 Israel appeared to indicate, tentatively, that it might be prepared to execute a full withdrawal from the Golan Heights in return for a comprehensive peace agreement with Syria; it was subsequently reported that the Government would put the issue to a referendum before making such a withdrawal. Bilateral negotiations between Israeli and Syrian delegations resumed in Washington later that month.

In February 1994 Israel and the PLO reached an agreement to share control of the two future international border crossings. It was reported that security arrangements for Jewish settlers in the Gaza Strip had also been decided, whereby three access routes to Jewish settlements were to remain under Israeli control. However, the boundaries of the Jericho enclave remained undefined. Talks followed on issues of the implementation of the first stage of Palestinian autonomy in the Gaza Strip and the Jericho area; the size, structure and jurisdiction of a future Palestinian police force; control of sea and air space; and the delineation of the Jericho enclave. In April Israel and the PLO signed an agreement concerning economic relations between Israel and the autonomous Palestinian entity during the five-year period leading to self-rule. Meeting in Cairo, on 4 May Israel and the PLO signed an agreement detailing arrangements for Palestinian self-rule in Gaza and Jericho. The accord provided for Israel's military withdrawal from the Gaza Strip and Jericho, and for the deployment there of a 9,000-strong Palestinian police force. A nominated Palestinian National Authority (PNA) was to assume the responsibilities of the Israeli military administration in Gaza and Jericho, although Israeli authorities were to retain control in matters of external security and foreign affairs. Elections for a Palestinian Council, which, under the terms of the Oslo accords, were to have taken place in Gaza and the West Bank in July, were now postponed until October. Israel's military withdrawal from Gaza and Jericho was completed on 13 May, and on 17 May the PLO formally assumed control of the Israeli Civil Administration's departments there. On 26–28 May the PNA held its inaugural meeting in Tunis, defining a political programme and distributing ministerial portfolios. Arafat made a symbolic return to Gaza City on 1 July—his first visit for 25 years—and the PNA was formally inaugurated in Jericho on 5 July. Meanwhile, negotiations continued with Israel on the extension of Palestinian authority and the redeployment of Israeli armed forces in the West Bank, and on the holding of Palestinian elections. In August Israel and the PLO signed an agreement extending the authority of the PNA to include education, health, tourism, social welfare and taxation.

On 25 July 1994 Israel and Jordan signed a joint declaration formally ending the state of war between them and further defining arrangements for future bilateral negotiations. In September Itzhak Rabin announced details of a plan for a partial withdrawal of Israeli armed forces from the occupied Golan Heights, after which a three-year trial period of Israeli-Syrian 'normalization' would ensue. The proposals were rejected by President Assad; however, the Syrian leader did state his willingness to work towards peace with Israel. In late September Rabin and King Hussein held talks in Aqaba, Jordan, with the aim of devising a timetable for a full Israeli-Jordanian peace treaty. Also in September Morocco, closely followed by Tunisia, became the second and third Arab states to establish diplomatic ties with Israel, and the six members of the Co-operation Council for the Arab States of the Gulf (the Gulf Co-operation Council, see p. 160) also announced their decision to revoke the subsidiary elements of the Arab economic boycott of Israel.

A World Bank-sponsored conference of international donors, held in Paris in September 1994, collapsed almost immediately, owing to a dispute between Israel and the Palestinians over Palestinian investment plans to fund projects in East Jerusalem. Israel regarded such plans as compromising negotiations on the final status of Jerusalem which, under the terms of the Declaration of Principles, were not due to begin before May 1996. Meeting in Oslo, Norway, shortly afterwards, Arafat and Peres negotiated a 15-point agreement aimed at accelerating economic aid to the PNA. Later in September 1994 Arafat and Rabin met at the Erez crossing point between Gaza and Israel to discuss the future Palestinian elections in the Gaza Strip and the West Bank. The PLO reportedly sought to elect a 100-member Palestinian Council, while Israel insisted that its size should be restricted to 25 members. Israel rejected Arafat's proposal for elections on 1 November as unrealistic; it was, however, agreed to meet again in October to negotiate a compromise. At the same time, Arafat agreed to 'take all measures' to prevent attacks on Israeli targets by opponents of the Oslo process. In late September, however, Rabin approved a plan to build some 1,000 new housing units at a Jewish settlement just inside the West Bank, in an apparent reversal of the moratorium he had imposed on new construction in 1992. The PLO claimed that this contravened the Declaration of Principles. In early October 1994 Hamas claimed responsibility for an attack in Jerusalem in which an Israeli soldier and a Palestinian civilian died. On the same day another Israeli soldier was abducted by Hamas fighters near Tel-Aviv, who subsequently demanded that Israel release the detained Hamas spiritual leader, Sheikh Ahmad Yassin, and other Palestinian prisoners in exchange for his life. Despite Palestinian action to detain some 300 Hamas members in the Gaza Strip, the kidnapped soldier was killed in the West Bank in mid-October. Shortly afterwards an attack by a Hamas suicide bomber in Tel-Aviv, in which 22 people died, prompted Israel to close its borders with the West Bank and the Gaza Strip for an indefinite period.

On 26 October 1994 Israel and Jordan signed a formal peace treaty, defining the border between the two countries and providing for a normalization of relations. The peace treaty was denounced by the Syrian Government, all elements of Palestinian opinion, and by some Islamists in Jordan.

In November 1994 a member of Islamic Jihad was killed in a car bomb attack in Gaza. The attack was blamed on the Israeli security forces by many Palestinians opposed to the Oslo accords. Three Israeli soldiers were subsequently killed in a suicide bombing in the Gaza Strip, for which Islamic Jihad claimed responsibility. It subsequently became clear that Israel's security concerns would continue to delay the redeployment of its armed forces in the West Bank and the holding of Palestinian elections, as Rabin stated, in December, that the elections would either have to take place in the continued presence of Israeli armed forces, or be postponed for a year. It was reported in that month that there had been a 10% increase in the number of Jewish settlers in the occupied West Bank during 1994. In January 1995 a suicide bombing (responsibility for which was claimed by Islamic Jihad) at Beit Lid, in which 21 Israeli soldiers and civilians died, and more than 60 were injured, seriously jeopardized the peace process. The Government again closed Israel's borders with the Gaza Strip and the West Bank, and postponed the planned release of some 5,500 Palestinian prisoners. An emergency meeting of the leaders of Egypt, Israel, Jordan and the PLO was convened in Cairo early the following month; the summit's final communiqué condemned acts of terror and violence, and expressed support for the Declaration of Principles and the wider peace process. US President Bill Clinton subsequently held a meeting with the Israeli and the Egyptian Ministers of Foreign Affairs and the PNA Minister of Planning and Economic Co-operation in Washington, after which Shimon Peres reportedly stated that any further expansion of Palestinian self-rule in the West Bank was conditional upon real progress by the PNA in suppressing terrorism. On 9 February, meanwhile, Israeli armed forces completed their withdrawal from Jordanian territories, in accordance with the bilateral peace treaty concluded in October 1994.

In March 1995 Arafat and Peres agreed, at talks in Gaza, to adopt 1 July as the date by which an agreement on the expansion of Palestinian self-rule in the West Bank should be concluded. Later in March it was announced that Israel and Syria had agreed to resume peace negotiations for the first time since February 1994. In May Syria and Israel were reported to have concluded a 'framework understanding on security arrangements', intended to facilitate discussions on security issues. Peres subsequently indicated that Israel had proposed that its forces should withdraw from the Golan Heights over a four-year period; Syria, however, had insisted that the withdrawal be effected over 18 months.

In April 1995 seven Israeli soldiers were killed, and more than 50 people injured, in two suicide bomb attacks in the Gaza Strip. The Palestinian police force was subsequently reported to have arrested as many as 300 members of Hamas and Islamic Jihad, which claimed responsibility for the attacks.

In June 1995 one of the most prominent members of Likud, David Levy (who had opposed Netanyahu's election as party leader in 1993), announced that he was to form a new party to contest the legislative elections scheduled for 1996. The division was reportedly the result of Levy's opposition to new selection procedures within Likud for general election candidates. Levy's new political movement, Gesher, was formally inaugurated later in June 1995.

Despite intensive negotiations, it proved impossible to conclude an agreement on the expansion of Palestinian self-rule in the West Bank by the target date of 1 July 1995. The principal obstacles remained the question of precisely to where Israeli troops in the West Bank would redeploy, and the exact nature of security arrangements for some 130,000 Jewish settlers who were to remain there. In August Hamas claimed responsibility for a suicide bomb attack on a bus in Jerusalem, which killed six people. On 28 September the Israeli-Palestinian Interim Agreement on the West Bank and the Gaza Strip was finally signed by Israel and the PLO. Its main provisions were the withdrawal of Israeli armed forces from a further six West Bank towns (Nablus, Ramallah, Jenin, Tulkaram, Qaqilya and Bethlehem), and a partial redeployment away from the town of Hebron; national Palestinian legislative elections to an 82-member Palestinian Council and for a Palestinian Executive President; and the release, in three phases, of Palestinians detained by Israel. In anticipation of a violent reaction against the Interim Agreement by so-called 'rejectionist' groups within the Occupied Territories, Israel immediately announced the closure of its borders with the Gaza Strip and the West Bank. Meanwhile, right-wing elements within Israel denounced the agreement, believing that too much had been conceded to the Palestinians.

On 4 November 1995 Itzhak Rabin was assassinated in Tel-Aviv by a Jewish student opposed to the peace process, in particular the Israeli withdrawal from the West Bank. The assassination caused a further marginalization of those on the extreme right wing of Israeli politics who had advocated violence as a means of halting the Oslo process, and provoked criticism of the opposition Likud, which, it was widely felt, had not sufficiently distanced itself from such extremist elements. The Minister of Foreign Affairs, Shimon Peres, was, with the agreement of Likud, invited to form a new government. The members of the outgoing administration—Labour, Meretz and Yi'ud—subsequently signed a new coalition agreement, and the Cabinet was formally approved by the Knesset in late November. In February 1996 Peres announced that elections to the Knesset and—for the first time—the direct election of the Prime Minister would take place in May 1996.

In spite of Rabin's assassination, Israeli armed forces completed their withdrawal from the West Bank town of Jenin on 13 November 1995, and during December they withdrew from Tulkaram, Nablus, Qaqilya, Bethlehem and Ramallah. With regard to Hebron, Israel and the PNA signed an agreement transferring jurisdiction in some 17 areas of civilian affairs from Israel to the PNA. At talks with Arafat at Erez in December, Peres confirmed that Israel would release some 1,000 Palestinian prisoners before the impending Palestinian legislative and presidential elections.

Peace negotiations between Israel and Syria resumed in December 1995 in Maryland, USA, followed by a second round in January 1996. Also in January King Hussein made a public visit to Tel-Aviv, during which Israel and Jordan signed a number of agreements relating to the normalization of economic and cultural relations.

Palestinian legislative and presidential elections were held in late January 1996, leading in principle to the final stage of the peace process, when Palestinian and Israeli negotiators would address such issues as Jerusalem, the rights of Palestinian refugees, the status of Jewish settlements in the Palestinian territories, and the extent of that autonomy. In February and March, however, more than 50 Israelis died as a result of suicide bomb attacks in Jerusalem, Ashkelon and Tel-Aviv, and talks were suspended. Israel again ordered the indefinite closure of the borders of the West Bank and the Gaza Strip, and demanded that the Palestinian authorities suppress the activities of Hamas and Islamic Jihad in the areas under their control. A hitherto unknown group, the 'Yahya Ayyash Units', claimed responsibility for the attacks, to avenge the assassination—allegedly by Israeli agents—of Ayyash, a leading member of Hamas, in January 1996. Yasser Arafat, now the elected Palestinian President, condemned the bombings, and in late February more than 200 members of Hamas were reported to have been detained by the Palestinian security forces. The attacks led Israel to impose even more stringent security measures, notably asserting the right of its armed forces to enter PNA-controlled areas when Israeli security was at stake. Furthermore, an agreement to redeploy troops from Hebron by 20 March was rescinded. For their part, the Palestinian authorities were reported to have held emergency talks with the leadership of

Hamas and Islamic Jihad, and to have outlawed the armed wings of these and other, unspecified Palestinian paramilitary groups.

The suicide bombings also undermined the talks taking place between Israeli and Syrian representatives in the USA, and in March the Israeli negotiators returned to Israel. Syria and Lebanon both declined an invitation to attend the so-called 'Summit of Peacemakers', held at the Egyptian resort of Sharm esh-Sheikh in March, at which some 27 Heads of State expressed their support for the Middle East peace process and pledged to redouble their efforts to combat terrorism. In April 1996 Israel and Turkey signed a number of military co-operation agreements, a development condemned by Syria as a threat to its own security and to that of all Arab and Islamic countries.

In April 1996 Israeli armed forces began a sustained campaign of intense air and artillery attacks on alleged Hezbollah positions in southern Lebanon and the southern suburbs of Beirut. The declared aim of the Israeli operation (code-named 'Grapes of Wrath') was to achieve the complete cessation of rocket attacks by Hezbollah on settlements in northern Israel. Some 400,000 Lebanese were displaced northwards, after the Israeli military authorities warned that they would be endangered by the offensive against Hezbollah. Moreover, the shelling by Israeli forces of a base of the UN peace-keeping force at Qana resulted in the deaths of more than 100 Lebanese civilians who had been sheltering there, and of four members of the UN force. What was termed a cease-fire 'understanding' took effect in late April, after more than two weeks of hostilities. This was effectively a compromise confining the conflict to the area of the security zone in southern Lebanon, recognizing both Hezbollah's right to resist Israeli occupation and Israel's right to self-defence; the 'understanding' also envisaged the establishment of an Israel-Lebanon Monitoring Group (ILMG), comprising Israel, Lebanon, Syria, France and the USA, to supervise the cease-fire.

Israel welcomed the decision of the Palestine National Council (PNC) in late April 1996 to amend the Palestinian National Charter (or PLO Covenant), removing all clauses demanding the destruction of Israel: the Israeli Government had demanded that the Covenant be amended as a precondition for participation in the final stage of peace negotiations with the PLO.

No party gained an outright majority of the 120 seats in the elections to the Knesset, held on 19 May 1996, but the Likud leader, Binyamin Netanyahu, achieved a marginal victory over Peres in the direct election for the Prime Minister. Prior to the legislative election a formal alliance between Likud, the Tzomet Party and Gesher had been announced. This alliance secured 32 seats, and Labour 34. The success of the ultra-orthodox Shas and the National Religious Party (NRP), with 10 seats and nine, respectively, was the key factor in determining that the new Government would be formed by Likud. Some 79.7% of the electorate were reported to have participated in the polls. Netanyahu proceeded to sign agreements between the Likud alliance and Shas, the NRP, Israel B'Aliyah, United Torah Judaism and the Third Way, to form a coalition which would command the support of 66 deputies in the Knesset. Moledet also agreed to support the Government, but did not formally enter the coalition. The new Government received the approval of the Knesset in mid-June. Its statement of policy excluded the possibility of granting Palestinian statehood or, with regard to Syria, of relinquishing *de facto* sovereignty of the occupied Golan Heights. It was subsequently reported that Netanyahu had postponed further discussion of the withdrawal of Israeli armed forces from the West Bank town of Hebron—where they provided security for some 400 Jewish settlers. Furthermore, Netanyahu reiterated his refusal to meet the Palestinian President. In July the likely stance of the new Government was underlined by the incorporation into the Cabinet, as Minister of Infrastructure, of Ariel Sharon—who had played a leading role in the creation and expansion of Jewish settlements in the West Bank. The PNA organized a short general strike at the end of the month, in protest at the refusal of the Israeli authorities to allow Palestinian Muslims to participate in Friday prayers at the al-Aqsa mosque in East Jerusalem, and also at a decision by the new Government to expand existing Jewish settlements in the West Bank.

The election of a Likud-led Government thus appeared to have particularly grave implications for the future of Israeli-Palestinian peace negotiations. In late May 1996 a joint meeting, in Gaza, of the Palestinian Council of Ministers and the Executive Committee of the PLO urged the incoming Israeli Government to implement all previous agreements and to commence the final stage of peace talks. In late June, in response to Likud's electoral victory, a summit meeting of all Arab leaders (with the exception of Iraq) was convened in Cairo. The meeting's final communiqué reiterated Israel's withdrawal from all occupied territories (including East Jerusalem) as a basic requirement for a comprehensive Middle East peace settlement. Netanyahu and Arafat did in fact meet in September, at the Erez crossing point, when they confirmed their commitment to the implementation of the Interim Agreement.

In September 1996 it was announced that Israel's Ministry of Defence had approved plans to construct some 1,800 new housing units at existing Jewish settlements in the West Bank causing many observers to conclude that the new Israeli Government had effectively halted the peace process by either abandoning or postponing many of the commitments inherited from its predecessor. Violent confrontations erupted between Palestinian security forces, Palestinian civilians and the Israeli armed forces, in which at least 50 Palestinians and 18 Israelis were killed and hundreds wounded. The direct cause of the disturbances was attributed to the decision of the Israeli Government to open the north end of the Hasmonean tunnel running beneath the al-Aqsa mosque in Jerusalem, although it appeared to be the inevitable culmination of Palestinian frustration at the Israeli Government's failure to implement agreements previously signed with the PNA, and there were fears of a new Palestinian *intifada*. The Israeli military authorities declared a state of emergency in the Gaza Strip and the West Bank, and threatened military intervention to suppress the disturbances. A special session of the UN Security Council was convened, and intense international diplomacy facilitated a crisis summit in Washington hosted by US President Clinton and attended by Netanyahu, Arafat and King Hussein of Jordan. The meeting reportedly achieved nothing, but in October it was announced that, following further US mediation, Israel had agreed to resume negotiations on the partial withdrawal of its armed forces from Hebron. Netanyahu subsequently stated that once the question of the redeployment from Hebron had been settled Israel would reopen its borders with the West Bank and the Gaza Strip—which had remained closed since February—and move quickly towards seeking a final settlement with the Palestinians.

In January 1997 Israel and the PNA finally concluded an agreement on the withdrawal of Israeli armed forces from Hebron. The principal terms of the accord were that Israeli forces should withdraw from 80% of the town within 10 days, and that the first of three subsequent redeployments from the West Bank should take place six weeks after the signing of the agreement, and the remaining two by August 1998. With regard to security arrangements for Jewish settlers in central Hebron, Palestinian police patrols would be armed only with pistols in areas close to the Jewish enclaves, while joint Israeli-Palestinian patrols would secure the heights above the enclaves. The 'final status' negotiations on borders, the Jerusalem issue, Jewish settlements and Palestinian refugees were to commence within two months of the signing of the agreement on Hebron. As guarantor of the agreement, the USA undertook to obtain the release of Palestinian prisoners, and to ensure that Israel continued to engage in negotiations for a Palestinian airport in the Gaza Strip and on safe passage for Palestinians between the West Bank and Gaza. The USA also undertook to ensure that the Palestinians would continue to combat terrorism, complete the revision of the Palestinian National Charter and consider Israeli requests to extradite Palestinians suspected of involvement in attacks in Israel.

While the conclusion of the agreement regarding Hebron marked the first significant progress in the peace process since Netanyahu's election as Prime Minister, negotiations with Syria remained suspended. In January 1997 Netanyahu urged Syria to exert pressure on Hezbollah to cease hostilities in Israel's self-declared security zone in southern Lebanon. In February, however, he denied speculation that Israel was considering a unilateral withdrawal from the security zone, which had intensified as a result of the deaths, in a helicopter accident, of 73 Israeli soldiers travelling to southern Lebanon.

Progress achieved through the agreement on Hebron was severely undermined in February 1997, when Israel announced that it was to proceed with the construction of 6,500 housing units at Har Homa in East Jerusalem. Tensions escalated in the following month, after Israel unilaterally decided to withdraw its armed forces from only 9% of the West Bank. Arafat denounced the decision and King Hussein accused Netanyahu of intentionally destroying the peace process. Increasing anti-Israeli sentiment reportedly motivated a Jordanian soldier to murder seven Israeli schoolgirls in Nayarim, an enclave between Israel and Jordan. Israeli intransigence over the Har Homa settlement prompted Palestinians to abandon the 'final status' talks, scheduled to begin on 17 March, and on the following day construction at the site began. Riots among Palestinians erupted immediately, and shortly afterwards Hamas carried out a bomb attack in Tel-Aviv, killing four and wounding more than 60 people. In response, the Israeli Government again ordered the closure of Israel's borders with the West Bank and the Gaza Strip. In late March the League of Arab States (the Arab League, see p. 232) voted to resume its economic boycott of Israel, suspend moves to establish diplomatic relations, and withdraw from multilateral peace talks. (Jordan, the PNA and Egypt were excluded from the resolution, owing to their binding bilateral agreements with Israel.) Meeting with with US President Clinton in Washington in early April, Netanyahu reiterated that he would not suspend the settlement programme. Rioting erupted in Hebron the following day, after a Palestinian was allegedly murdered by Jewish settlers. The disturbances subsided at the end of the month, and the Gaza Strip and the West Bank were reopened. During May the USA's chief Middle East negotiator, Dennis Ross, failed to achieve any progress towards a resumption of peace talks despite a nine-day mediation attempt.

Meanwhile, in April 1997 police investigators recommended that the Prime Minister be charged with fraud and breach of trust for his appointment, in January, of Roni Bar-On as Attorney-General. Bar-On had resigned within 12 hours of his appointment after it was alleged that his promotion had been made in order to facilitate a plea bargain for Aryeh Der'i, leader of the Shas party, who was the subject of separate corruption charges. It was suggested that, in return for Bar-On's appointment, Der'i had pledged his party's support for the Cabinet's decision regarding the withdrawal from Hebron. In May Der'i was indicted for obstruction of justice, but charges against Netanyahu were dismissed owing to lack of evidence. However, the Prime Minister's authority was further undermined by the subsequent resignation of the Minister of Finance, Dan Meridor. In June Ehud Barak, a former government minister and army chief of staff, was elected to replace Peres as Labour Party Chairman.

In June 1997 the US House of Representatives voted in favour of recognizing Jerusalem as the undivided capital of Israel and of transferring the US embassy there, from Tel-Aviv. The decision coincided with violent clashes between Palestinian civilians and Israeli troops in both Gaza and Hebron. Meanwhile, Yasser Arafat, fearing Israeli reoccupation of Hebron, assigned 200 police-officers to patrol the area.

In July 1997 the USA brokered an agreement between Israel and the Palestinians to resume peace talks the following month. At the end of July, however, on the eve of a planned visit to Israel by Dennis Ross, two Hamas suicide bombers killed 14 civilians and wounded more than 150 others in Jerusalem. Ross cancelled his visit and Israel suspended payment of tax revenues to the PNA and again closed off the Gaza Strip and the West Bank. Netanyahu insisted that the restrictions would remain until the Palestinians demonstrated a commitment to combat terrorism. Arafat subsequently convened a forum of Palestinian groups, during which he publicly embraced Hamas leaders and urged them, together with Islamic Jihad, to unite with the Palestinian people against Israeli policies. Israel reopened borders with the West Bank and Gaza in early September, but restrictions were reimposed three days later after suicide bombings in West Jerusalem killed eight people and wounded more than 150 others. The security crisis cast doubt on the viability of a planned visit by US Secretary of State Madeleine Albright in mid-September. However, Albright's visit was positively received; Israel released further Palestinian assets (one-third of tax revenues owed to the PNA had been released in mid-August), while the Palestinians announced the closure of 17 institutions affiliated to Hamas. In early October Netanyahu and Arafat met for the first time in eight months. Israel announced plans to release further dues to the PNA and to reopen the sealed borders. However, Israel failed to participate in a second round of negotiations, scheduled for that month, aimed at accelerating the 'final status' talks, and Netanyahu stated that further redeployments would not take place until Palestinians made further efforts to combat terrorism.

Meanwhile, relations between Jordan and Israel deteriorated in September 1997, after members of the Israeli intelligence force, Mossad, attempted to assassinate a Hamas leader, Khalid Meshaal, in Amman. In an attempt to preserve relations, intensive negotiations took place between Netanyahu, Crown Prince Hassan of Jordan and US officials. Several agreements regarding the release of prisoners ensued: in October Israel freed the Hamas spiritual leader, Sheikh Ahmad Yassin, in return for the release by Jordan of two Mossad agents arrested in connection with the attack on Meshaal; a further 12 Mossad agents were expelled by the Jordanian authorities following the release of 23 Jordanian and 50 Palestinian prisoners by Israel.

Renewed hostilities erupted in northern Israel in August 1997 after Hezbollah launched a rocket attack on civilians in Kiryat Shmona. The attack, made in retaliation for raids by Israeli commandos in which five Hezbollah members were killed, prompted further air-strikes by Israel in southern Lebanon. Violence escalated, with the shelling by the SLA of the Lebanese port of Sidon resulting in at least six deaths. Domestic pressure on the Israeli Government to withdraw from southern Lebanon increased after 12 Israeli marines, allegedly on a mission to assassinate Shi'ite leaders, were killed south of Sidon in September.

Bilateral negotiations between Israeli and Palestinian representatives resumed in November 1997. Israel offered to decelerate its construction of Jewish settlements in return for Palestinian approval of a plan to delay further redeployments of Israeli troops from the West Bank. At the same time, the Israeli Government announced plans to build 900 new housing units in the area. This virtual stalemate in the peace process prompted several Arab states to boycott the Middle East and North Africa economic conference, held in Doha, Qatar, in mid-November, which an Israeli delegation was scheduled to attend. Separate peace talks involving Albright, Netanyahu and Arafat were inconclusive. At the end of November the Israeli Cabinet agreed in principle to a partial withdrawal from the West Bank, but specified neither its timing nor its scale. Conflicting opinions within the Cabinet meant that Netanyahu failed to produce a conclusive redeployment plan to present at talks with Albright in Paris in December; furthermore, the Israeli Government had recently prevented PNA officials from conducting a census in East Jerusalem. Israeli and Palestinian officials none the less demonstrated their commitment to peace by signing a security memorandum.

In late 1998 divisions within the coalition Government obliged Netanyahu, in order to secure passage in the Knesset of the 1998 budget vote (effectively a demonstration of confidence in the Prime Minister), to grant concessions to various parties, in particular to right-wing members of the coalition. In January 1998 David Levy, the leader of Gesher, withdrew from the Government, citing dissatisfaction with the budget and with the slow rate of progress in the peace talks. Gesher's departure reduced Netanyahu's majority to only two votes, although the budget secured the approval of the Knesset, and Netanyahu subsequently survived a vote of 'no-confidence'. Meanwhile, Netanyahu announced that he would not make any further decisions regarding the peace process until the Palestinians had demonstrated further efforts to combat terrorism, reduced their security forces from 40,000 to 24,000 and amended their National Charter to recognize Israel's right to exist. The Israeli premier again failed, in January 1998, to present a plan of redeployment in talks with President Clinton in Washington. Netanyahu did express interest in a US proposal to withdraw troops from at least 10% of the land in several stages, but this was decisively rejected by Arafat. Several meetings during February between Israeli and Palestinian officials failed to break the deadlock over further redeployments of Israeli troops from the West Bank. At the end of the month Arafat rejected Netanyahu's appeals for a peace summit, stating that he would hold talks only after Israel had agreed to further redeployment and had fully implemented existing agreements. Progress had been further frustrated in early February, when the Ministry of the Interior approved plans to construct a new 132-home Jewish settlement in East Jerusalem.

Addressing the Knesset in March 1998, the UN Secretary-General, Kofi Annan, urged Israel to end 'provocative acts' towards the Palestinians, including the building of Jewish settlements. Meanwhile, the US envoy, Dennis Ross, visited the region, briefing Netanyahu, Arafat and Egypt's President Mubarak on a US peace proposal whereby Israel would redeploy from 13.1% of the West Bank over a 12-week period in exchange for specific security guarantees from the Palestinians. The proposal failed to revive the peace process, however, with Israel reportedly agreeing only to a phased redeployment from 9% of the territory. Violence had re-erupted on the West Bank, in the mean time, after three Palestinians were killed by Israeli soldiers near Hebron. Moreover, the assassination—allegedly by the Israeli secret services—of a senior Hamas official in late March precipitated widespread protests among Palestinians. Netanyahu warned that the risk of reprisal attacks on Israeli citizens would prevent further redeployments of Israeli troops from the Occupied Territories. In April two senior members of the Popular Front for the Liberation of Palestine (one of whom had been held without trial since 1992) were released from detention in Israel, after agreeing to renounce terrorism and violence.

In April 1998 Netanyahu and President Mubarak held their first meeting (in Cairo) since May 1997. President Mubarak reportedly advised Netanyahu to 'respond positively' to the US peace initiative. However, the Israeli Prime Minister rejected the proposal, which was publicly accepted by Arafat the following day. In May 1998 US Secretary of State Albright conducted separate rounds of talks with Netanyahu and Arafat in London, United Kingdom, with the aim of reviving negotiations on redeployments. The talks were inconclusive, and further meetings held in Washington later that month similarly failed to achieve a breakthrough. Meanwhile, celebrations to commemorate the 50th anniversary of the founding of the State of Israel provoked widespread rioting in the Occupied Territories.

In May 1998 the UN Committee Against Torture ruled for a second successive year that interrogation methods used by the Israeli security service, Shin Bet, were in contravention of the 1984 UN Convention against Torture and Other Cruel, Inhuman or Degrading Treatment or Punishment (which Israel had ratified in 1991). Shortly afterwards proceedings began at the Israeli Supreme Court in an unprecedented appeal case, brought by Palestinian detainees and two human rights groups, questioning the legality of Shin Bet's use of torture. (In September 1999 the Supreme Court ruled that the use of 'physical force' by Shin Bet during the interrogation of suspects was illegal. The ruling invalidated a 1987 decision that allowed the use of 'moderate physical pressure' against those accused of plotting terrorist attacks against Israel. Details of a report compiled by the State Comptroller in 1995 concerning Shin Bet's interrogation methods during the Palestinian *intifada* were published in early 2000. The report acknowledged that Palestinian prisoners had been 'systematically tortured' and that guide-lines allowing 'moderate physical pressure' had been exceeded.) A report published by a prominent human rights organization, Amnesty International, in September 1998 condemned both the Israeli and Palestinian authorities for alleged widespread human rights abuses. The report's demands included an end to imprisonment without trial, to judicial killings and to the legalized torture of detainees.

Details of the US peace plan were published in the Israeli newspaper *Ha'aretz* in June 1998. Although several Jewish settler groups threatened a campaign of civil disobedience in protest at any further redeployments from the West Bank, it became apparent that Netanyahu was under increasing pressure to accept the US initiative. Public opinion was reportedly shifting in favour of further redeployments, and in late June President Weizman (who had been elected for a second presidential term in March—defeating the candidate favoured by Netanyahu) angered Netanyahu by publicly demanding the dissolution of the Knesset and early elections so that Israelis might choose the future direction of peace negotiations. Meanwhile, further controversy arose when the Cabinet approved Netanyahu's draft plan whereby the municipal boundaries of Jerusalem would be extended to incorporate seven West Bank Jewish settlements—to create a 'Greater Jerusalem' covering six times the current area of the city. Arab leaders, including King Hussein, President Mubarak and Arafat, accused Netanyahu of seeking formally to annex parts of the West Bank, and the UN Security Council urged Israel to abandon the proposals. Arafat stated that the peace process was 'completely deadlocked', and that Palestinians could make no further concessions beyond those outlined in the US plan. During mid-1998 Netanyahu was the subject of allegations that he had intervened in the trial of Nahum Manbar, an Israeli business executive convicted of supplying toxic and chemical weapons material to Iran. Netanyahu denied claims that he had directly contacted the trial judge to demand a harsh sentence for Manbar, who

was sentenced to 16 years' imprisonment. The Ministry of Justice subsequently initiated an investigation into the affair. Netanyahu's domestic political standing was further undermined in late July, when the Labour Party (supported by some members of Netanyahu's coalition) secured a preliminary vote seeking the dissolution of the Knesset and early elections.

The first substantive senior-level meetings for several months between Israeli and Palestinian negotiators took place in Jerusalem in July 1998. However, Arafat withdrew his delegates in protest at what he described as Israel's 'obscure formulations' on the US peace plan. Israel had reportedly offered a compromise package, proposing redeployment from 10%, and partial redeployment from 3%, of the West Bank. By the end of August there were indications that the so-called '10+3' plan might lead to a revival of peace negotiations. However, the assassination of a settler rabbi in Hebron increased tensions on the West Bank, and the Israeli Government sealed off the town for several days. In late August a bomb attack in the centre of Tel-Aviv, believed to have been perpetrated by Hamas, injured some 18 people. In September Israel again closed its borders with the West Bank and Gaza, following warnings of imminent terrorist attacks in retaliation for the fatal shooting, by Israeli troops, of two leading Hamas members. Nevertheless, a US-mediated meeting between Netanyahu and Arafat held in Washington at the end of the month resulted in an agreement by the two leaders to attend a peace summit in mid-October, with the aim of finalizing agreement on further Israeli redeployments.

In October 1998 Ariel Sharon was redesignated Minister of Foreign Affairs and National Infrastructure. (The foreign affairs portfolio had been assumed by Netanyahu following David Levy's resignation in January.) Sharon's promotion was widely regarded as an attempt by Netanyahu to secure the support of right-wing nationalists and settler groups, since he was known to be opposed to redeployment from a further 13% of the West Bank.

On 23 October 1998, after nine days of intensive talks with President Clinton at the Wye Plantation, Maryland, USA, Netanyahu and Arafat finally signed an agreement that effectively outlined a three-month timetable for the implementation of the 1995 Interim Agreement and signalled the commencement of 'final status' talks, which were due to have begun in May 1996. The signing of this Wye River Memorandum, which broke a 19-month stalemate in the Israeli-Palestinian track of the Middle East peace process, was achieved despite a Palestinian grenade attack in Beersheba, in which at least 60 people were injured. With the mediation of Clinton and King Hussein of Jordan, Israel agreed to redeploy its troops from 13.1% of the West Bank, while the Palestinians agreed to intensify measures to prevent terrorism and to rewrite the Palestinian National Charter. In an effort to reassure Jewish settler groups in the West Bank, where there were demonstrations to protest against the 'land-for-security' deal, Netanyahu gave assurances that the construction of 1,025 new homes at the Har Homa settlement would proceed. On 11 November, after the postponement of four scheduled meetings (due to a bombing by Islamic Jihad in Jerusalem and Israeli fears of further terrorist attacks), the Israeli Cabinet approved the Wye Memorandum by a majority of eight votes to four. Netanyahu subsequently reiterated that a number of conditions would first have to be met by the Palestinians (primarily an annulment of clauses in the Palestinian National Charter demanding Israel's destruction), and threatened effective Israeli annexation of areas of the West Bank if a Palestinian state were to be declared on 4 May 1999. (Arafat continued to reassert his right to declare a Palestinian state on the expiry date of the interim stage defined in Oslo, an act Netanyahu claimed would fundamentally violate the Oslo accords.) In mid-November 1998 Arafat retracted a previous warning that the PLO would renew its armed struggle against Israel. On 17 November the Knesset ratified the Wye Memorandum by 75 votes to 19. Three days later the Israeli Government implemented the first stage of renewed redeployment from the West Bank, also releasing 250 Palestinian prisoners and signing a protocol allowing for the opening of an international airport at Gaza.

During December 1998 it became increasingly evident that divisions within Netanyahu's coalition over implementation of the Wye Memorandum were making government untenable. Attempts to avoid an early general election by offering to reappoint David Levy to the Government were frustrated when the Gesher leader refused the terms proposed by Netanyahu, and the administration effectively collapsed when the Minister of

Finance, Yaacov Ne'eman, announced his resignation. Shortly afterwards the Knesset voted to hold elections to the legislature and premiership in the spring of 1999. The impending election prompted the emergence of several new political parties and the realignment of political allegiances. Netanyahu's leadership was challenged by senior members of Likud, including Binyamin Begin, who left to form the New Herut party. In January 1999 Netanyahu dismissed Itzhak Mordechai as Minister of Defence, appointing Moshe Arens in his place. Speculation that Mordechai had been intending to leave Likud was apparently confirmed when he launched the new Centre Party.

Meanwhile, unrest in the West Bank and Gaza increased prior to a visit by President Clinton in December 1998. Palestinians demonstrated in support of almost 700 of their prisoners who began a nine-day hunger-strike to protest against Israel's failure to honour commitments made at Wye Plantation to release Palestinians detained on political charges. Clinton attended a meeting of the PNC, at which the removal from the Palestinian National Charter of all clauses seeking Israel's destruction was reaffirmed. At a meeting between Clinton, Arafat and Netanyahu at the Erez check-point, Netanyahu reiterated accusations that the Palestinians had not adequately addressed their security commitments and announced that he would not release Palestinian prisoners considered to have 'blood on their hands'. Netanyahu also repeated his demand that Arafat renounce his intention to declare Palestinian statehood in May 1999. Arafat, for his part, reasserted demands for a moratorium on the construction of Jewish settlements in disputed territory. Following the meeting, Netanyahu announced that the second phase of Israeli troop deployment envisaged by the Wye Memorandum, scheduled for 18 December, would not be undertaken. The Knesset subsequently voted to suspend implementation of the Wye Memorandum, effectively leading to a suspension of the peace process. In late December Arafat freed the Hamas spiritual leader, Sheikh Ahmad Yassin, from house arrest, prompting further Israeli claims that agreed anti-terrorism measures were not being implemented.

In January 1999 it was reported that US Secretary of State Albright would refuse to meet Ariel Sharon during a visit to the USA, owing to US frustration with Israel's 'freezing' of peace negotiations. The stalemate appeared likely to continue as violent clashes between Israelis and Palestinians again broke out in the West Bank. The US administration threatened to withhold US $1,200m. promised to Israel to fund its redeployment in the West Bank unless it complied with the terms of the Wye Memorandum. For several months President Clinton refused to hold a private meeting with Netanyahu, while agreeing to meet Arafat in March to discuss the Palestinian leader's threatened unilateral declaration of statehood on 4 May; the declaration was postponed at the end of April, following intense international pressure. Meanwhile, relations between Israel and the European Union (EU) deteriorated, owing to continuing disagreement over Likud's settlement programme and the status of Jerusalem. In March the EU strongly condemned Israeli instructions to foreign delegations not to visit the PLO's *de facto* headquarters in Jerusalem. Earlier in March the EU had provoked condemnation from Israeli officials by reaffirming that it regarded Jerusalem as a *corpus separatum* (in accordance with UN Resolution 181), which was outside Israeli sovereignty.

Although in March 1998 Ariel Sharon announced publicly that Israel still planned to assassinate the Hamas leader Khalid Meshaal, there were signs of an improvement in Israeli-Jordanian relations during 1998. In March Netanyahu and Crown Prince Hassan signed a series of bilateral trade agreements. In mid-April King Hussein and the Israeli Prime Minister met for the first time since the assassination attempt which had strained relations in 1997. In December 1998 Israel agreed to allow foreign airlines en route to Jordan to use Israeli airspace. There was widespread apprehension about the future of Israel's relations with Jordan following the death, in February 1999, of King Hussein (whose funeral was attended by Netanyahu). Nevertheless, the Israeli Government expected 'continuity' in its relations with Jordan under the new King Abdullah. In September of that year Israel commended the Jordanian authorities for their arrest of Khalid Meshaal and two other Hamas leaders.

Hostilities between Israeli forces and Hezbollah in southern Lebanon persisted throughout 1998. In that year some 23 Israeli soldiers were killed, and there was increasing pressure on Prime Minister Netanyahu, even from some Likud ministers, for a

unilateral withdrawal from the territory. On 1 April the Israeli Security Cabinet voted unanimously to adopt UN Resolution 425 (which called for an immediate withdrawal of Israeli troops from all Lebanese territory), provided that the Lebanese army gave security guarantees. However, both Lebanon and Syria demanded an unconditional withdrawal. At the end of May fighting in southern Lebanon was at its most intense for several months. In June, however, the first Israeli-Lebanese exchange of prisoners and bodies since July 1996 took place. Fighting escalated when, in August 1998, Hezbollah launched rocket attacks on northern Israel in retaliation for an Israeli helicopter attack in which a senior Lebanese military official died. Seven Israeli soldiers died in two attacks in November, leading Netanyahu to curtail a European tour in order to hold an emergency cabinet meeting on a possible withdrawal. In December an Israeli air attack in which eight Lebanese civilians were killed provoked condemnation from the ILMG, which declared it to be a violation of the cease-fire 'understanding' reached in April 1996. Following several Hezbollah attacks, in January 1999 Netanyahu reiterated previous warnings that in the event of further attacks, Israeli troops would target Lebanon's infrastructure. In February three Israeli army officers were killed during fighting with Hezbollah. A few days later the commander of the Israeli army unit for liaison with the SLA was killed in a bomb attack—the most senior Israeli officer to be killed in southern Lebanon since 1982. Israel responded with its heaviest air raids against Lebanon since the 1996 'Grapes of Wrath' operation, prompting fears of another major conflict. However, Israel's Minister of Defence stated that Israel had no intention of escalating the conflict as long as Syria refrained from encouraging Hezbollah rocket attacks on northern Israel.

In July 1998 it had been reported that Israel and Syria might resume talks on the issue of the Golan Heights, on the basis of a French initiative whereby Israel would accept a 'land-for-peace' formula in return for Syrian acceptance of Israel's security needs. However, in late July the Knesset approved preliminary legislation seeking a majority parliamentary vote and a referendum before Israel would withdraw from the territory; the vote was condemned in Syria. Tensions between the two countries increased in September when Israel publicly stated its intention to enter a military alliance with Turkey.

In April 1999 Aryeh Der'i (a close associate of Netanyahu) was sentenced to four years' imprisonment, having been found guilty of bribery, fraud and breach of public trust. His sentence was suspended pending appeal, thus enabling the Shas leader to campaign in the forthcoming elections.

By the time of the general election, held on 17 May 1999, Netanyahu and Ehud Barak were the only remaining candidates for the premiership, four others having withdrawn their candidacy. Following a decision by Itzhak Mordechai to transfer his support to Barak, who in March had established the 'One Israel' movement (including Gesher and the moderate Meimad party), victory for the Labour leader seemed certain. Barak was elected Prime Minister with 56.1% of the total votes cast. In the elections to the Knesset, Barak's One Israel alliance secured 26 seats, while Likud's strength declined from 32 seats to 19. Shas, meanwhile, increased its representation to 17 seats. The new Knesset contained an unprecedented 15 factions. Some 78.8% of the electorate were reported to have voted. Netanyahu subsequently resigned from both the Knesset and the Likud leadership, and in early September Ariel Sharon was elected as Likud's new Chairman.

Although Ehud Barak had received a clear mandate to form a government that would attempt to revive the stalled Middle East peace process, Israel's Prime Minister-elect committed himself only to seek a formula for regional peace. Barak stated that he would observe four 'security red lines' concerning negotiations with the Palestinians: Jerusalem would remain under Israeli sovereignty; there would be no return to the pre-1967 borders; most West Bank settlers would remain in settlements under Israeli sovereignty; and no 'foreign armies' would be based west of the Jordan river. Following complex negotiations, Barak forged a broad coalition of the Centre Party, Shas, Meretz, Israel B'Aliyah and the NRP (talks with Likud having collapsed), which was endorsed by the Knesset in early July. Barak himself took the defence portfolio, granting the foreign affairs ministry to David Levy; Itzhak Mordechai was made one of three Deputy Prime Ministers and assigned the transport portfolio, while Shimon Peres became Minister of Regional Co-operation.

In July 1999 the Speaker of the Palestinian Legislative Council became the first senior Palestinian official to address the Knesset. Meanwhile, Barak held a series of summit meetings with Arab and European leaders, culminating in discussions with US President Clinton in mid-July. The first direct talks between the new Israeli premier and Yasser Arafat were held at the Erez check-point in Gaza on 11 July, during which both leaders reaffirmed their commitment to peace. By late July, however, relations had deteriorated, after Barak expressed the desire to combine the Israeli land withdrawals agreed under the terms of the Wye Memorandum with 'final status' negotiations. The Palestinians were angered by this proposed delay in implementing the Wye agreement. In August Palestinian negotiators suspended discussions after Barak accused them of refusing to compromise, but negotiations resumed after Israel agreed to withdraw its demand to postpone further land withdrawals.

In early September 1999, during a visit to the region by US Secretary of State Albright, Barak and Arafat travelled to Egypt for talks at Sharm esh-Sheikh. On 4 September the two leaders signed the Sharm esh-Sheikh Memorandum (or Wye Two accords), which outlined a revised timetable for implementation of the outstanding provisions of the original Wye Memorandum and was thus intended to facilitate the resumption of 'final status' talks: a new target date—13 September 2000—was set for the conclusion of a comprehensive 'final status' settlement, with a framework agreement to be in place by 13 February. (One important change was the reduction, to 350, of the number of Palestinian prisoners that Israel was required to release.) Although the success of the deal was immediately threatened by two suicide bomb attacks in northern Israel, on 8 September the Knesset ratified the Wye Two accords. The following day Israel released some 200 Palestinian prisoners, and on 10 September a further 7% of the West Bank was transferred to Palestinian civilian control. A ceremony marking the launch of 'final status' negotiations between Israel and the Palestinians was held at the Erez check-point on 13 September, and a few days later it was reported that Barak and Arafat had held a secret meeting to discuss an agenda for such talks. Also in mid-September Israel signed an agreement with the USA to purchase 50 F-16 fighter aircraft. A further 151 Palestinian prisoners were released from Israeli custody in mid-October. On 25 October a southern 'safe passage' for Palestinians travelling between Gaza and Hebron was finally opened, under the terms of the Wye Memorandum. (King Abdullah of Jordan, who was a witness to the signing of the Sharm esh-Sheikh memorandum, made his first official visit to Israel in April 2000.)

In September 1999 Netanyahu and his wife were questioned by police following allegations, published in the daily *Yediot Aharanot*, that they had charged extensive private work on their residence to the Prime Minister's Office while Netanyahu was in power. Further allegations of the misuse of public funds emerged, and in October police reportedly seized several official gifts from Netanyahu's home and offices. (In late March 2000 the police recommended that Netanyahu should stand trial on charges of bribery, fraud, breach of trust and obstruction of justice, and that his wife should be charged with fraud and theft; however, in late September the Attorney-General announced that no prosecution would be brought against the Netanyahus, owing to insufficient evidence.)

In late September 1999 the Shas and Likud parties announced that they were to co-ordinate their policies on issues of national importance; however, Shas denied rumours that the party was about to join the opposition. (An ongoing dispute between Shas and the Government over the allocation of funds for Shas' education proposals regularly threatened Barak's new coalition; however, the crisis appeared to have been resolved after the announcement of the 2000 budget in December.) Meanwhile, Eliyahu Yishai, the Minister of Labour and Social Affairs, replaced Aryeh Der'i (who had resigned the leadership in June) as Chairman of Shas.

In the autumn of 1999 Barak encountered severe criticism by left-wing groups and Palestinians over his Government's apparent intention to continue to approve the expansion of Jewish settlements in the West Bank. (Since coming to power, the Government had issued tenders for some 2,600 new homes in such settlements.) Barak subsequently ruled that several of the 42 'outpost settlements' established in the West Bank under the Likud Government had been built illegally. After reaching a compromise with angry settler groups, 12 of the 'outposts' were dismantled in October.

In October 1999 Mauritania became the third member of the Arab League (after Egypt and Jordan) to establish full diplomatic relations with Israel. In early November Arafat, Barak and US President Clinton held talks in Oslo, Norway, after a ceremony to mark the fourth anniversary of Itzhak Rabin's assassination. Representatives of Israel and the PNA commenced talks on 'final status' issues on 8 November 1999 in the West Bank city of Ramallah; further rounds of talks were held during November and December. Prior to the discussions, three bombs had exploded in the Israeli town of Netanya, wounding at least 33 people. (Although no group claimed responsibility for the bombings, they followed an alleged warning by the military wing of Hamas of an escalation of violence in protest at Israeli settlement policies.) The redeployment of Israeli armed forces from a further 5% of the West Bank (due on 15 November) was delayed owing to a dispute over which areas were to be transferred. Relations between Israel and the Palestinians deteriorated again in early December, following an announcement that the Israeli Government had issued tenders for a further 500 Jewish homes to be built in the West Bank, although Barak, apparently under US pressure, subsequently refused to authorize the construction. Later that month Barak and Arafat met on Palestinian territory for the first time. At the end of December Israel released some 26 Palestinian 'security' prisoners as a 'goodwill gesture'.

On 6–7 January 2000 Israeli troops withdrew from a further 5% of the West Bank. However, in mid-January Israel announced the postponement of a third redeployment, agreed under Wye Two (and scheduled for 20 January), until Barak had returned from talks with Syrian representatives in the USA (see below). Meanwhile, some 20 people were wounded in a bomb explosion in northern Israel, believed to have been carried out by Palestinian militants. In early February Palestinian officials suspended peace negotiations with Israel, following the decision by the Israeli Cabinet to withdraw its armed forces from a sparsely-populated 6.1% of the West Bank. The redeployment from a further 6.1% of the West Bank took place on 21 March (Israel had on the previous day released 15 Palestinian prisoners), facilitating an official resumption of 'final status' talks. A ruling by Israel's Supreme Court, in early March, that the allocation of state-owned land on the basis of religion, nationality or ethnicity was illegal allowed Israeli Arabs to purchase land for the first time.

Meanwhile, in May 1999 senior Israeli commanders in southern Lebanon for the first time urged an immediate Israeli withdrawal. (Prime Minister-elect Barak had made a pre-election pledge to recall Israeli troops from Lebanon by July 2000.) In June 1999 the SLA completed a unilateral withdrawal from the Jezzine enclave. Later that month Barak was reportedly angered when the outgoing Netanyahu administration launched a series of air attacks on Lebanon, destroying Beirut's main power station and other infrastructure, in response to Hezbollah rocket attacks on northern Israel. In July Barak confirmed that he would propose to his Cabinet a unilateral withdrawal from Lebanon if no peace accord had been reached (in the context of an agreement with Syria over the Golan Heights) within one year. In December Israel apologized for an attack in which some 18 Lebanese schoolchildren were injured. The incident followed an increase in Hezbollah military action after the announcement of a resumption of Israeli-Syrian peace negotiations (see below). It was subsequently reported that Israel and Syria had reached an 'understanding in principle' to limit the fighting in southern Lebanon; the informal cease-fire did not endure, however, and in late January 2000 a senior SLA commander became the first Israeli soldier to be killed there for five months. At the end of January the deaths of another three of its soldiers led Israel to declare that peace talks with Syria would not resume until Syria took action to restrain Hezbollah. Attacks by Hezbollah escalated none the less, and in early February Israel retaliated with a massive series of bombing raids on Lebanese infrastructure. Israel announced a unilateral withdrawal from the 1996 'cease-fire' agreement, and there were once again fears of a major conflict. Following the killing of three Israeli soldiers by Hezbollah in mid-February 2000, the Israeli Security Cabinet approved wide powers for the Prime Minister to order immediate retaliatory bombing raids into Lebanon.

In late January 2000 a criminal investigation began into the financial affairs of the Israeli President, Ezer Weizman, following allegations that he had accepted some US $450,000 in donations from a French businessman while serving as a member of the Knesset (when he should have declared any additional income). Despite demands for his resignation, Weizman insisted that no favours had been granted in return for the donations. In early April the police declared that Weizman would not be prosecuted, owing to a lack of evidence. Weizman had announced that he would retire prior to the expiry of his second term of office in 2003, citing ill health; however, after the police investigation failed completely to exonerate him, the President stated in late May 2000 that he would resign on 10 July. Also in late January the State Comptroller accused the One Israel campaign team for the 1999 general election of serious financial irregularities. The Attorney-General subsequently ordered a criminal investigation into the financial activities of One Israel and several other parties; One Israel was required to pay a fine of NIS 13.5m. In early March 2000 Itzhak Mordechai took a leave of absence from the Government pending a police investigation into allegations that he had sexually harassed a female ministry employee. Mordechai denied the claims, but in late May he was arraigned on three charges of sexual harassment; he subsequently resigned as leader of the Centre Party, in which post he was succeeded by the Minister of Tourism, Amnon Lipkin-Shahak. In March 2001 Mordechai was found guilty of committing indecent assault against two of the three women who had brought charges; in May he received an 18-month suspended sentence.

A third round of 'final status' discussions opened in Eilat on 30 April 2000. The talks began acrimoniously, as Palestinian negotiators denounced a recent decision by the Israeli Government to approve construction of 174 new housing units in the West Bank. Maps presented by Israeli officials to the PNA in early May, defining Barak's interpretation of a future Palestinian state, were rejected by the Palestinians as 'utterly unacceptable'. Two days later Barak and Arafat held a crisis meeting in Ramallah, at which Barak proposed that Israel transfer to full PNA control three Arab villages situated close to Jerusalem, on condition that the third West Bank redeployment (due to be implemented in June) was postponed until after the conclusion of a final peace settlement. The Knesset approved the transfer in mid-May. The decision prompted the threatened withdrawal from Barak's Government, should the transfer take place, of the NRP, while Jewish settlers held a large-scale demonstration in Jerusalem. (Right-wing, religious and Russian immigrant parties saw the transfer as an unnecessary concession to the Palestinians). Meanwhile, large, and initially peaceful, demonstrations by Palestinians in support of a hunger-strike by Palestinians held in Israeli gaols escalated into violence on 15 May—declared by Palestinians as a 'day of rage'. Three days of violent gun battles in the West Bank between Israeli forces, Palestinian police and civilians resulted in the deaths of some seven Palestinians (including two policemen), while several Israeli soldiers and civilians were injured. In late May Barak ordered an end to 'secret' talks between Israeli and Palestinian officials in Stockholm, Sweden, after an Israeli child was seriously injured in a petrol bomb attack near Jericho. Barak also announced that an Israeli withdrawal from the Arab villages would not be implemented until the PNA took appropriate measures to curb the Palestinian unrest. By early June, however, Barak appeared to be willing to resume peace negotiations, after the PNA arrested several Palestinians believed to have been responsible for the recent violence. Later in the month Israel released three Palestinian prisoners as a 'gesture of goodwill'.

A major political crisis developed in mid-June 2000 when One Israel's largest coalition partner, the right-wing Shas, threatened to withdraw from the Government unless its demands regarding the peace process and the funding of its religious schools were met. After Barak capitulated to most of the party's demands, the four Shas ministers withdrew their resignations, thereby averting the collapse of the coalition; however, the return of Shas to the Government led to the departure of the two Meretz ministers, the Minister of Education, Yossi Sarid, and the Minister of Industry and Trade, Ran Cohen, both strong supporters of the Oslo peace process. In early July the former Shas leader, Aryeh Der'i, received a three-year term of imprisonment, having been found guilty of bribery and fraud; he began his sentence in September.

In early July 2000 Bill Clinton invited Barak and Arafat to attend a peace summit, to be held at the US presidential retreat at Camp David, in an attempt to reach a framework agreement for a final settlement. Immediately prior to the summit the Israeli Government was severely weakened when the three right-wing parties (Israel B'Aliyah, the NRP and Shas) withdrew their participation from the coalition, in protest at what they perceived to be Barak's readiness to concede more Israeli territory to the PNA. Barak was left without six Cabinet ministers (including the Minster of the Interior, Natan Sharansky) and narrowly survived a 'no confidence' motion in the Knesset. President Clinton opened the Camp David talks on 11 July, and, although no accord had been reached by their scheduled close on 19 July, he persuaded Israeli and Palestinian negotiators to remain at Camp David. However, despite intensive mediation efforts, the summit ended on 25 July without agreement. It was reported that significant progress had been made concerning the borders of a future Palestinian entity, and that some progress had been reached on the issue of Palestinian refugees. It had none the less proved impossible for Israeli and Palestinian negotiators to reach a compromise regarding the future status of Jerusalem. Barak had apparently offered the PNA municipal authority over certain parts of East Jerusalem and access to Islamic holy sites in the Old City, although Israel would retain full sovereignty. Arafat, meanwhile, had continued to demand a Palestinian state with East Jerusalem as its capital and sovereignty over the Islamic holy sites. In the final communiqué of the Camp David summit, both sides vowed to continue the pursuit of a 'final status' settlement and to avoid 'unilateral actions'—thereby implying that Arafat would not proceed to declare a Palestinian state after 13 September. Nevertheless, the failure of the talks led to fears of renewed violence in the West Bank and Gaza Strip.

In the presidential election held in the Knesset on 31 July 2000 the little-known Moshe Katsav, of Likud, unexpectedly defeated Barak's nominee, Shimon Peres, by 63 votes to 57 in a second round of voting (neither candidate having secured an outright majority in the first). Katsav was duly sworn in as the eighth President of Israel on 1 August, to serve an exceptional seven-year term. Immediately after the election Barak survived another 'no confidence' motion. However, in early August the Minister of Foreign Affairs, David Levy, announced his resignation, citing disagreements with Barak over the peace process (Levy had notably refused to attend the Camp David summit). The Minister of Public Security, Shlomo Ben-Ami, was subsequently appointed acting Minister of Foreign Affairs. (He was confirmed in this post in early November.) Later in the month Barak's long-serving Chief of Staff resigned his post. Also in August the Prime Minister announced proposals for legislation that would significantly reduce the influence of the Orthodox establishment in Israel, and in early September the Cabinet voted to abolish the Ministry of Religious Affairs.

At the end of July 2000 Clinton stated that the USA was considering the relocation of its embassy from Tel-Aviv to Jerusalem, apparently reflecting US frustration at what it regarded as Palestinian intransigence on the issue of the city's status. Israeli and Palestinian officials none the less resumed talks in an attempt to break the deadlock in the peace process, and the PNA came under mounting pressure from the international community to postpone a unilateral declaration of independence on 13 September. (Shortly before that date the Palestinian legislature voted to delay any such declaration for an indefinite period.) Meanwhile, in early August there were clashes between Muslims and Jews in Jerusalem, after Jewish extremists attempted to invade the al-Aqsa mosque. In mid-August it was reported that Barak had for the first time hinted at offering statehood to the Palestinians. During that month Israeli security services claimed to have uncovered a number of Palestinian 'terrorist squads', and more than 20 alleged militants, some of whom were believed to have links with the Saudi Arabian-born militant Islamist, Osama Bin Laden, were arrested.

In late September 2000 Barak and Arafat met, at the Israeli premier's home, for the first time since the failure of the Camp David summit. However, the resumption of contacts was swiftly overshadowed by a serious escalation of violence between Palestinians and Israelis in the West Bank and Gaza Strip, which threatened to bring a complete halt to the Middle East peace process and led to increased fears that a conflict might once again engulf the region. On 28 September a highly controversial visit by the Likud leader, Ariel Sharon, to the Temple Mount (or Haram ash-Sharif) in Jerusalem (the site of the Dome of the Rock and the al-Aqsa mosque) provoked violent protests by stone-throwing Palestinians, which quickly spread to other towns in the Palestinian territories. For the first time, moreover, Israeli Arabs clashed with security forces within Israel itself. The Israeli Government received international criticism for the severity of its response to the renewed Palestinian uprising—

widely termed the al-Aqsa *intifada*. On 7 October the UN Security Council issued a resolution condemning the 'excessive use of force' employed by Israeli security forces against Palestinian demonstrators. Intensive diplomatic efforts aimed at restoring calm, particularly by Egypt, the USA and France, failed to end the violent confrontations (which within a month had claimed at least 140 lives—all but eight of the dead were Palestinians—and wounded thousands more). Israel responded by closing the borders of the West Bank and Gaza Strip. Barak emphasized to Arafat his intention to suspend the peace process if the Palestinian unrest continued, and demanded that Arafat re-arrest about 65 militant Islamists who had recently been freed from Palestinian detention. Arafat, for his part, demanded an international inquiry into the causes of the violence. The crisis escalated in mid-October after Israeli forces launched rocket attacks on the headquarters of Arafat's Fatah movement in Ramallah, in response to the murder of two Israeli soldiers by a crowd of angry Palestinians. Following mediation by the UN Secretary-General, on 16–17 October an emergency summit meeting between Barak and Arafat was convened by President Clinton and hosted by President Mubarak at Sharm esh-Sheikh. At the close of the meeting Clinton announced that Israel and the Palestinians had agreed 'immediate concrete measures' to end the fighting. However, violence continued, and on 22 October Barak announced that Israel was to take what he termed a 'time-out' from the peace process. The declaration came as Barak undertook discussions with Likud (which opposes the Oslo process) on the formation of a 'national unity' government prior to the reconvening of the Knesset for the new parliamentary term; no compromise was reached, however, reportedly owing to Ariel Sharon's demand for a veto on all decisions relating to national security. Meanwhile, Arab leaders, meeting in emergency session in Cairo, declared that Israel bore full responsibility for the recent violence. Morocco, Tunisia and Oman announced that they had severed diplomatic relations with Israel, and Qatar broke off ties in November.

A suicide bomb attack perpetrated by Islamic Jihad on an Israeli military target in Gaza at the end of October 2000 apparently signalled a new campaign of violence by militant Islamist organizations, and led Israeli forces to declare a new strategy of targeting leading members of such groups, as well as senior Fatah members. In early November the Israeli Minister of Regional Co-operation, Shimon Peres, held crisis talks with Arafat in Gaza, at which the two sides were reported to have agreed a fragile cease-fire. On the following day, however, the truce was broken when a car bomb exploded in Jerusalem, killing two Israelis; Islamic Jihad claimed responsibility for the attack, while Barak held the PNA responsible through the recent release of dozens of Islamist militants. Also in early November Arafat requested US support in his appeal to the UN to provide an international peace-keeping force to protect Palestinians in the Occupied Territories. In mid-November Israel imposed what amounted to a complete economic blockade of the West Bank and Gaza Strip, in an effort to overcome increasing concerns over its national security. Later in the month the explosion of a bomb close to a bus carrying Israeli schoolchildren (as a result of which two people died and several children were injured) provoked public outrage and led Israel to launch further air raids against Fatah targets. Egypt responded by announcing in late November that it was recalling its ambassador to Israel. Meanwhile, Israeli officials again blamed the PNA for a car bomb attack in northern Israel. In early December a US-led investigative commission began inquiries into the Israeli–Palestinian clashes, which by now increasingly involved fighting between Jewish settlers and Palestinians in the West Bank and Gaza. In mid-December five Palestinian policemen were killed by Israeli forces during a gun battle in the Gaza Strip.

It was reported at the end of November 2000 that the Palestinians had rejected a partial peace plan put forward by Barak, whereby Israel would effect further troop redeployments from the West Bank in exchange for an agreement to postpone discussion of the remaining 'final status' issues. Although US-brokered talks between Israeli and Palestinian negotiators did resume in December, in an attempt to achieve a framework peace settlement prior to the expiry of Bill Clinton's term of office in late January 2001, the differences between the two sides remained apparently unbreachable. The outgoing US President had reportedly proposed to the two sides a far-reaching deal which included granting the PNA sovereignty over Islamic holy sites in the Old City of Jerusalem, while the area (also

comprising the Temple Mount) would remain under Israeli control. However, the talks stalled in late December 2000 following the deaths of two Israelis in two bomb explosions in Tel-Aviv and the Gaza Strip. At the end of the month an extremist Jewish settler, Rabbi Binyamin Kahane, and a senior Fatah official were both shot dead in the West Bank. In early January 2001 three bombs exploded in the northern Israeli town of Netanya, wounding more than 40 people. Discussions between Israeli and Palestinian representatives resumed in mid-January but were broken off a few days later, after the killing of a Jewish settler in the Gaza Strip; the attack resulted in revenge attacks on Palestinians by right-wing settlers. In late January the international fact-finding commission suspended its activities, owing to Israel's alleged refusal to co-operate in its work. Renewed attempts at breaking the deadlock in the peace process had failed by early February, when Israelis turned their attention to the election for the premiership. By this time more than 375 people (the majority of whom were Palestinians) had been killed since the beginning of the al-Aqsa *intifada* in September 2000.

At the end of November 2000 Barak unexpectedly called early prime ministerial elections for 2001, in an apparent attempt to secure his increasingly beleaguered Government. The date of the premiership election was subsequently set for February 2001 (ahead of legislative elections due in May 2003). The Likud leader, Ariel Sharon, immediately declared his candidacy for the premiership, as did Netanyahu (against whom corruption charges had recently been abandoned). The former Prime Minister urged the Knesset either to amend electoral legislation that prevents non-members of the Knesset standing for election, or to vote for the assembly's dissolution; however, he withdrew from the premiership contest in mid-December, after the Knesset voted against a bill to dissolve itself and thus force a general election in February 2001. Despite the widely held belief that the Minister of Regional Co-operation, Shimon Peres, was the only Labour politician likely to present a viable challenge to Sharon, Barak insisted that he would contest, and win, the election for Prime Minister.

Thus, the prime ministerial election, on 6 February 2001, was contested by Ariel Sharon and Ehud Barak, and resulted in an overwhelming victory for the Likud leader, with 62.4% of the votes cast; the rate of electoral participation was 62.3% of registered voters. Barak's defeat was compounded by the effective loss of the Israeli Arab vote—as the Arab parties had urged their supporters to boycott or abstain in the poll—and was interpreted as a decisive rejection by the majority of Israelis of the Oslo peace process. Sharon, who had during the election campaign undertaken to promote the return of domestic and regional stability, swiftly undertook the task of forming a broadly-based government of national unity, essentially in an effort to secure a political base in the Knesset (where Likud held only 19 of the 120 seats). Immediately following his election defeat, meanwhile, Barak resigned as Labour leader, leaving the party, already bitterly divided over the issue of participation in a government led by Sharon, in disarray. There was further confusion as it emerged a few days later that Barak (who remained Prime Minister in a 'caretaker' capacity pending the formation of a new cabinet) was considering accepting the post of Minister of Defence in a coalition administration and was thus apparently deferring his resignation. A little over a week later, however, as coalition talks continued, the defeated premier announced that he would not enter a government of national unity under Sharon and was intending to withdraw from political life 'for some time'; Barak none the less indicated that he would advise the Labour Party to finalize a unity government with Likud. In late February the party's central committee voted to join a coalition administration, despite the objections of prominent members including the outgoing Minister of Justice, Yossi Beilin, and Minister of Foreign Affairs, Shlomo Ben-Ami. This enabled Sharon to conclude coalition agreements principally with the religious and other parties of the right wing, and the unity Government was presented for Knesset approval one month after the prime ministerial election. The 26-member Cabinet (reportedly the largest in Israel's history) included the ultra-orthodox Shas (whose leader, Eliyahu Yishai, became Deputy Prime Minister and Minister of the Interior), Israel B'Aliyah (Natan Sharansky's appointment as Deputy Prime Minister and Minister of Construction and Housing was particularly well received in the Occupied Territories) and the extreme right-wing Haichud Haleumi-Israel B'Aitainu bloc; junior ministerial portfolios were allocated to United

Torah Judaism, to a member of the Centre Party (itself bitterly divided over the issue of joining the coalition) and to the moderate religious party Meimad. The finance and justice portfolios were notably taken, respectively, by Silvan Shalom (also a Deputy Prime Minister) and Meir Sheetrit of Likud, while Prime Minister Sharon assumed personal responsibility for immigrant absorption. Binyamin Ben-Eliezer of the Labour Party was named Minister of Defence, and Shimon Peres accepted the position of Deputy Prime Minister and Minister of Foreign Affairs.

While the new defence minister came to the Government with a reputation for an uncompromising stance, the appointment of Peres was a cause for cautious optimism for those, within Israel and beyond, who wished to see the Middle East peace process revived. Meanwhile, there was considerable uncertainty regarding the prospects for a continuation of the Oslo process under Ariel Sharon, and without the active engagement in Middle East diplomacy of the administration of Bill Clinton (whose term of office as US President had come to an end in January 2001).

In early March 2000 the Israeli Cabinet voted unanimously to withdraw its forces from southern Lebanon by 7 July, even in the absence of a peace agreement with Syria. The Lebanese Government responded by demanding that Israel also depart from a small area on the Syrian border known as Shebaa Farms. In mid-April Israel released 13 Lebanese prisoners who had been detained without trial for more than a decade, apparently as 'bargaining chips' for Israeli soldiers missing in Lebanon. Fighting between Israeli troops and Hezbollah intensified in May, and there were fears that further violence might follow an Israeli withdrawal after it was announced that Israel would not disarm the SLA. On 23 May Israel's Security Cabinet voted to accelerate the withdrawal of its remaining troops from southern Lebanon. By this date Hezbollah had taken control of about one-third of the territory following the evacuation by the SLA of outposts transferred to its control by the Israeli army; moreover, mass defections from the SLA were reported. Meanwhile, Lebanese citizens stormed the al-Khiam prison in the security zone and freed 144 inmates. The rapid departure of all Israeli forces from southern Lebanon was completed on 24 May, nearly six weeks before Barak's original July deadline. Israeli public opinion generally welcomed an end to the occupation, since about 900 Israelis had been killed in southern Lebanon since 1978. After the withdrawal there was an influx of refugees, as several thousands of SLA members and their families crossed the border into northern Israel, fearing reprisals should they remain in Lebanon. In mid-June the UN Security Council formally confirmed that Israel had completed its withdrawal from Lebanon in compliance with UN Resolution 425. UNIFIL's mandate was extended for a six-month period at the end of July (by which time UNIFIL personnel were patrolling the area vacated by Israeli forces, monitoring the line of withdrawal and providing humanitarian assistance), and again in late January 2001.

Meanwhile, Hezbollah reaffirmed in mid-2000 that it would pursue its armed campaign against Israel until Shebaa Farms was returned to Lebanese control. The al-Aqsa *intifada*, which erupted in late September, precipitated renewed operations by Hezbollah against the Israeli army. In early October three Israeli soldiers were kidnapped on the border with Lebanon by Hezbollah militants who were demanding the release of Lebanese and Palestinian prisoners held in Israel. One week later an Israeli army reservist was also captured by Hezbollah. Tensions escalated at the end of November when an Israeli soldier was killed by a Hezbollah bomb at Shebaa Farms; Israel responded by launching air raids on suspected Hezbollah targets. German-mediated attempts at securing an exchange of prisoners between Israel and Lebanon were reported in December.

Syria had welcomed the election of Ehud Barak to the Israeli premiership in May 1999. In July, at the inauguration of his Cabinet, Barak undertook to negotiate a bilateral peace with Syria, based on UN Resolutions 242 and 338: this was interpreted as a signal of his intention to return most of the occupied Golan Heights in exchange for peace and normalized relations. On 20 July Syria ordered a 'cease-fire' with Israel. However, it was not until early December that the two sides agreed to a resumption of negotiations from the point at which they had broken off in 1996, reportedly as a result of diplomatic efforts by US President Clinton and secret meetings between Israeli and Syrian officials. The Knesset subsequently approved the decision to resume talks, while Barak reasserted that any agreement concluded with Syria would be put to a national referendum.

President Clinton inaugurated peace discussions between Barak and the Syrian Minister of Foreign Affairs, Farouk ash-Shara', in Washington, DC, on 15 December 1999. The talks commenced amid rising tensions in southern Lebanon, and resulted only in an agreement to resume discussions in January 2000. Barak, meanwhile, was encountering growing opposition in Israel to a possible return of the Golan Heights to Syria. In late December 1999 it was reported that Israel and Syria had agreed an informal 'cease-fire' to curb hostilities in Lebanon. Barak and ash-Shara' attended further discussions (in which President Clinton played an active role) on 3–10 January 2000 in Shepherdstown, West Virginia. As a preliminary to the talks it was agreed that four committees would be established to discuss simultaneously the issues of borders, security, normalization of relations and water sharing. As further discussions proved inconclusive, the US administration presented a 'draft working document' to both sides, as the basis for a framework agreement. However, Syria announced that it required a commitment from Israel to withdraw from the Golan Heights before negotiations could resume. Israel, meanwhile, demanded the personal involvement of President Hafiz al-Assad in the peace process. In early January a demonstration was held in Tel-Aviv by some 10,000 Israelis opposed to any withdrawal from the Golan Heights; meanwhile, Israel B'Aliyah and the NRP threatened to leave Barak's coalition in any such event. On 17 January talks between Israel and Syria, which had been scheduled to reconvene two days later, were postponed indefinitely. Despite the intensification of the conflict in southern Lebanon (see above), and a Knesset vote in early March to change the majority required in the event of a referendum on an Israeli withdrawal from the Golan Heights from 50% of participants to 50% of the registered electorate, hopes of an imminent breakthrough in the Syrian track of the Middle East peace process were raised by the announcement, later in March, that Presidents Clinton and Assad were to meet in Geneva, Switzerland. However, the talks, on 26 March, broke down after only three hours, when it became apparent that the US President had brought with him no new Israeli proposals to offer to Syria regarding its demand for a full and unconditional withdrawal from the Golan Heights. In early April both Barak and Clinton appeared to acknowledge that official Israeli and Syrian positions on the border issue were irreconcilable, and Barak declared that his Government would resume the construction of Jewish settlements in the Golan Heights (following a declared suspension prior to the December 1999 talks). The prospect of further peace-making initiatives between Israel and Syria was further distanced by the death of President Assad in early June 2000. The Israeli premier was reported to have offered a veiled invitation to Assad's second son, Bashar—who assumed the Syrian presidency in July—to resume peace negotiations; however, although President Bashar al-Assad promised a continuation of his father's policies towards Israel, bilateral talks remained deadlocked, at least in the short term.

Meanwhile, in mid-April 2000 a visit to Israel by the Chinese President, Jiang Zemin, was overshadowed by US anger concerning a recent offer by Israel to sell military technology worth US $250m. to the People's Republic of China. After the US Congress threatened to reduce military aid to Israel, in mid-July the Israeli Government cancelled the contract. Meanwhile, in May Sri Lanka announced the resumption of diplomatic relations with Israel after a 20-year hiatus. In mid-June Israel and Turkey were reported to have signed a major defence agreement, worth some $1,000m.

Government

Supreme authority in Israel rests with the Knesset (Assembly), with 120 members elected by universal suffrage for four years (subject to dissolution), on the basis of proportional representation. The President, a constitutional Head of State, is elected by the Knesset for five years. (Moshe Katsav, who assumed the presidency in August 2000, was exceptionally elected for a seven-year term.) Executive power lies with the Cabinet, led by a directly-elected Prime Minister. The Cabinet takes office after receiving a vote of confidence in the Knesset, to which it is responsible. Ministers are usually members of the Knesset, but non-members may be appointed.

The country is divided into six administrative districts. Local authorities are elected at the same time as elections to the Knesset. There are 31 municipalities (including two Arab towns), 115 local councils (46 Arab and Druze) and 49 regional councils (one Arab) comprising representatives of 700 villages.

Defence

The Israel Defence Forces consist of a small nucleus of commissioned and non-commissioned regular officers, a contingent enlisted for national service, and a large reserve. Men are enlisted for 36 months of military service, and women for 21 months. Military service is compulsory for Jews and Druzes, but voluntary for Christians, Circassians and Muslims. Total regular armed forces in August 2000 numbered 172,500 (including 107,500 conscripts), comprising an army of 130,000, a navy estimated at 6,500 and an air force of 36,000; full mobilization to 597,500 can be quickly achieved with reserves of 425,000. State budget forecasts for 2000 allocated NIS 39,138m. to defence (equivalent to 20.7% of total expenditure).

Economic Affairs

In 1998, according to estimates by the World Bank, Israel's gross national product (GNP), measured at average 1996–98 prices, was US $96,483m., equivalent to $16,180 per head (or $16,861 per head on an international purchasing-power parity basis). During 1990–98, it was estimated, GNP per head increased, in real terms, at an average rate of 2.2% per year. Over the same period the population increased by an average of 3.5% per year. Israel's gross domestic product (GDP) increased, in real terms, by an average of 5.1% annually in 1990–99. Real GDP increased by 2.2% in 1999, and by an estimated 5.9% in 2000.

Agriculture (including hunting, forestry and fishing) contributed 2.2% of net domestic product (NDP) in 1995, and in 1999 engaged 2.3% of the employed labour force. Most agricultural workers live in large co-operatives (*kibbutzim*), of which there were 268 at December 1997, or co-operative smallholder villages (*moshavim*), of which there were 455. Israel is largely self-sufficient in foodstuffs. Citrus fruits constitute the main export crop. Other important crops are vegetables (particularly potatoes and tomatoes), wheat, melons and apples. The export of exotic fruits, winter vegetables and flowers has increased significantly in recent years. Poultry, livestock and fish production are also important. According to FAO data, agricultural output increased at an average annual rate of 0.8% in 1990–98; production declined by 7.0% in 1999, but increased by 2.1% in 2000.

Industry (comprising mining, manufacturing, construction and power) contributed 27.2% of NDP in 1995, and engaged 24.9% of the employed labour force in 1999. The State plays a major role in all sectors of industry, and there is a significant co-operative sector. Industrial production increased by an average of 5.9% annually in 1988–95.

The mining and manufacturing sectors together contributed 17.5% of NDP in 1995, and engaged 18.2% of the employed labour force in 1999; mining and quarrying employed about 0.2% of the working population in 1997. Israel has small proven reserves of petroleum (of some 3.9m. barrels), from which less than 500 barrels per day are currently produced; however, the discovery was reported in 1999 of potential new reserves in central Israel and off the southern coast. Some natural gas is also produced, and significant offshore gas discoveries were made in the south in 1999 and 2000. Phosphates, potash, bromides, magnesium and other salts are mined, and Israel is the world's largest exporter of bromine. Gold, in potentially commercial quantities, was discovered in 1988.

Manufacturing employed 19.3% of the working population in 1997. The principal branches of manufacturing, measured by gross revenue, in 1996 were food products, beverages and tobacco (accounting for 17.4% of the total), chemical, petroleum and coal products (15.0%), electrical machinery (12.1%), metal products (11.1%), scientific, photographic, optical equipment, etc. (8.0%), paper, publishing and printing (6.5%), textiles and clothing (5.6%), non-metallic mineral manufactures (5.4%), rubber and plastic products (5.1%) and non-electrical machinery (5.0%).

Energy is derived principally from imported petroleum and petroleum products; however, it is intended that natural gas should become Israel's principal energy source in the 21st century. Imports of mineral fuels comprised 5.8% of the total value of imports in 1999.

Services contributed 70.6% of NDP in 1995, and engaged 72.7% of the employed labour force in 1999. Tourism is an important source of revenue. However, the sector has been damaged by regional instability and a series of bomb attacks carried out by Islamist extremist groups in recent years. In 1999 some 2.3m. tourists visited Israel, and receipts from tourism totalled US $2,974m. in that year. Millennial celebrations in 2000 resulted in a large influx of tourists to Israel, although the upsurge in violence from late September once again deterred many foreign visitors. Financial services are also important: banking, insurance, real estate and business services together contributed 25.5% of NDP in 1995, and employed 14.1% of the working population in 1999.

In 1999 Israel recorded a visible trade deficit of US $4,408m., and there was a deficit of $1,881m. on the current account of the balance of payments. Excluding trade with the West Bank and the Gaza Strip, in 1999 the principal source of imports was the USA, which supplied 20.3% of imports to Israel; other major suppliers were the Belgo-Luxembourg Economic Union (BLEU), Germany, the United Kingdom, Switzerland and Italy. The USA was also the principal market for exports, taking 35.5% of Israeli exports in that year; other important purchasers were the United Kingdom and the BLEU. Israel is the world's largest supplier of polished diamonds. The principal exports in 1999 were basic manufactures (chiefly non-metallic mineral manufactures), machinery and transport equipment, chemicals and related products, and miscellaneous manufactured articles. The principal imports were machinery and transport equipment, basic manufactures (mainly non-metallic mineral manufactures), miscellaneous manufactured articles, and chemicals and related products.

In 1998 there was an overall budgetary deficit of NIS 8,698m. (equivalent to 2.1% of GDP). Government revenue each year normally includes some US $3,000m. in economic and military aid from the USA. At 31 December 1999 Israel's gross foreign debt amounted to $57,689m., of which $27,458m. was government debt. During 1990–99 consumer prices rose by an annual average rate of 10.5%. Annual inflation averaged 5.2% in 1999, and slowed to an average of 1.1% in 2000. In 2000 the unemployment rate was estimated at 8.8%.

The most significant factor affecting the Israeli economy in the 1990s was the mass influx of Jews from the former USSR, which led to a substantial increase in the population, additional flexibility in the labour market and growth in construction. In 1996, however, a period of economic slowdown began, reflecting an end to the demand boom and reduced tourism revenues following an increase in Islamist violence. By mid-1999, when the Government of Ehud Barak was elected, Israel was suffering a marked deceleration in economic growth and unemployment of about 9%; the Central Bureau of Statistics described 1999 as the worst economic year for a decade. However, following a revival of the Middle East peace process under Barak, by late 1999 a recovery was under way, with a significant improvement in activity reported and an increase in foreign investment. Moreover, inflation was at its lowest level since 1967. In May 1998 foreign-exchange restrictions were ended, allowing the shekel to become fully convertible. The sale of Bank Hapoalim—Israel's largest bank—in mid-2000 represented the first significant privatization undertaken by the Barak Government. The deregulation of the domestic telecommunications market was also undertaken, with the state telecommunications company scheduled for privatization. Budget proposals for 2001 were aimed at maintaining levels of growth, narrowing socio-economic divisions and expanding infrastructural investment. However, official growth estimates for 2001 were revised downwards, from more than 5% to 4%–4.5%, after the new *intifada* by Palestinians in the Occupied Territories from late September 2000 led to renewed instability both in Israel and the wider region, and prompted fears of reduced foreign investment and tourism revenues. Should discussions regarding both the Palestinian and (currently stalled) Syrian tracks of the Middle East peace process eventually result in a comprehensive, and enduring, regional peace settlement, Israel would be in a far better position to achieve its long-term economic growth potential.

Social Welfare

Israel has a comprehensive system of social welfare. Under the National Insurance Law, the State provides retirement pensions, benefits for industrial injury and maternity, and allowances for large families. The Histadrut (General Federation of Labour), to which about 85% of all Jewish workers in Israel belong, provides sickness benefits and medical care. The Ministry of Social Welfare provides for general assistance, relief grants, child care and other social services. In 1998, according to WHO data, Israel had 385 physicians per 100,000 inhabitants, 613 nurses per 100,000 and 18.6 midwives per 100,000 population. In 1999 there were 327 hospitals (of which 122 were private) and 37,442 beds. Of total forecast budgetary expenditure by the central Government in 2000, NIS 16,088m. (8.5%) was allocated to health, NIS 22,834m.(12.1%) to labour and welfare, and NIS 15,039m. (8.0%) to other social services.

Education

Israel has high standards of literacy—according to UNESCO, adult illiteracy averaged only 0.7% (males 0.4%; females 0.9%) in 1995—and advanced educational services. Free, compulsory education is provided for all children between five and 15 years of age. Primary education is provided for all those between five and 10 years of age. There is also secondary, vocational and agricultural education. Post-primary education comprises two cycles of three years. Enrolment at primary and secondary schools in 1995 was equivalent to 93% of children aged six to 17 (primary 98%; secondary 88%). There are six universities, one institute of technology (the Technion) and one institute of science (the Weizmann Institute), which incorporates a graduate school of science. In 2000 budgetary expenditure on education by the central Government was forecast at NIS 28,013m. (14.8% of total spending). In early 1999 legislation was approved to allow for the introduction of free education for pre-primary children.

Public Holidays

The Sabbath starts at sunset on Friday and ends at nightfall on Saturday. The Jewish year 5762 begins on 18 September 2001, and the year 5763 on 7 September 2002.

2001: 8–14 April (Passover—public holidays on first and last days of festival), 28 April (Independence Day), 28 May (Shavuot), 18–19 September (Rosh Hashanah, Jewish New Year), 27 September (Yom Kippur), 2–8 October (Succot).

2002: 28 March–3 April (Passover—see 2001), 17 April (Independence Day), 17 May (Shavuot), 7–8 September (Rosh Hashanah, Jewish New Year), 16 September (Yom Kippur), 21–27 September (Succot).

(The Jewish festivals and fast days commence in the evening of the dates given.)

Islamic holidays are observed by Muslim Arabs, and Christian holidays by the Christian Arab community.

Weights and Measures

The metric system is in force.

1 dunum = 1,000 sq metres.

Statistical Survey

Source: Central Bureau of Statistics, POB 13015, Hakirya, Romema, Jerusalem 91130; tel. 2-6592037; fax 2-6521340; e-mail yael@cbs.gov.il; internet www.cbs.gov.il.

Area and Population

AREA, POPULATION AND DENSITY

Area (sq km)	
Land	21,671
Inland water	474
Total	22,145*
Population (*de jure*; census results)†	
4 June 1983	4,037,620
4 November 1995	
Males	2,738,175
Females	2,810,348
Total	5,548,523
Population (*de jure*; official estimates at mid-year)†	
1998	5,964,500
1999	6,110,500
2000	6,275,400
Density (per sq km) at mid-2000†	283.4

* 8,550 sq miles. Area includes East Jerusalem, annexed by Israel in June 1967, and the Golan sub-district (1,154 sq km), annexed by Israel in December 1981.
† Including the population of East Jerusalem and Israeli residents in certain other areas under Israeli military occupation since June 1967. Beginning in 1981, figures also include non-Jews in the Golan sub-district, an Israeli-occupied area of Syrian territory. Census results exclude adjustment for underenumeration.

POPULATION BY RELIGION (estimates, 31 December 1999)

	Number	%
Jews	4,900,000	78.78
Muslims	936,000	15.05
Christians	131,000	2.11
Druze	101,000	1.62
Unclassified	152,000	2.44
Total	**6,220,000**	**100.00**

DISTRICTS (31 December 1998)

	Area (sq km)*	Population†	Density (per sq km)
Jerusalem‡	652	717,000	1,099.7
Northern§	4,478	1,026,700	229.3
Haifa	863	788,600	913.8
Central	1,276	1,358,200	1,064.4
Tel-Aviv	171	1,138,700	6,659.1
Southern	14,231	840,000	59.0
Total	**21,671**	**6,041,400**	**278.8**

* Excluding lakes, with a total area of 474 sq km.
† Excluding Israelis residing in Jewish localities in the West Bank and Gaza Strip, totalling 172,200.
‡ Including East Jerusalem, annexed by Israel in June 1967.
§ Including the Golan sub-district (area 1,154 sq km, population 33,000 at 31 December 1998), annexed by Israel in December 1981.

PRINCIPAL TOWNS (estimated population at 31 December 1998)

Jerusalem (capital) .	633,700*	Petach-Tikva	. .	159,400
Tel-Aviv—Jaffa .	348,100	Netanya	. .	154,900
Haifa . . .	265,700	Bat Yam	. .	137,000
Rishon LeZiyyon .	188,200	Ashdod	. .	155,800
Holon . . .	163,100	Bene Beraq	. .	133,900
Beersheba . .	163,700	Ramat Gan	. .	126,900

* Including East Jerusalem, annexed in June 1967.

BIRTHS, MARRIAGES AND DEATHS*

	Registered live births		Registered marriages		Registered deaths	
	Number	Rate (per 1,000)	Number	Rate (per 1,000)	Number	Rate (per 1,000)
1992 . .	110,062	21.5	32,769	6.4	33,327	6.5
1993 . .	112,330	21.3	34,856	6.6	33,027	6.3
1994 . .	114,543	21.2	36,035	6.7	33,535	6.2
1995 . .	116,886	21.1	35,990	6.5	35,348	6.4
1996 . .	121,333	21.3	36,081	6.3	34,658	6.1
1997 . .	124,478	21.4	37,611	6.5	36,106	6.2
1998 . .	130,080	21.8	40,137	6.7	36,927	6.2
1999† . .	131,936	21.7	n.a.	n.a.	37,242	6.1

* Including East Jerusalem.   † Provisional figures.

Expectation of life (years at birth, 1998): Males 76.1; Females 80.3.

IMMIGRATION*

	1997	1998	1999
Immigrants:			
on immigrant visas . . .	56,070	48,537	70,586
on tourist visas† . . .	9,756	8,089	6,104
Potential immigrants:			
on potential immigrant visas .	24	9	18
on tourist visas† . . .	371	95	58
Total	**66,221**	**56,730**	**76,766**

* Excluding immigrating citizens (3,905 in 1997; 3,255 in 1998; 3,226 in 1999) and Israeli residents returning from abroad.
† Figures refer to tourists who changed their status to immigrants or potential immigrants.

ECONOMICALLY ACTIVE POPULATION (sample surveys, '000 persons aged 15 years and over, excluding armed forces)*

	1997	1998	1999
Agriculture, hunting, forestry and fishing	48.9	47.5	49.6
Industry†	398.2	386.2	389.8
Electricity, gas and water supply	18.8	20.0	19.2
Construction.	146.2	131.4	120.3
Wholesale and retail trade; repair of motor vehicles, motorcycles and personal and household goods . . .	263.1	272.4	281.6
Hotels and restaurants . . .	75.5	80.6	90.1
Transport, storage and communications . . .	124.4	122.4	135.6
Financial intermediation . . .	73.6	72.8	73.7
Real estate, renting and business activities	204.4	216.7	224.7
Public administration and defence; compulsory social security	113.7	112.4	116.2
Education	246.2	262.2	267.8
Health and social work . . .	184.2	202.8	211.9
Other community, social and personal service activities . .	96.4	98.7	99.2
Private households with employed persons	32.4	32.4	40.1
Extra-territorial organizations and bodies.	1.3	2.2	1.8
Not classifiable by economic activity	12.9	11.6	14.6
Total employed . . .	**2,040.2**	**2,072.4**	**2,136.7**
Unemployed	169.8	193.4	208.5
Total labour force . . .	**2,210.0**	**2,266.0**	**2,345.3**
Males	1,240.0	1,255.7	1,285.1
Females	970.0	1,010.3	1,060.2

* Figures are estimated independently, so the totals may not be the sum of the component parts.
† Comprising mining and quarrying, and manufacturing.

Source: ILO, *Yearbook of Labour Statistics*.

Agriculture

PRINCIPAL CROPS ('000 metric tons)

	1997	1998	1999
Wheat	116	156	20*
Barley*	6	4	7
Potatoes.	277	333	333†
Groundnuts (in shell). . . .	23	24*	24†
Cottonseed	151	134	134†
Olives	19	45	45†
Cabbages	52	50†	50†
Tomatoes	386	493	463
Pumpkins, squash and gourds .	28	27	27
Cucumbers	102	115	115†
Peppers (green)	79	95	95
Onions (dry)	75	81	81†
Carrots	68	80†	80†
Other vegetables. . . .	337	349	349
Watermelons	319	334	334†
Melons	83	81	81†
Grapes	89	89	89†
Apples	111	103	103†
Peaches	48	47	47†
Oranges	327	313	385*
Tangerines, mandarins, clementines and satsumas .	118	82	125*
Lemons and limes . . .	22	21	17*
Grapefruit	435	377	335†
Avocados	79	66	66†
Bananas	114	109	109†
Strawberries.	15	16	16†
Other fruits and berries . .	127	133	134
Cotton (lint)	54	53	53†

* Unofficial figure.
† FAO estimate.

Source: FAO.

LIVESTOCK ('000 head, year ending September)

	1997	1998	1999*
Cattle	375	300*	300
Pigs*	165	163	163
Sheep	360	340	340
Goats	75	74	73
Chickens	23,470	25,340	25,340
Geese*	1,100	1,100	1,100
Turkeys	4,450	4,430	4,430
Ducks	200	200	200

* FAO estimate(s).

Source: FAO.

LIVESTOCK PRODUCTS ('000 metric tons)

	1997	1998	1999
Beef and veal	46	46*	46*
Mutton and lamb . . .	6†	5†	5*
Pig meat	12	12	12*
Poultry meat	265	264	264*
Cows' milk	1,159	1,186	1,186*
Sheep's milk	18	19	19*
Goats' milk	12	14	14*
Cheese	95	93	93
Butter	5	5*	5*
Hen eggs	92†	87	87*
Honey	3	3	3*

* FAO estimate(s).   † Unofficial figure(s).

Source: FAO.

Forestry

ROUNDWOOD REMOVALS ('000 cubic metres, excl. bark)

	1996	1997	1998
Sawlogs, veneer logs and logs for sleepers	37	40	40
Pulpwood	29	35	35
Other industrial wood	29	35	35
Fuel wood	10	14	14
Total	105	124	124

Source: FAO, *Yearbook of Forest Products*.

Fishing

('000 metric tons, live weight)

	1996	1997	1998
Capture	4,891	5,204	6,300
Carps, barbels, etc.	1,242	696	1,396
Aquaculture	17,553	18,264	18,556
Common carp	7,704	7,864	7,172
Tilapias	6,399	6,007	6,696
Rainbow trout	770	670	707
Gilthead seabream	633	1,326	1,643
Flathead grey mullet	1,232	1,562	1,476
Total catch	22,444	23,468	24,856

Note: Figures exclude crocodiles and alligators, recorded by number rather than weight. The number of American alligators caught was: 944 in 1996; 210 in 1997; 401 in 1998.

Source: FAO, *Yearbook of Fishery Statistics*.

Mining

('000 metric tons, unless otherwise indicated)

	1997	1998	1999
Crude petroleum ('000 barrels)*	36	36	n.a.
Natural gas (million cu m)*	20	20	n.a.
Kaolin*	40	40	40
Phosphate rock†	4,047	4,050	4,100*
Potash salts‡	1,488	1,500	1,750*
Salt (unrefined)*	800	800	900
Gypsum (crude)*	60	60	60

* Estimated production.
† Figures refer to beneficiated production. The phosphoric acid content (in '000 metric tons) was: 1,250 in 1997; 1,288 in 1998; 1,300 (estimate) in 1999.
‡ Figures refer to K_2O content.

Source: US Geological Survey.

Industry

SELECTED PRODUCTS
('000 metric tons, unless otherwise indicated)

	1992	1993	1994
Refined vegetable oils (metric tons)	56,463	57,558	45,447
Margarine	35.1	33.8	24.7
Wine ('000 litres)	12,373	12,733	n.a.
Beer ('000 litres)	51,078	58,681	50,750
Cigarettes (metric tons)	5,742	5,525	5,638
Newsprint (metric tons)	0	247	0
Writing and printing paper (metric tons)	66,334	65,426	65,790
Other paper (metric tons)	32,368	30,446	28,985
Cardboard (metric tons)	92,072	95,108	103,142
Rubber tyres ('000)	892	854	966
Ammonia (metric tons)	41,072	n.a.	n.a.
Ammonium sulphate (metric tons)	12,444	n.a.	n.a.
Sulphuric acid (metric tons)	138	n.a.	n.a.
Chlorine (metric tons)	33,912	35,241	37,555
Caustic soda (metric tons)	29,459	29,851	32,765
Polyethylene (metric tons)	128,739	144,147	126,979
Paints (metric tons)	58,963	57,429	53,260
Cement	3,960	4,536	4,800
Commercial vehicles (number)	852	836	1,260
Electricity (million kWh)	24,731	26,042	28,327

1996 ('000 metric tons, unless otherwise indicated): Margarine 35; Cigarettes (metric tons) 4,793; Chlorine 35; Caustic soda 41; Paints 58.0; Commercial vehicles (number) 1,199; (Source: UN, *Industrial Commodity Statistics Yearbook* and *Monthly Bulletin of Statistics*).
1997: Rubber tyres ('000) 792; Cement ('000 metric tons) 5,916.
1998: Commercial vehicles (number) 651 (Source: International Road Federation, *World Road Statistics*). Electricity (million kWh) 37,956 (Source: UN, *Monthly Bulletin of Statistics*.).
1999: Electricity (million kWh) 39,180 (Source: UN, *Monthly Bulletin of Statistics*).

Finance

CURRENCY AND EXCHANGE RATES

Monetary Units
100 agorot (singular: agora) = 1 new sheqel (plural: sheqalim) or shekel (NIS).

Sterling, Dollar and Euro Equivalents (29 December 2000)
£1 sterling = NIS 6.030;
US $1 = NIS 4.041;
€1 = NIS 3.760;
NIS 100 = £16.58 = $24.75 = €26.59.

Average Exchange Rate (NIS per US $)
1998   3.8001
1999   4.1397
2000   4.0773

STATE BUDGET (NIS million)

Revenue*	1998	1999†	2000†
Tax revenue‡	114,560	126,460	132,870
Taxes on income and profits	54,207	59,681	61,780
Companies	12,817	13,100	14,000
Individuals	41,390	45,200	47,780
Taxes on property	2,847	3,240	3,760
Taxes on goods and services	56,162	60,609	65,410
Value-added tax	39,962	42,170	46,320
Excises	6,960	7,360	8,440
Fuel	5,238	5,650	6,570
Purchase tax	8,069	8,610	9,310
Non-tax revenue	27,698	31,798	32,907
Interest	2,823	3,540	3,490
Loans from National Insurance Institute	5,550	6,320	5,490
Fees, royalties, pension provisions, etc.	11,176	12,571	13,223
Revenue for revenue-dependent expenditure	7,146	8,167	9,654
Total	142,258	158,258	165,777

Expenditure§	1998	1999†	2000†
General administration . . .	10,467	10,466	11,748
Defence	37,909	36,426	39,138
Public order	4,229	5,265	5,893
Education	23,769	26,258	28,013
Health	14,951	15,031	16,088
Labour and welfare	19,144	21,008	22,834
Other social services . . .	11,595	14,188	15,039
Housing	7,985	10,186	10,799
Economic services . . .	9,860	12,115	12,826
Manufacturing	3,329	4,039	3,926
Unallocable and other functions .	26,019	32,657	31,781
Interest	24,424	23,836	26,339
General transfers . . .	4,510	4,577	4,294
Reserves‖	—	7,417	4,449
Sub-total	157,943	173,414	183,360
Adjustment	5,582	4,642	5,567
Total	163,525	178,056	188,927
Current‖	156,438	161,761	174,772
Capital	7,087	9,164	9,743

* Excluding proceeds from sale of assets (NIS million): 5,094 in 1998; 4,590 (forecast) in 1999; 3,500 (forecast) in 2000. Also excluded are grants received from abroad (NIS million): 12,572 in 1998; 11,808 (forecast) in 1999; 12,260 (forecast) in 2000.

† Figures are forecasts.

‡ Excluding fees, classified as non-tax revenue.

§ Expenditure includes repayments to the National Insurance Institute (NIS million): 4,323 in 1998; 4,741 (forecast) in 1999; 5,095 (forecast) in 2000. It excludes the central Government's lending minus repayments (NIS million): –909 (forecast) in 1998; 97 (forecast) in 1999.

‖ Net transfers to reserves are included in current expenditure.

IMF, *Israel: Selected Issues and Statistical Appendix* (April 2000).

2001 (draft budget, NIS million): Revenue 191,200 (excl. grants received); Expenditure 199,400 (excl. lending minus repayments). Source: Ministry of Finance.

CENTRAL BANK RESERVES (US $ million at 31 December)

	1997	1998	1999
Gold*	0.4	0.0	0.0
IMF special drawing rights . .	0.0	0.3	0.2
Reserve position in IMF . .	0.0	0.0	89.9
Foreign exchange . . .	20,332.0	22,674.0	22,514.8
Total	20,332.5	22,674.3	22,604.9

* Valued at SDR 35 per troy ounce.

Source: IMF, *International Financial Statistics*.

MONEY SUPPLY (NIS million at 31 December)

	1997	1998	1999
Currency outside banks . . .	8,767	10,051	12,178
Demand deposits at deposit money banks	13,502	14,937	17,933
Total money (incl. others) . .	22,401	25,145	30,263

Source: IMF, *International Financial Statistics*.

COST OF LIVING
(Consumer Price Index, annual averages; base: 1990 = 100)

	1997	1998	1999
Food (incl. beverages) . . .	193.1	203.9	218.2
Fuel and light	204.2	213.6	228.1
Clothing (incl. footwear) . .	152.1	150.2	150.2
Rent	341.4	361.0	370.4
All items (incl. others) . . .	221.7	233.7	245.8

Source: ILO, *Yearbook of Labour Statistics*.

NATIONAL ACCOUNTS (NIS million at current prices)
National Income and Product (provisional)

	1993	1994	1995
Compensation of employees . .	97,937	120,626	142,990
Operating surplus	39,539	44,067	48,045
Domestic factor incomes . .	137,476	164,693	191,035
Consumption of fixed capital . .	26,908	32,698	38,780
Gross domestic product at factor cost	164,384	197,391	229,815
Indirect taxes	38,598	44,622	51,676
Less Subsidies	4,814	5,328	4,822
GDP in purchasers' values .	198,168	236,685	276,669
Factor income received from abroad	3,588	3,605	5,201
Less Factor income paid abroad .	8,916	10,281	12,676
Gross national product . .	192,840	230,009	269,194
Less Consumption of fixed capital .	26,908	32,697	38,780
National income in market prices	165,932	197,312	230,414
Other current transfers received from abroad	19,456	21,066	21,916
Less Other current transfers paid abroad	810	690	757
National disposable income .	184,579	217,688	251,573

Source: UN, *National Accounts Statistics*.

Expenditure on the Gross Domestic Product

	1997	1998	1999
Government final consumption expenditure	101,999	111,390	121,215
Private final consumption expenditure	208,833	227,081	248,606
Increase in stocks . . .	595	–95	5,493
Gross fixed capital formation .	76,916	76,953	82,366
Total domestic expenditure .	388,344	415,330	457,679
Exports of goods and services .	107,237	122,159	149,024
Less Imports of goods and services	145,552	154,694	189,257
GDP in purchasers' values .	350,029	382,795	417,446
GDP at constant 1995 prices .	288,104	295,673	302,205

Source: IMF, *International Financial Statistics*.

Net Domestic Product by Economic Activity (at factor cost)

	1997	1998	1999
Agriculture, hunting, forestry and fishing	3,302	4,179	4,419
Manufacturing, mining and quarrying	28,395	31,936	35,501
Electricity, gas and water . .	2,263	2,747	3,299
Construction	10,122	12,372	16,401
Wholesale and retail trade, restaurants and hotels . .	15,779	18,637	21,526
Transport, storage and communications . . .	10,379	11,653	13,122
Finance, insurance, real estate and business services . .	36,007	43,454	51,754
Government services . . .	31,293	40,365	48,297
Other community, social and personal services . . .	6,003	7,256	8,403
Statistical discrepancy . . .	471	418	363
Sub-total	144,014	173,017	203,085
Less Imputed bank service charge	6,064	6,611	8,855
Other adjustments (incl. errors and omissions)	–474	–1,713	–3,198
Total	137,476	164,693	191,032

Source: UN, *National Accounts Statistics*.

BALANCE OF PAYMENTS (US $ million)

	1997	1998	1999
Exports of goods f.o.b.	22,698	22,974	25,565
Imports of goods f.o.b.	−27,824	−26,199	−29,972
Trade balance	**−5,126**	**−3,225**	**−4,408**
Exports of services	8,326	9,103	10,326
Imports of services	−9,321	−9,793	−10,843
Balance on goods and services	**−6,120**	**−3,915**	**−4,925**
Other income received	2,120	2,861	3,429
Other income paid	−5,711	−5,982	−6,709
Balance on goods, services and income	**−9,711**	**−7,036**	**−8,205**
Current transfers received	6,374	6,680	7,134
Current transfers paid	−325	−607	−810
Current balance	**−3,662**	**−963**	**−1,881**
Capital account (net)	2,050	1,647	1,686
Direct investment abroad	−795	−972	−1,030
Direct investment from abroad	1,628	1,754	2,363
Portfolio investment assets	–	−309	−902
Portfolio investment liabilities	1,743	494	1,414
Other investment assets	1,638	−2,362	−2,924
Other investment liabilities	2,896	603	2,892
Net errors and omissions	1,585	3	−1,299
Overall balance	**7,083**	**−106**	**318**

Source: IMF, *International Financial Statistics*.

External Trade

PRINCIPAL COMMODITIES (US $ million)*

Imports c.i.f.†	1997	1998	1999
Food and live animals	1,654.6	1,560.8	1,526.9
Crude materials (inedible) except fuels	712.7	605.6	634.1
Mineral fuels, lubricants, etc.	1,884.0	1,431.2	1,818.1
Petroleum, petroleum products, etc.	1,875.4	1,424.2	1,807.9
Chemicals and related products	2,742.7	2,803.9	2,888.1
Organic chemicals	661.8	643.8	621.7
Basic manufactures	9,196.1	8,170.2	9,542.5
Paper, paperboard, etc.	486.1	495.6	500.9
Textile yarn, fabrics, etc.	793.5	802.0	789.1
Non-metallic mineral manufactures	5,631.3	4,679.0	6,250.8
Iron and steel	759.6	685.0	592.9
Machinery and transport equipment	9,499.1	9,445.6	10,969.2
Power-generating machinery and equipment	601.0	639.1	591.9
Machinery specialized for particular industries	647.3	713.7	767.2
General industrial machinery, equipment and parts	1,213.5	1,157.5	1,178.2
Office machines and automatic data-processing machines	1,167.3	1,179.3	1,421.4
Telecommunications and sound equipment	1,072.1	1,208.8	1,452.8
Other electrical machinery, apparatus, etc.	2,054.7	2,126.7	2,304.5
Road vehicles and parts‡	1,982.4	1,766.5	1,845.7
Other transport equipment and parts‡	612.3	474.4	1,149.0
Miscellaneous manufactured articles	2,614.3	2,679.7	2,988.8
Professional, scientific and controlling instruments, etc.	597.3	647.3	796.3
Total (incl. others)	29,084.4	27,469.8	31,090.0

Exports f.o.b.	1997	1998	1999
Food and live animals	903.2	866.7	835.8
Vegetables and fruit	578.3	587.6	567.4
Crude materials (inedible) except fuels	588.0	590.8	580.7
Chemicals and related products	3,287.1	3,372.3	3,534.2
Organic chemicals	806.2	843.1	904.0
Inorganic chemicals	421.7	501.7	510.0
Basic manufactures	8,296.5	7,973.2	9,375.6
Textile yarn, fabrics, etc.	448.4	475.6	480.1
Non-metallic mineral manufactures	6,875.1	6,440.5	7,853.7
Machinery and transport equipment	6,888.7	7,911.0	8,384.6
Machinery specialized for particular industries	506.6	568.2	619.6
General industrial machinery, equipment and parts	627.4	695.4	590.2
Office machines and automatic data-processing machines	1,117.2	1,330.0	1,392.3
Telecommunications and sound equipment	2,216.5	2,561.6	3,038.7
Other electrical machinery, apparatus, etc.	1,528.9	1,643.0	1,554.3
Road vehicles and other transport equipment and parts‡	586.6	815.4	908.9
Miscellaneous manufactured articles	2,454.9	2,530.7	2,889.3
Clothing (excl. footwear)	600.4	651.7	731.2
Professional, scientific and controlling instruments, etc.	755.9	787.9	931.7
Total (incl. others)	22,590.8	23,416.9	25,793.2

* The data exclude trade with the West Bank and the Gaza Strip. Including such transactions, the value of total trade (in US $ million) was: Imports c.i.f. (excl. military goods) 29,369.6 in 1997; 27,749.8 in 1998; 31,389.3 in 1999; Exports f.o.b. 24,256.3 in 1997; 25,052.9 in 1998; 27,493.5 in 1999.
† Figures exclude military goods. After deducting net returned imports, the value of total imports (in US $ million), excluding trade with the West Bank and the Gaza Strip, was: 30,781 in 1997; 29,341 in 1998; 33,159 in 1999 (Source: UN, *Monthly Bulletin of Statistics*).
‡ Data on parts exclude tyres, engines and electrical parts.

PRINCIPAL TRADING PARTNERS (US $ million)*

Imports (excl. military goods) c.i.f.	1997	1998	1999
Belgium-Luxembourg	3,618.7	2,871.1	3,527.5
Canada	294.3	316.1	306.8
France	1,099.5	1,125.6	1,221.2
Germany	2,786.7	2,417.7	2,524.0
Hong Kong	432.2	532.4	635.0
India	292.8	343.8	455.0
Italy	1,995.8	1,827.5	1,657.1
Japan	1,033.7	976.2	1,097.0
Netherlands	1,094.9	1,142.0	1,193.6
South Africa	306.8	274.1	275.7
Spain	600.9	623.1	579.8
Sweden	281.3	296.9	342.5
Switzerland-Liechtenstein	1,598.6	1,499.9	1,730.2
Turkey	355.4	443.1	557.1
United Kingdom	2,424.9	2,062.1	2,334.3
USA	5,444.8	5,386.0	6,317.0
Total (incl. others)	29,084.4	27,469.8	31,090.0

Exports	1997	1998	1999
Australia	243.6	237.2	280.3
Belgium-Luxembourg	1,114.4	1,103.1	1,381.3
Brazil	265.3	302.8	241.2
France	616.8	676.6	683.3
Germany	980.5	1,111.0	1,165.7
Hong Kong	1,182.9	796.9	1,052.1
India	367.4	334.5	536.3
Italy	624.3	736.8	720.6
Japan	1,022.0	758.3	839.1
Netherlands	982.6	1,116.0	976.0
Russia	255.9	184.6	106.4
Singapore	266.0	174.7	239.5
Spain	344.4	400.2	431.0
Switzerland-Liechtenstein	387.2	379.9	359.1
Turkey	256.8	287.3	338.3
United Kingdom	1,404.5	1,324.0	1,426.5
USA	7,256.5	8,334.5	9,162.4
Total (incl. others)	22,590.8	23,416.9	25,793.2

* Imports by country of purchase; exports by country of destination. The totals exclude trade with the West Bank and the Gaza Strip (US $ million): Imports c.i.f. 285 in 1997; 294 in 1998; 299 in 1999; Exports f.o.b. 1,666 in 1997, 1,660 in 1998; 1,700 in 1999.

Transport

RAILWAYS (traffic)

	1997	1998	1999
Freight ton-km (million)	992	1,049	1,128
Passenger-km (million)	346	383	529

ROAD TRAFFIC (motor vehicles in use at 31 December)

	1997	1998	1999
Private passenger cars	1,228,819	1,273,285	1,316,765
Taxis	11,563	12,644	13,836
Minibuses	15,239	15,881	16,240
Buses and coaches	11,095	11,141	11,303
Lorries, vans and road tractors	273,795	282,904	292,038
Special service vehicles	3,904	3,913	3,932
Motorcycles and mopeds	72,413	75,011	75,643

SHIPPING
Merchant Fleet (registered at 31 December)

	1996	1997	1998
Number of vessels	54	55	53
Displacement ('000 grt)	678.9	793.9	751.6

Source: Lloyd's Register of Shipping, *World Fleet Statistics.*

International Sea-borne Freight Traffic ('000 metric tons)

	1997	1998	1999
Goods loaded	12,215	13,489	12,875
Goods unloaded*	26,483	27,273	28,750

* Including traffic between Israeli ports.

CIVIL AVIATION (traffic on scheduled services)

	1995	1996	1997
Kilometres flown (million)	70	74	75
Passengers carried ('000)	3,453	3,695	3,754
Passenger-km (million)	11,412	11,793	11,776
Total ton-km (million)	2,103	2,179	2,195

Source: UN, *Statistical Yearbook.*

Tourism

TOURIST ARRIVALS ('000)*

Country of residence	1997	1998	1999†
Belgium	46.6	39.5	45.9
Canada	43.5	43.6	51.4
France	166.7	168.6	194.9
Germany	182.5	145.6	181.0
Italy	84.2	85.4	146.7
Jordan	46.9	52.9	59.8
Netherlands	77.7	73.9	90.4
Russia	69.7	61.5	55.4
United Kingdom	198.9	197.8	195.5
USA	420.7	451.0	515.2
Total (incl. others)	2,010.4	1,941.6	2,312.3

* Excluding arrivals of Israeli nationals residing abroad.
† Estimates.
Tourism receipts (US $ million): 2,813 in 1997; 2,637 in 1998; 2,974 in 1999.

Communications Media

	1995	1996	1997
Radio receivers ('000 in use)	2,700	3,000	3,070
Television receivers ('000 in use)	1,600	1,650	1,690
Telephones ('000 main lines in use)	2,343	2,539	2,656
Telefax stations (number in use)	140,000	n.a.	n.a.
Mobile cellular telephones (subscribers)	445,456	1,047,582	1,672,442
Daily newspapers:			
Number	34	34	n.a.
Average circulation ('000 copies)	1,500	1,650*	n.a.

* Estimate.
Book production (1992): 2,310 titles (excluding government publications); 9,368,000 copies.
Non-daily newspapers (1988): 80.
Other periodicals (1985): 807.
Sources: UNESCO, *Statistical Yearbook,* and UN, *Statistical Yearbook.*

Education

(estimates, 1999/00, unless otherwise indicated)

	Schools	Pupils	Teachers
Jewish			
Kindergarten	n.a.	310,000	n.a.
Primary schools	1,700	550,674	44,107*
Intermediate schools	453	188,122	15,987*
Secondary schools	792	258,584	31,830*
Vocational schools	320	100,657	n.a.
Agricultural schools	23	5,400	n.a.
Teacher training colleges	43	28,442	n.a.
Others (handicapped)	185	13,165	4,300†
Arab			
Kindergarten	n.a.	28,220	n.a.
Primary schools	366	165,724	9,829*
Intermediate schools	122	52,867	3,536*
Secondary schools	123	45,313	3,820*
Vocational schools	70	13,979	n.a.
Agricultural schools	2	614	n.a.
Teacher training colleges	3	2,621	n.a.
Others (handicapped)	39	2,253	604†

* 1997/98 figures.   † 1996/97 figures.

Directory

The Constitution

There is no written constitution. In June 1950 the Knesset voted to adopt a state constitution by evolution over an unspecified period. A number of laws, including the Law of Return (1950), the Nationality Law (1952), the State President (Tenure) Law (1952), the Education Law (1953) and the 'Yad-va-Shem' Memorial Law (1953), are considered as incorporated into the state Constitution. Other constitutional laws are: The Law and Administration Ordinance (1948), the Knesset Election Law (1951), the Law of Equal Rights for Women (1951), the Judges Act (1953), the National Service and National Insurance Acts (1953), and the Basic Law (The Knesset) (1958). The provisions of constitutional legislation that affect the main organs of government are summarized below:

THE PRESIDENT

The President is elected by the Knesset for a maximum of two five-year terms.*

Ten or more Knesset members may propose a candidate for the Presidency.

Voting will be by secret ballot.

The President may not leave the country without the consent of the Government.

The President may resign by submitting his resignation in writing to the Speaker.

The President may be relieved of his duties by the Knesset for misdemeanour.

The Knesset is entitled to decide by a two-thirds majority that the President is too incapacitated owing to ill health to fulfil his duties permanently.

The Speaker of the Knesset will act for the President when the President leaves the country, or when he cannot perform his duties owing to ill health.

* Moshe Katsav was elected to the presidency on 31 July 2000 for a seven-year term of office.

THE KNESSET

The Knesset is the parliament of the state. There are 120 members.

It is elected by general, national, direct, equal, secret and proportional elections.

Every Israeli national of 18 years or over shall have the right to vote in elections to the Knesset unless a court has deprived him of that right by virtue of any law.

Every Israeli national of 21 and over shall have the right to be elected to the Knesset unless a court has deprived him of that right by virtue of any law.

The following shall not be candidates: the President of the State; the two Chief Rabbis; a judge (shofet) in office; a judge (dayan) of a religious court; the State Comptroller; the Chief of the General Staff of the Defence Army of Israel; rabbis and ministers of other religions in office; senior state employees and senior army officers of such ranks and in such functions as shall be determined by law.

The term of office of the Knesset shall be four years.

The elections to the Knesset shall take place on the third Tuesday of the month of Marcheshvan in the year in which the tenure of the outgoing Knesset ends.

Election day shall be a day of rest, but transport and other public services shall function normally.

Results of the elections shall be published within 14 days.

The Knesset shall elect from among its members a Chairman and Vice-Chairman.

The Knesset shall elect from among its members permanent committees, and may elect committees for specific matters.

The Knesset may appoint commissions of inquiry to investigate matters designated by the Knesset.

The Knesset shall hold two sessions a year; one of them shall open within four weeks after the Feast of the Tabernacles, the other within four weeks after Independence Day; the aggregate duration of the two sessions shall not be less than eight months.

The outgoing Knesset shall continue to hold office until the convening of the incoming Knesset.

The members of the Knesset shall receive a remuneration as provided by law.

THE GOVERNMENT

The Government shall tender its resignation to the President immediately after his election, but shall continue with its duties until the formation of a new government. After consultation with representatives of the parties in the Knesset, the President shall charge one of the members with the formation of a government. The Government shall be composed of a Prime Minister (directly elected from May 1996, but from 2003 to revert to the previous system of election on a party basis) and a number of ministers from among the Knesset members or from outside the Knesset. After it has been chosen, the Government shall appear before the Knesset and shall be considered as formed after having received a vote of confidence. Within seven days of receiving a vote of confidence, the Prime Minister and the other ministers shall swear allegiance to the State of Israel and its Laws and undertake to carry out the decisions of the Knesset.

The Government

HEAD OF STATE

President: MOSHE KATSAV (took office 1 August 2000).

THE CABINET
(April 2001)

A coalition of Likud, Labour, Shas, Haichud Haleumi-Israel B'Aitainu, Israel B'Aliyah and Am Ehad.

Prime Minister and Minister of Immigrant Absorption: ARIEL SHARON (Likud).

Deputy Prime Minister and Minister of Foreign Affairs: SHIMON PERES (Labour).

Deputy Prime Minister and Minister of Finance: SILVAN SHALOM (Likud).

Deputy Prime Minister and Minister of Construction and Housing: NATAN SHARANSKY (Israel B'Aliyah).

Deputy Prime Minister and Minister of the Interior: ELIYAHU YISHAI (Shas).

Minister of Defence: BINYAMIN BEN-ELIEZER (Labour).

Minister of Labour and Social Affairs: SHLOMO BENIZRI (Shas).

Minister of Health: NISSIM DAHAN (Shas).

Minister of the Environment: TZACHI HANEGBI (Likud).

Minister of Industry and Trade: DALIA ITZIK (Labour).

Minister of National Infrastructure: AVIGDOR LIEBERMAN (Israel B'Aitainu).

Minister of Education: LIMOR LIVNAT (Likud).

Minister of Regional Co-operation: TZIPI LIVNI (Likud).

Minister of Public Security: UZI LANDAU (Likud).

Minister of Religious Affairs: ASHER OHANA (Shas).

Minister of Communications: REUVEN RIVLIN (Likud).

Minister of Justice: MEIR SHEETRIT (Likud).

Minister of Agriculture and Rural Development: SHALOM SIMHON (Labour).

Minister of Transport: EPHRAIM SNEH (Labour).

Minister of Science, Culture and Sport: MATAN VILNAI (Labour).

Minister of Tourism: RECHAVAM ZE'EVI (Haichud Haleumi).

Minister without Portfolio, responsible for Social Affairs Co-ordination: SHMUEL AVITAL (Am Ehad).

Minister without Portfolio, responsible for Government-Knesset Liaison: DAN NAVEH (Likud).

Minister without Portfolio, responsible for Jerusalem Affairs: ELIYAHU SUISSA (Shas).

Ministers without Portfolio: RA'ANAN COHEN (Labour), SALAH TARIF (Labour).

MINISTRIES

Office of the Prime Minister: POB 187, 3 Rehov Kaplan, Kiryat Ben-Gurion, Jerusalem 91919; tel. 2-6705511; fax 2-6512631; e-mail webmaster@pmo.gov.il; internet www.pmo.gov.il.

Ministry of Agriculture and Rural Development: POB 30, 14 Arnia St, Hakirya, Tel-Aviv 50200; tel. 3-9485561; fax 3-9485870; e-mail webmaster@moag.gov.il; internet www.moag.gov.il.

Ministry of Communications: 23 Jaffa St, Jerusalem 91999; tel. 2-6706320; fax 2-6706372; internet www.moc.gov.il.

Ministry of Construction and Housing: POB 18110, Kiryat Hamemshala (East), Jerusalem 91180; tel. 2-5847654; fax 2-5847250; e-mail webmaster@moch.gov.il; internet www.moch.gov.il.

Ministry of Defence: Kaplan St, Hakirya, Tel-Aviv 67659; tel. 3-5692010; fax 3-6916940; e-mail public@mod.gov.il; internet www.mod.gov.il.

Ministry of Economy and Planning: POB 13169, 3 Rehov Kaplan, Kiryat Ben-Gurion, Jerusalem 91131; tel. 2-6705111; fax 2-6705249.

Ministry of Education: POB 292, 34 Shivtei Israel St, Jerusalem 91911; tel. 2-5602222; fax 2-5602752; e-mail info@education.gov.il; internet www.education.gov.il.

Ministry of the Environment: POB 34033, 5 Kanfei Nesharim St, Givat Shaul, Jerusalem 95464; tel. 2-6553777; fax 2-6553752; e-mail sergio@environment.gov.il; internet www.environment.gov.il.

Ministry of Finance: POB 13191, 1 Rehov Kaplan, Kiryat Ben-Gurion, Jerusalem 91008; tel. 2-5317111; fax 2-5637891; e-mail webmaster@mof.gov.il; internet www.mof.gov.il.

Ministry of Foreign Affairs: Hakirya, Romema, Jerusalem 91950; tel. 2-5303111; fax 2-5303367; e-mail ask@israel-info.gov.il; internet www.mfa.gov.il.

Ministry of Health: POB 1176, 2 Ben-Tabai St, Jerusalem 91010; tel. 2-6705705; fax 2-6796491; e-mail pniot@matat.health.gov.il; internet www.health.gov.il.

Ministry of Immigrant Absorption: POB 13061, 13 Rehov Kaplan, Kiryat Ben-Gurion, Jerusalem 91006; tel. 2-6752696; fax 2-5618138; e-mail info@moia.gov.il; internet www.moia.gov.il.

Ministry of Industry and Trade: POB 299, 30 Rehov Agron, Jerusalem 94190; tel. 2-6220661; fax 2-6222412; e-mail dover@moit.gov.il; internet www.tamas.gov.il.

Ministry of the Interior: POB 6158, 2 Rehov Kaplan, Kiryat Ben-Gurion, Jerusalem 91008; tel. 2-6701411; fax 2-6701628; e-mail pniot@moin.gov.il; internet www.moin.gov.il.

Ministry of Justice: POB 1087, 29 Rehov Salahadin, Jerusalem 91010; tel. 2-6466666; fax 2-6287757; e-mail pniot@justice.gov.il; internet www.justice.gov.il.

Ministry of Labour and Social Welfare: POB 915, 2 Rehov Kaplan, Kiryat Ben-Gurion, Jerusalem 91008; tel. 2-6752311; fax 2-6752803; e-mail sar@molsa.gov.il.

Ministry of National Infrastructure: Ala Bldg, 216 Jaffa St, Jerusalem; e-mail pniot@mmi.gov.il; internet www.mni.gov.il; also responsible for **Israel Lands Administration:** POB 2600, 6 Shamai St, Jerusalem 94631; tel. 2-6208422; fax 2-6234960; e-mail pniot@mmi.gov.il; internet www.mmi.gov.il.

Ministry of Public Security: POB 18182, Bldg 3, Kiryat Hamemshala (East), Jerusalem 91181; tel. 2-5308003; fax 2-5847872; e-mail bp_meida@internet-zahav.net.

Ministry of Regional Co-operation: 8 Shaul Hamelech Blvd, Tel-Aviv 64733; tel. (3) 6955669; fax (3) 6086126; e-mail m_r_c@netvision.net.il.

Ministry of Religious Affairs: POB 13059, 7 Kanfei Nesharim St, Jerusalem 95464; tel. 2-5311182; fax 2-6513679; e-mail tzibor@religinfoserv.gov.il; internet www.religions.gov.il.

Ministry of Science, Culture and Sport: POB 49100, Kiryat Hamemshala, Hamizrachit, Bldg 3, Jerusalem 91490; tel. 2-5411100; fax 2-5811613; e-mail nps@most.gov.il; internet www.most.gov.il.

Ministry of Tourism: POB 1018, 24 Rehov King George, Jerusalem 91009; tel. 2-6754811; fax 2-6253407; e-mail pniot@tourism.gov.il; internet www.tourism.gov.il.

Ministry of Transport: Klal Bldg, 97 Jaffa St, Jerusalem 91000; tel. 2-6228211; fax 2-6228693; e-mail pniot@mot.gov.il; internet www.mot.gov.il.

Legislature

KNESSET

Speaker: AVRAHAM BURG.

General Election, 17 May 1999

Party	Valid votes cast	% of valid votes	Seats
Israel Ahat (One Israel)	670,484	20.3	26
Likud	468,103	14.1	19
Shas	430,676	13.0	17
Meretz-Democratic Israel	253,525	7.7	10
Israel B'Aliyah	171,705	5.2	6
Shinui	167,748	5.1	6
Centre Party	165,622	5.0	6
National Religious Party	140,307	4.2	5
United Torah Judaism	125,741	3.8	5
United Arab List	114,810	3.5	5
Haichud Haleumi (National Unity)	100,181	3.0	4
Hadash	87,022	2.6	3
Israel B'Aitainu (Israel Is Our Home)	86,153	2.6	4
Balad (National Democratic Alliance)	66,103	2.0	2
Am Ehad (One Nation)	64,143	1.9	2
Others*	197,093	6.0	—
Total	3,309,416†	100.0	120

* Including Penina Rosenblum (1.4%), Koah Lagimlaim (Power for Pensioners—1.1%), Mifleget Aleh Yarok (Green Leaf Party—1.0%), Third Way (0.8%), Ha Yerukim (Green Party—0.4%), Tiqva (Hope—0.2%), Casino Party (0.2%), Lev-Olim (Immigrants for Israel—0.2%), Negev Party (0.1%), Tzomet—Movement for Renewed Zionism (0.1%).

† Excluding 64,332 invalid votes.

According to Israel's General Election Committee, 78.7% of the 4.3m.-strong electorate participated in the legislative elections which were held on 17 May 1999. Voting to select the leader of the government took place at the same time as that to return deputies to the Knesset (the position of Prime Minister having become elective in 1996). On 28 November 2000 the Knesset voted in a first ballot to dissolve itself and hold fresh legislative elections (although officially not scheduled until May 2003). However, on 19 December 2000 the Knesset voted against holding general elections. Following the resignation of Ehud Barak on 10 December 2000, a special election for Prime Minister was held on 6 February 2001—the first time that a premiership election had been held separately from elections to the Knesset. Ariel Sharon, leader of Likud, secured 62.38% (1,698,077) of the valid votes cast, defeating the incumbent Prime Minister and leader of the Labour Party and its Israel Ahat (One Israel) alliance, Ehud Barak, who received 37.62% (1,023,944). The rate of voter participation was reported to be 62.3%.

Political Organizations

Agudat Israel: POB 513, Jerusalem; tel. 2-385251; fax 2-385145; orthodox Jewish party; stands for strict observance of Jewish religious law; Leaders AVRAHAM SHAPIRO, MENACHEM PORUSH.

Agudat Israel World Organization (AIWO): POB 326, Hacherut Sq., Jerusalem 91002; tel. 2-5384357; fax 2-5383634; f. 1912 at Congress of Orthodox Jewry, Kattowitz, Germany (now Katowice, Poland), to help solve the problems facing Jewish people all over the world; more than 500,000 mems in 25 countries; Chair. Rabbi J. M. ABRAMOWITZ (Jerusalem); Secs Rabbi MOSHE GEWIRTZ, Rabbi CHAIM WEINSTOCK.

Am Ehad (One Nation): Workers' and pensioners' party affiliated to Histadrut trade union federation; Leader AMIR PERETZ.

Balad (National Democratic Alliance): f. 1999; united Arab party; Leader AZMI BESHARA.

Centre Party: f. 1999; centrist electoral list, formed as an alternative to Likud and the Israel Labour Party; concerned primarily with the peace process and relations between religious and secular Jews; Leader DAN MERIDOR.

Council for Peace and Security: f. 1988 by four retd Israeli generals: Maj.-Gen. AHARON YARIV, Maj.-Gen. ORI ORR, Brig.-Gen. YORAM AGMON and Brig.-Gen. EPHRAIM SNEH; MOSHE AMIRAV of Shinui a founder mem.; aims: an Israeli withdrawal from the Occupied Territories in return for a peace treaty with the Arab nations.

Degel Hatora: 103 Rehov Beit Vegan, Jerusalem; tel. 2-6438106; fax 2-6418967; f. 1988 as breakaway from Agudat Israel; orthodox Western Jews; Chair. AVRAHAM RAVITZ.

Democratic Arab Party (DAP): Nazareth; tel. 6-6560937; fax 6-6560938; e-mail dap@g-ol.com; f. 1988; aims: to unify Arab political forces so as to influence Palestinian and Israeli policy; international recognition of the Palestinian people's right to self-determination; the withdrawal of Israel from all territories occupied in 1967, including East Jerusalem; the DAP also aims to achieve full civil equality between Arab and Jewish citizens of Israel, to eliminate discrimination and improve the social, economic and political conditions of the Arab minority in Israel; contested the 1999 elections as part of the coalition of the United Arab List; Dir MUHAMMAD DARAWSHE.

Gesher (Bridge): internet www.gesher.org.il; f. 1996; Leader DAVID LEVY.

Gush Emunim (Bloc of the Faithful): f. 1967; engaged in unauthorized establishment of Jewish settlements in the Occupied Territories; Leader Rabbi MOSHE LEVINGER.

Hadash (Democratic Front for Peace and Equality — Communist Party of Israel): 17 Tirtza St, Jaffa; tel. 3-6835252; fax 3-6824499; e-mail info@hadash.org.il; internet www.hadash.org.il; descended from the Socialist Workers' Party of Palestine (f. 1919); renamed Communist Party of Palestine 1921, Communist Party of Israel (Maki) 1948; pro-Soviet anti-Zionist group formed New Communist Party of Israel (Rakah) 1965; Jewish Arab membership; aims for a socialist system in Israel, a lasting peace between Israel and the Arab countries and the Palestinian Arab people, favours full implementation of UN Security Council Resolutions 242 and 338, Israeli withdrawal from all Arab territories occupied since 1967, formation of a Palestinian Arab state in the West Bank and Gaza Strip (with East Jerusalem as its capital), recognition of national rights of state of Israel and Palestine people, democratic rights and defence of working class interests, and demands an end to discrimination against Arab minority in Israel and against oriental Jewish communities; Gen. Sec. (Hadash) MUHAMAD BARAKE; Gen. Sec. (Communist Party) MUHAMMAD NAFAH.

Haichud Haleumi (National Unity): f. 1999; right-wing coalition comprising Herut, Moledet and Tekuma parties; in February 2000 Herut withdrew from the coalition, which subsequently merged with Israel B'Aitainu; Leader RECHAVAM ZE'EVI.

Herut (Freedom): f. 1948; reconstituted 1998; right-wing nationalist party; opposed to further Israeli withdrawal from the Occupied Territories; Leader ZE'EV BINYAMIN (BENNY) BEGIN.

Israel Ahat (One Israel): Ramat-Gan, Tel-Aviv; e-mail amuta@ehudbarak.co.il; f. 1999; electoral list comprising the Labour Party, Gesher and Meimad, formed prior to the 1999 election; Sec. RA'ANAN COHEN.

Israel B'Aitainu (Israel Is Our Home): f. 1999; right-wing immigrant party, formed as a rival to Israel B'Aliyah; Leader AVIGDOR LIEBERMAN.

Israel B'Aliyah: f. 1995; campaigns for immigrants' rights; Leader NATAN SHARANSKY.

Israel Labour Party: POB 62033, Tel-Aviv 61620; tel. 3-6899444; fax 3-6899420; e-mail avoda@inter.net.il; f. 1968 as a merger of the three Labour groups, Mapai, Rafi and Achdut Ha'avoda; a Zionist democratic socialist party; Sec.-Gen. and Acting Chair. RA'ANAN COHEN.

Kahane Chai (Kahane Lives): 111 Agripas St, Jerusalem; tel. 2-231081; f. 1977 as 'Kach' (Thus); right-wing religious nationalist party; advocates creation of a Torah state and expulsion of all Arabs from Israel and the annexation of the Occupied Territories; Leader Rabbi BINYAMIN ZEEV KAHANE.

Likud (Consolidation): 38 Rehov King George, Tel-Aviv 61231; tel. 3-5630666; fax 3-5282901; internet www.likud.org.il; f. September 1973; fmrly a parliamentary bloc of Herut (Freedom; f. 1948; Leader ITZHAK SHAMIR; Sec.-Gen. MOSHE ARENS), the Liberal Party of Israel (f. 1961; Chair. AVRAHAM SHARIR), Laam (For the Nation) (f. 1976; fmrly led by YIGAEL HURWITZ, who left the coalition to form his own party, Ometz, before the 1984 general election), Ahdut (a one-man faction, HILLEL SEIDEL), Tami (f. 1981; represents the interests of Sephardic Jews; Leader AHARON UZAN), which joined Likud in June 1987, and an independent faction (f. 1990; Leader ITZHAK MODAI), which formed the nucleus of a new Party for the Advancement of the Zionist Idea; Herut and the Liberal Party formally merged in August 1988 to form the Likud-National Liberal Movement; aims: territorial integrity (advocates retention of all the territory of post-1922 mandatory Palestine); absorption of newcomers; a social order based on freedom and justice, elimination of poverty and want; development of an economy that will ensure a decent standard of living; improvement of the environment and the quality of life; Leader of Likud ARIEL SHARON.

Meimad: internet www.meimad.org.il; moderate Jewish party; Leader Rabbi MICHAEL MELCHIOR.

Meretz (Vitality): Tel-Aviv; tel. 3-6360111; fax 3-5375107; e-mail information@meretz.org.il; internet www.meretz.org.il; an alliance of Ratz, Shinui and the United Workers' Party; stands for civil rights, electoral reform, welfarism, Palestinian self-determination, separation of religion from the state and a halt to settlement in the Occupied Territories; Leader YOSSI SARID.

Moledet (Homeland): 14 Rehov Yehuda Halevi, Tel-Aviv; tel. 3-654580; internet www.moledet.org.il; f. 1988; right-wing nationalist party; aims: the expulsion ('transfer') of the 1.5m. Palestinians living in the West Bank and Gaza Strip; united with Tehiya—Zionist Revival Movement (see below) in June 1994 as the Moledet—the Eretz Israel Faithful and the Tehiya; Leader Gen. RECHAVAM ZE'EVI.

Movement for the Advancement of the Zionist Idea (MAZI): f. 1990 as breakaway group of Likud; Leader ITZHAK MODAI.

National Religious Party (NRP): Jerusalem; tel. 2-377277; fax 2-377757; f. 1902; as the Mizrachi Organization within the Zionist Movement; present name adopted in 1956; stands for strict adherence to Jewish religion and tradition, and strives to achieve the application of religious precepts of Judaism in everyday life; it is also endeavouring to establish a Constitution for Israel based on Jewish religious law (the Torah); 126,000 mems; Leader ITZHAK LEVI; Sec.-Gen. ZEVULUN ORLEV.

New Liberal Party: Tel-Aviv; f. 1987 as a merger of three groups: Shinui-Movement for Change (f. 1974 and restored 1978, when Democratic Movement for Change split into two parties; centrist; Leader AMNON RUBINSTEIN), the Centre Liberal Party (f. 1986 by members of the Liberal Party of Israel; Leader ITZHAK BERMAN), and the Independent Liberal Party (f. 1965 by seven Liberal Party of Israel Knesset mems, after the formation of the Herut Movement and Liberal Party of Israel bloc; 20,000 mems; Chair. MOSHE KOL; Gen. Sec. NISSIM ELIAD); Leaders AMNON RUBINSTEIN, ITZHAK BERMAN and MOSHE KOL.

Poale Agudat Israel: f. 1924; working-class Orthodox Judaist party; Leader Dr KALMAN KAHANE.

Political Zionist Opposition (Ometz): f. 1982; one-man party, YIGAEL HURWITZ.

Progressive List for Peace: 5 Simtat Lane, Nes Tziona, Tel-Aviv; tel. 3-662457; fax 3-659474; f. 1984; Jewish-Arab; advocates recognition of the PLO and the establishment of a Palestinian state in the West Bank and the Gaza Strip; Leader MUHAMMAD MI'ARI.

Ratz (Civil Rights and Peace Movement): 21 Tchernihovsky St, Tel-Aviv 63291; tel. 3-5254847; fax 3-5255008; f. 1973; concerned with human and civil rights, opposes discrimination on basis of religion, gender or ethnic identification and advocates a peace settlement with the Arab countries and the Palestinians; Leader Mrs SHULAMIT ALONI.

Shas (Sephardic Torah Guardians): Beit Abodi, Rehov Hahida, Bene Beraq; tel. 3-579776; f. 1984 by splinter groups from Agudat Israel; ultra-orthodox Jewish party; Spiritual Leader Rabbi OVADIA YOSEF; Leader ELIYAHU YISHAI.

Shinui (Change): POB 20533, 100 Ha' Hashmona'im St, Tel-Aviv 67133; tel. 3-5620118; fax 3-5620139; e-mail shinui@shinui.org.il; internet www.shinui.org.il; f. 1974 as a new liberal party; combines an anti-religious coercion policy with a free-market economic philosophy; Leaders JOSEPH (TOMMY) LAPID, AVRAHAM PORAZ.

Tehiya—Zionist Revival Movement: 34 Rehov Hahaluts, Jerusalem; tel. 2-259385; f. 1979; aims: Israeli sovereignty over Judaea, Samaria, Gaza; extensive settlement programme; economic independence; uniting of religious and non-religious camps; opposes Camp David accords; united with Moledet in June 1994 (see above); Leaders GERSHON SHAFAT, GEULA COHEN, ELYAQIM HAEZNI, DAMI DAYAN.

Third Way: f. 1995; opposed to any transfer of the Golan Heights to Syria; Leader AVIGDOR KAHALANI.

Tiqva (Hope): f. 1999; campaigns for rights of new immigrants from former USSR; Leader ALEX TENCHER.

Tzomet (Crossroads): 22 Rehov Huberman, Tel-Aviv; tel. 3-204444; f. 1988; right-wing nationalist party; breakaway group from Tehiya party; Leader RAFAEL EITAN.

United Arab List: Arab party affiliated to Labour Party.

United Torah Judaism: electoral list of four minor ultra-orthodox parties (Moria, Degel Hatora, Poale Agudat Israel, Agudat Israel) formed, prior to 1992 election, to overcome the increase in election threshold from 1% to 1.5% and help to counter the rising influence of the secular Russian vote; contested 1999 election comprised of Degel Hatora and Agudat Israel; Spiritual Leader Rabbi ELIEZER SHACH.

United Workers' Party (Mapam): POB 1777, 2 Homa U'Migdal St, Tel-Aviv; tel. 3-6360111; fax 3-5375107; f. 1948; left-wing socialist-Zionist Jewish-Arab party; grouped in Labour-Mapam Alignment with Israel Labour Party from January 1969 until Sept. 1984 when it withdrew in protest over Labour's formation of a Government with Likud; member of the Socialist International; 77,000 mems; Chair. CHANAN EREZ; Sec.-Gen. VICTOR BLIT.

Yahad (Together): f. 1984; advocates a peace settlement with the Arab peoples and the Palestinians; joined the Labour Party parliamentary bloc in January 1987.

Yi'ud: f. 1994; breakaway group from the Tzomet Party.

A record 33 parties contested the 1999 general election, including Atid (Future; Leader RONI MILO), Casino Party (Leader EZRA TISSUNA), Organization for Democratic Action, Ale-Yarok (Green Leaf Party), Ha Yerukim (Green Party; Leader DEDI ZUCKER), Ihud Aravi (Arab Unity), Koah Lagimlaim (Power for Pensioners; Leader GIDEON BEN-ISRAEL), Lev-Olim (Immigrants for Israel), Men's Family Rights, Moreshet Avot (Tradition of the Fathers), Natural Law Party, New Arab Party (Leader MAKRAM HURI MAHUL), Penina Rosenblum, Progressive Centre Party (for Romanian immigrants), Tekuma (Revival; Leaders URI ARIEL, NATAN NATHANSON, BENI KATZOVER).

Diplomatic Representation

EMBASSIES IN ISRAEL

Argentina: 22nd Floor, Diamond Tower, 3A Jabotinsky St, Ramat-Gan, Tel-Aviv 52520; tel. 3-5759173; fax 3-5759178; e-mail embarg@netvision.net.il; Ambassador: VICENTE ESPECHE GIL.

Australia: Beit Europa, 4th Floor, 37 Shaul Hamelech Blvd, Tel-Aviv 64928; tel. 3-6950451; fax 3-6968404; Ambassador: IAN WILCOCK.

Austria: Beit Crystal, 12 Hahilazon, Ramat-Gan, Tel-Aviv 52522; tel. 3-6120924; fax 3-7510716; e-mail autambta@netvision.net.il; Ambassador: Dr WOLFGANG PAUL.

Belarus: 2 Rehov Kaufman, Tel-Aviv 68012; tel. 3-5102236; fax 3-5102235; Ambassador: MIKHAIL FARFEL.

Belgium: 12 Hahilazon, Ramat-Gan, Tel-Aviv 52522; tel. 3-6138130; fax 3-6138160; e-mail telaviv@diplobel.org; Ambassador: WILFRIED GEENS.

Bolivia: Apt 9, 5 Rehov Carmel, Mevasseret Zion 90805; tel. 2-5335195; fax 2-5335196; e-mail totora@netvision.net.il; Ambassador: Dr VÍCTOR TORRES ACHA.

Brazil: 2 Rehov Kaplan, Beit Yachin, 8th Floor, Tel-Aviv 64734; tel. 3-6919292; fax 3-6916060; Ambassador: JOSÉ NOGUEIRA FILHO.

Bulgaria: 9th Floor, 124 Ibn Gvirol, Tel-Aviv 62038; tel. 3-5241751; fax 3-5241798; e-mail bgemtlv@netvision.net.il; Ambassador: Prof. TSANKO YABLANSKI.

Cameroon: Tel-Aviv; tel. and fax 3-5190011; Chargé d'affaires a.i.: ETONNDI ESSOMBA.

Canada: 3 Nirim St, Tel-Aviv; tel. 3-6363300; fax 3-6363385; Ambassador: MICHAEL D. BELL.

Chile: 7 Havakook St, Tel-Aviv 63505; tel. 3-6020130; fax 3-6020133; e-mail echileil@inter.net.il; Ambassador: JOSÉ RODRÍGUEZ ELIZONDO.

China, People's Republic: Tel-Aviv; Ambassador: PAN ZHALIN.

Colombia: 52 Rehov Pinkas, Apt 26, Tel-Aviv 62261; tel. 3-5461717; fax 3-5461404; e-mail emcolis@netvision.net.il; Chargé d'affaires a.i.: (vacant).

Congo, Democratic Republic: Apt 5, 60 Hei Be'Iyar, Kikar Hamedina, Tel-Aviv 62198; tel. 3-452681; Ambassador: Gen. ELUKI MONGA AUNDU.

Costa Rica: 13 Rehov Diskin, Apt 1, Kiryat Wolfson, Jerusalem 92473; tel. 2-5666197; fax 2-5632591; e-mail emcri@netmedia.net.il; Ambassador: RODRIGO X. CARRERAS.

Côte d'Ivoire: South Africa Bldg, 25 Bezalel St, Ramat-Gan, Tel-Aviv; tel. 3-6126677; fax 3-6126688; e-mail ambcita@barak-online.net; Ambassador: LÉON H. KACOU ADOM.

Cyprus: 14th Floor, Top Tower, Dizengoff Centre, 50 Dizengoff St, Tel-Aviv 64322; tel. 3-5250212; fax 3-6290535; e-mail cyprus@netvision.net.il.

Czech Republic: POB 16361, 23 Rehov Zeitlin, Tel-Aviv 61664; tel. 3-6918282; fax 3-6918286; e-mail telaviv@embassy.mzv.cz; Ambassador DANIEL KUMERMANN.

Denmark: POB 21080, 23 Rehov Bnei Moshe, Tel-Aviv 61210; tel. 3-5442144; fax 3-5465502; e-mail mail@dk-embassy.org.il; internet www.dk-embassy.org.il; Ambassador: HANS MICHAEL KOFOED-HANSEN.

Dominican Republic: 19 Soutine St, Tel-Aviv 64684; tel. 3-5277073; fax 3-5277074; e-mail embajdom@netvision.net.il; Ambassador: Dr MANUEL MORALES-LAMA.

Ecuador: Asia House, 4 Rehov Weizman, Tel-Aviv 64239; tel. 3-6958764; fax 3-6913604; e-mail mecuaisr@infolink.net.il; Ambassador: LEONARDO RUILOVA.

Egypt: 54 Rehov Bazel, Tel-Aviv 62744; tel. 3-5464151; fax 3-5441615; Ambassador: MUHAMMAD ABD AL-AZIZ BASSIOUNI (withdrawn in November 2000).

El Salvador: POB 4005, Jerusalem 91039; tel. 2-6728411; fax 2-6733641; e-mail embasal@inter.net.il; internet www.el-salvador.org.il; Ambassador: RAFAEL A. ALFARO-PINEDA.

Ethiopia: 48 Darech Petach Tikva, Tel-Aviv 66184; tel. 3-6397831; fax 3-6397837; e-mail ethembis@netvision.net.il; Ambassador: FIT ZEWDIE OTTORO.

Finland: POB 39666, 40 Einstein St, Tel-Aviv 69101; tel. 3-7440303; fax 3-7440314; e-mail sanomat.tel@formin.fi; Ambassador: PASI PATOKALLIO.

France: 112 Tayeleth Herbert Samuel, Tel-Aviv 63572; tel. 3-5245371; fax 3-5270062; e-mail ambafran@actcom.co.il; internet www.ifta.co.il; Ambassador: JACQUES HUNTZINGER.

Germany: POB 16038, 19th Floor, 3 Rehov Daniel Frisch, Tel-Aviv 61160; tel 3-6931313; fax 3-6950608; e-mail ger_emb@netvision.net.il; internet www.germanemb.org.il; Ambassador: RUDOLF DRESSLER.

Greece: 47 Bodenheimer St, Tel-Aviv 62008; tel. 3-6055461; fax 3-6054374; Ambassador: Dr SOTIRIOS VAROUXAKIS.

Guatemala: Ackerstein Bldg, 103 Medinat Hayeudim, Herzliya Pituach, Herzliya B. 46130; tel. 9-9577335; fax 9-9518506; Ambassador: MARCO TULIO ZÚÑIGA.

Haiti: Tel-Aviv 64336; tel. 3-280285; Ambassador: FRANCK M. JOSEPH.

Holy See: 1 Netiv Hamazalot, Old Jaffa 68037; tel. 3-6835658; fax 3-6835659; e-mail vatge@netvision.net.il; Apostolic Nuncio: Mgr PIETRO SAMBI, Titular Archbishop of Belcastro.

Honduras: Tel-Aviv; tel. 3-5469506; fax 3-5469505; e-mail honduras@netvision.net.il; Ambassador: FRANCISCO LÓPEZ REYES.

Hungary: 18 Rehov Pinkas, Tel-Aviv 62661; tel. 3-5466860; fax 3-5468968; Ambassador: Dr ISTVÁN CSEJTEI.

India: 4 Rehov Kaufman, Tel-Aviv; tel. 3-5101431; fax 3-5101434; e-mail indemtel@netvision.net.il; Ambassador: RANJAN MATHAI.

Italy: Asia House, 4 Rehov Weizman, Tel-Aviv 64239; tel. 3-6964223; fax 3-6918428; e-mail italemb@netvision.net.il; internet www.italian-embassy-israel.org; Ambassador: GIAN PAOLO CAVARAI.

Japan: Asia House, 4 Rehov Weizman, Tel-Aviv 64239; tel. 3-6957292; fax 3-6910516; Ambassador: YUKATA KAWASHIMA.

Jordan: 12 Rehov Abba Hillel, Ramat-Gan, Tel-Aviv 52506; tel. 3-7517722; fax 3-7517713; e-mail jordan1@barak.net.il; Ambassador: ABDULLAH AL-KURDI.

Kazakhstan: 185 Rehov Hayarkon, Tel-Aviv 63453; tel. 3-5236776; fax 3-5239045; e-mail embacy@internet-zahav.net.

Korea, Republic: 38 Sderot Chen, Tel-Aviv 64166; tel. 3-6963244; fax 3-6963243; Ambassador: LEE CHANG-HO.

Latvia: 52 Pinkas St, Apt 51, Tel-Aviv 62261; tel. 3-5462438; fax 3-5444372; e-mail latvembi@netvision.net.il; Ambassador: JĀNIS LOVNIKS.

Liberia: 6 Shimon Frug, Ramat-Gan, Tel-Aviv 524282; tel. 3-728525; Ambassador: Maj. SAMUEL B. PEARSON, Jr.

Lithuania: 14th Floor, Top Tower, Dizengoff Centre, Tel-Aviv 64332; tel. 3-5288514; fax 3-5257265; e-mail erambizr@netvision.net.il; Ambassador: ROMAS JONAS MISIUNAS.

Mauritania: Tel-Aviv; Ambassador: AHMAD OULD TEGUEDDI.

Mexico: 25 Hamered St, 5th Floor, Trade Tower, Tel-Aviv 68125; tel. 3-5163938; fax 3-5163711; e-mail embamex@netvision.net.il; Ambassador: JUAN ANTONIO MATEOS.

Myanmar: 26 Rehov Hayarkon, Tel-Aviv 68011; tel. 3-5170760; fax 3-5171440; Ambassador: U KYAW MYINT.

Netherlands: Asia House, 4 Rehov Weizman, Tel-Aviv 64239; tel. 3-6957377; fax 3-6957370; e-mail nlgovtel@inter.net.il; Ambassador: H. R. R. V. FROGER.

Nigeria: POB 3339, 34 Gordon St, Tel-Aviv 61030; tel. 3-5222144; fax 3-5237886; Ambassador: E. EGBARA.

Norway: POB 17575, 40 Einstein St, Tel-Aviv 69101; tel. 3-7441490; fax 3-7441498; e-mail norambta@netvision.net.il; Ambassador: SVEIN OLE SAETHER.

Panama: 10 Rehov Hei Be'Iyar, Kikar Hamedina, Tel-Aviv 62998; tel. 3-6960849; fax 3-6910045; Ambassador: Prof. PAULINO C. ROMERO.

Peru: 37 Rehov Hamarganit, Shikun Vatikin, Ramat-Gan, Tel-Aviv 52584; tel. 3-6135591; fax 3-7512286; e-mail emperu@netvision.net.il; Ambassador: NICOLAS RONCAGLIOLO.

Philippines: POB 50085, 13th Floor, Textile Centre Bldg, 2 Rehov Kaufman, Tel-Aviv 68012; tel. 3-5175263; fax 3-5102229; e-mail filembis@netvision.net.il; Ambassador: ROSALINDA DE PERIO-SANTOS.

Poland: 16 Rehov Soutine, Tel-Aviv; tel. 3-5240186; fax 3-5237806; Ambassador: Chargé d'affaires a.i.: ZBIGNIEW ŻELAZOWSKI.

Portugal: 4 Rehov Weizman, Tel-Aviv; tel. 3-6956373; Ambassador: JOSÉ FILIPE MORAES CABRAL.

Romania: 24 Rehov Adam Hacohen, Tel-Aviv 64585; tel. 3-5230066; fax 3-5247379; Ambassador: Dr GHEORGHE POPESCU.

Russia: 120 Rehov Hayarkon, Tel-Aviv 63573; tel. 3-5226736; fax 3-5226744; Ambassador: MIKHAIL BOGDANOV.

Slovakia: POB 6459, 37 Jabotinsky St, Tel-Aviv 61064; tel. 3-5440066; fax 3-5449144; Ambassador Dr Maroš Šefčovič.

South Africa: POB 7138, 16th Floor, Top Tower, 50 Dizengoff St, Tel-Aviv 61071; tel. 3-5252566; fax 3-5252530; e-mail saemtel@isdn.net.il; internet www.safis.co.il; Ambassador: Johann Marx.

Spain: Dubnov Tower, 3 Rehov Daniel Frisch, 16th Floor, Tel-Aviv 64731; tel. 3-6965218; fax 3-6965217; Ambassador: Fermín Zelada Jurado.

Sweden: Asia House, 4 Rehov Weizman, Tel-Aviv 64239; tel. 3-6958111; fax 3-6958116; e-mail swembtlv@trendline.co.il; Ambassador: Anders Lidén.

Switzerland: 228 Rehov Hayarkon, Tel-Aviv 63405; tel. 3-5464455; fax 3-5464408; e-mail vertretung@tel.rep.admin.ch; Ambassador: Ernst Iten.

Turkey: 202 Rehov Hayarkon, Tel-Aviv 63405; tel. 3-35241101; fax 3-35240499; e-mail turquaz@netvision.net.il; Ambassador: Ahmet Üzümcü.

Ukraine: 50 Yirmiyagu, Tel-Aviv 62594; tel. 3-6040242; fax 3-6042512; Ambassador: Dmitro Ykhimovich Markov.

United Kingdom: 192 Rehov Hayarkon, Tel-Aviv 63405; tel. 3-7251222; fax 3-5243313; e-mail britemb@inter.net.il; internet www.britemb.org.il; Ambassador: Francis Cornish.

USA: 71 Rehov Hayarkon, Tel-Aviv 63903; tel. 3-5197575; fax 3-5173227; e-mail usisisr@usis.rog.il; Ambassador: Martin S. Indyk.

Uruguay: Tel-Aviv 62261; tel. 3-440411; Ambassador: Aníbal Díaz Mondino.

Venezuela: Textile Center, 2 Rehov Kaufman, 16th Floor, Tel-Aviv 61500; tel. 3-5176287; fax 3-5176210; Chargé d'affaires: Jorge Mendez Montilla.

Yugoslavia: Iderot Shaul Hamelech 8, Tel-Aviv 64733; tel. 3-6938412; fax 3-6938411; Charge d'affaires a.i.: Mirko Stefanović.

The Jewish Agency for Israel

POB 92, Jerusalem 91000; tel. 2-6202222; fax 2-6202303.

Organization: The governing bodies are the Assembly which determines basic policy, the Board of Governors which sets policy for the Agency between Assembly meetings and the Executive responsible for the day-to-day running of the Agency.

Chairman of Executive: Sallai Meridor.

Chairman of Board of Governors: Alex Grass.

Director-General: Aharon Abramowitz.

Secretary-General: Ilan Rubin.

Functions: According to the Agreement of 1971, the Jewish Agency undertakes the immigration and absorption of immigrants in Israel, including absorption in agricultural settlement and immigrant housing; social welfare and health services in connection with immigrants; education, youth care and training; neighbourhood rehabilitation through project renewal.

Budget (1999): US $350m.

Judicial System

The law of Israel is composed of the enactments of the Knesset and, to a lesser extent, of the acts, orders-in-council and ordinances that remain from the period of the British Mandate in Palestine (1922–48). The pre-1948 law has largely been replaced, amended or reorganized, in the interests of codification, by Israeli legislation. This legislation generally follows a pattern which is very similar to that operating in England and the USA.

Attorney-General: Elyaqim Rubenstein.

CIVIL COURTS

The Supreme Court: Sha'arei Mishpat St, Kiryat David Ben-Gurion, Jerusalem 91950; tel. 2-6759666; fax 2-6759648; e-mail marcia@supreme.court.gov.il; internet www.court.gov.il. This is the highest judicial authority in the state. It has jurisdiction as an Appellate Court over appeals from the District Courts in all matters, both civil and criminal (sitting as a Court of Civil Appeal or as a Court of Criminal Appeal). In addition it is a Court of First Instance (sitting as the High Court of Justice) in actions against governmental authorities, and in matters in which it considers it necessary to grant relief in the interests of justice and which are not within the jurisdiction of any other court or tribunal. The High Court's exclusive power to issue orders in the nature of *habeas corpus, mandamus,* prohibition and *certiorari* enables the court to review the legality of and redress grievances against acts of administrative authorities of all kinds and religious tribunals.

President of the Supreme Court: Aharon Barak.

Deputy-President of the Supreme Court: Shlomo Levin.

Justices of the Supreme Court: Yaacov Kedmi, Mrs Dorit Beinisch, Jacob Türkel, Mishael Cheshin, Mrs Tova Strasberg-Cohen, Theodore Or, Eliyahu Mazza, Itzhak England, Mrs Dalia Dorner, Itzhak Zamir, Abd ar-Rahman Zu'bi (acting), Eliezer Rivlin (acting), Hanoch Ariel (acting), Menachem Ilan (acting).

Registrars: Judge Michal Agmon; Attorney Hagit Mack-Kalmanowitch.

The District Courts: There are five District Courts (Jerusalem, Tel-Aviv, Haifa, Beersheba, Nazareth). They have residual jurisdiction as Courts of First Instance over all civil and criminal matters not within the jurisdiction of a Magistrates' Court, all matters not within the exclusive jurisdiction of any other tribunal, and matters within the concurrent jurisdiction of any other tribunal so long as such tribunal does not deal with them. In addition, the District Courts have appellate jurisdiction over appeals from judgments and decisions of Magistrates' Courts and judgments of Municipal Courts and various administrative tribunals.

Magistrates' Courts: There are 29 Magistrates' Courts, having criminal jurisdiction to try contraventions, misdemeanours and certain felonies, and civil jurisdiction to try actions concerning possession or use of immovable property, or the partition thereof whatever may be the value of the subject matter of the action, and other civil claims not exceeding one million shekels.

Labour Courts: Established in 1969. Regional Labour Courts in Jerusalem, Tel-Aviv, Haifa, Beersheba and Nazareth, composed of judges and representatives of the public. A National Labour Court in Jerusalem. The Courts have jurisdiction over all matters arising out of the relationship between employer and employee or parties to a collective labour agreement, and matters concerning the National Insurance Law and the Labour Law and Rules.

RELIGIOUS COURTS

The Religious Courts are the courts of the recognized religious communities. They have jurisdiction over certain defined matters of personal status concerning members of their respective communities. Where any action of personal status involves persons of different religious communities the President of the Supreme Court decides which Court will decide the matter. Whenever a question arises as to whether or not a case is one of personal status within the exclusive jurisdiction of a Religious Court, the matter must be referred to a Special Tribunal composed of two Justices of the Supreme Court and the President of the highest court of the religious community concerned in Israel. The judgments of the Religious Courts are executed by the process and offices of the Civil Courts. Neither these Courts nor the Civil Courts have jurisdiction to dissolve the marriage of a foreign subject.

Jewish Rabbinical Courts: These Courts have exclusive jurisdiction over matters of marriage and divorce of Jews in Israel who are Israeli citizens or residents. In all other matters of personal status they have concurrent jurisdiction with the District Courts.

Muslim Religious Courts: These Courts have exclusive jurisdiction over matters of marriage and divorce of Muslims who are not foreigners, or who are foreigners subject by their national law to the jurisdiction of Muslim Religious Courts in such matters. In all other matters of personal status they have concurrent jurisdiction with the District Courts.

Christian Religious Courts: The Courts of the recognized Christian communities have exclusive jurisdiction over matters of marriage and divorce of members of their communities who are not foreigners. In all other matters of personal status they have concurrent jurisdiction with the District Courts.

Druze Courts: These Courts, established in 1963, have exclusive jurisdiction over matters of marriage and divorce of Druze in Israel, who are Israeli citizens or residents, and concurrent jurisdiction with the District Courts over all other matters of personal status of Druze.

Religion

JUDAISM

Judaism, the religion of the Jews, is the faith of the majority of Israel's inhabitants. On 31 December 1999 Judaism's adherents totalled 4,900,000, equivalent to 78.78% of the country's population. Its basis is a belief in an ethical monotheism.

There are two main Jewish communities: the Ashkenazim and the Sephardim. The former are the Jews from Eastern, Central, or Northern Europe, while the latter originate from the Balkan countries, North Africa and the Middle East.

There is also a community of about 10,000 Falashas (Ethiopian Jews) who have been airlifted to Israel at various times since the fall of Emperor Haile Selassie in 1974.

The supreme religious authority is vested in the Chief Rabbinate, which consists of the Ashkenazi and Sephardi Chief Rabbis and the

Supreme Rabbinical Council. It makes decisions on interpretation of the Jewish law, and supervises the Rabbinical Courts. There are 8 regional Rabbinical Courts, and a Rabbinical Court of Appeal presided over by the two Chief Rabbis.

According to the Rabbinical Courts Jurisdiction Law of 1953, marriage and divorce among Jews in Israel are exclusively within the jurisdiction of the Rabbinical Courts. Provided that all the parties concerned agree, other matters of personal status can also be decided by the Rabbinical Courts.

There are 195 Religious Councils, which maintain religious services and supply religious needs, and about 405 religious committees with similar functions in smaller settlements. Their expenses are borne jointly by the State and the local authorities. The Religious Councils are under the administrative control of the Ministry of Religious Affairs. In all matters of religion, the Religious Councils are subject to the authority of the Chief Rabbinate. There are 365 officially appointed rabbis. The total number of synagogues is about 7,000, most of which are organized within the framework of the Union of Israel Synagogues.

Head of the Ashkenazi Community: The Chief Rabbi ISRAEL MEIR LAU.

Head of the Sephardic Community: Jerusalem; tel. 2-244785; The Chief Rabbi ELIAHU BAKSHI-DORON.

Two Jewish sects still loyal to their distinctive customs are:

The Karaites, a sect which recognizes only the Jewish written law and not the oral law of the Mishna and Talmud. The community of about 12,000, many of whom live in or near Ramla, has been augmented by immigration from Egypt.

The Samaritans, an ancient sect mentioned in 2 Kings xvii, 24. They recognize only the Torah. The community in Israel numbers about 500; about one-half of this number live in Holon, where a Samaritan synagogue has been built, and the remainder, including the High Priest, live in Nablus, near Mt Gerazim, which is sacred to the Samaritans.

ISLAM

The Muslims in Israel are mainly Sunnis, and are divided among the four rites of the Sunni sect of Islam: the Shafe'i, the Hanbali, the Hanafi and the Maliki. Before June 1967 they numbered approx. 175,000; in 1971, approx. 343,900. On 31 December 1999 the total Muslim population of Israel was 936,000.

Mufti of Jerusalem: POB 19859, Jerusalem; tel. 2-283528; Sheikh ABD AL-QADIR ABIDIN (also Chair. Supreme Muslim Council for Jerusalem). The Palestinian National Authority also claims the right to appoint the Mufti of Jerusalem and has named Sheikh AKRAM SA'ID SABRI as its choice.

There was also a total of 101,000 Druzes in Israel at 31 December 1999.

CHRISTIANITY

The total Christian population of Israel (including East Jerusalem) at 31 December 1999 was 131,000.

United Christian Council in Israel: POB 116, Jerusalem 91000; tel. 2-6714351; fax 2-6721349; e-mail kopp@galanet.net; f. 1956; 28 mems (churches and other bodies); Chair. CHARLES KOPP.

The Roman Catholic Church

Armenian Rite

The Armenian Catholic Patriarch of Cilicia is resident in Beirut, Lebanon.

Patriarchal Exarchate of Jerusalem: POB 19546, Via Dolorosa 36, Jerusalem 91190; tel. 2-6284262; fax 2-6272123; f. 1885; about 280 adherents (1998); Exarch Patriarchal ANTREAS BEDOGHOLIAN.

Chaldean Rite

The Chaldean Patriarch of Babylon is resident in Baghdad, Iraq.

Patriarchal Exarchate of Jerusalem: Chaldean Patriarchal Vicariate, POB 20108, 7 Chaldean St, Saad and Said Quarter, Jerusalem 91200; tel. 2-6284519; fax 7-6274614; Exarch Patriarchal Mgr PAUL COLLIN.

Latin Rite

The Patriarchate of Jerusalem covers Palestine, Jordan and Cyprus. At 31 December 1998 there were an estimated 77,000 adherents.

Bishops' Conference: Conférence des Evêques Latins dans les Régions Arabes, Notre Dame of Jerusalem Center, POB 20531, Jerusalem 91204; tel. 2-6288554; fax 2-6288555; e-mail evcat@palnet.com; f. 1967; Pres. His Beatitude MICHEL SABBAH; Patriarch of Jerusalem.

Patriarchate of Jerusalem: Patriarcat Latin, POB 14152, Jerusalem 91141; tel. 2-6282323; fax 2-6271652; e-mail latinpatr@isdn.co.il; Patriarch: His Beatitude MICHEL SABBAH; Vicar-General for Jerusalem: KAMAL HANNA BATHISH (Titular Bishop of Jericho);

Vicar-General for Israel: BOULOS G. MARCUZZO (Titular Bishop of Emmaus Nicopolis), Vicariat Patriarcal Latin, Street 6191/3, Nazareth 16100; tel. 6-6554075; fax 6-6452416; e-mail latinpatr@rannet.com.

Maronite Rite

The Maronite community, under the jurisdiction of the Maronite Patriarch of Antioch (resident in Lebanon), has about 7,000 members.

Patriarchal Exarchate of Jerusalem: Vicariat Maronite, POB 14219, 25 Maronite Convent St, Jaffa Gate, Jerusalem 91141; tel. 2-6282158; fax 2-6272821; about 504 adherents (1998); Exarch Patriarchal Mgr PAUL NABIL SAYAH (also the Archbishop of Haifa and the Holy Land).

Melkite Rite

The Greek-Melkite Patriarch of Antioch (MAXIMOS V HAKIM) is resident in Damascus, Syria.

Patriarchal Vicariate of Jerusalem: Patriarcat Grec-Melkite Catholique, POB 14130, Porte de Jaffa, Jerusalem 91141; tel. 2-6271968; fax 2-6286652; e-mail gcpjer@p_ol.com; about 3,300 adherents (1998); Vicars Patriarchal Mgr HILARION CAPUCCI (Titular Archbishop of Caesarea in Palestine), Mgr LUTFI LAHAM (Titular Archbishop of Tarsus).

Archbishop of Akka (Acre): Most Rev. PIERRE MOUALLEM, Archevêché Grec-Catholique, POB 279, 33 Hagefen St, 31002 Haifa; tel. 4-8523114; fax 4-8520798; e-mail mualem_p@rannet.com; 54,000 adherents at 31 December 1998.

Syrian Rite

The Syrian Catholic Patriarch of Antioch is resident in Beirut, Lebanon.

Patriarchal Exarchate of Jerusalem: Vicariat Patriarcal Syrien Catholique, POB 19787, 6 Chaldean St, Jerusalem 91191; tel. 2-6282657; fax 2-6284217; e-mail stjossc@l-ol.com; about 10,298 adherents (Dec. 2000); Exarch Patriarchal Mgr GRÉGOIRE PIERRE ABD AL-AHAD.

The Armenian Apostolic (Orthodox) Church

Patriarch of Jerusalem: TORKOM MANOOGIAN, St James's Cathedral, Jerusalem; tel. 2-6264853; fax 2-6264862 .

The Greek Orthodox Church

The Patriarchate of Jerusalem contains an estimated 260,000 adherents in Israel, the Israeli-occupied territories, Jordan, Kuwait, the United Arab Emirates and Saudi Arabia.

Patriarch of Jerusalem: (vacant), POB 19632-633, Greek Orthodox Patriarchate St, Old City, Jerusalem; tel. 2-6271657; fax 2-6282048.

The Anglican Communion

Episcopal Church in Jerusalem and the Middle East: POB 19122, St George's Cathedral Close, Jerusalem; tel. 2-6271670; fax (2) 6273847; e-mail ediosces@netvision.net.il; Bishop The Rt. Rev. RIAH ABU EL-ASSAL.

Other Christian Churches

Other denominations include the Coptic Orthodox Church (700 members), the Russian Orthodox Church, the Ethiopian Orthodox Church, the Romanian Orthodox Church, the Baptist Church, the Lutheran Church and the Church of Scotland.

The Press

Tel-Aviv is the main publishing centre. Largely for economic reasons, no local press has developed away from the main cities; hence all papers regard themselves as national. Friday editions, issued on Sabbath eve, are increased to as much as twice the normal size by special weekend supplements, and experience a considerable rise in circulation. No newspapers appear on Saturday.

Most of the daily papers are in Hebrew, and others appear in Arabic, English, French, Polish, Yiddish, Hungarian, Russian and German. The total daily circulation is 500,000–600,000 copies, or 21 papers per hundred people, although most citizens read more than one daily paper.

Most Hebrew morning dailies have strong political or religious affiliations. *Al-Hamishmar* is affiliated to Mapam, *Hatzofeh* to the National Religious Party—World Mizrachi. Most newspapers depend on subsidies from political parties, religious organizations or public funds. The limiting effect on freedom of commentary entailed by this party press system has provoked repeated criticism. There are around 400 other newspapers and magazines including some 50 weekly and 150 fortnightly; over 250 of them are in Hebrew, the remainder in 11 other languages.

The most influential and respected daily, for both quality of news coverage and commentary, is *Ha'aretz*. This is the most widely read of the morning papers, exceeded only by the popular afternoon press, *Ma'ariv* and *Yedioth Aharonoth*. The *Jerusalem Post* gives detailed and sound news coverage in English.

The Israeli Press Council (Chair. ITZHAK ZAMIR), established in 1963, deals with matters of common interest to the Press such as drafting the code of professional ethics which is binding on all journalists.

The Daily Newspaper Publishers' Association represents publishers in negotiations with official and public bodies, negotiates contracts with employees and purchases and distributes newsprint.

DAILIES

Al Anba (The News): Jerusalem Publications Ltd, POB 428, 37 Hillel St, Jerusalem; f. 1968; circ. 10,000.

Globes: POB 5126, Rishon le Zion 75150; tel. 3-9538888; fax 3-9525971; e-mail mailbox@globes.co.il; internet www.globes.co.il; f. 1983; evening; Hebrew; business, economics; CEO AMI EVEN; Editor-in-Chief HAGGAI GOLAN; circ. 40,000.

Ha'aretz (The Land): POB 233, 21 Salman Schocken St, Tel-Aviv 61001; tel. 3-5121110; fax 3-6815859; e-mail iht@haaretz.co.il; internet www.haaretz.co.il; f. 1918; morning; Hebrew; liberal, independent; Editor HANOCH MARMARI; circ. 65,000 (weekdays), 75,000 (weekends).

Hadashot (The News): 108 Igal Alon St, Tel-Aviv; 3-5120555; fax 3-5623084; late morning; Hebrew.

Al Hamishmar (The Guardian): Yton Vasefer Ltd, 2 Choma Umigdal St, Tel-Aviv 67771; tel. 3-378833; fax 3-5370037; f. 1943; morning; Hebrew; Editor-in-Chief ZVI TIMOR.

Hamodia (The Informer): POB 1306, Yehuda Hamackabbi 3, Jerusalem; tel. 2-5389255; fax 2-539108; e-mail moll@hamodia-mod.co.il; morning; Hebrew; also publishes weekly English-language edition; organ of Agudat Israel; Editors M. A. DRUCK, H. M. KNOPF; circ. 25,000.

Hatzofeh (The Watchman): POB 2045, 66 Hamasger St, Tel-Aviv; tel. 3-5622951; fax 3-5621502; f. 1938; morning; Hebrew; organ of the National Religious Party; Editor MOSHE ISHON; circ. 60,000.

Israel Nachrichten (News of Israel): 49 Tschlenow St, Tel-Aviv 66048; tel. 3-5372059; fax 3-6877142; f. 1974; morning; German; Editor ALICE SCHWARZ-GARDOS; circ. 20,000.

Al-Itihad (Unity): POB 104, Haifa; tel. 4-511296; fax 4-511297; f. 1944; Arabic; organ of Hadash; Editor AHMAD SA'AD; circ. 60,000.

The Jerusalem Post: POB 81, Romema, Jerusalem 91000; tel. 2-5315666; fax 2-5389527; e-mail jpedt@jpost.co.il; internet www.jpost.co.il; f. 1932; morning; English; independent; Pres. PAUL STASZEWSKI; Editor CARL SCHRAG; circ. 30,000 (weekdays), 50,000 (weekend edition); there is also a weekly international edition, circ. 70,000, and a weekly French-language edition, circ. 7,500.

Le Journal d'Israel: Tel-Aviv; tel. 3-33188; f. 1971; French; independent; Chief Editor J. RABIN; circ. 10,000; also overseas weekly selection; circ. 15,000.

Letzte Nyess (Late News): Tel-Aviv; tel. 3-35815; f. 1949; morning; Yiddish; Editor S. HIMMELFARB; circ. 23,000.

Ma'ariv (Evening Prayer): 2 Carlebach St, Tel-Aviv 61200; tel. 3-5632111; fax 3-5610614; f. 1948; mid-morning; Hebrew; independent; published by Modiin Publishing House; Editor OFFER NIMRODI; circ. 160,000 (weekdays), 270,000 (weekends).

Mabat: 8 Toshia St, Tel-Aviv 67218; tel. 3-5627711; fax 3-5627719; f. 1971; morning; Hebrew; economic and social; Editor S. YARKONI; circ. 7,000.

Nasha Strana (Our Country): 52 Harakeret St, Tel-Aviv 67770; tel. 3-370011; fax 3-5371921; f. 1970; morning; Russian; Editor S. HIMMELFARB; circ. 35,000.

Ash Shaab (The People): POB 19154, Jerusalem; tel. 2-289881.

Shearim (The Gates): POB 11044, 64 Frishman St, Tel-Aviv; tel. 3-242126; organ of the Poale Agudat Israel Party.

Al-Quds (Jerusalem): POB 19788, Jerusalem; tel. 2-6272663; fax 2-5855003; e-mail info@alquds.com; internet www.alquds.com; f. 1968; Arabic; circ. 60,000.

Uj Kelet: 49 Tchlenor St, Tel-Aviv; tel. 3-5371395; fax 3-377142; f. 1918; morning; Hungarian; independent; Editor D. DRORY; circ. 20,000.

Viata Noastra: 49 Tchlenor St, Tel-Aviv 61351; tel. 3-5372059; fax 3-6877142; e-mail erancourt@shani.co.il; f. 1950; morning; Romanian; Editor GEORGE EDRI; circ. 30,000.

Yated Ne'eman: POB 328, Bnei Brak; tel. 3-6170800; fax 3-6170801; e-mail let-edit@yatedneman.co.il; f. 1986; morning; religious; Editors Y. ROTH and N.GROSSMAN; circ. 25,000.

Yedioth Aharonoth (The Latest News): 2 Yehuda and Noah Mozes St, Tel-Aviv 61000; tel. 3-6972222; fax 3-6953950; f. 1939; evening;

independent; Editor-in-Chief MOSHE VARDI; circ. 300,000, Friday 600,000.

WEEKLIES AND FORTNIGHTLIES

Aurora: Aurora Ltd, POB 18066, Tel-Aviv 61180; tel. 3-5625216; fax 3-5625082; e-mail aurora@aurora-israel.co.il; internet www.aurora-israel.co.il; f. 1963; weekly; Spanish; for expatriates.

Bama'alah: 120 Kibbutz Gabuyot St, Tel-Aviv; tel. 3-6814488; fax 3-6816852; Hebrew; journal of the young Histadrut Movement; Editor ODED BAR-MEIR.

Bamahane (In the Camp): Military POB 1013, Tel-Aviv; f. 1948; military, illustrated weekly of the Israel Armed Forces; Hebrew; Editor-in-Chief YOSSEF ESHKOL; circ. 70,000.

Ethgar (The Challenge): 75 Einstein St, Tel-Aviv; twice weekly; Hebrew; Editor NATHAN YALIN-MOR.

Al Fajr (The Dawn): POB 19315, Jerusalem; tel. 2-271649; fax 2-273521; f. 1980; weekly; Editor-in-Chief MANNA SINIORA.

Glasul Populurui: Tel-Aviv; weekly of the Communist Party of Israel; Romanian; Editor MEÏR SEMO.

Harefuah (Medicine): POB 3566, 35 Jabotinsky St, Ramat-Gan, Tel-Aviv 52136; tel. 3-6100444; fax 3-5751616; f. 1920; fortnightly journal of the Israeli Medical Association; Hebrew with English summaries; Editor Y. ROTEM; circ. 12,000.

Hotam: Al-Hamishmar House, Choma U'Migdal St, Tel-Aviv; Hebrew.

Al-Hurriya (Freedom): 38 King George St, Tel-Aviv; Arabic weekly of the Herut Party.

Illustrirte WeltWoch: Tel-Aviv; f. 1956; weekly; Yiddish; Editor M. KARPINOVITZ.

Information Week: POB 1161, 13 Yad Harutzim St, Tel-Aviv 61116; tel. 3-6385858; fax 3-6889207; e-mail world@pc.co.il; internet www.people-and-computers.co.il; weekly; Man. Dirs DAHLIA PELLED, PELI PELED; Editor-in Chief PELI PELED.

The Israeli Tourist Guide Magazine: Tourist Guide Communications Ltd, POB 53333, Tel-Aviv 61533; tel. 3-5168282; fax 3-5168284; e-mail ishchori@touristguide.co.il; internet www.touristguide.co.il; weekly; Publisher and Editor ILAN SHCHORI; circ. 10,000.

Jerusalem Post International Edition: POB 81, Romema, Jerusalem 91000; tel. 2-5315666; fax 2-5389527; e-mail jpedt@jpost.co.il; internet www.jpost.co.il; f. 1959; weekly; English; overseas edition of the *Jerusalem Post* (q.v.); circ. 70,000 to 106 countries.

Jerusalem Report: POB 1805, Jerusalem 91017; tel. 2-5315440; fax 2-5379489; e-mail jrep@jreport.co.il; internet www.jrep.com; f. 1990; bi-weekly; English; CEO PAUL STASZEWSKI; Editor DAVID HOROVITZ; published by the *Jerusalem Post*; circ. 65,000 worldwide.

The Jerusalem Times: POB 20185, Jerusalem; tel. 2-6264883; fax 2-6264975; e-mail tjt@palnet.com; f. 1994; weekly; English; Editor HANNA SINIORA.

Kol Ha'am (Voice of the People): Tel-Aviv; f. 1947; Hebrew; organ of the Communist Party of Israel; Editor B. BALTI.

Laisha (For Women): POB 28122, 35 Bnei Brak St, Tel-Aviv 67132; tel. 3-6386969; fax 3-6386933; f. 1946; Hebrew; women's magazine; Editor MIRIAM NOFECH-MOSES; circ. 150,000.

Ma'ariv Lanoar: POB 20020, 2 Carlebach St, Tel-Aviv 67132; tel. 3-5632525; fax 3-5632030; e-mail maariv_lanoar@maariv.co.il; f. 1957; weekly for teenagers; Hebrew; Editor DANA BEN-NAFTALI; circ. 100,000.

MB (Mitteilungsblatt): POB 1480, Tel-Aviv 61014; tel. 3-5164461; fax 3-5164435; f. 1932; German monthly journal of the Irgun Olei Merkas Europa (The Association of Immigrants from Central Europe); Editor Prof. PAUL ALSBERG.

Al Mirsad (The Telescope): POB 1777, Tel-Aviv; tel. 3-266244; fax 3-664463; weekly; news and current affairs.

Otiot: Jerusalem; tel. 2-895097; fax 2-895196; f. 1987; weekly for children; English; Editor URI AUERBACH.

People and Computers: POB 11616, 13 Yad Harutzim St, Tel-Aviv 61116; tel. 3-6385888; fax 3-6889207; e-mail world@enet.co.il; internet www.enet.co.il; weekly; Hebrew; information technology; circ. 15,000.

Reshumot: Ministry of Justice, POB 1087, 29 Rehov Salahadin, Jerusalem 91010; f. 1948; Hebrew, Arabic and English; official government gazette.

Sada at-Tarbia (The Echo of Education): published by the Histadrut and Teachers' Association, POB 2306, Rehovot; f. 1952; fortnightly; Arabic; educational; Editor TUVIA SHAMOSH.

As-Sinnarah: Nazareth; weekly for Christians; Arabic; Editor-in-Chief LUFTI MASH'UR.

OTHER PERIODICALS

Adi 'Or: Miller Freeman (Israel) Ltd, POB 3441, Silver Bldg, 7 Abba Hillel St, Ramat-Gan, Tel-Aviv 52133; tel. 3-5750196; fax 3-

5754829; e-mail millisra@trendline.co.il; f. 1990; quarterly; jewellery; Publr CHAIM EVEN-ZOHAR.

Ariel: the Israel Review of Arts and Letters: Cultural and Scientific Relations Division, Ministry of Foreign Affairs, Jerusalem; Distributor: Youval Tal Ltd, POB 2160, Jerusalem 91021; tel. 2-6248897; fax 2-6245434; e-mail ariel-mail@usa.net; internet www.israel-mfa.gov.il; Editorial Office: 214 Jaffa Road, Jerusalem 91130; tel. 2-5381515; fax 2-538062; f. 1962; quarterly review of all aspects of culture in Israel; regular edns in English, Spanish, French, German, Arabic and Russian; occasional edns in other languages; Editor ASHER WEILL; Asst Editor ALOMA HALTER; circ. 30,000.

Asakim Vekalkala (Business and Economics): POB 20027, 84 Ha' Hashmonaim St, Tel-Aviv 61200; tel. 3-5631010; fax 3-5619025; monthly; Hebrew; Editor ZVI AMIT.

Avoda Urevacha Ubituach Leumi: POB 915, 2 Rehov Kaplan, Kiryat Ben-Gurion, Jerusalem 91008; f. 1949; monthly review of the Ministry of Labour and Social Welfare, and the National Insurance Institute, Jerusalem; Hebrew; Chief Editor AVNER MICHAELI; Editor MICHAEL KLODOVSKY; circ. 2,500.

Bitaon Heyl Ha'avir (Israel Air Force Magazine): Military POB 01560, Zahal; tel. 3-5694153; fax 3-5695806; e-mail iaf@inter.net.il; internet www.iaf.org.il; f. 1948; bi-monthly; Hebrew; Dep. Editor U. ETSION; Editor-in-Chief MERAV HALPERIN; circ. 30,000.

Al-Bushra (Good News): POB 6228, Haifa 31061; tel. 4-8385002; fax 4-8371612; f. 1935; monthly; Arabic; organ of the Ahmadiyya movement; Editor MUSA ASA'AD O'DEH.

Business Diary: Haifa; f. 1947; weekly; English, Hebrew; shipping movements, import licences, stock exchange listings, business failures, etc.; Editor G. ALON.

Challenge: POB 41199, Jaffa 61411; tel. 3-6839145; fax 3-6839148; e-mail oda@netvision.net.il; internet www.odaction.org/challenge/; f. 1989; magazine on the Israeli–Palestinian conflict, published by Hanitzotz Publishing House; bi-monthly; English; Editor-in-Chief RONI BEN EFRAT; Editor LIZ LEYH LEVAC; circ. 1,000.

Christian News from Israel: 30 Jaffa Rd, Jerusalem; f. 1949; half-yearly; English, French, Spanish; issued by the Ministry of Religious Affairs; Editor SHALOM BEN-ZAKKAI; circ. 10,000.

Divrei Haknesset: c/o The Knesset, Jerusalem; f. 1949; Hebrew; records of the proceedings of the Knesset; published by the Government Printer, Jerusalem; Editor DVORA AVIVI (acting); circ. 350.

Eastern Mediterranean Tourism and Travel: Israel Travel News Ltd, POB 3251, Tel-Aviv 61032; tel. 3-5251646; fax 3-5251605; f. 1979; monthly; English; circ. 19,515.

The Easy Way to do Business with Israel: POB 20027, Tel-Aviv; tel. 3-5612444; fax 3-5612614; published by Federation of Israeli Chambers of Commerce; Editor Y. SHOSTAK.

Eitanim (Popular Medicine): POB 16250, Merkez Kupat Holim, Tel-Aviv 62098; f. 1948; Hebrew; monthly; circ. 20,000.

Folk un Zion: POB 7053, Tel-Aviv 61070; tel. 3-5423317; f. 1950; bi-monthly; current events relating to Israel and World Jewry; Editor MOSHE KALCHHEIM; circ. 3,000.

Frei Israel: POB 8512, Tel-Aviv; progressive monthly; published by Asscn for Popular Culture; Yiddish.

Hamizrah Hehadash (The New East): Israel Oriental Society, The Hebrew University, Mount Scopus, Jerusalem 91905; tel. 2-5883633; e-mail ios49@hotmail.com; f. 1949; annual of the Israel Oriental Society; Middle Eastern, Asian and African Affairs; Hebrew with English summary; Editors HAIM GERBER, ELIE PODEH; circ. 1,500–2,000.

Hamionai (The Hotelier): Tel-Aviv; f. 1962; monthly of the Israel Hotel Asscn; Hebrew and English; Editor Z. PELTZ.

Hapraklit: POB 14152, 8 Wilson St, Tel-Aviv 61141; tel. 3-5614695; fax 3-561476; f. 1943; quarterly; Hebrew; published by the Israel Bar Asscn; Editor-in-Chief A. POLONSKI; Editor ARNAN GAVRIELI; circ. 7,000.

Hassadeh: POB 40044, 8 Shaul Hamelech Blvd, Tel-Aviv 61400; tel. 3-6929018; fax 3-6929979; f. 1920; monthly; review of Israeli agriculture; English and Hebrew; Publr GUY KING; Editor NAAMA DOTAN; circ. 13,000.

Hed Hagan: 8 Ben Saruk St, Tel-Aviv 62969; tel. 3-6922958; f. 1935; quarterly; Hebrew; educational; Editor MIRIAM SNAPIR; circ. 9,000.

Hed Hahinukh: 8 Ben Saruk St, Tel-Aviv 62969; tel. 3-5432911; fax 3-5432928; f. 1926; monthly; Hebrew; educational; published by the Israeli Teachers' Union; Editor DALIA LACHMAN; circ. 40,000.

Internet World (Israel): POB 1161, 13 Yad Harutzim St, Tel-Aviv 61116; tel. 3-6385858; fax 3-6889207; e-mail benrun@netvision.net.il; internet www.people-and-computers.co.il; 24 a year; computers and information technology; Man. Dirs DAHLIA PELLED, PELI PELED; Editor-in-Chief PELI PELED.

Israel Agritechnology Focus: 8 Twersky St, Tel-Aviv 61574; tel. 3-5628511; fax 3-5628512; f. 1993; quarterly; farming technology, agricultural company and investment news; Editor NICKY BLACKMAN.

Israel Economist: 6 Hazanowitz St, Jerusalem; tel. 2-234131; fax 2-246569; f. 1945; monthly; English; independent; political and economic; Editor BEN MOLLOV; Publisher ISRAEL KELMAN; also publishes *Keeping Posted* (diplomatic magazine), *Mazel and Brucha* (jewellers' magazine); annuals: *Travel Agents' Manual, Electronics, International Conventions in Israel, Arkia, In Flight,* various hotel magazines.

Israel Environment Bulletin: Ministry of the Environment, POB 34033, 5 Kanfei Nesharim St, Jerusalem 95464; tel. 2-6553777; fax 2-6535937; internet www.environment.gov.il; f. 1973; Editor SHOSHANA GABBAY; circ. 3,500.

Israel Exploration Journal: POB 7041, 5 Avida St, Jerusalem 91070; tel. 2-6257991; fax 2-6247772; e-mail ies@vms.huji.ac.il; internet www.hum.huji.ac.il/ies; f. 1950; quarterly; English; general and biblical archaelogy, ancient history and historical geography of Israel and the Holy Land; Editors S. ACHITUV, MIRIAM TADMOR; circ. 2,500.

Israel Export: POB 57500, 8 Twersky St, Tel-Aviv 61574; tel. and fax 3-5628512; f. 1993; annual; Editor NAOYA NAKAMURA.

Israel Export and Trade Journal: Tel-Aviv; f. 1949; monthly; English; commercial and economic; published by Israel Periodicals Co Ltd; Man. Dir ZALMAN PELTZ.

Israel Journal of Chemistry: POB 35409, Jerusalem 91352; tel. 2-6522226; fax 2-6522277; e-mail info@laserpages.net; internet www.laserpages.net; f. 1951; quarterly; published by Laser Pages Publishing Ltd; Editor Prof. H. LEVANON.

Israel Journal of Earth Sciences: POB 35409, Jerusalem 91352; tel. 2-6522226; fax. 2-6522277; e-mail info@laserpages.net; internet www.laserpages.net; f. 1951; quarterly; published by Laser Pages Publishing Ltd; Editor Prof. ALAN MATTHEWS.

Israel Journal of Mathematics: POB 39099, Jerusalem 91390; tel. 2-6586660; fax 2-5633370; e-mail magnes@vms.huji.ac.il; f. 1951; monthly, four vols of three issues per year; published by Magnes Press; Editor Prof. G. KALAI.

Israel Journal of Medical Sciences: 2 Etzel St, French Hill, Jerusalem 97853; tel. 2-5817727; fax 2-5815722; f. 1965; monthly; Editor-in-Chief Prof. MOSHE PRYWES; circ. 5,500.

Israel Journal of Plant Sciences: POB 35409, Jerusalem 91352; tel. 2-6522226; fax. 2-6522277; e-mail info@laserpages.net; internet www.laserpages.net; f. 1951 (as *Israel Journal of Botany*); quarterly; published by Laser Pages Publishing Ltd; Editor Prof. A. M. MAYER.

Israel Journal of Psychiatry and Related Sciences: Gefen Publishing House Ltd, POB 36004, Jerusalem 91360; tel. 2-5380247; fax 2-5388423; e-mail info@gefenpublishing.com; internet www.gefenbooks.com; f. 1963; quarterly; Editor-in-Chief Dr DAVID GREENBERG.

Israel Journal of Veterinary Medicine: POB 3076, Rishon Le-Zion 75130; tel. 9-7419929; fax 9-7431778; e-mail ivma@internet-zahav.net; internet www.isrvma.org; f. 1943; quarterly of the Israel Veterinary Medical Asscn; formerly *Refuah Veterinarith*; Editors G. SIMON, I. GLAS.

Israel Journal of Zoology: POB 35409, Jerusalem 91352; tel. 2-6522226; fax. 2-6522277; e-mail info@laserpages.net; internet www.laserpages.net; f. 1951; quarterly; published by Laser Pages Publishing Ltd; Editors Prof. ALAN DEGEN, Prof. MICHA ILAN.

Israel Law Review: Faculty of Law, Mount Scopus, Jerusalem 91905; tel. 2-5882520; fax 2-5823042; e-mail msilr@mscc.huji.ac.il; quarterly; published by the Israel Law Review Association.

Israel Press Service: POB 33188, Jerusalem 91330; tel. 2-6419783; fax 2-6439377; e-mail junes@netvision.net.il; f. 1956; English; Zionist; Editor JUNE SPITZER.

Israel-South Africa Trade Journal: Tel-Aviv; f. 1973; bi-monthly; English; commercial and economic; published by Israel Publications Corpn Ltd; Man. Dir Z. PELTZ.

Israels Aussenhandel: Tel-Aviv; tel. 3-5280215; f. 1967; monthly; German; commercial; published by Israel Periodicals Co Ltd; Editor PELTZ NOEMI; Man. Dir ZALMAN PELTZ.

Al-Jadid (The New): POB 104, Haifa; f. 1951; literary monthly; Arabic; Editor SALEM JUBRAN; circ. 5,000.

Journal d'Analyse Mathématique: f. 1955; 2 vols per year; published by Magnes Press; Editor Prof. L. ZALCMAN.

Kalkalan: Jerusalem; f. 1952; monthly; independent; Hebrew; commercial and economic; Editor J. KOLLEK.

Kibbutz Trends: Yad Tabenkin, Ramat Efal 52960; tel. 3-5301217; fax 3-5346376; e-mail yadtab@inter.net.il; f. 1991; quarterly; English language journal on kibbutz; Editors IDIT PAZ, NEIL HARRIS, ROCHELLE MASS; circ. 1,500.

Leshonenu: Academy of the Hebrew Language, POB 3449, Jerusalem 91034; tel. 2-6493555; fax 2-5617065; e-mail acad2u@vms.huji.ac.il; f. 1929; 4 a year; for the study of the Hebrew language and cognate subjects; Editor M. BAR-ASHER.

Leshonenu La'am: Academy of the Hebrew Language, POB 3449, Jerusalem 91034; tel. 2-6493555; fax 2-5617065; f. 1945; 4 a year; popular Hebrew philology; Editors C. E. COHEN, D. TALSHIR, Y. ÖFER.

Ma'arachot (Campaigns): POB 7026, Hakirya, 3 Albert Mendler St, Tel-Aviv 61070; tel. 3-5694345; fax 3-5694343; f. 1939; military and political bi-monthly; Hebrew; periodical of Israel Defence Force; Editors HAGGAI GOLAN, EFI MELZER.

Mada (Science): 8A Horkanya St, Jerusalem 91007; tel. 2-783203; fax 2-783784; f. 1955; popular scientific bi-monthly in Hebrew; published by Laser Pages Publishing Ltd; Editor-in-Chief Dr YACHIN UNNA; circ. 10,000.

Magallati (My Magazine): POB 28049, Tel-Aviv; tel. 3-371438; f. 1960; bi-monthly children's magazine; circ. 3,000.

Melaha Vetaassiya (Trade and Industry): Tel-Aviv; f. 1969; bi-monthly review of the Union of Artisans and Small Manufacturers of Israel; Hebrew; Man. Dir Z. PELTZ; circ. 8,500.

M'Lakha V'ta Asiya (Israel Industry): POB 11587, 40 Rembrandt St, Tel-Aviv; monthly; published by Israel Publications Corporation Ltd; circ. 8,500.

Moznaim (Balance): POB 7098, Tel-Aviv; tel. 3-6953256; fax 3-6919681; f. 1929; monthly; Hebrew; literature and culture; Editors ASHER REICH, AZRIEL KAUFMAN; circ. 2,500.

Na'amat: 93 Arlozorof St, Tel-Aviv 62098; tel. 3-6921111; fax 3-6912725; monthly; published by Histadrut; trade union issues.

Nekuda: Hebrew; organ of the Jewish settlers of the West Bank and Gaza Strip.

New Outlook: 9 Gordon St, Tel-Aviv 63458; tel. 3-5236496; fax 3-5232252; f. 1957; bi-monthly; Israeli and Middle Eastern Affairs; dedicated to the quest for Arab-Israeli peace; Editor-in-Chief CHAIM SHUR; Senior Editor DAN LEON; circ. 10,000.

News from Within: POB 31417, Jerusalem; tel. 2-6241159; fax 2-6253151; e-mail aicmail@trendline.co.il; internet www.aic.netgate .net; monthly; joint Israeli-Palestinian publication; political, economic, social and cultural; publ. by the Alternative Information Centre.

OTOT: 117 Ha' Hashmonaim St, Tel-Aviv; tel. 3-5615310; fax 3-5615281; e-mail igud@inter.net.il; f. 1975; monthly; Hebrew; advertising, marketing and communications; Editor-in-Chief YAIR FLADMANN; Editor RAYA RUBIN; circ. 4,000.

PC Magazine (Israel): PC Media, POB 11438, 13 Yad Harutzim St, Tel-Aviv 61114; tel. 3-6385810; fax 3-6889207; e-mail editor@pc.co.il; internet www.zdnet.co.il; f. 1992; monthly; Hebrew; information on personal computers; Man. Dirs DAHLIA PELLED, YEHUDA ELYADA; Editor-in-Chief YEHUDA ELYADA; circ. 13,500.

Proche-Orient Chrétien: POB 19079, Jerusalem 91190; tel. 2-6283285; fax 2-6280764; e-mail mafrpoc@steanne.org; f. 1951; quarterly on churches and religion in the Middle East; circ. 1,000.

Publish Israel: Olamot-Media Industries, POB 57285, Ben-Avigdor St, Tel-Aviv 61571; tel. 3-5622744; fax 3-5621808; e-mail olamot@ inter.net.il; f. 1998; six times a year; magazine for printers and publishers; Gen. Man. DAN SHEKEL; circ. 12,000.

Quarterly Review of the Israel Medical Assn (Mif'al Haverut Hutz—World Fellowship of the Israel Medical Assn): POB 33289, 39 Shaul Hamelech Blvd, Tel-Aviv 61332; tel. (3) 6955521; fax 3-6956103; quarterly; English; Editor-in-Chief YEHUDA SHOENFELD.

The Sea: POB 33706, Hane'emanim 8, Haifa; tel. 04-529818; every six months; published by Israel Maritime League; review of marine problems; Pres. M. POMROCK; Chief Editor M. LITOVSKI; circ. 5,000.

Shituf (Co-operation): POB 7151, 24 Ha'arba St, Tel-Aviv; f. 1948; bi-monthly; Hebrew; economic, social and co-operative problems in Israel; published by the Central Union of Industrial, Transport and Service Co-operative Societies; Editor L. LOSH; circ. 12,000.

Shivuk (Marketing): POB 20027, Tel-Aviv 61200; tel. 3-5631010; fax 3-5612614; monthly; Hebrew; publ. by Federation of Israeli Chambers of Commerce; Editor SARA LIPKIN.

Sinai: POB 642, Jerusalem 91006; tel. 2-6526231; fax 2-6526968; f. 1937; Hebrew; Torah science and literature; Editor Dr YITZCHAK RAPHAEL.

As-Sindibad: POB 28049, Tel-Aviv; tel. 3-371438; f. 1970; children's monthly; Arabic; Man. JOSEPH ELIAHOU; Editor WALID HUSSEIN; circ. 8,000.

Terra Santa: POB 14038, Jaffa Gate, Jerusalem 91140; tel. 2-6272692; fax 2-6286417; e-mail cicts@netmedia.net.il; f. 1921; every two months; published by the Custody of the Holy Land (the official custodians of the Holy Shrines); Italian, Spanish, French, English and Arabic editions published in Jerusalem, by the Franciscan Printing Press, German edition in Munich, Maltese edition in Valletta.

Tmuroth: POB 23076, 48 Hamelech George St, Tel-Aviv; f. 1960; monthly; Hebrew; organ of the Liberal Labour Movement; Editor S. MEIRI.

WIZO Review: Women's International Zionist Organization, 38 Sderot David Hamelech Blvd, Tel-Aviv 64237; tel. 3-6923805; fax 3-6923801; e-mail wreview@wizo.org; internet www.wizo.org; f. 1947; English edition (quarterly), Spanish and German editions (two a year); Editor HILLEL SCHENKER; circ. 20,000.

The Youth Times: POB 54065, Jerusalem; tel. 2-6273293; fax 2-6287893; e-mail youthtimes@jerusalem_times.com; f. 1998; monthly; Arabic and English; Editor-in-Chief HANIA BITAR.

Zion: POB 4179, Jerusalem 91041; tel. 2-5637171; fax 2-5662135; e-mail shazar@netvision.net.il; f. 1935; quarterly; published by the Historical Society of Israel; Hebrew, with English summaries; research in Jewish history; Editors R. I. COHEN, A. OPPENHEIMER, Y. KAPLAN; circ. 1,000.

Zraim: POB 40027, 7 Dubnov St, Tel-Aviv; tel. 3-691745; fax 3-6953199; f. 1953; Hebrew; journal of the Bnei Akiva (Youth of Tora Va-avoda) Movement; Editor URI AUERBACH.

Zrakor: Haifa; f. 1947; monthly; Hebrew; news digest, trade, finance, economics, shipping; Editor G. ALON.

PRESS ASSOCIATIONS

Daily Newspaper Publishers' Asscn of Israel: POB 51202, 74 Petach Tikva Rd, Tel-Aviv 61200; fax 3-5617938; safeguards professional interests and maintains standards, supplies newsprint to dailies; negotiates with trade unions, etc.; mems all daily papers; affiliated to International Federation of Newspaper Publishers; Pres. SHABTAI HIMMELFARB; Gen. Sec. BETZALEL EYAL.

Foreign Press Asscn: 9 Rehov Itamar Ben Avi, Tel-Aviv; tel. 3-6916143; fax 3-6961548; Chair. HOWARD GOLLER.

Israel Association of the Periodical Press (IAPP): 93 Arlozorof St, Tel-Aviv 62098; tel. 3-6921238; fax 3-6960155; e-mail lavied@ arg.huji.ac.il; Chair. DAVID LAVIE.

Israel Press Asscn: Sokolov House, 4 Kaplan St, Tel-Aviv.

NEWS AGENCIES

ITIM—The Israeli News Agency: 10 Tiomkin St, Tel-Aviv; tel. 3-5601011; fax 3-5605190; e-mail noy@itim.co.il; f. 1950; Editor-in-Chief HAIM NOY.

Jewish Telegraphic Agency (JTA): Israel Bureau, Jerusalem Post Bldg, Romema, Jerusalem 91000; tel. 2-610579; fax 2-536635; Dir DAVID LANDAU.

Palestine Press Service: Salah ad-Din St, East Jerusalem; Proprs IBRAHIM QARA'EEN, Mrs RAYMONDA TAWIL; only Arab news agency in the Occupied Territories.

Foreign Bureaux

Agence France-Presse: POB 1507, 206 Jaffa Rd, Jerusalem 91014; tel. 2-5373243; fax 2-5373873; e-mail afpjer@netvision.net.il; Correspondent LUC DE BAROCHEZ.

Agencia EFE (Spain): POB 37190, 18 Hilel St, Jerusalem 91371; tel. 2-6242038; fax 2-6242056; e-mail efeisrael@compuserv.com; Correspondent ELÍAS-SAMUEL SCHERBACOVSKY.

Agenzia Nazionale Stampa Associata (ANSA) (Italy): 30 Dizengoff St, Tel-Aviv 64332; tel. 3-6299319; fax 3-5250302; Bureau Chief SANDRO PARONE; 9 Lloyd George St, Jerusalem 93110; Correspondent GIORGIO RACCAH.

Associated Press (AP) (USA): POB 13172, 206 Jaffa Rd, Jerusalem; tel. 2-5385577; fax 2-5376083; Chief of Bureau DAN PERRY.

Deutsche Presse-Agentur (dpa) (Germany): 30 Ibn Gvirol St, Tel-Aviv 64078; tel. 3-6959007; fax 3-6969594; e-mail dpatlv@trend line.co.il; Correspondents Dr HEINZ-RUDOLF OTHMERDING, JEFF ABRAMOVITZ.

Jiji Tsushin-Sha (Japan): 9 Schmuel Hanagld, Jerusalem 94592; tel. 2-232553; fax 2-232402; Correspondent HIROKAZU OIKAWA.

Kyodo News Service (Japan): Tel-Aviv; tel. 3-6958185; fax 3-6917478; Correspondent HAJIME OZAKI.

Reuters (UK): 38 Hamasger St, Tel-Aviv 67211; tel. 3-5372211; fax 3-5372045; Jerusalem Capital Studios (JCS) 206 Jaffa Rd, Jerusalem 91131; tel. 2-5370502; fax 2-5374241; Chief of Bureau PAUL HOLMES.

United Press International (UPI) (USA): 138 Petach Tikva Rd, Tel-Aviv; Bureau Man. BROOKE W. KROEGER; Bureau Man. in Jerusalem LOUIS TOSCANO.

Informatsionnoye Telegrafnoye Agentstvo Rossii—Telegrafnoye Agentstvo Suverennykh Stran (ITAR—TASS) (Russia) is also represented.

Publishers

Achiasaf Ltd: POB 8414, Netanya 42504, tel. 9-8851390; fax 9-8851391; e-mail achiasaf@netvision.net.il; f. 1933; general; Man. Dir MATAN ACHIASAF.

Am Oved Publishers Ltd: POB 470, 22 Mazeh St, Tel-Aviv 61003; tel. 3-6291526; fax 3-6298911; e-mail info@am-oved.co.il; internet www.am-oved.co.il; f. 1942; fiction, non-fiction, reference books, school and university textbooks, children's books, poetry, classics, science fiction; Man. Dir YARON SADAN.

'Amihai' Publishing House Ltd: POB 8448, 19 Yad Harutzim St, Netanya Darom 42505; tel. 9-8859099; fax 9-8853464; e-mail oron@idc.ac.il; f. 1948; fiction, general science, linguistics, languages, arts; Dir YITZHAK ORON.

Arabic Publishing House: 93 Arlozorof St, Tel-Aviv; tel. 3-6921674; f. 1960; established by the Histadrut; periodicals and books; Gen. Man. GASSAN MUKLASHI.

Ariel Publishing House: POB 3328, 28 Nayadot St, Pisgat Ze'ev, Jerusalem 91033; tel. 2-524414; fax 2-436164; f. 1976; history, geology, religion, geography; CEO ELY SCHILLER.

Astrolog Publishing House: POB 11231, Hod Hasharon, Netanya 45111; tel. 9-7412044; fax 9-7442714; e-mail sarabm@netvision .net.il; f. 1994; general non-fiction, religion, alternative medicine; Man. Dir SARA BEN-MORDECHAI.

Bitan Publishers Ltd: POB 3068, Ramat-Hasharon 47130; tel. 3-6040089; fax 3-5404792; f. 1965; aeronautics, aviation, biography, child development, fiction, educational, literature and literary criticism, mysteries, leisure, travel, women's studies; Man. A. BITAN.

Carta, The Israel Map and Publishing Co Ltd: POB 2500, 18 Ha'uman St, Industrial Area, Talpiot, Jerusalem 91024; tel. 2-6783355; fax 2-6782373; e-mail cartaben@netvision.net.il; internet www.holyland-jerusalem.com; f. 1958; the principal cartographic publisher; Pres. and CEO SHAY HAUSMAN.

Dvir Publishing Co Ltd: POB 22383, 32 Schocken St, Tel-Aviv; tel. 3-6812244; fax 3-6826138; e-mail info@zmora.co.il; internet www.zmora.co.il; f. 1924; literature, science, art, education; Publr OHAD ZMORA.

Rodney Franklin Agency: POB 37727, 53 Mazeh St, Tel-Aviv 65789; tel. 3-5600724; fax 3-5600479; e-mail rodneyf@netvision .net.il; f. 1974; exclusive representative of various British and US publishers; Dir RODNEY FRANKLIN.

Gefen Publishing House Ltd: POB 36004, 6 Hatzvi St, Jerusalem 91360; tel. 2-5380247; fax 2-5388423; e-mail info@gefenpublishing .com; internet www.israelbooks.com; f. 1981; the largest publisher of English-language books; also publishes wide range of fiction and non-fiction. CEOs ILAN GREENFIELD, DROR GREENFIELD.

Globes Publishers: POB 18041, 127 Igal Alon St, Tel-Aviv 67443; tel. 3-6979797; fax 3-6910334; internet www.globes.co.il.

Gvanim: POB 11138, 29 Bar-Kochba St, Tel-Aviv 63427; tel. 3-5281044; fax 3-5283648; f. 1992; poetry, belles lettres, fiction; Man. Dir MARITZA ROSMAN.

Hakibbutz Hameuchad Publishing House Ltd: POB 1432, Bnei Brak, Tel-Aviv 51114; tel. 3-5785810; fax 3-5785811; f. 1940; general; Dir UZI SHAVIT.

Hanitzotz A-Sharara Publishing House: POB 41199, Jaffa 61411; tel. 3-6839145; fax 3-6839148; e-mail oda@netvision.net.il; internet www.hanitzotz.com; 'progressive' booklets and publications in Arabic, Hebrew and English; Publr SHIMON TZABAR; Editor-in-Chief RONI BEN EFRAT.

Hed Arzi (Ma'ariv) Publishing Ltd: 3A Yoni Netanyahu St, Or-Yehuda, Tel-Aviv 60376; tel. 3-5383333; fax 3-6343205; e-mail shimoni@hed-arzi.co.il; f. 1954 as Sifriat-Ma'ariv Ltd; later known as Ma'ariv Book Guild Ltd; general; Man. Dir. and Editor-in-Chief ELI SHIMONI.

Hod-Ami—Computer Books Ltd: POB 6108, Herzliya 46160; tel. 9-9564716; fax 9-9571582; e-mail info@hod-ami.co.il; internet www.hod-ami.co.il; f. 1984; computer science; CEO ITZHAK AMIHUD.

Intermedia Publishing Enterprises Ltd (IPE): POB 2121, 23 Hataas St, Kefar-Sava 44641; tel. 9-5608501; fax 9-5608513; e-mail freed@inter.net.il; f. 1993; business, education, English as a second language, journalism, health, nutrition, mathematics, medicine, philosophy, self-help; Man. Dir ARIE FRIED.

Israeli Music Publications Ltd: POB 7681, Jerusalem 94188; tel. 2-6251370; fax 2-6241378; e-mail khanukaev@pop.isracom.net.il; f. 1949; books on music, dance and musical works; Dir of Music Publications SERGEI KHANUKAEV.

Jerusalem Center for Public Affairs: 13 Tel Hai St, Jerusalem 92107; tel. 2-5619281; fax 2-5619112; e-mail jcenter@jcpa.org; internet www.jcpa.org; f. 1976; Jewish political tradition; publishes the Jewish Political Studies Review.

The Jerusalem Publishing House Ltd: POB 7147, 39 Tchernechovski St, Jerusalem 91071; tel. 2-5636511; fax 2-5634266; e-mail jphgagi@netvision.net.il; f. 1967; biblical research, history, encyclopaedias, archaeology, arts of the Holy Land, cookbooks, guidebooks, economics, politics; Dir SHLOMO S. GAFNI; Man. Editor RACHEL GILON.

The Jewish Agency—Department of Jewish Zionist Education: POB 10615, Jerusalem 91104; tel. 2-6216232; fax 2-6216230;

e-mail bookshop@jazo.org.il; f. 1945; education, Jewish philosophy, studies in the Bible, children's books published in Hebrew, English, French, Spanish, German, Swedish and Portuguese, Hebrew teaching material.

Jewish History Publications (Israel 1961) Ltd: POB 1232, 29 Jabotinsky St, Jerusalem 92141; tel. 2-5632310; f. 1961; encyclopedias, World History of the Jewish People series; Chair. ALEXANDER PELI.

Karni Publishers Ltd: 32 Zalman Schocken St, Tel-Aviv 66556; tel. 3-6812244; fax 3-6826138; e-mail info@zmora.co.il; internet www.zmora.co.il; f. 1951; biography, fiction, poetry, children's and educational books; Publr OHAD ZMORA.

Keter Publishing House Ltd: POB 7145, Givat Shaul B, Jerusalem 91071; tel. 2-6557822; fax 2-6536811; e-mail info@ keter-books.co.il; internet www.keter-books.co.il; f. 1959; original and translated works of fiction, encyclopedias, non-fiction, guidebooks and children's books; publishing imprints: Israel Program for Scientific Translations, Keter Books, Domino, Encyclopedia Judaica; Man. Dir YIPTACH DEKEL.

Kinneret Publishing House: 14 Habanai St, Holon 58850; tel. 3-5582252; fax 3-5582255; e-mail kinbooks@netvision.net.il; f. 1980; child development and care, cookery, dance, educational, humour, non-fiction, music, home-care, psychology, psychiatry, travel; Man. Dir YORAM ROS.

Kiryat Sefer: Tel-Aviv 65812; tel. 3-5660188; fax 3-5100227; f. 1933; concordances, dictionaries, textbooks, maps, scientific books; Dir AVRAHAM SIVAN.

Laser Pages Publishing Ltd: POB 35409, Merkaz Sapir 6/36, Givat Shaul, Jerusalem 91352; tel. 2-6522226; fax 2-6522277; e-mail info@laserpages.net; internet www.laserpages.net; scientific journals.

LB Publishing Co: POB 32056, Jerusalem 91000; tel. and fax 2-5664637; f. 1993; history, regional issues, religion; Pres. LILI BREZINER.

Magnes Press: The Hebrew University, POB 39099, Jerusalem 91390; tel. 2-6586656; fax 2-5633370; e-mail magnes@vms.huji.ac.il; f. 1929; biblical studies, Judaica, and all academic fields; Dir DAN BENOVICI.

MAP-Mapping and Publishing Ltd (Tel Aviv Books): POB 56024, 18 Tchernikhovski St, Tel-Aviv 61560; tel. 3-6203252; fax 3-5257725; e-mail info@mapa.co.il; f. 1985; maps, atlases, travel guides, textbooks and reference books; Man. Dir DANI TRACZ; Editor-in-Chief MOULI MELTZER.

Rubin Mass Ltd: POB 990, 7 Ha-Ayin-Het St, Jerusalem 91009; tel. 2-6277863; fax 2-6277864; e-mail rmass@inter.net.il; internet www.age.co.il/mas/index/htm; f. 1927; Hebraica, Judaica, export of all Israeli books and periodicals; Dir OREN MASS.

Ministry of Defence Publishing House: 107 Ha' Hashmonaim St, Tel-Aviv 67133; tel. 3-5655900; fax 3-5655994; e-mail publish@ attmail.com; internet www.modpublishing.co.il; f. 1939; military literature, Judaism, history and geography of Israel; Dir JOSEPH PERLOVITZ.

M. Mizrachi Publishing House Ltd: 106 Allenby St, Tel-Aviv 65815; tel. 3-5601579; fax 3-5660274; f. 1960; children's books, fiction, history, medicine, science; Dirs MEIR MIZRACHI, ISRAEL MIZRACHI.

Mosad Harav Kook: POB 642, 1 Maimon St, Jerusalem 91006; tel. 2-6526231; fax 2-6526968; f. 1937; editions of classical works, Torah and Jewish studies; Dir Rabbi M. KATZENELENBOGEN.

Otsar Hamoreh: c/o Israel Teachers' Union, 8 Ben Saruk, Tel-Aviv 62969; tel. 3-6922983; fax 3-6922988; f. 1951; educational; Man. Dir JOSEPH SALOMAN.

PC Media: POB 11438, 13 Yad Harutzim St, Tel-Aviv 61114; tel. 3-6385810; fax 3-6889207; e-mail pcmedia@pc.co.il; internet www.zdnet.co.il; information technology; Man. Dir DAHLIA PELLED.

Alexander Peli Jerusalem Publishing Co Ltd: POB 1232, 29 Jabotinsky St, Jerusalem 92141; tel. 2-5632310; f. 1961; encyclopedias, Judaica, history, the arts, educational material; Chair. ALEXANDER PELI.

Schocken Publishing House Ltd: POB 2316, 24 Nathan Yelin Mor St, Tel-Aviv 67015; tel. 3-5610130; fax 3-5622668; internet www.schocken.co.il; f. 1938; general; Dir Mrs RACHELI EDELMAN.

Shalem Press: 22A Hatzfira St, Jerusalem 93102; tel. 2-5662202; e-mail shalem@shalem.org.il; internet www.shalem.org.il; f. 1994; economics, political science, history, philosophy, cultural issues.

Shikmona Publishing Co Ltd: POB 7145, Givat Shaul B, Jerusalem 91071; tel. 2-6557822; fax 2-6536811; e-mail info@keter-books .co.il; internet www.keter-books.co.il; f. 1965; Zionism, archaeology, art, guidebooks, fiction and non-fiction; Man. Dir YIPTACH DEKEL.

Sifriat Poalim: POB 37068, Gate 3, 24 Kibbutz Galuiot St, Tel-Aviv 61369; tel. 3-5183143; fax 3-5183191; e-mail akantor@inter.net.il; internet www.dbook.co.il/images/poalim/default.html; f. 1939; general literature; Gen. Man. AVRAM KANTOR.

Sinai Publishing: 72 Allenby St, Tel-Aviv 65812; tel. 3-5163672; fax 3-5176783; f. 1853; Hebrew books and religious articles; Dir MOSHE SCHLESINGER.

Steinhart-Katzir: POB 8333, Netanya 42505; tel. 9-8854770; fax 9-8854771; e-mail skp@netvision.net.il; f. 1991; travel; Man. Dir OHAD SHARAV.

Tcehrikover Publishers Ltd: 12 Hasharon St, Tel-Aviv 66185; tel. 3-6870621; fax 3-6874729; e-mail barkay@inter.net.il; education, psychology, economics, psychiatry, literature, literary criticism, essays, history geography, criminology, art, languages, management; Man. Editor S. TCHERIKOVER.

Yachdav United Publishers Co Ltd: POB 20123, 29 Carlebach St, Tel-Aviv 67132; tel. 3-5614121; fax 3-5611996; e-mail tbpai@netvision.net.il; f. 1960; educational; Chair. EPHRAIM BEN-DOR; Exec. Dir AMNON BEN-SHMUEL.

Yavneh Publishing House Ltd: 4 Mazeh St, Tel-Aviv 65213; tel. 3-6297856; fax 3-6293638; e-mail yavneh@ibm.net; f. 1932; general; Dir NIRA PREISKEL.

Yeda Lakol Publications Ltd: POB 1232, 29 Jabotinsky St, Jerusalem 92141; tel. 2-5632310; f. 1961; encyclopaedias, Judaica, the arts, educational material, children's books; Chair. ALEXANDER PELI.

Yedioth Ahronoth Books: POB 37744, 3 Mikunis St, Tel-Aviv 61376; tel. 3-6888466; fax 3-5377820; e-mail books@yedioth.co.il; f. 1952; non-fiction, politics, Jewish religion, health, music, dance, fiction, education; Man. Dir DOV EICHENWALD; Editor-in-Chief ALIZA ZIGLER.

S. Zack and Co: 2 King George St, Jerusalem 94229; tel. 2-6257819; fax 2-6252493; e-mail zackpublishers@bezeqint.net; f. c. 1930; fiction, science, philosophy, Judaism, children's books, educational and reference books, dictionaries; Dir MICHAEL ZACK.

PUBLISHERS' ASSOCIATION

The Book Publishers' Association of Israel: POB 20123, 29 Carlebach St, Tel-Aviv 67132; tel. 3-5614121; fax 3-5611996; e-mail info@tbpai.co.il; internet www.tbpai.co.il; f. 1939; mems: 84 publishing firms; Chair. SHAI HAUSMAN; Man. Dir AMNON BEN-SHMUEL.

Broadcasting and Communications

TELECOMMUNICATIONS

Barak I.T.C.: Cibel Industrial Park, 15 Hamelacha St, Rosh Ha'ayin 48091; tel 3-9001900; fax 3-9001800; internet www.barak-online.net; f. 1998; Chair. MAIR LAISER; Pres. and CEO AVI PATIR.

Bezeq Israel Telecom: POB 1088, 15 Hazvi St, Jerusalem 91010; tel. 2-5395503; fax 2-5000410; e-mail bzq.spk@attmail.com; internet www.bezeq.co.il; 54.6% state-owned; scheduled for full privatization in 2001; launched own cellular network, Pelephone Communications Ltd, in 1986; total assets US $4,837m. (Dec. 1997); Chair ISRAEL TAPOOHI; Pres. and CEO AMI EREL.

> **Pelephone Communications Ltd:** 33 Hagvura St, Givatayim, Tel-Aviv 53483; tel. 3-5728881; fax 3-5728111; internet www.pelephone.co.il; Pres. and CEO YIGAL BAR-YOUSSEF.

Cellcom Israel: POB 3164, 3 Hagalim Blvd, Herzlia Pituach, Herzlia B, Netanya 46131; tel. 9-9599599; fax 9-9599700; internet www.cellcom.co.il; f. 1994; mobile telecommunications operator; Chair. S. PIOTRKOWSKY; Pres. and CEO JACOB PERRY.

ECI Telecom Ltd: POB 3038, 30 Hasivim St, Petach Tikva, Tel-Aviv 49133; tel. 3-9266555; fax 3-9266500; internet www.ecitele .com; Chair. JONATHON B. KOLBER; Pres. and Gen. Man. DAVID RUBNER.

Partner Communications Co: POB 435, Rosh Ha'ayin, Tel-Aviv 48103; tel. 3-9054888; fax 3-9054999; mobile telecommunications operator; f. 1998 when obtained licence to operate Israel's first GSM system; CEO AMIKAM COHEN; Man. Dir E. COHEN.

Vocal Tec: Tel-Aviv; Gen. Man. DORON SINGER.

BROADCASTING

Radio

Israel Broadcasting Authority (IBA) (Radio): POB 28080, Jerusalem 91280; tel. 2-240124; fax 2-257034; internet www.iba.org.il; f. 1948; state-owned station in Jerusalem with additional studios in Tel-Aviv and Haifa. IBA broadcasts six programmes for local and overseas listeners on medium, shortwave and VHF/FM in 16 languages; Hebrew, Arabic, English, Yiddish, Ladino, Romanian, Hungarian, Moghrabi, Persian, French, Russian, Bucharian, Georgian, Portuguese, Spanish and Amharic; Chair. MICHA YINON; Dir-Gen. URI PORAT; Dir of Radio (vacant); Dir External Services VICTOR GRAJEWSKY.

Galei Zahal: MPOB 01005, Zahal; tel. 3-5126666; fax 3-5126760; e-mail galatz@glz.co.il; internet www.glz.co.il; f. 1950; Israeli Defence Force broadcasting station, Tel-Aviv, with studios in Jerusalem;

broadcasts news, current affairs, music and cultural programmes on medium-wave and FM stereo, 24-hour in Hebrew; Dir ISACK TUNIK.

Kol Israel (The Voice of Israel): POB 1082, 21 Heleni Hamalka, Jerusalem 91010; tel. 2-6248715; fax 2-5383173; internet www .artificia.com/html/news.cgi; broadcasts music, news, and multilingual programmes for immigrants in Hebrew, Arabic, French and English on medium wave and FM stereo; Dir and Prog. Dir AMNON NADAV.

Television

Israel Broadcasting Authority (IBA): POB 7139, Jerusalem 91071; tel. 2-5301333; fax 2-292944; internet www.iba.org.il; broadcasts began in 1968; station in Jerusalem with additional studios in Tel-Aviv; one colour network (VHF with UHF available in all areas); one satellite channel; broadcasts in Hebrew, Arabic and English; Dir-Gen URI PORAT; Dir of Television YAIR STERN; Dir of Engineering RAFI YEOSHUA.

The Council of Cable TV and Satellite Broadcasting: 23 Jaffa Rd, Jerusalem 91999; tel. 2-6702210; fax 2-6702273; e-mail inbard @moc.gov.il; Chair. DORIT INBAR.

Israel Educational Television: Ministry of Education, 14 Klausner St, Tel-Aviv; tel. 3-6415270; fax 3-6427091; f. 1966 by Hanadiv (Rothschild Memorial Group) as Instructional Television Trust; began transmission in 1966; school programmes form an integral part of the syllabus in a wide range of subjects; also adult education; Gen. Man. AHUVA FAINMESSE; Dir of Engineering S. KASIF.

Second Channel TV and Radio Administration: 3 Kanfi Nesharim St, POB 34112, Jerusalem 95464; tel. 2-6556222; fax 2-6556287; e-mail channel2@netvision.net.il. f. 1991. Chair. Prof. GIDEON DORON; Man. Dir NACHMAN SHAI.

In 1986 the Government approved the establishment of a commercial radio and television network to be run in competition with the state system.

Finance

(cap. = capital; p.u. = paid up; dep. = deposits; m. = million; res = reserves; brs = branches; amounts in shekels)

BANKING

During 1991–98 the Government raised some US $3,995m. through privatization and the issuance of shares and convertible securities in the banking sector.

Central Bank

Bank of Israel: POB 780, Bank of Israel Bldg, Kiryat Ben-Gurion, Jerusalem 91007; tel. 2-6552211; fax 2-6528805; e-mail webmaster@bankisrael.gov.il; internet www.bankisrael.gov.il; f. 1954 as the Central Bank of the State of Israel; cap. 60m., res –7,850m., dep. 92,703m. (Dec. 1999); Gov. DAVID KLEIN; 2 brs.

Principal Israeli Banks

Arab-Israel Bank Ltd: POB 27, Nesher 20300; tel. (4) 8308222; fax (4) 8308250; total assets 3,198.4m., dep. 2,873.4m. (Dec. 1999); subsidiary of Bank Leumi le-Israel BM; Chair. D. EFRIMA; Gen. Man. Y. AZRAD.

Bank Hapoalim: POB 27, 50 Rothschild Blvd, Tel-Aviv 66883; tel. 3-5673333; fax 3-5607028; e-mail international@bnhp.co.il; internet www.bankhapoalim.co.il; f. 1921 as the Workers' Bank, name changed as above 1961; American-Israel Bank merged into the above 1999; privatized in June 2000; total assets 206,082m., dep. 175,456m. (Dec. 1999); Chair. SHLOMO NEHAMA; 338 brs in Israel and abroad.

Bank of Jerusalem Ltd: POB 2255, 2 Herbert Samuel St; tel. (2) 6706211; fax (2) 6246793; e-mail bankjer@netvision.net.il; private bank; total assets 4,578.1m., dep. 3,999.7m. (Dec. 1998); Chair. DAVID BLUMBERG; Man. Dir and Gen. Man. DAVID BARUCH.

Bank Leumi le-Israel BM: POB 2, 24–32 Yehuda Halevi St, Tel-Aviv 65546; tel. 3-5148111; fax 3-5661872; internet www.bankleumi .com; f. 1902 as Anglo-Palestine Co; renamed Anglo-Palestine Bank 1930; reincorporated as above 1951; 41.73% state-owned; total assets 199,350m., dep. 175,381m. (Dec. 1999); Chair. EITAN RAFF; Pres., CEO and Gen. Man. GALIA MAOR; 229 brs.

Euro-Trade Bank Ltd: POB 37318, 2 Yavne St, Tel-Aviv 61372; tel. 3-6216868; fax 3-6209062; e-mail eurotra@ibm.net; f. 1953; renamed Israel Building Bank Ltd 1978; name changed as above 1993; total assets 231,747m., dep. 177,889m. (Dec. 1998); Chair. Prof. BEN-ZION ZILBERFARB; Man. Dir JOSEPH PINCHASOF.

First International Bank of Israel Ltd: POB 29036, Shalom Mayer Tower, 9 Ahad Ha'am St, Tel-Aviv 62251; tel. 3-5196111; fax 3-5100316; e-mail yuvall@fibi.co.il; internet www.fibi.co.il; f. 1972 as a result of a merger between Foreign Trade Bank Ltd and Export Bank Ltd; total assets 48,912m., cap. 2,577m., dep. 40,698m. (Sept.

1999); Chair. YIGAL ARNON; Man. Dir and CEO SHLOMO PIOTRKOWSKY; 90 brs.

Industrial Development Bank of Israel Ltd: POB 33580, Asia House, 4 Weizman, Tel-Aviv 61334; tel. 3-6972727; fax 3-6972893; internet www.idbi.co.il; f. 1957; 61% state-owned; total assets 12,174.0m., dep. 11,805.3m. (Dec. 1999); Chair. SHLOMO BOROCHEV; Gen. Man. YEHOSHUA ICHILOV.

Investec Clali Bank Ltd: POB 677, 38 Rothschild Blvd, Tel-Aviv 61006; tel. 3-5645645; fax 3-5645210; e-mail irroni@igb.co.il; internet www.investec.co.il; f. 1934 as Palestine Credit Utility Bank Ltd, renamed Israel General Bank Ltd 1964; ownership transferred to Investec Bank Ltd (South Africa) in 1996; name changed as above 1999; total assets 5,856.7m., dep. 5,278.8m. (Dec. 1999); Chair. HUGH SYDNEY HERMAN; Man. Dir and CEO JONATHON IRRONI; 3 brs.

Israel Continental Bank Ltd: POB 37406, 65 Rothschild Blvd, Tel-Aviv 61373; tel. 3-5641616; fax 3-6200399; f. 1974; capital held jointly by Bank Hapoalim BM (63.3%) and Bank für Gemeinwirtschaft AG (36.7%); total assets 1,480.1m., dep. 1,174.5m. (Dec. 1999); Chair. AMIRAM SIVAN; Man. Dir P. HOREV; 3 brs.

Israel Discount Bank Ltd: 27 Yehuda Halevi St, Tel-Aviv 65136; tel. 3-5145555; fax 3-5145346; e-mail contact@discountbank.net; internet www.discountbank.net; f. 1935; 59.65% state-owned; cap p.u. 93m., dep. 105,729m. (Sept. 2000); Chair. ARIE MIENTKAVICH; some 160 brs in Israel and abroad.

Leumi Industrial Development Bank Ltd: POB 2, 13 Ahad Haam St, Tel-Aviv 61000; tel. 3-5149945; fax 3-5149897; f. 1944; subsidiary of Bank Leumi le-Israel BM; cap. and res 96.7m. (Dec. 2000); Chair. B. NAVEH; Gen. Man. M. ZIV.

Maritime Bank of Israel Ltd: POB 29373, 35 Ahad Ha'am St, Tel-Aviv 61293; tel. 3-5642222; fax 3-5642323; f. 1962; total assets 896.1m., cap. 6.0m., res 187.8m., dep. 822.5m. (Dec. 1999); Chair. SHIMON TOPOR; CEO and Gen. Man. DAVID LEVINSON.

Mercantile Discount Bank Ltd: POB 1292, 103 Allenby Rd, Tel-Aviv 61012; tel. 3-5647333; fax 3-5195833; e-mail mercant@netvision.net.il; internet www.mercantile.co.il; f. as Barclays Discount Bank Ltd in 1971 by Barclays Bank International Ltd and Israel Discount Bank Ltd to incorporate Israel brs of Barclays; Israel Discount Bank Ltd became the sole owner in February 1993; name changed as above April 1993; absorbed Mercantile Bank of Israel Ltd in 1997; total assets 10,864m., cap. 47.2m., res 25.6m., dep. 10,003.8m. (Dec. 1998); Chair. of Bd ARIE MIENTKAVICH; Gen. Man. Prof. SHALOM JOSEF HOCHMAN; 71 brs.

Union Bank of Israel Ltd: POB 2428, 6–8 Ahuzat Bayit St, Tel-Aviv 65143; tel. 3-5191111; fax 3-5191274; internet www.unionbank.co.il; f. 1951; 18.4% state-owned; total assets 15,994m., dep. 14,342m. (Dec. 1999); Chair. Z. ABELES; CEO and Gen. Man. B. OSHMAN; 28 brs.

United Mizrahi Bank Ltd: POB 309, 13 Rothschild Blvd, Tel-Aviv 61002; tel. 3-5679211; fax 3-5604780; e-mail info@mizrahi.co.il; internet www.mizrahi.co.il; f. 1923 as Mizrahi Bank Ltd; 1969 absorbed Hapoel Hamizrahi Bank Ltd and name changed as above; absorbed Finance and Trade Bank Ltd in 1990; 1.23% state-owned; total assets 61,738m., dep. 56,214m. (Dec. 1999); Pres. and CEO VICTOR MEDINA; 101 brs.

Mortgage Banks

Discount Mortgage Bank Ltd: POB 2844, 16–18 Simtat Beit Hashoeva, Tel-Aviv 61027; tel. 3-5643311; fax 3-5661704; f. 1959; subsidiary of Israel Discount Bank Ltd; cap. p.u. 1.3m., res 463.6m. (Dec. 1997); Chair. ARIE MIENTKAVICH; Man. M. ELDAR.

First International Mortgage Bank Ltd.: 39 Montefiore St, Tel-Aviv 65201; tel. 3-5643311; fax 3-5643321; f. 1922 as the Mortgage and Savings Bank, name changed as above 1996; subsidiary of First International Bank of Israel Ltd; cap. and res 334m. (Dec. 1996); Chair. SHLOMO PIOTRKOWSKY; Man. Dir P. HAMO; 50 brs.

Leumi Mortgage Bank Ltd: POB 69, 31–37 Montefiore St, Tel-Aviv 65201; tel. 3-5648448; fax 3-5648334; f. 1921 as General Mortgage Bank Ltd; subsidiary of Bank Leumi le-Israel BM; total assets 23,859.9m., dep. 21,391.4m. (Dec. 1999); Chair. A. ZELDMAN; Gen. Man. R. ZABAG; 6 brs.

Mishkan-Hapoalim Mortgage Bank Ltd: POB 1610, 2 Ibn Gvirol St, Tel-Aviv 61015; tel. 3-6970505; fax 3-6961379; f. 1950; subsidiary of Bank Hapoalim BM; total assets 8,289m., dep. 10,268.3m. (Dec. 1993); Chair. M. OLENIK; Man. Dir A. KROIZER; 131 brs.

Tefahot, Israel Mortgage Bank Ltd: POB 93, 9 Heleni Hamalka St, Jerusalem 91902; tel. 2-6755222; fax 2-6755344; f. 1945; subsidiary of United Mizrahi Bank Ltd; cap. and res 1,181m., total assets 18,973m. (Dec. 1994); Chair. DAVID BRODET; Man. Dir URI WÜRZBURGER; 60 brs.

STOCK EXCHANGE

The Tel-Aviv Stock Exchange: 54 Ahad Ha'am St, Tel-Aviv 65202; tel. 3-5677411; fax 3-5105379; e-mail spokesperson@tase .co.il; internet www.tase.co.il; f. 1953; Chair. Prof. YAIR E. ORGLER; Gen. Man. SAUL BRONFELD.

INSURANCE

The Israel Insurance Asscn lists 35 companies, a selection of which are listed below; not all companies are members of the association.

Ararat Insurance Co Ltd: Ararat House, 13 Montefiore St, Tel-Aviv 65164; tel. 3-640888; f. 1949; Co-Chair. AHARON DOVRAT, PHILIP ZUCKERMAN; Gen. Man. PINCHAS COHEN.

Aryeh Insurance Co of Israel Ltd: 9 Ahad Ha'am St, Tel-Aviv 65251; tel. 3-5141777; fax 3-5179337; e-mail aryeh@isdn.net.il; f. 1948; Chair. AVIGDOR KAPLAN.

Clal Insurance Co Ltd: POB 326, 42 Rothschild Blvd, Tel-Aviv 61002; tel. 3-627711; fax 3-622666; f. 1962; Pres. and CEO AVIGDOR KAPLAN; Man. Dir RIMON BEN-SHAOUL.

Hassneh Insurance Co of Israel Ltd: POB 805, 115 Allenby St, Tel-Aviv 61007; tel. 3-5649111; f. 1924; Man. Dir M. MICHAEL MILLER.

Israel Phoenix Assurance Co Ltd: 30 Levontin St, Tel-Aviv 65116; tel. 3-7141111; fax 3-5601242; e-mail yoni@phoenix.co.il; internet www.phoenix.co.il; f. 1949; Chair. of Bd JOSEPH D. HACKMEY; Man. Dir Dr ITAMAR BOROWITZ.

Maoz Insurance Co Ltd: Tel-Aviv; f. 1945; formerly Binyan Insurance Co Ltd; Chair. B. YEKUTIELI.

Menorah Insurance Co Ltd: Menorah House, 73 Rothschild Blvd, Tel-Aviv 65786; tel. 3-5260771; fax 3-5618288; f. 1935; Gen. Man. SHABTAI ENGEL.

Migdal Insurance Co Ltd: POB 37633, 26 Sa'adiya Ga'on St, Tel-Aviv 61375; tel. 3-5637637; part of Bank Leumi Group; f. 1934; Chair. S. GROFMAN; CEO U. LEVY.

Palglass Palestine Plate Glass Insurance Co Ltd: Tel-Aviv 65541; f. 1934; Gen. Man. AKIVA ZALZMAN.

Sahar Israel Insurance Co Ltd: POB 26222, Sahar House, 23 Ben-Yehuda St, Tel-Aviv 63806; tel. 3-5140311; f. 1949; Chair. G. HAMBURGER.

Samson Insurance Co Ltd: POB 33678, Avgad Bldg, 5 Jabotinsky St, Ramat-Gan, Tel-Aviv 52520; tel. 3-7521616; fax 3-7516644; f. 1933; Chair. E. BEN-AMRAM; Gen. Man. GIORA SAGI.

Sela Insurance Co Ltd: Tel-Aviv; tel. 3-61028; f. 1938; Man. Dir E. SHANI.

Shiloah Insurance Co Ltd: 3 Abba-Hillel St, Ramat-Gan, Tel-Aviv 52118; f. 1933; Gen. Man. Dr S. BAMIRAH; Man. Mme BAMIRAH.

Zion Insurance Co Ltd: POB 1425, 41–45 Rothschild Blvd, Tel-Aviv 61013; f. 1935; Gen. Man. MOTI ROSEN.

Trade and Industry

CHAMBERS OF COMMERCE

Federation of Bi-National Chambers of Commerce and Industry with and in Israel: POB 50196, 29 Hamered St, Tel-Aviv 61500; tel. 3-5173261; fax 3-5173283; federates: Israel-British Chamber of Commerce; Australia-Israel Chamber of Commerce; Chamber of Commerce and Industry Israel-Asia; Chamber of Commerce Israel-Belgique-Luxembourg; Canada-Israel Chamber of Commerce and Industry; Israel-Denmark Chamber of Commerce; Chambre de Commerce Israel-France; Chamber of Commerce and Industry Israel-Germany; Camera di Commercio Israeli-Italia; Israel-Japan Chamber of Commerce; Israel-Latin America, Spain and Portugal Chamber of Commerce; Netherlands-Israel Chamber of Commerce; Israel-Greece Chamber of Commerce; Israel-Bulgaria Chamber of Commerce; Israel-Ireland Chamber of Commerce; Handelskammer Israel-Schweiz; Israel-South Africa Chamber of Commerce; Israel-Sweden Chamber of Commerce; Israel-Hungary Chamber of Commerce; Israel-Romania Chamber of Commerce; Israel-Russia Chamber of Commerce; Israel-Poland Chamber of Commerce; Israel-Austria Chamber of Commerce; Israel-Ukraine Chamber of Commerce; Israel-Africa Chamber of Commerce; Israel-Jordan Chamber of Commerce; Israel-Egypt Chamber of Commerce; Israel-Morocco Chamber of Commerce; Israel-Moldova Chamber of Commerce; Israel-Norway Chamber of Commerce; Israel-Slovakia Chamber of Commerce; Israel-Portugal Chamber of Commerce; Israel-Finland Chamber of Commerce; Israel-Kazakhstan Chamber of Commerce; Israel-Turkey Chamber of Commerce; Israel-Thailand Chamber of Commerce; Chair. G. PROPPER.

Federation of Israeli Chambers of Commerce: POB 20027, 84 Ha 'Hashmonaim St, Tel-Aviv 67011; tel. 3-5631010; fax 3-5619025; e-mail chamber@tlv-chamber.org.il; internet www.tlv-chamber .org.il; co-ordinates the Tel-Aviv, Jerusalem, Haifa and Beersheba Chambers of Commerce; Pres. DAN GILLERMAN.

Haifa Chamber of Commerce and Industry (Haifa and District): POB 33176, 53 Haatzmaut Rd, Haifa 31331; tel. 4-8626364; fax 4-8645428; e-mail main@haifachamber.org.il; internet www.haifa

chamber.com; f. 1921; 700 mems; Pres. E. MELAMUD; S. GANTZ; Man. Dir D. MAROM.

Israel-British Chamber of Commerce: POB 50321, 29 Hamered St, Tel-Aviv 61502; tel. 3-5109424; fax 3-5109540; e-mail isrbrit@netvision.net.il; f. 1951; 350 mems; Chair. AMNON DOTAN; Exec. Dir FELIX KIPPER.

Jerusalem Chamber of Commerce: POB 2083, 10 Hillel St, Jerusalem 91020; tel. 2-6254333; fax 2-6254335; e-mail jerccom@inter.net.il; internet www.jerccom.co.il; f. 1908; c. 300 mems; Pres. JOSEPH PERLMAN.

Tel-Aviv-Jaffa Chamber of Commerce: POB 20027, 84 Ha 'Hashmonaim St, Tel-Aviv 61200; tel. 3-5631010; fax 3-5619025; f. 1919; 1,800 mems; Pres. DAN GILLERMAN.

INDUSTRIAL AND TRADE ASSOCIATIONS

Agricultural Export Co (AGREXCO): Tel-Aviv; state-owned agricultural marketing organization; Dir-Gen. AMOTZ AMIAD.

The Agricultural Union: Tel-Aviv; consists of more than 50 agricultural settlements and is connected with marketing and supplying organizations, and Bahan Ltd, controllers and auditors.

The Centre for International Agricultural Development Cooperation (CINADCO): Ministry of Agriculture and Rural Development, Agricultural Complex Rishon-Lezion, POB 30, Beit Dagan, Tel-Aviv 50200; tel. 3-9485760; fax 3-9485761; e-mail cinadco@moag.gov.il; Dir ZVI HERMAN.

Citrus Marketing Board: POB 80, Beit Dagan 50250; tel. 3-9683811; fax 3-9683838; e-mail cmbi@netvision.net.il; f. 1942; the central co-ordinating body of citrus growers and exporters in Israel; represents the citrus industry in international organizations; licenses private exporters; controls the quality of fruit; has responsibility for Jaffa trademarks; mounts advertising and promotion campaigns for Jaffa citrus fruit worldwide; carries out research and development of new varieties of citrus fruit, and 'environmentally friendly' fruit; Chair. D. KRITCHMAN; Gen. Man. M. DAVIDSON.

Farmers' Union of Israel: POB 209, 8 Kaplan St, Tel-Aviv; tel. 3-69502227; fax 3-6918228; f. 1913; membership of 7,000 independent farmers, citrus and winegrape growers; Pres. PESACH GRUPPER; Dir-Gen. SHLOMO REISMAN.

Flower Board of Israel: Tel-Aviv; e-mail help@fbi.org.il; internet www.fbi.org.il.

Fruit Board of Israel: POB 20117, 119 Rehov Ha 'Hashmonaim, Tel-Aviv 61200; tel. 3-5632929; fax 3-5614672; e-mail fruits@fruit.org.il; internet www.fruit.org.il; Dir-Gen. DANY BRUNER.

General Asscn of Merchants in Israel: Tel-Aviv; the organization of retail traders; has a membership of 30,000 in 60 brs.

Israel Cotton Production and Marketing Board Ltd: POB 384, Herzlia B'46103; tel. 9-9509491; fax 9-9509159.

Israel Diamond Exchange Ltd: POB 3222, Ramat-Gan, Tel-Aviv; tel. 3-5760211; fax 3-5750652; e-mail judi@isde.co.il; f. 1937; production, export, import and finance facilities; net exports (2000) US \$5,322m.; Pres. SHMUEL SCHNITZER.

Israel Export Institute: POB 50084, 29 Hamered St, Tel-Aviv 68125; tel. 3-5142830; fax 3-5142902; e-mail library@export.gov.il; internet www.export.gov.il; Dir-Gen. AMIR HAYEK.

Israel Journalists' Asscn: 4 Kaplan St, Tel-Aviv 64734; tel. 3-6956141; Man. Dir TUVIA SAAR.

Kibbutz Industries' Asscn: 8 Rehov Shaul Hamelech, Tel-Aviv 64733; tel. 3-6955413; fax 3-6951464; e-mail kiakia@netvision.co.il; liaison office for marketing and export of the goods produced by Israel's kibbutzim; Pres. GIORA MASAD.

Manufacturers' Asscn of Israel: POB 50022, Industry House, 29 Hamered St, Tel-Aviv 61500; tel. 3-5198787; fax 3-5162026; e-mail gendiv@industry.org.il; internet www.industry.org.il; 1,700 mem.-enterprises employing nearly 85% of industrial workers in Israel; Pres. ODED TYRAH.

National Federation of Israeli Journalists: POB 7009, 4 Kaplan St, Tel-Aviv 64734; tel. 3-6956141; fax 3-6951438.

UTILITIES

The Israel Electric Corporation Ltd and the **Mekorot (Israel National Water Co)** are two of Israel's largest state-owned companies, with total assets valued at US \$10,832m. and US \$1,978m., respectively, at the end of 1997.

Israel Electric Corporation Ltd (IEC): POB 8810, 2 Ha 'Haganah St, Haifa 31086; tel. 4-8548148; fax 4-8538149; internet www.israel-electric.co.il; Chair. GAD YA'ACOBI.

Mekorot (Israel National Water Co): 9 Lincoln St Development, Tel-Aviv 61201; tel. 3-6230806; fax 3-6230598; e-mail akanarek@mekorot.co.il; internet www.mekorot.co.il.

The Histadrut

Histadrut (General Federation of Labour in Israel): 93 Arlozorof St, Tel-Aviv 62098; tel. 3-6921513; fax 3-6921512; e-mail histint@netvision.net.il; f. 1920.

The General Federation of Labour in Israel, the Histadrut, is the largest labour organization in Israel. It strives to ensure the social security, welfare and rights of workers, and to assist in their professional advancement, while endeavouring to reduce the divisions in Israeli society. Membership of the Histadrut is voluntary, and open to all men and women of 18 years of age and above who live on the earnings of their own labour without exploiting the work of others. These include the self-employed and professionals, as well as housewives, students, pensioners and the unemployed. Workers' interests are protected through a number of occupational and professional unions affiliated to the Histadrut (see below). The organization operates courses for trade unionists and new immigrants, as well as apprenticeship classes. It maintains an Institute for Social and Economic Issues and the International Institute, one of the largest centres of leadership training in Israel, for students from Africa, Asia, Latin America and Eastern Europe, which includes the Levinson Centre for Adult Education and the Jewish-Arab Institute for Regional Co-operation. Attached to the Histadrut is Na'amat, a women's organization which promotes changes in legislation, operates a network of legal service bureaux and vocational training courses, and runs counselling centres for the treatment and prevention of domestic violence.

Chair: AMIR PERETZ.

Secretary-General: HAIM RAMON.

ORGANIZATION

In 1989 the Histadrut had a membership of 1,630,000. In addition some 110,000 young people under 18 years of age belong to the Organization of Working and Student Youth, a direct affiliate of the Histadrut.

All members take part in elections to the Histadrut Convention (Veida), which elects the General Council (Moetsa) and the Executive Committee (Vaad Hapoel). The latter elects the 41-member Executive Bureau (Vaada Merakezet), which is responsible for day-to-day implementation of policy. The Executive Committee also elects the Secretary-General, who acts as its chairman as well as head of the organization as a whole and chairman of the Executive Bureau. Nearly all political parties are represented on the Histadrut Executive Committee.

The Executive Committee has the following departments: Trade Union, Organization and Labour Councils, Education and Culture, Social Security, Industrial Democracy, Students, Youth and Sports, Consumer Protection, Administration, Finance and International.

TRADE UNION ACTIVITIES

Collective agreements with employers fix wage scales, which are linked with the retail price index; provide for social benefits, including paid sick leave and employers' contributions to sick and pension and provident funds; and regulate dismissals. Dismissal compensation is regulated by law. The Histadrut actively promotes productivity through labour management boards and the National Productivity Institute, and supports incentive pay schemes.

There are unions for the following groups: clerical workers, building workers, teachers, engineers, agricultural workers, technicians, textile workers, printing workers, diamond workers, metal workers, food and bakery workers, wood workers, government employees, seamen, nurses, civilian employees of the armed forces, actors, musicians and variety artists, social workers, watchmen, cinema technicians, institutional and school staffs, pharmacy employees, medical laboratory workers, X-ray technicians, physiotherapists, social scientists, microbiologists, psychologists, salaried lawyers, pharmacists, physicians, occupational therapists, truck and taxi drivers, hotel and restaurant workers, workers in Histadrut-owned industry, garment, shoe and leather workers, plastic and rubber workers, editors of periodicals, painters and sculptors and industrial workers.

Histadrut Trade Union Department: Dir SHLOMO SHANI.

ECONOMIC ACTIVITIES AND SOCIAL SERVICES

These include Hevrat Haovdim (employing 260,000 workers in 1983), Kupat Holim (the Sick Fund, covering almost 77% of Israel's population), seven pension funds, and Na'amat (see above).

Other Trade Unions

General Federation of West Bank Trade Unions: Sec.-Gen. SHAHER SAAD.

Histadrut Haovdim Haleumit (National Labour Federation): 23 Sprintzak St, Tel-Aviv 64738; tel. 3-6958351; fax 3-6961753; f. 1934; 170,000 mems; Chair. HIRSHZON ABRAHAM.

Histadrut Hapoel Hamizrahi (National Religious Workers' Party): 166 Ibn Gvirol St, Tel-Aviv 62023; tel. 3-5442151; fax 3-5468942; 150,000 mems in 85 settlements and 15 kibbutzim; Sec.-Gen. ELIEZER ABTABI.

Histadrut Poale Agudat Israel (Agudat Israel Workers' Organization): POB 11044, 64 Frishman St, Tel-Aviv; tel. 3-5242126; fax 3-5230689; has 33,000 members in 16 settlements and 8 educational insts.

Transport

RAILWAYS

Freight traffic consists mainly of grain, phosphates, potash, containers, petroleum and building materials. Rail service serves Haifa and Ashdod ports on the Mediterranean Sea, while a combined rail-road service extends to Eilat port on the Red Sea. Passenger services operate between the main towns: Nahariya, Haifa, Tel-Aviv and Jerusalem. In 1988 the National Ports Authority assumed responsibility for the rail system, although Israel Railways was expected to become a separate state concern in 1999. Bids to construct the first line of a US $1,400m. light railway network in Jerusalem (to be launched in 2004) were expected in 2000.

Israel Railways: POB 18085, Central Station, Tel-Aviv 61180; tel. 3-6937401; fax 3-6937480; in 1999 the total length of railway line was 663 km; Dir-Gen. A. UZANI; Gen. Man. EHUD HADAR.

Underground Railway

Haifa Underground Funicular Railway: 122 Hanassi Ave, Haifa 34633; tel. 4-8376861; fax 4-8376875; e-mail funicular@netvision.net.il; opened 1959; 2 km in operation; Man. AVI TELLEM.

ROADS

In 1999 there were 16,115 km of paved roads, of which 9,332 km were urban roads, 5,260 km were non-urban roads and 1,613 km were access roads.

Ministry of National Infrastructure: POB 13198, Public Works Dept, Jerusalem; tel. 2-584711; fax 2-823532.

SHIPPING

At 31 December 1998 Israel's merchant fleet consisted of 53 vessels amounting to 751,614 grt.

Haifa and Ashdod are the main ports in Israel. The former is a natural harbour, enclosed by two main breakwaters and dredged to 45 ft below mean sea-level. In 1965 the deep water port was completed at Ashdod which had a capacity of about 8.6m. tons in 1988.

The port of Eilat is Israel's gateway to the Red Sea. It is a natural harbour, operated from a wharf. Another port, to the south of the original one, started operating in 1965.

Israel Ports and Railways Authority (PRA): POB 20121, 74 Petach Tikva Rd, Tel-Aviv 61201; tel. 3-5657000; fax 3-5617142; e-mail dovf@israports.org.il; internet www.israports.org.il; f. 1961; to plan, build, develop, maintain and operate Israel's commercial ports and Israel Railways. A contract to upgrade Hayovel port, to the north of Ashdod, was awarded in mid-2000, involving new cargo and container quays, a breakwater extension and hinterland development; the first ship was scheduled to be handled at the new port in 2004. A proposed extension to Haifa port was also under way in 2001. Cargo traffic in 1999 amounted to 41.6m. tons; Chair. ARIEH RONA (acting); Dir-Gen. GIDEON SHAMIR.

Ofer Brothers (Management) Ltd: POB 1755, Haifa 31000; tel. 4-8610610; fax 4-8675666; runs cargo and container services; operates some 15 vessels; Chair. Y. OFER; Man. Dir E. ANGEL.

ZIM Israel Navigation Co Ltd: POB 1723, 7–9 Pal-Yam Ave, Haifa 31000; tel. 4-8652111; fax 4-8652956; e-mail zimpress@zim.co.il; internet www.zim.co.il; f. 1945; international integrated transportation system providing global door-to-door services; operates 85 vessels on three global services and 36 regional services; total cargo carried: 1,350,000 TEUs in 2000; Chair. U. ANGEL; Pres. and CEO Dr YORAM SEBBA.

CIVIL AVIATION

Israel Airports Authority: Ben-Gurion International Airport, Tel-Aviv; tel. 3-9710101; fax 3-9712436; internet www.ben-gurion-airport.co.il; Chair. TSVI SHALOM; Dir-Gen. AVI KOSTELITZ.

El Al Israel Airlines Ltd: POB 41, Ben-Gurion International Airport, Tel-Aviv 70100; tel. 3-9716111; fax 3-9716040; internet www.elal.com; f. 1948; 100% state-owned; total assets US $980m. (Dec. 1997); daily services to most capitals of Europe; over 20 flights weekly to New York; services to the USA, Canada, China, Egypt, India, Kenya, South Africa, Thailand and Turkey; Chair. JOSEPH CIECHANOVER; Pres. JOEL FELDSCHUH.

Arkia Israeli Airlines Ltd: POB 39301, Dov Airport, Tel-Aviv 61392; tel. 3-6902222; fax 3-6991390; e-mail income@arkia.co.il; internet www.arkia.co.il; f. 1980 through merger of Kanaf-Arkia Airlines and Aviation Services; scheduled passenger services linking Tel-Aviv, Jerusalem, Haifa, Eilat, Rosh Pina, Kiryat Shmona and Yotveta; charter services to European destinations; Chair. and CEO Prof. ISRAEL BOROVICH.

Tourism

In 1999 some 2,312,300 tourists visited Israel. Tourist receipts in that year totalled US $2,974m.

Ministry of Tourism: POB 1018, 24 Rehov King George, Jerusalem 91009; tel. 2-6754811; fax 2-6253407; e-mail pniot@tourism.gov.il; internet www.infotour.co.il; Minister of Tourism and Transport AMNON LIPKIN-SHAHAK; Dir-Gen. DAVID LITVAK.

Occupied Territories

THE GOLAN HEIGHTS

Location, Climate

The Golan Heights, a mountainous plateau which formed most of Syria's Quneitra Province (1,710 sq km) and parts of Dera'a Province, was occupied by Israel after the 1967 Arab–Israeli War. Following the Disengagement Agreement of 1974, Israel continued to occupy some 70% of the territory (1,176 sq km), valued for its strategic position and abundant water resources (the headwaters of the Jordan river have their source on the slopes of Mount Hermon). The average height of the Golan is approximately 1,200 m above sea-level in the northern region and about 300 m above sea-level in the southern region, near Lake Tiberias (the Sea of Galilee). Rainfall ranges from about 1,000 mm per year in the north to less than 600 mm per year in the southern region.

Administration

Prior to the Israeli occupation, the Golan Heights were incorporated by Syria into a provincial administration of which the city of Quneitra, with a population at the time of 27,378, was capital. The disengagement agreement that was mediated in 1974 by the US Secretary of State, Henry Kissinger, after the 1973 Arab–Israeli War, provided for the withdrawal of Israeli forces from Quneitra. Before they withdrew, however, Israeli army engineers destroyed the city. In December 1981 the Israeli Knesset enacted the Golan Annexation Law, whereby Israeli civilian legislation was extended to the territory of Golan, now under the administrative jurisdiction of the Commissioner for the Northern District of Israel. The Arab-Druze community of the Golan immediately responded by declaring a strike and appealed to the UN Secretary-General to force Israel to

rescind the annexation decision. At the seventh round of multilateral talks between Israeli and Arab delegations in Washington in August 1992, the Israeli Government of Itzhak Rabin for the first time accepted that UN Security Council Resolution 242, adopted in 1967, applied to the Golan Heights. In January 1999 the Knesset passed legislation which stated that any transfer of land under Israeli sovereignty (referring to the Golan Heights and East Jerusalem) was conditional on the approval of at least 61 of the 120 Knesset members and of the Israeli electorate in a subsequent national referendum. Following the election of Ehud Barak as Israel's Prime Minister in May 1999, peace negotiations between Israel and Syria were resumed in mid-December. However, in January 2000 the talks were postponed indefinitely after Syria demanded a written commitment from Israel to withdraw from the Golan Heights. The withdrawal of Israel from the disputed territory is one of Syria's primary objectives in any future peace agreement with Israel.

Demography and Economic Affairs

As a consequence of the Israeli occupation, an estimated 93% of the ethnically diverse Syrian population of 147,613, distributed across 163 villages and towns and 108 individual farms, was expelled. The majority were Arab Sunni Muslims, but the population also included Alawite and Druze minorities and some Circassians, Turcomen, Armenians and Kurds. Approximately 9,000 Palestinian refugees from the 1948 Arab–Israeli War also inhabited the area. At the time of the occupation, the Golan was a predominantly agricultural province, 64% of the labour force being employed in agriculture. Only one-fifth of the population resided in the administrative centres. By 1991 the Golan Heights had a Jewish population of about 12,000 living in 21 Jewish settlements (four new settlements had been created by the end of 1992), and a predominantly Druze population of some 16,000 living in the only six remaining villages, of which Majd ash-Shams is by far the largest. According to official figures, at the end of 1998 the Golan Heights had a total population of 33,000 (including 14,400 Jews, 16,400 Druze and 1,700 Muslims). The Golan Heights have remained largely an agricultural area, and, although many Druze now work in Israeli industry in Eilat, Tel-Aviv and Jerusalem, the indigenous economy relies almost solely on the cultivation of apples, for which the area is famous. The apple orchards benefit from a unique combination of fertile soils, abundance of water and a conducive climate.

EAST JERUSALEM

Location

Greater Jerusalem includes Israeli West Jerusalem (99% Jewish), the Old City and Mount of Olives, East Jerusalem (the Palestinian residential and commercial centre), Arab villages declared to be part of Jerusalem by Israel in 1967 and Jewish neighbourhoods constructed since 1967, either on land expropriated from Arab villages or in areas requisitioned as 'government land'. Although the area of the Greater Jerusalem district is 627 sq km, the Old City of Jerusalem covers just 1 sq km.

Administration

Until the 1967 Arab–Israeli War, Jerusalem had been divided into the new city of West Jerusalem—captured by Jewish forces in 1948—and the old city, East Jerusalem, which was part of Jordan. Israel's victory in 1967, however, reunited the city under Israeli control. Two weeks after the fighting had ended, on 28 June, Israeli law was applied to East Jerusalem and the municipal boundaries were extended by 45 km (28 miles). Jerusalem had been, in effect, annexed. Israeli officials, however, still refer to the 'reunification' of Jerusalem.

Demography and Economic Affairs

In June 1993 the Deputy Mayor of Jerusalem, Avraham Kahila, declared that the city now 'had a majority of Jews', based on population forecasts which estimated the Jewish population at 158,000 and the Arab population at 155,000. This was a significant moment for the Israeli administration, as this had been a long-term objective. Immediately prior to the June 1967 Arab–Israeli War, East Jerusalem and its Arab environs had an Arab population of approximately 70,000, and a small Jewish population in the old Jewish quarter of the city. By contrast, Israeli West Jerusalem had a Jewish population of 196,000. As a result of this imbalance, in the Greater Jerusalem district as a whole the Jewish population was in the majority even prior to the occupation of the whole city in 1967. Israeli policy following the occupation of East Jerusalem and the West Bank consisted of encircling the eastern sector of the city with Jewish settlements. In contrast to the more politically sensitive siting of Jewish settlements in the old Arab quarter of Jerusalem, the Government of Itzhak Rabin concentrated on the outer circle of settlement building. Official statistics for the end of 1998 reported that Greater Jerusalem had a total population of 633,700, of whom 433,600 (68%) were Jews. According to the Jerusalem Institute for Israel Studies, at the end of 1999 Greater Jerusalem had a total population of 646,000, of which about 66% were Jews. The same source estimates that the city's Arab population is increasing at a rate three times greater than the Jewish population.

The Old City, within the walls of which are found the ancient quarters of the Jews, Christians, Muslims and Armenians, has a population of approximately 25,500 Arabs and 2,600 Jews. In addition, there are some 600 recent Jewish settlers in the Arab quarter.

Many imaginative plans have been submitted with the aim of finding a solution to the problem of sharing Jerusalem between Arabs and Jews, including the proposal that the city be placed under international trusteeship, under the auspices of the UN. However, to make the implementation of such plans an administrative as well as a political quagmire, the Israeli administration, after occupying the whole city in June 1967, began creating 'facts on the ground'. Immediately following the occupation, all electricity, water and telephone grids in West Jerusalem were extended to the east. Roads were widened and cleared, and the Arab population immediately in front of the 'Wailing Wall' was forcibly evicted. Arabs living in East Jerusalem became 'permanent residents' and could apply for Israeli citizenship if they wished (in contrast to Arabs in the West Bank and Gaza Strip). However, few chose to do so. None the less, issued with identity cards (excluding the estimated 25,000 Arabs from the West Bank and Gaza Strip living illegally in the city), the Arab residents were taxed by the Israeli authorities, and their businesses and banks became subject to Israeli laws and business regulations. Now controlling approximately one-half of all land in East Jerusalem and the surrounding Palestinian villages (previously communally, or privately, owned by Palestinians), the Israeli authorities allowed Arabs to construct buildings on only 10%–15% of the land in the city; and East Jerusalem's commercial district has been limited to three streets.

Since the 1993 signing of the Declaration of Principles on Palestinian Self-Rule, the future status of Jerusalem and the continuing expansion of Jewish settlements in East Jerusalem have emerged as two of the most crucial issues affecting the peace process. In May 1999 the Israeli Government announced its refusal to grant Israeli citizenship to several hundred Arabs living in East Jerusalem, regardless of their compliance with the conditions stipulated under the Citizenship Law. In October of that year Israel ended its policy of revoking the right of Palestinians to reside in Jerusalem if they had spent more than seven years outside the city. Moreover, the Israeli Government announced in March 2000 that Palestinian residents of Jerusalem who had had their identity cards revoked could apply for their restoration.

At the Camp David summit meeting held between the Israelis and Palestinians in July 2000, the issue of who would have sovereignty over East Jerusalem in a future 'permanent status' agreement proved to be the principal obstacle to the achievement of a peace deal. It was reported in late July that the Israeli Government had offered the PNA municipal autonomy over certain areas of East Jerusalem (including access to the Islamic holy sites), although sovereignty would remain in Israeli hands; the proposals were rejected by Yasser Arafat. In late September 2000 the holy sites of East Jerusalem were the initial focal point of a renewed uprising by Palestinians against the Israeli authorities, which swiftly became known as the *Al-Aqsa intifada*.

EMERGING PALESTINIAN AUTONOMOUS AREAS

Introductory Survey

Location, Climate, Language, Religion, Flag, Capital

The Emerging Palestinian Autonomous Areas are located in the West Bank and the Gaza Strip. (For a more detailed description of the location of the Palestinian territories, see Government, below.) The West Bank lies in western Asia, to the west of the Jordan river and the Dead Sea. To the north and south is the State of Israel, to the west the State of Israel and the Gaza Strip. The Interim Agreement of September 1995 (see below) provides for the creation of a corridor, or safe passage, linking the Gaza Strip with the West Bank. A 'southern' safe passage between Hebron and Gaza was opened in October 1999. Precipitation ranges between 600 mm and 800 mm on the Mount Hebron massif and 200 mm in the Jordan Valley. Apart from the urban centres of Bethlehem (Beit Lahm) and Hebron (Al-Khalil) to the south, the majority of the Palestinian population is concentrated in the northern localities around Ramallah (Ram Allah), Nablus (Nabulus), Jenin (Janin) and Tulkarm. The Gaza Strip, lying beside the Mediterranean Sea and Israel's border with Egypt, covers an area of 371 sq km (143.2 sq miles). Annual average rainfall is 300 mm. The language of the Palestinians of the West Bank and the Gaza Strip is Arabic. The majority of the Palestinian population of the territories are Muslims. A Christian minority represents about 2% of the Palestinian population of the West Bank and the Gaza Strip. This minority, in turn, represents about 45% of all Palestinian Christians. The national flag (proportion 2 by 1) comprises three equal horizontal stripes of black, white and green, with a red triangle with its base corresponding to the hoist. Gaza City is the main population centre and the centre of administration for the Palestinian National Authority (PNA). In November 1988 the Palestine National Council (PNC) proclaimed Jerusalem as the capital of the newly-declared independent State of Palestine. Israel (q.v.) declares Jerusalem as its capital. In 1967 East Jerusalem was formally annexed by the Israeli authorities, although the annexation has never been recognized by the UN. The permanent status of Jerusalem remains subject to negotiation on so-called 'final status' issues under the Oslo accords.

Recent History

Until the end of the 1948 Arab–Israeli War, the West Bank formed part of the British Mandate of Palestine, before becoming part of the Hashemite Kingdom of Jordan under the Armistice Agreement of 1949. It remained under Jordanian sovereignty, despite Israeli occupation in 1967, until King Hussein of Jordan formally relinquished legal and administrative control on 31 July 1988. Under Israeli military occupation the West Bank was administered by a military government, which divided the territory into seven sub-districts. The Civil Administration, as it was later termed, did not extend its jurisdiction to the many Israeli settlements that were established under the Israeli occupation; settlements remained subject to the Israeli legal and administrative system. By February 2000 approximately 26.9% of the West Bank was under Israeli military control, with responsibility for civil administration transferred to the Palestinian authorities; about 12.1% was under full Palestinian control; and about 61% was under complete Israeli control.

An administrative province under the British Mandate of Palestine, Gaza was transferred to Egypt after the 1949 armistice and remained under Egyptian administration until June 1967, when it was invaded by Israel. Following Israeli occupation the Gaza Strip, like the West Bank, became an 'administered territory'. Until the provisions of the Declaration of Principles on Palestinian Self-Rule (see below) began to take effect, the management of day-to-day affairs was the responsibility of the area's Israeli military commander. Neither Israeli laws nor governmental and public bodies—including the Supreme Court—could review or alter the orders of the military command to any great extent. In 1993 an estimated 50% of the land area was under Israeli control, either through the establishment of Jewish settlements or through the closure of areas by the military authorities.

In accordance with the Declaration of Principles on Palestinian Self-Rule of September 1993, and the Cairo Agreement on the Gaza Strip and Jericho of May 1994, the Palestine Liberation Organization (PLO) assumed control of the Jericho area of the West Bank, and of the Gaza Strip, on 17 May 1994. In November and December 1995, under the terms of the Israeli-Palestinian Interim Agreement on the West Bank and the Gaza Strip signed by Israel and the PLO on 28 September 1995, Israeli armed forces withdrew from the West Bank towns of Nablus, Ramallah, Jenin, Tulkarm, Qalqilya and Bethlehem. (The Declaration of Principles, the Cairo Agreement, the Interim Agreement and associated accords are generally referred to collectively as the Oslo accords.) In late December 1995 the PLO assumed responsibility in some 17 areas of civil administration in the town of Hebron. Under the terms of the Interim Agreement, the PLO was eventually to assume full responsibility for civil affairs in the 400 surrounding villages, but the Israeli armed forces were to retain freedom of movement to act against potential hostilities there. In Hebron Israel effected a partial withdrawal of its armed forces in January 1997, but the Israeli authorities retained responsibility for the security of some 400 Jewish settlers there. Responsibility for security in the rest of Hebron passed to the Palestinian police force, but Israel retained responsibility for security on access roads. Israel was to retain control over a large area of the West Bank (including Jewish settlements, rural areas, military installations and the majority of junctions between Palestinian roads and those used by Israeli troops and settlers) until July 1997. Following the first phase of the redeployment and the holding, on its completion, of elections to a Palestinian Legislative Council and for a Palestinian executive President, Israel was to have completed a second redeployment from rural areas by July 1997. The Israeli occupation was to be maintained in Jewish settlements, military installations, East Jerusalem and the Jewish settlements around Jerusalem until the conclusion of 'final status' negotiations between Israel and the Palestinians, scheduled for May 1999.

Subsequent postponements, and further negotiations within the context of the Oslo accords, resulted in a new timetable for Israeli redeployment which envisaged two phases, subsequent to the Hebron withdrawal, to be completed by October 1997 and August 1998. Discussions on 'final status' issues—borders, the Jerusalem issue, Jewish settlements and Palestinian refugees—were to commence within two months of the signing of the agreement on Hebron. As guarantor of the Oslo accords, the USA undertook to obtain the release from Israeli custody of Palestinian prisoners, and to ensure that Israel continued to engage in negotiations for the establishment of a Palestinian airport in the Gaza Strip and for safe passage for Palestinians between the West Bank and Gaza. The USA also undertook to ensure that the Palestinians would continue to combat terrorism, complete the revision of the Palestinian National Charter (or PLO Covenant), adopted in 1964 and amended in 1968, and consider Israeli requests to extradite Palestinians suspected of involvement in attacks in Israel.

By July 1998, however, conflicting interpretations of the extent of both the phased and total final redeployment of Israeli armed forces (90% of the East Bank according to the Palestinians; less than 50% according to Israel) had resulted in a seemingly intractable impasse in the so-called Oslo peace process. Progress on redeployment had been impeded for some 15 months: this paralysis emerged from the decision of the Israeli Government of Binyamin Netanyahu, announced in February 1997, to begin construction of a new Jewish settlement at Jabal Abu Ghunaim (Har Homa), near Beit Sahur. Construction in this area was particularly controversial because, if completed, the new settlement would make it impossible to reach East Jerusalem from the West Bank without crossing Israeli territory, thereby prejudicing 'final status' negotiations concerning Jerusalem. In response, the Palestinians withdrew from 'final status' talks scheduled to commence in March. The immediate commencement of construction work at Jabal Abu Ghunaim provoked rioting among Palestinians and a resumption of attacks by the military wing of the Islamic Resistance Movement (Hamas) on Israeli civilian targets. The Israeli Cabinet responded by ordering a general closure of the West Bank and the Gaza Strip.

Both the Jabal Abu Ghunaim (Har Homa) construction and Israel's unilateral decision to redeploy its armed forces from only 9% of West Bank territory (announced in March 1997) were regarded by many observers as a vitiation of both the Oslo and the subsequent post-Hebron agreements. These were further undermined by the publication, in the Israeli daily newspaper *Ha'aretz*, of the results of a US study asserting that more than 25% of Jewish settlers' homes in the Gaza Strip and the West Bank were uninhabited (the Israeli Central Bureau of Statistics stated that only 12% of the settlements were unoccupied). *Ha'aretz* later reported that Israeli plans, evolved within the framework of the Oslo accords, to relinquish 90% of the West Bank had been revised to a 40% redeployment.

In June 1997 the US House of Representatives voted in favour of recognizing Jerusalem as the undivided capital of Israel and of transferring the US embassy to the city from Tel-Aviv. The vote (which US President Bill Clinton was known to oppose) coincided with violent clashes between Palestinian civilians and Israeli troops in Gaza and Hebron.

In late July 1997, following a series of meetings conducted by the US Department of State with representatives of the Israeli Government and of the Palestinian National Authority (PNA), it was announced that peace talks would resume in early August. At the end of July, however, on the eve of a scheduled visit by Dennis Ross, the US Special Envoy to the Middle East, to reactivate the negotiations, Hamas carried out a suicide bomb attack at a Jewish market in Jerusalem, in which 14 civilians were killed and more than 150 injured. Ross cancelled his visit and the Israeli Government immediately halted payment of tax revenues to the PNA and closed the Gaza Strip and the West Bank. In the aftermath of the bombing the Palestinian authorities undertook a campaign to detain members of Hamas and Islamic Jihad. The restrictions on access to the Palestinian territories were briefly relaxed at the beginning of September, in anticipation of a visit to the region by the US Secretary of State, Madeleine Albright, but a further suicide bomb attack in Jerusalem, in which eight people died, led to the reimposition of Israeli sanctions shortly afterwards; Hamas claimed responsibility for the attack. Albright's visit to the Middle East failed to reactivate the peace process. During her visit, she reportedly stated that Israel should halt the construction of Jewish settlements on Arab lands, cease confiscations of land and the demolition of Arab dwellings, and end its policy of confiscating Palestinian identity documents. While Albright endorsed Israeli Prime Minister Netanyahu's demand that the PNA take more effective measures to suppress the military wing of Hamas and other militant groups, US impatience at the Israeli Government's apparently provocative acts was demonstrated by the Secretary of State's criticism of Netanyahu's decision, announced in late September, to permit the construction of 300 Jewish homes in Efrat in the West Bank.

None the less, it was announced on 28 September 1997 that, as a result of US diplomatic efforts, Israeli and Palestinian officials had agreed to resume negotiations in early October. The first round of talks would focus on the outstanding issues of the Oslo accords, in particular the opening of an airport and seaport facilities in the Gaza Strip, the establishment of a safe corridor linking the Gaza Strip with the West Bank, and the release from Israeli detention of Palestinian prisoners. A second round of talks, in mid-October, would address issues of security co-operation between the Palestinian and the Israeli authorities, the long-delayed redeployment of Israeli armed forces from the West Bank, Israeli settlement expansion, and questions pertaining to 'final status' negotiations. Talks resumed on 7 October between Palestinian and Israeli negotiators on the outstanding issues of the Oslo accords, and the following day the Arafat and Netanyahu held their first meeting for eight months.

Meanwhile, the attempted assassination in Amman, in late September 1997, of Khalid Meshaal, the head of the Hamas political bureau in Jordan, provoked warnings of retaliation against Israel, even before official confirmation that agents of the Israeli security service, Mossad, had been responsible for the attack. In order to secure the release of its agents by the Jordanian authorities, Israel was obliged, at the beginning of October, to free a number of Arab political prisoners, most notably Sheikh Ahmad Yassin, the founder and spiritual leader of Hamas, who had been sentenced to life imprisonment in Israel in 1989 for complicity in attacks on Israeli soldiers. The release of Sheikh Yassin into Jordanian custody was swiftly followed by his return, on 6 October, to Gaza.

In December 1997, under further US pressure, it was reported that the Israeli Cabinet had agreed in principle to withdraw troops from an unspecified area of West Bank territory. In early January 1998 US Special Envoy Dennis Ross visited Israel, in a further attempt to break the deadlock regarding redeployment. However, the Israeli Government subsequently reiterated that it would not conduct such a redeployment until the Palestinian authorities had fulfilled a series of conditions, including requirements that the Palestinian leadership should adopt effective measures to counter terrorism, that it should reduce the strength of its security forces from 40,000 to 24,000, and that the Palestinian National Charter should be revised to recognize explicitly Israel's right to exist. There was further evidence of a hardening of the Israeli position as, prior to a summit meeting between Clinton and Netanyahu in Washington, DC, in late January, the Israeli Cabinet issued a communiqué detailing 'vital and national interests' in the West Bank (amounting to some 60% of the entire territory) that it was not prepared to relinquish; the document asserted that Israel would, among other areas, retain control of the territory surrounding Jerusalem. At the talks, it was reported that the USA was seeking to persuade Israel to effect a second withdrawal of its armed forces from some 12% of the West Bank over a period of 80 days, in exchange for the increased co-operation of the PNA on security issues. In late January, however, it was announced that direct contacts between Palestinian representatives and the Israeli Prime Minister had collapsed.

In late March 1998 it emerged that the USA planned to present new proposals regarding the withdrawal of Israeli armed forces at separate meetings, to be held in Europe, between the US Secretary of State and the PNA President and Israeli Prime Minister. Dennis Ross subsequently arrived in Jerusalem in order to clarify the latest US initiative. Although no details had been published, it appeared that the USA was proposing an Israeli withdrawal from slightly more than 13% of West Bank territory, and a suspension of settlement construction in return for further efforts by the PNA to combat militant organizations engaged in campaigns of violence against Israeli targets. Arafat sought an Israeli withdrawal from a further 30% of the West Bank, but there were indications that he might be prepared to accept an initial redeployment from some 13% of the territory. The Israeli Cabinet rejected the new US initiative; however, it was evident that, even if agreement could be reached on the extent of territory involved, the issue of whether a subsequent withdrawal should take place prior to the commencement of 'final status' negotiations remained far more contentious. At the end of March Madeleine Albright stated that the peace process was on the verge of collapse, and indicated that the USA was considering ending its involvement as a mediator. A month later, it emerged that, during a visit to Gaza City on behalf of the European Union (EU), the British Prime Minister, Tony Blair, had persuaded Arafat to attend a conference in London, United Kingdom, based on the most recent US initiative. Accordingly, in early May Blair hosted a summit meeting attended by Netanyahu, Arafat and Albright. At its conclusion the US Secretary of State invited Netanyahu and Arafat to attend a summit meeting with Bill Clinton in Washington, DC, to discuss the apparent US proposal that Israel and the Palestinians could proceed to 'final status' negotiations as soon as the scope of the next Israeli withdrawal from the West Bank had been agreed. However, the Israeli Government rejected the US initiative in advance of Clinton's direct participation, and further discussions involving Albright in mid-May achieved no progress. In June details of the latest US initiative were unofficially disclosed in the Israeli press: Israel would be required to agree to 'no significant expansion' of Jewish settlements and to relinquish slightly more than 13% of West Bank territory over a period of 12 weeks, in exchange for increased Palestinian co-operation. The adoption by the Israeli Cabinet later that month of a plan to extend the boundaries of Jerusalem and construct homes there for a further 1m. people prompted accusations by Palestinian officials that it amounted to a *de facto* annexation of territories that were officially subject to 'final status' negotiations.

On 7 July 1998 the UN General Assembly, despite objections from the USA and Israel, overwhelmingly approved a resolution to upgrade the status of the PLO at the UN. The new provision allowed the PLO to participate in debates, to co-sponsor resolutions, and to raise points of order during discussions of Middle East affairs.

On 19–22 July 1998 Israeli and Palestinian delegations held direct negotiations for the first time since March 1997. They discussed the most recent US initiative to reactivate the peace process, as disclosed in June; however, the proposal was deemed unacceptable by Israel. In August Netanyahu was reported to have presented a compromise plan to his Cabinet whereby Israel would effect a full redeployment from a further 10% of the West Bank and a partial withdrawal from 3% of the Judaean desert. Arafat gave a cautious welcome to the compromise plan. In late September Netanyahu and Arafat met for the first time since October 1997, in Washington, DC, and agreed to participate in a peace conference in the USA in the following month. The summit meeting, also attended by President Clinton, commenced at the Wye Plantation, Maryland, USA, on 15 October 1998, and culminated in the signing, on 23 October, of the Wye River Memorandum, which was intended to facilitate the implementation of the Oslo accords.

Under the terms of the Wye Memorandum, which was to be implemented within three months of its signing, Israel was to transfer a further 13.1% of West Bank territory from exclusive Israeli control to joint Israeli-Palestinian control. An additional 14% of the West Bank was to be transferred from joint Israeli-Palestinian control to exclusive Palestinian control. The Wye Memorandum also stipulated that negotiations with regard to a third Israeli redeployment (under the terms of the Oslo accords) should proceed concurrently with 'final status' discussions; that the Palestinians should reinforce anti-terrorism measures under the supervision of the US Central Intelligence Agency (CIA); that the strength of the Palestinian police force should be reduced by 25%; that the Palestinians should arrest 30 suspected terrorists; that Israel should carry out the phased release of 750 Palestinian prisoners (including political detainees); that the Palestine National Council (PNC) should annul those clauses of the PLO Covenant deemed to be anti-Israeli; that Gaza International Airport was to become operational with an Israeli security presence; and that an access corridor between the West Bank and the Gaza Strip should be opened. The Memorandum was endorsed by the Israeli Cabinet on 11 November and approved by the Knesset on 17 November. Three days later Israel redeployed its armed forces from about 500 sq km of the West Bank. Of this area, some 400 sq km came under exclusive Palestinian control for both civil and security affairs. In the remaining 100 sq km the PNA assumed responsibility for civil affairs, while Israel retained control over security affairs. At the same time, Israel released some 250 Palestinian prisoners (although a majority were non-political prisoners) and signed a protocol for the opening of Gaza International Airport: Israel retained the right to decide which airlines could use the airport, which was officially inaugurated by Arafat on 24 November. However, implementation of the Wye Memorandum did not proceed smoothly, with mutual accusations of failure to observe its terms.

In the weeks prior to a planned visit by Bill Clinton to Israel and the Gaza Strip in mid-December 1998, violent clashes erupted in the West Bank between Palestinians and the Israeli security forces. One cause of the unrest was a decision by the Israeli Cabinet to suspend further releases of Palestinian prisoners under the terms of the Wye Memorandum, and its insistence that no Palestinians convicted of killing Israelis, nor members of Hamas and Islamic Jihad, would be released. On 14 December, meanwhile, in the presence of President Clinton, the PNC voted to annul articles of the Palestinian National Charter that were deemed to be anti-Israeli. While the Israeli Prime Minister welcomed the vote, he insisted that several further conditions had to be met before Israel would implement the Wye Memorandum. At a summit meeting the following day between Clinton, Netanyahu and Arafat at the Erez check-point between Israel and the Gaza Strip, the Israeli premier reiterated Israel's stance regarding the release of Palestinian prisoners and further demanded that the Palestinians should cease incitement to violence and formally relinquish plans, reasserted by Arafat in November, for a unilateral declaration of Palestinian statehood on 4 May 1999, the original deadline as established by the Oslo accords. At the conclusion of the meeting Netanyahu announced that Israel would not proceed with the second scheduled redeployment of its armed forces (under the Wye Memorandum) on 18 December 1998, claiming once again that the Palestinians had failed to honour their commitments, and on 20 December the Israeli Cabinet voted to suspend implementation of the Wye Memorandum.

In January 1999 President Arafat came under intense international pressure to postpone any unilateral declaration of Palestinian statehood, at least until after the Israeli elections scheduled for May. Moreover, Arafat apparently considered that making such a declaration prior to the elections might actually improve Netanyahu's chances of re-election. In late January Arafat indicated that he might postpone a declaration of independence if he received certain assurances from Israel and the international community, particularly the USA and EU) regarding the issue of settlement expansion. In February the German Vice-Chancellor and Minister of Foreign Affairs, Joseph Fischer, led an EU delegation to the Palestinian territories; the visit coincided with mounting controversy arising from allegations of the misappropriation of EU funding to the PNA. Meanwhile, the Palestinian leader undertook numerous regional and international visits during February–April, as part of a campaign of intensive diplomacy. In late April PLO chief negotiators Mahmud Abbas and Saeb Erakat visited Washington, DC, in order to secure certain assurances from the USA in return for an extension of the 4 May deadline. In late April, following a meeting of the Palestinian Central Council, together with Hamas representatives, in Gaza, it was announced that a declaration on Palestinian statehood would be postponed until after the Israeli elections. The decision was applauded internationally, but provoked violent demonstrations among many Palestinians.

Palestinians cautiously welcomed the victory of Ehud Barak and the One Israel alliance in the Israeli elections of May 1999, and PNA officials immediately urged Barak to break the deadlock in the Middle East peace process. However, the new Israeli Prime Minister asserted immediately that he would not offer the Palestinians any fundamental concessions. After the elections there emerged a Palestinian consensus that a halt to Israel's programme of settlement expansion in the Occupied Territories (regarded by the Palestinians as an attempt to predetermine the 'final status' borders) must be a precondition for any meaningful resumption of talks. In early June Palestinians in the West Bank declared a 'day of rage' against continuing settlement construction there; the mass protests, which were particularly violent in Hebron, followed an announcement in late May that the population of the West Bank's largest Jewish settlement, Ma'aleh Edomin, was to be expanded from 25,000 to 50,000 settlers.

The first direct meeting between Arafat and Prime Minister Barak was held at the Erez check-point in July 1999. Both leaders reiterated their commitment to reviving the peace process; however, Arafat was reportedly alarmed by Barak's apparent opposition to full implementation of the Wye Memorandum and his seeming preoccupation with the Syrian component of the peace process (see below). Later that month, during a second meeting between the two leaders at Erez, Barak angered the Palestinians by seeking to win Arafat's approval to postpone implementation of the Wye Memorandum until it could be combined with 'final status' negotiations (thereby implying a 15-month delay in further Israeli troop redeployments). At the beginning of August Barak promised to bring forward the release of 250 Palestinian prisoners if Arafat agreed to a postponement. Discussions between the two delegations broke down the same day, as Arafat rejected the Israeli stance, but talks resumed in mid-August, when Israel agreed to pursue implementation of the Wye Memorandum.

Meeting at Sharm esh-Sheikh, Egypt, on 4 September 1999, during a visit to the region by Secretary of State Albright, Barak and Arafat signed the Sharm esh-Sheikh Memorandum (or Wye Two accords), outlining a revised timetable for implementation of the outstanding provisions of the original Wye agreement. Under the terms of the Memorandum, on 9 September some 200 Palestinian prisoners were released from Israeli custody, and the following day Israel transferred a further 7% of the West Bank to PNA control. A ceremonial opening of 'final status' negotiations between Israel and the Palestinians took place at the Erez check-point on 13 September 1999; shortly afterwards details emerged of a secret meeting between Barak and Arafat to discuss an agenda for such talks. However, in October the Palestinians' chief negotiator, Yasser Abd ar-Rabbuh, warned that the PNA would boycott 'final status' talks unless Israel ended its settlement expansion programme. In mid-October Barak, also under pressure from left-wing groups in Israel, responded by dismantling 12 'settlement outposts' in the West Bank which he deemed to be illegal. Meanwhile, Israel released a further 151 Palestinian prisoners, under the terms of Wye Two. The inauguration of the first 'safe passage' between the West Bank and Gaza Strip took place on 25 October. The opening had been delayed by almost a month owing to a dispute between the Israeli and Palestinian authorities over security arrangements for the 44-km route, linking the Erez check-point in the Gaza Strip to Hebron in the West Bank. Israel asserted that it would maintain almost complete control over the so-called 'southern route', including decisions on which Palestinians would be permitted to use it. In late October the killing of a Palestinian by Israeli soldiers resulted in several days of violence between Palestinians and Israeli security forces in the West Bank town of Bethlehem.

'Final status' negotiations between Israel and the PNA commenced in Ramallah on 8 November 1999, following a summit meeting, held earlier in the month in Oslo, Norway, between Arafat, Barak and Clinton. The opening of 'final status' talks had been threatened when three bombs exploded in northern Israel. (Israel claimed that Hamas was responsible, since the attack followed an alleged warning by the organization's military wing that it would intensify its activities in protest at Israel's settlement policies.) A further redeployment of Israeli armed forces from 5% of the West Bank, scheduled for 15 November, was postponed owing to disagreement over the areas to be transferred. Relations between the two sides worsened in early December when, amid reports that settlement activity had intensified under Barak, Palestinian negotiators walked out of 'final status' talks after demanding that Israel should end immediately its settlement programme. Apparently in response to US pressure, the Israeli Prime Minister subsequently announced a halt to settlement construction, at least for the course of the negotiations regarding a framework agreement on 'final status'. In late December Arafat conducted talks in Ramallah with Barak, who became the first Israeli premier to hold peace discussions on Palestinian territory. At the end of the month Israel released some 26 Palestinian 'security' prisoners as a 'gesture of goodwill'. On 6–7 January 2000 Israeli armed forces withdrew from a further 5% of the West Bank; however, Israel announced in mid-January that a third redeployment from some 6% of the territory (scheduled to take place on 20 January, according to Wye Two) would be postponed until Barak had returned from revived peace talks with Syrian representatives in the USA. During a meeting with Arafat on his return from the USA (where talks on the Israeli-Syrian track had collapsed), Barak was reported to have proposed that the deadline for reaching a framework agreement be postponed for two months. The approval by the Israeli Cabinet of a withdrawal of its troops from a sparsely-populated area of the West Bank led the PNA to break off negotiations in early February. In early March Israeli security forces in the Arab Israeli town of Tayibbah killed four members of Hamas' military wing, whom they alleged to be plotting terrorist actions within Israel. On 19–20 March Israel released 15 Palestinian prisoners, and the resumption of 'final status' talks was announced on 21 March. On the same day Israeli armed forces withdrew from a further 6.1% of the West Bank.

Meanwhile, in February the summary of an Israeli report concerning the interrogation methods adopted by Israel's security service, Shin Bet, during the Palestinian *intifada* (1988–92) was published for the first time. The report acknowledged that Palestinian prisoners, especially those in the Gaza Strip, had been 'systematically tortured' by Shin Bet officers.

On 15 February 2000 the PLO and the Vatican signed an 'historic' agreement aimed at strengthening ties between the Roman Catholic Church and a future Palestinian state; the document was strongly criticized by Israel. In late March Pope John Paul II undertook a highly publicized five-day visit to Israel and the Palestinian self-rule areas; in a symbolic address to displaced Palestinians at the Dheisheh refugee camp in the West Bank, the Pontiff affirmed what he termed their 'natural right to a homeland'.

In late February 2000 a visit to the Palestinian territories by the French Prime Minister, Lionel Jospin, became highly controversial, owing to remarks made by Jospin referring to Hezbollah's resistance in southern Lebanon as 'terrorism'. After giving a lecture at the Birzeit University in the West Bank, the French premier came under attack by angry students. Some 120 students were arrested after the protests escalated into violent confrontations between Palestinian civilians and the police and security forces. The PNA subsequently declared that all marches, rallies and public gatherings would henceforth require the prior consent of the police.

In mid-April 2000 Barak and Clinton held talks in Washington, DC, after which it was reported that Israel had agreed to Palestinian demands for greater US involvement in future discussions. The Israeli premier was subsequently reported to have indicated that a Palestinian entity could be established in

what was now PNA-controlled territory—covering 60%–70% of the West Bank—although Barak refused to speak of a Palestinian 'state'. Later in April Arafat met with Clinton in Washington, where he reportedly sought his intervention in halting Israel's settlement expansion programme. Israel and the PNA opened the third round of 'final status' talks at the Israeli port of Eilat on 30 April. Palestinian negotiators immediately denounced a recent decision by the Israeli Government to construct 174 new Jewish homes in the West Bank. Moreover, in early May the Palestinian rejected as 'utterly unacceptable' maps presented by Israeli officials that outlined Barak's vision of a future Palestinian entity. Shortly afterwards Barak and Arafat held a crisis meeting, mediated by Dennis Ross, in Ramallah, in the course of which Barak was reported to have proposed the transfer to full PNA control of three Palestinian villages close to Jerusalem, on condition that the third West Bank redeployment (scheduled to be implemented in June) be postponed until the conclusion of a final peace settlement. After Palestinian negotiators admitted that the 13 May deadline for reaching a framework agreement would not be met, 'final status' talks were suspended.

At the beginning of May 2000 as many as 1,000 Palestinians held in Israeli detention began a hunger strike. Palestinians in the West Bank and Gaza initiated mass protests in support of the prisoners' action; the demonstrations erupted into violence on 15 May (the anniversary of the declaration of the State of Israel in 1948), which was declared to be a 'day of rage'. Three days of violent gun battles ensued between Palestinian police and civilians and Israeli troops, in which seven Palestinians (including two policemen) were killed, and several hundred injured. Meanwhile, also on 15 May the PNA chief negotiator, Yasser Abd ar-Rabbuh, announced his resignation (which Arafat refused to accept), in protest at 'secret' talks being conducted between Israeli and Palestinian representatives in Stockholm, Sweden; Abd ar-Rabbuh claimed that he had not been informed about the discussions. Growing anger among Palestinians over the apparent unaccountability of the PNA leadership appeared to have contributed to the civil unrest. Arafat, however, refused to accept Abd ar-Rabbuh's resignation. On 21 May Israel suspended the Stockholm talks, after an Israeli child was killed in continuing violence in the West Bank. The Israeli Government also reversed its decision to transfer the three Arab villages to PNA control, demanding that Arafat take action to curb Palestinian unrest. Several Palestinians accused of involvement in the recent violence were subsequently detained by the PNA. The Palestinian prisoners called off their hunger strike at the end of the month.

Meanwhile, Palestinians welcomed the withdrawal of Israeli troops from southern Lebanon in late May 2000. Following a tour of Israel and the Palestinian areas by US Secretary of State Madeleine Albright in early June, on 15 June Clinton received Arafat for discussions in Washington, DC, in an attempt to reinvigorate the Israeli-Palestinian track of the Middle East peace process. Four days later Israel released three Palestinian prisoners as a 'goodwill gesture'. On 21 June, two days prior to the scheduled date, the PNA was reported to have agreed to a postponement of the third redeployment of Israeli forces from the West Bank. The Palestinian Central Council convened on 2 July, and after two days of discussions, stated that the PLO would declare a State of Palestine on or before 13 September.

In early July 2000 Bill Clinton invited Arafat and Barak to a peace summit, to be held at the US presidential retreat at Camp David, Maryland, on 11–19 July, with the hope that a framework agreement might be achieved. Despite intensive mediation efforts the Camp David talks, which were extended beyond their original deadline, ended without agreement on 25 July. Although progress had reportedly been made regarding the borders of a future Palestinian entity and the question of Palestinian refugees, disagreements over the future status of Jerusalem had been the principal obstacle to an accord. Israel was said to have offered the Palestinians municipal authority over certain parts of East Jerusalem, as well as access to the Islamic holy sites. PNA officials, however, demanded full sovereignty over the holy sites (in particular the al-Aqsa Mosque and the Dome of the Rock), with East Jerusalem as the capital of a Palestinian state. Nevertheless, in the summit's final communiqué Israel and the PNA pledged to continue peace negotiations and to avoid 'unilateral actions'—interpreted as Arafat's threat unilaterally to declare an independent Palestinian state. After a brief visit to Egypt for talks with President Hosni Mubarak,

Arafat returned to Gaza in late July, hailed by Palestinians for having maintained a firm stance on the Jerusalem issue. Meanwhile, an attempted invasion of the al-Aqsa Mosque by Jewish extremists resulted in confrontations between Jews and Muslims in Jerusalem; a similar incident occurred in early August. At the end of July the PNA leadership was angered by strong indications by US officials that the US administration was considering relocating its embassy from Tel-Aviv to Jerusalem. Travelling widely in Europe, the Middle East, Asia and South Africa in late July and during August, Arafat came under intense international pressure not to announce the establishment of a Palestinian state on 13 September. Meanwhile, during August about 23 Palestinians were arrested by Israeli security forces on charges of involvement in militant Islamist 'terrorist squads'. In early September Bill Clinton held separate talks with Arafat and Barak on the sidelines of the UN Millennium Summit in New York, USA. The Palestinian Central Council convened in Gaza on 9–10 September, and agreed to postpone the declaration of statehood for an indefinite period (although 15 November was reportedly designated as the intended date for the declaration of independence). Later in September negotiations between Israeli and Palestinian officials were resumed in the USA, and on 20 September an agreement was signed that would enable construction of the Gaza seaport to begin. On 26 September Barak and Arafat met at the Israeli premier's home for their first direct discussions since the Camp David summit.

From late September 2000 the West Bank and Gaza Strip became engulfed in the most serious violence in the territories for many years, as Palestinians demonstrated their frustration at the lack of progress in the talks with Israel and at their failure to achieve statehood. The violence was provoked on 28 September when Ariel Sharon, leader of Israel's right-wing Likud party, visited Temple Mount/Haram ash-Sharif in Jerusalem—the site of the al-Aqsa Mosque and the Dome of the Rock—flanked by Israeli security guards. Sharon's visit to the Islamic holy sites provoked violent protests by stone-throwing Palestinians, to which Israeli security forces responded forcefully. While intensive diplomatic attempts were made to curb the violence, the clashes spread rapidly to other Palestinian towns and the death toll continued to rise: by the end of October at least 140 people had died—all but eight of whom were Palestinians, including several teenagers—and thousands had been wounded. The perceived plight of the Palestinians received considerable support from the international community, and there were widespread protests in other Arab capitals.

On 4 October 2000 Arafat and Barak travelled to Paris, France, for negotiations led by the US Secretary of State. However, a tense series of proximity discussions and direct encounters failed notably to agree on the composition of an international commission of inquiry into the causes of the violence, and while Yasser Arafat and Madeleine Albright travelled to Egypt to continue talks at Sharm-esh Sheikh the following day, Barak returned direct to Israel. Israeli armed forces subsequently sealed off the borders of the West Bank and Gaza Strip. (The closure was originally imposed for a three-day period, until the conclusion of the Jewish commemoration of Yom Kippur, but was not rescinded as violence continued.) On 7 October the UN Security Council issued a resolution condemning the 'provocation carried out' at Temple Mount/Haram ash-Sharif and the 'excessive use of force' employed by the Israeli security forces against Palestinians. Two days later the UN Secretary-General, Kofi Annan, arrived in the region, as international peace initiatives (variously involving the UN, the USA, Russia, the EU, Egypt, Jordan and Syria) intensified. Meanwhile, Israel accused Arafat of failing to intervene to halt the violence, as members of Arafat's own organization, Fatah, joined Hamas and other militant groups in what swiftly became known as the al-Aqsa *intifada*. Tensions escalated in mid-October after the Israeli army launched rocket attacks on Arafat's headquarters in the West Bank and Gaza, in retaliation for the murder of two Israeli soldiers by Palestinians in Ramallah. In an attempt to prevent the crisis from escalating into a major regional conflict, a summit meeting between Barak and Arafat, brokered by US President Bill Clinton, was convened on 16–17 October at the Egyptian resort of Sharm esh-Sheikh, at the end of which Clinton announced that the Israeli and Palestinian leaders had agreed the terms of a 'truce' to halt the spiralling violence. The two sides had also reportedly agreed on the formation of a US-appointed fact-finding committee to investigate the clashes. Barak, however, demanded that Arafat rearrest some 65 mili-

tant Islamists whom the PNA had freed in early October. The fragile truce did not hold, and, amid further violence in the West Bank and Gaza, the League of Arab States (the Arab League, see p. 232) held an emergency summit meeting in the Egyptian capital on 21–22 October, issuing a strong condemnation of Israel's actions towards the Palestinians. Barak responded by announcing that Israel was calling a what he termed a 'time-out' in the peace process.

At the end of October 2000 Islamic Jihad claimed responsibility for a suicide bombing on an Israeli army post in Gaza. The attack signalled a new campaign against Israeli forces by militant Palestinian organizations opposed to the Oslo accords. Israel responded by launching air strikes on Fatah military bases, and declared that henceforth it would target leading officials of militant Islamist groups suspected of involvement in terrorism. On 1 November Arafat held a crisis meeting in Gaza with the Israeli Minister for Regional Co-operation, Shimon Peres, and the two sides were reported to have agreed a cease-fire, based on the truce brokered in Egypt in October. The 'cease-fire' was short-lived, however, as on the following day a car bomb exploded in Jerusalem, killing two Israelis. Although Islamic Jihad claimed responsibility for the attack, Barak accused the PNA of being indirectly culpable by its recent release of Islamist prisoners. In early November President Clinton appointed the five-member international commission of inquiry, chaired by former US Senator George Mitchell; however, some Palestinians expressed concern that the commission was incomplete, since no representative of Russia or of the Non-aligned countries had been appointed. Meeting with Clinton in the USA shortly afterwards, Arafat demanded that the USA support Palestinian requests for a UN peace-keeping force in the West Bank and Gaza; Barak was opposed to the establishment of such a force. Prior to the meeting, a senior Fatah representative in the West Bank was killed by Israeli troops. In mid-November Israel reinforced its closure of the West Bank and Gaza Strip and imposed an economic blockade on the territories. Meanwhile, the UN High Commissioner for Human Rights, Mary Robinson, completed a fact-finding mission to the region; her final report expressed concerns regarding the deterioration of human rights in the Palestinian territories and recommended the presence there of international monitors. Violence escalated in late November, when Israel launched air-strikes against PNA offices in Gaza, in reprisal for the deaths of two people in the bombing of a school bus for Jewish settlers. Two days later another two Israelis were killed in a car bombing perpetrated by Palestinian militants in northern Israel, apparently in retaliation for the deaths of four Fatah officials.

Despite the ongoing violence, Israeli-Palestinian negotiations were resumed in late November 2000, partly as a result of Russian diplomatic efforts. At the end of the month the PNA rejected a partial peace plan, announced by Barak, whereby Israel would withdraw its armed forces from additional West Bank territory on condition that the PNA agree to postpone any discussion of the remaining 'final status' issues. Violent confrontations between Palestinian police and civilians and Israeli troops in the West Bank and Gaza persisted throughout December. In that month Israeli settlers increasingly became the target of Palestinian attacks, while Palestinians frequently used automatic weapons against Israeli troops. Under pressure from the USA, in early December Israel eased some of the economic sanctions imposed on the Palestinian territories at the outbreak of the crisis. In mid-December the US-led commission of inquiry began conducting investigations into the violence. Shortly afterwards five Palestinian policemen were killed by Israeli forces during a gun battle in the Gaza Strip.

Meanwhile, the USA was evidently keen to continue negotiations aimed at reaching a framework agreement on permanent status prior to the expiry of President Clinton's term of office in January 2001. (By this time indications were strong that George W. Bush, who had been elected to the US presidency in November 2000, would be less actively engaged in the Middle East peace process than Clinton.) Moreover, Barak was under increasing pressure from his supporters to conclude a peace deal with the PNA, in order to minimize the chances of a victory for Ariel Sharon in the Israeli premiership election scheduled for February 2001. A further round of peace talks opened in mid-December 2000, at which the US President was reported to have proposed a peace deal that included plans for a future Palestinian state covering the Gaza Strip and some 95% of the West Bank, as well as granting the Palestinians sovereignty over the Islamic holy sites in the Old City of Jerusalem. However, the

US plan also required that Palestinians renounce the right of return for 3.7m. refugees to Israel, which the PNA and other Arab states deemed unacceptable. The negotiations broke down in late December after two Israelis died in bombings carried out by Palestinian militants in Tel-Aviv and the Gaza Strip. Tensions increased further at the end of the month, when a prominent Jewish settler and a senior member of Fatah were both shot dead in the West Bank. In early January 2001 Arafat visited Washington, DC, to seek official clarification of the Clinton proposals. (Israel was reported to have cautiously accepted the plan as a basis for further talks.) Meanwhile, following a car bomb explosion in northern Israel, the Israeli authorities once again tightened their blockade of the West Bank and Gaza. Israel subsequently confirmed its policy of assassinating local Palestinian officials who were regarded as endangering Israeli society. Israeli-Palestinian discussions aimed at securing a breakthrough prior to the Israeli premiership election opened at the Egyptian resort of Taba on 21 January. However, Israel suspended the talks two days later, after two Israeli civilians were killed in a gun attack, for which Hamas claimed responsibility, in the West Bank. Shortly afterwards the international inquiry committee suspended its sessions, accusing the Israeli Government of failing to co-operate.

The success of Ariel Sharon in the Israeli premiership election in early February 2001 provoked violent demonstrations by Palestinians in the West Bank and Gaza, in protest at the election of a man whom (as Israel's Minister of Defence at that time) they blamed for the massacre of Palestinian refugees in Lebanese camps in 1982 (see the chapter on Israel). Immediately after Sharon's election Palestinian militants carried out a car bombing in Jerusalem. A few days later another senior Fatah official was assassinated by Israeli security forces. In mid-February a Palestinian bus driver, apparently acting alone, launched an attack on Israeli soldiers and civilians in Tel-Aviv, killing nine people. Israel responded by again closing the West Bank and Gaza Strip. According to the Palestine Red Crescent Society, by late February 2001 at least 360 Palestinians had been killed and more than 11,000 injured since the start of the al-Aqsa *intifada*.

After Barak's victory in May 1999, one of Arafat's principal concerns was the Israeli concentration of efforts on the Lebanese and, especially, Syrian elements of the Middle East peace process. Any possibility of a breakthrough in Israeli-Syrian negotiations (which resumed in early December) would leave the Palestinians in a position of isolation. In mid-June Arafat was reported to have accused both the Jordanian and Syrian leaders of having abandoned the PNA. In August a political crisis developed after the Syrian Deputy Prime Minister and Minister of Defence, Maj.-Gen. Mustafa Tlass, was reported to have made highly insulting remarks about Yasser Arafat—including a claim that Arafat had 'sold Jerusalem and the Arab nation' in peace deals concluded with Israel since 1993—leading to Palestinian demands for the Syrian minister's resignation, and the issuing, by Fatah, of a death warrant for him. Despite Arafat's poor relations with the Syrian regime, he attended the funeral of President Hafiz al-Assad in June 2000.

Palestinians reacted to the death of King Hussein of Jordan on 7 February 1999 with public grief—about 65% of the Kingdom's inhabitants are believed to be of Palestinian origin—especially in the West Bank, which King Hussein ruled for 15 years until June 1967. For Arafat, the death of Hussein was a political disaster since the King had frequently supported him when the peace process with Israel appeared to be on the verge of collapse. Arafat subsequently surprised many Jordanians by proposing the establishment of a Palestinian-Jordanian confederation. The proposal (which had been put forward as part of a peace initiative in 1985, but was rejected by King Hussein) was not welcomed in Jordan, where it was considered to be premature while the West Bank was still largely under Israeli occupation.

Elections to a Palestinian Legislative Council (PLC) took place on 20 January 1996. Some 79% of the estimated 1m. eligible Palestinian voters were reported to have participated in the elections, returning 88 deputies to the 89-seat Council. (One seat was automatically reserved for the president of the Council's executive body—the Palestinian President.) Yasser Arafat took 88.1% of the votes cast at the concurrent election for a Palestinian Executive President (Arafat was opposed by one other candidate, Samiha Khalil), and took office as President on 12 February 1996. Deputies returned to the PLC automatically became members of the PNC, the existing 483 members

of which were subsequently permitted to return from exile by the Israeli authorities. The PLC held its first session in Gaza City on 7 March, electing Ahmad Quray as its Speaker.

At the 21st session of the PNC, held in Gaza City on 22–24 April 1996, the PNC voted to amend the Palestinian National Charter by annulling those clauses that sought the destruction of the State of Israel. The PNC also voted to amend all clauses contained within the Charter that were not in harmony with the agreement of mutual recognition concluded by Israel and the PLO in September 1993. At the end of its session the PNC elected a new Executive Committee, and in May 1996 President Arafat appointed a Palestinian Cabinet. The appointments were approved by the PLC in July.

In April 1997 Arafat's audit office disclosed what it had found to be the misappropriation by PNA ministers of some US $326m. of public funds. The PNA General Prosecutor, Khalid al-Qidram, resigned in response to the findings, and was reportedly placed under house arrest in June. The Cabinet submitted its resignation in August (in accordance with the findings of a parliamentary committee appointed by Arafat to investigate the affair, which had concluded that the Cabinet should be dissolved and some of its members prosecuted); however, this was not accepted by the President until December, when it was announced that ministers would remain in office in a provisional capacity until new ministerial appointments were made in early 1998. In March the PLC threatened to conduct a vote of 'no-confidence' in President Arafat's leadership in protest at alleged corruption within the PNA, as well as at the prolonged delay in approval of budget proposals for 1998 and at the failure to hold local government elections. (There was speculation that the PNA had deferred local elections because it was concerned that the results would reveal widespread dissatisfaction at the way in which peace negotiations with Israel were being conducted.) The Cabinet resigned in June, apparently in order to obstruct a renewed attempt by the PLC to institute a motion of 'no-confidence' in it. The new Cabinet, appointed by Arafat in August, included several new ministers; however, only one minister of the outgoing administration was actually dismissed, and two prominent ministers immediately resigned, on the grounds that the reshuffle had failed adequately to address the shortcomings of the PNA. The new Cabinet was also criticized by officials of the principal international organizations granting funds to the PNA. During September 1998 the chief negotiator at the peace talks and Minister of Local Government, Saeb Erakat, and the Minister of State for the Environment, Yousuf Abu Saffieh, were both persuaded by Arafat to withdraw their resignations, tendered in protest at inefficiency and incompetence within the PNA. In October the PNA was again accused of financial mismanagement, after customs revenues amounting to some US $70m. allegedly failed to be deposited at the PNA treasury. In November, nevertheless, donors agreed to grant the PNA more than US $3,000m., to be disbursed over the next five years.

In addition to persistent allegations of corruption within the PNA, President Arafat himself has at times been the target of accusations of autocracy from other members of the Palestinian leadership. Furthermore, there have been frequent claims that the Palestinian security forces have resorted to intimidation and torture in their treatment of detainees. Such allegations were contained in a report published by the US-based Human Rights Watch in 1998. In February of that year, in its annual report, the Palestinian Independent Commission for Citizens' Rights accused Palestinian security personnel of the mistreatment of prisoners.

In February 1998 Arafat instigated firm action to suppress popular demonstrations in support of Iraq, which was under threat of military action by the USA as a result of the dispute over UN-conducted weapons inspections (see the chapter on Iraq). It was reported that many members of Arafat's own political movement, Fatah, had been arrested for flouting a ban on such protests, and that the publication and broadcasting of reports in support of President Saddam Hussein of Iraq had been forbidden.

US officials were reported to have confirmed in March 1998 that the CIA was assisting the Palestinian security forces in the spheres of espionage, information-gathering and interrogation in an attempt to reassure the Israeli Government of the PNA's ability to take effective action against groups involved in attacks on Israeli targets. Later that month the death of a senior Hamas official provoked a serious deterioration in relations between the Islamist organization and the PNA. Hamas accused the PNA of colluding with the Israeli authorities in the killing of Muhi ad-Din Sharif, and its threats to wreak revenge on Israeli citizens prompted the PNA to arrest many of its members. In April, however, Hamas's political leader in Jordan retracted the allegation that the PNA had collaborated with Israel. In October the PNA detained 11 journalists who had attempted to obtain an interview with the spiritual leader of Hamas, Sheikh Ahmad Yassin (who was subsequently placed under house arrest); Palestinian police also arrested an outspoken cleric and Islamic Jihad's chief spokesman for publicly criticizing the newly-signed Wye Memorandum. In subsequent weeks several radio and television stations, as well as press offices, were closed down by the PNA, and numerous journalists were imprisoned on various charges. There was also a marked increase in self-censorship in the state-controlled and pro-Government media.

In January 1999 the PLC approved a motion urging an end to political detentions and the release of all those imprisoned on exclusively political charges. The motion further demanded the formation of a special committee to assess the case of every political prisoner in the Palestinian territories and to recommend which prisoners should be released: the committee was duly appointed in February, under the chairmanship of the Minister of Justice. Meanwhile, the PNA responded to the PLC's immediate demands by releasing 37 political prisoners. However, in late January many detainees linked to Hamas and Islamic Jihad began a hunger strike in Jericho and Nablus, in protest at their continued detention without trial. In early February some 3,000 protesters marched to the PNA headquarters, accusing the Palestinian leadership of 'subservience to Israel and the CIA' (under the terms of the Wye Memorandum, the CIA was to monitor the PNA's compliance with the security provisions as part of a trilateral committee involving the PNA and Israel), and throughout the month thousands of Palestinians—mostly Hamas supporters—demonstrated in support of the detainees.

Also in February 1999 a Gaza-based police chief, known to be an opponent of Hamas, alleged that the organization had received some US \$35m. from Iran in order to carry out suicide bombings against Israeli targets. Both Iran and Hamas leaders strongly denied the allegations. Relations between the PNA and Hamas were further strained following the murder of a Palestinian intelligence officer in Rafah. In March a security agent and former member of Hamas' military wing was sentenced to death for the killing, while two accomplices received lengthy prison sentences. The verdict provoked serious clashes between Palestinian police and protesters in the Gaza Strip, during which two youths were shot dead by police; Arafat was forced to curtail an official visit to Jordan to address the domestic security crisis. Security surrounding the President was intensified in June, after a group of Palestinian dissidents calling themselves 'the Free Officers and the Honest People of Palestine' released a statement accusing leading Palestinian officials of corruption and of collaboration with Israel, and containing a veiled threat to assassinate the President; nine arrests were subsequently made.

In August 1999 a Palestinian national dialogue conference was held in Cairo, Egypt, between representatives of Arafat's Fatah movement and the Popular Front for the Liberation of Palestine (PFLP). Later in August Arafat and the Secretary-General of the Democratic Front for the Liberation of Palestine (DFLP), Naif Hawatmeh, met, also in Cairo, for the first time since 1993. At the end of the month representatives of nine Palestinian political factions, meeting in Ramallah, agreed on an agenda for a comprehensive national dialogue; Hamas and Islamic Jihad, however, refused to enter the dialogue. (In late August 1999 the PNA reportedly arrested several suspected activists of these two organizations in the West Bank and the Gaza Strip, while the Jordanian authorities closed Hamas' offices in Amman.) It was reported in September that the leader of the PFLP, George Habash, was to resign. In late September the organization's deputy leader, Abu Ali Moustafa, was permitted by the Israeli Government to return to the West Bank from exile in Jordan, in order to participate in reconciliation talks with Arafat. However, although in late October Israeli officials had also reportedly granted an entry permit to the DFLP leader, they subsequently cancelled Hawatmeh's right of return. (Habash finally stepped down in late April 2000, and Ali Abu Moustafa was elected as the new PFLP leader in early July.)

In October 1999 Arafat issued a presidential decree granting ministerial status to the Chairman of the Palestinian Public Control Commission. In November 20 leading Palestinian intellectuals (including members of the PLC) issued a joint statement in which they criticized alleged corruption, mismanagement and abuse of power within the PNA, and accused Palestinian officials of ineffectiveness in the peace talks with Israel. The authorities responded by launching a crack-down on Arafat's critics, detaining several of the document's signatories or placing them under house arrest (they were later released on bail). In December a PLC member who had signed the anti-corruption manifesto was wounded by unidentified gunmen in Nablus. The establishment, announced in January 2000, of a Higher Council for Development, under Arafat's chairmanship was welcomed by foreign donors as a major step towards ending corruption and mismanagement within the Palestinian administration.

On 2–3 February 2000 the Palestinian Central Council convened in Gaza. Eight political organizations were represented, although Hamas and Islamic Jihad boycotted the sessions. PFLP members chose not to attend, having presented their positions beforehand. The meeting's final communiqué urged Arafat to declare an independent Palestinian state by September of that year (see above).

In mid-March 2000 the Minister of Social Affairs, Intisar al-Wasir, tendered her resignation, following a reduction in the funds to be allocated to her ministry. Arafat refused to accept the minister's resignation. Two separate incidents were reported in that month in which senior Palestinian officials were allegedly assaulted by members of the security forces. Meanwhile, in late 1999 the US-based Human Rights Watch had urged Arafat to take action in order to increase press freedom. At the end of May 2000 the chief news editor at the Voice of Palestine radio station, Fathi Barqawi, was arrested after publicly criticizing the PNA's 'secret talks' with Israel in Sweden. During May and June the PNA intensified its crack-down on political activists and journalists who were critical of Arafat's administration; four television and two radio stations were reportedly shut down, and a number of journalists, among them members of Fatah and the PFLP, were detained (although most were later released). At the end of July security forces in Gaza arrested Abd al-Aziz ar-Rantisi, a leading Hamas official, on charges including incitement and defamation.

After Palestinians began a new *intifada* against Israeli occupation in late September 2000 (see above), some analysts suggested that Arafat's influence over Palestinians in the West Bank and Gaza might be waning, as other Fatah leaders began to pursue their own agendas and became increasingly outspoken against the President. In particular, the leader of Fatah in the West Bank, Marwan Barghouti, was said to attract considerable support among Palestinians there. In early December a court in Nablus sentenced to death a Palestinian who had been convicted of collaborating with Israeli secret services in the assassination of a Hamas commander. The harsh sentence signalled a change in policy by the PNA, which in January 2001 carried out the executions, by firing squad, of two alleged collaborators. The executions were criticized by human rights organizations in the Palestinian self-rule areas and internationally. In mid-January Hisham Mekki, the Chairman of Palestinian Satellite Television and a director of the state broadcasting corporation (who had been a close associate of Arafat), was assassinated by unidentified gunmen in Gaza. A militant Palestinian group, the al-Aqsa Martyrs Brigade, claimed responsibility for the killing, and accused the President of failing to end official corruption. The PNA, for its part, accused Palestinian collaborators with Israel of being behind the attack; Israel vehemently denied the claim.

Government

In accordance with the Declaration of Principles on Palestinian Self-Rule of September 1993, and the Cairo Agreement on the Gaza Strip and Jericho, the PLO assumed control of the Jericho area of the West Bank and of the Gaza Strip on 17 May 1994. In November and December 1995, under the terms of the Israeli-Palestinian Interim Agreement on the West Bank and the Gaza Strip signed by Israel and the PLO on 28 September 1995, Israeli armed forces withdrew from the West Bank towns of Nablus, Ramallah, Jenin, Tulkarm, Qalqilya and Bethlehem. In late December the PLO assumed responsibility in some 17 areas of civil administration in the town of Hebron. The Interim Agreement divided the West Bank into three zones: Areas A, B and C. As of July 1998, the PNA had sole jurisdiction and security control in Area A (2% of the West Bank), but Israel retained authority over movement into and out of the Area. In Area B (26% of the West Bank) the PNA had some limited authority while Israel maintained a security presence and 'over-riding security responsibility'. Area C, the remaining 72% of the West Bank, was under Israeli military occupation. In accordance with the Wye Memorandum of October 1998 (see Recent History, above), Israel effected a further redeployment of its armed forces from approximately 500 sq km of West Bank territory in November. Of this, about 400 sq km became Area A territory and the remainder Area B territory. After full implementation of the Wye Memorandum Area A will constitute 17.2% of the West Bank, Area B 23.9% and Area C 58.9%. The Sharm esh-Sheikh Memorandum of September 1999 (see Recent History) was intended to facilitate completion of outstanding commitments under agreements previously signed, as well as to enable the resumption of 'final status' talks. By February 2000 approximately 26.9% of the West Bank was under Israeli military control, with responsibility for civil administration transferred to the Palestinian authorities; about 12.1% was under full Palestinian control; and about 61% was under complete Israeli control. The total area of the West Bank over which the PNA will eventually assume control, and the extent of its jurisdiction there, remain subject to 'final status' negotiations with Israel.

Defence

Paramilitary forces in the Gaza Strip and in the areas of the West Bank where the PNA has assumed responsibility for security totalled an estimated 35,000 in August 2000. They included a Public Security Force of 14,000 (Gaza 6,000, West Bank 8,000); a Civil Police Force of 10,000 (Gaza 4,000, West Bank 6,000); a Preventive Security Force of 3,000 (Gaza 1,200, West Bank 1,800); a General Intelligence Force of 3,000; a Military Intelligence Force of 500; and a Presidential Security Force of 1,000. In addition, there are small forces belonging to Coastal Police, Civil Defence, Air Force, a Customs and Excise Police Force and a University Security Service. Units of the Palestine National Liberation Army (PNLA) are garrisoned in various countries in the Middle East and North Africa. The security budget of the Gaza Strip and the Palestinian Autonomous Areas of the West Bank was estimated at US $500m. in 1999.

Economic Affairs

In 1998, according to estimates by the World Bank, the gross national product (GNP) of the West Bank and the Gaza Strip, measured at average 1996–98 prices, was US $4,263m., equivalent to $1,560 per head. Expressed in Israeli new shekels at constant 1986 prices, the IMF estimated that the GNP of the West Bank and the Gaza Strip declined at an average annual rate of 0.8%, and that GNP per head declined at an average annual rate of 5.4%, in 1995–97. Over the same period the population increased by an estimated annual average rate of 5.0%. The World Bank estimated population growth averaging 4.5% annually in 1990–98. GNP totalled an estimated US $4,559m. ($1,610 per head) in 1999. The IMF estimates that in 1995–97 the gross domestic product (GDP) of the West Bank and Gaza declined, in real terms, at an average annual rate of 1.3%. According to the PNA, GDP increased by 7.0% in 1998 and by an estimated 6.0% in 1999.

Agriculture and fishing contributed 9.5% of the GDP of the West Bank and the Gaza Strip in 1998. In 1999 agriculture (including hunting, forestry and fishing) engaged an estimated 12.7% of the employed labour force of the West Bank and Gaza Strip. Although the agricultural sector is focused mainly on supplying local needs, about one-half of Palestinian exports are derived from agricultural production. Citrus fruits are the principal export crop, and horticulture also makes a significant contribution to trade. Other important crops are tomatoes, cucumbers, olives, potatoes and grapes.

Industry (mining and quarrying, manufacturing, electricity and water supply and construction) contributed 31.2% of the GDP of the West Bank and the Gaza Strip in 1998. The industrial sector (including gas utilities) engaged an estimated 38.4% of the employed labour force of the West Bank and Gaza in 1999; construction alone accounted for 10.8% of GDP and employed some 19.9% of the working population.

Mining and quarrying contributed 0.7% of the GDP of the West Bank and the Gaza Strip in 1998, and engaged an estimated 0.3% of the total labour force in 1999. Two significant gas fields were discovered off the Gaza coast in mid-1999.

Manufacturing contributed 17.8% of the GDP of the West Bank and the Gaza Strip in 1998. In 1999 an estimated 15.3% of the total labour force of the West Bank and Gaza Strip were employed in the sector. Palestinian manufacturing is character-ized by small-scale enterprises which typically engage in food-processing and the production of textiles and footwear. The frequent closure of the West Bank and the Gaza Strip by the Israeli authorities has prompted the development of free-trade industrial zones on the Palestinian side of the boundaries separating Israel from the territories: Israeli and Palestinian enterprises can continue to take advantage of low-cost Palestinian labour at times of closure, and the zones also benefit from tax exemptions and export incentives.

In the West Bank there is no utility supplying electric power apart from the Jerusalem District Electric Company, which supplies Jerusalem, Bethlehem, Ramallah and Al-Birah. Most municipalities in the Gaza Strip purchase electricity from the Israel Electric Corporation. However, the Palestine Electric Company—established in 1999—is constructing a power plant in Gaza, while the National Electric Company—created in 2000—plans to build a second power plant in the West Bank.

In 1998 the services sector contributed 59.3% of the GDP of the West Bank and the Gaza Strip. Within the services sector, real estate and business services contributed 11.7% of GDP, and wholesale and retail trade 12.8%. In 1999 the services sector engaged an estimated 48.9% of the employed labour force of the West Bank and the Gaza Strip. In that year some 14.6% of the working population were employed in the wholesale and retail trade, and 11.2% in public administration and defence.

In 1998, according to IMF estimates, the West Bank and the Gaza Strip recorded a deficit on trade in goods and services of US $1,839m. and a deficit of $748m. on the current account of the balance of payments. In 1997 the value of exports (f.o.b.) to Israel was estimated at $358m., while the value of imports from Israel amounted to an estimated $1,803m. In the absence of seaport facilities and of an airport (Gaza International Airport was opened in November 1998 and has frequently been closed by the Israeli authorities) foreign trade (in terms of value) has been conducted almost exclusively with Israel since occupation. Most Palestinian exports are of agricultural or horticultural products. One notable feature of this trade is that Palestinian goods have often in the past been exported to Israel, and subsequently re-exported as originating in Israel.

In 1998, according to data published by the IMF, the PNA recorded an overall budget deficit of US $144.7m., equivalent to some 3.4% of GDP. The annual rate of inflation in the West Bank and the Gaza Strip averaged 5.4% in 1996–2000; consumer prices increased by an average of 5.5% in 1999, but inflation slowed to an average of 2.8% in 2000. Preliminary figures published by the PNA estimated that 11.8% of the labour force were unemployed in 1999.

The prospects for an improvement in economic conditions in the Emerging Palestinian Autonomous Areas, which remain highly dependent on Israel, are inextricably linked to the full implementation of the Oslo accords (see Recent History, above) and the outcome of 'final status' negotiations between the PNA and Israel. The two most striking examples of this economic dependency are the large number of Palestinian workers employed in Israel, and the reliance of the trade sector on Israel as a market for exports and source of imports, and—to a lesser extent—as a conduit for wider international trade. The underdevelopment of Palestinian agriculture and industry is a consequence of the Israeli occupation, when investment became orientated towards residential construction at the expense of these sectors. Agriculture remains focused mainly on meeting local demand, although the sector supplies the bulk of Palestinian exports and there is proven demand for Palestinian products beyond the Israeli market. The expansion of Palestinian agriculture is also limited by problems with irrigation: access to water supplies is subject to 'final status' negotiations with Israel. Economic conditions in the West Bank and Gaza have deteriorated markedly since 1993, largely as a result of frequent border closures enforced by the Israeli authorities in reprisal for terrorist attacks by militant Islamist groups which reject the Oslo accords. Such closures lead to an immediate rise in the already high rate of unemployment among Palestinians, increase transportation costs for Palestinian goods and, at times, halt trade entirely. The Oslo accords provide for the development of seaport facilities, the opening of Gaza International Airport and the opening of a safe passage linking the Gaza Strip with the West Bank. By February 2001 the provision for a seaport at Gaza had still not been implemented (although in April 2000 a contract to construct the port was signed by the PNA and a Franco-Dutch consortium). Since 1998 the aim of the PNA has been to achieve current budget surpluses, and to focus public expenditure on health, education and on investment in infrastructure. In 2000, for the first time, the PNA forecast a balanced budget, with both revenue and expenditure set at US $1,386m. In early 2000 the PNA announced the creation of a Palestinian Investment Fund and a Higher Council for Development, the latter being charged with the preparation of a comprehensive privatization strategy by May. However, in the context of the renewed Palestinian *intifada*, in November 2000 the Israeli authorities imposed a complete economic blockade on the West Bank and Gaza, and halted the payment of tax transfers to the PNA. The closure quickly reversed any recent economic successes: in the first half of 2000 unemployment had been reported to be declining, GDP growth was strong, and private-sector investment was increasing sharply. By January 2001, however, economic losses as a result of the blockade were estimated at more than US $1,000m.; furthermore, long-term investment programmes were being replaced by short-term projects aimed at reducing soaring levels of both unemployment and poverty. In October 2000 Arab states pledged aid worth US $1,000m., although by late January 2001 the PNA had reportedly received only $237m. In November 2000 the European Union authorized the payment of $23m. from its special cash facility to the PNA, in an attempt to ease the chronic economic situation. In December the World Bank also announced that it was to grant $12m. for an Emergency Response Programme.

Social Welfare

Programmes operated by the United Nations Relief and Works Agency for Palestine Refugees in the Near East (UNRWA) form the basis of the social welfare system in the West Bank and the Gaza Strip, since about 45% of the population there are registered refugees. UNRWA assists refugee families principally by providing direct material and financial support to those in special hardship. Following the signing of the Declaration of Principles on Palestinian Self-Rule in 1993, UNRWA introduced a Peace Implementation Programme in order to improve infrastructure, create employment and improve conditions among Palestinian refugees. An Income Generation Programme provides working capital at commercial rates to small enterprises to assist in the creation of sustainable employment and in the elimination of poverty. In the Gaza Strip, where UNRWA's income-generation efforts are concentrated, the programme is the largest and most successful of its kind.

Palestinians working for Israeli employers are required to participate in Israel's national social security scheme. However, taxes deducted from Palestinian workers finance only very limited benefits to Palestinians as residency in Israel is a requirement to qualify for most Israeli schemes. The PNA administers a pension scheme for public sector employees, who represent about 15% of the work-force.

UNRWA provides primary health care through 34 facilities in the West Bank and 16 in the Gaza Strip. Health staff number 665 in the West Bank and 915 in the Gaza Strip. Primary services include outpatient care, disease prevention and control, maternal and child health care and family planning. UNRWA also assists with secondary care by means of contractual agreements with non-governmental and private hospitals, or through the partial reimbursement of treatment costs. UNRWA operates a 43-bed hospital in Qalqilya, West Bank. According to the PCBS, in 1999 there were nine PNA-operated hospitals in the West Bank, and six in the Gaza Strip. Since 1994 the Government has sought to expand health care facilities in the Palestinian territories. According to government figures, there were 369 primary health care centres in 1998, compared with 207 in 1994.

Health services are also provided by the Israeli Civil Administration (excluding those areas where civil jurisdiction has been transferred to the PNA), private voluntary organizations and private, profit-seeking organizations. Institutions operated by the Israeli Civil Administration in the West Bank derive from Jordanian systems. Until 1974, when a Government Health Insurance (GHI) system was introduced, residents of the West Bank were entitled to free health care from these facilities. Now only members of the GHI scheme may receive comprehensive care at government facilities without charge. Prenatal care and preventive services are provided by the Civil Administration free of charge to all children under the age of three years.

Education

Since 1950 UNRWA has provided education services to all Palestinian refugees. The focus of UNRWA's education programme is basic primary and junior secondary schooling, offered free of charge to all refugee children and youth in accordance with local systems. In the 1997/98 school year UNRWA operated 267 schools in the West Bank and the Gaza Strip. The number of pupils receiving education through the UNRWA programme in that year was 200,886. Education personnel numbered 3,682. In addition, UNRWA operated four vocational training centres and provided 410 university scholarships.

In 1999/2000 a total of 77,402 pupils attended 843 pre-primary institutions, and 792,990 attended 1,259 primary institutions. In the same year 72,550 students attended secondary institutions. The number of students attending universities or equivalent third-level institutions was 44,987.

Public Holidays

2001: 1 January (Fatah Day), 6 March* (Id al-Adha, Feast of the Sacrifice), 15 November (Independence Day), 17 December* (Id al-Fitr, end of Ramadan).

2002: 1 January (Fatah Day), 23 February* (Id al-Adha, Feast of the Sacrifice), 15 November (Independence Day), 6 December* (Id al-Fitr, end of Ramadan).

* These holidays are dependent on the Islamic lunar calendar and may vary by one or two days from the dates given.

Christian holidays are observed by the Christian Arab community.

Statistical Survey of the West Bank and the Gaza Strip

Source (unless otherwise indicated): Palestinian Central Bureau of Statistics (PCBS), POB 1647, Ramallah, West Bank, Palestine; tel. 2-2406340; fax 2-2406343; e-mail diwan@pcbs.pna.org; internet www.pcbs.org.

Note: Unless otherwise indicated, data include East Jerusalem, annexed by Israel in 1967.

Area and Population

AREA, POPULATION AND DENSITY

Area (sq km) .		6,004*
Population (census of 9 December 1997)†		
Males .		1,470,506
Females		1,425,177
Total		2,895,683
Population (official estimates at mid-year)		
1998		2,897,452
1999		3,019,704
2000		3,150,056
Density (per sq km) at mid-2000†		524.7

* 2,318.2 sq miles. The total comprises: West Bank 5,633 sq km (2,175 sq miles); Gaza Strip 371 sq km (143.2 sq miles).

† Figures include an estimate of 210,209 for East Jerusalem and an adjustment of 83,805 for estimated underenumeration. The total comprises 1,873,476 (males 951,693; females 921,783) in the West Bank (including East Jerusalem) and 1,022,207 (males 518,813; females 503,394) in the Gaza Strip. The data exclude Jewish settlers. According to official Israeli estimates, the population of Israelis residing in Jewish localities in the West Bank (excluding East Jerusalem) and Gaza Strip was 172,200 at 31 December 1998.

GOVERNORATES (official estimates, mid-2000)

	Area (sq km)	Popu-lation*	Density (per sq km)
West Bank			
Janin (Jenin)	578	216,126	373.9
Tubas	349	39,239	112.4
Tulkarm	244	142,865	585.5
Qalqilya.	165	78,029	472.9
Salfit	205	52,137	254.3
Nabulus (Nablus) . . .	612	278,317	454.8
Ram Allah (Ramallah) and Al-Birah	847	231,690	273.5
Al-Quds (Jerusalem)† . .	341	354,417	1,039.3
Ariha (Jericho) . . .	652	35,352	54.2
Beit Lahm (Bethlehem) . .	632	147,121	232.8
Al-Khalil (Hebron) . . .	1,008	436,637	433.2
Gaza Strip			
North Gaza	64	209,768	3,287.9
Gaza	71	404,973	5,736.2
Deir al-Balah . . .	62	164,919	2,681.6
Khan Yunus (Khan Yunis) . .	117	222,157	1,895.5
Rafah	58	136,309	2,362.4
Total	6,004	3,150,056	524.7

* Figures exclude Jewish settlers.

† The figure refers only to the eastern sector of the city.

PRINCIPAL LOCALITIES
(estimated population at mid-2000, excluding Jewish settlers)

West Bank

Al-Quds (Jerusalem)	228,152*	Adh-Dhahiriya .	22,989
Al-Khalil (Hebron) .	133,586	Ar-Ram and Dahiyat	
Nabulus (Nablus) .	110,966	al-Bareed . .	21,027
Tulkarm . .	37,589	Ram Allah (Ramallah) .	20,318
Qalqilya . .	35,791	Halhul . . .	17,545
Yattah (Yatta) .	34,485	Dura . . .	17,345
Al-Birah . .	31,545	Ariha (Jericho) .	16,546
Janin (Jenin) . .	29,526	Qabatiya . . .	16,261
Beit Lahm (Bethlehem)	24,444		

Gaza Strip

Ghazzah (Gaza) .	328,077	Beit Lahya .	44,898
Rafah . . .	104,192†	Deir al-Balah . .	39,311
Khan Yunus (Khan		Bani Suhayla . .	26,017
Yunis) . .	100,118	Beit Hanun . .	24,271
Jabalyah . .	62,495	Tel as-Sultan Camp .	19,243
An-Nuseirat . .	50,904	Al-Maghazi Camp .	19,188

* The figure refers only to the eastern sector of the city.

† Including the population of an associated refugee camp.

BIRTHS AND DEATHS (estimated)*

	1997	1998
Live births*		
West Bank	73,586	74,891
Gaza Strip	45,214	46,844
Deaths		
West Bank	8,686	8,788
Gaza Strip	4,630	4,689

* Excluding Jewish settlers.

Source: Ministry of Health, *Annual Report*.

MARRIAGES (number registered)

	1997	1998	1999
West Bank	15,883	16,285	16,099
Gaza Strip	7,609	8,115	8,775

ECONOMICALLY ACTIVE POPULATION*
('000 persons aged 10 years and over, labour force survey, 1999)

	Males	Females	Total
Agriculture, hunting, forestry and fishing	47	28	75
Mining and quarrying	2	—	2
Manufacturing	79	11	90
Electricity, gas and water supply	1	—	1
Construction	132	1	133
Wholesale and retail trade	80	6	86
Hotels and restaurants	15	—	15
Transport, storage and communications	28	1	29
Financial intermediation	4	1	5
Real estate, renting and business activities	8	2	10
Public administration and defence	61	5	66
Education	27	23	50
Health and social work	12	7	19
Other community, social and personal service activities	4	1	5
Extra-territorial organizations and bodies	2	1	3
Total employed	502	87	589
Unemployed	67	11	78
Total labour force	569	98	667
West Bank	387	75	462
Gaza Strip	182	23	205

* Figures refer to Palestinians only.

Agriculture

PRINCIPAL CROPS ('000 metric tons, year ending September)

	1995/96	1996/97	1997/98
Wheat	30.9	28.3	36.5
Barley	20.4	14.2	15.7
Maize	7.5	9.0	5.1
Potatoes	54.6	45.0	58.7
Olives	130.5	50.7	98.1
Cabbages	10.7	14.5	14.3
Tomatoes	122.5	140.7	153.7
Cauliflower	16.0	15.2	20.4
Squash	41.5	44.3	39.2
Cucumbers	91.3	106.6	100.7
Aubergines (Eggplants)	30.7	43.0	36.3
Hot pepper	11.4	15.7	14.6
Onions	23.3	39.6	19.8
Okra	9.5	4.3	2.9
Jew's mallow	16.3	11.9	13.5
Watermelons	7.6	15.5	19.8
Musk-melons	4.0	11.8	9.0
Grapes	57.0	52.8	56.9
Plums	12.4	0.8	5.6
Oranges*	117.1	114.6	101.5
Mandarins and clementines	23.9	20.8	18.9
Lemons	15.9	24.5	27.2
Grapefruit	6.6	8.5	10.0
Bananas	19.8	23.1	20.6
Figs	8.6	6.5	6.8
Guava	14.7	12.9	15.0
Almonds	8.4	6.5	5.1

* Valencia, Shamouti and navel oranges.

LIVESTOCK ('000 head, year ending September)*

	1995/96	1996/97	1997/98
Cattle	19.3	21.0	22.1
Sheep	634.5	504.9	538.0
Goats	272.6	267.1	252.3
Chickens	27,196	37,481	40,611

* Including estimates for the Gaza Strip.

Fishing

Gaza Strip (metric tons, live weight)

	1996	1997	1998
Bogue	9	81	162
Jack and horse mackerels	90	100	115
Sardinellas	978	2,483	1,780
Little tunny	90	59	61
Chub mackerel	130	120	337
Shrimps and prawns	55	161	161
Cuttlefish and bobtail squids	62	98	144
Total catch (incl. others)	2,493	3,791	3,625

Source: FAO, *Yearbook of Fishery Statistics*.

Finance

CURRENCY AND EXCHANGE RATES

At present there is no domestic Palestinian currency in use. The Israeli shekel, the Jordanian dinar and the US dollar all circulate within the West Bank and the Gaza Strip.

BUDGET OF THE PALESTINIAN AUTHORITY
(estimates, US $ million)

Revenue	1996	1997	1998
Domestic revenue	264.6	329.4	321.1
Tax revenue	178.8	210.9	224.3
Income tax	52.4	66.0	68.4
Value-added tax	65.8	75.0	80.6
Other receipts	85.8	118.5	96.8
Revenue clearances*	419.6	496.0	542.0
Value-added tax	216.7	216.5	202.1
Petroleum excise	100.4	111.3	106.8
Total	684.2	825.4	863.1

Expenditure†	1996	1997	1998
Current expenditure	779.3	863.2	802.6
Wages and salaries	402.5	470.9	466.8
Civil service	246.5	273.4	286.0
Police force	156.0	197.5	180.9
Other purposes	376.8	392.3	335.8
Capital expenditure	173.6	214.4	204.7
Total	952.9	1,077.6	1,007.3

* Figures refer to an apportionment of an agreed pool of selected tax revenues arising as a result of the *de facto* customs union between Israel and the Palestinian territories. Israel is the collecting agent for these receipts and periodically makes transfers to the Palestinian Authority.
† Excluding the cost of foreign-financed employment programmes (estimates, US $ million): 49.2 in 1996; 5.7 in 1997; 0.5 in 1998.
Source: IMF, *West Bank and Gaza Strip: Economic Developments in the Five Years Since Oslo (1999)*.

1999 (estimates, US $ million): Total revenue 1,589; Total expenditure 1,740.
2000 (estimates, US $ million): Total revenue 1,386; Total expenditure 1,386 (Current 940; Capital 446).

COST OF LIVING
(Consumer Price Index; base: 1996 = 100)

	1998	1999	2000
Food	113.9	119.3	121.2
Beverages and tobacco	117.1	126.9	130.2
Textiles, clothing and footwear	121.9	123.2	125.9
Housing	109.4	116.7	126.5
All items (incl. others)	113.6	119.9	123.3

NATIONAL ACCOUNTS
(US $ million at current prices)

Expenditure on the Gross Domestic Product

	1996	1997	1998
Government final consumption expenditure	852.4	893.6	905.5
Private final consumption expenditure	4,159.5	4,196.9	4,208.8
Increase in stocks . . .	63.1	85.8	64.4
Gross fixed capital formation . .	1,222.0	1,339.1	1,658.1
Statistical discrepancy* . . .	72.8	126.8	3.6
Total domestic expenditure	6,369.9	6,642.2	6,840.4
Exports of goods and services . .	838.9	812.6	1,017.7
Less Imports of goods and services	3,327.8	3,399.2	3,553.9
GDP in purchasers' values .	3,881.1	4,055.7	4,304.2

* Referring to the difference between the sum of the expenditure components and official estimates of GDP, compiled from the production approach.

Gross Domestic Product by Economic Activity

	1996	1997	1998
Agriculture and fishing . .	344.5	338.4	364.1
Mining and quarrying . .	25.9	26.5	25.5
Manufacturing . . .	708.2	672.3	681.3
Electricity and water supply .	59.2	73.5	76.1
Construction . . .	335.6	390.4	411.2
Wholesale and retail trade .	543.3	461.1	490.1
Hotels and restaurants . .	74.6	62.2	66.9
Transport, storage and communications . .	127.7	112.7	183.9
Financial intermediation . .	79.8	101.6	122.4
Real estate and business services*	400.3	437.8	446.6
Education . . .	175.2	245.0	260.4
Health and social work . .	129.8	105.8	122.9
Public administration and defence	424.6	432.0	403.6
Other community, social and personal services . . .	31.8	23.8	30.7
Domestic services of households	6.3	6.9	7.8
Public-owned enterprises . .	65.4	114.5	130.8
Sub-total . . .	3,532.2	3,604.7	3,824.3
Customs duties . . .	196.3	263.0	286.8
Value-added tax on imports (net)	216.6	273.0	292.1
Less Imputed bank service charges	64.1	85.0	99.0
GDP in purchasers' values .	3,881.1	4,055.7	4,304.2

* Including imputed rents of owner-occupied dwellings (estimated at around 60%).

BALANCE OF PAYMENTS
(provisional, US $ million, excluding East Jerusalem)

	1995	1996
Exports of goods f.o.b.	417.7	449.5
Imports of goods f.o.b.	−1,783.7	−2,123.2
Trade balance	−1,366.0	−1,673.7
Exports of services	132.0	132.7
Imports of services	−228.7	−244.8
Balance on goods and services . .	−1,462.6	−1,785.8
Other income received	550.4	487.7
Other income paid	−15.7	−18.8
Balance on goods, services and income	−927.9	−1,316.9
Current transfers received . . .	439.7	532.2
Current transfers paid	−85.7	−71.5
Current balance	−573.9	−856.2
Capital account (net)	237.2	271.3
Direct investment abroad . . .	n.a.	−52.4
Direct investment from abroad . .	n.a.	199.5
Portfolio investment assets . . .	n.a.	−19.2
Portfolio investment liabilities . .	n.a.	3.0
Other investment (net)	n.a.	96.5
Net errors and omissions . . .	n.a.	440.4
Overall balance	n.a.	83.0

External Trade

PRINCIPAL COMMODITIES (US $ '000)

Imports c.i.f.	1998	1999*	2000*
Food and live animals . .	447,195	533,787	576,490
Beverages and tobacco . .	97,494	116,372	125,682
Crude materials (inedible) except fuels . . .	67,185	80,194	86,610
Mineral fuels, lubricants, etc.. .	409,881	489,247	528,387
Animal and vegetable oils and fats	19,558	23,345	25,213
Chemicals and related products	189,739	226,479	244,597
Basic manufactures . . .	565,422	674,906	728,899
Machinery and transport equipment . . .	386,625	461,488	498,407
Miscellaneous manufactured articles	175,642	209,652	226,424
Other commodities and transactions . . .	14,363	17,144	18,516
Total . . .	2,375,102	2,835,000	3,061,800

* Estimates.

Exports f.o.b.	1998	1999*	2000*
Food and live animals . . .	61,793	64,019	66,260
Beverages and tobacco . . .	25,432	26,348	27,270
Crude materials (inedible) except fuels	17,566	18,199	18,836
Mineral fuels, lubricants, etc.. .	7,008	7,260	7,515
Animal and vegetable oils and fats	5,343	5,535	5,729
Chemicals and related products	24,631	25,518	26,412
Basic manufactures . . .	164,865	170,804	176,783
Machinery and transport equipment . . .	20,739	21,486	22,238
Miscellaneous manufactured articles	64,397	66,717	69,052
Other commodities and transactions	1,080	1,119	1,158
Total	392,854	407,007	421,252

* Estimates.

Transport

ROAD TRAFFIC
(registered motor vehicles holding Palestinian licence, December 1999)

	West Bank	Gaza Strip	Total
Private cars	62,268	36,469	98,737
Taxis	7,571	1,173	8,744
Buses and minibuses . .	846	157	1,003
Trucks and commercial cars .	15,604	8,445	24,049
Motorcycles and scooters . .	54	211	265
Tractors	2,720	1,279	3,999
Special service and other vehicles	127	133	260
Total	89,190	47,867	137,057

Tourism

ARRIVALS OF VISITORS AT HOTELS*

	1997	1998	1999
Total	220,850	214,220	316,871

* Including Palestinians (10,828 in 1997; 14,441 in 1998).

Communications Media

	1996	1997	1998
Book production*:			
Titles	114	n.a.	n.a.
Copies ('000)	571	n.a.	n.a.
Telephones in use	n.a.	95,729†	167,271

* Source: UNESCO, *Statistical Yearbook*.   † At August.
Telephones in use: 222,198 in 1999.

Education

(1999/2000)

	Institutions	Teachers	Students
Pre-primary	843	2,874	77,402
Primary	1,259*	}	792,990
Secondary:		29,186 {	
General	499†	}	69,788
Vocational	9		2,762
Higher:			
Universities, etc.. . .	12	1,822	44,987
Distance-learning . .	1	715	20,981
Other	17	467	5,157

* Schools for primary education only.
† Including schools for primary and secondary education, and including 30
schools providing both general and vocational education.

Directory

Administration

PALESTINIAN NATIONAL AUTHORITY

Appointed in May 1994, the Palestinian National Authority (PNA) has assumed some of the civil responsibilities formerly exercised by the Israeli Civil Administration in the Gaza Strip and parts of the West Bank.

CABINET
(May 2001)

Acting Minister of the Interior: YASSER ARAFAT (Fatah).

Minister of Civil Affairs: JAMIL AT-TARIFI (Fatah).

Minister of Planning and International Co-operation: Dr NABIL SHAATH (Fatah).

Minister of Finance: MUHAMMAD ZOHDI AN-NASHASHIBI (Independent).

Minister of Justice: FURAYH ABU MIDDAYN (Fatah).

Minister of Youth and Sports: (vacant).

Minister of Culture and Information: YASSER ABD AR-RABBUH (Democratic Union).

Minister of Awqaf (Religious Endowments): (vacant).

Minister of Local Government: Dr SAEB ERAKAT (Fatah).

Minister of Social Affairs: INTISAR AL-WASIR (Fatah).

Minister of Housing: Dr ABD AR-RAHMAN HAMAD (Fatah).

Minister of Posts and Telecommunications: IMAD AL-FALOUJI (Islamist).

Minister of Public Works: AZZAM AL-AHMAD (Fatah).

Minister of Supply: ABD AL-AZIZ SHAHEEN (Fatah).

Minister of Health: Dr RIYAD AZ-ZAANOUN (Fatah).

Minister of Education: (vacant).

Minister of Higher Education: Dr MUNTHER SALAH (Independent).

Minister of Transport: ALI AL-KAWASMEH (Fatah).

Minister of Economy and Trade: MAHER AL-MASRI (Fatah).

Minister of Industry: SAADI AL-KARNAZ.

Minister of Non-Governmental Organizations: HASSAN ASFOUR.

Minister of Labour: RAFIK AN-NATSHA.

Minister of Tourism and Antiquities: METRI ABU ATTIA.

Minister of Prisoners' Affairs: HISHAM ABD AR-RAZZAK.

Minister of Agriculture: HEKMAT ZAID.

Minister of Parliamentary Affairs: NABIL AMR.

Ministers without Portfolio: Dr NABIL QAIS (with responsibility for the Bethlehem 2000 project), ZIAD ABU ZIAD (with responsibility for Settlements), SALAH AT-TAMARI, JIRAR QUDWA.

MINISTRIES

Ministry of Agriculture: POB 197, Ramallah; tel. (2) 2961080; fax (2) 2961212; e-mail moa@planet.edu.

Ministry of Awqaf (Religious Endowments): POB 54825, Jerusalem; tel. (2) 6282085; fax (2) 2986401.

Ministry of Civil Affairs: Ramallah; tel. (2) 2987336; fax (2) 2987335.

Ministry of Culture: POB 147, Ramallah; tel. (2) 2986205; fax (2) 2986204; e-mail moc@gov.ps; internet www.moc.gov.ps.

Ministry of Economy and Trade: POB 1629, Ramallah; tel. (2) 2982370; fax (2) 2347182.

Ministry of Education: POB 576, Ramallah; tel. (2) 2983254; fax (2) 2983261; e-mail moe@planet.com; internet www.moe.gov.ps.

Ministry of Environmental Affairs: POB 3841, Ramallah; tel. (2) 2403495; fax (2) 2403494; e-mail mena@hally.net; internet www.mena.gov.ps; Eth-Thawra St, Gaza; tel. (8) 2822000; fax (8) 2847198.

Ministry of Finance: Sateh Marhaba, Al-Birah/Ramallah; tel. (2) 2400372; fax (2) 2405880; e-mail mofdep@planet.edu; POB 4007, Gaza; tel. (8) 2829243; fax (8) 2820696.

Ministry of Health: POB 14, Nablus; tel. (9) 2384772; fax (9) 2384777; e-mail pnamoh@palnet.com; internet www.moh.gov.ps; POB 1035, Gaza; tel. (8) 2829173; fax (8) 2826295; e-mail mohgaza@palnet.com; internet www.palnet.com/health/welcome.html.

Ministry of Higher Education: POB 17360, Ramallah; tel. (2) 2982600; fax (2) 2954518; e-mail minhed@planet.edu; internet www.mohe.gov.ps.

Ministry of Housing: POB 4034, Gaza; tel. (8) 2822233; fax (8) 2822235.

Ministry of Industry: POB 2073, Ramallah; tel. (2) 2987641; fax (2) 2987640; POB 4053, Gaza; tel. (8) 2826463; fax (8) 2824884; e-mail pnaindus@p-i-s.com; internet www.industry.pna.net.

Ministry of Information: POB 224, Al-Birah/Ramallah; tel. (2) 2986465; fax (2) 2954043; Gaza; tel. (8) 2866888; fax (8) 2821672; e-mail postmaster@mininfo.pna.org; internet www.pna.org/mininfo.

Ministry of the Interior: Gaza; tel. (8) 2829185; fax (8) 2862500.

Ministry of Jerusalem Affairs: POB 20479, Jerusalem; tel. (2) 6273330; fax (2) 6286820.

Ministry of Justice: Gaza; tel. (8) 2822231; fax (8) 2867109.

Ministry of Labour: POB 350, Ramallah Industrial Zone, Ramallah; tel. (2) 2900375; fax (2) 2900607; e-mail narman@gov.ps; internet www.mol.gov.ps; POB 4021, Gaza; tel. (8) 2829146; fax (8) 2822400.

Ministry of Local Government: Jericho; tel. (2) 2321260; fax (2) 2321240; internet www.p-ol.com/~molg.

Ministry of Planning and International Co-operation: Ramallah; tel. (2) 5747045; fax (2) 5747046; POB 4017, Gaza; tel. (8) 2829260; fax (8) 2824090; e-mail info@nmopic.pna.net; internet www.mopic.gov.ps.

Ministry of Posts and Telecommunications: Ramallah; tel. (2) 9986555; fax (2) 9986556; Gaza; tel. (8) 2829171; fax (8) 2824555.

Ministry of Public Works: Gaza; tel. (8) 2829232; fax (8) 2823653; e-mail mopgaza@palnet.com.

Ministry of Social Affairs: POB 3525, Ramallah; tel. (2) 2986181; fax (2) 2985239.

Ministry of Supply: Gaza; tel. (8) 2824324; fax (8) 2826430.

Ministry of Tourism and Antiquities: POB 534, Bethlehem; tel. (2) 2741581; fax (2) 2743753; e-mail minister@visit-palestine.com; internet www.visit-palestine.com.

Ministry of Transport: POB 399, Ramallah; tel. (2) 2986945; fax (2) 2986943.

Ministry of Youth and Sports: POB 52, Ramallah; tel. (2) 2985981; fax (2) 2985991.

President

President: YASSER ARAFAT (took office 12 February 1996).

The first election for a Palestinian Executive President was contested on 20 January 1996 by two candidates: Yasser Arafat and Samiha Khalil. Arafat received 88.1% of the votes cast and Samiha Khalil 9.3%. The remaining 2.6% of the votes cast were spoilt.

Legislature

PALESTINIAN LEGISLATIVE COUNCIL

Speaker: AHMAD QURAY.

General Election, 20 January 1996

Party	Seats
Fatah	54
Independent Fatah	12
Independent Islamists	4
Popular Front for the Liberation of Palestine (PFLP)	1
Palestinian Democratic Union (FIDA)	1
Independents	16
Total	**88***

* The total number of seats in the Palestinian Legislative Council—including one which is automatically reserved for the Palestinian President—is 89.

The first Palestinian legislative elections took place in 16 multi-member constituencies—including East Jerusalem—on 20 January 1996. Some 79% of the estimated 1m. eligible Palestinian voters were reported to have participated in the elections. Prior to the polls European Union observers criticized the election commission appointed by Yasser Arafat—and, indeed, Arafat himself—for late alterations to electoral procedure, which, it was felt, might prejudice the prospects of some candidates. Some irregularities were reported during voting, but these were not regarded as sufficiently serious to compromise the final outcome. The elections were officially boycotted by all sections of the so-called Palestinian 'rejectionist' opposition, including Hamas and Islamic Jihad, although Hamas did endorse a list of 'approved' candidates for those voters who chose not to boycott the elections. All deputies elected to the Palestinian Legislative Council (PLC) automatically became members of the Palestine National Council (PNC), the existing 483 members of which were subsequently permitted to return from exile by the Israeli authorities, in order, among other things, to consider amendments to the Palestinian National Charter, which has in many ways been superseded by the agreements concluded between Israel and the PLO since September 1993. Under Palestinian legislation, the tenure of the PLC is scheduled to expire after the Israeli Government has implemented all of its outstanding obligations under the terms of the Interim Agreement of 1995 (see Recent History, above).

Political Organizations

Palestine Liberation Organization (PLO): Gaza City; after the conclusion of the Cairo Agreement on the Gaza Strip and Jericho, signed by the PLO and Israel on 4 May 1994, the PLO gradually transferred its administrative infrastructure and its officers from Tunis, Tunisia, to the Gaza Strip; f. 1964; the supreme organ of the PLO is the Palestine National Council (PNC; Speaker SALIM AZ-ZA'NUN), while the PLO Executive Committee (Chair. YASSER ARAFAT; Sec. MAHMUD ABBAS) deals with day-to-day business. Fatah (the Palestine National Liberation Movement) joined the PNC in 1968, and all the guerrilla organizations joined the Council in 1969. In 1973 the Palestinian Central Council (PCC; Chair. SALIM AZ-ZA'NUN) was established to act as an intermediary between the PNC and the Executive Committee. This 95-member Council meets when the PNC is not in session and approves major policy decisions on its behalf. Chair. YASSER ARAFAT.

The most important guerrilla organizations are:

Fatah (The Palestine National Liberation Movement): e-mail fateh@fateh.org; internet www.fateh.net; f. 1957; the largest single Palestinian movement, embraces a coalition of varying views from conservative to radical; Leader YASSER ARAFAT; Sec.-Gen. FAROUK KADDOUMI; Central Cttee (elected by Fatah's 530-member Congress, 31 May 1980): YASSER ARAFAT, SALAH KHALAF, FAROUK KADDOUMI, MAHMUD ABBAS, KHALID AL-HASSAN, HAYIL ABD AL-HAMID, MUHAMMAD GHUNAIM, SALIM AZ-ZA'NUN, RAFIQ AN-NATSHAH, HANI AL-HASAN.

Popular Front for the Liberation of Palestine (PFLP): Box 12144, Damascus, Syria; f. 1967; Marxist-Leninist; publ. *Democratic Palestine* (monthly, in English); Leader ABU ALI MOUSTAFA; in 1994 the PFLP announced the formation of the Democratic National Action Front (DNAF), which it described as an open political, popular forum, an extension of the PFLP.

Democratic Front for the Liberation of Palestine (DFLP): Damascus, Syria; Marxist; split from the PFLP in 1969; Sec.-Gen. NAIF HAWATMEH.

Arab Liberation Front (ALF): f. 1968; Iraqi-backed; Leader MAHMOUD ISMAIL.

Palestinian Popular Struggle Front (PPSF): f. 1967; Sec.-Gen. Dr SAMIR GHOUSHA.

Hezb ash-Sha'ab (Palestine People's Party): e-mail shaab@palpeople.org; internet www.palpeople.org; formerly Palestine Communist Party, admitted to the PNC at its 18th session in 1987; Sec.-Gen. SULAYMAN AN-NAJJAB.

Palestine Liberation Front (PLF): split from PFLP-GC in April 1977; the PLF split into two factions at the end of 1983, both of which retained the name PLF; one faction (leader MUHAMMAD 'ABU' ABBAS) based in Tunis, Tunisia, and Baghdad, Iraq, and remaining nominally loyal to Yasser Arafat; the other faction belonging to the anti-Arafat National Salvation Front and having offices in Damascus, Syria, and Libya. A third group derived from the PLF was reported to have been formed by its Central Cttee Secretary, Abd al-Fattah Ghanim, in June 1986. At the 18th session of the PNC, a programme for the unification of the PLF was announced, with Talaat Yaqoub (died November 1988) named as Secretary-General and 'Abu Abbas' appointed to the PLO Executive Committee, while unification talks were held. The merging of the two factions was announced in June 1987, with 'Abu Abbas' becoming Deputy Secretary-General.

Palestinian Democratic Union (FIDA): split from the DFLP in March 1990; Leader YASSER ABD AR-RABBUH; Sec.-Gen. SALEH RA'FAT.

The anti-Arafat **National Salvation Front** includes the following organizations:

Popular Front for the Liberation of Palestine—General Command (PFLP—GC): Damascus, Syria; split from the PFLP in 1968; pro-Syrian; Leader AHMAD JIBRIL.

Popular Front for the Liberation of Palestine—National General Command: Amman, Jordan; split from the PFLP-GC in 1999; aims to co-operate with the PNA; Leader ATIF YUNUS.

As-Saiqa (Vanguard of the Popular Liberation War): f. 1968; Syrian-backed; Leader ISSAM AL-QADI.

Palestine Revolutionary Communist Party: Damascus, Syria; Sec.-Gen. ARBI AWAD.

Alliance of Palestinian Forces: f. 1994; 10 members representing the PFLP, the DFLP, the PLF, the PPSF, the Palestine Revolutionary Communist Party and the PFLP-GC; opposes the Declaration of Principles on Palestinian Self-Rule signed by Israel and the PLO in September 1993, and subsequent agreements concluded within its framework. The **Fatah Revolutionary Council**, headed by Sabri Khalil al-Banna, alias 'Abu Nidal', split from Fatah in 1973. Its headquarters were formerly in Baghdad, Iraq, but the office was closed down and its staff expelled from the country by the Iraqi authorities in November 1983; a new base was established in Damascus, Syria, in December. Al-Banna was readmitted to Iraq in 1984, having fled Syria. With 'Abu Musa' (whose rebel Fatah group is called **Al-Intifada**, or 'Uprising'), 'Abu Nidal' formed a joint rebel Fatah command in February 1985, and both had offices in Damascus until June 1987, when those of 'Abu Nidal' were closed by the Syrian Government. In 1989 the Fatah Revolutionary Council was reported to have disintegrated, and in June 1990 forces loyal to Abu Nidal surrendered to Fatah forces at the Rashidiyeh Palestinian refugee camp near Tyre, northern Lebanon.

The Islamic fundamentalist organizations, Islamic Jihad (Gen. Sec. RAMADAN ABDALLAH SHALLAH) and the Islamic Resistance Movement (Hamas; Spiritual Leader Sheikh AHMAD YASSIN), are also active in the Gaza Strip and the West Bank, where they began to play an increasingly prominent role in the *intifada* during 1989. Like the organizations represented in the Alliance of Palestinian Forces, they are strongly opposed to the Declaration of Principles on Palestinian Self-Rule. The formation of the Right Movement for Championing the Palestinian People's Sons by former members of Hamas was announced in April 1995. The Movement, based in Gaza City, was reported to support the PNA.

Diplomatic Representation

Countries with which the PLO maintains diplomatic relations include:

Afghanistan, Albania, Algeria, Angola, Austria, Bahrain, Bangladesh, Benin, Bhutan, Botswana, Brunei, Bulgaria, Burkina Faso, Burundi, Cambodia, Cameroon, Cape Verde, Central African Republic, Chad, China (People's Rep.), Comoros, Congo (Dem. Rep.), Congo (Rep.), Cuba, Cyprus, Czech Republic, Djibouti, Egypt, Equatorial Guinea, Ethiopia, Gabon, Gambia, Ghana, Guinea, Guinea-Bissau, Hungary, India, Indonesia, Iran, Iraq, Jordan, Korea (Dem. People's Rep.), Kuwait, Laos, Lebanon, Libya, Madagascar, Malaysia, Maldives, Mali, Malta, Mauritania, Mauritius, Mongolia, Morocco, Mozambique, Nepal, Nicaragua, Niger, Nigeria, Norway, Oman, Pakistan, Philippines, Poland, Qatar, Romania, Russia, Rwanda, São Tomé and Príncipe, Saudi Arabia, Senegal, Seychelles, Sierra Leone, Somalia, Sri Lanka, Sudan, Swaziland, Sweden, Tanzania, Togo, Tunisia, Turkey, Uganda, United Arab Emirates, Vanuatu, the Vatican City, Viet Nam, Yemen, Yugoslavia, Zambia, Zimbabwe.

The following states, while they do not recognize the State of Palestine, allow the PLO to maintain a regional office: Belgium, Brazil, France, Germany, Greece, Italy, Japan, the Netherlands, Portugal, Spain, Switzerland, the United Kingdom.

A Palestinian passport has been available for residents of the Gaza Strip and the Jericho area only since April 1995. In September 1995 the passport was recognized by 29 states, including: Algeria, Bahrain, Bulgaria, China (People's Rep.), Cyprus, Egypt, France, Germany, Greece, India, Israel, Jordan, Malta, Morocco, the Netherlands, Pakistan, Qatar, Romania, Saudi Arabia, South Africa, Spain, Sweden, Switzerland, Tunisia, Turkey, the United Arab Emirates, the United Kingdom and the USA.

Judicial System

In the Gaza Strip, the West Bank towns of Jericho, Nablus, Ramallah, Jenin, Tulkarm, Qalqilya, Bethlehem and Hebron, and in other, smaller population centres in the West Bank, the PNA has assumed limited jurisdiction with regard to civil affairs. However, the situation is confused owing to the various and sometimes conflicting legal systems which have operated in the territories occupied by Israel in 1967: Israeli military and civilian law; Jordanian law; and acts, orders-in-council and ordinances that remain from the period of the British Mandate in Palestine. Religious and military courts have been established under the auspices of the PNA. In February 1995 the PNA established a Higher State Security Court in Gaza to decide on security crimes both inside and outside the PNA's area of jurisdiction; and to implement all valid Palestinian laws, regulations, rules and orders in accordance with Article 69 of the Constitutional Law of the Gaza Strip of 5 March 1962. As of June 1998 the PLC had drafted a total of 43 laws, of which nine had been approved by the President and enacted.

General Prosecutor of the PNA: ZUHEIR AS-SURANI.

The Press

NEWSPAPERS

Al-Ayyam al-Arabi: Ramallah; f. 1999; daily newspaper published by PNA; Editor-in-Chief SALIM SALAMAH.

Filastin ath-Thawra (Palestine Revolution): normally published in Beirut, but resumed publication from Cyprus in November 1982; weekly newspaper of the PLO.

Al-Hadaf: organ of the PFLP; weekly.

Al-Haria (Liberation): organ of the DFLP.

Al-Hayat al-Jadidah: West Bank; e-mail alhayat@p-ol.com; internet www.alhayat-j.com; f. 1994; weekly; Editor NADIL AMR.

Al-Istiqal: Gaza City; organ of Islamic Jihad; weekly.

Ar-Risala (Letter): Gaza City; organ of the Islamist Construction and Democracy Party; weekly; Editor-in-Chief GHAZI HAMAD.

Al-Watan: Gaza City; supports Hamas; weekly.

PERIODICALS

Filastin (Palestine): Gaza City; f. 1994; weekly.

Palestine Report: Jerusalem Media and Communications Centre, POB 25047, Nablus Rd, Jerusalem; tel. (2) 5819777; fax (2) 5829534; e-mail palreport@jmcc.org; internet www.jmcc.org/media/reportonline; f. 1990; English; weekly; current affairs.

Shu'un Filastiniya (Palestine Affairs): POB 5614, 92 Gr. Afxentiou St, Nicosia, Cyprus; tel. 461140; monthly.

NEWS AGENCY

Wikalat Anbaa' Filastiniya (WAFA, Palestine News Agency): Gaza City; tel. (8) 2824056; fax (8) 2824046; e-mail wafa15@palnet.com; internet www.wafa.pna.net; formerly based in Beirut, but resumed activities in Cyprus and Tunis, November 1982; official PLO news agency; Editor ŽIAD ABD AL-FATTAH.

Broadcasting and Communications

TELECOMMUNICATIONS

Palestine Telecommunications Co PLC (PalTel): POB 1570, Nablus; tel. (9) 2376225; fax (9) 2376227; e-mail paltel@palnet.net; internet www.paltel.net; f. 1995; privately-owned monopoly; launched cellular telephone service (Palcel) in 1999; Chair. HATEM AL-HALAWANI; Dir-Gen. WALID IRSHAID.

Palcel: 65% owned by PalTel, 35% state-owned; CEO DAVID BOSWORTH.

BROADCASTING

Palestinian Broadcasting Corpn (PBC): Um Ash-Sharyet, Ramallah; tel. (2) 2959899; fax (2) 2959893; e-mail pbc@planet.edu; Chair. RADWAN ABU AYYASH.

Sawt Filastin (Voice of Palestine): c/o Police HQ, Jericho; tel. (2) 921220; internet www.bailasan.com/pinc; f. 1994; official radio station of the PNA; broadcasts in Arabic from Jericho and Ramallah; Dir. RADWAN ABU AYYASH.

Palestine Television: f. 1994; broadcasts from Ramallah and Gaza City; Dir. RADWAN ABU AYYASH.

Finance

(cap. = capital; dep. = deposits; brs = branches; m. = million)

BANKING

Palestine Monetary Authority

It is intended to develop the Palestine Monetary Authority (PMA), which was established in December 1994, into the Central Bank of Palestine. In July 1995 the PMA began to license, inspect and supervise the Palestinian and foreign commercial banks operating in the Gaza Strip and the Jericho enclave in the West Bank at that time. In December 1995 the PMA assumed responsibility for 13 banks in the Palestinian Autonomous Areas over which the Central Bank of Israel had hitherto exercised control. Three currencies circulate in the Palestinian economy—the Jordanian dinar, the Israeli shekel and the US dollar. The PMA, which is seeking a reserve base of US $10m. from donors, currently has no right of issue. According to the PMA, there were 22 banks with a total of 115 branches operating in the West Bank and the Gaza Strip in December 1999. In November 1999 the banks' deposit base amounted to US $2,845m. Gov. FOUAD HAMDI BESEISO; Nablus Rd, Ramallah; tel. (2) 2964786; fax (2) 2959922; e-mail info@pma

-ram.pna.net; POB 4026, An Nassera St, Gaza; tel. (8) 2825713; fax (8) 2824487; e-mail pmgaza@palnet.com; internet www.pma-palestine.org.

National Banks

Bank of Palestine Ltd: POB 50, Omar al-Mukhtar St, Gaza City; tel. (8) 2826818; fax (8) 2828973; e-mail info@bankofpalestine.com; internet www.bankofpalestine.com; f. 1960; cap. US $15.2m., dep. US $196.5m., res US $1.8m., total assets US $219.4m. (Dec. 1999); Pres., Chair. and Gen. Man. HASHEM ATA SHAWA; 15 brs in West Bank and Gaza Strip.

Commercial Bank of Palestine PLC: POB 1799, Michael Tanous Bldg, Alawda St, Ramallah; tel. (2) 2954141; fax (2) 2953888; e-mail cbp@cbpal.palnet.com; f. 1992; total assets US $87m.; Gen. Man. KHALID MUHAMMAD GHABEISH.

Palestine International Bank: Al-Birah/Ramallah; tel. (2) 9983300; fax (2) 9983333; f. 1996; cap. US $20m.

Investment Banks

Arab Palestinian Investment Bank: POB 1260, Al-Harji Bldg, Ramallah; tel. (2) 2987126; fax (2) 2987125; e-mail apibank@palnet.com; f. 1996; Arab Bank of Jordan has a 51% share; cap. p.u. US $15m.

Jerusalem Development and Investment Bank: POB 2471, Main St, Ramallah; tel. (2) 2961750; fax (2) 2961753; e-mail qudsbkhq@palnet.com; f. 1996; merchant bank; 3 brs.

Palestine Investment Bank PLC: POB 3675, Al-Helal St, Al-Birah/Ramallah; tel. (2) 2987880; fax (2) 2987881; e-mail pibc@alami.net; f. 1995 by the PNA; some shareholders based in Jordan and the Gulf states; cap. p.u. US $20m.; provides full commercial and investment banking services throughout the Gaza Strip and the West Bank; Chair. ABD AL-KADIR AL-QADI; Man. Dir HANI AL-QADI; 6 brs.

Islamic Banks

Arab Islamic Bank: POB 631, Nablus St, Ramallah; tel. (2) 2980060; fax (2) 2980065; e-mail aib@p-ol.com; internet www.p-ol.com/~alb; Regional Man. MAHER AL-KABABJI; 6 brs.

Palestine Islamic Bank: POB 1244, Omar al-Mukhtar St, Gaza City; tel. (8) 2825259; fax (8) 2825269.

Foreign Banks

Arab Bank PLC (Jordan): Regional Management: POB 1476, Ramallah; tel. (2) 2982400; fax (2) 2982444; e-mail arabbank@palnet.com; internet www.arabbank.com; f. 1930; dep. of some US $1,800m. held by 18 brs in the West Bank and the Gaza Strip at Jan. 2001; Senior Exec. Vice-Pres. SHUKRY BISHARA; 13 brs.

Bank of Jordan PLC: POB 1328, Bahour Bldg, Al-Quds St, Ramallah; tel. (2) 2952702; fax (2) 2952705; e-mail bojreg@palnet.com; internet www.boj.com.jo; Chair. TAWFIK FAKHOURY; 4 brs.

Cairo Amman Bank (Jordan): POB 1870, Ramallah; tel. (2) 2983500; fax (2) 2952764; e-mail cabl@attmail.com; internet www.ca-bank.com; Regional Man. MAZEN ABU HAMDEN; 11 brs.

Jordan National Bank PLC: POB 550, Al-Quds St, Ramallah; tel. (2) 2959345; fax (2) 2959341; e-mail jnb@palnet.com; internet www.ahli.com; f. 1995; Chair. ABD AL-QADER M. TASH; Regional Man. HANNA GHATTAS; 6 brs.

Other foreign banks include ANZ Grindlays Bank Ltd, the Arab Real Estate Bank (Egypt), the Development and Agricultural Credit Bank (Egypt), HSBC Bank Middle East (United Kingdom), the Jordan Gulf Bank, the Jordan Kuwait Bank, the Housing Bank (Jordan) and the Union Bank for Savings and Investment (Jordan).

STOCK EXCHANGE

Palestine Securities Exchange (PSE): POB 128, Nablus; tel. (9) 2375946; fax (9) 2375945; e-mail psexchng@palnet.com; internet www.p-s-e.com; f. 1997; Chair. SABEIH MASRI; Gen. Man. NAIM KHUSHASHI.

INSURANCE

A very small insurance industry exists in the West Bank and Gaza.

Arab Insurance Establishment Co Ltd (AIE): POB 166, Nablus; tel. (9) 2384040; fax (9) 2384032; f. 1975; Man. Dir IBRAHIM ABD AL-HADI.

Gaza Ahliea Insurance Co: POB 1214, Remal-Gaza; tel. (8) 2824045; fax (8) 2824015; e-mail gaicnet@mail.palnet.com; f. 1994; Chair. and Gen. Man. Dr MUHAMMAD AS-SEBA'WI; 6 brs.

National Insurance Co: POB 1819, 34 Municipality St, Al-Birah/Ramallah; tel. (2) 2983800; fax (2) 2958160; f. 1992; Chair. MUHAMMAD MAHMOUD MASROUJI; Gen. Man. AZIZ MAHMOUD ABD AL-JAWAD; 7 brs.

DEVELOPMENT FINANCE ORGANIZATIONS

Arab Palestinian Investment Co. Ltd: tel. (2) 2984242; fax (2) 2984243; e-mail apic@apic.com.jo; internet www.apic-pal.com.

Palestine Development & Investment Co (PADICO): Chair. MUNIB AL-MASRI.

Palestinian Economic Council for Development and Reconstruction (PECDAR): POB 54910, Dahiyat Al-Barid, Jerusalem; tel. (2) 2362300; fax (2) 2347041; e-mail info@pecdar.pna.net; internet www.pecdar.org; privately-owned; Dir-Gen. MUHAMMAD ISHTAYAH.

Trade and Industry

CHAMBERS OF COMMERCE

Bethlehem Chamber of Commerce and Industry: POB 59, Bethlehem; tel. (2) 2742742; fax (2) 2764402; e-mail beth-chamber@excite.com; f. 1952; 2,500 mems.

Hebron Chamber of Commerce, Industry and Agriculture: POB 272, Hebron; tel. (2) 2228221; fax (2) 2227490; internet www.pal-chambers.com; f. 1954; 4,900 mems.

Jenin Chamber of Commerce, Industry and Agriculture: Jenin; tel. (4) 2501107; fax (4) 2503388; f. 1953; 3,800 mems.

Jericho Commercial, Industrial and Agricultural Arab Chamber: POB 91, Jericho; tel. (2) 2323313; fax (2) 2322394; e-mail jercom@palnet.com; f. 1953; 400 mems.

Jerusalem Arab Chamber of Commerce and Industry: Jerusalem; tel. (2) 6282351; fax (2) 6272615; 2,050 mems.

Nablus Chamber of Commerce and Industry: POB 35, Nablus; tel. (9) 2380335; fax (9) 2377605; e-mail nablus@palnet.com; internet www.pal-chambers.com; f 1941; 4,800 mems.

Palestine Chamber of Commerce in the Gaza Strip: POB 33, Sabra Quarter, Gaza; tel. and fax (8) 2864588; e-mail gazacham@palnet.com; internet www.g77tin.org/pccghp.html; f. 1954; Chair. MUHAMMAD AL-QUDWAH; 8,000 mems.

Palestinian-European Chamber of Commerce: tel. (2) 894883.

Qalqilya Chamber of Commerce, Industry and Agriculture: POB 13, Qalqilya; tel. (9) 2941473; fax (9) 2940164; f. 1972; 1,068 mems.

Ramallah Chamber of Commerce and Industry: POB 256, Al-Birah/Ramallah; tel. (2) 2956043; fax (2) 2955052; e-mail ramcom@palnet.com; internet www.pal-chambers.com; f. 1950; Chair. MUHAMMAD AHMAD AMIN; Vice-Chair. YOUSUF ASH-SHARIF; 3,100 mems.

Tulkarm Chamber of Commerce, Industry and Agriculture: POB 51, Tulkarm; tel. (9) 2671010; fax (9) 2675623; e-mail tulkarem@palnet.com; f. 1945; 980 mems.

TRADE AND INDUSTRIAL ORGANIZATIONS

Union of Industrialists: POB 1296, Gaza; tel. (8) 2866222; fax (8) 2862013; Chair MUHAMMAD YAZIJI.

UTILITIES
Electricity

National Electric Co (NEC): West Bank; f. 2000.

Palestine Electric Co (PEC): Gaza; f. 1999; Chair. SAID KHOURY; Man. Dir SAMIR SHAWWA.

Water

Palestinian Water Authority (PWA): Gaza; internet www.pwa.pna.org; Dir Eng. NABIL ASH-SHARIF.

Transport

CIVIL AVIATION

Palestinian Civil Aviation Authority (PCAA): Gaza International Airport, Gaza; e-mail capf@rannet.com; internet www.palestinianair.com; Gaza International Airport was formally inaugurated in November 1998 to operate services by Palestinian Airlines (its subsidiary), Egypt Air and Royal Jordanian Airline; Royal Air Maroc began to operate a service from February 1999; airlines currently operate services to Amman, Abu Dhabi, Cairo, Doha, Dubai and Jeddah, and intend to expand their network to European countries; Chair. and Dir-Gen. FAYEZ ZAIDAN.

Palestinian Airlines: POB 4043, Gaza; tel. (8) 2827834; fax (8) 2821309; e-mail samipf@palnet.com; internet www.palestinianair.com; f. 1995; state-owned; Chair. and Dir-Gen. FAYEZ ZAIDAN; Vice-Pres. RAJAIE DAOUDI.

Tourism

Although the tourist industry in the West Bank was virtually destroyed as a result of the 1967 Arab-Israeli war, by the late 1990s the sector was expanding significantly, with a number of hotels being opened or under construction. Much of the tourism in the West Bank centres around the historical and biblical sites of Jerusalem and Bethlehem. In 2000 it was anticipated that a considerable part of tourist revenues would be generated by the Bethlehem 2000 Project, which has enabled the centre of that town to be redeveloped and modernized. However, a renewed outbreak of violence between Palestinians and Israelis in the West Bank and Gaza Strip in late 2000 has severely hampered the continued recovery of the tourist industry.

Ministry of Tourism and Antiquities: POB 534, Bethlehem; tel. (2) 2741581; fax (2) 2743753; e-mail mota@visit-palestine.com; internet www.visit-palestine.com.

Bethlehem 2000: POB 2000, Bethlehem; tel. (2) 2742224; fax (2) 2742227; e-mail info@bethlehem 2000.org; internet www.bethlehem2000.org.

Near East Tourist Agency: POB 19015, 18 Azzahra St, Jerusalem; tel. (2) 6282515; fax (2) 6282415; e-mail operations@netours.com.

ITALY

Introductory Survey

Location, Climate, Language, Religion, Flag, Capital

The Italian Republic comprises a peninsula, extending from southern Europe into the Mediterranean Sea, and a number of adjacent islands. The two principal islands are Sicily, to the south-west, and Sardinia, to the west. The Alps form a natural boundary to the north, where the bordering countries are France to the north-west, Switzerland and Austria to the north and Slovenia to the north-east. The climate is temperate in the north and Mediterranean in the south, with mild winters and long, dry summers. The average temperature in Rome is 7.4°C (45.3°F) in January and 25.7°C (78.3°F) in July. The principal language is Italian. German and Ladin are spoken in the Alto Adige region on the Austrian border, and French in the Valle d'Aosta region (bordering France and Switzerland), while in southern Italy there are Greek-speaking and Albanian minorities. A language related to Catalan is spoken in north-western Sardinia. Almost all of the inhabitants profess Christianity: more than 90% are adherents of the Roman Catholic Church. There is freedom of expression for other Christian denominations and for non-Christian religions. The national flag (proportions 3 by 2) has three equal vertical stripes, of green, white and red. The capital is Rome.

Recent History

The Kingdom of Italy, under the House of Savoy, was proclaimed in 1861 and the country was unified in 1870. Italy subsequently acquired an overseas empire, comprising the African colonies of Eritrea, Italian Somaliland and Libya. Benito Mussolini, leader of the Fascist Party, became Prime Minister in October 1922 and assumed dictatorial powers in 1925–26. Relations between the Italian State and the Roman Catholic Church, a subject of bitter controversy since Italy's unification, were codified in 1929 by a series of agreements, including the Lateran Pact, which recognized the sovereignty of the State of the Vatican City (q.v.), a small enclave within the city of Rome, under the jurisdiction of the Pope. Under Mussolini, Italian forces occupied Ethiopia in 1935–36 and Albania in 1939. Italy supported the fascist forces in the Spanish Civil War of 1936–39, and from June 1940 supported Nazi Germany in the Second World War. In 1943, however, as forces from the allied powers invaded Italy, the fascist regime collapsed. In July of that year King Victor Emmanuel III dismissed Mussolini, and the Fascist Party was dissolved.

In April 1945 German forces in Italy surrendered and Mussolini was killed. In June 1946, following a referendum, the monarchy was abolished and Italy became a republic. Until 1963 the Partito della Democrazia Cristiana (DC—Christian Democratic Party) held power unchallenged, while industry expanded rapidly, supported by capital from the USA. By the early 1960s, however, public discontent was increasing, largely owing to low wage rates and a lack of social reform. In the general election of 1963 the Partito Comunista Italiano (PCI—Italian Communist Party), together with other parties of the extreme right and left, made considerable gains at the expense of the DC. During the next decade there was a rapid succession of mainly coalition Governments, involving the DC and one or more of the other major non-communist parties.

Aldo Moro's coalition Government of the DC and the Partito Repubblicano Italiano (PRI—Italian Republican Party), formed in November 1974, resigned in January 1976, following the withdrawal of support by the Partito Socialista Italiano (PSI—Italian Socialist Party). After the failure of a minority DC administration, general elections to both legislative chambers took place in June, at which the PCI won 228 seats in the 630-member Chamber of Deputies. The DC remained the largest party, but could no longer govern against PCI opposition in the legislature. However, the DC continued to insist on excluding the PCI from power, and in July formed a minority Government, with Giulio Andreotti as Prime Minister. He relied on the continuing abstention of PCI deputies to introduce severe austerity measures, in response to the economic crisis. In January 1978 the minority Government was forced to resign, owing to pressure from the PCI, which wanted more active participation

in government (since July 1977 the PCI had been allowed to participate in policy-making but had no direct role in government). In March, however, Andreotti formed a new, almost identical Government, with PCI support. In May of the same year Aldo Moro was murdered by the Brigate Rosse (Red Brigades), a terrorist group (In June 2000 a suspected former member of the Brigate Rosse was arrested in France in connection with Moro's murder). In the following month the President, Giovanni Leone, resigned as a result of allegations of corruption. In July Alessandro Pertini was inaugurated as the first socialist President of the Republic.

The Andreotti administration collapsed in January 1979, when the PCI withdrew from the official parliamentary majority. A new coalition Government, formed by Andreotti in March, lasted only 10 days before being defeated on a vote of 'no confidence'. Following elections in June, at which its representation in the Chamber of Deputies declined to 201 seats, the PCI returned to the role of opposition.

In August 1979 Francesco Cossiga, a former Minister of the Interior, formed a minority 'government of truce', composed of the DC, the Partito Liberale Italiano (PLI—Italian Liberal Party) and the Partito Socialista Democratico Italiano (PSDI—Italian Social Democratic Party), relying on the abstention of the PSI to remain in office. However, the new Government was continually thwarted by obstructionism in Parliament. In April 1980 Cossiga formed a majority coalition, comprising members of the DC, the PRI and the PSI. The deliberate exclusion of the PCI from the Government led to an open campaign by its deputies in the legislature to force the resignation of the new coalition. In September the Government resigned after losing a vote on its economic programme. A four-party coalition Government assembled by Arnaldo Forlani, the Chairman of the DC, was swiftly beset with allegations of corruption. In May 1981 the Government was forced to resign, after it became known that more than 1,000 of Italy's foremost establishment figures belonged to a secret masonic lodge, P-2 ('Propaganda Due'), which had extensive criminal connections both in Italy and abroad. The lodge was linked with many political and financial scandals and with right-wing terrorism, culminating in mid-1982 with the collapse of one of Italy's leading banks, Banco Ambrosiano, and the death of its President, Roberto Calvi. In January 1989 a Milan court ruled that Calvi had been murdered, and in April it was announced that Licio Gelli, the former head of P-2, and 34 other people were to be tried on charges related to the Banco Ambrosiano bankruptcy. In March 1991 it was announced that Carlo De Benedetti, one of Italy's most prominent financiers, had been charged with fraudulent bankruptcy in connection with the collapse of the bank. In April 1992, along with more than 30 other defendants, both De Benedetti and Gelli were convicted on charges relating to the bank scandal. In April 1998 De Benedetti was cleared on appeal of the fraud charges, while Gelli was sentenced to 12 years' imprisonment.

In June 1981 Senator Giovanni Spadolini, leader of the PRI, formed a five-party coalition Government, thus becoming the first non-DC Prime Minister since 1946. Spadolini resigned in November 1982, following a dispute over economic policy. Amintore Fanfani, a former DC Prime Minister, formed a new, four-party coalition in December. This administration lasted until April 1983, when the PSI withdrew its support. A general election was held in June, at which the DC lost considerable support, winning only 32.9% of the votes for the Chamber of Deputies. The PSI increased its share of the votes to 11.4%, and its leader, Bettino Craxi, was subsequently appointed Italy's first socialist Prime Minister, at the head of a five-party coalition.

In July 1985 Cossiga succeeded Alessandro Pertini as President of the Republic. In June 1986 the Government lost a vote of confidence in the Chamber of Deputies, thus bringing to an end Italy's longest administration (1,060 days) since the Second World War. Craxi resigned, and President Cossiga nominated the former DC Prime Minister, Giulio Andreotti, to attempt to form a new government. However, the refusal of other parties to support Andreotti led to Craxi's return to power in July, on condition that he transfer the premiership to a DC member in March 1987.

Craxi duly submitted his resignation, and that of his Government, in March 1987. Several attempts to form a coalition failed, and a general election was held in June. The DC obtained 34.3% of the votes cast, and the PSI increased its share to 14.3%. With 26.6% of the votes, the PCI suffered its worst post-war electoral result, and lost 21 seats in the Chamber of Deputies. The Federazione dei Verdi (Green Party) received 2.5% of the votes and entered the Chamber for the first time, occupying 13 seats. Giovanni Goria, a DC member and the former Minister of the Treasury, became Prime Minister of a five-party coalition Government. By the end of the year, however, the Government had lost considerable support, following a series of strikes and other economic problems. Goria offered his resignation in November (following the withdrawal of the PLI from the coalition) and again in February 1988, but it was rejected both times by President Cossiga; Goria finally resigned in March. After five weeks of inter-party talks, Ciriaco De Mita, the Secretary-General of the DC, formed a coalition with the same five parties that had served in Goria's administration. In May the Government's decision to grant a measure of autonomy to the Alto Adige region (Südtirol), on the north-eastern border with Austria, prompted a series of bombings, perpetrated by German-speaking extremists in the region. At provincial elections held in the Alto Adige region in November, the neo-fascist Movimento Sociale Italiano-Destra Nazionale (MSI-DN, Italian Social Movement-National Right), almost doubled its share of the votes, thus replacing the DC as the largest Italian-language grouping in the region.

Severe criticism by Craxi of De Mita's premiership led to the collapse of the coalition Government in May 1989. In June President Cossiga nominated De Mita to form a new government, but he was unsuccessful and it was not until late July that the coalition partners of the outgoing Government agreed to form a new administration, with Andreotti as Prime Minister (for the sixth time).

In February 1990, as a result of an internal party dispute, De Mita resigned from the presidency of the DC. Supporters of De Mita, who together constituted a left-wing alliance within the DC, also withdrew from party posts, but pledged their continued support for the Andreotti Government. However, the cohesion of the coalition Government was threatened in early 1990 by the response of the PRI to a decree (issued in late 1989) that aimed, for the first time, to impose restrictions on immigration levels. The PRI demanded more stringent legislation, but the Government's proposals received parliamentary approval in late February 1990.

In November 1989 the Central Committee of the PCI, which had suffered a recent series of electoral reverses, renounced the party's communist identity and began a process of transforming the PCI into a mass social democratic party. In early 1991 the PCI was renamed the Partito Democratico della Sinistra (PDS—Democratic Party of the Left). A minority of members of the former PCI refused to join the PDS, and in May they formed the Rifondazione Comunista (RC—Reconstructed Communism).

Andreotti resigned the premiership in March 1991, accused by the PSI of failing to implement effectively policies on key issues. President Cossiga none the less nominated Andreotti to form a new Government. The new administration (the 50th in Italy since the Second World War) initially comprised the same five coalition partners, but, before the Government was sworn in, the three PRI members withdrew, dissatisfied with the portfolios that they had been allocated. The new Government, now a four-party coalition, nevertheless received a parliamentary vote of confidence.

In September 1991, apparently in response to widespread nationalist fervour in parts of Eastern Europe, German-speaking separatists from the Alto Adige region made demands for greater autonomy from Italy. In the same month the Union Valdôtaine, the nationalist party governing the Aosta Valley (on the borders of France and Switzerland), announced that it was planning a referendum on secession. Demands for greater autonomy were also made in Sardinia, following a resurgence of activism by militant separatists there. The growing influence of the Lega Nord (Northern League), a grouping of regionalist parties which denounced the 'southern hegemony' of the central Government, was demonstrated at municipal elections in the important industrial city of Brescia (in Lombardy) in November, when the Lega Lombarda narrowly defeated the DC, hitherto the city's governing party. (In January 1992 the Italian Govern-

ment, in an attempt to end a long-standing dispute with Austria over the Alto Adige area, agreed to grant further autonomy to the region.)

In February 1992 President Cossiga dissolved the legislature and announced that a general election would take place on 5 April. The election campaign was marred by the murder of Salvatore Lima, an associate of Andreotti (see below). At the election support for the DC was reduced to less than 30% of votes cast. The PDS won 16.1% of votes cast for the Chamber of Deputies, while the PSI received 13.6%. The Lega Nord, led by Umberto Bossi, performed well in northern Italy, as did a new anti-Mafia political party, La Rete per il Partito Democratico (Democratic Network Party), in the south.

Following the general election, the Prime Minister announced his resignation. Although his mandate did not expire until July 1992, President Cossiga also resigned. In May 1991 Cossiga was succeeded by Oscar Luigi Scalfaro, the newly-elected President of the Chamber of Deputies. In the following month Giuliano Amato, of the PSI, was appointed Prime Minister. The new Council of Ministers comprised mainly members of the PSI and DC, with the remaining portfolios being allocated to the PSDI, PLI and non-party politicians. The incoming coalition was thus composed of the same four parties as the previous Government. The new administration's programme of drastic reductions in public expenditure led to large-scale anti-Government protests later in the year.

Meanwhile, the extent of a corruption scandal, which had been uncovered in Milan in 1992, continued to widen. It was alleged that politicians (mainly of the PSI and DC) and government officials had accepted bribes in exchange for the awarding of large public contracts. Among those accused of corruption was senior PSI official Gianni De Michelis, a former Minister of Foreign Affairs. The Government's credibility was seriously undermined in February 1993 when the Minister of Justice, Claudio Martelli of the PSI, was obliged to resign, after being placed under formal investigation for alleged complicity in the collapse in 1982 of Banco Ambrosiano. Shortly afterwards Craxi resigned as Secretary-General of the PSI, although he continued to deny accusations of fraud. (He was replaced by Giorgio Benvenuto, formerly General Secretary of the Unione Italiana del Lavoro trade union and Director-General of the Ministry of Finance.) The Prime Minister's difficulties were compounded at the end of the month when the Ministers of Finance and of Health resigned, again following accusations of corruption. In March five DC politicians, including Andreotti, were subject to investigation of their alleged links with the Mafia. The Government's position became increasingly untenable, but President Scalfaro appealed to Amato to remain in office until impending referendums on constitutional reform had taken place. Later in March the Ministers of Finance and of Agriculture were forced to resign, following accusations of corruption.

In April 1993 referendums were held throughout Italy on a number of proposed changes to the Constitution, including an amendment providing for the election by majority vote of 75% of the 315 elective seats in the Senate (the remainder would be elected under a system of proportional representation); the ending of state funding of political parties; and the establishment of an environmental regulator. These amendments, which were introduced in an attempt to prevent electoral malpractice and, in particular, interference by the Mafia and similar illegal organizations, were approved by a large majority. (In August Parliament approved a similar system for elections to the Chamber of Deputies.) Amato resigned as Prime Minister shortly after the referendums, and Carlo Azeglio Ciampi was subsequently invited by President Scalfaro to form a new government. Ciampi, hitherto Governor of the Bank of Italy, was the first non-parliamentarian to be appointed to the position. He stated that the priority of his Government, chosen without consultation with party leaders, was the implementation of electoral reform and the resolution of the country's economic problems by means of a programme of privatization and the reduction of the budget deficit. The new notional coalition comprised the four parties of the outgoing administration, but also included the PDS, the PRI and the Federazione dei Verdi. However, the PDS and the Federazione dei Verdi immediately withdrew their ministers from the coalition, in protest at the new Government's refusal to revoke Craxi's parliamentary immunity from prosecution, although they subsequently continued to support Ciampi's Government. In August the Chamber of Deputies voted to allow Craxi to be investigated by magistrates on four charges of corruption. In May the Senate approved the removal of Andreotti's parliamentary immunity, to allow investigations into his alleged association with the Mafia; his arrest, however, remained prohibited. On the same day the Chamber of Deputies voted overwhelmingly to abolish parliamentary immunity in cases of corruption and serious crime.

Giorgio Benvenuto resigned as Secretary-General of the PSI in May 1993, owing to the party's opposition to his proposals for reform. He was replaced by another trade unionist, Ottaviano del Turco. The PLI also elected a new party leader, Raffaele Costa, the Minister of Transport, in that month, following the arrest of former Secretary-General Renato Altissimo on corruption charges in March. Investigations began into the activities of the former DC Prime Minister Arnaldo Forlani in April. In May corruption investigations extended to encompass politicians of the PDS and PRI, as arrests of leading political and business figures multiplied. At the end of the month demonstrations were held throughout the country to protest at financial corruption and the involvement of politicians in organized crime.

Municipal elections in a number of cities in June 1993 confirmed the advance of the new parties, La Rete and the federalist Lega Nord (which was victorious in Milan), at the expense of their more established rivals. Of the latter only the PDS maintained its support, and even made some gains in the north and centre of the country.

In September 1993 Diego Curto, head of Milan's commercial court, became the first member of the judiciary to be investigated in connection with the corruption scandals. A senior member of the PDS was also arrested and charged with receiving a bribe from a construction company, as the financial affairs of the former communist party became the focus of scrutiny. At the end of the month Andreotti was charged with having provided the Sicilian Mafia (the Cosa Nostra) with political protection in exchange for votes in Sicily, and with complicity in the murder of an investigative journalist who had allegedly discovered evidence linking Andreotti with the Mafia. (He was acquitted of both charges in late 1999, following trials lasting some four years.) In November 1993 Senator Giuseppe Leoni, a founding member of the Lega Nord, resigned after a judicial inquiry was initiated into the illegal funding of his electoral campaign.

In January 1994 Ciampi offered his resignation to President Scalfaro following a parliamentary debate that exposed deep divisions over the timing of a general election. Scalfaro dissolved Parliament, but requested that Ciampi remain in office until the forthcoming legislative elections, which were to take place in March under the new electoral system. In late January Silvio Berlusconi, the principal shareholder in and former manager of the media-based Fininvest, Italy's third-largest private business group, announced the formation of a right-wing organization, Forza Italia (Come on, Italy!), to contest the elections. The liberal wing of the DC, which was now entirely discredited by corruption scandals, relaunched itself as the centrist Partito Popolare Italiano (PPI—Italian People's Party). In subsequent weeks, parties of the left, right and centre sought to form alliances capable of gaining a majority in the Chamber of Deputies; seven parties, including the PDS, RC, the Federazione dei Verdi and La Rete, formed I Progressisti (the Progressives); the Polo per le Libertà e del Buon Governo (hereafter referred to as the Polo per le Libertà—known in English as the Freedom Alliance), was formed by the Lega Nord, Forza Italia and the Alleanza Nazionale (AN—National Alliance, a new party led by Gianfranco Fini and incorporating members of the neo-fascist MSI-DN), under the leadership of Berlusconi; the centre-right Patto per l'Italia (Pact for Italy), comprised Mario Segni's Patto Segni and the PPI. The election campaign intensified against a background of judicial investigations and mutual accusations of media bias and malpractice. Meanwhile, Berlusconi's popularity increased notably, despite the arrest of a number of senior Fininvest executives (including his brother) on suspicion of financial malpractice.

At the elections, held at the end of March 1994, the Polo per le Libertà alliance won an outright majority in the Chamber of Deputies, obtaining 366 of the 630 seats, and was only three seats short of an outright majority in the elections to the Senate, winning 156 of the 315 seats. The Progressisti took 213 seats in the Chamber of Deputies and 122 seats in the Senate, while the Patto per l'Italia won a disappointing 46 and 31 seats respectively. In spite of the success of Berlusconi's alliance, major differences existed between the parties in the right-wing electoral grouping. Berlusconi selected his own candidates from the precarious alliance for the usually impartial posts of Presi-

dent of the Chamber of Deputies and President of the Senate, using the threat of calling new elections to ensure that they were elected in the second round of voting. In late April Berlusconi was invited by President Scalfaro to form a Government. The new Council of Ministers, announced in May, included five members of the AN, two of whom were members of the neo-fascist MSI-DN. The appointment of neo-fascists to the Government caused alarm in the European Parliament, where, in an attempt to dissuade Berlusconi from making such appointments, a resolution had been approved demanding that Italy respect democratic values. In addition, Berlusconi was criticized for appointing Roberto Maroni of the Lega Nord as Minister of the Interior. Berlusconi's popularity none the less increased and Forza Italia won 30.6% of the votes at elections to the European Parliament held in mid-June. The PDS won only 19.1% of the votes, and its leader, Achille Occhetto, resigned. (Massimo D'Alema was elected as the new General Secretary in July.)

In July 1994 Craxi and the former Deputy Prime Minister and Minister of Justice, Claudio Martelli, were both sentenced to eight-and-a-half years' imprisonment for fraudulent bankruptcy in relation to the collapse of Banco Ambrosiano in 1982. Craxi was sentenced *in absentia*, allegedly too ill to return for trial from his holiday home in Tunisia. (In July 1995 two international warrants were issued for his arrest, and when he failed to return to Italy he was formally declared a fugitive from justice.) In all, 32 politicians and business figures, including former Prime Minister Forlani, stood trial on charges of illegal party financing and fraud. In July 1994 an emergency decree was issued by Berlusconi abolishing pre-trial preventive detention of bribery and corruption suspects as the number of detainees had escalated since the corruption investigations began in 1992. The decree was rescinded, however, following public protest and the resignation of the magistrates in Milan in charge of anti-corruption cases. The magistrates withdrew their resignations two days later. (In August 1995 the Chamber of Deputies approved an amendment to legislation on preventive detention, limiting its use to those under investigation for crimes punishable by sentences of more than four years' imprisonment, effectively impeding the detention of corruption suspects, who could receive a maximum sentence of three years in prison.) Shortly afterwards two Fininvest employees were arrested on charges of bribing the finance police, 23 of whose senior members were also taken into custody. The arrests, together with ongoing controversy regarding the appropriateness of the extent of the Prime Minister's media holdings, fuelled concern about Berlusconi's continued involvement in Fininvest and his unresolved conflict of business and political interests.

In November 1994 Berlusconi was formally notified that he was under investigation for bribery. In the following month Antonio Di Pietro, the most high-profile of the magistrates in Milan and one of the most popular public figures in Italy, resigned from his post in protest at increasing government interference in the work of the judiciary in Milan. The failure of the Prime Minister to resolve his conflict of interests, together with the growing tension between the Government and the judiciary, undermined the integrity of the Government and precipitated the disintegration of the coalition. Berlusconi resigned in order to avoid probable defeat in three votes of 'no confidence' proposed by the Lega Nord and opposition parties. In January 1995 Lamberto Dini, the Minister of the Treasury and a former Director-General of the Bank of Italy, was invited to form an interim government. Dini appointed a Council of Ministers comprised of technocrats, and pledged to hold elections once he had implemented a programme to improve public finances, reform the state pension system, introduce new regional electoral laws, and establish controls on media ownership and its use during electoral campaigns. Dini secured parliamentary approval for legislation reforming regional electoral procedures and for a supplementary budget, largely through recourse to parliamentary votes of confidence.

New political alliances emerged in 1995 in preparation for legislative elections. In January the MSI-DN was officially disbanded and most of its members were absorbed in the AN. The AN leader, Gianfranco Fini, distanced the party from its neo-fascist past, denouncing racism and anti-Semitism, in an attempt to widen support. The PSI had been dissolved in November 1994 and reformed as the Socialisti Italiani (Italian Socialists), under the leadership of Enrico Bosselli. In February 1995 Romano Prodi, a respected business executive and a former head of the state industrial and banking holding, Istituto per la Ricostruzione Industriale (Iri, which closed in June 2000), , offered to lead the centre-left parties to challenge Berlusconi in the coming elections. In the same month Rocco Buttiglione, leader of the centrist PPI, won the support of the majority of his party to seek an alliance with Berlusconi, but the PPI effectively split in March, after the party's national executive rejected the alliance with Berlusconi. The PPI national executive subsequently elected Gerardo Bianco as its Secretary-General in place of Buttiglione, who had disregarded calls for his resignation. (In January 1997 Franco Marini was elected to replace Bianco.) In July 1995 Buttiglione and his allies formed a new centre-right party, the Cristiani Democratici Uniti (CDU—United Christian Democrats). In the same month the PDS formally endorsed Prodi as leader of the centre-left electoral alliance, subsequently named L'Ulivo (The Olive Tree). Divisions within the Lega Nord also emerged, and in February a breakaway group was formed under the leadership of Roberto Maroni, who was in favour of forming an alliance with Berlusconi.

In March 1995 it was formally announced that Berlusconi was to be subject to further investigation on charges of financial irregularities. Moreover, his Polo per le Libertà, was defeated by the centre-left parties in nine of the 15 regional elections held in April, despite obtaining 40.7% of the votes cast (compared with 40.5% won by parties of the centre-left). The PDS won the largest share of the votes (24.6%), followed by Forza Italia (22.4%) and the AN (14.1%).

In June 1995 12 referendums were held on issues including media ownership, trade union and electoral reform, retailing and crime. Significantly, the majority of the voters who participated in the referendums on media ownership approved the retention of laws permitting an individual to own more than one commercial television channel and preserving the existing monopoly on television advertising. Furthermore, the majority of voters supported the partial privatization of the state-owned RAI broadcasting company, control of which had become increasingly contentious since the resignation of its board of directors in mid-1994, in protest at a government decree that increased government control over the appointment of directors. Another important outcome was the endorsement of proposed reforms to trade unions, restricting the unions' power of representation and effectively reducing the dominance of the three largest trade union federations.

In July 1995 Dini again successfully sought recourse to parliamentary votes of confidence to secure the approval of pension reforms that had been agreed with trade union leaders in May. In August the pension reform programme received parliamentary approval. However, Dini's premiership was threatened in October when the Minister of Justice, Filippo Mancuso, refused to resign from the Council of Ministers following the approval in the Senate of a motion of 'no confidence' in him which had been prompted by his allegedly ruthless vendetta against anti-corruption magistrates in Milan. Since Dini was constitutionally unable to remove a minister from office without submitting the Government's resignation, Scalfaro intervened and revoked Mancuso's mandate, appointing Dini as interim Minister of Justice. Dini's administration remained precarious, however, and shortly afterwards Berlusconi allied himself with Mancuso and proposed a motion of 'no confidence' in the Government, claiming the support of the RC. The Government narrowly defeated the motion, after having forged an agreement whereby RC deputies abstained from the vote on condition that Dini resign as Prime Minister by the end of the year.

In October 1995 anti-corruption magistrates in Milan issued arrest warrants for 20 army officers who had allegedly received bribes for contracts. (It was estimated that as many as 2,500 military personnel were subsequently subject to investigation on charges of corruption.) Also in October, at the end of a trial concerning the illegal funding of political parties, all 22 defendants were convicted, including former Prime Ministers Craxi (*in absentia*) and Forlani, who were sentenced to four years' and 28 months' imprisonment respectively; Umberto Bossi received a suspended sentence.

In November 1995 Dini secured parliamentary approval for the draft budget for 1996, despite initial opposition from the Lega Nord, which had made its support of the budget conditional on the Government's approval of new measures against illegal immigrants. (The Government had in fact approved a controversial decree restricting immigration and imposing harsh sanctions on illegal immigrants as the budget debate began; however, the decree's contents were made public only after the budget debate had concluded.) At the end of the month the Chamber of Deputies approved legislation regulating political parties' access to RAI.

On 30 December 1995 Dini submitted his resignation to the President. Scalfaro rejected the resignation, however, and asked Dini to continue in a caretaker capacity pending a parliamentary debate to resolve the political crisis and determine the future of the Government. In January 1996 the AN tabled a resolution demanding Dini's resignation, which it was expected to win with the support of parties of the extreme left. Scalfaro was thus obliged to accept Dini's resignation, which he submitted prior to the vote. In February, following an unsuccessful attempt by Antonio Maccanico, a bureaucrat and a former Chairman of Italy's powerful merchant bank, Mediobanca, to form a government, Scalfaro dissolved Parliament and asked Dini to remain as interim Prime Minister until a general election in April.

At the legislative elections, held on 21 April 1996, Romano Prodi's L'Ulivo alliance (dominated by the PDS, but also including the PPI and Dini's newly-formed centrist, Rinnovamento Italiano—Italian Renewal) narrowly defeated the Polo per le Libertà, securing 284 of the 630 seats in the Chamber of Deputies and 157 of the 315 elective seats in the Senate; the Polo per le Libertà won 246 seats in the Chamber of Deputies and 116 seats in the Senate. Both the Lega Nord and the RC, neither of which had allied with any grouping, increased their parliamentary representation, respectively obtaining 59 and 35 seats in the Chamber of Deputies and 27 and 10 seats in the Senate. President Scalfaro invited Prodi to form a government; Prodi announced his intention to introduce educational and constitutional reforms, reduce unemployment, address the contentious issue of media ownership and persevere with a policy of economic austerity. Massimo D'Alema, the influential General Secretary of the PDS, elected not to serve in the new Council of Ministers; however, his second-in-command, Walter Veltroni, was appointed Deputy Prime Minister. In late May Prodi assumed full powers, following votes of confidence in the Chamber of Deputies and in the Senate. Although the RC agreed to support the Government in the vote of confidence in the Chamber of Deputies, its Secretary-General, Fausto Bertinotti, emphasized that his party could express only 'conditional confidence' in the new administration, and in subsequent months he successfully forced the Government to accede to many RC demands in return for providing crucial parliamentary support.

In May 1996 Umberto Bossi of the Lega Nord announced the formation of an 11-member 'Government of the Independent Republic of Padania' (a territory comprising the regions of Liguria, Emilia-Romagna, Lombardy, Piedmont and the Veneto). The concept of the creation of a 'Republic of Padania' was generally regarded with scepticism, although many inhabitants of the northern regions were in favour of greater local autonomy. At local elections in June the Lega Nord's share of the vote declined in the strategic cities of Pavia and Lodi, and it came third in mayoral elections in Mantua (the designated capital of 'Padania'). In September Bossi's credibility was damaged further by the expulsion from the party of Irene Pivetti (a highly-regarded Lega Nord member and former President of the Chamber of Deputies) for publicly supporting a less extreme policy of local autonomy. In addition, a well-publicized rally in Venice to mark the formal independence of 'Padania' was attended by only 50,000 people, compared with some 150,000 people who participated in an anti-secession demonstration held concurrently in Milan. Shortly afterwards Bossi was placed under investigation, and his offices were searched for anti-constitutional material.

Meanwhile the former magistrate, Antonio Di Pietro, countered a series of allegations that he had abused his position within the judiciary to extort favours and had been personally responsible for discrediting Berlusconi in an attempt to further his own political ambitions. In March 1996, after a court in Brescia dismissed charges against Di Pietro, Berlusconi's brother, Paolo, and Cesare Previti, a former Minister of Defence and a lawyer for Fininvest, were placed under investigation for allegedly attempting to discredit him. (However, in January 1997 they were acquitted.) Although Di Pietro had been appointed Minister of Public Works in May 1996, by November he had resigned from the post, in protest at renewed investigations into his affairs. In December the Court of Review ruled that raids on Di Pietro's home and offices by the Finance Police (suspected of seeking vengeance on Di Pietro for his earlier investigations into their affairs) were 'unjustified and illegitimate'. In November Romano Prodi was himself placed under investigation for alleged abuse of office while head of the state holding company, Iri, during 1993–94; the Prime Minister dismissed the allegations and pledged to co-operate fully with the inquiry.

The Prodi administration experienced difficulty in reaching political consensus over constitutional reform. In July 1996, after lengthy negotiations, the Government reportedly reached agreement with the Polo per le Libertà on the establishment of a bicameral commission charged with advising Parliament on constitutional revision. In mid-July the Government had presented draft legislation on media reform that, appearing to adopt a lenient interpretation of the Constitutional Court's ruling, would allow Berlusconi's Mediaset media concern to convert one of its three television channels to cable or satellite (or else reduce its share of the terrestrial audience) rather than to divest it. The draft legislation also envisaged the establishment of a telecommunications and media regulator, while the RAI broadcasting group would be obliged to convert one of its channels to a regional network. However, the reforms failed to receive parliamentary approval prior to the date set by the Constitutional Court (late August), and, in the absence of new legislation, the Court ruled that its proposal to reduce the proportion of television companies held by any one group from 25% to 20% would take effect. It consequently announced that it would block the transmission of one of Mediaset's channels as of 22 December. In early December Massimo D'Alema, who had increasingly been acknowledged as the principal strategist in the Government, successfully exploited Berlusconi's vulnerability with regard to both media legislation and to the judicial investigations into his affairs (see below). D'Alema secured the temporary postponement (until 30 May 1997 at the earliest) of the Constitutional Court's decision to enforce its broadcasting ruling, and, in addition, suggested that the Government might support the introduction of judicial reforms that could result in extensive plea-bargaining in corruption cases. In return, Berlusconi agreed to collaborate with the Government and support the rapid conversion of numerous decrees into law. (In September the Constitutional Court had ruled that the widespread practice of renewing decrees without substantially altering their content was illegal; it declared that decrees issued by the Prodi administration, as well as those inherited from previous Governments, would no longer be renewable.) In January 1997 the continuing co-operation of the Polo per le Libertà enabled the Senate to approve the creation of a 70-member bicameral commission on constitutional reform, with D'Alema as its elected President. In June the commission presented its recommendations, which included a directly-elected President, a reduction in the size of the Chamber of Deputies and the Senate and greater regional financial autonomy. Referendum procedures were also to be amended following the invalidation of seven referendums due to low participation in May.

In October 1997 the RC announced that it would oppose the 1998 budget thus leaving the Government without a legislative majority. Following the failure of negotiations in which the Secretary-General of the RC, Fausto Bertinotti, demanded policy changes in exchange for their continued support, Prodi offered his resignation to Scalfaro. He remained as caretaker Prime Minister, however, and continued attempts to resolve the issue with Scalfaro and Bertinotti. A one-year political pact was subsequently announced, which included significant concessions from Bertinotti, who agreed to the adoption of measures to secure EMU qualification, while Prodi was forced to compromise on pension reform. Scalfaro declared his rejection of Prodi's resignation and Prodi subsequently won a parliamentary vote of confidence.

In January 1996 Berlusconi, along with his brother Paolo and nine others, went on trial in Milan charged with either giving or receiving bribes between 1989 and 1991. In January 1997 the trial was declared invalid, following the resignation of the presiding judge who had been accused of bias; a new trial began in February. In December Berlusconi was found guilty, although an initial prison sentence was quashed and a fine imposed. Later that month Berlusconi and Cesare Previti were ordered to stand trial on charges relating to allegations that they had accumulated funds with the intention of bribing judges. Berlusconi also faced charges of making illicit payments, via Fininvest, to Craxi and the PSI in 1991, and of maintaining links with the Sicilian Mafia.

At the Lega Nord party congress in February 1997 Bossi advocated consensual secession and in May the Lega Nord organized a referendum to determine the level of popular support for 'Padania'. Despite media reports that participation

levels had been low, Bossi claimed that 5m. had voted, of whom 99% supported an independent 'Republic of Padania'. In local elections in April, however, the Lega Nord had suffered a sharp decline in support, losing control of Gorizia, Pavia and Mantua. In September 15,000 secessionists demonstrated in Venice in support of the 'Republic of Padania'. However, later that month anti-secession rallies attracted hundreds of thousands of supporters in Milan and Venice. In October elections to a 200-seat constituent assembly in the 'Republic of Padania', organized by the Lega Nord, were contested by 63 parties. The assembly held its first session in November. In January 1998 Bossi received a one-year suspended prison sentence for inciting criminal acts during a party meeting in 1995; in July 1998 he received a second sentence, of seven months, for resistance to authority and offensive behaviour.

Following the escape from the country in May 1998 of a leading mafioso who was to be imprisoned for drugs-trafficking and the disappearance of Licio Gelli on the eve of his incarceration for his involvement in the Banco Ambrosiano scandal (see above), the Minister of Justice, Giovanni Maria Flick, offered to resign; Prodi, however, refused to accept his resignation. As a result of the high-profile criminal escapes (both men were later recaptured) and the theft of three valuable works of art from the National Gallery of Modern Art in Rome, a parliamentary motion of 'no confidence' was introduced by the opposition against Flick and the Minister of the Interior, Giorgio Napolitano, in late May; the motion was soundly defeated. In May 1998 the RC's opposition to a parliamentary vote regarding the admission of Hungary, Poland and the Czech Republic into NATO (see p. 241) led to the party withdrawing its support for the Government. Prodi subsequently called a confidence vote, through which he sought, and gained by a narrow majority, the support of Parliament. Inter-party talks on the proposed constitutional reforms ended in June without any agreement, the principal area of contention being the issue of presidential powers. Berlusconi, in particular, opposed any alteration of the presidential mandate and demanded greater reform of the judiciary, including a curb on the power of the magistrates. There appeared to be little possibility of the talks resuming in the near future.

In July 1998 Berlusconi received two further sentences for fraud; he was still awaiting trial for another five offences. The sentences, however, were not to be enforced as the former Prime Minister was protected by parliamentary immunity. In the same month warrants were issued for the arrest of 113 people on corruption charges, including local administration officials and 20 Guardi di Finanza. Further allegations against Berlusconi were uncovered in August when a witness in an unrelated corruption trial accused him of money laundering for the Mafia; Berlusconi strenuously denied the charge. In November legislation, which had been passed in 1997 and which favoured defendants in Mafia trials by disallowing testimony given before the start of legal proceedings, was overturned.

The 1999 budget provoked a political crisis in October 1998. The RC again withdrew its support for the Government and opposed the budget, which necessitated a parliamentary vote of confidence. The Government lost the motion by one vote and Prodi was forced to resign. Following an unsuccessful attempt by Prodi to form a new government, the leader of the Democratici di Sinistra (DS, as the PDS had been renamed), Massimo D'Alema, was asked to assume the premiership. On 22 October D'Alema announced the formation of a coalition Government, composed of members of the DS, the Federazione dei Verdi, the Partito dei Comunisti Italiani (PdCI), the Unione Democratica per la Repubblica (UDR—Democratic Union for the Republic, a centrist political movement, created in February by former President Francesco Cossiga), the PPI, the Socialisti Democratici Italiani (SDI—Italian Democratic Socialists, formed earlier that year following merger of the Italian Socialists and the Social Democratic Party) and Rinnovamento Italiano. In an effort to revive the process of constitutional reform, D'Alema appointed former Prime Minister Giuliano Amato to the new post of Minister of Institutional Reforms. Rosa Russo Jervolino of the PPI replaced Giorgio Napolitano as Minister of the Interior, and, in what was regarded as a somewhat controversial move, a communist, Oliviero Diliberto, was appointed as Minister of Justice.

In mid-May 1999 Carlo Azeglio Ciampi, the former Minister of the Treasury and of the Budget, was elected to succeed Scalfaro as President, at the end of his mandate. Giuliano Amato, formerly the Minister of Constitutional Reform, succeeded Ciampi as Minister of the Treasury and of the Budget. In that month, Massimo D'Antona, an adviser to the Minister of Employment and Social Welfare, Antonio Bassolino, was shot dead outside his home in Rome. Responsibility was claimed by the Brigate Rosse (the terrorist grouping was believed to have been inactive since the late 1980s), which, in a document sent to a newspaper in Rome, cited D'Antona's involvement in formulating a series of labour reforms (which were approved by the Government the day after his murder) creating more flexibility between the Government and trade unions, together with Italy's involvement in the NATO action in Kosovo (see below) as the reasons for his murder. In May 2000 a trade union employee, Alessandro Geri, was arrested in connection with and subsequently charged with complicity in D'Antona's murder; Geri was further charged with membership of a subversive organization, theft, and the illegal possession of firearms. In June 1999 Bassolino resigned in order to devote all of his time to his role as Mayor of Naples, and a minor government-reorganization ensued. Among the new appointees were Cesare Salvi as Minister of Employment and Social Welfare, and Antonio Maccanico as Minister of Constitutional Reform. In June municipal and provincial elections resulted in a number of defeats for the governing coalition, most notably in the leftist stronghold of Bologna, where a right-wing candidate won (by a narrow majority) for the first time since 1945; elections to the European Parliament in June 1999 also showed increased support for right-wing parties.

Meanwhile, in March 1999, Berlusconi was acquitted on charges of tax fraud; his conviction for making illicit payments to Craxi and the PSI was overturned in October. In November, however, Berlusconi was ordered to stand trial on charges of bribery and of false accounting linked to funds allegedly used as bribes. In June a new trial had been ordered against Craxi on charges of illegal party financing, although he remained in exile in Tunisia and was reportedly too ill to return. In October, D'Alema announced that he had no objection to Craxi's returning to Italy on medical grounds, and in November a Milan court ruled that Craxi could return to Italy for treatment and serve his sentence under house arrest rather than in prison. However, Craxi maintained that he would not return to Italy unless he received an official pardon, and he died in exile in January 2000.

In September 1999 four Italian generals were indicted on charges of crimes against the Constitution and high treason; five other military officials were accused of giving false testimony. The charges followed the publication of a report by the investigating magistrate alleging that a passenger aircraft that had crashed in southern Italy in 1980, killing all 81 passengers, had been caught in a confrontation between NATO and Libyan fighter aircraft; the wreckage of a Libyan jet had been officially said to have been found three weeks after that of the civilian craft, and it was believed that the military had sought to confuse crash investigators as to when the Libyan plane had actually come down. The trial of the nine military officials commenced in September 2000.

In October 1999 D'Alema announced plans to renew and strengthen the ruling coalition, with the addition of I Democratici per l'Ulivo (The Democrats for the Olive Tree—hereafter referred to as the Democratici), founded by Prodi in February. The parties of the coalition were divided over this proposal, and the SDI and the UDR, in particular, announced their intention to withdraw their support if the changes were implemented. D'Alema stated that he would be forced to resign if his reforms did not proceed, but this was averted when centre-left candidates won all five seats (including the seat for Bologna vacated by Romano Prodi, who had become President of the European Commission) at by-elections in November, thus strengthening the governing coalition and effectively demonstrating confidence in the Government following the poor results at the local and European elections in June. However, in mid-December, as a result of the ongoing disputes within the governing coalition and the subsequent withdrawal of support by the Trifoglio (Clover) alliance (including the SDI and the UDR), D'Alema tendered his resignation. He was subsequently asked by Ciampi to form a new government. The SDI left the coalition, and the Democratici and the Unione Democratici per l'Europa (UDEUR—Union of Democrats for the Republic) joined. Eight new ministers were appointed, including Enzo Bianco of the Democratici as Minister of the Interior, and Sergio Mattarella, previously Deputy Prime Minister (a post abolished in the new administration), as Minister of Defence. The new Government was subsequently endorsed in a vote of confidence in the Chamber of Deputies by 310 votes to 287.

In March 2000 it was announced that an investigation was to be carried out into the financial affairs of Donatella Dini, the wife of the Minister of Foreign Affairs, Lamberto Dini. It was alleged that Dini was involved in tax evasion and fraud. It was subsequently reported, in June, that Donatella Dini was also being investigated on charges of corruption and bribery; she was accused of illegally assisting a US company to obtain a 30,000m. lire state-approved loan. At regional elections held on 16 April, which Berlusconi had characterized as a test of the national Government's popularity, the ruling centre-left coalition was defeated by a centre-right alliance composed of Berlusconi's Forza Italia and Bossi's Lega Nord. The centre-right won 51% of the vote and eight regions compared with 45% of the votes and seven regions for the centre-left. The next day D'Alema's offer of resignation was declined by President Ciampi, who suggested he seek a confidence vote in Parliament. However, in an attempt to avert a general election, which would follow a predicted vote of 'no confidence', D'Alema resigned on 19 April. The Minister of Treasury and the Budget and former Prime Minister, Giuliano Amato, was appointed in his place, and a new Government, a coalition of eight parties, comprising five new ministers, was sworn in on 26 April. The new Government survived a vote of confidence three days later, by 319 votes to 298. Also in that month legislation attempting to reduce the number of strikes was approved by the Senate. Measures adopted included a minimum 10-day notice period, the imposition of fines for illegal strike action, and the guarantee that 50% of essential public services would continue to function during a strike.

Seven referendums held in late May 2000 were deemed invalid as the turn-out did not meet the required 50%. Measures submitted to the electorate included the abolition of proportional representation (which had also been the subject of a referendum that had subsequently been declared invalid in April 1999) and of state funding of political parties. The 32% turn-out was interpreted by opposition parties as reflecting a lack of support for the new Government, and calls were made by Berlusconi for Amato to stand down. Earlier that month, at a first appeal, a court acquitted Berlusconi of one charge of bribing tax inspectors involved in the auditing of his company, Fininvest, in 1998, and invoked the statute of limitations (on the grounds that too much time had elapsed since the perpetration of the crimes) to overturn his convictions on three similar counts. Moreover in mid-June Berlusconi was further acquitted of bribery charges relating to his acquisition of the Mondadori publishing company in 1991.

In late September 2000 Amato announced that he would resign as Prime Minister shortly before the parliamentary elections, scheduled to take place in May 2001, in favour of the Mayor of Rome and Democratici per l'Ulivo member, Francesco Rutelli. Amato argued that Rutelli's growing popularity among the Italian electorate would increase the centre-left coalition's chances of defeating Berlusconi's centre-right alliance at the elections. The following month Rutelli was endorsed as the centre-left's official candidate for Prime Minister in the forthcoming elections. Rutelli stood down as Mayor of Rome in early January 2001 to concentrate on his election campaign. The announcement of Rutelli's candidacy led to accusations of nepotism by opposition members, and an inquiry was subsequently opened into allegations that government members had abused their positions to provide employment for friends and relatives. Earlier in September Lombardy's Regional Council announced that it was to hold a referendum, in conjunction with the parliamentary elections in 2001, on the possible transfer of powers from the national capital, Rome, to the regional capital, Milan; competencies expected to be brought under local control included health, education, trade and law and order. The move, which was supported by the Lega Nord and Forza Italia, was strongly condemned by Amato as well as by the centre-right coalition partner, the AN. In early October Piedmont's administration in turn announced its intention to hold a referendum on possible devolution. Moreover, later that month the President of the Veneto Regional Council, Giancarlo Galan, a Forza Italia member, called for a referendum to be held on proposals that the region be granted sovereignty over its 'foreign policy', immigration laws, and the collection of taxes, as well as education and health. The Government announced in early November, however, that referendums could only be declared by central Government.

In mid-October 2000 a state of emergency was announced by the Government in the north-west provinces of Liguria, Piedmont and Valle d'Aosta, following serious flooding in which some 31 people were killed and thousands of people were displaced. In mid-November national measures were announced to prevent the spread of bovine spongiform encephalopathy (BSE) in cattle and its human variant, Creutzfeldt-Jakob disease—vCJD. The Italian Government announced the imposition of a ban on all French cattle over the age of 18 months, and of all French beef sold on the bone, as well as a ban on the use of feed containing animal protein. Moreover, from January 2001 tests detecting BSE were to be carried out on all Italian cattle over 24 months of age. However following the discovery in January of Italy's first two cases of BSE, the ban on imports of French beef was lifted. On 9 March 2001 the Italian Parliament was dissolved by President Ciampi in anticipation of the legislative elections.

At legislative elections held on 13 May 2001, the right-wing Casa delle Libertà alliance, led by Berlusconi, gained a majority in both the Senate and the Chamber of Deputies, defeating Rutelli's left-wing L'Ulivo alliance. The Casa delle Libertà gained 177 seats in the Senate (compared with the 128 secured by L'Ulivo), and 368 in the Chamber of Deputies (compared with 242 for L'Ulivo). Amato's Government was to remain in power as a caretaker administration until the Prime Minister-elect, Berlusconi, named his Government; this was expected to take place before 13 June.

Despite mass trials of Mafia suspects in the late 1980s, the Italian Government continued to experience problems in dealing with organized crime. In 1992 the murders of Salvatore Lima, a Sicilian politician and member of the European Parliament, Giovanni Falcone, a prominent anti-Mafia judge, and that of his colleague, Paolo Borsellino, provoked renewed public outrage. In August the powers of the police and of the judiciary were strengthened, in a fresh attempt to combat the Mafia. During 1992 hundreds of suspects were detained. In January 1993 the capture of Salvatore Riina, the alleged head of the Sicilian Mafia who had eluded the security forces for more than 20 years, was regarded as a significant success in the Government's campaign against organized crime. In the following month Rosetta Cutolo, leader of a faction of the Camorra (the Neapolitan Mafia), was also arrested. In 1993 the judiciary mounted a campaign to seize Mafia funds. In the course of the year several suspects, alleged to be leading figures in the world of organized crime, were arrested. Among these were Paolo Benedetto, regarded as the leader of the Mafia in Catania, Giuseppe Pulvirenti, alleged to be another principal figure of the Mafia in Eastern Sicily, and Michele Zaza, the alleged head of the Camorra. In March 1994 the Governments of Italy and France pledged to increase co-operation in the sharing of intelligence to combat Mafia activities, and in October a similar agreement was signed with Russia to fight organized crime and drugs-trafficking. A sudden increase in Mafia-related violence in Sicily during March 1995 was largely attributed to attempts to intimidate potential informers. Numerous alleged mafiosi were arrested in the following months, including Leoluca Bagarella, the alleged head of the Sicilian Mafia, in June, and some 150 suspected members of the Calabrian Mafia in July. In November Francesco Musotto, a senior politician in Palermo and an ally of Berlusconi, was arrested and charged with assisting high-ranking members of the Sicilian Mafia to evade capture over a four-year period. In January 1996 Marcello Dell'Utri, a leading Forza Italia politician, was reported to be subject to investigation on charges of links with the Mafia. (In December Dell'Utri received a custodial sentence of three years for the falsification of invoices and financial fraud while Chairman and Managing Director of Berlusconi's company, Publitalia.) Following the arrests of a number of senior mafiosi in 1996, in March 1997 more than 70 alleged members of the Mafia were arrested in Sicily and later that month a further 70 suspected members of the Calabrian Mafia were detained. In July troops were dispatched to Naples to help the security forces, owing to violent territorial disputes between rival Mafia groups. In September 24 influential members of the Mafia, including Salvatore Riina and Pietro Aglieri (who had been arrested in June), were sentenced to life imprisonment for their part in the murder of Giovanni Falcone. Several senior Mafia figures were arrested in 1998, including Vito Vitale, the alleged head of the Mafia in Trapani, Sicily, and Francesco Schiavone, the leader of the Camorra. During the year more than 100 people were arrested on suspicion of having links with the Mafia, and in March the Government voted unanimously to oust a junior minister following allegations that he had links

with the Mafia. The withdrawal of troops installed in Sicily following the murders of Paolo Borsellino and Giovanni Falcone in 1992, was completed in June 1998. In the following month 18 people, including Salvatore Riina, were convicted of complicity in the murder of Salvatore Lima in 1992; this constituted Riina's 13th sentence of life imprisonment. In January 1999 D'Alema announced that the army was to return to Sicily to assist in operations against the Mafia, only six months after its withdrawal had been completed; some 500 troops were to guard public buildings, thereby allowing police to concentrate on countering organized crime. In March Giuseppe Piromalli, a leader of the Calabrian Mafia, was captured; he had been sentenced, *in absentia*, to life imprisonment in 1991 for murder, and was also accused of extortion. In April 1999 an official of the treasury ministry was arrested on charges of external complicity with the Mafia; he was the first serving government member to be taken into preventive detention. Further arrests were made during 1999, and in December 17 Mafia members were sentenced to life imprisonment for the murder of Paolo Borsellino in 1992. In January 2000, Riina was sentenced to life imprisonment for, amongst other charges, the bombing of the Uffizi Gallery in Florence in May 1993 in which six people were killed. In February 2001 Vincenzo Virga, the financial head of the Sicilian Mafia, who had been in hiding since 1994, was arrested. Benedetto Spera, reputedly the closest colleague of the head of the Sicilian Mafia, Bernardo Provenzano, had also been arrested at the end of January; Spera had been convicted *in absentia* for his role in the 1992 murders of Giovanni Falcone and Paolo Borsellino.

Emergency measures were decreed in November 2000 in an attempt to prevent the early release from prison of those accused of Mafia-related crimes. The laws followed the discharging of 10 prisoners accused of involvement in murders attributed to the Mafia, on technical grounds. Magistrates were granted greater powers in determining the length of preventive detention for suspects and a ban on plea bargaining was introduced. In December 2000 a UN conference on organized crime opened in Palermo, in the wake of the publication of a report implicating some 329 politicians, business executives and law enforcers in Mafia-related activities.

Italy's foreign policy has traditionally been governed by its firm commitment to Europe, notably through its membership of the European Community (EC—now the European Union, EU, see p. 181) and NATO. The Treaty on European Union was ratified by the Italian legislature in October 1992. On 1 January 1999 Italy joined the single European currency, the euro.

In July 1991, following the escalation of hostilities in the neighbouring Yugoslav republic of Slovenia, the Italian Government temporarily deployed military personnel in the north-east of Italy and reinforced border posts in the region. Italy gave firm support to the EC's efforts to find a peaceful solution to the Yugoslav crisis. In January 1992 President Cossiga became the first European Head of State to visit Croatia and Slovenia since the former Yugoslav republics' recognition as independent states by the EC. In May the Italian Government was obliged to declare a state of emergency, following an influx of thousands of refugees from Bosnia and Herzegovina. The victory of Berlusconi's right-wing alliance in the general election in March 1994 was met with unease by the European Parliament due to the neo-fascist element of the grouping. In May Italy was refused a place on the international 'Contact Group' formed to facilitate a cease-fire in Bosnia and Herzegovina, following alleged statements by AN members reviving claims to territories of the former Yugoslavia. In July relations between Italy and Slovenia deteriorated, following a threat by the Italian Government to veto Slovenian membership of the EU if some form of non-monetary compensation were not given to the ethnic Italians who were dispossessed when Slovenia (then part of the former Yugoslavia) was awarded the Italian territory of Istria as part of the post-1945 peace settlement. Slovenia subsequently conceded that legislation would be amended to allow foreign nationals to acquire property in Slovenia, and in March 1995 the Italian Government withdrew its veto on Slovenian negotiations to become a member of the EU. In February 1998 Italy and Slovenia agreed a set of compensation measures for those Italians expelled from Slovenia at the end of the Second World War.

In May 1995 a contingent of some 500 troops was deployed along Italy's south-eastern coast in an attempt to halt a sudden influx of illegal immigrants, primarily from Albania and Montenegro. It was estimated that as many as 10,000 foreign nationals had entered Italy illegally via this route during the previous six months. Controversial legislation was approved in November restricting immigration and imposing harsh sanctions on illegal immigrants. As a result of the deteriorating political situation within Albania, large numbers of refugees arrived in Italy throughout 1997, and in March a state of emergency was declared for three months. Following a visit by Prodi, an Italian-led multi-national peace-keeping force, known as Operation Alba, was deployed in Albania in April, with a three-month mandate to facilitate the distribution of humanitarian aid. In June Italy was forced to recall two successive ambassadors to Albania, following comments that they were alleged to have made regarding the Albanian political situation. At the end of July, at an international conference in Rome, it was decided that Italian security aid to Albania would continue after the withdrawal of the international force and that co-operation on border control would be extended until October. At the end of August it was announced that the repatriation of refugees would be delayed until November. In October it was agreed to establish a joint office to combat organized crime, and in December Italy and Albania signed an aid agreement.

In June 1997 the Government announced the creation of a commission to investigate claims that members of an Italian paratroop regiment attached to the UN peace mission in Somalia (UNOSOM) had tortured, sexually assaulted and murdered unarmed Somalis in the early 1990s. The commission issued a report in August, which declared that the abuses had taken place but were not widespread. Later that month the inquiry was reopened, following allegations by a former member of the regiment that senior figures had been aware of the misconduct and that an investigative journalist had uncovered proof of their involvement prior to her murder in Somalia in March 1993. Further investigations failed to confirm alleged incidents of abuse, and a second report, issued in May 1998, again concluded that abuse had taken place but had not been widespread. The senior officers involved were criticized for failing to ensure that orders and instructions were obeyed and for tolerating unacceptable behaviour; 12 of them were subsequently disciplined. An association representing the victims of violence in the armed forces criticized the commission for failing to visit Somalia and for basing its findings on an incomplete investigation.

Following Italy's accession to the EU's Schengen agreement on cross-border travel (see p. 194) in late October 1997, large numbers of refugees, mainly Turkish and Iraqi Kurds, began arriving in southern Italy, provoking concern from Italy's EU partners. These concerns were partially alleviated by the initial approval, in November, of a bill designed to facilitate the deportation of illegal immigrants. However, the concerns resurfaced in January 1998, following comments by President Scalfaro, who proclaimed that Italy had an 'open arms' policy towards refugees. On 1 April 1998 the Schengen agreement, which had previously only been applicable to air travel between Italy and the other EU member states, was fully implemented, opening the borders with Austria and France. In order to comply with the terms of the agreement, a new law had been promulgated in February, providing for the detention, prior to forcible repatriation, of illegal immigrants; previously they had been given unenforced expulsion orders and released. In August the discovery of ambiguities in the new immigration law, which would enable immigrants to be released if their country of origin could not be determined, led to renewed fears of a 'flood' of immigrants. In February 1999 legislation was approved allowing for the detention of illegal immigrants arriving in Italy without making an asylum application; previously they had been given 15 days to leave before being expelled, and it was considered many used this period to find employment in the 'black' economy and go into hiding.

In March 1999, as the conflict in the Serbian province of Kosovo deepened (see the chapter on Yugoslavia), Italian bases were used for NATO bombing raids on Yugoslavia. However, political opinion within Italy was strongly in favour of a diplomatic solution, and the Chamber of Deputies overwhelmingly endorsed a motion urging the reopening of negotiations and an immediate suspension of the bombing. In early April the RC threatened to withdraw from the Government unless there was an unconditional end to the NATO action; D'Alema averted a crisis in May by proposing a compromise resolution seeking the suspension of the bombing raids only if a UN Security Council resolution to end the conflict was achieved with Russian and Chinese backing. In April the Senate had approved the deployment of 2,000 Italian troops in Albania to aid the humanitarian mission although they refused to sanction any military ground

intervention in Yugoslavia; by mid-1999 some 5,500 Italians had been deployed in Kosovo as part of a NATO contingent in the region. In March Italy had launched a programme of humanitarian aid for Kosovan refugees in Albania, and a large number of Kosovan refugees also arrived in Italy. However, in July Italy announced that as the conflict in Kosovo had ended those arriving from the region would no longer be accorded refugee status, but would be regarded as illegal immigrants. In early January 2001 the Minister of Defence, Sergio Mattarella, requested that NATO impose a temporary ban on the use of depleted uranium (DU) as a weapons component, following alleged evidence that deaths of veterans of NATO operations in the Balkans, including a number of former Italian military personnel, were linked to exposure to DU. NATO subsequently announced that a full examination of the use of DU weapons would be undertaken.

Diplomatic relations were established at ambassadorial level with the Democratic People's Republic of Korea in early January 2000. In February comments by the German Chancellor, Gerhard Schröder, warning against the dangers of a possible return to power of neo-fascist groups in Italy, angered the Italian Government, which requested that the remarks be withdrawn. Schröder's comments that this could lead to isolation for Italy in Europe, were thought to refer to the possible involvement of the right-wing AN in government, were Berlusconi's centre-right alliance to be successful in the legislative elections, scheduled for 2001. The AN had participated in Berlusconi's Government in 1994.

Government

Under the 1948 Constitution, legislative power was held by the bicameral Parliament, elected by universal suffrage for five years (subject to dissolution) on the basis of proportional representation. A referendum held in April 1993 supported the amendment of the Constitution to provide for the election of 75% of the members of the Senate by a simple plurality and the remainder under a system of proportional representation, and provided for further electoral reform. In August Parliament approved a similar system for elections to the Chamber of Deputies. The Senate has 315 elected members (seats allocated on a regional basis) and 10 life Senators. The Chamber of Deputies has 630 members. The minimum voting age is 25 years for the Senate and 18 years for the Chamber. The two houses have equal power.

The President of the Republic is a constitutional Head of State elected for seven years by an electoral college comprising both Houses of Parliament and 58 regional representatives. Executive power is exercised by the Council of Ministers. The Head of State appoints the President of the Council (Prime Minister) and, on the latter's recommendation, other ministers. The Council is responsible to Parliament.

The country is divided into 20 regions, of which five (Sicily, Sardinia, Trentino-Alto Adige, Friuli-Venezia Giulia and Valle d'Aosta) enjoy a special status. There is a large degree of regional autonomy. Each region has a Regional Council elected every five years by universal suffrage and a Giunta regionale responsible to the regional council. The Regional Council is a legislative assembly, while the Giunta holds executive power. The regions are subdivided into a total of 95 provinces.

In June 1997 a parliamentary commission on constitutional reform, which had been established in January, announced its recommendations, which included: a directly-elected President for a six-year term with overall control of foreign and defence policy; a reduction of the Chamber of Deputies from 630 to 400 members and of the Senate from 315 to 200 members; greater financial autonomy for the regional councils; and a second round of voting for seats allocated on the basis of a simple plurality. The commission's recommendations required approval by both the Chamber of Deputies and the Senate prior to endorsement at a national referendum. A referendum, held in May 2000, at which the electorate were required to vote on abolishing proportional representation, was deemed to be invalid due to low turnout.

Defence

Italy has been a member of the North Atlantic Treaty Organisation (NATO—see p. 241) since 1949. In August 2000 it maintained armed forces totalling 250,600 (conscripts numbered an estimated 111,888), including an army of 153,000, a navy of 38,000 and an air force of 59,600. There were also paramilitary forces numbering 252,500 men (including 110,000 Carabinieri). Military service lasts 10 months in all the services. However, in 1999 the Government approved a draft law phasing out military conscription by 2005 and introducing women soldiers. The law, which would replace the current defence force with a professional army of some 190,000, was approved by the legislature in June 2000. The 2000 state budget allocated 32,800,000m. lire to defence.

Economic Affairs

In 1998, according to estimates by the World Bank, Italy's gross national product (GNP), measured at average 1996–98 prices, was US $1,157,001m., equivalent to $20,090 per head (or $20,365 per head on an international purchasing-power parity basis). During 1990–98, it was estimated, GNP per head increased, in real terms, at an average annual rate of 1.0%. Over the same period the population increased by an average of 0.2% per year. In 1999 estimated GNP was $1,136,000m. ($19,710 per head). Italy's gross domestic product (GDP) increased, in real terms, by an average of 1.2% per year in 1990–99. Real GDP increased by 2.9% in 1995, by 0.6% in 1996 and by 1.5% in 1997.

Agriculture (including forestry and fishing) contributed 3.0% of GDP in 1999. In that year 5.4% of the employed labour force were engaged in the agricultural sector. The principal crops are sugar beet, maize, grapes, wheat and tomatoes. Italy is a leading producer and exporter of wine. During 1995–99 the real GDP of the agricultural sector increased at an average rate of 2.3% per year.

Industry (including mining, manufacturing, construction and power) contributed 28.4% of GDP in 1999; 32.3% of the employed labour force were engaged in industrial activities in that year. The State has traditionally played a major role in the development of heavy industry. In 1990–94 industrial GDP increased, in real terms, at an annual average rate of only 0.3% per year; this increased to 1.0% per year in 1995–99.

The major product of the mining sector is petroleum, followed by rock salt, talc, fluorspar and barytes. Italy also has reserves of lignite, lead and zinc. Reserves of epithermal gold in Sardinia were discovered in 1996. Mining GDP increased at an average rate of 1.0% per year during 1995–99.

Manufacturing contributed about 20% of GDP in the early 1990s, according to World Bank estimates; 23.6% of the employed labour force were engaged in mining and manufacturing (excluding the energy sector) in 1999. The most important branches of manufacturing in 1994, measured by gross value of output, were non-electric machinery (accounting for 12.2% of the total), metals and metal products (11.7%), food products (10.5%), chemical products (9.0%) and refined petroleum products (8.1%). In 1995–99 the GDP of the construction sector increased, in real terms, at an average annual rate of 0.5%. More than 80% of energy requirements are imported. In 1988 58% of requirements were derived from petroleum; coal-fired electricity generating stations provided 14.6%, natural gas-fired stations provided 12.6%, and nuclear power stations provided 4.6%. In late 1996 plans were announced for the construction of an integrated gasification and combined cycle power plant. In 1998 imports of mineral fuels and lubricants accounted for 5.6% of the value of total imports.

Services engaged 62.2% of the employed labour force in 1999 and accounted for 68.6% of GDP in that year. The combined GDP of the services sector increased, in real terms, at an estimated average rate of 1.2% per year in 1990–94 and by 1.5% per year in 1995–99. Tourism is an important source of income, and in 1999 a total of 32.1m. foreigners visited Italy. Tourist receipts totalled US $29,714m. in 1997. There were 1.8m. hotel beds in 1998.

In 1999 Italy recorded a visible trade surplus of US $20,383m., and a surplus of $6,304m. on the current account of the balance of payments. In that year the principal source of imports (19.0%) was Germany; other major suppliers were France (12.5%), the Netherlands (6.2%) and the United Kingdom (6.1%). Germany was also the principal market for exports (16.5%); other major purchasers in that year were France (13.0%), the USA (9.5%), the United Kingdom (7.1%) and Spain (6.3%). In 1999 Italy's fellow members of the European Union (EU—see p. 181) purchased 57.4% of its exports. The principal exports in 1998 were machinery and transport equipment, clothing and footwear, basic manufactures, and chemicals and related products. The principal imports were machinery and transport equipment, basic manufactures, chemicals and related products, and food and live animals.

The budgetary deficit for 1998 was equivalent to 3.5% of annual GDP. At the end of 1999 Italy's total accumulated government debt was equivalent to 114.9% of annual GDP. The

annual rate of inflation averaged 3.8% in 1990–99; it averaged 2.0% in 1997, 1.8% in 1998 and 1.7% in 1999. As a percentage of the total labour force, unemployment was 11.3% in 1999. According to government sources, unemployment was 10.0% in October 2000, the lowest level in eight years.

Italy is a member of the EU, the Organisation for Economic Co-operation and Development (OECD, p. 247) and the Central European Initiative (p. 316).

Italy has long-term structural problems, principally the underdevelopment of the southern part of the country, a low level of agricultural productivity, and heavy dependence on imported energy supplies. From mid-1995 government economic policy was directed towards meeting the economic convergence criteria for European economic and monetary union (EMU). Despite a continuing high level of public debt, Italy was among the first countries to adopt a single European currency, the euro, in January 1999. The Government proposed to reduce its level of public debt to 107% of GDP by 2001 and to 60% of GDP by 2016; in 2000 public debt represented 112.1% of GDP (compared with 144.9% in 1999). In February 2000 it was announced that the gas market was to be liberalized by January 2003 to comply with EU regulations, putting an end to the monopoly held by the principal producer and distributor of gas and petroleum, Eni. The European Commission also insisted on the closure of the state holding company, Iri, at the end of June 2000, as its operations contravened rules prohibiting state aid to industry. The privatization programme proceeded with the partial sale of government stakes in Eni and Enel (electricity), as well as the sale of the remainder of its stake in Telecom Italia (telecommunications, largely privatized in 1997), which was due to take place in early 2001. The programme had been accelerated in an attempt to make up a shortfall in revenue needed to meet debt reduction pledges, following the sale of third-generation mobile telephone licences held in October 2000, which generated less income than had been expected. Draft budget proposals for 2001, presented in September 2000, included substantial tax reductions as well as increases in benefit payments, which were to be funded through the implementation of a more efficient tax collection system. Since 1996 significant structural reform of taxations had been introduced, including the reduction of corporate taxes and the expansion of the tax base, including the introduction of capital gains tax in 1998. The increased revenue generated by these improvements was also expected to reduce the budget deficit from 1.3% of GDP in 2000 to 0.8% of GDP in 2001. GDP was projected to increase by 2.9% in that year (compared with 2.8% in 2000). However, Italy's economy needed structural economic reforms, including the reduction of the state's onerous pension liabilities and the creation of a more flexible work-force in order to promote long-term prosperity. Growth was threatened by high international petroleum prices, which have already had an adverse effect on inflation, owing to Italy's dependence on imported energy, rising European interest rates and by a deceleration in the US economy.

Social Welfare

Italy has a comprehensive system of social benefits covering unemployment and disability as well as retirement pensions and family allowances. These benefits are all provided by the social security system (Istituto Nazionale della Previdenza Sociale). There is also an industrial injuries scheme, operated by the Istituto Nazionale per l'Assicurazione contro gli Infortuni sul Lavoro. Legislation approved in August 1995 allowed for the separation of state pensions from all other social security payments and introduced a contributions-based pension with a minimum retirement age of 52 years, rising gradually to 57 years by 2008 (with 35 and 40 years' contributions respectively).

A comprehensive national health service, aiming to provide free medical care for all citizens, was introduced in 1980. However, minimum charges are still made for essential medicines, medical examinations and hospital treatment. All workers are eligible for benefits under a unified national medical insurance scheme. In 1997 Italy had a total of 334,613 hospital beds: equivalent to 5.8 per 1,000 head of population. In that year there were 114,756 physicians working in Italy (2.0 per 1,000 head of population). In 1992 the state budget allocated 91,624,000m. lire to health. In 1996, according to the IMF, current expenditure on social security and welfare by the central Government (including social security funds) was 360,800,000m. lire (39.1% of total current spending).

Education

Education is free and compulsory between the ages of six and 14 years. The curricula of all Italian schools are standardized by the Ministry of Education. After primary school, for children aged six to 10 years, the pupil enters the lower secondary school (scuola media unificata). An examination at the end of three years leads to a lower secondary school certificate, which gives access to all higher secondary schools. Pupils wishing to enter a classical lycée (liceo classico) must also pass an examination in Latin.

Higher secondary education is provided by classical, artistic and scientific lycées, training schools for elementary teachers and technical and vocational institutes (industrial, commercial, nautical, etc.). After five years at a lycée, the student sits an examination for the higher secondary school certificate (maturità), which allows automatic entry into any university faculty. Special four-year courses are provided at the teachers' training schools and the diploma obtained permits entry to a special university faculty of education, the magistero, and a few other faculties. The technical institutes provide practical courses that prepare students for a specialized university faculty.

In 1996 the total enrolment at primary and secondary schools was equivalent to 97% of the school-age population. Primary enrolment in that year was equivalent to 100% of all children in the relevant age-group, while the comparable ratio for secondary enrolment was 95%. In 1995 the average rate of adult illiteracy was estimated at 1.8% (males 1.3%; females 2.2%).

University courses last for a minimum of four years. Study allowances are awarded to students according to their means and merit. In 1992 government expenditure on education (including higher education) was 80,268,000m. lire (equivalent to 5.4% of GNP).

Public Holidays

2001: 1 January (New Year's Day), 6 January (Epiphany), 16 April (Easter Monday), 25 April (Liberation Day), 1 May (Labour Day), 15 August (Assumption), 1 November (All Saints' Day), 8 December (Immaculate Conception), 25 December (Christmas Day), 26 December (St Stephen).

2002: 1 January (New Year's Day), 6 January (Epiphany), 1 April (Easter Monday), 25 April (Liberation Day), 1 May (Labour Day), 15 August (Assumption), 1 November (All Saints' Day), 8 December (Immaculate Conception), 25 December (Christmas Day), 26 December (St Stephen).

There are also numerous local public holidays, held on the feast day of the patron saint of each town.

Weights and Measures

The metric system is in force.

Statistical Survey

Source (unless otherwise stated): Istituto Nazionale di Statistica, Via Cesare Balbo 16, 00184 Rome;
tel. (06) 46731; fax (06) 46733101; e-mail dipdiff@istat.it; internet www.istat.it.

Area and Population

AREA, POPULATION AND DENSITY

Area (sq km)	301,338*
Population (census results)	
25 October 1981	
Males	27,506,354
Females	29,050,557
Total	56,556,911
20 October 1991	56,778,031
Population (official estimates at 31 December)	
1997	57,563,354
1998	57,612,615
1999	57,679,895
Density (per sq km) at 31 December 1999	191.4

* 116,346 sq miles.

REGIONS (31 December 1999)

Region	Area (sq km)	Population	Regional capital	Population of capital
Abruzzo . .	10,798	1,279,016	L'Aquila	69,839
Basilicata . .	9,992	606,183	Potenza	69,735
Calabria . .	15,080	2,050,478	Catanzaro	96,700
Campania . .	13,595	5,780,958	Napoli (Naples)	1,002,619
Emilia-Romagna .	22,124	3,981,146	Bologna	381,161
Friuli-Venezia Giulia . .	7,855	1,185,172	Trieste	216,459
Lazio . . .	17,207	5,264,077	Roma (Rome)	2,643,581
Liguria .	5,421	1,625,870	Genova (Genoa)	636,104
Lombardia (Lombardy) .	23,861	9,065,440	Milano (Milan)	1,300,977
Marche . .	9,694	1,460,999	Ancona	98,329
Molise . . .	4,438	327,987	Campobasso	51,413
Piemonte (Piedmont) .	25,399	4,287,465	Torino (Turin)	903,705
Puglia . . .	19,362	4,085,239	Bari	331,848
Sardegna (Sardinia) .	24,090	1,651,888	Cagliari	165,926
Sicilia (Sicily) .	25,708	5,087,794	Palermo	683,794
Toscana (Tuscany) .	22,997	3,536,392	Firenze (Florence)	376,662
Trentino-Alto Adige .	13,607	936,256	Bolzano (Bozen)*	97,232
			Trento (Trent, Trient)*	104,906
Umbria .	8,456	835,488	Perugia	156,673
Valle d'Aosta .	3,263	120,343	Aosta	34,741
Veneto . . .	18,392	4,511,714	Venezia (Venice)	277,305

* Joint regional capitals.

PRINCIPAL TOWNS (population at 31 December 1999)

Roma (Rome, the capital) . .	2,643,581	Perugia . . .	156,673
Milano (Milan) .	1,300,977	Foggia	154,891
Napoli (Naples) .	1,002,619	Salerno . . .	142,055
Torino (Turin) .	903,705	Reggio nell' Emilia .	143,664
Palermo . .	683,794	Ravenna . .	138,122
Genova (Genoa) .	636,104	Ferrara . . .	132,127
Bologna . .	381,161	Rimini . . .	131,,062
Firenze (Florence) .	376,662	Siracusa (Syracuse) .	126,282
Catania . .	337,862	Sassari . . .	120,803
Bari . . .	331,848	Monza . . .	119,516
Venezia (Venice) .	277,305	Bergamo . .	117,837
Messina . .	259,156	Pescara . . .	115,698
Verona . .	255,268	Latina . . .	114,099
Trieste . .	216,459	Vicenza . . .	109,738
Padova (Padua) .	211,391	Terni . . .	107,770
Taranto . .	208,214	Forlí . . .	107,475
Brescia . .	191,317	Trento (Trent, Trient) . .	104,906
Reggio di Calabria .	179,617	Novara . . .	102,237
Modena . .	176,022	Piacenza . .	98,384
Prato . . .	172,473	Ancona . .	98,329
Parma . .	168,717	Lecce . . .	98,208
Cagliari . .	165,926	Bolzano (Bozen) .	97,232
Livorno (Leghorn) .	161,673		

BIRTHS, MARRIAGES AND DEATHS

	Registered live births		Registered marriages		Registered deaths	
	Number	Rate (per 1,000)	Number	Rate (per 1,000)	Number	Rate (per 1,000)
1992 . .	560,768	9.9	303,785	5.3	541,418	9.5
1993 . .	538,168	9.4	292,632	5.1	543,433	9.5
1994 . .	527,406	9.2	285,112	5.0	548,081	9.6
1995 . .	525,609	9.2	290,009	5.1	566,690	9.7
1996 . .	528,103	9.2	278,611	4.9	554,576	9.7
1997 . .	528,901*	9.2	277,738	4.8	561,207	9.6
1998† .	515,439	9.0	276,570	4.8	569,418	9.9
1999† .	523,463	9.1	275,250	4.8	565,838	9.8

* Estimate.
† Provisional figures.

Expectation of life (years at birth, 1994): Males 74.3; Females 80.7.
Source: UN, *Demographic Yearbook*.

EMIGRATION

Destination	1994	1995	1996
Belgium	3,845	2,177	1,870
France	5,181	3,371	3,448
Germany	21,407	10,816	10,805
Switzerland	10,449	4,560	5,149
United Kingdom	3,515	2,787	3,666
Other European countries . .	6,380	6,780	8,049
Argentina	1,936	1,592	1,478
Brazil	636	641	770
Canada	1,082	693	706
USA	4,135	3,043	3,939
Venezuela	632	433	484
Oceania	866	692	656
Other countries	5,484	5,718	6,590
Total	65,548	43,303	47,610

ECONOMICALLY ACTIVE POPULATION*
(annual averages, '000 persons aged 15 years and over)

	1997	1998	1999
Agriculture, hunting and forestry .	1,201	1,156	1,089
Fishing	44	45	46
Mining and quarrying . . .	67	74	70
Manufacturing	4,839	4,921	4,928
Electricity, gas and water supply	191	191	176
Construction.	1,564	1,544	1,575
Wholesale and retail trade; repair of motor vehicles, motorcycles and personal and household goods	3,234	3,266	3,308
Hotels and restaurants . . .	691	676	739
Transport, storage and communications	1,099	1,097	1,133
Financial intermediation . . .	647	673	671
Real estate, renting and business activities	1,153	1,217	1,336
Public administration and defence; compulsory social security	1,924	1,939	1,943
Education	1,430	1,426	1,445
Health and social work . . .	1,261	1,281	1,289
Other community, social and personal service activities . .	849	878	898
Private households with employed persons	202	215	201
Extra-territorial organizations and bodies.	17	18	17
Total employed	20,413	20,618	20,864
Unemployed	2,688	2,745	2,669
Total labour force	23,101	23,363	23,533
Males	14,515	14,586	14,596
Females	8,586	8,776	8,937

Source: ILO, *Yearbook of Labour Statistics*.

Agriculture

PRINCIPAL CROPS ('000 metric tons)

	1997	1998	1999
Wheat	6,758	8,338	7,762
Rice (paddy)	1,442	1,407	1,363
Barley	1,180	1,359	1,318
Maize	10,005	9,055	10,014
Oats	311	363	332
Sorghum	174	160	207
Potatoes	2,020	2,195	2,080
Soybeans (Soya beans) . . .	1,146	1,231	870
Sunflowers	488	466	434
Olives	3,591	2,549	3,881
Cabbages	300	304	313
Artichokes	521	509	472
Tomatoes	5,575	5,366	6,844
Cauliflowers	494	494	508
Pumpkins, squash and gourds .	465	465	285
Aubergines (Egg-plants) . . .	361	258	252
Onions (dry)	447	451	460
Green beans	193	191	193
Carrots	458	472	507
Broccoli	171	173	180
Fennel	503	508	490
Salad (fresh)	919	854	849
Celery	n.a.	141	125
Peppers	357	246	243
Courgettes	465	340	252
Strawberries	161	81	83
Watermelons	590*†	590*‡	471
Melons	520	417	409
Grapes	8,058	9,257	9,362
Sugar beet	13,803	13,382	13,971
Apples	1,967	2,143	2,343
Pears	589	965	812
Peaches and nectarines . . .	1,158	1,426	1,765
Apricots	103	136	212
Plums	114	149	189
Oranges	1,824	1,294	1,810
Lemons and limes	574	460	523
Mandarins and clementines . .	502	422	591
Almonds (in the shell) . . .	105	88	104
Hazelnuts	90	117	118
Tobacco	131	132	n.a.

* Source: FAO, *Production Yearbook*.
† Unofficial figure.   ‡ FAO estimate.

LIVESTOCK ('000 head, year ending September)

	1997	1998	1999
Horses*	305	288	288
Mules*	12	11	11
Asses*	25	23	23
Cattle	7,163	7,166	7,150
Buffaloes	150	162	170
Pigs	8,171	8,281	8,225
Sheep	10,943	10,894	10,770
Goats	1,419	1,347	1,365
Chickens	108,345†	115,000*	106,000*
Turkeys*	25,000	26,000	25,000

* FAO estimate(s).
† Provisional figure.
Source: FAO.

LIVESTOCK PRODUCTS ('000 metric tons)

	1997	1998	1999
Beef and veal	1,159	1,111	1,164
Mutton and lamb	72	70	70
Goat meat	4	3	4
Pig meat	1,396	1,412	1,472
Horse meat	53	50	50
Poultry meat	1,134	1,154	1,154
Other meat	242	244	242
Cows' milk	11,319	11,236*	11,236†
Buffaloes' milk	144	89	89†
Sheeps' milk	759	780†	780†
Goats' milk	133*	131*	131†
Butter	93	91	91†
Cheese	949	910	910
Hen eggs	775*	783*	786*
Wool: greasy	11	11	11†

* Provisional figure.
† FAO estimate.
Source: FAO.

Forestry

ROUNDWOOD REMOVALS ('000 cubic metres, excl. bark)

	1997	1998
Sawlogs, veneer logs and logs for sleepers	2,169	2,533
Pulpwood	820	984
Other industrial wood	799	871
Fuel wood	5,140	5,183
Total	8,928	9,570

SAWNWOOD PRODUCTION
('000 cubic metres, incl. railway sleepers)

	1996	1997	1998
Coniferous (softwood)	750	788	700
Broadleaved (hardwood)	900	963	900
Total	1,650	1,751	1,600

Source: FAO, *Yearbook of Forest Products*.

Fishing

('000 metric tons, live weight)

	1996	1997	1998
Capture	365.9	341.0	315.6
European hake	30.7	18.0	13.2
European pilchard	42.1	38.2	36.4
European anchovy	40.5	53.4	44.4
Mediterranean mussel	22.2	21.4	39.0
Striped venus	36.7	28.6	28.8
Aquaculture	209.4	211.7	246.6
Rainbow trout	48.0	51.0	48.0
Mediterranean mussel	105.0	103.0	130.0
Clams	40.3	40.0	48.8
Total catch	575.3	552.7	562.2

Note: Figures exclude aquatic plants ('000 metric tons): 6.9 (capture 1.9, aquaculture 5.0) in 1996; 7.0 (capture 2.0, aquaculture 5.0) in 1997; 5.0 (capture 2.0, aquaculture 3.0) in 1998.
Source: FAO, *Yearbook of Fishery Statistics*.

Mining

('000 metric tons)

	1997	1998	1999
Lead concentrates*	17.6	10.1	9.7
Zinc concentrates*	15.4	5.2	—
Barytes	26.7	31.8	24.6
Fluorspar	105.8	104.2	46.9
Petroleum	5,892.0	5,560.1	5,049.4
Natural gas (million cu m)	19,123.4	18,981.3	17,635.2
Lignite	222.4	93.7	—
Salt	3,594.5	3,413.5	3,338.1
Talc	140.8	133.6	123.5

* Figures refer to gross weight of ores and concentrates.

Industry

SELECTED PRODUCTS
('000 metric tons, unless otherwise indicated)

	1997	1998	1999
Wine ('000 hectolitres)	n.a.	56,896.0	n.a.
Pig iron	11,377.9	10,792.7	10,664.5
Steel	25,769.2	25,782.3	24,780.4
Rolled iron	23,894.1	23,367.8	23,463.4
Other iron and steel-finished manufactures	3,197.8	3,279.4	3,277.9
Iron alloys and *spiegel-eisen* special pig irons	154.4	150.4	92.9
Fuel oil	16,766.3	17,630.3	15,688.9
Sulphuric acid at 50° Bé	2,214.3	2,013.4	1,627.2
Synthetic organic dyes	26.6	n.a.	n.a.
Caustic soda	855.3	722.0	810.0
Cotton yarn	266.4	262.4	239.3
Natural methane gas (million cu m)	19,123.4	18,981.3	17,635.2
Passenger motor cars ('000)	1,562.9	1,378.5	1,384.3
Lorries (Trucks) ('000)	258.5	282.4	291.3
Hydroelectric power (million kWh)*	46.7	47.6	51.8
Thermoelectric power (million kWh)*	200.9	208.0	209.1

* Net production.

Finance

CURRENCY AND EXCHANGE RATES

Monetary Units
100 centèsimi (singular: centèsimo) = 1 Italian lira (plural: lire).

Sterling, Dollar and Euro Equivalents (29 December 2000)
£1 sterling = 3,105.1 lire;
US $1 = 2,080.9 lire;
€1 = 1,936.3 lire;
10,000 lire = £3.221 = $4.806 = €5.165.

Average Exchange Rate (lire per US $)
1998   1,736.2
1999   1,817.4
2000   2,106.3

Note: Since the introduction of the euro, with Italian participation, on 1 January 1999, a fixed exchange rate of €1 = 1,936.27 lire has been in operation.

STATE BUDGET ('000 million lire)*

Revenue†	1996	1997	1998
Taxation	760,405	825,816	785,366
Taxes on income, profits, etc.	266,400	295,646	254,751
Social security contributions .	276,648	293,122	261,822
Domestic taxes on goods and			
services.	189,958	210,105	243,316
Other current revenue . .	38,406	57,217	58,828
Entrepreneurial and property			
income	12,304	21,785	23,211
Capital revenue	3,033	4,866	4,375
Adjustment	11	—	—
Total	801,855	887,899	848,569

Expenditure‡	1996	1997	1998
Current expenditure . . .	876,233	891,116	858,902
Expenditure on goods and			
services.	172,657	164,270	177,216
Wages and salaries . .	132,571	137,371	143,161
Interest payments . . .	191,036	177,703	151,010
Subsidies and other current			
transfers	512,540	549,143	530,676
Capital expenditure . . .	51,271	49,963	49,510
Acquisition of fixed capital			
assets	11,591	12,457	14,414
Capital transfers . . .	39,680	37,506	35,096
Domestic	39,402	37,258	34,791
Total	927,504	941,079	923,813

* Figures represent the consolidated operations of the Central Government, comprising the General Account Budget and the budgets of three autonomous agencies and 12 social security institutions. Data exclude the accounts of the Deposit and Loan Fund and miscellaneous extrabudgetary agencies.
† Excluding grants received ('000 million lire): 9,293 in 1996; 8,637 in 1997; 8,668 in 1998.
‡ Excluding lending minus repayments ('000 million lire): 16,363 in 1996; 15,737 in 1997; 15,401 in 1998.

Source: IMF, *Government Finance Statistics Yearbook*.

INTERNATIONAL RESERVES (US $ million at 31 December)*

	1998	1999	2000
Gold†	24,711	22,880	21,635
IMF special drawing rights . .	111	168	238
Reserve position in IMF . . .	4,330	3,546	2,906
Foreign exchange . . .	25,447	18,623	22,423
Total	54,599	45,217	47,202

* Excluding deposits made with the European Monetary Institute (now the European Central Bank).
† Valued at market-related prices.

Source: IMF, *International Financial Statistics*.

MONEY SUPPLY ('000 million lire at 31 December)*

	1998	1999	2000
Currency outside banks . .	126,540	71,960	76,420
Demand deposits at commercial			
banks	601,150	385,300	407,890
Total money	727,690	457,260	484,310

* Figures are rounded to the nearest 10,000 million lire.
Source: IMF, *International Financial Statistics*.

COST OF LIVING (Consumer Price Index; base: 1990 = 100)

	1997	1998	1999
Food (incl. beverages) . .	130.9	132.4	132.9
Fuel and light	132.8	132.1	130.2
Clothing (incl. footwear) . .	131.7	135.2	137.7
Rent	163.4	171.9	177.6
All items (incl. others) . .	135.5	138.0	140.3

Source: ILO, *Yearbook of Labour Statistics*.

NATIONAL ACCOUNTS ('000 million lire at current prices)
National Income and Product

	1994	1995	1996
Compensation of employees . .	698,174	727,779	768,358
Operating surplus . . .	572,440	637,567	676,120
Domestic factor incomes . .	1,270,614	1,365,346	1,444,478
Consumption of fixed capital .	203,398	219,629	231,781
Gross domestic product (GDP)			
at factor cost . . .	1,474,012	1,584,975	1,676,259
Indirect taxes	204,154	221,181	234,685
Less Subsidies	39,500	35,138	37,450
GDP in purchasers' values .	1,638,666	1,771,018	1,873,494
Factor income received from			
abroad	46,355	55,657	59,574
Less Factor income paid abroad	73,697	81,526	83,790
Gross national product . .	1,611,324	1,745,149	1,849,278
Less Consumption of fixed capital	203,398	219,629	231,781
National income in market			
prices	1,407,926	1,525,520	1,617,497
Other current transfers from			
abroad	19,774	21,455	22,109
Less Other current transfers paid			
abroad	31,072	29,173	33,659
National disposable income .	1,396,628	1,517,802	1,605,947

Expenditure on the Gross Domestic Product*

	1997	1998	1999
Government final consumption			
expenditure	369,455	381,634	395,629
Private final consumption			
expenditure	1,158,922	1,210,066	1,257,113
Increase in stocks . . .	15,361	25,699	30,132
Gross fixed capital formation . .	359,624	381,152	402,659
Total domestic expenditure .	1,903,362	1,998,551	2,085,533
Exports of goods and services .	524,445	547,238	543,048
Less Imports of goods and services	443,957	478,086	500,416
GDP in purchasers' values . .	1,983,850	2,067,703	2,128,165
GDP at constant 1995 prices .	1,839,624	1,867,796	1,894,407

* Figures are rounded to the nearest 100,000 million lire.

Gross Domestic Product by Economic Activity

	1997	1998	1999
Agriculture, forestry, hunting and			
fishing	58,081	58,064	58,865
Energy and water	54,593	56,894	57,652
Industrial transformations* . .	387,181	401,835	406,243
Construction	91,478	92,333	94,722
Trade, restaurants and hotels† .	312,035	322,796	332,374
Transport, storage and			
communications . . .	133,464	142,544	146,610
Other private services . .	457,423	474,825	488,849
Government services . . .	362,569	370,998	381,663
Sub-total	1,856,824	1,920,288	1,966,976
Import duties	206,557	225,550	238,667
Less Imputed bank service charge	79,531	78,135	77,478
GDP in purchasers' values .	1,983,850	2,067,703	2,128,165

* Mining and manufacturing, excluding energy.
† Including repair services.

BALANCE OF PAYMENTS (US $ million)

	1997	1998	1999
Exports of goods f.o.b. . .	240,404	242,572	230,829
Imports of goods f.o.b. . .	−200,527	−206,941	−210,445
Trade balance . . .	39,878	35,631	20,383
Exports of services . . .	66,991	67,549	61,464
Imports of services . . .	−59,227	−63,379	−58,672
Balance on goods and services	47,642	39,801	23,176
Other income received . .	45,734	51,319	45,942
Other income paid . . .	−56,936	−63,636	−57,434
Balance on goods, services and income	36,440	27,483	11,683
Current transfers received . .	15,552	14,402	16,729
Current transfers paid . .	−19,588	−21,887	−22,108
Current balance . . .	32,403	19,998	6,304
Capital account (net). . .	3,434	2,358	2,933
Direct investment abroad. .	−10,414	−12,407	−6,746
Direct investment from abroad	3,700	2,635	6,783
Portfolio investment assets .	−61,857	−109,064	−129,624
Portfolio investment liabilities	73,375	111,987	104,607
Financial derivatives assets .	−1,118	−850	161
Financial derivatives liabilities	1,273	1,041	1,709
Other investment assets . .	−25,541	−21,232	−32,573
Other investment liabilities .	13,703	9,816	37,751
Net errors and omissions . .	−15,810	−25,754	644
Overall balance . . .	13,150	−21,472	−8,051

Source: IMF, *International Financial Statistics*.

External Trade

Note: Data refer to the trade of Italy (excluding San Marino and the commune of Campione). The figures include trade in second-hand ships, and stores and bunkers for foreign ships and aircraft, but exclude manufactured gas, surplus military equipment, war reparations and repayments and gift parcels by post. Also excluded are imports of military goods and exports of fish landed abroad directly from Italian vessels.

PRINCIPAL COMMODITIES (distribution by SITC, '000 million lire)

Imports c.i.f.	1996	1997	1998
Food and live animals . .	30,539.6	31,866.6	32,601.5
Crude materials (inedible) except fuels . .	21,544.9	23,462.4	23,082.9
Mineral fuels and lubricants .	26,875.6	28,124.4	20,853.1
Petroleum and petroleum products	24,505.6	25,293.4	18,406.2
Crude petroleum . . .	17,383.1	18,631.8	13,720.6
Refined petroleum products .	6,584.6	5,869.4	3,958.2
Chemicals and related products . . .	41,769.7	46,461.8	48,270.0
Organic chemicals . . .	12,346.6	13,583.4	13,650.9
Medicinal and pharmaceutical products	7,137.5	8,160.4	9,431.6
Artificial resins and plastic materials, and cellulose esters and ethers	8,865.6	9,840.8	9,742.8
Products of polymerization etc.	7,183.6	7,817.2	7,830.0
Basic manufactures . .	51,918.3	58,235.8	62,254.6
Textile yarn, fabrics, etc. . .	9,497.0	11,048.2	11,446.1
Iron and steel	12,219.0	13,894.9	15,784.7
Non-ferrous metals . . .	8,189.8	9,489.0	9,782.7
Machinery and transport equipment . .	96,782.3	110,505.2	126,302.0
Machinery specialized for particular industries . .	7,324.8	7,594.6	8,975.1
Office machines and automatic data-processing equipment .	11,568.8	12,159.8	13,270.1
Telecommunications and sound recording and reproducing apparatus and equipment . .	7,013.6	9,709.1	11,588.7

Imports c.i.f. — *continued*	1996	1997	1998
Other electrical machinery, apparatus, etc. . . .	17,118.6	18,281.0	18,984.7
Road vehicles and parts . .	31,517.4	38,855.8	44,055.7
Passenger motor cars (excl. buses)	22,309.3	28,665.8	31,385.2
Miscellaneous manufactured articles . . .	30,786.4	35,456.0	38,197.4
Clothing and accessories (excl. footwear)	7,761.7	9,129.5	10,146.9
Special transactions and commodities not classified according to kind . .	15,043.7	16,893.1	16,489.3
Gold, non-monetary (excluding gold ores and concentrates) . .	6,264.3	7,181.9	7,140.6
Total (incl. others) . . .	321,285.8	357,586.7	374,283.1

Exports f.o.b.	1996	1997	1998
Food and live animals . .	20,334.6	21,168.9	21,645.1
Chemicals and related products . . .	30,510.5	33,770.4	35,073.4
Basic manufactures . .	82,784.9	87,742.9	89,893.5
Textile yarn, fabrics, etc. . .	20,370.6	22,119.4	22,635.7
Non-metallic mineral manufactures . . .	13,870.5	14,713.3	15,073.4
Iron and steel	11,806.0	12,523.1	12,639.7
Other manufactures of metals .	15,732.2	16,384.4	17,105.0
Machinery and transport equipment . . .	148,904.3	154,589.7	164,055.2
Machinery specialized for particular industries . .	28,209.9	30,245.0	28,929.6
General industrial machinery and equipment	39,811.8	41,526.6	44,094.4
Electrical machinery, apparatus, etc. (excl. telecommunications and sound equipment) . .	23,297.2	24,107.8	24,837.1
Domestic electrical equipment .	8,449.8	8,974.3	9,194.1
Road vehicles and parts . .	30,939.2	31,633.5	33,994.5
Passenger motor cars (excl. buses)	12,109.9	10,993.6	11,956.8
Miscellaneous manufactured articles . . .	87,867.8	91,424.8	91,026.5
Furniture and parts thereof .	13,766.3	2,630.5	2,273.1
Clothing and accessories (excl. footwear) . . .	24,946.8	25,543.9	25,643.4
Outer garments and other articles, knitted or crocheted, not elastic nor rubberized .	23,482.8	24,023.4	24,150.5
Footwear	13,838.1	14,009.1	13,490.1
Jewellery, goldsmiths' and silversmiths' wares, etc. .	7,637.5	8,205.1	8,237.4
Total (incl. others) . . .	388,885.1	409,128.3	420,764.1

PRINCIPAL TRADING PARTNERS ('000 million lire)*

Imports c.i.f.	1997	1998	1999
Algeria	5,053.0	4,442	5,424
Austria	8,313.9	9,305	9,586
Belgium-Luxembourg . .	16,750.4	18,315	17,557
China, People's Republic . .	7,515.5	8,407	9,682
France	47,580.3	50,135	49,271
Germany	64,640.9	71,935	74,950
Ireland	n.a.	4,200	5,551
Japan	7,180.3	8,222	9,987
Libya	7,592.4	5,515	6,000
Netherlands	22,063.3	23,479	24,682
Russia	7,280.1	6,462	8,153
Saudi Arabia . . .	3,662.3	2,412	2,133
South Africa . . .	n.a.	4,152	4,292
Spain	17,037.7	17,374	16,958
Sweden	5,029.5	5,832	6,116
Switzerland . . .	13,745.7	15,177	15,088
United Kingdom . . .	24,115.4	24,427	23,948
USA	17,382.7	18,895	19,408
Total (incl. others) . . .	357,586.7	378,783	394,271

Exports f.o.b.		1997	1998	1999
Austria		9,323.9	9,810	9,764
Belgium-Luxembourg	. .	11,141.8	11,683	11,680
Brazil	.	5,988.0	5,738	4,655
China, People's Republic .	.	4,305.5	3,567.5	3,551
France	.	50,071.6	55,009	54,516
Germany	.	67,388.1	70,924	69,119
Greece	.	8,055.1	8,528	8,597
Hong Kong	.	6,817.5	5,346	4,955
Japan	.	8,028.0	7,010	6,793
Netherlands	.	11,714.5	12,352	12,016
Poland	.	6,347.0	6,715.8	6,690
Portugal	.	5,479.3	6,058	6,248
Russia	.	6,556.8	5,406	3,338
Spain	.	21,334.4	24,944	26,609
Sweden	.	n.a.	4,588	4,515
Switzerland	.	13,901.9	14,682.9	14,827
Turkey	.	7,481.0	7,104.6	5,503
United Kingdom . . .	.	29,272.2	30,861	29,801
USA	.	32,191.2	36,797	39,803
Total (incl. others) . .	.	409,128.3	426,183	419,124

* Imports by country of production; exports by country of consumption.

Transport

STATE RAILWAYS (traffic)

		1997	1998	1999
Passenger journeys ('000)	. .	444,440	425,881	432,261
Passenger-km (million)	. .	43,591	41,392	40,971
Freight ton-km (million) .	.	25,228	24,704	23,781

ROAD TRAFFIC (vehicles in use at 31 December)

		1995	1996	1997
Passenger motor cars	. .	30,301,424	30,467,173	30,741,953
Buses and coaches	. . .	75,023	83,182	84,177
Goods vehicles	. . .	2,788,432	3,094,563	3,169,538

1999: Passenger motor cars 31,953,247; Buses and coaches 85,509; Goods vehicles 3,217,060.

SHIPPING

Merchant Fleet (registered at 31 December)

		1996	1997	1998
Number of vessels	. . .	1,348	1,324	1,329
Displacement ('000 grt)	. .	6,594	6,194	6,819

Source: Lloyd's Register of Shipping, *World Fleet Statistics*.

International Sea-borne Freight Traffic

	1993	1994	1995
Vessels entered ('000 nrt) .	168,545	180,175	181,733
Vessels cleared ('000 nrt) . .	84,044	91,288	96,505
Goods loaded ('000 metric tons) .	51,420	50,247	48,250
Goods unloaded ('000 metric tons) .	222,060	226,220	234,120

Source: UN, *Statistical Yearbook* and *Monthly Bulletin of Statistics*.
1996 ('000 metric tons): Goods loaded 59,218; Goods unloaded 248,063.

CIVIL AVIATION (traffic on scheduled services)

		1995	1996	1997
Kilometres flown (million)	. .	260	293	326
Passengers carried ('000) .	. .	23,396	25,868	27,241
Passenger-km (million)	. .	33,264	36,140	37,734

Tourism

	1996	1997	1998
Foreign tourist arrivals . .	29,324,237	29,903,670	30,941,982
Amount spent US $ million . .	30,017	29,714	n.a.

1999: 32,094,436 tourist arrivals.
Number of hotel beds: 1,772,096 in 1997; 1,782,382 in 1998.
Source: partly, World Tourism Organization, *Yearbook of Tourism Statistics*.

TOURIST ARRIVALS BY COUNTRY OF ORIGIN

		1996	1997	1998
Austria	.	1,618,326	1,615,797	1,628,362
Belgium	.	638,864	630,801	646,416
France	.	2,295,973	2,251,462	2,252,844
Germany	.	8,462,818	8,500,137	8,643,819
Japan	.	2,173,964	2,169,234	2,017,742
Netherlands	.	814,137	872,995	912,859
Switzerland	.	1,342,214	1,336,851	1,338,256
United Kingdom . . .	.	1,686,642	1,771,730	1,969,134
USA	.	2,884,149	3,168,636	3,585,823
Total (incl. others) . .	.	29,324,237	29,963,670	30,941,982

Source: World Tourism Organization, *Yearbook of Tourism Statistics*.

Communications Media

	1995	1996	1997
Telephones ('000 mainlines in use)	24,854	25,259	25,698
Telefax stations (number in use)	1,500,000	1,650,000	1,800,000
Mobile cellular telephones			
(subscribers)	3,923,000	6,422,000	11,737,904
Radio receivers ('000 in use) . .	47,000	50,000	50,500
Television receivers ('000 in use) .	25,500	30,000	30,000
Book production (titles) . .	34,470	35,236	n.a.
Daily newspapers:			
Number of titles . . .	76	78	n.a.
Average circulation ('000) . .	5,722	5,960	n.a.
Non-daily newspapers:			
Number of titles . . .	274	n.a.	n.a.
Average circulation ('000) . .	2,132	n.a.	n.a.

Source: UNESCO, *Statistical Yearbook* and UN, *Statistical Yearbook*.

Education

(1998/99, provisional)

		Schools	Teachers	Students
Pre-primary	.	25,666	139,132	1,577,696
Primary	.	19,073	281,909	2,859,379
Secondary:				
Scuola Media . . .	.	8,695	208,620	1,775,009
Secondaria Superiore . .	.	6,883	295,482	2,543,750
of which:				
Technical* . . .	.	2,966	139,392	1,113,794
Vocational* . . .	.	1,690	68,957	507,125
Teacher training* . .	.	762	22,317	200,305
Art Licei*	.	312	13,481	93,429
Classical, linguistic and				
scientific Licei* . .	.	2,158	68,854	747,107
Higher	.	56†	48,933	1,573,052

* Data refer to the 1995/96 academic year.
† Data refers to 1994/95 academic year.

Directory

The Constitution*

The Constitution of the Italian Republic was approved by the Constituent Assembly on 22 December 1947 and came into force on 1 January 1948 (and was amended in April 1993). The fundamental principles are declared in Articles 1–12, as follows:

Italy is a democratic republic based on the labour of the people.

The Republic recognizes and guarantees as inviolable the rights of its citizens, either as individuals or in a community, and it expects, in return, devotion to duty and the fulfilment of political, economic and social obligations.

All citizens shall enjoy equal status and shall be regarded as equal before the law, without distinction of sex, race, language or religion, and without regard to the political opinions which they may hold or their personal or social standing.

It shall be the function of the Republic to remove the economic and social inequalities which, by restricting the liberty of the individual, impede the full development of the human personality, thereby reducing the effective participation of the citizen in the political, economic and social life of the country.

The Republic recognizes the right of all citizens to work and shall do all in its power to give effect to this right.

The Republic, while remaining one and indivisible, shall recognize and promote local autonomy, fostering the greatest possible decentralization in those services which are administered by the State, and subordinating legislative methods and principles to the exigencies of decentralized and autonomous areas.

The State and the Catholic Church shall be sovereign and independent, each in its own sphere. Their relations shall be governed by the Lateran Pact (Patti Lateranensi), and any modification in the pact agreed upon by both parties shall not necessitate any revision of the Constitution.

All religious denominations shall have equal liberty before the law, denominations other than the Catholic having the right to worship according to their beliefs, in so far as they do not conflict with the common law of the country.

The Republic shall do all in its power to promote the development of culture and scientific and technical research. It shall also protect and preserve the countryside and the historical and artistic monuments which are the inheritance of the nation.

The juridical system of the Italian Republic shall be in conformity with the generally recognized practice of international law. The legal rights of foreigners in the country shall be regulated by law in accordance with international practice.

Any citizen of a foreign country who is deprived of democratic liberty such as is guaranteed under the Italian Constitution, has the right of asylum within the territory of the Republic in accordance with the terms of the law, and his extradition for political offences will not be granted.

Italy repudiates war as an instrument of offence against the liberty of other nations and as a means of resolving international disputes. Italy accepts, under parity with other nations, the limitations of sovereignty necessary for the preservation of peace and justice between nations. To that end, it will support and promote international organizations.

The Constitution is further divided into Parts I and II, in which are set forth respectively the rights and responsibilities of the citizen and the administration of the Republic.

PART ONE

Civic Clauses

Section I (Articles 13–28). The liberty of the individual is inviolable and no form of detention, restriction or inspection is permitted unless it be for juridical purposes and in accordance with the provisions of the law. The domicile of a person is likewise inviolable and shall be immune from forced inspection or sequestration, except according to the provisions of the law. Furthermore, all citizens shall be free to move wheresoever they will throughout the country, and may leave it and return to it without let or hindrance. Right of public meeting, if peaceful and without arms, is guaranteed. Secret organizations of a directly or indirectly political or military nature are, however, prohibited.

Freedom in the practice of religious faith is guaranteed.

The Constitution further guarantees complete freedom of thought, speech and writing, and lays down that the Press shall be entirely free from all control or censorship. No person may be deprived of civic or legal rights on political grounds.

The death penalty is not allowed under the Constitution except in case of martial law. The accused shall be considered 'not guilty' until he is otherwise proven. All punishment shall be consistent with humanitarian practice and shall be directed towards the re-education of the criminal.

Ethical and Social Clauses

Section II (Articles 29–34). The Republic regards the family as the fundamental basis of society and considers the parents to be responsible for the maintenance, instruction and education of the children. The Republic shall provide economic assistance for the family, with special regard to large families, and shall make provision for maternity, infancy and youth, subject always to the liberty and freedom of choice of the individuals as envisaged under the law.

Education, the arts and science shall be free, the function of the State being merely to indicate the general lines of instruction. Private entities and individuals shall have the right to conduct educational institutions without assistance from the State, but such non-state institutions must ensure to their pupils liberty and instruction equal to that in the state schools. Institutions of higher culture, universities and academies shall be autonomous within the limitations prescribed by the law.

Education is available to all and is free and obligatory for at least eight years. Higher education for students of proven merit shall be aided by scholarships and other allowances made by the Republic.

Economic Clauses

Section III (Articles 35–47). The Republic shall safeguard the right to work in all its aspects, and shall promote agreement and co-operation with international organizations in matters pertaining to the regulation of labour and the rights of workers. The rights of Italian workers abroad shall be protected.

All workers shall be entitled to remuneration proportionate to the quantity and quality of their work, and in any case shall be ensured of sufficient to provide freedom and a dignified standard of life for themselves and their families.

The maximum working hours shall be fixed by law, and the worker shall be entitled to a weekly day of rest and an annual holiday of nine days with pay.

Women shall have the same rights and, for equal work, the same remuneration as men. Conditions of work shall be regulated by their special family requirements and the needs of mother and child. The work of minors shall be specially protected.

All citizens have the right to sickness, unemployment and disability maintenance.

Liberty to organize in trade unions is guaranteed and any union may register as a legal entity, provided it is organized on a democratic basis. The right to strike is admitted within the limitations of the relevant legislation.

Private enterprise is permitted in so far as it does not run counter to the well-being of society nor constitute a danger to security, freedom and human dignity.

Ownership of private property is permitted and guaranteed within the limitations laid down by the law regarding the acquisition, extent and enjoyment of private property. Inheritance and testamentary bequests shall be regulated by law.

Limitation is placed by law on private ownership of land and on its use, with a view to its best exploitation for the benefit of the community.

The Republic recognizes the value of mutual co-operation and the right of the workers to participate in management.

The Republic shall encourage all forms of saving, by house purchase, by co-operative ownership and by investment in the public utility undertakings of the country.

Political Clauses

Section IV (Articles 48–54). The electorate comprises all citizens, both men and women, who have attained their majority. Voting is free, equal and secret, and its exercise is a civic duty. All citizens have the right to associate freely together in political parties, and may also petition the Chambers to legislate as may be deemed necessary.

All citizens of both sexes may hold public office on equal terms.

Defence of one's country is a sacred duty of the citizen, and military service is obligatory within the limits prescribed by law. Its fulfilment shall in no way prejudice the position of the worker nor hinder the exercise of political rights. The organization of the armed forces shall be imbued with the spirit of democracy.

All citizens must contribute to the public expenditure, in proportion to their capacity.

All citizens must be loyal to the Republic and observe the terms of the law and the Constitution.

PART TWO

Sections I, II and III (Articles 55–100). These sections are devoted to a detailed exposition of the Legislature and legislative procedure of the Republic.

Parliament shall comprise two Chambers, namely the Chamber of Deputies (Camera dei Deputati) and the Senate of the Republic (Senato).

The Chamber of Deputies is elected by direct universal suffrage, the number of Deputies being 630. All voters who on the day of the elections are 25 years of age, may be elected Deputies.

Three-quarters of the seats are allocated on the basis of a simple plurality and the remaining one-quarter by proportional representation.

The Senate of the Republic is elected on a regional basis, the number of eligible Senators being 315. No region shall have fewer than seven Senators. Valle d'Aosta has only one Senator.

Three-quarters of the seats are allocated on the basis of a simple plurality and the remaining one-quarter by proportional representation.

The Chamber of Deputies and the Senate of the Republic are elected for five years.

The term of each House cannot be extended except by law and only in the case of war.

Members of Parliament shall receive remuneration fixed by law.

The President of the Republic must be a citizen of at least fifty years of age and in full enjoyment of all civic and political rights. The person shall be elected for a period of seven years (Articles 84–85).

The Government shall consist of the President of the Council and the Ministers who themselves shall form the Council. The President of the Council, or Prime Minister, shall be nominated by the President of the Republic, who shall also appoint the ministers on the recommendation of the Prime Minister (Article 92).

Section IV (Articles 101–113). Sets forth the judicial system and procedure.

Section V (Articles 114–133). Deals with the division of the Republic into regions, provinces and communes, and sets forth the limits and extent of autonomy enjoyed by the regions. Under Article 131 the regions are enumerated as follows:

Piemonte (Piedmont)	Marche
Lombardia (Lombardy)	Lazio
Veneto	Abruzzo
Liguria	Molise
Emilia-Romagna	Campania
Toscana (Tuscany)	Puglia
Umbria	Basilicata
Calabria	Trentino-Alto Adige†
Sicilia (Sicily)†	Friuli-Venezia Giulia†
Sardegna (Sardinia)†	Valle d'Aosta†

The final articles provide for the establishment of the Corte Costituzionale to deal with constitutional questions and any revisions which may be found necessary after the Constitution has come into operation.

* In June 1997 a parliamentary commission on constitutional reform, which had been established in January, announced its recommendations, which included: a directly-elected President for a six-year term with responsibility for foreign and defence policy; a reduction of the Chamber of Deputies from 630 to 400 members and of the Senate from 315 to 200 members; greater financial autonomy for the regions; and a second round of voting for seats allocated on the basis of a simple plurality. The recommendations required approval by both the Chamber of Deputies and the Senate prior to endorsement at a national referendum.

† These five regions have a wider form of autonomy, based on on constitutional legislation specially adapted to their regional characteristics (Article 116). Each region shall be administered by a Regional Council, in which is vested the legislative power and

which may make suggestions for legislation to the Chambers, and the Giunta regionale, which holds the executive power (Article 121).

The Government

(May 2001)

HEAD OF STATE

President of the Republic: CARLO AZEGLIO CIAMPI (inaugurated 18 May 1999).

COUNCIL OF MINISTERS*

A coalition of the Democratici di Sinistra (DS), the Partito Popolare Italiano (PPI), I Democratici per l'Ulivo (Democratici), the Partito dei Comunisti Italiani (PdCI), the Federazione dei Verdi (Verdi), the Rinnovamento Italiano (RI), the Socialisti Democratici Italiani, the Unione Democratici per l'Europa (UDEUR) and Independents (Ind.).

* The Prime Minister, Giuliano Amato, and the Council of Ministers, resigned on 31 May 2001, but were to remain as a caretaker administration pending the formation of a new government by Prime Minister-elect, Silvio Berlusconi.

Prime Minister: GIULIANO AMATO (Ind.)

Minister of Foreign Affairs: Prof. LAMBERTO DINI (RI).

Minister of the Interior: ENZO BIANCO (Democratici).

Minister of Justice: PIERO FRANCO FASSINO (DS).

Minister of the Treasury and of the Budget: VINCENZO VISCO (DS).

Minister of Finance: OTTAVIANO DEL TURCO (SDI).

Minister of Defence: SERGIO MATTARELLA (PPI).

Minister of Education: TULLIO DE MAURO (Ind.).

Minister of Public Works: NERIO NESI (PdCi).

Minister of Culture: GIOVANNA MELANDRI (DS).

Minister of Agriculture: ALFONSO PECORARO SCANIO (Verdi).

Minister of Transport: PIER LUIGI BERSANI (DS).

Minister of Communications: SALVATORE CARDINALE (UDEUR).

Minister of Industry, Commerce and Handicrafts and Foreign Trade: ENRICO LETTA (PPI).

Minister of Employment and Social Welfare: CESARE SALVI (DS).

Minister of Health: UMBERTO VERONESI (Ind.).

Minister of the Environment: WILLER BORDON (Democratici).

Minister of Universities and Scientific Research: ORTENSIO ZECCHINO (PPI).

Ministers without Portfolio:

Institutional Reforms: ANTONIO MACCANICO (Democratici).

Social Solidarity: LIVIA TURCO (DS).

Equal Opportunities: KATIA BELLILLO (PdCI).

Public Administration: FRANCO BASSANINI (DS).

Regional Affairs: AGAZIO LOIERO (UDEUR).

European Policies: GIANNI FRANCESCO MATTIOLI (Verdi).

Relations with Parliament: PATRIZIA TOIA (PPI).

MINISTRIES

Office of the President: Palazzo del Quirinale, 00187 Rome; tel. (06) 46991; fax 46992384.

Office of the Prime Minister: Palazzo Chigi, Piazza Colonna 370, 00186 Rome; tel. (06) 67791; fax (06) 6783998; internet www.palazzochigi.it.

Ministry of Agriculture: Via XX Settembre, 00187 Rome; tel. (06) 46651; fax (06) 4742314.

Ministry of Communications: Viale America 201, 00144 Rome; tel. (06) 54441; fax (06) 5407728; e-mail mincom@tin.it; internet www.comunicazioni.it.

Ministry of Culture: Via del Collegio Romano 27, 00186 Rome; tel. (06) 67231; fax (06) 6793156; internet www.beniculturali.it.

Ministry of Defence: Via XX Settembre 8, 00187 Rome; tel. (06) 4882126; fax (06) 4747775.

Ministry of Education: Viale Trastevere 76A, 00153 Rome; tel. (06) 58491; fax (06) 5803381; internet www.istruzione.it.

Ministry of Employment and Social Welfare: Via Flavia 6, 00187 Rome; tel. (06) 46831; fax (06) 47887174; internet www.minlavoro.it.

Ministry of the Environment: Via Cristoforo Colombo 44, 0144 Rome; tel. (06) 70361; fax (06) 6790130; internet www.scn .minambiente.it.

Ministry of Finance: Viale Europa 242, 00144 Rome; tel. (06) 59971; fax (06) 5910993; internet www.finanze.it.

Ministry of Foreign Affairs: Piazzale della Farnesina 1, 00194 Rome; tel. (06) 36911; fax (06) 3236210; e-mail info@mincomes.it; internet www.esteri.it.

Ministry of Foreign Trade: Viale America 341, 00144 Rome; tel. (06) 59931; fax (06) 59647531; e-mail info@mincomes.it; internet www.mincomes.it.

Ministry of Health: Piazzale dell'Industria 20, 00144 Rome; tel. (06) 59941; fax (06) 59647749; internet www.sanita.it.

Ministry of Industry, Commerce and Handicrafts and Foreign Trade: Via Molise 2, 00187 Rome; tel. (06) 47051; fax (06) 47052215; internet www.minindustria.it.

Ministry of the Interior: Piazzale del Viminale, 00184 Rome; tel. (06) 4651; fax (06) 4741717; internet www.mininterno.it.

Ministry of Justice: Via Arenula 71, 00186 Rome; tel. (06) 68851; fax (06) 6875419; internet www.giustizia.it.

Ministry of Public Works: Piazza Porta Pia 1, 00198 Rome; tel. (06) 4412; fax (06) 867187; internet www.llpp.it.

Ministry of Transport: Piazza della Croce Rossa 1, 00161 Rome; tel. (06) 44101; fax (06) 8415693; internet www .trasportinavigazione.it.

Ministry of the Treasury and of the Budget: Via XX Settembre 97, 00187 Rome; tel. (06) 647611; fax (06) 5913751; internet www .tesoro.it.

Ministry of Universities and Scientific Research: Piazza J. F. Kennedy 20, 00144 Rome; tel. (06) 59911; fax (06) 59912967; internet www.murst.it.

Legislature

PARLAMENTO
(Parliament)

Senato
(Senate)

President: MARCELLO PERA.

General Election, 13 May 2001

Parties/Alliances	Percentage of votes for seats elected by proportional representation*	Total seats
Casa delle Libertà†	42.5	177
L'Ulivo and Südtiroler Volkspartei (SVP)‡	38.7	128
Rifondazione Comunista	5.0	3
Democrazia Europea	3.2	2
Lista Di Pietro	3.4	1
Lista Bonino	2.0	—
Movimento Sociale—Fiamma Tricolore .	1.0	—
Others	4.2	4
Total§	**100.0**	**315**

* Figures refer to seats elected by proportional representation (25% of the total); percentages for the remaining 75% of seats, elected by majority vote, are not available.
† Centre-right grouping including Forza Italia, the Alleanza Nazionale (AN), the Centro Cristiano Democratico (CCD), the Cristiani Democratici Uniti (CDU), the Lega Nord per l'Indipendenza della Padania, and the Nuovo Partito Socialista Italiano.
‡ Centre-left alliance comprising the Democratici di Sinistra (DS), the Partito Popolare Italiano (PPI), the Rinnovamento Italiano (RI), the Federazione dei Verdi (FV), the Partito dei Comunisti Italiani (PdCI), the Democratici per l'Ulivo, the Socialisti Democratici Italiani (SDI) and the Unione Democratici per l'Europa (UDEUR).
§ In addition to the 315 elected members, there are 10 life members.

Camera dei Deputati
(Chamber of Deputies)

President: PIER FERDINANDO CASINI.

General Election, 13 May 2001

Parties/Alliances	Percentage of votes for seats elected by proportional representation*	Total seats
Casa delle Libertà	49.4	368
Forza Italia	29.4	
Alleanza Nazionale (AN)	12.0	
Lega Nord	3.9	
Biancofiore†	3.2	
Nuovo Partito Socialista Italiano . .	0.9	
L'Ulivo	35.0	242
Democratici di Sinistra (DS) . . .	16.6	
Partito dei Comunisti Italiani (PdCI) .	1.7	
Margherita‡	14.5	
Girasole§	2.2	
Rifondazione Comunista	5.0	11
Lista Di Pietro	3.9	—
Democrazia Europea	2.4	—
Lista Bonino	2.3	—
Movimento Sociale—Fiamma Tricolore .	0.4	1
Others	1.6	1
Ulivo—Sudtiroler Volkspartei (SVP) .	—	8
Total	**100.0**	**630**

* Figures refer to seats elected by proportional representation (25% of the total); percentages for the remaining 75% of seats, elected by majority vote, are not available.
† Coalition of the Cristiani Democratici Uniti (CDU) and the Centro Cristiano Democratico (CCD).
‡ Coalition of the Partito Popolare Italiano (PPI), the Unione Democratici per l'Europa (UDEUR) and Rinnovamento Italiano.
§ Coalition of the Federazione dei Verdi and the Socialisti Democratici Italiani (SDI).

Political Organizations

Alleanza Nazionale (AN) (National Alliance): Via della Scrofa 39, 00186 Rome; tel. (06) 688171; fax (06) 688172; internet www .alleanza-nazionale.it; f. 1994; in early 1995 absorbed the neo-fascist Movimento Sociale Italiano-Destra Nazionale (MSI-DN, f. 1946); Sec.-Gen. GIANFRANCO FINI; 400,000 mems.

Associazione Riformatori per l'Europa (Association of Reformists for Europe) Largo A. Sarti 4, 00196 Rome; tel. (06) 36001070; fax (06) 36001231; Spokesman GIORGIO BENVENUTO.

Autonomisti per l'Europa (APE) (Autonomists for Europe): Via Pozzo Strada 19, 10139 Turin; tel. (011) 531274; fax (011) 534957; internet www.fedaralisti.net; Pres. DOMENICO COMINO.

Cattolici Liberali (Liberal Catholics): Piazza San Salvatore in Lauro 15, 00186 Rome; tel. (06) 68805651; fax (06) 68805706; Pres. ALBERTO MICHELINI.

Centro Cristiano Democratico (CCD) (Christian-Democratic Centre): Via dei Due Macelli 66, Rome; tel. (06) 69791001; fax (06) 6795940; e-mail direzione@ccd.it; internet www.ccd.it; advocates centre-right policies; Pres. PIERFERDINANDO CASINI.

Il Centro-Unione Populare Democratica (The Popular Democratic Centre-Union): Piazza C. Battisti 30, 38100 Trento; tel. and fax (0461) 260416; Pres. RENZO GUBERT.

Coalizione Christiana (Christian Coalition): Via U. Bassi 20, 00152 Rome; tel. (06) 58340843; fax (06) 58179926; e-mail consorzio .esteuropa@flashnet.it; Gen. Sec. DEMETRIO ERRIGO.

Coordinamento Nazionale dei Repubblicani per l'Unità della Sinistra Democratica (National Co-ordination of Republicans for the Unity of the Democratic Left): Via del Tritone 62c, 00187 Rome; tel. and fax (06) 69940909. Gen. Sec. GIORGIO BOGI.

Cristiani Democratici Uniti (CDU) (United Christian Democrats): Piazza del Gesù 46, 00186 Rome; tel. (06) 6775204; fax 6785956; e-mail cdu@wmail.axnet.it; internet www.cdu.it; f. 1995 after split with Partito Popolare Italiano; advocates centre-right policies; Sec.-Gen. ROCCO BUTTIGLIONE.

Cristiano Democratici Europei (European Christian Democrats): Via dei Pontefici 3, 00186 Rome; tel. (06) 68199913; fax (06) 68134196; Pres. ALESSANDRO MELUZZI; Gen. Sec. STEFANO PEDICA.

I Democratici per l'Ulivo (The Democrats for the Olive Tree): Piazza SS Apostoli 73, Rome; tel. (06) 695191; fax (06) 69781764; internet www.democraticiperlulivo.it; f. 1999; Pres. ARTURO PARISI.

Democratici di Sinistra (DS) (Democrats of the Left): Via delle Botteghe Oscure 4, 00186 Rome; tel. (06) 67111; fax (06) 6711596; e-mail ufficio.stampa@democraticidisinistra.it; internet www .dsonline.it; f. 1921 as the Partito Comunista Italiano (PCI) (Italian

Communist Party); name changed to Partito Democratico della Sinistra 1991; name changed as above 1998; advocates a democratic and libertarian society; Gen. Sec. WALTER VELTRONI; approx. 1.4m. mems.

Democrazia Europea: Corso Vittorio Emanuele 326, 00186 Rome; tel. (06) 6872543; fax (06) 68214906; internet www.democraziaeuropea.it; Leader SERGIO D'ANTONI.

Federalisti (the Federalists): Via P. Micca 4, 21047 Saronno; tel. and fax (02) 96700677; Pres. DACIRIO GHIDORZI GHIZZI.

Federazione dei Liberali Italiani (Federation of Italian Liberals): Via Laurina 20, 00187 Rome; tel. and fax (06) 32110200; Pres. VALERIO ZANONE; Gen. Sec. RAFAELLO MORELLI.

Federazione del Sud—AT6 Lega d'Azione Meridionale (Federation of the South—AT6 Southern League of Action): Via Poli 13, 00187 Rome; tel. (06) 67604877; fax (06) 67604876; internet www.listacito.8m.com; Pres. GIANCARLO CITO.

Federazione dei Verdi (Verdi) (Green Party): Via Antonio Salandra 6, 00187 Rome; tel. (06) 4203061; fax (06) 42004600; e-mail federazione@verdi.it; internet www.verdi.it; f. 1986; advocates environmentalist and anti-nuclear policies; branch of the European Green movement; Leader GRAZIA FRANCESCATO.

Forum Popolare Federalista per l'Assemblea Costituente (People's Federalist Forum for the Constituent Assembly): Piazza Rondanini 29, 00186 Rome; tel. and fax (06) 6872055; Spokesman GIOVANNI DI BELLO.

Forza Italia (Come on, Italy!): Via dell'Umiltà 36, 00187 Rome; tel. (06) 67311; fax (06) 6788255; e-mail lettere@forza-italia.it; internet www.forza-italia.it; f. 1993; advocates principles of market economy; Leader SILVIO BERLUSCONI.

Italia dei Valori—Lista Di Pietro (Italy for Values—Di Pietro List): Via Milano 13, 21052 Busto Arsizio; tel. (0331) 624412; fax (0331) 624783; internet www.antoniodipietro.org; Pres. ANTONIO DI PIETRO.

Italia Democratica (Democratic Italy): Viale Col di Lana 12, 20136 Milan; tel. (02) 8392338; fax (02) 8356459; internet www.italiademocratica.it; Gen. Sec. NANO DELLA CHIESA.

Italia Federale (Federal Italy): Via del Parlamento 9, 00186 Rome; tel. (06) 67603240; fax (06) 67602611; internet www.irenet.it; Pres. IRENE PIVETTI.

La Rete per il Partito Democratico (The Democratic Party Network): Via Marianna Dionigi 29, 00193 Rome; tel. (06) 67064232; internet www.larete.it; f. 1991; anti-Mafia party; Pres. LEOLUCA ORLANDO.

Lega Autonomia Veneta—Lega delle Regioni (League for the Autonomy of Veneto—League for the Regions): Via Rossarol 22, 30175 Marghera; tel. and fax (041) 935736; e-mail venetonordest@hotmail.com; Gen. Sec. MARIO RIGO.

Lega Nord per l'Indipendenza della Padania (Northern League for the Independence of Padania): Via C. Bellerio 41, 20161 Milan; tel. (02) 662341; fax (02) 66234266; e-mail webmaster@leganord.org; internet www.leganord.org; f. 1991; advocates federalism and transfer of control of resources to regional govts; in 1996 declared the 'Independent Republic of Padania'; opposes immigration; Pres. STEFANO STEFANI; Sec. UMBERTO BOSSI.

Liberal Sgarbi: Via Carlo Dolci 38, 20122 Milan; tel. (02) 4237947; fax (02) 55181921; internet www.sgarbilibertari.it; Pres. VITTORIO SGARBI.

Movimento Cristiano-Sociali (Christian-Social Movement): Piazza Adriana 5, 00193 Rome; tel. (06) 68300537; fax (06) 68300539; e-mail movcs@tin.it; Pres. DOMENICO LUCÀ.

Movimento dei Comunisti Unitari (Movement of Unitary Communists): Via della Colonna Antonina 41, 00186 Rome; tel. (06) 6790293; fax (06) 6788498; internet www.comunisti.org; Gen. Sec. FAMIANO CRUCIANELLI.

Movimento Italiano Demcoratico (Italian Demcoratic Movement): Via del Tritone 61, 00187 Rome; tel. (06) 6796912; fax (06) 6796915; Pres. SERGIO BERLINGUER; Gen. Sec. CARMELO PUJIA.

Movimento per le Riforme Istituzionali (Movement for Institutional Reforms): Piazza Campitelli 1, 00186 Rome; tel. (06) 6990328; e-mail coalizione@iol.it; internet www.movimentoriforme.com; Gen. Sec. GIULIANA OLCESE.

Movimento Sociale–Fiamma Tricolore (Social Movement of the Tricolour Flame): Via Simon de Saint Bon 89, 00195 Rome; tel. (06) 3701756; fax (06) 3720376; e-mail fiamma@msifiammatric.it; internet www.msifiammatric.it; f. 1996; electoral alliance incorporating former mems of neo-fascist Movimento Sociale Italiano-Destra Nazionale; Nat. Sec. PINO RAUTI.

Movimento per l'Ulivo (Movement for the Olive Tree alliance): Largo Pietro di Brazzà 26, 00187 Rome; tel. (06) 6990200; fax (06) 69920457; internet www.perlulivo.it; Gen. Sec. MARINA MAGISTRELLI.

Movimento Unitario Pensionati—Uomini Vivi (Unitary Pensioners Movement—Living Men): Via Boezio 17, 00193 Rome; tel. (06) 6878628; fax (06) 6878697; Pres. GIUSEPPE POLINI; Sec. BALILLA TATA.

Nuovo Partito Socialista Italiano (New Italian Socialist Party): Via dei Pontefici 3, 00186 Rome; tel. (06) 68892583; fax (06) 6892000; Sec. GIANNI DE MICHELIS.

Partito dei Comunisti Italiani (PdCI) (Party of Italian Communists): Corso Vittorio Emanuele II 209, 00186 Rome; tel. (06) 6862721; fax (06) 68627230; e-mail direzionenazionale@comunisti-italiani.it; internet www.comunisti-italiani.it; f. 1998; Chair. ARMANDO COSSUTTA.

Patito Federalista (Federalist Party): Via Soperga 39, 20127 Milan; tel. (02) 26826465; fax (02) 26826788; Sec. UMBERTO GIOVINE.

Partito Popolare Italiano (PPI) (Italian People's Party): Piazza del Gesù 46, 00186 Rome; tel. (06) 699591; fax (06) 6790449; e-mail ufficiostampa@pronet.it; internet www.popolari.it; f. 1994 as the successor to the Partito della Democrazia Cristiana (DC) (Christian Democrat Party; f. 1943); while extending its appeal to voters of all classes, the party attempts to maintain a centre position; Sec.-Gen. PIERLUIGI CASTAGNETTI.

Partito Repubblicano Italiano (PRI) (Italian Republican Party): Corso Vittorio Emanuele 326, 00186 Rome; tel. (06) 6865044; fax (06) 6893002; internet www.pri.it; f. 1897; followers of the principles of Mazzini (social justice in a modern free society) and modern liberalism; Pres. GUGLIELMO NEGRI; Gen. Sec. GIORGIO LA MALFA; 110,000 mems.

Partito della Rifondazione Comunista (PRC) (Reconstructed Communism): Viale del Policlinico 131, 00161 Rome; tel. (06) 441821; fax (06) 44239490; e-mail direzione.prc@rifondazione.it; internet www.rifondazione.it; f. 1991 by former members of the Partito Comunista Italiano (Italian Communist Party); Sec.-Gen. FAUSTO BERTINOTTI.

Partitu Sardu—Partito Sardo d'Azione (Sardinian Action Party): Via Roma 231, 09123 Cagliari; tel. (070) 657599; fax (070) 657779; Pres. LORENZO PALERMO; Sec. GIACOMO SANNA.

Patto Segni Liberaldemocratici (Segni's Pact—Liberal Democrats): Via Belsiana 100, 00187 Rome; tel. (06) 6780840; fax (06) 6789890; e-mail edpatto@tin.it; internet www.pattosegni.it; f. 1993; liberal party, advocating institutional reform; Leader MARIO SEGNI.

Pensionati Nord (Pensioners of the North): Via Silvio Pellico 8, 20121 Milan; tel. (02) 866593; fax (02) 8057079; e-mail pensionati.nord@tiscalinet.it; Sec. ROBERTO BERNARDELLI.

Pour la Vallée d'Aoste (For the Aosta Valley): Via Festaz 47, 11100 Aosta; tel. and fax (0165) 41055; pres. CESARE DUJANY; Sec. ILARIO LANIVI.

Riforme e Libertà (Reforms and Freedom): Via Cornaggia 9, 20123 Milan; internet www.liberta.com; Pres. GUILIO SAVELLI.

Rinnovamento Italiano (Italian Renewal): Via di Ripetta 142, 00186 Rome; tel. (06) 68808380; fax (06) 68808480; e-mail informa@rinnovamento.it; internet www.rinnovamento.it; f. 1996; centrist; Leader Prof. LAMBERTO DINI.

Socialisti Democratici Italiani (SDI) (Italian Democratic Socialists): Piazza S. Lorenzo in Lucina 26, 00186 Rome; tel. (06) 68307666; fax (06) 68307659; e-mail socialisti@nexus.it; internet www.socialisti.org; f. 1892 as Partito Socialista Italiano (PSI); in 1966 merged with the Social Democratic Party to form the United Socialist Party, but in 1969 the Social Democrats broke away; name changed to Socialisti Italiani in 1994; in 1998 re-merged with Social Democratic Party, name changed as above; centre-left; it adheres to the Socialist International and believes that socialism is inseparable from democracy and individual freedom; Pres. ENRICO BOSSELLI.

Südtiroler Volkspartei (SVP) (South Tyrol People's Party): Brennerstrasse 7A, 39100 Bozen/Bolzano; tel. (0471) 304020; fax (0471) 981473; e-mail info@svpartei.org; internet www.svpartei.org; regional party of the German and Ladin-speaking people in the South Tyrol; Pres. SIEGFRIED BRUGGER; Gen. Sec. THOMAS WIDMANN.

L'Ulivo (The Olive Tree): Via della Dogana Vecchia 27, 00186 Rome; tel. (06) 68808860; e-mail info@ulivo.it; internet www.ulivo.it; f. 1995; centre-left alliance comprising the Partito Democratico della Sinistra (renamed Democratici di Sinistra in 1998), the Partito Popolare Italiano, the Südtiroler Volkspartei, the Unione Democratica, the Lista Romano Prodi, the Rinnovamento Italiano and the Federazione dei Verdi; Leader Prof. ROMANO PRODI.

Union Autonomista Ladina (Autonomist Ladin Movement): Via Pilat 8, 38039 Vigo di Fassa; tel. (0462) 763396; fax (0462) 763407; Pres. GINO FONTANA; Sec. GIUSEPPE DETOMAS.

Union Valdôtaine (Aosta Valley Union): Ave. des Maquisards 27/29, 11100 Aosta; tel. (0165) 235181; fax (0165) 364289; internet www.unionvaldotaine.org; Pres. AUGUSTE ROLLANDIN.

Unione Democratici per l'Europa (UDEUR) (Union of Democrats for Europe): Largo Arenula 34, 00186 Rome; tel. (06) 684241; fax (06) 6872593; e-mail udeur@udeur.org; internet www.udeur.org; f. 1999; Pres. IRENE PIVETTI; Sec. CLEMENTE MASTELLA.

Unione Liberale di Centro (Centre-Liberal Union): Via del Tritone 62c, 00187 Rome; tel. and fax (06) 69921932; Gen. Sec. RAFFAELE COSTA; Pres. PIERLUIGI FLORIO.

Unione per la Repubblica (Union for the Republic): Via Cicerone 44, 00193 Rome; tel. (06) 36003745; fax (06) 32609549; Sec. ANGELO SANZA; Pres. FRANCESCO COSSIGA.

Veneti d'Europa (Inhabitants of the Veneto region for Europe): Viale della Navigazione Interna 23, 35129 Padua; tel. (049) 7800702; fax (049) 7803077; internet www.vde.it; Pres. FABRIZIO COMENCINI; Gen. Sec. ETTORE BEGGIATO.

Diplomatic Representation

EMBASSIES IN ITALY

Afghanistan: Via Nomentana, 120, 00161 Rome; tel. (06) 8611009; fax (06) 86322939; Chargé d'affaires a.i.: HAMIDULLAH NASSER-ZIA.

Albania: Via Asmara 3-5, 00199 Rome; tel. (06) 86218214; fax (06) 86216005; Ambassador: LEONTIEV ÇUÇI.

Algeria: Via Barnaba Oriani 26, 00197, Rome; tel. (06) 80687620; fax (06) 8083436; Ambassador: HOCINE MEGHAR.

Angola: Via Filippo Bernardini 21, 00165 Rome; tel. (06) 39366902; fax (06) 634960; Ambassador: BOAVENTURA DA SILVA CARDOSO.

Argentina: Piazza dell'Esquilino 2, 00185 Rome; tel. (06) 4742551; fax (06) 4744756; Ambassador: ELSA DIANA ROSA KELLY.

Armenia: Via dei Colli della Farnesina 174, 00194 Rome; tel. (06) 3296638; fax (06) 3297763; e-mail gaghikb@tin.it; internet www.space.tin.it/associazioni/gbaghdas; Ambassador: GAGHIK BAGHDASSARIAN.

Australia: Via Alessandria 215, 00198 Rome; tel. (06) 852721; fax (06) 85272300; e-mail pbaffairs@australian_embassy.it; internet www.australian-embassy.it; Ambassador: WILLIAM RORY STEELE.

Austria: Via G. B. Pergolesi 3, 00198 Rome; tel. (06) 8440141; fax (06) 8543286; e-mail austrianembassyrome@rmnet.it; internet www.austria.it; Ambassador: GÜNTER BIRBAUM.

Bangladesh: Via Antonio Bertoloni 14, 00197 Rome; tel. (06) 8083595; fax (06) 8084853; Ambassador: MOHAMMAD ZIAUDDIN.

Belarus: Via della Giuliana 113, 00195 Rome; tel. (06) 39741268; fax (06) 3724634; Ambassador: NATALYA DROZD.

Belgium: Via dei Monti Parioli 49, 00197 Rome; tel. (06) 3609511; fax (06) 3226935; Ambassador: PATRICK NOTHOMB.

Bolivia: Via Brenta 2A, 00198 Rome; tel. (06) 8841001; fax (06) 8840740; Ambassador: DAVID BLANCO ZABALA.

Bosnia and Herzegovina: Via G. Bazzoni 3, 00195 Rome; tel. (06) 3728509; fax (06) 3728548; Ambassador: MIROSLAV PALAMETA.

Brazil: Palazzo Pamphili, Piazza Navona 14, 00186 Rome; tel. (06) 683981; fax (06) 6867858; internet www.web.tin.it/brasile; Ambassador: PAULO TARSO FLECHA DE LIMA.

Bulgaria: Via Pietro P. Rubens 21, 00197 Rome; tel. (06) 3224640; fax (06) 3226122; Ambassador: DIMITAR ILIEV LASAROV.

Burkina Faso: Via Alessandria 26, 00198 Rome; tel. (06) 44250052; fax (06) 44250042; internet www.airafrique.it/burkinafaso.htm; Ambassador: NOELLIE MARIE BEATRICE DAMIBA.

Cameroon: Via Siracusa 4–6, 00161 Rome; tel. (06) 44291285; fax (06) 44291323; Ambassador: MICHAEL TABONG KIMA.

Canada: Via G. B. de Rossi 27, 00161 Rome; tel. (06) 445981; fax (06) 44598760; e-mail rome@dfaitmaeci.gc.ca; internet www.canada.it; Ambassador: ROBERT R. FOWLER.

Cape Verde: Via Giosuè Carducci 4, 00187 Rome; tel. (06) 4744678; fax (06) 4744643; Ambassador: ELVIO GONÇALVES NAPOLEÃO FERNANDES.

Chile: Via Po 23, 00198 Rome; tel. (06) 8841449; fax (06) 8812348; e-mail embachite.italia@flashnet.it; Ambassador: JOSÉ GOÑI.

China, People's Republic: Via Bruxelles 56, 00198 Rome; tel. (06) 8848186; fax (06) 85352891; Ambassador: CHENG WENDONG.

Colombia: Via Giuseppe Pisanelli 4, 00196 Rome; tel. (06) 3612131; fax (06) 3225798; Ambassador: FABIO VALENCIA COSIO.

Congo, Democratic Republic: Via Barberini 3, 00187 Rome; tel. (06) 42010779; fax (06) 7480240; Ambassador: EDOUARD UMBA ILUNGA.

Congo, Republic: Via Ombrone 8–10, 00198 Rome; fax (06) 41400218; Ambassador: MAMADOU KAMARA DEKAMO.

Costa Rica: Via B. Eustachio 22, 00161 Rome; tel. (06) 44251042; fax (06) 44251048; internet www.mix.it/utenti/embcosta; Ambassador: MANUEL HERNÁNDEZ GUTIÉRREZ.

Côte d'Ivoire: Via Guglielmo Saliceto 8, 00161 Rome; tel. (06) 44231129; fax (06) 44292531; Chargé d'affaires a.i.: RICHOLO ZOUINGNAM.

Croatia: Via L. Bodio 74–76, 00191 Rome; tel. (06) 36307650; fax (06) 36303405; Ambassador: DRAGO KRALJEVIĆ.

Cuba: Via Licinia 7, 00153 Rome; tel. (06) 5755984; fax (06) 5745445; internet www.elabora95.it/ambasciatadicuba; Ambassador: MARÍA DE LOS ANGELES FLOREZ PRIDA.

Cyprus: Via Francesco Denza 15, 00197 Rome; tel. (06) 8088365; fax (06) 8088338; e-mail emb.rome@flashnet.it; Ambassador: ALEXANDROS N. ZENON.

Czech Republic: Via dei Gracchi 322, 00192 Rome; tel. (06) 3244459; fax (06) 3244466; Ambassador: HANA ŠEVČÍKOVÁ.

Denmark: Via dei Monti Parioli 50, 00197 Rome; tel. (06) 3200441; fax (06) 3610290; e-mail ambadane@iol.it; Ambassador: GUNNAR RIBERHOLDT.

Dominica: Via Laurentina 767, 00143 Rome; tel. and fax (06) 5010643; Ambassador: HANNELORE BENJAMIN.

Dominican Republic: Via Domenico Chelini 10, 00197 Rome; tel. (06) 8074665; fax (06) 8074791; Ambassador: LEONARDO MATOS BERRIDO.

Ecuador: Via Antonio Bertoloni 8, 00197 Rome; tel. (06) 8076272; fax (06) 8078209; e-mail mecuroma@flashnet.it; Ambassador: ARTURO GANGOTENA GUARDERAS.

Egypt: Villa Savoia, Via Salaria 267, 00199 Rome; tel. (06) 8440191; fax (06) 8554424; Ambassador: NEHAD IBRAHIM ABD AL-LATIF.

El Salvador: Via G. Castellini 13, 00197 Rome; tel. (06) 8076605; fax (06) 8079726; Ambassador: JOSÉ SAGUER SAPRISSA.

Eritrea: Via Boncompagni 16B, 00187 Rome; tel. (06) 42741293; fax (06) 42086806; Ambassador: PIETROS FESSAHAZION.

Estonia: Viale Liegi 28, int. 5, 00198 Rome; tel. (06) 8440751; fax (06) 844075119; e-mail saatkond@rooma.vm.ee; Ambassador: JAAK JÕERÜÜT.

Ethiopia: Via Andrea Vesalio 16–18, 00161 Rome; tel. (06) 4402602; fax (06) 4403676; Ambassador: HALIMA MOHAMMED.

Finland: Via Lisbona 3, 00198 Rome; tel. (06) 852231; fax (06) 8540362; e-mail ambasciata.di.finlandia@interbusiness.it; internet www.finland.it/info/ambasciata; Ambassador: DIETER VITZTHUM.

France: Piazza Farnese 67, 00186 Rome; tel. (06) 686011; fax (06) 68601360; internet www.france-italia.it; Ambassador: JACQUES BLOT.

Gabon: Via Mercalli 25, 00197 Rome; tel. (06) 80691390; fax (06) 80691504; Ambassador: MARCEL IBINGA-MAGWANGU.

Georgia: Palazzo Pierret, Piazza di Spagna 20, 00187 Rome; tel. (06) 69941972; fax (06) 69941942; Ambassador: RUSSADAN LORTKIPANIDZE.

Germany: Via San Martino della Battaglia 4, 00185 Rome; tel. (06) 49213; fax (06) 4452672; internet www.ambgermania.it; Ambassador: FRITJOF VON NORDENSKJÖLD.

Ghana: Via Ostriana 4, 00199 Rome; tel. (06) 86217191; fax (06) 86325762; Ambassador: AANAA NAMUA ENIN.

Greece: Via Mercadente 36, 00198 Rome; tel. (06) 8549630; fax (06) 8415927; e-mail gremroma@tin.it; Ambassador: CONSTANTIN YEROCOSTOPOULOS.

Guatemala: Via dei Colli della Farnesina 128, 00194 Rome; tel. (06) 36307392; fax 3291639; e-mail embaguate.ita@flashnet.it; Ambassador: MARIO ALBERTO CARRERA.

Guinea: Via Adelaide Ristori 9/13, 00197 Rome; tel. and fax (06) 8078989; Chargé d'affaires a.i.: SOUHAIB DEEN BANGOURA.

Haiti: 1st floor, Via Ottaviano 32, 00192 Rome; tel. (06) 39723362; fax (06) 39737764; Chargé d'affaires a.i.: JEAN-WALNARD DORNEVAL.

Holy See: Via Po 27–29, 00198 Rome; tel. (06) 8546287; fax (06) 8549725; Apostolic Nuncio: Most Rev. ANDREA CORDERO LANZA DI MONTEZEMOLO, Titular Archbishop of Tuscania.

Honduras: Via Giambattista Vico 40, 00196 Rome; tel. (06) 3207236; fax (06) 3207973; e-mail ambhond@tin.it; Ambassador: SALOMÉ CASTELLANOS DELGADO.

Hungary: Via dei Villini 14, 00161 Rome; tel. (06) 44230567; fax (06) 4403270; internet www.web.tin.it/huembit; Ambassador: ENIKI GYORI.

India: Via XX Settembre 5, 00187 Rome; tel. (06) 4884642; fax (06) 4819539; Ambassador: SIDDHARTH SINGH.

Indonesia: Via Campania 55, 00187 Rome; tel. (06) 4200911; fax (06) 4880280; Ambassador: SOENDROE RACHMAD.

Iran: Via Nomentana 361, 00162 Rome; tel. (06) 86328485; fax (06) 86328492; e-mail embassiran_rome@hotmail.com; Ambassador: ALI AHANI.

Ireland: Piazza di Campitelli 3, 00186 Rome; tel. (06) 6979121; fax (06) 6792354; Ambassador: JOSEPH SMALL.

Israel: Via M. Mercati 12, 00197 Rome; tel. (06) 36198500; fax (06) 36198555; e-mail israel.roma@agora.stm.it; internet www.israel.amb.it; Ambassador: YEHUDA MILLO.

Japan: Via Quintino Sella 60, 00187 Rome; tel. (06) 487991; fax (06) 4873316; internet www.ambasciatajp.it; Ambassador: AKIRA HAYASHI.

Jordan: Via G. Marchi 1B, 00161 Rome; tel. (06) 86205303; fax (06) 8606122; Ambassador: OMAR ABDEL MUNIM AL RIFAEE.

Kazakhstan: Piazza Farnese 101, 00186 Rome; tel. (06) 68808640; fax (06) 68891360; e-mail kazakhstan.emb@agora.stm.it; Ambassador: OLZHAS SULEYMENOV.

Kenya: Via Archimede 164, 00197 Rome; tel. (06) 8082714; fax (06) 8082707; Chargé d'affaires a.i.: BETTY C. KIMURGOR.

Korea, Democratic People's Republic: Via Ludovico di Savoia 23, 00185 Rome; tel. (06) 77209094; fax (06 77209111; Ambassador: KIM HUNG RIM.

Korea, Republic: Via Barnaba Oriani 30, 00197 Rome; tel. (06) 8088769; fax (06) 80687794; Ambassador: KIM SUK-HYUN.

Kuwait: Via Archimede 124, 00197 Rome; tel. (06) 8078415; fax (06) 8076651; Ambassador: GHAZI AR-RAYES.

Latvia: Viale Liegi 42, 00198 Rome; tel. (06) 8841227; fax (06) 8841239; e-mail segrom@micanet.it; Ambassador: MĀRTIŅŠ PERTS.

Lebanon: Via Giacomino Carissimi 38, 00198 Rome; tel. (06) 8537211; fax (06) 8411794; Ambassador: SAMIR EL-KHOURY.

Lesotho: Via Serchio 8, 00198 Rome; tel. (06) 8542496; fax (06) 8542527; e-mail les.rome@flashnet.it; Ambassador: RACHEL R. MATHABO NTSINYI.

Liberia: Via A. Vivaldi 13, 00199 Rome; tel. (06) 86329034; fax (06) 86384898; Chargé d'affaires a.i.: KRONYANH MOSES WEEFUR.

Libya: Via Nomentana 365, 00162 Rome; tel. (06) 86320951; fax (06) 86205473; Ambassador: ABDULATI IBRAHIM ALOBIDI.

Lithuania: Viale di Villa Grazioli 9, 00198 Rome; tel. (06) 8559052; fax (06) 8559053; e-mail ltemb@tin.it; Ambassador: ROMANAS PODAGÉLIS.

Luxembourg: Via S. Croce in Gerusalemme 90, 00185 Rome; tel. (06) 77201177; fax (06) 77201055; Ambassador: PAUL FABER.

Macedonia, former Yugoslav republic: Via Bruxelles 73–75, 00198 Rome; tel. (06) 84241109; fax (06) 84241131; e-mail repmaced@ats.it; Ambassador: VIKTOR GABER.

Madagascar: Via Riccardo Zandonai 84A, 00194 Rome; tel. (06) 36307797; fax (06) 3294306; Ambassador: GEORGES RUPHIN.

Malaysia: Via Nomentana 297, 00162 Rome; tel. (06) 8415764; fax (06) 8555040; Ambassador: SHAMSUDDIN BIN ABDULLAH.

Mali: Via Nomentana 13, 00100 Rome; Ambassador: IBRAHIM BOCAR DAGA.

Malta: Lungotevere Marzio 12, 00186 Rome; tel. (06) 6879990; fax (06) 6892687; e-mail maltaembassy.rome@magnet.mt; internet www.foreign.govt.mt; Ambassador: JOSEPH CASSAR.

Mauritania: Via Giovanni Paisiello 26, 00198 Rome; tel. (06) 85351530; fax (06) 85351441; Ambassador: MELANINE OULD MOCTAR NECHE.

Mexico: Via Lazzaro Spallanzani 16, 00161 Rome; tel. (06) 441151; fax (06) 4403876; e-mail emexport@tin.it; internet www.target.it/messico; Ambassador: MARIO MOYA PALENCIA.

Moldova: Via Montebello 8, 00185 Rome; tel. and fax (06) 47881092; Ambassador: VALENTIN CIUMAC.

Monaco: Via Bertoloni 36, 00197 Rome; tel. (06) 8083361; fax (06) 8077692; Ambassador: HENRI FISSORE.

Morocco: Via Lazzaro Spallanzani 8, 00161 Rome; tel. (06) 4402524; fax (06) 4402695; Ambassador: AZIZ MEKOUAR.

Mozambique: Via Filippo Corridoni 14, 00195 Rome; tel. (06) 37514852; fax (06) 37514699; Chargé d'affaires a.i.: ANANIAS BENJAMIN SIGAUQUE.

Myanmar: Via Gioacchino Rossini 18, 00198 Rome; tel. (06) 8549374; fax (06) 8413167; Ambassador: MYINT U PHONE.

Netherlands: Via Michele Mercati 8, 00197 Rome; tel. (06) 3221141; fax (06) 3221440; e-mail nlgovrom@tin.it; internet www.olanda.it; Ambassador: RONALD HENRY LOUDON.

New Zealand: Via Zara 28, 00198 Rome; tel. (06) 4417171; fax (06) 4402984; e-mail nzemb.rom@flashnet.it; Ambassador: PETER ROBERT BENNETT.

Nicaragua: Via Brescia 16, 00198 Rome; tel. (06) 8413471; fax (06) 8841695; Ambassador: ALEJANDRO MEJA FERRETTI.

Niger: Via Antonio Baiamonti 10, 00195 Rome; tel. and fax (06) 3729013; Ambassador: ADAMOU CHEKOU.

Nigeria: Via Orazio 14–18, 00193 Rome; tel. (06) 6896243; fax (06) 6832528; Ambassador: ETIM JACK OKPOYO.

Norway: Via delle Terme Deciane 7, 00153 Rome; tel. and fax (06) 5717031; Ambassador: GEIR GRUNG.

Oman: Via della Camilluccia 625, 00135 Rome; tel. (06) 36300517; fax (06) 3296802; Ambassador: YAHYA BIN ABDULLAH BIN SALIM AL-IRAIMY.

Pakistan: Via della Camilluccia 682, 00135 Rome; tel. (06) 36301775; fax (06) 36301936; e-mail pareprom@forobit.it; Ambassador: HILALYA A. ZAFAR.

Panama: Viale Regina Margherita 239, 00198 Rome; tel. (06) 44252173; fax (06) 44252237; Ambassador: ROBERTO ALFARO EDTRIPEAUT.

Paraguay: Via Salaria 237B, 00199 Rome; tel. (06) 8848150; fax (06) 8558739; Ambassador: LILIA ROMERO PEREIRA.

Peru: Via Siacci 4, 00197 Rome; tel. (06) 80691510; fax (06) 8073216; e-mail amb.peru@agora.stm.it; Ambassador: ANA MARÍA DEUSTUA.

Philippines: Viale delle Medaglie d'Oro 112, 00136 Rome; tel. (06) 39746621; fax (06) 39740872; e-mail ph1@agora.it; Ambassador: PHILIPPE J. LHUILLIER.

Poland: Via Pietro Paolo Rubens 20, 00197 Rome; tel. (06) 3224455; fax (06) 3217895; Ambassador: MACIEJ GORSKI.

Portugal: Viale Liegi 21–23, 00198 Rome; tel. (06) 844801; fax (06) 8417404; Ambassador: JOSÉ CESAR PAULOURO DAS NEVES.

Qatar: Via Antonio Bosio 14, 00161 Rome; tel. (06) 44249450; fax (06) 44245273; Ambassador: ALI FAHAD AL SHAHAWANI AL-HAJERI.

Romania: Via Nicolò Tartaglia 36, 00197 Rome; tel. (06) 8084529; fax (06) 8084995; Ambassador: SERBAN STATI.

Russia: Via Gaeta 5, 00185 Rome; tel. (06) 4941680; fax (06) 491031; Ambassador: NIKOLAI NIKOLAYEVICH SPASSKII.

San Marino: Via Eleonora Duse 35, 00197 Rome; tel. (06) 8084567; fax (06) 8070072; Ambassador: BARBARA PARA.

Saudi Arabia: Via G. B. Pergolesi 9, 00198 Rome; tel. (06) 844851; fax (06) 8551781; e-mail relazioni.esterne@arabia-saudita.it; internet www.arabia-saudita.it; Ambassador: MUHAMMAD BIN NAWAF BIN ABDUL AZIZ AL-SAUD.

Senegal: Via Giulia 66, 00186 Rome; tel. (06) 6872381; fax (06) 6865212; Ambassador: MAME BALLA SY.

Slovakia: Via dei Colli della Farnesina 144, 00194 Rome; tel. (06) 367151; fax (06) 3615265; Ambassador: JOSEF MIKLOSKO.

Slovenia: Via Leonardo Pisano 10, 00197 Rome; tel. (06) 8081075; fax (06) 8081471; Ambassador: PETER ANDREJ BEKEŠ.

South Africa: Via Tanaro 14, 00198 Rome; tel. (06) 852541; fax (06) 85254300; e-mail sae@flashnet.it; internet www.sudafrica.it; Ambassador: ANTHONY LE CLERK MONGALO.

Spain: Palazzo Borghese, Largo Fontenella Borghese 19, 00186 Rome; tel. (06) 6878172; fax (06) 6872256; e-mail embaspagna.roma@pronet.it; Ambassador: JOSÉ DE CARVAJAL SALIDO.

Sri Lanka: Via Giuseppe Cuboni 6–8, 00197 Rome; tel. (06) 3224202; fax (06) 3224193; e-mail mc7785@mclink.it; Ambassador: THELMUTH HARRIS WILHELM WOUTERSZ.

Sudan: Via Lazzaro Spallanzani 24, 00161 Rome; tel. (06) 4403609; fax (06) 4402358; Ambassador: ANDREW MAKUR THOU.

Sweden: Piazza Rio de Janeiro 3, 00161 Rome; tel. (06) 441941; fax (06) 44194760; Ambassador: ROLF GORAN KRISTOFFER BERG.

Switzerland: Via Barnaba Oriani 61, 00197 Rome; tel. (06) 809571; fax (06) 8088510; Ambassador: ALEXEI LAUTENBERG.

Syria: Piazza dell'Ara Coeli 1, 00186 Rome; tel. (06) 6797791; fax (06) 6794989; Chargé d'affaires a.i.: NABILA CHAALAN.

Tanzania: Via C. Becaria 88, 00196 Rome; tel. (06) 36005234; fax (06) 3216611; Ambassador: COSTA RICKY MAHALU.

Thailand: Via Nomentana 132, 00162 Rome; tel. (06) 86204381; fax (06) 86208399; e-mail thai.em.rome@pn.itnet.it; Ambassador: SOMBOON SANGIAMBUT.

Tunisia: Via Asmara 7, 00199 Rome; tel. (06) 8603060; fax (06) 86218204; Ambassador: AZOUZ ENNIFAR.

Turkey: Via Palestro 28, 00185 Rome; tel. (06) 4469933; fax (06) 4941526; Ambassador: NECATI UTKAN.

Uganda: Via Ennio Quirino Visconti 8, 00193 Rome; tel. (06) 3225220; fax (06) 3203174; Ambassador: VINCENT KIRABOKYAMARIA.

Ukraine: Via Guido d'Arezzo 9, 00198 Rome; tel. (06) 8412630; fax (06) 8547539; Ambassador: BORYS GUDYAMA.

United Arab Emirates: Via della Camilluccia 551, 00135 Rome; tel. (06) 36306100; fax (06) 36306155; Ambassador: MUHAMMAD FAHD ABDULRAHMAN ADH-DHAIM.

United Kingdom: Via XX Settembre 80A, 00187 Rome; tel. (06) 42200001; fax (06) 48903217; e-mail info@rome.mail.fco.gov.uk; internet www.britain.it; Ambassador: JOHN SHEPHERD.

USA: Via Vittorio Veneto 119A, 00187 Rome; tel. (06) 46741; fax (06) 46742356; internet www.usis.it; Ambassador: THOMAS FOGLIETTA.

Uruguay: Via Vittorio Veneto 183, 00187 Rome; tel. (06) 4821776; fax (06) 4823695; Ambassador: CARLOS BRUGNINI.

Uzbekistan: Via Tolmino 12, 00198 Rome; tel. (06) 8542456; fax (06) 8541020; e-mail uzbembass@tiskalinet.it; internet www.uzbekistanitalia.com; Chargé d'affaires a.i.: KHURSHID M. BABASHEV.

Venezuela: Via Nicolò Tartaglia 11, 00197 Rome; tel. (06) 8079464; fax (06) 8084410; Ambassador: FERNANDO GERBASI.

Viet Nam: Via Clitunno 34–36, 00198 Rome; tel. (06) 8543223; fax (06) 8548501; Chargé d'affaires a.i.: NGUYEN HOANG THANH.

Yemen: Viale Regina Margherita 1, 00198 Rome; tel. (06) 8416711; fax (06) 8416801; Chargé d'affaires a.i.: MOSLEH ALI SAAD HAJAR.

Yugoslavia: Via dei Monti Parioli 20, 00197 Rome; tel. (06) 3200805; fax (06) 3200868; Chargé d'affaires a.i.: MIODRAG LEKIĆ.

Zimbabwe: Via Virgilio 8, 00193 Rome; tel. (06) 68807781; fax (06) 68308324; Ambassador: MARY MARGARET MUCHADA.

Judicial System

The Constitutional Court was established in 1956 and is an autonomous constitutional body, standing apart from the judicial system. Its most important function is to pronounce on the constitutionality of legislation both subsequent and prior to the present Constitution of 1948. It also judges accusations brought against the President of the Republic or ministers.

At the base of the system of penal jurisdiction are the Preture (District Courts), where offences carrying a sentence of up to four years' imprisonment are tried. Above the Preture are the Tribunali (Tribunals) and the Corti di Assise presso i Tribunali (Assize Courts attached to the Tribunals), where graver offences are dealt with. From these courts appeal lies to the Corti d'Appello (Courts of Appeal) and the parallel Corti di Assise d'Appello (Assize Courts of Appeal). Final appeal may be made, on juridical grounds only, to the Corte Suprema di Cassazione.

Civil cases may be taken in the first instance to the Giudici Conciliatori (Justices of the Peace), Preture or Tribunali, according to the economic value of the case. Appeal from the Giudici Conciliatori lies to the Preture, from the Preture to the Tribunali, from the Tribunali to the Corti d'Appello, and finally, as in penal justice, to the Corte Suprema di Cassazione on juridical grounds only.

Special divisions for cases concerning labour relations are attached to civil courts. Cases concerned with the public service and its employees are tried by Tribunali Amministrativi Regionali and the Consiglio di Stato. Juvenile courts have criminal and civil jurisdiction.

A new penal code was introduced in late 1989.

Consiglio Superiore della Magistratura (CSM): Piazza dell'Indipendenza 6, 00185 Rome; f. 1958; tel. (06) 444911; supervisory body of judicial system; 33 mems.

President: The President of the Republic.

CONSTITUTIONAL COURT

Corte Costituzionale: Palazzo della Consulta, Piazza del Quirinale 41, 00187 Rome; tel. (06) 46981; fax (06) 4825706; e-mail c.costit@mclink.it; internet www.cortecostituzionale.it; consists of 15 judges, one-third appointed by the President of the Republic, one-third elected by Parliament in joint session, one-third by the ordinary and administrative supreme courts.

President: CESARE MIRABELLI.

ADMINISTRATIVE COURTS

Consiglio di Stato: Palazzo Spada, Piazza Capo di Ferro 13, 00186 Rome; tel. (06) 68271; fax (06) 6827534; established in accordance with Article 10 of the Constitution; has both consultative and judicial functions.

President: RENATO LASCHENA.

Corte dei Conti: Via Antonio Baiamonti 25, 00195 Rome; tel. (06) 38761; fax (06) 38763477; e-mail uric@corteconti.it, and Via Barberini 38, Rome; functions as the court of public auditors for the state.

President: FRANCESCO STADERINI.

SUPREME COURT OF APPEAL

Corte Suprema di Cassazione: Palazzo di Giustizia, 00193 Rome; tel. (06) 68831; fax (06) 6883420; supreme court of civil and criminal appeal.

First President: ANDREA VELA.

Religion

More than 90% of the population of Italy are adherents of the Roman Catholic Church. Under the terms of the Concordat formally ratified in June 1985, Roman Catholicism was no longer to be the state religion, compulsory religious instruction in schools was abolished and state financial contributions reduced. The Vatican City's sovereign rights as an independent state, under the terms of the Lateran Pact of 1929, were not affected.

Several Protestant churches also exist in Italy, with a total membership of about 50,000. There is a small Jewish community, and in 1987 an agreement between the State and Jewish representatives recognized certain rights for the Jewish community, including the right to observe religious festivals on Saturdays by not attending school or work. In March 2000 Jehovah's Witnesses and Buddhism were officially recognized as religions by the Italian legislature.

CHRISTIANITY

The Roman Catholic Church

For ecclesiastical purposes, Italy comprises the Papal See of Rome, the Patriarchate of Venice, 58 archdioceses (including six directly responsible to the Holy See), 157 dioceses (including seven within the jurisdiction of the Pope, as Archbishop of the Roman Province, and 17 directly responsible to the Holy See), two territorial prelatures (including one directly responsible to the Holy See) and seven territorial abbacies (including four directly responsible to the Holy See). Almost all adherents follow the Latin rite, but there are two dioceses and one abbacy (all directly responsible to the Holy See) for Catholics of the Italo-Albanian (Byzantine) rite.

Bishops' Conference: Conferenza Episcopale Italiana, Circonvallazione Aurelia 50, 00165 Rome; tel. (06) 663981; fax (06) 6623037; f. 1985; Pres. HE Cardinal CAMILLO RUINI, Vicar-General of Rome.

Primate of Italy, Archbishop and Metropolitan of the Roman Province and Bishop of Rome: His Holiness Pope JOHN PAUL II.

Patriarch of Venice: HE Cardinal MARCO CÉ.

Archbishops:
Acerenza: Most Rev. MICHELE SCANDIFFIO.
Amalfi-Cava de'Tirreni: (vacant).
Ancona-Osimo: Most Rev. FRANCO FESTORAZZI.
Bari-Bitonto: Most Rev. FRANCESCO CACUCCI.
Benevento: Most Rev. SERAFINO SPROVIERI.
Bologna: HE Cardinal GIACOMO BIFFI.
Brindisi-Ostuni: Most Rev. SETTIMIO TODISCO.
Cagliari: Most Rev. OTTORINO PIETRO ALBERTI.
Camerino-San Severino Marche: Most Rev. ANGELO FAGIANI.
Campobasso-Boiano: Most Rev. ARMANDO DINI.
Capua: Most Rev. BRUNO SCHETTINO.
Catania: Most Rev. LUIGI BOMMARITO.
Catanzaro-Squillace: Most Rev. ANTONIO CANTISANI.
Chieti-Vasto: Most Rev. EDOARDO MENICHELLI.
Cosenza-Bisignano: Most Rev. GIUSEPPE AGOSTINO.
Crotone-Santa Severina: Most Rev. ANDREA MUGIONE.
Fermo: Most Rev. GENNARO FRANCESCHETTI.
Ferrara-Comacchio: Most Rev. CARLO CAFFARRA.
Florence: HE Cardinal SILVANO PIOVANELLI.
Foggia-Bovino: Most Rev. DOMENICO UMBERTO D'AMBROSIO.
Gaeta: Most Rev. PIER LUIGI MAZZONI.
Genoa: HE Cardinal DIONIGI TETTAMANZI.
Gorizia: Most Rev. DINO DE ANTONI.
Lanciano-Ortona: Most Rev. ENZO D'ANTONIO.
L'Aquila: Most Rev. GIUSEPPE MOLINARI.
Lecce: Most Rev. COSMO FRANCESCO RUPPI.
Lucca: Most Rev. BRUNO TOMMASI.
Manfredonia-Vieste: Most Rev. VINCENZO D'ADDARIO.
Matera-Irsina: Most Rev. ANTONIO CILIBERTI.
Messina-Lipari-Santa Lucia del Mela: Most Rev. GIOVANNI MARRA.
Milan: HE Cardinal CARLO MARIA MARTINI.
Modena-Nonantola: Most Rev. BENITO COCCHI.
Monreale: Most Rev. PIO VITTORIO VIGO.
Naples: HE Cardinal MICHELE GIORDANO.
Oristano: Most Rev. PIER GIULIANO TIDDIA.
Otranto: (vacant).
Palermo: HE Cardinal SALVATORE DE GIORGI.
Perugia-Città della Pieve: Most Rev. GIUSEPPE CHIARETTI.
Pescara-Penne: Most Rev. FRANCESCO CUCCARESE.
Pisa: Most Rev. ALESSANDRO PLOTTI.
Potenza-Muro Lucano-Marsico Nuovo: Most Rev. ENNIO APPIGNANESI.
Ravenna-Cervia: Most Rev. LUIGI AMADUCCI.
Reggio Calabria-Bova: Most Rev. VITTORIO LUIGI MONDELLO.
Rossano-Cariati: Most Rev. ANDREA CASSONE.
Salerno-Campagna-Acerno: Most Rev. GERARDO PIERRO.
Sant'Angelo dei Lombardi-Conza-Nusco-Bisaccia: Most Rev. SALVATORE NUNNARI.
Sassari: Most Rev. SALVATORE ISGRÓ.
Siena-Colle di Val d'Elsa-Montalcino: Most Rev. GAETANO BONICELLI.
Sorrento-Castellammare di Stabia: Most Rev. FELICE CECE.
Spoleto-Norcia: Most Rev. RICCARDO FONTANA.
Syracuse: Most Rev. GIUSEPPE COSTANZO.
Taranto: Most Rev. BENIGNO LUIGI PAPA.
Trani-Barletta-Bisceglie: Most Rev. GIOVANNI BATTISTA PICHIERRI.
Trento: Most Rev. LUIGI BRESSAN.
Turin: HE Cardinal SEVERINO POLETTO.
Udine: Most Rev. ALFREDO BATTISTI.
Urbino-Urbania-Sant'Angelo in Vado: (vacant).
Vercelli: Most Rev. ENRICO MASSERONI.

Azione Cattolica Italiana (ACI) (Catholic Action): Via della Conciliazione 1, 00193 Rome; tel. (06) 6868751; fax (06) 68802088; in Italy there are numerous apostolic lay organizations, prominent among which is Italian Catholic Action, which has a total membership of 1m.; National Presidency is the supreme executive body and co-ordinator of the different branches of Catholic Action; Pres. Dott.ssa PAOLA BIGNARDI; Sec.-Gen. Prof. DOMENICO ZAPPONE.

Protestant Churches

Federazione delle Chiese Evangeliche in Italia (Federation of the Protestant Churches in Italy): Via Firenze 38, 00184 Rome; tel. (06) 4825120; fax (06) 4828728; e-mail fcei@fcei.it; the Federation was formed in 1967; total mems more than 50,000; Pres. Dott. GIANNI LONG; Sec. LUCA MARIA NEGRO; includes the following organizations:

Chiesa Apostolica d'Italia

Chiesa Evangelica Luterana in Italia (Lutheran Church): Via Toscana 7, 00187 Rome; tel. (06) 4880394; fax (06) 4874506; Dean JÜRGEN ASTFALK; 20,100 mems.

Chiesa Evangelica Metodista in Italia (Evangelical Methodist Church): Via Firenze 38, 00184 Rome; tel. (06) 4743695; fax (06) 47881267; e-mail metodismo@tin.it; f. 1861; Pres. Pastor VALDO BENECCHI; 4,000 mems.

Comunione delle Chiese Libere

Comunità Ecumenica di Ispra-Varese

Comunità Evangelica di Confessione Elvetica

Esercito della Salvezza (Salvation Army): Via degli Apuli 39, 00185 Rome; tel. (06) 4462614; fax (06) 490078; Officer Commanding for Italy Lt-Col DAVID ARMISTEAD; 15 regional centres.

Fiumi di Vita

Tavola Valdese (Waldensian Church): Via Firenze 38, 00184 Rome; tel. (06) 4745537; fax (06) 47885308; e-mail tvmode@tin.it; internet www.chiesavaldese.org; Moderator GIANNI GENRE; Sec.-Treas. ROSELLA PANZIRONI; 25,000 mems.

Unione Cristiana Evangelica Battista d'Italia (Italian Baptist Union): Piazza San Lorenzo in Lucina 35, 00186 Rome; tel. (06) 6876124; fax (06) 6876185; e-mail ucebit@tin.it; f. 1873; Pres. ALDO CASONATO; 5,000 mems.

Associated Organization

Seventh-day Adventists: Lungotevere Michelangelo 7, 00192 Rome; tel. (06) 3609591; fax (06) 36095952; e-mail uicca@avventisti.org; internet www.avventisti.org; f. 1929; represents 90 communities in Italy and Malta; Supt LUCIO ALTIN; Sec. IGNAZIO BARBUSCIA.

JUDAISM

The number of Jews was estimated at 30,000 in 1997.

Union of Italian Jewish Communities: Lungotevere Sanzio 9, 00153 Rome; tel. (06) 5803667; fax (06) 5899569; f. 1930; represents 21 Jewish communities in Italy; Pres. AMOS LUZZATTO; Chief Rabbi of Rome Dott. ELIO TOAFF.

Rabbinical Council: Chief Rabbi Dott. ELIO R. TOAFF; Via Catalana 1A, Rome; Rabbi Dott. GIUSEPPE LARAS (Via Guastalla 19, Milan), Rabbi Dott. ELIA RICHETTI (Via Guastalla 19, Milan).

BAHÁ'Í FAITH

Assemblea Spirituale Nazionale: Via Stoppani 10, 00197 Rome; tel. (06) 8079647; fax (06) 8070184; e-mail segreteria@bahai.it; internet www.bahai.it; mems resident in 330 localities.

The Press

Relative to the size of Italy's population, the number of daily newspapers is rather small (78 in 1996). The average total circulation of daily newspapers in 1996 was 5,960,000 copies per issue; sales in the north and centre of the country accounted for 80% of this figure, and those in the south for 20%.

Rome and Milan are the main press centres. The most important national dailies are *Corriere della Sera* in Milan and Rome and *La Repubblica* in Rome, followed by Turin's *La Stampa*, *Il Sole 24 Ore* in Milan, the economic and financial newspaper with the highest circulation in Europe, *Il Messaggero* in Rome, *Il Resto del Carlino* in Bologna, *La Nazione* in Florence, and *Il Giornale* and *Il Giorno*, which circulate mainly in the north.

In 1993 there were about 10,000 periodical titles, with a combined annual circulation of some 4,036m. Many illustrated weekly papers and magazines maintain very high levels of circulation, with *TV Sorrisi e Canzoni* and *Famiglia Cristiana* enjoying the highest figures. Other very popular general-interest weeklies are *Gente* and *Oggi*. Among the serious and influential magazines are *Panorama* and *L'Espresso*.

PRINCIPAL DAILIES

Ancona

Corriere Adriatico: Via Berti 20, 60126 Ancona; tel. (071) 4581; fax (071) 42980; f. 1860; Dir SESTO EGIDI; circ. 29,349.

Bari

La Gazzetta del Mezzogiorno: Viale Scipione l'Africano 264, 70124 Bari; tel. (080) 5470200; fax (080) 5470488; internet www.gdmland.it; f. 1928; independent; Man. Dir PASQUALE PATRUNO; circ. 82,398.

Ii Quotidiano di Bari: Piazza A. Moro 31, 70121 Bari; tel. (080) 5240110; fax (080) 5245486; Dir MATTEO TATARELLA.

Bergamo

L'Eco di Bergamo: Viale Papa Giovanni XXIII 118, 24121 Bergamo; tel. (035) 386111; fax (035) 386217; e-mail redazione@eco.bg.it; internet www.eco.bg.it; f. 1880; Catholic; Man. Dr ETTORE ONGIS; circ 68,449.

Il Nuovo Giornale di Bergamo: Vis S. Bernardino 120, 24126 Bergamo; tel. (035) 4243161; fax (035) 4243160; Dir SERGIO CARRARO.

Bologna

Il Resto del Carlino: Via Enrico Mattei 106, 40138 Bologna; tel. (051) 6006111; fax (051) 532990; internet www.ilrestodelcarlino.it; f. 1885; independent; Dir MARCO LEONELLI; circ. 232,866.

Bolzano/Bozen

Alto Adige: Via Volta 10, 39100 Bozen; tel. (0471) 904111; fax (0471) 9042663; e-mail altoadi@tin.it; internet www.altoadige.it; f. 1945; independent; Dir GIAMPAOLO VISETTI; circ. 53,674.

Dolomiten: Weinbergweg 7, 39100 Bozen; tel. (0471) 925111; fax 925440; e-mail dolomiten@athesia.it; internet www.dolomiten.it; f. 1926; independent; German language; Dir Dr TONI EBNER; circ. 56,500.

Il Mattino di Bolzano e Provincia: Via Dante 5, 39100 Bozen; tel. (0471) 990711; fax (0471) 990729; internet www.ilmattinobz.it; Dir PAOLO GHEZZI.

Brescia

Bresciaoggi Nuovo: Via Eritrea 20a, 25126 Brescia; tel. (030) 2294260; fax (030) 2294229; internet www.bresciaoggi.it; f. 1974; Dir MAURIZIO CATTANEO; circ. 18,500.

Il Giornale di Brescia: Via Solferino 22, 25121 Brescia; tel. (030) 37901; fax (030) 292226; f. 1945; Editor GIAN BATTISTA LANZANI; Man. Dir FRANCESCO PASSERINI GLAZEL; circ. 72,301.

Cagliari

L'Unione Sarda: Viale Regina Elena 14, 09124 Cagliari; tel. (070) 60131; fax (070) 6013306; e-mail unione@unionesarda.it; internet www.unionesarda.it; f. 1889; independent; Dir MARIO SECHI; circ. 81,810.

Catania

La Sicilia: Viale Odorico da Pordenone 50, 95126 Catania; tel. (095) 330544; fax (095) 336466; internet www.lasicilia.it; f. 1945; independent; Dir Dott. MARIO CIANCIO SANFILIPPO; circ. 87,942.

Como

Il Corriere: Via Vittorio Emanuele II 115, 202100 Como; tel. (031) 337788; fax (031) 3377823; Dir MARIO RAPISARDA.

La Provincia di Como: Via Paoli 21, 22100 Como; tel. (031) 582311; fax (031) 505003; e-mail laprovincia@laprovincia.it; f. 1892; independent; Dir GIGI RIVA; circ. 49,711.

Cremona

La Provincia di Cremona: Via delle Industrie 2, 26100 Cremona; tel. (0372) 4981; fax (0372) 28487; internet www.cremonaonline.it; f. 1946; independent; Pres. MARIO MAESTRONI; Man. Dir ENRICO PIRONDINI; circ. 26,777.

Ferrara

La Nuova Ferrara: Via Baruffaldi 22, 44100 Ferrara; tel. (0532) 214211; fax (0532) 247689; internet www.lanuovaferrara.it; f. 1989; independent; Man. Dir VALENTINO PESCI; circ. 11,886.

Foggia

Foggia Sera: Corso Roma 204b, 71100 Foggia; tel. (0881) 632259; fax (0881) 661534; Dir MATTEO TATARELLA.

Il Quotidiano di Foggia: Corso Roma 204b, 71100 Foggia; (0881) 686967; fax (0881) 777812; Dir MATTEO TATARELLA.

Florence

La Nazione: Via Ferdinando Paolieri 2, 50121 Florence; tel. (055) 87951; fax (055) 2343646; internet www.lanazione.it; f. 1859; independent; Dir UMBERTO CECCHI; circ. 258,794.

Genoa

L'Avvisatore Marittimo: Piazza Piccapietra 21, 16121 Genoa; tel. (010) 545341; fax (010) 5453436; e-mail avvmar@tin.it; internet www.avvmar.it; f. 1925; shipping and financial; Editor SANDRO GRIMALDI; circ. 2,400.

Corriere Mercantile: Via Archimede 169, 16142 Genoa; tel. (010) 53691; fax (010) 504148; f. 1824; political and financial; independent; Editor MIMMO ANGELI; circ. 17,000.

Il Secolo XIX: Piazza Piccapietra 21, 16122 Genoa; tel. (010) 53881; fax (010) 5306759; internet www.ilsecoloXIX.it; f. 1886; independent; Dir ANTONIO DI ROSA; circ. 181,617.

Lecce

Quotidiano di Lecce, Brindisi e Taranto: Via dei Mocenigo 25–29, 73100 Lecce; tel. (0832) 3382000; fax (0832) 338244; f. 1979; Dir GIANCARLO MINICUCCI; circ. 26,502.

Leghorn/Livorno

Il Tirreno: Viale Alfieri 9, 57124 Livorno; tel. (0586) 220111; fax (0586) 220717; e-mail iltirreno@petrurianet.it; internet www.iltirreno.it; f. 1978; independent; Dir SANDRA BONSANTI; circ. 130,000.

Mantua

Gazzetta di Mantova: Via Fratelli Bandiera 32, 46100 Mantua; tel. (0376) 3031; fax (0376) 303263; internet www.gazzettadimantova.it; f. 1664; independent; Dir BRUNO MANFELLOTTO; circ. 42,684.

Messina

Gazzetta del Sud: Uberto Bonino 15C, 98124 Messina; tel. (090) 2261; fax (090) 2936359; internet www.gazzettadelsud.it; f. 1952; independent; Dir NINO CALARCO; circ. 92,722.

Milan

Avvenire: Piazza Carbonari 3, 20125 Milan; tel. (02) 67801; fax (02) 6780208; internet www.avvenire.it; f. 1968; Catholic; Man. Dir DINO BOFFO; circ. 138,000.

Corriere della Sera: Via Solferino 28, 20121 Milan; tel. (02) 6339; fax (02) 29009668; internet www.corriere.it; f. 1876; independent; contains weekly supplement, *Sette*; Dir FERRUCCIO DE BORTOLI; circ. 720,239.

Il Foglio: Largo Corsia dei Servi 3, 20122 Milan; tel. (02) 7712951; internet www.ilfoglio.it; Dir GIULIANO FERRARA.

La Gazzetta dello Sport: Via Solferino 28, 20121 Milan; tel. (02) 6353; fax (02) 29009668; e-mail gasport@rcs.it; internet www.gazzetta.it; f. 1896; sport; Dir CANDIDO CANNAVÒ; circ. 426,000.

Il Giornale: Via Gaetano Negri 4, 20123 Milan; tel. (02) 85661; fax (02) 72023859; e-mail segretaria@ilgiornale.it; internet www.ilgiornale.com; f. 1974; independent, controlled by staff; Editor MARIO CERVI; circ. 210,000.

Il Giorno: Via Stradivari 4, 20131 Milan; tel. (02) 277991; fax (02) 27799537; e-mail ilgiorno@ilgiorno.it; internet www.ilgiorno.it; Man. Dir UMBERTO MARCHESINI; circ. 255,377.

Il Sole 24 Ore: Via Paolo Lomazzo 52, 20154 Milan; tel. (02) 30221; fax (02) 312055; internet www.ilsole24ore.com; f. 1865; financial, political, economic; Dir ERNESTO AUCI; circ. 400,000.

Modena

Nuova Gazzetta di Modena: Via Ricci 56, 41100 Modena; tel. (059) 247311; fax (059) 226533; internet www.gazzettadimodena.it; Dir ANTONIO MASCOLO; circ. 14,710.

Naples

Corriere del Mezzogiorno: Vico II san Nicola alla dogana 9, 80133 Naples; tel. (081) 7602001; fax (081) 5802779; internet www.corrieredelmezzogiorno.it; Dir MARCO DEMARCO.

Il Giornale di Napoli: Piazza M. Serao 19, 80132 Naples; tel. (081) 2458111; f. 1985; Editor ROBERTO TUMBARELLO; circ. 11,000.

Il Mattino: Via Chiatamone 65, 80121 Naples; tel. (081) 7947111; fax (081) 7947288; internet www.ilmattino.it; f. 1892, reformed 1950; independent; Dir PAOLO GAMBESCIA; circ. 207,040.

Padua

Il Mattino di Padova: Via Pelizzo 3, 35100 Padua; tel. (049) 8083411; fax (049) 8079067; internet www.mattinopadova.it; f. 1978; Dir FABIO BARBIERI; circ. 37,252.

Palermo

Giornale di Sicilia: Via Lincoln 21, 90133 Palermo; tel. (091) 6627111; fax (091) 6627280; internet www.gds.it; f. 1860; independent; Dir ANTONIO ARDIZZONE; circ. 89,880.

Parma

Gazzetta di Parma: Via Emilio Casa 5A, 43100 Parma; tel. (0521) 2251; fax (0521) 285515; internet www.gazzettadiparma.it; f. 1735; Dir GIULIANO MOLOSSI; circ. 59,710.

Pavia

La Provincia Pavese: Viale Canton Ticino 16–18, 27100 Pavia; tel. (0382) 434511; fax (0382) 473875; e-mail info@laprovincia.pv.it; internet www.laprovincia.pv.it; f. 1870; independent; Dir ROBERTO GALLI; circ. 33,793.

Perugia

Corriere dell'Umbria: Via Pievaiola km 5.7, 06100 Perugia; tel. (075) 52731; fax (075) 5273259; internet www.corr.it; f. 1983; independent; Editor FEDERICO FIORAVANTI; circ. 23,000.

Pescara

Il Centro: Corso Vittorio Emanuele 372, 65122 Pescara; tel. (085) 20521; fax (085) 4212460; e-mail ilcentro@micso.it; internet www.ilcentro.it; f. 1986; independent; Dir ANTONIO DEL GIUDICE; circ. 38,655.

Piacenza

Libertà: Via Benedettine 68, 29100 Piacenza; tel. (0523) 393939; fax (0523) 393962; e-mail info@liberta; internet www.liberta.it; f. 1883; Dir GAETANO RIZZUTO; circ. 37,445.

Reggio Emilia

Gazzetta di Reggio: Via Isonzo 72, 42100 Reggio Emilia; tel. (0552) 501511; fax (0522) 517301; internet www.gazzettadireggio.it; f. 1860; Dir ENRICO GRAZIOLI; circ. 19,563.

Rimini

Corriere di Romagna: Piazza Tre Martiri 43a, 47900 Rimini; tel. (0541) 354111; fax (0541) 351499; Dir CLAUDIO CASALI.

Rome

Corriere dello Sport: Piazza Indipendenza 11B, 00185 Rome, tel. (06) 49921; fax (06) 4992690; f. 1924; 13 regional editions; Editor ITALO UCI; circ. 270,307.

Il Giornale d'Italia: Via Boezio 17, 00193 Rome; tel. (06) 6878628; fax (06) 6878697; Dir MASSIMO BASSOLI; circ. 25,000.

Il Manifesto: Via Tomacelli 146, 00186 Rome; tel. (06) 687191; fax (06) 68719573; e-mail redazione@ilmanifesto.mir.it; internet www.ilmanifesto.it; f. 1971; splinter communist; Dir RICCARDO BARENGHI; circ. 55,000.

Il Messaggero: Via del Tritone 152, 00187 Rome; tel. (06) 47201; fax (06) 4720300; internet www.ilmessaggero.it; f. 1878; independent; Dir PAOLO GRALDI; circ. 260,000.

L'Opinione: Via del Corso 117, 00186 Rome; tel. (06) 69200880; fax (06) 6787573; internet www.opinione.it; f. 1977; independent; Man. Editor ARTURO DIACONALE; circ. 5,000.

Il Popolo: Via del Gesú 62, 00186 Rome; tel. (06) 695071; fax (06) 69942377; f. 1944; organ of the PPI; Dir FRANCESCO SAVERIO GAROFANI; circ. 6,000.

La Repubblica: Piazza dell'Indipendenza 11B, 00185 Rome; tel. (06) 49821; fax (06) 49822923; e-mail larepubblica@repubblica.it; internet www.repubblica.it; f. 1976; left-wing; Publr Editoriale L'Espresso; Editor-in-Chief EZIO MAURO; circ. 662,000.

Secolo d'Italia: Via della Scrofa 43, 00186 Rome; tel. (06) 6833889; fax (06) 6861598; f. 1951; organ of the AN; Editor GENNARO MALGIERI; circ. 15,000.

Il Tempo: Piazza Colonna 366, 00187 Rome; tel. (06) 675881; fax (06) 6758869; internet www.iltempo.it; f. 1944; right-wing; Editor GIUSEPPE SANZOTTA; circ. 100,000.

L'Unità: Via dei Due Macelli 23/13, 00187 Rome; tel. (06) 699961; fax (06) 6783555; e-mail unitaedi@unita.it; internet www.unita.it; f. 1924; Dir FURIO COLOMBO; circ. 137,000.

Sassari

La Nuova Sardegna: Via Porcellana 9, 07100 Sassari; tel. (079) 222400; fax (079) 236293; internet www.lanuovasardegna.it; f. 1892; independent; Editor LIVIO LIUZZI; circ. 65,000.

Taranto

Corriere del Giorno di Puglia e Lucania: Piazza Maria Immacolata 30, 74100 Taranto; tel. (099) 4553111; fax (099) 4538322; f. 1947; Dir CLEMENTE SELVAGGIO; circ. 3,500.

Trent

l'Adige: Via Missioni Africane 17, 38100 Trent; tel. (0461) 886111; fax (0461) 886263; internet www.ladige.it; f. 1946; independent; Dir Dott. PAOLO GHEZZI; circ. 25,450.

Treviso

La Tribuna di Treviso: Corso del Popolo 42, 31100 Treviso; tel. (0422) 417611; fax (0422) 579212; internet www.tribunatreviso.it; f. 1978; independent; Dir FABIO BARBIERI; circ. 25,641.

Trieste

Il Piccolo (Giornale di Trieste): Via Guido Reni 1, 34123 Trieste; tel. (040) 3733111; fax (040) 3733243; e-mail piccolo@ilpiccolo.it; internet www.ilpiccolo.it; f. 1881; independent; Dir ALBERTO STATERA; circ. 52,544.

Primorski Dnevnik: Via dei Montecchi 6, 34137 Trieste; tel. (040) 7786300; fax (040) 772418; e-mail redakcija@primorski.it; internet www.primorski.it; f. 1945; Slovene; Editor-in-Chief BOJAN BREZIGAR; circ. 10,000.

Turin

La Stampa: Via Marenco 32, 10126 Turin; tel. (011) 656811; fax (011) 655306; e-mail lettere@lastampa.it; internet www.lastampa.it; f. 1868; independent; Dir MARCELLO SORGI; circ. 500,000.

Udine

Messaggero Veneto: Viale Palmanova 290, 33100 Udine; tel. (0432) 5271; fax (0432) 523072; e-mail messven@messaggeroveneto.it; internet www.messaggeroveneto.it; f. 1946; Editor SERGIO BARALDI; circ. 60,309.

Varese

La Prealpina: Viale Tamagno 13, 21100 Varese; tel. (0332) 275700; fax (0332) 275701; e-mail prealpina@betanet.it; internet www.laprealpinagiorn.it; f. 1888; Dir MINO DURAND; circ. 38,000.

Venice

Il Gazzettino: Via Torino 110, 30172 Venezia-Mestre; tel. (041) 665111; fax (041) 665386; internet www.gazzettino.it; f. 1887; independent; Dir GIULIO GIUSTINIANI; circ. 139,000.

La Nuova Venezia: Via Verdi 30, 30171 Mestre; tel. (041) 5074611; fax (041) 958856; internet www.nuovavenezia.it; Dir FABIO BARBIERI; circ. 13,000.

Verona

L'Arena: Vicolo Stella 11, 37121, Verona; tel. (045) 8094899; fax (045) 597966; internet www.larena.it; f. 1866; independent; Editor-in-Chief Dr MINO ALLIONE; Man. Dir Ing. ALESSANDRO ZELGER; circ. 67,746.

Vicenza

Il Giornale di Vicenza: Viale S. Lazzaro 89, 36100 Vicenza; tel. (0444) 396311; fax (0444) 570117; internet www.ilgiornaledivicenza.it; f. 1946; Editor LUIGI BACIALLI; circ. 47,000.

SELECTED PERIODICALS

Fine Arts

Casabella: Via Trentacoste 7, 20134 Milan; tel. (02) 215631; fax (02) 21563260; e-mail casabella@mondadori.it; f. 1938; 10 a year; architecture and interior design; Editor FRANCESCO DAL CO; circ. 43,000.

Domus: Via A. Grandi 5/7, 20089 Rozzano, Milan; tel. (02) 824721; fax (02) 82472386; e-mail domus@edidomus.it; internet www.edidomus.it; f. 1928; 11 a year; architecture, interior design and art; Editor FRANÇOIS BURKHARDT; circ. 53,000.

Graphicus: Via Morgari 36B, 10125 Turin; tel. (011) 6690577; fax (011) 6689200; e-mail graphicus@arpnet.it; internet www.arpnet.it/prograf; f. 1911; 10 a year; printing and graphic arts; Dir ANGELO DRAGONE; Editor LUCIANO LOVERA; circ. 7,200.

L'Illustrazione Italiana: Via Nino Bixio 30, 20129 Milan; tel. (02) 2043941; fax (02) 2046507; f. 1873; quarterly; fine arts; Editor MASSIMO CAPRARA.

Interni: Via Trentacoste 7, 20134 Milan; tel. (02) 215631; fax (02) 26410847; e-mail interni@mondadori.it; monthly; interior decoration and design; Editor GILDA BOLARDI; circ. 40,000.

Lotus International: Via Trentacoste 7, 20134 Milan; tel. (02) 21563240; fax (02) 26410847; e-mail lotus@mondadori.it; f. 1963; quarterly; architecture, town-planning; Editor PIERLUIGI NICOLIN.

Rivista Italiana di Musicologia: Leo S. Olschki, Viuzzo del Pozzetto, 50126 Florence; tel. (055) 6530684; fax (055) 6530214; f. 1966; twice a year; musicology; Editor ENRICO FUBINI.

Il Saggiatore Musicale: Leo S. Olschki, Viuzzo del Pozzetto, 50126 Florence; tel. (055) 6530684; fax (055) 6530214; f. 1994; twice a year; musicology; Editor GIUSEPPINA LA FACE BIANCONI.

Storia dell'Arte: Viale Carso 46, 00195 Rome; tel. (0361) 3729220; fax (0361) 3251055; f. 1969; quarterly; art history; Dirs MAURIZIO CALVESI, ORESTE FERRARI, ANGIOLA M. ROMANINI; circ. 1,200.

Studi Musicali: Leo S. Olschki, Viuzzo del Pozzetto, 50126 Florence; tel. (055) 6530684; fax (055) 6530214; f. 1972; twice a year; musicology; Editor BRUNO CAGLI.

General, Literary and Political

Archivio Storico Italiano: Leo S. Olschki, Viuzzo del Pozzetto, 50126 Florence; tel. (055) 6530684; fax (055) 6530214; f. 1842; quarterly; history; Editor GIULIANO PINTO.

Belfagor: Leo S. Olschki, Viuzzo del Pozzetto, 50126 Florence; tel. (055) 6530684; fax (055) 6530214; f. 1946; every 2 months; historical and literary criticism; Editor CARLO FERDINANDO RUSSO; circ. 2,500.

La Bibliofilia: Leo S. Olschki, Viuzzo del Pozzetto, 50126 Florence; tel. (055) 6530684; fax (055) 6530214; f. 1899; every 4 months; bibliography, history of printing; Editor LUIGI BALSAMO.

L'Espresso: Via Po 12, 00198 Rome; tel. (06) 84781; fax (06) 8550246; e-mail segred@espresso.it; internet www.espressoedit.it; weekly; independent left; political; illustrated; Dir GIULIO ANSELMI; circ. 381,000.

Famiglia Cristiana: Via Giotto 36, 20145 Milan; tel. (02) 48071; fax (02) 48008247; e-mail famigliacristiana@stpauls.it; internet www.stpauls.it; f. 1931; weekly; Catholic; illustrated; Dir FRANCO PIERINI; circ. 1,053,240.

Francofonia: Leo S. Olschki, Viuzzo del Pozzetto, 50126 Florence; tel. (055) 6530684; fax (055) 6530214; f. 1981; twice a year; French language; Editor ADRIANO MARCHETTI.

Gazzetta del Lunedì: Via Archimede 169, 16142 Genoa; tel. (010) 53691; f. 1945; weekly; political; Dir MIMMO ANGELI; circ. 83,315.

Gente: Viale Sarca 235, 20126 Milan; tel. (02) 27751; f. 1957; weekly; illustrated political, cultural and current events; Editor Dott. RENDINI; circ. 789,906.

Giornale della Libreria: Viale Vittorio Veneto 24, 20124 Milan; tel. (02) 29006965; fax (02) 654624; e-mail bibliografica@bibliografica.it; f. 1888; monthly; organ of the Associazione Italiana Editori; bibliographical; Editor FEDERICO MOTTA; circ. 5,000.

Lettere Italiane: Leo S. Olschki, POB 66, 50100 Florence; tel. (055) 6530684; fax (055) 6530214; f. 1949; quarterly; literary; Dirs VITTORE BRANCA, CARLO OSSOLA.

Mondo Economico: Via Paolo Lomazzo 51, 20154 Milan; tel. (02) 331211; fax (02) 316905; f. 1948; weekly; economics; business, finance; Editor ENRICO SASSOON; circ. 85,752.

Il Mulino: Strada Maggiore 37, 40125 Bologna; tel. (051) 222419; fax (051) 6486014; e-mail ilmulino@mulino.it; internet www.mulino.it; f. 1951; every 2 months; culture and politics; Editor ALESSANDRO CAVALLI.

Oggi: Via A. Rizzoli 2, 20132 Milan; tel. (02) 25841; fax (02) 27201485; f. 1945; weekly; topical, literary; illustrated; Dir PAOLO OCCHIPINTI; circ. 727,965.

Panorama: Arnoldo Mondadori Editore SpA, Via Marconi 27, 20090 Segrate, Milan; tel. (02) 75421; fax (02) 75422769; internet www.mondadori.com/panorama; f. 1962; weekly; current affairs; Dir CARLO ROSSELLA; circ. 540,000.

Il Pensiero Politico: Leo S. Olschki, Viuzzo del Pozzetto, 50126 Florence, tel. (055) 6530684; fax (055) 6530214; f. 1968; every 4 months; political and social history; Editor SALVO MASTELLONE.

Rassegna Storica Toscana: Leo S. Olschki, Viuzzo del Pozzetto, 50126 Florence; tel. (055) 6530684; fax (055) 6530214; f. 1955; twice a year; Tuscan history; Editors LUIGI LOTTI, SANDRO ROGARI.

Rivista di Storia della Filosofia: Via de Togni 7, 20123 Milan; tel. (02) 8052538; fax (02) 8053948; f. 1946; quarterly; philosophy.

Scuola e Didattica: Via L. Cadorna 11, 25186 Brescia; tel. (030) 29931; e-mail lascuola@tin.it; 19 a year; education; Editor GIUSEPPE VICO.

Selezione dal Reader's Digest: Via Alserio 10, 20173 Milan; tel. (02) 69871; fax (02) 66800070; e-mail readerd@hbox.vol.it; internet www.readersdigest.com; monthly; Editor-in-Chief CLAUDIO PINA (acting); circ. 521,432.

Visto: Via Rizzoli 4, 20132 Milan; tel. (02) 2588; fax (02) 25843683; f. 1989; illustrated weekly review; Editor-in-Chief MARCELLO MINERBI; circ. 342,850.

Zett-Volksbole: Weinbergweg 7, 39100 Bozen; tel. (0471) 200400; fax (0471) 200462; e-mail zett@athesia.it; f. 1989; German language; circ. 34,000.

Religion

Città di Vita: Piazza Santa Croce 16, 50122 Florence; tel. and fax (055) 242783; e-mail cittadivita@dada.it; internet www.casa.dada.it/cittadivita; f. 1946; every 2 months; cultural review of religious research in theology, art and science; Dir P. M. GIUSEPPE ROSITO; circ. 2,000.

La Civiltà Cattolica: Via di Porta Pinciana 1, 00187 Rome; tel. (06) 6979201; fax (06) 69792022; f. 1850; fortnightly; Catholic; Editor GIAN PAOLO SALVINI.

Humanitas: Via G. Rosa 71, 25121 Brescia; tel. (030) 46451; fax (030) 2400605; f. 1946; every 2 months; religion, philosophy, science, politics, history, sociology, literature, etc.; Dir STEFANO MINELLI.

Protestantesimo: Via Pietro Cossa 42, 00193 Rome; tel. (06) 3210789; fax (06) 3201040; e-mail fvt.protest@chiesavaldese.org; internet www.chiesavaldese.org/facolta/protestantesimo; f. 1946;

quarterly; theology and current problems, book reviews; Prof. SERGIO ROSTAGNO.

La Rivista del Clero Italiano: Largo Gemelli 1, 20123 Milan; tel. (02) 72342335; fax (02) 72342260; f. 1920; monthly; Dir BRUNO MAGGIONI.

Rivista di Storia della Chiesa in Italia: c/o Herder Editrice e Libreria, Piazza Montecitorio 117, 00187 Rome; f. 1947; twice a year; Editor PIETRO ZERBI.

Rivista di Storia e Letteratura Religiosa: Leo S. Olschki, Viuzzo del Pozzetto, 50126 Florence; tel. (055) 6530684; fax (055) 6530214; f. 1965; every 4 months; religious history and literature; Dir FRANCO BOLGIANI.

Science and Technology

L'Automobile: Viale Regina Margherita 290, 00198 Rome; tel. (06) 441121; fax (06) 44231160; e-mail lea.srl@iol.it; f. 1945; monthly; motor mechanics, tourism; Dir CARLO LUNA; circ. 1,083,210.

Gazzetta Medica Italiana-Archivio per le Scienze Mediche: Corso Bramante 83–85, 10126 Turin; tel. (011) 678282; fax (011) 674502; e-mail minmed@tin.it; internet www.medialog.it/minmed; six a year; medical science; Dir ALBERTO OLIARO; circ. 2,900.

Il Medico d'Italia: Rome; tel. (06) 36000710; fax (06) 6876739; weekly; medical science; Editor-in-Chief Dott. ANDREA SERMONTI.

Minerva Medica: Corso Bramante 83–85, 10126 Turin; tel. (011) 678282; fax (011) 674502; e-mail minmed@tin.it; internet www.minervamedica.it; 10 a year, medical science; Dir ALBERTO OLIARO; circ. 4,900.

Monti e Boschi: Via Emilia Levante 31/2, 40139 Bologna; tel. (051) 492211; internet www.agriline.it/edagri; f. 1949; 2 a month; ecology and forestry; Publr Edagricole; Editor UMBERTO BAGNARESI; circ. 16,700.

Motor: Piazza Antonio Mancini 4G, 00196 Rome; tel. (06) 3233195; fax (06) 3233309; f. 1942; monthly; motor mechanics; Dir S. FAVIA DEL CORE; circ. 12,500.

Nuncius: Leo S. Olschki, Viuzzo del Pozzetto, 50126 Florence; tel. (055) 6530684; fax (055) 6530214; f. 1976; twice a year; history of science; Dir P. GALLUZZI.

Physis: Leo S. Olschki, Viuzzo del Pozzetto, 50126 Florence; tel. (055) 6530684; fax (055) 6530214; f. 1959; twice a year; history of science; Editors V. CAPPELLETTI, G. CIMINO.

Rivista Geografica Italiana: Via Curtatone 1, 50123 Florence; tel. (055) 2710445; fax (055) 2710424; f. 1894; quarterly geographical review; Editor PAOLO DOCCIOLI.

Women's Publications

Amica: Via Rizzoli 2, 20132 Milan; tel. (02) 2588; f. 1962; weekly; Editor G. MAZZETTI; circ. 196,244.

Anna: Via Civitavecchia 102, Milan; tel. (02) 25843213; f. 1932; weekly; Editor M. VENTURI; circ. 549,227.

Confidenze: Arnoldo Mondadori Editore SpA, Via Mondadori, 20090 Segrate, Milan; tel. (02) 75421; fax (02) 75422806; e-mail cassinoni@mondadori.it; f. 1946; weekly; Dir LAURA PAVESE; circ. 303,178.

Gioia: Viale Sarca 235, 20126 Milan; tel. (02) 66191; fax (02) 66192717; f. 1938; weekly; Dir VERA MONTANARI; circ. 432,326.

Grazia: Arnoldo Mondadori Editore SpA, Via Marconi 27, 20090 Segrate, Milan; tel. (02) 75422390; fax (02) 75422515; e-mail grazia@mondadori; f. 1938; weekly; Dir CARLA VANNI; circ. 377,804.

Intimità della Famiglia: Via Borgogna 5, 20122 Milan; tel. (02) 781051; weekly; published by Cino del Duca; Dir G. GALLUZZO; circ. 424,946.

Vogue Italia: Piazza Castello 27, 20121 Milan; tel. (02) 85611; fax (02) 870686; monthly; Editor FRANCA SOZZANI; circ. 73,773.

Miscellaneous

Annali della Scuola Normale Superiore di Pisa: Scuola Normale Superiore, Pisa; tel. (050) 509111; fax (050) 563513; f. 1871; quarterly; mathematics, philosophy, philology, history, literature; Editor (Mathematics) Prof. EDOARDO VESENTINI; Editor (literature and philosophy) Prof. GIUSEPPE NENCI; circ. 1,300.

Cooperazione Educativa: La Nuova Italia, Via dei Piceni 16, 00185 Rome; tel. (06) 4457228; fax (06) 4460386; f. 1952; monthly; education; Dir MIRELLA GRIEG.

Lares: Leo S. Olschki, Viuzzo del Pozzetto, 50126 Florence; tel. (055) 6530684; fax (055) 6530214; f. 1912; quarterly; folklore; Editor GIOVANNI BATTISTA BRONZINI.

Il Maestro: Clivo Monte del Gallo 48, 00165 Rome; tel. (06) 634651; fax (06) 39375903; f. 1945; monthly; Catholic teachers' magazine; Dir MARIANGELA PRIORESCHI.

Quattroruote: Via A. Grandi 5/7, 20089 Rozzano, Milan; tel. (02) 824721; fax (02) 57500416; f. 1956; motoring; monthly; Editor MAURO COPPINI; circ. 662,000.

NEWS AGENCIES

AdnKronos: Via Ripetta 73, 00186 Rome; tel. (06) 324961; fax (06) 32002204; internet www.adnkronos.com; Dir. GIUSEPPE MARRA.

Agenzia Giornalistica Italia (AGI): Via Cristoforo Colombo 98, 00147 Rome; tel. (06) 519961; fax (06) 51996201; internet www.agenziaitalia.it; Gen. Man. EUGENIO PALMIERI.

Agenzia Nazionale Stampa Associata (ANSA): Via della Dataria 94, 00187 Rome; tel. (06) 67741; fax (06) 69792911; e-mail webmaster@ansa.it; internet www.ansa.it; f. 1945; 22 regional offices in Italy and 90 brs all over the world; service in Italian, Spanish, French, English; Pres. UMBERTO CUTTICA; Man. Dir and Gen. Man. PIERLUIGI MAGNASCHI; Chief Editor BRUNO CASELLI.

Asca: Via Due Macelli 23, 00187 Rome; tel. (06) 69792911; fax (06) 6783535; internet www.asca.it; Dir. CLAUDIO SONZOGNO.

Documentazioni Informazioni Resoconti (Dire): Via della Mercede 33, 00187 Rome; tel. (06) 6920921; fax (06) 699 41767; internet www.dire.it; Dir. ADRIANO PANICCIA.

Inter Press Service International Association (IPS): Via Panisperna 207, 00184 Rome; tel. (06) 4871363; fax (06) 4817877; e-mail romaser@ips.org; internet www.ips.org; f. 1964; international daily news agency; Dir-Gen. PATRICIA A. MADE.

Foreign Bureaux

Agencia EFE (Spain): Via dei Canestrari 5, 00186 Rome; tel. (06) 6834087; fax (06) 6874918; Bureau Chief JAIME CASTILLO.

Agence France-Presse (AFP): Piazza Santi-Apostoli 66, 00187 Rome; tel. (06) 6793588; fax (06) 6793623; e-mail afp-rome@afp.com; internet www.afp.com; Bureau Chief PATRICK CRAMPONT.

Associated Press (AP) (USA): Piazza Grazioli 5, 00186 Rome; tel. (06) 6798382; fax (06) 6784591; internet www.ap.org/italia; Bureau Chief DENNIS F. REDMONT.

Česká tisková kancelář (ČTK) (Czech Republic): Via di Vigna Stelluti 150/13, 00191 Rome; tel. (06) 3270777.

Deutsche Presse-Agentur (dpa) (Germany): Via della Mercede 55, Int. 15, 00187 Rome; tel. (06) 6789810; fax (06) 6841598; Bureau Chief LÁSZLÓ TRANKOVITS.

Informatsionnoye Telegrafnoye Agentstvo Rossii—Telegrafnoye Agentstvo Suverennykh Stran (ITAR—TASS) (Russia): Viale dell'Umanesimo 172, 00144 Rome; tel. (06) 5912882; fax (06) 5925711; e-mail latyzeva@hotmail.com; Correspondent SERGEI BATYREV.

Kyodo Tsushin (Japan): Rome; tel. (06) 8440709; internet home.kyodo.co.jp; Bureau Chief KATSUO UEDA.

Magyar Távirati Iroda (MTI) (Hungary): Villino 22, Capena, Castello di Sorano, 00060 Rome; tel. (06) 8441309; Correspondent ISTVÁN GÓZON.

Reuters (United Kingdom): Corso Italia 39, 00198 Rome; tel. (06) 8540111; fax (06) 8540568; Bureau Chief STEVE PAGANI.

United Press International (UPI) (USA): Via della Mercede 55, 00187 Rome; tel. (06) 6795747; fax (06) 6781540; Correspondent CHARLES RIDLEY.

Xinhua (New China) News Agency (People's Republic of China): Via Bruxelles 59, 00198 Rome; tel. (06) 865028; fax (06) 8450575; Bureau Chief HUANG CHANGRUI.

CNA (Taiwan) and Jiji Tsushin (Japan) are also represented.

PRESS ASSOCIATIONS

Associazione della Stampa Estera in Italia: Via della Mercede 55, 00186 Rome; tel. (06) 675911; fax (06) 67591262; foreign correspondents' asscn; Pres. ANTONIO PELAYO; Sec. SANTIAGO FERNÁNDEZ ARDANAZ.

Federazione Italiana Editori Giornali (FIEG): Via Piemonte 64, 00187 Rome; tel. (06) 4881683; fax (06) 4871109; e-mail fiegroma@iol.it; internet www.fieg.it; f. 1950; association of newspaper publishers; Pres. MARIO CIANCIO SANFILIPPO; Dir-Gen. SEBASTIANO SORTINO; 268 mems.

Federazione Nazionale della Stampa Italiana: Corso Vittorio Emanuele II 349, 00186 Rome; tel. (06) 6833879; fax (06) 6871444; internet www.fnsi.it; f. 1877; 17 affiliated unions; Pres. LORENZO DEL BOCA; Nat. Sec. PAOLO SERVENTI LONGHI; 16,000 mems.

Unione Stampa Periodica Italiana (USPI): Viale Bardanzellu 95, 00155 Rome; tel. (06) 4065941; fax (06) 4066859; internet www.uspi.it; Pres. MARIO NEGRI; Gen. Sec. FRANCESCO SAVERIO VETERE; 4,500 mems.

Publishers

There are more than 300 major publishing houses and many smaller ones.

Bologna

Gruppo Calderini Edagricole: Via Emilia Levante 31/2, 40139 Bologna; tel. (051) 62267; fax (051) 490200; e-mail comunica@ calderini.it; internet www.edagricole.it; group includes Calderini (f. 1960; art, sport, electronics, mechanics, university and school textbooks, travel guides, nursing, architecture) and Edagricole; (f. 1935; agriculture, veterinary science, gardening, biology, textbooks); Pres. Prof. GIORGIO AMADEI; Man. Dir GIOVANNA VILLANI PERDISA.

Nuova Casa Editrice Licinio Cappelli GEM SrL: Via Farini 14, 40124 Bologna; tel. (051) 239060; fax (051) 239286; f. 1848; medical science, history, politics, literature, textbooks; Chair. and Man. Dir MARIO MUSSO.

Editrice CLUEB: Via Marsala 31, 40126 Bologna; tel. (051) 220736; fax (051) 237758; e-mail clueb@clueb.com; internet www.clueb.com; f. 1959; education, arts, business, history, literature; Man. Dir LUIGI GUARDIGLI.

Società Editrice Il Mulino: Strada Maggiore 37, 40125 Bologna; tel. (051) 256011; fax (051) 256034; e-mail info@mulino.it; f. 1954; politics, history, philosophy, social sciences, linguistics, literary criticism, law, music, theatre, psychology, economics, journals; Gen. Man. GIOVANNI EVANGELISTI.

Zanichelli Editore SpA: Via Irnerio 34, 40126 Bologna; tel. (051) 293111; fax (051) 249782; e-mail zanichelli@zanichelli.it; internet www.zanichelli.it; f. 1859; educational, history, literature, philosophy, mathematics, science, technical books, law, psychology, architecture, reference books, dictionaries, atlases, earth sciences, linguistics, medicine, economics, etc.; Chair. and Gen. Man. FEDERICO ENRIQUES; Vice-Chair. and Man. Dir LORENZO ENRIQUES.

Brescia

Editrice La Scuola SpA: Via Cadorna 11, Brescia; tel. (030) 29931; fax (030) 2993299; e-mail lascuola@tin.it; internet www.lascuola.it; f. 1904; educational magazines, educational textbooks, audiovisual aids and toys; Chair. Dott. Ing. LUCIANO SILVERI; Man. Dir Rag. GIUSEPPE COVONE.

Florence

Casa Editrice Bonechi: Via dei Cairoli 18B, 50131 Florence; tel. (055) 576841; fax (055) 5000766; e-mail bonechi@bonechi.it; internet www.bonechi.it; f. 1973; art, travel, cooking, CD-Rom; Pres. GIAMPAOLO BONECHI.

Cremonese: Borgo Santa Croce 17, 50122 Florence; tel. (055) 2476371; fax (055) 2476372; e-mail cremonese@ed-cremonese.it; internet www.ed-cremonese.it; f. 1929; history, reference, engineering, science, textbooks, architecture, mathematics, aviation; Chair. ALBERTO STIANTI.

Giunti Editore: Via Bolognese 165, 50139 Florence; tel. (055) 66791; fax (055) 6679298; f. 1839; art, psychology, literature, science, law; Dir Dott. SERGIO GIUNTI.

Casa Editrice Felice Le Monnier: Via A. Meucci 2, 50015 Grassina, Florence; tel. (055) 64910; fax (055) 643983; e-mail monnier@ tin.it; f. 1836; academic and cultural books, textbooks, dictionaries; Man. Dirs Dott. VANNI PAOLETTI, Dott. GUGLIELMO PAOLETTI, Dott. SIMONE PAOLETTI.

La Nuova Italia Editrice SpA: Via Ernesto Codignola 1, 50018 Florence; tel. (055) 75901; fax (055) 7590208; f. 1926; biography, psychology, philosophy, philology, education, history, politics, belles-lettres, art, music and science; Man. Dirs FEDERICO CODIGNOLA, CARMELO SAMBUGAR.

Casa Editrice Leo S. Olschki: CP 66, 50100 Florence; tel. (055) 6530684; fax (055) 6530214; e-mail celso@olschki.it; internet www.olschki.it; f. 1886; reference, periodicals, textbooks, humanities; Man. ALESSANDRO OLSCHKI.

Vallecchi Editore SpA: Via Il Prato 21, 50123 Florence; tel. (055) 290765; fax (055) 293477; f. 1913; art, fiction, literature, essays, media; Pres. PIERO SUSMEL.

Genoa

Casa Editrice Marietti SpA: Via Piandilucco 7, 16155 Genoa; tel. (010) 6984226; fax (010) 667092; e-mail marinetti1820@split.it; f. 1820; liturgy, theology, fiction, history, politics, literature, philosophy, art, children's books; Editor CARLA VILLATA.

Milan

Adelphi Edizioni SpA: Via S. Giovanni sul Muro 14, 20121 Milan; tel. (02) 725731; fax (02) 89010337; f. 1962; classics, philosophy, biography, music, art, psychology, religion and fiction; Pres. ROBERTO CALASSO.

Editrice Ancora: Via G. B. Niccolini 8, 20154 Milan; tel. (02) 3456081; fax (02) 345608; e-mail editrice@ancora-libri.it; internet www.ancora-libri.it; f. 1934; religious, educational; Dir GILBERTO ZINI.

Franco Angeli Srl: Viale Monza 106, CP 17130, 20127 Milan; tel. (02) 2827651; fax (02) 2891515; f. 1956; general; Man. Dir FRANCO ANGELI.

Bramante Editrice: Viale Bianca Maria 19, 20122 Milan; tel. (02) 760759; fax (02) 780904; f. 1958; art, history, encyclopaedias, natural sciences, interior decoration, arms and armour, music; Chair. Dott. GUIDO CERIOTTI.

Feltrinelli SpA: Via Andegari 6, 20121 Milan; tel. (02) 808346; f. 1954; fiction, juvenile, science, technology, textbooks, poetry, art, music, history, literature, political science, philosophy, reprint editions of periodicals; Chair. INGE FELTRINELLI; Man. Dir GIUSEPPE ANTONINI.

Garzanti Editore: Via Gasparotto 1, 20124 Milan; tel. (02) 674161; fax (02) 67416292; internet www.garzanti.it; f. 1938; literature, poetry, science, art, history, politics, encyclopaedias, dictionaries, scholastic and children's books; Chair. GIOVANNI MERLINI; Gen. Man. MARCO BENDINELLI.

Casa Editrice Libraria Ulrico Hoepli: Via Hoepli 5, 20121 Milan; tel. (02) 864871; fax (02) 8052886; f. 1870; grammars, art, technical, scientific and school books, encyclopaedias; Chair. ULRICO HOEPLI; Man. Dir GIANNI HOEPLI.

Longanesi e C. SpA: Corso Italia 13, 20122 Milan; tel. (02) 8692142; fax (02) 72000306; f. 1946; art, history, philosophy, fiction; Pres. S. PASSIGLI; Man. Dir M. SPAGNOL.

Massimo: Viale Bacchiglione 20A, 20139 Milan; tel. (02) 55210800; fax (02) 55211315; f. 1950; fiction, biography, history, social science, philosophy, pedagogy, theology, school texts; Chair. CESARE CRESPI.

Arnoldo Mondadori Editore SpA: Via Mondadori 1, 20090 Segrate, Milan; tel. (02) 75421; fax (02) 75422302; internet www .mondadori.com; f. 1907; books, magazines and online publishing; Chair. LEONARDO MONDADORI; Man. Dir MAURIZIO COSTA.

Edizioni Bruno Mondadori: Via Archimede 23, 20129 Milan; tel. (02) 748231; fax (02) 74823362; f. 1946; textbooks and educational books; Chair. ROBERTA MONDADORI; Man. Dir ROBERTO GULLI; Dir AGOSTINO CATTANEO.

Gruppo Ugo Mursia Editore SpA: Via Tadino 29, 20124, Milan; tel. (02) 205720601; fax (02) 205720215; e-mail info@mursia.com; internet www.mursia.com; f. 1955; general fiction and non-fiction, textbooks, reference, art, history, nautical books, philosophy, biography, sports, children's books; Gen. Man. FIORENZA MURSIA.

Gruppo Editoriale RCS SpA: Via Mecenate 91, 20138 Milan; tel. (02) 50951; fax (02) 5065361; internet www.rcs.it/libri; f. 1947; juveniles, education, textbooks, reference, literature, art books; Chair. CLAUDIO CALABI; CEO GIANNI VALLARDI.

> **Bompiani:** e-mail sgarbi@rcs.it; f. 1929; modern literature, biographies, theatre, science, art, history, classics, dictionaries, pocket books; Dir MARIO ANDREOSE.

> **Etas Srl:** technical periodicals and books; Man. Dir Dott. GIORGIO ORSI.

> **Rizzoli:** f. 1929; newspapers, magazines and books; Dir-Gen. GIOVANNI UNGARELLI; Man. Dir GIORGIO FATTORI.

> **Sonzogno:** f. 1861; fiction, non-fiction, illustrated, manuals; Dir MARIO ANDREOSE.

Riccardo Ricciardi Editore SpA: c/o Arnoldo Mondadori Editore, Via Mondadori 1, 20090 Segrate, Milan; tel. (02) 75421; f. 1907; classics, philology, history, literature; Gen. Man. GIAN ARTURO FERRARI.

Casa Ricordi SpA: Via Berchet 2, 20121 Milan; tel. (02) 88812206; fax (02) 88812212; f. 1808; academic, art, music; Chair. GIANNI BABINI; Man. Dir MIMMA GUASTONI.

Rusconi Libri Srl: Viale Sarca 235, 20126 Milan; tel. (02) 66191; fax (02) 66192758; f. 1969; non-fiction including history, biography, music, philosophy, archaeology, religion, needlecraft, embroidery and art; Pres. ALBERTO RUSCONI; Editorial Dir ALBERTO CONFORTI.

Il Saggiatore: Via Melzo 9, 20129 Milan; tel. (02) 29403460; fax (02) 29513061; e-mail info@saggiatore.it; art, fiction, social sciences; Pres. LUCA FORMENTON.

Adriano Salani Editore Srl: Corso Italia 13, 20122 Milan; tel. (02) 8693238; fax (02) 72018806; e-mail longaec@micronet.it; internet www.salani.it; f. 1988; fiction, children's books; Editor MARIAGRAZIA MAZZITELLI.

Edizioni San Paolo: Piazza Soncino 5, 20092 Cinisello Balsamo— Milan; tel. (02) 660751; fax (02) 66075211; e-mail sanpaoloedizioni @stpauls.it; internet www.sanpaolo.org.it; f. 1914; religious; Gen. Man. VINCENZO SANTARCANGELO.

SEDES SpA-Ghisetti e Corvi Editori: Corso Concordia 7, 20129 Milan; tel. (02) 76006232; fax (02) 76009468; e-mail sedes.spa@ gpa.it; internet www.sedes.gpa.it; f. 1937; educational textbooks.

Selezione dal Reader's Digest SpA: Via Alserio 10, 20173 Milan; tel. (02) 69871; fax (02) 6987401; f. 1948; educational, reference, general interest; Man. Dir CHARLES J. LOBKOWICZ.

Sugarco Edizioni Srl: Via E. Fermi 9, 21040 Carnago; tel. (0331) 985511; fax (0331) 985385; f. 1957; fiction, biography, history, philosophy, guidebooks, Italian classics; Chair. Prof. SERGIO CIGADA; Gen. Man. OLIVIERO CIGADA.

Casa Editrice Luigi Trevisini: Via Tito Livio 12, 20137 Milan; tel. (02) 5450704; fax (02) 55195782; f. 1849; school textbooks; Dirs LUIGI TREVISINI, GIUSEPPINA TREVISINI.

Vita e Pensiero: Largo A. Gemelli 1, 20123 Milan; tel. (02) 72342335; fax (02) 72342260; f. 1918; publisher to the Catholic University of the Sacred Heart; cultural, scientific books and magazines.

Naples

Idelson Gnocchi Editore Srl: Via Alcide De Gasperi 55, 80133 Naples; tel. (081) 5524733; fax (081) 5518295; e-mail idelgno@tin.it; internet www.idelson-gnocchi.com; f. 1908; medicine, psychology, biology; CEO GUIDO GNOCCHI.

Liguori Editore Srl: Via Posillipo 394, 80123 Naples; tel. (081) 7206111; fax (081) 7206244; e-mail liguori@liguori.it; f. 1949; linguistics, mathematics, engineering, economics, law, history, philosophy, sociology; Man. Dir Dott. GUIDO LIGUORI.

Edizioni Scientifiche Italiane SpA: Via Chiatamone 7, 80121 Naples; tel. (081) 7645443; fax (081) 7646477; f. 1945; literature, arts, history, Science; Pres. PIETRO PERLINGIERI.

Novara

Instituto Geografico De Agostini SpA: Via Giovanni da Verrazano 15, 28100 Novara; tel. (0321) 4241; fax (0321) 471286; e-mail ufficio.stampa@deagostini.it; internet www.deagostini.it; geography, maps, encyclopaedias, dictionaries, art, literature, textbooks, science; Chair. ANTONIO BELLONI; CEO PIETRO BOROLI.

Padua

CEDAM—Casa Editrice Dr A. Milani: Via Jappelli 5/6, 35121 Padua; tel. (049) 3239111; fax (049) 8239111; e-mail info@cedam.com; internet www.cedam.com; f. 1902; law, economics, political and social sciences, engineering, science, medicine, literature, philosophy, textbooks; Dirs ANTONIO MILANI, CARLO PORTA.

Libreria Editrice Gregoriana: Via Roma 82, 35122 Padua; tel. (049) 8758455; f. 1922; *Lexicon Totius Latinitatis*, religion, philosophy, psychology, social studies; Dir DON GIANCARLO MINOZZI.

Piccin Nuova Libraria SpA: Via Altinate 107, 35121 Padua; tel. (049) 655566; fax (049) 8750693; e-mail infopiccinonline.com; internet ww.piccinonline.com; f. 1980; scientific and medical textbooks and journals; Man. Dir Dott. MASSIMO PICCIN.

Rome

Armando Armando Srl: Viale Trastevere 236, 00153 Rome; tel. (06) 5806420; fax (06) 5818564; e-mail armando@palomar.it; internet www.armando.it; f. 1950; philosophy, psychology, social sciences, languages, ecology, education; Man. Dir ENRICO JACOMETTI.

Edizioni d'Arte di Carlo E. Bestetti & C. Sas: Via di San Giacomo 18, 00187 Rome; tel. (06) 6790174; f. 1947; art, architecture, industry; Man. Dir CARLO BESTETTI.

AVE (Anonima Veritas Editrice): Via Aurelia 481, 00165 Rome; tel. (06) 6633041; fax (06) 6620207; f. 1935; theology, sociology, pedagogy, psychology, essays, learned journals, religious textbooks; Man. Dir ANTONIO SANTANGELO.

Vito Bianco Editore: Via Messina 31, 00198 Rome; tel. (06) 8443151; fax (06) 8417595; various, especially marine publications; Chair. Dott. VITO BIANCO.

Edizioni Borla Srl: Via delle Fornaci 50, 00165 Rome; tel. (06) 39376728; fax (06) 39376620; e-mail borla@edizioni-borla.it; internet www.edizioni-borla.it; f. 1863; religion, philosophy, psychoanalysis, ethnology, literature; Man. Dir VINCENZO D'AGOSTINO.

Bulzoni Editore—Le edizioni universitarie d'Italia: Via dei Liburni 14, 00185 Rome; tel. (06) 4455207; fax (06) 4450355; f. 1969; science, arts, fiction, textbooks; Man. Dir MARIO BULZONI.

Editrice Ciranna: Via Capograssa 115, 04010 Borgo S. Michele; tel. and fax (0773) 250746; f. 1940; school textbooks; Man. Dir LIDIA FABIANO.

Edizioni Europa: Via G.B. Martini 6, 00198 Rome; tel. (06) 8449124; f. 1944; essays, literature, art, history, politics, music, economics; Chair. Prof. PIER FAUSTO PALUMBO.

Hermes Edizioni Srl: Via Flaminia 109, 00196 Rome; tel. (06) 3201656; fax (06) 3236277; e-mail info@ediz-mediterranee.com; internet www.ediz-mediterranee.com; f. 1979; alternative medicine, astrology, nature, dietetics, sports; Gen. Man. GIOVANNI CANONICO.

Jandi Sapi Editori Srl: Via Crescenzio 62, 00193 Rome; tel. (06) 68805515; fax (06) 6832612; e-mail info@jandisapi.com; internet www.jandisapi.com; f. 1941; industrial and legal publications, art books.

Giuseppe Laterza e Figli SpA: Via di Villa Sacchetti 17, 00197 Rome; tel. (06) 3218393; fax (06) 3223853; f. 1885; belles-lettres, biography, reference, religion, art, classics, history, economics, philosophy, social science; Man. Dir VITO LATERZA; Editorial Dirs ALESSANDRO LATERZA, GIUSEPPE LATERZA.

Edizioni Lavoro: Via G.M. Lancisi 25, 00161 Rome; tel. (06) 44251174; fax (06) 44251177; e-mail edizionilavoro@tiscalinet.it; f. 1982; history, politics, political philosophy, sociology, religion, African literature; Chair. PIETRO GELARDI; Man. Dir MARIO BERTIN.

Guida Monaci SpA: Via Salaria 1319, 00138 Rome; tel. (06) 8887777; fax (06) 8889996; e-mail guida.monaci@italybygm.it; internet www.italybygm.it; f. 1870; commercial and industrial, financial, administrative and medical directories; Dir Ing. GIANCARLO ZAPPONINI.

Fratelli Palombi Srl: Via dei Gracchi 181-185, 00192 Rome; tel. (06) 3214150; fax (06) 3214752; e-mail flli.palombi@mail.sth.it; f. 1914; history, art, etc. of Rome; Man. Dir Dott. MARIO PALOMBI.

Angelo Signorelli: Via Falconieri 84, 00152 Rome; tel. (06) 5314942; fax (06) 531492; f. 1912; science, general literature, textbooks; Man. Dirs GIORGIO SIGNORELLI, GILBERTA ALPA.

Società Editrice Dante Alighieri Srl: Via Timavo 3, 00195 Rome; tel. (06) 3725870; fax (06) 37514807; f. 1928; school textbooks, science and general culture; Pres. and Man. Dir SILVANO SPINELLI.

Edizioni Studium: Via Cassiodoro 14, 00193 Rome; tel. (06) 6865846; fax (06) 6875456; e-mail edizionistudium@libero.it; f. 1927; philosophy, literature, sociology, pedagogy, religion, economics, law, science, history, psychology; periodical *Studium*.

Stresa

Edizioni Rosminiane Sodalitas Sas: Centro Internazionale di Studi Rosminiani, Corso Umberto I 15, 28838 Stresa; tel. (0323) 30091; fax (0323) 31623; e-mail edizioni@rosmini.it; f. 1925; philosophy, theology, *Rivista Rosminiana* (quarterly); Dir Prof. PIER PAOLO OTTONELLO.

Turin

Bollati Boringhieri Editore: Corso Vittorio Emanuele II 86, 10121 Turin; tel. (011) 5591711; fax (011) 543024; e-mail info@bollatiboringhieri.it; internet www.bollatiboringhieri.it; f. 1957; history, economics, natural sciences, psychology, social and human sciences, fiction and literary criticism; Chair. ROMILDA BOLLATI.

Giulio Einaudi Editore SpA: Via Umberto Biancamano 2, CP 245, 10121 Turin; tel. (011) 56561; fax (011) 542903; internet www.einaudi.it; f. 1933; fiction, classics, general; Chair. ROBERTO CERATI; Gen. Man. VITTORIO BO.

Giorgio Giappichelli Editore Srl: Via Po 21, 10124 Turin; tel. (011) 8153511; fax (011) 8125100; e-mail giappi@venturanet.it; f. 1921; university publications on law, economics, politics and sociology.

Lattes S. e C. Editori SpA: Via Confienza 6, 10121 Turin; f. 1893; tel. (011) 5625335; fax (011) 5625070; technical, textbooks; Pres. MARIO LATTES.

Levrotto e Bella, Libreria Editrice Universitaria: Corso Vittorio Emanuele II 26, 10123 Turin; tel. (011) 8121205; fax (011) 8124025; f. 1911; university textbooks; Man. Dir Dott. ELISABETTA GUALINI.

Loescher: Via Vittorio Amedeo II 18, 10121 Turin; tel. (011) 5654111; fax (011) 5625822; e-mail loescher@inrete.it; f. 1867; school textbooks, general literature, academic books; Chair. LORENZO ENRIQUES.

Edizioni Minerva Medica: Corso Bramante 83–85, 10126 Turin; tel. (011) 678282; fax (011) 674502; e-mail minmed@tin.it; internet www.minervamedica.it; medical books and journals; Pres. ALBERTO OLIARO.

Petrini Editore: Strada del Portone 179, 10095 Grugliasco, Turin; tel. (011) 3158768; fax (011) 3158710; e-mail petrini@petrini.it; internet www.petrini.it; f. 1872; school textbooks.

Rosenberg & Sellier: Via Andrea Doria 14, 10123 Turin; tel. (011) 8127808; fax (011) 8127820; f. 1883; philology, social sciences, philosophy, linguistics, scientific journals; Chair. and Man. Dir UGO GIANNI ROSENBERG.

Società Editrice Internazionale SpA (SEI): Corso Regina Margherita 176, 10152 Turin; tel. (011) 52271; fax (011) 5211320; e-mail seito@inrete.it; f. 1908; textbooks, religion, history, education, multimedia; Head of Editorial Dept ROBERTO GIULIDORI.

Unione Tipografico-Editrice Torinese (UTET): Corso Raffaello 28, 10125 Turin; tel. (011) 2099111; fax (011) 2099394; e-mail utet@utet.it; internet www.utet.it; f. 1791; university and specialized editions on history, geography, art, literature, economics, law, sciences, encyclopaedias, dictionaries, etc.; Pres. Prof. CESARE MERLINI.

Venice

Alfieri Edizioni d'Arte: San Marco 1991, Cannaregio 6099, 30124 Venice; tel. (041) 5223323; f. 1939; modern art, Venetian art, architecture, periodicals; Chair. GIORGIO FANTONI; Gen. Man. MASSIMO VITTA ZELMAN.

Marsilio Editori: Marittima, Fabbricato 205, 30135 Venice; tel. (041) 2406511; fax (041) 5238352; e-mail info@marsilioeditori.it; internet www.marsilioeditori.it; f. 1961; fiction, non-fiction, history of art, catalogues, cartography; Man. Dirs Dott. EMANUELA BASSETTI, Prof. CESARE DE MICHELIS.

Verona

Giorgio Bertani Editore Srl: Via Interr. Acqua Morta 31, 37129 Verona; tel. (045) 8011345; fax (045) 8350402; f. 1973; politics, literature, anthropology, sociology, theatre, cinema, geography, humanities, history of Verona and Veneto, psychology, cultural journals; Man. Dir MARIO QUARANTA; Editorial Dir GIORGIO BERTANI.

Arnoldo Mondadori Editore: Via Arnoldo Mondadori 15, 37131 Verona; tel. (045) 934602; fax (045) 934566; e-mail forestan@ mondadori.it; f. 1912; children and young adults' books; Man. Dir MARGHERITA FORESTAN.

Vicenza

Neri Pozza Editore SpA: Contrà Oratorio dei Servi 19–21, 36100 Vicenza; tel. (0444) 320787; fax (0444) 324613; e-mail neri.pozza@ goldnet.it; internet www.neripozza.it; f. 1946; art, fiction, history, politics; Pres. MINO ALLIONE; Dir GIUSEPPE RUSSO.

Government Publishing House

Istituto Poligrafico e Zecca dello Stato: Piazza Verdi 10, 00198 Rome; tel. (06) 85081; fax (06) 85082517; e-mail infoipzs@ipzs.it; f. 1928; art, literary, scientific, technical books and reproductions; Chair. Dott. MICHELE TEDESCHI; Gen. Dir Dott. SALVATOR FICAIO.

PUBLISHERS' ASSOCIATION

Associazione Italiana Editori: Via delle Erbe 2, 20121 Milan; tel. (02) 86463091; fax (02) 89010863; Via Crescenzio 19, 00193 Rome; tel. (06) 8806298; fax (06) 6872426; e-mail aie@aie.it; internet www.aie.it; f.1869; Pres. FEDERICO MOTTA; Dir IVAN CECCHINI.

Broadcasting and Communications

L'Autorità per le Garanzie nelle Communicazioni (AGC): Centro Direzionale, Isola B5, Naples; tel. (081) 7507111; fax (081) 7507616; e-mail info@agcom.it; internet www.agcom.it; regulatory body for broadcasting and telecommunications; Pres. ENZO CHELI.

TELECOMMUNICATIONS

Omnitel Pronto Italia: Via dei Boccabelli 5, 00143 Rome; tel. (06) 5004387; e-mail ufficio.stampa@omnitel.it; internet www.omnitel.it; f. 1995; operates mobile network; Chair. ANTONIO TESONE; CEO ROBERTO COLANINNO.

Telecom Italia SpA: Via Flaminia 186, 00196 Rome; tel. (06) 36881; internet www.telecomitalia.it; Italy's leading telecommunications operator; merged with Società Finanziaria Telefonica SpA (STET) in 1997; 52% owned by Olivetti SpA; 3.46% state-owned; Chair. and CEO ROBERTO COLANINNO.

Telecom Italia Mobile SpA (TIM): Via Luigi Rizzo 22, 00136 Rome; tel. (06) 39001; internet www.tim.it; f. 1995 after split from Telecom Italia SpA; Italy's leading mobile telecommunications operator; 60% owned by Telecom Italia SpA; Pres. BERARDINO LIBONATI; Man. Dir UMBERTO DE JULIO.

Tiscali SpA: Piazza del Carmine 22, 09124 Cagliari; tel. (070) 605161.

WIND Telecomunicazioni SpA: Via Dalmazia 15, 00198 Rome; tel. (06) 83111; internet www.wind.it; f. 1997; owned by ENEL (51%), Deutsche Telekom (24.5%) and France Telecom (24.5%); mobile and fixed-line services.

BROADCASTING

Radio

In April 1975 legislation was adopted to ensure the political independence of Radiotelevisione Italiana (RAI). The state monopoly on broadcasting was abolished in 1976; more than 2,100 private local radio stations had begun broadcasting by 1995.

Radiotelevisione Italiana (RAI): Viale Mazzini 14, 00195 Rome; tel. (06) 3878; fax (06) 3725680; internet www.rai.it; f. 1924; a public share capital company; programmes comprise the national programme (general), Second Programme (recreational), Third Programme (educational); there are also regional programmes in Italian and in the languages of ethnic minorities; the foreign and overseas service (Radio Ronia) broadcasts in 27 languages; Pres. ROBERTO ZACCARIA; Dir Gen. PIER LUIGI CELLI.

Rundfunk Anstalt Südtirol (RAS): Europaallee 164A, 39100 Bozen; tel. (0471) 546666; fax (0471) 200378; e-mail info@ras.bz.it; internet www.raz.bz.it; f. 1975; relays television and radio broadcasts from Germany, Austria and Switzerland to the population of South Tyrol; Pres. HELMUTH HENDRICH; Man. Dir KLAUS GRUBER.

Television

Sixteen private stations have nationwide networks. In 1995 there were about 900 privately-operated television stations, mostly offering a local service.

Radiotelevisione Italiana (RAI): Viale Mazzini 14, 00195 Rome; tel. (06) 38781; fax (06) 3226070; internet www.rai.it; f. 1924; operates three channels, RAI Uno, RAI Due and RAI Tre; also broadcasts local programmes in Italian and in German for the Alto Adige; Pres. ROBERTO ZACCARIA; Dir.-Gen. PIER LUIGI CELLI.

Rundfunk Anstalt Südtirol (RAS): (see Radio).

Finance

(cap. = capital; p.u. = paid up; res = reserves; dep. = deposits; m. = million; brs = branches; amounts in lire or euros (€))

The number of banks in Italy fell during the 1990s, from 1,156 in 1990 to 921 in 1998, owing to an increasing number of mergers. In 1990 a programme of privatization of state-controlled banks was initiated and in November 1999 the last state-controlled bank was divested. There are more than 100 private banks, and a large number of co-operative and savings banks (*banche popolari, casse di risparmio, casse rurali*) of widely ranging size and importance. In addition, there are some 90 specialized credit institutions which provide medium-and long-term finance, together with other services outside the scope of the banks.

BANKING

Central Bank

Banca d'Italia: Via Nazionale 91, 00184 Rome; tel. (06) 47921; fax (06) 47922983; internet www.bancaditalia.it; f. 1893; cap. €0.2m., res €10,316m., dep. €44,043m. (Dec. 1999); since 1926 the Bank has had the sole right to issue notes in Italy; Gov. ANTONIO FAZIO; Dir-Gen. VINCENZO DESARIO; 85 brs.

Major Commercial Banks

Banca Agricola Mantovana SpA: Corso Vittorio Emanuele 30, 46100 Mantua; tel. (0376) 3311; fax (0376) 331261; e-mail intel.rcl@bam.it; internet www.bam.it; f. 1871; cap. 585,935m. lire, res 906,442m. lire, dep. 15,907,582m. lire (Dec. 1998); Chair. PIERMARIA PACCHIONI; Gen. Man. MARIO PETRONI; 194 brs.

Banca Antoniana-Popolare Veneta Scarl: Via Verdi 13–15, 35122 Padua; tel. (049) 839111; fax (049) 839695; e-mail esterbap@ tin.it; internet www.antonveneta.it; f. 1893; July 1996 merged with Banca Popolare di Verona Scarl; cap. and res 4,097,130m. lire, dep. 25,650,878m.lire (Dec. 1999); Pres. Dott. DINO MARCHIORELLO; Gen. Man. Dott. SILVANO PONTELLO; 591 brs.

Banca Carige SpA (Cassa di Risparmio di Genova e Imperia): Via Cassa di Risparmio 15, 16123 Genoa; tel. (010) 5792041; fax (010) 280013; e-mail carige@carige.it; internet www.carige.it; f. 1846; cap. 1,970,173m. lire res 552,125m. lire dep. 15,324,140m. lire (Dec. 1999); Chair. Prof. FAUSTO CUOCOLO; Gen. Man. Dott. GIOVANNI BERNESCHI; 245 brs.

Banca Cassa di Risparmio di Torino SpA: Via XX Settembre 31, 10121 Turin; tel. (011) 6621; fax (011) 638203; internet www .bancacrt.it; f. 1827; cap. 1,000,000m. lire, res 1,041,688m. lire, dep. 29,547,456m. lire (Dec. 1999); Chair. GIORGIO GIOVANDO; Gen. Man. EDOARDO MASSAGLIA; 437 brs.

Banca Commerciale Italiana SpA: Piazza della Scala 6, 20121 Milan; tel. (02) 88501; fax (02) 88503026; internet www.bci.it; f. 1894; cap. 1,794,759m. lire, res 6,424,937m. lire, dep. 154,723,475m. lire (Dec. 1998); Chair. LUIGI LUCCHINI; CEO LINO BENASSI; 1,019 brs.

Banca Intesa SpA: Via Monte di Pietà 8, 20121 Milan; tel. (02) 88441; fax (02) 72397326; internet www.bancaintesa.it; f. 1998 by integration of Banco Ambrosiano Veneto SpA and CARIPLO SpA; cap. 5,405,739m. lire, res 12,432,816m. lire, dep. 481,063,658m. lire (Dec. 1999); Chair. GIOVANNI BAZOLI; Man. Dir and CEO CARLO SALVATORI.

Banca Lombarda SpA: Via Cefalonia 62, 25175 Brescia; tel. (030) 24331; fax (030) 2433802; e-mail info@bancalombarda.com; internet www.bancalombarda.it; f. 1998 by merger of Banca San Paolo di Brescia SpA into CAB SpA; cap. 251,059m. lire, res 1,479,876m. lire, dep. 28,827,820m. lire (Dec. 1999); Chair. GINO TROMBI; Gen. Man. BRUNO DEGRANDI.

Banca delle Marche SpA: Via Alessandro Ghislieri 6, 60035 Jesi; tel. (0731) 5391; fax (0731) 539328; e-mail info@bancamarche.it; internet www.bancamarche.it; f. 1994; cap. 665,960m. lire, res. 388,497m. lire, dep. 11,286,163m. lire (Dec. 1999); Chair. BRUNO BRUSCIOTTI; Gen. Man. ALBERTO COSTANTINI; 216 brs.

Banca Monte dei Paschi di Siena SpA: Piazza Salimbeni 3, 53100 Siena; tel. (0577) 294111; fax (0577) 294313; internet www.mps.it; f. 1472; joint stock company; cap. 978,414m. lire, res 3,468,131m. lire dep. 46,708,237m. lire (Dec. 1999); Chair. PIER LUIGI FABRIZI; CEO and Gen. Man. DIVO GRONCHI; 829 brs.

Banca Nazionale del Lavoro SpA: Via Vittorio Veneto 119, 00187 Rome; tel. (06) 47021; fax (06) 47027298; e-mail press.bnl@bnl.it; internet www.bnl.it; f. 1913; cap. 2,121,024m. lire, res 3,759,853m.lire, dep. 125,898,755m. lire (Dec. 1999); Pres. Dr LUIGI ABETE; Man. D. CROFF; 681 brs incl. 8 overseas brs.

Banca Popolare Commercio e Industria Scarl: POB 10167, Via della Moscova 33, 20121 Milan; tel. (02) 62751; fax (02) 6275640; e-mail intbkg@bpci.it; internet www.bpci.it; f. 1888; cap. 241,105m., res 578,846m., dep. 9,058,110m. (Dec. 1999); Chair. and Man. Dir GIUSEPPE VIGORELLI; Gen. Man. CARLO PORCARI; 95 brs.

Banca Popolare dell'Emilia Romagna Scrl: Via San Carlo 8/20, 41100 Modena; tel. (059) 202111; fax (059) 220537; e-mail relest@bper.it; internet www.bperbank.it; f. 1867; cap. 166,058m. lire, res 1,726,253m. lire, dep. 20,945,036m. lire (Dec. 1999); Chair. Dott. CARLO BALDONI; Gen. Man. Dott. GUIDO LEONI; 204 brs.

Banca Popolare di Bergamo-Credito Varesino Scarl: Piazza Vittorio Veneto 8, 24122 Bergamo; tel. (035) 392111; fax (035) 221417; e-mail info@bpb.it; internet www.bpb.it; f. 1869; co-operative bank; cap. 526,629m. lire, res 1,936,646m. lire, dep. 45,066,427m. lire (Dec. 1999); Chair. E. ZANETTI; CEO and Gen. Man. G. CATTANEO; 320 brs.

Banca Popolare di Lodi: Via Polenghi Lombardo 13, 26900 Lodi; tel. (0371) 580111; fax (0371) 580762; internet www.poplodi.it; f. 1864; cap. 334,891m. lire, res 725,574m. lire, dep. 14,471,822m. lire (Dec. 1998); Chair. GIOVANNI BENEVENTO; CEO GIANPIERO FIORANI; 156 brs.

Banca Popolare di Milano Scarl: Piazza F. Meda 4, 20121 Milan; tel. (02) 77001; fax (02) 77002156; e-mail bipiemme@bpm.it; internet www.bpm.it; f. 1865; cap. €698m., res €783m., dep. €21,373m. (Dec. 1999); Pres. PAOLO BASSI; Gen. Man. ERNESTO PAOLILLO; 483 brs.

Banca Popolare di Novara Scarl: Via Carlo Negroni 12, 28100 Novara; tel. (0321) 662111; fax (0321) 662100; e-mail pronto@bpn.it; internet www.bpn.it; f. 1871; co-operative bank; cap. 1,186,852m. lire, res 1,198,589m. lire, dep. 36,835,000m. lire (Dec. 1999); Chair. SIRO LOMBARDINI; Man. Dir PIERO LUIGI MONTANI; 518 brs.

Banca Popolare di Sondrio Scarl: Piazza Garibaldi 16, 23100 Sondrio; tel. (0342) 528111; fax (0342) 528204; internet www .popso.it; f. 1871; cap. 343,915m. lire, res 668,663m. lire, dep. 9,794,877m. lire (Dec. 1998); Chair. and CEO PIERO MELAZZINI; 144 brs.

Banca Popolare di Verona—Banco S. Geminiano e S. Prospero: Piazza Nogara 2, 37100 Verona; tel. (045) 8675111; fax (045) 8675474; internet www.bpv.it; f. 1867; cap. 1,170,249m. lire, res 1,756,823m. lire, dep. 40,533,795m. lire (Dec. 1999); Pres. Prof. CARLO FRATTA PASINI; Gen. Man. FRANCO NALE; 368 brs and agencies.

Banca Popolare di Vicenza Scparl: Via Battaglione Framarin 18, 36100 Vicenza; tel. (0444) 339111; fax (0444) 329364; e-mail info@popvi.it; internet www.popvi.it; f. 1866; cap. 256,956m. lire, res 2,546,811m. lire, dep. 7,924,743m. lire (Dec. 1998); Chair. GIANNI ZONIN; Gen. Man. GIUSEPPE GRASSANO; 130 brs.

Banca Regionale Europea Spa: Via Monte di Pietà 7, 20121 Milan; tel. (02) 721211; fax (02) 865413; e-mail breestero@tin.it; internet www.brebanca.it; cap. 850,000m. lire, res 369,259m. lire, dep. 10,200,629m. lire (Dec. 1998); Chair. MARIO CERA; Gen. Man. PIERLUIGI GARDELLA; 253 brs.

Banca di Roma: Via Marco Minghetti 17, 00187 Rome; tel. (06) 54451; fax (06) 54453154; e-mail wweb@bancaroma.it; internet www.bancaroma.it; f. 1992 by merger; cap. 2,675,008m., res 7,645m. lire, dep. 144,218m. lire (Dec. 1999); Chair. CESARE GERONZI; Man. Dir ANTONIO NOTTOLA; 1,260 local brs, 20 overseas brs.

Banca Toscana SpA: Via Leone Pancaldo 4, 50127 Florence; tel. (055) 43911; fax (055) 4360061; e-mail international.dept@ bancatoscana.it; internet www.bancatoscana.it; f. 1904; cap. 294,400m. lire, res 1,445,616m. lire, dep. 22,176,881m. lire (Dec. 1998); Pres. PAOLO MOTTURA; Gen. Man. and CEO FRANCESCO ARRIGONI; 330 brs.

Banco di Napoli SpA: Via Toledo 177–178, 80132 Naples; tel. (081) 7911111; fax (081) 5801390; e-mail bninfo@tin.it; internet www.bancodinapoli.it; f. 1539; chartered public institution; cap. 1,992,175m. lire, res. 998,143m. lire, dep. 53,700,083m. lire (Dec. 1999); Chair. Dott. GIUSEPPE FALCONE; Central Man. PIETRO CUZZONI; 757 brs.

Banco di Sardegna SpA: Viale Umberto 36, 07100 Sassari; tel. (079) 226000; fax (079) 226015; www.bancosardegna.it; f. 1953; cap. 206,611m. lire, res 976,393m. lire, dep. 16,336,191m. lire (Dec. 1999); Chair. Prof. SEBASTIANO BRUSCO; Gen. Man. NATALINO OGGIANO; 235 brs.

Banco di Sicilia SpA: Via Generale Magliocco 1, 90141 Palermo; tel. (091) 6081111; fax (091) 6085051; internet www.bancodisicilia.it; f. 1860; cap. 2,471,083m. lire, res 34,263m. lire, dep. 49,761,828m. lire (Dec. 1999); Chair. and Pres. SABINO CASSESE; Gen. Man. CESARE CALETTI; 646 brs.

BIPOP-CARIRE SpA: Via Leonardo da Vinci 74, 25122 Brescia; tel. (030) 39931; fax (030) 396313; e-mail info@bipop.it; internet www. bipop.it; f. 1999 by merger of Banca Popolare di Brescia and Cassa di Risparmio di Reggio Emilia; cap. 808,309m. lire, res 983,817m. lire, dep. 18,996,024m. lire (Dec. 1999); Chair. GIACOMO FRANCESCHETTI; Gen. Man. BRUNO SONZOGNI; 69 brs.

Cariverona Banca SpA (Cassa di Risparmio di Verona, Vicenza, Belluno e Ancona SpA): Via G. Garibaldi 2, 37121 Verona; tel. (045) 8081111; fax (045) 8033679; e-mail carimail@ cariverona.it; internet www.cariverona.it; f. 1825; cap. 1,955,587m. lire, res 792,388m. lire, dep. 25,871,049m. lire (Dec. 1999); Chair. EUGENIO CAPONI; Gen. Man. MASSIMO BIANCONI; 485 brs.

Cassa di Risparmio di Firenze SpA: Via Bufalini 4/6, 50122 Florence; tel. (055) 26121; fax (055) 679986; e-mail estero@ carifirenze.it; internet www.carifirenze.it; f. 1829; cap. 1,063,832m. lire, res 230,235m. lire, dep. 16,709,610m. lire (Dec. 1999); Chair. and Pres. AURELIANO BENEDETTI; Gen. Man. LINO MOSCATELLI; 259 brs.

Cassa di Risparmio di Padova e Rovigo SpA: POB 1088, Corso Garibaldi 22/26, 35122 Padua; tel. (049) 8368111; fax (049) 8228540; e-mail mk@carip50.it; internet www.cariparo.it; f. 1822; cap. 534,666m. lire, res 1,371,372m.lire, dep. 17,608,712m. lire (Dec. 1998); Pres. ORAZIO ROSSI; Man. Dir PIO BUSSOLOTTO; 227 brs.

Cassa di Risparmio di Parma e Piacenza SpA: Via Università 1, 43100 Parma; tel. (0521) 912111; fax (0521) 912976; internet www.cariprpc.it; f. 1860; cap. 1,187,500m. lire, res 566,699m. lire, dep. 21,712,719m. lire (Dec. 1998); Chair. GIUSEPPE CONTINO; Gen. Man. FABRIZIO AMPOLLINI; 300 brs.

Cassa di Risparmio in Bologna SpA: Via Farini 22, 40124 Bologna; tel. (051) 6454111; fax (051) 6454366; internet www .carisbo.it; f. 1837; cap. 1,196,029m. lire, res 858,248m. lire, dep. 22,294,649m. lire (Dec. 1999); Chair. GIANGUIDO S. MORSIANI; Gen. Man. PAOLO LELLI; 169 brs.

Credito Bergamasco SpA: Largo Porta Nuova 2, 24122 Bergamo; tel. (035) 393111; fax (035) 393144; e-mail dip.internazionale@ creberg.it; internet www.creberg.it; f. 1891; cap. €185m., res €368m., dep. €6,871m. (Dec. 1999); Pres. CESARE ZONCA; Man. Dir FRANCO NALE; 200 brs.

Credito Emiliano SpA: Via Emilia S. Pietro 4, 42100 Reggio-Emilia; tel. (0522) 4501; fax (0522) 433969; e-mail int@credem.it; internet www.credem.it; f. 1910; cap. €264m., res €224m., dep. €8,542m. (Dec. 1999); Pres. GIORGIO FERRARI; Man. Dir FRANCO BIZZOCCHI; 233 brs.

Deutsche Bank SpA: Via Borgogna 8, 20122 Milan; tel. (02) 77951; fax (02) 40242636; internet www.deutsche-bank.it; f. 1918 as Banca dell'Italia Meridionale; in 1923 name changed to Banca d'America e d'Italia SpA, and as above in 1994; cap. 596,889m. lire, res 1,202,105m. lire, dep. 22,294,158m. (Dec. 1999); Pres. GIUSEPPE VITA; Man. Dir GIANNI TESTONI; 256 brs.

Mediocredito Centrale SpA: Via Piemonte 51, 00187 Rome; tel. (06) 47911; e-mail mediocredito@mcc.it; internet www.mcc.it; f. 1952; owned by Gruppo Bancaroma banking group; cap. 2,757,712m. lire, res 340,302m. lire, dep. 11,664,020m. lire (Dec. 1999); Chair. FRANCO CARRARO; CEO MARIO MAURO.

ROLO BANCA 1473 SpA: POB 775, Via Zamboni 20, 40126 Bologna; tel. (051) 6408111; fax (051) 6408377; e-mail posta@ rolobanca.it; internet www.rolobanca.it; f. 1896 as Piccolo Credito Romagnolo; cap. 438,604m. lire, res 3,799,948m. lire, dep. 68,823,571m.lire (Dec. 1998); Pres. ARISTIDE CANOSANI; Gen. Man. CESARE FARSETTI; 344 brs.

SANPAOLO IMI SpA: Piazza San Carlo 156, 10121 Turin; tel. (011) 5551; e-mail investor.relation@sanpaoloimi.com; internet www.sanpaoloimi.com; f. 1563 as Istituto Bancario San Paolo di Torino SpA, merged with Istituto Mobiliare Italiano SpA 1998; cap. €3,926m., res €1,921m., dep. €85,512m. (Dec. 1999); Chair. LUIGI ARCUTI; Man. Dirs LUIGI MARANZIANA, RAINER STEFANO MASERA; 1,427 brs.

UniCredito Italiana SpA: Piazza Cordusio, 20123 Milan; tel. (02) 88621; fax (02) 88623034; e-mail info@unicredito.it; internet www .unicredito.it; f. 1870; cap. 2,488,086m. lire, res 12,434,910m. lire, dep. 276,512,441m. lire (Dec. 1999); Chair. LUCIO RONDELLI; CEO ALESSANDRO PROFUMO; 973 brs.

FINANCIAL INSTITUTIONS

CENTROBANCA (Banca Centrale di Credito Popolare) SpA: Corso Europa 20, 20122 Milan; tel. (02) 77811; fax (02) 784372; e-mail comunica@centrobanca.it; internet www.centrobanca.it; f. 1946; central organization for medium- and long-term operations of Banche Popolari (co-operative banks) throughout Italy; cap. 309,803m.lire, res 354,682m. lire, dep. 15,205,917m. lire (Dec. 1999); Pres. PAOLO GIORGIO BASSI; Gen. Man. GIAN GIACOMO FAVERIO.

CREDIOP SpA: Via XX Settembre 30, 00187 Rome; tel. (06) 47711; fax (06) 47715952; e-mail crediop@crediop.it; internet www .crediop.it; f. 1919; newly incorporated 1996; cap. 872,500m. lire, res 55,365m. lire, dep. 31,097,474m. lire (Dec. 1998); Pres. ANTONIO PEDONE; Man. Dir MAURO CICCHINÉ.

EFIBANCA—Ente Finanziario Interbancario SpA: Via Po 28–32, 00198 Rome; tel. (06) 85991; fax (06) 8599250; e-mail efibanca@ntt.it; internet www.efibancaspa.it; f. 1939; cap. 316,113m. lire, res 481,638m. lire, dep. 13,636,587m. lire (Dec. 1998); Chair. PIETRO RASTELLI; Gen. Man. VALERIO LATTANZI; 8 brs.

ICCRI Banca Federale Europea SpA: Via Boncompagni 71h, 00187 Rome; tel. (06) 47151; fax (06) 47153579; internet www.iccri.it; f. 1919 as Istituto di Credito delle Casse di Risparmio Italiane, name changed in 1999; cap. 462,000m.lire, res 183,487m. lire, dep. 14,809,395m. lire (Dec. 1999); CEO ERNESTO MONTI.

INTERBANCA SpA: Corso Venezia 56, 20121 Milan; tel. (02) 77311; fax (02) 784321; f. 1961; cap. 27,900m. lire, res 436,734m.lire, dep. 11,691,009m. lire (Dec. 1999); Chair. ANTONIO CEOLA; Gen. Man. MARIO GABRIELE; 10 brs.

Istituto Centrale delle Banche di Credito Cooperativo (ICCREA SpA): Via Torino 146, 00184 Rome; tel. (06) 47161; fax (06) 4747155; f. 1963; cap. 320,000m., res 6,250m., dep. 9,989,184m. (Dec. 1997); Pres. GIORGIO CLEMENTI; Gen. Man. ALFREDO NERI; 5 brs.

Mediobanca—Banca di Credito Finanziario SpA: Piazzetta Enrico Cuccia 1, 20121 Milan; tel. (02) 88291; fax (02) 8829367; internet www.mediobanca.it; f. 1946; cap. 595,946m. lire, res 5,046,128m. lire., dep. 32,962,867m.lire (June 2000); Chair. FRANCESCO CINGANO; Man. Dir VINCENZO MARANGHI.

BANKERS' ORGANIZATIONS

Associazione Bancaria Italiana: Piazza del Gesù 49, 00186 Rome; tel. (06) 67671; fax (06) 6767457; internet www.abi.it; Via della Posta 3, 20123 Milan; tel. (02) 86450695; fax (02) 878684; f. 1919; Pres. MAURIZIO SELLA; Gen. Man. Dott. GIUSEPPE ZADRA; membership (1,032 mems) is comprised of the following institutions: banks authorized to gather savings from the general public and exercise credit business as well as to perform other financial activities; brs and representative offices of foreign banks; asscns of banks or financial intermediaries; financial intermediaries engaging in one or more of the activities subject to mutual recognition under the Second Banking Directive or other financial activities subject to public prudential supervison.

Associazione fra le Casse di Risparmio Italiane: Viale di Villa Grazioli 23, 00198 Rome; tel. (06) 855621; fax (06) 8540192; internet www.acri.it; f. 1912; Chair. Dott. GIUSEPPE GUZZETTI; Gen. Man. STEFANO MARCHETTINI.

Associazione fra gli Istituti Regionale Di Mediocredito: Piazza della Marina 1, 00196 Rome; tel. (06) 3225150; fax (06) 3225135; Pres. Prof. ANGELO CALOIA; Gen. Man. Dott. ANTONIO DE VITO.

Associazione Italiana per il Factoring: Via Cerva 9, 20122 Milan; tel. (02) 76020127; fax (02) 76020159; e-mail posta@ assifact.it; internet www.assifact.it; Pres. Avv. GIORGIO BONDIOLI; Sec.-Gen. Prof. ALESSANDRO CARRETTA.

Associazione Nazionale Banche Private—ASSBANK: Corso Monforte 34, 20122 Milan; tel. (02) 777241; fax (02) 77724599; e-mail assbank@assbank.it; internet www.assbank.it; Pres. Dott. Prof. TANCREDI BIANCHI; Dir-Gen. Dott. EDMONDO FONTANA.

Associazione Nazionale fra le Banche Popolari: Piazza Venezia 11, 00187 Rome; tel. (06) 695351; Pres. Prof. SIRO LOMBARDINI; Dir-Gen. Dott. GIORGIO CARDUCCI.

Associazione Nazionale fra gli Istituti di Credito Agrario (ANICA): Via A. Bertoloni 3, 00197 Rome; tel. (06) 8077506; fax (06) 8077506; f. 1946; Pres. Prof. GIUSEPPE GUERRIERI; Sec.-Gen. Dott. ERNESTO DE MEDIO.

Associazione Sindacale fra le Aziende del Credito—ASSICREDITO: Via G. Paisiello 5, 00198 Rome; tel. (06) 854591; f. 1947; Dir Dott. GIUSEPPE CAPO.

Associazione Italiana delle Società Edenti Digestione Mobiliare ed Immobiliare: Via In Lucina 12, 00186 Rome; tel. (06) 6893203; fax (06) 6893262; Pres. Prof. GUSTAVO VISENTINI; Sec. Gen. Prof. GUIDO CAMMARANO.

Associazione Italiana Leasing—ASSILEA: Piazza di Priscilla 4, 00199 Rome; tel. (06) 86211271; fax (06) 86211214; e-mail info@ assilea.it; internet www.assilea.it; Pres. Dott. ANTONIO DATTOLO.

STOCK EXCHANGES

Commissione Nazionale per le Società e la Borsa (CONSOB) (Commission for Companies and the Stock Exchange): Via Isonzo 19, 00198 Rome; tel. (06) 84771. 1974; regulatory control over cos quoted on stock exchanges, convertible bonds, unlisted securities, insider trading, all forms of public saving except bank deposits and mutual funds; Chair. LUIGI SPAVENTA; there are 10 stock exchanges, of which the following are the most important:

Genoa: Borsa Valori, Via G. Boccardo 1, Genoa; tel. (010) 590920; f. 1855; Pres. LUCIANO GAMBAROTTA.

Borsa Italiana (Italian Stock Exchange): Piazza degli Affari 6, 20123 Milan; tel. (02) 72426202; fax (02) 72004333; internet www.borsaitalia.it; Pres. ANGELO TANTAZZI; Dir-Gen. MASSIMO CAPUANO.

Naples: Borsa Valori, Palazzo Borsa, Piazza Bovio, Naples; tel. (081) 269151; Pres. GIORGIO FOCAS.

Rome: Borsa Valori, Via dei Burro 147, 00186 Rome; tel. (06) 6792701; f. 1821; Pres. ALBERTO BORTI.

Turin: Borsa Valori, Via San Francesco da Paola 28, Turin; tel. (011) 547743; fax (011) 5612193; f. 1850; Pres. Dott. FRANCO CELLINO.

INSURANCE

Alleanza Assicurazioni SpA: Viale Luigi Sturzo 35, 20154 Milan; tel. (02) 62961; fax (02) 653718; e-mail info@alleanzaassicurazioni.it; f. 1898; life insurance; subsidiary of Assicurazioni Generali (q.v.); cap. €423.1m. (December 1999); Chair. Dott. SANDRO SALVATI.

Allianz Subalpina SpA: Via Alfieri 22, 10121 Turin; tel. (011) 5161431; fax (011) 5627246; f. 1928; cap. 40,910.6m. (Dec. 1998); Chair. Dott. GIULIO BASEGGIO; Man. Dir Dott. ROBERTO GAVAZZI.

Assicuratrice Edile SpA: Via A. De Togni 2, 20123 Milan; tel. (02) 480411; fax (02) 48041292; e-mail cauzioni@assedile.it; internet www.assedile.it; f. 1960; cap. 16,000m. (Jan. 2000); Chair. CHRISTIAN HUOT; Man. Dir ANTOINE NINU.

Assicurazioni Generali SpA: Piazza Duca degli Abruzzi 2, 34132 Trieste; tel. (040) 6711; fax (040) 671600; f. 1831; cap. 1,603,250m. (1994); Chair. (vacant).

Le Assicurazioni d'Italia (ASSITALIA) SpA: Corso d'Italia 33, 00198 Rome; tel. (06) 84831; fax (06) 84833142; f. 1923; cap. 150,000m. (Dec. 1990); Pres. Avv. PIER LUIGI CASSIETTI; Gen. Man. Prof. Avv. VINCENZO MUNGARI.

Aurora Assicurazioni SpA: Via R. Montecuccoli 20, 20147 Milan; tel. (02) 41441; fax (02) 48300451; f. 1947; cap. 50,000m. (Dec. 1990); Chair. Avv. EMILIO DUSI; Gen. Man. Dott. GIACOMO NURRA.

BNC Assicurazioni SpA: Via S. Martino della Battaglia 4, 00185 Rome; tel. (06) 44761; fax (06) 44763343; f. 1927; cap. 157,360m. (Dec. 1996); Pres. Dott. LUCA A. BERTOLA; Dir-Gen. Dott. RICCARDO ROMUSSI.

Compagnia Assicuratrice Unipol SpA: Via Stalingrado 45, 40128 Bologna; tel. (051) 6097111; fax (051) 375349; f. 1961; cap. 261,680m. (Sept. 1999); Chair. GIOVANNI CONSORTE; Vice-Chair. IVANO SACCHETTI.

Compagnia di Assicurazioni di Milano SpA: Via del Lauro 7, 20121 Milan; tel. (02) 88401; fax (02) 88402389; f. 1825; cap. 175,333m. (Dec. 1996); Pres. Dott. AMATO MOLINARI; Dir-Gen. Ing. LUCIANO PASQUALI.

Dival Vita SpA: Piazza Erculea 13, 20122 Milan; tel. (02) 85751; fax (02) 8575266; f. 1975; cap. 175,000m. (Dec. 1996); Pres. Dott. GIULIO BASEGGIO; Dir-Gen. ENZO ZENI.

FATA (Fondo Assicurativo Tra Agricoltori) SpA: Via Urbana 169/A, 00184 Rome; tel. (06) 47651; fax (06) 4871187; f. 1927; cap. 20,000m. (Dec. 1990); Chair. GIANCARLO BUSCARINI; Man. Dir FRANCO RIZZI.

La Fiduciaria: Via A. Finelli 8, 40126 Bologna; tel. (051) 6307011; fax (051) 243030; f. 1970; cap. 11,508m. (June 1992); Chair. JEAN PAUL GALBRUN; Man. Dir Dott. Ing. SERGIO BEDINI.

La Fondiaria SpA: Piazza della Libertà 6, 50129 Florence; tel. (055) 47941; fax (055) 476026; f. 1879; cap. 390,160m. (1996); Pres. ALBERTO PECCI; Gen. Man. AMATO LUIGI MOLINARI.

Istituto Nazionale delle Assicurazioni SpA (INA): Via Sallustiana 51, 00187 Rome; tel. (06) 47221; fax (06) 47224559; internet www.gruppoina.it; f. 1912; Chair. Dott. SERGIO SIGLIENTI; Man. Dir LINO BENASSI.

ITAS, Istituto Trentino-Alto Adige per Assicurazioni: Via Mantova 67, 38100 Trent; tel. (0461) 982112; fax (0461) 980297; f. 1821; cap. 60,000m. (Dec. 1996); Chair. Dott. EDO BENEDETTI; Gen. Man. Dott. ETTORE LOMBARDO.

Lavoro e Sicurtà SpA: Piazza Erculea 13–15, 20122 Milan; tel. (02) 85751; fax (02) 72021420; f. 1963; cap. 20,000m. (Dec. 1990); Chair. ENZO ZENI; Man. Dir ENRICO ORLANDO.

Lloyd Adriatico SpA: Largo Ugo Irneri 1, 34143 Trieste; tel. (040) 77811; fax (040) 7781311; f. 1936; cap. 60,000m. (Dec. 1990); Chair.

Dott. HELMUT PERLET; Vice-Chair. Dott. GIOVANNI GABRIELLI; Man. Dir Dott. ENRICO TOMASO CUCCHIANI.

Lloyd Italico Assicurazioni SpA: Via Fieschi 9, 16121 Genoa; tel. (010) 53801; fax (010) 592856; e-mail lloydita@lia.it; internet www.lloyditalico.it; f. 1983; cap. 61,500m. (Dec. 1990); Chair. JENS E. CHRISTENSEN; Man. Dir GIORGIO E. FUSELLI.

Mediolanum Vita SpA: Palazzo Meucci, Via Francesco Sforza 15, 20080 Basiglio; tel. (02) 90491; fax (02) 90492427; f. 1972; cap. 170,000m. (Dec. 1996); Pres. Dott. ALFREDO MESSINA.

La Nationale Assicurazioni SpA: Piazza del Porto di Ripetta 1, 00186 Rome; tel. (06) 682801; fax (06) 6834089; f. 1962; cap. 30,000m. (1992); Pres. JEAN PAUL GALBRUN; Vice-Pres. PIER UGO ANDREINI.

Norditalia Assicurazioni SpA: Viale Certosa 222, 20156 Milan; tel. (02) 30761; fax (02) 3086125; f. 1963; cap. 165,300m. (Dec. 1997); Pres. Ing. OLIVIERO TAROLLI; Man. Dir Dott. FERDINANDO MENCONI.

Nuova Tirrena SpA: Via Massimi 158, 00136 Rome; tel. (06) 30181; fax (06) 30183613; f. 1929; cap. 230,250m. (Dec. 1996); Pres. Rag. FRANCESCO TORRI; Dir-Gen. Dott. LUCIANO BECCHIO.

RAS—Riunione Adriatica di Sicurtà: Corso Italia 23, 20122 Milan; tel. (02) 72161; f. 1838; cap. 217,000m., res 1,932,599m. (Dec. 1991); Chair. and Man. Dir Dott. UMBERTO ZANNI.

SAI—Società Assicuratrice Industriale SpA: Corso Galileo Galilei 12, 10126 Turin; tel. (011) 65621; fax (011) 6562685; f. 1921; cap. 165,000m. (Dec. 1990); Chair. Dott. Ing. SALVATORE LIGRESTI; Gen. Man. Dott. GIORGIO BRINATTI.

SARA Assicurazioni SpA: Via Po 20, 00198 Rome; tel. (06) 84751; fax (06) 8475223; f. 1924; cap. 60,750m. (June 1994); Chair. ROSARIO ALESSI; Gen. Man. Dott. MARCO ROCCA.

Società Cattolica di Assicurazione: Lungadige Cangrande 16, 37126 Verona; tel. (045) 8391111; fax (045) 8391112; f. 1896; cap. 78,150m. (June 1994); Chair. Ing. GIULIO BISOFFI; Gen. Man. Dott. EZIO PAOLO REGGIA.

Società Italiana Cauzioni SpA (SIC): Via Crescenzio 12, 00193 Rome; tel. (06) 688121; fax (06) 6874418; e-mail sic.dirgen@sic-spa.it; internet www.sic-spa.it; f. 1948; cap. 35,000m. (Oct. 1998); Chair. GIANLUCA BOCCIA; Gen. Man. GIORIO CIMAGALLI.

Società Reale Mutua di Assicurazioni: Via Corte d'Appello 11, 10122 Turin; tel. (011) 431111; fax (011) 4350966; e-mail webmaster@realmutua.it; internet www.realmutua.it; f. 1828; total assets 8,195,584m. (1998); Chair. CARLO ALBANI CASTELBARCO VISCONTI; Gen. Man. Dott. PIERO CASTELLI.

Toro Assicurazioni SpA: Via Arcivescovado 16, 10121 Turin; tel. (011) 51631; fax (011) 543587; f. 1833; cap. 159,510m. (Dec. 1998); Chair. BENEDETTO SALAROLI; Man. Dir Rag. FRANCESCO TORRI.

UAP Italiana SpA: Via Leopardi 15, 20123 Milan; tel. (02) 480841; fax (02) 48084331; f. 1956; cap. 8,211m. (Dec. 1990); Chair. and Man. Dir Dott. PIERRE MERCIER.

Unione Italiana di Riassicurazione SpA: Via dei Giuochi Istmici 40, 00194 Rome; tel. (06) 323931; fax (06) 36303398; f. 1922; cap. 100,000m. (Dec. 1990); Chair. Avv. LORENZO PALLESI.

Universo Assicurazioni SpA: Via del Pilastro 52, 40127 Bologna; tel. (051) 6371111; fax (051) 6371401; f. 1972; cap. 62,500m. (Dec. 1990); Chair. Dott. GIUSEPPE SOLINAS; Gen. Man. Dott. GIORGIO DI GIANSANTE.

Vittoria Assicurazioni SpA: Via Caldera 21, 20153 Milan; tel. (02) 482191; fax (02) 48203693; f. 1921; cap. 30,000m. (Dec. 1990); Chair. Prof. LUIGI GUATRI; Man. Dir Rag. ROBERTO GUARENA.

Winterthur Assicurazioni SpA: Piazza Missori 2, 20122 Milan; tel. (02) 85471; fax (02) 8547701; f. 1919; cap. 223,000m. (Dec. 1996); Pres. Dott. LUIGO CAPÉ; Dir-Gen. Dott. FABRIZIO RINDI.

INSURANCE ASSOCIATION

Associazione Nazionale fra le Imprese Assicuratrici (ANIA): Piazza S. Babila 1, 20122 Milan; tel. (02) 77641; fax (02) 780870; e-mail info@ania.it; f. 1944; Pres. Dott. ALFONSO DESIATA; Dir Gen. Dott. MARIO ORIO; 210 mems.

Trade and Industry

GOVERNMENT AGENCIES

Autorità garante della concorrenza e del mercato (Regulatory authority for competition and markets): Via Liguria 26, 00187 Rome; tel. (06) 481621; fax (06) 48162256; e-mail antitrust@agcm.it; internet www.agcm.it; Pres. GIUSEPPE TESAURO; Sec. Gen. RITA CICCONE.

Istituto Nazionale per il Commercio Estero (ICE) (National Institute for Foreign Trade): Via Liszt 21, 00144 Rome; tel. (06) 59921; fax (06) 59926899; e-mail ice@ice.it; f. 1919; govt agency for the promotion of foreign trade; Chair. and CEO Prof. FABRIZIO ONIDA.

CHAMBERS OF COMMERCE

Unione Italiana delle Camere di Commercio, Industria, Artigianato e Agricoltura (Italian Union of Chambers of Commerce, Industry, Crafts and Agriculture): Piazza Sallustio 21, 00187 Rome; tel. (06) 47041; f. 1954 to promote the development of chambers of commerce, industry, trade and agriculture; Pres. DANILO LONGHI; Sec.-Gen. Dott. GIUSEPPE CERRONI.

INDUSTRIAL AND TRADE ASSOCIATIONS

Confederazione Generale dell'Industria Italiana—CONFINDUSTRIA (General Confederation of Italian Industry): Viale dell'Astronomia 30, EUR, 00144 Rome; tel. (06) 59031; fax (06) 5919615; e-mail confindustria@confindustria.it; internet www.confindustria.it; f. 1910, re-established 1944; mems: 107 territorial asscns and 110 branch asscns, totalling 111,000 firms and 4.5m. employees; office in Brussels; Pres. ANTONIO D'AMATO; Dir-Gen. STEFANO PARISI.

Principal Affiliated Organizations

Associazione degli Industriali della Birra e del Malto (Brewers): Viale di Val Fiorita 90, 00144 Rome; tel. (06) 543932; fax (06) 5912910; Pres. Dott. RUDI PERONI; Dir Avv. STEFANO GENOVESE.

Associazione Industrie per l'Aerospazio, i Sistemi e la Difesa (AIAD) (Aerospace, Systems and Defence Industries): Via Nazionale 200, 00184 Rome; tel. (06) 4880247; fax (06) 4827476; e-mail aiad@aiad.it; internet www.aiad.it; f. 1947; Pres. Dott. Ing. CORRADO ANTONINI; Sec. Gen. CARLO FESTUCCI.

Associazione Italiana delle Industrie della Filiera Tessile Abbigliamento (Clothing and Knitwear Manufacturers): Viale Sarca 223, 20126 Milan; tel. (02) 66103391; fax (02) 66103670; e-mail info@sistemamodaitalia.it; internet www.sistemamodaitalia.it; f. 1945; produces weekly, fortnightly and annual periodicals; Pres. VITTORIO GIULINI.

Associazione Italiana Industrie Prodotti Alimentari (AIIPA) (Food Manufacturers): Corso di Porta Nuova 34, 20121 Milan; tel. (02) 654184; fax (02) 654822; f. 1946; Pres. EMILIO LAVAZZA; Dir Dott. GIOVANNI FRANCO CRIPPA; 300 mems.

Associazione Italiana Tecnico Economica del Cemento (AITEC) (Cement): Piazza G. Marconi 25, 00144 Rome; tel. (06) 54210237; fax (06) 5915408; Viale Milanofiori, Strada 1, Pal. F2, 20090 Milan; f. 1959; Pres. GIACOMO MARAZZI.

Associazione Mineraria Italiana (Mining): Via delle Tre Madonne 20, 00197 Rome; tel. (06) 8073045; fax (06) 8073385; f. 1144; Pres. Ing. GUGLIELMO MOSCATO; Dir-Gen. Dott. FRANCESCO SAVERIO GUIDI; 150 mems.

Associazione Nazionale Costruttori Edili (ANCE) (Builders): Via Guattani 16, 00161 Rome; tel. (06) 84567; fax (06) 44232832; e-mail info@ance.it; internet www.ance.it; f. 1946; Pres. CLAUDIO DE ALBERTIS; Man. Dir CARLO FERRONI; mems: 19,000 firms in 101 provincial and 20 regional asscns.

Associazione Nazionale delle Fonderie—ASSOFOND (Foundries): Via Copernico 54, 20090 Trezzano Sul Naviglio; tel. (02) 48400967; fax (02) 48401282; e-mail assofond@ronet.it; f. 1948; Pres. GIAN PAOLO MORA.

Associazione Nazionale dell'Industria Farmaceutica—FARMINDUSTRIA (Pharmaceutical Industry): Largo del Nazareno 3/8, 00187 Rome; tel. (06) 675801; fax (06) 6786494; internet www.farmindustria.it; f. 1978; Pres. Dott. GIANPIETRO LEONI; Dir Dott. IVAN CAVICCHI; 208 mem. firms.

Associazione Nazionale fra Industrie Automobilistiche (ANFIA) (Motor Vehicle Industries): Corso Galileo Ferraris 61, 10128 Turin; tel. (011) 5546511; fax (011) 545986; e-mail anfia@anfia.it; internet www.anfia.it; f. 1912; Pres. Dott. CARLO SINCERI; Dir-Gen. Dott. EMILIO DI CAMILLO; 250 mems.

Associazione Nazionale Italiana Industrie Grafiche, Cartotecniche e Trasformatrici (Printing and Paper-Converting Industries): Piazza Conciliazione 1, 20123 Milan; tel. (02) 4981051; fax (02) 4816947; e-mail info@assografici.it; internet www.assografici.it; f. 1946; Pres. Ing. EMANUELE PIOVANO; Gen. Dir Dott. CLAUDIO COVINI; 1,200 mems.

Federazione delle Associazioni Nazionali dell'Industria Meccanica Varia ed Affine (ANIMA) (Federation of Italian Mechanical and Engineering Industry Associations): Via L. Battistotti Sassi 11/B, 20133 Milan; tel. (02) 73971; fax (02) 7397316; internet www.anima-it.com; f. 1945; Pres. LUIGI CAZZANIGA; Sec.-Gen. Dott. Ing. ENRICO MALCOVATI; 1,500 mems.

Federazione Italiana Industriali Produttori Esportatori ed Importatori di Vini, Acquaviti, Liquori, Sciroppi, Aceti ed Affini—FEDERVINI (Producers, Importers and Exporters of Wines, Brandies, Liqueurs, Syrups, Vinegars and Allied Products): Via Mentana 2B, 00185 Rome; tel. (06) 4941630; fax (06) 4941566; e-mail federvini@foodarea.it; f. 1921; Pres. LUIGI ROSSI DI MONTELERA; Dir-Gen. FEDERICO CASTELLUCCI.

Federazione Nazionale dell'Industria Chimica—FEDER-CHIMICA (Chemical Industry): Via Giovanni da Procida 11, 20121 Milan; tel. (02) 345651; fax (02) 34565310; Viale Pasteur 10, 00144 Rome; tel. (06) 542731; fax (06) 542732; e-mail federchimica@federchimica.it; internet www.federchimica.it; f. 1945; Pres. Dott. GIORGIO SQUINZI; Dir-Gen. Dott. GUIDO VENTURINI.

Federazione Nazionale Industrie Elettrotecniche ed Elettroniche (ANIE) (Electrotechnic and Electronic Industries): Via Gattamelata 34, 20149 Milan; tel. (02) 32641; fax (02) 3264212; e-mail info@anie.it; internet www.anie.it; Pres. RAFFAELE PALIERI; Sec.-Gen. CLAUDIO GATTI.

Unione Industriali Pastai Italiani—UNIPI (Pasta Manufacturers): Via Po 102, 00198 Rome; tel. (06) 8543291; fax (06) 8415132; e-mail unipi@unipi-pasta.it; internet www.unipi-pasta.it; Pres. Dott. MARIO RUMMO; Dir RAFFAELLO RAGAGLINI.

Unione Nazionale Cantieri e Industrie Nautiche ed Affini (UCINA) (Shipyard and Nautical Industries): Piazzale Kennedy 1, 16129 Genoa; tel. (010) 5769811; fax (010) 5531104; e-mail ucina@ucina.it; internet www.ucina.it; Pres. Dott. PAOLO VITELLI; Sec.-Gen. Dott. Ing. LORENZO POLLICARDO.

Unione Petrolifera (Petroleum Industries): Via Giorgione 129, 00147 Rome; tel. (06) 5423651; fax (06) 59602925; e-mail info@unionepetrolifera.it; internet www.unionepetrolifera.it; f. 1948; Pres. Dott. PASQUALE DE VITA; Dir-Gen. Dott. PIETRO DE SIMONE; 36 mems.

Others

Associazione Nazionale Comuni Italiani (ANCI): Via dei Prefetti 46, 00186 Rome; tel. (06) 680091; fax (06) 68009202; e-mail baroni@anci.it; internet www.anci.it; Pres. Dott. LEONARDO DOMENICI; Dir-Gen. Dott. FABIO MELILLI.

Associazione Nazionale fra i Concessionari del Servizio di Riscossione del Tributi (ASCOTRIBUTI) (Services relating to Collection of Payments): Via Parigi 11, 00185 Rome; tel. (06) 485764; fax (06) 4828184; Pres. RICCARDO TRIGLIA; Dir-Gen. Dott. GERARDO CHIRO.

Associazione Sindacale per le Aziende Petrochimiche e Collegate a Partecipazione Statale (State-controlled Petrochemical Cos): Via Due Macelli 66, 00187 Rome; tel. (06) 67341; fax (06) 6734242; f. 1960; draws up labour and union contracts and represents the cos in legal matters; Pres. Avv. GUIDO FANTONI; Vice-Pres. and Dir-Gen. Dott. MODESTINO FUSCO.

Associazione fra le Società Italiane per Azioni—ASSONIME (Limited Cos): Piazza Venezia 11, 00187 Rome; tel. (06) 695291; fax (06) 6790487; e-mail assonime@assonime.it; internet www.assonime.it; f. 1911; Pres. Dott. UMBERTO ZANNI; Dir-Gen. STEFANO MICOSSI.

Confederazione Generale della Agricoltura Italiana—CONFAGRICOLTURA (General Agricultural): Corso Vittorio Emanuele II 101, 00186 Rome; tel. (06) 68521; fax (06) 68308578; e-mail immco@mail.confagricoltura.it; internet www.confagricoltura.it; f. 1945; Pres. Dott. AUGUSTO BOCCHINI; Dir-Gen. VITO BIANCO.

CONFCOMMERCIO—Confederazione Generale Italiana del Commercio, del Turismo, dei Servizi e delle Piccole e Medie Industrie (Commerce, Tourism, Services and Small and Medium-sized Industry): Piazza G.G. Belli 2, 00153 Rome; tel. (06) 58661; fax (06) 5809425; e-mail confcommercio@confcommercio.it; internet www.confcommercio.it; f. 1946; Pres. Dott. SERGIO BILLÈ; Sec.-Gen. Dott. GIUSEPPE CERRONI.

Confederazione Italiana della Piccola e Media Industria Privata—CONFAPI (Small and Medium Private Industry): Via della Colonna Antonina 52, 00186 Rome; tel. (06) 690151; fax (06) 6791488; e-mail mail@confapi.it; internet www.confapi.it; f. 1947; Pres. LUCIANO BOLZONI; Dir-Gen. Dott. SANDRO NACCARELLI; 55,000 mems.

Confederazione Italiana della Proprietà Edilizia—CONFEDILIZIA (Property and Building): Via Borgognona 47, 00187 Rome; tel. (06) 6793489; fax (06) 6793447; Pres. Avv. CORRADO SFORZA FOGLIANI; Sec.-Gen. Avv. GIORGIO SPAZIANI TESTA.

Delegazione Sindacale Industriale Autonoma della Valle d'Aosta (Autonomous Industrial Delegation of the Valle d'Aosta): Via G. Elter 6, 11100 Aosta; Pres. Dott. ETTORE FORTUNA; Sec. Dott. ROBERTO ANSALDO.

Federazione Associazioni Industriali (Industrial Asscns): Via Petitti 16, 20149 Milan; tel. (02) 326721; fax (02) 33003819; Pres. Dott. DINO FENZI; Dir-Gen. Dott. UMBERTO MALTAGLIATI.

Federazione delle Associazioni Italiane Alberghi e Turismo—FEDERALBERGHI (Hotels and Tourism): Via Toscana 1, 00187 Rome; tel. (06) 42741151; fax (06) 42871197; f. 1950; Pres. AMATO RAMONDETTI; Gen. Man. ALESSANDRO CIANELLA; 30,000 mems.

UNAPACE Via Ombrone 2G, 00198 Rome; tel. (06) 8537281; fax (06) 85356431; internet www.unapace.it; f. 1946; represents the interests of concerns producing and/or offering electricity; Pres. Dott. FRANCO BRUNETTI; Dir-Gen. FRANCESCO DE LUCA.

UTILITIES

Autorità per l'Energia Elettrica e il Gas: Piazza Cavour 5, 20121 Milan; tel. (02) 655651; fax (02) 29014219; e-mail milano@autorita.energia.it; internet www.autorita.energia.it; regulatory authority; Pres. PIPPO RANCI.

Electricity

Ente Nazionale per l'Energia Elettrica (Enel): Via Giovanni Battista Martini 3, 00198 Rome; tel. (06) 85091; fax (06) 85092162; f. 1962 to generate and distribute electrical power throughout various areas of the country and to work in conjunction with the Ministry of Industry; 34.5% privatized in 1999; further divestment of government stake planned for 2001; Chair. CHICO TESTA; CEO FRANCO TATO.

Gas

In February 2000 the Government announced that the gas market was to be liberalized by January 2003 to comply with European Union regulations.

Snam: Piazza Vanoni 1, 20097 San Donato Milanese; tel. (02) 5201; fax (02) 52043226; subsidiary of Ente Nazionale Idrocarburi (Eni); primary supplier of natural gas in Italy; Chair. ANGELO FERRARI.

TRADE UNIONS

There are three main federations of Italian trade unions, CGIL, CISL and UIL, all of which have close ties with political parties. The CGIL was formerly dominated by the Partito Comunista Italiano (Italian Communist Party, now the Democratici di Sinistra—Democrats of the Left), the CISL has links with the Partito Popolare Italiano (Italian Popular Party, formerly Partito della Democrazia Cristiana (Christian Democrat Party) and the UIL is associated with the socialists.

National Federations

Confederazione Autonoma Italiana del Lavoro (CONFAIL): Viale Abruzzi 38, 20131 Milan; tel. (02) 29404554; fax (02) 29525692; e-mail info@confail.org; internet www.confail.org; Gen. Sec. EVANGELISTA ZACCARIA.

Confederazione Autonoma Sindacati Artigiani (CASARTIGIANI): Via Flaminio Ponzio 2, 00153 Rome; tel. (06) 5758081; f. 1958; federation of artisans' unions and regional and provincial asscns; Pres. GIACOMO BASSO.

Confederazione Generale Italiana dell'Artigianato (CONFARTIGIANATO) (Artisans): Via di S. Giovanni in Laterano 152, 00184 Rome; tel. (06) 703741; fax (06) 70452188; e-mail confartigianato@confartigianato.it; internet www.confartigianato.it; f. 1945; independent; 170 mem. unions; 600,000 associate enterprises; Pres. IVANO SPALANZANI.

Confederazione Generale Italiana del Lavoro (CGIL) (General Union of Italian Workers): Corso d'Italia 25, 00198 Rome; tel. (06) 84761; fax (06) 8845683; e-mail segreteria.cofferati@mail.cgil.it; internet www.cgil.it; f. 1944; federation of 17 unions; Sec.-Gen. SERGIO COFFERATI; 5,247,201 mems.

Confederazione Italiana Dirigenti di Azienda (CIDA): Via Nazionale 75, 00184 Rome; tel. (06) 4888241; fax (06) 4873994; e-mail dirigenti@tin.it; internet www.cida.it; federation of six managers' unions; Pres. Dott. GIAN PAOLO CARROZZA; Sec.-Gen. Dott. GIOVANNI CARDEGNA.

Confederazione Italiana Lavoratori Democratici Indipendenti (CILDI): Via dell'Impruneta 15, 00192 Rome; tel. (06) 5002444; fax (06) 5003196; Gen. Sec. VINCENZO CACI.

Confederazione Italiana Lavoratori Liberi (CONFIL): Via di Campo Marzio 46, 00186 Rome; tel. (06) 6872508; fax (06) 6872509; Gen. Sec. FRANCESCO BRUNETTI.

Confederazione Italiana dei Professionisti e Artisti (CIPA) (Artists and Professional People): Rome; tel. (06) 461849; federation of 19 unions; Pres. Rag. SERGIO SPLENDORI.

Confederazione Italiana Sindacati Addetti ai Servizi (CISAS): Via Sapri 6, 00185 Rome; tel. (06) 4466618; fax (06) 4466617; internet www.cisas.org; Gen. Sec. ONOFRIO DANIELLO.

Confederazione Italiana dei Sindacati Autonomi Lavoratori (CISAL): Viale Giulio Cesare 21, 00192 Rome; tel. (06) 3207941; fax (06) 3212521; internet www.cisal.org; f. 1957; affiliated to Confédération Européenne des Syndacats Independents; federation of 45 unions; Sec.-Gen. GIUSEPPE CARBONE; 1,500,000 mems.

Confederazione Italiana Sindacati Lavoratori (CISL): Via Po 21, 00198 Rome; tel. (06) 84731; fax (06) 8546076; e-mail cisl@cisl.it; 8413782; internet www.cisl.it; f. 1950; affiliated to the International Confederation of Free Trade Unions and the European Trade Union

Confederation; federation of 17 unions; Sec.-Gen. SERGIO D'ANTONI; 3,800,000 mems.

Confederazione Nazionale dell'Artigianato e delle Piccole Imprese (CNA): Via G. A. Guattani 13, 00161 Rome; tel. (06) 441881; fax (06) 44249513; e-mail cna@cna.it; internet www.cna.it; provincial asscns; Pres. FILIPPO MINOTTI; Gen. Sec. Dott. GIAN CARLO SANGALLI.

Confederazione dei Sindacati Autonomi dei Lavoratori (CONFSAL): Viale Trasevere 60, 00153 Rome; tel. (06) 5899553; fax (06) 5818218; e-mail info@confsal.it; internet www.confsal.it; Pres. CARMINE GALLOTTA.

Confederazione Unitaria Quadri (CUQ): Via XX Settembre 58, 10121 Turin; tel. (011) 5612042; fax (011) 5620362; e-mail confquadri@tin.it; Pres. CARLO CAPELLARO.

Confederazione Unitaria Sindacati Autonomi Lavoratori (CUSAL): Via di Campo Marzio 46, 00186 Rome; tel. (06) 6872508; fax (06) 6872509; Pres. DOMENICO MANNO; Gen. Sec. FRANCESCO BRUNETTI.

Coordinamento Sindacale Autonomo (CSA): Via Avicenna 40, 00146 Rome; tel. (06) 5585292; fax (06) 5576903; Gen. Man. ANTONIO MARRONE.

Federazione fra le Associazioni e i Sindacati Nazionali dei Quadri Direttivi dell'amministrazione dello Stato (DIRSTAT): Via Ezio 12, 00192 Rome; tel. (06) 3211535; fax (06) 3212690; f. 1948; federation of 33 unions and asscns of civil service executives and officers; Sec.-Gen. ARCANGELO D'AMBROSIO; Treas. Dott. SERGIO DI DONNA.

Unione Generale del Lavoro (UGL): Via Margutta 19, 00187 Rome; tel. (06) 324821; fax (06) 324820; e-mail ugl@ugl.it; internet www.ugl.it; f. 1950 as CISNAL, name changed as above 1995; upholds traditions of national syndicalism; federation of 64 unions, 77 provincial unions; Gen. Sec. STEFANO CETICA; 2,137,979 mems.

Unione Italiana del Lavoro (UIL): Via Lucullo 6, 00187 Rome; tel. (06) 4753210; fax (06) 4753295; e-mail segretariagenerale@uil.it; internet www.uil.it; f. 1950; Socialist, Social Democrat and Republican; affiliated to the International Confederation of Free Trade Unions and European Trade Union Confederation; 18 national trade union federations and 108 provincial union councils; Gen. Sec. LUIGI ANGELETTI; 1,758,729 mems.

Unione Italiana Quadri (UNIONQUADRI): Via A. Gramsci 34, 00197 Rome; tel. (06) 3611683; fax (06) 3225558; e-mail uquadri@tin.it; internet www.unionquadri.it; Pres. CORRADO ROSSITTO; Sec. ANTONIO DIONESALVI.

Principal Unions
Banking and Insurance

Federazione Autonoma Bancari Italiana (FABI) (Bank, Tax and Finance Workers): Via Tevere 46, 00198 Rome; tel. (06) 8415751; fax (06) 8559220; f. 1948; independent; Sec.-Gen. GIANFRANCO STEFFANI; 69,000 mems.

Federazione Autonoma Lavoratori Casse di Risparmio Italiane (FALCRI) (Savings Banks Workers): Via Mercato 5, Milan; tel. (02) 86460536; Via Carducci 4, Rome; Sec.-Gen. DAVIDE CATTANEO.

Federazione Italiana Bancari e Assicuratori (FIBA): Via Modena 5, 00184 Rome; tel. (06) 4741245; fax (06) 4746136; internet www.fiba.it; affiliated to the CISL; Gen. Sec. ELIGIO BONI; 58,980 mems.

Federazione Italiana Sindacale Lavoratori Assicurazioni Credito (Employees of Credit Institutions): Via Vicenza 5A, 00184 Rome; tel. (06) 448841; fax (06) 4457356; e-mail fisac.ced@mail.cgil.it; internet www.cgil.it/fisac; affiliated to the CGIL; Sec. NICOLETTA ROCCHI; 60,000 mems.

Federazione Nazionale Assicuratori (FNA) (Insurance Workers): Via Vincenzo Monti 25, Milan; Via Val Montebello 104, Rome; independent; Pres. LUIGI FERAZZI; Sec.-Gen. EZIO MARTONE.

Unione Italiana Lavoratori Credito e Assicurazioni (UILCA) (Credit and Assurance Co Workers): Via Lombardia 30, 00187 Rome; tel. (06) 4872132; fax (06) 484704; affiliated to the UIL; Sec. Gen. ELIO PORINO; 37,453 mems.

Building and Building Materials

Federazione Autonoma Italiana Lavoratori Cemento, Legno, Edilizia ed Affini (FAILCLEA) (Workers in Cement, Wood, Construction and Related Industries): c/o CISAL, Viale Giulio Cesare 21, 00192 Rome; affiliated to the CISAL; Sec. ENZO BOZZI.

Federazione Italiana Lavoratori delle Costruzioni a Affini (FILCA) (Building Industries' Workers): Via dei Mille 23, Rome; tel. (06) 497801; e-mail bonanni@filca.cisl.it; internet www.filca.cisl.it; f. 1955; affiliated to the CISL; Sec.-Gen. CESARE REGENZI; 188,009 mems.

Federazione Italiana Lavoratori Legno, Edili, Industrie Affini ed Estrattive (FILLEA) (Wood-workers, Construction Workers and Allied Trades): Via G. B. Morgagni 27, 00161 Rome; tel. (06) 441141; fax (06) 44235849; e-mail fillea@mail.cgil.it; internet www.cgil.it/fillea; affiliated to the CGIL; Sec.-Gen. CARLA CANTONE; 434,154 mems.

Federazione Nazionale Costruzioni (Construction): Lungotevere Sanzio 5, Rome; tel. (06) 585511; fax (06) 5815184; affiliated to the UGL; Sec. EGIDIO SANGUE.

Federazione Nazionale Lavoratori Edili Affini e del Legno (FeNEAL) (Builders and Woodworkers): Via Alessandria 171, 00198 Rome; tel.(06) 8547393; fax (06) 8547423; affiliated to the UIL; Sec.-Gen. FRANCO MARABOTTINI; 106,698 mems.

Chemical, Mining and Allied Industries

Federazione Lavoratori Energia Risorse Chimica Affini (FLERiCA) (Chemical and Allied Workers): Via Bolzano 16, Rome; tel. (06) 85565415; fax (06) 85565414; e-mail federazione@flerica.cisl.it; internet flerica.cisl.it; affiliated to the CISL; Sec.-Gen. ANTONINO SCALFARO.

Federazione Nazionale Chimici (Chemicals): Via Manin 53, Rome; tel. (06) 4742703; fax (06) 4746051; affiliate to the UGL; Sec. DOMENICO SCOPELLITI.

Unione Italiana Lavoratori Chimici, Energia e Manufatturiero (UILCEM) (Chemicals, Energy and Manufacturing Workers): Via Bolzano 16, 00198 Rome; tel. (06) 85565305; fax (06) 8417002; e-mail uilcem@uil.it; affiliated to the UIL; Sec.-Gen. ROMANO BELLISSIMA; 84,649 mems.

Clothing and Textiles

Federazione Italiana Lavoratori Tessili Abbigliamento, Calzaturieri (FILTEA) (Textile and Clothing Workers and Shoe Manufacturers): Via Leopoldo Serra 31, 00153 Rome; tel. (06) 5811380; fax (06) 5803182; e-mail filtea@uni.net; internet www.uni.net/filtea; f. 1966; affiliated to the CGIL; Gen. Sec. AGOSTINO MEGALE; 150,000 mems.

Federazione Italiana dei Lavoratori Tessili e Abbigliamento (FILTA-CISL): Via Goito 39, 00185 Rome; tel. (06) 44701263; fax (06) 4462544; e-mail fltnazio@tin.it; internet www.rcnet.net/evoluzione3/cisl; affiliated to the CISL; Gen. Sec. AUGUSTA RESTELLI; 125,084 mems.

Unione Italiana Lavoratori Tessili, Abbigliamento e Calzaturieri (UILTA): Via del Viminale 43, 00184 Rome; tel. (06) 4883486; fax (06) 4819421; affiliated to the UIL; Sec.-Gen. PASQUALE ROSSETTI.

Engineering and Metallurgy

Federazione Impiegati Operai Metallurgici (FIOM-CGIL) (Metalworkers): Corso Trieste 36, 00198 Rome; tel. (06) 852621; fax (06) 85303079; e-mail fiom@cgil.it; internet www.cgil.it/fiom; f. 1902; affiliated to the CGIL; Sec. CLAUDIO SABATTINI; 400,000 mems.

Federazione Italiana Metalmeccanici (FIM) (Metal Mechanic Workers): Corso Trieste 36, 00198 Rome; tel. (06) 84711; fax (06) 8471305; internet www.cisl.it/fim; affiliated to the CISL; Sec.-Gen. GIANNI ITALIA; 277,789 mems.

Federazione Nazionale Metalmeccanici: Via Amadeo 23, Rome; tel. (06) 4741808; fax (06) 4881236; affiliated to the UGL; Sec. DOMENICO FRESILLI.

Sindacato Nazionale Ingegneri Liberi Professionisti Italiana (SNILPI) (Liberal Professionals-Engineers): Via Salaria 292, 00199 Rome; Pres. Dott. Ing. LUIGI LUCHERINI; Sec.-Gen. Dott. Ing. GIUSEPPE MILONE.

Unione Italiana Lavoratori Metalmeccanici (UILM) (Metalworkers): Corso Trieste 36, 00198 Rome; tel. (06) 852621; fax (06) 85262203; e-mail uilm@uil.it; f. 1950; affiliated to the UIL; Sec.-Gen. TONINO REGAZZI; 100,534 mems.

Food and Agriculture

Confederazione Italiana Coltivatori (Farmers): Via Mariano Fortuny 20, 00196 Rome; tel. (06) 3227008; fax (06) 3208364; independent; Pres. GIUSEPPE AVOLIO; Vice-Pres. MASSIMO BELLOTTI.

Confederazione Italiana Dirigenti, Quadri e Impiegati dell' Agricoltura (CONFEDERDIA): Viale Beethoven 48, 00144 Rome; tel. (06) 5912808; fax (06) 5915014; e-mail confederdia@confederdia.it; internet www.confederdia.it; Pres. LUCIANO BOZZATO; Gen. Sec. TOMMASO BRANDONI.

Confederazione Nazionale Coltivatori Diretti (CONACOLTIVATORI) (Small-holders): Via XXIV Maggio 43, 00187 Rome; tel. (06) 46821; e-mail coldiretti@coldiretti.it; independent; Pres. PAOLO BEDONI; Sec.-Gen. Dott. FRANCO PASQUALI.

Federazione Italiana Salariati Braccianti Agricoli e Maestranze Specializzate (FISBA) (Permanent Unskilled and Skilled Agricultural Workers): Via Tevere 20, 00198 Rome; tel. (06) 8415455; f. 1950; Sec. ALBINO GORINI; 347,265 mems.

Federazione Lavoratori dell'Agroindustria (Workers in the Agricultural Industry): Via Leopoldo Serra 31, 00153 Rome; tel. (06)

585611; fax (06) 5880585; e-mail flai@mail.cgil.it; internet www.cgil.it/flai; f. 1988; affiliated to the CGIL; Sec.-Gen. GIANFRANCO BENZI; 438,000 mems.

Federazione Nazionale Coltivatori (Farmers): Via Massacciuccoli 8, Rome, tel. (06) 86219310; fax (06) 8621910; affiliated to the UGL; Sec. ROMANO BECHERINI.

Unione Coltivatori Italiana (UCI) (Farmers): Via in Lucina 10, 00186 Rome; tel. (06) 6871043; Pres. VINCENZO PANDOVINO.

Unione Generale Coltivatori (UGC): Via Tevere 44, 00198 Rome; tel. (06) 8552383; fax (06) 8553891; affiliated to the CISL; Pres. GAVINO DERUDA; 151,625 mems.

Unione Italiana Lavoratori Agroalimentari (UILA-UIL) (Food Workers): Via Savoia 80, 00198 Rome; tel. (06) 85301610; fax (06) 85303253; e-mail uila@uil.it; affiliated to the UIL; Sec. STEFANO MANTEGAZZA.

Unione Italiana Mezzadri e Coltivatori Diretti (UIMEC) (Land Workers): Via Tirso 26, 00198 Rome; tel. (06) 8418044; fax (06) 8413968; affiliated to the UILA-UIL; Sec. FURIO VENARUCCI; 100,000 mems.

Medical

Confedrazione Italiana Sindacati Medici Dirigenti (COSMED) (Doctors): c/o Anaao Assomed, via Barberini 3, 00187 Rome; tel. (06) 4820154; fax (06) 48903523; Man. SERAFINO ZUCCHELLI.

Federazione Italiana Servizi Territoriali (FIST) (Hospital and Regional Municipal Workers' Unions): Via Lancisi 25, 00161 Rome; tel. (06) 4425981; fax (06) 44230114; e-mail fist@cisl.it; internet www.mclink.it/com/fist; affiliated to the CISL; Sec.-Gen. ERMENEGILDO BONFANTI; 250,000 mems.

Federazione Nazionale Medici (Doctors): Via Amendola 7, Rome; tel. (06) 4870444; fax (06) 4874323; e-mail federmed@flashnet.it; affiliated to the UGL; Sec.-Gen. GIOVANNI PALOMBI.

Public Services

Confederazione dei Quadri Direttivi e Dirigenti della Funzione Pubblica (CONFEDIR) (Public Office Managers) Arco dei Banchi 8, 00186 Rome; tel. and fax (06) 68803688; Gen. Sec. ROBERTO CONFALONIERI.

Federazione Italiana Lavoratori Esattoriali (FILE) (Tax Collectors): Via Galileo Galilei 35, 00185 Rome; tel. (06) 70495198; fax (06) 77200528; affiliated to the UIL; Sec.-Gen. ANTONIO BARBERA.

Federazione Lavoratori Aziende Elettriche Italiane (FLAEI) (Workers in Italian Electrical Undertakings): Via Salaria 83, 00198 Rome; tel. (06) 8440421; fax (06) 8548458; e-mail nazionale@flaei.org; internet www.flaie.cds.it; f. 1948; affiliated to the CISL; Sec. ARSENIO CAROSI; 32,000 mems.

Federazione Lavoratori del Pubblico Impiego (FPI) (Public Sector Workers): Via Po 102, 00198 Rome; tel. (06) 852381; e-mail fpi@interbusiness.it; internet www.fpi.cisl.it; affiliated to the CISL; Sec.-Gen. RINO TARELLI.

Federazione Nazionale Energia (Energy): Via Filiberto 125; Rome tel. (06) 7005935; fax (06) 7003451; affiliated to the UGL; Sec. LUIGI DE NARDIS.

Federazione Nazionale Enti Locali (Employees of Local Authorities): Via Amendola 5, Rome; tel. (06) 4743418; fax (06) 4743853; affiliated to the UGL; Sec. GUIDO ANDERSON.

Federazione Nazionale Enti Pubblici (Public Employees): Via del Corea 13, Rome; tel. (06) 59056508; fax (06) 3226052; f. 1962; affiliated to the UGL; Gen. Sec. GIANFRANCO SCHETTINO.

Federazione Nazionale Lavoratori Funzione Pubblica: Via Leopoldo Serra 31, 00153 Rome; tel. (06) 585441; fax (06) 5836970; e-mail fp@cgil.it; internet www.cgil.it/fp; affiliated to the CGIL, Public Services International, and European Public Services Union (EPSU); Sec.-Gen. LAIMER ARMUZZI.

Federazione Nazionale Lavoratori Energia (Gas, Water and Electricity): Via Piemonte 32, 00187 Rome; tel. (06) 4620091; fax 4824246; e-mail casali-stampa@uni.net; internet www.cgil.it/fnle; affiliated to the CGIL; Sec. GIACOMO BERNI; 72,000 mems.

Federazione Nazionale Sanità (Sanitary Workers): Via Farini 16, Rome; tel. (06) 4814678; fax (06) 4814651; affiliated to the UGL; Sec. SALVATORE GALIZIA.

Unione Italiana Lavoratori Enti Locali (UILEE.LL.) (Local Authority Employees): Via Genova 24, 00184 Rome; tel. (06) 4873423; fax (06) 4873932; e-mail entilocali@uil.it; affiliated to the UIL; Gen. Sec. FABRIZIO LUCARINI; 89,179 mems.

Unione Italiana Lavoratori degli Organi Costituzionali (Employees of Constitutional Bodies): Via del Corso 173, 00186 Rome; tel. (06) 67609118; fax (06) 67604890; affiliated to the UIL; Sec.-Gen. SILVANO SGREVI.

Unione Italiana Lavoratori Pubblico Amministrazione (UILPA) (Public Office Workers): Via Emilio Lepido 46, 00175 Rome; tel. (06) 71588888; fax (06) 71582046; e-mail uilpa@uil.it; affiliated to the UIL; Sec.-Gen. SALVATORE BOSCO; 67,702 mems.

Unione Italiana Lavoratori Sanità (UIL Sanità) (Sanitary Workers): Via Nemorense 18, 00199 Rome; tel. (06) 8550164; fax (06) 8416777; e-mail uilsanita@uil.it; affiliated to UIL; Sec.-Gen. CARLO FIORDALISO; 98,669 mems.

Teachers

Cisl-Scuola (School Teachers): Via Bargoni 8, 00153 Rome; tel. (06) 583111; fax (06) 5881713; affiliated to the CISL; Sec.-Gen. DANIELA COLTURANI.

Cisl-Università (University Teachers): Via Rovereto 11, 00198 Rome; tel. (06) 8840772; fax (06) 8844977; affiliated to the CISL; Sec.-Gen. GIUSEPPE ACOCELLA.

Federazione Italiana Scuola Università e Ricerca (University Teachers): Via S. Croce in Gerusalemme 107, 00185 Rome; tel. (06) 757941; affiliated to the CISL; Gen. Sec MARIO GIOVANNI GAROFALO; 184,235 mems.

Federazione Nazionale Scuola ed Università (School and University Teachers): Via Manin 53, Rome; tel. (06) 4741200; fax (06) 4874738; affiliated to the UGL; Sec. ORESTE TOFANI.

Sindacato Nazionale Scuola (School Teachers): Via Leopoldo Serra 31, Rome; tel. (06) 585480; e-mail mail@cgilscuola.it; internet www.cgilscuola.it; affiliated to the CGIL; 97,149 mems (1997).

Unione Italiana Lavoratori Scuola (UIL Scuola) (School Workers): Via Marino Laziale 44, 00179 Rome; tel. (06) 7846941; fax (06) 7842858; e-mail uilscuola@uil.it; affiliated to the UIL; Sec.-Gen. MASSIMO DI MENNA; 59,402 mems.

Tourism and Entertainments

Federazione Informazione Spettacolo e Telecomunicazioni (FISTEL) (Actors, Artists and Media Workers): Via Palestro 30, 00185 Rome; tel. (06) 492171; fax (06) 4457330; affiliated to the CISL; Sec.-Gen. FULVIO GIACOMASSI; 43,388 mems.

Federazione Italiana Lavoratori Commercio Albergo Mensa e Servizi (FILCAMS) (Hotel and Catering Workers): Via Leopoldo Serra 31, 00153 Rome; tel. (06) 5885102; fax (06) 5885323; f. 1960; affiliated to the CGIL; Sec.-Gen. ALDO AMORETTI; 189,000 mems.

Federazione Italiana Personale Aviazione Civile (Aviation Employees): Via Ostiense 224, Rome; affiliated to the CGIL; Sec. PIERRO TORINO.

Federazione Italiana Sindacati Addetti Servizi Commerciali Affini e del Turismo (FISASCAT-CISL) (Commercial and Tourist Unions): Via Livenza 7, 00198 Rome; tel. (06) 8541042; fax (06) 8558057; internet www.reale.it/fisascat; Sec.-Gen. GIANNI BARATTA; 116,000 mems.

Federazione Nazionale Informazione e Spettacolo (Actors, Artists and Media Workers): Via Margutta 19, Rome; tel. (06) 324821; fax (06) 323420; affiliated to the UGL; Sec. GIANNI IMPROTA.

Sindacato Attori Italiani (SAI) (Actors): Via Ofanto 18, 00198 Rome; tel. (06) 8411288; fax (06) 8546780; e-mail sai-slc@cgil.it; internet www.cgil.it/sai-slc; affiliated to the CGIL; Sec.-Gen. MASSIMO GHINI.

Unione Italiana Lavoratori Turismo Commercio e Servizi (UILTuCS): Via Alessandria 112, 00198 Rome; tel. (06) 44251279; fax (06) 44251309; e-mail uiltucs@uil.it; f. 1977; affiliated to the UIL; Gen. Sec. BRUNO BOCO; 75,042 mems.

Transport and Telecommunications

Federazione Italiana dei Postelegrafonici (Postal, Telegraph and Telephone Workers): Via Cavour 185, 00187 Rome; tel. (06) 461321; affiliated to the CGIL; Sec. GIUSEPPE MASTRACCHI; 35,000 mems.

Federazione Italiana Trasporti Settore Marittimi (Italian Maritime): Via Boncompagni 19, 00187 Rome; tel. (06) 4689216; fax (06) 4825233; affiliated to the International Transport Workers' Federation; Gen. Sec. REMODI FIORE.

Federazione Italiana Sindacati dei Trasporti (FILT-CGIL): Via G. B. Morgagni 27, 00161 Rome; tel. (06) 442961; fax (06) 44293313; e-mail filt@mail.cgil.it; affiliated to the CGIL; Sec. PAOLO BRUTTI.

Federazione Italiana Trasporti (FIT): Via Boncompagni 19, 00187 Rome; tel. (06) 4689235; fax (06) 4825404; f. 1950; affiliated to the CISL; National Sec. LUIGI VAGLICA; 40,000 mems.

Federazione Nazionale Comunicazioni (Communications): Via Volturno 40, Rome; tel. (06) 4746714; fax (06) 49384693; affiliated to the UGL; Sec. SERAFINO CABRAS.

Federazione Nazionale Trasporti (Transport): Via Margutta 19, Rome; tel. (06) 324821; fax (06) 3232420; affiliated to the UGL; Sec. PAOLO SEGARELLI.

Federazione dei Sindacati Dipendenti Aziende di Navigazione (FEDERSINDAN): Rome; independent; Sec.-Gen. Dott. GIUSEPPE AURICCHIO.

Sindacato Lavoratori Communicazione (SLC) (Communications Workers): Piazza Sallustio 24, 00187 Rome; tel. (06) 421071; fax (06) 4824325; e-mail slc.sal@mail.cgil.it; internet www.cgil.it/slc; affiliated to the CGIL; Gen. Sec. FULVIO FAMMONI.

SLP—Federazione Lavoratori Poste e Appalti (Postal Workers): Via dell'Esquilino 38, 00185 Rome; internet www.slp-cisl.it; affiliated to the CISL; Sec.-Gen. ANTONINO SORGI.

UIL TRASPORTI (Transport Workers): Via Salaria 44, 00198 Rome; tel. (06) 852511; fax (06) 85350501; e-mail uiltrasporti@uil.it; affiliated to the UIL; Sec. SANDRO DEGNI; 103,687 mems.

Unione Italiana Lavoratori Postelegrafonici (UILPOST) (Post, Telegraph and Telephone Workers): Via Sallustiana 15, 00187 Rome; tel. (06) 4871213; fax (06) 4814403; e-mail uilpost@uil.it; affiliated to the UIL; Sec.-Gen. PAOLO TULLO; 30,853 mems.

Unione Italiana Lavoratori Telecomunicazioni (UILTE) (Telecommunications): Via Po 102, 00198 Rome; tel. (06) 8415654; fax (06) 8543179; e-mail segretaria@uilte.it; affiliated to the UIL; Sec.-Gen. LUIGI FERRANDO; 17,468 mems.

Miscellaneous

Federazione Nazionale Pensionati (FNP) (Pensioners): Via Castelfidardo 47, 00185 Rome; tel. (06) 448811; fax (06) 4452608; e-mail andrea.pellicari@fnp.cisl.it; internet fnp.cisl.it; f. 1952; affiliated to the CISL; Sec. CARMELO MUSCOLIMO; 1,180,000 mems.

Federazione Nazionale Pensionati dell'Unione Generale del Lavoro (Pensioners): Via Margutta 19, 00187 Rome; tel. (06) 32482248; fax (06) 3612027; e-mail pensionati@ugl.it; internet www.pensionatiugl.it; affiliated to the UGL.

Federazione Nazionale Terziario (Service Sector Workers): Via Margutta 19, 00187 Rome; tel. (06) 324821; fax (06) 3232420; affiliated to the UGL; Sec. LUIGI GABRIELE.

Sindacato Pensionati Italiani (Pensioners): Via Frentani 4A, 00185 Rome; tel. (06) 444811; fax (06) 4440941; e-mail spi.segretaria@mail.cgil.it; f. 1948; affiliated to the CGIL; Sec.-Gen. RAFFAELE MINELLI; 2,876,463 mems.

Unione Italiana Lavoratori Pensionati (UILP) (Pensioners): Via Po 162, 00198 Rome; tel. (06) 852591; fax (06) 8548632; e-mail uilpensionati@uil.it; affiliated to the UIL; Sec.-Gen. SILVANO MINIATI; 429,697 mems.

Unione Italiana Lavoratori Stampa, Informazione e Cultura (UILSIC) (Press, Media and Culture): Via Belisario 7, 00187 Rome; tel. (06) 42881974; fax (06) 42744897; affiliated to the UIL; Sec.-Gen. BRUNO DI COLA.

Co-operative Unions

Associazione Generale delle Cooperative Italiane (AGCI): Via A. Bargoni, 00153 Rome; tel. (06) 583271; fax (06) 58327210; e-mail agicimail@tin.it; internet www.agci.it; f. 1952; Pres. MAURIZIO ZAFFI.

Confederazione Cooperative Italiane (CONFCOOPERATIVE): Borgo S. Spirito 78, 00193 Rome; tel. (06) 680001; fax (06) 6868595; e-mail confcooperative@confcooperative.it; internet www.confcooperative.it; f. 1919; federation of co-operative unions; Pres. LUIGI MARINO; Sec.-Gen. VINCENZO MANNINO.

Lega Nazionale delle Cooperative e Mutue (National League of Co-operative and Friendly Societies): Via Guattani 9, 00161 Rome; tel. (06) 84439391; fax (06) 84439370; e-mail presidenza@legacoop.it; internet www.legacoop.it; f. 1886; 9 affiliated unions; Pres. IVANO BARBERINI.

Unione Nazionale Cooperative Italiane: Via San Sotero 32, 00165 Rome; tel. (06) 39366729; fax (06) 39375080; e-mail uncinazionale@mclink.it; internet www.uncinazionale.it; Pres. LUCIANO D'ULIZIA.

Transport

Direzione Generale della Motorizzazione Civile e del Trasporti in Concessione: Via Giuseppe Caraci 36, 00157 Rome; tel. (06) 41581; fax (06) 41582211; controls road transport and traffic, and public transport services (railways operated by private cos, motor-buses, trolley-buses, funicular railways and inland waterways); Dir-Gen. Dott. GIORGIO BERRUTI.

RAILWAYS

The majority of Italian lines are controlled by an independent state-owned corporation. In 1998 the total length of the network was 16,031 km, of which 10,359 km were electrified. Apart from the state railway system there are 27 local and municipal railway companies, many of whose lines are narrow gauge. There are metro systems in Rome, Milan and Naples; a metro system is also planned for Turin. A high-speed service is planned on the following routes: Rome–Milan–Turin, Naples–Rome, Milan–Genoa and Milan–Venice. In 1991 TAV, a semi-private company for the creation of a high-speed train network, was established; from 1998 it was wholly-owned by Ferrovie dello Stato. Work on the following lines was to be completed by 2006: Naples–Rome and Rome–Milan. In January 2001 it was announced that plans had been approved for the construction of a 52 km rail tunnel under the Alps linking France with Italy. Due to be completed in 2015, the tunnel was to be part of a new high-speed rail link between Turin and Lyons in France.

Ferrovie dello Stato SpA: Piazza della Croce Rossa 1, 00161 Rome; tel. (06) 84903758; fax (06) 84905186; Pres. C. DEMATTÈ; Man. Dir GIANCARLO CIMOLI.

ROADS

In 1997 there were an estimated 654,676 km of roads in Italy, including 46,043 km of major roads, 113,924 km of secondary roads and 6,957 km of motorway. All the *autostrade* (motorways) are toll roads except for the one between Salerno and Reggio Calabria and motorways in Sicily. By law ANAS is responsible for the planning, construction and management of the motorway network. Plans were announced in 1996 for the privatization of the motorway network and for the construction of a bridge linking Sicily to the Italian mainland. The 13-km Mount Frejus highway tunnel, linking Italy and France through the Alps, opened in 1980.

Autostrade SpA: Via Alberto Berganini 50, 00159 Rome; tel. (06) 43632121; fax (06) 43632131; e-mail info@autostrade.it; internet www.autostrade.it; maintenance and management of motorway network.

Ente Nazionale per le Strade (National Road Board): Via Monzambano 10, 00185 Rome; tel. (06) 44461; f. 1928 as Azienda Nazionale Autonoma delle Strade, name changed as above 1995; responsible for the administration of state roads and their improvement and extension; Pres. GIUSEPPE D'ANGIOLINO.

SHIPPING

In 1998 the Italian merchant fleet (1,329 vessels) had a displacement of 6,818,632 grt.

Direzione Generale della Marina Mercantile: Via dell'Arte 16, 00144 Rome.

Genoa

Costa Crociere: Via Gabriele D'Annunzio 2, 16121 Genoa; tel. (010) 54831; fax (010) 5483290; passenger and cargo service; Mediterranean–North, Central and South America; Caribbean cruises; Chair. NICOLA COSTA.

'Garibaldi' Società Cooperativa di Navigazione Srl: Piazza Dante 8, 16121 Genoa; tel. (010) 581635; fax (010) 5702386; f. 1918; tanker and cargo services; Pres. GIAN FRANCO VIALE.

'Italia di Navigazione' SpA: Torre WTC, Via de Marini 1, Genoa; tel. (010) 24021; fax (010) 2402386; f. 1932; freight services to Mediterranean, and North, South and Central America; Chair. ANTONIO D'AMICO; CEO CESARE D'AMICO.

Messina, Ignazio and C. SpA: Via G. d'Annunzio 91, 16121 Genoa; tel. (010) 53961; fax (010) 5396264; e-mail info@messinaline.it; internet www.messinaline.it; services to Arabian Gulf, India, Pakistan, Nigeria, North, East, South and West Africa, Libya and Near East, Red Sea, Malta, Europe; Chair. GIANFRANCO MESSINA.

Navigazione Alta Italia, SpA: Via Corsica 19, 16128 Genoa; tel. (010) 56331; f. 1906; worldwide dry and bulk cargo; Chair. and Man. Dir SEBASTIANO CAMELI; Gen. Man. ROMANO GUGLIELMINI.

Naples

Garolla Fratelli SpA: Pontile Falvio Giola 45, 80133 Naples; tel. (081) 5534477; Chair. R. GAROLLA; Dirs F. GAROLLA, C. GAROLLA.

Fratelli Grimaldi Armatori: Via M. Campodisola 13, 80133 Naples; tel. (081) 205466; passenger, cargo, containers and tramp to Europe, Middle East, South, Central and North America; Dirs M. GRIMALDI, G. GRIMALDI, A. GRIMALDI, U. GRIMALDI.

Tirrenia di Navigazione SpA: Head Office: Palazzo Sirignano, Rione Sirignano 2, 80121 Naples; tel. (081) 7201111; fax (081) 7201441; Man. Dir and Dir-Gen. FRANCO PECORINI.

Palermo

Sicilia Regionale Marittima SpA—SIREMAR: Via Principe di Belmonte, 90139 Palermo; tel. (091) 582688; fax (091) 582267; ferry services; Pres. Dott GIUSEPPE RAVERA; Man. Dir CARLO COSTA.

Sicula Oceanicas SA—SIOSA: Via Mariano Stabile 179, 90139 Palermo; tel. (091) 217939; f. 1941; cruises, passenger and cargo; Italy to North Europe, South, Central, North America; Dir G. GRIMALDI.

Rome

D'Amico Fratelli, Armatori, SpA: Via Liguria 36, 00187 Rome; tel. (06) 4671; e-mail damiship@tin.it; dry cargo and tankers; Dirs GIUSEPPE D'AMICO, VITTORIO D'AMICO.

Trieste

Fratelli Cosulich SpA: Piazza S. Antonio 4, 34122 Trieste; tel. (040) 6797111; fax (040) 630844; f. 1854; shipowners and shipping agents; domestic network and cargo to Near East, Red Sea, Hong Kong, Singapore, New York and Zürich; Chair. and Man. Dir GEROLIMICH COSULICH.

Lloyd Triestino di Navigazione SpA: Palazzo della Marineria, Passeggio S. Andrea 4, 34123 Trieste; tel. (040) 3180111; fax (040) 3180296; e-mail headoffice@lloydtriestino.it; internet www .lloydtriestino.it; f. 1836; cargo services by container, roll on/roll off and conventional vessels to Africa, Australasia and Far East; privatized 1998; Pres. CHENG YUNG-FA; Vice-Pres. PIER LUIGI MANESCHI; Man. Dir BRONSON HSIEH.

Venice

Adriatica di Navigazione SpA: Zattere 1411, CP 705, 30123 Venice; tel. (041) 781611; fax (041) 781894; e-mail adrnav@ interbusiness.it; internet www.adriatica.it; f. 1937; passenger services from Italy, Albania, Croatia and Yugoslavia; Pres. GIORGIO GROSSO; Man. Dir ANTONIO CACUCCI.

SHIPPING ASSOCIATION

Confederazione Italiana Armatori—CONFITARMA: Piazza S. Apostoli 66, 00187 Rome; tel. (06) 6991261; fax (06) 6789473; f. 1901; shipowners' asscn; Pres. PAOLO CLERICI; Dir-Gen. LUIGI PERISSICH; 140 mems.

CIVIL AVIATION

National Airline

Alitalia (Linee Aeree Italiane): Viale Alessandro Marchetti 111, 00148 Rome; tel. (06) 65621; fax (06) 7093065; internet www .alitalia.com; f. 1946; state-owned; international services throughout Europe and to Africa, North and South America, the Middle East, the Far East and Australia; Chair. FAUSTO CERETI; CEO FRANCESCO MENGOZZI.

Other Airlines

Air Dolomiti: Via Senatore Augusto Tambarin 36, 34077 Ronchi dei Legionari; tel. (0481) 477711.

Air Europe: Via Carlo Noè 3, 21013 Gallarate; tel. (0331) 713111; fax (0331) 713850; e-mail marketing@aireurope.it; internet www .aireurope.it; f. 1988; international charter flights; Man. Dir ISABELLA ANTONELLO.

Air One: Via Sardegna 14, 00187 Rome; tel. (06) 478761; fax (06) 4820399; internet www.flyairone.it; f. 1983 as Aliadratica, adopted current name in 1995; private co; domestic flights; Chair GIOVANNI SEBASTIANI; Pres. CARLO TOTO.

Air Sicilia: Via G. La Rosa 13, 95041 Caltagirone; tel. (0993) 58015; fax (0993) 23273; internet www. airsicilia.it.

Alpi Eagles: Via Encrco Mattei 1c, 30020 Margon; tel. (041) 5997777; fax (041) 5997707.

Azzurair: Via Pietro Paleocapa 3d, 24121 Bergamo; tel. (035) 4160311; fax (035) 4160330; e-mail paola.garofalo@ azzurraair.it; internet www.azzurraair.it; f. 1995; scheduled and chartered European flights; CEO DOMINIC R. ATTARD.

Eureca: Hangar 39, Aeroporto, 24050 Orio al Serio; tel. (035) 4203911; internet www.eureca.it.

Gandalfair: Via Aeroporto 13, 24050 Orio al Serio; tel. (035) 4595011; internet www.gandalfair.it.

Meridiana SpA: Zona Industriale A, 07026 Olbia, Sardinia; tel. (0789) 52600; fax (0789) 23661; e-mail anna.sacripanti@meridiana .it; internet www.meridiana.it; f. 1963; scheduled and charter services throughout Italy and Europe; Pres. and Man. Dir FRANCO TRIVI.

Tourism

A great number of tourists are attracted to Italy by its Alpine and Mediterranean scenery, sunny climate, Roman archaeological remains, medieval and Baroque churches, Renaissance towns and palaces, paintings and sculpture and famous opera houses. Each of the 95 provinces has a Board of Tourism; there are also about 300 Aziende Autonome di Cura, Soggiorno e Turismo, with information about tourist accommodation and health treatment, and about 2,000 Pro Loco Associations concerned with local amenities. In 1999 a total of 32.1m. foreign visitors (including excursionists) arrived in Italy; tourist receipts totalled US \$29,714m. in 1997.

Compagnia Italiana Turismo: Via Nazionale 196, 00184 Rome; tel. (06) 48787294; fax (06) 4819120.

Dipartimento del Turismo—Ministry of Industry, Commerce and Handicrafts and Foreign Trade: Presidenza del Consiglio dei Ministri, Via della Ferratella in Laterano 51, 00184 Rome; tel. (06) 77321; fax (06) 77209808; Dir-Gen. Dott. STEFANO LANDI.

Ente Nazionale Italiano per il Turismo (ENIT) (Italian State Tourist Board): Via Marghera 2, 00185 Rome; tel. (06) 49711; fax (06) 4463379; e-mail sedecentrale.enit@interbusiness.it; f. 1919; Chair. AMEDEO OTTAVIANI; Dir-Gen. PIERGIORGIO TOGNI.

JAMAICA

Introductory Survey

Location, Climate, Language, Religion, Flag, Capital

Jamaica is the third largest island in the Caribbean Sea, lying 145 km (90 miles) to the south of Cuba and 160 km (100 miles) to the south-west of Haiti. The climate varies with altitude, being tropical at sea-level and temperate in the mountain areas. The average annual temperature is 27°C (80°F) and mean annual rainfall is 198 cm (78 ins). The official language is English, although a local patois is widely spoken. The majority of the population belong to Christian denominations, the Church of God being the most numerous. The national flag (proportions 2 by 1) consists of a diagonal yellow cross on a background of black (hoist and fly) and green (above and below). The capital is Kingston.

Recent History

Jamaica, a British colony from 1655, was granted internal self-government in 1959, and full independence, within the Commonwealth, was achieved on 6 August 1962. Jamaica formed part of the West Indies Federation between 1958 and 1961, when it seceded, following a referendum. The Federation was dissolved in May 1962. The two dominant political figures after the Second World War were the late Sir Alexander Bustamante, leader of the Jamaica Labour Party (JLP), who retired as Prime Minister in 1967, and Norman Manley, a former Premier and leader of the People's National Party (PNP), who died in 1969. The JLP won the elections of 1962 and 1967 but, under the premiership of Hugh Shearer, it lost the elections of February 1972 to the PNP, led by Michael Manley, the son of Norman Manley. Michael Manley advocated democratic socialism and his Government put great emphasis on social reform and economic independence.

The early 1970s were marked by escalating street violence and crime, with gang warfare rife in the deprived areas of Kingston. More than 160 people were killed in the first half of 1976, and in June the Government declared a state of emergency (which remained in force until June 1977). Despite the unrest, high unemployment and severe economic stagnation, the PNP was returned to power in December 1976 with an increased majority. By January 1979, however, there was again widespread political unrest, and violent demonstrations signalled growing discontent with the Manley administration. In February 1980, in the context of a worsening economic crisis, Manley rejected the stipulation of the International Monetary Fund (IMF) that economic austerity measures be undertaken, as a condition of its making further loans to Jamaica. He called a general election to seek support for his economic policies and his decision to end dependence on the IMF. The electoral campaign was one of the most violent in Jamaica's history. In the October election the JLP received about 57% of the total votes and won 51 of the 60 seats in the House of Representatives. Edward Seaga, the leader of the JLP, became Prime Minister; he supported closer political and economic links with the USA and the promotion of free enterprise. Seaga severed diplomatic relations with Cuba in October 1981, and secured valuable US financial support for the economy. Negotiations on IMF assistance were resumed.

In November 1983, before the completion of a new electoral roll, Seaga announced that an election would take place in mid-December. Only four days were allowed for the nomination of candidates, and the PNP, unable to present candidates at such short notice, refused to participate and declared the elections void. The JLP, opposed in only six constituencies (by independent candidates), won all 60 seats in the House of Representatives and formed a one-party legislature.

Devaluations of the Jamaican dollar and the withdrawal of food subsidies provoked demonstrations and sporadic violence in 1984, as the prices of foodstuffs and energy increased by between 50% and 100%. Despite government attempts to offset the effects of these economic austerity measures, imposed at the instigation of the IMF, unemployment, together with the consequences of illicit trading in drugs, contributed to a rise in the incidence of crime and violence, especially in Kingston. In 1985 another increase in fuel prices precipitated further violent demonstrations in the capital and industrial unrest in the public sector. In May 1986 Seaga defied recommendations by the IMF and other aid agencies, and introduced an expansionary budget for 1986/87, in an attempt to stimulate economic growth.

Municipal elections took place in July 1986, having been postponed three times. The PNP obtained control of 11 of the 13 municipalities in which polling took place, winning 57% of the total votes. A significant increase in drugs-related violence in mid-1987 prompted the Government to announce more severe punishments for drugs-related offences.

In September 1988 Jamaica was struck by 'Hurricane Gilbert', the most damaging storm in the country's recorded history. More than 100,000 homes were destroyed, while the economy, particularly the agriculture sector, was severely disrupted. Seaga's successful efforts to secure international aid won him some initial support, but this soon declined, particularly following controversy over the alleged preferential allocation of relief resources to JLP supporters.

After a brief, and relatively peaceful, campaign, a general election took place in February 1989. The PNP received about 56% of the votes cast, thereby securing 45 of the 60 seats in the House of Representatives. Manley, who had developed a more moderate image during his years in opposition, again became Prime Minister. The Government conceded the necessity for a devaluation of the Jamaican dollar, which was announced in October. Unusually for Jamaican politics, the two main parties achieved a limited consensus on the pursuit of an economic policy of austerity, despite its unpopularity. There was also agreement that further action should be taken against the drugs trade. The Government was particularly anxious to prevent the use of Jamaican shipping and aviation for the smuggling of illegal drugs, and demanded increased security measures, despite the consequent impediment to normal trade movements.

At local elections in March 1990, the PNP won control of 12 of the 13 local councils, obtaining some 60% of the votes cast. During 1990 there was disagreement within the opposition JLP: five MPs criticized Seaga's alleged autocratic leadership, and were banned by him from standing as JLP candidates at the next general election. New economic adjustment measures (including a further devaluation of the Jamaican dollar) were adopted in January, in order to secure another IMF stand-by arrangement. In June a five-year economic development plan was announced, as part of the Government's programme of deregulation and reform. However, the cost of living continued to rise, prompting industrial unrest in late 1991.

In December 1991 controversy surrounding the waiving of taxes worth some US $30m. that were owed to Jamaica by an international petroleum company, Shell, resulted in the resignation of Horace Clarke, the Minister of Mining and Energy, and Percival Patterson, the Deputy Prime Minister, amid opposition allegations of corruption and misconduct. Patterson requested not to be included in the new Cabinet (which was reorganized following the scandal), but remained as Chairman of the PNP. In March 1992 Manley announced his resignation, owing to ill health, from the premiership and from the presidency of the PNP. Patterson was subsequently elected as Manley's successor by members of the PNP, and was appointed Prime Minister at the end of the month.

During 1992 there was a marked increase in violent crime, much of which appeared to be politically motivated. Speculation that the Government would organize an early general election intensified in the first few months of 1993, following reports that public support for the JLP had diminished considerably. Patterson's PNP duly secured 52 of the 60 seats in the House of Representatives at a general election contested on 30 March 1993. The scale of the PNP victory was widely attributed to the success of Patterson's populist overtures to the island's majority population of African origin, and a perceived shift in political influence away from the capital, traditionally a power base of the JLP (which won the remaining eight seats). In April Patterson announced plans to reform and modernize the electoral system. However, allegations of electoral malpractice and demands by the JLP for an official inquiry into suspected procedural abuses

2170

were rejected by the PNP, prompting the JLP to boycott the official opening of Parliament later in the month. By February 1994 attempts at electoral reform had been undermined by the resignation of the Chairman of the Electoral Advisory Committee (EAC), and by the failure of the EAC to appoint a new Director of Elections. Demands for constitutional and electoral reform continued, and the JLP repeatedly accused the Government of seeking to delay progress towards any such reforms. Proposals drafted in late 1994 recommended the establishment of a permanent electoral commission to supervise elections, the publication of a revised register of voters every six months, and rules governing political campaigning and the nomination of candidates. An electronic voter registration system was installed in 1996 and new electoral rolls were completed in late 1997.

Industrial relations deteriorated in 1994, and there was further industrial unrest in 1995, as workers in both the public and private sectors argued for large pay increases to compensate for high rates of inflation. Meanwhile, the country's poor economic performance (particularly its high inflation rate and increasing trade deficit) and an increase in violent crime in Kingston compounded widespread dissatisfaction with the Government.

In early 1995 widespread dissatisfaction with the leadership of Edward Seaga of the JLP was reported among party members. However, Seaga survived an attempt to remove him as leader of the party in March, and in September the party leadership dismissed the main critics of Seaga as prospective parliamentary candidates for the JLP. In October Bruce Golding, who had resigned as Chairman of the JLP in February after disagreements with Seaga, announced the formation of a political party, the National Democratic Movement (NDM). The NDM, which aimed to achieve constitutional reform, including the introduction of an elected, executive president, gathered support from former members of both the JLP and the PNP.

In an effort to stabilize the economy, and, in particular, to address the problem of continuing industrial unrest, in 1996 the Government sought the agreement of a 'social contract' with trade unions and the private sector. In return for a commitment to increase its efforts to reduce inflation, the Government hoped to secure an undertaking from the labour organizations to moderate their wage demands. In July the Government implemented a 60% increase in the minimum wage. However, efforts to establish a 'social contract' continued to be frustrated during 1997 owing to trade union intransigence concerning demands for salary increases.

A general election was held on 18 December 1997, at which the PNP won 56% of the votes cast and 50 of the 60 seats in the House of Representatives. The JLP obtained 39% of the votes and secured 10 seats, but the NDM, which won 5% of the votes, failed to gain parliamentary representation. It was estimated that 67% of the electorate participated in the election. Patterson, who was subsequently sworn in as Prime Minister for a third consecutive term, appointed a new Cabinet in January 1998 and announced plans for Jamaica to become a republic within five years; a referendum on proposed constitutional reform was expected to be held in 2001.

Local elections, which had been repeatedly postponed since 1993 following allegations of electoral malpractice, finally took place in September 1998. The PDP gained control of all 13 local councils, one of which had previously been controlled by the JLP. The NDM, which had called for the introduction of further electoral reforms in order to prevent procedural abuses, did not contest the elections, while Seaga resigned from the JLP leadership for three months in protest at the party's decision to contest the elections; Seaga opposed the decision on the grounds of possible electoral malpractice.

In 1998 and 1999 there were many public protests against police actions and the deepening economic crisis, several of which resulted in riots. The continuing unrest led to the imposition of a curfew in Kingston in October 1998. In the same month a firebomb attack was made on Parliament although no-one was hurt. There was further unrest in April 1999 following the announcement made in the 1999/2000 budget proposals of a significant increase in the price of diesel. The JLP and NDM, while initially helping to organize the protests, disassociated themselves from the subsequent violence, in which eight people were killed and many businesses were burnt or looted. The Government later agreed to reduce the proposed increase. In July the authorities announced that army personnel were to be deployed on patrols in greater Kingston in an attempt to combat the high incidence of criminal activity, the majority of which was reportedly related to drugs-trafficking. In October the British

Government announced that it would contribute £2.9m. in grant assistance towards a programme to reform and modernize the Jamaican police force. In early September 2000 the Jamaican Government announced the establishment of a specialized police unit to combat organized crime. In October 2000 an investigation was initiated in response to widespread allegations of corruption in the police force, which included involvement in drugs-trafficking and the illicit recording of ministerial telephone conversations.

In July 1999 the JLP's central executive voted to suspend the party's deputy leader, Mike Henry. Henry, who was replaced by Dwight Nelson, had been accused of publicly criticizing Seaga earlier in the year. In November the recently-established pressure group, Citizens for Civil Society (CCS), organized a demonstration to protest at what it termed Seaga's 'ineffective' leadership of the opposition and to demand his resignation. In the same month the CCS staged a protest march to demand the dismissal of the Minister of National Security and Justice, Keith (K. D.) Knight, whom the CCS held responsible for the country's high crime rate, and that of the Minister of Finance and Planning, Dr Omar Davies, whom the CCS accused of mishandling the economy. The country's police federation, however, indicated its support for Knight, while Prime Minister Patterson criticized the CCS's tactic of organizing protest marches, which he claimed diverted the attention of the security forces from their anti-crime activities.

In February 2000 the Ministry of Industry and Investment merged with the Ministry of Commerce and Technology. On 25 November Sir Florizel Augustus Glasspole, who had been Governor-General in 1973–1991, died.

A decision reached in November 1993 by the Judicial Committee of the Privy Council in the United Kingdom (in its capacity as the final court of appeal for the Jamaican legal system) to commute to life imprisonment the death sentences imposed on two Jamaicans in 1979, in recognition of their prolonged suffering in anticipation of execution, threw doubt on the legal position of many similarly-sentenced prisoners in Jamaica and other Caribbean Commonwealth countries, given the recommendation of the Judicial Committee that all executions not effected within five years of sentencing should be subject to review, with a recommendation for commutation. In January 1998 Jamaica withdrew from a UN treaty that had hitherto allowed prisoners sentenced to death to appeal for a review by the UN Commission on Human Rights and later that year it also withdrew from the Organization of American States' Inter-American Court of Human Rights. In mid-February 2001, following legislative approval in November 2000, Patterson and 10 other Caribbean leaders signed an agreement to establish a Caribbean Court of Justice, based in Trinidad and Tobago. The Court was to replace the Privy Council as the final court of appeal, and would allow for the executions of convicted criminals. The JLP opposed the move, and demanded that a referendum be held on the issue.

In early March 2001 the PNP was defeated by the JLP in a by-election in North-East St Ann, traditionally a stronghold of the governing party.

Relations between Jamaica and the USA have been hampered by persistent demands by the USA for the eradication of Jamaica's marijuana crop. In May 1997, after months of negotiation, the two countries concluded a counter-narcotics agreement, permitting US drugs-enforcement agents to pursue suspected drugs-traffickers in Jamaican airspace and territorial waters. In August 1999 a Jamaican delegation visited the USA to discuss the prospect of increasing US assistance in measures aimed at combating crime.

Diplomatic relations with Cuba were resumed in mid-1990, and in February 1994 the two countries agreed a maritime border delimitation treaty. Relations with Cuba were consolidated further during a visit to that country in mid-1997 by Prime Minister Patterson and in mid-1998 when President Castro visited Jamaica.

Government

The Head of State is the British monarch, who is represented locally by the Governor-General, who is appointed on the recommendation of the Prime Minister in consultation with the Leader of the Opposition. The Governor-General acts, in almost all matters, on the advice of the Cabinet.

Legislative power is vested in the bicameral Parliament: the Senate, with 21 appointed members, and the House of Representatives, with 60 elected members. Thirteen members of the Senate are appointed by the Governor-General on the advice of the Prime Minister and eight on the advice of the Leader of the Opposition. Members of the House are elected by universal adult suffrage for five years (subject to dissolution). Executive power lies with the Cabinet. The Prime Minister is appointed from the House of Representatives by the Governor-General, and is the leader of the party that holds the majority of seats in the House of Representatives. The Cabinet is responsible to Parliament.

Defence

In August 2000 the Jamaica Defence Force consisted of 2,830 men on active service, including an army of 2,500, a coastguard of 190 and an air wing of 140 men. There are reserves of some 953. Defence expenditure in 2000 was budgeted at J \$2,100m.

Economic Affairs

In 1998, according to estimates by the World Bank, Jamaica's gross national product (GNP), measured at average 1996–98 prices, was US \$4,481m., equivalent to US \$1,740 per head (or US \$3,344 per head on an international purchasing-power parity basis). During 1990–98 GNP per head was estimated to have increased, in real terms, by an average of 0.7% per year. Over the same period, the population increased at an average annual rate of 1.0%. Jamaica's gross domestic product (GDP) increased, in real terms, at an average annual rate of 0.1% in 1990–99; GDP declined by 0.5% in 1998 and by an estimated 0.4% in 1999.

Agriculture (including forestry and fishing) contributed an estimated 6.9% of GDP in 1999, and engaged an estimated 21.0% of the economically active population in 1998. The principal cash crops are sugar cane (sugar accounted for an estimated 6.3% of total export earnings in 1998/99), bananas, coffee, citrus fruit and cocoa. The cultivation of vegetables, fruit and rice is being encouraged, in an attempt to reduce imports and diversify agricultural exports. According to the World Bank, agricultural GDP increased at an average annual rate of 2.3% in 1990–99, by 0.2% in 1998 and by an estimated 1.7% in 1999. In November of that year the Inter-American Development Bank (IDB—see p. 212) approved a US \$22m. loan to the Ministry of Agriculture to improve competitiveness in the sector.

Industry (including mining, manufacturing, public utilities and construction) contributed an estimated 27.7% of GDP in 1999, and engaged 18.2% of the economically active population in 1998. According to the World Bank, industrial GDP declined at an average rate of 0.6% per year in 1990–99. The sector declined by 1.4% in 1998 and by an estimated 0.1% in 1999.

Mining and quarrying contributed an estimated 4.6% of GDP in 1998, but engaged only 0.5% of the active labour force. Mining is the principal productive sector of the economy, and in 1998/99 bauxite and its derivative, alumina (aluminium oxide), accounted for an estimated 43.2% of total export earnings. Bauxite, of which Jamaica is one of the world's leading producers, is the major mineral mined, but there are also reserves of marble, gypsum, limestone, silica and clay. Bauxite production fell slightly in 2000, to 11.3m. metric tons, but was expected to increase in 2001. Alumina output rose to 3.6m. tons in 2000; production was forecast to rise further in 2001.

Manufacturing contributed an estimated 12.4% of GDP in 1999, and engaged some 8.9% of the active labour force in 1998. Much of the activity in the sector is dependent upon the processing of agricultural products and bauxite. Petroleum-refining is also important. The export of garments, mainly to the USA, became increasingly important during the 1980s, providing an estimated 11.9% of total export earnings in 1998/99. According to the World Bank, manufacturing GDP increased at an average annual rate of 1.8% during 1989–99, but declined by an estimated 3.9% in 1998 and by an estimated 0.9% in 1999.

Energy is derived principally from imported hydrocarbon fuels. Most of Jamaica's petroleum requirements are fulfilled by imports from Venezuela and Mexico. Imports of mineral fuels and lubricants accounted for an estimated 9.8% of the total value of merchandise imports in 1998/99. In March 2001 the Government sold 80% of the country's electricity company, Jamaica Public Service Co, to the US-based Mirant Corporation.

The services sector contributed an estimated 65.4% of GDP in 1999, and engaged some 60.7% of the active labour force in 1998. The principal earner of foreign exchange is tourism. Tourist arrivals exceeded 1m. for the first time in 1987 and totalled an estimated 1.2m. in 1998. The largest proportion of tourists is from the USA (67.7% in 1998). Earnings from tourism

reached an estimated US \$1,300m. in 2000. According to the World Bank, the GDP of the services sector increased at an average annual rate of 0.9% in 1989–99. The sector increased by 0.2% in 1998 and decreased by an estimated 0.1% in 1999.

In 1999 Jamaica recorded a visible trade deficit of US \$1,137.7m., and there was a deficit of US \$255.7m. on the current account of the balance of payments. In 1998 the principal source of imports (50.9%) was the USA. Other major suppliers in that year were Trinidad and Tobago, Japan and the United Kingdom. In that year the United Kingdom was the principal market for exports (12.1%), while Canada, Norway and the USA were among other important purchasers. The principal exports in 1998/99 were bauxite and alumina, garments, sugar and bananas. The principal imports in 1998/99 were raw materials, consumer goods (including food), capital goods (notably machinery and transport equipment) and mineral fuels. The illegal production of hemp (marijuana) is also believed to generate significant export revenue.

In the financial year ending 31 March 1999 Jamaica's overall budget deficit was estimated at J \$19,171m. Total external debt in 1999 was US \$4,069m. In that year the cost of debt-servicing was US \$674m., and in the budget for 1999/2000 some 62% of total expenditure was allocated to debt-servicing. The average annual rate of inflation was 29.6% in 1990–98, and stood at 6.0% in 1999 and 8.2% in 2000. Some 15.5% of the labour force were unemployed in 1998.

Jamaica is a founding member of the Caribbean Community and Common Market (CARICOM—see p. 142) and of the IDB (see p. 212).

The Jamaican economy, which was hampered in the 1990s by persistent fiscal imbalances and a high rate of inflation, was severely affected by a crisis in the financial sector in 1995–96. State intervention in troubled banks and insurance companies proved extremely costly and led to an increased fiscal deficit (reaching the equivalent of some 12% of GDP in 1998). Considerable progress was none the less made in reforming the financial sector in the late 1990s, while the Government continued to implement a policy of privatization of state assets and of increased trade liberalization. In the late 1990s bauxite and alumina production rose significantly, although weak international market prices meant that the sector's improved productivity did not create increased revenue. Following the re-opening of the US-owned Kaiser Aluminium bauxite refinery in late 2000, the industry was expected to resume shipments of some 400,000 metric tons per year. The sugar and coffee industries were both affected by aberrant climatic conditions and a lack of investment. However, output of some 300,000 tons of sugar was predicted for 2001/02: a significant increase on the 216,000 tons produced in the previous season. Despite the adverse conditions, the Government's stringent monetary policy succeeded in reducing the rate of increase in consumer prices from 31% in 1995/96 to 6.0% in 1999, although this increased to 8.2% in 2000. Although a lower inflation rate resulted in lower wage demands, industrial unrest increased in 1998 and the Government was criticized for inhibiting economic growth; GDP declined, in real terms, in 1996/97, 1997/98 and 1998/99, and was expected to register growth of only 1.0% in 1999/2000. In March 1999 the Government announced that it was to introduce a significant rise in the price of diesel in order to increase revenue from taxation. The announcement prompted widespread protests, which were estimated to have cost the economy between J \$10,250m. and J \$14,250m., thereby revealing the extent to which the Jamaican economy remains highly vulnerable to domestic and external pressures. In 2000 Jamaica entered into a Staff Monitored Programme (SMP) with the International Monetary Fund, which the Government believed would encourage foreign investment.

Social Welfare

Social welfare is undertaken by the Government. The Social Development Commission arranges and co-ordinates social welfare in the villages. Contributory national insurance and housing trust schemes are administered by the Government. In 1996 Jamaica had 24 public hospitals and 371 health centres. In the same year there were 140.1 physicians and 64.5 nurses per 100,000 inhabitants.

Education

Primary education is compulsory in certain districts, and free education is ensured. The education system (which begins at six years of age) consists of a primary cycle of six years, followed by two secondary cycles of three and four years, respectively.

In 1998 enrolment at primary schools included 95.6% of children in the relevant age-group (males 95.5%; females 95.7%), while enrolment at secondary schools was equivalent to only 69.8% of children in the appropriate age-group (males 67.5%; females 72.1%). In 1990 an estimated 1.6% of the adult population had received no schooling, and in 2000 it was estimated that some 13.3% of the adult population were illiterate. Higher education is provided by technical colleges and by the University of the West Indies, which has five faculties situated at its Mona campus in Kingston. Education was declared the first priority for special attention in the 1999/2000 budget proposals. Government expenditure on education during the financial year 1997/98 was estimated to be some J $16,400m., representing about 19% of total budgetary expenditure.

Public Holidays

2001: 1 January (New Year's Day), 28 February (Ash Wednesday), 13 April (Good Friday), 16 April (Easter Monday), 23 May (Labour Day), 5 August (Emancipation Day), 6 August (Independence Day), 15 October (National Heroes' Day), 25 December (Christmas Day), 26 December (Boxing Day).

2002: 1 January (New Year's Day), 13 February (Ash Wednesday), 29 March (Good Friday), 1 April (Easter Monday), 23 May (Labour Day), 4 August (Emancipation Day), 5 August (Independence Day), 21 October (National Heroes' Day), 25 December (Christmas Day), 26 December (Boxing Day).

Weights and Measures

Both the imperial and the metric systems are in use.

Statistical Survey

Sources (unless otherwise stated): Statistical Institute of Jamaica, 9 Swallowfield Rd, Kingston 5, Jamaica; tel. 926-2175; fax 926-4859; e-mail statinja@infochan.com; internet www.statinja.com; Jamaica Information Service, 58A Half Way Tree Rd, POB 2222, Kingston 10, Jamaica; tel. 926-3740; fax 926-6715; e-mail jis@jis.gov.jm; internet www.jis.gov.jm.

Area and Population

AREA, POPULATION AND DENSITY

Area (sq km)	10,991*
Population (census results)	
8 June 1982	2,205,507
7 April 1991	
Males	1,134,386
Females	1,180,093
Total	2,314,479
Population (official estimates at mid-year)	
1996	2,515,000
1997	2,554,000
1998	2,576,000
Density (per sq km) at mid-1998	234.4

* 4,243.6 sq miles.

PARISHES

	Area (sq miles)	Population (estimates, 1994)	Parish capitals (with population at 1991 census)
Kingston . .	8.406 ⎫	697,000	Kingston M.A. (587,800)
St Andrew . .	166.308 ⎭		
St Thomas . .	286.800	88,900	Morant Bay (9,600)
Portland . .	314.347	78,500	Port Antonio (13,200)
St Mary . .	235.745	113,700	Port Maria (7,700)
St Ann . .	468.213	154,500	St Ann's Bay (10,500)
Trelawny . .	337.651	74,100	Falmouth (8,000)
St James . .	229.728	166,000	Montego Bay (83,400)
Hanover . .	173.855	66,600	Lucea (5,400)
Westmoreland .	311.604	130,500	Savanna La Mar (16,600)
St Elizabeth .	468.085	146,600	Black River (3,600)
Manchester .	320.482	173,100	Mandeville (39,400)
Clarendon . .	461.864	222,500	May Pen (46,800)
St Catherine .	460.396	370,600	Spanish Town (92,400)
Total . . .	4,243.484	2,482,600	—

BIRTHS, MARRIAGES AND DEATHS*

	Registered live births		Registered marriages		Registered deaths	
	Number	Rate (per 1,000)	Number	Rate (per 1,000)	Number	Rate (per 1,000)
1990 . .	59,606	24.7	13,037	5.4	12,174	5.0
1991 . .	59,879	25.3	13,254	5.6	13,319	5.6
1992 . .	56,276	23.5	13,042	5.6	13,225	5.5
1993 . .	58,627	24.0	14,352	5.9	13,927	5.7
1994 . .	57,404	23.2	15,171	6.1	13,503	5.5
1995 . .	57,607	23.0	16,515	6.6	12,776	5.1
1996 . .	57,370	22.8	18,708	7.4	14,854	5.9

* Data are tabulated by year of registration rather than by year of occurrence.

Source: partly UN, *Demographic Yearbook*.

Expectation of life (estimates, years at birth, 1998): 75.0 (males 73.0; females 77.0) (Source: UNDP, *Human Development Report*).

ECONOMICALLY ACTIVE POPULATION*
('000 persons aged 10 years and over, 1998)

	Males	Females	Total
Agriculture, forestry and fishing .	160.5	39.6	200.1
Mining and quarrying . . .	4.5	0.7	5.2
Manufacturing	55.7	29.1	84.8
Electricity, gas and water . .	4.0	1.7	5.7
Construction	75.8	2.6	78.4
Trade, restaurants and hotels .	77.2	127.2	204.4
Transport, storage and communications . . .	46.6	11.3	57.9
Financing, insurance, real estate and business services . . .	27.5	30.4	57.9
Community, social and personal services	101.0	157.6	258.6
Activities not adequately defined .	0.9	0.4	1.3
Total employed	553.7	400.6	954.3
Unemployed	61.4	113.5	175.0
Total labour force	615.1	514.1	1,129.3

Source: ILO, *Labour Statistics Yearbook*.

Agriculture

PRINCIPAL CROPS ('000 metric tons)

	1997	1998	1999
Sweet potatoes	23	27	25
Cassava	14	15	17
Yams	213	198	196
Other roots and tubers* . . .	45	45	45
Coconuts*	115	115	115
Pumpkins, squash and gourds* .	42	42	42
Sugar cane	2,413	2,284†	2,312
Oranges*	72	72	72
Lemons and limes* . . .	24	24	24
Grapefruit and pomelo* . . .	42	42	42
Bananas*	130	130	130
Plantains*	34	34	34
Coffee (green)	3	2†	2†
Cocoa beans	2	2	1
Tobacco (leaves)†	2	2	2

* FAO estimate(s).　† Unofficial figure.

Source: FAO.

LIVESTOCK (FAO estimates, '000 head, year ending September)

	1997	1998	1999
Horses	4	4	4
Mules	10	10	10
Asses	23	23	23
Cattle	400	400	400
Pigs	180	180	180
Sheep	2	2	1
Goats	440	440	440

Poultry (FAO estimates, million): 10 in 1997; 10 in 1998; 10 in 1999.

Source: FAO.

LIVESTOCK PRODUCTS ('000 metric tons)

	1997	1998	1999
Beef and veal	15	14	15
Goat meat*	2	2	2
Pig meat	7	7	7
Poultry meat	59	63	73
Cows' milk*	53	53	53
Hen eggs*	28	28	28

* FAO estimate(s).

Source: FAO.

Forestry

ROUNDWOOD REMOVALS ('000 cubic metres, excl. bark)

	1996	1997	1998
Sawlogs, veneer logs and logs for sleepers	42	42	42
Other industrial wood	1	1	1
Fuel wood	300	300	300
Total	343	343	343

Source: FAO, *Yearbook of Forest Products*.

SAWNWOOD PRODUCTION ('000 cubic metres, incl. railway sleepers)

	1996	1997	1998
Total	12	12	12

Source: FAO, *Yearbook of Forest Products*.

Fishing

('000 metric tons, live weight)

	1996	1997	1998
Capture	12.8	8.4	6.7
Nile tilapia	0.7*	0.6	0.6
Marine fishes	8.8*	5.6	4.2
Stromboid conchs	2.9	1.8	1.7
Aquaculture*	3.1	3.1	3.4
Nile tilapia*	2.8	2.8	3.0
Total catch	15.9	11.5	10.1

* FAO estimate.

Source: FAO, *Yearbook of Fishery Statistics*.

Mining

('000 metric tons)

	1996	1997	1998
Bauxite*	11,757	11,987	12,675
Alumina	3,365	3,394	3,440
Crude Gypsum	251	132	154

* Dried equivalent of crude ore.

Industry

SELECTED PRODUCTS

	1997	1998	1999
Edible oil ('000 litres)	13,712	14,038	15,976
Flour (metric tons)	147,961	135,859	130,885
Sugar (metric tons)	232,798	182,761	201,319
Molasses (metric tons)	92,158	97,865	85,120
Rum ('000 litres)	22,362	22,171	19,709
Beer and stout ('000 litres)	67,434	66,933	65,573
Animal feed (metric tons)	186,955	191,765	232,351
Fertilizers (metric tons)	n.a.	27,918	43,897
Fuel oil ('000 litres)	382,134	399,018	284,967
Asphalt ('000 litres)	15,722	3,708	5,508
Gasoline (petrol) ('000 litres)	143,061	146,224	86,683
Kerosene, turbo and jet fuel ('000 litres)	72,486	52,690	41,397
Auto diesel oil ('000 litres)	159,013	150,109	102,336
Cement ('000 metric tons)	588,118	588,001	503,053

Electric energy (million kWh): 6,038 in 1996.

Finance

CURRENCY AND EXCHANGE RATES

Monetary Units
100 cents = 1 Jamaican dollar (J $).

Sterling, US Dollar and Euro Equivalents (29 December 2000)
£1 sterling = J $67.768;
US $1 = J $45.415;
€1 = J $42.259;
J $1,000 = £14.76 = US $22.02 = €23.66.

Average Exchange Rate (J $ per US $)
1998   36.550
1999   39.044
2000   42.701

BUDGET (J $ million, year ending 31 March)*

Revenue†	1996/97	1997/98	1998/99‡
Tax revenue	55,191	59,224	66,971
Taxes on income and profits	21,646	23,297	25,844
Taxes on production and consumption	17,139	18,415	20,974
Taxes on international trade	16,006	17,513	20,154
Bauxite levy	2,798	2,872	2,787
Other current revenue	3,310	3,097	3,085
Capital revenue	727	508	602
Total	62,026	65,701	73,444

Expenditure	1996/97	1997/98	1998/99‡
Current expenditure	64,225	73,260	85,764
Wages and salaries	24,043	29,066	31,913
Other goods and services			
Pensions	12,902	19,631	19,262
Other current transfers			
Interest payments	27,280	24,564	34,889
Capital expenditure	13,498	13,128	7,503
Unallocated expenditure (net)	329	—	—
Total	78,052	86,388	93,267

* Figures refer to budgetary transactions of the central Government, excluding the operations of the National Insurance Fund and other government units with individual budgets.
† Excluding grants received (J $ million): 1,060 in 1996/97; 725 in 1997/98; 652‡ in 1998/99.
‡ Preliminary.

Source: IMF, *Jamaica: Selected Issues* (February 2000).

INTERNATIONAL RESERVES (US $ million, at 31 December)

	1998	1999	2000
IMF special drawing rights . .	0.7	0.7	0.1
Foreign exchange . . .	708.8	553.8	1,053.4
Total	709.5	554.5	1,053.5

Source: IMF, *International Financial Statistics*.

MONEY SUPPLY (J $ million at 31 December)

	1998	1999	2000
Currency outside banks . .	13,504	17,821	17,607
Demand deposits at commercial banks	23,160	27,221	30,289
Total money	36,664	45,042	47,897

Source: IMF, *International Financial Statistics*.

COST OF LIVING (Consumer Price Index; base: 1990 = 100)

	1996	1997	1998
Food (incl. beverages) . .	688.0	742.0	794.2
Fuel and household supplies .	679.8	743.1	793.9
Clothing (incl. footwear) . .	690.2	804.0	846.4
Rent and household operation .	316.5	427.2	512.0
All items (incl. others) . .	669.5	734.2	797.5

Source: ILO, *Labour Statistics Yearbook*.

NATIONAL ACCOUNTS (J $ million at current prices)
Expenditure on the Gross Domestic Product

	1997	1998	1999*
Government final consumption expenditure	39,871	45,882	47,997
Private final consumption expenditure	159,593	166,731	176,335
Increase in stocks . . .	602	425	330
Gross fixed capital formation .	76,494	72,589	78,425
Total domestic expenditure .	276,560	285,627	303,087
Exports of goods and services . .	103,466	104,038	120,895
Less Imports of goods and services	137,264	142,266	147,449
GDP in purchasers' values .	242,762	257,392	276,533
GDP at constant 1986 prices .	17,920	17,828	17,757

* Estimates.
Source: IMF, *International Financial Statistics*.

Gross Domestic Product by Economic Activity

	1996	1997	1998*
Agriculture, forestry and fishing .	16,893	17,629	18,535
Mining and quarrying . .	11,915	12,264	11,341
Manufacturing . . .	33,976	35,375	35,014
Electricity and water . .	4,599	4,855	5,323
Construction	23,598	25,517	26,320
Wholesale and retail trade .	45,812	50,463	53,333
Hotels, restaurants and clubs .	3,746	4,214	4,634
Transport, storage and communication . . .	21,876	24,471	27,390
Finance, insurance, real estate and business services . .	28,383	27,848	30,089
Producers of government services .	23,053	26,703	29,327
Household and private non-profit services	1,341	1,484	1,404
Other community, social and personal services . . .	4,229	4,963	5,664
Sub-total	219,421	235,786	248,374
Value-added tax	16,965	17,463	19,344
Less Imputed bank service charge .	16,311	15,263	16,595
GDP in purchasers' values .	220,074	237,986	251,123

* Preliminary.

Source: IMF, *Jamaica: Selected Issues* (February 2000).

BALANCE OF PAYMENTS (US $ million)

	1997	1998	1999
Exports of goods f.o.b. . .	1,700.3	1,613.4	1,489.9
Imports of goods f.o.b. . . .	−2,832.6	−2,743.9	−2,627.6
Trade balance	−1,132.3	−1,130.5	−1,137.7
Exports of services . . .	1,714.6	1,786.1	1,865.8
Imports of services . . .	−1,225.8	−1,284.9	−1,300.6
Balance on goods and services	−643.5	−629.3	−572.5
Other income received . .	147.3	156.3	165.8
Other income paid . . .	−439.2	−464.4	−498.3
Balance on goods, services and income	−935.4	−937.4	−905.0
Current transfers received . .	705.7	732.1	756.3
Current transfers paid . .	−80.9	−97.1	−107.0
Current balance . . .	−310.6	−302.4	−255.7
Capital account (net) . . .	16.9	15.5	13.1
Direct investment abroad . .	−56.6	−82.0	−94.9
Direct investment from abroad .	203.3	369.1	523.7
Portfolio investment (net) . .	5.7	7.0	4.9
Other investment assets . .	−113.2	−59.1	−122.7
Other investment liabilities . .	124.3	102.2	−138.4
Net errors and omissions . .	−40.2	−6.4	−66.4
Overall balance . . .	−170.4	43.9	−136.4

Source: IMF, *International Financial Statistics*.

External Trade

PRINCIPAL COMMODITIES (US $ million, year ending 31 March)

Imports c.i.f.	1996/97	1997/98	1998/99*
Consumer goods	748	933	918
Foods	221	271	275
Non-durable goods .	230	286	291
Durable goods . . .	297	376	352
Fuels	467	371	286
Raw materials . . .	1,150	1,213	1,182
Capital goods . . .	577	623	547
Construction materials . .	131	173	158
Transport equipment . .	171	189	120
Other machinery . . .	275	261	269
Total	2,942	3,140	2,933

Exports f.o.b.	1996/97	1997/98	1998/99*
Agricultural products . .	90	85	64
Bananas	44	44	33
Coffee	33	31	17
Minerals	667	729	670
Bauxite	79	72	83
Alumina	588	657	587
Manufactures . . .	488	428	401
Sugar	122	81	98
Clothing	242	224	186
Other	444	461	416
Total	1,689	1,703	1,551

* Estimates.
Source: IMF, *Jamaica: Selected Issues* (February 2000).

PRINCIPAL TRADING PARTNERS (US $ million)

Imports c.i.f.	1996	1997	1998
Canada	88	94	95
Japan	164	217	200
Trinidad and Tobago . .	248	245	230
United Kingdom . . .	114	117	115
USA	1,531	1,504	1,523
Venezuela	67	66	46
Total (incl. others) . .	2,934	3,128	2,992

Exports f.o.b.	1996	1997	1998
Canada	164	195	151
Japan	31	32	17
Norway	91	80	88
United Kingdom . . .	184	186	159
USA	511	463	52
Total (incl. others) . . .	1,387	1,387	1,316

Source: IMF, *Jamaica: Selected Issues* (February 2000).

Transport

RAILWAYS (traffic)

	1988	1989	1990
Passenger-km ('000)	36,146	37,995	n.a.
Freight ton-km ('000) . . .	115,076	28,609	1,931

Source: Jamaica Railway Corporation.

ROAD TRAFFIC ('000 motor vehicles in use)

	1995	1996	1997
Passenger cars	104.0	120.7	156.8
Commercial vehicles . . .	49.1	52.8	56.1

Source: UN, *Statistical Yearbook.*

SHIPPING

Merchant Fleet (registered at 31 December)

	1996	1997	1998
Number of vessels	11	12	9
Total displacement ('000 grt) . .	9.3	9.6	3.6

Source: Lloyd's Register of Shipping, *World Fleet Statistics.*

International Sea-borne Freight Traffic (estimates, '000 metric tons)

	1989	1990	1991
Goods loaded	7,711	8,354	8,802
Goods unloaded	5,167	5,380	5,285

Source: Port Authority of Jamaica.

CIVIL AVIATION (traffic on scheduled services)

	1995	1996	1997
Kilometres flown (million) . .	12	17	22
Passengers carried ('000) . .	1,060	1,322	1,400
Passenger-km (million) . .	1,583	2,107	2,677
Total ton-km (million) . .	166	216	264

Source: UN, *Statistical Yearbook.*

Tourism

VISITOR ARRIVALS BY COUNTRY OF ORIGIN

	1996	1997	1998
Canada	102,215	99,216	109,802
USA	773,846	804,361	829,330
United Kingdom	114,417	116,390	116,552
Italy	23,969	21,028	17,718
Germany	36,509	33,480	43,018
Total (incl. others) . . .	1,162,449	1,192,194	1,225,287

Receipts from tourism (US $ million): 1,092 in 1996; 1,131 in 1997; 1,197 in 1998.

Source: mainly World Tourism Organization, *Yearbook of Tourism Statistics.*

Communications Media

	1995	1996	1997
Radio receivers ('000 in use) . .	1,080	1,200	1,215
Television receivers ('000 in use) .	400	450	460
Telephones (main lines in use, '000)*	292	353	n.a.
Mobile cellular telephones (subscribers)*	45,178	54,640	n.a.
Daily newspapers (number) . .	3	3	n.a.
Circulation (estimates, '000) .	160	158	n.a.

Telefax stations (number in use)*: 1,567 in 1992.

* Year beginning 1 April.

Sources: UNESCO, *Statistical Yearbook*, and UN, *Statistical Yearbook.*

Education

	Institutions	Teachers	Students
Pre-primary*	1,681	4,158†	133,687†
Primary‡	—	9,512†	293,863†
Secondary§	—	10,931	235,071
Tertiary‖	1	418	8,191

* Figures for 1990/91.
† Public sector only.
‡ Figures for 1996/97.
§ Figures for 1992/93.
‖ Figures for 1995/96.

Source: UNESCO, *Statistical Yearbook.*

Directory

The Constitution

The Constitution came into force at the independence of Jamaica on 6 August 1962. Amendments to the Constitution are enacted by Parliament, but certain entrenched provisions require ratification by a two-thirds majority in both chambers of the legislature, and some (such as a change of the head of state) require the additional approval of a national referendum.

HEAD OF STATE

The Head of State is the British monarch, who is locally represented by a Governor-General, appointed by the British monarch, on the recommendation of the Jamaican Prime Minister in consultation with the Leader of the Opposition party.

THE LEGISLATURE

The Senate or Upper House consists of 21 Senators of whom 13 will be appointed by the Governor-General on the advice of the Prime Minister and eight by the Governor-General on the advice of the Leader of the Opposition. (Legislation enacted in 1984 provided for eight independent Senators to be appointed, after consultations with the Prime Minister, in the eventuality of there being no Leader of the Opposition.)

The House of Representatives consists of 60 elected members called Members of Parliament.

A person is qualified for appointment to the Senate or for election to the House of Representatives if he or she is a citizen of Jamaica or other Commonwealth country, of the age of 21 or more and has been ordinarily resident in Jamaica for the immediately preceding 12 months.

THE PRIVY COUNCIL

The Privy Council consists of six members appointed by the Governor-General after consultation with the Prime Minister, of whom at least two are persons who hold or who have held public office. The functions of the Council are to advise the Governor-General on the exercise of the Royal Prerogative of Mercy and on appeals on disciplinary matters from the three Service Commissions.

THE EXECUTIVE

The Prime Minister is appointed from the House of Representatives by the Governor-General, and is the leader of the party that holds the majority of seats in the House of Representatives. The Leader of the party is voted in by the members of that party. The Leader of the Opposition is voted in by the members of the Opposition party.

The Cabinet consists of the Prime Minister and not fewer than 11 other ministers, not more than four of whom may sit in the Senate. The members of the Cabinet are appointed by the Governor-General on the advice of the Prime Minister.

THE JUDICATURE

The Judicature consists of a Supreme Court, a Court of Appeal and minor courts. Judicial matters, notably advice to the Governor-General on appointments, are considered by a Judicial Service Commission, the Chairman of which is the Chief Justice, members being the President of the Court of Appeal, the Chairman of the Public Service Commission and three others.

CITIZENSHIP

All persons born in Jamaica after independence automatically acquire Jamaican citizenship and there is also provision for the acquisition of citizenship by persons born outside Jamaica of Jamaican parents. Persons born in Jamaica (or persons born outside Jamaica of Jamaican parents) before independence who immediately prior to independence were citizens of the United Kingdom and colonies also automatically become citizens of Jamaica.

Appropriate provision is made which permits persons who do not automatically become citizens of Jamaica to be registered as such.

FUNDAMENTAL RIGHTS AND FREEDOMS

The Constitution includes provisions safeguarding the fundamental freedoms of the individual, irrespective of race, place of origin, political opinions, colour, creed or sex, subject only to respect for the rights and freedoms of others and for the public interest. The fundamental freedoms include the rights of life, liberty, security of the person and protection from arbitrary arrest or restriction of movement, the enjoyment of property and the protection of the law, freedom of conscience, of expression and of peaceful assembly and association, and respect for private and family life.

The Government

Head of State: HM Queen Elizabeth II (succeeded to the throne 6 February 1952).

Governor-General: Sir Howard Felix Hanlan Cooke (appointed 1 August 1991).

PRIVY COUNCIL OF JAMAICA

Dr Vernon Lindo, Ewart Forrest, G. Owen, W. H. Swaby, Dr Douglas Fletcher.

CABINET
(April 2000)

Prime Minister: Percival James Patterson.

Deputy Prime Minister and Minister of Land and the Environment: Seymour Mullings.

Minister of Finance and Planning: Dr Omar Davies.

Minister of Labour and Social Security: Donald Buchanan.

Minister of Tourism and Sport: Portia Simpson-Miller.

Minister of Local Government, Youth and Community Development: Arnold Bertram.

Minister of National Security and Justice: Keith (K. D.) Knight.

Minister of Agriculture: Roger Clarke.

Minister of Foreign Affairs: Dr Paul Robertson.

Minister of Foreign Trade: George Anthony Hylton.

Minister of Mining and Energy: Robert Pickersgill.

Minister of Health: John Junor.

Minister of Education and Culture: Burchell Whiteman.

Minister of Transportation and Works: Dr Peter Phillips.

Minister of Water and Housing: Dr Karl Blythe.

Minister of Industry, Commerce and Technology: Phillip Paulwell.

Minister of Information: Maxine Henry-Wilson.

MINISTRIES

Office of the Governor-General: King's House, Hope Rd, Kingston 10; tel. 927-6424.

Office of the Prime Minister: Jamaica House, 1 Devon Rd, POB 272, Kingston 10; tel. 927-9941; fax 929-0005; e-mail pmo@opm.gov.jm.

Ministry of Agriculture: Hope Gardens, Kingston 6; tel. 927-1731; fax 927-1904.

Ministry of Education and Culture: 2 National Heroes Circle, Kingston 4; tel. 922-1400; fax 922-9371; internet www.moec.gov.jm.

Ministry of Finance and Planning: 30 National Heroes Circle, Kingston 4; tel. 922-8600; fax 922-7097; e-mail info@mof.gov.jm; internet www.mof.gov.jm.

Ministry of Foreign Affairs and Foreign Trade: 21 Dominica Drive, POB 624, Kingston 5; tel. 926-4220; fax 929-6733; e-mail mfaftjam@cwjamaica.com; internet www.mfaft.gov.jm.

Ministry of Health: Oceana Hotel Complex, 2–4 King St, Kingston; tel. 967-1100; fax 967-7293; internet www.moh.gov.jm.

Ministry of Industry, Commerce and Technology: PCJ Bldg, 36 Trafalgar Rd, Kingston 10; tel. 929-8990; fax 960-1623; e-mail admin@mct.gov.jm; internet www.mct.gov.jm.

Ministry of Labour and Social Security: 1F North St, POB 10, Kingston; tel. 922-3904; fax 924-9560; e-mail manpower@minlab.gov.jm; internet www.minlab.gov.jm.

Ministry of Land and the Environment: 2 Hagley Park Rd, Kingston 10; tel. 926-1590; fax 926-2591; e-mail mehsys@hotmail.com.

Ministry of Local Government, Youth and Community Development: 85 Hagley Park Rd, Kingston 10; tel. 754-0994; fax 960-0725.

Ministry of Mining and Energy: PCJ Bldg, 36 Trafalgar Rd, Kingston 10; tel. 926-9170; fax 968-2082; e-mail hmme@cwjamaica.com.

Ministry of National Security and Justice: Mutual Life Bldg, North Tower, 2 Oxford Rd, Kingston 5; tel. 906-4909; fax 906-1713; e-mail information@mnsj.gov.jm; internet www.mnsj.gov.jm.

Ministry of Tourism and Sport: 64 Knutsford Blvd, Kingston 5; tel. 920-4956; fax 920-4944; e-mail opmt@cwjamaica.com.

Ministry of Transportation and Works: 1C–1F Pawsey Place, Kingston 5; tel. 754-1900; fax 927-8763; e-mail ps@mtw.gov.jm; internet www.mtw.gov.jm.

Ministry of Water and Housing: 7th Floor, Island Life Bldg, 6 St Lucia Ave, Kingston 5; tel. 754-0971; fax 754-0975; e-mail prumow@cwjamaica.com.

Legislature

PARLIAMENT

Houses of Parliament: Gordon House, Duke St, Kingston; tel. 922-0200.

Senate

President: SYRINGA MARSHALL-BURNETT.
Vice-President: NOEL MONTEITH.
The Senate has 20 other members.

House of Representatives

Speaker: VIOLET NEILSON.
Deputy Speaker: O'NEIL T. WILLIAMS.

General Election, 18 December 1997*

	Votes cast	Seats
People's National Party (PNP) . . .	441,739	50
Jamaica Labour Party (JLP) . . .	312,471	10
National Democratic Movement (NDM) .	38,430	—
Total	792,640	60

* Following a by-election in the North-East St Ann constituency on 8 March 2001, the JLP increased its parliamentary representation to 11 seats, thus reducing the PNP's representation in the House of Representatives to 49.

Political Organizations

Jamaica Labour Party (JLP): 20 Belmont Rd, Kingston 5; tel. 929-1183; fax 968-0873; e-mail jlp@colis.com; internet www.thejlp.com; f. 1943; supports free enterprise in a mixed economy and close co-operation with the USA; Leader EDWARD SEAGA; Deputy Leader DWIGHT NELSON.

National Democratic Movement (NDM): NDM House, 3 Easton Ave, Kingston 5; e-mail mail@ndmjamaica.org; internet www .ndmjamaica.org; f. 1995; advocates a clear separation of powers between the central executive and elected representatives; supports private investment and a market economy; Pres. (vacant); Chair. STAFFORD HAUGHTON.

Natural Law Party: c/o 21st Century Integrated Medical Centre, Shop OF3, Overton Plaza, 49 Union St, Montego Bay; tel. 971-9107; fax 971-9109; e-mail nlp@cwjamaica.com; internet www.natural-law-party.org/jamaica/; f. 1996; Leader Dr. LEO CAMPBELL.

People's National Party (PNP): 89 Old Hope Rd, Kingston 5; tel. 978-1337; fax 927-4389; internet www.pnp.org.jm; f. 1938; socialist principles; affiliated with the National Workers' Union; Leader PERCIVAL J. PATTERSON; Gen. Sec. MAXINE HENRY-WILSON; First Vice-Pres. PETER PHILLIPS.

In 1999 a pressure group, **Citizens for a Civil Society (CCS)**, was formed by Daryl Vaz to lobby the Government on specific issues.

Diplomatic Representation

EMBASSIES AND HIGH COMMISSIONS IN JAMAICA

Argentina: Dyoll Bldg, 40 Knutsford Blvd, Kingston 5; tel. 926-5588; fax 926-0580; e-mail embargen@kasnet.com; Ambassador: ALFREDO ALCORTA.

Brazil: PCMB Bldg, 3rd Floor, 64 Knutsford Blvd, Kingston 5; tel. 929-8607; fax 929-1259; e-mail brasking@infochan.com; Ambassador: SÉRGIO ARRUDA.

Canada: 3 West Kings House Rd, POB 1500, Kingston 10; tel. 926-1500; e-mail kngtn@dfait-maeci.gc.ca; High Commissioner: JOHN ROBINSON.

Chile: Island Life Centre, 5th Floor, South 6th St, Lucia Ave, Kingston; tel. 968-0260; fax 968-0265; e-mail chilejam@cwjamaica.com; Ambassador: FERNANDO PARDO HUERTA.

China, People's Republic: 8 Seaview Ave, Kingston 10; tel. 927-0850; Ambassador: LI SHANGSHENG.

Colombia: Victoria Mutual Bldg, 3rd Floor, 53 Knutsford Blvd, Kingston 5; tel. 929-1702; fax 929-1701; Ambassador: RICARDO VARGAS TAYLOR.

Costa Rica: Belvedere House, Beverly Drive, Kingston 5; tel. 927-5988; fax 978-3946; e-mail cr_emb_jam@hotmail.com; Ambassador: RODRIGO CASTRO ECHEVERRIA.

Cuba: 9 Trafalgar Rd, Kingston 5; tel. 978-0931; fax 978-5372; Ambassador: DARÍO DE URRA.

France: 13 Hillcrest Ave, POB 93, Kingston 6; e-mail albert.salon@diplomatie.fr; Ambassador: ALBERT SALON.

Germany: 10 Waterloo Rd, POB 444, Kingston 10; tel. 926-6728; fax 929-8282; e-mail germanemb@cwjamaica.com; Ambassador: ADOLF EDERER.

Haiti: 2 Monroe Rd, Kingston 6; tel. 927-7595; Chargé d'affaires: ANDRÉ L. DORTONNE.

India: 4 Retreat Ave, POB 446, Kingston 6; tel. 927-0486; fax 978-2801; High Commissioner: V. B. SONI.

Italy: 10 Rovan Drive, Kingston 6; tel. 978-1273; fax 978-0675; Ambassador: STEFANO CANAVESIO.

Japan: Mutual Life Centre, North Tower, 6th Floor, 2 Oxford Rd, Kingston 10; tel. 929-3338; fax 968-1373; Ambassador: TAKASHI MATSUMOTO.

Korea, Democratic People's Republic: Kingston; tel. 927-7087; Ambassador: HAN PONG GU.

Mexico: PCJ Bldg, 36 Trafalgar Rd, Kingston 10; tel. 926-6891; fax 929-7995; e-mail mexico.j@cwjamaica.com; Ambassador: JOSE LUIS VALLARTA MARRON.

Netherlands: Victoria Mutual Bldg, 53 Knutsford Blvd, Kingston 5; tel. 926-2026; fax 926-1248; e-mail rnekst@cwjamaica.com; Ambassador: E. W. P. KLIPP.

Nigeria: 5 Waterloo Rd, Kingston 10; tel. 926-6400; fax 968-7371; e-mail nhckingston@mail-infochan.com; High Commissioner: FLORENTINA ADENIKE UKONGA.

Panama: 1 St Lucia Ave, Spanish Court, Office 26, Kingston 5; tel. 968-2928; fax 960-1618; Chargé d'affaires: JOSÉ DE JESÚS MARTÍNEZ.

Russia: 22 Norbrook Drive, Kingston 8; tel. 924-1048; Ambassador: IGOR YAKOVLEV.

Spain: 25 Dominica Drive, 10th Floor, Kingston 5; tel. 929-6710; Ambassador: FERNANDO DE LA SERNA INCIARTE.

Trinidad and Tobago: First Life Bldg, 3rd Floor, 60 Knutsford Blvd, Kingston 5; tel. 926-5730; fax 926-5801; e-mail t&thckgn@infochan.com; High Commissioner: DENNIS FFANCIS.

United Kingdom: 28 Trafalgar Rd, POB 575, Kingston 10; tel. 926-9050; fax 929-7869; e-mail bhckingston@cw.com; High Commissioner: ANTONY F. SMITH.

USA: Mutual Life Centre, 2 Oxford Rd, Kingston 5; tel. 929-4850; Ambassador: STANLEY L. MCLELLAND.

Venezuela: Petroleum Corpn of Jamaica Bldg, 3rd Floor, 36 Trafalgar Rd, Kingston 10; tel. 926-5510; fax 926-7442; Chargé d'affaires a.i.: NÉSTOR CASTELLANOS.

Judicial System

The Judicial System is based on English common law and practice. Final appeal is to the Judicial Committee of the Privy Council in the United Kingdom, although in 2001 the Jamaican Government signed an agreement to establish a Caribbean Court of Justice to fulfil this function.

Justice is administered by the Privy Council, Court of Appeal, Supreme Court (which includes the Revenue Court and the Gun Court), Resident Magistrates' Court (which includes the Traffic Court), two Family Courts and the Courts of Petty Sessions.

Judicial Service Commission: Office of the Services Commissions, 63–67 Knutsford Blvd, Kingston 5; advises the Governor-General on judicial appointments, etc.; chaired by the Chief Justice.

Attorney-General: ARNOLD J. NICHOLSON.

SUPREME COURT

Public Building E, 134 Tower St, POB 491, Kingston; tel. 922-8300; fax 967-0669; e-mail webmaster@sc.gov.jm; internet www.sc.gov.jm.

Chief Justice: LENSLEY H. WOLFE.
Senior Puisne Judge: LLOYD B. ELLIS.
Master: CAROL BESWICK.
Registrar: CHRISTINE MCDONALD.

COURT OF APPEAL
POB 629, Kingston; tel. 922-8300.

President: R. CARL RATTRAY.
Registrar: G. P. LEVERS.

Religion

CHRISTIANITY

There are more than 100 Christian denominations active in Jamaica. According to the 1982 census, the largest religious bodies were the

Church of God, Baptists, Anglicans and Seventh-day Adventists. Other denominations include the Methodist and Congregational Churches, the Ethiopian Orthodox Church, the Disciples of Christ, the Moravian Church, the Salvation Army and the Society of Friends (Quakers).

Jamaica Council of Churches: 14 South Ave, Kingston 10; tel. 926-0974; e-mail jchurch_99@yahoo.com; f. 1941; 10 member churches and three agencies; Pres. Rev. STANLEY CLARKE; Gen. Sec. NORMAN MILLS.

The Anglican Communion

Anglicans in Jamaica are adherents of the Church in the Province of the West Indies, comprising eight dioceses. The Archbishop of the Province is the Bishop of the North East Caribbean and Aruba. The Bishop of Jamaica, whose jurisdiction also includes Grand Cayman (in the Cayman Islands), is assisted by three suffragan Bishops (of Kingston, Mandeville and Montego Bay). The 1982 census recorded 154,548 Anglicans.

Bishop of Jamaica: Rt Rev. NEVILLE WORDSWORTH DE SOUZA, Church House, 2 Caledonia Ave, Kingston 5; tel. 926-6609; fax 968-0618.

The Roman Catholic Church

Jamaica comprises the archdiocese of Kingston in Jamaica (also including the Cayman Islands), and the dioceses of Montego Bay and Mandeville. At 31 December 1998 the estimated total of adherents in Jamaica and the Cayman Islands was 113,523, representing about 4.3% of the total population. The Archbishop and Bishops participate in the Antilles Episcopal Conference (currently based in Port of Spain, Trinidad and Tobago).

Archbishop of Kingston in Jamaica: Most Rev. EDGERTON ROLAND CLARKE, Archbishop's Residence, 21 Hopefield Ave, POB 43, Kingston 6; tel. 927-9915; fax 927-4487; e-mail rcabkgn@cwjamaica.com.

Other Christian Churches

Assembly of God: Evangel Temple, 3 Friendship Park Rd, Kingston 3; tel. 928-2728; Pastor WILSON.

Baptist Union: 6 Hope Rd, Kingston 10; tel. 926-1395; fax 968-7832; e-mail jbuaid@mail.infochan.com; internet www.jbu.org.jm; Pres. Rev. NEVILLE CALLAM; Gen. Sec. Rev. KARL JOHNSON .

Church of God in Jamaica: 35A Hope Rd, Kingston 10; tel. 927-8128; 400,379 adherents (1982 census).

First Church of Christ, Scientist: 17 National Heroes Circle, C.S.O., Kingston 4.

Methodist Church (Jamaica District): 143 Constant Spring Rd, POB 892, Kingston 8; tel. and fax 924-2560; f. 1789; 18,284 mems; Chair. Rev. BRUCE B. SWAPP; Synod Sec. Rev. GILBERT G. BOWEN.

Moravian Church in Jamaica: 3 Hector St, POB 8369, Kingston 5; tel. 928-1861; fax 928-8336; f. 1754; 30,000 mems; Pres. Rev. STANLEY G. CLARKE.

Seventh-day Adventist Church: 56 James St, Kingston; tel. 922-7440; f. 1901; 150,722 adherents (1982 census); Pastor Rev. E. H. THOMAS.

United Church in Jamaica and the Cayman Islands: 12 Carlton Cres., POB 359, Kingston 10; tel. 926-8734; fax 929-0826; f. 1965 by merger of the Congregational Union of Jamaica (f. 1877) and the Presbyterian Church of Jamaica and Grand Cayman to become United Church of Jamaica and Grand Cayman; merged with Disciples of Christ in Jamaica in 1992 when name changed as above; 20,000 mems; Gen. Sec. Rev. MAITLAND EVANS.

RASTAFARIANISM

Rastafarianism is an important influence in Jamaican culture. The cult is derived from Christianity and a belief in the divinity of Ras (Prince) Tafari Makonnen (later Emperor Haile Selassie) of Ethiopia. It advocates racial equality and non-violence, but causes controversy in its use of 'ganja' (marijuana) as a sacrament. The 1982 census recorded 14,249 Rastafarians (0.7% of the total population). Although the religion is largely unorganized, there are some denominations.

Royal Ethiopian Judah Coptic Church: Kingston; not officially incorporated, on account of its alleged use of marijuana; Leader ABUNA S. WHYTE.

BAHÁ'Í FAITH

National Spiritual Assembly: 208 Mountain View Ave, Kingston 6; tel. 927-7051; fax 978-2344; incorporated in 1970; 6,300 mems resident in 368 localities.

ISLAM

At the 1982 census there were 2,238 Muslims.

JUDAISM

The 1991 census recorded 250 Jews.

United Congregation of Israelites: 92 Duke St, Kingston; tel. 927-7948; fax 978-6240; f. 1655; *c.* 250 mems; Spiritual Leader and Sec. ERNEST H. DE SOUZA; Pres. WALLACE R. CAMPBELL.

The Press

DAILIES

Daily Gleaner: 7 North St, POB 40, Kingston; tel. 922-3400; fax 922-2058; e-mail ads@jamaica-gleaner.com; internet www.jamaica-gleaner.com; f. 1834; morning; independent; Chair. and Man. Dir OLIVER CLARKE; Editor-in-Chief GARFIELD GRANDISON; circ. 44,000.

Daily Star: 7 North St, POB 40, Kingston; tel. 922-3400; evening; Editor LEIGHTON LEVY; circ. 49,500.

Jamaica Herald: 29 Molynes Rd, Kingston 10; tel. 968-7721; fax 968-7722; Man. Editor FRANKLIN MCKNIGHT.

Jamaica Observer: 2 Fagan Ave, Kingston 8; tel. 931-5188; fax 931-5190; internet www.jamaicaobserver.com; f. 1993; Chair. GORDON 'BUTCH' STEWART; CEO Dr GEORGE T. PHILLIP.

PERIODICALS

Caribbean Challenge: 55 Church St, POB 186, Kingston; tel. 922-5636; f. 1957; monthly; Editor JOHN KEANE; circ. 18,000.

Caribbean Shipping: Creative Communications Inc, Kingston; tel. 968-7279; fax 926-2217; 2 a year.

Catholic Opinion: 21 Hopefield Ave, POB 43, Kingston 6; tel. 927-9915; fax 927-4487; e-mail rcabkgn@cwjamaica.com; 6 a year; religious; Editor Rev. MICHAEL LEWIS.

Children's Own: 7 North St, POB 40, Kingston; weekly during term time; circ. 120,188.

Government Gazette: POB 487, Kingston; f. 1868; Govt Printer RALPH BELL; circ. 1,350.

Inquirer: 7 11 West St, Kingston; tel. 922-3952; weekly; current affairs.

Jamaica Churchman: 2 Caledonia Ave, Kingston 5; tel. 926-6608; quarterly; Editor BARBARA GLOUDON; circ. 7,000.

Jamaica Journal: 4 Camp Rd, Kingston 4; tel. 929-4048; fax 926-8817; f. 1967; 3 a year; literary, historical and cultural review; publ. by Instit. of Jamaica Publs Ltd; Man. Dir PATRICIA ROBERTS; Editor LEETA HEARNE.

Jamaica Weekly Gleaner: 7 North St, POB 40, Kingston; tel. 922-3400; weekly; overseas; Chair. and Man. Dir OLIVER CLARKE; circ. 13,599.

The Siren: 1 River Bay Rd, PO Box 614, Montego Bay, St James; tel. 952-0997; f. 1990; weekly.

Sunday Gleaner: 7 North St, POB 40, Kingston; tel. 922-3400; weekly; Editor-in-Chief GARFIELD GRANDISON; circ. 488,000.

Sunday Herald: 86 Hagley Park Rd, Kingston 10; tel. 901-5022; fax 937-7313; f. 1997; weekly; Editor FRANKLYN MCKNIGHT; circ. 20,000.

Swing: 102 East St, Kingston; f. 1968; monthly; entertainment and culture; Editor ANDELL FORGIE; circ. 12,000.

The Vacationer: POB 614, Montego Bay; tel. 952-6006; f. 1987; monthly; Man. Editor EVELYN L. ROBINSON; circ. 8,000.

The Visitor Vacation Guide: 82 Barnett St, POB 1258, Montego Bay; tel. 952-5253; fax 952-6513; weekly; Editor LLOYD B. SMITH.

Weekend Star: 7 North St, POB 40, Kingston; tel. 922-3400; weekly; Editor LOLITA TRACEY-LONG; circ. 400,000.

The Western Mirror: 82 Barnett St, POB 1258, Montego Bay; tel. 952-5253; fax 952-6513; e-mail westernmirror@mail.infochan.com; f. 1980; 2 a week; Man. Dir and Editor LLOYD B. SMITH; circ. 16,000.

West Indian Medical Journal: Faculty of Medical Sciences, University of the West Indies, Kingston 7; tel. 927-1214; fax 927-1846; f. 1951; quarterly; Editor-in-Chief Dr. E. N. BARTON; circ. 2,000.

PRESS ASSOCIATION

Press Association of Jamaica (PAJ): 5 East Ave, Kingston; tel. 926-7584; f. 1943; 240 mems; Pres. DESMOND ALLEN; Sec. MONICA DIAS.

NEWS AGENCIES

Jampress Ltd: 3 Chelsea Ave, Kingston 10; tel. 926-8428; fax 929-6727; e-mail jamnews@infochan.com; f. 1984; govt news agency; Exec. Dir DESMOND ALLEN.

Foreign Bureaux

Inter Press Service (IPS) (Italy): Suite 1G, 2-6 Melmac Ave, Kingston 5; tel. 960-0604; fax 929-6889; Regional Editor CORINNE BARNES.

Associated Press (USA) and CANA (Caribbean News Agency) are also represented.

Publishers

Caribbean Publishing Co Ltd: Kingston; tel. 925-3228.

Jamaica Publishing House Ltd: 97 Church St, Kingston; tel. 967-3866; fax 922-5412; e-mail jph@jol.com.jm; f. 1969; wholly-owned subsidiary of Jamaica Teachers' Asscn; educational, English language and literature, mathematics, history, geography, social sciences, music; Chair. WOODBURN MILLER; Man. ELAINE R. STENNETT.

Kingston Publishers Ltd: 7 Norman Road, Suite 10, LOJ Industrial Complex, Kingston CSO; tel. 928-8898; fax 928-5719; f. 1970; educational textbooks, general, travel, atlases, fiction, non-fiction, children's books; Chair. L. MICHAEL HENRY.

Western Publishers Ltd: 82 Barnett St, POB 1258, Montego Bay; tel. 952-5253; fax 952-6513; e-mail westernmirror@mail.infochan.com; f. 1980; Man. Dir and Editor-in-Chief LLOYD B. SMITH.

Government Publishing House

Jamaica Printing Services: 77 Duke St, Kingston; tel. 967-2250; Chair. EVADNE STERLING; Man. RALPH BELL.

Broadcasting and Communications

TELECOMMUNICATIONS

In September 1999 the Government announced a three-year transition period to a fully competitive telecommunications sector. The sector was to be regulated by the Office of Utilities Regulation (see Utilities).

Cable & Wireless Jamaica Ltd: 7 Cecilio Ave, Kingston 10; tel. 926-9450; fax 929-9530; f. 1989; in 1995 merged with Jamaica Telephone Co Ltd and Jamaica International Telecommunications Ltd, name changed as above 1995; 79% owned by Cable & Wireless; Pres. E. MILLER.

Cellular One Caribbean: Kingston; mobile cellular telephone operator; licence granted Dec. 1999.

Mossel Ltd: Kingston; mobile cellular telephone operator; Irish owned; licence granted Jan. 2000.

BROADCASTING

Television

CVM Television: 69 Constant Sprint Rd, Kingston 10; tel. 931-9400; fax 931-9417; e-mail manager@cvmtv.com.

Love Television: Kingston; f. 1997; religious programming; owned by religious Media Ltd.

Television Jamaica Limited (TVJ): 5–9 South Odeon Avenue, POB 100, Kingston 10; tel. 926-5620; fax 929-1029; e-mail tvjadmin@cwjamaica.com; internet www.radiojamaica.com; f. 1959 as Jamaica Broadcasting Corporation; privatized 1997, name changed as above; island-wide VHF transmission, 24 hrs a day; Gen. Man. MARCIA FORBES.

Radio

Educational Broadcasting Service: Multi-Media Centre, 37 Arnold Road, Kingston 4; tel. 922-9370; f. 1964; radio broadcasts during school term; Pres. OUIDA HYLTON-TOMLINSON.

Independent Radio: 6 Bradley Ave, Kingston 10; tel. 968-4880; fax 968-9165; commercial radio station; broadcasts 24 hrs a day on FM; Gen. Man. NEWTON JAMES.

IRIE FM: Coconut Grove, POB 282, Ocho Rios, St Ann; tel. 974-5051; fax 968-8332; f. 1991; commercial radio station; plays only raggae music.

Island Broadcasting Services Ltd: 41B Half Way Tree Rd, Kingston 5; tel. 929-1344; fax 929-1345; commercial; broadcasts 24 hrs a day on FM; Exec. Chair. NEVILLE JAMES.

KLAS-FM: 81 Knutsford Blvd, Kingston 5; f. 1991; commercial radio station.

Love 101: Kingston; f. 1997; commercial radio station, broadcasts religious programming on FM; owned by Religious Media Ltd.

Radio Jamaica Ltd (RJR): Broadcasting House, 32 Lyndhurst Rd, POB 23, Kingston 5; tel. 926-1100; fax 929-7467; e-mail rjr@radiojamaica.com; internet www.radiojamaica.com; f. 1947; commercial, public service; three channels:

    RJR Supreme '94: broadcasts on AM and FM, island-wide, 24 hrs a day; Exec. Producer NORMA BROWN-BELL.

    FAME FM: broadcasts on FM, island-wide, 24 hrs a day; Exec. Producer FRANCOIS ST. JUSTE.

    Radio 2: broadcasts on FM, island-wide, 24 hrs a day; Media Services Man. DONALD TOPPING.

Other stations broadcasting include Hot 102, Power 106 FM, Roots FM and TBC FM.

Finance

(cap. = capital; p.u. = paid up; res = reserves; dep. = deposits; m. = million; brs = branches; amounts in Jamaican dollars)

BANKING

Central Bank

Bank of Jamaica: Nethersole Place, POB 621, Kingston; tel. 922-0752; fax 922-0854; e-mail info@boj.org.jm; internet www.boj.org.jm;

f. 1960; cap. 4.0m., res 159.9m., dep. 51,793.3m. (Dec. 1998); Gov. DERICK LATIBEAUDIÈRE.

Commercial Banks

Bank of Nova Scotia Jamaica Ltd (Canada): Scotiabank Centre Bldg, cnr Duke and Port Royal Sts, POB 709, Kingston; tel. 922-1000; fax 924-9294; f. 1967; cap. 1,463.6m., res 4,114.0m., dep. 47,628.4m. (Dec. 1998); Chair. BRUCE R. BIRMINGHAM; Man. Dir WILLIAM E. CLARKE; 36 brs.

CIBC Jamaica Ltd (Canada): CIBC Centre, 23–27 Knutsford Blvd, POB 762, Kingston 5; tel. 929-9310; fax 929-7751; 57% owned by Canadian Imperial Bank of Commerce; cap. 96.7m., res 516.2m., dep. 8,153.1m. (Oct. 1997); Man. Dir A. W. WEBB; 12 brs.

Citibank, NA (USA): 63–67 Knutsford Blvd, POB 286, Kingston 5; tel. 926-3270; fax 929-3745.

National Commercial Bank Jamaica Ltd: 'The Atrium', 32 Trafalgar Rd, POB 88, Kingston 10; tel. 929-9050; fax 929-8399; internet www.jncb.com; f. 1977; merged with Mutual Security Bank in 1996; cap. 433.0m., res 1,811.6m., dep. 67,471.9m. (Sept. 1998); Chair. GLORIA D. KNIGHT; Man. Dir REX JAMES; 33 brs.

Trafalgar Commercial Bank Ltd: 60 Knutsford Blvd, Kingston 5; tel. 968-5119.

Union Bank of Jamaica Ltd: 17 Dominica Dr., Kingston 5; tel. 960-1350; fax 960-2332; f. 2000 by merger of Citizens Bank Ltd, Eagle Commercial Bank Ltd, Island Victoria Bank Ltd, and Workers' Savings and Loan Bank; bought by the Royal Bank of Trinidad and Tobago in 2001; 6 brs.

Development Banks

Jamaica Mortgage Bank: 33 Tobago Ave, POB 950, Kingston 5; tel. 929-6350; fax 968-5428; f. 1971 by the Jamaican Govt and the US Agency for Int. Devt; govt-owned statutory org. since 1973; intended to function primarily as a secondary market facility for home mortgages and to mobilize long-term funds for housing devts in Jamaica; also insures home mortgage loans made by approved financial institutions, thus transferring risk of default on a loan to the Govt; Chair. PETER THOMAS; Man. Dir EVERTON HANSON.

National Development Bank of Jamaica Ltd: 11A–15 Oxford Rd, POB 8309, Kingston 5; tel. 929-6124; fax 929-6996; e-mail ndb@ndbjam.com; internet www.ndbjam.com; replaced Jamaica Development Bank, f. 1969; provides funds for medium- and long-term devt-orientated projects in the tourism, industrial, agro-industrial and mining sectors through financial intermediaries; Pres. NATAN RICHARDS; Chair. HUNTLEY MANHERTZ.

    Agricultural Credit Bank of Jamaica: 11A–15 Oxford Rd, POB 466, Kingston 5; tel. 929-4010; fax 929-6055; f. 1981; provides loans to small farmers through co-operative banks; Man. Dir KINGSLEY THOMAS; Chair. ARTHUR BARRET.

Trafalgar Development Bank: The Towers, 3rd Floor, 25 Dominica Drive, Kingston 5; tel. 929-4760; e-mail tdbhrgen@cwjamaica.com.

Other Banks

National Export-Import Bank of Jamaica Ltd: 48 Duke St, POB 3, Kingston; tel. 922-9690; fax 922-9184; e-mail eximjam@cwjamaica.com; replaced Jamaica Export Credit Insurance Corpn; finances import and export of goods and services; Chair. Dr OWEN JEFFERSON.

National Investment Bank of Jamaica Ltd: 11 Oxford Rd, POB 889, Kingston 5; tel. 960-9691; fax 920-0379; e-mail nibj@infochan.com; Chair. DAVID COORE; Pres. Dr GAVIN CHEN.

Banking Association

Jamaica Bankers' Association: POB 1079, Kingston; tel. 929-9050; fax 929-8399; Pres. PETER MOSES.

Financial Sector Adjustment Company

FINSAC Ltd: 76 Knutsford Blvd, POB 54, Kingston 5; tel. 906-1809; fax 906-1822; e-mail info@FINSAC.com; internet finsac.com; f. 1997; state-owned; intervenes in the banking and insurance sectors to restore stability in the financial sector.

STOCK EXCHANGE

Jamaica Stock Exchange Ltd: 40 Harbour St, Kingston; tel. 967-3271; fax 922-6966; f. 1968; 50 listed cos (1995); Chair. RITA HUMPHRIES-LEWIN; Gen. Man. C. WAIN ITON.

INSURANCE

Office of the Superintendent of Insurance: 51 St Lucia Ave, POB 800, Kingston 5; tel. 926-1790; fax 968-4346; f. 1972; regulatory body; Superintendent ERROL MCLEAN (acting).

Jamaica Association of General Insurance Companies: 58 Half Way Tree Rd, POB 459, Kingston 10; tel. 929-8404; e-mail jagic@cwjamaica.com; Man. GLORIA M. GRANT; Chair. LESLIE CHUNG.

Principal Companies

British Caribbean Insurance Co Ltd: 36 Duke St, POB 170, Kingston; tel. 922-1260; fax 922-4475; internet www.bcicdirect.com; f. 1962; general insurance; Gen. Man. LESLIE W. CHUNG.

First Life Insurance Group: 60 Knutsford Blvd, Kingston 5; tel. 926-3700; fax 929-8523; e-mail info@firstlife.com.jm; internet www.firstlife.com.jm; division of the Pan-Jamaican Investment Trust Group; all branches.

Globe Insurance Co of the West Indies Ltd: 17 Dominica Drive, POB 401, Kingston 5; tel. 926-3720; fax 929-2727; Gen. Man. R. E. D. THWAITES.

Guardian Holdings: Kingston; pension and life policies.

Insurance Co of the West Indies Ltd (ICWI): 2 St Lucia Ave, POB 306, Kingston 5; tel. 926-9182; fax 929-6641; Chair. DENNIS LALOR; CEO KENNETH BLAKELEY.

Island Life Insurance Co: 6 St Lucia Ave, Kingston 5; tel. 968-6874; e-mail ceo@islandlife-ja-com.jm; 64% owned by Barbados Mutual Life Assurance Co; 26% owned by FINSAC.

Jamaica General Insurance Co Ltd: 9 Duke St, POB 408, Kingston; tel. 922-6420; fax 922-2073; Man. Dir A. C. LEVY.

Life of Jamaica Ltd: 28–48 Barbados Ave, Kingston 5; tel. 929-8920; fax 929-4730; f. 1970; life and health insurance, pensions; Pres. R. D. WILLIAMS.

NEM Insurance Co (Jamaica) Ltd: NEM House, 9 King St, Kingston; tel. 922-1460; fax 922-4045; fmrly the National Employers' Mutual General Insurance Asscn; Gen. Man. NEVILLE HENRY.

Trade and Industry

GOVERNMENT AGENCIES

Jamaica Commodity Trading Co Ltd: 8 Ocean Blvd, POB 1021, Kingston; tel. 922-0971. 1981 as successor to State Trading Corpn; oversees all importing on behalf of state; Chair. DAVID GAYNAIR; Man. Dir ANDREE NEMBHARD.

Jamaica Information Service (JIS): 58A Half Way Tree Rd, POB 2222, Kingston 10; tel. 926-3741; fax 920-7427; e-mail jis@jis.gov.jm; internet www.jis.gov.jm; f. 1963; information agency for govt policies and programmes, ministries and public sector agencies; CEO CARMEN E. TIPLING.

DEVELOPMENT ORGANIZATIONS

Agricultural Development Corpn (ADC) Group of Companies: Mais House, Hope Rd, POB 552, Kingston; tel. 977-4412; fax 977-4411; f. 1989; manages and develops breeds of cattle, provides warehousing, cold storage, offices and information for exporters and distributors of non-traditional crops and ensures the proper utilization of agricultural lands under its control; Chair. Dr ASTON WOOD; Gen. Man. DUDLEY IRVING.

Coffee Industry Development Co: Marcus Garvey Drive, Kingston 15; tel. 923-5645; fax 923-7587; e-mail cofeboard-jam@cwjamaica.com; f. 1981; to implement coffee devt and rehabilitation programmes financed by international aid agencies; Sec. JOYCE CHANG.

Jamaica Promotions Corpn (JAMPRO): 35 Trafalgar Rd, Kingston 10; tel. 929-7190; fax 960-8082; e-mail jampro@investjamaica.com; f. 1988 by merger of Jamaica Industrial Development Corpn, Jamaica National Export Corpn and Jamaica Investment Promotion Ltd; trade and investment promotion agency; Pres. PATRICIA FRANCIS; Chair. JOSEPH A. MATALON.

National Development Agency Ltd: Kingston; tel. 922-5445.

Planning Institute of Jamaica: 8 Ocean Blvd, Kingston Mall; tel. 967-3690; fax 967-3688; e-mail doccen@mail.colis.com; f. 1955 as the Central Planning Unit; adopted current name in 1984; monitoring performance of the economy and the social sector; publishing of devt plans and social surveys; Dir-Gen. WESLEY HUGHES.

Urban Development Corpn: The Office Centre, 8th Floor, 12 Ocean Blvd, Kingston; tel. 922-8310; fax 922-9326; f. 1968; responsibility for urban renewal and devt within designated areas; Chair. Dr VINCENT LAWRENCE; Gen. Man. IVAN ANDERSON.

CHAMBERS OF COMMERCE

Associated Chambers of Commerce of Jamaica: 7–8 East Parade, POB 172, Kingston; tel. 922-0150; f. 1974; 12 associated Chambers of Commerce; Pres. RAY CAMPBELL.

Jamaica Chamber of Commerce: 7–8 East Parade, POB 172, Kingston; tel. 922-0150; fax 924-9056; f. 1779; 450 mems; Pres. HOWARD HAMILTON.

INDUSTRIAL AND TRADE ASSOCIATIONS

Cocoa Industry Board: Marcus Garvey Drive, POB 1039, Kingston 15; tel. 923-6411; fax 923-5837; e-mail cocoajam@cwjamaica.com; f. 1957; has statutory powers to regulate and develop the industry;

owns and operates four central fermentaries; Chair. JOSEPH SUAH; Man. and Sec. NABURN NELSON.

Coconut Industry Board: 18 Waterloo Rd, Half Way Tree, Kingston 10; tel. 926-1770; fax 968-1360; f. 1945; 9 mems; Chair. R. A. JONES; Gen. Man. JAMES S. JOYLES.

Coffee Industry Board: Marcus Garvey Drive, POB 508, Kingston 15; tel. 923-5850; fax 923-7587; e-mail cibcommercial@cwjamaica.com; internet www.jamaicancoffee.gov.jm; f. 1950; 9 mems; has wide statutory powers to regulate and develop the industry; Chair. RICHARD DOWNER; CEO GONZALO HERNÁNDEZ.

Jamaica Bauxite Institute: Hope Gardens, POB 355, Kingston 6; tel. 927-2073; fax 927-1159; f. 1975; adviser to the Govt in the negotiation of agreements, consultancy services to clients in the bauxite/alumina and related industries, laboratory services for mineral and soil-related services, Pilot Plant services for materials and equipment testing, research and development; Chair. CARLTON DAVIS.

Jamaica Export Trading Co Ltd: 6 Waterloo Rd, POB 645, Kingston 10; tel. 929-4390; fax 926-1608; e-mail jetcoja@infochan.com; f. 1977; export trading in non-traditional products, incl. spices, fresh produce, furniture, garments, processed foods, minerals, etc.; Chair. JOSEPH A. MATALON; Man. Dir HERNAL HAMILTON.

Sugar Industry Authority: 5 Trevennion Park Rd, POB 127, Kingston 5; tel. 926-5930; fax 926-6149; e-mail sia@cwjamaica.com; f. 1970; statutory body under portfolio of Ministry of Agriculture; responsible for regulation and control of sugar industry and sugar marketing; conducts research through Sugar Industry Research Institute; Exec. Chair. ANDRÉE NEMBHARD.

Trade Board: 107 Constant Spring Rd, Kingston 10; tel. 969-0478; Admin. JEAN MORGAN.

EMPLOYERS' ORGANIZATIONS

All-Island Banana Growers' Association Ltd: Banana Industry Bldg, 10 South Ave, Kingston 4; tel. 922-5492; fax 922-5497; f. 1946; 1,500 mems (1997); Chair. BOBBY POTTINGER; Sec. I. CHANG.

All-Island Jamaica Cane Farmers' Association: 4 North Ave, Kingston 4; tel. 922-3010; fax 922-2077; f. 1941; registered cane farmers; 27,000 mems; Chair. KENNETH A. HAUGHTON; Man. DAVID BELINFANTI.

Banana Export Co (BECO): 1A Braemar Ave, Kingston 10; tel. 927-3402; fax 978-6096; f. 1985 to replace Banana Co of Jamaica; oversees the devt of the banana industry; Chair. Dr MARSHALL HALL.

Citrus Growers' Association Ltd: Kingston; tel. 922-8230; fax 922-2774; f. 1944; 13,000 mems; Chair. IVAN H. TOMLINSON.

Jamaica Association of Sugar Technologists: c/o Sugar Industry Research Institute, Kendal Rd, Mandeville; tel. 962-2241; fax 962-1288; e-mail maureenwil@hotmail.com; f. 1936; 275 mems; Pres. GILBERT THORNE; Sec. Dr MAUREEN R. WILSON.

Jamaica Exporters' Association (JEA): 13 Dominica Drive, POB 9, Kingston 5; tel. 960-1675; fax 960-1465; e-mail sbed@cwjamaica.com; internet www.exportjamaica.org; Pres. KARL JAMES; Exec. Dir PAULINE GRAY.

Jamaica Livestock Association: Newport East, POB 36, Kingston; f. 1941; tel. 922-7130; fax 923-5046; 7,316 mems; Chair. Dr JOHN MASTERTON; Man. Dir and CEO HENRY J. RAINFORD.

Jamaica Manufacturers' Association Ltd: 85A Duke St, Kingston; tel. 922-8869; fax 922-0051; e-mail jma@toj.com; f. 1947; 400 mems; Pres. SAMEER YOUNIS.

Jamaica Producers' Group Ltd: 6A Oxford Rd, POB 237, Kingston 5; tel. 926-3503; fax 929-3636; e-mail cosecretary@jpjamaica.com; f. 1929; fmrly Jamaica Banana Producers' Asscn; Chair. C. H. JOHNSTON; Man. Dir Dr MARSHALL HALL.

Private Sector Organization of Jamaica (PSOJ): 39 Hope Rd, POB 236, Kingston 10; tel. 927-6238; fax 927-5137; federative body of private business individuals, cos and asscns; Pres. CLIFTON CAMERON; Exec. Dir CHARLES A. ROSS.

Small Businesses' Association of Jamaica (SBAJ): 2 Trafalgar Rd, Kingston 5; tel. 927-7071; fax 978-2738; Pres. ALBERT GRAY; Exec. Dir ESME L. BAILEY.

Sugar Manufacturing Corpn of Jamaica Ltd: 5 Trevennion Park Rd, Kingston 5; tel. 926-5930; fax 926-6149; established to represent the sugar manufacturers in Jamaica; deals with all aspects of the sugar industry and its by-products; provides liaison between the Govt, the Sugar Industry Authority and the All-Island Jamaica Cane Farmers' Asscn; 9 mems; Chair. CHRISTOPHER BOVELL; Gen. Man. DERYCK T. BROWN.

UTILITIES
Regulatory Authority

Office of Utilities Regulation (OUR): PCJ Resource Centre, 36 Trafalgar Rd, Kingston 10; tel. 960-6474; fax 968-8703; e-mail office@our.org.jm; internet www.our.org.jm; f. 1995; regulates provision of services in the following sectors: water, electricity, telecommunications, public passenger transportation, sewerage; Dir-Gen. WINSTON HAY.

Electricity

Jamaica Public Service Co (JPSCo): Dominion Life Bldg, 6 Knutsford Blvd, POB 54, Kingston 5; tel. 926-3190; fax 968-3337; responsible for the generation and supply of electricity to the island; 80% sold to Mirant Corpn (USA) in March 2001; Chair. GORDON SHIRLEY; Man. Dir DERRICK DYER.

Water

National Water Commission: 4A Marescaux Rd, Kingston 5; tel. 929-3540; internet www.nwcjamaica.com; statutory body; provides potable water and waste water services.

Water Resources Authority: Hope Gardens, POB 91, Kingston 7; tel. 927-0077; fax 977-0179; e-mail wra@colis.com; internet www .wra-ja.org; f. 1996; manages, protects and controls allocation and use of water supplies.

TRADE UNIONS

Bustamante Industrial Trade Union (BITU): 98 Duke St, Kingston; tel. 922-2443; fax 967-0120; f. 1938; Pres. HUGH SHEARER; Gen. Sec. GEORGE FYFFE; 60,000 mems.

National Workers' Union of Jamaica (NWU): 130–132 East St, Kingston 16; tel. 922-1150; e-mail nwyou@toj.com; f. 1952; affiliated to the International Confederation of Free Trade Unions, etc.; Pres. CLIVE DOBSON; Gen. Sec. LLOYD GOODLEIGH; 10,000 mems.

Trades Union Congress of Jamaica: 25 Sutton St, POB 19, Kingston; tel. 922-5313; fax 922-5468; affiliated to the Caribbean Congress of Labour and the International Confederation of Free Trade Unions; Pres. E. SMITH; Gen. Sec. HOPETON CRAVEN; 20,000 mems.

Principal Independent Unions

Dockers' and Marine Workers' Union: 48 East St, Kingston 16; tel. 922-6067; Pres. MILTON A. SCOTT.

Industrial Trade Union Action Council: 2 Wildman St, Kingston; Pres. RODERICK FRANCIS; Gen. Sec. KEITH COMRIE.

Jamaica Federation of Musicians' and Artistes' Unions: POB 1125, Montego Bay 1; tel. 952-3238; f. 1958; Pres. HEDLEY H. G. JONES; Sec. CARL AYTON; 2,000 mems.

Jamaica Local Government Officers' Union: c/o Public Service Commission, Knutsford Blvd, Kingston 5; Pres. E. LLOYD TAYLOR.

Jamaica Teachers' Association: 97 Church St, Kingston; tel. 922-1385; fax 922-3257; e-mail jta@toj.com; Pres. PATRICK SMITH.

Master Printers' Association of Jamaica: Kingston; f. 1943; 44 mems; Pres. HERMON SPOERRI; Sec. RALPH GORDON.

National Union of Democratic Teachers (NUDT): Kingston; tel. 922-3902; f. 1978; Pres. and Gen. Sec. HOPETON HENRY.

Union of Schools, Agricultural and Allied Workers (USAAW): 2 Wildman St, Kingston; tel. 967-2970; f. 1978; Pres. IAN HINES.

United Portworkers' and Seamen's Union: Kingston.

University and Allied Workers' Union (UAWU): Students' Union, University of West Indies, Mona; tel. 927-7968; affiliated to the WPJ; Gen. Sec. Dr TREVOR MUNROE.

There are also 35 associations registered as trade unions.

Transport

RAILWAYS

There are about 339 km (211 miles) of railway, all standard gauge, in Jamaica. Most of the system is operated by the Jamaica Railway Corpn, which is subsidized by the Government. The main lines are from Kingston to Montego Bay, and Spanish Town to Ewarton and Port Antonio. Passenger services were suspended in 1992; operations were scheduled to resume in 2000. There are four railways for the transport of bauxite.

Jamaica Railway Corpn (JRC): 142 Barry St, POB 489, Kingston; tel. 922-6620; fax 922-4539; f. 1845 as Jamaica Railway Co, the earliest British colonial railway; transferred to JRC in 1960; govt-owned, but autonomous, statutory corpn until 1990, when it was partly leased to Alcan Jamaica Co Ltd as the first stage of a privatization scheme; 207 km of railway; Chair. W. TAYLOR; Gen. Man. OWEN CROOKS.

Alcoa Railroads: Alcoa Minerals of Jamaica Inc, May Pen PO; tel. 986-2561; fax 986-2026; 43 km of standard-gauge railway; transport of bauxite; Superintendent RICHARD HECTOR; Man. FITZ CARTY (Railroad Operations and Maintenance).

Kaiser Jamaica Bauxite Co Railway: Discovery Bay PO, St Ann; tel. 973-2221; 25 km of standard-gauge railway; transport of bauxite; Gen. Man. GENE MILLER.

ROADS

Jamaica has a good network of tar-surfaced and metalled motoring roads. According to estimates by the International Road Federation, there were 19,000 km of roads in 1998, of which 70.7% were paved. A five-year programme to improve the condition of all arterial and secondary roads and 30% of minor roads was to begin in 1999. In September 1999 plans were announced for a 290 km-highway system linking major cities.

SHIPPING

The principal ports are Kingston, Montego Bay and Port Antonio. The port at Kingston has four container berths, and is a major transhipment terminal for the Caribbean area. Jamaica has interests in the multinational shipping line WISCO (West Indies Shipping Corpn—based in Trinidad and Tobago). Services are also provided by most major foreign lines serving the region.

Port Authority of Jamaica: 15–17 Duke St, Kingston; tel. 922-0290; fax 924-9437; e-mail pajmktg@infochan.com; internet www .seaportsofjamaica.com; f. 1966; Govt's principal maritime agency; responsible for monitoring and regulating the navigation of all vessels berthing at Jamaican ports, for regulating the tariffs on public wharves, and for the devt of industrial Free Zones in Jamaica; Pres. and Chair. NOEL HYLTON.

Kingston Free Zone Co Ltd: 27 Shannon Drive, POB 1025, Kingston 15; tel. 923-5274; fax 923-6023; f. 1976; subsidiary of Port Authority of Jamaica; management and promotion of an export-orientated industrial free trade zone for cos from various countries; Gen. Man. OWEN HIGGINS.

Montego Bay Export Free Zone: c/o Port Authority of Jamaica, 15–17 Duke St, Kingston; tel. 922-0290.

Shipping Association of Jamaica: 4 Fourth Ave, Newport West, POB 1050, Kingston 15; tel. 923-3491; fax 923-3421; e-mail shipping .assoc@cwjamaica.com; f. 1939; 63 mems; an employers' trade union which regulates the supply and management of stevedoring labour in Kingston; represents members in negotiations with govt and trade bodies; Pres. GRANTLEY STEPHENSON; Gen. Man. ALVIN C. HENRY.

Principal Shipping Companies

Jamaica Freight and Shipping Co Ltd (JFS): 80–82 Second St, Port Bustamante, POB 167, Kingston 13; tel. 923-9371; fax 923-4091; e-mail cshaw@toj.com; cargo services to and from the USA, Caribbean, Central and South America, the United Kingdom, Japan and Canada; Exec. Chair. CHARLES JOHNSTON; Man. Dir GRANTLEY STEPHENSON.

Petrojam Ltd: 96 Marcus Garvey Drive, POB 241, Kingston; tel. 923-8727; fax 923-5698; Man. Dir STEPHEN WEDDERBURN (acting).

Portcold Ltd: 122 Third St, Newport West, Kingston 13; tel. 923-7425; fax 923-5713; Chair. and Man. Dir ISHMAEL E. ROBERTSON.

CIVIL AVIATION

There are two international airports linking Jamaica with North America, Europe, and other Caribbean islands. The Norman Manley International Airport is situated 22.5 km (14 miles) outside Kingston. The Donald Sangster International Airport is 5 km (3 miles) from Montego Bay. A J $800m.-programme to expand and improve the latter was under consideration in 2001.

Air Jamaica Ltd: 72–76 Harbour St, Kingston; tel. 922-3460; fax 922-0107; internet www.airjamaica.com; f. 1968; privatized in 1994; services within the Caribbean and to Canada (in asscn with Air Canada), the USA and the United Kingdom; Chair. GORDON 'BUTCH' STEWART; CEO CHRISTOPHER ZACCA.

Air Jamaica Express: Tinson Pen Aerodrome, Kingston 11; tel. 923-6664; fax 937-3807; previously known as Trans-Jamaican Airlines; internal services between Kingston, Montego Bay, Negril, Ocho Rios and Port Antonio; Chair. GORDON 'BUTCH' STEWART; Man. Dir PAULO MOREIRA.

Airports Authority of Jamaica: Victoria Mutual Bldg, 53 Knutsford Blvd, POB 567, Kingston 5; tel. 926-1622; fax 929-8171; Chair. CEZLEY SAMPSON; Pres. LUCIEN RATTRAY.

Civil Aviation Authority: 4 Winchester Rd, Kingston 10; tel. 960-3948; fax 920-0194; e-mail jcivav@cwjamaica.com; internet www.jcaa.gov.jm.

Tourism

Tourists, mainly from the USA, visit Jamaica for its beaches, mountains, historic buildings and cultural heritage. In 2000 there were an estimated 2,018,347 'stop over' visitors (of whom 812,572 were cruise-ship passengers). Tourist receipts were estimated to be US $1,300m. in that year. In 1995 there were some 29,376 hotel rooms. In 2000 a US $125m. luxury resort opened in Montego Bay.

Jamaica Tourist Board (JTB): ICWI Bldg, 2 St Lucia Ave, Kingston 5; tel. 929-9200; fax 929-9375; internet www.jamaicatravel.com; f. 1955; a statutory body set up by the Govt to develop all aspects of the tourist industry through marketing, promotional and advertising efforts; Chair. Adrian Robinson; Dir of Tourism Fay Pickersgill.

Jamaica Hotel and Tourist Association (JHTA): 2 Ardenne Rd, Kingston 10; tel. 926-2796; fax 929-1054; e-mail info@jhta.org; internet www.jobsnmore.com; f. 1961; trade asscn for hoteliers and other cos involved in Jamaican tourism; Pres. James Samuels; Exec. Dir Camille Needham.

JAPAN

Introductory Survey

Location, Climate, Language, Religion, Flag, Capital

Japan lies in eastern Asia and comprises a curved chain of more than 3,000 islands. Four large islands, named (from north to south) Hokkaido, Honshu, Shikoku and Kyushu, account for about 98% of the land area. Hokkaido lies just to the south of Sakhalin, a large Russian island, and about 1,300 km (800 miles) east of Russia's mainland port of Vladivostok. Southern Japan is about 150 km (93 miles) east of the Republic of Korea. Although summers are temperate everywhere, the climate in winter varies sharply from cold in the north to mild in the south. Temperatures in Tokyo range from –6°C (21°F) to 30°C (86°F). Typhoons and heavy rains are common in summer. The language is Japanese. The major religions are Shintoism and Buddhism, and there is a Christian minority. The national flag (proportions 10 by 7) is white, with a red disc (a sun without rays) in the centre. The capital is Tokyo.

Recent History

Following Japan's defeat in the Second World War, Japanese forces surrendered in August 1945. Japan signed an armistice in September, and the country was placed under US military occupation. A new democratic constitution, which took effect from May 1947, renounced war and abandoned the doctrine of the Emperor's divinity. Following the peace treaty of September 1951, Japan regained its independence on 28 April 1952, although it was not until 1972 that the last of the US-administered outer islands were returned to Japanese sovereignty.

In November 1955 rival conservative groups merged to form the Liberal-Democratic Party (LDP). Nobusuke Kishi, who became Prime Minister in February 1957, was succeeded by Hayato Ikeda in July 1960. Ikeda was replaced by Eisaku Sato in November 1964. Sato remained in office until July 1972, when he was succeeded by Kakuei Tanaka.

Tanaka's premiership was beset by problems, leading to his replacement by Takeo Miki in December 1974. Tanaka was subsequently accused of accepting bribes from the Marubeni Corporation, and he was arrested in July 1976. The LDP lost its overall majority in the House of Representatives (the lower house of the Diet) at a general election held in December 1976. Miki resigned and was succeeded by Takeo Fukuda. However, Mayayoshi Ohira defeated Fukuda in the LDP presidential election of November 1978, and replaced him as Prime Minister in December. Ohira was unable to win a majority in the lower house at elections in October 1979. In May 1980 the Government was defeated in a motion of 'no confidence', forcing the dissolution of the lower house. Ohira died before the elections in June, when the LDP won 284 of the 511 seats, despite obtaining only a minority of the votes cast. In July Zenko Suzuki, a relatively little-known compromise candidate, was elected President of the LDP, and subsequently appointed Prime Minister. In November 1981 Suzuki reorganized the Cabinet, distributing major posts among the five feuding LDP factions. The growing factionalism of the LDP and the worsening economic crisis prompted Suzuki's resignation as Prime Minister and LDP President in October 1982. He was succeeded by Yasuhiro Nakasone.

At elections in June 1983 for one-half of the seats in the House of Councillors (the upper house of the Diet), a new electoral system was used. Of the 126 contested seats, 50 were filled on the basis of proportional representation. As a result, two small parties entered the House of Councillors for the first time. The LDP increased its strength from 134 to 137 members in the 252-seat chamber. This result was seen as an endorsement of Nakasone's policies of increased expenditure on defence, closer ties with the USA and greater Japanese involvement in international affairs.

In October 1983 the former Prime Minister, Kakuei Tanaka, was found guilty of accepting bribes. However, Tanaka refused to relinquish his legislative seat (he had already resigned from the LDP). The opposition parties therefore led a boycott of the Diet, forcing Nakasone to call a premature general election in December 1983. The Komeito (Clean Government Party), the Democratic Socialist Party (DSP) and the Japan Socialist Party (JSP) gained seats, at the expense of the Communists and the New Liberal Club (NLC). The LDP, which had performed badly in the election, formed a coalition with the NLC (which had split from the LDP over the Tanaka affair in 1976) and several independents. Nakasone remained President of the LDP, after promising to reduce Tanaka's influence. Following the trial of Tanaka, reforms were introduced, whereby cabinet members were required to disclose the extent of their personal assets.

Nakasone called another premature general election for July 1986, which coincided with elections for one-half of the seats in the House of Councillors. In the election to the House of Representatives, the LDP obtained its highest level of electoral support since 1963, and won a record 304 of the 512 seats. The increased LDP majority was achieved largely at the expense of the JSP and the DSP, thus enabling the LDP to dispense with its coalition partner, the NLC (which disbanded in August and rejoined the LDP). In September the leaders of the LDP agreed to alter by-laws to allow party presidents one-year extensions beyond the normal limit of two terms of two years each. Nakasone was thus able to retain the posts of President of the LDP and Prime Minister until October 1987.

In July 1987 the Secretary-General of the LDP, Noboru Takeshita, left the Tanaka faction, with 113 other members, and announced the formation of a major new grouping within the ruling party. In the same month Tanaka's political influence was further weakened when the Tokyo High Court upheld the decision, taken in 1983, declaring him guilty of accepting bribes. (In February 1995 this ruling was upheld by the Supreme Court.)

In October 1987 Nakasone nominated Takeshita as his successor. The Diet was convened and Takeshita was formally elected as Prime Minister in November. In the new Cabinet, Takeshita maintained a balance among the five major factions of the LDP, retaining only two members of Nakasone's previous Cabinet, but appointing four members of the Nakasone faction to senior ministerial posts (including Nakasone's staunch ally, Sosuke Uno, as Minister of Foreign Affairs).

The implementation of a programme of tax reforms was one of the most important issues confronting Takeshita's Government. In June 1988 the proposed introduction of a new indirect tax (a general consumption tax, or a form of value-added tax) aroused widespread opposition. In the same month the Prime Minister and the LDP suffered a serious set-back when several leading figures in the party, including Nakasone, Shintaro Abe, Kiichi Miyazawa and Takeshita himself, were alleged to have been indirectly involved in share-trading irregularities with the Recruit Cosmos Company. In November, shortly after the LDP had agreed to establish a committee to investigate the Recruit scandal, the House of Representatives approved proposals for tax reform (which constituted the most wide-ranging revision of the tax system for 40 years). Three cabinet ministers and the Chairman of the DSP were subsequently forced to resign, owing to their alleged involvement in the Recruit affair.

In January 1989 Emperor Hirohito, who had reigned since 1926, died after a long illness, thus ending the Showa era. He was succeeded by his son, Akihito, and the new era was named Heisei ('achievement of universal peace').

In April 1989, as the allegations against politicians widened to include charges of bribery and malpractice, Takeshita announced his resignation. He was subsequently found to have accepted donations worth more than 150m. yen from the Recruit organization. Takeshita nominated Sosuke Uno as his successor. Uno was elected Prime Minister by the Diet on 2 June; a new Cabinet was appointed on the same day. Uno thus became the first Japanese Prime Minister since the foundation of the LDP not to command his own political faction. In May, following an eight-month investigation undertaken by the LDP's special committee, public prosecutors indicted 13 people. Nakasone resigned from his faction and from the LDP, assuming responsibility for the Recruit affair, but did not relinquish his seat in the Diet.

Within a few days of Uno's assumption of office, a Japanese magazine published allegations of sexual impropriety involving the Prime Minister, which precipitated demands for his resignation. Serious losses suffered by the LDP in Tokyo's municipal elections in July 1989 further discredited Uno. As a result of a considerable increase in support for the JSP, led by Takako Doi, the LDP lost its majority in the upper house for the first time in its history. Uno's offer to resign was accepted by the LDP, which in August chose the relatively unknown Toshiki Kaifu, a former Minister of Education, to replace Uno as the party's President and as the new Prime Minister. Although the House of Councillors' ballot rejected Kaifu as the new Prime Minister in favour of Takako Doi, the decision of the lower house was adopted, in accordance with stipulations embodied in the Constitution. This was the first time in 41 years that the two houses of the Diet had disagreed over the choice of Prime Minister. In October Kaifu was re-elected as President of the LDP for a further two-year term.

At a general election held in February 1990, the LDP was returned to power with an unexpectedly large measure of support, securing 275 of the 512 seats in the lower house. In December Toshiyuki Inamura, a former cabinet minister, resigned from the LDP after charges of large-scale tax evasion and complicity in a new stock-manipulation scandal were brought against him. A prison sentence with hard labour, which he received in November 1991, was regarded as a deterrent to other politicians from engaging in financial corruption. In January 1991 the JSP changed its English name to the Social Democratic Party of Japan (SDPJ) and Makato Tanabe later replaced Takako Doi as Chairman of the party. In September senior LDP officials forced Kaifu to abandon proposals for electoral reform and the Takeshita faction of the LDP subsequently withdrew its support for the Prime Minister. Sponsored by the faction, the former Minister of Finance, Kiichi Miyazawa, was elected President of the LDP in October, and in November the Diet endorsed his appointment as Prime Minister. New allegations of involvement in the Recruit affair, publicized by the SDPJ in December 1991, seriously undermined Miyazawa's position.

In early 1992 public disgust at official corruption was registered at two prefectural by-elections to the upper house, when the LDP lost seats, which had previously been considered secure, to Rengo-no-kai (the political arm of RENGO, the trade union confederation). However, the anti-Government alliance, which had supported Rengo-no-kai, disintegrated in May over the issue of the authorization of Japanese involvement in UN peace-keeping operations. Members of the SDPJ attempted to obstruct the vote in the lower house by submitting their resignations *en masse*. The Speaker, however, ruled that these could not be accepted during the current Diet session. The successful passage through the Diet of the legislation on international peace-keeping improved the Government's standing, and in elections to the upper house in July the LDP won 69 of the 127 seats contested. The SDPJ, by contrast, lost 25 of its 46 seats; the Komeito increased its total strength from 20 to 24 seats, but Rengo-no-kai failed to win any seats, owing to the dissolution of the informal coalition it had facilitated between the SDPJ and the DSP. The Japan New Party (JNP), founded only two months prior to the election by LDP dissidents, secured four seats. A formal split within the Takeshita faction took place in December 1992. The new faction was to be led nominally by Tsutomu Hata, the Minister of Finance, although it was widely recognized that Ichiro Ozawa held the real power in the grouping.

Electoral reform was a major political issue in the first half of 1993. While the LDP favoured a single-member constituency system, the opposition parties proposed various forms of proportional representation. The LDP's lack of a majority in the upper house rendered it unable to enforce any reforms without the agreement of the opposition parties. Within the LDP itself there was conflict over whether or not to compromise with opposition parties. In June the lower house adopted a motion of 'no confidence' against the Government, after the LDP refused to modify its reform proposals to meet opposition demands. Numerous LDP members opposed the Government or abstained. The Ozawa-Hata group, comprising 44 former LDP members, immediately established a new party, the Shinseito (Japan Renewal Party, JRP), in order to contest the forthcoming general election. Another new party, the New Party Sakigake, was also formed by LDP Diet members. In the election to the House of Representatives, held in July, the LDP won 223 of the 511 seats, and was thus 33 seats short of a majority. Miyazawa resigned as Prime Minister and a coalition Government was formed. On 6 August Morihiro Hosokawa, the leader of the JNP, was elected Prime Minister, defeating the new President of the LDP, Yohei Kono.

In late 1993 three senior politicians, Noboru Takeshita, Ichiro Ozawa and Kishiro Nakamura (a former Minister of Construction), were implicated in a scandal involving payments from construction companies in return for awarding building contracts. Ozawa claimed that the payments were legal, since none had exceeded 1.5m. yen. In January 1994 the Public Prosecutor's office began investigations into bribery allegations against Nakamura and Hideo Watanabe, the former Minister of Posts and Telecommunications.

In November 1993 four items of electoral reform legislation were passed by a majority of 270 to 226 votes in the House of Representatives (they were opposed by the LDP). In January 1994, however, the reform bills were defeated in the upper house, but Hosokawa, (who had threatened to resign if the legislation were not passed), subsequently reached agreement with the LDP on modifications to the reform bills (see below).

Hosokawa resigned as Prime Minister in April 1994. Tsutomu Hata was subsequently appointed Prime Minister, at the head of a minority Government that excluded the SDPJ and the New Party Sakigake. Hata was obliged to resign in June, however, owing to his continued failure to command a viable majority in the Diet, and a new coalition of the SDPJ, the LDP and the New Party Sakigake took office. Tomiichi Murayama, the leader of the SDPJ, became Prime Minister, and Kono was appointed Deputy Prime Minister and Minister of Foreign Affairs.

In July 1994 Murayama recognized the constitutional right to the existence of Japan's Self-Defence Forces (SDF, the armed forces), thereby effectively contradicting official SDPJ policy on the issue. (The SDPJ amended its policy to accord with Murayama's statement in September.) In December nine opposition parties, including the JNP, the JRP, the DSP and the Komeito, amalgamated to form a new political party, the Shinshinto (New Frontier Party, NFP). A faction of Komeito remained outside the new party and was renamed Komei. Kaifu, the former LDP Prime Minister, was elected leader of the NFP; Ozawa was appointed Secretary-General.

The creation of the NFP was widely perceived to be a response to the approval by the Diet in November 1994 of the electoral reform bills first proposed in 1993, which appeared to favour larger political parties. Under the terms of the new law, the House of Representatives was to be reduced to 500 seats, comprising 300 single-seat constituencies and 200 seats determined by proportional representation; the proportional-representation base was to be divided into 11 regions, and a party would qualify for a proportional-representation seat if it received a minimum of 2% of the vote; donations amounting to 500,000 yen annually per private sector corporation to individual politicians were permitted, but this was to be phased out after five years; restrictions on corporate donations would be subsidized by the State; door-to-door campaigning was to be permitted and an independent body would draw up new electoral boundaries. In June 1995 the first distribution of public money to political parties took place.

In January 1995 a massive earthquake in the Kobe region caused thousands of deaths and severe infrastructural damage. The Government was severely criticized (and subsequently acknowledged responsibility) for the poor co-ordination of the relief operation. In March a poisonous gas, sarin, was released into the Tokyo underground railway system, killing 12 people and injuring more than 5,000. A religious sect, Aum Shinrikyo, was accused of perpetrating the attack. Following a further gas attack in Yokohama in April, a number of sect members were detained by the authorities. In June Shoko Asahara, the leader of Aum Shinrikyo, was indicted on a charge of murder. The sect was declared bankrupt in March 1996 and the trial of Asahara opened in the following month. In September Asahara and two other members of the sect were instructed to pay some US $7.3m. in compensation to victims of the Tokyo incident. The sect was later denied legal status as a religious organization.

Participation in the elections to the House of Councillors, held in July 1995, was low. With one-half of the 252 seats being contested, the LDP won only 49 seats, the SDPJ 16 and the New Party Sakigake three, whereas the NFP, benefiting from the support of the Soka Gakkai religious organization, won 40 seats. In September Ryutaro Hashimoto, the Minister of International Trade and Industry, was elected leader of the LDP, after Yohei Kono announced that he would not seek re-election.

Conflict in the Diet escalated between February and June 1995 over government plans, announced in June 1994, to issue a resolution to commemorate the 50th anniversary of the ending of the Second World War. The resolution was to constitute an apology to countries whose citizens had suffered from the actions of the Japanese army during the war. The New Party Sakigake threatened to withdraw from the coalition if an apology were not made, while a group of 160 LDP Diet members, led by Seisuke Okuno, objected to the definition of Japan as an aggressor. A resolution was finally passed in June 1995, despite a boycott of the vote by the NFP.

In December 1995 Toshiki Kaifu was succeeded by Ichiro Ozawa as leader of the NFP. In January 1996 Tomiichi Murayama resigned as Prime Minister; he was, however, re-elected Chairman of the SDPJ. The LDP leader, Ryutaro Hashimoto, was elected Prime Minister on 11 January. A coalition Cabinet, largely dominated by the LDP, was formed.

In March 1996 the New Socialist Party (NSP) was formed by left-wing defectors from the SDPJ. Osamu Yatabe was elected Chairman of the NSP and Tetsuo Yamaguchi was appointed Secretary-General. In mid-1996, in an attempt to strengthen their electoral bases, particularly in the new single-member districts, there was a further realignment of political parties. In August Shoichi Ide and Hiroyuki Sonoda were elected Leader and Secretary-General, respectively, of the New Party Sakigake following the resignations of Masayoshi Takemura and Yukio Hatoyama. Hatoyama left the party and founded the Democratic Party of Japan (DPJ), with other dissident members of the New Party Sakigake and individual members of the SDPJ and NFP.

A general election was held in October 1996. The LDP won 239 of the 500 seats in the House of Representatives, while the NFP secured 156, the DPJ 52, the Japan Communist Party (JCP) 26, the SDPJ 15, and the New Party Sakigake two seats. Four deputies, who were elected as independents, subsequently formed a new party called the 21st Century. In November Ryutaro Hashimoto was re-elected Prime Minister, and formed the first single-party Cabinet since 1993.

Soon after the election several government ministers and party leaders were implicated in various official corruption scandals. In December 1996 the former Prime Minister, Tsutomu Hata, left the NFP and formed a new party, called Taiyoto (Sun Party), together with 12 other dissident NFP members. In late December Takako Doi was formally appointed Chairwoman of the SDPJ (she had been acting Chairwoman since the dissolution of the House of Representatives in September).

In early 1997 the Government established several commissions, charged with devising a comprehensive programme of administrative and economic reforms. A reduction in government bureaucracy and public expenditure was envisaged, and details of a series of financial deregulation measures were announced in February, including the transfer of the Ministry of Finance's supervisory role to an independent agency in mid-1998. The Government's management of the nuclear programme was comprehensively reviewed, following two accidents at plants in December 1995 and March 1997. Allegations that a further 11 unreported radiation leaks had occurred over the previous three years served to heighten public disquiet over Japan's nuclear research and development programme.

In mid-1997 Hosokawa resigned from the NFP, reportedly owing to dissatisfaction with Ozawa's leadership. (In December Hosokawa formed a new party—From Five.) In addition, the NFP lost all of its seats in elections to the Tokyo Metropolitan Assembly, held in July. The LDP and the JCP, by contrast, increased their representation in the Assembly. By September the LDP had regained its majority in the House of Representatives, following a series of defections by members of the NFP. In December a much-reduced NFP was dissolved. Six new parties were founded by former NFP members, and a significant political realignment took place. In January 1998 six opposition parties, including the DPJ, formed a parliamentary group, Minyuren, which constituted the largest opposition bloc in the Diet. In March the parties comprising Minyuren agreed on their integration into the DPJ, formally establishing a new DPJ, with Naoto Kan as its President, in the following month.

Meanwhile, during 1997 various circumstances, including continuing financial corruption, an increase in the rate of the unpopular consumption tax, from 3% to 5%, a decrease in public expenditure (as part of the Government's fiscal reforms, which resulted in a significant weakening in consumer demand) and the collapse of several prominent financial institutions, together with the threat of further bankruptcies, contributed to the development of an economic crisis. The Government announced a series of measures designed to encourage economic growth, including a reduction in taxes and, in a major reversal of policy, the use of public funds to support the banking system. In January 1998 the Diet reconvened earlier than scheduled, in order to approve the budget for 1998/99, as well as supplementary budget proposals incorporating the tax reductions. In late January 1998 two senior officials from the Ministry of Finance were arrested on suspicion of accepting bribes from banks. The Minister of Finance, Hiroshi Mitsuzuka, resigned, accepting full moral responsibility for the affair. As more banks and other financial institutions became implicated in the bribery scandal, the central bank initiated an internal investigation into its own operations. In March the Governor resigned after a senior bank executive was arrested amid further allegations of bribery. Trials of those implicated in the financial scandals took place in 1998 and 1999.

A number of financial deregulation measures, including the liberalization of brokerage commissions and the removal of foreign-exchange controls, came into effect on 1 April 1998, as part of Japan's 'Big Bang' reform process. The economy continued to stagnate, however, despite the launch of a series of economic stimulus programmes, and Hashimoto's administration was widely criticized for its slow reaction to the economic crisis. In June the SDPJ and the New Party Sakigake withdrew from their alliance with the ruling LDP.

The LDP performed poorly in elections for one-half of the seats in the House of Councillors in July 1998, retaining only 44 of its 61 seats contested, while the DPJ won 27 seats, increasing its representation to 47 seats, and the JCP became the third-largest party in the upper house, taking 15 seats. Hashimoto resigned as Prime Minister and President of the LDP and was succeeded by Keizo Obuchi, hitherto Minister for Foreign Affairs. Obuchi was elected Prime Minister on 30 July.

Obuchi's Government was designated an 'economic reconstruction' Cabinet, but as it comprised a large number of hereditary politicians doubts arose about its commitment to comprehensive economic reform. Kiichi Miyazawa, the former Prime Minister, was appointed Minister of Finance. In his inaugural policy speech, Obuchi announced the establishment of an Economic Strategy Council and promised substantial tax cuts. As Japan's economic situation worsened, political disputes over banking reform dominated the following months, with the Government reluctant to commit itself to the closure of failing banks. Following weeks of negotiations, in October 1998 the Diet approved banking legislation that included provisions for the nationalization of failing banks, as demanded by the opposition.

Shinto Heiwa and Komei merged in November 1998 to form New Komeito, which thus became the second-largest opposition party. Also in that month Fukushiro Nukaga, the Director-General of the Defence Agency, resigned from the Government to assume responsibility for a procurement scandal involving his agency. In mid-November the LDP and the Liberal Party (LP) reached a basic accord on the formation of a coalition, which would still remain short of a majority in the upper house. In January 1999 agreement was reached on coalition policies, including measures to reduce the influence of bureaucrats on the legislative process. The LP appeared to have won concessions on a number of proposals that it wanted to be submitted for consideration by the Diet in forthcoming sessions. The Cabinet was reshuffled to include the LP, with the number of ministers reduced from 20 to 18 (excluding the Prime Minister). The leader of the LP, Ichiro Ozawa, had refused a cabinet position. At the end of January the Government adopted an administrative reform plan, which aimed to reduce further the number of cabinet ministers and public servants and to establish an economic and fiscal policy committee. Draft legislation on the implementation of the plan was introduced in the Diet in April.

At local elections in April 1999, 11 of the 12 governorships contested were won by the incumbents, all standing as independents. At the gubernatorial election for Tokyo, the convincing victory of Shintaro Ishihara, a nationalist writer and a former Minister of Transport under the LDP (although now unaffiliated), was regarded as an embarrassment for the ruling party. Ishihara immediately provoked controversy, making inflammatory comments about the 1937 Nanjing massacre and criticizing the Chinese Government, which responded angrily, prompting the Japanese Government to distance itself publicly from the new Governor's remarks. In November the Chinese Government also expressed its concern regarding an unofficial visit by Ishihara to Taiwan, which had recently suffered a major earthquake. Ishihara also angered the People's Republic of China by visiting Taiwan in May 2000 for the inauguration of the latter's new President, Chen Shui-bian, despite having refused an invitation to visit China as part of celebrations to mark the anniversary of the establishment of relations between Beijing and Tokyo.

In June 1999 the Government voted to grant official legal status to the *de facto* national flag (*Hinomaru*) and anthem (*Kimigayo*), despite considerable opposition owing to their association with Japan's militaristic past. The necessary legislation became effective in mid-August, following approval by the Diet. Also approved was controversial legislation allowing police investigators, in certain circumstances, to monitor the telephones of suspected criminals. Meanwhile, in July New Komeito agreed to join the ruling LDP-LP coalition, giving the Government a new majority in the upper house and expanding its control in the lower house to more than 70% of the seats. Negotiations on policy initiatives proved difficult, however, and were still continuing in September, owing to differences over a number of contentious issues such as constitutional revision and New Komeito's opposition to a reduction in the number of seats in the lower house, as favoured by the LP. Obuchi was re-elected President of the LDP in September. Naoto Kan was replaced as President of the DPJ by Yukio Hatoyama, hitherto Secretary-General of the party.

At the end of September 1999 a serious accident at a uranium-processing plant at Tokaimura, which temporarily raised levels of radiation to 15 times the normal level and appeared to have been caused by human error and poor management, severely undermined public confidence in the safety of Japan's nuclear industry. Furthermore, in November it was revealed that 15 of 17 nuclear facilities recently inspected by government officials had failed to meet legal health and safety standards. In December the Diet enacted legislation aimed at preventing accidents and improving procedures for the management of any future incidents at nuclear power facilities. In February 2000 the Government announced that 439 people had been exposed to radiation in the Tokaimura accident, far more than the 69 recorded in the initial report. Two workers from the plant subsequently died from radiation exposure. In September 2000 compensation was agreed for the victims of the accident. Former staff at the plant were arrested in October and charged with negligence resulting in death for illegally changing safety procedures in order to cut costs in September 1999. In November 2000 the plant was authorized to be reopened.

A new Cabinet was appointed in October 1999. Notably, Michio Ochi was appointed Chairman of the Financial Reconstruction Commission. The LP and New Komeito each received one cabinet post. A basic accord on coalition policy included an agreement to seek a reduction in the number of seats in the House of Representatives, initially by 20 and subsequently by a further 30. A Vice-Minister at the Defence Agency resigned shortly after being appointed, following widespread criticism of his suggestion that Japan should arm itself with nuclear weapons. Obuchi, whose judgement in the affair was questioned, subsequently apologized to the nation in a speech to the Diet.

Trials continued in 1997–99 of members of Aum Shinrikyo, the cult accused of perpetrating the sarin gas attack on the Tokyo underground railway system in March 1995. In September 1999 Masato Yokoyama, a leading member of the cult, became the first of those accused to receive the death sentence. In late 1999, as the Diet considered and subsequently enacted legislation aimed at curbing its activities, Aum Shinrikyo issued a series of statements in an apparent attempt to avert any restriction on the cult or seizure of its assets. The leaders of the cult announced a suspension of all external activities from October, and in December acknowledged its culpability for a number of crimes, including the 1995 gas attack. Moreover, in January 2000 the cult announced that it was changing its name to Aleph and renouncing its leader, Shoko Asahara, who was still being tried for his part in the gas attack. In February, following a police raid on Aum Shinrikyo premises, it was revealed that a number of major companies and government agencies had placed orders for computer software with a firm believed to be major source of revenue for the cult; the Defence Agency subsequently announced that it was to abandon software purchased from the company for use by the Self-Defence Forces.

In December 1999 a political crisis was averted when Ozawa was persuaded not to withdraw the LP from the ruling coalition, as he had threatened, over a delay in the proposal of legislation to reduce the number of seats in the lower house. The ruling parties had earlier agreed also to postpone the consideration of a proposal to expand Japan's participation in UN peace-keeping activities. In early 2000 the ruling coalition passed the controversial legislation on the reduction in seats through the Diet, despite an opposition boycott, which continued for some two weeks. Political observers speculated that the opposition had hoped to force Obuchi to dissolve the House of Representatives and call elections, which were due to be held by 19 October. Meanwhile, multi-party committees were established in both houses in January, which were to review the Constitution over a period of five years. In late February Michio Ochi was forced to resign from the Cabinet over remarks that suggested he would be lenient on banking reform. In March a number of incidents of police misconduct at a senior level resulted in disciplinary action being taken against the chief of the National Police Agency.

Discord within the coalition increased, and on 1 April 2000 the LP withdrew from the Government. Shortly afterwards, 26 members of the LP formed Hoshuto (New Conservative Party). On the following day, however, Keizo Obuchi suffered a stroke and went into a coma from which he never regained consciousness. The Government was criticized for not releasing the news of Obuchi's condition (it was not reported in the media for at least 24 hours) even though the country had effectively been without a premier. Chief Cabinet Secretary Mikio Aoki became Acting Prime Minister, claiming that Obuchi had specifically asked him to fulfil the role, but the LDP elected Yoshiro Mori, the Secretary-General, as party President; he was subsequently elected Prime Minister by both houses of the Diet. Mori immediately affirmed his commitment to the economic and political reform initiatives of his predecessor and in early April formed a coalition with New Komeito and Hoshuto. All ministers from the Obuchi administration were retained. During that month both Seiroku Kajiyama (a former Chief Cabinet Secretary) and Noboru Takeshita, the former Prime Minister, announced their retirement from politics and from the LDP; both men died shortly afterwards. Former Prime Minister Ryutaro Hashimoto was appointed head of the Takeshita faction of the LDP, which had been led by Obuchi prior to his stroke.

Following his appointment as Prime Minister, Mori made a number of controversial public statements, expressing imperialist views. Heavy criticism from the opposition and the media forced him to issue apologies although he did not retract his remarks. Shortly prior to the elections, the media declared that some 50% of the electorate remained undecided on how to vote; Mori expressed the view that these voters should 'sleep in' on election day, later claiming that his intent was to urge unaligned voters to abstain rather than vote against the LDP, although some concern was expressed as Japan tried to combat voter apathy. In the election, held on 25 June 2000 and at which the number of seats in the House of Representatives was reduced from 500 to 480, the LDP won the most seats, although its representation was reduced to 233 and many of its key political figures, including current and former cabinet ministers, lost their seats, particularly in metropolitan areas. The DPJ increased its representation to 127 seats, New Komeito won 31 seats, the LP 22 seats, Hoshuto 20 seats and the SDPJ 19 seats. The LDP benefited from the electoral system, which gave rural areas (where the LDP has strong support) disproportionately high representation. Tradition and family connections remained important, with two candidates (the brother of Noboru Takeshita and the daughter of Keizo Obuchi) winning seats despite their lack of political experience. The participation rate was 62.5%. Although remaining in power, the LDP faced serious problems, among the most prominent of which related to the suitability of its leadership, Mori having made numerous political gaffes and public errors of protocol. Nevertheless, Mori was returned as Prime Minister and announced the composition of his new Cabinet in July.

Meanwhile, in February 2000 Governor Ishihara of Tokyo proposed that a tax be levied on major banks based on the size of their business rather than their profits; he was criticized by the central Government, which had previously been the only body able to introduce taxes. Ishihara attracted criticism from the foreign residents of Tokyo, and from neighbouring countries, in April when, in an address to members of the Self-Defence Forces, he blamed foreign residents for a number of serious crimes and referred to them as *sangokujin*, a derogatory wartime term for people from Taiwan and Korea.

In October 2000 an amendment to the voting system, under which electors would choose to vote either for a party or for an individual candidate, was proposed by the governing coalition. The opposition strongly criticized the proposed changes and, following the Government's insistence that they be passed through the Diet, commenced a boycott of proceedings. The bill was approved in the House of Representatives despite the boycott, which lasted 18 days and ended following an agreement between the Government and the opposition to debate the proposed legislation in the House of Representatives. It was enacted in late October. Meanwhile, Juro Saito resigned as President of the House of Councillors, owing to his failure successfully to mediate in the dispute. He was replaced by the former Minister of Education, Yutaka Inoue.

Corruption was a major issue throughout 2000, particularly the taking of bribes, revelations of which resulted in several resignations. Among the most serious incidents was a 'cash for questions' scandal involving an insurance company. One LDP member resigned and another was arrested in connection with the affair in November, and in January 2001 Fukushiro Nukaga, the Minister of State for Economy, Industry and Information Technology, resigned, having earlier admitted that he had accepted bribes from the firm. An LDP ally of Yoshiro Mori, Masakuni Murakami, was implicated in the case and arrested in March. In October 2000 Hidenao Nakagawa, Minister of State, Chief Cabinet Secretary, Director-General of the Okinawa Development Agency and Minister in Charge of Information Technology, resigned after it was alleged, *inter alia*, that he had links to a right-wing activist. In the following month the former Minister of Construction, Eiichi Nakao, acknowledged in court that he had taken bribes in 1996 in exchange for the allocation of public works contracts.

The high incidence of corruption further undermined Mori, and during October 2000 the Prime Minister came under increasing pressure to resign after it was alleged in a magazine that some years previously he had been arrested for violation of an anti-prostitution law. Mori denied the allegation and sued the publication for libel. Later that month, during a meeting with Tony Blair, the British Prime Minister, Mori reportedly suggested that the Democratic People's Republic of Korea could release Japanese hostages (see below) to a third country in order to avoid any admission of their existence. Harsh criticism ensued, and subsequent attempts to mitigate the situation, by claiming that the remarks referred to an episode from the past, proved unsuccessful. In mid-November the opposition launched a motion of 'no confidence' in the Prime Minister. Furthermore, LDP member Koichi Kato publicly criticized Mori and declared himself ready to form a government. The Prime Minister won the vote, however, following threats by the party leadership that rebels voting against Mori would be expelled from the LDP. In early December, Mori suffered a set-back when his strong ally, Hiromu Nonaka, resigned as Secretary-General of the LDP and retired from politics. His nominated successor, Makoto Koga, subsequently assumed the role.

A major cabinet reorganization was effected in December 2000, and substantial changes were made to the government structure. The number of ministries was to be reduced from 23 to 13, mainly through mergers, and various state agencies were absorbed into the newly-created Cabinet Office. (Legislation providing for these changes had been approved in June 1998.) The new structure was not fully implemented until January 2001, following an administrative reform. Notable appointments to the new Cabinet included the leader of the largest LDP faction and former Prime Minister, Ryutaro Hashimoto, and Hakuo Yanagisawa, the former Director-General of the Financial Reconstruction Commission. The former was appointed Minister of State for the Development of Okinawa and the Settlement of the Northern Territories, and the latter became Minister of State for Financial Affairs. Both men were well-respected and enjoyed considerable political support, and their appointment was seen as an attempt by Mori to strengthen his position. During December 2000, however, photographs showing the Prime Minister in the company of an alleged gangster and convicted murderer were published. In the same month, and again in January 2001, senior officials of the party were implicated in a bribery scandal (see above). Mori won another vote of confidence in March, but in early April announced his intention to resign. In late April Junichiro Koizumi, a former Minister of Health and Welfare, defeated two other candidates, including Ryutaro Hashimoto, to secure the presidency of the ruling LDP and thus the post of Prime Minister. A cabinet reorganization followed.

Meanwhile, in November 2000 Fusaka Shigenobu, the founder of the extremist left-wing Japanese Red Army which had been responsible for a number of terrorist attacks during the 1970s, was arrested in Tokyo. She was detained on suspicion of the seizure of the French embassy in The Hague, the Netherlands, in 1974, and subsequently indicted on various related charges. A number of other members had been repatriated from various countries since 1995, and now faced trials for terrorism. Japan hoped to obtain the extradition from the Democratic People's Republic of Korea, in return for economic aid, of more Red Army members, who had hijacked a Japanese aircraft and forced it to fly to Pyongyang in 1970 (later being granted political asylum).

From the mid-1990s Japan's growing trade surplus with the USA became a matter of increasing concern for the US authorities. In October 1994 trade agreements in three of the four main areas under bilateral discussion were signed. Negotiations concerning the automobile trade resulted in the signing of an agreement with the USA in June 1995. However, an increase in the export of Japanese vehicles to the USA in 1997, and a concomitant rise in the US trade deficit with Japan, caused growing tension between the two countries. Negotiations in April and June focused on trade issues. In September an agreement to reform Japanese port operations was concluded shortly after the USA imposed large fines on Japanese companies for employing restrictive harbour practices. Negotiations on increased access to airline routes were successfully concluded in January 1998. However, relations were again strained by trade disputes in 1998, with Japan's high tariffs on rice, in the forestry and fisheries sectors, and low-priced steel exports being of particular concern to the USA. Tension also arose over the USA's repeated criticism that Japan was not doing enough to stimulate its own economy and alleviate the Asian economic crisis. During a visit to Japan in November 1998, President Clinton urged the Government rapidly to implement measures to encourage domestic demand, reform the banking sector and liberalize its markets. Meanwhile, Japan's trade surplus with the USA continued to increase, and in 1998 reached its highest level since 1987. In May 1999, during a visit by Prime Minister Obuchi to the USA (the first such official state visit in 12 years), Clinton praised Obuchi's efforts to promote economic recovery and welcomed Japanese plans for further deregulation in several sectors. Meanwhile, a dispute over Japanese steel exports had escalated. A ruling, in April 1999, by the US Department of Commerce that Japan had 'dumped' hot-rolled steel into the US market was endorsed, in June, by the US International Trade Commission, and punitive duties were subsequently imposed. In November Japan announced its intention to bring a complaint before the World Trade Organization (WTO) against the US ruling. Relations between the two countries deteriorated in mid-2000, following the expansion by Japan of its hunting of whales as part of a 'scientific research' programme. The USA subsequently banned Japan from future access to its territorial waters and threatened to impose sanctions on Japanese food imports. Japan warned that if any such sanctions were imposed, it would take the dispute to the WTO. The International Whaling Commission subsequently refused a bid by Japan to hold its next meeting in the country.

Together with trade issues, Japan's bilateral security arrangements with the USA, concluded by treaty in 1951, continued to be the focus of US-Japanese relations. The treaty granted the use of military bases in Japan to the USA, in return for a US commitment to provide military support to Japan in the event of external aggression. In January 1992, the 'Tokyo declaration on the US-Japan global partnership' was issued, whereby the two countries undertook to co-operate in promoting international security and prosperity. In February 1993 Japan and the USA reaffirmed their security relationship, with the USA agreeing to protect Japan from the threat posed by potential nuclear proliferation around the world.

The presence of the US forces in Japan provoked much debate in the mid-1990s. In November 1995 three US servicemen were arrested and subsequently imprisoned for the rape of a schoolgirl in Okinawa. Considerable civil unrest ensued and legal proceedings were initiated against the Governor of Okinawa, Masahide Ota, following his refusal to renew the leases for US military installations in the region. Protracted negotiations between the two countries resulted in the USA agreeing, in December 1996, to release 21% of the land used for US military purposes in Okinawa, and to build a floating offshore helicopter base to replace the air base at Futenma. In April 1997 it was proposed to relocate several of the US bases to other prefectures. In December, in a non-binding referendum held in Nago, Okinawa, to assess public opinion concerning the construction of the offshore helicopter base, the majority of voters rejected the proposal, prompting the resignation of the Mayor of Nago. Governor Ota stated his opposition to the proposed base, a position also adopted by the new Mayor, elected in February 1998. In November 1998 Keiichi Inamine defeated Ota in the Okinawa gubernatorial elections. Inamine, who had been supported by the LDP, presented an alternative solution, proposing that a military-commercial airport be built in northern Okinawa and leased to the USA for a period of 15 years. In December 1998 a US military site was the first of the 11 bases to be returned under the 1996 agreement. In December 1999 Inamine's proposal for the relocation of the Futenma air base was approved by both the local authorities and the Japanese Government, with the Henoko district of Nago chosen as the site for the new airport; at the same time funding was allocated for a 10-year development plan for northern Okinawa. Negotiations with the US Government, which opposed any time limit on its use of the airport, took place in October 2000; no progress was made.

In September 1997 revised Guidelines for Japan-US Defense Co-operation (first compiled in 1978) were issued. The Guidelines envisaged enhanced military co-operation between the USA and Japan, not only on Japanese territory, but also in situations in unspecified areas around Japan. In April 1998 the LDP Government approved legislation on the implementation of the revised Guidelines, which was enacted in May 1999, prompting criticism from China and Russia. Its approval was ensured by an agreement between the LDP, the LP, and New Komeito to exclude a clause that would have allowed the inspection of unidentified foreign ships by the SDF, with the aim of enforcing economic sanctions. In August 1999 the Japanese Government formally approved a memorandum of understanding with the USA stipulating details of joint technical research on the development of a theatre missile defence system, which aims to detect and shoot down incoming ballistic missiles within a 3,000-km radius. The Defence Agency estimated that Japan would have to allocate up to 30,000m. yen to the controversial research project over a five-year period.

From 1982 Japan remained under pressure from the USA to increase its defence expenditure and to assume greater responsibility for security in the Western Pacific area. In December 1990 the Government announced a new five-year programme to develop the country's defence capability. The new programme also envisaged that Japan would assume a greater share of the cost of maintaining the US troops stationed in Japan. In November 1995 the Cabinet approved a new national defence programme, which envisaged a 20% reduction in troops and confirmed Japan's security co-operation with the USA. In November 2000 the Japanese House of Representatives approved a five-year agreement, to commence in April 2001, to reduce host nation spending for US forces stationed in Japan. Relations between Japan and the USA deteriorated in February 2001 when a Japanese trawler sank, killing the entire crew, following a collision with a US submarine off Hawaii. The revelation that a civilian had been at the controls of the submarine at the time caused fury in Japan, as did reports that Yoshiro Mori had insisted on finishing a game of golf before dealing with the situation. The USA subsequently appointed the navy's second-in-command as a special envoy to Japan, who travelled to Tokyo at the end of the month to apologize in person and to brief the Japanese Prime Minister on the progress of investigations into the accident. The captain of the submarine also apologized to the families of those who had died, but resentment over the US military presence in Japan remained.

In September 1990 Japan contributed to the international effort to force an unconditional Iraqi withdrawal from Kuwait. A controversial LDP-sponsored Peace Co-operation Bill, which provided for the dispatch to the Persian (Arabian) Gulf area of some 2,000 non-combatant personnel, was withdrawn in November after it encountered severe political opposition. In January 1991, following repeated US demands for a greater financial commitment to the Gulf crisis (and a swifter disbursement of moneys already pledged), the Japanese Government announced plans substantially to increase its contribution and to provide aircraft for the transportation of refugees in the region. Opposition to the proposal was again vociferous. The Government secured the support of several centrist parties, by

pledging that any financial aid from Japan would be employed in a 'non-lethal' capacity, and legislation to approve the new contribution was adopted by the Diet in March.

In June 1992 controversial legislation to permit the SDF to participate in UN peace-keeping operations was approved. Their role, however, was to be confined to logistical and humanitarian tasks, unless a special dispensation from the Diet were granted. In September members of the SDF were dispatched to serve in the UN Transitional Authority in Cambodia (UNTAC). Japanese troops participated in further UN peace-keeping operations in Mozambique, in 1993, and, under Japanese command, on the Rwandan-Zairean border, in 1994. Legislation was approved in November 1994 to enable Japanese forces to be deployed overseas if the Government believed the lives of Japanese citizens to be at risk. In September Japan reiterated its desire to be a permanent member of the UN Security Council, particularly in view of its status as the world's largest donor of development aid and the second-largest contributor (after the USA) to the UN budget. In October 1996 the UN General Assembly voted to allocate to Japan a non-permanent seat on the Security Council, to be held for a two-year period from January 1997. In the late 1990s the Japanese Government was campaigning for a greater proportion of senior-level positions within the UN to be allocated to Japanese personnel. Draft legislation on an expansion of SDF participation in UN peace-keeping operations was to be considered by the Japanese Diet in early 2000. In November of that year Japan's announcement that it hoped to reduce expenditure on its foreign aid programme by 3% in 2001/02 prompted concern from the UN. Japan intensified its campaign to obtain a permanent seat on the UN Security Council in January 2001, when Yoshiro Mori visited South Africa, Kenya and Nigeria, on the first ever trip by a serving Japanese Prime Minister to sub-Saharan Africa. He hoped to obtain support for the bid in return for economic assistance.

Stability in East and South-East Asia remained a vital consideration in Japanese foreign policy, since Japan continued to depend on Asia for much of its foreign trade, including imports of raw materials. Despite the signing of a treaty of peace and friendship with the People's Republic of China in 1978, relations deteriorated in the late 1980s after China expressed concern at Japan's increased defence expenditure and its more assertive military stance. Japanese aid to China was suspended in June 1989, following the Tiananmen Square massacre in Beijing, and was not resumed until November 1990, after the Chinese Government abandoned a state of martial law. Relations between the two countries were strengthened by the visits to China by Emperor Akihito in October 1992, the first-ever Japanese imperial visit to China, and by Prime Minister Hosokawa in March 1994. However, in August of that year Japan announced the suspension of economic aid to China, following renewed nuclear testing by the Chinese Government. The provision of economic aid was resumed in early 1997, following the declaration of a moratorium on Chinese nuclear testing.

In July 1996 Japan's relations with both China and Taiwan were strained when a group of nationalists, the Japan Youth Federation, constructed a lighthouse and war memorial on the Senkaku Islands (or Diaoyu Islands in Chinese), a group of uninhabited islands situated in the East China Sea, to which all three countries laid claim. The situation was further aggravated in September by the accidental drowning of a Hong Kong citizen during a protest near the islands against Japan's claim. In October a flotilla of small boats, operated by activists from Taiwan, Hong Kong and Macau, raised the flags of China and Taiwan on the disputed islands. The Japanese Government sought to defuse tensions with China and Taiwan by withholding official recognition of the lighthouse; it did not, however, condemn those who had constructed the controversial buildings. In May 1997 China expressed serious concern, when a member of the Japanese Diet landed on one of the disputed islands. The Japanese Government distanced itself from the action.

In September 1997 Hashimoto visited China to commemorate the 25th anniversary of the normalization of relations between the two countries. China expressed concern at the revised US-Japanese security arrangements, following a statement by a senior Japanese minister that the area around Taiwan might be covered under the new guidelines. Procedures for the removal of chemical weapons, deployed in China by Japanese forces during the Second World War, were also discussed. During a visit to Japan by the Chinese Premier, Li Peng, in November, a bilateral fisheries agreement was signed. In November 1998, during a six-day state visit by President Jiang Zemin, Obuchi and Zemin issued (but declined to sign) a joint declaration on friendship and co-operation, in which Japan expressed deep remorse for past aggression against China. China, however, was reported to be displeased by the lack of a written apology, and remained concerned by the implications of US-Japanese defence arrangements regarding Taiwan. A subsequent US-Japanese agreement to initiate joint technical research on the development of a theatre missile defence system, followed by the Japanese Diet's approval, in May 1999, of legislation on the implementation of the revised US-Japanese defence guidelines (see above), provoked severe criticism from China, despite Japan's insistence that military co-operation with the USA was purely defensive. In July a meeting in Beijing between Obuchi and the Chinese Premier, Zhu Rongji, resulted in the formalization of a bilateral agreement on China's entry to the WTO, following several months of intense negotiations on the liberalization of trade in services. In August 2000 China withdrew permission for the Japanese Minister of Transport, Hajime Morita, to visit the People's Republic in September, owing to scheduling difficulties with Chinese officials. The Japanese media, however, attributed the Chinese change of attitude to a recent visit by Morita to a shrine honouring Japan's war dead, including those convicted of war crimes. Zhu Rongji visited Japan in October, and admitted that his failure to demand an apology for the host country's wartime conduct had attracted criticism in China.

In January 1993, meanwhile, Prime Minister Miyazawa toured four member countries of the Association of South East Asian Nations (ASEAN, see p. 134), during which he advocated an expansion of political and economic co-operation in the region. A visit by Prime Minister Hashimoto to ASEAN countries in January 1997 aimed to strengthen economic and security relations with the member countries. During 1998 Japan was widely criticized for its slow response to the Asian economic crisis. The weakness of the Japanese currency adversely affected financial markets throughout Asia, undermining efforts to stimulate regional economic recovery. As a result of increasing international pressure, in October the Japanese Government announced a US $30,000m. aid 'package' for Asian countries. In November the USA and Japan presented a joint initiative for growth and economic recovery in Asia, and in the following month Japan pledged further aid, to be disbursed over a three-year period.

Attempts to establish full diplomatic relations with the Democratic People's Republic of Korea (DPRK) in early 1991 were hindered by the DPRK's demands for financial reparations for the Japanese colonization of the country during 1910–45 and by the DPRK's refusal to allow International Atomic Energy Agency inspectors access to its nuclear facilities. Relations improved in 1995 and 1996 after Japan provided emergency aid to the DPRK when serious food shortages were reported. Concerns that the DPRK had developed a missile capable of reaching Japanese territory resulted in the suspension of food aid in mid-1996, but, following bilateral negotiations in August 1997, at which it was agreed to reopen discussions aimed at restoring full diplomatic relations, provision of food aid resumed in October. Agreement was also reached concerning the issue of visits to relatives in Japan by the estimated 1,800 Japanese nationals resident in the DPRK. The first such visits took place in November. However, food aid and normalization talks were suspended in mid-1998, following the testing by the DPRK of a suspected missile over Japanese territory. Tensions were exacerbated in March 1999, when two suspected North Korean spy ships, which had infiltrated Japanese waters, were pursued and fired on by Japanese naval forces. In mid-1999 it was reported that Japanese components had been used by the DPRK for the construction of weapons and other military equipment. Relations improved following the DPRK's agreement with the USA, in September, to suspend its reported plans to test a new long-range missile. In October, following unofficial talks between Japanese and North Korean government officials in Singapore, Japan lifted a ban on charter flights to the DPRK. In December the Japanese Government announced that it would resume the provision of food aid. Later that month intergovernmental preparatory talks on re-establishing diplomatic relations were held in Beijing, after Japanese and North Korean Red Cross officials reached an agreement on humanitarian issues. Most notably, the Red Cross organization of the DPRK promised to urge its Government to co-operate in an investigation into the fate of some 10 missing Japanese nationals, believed by the Japanese Government to have been abducted by

North Korean agents in the 1970s and 1980s. Full negotiations on the establishment of diplomatic relations were held in April 2000, and several further rounds of talks took place during the year, despite an announcement by Japan in September that normal bilateral relations would not be restored until the cases of Japanese citizens allegedly abducted by North Korean agents had been solved. In October, however, a further round of negotiations took place in Beijing, China. Meanwhile, in September the long-delayed third series of visits to their homeland by the Japanese wives of North Korean men took place.

The Japanese Government criticized India and Pakistan for conducting nuclear tests in mid-1998, and suspended grants of non-humanitarian aid and loans to both countries in response to the tests. A series of missile tests carried out by India and Pakistan in April 1999 again provoked criticism from Japan. Following a visit to India by the Japanese Prime Minister in August 2000, differences over nuclear testing were set aside in favour of enhanced security, defence and research co-operation between Japan and India.

Relations with the Republic of Korea were strained during 1996–98 for various reasons, principally concerning territorial and fishing disputes. Relations improved, however, during a four-day state visit by President Kim Dae-Jung to Japan in October 1998, when a joint declaration was signed, in which Japan apologized for the suffering inflicted on the Korean people during Japanese colonial rule. Japan also pledged substantial aid to the Republic of Korea to stimulate economic recovery. In November the two countries concluded negotiations on the renewal of their bilateral fisheries agreement, which came into effect in January 1999. An agreement to modify some of the terms of the accord was reached in March 1999, following a series of differences over its implementation. Increased co-operation was emphasized during a visit by Obuchi to the Republic of Korea later that month, when both countries agreed to strengthen bilateral economic relations, and Japan pledged further aid.

The actions of the Japanese army in the Second World War proved to be a contentious issue from the mid-1990s, both domestically and in Japan's relations with neighbouring Asian countries, in the context of the 50th anniversary, in August 1995, of the surrender of Japanese forces. In November 1994 an international ruling that Asian women, used for sexual purposes by the Japanese army during the Second World War ('comfort women'), should receive compensation was rejected by the Japanese Government, which insisted that the issue of reparation payments to individuals had been fully covered under the terms of the peace treaty of 1951. Japan also applied this policy to claims for compensation made by former prisoners of war belonging to the Allied forces. In February 1995 Prime Minister Murayama publicly acknowledged that Japan was responsible, in part, for the post-war division of the Korean peninsula. He was forced to retract the statement, however, following bitter controversy in the Diet. In June a resolution was passed apologizing for Japanese actions in the war, despite considerable disagreement in the Diet. However, countries whose citizens had been prisoners of the Japanese army criticized the resolution as being insufficiently explicit. In August 1996 the first compensation payments, accompanied by a letter of apology from Prime Minister Hashimoto, were made from a private fund to four Philippine victims, who had been used as 'comfort women' during the war. The majority of groups representing South Korean victims refused to accept payment from the fund, demanding that compensation be forthcoming from official, rather than private, sources. In April 1998, however, a Japanese district court ordered the Government to pay compensation to three former 'comfort women' from the Republic of Korea. Another group of South Korean 'comfort women' was refused the right to compensation by the Japanese High Court in November 2000. In late 1999 a lawsuit was filed in the US state of California against several large Japanese corporations on behalf of former prisoners of war and civilians from various countries, who alleged that the companies had profited from their forced labour during the Second World War. In November 2000 one of these corporations agreed to pay compensation to Chinese forced labourers used during the War.

Japan's relations with Russia have been dominated by the issue of the Northern Territories, four small islands situated close to Hokkaido, which were annexed in 1945 by the USSR. Both countries claim sovereignty over the islands, and there has been no substantial progress towards resolving the situation since 1956, when Japan and the USSR resumed diplomatic relations. In February 1992 a joint Japanese-Russian working group began discussions about a prospective peace treaty (formally ending the Second World War), and meetings on the issue took place in 1992 and 1993. However, relations between the two countries deteriorated, following the disposal of nuclear waste in Japanese waters by Russian ships in November, and Russia's decision, in August 1994, to open fire on Japanese vessels, that were alleged to have been fishing in Russian waters. Bilateral negotiations over the status of the disputed territory opened in March 1995. In November 1996 Japan indicated that it was prepared to resume the disbursement of an aid 'package', withheld since 1991, and in May 1997 the Japanese Government abandoned its opposition to Russia's proposed membership of the G-7 group. Russian plans for joint development of the mineral and fishing resources of the disputed territory were followed, in July, by an outline agreement on the jurisdiction of the islands. Later in that month a new diplomatic policy was forged, based on 'trust, mutual benefit and long-term prospects'. At an informal summit meeting in November, the two parties agreed to work towards the conclusion of a formal peace treaty by the year 2000. Negotiations resulted in the conclusion of a framework fisheries agreement in December 1997. The Japanese Government offered considerable financial aid to Russia during a visit by President Yeltsin to Japan in April 1998, and agreement was reached on the expansion of economic co-operation. In November Prime Minister Obuchi and Yeltsin signed a joint declaration on bilateral relations in Moscow. During Obuchi's visit Yeltsin reportedly submitted proposals on the resolution of the territorial dispute, in response to suggestions made by Hashimoto in April. Although it had been agreed that the contents of the proposals should not be made public, it was widely reported that both countries still claimed sovereignty over the islands, with Japan advocating a transitional period of Russian administrative control. Agreement was reached on the establishment of subcommissions to examine issues of border delimitation and joint economic activity on the disputed islands. However, little progress was achieved by the subcommissions during 1999. In September Japan agreed to resume lending to Russia, which had been suspended since the Russian Government had effectively devalued the rouble and defaulted on some of its debts in mid-1998. At the same time an accord was concluded on improved access to the disputed islands for former Japanese inhabitants. Negotiations achieved little progress during 2000, a major obstacle being the issue of how many of the islands should be returned. Despite Russian President Vladimir Putin's repudiation of Japan's claim to any of the islands during his first official visit to Tokyo in September, Russia subsequently offered to abide by a 1956 declaration that it would relinquish two of the islands after the signature of a peace treaty, but Japan initially rejected this partial solution. Discussions scheduled to be held in March 2001 in Irkutsk in the Russian Federation, however, were expected to discuss the possibility of basing a treaty on the declaration. Meanwhile, in November 2000 a former Japanese naval officer on trial in Tokyo admitted spying for Russia. There was outrage in Japan at the fact that the crime carried possible punishments that were perceived as being extremely lenient in relation to the severity of the offence.

Japan's urgent need for new oil supplies prompted the visit to the country in October 2000 of the Iranian President, Muhammad Khatami, the first by an Iranian Head of State since that country's revolution of 1979. The trip culminated in Japan's securing negotiation rights over the world's largest undeveloped oilfield, in Iran.

In November 2000 the Peruvian President, Alberto Fujimori, arrived in Tokyo from where he submitted his resignation by fax, following increasing allegations of domestic corruption. In December Japan announced that Fujimori possessed dual nationality as his father had been a Japanese citizen, and that he was therefore entitled to remain indefinitely in the country. In March 2001, however, the Peruvian authorities charged Fujimori with criminal abuse of power and requested his extradition. Japan refused, despite Peruvian warnings of serious consequences if the former President did not return.

Government

Under the Constitution of 1947, the Emperor is Head of State but has no governing power. Legislative power is vested in the bicameral Diet, comprising the House of Representatives (lower house), whose members are elected for a four-year term, and the House of Councillors (upper house), members of which are elected for six years, one-half being elected every three years.

The House of Representatives comprises 480 seats—300 single-seat constituencies and 180 determined by proportional representation—and there are 252 seats in the House of Councillors. The number of seats in the House of Representatives was reduced from 500 for the 2000 elections; the reduction was in the number of seats determined by proportional representation. There is universal suffrage for all adults from 20 years of age. Executive power is vested in the Cabinet, which is responsible to the Diet. The Emperor appoints the Prime Minister (on designation by the Diet), who appoints the other Ministers in the Cabinet.

Japan has 47 prefectures, each administered by an elected Governor.

Defence

Although the Constitution renounces war and the use of force, the right of self-defence is not excluded. Japan maintains ground, maritime and air self-defence forces. Military service is voluntary. The USA provides equipment and training staff and also maintains bases in Japan. US forces in Japan totalled 39,750 at 1 August 2000. The total strength of the Japanese Self-Defence Forces at 1 August 2000 was some 236,700: army 148,500, navy 42,600, air force 44,200 and central staff 1,400. Government expenditure on defence under revised projections for the 1999/2000 general account budget was 4,915,000m. yen.

Economic Affairs

In 1998, according to estimates by the World Bank, Japan's gross national product (GNP), measured at average 1996–98 prices, was US $4,089,140m., equivalent to $32,350 per head (or $23,592 per head on an international purchasing-power parity basis). During 1990–98, it was estimated, GNP per head increased, in real terms, by an average of 1.3% per year. Over the same period, the population increased by an average of 0.3% per year. In 1999 GNP was $4,078,900m., equivalent to $32,230 per head. In 1990–99 GDP increased at an average annual rate of 1.7%, in real terms. Real GDP rose by 1.6% in 1997, but declined by 2.5% in 1998, before increasing by 0.2% in 1999.

In 1998 agriculture (including forestry and fishing) contributed 1.7% of GDP. In 1999 5.2% of the employed labour force were engaged in the sector. The principal crops are rice, potatoes, cabbages, sugar beets, and citrus fruits. During 1990–95, according to the World Bank, agricultural GDP declined at an average rate of 2.2% annually. According to the FAO, agricultural production decreased by 1.4% annually between 1996 and 1998.

Industry (including mining, manufacturing, construction and utilities) contributed 34.5% of GDP in 1998. In 1999 31.9% of the employed labour force were engaged in the industrial sector. During 1990–95, according to the World Bank, industrial GDP remained constant. Industrial production increased by 2.3% in 1996 and by 3.6% in 1997, but declined sharply in 1998, falling by 7.1%. In 1999 the decline decelerated, with production decreasing by 2.7% year-on-year in October of that year. Following an apparent improvement in 2000, however, by early 2001 industrial output was reported to be contracting sharply once again.

Mining and quarrying contributed 0.2% of GDP in 1998. Less than 0.1% of the employed labour force were engaged in the sector in 1999. While the domestic output of limestone and sulphur is sufficient to meet domestic demand, all of Japan's requirements of bauxite, crude petroleum and iron ore, and a high percentage of its requirements of copper ore and coking coal are met by imports.

In 1998 manufacturing contributed 22.6% of GDP, and in 1999 20.9% of the employed labour force were engaged in the sector. According to the World Bank, manufacturing GDP increased by an average of 4.7% per year in 1985–92. The most important branches of manufacturing are machinery and transport equipment, electrical and electronic equipment, and iron and steel.

Japan imports most of its energy requirements, with imports of petroleum and petroleum products comprising 9.5% of the value of total imports in 1998. Nuclear energy accounted for 31.7% of electricity output in 1996. There are proposals to construct a further 20 nuclear reactors by 2010. In October 2000 Japan secured negotiation rights over the world's largest undeveloped oilfield, in Iran.

The services sector contributed 63.8% of GDP in 1998, and engaged 62.9% of the employed labour force in 1999. According to the World Bank, the GDP of the services sector increased by an average of 2.3% annually in 1990–95. Tourist receipts, totalling US $3,428m. in 1999, are an important source of revenue.

In 1999 Japan recorded a trade surplus of US $123,320m., and there was a surplus of $106,870m. on the current account of the balance of payments. In 1998 the principal source of imports was the USA (23.9%), which was also the principal market for exports (30.5%). Other major suppliers in that year were the People's Republic of China, Australia and the Republic of Korea. Other major purchasers of Japanese exports were Taiwan, Hong Kong and China. The principal imports in 1998 were machinery and transport equipment, miscellaneous manufactured articles, petroleum and petroleum products, food and live animals, and basic manufactures. The principal exports in that year were non-electric and electrical machinery, and transport equipment.

Projections for the financial year ending 31 March 2001 envisaged a deficit of 32,610,000m. yen on the general account budget. (In the previous year the deficit was equivalent to 8.0% of GDP.) The annual rate of inflation averaged 1.0% in 1990–99. Consumer prices declined by 0.3% in 1999 and by 0.4% in 2000. The rate of unemployment was 4.9% of the labour force in January 2001.

Japan is a member of the Asia-Pacific Economic Co-operation (APEC, see p. 128) forum, the Asian Development Bank (ADB, see p. 131), the Organisation for Economic Co-operation and Development (OECD, see p. 247) and the World Trade Organization (WTO, see p. 292).

Following a period of rapid economic expansion in the 1980s, Japan underwent a severe recession during the early 1990s, resulting from the collapse of asset prices. Prospects for growth improved, following the implementation of stimulus measures in the mid-1990s. In 1997 and 1998, however, the economy contracted significantly, and Japan again entered a recession. Investor confidence was low, owing to the weakness of the country's financial institutions and to the revelation of several corruption scandals. Domestic demand also declined sharply. Fiscal stimulus measures had little effect. Despite some signs of improvement during 1999 and the first half of 2000, as production levels and exports increased, by the third quarter of 2000 another recession appeared likely. Consumer demand remained low, while unemployment had reached its highest level since the Second World War. Political instability and a lack of confidence in the Government's commitment to reform contributed to the Japanese stock market's decline by 30% during 2000, and a further fall in the index to its lowest level for over 15 years in March 2001. The economic deceleration in the USA was a major factor, owing to its position as Japan's major trading partner. The US situation also had an indirect adverse effect on Japan's regional trade, as other Asian countries reliant on extensive export revenue from the USA found their purchasing power for Japanese goods reduced. Consolidation was widespread in the financial sector in 2000, and bankruptcies of high-profile organizations continued. In September 2000 the Government announced a programme of economic stimulus measures (the 10th such 'package' in eight years). Of the total allocation of 4,000,000m. yen, a sum of 300,000m. yen was to be spent on increasing information technology literacy, while 2,500,000m. yen was to be allocated to social infrastructure projects. Analysts were concerned, however, about the effect of increased spending on the rising level of public debt, which by early 2001 was equivalent to more than 125% of GDP. In early 2001, however, the depreciation of the yen against the US dollar and the euro was seen as a welcome boost for the economy. Nevertheless, recession seemed to be unavoidable. In March, as the economic situation worsened, the Government announced plans to buy back shares in Japanese banks that had been sold by the institutions in order to cover losses from bad loans. It also proposed tax cuts and a reduction in interest rates. A further range of emergency economic measures, focusing on structural reforms of the financial sector, was announced in early April 2001. Observers doubted, however, that the measures would be sufficient to restore confidence in the economy. In late April Junichiro Koizumi was appointed Prime Minister, having pledged effectively to address the problem of the country's debt burden, to give priority to corporate restructuring rather than to short-term economic growth, to compel the closure of businesses with excessive bad debts and to transfer the state-managed postal savings system to the private sector.

Social Welfare

Social welfare benefits are provided through three schemes: the Welfare Insurance system, which insures private sector employees; Mutual Aid Associations, which are responsible for public sector workers; and the National Pension and National Health systems, which cover self-employed people and agricultural workers. A basic pension is provided to almost all of the population through these schemes, and a universal health insurance system was introduced in 1961. The Government subsidizes the cost of medical care for the elderly and the self-employed. Significant changes to the social welfare system were proposed in the late 1990s, with an increase in the cost of insurance and a reduction in government subsidies envisaged. A new nursing care insurance scheme was to be introduced in April 2000. Legislation to introduce defined contribution pensions was expected to be passed in 2001. In 1999 Japan had 9,286 hospitals, with a total of 1,872,518 beds. In 1998 there were 248,611 physicians and 88,061 dentists working in the country. According to initial forecasts for the general account budget, government expenditure on social security was expected to amount to 16,767,000m. yen for the 2000/01 financial year.

Education

A kindergarten (*yochien*) system provides education for children aged between three and five years of age, although the majority of kindergartens are privately controlled. Education is compulsory between the ages of six and 15. Elementary education, which begins at six years of age, lasts for six years. Lower secondary education lasts for a further three years. In 1999 more than 11.7m. children aged six to 15 were enrolled in compulsory education, while 4.2m. of those aged 15 to 18 received upper secondary education. Upper secondary schools provide a three-year course in general topics, or a vocational course in subjects such as agriculture, commerce, fine art and technical studies. There are four types of institution for higher education. Universities (*daigaku*) offer a four-year degree course, as well as postgraduate courses. In 1999 there were 622 graduate schools and universities in Japan. Junior colleges (*tanki-daigaku*) provide less specialized two- to three-year courses. In 1999 there were 585 junior colleges in Japan. Both universities and junior colleges offer facilities for teacher-training. Colleges of technology (*koto-senmon-gakko*), of which there were 62 in 1999, offer a five-year specialized training. Since 1991 colleges of technology have been able to offer short-term advanced courses. Special training colleges (*senshu-gakko*) offer advanced courses in technical and vocational subjects, lasting for at least one year. Initial forecasts for the 1999/2000 general account budget envisaged government expenditure of 6,473,100m. yen on education and science.

Public Holidays

2001: 1 January (New Year's Day), 8 January (Coming of Age Day), 11 February (National Foundation Day), 20 March (Vernal Equinox Day), 29 April (Greenery Day), 3 May (Constitution Memorial Day), 5 May (Children's Day), 20 July (Marine Day), 15 September (Respect for the Aged Day), 23 September (Autumnal Equinox), 8 October (Sports Day), 3 November (Culture Day), 23 November (Labour Thanksgiving Day), 23 December (Emperor's Birthday).

2002: 1 January (New Year's Day), 14 January (Coming of Age Day), 11 February (National Foundation Day), 20 March (Vernal Equinox Day), 29 April (Greenery Day), 3 May (Constitution Memorial Day), 5 May (Children's Day), 20 July (Marine Day), 15 September (Respect for the Aged Day), 23 September (Autumnal Equinox), 14 October (Sports Day), 3 November (Culture Day), 23 November (Labour Thanksgiving Day), 23 December (Emperor's Birthday).

Weights and Measures

The metric system is in force.

Statistical Survey

Source (unless otherwise stated): Statistics Bureau, Management and Co-ordination Agency, 19-1, Wakamatsu-cho, Shinjuku-ku, Tokyo 162-8668; tel. (3) 5273-1145; fax (3) 5273-1181; e-mail standard@stat.go.jp; internet www.stat.go.jp.

Area and Population

AREA, POPULATION AND DENSITY

Area (sq km)	377,855*
Population (census results)†	
1 October 1990	123,611,167
1 October 1995	
Males	61,574,398
Females	63,995,848
Total	125,570,246
Population (official estimates at mid-year)	
1998	126,413,000
1999	126,650,000
2000	126,870,000
Density (per sq km) at mid-2000	335.8

* 145,891 sq miles.
† Excluding foreign military and diplomatic personnel and their dependants.

PRINCIPAL CITIES (population at census of 1 October 1995)*

Tokyo (capital)†	7,967,614	Fukuyama . .	374,517
Yokohama . . .	3,307,136	Fujisawa . .	368,651
Osaka . . .	2,602,421	Takatsuki . .	362,270
Nagoya . . .	2,152,184	Iwaki . .	360,598
Sapporo . . .	1,757,025	Asahikawa . .	360,568
Kyoto . . .	1,463,822	Machida . .	360,525
Kobe . . .	1,423,792	Nara . .	359,218
Fukuoka . .	1,284,795	Nagano . .	358,516
Kawasaki . .	1,202,820	Toyohashi . .	352,982
Hiroshima . .	1,108,888	Suita . .	342,760
Kitakyushu . .	1,019,598	Toyota . .	341,079
Sendai . .	971,297	Takamatsu . .	331,004
Chiba . . .	856,878	Koriyama . .	326,833
Sakai . . .	802,993	Toyama . .	325,375
Kumamoto. .	650,341	Kawagoe . .	323,353
Okayama . .	615,757	Okazaki . .	322,621
Sagamihara .	570,597	Kochi . .	321,999
Hamamatsu . .	561,606	Tokorozawa . .	320,406
Kagoshima . .	546,282	Kashiwa . .	317,750
Funabashi . .	540,817	Akita . .	311,948
Higashiosaka . .	517,232	Naha . .	301,890
Hachioji . .	503,363	Miyazaki . .	300,068
Niigata . .	494,769	Hakodate . .	298,881
Amagasaki . .	488,586	Koshigaya . .	298,253
Shizuoka . .	474,092	Aomori . .	294,167
Himeji. . .	470,986	Akashi . .	287,606
Matsudo . .	461,503	Morioka . .	286,478
Matsuyama . .	460,968	Yokkaichi . .	285,779
Kanazawa . .	453,975	Fukushima . .	285,754
Urawa. . .	453,300	Maebashi . .	284,788
Kawaguchi . .	448,854	Kasugai . .	277,589
Ichikawa . .	440,555	Ichihara . .	277,061
Nagasaki . .	438,635	Yao . .	276,664
Utsunomiya . .	435,357	Otsu . .	276,332
Omiya. . .	433,755	Tokushima . .	268,706
Yokosuka . .	432,193	Ichinomiya . .	267,362
Oita . . .	426,979	Kakogawa . .	260,567
Kurashiki . .	422,836	Shimonoseki . .	259,795
Gifu . . .	407,134	Neyagawa . .	258,443
Hirakata . .	400,144	Ibaraki . .	258,233
Toyonaka . .	398,908	Fukui . .	255,604
Wakayama . .	393,885	Yamagata . .	254,488
Nishinomiya . .	390,389	Hiratsuka . .	253,822

* Except for Tokyo, the data for each city refer to an urban county (*shi*), an administrative division which may include some scattered or rural population as well as an urban centre.
† The figure refers to the 23 wards (*ku*) of the old city. The population of Tokyo-to (Tokyo Prefecture) was 11,773,605.

BIRTHS, MARRIAGES AND DEATHS*

	Registered live births		Registered marriages†		Registered deaths	
	Number	Rate (per 1,000)	Number	Rate (per 1,000)	Number	Rate (per 1,000)
1991 .	1,223,245	9.9	742,264	6.0	829,797	6.7
1992 .	1,208,989	9.8	754,441	6.1	856,643	6.9
1993 .	1,188,282	9.6	792,658	6.4	878,532	7.1
1994 .	1,238,328	10.0	782,738	6.3	875,933	7.1
1995 .	1,187,064	9.6	791,888	6.4	922,139	7.4
1996 .	1,206,555	9.7	795,080	6.4	896,211	7.2
1997 .	1,191,665	9.5	775,651	6.2	913,402	7.3
1998 .	1,203,147	9.6	784,595	6.3	936,484	7.5
1999 .	1,177,669	9.4	762,011	6.1	982,031	7.8

* Figures relate only to Japanese nationals in Japan.
† Data are tabulated by year of registration rather than by year of occurrence.

Expectation of life (years at birth, 1999): Males 77.10; Females 83.99.

ECONOMICALLY ACTIVE POPULATION*
(annual averages, '000 persons aged 15 years and over)

	1997	1998	1999
Agriculture and forestry . .	3,240	3,170	3,070
Fishing and aquatic culture . .	260	260	280
Mining and quarrying . .	70	60	60
Manufacturing . . .	14,420	13,820	13,450
Electricity, gas and water. . .	360	370	380
Construction	6,850	6,620	6,570
Wholesale and retail trade and restaurants	14,750	14,830	14,830
Transport, storage and communications	4,120	4,050	4,060
Financing, insurance, real estate and business services . . .	5,750	5,930	5,990
Community, social and personal services (incl. hotels) . .	15,410	15,660	15,520
Activities not adequately defined .	340	360	410
Total employed	65,570	65,140	64,620
Unemployed	2,300	2,790	3,170
Total labour force . . .	67,870	67,930	67,790
Males	40,270	40,260	n.a.
Females	27,600	27,670	n.a.

* Figures are rounded to the nearest 10,000 persons.

2000 ('000 persons): Total employed 64,460; Unemployed 3,200; Total labour force 67,660.

Agriculture

PRINCIPAL CROPS ('000 metric tons)

	1997	1998	1999
Wheat	573	570*	583
Rice (paddy)	12,531	11,200*	9,159†
Barley	193	144	205
Potatoes	3,395	3,073	2,963
Sweet potatoes	1,130	1,139	1,008
Yams	183	179	200‡
Taro (Coco yam)	270	258	248
Other roots and tubers	55	76	74
Dry beans	105	102	102
Soybeans (Soya beans)	145	158	187
Cabbages	1,502	1,407	1,471
Tomatoes	780	764	769
Cauliflowers	122	102	116
Pumpkins, squash and gourds	247	258	266
Cucumbers and gherkins	792	746	766
Aubergines (Eggplants)	475	459	473
Chillies and peppers (green)	169	160	165
Onions (dry)	1,257	1,355	1,205
Green beans	71	66	60‡
Carrots	716	648	677
Other vegetables	6,818	6,404	6,506
Watermelons	614	603	595
Melons	319	320‡	320‡
Grapes	251	233	242
Sugar cane	1,445	1,666	1,571
Sugar beets	3,685	4,164	3,787
Apples	993	879	928
Pears	428	410	416
Peaches and nectarines	175	170	158
Plums	136	96	119
Oranges	133	123	118‡
Tangerines, mandarins, clementines and satsumas	1,555	1,194	1,447
Other citrus fruit	281	280	258
Strawberries	200	181	203
Other fruits and berries	341	341‡	299
Tea (green)	91	91‡	89
Tobacco (leaves)	69	64	65

* Unofficial figure.
† Brown rice only.
‡ FAO estimate.
Source: partly FAO.

LIVESTOCK ('000 head at 30 September)

	1997	1998	1999
Horses*	30	28	28
Cattle	4,750	4,708	4,658
Pigs	9,823	9,904	9,879
Sheep	16	16*	16*
Goats	29	29*	29*
Poultry	307,351	303,022	286,250

* FAO estimate(s).
Source: partly FAO.

LIVESTOCK PRODUCTS ('000 metric tons)

	1997	1998	1999
Beef and veal	530	529	540
Pig meat	1,283	1,286	1,277
Poultry meat	1,034	1,030	1,036
Cows' milk	8,645	8,572	8,460
Butter	87	84	86
Cheese	114	124	124
Poultry eggs	2,566	2,542	2,526
Honey	3	3	3*
Raw silk	2	1	0.6
Cattle hides (fresh)	34†	33†	33†

* FAO estimate(s).   † Unofficial figures.
Source: partly FAO.

Forestry

ROUNDWOOD REMOVALS ('000 cubic metres, excl. bark)

	1996	1997	1998
Sawlogs, veneer logs and logs for sleepers	16,382	15,637	13,556
Pulpwood	5,658	5,517	5,421
Other industrial wood	429	397	339
Fuel wood	749	777	777
Total	23,218	22,328	20,093

Source: partly FAO, *Yearbook of Forest Products*.

SAWNWOOD PRODUCTION
(FAO estimates, '000 cubic metres, incl. railway sleepers)

	1996	1997	1998
Coniferous (softwood)	22,771	20,719	17,788
Broadleaved (hardwood)	1,073	990	837
Total	23,844	21,709	18,625

Source: FAO, *Yearbook of Forest Products*.

Fishing

('000 metric tons, live weight)

	1996	1997	1998
Capture	5,936.1	5,916.1	5,259.1
Chum salmon (Keta or Dog salmon)	299.8	269.2	206.6
Alaska (Walleye) pollock	331.2	338.8	316.0
Atka mackerel	181.5	206.8	241.0
Pacific saury (Skipper)	229.2	290.8	145.0
Japanese jack mackerel	330.4	323.1	311.3
Japanese pilchard (sardine)	319.4	284.1	167.1
Japanese anchovy	345.5	233.1	470.6
Skipjack tuna (Oceanic skipjack)	286.7	311.5	385.4
Chub mackerel	760.4	849.0	511.2
Yesso scallop	271.1	261.2	287.8
Japanese flying squid	444.2	366.0	181.2
Aquaculture	829.4	806.5	766.8
Pacific cupped oyster	222.9	218.1	199.5
Yesso scallop	265.6	254.1	226.1
Total catch*	6,765.5	6,722.7	6,025.9

* Excluding aquatic mammals (including whales, see below).
Source: FAO, *Yearbook of Fishery Statistics*.

WHALING*

	1996	1997	1998
Number of whales caught	18,255	20,710	13,883

* Figures include whales caught during the Antarctic summer season beginning in the year prior to the year stated.

Aquatic plants ('000 metric tons): 674.1 (capture 154.1, aquaculture 520.1) in 1996; 683.2 (capture 149.9, aquaculture 533.3) in 1997; 640.6 (capture 116.9, aquaculture 523.7) in 1998.

Source: FAO, *Yearbook of Fishery Statistics*.

Mining

('000 metric tons, unless otherwise indicated)

	1997	1998	1999
Hard coal	4,274	3,663	3,906
Zinc ore*	72	68	64
Iron ore†	4	2	2
Silica stone	18,124	16,236	15,548
Limestone	201,399	183,955	180,193
Copper ore (metric tons)* . .	932	1,070	1,038
Lead ore (metric tons)* . .	5,227	6,198	6,074
Gold ore (kg)* . . .	8,384	8,601	9,405
Crude petroleum (million litres)	842	792	730
Natural gas (million cu m) . .	2,280	2,301	2,280

* Figures refer to the metal content of ores.
† Figures refer to gross weight. The estimated iron content is 54%.

Industry

SELECTED PRODUCTS
('000 metric tons, unless otherwise indicated)

	1997	1998	1999
Refined sugar	2,311	n.a.	n.a.
Cotton yarn—pure (metric tons) .	169,141	160,381	157,941
Cotton yarn—mixed (metric tons) .	14,378	13,046	13,059
Woven cotton fabrics—pure and mixed (million sq m) . .	917	842	774
Flax, ramie and hemp yarn (metric tons)	1,411	682	998
Linen fabrics ('000 sq m) . .	4,039	3,070	3,577
Woven silk fabrics—pure and mixed ('000 sq m) . .	55,381	40,440	34,564
Wool yarn—pure and mixed (metric tons) . . .	62,439	46,637	41,997
Woven woollen fabrics—pure and mixed ('000 sq m)[1] . .	246,966	212,862	199,058
Rayon continuous filaments (metric tons)	43,374	40,127	33,980
Acetate continuous filaments (metric tons) . . .	29,900	27,762	24,204
Rayon discontinuous fibres (metric tons)	110,796	96,611	77,294
Acetate discontinuous fibres (metric tons)[2] . . .	76,036	71,989	80,536
Woven rayon fabrics—pure and mixed (million sq m)[1] . .	416.3	361	325
Woven acetate fabrics—pure and mixed (million sq m)[1] . .	39.4	28	27
Non-cellulosic continuous filaments (metric tons) .	736,476	683,458	664,280
Non-cellulosic discontinuous fibres (metric tons) .	825,847	803,558	754,033
Woven synthetic fabrics (million sq m)[1,3]	2,040.6	1,743	1,581
Leather footwear ('000 pairs)[4]	47,573	42,573	37,546
Mechanical wood pulp . . }	11,490.7	10,919	10,990
Chemical wood pulp[5] . . }			
Newsprint	3,192.3	3,265	3,295
Other printing and writing paper .	11,092.4	10,887	11,330
Other paper	3,983	3,704	3,769
Paperboard	12,746.8	12,031	12,338
Synthetic rubber	1,591.9	1,520	1,577
Motor vehicle tyres ('000) . .	170,800	166,956	171,083
Rubber footwear ('000 pairs) . .	19,052	13,954	12,775
Ethylene—Ethene . . .	7,416.1	7,076	7,687
Propylene—Propene . . .	5,408.6	5,101	5,520
Benzene—Benzol . . .	4,502.0	4,203	4,459
Toluene—Toluol . . .	1,418.7	1,349	1,488
Xylenes—Xylol . . .	4,634.0	4,340	4,641
Ethyl alcohol—95% (kilolitres) .	283,319	265,027	263,633
Sulphuric acid—100% . .	6,828	6,739	6,493
Caustic soda—Sodium hydroxide .	4,391	4,252	4,345
Soda ash—Sodium carbonate .	801.2	722	722
Ammonium sulphate . .	1,779.8	1,618	1,716
Nitrogenous fertilizers (a)[6] .	854	762	751
Phosphate fertilizers (b)[6] . .	472	422	399
Liquefied petroleum gas . .	5,904	4,777	4,871
Naphtha (million litres) . .	19,234	18,003	17,978

— continued	1997	1998	1999
Motor spirit—Gasoline (million litres)[7]	53,534	55,316	56,316
Kerosene (million litres) . .	27,620	27,685	26,669
Jet fuel (million litres) . .	9,224	10,526	10,451
Gas oil (million litres) . .	48,153	46,071	44,536
Heavy fuel oil (million litres) .	74,297	71,782	69,305
Lubricating oil (million litres) .	2,833	2,630	2,693
Petroleum bitumen—Asphalt .	5,886	5,492	5,596
Coke-oven coke . . .	41,224	39,568	36,473
Cement	91,938	81,328	80,120
Pig-iron	78,519	74,981	74,520
Ferro-alloys[8] . . .	1,004.4	903	847
Crude steel	104,545	93,548	94,192
Aluminium—unwrought:			
primary	363	309	311
Electrolytic copper . . .	1,278.7	1,277	342
Refined lead—unwrought (metric tons)	227,953	227,571	227,122
Electrolytic, distilled and rectified zinc—unwrought (metric tons) .	603,112	607,899	633,383
Calculating machines ('000) . .	3,238	2,705	2,402
Video disk players ('000) . .	1,214.5	171	43
Television receivers ('000)[9] . .	6,672	5,569	3,444
Merchant vessels launched ('000 grt)	9,963	10,563	n.a.
Passenger motor cars ('000) . .	8,491.4	8,056	8,100
Lorries and trucks ('000) . .	2,421.4	1,937	1,746
Motorcycles, scooters and mopeds ('000)	2,675.7	2,636	2,252
Cameras ('000)	12,275	11,977	10,326
Watches and clocks ('000)[10] .	541,070	594,963	552,269
Construction: new dwellings started ('000) . . .	1,387.0	n.a.	n.a.
Electric energy (million kWh)[11] .	1,037,938	1,046,288	n.a.

[1] Including finished fabrics.
[2] Including cigarette filtration tow.
[3] Including blankets made of synthetic fibres.
[4] Sales.
[5] Including pulp prepared by semi-chemical processes.
[6] Figures refer to the 12 months ending 30 June of the year stated and are in terms of (a) nitrogen, 100%, and (b) phosphoric acid, 100%.
[7] Including aviation gasoline.
[8] Including silico-chromium.
[9] Figures refer to colour television receivers only.
[10] Including watch and clock movements.
[11] Twelve months beginning 1 April of the year stated.

Source: partly UN, *Industrial Commodity Statistics Yearbook*.

Finance

CURRENCY AND EXCHANGE RATES

Monetary Units
100 sen = 1 yen.

Sterling, Dollar and Euro Equivalents (29 December 2000)
£1 sterling = 171.45 yen;
US $1 = 114.90 yen;
€1 = 106.91 yen;
1,000 yen = £5.832 = $8.703 = €9.353.

Average Exchange Rate (yen per US $)
1998	130.91
1999	113.91
2000	107.77

BUDGET ('000 million yen, year ending 31 March)*

Revenue	1998/99	1999/2000†	2000/01‡
Tax revenue	47,824	44,094	47,148
Individual income tax . .	16,996	15,067	18,680
Corporate income tax . .	11,423	9,799	9,947
Consumption tax . . .	10,074	10,376	9,856
Liquor tax	1,898	1,867	1,860
Gasoline tax	1,998	2,045	2,078
Tobacco tax	1,046	896	900
Stamp duties	1,068	1,584	1,511
Other receipts	4,651	3,766	3,718
Total	54,083	49,444	52,377

Expenditure	1998/99	1999/2000†	2000/01‡
Defence	4,956	4,915	4,936
Social security . . .	15,658	19,112	16,767
Public works. . . .	13,034	12,235	9,931
Servicing of national debt‖ .	17,699	20,272	21,965
Interest payments . .	10,796	10,907	10,743
Transfer of local allocation tax to			
local governments . . .	14,305	12,444	14,930
Total (incl. others) . . .	84,392	89,019	84,987

* Figures refer only to the operations of the General Account budget. Data exclude transactions of other accounts controlled by the central Government: two mutual aid associations and four special accounts (including other social security funds).

† Revised forecasts.

‡ Initial forecasts.

§ Provisional.

‖ Including the repayment of debt principal and administrative costs.

Source: IMF, *Japan: Economic and Policy Developments* (November 2000).

INTERNATIONAL RESERVES (US $ million at 31 December)

	1997	1998	1999
Gold*	1,144	1,194	1,164
IMF special drawing rights . .	2,638	2,663	2,656
Reserve position in IMF . .	9,144	9,593	6,552
Foreign exchange . . .	207,866	203,215	277,708
Total	220,792	216,665	288,080

* Valued at SDR 35 per troy ounce.

Source: IMF, *International Financial Statistics*.

MONEY SUPPLY ('000 million yen at 31 December)*

	1997	1998	1999
Currency outside banks . . .	52,730	54,310	59,400
Demand deposits at deposit money			
banks.	151,550	160,090	180,130
Total money	204,280	214,400	239,540

* Figures are rounded to the nearest 10,000 million yen.

Source: IMF, *International Financial Statistics*.

COST OF LIVING

(Consumer Price Index; average of monthly figures; base: 1995 = 100)

	1998	1999	2000
Food (incl. beverages) . .	103.1	102.6	100.6
Housing.	103.6	103.5	103.7
Rent	103.5	n.a.	n.a.
Fuel, light and water charges .	102.9	101.3	102.9
Clothing and footwear . .	104.8	104.6	103.5
Miscellaneous	102.7	103.7	103.3
All items	102.5	102.2	101.5

NATIONAL ACCOUNTS ('000 million yen at current prices)

National Income and Product

	1996	1997	1998
Compensation of employees . .	279,620	285,437	282,541
Operating surplus . . .	104,192	103,015	90,612
Domestic factor incomes . .	383,812	388,452	373,154
Consumption of fixed capital . .	79,993	81,836	83,194
Inventory valuation adjustment .	−973	1,645	1,398
Gross domestic product (GDP)			
at factor cost	462,832	471,933	457,746
Indirect taxes	41,062	41,374	43,801
Less Subsidies	3,585	3,661	3,048
GDP in purchasers' values .	500,310	509,645	498,499
Factor income received from			
abroad	25,675	28,463	29,133
Less Factor income paid abroad .	20,218	21,972	21,918
Gross national product (GNP) .	505,767	516,137	505,714
Inventory valuation adjustment .	973	−1,645	−1,398
Less Consumption of fixed capital .	79,993	81,836	83,194
National income in market			
prices	426,747	432,656	421,122
Other current transfers from			
abroad	655	727	719
Less Other current transfers paid			
abroad	1,632	1,799	1,865
National disposable income .	425,770	431,585	419,975

Expenditure on the Gross Domestic Product

	1996	1997	1998
Government final consumption			
expenditure	48,423	49,555	50,676
Private final consumption			
expenditure	299,341	305,907	304,766
Increase in stocks . . .	2,443	2,559	−253
Gross fixed capital formation .	147,425	145,609	133,593
Total domestic expenditure .	497,632	503,629	488,783
Exports of goods and services . .	49,700	56,332	55,324
Less Imports of goods and services	47,022	50,316	45,607
GDP in purchasers' values .	500,310	509,645	498,499
GDP at constant 1990 prices .	485,219	492,954	480,587

Gross Domestic Product by Economic Activity

	1996	1997	1998
Agriculture, hunting, forestry and			
fishing	9,385.4	8,656.5	8,619.0
Mining and quarrying . . .	1,083.7	1,057.7	995.3
Manufacturing	122,525.6	124,493.8	117,215.6
Electricity, gas and water. . .	14,151.4	14,715.8	15,049.3
Construction.	51,361.9	49,923.1	46,121.6
Wholesale and retail trade . .	60,225.5	61,631.2	58,581.6
Transport, storage and			
communications . . .	33,177.2	33,357.1	32,623.3
Finance and insurance . . .	23,597.0	25,365.5	24,582.2
Real estate*	66,112.1	68,818.9	70,237.2
Public administration . . .	39,807.3	40,762.9	41,527.9
Other services	99,405.3	101,405.5	103,648.6
Sub-total	520,832.2	530,188.1	519,201.5
Import duties	3,159.7	3,254.0	3,032.9
Less Imputed bank service charge .	20,640.9	22,035.6	21,749.2
Value-added tax	−2,068.6	−3,405.9	−3,384.3
Inventory valuation adjustment .	−972.6	1,644.8	1,398.4
GDP in purchasers' values .	500,309.7	509,645.3	498,499.3

* Including imputed rents of owner-occupied dwellings.

BALANCE OF PAYMENTS (US $ million)*

	1997	1998	1999
Exports of goods f.o.b. . .	409,240	374,040	403,690
Imports of goods f.o.b. . .	−307,640	−251,660	−280,370
Trade balance . . .	101,600	122,390	123,320
Exports of services . .	69,300	62,410	61,000
Imports of services . .	−123,450	−111,830	−115,160
Balance on goods and services	47,450	72,970	69,160
Other income received .	222,150	209,580	188,270
Other income paid . .	−166,410	−153,010	−138,430
Balance on goods, services and income	103,190	129,540	119,000
Current transfers received .	6,010	5,530	6,210
Current transfers paid .	−14,840	−14,370	−18,350
Current balance . .	94,350	120,700	106,870
Capital account (net) . .	−4,050	−14,450	−16,470
Direct investment abroad . .	−26,060	−24,620	−22,270
Direct investment from abroad .	3,200	3,270	12,310
Portfolio investment assets .	−47,060	−95,240	−154,410
Portfolio investment liabilities	79,190	56,060	126,930
Financial derivatives assets .	−24,160	−18,490	−12,430
Financial derivatives liabilities .	20,770	17,640	17,530
Other investment assets . .	−191,960	37,940	266,340
Other investment liabilities .	68,030	−93,330	−265,120
Net errors and omissions .	34,310	4,360	16,970
Overall balance . . .	6,570	−6,160	76,260

* Figures are rounded to the nearest $10 million.
Source: IMF, *International Financial Statistics*.

JAPANESE DEVELOPMENT ASSISTANCE
(net disbursement basis, US $ million)*

	1996	1997	1998
Official:			
Bilateral assistance:			
Grants	5,438	4,985	4,901
Grant assistance . .	3,254	3,029	3,082
Technical assistance .	2,184	1,956	1,819
Loans	2,769	1,568	3,652
Total	8,207	6,553	8,553
Contributions to multilateral institutions . . .	1,232	2,806	2,087
Total	9,439	9,359	10,640
Other official flows:			
Export credits . . .	−282	−382	1,806
Direct investment and others .	1,572	4,236	6,921
Transfers to multilateral institutions . . .	−343	121	2,076
Total	947	3,975	10,804
Total official . .	10,386	13,334	21,444
Private flows:			
Export credits . . .	−485	—	−2,638
Direct investment and others .	28,554	17,363	3,450
Transfers to multilateral institutions . . .	−599	−1,411	−4,556
Grants from private voluntary agencies . . .	232	223	203
Total private . .	27,701	16,175	−3,541
Grand total . . .	38,087	29,509	17,902

* Excluding aid to Eastern Europe.

External Trade

PRINCIPAL COMMODITIES (million yen)

Imports c.i.f.	1996	1997	1998
Food and live animals . . .	5,035,626	5,046,986	4,776,723
Meat and meat preparations . .	1,019,115	915,900	882,043
Fresh, chilled or frozen meat .	863,578	775,755	726,862
Fish and fish preparations* .	1,813,403	1,835,845	1,642,455
Fresh and simply preserved fish*	1,550,225	1,547,952	1,393,774
Crude materials (inedible) except fuels . .	3,213,407	3,454,710	2,763,448
Wood, lumber and cork . .	1,046,240	1,075,976	633,900
Metalliferous ores and metal scrap .	898,285	1,039,905	957,671
Mineral fuels, lubricants, etc.	6,587,732	7,542,456	5,623,159
Coal, coke and briquettes . .	764,248	843,871	817,410
Coal (excl. briquettes) . .	751,235	823,254	800,973
Petroleum and petroleum products.	4,495,001	5,055,074	3,464,122
Crude and partly refined petroleum . . .	3,644,237	4,217,388	2,930,364
Petroleum products . .	850,764	837,687	533,758
Gas (natural and manufactured) .	1,328,483	1,643,510	1,344,628
Liquefied natural gas . .	940,157	1,155,447	1,016,015
Chemicals	2,535,616	2,840,862	2,726,207
Chemical elements and compounds	1,068,831	1,210,595	1,141,736
Organic chemicals . . .	718,293	816,719	751,285
Basic manufactures . .	4,252,168	4,614,046	3,876,514
Non-ferrous metals . . .	1,008,961	1,214,848	1,062,557
Machinery and transport equipment . . .	9,547,514	10,419,566	10,124,039
Non-electric machinery . .	3,549,905	3,988,996	3,852,984
Office machines . . .	2,052,739	2,264,082	2,135,626
Electronic computers, etc. .	2,017,741	2,226,968	2,097,883
Electrical machinery, apparatus, etc.	4,270,914	4,656,462	4,506,541
Telecommunications apparatus .	1,157,035	1,167,487	464,630
Thermionic valves, tubes, etc. .	1,440,550	1,555,735	1,407,104
Electronic integrated circuits .	1,274,432	1,336,389	1,203,772
Transport equipment . . .	1,726,695	1,774,107	1,764,514
Road motor vehicles and parts† .	1,152,136	974,013	746,508
Passenger cars (excl. buses) .	1,114,738	947,076	725,463
Miscellaneous manufactured articles . . .	5,552,871	5,712,187	5,334,622
Clothing (excl. footwear) . .	2,130,254	2,011,081	1,911,875
Non-knitted textile clothing (excl. accessories and headgear) . . .	1,076,212	995,303	900,294
Knitted clothing and accessories (excl. headgear) . .	839,136	831,634	842,711
Scientific instruments, watches, etc.	913,479	1,056,727	1,047,886
Total (incl. others)‡ . .	37,993,421	40,956,183	36,653,647

* Including crustacea and molluscs.
† Excluding tyres, engines and electrical parts.
‡ Including re-imports not classified according to kind (million yen): 470,549 in 1996; 492,501 in 1997.

Exports f.o.b.	1996	1997	1998
Chemicals	3,138,595	3,623,238	3,556,169
Chemical elements and compounds	1,292,035	1,433,561	1,441,502
Organic chemicals . . .	1,105,742	1,224,945	1,235,814
Basic manufactures . .	4,948,022	5,597,637	5,497,008
Iron and steel	1,654,761	1,929,427	1,940,480
Universals, plates and sheets .	1,046,410	1,204,859	1,131,592
Machinery and transport equipment . . .	31,067,331	35,139,832	34,910,422
Non-electric machinery . .	11,049,869	12,130,058	11,403,171
Power-generating machinery .	1,533,316	1,565,303	1,068,380
Internal combustion engines .	1,322,088	1,343,683	1,317,122
Office machines . . .	3,188,509	3,825,611	3,651,780
Automatic data-processing machines	1,725,121	2,230,196	2,045,374
Metalworking machinery . .	924,549	973,443	931,681

Exports f.o.b. — *continued*	1996	1997	1998
Electrical machinery, apparatus,			
etc.	10,879,513	12,040,586	11,749,243
Switchgear	1,134,508	1,290,153	1,283,783
Telecommunications apparatus	2,527,681	2,849,847	3,017,392
Visual apparatus	972,669	1,094,334	1,250,978
Thermionic valves, tubes, etc.	3,881,188	4,065,636	3,702,842
Electronic integrated circuits	2,404,863	2,433,460	2,221,390
Transport equipment	9,137,949	10,969,188	11,758,008
Road motor vehicles and parts*	5,513,795	7,112,326	7,795,170
Passenger cars (excl. buses)	4,351,105	5,765,320	6,549,542
Lorries and trucks (incl. ambulances)	1,088,091	1,266,412	1,205,662
Parts for cars, buses, lorries, etc.*	1,840,529	1,789,497	1,637,427
Ships and boats	1,046,298	1,191,894	1,321,476
Miscellaneous manufactured articles	3,688,496	4,286,642	4,049,204
Scientific instruments, watches, etc.	2,094,555	2,426,917	2,346,406
Scientific instruments and photographic equipment	1,894,539	2,211,045	2,140,560
Total (incl. others)†	44,731,311	50,937,992	50,645,004

* Excluding tyres, engines and electrical parts.
† Including re-exports not classified according to kind (million yen): 1,075,954 in 1996; 1,350,205 in 1997.

PRINCIPAL TRADING PARTNERS (million yen)*

Imports c.i.f.	1996	1997	1998
Australia	1,548,244	1,763,289	1,699,787
Brazil	408,469	452,538	380,798
Canada	1,100,532	1,184,589	1,003,009
China, People's Republic	4,399,676	5,061,673	4,844,135
France	681,329	698,170	748,223
Germany	1,540,869	1,501,333	1,396,784
Indonesia	1,653,175	1,769,383	1,416,287
Italy	735,462	715,892	668,700
Korea, Republic	1,735,329	1,762,757	1,577,250
Malaysia	1,278,512	1,375,091	1,133,201
Philippines	492,025	606,485	578,823
Russia	428,365	483,129	377,680
Saudi Arabia	1,160,376	1,443,485	936,587
Singapore	796,741	710,083	616,287
Switzerland	387,720	414,764	393,249
Taiwan	1,627,657	1,510,932	1,336,327
Thailand	1,111,154	1,157,321	1,068,174
United Arab Emirates	1,253,019	1,491,484	1,088,900
United Kingdom	779,946	869,290	764,405
USA	8,630,976	9,149,282	8,778,119
Total (incl. others)	37,993,421	40,956,183	36,653,647

Exports f.o.b.	1996	1997	1998
Australia	806,023	962,352	1,049,010
Canada	557,391	738,101	828,244
China, People's Republic	2,382,363	2,630,721	2,620,905
France	586,045	681,654	807,699
Germany	1,980,878	2,177,647	2,489,115
Hong Kong	2,759,968	3,297,762	3,335,452
Indonesia	986,013	1,230,176	560,059
Korea, Republic	3,192,333	3,153,288	2,004,542
Malaysia	1,668,420	1,755,532	1,216,122
Netherlands	1,006,985	1,186,043	1,417,425
Panama	641,976	806,199	797,923
Philippines	914,733	1,051,252	948,199
Singapore	2,259,586	2,449,630	1,929,646
Taiwan	2,825,133	3,335,154	3,340,382
Thailand	1,987,969	1,764,366	1,222,137
United Kingdom	1,358,043	1,658,787	1,904,876
USA	12,177,119	14,168,941	15,470,006
Total (incl. others)	44,731,311	50,937,992	50,645,004

* Imports by country of production; exports by country of last consignment.

Transport

RAILWAYS (traffic, year ending 31 March)

	1996/97	1997/98	1998/99
National railways:			
Passengers (million)	8,997	8,859	8,764
Freight ton-km (million)	24,601	24,301	22,643
Private railways:			
Passengers (million)	13,596	13,339	13,249
Freight ton-km (million)	366	317	277

ROAD TRAFFIC ('000 motor vehicles in use at 31 December)

	1997	1998	1999
Cars	48,611	49,896	51,165
Buses and coaches	240	238	236
Goods vehicles	21,156	20,684	20,326
Tractors and trailers	128	130	131
Total	70,135	70,948	71,858

SHIPPING

Merchant Fleet (registered at 31 December)

	1996	1997	1998
Number of vessels	9,399	9,310	8,922
Total displacement ('000 grt)	19,201	18,516	17,780

Source: Lloyd's Register of Shipping, *World Fleet Statistics*.

International Sea-borne Traffic

	1997	1998	1999
Vessels entered:			
Number	66,466	63,950	65,593
Total displacement ('000 net tons)	438,111	425,193	446,482
Goods ('000 metric tons):			
Loaded	119,253	118,185	n.a.
Unloaded	794,177	763,251	746,530

CIVIL AVIATION (traffic on scheduled services)

	1995	1996	1997
Kilometres flown (million)	692	727	777
Passengers carried ('000)	91,797	95,914	94,998
Passenger-km (million)	129,981	141,812	151,048
Total ton-km (million)	17,922	19,142	20,627

Source: UN, *Statistical Yearbook*.

Tourism

FOREIGN VISITORS BY COUNTRY OF ORIGIN

	1997	1998	1999
Australia	101,460	123,681	135,303
Canada	94,171	106,884	106,734
China, People's Republic	260,627	267,180	294,937
Korea, Republic	1,010,571	724,445	942,674
Taiwan	820,234	843,088	931,411
United Kingdom	400,496	484,788	393,272
USA	621,737	666,700	697,630
Total (incl. others)	4,218,208	4,106,057	4,437,863

Receipts from tourism (US $ million): 4,326 in 1997; 3,742 in 1998; 3,428 in 1999.

Source: Japan National Tourist Organization.

Communications Media

	1996	1997	1998
Radio receivers ('000 in use) . .	120,000	120,500	n.a.
Television receivers ('000 in use) .	85,900	86,500	n.a.
Telephones ('000 subscriptions)* .	61,500	60,400	58,600
Mobile cellular telephones ('000 in use)*	20,900	31,500	41,500
Telefax stations ('000 in use) . .	14,300	n.a.	n.a.
Book production:			
Titles	63,054	65,438	65,513
Copies (million)	1,506	1,508	1,432
Daily newspapers:			
Number	122	n.a.	121
Circulation ('000 copies). . .	72,705	n.a.	72,410

1999: Book production 65,026 titles (1,368 million copies); Daily newspapers 121.

* Twelve months beginning 1 April of year stated.

Sources: Foreign Press Center, *Facts and Figures of Japan*, and UNESCO, *Statistical Yearbook*.

Education

(1999)

	Institutions	Teachers	Students
Elementary schools	24,188	411,439	7,500,317
Lower secondary schools . . .	11,220	262,226	4,243,762
Upper secondary schools . . .	5,481	271,210	4,211,826
Colleges of technology . . .	62	4,433	56,436
Junior colleges	585	18,206	377,852
Graduate schools and universities	622	147,579	2,701,104

Directory

The Constitution

The Constitution of Japan was promulgated on 3 November 1946 and came into force on 3 May 1947. The following is a summary of its major provisions, with subsequent amendments:

THE EMPEROR

Articles 1–8. The Emperor derives his position from the will of the people. In the performance of any state act as defined in the Constitution, he must seek the advice and approval of the Cabinet, though he may delegate the exercise of his functions, which include: (i) the appointment of the Prime Minister and the Chief Justice of the Supreme Court; (ii) promulgation of laws, cabinet orders, treaties and constitutional amendments; (iii) the convocation of the Diet, dissolution of the House of Representatives and proclamation of elections to the Diet; (iv) the appointment and dismissal of Ministers of State, the granting of amnesties, reprieves and pardons, and the ratification of treaties, conventions or protocols; (v) the awarding of honours and performance of ceremonial functions.

RENUNCIATION OF WAR

Article 9. Japan renounces for ever the use of war as a means of settling international disputes.

Articles 10–40 refer to the legal and human rights of individuals guaranteed by the Constitution.

THE DIET

Articles 41–64. The Diet is convened once a year, is the highest organ of state power and has exclusive legislative authority. It comprises the House of Representatives (500 seats—300 single-seat constituencies and 200 determined by proportional representation) and the House of Councillors (252 seats). The members of the former are elected for four years whilst those of the latter are elected for six years and election for one-half of the members takes place every three years. If the House of Representatives is dissolved, a general election must take place within 40 days and the Diet must be convoked within 30 days of the date of the election. Extraordinary sessions of the Diet may be convened by the Cabinet when one-quarter or more of the members of either House request it. Emergency sessions of the House of Councillors may also be held. A quorum of at least one-third of the Diet members is needed to carry out parliamentary business. Any decision arising therefrom must be passed by a majority vote of those present. A bill becomes law having passed both Houses, except as provided by the Constitution. If the House of Councillors either vetoes or fails to take action within 60 days upon a bill already passed by the House of Representatives, the bill becomes law when passed a second time by the House of Representatives, by at least a two-thirds majority of those members present.

The Budget must first be submitted to the House of Representatives. If, when it is approved by the House of Representatives, the House of Councillors votes against it or fails to take action on it within 30 days, or failing agreement being reached by a joint committee of both Houses, a decision of the House of Representatives shall be the decision of the Diet. The above procedure also applies in respect of the conclusion of treaties.

THE EXECUTIVE

Articles 65–75. Executive power is vested in the Cabinet, consisting of a Prime Minister and such other Ministers as may be appointed. The Cabinet is collectively responsible to the Diet. The Prime Minister is designated from among members of the Diet by a resolution thereof.

If the House of Representatives and the House of Councillors disagree on the designation of the Prime Minister, and if no agreement can be reached even through a joint committee of both Houses, provided for by law, or if the House of Councillors fails to make designation within 10 days, exclusive of the period of recess, after the House of Representatives has made designation, the decision of the House of Representatives shall be the decision of the Diet.

The Prime Minister appoints and may remove other Ministers, a majority of whom must be from the Diet. If the House of Representatives passes a no-confidence motion or rejects a confidence motion, the whole Cabinet resigns, unless the House of Representatives is dissolved within 10 days. When there is a vacancy in the post of Prime Minister, or upon the first convocation of the Diet after a general election of members of the House of Representatives, the whole Cabinet resigns.

The Prime Minister submits bills, reports on national affairs and foreign relations to the Diet. He exercises control and supervision over various administrative branches of the Government. The Cabinet's primary functions (in addition to administrative ones) are to: (a) administer the law faithfully; (b) conduct State affairs; (c) conclude treaties subject to prior (or subsequent) Diet approval; (d) administer the civil service in accordance with law; (e) prepare and present the budget to the Diet; (f) enact Cabinet orders in order to make effective legal and constitutional provisions; (g) decide on amnesties, reprieves or pardons. All laws and Cabinet orders are signed by the competent Minister of State and countersigned by the Prime Minister. The Ministers of State, during their tenure of office, are not subject to legal action without the consent of the Prime Minister. However, the right to take that action is not impaired.

Articles 76–95. Relate to the Judiciary, Finance and Local Government.

AMENDMENTS

Article 96. Amendments to the Constitution are initiated by the Diet, through a concurring vote of two-thirds or more of all the members of each House and are submitted to the people for ratification, which requires the affirmative vote of a majority of all votes cast at a special referendum or at such election as the Diet may specify.

Amendments when so ratified must immediately be promulgated by the Emperor in the name of the people, as an integral part of the Constitution.

Articles 97–99 outline the Supreme Law, while Articles 100–103 consist of Supplementary Provisions.

Note: In February 2000 legislation was enacted to provide for a reduction in the number of seats in the House of Representatives to 480, comprising 300 single-seat constituencies and 180 seats determined by proportional representation.

The Government

HEAD OF STATE

His Imperial Majesty AKIHITO, Emperor of Japan (succeeded to the throne 7 January 1989).

THE CABINET
(May 2001)

A coalition of the Liberal Democratic Party (LDP), Hoshuto and New Komeito. All ministers were members of the LDP, unless otherwise specified.

Prime Minister: JUNICHIRO KOIZUMI.

Minister of Public Management, Home Affairs, Posts and Telecommunications: TORANOSUKE KATAYAMA.

Minister of Justice: MAYUMI MORIYAMA.

Minister of Foreign Affairs: MAKIKO TANAKA.

Minister of Finance: MASAJURO SHIOKAWA.

Minister of Education, Culture, Sports, Science and Technology: ATSUKO TOYAMA (non-politician).

Minister of Health, Labour and Welfare: CHIKARA SAKAGUCHI (New Komeito).

Minister of Agriculture, Forestry and Fisheries: TSUTOMU TAKEBE.

Minister of Economy, Trade and Industry: TAKEO HIRANUMA.

Minister of Land, Infrastructure and Transport: CHIKAGE OGI (Hoshuto).

Minister of the Environment: YORIKO KAWAGUCHI (non-politician).

Minister of State and Chief Cabinet Secretary (Gender Equality): YASUO FUKUDA.

Minister of State and Chairman of the National Public Safety Commission: JIN MURAI.

Minister of State and Director-General of the Defence Agency: GEN NAKATANI.

Minister of State for Development of Okinawa and Northern Territories Affairs, Science and Technology Policy: KOJI OMI.

Minister of State (Financial Services Agency): HAKUO YANAGI-SAWA.

Minister of State (Economic and Fiscal Policy, IT Policy): HEIZO TAKENAKA (non-politician).

Minister of State (Administrative Reform, Regulatory Reform): NOBUTERU ISHIHARA.

MINISTRIES

Imperial Household Agency: 1-1, Chiyoda, Chiyoda-ku, Tokyo 100-8111; tel. (3) 3213-1111; fax (3) 3282-1407; e-mail information@ kunaicho.go.jp; internet www.kunaicho.go.jp.

Prime Minister's Office: 1-6-1, Nagata-cho, Chiyoda-ku, Tokyo 100-8914; tel. (3) 3581-2361; fax (3) 3581-1910; internet www.kantei .go.jp.

Cabinet Office: 1-6-1, Nagata-cho, Chiyoda-ku, Tokyo 100-8914; tel. (3) 5253-2111; internet www.cao.go.jp.

Ministry of Agriculture, Forestry and Fisheries: 1-2-1, Kasumi-gaseki, Chiyoda-ku, Tokyo 100-8950; tel. (3) 3502-8111; fax (3) 3592-7697; e-mail white56@sc.maff.go.jp; internet www.maff.go.jp.

Ministry of Economy, Trade and Industry: 1-3-1, Kasumigaseki, Chiyoda-ku, Tokyo 100-8901; tel. (3) 3501-1511; fax (3) 3501-6942; e-mail webmail@meti.go.jp; internet www.meti.go.jp.

Ministry of Education, Culture, Sports, Science and Technology: 3-2-2, Kasumigaseki, Chiyoda-ku, Tokyo 100-8959; tel. (3) 3581-4211; fax (3) 3595-2017; internet www.mext.go.jp.

Ministry of the Environment: 1-2-2, Kasumigaseki, Chiyoda-ku, Tokyo 100-8975; tel. (3) 3581-3351; fax (3) 3502-0308; e-mail moe@eanet.go.jp; internet www.env.go.jp.

Ministry of Finance: 3-1-1, Kasumigaseki, Chiyoda-ku, Tokyo 100-8940; tel. (3) 3581-4111; fax (3) 5251-2667; e-mail info@mof.go.jp; internet www.mof.go.jp.

Ministry of Foreign Affairs: 2-2-1, Kasumigaseki, Chiyoda-ku, Tokyo 100-8919; tel. (3) 3580-3311; fax (3) 3581-2667; e-mail webmaster@mofa.go.jp; internet www.mofa.go.jp.

Ministry of Health, Labour and Welfare: 1-2-2, Kasumigaseki, Chiyoda-ku, Tokyo 100-8916; tel. (3) 5253-1111; fax (3) 3501-2532; internet www.mhlw.go.jp.

Ministry of Justice: 1-1-1, Kasumigaseki, Chiyoda-ku, Tokyo 100-8977; tel. (3) 3580-4111; fax (3) 3592-7011; e-mail webmaster@ moj.go.jp; internet www.moj.go.jp.

Ministry of Land, Infrastructure and Transport: 2-1-3, Kasu-migaseki, Chiyoda-ku, Tokyo 100-8989; tel. (3) 5253-8111; fax (3) 3580-7982; e-mail webmaster@mlit.go.jp; internet www.mlit.go.jp.

Ministry of Public Management, Home Affairs, Posts and Telecommunications: 2-1-2, Kasumigaseki, Chiyoda-ku, Tokyo 100-8926; tel. (3) 5253-5111; fax (3) 3504-0265; internet www .soumu.go.jp.

Defence Agency: 5-1 Ichigaya, Honmura-cho, Shinkuju-ku, Tokyo 162-8801; tel. (3) 3268-3111; e-mail info@jda.go.jp; internet www.jda.go.jp.

National Public Safety Commission: 2-1-2, Kasumigaseki, Chi-yoda-ku, Tokyo 100-8974; tel. (3) 3581-0141; internet www.npsc.go.jp.

Legislature

KOKKAI
(Diet)

The Diet consists of two Chambers: the House of Councillors (upper house) and the House of Representatives (lower house). The members of the House of Representatives are elected for a period of four years (subject to dissolution). Following the enactment of reform legislation in December 1994, the number of members in the House of Representatives was reduced to 500 (from 511) at the general election of October 1996. Further legislation was enacted in February 2000, reducing the number of members in the House of Representatives to 480, comprising 300 single-seat constituencies and 180 seats determined by proportional representation. For the House of Councillors, which has 252 members, the term of office is six years, with one-half of the members elected every three years.

House of Councillors

Speaker: YUTAKA INOUE.

Party	Seats after elections*	
	23 July 1995	12 July 1998
Liberal-Democratic Party	110	102
Democratic Party of Japan	—	47
New Frontier Party (Shinshinto)†	56	—
Japanese Communist Party	14	23
Komei‡	11	22
Social Democratic Party of Japan§	38	13
Liberal Party	—	12
Kaikaku (Reform) Club	—	3
New Party Sakigake‖	3	3
Dai-Niin Club	2	1
Independents	12	26
Other parties	6	—
Total	**252**	**252**

* One-half of the 252 seats are renewable every three years. At each election, 50 of the 126 seats are allocated on the basis of proportional representation.
† In December 1997 the New Frontier Party (Shinshinto) was dissolved. Six new parties were formed, two of which subsequently merged with the Taiyo Party (Sun Party) to form the Minseito. In April 1998 the Minseito was integrated into the Democratic Party of Japan, together with the Democratic Reform League and the Shinto Yuai.
‡ Renamed New Komeito in November 1998 following merger with Shinto Heiwa.
§ Formerly the Japan Socialist Party.
‖ Dissolved October 1998; new party (Party Sakigake) formed; absorbed by Democratic Party of Japan in March 2001.

House of Representatives

Speaker: TAMISUKI WATANUKI.

General Election, 25 June 2000

Party	Seats
Liberal-Democratic Party	233
Democratic Party of Japan	127
New Komeito	31
Liberal Party	22
Japanese Communist Party	20
Social Democratic Party of Japan§	19
Hoshuto	7
Independents and others	21
Total	**480**

§ See footnotes to House of Councillors.

Political Organizations

The Political Funds Regulation Law provides that any organization wishing to support a candidate for an elective public office must be registered as a political party. There are more than 10,000 registered parties in the country, mostly of local or regional significance.

21st Century: 1-7-1, Nagato-cho, Chiyoda-ku, Tokyo; tel. (3) 3581-5111; f. 1996 by four independent mems of House of Representatives; Chair. HAJIME FUNADA.

Dai-Niin Club: Rm 531, Sangiin Kaikan, 2-1-1, Nagata-cho, Chi-yoda-ku, Tokyo 100-0014; tel. (3) 3508-8531; e-mail info@niinkuraba .gr.jp; successor to the Green Wind Club (Ryukufukai), which originated in the House of Councillors in 1946–47.

Democratic Party of Japan—DPJ: 1-11-1, Nagata-cho, Chiyoda-ku, Tokyo 100-0014; tel. (3) 3595-9988; e-mail democrat@smn.co.jp; internet www.dpj.or.jp/index-e.html; f. 1998 by the integration into the original DPJ (f. 1996) of the Democratic Reform League, Minseito and Shinto Yuai; advocates a cabinet formed and controlled by the people; absorbed Party Sakigake in March 2001; Pres. YUKIO HATOYAMA; Sec.-Gen. TSUTOMU HATA.

Hoshuto (New Conservative Party): Tokyo; f. 2000 by 26 fmr mems of LP; Head CHIKAGE OGI; Sec.-Gen. TAKESHI NODA.

Japanese Communist Party—JCP: 4-26-7, Sendagaya, Shibuya-ku, Tokyo 151-8586; tel. (3) 3403-6111; fax (3) 3746-0767; e-mail intl@jcp.or.jp; internet www.jcp.or.jp; f. 1922; 370,000 mems (1999); Chair. of the Presidium TETSUZO FUWA; Head of Secr. KAZUO SHII.

Kaikaku (Reform) Club: Sabo Kaikan Bldg, 2-7-5, Hirakawa-cho, Chiyoda-ku, Tokyo 102-0093; tel. (3) 5211-3331; f. 1997; Pres. TATSUO OZAWA.

Liberal Party: Kokusai Kogyo Bldg, 2-2-12, Akasaka, Minato-ku, Tokyo 107-0052; tel. (3) 5562-7111; internet www.jiyuto.or.jp; f. 1998; Pres. ICHIRO OZAWA; Sec.-Gen. HIROHISA FUJII.

Liberal-Democratic Party—LDP (Jiyu-Minshuto): 1-11-23, Nagata-cho, Chiyoda-ku, Tokyo 100-0014; tel. (3) 3581-6211; e-mail koho@ldp.jimin.or.jp; internet www.jimin.or.jp/jimin/title.html; f. 1955; advocates the establishment of a welfare state, the promotion of industrial development, the improvement of educational and cultural facilities and constitutional reform as needed; follows a foreign policy of alignment with the USA; 2,774,460 mems (Oct. 1994); Pres. JUNICHIRO KOIZUMI; Sec.-Gen. TAKU YAMASAKI; Chair. of Gen. Council MITSUO HORIUCHI.

New Komeito: 17, Minami-Motomachi, Shinjuku-ku, Tokyo 160-0012; tel. (3) 3353-0111; e-mail newkomeito@gorilla.or.jp; internet www.newkomeito.or.jp/; f. 1964 as Komeito, renamed as Komei 1994 following defection of a number of mems to the New Frontier Party (Shinshinto, dissolved Dec. 1997); absorbed Reimei Club Jan. 1998; renamed as above Nov. 1998 following merger of Komei and Shinto Heiwa; advocates political moderation, humanism and globalism, and policies respecting 'dignity of human life'; 330,000 mems (1999); Representative TAKENORI KANZAKI; Sec.-Gen. TETSUZO FUYUSHIBA.

New Socialist Party: Sanken Bldg, 6th Floor, 4-3-7, Hachobori, Chuo-ku, Tokyo 104-0032; tel. (3) 3551-3980; e-mail honbu@sinsyakai.or.jp; internet www.sinsyakai.or.jp; f. 1996 by left-wing defectors from SDPJ; opposed to US military bases on Okinawa and to introduction in 1996 of new electoral system; Chair. OSAMU YATABE; Sec.-Gen. KIMIKO KURIHARA.

Sangiin Club: Tokyo; f. 1998; Leader MOTOO SHIINA.

Social Democratic Party of Japan—SDPJ (Shakai Minshuto): 1-8-1, Nagata-cho, Chiyoda-ku, Tokyo 100-0014; tel. (3) 3580-1171; fax (3) 3580-0691; e-mail sdpjmail@omnics.co.jp; internet www.omnics.co.jp/politics/SDPJ/SDPJ-E.html; f. 1945 as the Japan Socialist Party (JSP); adopted present name in 1996; seeks the establishment of collective non-aggression and a mutual security system, including Japan, the USA, the CIS and the People's Republic of China; 115,000 mems (1994); Chair. TAKAKO DOI; Sec.-Gen. SADAO FUCHIGAMI.

Diplomatic Representation

EMBASSIES IN JAPAN

Afghanistan: Olympia Annex Apt 503, 6-31-21, Jingumae, Shibuya-ku, Tokyo 150-0001; tel. (3) 3407-7900; fax (3) 3400-7912; Chargé d'affaires a.i.: RAHMATULLAH AMIR.

Algeria: 2-10-67, Mita, Meguro-ku, Tokyo 153-0062; tel. (3) 3711-2661; fax (3) 3710-6534; e-mail ambalgto@twics.com; Ambassador: BOUDJEMAA DELMI.

Argentina: 2-14-14, Moto Azabu, Minato-ku, Tokyo 106-0046; tel. (3) 5420-7101; fax (3) 5420-7109; Ambassador: ALFREDO VICENTE CHIARADIA.

Australia: 2-1-14, Mita, Minato-ku, Tokyo 108-8361; tel. (3) 5232-4111; fax (3) 5232-4149; internet www.australia.or.jp; Ambassador: PETER C. GREY.

Austria: 1-1-20, Moto Azabu, Minato-ku, Tokyo 106-0046; tel. (3) 3451-8281; fax (3) 3451-8283; e-mail austria@gol.com; internet www.austria.or.jp; Ambassador: HANS DIETMAR SCHWEISGUT.

Bangladesh: 4-15-15, Meguro, Meguro-ku, Tokyo 153-0063; tel. (3) 5704-0216; fax (3) 5704-1696; Ambassador: S. M. RASHED AHMED.

Belarus: 4-14-12, Shirogane K House, Shirogane, Minato-ku, Tokyo 108-0072; tel. (3) 3448-1623; fax (3) 3448-1624; e-mail belarus@japan.co.jp; Ambassador: PETR K. KRAVCHANKA.

Belgium: 5, Niban-cho, Chiyoda-ku, Tokyo 102-0084; tel. (3) 3262-0191; fax (3) 3262-0651; e-mail tokyo@diplobel.org; Ambassador: Baron PATRICK NOTHOMB.

Bolivia: Kowa Bldg, No. 38, Room 804, 4-12-24, Nishi Azabu, Minato-ku, Tokyo 106-0031; tel. (3) 3499-5441; fax (3) 3499-5443; e-mail emboltk@interlink.or.jp; Ambassador: EUDORO GALINDO ANZE.

Brazil: 2-11-12, Kita Aoyama, Minato-ku, Tokyo 107-0061; tel. (3) 3404-5211; fax (3) 3405-5846; internet www.brasemb.or.jp; Ambassador: FERNANDO GUIMARÃES REIS.

Brunei: 6-5-2, Kita Shinagawa, Shinagawa-ku, Tokyo 141-0001; tel. (3) 3447-7997; fax (3) 3447-9260; Ambassador: Dato' MALAI AHMAD MURAD MASHOR.

Bulgaria: 5-36-3, Yoyogi, Shibuya-ku, Tokyo 151-0053; tel. (3) 3465-1021; fax (3) 3465-1031; Ambassador: PETUR ANDONOV.

Burkina Faso: Apt 301, Hiroo Glisten Hills, 3-1-17, Hiroo, Shibuya-ku, Tokyo 150; tel. (3) 3400-7919; fax (3) 3400-6945; Ambassador: W. RAYMOND EDOUARD OUÉDRAOGO.

Burundi: 6-5-3, Kita-Shinagawa, Shinagawa-ku, Tokyo 141; tel. (3) 3443-7321; fax (3) 3443-7720; Ambassador: GABRIEL NDIHOKUBWAYO.

Cambodia: 8-6-9, Akasaka, Minato-ku, Tokyo 107-0052; tel. (3) 5412-8521; fax (3) 5412-8526; e-mail kpnarin@iac.co.jp; internet embassy.kcom.ne.jp/cambodia/index.htm; Ambassador: ING KIETH.

Cameroon: 3-27-16, Nozawa, Setagaya-ku, Tokyo 154-0003; tel. (3) 5430-4381; fax (3) 5430-6489; e-mail ambacamtokyo@gol.com; Chargé d'affaires a.i: ANDRÉ-MARIE ATANGANA-ZANG.

Canada: 7-3-38, Akasaka, Minato-ku, Tokyo 107-8503; tel. (3) 5412-6200; fax (3) 5412-6249; internet www.canadanet.or.jp; Ambassador: LEONARD J. EDWARDS.

Chile: Nihon Seimei Akabanebashi Bldg, 8th Floor, 3-1-14, Shiba, Minato-ku, Tokyo 105-0014; tel. (3) 3452-7561; fax (3) 3452-4457; e-mail chile@twics.com; internet www.oficom-chile.gol.com; Ambassador: OSCAR FUENTES.

China, People's Republic: 3-4-33, Moto Azabu, Minato-ku, Tokyo 106-0046; tel. (3) 3403-3380; fax (3) 3403-3345; Ambassador: CHEN JIAN.

Colombia: 3-10-53, Kami Osaki, Shinagawa-ku, Tokyo 141-0021; tel. (3) 3440-6451; fax (3) 3440-6724; internet embassy.kcom.ne.jp/colombia/index.html; Ambassador: RICARDO GUTIÉRREZ.

Congo, Democratic Republic: Harajuku Green Heights, Room 701, 3-53-17, Sendagaya, Shibuya-ku, Tokyo 151-0051; tel. (3) 3423-3981; fax (3) 3423-3984; Chargé d'affaires: NGAMBANI ZI-MIZELE.

Costa Rica: Kowa Bldg, No. 38, Room 901, 4-12-24, Nishi Azabu, Minato-ku, Tokyo 106-0031; tel. (3) 3486-1812; fax (3) 3486-1813; Chargé d'affaires a.i.: ANA LUCÍA NASSAR SOTO.

Côte d'Ivoire: 2-19-12, Uehara, Shibuya-ku, Tokyo 151-0064; tel. (3) 5454-1401; fax (3) 5454-1405; e-mail ambacijp@gol.com; Ambassador: PATRICE KOFFI ANOH.

Croatia: 3-3-100, Hiroo, Shibuya-ku, Tokyo 150-0012; tel. (3) 5469-3014; fax (3) 5469-3015; e-mail veltok@hpo.net; Chargé d'Affaires a.i.: DAVOR LJUBANOVIĆ.

Cuba: 4-11-12, Shimo Meguro, Meguro-ku, Tokyo 153-0064; tel. (3) 3716-3112; fax (3) 3716-4334; Ambassador: ERNESTO MELÉNDEZ BACHS.

Czech Republic: 2-16-14, Hiroo, Shibuya-ku, Tokyo 150-0012; tel. (3) 3400-8122; fax (3) 3400-8124; e-mail tokyo@embassy.mzv.cz; internet embassy.kcom.ne.jp/czech; Ambassador: KAREL ZEBRAKOVSKY.

Denmark: 29-6, Sarugaku-cho, Shibuya-ku, Tokyo 150-0033; tel. (3) 3496-3001; fax (3) 3496-3440; e-mail embassy.tokyo@denmark.or.jp; internet www.denmark.or.jp; Ambassador: PETER BRÜCKNER.

Djibouti: 5-18-10, Shimo Meguro, Meguro-ku, Tokyo 153-0064; tel. (3) 5704-0682; fax (3) 5725-8305; Ambassador: RACHAD AHMED SALEH FARAH.

Dominican Republic: Kowa Bldg, No. 38, Room 904, 4-12-24, Nishi Azabu, Minato-ku, Tokyo 106-0031; tel. (3) 3499-6020; fax (3) 3499-2627.

Ecuador: Kowa Bldg, No. 38, Room 806, 4-12-24, Nishi Azabu, Minato-ku, Tokyo 106-0031; tel. (3) 3499-2800; fax (3) 3499-4400; internet embassy.kcom.ne.jp/ecuador/index.html; Ambassador: MARCELO AVILA.

Egypt: 1-5-4, Aobadai, Meguro-ku, Tokyo 153-0042; tel. (3) 3770-8022; fax (3) 3770-8021; internet embassy.kcom.ne.jp/egypt/index.html; Ambassador: NABIL FAHMY.

El Salvador: Kowa Bldg, No. 38, 8th Floor, 4-12-24, Nishi Azabu, Minato-ku, Tokyo 106-0031; tel. (3) 3499-4461; fax (3) 3486-7022; e-mail embesal@gol.com; Ambassador: RICARDO PAREDES-OSORIO.

Estonia: Akasaka Royal Office Bldg, 3rd Floor, 6-9-17, Akasaka, Minato-ku, Tokyo 107; tel. (3) 5545-7171; fax (3) 5545-7172; e-mail embassy.tokyo@mfa.ee; Ambassador: MARK SINISOO.

Ethiopia: 1-14-15, Midorigaoka, Meguro-ku, Tokyo 152-0034; tel. (3) 5420-6860; fax (3) 5420-6866; ethioemb@gol.com; Ambassador: MAHDI AHMED.

Fiji: Noa Bldg, 14th Floor, 3-5, 2 Chome, Azabudai, Minato-ku, Tokyo 106-0041; tel. (3) 3587-2038; fax (3) 3587-2563; e-mail fijiemb@hotmail.com; Ambassador: Ratu SEREMAIA CAVUILATI.

Finland: 3-5-39, Minami Azabu, Minato-ku, Tokyo 106-8561; tel. (3) 5447-6000; fax (3) 5447-6042; e-mail info@finland.or.jp; internet www.finland.or.jp; Ambassador: MATTI PEKKA LINTU.

France: 4-11-44, Minami Azabu, Minato-ku, Tokyo 106-8514; tel. (3) 5420-8800; fax (3) 5420-8917; e-mail ambafrance.tokyo@diplomatie.fr; internet www.ambafrance.or.jp; Ambassador: MAURICE GOURDAULT-MONTAGNE.

Gabon: 1-12-11, Kami Osaki, Shinagawa-ku, Tokyo 141; tel. (3) 3448-9540; fax (3) 3448-1596; Ambassador: VINCENT BOULÉ.

Germany: 4-5-10, Minami Azabu, Minato-ku, Tokyo 106-0047; tel. (3) 3473-0151; fax (3) 3473-4243; e-mail germtoky@rosenet.ne.jp; internet www.germanembassy-japan.org; Ambassador: Dr UWE KAESTNER.

Ghana: 1-5-21, Nishi Azabu, Minato-ku, Tokyo 106-0031; tel. (3) 5410-8631; fax (3) 5410-8635; e-mail mission@ghanaembassy.or.jp; internet www.ghanaembassy.or.jp; Ambassador: TOGBI KPORKU III.

Greece: 3-16-30, Nishi Azabu, Minato-ku, Tokyo 106-0031; tel. (3) 3403-0871; fax (3) 3402-4642; e-mail greekemb@gol.com; Ambassador: ELIAS KATSAREAS.

Guatemala: Kowa Bldg, No. 38, Room 905, 4-12-24, Nishi Azabu, Minato-ku, Tokyo 106-0031; tel. (3) 3400-1830; fax (3) 3400-1820; e-mail embguate@twics.com; Ambassador: ROBERTO ANTONIO CASTELLANOS LÓPEZ.

Guinea: 12-9, Hachiyama-cho, Shibuya-ku, Tokyo 150-0035; tel. (3) 3724-2418; fax (3) 3770-4643; Ambassador: RAFIOU BARRY.

Haiti: Kowa Bldg, No. 38, Room 906, 4-12-24, Nishi Azabu, Minato-ku, Tokyo 106; tel. (3) 3486-7096; fax (3) 3486-7070; Ambassador: MARCEL DURET.

Holy See: Apostolic Nunciature, 9-2, Sanban-cho, Chiyoda-ku, Tokyo 102-0075; tel. (3) 3263-6851; fax (3) 3263-6060; Apostolic Nuncio: Most Rev. AMBROSE B. DE PAOLI, Titular Archbishop of Lares.

Honduras: Kowa Bldg, No. 38, Room 802, 8th Floor, 4-12-24, Nishi Azabu, Minato-ku, Tokyo 106-0031; tel. (3) 3409-1150; fax (3) 3409-0305; e-mail honduras@interlink.or.jp; Ambassador: EDGARDO SEVILLA IDIÁQUEZ.

Hungary: 2-17-14, Mita, Minato-ku, Tokyo 108-0073; tel. (3) 3798-8801; fax (3) 3798-8812; e-mail huembtio@attmail.com; Ambassador: Dr ZOLTÁN SÚDY.

India: 2-2-11, Kudan Minami, Chiyoda-ku, Tokyo 102-0074; tel. (3) 3262-2391; fax (3) 3234-4866; internet embassy.kcom.ne.jp/embnet/india.html; Ambassador: SIDDHARTH SINGH.

Indonesia: 5-2-9, Higashi Gotanda, Shinagawa-ku, Tokyo 141-0022; tel. (3) 3441-4201; fax (3) 3447-1697; Ambassador: SOEMADI D. M. BROTODININGRAT.

Iran: 3-10-32, Minami Azabu, Minato-ku, Tokyo 106-0047; tel. (3) 3446-8011; fax (3) 3446-9002; Ambassador: ALI MAJEDI.

Iraq: 8-4-7, Akasaka, Minato-ku, Tokyo 107-0052; tel. (3) 3423-1727; fax (3) 3402-8636; Chargé d'affaires a.i.: MUHSIN M. ALI.

Ireland: Ireland House, 2-10-7, Kojimachi, Chiyoda-ku, Tokyo 102-0083; tel. (3) 3263-0695; fax (3) 3265-2275; internet embassy.kcom.ne.jp/ireland/index.html; Ambassador: DECLAN O'DONOVAN.

Israel: 3, Niban-cho, Chiyoda-ku, Tokyo 102-0084; tel. (3) 3264-0911; fax (3) 3264-0791; e-mail israel@gol.com; internet www.israelembassy-tokyo.com; Ambassador: MOSHE BEN-YAACOV.

Italy: 2-5-4, Mita, Minato-ku, Tokyo 108-8302; tel. (3) 3453-5291; fax (3) 3456-2319; e-mail itembtky@gol.com; internet sunsite.sut.ac.jp/embitaly; Ambassador: GABRIELE MENEGATTI.

Jamaica: Toranomon Yatsuka Bldg, 2nd Floor, 1-1-11, Atago, Minato-ku, Tokyo 105-0002; tel. (3) 3435-1861; fax (3) 3435-1864; e-mail info@jamaicaemb-tokyo.com; Ambassador: Dr EARL A. CARR.

Jordan: Chiyoda House, 4th Floor, 2-17-8, Nagata-cho, Chiyoda-ku, Tokyo 100-0014; tel. (3) 3580-5856; fax (3) 3593-9385; internet www2.giganet.net/private/users/emb-jord; Ambassador: SAMIR NAOURI.

Kenya: 3-24-3, Yakumo, Meguro-ku, Tokyo 152-0023; tel. (3) 3723-4006; fax (3) 3723-4488; e-mail kenrepj@ma.kcom.ne.jp; internet embassy.kcom.ne.jp/kenya; Ambassador: MARY DONDE OCHINGA.

Korea, Republic: 1-2-5, Minami Azabu, Minato-ku, Tokyo 106-0047; tel. (3) 3452-7611; fax (3) 5232-6911; internet embassy.kcom.ne.jp/korea/index.html; Ambassador: KIM SUK-KYU.

Kuwait: 4-13-12, Mita, Minato-ku, Tokyo 108-0073; tel. (3) 3455-0361; fax (3) 3456-6290; internet kuwait-embassy.or.jp; Ambassador: WALID ALI AL-KHOBAIZI.

Laos: 3-3-22, Nishi Azabu, Minato-ku, Tokyo 106-0031; tel. (3) 5411-2291; fax (3) 5411-2293; Ambassador: THONGSAY BODHISANE.

Lebanon: Chiyoda House, 5th Floor, 2-17-8, Nagata-cho, Chiyoda-ku, Tokyo 100-0014; tel. (3) 3580-1227; fax (3) 3580-2281; e-mail ambaliba@japan.co.jp; Ambassador: JAAFAR MOAWI.

Liberia: Sugi Terrace 201, 3-13-11, Okusawa, Setagaya-ku, Tokyo 158; tel. (3) 3726-5711; fax (3) 3726-5712; Chargé d'affaires a.i.: HARRY TAH FREEMAN.

Libya: 10-14, Daikanyama-cho, Shibuya-ku, Tokyo 150-0034; tel. (3) 3477-0701; fax (3) 3464-0420; Secretary of the People's Bureau: SULAIMAN ABU BAKER BADI (acting).

Luxembourg: Niban-cho TS Bldg, 4th Floor, 2-1, Niban-cho, Chiyoda-ku, Tokyo 102-0084; tel. (3) 3265-9621; fax (3) 3265-9624; internet www.luxembourg.or.jp; Ambassador: PIERRE GRAMEGNA.

Madagascar: 2-3-23, Moto Azabu, Minato-ku, Tokyo 106; tel. (3) 3446-7252; fax (3) 3446-7078; Ambassador: CYRILLE FIDA.

Malawi: Takanawa-Kaisei Bldg, 7th Floor, 3-4-1, Takanawa, Minato-ku, Tokyo 108-0074; tel. (3) 3449-3010; fax (3) 3449-3220; e-mail malawi@mx1.ttcn.ne.jp; internet embassy.kcom.ne.jp/malawi; Ambassador: BRIGHT S. M. MANGULAMA.

Malaysia: 20-16, Nanpeidai-cho, Shibuya-ku, Tokyo 150-0036; tel. (3) 3476-3840; fax (3) 3476-4971; Ambassador: Datuk H. M. KHATIB.

Marshall Islands: Meiji Park Heights 101, 9-9, Minamimoto-machi, Shinjuku-ku, Tokyo 106; tel. (3) 5379-1701; fax (3) 5379-1810; Ambassador: MACK T. KAMINAGA.

Mauritania: 5-17-5, Kita Shinagawa, Shinagawa-ku, Tokyo 141-0001; tel. (3) 3449-3810; fax (3) 3449-3822; Ambassador: BA ALIOU IBRA.

Mexico: 2-15-1, Nagata-cho, Chiyoda-ku, Tokyo 100-0014; tel. (3) 3581-1131; fax (3) 3581-4058; e-mail embamex@twics.com; internet embassy.kcom.ne.jp/mexico/index.html; Ambassador: MANUEL URIBE CASTAÑEDA.

Micronesia: Reinanzaka Bldg, 2nd Floor, 1-14-2, Akasaka, Minato-ku, Tokyo 107-0052; tel. (3) 3585-5456; fax (3) 3585-5348; e-mail fsmemb@fsmemb.or.jp; Ambassador: ALIK L. ALIK.

Mongolia: Pine Crest Mansion, 21-4, Kamiyama-cho, Shibuya-ku, Tokyo 150-0047; tel. (3) 3469-2088; fax (3) 3469-2216; e-mail embmong@gol.com; internet embassy.kcom.ne.jp/mongolia/index.html; Ambassador: SODOVJAMTSYN KHURELBAATAR.

Morocco: Silva Kingdom Bldg, 5th–6th Floors, 3-16-3, Sendagaya, Shibuya-ku, Tokyo 151-0051; tel. (3) 3478-3271; fax (3) 3402-0898; Ambassador: SAAD EDDIN TAIB.

Mozambique: 33-3, Ohyama-cho, Shibuya-ku, Tokyo 151; tel. (3) 3485-7621; fax (3) 3485-7622; Chargé d'affaires a.i.: ARTUR JOSSEFA JAMO.

Myanmar: 4-8-26, Kita Shinagawa, Shinagawa-ku, Tokyo 140-0001; tel. (3) 3441-9291; fax (3) 3447-7394; Ambassador: U SOE WIN.

Nepal: 7-14-9, Todoroki, Setagaya-ku, Tokyo 158-0082; tel. (3) 3705-5558; fax (3) 3705-8264; e-mail nepembjp@big.or.jp; Ambassador: KEDAR BHAKTA MATHEMA.

Netherlands: 3-6-3, Shiba Koen, Minato-ku, Tokyo 105-0011; tel. (3) 5401-0411; fax (3) 5401-0420; e-mail nlgovtok@oranda.or.jp; internet www.oranda.or.jp; Ambassador: EGBERT F. JACOBS.

New Zealand: 20-40, Kamiyama-cho, Shibuya-ku, Tokyo 150-0047; tel. (3) 3467-2271; fax (3) 3467-2278; e-mail nzemb@gol.com; internet embassy.kcom.ne.jp/newzealand; Ambassador: PHILIP GIBSON.

Nicaragua: Kowa Bldg, No. 38, Room 903, 9th Floor, 4-12-24, Nishi Azabu, Minato-ku, Tokyo 106; tel. (3) 3499-0400; fax (3) 3499-3800; Ambassador: Dr HARRY BODÁN-SHIELDS.

Nigeria: 5-11-17, Shimo-Meguro, Meguro-ku, Tokyo 153-0064; tel. (3) 5721-5391; fax (3) 5721-5342; internet www.crisscross.com/users/nigeriaemb/home.htm; Ambassador: EMMANUEL OSEIMIEGHA OTIOTIO.

Norway: 5-12-2, Minami Azabu, Minato-ku, Tokyo 106-0047; tel. (3) 3440-2611; fax (3) 3440-2620; e-mail embassy@norway.or.jp; internet www.norway.or.jp; Ambassador: ODD FOSSEIDBRÅTEN.

Oman: 2-28-11, Sendagaya, Shibuya-ku, Tokyo 151-0051; tel. (3) 3402-0877; fax (3) 3404-1334; e-mail omanemb@gol.com; Ambassador: MOHAMMED ALI AL-KHUSAIBY.

Pakistan: 2-14-9, Moto Azabu, Minato-ku, Tokyo 106-0046; tel. (3) 3454-4861; fax (3) 3457-0341; e-mail pakemb@gol.com; Ambassador: TOUQIR HUSSAIN.

Palau: 1-1, Katamachi, Shinjuku-ku, Tokyo 160-0001; tel. (3) 3354-5500; Ambassador: MASAO SALVADOR.

Panama: Kowa Bldg, No. 38, Room 902, 4-12-24, Nishi Azabu, Minato-ku, Tokyo 106-0031; tel. (3) 3499-3741; fax (3) 5485-3548; e-mail panaemb@gol.com; internet embassy.kcom.ne.jp/panama/top-j; Ambassador: JOSÉ A. SOSA.

Papua New Guinea: Mita Kokusai Bldg, Room 313, 3rd Floor, 1-4-28, Mita, Minato-ku, Tokyo 108; tel. (3) 3454-7801; fax (3) 3454-7275; Ambassador: AIWA OLMI.

Paraguay: Kowa Bldg, No. 38, Room 701, 4-12-24, Nishi Azabu, Minato-ku, Tokyo 106; tel. (3) 5485-3101; fax (3) 5485-3103; e-mail embapar@gol.com; internet embassy.kcom.ne.jp/paraguay/index.htm; Ambassador: Dr MIGUEL A. SOLANO LÓPEZ.

Peru: 4-4-27, Higashi, Shibuya-ku, Tokyo 150-0011; tel. (3) 3406-4243; fax (3) 3409-7589; e-mail 1-tokio@ma.kcom.ne.jp; Ambassador: JUAN AURICH MONTERO (acting).

Philippines: 5-15-5, Roppongi, Minato-ku, Tokyo 106-8537; tel. (3) 5562-1600; e-mail phpjp@gol.com; internet www.rptokyo.org; Ambassador: ROMEO ABELARDO ARGUELLES.

Poland: 4-5-14, Takanawa, Minato-ku, Tokyo 108-0074; tel. (3) 3280-2882; fax (3) 3280-2362; Ambassador: JERZY POMIANOWSKI.

Portugal: Kamiura-Kojimachi Bldg, 5th Floor, 3-10-3, Kojimachi, Chiyoda-ku, Tokyo 102-0083; tel. (3) 5212-7322; fax (3) 5226-0616; e-mail embportj@ma.kcom.ne.jp; internet www.pnsnet.co.jp/users/cltembpt; Ambassador: MANUEL GERVÁSIO DE ALMEIDA LEITE.

Qatar: 6-8-7, Akasaka, Minato-ku, Tokyo 107-0052; tel. (3) 3224-3911; Ambassador: RIYADH ALI AL-ANSARI.

Romania: 3-16-19, Nishi Azabu, Minato-ku, Tokyo 106-0031; tel. (3) 3479-0311; fax (3) 3479-0312; e-mail romembjp@gol.com; internet www2.gol.com/users/romembjp/; Ambassador: ION PASCU.

Russia: 2-1-1, Azabu-dai, Minato-ku, Tokyo 106-0041; tel. (3) 3583-4224; fax (3) 3505-0593; internet embassy.kcom.ne.jp/russia/index.html; Ambassador: ALEKSANDR N. PANOV.

Rwanda: Kowa Bldg, No. 38, 4-12-24, Nishi Azabu, Minato-ku, Tokyo 106; tel. (3) 3486-7801; fax (3) 3409-2434; Ambassador: MATANGUHA ZEPHYR.

Saudi Arabia: 1-8-4, Roppongi, Minato-ku, Tokyo 106-0032; tel. (3) 3589-5241; Ambassador: MUHAMMAD BASHIR KURDI.

Senegal: 1-3-4, Aobadai, Meguro-ku, Tokyo 153-0042; tel. (3) 3464-8451; fax (3) 3464-8452; Ambassador: Aladji AMADOU THIAM.

Singapore: 5-12-3, Roppongi, Minato-ku, Tokyo 106-0032; tel. (3) 3586-9111; fax (3) 3582-1085; Ambassador: LIM CHIN BENG.

Slovakia: POB 35, 2-16-14, Hiroo, Shibuya-ku, Tokyo 150-8691; tel. (3) 3400-8122; fax (3) 3406-6215; e-mail zutokio@twics.com; internet embassy.kcom.ne.jp/slovakia/index.html; Ambassador: MIKULÁŠ SEDLÁK.

Slovenia: 7-5-15, Akasaka, Minato-ku, Tokyo 107-0052; tel. (3) 5570-6275; fax (3) 5570-6075; Ambassador JANEZ PREMOŽE.

South Africa: 414 Zenkyoren Bldg, 4th Floor, 2-7-9, Hirakawa-cho, Chiyoda-ku, Tokyo 102-0093; tel. (3) 3265-3366; fax (3) 3265-1108; e-mail sajapan@rsatk.com; internet www.rsatk.com; Ambassador: KARAMCHUND MACKERDHUJ.

Spain: 1-3-29, Roppongi, Minato-ku, Tokyo 106-0032; tel. (3) 3583-8531; fax (3) 3582-8627; e-mail embspjp@mail.mae.es; Ambassador: JUAN LEÑA CASAS.

Sri Lanka: 2-1-54, Takanawa, Minato-ku, Tokyo 108-0074; tel. (3) 3440-6911; fax (3) 3440-6914; e-mail lankaemb@sphere.ne.jp; internet embassy.kcom.ne.jp/srilanka; Ambassador: NEVILLE PIYADIGAMA.

Sudan: Kindai-Shisetsu Bldg 2F-3F, 1-13-4, Aobadai, Meguro-ku, Tokyo 153; tel. (3) 3476-0811; fax (3) 3476-0814; Ambassador: KHADIR HARON.

Sweden: 1-10-3-100, Roppongi, Minato-ku, Tokyo 106-0032; tel. (3) 5562-5050; fax (3) 5562-9095; e-mail ambassaden.tokyo@foreign.ministry.se; internet www.twics.com/~swedemb; Ambassador: KRISTER KUMLIN.

Switzerland: 5-9-12, Minami Azabu, Minato-ku, Tokyo 106-8589; tel. (3) 3473-0121; fax (3) 3473-6090; e-mail vertretung@tok.rep.admin.ch; Ambassador: JOHANNES J. MANZ.

Syria: Homat Jade, 6-19-45, Akasaka, Minato-ku, Tokyo 107-0052; tel. (3) 3586-8977; fax (3) 3586-8979; Chargé d'affaires a.i.: HAMZAH HAMZAH.

Tanzania: 4-21-9, Kami Yoga, Setagaya-ku, Tokyo 158-0098; tel. (3) 3425-4531; fax (3) 3425-7844; e-mail tzrepjp@gol.com; Ambassador: ELLY E. E. MTANGO.

Thailand: 3-14-6, Kami Osaki, Shinagawa-ku, Tokyo 141-0021; tel. (3) 3447-2247; fax (3) 3442-6750; e-mail thaitke@crisscross.com; Ambassador: CHAWAT ARTHAYUKTI.

Tunisia: 1-18-8, Wakaba, Shinjuku-ku, Tokyo 160-0011; tel. (3) 3353-4111; fax (3) 3225-4387; Ambassador: SALAH HANNACHI.

Turkey: 2-33-6, Jingumae, Shibuya-ku, Tokyo 150-0001; tel. (3) 3470-5131; fax (3) 3470-5136; Ambassador: YAMAN BAŞKUT.

Uganda: 39-15, Oyama-cho, Shibuya-ku, Tokyo 151-0065; tel. (3) 3465-4552; fax (3) 3465-4970; e-mail ugabassy@crisscross.com.

Ukraine: 6-5-26, Kita Shinagawa, Shinagawa-ku, Tokyo 141-0001; tel. (3) 3445-9229; fax (3) 3447-6768; e-mail ukremb@rose.ocn.ne.jp; Chargé d'affaires a.i.: VOLODYMYR RIABTSEV.

United Arab Emirates: 9-10, Nanpeidai-cho, Shibuya-ku, Tokyo 150-0036; tel. (3) 5489-0804; fax (3) 5489-0813; e-mail uae-emb@onyx.dti.ne.jp; Ambassador: AHMAD ALI HAMAD AL-MUALLA.

United Kingdom: 1, Ichiban-cho, Chiyoda-ku, Tokyo 102-8381; tel. (3) 5211-1100; fax (3) 5275-3164; e-mail embassy@tokyo.mail.fco.gov.uk; internet www.uknow.or.jp; Ambassador: Sir STEPHEN GOMERSALL.

USA: 1-10-5, Akasaka, Minato-ku, Tokyo 107-8420; tel. (3) 3224-5000; e-mail ustkyecn@ppp.bekkoame.or.jp; internet usembassy.state.gov/posts/ja1/wwwhmain.html; Ambassador: THOMAS S. FOLEY.

Uruguay: Kowa Bldg, No. 38, Room 908, 4-12-24, Nishi Azabu, Minato-ku, Tokyo 106-0031; tel. (3) 3486-1888; fax (3) 3486-9872; Ambassador: ZULMA GUELMAN.

Venezuela: Kowa Bldg, No. 38, Room 703, 4-12-24, Nishi Azabu, Minato-ku, Tokyo 106-0031; tel. (3) 3409-1501; fax (3) 3409-1505; e-mail embavene@interlink.or.jp; internet sunsite.sut.ac.jp/embassy/venemb/embvenez.html; Ambassador: Dr CARLOS ENRIQUE NONES.

Viet Nam: 50-11, Moto Yoyogi-cho, Shibuya-ku, Tokyo 151-0062; tel. (3) 3466-3313; fax (3) 3466-3391; Ambassador: NGUYEN TAM CHIEN.

Yemen: Kowa Bldg, No. 38, Room 807, 4-12-24, Nishi Azabu, Minato-ku, Tokyo 106-0031; tel. (3) 3499-7151; fax (3) 3499-4577; Chargé d'affaires a.i.: ABDULRAHMAN M. AL-HOTHI.

Yugoslavia: 4-7-24, Kita Shinagawa, Shinagawa-ku, Tokyo 140-0001; tel. (3) 3447-3571; fax (3) 3447-3577; e-mail embtokyo@twics.com; internet www.twics.com/~embtokyo/home.htm; Ambassador: Dr RADOSLAV BULAJIĆ.

Zambia: 1-10-2, Ebara, Shinagawa-ku, Tokyo 142-0063; tel. (3) 3491-0121; fax (3) 3491-0123; e-mail zamet@crisscross.com; Ambassador: ELIAS MARKO CHISHA CHIPIMO.

Zimbabwe: 5-9-10, Shiroganedai, Minato-ku, Tokyo 108; tel. (3) 3280-0331; fax (3) 3280-0466; e-mail zimtokyo@chive.ocn.ne.jp; Ambassador: Dr ANDREW H. MTETWA.

Judicial System

The basic principles of the legal system are set forth in the Constitution, which lays down that judicial power is vested in the Supreme Court and in such inferior courts as are established by law, and enunciates the principle that no organ or agency of the Executive shall be given final judicial power. Judges are to be independent in the exercise of their conscience, and may not be removed except by public impeachment, unless judicially declared mentally or physically incompetent to perform official duties. The justices of the Supreme Court are appointed by the Cabinet, the sole exception being the Chief Justice, who is appointed by the Emperor after designation by the Cabinet.

The Court Organization Law, which came into force on 3 May 1947, decreed the constitution of the Supreme Court and the establishment of four types of lower court—High, District, Family (established 1 January 1949) and Summary Courts. The constitution and functions of the courts are as follows:

SUPREME COURT

4-2, Hayabusa-cho, Chiyoda-ku, Tokyo 102-8651; tel. (3) 3264-8111; fax (3) 3221-8975; internet www.courts.go.jp.

This court is the highest legal authority in the land, and consists of a Chief Justice and 14 associate justices. It has jurisdiction over Jokoku (Jokoku appeals) and Kokoku (Kokoku appeals), prescribed in codes of procedure. It conducts its hearings and renders decisions through a Grand Bench or three Petty Benches. Both are collegiate bodies, the former consisting of all justices of the Court, and the latter of five justices. A Supreme Court Rule prescribes which cases are to be handled by the respective Benches. It is, however, laid down by law that the Petty Bench cannot make decisions as to the constitutionality of a statute, ordinance, regulation, or disposition, or as to cases in which an opinion concerning the interpretation and application of the Constitution, or of any laws or ordinances, is at variance with a previous decision of the Supreme Court.

Chief Justice: SHIGERU YAMAGUCHI.

Secretary-General: YUKIO HORIGOME.

LOWER COURTS

High Court

A High Court conducts its hearings and renders decisions through a collegiate body, consisting of three judges, though for cases of insurrection the number of judges must be five. The Court has jurisdiction over the following matters:

Koso appeals from judgments in the first instance rendered by District Courts, from judgments rendered by Family Courts, and from judgments concerning criminal cases rendered by Summary Courts.

Kokoku appeals against rulings and orders rendered by District Courts and Family Courts, and against rulings and orders concerning criminal cases rendered by Summary Courts, except those coming within the jurisdiction of the Supreme Court.

Jokoku appeals from judgments in the second instance rendered by District Courts and from judgments rendered by Summary Courts, except those concerning criminal cases.

Actions in the first instance relating to cases of insurrection.

Presidents: TOKUJI IZUMI (Tokyo), YOSHIO OKADA (Osaka), REISUKE SHIMADA (Nagoya), TOYOZO UEDA (Hiroshima), TOSHIMARO KOJO (Fukuoka), FUMIYA SATO (Sendai), KAZUO KATO (Sapporo), FUMIO ARAI (Takamatsu).

District Court

A District Court conducts hearings and renders decisions through a single judge or, for certain types of cases, through a collegiate body of three judges. It has jurisdiction over the following matters:

Actions in the first instance, except offences relating to insurrection, claims where the subject matter of the action does not exceed 900,000 yen, and offences liable to a fine or lesser penalty.

Koso appeals from judgments rendered by Summary Courts, except those concerning criminal cases.

Kokoku appeals against rulings and orders rendered by Summary Courts, except those coming within the jurisdiction of the Supreme Court and High Courts.

Family Court

A Family Court handles cases through a single judge in case of rendering judgments or decisions. However, in accordance with the provisions of other statutes, it conducts its hearings and renders decisions through a collegiate body of three judges. A conciliation is effected through a collegiate body consisting of a judge and two or more members of the conciliation committee selected from among citizens.

It has jurisdiction over the following matters:

Judgment and conciliation with regard to cases relating to family as provided for by the Law for Adjudgment of Domestic Relations.

Judgment with regard to the matters of protection of juveniles as provided for by the Juvenile Law.

Actions in the first instance relating to adult criminal cases of violation of the Labour Standard Law, the Law for Prohibiting Liquors to Minors, or other laws especially enacted for protection of juveniles.

Summary Court

A Summary Court handles cases through a single judge, and has jurisdiction in the first instance over the following matters:

Claims where the value of the subject matter does not exceed 900,000 yen (excluding claims for cancellation or change of administrative dispositions).

Actions which relate to offences liable to a fine or lesser penalty, offences liable to a fine as an optional penalty, and certain specified offences such as habitual gambling and larceny.

A Summary Court cannot impose imprisonment or a graver penalty. When it deems proper the imposition of a sentence of imprisonment or a graver penalty, it must transfer such cases to a District Court, but it can impose imprisonment with labour not exceeding three years for certain specified offences.

Religion

The traditional religions of Japan are Shintoism and Buddhism. Neither is exclusive, and many Japanese subscribe at least nominally to both. Since 1945 a number of new religions (Shinko Shukyo) have evolved, based on a fusion of Shinto, Buddhist, Daoist, Confucian and Christian beliefs. In 1995 there were some 184,000 religious organizations registered in Japan, according to the Ministry of Education.

SHINTOISM

Shintoism is an indigenous religious system embracing the worship of ancestors and of nature. It is divided into two cults: national Shintoism, which is represented by the shrines; and sectarian Shintoism, which developed during the second half of the 19th century. In 1868 Shinto was designated a national religion and all Shinto shrines acquired the privileged status of a national institution. Complete freedom of religion was introduced in 1947, and state support of Shinto was prohibited. In the mid-1990s there were 81,307 shrines, 90,309 priests and 106.6m. adherents.

BUDDHISM

World Buddhist Fellowship: Rev. Fuji Nakayama, Hozenji Buddhist Temple, 3-24-2, Akabane-dai, Kita-ku, Tokyo.

CHRISTIANITY

In 1993 the Christian population was estimated at 1,050,938.

National Christian Council in Japan: Japan Christian Centre, 2-3-18-24, Nishi Waseda, Shinjuku-ku, Tokyo 169-0051; tel. (3) 3203-0372; fax (3) 3204-9495; e-mail ncc-j@jca.apc.org; internet www.jca.apc.org/ncc-j; f. 1923; 14 mems (churches and other bodies), 19 assoc. mems; Chair. Reiko Suzuki; Gen. Sec. Rev. Kenichi Otsu.

The Anglican Communion

Anglican Church in Japan (Nippon Sei Ko Kai): 65, Yarai-cho, Shinjuku-ku, Tokyo 162; tel. (3) 5228-3171; fax (3) 5228-3175; e-mail general-sec.po@nskk.org; internet www.nskk.org; f. 1887; 11 dioceses; Primate of Japan Most Rev. John Jun'ichiro Furumoto, Bishop of Kobe; Gen. Sec. Rev. Samuel I. Koshiishi; 57,782 mems (1999).

The Orthodox Church

Japanese Orthodox Church (Nippon Haristosu Seikyoukai): Holy Resurrection Cathedral (Nicolai-Do), 4-1-3, Kanda Surugadai, Chiyoda-ku, Tokyo 101; tel. (3) 3291-1885; fax (3) 3291-1886; e-mail ocj@gol.com; three dioceses; Archbishop of Tokyo, Primate and Metropolitan of All Japan Most Rev. Theodosius; 24,821 mems.

Protestant Church

United Church of Christ in Japan (Nihon Kirisuto Kyodan): Japan Christian Center, Room 31, 2-3-18, Nishi Waseda, Shinjuku-ku, Tokyo 169-0051; tel. (3) 3202-0541; fax (3) 3207-3918; f. 1941; union of 34 Congregational, Methodist, Presbyterian, Reformed and other Protestant denominations; Moderator Rev. Seishi Ojima; Gen. Sec. Rev. Sadao Ozawa; 205,735 mems (1997).

The Roman Catholic Church

Japan comprises three archdioceses and 13 dioceses. There were an estimated 443,644 adherents at 31 December 1998.

Catholic Bishops' Conference of Japan (Chuo Kyogikai): 2-10-10, Shiomi, Koto-ku, Tokyo 135-8585; tel. (3) 5632-4411; fax (3) 5632-4457; e-mail cbcj-has@ja2.so-net.ne.jp; internet www02.so-net.ne.jp/~catholic; Pres. Most Rev. Francis Xavier Kaname Shimamoto, Archbishop of Nagasaki.

Archbishop of Nagasaki: Most Rev. Francis Xavier Kaname Shimamoto, Archbishop's House, 1-1, Hashiguchi-machi, Nagasaki-shi, Nagasaki-ken 852-8114; tel. (95) 843-4188; fax (95) 843-4322.

Archbishop of Osaka: Most Rev. Leo Jun Ikenaga, Archbishop's House, 2-24-22, Tamatsukuri, Chuo-ku, Osaka 540-0004; tel. (6) 6941-9700; fax (6) 6946-1345.

Archbishop of Tokyo: Most Rev. Peter Takeo Okada, Archbishop's House, 3-16-15, Sekiguchi, Bunkyo-ku, Tokyo 112-0014; tel. (3) 3943-2301; fax (3) 3944-8511.

Other Christian Churches

Japan Baptist Convention: 1-2-4, Minami Urawa, Urawa-shi, Saitama 336-0017; tel. (48) 883-1091; fax (48) 883-1092; e-mail bapjo@mua.biglobe.ne.jp; f. 1947; Pres. Rev. Hidetsugu Ando; Gen. Sec. Rev. Seiya Yamashita; 33,012 mems (March 1998).

Japan Baptist Union: 2-3-18, Nishi Waseda, Shinjuku-ku, Tokyo 169-0051; tel. (3) 3202-0053; fax (3) 3202-0054; e-mail DQK10166@nifty.ne.jp; f. 1958; Moderator Kunihiko Amano; Gen. Sec. Kazuo Oya; 4,819 mems.

Japan Evangelical Lutheran Church: 1-1, Sadohara-cho, Ichigaya-shi, Shinjuku-ku, Tokyo 162-0842; tel. (3) 3260-8631; fax (3) 3268-3589; e-mail m-uno@jelc.or.jp; internet www.jelc.or.jp; f. 1893; Moderator Rev. Jun Koizumi; Gen. Sec. Rev. Masanori Uno; 22,246 mems (March 1996).

Korean Christian Church in Japan: Room 52, Japan Christian Center, 2-3-18, Nishi Waseda, Shinjuku-ku, Tokyo 169-0051; tel. (3) 3202-5398; fax (3) 3202-4977; e-mail kccj@kb3.so-net.ne.jp; f. 1909; Moderator Kim Duk-Hwa; Gen. Sec. Kang Young-Il; 10,000 mems (1994).

Among other denominations active in Japan are the Christian Catholic Church, the German Evangelical Church and the Tokyo Union Church.

OTHER COMMUNITIES

Bahá'í Faith

The National Spiritual Assembly of the Bahá'ís of Japan: 7-2-13, Shinjuku, Shinjuku-ku, Tokyo 160-0022; tel. (3) 3209-7521; fax (3) 3204-0773; e-mail nsajpn@att.ne.jp; internet www.bahaijp.org.

Judaism

Jewish Community of Japan: 8-8 Hiro, 3-Chome, Shibuya-ku, Tokyo 150-0012; tel. (3) 3400-2559; e-mail jccjapan@gol.com; internet jewish.japan.co.jp; Leader Rabbi Elliott M. Marmon.

Islam

Islam has been active in Japan since the late 19th century. There is a small Muslim community, maintaining several mosques, including those at Kobe, Nagoya, Chiba and Isesaki, the Arabic Islamic Institute and the Islamic Center in Tokyo. The construction of Tokyo Central mosque was ongoing in 1999.

Islamic Center, Japan: 1-16-11, Ohara, Setagaya-ku, Tokyo 156-0041; tel. (3) 3460-6169; fax (3) 3460-6105; e-mail islamcpj@islamcenter.or.jp; internet www.islamcenter.or.jp; f. 1965; Chair. Dr Salih Samarrai.

The New Religions

Many new cults have emerged in Japan since the end of the Second World War. Collectively these are known as the New Religions (Shinko Shukyo), among the most important of which are Tenrikyo, Omotokyo, Soka Gakkai, Rissho Kosei-kai, Kofuku-no-Kagaku, Agonshu and Aum Shinrikyo. (Following the indictment on charges of murder of several members of Aum Shinrikyo, including its leader, Shoko Asahara, the cult lost its legal status as a religious organization in 1996. In January 2000 the cult announced its intention to change its name to Aleph. At that time it named a new leader, TATSUKO MURAOKA.)

Kofuku-no-Kagaku (Institute for Research in Human Happiness): Tokyo; f. 1986; believes its founder to be reincarnation of Buddha; 8.25m. mems; Leader RYUHO OKAWA.

Rissho Kosei-kai: 2-11-1, Wada Suginami-ku, Tokyo 166-8537; tel. (3) 3380-5185; fax (3) 3381-9792; internet www.kosei-kai.or.jp; f. 1938; Buddhist lay organization based on the teaching of the Lotus Sutra, active inter-faith co-operation towards peace; Pres. Rev. Dr NICHIKO NIWANO; 6.3m. mems with 245 brs world-wide (2000).

Soka Gakkai: 32, Shinano-machi, Shinjuku-ku, Tokyo 160-8583; tel. (3) 5360-9830; fax (3) 5360-9885; e-mail webmaster@ sokagakkai.or.jp; internet www.sokagakkai.or.jp; f. 1930; society of lay practitioners of the Buddhism of Nichiren; membership of 8.21m. households (2000); group promotes activities in education, international cultural exchange and consensus-building towards peace, based on the humanist world view of Buddhism; Hon. Pres. DAISAKU IKEDA; Pres. EINOSUKE AKIYA.

The Press

In December 1999 there were 121 daily newspapers in Japan. Their average circulation was the highest in the world, and the circulation per head of population was also among the highest, at 573 copies per 1,000 inhabitants in 1999. The large number of weekly news journals is a notable feature of the Japanese press. At December 1998 a total of 2,763 periodicals were produced, 85 of which were weekly publications. Technically the Japanese press is highly advanced, and the major newspapers are issued in simultaneous editions in the main centres.

The two newspapers with the largest circulations are the *Yomiuri Shimbun* and *Asahi Shimbun*. Other influential papers include *Mainichi Shimbun*, *Nihon Keizai Shimbun*, *Chunichi Shimbun* and *Sankei Shimbun*.

NATIONAL DAILIES

Asahi Shimbun: 5-3-2, Tsukiji, Chuo-ku, Tokyo 104-8011; tel. (3) 3545-0131; fax (3) 3545-0358; internet www.asahi.com; f. 1879; also published by Osaka, Seibu and Nagoya head offices and Hokkaido branch office; Pres. SHINICHI HAKOSHIMA; Dir and Exec. Editor KIYOFUKU CHUMA; circ. morning 8.3m., evening 4.1m.

Mainichi Shimbun: 1-1-1, Hitotsubashi, Chiyoda-ku, Tokyo 100-8051; tel. (3) 3212-0321; fax (3) 3211-3598; internet www.mainichi .co.jp; f. 1882; also published by Osaka, Seibu and Chubu head offices, and Hokkaido branch office; Pres. AKIRA SAITO; Man. Dir and Editor-in-Chief ATSUMU KIDO; circ. morning 4.0m., evening 1.8m.

Nihon Keizai Shimbun: 1-9-5, Otemachi, Chiyoda-ku, Tokyo 100-8066; tel. (3) 3270-0251; fax (3) 5255-2661; internet www.nikkei .co.jp; f. 1876; also published by Osaka head office and Sapporo, Nagoya and Seibu branch offices; Pres. TAKUHIKO TSURUTA; Dir and Man. Editor YASUO HIRATA; circ. morning 3.0m., evening 1.7m.

Sankei Shimbun: 1-7-2, Otemachi, Chiyoda-ku, Tokyo 100-8077; tel. (3) 3231-7111; internet www.sankei.co.jp; f. 1933; also published by Osaka head office; Man. Dir and Editor NAGAYOSHI SUMIDA; circ. morning 2.0m., evening 905,771.

Yomiuri Shimbun: 1-7-1, Otemachi, Chiyoda-ku, Tokyo 100-8055; tel. (3) 3242-1111; e-mail webmaster@yomiuri.co.jp; internet www.yomiuri.co.jp; f. 1874; also published by Osaka, Seibu and Chubu head offices, and Hokkaido and Hokuriku branch offices; Pres. and Editor-in-Chief TSUNEO WATANABE; circ. morning 10.2m., evening 4.3m.

PRINCIPAL LOCAL DAILIES

Tokyo

Asahi Evening News : 5-3-2, Tsukiji, Chuo-ku, Tokyo 104-8011; tel. (3) 5540-7641; fax (3) 3542-6172; f. 1954; evening; English; Exec. Editor TAKAHIRO ODA; Man. Editor MANABU HARA; circ. 38,800.

Daily Sports: 1-20-3, Osaki, Shinagawa-ku, Tokyo 141-8585; tel. (3) 5434-1752; f. 1948; morning; Dir YOSHIHIKO SHIMOMURA; circ. 400,254.

The Daily Yomiuri: 1-7-1, Otemachi, Chiyoda-ku, Tokyo 100-8055; tel. (3) 3242-1111; f. 1955; morning; Editor ICHIRO TANIGUCHI; circ. 49,030.

Dempa Shimbun: 1-11-15, Higashi Gotanda, Shinagawa-ku, Tokyo 141-8790; tel. (3) 3445-6111; fax (3) 3444-7515; f. 1950; morning; Pres. TETSUO HIRAYAMA; Man. Editor TOSHIO KASUYA; circ. 298,000.

Hochi Shimbun: 4-6-49, Konan, Minato-ku, Tokyo 108-8485; tel. (3) 5479-1111; internet www.yomiuri.co.jp/hochi/home.htm; f. 1872; morning; Pres. MASARU FUSHIMI; Man. Editor TATSUE AOKI; circ. 764,445.

The Japan Times: 4-5-4, Shibaura, Minato-ku, Tokyo 108-8071; tel. (3) 3453-5312; internet www.japantimes.co.jp; f. 1897; morning;

English; Chair. and Pres. TOSHIAKI OGASAWARA; Dir and Editor-in-Chief YUTAKA MATAEBARA; circ. 61,929.

The Mainichi Daily News: 1-1-1, Hitotsubashi, Chiyoda-ku, Tokyo 100-8051; tel. (3) 3212-0321; f. 1922; morning; English; also publ. from Osaka; Man. Editor TETSUO TOKIZAWA; combined circ. 49,200.

Naigai Times: 1-1-15, Ariake, Koto-ku, Tokyo 135-0063; tel. (3) 5564-7021; f. 1949; evening; Pres. MITSUGU ONDA; Vice-Pres. and Editor-in-Chief MASAHIRO MORITA; circ. 298,000.

Nihon Kaiji Shimbun (Japan Maritime Daily): 5-19-2, Shimbashi, Minato-ku, Tokyo 105-0004; tel. (3) 3436-3221; internet www.jmd.co.jp; f. 1942; morning; Man. Editor MINORU TAKASHIMIZU; circ. 55,000.

Nihon Kogyo Shimbun: 1-7-2, Otemachi, Chiyoda-ku, Tokyo 100-8125; tel. (3) 3231-7111; internet www.jij.co.jp; f. 1933; morning; industrial, business and financial; Man. Editor YASUSHI KITANO; circ. 407,125.

Nihon Nogyo Shimbun (Agriculture): 2-3, Akihabara, Taito-ku, Tokyo 110-8722; tel. (3) 5295-7411; fax (3) 3253-0980; f. 1928; morning; Man. Editor YASUNORI INOUE; circ. 423,840.

Nihon Sen-i Shimbun (Textile and Fashion): 1-13-12, Nihonbashi-muromachi, Chuo-ku, Tokyo 103-0022; tel. (3) 3270-1661; fax (3) 3246-1858; f. 1943; morning; Man. Editor KIYOSHIGE SEIRYU; circ. 124,000.

Nikkan Kogyo Shimbun (Industrial Daily News): 1-8-10, Kudan-kita, Chiyoda-ku, Tokyo 102-8181; tel. (3) 3222-7111; fax (3) 3262-6031; internet www.nikkan.co.jp; f. 1915; morning; Man. Editor HIDEO WATANABE; circ. 533,145.

Nikkan Sports News: 3-5-10, Tsukiji, Chuo-ku, Tokyo 104-8055; tel. (3) 5550-8888; fax (3) 5550-8901; internet www.nikkansport-s.com; f. 1946; morning; Man. Editor YUKIHIRO MORI; circ. 993,240.

Sankei Sports: 1-7-2, Otemachi, Chiyoda-ku, Tokyo 100-8077; tel. (3) 3231-7111; internet www.xusxus.com; f. 1963; morning; Man. Editor YUKIO INADA; circ. 809,245.

Shipping and Trade News: Tokyo News Service Ltd, Tsukiji Hamarikyu Bldg, 5-3-3, Tsukiji, Chuo-ku, Tokyo 104-8004; tel. (3) 3542-6511; fax (3) 3542-5086; internet www.tvguide.or.jp; f. 1949; English; Man. Editor TAKASHI INOUE; circ. 15,000.

Sports Nippon: 2-1-30, Ecchujima, Koto-ku, Tokyo 135-8735; tel. (3) 3820-0700; internet www.mainichi.co.jp/suponichi; f. 1949; morning; Man. Editor SUSUMU KOMURO; circ. 929,421.

Suisan Keizai Shimbun (Fisheries): 6-8-19, Roppongi, Minato-ku, Tokyo 106-0032; tel. (3) 3404-6531; fax (3) 3404-0863; f. 1948; morning; Man. Editor KOSHI TORINOUMI; circ. 61,000.

Tokyo Chunichi Sports: 2-3-13, Kohnan, Minato-ku, Tokyo 108-8010; tel. (3) 3471-2211; f. 1956; evening; Head Officer TETSUO TANAKA; circ. 330,431.

Tokyo Shimbun: 2-3-13, Kohnan, Minato-ku, Tokyo 108-8010; tel. (3) 3471-2211; fax (3) 3471-1851; internet www.tokyo-np.co.jp; f. 1942; Man. Editor KUNIHIRO TAKABA; circ. morning 655,970, evening 354,191.

Tokyo Sports: 2-1-30, Ecchujima, Koto-ku, Tokyo 135-8721; tel. (3) 3820-0801; f. 1959; evening; Man. Editor YASUO SAKURAI; circ. 1,321,250.

Yukan Fuji: 1-7-2, Otemachi, Chiyoda-ku, Tokyo 100-8077; tel. (3) 3231-7111; fax (3) 3246-0377; internet www.zakzak.co.jp; f. 1969; evening; Man. Editor MASAMI KATO; circ. 268,984.

Osaka District

Daily Sports: 1-18-11, Edobori, Nishi-ku, Osaka 550-0002; tel. (6) 6443-0421; f. 1948; morning; Man. Editor TOSHIAKI MITANI; circ. 562,715.

The Mainichi Daily News: 3-4-5, Umeda, Kita-ku, Osaka 530-8251; tel. (6) 6345-1551; f. 1922; morning; English; Man. Editor KATSUYA FUKUNAGA.

Nikkan Sports: 5-92-1, Hattori-kotobuki-cho, Toyonaka 561-8585; tel. (6) 6867-2811; internet www.nikkansports.com/osaka; f. 1950; morning; Man. Editor KATSUO FURUKAWA; circ. 513,498.

Osaka Shimbun: 2-4-9, Umeda, Kita-ku, Osaka 530-8279; tel. (6) 6343-1221; internet www.osakanews.com; f. 1922; evening; Man. Editor KAORU YURA; circ. 88,887.

Osaka Sports: Osaka Ekimae Daiichi Bldg, 4th Floor, 1-3-1-400, Umeda, Kita-ku, Osaka 530-0001; tel. (6) 6345-7657; f. 1968; evening; Head Officer KAZUOMI TANAKA; circ. 470,660.

Sankei Sports: 2-4-9, Umeda, Kita-ku, Osaka 530-8277; tel. (6) 6343-1221; f. 1955; morning; Man. Editor MASAKI YOSHIDA; circ. 552,519.

Sports Nippon: 3-4-5, Umeda, Kita-ku, Osaka 530-8278; tel. (6) 6346-8500; f. 1949; morning; Man. Editor HIDETOSHI ISHIHARA; circ. 477,300.

Kanto District

Chiba Nippo (Chiba Daily News): 4-14-10, Chuo, Chuo-ku, Chiba 260-0013; tel. (43) 222-9211; internet www.chibanippo.co.jp; f. 1957; morning; Man. Editor NOBORU HAYASHI; circ. 190,187.

Ibaraki Shimbun: 2-15, Kitami-machi, Mito 310-8686; tel. (292) 21-3121; internet www1.sphere.ne.jp/iba-news; f. 1891; morning; Pres. and Editor in Charge TADANORI TOMOSUE; circ. 117,449.

Jomo Shimbun: 1-50-21, Furuichi-machi, Maebashi 371-8666; tel. (272) 54-9911; internet www.web-jumps.com; f. 1887; morning; Man. Editor MUTSUO ODAGIRI; circ. 296,111.

Joyo Shimbun: 2-7-6, Manabe, Tsuchiura 300-0051; tel. (298) 21-1780; internet www.tsukuba.com; f. 1948; morning; Pres. MINEO IWANAMI; Man. Editor AKIRA SAITO; circ. 88,700.

Kanagawa Shimbun: 6-145, Hanasaki-cho, Nishi-ku, Yokohama 220-8588; tel. (45) 411-7450; internet www.kanagawa-np.co.jp; f. 1942; morning; Dir and Man. Editor TADASHI ITO; circ. 237,149.

Saitama Shimbun: 6-12-11, Kishi-machi, Urawa 336-8686; tel. (48) 862-3371; internet www.saitama-np.co.jp; f. 1944; morning; Man. Editor YOTARO NUMATA; circ. 162,071.

Shimotsuke Shimbun: 1-8-11, Showa, Utsunomiya 320-8686; tel. (286) 25-1111; internet www.shimotsuke.co.jpf. 1884; morning; Man. Dir and Editor-in-Chief EISUKE TODA; circ. 306,072.

Tohoku District
(North-east Honshu)

Akita Sakigake Shimpo: 1-1, San-no-rinkai-cho, Akita 010-8601; tel. (188) 88-1800; fax (188) 23-1780; internet www.sakigake.co.jp; f. 1874; Man. Editor SHIGEAKI MAEKAWA; circ. 262,289.

Daily Tohoku: 1-3-12, Joka, Hachinohe 031-8601; tel. (178) 44-5111; f. 1945; morning; Exec. Dir and Man. Editor UICHI IZUMIYAMA; circ. 105,721.

Fukushima Mimpo: 13-17, Otemachi, Fukushima 960-8602; tel. (245) 31-4111; internet www.fukushima-minpo.co.jp; f. 1892; Pres. and Editor-in-Chief TSUTOMU HANADA; circ. morning 308,353, evening 9,489.

Fukushima Minyu: 4-29, Yanagimachi, Fukushima 960-8648; tel. (245) 23-1191; internet www.minyu.cc.jp; f. 1895; Man. Editor KENJI KANNO; circ. morning 201,414, evening 6,066.

Hokuu Shimpo: 3-2, Nishi-dori-machi, Noshiro 016-0891. (185) 54-3150; f. 1895; morning; Chair. KOUICHI YAMAKI; circ. 31,490.

Ishinomaki Shimbun: 2-1-28, Sumiyoshi-machi, Ishinomaki 986; tel. (225) 22-3201; f. 1946; evening; Man. Editor MASATOSHI SATO; circ. 13,050.

Iwate Nichi-nichi Shimbun: 60, Minami-shin-machi, Ichinoseki 021-8686; tel. (191) 26-5114; internet www.isop.ne.jp/iwanichi; f. 1923; morning; Pres. TAKESHI YAMAGISHI; Man. Editor SEIICHI WATANABE; circ. 59,850.

Iwate Nippo: 3-7, Uchimaru, Morioka 020-8622; tel. (196) 53-4111; internet www.iwate-np.co.jp; f. 1876; Man. Editor HIROSHI MIURA; circ. morning 226,998, evening 226,565.

Kahoku Shimpo: 1-2-28, Itsutsubashi, Aoba-ku, Sendai 980-8660; tel. (22) 211-1111; fax (22) 224-7947; internet www.kahoku.co.jp; f. 1897; Exec. Dir and Man. Editor MASAHIKO ICHIRIKI; circ. morning 503,318, evening 133,855.

Mutsu Shimpo: 2-1, Shimo-shirogane-cho, Hirosaki 036-8356; tel. (172) 34-3111; f. 1946; morning; Man. Editor YUJI SATO; circ. 53,500.

Shonai Nippo: 8-29, Baba-cho, Tsuruoka 997-8691; tel. (235) 22-1480; f. 1946; morning; Pres. SHOJI KON-NO; Exec. Dir and Editor-in-Chief MASATOSHI MATSUNOKI; circ. 22,500.

To-o Nippo: 78, Kanbayashi, Yatsuyaku, Aomori 030-0180; tel. (177) 39-1111; internet www.toonippo.co.jp; f. 1888; Exec. Dir and Man. Editor TAKAO SHIOKOSHI; circ. morning 262,590, evening 258,570.

Yamagata Shimbun: 2-5-12, Hatago-cho, Yamagata 990-0047; tel. (236) 22-5271; internet www.yamagata-np.co.jp; f. 1876; Dir and Man. Editor YOUSUKE KUROSAWA; circ. morning 227,919, evening 227,917.

Yonezawa Shimbun: 3-3-7, Monto-cho, Yonezawa 992-0039; tel. (238) 22-4411; f. 1879; morning; Man. Dir and Editor-in-Chief MAKOTO SATO; circ. 13,750.

Chubu District
(Central Honshu)

Chubu Keizai Shimbun: 4-4-12, Meieki, Nakamura-ku, Nagoya 450-8561; tel. (52) 561-5215; f. 1946; morning; Man. Editor NORIMITSU INAGAKI; circ. 97,000.

Chukyo Sports: Chunichi Kosoku Offset Insatsu Bldg, 4-3-9, Kinjo, Naka-ku, Nagoya 460-0847; tel. (52) 982-1911; f. 1968; evening; circ. 289,430; Head Officer OSAMU SUETSUGU.

Chunichi Shimbun: 1-6-1, Sannomaru, Naka-ku, Nagoya 460-8511; tel. (52) 201-8811; internet www.chunichi.ne.jp; f. 1942; Man. Editor NOBUAKI KOIDE; circ. morning 2.7m., evening 748,635.

Chunichi Sports: 1-6-1, Sannomaru, Naka-ku, Nagoya 460-8511; tel. (52) 201-8811; f. 1954; evening; Head Officer KATSUHIKO SAKAI; circ. 643,644.

Gifu Shimbun: 10, Imakomachi, Gifu 500-8577; tel. (582) 64-1151; internet www.jic-gifu.or.jp/np; f. 1879; Exec. Dir and Man. Editor TADASHI TANAKA; circ. morning 170,176, evening 31,775.

Higashi-Aichi Shimbun: 62, Torinawate, Shinsakae-machi, Toyohashi 441-8666; tel. (532) 32-3111; f. 1957; morning; Man. Editor HARUO INOUE; circ. 52,300.

Nagano Nippo: 3-1323-1, Takashima, Suwa 392-8611; tel. (266) 52-2000; f. 1901; morning; Exec. Dir and Man. Editor KENJIRO BANZAI; circ. 73,000.

Nagoya Times: 1-3-10, Marunouchi, Naka-ku, Nagoya 460-8530; tel. (52) 231-1331; f. 1946; evening; Man. Editor NAOKI KITO; circ. 146,137.

Shinano Mainichi Shimbun: 657, Minamiagata-machi, Nagano 380-8546; tel. (26) 236-3000; fax (26) 236-3197; internet www.shinmai.co.jp; f. 1873; Man. Editor SEIICHI INOMATA; circ. morning 469,801, evening 55,625.

Shizuoka Shimbun: 3-1-1, Toro, Shizuoka 422-8033; tel. (54) 284-8900; internet www.sbs-np.co.jp; f. 1941; Dir and Man. Editor SEIJI HARADA; circ. morning 726,755, evening 726,676.

Yamanashi Nichi-Nichi Shimbun: 2-6-10, Kitaguchi, Kofu 400-8515; tel. (552) 31-3000; internent www.sannichi.co.jp; f. 1872; morning; Man. Editor MATSUO MORIMOTO; circ. 203,880.

Hokuriku District
(North Coastal Honshu)

Fukui Shimbun: 1-1-14, Haruyama, Fukui 910-8552; tel. (776) 23-5111; internet www.fukuishimbun.co.jp; f. 1899; morning; Man. Editor MITSUSHI ASANO; circ. 201,450.

Hokkoku Shimbun: 2-5-1, Kohrinbo, Kanazawa 920-8588; tel. (762) 63-2111; internet www.hokkoku.co.jp; f. 1893; Man. Editor HAJIME MURAHAMA; circ. morning 328,532, evening 97,051.

Hokuriku Chunichi Shimbun: 2-7-15, Kohrinbo, Kanazawa 920-8573; tel. (762) 61-3111; internet www.hokuriku.chunichi.co.jp; f. 1960; Man. Editor KANJI KOMIYA; circ. morning 116,719, evening 12,820.

Kitanippon Shimbun: 2-14, Azumi-cho, Toyama 930-8680; tel. (764) 45-3300; internet www.kitanippon.co.jp; f. 1940; Dir and Man. Editor RYUICHI KITAGAWA; circ. morning 223,033, evening 29,959.

Niigata Nippo: 258-24, Sanban-cho, Nishibori-dori, Niigata 951-8620; tel. (25) 378-9111; internet www.niigata-inet.or.jp/nippo; f. 1942; Dir and Man. Editor GEN HOSHINO; circ. morning 495,458, evening 67,235.

Toyama Shimbun: 5-1, Otemachi, Toyama 930-8520; tel. (764) 91-8111; internet www.toyama.hokkoku.co.jp; f. 1923; morning; Man. Editor SACHIO MIYAMOTO; circ. 42,988.

Kinki District
(West Central Honshu)

Daily Sports: 1-5-7, Higashi-Kawasaki-cho, Chuo-ku, Kobe 650-0044; tel. (78) 362-7100; morning; Man. Editor HIROHISA KARUO.

Ise Shimbun: 34-6, Hon-cho, Tsu 514-0831; tel. (592) 24-0003; internet www.isenp.co.jp; f. 1878; morning; Man. Editor FUJIO YAMAMOTO; circ. 100,550.

Kii Minpo: 100, Akitsu-machi, Tanabe 646-8660; tel. (739) 22-7171; internet www.aikis.or.jp/~agara-km; f. 1911; evening; Man. Editor SOCHI TANIKAWA; circ. 38,065.

Kobe Shimbun: 1-5-7, Higashi-Kawasaki-cho, Chuo-ku, Kobe 650-8571; tel. (78) 362-7100; internet www.kobe-np.co.jp; f. 1898; Man. Editor YASUO ISHIYAMA; circ. morning 539,498, evening 271,627.

Kyoto Shimbun: 239, Shoshoi-machi, Ebisugawa-agaru, Karasuma-dori, Nakagyo-ku, Kyoto 604-8577; tel. (75) 241-5430; internet www.kyoto-np.co.jp; f. 1879; Man. Editor OSAMU SAITO; circ. morning 505,723, evening 319,313.

Nara Shimbun: 606, Sanjo-machi, Nara 630-8686; tel. (742) 26-1331; internet www.nara-shimbun.com; f. 1946; morning; Dir and Man. Editor SADAYUKI HAYASHI; circ. 118,064.

Chugoku District
(Western Honshu)

Chugoku Shimbun: 7-1, Dobashi-cho, Naka-ku, Hiroshima 730-8677; tel. (82) 236-2111; fax (82) 236-2321; e-mail denshi@hiroshima-cdas.or.jp; internet www.chugoku-np.co.jp; f. 1892; Dir and Man. Editor MASAOMI MIYAKE; circ. morning 735,460, evening 94,526.

Nihonkai Shimbun: 2-137, Tomiyasu, Tottori 680-8678; tel. (857) 21-2888; internet www.nnn.co.jp; f. 1976; morning; Man. Editor KENJI SAEKI; circ. 101,768.

Okayama Nichi-Nichi Shimbun: 6-30, Hon-cho, Okayama 700-8678; tel. (86) 231-4211; f. 1946; evening; Man. Dir and Man. Editor TAKASHI ANDO; circ. 45,000.

San-In Chuo Shimpo: 383, Tono-machi, Matsue 690-8668; tel. (852) 32-3440; f. 1942; morning; Man. Editor MASAMI MOCHIDA; circ. 171,315.

Sanyo Shimbun: 2-1-23, Yanagi-machi, Okayama 700-8634; tel. (86) 231-2210; internet www1.meshnet.ne.jp/sanyo-np; f. 1879; Man. Dir and Man. Editor TAKAMASA KOSHIMUNE; circ. morning 451,837, evening 71,324.

Ube Jiho: 3-6-1, Kotobuki-cho, Ube 755-8557; tel. (836) 31-1511; f. 1912; evening; Exec. Dir and Man. Editor KAZUYA WAKI; circ. 42,550.

Yamaguchi Shimbun: 1-1-7, Higashi-Yamato-cho, Shimonoseki 750-8506; tel. (832) 66-3211; internet www.minato-yamaguchi.co.jp; f. 1946; morning; Man. Editor SHOICHI SASAKI; circ. 84,000.

Shikoku Island

Ehime Shimbun: 1-12-1, Otemachi, Matsuyama 790-8511; tel. (899) 35-2111; internet www.ehime-np.co.jp; f. 1941; morning; Man. Editor RYOJI YANO; circ. 319,284.

Kochi Shimbun: 3-2-15, Hon-machi, Kochi 780-8572; tel. (888) 22-2111; internet www.kochinews.co.jp; f. 1904; Dir and Man. Editor KENGO FUJITO; circ. morning 233,319, evening 146,276.

Shikoku Shimbun: 15-1, Nakano-machi, Takamatsu 760-8572; tel. (878) 33-1111; internet www.shikoku-np.co.jp; f. 1889; morning; Man. Editor SHIGEHARA TANAKA; circ. 208,816.

Tokushima Shimbun: 2-5-2, Naka-Tokushima-cho, Tokushima 770-8572; tel. (886) 55-7373; fax (866) 54-0165; internet www.topics.or.jp; f. 1941; Dir and Man. Editor HIROSHI MATSUMURA; circ. morning 251,001, evening 51,364.

Hokkaido Island

Doshin Sports: 3-6, Ohdori-Nishi, Chuo-ku, Sapporo 060-8711; tel. (11) 241-1230; internet douspo.aurora-net.or.jp; f. 1982; morning; Pres. YOSHIAKI KODAMA; circ. 141,128.

Hokkai Times: 10-6, Nishi, Minami-Ichijo, Chuo-ku, Sapporo 060; tel. (11) 231-0131; f. 1946; Man. Editor KOKI ITO; circ. morning 120,736.

Hokkaido Shimbun: 3-6, Ohdori-Nishi, Chuo-ku, Sapporo 060-8711; tel. (11) 221-2111; internet www.aurora-net.or.jp; f. 1942; Man. Editor RYOZO ODAGIRI; circ. morning 1.2m., evening 740,264.

Kushiro Shimbun: 7-3, Kurogane-cho, Kushiro 085-8650; tel. (154) 22-1111; internet www.hokkai.or.jp/senshin/index.html; f. 1955; morning; Man. Editor YUTAKA ITO; circ. 65,200.

Muroran Mimpo: 1-3-16, Hon-cho, Muroran 051-8550; tel. (143) 22-5121; internet www.swan-bay.ne.jp/~muromin; f. 1945; Man. Editor TSUTOMU KUDO; circ. morning 60,300, evening 52,500.

Nikkan Sports: 3-1-30, Higashi, Kita-3 jo, Chuo-ku, Sapporo 060-0033; tel. (11) 242-3900; fax (11) 231-5470; internet www.kita-nikkan .co.jp; f. 1962; morning; Pres. SATOSHI KATO; circ. 160,355.

Tokachi Mainichi Shimbun: 8-2, Minami, Higashi-Ichijo, Obihiro 080-8688; tel. (155) 22-2121; fax (155) 25-2700; internet www .tokachi.co.jp; f. 1919; evening; Dir and Man. Editor MASAO MATSUDA; circ. 87,581.

Tomakomai Mimpo: 3-1-8, Wakakusa-cho, Tomakomai 053-8611; tel. (144) 32-5311; internet www1.tomakomai.or.jp/minpo; f. 1950; evening; Dir and Man. Editor RYUICHI KUDO; circ. 60,676.

Yomiuri Shimbun: 4-1, Nishi, Kita-4 jo, Chuo-ku, Sapporo 060-8656; tel. (11) 242-3111; f. 1959; Head Officer TSUTOMU IKEDA; circ. morning 261,747, evening 81,283.

Kyushu Island

Kagoshima Shimpo: 7-28, Jonan-cho, Kagoshima 892-8551; tel. (99) 226-2100; f. 1959; morning; Dir and Man. Editor JUNSUKE KINO-SHITA; circ. 39,787.

Kumamoto Nichi-Nichi Shimbun: 2-33, Kamitori-cho, Kumamoto 860-8505; tel. (96) 327-3111; internet www.kumanichi.co.jp; f. 1942; Man. Editor HIROSHI KAWARABATA; circ. morning 385,700, evening 100,948.

Kyushu Sports: Fukuoka Tenjin Centre Bldg, 2-14-8, Tenjin-cho, Chuo-ku, Fukuoka 810-0001; tel. (92) 781-7401; f. 1966; morning; Head Officer HIROSHI MITOMI; circ. 471,740.

Minami Nippon Shimbun: 1-2, Yasui-cho, Kagoshima 892-8684; tel. (99) 225-9702; fax (99) 224-1490; e-mail tuusin@po.minc.ne.jp; internet www.minaminippon.co.jp; f. 1881; Man. Editor KEITEN NISHIMURA; circ. morning 401,938, evening 27,959.

Miyazaki Nichi-Nichi Shimbun: 1-1-33, Takachihodori, Miyazaki 880-8570; tel. (985) 26-9315; internet www.the-miyanichi.co.jp; f. 1940; morning; Man. Editor MASAAKI MINAMIMURA; circ. 236,083.

Nagasaki Shimbun: 3-1, Morimachi, Nagasaki 852-8601; tel. (958) 44-2111; internet www.nagasaki-np.co.jp; f. 1889; Dir and Man. Editor KOJI UMEHARA; circ. morning 200,128.

Nankai Nichi-Nichi Shimbun: 10-3, Nagahama-cho, Naze 894-8601; tel. (997) 53-2121; internet www.amami.or.jp/nankai; f. 1946; morning; Man. Editor TERUMI MATSUI; circ. 24,038.

Nishi Nippon Shimbun: 1-4-1, Tenjin, Chuo-ku, Fukuoka 810-8721; tel. (92) 711-5555; internet www.nishinippon.co.jp; f. 1877; Exec. Dir and Man. Editor TAKAMICHI TAMAGAWA; circ. morning 834,800, evening 188,444.

Nishi Nippon Sports: 1-4-1, Tenjin, Chuo-ku, Fukuoka 810; tel. (92) 711-5555; f. 1954; Man. Editor KENJI ISHIZAKI; circ. 184,119.

Oita Godo Shimbun: 3-9-15, Fudai-cho, Oita 870-8605; tel. (975) 36-2121; internet www.oita-press.co.jp; f. 1886; Dir and Man. Editor MASAKATSU TANABE; circ. morning 242,139, evening 242,117.

Okinawa Times: 2-2-2, Kumoji, Naha 900-8678; tel. (98) 860-3000; internet www.okinawatimes.co.jp; f. 1948; Pres. and Editor-in-Chief RYOICHI TOYOHIRA; circ. morning 204,420, evening 204,420.

Ryukyu Shimpo: 1-10-3, Izumisaki, Naha 900-8525; tel. (98) 865-5111; internet www.ryukyushimpo.co.jp; f. 1893; Man. Editor TOMOKAZU TAKAMINE; circ. 200,936.

Saga Shimbun: 3-2-23, Tenjin, Saga 840-8585; tel. (952) 28-2111; fax (952) 29-4829; internet www.saga-s.co.jp; f. 1884; morning; Man. Editor TERUHIKO WASHIZAKI; circ. 138,079.

Yaeyama Mainichi Shimbun: 614, Tonoshiro, Ishigaki 907-0004; tel. (9808) 2-2121; internet www.cosmos.ne.jp/~mainichi; f. 1950; morning; Exec. Dir and Man. Editor YOSHIO UECHI; circ. 14,500.

WEEKLIES

An-An: Magazine House, 3-13-10, Ginza, Chuo-ku, Tokyo 104-03; tel. (3) 3545-7050; fax (3) 3546-0034; f. 1970; fashion; Editor MIYOKO YODOGAWA; circ. 650,000.

Asahi Graphic: Asahi Shimbun Publishing Dept, 5-3-2, Tsukiji, Chuo-ku, Tokyo 104-11; tel. (3) 3545-0131; f. 1923; pictorial review; Editor KIYOKAZU TANNO; circ. 120,000.

Diamond Weekly: Diamond Inc, 1-4-2, Kasumigaseki, Chiyoda-ku, Tokyo 100; tel. (3) 3504-6250; f. 1913; economics; Editor YUTAKA IWASA; circ. 78,000.

Focus: Shincho-Sha, 71, Yaraicho, Shinjuku-ku, Tokyo 162; tel. (3) 3266-5271; fax (3) 3266-5390; politics, economics, sport; Editor KAZUMASA TAJIMA; circ. 850,000.

Friday: Kodan-Sha Co Ltd, 2-12-21, Otowa, Bunkyo-ku, Tokyo 112; tel. (3) 5395-3440; fax (3) 3943-8582; current affairs; Editor-in-Chief TETSU SUZUKI; circ. 1m.

Hanako: Magazine House, 3-13-10, Ginza, Chuo-ku, Tokyo 104-03; tel. (3) 3545-7070; fax (3) 3546-0994; f. 1988; consumer guide; Editor KOJI TOMONO; circ. 350,000.

Nikkei Business: Nikkei Business Publications Inc, 2-7-6, Hirakawa-cho, Chiyoda-ku, Tokyo 102-8622; tel. (3) 5210-8101; fax (3) 5210-8520; internet www.nikkeibp.co.jp; f. 1969; Editor-in-Chief HIROTOMO NOMURA; circ. 350,000.

Shukan Asahi: Asahi Shimbun Publishing Dept, 5-3-2, Tsukiji, Chuo-ku, Tokyo 104-11; tel. (3) 3545-0131; f. 1922; general interest; Editor-in-Chief CHIAHI OMORI; circ. 482,000.

Shukan Bunshun: Bungei-Shunju Ltd, 3-23, Kioicho, Chiyoda-ku, Tokyo 102; tel. (3) 3265-1211; f. 1959; general interest; Editor KIYONDO MATSUI; circ. 800,000.

Shukan Gendai: Kodan-Sha Co Ltd, 2-12-21, Otowa, Bunkyo-ku, Tokyo 112; tel. (3) 5395-3438; fax (3) 3943-7815; f. 1959; general; Editor-in-Chief TETSU SUZUKI; circ. 930,000.

Shukan Josei: Shufu-To-Seikatsu Sha Ltd, 3-5-7, Kyobashi, Chuo-ku, Tokyo 104; tel. (3) 3563-5130; fax (3) 3563-2073; f. 1957; women's interest; Editor HIDEO KIKUCHI; circ. 638,000.

Shukan Post: Shogakukan Publishing Co Ltd, 2-3-1, Hitotsubashi, Chiyoda-ku, Tokyo 101-01; tel. (3) 3230-5951; f. 1969; general; Editor NORIMICHI OKANARI; circ. 696,000.

Shukan Shincho: Shincho-Sha, 71, Yarai-cho, Shinjuku-ku, Tokyo 162-8711; tel. (3) 3266-5311; fax (3) 3266-5622; f. 1956; general interest; Editor HIROSHI MATSUDA; circ. 521,000.

Shukan SPA: Fuso-Sha Co, 1-15-1, Kaigan, Minato-ku, Tokyo 105; tel. (3) 5403-8875; f. 1952; general interest; Editor-in-Chief TOSHIHIKO SATO; circ. 400,000.

Shukan ST: Japan Times Ltd, 4-5-4, Shibaura, Minato-ku, Tokyo 108-0023; tel. (3) 3452-4077; fax (3) 3452-3303; e-mail shukanst@japantimes.co.jp; f. 1951; English and Japanese; Editor MITSURU TANAKA; circ. 150,000.

Shukan Yomiuri: Yomiuri Shimbun Publication Dept, 1-2-1, Kiyosumi, Koto-ku, Tokyo 135; tel. (3) 5245-7001; f. 1938; general interest; Editor SHINI KAGEYAMA; circ. 453,000.

Sunday Mainichi: Mainichi Newspapers Publishing Dept, 1-1-1, Hitotsubashi, Chiyoda-ku, Tokyo 100-51; tel. (3) 3212-0321; fax (3) 3212-0769; f. 1922; general interest; Editor KENJI MIKI; circ. 237,000.

Tenji Mainichi: Mainichi Newspapers Publishing Dept, 3-4-5, Umeda, Osaka; tel. (6) 6346-8386; fax (6) 6346-8385; f. 1922; in Japanese braille; Editor TADAMITSU MORIOKA; circ. 12,000.

Weekly Economist: Mainichi Newspapers Publishing Dept, 1-1-1, Hitotsubashi, Chiyoda-ku, Tokyo 100-51; tel. (3) 3212-0321; f. 1923; Editorial Chief NOBUHIRO SHUDO; circ. 120,000.

Weekly Toyo Keizai: Toyo Keizai Inc, 1-2-1, Hongoku-cho, Nihonbashi, Chuo-ku, Tokyo 103-8345; tel. (3) 3246-5470; fax (3) 3270-0159; f. 1895; business and economics; Editor TOSHIKI OTA; circ. 62,000.

PERIODICALS

All Yomimono: Bungei-Shunju Ltd, 3-23, Kioicho, Chiyoda-ku, Tokyo 102; tel. (3) 3265-1211; fax (3) 3239-5481; f. 1930; monthly; popular fiction; Editor KOICHI SASAMOTO; circ. 95,796.

Any: 1-3-14, Hirakawa-cho, Chiyoda-ku, Tokyo 102; tel. (3) 5276-2200; fax (3) 5276-2209; f. 1989; every 2 weeks; women's interest; Editor YUKIO MIWA; circ. 380,000.

Asahi Camera: Asahi Shimbun Publishing Dept, 5-3-2, Tsukiji, Chuo-ku, Tokyo 104-8011; tel. (3) 3545-0131; fax (3) 5565-3286; f. 1926; monthly; photography; Editor HIROSHI HIROSE; circ. 90,000.

Balloon: Shufunotomo Co Ltd, 2-9, Kanda Surugadai, Chiyoda-ku, Tokyo 101; tel. (3) 3294-1132; fax (3) 3291-5093; f. 1986; monthly; expectant mothers; Dir MARIKO HOSODA; circ. 250,000.

Brutus: Magazine House, 3-13-10, Ginza, Chuo-ku, Tokyo 104-03; tel. (3) 3545-7000; fax (3) 3546-0034; f. 1980; every 2 weeks; men's interest; Editor KOICHI TETSUKA; circ. 250,000.

Bungei-Shunju: Bungei-Shunju Ltd, 3-23, Kioicho, Chiyoda-ku, Tokyo 102-8008; tel. (3) 3265-1211; fax (3) 3221-6623; internet bunshun.topica.ne.jp; f. 1923; monthly; general; Pres. MASARU SHIRAISHI; Editor KIYONDO MATSUI; circ. 656,000.

Business Tokyo: Keizaikai Bldg, 2-13-18, Minami-Aoyama, Minato-ku, Tokyo 105; tel. (3) 3423-8500; fax (3) 3423-8505; f. 1987; monthly; Dir TAKUO IDA; Editor ANTHONY PAUL; circ. 125,000.

Chuokoron: Chuokoron-Sha Inc, 2-8-7, Kyobashi, Chuo-ku, Tokyo 104; tel. (3) 3563-1866; fax (3) 3561-5920; f. 1887; monthly; general interest; Chief Editor KAZUHO MIYA; circ. 100,000.

Clique: Magazine House, 3-13-10, Ginza, Chuo-ku, Tokyo 104-03; tel. (3) 3545-7080; fax (3) 3546-0034; f. 1989; every 2 weeks; women's interest; Editor TAKAKO NOGUCHI; circ. 250,000.

Croissant: Magazine House, 3-13-10, Ginza, Chuo-ku, Tokyo 104-03; tel. (3) 3545-7111; fax (3) 3546-0034; f. 1977; every 2 weeks; home; Editor MASAAKI TAKEUCHI; circ. 600,000.

Fujinkoron: Chuokoron-Sha Inc, 2-8-7, Kyobashi, Chuo-ku, Tokyo 104; tel. (3) 3563-1866; fax (3) 3561-5920; f. 1916; women's literary monthly; Editor YUKIKO YUKAWA; circ. 185,341.

Geijutsu Shincho: Shincho-Sha, 71, Yarai-cho, Shinjuku-ku, Tokyo 162-8711; tel. (3) 3266-5381; fax (3) 3266-5387; e-mail geishin@shinchosha.co.jp; f. 1950; monthly; fine arts, music, architecture, films, drama and design; Editor-in-Chief MIDORI YAMAKAWA; circ. 65,000.

Gendai: Kodan-Sha Ltd, 2-12-21, Otowa, Bunkyo-ku, Tokyo 112; tel. (3) 5395-3517; fax (3) 3945-9128; f. 1966; monthly; cultural and political; Editor SHUNKICHI YABUKI; circ. 250,000.

Gunzo: Kodan-Sha Ltd, 2-12-21, Otowa, Bunkyo-ku, Tokyo 112; tel. (3) 5395-3501; fax (3) 5395-5626; f. 1946; literary monthly; Editor KATSUO WATANABE; circ. 30,000.

Hot-Dog Press: Kodan-Sha Ltd, 2-12-21, Otowa, Bunkyo-ku, Tokyo 112-01; tel. (3) 5395-3473; fax (3) 3945-9128; every 2 weeks; men's interest; Editor ATSUHIDE KOKUBO; circ. 650,000.

Ie-no-Hikari (Light of Home): Ie-no-Hikari Asscn, 11, Ichigaya Funagawaramachi, Shinjuku-ku, Tokyo 162-8448; tel. (3) 3266-9013; fax (3) 3266-9052; e-mail hikari@mxd.meshnet.or.jp; internet www.mediagalaxy.co.jp/ienohikarinet; f. 1925; monthly; rural and general interest; Pres. SHUZO SUZUKI; Editor KAZUO NAKANO; circ. 928,000.

Japan Company Handbook: Toyo Keizai Inc, 1-2-1, Nihonbashi Hongoku-cho, Chuo-ku, Tokyo 103-8345; tel. (3) 3246-5655; fax (3) 3241-5543; e-mail sub@toyokeizai.co.jp; internet www.toyokeizai.co.jp; f. 1974; quarterly; English; Editor FUSAKAZU IZUMURA; total circ. 100,000.

Japan Quarterly: Asahi Shimbun Publishing Co, 5-3-2, Tsukiji, Chuo-ku, Tokyo 104-8011; tel. (3) 5541-8699; fax (3) 5541-8700; e-mail jpnqtrly@mx.asahi-np.co.jp; f. 1954; English; political, economic and cultural; Editor-in-Chief TAKENOBU ETSUO; circ. 10,000.

Jitsugyo No Nihon: Jitsugyo No Nihon-Sha Ltd, 1-3-9, Ginza, Chuo-ku, Tokyo 104; tel. (3) 3562-1967; fax (3) 2564-2382; f. 1897; monthly; economics and business; Editor TOSHIO KAWAJIRI; circ. 60,000.

Junon: Shufu-To-Seikatsu Sha Ltd, 3-5-7, Kyobashi, Chuo-ku, Tokyo 104; tel. (3) 3563-5132; fax (3) 5250-7081; f. 1973; monthly; television and entertainment; circ. 560,000.

Kagaku (Science): Iwanami Shoten Publishers, 2-5-5, Hitotsubashi, Chiyoda-ku, Tokyo 102; tel. (3) 5210-4070; fax (3) 5210-4073; f. 1931; Editor NOBUAKI MIYABE; circ. 29,000.

Kagaku Asahi: Asahi Shimbun Publishing Dept, 5-3-2, Tsukiji, Chuo-ku, Tokyo 104-8011; tel. (3) 5540-7810; fax (3) 3546-2404; f. 1941; monthly; scientific; Editor TOSHIHIRO SASAKI; circ. 105,000.

Keizaijin: Kansai Economic Federation, Nakanoshima Center Bldg, 6-2-27, Nakanoshima, Kita-ku, Osaka 530-6691; tel. (6) 6441-0105; fax (6) 6443-5347; internet www.kankeiren.or.jp; f. 1947; monthly; economics; Editor M. YASUTAKE; circ. 2,600.

Lettuce Club: SS Communications, 11-2, Ban-cho, Chiyoda-ku, Tokyo 102; tel. (3) 5276-2151; fax (3) 5276-2229; f. 1987; every 2 weeks; cookery; Editor MITSURU NAKAYA; circ. 800,000.

Money Japan: SS Communications, 11-2, Ban-cho, Chiyoda-ku, Tokyo 102; tel. (3) 5276-2220; fax (3) 5276-2229; f. 1985; monthly; finance; Editor TOSHIO KOBAYASHI; circ. 500,000.

Popeye: Magazine House, 3-13-10, Ginza, Chuo-ku, Tokyo 104-8003; tel. (3) 3545-7160; fax (3) 3546-0034; f. 1976; every 2 weeks; fashion, teenage interest; Editor SHINICHIRO ONODERA; circ. 320,000.

President: President Inc, Bridgestone Hirakawacho Bldg, 2-13-12, Hirakawa-cho, Chiyoda-ku, Tokyo 102; tel. (3) 3237-3737; fax (3) 3237-3748; internet www.president.co.jp; f. 1963; monthly; business; Editor KAYOKO ABE; circ. 263,308.

Ray: Shufunotomo Co Ltd, 2-9, Kanda Surugadai, Chiyoda-ku, Tokyo 101; tel. (3) 3294-1163; fax (3) 3291-5093; f. 1988; monthly; women's interest; Editor TATSURO NAKANISHI; circ. 450,000.

Ryoko Yomiuri: Ryoko Yomiuri Publications Inc, 2-2-15, Ginza, Chuo-ku, Tokyo 104; tel. (3) 3561-8911; fax (3) 3561-8950; f. 1966; monthly; travel; Editor TETSUO KINUGAWA; circ. 470,000.

Sekai: Iwanami Shoten Publishers, 2-5-5, Hitotsubashi, Chiyoda-ku, Tokyo 101; tel. (3) 5210-4141; fax (3) 5210-4144; internet www.iwanami.co.jp/sekai; f. 1946; monthly; review of world and domestic affairs; Editor ATSUSHI OKAMOTO; circ. 120,000.

Shinkenchiku: Shinkenchiku-Sha Co Ltd, 2-31-2, Yushima, Bunkyo-ku, Tokyo 113-8501; tel. (3) 3811-7101; fax (3) 3812-8229; e-mail ja-business@japan-architecture.co.jp; internet www.japan-architect.co.jp; f. 1925; monthly; architecture; Editor YASUHIRO TERAMATSU; circ. 87,000.

Shiso (Thought): Iwanami Shoten Publishers, 2-5-5, Hitotsubashi, Chiyoda-ku, Tokyo 101-8002; tel. (3) 5210-4055; fax (3) 5210-4037; e-mail shiso@iwanami.co.jp; internet www.iwanami.co.jp/shiso; f. 1921; monthly; philosophy, social sciences and humanities; Editor KIYOSHI KOJIMA; circ. 20,000.

Shosetsu Shincho: Shincho-Sha, 71, Yarai-cho, Shinjuku-ku, Tokyo 162-8711; tel. (3) 3266-5241; fax (3) 3266-5412; internet www.shincho.net/magazines/shosetsushincho; f. 1947; monthly; literature; Editor-in-Chief TSUYOSHI MENJO; circ. 80,000.

Shufunotomo: Shufunotomo Co Ltd, 2-9, Kanda Surugadai, Chiyoda-ku, Tokyo 101; tel. (3) 5280-7531; fax (3) 5280-7431; f. 1917; monthly; home and lifestyle; Editor KYOKO FURUTO; circ. 450,000.

So-en: Bunka Publishing Bureau, 4-12-7, Hon-cho, Shibuya-ku, Tokyo 151; tel. (3) 3299-2531; fax (3) 3370-3712; f. 1936; fashion monthly; Editor KEIKO SASAKI; circ. 270,000.

NEWS AGENCIES

Jiji Tsushin (Jiji Press Ltd): Shisei Bldg, 1-3, Hibiya Park, Chiyoda-ku, Tokyo 100-8568; tel. (3) 3591-1111; e-mail info@jiji.co.jp; internet www.jiji.co.jp; f. 1945; Pres. MASATOSHI MURAKAMI; Man. Editor KUNIJI OGURO.

Kyodo Tsushin (Kyodo News): 2-2-5, Toranomon, Minato-ku, Tokyo 105-8474; tel. (3) 5573-8180; fax (3) 5573-8184; e-mail kokusai@hq.kyodo.co.jp; internet www.kyodo.co.jp; f. 1945; Pres. ICHIRO SAITA; Man. Editor MAKATO NII.

Radiopress Inc: R-Bldg Shinjuku, 33-8, Wakamatsu-cho, Shinjuku-ku, Tokyo 162-0056; tel. (3) 5273-2171; fax (3) 5273-2180; e-mail rptokyo@oak.ocn.ne.jp; f. 1945; provides news from China, the former USSR, Democratic People's Repub. of Korea, Viet Nam and elsewhere to the press and govt offices; Pres. YOSHITOMO TANAKA.

Sun Telephoto: Palaceside Bldg, 1-1-1, Hitotsubashi, Chiyoda-ku, Tokyo 100-0003; tel. (3) 3213-6771; e-mail webmaster@suntele.co.jp; internet www.suntele.co.jp; f. 1952; Pres. KOZO TAKINO; Man. Editor KIYOSHI HIRAI.

Foreign Bureaux

Agence France-Presse (AFP): Asahi Shimbun Bldg, 11th Floor, 5-3-2, Tsukiji, Chuo-ku, Tokyo 104-0045; tel. (3) 3545-3061; fax (3) 3546-2594; Bureau Chief PHILIPPE RIES.

Agencia EFE (Spain): Kyodo Tsushin Bldg, 9th Floor, 2-2-5, Toranomon, Minato-ku, Tokyo 105-0001; tel. (3) 3585-8940; fax (3) 3585-8948; Bureau Chief CARLOS DOMÍNGUEZ.

Agenzia Nazionale Stampa Associata (ANSA) (Italy): Kyodo Tsushin Bldg, 9th Floor, 2-2-5, Toranomon, Minato-ku, Tokyo 105-0001; tel. (3) 3584-6667; fax (3) 3584-5114; Bureau Chief ALBERTO ZANCONATO.

Antara (Indonesia): Kyodo Tsushin Bldg, 9th Floor, 2-2-5, Toranomon, Minato-ku, Tokyo 105-0001; tel. (3) 3584-4234; fax (3) 3584-4591; Correspondent MARIA ANDRIANA.

Associated Press (AP) (USA): Asahi Shimbun Bldg, 11th Floor, 5-3-2, Tsukiji, Chuo-ku, Tokyo 104-0045; tel. (3) 3545-5902; fax (3) 3545-0895; internet www.ap.org; Bureau Chief JAMES C. LAGIER.

Central News Agency (Taiwan): 3-7-3-302, Shimo-meguro, Meguro-ku, Tokyo 153-0064; tel. (3) 3495-2046; fax (3) 3495-2066; Bureau Chief CHANG FANG MIN.

Deutsche Presse-Agentur (dpa) (Germany): Nippon Press Center, 3rd Floor, 2-2-1, Uchisaiwai-cho, Chiyoda-ku, Tokyo 100-0011; tel. (3) 3580-6629; fax (3) 3593-7888; Bureau Chief LARS NICOLAYSEN.

Informatsionnoye Telegrafnoye Agentstvo Rossii—Telegrafnoye Agentstvo Suverennykh Stran (ITAR—TASS) (Russia): 1-5-1, Hon-cho, Shibuya-ku, Tokyo 151-0071; tel. (3) 3377-0380; fax (3) 3378-0606; Bureau Chief VASILII GOLOVNIN.

Inter Press Service (IPS) (Italy): 1-15-19, Ishikawa-machi, Ota-ku, Tokyo 145-0061; tel. (3) 3726-7944; fax (3) 3726-7896; Correspondent SUVENDRINI KAKUCHI.

Magyar Távirati Iroda (MTI) (Hungary): 1-3-4-306, Okamoto, Setagaya-ku, Tokyo 157-0076; tel. (3) 3708-3093; fax (3) 3708-2703; Bureau Chief JÁNOS MARTON.

Reuters (UK): Shuwa Kamiya-cho Bldg, 5th Floor, 4-3-13, Toranomon, Minato-ku, Tokyo 105-0001; tel. (3) 3432-4141; fax (3) 3433-2921; Editor WILLIAM SPOSATO.

Rossiiskoye Informatsionnoye Agentstvo—Novosti (RIA—Novosti) (Russia): 3-9-13 Higashi-gotanda, Shinagawa-ku, Tokyo 141-0022; tel. (3) 3441-9241; fax (3) 3447-3538; Bureau Chief ANDREI ILIACHENKO.

United Press International (UPI) (USA): Ferrare Bldg, 4th Floor, 1-24-15, Ebisu, Shibuya-ku, Tokyo 150-0013; tel. (3) 5421-1333; fax (3) 5421-1339; Bureau Chief RUTH YOUNGBLOOD.

Xinhua (New China) News Agency (People's Republic of China): 3-35-23, Ebisu, Shibuya-ku, Tokyo 150-0013; tel. (3) 3441-3766; fax (3) 3446-3995; Bureau Chief WANG DAJUN.

Yonhap (United) News Agency (Republic of Korea): Kyodo Tsushin Bldg, 2-2-5, Toranomon, Minato-ku, Tokyo 105-0001; tel. (3) 3584-4681; fax (3) 3584-4021; f. 1945; Bureau Chief MOON YOUNG SHIK.

PRESS ASSOCIATIONS

Foreign Correspondents' Club of Japan: 20th Floor, 1-7-1, Yuraku-cho, Chiyoda-ku, Tokyo 100-0006; tel. (3) 3211-3161; fax (3) 3211-3168; e-mail katayama@fccj.or.jp; internet www.fccj.or.jp; f. 1945; 193 companies; Pres. ROGER SCHREFFLER; Man. KENJI KATAYAMA.

Foreign Press Center: Nippon Press Center Bldg, 6th Floor, 2-2-1, Uchisaiwai-cho, Chiyoda-ku, Tokyo 100-0011; tel. (3) 3501-3401; fax (3) 3501-3622; internet www.nttls.co.jp/fpc; f. 1976; est. by the Japan Newspaper Publrs' and Editors' Asscn and the Japan Fed. of Economic Orgs; provides services to the foreign press; Pres. YOSHIO HATANO; Man. Dir MASAHIKO ISHIZUKA.

Nihon Shinbun Kyokai (The Japan Newspaper Publishers and Editors Asscn): Nippon Press Center Bldg, 2-2-1, Uchisaiwai-cho, Chiyoda-ku, Tokyo 100-8543; tel. (3) 3591-3462; fax (3) 3591-6149; e-mail s_intl@pressnet.or.jp; internet www.pressnet.or.jp; f. 1946; mems include 153 companies (110 daily newspapers, 5 news agencies and 38 radio and TV companies); Chair. TSUNEO WATANABE; Man. Dir and Sec.-Gen. SHIGEMI MURAKAMI.

Nihon Zasshi Kyokai (Japan Magazine Publishers Asscn): 1-7, Kanda Surugadai, Chiyoda-ku, Tokyo 101-0062; tel. (3) 3291-0775; fax (3) 3293-6239; f. 1956; 85 mems; Pres. HARUHIKO ISHIKAWA; Sec. GENYA INUI.

Publishers

Akane Shobo Co Ltd: 3-2-1, Nishikanda, Chiyoda-ku, Tokyo 101-0065; tel. (3) 3263-0641; fax (3) 3263-5440; f. 1949; juvenile; Pres. MASAHARU OKAMOTO.

Akita Publishing Co Ltd: 2-10-8, Iidabashi, Chiyoda-ku, Tokyo 102-8101; tel. (3) 3264-7011; fax (3) 3265-5906; f. 1948; social sciences, history, juvenile; Chair. SADAO AKITA; Pres. SADAMI AKITA.

ALC Press Inc: 2-54-12, Eifuku, Suginami-ku, Tokyo 168-0064; tel. (3) 3323-1101; fax (3) 3327-1022; e-mail menet@alc.co.jp; internet www.alc.co.jp; f. 1969; linguistics, educational materials, dictionary, juvenile; Pres. TERUMARO HIRAMOTO.

Asahi Shimbun Publications Division: 5-3-2, Tsukiji, Chuo-ku, Tokyo 104-8011; tel. (3) 3545-0131; fax (3) 5540-7682; f. 1879; general; Pres. MUNEYUKI MATSUSHITA; Dir of Publications HISAO KUWASHIMA.

Asakura Publishing Co Ltd: 6-29, Shin Ogawa-machi, Shinjuku-ku, Tokyo 162-8707; tel. (3) 3260-0141; fax (3) 3260-0180; e-mail edit@asakura.co.jp; internet www.asakura.co.jp; f. 1929; natural science, medicine, social sciences; Pres. KUNIZO ASAKURA.

Baifukan Co Ltd: 4-3-12, Kudan Minami, Chiyoda-ku, Tokyo 102-8260; tel. (3) 3262-5256; fax (3) 3262-5276; f. 1924; engineering, natural and social sciences, psychology; Pres. ITARU YAMAMOTO.

Baseball Magazine-Sha: 3-10-10, Misaki-cho, Chiyoda-ku, Tokyo 101-8381; tel. (3) 3238-0081; fax (3) 3238-0106; internet www.bbm-japan.com; f. 1946; sports, physical education, recreation, travel; Chair. TSUNEO IKEDA; Pres. TETSUO IKEDA.

Bijutsu Shuppan-Sha Ltd: Inaoka Kudan Bldg, 6th Floor, 2-36, Kanda Jimbo-cho, Chiyoda-ku, Tokyo 101-8417; tel. (3) 3234-2151; fax (3) 3234-9451; f. 1905; fine arts, graphic design; Pres. ATSUSHI OSHITA.

Bonjinsha Co Ltd: 1-3-13, Hirakawa-cho, Chiyoda-ku, Tokyo 102-0093; tel. (3) 3263-3959; fax (3) 3263-3116; f. 1973; Japanese language teaching materials; Pres. HISAMITSU TANAKA.

Bungeishunju Ltd: 3-23, Kioi-cho, Chiyoda-ku, Tokyo 102-8008; tel. (3) 3265-1211; fax (3) 3239-5482; internet www.bunshun.co.jp; f. 1923; fiction, general literature, recreation, economics, sociology; Dir MASARU SHIRAISHI.

Chikuma Shobo: Komuro Bldg, 2-5-3, Kuramae, Taito-ku, Tokyo 111-8755; tel. (3) 5687-2680; fax (3) 5687-2685; f. 1940; general literature, fiction, history, juvenile, fine arts; Pres. AKIO KIKUCHI.

Child-Honsha Co Ltd: 5-24-21, Koishikawa, Bunkyo-ku, Tokyo 112-8512; tel. (3) 3813-3781; fax (3) 3813-3765; f. 1930; juvenile; Pres. YOSHIAKI SHIMAZAKI.

Chuokoron-Shinsha Inc: 2-9-2, Kyobashi, Chuo-ku, Tokyo 104-0031; tel. (3) 3563-1261; fax (3) 3561-5920; f. 1886; philosophy, history, sociology, general literature; Chair. MASAKO SHIMANAKA; Pres. JIN NAKAMURA.

Corona Publishing Co Ltd: 4-46-10, Sengoku, Bunkyo-ku, Tokyo 112-0011; tel. (3) 3941-3131; fax (3) 3941-3137; e-mail info@coronasha.co.jp; internet www.coronosha.co.jp; f. 1927; electronics business publs; Pres. TATSUMI GORAI.

Dempa Publications Inc: 1-11-15, Higashi Gotanda, Shinagawa-ku, Tokyo 141-0022; tel. (3) 3445-6111; fax (3) 3445-6101; f. 1950; electronics, personal computer software, juvenile, trade newspapers; Pres. TETSUO HIRAYAMA.

Diamond Inc: 6-12-17, Jingumae, Shibuya-ku, Tokyo 150-8409; tel. (3) 5778-7203; fax (3) 5778-6612; e-mail mitachi@diamond.co.jp; internet www.diamond.co.jp; f. 1913; business, management, economics, financial; Pres. YUTAKA IWASA.

Dohosha Ltd: TAS Bldg, 2-5-2, Nishikanda, Chiyoda-ku, Tokyo 101-0065; tel. (3) 5276-0831; fax (3) 5276-0840; e-mail intl@doho-sha.co.jp; internet www.doho-sha.co.jp; f. 1997; general works, architecture, art, Buddhism, business, children's education, cooking, flower arranging, gardening, medicine.

Froebel-Kan Co Ltd: 6-14-9, Honkomagome, Bunkyo-ku, Tokyo 113-8611; tel. (3) 5395-6614; fax (3) 5395-6627; e-mail soumu@froebel-kan.co.jp; internet www.froebel-kan.co.jp; f. 1907; juvenile, educational; Pres. KENNOSUKE ARAI; Dir HARRY IDICHI.

Fukuinkan Shoten Publishers Inc: 6-6-3, Honkomagome, Bunkyo-ku, Tokyo 113-8686; tel. (3) 3942-2151; fax (3) 3942-1401; f. 1952; juvenile; Pres. SHIRO TOKITA; Chair. KATSUMI SATO.

Gakken Co Ltd: 4-40-5, Kamiikedai, Ohta-ku, Tokyo 145-8502; tel. (3) 3726-8111; fax (3) 3493-3338; f. 1946; juvenile, educational, art, encyclopaedias, dictionaries; Pres. KAZUHIKO SAWADA.

Graphic-sha Publishing Co Ltd: 1-9-12, Kudan Kita, Chiyoda-ku, Tokyo 102-0073; tel. (3) 3263-4318; fax (3) 3263-5297; e-mail info@graphicsha.co.jp; internet www.graphicsha.co.jp; f. 1963; art, design, hobbies; Pres. SEIICHI SUGAYA.

Gyosei Corpn: 4-30-16, Ogikubo, Suginami-ku, Tokyo 167-8088; tel. (3) 5349-6666; fax (3) 5349-6677; e-mail business@gyosei.co.jp; internet www.gyosei.co.jp; f. 1893; law, education, science, politics, business, art, language, literature, juvenile; Pres. MOTOO FUJISAWA.

Hakusui-Sha Co Ltd: 3-24, Kanda Ogawa-machi, Chiyoda-ku, Tokyo 101-0052; tel. (3) 3291-7821; fax (3) 3291-7810; f. 1915; general literature, science and languages; Pres. KAZUKI FUJIWARA.

Hayakawa Publishing Inc: 2-2, Kanda-Tacho, Chiyoda-ku, Tokyo 101-0046; tel. (3) 3252-3111; fax (3) 3254-1550; f. 1945; science fiction, mystery, autobiography, literature, fantasy; Pres. HIROSHI HAYAKAWA.

Heibonsha Ltd Publishers: 2-29-4 Hakusan, Bunkyo-ku, Tokyo 112-0001; tel. (3) 3818-0641; fax (3) 3818-0754; internet www.heibonsha.co.jp; f. 1914; encyclopaedias, art, history, geography, literature, science; Pres. NAOTO SHIMONAKA.

Hirokawa Publishing Co: 3-27-14, Hongo, Bunkyo-ku, Tokyo 113-0033; tel. (3) 3815-3651; fax (3) 5684-7030; f. 1925; natural sciences, medicine, pharmacy, nursing, chemistry; Pres. SETSUO HIROKAWA.

Hoikusha Publishing Co: 1-6-12, Kawamata, Higashi, Osaka 577-0063; tel. (6) 6788-4470; fax (6) 6788-4970; internet www.hoikusha.co.jp; f. 1947; natural science, juvenile, fine arts, geography; Pres. YUKI IMAI.

Hokuryukan Co Ltd: 3-8-14, Takanawa, Minato-ku, Tokyo 108-0074; tel. (3) 5449-4591; fax (3) 5449-4950; e-mail hk-ns@mk1.macnet.or.jp; internet www.macnet.or.jp/co/hk-ns; f. 1891; natural science, medical science, juvenile, dictionaries; Pres. HISAKO FUKUDA.

The Hokuseido Press: 3-32-4, Honkomagome, Bunkyo-ku, Tokyo 113-0021; tel. (3) 3827-0511; fax (3) 3827-0567; f. 1914; regional non-fiction, dictionaries, textbooks; Pres. MASAZO YAMAMOTO.

Ie-No-Hikari Association: 11, Funagawara-cho, Ichigaya, Shinjuku-ku, Tokyo 162-8448; tel. (3) 3266-9000; fax (3) 3266-9048; e-mail hikari@mxd.meshnet.or.jp; internet www.mediagalaxy.co.jp/ienohikarinet; f. 1925; social science, agriculture; Chair. SHUZO SUZUKI; Pres. KATSURO KAWAGUCHI.

Igaku-Shoin Ltd: 5-24-3, Hongo, Bunkyo-ku, Tokyo 113-8719; tel. (3) 3817-5610; fax (3) 3815-4114; e-mail info@igaku-shoin.co; internet www.igaku-shoin.co.jp; f. 1944; medicine, nursing; Pres. YU KANEHARA.

Institute for Financial Affairs Inc (KINZAI): 19, Minami-Motomachi, Shinjuku-ku, Tokyo 160-8519; tel. (3) 3358-1161; fax (3) 3359-7947; e-mail JDI04072@nifty.ne.jp; internet www.kinzai.or.jp; f. 1950; finance and economics, banking laws and regulations, accounting; Pres. MASATERU YOSHIDA.

Ishiyaku Publishers Inc: 1-7-10, Honkomagome, Bunkyo-ku, Tokyo 113-8612; tel. (3) 5395-7600; fax (3) 5395-7606; e-mail dev-mdp@nna.so-net.ne.jp; internet www.so-net.ne.jp/medipro/isyk; f. 1921; medicine, dentistry, rehabilitation, nursing, nutrition and pharmaceutics; Pres. KATSUJI FUJITA.

Iwanami Shoten, Publishers: 2-5-5, Hitotsubashi, Chiyoda-ku, Tokyo 101-8002; tel. (3) 5210-4000; fax (3) 5210-4039; internet www.iwanami.co.jp; f. 1913; natural and social sciences, literature, fine arts, juvenile, dictionaries; Pres. NOBUKAZU OTSUKA.

Japan Broadcast Publishing Co Ltd: 41-1, Udagawa-cho, Shibuya-ku, Tokyo 150-8081; tel. (3) 3464-7311; fax (3) 3780-3353; e-mail webmaster@npb.nhk-grp.co.jp; internet www.nhk-grp.co.jp/npb; f. 1931; foreign language textbooks, gardening, home economics, sociology, education, art, juvenile; Pres. TATSUO ANDO.

Japan External Trade Organization (JETRO): 2-2-5, Toranomon, Minato-ku, Tokyo 105-8466; tel. (3) 3582-5512; fax (3) 3582-5662; internet www.jetro.go.jp; f. 1958; trade, economics, investment; Pres. SHOJI ISAKI.

Japan Publications Trading Co Ltd: 1-2-1, Sarugaku-cho, Chiyoda-ku, Tokyo 101-0064; tel. (3) 3292-3751; fax (3) 3292-0410; e-mail jpt@po.iijnet.or.jp; internet www.jptco.co.jp; f. 1942; general works, art, health, sports; Pres. SATOMI NAKABAYASHI.

The Japan Times Ltd: 4-5-4, Shibaura, Minato-ku, Tokyo 108-0023; tel. (3) 3453-2013; fax (3) 3453-8023; e-mail jt-books@kt.rim.or.jp; internet bookclub.japantimes.co.jp; f. 1897; linguistics, culture, business; Pres. TOSHIAKI OGASAWARA.

Japan Travel Bureau Inc: Shibuya Nomura Bldg, 1-10-8, Dogenzaka, Shibuya-ku, Tokyo 150-8558; tel. (3) 3477-9521; fax (3) 3477-9538; internet www.jtb.co.jp; f. 1912; travel, geography, history, fine arts, languages; Vice-Pres. MITSUMASA IWATA.

Jimbun Shoin: 9, Nishiuchihata-cho, Takeda, Fushimi-ku, Kyoto 612-8447; tel. (75) 603-1344; fax (75) 603-1814; e-mail edjimbun@mbox.kyoto-inet.or.jp; internet www.jimbunshoin.co.jp; f. 1922; general literature, philosophy, fiction, social science, religion, fine arts; Pres. MUTSUHISA WATANABE.

Kadokawa Shoten Publishing Co Ltd: 2-13-3, Fujimi, Chiyoda-ku, Tokyo 102-0071; tel. (3) 3238-8611; fax (3) 3238-8612; f. 1945; literature, history, dictionaries, religion, fine arts, books on tape, compact discs, CD-ROM, comics, animation, video cassettes, computer games; Pres. TSUGUHIKO KADOKAWA.

Kaibundo Publishing Co Ltd: 2-5-4, Suido, Bunkyo-ku, Tokyo 112-0005; tel. (3) 5684-6289; fax (3) 3815-3953; e-mail LED04737@nifty.ne.jp; f. 1914; marine affairs, natural science, engineering, industry; Pres. YOSHIHIRO OKADA.

Kaiseisha Publishing Co Ltd: 3-5, Ichigaya Sadohara-cho, Shinjuku-ku, Tokyo 162-8450; tel. (3) 3260-3229; fax (3) 3260-3540; e-mail foreign@kaiseisha.co.jp; internet www.kaiseisha.co.jp; f. 1936; juvenile; Pres. MASAKI IMAMURA.

Kanehara & Co Ltd: 2-31-14, Yushima, Bunkyo-ku, Tokyo 113-8687; tel. (3) 3811-7185; fax (3) 3813-0288; f. 1875; medical, agricultural, engineering and scientific; Pres. SABURO KOMURO.

Kenkyusha Ltd: 2-11-3, Fujimi, Chiyoda-ku, Tokyo 102-8152; tel. (3) 3288-7711; fax (3) 3288-7821; e-mail kenkyusha-hanbai@in.aix.or.jp; internet www2.aix.or.jp/kenkyusha; f. 1907; bilingual dictionaries; Pres. KATSUYUKI IKEGAMI.

Kinokuniya Co Ltd: 5-38-1, Sakuragaoka, Setagaya-ku, Tokyo 156-8691; tel. (3) 3439-0172; fax (3) 3439-0173; e-mail publish@kinokuniya.co.jp; internet www.kinokuniya.co.jp; f. 1927; humanities, social science, natural science; Pres. OSAMU MATSUBARA.

Kodansha International Ltd: 1-17-14, Otowa, Bunkyo-ku, Tokyo 112-8652; tel. (3) 3944-6492; fax (3) 3944-6323; e-mail sales@kodansha-intl.co.jp; f. 1963; art, business, cookery, crafts, gardening, language, literature, martial arts; Pres. SAWAKO NOMA.

Kodansha Ltd: 2-12-21, Otowa, Bunkyo-ku, Tokyo 112-8001; tel. (3) 5395-3574; fax (3) 3944-9915; f. 1909; fine arts, fiction, literature, juvenile, comics, dictionaries; Pres. SAWAKO NOMA.

Kosei Publishing Co Ltd: 2-7-1, Wada, Suginami-ku, Tokyo 166-8535; tel. (3) 5385-2309; fax (3) 5385-2331; e-mail kspub@mail.kosei-shuppan.co.jp; internet www.kosei-shuppan.co.jp; f. 1966; general works, philosophy, religion, history, pedagogy, social science, art, juvenile; Pres. TEIZO KURIYAMA.

Kyoritsu Shuppan Co Ltd: 4-6-19, Kohinata, Bunkyo-ku, Tokyo 112-8700; tel. (3) 3947-2511; fax (3) 3947-2539; e-mail kyoritsu@po.iijnet.or.jp; internet www.kyoritsu-pub.co.jp; f. 1926; scientific and technical; Pres. MITSUAKI NANJO.

Maruzen Co Ltd: 3-9-2, Nihonbashi, Chuo-ku, Tokyo 103-8244; tel. (3) 3272-0521; fax (3) 3272-0693; internet www.maruzen.co.jp; f. 1869; general works; Pres. SEISHIRO MURATA.

Medical Friend Co Ltd: 3-2-4, Kudan Kita, Chiyoda-ku, Tokyo 102-0073; tel. (3) 3264-6611; fax (3) 3261-6602; f. 1947; medical and allied science, nursing; Pres. KAZUHARU OGURA.

Minerva Shobo: 1, Tsutsumi dani-cho, Hinooka, Yamashina-ku, Kyoto 607-8494; tel. (75) 581-5191; fax (75) 581-0589; e-mail info@minervashobo.co.jp; internet www.minervashobo.co.jp; f. 1948; general non-fiction and reference; Pres. NOBUO SUGITA.

Misuzu Shobo Ltd: 5-32-21, Hongo, Bunkyo-ku, Tokyo 113-0033; tel. (3) 3815-9181; fax (3) 3818-8497; f. 1947; general, philosophy, history, psychiatry, literature, science, art; Pres. KEIJI KATO.

Morikita Shuppan Co Ltd: 1-4-11, Fujimi, Chiyoda-ku, Tokyo 102-0071; tel. (3) 3265-8341; fax (3) 3264-8709; e-mail info@morikita.co.jp; internet www.morikita.co.jp; f. 1950; natural science, engineering; Pres. HAJIME MORIKITA.

Nakayama-Shoten Co Ltd: 1-25-14, Hakusan, Bunkyo-ku, Tokyo 113-8666; tel. (3) 3813-1101; fax (3) 3816-1015; e-mail eigyo@nakayamashoten.co.jp; internet www.nakayamashoten.co.jp; f. 1948; medicine, biology, zoology; Pres. TADASHI HIRATA.

Nanzando Co Ltd: 4-1-11, Yushima, Bunkyo-ku, Tokyo; tel. (3) 5689-7868; fax (3) 5689-7869; e-mail info@nanzando.com; internet www.nanzando.com; medical reference, paperbacks; Pres. HAJIME SUZUKI.

Nigensha Publishing Co Ltd: 2-2, Kanda Jimbo-cho, Chiyoda-ku, Tokyo 101-8419; tel. (3) 5210-4733; fax (3) 5210-4723; e-mail sales@nigensha.co.jp; internet www.nigensha.co.jp; f. 1953; calligraphy, fine arts, art reproductions, cars, watches; Pres. TAKAO WATANABE.

Nihon Keizai Shimbun Inc, Publications Bureau: 1-9-5, Otemachi, Chiyoda-ku, Tokyo 100-0004; tel. (3) 3270-0251; fax (3) 5255-2864; f. 1876; economics, business, politics, fine arts, video cassettes, CD-ROM; Pres. TOYOHIKO KOBAYASHI.

Nihon Vogue Co Ltd: 3-23, Ichigaya Honmura-cho, Shinjuku-ku, Tokyo 162-8705; tel. (3) 5261-5081; fax (3) 3269-8726; e-mail wada-t@tezukuritown.com; internet www.creators-guild.co.jp; f. 1954; quilt, needlecraft, handicraft, knitting, decorative painting, pressed flowers; Pres. NOBUAKI SETO.

Nippon Jitsugyo Publishing Co Ltd: 3-2-12, Hongo, Bunkyo-ku, Tokyo 113-0033; tel. (3) 3814-5651; fax (3) 3818-2723; e-mail int@njg.co.jp; internet www.njg.co.jp; f. 1950; business, management, finance and accounting, sales and marketing; Chair. and CEO YOICHIRO NAKAMURA.

Obunsha Co Ltd: 78, Yarai-cho, Shinjuku-ku, Tokyo 162-0805; tel. (3) 3266-6000; fax (3) 3266-6291; f. 1931; internet www.obunsha.co.jp; textbooks, reference, general science and fiction, magazines, encyclopaedias, dictionaries; software; audio-visual aids; CEO FUMIO AKAO.

Ohm-Sha Ltd: 3-1, Kanda Nishiki-cho, Chiyoda-ku, Tokyo 101-8460; tel. (3) 3233-0641; fax (3) 3233-2426; e-mail kaigaika@ohmsha.co.jp; internet www.ohmsha.co.jp; f. 1914; engineering, technical and scientific; Pres. SEIJI SATO; Dir M. MORI.

Ondorisha Publishers Ltd: 11-11, Nishigoken-cho, Shinjuku-ku, Tokyo 162-8708; tel. (3) 3268-3101; fax (3) 3235-3530; f. 1945; knitting, embroidery, patchwork, handicraft books; Pres. HIDEAKI TAKEUCHI.

Ongaku No Tomo Sha Corpn (ONT): 6-30, Kagurazaka, Shinjuku-ku, Tokyo 162-0825; tel. (3) 3235-2111; fax (3) 3235-2119; internet www.ongakunotomo.co.jp; f. 1941; compact discs, videograms, music magazines, music books, music data, music textbooks; Pres. JUN MEGURO.

PHP Institute Inc: 11, Kitanouchi-cho, Nishikujo, Minami-ku, Kyoto 601-8411; tel. (75) 681-4431; fax (75) 681-9921; internet www.php.co.jp; f. 1946; social science; Pres. MASAHARU MATSUSHITA.

Poplar Publishing Co Ltd: 5, Suga-cho, Shinjuku-ku, Tokyo 160-8565; tel. (3) 3357-2216; fax (3) 3351-0736; e-mail henshu@poplar.co.jp; internet www.poplar.co.jp; f. 1947; children's; Pres. HARUO TANAKA.

Sanseido Co Ltd: 2-22-14, Misaki-cho, Chiyoda-ku, Tokyo 101-8371; tel. (3) 3230-9411; fax (3) 3230-9547; f. 1881; dictionaries, educational, languages, social and natural science; Chair. HISANORI UENO; Pres. TOSHIO GOMI.

Sanshusha Publishing Co Ltd: 1-5-34, Shitaya, Taito-ku, Tokyo 110-0004; tel. (3) 3842-1711; fax (3) 3845-3965; e-mail maeda_k@sanshusha.or.jp; internet www.sanshusha.co.jp; f. 1938; languages, dictionaries, philosophy, sociology, electronic publishing (CD-ROM); Pres. KANJI MAEDA.

Seibundo-Shinkosha Co Ltd: 3-3-1, Hongo, Bunkyo-ku, Tokyo 113-0033; tel. (3) 5800-5775; fax (3) 5800-5773; f. 1912; technical, scientific, design, general non-fiction; Pres. MINORU TAKITA.

Sekai Bunka Publishing Inc: 4-2-29, Kudan-Kita, Chiyoda-ku, Tokyo 102-8187; tel. (3) 3262-5111; fax (3) 3221-6843; internet www.sekaibunka.com; f. 1946; history, natural science, geography, education, art, literature, juvenile; Pres. TSUTOMU SUZUKI.

Shincho-Sha Co Ltd: 71, Yarai-cho, Shinjuku-ku, Tokyo 162-8711; tel. (3) 3266-5411; fax (3) 3266-5534; e-mail shinchosha@webshincho.com; internet www.webshincho.com; f. 1896; general literature, fiction, non-fiction, fine arts, philosophy; Pres. TAKANOBU SATO.

Shinkenchiku-Sha Co Ltd: 2-31-2, Yushima, Bunkyo-ku, Tokyo 113-8501; tel. (3) 3811-7101; fax (3) 3812-8229; e-mail ja-business@japan-architect.co.jp; internet www.japan-architect.co.jp; f. 1925; architecture; Pres. NOBUYUKI YOSHIDA.

Shogakukan Inc: 2-3-1, Hitotsubashi, Chiyoda-ku, Tokyo 101-8001; tel. (3) 3230-5526; fax (3) 3288-9653; internet www.shogakukan.co.jp; f. 1922; juvenile, education, geography, history, encyclopaedias, dictionaries; Pres. MASAHIRO OHGA.

Shokabo Publishing Co Ltd: 8-1, Yomban-cho, Chiyoda-ku, Tokyo 102-0081; tel. (3) 3262-9166; fax (3) 3262-7257; e-mail info@shokabo.co.jp; internet www.shokabo.co.jp; f. 1895; natural science, engineering; Pres. TATSUJI YOSHINO.

Shokokusha Publishing Co Ltd: 25, Saka-machi, Shinjuku-ku, Tokyo 160-0002; tel. (3) 3359-3231; fax (3) 3357-3961; e-mail eigyo@shokokusha.co.jp; f. 1932; architectural, technical and fine arts; Pres. TAISHIRO YAMAMOTO.

Shueisha Inc: 2-5-10, Hitotsubashi, Chiyoda-ku, Tokyo 101-8050; tel. (3) 3230-6320; fax (3) 3262-1309; f. 1925; literature, fine arts, language, juvenile, comics; Pres. and CEO TAMIO KOJIMA.

Shufunotomo Co Ltd: 2-9, Kanda Surugadai, Chiyoda-ku, Tokyo 101-8911; tel. (3) 5280-7567; fax (3) 5280-7568; e-mail international@shufunotomo.co.jp; internet www.shufunotomo.co.jp; f. 1916; domestic science, fine arts, gardening, handicraft, cookery and magazines; Chair. HARUHIKO ISHIKAWA; Pres. YASUHIKO ISHIKAWA.

Shunju-Sha: 2-18-6, Soto-Kanda, Chiyoda-ku, Tokyo 101-0021; tel. (3) 3255-9614; fax (3) 3255-9370; f. 1918; philosophy, religion, literary, economics, music; Pres. AKIRA KANDA; Man. RYUTARO SUZUKI.

Taishukan Publishing Co Ltd: 3-24, Kanda-Nishiki-cho, Chiyoda-ku, Tokyo 101-8466; tel. (3) 3294-2221; fax (3) 3295-4107; internet www.taishukan.co.jp; f. 1918; reference, Japanese and foreign languages, sports, dictionaries, audio-visual aids; Pres. SHIGEO SUZUKI.

Tanko Weatherhill Inc: 39-1, Ichigaya Yanagi-cho, Shinjuku-ku, Tokyo 162; tel. (3) 5269-2371; fax (3) 5269-7266; f. 1962; arts, crafts, architecture, gardening, language, history, zen and Eastern philosophy, sports, travel; Pres. YOSHIHARU NAYA.

Tankosha Publishing Co Ltd: 19-1, Miyanishi-cho Murasakino, Kita-ku, Kyoto 603-8691; tel. (75) 432-5151; fax (75) 432-0273; e-mail tankosha@magical.egg.or.jp; internet tankosha.topica.ne.jp; f. 1949; tea ceremony, fine arts, history; Pres. YOSHITO NAYA.

Teikoku-Shoin Co Ltd: 3-29, Kanda Jimbo-cho, Chiyoda-ku, Tokyo 101-0051; tel. (3) 3262-0834; fax (3) 3262-7770; e-mail kenkyu@teikokushoin.co.jp; f. 1926; geography, atlases, maps, textbooks; Pres. MUTSUO SHIRAHAMA.

Tokai University Press: 2-28-4, Tomigaya, Shibuya-ku, Tokyo 151-8677; tel. (3) 5478-0891; fax (3) 5478-0870; f. 1962; social science, cultural science, natural science, engineering, art; Pres. TATSURO MATSUMAE.

Tokuma Shoten Publishing Co Ltd: 1-1-16, Higashi Shimbashi, Minato-ku, Tokyo 105-8055; tel. (3) 3573-0111; fax (3) 3573-8788; e-mail info@tokuma.com; internet www.tokuma.com; f. 1954; Japanese classics, history, fiction, juvenile; Pres. YASUYOSHI TOKUMA.

Tokyo News Service Ltd: Tsukiji Hamarikyu Bldg, 5-3-3, Tsukiji, Chuo-ku, Tokyo 104; tel. (3) 3542-6511; fax (3) 3545-3628; f. 1947; shipping, trade and television guides; Pres. T. OKUYAMA.

Tokyo Shoseki Co Ltd: 2-17-1, Horifune, Kita-ku, Tokyo 114-8524; tel. (3) 5390-7513; fax (3) 5390-7409; internet www.tokyo-

shoseki.co.jp; f. 1909; textbooks, reference books, cultural and educational books; Pres. YOSHIKATSU KAWAUCHI.

Tokyo Sogen-Sha Co Ltd: 1-5, Shin-Ogawa-machi, Shinjuku-ku, Tokyo 162-0814; tel. (3) 3268-8201; fax (3) 3268-8230; f. 1954; mystery and detective stories, science fiction, literature; Pres. YASUNOBU TOGAWA.

Toyo Keizai Inc: 1-2-1, Nihonbashi, Hongoku-cho, Chuo-ku, Tokyo 103-8345; tel. (3) 3246-5661; fax (3) 3231-0906; internet www.toyokeizai.co.jp; f. 1895; economics, business, finance and corporate, information; Pres. JUNJI ASANO.

Tuttle Publishing Co Inc: RK Bldg, 2-13-10 Shimo Meguro, Meguro-ku, Tokyo 153-0064, tel. (3) 5437-0171; fax (44) 5437-0755; e-mail tuttle@gol.com; f. 1948; books on Japanese and Asian religion, history, social science, arts, languages, literature, juvenile, cookery; Pres. ERIC OEY.

United Nations University Press: 5-53-70, Jingumae, Shibuya-ku, Tokyo 150-8925; tel. (3) 3499-2811; fax (3) 3499-2828; f. 1975; social sciences, humanities, pure and applied natural sciences; Rector HANS J. H. VAN GINKEL.

University of Tokyo Press: 7-3-1, Hongo, Bunkyo-ku, Tokyo 113-8654; tel. (3) 3811-0964; fax (3) 3815-1426; e-mail info@utp.or.jp; f. 1951; natural and social sciences, humanities; Japanese and English; Chair. MASARU NISHIO; Man. Dir TADASHI YAMASHITA.

Yama-Kei Publishers Co Ltd: 1-1-33, Shiba-Daimon, Minato-ku, Tokyo 105-0012; tel. (3) 3436-4021; fax (3) 3438-1949; f. 1930; natural science, geography, mountaineering; Pres. YOSHIMITSU KAWASAKI.

Yohan: 3-14-9, Okubo, Shinjuku-ku, Tokyo 169-0072; tel. (3) 3208-0181; fax (3) 3209-0288; internet www.yohan.co.jp; f. 1963; social science, language, art, juvenile, dictionary; Pres. MASANORI WATANABE.

Yuhikaku Publishing Co Ltd: 2-17, Kanda Jimbo-cho, Chiyoda-ku, Tokyo 101-0051; tel. (3) 3264-1312; fax (3) 3264-5030; f. 1877; social sciences, law, economics; Pres. TADATAKA EGUSA.

Yuzankaku Shuppan: 2-6-9, Fujimi, Chiyoda-ku, Tokyo 102; tel. (3) 3262-3231; fax (3) 3262-6938; e-mail yuzan@cf.mbn.or.jp; internet www.nepto.co.jp/yuzankaku; f. 1916; history, fine arts, religion, archaeology; Pres. KEIKO NAGASAKA.

Zoshindo Juken Kenkyusha Co Ltd: 2-19-15, Shinmachi, Nishi-ku, Osaka 550-0013; tel. (6) 6532-1581; fax (6) 6532-1588; e-mail zoshindo@mbox.inet-osaka.or.jp; internet www.zoshindo.co.jp; f. 1890; educational, juvenile; Pres. AKITAKA OKAMATO.

Government Publishing House

Government Publications' Service Centre: 1-2-1, Kasumigaseki, Chiyoda-ku, Tokyo 100-0013; tel. (3) 3504-3885; fax (3) 3504-3889.

PUBLISHERS' ASSOCIATIONS

Japan Book Publishers Association: 6, Fukuro-machi, Shinjuku-ku, Tokyo 162-0828; tel. (3) 3268-1301; fax (3) 3268-1196; f. 1957; 499 mems; Pres. TAKAO WATANABE; Exec. Dir TOSHIKAZU GOMI.

Publishers' Association for Cultural Exchange, Japan: 1-2-1, Sarugaku-cho, Chiyoda-ku, Tokyo 101-0064; tel. (3) 3291-5685; fax (3) 3233-3645; e-mail office@pace.or.jp; internet www.pace.or.jp; f. 1953; 135 mems; Pres. Dr TATSURO MATSUMAE; Man. Dir YASUKO KORENAGA.

Broadcasting and Communications

TELECOMMUNICATIONS

International Digital Communications: 5-20-8, Asakusabashi, Taito-ku, Tokyo 111; tel. (3) 5820-5080; fax (3) 5820-5363; f.1985; 53% owned by Cable and Wireless Communications (UK); Pres. SIMON CUNNINGHAM.

Japan Telecom Co Ltd: 4-7-1, Hatchobori, Chuo-ku, Tokyo 104-8508; tel. (3) 5540-8417; fax (3) 5540-8485; internet www.japan-telecom.co.jp; 30% owned by alliance of British Telecommunications PLC (UK) and American Telegraph and Telephone Corpn (USA); Pres. HARUO MURAKAMI.

KDDI Corpn: KDDI Bldg, 2-3-2, Nishi Shinjuku, Shinjuku-ku, Tokyo 163-03; tel. (3) 3347-7111; fax (3) 3347-6470; internet www.kddi.com; f. 2000 by merger of DDI Corpn, Kokusai Denshin Denwa Corpn (KDD) and Nippon Idou Tsushin Corpn (IDO); major international telecommunications carrier; Chair. JIRO USHIO; Pres. YUSAI OKUYAMA.

Nippon Telegraph and Telephone Corpn: 2-3-1, Otemachi, Chiyoda-ku, Tokyo 100-0004; tel. (3) 5359-2122; e-mail hyamada@yamato.ntt.jp; operates local, long-distance and international services; largest telecommunications co in Japan; Chair. SHIGEO SAWADA; Pres. JUN-ICHIRO MIYAZU.

Tokyo Telecommunication Network Co Inc: 4-9-25, Shibaura, Minato-ku, Tokyo 108; tel. (3) 5476-0091; fax (3) 5476-7625.

NTT DoCoMo, KDDI, Digital Phone and Digital TU-KA operate mobile telecommunication services in Japan.

BROADCASTING

Nippon Hoso Kyokai, NHK (Japan Broadcasting Corporation): 2-2-1, Jinnan, Shibuya, Tokyo 150-8001; tel. (3) 3465-1111; fax (3) 3469-8110; e-mail webmaster@www.nhk.or.jp; internet www.nhk.or.jp; f. 1925; sole public broadcaster; operates five TV channels (incl. two satellite services), three radio channels and three worldwide services, NHK World TV, NHK World Premium and NHK World Radio Japan; headquarters in Tokyo, regional headquarters in Osaka, Nagoya, Hiroshima, Fukuoka, Sendai, Sapporo and Matsuyama; Pres. KATSUJI EBISAWA.

National Association of Commercial Broadcasters in Japan (NAB-J): 3-23, Kioi-cho, Chiyoda-ku, Tokyo 102-8577; tel. (3) 5213-7727; fax (3) 5213-7730; internet www.nab.or.jp; f. 1951; asscn of 201 companies (133 TV cos, 110 radio cos). Among these companies, 42 operate both radio and TV, with 664 radio stations and 8,315 TV stations (incl. relay stations). Pres. SEIICHIRO UJIIE; Exec. Dir AKIRA SAKAI.

In June 2000 there were a total of 99 commercial radio broadcasting companies and 127 commercial television companies operating in Japan. Some of the most important companies are:

Asahi Hoso—Asahi Broadcasting Corpn: 2-2-48, Ohyodo-Minami, Kita-ku, Osaka 531-8501; tel. (6) 6458-5321; fax (6) 6458-3672; internet www.asahi.co.jp; Pres. TOSHIHARU SHIBATA.

Asahi National Broadcasting Co Ltd—TV Asahi: 1-1-1, Roppongi, Minato-ku, Tokyo 106; tel. (3) 3587-5412; fax (3) 3586-6369; internet www.tv-asahi.co.jp; f. 1957; Pres. KUNIO ITO.

Bunka Hoso—Nippon Cultural Broadcasting, Inc: 1-5, Wakaba, Shinjuku-ku, Tokyo 160-8002; tel. (3) 3357-1111; fax (3) 3357-1140; internet www.joqr.co.jp; f. 1952; Pres. SHIGEKI SATO.

Chubu-Nippon Broadcasting Co Ltd: 1-2-8, Shinsakae, Naka-ku, Nagoya 460-8405; tel. (052) 241-8111; fax (052) 259-1303; internet www.cbc-nagoya.co.jp; Pres. KEN-ICHI YOKOYAMA.

Fuji Television Network, Inc: 2-4-8, Daiba, Minato-ku, Tokyo 137-8088; tel. (3) 5500-8888; fax (3) 5500-8027; internet www.fujitv.co.jp; f. 1958; Pres. HISASHI HIEDA.

Kansai Telecasting Corpn: 2-1-7, Ogimachi, Kita-ku, Osaka 530-8408; tel. (6) 6314-8888; internet www.ktv.co.jp; Pres. NOBUO MAKIHATA.

Mainichi Broadcasting System, Inc: 17-1, Chayamachi, Kita-ku, Osaka 530-8304; tel. (6) 6359-1123; fax (6) 6359-3503; internet mbs.co.jp; Chair. and CEO MORIYOSHI SAITO; Pres. AKIRA YANASE.

Nippon Hoso—Nippon Broadcasting System, Inc: 2-4-8, Daiba, Minato-ku, Tokyo 137-8686; tel. (3) 5500-1234; internet www.jolf.co.jp; f. 1954; Pres. MICHIYASU KAWAUCHI.

Nippon Television Network Corpn (NTV): 14, Niban-cho, Chiyoda-ku, Tokyo 102-8004; tel. (3) 5275-1111; fax (3) 5275-4501; internet www.ntv.co.jp; f. 1953; Pres. SEIICHIRO UJIIE.

Okinawa Televi Hoso—Okinawa Television Broadcasting Co Ltd: 1-2-20, Kumoji, Naha 900-8588; tel. (988) 63-2111; fax (988) 61-0193; f. 1959; Pres. BUNKI TOMA.

Radio Tampa—Nihon Short-Wave Broadcasting Co: 1-9-15, Akasaka, Minato-ku, Tokyo 107-8373; tel. (3) 3583-8151; fax (3) 3583-7441; internet www.tampa.co.jp; f. 1954; Pres. TAMIO IKEDA.

Ryukyu Hoso—Ryukyu Broadcasting Co: 2-3-1, Kumoji, Naha 900-8711; tel. (98) 867-2151; fax (98) 864-5732; internet www.cosmos.ne.jp/rbc; f. 1954; Pres. YOSHIO ISHIGAKE.

Television Osaka, Inc: 1-2-18, Otemae, Chuo-ku, Osaka 540-8519; tel. (6) 6947-0019; fax (6) 6946-9796; internet www.tv-osaka.co.jp; Pres. MAKOTO FUKAGAWA.

Television Tokyo Channel 12 Ltd: 4-3-12, Toranomon, Minato-ku, Tokyo 105-8012; tel. (3) 3432-1212; fax (3) 5473-3447; internet www.tv-tokyo.co.jp; f. 1964; Pres. YUTAKA ICHIKI.

Tokyo-Hoso—Tokyo Broadcasting System, Inc (TBS): 5-3-6, Akasaka, Minato-ku, Tokyo 107-8006; tel. (3) 3746-1111; fax (3) 3588-6378; internet www.tbs.co.jp/index.html; f. 1951; Chair. HIROSHI SHIHO; Pres. YUKIO SUNAHARA.

Yomiuri Televi Hoso—Yomiuri Telecasting Corporation: 2-2-33, Shiromi, Chuo-ku, Osaka 540-8510; tel. (6) 6947-2111; internet www.ytv.co.jp; f. 1958; 20 hrs colour broadcasting daily; Pres. TOMONARI DOI.

Satellite, Cable and Digital Television

In addition to the two broadcast satellite services that NHK introduced in 1989, a number of commercial satellite stations are in operation. Cable television is available in many urban areas, and in 1996/97 there were some 12.6m. subscribers to cable services in Japan. Satellite digital television services, which first became available in 1996, are provided by Japan Digital Broadcasting Services (f. 1998 by the merger of PerfecTV and JSkyB)

and DirecTV. Terrestrial digital services were scheduled to be introduced by 2000.

Finance

(cap. = capital; p.u. = paid up; res = reserves; dep. = deposits; m. = million; brs = branches; amounts in yen)

BANKING

Japan's central bank and bank of issue is the Bank of Japan. More than one-half of the credit business of the country is handled by 136 private commercial banks, seven trust banks and three long-term credit banks, collectively designated 'All Banks'. At October 1998 the private commercial banks had total assets of 641,000,000m. yen, the trust banks had total assets of 62,000,000m. yen and the long-term credit banks had total assets of 72,000,000m. yen.

Of the former category, the most important are the city banks, of which there are 10, some of which have a long and distinguished history, originating in the time of the *zaibatsu*, the private entrepreneurial organizations on which Japan's capital wealth was built before the Second World War. Although the *zaibatsu* were abolished as integral industrial and commercial enterprises during the Allied Occupation, the several businesses and industries which bear the former *zaibatsu* names, such as Mitsubishi, Mitsui and Sumitomo, continue to flourish and to give each other mutual assistance through their respective banks and trust corporations.

Among the commercial banks, the Bank of Tokyo-Mitsubishi specializes in foreign-exchange business, while the Industrial Bank of Japan finances capital investment by industry. Shinsei Bank and Nippon Credit Bank also specialize in industrial finance; the work of these three privately-owned banks is supplemented by the government-controlled Development Bank of Japan.

The Government has established a number of other specialized institutions to provide services that are not offered by the private banks. Thus the Japan Bank for International Cooperation advances credit for the export of heavy industrial products and the import of raw materials in bulk. A Housing Loan Corporation assists firms in building housing for their employees, while the Agriculture, Forestry and Fisheries Finance Corporation provides loans to the named industries for equipment purchases. Similar services are provided for small enterprises by the Japanese Finance Corporation for Small Business.

An important financial role is played by co-operatives and by the many small enterprise institutions. Each prefecture has its own federation of co-operatives, with the Central Co-operative Bank of Agriculture and Forestry as the common central financial institution. This bank also acts as an agent for the government-controlled Agriculture, Forestry and Fisheries Finance Corporation.

There are also two types of private financial institutions for small business. There were 342 Credit Co-operatives, with total assets of 22,000,000m. yen, and 400 Shinkin Banks (credit associations), with total assets of 113,000,000m. yen at October 1998, which lend only to members. The latter also receive deposits.

The most common form of savings is through the government-operated Postal Savings System, which collects small savings from the public by means of the post office network. Total deposits amounted to 248,000,000m. yen in November 1998. The funds thus made available are used as loan funds by government financial institutions, through the Ministry of Finance's Trust Fund Bureau.

Clearing houses operate in each major city of Japan, and total 182 institutions. The largest are those of Tokyo and Osaka.

In June 1998 the Financial Supervisory Agency was established to regulate Japan's financial institutions.

Central Bank

Nippon Ginko (Bank of Japan): 2-1-1, Hongoku-cho, Nihonbashi, Chuo-ku, Tokyo 100-8630; tel. (3) 3279-1111; fax (3) 5203-8703; internet www.boj.or.jp; f. 1882; cap. and res 3,351,339m., dep. 31,404,614m. (March 2000); Gov. MASARU HAYAMI; Dep. Govs SAKUYA FUJIWARA, YUTAKA YAMAGUCHI; 33 brs.

Principal Commercial Banks

Asahi Bank Ltd: 1-1-2, Otemachi, Chiyoda-ku, Tokyo 100-8106; tel. (3) 3287-2111; fax (3) 3212-3484; internet www.asahibank.co.jp; f. 1945 as Kyowa Bank Ltd; merged with Saitama Bank Ltd (f. 1943) in 1991; adopted present name in 1992; cap. 401,446m., res 986,658m., dep. 21,897,556m. (March 2000); Chair. TADASHI TANAKA; Pres. TATSURO ITOH; 424 brs.

Ashikaga Bank Ltd: 4-1-25, Sakura, Utsunomiya, Tochigi 320-8610; tel. (286) 22-0111; e-mail ashigin@ssctnet.or.jp; internet www.ashikagabank.co.jp; f. 1895; cap. 58,536m., res 79,539m., dep. 5,328,279m. (March 1999); Chair. HISAO MUKAE; Pres. YOSHIO YANAGITA; 140 brs.

Bank of Fukuoka Ltd: 2-13-1, Tenjin, Chuo-ku, Fukuoka 810-8727; tel. (92) 723-2131; fax (92) 711-1746; f. 1945; cap. 57,365m., res 246,046m., dep. 5,856,544m. (March 1999); Chair. TOYOHIKO GOTO; Pres. RYOJI TSUKUDA; 189 brs.

Bank of Tokyo-Mitsubishi Ltd: 2-7-1, Marunouchi, Chiyoda-ku, Tokyo 100-8388; tel. (3) 93240-1111; fax (3) 93240-4197; internet www.btm.co.jp; f. 1996 as a result of merger between Bank of Tokyo Ltd (f. 1946) and Mitsubishi Bank Ltd (f. 1880); specializes in international banking and financial business; cap. 785,970m., res 1,855,717m., dep. 46,102,053m. (March 2000); Chair. SATORU KISHI; Pres. SHIGEMITSU MIKI; 805 brs.

Bank of Yokohama Ltd: 3-1-1, Minatomirai, Nishi-ku, Yokohama, Kanagawa 220-8611; tel. (45) 225-1111; fax (45) 225-1160; e-mail intldept@boy.co.jp; internet www.boy.co.jp; f. 1920; cap. 184,800m., res 244,928m., dep. 8,853,324m. (March 2000); Chair. TAKASHI TANAKA; Pres. SADAAKI HIRASAWA; 193 brs.

Chiba Bank Ltd: 1-2, Chiba-minato, Chuo-ku, Chiba 260-8720; tel. (43) 245-1111; e-mail 76374822@people.or.jp; internet www .chibabank.co.jp; f. 1943; cap. 106,888m., res 194,702m., dep. 6,870,950m. (March 2000); Chair. TAKASHI TAMAKI; Pres. TSUNEO HAYAKAWA; 163 brs.

Dai-Ichi Kangyo Bank Ltd: 1-1-5, Uchisaiwai-cho, Chiyoda-ku, Tokyo 100-0011; tel. (3) 3596-1111; fax (3) 3596-2179; internet www.dkb.co.jp; f. 1971; jt holding co established with Fuji Bank Ltd and Nippon Kogyo Ginko in September 2000, prior to full merger by early 2002; cap. 858,784m., res 1,519,755m., dep. 40,012,121m. (March 2000); Pres. and CEO KATSUYUKI SUGITA; 353 brs.

Daiwa Bank Ltd: 2-2-1, Bingo-machi, Chuo-ku, Osaka 540-8610; tel. (6) 6271-1221; internet www.daiwabank.co.jp; f. 1918; cap. 465,158m., total funds 25,296,807m. (March 2000); Pres. TAKASHI KAIHO; 182 brs.

Fuji Bank Ltd: 1-5-5, Otemachi, Chiyoda-ku, Tokyo 100-0004; tel. (3) 3216-2211; internet www.fujibank.co.jp; f. 1880; jt holding co with Dai-Ichi Kangyo Bank Ltd and Nippon Kogyo Ginko established Sept. 2000, prior to full merger by early 2002; cap. 1,039,543m., res 1,239,276m., dep. 38,961,618m. (March 2000); Chair. TORU HASHIMOTO; Pres. YOSHIRO YAMAMOTO; 293 brs.

Hokuriku Bank Ltd: 1-2-26, Tsutsumichodori, Toyama 930-8637; tel. (764) 423-7111; fax (3) 3242-0541; e-mail kokusaibu@hokugin .co.jp; internet www.hokugin.co.jp; f. 1877; cap. 120,842m., res 125,439m., dep. 5,201,203m. (March 2000); Pres. SHINICHIRO INUSHIMA; 191 brs.

Japan Net Bank: internet www.japannetbank.co.jp; f. 2000; Japan's first internet-only bank.

Joyo Bank Ltd: 2-5-5, Minamimachi, Mito-shi, Ibaraki 310-0021; tel. (29) 231-2151; fax (29) 255-6522; e-mail joyointl@po.net-ibaraki .ne.jp; internet www.joyobank.co.jp; f. 1935; cap. 85,113m., res 277,802m., dep. 6,049,079m. (March 2000); Chair. ITARU ISHIKAWA; Pres. TORANOSUKE NISHINO; 186 brs.

Sakura Bank Ltd: 1-3-1, Kudan-Minami, Chiyoda-ku, Tokyo 100-8611; tel. (3) 3230-3111; fax (3) 3221-1084; internet www.sakura .co.jp; f. 1990; to merge with Sumitomo Bank Ltd by April 2001; cap. 1,042,706m., res 967,687m., dep. 38,654,872m. (March 2000); Chair. MASAHIRO TAKASAKI; Pres. AKISHIGE OKADA; 486 brs.

Sanwa Bank Ltd: 3-5-6, Fushimi-machi, Chuo-ku, Osaka 541-8530; tel. (6) 6206-8111; fax (6) 6229-1066; internet www.sanwabank.co.jp; f. 1933; plan to establish a jt holding co with Tokai Bank Ltd and Toyo Trust and Banking Co Ltd announced Oct. 2000; cap. 1,574,796m., res 253,547m., dep. 39,456,135m. (March 1999); Chair. HIROSHI WATANABE; Pres. K. MUROMACHI; 1,144 brs.

Shizuoka Bank Ltd: 1-10, Gofuku-cho, Shizuoka 420-8761; tel. (54) 345-5411; fax (3) 3246-1483; internet www.shizuokabank.co.jp; f. 1943; cap. 90,845m., res 145,729m., dep. 6,646,475m. (March 1999); Chair. SOICHIRO KAMIYA; Pres. YASUO MATSUURA; 199 brs.

Sumitomo Bank Ltd: 4-6-5, Kitahama, Chuo-ku, Osaka 541-0041; tel. (6) 6227-2111; internet www.sumitomobank.co.jp; f. 1895; to merge with Sakura Bank Ltd by April 2001; cap. 752,848m., res 797,936m., dep. 41,640,312m. (March 2000); Chair. TOSHIO MORIKAWA; Pres. YOSHIFUMI NISHIKAWA; 351 brs.

Tokai Bank Ltd: 3-21-24, Nishiki, Naka-ku, Nagoya 460-8660; tel. (52) 211-1111; fax (52) 211-0931; internet www.csweb.co.jp/tbkj; f. 1941; plan to establish a jt holding co with Sanwa Bank Ltd and Toyo Trust and Banking Co Ltd announced Oct. 2000; cap. 723,138m., res 857,785m., dep. 24,908,793m. (March 2000); Chair. SATORU NISHIGAKI; Pres. HIDEO OGASAWARA; 276 brs.

Principal Trust Banks

Chuo Mitsui Trust and Banking Co Ltd: 1-7-1, Kyobashi, Chuo-ku, Tokyo 104-8345; tel. (3) 3567-1451; fax (3) 3562-6902; internet www.chuomitsui.co.jp; f. 1962 as Chuo Trust and Banking Co Ltd, name changed as above in 2000, following merger with Mitsui Trust and Banking Co Ltd; cap. 170,966m., res 166,803m., dep. 3,594,827m. (March 2000); Chair. HISAO MURAMOTO; Pres. KIICHIRO FURUSAWA; 169 brs.

Mitsubishi Trust and Banking Corporation: 1-4-5, Marunouchi, Chiyoda-ku, Tokyo 100-0005; tel. (3) 3212-1211; fax (3) 3284-1326;

internet www.mitsubishi-trust.co.jp; f. 1927; cap. 192,793m., res 346,376m., dep. 10,216,797m. (March 2000); Chair. HIROSHI HAYASHI; Pres. TOYOSHI NAKANO; 54 brs.

Sumitomo Trust and Banking Co Ltd: 4-5-33, Kitahama, Chuo-ku, Osaka 540-8639; tel. (6) 6220-2121; fax (6) 6220-2043; e-mail ipda@sumitomotrust.co.jp; internet www.sumitomotrust.co.jp; f. 1925; cap. 282,068m., res 300,710m., dep. 8,391,773m. (March 2000); Chair. HITOSHI HURAKAMI; Pres. ATSUSHI TAKAHASHI; 57 brs.

Toyo Trust and Banking Co Ltd: 1-4-3, Marunouchi, Chiyoda-ku, Tokyo 100-0005; tel. (3) 3287-2211; fax (3) 3201-1448; f. 1959; plan to establish a jt holding co with Sanwa Bank Ltd and Tokai Bank Ltd announced Oct. 2000; cap. 280,471m., res 263,357m., dep. 3,952,347m. (March 2000); Chair. MITSUO IMOSE; Pres. J. YOKOSUGA; 56 brs.

Yasuda Trust and Banking Co Ltd: 1-2-1, Yaesu, Chuo-ku, Tokyo 103-0028; tel. (3) 3278-8111; fax (3) 3278-0904; internet www.ytb.co.jp; f. 1925; cap. 337,231m., res 213,724m., dep. 3,663,667m. (March 1999); Chair. KAZUHIKO KASAI; Pres. and CEO TAKAHIKO KIMINAMI; 50 brs.

Long-Term Credit Banks

Aozora: 1-13-10, Kudan-kita, Chiyoda-ku, Tokyo 102-8660; tel. (3) 3263-1111; fax (3) 3239-8065; e-mail sora@aozora.co.jp; internet www.aozora.co.jp; f. 1957; nationalized Dec. 1998, sold to consortium led by Softbank Corpn in Aug. 2000; frmrly The Nippon Credit Bank, name changed as above 2001; cap. 353,114m., res 114,047m., dep. 8,029,300m. (March 2000); Pres. YOSHINOBU KOTERA (acting); 17 brs.

Nippon Kogyo Ginko (The Industrial Bank of Japan Ltd): 1-3-3, Marunouchi, Chiyoda-ku, Tokyo 100-8210; tel. (3) 3214-1111; fax (3) 3201-7643; internet www.ibjbank.co.jp; f. 1902; jt holding co with Dai-Ichi Kangyo Bank Ltd and Fuji Bank Ltd established in Sept. 2000, prior to full merger by early 2002; medium- and long-term financing; cap. 673,605m., res 650,501m., dep. 28,041,940m. (March 1999); Pres. and CEO MASAO NISHIMURA; 23 domestic brs, 20 overseas brs.

Shinsei Bank Ltd: 2-1-8, Uchisaiwai-cho, Chiyoda-ku, Tokyo 100-8501; tel. (3) 5511-5111; fax (3) 5511-8138; internet www .shinseibank.co.jp; f. 1952 as The Long-Term Credit Bank of Japan; nationalized Oct. 1998, sold to Ripplewood Holdings (USA), renamed as above June 2000; cap. 180,853m., res 569,856m., dep. 10,116,726m. (March 2000); Chair. MASAMOTO YASHIRO; 23 brs.

Co-operative Bank

Zenshinren Bank: 3-8-1, Kyobashi, Chuo-ku, Tokyo 104-0031; tel. (3) 3563-4111; fax (3) 3563-7554; internet www.shinkin.co.jp; f. 1950; cap. 249,998m., res 322,658m., dep. 19,293,301m. (March 2000); Chair. KEIKICHI KATO; Pres. YASUTAKA MIYAMOTO; 17 brs.

Principal Government Credit Institutions

Agriculture, Forestry and Fisheries Finance Corporation: Koko Bldg, 1-9-3, Otemachi, Chiyoda-ku, Tokyo 100-0004; tel. (3) 3270-2261; e-mail intl@afc.go.jp; internet www.afc.go.jp; f. 1953; finances mainly plant and equipment investment; Gov. TOSHIHIKO TSURUOKA; Dep. Gov. (vacant); 21 brs.

Development Bank of Japan: 1-9-1, Otemachi, Chiyoda-ku, Tokyo 100-0004; tel. (3) 3244-1770; fax (3) 3245-1938; e-mail safukas@dbj.go.jp; internet www.dbj.go.jp; f. 1951 as the Japan Development Bank; renamed Oct. 1999 following consolidation with the Hokkaido and Tohoku Development Finance Public Corpn; provides long-term loans; subscribes for corporate bonds; guarantees corporate obligations; invests in specific projects; borrows funds from Govt and abroad; issues external bonds and notes; provides market information and consulting services for prospective entrants to Japanese market; cap. US $9,111.4m. (March 2000), res 455,768m. (March 1999), dep. 15,096,100m. (March 1998); Gov. TAKESHI KOMURA; Dep. Govs KUNITAKA KAJITA, TAKASHI MATSUKAWA; 10 domestic brs, 6 overseas brs.

Housing Loan Corporation: 1-4-10, Koraku, Bunkyo-ku, Tokyo 112-8570; tel. (3) 3812-1111; fax (3) 5800-8257; internet www .jyukou.go.jp; f. 1950 to provide long-term capital for the construction of housing at low interest rates; cap. 97,200m. (1994); Pres. SUSUMU TAKAHASHI; Vice-Pres. HIROYUKI ITOU; 12 brs.

Japan Bank for International Cooperation (JBIC): 1-4-1, Otemachi, Chiyoda-ku, Tokyo 100-8144; tel. (3) 5218-3101; fax (3) 5218-3955; internet www.jbic.go.jp; f. 1999 by merger of The Export-Import Bank of Japan (f. 1950) and The Overseas Economic Co-operation Fund (f. 1961); governmental financial institution, responsible for Japan's external economic policy and co-operation activities; cap. 6,679,944m. (March 2000); Gov. HIROSHI YASUDA.

Japan Finance Corporation for Small Business: Koko Bldg, 1-9-3, Otemachi, Chiyoda-ku, Tokyo 100-0004; tel. (3) 3270-1271; internet www.jfs.go.jp; f. 1953 to supply long-term operating funds to small businesses (capital not more than 100m., or not more than

300 employees) which are not easily secured from ordinary private financial institutions; cap. 274,915m. (Feb. 1999) wholly subscribed by Govt; Gov. TOMIO TSUTSUMI; Vice-Gov. SOHEI HIDAKA; 58 brs.

National Life Finance Corporation: Koko Bldg, 1-9-3, Otemachi, Chiyoda-ku, Tokyo 100-0004; tel. (3) 3270-1361; internet www.kokukin.go.jp; f. 1999 following consolidation of The People's Finance Corpn (f. 1949 to provide business funds, particularly to small enterprises unable to obtain loans from banks and other private financial institutions) and the Environmental Sanitation Business Finance Corpn (f. 1967 to improve sanitary facilities); cap. 290,771m. (March 2000); Gov. MAMORU OZAKI; Dep. Gov. MASAAKI TSUCHIDA; 152 brs.

Norinchukin Bank (Central Co-operative Bank for Agriculture, Forestry and Fisheries): 1-13-2, Yuraku-cho, Chiyoda-ku, Tokyo 100; tel. (3) 3279-0111; fax (3) 3218-5177; internet www.nochubank.or.jp; f. 1923; main banker to agricultural, forestry and fisheries co-operatives; receives deposits from individual co-operatives, federations and agricultural enterprises; extends loans to these and to local govt authorities and public corpns; adjusts excess and shortage of funds within co-operative system; issues debentures, invests funds and engages in other regular banking business; cap. 1,124,999m., res 222,951m., dep. 38,181,177m. (March 1999); Pres. KENICHI KAKUDOH; Dep. Pres. MITSUO NAITO; 39 brs.

Shoko Chukin Bank (Central Co-operative Bank for Commerce and Industry): 2-10-17, Yaesu, Chuo-ku, Tokyo 104-0028; tel. (3) 3272-6111; fax (3) 3274-1257; e-mail JDK06560@nifty.ne.jp; internet www.shokochukin.go.jp; f. 1936 to provide general banking services to facilitate finance for smaller enterprise co-operatives and other organizations formed mainly by small- and medium-sized enterprises; issues debentures; cap. 474,865m., res 24,410m., dep. 12,947,345m. (March 2000); Pres. YUKIHARU KODAMA; Dep. Pres. SHIGENORI SHIODA; 99 brs.

Other government financial institutions include the Japan Finance Corpn for Municipal Enterprises, the Small Business Credit Insurance Corpn and the Okinawa Development Finance Corpn.

Principal Foreign Banks

In March 1999 there were 88 foreign banks operating in Japan.

ABN AMRO Bank NV (Netherlands): Shiroyama J. T. Mori Bldg, 4-3-1, Toranomon, Minato-ku, Tokyo 105-6013; tel. (3) 5405-6501; fax (3) 5405-6900; Country Man. (Japan) MICHIEL F. KERBERT.

Bangkok Bank Public Co Ltd (Thailand): Bangkok Bank Bldg, 2-8-10, Nishi Shinbashi, Minato-ku, Tokyo 105-0003; tel. (3) 3503-3333; fax (3) 3502-6420; Senior Vice-Pres. and Gen. Man. (Japan) THAWEE PHUANGKETKEOW; br. in Osaka.

Bank of America NA: Ark Mori Bldg, 34th Floor, 1-12-32, Akasaka, Minato-ku, Tokyo 107; tel. (3) 3587-3155; fax (3) 3587-3460; Sr Vice-Pres. & Regional Man. Japan, Australia and Korea ARUN DUGGAL.

Bank of India: Mitsubishi Denki Bldg, 2-2-3, Marunouchi, Chiyoda-ku, Tokyo 100-0005; tel. (3) 3212-0911; fax (3) 3214-8667; e-mail boitok@gol.com; CEO (Japan) A. C. MAHAJAN; br. in Osaka.

Bank Negara Indonesia (Persero): Kokusai Bldg, 3-1-1, Marunouchi, Chiyoda-ku, Tokyo 100-0005; tel. (3) 3214-5621; fax (3) 3201-2633; e-mail tky-br@ptbni.co.jp; Gen. Man. SURYO DANISWORO.

Bank One NA (USA): Hibiya Central Bldg, 7th Floor, 1-2-9, Nishi Shinbashi, Minato-ku, Tokyo 105; tel. (3) 3596-8700; fax (3) 3596-8744; Sr Vice-Pres. and Gen. Man. YOSHIO KITAZAWA.

Barclays Bank PLC (UK): Urbannet Otemachi Bldg, 15th Floor, 2-2-2, Otemachi, Chiyoda-ku, Tokyo 100-31; tel. (3) 5255-0011; fax (3) 5255-0102; Chair. SHIJURO OGATA; Pres. YOICHI KAMINA.

Bayerische Hypo- und Vereinsbank AG (Germany): Otemachi 1st Sq. East Tower, 17th Floor, 1-5-1, Otemachi, Chiyoda-ku, Tokyo 100-0004; tel. (3) 3284-1341; fax (3) 3284-1370; Exec. Dirs Prof. PETER BARON, KENJI AKAGI.

BNP Paribas (France): Shiroyama JT Mori Bldg, 23rd Floor, 4-3-1, Toranomon, Minato-ku, Tokyo 105-6023; tel. (3) 5473-3520; fax (3) 5473-3510; CEO (Japan) ERIC MARTIN; br. in Osaka.

Chase Manhattan Bank (USA): Akasaka Park Bldg, 11th–13th Floors, 5-2-20, Akasaka, Minato-ku, Tokyo 107; tel. (3) 5570-7500; fax (3) 5570-7960; Man. Dir and Gen. Man. NORMAN J. T. SCOTT; br. in Osaka.

Citibank NA (USA): Pan Japan Bldg, 1st Floor, 3-8-17, Akasaka, Minato-ku, Tokyo 107; tel. (3) 3584-6321; fax (3) 3584-2924; Country Corporate Officer MASAMOTO YASHIRO; 20 brs.

Commerzbank AG (Germany): Nippon Press Center Bldg, 2nd Floor, 2-2-1, Uchisaiwai-cho, Chiyoda-ku, Tokyo 100-0011; tel. (3) 3502-4371; fax (3) 3508-7545; e-mail cbkjapan@gol.com; Gen. Mans BURKHARDT FIGGE, FRANÇOIS DE BELSUNCE.

Crédit Agricole Indosuez (France): Indosuez Bldg, 3-29-1, Kanda Jimbo-cho, Chiyoda-ku, Tokyo 101; tel. (3) 3261-3001; fax (3) 3261-0426; Sr Country Exec. FRANÇOIS BEYER.

Deutsche Bank AG (Germany): Sanno Park Tower, 2-11-1 Nagatacho, Chiyoda-ku, Tokyo 100-6171; tel. (3) 5156-6000; fax (3) 5156-

6001; CEO and Chief Country Officer JOHN MACFARLANE; brs in Osaka and Nagoya.

The Hongkong and Shanghai Banking Corpn Ltd (Hong Kong): HSBC Bldg, 3-11-1, Nihonbashi, Chuo-ku, Tokyo 103-0027; tel. (3) 5203-3000; fax (3) 5203-3039; CEO NICHOLAS A. NICOLOV; br in Osaka.

International Commercial Bank of China (Taiwan): Togin Bldg, 1-4-2, Marunouchi, Chiyoda-ku, Tokyo 100; tel. (3) 3211-2501; fax (3) 3216-5686; Sr Vice-Pres. and Gen. Man. SHIOW-SHYONG LAI; br. in Osaka.

Korea Exchange Bank (Republic of Korea): Shin Kokusai Bldg, 3-4-1, Marunouchi, Chiyoda-ku, Tokyo 100; tel. (3) 3216-3561; fax (3) 3214-4491; f. 1967; Acting Gen. Man. CHAE KYOON-JUNG; brs in Osaka and Fukuoka.

Lloyds TSB Bank PLC (UK): Akasaka Twin Tower New Bldg, 2-11-7, Akasaka, Minato-ku, Tokyo 107; tel. (3) 3589-7700; fax (3) 3589-7722; Principal Man. (Japan) KAH HIN LIM.

Morgan Guaranty Trust Co of New York (USA): Akasaka Park Bldg, 5-2-20, Akasaka, Minato-ku, Tokyo 107-6151; tel. (3) 5573-1100; Man. Dir TAKESHI FUJIMAKI.

National Bank of Pakistan: 20 Mori Bldg, 3rd Floor, 2-7-4, Nishi Shinbashi, Minato-ku, Tokyo 105; tel. (3) 3502-0331; fax (3) 3502-0359; f. 1949; Pres. SARDAR MUHAMMAD KHAWAJA.

Oversea-Chinese Banking Corpn Ltd (Singapore): Akasaka Twin Tower, 15th Floor, 2-17-22, Akasaka, Minato-ku, Tokyo 107-0052; tel. (3) 5570-3421; fax (3) 5570-3426; Gen. Man. YEO WEE GHEE.

Société Générale (France): Ark Mori Bldg, 1-12-32, Akasaka, Minato-ku, Tokyo 107; tel. (3) 5549-5800; fax (3) 5549-5729; Chief Exec. BRIAN KAYE; br. in Osaka.

Standard Chartered Bank (UK): 21st Floor, Sanno Park Tower, 2-11-1, Nagata-cho, Chiyoda-ku, Tokyo 100-6155; tel. (3) 5511-1200; fax (3) 5511-9333; Chief Exec. (Japan) JULIAN WYNTER.

State Bank of India: 352 South Tower, Yuraku-cho Denki Bldg, 1-7-1, Yuraku-cho, Chiyoda-ku, Tokyo 100; tel. (3) 3284-0085; fax (3) 3201-5750; e-mail sbitok@gol.com; internet www.sbijapan.com; CEO M. RANGARAJAN; br. in Osaka.

UBS AG: East Tower, Otemachi 1st Sq., 1-5-1, Otemachi, Chiyoda-ku, Tokyo 100-0004; tel. (3) 5293-3000; fax (3) 5293-3456; Man. TAKAO SAKOH.

Union de Banques Arabes et Françaises (UBAF) (France): Sumitomo Jimbocho Bldg, 8th Floor, 3-25, Kanda Jimbocho, Chiyoda-ku, Tokyo 101-0051; tel. (3) 3263-8821; fax (3) 3263-8820; e-mail bonin@ubaf.co.jp; Gen. Man. (Japan) PHILIPPE L. BONIN; br. in Osaka.

Westdeutsche Landesbank (Germany): Fukoku Seimei Bldg, 2-2-2, Uchisaiwaicho, Chiyoda-ku, Tokyo 100-0011; tel. (3) 5510-6200; fax (3) 5510-6299; Gen. Man. PETER CLERMONT.

Bankers' Associations

Japanese Bankers Association: 1-3-1, Marunouchi, Chiyoda-ku, Tokyo 100-8216; tel. (3) 3216-3761; fax (3) 3201-5608; internet www.zenginkyo.or.jp; f. 1945; fmrly Federation of Bankers Associations of Japan; 143 full mems, 43 associate mems, 72 special mems; Chair. YOSHIFUMI NISHIKAWA.

Tokyo Bankers Association, Inc: 1-3-1, Marunouchi, Chiyoda-ku, Tokyo 100-8216; tel. (3) 3216-3761; fax (3) 3201-5608; f. 1945; 121 mem. banks; conducts the above Association's administrative business; Chair. YOSHIFUMI NISHIKAWA; Vice-Chair. AKIRA KANNO.

National Association of Labour Banks: 2-5-15, Kanda Surugadai, Chiyoda-ku, Tokyo 101-0062; tel. (3) 3295-6721; fax (3) 3295-6752; Pres. TETSUEI TOKUGAWA.

Regional Banks Association of Japan: 3-1-2, Uchikanda, Chiyoda-ku, Tokyo 101-0047; tel. (3) 3252-5171; fax (3) 3254-8664; f. 1936; 64 mem. banks; Chair. SADAAKI HIROSAWA.

Second Association of Regional Banks: 5, Sanban-cho, Chiyoda-ku, Tokyo 102-0075; tel. (3) 3262-2181; fax (3) 3262-2339; f. 1989 (fmrly National Asscn of Sogo Banks); 65 commercial banks; Chair. MASANAO TAKEI.

STOCK EXCHANGES

Fukuoka Securities Exchange: 2-14-2, Tenjin, Chuo-ku, Fukuoka 810-0001; tel. (92) 741-8231; Pres. FUBITO SHIMOMURA.

Hiroshima Stock Exchange: 14-18, Kanayama-cho, Naka-ku, Hiroshima 730-0022; tel. (82) 541-1121; f. 1949; 20 mems; Pres. MASARU NANKO.

Kyoto Securities Exchange: 66, Tachiuri Nishimachi, Shijodori, Higashitoin Higashi-iru, Shimogyo-ku, Kyoto 600-8007; tel. (75) 221-1171; Pres. IICHI NAKAMURA.

Nagoya Stock Exchange: 3-3-17, Sakae, Naka-ku, Nagoya 460-0008; tel. (52) 262-3172; fax (52) 241-1527; e-mail kikaku@nse.or.jp; internet www.nse.or.jp; f. 1949; Pres. HIROSHI FUJITA; Sr Exec. Dir KAZUNORI ISHIMOTO.

Niigata Securities Exchange: 1245, Hachibancho, Kami-Okawa-maedori, Niigata 951-8068; tel. (252) 222-4181; Pres. KYUUZOU NAKATA.

Osaka Securities Exchange: 1-6-10, Kitahama, Chuo-ku, Osaka 541-0041; tel. (6) 4706-0875; fax (6) 6231-2639; internet www.ose.or.jp; f. 1949; 103 regular mems, 5 special participants; Chair. HIROTARO HIGUCHI; Pres. GORO TATSUMI.

Sapporo Stock Exchange: 5-14-1, Nishi, Minami Ichijo, Chuo-ku, Sapporo 060-0061; tel. (11) 241-6171; Pres. YOSHIRO ITOH.

Tokyo Stock Exchange: 2-1, Nihonbashi, Kabuto-cho, Chuo-ku, Tokyo 103-8220; tel. (3) 3666-0141; fax (3) 3663-0625; internet www.tse.or.jp; f. 1949; 120 mems (incl. 23 foreign mems) (June 1999); Pres. and CEO MITSUHIDE YAMAGUCHI; Deputy Pres. KEN-ICHI ISAKA, TAKUO TSURUSHIMA.

Supervisory Body

The Securities and Exchange Surveillance Commission: 3-1-1, Kasumigaseki, Chiyoda-ku, Tokyo 100; tel. (3) 3581-7868; fax (3) 5251-2136; f. 1992 for the surveillance of securities and financial futures transactions; Chair. TOSHIHIRO MIZUHARA.

INSURANCE
Principal Life Companies

Aetna Heiwa Life Insurance Co Ltd: 3-2-16, Ginza, Chuo-ku, Tokyo 104-8119; tel. (3) 3563-8111; fax (3) 3374-7114; f. 1907; Pres. BARRY S. HALPERN.

American Family Life Assurance Co of Columbus AFLAC Japan: Shinjuku Mitsui Bldg, 12th Floor, 2-1-1, Nishishinjuku, Shinjuku-ku, Tokyo 163-0456; tel. (3) 3344-2701; fax (3) 0424-41-3001; f. 1974; Chair. YOSHIKI OTAKE; Pres. HIDEFUMI MATSUI.

American Life Insurance Co (Japan): 1-1-3, Marunouchi, Chiyoda-ku, Tokyo 100-0005; tel. (3) 3284-4111; fax (3) 3284-3874; f. 1972; Chair. HIROSHI FUJINO; Pres. SEIKI TOKUNI.

Aoba Life Insurance Co Ltd: 3-6-30, Aobadai, Meguro-ku, Tokyo 153-8523; tel. (3) 3462-0007; fax (3) 3780-8169; Pres. TAKASHI KASA-GAMI.

Asahi Mutual Life Insurance Co: 1-7-3, Nishishinjuku, Shinjuku-ku, Tokyo 163-8611; tel. (3) 3342-3111; fax (3) 3346-9397; internet www.asahi-life.co.jp; f. 1888; Pres. YUZURU FUJITA.

AXA Nichidan Life Insurance Co Ltd: 1-2-19 Higashi, Shibuya-ku, Tokyo 150-8020; tel. (3) 3407-6231; fax (3) 5466-7131; internet www.axa-nichidan.co.jp; Pres. MICHAEL W. SHORT.

Cardif Assurance Vie: 3-25-2, Toranomon, Minato-ku, Tokyo 105-0001; tel. (3) 5776-6230; fax (3) 5776-6236; f. 2000; Pres. ATSUSHI SAKAUCHI.

Chiyoda Mutual Life Insurance Co: 2-19-18, Kamimeguro, Meguro-ku, Tokyo 153-8611; tel. (3) 5704-5111; fax (3) 3719-6605; internet www.chiyoda-life.co.jp; f. 1904; declared bankrupt October 2000; Pres. REIJI YONEYAMA.

Chiyodakasai EBISU Life Insurance Co Ltd: Ebisu MF Bldg, 6th Floor, 4-6-1, Ebisu Shibuya-ku, Tokyo 150-0013; tel. (3) 5420-8282; fax (3) 5420-8273; f. 1996; Pres. SHIGEJI MINOSHIMA.

Daido Life Insurance Co: 1-2-1, Edobori Nishi-ku, Osaka City, Osaka 550-0002; tel. (6) 6447-6111; fax (6) 6447-6315; f. 1902; Pres. NAOTERU MIYATO.

Daihyaku Mutual Life Insurance Co: 3-1-4, Shibuya, Shibuya-ku, Tokyo 150-8670; tel. (3) 3498-2294; fax (3) 3400-9313; e-mail kikaku@daihyaku-life.co.jp; internet www.daihyaku-life.co.jp; f. 1914; declared bankrupt June 2000; Pres. MITSUMASA AKIYAMI.

Dai-ichi Mutual Life Insurance Co: 1-13-1, Yuraku-cho, Chiyoda-ku, Tokyo 100-0006; tel. (3) 3216-1211; fax (3) 5221-3221; f. 1902; Chair. TAKAHIDE SAKURAI; Pres. TOMIJIRO MORITA.

Dai-Tokyo Happy Life Insurance Co Ltd: Shijuku Square Tower, 17th Floor, 6-22-1, Nishishinjuku, Shinjuku-ku, Tokyo 163-1131; tel. (3) 5323-6411; fax (3) 5323-6419; f. 1996; Pres. HITOSHI HASUNUMA.

DIY Life Insurance Co Ltd: 5-68-2, Nakano, Nakano-ku, Tokyo 164-0001; tel. (3) 5345-7603; fax (3) 5345-7608; f. 1999; Pres. HITOSHI KASE.

Dowa Life Insurance Co Ltd: 1-28-44, Shinkawa, Chuo-ku, Tokyo 104-0033; tel. (3) 3555-8870; fax (3) 3555-6876; f. 1996; Pres. KIMIO HARUNA.

Fuji Life Insurance Co Ltd: 1-18-17, Minamisenba, Chuo-ku, Osaka-shi 542-0081; tel. (6) 6261-0284; fax (6) 6261-0113; f. 1996; Pres. YOSHIAKI YONEMURA.

Fukoku Mutual Life Insurance Co: 2-2-2, Uchisaiwai-cho, Chiyoda-ku, Tokyo 100-0011; tel. (3) 3508-1101; fax (3) 3597-0383; f. 1923; Chair. TAKASHI KOBAYASHI; Pres. TOMOFUMI AKIYAMA.

GE Edison Life Insurance Co: Shibuya Markcity, 1-12-1, Dogen-zaka, Shibuya-ku, Tokyo 150-8674; tel. (3) 5457-8100; fax (3) 5457-8017; Chair. MICHAEL D. FRAIZER; Pres. YASUHIRO ISHIZAKA.

INA Himawari Life Insurance Co Ltd: 2-1-1, Nishi-Shinjuku, Shinjuku-ku, Tokyo 163-0434; tel. (3) 3348-7011; fax (3) 3348-5723; f. 1981; Chair. WILLIAM M. CLOWES; Pres. TAKASHI TAKEBAYASHI.

ING Life Insurance Co Ltd: 26th Floor, New Otani Garden Court, 4-1, Kioi-cho, Chiyoda-ku, Tokyo 102-0094; tel. (3) 5210-0300; fax (3) 5210-0430; f. 1985; Pres. MAKOTO CHIBA.

Koa Life Insurance Co Ltd: 7-13-10, Ginza, Chuo-ku, Tokyo 104-0061; tel. (3) 3248-3800; fax (3) 3544-5171; f. 1996; Pres. AKIO OKADA.

Kyoei Kasai Shinrai Life Insurance Co Ltd: J. City Bldg, 5-8-20, Takamatsu, Nerima-ku, Tokyo 179-0075; tel. (3) 5372-2100; fax (3) 5372-7701; f. 1996; Pres. YOSHIHIRO TOKUMITSU.

Kyoei Life Insurance Co Ltd: 4-4-1, Nihonbashi, Hongoku-cho, Chuo-ku, Tokyo 103-0021; tel. (3) 3270-8511; fax (3) 3231-8363; f. 1947; declared bankrupt Oct. 2000; Pres. SHOICHI OTSUKA.

Manulife Century Life Insurance Co: 4-34-1, Kokuryo, Chofu, Tokyo 182-8621; tel. (3) 2489-8090; fax (3) 2489-8134; e-mail david_horman@manulife.com; internet www.manulife.co.jp; f. 1999; Pres. DAVID HORMAN.

Meiji Life Insurance Co: 2-1-1, Marunouchi, Chiyoda-ku, Tokyo 100-0005; tel. (3) 3283-8111; fax (3) 3215-5219; internet www.meiji-life.co.jp; f. 1881; Chair. KENJIRO HATA; Pres. RYOTARO KANEKO.

Mitsui Mirai Life Insurance Co Ltd: Mitsui Kaijyo Nihonbashi Bldg, 1-3-16, Nihonbashi, Chuo-ku, Tokyo 103-0027; tel. (3) 5202-2811; fax (3) 5202-2997; f. 1996; Pres. KATSUYA WATANABE.

Mitsui Mutual Life Insurance Co: 1-2-3, Otemachi, Chiyoda-ku, Tokyo 100-8123; tel. (3) 3211-6111; fax (3) 5252-7265; internet www.mitsui-seimei.co.jp; f. 1927; Chair. KOSHIRO SAKATA; Pres. AKIRA MIYAKE.

Nichido Life Insurance Co Ltd: 4-2-3, Toranomon, Minato-ku, Tokyo 105-0001; tel. (3) 5403-1700; fax (3) 5403-1707; f. 1996; to merge with Tokio Marine Life Insurance Co in 2002; Pres. YOSHIAKI MIYAMOTO.

NICOS Life Insurance Co Ltd: Hongo MK Bldg, 1-28-34, Hongo, Bunkyo-ku, Tokyo 113-8414; tel. (3) 5803-3111; fax (3) 5803-3199; internet www.nicos-life.co.jp; f. 1986; Pres. RENE MULLER.

Nippon Fire Partner Life Insurance Co Ltd: 3-4-2, Tsukiji, Chuo-ku, Tokyo 104-8407; tel. (3) 5565-8080; fax (3) 5565-8365; f. 1996; Pres. HIRONOBU HARA.

Nippon Life Insurance Co (Nissay): 3-5-12, Imabashi, Chuo-ku, Osaka 541-8501; tel. (6) 6209-4500; f. 1889; Chair. JOSEI ITOH; Pres. IKUO UNO.

Orico Life Insurance Co Ltd: Sunshine 60, 26th Floor, 3-1-1, Higashi Ikebukuro, Toshima-ku, Tokyo 170-6026; tel. (3) 5391-3051; fax (3) 5391-3060; f. 1990; Chair. HIROSHI ARAI; Pres. TAKASHI SATO.

ORIX Life Insurance Corpn: Shinjuku Chuo Bldg, 5-17-5, Shin-juku, Shinjuku-ku, Tokyo 160-0022; tel. (3) 5272-2700; fax (3) 5272-2720; f. 1991; Chair. SHOGO KAJINISHI; Pres. SHINOBU SHIRAISHI.

Prudential Life Insurance Co Ltd: 1-7, Kojimachi, Chiyoda-ku, Tokyo 102-0083; tel. (3) 3221-0961; fax (3) 3221-2305; f. 1987; Chair. KIYOFUMI SAKAGUCHI; Pres. ICHIRO KONO.

Saison Life Insurance Co Ltd: Sunshine Sixty Bldg, 39th Floor, 3-1-1, Higashi Ikebukuro, Toshima-ku, Tokyo 170-6067; tel. (3) 3983-6666; fax (3) 2980-0598; internet www.saison-life.co.jp; f. 1975; Chair. and Pres. TOSHIO TAKEUCHI.

Skandia Life Insurance Co (Japan) Ltd: 5-6-6, Hiroo, Shibuya-ku, Tokyo 150-0012; tel. (3) 5488-1500; fax (3) 5488-1501; f. 1996; Pres. SUMIO SHIMOYAMA.

Sony Life Insurance Co Ltd: 1-1-1, Minami-Aoyama, Minato-ku, Tokyo 107-8585; tel. (3) 3475-8811; fax (3) 3475-8914; Chair. TSUNAO HASHIMOTO; Pres. KEN IWAKI.

Sumitomo Life Insurance Co: 7-18-24, Tsukiji, Chuo-ku, Tokyo 104-8430; tel. (3) 5550-1100; fax (3) 5550-1160; f. 1907; Chair. TOSHIOMI URAGAMI; Pres. KOICHI YOSHIDA.

Sumitomo Marine Yu-Yu Life Insurance Co Ltd: 2-27-1, Shin-kawa, Chuo-ku, Tokyo 104-0033; tel. (3) 5541-3111; fax (3) 5541-3976; f. 1996; Pres. KATSUHIRO ISHII.

Taisho Life Insurance Co Ltd: 1-9-1, Yurakucho, Chiyoda-ku, Tokyo 100-0006; tel. (3) 3281-7651; fax (3) 5223-2299; f. 1913; Pres. GEN SHIMURA.

Taiyo Mutual Life Insurance Co: 2-11-2, Nihonbashi, Chuo-ku, Tokyo 103-0027; tel. (3) 3272-6211; fax (3) 3272-1460; Pres. MASAHIRO YOSHIIKE.

Tokio Marine Life Insurance Co Ltd: Tokio Marine New Bldg, 1-2-1, Marunouchi, Chiyoda-ku, Tokyo 100-0005; tel. (3) 5223-2111; fax (3) 5223-2165; internet www.tokiomarine-life.co.jp; f. 1996; to merge with Nichido Life Insurance Co in 2002; Pres. SUKEAKI OHTA.

Tokyo Mutual Life Insurance Co: 1-5-2, Uchisaiwai-cho, Chi-yoda-ku, Tokyo 100-8555; tel. (3) 3504-2211; fax (3) 3593-0785; f. 1895; Pres. KENICHI NAKAMURA.

Yamato Mutual Life Insurance Co: 1-1-7, Uchisaiwai-cho, Chi-yoda-ku, Tokyo 100-0011; tel. (3) 3508-3111; fax (3) 3508-3118; f. 1911; Pres. KEIJI NONOMIYA.

Yasuda Mutual Life Insurance Co: 1-9-1, Nishi-Shinjuku, Shinjuku-ku, Tokyo 169-8701; tel. (3) 3342-7111; fax (3) 3349-8104; f. 1880; Chair. YUJI OSHIMA; Pres. MIKIHIKO MIYAMOTO.

Zurich Life Insurance Co Ltd: Shinanomachi Rengakan, 35, Shinanomachi, Shinjuku-ku, Tokyo 160-0016; tel. (3) 5361-2700; fax (3) 5361-2728; f. 1996; Pres. KENICHI NOGAMI.

Principal Non-Life Companies

ACE Insurance: Arco Tower, 1-8-1, Shimomeguro, Meguro-ku, Tokyo 153-0064; tel. (3) 5740-0600; fax (3) 5740-0608; internet www.ace-insurance.co.jp; f. 1999; Chair. FUMIO TOKUHIRA; Pres. TAKASHI ONAWA.

Allianz Fire and Marine Insurance Japan Ltd: MITA N. N. Bldg, 4th Floor, 4-1-23, Shiba, Minato-ku, Tokyo 108-0014; tel. (3) 5442-6500; fax (3) 5442-6509; e-mail admin@allianz.co.jp; f. 1990; Chair. HEINZ DOLLBERG; Pres. ALEXANDER ANKEL.

The Asahi Fire and Marine Insurance Co Ltd: 2-6-2, Kaji-cho, Chiyoda-ku, Tokyo 101-8655; tel. (3) 3254-2211; fax (3) 3254-2296; e-mail asahifmi@blue.ocn.ne.jp; f. 1951; Pres. MORIYA NOGUCHI.

AXA Non-Life Insurance Co Ltd: Ariake Frontier Bldg, Tower A, 3-1-25, Ariake Koto-ku, Tokyo 135-0063; tel. (3) 3570-8900; fax (3) 3570-8911; f. 1998; Pres. GUY MARCILLAT.

The Chiyoda Fire and Marine Insurance Co Ltd: 1-28-1, Ebisu, Shibuya-ku, Tokyo 150-8488; tel. (3) 5424-9288; fax (3) 5424-9382; bought by Dai-Tokyo Fire and Marine Insurance Co in 2000, to combine in April 2001; f. 1897; Pres. KOJI FUKUDA.

The Daido Fire and Marine Insurance Co Ltd: 1-12-1, Kumoji, Naha-shi, Okinawa 900-8586; tel. (98) 867-1161; fax (98) 862-8362; f. 1971; Pres. MUNEMASA URA.

The Daiichi Mutual Fire and Marine Insurance Co: 5-1, Niban-cho, Chiyoda-ku, Tokyo 102-0084; tel. (3) 3239-0011; fax (3) 5999-0375; f. 1949; collapsed May 2000.

The Dai-ichi Property and Casualty Insurance Co Ltd: 1-2-10, Hirakawa-cho, Chiyoda-ku, Tokyo 102-0093; tel. (3) 5213-3124; fax (3) 5213-3306; f. 1996; Pres. TSUYOSHI SHINOHARA.

The Dai-Tokyo Fire and Marine Insurance Co Ltd: 3-25-3, Yoyogi, Shibuya-ku, Tokyo 151-8530; tel. (3) 5371-6122; fax (3) 5371-6248; internet www.daitokyo.index.or.jp; f. 1918; bought Chiyoda Fire and Marine Insurance Co in 2000, to combine in April 2001; Chair. HAJIME OZAWA; Pres. AKIRA SESHIMO.

The Dowa Fire and Marine Insurance Co Ltd: St Luke's Tower, 8-1, Akashi-cho, Chuo-ku, Tokyo 104-8556; tel. (3) 5550-0254; fax (3) 5550-0318; internet www.dowafire.co.jp; f. 1944; Chair. MASAO OKAZAKI; Pres. SHUICHIRO SUDO.

The Fuji Fire and Marine Insurance Co Ltd: 1-18-11, Minami-senba, Chuo-ku, Osaka 542-8567; tel. (6) 6271-2741; fax (6) 6266-7115; internet www.fujikasai.co.jp; f. 1918; Pres. YASUO ODA.

The Japan Earthquake Reinsurance Co Ltd: Kobuna-cho, Fuji Plaza, 4th Floor, 8-1, Nihonbashi, Kobuna-cho, Chuo-ku, Tokyo 103-0024; tel. (3) 3664-6107; fax (3) 3664-6169; e-mail jishin-a@db3.so-net.or.jp; f. 1966; Pres. KAZUMOTO ADACHI.

JI Accident & Fire Insurance Co Ltd: A1 Bldg, 20-5, Ichiban-cho, Chiyoda-ku, Tokyo 102-0082; tel. (3) 3237-2045; fax (3) 3237-2250; internet www.jihoken.co.jp; f. 1989; Pres. TSUKASA IMURA.

The Koa Fire and Marine Insurance Co Ltd: 3-7-3, Kasumiga-seki, Chiyoda-ku, Tokyo 100-0013; tel. (3) 3593-7711; fax (3) 3593-7325; internet www.koa.co.jp; f. 1944; plans to merge with The Nippon Fire and Marine Insurance Co Ltd; Chair. TERUHIKO TATSUUMA; Pres. MUTUHARU OKAMOTO.

The Kyoei Mutual Fire and Marine Insurance Co: 1-18-6, Shimbashi, Minato-ku, Tokyo 105-8604; tel. (3) 3504-2335; fax (3) 3508-7680; e-mail reins.intl@kyoeikasai.co.jp; internet www.kyoeikasai.co.jp; f. 1942; Chair. HIDEJI SUZUKI; Pres. WATARU OZAWA.

Meiji General Insurance Co Ltd: 2-11-1, Kanda-tsukasa-cho, Chiyoda-ku, Tokyo 101-0048; tel. (3) 3257-3141; fax (3) 3257-3295; internet meiji-general.aaapc.co.jp; f. 1996; Pres. FUJIO MIYAZAKI.

Mitsui Marine and Fire Insurance Co Ltd: 3-9, Kanda Surugadai, Chiyoda-ku, Tokyo 101-8011; tel. (3) 3259-3111; fax (3) 3291-5467; internet www.mitsuimarine.co.jp; f. 1918; Pres. TAKEO INOKUCHI.

Mitsui Seimei General Insurance Co Ltd: 2-1-1, Toranomon, Minato-ku, Tokyo 105-0001; tel. (3) 3224-2830; fax (3) 3224-2677; f. 1996; Pres. KIYOSHI MATSUOKA.

The Nichido Fire and Marine Insurance Co Ltd: 5-3-16, Ginza, Chuo-ku, Tokyo 104-0061; tel. (3) 3289-1066; fax (3) 3574-0646; e-mail nichido@mu2.so-net.ne.jp; internet www.mediagalaxy.co.jp/nichido; f. 1914; Chair. IKUO EGASHIRA; Pres. TAKASHI AIHARA.

The Nippon Fire and Marine Insurance Co Ltd: 2-2-10, Nihonbashi, Chuo-ku, Tokyo 103-8255; tel. (3) 3272-8111; fax (3) 5229-3385; internet www.nihonkasai.co.jp; f. 1892; plans to merge with The Koa Fire and Marine Insurance Co Ltd; Pres. and CEO KEN MATSUZAWA.

The Nissan Fire and Marine Insurance Co Ltd: 2-9-5, Kita-Aoyama, Minato-ku, Tokyo 107-8654; tel. (3) 3746-6516; fax (3) 3470-1308; e-mail webmas@nissan-ins.co.jp; internet www.nissan-ins.co.jp; f. 1911; Chair. FUMIYA KAWATE; Pres. RYUTARO SATO.

Nissay General Insurance Co Ltd: Shinjuku NS Bldg, 25th Floor, 2-4-1, Nishi-Shinjuku, Shinjuku-ku, Tokyo 163-0888; tel. (3) 5325-7932; fax (3) 5325-8149; f. 1996; Pres. TADAO NISHIOKA.

The Nisshin Fire and Marine Insurance Co Ltd: 2-3 Kanda Surugadai, Chiyoda-ku, Tokyo 100-8329; tel. (3) 5282-5534; fax (3) 5282-5582; e-mail nisshin@mb.infoweb.ne.jp; internet www.nisshinfire.co.jp; f. 1908; Pres. MICHIO NODA.

Saison Automobile and Fire Insurance Co Ltd: Sunshine 60 Bldg, 3-1-1, Higashi Ikebukuro, Toshima-ku, Tokyo 170-6068; tel. (3) 3988-2572; fax (3) 3980-7367; internet www.saison.ne.jp/sonpo; f. 1982; Pres. TOMONORI KANAI.

Secom General Insurance Co Ltd: 2-6-2, Hirakawa-cho, Chiyoda-ku, Tokyo 103-8645; tel. (3) 5216-6129; fax (3) 5216-6149; internet www.secom-sonpo.co.jp; Pres. SEIJI YAMANAKA.

Sony Assurance Inc.: Aromia Square 11F, 5-37-1, Kamata, Ota-ku, Tokyo 144-8721; tel. (3) 5744-0300; fax (3) 5744-0480; internet www.sonysonpo.co.jp; f. 1999; Pres. SHINIEH YAMAMOTO.

The Sumi-Sei General Insurance Co Ltd: Sumitomo Life Yotsuya Bldg, 8-2, Honshio-cho, Shinjuku-ku, Tokyo 160-0003; tel. (3) 5360-6229; fax (3) 5360-6991; f. 1996; Chair. HIDEO NISHIMOTO; Pres. HIDEKI ISHII.

The Sumitomo Marine and Fire Insurance Co Ltd: 2-27-2, Shinkawa, Chuo-ku, Tokyo 104-8252; tel. (3) 3297-6663; fax (3) 3297-6882; internet www.sumitomomarine.co.jp; f. 1944; Chair. TAKASHI ONODA; Pres. HIROYUKI UEMURA.

The Taisei Fire and Marine Insurance Co Ltd: 4-2-1, Kudan-Kita, Chiyoda-ku, Tokyo 102-0073; tel. (3) 3222-3096; fax (3) 3234-4073; e-mail saiho@taiseikasai.co.jp; internet www.taiseikasai.co.jp; f. 1950; Pres. ICHIRO OZAWA.

Taiyo Fire and Marine Insurance Co Ltd: 7-7, Niban-cho, Chiyoda-ku, Tokyo 102-0084; tel. (3) 5226-3117; fax (3) 5226-3133; f. 1951; Chair. YUJI YAMASHITA; Pres. TSUNAIE KANIE.

The Toa Reinsurance Co Ltd: 3-6, Kanda Surugadai, Chiyoda-ku, Tokyo 101-8703; tel. (3) 3253-3177; fax (3) 3253-5298; f. 1940; Dir TAKAYA IMASHIMIZU.

The Tokio Marine and Fire Insurance Co Ltd (Tokio Kaijo): 1-2-1, Marunouchi, Chiyoda-ku, Tokyo 100-8050; tel. (3) 3285-1900; fax (3) 5223-3040; internet www.tokiomarine.co.jp; f. 1879; Chair. SHUNJI KONO; Pres. KOUKEI HIGUCHI.

The Yasuda Fire and Marine Insurance Co Ltd: 1-26-1, Nishi-Shinjuku, Shinjuku-ku, Tokyo 160-8338; tel. (3) 3349-3111; fax (3) 5381-7406; internet www.yasuda.co.jp; f. 1887; Chair. KOICHI ARIYOSHI; Pres. HIROSHI HIRANO.

The Yasuda General Insurance Co Ltd: Shinjuku MAYNDS Tower, 29th Floor, 2-1-1, Yoyogi, Shibuya-ku, Tokyo 151-0053; tel. (3) 5352-8129; fax (3) 5352-8213; e-mail uwdept@mx7.mesh.ne.jp; f. 1996; Chair. SHIGEO FUJINO; Pres. IEJI YOSHIOKA.

The Post Office also operates life insurance and annuity plans.

Insurance Associations

The Life Insurance Association of Japan (Seimei Hoken Kyokai): New Kokusai Bldg, 3-4-1, Marunouchi, Chiyoda-ku, Tokyo 100-0005; tel. (3) 3286-2652; fax (3) 3286-2630; f. 1908; 47 mem. cos; Chair. TOMIJIRO MORITA; Senior Man. Dir SHIGERU SUWA.

The Marine and Fire Insurance Association of Japan Inc (Nihon Songai Hoken Kyokai): Non-Life Insurance Bldg, 2-9, Kanda Awaji-cho, Chiyoda-ku, Tokyo 101-8335; tel. (3) 3255-1437; fax (3) 3255-1234; e-mail kokusai@sonpo.or.jp; internet www.sonpo.or.jp; f. 1946; 35 mems; Chair. TAKEO INOKUCHI; Exec. Dir NOBORU ARAKI.

Property and Casualty Insurance Rating Organization of Japan: Banzai Bldg, 2-31-19, Shiba, Minato-ku, Tokyo 105-0014; tel. (3) 5441-1228; fax (3) 5441-1274; e-mail sohki@sonsan.or.jp; internet www.sonsan.or.jp; f. 1948; 53 mems; Pres. TAKASHI MUKAIBO; Senior Man. Dir. TAKEYOSHI KATSURADA.

Trade and Industry

CHAMBERS OF COMMERCE AND INDUSTRY

The Japan Chamber of Commerce and Industry (Nippon Shoko Kaigi-sho): 3-2-2, Marunouchi, Chiyoda-ku, Tokyo 100-0005; tel. (3) 3283-7851; fax (3) 3216-6497; e-mail info@jcci.or.jp; internet www.jcci.or.jp/home-e; f. 1922; the cen. org. of all chambers of commerce and industry in Japan; mems 521 local chambers of commerce and industry; Chair. KOSAKU INABA; Pres. SHOICHI TANIMURA.

Principal chambers include:

Kobe Chamber of Commerce and Industry: 6-1, Minatojima-nakamachi, Chuo-ku, Kobe 650-0046; tel. (78) 303-5806; fax (78)

303-2312; e-mail info@kcci.hyogo-iic.ne.jp; f. 1878; 14,000 mems; Chair. HIROSHI OHBA; Pres. HIROSHI MIYAMICHI.

Kyoto Chamber of Commerce and Industry: 240, Shoshoi-cho, Ebisugawa-agaru, Karasumadori, Nakakyo-ku, Kyoto 604-0862; tel. (75) 212-6450; fax (75) 251-0743; e-mail kyoto@kyo.or.jp; f. 1882; 13,008 mems; Chair. KAZUO INAMORI; Pres. OSAMU KOBORI.

Nagoya Chamber of Commerce and Industry: 2-10-19, Sakae, Naka-ku, Nagoya, Aichi 460-8422; tel. (52) 223-5722; fax (52) 232-5751; f. 1881; 20,622 mems; Chair. SEITARO TANIGUCHI; Pres. YOSHIKI KOBAYASHI.

Naha Chamber of Commerce and Industry: 2-2-10, Kume Naha, Okinawa; tel. (98) 868-3758; fax (98) 866-9834; e-mail cci-naha@cosmos.ne.jp; f. 1927; 4,874 mems; Chair. AKIRA SAKIMA; Pres. KOSEI YONEMURA.

Osaka Chamber of Commerce and Industry: 2-8, Hommachi-bashi, Chuo-ku, Osaka 540-0029; tel. (6) 6944-6400; fax (6) 6944-6248; e-mail intl@osaka.cci.or.jp; internet www.osaka.cci.or.jp; f. 1878; 36,666 mems; Chair. WA TASHIRO; Pres. TAKAO OHNO.

Tokyo Chamber of Commerce and Industry: 3-2-2, Marunouchi, Chiyoda-ku, Tokyo 100-0005; tel. (3) 3283-7756; fax (3) 3216-6497; e-mail webmaster@tokyo-cci.or.jp; f. 1878; 118,642 mems; Chair. KOSAKU INABA; Pres. SHOICHI TANIMURA.

Yokohama Chamber of Commerce and Industry: Sangyo Boueki Center Bldg, Yamashita-cho, Naka-ku, Yokohama 231-8524; tel. (45) 671-7472; fax (45) 671-7410; e-mail yccisomz@mb.infoweb.ne.jp; f. 1880; 17,673 mems; Chair. KOJIRO TSUSHIMA; Pres. SHIRO SAITOH.

INDUSTRIAL AND TRADE ASSOCATIONS
General

The Association for the Promotion of International Trade, Japan (JAPIT): 1-26-5, Toranomon, Minato-ku, Tokyo; tel. (3) 3506-8261; fax (3) 3506-8260; f. 1954 to promote trade with the People's Repub. of China; 700 mems; Chair. YOSHIO NAKATA; Pres. YOSHIO SAKURAUCHI.

Industry Club of Japan: 1-4-6, Marunouchi, Chiyoda-ku, Tokyo; tel. (3) 3281-1711; f. 1917 to develop closer relations between industrialists at home and abroad and promote expansion of Japanese business activities; c. 1,600 mems; Pres. GAISHI HIRAIWA; Exec. Dir KOUICHIROU SHINNO.

Japan Association of Corporate Executives (Keizai Doyukai): Nippon Kogyo Club Bldg, 1-4-6, Marunouchi, Chiyoda-ku, Tokyo 100-0005; tel. (3) 3211-1271; fax (3) 3213-2946; internet www.doyukai.or.jp; f. 1946; mems: c. 1,493 corporate executives concerned with national and international economic and social policies; Chair. YOTARO KOBAYASHI.

Japan Commercial Arbitration Association: Taishoseimei Hibiya Bldg, 1-9-1, Yurakucho, Chiyoda-ku, Tokyo 100; tel. (3) 3287-3061; fax (3) 3287-3064; f. 1950; 1,012 mems; provides facilities for mediation, conciliation and arbitration in international trade disputes; Pres. KOSAKU INABA.

Japan External Trade Organization (JETRO): 2-2-5, Toranomon, Minato-ku, Tokyo 105-8466; tel. (3) 3582-5511; fax (3) 3582-5662; e-mail seh@jetro.go.jp; internet www.jetro.go.jp; f. 1958; information for international trade, investment, import promotion, exhibitions of foreign products; Chair. and CEO NOBORU HATAKEYAMA; Pres. YOSIHIKO SAEKI.

Japan Federation of Economic Organizations (KEIDANREN): 1-9-4, Otemachi, Chiyoda-ku, Tokyo 100-8188; tel. (3) 3279-1411; fax (3) 5255-6253; f. 1946; to merge with Japan Federation of Employers' Associations (Nikkeiren) by May 2001; private non-profit asscn researching domestic and international economic problems and providing policy recommendations; mems: 120 industrial orgs, 1,007 corpns (1999); Chair. TAKASHI IMAI; Pres. KOZO UCHIDA.

Japan Federation of Smaller Enterprise Organizations (JFSEO) (Nippon Chusokigyo Dantai Renmei): 2-8-4, Nihonbashi, Kayaba-cho, Chuo-ku, Tokyo 103-0025; tel. (3) 3669-6862; f. 1948; 18 mems and c. 1,000 co-operative socs; Pres. MASATAKA TOYODA; Chair. of Int. Affairs SEIICHI ONO.

Japan General Merchandise Exporters' Association: 2-4-1, Hamamatsu-cho, Minato-ku, Tokyo; tel. (3) 3435-3471; fax (3) 3434-6739; f. 1953; 40 mems; Pres. TADAYOSHI NAKAZAWA.

Japan Productivity Center for Socio-Economic Development (JPC-SED) (Shakai Keizai Seisansei Honbu): 3-1-1, Shibuya, Shibuya-ku, Tokyo 150-8307; tel. (3) 3409-1112; fax (3) 3409-1986; f. 1994 following merger between Japan Productivity Center and Social Economic Congress of Japan; 10,000 mems; concerned with management problems and research into productivity; Chair. MASAO KAMEI; Pres. ARIO ORITA.

Nihon Boeki-Kai (Japan Foreign Trade Council, Inc): World Trade Center Bldg, 6th Floor, 2-4-1, Hamamatsu-cho, Minato-ku, Tokyo 105-6106; tel. (3) 3435-5952; fax (3) 3435-5969; e-mail jftc001@infotokyo.or.jp; internet www.fjt.co.jp/JFTC; f. 1947; 251 mems; Chair. MINORU MUROFUSHI; Exec. Man. Dir MIKIO KOJIMA; Man. Dir HISAO IKEGAMI.

Chemicals

Federation of Pharmaceutical Manufacturers' Associations of Japan: Tokyo Yakugyo Bldg, 2-1-5, Nihonbashi Honcho, Chuo-ku, Tokyo 103-0023; tel. (3) 3270-0581; fax (3) 3241-2090; Pres. TADASHI SUZUKI.

Japan Chemical Industry Association: Tokyo Club Bldg, 3-2-6, Kasumigaseki, Chiyoda-ku, Tokyo 100-0013; tel. (3) 3580-0751; fax (3) 3580-0764; f. 1948; 266 mems; Pres. AKIRA MIURA.

Japan Cosmetic Industry Association: Hatsumei Bldg, 2-9-14, Toranomon, Minato-ku, Tokyo 105-0001; tel. (3) 3502-0576; fax (3) 3502-0829; f. 1959; 630 mem. cos; Chair. KINZO OZAWA.

Japan Gas Association: 1-15-12, Toranomon, Minato-ku, Tokyo 105-0001; tel. (3) 3502-0116; fax (3) 3502-3676; f. 1947; Chair. SHINICHIRO RYOKI; Vice-Chair. and Sr Man. Dir KOSHIRO GODA.

Japan Perfumery and Flavouring Association: Nitta Bldg, 8-2-1, Ginza, Chuo-ku, Tokyo 104-0061; tel. and fax (3) 3571-3855; f. 1947; Chair. KINZO OGAWA.

Photo-Sensitized Materials Manufacturers' Association: JCII Bldg, 25, Ichiban-cho, Chiyoda-ku, Tokyo 102-0082; tel. (3) 5276-3561; fax (3) 5276-3563; f. 1948; Pres. MASAYUKI MUNEYUKI.

Fishing and Pearl Cultivation

Japan Fisheries Association (Dainippon Suisankai): Sankaido Bldg, 1-9-13, Akasaka, Minato-ku, Tokyo 107-0052; tel. (3) 3585-6683; fax (3) 3582-2337; Pres. HIROYA SANO.

Japan Pearl Export and Processing Co-operative Association: 3-7, Kyobashi, Chuo-ko, Tokyo; f. 1951; 130 mems.

Japan Pearl Exporters' Association: 122, Higashi-machi, Chuo-ku, Kobe; tel. (78) 331-4031; fax (78) 331-4345; e-mail jpeakobe@lime.ocn.ne.jp; internet www.japan-pearl.com; f. 1954; 67 mems; Pres. CHIAKI NISHIOKA.

Paper and Printing

Japan Federation of Printing Industries: 1-16-8, Shintomi, Chuo-ku, Tokyo 104; tel. (3) 3553-6051; fax (3) 3553-6079; Pres. HIROMICHI FUJITA.

Japan Paper Association: Kami Parupu Bldg, 3-9-11, Ginza, Chuo-ku, Tokyo 104-8139; tel. (3) 3248-4801; fax (3) 3248-4826; f. 1946; 54 mems; Chair. MASAO KOBAYASHI; Pres. KIYOSHI SAKAI.

Japan Paper Exporters' Association: Kami Parupu Bldg, 3-9-11, Ginza, Chuo-ku, Tokyo 104-8139; tel. (3) 3248-4831; fax (3) 3248-4834; f. 1952; 43 mems; Chair. KENTARO NAGAOKA.

Japan Paper Importers' Association: Kami Parupu Bldg, 3-9-11, Ginza, Chuo-ku, Tokyo 104-8139; tel. (3) 3248-4832; fax (3) 3248-4834; f. 1981; 32 mems; Chair. NOBUO KATSUMATA.

Japan Paper Products Manufacturers' Association: 4-2-6, Kotobuki, Taito-ku, Tokyo; tel. (3) 3543-2411; f. 1949; Exec. Dir KIYOSHI SATOH.

Mining and Petroleum

Asbestos Cement Products Association: Takahashi Bldg, 7-10-8, Ginza, Chuo-ku, Tokyo; tel. (3) 3571-1359; f. 1937; Chair. KOSHIRO SHIMIZU.

Japan Cement Association: Hattori Bldg, 1-10-3, Kyobashi, Chuo-ku, Tokyo 104-0031; tel. (3) 3561-8632; fax (3) 3567-8570; f. 1948; 20 mem. cos; Chair. KAZUTSUGU HIRAGA; Exec. Man. Dir HIROFUMI YAMASHITA.

Japan Coal Association: Hibiya Park Bldg, 1-8-1, Yuraku-cho, Chiyoda-ku, Tokyo 100; tel. (3) 3271-3481; fax (3) 3214-0585; Chair. TADASHI HARADA.

Japan Mining Industry Association: Shuwa Toranomon Bldg, No. 3, 1-21-8 Toranomon, Minato-ku, Tokyo 105-0001; tel. (3) 3502-7451; fax (3) 3591-9841; f. 1948; 60 mem. cos; Chair. SHINPEI MIYAMURA; Pres. A. SHINOZAKI; Dir-Gen. H. HIYAMA.

Japan Petroleum Development Association: Keidanren Bldg, 1-9-4, Otemachi, Chiyoda-ku, Tokyo 100; tel. (3) 3279-5841; fax (3) 3279-5844; f. 1961; Chair. TAMOTSU SHOYA.

Metals

Japan Aluminium Association (JAA): Tsukamoto-Sozan Bldg, 4-2-15, Ginza, Chuo-ku, Tokyo 104-0061; tel. (3) 3538-0221; fax (3) 3538-0233; f. 1999 by merger of Japan Aluminium Federation and Japan Light Metal Association; Chair. NOBUAKI FUJII.

Japan Brass Makers' Association: 1-12-22, Tsukiji, Chuo-ku, Tokyo 104-0045; tel. (3) 3542-6551; fax (3) 3542-6556; e-mail jbmajwcc@copper-brass.gr.jp; internet www.copper-brass.gr.jp; f. 1948; 62 mems; Pres. S. SATO; Man. Dir J. HATANO.

Japan Iron and Steel Exporters' Association: Tekko Kaikan Bldg, 3-2-10, Nihonbashi Kayaba-cho, Chuo-ku, Tokyo 103-0025; tel. (3) 3669-4818; fax (3) 3661-0798; f. 1953; mems 17 mfrs, 27 dealers; Chair. AKIRA CHIHAYA.

The Japan Iron and Steel Federation: Keidanren Bldg, 1-9-4, Otemachi, Chiyoda-ku, Tokyo 100-0004; tel. (3) 3279-3612; fax (3) 3245-0144; internet www.jisf.or.jp; f. 1948; Chair. AKIRA CHIHAYA.

Japan Stainless Steel Association: Tekko Bldg, 3-2-10, Nihonbashi Kayaba-cho, Chuo-ku, Tokyo 103; tel. (3) 3669-4431; fax (3) 3669-4431; e-mail yabe@jssa.gr.jp; internet www.jssa.gr.jp; Pres. MIKIO KATOH; Exec. Dir TAKEO YABE.

The Kozai Club: Tekko Bldg, 3-2-10, Nihonbashi Kayaba-cho, Chuo-ku, Tokyo 103-0025; tel. (3) 3669-4815; fax (3) 3667-0245; f. 1947; mems 39 mfrs, 69 dealers; Chair. AKIRA CHIHAYA.

Steel Castings and Forgings Association of Japan (JSCFA): Uchikanda DNK Bldg, 2-15-2, Uchikanda, Chiyoda-ku, Tokyo 101-0047; tel. (3) 3255-3961; fax (3) 3255-3965; e-mail jscfa@aqua.famille.ne.jp; f. 1972; mems 48 cos, 54 plants; Exec. Dir SADAO HARA.

Machinery and Precision Equipment

Electronic Industries Association of Japan: 3-2-2, Marunouchi, Chiyoda-ku, Tokyo 100-0005; tel. (3) 3213-5861; fax (3) 3213-5863; e-mail pao@eiaj.or.jp; internet www.eiaj.or.jp; f. 1948; 540 mems; Chair. FUMIO SATO.

Japan Camera Industry Association: JCII Bldg, 25, Ichibancho, Chiyoda-ku, Tokyo 102-0082; tel. (3) 5276-3891; fax (3) 5276-3893; f. 1954; Pres. FUJIO MITARAI.

Japan Clock and Watch Association: Kudan Sky Bldg, 1-12-11, Kudan-kita, Chiyoda-ku, Tokyo 102-0073; tel. (3) 5276-3411; fax (3) 5276-3414; Chair. CHUHICHI INOUE.

Japan Electric Association: 1-7-1, Yuraku-cho, Chiyoda-ku, Tokyo 100-0006; tel. (3) 3216-0551; fax (3) 3214-6005; f. 1921; 4,610 mems; Pres. TATSUO KAWAI.

Japan Electric Measuring Instruments Manufacturers' Association (JEMIMA): 1-9-10, Toranomon, Minato-ku, Tokyo 105-0001; tel. (3) 3502-0601; fax (3) 3502-0600; e-mail oshima-y@jemima.or.jp; internet www.jemima.or.jp; 143 mems; Gen. Man. YOSHIO OSHIMA.

Japan Electrical Manufacturers' Association: 2-4-15, Nagata-cho, Chiyoda-ku, Tokyo 100-0014; tel. (3) 3581-4841; fax (3) 3593-3198; f. 1948; 245 mems; Chair. TSUTOMU KANAI.

Japan Energy Association: Houwa Mita Tsunasaka Bldg, 2-7-7, Mita, Minato-ku, Tokyo 108-0073; tel. (3) 3451-1651; fax (3) 3451-1360; e-mail common@jea-wec.or.jp; internet www.jea-wec.or.jp; f. 1950; 143 mems; Chair. SHIGE-ETSU MIYAHARA; Exec. Dir HAJIME MURATA.

Japan Machine Tool Builders' Association: Kikai Shinko Bldg, 3-5-8, Shiba Koen, Minato-ku, Tokyo 105-0011; tel. (3) 3434-3961; fax (3) 3434-3763; f. 1951; 112 mems; Chair. TOYO KATO; Exec. Dir S. ABE.

Japan Machinery Center for Trade and Investment (JMC): Kikai Shinko Bldg, 3-5-8, Shiba Koen, Minato-ku, Tokyo 105-0011; tel. (3) 3431-9507; fax (3) 3436-6455; Pres. ISAO YONEKURA.

The Japan Machinery Federation: Kikai Shinko Bldg, 3-5-8, Shiba Koen, Minato-ku, Tokyo 105-0011; tel. (3) 3434-5381; fax (3) 3434-2666; f. 1952; Pres. SHOICHI SADA; Exec. Vice-Pres. SHINICHI NAKANISHI.

Japan Machinery Importers' Association: Koyo Bldg, 8th Floor, 1-2-11, Toranomon, Minato-ku, Tokyo 105-0001; tel. (3) 3503-9736; fax (3) 3503-9779; f. 1957; 94 mems; Pres. ISAO YONEKURA.

Japan Microscope Manufacturers' Association: c/o Olympus Optical Co Ltd, 2-43-2, Hatagaya, Shibuya-ku, Tokyo 151-0072; tel. (3) 3377-2139; fax (3) 3377-2139; e-mail jmma@olympus.co.jp; f. 1954; 31 mems; Chair. T. SHIMOYAMA.

Japan Motion Picture Equipment Industrial Association: Kikai Shinko Bldg, 3-5-8, Shiba Koen, Minato-ku, Tokyo 105; tel. (3) 3434-3911; fax (3) 3434-3912; Pres. MASAO SHIKATA; Gen. Sec. TERUHIRO KATO.

Japan Optical Industry Association: Kikai Shinko Bldg, 3-5-8, Shiba Koen, Minato-ku, Tokyo 105-0011; tel. (3) 3431-7073; f. 1946; 200 mems; Chair. SHIGEO ONO; Exec. Dir M. SUZUKI.

The Japan Society of Industrial Machinery Manufacturers: Kikai Shinko Bldg, 3-5-8, Shiba Koen, Minato-ku, Tokyo 105-0011; tel. (3) 3434-6821; fax (3) 3434-4767; e-mail obd@jsim.or.jp; internet www.jsim.or.jp; f. 1948; 213 mems; Exec. Man. Dir KOJI FUJISAKI; Pres. KENTARO AIKAWA.

Japan Textile Machinery Association: Kikai Shinko Bldg, Room 310, 3-5-8, Shiba Koen, Minato-ku, Tokyo 105; tel. (3) 3434-3821; fax (3) 3434-3043; f. 1951; Pres. YOSHITOSHI TOYODA.

Textiles

Central Raw Silk Association of Japan: 1-9-4, Yuraku-cho, Chiyoda-ku, Tokyo; tel. (3) 3214-5777; fax (3) 3214-5778.

Japan Chemical Fibers Association: Seni Kaikan, 3-1-11, Nihonbashi-Honcho, Chuo-ku, Tokyo 103-0023; tel. (3) 3241-2311; fax (3) 3246-0823; f. 1948; 43 mems, 13 assoc. mems; Pres. KAZUMOTO YAMAMOTO; Dir-Gen. KAZUHIKO MORIYA.

Japan Cotton and Staple Fibre Weavers' Association: 1-8-7, Nishi-Azabu, Minato-ku, Tokyo; tel. (3) 3403-9671.

Japan Silk Spinners' Association: f. 1948; 95 mem. firms; Chair. ICHIJI OHTANI.

Japan Spinners' Association: Mengyo Kaikan Bldg, 2-5-8, Bingo-machi, Chuo-ku, Osaka 541-0051; tel. (6) 6231-8431; fax (6) 6229-1590; e-mail spinas@cotton.or.jp; internet www.jsa-jp.org/; f. 1948; Exec. Dir KIYONORI MAYUMI.

Transport Machinery

Japan Association of Rolling Stock Industries: Awajicho Suny Bldg, 1-2, Kanda-Sudacho, Chiyoda-ku, Tokyo 101-0041; tel. (3) 3257-1901.

Japan Auto Parts Industries Association: 1-16-15, Takanawa, Minato-ku, Tokyo 108-0074; tel. (3) 3445-4211; fax (3) 3447-5372; e-mail japiaint@green.am.egg.or.jp; f. 1948; 530 mem. firms; Chair. TSUNEO ISHIMARU; Exec. Dir K. SHIBASAKI.

Japan Automobile Manufacturers Association, Inc: Otemachi Bldg, 1-6-1, Otemachi, Chiyoda-ku, Tokyo 100-0004; tel. (3) 5219-6651; fax (3) 3287-2072; f. 1967; 13 mem. firms; Chair. YOSHIFUMI TSUJI; Exec. Man. Dir TAKAO TOMINAGA.

Japan Bicycle Manufacturers' Association: 1-9-3, Akasaka, Minato-ku, Tokyo 107; tel. (3) 3583-3123; fax (3) 3589-3125; f. 1955.

Japan Ship Exporters' Association: Nippon-Zaidan Bldg, 1-15-16, Toranomon, Minato-ku, Tokyo 105-0001; tel. (3) 3502-2094; fax (3) 3508-2058; e-mail postmaster@jsea.or.jp; 38 mems; Exec. Man. Dir YUICHI WATANABE.

Japanese Marine Equipment Association: Bansui Bldg, 1-5-16, Toranomon, Minato-ku, Tokyo 105-0001; tel. (3) 3502-2041; fax (3) 3591-2206; e-mail info@jsmea.or.jp; internet www.jsmea.or.jp; f. 1956; 240 mems; Pres. TADAO YAMAOKA.

Japanese Shipowners' Association: Kaiun Bldg, 2-6-4, Hirakawa-cho, Chiyoda-ku, Tokyo 102-0093; tel. (3) 3264-7171; fax (3) 3262-4760; Pres. KENTARO KAWAMURA.

Shipbuilders' Association of Japan: 1-15-16, Toranomon, Minato-ku, Tokyo 105-0001; tel. (3) 3502-2010; fax (3) 3502-2816; f. 1947; 21 mems; Chair. TOSHIO KAMEI; Exec. Man. Dir NOBUTAKA NAMBU.

Society of Japanese Aerospace Companies Inc (SJAC): Toshin-Tameike Bldg, 2nd Floor, 1-1-14, Akasaka, Minato-ku, Tokyo 107-0052; tel. (3) 3585-0511; fax (3) 3585-0541; e-mail miwas@interlink.or.jp; internet www.sjac.or.jp/; f. 1952; reorg. 1974; 125 mems, 40 assoc. mems; Chair. TOSHIFUMI TAKEI; Pres. TAKATOSHI HOSOYA.

Miscellaneous

Communications Industry Association of Japan (CIA-J): Sankei Bldg, 1-7-2, Otemachi, Chiyoda-ku, Tokyo 100-0004; tel. (3) 3231-3005; fax (3) 3231-3110; e-mail admin@ciaj.or.jp; internet www.ciaj.or.jp; f. 1948; non-profit org. of telecommunications equipment mfrs; 236 mems; Chair. TADASHI SEKIZAWA; Pres. YUTAKA HAYASHI.

Japan Canners' Association: Yurakuchu Denki Bldg, 1-7-1, Yuraku-cho, Chiyoda-ku, Tokyo 100-0006; tel. (3) 3213-4751; fax (3) 3211-1430; Pres. KEINOSUKE HISAI.

Japan Hardwood Exporters' Association: Matsuda Bldg, 1-9-1, Ironai, Otaru, Hokkaido 047; tel. (134) 23-8411; fax (134) 22-7150; 7 mems.

Japan Lumber Importers' Association: Yushi Kogyo Bldg, 3-13-11, Nihonbashi, Chuo-ku, Tokyo 103; tel. (3) 3271-0926; fax (3) 3271-0928; f. 1950; 130 mems; Pres. SHOICHI TANAKA.

Japan Plastics Industry Federation: Kaseihin-Kaikan, 5-8-17, Roppongi, Minato-ku, Tokyo 106-0032; tel. (3) 3586-9761; fax (3) 3586-9760; Chair. HIDEO MORI.

Japan Plywood Manufacturers' Association: Meisan Bldg, 1-18-17, Nishi-Shimbashi, Minato-ku, Tokyo 105; tel. (3) 3591-9246; fax (3) 3591-9240; f. 1965; 92 mems; Pres. HIROSHI INOUE.

Japan Pottery Manufacturers' Federation: Toto Bldg, 1-1-28, Toranomon, Minato-ku, Tokyo; tel. (3) 3503-6761.

The Japan Rubber Manufacturers Association: Tobu Bldg, 1-5-26, Moto Akasaka, Minato-ku, Tokyo 107-0051; tel. (3) 3408-7101; fax (3) 3408-7106; f. 1950; 132 mems; Pres. YOICHIRO KAIZAKI.

Japan Spirits and Liquors Makers' Association: Koura Dai-ichi Bldg, 7th Floor, 1-1-6, Nihonbashi-Kayaba-cho, Chuo-ku, Tokyo 103; tel. (3) 3668-4621.

Japan Sugar Import and Export Council: Osima Bldg 1-3, Nihonbashi Koamicho, Chuo-ku, Tokyo; tel. (3) 3571-2362; fax (3) 3571-2363; 16 mems.

Japan Sugar Refiners' Association: 5-7, Sanban-cho, Chiyoda-ku, Tokyo 102; tel. (3) 3288-1151; fax (3) 3288-3399; f. 1949; 17 mems; Sr Man. Dir KATSUYUKI SUZUKI.

Japan Tea Exporters' Association: 17, Kitaban-cho, Shizuoka, Shizuoka Prefecture 420-0005; tel. (54) 271-3428; fax (54) 271-2177; e-mail japantea@nyc.odn.ne.jp; 32 mems.

Japan Toy Association: 4-22-4, Higashi-Komagata, Sumida-ku, Tokyo 130; tel. (3) 3829-2513; fax (3) 3829-2549; Chair. MAKOTO YAMA-SHINA.

Motion Picture Producers' Association of Japan, Inc: Tokyu Ginza Bldg, 2-15-2, Ginza, Chuo-ku, Tokyo 104-0061; tel. (3) 3547-1800; fax (3) 3547-0909; e-mail eiren@mc.neweb.ne.jp; internet www2.neweb.ne.jp/wd/eiren; Pres. ISAO MATSUOKA.

EMPLOYERS' ORGANIZATION

Japan Federation of Employers' Associations (Nikkeiren) (Nihon Keieisha Dantai Renmei): Palace Bldg, 6/F, 1-1, Marunouchi, 1-chome, Chiyoda-ku, Tokyo 100-0005; tel. (3) 3213-4454; fax (3) 3213-4455; e-mail intldiv@nikkeiren.or.jp; f. 1948; to merge with the Japan Federation of Economic Organizations (KEIDANREN) in May 2001; 108 mem. asscns; Chair. HIROSHI OKUDA; Dir-Gen. MICHIO FUKUOKA.

UTILITIES

Electricity

Chubu Electric Power Co Inc: 1, Higashi-Shincho, Higashi-ku, Nagoya 461-8680; tel. (52) 951-8211; fax (52) 962-4624; internet www.chuden.co.jp; Chair. KOHEI ABE; Pres. HIROJI OTA.

Chugoku Electric Power Co Inc: 4-33, Komachi, Naka-ku, Hiroshima 730-8701; tel. (82) 241-0211; fax (82) 523-6185; e-mail angel@inet.energia.co.jp; internet www.energia.co.jp; f. 1951; Chair. KOKI TADA; Pres. SHITOMI TAKASU.

Hokkaido Electric Power Co Inc: internet www.hepco.co.jp; Chair. KAZUO TODA; Pres. SEIJI IZUMI.

Hokuriku Electric Power Co Inc: internet www.rikuden.co.jp.

Kansai Electric Power Co Inc: 3-3-22, Nakanoshima, Kita-ku, Osaka 530-8270; tel. (6) 6441-8821; fax (6) 6441-8598; e-mail postmaster@kepco.co.jp; internet www.kepco.co.jp; Chair. YOSHIHISA AKIYAMA; Pres. H. ISHIKAWA.

Kyushu Electric Power Co Inc: 2-1-82, Watanabe-dori, Chuo-ku, Fukuoka 810-8726; tel. (92) 726-1649; fax (92) 731-8719; internet www.kyuden.co.jp; ; Chair. MICHISADA KAMATA.

Shikoku Electric Power Co Inc: 2-5, Marunouchi, Takamatsu 760-8573; tel. (878) 21-5061; fax (878) 26-1250; e-mail postmaster@yonden.co.jp; internet www.yonden.co.jp; Chair. HIROSHI YAMAMOTO; Pres. KOZO KONDO.

Tohoku Electric Power Co Inc: 3-7-1, Ichiban-cho, Aoba-ku, Sendai 980; tel. (22) 225-2111; fax (22) 222-2881; e-mail webmaster@tohoku-epco.co.jp; internet www.tohoku-epco.co.jp; Chair. TERUYUKI AKEMA; Pres. TOSHIAKI YASHIMA.

Tokyo Electric Power Co Inc: 1-1-3, Uchisaiwai-cho, Chiyoda-ku, Tokyo 100; tel. (3) 3501-8111; fax (3) 3592-1795; internet www.tepco.co.jp; Chair. SHOH NASU; Pres. N. MINAMI.

Gas

Osaka Gas Co Ltd: e-mail intlstaff@osakagas.co.jp; internet www.osakagas.co.jp.

Toho Gas Co Ltd: 19-18, Sakurada-cho, Atsuta-ko, Nagoya 456; tel. (52) 871-3511; internet www.tohogas.co.jp; f. 1922; Chair SUSUMU OGAWA; Pres. SADAHIKO SIMIZU.

Tokyo Gas Co Inc: 1-5-20, Kaigan, Minato-ku, Tokyo 105; tel. (3) 3433-2111; fax (3) 5472-5385; internet www.tokyo-gas.co.jp; f. 1885; Chair. HIROSHI WATANABE; Pres. H. UEHARA.

CO-OPERATIVE ORGANIZATION

Nikkenkyo (Council of Japan Construction Industry Employees' Unions): Moriyama Bldg, 1-31-16, Takadanobaba, Shinjuku-ku, Tokyo 169; tel. (3) 5285-3870; fax (3) 5285-3879; Pres. NOBORU SEKIGUCHI.

TRADE UNIONS

A feature of Japan's trade union movement is that the unions are usually based on single enterprises, embracing workers of different occupations in that enterprise. In June 1994 there were 32,581 unions; union membership stood at 12.5m. workers in 1996. In November 1989 the two largest confederations, SOHYO and RENGO, merged to form the Japan Trade Union Confederation (JTUC–RENGO).

Japanese Trade Union Confederation (JTUC–RENGO): 3-2-11, Kanda Surugadai, Chiyoda-ku, Tokyo 101-0062; tel. (3) 5295-0526; fax (3) 5295-0548; e-mail jtuc-kokusai@sv.rengo-net.or.jp;

internet www.jtuc-rengo.or.jp; f. 1989; 7.7m. mems; Pres. ETSUYA WASHIO.

Principal Affiliated Unions

Ceramics Rengo (All-Japan Federation of Ceramics Industry Workers): 3-11, Heigocho, Mizuho-ku, Nagoya-shi, Aichi 467; tel. (52) 882-4562; fax (52) 882-9960; 30,083 mems; Pres. TSUNEYOSHI HAYAKAWA.

Chain Rokyo (Chain-store Labour Unions' Council): 3rd Floor, 2-29-8, Higashi-ikebukuro, Toshima-ku, Tokyo 170; tel. (3) 5951-1031; fax (3) 5951-1051; 40,015 mems; Pres. TOSHIFUMI HIRANO.

CSG Rengo (Japanese Federation of Chemical, Service and General Workers' Unions): Yuai Bldg, 8th Floor, 2-20-12, Shiba, Minato-ku, Tokyo 105; tel. (3) 3453-3801; fax (3) 3454-2236; f. 1951; 228,137 mems; Pres. DAISAKU KOUCHIYAMA.

Denki Rengo (Japanese Electrical, Electronic & Information Union): Denkirengo Bldg, 1-10-3, Mita, Minato-ku, Tokyo 108-8326; tel. (3) 3455-6911; fax (3) 3452-5406; internet www.jeiu.or.jp/index; f. 1953; 810,000 mems; Pres. KATSUTOSHI SUZUKI.

Denryoku Soren (Federation of Electric Power Related Industry Workers' Unions of Japan): Shiba 2nd AMEREX Bldg, 4th Floor, 4-5-10, Shiba, Minato-ku, Tokyo 108-0014; tel. (3) 3454-0231; fax (3) 3798-1470; 258,935 mems; Pres. JIRO TERADA.

Dokiro (Hokkaido Seasonal Workers' Union): Hokuro Bldg, Kita 4, Nishi 12, Chuo-ku, Sapporo, Hokkaido 060; tel. (11) 261-5775; fax (11) 272-2255; 19,063 mems; Pres. YOSHIZO ODAWARA.

Gomu Rengo (Japanese Rubber Workers' Union Confederation): 2-3-3, Mejiro, Toshima-ku, Tokyo 171; tel. (3) 3984-3343; fax (3) 3984-5862; 60,070 mems; Pres. YASUO FURUKAWA.

Hitetsu Rengo (Japanese Metal Mine Workers' Union): Gotanda Metalion Bldg, 5-21-15, Higashi-gotanda, Shinagawa-ku, Tokyo 141; tel. (3) 5420-1881; fax (3) 5420-1880; 23,500 mems; Pres. SHOUZOU HIMENO.

Insatsu Roren (Federation of Printing Information Media Workers' Unions): Yuai-kaikan, 7th Floor, 2-20-12, Shiba, Minato-ku, Tokyo 105-0014; tel. (3) 5442-0191; fax (3) 5442-0219; 22,303 mems; Pres. HIROFUMI NAKABAYASHI.

JA Rengo (All-Japan Agriculture Co-operative Staff Members' Union): 964-1, Toyotomicho-mikage, Himeji-shi, Hyogo 679-21; tel. and fax (792) 64-3618; 2,772 mems; Pres. YUTAKA OKADA.

Jichi Roren (National Federation of Prefectural and Municipal Workers' Unions): 1-15-22, Oji-honcho, Kita-ku, Tokyo 114; tel. and fax (3) 3907-1584; 5,728 mems; Pres. NOBUO UENO.

Jichiro (All-Japan Prefectural and Municipal Workers' Union): Jichiro Bldg, 1, Rokubancho, Chiyoda-ku, Tokyo 102-0085; tel. (3) 3263-0263; fax (3) 5210-7422; f. 1951; 1,030,000 mems; Pres. MORISHIGE GOTO.

Jidosha Soren (Confederation of Japan Automobile Workers' Unions): U-Life Center, 1-4-26, Kaigan, Minato-ku, Tokyo 105-8523; tel. (3) 3434-7641; fax (3) 3434-7428; internet www.jaw.or.jp; f. 1972; 778,000 mems; Pres. TADAYOSHI KUSANO.

Jiunro (Japan Automobile Drivers' Union): 2-3-12, Nakameguro, Meguro-ku, Tokyo 153; tel. (3) 3711-9387; fax (3) 3719-2624; 1,958 mems; Pres. SADAO KANEZUKA.

JR-Rengo (Japan Railway Trade Unions Confederation): TOKO Bldg, 9th Floor, 1-8-10, Nihonbashi-muromachi, Chuo-ku, Tokyo 103; tel. (3) 3270-4590; fax (3) 3270-4429; 78,418 mems; Pres. KAZUAKI KUZUNO.

JR Soren (Japan Confederation of Railway Workers' Unions): Meguro-satsuki Bldg, 3-2-13, Nishi-gotanda, Shinagawa-ku, Tokyo 141-0031; tel. (3) 3491-7191; fax (3) 3491-7192; 93,000 mems; Pres. MITUMARU SHIBATA.

Jyoho Roren (Japan Federation of Telecommunications, Electronic Information and Allied Workers): Zendentsu-rodo Bldg, 3-6, Kanda Surugadai, Chiyoda-ku, Tokyo 101-0062; tel. (3) 3219-2231; fax (3) 3253-3268; 265,132 mems; Pres. KAZUO SASAMORI.

Kagaku League 21 (Japanese Federation of Chemistry Workers' Unions): Senbai Bldg, 5-26-30, Shiba, Minato-ku, Tokyo 108-8389; tel. (3) 3452-5591; fax (3) 3454-7464; formed by merger of Goka Roren and Zenkoku Kagaku; 104,000 mems; Pres. KATUTOSHI KATO.

Kagaku Soren (Japanese Federation of Chemical Workers' Unions): Kyodo Bldg, 7th Floor, 2-4-10, Higashi-shinbashi, Minato-ku, Tokyo 105; tel. (3) 5401-2268; fax (3) 5401-2263; Pres. HIROKAZU IWASAKI.

Kaiin Kumiai (All-Japan Seamen's Union): 7-15-26, Roppongi, Minato-ku, Tokyo 106-0032; tel. (3) 5410-8330; fax (3) 5410-8336; 40,000 mems; Pres. SAKAE IDEMOTO.

Kamipa Rengo (Japanese Federation of Pulp and Paper Workers' Unions): 2-12-4, Kita Aoyama, Minato-ku, Tokyo 107-0061; tel. (3) 3402-7656; fax (3) 3402-7659; 50,858 mems; Pres. TUNEO MUKAI.

Kensetsu Rengo (Japan Construction Trade Union Confederation): Yuai Bldg, 7th Floor, 2-20-12, Shiba, Minato-ku, Tokyo 105; tel. (3)

3454-0951; fax (3) 3453-0582; 13,199 mems; Pres. MASAYASU TERA-SAWA.

Kinzoku Kikai (National Metal and Machinery Workers' Unions of Japan): 6-2, Sakuraokacho, Shibuya-ku, Tokyo 150-0031; tel. (3) 3463-4231; fax (3) 3463-7391; f. 1989; 205,082 mems; Pres. MASAOKI KITAURA.

Kokko Soren (Japan General Federation of National Public Service Employees' Unions): 1-2-1, Kasumigaseki, Chiyoda-ku, Tokyo 100; tel. (3) 3508-4990; fax (3) 5512-7555; 40,370 mems; Pres. MARU-YAMA KENZO.

Koku Domei (Japanese Confederation of Aviation Labour): Nikko-kiso Bldg, 2nd Floor, 1-6-3, Haneda-kuko, Ota-ku, Tokyo 144; tel. (3) 3747-7642; fax (3) 3747-7647; 16,310 mems; Pres. KATSUMI UTAGAWA.

Kokuzei Roso (Japanese Confederation of National Tax Unions): R154, Okurasho Bldg, 3-1-1, Kasumigaseki, Chiyoda-ku, Tokyo 100; tel. (3) 3581-2573; fax (3) 3581-3843; 40,128 mems; Pres. TATSUO SASAKI.

Kotsu Roren (Japan Federation of Transport Workers' Unions): Yuai Bldg, 3rd Floor, 2-20-12, Shiba, Minato-ku 105-0014; tel. (3) 3451-7243; fax (3) 3454-7393; 97,239 mems; Pres. SHIGEO MAKI.

Koun-Domei (Japanese Confederation of Port and Transport Workers' Unions): 5-10-2, Kamata, Ota-ku, Tokyo 144-0052; tel. (3) 3733-5285; fax (3) 3733-5280; f. 1987; 1,888 mems; Pres. SHOSHIRO NAKANISHI.

Leisure Service Rengo (Japan Federation of Leisure Service Industries Workers' Unions): Zosen Bldg, 4th Floor, 3-5-6, Misaki-cho, Chiyoda-ku, Tokyo 101-0061; tel. (3) 3230-1724; fax (3) 3239-1553; 47,601 mems; Pres. HIROSHI SAWADA.

NHK Roren (Federation of All-NHK Labour Unions): NHK, 2-2-1, Jinnan, Shibuya-ku, Tokyo 150; tel. (3) 3485-6007; fax (3) 3469-9271; 12,526 mems; Pres. YASUZO SUDO.

Nichirinro (National Forest Workers' Union of Japan): 1-2-1, Kasu-migaseki, Chiyoda-ku, Tokyo 100; tel. (3) 3580-8891; fax (3) 3580-1596; Pres. KOH IKEGAMI.

Nikkyoso (Japan Teachers' Union): Japan Education Hall, 2-6-2, Hitotsubashi, Chiyoda-ku, Tokyo 101-0003; tel. (3) 3265-2171; fax (3) 3230-0172; internet www.jtu-net.or.jp; f. 1947; 377,014 mems; Pres. NAGAKAZU SAKAKIBARA.

Rosai Roren (National Federation of Zenrosai Workers' Unions): 2-12-10, Yoyogi, Shibuya-ku, Tokyo 151; tel. (3) 3299-0161; fax (3) 3299-0126; 2,091 mems; Pres. TADASHI TAKACHI.

Seiho Roren (National Federation of Life Insurance Workers' Unions): Tanaka Bldg, 3-19-5, Yushima, Bunkyo-ku, Tokyo 113-0034; tel. (3) 3837-2031; fax (3) 3837-2037; 414,021 mems; Pres. YOHTARU KOHNO.

Seiroren (Labour Federation of Government Related Organiza-tions): Hasaka Bldg, 4th-6th Floors, 1-10-3, Kanda-ogawacho, Chi-yoda-ku, Tokyo 101; tel. (3) 5295-6360; fax (3) 5295-6362; Chair. MITSURU WATANABE.

Sekiyu Roren (Japan Confederation of Petroleum Industry Workers' Union): NKK Bldg, 7th Floor, 2-18-2, Nishi-shinbashi, Minato-ku, Tokyo 105; tel. (3) 3578-1315; fax (3) 3578-3455; 28,807 mems; Pres. HIROSHI MOCHIMARU.

Sen'i Seikatsu Roren (Japan Federation of Textile Clothing Workers' Unions of Japan): Katakura Bldg, 3-1-2, Kyobashi, Chuo-ku, Tokyo 104; tel. (3) 3281-4806; fax (3) 3274-3165; 4,598 mems; Pres. KATSUYOSHI SAKAI.

Shigen Roren (Federation of Japanese Metal Resources Workers' Unions): Roppongi Azeria Bldg, 1-3-8, Nishi-azabu, Minato-ku, Tokyo 106; tel. (3) 3402-6666; fax (3) 3402-6667; Pres. MINORU TAKAHASHI.

Shin Unten (F10-Drivers' Craft Union): 4th Floor, 3-25-6, Negishi, Taito-ku, Tokyo 110; tel. (3) 5603-1015; fax (3) 5603-5351; 4,435 mems; Pres. SHOHEI SHINOZAKI.

Shinkagaku (National Organization of All Chemical Workers): MF Bldg, 2nd Floor, 2-3-3, Fujimi, Chiyoda-ku, Tokyo 102; tel. (3) 3239-2933; fax (3) 3239-2932; 8,400 mems; Pres. HISASHI YASUI.

Shinrin Roren (Japanese Federation of Forest and Wood Workers' Unions): 3-28-7, Otsuka, Bunkyo-ku, Tokyo 112; tel. (3) 3945-6385; fax (3) 3945-6477; 13,928 mems; Pres. AGATSUMA MINORU.

Shitetsu Soren (General Federation of Private Railway Workers' Unions): 4-3-5, Takanawa, Minato-ku, Tokyo 108-0074; tel. (3) 3473-0166; fax (3) 3447-3927; f. 1947; 140,179 mems; Pres. RYOICHI IKE-MURA.

Shogyo Roren (Japan Federation of Commercial Workers' Unions): New State Manor Bldg, 3rd Floor, 2-23-1, Yoyogi, Shibuya-ku, Tokyo 151-0053; tel. (3) 3370-4121; fax (3) 3370-1640; 120,000 mems; Pres. MITSUO NAGUMO.

Shokuhin Rengo (Japan Federation of Foods and Tobacco Workers' Unions): Hiroo Office Bldg, 8th Floor, 1-3-18, Hiroo, Shibuya-ku, Tokyo 150; tel. (3) 3446-2082; fax (3) 3446-6779; f. 1991; 116,370 mems; Pres. SHIGERU MASUDA.

Shokuhin Rokyo (Food Industry Workers' Union Council (FIWUC)): ST Bldg, 6th Floor, 4-9-4, Hatchyoubori, Chuo-ku, Tokyo 104; tel. (3) 3555-7671; fax (3) 3555-7760; Pres. TAROU FUJIE.

Sonpo Roren (Federation of Non-Life Insurance Workers' Unions of Japan): Kanda MS Bldg, 4th Floor, 27, Kanda-higashimatsushi-tacho, Chiyoda-ku, Tokyo 101; tel. (3) 5295-0071; fax (3) 5295-0073; Pres. KUNIO MATSUMOTO.

Tanro (Japan Coal Miners' Union): Hokkaido Rodosha Bldg, 2nd Floor, Kita-11, Nishi-4, Kita-ku, Sapporo-shi, Hokkaido 001; tel. (11) 717-0291; fax (11) 717-0295; 1,353 mems; Pres. KAZUO SAKUMA.

Tanshokukyo (Association of Japan Coal Mining Staff Unions): 2-30, Nishiminatomachi, Omuta-shi, Fukuoka 836; tel. (944) 52-3883; fax (944) 52-3853; Pres. KEIZO UMEKI.

Tekko Roren (Japan Federation of Steel Workers' Unions): I&S Riverside Bldg, 4th Floor, 1-23-4, Shinkawa, Chuo-ku, Tokyo 104-0033; tel. (3) 3555-0401; fax (3) 3555-0407; 150,000 mems; Pres. TAKESHI OGINO.

Tokei Roso (Statistics Labour Union Management and Co-ordina-tion Agency): 19-1, Somucho, Wakamatsucho, Shinjuku-ku, Tokyo 162; tel. (3) 3202-1111; fax (3) 3205-3850; Pres. TOSHIAKI MAGARA.

Toshiko (The All-Japan Municipal Transport Workers' Union): 3-1-35, Shibaura, Minato-ku, Tokyo 108; tel. (3) 3451-5221; fax (3) 3452-2977; 43,612 mems; Pres. SHUNICHI SUZUKI.

Unyu Roren (All-Japan Federation of Transport Workers' Union): Zennittsu Kasumigaseki Bldg, 5th Floor, 3-3-3, Kasumigaseki, Chi-yoda-ku, Tokyo 100-0013; tel. (3) 3503-2171; fax (3) 3503-2176; f. 1968; 143,084 mems; Pres. KAZUMARO SUZUKI.

Zeikan Roren (Federation of Japanese Customs Personnel Labour Unions): 3-1-1, Kasumigaseki, Chiyoda-ku, Tokyo 100; tel. and fax (3) 3593-1788; Pres. RIKIO SUDO.

Zen Insatsu (All-Printing Agency Workers' Union): 3-59-12, Nishi-gahara, Kita-ku, Tokyo 114; tel. (3) 3910-7131; fax (3) 3910-7155; 5,431 mems; Chair. TOSHIO KATAKURA.

Zen Yusei (All-Japan Postal Labour Union): 1-20-6, Sendagaya, Shibuya-ku, Tokyo 151; tel. (3) 3478-7101; fax (3) 5474-7085; 77,573 mems; Pres. NOBUAKI IZAWA.

Zenchuro (All-Japan Garrison Forces Labour Union): 3-41-8, Shiba, Minato-ku, Tokyo 105; tel. (3) 3455-5971; fax (3) 3455-5973; Pres. EIBUN MEDORUMA.

Zendensen (All- Japan Electric Wire Labour Union): 1-11-6, Hatan-odai, Shinagawa-ku, Tokyo 142; tel. (3) 3785-2991; fax (3) 3785-2995; Pres. NAOKI TOKUNAGA.

Zen-eien (National Cinema and Theatre Workers' Union): Hibiya Park Bldg, 1-8-1, Yurakucho, Chiyoda-ku, Tokyo 100; tel. (3) 3201-4476; fax (3) 3214-0597; Pres. SADAHIRO MATSUURA.

Zengin Rengo (All-Japan Federative Council of Bank Labour Unions): R904, Kyodo Bldg, 16-8, Nihonbashi-Kodenmacho, Chuo-ku, Tokyo 103; tel. and fax (3) 3661-4886; 32,104 mems; Pres. KIKUO HATTORI.

Zenjiko Roren (National Federation of Automobile Transport Wor-kers' Unions): 3-7-9, Sendagaya, Shibuya-ku, Tokyo 151; tel. (3) 3408-0875; fax (3) 3497-0107; Pres. OSAMU MIMASHI.

Zenkairen (All-Japan Shipping Labour Union): Shinbashi Ekimae Bldg, No. 1, 8th Floor, 2-20-15, Shinbashi, Minato-ku, Tokyo 105; tel. (3) 3573-2401; fax (3) 3573-2404; Chair. MASAHIKO SATO.

Zenkin Rengo (Japanese Federation of Metal Industry Unions): Yuai Bldg, 5th Floor, 2-20-12, Shiba, Minato-ku, Tokyo 105-0014; tel. (3) 3451-2141; fax (3) 3452-0239; f. 1989; 310,818 mems; Pres. MITSURO HATTORI.

Zenkoku Gas (Federation of Gas Workers' Unions of Japan): 5-11-1, Omori-nishi, Ota-ku, Tokyo 143; tel. (3) 5493-8381; fax (3) 5493-8216; 31,499 mems; Pres. AKIO HAMAUZU.

Zenkoku Keiba Rengo (National Federation of Horse-racing Workers): 2500, Mikoma, Miho-mura, Inashiki-gun, Ibaragi 300-04; tel. (298) 85-0402; fax (298) 85-0416; Pres. TOYOHIKO OKUMURA.

Zenkoku Nodanro (National Federation of Agricultural, Forestry and Fishery Corporations' Workers' Unions): 1-5-8, Hamamatsu-cho, Minato-ku, Tokyo 105; tel. (3) 3437-0931; fax (3) 3437-0681; 26,010 mems; Pres. SHIN-ICHIRO OKADA.

Zenkoku Semento (National Federation of Cement Workers' Unions of Japan): 5-29-2, Shinbashi, Minato-ku, Tokyo 105; tel. (3) 3436-3666; fax (3) 3436-3668; Pres. KIYONORI URAKAWA.

Zenkoku-Ippan (National Council of General Amalgamated Workers' Unions): Zosen Bldg, 5th Floor, 3-5-6, Misakicho, Chiyoda-ku, Tokyo 101-0061; tel. (3) 3230-4071; fax (3) 3230-4360; 54,708 mems; Pres. YASUHIKO SATO.

Zenkyoro (National Race Workers' Union): Nihon Kyoiku Kaikan, 7th Floor, 2-6-2, Hitotsubashi, Chiyoda-ku, Tokyo 101; tel. (3) 5210-5156; fax (3) 5210-5157; 24,720 mems; Pres. SHIMAKO YOSHIDA.

Zennitto (Japan Painting Workers' Union): Shin-osaka Communi-cation Plaza, 1st Floor, 1-6-36, Nishi-miyahara, Yodogawa-ku,

Osaka-shi, Osaka 532; tel. (6) 6393-8677; fax (6) 6393-8533; Pres. SEIICHI UOZA.

Zenrokin (Federation of Labour Bank Workers' Unions of Japan): Nakano Bldg, 3rd Floor, 1-11, Kanda-Awajicho, Chiyoda-ku, Tokyo 101; tel. (3) 3256-1015; fax (3) 3256-1045; Pres. EIICHI KAKU.

Zensen (Japanese Federation of Textile, Garment, Chemical, Commercial, Food and Allied Industries Workers' Unions): 4-8-16, Kudanminami, Chiyoda-ku, Tokyo 102-0074; tel. (3) 3288-3723; fax (3) 3288-3728; e-mail kokusai@zensen.or.jp; f. 1946; 1,246 affiliates; 619,901 mems; Pres. TSUYOSHI TAKAGI.

Zensuido (All-Japan Water Supply Workers' Union): 1-4-1, Hongo, Bunkyo-ku, Tokyo 113; tel. (3) 3816-4132; fax (3) 3818-1430; 33,522 mems; Pres. KAZUMASA KATO.

Zentanko (National Union of Coal Mine Workers): Yuai Bldg, 6th Floor, 2-20-12, Shiba, Minato-ku, Tokyo 105; tel. (3) 3453-4721; fax (3) 3453-6457; Pres. AKIRA YASUNAGA.

Zentei (Japan Postal Workers' Union): 1-2-7, Koraku, Bunkyo-ku, Tokyo 112-0004; tel. (3) 3812-4260; fax (3) 5684-7201; 156,784 mems; Pres. SUSUMU TAKATO.

Zenzohei (All-Mint Labour Union): 1-1-79, Temma, Kita-ku, Osaka-shi, Osaka 530; tel. and fax (6) 6354-2389; Pres. CHIKASHI HIGUCHI.

Zenzosen-kikai (All-Japan Shipbuilding and Engineering Union): Zosen Bldg, 6th Floor, 3-5-6, Misakicho, Chiyoda-ku, Tokyo 101; tel. (3) 3265-1921; fax (3) 3265-1870; Pres. YOSHIMI FUNATSU.

Zosen Juki Roren (Japan Confederation of Shipbuilding and Engineering Workers' Unions): Yuai Kaikan Bldg, 4th Floor, 2-20-12, Shiba, Minato-ku, Tokyo 105-0014; tel. (3) 3451-6783; fax (3) 3451-6935; e-mail zosenjuki@mth.biglobe.ne.jp; 116,844 mems; Pres. MASAYUKI YOSHII.

Transport

RAILWAYS

Japan Railways (JR) Group: 1-6-5, Marunouchi, Chiyoda-ku, Tokyo 100-0005; tel. (3) 3215-9649; fax (3) 3213-5291; internet www.japanrail.com; fmrly the state-controlled Japanese National Railways (JNR); reorg. and transferred to private-sector control in 1987; the high-speed Shinkansen rail network consists of the Tokaido line (Tokyo to Shin-Osaka, 552.6 km), the Sanyo line (Shin-Osaka to Hakata, 623.3 km), the Tohoku line (Tokyo to Morioka, 535.3 km) and the Joetsu line (Omiya to Niigata, 303.6 km). The 4-km link between Ueno and Tokyo stations was opened in June 1991. The Yamagata Shinkansen (Fukushima to Yamagata, 87 km) was converted in 1992 from a conventional railway line. It is operated as a branch of the Tohoku Shinkansen with through trains from Tokyo, though not at full Shinkansen speeds. In 1997 the total railway route length was about 36,634 km.

Central Japan Railway Co: Yaesu Center Bldg, 1-6-6, Yaesu, Chuo-ku, Tokyo 103-8288; tel. (3) 3274-9727; fax (3) 5255-6780; e-mail jrtt@mxa.mesh.ne.jp; internet www.jr-central.co.jp; scheduled for privatization in 2001; Chair. HIROSHI SUDA; Pres. YOSHIYUKI KASAI.

East Japan Railway Co: 2-2-2, Yoyogi, Shibuya-ku, Tokyo 151-8578; tel. (3) 5334-1151; fax (3) 5334-1110; internet www.jreast.co.jp; scheduled for privatization in 2001; Chair. S. YAMANOUCHI; Pres. MASATAKE MATSUDA.

Hokkaido Railway Co: West 15-chome, Kita 11-jo, Chuo-ku, Sapporo 060-8644; tel. (11) 700-5717; fax (11) 700-5719; e-mail keieki@jrhokkaido.co.jp; internet www.jrhokkaido.co.jp; Chair. YOSHIHIRO OHMORI; Pres. SHINICHI SAKAMOTO.

Japan Freight Railway Co: 2-3-19, Koraku, Bynkyo-ku, Tokyo 112-0004; tel. (3) 3816-9722; internet www.jrfreight.co.jp; Chair. MASASHI HASHIMOTO; Pres. YASUSHI TANAHASHI.

Kyushu Railway Co: 1-1, Hakataeki-Chuogai, Hakata-ku, Fukuoka 812-8566; tel. (92) 474-2501; fax (92) 474-9745; internet www.jrkyushu.co.jp; Chair. Y. ISHII; Pres. K. TANAKA.

Shikoku Railway Co: 8-33, Hamano-cho, Takamatsu, Kagawa 760-8580; tel. (87) 825-1622; fax (87) 825-1623; internet www.jr-shikoku.co.jp; Chair. HIROATSU ITO; Pres. TOSHIYUKI UMEHARA.

West Japan Railway Co: 2-4-24, Shibata, Kita-ku, Osaka 530-8341; tel. (6) 6375-8981; fax (6) 6375-8919; e-mail wjr01020@mxy.meshnet.or.jp; internet www.westjr.co.jp; scheduled for privatization in 2001; Chair. MASATAKA IDE; Pres. SHOJIRO NANYA.

Other Principal Private Companies

Hankyu Corpn: 1-16-1, Shibata, Kita-ku, Osaka 530-8389; tel. (6) 6373-5092; fax (6) 6373-5670; e-mail koho@hankyu.co.jp; internet www.hankyu.co.jp; f. 1907; links Osaka, Kyoto, Kobe and Takarazuka; Chair. KOHEI KOBAYASHI; Pres. T. OHASHI.

Hanshin Electric Railway Co Ltd: 1-1-24, Ebie, Fukushima-ku, Osaka 553; tel. (6) 6457-2123; f. 1899; Chair. S. KUMA; Pres. M. TEZUKA.

Keihan Electric Railway Co Ltd: 1-2-27, Shiromi, Chuo-ku, Osaka 540; tel. (6) 6944-2521; fax (6) 6944-2501; internet www.keihan.co.jp; f. 1906; Chair. MINORU MIYASHITA; Pres. A. KIMBA.

Keihin Express Electric Railway Co Ltd: 2-20-20, Takanawa, Minato-ku, Tokyo 108-8625; tel. (3) 3280-9120; fax (3) 3280-9199; internet www.keikyu.co.jp; f. 1899; Chair. ICHIRO HIRAMATSU; Pres. M. KOTANI.

Keio Electric Railway Co Ltd: 1-9-1, Sekido, Tama City, Tokyo 206-8052; tel. (42) 337-3106; fax (42) 374-9322; internet www.keio.co.jp; f. 1913; Chair. K. KUWAYAMA; Pres. H. NISHIYAMA.

Keisei Electric Railway Co Ltd: 1-10-3, Oshiage, Sumida-ku, Tokyo 131; tel. (3) 3621-2242; fax (3) 3621-2233; internet www.keisei.co.jp; f. 1909; Chair. (vacant); Pres. M. SATO.

Kinki Nippon Railway Co Ltd: 6-1-55, Uehommachi, Tennoji-ku, Osaka 543-8585; tel. (6) 6775-3444; fax (6) 6775-3468; internet www.kintetsu.co.jp; f. 1910; Chair. WA TASHIRO; Pres. AKIO TSUJII.

Nagoya Railroad Co Ltd: 1-2-4, Meieki, Nakamura-ku, Nagoya-shi 450; tel. (52) 571-2111; fax (52) 581-6060; e-mail info@meitetsu.co.jp; internet www.meitetsu.co.jp; Chair. S. TANIGUCHI; Pres. S. MINOURA.

Nankai Electric Railway Co Ltd: 5-1-60, Namba, Chuo-ku, Osaka 542; tel. (6) 6644-7121; internet www.nankai.co.jp; Pres. SHIGERU YOSHIMURA; Vice-Pres. K. OKAMOTO.

Nishi-Nippon Railroad Co Ltd: 1-11-17, Tenjin-cho, Chuo-ku, Fukuoka 810; tel. (92) 761-6631; fax (92) 722-1405; internet www.nnr.co.jp; serves northern Kyushu; Chair. H. YOSHIMOTO; Pres. G. KIMOTO.

Odakyu Electric Railway Co Ltd: 1-8-3, Nishi Shinjuku, Shinjuku-ku, Tokyo 160; tel. (3) 3349-2151; fax (3) 3346-1899; internet www.odakyu-group.co.jp; f. 1948; Chair. TATSUZO TOSHIMITSU; Pres. M. KITANAKA.

Sanyo Electric Railway Co Ltd: 3-1-1, Oyashiki-dori, Nagata-ku, Kobe 653; tel. (78) 611-2211; Pres. T. WATANABE.

Seibu Railway Co Ltd: 1-11-1, Kasunokidai, Tokorozawa-shi, Saitama 359; tel. (429) 26-2035; fax (429) 26-2237; internet www.seibu-group.co.jp/railways; f. 1894; Pres. YOSHIAKI TSUTSUMI.

Tobu Railway Co Ltd: 1-1-2, Oshiage, Sumida-ku, Tokyo 131-8522; tel. (3) 3621-5057; internet www.tobu.co.jp; f. 1897; Chair. KAICHIRO NEZU; Pres. TAKASHIGE UCHIDA.

Tokyo Express Electric Railway Co Ltd: 5-6, Nanpeidai-cho, Shibuya-ku, Tokyo 150; tel. (3) 3477-6111; fax (3) 3496-2965; e-mail public@tokyu.co.jp; internet www.tokyu.co.jp; f. 1922; Pres. S. SHIMUZU.

Principal Subways, Monorails and Tunnels

Subway services operate in Tokyo, Osaka, Kobe, Nagoya, Sapporo, Yokohama, Kyoto, Sendai and Fukuoka with a combined network of about 500 km. Most new subway lines are directly linked with existing private railway terminals which connect the cities with suburban areas.

The first commercial monorail system was introduced in 1964 with straddle-type cars between central Tokyo and Tokyo International Airport, a distance of 13 km. In 1988 the total length of monorail was 38.6 km.

In 1985 the 54-km Seikan Tunnel (the world's longest undersea tunnel), linking the islands of Honshu and Hokkaido, was completed. Electric rail services through the tunnel began operating in March 1988.

Fukuoka City Subway: Fukuoka Municipal Transportation Bureau, 2-5-31, Daimyo, Chuo-ku, Fukuoka 810-0041; tel. (92) 732-4107; fax (92) 721-0754; internet subway.city.fukuoka.jp; 2 lines of 17.8 km open; Dir KENNICHIROU NISHI.

Kobe Rapid Transit: 6-5-1, Kanocho, Chuo-ku, Kobe 650; tel. (78) 331-8181; Dir YASUO MAENO.

Kyoto Rapid Transit: 48, Bojocho Mibu, Nakakyo-ku, Kyoto 604; tel. (75) 822-9115; fax (75) 822-9240; Chair. T. TANABE.

Nagoya Underground Railway: Nagoya Municipal Transportation Bureau, City Hall Annex, 3-1-1, Sannomaru, Naka-ku, Nagoya 460-8508; tel. (52) 972-3812; fax (52) 972-3849; internet www.kotsu.city.nagoya/index-e.htm; 76.5 km open (1998); Dir-Gen. KATSUYOSHI TAKAGI.

Osaka Monorail: 5-1-1, Higashi-machi, Shin-Senri, Toyonakashi, Osaka 565; tel. (6) 871-8280; fax (6) 871-8284; Gen. Man. S. OKA.

Osaka Underground Railway: Osaka Municipal Transportation Bureau, 1-11-53, Kujominami, Nishi-ku, Osaka 550; tel. (6) 6582-1101; fax (6) 6582-7997; f. 1933; 120 km open in 1998; the 6.6 km computer-controlled 'New Tram' service began between Suminoe-koen and Nakafuto in 1981; a seventh line between Kyobashi and Tsurumi-ryokuchi was opened in 1990; Gen. Man. HARUMI SAKAI.

Sapporo Transportation Bureau: Higashi, 2-4-1, Oyachi, Atsubetsu-ku, Sapporo 004; tel. (11) 896-2708; fax (11) 896-2790; f. 1971; 3 lines of 53 km open in 1993/94; Dir T. IKEGAMI.

Sendai City Subway: Sendai City Transportation Bureau, 1-4-15, Kimachidori, Aoba-ku, Sendai-shi, Miyagi-ken 980-0801; tel. (22) 224-5502; fax (22) 224-6839; internet www.comminet.or.jp/~kotsu-s; 15.4 km open; Dir T. IWAMA.

Tokyo Underground Railway: Teito Rapid Transit Authority, 3-19-6, Higashi Ueno, Taito-ku, Tokyo 110-0015; tel. (3) 3837-7046; fax (3) 3837-7048; internet www.tokyometro.go.jp; f. 1941; Pres. KIYOSHI TERASHIMA; 171.5 km open; and Transportation Bureau of Tokyo Metropolitan Govt, 2-8-1, Nishi-shinjuku, Shinjuku-ku, Tokyo 163-8001; tel. (3) 5321-1111; fax (3) 5388-1650; f. 1960; Dir-Gen. K. KATO; 90 km open.

Yokohama Rapid Transit: Municipal Transportation Bureau, 1-1, Minato-cho, Naka-ku, Yokohama 231-80; tel. (45) 671-3201; fax (45) 664-3266; 33 km open; Dir-Gen. MICHINORI KISHIDA.

ROADS

In December 1997 Japan's road network extended to an estimated 1,152,207 km, including 6,114 km of motorways and 53,356 km of highways. In May 1999 work was completed on a 29-year project to construct three routes, consisting of a total of 19 bridges, between the islands of Honshu and Shikoku across the Seto inland sea, at a cost of some US $25,000m.

There is a national omnibus service, 60 publicly-operated services and 298 privately-operated services.

Japan Highway Public Corpn: 3-3-2, Kasumigaseki, Chiyoda-ku, Tokyo 100-8979; tel. (3) 3506-0111.

SHIPPING

Shipping in Japan is subject to the supervision of the Ministry of Transport. At 31 December 1998 the Japanese merchant fleet (8,922 vessels) had a total displacement of 17,780,396 grt. The main ports are Tokyo, Yokohama, Nagoya and Osaka. The rebuilding of the port at Kobe, severely damaged by an earthquake in January 1995, was completed in 1997.

Principal Companies

Daiichi Chuo Kisen Kaisha: Dowa Bldg, 3-5-15, Nihonbashi, Chuo-ku, Tokyo 103; tel. (3) 3278-6745; fax (3) 3278-6746; f. 1960; liner and tramp services; Pres. MAHIKO SAOTOME.

Iino Kaiun Kaisha Ltd: Iino Bldg, 2-1-1, Uchisaiwai-cho, Chiyoda-ku, Tokyo 100; tel. (3) 3506-3037; fax (3) 3508-4121; f. 1918; cargo and tanker services; Chair. T. CHIBA; Pres. A. KARINO.

Kansai Kisen KK: Osaka Bldg, 3-6-32, Nakanoshima, Kita-ku, Osaka 552; tel. (6) 6574-9131; fax (6) 6574-9149; f. 1942; domestic passenger services; Pres. TOSHIKAZU EGUCHI.

Kawasaki Kisen Kaisha Ltd (K Line): 1-2-9, Nishi Shinbashi, Minato-ku, Tokyo 105-8421; tel. (3) 3595-5082; fax (3) 3595-5001; e-mail otaki@email.kline.co.jp; internet www.kline.co.jp; f. 1919; containers, cars, LNG, LPG and oil tankers, bulk carriers; Chair. of Bd I. SHINTANI; Exec. Vice-Pres. Z. WAKABAYASHI.

Nippon Yusen Kaisha (NYK) Line: 2-3-2, Marunouchi, Chiyoda-ku, Tokyo 100-0005; tel. (3) 3284-5151; fax (3) 3284-6361; e-mail prteam@jp.nykline.com; internet www.nykline.com; f. 1885; merged with Showa Line Ltd in 1998; world-wide container, cargo, pure car and truck carriers, tanker and bulk carrying services; Chair. JIRO NEMOTO; Pres. KENTARO KAWAMURA.

Nissho Shipping Co Ltd: 33, Mori Bldg, 7th Floor, 3-8-21, Tora-nomon, Minato-ku, Tokyo 105; tel. (3) 3438-3511; fax (3) 3438-3566; f. 1943; Pres. MINORU IKEDA.

OSK Mitsui Ltd: Shosen Mitsui Bldg, 2-1-1, Toranomon, Minato-ku, Tokyo 105-91; tel. (3) 3587-7092; fax (3) 3587-7734; f. 1942; merged with Navix Line Ltd in 1999; world-wide container, liner, tramp, and specialized carrier and tanker services; Chair. SUSUMU TEMPORIN; Pres. MASAHARU IKUTA.

Ryukyu Kaiun KK: 1-24-11, Nishi-machi, Naha, Okinawa 900; tel. (98) 868-8161; fax (98) 868-8561; cargo and passenger services on domestic routes; Pres. M. AZAMA.

Taiheiyo Kaiun Co Ltd: Mitakokusai Bldg, 23rd Floor, 1-4-28, Minato-ku, Tokyo 100; tel. (3) 5445-5805; fax (3) 5445-5806; f. 1951; cargo and tanker services; Pres. SANROKURO YAMAJI.

CIVIL AVIATION

There are international airports at Tokyo, Osaka and Narita. In 1991 the Government approved a plan to build five new airports, and to expand 17 existing ones. This project was expected to take five years to complete and to cost US $25,000m. There are proposals to build new airports at Shizuoka, Nagoya and Kobe. In September 1994 the world's first offshore international airport (Kansai Interna-tional Airport) was opened in Osaka Bay. In December 1999 work began on the construction of a second runway at Narita, which was scheduled to be completed in 2002. At March 1999 a total of 85 airports were in operation.

Air Do: 6, Nishi, Kita 5, Chuo-ku, Sapporo; tel. (11) 252-5533; fax (11) 252-5580; e-mail postbear@airdo.co.jp; internet www.airdo.co.jp; f. 1996; domestic service between Tokyo and Sapporo; Pres. AKIRA NAKAMURA.

Air Nippon: 3-5-10, Haneda Airport, Ota-ku, Tokyo 144-0041; tel. (3) 5462-1911; fax (3) 5462-1941; internet www.ananet.or.jp/ank; f. 1974; formerly Nihon Kinkyori Airways; international and domestic passenger services; Pres. and CEO YUZURU MASUMOTO.

All Nippon Airways—ANA: 3-5-10 Haneda Airport, Ota-ku, Tokyo 144-0041; tel. (3) 5756-5675; fax (3) 5756-5679; internet www.ana.co.jp; f. 1952; operates domestic passenger and freight services; scheduled international services to the Far East, Australasia, the USA and Europe; charter services world-wide; Pres. and CEO KICHI-SABURO NOMURA.

Hokkaido Air System: Hokkadama-cho Airport, Sapporo-shi, Shi-gashi-ku, Sapporo 063; tel. (11) 781-1247; fax (11) 784-1716; internet www.hac-air.co.jp; f. 1997; domestic services on Hokkaido; Pres. TAKESHI KANDI.

JALways Co Ltd: JAL Bldg, 18th Floor, 2-4-11, Higashi-Shina-gawa, Shinagawa-ku, Tokyo 140-8647; tel. (3) 5460-6830; fax (3) 5460-6839; e-mail jazgz@jaz.jalgroup.or.jp; internet www.jalways.co.jp; f. 1990; subsidiary of JAL; domestic and international sched-uled and charter services; Chair. JIRO SAGARA; Pres. YUKIO OHTANI.

Japan Air Commuter: 8-2-2, Fumoto, Mizobe-cho, Aira-gun, Kago-shima 899-64; tel. (995) 582151; fax (995) 582673; e-mail info@jac.co.jp; internet www.jac.co.jp; f. 1983; subsidiary of Japan Air System; domestic services; Chair. YOSHITOMI ONO.

Japan Air System: JAS M1 Bldg, 3-5-1, Haneda Airport, Ota-ku, Tokyo 144-0041; tel. (3) 5756-4022; fax (3) 5473-4109; internet www.jas.co.jp; f. 1971; domestic and international services; plans to co-ordinate services with Northwest Airlines (USA) announced in 1995; Chair. TAKESHI MASHIMA; Pres. HIROMI FUNABIKI.

Japan Airlines Co Ltd—JAL (Nihon Koku Kabushiki Kaisha): JAL Bldg, 2-4-11, Higashi-Shinagawa, Shinagawa-ku, Tokyo 140; tel. (3) 5460-3121; fax (3) 5460-3936; internet www.jal.co.jp; f. 1951; fully transferred to private-sector control in 1987; domestic and international services to Australasia, the Far East, North America, South America and Europe; Pres. ISAO KANEKO.

Japan Asia Airways Co: JAL Bldg, 19th Floor, 2-4-11. Higashi-shinagawa, Shinagawa-ku, Tokyo 140-0002; tel. (3) 5460-7285; fax (3) 5460-7286; e-mail jaabz@jaa.jalgroup.or.jp; internet www.japanasia.co.jp; f. 1975; subsidiary of JAL; international services from Tokyo, Osaka, Nagoya and Okinawa to Hong Kong and Taiwan; Chair. TEIICHI KURIBAYASHI; Pres. OSAMU IGARASHI.

Japan TransOcean Air: 3-24, Yamashita-cho, Naha-shi, Okinawa 900; tel. (988) 572112; fax (988) 582581; internet www.jal.co.jp/jta; f. 1967, present name since 1993; subsidiary of JAL; inter-island service in Okinawa; Chair. KEIICHI INAMINE; Pres. MICHIO OKUNO.

Nakanihon Airline Service—NAL: Nagoya Airport, Toyoyama-cho, Nishi Kasugai-gun, Aichi 480-0202; tel. (568) 285405; fax (568) 285415; internet www.nals.co.jp; f. 1988; regional and domestic serv-ices; Pres. TAKEHIKO KAITO.

Skymark Airlines: POB 116, Haneda Airport, Ota-ku, Tokyo 144-6591; tel. (3) 5757-9555; fax (3) 5757-7161; e-mail info@skymark.co.jp; internet www.skymark.co.jp; f. 1997; domestic services; Chair. HIDEO SAWADA; Pres TAKASHI IDE.

Tourism

The ancient capital of Kyoto, pagodas and temples, forests and mountains, traditional festivals and the classical Kabuki theatre are some of the many tourist attractions of Japan. In 1999 there were 4,437,863 foreign visitors to Japan, and receipts from tourism totalled US $3,428m.

Department of Tourism: 2-1-3, Kasumigaseki, Chiyoda-ku, Tokyo 100; tel. (3) 3580-4488; fax (3) 3580-7901; f. 1946; a dept of the Ministry of Transport; Dir-Gen. KIMITAKA FUJINO.

Japan National Tourist Organization: Tokyo Kotsu Kaikan Bldg, 2-10-1, Yuraku-cho, Chiyoda-ku, Tokyo 100-0006; tel. (3) 3216-1901; fax (3) 3216-1846; internet www.jnto.go.jp; Pres. HIDEAKI MUKAIYMA.

Japan Travel Bureau Inc: 1-6-4, Marunouchi, Chiyoda-ku, Tokyo 100-0005; tel. (3) 3284-7028; f. 1912; 10,297 mems; Chair. I. MATSU-HASHI; Pres. R. FUNAYAMA.

JORDAN

Introductory Survey

Location, Climate, Language, Religion, Flag, Capital

The Hashemite Kingdom of Jordan is an almost land-locked state in western Asia. It is bordered by Israel and the Emerging Palestinian Autonomous Areas to the west, by Syria to the north, by Iraq to the east and by Saudi Arabia to the south. The port of Aqaba, in the far south, gives Jordan a narrow outlet to the Red Sea. The climate is hot and dry. The average annual temperature is about 15°C (60°F) but there are wide diurnal variations. Temperatures in Amman are generally between –1°C (30°F) and 32°C (90°F). More extreme conditions are found in the valley of the River Jordan and on the shores of the Dead Sea (a lake on the Israeli-Jordanian frontier), where the temperature may exceed 50°C (122°F) in summer. The official language is Arabic. More than 90% of the population are Sunni Muslims, while there are small communities of Christians and Shi'i Muslims. The national flag (proportions 2 by 1) has three equal horizontal stripes, of black, white and green, with a red triangle, containing a seven-pointed white star, at the hoist. The capital is Amman.

Recent History

Palestine (including the present-day West Bank of Jordan) and Transjordan (the East Bank) were formerly parts of Turkey's Ottoman Empire. During the First World War (1914–18), when Turkey was allied with Germany, the Arabs under Ottoman rule rebelled. British forces, with Arab support, occupied Palestine and Transjordan in 1917–18, when the Turks withdrew. British occupation continued after the war, when the Ottoman Empire was dissolved. In 1920 Palestine and Transjordan were formally placed under British administration by a League of Nations mandate. In 1921 Abdullah ibn Hussein, a member of the Hashimi (Hashemite) dynasty of Arabia, was proclaimed Amir (Emir) of Transjordan. In the same year, his brother, Faisal, became King of neighbouring Iraq. The two new monarchs were sons of Hussein ibn Ali, the Sharif of Mecca, who had proclaimed himself King of the Hejaz (now part of Saudi Arabia) in 1916. The British decision to nominate Hashemite princes to be rulers of Iraq and Transjordan was a reward for Hussein's co-operation in the wartime campaign against Turkey.

Under the British mandate, Transjordan (formally separated from Palestine in 1923) gained increasing autonomy. In 1928 the United Kingdom acknowledged the nominal independence of Transjordan, although retaining certain financial and military powers. Amir Abdullah followed a generally pro-British policy and supported the Allied cause in the Second World War (1939–45). The mandate was terminated on 22 March 1946, when Transjordan attained full independence. On 25 May Abdullah was proclaimed King, and a new Constitution took effect.

When the British Government terminated its mandate in Palestine in May 1948, Jewish leaders there proclaimed the State of Israel, but Palestinian Arabs, with military support from Arab states, opposed Israeli claims and hostilities continued until July. Transjordan's forces occupied about 5,900 sq km of Palestine, including East Jerusalem, and this was confirmed by the armistice with Israel in April 1949. In June the country was renamed Jordan, and in April 1950, following a referendum, King Abdullah formally annexed the West Bank territory, which contained many Arab refugees from Israeli-held areas.

In July 1951 King Abdullah was assassinated in Jerusalem by a Palestinian belonging to an extremist Islamist organization. Abdullah was succeeded by his eldest son, Talal ibn Abdullah, hitherto Crown Prince. However, in August 1952, because of Talal's mental incapacity, the crown passed to his son, Hussein ibn Talal, then 16 years of age. King Hussein formally took power in May 1953.

In March 1956, responding to Arab nationalist sentiment, King Hussein dismissed the British army officer who had been Chief of Staff of the British-equipped and -financed Arab Legion (the Jordanian armed forces) since 1939. Jordan's treaty relationship with the United Kingdom was ended in March 1957, and British troops completed their withdrawal from Jordan in July.

The refugee camps in the West Bank became the centre of Palestinian resistance to Israel, and during the 1950s there were numerous attacks on Israeli territory by groups of Palestinian *fedayeen* ('martyrs'). In September 1963 the creation of a unified 'Palestinian entity' was approved by the Council of the League of Arab States (the Arab League, see p. 232), and the first congress of Palestinian groups was held in the Jordanian sector of Jerusalem in May–June 1964, during which the participants unanimously agreed to form the Palestine Liberation Organization (PLO), which would be financed by the Arab League and would recruit military units to form a Palestine Liberation Army (PLA). The principal Palestinian guerrilla organization within the PLO was the Palestine National Liberation Movement, known as Fatah ('Conquest'), led by Yasser Arafat from 1968. However, King Hussein regarded the establishment of the PLO as a threat to Jordanian sovereignty, and from the outset refused to allow the PLA to train in Jordan or the PLO to levy taxes from Palestinian refugees residing in his country.

In April 1965 Hussein nominated his brother Hassan ibn Talal to be Crown Prince, thus excluding his own children from succession to the throne. King Hussein's personal rule was severely challenged when, during the Six-Day War in June 1967, Israel made substantial military gains, including possession of the whole of Jerusalem (which was incorporated into Israel) and the West Bank; the latter became an Israeli 'administered territory'. The influx of Palestinian refugees into the East Bank bolstered the strength of the PLO, which continued armed raids on the Israeli-administered territories, thereby challenging the personal authority of King Hussein and the sovereignty of the Jordanian Government (up to 60% of Jordan's population are Palestinian, and more than 1m. Palestinians live in the West Bank). King Hussein responded by expelling the guerrilla groups, after a civil war which lasted from September 1970 to July 1971. Aid to Jordan from Kuwait and other wealthy Arab states, suspended after the expulsion of the Palestinian fighters, was only restored following Jordan's military support for Syria during the 1973 Arab–Israeli War. At an Arab summit meeting in Rabat, Morocco, in October 1974 King Hussein supported a unanimous resolution recognizing the PLO as the 'sole legitimate representative of the Palestinian people' and giving the organization the right to establish an independent national authority on any piece of Palestinian land to be liberated.

In November 1974, as a response to this resolution, both chambers of the Jordanian National Assembly (which had equal representation for the East and West Banks) approved constitutional amendments that empowered the King to dissolve the Assembly and to postpone elections for up to 12 months. The Assembly was dissolved later that month, although it was briefly reconvened in February 1976, when it approved a constitutional amendment giving the King power to postpone elections indefinitely and to convene the Assembly as required. A royal decree of April 1978 provided for the creation of a National Consultative Council, with 60 members appointed for a two-year term by the King, on the Prime Minister's recommendation, to debate proposed legislation.

A proposal, put forward by US President Ronald Reagan in September 1982, for an autonomous Palestinian authority on the West Bank, in association with Jordan, was rejected by Yasser Arafat following talks with King Hussein. In January 1984, however, the King responded by dissolving the National Consultative Council and recalling the National Assembly for the first time since 1967—in effect creating the kind of Palestinian forum envisaged by the Reagan initiative. Israel allowed the surviving West Bank deputies to attend the Assembly, which approved constitutional amendments enabling elections to be held in the East Bank and West Bank deputies to be chosen by the Assembly itself. After discussions with the PLO leader in January 1984 on a joint Palestinian-Jordanian peace initiative, King Hussein's proposals for negotiations, based on UN Security Council Resolution 242 (the resolution, adopted in November 1967, sought to return the region's territorial boundaries to the pre-Six-Day War status, but incorporated implicit recognition of an Israeli state), met with a non-com-mittal response from the Palestine National Council (PNC), which convened in Amman in November. President Hosni Mubarak of Egypt gave his support to Hussein's proposals, following the resumption of diplomatic relations between the two countries in September. In February 1985 King Hussein and Yasser Arafat announced the terms of a joint Jordanian-Palestinian agreement, proposing a confederated state of Jordan and Palestine to be reached through the convening of a conference of all concerned parties in the Middle East, including the PLO.

In July 1985 Israel rejected a list of seven Palestinians, five of whom were members of the PLO or had links with the PNC, whom King Hussein had presented to the USA as candidates for a joint Jordanian-Palestinian delegation to preliminary peace talks. Further progress was hampered by a series of terrorist incidents in which the PLO was implicated, thereby giving Israel further cause to reject the PLO as a credible partner in peace negotiations. King Hussein was under increasing pressure to advance the peace process, if necessary without PLO participation. In September President Reagan revived his 1984 plan to sell military equipment to the value of some US $1,900m. to Jordan. The proposal was approved by the US Congress on the condition that Jordan enter into direct talks with Israel before 1 March 1986. However, such talks were obstructed by a gradual *rapprochement* between Jordan and Syria, both of which supported a Middle East peace settlement through an international conference, having recently rejected 'partial and unilateral' solutions.

Frustrated by the lack of co-operation from Yasser Arafat in advancing the aims of the Jordanian-PLO peace initiative, King Hussein publicly severed political links with the PLO on 19 February 1986. Arafat was subsequently ordered to close his main PLO offices in Jordan by 1 April. The PLO's activities were henceforth to be restricted even further, and a number of Fatah officers loyal to Arafat were expelled. In July the Jordanian authorities closed all 25 Fatah offices in Amman; only 12 bureaux belonging to the PLO remained.

Despite the termination of political co-ordination with the PLO, Jordan continued to reject Israeli requests for direct peace talks that excluded a form of PLO representation. However, Jordan's subsequent efforts to strengthen its influence in the Israeli-occupied territories (Occupied Territories), and to foster a Palestinian constituency there independent of Arafat's PLO, coincided with Israeli measures to grant a limited autonomy to Palestinians in the West Bank. In March 1986 the Jordanian House of Representatives approved a draft law increasing the number of seats in the House from 60 to 142 (71 seats each for the East and West Banks), thereby providing for greater representation for West Bank Palestinians in the National Assembly. In August, with Israeli support, Jordan announced a five-year development plan, valued at US $1,300m., for the West Bank and the Gaza Strip; the plan was condemned by Arafat and West Bank Palestinians as representing a normalization of relations with Israel. Support for Arafat among Palestinians in the Occupied Territories, and in Jordan, was consolidated as he re-established himself at the head of a reunified PLO at the 18th session of the PNC in April 1987 (when the Jordan-PLO accord of 1985 was formally abrogated).

In May 1987, following several secret meetings with King Hussein, the Israeli Minister of Foreign Affairs, Shimon Peres, claimed to have made significant progress on the crucial issue of Palestinian representation at a Middle East peace conference, and to have the consent of Egypt, Jordan and the USA to convene an international conference including the five permanent members of the UN Security Council and a delegation of Palestinians who rejected terrorism and accepted Security Council Resolutions 242 and 338 (the latter defined the terms of immediate peace following the October 1973 Arab–Israeli war) as the basis for negotiations. The Jordanian Prime Minister, Zaid ar-Rifai, confirmed his country's willingness to participate in a joint Jordanian-Palestinian delegation including the PLO, provided that the organization complied with the stated conditions. However, Israel's Prime Minister, Itzhak Shamir, was opposed in principle to an international peace conference and reiterated his alternative proposal of direct regional talks excluding the PLO, and Peres failed to secure the support of a majority of the Israeli Cabinet for his proposals.

At the first full meeting of the Arab League for eight years, convened in Amman in November 1987, King Hussein pursued an agenda of greater Arab unity in support of Iraq in the war with Iran. Prior to the summit, Jordan restored full diplomatic relations with Libya (severed in 1984), which had modified its

support for Iran. However, King Hussein's appeal for Egypt to be restored to membership of the League (suspended following the peace treaty with Israel in 1979) was resisted by Libya and Syria, although 11 Arab states subsequently re-established diplomatic relations. Jordan also announced the resumption of co-operation with the PLO at the meeting.

These achievements were soon overshadowed by the Palestinian *intifada* (uprising), which erupted in the West Bank and Gaza Strip in December 1987, in protest at the continued Israeli occupation and the seemingly indifferent attitude of Arab League states to the Palestinians' plight. The *intifada*, and the Israelis' increasingly violent attempts at its suppression, increased international support for the PLO and Palestinian national rights. At an extraordinary meeting of the Arab League held in the Algerian capital in June 1988, King Hussein gave the *intifada* his unconditional support and insisted that the PLO must represent the Palestinians at any future peace conference. Furthermore, in accordance with agreements reached at the meeting, Jordan cancelled the West Bank development plan and severed Jordan's legal and administrative links with the territory. Jordan's disengagement from the West Bank effectively rendered a proposal put forward earlier in the year by the US Secretary of State, George Shultz, for an international peace conference at which there would be no PLO representation or joint Jordanian-Palestinian delegation, redundant.

On 15 November 1988 the PNC, meeting in Algiers, proclaimed the establishment of an independent State of Palestine and, for the first time, endorsed UN Security Council Resolution 242 as a basis for a Middle East peace settlement, thus implicitly recognizing Israel. Jordan and 60 other countries recognized the new state. In December Yasser Arafat addressed a special session of the UN General Assembly in Geneva, where he renounced violence on behalf of the PLO. The USA subsequently opened a dialogue with the PLO, and it appeared that Israel would have to negotiate directly with the organization if it sought a solution to the Palestinian question, while Jordan's future role in the peace process was likely to be reduced.

In April 1989 there was rioting in several cities, after the Jordanian Government imposed sizeable price increases on basic goods and services. The riots led to the resignation of Zaid ar-Rifai (the Prime Minister since 1985) and his Cabinet. Field Marshal Sharif Zaid ibn Shaker, a cousin of the King who had been Commander-in-Chief of the Jordanian Armed Forces in 1976–88, was appointed Prime Minister at the head of a new Cabinet. While King Hussein refused to make any concessions regarding the price increases (which had been imposed in accordance with IMF recommendations), he announced that a general election would be held for the first time since 1967. The election to the 80-seat House of Representatives, which proceeded in November 1989, was contested by 647 candidates, mostly independents, as the ban on political parties (in force since 1963) remained. However, the Muslim Brotherhood was able to present candidates for election, owing to its legal status as a charity rather than a political party. At the election the Muslim Brotherhood won 20 seats, while 12–14 seats were won by independent Islamic candidates who supported the Brotherhood. It was estimated that Palestinian or Arab nationalist candidates won seven seats and that 'leftist' candidates won four. The remaining seats were won by broadly pro-Government candidates. The strength of support for opposition candidates was unexpected, especially since a disproportionately large number of seats had been assigned to rural areas from which the Government had traditionally drawn most support. In December King Hussein appointed Mudar Badran as Prime Minister, a post he had previously held in 1976–79 and 1980–84. The Muslim Brotherhood declined participation in the new Cabinet after its demand for the education portfolio was rejected. However, the Government included three independent Muslim deputies and three 'leftists', all of whom were regarded as members of the opposition; four appointees were described as independent nationalists close to the State, while another six had held office in the outgoing administration. The new Government, whose Prime Minister affirmed continuing support for prevailing austerity measures, received a vote of confidence from the House of Representatives in January 1990. Prior to the vote, Badran pledged to abolish martial law (which had been suspended in December 1989) within four to six months, and to liberalize the judicial system. In January 1991 King Hussein reshuffled the Cabinet to include five members of the Muslim Brotherhood, one of whom received the education portfolio.

In November 1989 King Hussein had announced his intention to appoint a royal commission to devise a national charter that would legalize political parties. In April 1990 the King named the 60-member commission, under the chairmanship of a former Prime Minister, Ahmad Ubeidat. The commission's draft national charter was approved by the King in January 1991, and further endorsed by the King and leading political figures in June. Meanwhile, in January 1990 Badran had announced the abolition of the anti-communism law in force since 1954.

Jordan was deeply affected by Iraq's invasion of Kuwait in August 1990, and the consequent imposition of economic sanctions by the UN against Iraq: Iraq was Jordan's principal trading partner, and Jordan relied on supplies of Iraqi petroleum. Although King Hussein condemned Iraq's invasion of Kuwait, he was slow to do so, and hoped for an 'Arab solution' to the crisis. There was considerable support for Saddam Hussein among the Jordanian population, particularly among Palestinians. King Hussein was critical of the large, US-led deployment of multinational military forces in Saudi Arabia and the region of the Persian (Arabian) Gulf, and throughout the closing months of 1990 he visited numerous Middle East and other capitals in an attempt to avert a war that could be potentially disastrous for Jordan. Jordan's response to the Gulf crisis prompted the USA to review its military and economic assistance to Jordan and led to a deterioration in Jordan's relations with Egypt and Saudi Arabia, both of which contributed to the US-led force. However, diplomatic relations between Jordan and Iran were re-established (having been severed in 1981).

In the early stages of the Gulf crisis Jordan experienced the additional problem of a large-scale influx of refugees from Iraq and Kuwait, many of whom were seeking passage through Jordan in order to return to the Indian sub-continent and South East Asia. According to Jordanian officials, about 470,000 foreigners fled to Jordan in the five weeks following the Iraqi invasion of Kuwait. In addition to the foreign influx, large numbers of Jordanian nationals returned from the Gulf region. Some 300,000 of these expatriates remained in Jordan after the liberation of Kuwait in February 1991, fearing reprisals in Kuwait, where most Jordanian and Palestinian residents were regarded by the authorities as collaborators with the Iraqi occupation forces.

In the months following the end of the Gulf War Jordan concentrated on attempts to revive its shattered economy and on improving its relations with Arab neighbours, particularly Saudi Arabia. In response to Jordanian co-operation in the arrest of a Saudi dissident, Muhammad al-Fassi, in Amman, Saudi Arabia revoked a ban on the entry of Jordanian transport vehicles into its territory, and trade between Jordan and Saudi Arabia was resumed. However, high-level ministerial contacts were not renewed until mid-1995. Although King Hussein was apparently rebuffed in an attempt to meet King Fahd during a visit to Saudi Arabia in early 1996, the Jordanian leader emphasized the improvement that was taking place in bilateral relations.

Meanwhile, Jordan secured the approval of the USA by agreeing to join with a Palestinian delegation at the Middle East peace conference which opened in Madrid, Spain, in October 1991. Subsequent talks in Washington, DC, and Moscow, Russia, between the Israeli and the joint Jordanian-Palestinian delegations remained deadlocked with regard to substantive issues until September 1993, when Israel and the PLO agreed to a declaration of principles regarding Palestinian self-rule in the Occupied Territories. On the signing of the Declaration of Principles, which King Hussein welcomed, the joint Jordanian-Palestinian delegation was disbanded, and Jordan and Israel concluded an agreement that defined the agenda for subsequent bilateral negotiations within the context of the Middle East peace conference. The negotiations were to address the following issues: refugees and displaced persons; security; water resources; the demarcation of the border between Jordan and Israel; and future bilateral co-operation.

In 1991 Jordan and the PLO had agreed on the principle of confederation between Jordan and whatever Palestinian entity ultimately emerged from the Middle East peace process; and in July 1993 Jordan and the PLO agreed to form six committees to discuss relations between Jordan and the Occupied Territories during a period of transitional Palestinian self-rule. Within the terms of the Declaration of Principles, however, Jordan was formally excluded from the discussion of some of the issues—henceforth to be dealt with bilaterally by Israeli and Palestinian authorities—which the committees had already begun to

address. Under the Declaration of Principles, Jordan was to be invited to join a joint Israeli-Palestinian Liaison Committee to determine procedures for the return of Palestinians displaced from the West Bank and Gaza Strip in 1967. However, Jordan stated its unwillingness to join such a committee, since it had not been consulted about its establishment. In January 1994, after King Hussein had twice warned that Jordan might otherwise pursue its own agenda in the ongoing peace talks with Israel, the PLO agreed to sign a comprehensive economic co-operation agreement with Jordan, and to establish a joint committee to co-ordinate financial policy in the Palestinian territories. In the same month Jordan signed a draft security accord with the PLO. Yasser Arafat visited Amman immediately following the signing of the Cairo Agreement on the Gaza Strip and Jericho by Israel and the PLO in May (see the chapter on Israel), but King Hussein reportedly remained disappointed at the PLO's failure to liaise fully with Jordan in the peace process.

On 25 July 1994 King Hussein and the Prime Minister of Israel, Itzhak Rabin, meeting in the US capital, signed the Washington Declaration, which formally ended the state of war that had existed between Jordan and Israel since 1948. It was the first time that King Hussein had publicly met an Israeli premier. In October Jordan and Israel signed a full peace treaty settling outstanding issues of contention between them and providing, *inter alia*, for the establishment of diplomatic relations and for talks on economic and security co-operation. The official normalization of relations between Jordan and Israel had been completed by 18 January 1996. In Jordan the peace treaty was opposed by Islamist militants, and it was also criticized by Syria. The PLO leadership complained that the peace treaty undermined Palestinian claims to sovereignty over Jerusalem. None the less, in January 1995 the PLO and Jordan signed an agreement that regulated relations between Jordan and the Emerging Palestinian Autonomous Areas with regard to economic affairs, finance, banking, education, transport, telecommunications, information and administration. At the same time, the PLO acknowledged Jordan's custodianship of the Muslim holy places in Jerusalem for as long as Jordan recognized and supported Palestinian claims to sovereignty over East Jerusalem.

Meanwhile, in June 1991 Taher al-Masri was appointed to replace Mudar Badran as Prime Minister. However, in the period preceding the opening of the National Assembly in December, it became clear that al-Masri could not command majority support in the legislature; he was forced to resign in November, whereupon Sharif Zaid ibn Shaker again assumed the premiership. An extraordinary session of the House of Representatives was convened in June 1992 to debate new laws regarding political parties and the press. In July the House adopted legislation whereby, subject to certain conditions, political parties were formally legalized. In May King Hussein appointed Abd as-Salam al-Majali, the head of the Jordanian delegation to the Middle East peace conference, as Prime Minister in a new Government, which was regarded as a transitional administration pending legislative elections to be held before November 1993.

In August 1993 King Hussein unexpectedly dissolved the House of Representatives, provoking criticism from some politicians who had expected the House to debate proposed amendments to Jordan's electoral law. Changes in voting procedures at the general election were announced by the King in that month: voters were to be allowed to cast one vote only, rather than, as before, multiple votes equal to the number of candidates contesting a given constituency. Some 68% of the electorate were reported to have participated in Jordan's first multi-party general election, held on 8 November. By far the largest number of deputies returned to the House of Representatives were independent centrists loyal to the King. The Islamic Action Front (IAF, the political wing of the Muslim Brotherhood), which emerged as the second largest party in the House of Representatives, maintained that the new electoral law had prevented it from winning more seats. A new Senate was appointed by the King on 18 November, and a new Cabinet, again under Abd as-Salam al-Majali, was announced in December.

An extensive reorganization of the Government followed the dismissal in January 1995 of al-Majali as Prime Minister. Sharif Zaid ibn Shaker once again assumed the premiership. Islamic and left-wing groups failed to gain significant popular support at municipal elections held in July, most elected candidates being largely pro-Government or independent. The IAF attributed its poor performance to a low level of voter participation, and to official harassment of its members during the campaign.

King Hussein implemented an extensive cabinet reshuffle in February 1996, appointing Abd al-Karim al-Kabariti, hitherto Minister of Foreign Affairs, as Prime Minister. (Kabariti retained the foreign affairs portfolio, and also assumed responsibility for defence.) In mid-August rioting erupted in southern Jordan after the Government imposed a sharp increase in the price of bread. The unrest quickly spread to other parts of the country, including impoverished areas of the capital, and was regarded as the greatest challenge to King Hussein's rule since the rioting over fuel prices in 1989. King Hussein responded by suspending the legislature and deploying the army in order to suppress the worst disturbances. In December 1996 the Government announced its commitment to certain reforms of electoral legislation before the next general election.

Kabariti was unexpectedly dismissed by King Hussein in March 1997, reportedly as a result of disagreement between the King and Prime Minister on issues relating to Jordan's policies towards Israel. Abd as-Salam al-Majali again assumed the premiership, taking the defence portfolio in the new Cabinet.

In July 1997 the IAF announced its intention to boycott the forthcoming parliamentary elections, in protest at what it regarded as the Government's overly concessionary policies towards Israel and at recent restrictive amendments to press legislation. Several other parties also boycotted the polls. Many of the 524 candidates at the elections, which took place on 4 November, were independents or tribal leaders campaigning on local issues. In all, 62 of the 80 seats in the new House of Representatives were won by pro-Government candidates (including two members of the recently-formed National Constitutional Party); 10 seats were secured by nationalist and left-wing candidates and eight by independent Islamists. The overall level of voter participation was reported to have been 54.6%, and was declared by the Government to be an endorsement of the country's electoral system and of the policies of King Hussein. However, there were reports that the level of turn-out was only 20% in some districts of Amman, and that the majority of Jordan's Palestinians had not voted. A new Senate was appointed by the King on 22 November. The Government was reorganized in February 1998. In July widespread public discontent arising from severe water shortages and the contamination of water supplies in Amman prompted the resignation of the Minister of Water and Irrigation. In August Fayez at-Tarawneh was appointed Prime Minister, in place of al-Majali (who had also been criticized for failing to address the water crisis); a new Cabinet was subsequently named.

Meanwhile, in July 1998 King Hussein began to undergo treatment for cancer in the USA. In August he issued a royal decree transferring responsibility for certain executive duties, including the appointment of ministers, to his brother, Crown Prince Hassan. On King Hussein's return to Jordan in January 1999, amid official assurances that his health had been restored, the King prompted renewed speculation about the royal succession by appointing Crown Prince Hassan as his 'deputy'. On 24 January King Hussein issued a royal decree naming his eldest son, Abdullah, as Crown Prince of Jordan. Although Crown Prince Hassan had been regent since 1965, it was reported that King Hussein was dissatisfied with his brother's handling of Jordanian affairs during his absence, in particular his attempts to involve himself in military matters. King Hussein had also accused his brother's supporters of slandering his immediate family, fuelling rumours that serious divisions had emerged within the royal family. Two days later the King left Jordan for emergency treatment in the USA, following a rapid deterioration in his health. King Hussein returned to Amman on 5 February and was pronounced dead on 7 February. The new Crown Prince was sworn in, as King Abdullah ibn al-Hussein of Jordan, on the same day. Prince Hamzeh ibn Hussein, the youngest son of King Hussein, became the new Crown Prince of Jordan.

In March 1999 King Abdullah announced the formation of a new Cabinet. Abd ar-Raouf ar-Rawabdeh, a former Deputy Prime Minister and mayor of Amman, replaced Fayez at-Tarawneh as Prime Minister and Minister of Defence; Abd al-Karim al-Kabariti was appointed Chief of the Royal Court. Ar-Rawabdeh's Cabinet contained eight ministers from the outgoing administration, including those responsible for the key portfolios of the interior, finance and foreign affairs, although several ministers regarded as loyal to Prince Hassan were replaced. In his letter of appointment to ar-Rawabdeh, King Abdullah prescribed 'fundamental reforms', including a strengthening of the rule of law and further democratization, as well as economic reforms to address the serious problems of poverty and unemployment in Jordan. The new Government won a strong vote of confidence from the National Assembly in early April, while opposition groups expressed cautious loyalty to the new King. The Muslim Brotherhood called for an open dialogue with the Government, and its political wing, the IAF, indicated that it would participate in municipal elections scheduled for July. However, the IAF did not join the Popular Participation Bloc, a new grouping of 13 leftist, Baathist and pan-Arab parties subsequently formed to contest the municipal elections, owing to a disagreement regarding quotas of candidates to be presented by each party.

All censorship of the foreign press was removed in April 1999. In the previous month King Abdullah had met with members of the Jordan Press Association, and Prime Minister ar-Rawabdeh encouraged members to propose amendments to the controversial Press and Publications Law. In June the Government agreed to amend part of the Law, in order to ease certain restrictions on journalists. Meanwhile, also in March King Abdullah released almost 500 prisoners as part of a recent amnesty law. In its annual report, released in April, the Arab Human Rights Organization in Jordan criticized the Government for an increase in human rights violations, including arrests of journalists and harsh treatment of prisoners held in detention centres. Moreover, a report published in June by Amnesty International alleged numerous cases of torture in Jordanian prisons.

The final results of municipal elections, held throughout Jordan in July 1999, indicated that independent and tribal candidates had secured the most seats. Islamists too were successful in their traditional urban strongholds: the IAF, which notably increased its presence on the Amman municipal council, announced subsequently that it would contest the general election due in 2001 if there were a change in the electoral law meanwhile. The overall level of participation by voters was around 59%; voting in some areas was marred by violence, as a result of which two people were killed. In September the Government agreed in principle to some of the opposition's demands regarding electoral reform; these included an increase in the number of seats in the House of Representatives from 80 to 120, and the division of the country into 80 electoral districts. (By late 2000, however, little progress appeared to have been made regarding this issue.)

In December 1999 King Abdullah appointed an Economic Consultative Council to supervise implementation of the Five-Year Plan for 1999–2003. In mid-January 2000 Abd al-Karim al-Kabariti, a long-standing rival of ar-Rawabdeh, resigned as Chief of the Royal Court for unspecified reasons. He was replaced by former premier Fayez at-Tarawneh (who had held the post during 1998). A reorganization of the Government followed shortly after: the new Cabinet, which included seven new ministers, was dominated by technocrats and supporters of the Prime Minister, and the key ministries remained unchanged. In late February the Deputy Prime Minister and Minister of Planning, Dr Rima Khalaf al-Hunaidi, announced her resignation, owing to alleged differences with the Government regarding economic reforms. Taleb Rifai was appointed as the new Minister of Planning in early May. Meanwhile, in mid-February a parliamentary committee charged with investigating allegations of corruption made against ar-Rawabdeh and his son Issam (both had been accused by a parliamentary deputy of having sought a US $20m. bribe from a Gulf businessman in return for securing approval to build a tourism complex in Jordan) cleared both the Prime Minister and his son of any wrongdoing.

In mid-February 2000 more than 3,000 people in Amman took part in a demonstration demanding that the National Assembly revoke the article in Jordan's penal code concerned with so-called 'honour killings'. The protest appeared to be led by King Abdullah's half-brother, Prince Ali, and the King's cousin and adviser on tribal affairs, Prince Ghazi bin Muhammad. The Government had recently attempted to persuade deputies to repeal the article—which protects those who murder female relatives in the name of 'family honour'—and to introduce harsh punishment for such crimes. The conservative establishment, however, believed that any change in the law would encourage adultery. In its annual report for 2000, the US-based Human Rights Watch condemned the practice of 'honour killings' as a violation of human rights. Later in February a majority of deputies in the House of Representatives submitted a petition to the Speaker, Abd al-Hadi al-Majali, demanding the implementation of *Shari'a* (Islamic) law in order to reduce corruption and nepotism in public office.

In mid-April 2000 a group of deputies in the House of Representatives, among them al-Majali and the Chairman of the Economic and Finance Committee, Ali Abu ar-Ragheb, urged King Abdullah to dismiss the ar-Rawabdeh Government for its failure to implement reforms and for violating public freedoms; they also called for the establishment of a 'parliamentary government' of deputies. At the same time opposition groups accused the Government of using excessive force in controlling public dissent. Although the King responded by expressing his confidence in the Prime Minister, in mid-June Abdullah dismissed ar-Rawabdeh, appointing the more liberal ar-Ragheb in his place. A new Cabinet was subsequently appointed, including nine Palestinians and three Islamists together with several ministers from the outgoing administration. A leading member of the IAF, Abd ar-Rahim al-Akour, was named as Minister of Municipal, Rural and Environmental Affairs, which led the IAF to suspend his party membership. King Abdullah stated that the priorities of the new Government (which secured a strong vote of confidence in the National Assembly in mid-July) were to end corruption, to introduce electoral legislation prior to the parliamentary elections scheduled for late 2001, and to accelerate the economic reform programme.

In late August 2000 King Abdullah was said to have called for the formation of a royal committee whose task would be to implement a 'drastic review' of the country's judicial system. At the end of September former Prime Ministers Ahmad Ubeidat and Taher al-Masri established a new political bloc, the Arab Democratic Front. Al-Majali was re-elected Speaker of the House of Representatives in late November. In mid-January 2001 the Government was forced to reverse a decision to increase fuel prices, following opposition from deputies who cited the widespread deterioration in living standards. In late January an Anti-Normalization Committee, composed of trade union activists opposed to Jordan's peace treaty with Israel, issued a list of organizations and public figures considered to have links with Israel (for further details, see below). Several leaders of the Committee, including its leader, Ali Abu as-Sukkar, were arrested by the Jordanian authorities, provoking condemnation by the Muslim Brotherhood. All the trade unionists were released on bail at the end of February, pending trial.

Meanwhile, in September 1997 relations with Israel were severely undermined when the head of the political bureau of the Islamist group Hamas, Khalid Meshaal, was the victim of an assassination attempt in Amman by agents of the Israeli intelligence service, Mossad. Following intensive negotiations involving Crown Prince Hassan, the Israeli Prime Minister, Binyamin Netanyahu, and US officials resulted in an agreement in October whereby Israel freed the Hamas spiritual leader, Sheikh Ahmad Yassin, in return for which Jordan released two Mossad agents arrested in connection with the attempt on Meshaal's life. A further 12 Mossad agents were expelled from Jordan following the release from Israeli custody of 23 Jordanian and 50 Palestinian detainees. The Mossad chief, Danny Yatom, resigned in February 1998 and was replaced by Ephraim Halevy, who had played an important role in the negotiations leading to the 1994 peace treaty between Israel and Jordan. The Jordanian Crown Prince and Israeli premier signed several bilateral trade agreements in March 1998, and in the following month King Hussein met with Netanyahu for the first time since the attempted assassination of Meshaal; in March, however, the Israeli Minister of National Infrastructure, Ariel Sharon, had angered Jordan by stating publicly that Israel still intended to kill Meshaal (although Sharon later retracted his remarks). King Hussein's mediation at the US-brokered peace summit held between the Israeli and Palestinian leaders in October was crucial to the signing of the Wye Memorandum (see the chapter on Israel). In December Israel agreed to open its airspace to foreign airlines *en route* for Jordan.

Upon his accession in February 1999 King Abdullah assured Israel that he was, like his father, committed to the Middle East peace process. None the less, Netanyahu's first official visit to Amman to meet the new King, in late February, was largely overshadowed by recent comments made by the Israeli premier to the effect that Jordan intended to strengthen its links with Iraq at the expense of improving relations with Israel. In July King Abdullah held talks with the new Israeli Prime Minister, Ehud Barak; discussions reportedly focused on ways to revive the peace process, as well as other bilateral concerns. King Abdullah welcomed the reactivation of the stalled Wye Memor-

andum by the signing (to which he was a witness) of the Sharm esh-Sheikh Memorandum (Wye Two—see the chapter on Israel) by Barak and Arafat in September 1999.

There was considerable speculation at the time of the Wye Two agreement that recent efforts to bring an end to Hamas' political activities in Jordan had been motivated by a consensus among the Jordanian, Palestinian, Israeli and US authorities on the need to contain potential Islamist opposition to a revival of the peace process. In August 1999 Hamas' offices in Amman were closed down by the Jordanian security forces, following claims by the authorities that the offices were being used for illegal political activities by non-Jordanian groups. The home of the Hamas bureau chief, Khalid Meshaal, was also raided, while some 15 Hamas officials were detained and arrest warrants were issued for a further five leading members of the organization. In late September three of the five (including Meshaal and the Hamas spokesman, Ibrahim Ghosheh) were arrested on their return to Amman from Iran, on charges of involvement in illicit political activities and the illegal possession of firearms; one of the men, a Yemeni national, was liable to immediate deportation. Further charges, which could carry the death penalty, were brought against Meshaal and Ghosheh in early October. In early November another senior Hamas official was arrested, amid reports that the organization had rejected an offer by the Jordanian Government to release the detained activists provided they agreed to cease all political activity and that their leaders left the country. Later in the month the Jordanian authorities released some 24 Hamas officials, including four leaders (including Meshaal and Ghosheh) who were immediately flown to Qatar. An appeal against this effective deportation, lodged by the four leaders at Jordan's Higher Court of Justice in January 2000, was rejected in late June; a further appeal was expected. In mid-November, during talks with Khalid Meshaal in Qatar, Jordan's Prime Minister, Ali Abu ar-Ragheb, reportedly reiterated the conditions under which the Hamas leaders would be allowed to return to Jordan. Meanwhile, in December 1999 16 people were arrested on charges of plotting attacks against US and tourist targets in Jordan. The detainees were alleged to be members of the al-Qa'idah (Base) organization, which has links with the Saudi-born militant Islamist, Osama bin Laden. Trial proceedings began against the 16 in Amman in early May 2000; a further 12 members of al-Qa'idah were tried *in absentia*. In mid-September six of the defendants were sentenced to death, having been convicted of charges including membership of al-Qa'idah and the manufacture of explosives; 16 were condemned to various terms of imprisonment, while six defendants were acquitted. The Jordanian authorities arrested a number of suspected Islamist fundamentalists in mid-July 2000, apparently in response to a warning that the US embassy in Amman was vulnerable to attacks by militant groups.

King Abdullah postponed his first visit to Israel in mid-February 2000, apparently in protest at recent Israeli bombing raids against infrastructure targets in Lebanon (although Jordanian officials cited the lack of progress in the Middle East peace process as the reason for the delay). Abdullah finally visited Israel in April, when he held short discussions with Ehud Barak regarding the peace process as well as water management and other bilateral issues.

In advance of the Israeli-Palestinian peace talks held at the US presidential retreat at Camp David, Maryland, in July 2000, Prime Minister ar-Ragheb emphasized that the Jordanian Government would not accept any more Palestinian refugees and that it supported their right of return to their homeland. (Recent reports had implied that Jordan was being considered as a possible home for those displaced persons currently in refugee camps in Lebanon.) In August King Abdullah reiterated that Jordan would not accept Israeli or international sovereignty over the Islamic holy sites in East Jerusalem, an issue that was a major obstacle to progress at Camp David.

King Abdullah participated in the intense diplomatic efforts aimed at restoring peace in the region following the outbreak of violence in the West Bank and Gaza provoked by a controversial visit by Ariel Sharon (now leader of the Likud party in Israel) to the site of Temple Mount/Haram ash-Sharif in late September 2000. In mid-October the King attended the US-brokered summit meeting between Ehud Barak and Yasser Arafat in Sharm esh-Sheikh, Egypt. As violence between Palestinians and Israeli security forces escalated, Jordan came under growing pressure from other Arab states to sever diplomatic ties with Israel, while large-scale public demonstrations against

Israeli and US policies towards the Palestinians were held in Amman and in Jordan's refugee camps. One 'anti-normalization' protest held in early October resulted in violent confrontations between protesters and police, in which 69 policemen were wounded. The Government subsequently issued a ban on demonstrations, and several protesters were detained. Meanwhile, Jordan delayed the dispatch of its new ambassador to Israel, owing to the deteriorating situation in the West Bank and Gaza; also in October 30 parliamentary deputies signed a petition demanding the expulsion of the Israeli ambassador in Amman. In late October Jordanian police used tear gas and water cannons to disperse thousands of protesters who had gathered on Jordan's border with the West Bank in support of the right of return for Palestinian refugees. In mid-November the Israeli Vice-Consul in Amman was injured in a gun attack by militant Islamists; another Israeli diplomat was wounded in a similar attack in early December. In late November, meanwhile, King Abdullah appealed to the USA to intervene in order to halt 'Israeli aggressive practices' which threatened to destroy the prospects for Middle East peace. Abdullah expressed his hopes that the peace process would continue following the election of the hard-line Ariel Sharon as Israeli Prime Minister in early February 2001 and appealed to the new US administration under President George W. Bush to engage actively in efforts to bring an end to the violence.

Jordan's relations with the USA in the early 1990s were frequently strained by US allegations of Jordanian assistance to Iraq in circumventing the UN trade embargo, as well as Jordan's vocal criticism of US-led policies towards Iraq. In July 1993 the USA reportedly informed Jordan that it must make payments to the UN Compensation Fund for Kuwait if it continued to receive deliveries of petroleum from Iraq. In September, however, US President Bill Clinton announced that some US $30m. in economic and military aid to Jordan was to be released in recognition of the country's enforcement of sanctions against Iraq and of its role in the Middle East peace process. In early 1994 renewed tensions emerged with the USA over the Jerusalem issue and the US-led naval blockade of Jordan's only port at Aqaba. In August 1995, as King Hussein formally severed political ties with Iraq (see below), Clinton promised to support Jordan in the event of any threat to its security; however, the USA failed to persuade Jordan to sever all economic links with Iraq. In January 1996 the USA offered Jordan $300m. in military aid, and an expansion of bilateral military co-operation was announced in March. In June 1997 the USA pledged $100m. in economic aid to Jordan, reportedly in recognition of Jordan's contributions to the regional peace process; an assistance fund was established in August. In the same month Jordan signed a debt-rescheduling agreement with the USA, in accordance with an agreement reached in May by members of the 'Paris Club' of Western official creditors to reschedule approximately $400m. of Jordanian debt. During a visit to Washington, DC, in March 1998 King Hussein reiterated demands that the USA exert pressure on Israel to make concessions over the West Bank. The King also proposed Jordan's participation in future negotiations between US and Iraqi officials.

In May 1999 King Abdullah began a three-week tour of the USA and several European capitals. Prior to the visit, the King had announced that, in anticipation of a summit of leaders of the Group of Eight (G-8) industrialized countries, due to be held in Germany in June, he would be seeking US support for an agreement by Western countries to write off as much as 50% of Jordan's debt. He achieved some success when, in late May (two days after a meeting with President Clinton) the 'Paris Club' agreed to reschedule about US $800m. of Jordanian debt. In June the G-8 leaders recommended arrangements for debt-reduction for Jordan, and King Abdullah acknowledged the USA's role in the decision. In mid-2000 King Abdullah held a series of meetings with President Clinton and senior US officials to discuss the Middle East peace process and bilateral trade. During a visit by the King to Washington, DC, in late October, Jordan and the USA signed a free-trade agreement.

After August 1995, when Jordan granted political asylum to the two sons-in-law of the Iraqi President, Saddam Hussein, and their wives (see the chapter on Iraq), King Hussein became more openly critical of the Iraqi regime, although Jordan continued to provide Iraq with a crucial external economic link. In October King Hussein denounced the presidential election in Iraq as a farce; he was reported to have established contact with Iraqi opposition groups in London, United Kingdom, and to have proposed a congress in Amman in order to discuss

political change in Iraq. Jordan's new policy towards Iraq provoked some suspicion in Egypt and Syria that it might lead to a further US-backed strategic reorientation in the region, bringing together the USA, Israel, Turkey and Jordan in a military alliance designed to protect Israeli and US interests. In December 1997 Jordan recalled its chargé d'affaires in Baghdad and expelled a number of Iraqi diplomats from Jordan in protest at the execution of four Jordanians by the Iraqi authorities. Later in December, none the less, the two countries signed an agreement whereby Iraq was to supply 4.8m. metric tons of crude petroleum and refined petroleum products to Jordan in 1998. In January 1998 more than 50 Jordanian detainees were released by Iraq as a 'goodwill gesture'.

In response to critical confrontations between Iraq and the UN in the course of 1998 over the issue of weapons inspections, Jordan indicated that it would not allow its territory or airspace to be used for air-strikes against Iraq. King Hussein consistently advocated a resolution of the crises by diplomatic means, whilst urging Iraq to comply with all pertinent UN resolutions. This position allowed Jordan to improve its relations with some Arab states, notably Egypt. In February riot police in Amman and Ma'an dispersed mass protests against the US-led military build-up in the Gulf. (The demonstrations were organized by various Islamist groups and trade unions, in defiance of an official ban on pro-Iraq protests.) Jordan strongly condemned the air-strikes carried out against Iraq by US and British forces in December, and in early 1999 the Jordanian National Assembly voted in favour of an end to the UN embargo against Iraq.

King Abdullah made attempts to improve Jordan's relations with Iraq following his accession in February 1999. However, in early June 2000 Jordan condemned the execution by Iraq of a Jordanian national charged with spying for the US Central Intelligence Agency (CIA). Tensions were eased somewhat following a visit to Amman in mid-July by Iraqi Vice-President Taha Yassin Ramadan. At the end of November it was reported that the resumption of commercial flights between Amman and Baghdad was imminent; following objections by the UN, however, in mid-December the Jordanian authorities decided not to resume regular flights. In early November Prime Minister ar-Ragheb undertook an official visit to Iraq—the first visit by a Jordanian premier since 1991—and the two states agreed to increase the value of their trade agreement from US $300m. in 2000 to $450m. in 2001. Jordan condemned the air-strikes launched on Baghdad by US and British air forces in mid-February 2001.

Meanwhile, King Abdullah sought to strengthen relations with other Arab states. His first major foreign visit was to Egypt for talks with President Mubarak in March 1999. (Jordan and Egypt had signed an agreement in December 1998 providing for the establishment of a free-trade zone by 2005.) During April 1999 the new King visited Saudi Arabia, Libya, Morocco, the United Arab Emirates and Kuwait. Jordan's embassy in Kuwait had been reopened in March, following the restoration of full diplomatic relations between the two countries (which had been severed in 1990), and in September 1999 the *rapprochement* was apparently confirmed as King Abdullah again visited Kuwait. Kuwait subsequently announced an end to a nine-year ban on the sale of Jordanian newspapers. In October Kuwait returned an ambassador to Amman (the post having been vacant since the Gulf crisis of 1990–91). It was reported in early 2000 that Kuwait's Amir intended to visit Jordan for the first time since 1990. King Abdullah became the first Jordanian monarch to visit Lebanon for more than 30 years when, in September 1999, he held discussions with senior officials there regarding both the Middle East peace process and bilateral issues including a planned free trade agreement between the two countries.

President Hafiz al-Assad of Syria led a high-level Syrian delegation at King Hussein's funeral in February 1999, since when Jordan's relations with Syria have improved significantly. In May it was announced that Syria would supply Jordan with water in order to ease the summer drought. In June Jordan refused to participate in joint Turkish-Israeli naval exercises, scheduled for July; similar exercises in 1998 had created a diplomatic crisis with Syria. In August the first senior Syrian delegation for almost a decade visited Amman for a session of the Jordanian-Syrian Higher Committee; the meeting resulted in a bilateral accord that officials hoped might double the volume of trade between the two countries. Later in the month Syria was reported to have agreed to end the ban (imposed in 1994) on the free circulation of Jordanian newspapers and publications.

King Abdullah made an unscheduled visit to Syria in July 1999, amid Jordanian concerns that any peace agreement concluded by Israel and Syria could damage the Palestinians' position and effectively isolate them in future negotiations. None the less, following the resumption of negotiations on the Syria-Israel track of the peace process in December 1999, Abdullah urged Israel to make concessions to Syria in order to increase the likelihood of a bilateral settlement being reached. King Abdullah attended the funeral of President Assad in June 2000, and acted swiftly to forge close relations with the new Syrian President, Bashar al-Assad. In late November Syria confirmed that it had upgraded its diplomatic representation in Amman to ambassadorial status, and the Syrian state airline resumed regular flights to Amman after a hiatus of more than 20 years. The Syrian authorities declared in January 2001 that all Jordanian prisoners held in Syria would be released in the near future.

Government

Jordan is a constitutional monarchy. Legislative power is vested in a bicameral National Assembly: the Senate (House of Notables) has 40 members, appointed by the King for eight years (one-half of the members retiring every four years), while the House of Representatives (House of Deputies) has 80 members, elected by universal adult suffrage for four years. Executive power is vested in the King, who governs with the assistance of an appointed Council of Ministers, responsible to the Assembly.

There are eight administrative provinces, of which three have been occupied by Israel since June 1967.

Defence

The total strength of the Jordanian armed forces in August 2000 was estimated at 103,880. The army had 90,000 men, the air force 13,400 and the navy (coastguard) an estimated 480. Reserve forces numbered 35,000 (30,000 in the army). Paramilitary forces numbered an estimated 45,000 men, comprising a Civil Militia of 35,000 and a Public Security Force of 10,000. Military service is based on selective conscription. Defence expenditure in 1999 amounted to JD 403m.

Economic Affairs

In 1998, according to estimates by the World Bank, the East Bank of Jordan's gross national product (GNP), measured at average 1996–98 prices, was US $5,252m., equivalent to $1,150 per head (or $2,615 per head on an international purchasing-power parity basis). During 1990–98, it was estimated, GNP per head increased, in real terms, at an average rate of 2.1% per year. Over the same period, the population increased by an average of 5.2% per year. GNP totalled $7,000m. in 1999, equivalent to $1,500 per head. The East Bank's gross domestic product (GDP) increased, in real terms, by an average of 4.8% per year in 1990–99. GDP growth was 2.0% in 1999.

Agriculture (including hunting, forestry and fishing) contributed about 3.0% of Jordan's GDP in 1998. An estimated 6.1% of the country's labour force were employed in the sector in 1999. The principal cash crops are vegetables, fruit and nuts, which accounted for about 7.4% of export earnings in 1999. Wheat production is also important. During 1990–99 agricultural GDP decreased by an average of 4.6% per year. Agricultural production declined by 20.8% in 1999, owing to severe drought in that year, although output increased by an estimated 16.5% in 2000.

Industry (including mining, manufacturing, construction and power) provided an estimated 24.9% of GDP in 1998. In 1999 about 22.2% of the country's active labour force were employed in the industrial sector. During 1990–99 industrial GDP increased by an average of 6.2% per year.

Mining and quarrying contributed an estimated 3.5% of GDP in 1998. The sector employed about 1.5% of the total labour force in 1999. Phosphates and potash are the major mineral exports, together accounting for about 22.9% of total export earnings in 1999. Jordan also has reserves of oil-bearing shale, but exploitation of this resource is at present undeveloped. The GDP of the mining sector increased by 5.4% in 1997, but declined by an estimated 5.9% in 1998.

Manufacturing provided an estimated 14.9% of GDP in 1998, and engaged about 11.6% of the employed labour force in 1999. In 1997 the most important branches of manufacturing, measured by gross value of output, were food, beverages and tobacco (accounting for 25.3% of the total), refined petroleum products (17.4%), chemicals (11.0%), non-metallic mineral products (9.1%) and metal products (7.2%). Manufacturing GDP increased by an annual average of 6.5% in 1990–98.

Energy is derived principally from imported petroleum, but attempts are being made to develop alternative sources of power, including wind and solar power. Imports of mineral fuels comprised 12.1% of the total value of imports in 1999.

Services (including wholesale and retail trade, restaurants and hotels, transport, financing and community, social and personal services) accounted for some 72.1% of Jordan's GDP in 1998. In 1999 an estimated 71.7% of the total employed labour force were engaged in the service sector. During 1990–98 the GDP of the service sector increased by an average of 5.5% per year.

In 1999 Jordan recorded a visible trade deficit of US $1,460.1m., while there was a surplus of $404.9m. on the current account of the balance of payments. In 1999 Iraq was the principal source of imports and was also a significant market for exports. In that year the principal export market was India. Other major trading partners were Germany, Saudi Arabia and the USA. The principal exports in 1999 were chemicals, minerals and basic manufactures, while the principal imports were machinery and transport equipment, food and live animals and basic manufactures.

In 1999 there was a budget deficit of JD 223.6m., equivalent to 4.2% of GDP in that year. Jordan's external debt totalled US $8,485m. at the end of 1998, of which US $7,388m. was long-term public debt. In that year the cost of debt-servicing was equivalent to 16.4% of the value of exports of goods and services. The annual rate of inflation averaged 3.8% in 1990–99. Inflation slowed to an average of 0.6% in 1999, from 3.1% in 1998. Unemployment was officially put at 16% of the labour force in 1999, but unofficially estimated to be 20%–30%.

Jordan is a member of the Council of Arab Economic Unity (p. 163), the Arab Co-operation Council (p. 306), the Arab Monetary Fund (p. 126) and the World Trade Organization (see p. 292). In September 1999 the Jordanian parliament ratified the Jordanian-European Partnership Agreement (signed with the European Union in November 1997), which allows for the creation of a duty-free zone and for the abolition of import duties by 2010.

Since the early 1990s the Jordanian economy has been constrained by a heavy burden of foreign debt and by the loss, owing to the imposition of UN sanctions, of its vital Iraqi market. Nevertheless, the conclusion of a peace treaty with Israel in 1994 created new opportunities in tourism, transport and banking, and facilitated co-operation in areas such as water management. Furthermore, an improvement in relations with other Arab states afforded new trading and co-operation opportunities. Jordan has implemented an IMF-supported adjustment and reform programme with the aim of reducing state intervention in industry and, through privatization, raising funds to support the repayment of foreign debt. In order to encourage foreign investment, all foreign-exchange restrictions were revoked in June 1997. By early 2001 the restructuring of a number of state enterprises was under way, notably in the utilities, transport, postal and telecommunications sectors. Jordan is deemed to have brought its external debt under control, a process facilitated by a series of debt-relief measures by Western official creditors in the late 1990s (see Recent History); however, the IMF has recommended a faster pace of structural reform, as well as reform of the tax system and the introduction of new banking legislation. A value-added tax was scheduled to be introduced in 2001. In January of that year the Aqaba region was accorded the status of a Special Economic Zone, which the Government hoped would attract investment worth US $6,000m. and create as many as 70,000 new jobs by 2020. By 2000 the Jordanian economy was emerging from four years of stagnation, although the growth rate was deemed to be insufficient to reduce unemployment and raise living standards. In June the new Government under Ali Abu ar-Ragheb stated that one of its priorities would be to accelerate the IMF-sponsored reforms. However, although the IMF required GDP growth of 3%–4% per year under the 1999–2003 Five Year Plan, by mid-2000 the projection for that year's growth had been revised to 2.5%, and there were subsequently fears that the economy would be further depressed as a consequence of the renewed Palestinian *intifada*.

Social Welfare

There is at present no comprehensive welfare scheme but the Government administers medical and health services. In 1999 Jordan had 84 hospital establishments, providing 8,726 beds.

There were 11,090 registered physicians in 1999. A new Social Security Law, providing security for both employers and employees, was put into effect in 1978 and extended in 1981. In 1999 the Government announced plans for the introduction of a national health service, scheduled for completion in 2010. In 2000 the Government, with World Bank assistance, was formulating a 'social productivity package', to include the provision of financial aid directly to the poor and improvements to infrastructure in deprived areas. Of total budgetary expenditure by the central Government in 1997, JD 172.2m. (10.2%) was for health services, and a further JD 298.9m. (17.8%) for social security and welfare.

In June 2000 there were 1,570,192 Palestinian refugees in Jordan and a further 583,009 in the West Bank registered with the UN Relief and Works Agency for Palestine Refugees in the Near East (UNRWA).

Education

Primary education, beginning at six years of age, is free and compulsory. This 10-year preparatory cycle is followed by a two-year secondary cycle. UNRWA provides schooling for Palestinian refugees. In 19998/99, at the primary level, there were 46,900 teachers and 1,135,100 pupils. At the secondary level (including both general and vocational education) there were 13,400 teachers and 165,500 pupils in 1998/99. In 1996/97 there were 5,275 teachers and 112,959 pupils engaged in higher

education. In 1998 there were 4,478 schools and 21 universities in Jordan. Budgetary expenditure on education by the central Government in 1997 was JD 245.1m. (14.6% of total spending).

Public Holidays

2001: 15 January (Arbor Day), 30 January (King Abdullah's Birthday), 6 March* (Id al-Adha, Feast of the Sacrifice), 22 March (Arab League Day), 26 March* (Muharram, Islamic New Year), 25 May (Independence Day), 4 June* (Mouloud, birth of Muhammad), 9 June (King Abdullah's Accession), 15 October* (Leilat al-Meiraj, ascension of Muhammad), 14 November (the late King Hussein's Birthday); 17 December* (Id al-Fitr, end of Ramadan).

2002: 15 January (Arbor Day), 30 January (King Abdullah's Birthday), 23 February* (Id al-Adha, Feast of the Sacrifice), 15 March* (Muharram, Islamic New Year), 22 March (Arab League Day), 24 May* (Mouloud, birth of Muhammad), 25 May (Independence Day), 9 June (King Abdullah's Accession), 4 October* (Leilat al-Meiraj, ascension of Muhammad), 14 November (the late King Hussein's Birthday), 6 December* (Id al-Fitr, end of Ramadan).

* These holidays are dependent on the Islamic lunar calendar and may vary by one or two days from the dates given.

Weights and Measures

The metric system is in force. In Jordan the dunum is 1,000 sq m (0.247 acre).

Statistical Survey

Source: Department of Statistics, POB 2015, Amman; tel. (6) 5342171; fax (6) 5333518; e-mail stat@dos.gov.jo; internet www.dos.gov.jo.

Area and Population

AREA, POPULATION AND DENSITY (East and West Banks)

Area (sq km)	97,740*
Population (UN estimates at mid-year)	
1997†	6,126,000
1998†	6,304,000
1999‡	6,482,000
Density (per sq km) at mid-1999	66.3

* 37,738 sq miles.
† Source: UN, *World Population Prospects: The 1998 Revision.*
‡ Source: UN, *Population and Vital Statistics Report.*

(East Bank only)

Area (sq km)	89,342*
Population (census results)	
10–11 November 1979	2,100,019
10 December 1994	
Males	2,135,883
Females	1,959,696
Total	4,095,579
Population (official estimates at 31 December)	
1998	4,755,800
1999	4,900,000
2000	5,039,000
Density (per sq km) at 31 December 2000 . . .	56.4

* 34,495 sq miles.

GOVERNORATES
(East Bank only; estimated population at 31 December 1999)

	Area (sq km)	Population	Density (per sq km)
Amman	8,231	1,864,500	226.5
Irbid	1,621	874,200	539.3
Zarqa	4,080	770,800	188.9
Balqa	1,076	321,400	298.7
Mafraq	26,435	225,900	8.5
Karak	3,217	197,000	61.2
Jarash	402	144,100	358.5
Madaba	2,008	125,000	62.3
Ajloun	412	108,800	264.1
Aqaba	6,583	98,500	15.0
Ma'an	33,163	95,600	2.9
Tafilah	2,114	74,500	35.2
Total	89,342	4,900,000	54.8

PRINCIPAL TOWNS (including suburbs)

Population at 31 December 1991: Amman (capital) 965,000; Zarqa 359,000; Irbid 216,000; Russeifa 115,500.

BIRTHS, MARRIAGES AND DEATHS (East Bank only)*

	Registered live births		Registered marriages		Registered deaths	
	Number	Rate (per 1,000)	Number	Rate (per 1,000)	Number	Rate (per 1,000)
1992 . .	125,395	n.a.	37,216	n.a.	11,820	n.a.
1993 . .	134,489	n.a.	40,391	n.a.	11,915	n.a.
1994 . .	140,444	34.5	36,132	8.9	12,290	3.0
1995 . .	141,319	33.5	35,501	8.4	13,018	3.1
1996 . .	142,404	32.6	34,425	7.9	13,302	3.0
1997 . .	130,633	28.4	37,278	8.1	13,190	2.9
1998 . .	133,714	28.1	39,376	8.3	13,552	2.8
1999 . .	135,300†	28.0	39,400†	8.2	13,900†	2.9

* Data are tabulated by year of registration rather than by year of occurrence. Registration of births and marriages is reported to be complete, but death registration is incomplete. Figures exclude foreigners, but include registered Palestinian refugees.
† Figures are rounded.

Expectation of life (years at birth, 1998): Males 68.0; Females 70.0.

ECONOMICALLY ACTIVE POPULATION (Jordanians only)

	1990	1991	1992
Agriculture	38,266	40,848	44,400
Mining and manufacturing . .	53,468	56,856	61,800
Electricity and water . . .	6,815	7,176	6,600
Construction	51,895	54,096	60,000
Trade	52,944	56,856	63,000
Transport and communications .	44,557	48,576	52,200
Financial and insurance services .	16,774	17,664	19,800
Social and administrative services	259,478	269,928	292,200
Total employed . . .	524,197	552,000	600,000
Unemployed	106,000	128,000	106,000
Total civilian labour force . .	630,197	680,000	706,000

Source: Ministry of Labour, *Annual Report.*

Agriculture

PRINCIPAL CROPS (East Bank only; '000 metric tons)

	1997	1998	1999
Wheat	42	36	9
Barley	43	45	5
Potatoes	95	88	96
Olives	57	138	38
Cabbages	14	15	35*
Tomatoes	324	300	293
Cauliflowers	27	48	49
Pumpkins, squash and gourds .	29	37	36
Cucumbers and gherkins . .	59	90	66
Eggplants (Aubergines) . .	40	53	44
Green peppers	19	24	24†
Onions (dry)	18	21	28
Green beans	14	18	11
Other vegetables	96	104	95
Watermelons	105	90	121
Melons	19	17	17†
Grapes	18	18	18
Apples	31	39	31
Oranges	29	38	18
Tangerines, mandarins, clementines and satsumas . .	87	55	33
Lemons and limes . . .	45	43	24
Bananas	18	24	24†
Other fruits and berries . .	55	48	48
Tobacco (leaves)	2	2	2†

* Unofficial figure.　　† FAO estimate.
Source: FAO.

LIVESTOCK (East Bank only; '000 head, year ending September)

	1997	1998	1999
Horses*	4	4	4
Mules*	3	3	3
Asses*	18	18	18
Cattle	52	56	57
Camels*	18	18	18
Sheep	2,144	1,935	1,581
Goats	782	650	631

* FAO estimate(s).

Poultry (million): 23 in 1997; 24 in 1998 (FAO estimate); 25 in 1999 (FAO estimate).

Source: FAO.

LIVESTOCK PRODUCTS (East Bank only; '000 metric tons)

	1997	1998	1999
Beef and veal	4	3	4
Mutton and lamb	9	15	13
Goat meat	3	4	3
Poultry meat	98	93	111
Cows' milk	115	123	141
Sheeps' milk	35	31	20
Goats' milk	20	16	12
Cheese	4	4	2
Hen eggs	51	51	48
Greasy wool	4	4	4
Sheepskins	1*	1*	—

* FAO estimate(s).

Source: FAO.

Forestry

ROUNDWOOD REMOVALS ('000 cubic metres, excluding bark)

	1996	1997	1998
Industrial wood	4	4	4
Fuel wood	6	7	7
Total	10	11	11

Source: FAO, *Yearbook of Forest Products*.

Fishing

(metric tons, live weight)

	1996	1997	1998
Capture	440	450	470
Freshwater fishes . .	350	350	350
Tunas	n.a.	n.a.	70
Other marine fishes . .	90	100	50
Aquaculture	181	200	293
Freshwater fishes . .	181	200	293
Total catch	621	650	763

Source: FAO, *Yearbook of Fishery Statistics*.

Mining

('000 metric tons)

	1994	1995	1996
Crude petroleum	1.2	1.5	1.9
Phosphate rock . . .	4,216.5	4,983.9	5,424.2
Potash salts* . . .	1,550.3	1,780.0	1,765.5
Salt (unrefined) . . .	19	57	50

* Figures refer to the K_2O content.

Industry

SELECTED PRODUCTS ('000 metric tons, unless otherwise indicated)

	1994	1995	1996
Liquefied petroleum gas . .	126	138	133
Motor spirit (petrol) . . .	471	483	500
Aviation gasoline . . .	20*	30	32
Kerosene	222	215	202
Jet fuels	198	244	298
Distillate fuel oils . . .	859	872	853
Residual fuel oils . . .	901	995	1,020
Lubricating oils . . .	24	25	27
Petroleum bitumen (asphalt) .	136	129	141
Nitrogenous fertilizers (a)† .	135	131	121
Phosphate fertilizers (b)† . .	750	729	671
Potassic fertilizers (c)† . .	930	1,068	1,059
Cement	3,392	3,415	3,512
Cigarettes (million) . . .	4,191	3,675	4,738
Electricity (million kWh) . .	5,075	5,616	6,058

* Estimated production.

† Production in terms of (a) nitrogen; (b) phosphoric acid; and (c) potassium oxide.

Source: UN, *Industrial Commodity Statistics Yearbook*.

1997: Cement ('000 metric tons) 3,252; Electricity (million kWh) 5,940.
1998: Cement ('000 metric tons) 2,652; Electricity (million kWh) 6,336.
1999: Electricity (million kWh) 6,828.

Source: UN, *Monthly Bulletin of Statistics*.

Finance

CURRENCY AND EXCHANGE RATES

Monetary Units
1,000 fils = 1 Jordanian dinar (JD).

Sterling, Dollar and Euro Equivalents (29 December 2000)
£1 sterling = JD 1.0580;
US $1 = 709.0 fils;
€1 = 659.7 fils;
JD 100 = £94.52 = $141.04 = €151.58.

Exchange Rate
An official mid-point rate of US $1 = 709 fils (JD1 = $1.4104) has been maintained since October 1995.

BUDGET (East Bank only; JD million)*

Revenue†	1997	1998	1999
Taxation	798.0	858.6	884.2
Taxes on income and profits .	150.0	139.6	152.8
Corporations	96.6	84.1	94.2
Individuals	33.5	35.4	35.7
Taxes on domestic transactions	375.0	407.5	435.0
General sales tax . . .	315.0	350.3	372.5
Taxes on foreign trade . .	246.0	294.3	279.3
Customs duties . . .	240.0	288.4	274.0
Other revenue	597.0	637.9	701.1
Licences	32.0	24.2	24.9
Fees	166.0	167.9	172.4
Interest and profits . . .	19.0	152.3	197.4
Total	1,395.0	1,496.5	1,585.3

Expenditure‡	1997	1998	1999
Wages and salaries . . .	351.0	339.0	343.4
Purchases of goods and services	77.0	63.1	72.6
Interest payments . . .	238.0	247.7	278.1
Food subsidies . . .	71.0	38.0	15.0
Other transfers . . .	283.0	371.4	376.7
Pensions . . .	213.0	235.0	238.5
Decentralized agencies . .	43.0	62.7	66.8
University and municipalities	—	43.0	43.0
Defence and security . . .	444.0	491.0	512.1
Total	1,776.0	2,010.1	1,942.1
Current	1,489.0	1,664.6	1,643.1
Capital§	287.0	365.5	299.0

* Figures represent a consolidation of the Current, Capital and Development Plan Budgets of the central Government. The data exclude the operations of the Health Security Fund and of other government agencies with individual budgets.

† Excluding foreign grants received (JD million): 225.0 in 1997; 203.0 in 1998; 198.5 in 1999.

‡ Excluding lending minus repayments (JD million): −1.0 in 1997; 45.0 in 1998; 65.3 in 1999.

§ Includes overdue settlements and arrears on public sector.

Source: IMF, Ministry of Finance.

INTERNATIONAL RESERVES (US $ million at 31 December)

	1997	1998	1999
Gold*	200.7	204.3	120.0
IMF special drawing rights . .	0.2	0.8	0.3
Foreign exchange . . .	2,200.1	1,749.6	2,628.8
Total	2,401.0	1,954.7	2,749.1

* National valuation.

Source: IMF, *International Financial Statistics*.

MONEY SUPPLY (JD million at 31 December)

	1997	1998	1999
Currency outside banks . .	987.6	952.8	1,106.6
Demand deposits at commercial banks	636.1	648.5	658.0
Total money (incl. others) . .	1,626.1	1,612.6	1,766.1

Source: IMF, *International Financial Statistics*.

COST OF LIVING (Consumer Price Index; base: 1990 = 100)

	1997	1998	1999
Food (incl. beverages) . . .	144.1	149.8	148.5
Electricity, gas and other fuels	130.0	131.4	131.5
Clothing (incl. footwear) . .	151.4	157.1	165.5
Rent	122.8	125.0	126.1
All items (incl. others) . .	135.1	139.3	140.1

Source: ILO, *Yearbook of Labour Statistics*.

NATIONAL ACCOUNTS (East Bank only; JD million at current prices)
Expenditure on the Gross Domestic Product

	1997	1998	1999
Government final consumption expenditure . . .	1,316.8	1,365.0	1,408.4
Private final consumption expenditure . . .	3,451.1	3,689.5	3,740.7
Increase in stocks . . .	−3.3	35.6	35.6
Gross fixed capital formation .	1,325.1	1,182.9	1,153.9
Total domestic expenditure .	6,089.7	6,273.0	6,338.6
Exports of goods and services	2,532.8	2,515.7	2,505.0
Less Imports of goods and services	3,676.7	3,608.7	3,550.6
GDP in purchasers' values .	4,945.8	5,180.0	5,293.0
GDP at constant 1985 prices .	2,764.5	2,824.9	n.a.

Source: IMF, *International Financial Statistics*

Gross Domestic Product by Economic Activity

	1996	1997	1998*
Agriculture, hunting, forestry and fishing	158.6	148.3	144.8
Mining and quarrying . . .	153.7	169.9	170.4
Manufacturing	570.0	621.6	726.7
Electricity and water . . .	104.4	117.8	121.2
Construction	254.8	224.2	195.5
Wholesale and retail trade, restaurants and hotels . . .	493.9	582.7	609.9
Transport, storage and communications . . .	642.7	672.9	717.0
Finance, insurance, real estate and business services . . .	882.3	918.5	979.2
Government services . . .	827.4	896.2	943.2
Other community, social and personal services . . .	147.0	177.8	196.5
Private non-profit services to households	51.5	52.9	56.1
Domestic services of households	5.3	5.2	6.6
Sub-total	4,291.6	4,588.0	4,867.1
Less Imputed bank service charge	77.3	81.0	107.5
GDP at factor cost . . .	4,214.3	4,507.0	4,759.6
Indirect taxes, *less* subsidies .	768.2	685.6	886.4
GDP in purchasers' values .	4,982.5	5,192.6	5,645.9

*Preliminary figures.

BALANCE OF PAYMENTS (US $ million)

	1997	1998	1999
Exports of goods f.o.b. . . .	1,835.5	1,802.4	1,831.9
Imports of goods f.o.b. . . .	−3,648.5	−3,403.9	−3,292.0
Trade balance	−1,813.0	−1,601.6	−1,460.1
Exports of services . . .	1,736.8	1,825.1	1,701.7
Imports of services . . .	−1,537.2	−1,783.8	−1,698.0
Balance on goods and services	−1,613.4	−1,560.2	−1,456.4
Other income received . .	248.2	306.9	301.1
Other income paid . . .	−457.0	−445.0	−455.6
Balance on goods, services and income	−1,822.1	−1,698.3	−1,610.9
Current transfers received . .	2,096.1	1,984.3	2,321.3
Current transfers paid . .	−244.6	−271.9	−305.5
Current balance . . .	29.3	14.1	404.9
Capital account (net) . . .	163.8	81.1	90.3
Direct investment abroad . . .	—	—	−4.5
Direct investment from abroad .	360.9	310.0	158.0
Other investment assets . .	16.4	−80.3	−73.5
Other investment liabilities .	−135.0	−407.1	353.9
Net errors and omissions . .	−160.8	−454.0	−10.2
Overall balance . . .	274.6	−536.1	972.9

Source: IMF, *International Financial Statistics*.

External Trade

PRINCIPAL COMMODITIES (distribution by SITC, US $ million)

Imports c.i.f.	1997	1998	1999
Food and live animals . . .	761.0	750.6	682.8
Crude materials (inedible) except fuels	118.4	125.0	119.0
Mineral fuels, lubricants, etc. . .	541.5	355.2	450.0
Crude petroleum . . .	410.4	254.5	311.0
Animal and vegetable oils and fats	136.6	81.3	63.0
Chemicals	477.2	488.3	471.4
Basic manufactures . . .	625.1	614.6	551.8
Machinery and transport equipment	1,148.3	1,095.7	1,022.4
Miscellaneous manufactured articles	209.3	246.9	254.8
Total (incl. others) . . .	4,101.7	3,828.5	3,716.8

Exports f.o.b.	1997	1998	1999
Natural calcium phosphates .	189.8	197.1	162.4
Natural potassic salts, crude .	139.1	157.5	177.7
Chemicals	472.6	456.0	497.2
Fertilizers	134.7	145.8	110.3
Cement	47.2	22.8	23.4
Vegetables, fruit and nuts .	129.0	151.1	110.3
Basic manufactures . . .	155.2	141.2	153.2
Machinery and transport equipment . . .	49.0	64.0	95.9
Miscellaneous manufactured articles	80.4	110.4	109.4
Total (incl. others) . . .	1,505.2	1,475.9	1,482.9

Source: Central Bank of Jordan.

PRINCIPAL TRADING PARTNERS
(countries of consignment, US $ million)

Imports c.i.f.	1997	1998	1999
Argentina	82.0	87.9	69.4
Australia	36.6	32.0	52.1
Belgium-Luxembourg . . .	54.0	67.7	42.6
Brazil	46.9	35.2	23.4
China, People's Republic . . .	102.0	101.5	118.1
Egypt	36.3	44.5	41.1
France	142.9	147.8	144.3
Germany	411.9	374.9	361.1
India	76.6	69.0	59.7
Indonesia	44.4	60.4	41.9
Iraq	513.8	332.4	417.5
Italy	241.9	188.7	153.0
Japan	208.3	224.2	234.5
Korea, Republic . . .	95.6	127.9	161.6
Malaysia	121.3	60.9	48.4
Netherlands	94.2	93.6	74.4
Russia	48.2	84.4	61.1
Saudi Arabia	145.5	143.2	151.2
Spain	52.1	54.6	44.8
Switzerland	89.8	74.1	67.9
Syria	83.9	43.4	49.1
Turkey	105.4	172.0	77.5
Ukraine	39.0	47.0	62.0
United Kingdom	197.0	195.0	175.4
USA	387.8	364.0	366.2
Total (incl. others) . . .	4,101.7	3,828.5	3,716.4

Source: Central Bank of Jordan.

Exports f.o.b.	1997	1998	1999
Bahrain	16.5	18.5	14.8
China, People's Republic . .	19.2	16.3	35.6
India	139.0	165.0	254.7
Indonesia	25.7	25.8	26.1
Iran	7.4	28.9	8.8
Iraq	200.4	149.7	113.3
Italy	19.1	19.8	18.0
Japan	18.0	14.2	15.0
Korea, Republic . . .	27.3	13.3	11.7
Lebanon	40.2	42.3	31.6
Malaysia	21.0	21.2	29.0
Netherlands	24.3	32.3	17.7
Philippines	17.1	9.7	8.0
Qatar	30.4	26.8	22.2
Saudi Arabia	198.4	146.3	140.5
Sudan	16.2	15.3	16.6
Syria	36.2	21.6	18.7
Turkey	23.1	6.0	14.3
United Arab Emirates . .	78.2	81.8	87.1
Yemen	18.8	16.4	16.2
Total (incl. others) . . .	1,505.2	1,475.9	1,482.9

Source: Central Bank of Jordan

Transport

RAILWAYS (traffic)

	1996	1997	1998
Passenger-km (million) . . .	1	2	2
Freight ton-km (million) . . .	735	625	596

Source: UN, *Statistical Yearbook*.

ROAD TRAFFIC (motor vehicles in use at 31 December)

	1994	1995	1996
Passenger cars	180,453	188,238	213,874
Buses and coaches . . .	6,943	7,604	10,309
Lorries and vans	63,163	69,090	68,844
Motorcycles and mopeds . .	384	368	369

Source: IRF, *World Road Statistics*.

1997 (motor vehicles in use): 202,100 passenger cars; 85,100 commercial vehicles.
1998 (motor vehicles in use): 200,000 passenger cars; 106,900 commercial vehicles.
Source: UN, *Statistical Yearbook*.

SHIPPING

Merchant Fleet (registered at 31 December)

	1996	1997	1998
Number of vessels	4	7	10
Displacement (grt) . . .	40,829	42,799	42,100

Source: Lloyd's Register of Shipping, *World Fleet Statistics*.

International Sea-borne Freight Traffic ('000 metric tons)

	1996	1997	1998
Goods loaded	7,396.4	7,534.8	7,310.3
Goods unloaded	4,612.5	4,778.3	5,333.7

CIVIL AVIATION (traffic on scheduled services)

	1995	1996	1997
Kilometres flown (million) . .	38	42	40
Passengers carried ('000) . .	1,270	1,299	1,353
Passenger-km (million) . . .	4,395	4,750	4,900
Total ton-km (million) . . .	664	731	721

Source: UN, *Statistical Yearbook*.

Passengers carried ('000): 1,187 in 1998; 1,252 in 1999; 1,283 in 2000. (Source: partly Royal Jordanian Airline).

Tourism

ARRIVALS BY NATIONALITY ('000)*

	1996	1997	1998
Egypt	803.3	600.5	373.4
Iraq	187.0	264.5	327.3
Israel	121.2	125.6	119.3
Kuwait	47.5	55.5	82.2
Lebanon	67.8	59.5	63.1
Saudi Arabia . . .	459.1	477.8	608.5
Syria	688.7	717.1	946.5
Turkey	100.0	90.8	91.2
USA	86.1	85.8	87.6
Total (incl. others)	3,163.6	3,067.9	3,303.1

* Including pilgrims and excursionists (same-day visitors). The total number of tourist arrivals (in '000) was: 1,102.8 in 1996; 1,127.0 in 1997; 1,256.4 in 1998.

Source: World Tourism Organization, *Yearbook of Tourism Statistics*.

Tourism receipts (US $ million): 743.4 in 1996; 773.8 in 1997; 852.6 in 1998.

1999: Tourist arrivals 1,357,822; Tourism receipts (JD million) 564.1.

Source: Ministry of Tourism and Antiquities.

Communications Media

(East Bank only)

	1994	1995	1996
Radio receivers ('000 in use) .	1,265	1,350	1,600
Television receivers ('000 in use) .	405	430	480
Telephones ('000 main lines in use)*	317.3	328.3	356.2
Telefax stations ('000 in use)† .	31	32	35
Mobile telephones (subscribers)†	1,446	11,500	n.a.
Book production: titles . .	n.a.	465	511
Daily newspapers:			
Number of titles . . .	4	4	4
Average circulation ('000 copies)	250	250	250
Non-daily newspapers:			
Number of titles . . .	21	34	41
Average circulation ('000 copies)	60	90	95

1997 ('000 in use): Radio receivers 1,660; Television receivers 500; Telephones ('000 main lines in use) 404.3*.

1998 Telephones ('000 main lines in use) 508.6*.

1999 Telephones ('000 main lines in use) 564.7*.

* Source: Jordanian Department of Statistics.

† Source: UN, *Statistical Yearbook* (data on telefax stations are estimates).

Source (unless otherwise indicated): UNESCO, *Statistical Yearbook*.

Education

(East Bank, 1997/98 unless otherwise indicated)

	Schools	Teachers	Pupils
Pre-primary	932	3,346	69,425
Primary	2,623	45,367	1,121,866
Secondary: general . . .	n.a.	6,309*	115,307
Secondary: vocational . .	n.a.	2,306*	39,701
Higher†	n.a.	5,275	112,959
of which universities . .	n.a.	3,982	89,010

* 1995/96 figure.

† 1996/97 figures.

Source: mainly UNESCO, *Statistical Yearbook*.

Directory

The Constitution

The revised Constitution was approved by King Talal I on 1 January 1952.

The Hashemite Kingdom of Jordan is an independent, indivisible sovereign state. Its official religion is Islam; its official language Arabic.

RIGHTS OF THE INDIVIDUAL

There is to be no discrimination between Jordanians on account of race, religion or language. Work, education and equal opportunities shall be afforded to all as far as is possible. The freedom of the individual is guaranteed, as are his dwelling and property. No Jordanian shall be exiled. Labour shall be made compulsory only in a national emergency, or as a result of a conviction; conditions, hours worked and allowances are under the protection of the state.

The Press, and all opinions, are free, except under martial law. Societies can be formed, within the law. Schools may be established freely, but they must follow a recognized curriculum and educational policy. Elementary education is free and compulsory. All religions are tolerated. Every Jordanian is eligible for public office, and choices are to be made by merit only. Power belongs to the people.

THE LEGISLATIVE POWER

Legislative power is vested in the National Assembly and the King. The National Assembly consists of two houses: the Senate and the House of Representatives.

THE SENATE

The number of Senators is one-half of the number of members of the House of Representatives. Senators must be unrelated to the King, over 40, and are chosen from present and past Prime Ministers and Ministers, past Ambassadors or Ministers Plenipotentiary, past Presidents of the House of Representatives, past Presidents and members of the Court of Cassation and of the Civil and *Shari'a* Courts of Appeal, retired officers of the rank of General and above, former members of the House of Representatives who have been elected twice to that House, etc. . . They may not hold public office. Senators are appointed for four years. They may be reappointed. The President of the Senate is appointed for two years.

THE HOUSE OF REPRESENTATIVES

The members of the House of Representatives are elected by secret ballot in a general direct election and retain their mandate for four years. General elections take place during the four months preceding the end of the term. The President of the House is elected by secret ballot each year by the Representatives. Representatives must be Jordanians of over 30, they must have a clean record, no active business interests, and are debarred from public office. Close relatives of the King are not eligible. If the House of Representatives is dissolved, the new House shall assemble in extraordinary session not more than four months after the date of dissolution. The new House cannot be dissolved for the same reason as the last.

GENERAL PROVISIONS FOR THE NATIONAL ASSEMBLY

The King summons the National Assembly to its ordinary session on 1 November each year. This date can be postponed by the King for two months, or he can dissolve the Assembly before the end of its three months' session. Alternatively, he can extend the session up to a total period of six months. Each session is opened by a speech from the throne.

Decisions in the House of Representatives and the Senate are made by a majority vote. The quorum is two-thirds of the total number of members in each House. When the voting concerns the Constitution, or confidence in the Council of Ministers, 'the votes shall be taken by calling the members by name in a loud voice'. Sessions are public, though secret sessions can be held at the request of the Government or of five members. Complete freedom of speech, within the rules of either House, is allowed.

The Prime Minister places proposals before the House of Representatives; if accepted there, they are referred to the Senate and finally sent to the King for confirmation. If one house rejects a law while the other accepts it, a joint session of the House of Representatives and the Senate is called, and a decision made by a two-thirds majority. If the King withholds his approval from a law, he returns it to the Assembly within six months with the reasons for his dissent; a joint session of the Houses then makes a decision, and if the law is accepted by this decision it is promulgated. The Budget is submitted to the National Assembly one month before the beginning of the financial year.

THE KING

The throne of the Hashemite Kingdom devolves by male descent in the dynasty of King Abdullah ibn al-Hussein. The King attains his majority on his eighteenth lunar year; if the throne is inherited by a minor, the powers of the King are exercised by a Regent or a Council of Regency. If the King, through illness or absence, cannot perform his duties, his powers are given to a Deputy, or to a Council of the Throne. This Deputy, or Council, may be appointed by Iradas (decrees) by the King, or, if he is incapable, by the Council of Ministers.

On his accession, the King takes the oath to respect and observe the provisions of the Constitution and to be loyal to the nation. As Head of State he is immune from all liability or responsibility. He approves laws and promulgates them. He declares war, concludes peace and signs treaties; treaties, however, must be approved by the National Assembly. The King is Commander-in-Chief of the navy, the army and the air force. He orders the holding of elections; convenes, inaugurates, adjourns and prorogues the House of Representatives. The Prime Minister is appointed by him, as are the President and members of the Senate. Military and civil ranks are also granted, or withdrawn, by the King. No death sentence is carried out until he has confirmed it.

MINISTERS

The Council of Ministers consists of the Prime Minister, President of the Council, and of his ministers. Ministers are forbidden to become members of any company, to receive a salary from any company, or to participate in any financial act of trade. The Council of Ministers is entrusted with the conduct of all affairs of state, internal and external.

The Council of Ministers is responsible to the House of Representatives for matters of general policy. Ministers may speak in either House, and, if they are members of one House, they may also vote in that House. Votes of confidence in the Council are cast in the House of Representatives, and decided by a two-thirds majority. If a vote of 'no confidence' is returned, the ministers are bound to resign. Every newly-formed Council of Ministers must present its programme to the House of Representatives and ask for a vote of confidence. The House of Representatives can impeach ministers, as it impeaches its own members.

AMENDMENTS

Two amendments were passed in November 1974 giving the King the right to dissolve the Senate or to take away membership from any of its members, and to postpone general elections for a period not to exceed a year, if there are circumstances in which the Council of Ministers feels that it is impossible to hold elections. A further amendment in February 1976 enabled the King to postpone elections indefinitely. In January 1984 two amendments were passed, allowing elections 'in any part of the country where it is possible to hold them' (effectively, only the East Bank) and empowering the National Assembly to elect deputies from the Israeli-held West Bank.

The Government

HEAD OF STATE

King ABDULLAH IBN AL-HUSSEIN (succeeded to the throne on 7 February 1999).

CABINET*
(April 2001)

Prime Minister and Minister of Defence: Eng. ALI ABU AR-RAGHEB.

Deputy Prime Minister and Minister of the Interior: Dr AWAD KHLEIFAT.

Deputy Prime Minister, Minister of Transport and Minister of State for Cabinet Affairs: Dr SALEH IRSHEIDAT.

Deputy Prime Minister and Minister of Justice: FARIS AN-NABULSI.

Deputy Prime Minister and Minister of State for Economic Affairs: Dr MUHAMMAD AL-HALAIQA.

Minister of Awqaf (Religious Endowments) and Islamic Affairs: Dr ABD AS-SALAM AL-ABBADI.

Minister of Health: Dr TARIQ SUHEIMAT.

Minister of Foreign Affairs: ABD AL-ILAH AL-KHATIB.

Minister of Tourism and Antiquities: AQEL BELTAJI.

Minister of Finance: Dr MICHEL MARTO.

Minister of Labour: EID AL-FAYEZ.

Minister of Public Works and Housing: Eng. HOSNI ABU GHEIDA.

Minister of Youth and Sports: SA'ID SHUQUM.

Minister of Energy and Mineral Resources: Eng. WA'IL SABRI.

Minister of Information: Dr TALEB AR-RIFAI.

Minister of Education: Dr KHALID TOUQAN.

Minister of Municipal, Rural and Environmental Affairs: ABD AR-RAHIM AL-AKOUR.

Minister of Culture: MAHMOUD AL-KAYED.

Minister of Agriculture: ZUHEIR ZANNOUNEH.

Minister of Industry and Trade: WASIF AZAR.

Minister of Planning: JAWAD AL-HADID.

Minister of Water and Irrigation: Eng. HATIM AL-HALAWANI.

Minister of Social Development: TAMAM AL-GHOUL.

Minister of Post and Telecommunications: Dr FAWWAZ HATIM AZ-ZU'BI.

Minister of State: Dr ADEL ASH-SHREIDAH.

Minister of State for Administrative Development: Dr MUHAMMAD DHUNEIBAT.

Minister of State for Parliamentary Affairs: YOUSUF AD-DALABIH.

Minister of State for Legal Affairs: DAIFALLAH SALEM AL-MASA'IDAH.

* The Head of Intelligence and the Governor of the Central Bank also have full ministerial status.

MINISTRIES

Office of the Prime Minister: POB 80, Amman; tel. (6) 4641211; fax (6) 4642520; e-mail pmic@pm.gov.jo; internet www.pm.gov.jo.

Ministry of Agriculture: POB 2099, Amman; tel. (6) 5686151; fax (6) 5686310; e-mail agri@moa.gov.jo; internet www.moa.gov.jo.

Ministry of Awqaf (Religious Endowments) and Islamic Affairs: POB 659, Amman; tel. (6) 5666141; fax (6) 5602254.

Ministry of Culture: POB 6140, Amman; tel. (6) 5696588; fax (6) 5696598.

Ministry of Defence: POB 80, Amman; tel. (6) 4641211; fax (6) 4642520.

Ministry of Development Affairs: POB 1577, Amman; tel. (6) 4644361; fax (6) 4648825.

Ministry of Education: POB 1646, Amman 11118; tel. (6) 5607181; fax (6) 5666019; e-mail moe@amra.nic.gov.jo; internet www.moe.gov.jo.

Ministry of Energy and Mineral Resources: POB 2310, Amman; tel. (6) 5863326; fax (6) 5818336; e-mail memr@amra.nic.gov.jo; internet www.nic.gov.jo/memr/memr.html.

Ministry of Finance: POB 85, Amman 11118; tel. (6) 4636321; fax (6) 4643132; e-mail webmaster@mof.gov.jo; internet www.mof.gov.jo.

Ministry of Foreign Affairs: POB 35217, Amman 11180; tel. (6) 4644361; fax (6) 4648825.

Ministry of Health: POB 86, Amman; tel. (6) 5665131; fax (6) 5665232.

Ministry of Industry and Trade: POB 2019, Amman; tel. (6) 5607191; fax (6) 5603721; e-mail info@mit.gov.jo; internet www.mit.gov.jo.

Ministry of Information: POB 1854, Amman; tel. (6) 4641467; fax (6) 4648895.

Ministry of the Interior: POB 100, Amman; tel. (6) 4638849; fax (6) 5606908.

Ministry of Justice: POB 6040, Amman; tel. (6) 4653533; fax (6) 4643197; e-mail moj@amra.nic.gov.jo.

Ministry of Labour: POB 8160, Amman; tel. (6) 5607481; fax (6) 5667193.

Ministry of Municipal, Rural and Environmental Affairs: POB 1799, Amman; tel. (6) 4641393; fax (6) 4640404.

Ministry of Planning: POB 555, Amman 11118; tel. (6) 4641460; fax (6) 4649341; e-mail mop@mop.gov.jo; internet www.mop.gov.jo.

Ministry of Post and Telecommunications: POB 9903, Amman 11191; tel. (6) 5859001; fax (6) 5825262; e-mail cio@mopc.gov.jo; internet www.mopc.gov.jo.

Ministry of Public Works and Housing: POB 1220, Amman; tel. (6) 5850470; fax (6) 5857590; e-mail mhpw@amra.nic.gov.jo.

Ministry of Social Development: POB 6720, Amman; tel. (6) 5931391; fax (6) 5673198.

Ministry of Tourism and Antiquities: POB 224, Amman 11118; tel. (6) 4642311; fax (6) 4648465; e-mail tourism@mota.gov.jo; internet www.mota.gov.jo.

Ministry of Transport: POB 35214, Amman; tel. (6) 5518111; fax (6) 5527233; e-mail mot1@go.com.jo.

Ministry of Water and Irrigation: POB 2412, Amman; tel. (6) 5680100; fax (6) 5679143.

Ministry of Youth and Sports: POB 1794, Amman; tel. (6) 5604701; fax (6) 5604717.

Legislature

MAJLIS AL-UMMA
(National Assembly)

Senate

Speaker: ABD AL-HADI AL-MAJALI.

The Senate (House of Notables) consists of 40 members, appointed by the King. A new Senate was appointed by the King on 22 November 1997.

House of Representatives

Speaker: SAED HAYEL AS-SROUR.

General Election, 4 November 1997*

Party/Group	Seats
Pro-Government†	60
Independent nationalists and leftists	10
Independent Islamists	8
National Constitutional Party (NCP)	2
Total	**80**

* The 1997 general election was boycotted by all the principal opposition parties in Jordan, including the Islamic Action Front (which had emerged as the largest single party in the House of Representatives after the 1993 elections).
† Excluding NCP.

Political Organizations

Political parties were banned before the elections of July 1963. In September 1971 King Hussein announced the formation of a Jordanian National Union, which was the only legal political organization. Communists, Marxists and 'other advocates of imported ideologies' were ineligible for membership. In March 1972 the organization was renamed the Arab National Union. In April 1974 King Hussein dissolved the executive committee of the Arab National Union, and accepted the resignation of the Secretary-General. In February 1976 the Cabinet approved a law abolishing the Union, membership of which was about 100,000. A royal commission was appointed in April 1990 to draft a National Charter, one feature of which was the legalization of political parties. In January 1991 King Hussein approved the National Charter, which was formally endorsed in June. In July 1992 the House of Representatives adopted draft legislation which formally permitted the establishment of political parties, subject to certain conditions. In the same month a joint session of the Senate and the House of Representatives was convened to debate amendments to the new legislation, proposed by the Senate. The political parties which achieved representation in the general election of November 1993 were: the Islamic Action Front (Sec.-Gen. Dr ABD AL-LATIF ARABIYAT; Dep. Sec.-Gen. HAMZEH MANSUR); al-Mustaqbal (Future) Party (Sec.-Gen. SULEIMAN ARAR); the Jordanian Arab Socialist Baath Party (Sec.-Gen. TAYSEER SAL-AMEH AL-HOMSI); al-Yakatha (Reawakening) Party; al-Ahd (Pledge) Party; the Jordan National Alliance; the Jordan People's Democratic Party (Leader TAYSIR AZ-ZABRI; Sec.-Gen. SALEM NAHHAS); the Jordan Social Democratic Party; and the Jordanian Arab Democratic Party. In May 1997 nine centre parties, including al-Ahd (Pledge) and the Jordan National Alliance, announced that they had united to form the National Constitutional Party (NCP; Sec.-Gen. ABD AL-HADI MAJALI), which became Jordan's largest political grouping. The formation of the NCP, together with the establishment in 1996 of the Unionist Arab Democratic Party (a coalition of three leftist parties), reduced the total number of political parties from 24 to 14. In July 1997 the establishment of a new Jordanian political party, the Popular Democratic Pan-Arab Movement, was announced. In May 1999 the Popular Participation Bloc was established to contest the municipal elections, held in July; it was a new grouping of 13 leftist, Baathist and pan-Arab parties. The formation of two new political parties was announced in late 1999: the New Generations Party (centrist green party; Leader ZAHI KARIM) and the Jordanian Arab New Dawn Party.

Diplomatic Representation

EMBASSIES IN JORDAN

Algeria: POB 830375, Amman 11183; tel. (6) 4641271; fax (6) 4616552; Ambassador: HAMID CHEBIRA.

Australia: POB 35201, Amman 11180; tel. (6) 5930246; fax (6) 5932160; e-mail ausemb@nets.com.jo; Ambassador: IAN W. RUSSELL.

Austria: POB 830795, 36 Mithqal al-Fayez St, Jabal Amman 11183; tel. (6) 4644635; fax (6) 4612725; e-mail austemb@go.com.jo; Ambassador: Dr PHILIPP HOYOS.

Bahrain: POB 5220, Zahran, Amman; tel. (6) 5664148; fax (6) 5664190; Ambassador: MUHAMMAD SEIF JABER AL-MSALLAM.

Belgium: POB 942, Amman 11118; tel. (6) 5932683; fax (6) 5930487; e-mail belgica@nol.com.jo; Ambassador: MARC DO SCHOUTHEETE.

Bosnia and Herzegovina: POB 850836, Amman 11185; tel. (6) 5856921; fax (6) 5856923; e-mail bosnia@go.com.jo; Chargé d'affaires: IBRAHIM EFENDIĆ.

Brazil: POB 5497, Amman 11183; tel. (6) 4642183; fax (6) 4641328; e-mail jorbrem@go.com.jo; Ambassador: SERGIO HENRIQUE NABUCO DE CASTRO.

Brunei: POB 851752, Amman; tel. (6) 5928021; fax (6) 5928024; e-mail bruneijo@go.com.jo; Ambassador: DATO ABDOUL SAMAN KAHAR.

Bulgaria: POB 950578, Amman 11195; tel. (6) 5529391; fax (6) 5539393; Chargé d'affaires: NIKOLAY NIKOLOV.

Canada: POB 815403, Amman 11180; tel. (6) 5666124; fax (6) 5689227; Ambassador: RODERICK BEALL.

Chile: POB 830663, 71 Suez St, Abdoun, Amman 11183; tel. (6) 5923360; fax (6) 5924263; e-mail echilejo@go.com.jo; Ambassador: ALVREDO TABIA.

China, People's Republic: POB 7365, Amman 11118; tel. (6) 5516136; fax (6) 5518713; Ambassador: QIU SHENGYUN.

Czech Republic: POB 2213, Amman 11118; tel. (6) 5927051; fax (6) 5927053; e-mail amman@embassy.mzv.cz; Ambassador: TOMAS SMETANKA.

Denmark: POB 222, 24 Sharif Abd-al Hamid Sharaf St, Shmeisani, Amman 11118; tel. (6) 5604644; fax (6) 5604664; e-mail dancons@kawar.com.jo; Ambassador OLE WØHLERS OLSEN.

Egypt: POB 35178, Amman 11180; tel. (6) 5605175; fax (6) 5604082; Ambassador: MUHAMMAD HIJAZI.

France: POB 5348, Amman 11183; tel. (6) 4641273; fax (6) 4659606; e-mail ambafr@joinnet.com.jo; internet www.ambafrance.org.jo; Ambassador: BERNARD EMIÉ.

Germany: POB 183, Benghazi St, Jabal Amman; tel. (6) 5930351; fax (6) 5932887; e-mail germaemb@go.com.jo; Ambassador: Dr MARTIN SCHNELLER.

Greece: POB 35069, Amman 11180; tel. (6) 5672331; fax (6) 5696591; e-mail greekemb@nol.com.jo; Ambassador: CONSTANTIN KARBETSIS.

Holy See: POB 142916, Amman 11814; tel. (6) 5929934; fax (6) 5929931; e-mail nuntius@nol.com.jo; Apostolic Nuncio: Most Rev. FERNANDO FILONI, Titular Archbishop of Volturno.

Hungary: POB 3441, Amman 11181; tel. (6) 5925614; fax (6) 5930836; e-mail huembamm@nol.com.jo; Chargé d'Affaires: Dr ATTIAL SZANTO.

India: POB 2168, 1st Circle, Jabal Amman; tel. (6) 4622098; fax (6) 4659540; e-mail indembjo@firstnet.com.jo; Ambassador: HER CHARAN SINGH DHODY.

Indonesia: POB 811784, South Um-Uthaina, 6th Circle, Amman 11181; tel. (6) 5513232; fax (6) 5528380; e-mail amman96@go.com.jo; Ambassador: EDHIMURTI SUNOKO.

Iran: POB 173, Jabal Amman; tel. (6) 4641281; fax (6) 4641383; e-mail emb@go.com.jo; Ambassador: NOSRATOLLAH TAGIK.

Iraq: POB 2025, 1st Circle, Jabal Amman; tel. (6) 4623175; fax (6) 4619172; Ambassador: Dr SABAH YASEEN ALI.

Israel: POB 950866, Amman 11195; tel. (6) 5524680; fax (6) 5524689; e-mail isrem@go.com.jo; Ambassador: Dr ODED ERAN.

Italy: POB 9800, Jabal Luweibdeh, Amman 11191; tel. (6) 4638185; fax (6) 4659730; e-mail italemb1@go.com.jo; internet www.italembamman.org; Ambassador: STEFANO JEDRKIEWICZ.

Japan: POB 2835, Amman 11191; tel. (6) 5931487; fax (6) 5930355; e-mail mail@embjapan.org.jo; Ambassador: KOICHI MATSUMOTO.

Korea, Democratic People's Republic: Amman; tel. (6) 5666349; Ambassador: (vacant).

Korea, Republic: POB 3060, Amman 11181; tel. (6) 5930745; fax (6) 5930280; e-mail skorea@go.com.jo; Ambassador: LEE KYUNG-WOO.

Kuwait: POB 2107, Jabal Amman; tel. (6) 5675135; fax (6) 5699217; Ambassador FAYSAL AL-MESHA'AN.

Lebanon: POB 811779, 2nd Circle, Jabal Amman 11181; tel. and fax (6) 5929111; Ambassador: HABIB ALAM UDDIN.

Morocco: POB 2175, Amman 11183; tel. (6) 5921771; fax (6) 5926069; Ambassador: MESDI ALOUI.

Netherlands: POB 94136, Amman 11194; tel. (6) 5930581; fax (6) 5930214; e-mail nlammcom@index.com.jo; Ambassador: Mrs M. DE KWAASTENIET.

Norway: POB 830510, 25 Damascus St, Abdoun, Amman 11183; tel. (6) 5931646; fax (6) 5931650; e-mail embamm@mfa.no; Ambassador JAN G. JØLLE.

Oman: POB 20192, Amman 11110; tel. (6) 5686155; fax (6) 5689404; Ambassador: HAMAD BIN HILAL AL-MA'MARI.

Pakistan: POB 1232, Amman; tel. (6) 4622787; fax (6) 4611633; e-mail pakembjo@go.com.jo; Ambassador: TARIQ FATEMI.

Poland: POB 2124, 3rd Circle, 1 Mai Zayadeh St, Jabal Amman; tel. (6) 4637153; fax (6) 4618744; e-mail polemb@nol.com.jo; Chargé d'affaires: MARIUSZ WOŹNIAK.

Qatar: POB 5098, Amman 11183; tel. (6) 5607311; fax (6) 5607350; e-mail qeamman@jonet.com; Ambassador: Sheikh ABD AL-RAHMAN BIN JASSIM BIN MUHAMMAD ATH-THANI.

Romania: POB 2869, 21 Abdullah Bin Massoud St, Shmeisani, Amman; tel. (6) 5667738; fax (6) 5684018; e-mail romania@go.com.jo; Ambassador: IOAN AGAFICIOAIA.

Russia: POB 2187, Amman 11181; tel. (6) 4641158; fax (6) 4647448; e-mail russjo@nets.com.jo; Ambassador: IVANOV GALITSIM.

Saudi Arabia: POB 2133, 5th Circle, Jabal Amman; tel. (6) 5924154; fax (6) 5921154; Chargé d'affaires: ABDULLAH SULEIMAN AL-HAMDAN.

South Africa: POB 851508, Sweifieh 11185, Amman; tel. (6) 5921194; fax (6) 5920080; e-mail saembjor@index.com.jo; Ambassador: Dr VINCENT T. ZULU.

Spain: Zahran St, POB 454, Amman 11118; tel. (6) 4614166; fax (6) 4614173; e-mail embespjo@mail.mae.es; Ambassador: EUDALDO MIRAPEIX MARTÍNEZ.

Sri Lanka: POB 830731, Amman 11183; tel. (6) 5820611; fax (6) 5820615; e-mail lankaemb@go.com.jo; Ambassador: AHMAD SABRAL-LAHKHAN.

Sudan: Jabal Amman; tel. (6) 5624145; Ambassador: AHMAD DIAB.

Sweden: POB 830536, 4th Circle, Amman 11183; tel. (6) 5931177; fax (6) 5930179; e-mail sweamman@go.com.jo; Ambassador: KLAS GIEROW.

Switzerland: POB 5341, Amman 11183; tel. (6) 5931416; fax (6) 5930685; e-mail swiemamm@go.com.jo; Ambassador: ROLF BODEN MULLER.

Syria: POB 1733, Amman 11118; tel. (6) 4641935; fax (6) 4651945; Ambassador: ABD AL -FATAH AMURA.

Tunisia: POB 7185, Amman 11195; tel. (6) 5674307; fax (6) 5605790; Ambassador: MUHAMMAD HABIB KAABACHI.

Turkey: POB 2062, Islamic College St, 2nd Circle, Jabal Amman 11181; tel. (6) 4641251; fax (6) 4612353; e-mail tcammanbe@index .com.jo; Ambassador: TUNCER TOPUR.

United Arab Emirates: POB 2623, Amman 11181; tel. (6) 5934780; fax (6) 5932666; Ambassador: AHMAD ALI NASSER ALI AZ-ZU'ABI.

United Kingdom: POB 87, Abdoun Amman 11118; tel. (6) 5923100; fax (6) 5923759; e-mail info@britain.org.jo; internet www.britain .org.jo; Ambassador: EDWARD CHAPLIN.

USA: POB 354, Amman 11118; tel. (6) 5920101; fax (6) 5920121; e-mail administration@usembassy-amman.org.jo; Ambassador: WILLIAMS J. BURNS.

Yemen: POB 3085, Amman 11181; tel. (6) 4642381; fax (6) 4647425; Ambassador: HASSAN AHMAD AL-LOZI.

Yugoslavia: POB 5227, Amman 11183; tel. (6) 4647593; fax (6) 4647605; e-mail yugoembjo@nets.com.jo; Ambassador: OLIVER V. POTEZICA.

Judicial System

With the exception of matters of purely personal nature concerning members of non-Muslim communities, the law of Jordan was based on Islamic Law for both civil and criminal matters. During the days of the Ottoman Empire, certain aspects of Continental law, especially French commercial law and civil and criminal procedure, were introduced. Due to British occupation of Palestine and Transjordan from 1917 to 1948, the Palestine territory has adopted, either by statute or case law, much of the English common law. Since the annexation of the non-occupied part of Palestine and the formation of the Hashemite Kingdom of Jordan, there has been a continuous effort to unify the law.

Court of Cassation. The Court of Cassation consists of seven judges, who sit in full panel for exceptionally important cases. In most appeals, however, only five members sit to hear the case. All cases involving amounts of more than JD 100 may be reviewed by this Court, as well as cases involving lesser amounts and cases which cannot be monetarily valued. However, for the latter types of cases, review is available only by leave of the Court of Appeal, or, upon refusal by the Court of Appeal, by leave of the President of the Court of Cassation. In addition to these functions as final and Supreme Court of Appeal, the Court of Cassation also sits as High Court of Justice to hear applications in the nature of habeas corpus, mandamus and certiorari dealing with complaints of a citizen against abuse of governmental authority.

Courts of Appeal. There are two Courts of Appeal, each of which is composed of three judges, whether for hearing of appeals or for dealing with Magistrates Courts' judgments in chambers. Jurisdiction of the two Courts is geographical, with the Court for the Western Region (which has not sat since June 1967) sitting in Jerusalem and the Court for the Eastern Region sitting in Amman. The regions are separated by the Jordan river. Appellate review of the Courts of Appeal extends to judgments rendered in the Courts of First Instance, the Magistrates' Courts, and Religious Courts.

Courts of First Instance. The Courts of First Instance are courts of general jurisdiction in all matters civil and criminal except those specifically allocated to the Magistrates' Courts. Three judges sit in all felony trials, while only two judges sit for misdemeanour and civil cases. Each of the seven Courts of First Instance also exercises appellate jurisdiction in cases involving judgments of less than JD 20 and fines of less than JD 10, rendered by the Magistrates' Courts.

Magistrates' Courts. There are 14 Magistrates' Courts, which exercise jurisdiction in civil cases involving no more than JD 250 and in criminal cases involving maximum fines of JD 100 or maximum imprisonment of one year.

Religious Courts. There are two types of religious court: The *Shari'a* Courts (Muslims): and the Ecclesiastical Courts (Eastern Orthodox, Greek Melkite, Roman Catholic and Protestant). Jurisdiction extends to personal (family) matters, such as marriage, divorce, alimony, inheritance, guardianship, wills, interdiction and, for the Muslim community, the constitution of Waqfs (Religious Endowments). When a dispute involves persons of different religious communities, the Civil Courts have jurisdiction in the matter unless the parties agree to submit to the jurisdiction of one or the other of the Religious Courts involved.

Each *Shari'a* (Muslim) Court consists of one judge (*Qadi*), while most of the Ecclesiastical (Christian) Courts are normally composed of three judges, who are usually clerics. *Shari'a* Courts apply the doctrines of Islamic Law, based on the Koran and the *Hadith* (Precepts of Muhammad), while the Ecclesiastical Courts base their law on various aspects of Canon Law. In the event of conflict between any two Religious Courts or between a Religious Court and a Civil Court, a Special Tribunal of three judges is appointed by the President of the Court of Cassation, to decide which court shall have jurisdiction. Upon the advice of experts on the law of the various communities, this Special Tribunal decides on the venue for the case at hand.

Religion

Over 80% of the population are Sunni Muslims, and the King can trace unbroken descent from the Prophet Muhammad. There is a Christian minority, living mainly in the towns, and there are smaller numbers of non-Sunni Muslims.

ISLAM

Chief Justice and President of the Supreme Muslim Secular Council: Sheikh IZZEDIN AL-KHATIB AT-TAMIMI.

Director of Shari'a Courts: Sheikh SUBHI AL-MUWQQAT.

Mufti of the Hashemite Kingdom of Jordan: Sheikh MUHAMMAD ABDO HASHEM.

CHRISTIANITY

The Roman Catholic Church

Latin Rite

Jordan forms part of the Patriarchate of Jerusalem (see chapter on Israel).

Vicar-General for Transjordan: Mgr SELIM SAYEGH (Titular Bishop of Aquae in Proconsulari), Latin Vicariate, POB 851379, Amman 11185; tel. (6) 5929546; fax (6) 5920548; e-mail proffice@joinnet.com.jo.

Melkite Rite

The Greek-Melkite archdiocese of Petra (Wadi Musa) and Philadelphia (Amman) contained 31,200 adherents at 31 December 1998.

Archbishop of Petra and Philadelphia: Most Rev. GEORGES EL-MURR, Archevêché Grec-Melkite Catholique, POB 2435, Jabal Amman 11181; tel. (6) 4624757; fax (6) 4628560.

Syrian Rite

The Syrian Catholic Patriarch of Antioch is resident in Beirut, Lebanon.

Patriarchal Exarchate of Jerusalem: Mont Achrafieh, POB 510393, Rue Barto, Amman; e-mail stjossc@l-ol.com; Exarch Patriarchal Mgr GRÉGOIRE PIERRE ABD AL-AHAD.

The Anglican Communion

Within the Episcopal Church in Jerusalem and the Middle East, Jordan forms part of the diocese of Jerusalem. The President Bishop of the Church is the Bishop in Jerusalem (see the chapter on Israel).

Assistant Bishop in Amman: Rt Rev. ELIA KHOURY, POB 598, Amman.

Other Christian Churches

The Coptic Orthodox Church, the Greek Orthodox Church (Patriarchate of Jerusalem) and the Evangelical Lutheran Church in Jordan are also active.

The Press

Jordan Press Association (JPA): Amman; Pres. RAKAN AL-MAJALI; Vice-Pres. TARIQ MUMANI; Sec.-Gen. NIDAL MANSUR.

DAILIES

Al-Akhbar (News): POB 62420, Amman; f. 1976; Arabic; publ. by the Arab Press Co; Editor RACAN EL-MAJALI; circ. 15,000.

Al-Aswaq (Markets): POB 11117, Amman 11123; tel. (6) 5157690; fax (6) 5154390; f. 1992; Editor MUSTAFA ABU LIBDEH; circ. 40,000.

Ad-Dustour (The Constitution): POB 591, Amman; tel. (6) 5664153; fax (6) 5667170; e-mail dustour@go.com.jo; internet www.addustour.com; f. 1967; Arabic; publ. by the Jordan Press and Publishing Co; owns commercial printing facilities; Chair. KAMEL ASH-SHERIF; Editor NABIL ASH-SHARIF; Man. Dir SAIF ASH-SHARIF; circ. 100,000.

Al-Mithaq: Amman; f. 1993; Arabic.

Ar-Rai (Opinion): POB 6710, Queen Rania St, Amman 11118; tel. (6) 5667171; fax (6) 5676581; e-mail alrai@jpf.com.jo; internet www.alrai.com; f. 1971; morning; Arabic; independent; published by Jordan Press Foundation; Chair. Dr KHALED KARAKI; Gen. Dir MUHAMMAD AL-AMAD; Editor-in-Chief SULAYMAN AL-QUDA; circ. 90,000.

Arab Daily: Amman; f. 1999; English.

The Jordan Times: POB 6710, Amman 11118; tel. (6) 5696331; fax (6) 5696183; e-mail jotimes@jpf.com.jo; internet www.jordantimes.com; f. 1975; English; published by Jordan Press Foundation; Editor-in-Chief RANA SABBAGH-GARGOUR (acting); circ. 10,000.

Sawt ash-Shaab (Voice of the People): POB 3037, Amman; tel. (6) 5667101; fax (6) 5667993; f. 1983; Arabic; Editor-in-Chief: HASHEM KHAISAT; circ. 30,000.

WEEKLIES

Al-Majd: POB 926856, Amman 11110; tel. (6) 5530553; fax (6) 5530352; f. 1994; Editor FAHD AR-RIMAWI; circ. 10,000.

PERIODICALS

Akhbar al-Usbou (News of the Week): POB 605, Amman; tel. (6) 5677881; fax (6) 5677882; f. 1959; weekly; Arabic; economic, social, political; Chief Editor and Publr ABD AL-HAFIZ MUHAMMAD; circ. 50,000.

Al-Ghad al-Iqtisadi: Media Services International, POB 9313, Amman 11191; tel. (6) 5645380; fax (6) 5648298; fortnightly; English; economic; Chief Editor RIAD AL-KHOURI.

Arabia Online: POB 91128, Amman 11191; tel. (6) 5154238; fax (6) 5154239; e-mail info@arabia.com; internet www.arabia.com; f. 1995; monthly; Arabic; information technology; Editor-in-Chief KHALDOON TABAZA.

Huda El-Islam (The Right Way of Islam): POB 659, Amman; tel. (6) 5666141; f. 1956; monthly; Arabic; scientific and literary; published by the Ministry of Awqaf and Islamic Affairs; Editor Dr AHMAD MUHAMMAD HULAYYEL.

Jordan: POB 224, Amman; f. 1969; published quarterly by Jordan Information Bureau, Washington; circ. 100,000.

Jordan Today: Media Services International, POB 9313, Amman 11191; tel. (6) 652380; fax (6) 648298; e-mail star@arabia.com; internet www.corp.arabia.com/JordanToday; f. 1995; monthly; English; tourism, culture and entertainment; Editor-in-Chief ZEID NASSER.

Al-Liwa' (The Standard): POB 3067, 2nd Circle, Jabal Amman 11181; tel. (6) 5642770; fax (6) 5656324; f. 1972; weekly; Arabic; Editor-in-Chief Hassan at-Tal; Man. Dir Muhammad H. Al; circ. 15,000.

Military Magazine: Army Headquarters, Amman; f. 1955; quarterly; dealing with military and literary subjects; published by Armed Forces.

Royal Wings: POB 302, Amman; tel. (6) 5672872; fax (6) 5672527; bi-monthly; Arabic and English; magazine for Royal Jordanian Airline; circ. 40,000.

As-Sabah (The Morning): POB 2396, Amman; weekly; Arabic; circ. 6,000.

Shari'a: POB 585, Amman; f. 1959; fortnightly; Islamic affairs; published by Shari'a College; circ. 5,000.

Shihan: POB 96-654, Amman; tel. (6) 5601511; fax (6) 5656324; e-mail shihan@go.com.jo; internet www.access2arabia.com/shihan; weekly; Arabic; Editor-in-Chief Hassan at-Tal.

The Star: Media Services International, POB 9313, Amman 11191; tel. (6) 5645380; fax (6) 5648298; e-mail star@arabia.com; f. 1982, formerly The Jerusalem Star; weekly; English and French; Publr and Editor-in-Chief Osama ash-Sherif; circ. 9,000.

World Travel Gazette (WTG): POB 658, Amman; tel. (6) 5665091; fax (6) 5667933; Arabic.

NEWS AGENCIES

Jordan News Agency (PETRA): POB 6845, Amman; tel. (6) 5644455; e-mail petra@petranews.gov.jo; internet www.petra.gov.jo; f. 1965; government-controlled; Dir-Gen. Abdullah al-Utum.

Foreign News Bureaux

Agence France-Presse (AFP): POB 3340, Amman 11181; tel. (6) 4642976; fax (6) 4654680; e-mail randa@afp.index.com.jo; Bureau Man. Mrs Randa Habib.

Agenzia Nazionale Stampa Associata (ANSA) (Italy): POB 35111, Amman; tel. (6) 5644092; Correspondent John Halabi.

Associated Press (AP) (USA): POB 35111, Amman 11180; tel. (6) 4614660; fax (6) 4614661; e-mail jamal-halaby@ap.org; Correspondent Jamal Halaby.

Deutsche Presse Agentur (dpa) (Germany): POB 35111, Amman; tel. (6) 5623907; Correspondent John Halabi.

Reuters (UK): POB 667, Amman; tel. (6) 5623776; fax (6) 5619231; Bureau Chief Jack Redden.

Informatsionnoye Telegrafnoye Agentstvo Rossii—Telegrafnoye Agentstvo Suverennykh Stran (ITAR—TASS) (Russia): Jabal Amman, Nabich Faris St, Block 111/83 124, Amman; Correspondent Nikolai Lebedinsky.

Central News Agency (Taiwan), Iraqi News Agency, Kuwait News Agency (KUNA), Middle East News Agency (Egypt), Qatar News Agency, Saudi Press Agency and UPI (USA) also maintain bureaux in Amman.

Publishers

Alfaris Publishing and Distribution Co: POB 9157, Petra Centre, A. H. Shoman St, Shmeisani, Amman 11191; tel. (6) 5605432; fax (6) 5685501; e-mail mkayyali@nets.com.jo; internet www.kayyalibooks.com; Dir Maher Said Kayyali.

Aram Studies Publishing and Distribution House: POB 997, Amman 11941; tel. (6) 835015; fax (6) 835079; art, finance, health, management, science, business; Gen. Dir Saleh Abousba.

El-Nafa'es: POB 211511, Al-Abdali, Amman 11121; tel. (6) 5693940; fax (6) 5693941; e-mail alnafaes@hotmail.com; f. 1990; education, Islamic.

Jordan Book Centre Co Ltd: POB 301, Al-Jubeiha, Amman 11941; tel. (6) 5151882; fax (6) 5152016; e-mail jbc@go.com.jo; f. 1982; fiction, business, economics, computer science, medicine, engineering, general non-fiction; Man. Dir J. J. Sharbain.

Jordan Distribution Agency Co Ltd: POB 375, Amman 11118; tel. (6) 4630191; fax (6) 4635152; e-mail jda@go.com.jo; internet www.jda-jo.com; f. 1951; history; Chair. and Gen. Man. Raja Elissa; Dir Nadia Elissa.

Jordan House for Publication: POB 1121, Basman St, Amman; tel. (6) 24224; fax (6) 51062; f. 1952; medicine, nursing, dentistry; Man. Dir Mursi el-Ashkar.

Jordan Press Foundation: POB 6710, Amman 11118; tel. (6) 5667171; fax (6) 5661242; e-mail alrai@jpf.com.jo; internet www .alrai.com.jo; f. 1975; publishes Ar-Rai (daily) and the Jordan Times (daily); Chair. Dr Khaled Karaki; Gen. Dir Muhammad Amad.

Jordan Press and Publishing Co Ltd: POB 591, Amman; tel. (6) 5664153; fax (6) 5667170; e-mail dustour@go.com.jo; f. 1967 by Al-Manar and Falastin dailies; publishes Ad-Dustour (daily), Ad-Dus-

tour Sport (weekly) and The Star (English weekly); Chair. Kamel ash-Sharif; Dir-Gen Seif ash-Sherif.

At-Tanwir al-Ilmi (Scientific Enlightenment Publishing House): POB 4237, Al-Mahatta, Amman 11131; tel. and fax (6) 4899619; e-mail taisir@yahoo.com; education,engineering, philosophy, science, sociology; Owner Dr Taisir Subhi Mahmoud.

Other publishers in Amman include: Dairat al-Ihsaat al-Amman, George N. Kawar, Al-Matbaat al-Hashmiya and The National Press.

Broadcasting and Communications

TELECOMMUNICATIONS

Telecommunications Regulatory Commission (TRC): POB 850967, Amman 11185; tel. (6) 5862020; fax (6) 5863641; e-mail webmaster@trc.gov.jo; internet www.trc.gov.jo; f. 1995; Dir-Gen. Mamoun Balqar.

Jordan Mobile Telephone Services Company (JMTS—Fastlink): 25 Said Abujaber St, Um-Uthaina, Amman; tel. (6) 5512010; fax (6) 5673242; e-mail jumanat@fastlink.com.jo; f. 1994; private co; since 1995 operates Jordan's first mobile telecommunications network.

Jordan Telecommunications Company (JTC): POB 1689, Amman 11118; tel. (6) 4638301; fax (6) 4649882; f. 1971; formerly Jordan Telecommunications Corpn; 60% govt-owned; 40% privately-owned; Chair. Shabib Ammari; Man. Dir Walid Dweik.

MobileCom: Amman; f. 2000; subsidiary of Jordan Telecommunications Company; provides cellular telecommunications service.

BROADCASTING

Radio and Television

Jordan Radio and Television Corporation (JRTV): POB 1041, Amman; tel. (6) 773111; fax (6) 751503; e-mail general@jrtv .gov.jo; internet www.jrtv.com; f. 1968; government TV station broadcasts for 90 hours weekly in Arabic and English; in colour; advertising accepted; Dir-Gen. Ihsan Ramzi Shikim; Dir of Television Nasser Judeh; Dir of Radio Hashim Khuraysat.

Finance

(cap. = capital; p.u. = paid up; dep. = deposits; m. = million;
res = reserves; brs = branches; JD = Jordanian dinars)

BANKING

Central Bank

Central Bank of Jordan: POB 37, King Hussein St, Amman 11118; tel. (6) 4630301; fax (6) 4638889; e-mail redp@cbj.gov.jo; internet www.cbj.gov.jo; f. 1964; cap. JD 18m., res JD 60.1m., dep. JD 2,992.5m. (Dec. 2000); Gov. and Chair. Ummaya Toukan; Dep. Govs Ahmad Moustafa, Saleh at-Tayeh.

National Banks

Arab Bank PLC: POB 950545, Shmeisani, Amman 11195; tel. (6) 5607231; fax (6) 5606793; e-mail international@arabbank.com.jo; internet www.arabbank.com; f. 1930; cap. JD 146.9m., res JD 1,750.9m., dep. JD 16,712.1m. (Dec. 1999); Chair. and CEO Abd al-Majid Shoman; Pres. and Dep. Chair. Khalid Shoman; 96 brs in Jordan, 62 brs abroad.

Bank of Jordan PLC: POB 2140, Shmeisani, Amman 11181; tel. (6) 5696277; fax (6) 5696291; e-mail boj@go.com.jo; internet www.boj.com.jo; f. 1960; cap. JD 21m., res JD 14.1m., dep. JD 553.8m. (Dec. 1999); Chair. Tawfik Shaker Fakhouri; Gen. Man. Muhammad J. Qassim (acting); 64 brs.

Cairo Amman Bank: POB 950661, Cairo Amman Bank Bldg, Wadi Saqra St, Amman 11195; tel. (6) 4616910; fax (6) 4642890; e-mail cainfo@ca-bank.com.jo; internet www.ca-bank.com; f. 1960; cap. JD 20m., res JD 27.6m., dep. JD 769.3m. (Dec. 1999); Chair. Khaled al -Masri; Gen. Man. Yazid al-Mufti; 64 brs in Jordan, 19 brs abroad.

Export and Finance Bank: POB 941283, Issam Ajlouni St, Amman 11194; tel. (6) 5694250; fax (6) 5692062; e-mail info@efbank .com.jo; internet www.efbank.com.jo; f. 1995; cap. JD 22m., res JD 2.9m., dep. JD 103.6m. (Dec. 1999); Chair. and CEO Muhammad Ali Al-Husry; Gen. Man. Hakoub Bannayan (acting).

Jordan Gulf Bank: POB 9989, Shmeisani-Al Burj Area, Amman 11191; tel. (6) 5603931; fax (6) 5664110; e-mail jgb@jgbank.com.jo; f. 1977; cap JD 33m., res JD –0.1m., dep JD 253.8m. (Dec. 1999); Chair. Nabeel Yousuf Barakat; Gen. Man. Fayez Abu al-Enein; 33 brs.

Jordan Islamic Bank for Finance and Investment: POB 926225, Shmeisani, Amman 11110; tel. (6) 5666325; fax (6) 5666326; e-mail jib@islamicbank.com.jo; internet www.jordanislamicbank .com; f. 1978; cap. JD 22m., res JD 27m., dep. JD 647m. (Dec. 1999);

Chair. MAHMOUD HASSOUBAH; Vice-Chair. and Gen. Man. MUSA A. SHIHADEH; 63 brs.

Jordan Kuwait Bank: POB 9776, Amman 11191; tel. (6) 5688814; fax (6) 5695604; e-mail webmaster@jkbank.com.jo; internet www.jordan-kuwait-bank.com; f. 1976; cap. JD 20m., res JD 15.3m., dep. JD 328.5m. (Dec. 1999); Chair. FAISAL HAMAD AL-AYYAR; Gen. Man. MUHAMMAD YASSER AL-ASMAR; 31 brs in Jordan, 1 br. abroad.

Jordan National Bank PLC: POB 3103, Queen Noor St, Shmeisani, Amman 11181; tel. (6) 5622283; fax (6) 5622281; e-mail jnb@go .com.jo; internet www.ahli.com; f. 1955; cap. JD 42m., res JD 30.6m., dep. JD 826.4m. (Dec. 1999); Chair. and CEO Dr RAJAI AL-MUASHER; Dep. CEO and Gen. Man. NABIL WAHBAH; 55 brs in Jordan, 4 brs in Lebanon, 1 br. in Cyprus and 5 brs in the West Bank.

Middle East Investment Bank: POB 560, 30 Prince Shaker bin Zeid St, Shmeisani, Amman 11118; tel. (6) 5695470; fax (6) 5693410; e-mail meibsg@meib.com; internet www.meib.com; f. 1981; cap. JD 10m., res 1.9m., dep. 41.9m. (Dec. 1998); Chair. MUHAMMAD ALI MANGO; Gen. Man. WALID AS-SOUS (acting); 21 brs.

Foreign Banks

ANZ Grindlays Bank: POB 9997, Shmeisani, Amman 11191; tel. (6) 5607201; fax (6) 5679115; e-mail zahranm@anz.com; internet www.anz.com; cap. p.u. JD 10m., dep. JD 203m., total assets JD 229m. (Dec. 1998); Gen. Man. DIVED MANSON; 6 brs.

Arab Banking Corpn: POB 926691, ABC Bldg, Al-Malekah Noor St, Amman 11110; tel. (6) 5664183; fax (6) 5686291; e-mail info@abc.com.jo; internet www.abc.com.jo; f. 1990; cap. p.u. JD 20m., res JD 3.0m., dep. JD 217.8m., total assets JD 254.2m. (Dec. 1999); Chair. ABD AL-WAHAB AT-TAMMAR; Dep. Chair. and Gen. Man. JAWAD HADID; 22 brs.

Arab Land Bank (Egypt): POB 6729, Queen Musbah St, 3rd Circle, Jabal Amman 11118; tel. (6) 4646271; fax (6) 4646274; e-mail arlb@go.com.jo; internet www.arakari.com.jo; f. 1976; wholly-owned subsidiary of the Central Bank of Egypt; cap. JD 10m., dep. JD 103.3m., res JD 5.5m., total assets JD 136.1m. (Dec. 1997); Chair. ALA AL-ALOSSIYA; Gen. Man. SAMIR MAHDI; 23 brs in Jordan, 4 brs abroad.

Citibank NA (USA): POB 5055, Prince Muhammad St, Jabal Amman 11183; tel. (6) 4644065; fax (6) 4658693; internet www .citibank.com/jordan; f. 1974; cap. p.u. JD 5m., dep. JD 56.2m., total assets JD 75.4m. (Dec. 1992); Chair. and CEO JOHN S. REED; Gen. Man. SUHEIR AL-ALI; 3 brs.

HSBC Bank Middle East (United Kingdom): POB 925286, Khalid Bin Walid St, Jebel Hussein, Amman 11110; tel. (6) 5607471; fax (6) 5682047; f. 1889; cap. JD 5m., dep. JD 150m., total assets JD 169m. (Dec. 1994); Chair. Sir JOHN BOND; Gen. Man. ROBERT JAMES BRAY; 4 brs.

Islamic International Arab Bank: POB 925802, Amman 11110; tel. (6) 5694901; fax (6) 5694914; f. 1997; cap p.u. JD 40m; Chair. KHALED SHOMAN; Gen. Man. JAMEEL AD-DASOQI; 8 brs.

Rafidain Bank (Iraq): POB 1194, Amman 11118; tel. (6) 4624365; fax (6) 4658698; f. 1941; cap. p.u. JD 5m., res JD 2.1m., dep. JD 31.4m. (Dec. 1992); Pres. and Chair. DHIA HABEEB AL-KHAYOON; Gen. Man. ABD AL-HUSSEIN MAJID AL-MUKHTAR; 4 brs.

Bank Al-Mashrek (Lebanon) also has a branch in Amman.

Specialized Credit Institutions

Agricultural Credit Corporation: POB 77, Amman; tel. (6) 5661105; fax (6) 5698365; e-mail agri-cc@nets.com.jo; f. 1959; cap. p.u. JD 24m., res JD 7.5m., total assets JD 96.4m. (Dec. 1997); Chair. MEGHIM AL-KHRIESHA; Dir-Gen. NIMER AN-NABULSI; 20 brs.

Arab Jordan Investment Bank: POB 8797, Arab Jordan Investment Bank Bldg, Shmeisani Commercial Area, Amman 11121; tel. (6) 5607126; fax (6) 5681482; e-mail ajib@go.com.jo; internet www .ajib.com; f. 1978; cap. JD 20m., res JD 11.3m., dep. JD 252.5m. (Dec. 1998); Chair. and CEO ABD AL-KADER AL-QADI; 17 brs in Jordan, 2 brs abroad.

Cities and Villages Development Bank: POB 1572, Amman; tel. (6) 5668151; fax (6) 5668153; e-mail cvdb100@hotmail.com; f. 1979; cap. p.u. JD 25m., res JD 14.5m., total assets JD 66.5m. (Dec. 1998); Gen. Man. Dr IBRAHIM AN-NSOUR; 4 brs.

Housing Bank for Trade and Finance: POB 7693, Parliament St, Abdali, Amman 11118; tel. (6) 5607315; fax (6) 5678121; e-mail hbho@go.com.jo; internet www.iskanbank.com.jo; f. 1973; cap. JD 100m., res JD 124.5m., dep. JD 1,253.8m. (Dec. 1999); Chair. ZUHAIR KHOURI; Gen. Man. ABDUL QADER DWEIK; 104 brs in Jordan; 1 br. abroad.

Industrial Development Bank: POB 1982, Islamic College St, Jabal Amman, Amman 11118; tel. (6) 4642216; fax (6) 4647821; e-mail idb@indevbank.com.jo; internet www.indevbank.com.jo; f. 1965; cap. JD 24m., res JD 21.7m. dep. JD 34.9m. (Dec. 1999); Chair. MOFLEH AKEL; Gen. Man. Dr MAHER AL-WAKED; 3 brs.

Jordan Co-operative Organization: POB 1343, Amman; tel. (6) 5665171; f. 1968; cap. p.u. JD 5.2m., dep. JD 11.5m., res JD 6.8m. (Nov. 1992); Chair. and Dir-Gen. JAMAL AL-BEDOUR.

Jordan Investment Corporation (JIC): Amman; state-owned; Dir-Gen. MUHAMMAD BATAYNEH.

Jordan Investment and Finance Bank (JIFBANK): POB 950601, Issam Ajlouni St, Shmeisani, Amman 11195; tel. (6) 5665145; fax (6) 5681410; e-mail jifbank@index.com.jo; internet www.jifbank.com; f. 1982 as Jordan Investment and Finance Corpn, name changed 1989; cap. JD 20m., res JD 3.7m., dep. JD 238.1m. (Dec. 1998); Chair. NIZAR JARDANEH; Man. Dir BASIL JARDANEH; 7 brs.

Social Security Corporation: POB 926031, Amman 11110; tel. (6) 4643000; fax (6) 4610014; f. 1978; Dir-Gen. Dr SAFWAN TOQAN.

Union Bank for Savings and Investment: POB 35104, Prince Shaker Bin Zeid St, Shmeisani, Amman 11180; tel. (6) 5607011; fax (6) 5666149; e-mail info@unionbankjo.com; internet www .unionbankjo.com; f. 1978 as Arab Finance Corpn, named changed 1991; cap. JD 20m., res 9.1m., dep. 191.9m. (Dec. 1999); Chair. and Gen. Man. ISAM AS-SALFITI; 14 brs.

STOCK EXCHANGE

Amman Stock Exchange (ASE): POB 212466, 4th Floor, Hamzeh Center, Issam Ajlouni St, Shmeisani, Amman 11121; tel. (6) 5664109; fax (6) 5664071; e-mail info@ammanstockex.com; internet www.ase.com.jo; f. 1978 as Amman Financial Market; name changed March 1999; privately-run; CEO JALIL TARIF; Gen. Man. WAHIB SHAIR.

INSURANCE

Jordan Insurance Co Ltd: POB 279, Company's Bldg, 3rd Circle, Jabal Amman, Amman; tel. (6) 4634161; fax (6) 4637905; e-mail jicjo@go.com.jo; f. 1951; cap. p.u. JD 5m.; Chair. KHALDUN ABU HASSAN; 6 brs (3 in Saudi Arabia, 3 in the United Arab Emirates).

Middle East Insurance Co Ltd: POB 1802, Al Kindy St, Um Uthaina 5th Circle, Jabal Amman, Amman; tel. (6) 5527100; fax (6) 5527801; e-mail meico@go.com.jo; internet www.meico.com.jo; f. 1963; cap. p.u. US $3.7m.; Chair. SAMIR KAWAR; 1 br. in Saudi Arabia.

National Ahlia Insurance Co: POB 6156-2938, Sayed Qutub St, Shmeisani, Amman 11118; tel. (6) 5671169; fax (6) 5684900; e-mail info@nationalahlia.com; internet www.nationalahlia.com; f. 1965; cap. p.u. JD 2m.; Chair. MUSTAFA ABU GOURA; Gen. Man. GHALEB ABU GOURA.

United Insurance Co Ltd: POB 7521, United Insurance Bldg, King Hussein St, Amman; tel. (6) 4648513; fax (6) 4629417; e-mail uic@go.com.jo; internet www.unitedi.com; f. 1972; all types of insurance; cap. JD 2m.; Gen. Man. N. AZAR.

There are 17 local and one foreign insurance company operating in Jordan.

Trade and Industry

DEVELOPMENT ORGANIZATIONS

Amman Development Corporation: POB 926621, Amman; tel. (6) 5629471; f. 1979; development of services in the Amman municipality by constructing and running real estate; industrial and other complexes; Dir Gen. SAMI AR-RASHID.

Jordan Valley Authority: POB 2769, Amman; tel. (6) 5689400; fax (6) 5689916; e-mail jvadewan2@mwi.gov.jo; f. 1977 as a governmental organization responsible for the integrated social and economic development of the Jordan Valley. Projects in Stage I of the Jordan Valley Development Plan were completed in 1979. In 1988 the JVA was incorporated into the Ministry of Water and Irrigation. By late 2000 completed infrastructure projects included 2,205 km of roads, 2,223 housing units, 90 schools, 15 health centres, 16 local government buildings, 4 marketing centres, 2 tomato paste factories, 1 cold storage facility and several workshops. Electricity is now provided to all towns and villages in the valley from the national network and potable water is supplied to them from tube wells. Many of the Stage II irrigation projects are now completed. These include the construction of the King Talal, Wadi Arab, Kafrein and Karamah dams; the extension of the King Abdullah Canal to total 110.5 km in length; the construction of major municipal water projects in Amman and Irbid; the construction and conversion of a surface irrigation system into a pressurized pipe system covering an irrigated area of 25,000 ha; the development of groundwater resources and subsurface drainage systems. Projects under way include the construction of the Al-Wehdeh, Tanour and Wala dams, as well as the Mujeb dam and diversion weir. Future developments in tourist and industrial infrastructure will include the development of the Dead Sea East shore, Christ's baptism site on the Jordan river, and industrial free zones; Sec.-Gen. AVEDIS SERPEKIAN.

CHAMBERS OF COMMERCE AND INDUSTRY

Amman Chamber of Commerce: POB 1800, Amman 11118; tel. (6) 5666151; e-mail aci@amra.nic.gov.jo; f. 1923; Pres. HAIDER MURAD; Sec.-Gen. MUHAMMAD AL-MUHTASSEB.

Amman Chamber of Industry: POB 1800, Amman; tel. (6) 5643001; fax (6) 5647852; e-mail aci@aci.org.jo; internet www .aci.org.jo; f. 1962; 7,500 industrial companies registered (1999); Pres. KHALDUN ABU HASSAN; Dir.-Gen. Dr MUHAMMAD SMADI.

Federation of the Jordanian Chambers of Commerce: Amman; e-mail fjcc@go.com.jo; internet www.fjcc.com; Pres. HAIDER MURAD.

UTILITIES
Electricity

Jordanian Electric Power Company (JEPCO): POB 618, Amman 11118; tel. (6) 4636381; fax (6) 4648482; e-mail jepco@go .com.jo; privately-owned; Chair. ISSAM BDEIR; Gen. Man. Eng. MARWAN BUSHNAQ.

Central Electricity Generating Company (CEGCO): POB 3148, Amman 11181; tel (6) 5865171; fax (6) 5820975; electricity generation; govt-owned; scheduled for privatization.

Electricity Distribution Company (EDCO): POB 2310, Orthodox St, 7th Circle, Jabal Amman; tel. (6) 5858615; fax (6) 5818336; e-mail wadah@nepco.com.jo; electricity distribution; govt-owned; scheduled for privatization.

National Electric Power Company (NEPCO): POB 2310, Amman 11118; tel. (6) 5858615; fax (6) 5818336; e-mail info@nepco .com.jo; internet www.nepco.com.jo; f. 1996; formerly Jordan Electricity Authority; electricity transmission; govt-owned; scheduled for privatization; Man. Dir Eng. MUHAMMAD AZZAM.

Water

Water Authority of Jordan (WAJ): Amman.

TRADE UNIONS

The General Federation of Jordanian Trade Unions: POB 1065, Amman; tel. (6) 5675533; f. 1954; 33,000 mems; member of Arab Trade Unions Confederation; Chair. KHALIL ABU KHURMAH; Gen. Sec. ABD AL-HALIM KHADDAM.

There are also a number of independent unions, including:

Drivers' Union: POB 846, Amman; tel. (6) 4765637; fax (6) 4765829; Sec.-Gen. MAHMOUD ABD AL-HADI HAMMAD.

Jordan Engineers' Association (JEA): Amman; Pres. AZZAM HUNEIDI; Sec.-Gen. LEITH SHBEILAT.

Union of Petroleum Workers and Employees: POB 1346, Amman; Sec.-Gen. BRAHIM HADI.

Transport

RAILWAYS

Aqaba Railways Corporation (ARC): POB 50, Ma'an; tel. (3) 2132114; fax (3) 2131861; f. 1975; length of track 292 km (1,050-mm gauge); scheduled for privatization; Dir-Gen. ABDULLAH KHAWALDIH.

Formerly a division of the Hedjaz–Jordan Railway (see below), the Aqaba Railway was established as a separate entity in 1972; it retains close links with the Hedjaz but there is no regular through traffic between Aqaba and Amman. It comprises the 169-km line south of Menzil (leased from the Hedjaz–Jordan Railway) and the 115-km extension to Aqaba, opened in October 1975, which serves phosphate mines at el-Hasa and Wadi el-Abyad.

Hedjaz–Jordan Railway (administered by the Ministry of Transport): POB 4448, Amman; tel. (6) 4895414; fax (6) 4894117; f. 1902; length of track 496 km (1,050-mm gauge); Chair. MUHAMMAD KAL-ALDAH; Dir-Gen. A. ABOU-ALFEILAT.

This was formerly a section of the Hedjaz Railway (Damascus to Medina) for Muslim pilgrims to Medina and Mecca. It crosses the Syrian border and enters Jordanian territory south of Dera'a, and runs for approximately 366 km to Naqb Ishtar, passing through Zarka, Amman, Qatrana and Ma'an. Some 844 km of the line, from Ma'an to Medina in Saudi Arabia, were abandoned for over sixty years. Reconstruction of the Medina line, begun in 1965, was scheduled to be completed in 1971 at a cost of £15m., divided equally between Jordan, Saudi Arabia and Syria. However, the reconstruction work was suspended at the request of the Arab states concerned, pending further studies on costs. The line between Ma'an and Saudi Arabia (114 km) is now completed, as well as 15 km in Saudi Arabia as far as Halet Ammar Station. A new 115-km extension to Aqaba (owned by the Aqaba Railway Corporation (see above) was opened in 1975. In 1987 a study conducted by Dorsch Consult (Federal Republic of Germany) into the feasibility of reconstructing the Hedjaz Railway to high international specifications to connect Saudi Arabia, Jordan and Syria, concluded that the reopening of the

Hedjaz line would be viable only if it were to be connected with European rail networks. In August 1999 an express rail link between Amman and the Syrian capital, Damascus, was inaugurated.

ROADS

Amman is linked by road with all parts of the kingdom and with neighbouring countries. All cities and most towns are connected by a two-lane paved road system. In addition, several thousand km of tracks make all villages accessible to motor transport. In 1998 the total road network of the East Bank of Jordan was an estimated 7,133 km: 2,906 km of main roads, 2,000 km of secondary roads (both types asphalted) and 2,227 km of other roads. Jordan's total road network in 1999 was an estimated 7,200 km.

Joint Land Transport Co: Amman; joint venture of Govts of Jordan and Iraq; operates about 750 trucks.

Jordanian-Syrian Land Transport Co: POB 20686, Amman; tel. (6) 5661134; fax (6) 5669645; f. 1976; transports goods between ports in Jordan and Syria; Chair. and Gen. Man. HAMDI AL-HABASHNEH.

SHIPPING

The port of Aqaba is Jordan's only outlet to the sea and has more than 20 modern and specialized berths, and one container terminal (540 m in length). The port has 299,000 sq m of storage area, and is used for Jordan's international trade and regional transit trade (mainly with Iraq). There is a ferry link between Aqaba and the Egyptian port of Nuweibeh.

Jordanian Ports Corporation (JPC): POB 115, Aqaba 77110; tel. (3) 2014031; fax (3) 2016204; e-mail ports@amra.nic.gov.jo; Dir-Gen. Eng. ABDULLAH ABU ALIM.

Arab Bridge Maritime Co: Aqaba; f. 1987; joint venture by Egypt, Iraq and Jordan to improve economic co-operation; an extension of the company that established a ferry link between Aqaba and the Egyptian port of Nuweibeh in 1985; Chair. Eng. KHALID SALEH AMAR; Dir-Gen. TAWFIQ GRACE AWADALLA.

Arrow Trans Shipping SA: POB 926567, Amman; tel. (6) 692620; fax (6) 693324.

Assaf Shipping Co SA: POB 2637, Irbid 21110; tel. (2) 7279117; fax (2) 7261329; e-mail reefer_assaf@yahoo.com.

T. Gargour & Fils: POB 419, 4th Floor, Da'ssan Commercial Centre, Wasfi at-Tal St, Amman; tel. (6) 5524142; fax (6) 5530512; e-mail tgf@tgf.com.jo; f. 1928; shipping agents and owners; Chair. JOHN GARGOUR.

Hijezi & Ghosheh Co: POB 183292, Amman; tel. (6) 386166.

Jordan National Shipping Lines Co Ltd: POB 5406, Nasir Ben Jameel St, Wadi Saqra, Amman 11183; tel. (6) 5511500; fax (6) 5515119; e-mail jnl@go.com.jo; internet www.jnsl-jo.com; POB 557, Aqaba; tel. (3) 2018739; fax (3) 318738; 75% govt-owned; service from Antwerp, Bremen and Tilbury to Aqaba; daily passenger ferry service to Egypt; land transportation to destinations in Iraq and elsewhere in the region; Chair. MUHAMMAD SMADI; Gen. Man. Eng. AKEF ABU TAYEH.

Amin Kawar & Sons Co W.L.L.: POB 222, 24 Abd al-Hamid Sharaf St, Shmeisani, Amman 11118; tel. (6) 5603703; fax (6) 5672170; e-mail kawar@kawar.com.jo; internet www.kawar.com.jo; chartering, re-forwarding and shipping agents; Chair. TAWFIQ A. KAWAR; Gen. Man. GHASSOUB F. KAWAR; Liner Man. JAMIL SAID.

Al-Mansour Marine Transportation and Trading Co: POB 960359, Amman; tel. (6) 697958; fax (6) 702352.

Orient Shipping Co Ltd: POB 207, Amman 11118; tel. (6) 5641695; fax (6) 5651567.

Petra Navigation and International Trading Co Ltd: POB 8362, White Star Bldg, King Hussein St, Amman 11121; tel. (6) 5607021; fax (6) 5601362; e-mail petra@armoush.com.jo; general cargo, ro/ro and passenger ferries; Chair. MAJED ARMOUSH.

Salam International Transport and Trading Co: King Hussein St, Abdali, Amman 11121; tel. (6) 5607021.

Syrian-Jordanian Shipping Co: POB 148, rue Port Said, Latakia, Syria; tel. (41) 471635; fax (41) 470250; Chair. OSMAN LEBBADI.

PIPELINES

Two oil pipelines cross Jordan. The former Iraq Petroleum Co pipeline, carrying petroleum from the oilfields in Iraq to Haifa, has not operated since 1967. The 1,717-km (1,067-mile) pipeline, known as the Trans-Arabian Pipeline (Tapline), carries petroleum from the oilfields of Dhahran in Saudi Arabia to Sidon on the Mediterranean seaboard in Lebanon. Tapline traverses Jordan for a distance of 177 km (110 miles) and has frequently been cut by hostile action. Tapline stopped pumping to Syria and Lebanon at the end of 1983, when it was first due to close. It was later scheduled to close in 1985, but in September 1984 Jordan renewed an agreement to receive Saudi Arabian crude oil through Tapline. The agreement can be cancelled by either party at two years' notice.

CIVIL AVIATION

There are international airports at Amman and Aqaba. The Queen Alia International Airport at Zizya, 40 km south of Amman, was opened in 1983.

Civil Aviation Authority: POB 7547, Amman; tel. (6) 4892282; fax (6) 4891653; e-mail caa@amra.nic.gov.jo; f. 1950; Dir-Gen. Capt. JIHAD IRSHAID.

Royal Jordanian Airline: Head Office: POB 302, Housing Bank Commercial Centre, Shmeisani, Amman 11118; tel. (6) 5607300; fax (6) 5672527; e-mail rj@rja.com.jo; internet www.rja.com.jo; f. 1963; govt-owned, but scheduled for partial privatization in 2000; scheduled and charter services to Middle East, North Africa, Europe, USA and Far East; Chair. WALID ASFOUR; Pres. and CEO NADER DAHABI.

Arab Wings Co Ltd: POB 341018, Amman 11134; tel. (6) 4893901; fax (6) 4893158; e-mail info@arabwings.com.jo; internet www.arabwings.com.jo; f. 1975; subsidiary of Royal Jordanian; executive jet charter service, air ambulances, priority cargo; Man. Dir AHED QUNTAR.

Royal Wings Co Ltd: POB 314018, Amman 11134; tel. (6) 4875206; fax (6) 4875656; e-mail info@royalwings.com.jo; internet www.royalwings.com.jo; f. 1996; subsidiary of Royal Jordanian; operates scheduled and charter regional and domestic services; Man. Dir AHED QUNTAR.

Tourism

The ancient cities of Jerash and Petra, and Jordan's proximity to biblical sites, have encouraged tourism. In the late 1990s the development of Jordan's Dead Sea coast was under way; owing to the Sea's mineral-rich waters, the growth of curative tourism is anticipated. The Red Sea port of Aqaba is also undergoing a major programme of development, with a view to becoming a centre for diving holidays. In 1999 there were an estimated 1.4m. tourists. Income from tourism in that year was JD 564.1m.

Ministry of Tourism and Antiquities: POB 224, Amman 11118; tel. (6) 4642311; fax (6) 4648465; e-mail tourism@mota.gov.jo; internet www.mota.gov.jo; f. 1952; Minister of Tourism and Antiquities AQEL BELTAJI; Sec.-Gen. MUHAMMAD AFFASH AL-ADWAN.

Jordan Tourism Board: POB 830688, Amman 11183; tel. (6) 5678294; fax (6) 5678295; f. 1997; e-mail jtb@nets.com.jo; internet www.see-jordan.com; Man. Dir MARWAN KHOURY.

INDEX OF INTERNATIONAL ORGANIZATIONS

(Main reference only)

Major Titles from Europa

The European Union Encyclopedia and Directory

- The very latest information on the European Union
- Charts the Union's development from its creation, through the Treaty of Amsterdam, to present day policies and activities
- Includes an A-Z section, introductory articles, a statistical section and an extensive directory, including details of all major European Union institutes and their official bodies
- Details MEPs, their political groups and national parties, members of major committees, Directorates-General and other Commission bodies

The Environment Encyclopedia and Directory

- Provides an A-Z section of key terms relating to the environment
- A directory section organized alphabetically by country lists main governmental and non-governmental organizations, both national and international
- A series of maps show areas of pollution, rainforest and other environmental features both regionally and world-wide
- Includes an extensive bibliography of relevant periodicals
- A Who's Who section of people actively involved with environmental organizations

The Directory of University Libraries in Europe

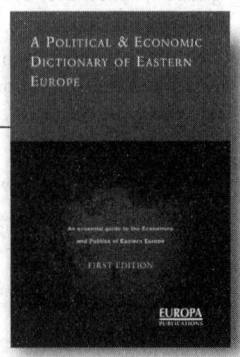

- Extensive information on central and other university libraries of European universities and, where appropriate, details of attached institutes and research centres
- Almost 4,000 entries, with full contact details, including the names of chief librarians and other relevant staff, and further information such as size and composition of library holdings, on-line subscription details and details of libraries' own publications
- Fully indexed

The Territories of the Russian Federation

- This new reference survey provides much needed up-to-date information on the 89 constituent units of the Russian Federation
- Over 300 pages of 100 current maps, analysis, statistics and detailed information
- Provides comprehensive individual territory surveys
- Includes a chronology of Russia, an essay on the economic perspective of the Russian federative system and an introduction to the structure of the Federal Government

A Political & Economic Dictionary of Eastern Europe

- A new dictionary written by a respected team of reference book compilers
- Over 1,000 concise entries concerning the politics and economics of central, eastern and south-eastern Europe, trans-Caucasus and the Russian Federation
- Information is provided on the countries, regions, ethnic groups, political parties, prime ministers, presidents and other prominent politicians, business organizations, geographical features, religions and border disputes
- Includes separate articles on each country, and on its economy

A Dictionary of Human Rights

By David Robertson

- Over 200 mini articles, arranged alphabetically and extensively cross-referenced
- Explanations of the terms, issues, organizations and laws occurring within the subject of human rights
- Outlines the significance of eminent thinkers, such as Locke, Cardozo and Nozick
- Contains extracts of leading documents, such as the Declaration of the Rights of Man and of the Citizen and the Convention on the Rights of the Child

For further information on any of the above titles contact our marketing department on:

tel. + 44 (0) 20 7842 2110   fax. + 44 (0) 20 7842 2249

e-mail info.europa@tandf.co.uk   www.europapublications.co.uk

Other Titles from Europa

Political Chronologies of the World Series

- Each of the six volumes profiles the major events in the histories of the region
- Includes an individual chronology for each country
- The chronologies provide concise details of events from early history to the mid-twentieth century and present greater detail on more recent events
- Available individually or as a six-volume set

A Political Chronology of Europe
A Political Chronology of Central, South and East Asia
A Political Chronology of the Middle East
A Political Chronology of Africa
A Political Chronology of South-East Asia and Oceania
A Political Chronology of the Americas

The International Who's Who of Women

- Over 5,500 detailed biographies of the most talented and distinguished women in the world today
- Includes women from all occupations, from Heads of State to supermodels
- Over 500 new entries for this edition
- Includes an extensive index by profession
- A must for libraries and press offices

Gutteridge and Megrah's Law of Bankers' Commerical Credits

- Presents a systematic study of the law of bankers' commercial credits
- Includes a table of cases and statutes relevant to bankers' commercial credits
- Provides information on the types of credit, mechanism and operation
- Discusses the legal aspects; relationship between buyer and seller; bankers' security

A Dictionary of Modern Politics

By David Robertson
- A thorough guide to the complex terminology and ideology which surrounds the world of politics
- Over 500 definitions/mini essays
- Defines political theories, ideas and "isms"
- Explains highly specialized terms
- Invaluable for anyone concerned with politics and current affairs

The International Directory of Government

- The definitive guide to people in power world-wide
- Details over 17,500 government ministries, departments, agencies, corporations and their connected bodies and people who work within them
- Also includes an outline of the each country's legislature and governmental system
- Explains the constitutional position of the head of state
- Entries contain: name and title of principal officials, postal and e-mail address, telephone, telex and fax numbers, and an outline of each organization's activities

International Relations Research Directory

- Directory information on every major research institute concerned with international relations throughout the world
- Provides details of institutes names, address, telephone, fax and e-mail, principal officers, date of foundation, activities and publications
- Lists periodicals and journals in the field of international relations with details of name, address, telephone, fax and e-mail, editor, publisher, date of foundation, subject of coverage, frequency and circulation

Who's Who in International Affairs

- Provides up-to-date biographical information on more than 7,000 principal figures in the fields of international politics, economics, legal, medical, cultural and scientific affairs
- Fully indexed by organization and nationality, it is a useful directory of international organizations as well as an invaluable A-Z guide of leading personalities
- Each entry contains, where available, name, nationality, date of birth, family details, education, career details, publications, contact address, telephone, fax numbers, e-mail addresses and leisure interests

Profiles of People in Power: the World's Government Leaders

- Individual country sections explain the types of government; the respective roles of the head of state, the head of government and the legislature
- Lists the most recent heads of state and head of goverment, with dates of office
- Biographical profiles of the current head of state and head of government and other significant past leaders who remain an active political presence
- Photographic section of many of the world's political leaders

Europa's Regional Surveys of the World

A unique series of regularly revised reference titles aimed at businesses, libraries, universities, government departments, embassies, newspapers and international organizations

'Europa's Regional Surveys of the World are justly renowned for their exceptionally high levels of production, content and accuracy.' Reference Reviews

South America, Central America and the Caribbean

- An incomparable source of factual and statistical information for this vast region
- Reflects the very latest political and economic developments
- Includes contributions from over 30 leading authorities on Latin American and Caribbean affairs
- Provides a systematic survey of each country
- Enlightened commentary on topical issues, such as international trade and the banana war, the environment and the drug crisis

Africa South of the Sahara

- A one-volume library of essential data on all the countries of Sub-Saharan Africa
- Over 1,200 pages of economic and demographic statistics, wide-ranging directory material and authoritative articles
- Contributions from 50 leading experts on African affairs
- Incisive analysis and the latest available information
- Includes details of international organizations active in the region

Central and South Eastern Europe

- This title is one of the two new successor volumes to Europa's award-winning Eastern Europe and the Commonwealth of Independent States
- Includes country-by-country surveys, political, economic and social information
- Detailed articles by acknowledged experts cover issues of regional importance such as integration with the West, social policy and religion, the Macedonian Question
- Coverage of regional organizations, research institutes and periodicals
- A select bibliography and a political profile section

Western Europe

- Over 660 pages of statistics, directory and analytical information
- Introductory essays on the region cover political, economic and social issues ranging from the impact of the European Union to Western Europe's environmental politics and its relations with the wider world
- Acknowledged authorities write on regional and country-specific topics
- Chronologies detailing the history of each country

Eastern Europe, Russia and Central Asia

- This title is one of the two successor volumes to the award-winning Eastern Europe and the Commonwealth of Independent States
- Includes country-by-country surveys, political, economic and social information
- Articles by acknowledged authorities covering regional issues such as the politics of energy and the environment
- Coverage of regional organizations, institutes and periodicals
- A select bibliography and a political profile section

The Middle East and North Africa

- Covers the Middle Eastern world from Algeria to Yemen
- Draws together the events of the past twelve months
- Provides comprehensive information on the United Nations and all major international organizations operating in the area
- A detailed calendar of events, expert articles, up to date statistics and directory information
- An invaluable reference source in business matters relating to the area

The Far East and Australasia

- A systematic survey of all the countries of East Asia, South Asia, South-East Asia, Australasia and the Pacific Islands
- Essential for anyone with a professional interest in this part of the world, the book keeps you up to date with current economic and political developments
- Presents over 1,400 pages of statistics, directory information and expert analysis
- Provides details of all major international organizations active in the region

The USA and Canada

- Invaluable reference guide to the political, economic and social affairs of these two powerful North American nations
- Contributions from over 30 acknowledged authorities
- Specially commissioned articles cover issues such as the USA and the United Nations, Aboriginal Peoples in North America, the Canadian Economy
- Includes wide-ranging statistics and directory information
- Provides geographical and historical introductions to each state/province, data on the economies, and a comprehensive governmental and legislative directory section

For further information on any of the above titles contact our marketing department on:

tel. + 44 (0) 20 7842 2110   fax. + 44 (0) 20 7842 2249

e-mail info.europa@tandf.co.uk   www.europapublications.co.uk

EUROPA PUBLICATIONS
Taylor & Francis Group

Greenland
Sea

Laptev
Sea

Barents
Sea

Kara
Sea

Central
Siberian Plain

Denmark Strait

Arctic Circle

Norwegian
Sea

Scandinavia

West
Siberian
Plain Ob

S i b e r i a

Khrebet Cherskorgo

Lena

North
Sea

Baltic Sea

Volga

Ural Mountains

ASIA

Sea of
Okhotsk

British
Isles

North European
Plain

EUROPE

Carpathian Mts

Alps

Danube

Lake
Balkhash

Altai

Lake
Baikal

Manchurian
Plain

Bay of
Biscay

Balkan Mts

Black Sea

Aral
Sea

Tien Shan

Gobi
Desert

Sea of
Japan

Iberian
Peninsula

Mediterranean Sea

Anatolia

Caspian
Sea

Pamirs

Hindu Kush

K2 Kunlun Mountains
8611m

Yellow River

East
China
Sea

Japan

Atlas Mtns

Iranian
Plateau

Zagros Mountains

Plateau
of Tibet

Yangtze

Tropic of Cancer

S a h a r a

Hoggar

Libyan Desert

Nile

The Gulf

Himalayas

Mt Everest
8848m

Philippine
Sea

Tibesti

Red Sea

Arabian
Peninsula

Thar
Desert

Ganges

Deccan

AFRICA

Sahel

Niger

Lake Chad

Ethiopian
Highlands

Gulf of Aden

Horn of
Africa

Arabian
Sea

Western Ghats

Eastern Ghats

Bay of
Bengal

Mekong

South
China
Sea

Equator

Gulf of
Guinea

Adamawa
Highland

Congo
Basin

Congo

Rift Valley

Rift Valley

Lake Victoria
Kilimanjaro
5895m

Lake Tanganyika

Sri
Lanka

Borneo

New
Guinea

ATLANTIC

OCEAN

Lake Nyasa

Zambezi

Mozambique Channel

INDIAN

Timor
Sea

Namib Desert

Tropic of Capricorn

Kalahari
Desert

OCEAN

AUSTRALIA

Great
Sandy Desert

Great Dividing Range

Drakensberg

Great Victoria Desert

Nullarbor
Plain

Darling

Cape
Basin

Antarctic Circle

A n t a r c t i c a